CONGRESSIONAL QUARTERLY

2000

ALMANAC®

106TH CONGRESS
2ND SESSION

VOLUME LVI

Congressional Quarterly Inc.

1414 22nd Street N.W.
Washington, D.C. 20037

CONGRESSIONAL QUARTERLY 2000 ALMANAC

Congressional Quarterly Inc.

Congressional Quarterly Inc. is a publishing and information services company and the recognized national leader in political journalism. For more than half a century, CQ has served clients in the fields of business, government, news and education with complete, timely and nonpartisan information on Congress, politics and national issues.

The flagship publication is the CQ Weekly, a news magazine on Congress and its legislative activities. The award-winning reporters and editors of CQ Weekly are top experts in their subject specialties. They track legislation as it is created in subcommittee, committee, floor, House-Senate conferences and leadership offices, providing detail and analysis unavailable anywhere else.

The CQ Daily Monitor is a morning news report on Congress and the scheduled hearings and markups of congressional committees. It provides a comprehensive breaking news report of everything that just happened or is about to happen on Capitol Hill.

CQ now offers the most comprehensive, detailed and up-to-the-minute legislative tracking information on the World Wide Web. CQ.com On Congress is an Internet service with immediate access to exclusive CQ coverage of bill action, votes, schedules and member profiles, with direct links to relevant texts of bills, committee reports, testimony and verbatim transcripts.

CQ also publishes specialized publications on campaign politics and trends: Campaigns & Elections magazine is a monthly trade journal for candidates and campaign consultants, and Campaign Insider is a weekly fax newsletter for political professionals.

CQ serves the academic and education markets with a special weekly publication — The CQ Researcher — which focuses each week on a single topic of current interest.

Also CQ Press publishes a variety of books, including political science textbooks, to keep journalists, scholars and the public abreast of developing issues and events. This includes a line of print and web-based directories, such as the Congressional Staff Directory, plus reference books on the federal government, national elections and politics.

The Congressional Quarterly Almanac®, published annually, provides a legislative history for each session of Congress. Congress and the Nation, published every four years, provides a record of government for a presidential term.

Library of Congress Catalog Number 47-41081
ISBN: 1-56802-636-6 ISSN: 0095-6007

CONGRESSIONAL QUARTERLY OFFERS A COMPLETE LINE OF PUBLICATIONS AND RESEARCH SERVICES.

The CQ Almanac

"The story of Congress is the sum of the work of these members on the floor, in the lobbies, in committees in Washington and on the road, at home and abroad, in session and during recess."

More than 50 years ago, CQ founders Henrietta and Nelson Poynter prefaced the 1946 edition of the CQ Almanac with those words. They had only recently initiated the unprecedented task of compiling the only complete reference work on the actions of each session of Congress.

A half century later, Congressional Quarterly Inc. is proud to maintain the Poynter legacy and Poynter mission. This 2000 edition of the CQ Almanac, edited by CQ Weekly Assistant Managing Editor Jan Austin and Production Editor Melinda W. Nahmias, covers the actions, votes and other deeds of the second session of the 106th Congress. It provides a collection of articles from CQ Weekly, our award-winning, flagship news magazine, with stories tracking some 80 pieces of legislation that saw action at the full committee or floor level.

The Almanac also pulls together all the recorded votes in the House and Senate, important presidential statements and responses from members of Congress, and public laws. It includes the annual CQ Vote Studies, which provide exclusive statistical analyses of presidential support, party unity and voting participation.

The 2000 edition includes reports on the tumultuous presidential election and the difficulties faced by both parties in organizing for the 107th Congress.

Bills covered in this edition — selected by Congressional Quarterly's editors as the most significant of the year — range from granting permanent normal trade status to China, to auto-safety legislation enacted in the wake of the massive Firestone tire recall, to the year-end omnibus appropriations package and Republican efforts, stymied by President Clinton, to repeal the estate tax and do away with the "marriage penalty."

The book covers the 13 regular appropriations bills, the budget resolution, reauthorization of the Defense Department and the failure to reconcile significantly different House and Senate bills to protect patients enrolled in managed-care health plans.

Most sections begin with a brief introduction, followed by articles from the CQ Weekly arranged in chronological order and marked with the date of the magazine in which they appeared.

In the back, you will find a number of appendixes, including:

- **Congress and Its Members:** A 11-page glossary of terms that arise in discussing Congress and legislation and a list of members of the House and Senate in the second session of the 106th Congress.
- **Vote studies.** CQ's popular study of the roll call votes cast in Congress during the year. Separate studies analyze the level of presidential support, party unity and member participation during the year.
- **Key votes.** An account of the votes chosen by the CQ editors as most critical in determining the outcome of congressional action on major issues during the year.
- **Texts.** Presidential statements, Republican responses and materials from the Democratic and Republican nominating conventions.
- **Public laws.** A detailed list of all the bills enacted into law during the year.
- **Roll call votes.** A complete set of roll call vote charts for both chambers.

CQ produces the Almanac for public policy specialists, scholars, journalists and all interested citizens and students of the U.S. legislative system. As the Poynters wrote at the very beginning: "Congressional Quarterly presents the facts in as complete, concise and unbiased form as we know how. The editorial comment on the acts and votes of Congress, we leave to our subscribers."

David Rapp
Executive Editor

CQ

"By providing a link between the local newspaper and Capitol Hill we hope Congressional Quarterly can help to make public opinion the only effective pressure group in the country. Since many citizens other than editors are also interested in Congress, we hope that they too will find Congressional Quarterly an aid to a better understanding of their government.

Foreword, Congressional Quarterly, Vol. I, 1945
Henrietta Poynter, 1901-1968
Nelson Poynter, 1903-1978

SUMMARY TABLE OF CONTENTS

Table of Contents

Chapter 1 – Inside Congress

Chapter 2 – Appropriations

Chapter 3 – Abortion

Chapter 4 – Agriculture

Chapter 5 – Banking & Finance

Chapter 6 – Budget

Chapter 7 – Congressional Affairs

Chapter 8 – Defense

Chapter 9 – Education

Chapter 10 – Energy & Environment

Chapter 11 – Foreign Policy

Chapter 12 – Health

Chapter 13 – Industry & Regulation

Chapter 14 – Labor & Employment

Chapter 15 – Law & Judiciary

Chapter 16 – Science

Chapter 17 – Social Policy

Chapter 18 – Taxes

Chapter 19 – Telecommunications

Chapter 20 — Trade

Chapter 21 — Transportation & Infrastructure

Chapter 22 — Veterans Affairs

Appendixes

Congress and Its Members

Vote Studies

Key Votes

Texts

Roll Call Votes

Chapter 1

INSIDE CONGRESS

Parties' Ambitious Agendas Make Little Headway in 106th

SUMMARY

For the 106th Congress, more turned out to be less. Two months added to the legislative calendar did not help lawmakers emerge from a morass that produced few accomplishments. While President Clinton has already signed more than 370 laws this year — double the number enacted last year — dozens of those measures were to name post offices and public buildings.

Republican leaders began the year with an impressive agenda that included proposals for a series of targeted tax breaks and initiatives aimed at giving state and local officials more control over federal education dollars. Ultimately, those and other issues were not resolved. Democrats did not fare any better in enacting key objectives such as expanding Medicare to provide prescription drugs for beneficiaries and increasing the minimum wage.

"It's kind of slim pickings," said Sarah Binder, assistant professor of political science at George Washington University, in a Dec. 13 interview. "I'm hard-pressed to say [lawmakers] were terribly productive."

Presidential politics jammed the legislative gears a bit, but there were other factors to blame for the less-than-productive session. "Institutional dynamics" wreaked as much havoc as political ones, Binder said. For example, House and Senate Republicans could not agree how to proceed on politically difficult measures such as broader federal regulation of managed-care plans, which died in a House-Senate conference. While House Republicans pushed legislation they knew could pass with their razor-thin majority, Senate Republicans were less eager to engage in the procedural wrangling necessary to move their priorities. Senate Democrats mastered the art of the filibuster and used it well, slowing the Senate to a crawl when they disagreed with how

Majority Leader Trent Lott, R-Miss., was running the show.

Few moderates emerged to bridge differences between the parties on such difficult topics as gun control and patients' rights. Congress sputtered through the budget process in fits and starts until Dec. 15, when it concluded work on the fiscal 2001 budget. The omnibus package (HR 4577) included four appropriations bills and a measure to give Medicare providers about $35 billion more in payments over the next five years.

The budget debate intensified shortly before the scheduled Oct. 6 adjournment, when Republicans decided to reverse the pattern of earlier years when they basically gave in to Clinton's spending demands. As a result, the two sides battled bitterly over the final appropriations measures, passing 22 continuing resolutions while they tried to finish their work.

Earlier this month, House Majority Whip Tom Delay, R-Texas, suggested the best way to end the session was with a 10-month continuing resolution that would fund at fiscal 2000 levels all programs and agencies covered by the four unfinished appropriations bills. His suggestion was rejected by Democrats and Republicans alike, but lawmakers on both sides did agree to break the caps imposed by the 1997 Balanced Budget Act (PL 105-33) and set new discretionary spending limits.

The Crown Jewel

Perhaps the year's most impressive accomplishment was passage of legislation to give China permanent normal trade status, which applies the same tariff rates to Chinese imports as those on goods from most U.S. trading partners. Clinton made the bill a priority during his final year in office, and business leaders — particularly those in the high-tech and agriculture sectors — helped push a skeptical House and mostly gridlocked Senate to take action. Passage also meant the United States would support China's efforts to join the World Trade Organization. The first major legislation in six years to expand U.S. trade also became law as Congress cleared a measure to lower import tariffs and remove quotas on certain goods — mainly apparel made with U.S. cloth and yarn — from sub-Saharan Africa, Central America and the Caribbean.

Republicans got two important pieces of their tax strategy — repeal of the estate tax and the so-called marriage penalty — through both chambers, but failed to override Clinton vetoes. Both sides did agree to lift the limit on how much outside income retirees between ages 65 and 69 may earn and still collect full Social Security benefits.

Health care was a hot-button issue in Congress and on the campaign

Session's Highlights

Congress did:

- Break the 1997 budget caps and put new discretionary spending limits into law.
- Repeal the Social Security "earnings test."
- Initiate a $7.8 billion federal-state project to restore Florida's Everglades.
- Reauthorize the Strategic Petroleum Reserve and create a home heating oil reserve in the Northeast.
- Provide $1.3 billion in supplemental aid to Colombia to combat drug traffickers and left-wing guerrillas.
- Significantly increase the number of non-immigrant (H-1B) visas available for highly skilled workers.
- Reauthorize the Federal Aviation Administration and guarantee a spending boost for airport construction.
- Require tire manufacturers to give federal regulators data on possible defects and require the government to devise a crash test for auto rollovers.
- Grant permanent normal trade relations status to products from China.
- Revamp the system for taxing income earned abroad.
- Authorize the use of electronic signatures to close business deals over the Internet.
- Reauthorize the Violence Against Women Act.
- Reauthorize the Older Americans Act.
- Reimburse Medicare providers for cuts made in a 1997 law.
- Establish programs to boost home ownership among low- and moderate-income families.

Congress did not:

- Expand patients' rights in managed-care plans.
- Provide prescription drug coverage for Medicare beneficiaries.
- Tighten federal restrictions on gun sales.
- Stiffen penalties for juvenile offenders.
- Repeal the "marriage penalty" in tax law.
- Repeal the estate tax.
- Increase the minimum wage.
- Protect the privacy of medical records.
- Overhaul the national system for organ allocation.
- Deregulate the electric power industry.
- Expand federal hate crime laws to include gender, sex ual orientation and disability.
- Enact an overhaul of the nation's bankruptcy laws.
- Reauthorize the Elementary and Secondary Education Act, the main source of federal aid to public schools.
- Federalize compensation rules for asbestos exposure.
- Overhaul the superfund hazardous waste program.
- Block the designation of new national monuments.
- Ban "partial birth" abortions.
- Ban physician-assisted suicide.
- Facilitate the temporary storage of nuclear waste.
- Expand education savings accounts.
- Ban the clean-burning gasoline additive MTBE, a suspected carcinogen.
- Overhaul the Export Administration Act.

trail, but lawmakers could not agree on how to give patients broader latitude to appeal health insurers' decisions. Republicans and Democrats both wanted to add a prescription drug benefit to Medicare, but disagreed on the best way to accomplish it. A GOP-backed bill relying on the private sector to develop coverage squeaked through the House — giving Republicans political cover in the November elections — but was dead on arrival in the Senate.

Congress failed to take action to protect the confidentiality of individual medical records. Some lawmakers had hoped to pass a narrowly tailored provision aimed at preventing bias based on genetic traits as part of the fiscal 2001 Labor, Health and Human Services, and Education spending bill, but the language was removed in endgame negotiations.

While a comprehensive overhaul of the nation's campaign finance system eluded Congress, lawmakers passed and Clinton signed the first change in federal election law in two decades. The new law closed the loophole on so-called 527 political action committees. The fundraising groups, organized under section 527 of the tax code, spent millions of dollars on elections but were not required to disclose their donors or expenditures as long as they did not expressly advocate the election or defeat of a candidate.

Congress was unable to raise the minimum wage, even though both chambers passed bills that would have increased the wage by $1, to $6.15 an hour. House and Senate leaders were unable to iron out their differences — most notably between the two-year phase-in passed by the House and the three-year time frame agreed to by the Senate.

On the environmental front, Congress had one of its few major successes — clearing legislation that authorized the first $1.4 billion of a $7.8 billion, 35-year federal-state project to restore Florida's Everglades. Lawmakers failed to move legislation that would have banned the clean-burning gasoline additive methyl tertiary butyl ether — a suspected carcinogen found to be leaking from underground tanks in some 30 states — because they could not forge a compromise that could satisfy both the petroleum industry and agricultural interests promoting a corn-based substitute.

Congress also failed to move the Conservation and Reinvestment Act (CARA), which enjoyed strong bipartisan support because it would have guaranteed about $3 billion annually in offshore drilling royalties for federal-state conservation programs. However, some $400 million for coastal conservation programs was added to the fiscal 2001 Commerce-Justice-State spending bill.

Continued on p. 1-6

Clinton's Use of the Veto

President Clinton vetoed 37 bills during his two terms, including 14 appropriations bills. Congress overrode him only twice, enacting measures, in bold below, to limit shareholder lawsuits (PL 104-67) and to restore military construction spending that Clinton had struck using his short-lived, line-item veto power (PL 105-159).

BILL	DESCRIPTION	VETOED	CONGRESSIONAL RESPONSE
	1995		
HR 1158	FY95 supplemental spending/rescissions	June 7	
S 21	Lift Bosnia arms embargo	Aug. 11	
HR 1854	FY96 legislative branch spending	Oct. 3	
HR 2586	Temporary increase in public debt limit	Nov. 13	
H J Res 115	FY96 continuing appropriations	Nov. 13	
HR 2491	$245 billion tax cut over seven years	Dec. 6	
HR 1977	FY96 Interior spending	Dec. 18	House sustained, 239-177
HR 2099	FY96 VA-HUD spending	Dec. 18	
HR 2076	FY96 Commerce-Justice-State spending	Dec. 19	House sustained, 240-159
HR 1058	**Limitation on lawsuits by disgruntled shareholders**	**Dec. 19**	**House overrode, 319-100** **Senate overrode, 68-30**
HR 1530	FY96 defense authorization	Dec. 28	House sustained, 240-156
	1996		
HR 4	Welfare system overhaul	Jan. 10	
HR1833	Ban on "partial birth" abortion	April 10	House overrode, 285-137 Senate sustained, 57-41
HR1561	State Department authorization	April 12	House sustained,234-188
HR 956	Limit on awards in product liability lawsuits	May 2	House sustained, 258-163
HR 743	Ease regulation of labor-management teams	July 30	
HR 2909	Land acquisition in wildlife refuge	Oct. 2	
	1997		
HR 1469	FY97 supplemental spending	June 9	
HR 1122	Ban on "partial-birth" abortion	Oct. 10	House overrode, 296-132 Senate sustained, 64-36
HR 2631	**Restore spending struck by line-item veto from FY98 military construction law**	**Nov. 13**	**House overrode, 347-69** **Senate overrode, 78-20**
	1998		
S 1502	District of Columbia school vouchers	May 20	
HR 2709	Punish nations giving missile aid to Iran	June 23	
HR 2646	Expand education savings account benefits	July 21	
HR 4101	FY99 agriculture spending	Oct. 7	
HR 1757	State Department authorization	Oct. 21	
	1999		
HR 2488	$792 billion tax cut over 10 years	Sept. 23	
HR 2587	FY00 District of Columbia spending	Sept. 28	
HR 2606	FY00 foreign operations spending	Oct. 18	
HR 2670	FY00 Commerce-Justice-State spending	Oct. 25	
HR 3064	FY00 D.C./Labor-HHS-Education spending	Nov. 3	
	2000		
S 1287	Rules for Nevada nuclear waste storage site	April 25	Senate sustained 64-35
HR 4810	Alleviate tax code's "marriage penalty"	Aug. 5	House sustained, 270-158
HR 8	Repeal of taxes on estates, gifts and trusts	Aug. 31	House sustained, 274-157
HR 4733	FY01 energy and water spending	Oct. 11	
HR 4516	FY01 Treasury-Postal Service and legislative branch spending	Oct. 30	
HR 4392	FY01 intelligence authorization	Nov. 4	
HR 2415	Consumer bankruptcy overhaul	Dec. 19	(Congress had adjourned)

NOTE: Does not include line-item vetoes, which were permitted under a 1996 law (PL 104-130) that was struck down by the Supreme Court in *City of New York v. Clinton* in 1998.

Second Session by the Numbers

The second session of the 106th Congress began on Jan. 24, 2000. The Senate adjourned sine die at 8:03 p.m on Dec. 15, 2000; the House adjourned sine die at 8:41 p.m. the same day.

The following is a statistical portrait of the two chambers of Congress over the past decade:

		2000	1999	1998	1997	1996	1995	1994	1993	1992	1991
Days in Session	Senate	141	162	143	153	132	211	138	153	129	158
	House	135	137	119	132	122	168	123	142	123	154
Time in Session (hours)	Senate	1,018	1,184	1,095	1,093	1,037	1,839	1,244	1,270	1,091	1,201
	House	1,054	1,125	999	1,004	919	1,525	905	982	857	939
Avg. Length Daily Session (hours)	Senate	7.2	7.3	7.7	7.1	7.9	8.7	9.0	8.3	8.5	7.6
	House	7.8	8.2	8.4	7.6	7.5	9.1	7.4	6.9	7.0	6.1
Public Laws Enacted		410	170	241	153	245	88	255	210	347	243
Bills/Resolutions Introduced	Senate	1,546	2,352	1,321	1,839	860	1,801	999	2,178	1,544	2,701
	House	2,701	4,241	2,253	3,662	1,899	3,430	2,104	4,543	2,714	5,057
	TOTAL	**4,247**	**6,593**	**3,574**	**5,501**	**2,759**	**5,231**	**3,103**	**6,721**	**4,258**	**7,758**
Recorded Votes	Senate	298	374	314	298	306	613	329	395	270	280
	House[1]	603	611	547	640	455	885	507	615	488	444
	TOTAL	**901**	**985**	**861**	**938**	**761**	**1,498**	**836**	**1,010**	**758**	**724**
Vetoes		7[2]	5	5	3[3]	6	11	0	0	21[2]	4[2]

SOURCE: Congressional Record

[1] includes quorum calls

[2] includes pocket vetoes

[3] does not include line-item vetoes

Continued from p. 1-4

In a nod to the nation's rapidly expanding aviation system, Congress cleared a three-year, $40 billion bill reauthorizing the Federal Aviation Administration and guaranteeing a huge spending increase for airport construction. The measure permits airports to increase local fees on airline tickets and eases flight restrictions at some of the nation's most congested airports, including Ronald Reagan Washington National Airport, a popular weekend departure point for lawmakers. ◆

Chapter 2

APPROPRIATIONS

Longest Appropriations Cycle in Five Years Ends With Omnibus Spending Bill

BoxScore

Year-End Omnibus Package

2001 Fiscal Year

- **Bill:** HR 4577 — PL 106-554
- **Legislative action: House** adopted the conference report (H Rept 106-1033), 292-60, on Dec. 15.

Senate cleared the bill by voice vote Dec. 15.

President signed the bill Dec. 21.

SUMMARY

Congress was unable to avert its annual pileup of overdue appropriations bills at the end of the session. With election-year partisanship at a fever pitch, the fiscal 2001 appropriations impasse lumbered into a lame-duck session that lasted until mid-December, when an omnibus package was used to close the books on four spending bills and move other unrelated legislation.

Republicans claimed victory by arguing that in the final weeks of negotiations, they had curtailed billions in White House spending demands. Still, Congress ended up spending about $10 billion more than the president requested at the beginning of the year.

Abandoned spending restraints, hostile fights over policy riders, missed deadlines and an end-of-session backlog of unfinished bills have become common features in the annual appropriations process, and this year was no different.

Republican leaders had hoped they could break the cycle with an accelerated timetable, and they got off to a good start when Congress adopted its fiscal 2001 budget resolution (H Con Res 290) by the April 15 deadline. But appropriators on both sides of the aisle warned that the budget's tight fiscal restraints — it called for a less-than-inflation increase in discretionary spending to no more than $600.3 billion — would doom any chance of clearing realistically funded bills that President Clinton would sign.

The critics turned out to be right. Republican leaders tried to hold the line on spending, but when it became clear the budget resolution's spending limit would be ignored, the dam broke. Members of both parties padded the appropriations bills with hundreds of special projects. And with both Republicans and Democrats equally eager in an election year to push for big increases for education, health research and other social programs, the tab rose to far more than Clinton's initial budget request of about $625 billion in February, a total Republicans had blasted as recklessly excessive. In the end, Congress approved about $10 billion more.

The biggest budget fight of the year, not surprisingly, was over education. The dispute was the primary cause of the lame-duck session. Republicans pushed for more block grants and local control, while Democrats backed Clinton's proposals to target funds to hire new teachers and for school construction. In the end, both sides got some, but not all, of what they wanted in a lame-duck fight that dragged into mid-December.

The final appropriations bill wrapped together the spending bills for the departments of Labor, Health and Human Services and Education; the legislative branch; and the Treasury and Postal Service. It also made needed technical changes to a previously-cleared bill for the departments of Commerce, Justice and State and the federal judiciary that had been cleared but never sent to the president.

Omnibus Spending Deal Clears As White House Settles for Less

DECEMBER 16 — Bill Clinton did not have to retreat often during his six years of budgetary battle with a Republican Congress, but that was the posture he found himself in during the final legislative fight of his presidency.

The GOP leadership — suddenly emboldened when Republican Gov. George W. Bush of Texas emerged as the presidential victor after five weeks of legal challenges — insisted the week of Dec. 11 on an array of concessions from the president with just five weeks left in the White House. And Clinton, who had hoped that a victory by Vice President Al Gore would give him some leverage in the lame-duck session, gave in on a range of issues, including spending on social programs, immigration restrictions and a last-hour environmental dispute.

The deal, finally sealed the afternoon of Dec. 15, was written into the conference report for the fiscal 2001 appropriations bill (HR 4577) covering the departments of Labor, Health and Human Services, and Education. That evening the House voted to adopt the sweeping package, 292-60; the Senate had agreed to automatically clear it on a voice vote, effectively bringing the 106th Congress to an anticlimactic end. *(Vote 603, H-190)*

Overall, the package would appropriate about $384 billion — $127 billion of it discretionary — because Clinton was compelled to accept about $5 billion less than he had won in agreements, and even in some laws he had signed, earlier in the year.

It had not taken Clinton and the GOP as long to finish an annual appropriations cycle since the first year of GOP control, in 1995, when a standoff produced two government shutdowns and kept the fiscal 1996 budget debate alive into the following spring. *(1996 Almanac, p. 10-5)*

The "omnibus" legislation also reiterates two other spending measures — for the legislative branch and for the Treasury Department, White House operations and the Postal Service — that Clinton had vetoed before the election, protesting that Congress had sent him the pair as a package (HR 4516) "at a time when the business of the American people remains unfinished."

To complete all of the appropriations business for fiscal 2001, which began on Oct. 1, the omnibus package also included language to alter legislation (HR 4942) already cleared by Congress to finance the Commerce, Justice and State departments (CJS) and the judiciary. The revisions give Clinton only part of the looser immigration rules he had been insisting on before Election Day, when he threatened to veto the CJS measure unless it provided what he sought. *(CJS, p. 2-23)*

The president's biggest victory was that the omnibus measure includes a $25.9 billion, 10-year package of tax breaks and other initiatives designed to boost distressed urban and rural communities — but Clinton won that in large measure because it was also a top priority of House Speaker J. Dennis Hastert, R-Ill. It will be the only significant tax cut of the year.

After months of negotiations, Congress and the White House also agreed to give about $35 billion more in the next five years to hospitals, managed-care plans, nursing homes and others who provide services under Medicare, the federal medical insurance plan for the elderly and disabled.

Enacting the package would bring the discretionary spending grand total for fiscal 2001 to approximately $635 billion. That would be approximately $10 billion, or 2 percent, more than Clinton requested; $24 billion, or 4 percent, more than the amount that would be needed to maintain current programs at the rate of inflation; $35 billion, or 6 percent, more than the limit authorized by the fiscal 2001 budget resolution (H Con Res 290); and $94 billion, or 17 percent, more than the statutory cap set in the budget-balancing reconciliation law (PL 105-33) of three years ago. *(1997 Almanac, p. 2-47)*

Some Wins for Clinton

Despite its concessions, the administration described the final measure as a victory, especially on the domestic policy front. And while Clinton's victories may have been less sweeping than in his past battles with the GOP Congress, there were still plenty of them, in part because in this election year the Republicans themselves were willing to accept, more readily than usual, more spending for hiring teachers, repairing schools, conducting biomedical research, financing loans for low-income college students and other programs.

"This historic new investment is the culmination of President Clinton's eight-year commitment to strengthening America's education system," said White House spokesman Jake Siewert.

As in the past, much of the fight over domestic priorities was conducted in the writing of the Labor-HHS-Education package.

In its final form, that package contains $108.9 billion in discretionary budget authority, not counting advance appropriations — an increase of about $12 billion over fiscal 2000, but $3.6 billion less than Clinton and the GOP had agreed to spend in October. Although Clinton did not get everything he sought, spending would increase significantly in the major funding categories, and its total would be almost $3 billion more than Clinton originally requested in February. All year long, the disagreements over the bill were less about its overall spending level than about the priorities for the additional money.

The final package would boost federal education spending by a record $6.5 billion — an 18 percent increase over last year's funding levels and the biggest increase since the Department of Education was created in 1979. It also includes a $2.5 billion increase in funding for the National Institutes of Health, just shy of the $2.7 billion increase appropriators wanted for biomedical research.

"I think it came out better than most members thought it would," Barney Frank, D-Mass., said after a meeting House Democrats had Dec. 15 with White House Chief of Staff John D. Podesta and Office of Management and Budget Director Jack Lew. "There were standing ovations. It was a very upbeat situation."

Among those endorsing the deal was Sen. Joseph I. Lieberman of Connecticut, the 2000 Democratic nominee for vice president. Upon returning to the Capitol on Dec. 14, the day after Gore conceded, Lieberman signaled to other Democrats that the time for budget haggling this year was over.

"We ought to start fresh next year," he said. "This has been another long count, but it ought to end, and it ought to end with an accomplishment."

Still, many Democratic negotiators were frustrated that agreements they thought they had struck before the election were abandoned. "And now, we are being told that we have committed a mortal sin and we are all going to go to hell because we passed a Labor-Health-Education program that was a few billion dollars above the president's request," David R. Obey of Wisconsin, the top Democrat on the House Appropriations Committee, said on the floor Dec. 11. He ended up voting for the package, he said Dec. 15, because he concluded he could not win a better deal.

Republicans also groused about the price tag of the bill, but they supported it anyway. "I'm prepared to go along with that figure, although very, very reluctantly," Arlen Specter, R-Pa., chairman of the Senate Appropriations Labor-HHS-Education Subcommittee, said on the Senate floor Dec. 15.

Steller Distraction

And although he had been publicly fretting for months about the lack of a fiscal timetable for finishing the appropriations bills, Senate Appropriations Committee Chairman Ted Stevens, R-Alaska, was the last lawmaker to hold the session-ending package hostage.

For days, Stevens insisted that the measure impede or reverse the Commerce Department's decision to invoke the Endangered Species Act and limit pollock and cod fishing near the Alaskan coast, which the agency said was necessary to protect the food supply of the Steller sea lion, an endangered species.

Ultimately, Stevens agreed to language requiring a review of environmental data on the issue and prohibiting a reduction in the allowable catch of any fishery by more than 10 percent. He also won a $20 million appropriation to study whether sea lions are being killed by other mammals — Stevens suspects killer whales are responsible for the sea lions' fate — and $30 million to repay those harmed economically by sea lion protection efforts.

Without such a deal, the administration's decision "will create ghost towns in my state along the shore from Kodiak all the way out along the Aleutian chain," he said on the floor Dec. 14. "Primarily, those are native villages. They are not enormous factory trawlers."

Stevens also complained that the final deal did not exempt defense spending from a 0.2 percent across-the-board cut in previously agreed-upon discretionary spending.

The Final CR

To make sure the government keeps running uninterrupted, the House and Senate by voice vote Dec. 15 cleared a continuing resolution (H J Res 133) to keep programs operating until Dec. 21, by which time they expect the deal to have been signed into law. It was the 21st such stopgap measure, or CR, produced by Congress since the new budget year began Oct. 1. The last one to face a roll-call vote at the Capitol (H J Res 128) kept the government operating Dec. 8-11. The House passed it 284-37. *(Vote 602, p. H-190)*

Negotiators say the deal began to jell that weekend, in a series of meetings between Obey and House Appropriations Committee Chairman C.W. Bill Young, R-Fla. Those talks were followed by a Dec. 11 meeting between Clinton and the top congressional leaders of both parties. That yielded a spending total for the Labor-HHS package, but it took negotiators the rest of the week to hash out the details.

Hastert said at a Dec. 14 news conference that he believed the delay in settling the winner of the presidential election kept Congress from finishing its work sooner. Both parties were "posturing to make sure that their president or candidate would have the best advantage in whatever happens in this budget," Hastert said. "I think probably Monday when we met with the president, the indications were that this thing was going to be over one way or another very soon, and it was time to move."

Sen. Larry E. Craig, R-Idaho, said he encouraged the leadership before the election to delay final action on the Labor-HHS bill in hopes that it might strengthen the hand of congressional Republicans. "I, quite early on," said Craig, "urged the leadership to look at a lame duck [session] if necessary, because I believed that ultimately a lame duck would . . . decrease the ability of the president to leverage us. I think that's probably happened to some extent."

Rep. John E. Sununu, R-N.H., said he believes most rank-and-file members were ready the entire week to accept the product of their leaders' negotiations and go home. "I think that over the last few days, whatever came to the floor was going to pass," Sununu said Dec. 15.

High-Speed Funding Derailed

Besides the Alaskan sea lions imbroglio, the other dust-up that briefly appeared to imperil — or at least delay — the package involved another parochial concern: the absence in the bill of a proposal to create a tax credit to assist Amtrak in raising $10 billion to develop additional high-speed train routes. The cost to the government would be $3.3 billion over 10 years, according to the Joint Committee on Taxation.

Senators from the Northeast briefly pledged to fight, then filibuster, the conference agreement, but they relented when they won pledges from Senate leaders of both parties to pursue the idea early in the 107th Congress.

The Amtrak provision — which had made it into a package (HR 2614) that in October was viewed as the wrap-up bill for the year — was among dozens that had traveled far through the legislative maze this year, only to be left on the drafting room floor in the final hours. Negotiators said they received hundreds of request for such add-ons.

One policy rider that survived was an overhaul (HR 4541) of the Commodity Exchange Act to permit the trading of single stock futures, and to clarify the rules for a type of over-the-counter derivative known as a swap. Securities industry executives have warned that if the measure is not enacted they will lose business to foreign exchanges.

Another reauthorizes the Even Start family literacy program for five years, making it among the few programs under the 1965 Elementary and Secondary Education Act reauthorized in the 106th Congress. The Even Start provision keeps most of the structural changes in the House-passed version (HR 3222), including more state oversight and better training for instructors, but it drops a controversial "charitable choice" provision that would have allowed faith-based literacy programs to receive federal funds.

Another provision, pushed by Senate Commerce Committee Chairman John McCain, R-Ariz., and Rep. Ernest Istook, R-Okla., would require schools to have Internet filtering devices or software on their computer networks to block access to pornography in order to receive federal funding for high-speed Internet service and technology purchases. The provision faces a likely challenge from the American Civil Liberties Union as a violation of the constitutional protection of free speech.

The package includes $50 million in research funding to find ways to prevent medical errors. This increase, for the Agency for Healthcare Research and Quality, was the only medical error initiative Republicans and Democrats could agree on this year, but the debate over other steps to reduce the number of mistakes is sure to resurface next year.

Many more provisions were left out. Among them:

- **Minimum wage.** Republicans acknowledge that many members of their conference support increasing the minimum wage but say this issue will have to wait until next year. Both the House and Senate had passed bills to raise the wage by $1, although on different timetables.
- **Ergonomics.** The bill was silent on one of the biggest controversies that derailed the October agreement: the rules to limit repetitive motion injuries in the workplace, issued by the Occupational Safety and Health Administration. Republicans were trying to add language that would allow the new president to kill the rule, which is strongly opposed by employers, but decided to save their repeal efforts for the 107th Congress.
- **Middle East funds.** An administration request for $750 million in emergency funds for Israel, Jordan and Egypt was never seriously considered for inclusion.
- **Child support.** Nancy L. Johnson, R-Conn., and Benjamin L. Cardin, D-Md., pushed unsuccessfully to attach their House-passed bill (HR 4678) that would allow low-income parents to keep more of the child support that is collected by state agencies. The bill will probably resurface next year when Congress turns to the reauthorization of the 1996 welfare overhaul (PL 104-193).
- **Genetic testing.** The bill excluded two provisions in the Senate version of the Labor-HHS bill that would have prevented the use of genetic

testing to discriminate against people when they apply for jobs or health insurance coverage.

In the Fine Print: Faith-Based Groups Get Funds For Drug Addicts

JANUARY 6, 2001— Giant spending packages that are the finales for so many congressional sessions almost always serve as vehicles — in some cases, hiding places — for dozens of the narrow but fervent wishes of lawmakers. These measures are generally so cumbersome, and so hastily cobbled together, that even the people most closely involved in the drafting are sometimes surprised days or weeks later to learn of items that have wormed their way in.

The legislation that ended the 106th Congress was no exception. Pork-barrel politicking, as always, provided part of the filler, but some important policy changes were included along with some amusingly narrow items.

President Clinton signed the bill (HR 4577 — PL 106-554) on Dec. 21, six days after it had been unveiled in its final form to Congress, which cleared it within hours. The law is the final word on four of the fiscal 2001 appropriations measures: Labor-HHS-Education, Commerce-Justice-State (CJS), Treasury-Postal Service and the legislative branch. In addition, it provides a significant boost in federal payments to Medicare providers and enacts a community renewal initiative embraced by both the president and House Speaker J. Dennis Hastert, R-Ill.

Among the other provisions in the package:

- **Religious help.** For the first time, faith-based organizations will be allowed to receive federal funds to provide substance abuse treatment. If a person seeking treatment objects to the religious nature of the program, the administering agency will be required to provide an alternative. Administrators of federal treatment funds are barred from demanding that a treatment facility change its governance, or remove religious symbols or art.
- **Federal retirement benefits.** A 0.5 percent increase in contributions required from participants in the federal employment retirement system was rolled back. The increase was enacted in the budget-balancing law (PL 105-33) of four years ago. *(1997 Almanac, p. 2-47)*
- **Snowmobiles.** The law bars the National Park Service from enforcing a new rule banning the use of snowmobiles in national parks until July 31, giving the incoming Bush administration time to decide whether to alter or block the rule. A similar proposal was considered, but ultimately dropped, in the debate on the fiscal 2001 Interior appropriations law (PL 106-291).
- **Candidate flights.** The law dropped Republican language in the House version of the Treasury-Postal Service measure to require congressional candidates to report their use of government aircraft for campaign trips, an essentially moot point given that the bill was cleared after the election to the Senate of first lady Hillary Rodham Clinton, D-N.Y.
- **Gambling.** The law bars gaming on cruise ships that depart from and return to Hawaii, a provision that Sen. John McCain, R-Ariz., described as a special favor for the one company, American Classic Voyages, that operates out of the state but does not have gambling on board.
- **Diamonds.** A prohibition on the importation of "conflict diamonds" — those used to finance wars — from several African nations was stripped from the CJS bill that Congress had cleared earlier. Clinton signed that legislation (PL 106 —553) after that and several other changes were made, particularly on immigration policy.
- **Computer donations.** The law extends through 2003 the tax deductions for computers donated to schools and expands the program to include business donations to libraries and to allow the write-off for machines as old as three years.
- **Water projects.** The bill contains a long list of water projects demanded by outgoing House Transportation Committee Chairman Bud Shuster, R-Pa. He had pledged to fight enactment of the Florida Everglades restoration measure (PL 106-541) unless he got his way on a list of water and sewer projects totaling almost $400 million. Shuster dropped his opposition to the Everglades bill after getting assurances from House leaders that his projects would be funded.
- **Other projects.** The fiscal 2001 appropriations law (PL 106-377) for veterans, housing, environmental and space programs included more than $1 billion in earmarks for 1,183 pet projects, but apparently the list did not satisfy all lawmakers. The wrap-up law provides $66 million more for 74 additional community economic development projects.
- **Capital real estate.** A $5,000 tax credit for first-time home buyers in Washington, D.C., was extended through 2003.
- **Secret Service.** The organization that investigates counterfeiting and protects the president, his family, former presidents and foreign dignitaries was given an unusually large spending increase of 20 percent, to $833 million.
- **Small Business Administration.** Virtually all the existing programs of the agency were reauthorized through fiscal 2003. The per-loan guarantee limit was raised to $1 million, from $750,000. A new program was created to strengthen the technological competitiveness of small businesses.
- **Condoms.** The Health and Human Services Department was ordered to study condom labels to determine if their information about condoms' ability to prevent sexually transmitted diseases are accurate.
- **Alternative health.** The law provides $89 million for the National Center for Complementary and Alternative Medicine, and encourages the center to study the health benefits of cranberry juice because "the conferees are aware of the health benefits of cranberries and cranberry juice products in maintaining urinary tract health." ◆

Appropriations Mileposts

Fiscal 2001
(as of December 16, 2000)

Bill	House	Senate	Final
Agriculture (HR 4461 — conference report: H Rept 106-948)	Adopted conference report on HR 4461 10/11/00	Cleared HR 4461 10/18/00	President signed (PL 106-387) 10/28/00
Commerce-Justice-State (HR 4942 — conference report: H Rept 106-1005)	Adopted conference report on HR 4942 10/26/00	Cleared HR 4942 10/27/00	President signed (PL 106-553) 12/21/00
Defense (HR 4576 — conference report: H Rept 106-754)	Adopted conference report on HR 4576 7/19/00	Cleared HR 4576 7/27/00	President signed (PL 106-259) 8/9/00
District of Columbia (HR 5633)	Passed HR 5633 11/14/00	Cleared HR 5633 11/14/00	President signed (PL 106-522) 11/22/00
Energy, Water Development (HR 4635 — conference report: H Rept 106-988)	Adopted conference report on HR 4635 10/19/00	Cleared HR 4635 10/19/00	President signed (PL 106-377) 10/27/00
Foreign Operations (HR 4811 — conference report: H Rept 106-997)	Adopted conference report on HR 4811 10/25/00	Cleared HR 4811 10/25/00	President signed (PL 106-429) 11/6/00
Interior (HR 4578 — conference report: H Rept 106-914)	Adopted conference report on HR 4578 10/3/00	Cleared HR 4578 10/5/00	President signed (PL 106-291) 10/11/00
Labor-HHS-Education (HR 4577 — conference report: H Rept 106-1033)	Adopted conference report on HR 4577 12/15/00	Cleared HR 4577 12/15/00	President signed (PL 106-554) 12/21/00
Legislative Branch (HR 4577 — conference report: H Rept 106-1033)	Adopted conference report on HR 4577 12/15/00	Cleared HR 4577 12/15/00	President signed (PL 106-554) 12/21/00
Military Construction (HR 4425 — conference report: H Rept 106-710)	Adopted conference report on HR 4425 6/29/00	Cleared HR 4425 6/30/00	President signed (PL 106-246) 7/13/00
Transportation (HR 4475 — conference report: H Rept 106-940)	Adopted conference report on HR 4475 10/6/00	Cleared HR 4475 10/6/00	President signed (PL 106-346) 10/23/00
Treasury-Postal Service (HR 4577 — conference report: H Rept 106-1033)	Adopted conference report on HR 4577 12/15/00	Cleared HR 4577 12/15/00	President signed (PL 106-554) 12/21/00
VA-HUD (HR 4635 — conference report: H Rept 106-988)	Adopted conference report on HR 4635 10/19/00	Cleared HR 4635 10/19/00	President signed (PL 106-377) 10/27/00
21st Fiscal 2001 Continuing Appropriations (H J Res 133)	Passed H J Res 133 12/15/00	Cleared H J Res133 12/15/00	President signed (PL 106-543) 12/15/00

Agriculture Spending Bill Sparks Fiery Debate On International Sanctions

SUMMARY

Lawmakers grudgingly resolved their differences on the fiscal 2001 agriculture appropriations bill, which had been stalled for months by controversies over drug re-importation and provisions to ease economic sanctions against Cuba and other countries. They added $3.6 billion in emergency aid to farmers before sending the $78.5 billion bill to President Clinton, who signed it Oct. 28.

Traditionally one of the least controversial appropriations bills, the agriculture measure became a vehicle for fiery rhetoric reminiscent of the Cold War era after farm-state Republicans added language by Rep. George Nethercutt, R-Wash., to remove sanctions on food and medicine exports to Cuba, Iran, Libya, North Korea and Sudan.

Democrats joined many of the GOP rank and file in forcing a showdown with conservative Republican House leaders, most notably Majority Whip Tom DeLay, R-Texas, and Cuban-born Republican Reps. Lincoln Diaz-Balart and Ileana Ros-Lehtinen of Florida, who staunchly oppose improving ties with the communist regime of Fidel Castro.

After months of negotiations — some of which played out during the dispute over repatriating 7-year-old Cuban shipwreck victim Elián González — the sides compromised, allowing exports but barring public or private U.S. financing of Cuban agricultural purchases. The final bill language, crafted by House Republican leaders, also codified travel restrictions, previously implemented by executive order, that prevent most Americans from visiting Cuba. Because the language is contained in an annual spending bill, it amounts to a one-year travel ban that could be renewed or struck in the fiscal 2002 bill.

Concern over rising prescription drug prices led to language in the bill allowing pharmacists and drug wholesalers to re-import U.S. prescription drugs that are sold abroad for less than they cost in the United States. Previously, only drugmakers could re-import the products.

Republicans saw the provision, by Sen. James M. Jeffords, R-Vt., as preferable to creating a defined Medicare drug benefit. Democrats decried the final compromise — again brokered by the House Republican leadership — charging it contained language that could be exploited by drugmakers to keep prices high. Clinton strongly criticized the drug language but stopped short of threatening to veto the bill.

The final bill also lifted two caps that restricted participation in the food stamp program, providing more generous exemptions for housing costs and car ownership. The changes are expected to allow approximately 500,000 people who currently do not qualify for the program to receive food stamps, at a cost of about $1.6 billion over five years.

Another provision, by Sen. Robert C. Byrd, D-W.Va., redirected tens of millions of dollars in anti-dumping duties and countervailing tariffs assessed on foreign companies to "injured parties" in the United States instead of the U.S. Treasury. Byrd said the amendment will help small agricultural producers, but critics complained it is just as likely to help the domestic steel industry and its unions.

The bill's $3.6 billion in emergency spending includes $1.1 billion for forest firefighting efforts and cleanup in Western states. The measure also contains provisions to aid dairy farmers, apple, citrus and potato producers, cranberry growers, beekeepers and the wool and mohair industry.

The bill provided $9.5 billion for child nutrition programs, $1.7 billion for crop insurance, $1.3 billion for farm assistance and $873 million for conservation programs.

Box Score — Agriculture — 2001 Fiscal Year

- **Bill:** HR 4461 — PL 106-387
- **Legislative action: House** passed HR 4461 (H Rept 106-619), 339-82, on July 11.

Senate passed HR 4461, 79-13, on July 20, after substituting the text of S 2536 (S Rept 106-288).

House adopted the conference report (H Rept 106-948), 340-75, on Oct. 11.

Senate cleared the bill, 86-8, on Oct. 18.

President signed HR 4461 on Oct. 28.

Bills Advance Quickly in Both Chambers

MAY 6 — The agriculture spending bill lived up to its reputation for fast starts May 4, winning approval from both the House and Senate Agriculture Appropriations subcommittees the same day.

The House Agriculture Appropriations Subcommittee approved, by voice vote, a $75.1 billion draft fiscal 2001 spending measure for agriculture, rural development, and food and nutrition programs, including $14.4 billion in discretionary spending. The full committee is scheduled to mark up the bill May 10.

Hours later, the Senate Agriculture Appropriations Subcommittee approved, by voice vote, a $75.3 billion draft spending package that includes $14.8 billion for discretionary spending. The full Senate committee has scheduled a May 9 markup of the legislation.

For all of that, floor fights are likely over spending priorities and riders dealing with such issues as international sanctions, egg safety, child nutrition programs and government research.

"You're attaching items that you know blessed well will invite a veto . . . and I will watch with interest,"

David R. Obey, D-Wis., ranking member of the House Appropriations Committee, warned Republicans during debate on a GOP-sponsored amendment to block money from being used to implement the 1997 Kyoto protocol on global warming. The amendment was adopted, 9-6, along party lines.

The pace reflected lawmakers' desire to move quickly on legislation that usually is free of the kind of partisan riders that can stall other spending bills.

The Clinton administration had requested $76.8 billion in new budget authority for agriculture this year, including $15.5 billion in discretionary spending. Both House and Senate appropriators dismissed the possibility of matching the request because of tight congressional budget caps.

"This is the toughest allocation we've faced since I've been chairman," said Joe Skeen, R-N.M., who heads the House Agriculture Appropriations panel.

Both panels focused most of their attention on a series of special-interest provisions that are likely to spark more debate as the bills move to full committee and floor action.

Chief among them is a proposal to exempt exports of food and medicine from current and future U.S. sanctions. Farm-state lawmakers, with the support of business and agriculture groups, argue that sanctions deprive U.S. exporters of access to overseas markets, including Cuba, North Korea and Iran. A Senate-passed provision that would have rolled back sanctions was dropped last year from the fiscal 2000 agriculture spending bill in conference.

The House Appropriations subcommittee accepted, by voice vote, an amendment offered by George Nethercutt, R-Wash., that would unilaterally lift medical and agricultural sanctions on certain countries, including Cuba. The approval came despite concerns from some lawmakers that Congress should not be dealing with trade and foreign policy through appropriations bills. Staunch foes of Cuban leader Fidel Castro are expected to strenuously oppose the effort, which comes in the midst of the Elián González custody case.

"I feel this is critically important," Nethercutt said, acknowledging the prospect for a heated floor fight. "This would open commodity markets around the world, valued at $7 billion. There is no reason they should be closed to farmers."

Democrat Byron L. Dorgan of North Dakota echoed those sentiments in the Senate Appropriations subcommittee, saying he would work with John Ashcroft, R-Mo., and Christopher J. Dodd, D-Conn., to revive a similar Senate provision. The Senate panel did not include sanctions language in its draft bill.

House appropriators also accepted an amendment that would impose restrictions on a Clinton administration proposal to increase the testing of eggs for salmonella bacteria. The amendment, offered by Jack Kingston, R-Ga., was accepted by a 10-5 vote; it would bar federal regulators from removing eggs from the market unless salmonella was found on the eggs themselves. The Clinton administration plan calls for pasteurizing or removing eggs if salmonella is found anywhere on the farm or facility where the eggs were produced.

The House panel offered a break to citrus producers by accepting, on a voice vote, an amendment by Allen Boyd, D-Fla., that would change the way the government reimburses growers from losses caused by citrus canker. The blight caused the destruction of some 180,000 orange and grapefruit trees between 1995 and 1999. Current policy reimburses growers only for the cost of the tree.

The change would require the Department of Agriculture (USDA) to take lost production into account, too. Separate money for citrus canker-related losses is included in the stalled fiscal 2000 supplemental spending measure.

Another House-accepted amendment, offered by Henry Bonilla, R-Texas, and accepted by voice vote, would place legislative conditions on USDA rules that permit school lunch programs to replace meat with soyburgers, tofu and other soy products. The amendment, backed by the meat industry, would require the soy products to be fortified with iron and zinc and mandate that lunch programs inform children when lunch items contain significant amounts of soy. The National Cattlemen's Beef Association contends that meat products that have soy added to them could damage beef's reputation.

The House Appropriations subcommittee also approved an amendment by Jo Ann Emerson, R-Mo., that would bar funding for implementing Kyoto protocol measures that are not found anywhere in U.S. law, including carbon emissions trading programs. Emerson said the language was necessary because the Clinton administration has repeatedly flouted congressional bans on implementing the 1997 treaty, which has never been submitted to the Senate for approval.

"It gives better direction on what taxpayer money can and cannot do for implementation of the treaty," Emerson said.

However, angry Democrats accused Emerson and other Republicans of trying to implement scientific conclusions in a spending bill. Maurice D. Hinchey, D-N.Y., said the language also could be at odds with existing clean air laws.

No such amendment was offered in the Senate Appropriations subcommittee. However, Chairman Thad Cochran, R-Miss., said it was likely that he and other members would offer amendments at the May 9 full committee markup.

Panels Approve Bills After Debates On Tobacco Suits, Foreign Sanctions

MAY 13 — The agriculture appropriations bill became the vehicle for heated debates over tobacco litigation and international sanctions the week of May 8, as Senate and House Appropriations committees approved rival versions of the fiscal 2001 spending plan.

The Senate Appropriations Committee on May 9 approved, by voice vote, a $75.3 billion bill (S 2536) for agriculture, rural development and food and nutrition programs that includes $14.8 billion in discretionary spending.

The Senate panel added $1.4 billion in fiscal 2000 "emergency" spending for agricultural disasters, part of a package of supplemental funds that was added to three fiscal 2001 appropriations bills. *(Supplemental, p. 2-162)*

The following day the House Appropriations Committee gave voice vote approval to a $75.4 billion spending bill that includes $14.5 billion in discretionary spending.

For some two hours, members debated a provision that would lift economic sanctions to allow shipments of food and medicine to countries accused of sponsoring terrorism. Despite efforts by House Majority Whip Tom DeLay, R-Texas, and some other conservative Republicans, the language was retained. The Senate version contains similar language.

The rancor over sanctions and a number of other provisions during the two committee markups portends more fights as the bills move to the floors of their respective chambers, probably the week of May 15.

Some fiscal conservatives are expected to question whether all of the emergency spending in the Senate bill really is for emergencies, and whether it could force reductions in other farm payments because of tight budget caps. "At some point, even for agriculture, enough is enough," said Senate Budget Committee Chairman Pete V. Domenici, R-N.M., who is also a member of the Appropriations panel.

Significant parts of the supplemental agriculture emergency spending package include $450 million for livestock assistance, $443 million for dairy assistance, $80 million for rural community facilities, and $50 million for water and waste facilities.

Debate Over Funds Transfer

Much of the debate during the Senate markup centered on a Republican-backed provision that would prevent the Department of Justice from receiving money from other federal agencies to help it press its lawsuit against the tobacco industry to recover the government's costs of treating smoking-related illnesses.

An amendment by Ernest F. Hollings, D-S.C., to strike the language failed, 11-14, along party lines, after Democrats accused Republicans of using the provision to protect the tobacco industry. Hollings said denying the funds could jeopardize the Justice Department's case and hinder prosecution of other government lawsuits.

"This is a highly unusual initiative," he said. "I want to continue the tobacco case, and you don't want to do it."

"This has nothing to do with the tobacco case," Appropriations Committee Chairman Ted Stevens, R-Alaska, angrily responded. "[The Justice Department] had no right to take money Congress appropriated for other purposes."

The language in the bill would repeal a provision in the fiscal 1995 Commerce-Justice-State appropriations bill (PL 103-317) stating that, in high-cost cases, Justice can draw funds from governmental agencies represented in the action. *(1994 CQ Almanac, p. 483)*

Stevens said the measure was intended strictly to reimburse the Justice Department for defending various agencies. He accused the department of flouting the intent of the bill's language by ordering the departments of Defense, Veterans Affairs, and Health and Human Services since September to pay a total of $10 million to pursue the tobacco case. Democrats, including Richard J. Durbin of Illinois and Frank R. Lautenberg of New Jersey, said the department had acted appropriately.

Senate Republicans were united on the transfer of funds, but the issue of international sanctions is dividing GOP lawmakers in both chambers and could become the focus of a floor fight over whether such language belongs in either appropriations bill.

DeLay offered an amendment during the House Appropriations markup to strip the bill of language that would unilaterally lift medical and agricultural sanctions on Cuba, North Korea, Libya, Iran and Sudan.

The language, first offered by George Nethercutt, R-Wash., and adopted by the House Agriculture Appropriations Subcommittee on May 4, enjoys bipartisan support, particularly from farm-state lawmakers whose constituents have been hurt by low commodity prices and are seeking new markets.

Similar language was offered in the Senate Appropriations Committee on May 9 by Byron L. Dorgan, D-N.D., and was adopted with little debate.

"I believe in exporting American values. I strongly support expanded trade . . . but trade is not a moral imperative superior to all other considerations," said DeLay, who succeeded last year in stripping similar language out of the fiscal 2000 agriculture appropriations bill.

Nethercutt and others argued that withholding food and medicine was an inappropriate and lamentable foreign policy tool. Democrats also criticized DeLay for supporting tough sanctions against nations such as Cuba while supporting permanent normal trade relations with China. DeLay's amendment was rejected, 24-35.

The sanctions issue is expected to resurface during floor debate on the bill's spending measures. Several lawmakers said Republican leaders may raise a point of order to block a vote on the provision, arguing that an appropriations bill is not the proper legislative vehicle for such policy matters.

Senate Foreign Relations Committee Chairman Jesse Helms, R-N.C., raised that prospect in a May 10 letter to his House counterpart, International Relations Committee Chairman Benjamin A. Gilman, R-N.Y., stating, "I wish to reiterate my insistence that any 'sanctions reform' measure must be considered only as part of an authorization bill."

The House Appropriations Committee also:

- Rejected, 20-24, an amendment by Rosa DeLauro, D-Conn., to add $14.4 million for the Department of Agriculture's Food Safety and Inspection Service. The amendment was in response to Republican efforts to impose legislative conditions on a new Clinton administration proposal for egg safety.
- Adopted, 26-22, an amendment by Maurice D. Hinchey, D-N.Y., and James T. Walsh, R-N.Y., that would provide $115 million in emergency payments to apple and potato growers.
- Adopted, 25-23, another Hinchey amendment that would provide $57 million in new budget authority for the Agriculture Department's Rural Community Advancement Program.

Fight Over Cuba Sanctions Delays Action

MAY 27 — A showdown over whether to continue trade sanctions against Cuba and a series of procedural disputes halted progress on the fiscal 2001 agriculture appropriations bill in the House and Senate the week of May 22, dashing lawmakers' hopes of approving either version of the measure before the Memorial Day recess.

House Republican leaders May 25 deferred action on the spending measure (HR 4461) by pulling a rule (H Res 513) designed to kill a controversial provision that proposed allowing food and medicine sales to Cuba, Iran, Libya, North Korea and Sudan.

The provision, sponsored by George Nethercutt, R-Wash., is opposed by Republican leaders, who favor keeping sanctions in place, especially in the case of Cuba. However, many Democrats and farm-state Republicans support the measure, either on humanitarian grounds or because they think it will open up new markets for American farmers hurt by low commodities prices.

House GOP leaders "are not giving us a fair shake," Nethercutt said in a May 25 interview. "I think it's the will of the House and the will of the country to have this policy change."

A 'Cuba Carve-Out'

House Majority Leader Dick Armey, R-Texas, indicated that there could be a number of solutions to the impasse, including adoption of "Cuba carve-out" language that would lift sanctions on the other four nations but leave intact those imposed on Cuba.

"We're continuing to work on a variety of approaches," Armey told reporters May 23. "We need to sit down with the principals and have a heartfelt discussion."

While the sanctions language is less controversial in the Senate, progress on the agriculture spending bill (S 2536) in that chamber was also halted by broader disputes over judicial and executive nominations and by the insistence of Minority Leader Tom Daschle, D-S.D., that the Senate act only on House-passed spending measures.

Both the House and Senate are expected to turn their attention back to the agriculture bill the week of June 5. The House version would designate $75.4 billion for agriculture, rural development, food and nutrition programs, including $14.5 billion in discretionary spending. The Senate version calls for $75.3 billion in total spending, including $14.8 billion in discretionary accounts.

The Senate bill contains its share of controversial provisions, including Republican-backed language that would prevent the Justice Department from receiving money from other federal agencies to help press its lawsuit against the tobacco industry seeking to recover the government's costs of treating smoking-related illnesses.

The Senate bill also includes $1.3 billion in fiscal 2000 "emergency" spending for agricultural disasters, part of a package of supplemental funds that was added to three fiscal 2001 appropriations bills.

The lack of progress on the fiscal 2001 agriculture spending bill in the House can be partly attributed to GOP leaders' focus on maintaining party discipline for the much-watched May 24 vote to grant permanent normal trading privileges to China.

The Republican majority did not have time to poll its members on the sanctions issue, and congressional staff aides said May 25 that they were only beginning to turn their attention to whip counts.

Procedural Hurdle

Nonetheless, the House leadership tried to erect a major procedural hurdle to the Nethercutt provision on the night of May 24, when the Rules Committee reported a rule that would have allowed the sanctions language to be dropped from the bill without a vote. House leaders pulled the rule the next morning as they rushed to finish a series of bills before the Memorial Day recess.

Sanctions on Cuba have become an especially volatile issue in the wake of the furor surrounding the Elián González case and whether the 6-year-old Cuban boy should be granted political asylum or returned to Cuba with his father.

House Majority Whip Tom DeLay, R-Texas, most notably, has argued that expanding trade to totalitarian regimes such as Fidel Castro's is morally unacceptable, and other congressional leaders have expressed reservations about incorporating significant policy decisions in spending bills. But an amendment by DeLay to remove the sanctions language in the House Appropriations Committee was rejected May 10, 24-35.

Nethercutt said May 25 that although he initially was inclined to support a compromise, he now insists on a stand-alone vote for his provision. He cited independent vote tallies in various media indicating that he could have as many as 280 supporters.

"We've been talking to our allies and have been receiving a lot of encouragement and support for defeating the rule," Nethercutt said, adding that he has not spoken directly to House GOP leaders since the week of May 15.

In a symbolic show of support, three senators who inserted a provision nearly identical to Nethercutt's in the Senate agriculture appropriations bill issued a statement saying they would continue fighting for the proposal. Senators voted against tabling a motion to lift the sanctions last year, but House Republican leaders succeeded in removing that language during the conference on the fiscal 2000 agriculture spending bill.

"We want it understood that it is our intent to wage an aggressive fight to eliminate all sanctions on food and medicine now," Sens. Byron L. Dorgan, D-N.D., John Ashcroft, R-Mo., and Slade Gorton, R-Wash., said in a May 24 statement.

Offsets a Problem

Offsets are another issue hindering progress on the agriculture bill. The rule for the appropriations measure established budgetary offsets for $115 million in emergency payments to apple and potato growers that were approved by the House Appropriations Committee on May 10. However, Democrats on the appropriations panel complained that the offsets would cut the number of acres that could be enrolled in the federal wetlands reserve program.

The offsets would also cut $24 million from the Department of Agriculture's Rural Community Advancement Program, reduce Food and Drug Administration salaries and expenses by $14 million, and trim $5 million for agricultural inspections at border crossings.

David R. Obey of Wisconsin, the ranking Democrat on the House Appropriations Committee, said the cuts, combined with the Rules Committee's procedural maneuvering on the sanctions issue, would stoke Democratic opposition to the bill.

"There are a lot of reasons this bill has problems," he said in a May 25 interview. Obey said he would probably offer an amendment on the House floor that would add $13.7 million to the bill to investigate market concentration and anti-competitive behavior in agriculture industries.

House Debate Centers on Sugar Price Supports

JULY 1 — The fiscal 2001 agriculture appropriations bill became the field for a House battle over the government's sugar price-support program June 29, but sugar-state lawmakers were able to block on procedural grounds an effort to limit the U.S. subsidies for domestic growers.

The nearly two-hour-long debate punctuated a day of slow deliberations over the long-stalled spending measure (HR 4461). Lawmakers also sparred over a passel of amendments dealing with issues such as government efforts to control pests and diseases and the merits of bioengineered crops.

Debate over the agriculture bill was halted so the House could consider other pressing business before lawmakers returned to their districts for the July Fourth recess. House Majority Leader Dick Armey, R-Texas, said the bill will come back to the floor "at a later time."

As approved by the House Appropriations Committee, the bill would provide $75.4 billion for agriculture, rural development and food and nutrition programs, including $14.5 billion in discretionary spending. A Senate version (S 2536 – S Rept 106-288), approved by that chamber's Appropriations Committee, would provide $75.3 billion in spending, including $14.8 billion in discretionary spending authority.

The House debate largely left intact the spending priorities that were approved by House Appropriations on May 10. The bill faces a threatened veto from the Clinton administration, which contends that would underfund critical programs in areas such as food safety, conservation and environmental programs.

The House approved only $6 million of the administration's $28 million request for Agriculture Department food inspection efforts and approved a $26 million cut to the Environmental Quality Incentives Program, which helps farmers and ranchers improve their operations and comply with clean water laws.

The White House also objects to Republican language in the bill that would bar funding for implementing provisions of the Kyoto protocol on climate change that are not found anywhere in U.S. law, as well as language that would weaken a Clinton administration initiative to strengthen the testing of eggs for salmonella.

Action on the agriculture bill had been delayed for more than a month as farm-state lawmakers and House GOP leaders argued over a provision authored by George Nethercutt, R-Wash., to lift food and medicine sanctions on Cuba and four other "rogue" nations. The leaders were intent on keeping the sanctions in place but could not muster enough votes to overcome a coalition of Democrats and farm-state Republicans who favored the language on humanitarian grounds and because it could open new export markets.

The bill was cleared for general debate after the House the night of June 28 adopted, 232-179, a rule (H Res 538) allowing the language to be removed on a point of order and inserted later into the House-Senate agriculture conference report. *(Vote 358, p. H-112)*

Sugar Debate

Under the sugar program, which has become a perennial point of contention in agriculture spending debates, the government sets a high price on sugar, as well as quotas on imported sugar, to guarantee U.S. producers a certain price on their crop. The program supports both sugar cane growers in the South and Hawaii at 18 cents per pound, and sugar beet growers in the upper Midwest at 22 cents.

The purchases have led to discrepancies between domestic and world sugar prices. Currently, world sugar prices on commodity markets range from 8 to 9 cents per pound, while U.S. prices hover between 18 and 19 cents per pound.

Program supporters used a point of order that prohibits legislative language on an appropriations bill to strike an amendment by Dan Miller, R-Fla., to limit Agriculture Department purchases of raw or refined sugar to $54 million — the amount spent on sugar purchases in fiscal 2000. But the unsuccessful language sparked a prolonged floor debate over the purchases, a practice last authorized in the 1996 farm bill (PL 104-127). *(1996 Almanac, p. 3-15)*

Miller and other critics, such as Barney Frank, D-Mass., denounced the program as a way of propping up prices for well-heeled sugar cane and beet planters. They argued that the purchases also encourage overproduction of sugar cane and consequent environmental damage from agricultural runoff in the Florida Everglades.

"What is it about sugar that repels the free-market ethic?" Frank asked, complaining that cranberry product manufacturers in his state, such as Ocean Spray Cranberries Inc., were being hurt by artificially high sugar prices. "Is sugar some alien substance that repels the concept of demand and supply?"

Miller and Frank cited a recent General Accounting Office report estimating that the sugar purchases cost consumers $1.9 billion in 1990.

But sugar-state lawmakers, such as David Minge, D-Minn., and Earl Pomeroy, D-N.D., questioned that figure and argued that price supports were consistent with other recent government action to aid distressed farmers, such as purchases of surplus wheat and assistance to dairy producers. They also depicted the vast majority of sugar producers as small and midsize farmers.

"It's about family farmers struggling to hang on," said Pomeroy, whose state is a prime sugar-beet producing region. Pomeroy argued that limiting purchases would lead to a glut of foreign sugar entering U.S. markets, which in turn would bring about price volatility.

Blight Money

In other action, House Republicans succeeded in striking on a point of order an amendment by Marcy Kaptur of Ohio, ranking Democrat on the Appropriations Agriculture, Rural Development, FDA and Related Agencies Subcommittee, that would increase funding for the Agriculture Department's Animal and Plant Health Inspection Service by $53 million, the level in President Clinton's fiscal 2001 budget request. GOP lawmakers objected be-

GOP Leaders Yield on Cuba Sanctions

JULY 1 — Facing certain defeat, House Republican leaders have agreed to ease nearly four decades of sanctions against Fidel Castro, accepting a provision that would allow food and medicine sales to Cuba and four other unfriendly nations.

After nearly six hours of haggling that lasted into the early hours of June 27, GOP leaders accepted a compromise on language offered by George Nethercutt, R-Wash., as part of the fiscal 2001 agriculture appropriations bill (HR 4461). Supporters, chiefly farm-state lawmakers, said the change would open agricultural markets worth about $7 billion per year.

The language would lift sanctions on sales of food and medicine to Cuba, North Korea, Libya, Sudan and Iran. But at the insistence of Cuban-American lawmakers, the deal would deny Cuba eligibility for U.S. bank loans or government credits to finance purchases. And the import ban on Cuban goods, such as cigars and sugar, would remain in place.

"This is a fundamental shift in U.S. foreign policy and a new day for agriculture," Nethercutt said at a June 27 news conference. "This July Fourth, our farmers will have a new independence day to celebrate."

Republican Reps. Lincoln Diaz-Balart and Ileana Ros-Lehtinen of Florida also claimed victory because they succeeded in getting an agreement to write into law existing restrictions on travel to Cuba by U.S. citizens. Federal rules currently limit travel to certain groups, such as religious leaders, musicians and journalists. "This agreement is much better for us than current law. No credits for Castro, and no tourism either," Ros-Lehtinen said.

To get the agriculture appropriations bill moving, Republican leaders promised to find a new vehicle for the Nethercutt language. Their first preference was a supplemental spending package that was added to the conference report on the fiscal 2001 military construction spending bill (HR 4425).

But procedural wrangling and a threatened Senate filibuster made it more likely that they will add Nethercutt's language to the conference report on the agriculture bill in negotiations with the Senate.

Support for lifting sanctions is considerably stronger in the Senate, which voted overwhelmingly last year to add language to its version of the fiscal 2000 agriculture appropriations bill. However, the language was dropped in conference because of opposition from House conservatives led by Majority Whip Tom DeLay, R-Texas.

Bug Smashing

House leaders depicted this year's move as pragmatic, noting that Nethercutt had assembled broad support from farm-state lawmakers and Democrats who long opposed the sanctions on humanitarian grounds. Nethercutt had said he had as many as 280 votes for his measure.

"When people have the votes, people have the votes," said House Majority Leader Dick Armey, R-Texas. "Sometimes you're the windshield, sometimes you're the bug. This time, I'm the bug." DeLay, rebuffed in a May 10 attempt to strip the language out of the bill in the Appropriations Committee, sent Chief Deputy Whip Roy Blunt, R-Mo., to the final negotiations.

The reversal on sanctions marked a major concession for congressional Republicans, who for years beat back attempts by Democrats to improve ties with Castro's regime.

It also gave a boost to the political fortunes of Nethercutt, who is locked in a tough re-election fight in a swing district that is a wheat-producing hub. House GOP leaders, trying to protect their slim six-seat majority, have repeatedly stressed the importance of helping Nethercutt, even as they chafed at his insistence on bringing up the sanctions language. "We would not be here if George had blinked," said John A. Boehner, R-Ohio, a supporter of the sanctions language.

Nethercutt also had support from the U.S. Chamber of Commerce, which has actively lobbied to expand trade with Cuba. Hotel chains, among other businesses, would like access to the country and its expanding tourism.

Sen. Christopher J. Dodd, D-Conn., who last year unsuccessfully tried to attach language to a foreign aid bill to allow Americans to freely travel to Cuba, termed the House deal "a clear-cut case of one hand giving while the other takes away."

President Clinton said at a June 28 White House news conference that he would sign legislation lifting food and medicine sanctions on Cuba, but questioned whether the House-negotiated deal would really lead to increased sales to Cuba and fit with U.S. foreign-policy objectives.

"I don't believe that we can change the law until there is a bipartisan majority which believes that there has been some effort on the part of the Cuban government to reach out to us as well," Clinton said. The White House has argued that Nethercutt's language could hinder future presidents' ability to levy sanctions without the approval of Congress.

Because the language lifting sanctions is part of an appropriations bill, it would have to be renewed each year, raising the prospect of annual floor fights. Nethercutt and his allies see ways around this hurdle, possibly by seeking authorizing language next year from a sympathetic House Agriculture Committee.

Advocates of improving ties may seek to further clarify or expand terms of the deal, perhaps by allowing cash-strapped Cuba to barter for U.S. commodities with sugar, citrus products or rum.

cause the amendment designated the funding as emergency spending, and thus outside the bill's spending caps.

Kaptur said the extra money was necessary because of a series of blights, including citrus canker in Florida, plum pox in Pennsylvania and neighboring states, and a recurrence of bovine tuberculosis in the Midwest. Republicans, such as Tom Latham of Iowa, responded that the Agriculture Department already has the authority to provide money to address some of the problems.

The House also rejected on a point of order an amendment by John F. Tierney, D-Mass., to earmark $500,000 for an Agriculture Department study of the health risks associated with genetically modified foods. Opponents, led by Nick Smith, R-Mich., argued that more studies on the products could stoke consumer fears about their safety.

Tierney said consumers needed assurances that genetically altered crops that make their way into snack foods, cereals and other products do not pose human health risks, such as inducing allergies. He questioned whether Food and Drug Administration guidelines, which allow manufacturers to conduct safety tests, were sufficient.

"We need confidence in these genetically engineered foods. [The study] should tell us what kind of regulatory system we should have," Tierney said.

Smith maintained that recent studies by the National Research Council and the House Science Basic Research Subcommittee, which he chairs, each concluded that genetically modified products do not pose any special human health risks. "I'm concerned that over-regulating would stifle the production of these products," Smith said.

A point of order killed Tierney's proposal as legislative language on a spending bill.

Other Amendments

In other action, the House:

• Adopted, by voice vote, an amendment by Bart Stupak, D-Mich., and Sherwood Boehlert, R-N.Y., to redirect $20 million from an Agriculture Department's international commodity donation program to the department's nutrition program for the elderly, which oversees the popular "Meals on Wheels" program.

Boehlert said the move was necessary because funding for Meals on Wheels has been flat in recent years, despite an increase in the number of indigent elderly people. Kaptur objected to the amendment because it took money away from the so-called PL-480, or "Food for Peace," program, which subsidizes agricultural exports and promotes sustainable agriculture practices in recipient countries.

• Adopted, by voice vote, an amendment by Robin Hayes, R-N.C., to overturn a 1993 ban on using Agriculture Department funds to study medical uses for tobacco. Congress already mandated $3 million for tobacco-related medical research in a crop insurance bill (HR 2559 — H Rept 106-639) that passed both chambers in May.

Hayes pointed to recent developments that have allowed scientists to cultivate proteins in genetically modified tobacco plants for a vaccine to fight cervical cancer. The language would not appropriate additional money for research, but would allow future funding.

• Adopted, by voice vote, an amendment by Marion Berry, D-Ark., to take $693,000 from Agriculture Department salaries to provide technical assistance in resource conservation to farmers. Berry and Charles W. Stenholm, D-Texas, said the move reflected farm-state lawmakers' dissatisfaction with the department for not objecting to a new Environmental Protection Agency plan to clean up polluted waterways.

The plan, known as "Total Maximum Daily Load," requires states to submit strategies to clear up waterways. Landowners along polluted rivers and streams would be required to obtain pollution discharge permits if the EPA determined that they were contributing to environmental problems and that states were not taking adequate steps.

• Rejected, by voice vote, an amendment by Mark Sanford, R-S.C., to cut $14 million from special agricultural research grants. Sanford said the grants go primarily to fund "pork barrel" spending in key lawmakers' districts. Tom Latham, R-Iowa, Nita M. Lowey, D-N.Y., and others defended the grants, saying they helped fund projects on breast cancer prevention and pest control.

• Adopted, by voice vote, an amendment by Eva Clayton, D-N.C., to increase funding for historically black colleges and universities by $6.8 million.

Funding for the colleges has remained flat for the past four years. The amendment would add $4 million to research activities, currently funded at $30.6 million, and $3 million to extension activities, currently funded at $26.8 million.

• Adopted, by voice vote, an amendment by Clayton to earmark $5.4 million of Agriculture Department rural development funds to help provide modular housing for low-income elderly families whose homes were destroyed by Hurricane Floyd.

House Democrats complained that tight congressional budget caps gave short shrift to critical farmer assistance programs in the bill at a time when the U.S. agriculture industry is reeling from low commodities prices.

Subcommittee Chairman Joe Skeen, R-N.M., urged members to support the measure, noting that his panel had made tough but fair funding decisions.

"This bill will deliver benefits to your constituents every day, no matter what kind of district you represent," Skeen said.

House Passes Bill After Sparring Over Food Safety, Environment

JULY 15 — After two months of delays, the House passed the fiscal 2001 agriculture appropriations bill (HR 4461 — H Rept 106-619) on July 11 amid signs the spending package is headed for a contentious House-Senate conference and a possible presidential veto.

The 339-82 vote concluded two days of debate over proposals to ease Food and Drug Administration (FDA) rules for importing drugs and to address rising prescription-drug prices. *(Vote 385, p. H-120)*

Lawmakers also sparred over amendments dealing with the Department of Agriculture's predator control program and the agency's food safety efforts. The House began debating the bill June 29, but cut off deliberations so it could consider other business before the July Fourth recess.

"This bill has a long way to go before it is going to receive a presidential signature," said David R. Obey of Wisconsin, ranking Democrat on the Appropriations Committee. Obey and other Democrats complained that tight congressional budget caps prevented adequate funding of food safety, conservation, rural development and pest control programs.

The White House has signaled that these concerns — plus language in the bill that would modify an administration plan to strengthen egg safety rules and restrict implementation of the Kyoto treaty on global warming and environmental change — are likely to prompt a veto.

The $75.4 billion bill includes $14.5 billion in discretionary spending. The Senate version (S 2536 — S Rept 106-288) would provide $75.3 billion, including $14.8 billion in discretionary spending authority. The Senate is expected to take up its measure later this month.

A provision written by George Nethercutt, R-Wash., that would lift sanctions on food and medicine sales to Cuba and four other unfriendly nations was lifted from the bill, as expected, on a point of order July 10. The procedural move was part of a deal between Nethercutt and House Republican leaders that called for removing the language — which had delayed full House consideration of the bill since it was approved by the House Appropriations Committee on May 10 — and re-inserting it during a House-Senate conference.

Cuban-American lawmakers and GOP leaders strenuously oppose easing any restrictions on the regime of Fidel Castro but find themselves at odds with a large number of farm-state Republicans, whose constituents see the countries in question as potential markets that could generate upwards of $7 billion per year in sales.

Democrats complained the Nethercutt deal was the product of back-room negotiations that avoided any public discussion of the sanctions. About three hours after the sanctions language was removed, Charles B. Rangel, D-N.Y., tried to revive the issue.

He introduced an amendment that would have effectively lifted the sanctions by preventing any money in the appropriations bill from being used to enforce them. "This would allow us to at least do publicly on the House floor what so many said was going to be done privately in the conference," Rangel said. His amendment was struck on a point of order after opponents argued it was not germane.

Support for lifting the sanctions is stronger in the Senate, though Republican leaders in that chamber also have expressed misgivings. Proponents — most notably Byron L. Dorgan, D-N.D., and John Ashcroft, R-Mo. — have vowed to press when they go to conference for more liberalized relations with Cuba than the House agreement contemplates.

Prescription Drug Debate

The House passage June 28 of a GOP bill (HR 4860) to provide prescription drug benefits to seniors prompted lively debate during July 10 consideration of the agriculture bill as lawmakers tried to position themselves on an important election-year issue.

A number of lawmakers recounted stories of border-hopping seniors from their districts who were forced to travel to Canada or Mexico to purchase drugs that cost many times more in the United States. The House adopted two provisions that would make it easier to bring cheaper drugs into the country. They were:

- An amendment by Joseph Crowley, D-N.Y., adopted 363-12, that would overturn FDA prohibitions on U.S. citizens who travel to foreign countries to purchase prescription drugs solely for personal use. *(Vote 375, p. H-118)*
- An amendment by Tom Coburn, R-Okla., adopted 370-12, that would prevent the use of federal money to issue FDA warning notices discouraging the importation of drugs that are legally available in the United States. *(Vote 377, p. H-118)*

The Food, Drug and Cosmetic Act of 1938 prohibits the re-importation of American-made prescription drugs. The FDA sometimes sends warning letters to individuals caught in the act by Customs officials, but the agency has the discretion to look the other way if the drugs are intended for personal use and not for resale.

"Everybody in this country is paying too much for drugs," said Coburn, a physician. "This is a small step that would help. It is not even one of the major ones."

Crowley said a drug-pricing survey he conducted in his Queens, N.Y., district found serious discrepancies between what consumers pay in the United States and elsewhere. Typical, he said, was a constituent who paid nearly $400 for a three-month supply of the popular anti-heartburn drug Prilosec that could be purchased for $107 in Mexico and $184 in Canada.

Opponents of the amendments raised concerns that the two proposals could undercut FDA efforts to track drug safety and create the impression that all drugs purchased on foreign soil are safe.

The agency itself said the amendments could compromise its ability to protect consumers. "We have concerns that steps like this may undermine the agency's ability to protect against substandard, counterfeit and poorly manufactured drugs," FDA spokesman Brad Stone said in a July 12 interview.

Two other provisions dealing with prescription drugs were withdrawn after Joe Skeen, R-N.M., chairman of the Agriculture Appropriations Subcommittee, raised points of order:

- An amendment by Tom Allen, D-Maine, to require drugmakers to disclose how much taxpayers helped fund the development of new products through biomedical research at institutions such as the National Institutes of Health.
- An amendment by Sherrod Brown, D-Ohio, that would have barred the FDA from approving a new drug unless its manufacturer disclosed the average price it was charging in every developed country where the product was being marketed.

Predator Eradication

The Department of Agriculture's Wildlife Services Program, which provides federal subsidies for eradicating coyotes, wolves, mountain lions and other livestock predators — mostly in Western states — drew protests from some Eastern lawmakers, but an amendment by Peter A. DeFazio, D-Ore., Charles Bass, R-N.H., and Constance A. Morella, R-Md., that would have cut $7 million from the program, was rejected, 190-228, on July 11. *(Vote 382, p. H-120)*

DeFazio questioned why taxpayers should pay for predator control services on private ranches and added that some of the techniques used — such as cyanide poisoning — were cruel and posed dangers for humans. Defenders of the program said it was needed to control wildlife and prevent animal attacks on humans.

Egg Initiative Scrambled

The House also kept controversial language in the bill that would weaken a Clinton administration initiative to craft new FDA requirements for testing salmonella in eggs. The language would bar federal regulators from removing eggs from the market unless salmonella was found on the eggs themselves. The administration proposal calls for pasteurizing or destroying eggs if salmonella is found anywhere at the facility where they are produced.

Jack Kingston, R-Ga., author of the provision, said egg producers were negotiating with the FDA on changing the proposed requirements, and the language could be stripped from the bill if the two sides reach a compromise.

In other action, the House:

• Rejected, 182-187, a Coburn amendment to prohibit the use of federal funds for testing, developing or approving abortion-inducing drugs such as the French-made RU-486. *(Vote 373, p. H-118)*

The House approved similar amendments offered by Coburn in the fiscal 1998 and 1999 agriculture appropriations bills, but the restrictions were stripped out of both bills in conference. This year's outcome was influenced by the absence of 66 members who missed the vote.

• Rejected, 77-301, an amendment by Steve Chabot, R-Ohio, Ed Royce, R-Calif., and Bass to prohibit the use of funds for the Department of Agriculture's Market Access Program. *(Vote 376, p. H-118)*

The program is providing $90 million in subsidies to 65 U.S. trade groups in fiscal 2000 to promote agricultural exports abroad. Amendment supporters said the subsidies amount to corporate welfare and questioned why groups such as mink producers are allowed to apply for funding. Supporters of the program, such as Skeen, said it primarily helps small and independent producers get access to foreign markets.

• Rejected, 166-255, an amendment by Mark Sanford, R-S.C., to prohibit use of funds to make payments to producers of wool and mohair. *(Vote 383, p. H-120)*

Sanford argued that the recently enacted crop insurance reform bill (PL 106-224) authorizes $10 million for wool and mohair payments and that spending additional taxpayer funds would be perpetuating a wasteful, outdated subsidy dating to World War II, when the materials were used to make uniforms. Supporters of the program, such as Charles W. Stenholm, D-Texas, said the amendment was mean-spirited because it would eliminate subsidies for a small group of agricultural producers.

• Accepted, by voice vote, an amendment by Brown that would require the FDA to allocate $3 million from its overall budget to study how the use of antibiotics to promote growth and disease resistance in livestock can breed resistant strains of E. coli, salmonella and other harmful bacteria that may be passed on to humans through food.

• Rejected, 59-323, a Sanford amendment to block a $6 million pilot program to determine whether providing breakfast at school to all children — regardless of income — affects grades, attendance and behavior. *(Vote 378, p. H-118)*

Sanford said the program could lead to expensive efforts to provide free breakfasts for every pupil nationwide. Defenders of the program, such as Lynn Woolsey, D-Calif., said it was necessary to understand the benefits of a universal school breakfast program.

• Rejected, 168-253, an amendment by Dan Burton, R-Ind., to prohibit the granting of conflict-of-interest waivers to scientists who sit on FDA advisory committees for vaccine policies and also have financial ties to the drug industry. *(Vote 384, p. H-120)*

Senate-Passed Bill Adds Heavily to Emergency Funds

JULY 22 — After a heated debate that pitted farm-state lawmakers against fiscal conservatives, the Senate on July 20 added $900 million in new disaster spending to its version of a fiscal 2001 agriculture appropriations bill (HR 4461), then passed the measure by a vote of 79-13. *(Vote 225, p. S-40)*

The extra spending came on top of $1.1 billion in emergency aid already designated in the bill, and another $7.1 billion in fiscal 2000 economic assistance for farmers hit by low commodity prices that was included in a recently enacted crop insurance bill (PL 106-224). Since 1998, Congress has provided more than $15 billion in emergency farm aid through the appropriations process.

The move to add yet more emergency spending to the appropriations bill, through a package of 15 amendments, came at the end of a day and a half of slow debate and prompted loud protests from some Republicans. They complained that Congress had already spent enough on relief for farmers and was breaking previously agreed-to spending caps.

"The level of scratching and clawing to get into the pockets of the federal government is at a level I have never experienced in 22 years [here]," said Phil Gramm, R-Texas, who likened the extra spending to "a bidding war to buy votes in rural America."

Farm-state lawmakers, such as Kent Conrad, D-N.D., defended the extra aid, saying it would provide relief to farmers in more than a dozen states hit by weather-related disasters, as well as losses to citrus, apple and potato crops and livestock that were not covered by the earlier relief packages. The largest portion of the package — $450 million to compensate farmers for losses from flooding in the Great Plains and drought in the South — was offered by Conrad and fellow North Dakota Democrat Byron L. Dorgan.

"The fact is there are real disasters and real emergencies," Conrad said. "It's perverse, but it's happened — hundreds of millions of dollars of damage in my state alone, and others are affected."

Emergency Aid or Pork?

The en bloc amendments were introduced by Senate Agriculture, Rural Development and Related Agencies Appropriations Subcommittee Chairman Thad Cochran, R-Miss., who said they reflected newly identified emergencies in farm country that could not be addressed in earlier legislation.

Opponents, including Gramm,

Budget Committee Chairman Pete V. Domenici, R-N.M., and John McCain, R-Ariz., attempted to strike the amendments on a point of order, arguing that the extra spending violated congressional budget caps. Cochran then tried to waive the point of order, setting off an animated, sometimes heated 20-minute conference on the floor involving Gramm, Majority Leader Trent Lott, R-Miss., Minority Leader Tom Daschle, D-S.D. and Appropriations Committee Chairman Ted Stevens, R-Alaska.

Stevens finally brokered a compromise that allowed for a single vote on the amendments and a concession that no more emergency spending would be added to the bill. The amendments were adopted by voice vote. However, Stevens indicated that he may seek to add more emergency spending in a House-Senate conference on the measure to address the depletion of fisheries in his home state.

Spending designated as an emergency does not count against congressionally mandated budget caps.

Precise totals reflecting the bill, as amended on the floor, were not available July 21. As reported by committee, the Senate bill would provide $75.3 billion for agriculture, rural development, food and nutrition programs in fiscal 2001, including $14.8 billion in discretionary spending. The House version, passed July 11 by 339-82, would provide $75.4 billion, including $14.5 billion in discretionary spending.

The additional emergency spending could further complicate House and Senate conferees' efforts to reconcile their differing versions of the spending package. The conference already faces a fight over language House negotiators plan to insert that would lift food and medicine sanctions on Cuba and four other unfriendly nations, but would restrict Cuba's financing of U.S. agricultural purchases.

The Senate bill contains language lifting the sanctions with no such conditions.

Prior to the fight over the emergency spending, the Senate, for nearly three hours, debated a food-safety proposal prompted by a dispute over Department of Agriculture (USDA) meat and poultry inspection standards.

Senators narrowly rejected, 48-49, an amendment by Tom Harkin, D-Iowa, that would have allowed the USDA to refuse to place its inspection seal on meat and poultry that did not pass microbial tests for salmonella. The lack of a USDA seal would prevent the meat from being shipped interstate. *(Vote 221, p. S-40)*

The amendment was prompted by a dispute between the USDA and Supreme Beef Processors Inc., a Texas supplier of ground beef to the government-subsidized school lunch program.

In June, a federal judge in Texas blocked the agency from using the tests to levy sanctions, siding with meatpacking industry arguments that salmonella levels are not a fair criterion for measuring the cleanliness of a plant. Supreme Beef had failed four such tests.

"The decision in Texas now threatens the very foundation of our country's efforts to produce products with lower levels of microbiological pathogens," Harkin said.

Cochran argued that Harkin's language essentially would have the Senate overturn the court decision before USDA had even decided whether to appeal. A Cochran attempt to table the amendment failed, 49-49, as six Republicans joined Democrats in backing the measure, seen as putting more pressure on the meatpacking industry. *(Vote 218, p. S-39)*

Sugar Subsidies

Debate over Harkin's food-safety amendment was interrupted by a flap over a perennial point of contention in agriculture spending bills: the government's sugar price support program.

The Senate tabled, or killed, 65-32, a McCain amendment that would have cut off funding for federal sugar purchases in fiscal 2001. McCain argued that sugar subsidies and mandatory import quotas cause U.S. consumers to pay close to $2 billion annually in inflated sugar prices. He said the lion's share of government subsidies goes to large producers, who also happen to be major political donors. Senators from sugar-producing states, such as John B. Breaux, D-La., blamed the high prices on manufacturers of candy, ice cream and other food products that use sugar. *(Vote 219, p. S-39)*

Under the sugar program, the government sets a floor under sugar prices through an annual loan rate, as well as quotas on imported sugar, to guarantee U.S. producers a certain price for their crop. The program supports sugar cane growers in the South and Hawaii at 18 cents per pound, and sugar beet growers in the upper Midwest at 22 cents.

Prescription Drugs

The Senate began debate on the spending bill July 19 by adding language that would make it easier to import prescription drugs approved by the Food and Drug Administration (FDA). Senators adopted, 74-21, an amendment by James M. Jeffords, R-Vt., and Dorgan that would allow pharmacists and drug wholesalers to import drugs that had been shipped to nations, including Canada and Mexico, that cap the price of medications. *(Vote 217, p. S-39)*

Jeffords argued that price increases have threatened the well-being of consumers who do not have health insurance that covers drugs. The amendment was based on legislation (S 2520) Jeffords introduced earlier this year with Paul Wellstone, D-Minn.

"The best medicines in the world will not help a person who cannot afford them," Jeffords said. "[The problem is that] Americans pay by far the highest prices in the world for prescription drugs."

Before adopting the Jeffords amendment, the Senate adopted, 96-0, a Cochran amendment that would allow the drug imports only if the Department of Health and Human Services (HHS) certified that they would not pose a risk to public health and would significantly reduce costs to American consumers. Some Democrats questioned whether the Cochran amendment was necessary but voted for it to show support for the underlying Jeffords amendment. *(Vote 216, p. S-39)*

The 1938 Food, Drug and Cosmetic Act currently allows only drug manufacturers to import pharmaceuticals. Individuals are technically forbidden to cross borders to buy cheaper drugs, though the prohibition frequently is not enforced.

The prescription drug issue has been the object of a fierce lobbying battle since the House on July 10 adopted two amendments addressing prescription-drug prices in its version of the agriculture appropriations bill. The drug industry, already engulfed in a separate debate over a proposed Medicare prescription drug benefit, took out full-page newspaper advertisements following the House votes. The ads raised the prospect that a flood of imported drugs could jeopardize patient safety. Pharmaceutical company executives, such as Pfizer Inc. Chairman and Chief Executive Officer William C. Steere Jr., were seen buttonholing senators in the halls of the Capitol before the debate.

Jeffords and Dorgan sought to address safety concerns by including language in their amendment specifying that the drugs be made in FDA-approved facilities and that imports be subject to strict shipping regulations. However, lawmakers such as Bill Frist, R-Tenn., Orrin G. Hatch, R-Utah, and Breaux questioned whether the FDA and its parent agency, HHS, could handle the added responsibilities.

"They simply cannot police the world in making absolutely sure these are not counterfeit drugs coming back in, and because of this, I find it very hard to support the underlying [amendment]," said Frist, a heart surgeon.

Other Amendments

In other action, the Senate:

• Adopted, 72-24, an amendment by Arlen Specter, R-Pa., to authorize Amtrak to lease vehicles from the General Services Administration (GSA). Specter said the Amtrak Reform and Accountability Act of 1997, which is gradually privatizing the passenger rail carrier, unintentionally made Amtrak ineligible for GSA leasing, a move that could cost it $15 million in lost aid per year. Opponents said the goal of the act was to wean Amtrak from subsidies. *(Vote 223, p. S-40)*

• Tabled, 51-47, a Wellstone amendment to shift $3.95 million from the USDA's Economic Research Service to its Grain Inspection, Packers and Stockyards Administration. Wellstone said the shift was necessary to study anti-competitive behavior in the meatpacking industry. Cochran offered the motion to table, saying the Senate should not determine whether the USDA had enough money for such studies. *(Vote 220, p. S-40)*

• Adopted, 90-6, a Wellstone amendment to provide $500,000 to the USDA to study a decline in participation in the food stamp program and problems that households with eligible children may have experienced in obtaining food stamps.

Wellstone said there had been a 30 percent decline in food stamp participation over the past five years, but not a corresponding decline in poverty. *(Vote 222, p. S-40)*

Conferees Address Cuba Sanctions, Drug Imports in Compromise Bill

OCTOBER 7 — After two days of often rancorous debate, House and Senate conferees agreed to a compromise version of a fiscal 2001 agriculture appropriations bill (HR 4461) on Oct. 5, clearing the way for expected House and Senate passage the week of Oct. 9.

Conferees accepted two amendments drafted by House Republican leaders dealing with the controversial issues of food and medicine sanctions — primarily aimed at Cuba — and the re-importation of prescription drugs. Despite complaints from Democrats that they had been left out of the process, Republican leaders predicted that the overall spending package — which now contains $78.5 billion for farm programs, rural development and the Food and Drug Administration — will win approval in both chambers.

"It has an awful lot of money for agriculture . . . enough to gag a horse," Senate Majority Leader Trent Lott, R-Miss., told reporters Oct. 4.

President Clinton criticized the sanctions and re-importation measures Oct. 6, but stopped short of threatening to veto the bill. Clinton told reporters the Cuba language contained "unwarranted" restrictions, adding he was "deeply disappointed" with the drug re-importation measure. "I want to reserve some room for judgment when we have a chance to review the actual language," he said.

Tempers boiled several times during nearly eight hours of conference debate Oct. 5. After one heated exchange between House Appropriations Committee Chairman C.W. Bill Young, R-Fla., and ranking Democrat David R. Obey of Wisconsin over extraneous provisions being added to the bill, the conference recessed for one hour.

Conferees agreed on a total spending package that would include $15 billion in discretionary spending. The lawmakers approved a total of $3.6 billion in "emergency" aid, including $2.1 billion in relief for farmers hurt by economic and weather-related losses that was included in the Senate version of the bill. Another $1.1 billion was designated for this year's forest fire fighting efforts and cleanup in Western states.

Also included in the emergency spending was the lifting of two caps that restrict participation in the food stamp program — a move expected to cost $66 million in fiscal 2001 and $1.6 billion over five years.

The sanctions and re-importation provisions that held up progress on the bill for more than two months continued to be a point of bitter debate as Democrats derided GOP leaders for meddling in the appropriations process.

Democratic conferees especially criticized GOP House leaders, charging they watered down language in the drug-importation provision so it can be exploited by pharmaceutical companies to keep prices high. The amendment would, for the first time, give pharmacists and wholesalers the right to re-import U.S. prescription drugs that are sold abroad for less than they cost in the United States — a move most Republicans see as more palatable than creating a defined Medicare drug benefit.

"If I was a drug company lobbyist, I would ask my employer for a raise if this passes," Obey said.

Republicans said the amendment is a practical solution to rising drug prices — a potent election-year issue. Rep. Jo Ann Emerson, R-Mo., pointed to provisions in the amendment that would give the Department of Health and Human Services latitude to determine from which countries drugs can be re-imported and establish a regimen for testing the products.

"I can tell you, the drug companies are not happy about this," Emerson said.

Democrats, nonetheless, offered four amendments they said would toughen the language and ensure that drug prices would fall. Of particular concern are what they said are "loopholes" in the GOP amendment that would allow drug companies to enter into contracts that would give preferential prices to foreign buyers but discriminate against U.S. importers. Each amendment was rejected by House conferees, 6-9, on identical, party-line votes.

Senate conferees added a country-of-origin labeling requirement offered by Christopher S. Bond, R-Mo., that was rejected by House conferees, who argued it would do little but scare consumers. The overall drug re-importation amendment was then agreed to by voice vote.

Cuba Si, Sort Of

Debate on food and medicine sanctions, particularly as they relate to Cuba, was equally intense. The provision, originally authored by Rep. George Nethercutt, R-Wash., and modified by House GOP leaders, would lift sanctions first imposed on the regime of Fidel Castro in 1962 — a move favored by a large number of farm-state Republicans and Democrats.

However, to gain the support of powerful Castro critics such as House Majority Whip Tom DeLay, R-Texas, the amendment would also bar public and private U.S. financing of Cuban agricultural purchases and write into law travel restrictions now implemented by executive order. Currently, 12 categories of "exempt" groups can travel to Cuba, including humanitarian and church groups, musicians and artists.

"I will be the first to acknowledge it is not the perfect package, but it is the package necessary to get it though the majority side of the House of Representatives," Nethercutt said.

The amendment also would allow sales of food and medicine to Libya, North Korea, Iran and Sudan by permitting U.S. subsidies for agricultural and other exports. It would make it more difficult for future presidents to impose embargoes on food and medicine without the consent of Congress.

The amendment language would require Cuba to make cash purchases or obtain credit from a third country or foreign bank. U.S. banks could participate only as intermediaries serving, for example, as collection or payment agents for U.S. exporters.

The U.S.-Cuba Trade and Economic Council, which backs the provision, estimated it could spur up to $45 million in trade in its first year. The Castro regime, however, bitterly criticized the amendment, saying it would actually intensify the "economic war" on Cuba instead of increasing trade.

Democrats and Republican Sen. Arlen Specter, R-Pa., criticized the travel restrictions as unnecessarily punitive, noting they would prevent ordinary Americans from traveling freely. "This impinges on a basic human right," Obey said, likening the restriction to those imposed on Soviet Jews during the Cold War.

Democrats, including Rep. Maurice D. Hinchey of New York and Sen. Richard J. Durbin of Illinois, offered amendments to strike the travel ban and loosen the financing restrictions. Byron L. Dorgan of North Dakota also offered an amendment urging conferees to adopt the less-restrictive language on Cuba that senators passed last year. All of the amendments were rejected along party lines.

Nethercutt argued that the report language would actually increase travel to Cuba because it would boost the number of groups exempt from the ban and allow farmers to travel there to strike new trade agreements.

The practical effect of the travel restriction is a one-year ban for non-exempt Americans, because the provision is contained in an appropriations bill and has to be renewed annually. The issue may become less controversial after the presidential elections — both parties are loath to offend Cuban-Americans, most of whom oppose improving ties with Castro and are an important voting bloc in Florida, now considered a tossup state.

Easing Food Stamp Caps

Before dealing with drug re-importation and Cuba, conferees raised two financial caps, a move that will make it easier for hundreds of thousands of people to participate in the federal food stamp program.

An amendment offered by James T. Walsh, R-N.Y., and accepted by voice vote added the Hunger Relief Act (HR 3192) to the emergency spending section of the bill, despite objections by Republican lawmakers, particularly Senate Agriculture Appropriations Subcommittee Chairman Thad Cochran of Mississippi and Rep. Jack Kingston of Georgia, who argued it was too costly.

The measure would modify food stamp eligibility rules put in place during the 1996 welfare overhaul (PL 104-193). *(1996 CQ Almanac, p. 6-3)*

Current law prohibits food stamp recipients from owning a car worth more than $4,650 or paying monthly housing costs of more than $275, according to Walsh. The amendment would allow states to set their own caps for the vehicle allowance and gradually raise the housing cap to $340 per month over five years. After that, the cap would be indexed annually to reflect inflation. Walsh said the changes would allow approximately 500,000 Americans who currently do not receive food stamps to qualify for the program, at a cost of about $1.6 billion over five years.

Food stamp program enrollment has declined by more than 30 percent over the past four years due partly to the robust economy, and because some states have tightened their eligibility requirements. However, the government estimates that one in 10 Americans continue to go hungry. Officials say many people are unaware they are eligible.

Turf Battle Ahead?

Conferees weighed in on unfair trade practices — and may have triggered a jurisdictional fight with the House Ways and Means Committee — by accepting an amendment by Senate Appropriations Committee ranking Democrat Robert C. Byrd of West Virginia. The amendment, patterned on a bill (S 61) by Sen. Mike DeWine, R-Ohio, would redirect tens of millions of dollars in anti-dumping duties assessed on foreign companies by the Treasury to "injured parties" in the United States.

Byrd depicted the amendment as a way of helping beef, apple and mushroom producers fight subsidized agricultural imports. However, critics complained the measure also would help steel companies and their unions. House Appropriations Committee Chairman Young objected to the provision, saying it would be "blue-slipped," or subject to a point of order, by Ways and Means because it dealt with trade issues. However, Byrd argued the spending bill was the proper venue.

"This is the right time, the right place, the right bill," Byrd said.

House conferees accepted Byrd's language, 7-6. However, Ways and Means Chairman Bill Archer, R-Texas, sent Young a letter on Oct. 4 insisting the language be deleted from the bill. The provision faced the prospect of being struck before the conference report was filed.

In other action, conferees:

• Rejected an effort by Young to strike language that would make it easier for sugar beet and cane growers to receive penalty-free government loans. Young said the measure had been mysteriously inserted into the draft conference agreement without being part of either the House or Senate agriculture appropriations bill and with no lawmaker claiming authorship. Rep. Allen Boyd, D-Fla., and other lawmakers representing cane and beet growers said current law does not restrict the availability of penalty-free loans for any other commodity.

• Accepted a substitute amendment by Cochran to an amendment by Senate Agriculture Appropriations Subcommittee ranking Democrat Herb Kohl of Wisconsin that would restore $711,000 in Agriculture Department salaries. The House cut the money after angry farm-state lawmakers protested the department's failure to object to new Environmental Protection Agency plans to clean up polluted waterways.

House Adopts Conference Report; Clinton Indicates Support

OCTOBER 14 — With President Clinton signaling support, the House on Oct. 11 overwhelmingly adopted the conference report on a $78.5 billion fiscal 2001 agriculture appropriations bill (HR 4461) loaded with special provisions for farmers and other rural constituencies.

The 340-75 vote followed another heated debate between Republicans and Democrats over language easing sanctions on sales of food and medicine primarily aimed at Cuba and language that would loosen restrictions on re-importing prescription drugs. *(Vote 525, p. H-166)*

The two issues had stymied progress for months on the bill, which traditionally is one of the least controversial appropriations measures and one of the first to pass both chambers. Clinton criticized the Republican-crafted provisions on Oct. 6 and hinted he might veto the entire spending bill. However, the White House announced Oct. 11 that Clinton would sign the measure despite misgivings over the two issues.

The Senate plans to vote on the conference report Oct. 18.

House Democrats unsuccessfully tried a procedural maneuver to amend the rule to strike the drug re-importation language and substitute a provision establishing a Medicare prescription drug benefit. Democrats complained they had been thwarted by the GOP from considering the drug benefit plan through the normal legislative process and depicted the effort as a last chance during the 106th Congress to take significant action to address rising drug prices. The tactic was rejected, 214-201, largely along party lines. *(Vote 524, p. H-166)*

Democrats later echoed the White House in saying they would support the overall conference report because of the substantial amount of aid it would deliver to rural America.

"It is my fond hope that some day soon, we will have an honest conference on an agricultural bill with input from the administration and from this side of the aisle in a true, bipartisan result, but not today," said Charles W. Stenholm, D-Texas.

The conference report designates $78.5 billion in spending for agriculture, rural development and the Food and Drug Administration — a boost from the $75.7 billion in the Senate bill and the $75.4 billion in the House version. Discretionary spending totals $18.7 billion, an increase over the $14.5 billion in the House measure and $14.8 billion in the Senate version.

The report contains $9.5 billion for child nutrition programs, $1.7 billion for crop insurance and $873 million for conservation programs.

It also calls for $3.6 billion in emergency aid to farmers hurt by low commodity prices and bad weather, including $1.1 billion for this year's forest firefighting efforts and cleanup in Western states.

To assure widespread support from both parties, appropriators included targeted provisions for several constituencies. Dairy producers hurt by historically low milk prices would get $473 million — a cause championed by Herb Kohl of Wisconsin, ranking Democrat on the Senate Agriculture Appropriations Subcommittee, and David R. Obey of Wisconsin, ranking Democrat on the House Appropriations Committee. Some $100 million of that amount would go to Wisconsin dairy farmers.

The report also calls for $20 million each in emergency assistance for wool and mohair producers, beekeepers and cranberry growers. Apple and potato producers would receive $138 million for market losses, while citrus producers would get $58 million for lost production and trees affected by citrus canker.

The Cuba Debate

While many provisions were agreed to with no discussion, the Cuba and drug re-importation proposals aroused significant debate. Farm-state Republicans and Democrats expressed displeasure with the Cuba language, which would lift an embargo on food exports first imposed in 1962 and codify travel restrictions to the island nation now implemented by executive order. Democrats object to tightening the travel restrictions, a move designed to mollify Cuban-Americans, a key voting bloc in Florida, now considered a toss-up state in the presidential election.

"This is workable, notwithstanding the people who might say nay about it," said Republican George Nethercutt of Washington, who wrote the original Cuba language.

On drug re-importation, Democrats denounced the conference report language as a sham filled with loopholes that would allow drug companies to negotiate advantageous pricing agreements. Supporters said the language would deliver lower drug prices by allowing pharmacists and wholesalers to import U.S.-made pharmaceuticals that cost less abroad than in the United States.

Agriculture Spending Highlights

Where the Money Goes

HR 4461 — Conference Report: H Rept 106-948

Spending Synopsis

The conference report on the $78.5 billion bill, adopted Oct. 11 by the House, would appropriate $3 billion more than the House measure, $2.8 billion more than the Senate version and $1.3 billion more than President Clinton requested. Conferees agreed to spend some $59.8 billion for entitlements, including $20.1 billion for the food stamp program — $2 billion less than Clinton's request and $1.1 billion less than the House and Senate versions.

The report also would provide $9.5 billion for child nutrition programs and $4.1 billion for the Special Supplemental Food Program for Women, Infants and Children.

• Emergency spending

The report includes $3.6 billion in emergency spending for agricultural disasters and other purposes, $1.5 billion more than the Senate version; the House-passed bill called for only $115 million in emergency funding. Another $1.1 billion was designated for this year's fire fighting efforts in Western states. The emergency farm relief is in addition to $7.1 billion contained in the crop insurance bill (PL 106-224) signed by Clinton on June 20.

• Rural aid programs

The agreement would appropriate $1.3 billion — $146 million above the fiscal 2000 level — to support $5.1 billion in low-income rural housing loans. Conferees also agreed to spend $763 million for the Rural Community Advancement Program, which consolidates several development efforts, and $108 million — roughly equal to fiscal 2000 funding — for the Rural Utilities Service, which administers several electric, telecommunications and waste disposal programs.

Hot-Button Issues

△ **Food, medicine exports.** The provision, authored by Rep. George Nethercutt, R-Wash., and modified by House GOP leaders, would lift food and medicine sanctions first imposed on Cuba in 1962. It would bar public or private U.S. financing of Cuban agricultural purchases and write into law rules now implemented by executive order that bar travel to Cuba. The language would also allow sales of food and medicine to Libya, North Korea, Iran and Sudan, and make it tougher for future presidents to impose embargoes without the consent of Congress.

△ **Drug re-importation.** Language in the report would allow pharmacies and wholesalers to buy American-made prescription drugs that are sold abroad for less than they cost in the United States and re-import them. Republicans say the provision — which would allot $23 million to monitor drug re-imports — is a practical solution to rising drug prices. Democrats argued it contains loopholes that could keep prices high.

△ **Anti-dumping duties.** Conferees accepted an amendment by Sen. Robert C. Byrd, D-W.Va., to redirect tens of millions of dollars in anti-dumping duties assessed on foreign companies to "injured parties" in the United States. Byrd said the provision would help agricultural interests, while opponents said it is aimed more at aiding steel companies and their unions.

(figures are in thousands of dollars of new budget authority)

	Fiscal 2000 Appropriations	Fiscal 2001 Clinton Request	House Bill	Senate Bill	Conference Report
Agricultural Programs	$35,436,305	$34,740,299	$34,483,961	$34,506,850	$34,690,867
Conservation Programs	804,158	878,010	817,811	867,565	873,478
Rural Economic, Community Dev. Programs	2,187,507	2,587,610	2,407,744	2,512,229	2,486,598
Domestic Food Programs	35,044,106	36,205,658	35,230,359	35,213,590	34,116,590
Foreign Assistance and Related Programs	1,055,669	1,090,765	1,049,364	1,090,602	1,092,602
FDA and Related Agencies	1,112,011	1,283,255	1,171,255	1,165,973	1,167,874
General Provisions	2,250	—	119	—	30,000
Loan authorizations	*($10,712,421)*	*($12,642,442)*	*($12,299,691)*	*($11,387,371)*	*($11,906,152)*
GRAND TOTAL	**$84,312,546**	**$76,785,597**	**$75,264,494**	**$75,356,809***	**$78,144,809**
Total Adjusted for scorekeeping	**($75,898,740)**	**($77,210,686)**	**($75,421,583)**	**($75,702,898)**	**($78,460,898)**

* Does not include approximately $2.1 billion in emergency aid.

TABLE: House and Senate Appropriations committees.

Senate Clears Bill; President's Signature Expected

OCTOBER 21 — After serving as the vehicle for months of fiery debate over international economic sanctions and drug re-importation, the fiscal 2001 agriculture appropriations bill (HR 4461) overcame its final legislative hurdle when the Senate cleared the conference report Oct. 18.

Despite the lopsided 86-8 vote, lawmakers sparred over the levels of spending for a variety of agriculture programs. Some also expressed their lingering displeasure with provisions that would ease sanctions on sales of food and medicine to Cuba and four other countries and codify restrictions on travel to the island nation. *(Vote 277, p. S-50)*

The conference report would appropriate $78.5 billion for agriculture, rural development and the Food and Drug Administration — an increase over both the $75.7 billion Senate bill and the $75.4 billion House version. Included is $3.6 billion in emergency aid to farmers hurt by low commodity prices and inclement weather. President Clinton is expected to sign the bill.

The report also contains language that would allow pharmacists and drug wholesalers to re-import American prescription drugs from countries where they are sold for less than in the United States. Currently, only drugmakers are allowed to re-import their products.

John McCain, R-Ariz., derided the inclusion of what he said was $300 million in "pork barrel spending" in the bill and presented a list of "Top 10 Porkbusters." They include $1.05 million for sunflower research in Fargo, N.D., $5 million for an insect hatching facility in Stoneville, Miss., and $300,000 for manure management systems in Florence, S.C.

"What I object to is the way these projects have been selectively identified and prioritized for earmarks, mostly for purely political interest, rather than for the national interest," McCain said.

Tom Harkin, D-Iowa, and other lawmakers defended the projects, saying they were important to agriculture and thus are in the national interest.

"There is nothing wrong with the government providing federal funds to help identify better ways of dealing with these problems in agriculture," said Agriculture Appropriations Subcommittee Chairman Thad Cochran, R-Miss.

Before the vote, Pat Roberts, R-Kan., said he and other farm-state senators would work next year to remove restrictions in the bill that would prevent most Americans from traveling to Cuba and block U.S. and multilateral lending to finance Cuban agricultural purchases.

House Republican leaders added the provisions to mollify conservatives and many Cuban-American voters upset about the prospect of improved ties with the regime of dictator Fidel Castro.

"Compared to what we should be doing, this is one step forward, several steps to the side and one step back," Roberts said.

As the Senate debated the bill, Castro led a large demonstration — estimated at 800,000 people — through the streets of Havana and vowed not to buy any American goods until the restrictions are lifted. "In practice, it will be totally impossible to buy food and medicine from the United States" under the financing restrictions, complained an editorial published Monday in state newspapers. ◆

After Protracted Immigration Dispute, Congress Wraps CJS Bill Into Omnibus Package

Box Score 2001 Fiscal Year

Commerce-Justice-State

- **Bill:** HR 4942 — PL 106-553
- **Legislative action: House** passed HR 4690 (H Rept 106-680), 214-195, on June 26.

Senate committee approved HR 4690 (S Rept 106-404), 28-0, on July 18.

House adopted the conference report on HR 4942 (H Rept 106-1005), 206-198, on Oct. 26.

Senate cleared the bill, 48-43, on Oct. 27.

President signed the bill on Dec. 21.

SUMMARY

Negotiations continued into December on the fiscal 2001 spending bill for the departments of Commerce, Justice, State (CJS) and the federal judiciary — despite the fact the Senate had cleared the measure in late October. The main stumbling block was a package of unrelated immigration provisions sought by the Clinton administration and congressional Democrats. In the end, the bill was sent to the White House separately, while the immigration provisions were included in the year-end omnibus (HR 4577).

The final Commerce, Justice, State bill appropriated nearly $40 billion, including $21.1 billion for the Justice Department, $5.2 billion for the Commerce Department, $6.6 billion for the State Department and $4.3 billion for the federal judiciary. Virtually all the spending fights that took place during the bill's consideration were solved by adding more money.

The bill's path was convoluted almost from the outset. The House passed a $37.4 billion version (HR 4690) in June, and Senate appropriators approved a $36.7 billion version July 18. But instead of taking the bill to the Senate floor, where Democrats were waiting with amendments on gun control and immigration, House and Senate Republicans held informal negotiations to hammer out a compromise. The resulting bill was brought to both chambers and cleared as part of the conference report on the District of Columbia spending bill (HR 4942).

Though the $39.9 billion CJS measure gave the president nearly all the fiscal 2001 funding he requested, it remained under a veto threat. Democrats had prevailed on Clinton to promise to veto the bill unless it included a set of immigration provisions granting amnesty to certain illegal immigrants, making it easier for some Central American aliens to become permanent residents, and allowing residency applicants whose visas had expired to remain in the country while their applications were pending. Republican leaders waited to send the measure to the White House while they negotiated over the proposed immigration changes. After a long fight, both sides accepted a few, less-sweeping immigration changes, which were added to the omnibus bill. *(Immigration relief, p. 15-14)*

Democrats also had bitterly fought a Republican plan to block the Justice Department from getting money for its lawsuit against tobacco companies. While a federal court threw out part of the department's historic lawsuit in September, the court did allow the department to proceed with racketeering charges against tobacco companies. The final version of the CJS bill does not include the $23 million Attorney General Janet Reno said it would take to prosecute the case, but it also does not include provisions backed by Republicans that would have blocked the suit entirely.

Though Republicans in both chambers wanted to slash funding for international peacekeeping, the final bill gave Clinton $846 million — more than he requested. Restrictions added by the House appropriators to bar U.S. funding for peacekeeping forces in several parts of Africa were dropped from the bill.

The bill also included provisions to create 10 new district court judgeships and allow judges to get a cost of living increase this year so long as members of Congress get one.

House Panel Approves CJS Bill

JUNE 10 — As the fiscal 2001 appropriations bill for the departments of Commerce, Justice and State begins to work its way through Congress, it brings to mind the 1976 documentary on the rock group Led Zeppelin: "The Song Remains the Same."

The House Appropriations Subcommittee that funds the three departments and the federal judiciary approved its unnumbered version of the bill by voice vote June 6. The $34.9 billion measure is expected to be considered by the full panel the week of June 12. It would provide $20.3 billion for Justice, $4.4 billion for Commerce and $6.4 billion for the State Department and international broadcasting.

The bill has shed some of the controversial items that caused problems last year, such as money for the 2000 census or payment of back dues to the United Nations. But other difficulties from the past have resurfaced, making it likely that the bill will be among the last to be cleared this year.

Among other things, the bill does not include funding to allow the Justice Department to pursue its lawsuit against tobacco companies, and it would prohibit Justice from taking funds from other departments to initiate prosecutions. The Justice Department last year filed suit against tobacco companies to recover some federal health care costs associated with smoking-related illnesses.

Appropriations Subcommittee Chairman Harold Rogers, R-Ky., acknowledged that the proposed cuts would not be popular, but he said the bill "represents our best take on matching needs with scarce resources."

The $34.9 billion represents a $2.7 billion reduction from President Clinton's request, including $405 million from the State Department, $530 million from the National Oceanic and Atmospheric Administration (NOAA), $241 million from international peacekeeping and $201.6 million from the Small Business Administration.

As in prior years, the bill seeks to terminate the Advance Technology Program, which provides seed money for technology research aimed at developing commercial products, for a savings of $198.6 million. It also would terminate the North-South and East-West centers for a savings of about $15 million. The centers, affiliated with universities, aim to foster better relations between the United States and South America and Asia and the Pacific. The House has routinely tried to kill these programs, only to see their funding restored in conference.

Republicans also took their annual swipe at the Legal Services Corporation, the government entity that helps provide legal aid to the poor. The draft bill would appropriate $141 million for the program, $199 million below the president's request and $164 million below the fiscal 2000 level. Each year since the GOP took control of the House in 1995, the Appropriations panel has cut Legal Services funding and the full House has restored it.

"We are simply not meeting our responsibilities," David R. Obey of Wisconsin, ranking Democrat on the full Appropriations panel, said of the cuts. "To me, the issue is whether we get real early, or get real late."

Tough Choices

Rogers said that with the constraint of tight budget caps, appropriators and the Clinton administration need to make difficult decisions.

As an example, he cited the proposed cut of $241 million in the president's request for international peacekeeping efforts. The bill would appropriate $498 million for the U.S. contribution, the same as in fiscal 2000.

"We can cut back on some of these non-performing missions," Rogers said, noting that he had recently returned from a trip to Western Sahara where the situation "is going nowhere." A U.N.-brokered plebiscite there on independence from Morocco has been delayed since 1990 in a stalemate over who should be allowed to vote.

Obey called the proposed peacekeeping cut a "gross dereliction of duty" and said that it would force the administration to decide "which people will die and which won't."

Said Appropriations Chairman C.W. Bill Young, R-Fla., "We know this is not easy. The House passed a budget, and we have to stay within that budget, at least until something changes."

Justice Increases

Virtually the only area designated for increases was the Justice Department, whose proposed $20.3 billion appropriation would be $1.75 billion more than in fiscal 2000 and $128 million more than Clinton requested.

The Immigration and Naturalization Service (INS) — despite widespread criticism of its management — would receive an increase of $410 million to a total of $4.67 billion, about $130 million less than Clinton requested.

The bill would appropriate $4 billion in grants to states and localities, including $523 million for the Local Law Enforcement block grant and $686 million for grants to states that require prisoners to serve at least 85 percent of their sentences.

The bill would fully fund the $683 million requested by the administration for prison construction. But the bill does not include the "forward" funding of $791 million for fiscal 2002 and $535 million for fiscal 2003 that was included in the president's budget. A spokeswoman said the committee does not like to fund programs beyond one fiscal year.

The bill would fund only a small portion of the president's gun enforcement initiative. The panel approved the $14.5 million requested by Clinton to hire 113 additional federal prosecutors to handle firearms violations. The bill would not fund the $150 million requested for grants to states and localities to hire more prosecutors for gun crimes. Republicans said they were concerned that the money would broaden Clinton's Community Oriented Policing Services (COPS) program, which the GOP has funded reluctantly. It also does not include $50 million for smaller grant programs and for research on "smart gun" technology.

Unlike in previous years, when the panel proposed to dramatically cut COPS funding, the fiscal 2001 bill would appropriate $595 million, the same as in fiscal 2000.

The bill would provide $3.2 billion for the FBI, virtually the president's full request, and $1.4 billion for the Drug Enforcement Administration, an increase of about $77 million over the president's budget.

The Commerce Department would sustain deep cuts: The bill would provide $287 million less than in fiscal 2000. The department also would not get the $4.5 billion for 2000 census operations that was a one-time cost in last year's bill. Particularly hard hit was the request for coastal and atmospheric programs at NOAA, which the panel cut by $530 million. "We simply can't afford [them], and [they] aren't authorized," Rogers said.

The National Institute of Standards and Technology would be cut to $422 million, $216 million below fiscal 2000 and $290 million less than the administration's request.

The State Department would receive the full $1.06 billion requested for security improvements at embassies around the world, which would go toward upgrading some buildings and replacing others.

The panel cut $201.6 million from the president's request for the Small Business Administration. The $856.2 million for the SBA, Rogers said, includes $276 million for disaster relief.

House Committee Approves Bill After Battle Over Peacekeeping

JUNE 17 — An impassioned fight over how much the United States should contribute to international peacekeeping forces contributed to a lengthy and deeply partisan House markup of the fiscal 2001 appropriations bill for the departments of Commerce, Justice and State (CJS).

The peacekeeping split and similar fights over gun law enforcement and a tobacco lawsuit virtually guarantee a space for the measure in the final omnibus spending package expected from Congress at the end of the session.

The House Appropriations Committee approved by voice vote June 14 an unnumbered $37.4 billion fiscal 2001 spending bill for the three departments and the federal judiciary. The bill could be on the floor the week of June 19.

But the voice vote belied the intensity of the six-hour markup, where Democrats spent hours highlighting their policy differences with the GOP. House and Senate Democrats are sure to keep up the pressure on these issues throughout the process. The White House has threatened a veto.

The committee considered 19 amendments and held 13 roll call votes. Republicans defeated all attempts by Democrats to increase spending for various programs, sometimes by narrow margins.

As approved by the committee, the bill would appropriate $2.2 billion less than President Clinton requested for fiscal 2001. (That does not include $11.3 billion in "advance appropriations" he requested for future fiscal years.) It would provide $20.4 billion for the Justice Department, $4.4 billion for the Commerce Department and $6.4 billion for the State Department and international broadcasting.

Harold Rogers, R-Ky., chairman of the CJS Appropriations Subcommittee, called the measure a "solid bill," especially considering the "tight funding limits" the committee had to work with. "If you like a lot of increased spending, you're not going to like this bill," he said. He quoted comedian Red Skelton in defending a bill that has so many cuts in so many places: "Bad breath is better than no breath at all."

Democrats argued that the committee was producing a bill with a short shelf-life. David R. Obey of Wisconsin, ranking Democrat on the full Appropriations Committee, said members were "grinding our way through the House on bills that will have to be changed drastically to get the signature of the president."

Jose E. Serrano of New York, ranking Democrat on the subcommittee, said the bill "starves important core functions" at the departments. "Obviously, those resources are inadequate to do the job," he said.

Peacekeeping Battle

Clinton requested nearly $739 million for peacekeeping, which is the amount that the administration expects the United Nations to assess the United States. The committee bill would appropriate $498 million, the same as in fiscal 2000.

The committee rejected, 26-27, an amendment by Julian C. Dixon, D-Calif., that would have added $241 million to the peacekeeping account to match the president's request.

Rogers objected, arguing that as a part of a deal last year in which Congress agreed to pay off the U.S. debt to the United Nations, the administration agreed that peacekeeping would be capped at $498 million. "You'll have to discipline yourselves," Rogers said of the administration. He said peacekeepers should be deployed only "in a place where there's a peace to keep. . . . The moneys in this bill are for peacekeeping, not for war fighting."

The Dixon amendment also would have stripped language from the committee report accompanying the bill that would deny funds to several specific peacekeeping missions. The report said the $498 million did not include any of the funds requested for Tajikistan, Democratic Republic of the Congo, Western Sahara or Sierra Leone.

The report also rules out funding for a new peacekeeping mission planned for Ethiopia and Eritrea.

"Somehow peacekeeping in Africa is different from peacekeeping in Europe," said Jesse L. Jackson Jr., D-Ill. He urged members to vote for the amendment because "it says that African life is just as important as life in Europe."

The committee also turned back, 18-34, an amendment by Democrat Nita M. Lowey of New York that would have removed a requirement that the bill would place on the U.S. general contribution to the United Nations. The measure would condition release of $100 million on a report from the State Department saying that the United Nations had not exceeded its budget.

Guns and Tobacco

The remainder of the markup highlighted sharp differences between the parties on domestic priorities. Democrats offered many amendments knowing they would lose but putting their objections into the record.

Serrano offered an amendment to increase funding for the Legal Services Corporation to the fiscal 2000 level of $305 million. It was narrowly rejected, 26-27, and Democrats are sure to offer it again on the floor. The bill would appropriate $141 million for Legal Services, which helps provide legal assistance for the poor. Clinton requested $340 million.

Rogers said he was sympathetic to the effort, but warned that because Serrano did not include any offsets in his amendment, the increase would push the bill over its allocation and make it difficult to bring to the floor.

Rogers was less receptive to an amendment offered by Lowey that would have set aside $150 million in block grant funds for state and local governments to be used for hiring prosecutors to improve the enforcement of gun laws. The program was part of the gun enforcement initiative that Clinton included in his fiscal 2001 budget proposal. The committee defeated the amendment, 18-31.

Rogers said the block grant, which would get $523 million under his bill, permits the use of funds for hiring prosecutors, adding that the amendment was merely "political spin" on the volatile gun issue.

While most Democrats have been trying to pass stricter gun laws, Republicans and the National Rifle Association have argued that the key to reducing gun violence is to enforce existing laws. The Clinton administration responded with a $215.9 million enforcement package, only part of which would be funded by the CJS bill.

The only part of the package specifically included in the committee-approved bill was $14.5 million for hiring additional federal attorneys to prosecute firearms crimes.

Democrats also objected to provisions that they argued would make it difficult for the Justice Department to carry out its lawsuit against major tobacco companies. Last year the department sued nine tobacco manufacturers to recover federal health care costs associated with smoking-related diseases.

The bill would allow Justice to take funds from other departments to pay for lawsuits to defend the government but not for lawsuits initiated by the government. Rogers said the provision was not directed at the tobacco suit. "There's no prohibition in this bill against the lawsuit," he said.

Rosa DeLauro, D-Conn., offered an amendment to strip the language from the bill, saying it was intended to block the lawsuit. "The industry should not be awarded special protections at the cost of public health," DeLauro said.

The committee rejected the amendment, 19-30, with three Republicans voting for it — including full committee Chairman C.W. Bill Young, R-Fla. Two Southern Democrats, David E. Price of North Carolina and Allen Boyd of Florida, were opposed.

It was the last amendment considered by the committee, and it prompted some of the more vociferous debate.

Rogers said the bill language was designed to make sure that Justice was not indiscriminately raiding the coffers of other agencies to pay for its lawsuits.

Obey responded: "This language is in this bill to protect the tobacco companies' butt." He implored members to "say no to the lies [told by tobacco companies], say no to that political power. Tell them to go to hell."

After the markup, Obey said the bill would make it almost impossible for Justice to continue its lawsuit. The bill does not include any extra money for the suit. Under the bill, if the department needs funds for the lawsuit, it must notify appropriators at least 15 days before funds are transferred from another account. Obey noted that the request would have to get past Rogers, who comes from one of the nation's top tobacco states.

Other Amendments

Most Republicans were unsympathetic to other attempts by Democrats to boost funding in the bill.

Despite an impassioned plea from DeLauro and Lowey, the committee rejected, 24-28, an attempt to include $28.7 million in the bill to help lobster fishermen in New York and Connecticut. Long Island Sound has lost much of its lobster population, they said, leaving lives and local economies in shambles. "Their catch is zero. Their livelihood is gone," said Lowey.

But Rogers said the lobster fishermen would be taken care of in the fiscal 2000 supplemental spending bill. *(Supplemental, p. 2-162)*

Obey had no luck winning approval of an amendment that would have added $22 million to international trade compliance programs. The committee rejected it, 24-29.

He said that while he had not supported the China trade bill (HR 4444) recently passed on the House floor, it was critical that compliance agencies get enough money to enforce the deal.

This issue may come back: Jim Kolbe, R-Ariz., said he had voted for the trade agreement and believed "there was a very strongly implied commitment" to strengthen compliance enforcement. Kolbe said he would work with Obey and others on a compromise.

Obey also lost, 19-26, an attempt to add about $50 million to the budgets for antitrust activities at the Justice Department and the Federal Trade Commission. Obey said that with the recent rash of mergers and acquisitions, the additional money was needed to keep the United States from converting from a "capitalist society into an oligopoly."

Sam Farr, D-Calif., tried to increase funds for the National Oceanic and Atmospheric Administration, which was hard hit in the GOP bill. His amendment to add $85 million to operations and research programs failed, 22-28.

Lowey offered an amendment to add $79 million to a program that would help public television stations convert to digital programming by the federal deadline of 2003. The bill would appropriate $31 million for the Public Television Facilities Program. Lowey's amendment was defeated, 20-31.

Serrano also lost, 17-35, an attempt to add $77.4 million to civil rights enforcement programs at the Justice Department.

He won adoption, by voice vote, of an amendment that would allow Guam to get more funds under the local law enforcement block grant program. Currently, the South Pacific territories of Guam, American Samoa and the Commonwealth of the Northern Mariana Islands are considered one state for purposes of the grant. His amendment would take Guam out of that group and allow it to be considered separately.

House Votes To Allow Justice To Tap Funds From Other Agencies

JUNE 24 — The House on June 23 easily agreed to allow the Justice Department to obtain funds from other agencies to prosecute its lawsuit against tobacco companies, which it filed last year to recover federal health care costs attributed to smoking-related illnesses.

The action came as the House debated the $37.4 billion fiscal 2001 appropriations bill (HR 4690) for the departments of Commerce, Justice and State (CJS).

By a vote of 215-183, the House adopted an amendment that would specifically exempt the tobacco lawsuit from a provision in the bill barring reimbursement to Justice from other departments for lawsuits in which the government is the plaintiff. It was the second victory in a week for anti-tobacco forces in the House. Earlier, the House agreed to allow the Department of Veterans Affairs (VA) to give Justice $4 million for its part of the lawsuit. *(Vote 319, p. H-104)*

The House did not complete work on the CJS bill and is expected to return to it June 26. Still pending is a battle over how much the United States should contribute to international peacekeeping. The Clinton administration has requested $739 million, but the bill would provide $498 million.

The lion's share of the bill's funds would go to the Justice Department: $20.4 billion. Most of the two days of debate June 22-23 focused on Justice programs. Members adopted an amendment to more than double appropriators' recommendation for funding for the Legal Services Corporation, which provides legal aid to the poor, and a measure to discourage the Justice Department from using secret evidence in its prosecutions.

Republicans rejected or ruled out of order a series of Democratic amendments that aimed to increase funding for one of the Clinton administration's high-priority programs, the Community Oriented Policing Services (COPS). The bill would appropriate $595 million for the program, $740 million less than Clinton requested.

Even as members worked on the measure, the Clinton administration formally issued a veto threat: "Given the severe underfunding of critical programs . . . the president's senior advisers would recommend that he veto the bill if it were presented to him in its current form."

Tobacco Lawsuit

As approved by the Appropriations Committee, the CJS bill would have prohibited any other department from giving funds to Justice to pursue a lawsuit, unless the government was the defendant.

The amendment adopted by the House, sponsored by Henry A. Waxman, D-Calif., would exempt from this restriction any litigation filed before Jan. 1, 2000, that has already received funds from other departments. It applies only to the tobacco lawsuit.

At issue is a 1994 law (PL 103-317) that allows Justice to help pay for its activities with funds from other departments. CJS Appropriations Subcommittee Chairman Harold Rogers, R-Ky., argued that the provision was enacted to allow Justice to get funds to fight a multibillion-dollar lawsuit filed by defense contractors after the Defense Department cancelled production of the A-12 bomber plane in 1991. *(1994 Almanac, p. 483; 1991 Almanac, p. 431)*

When Congress did not include funds in last year's CJS bill for the tobacco lawsuit, which Justice estimates could cost $20 million, the department sought funds from Defense, the VA and the Department of Health and Human Services, all of which would be reimbursed if the lawsuit were successful.

Rogers and others argued that this would give the Justice Department too much power to interfere with other departments' budgets, a power Congress prefers to reserve for itself. He argued that the $148 million in the bill for routine salaries of more than 1,000 Justice attorneys could easily pay for the lawsuit.

"This [law] was for defense, but the Justice Department has violated it and you want to reward them for it," Rogers scolded Democrats.

"This amendment jeopardizes the appropriations authority granted in the Constitution," said Robin Hayes, R-N.C.

But Waxman urged members to "stand with our veterans and our seniors and stand up to the tobacco companies."

Said James V. Hansen, R-Utah, one of 55 Republicans to vote for the amendment: "I believe the time has come to demand responsibility, and that's why I'm supporting this amendment." Thirty-five Democrats opposed it.

Legal Services

In contrast to the sharp exchange over tobacco, the annual debate over funding for Legal Services was lackluster and relatively short. Members adopted by voice vote an amendment, sponsored by CJS Appropriations Subcommittee ranking Democrat Jose E. Serrano of New York, to add $134 million to the agency's budget, bringing the total to $275 million for fiscal 2001. That is $30 million less than the fiscal 2000 level and $65 million less than Clinton requested. Democrats said they hoped the Senate would find more money for the agency.

As in prior years, the House Appropriations Committee had slashed the agency's funding to $141 million.

Serrano's amendment proposed to offset the increase with cuts to a variety of other programs, from diplomatic and consular services to Bureau of Prisons salaries and expenses. "The House has repeatedly rejected $141 million as insufficient for the work of the Legal Services Corporation," Serrano said.

"If this amendment is defeated, there will be no equal justice in America," said amendment cosponsor Jim Ramstad, R-Minn.

George W. Gekas, R-Pa., was one of two members who spoke against the amendment. Gekas, chairman of the Judiciary subcommittee with jurisdiction over Legal Services, argued that the agency had done too poor a job documenting its workload to justify continuing its budget at current levels.

Secret Evidence

While little money was at stake, the debate over the use of secret evidence was one of the most impassioned on the bill. The House on June 22 adopted an amendment to strike a largely symbolic amount — $173,000 — from the Bureau of Prisons account. The vote was 239-173. *(Vote 315, p. H-102)*

At issue was a practice by the Immigration and Naturalization Service, in some immigration cases, to incarcerate immigrants suspected of terrorism without disclosing the charges to them or the evidence against them. The agency has the authority to do so under the 1996 anti-terrorism law (PL 104-132). *(1996 Almanac, p. 5-18)*

The amendment, offered by Tom Campbell, R-Calif., and Minority Whip David E. Bonior, D-Mich., took $173,000 from the Bureau of Prisons, an amount calculated to represent what would be used to incarcerate the eight immigrants that Campbell and Bonior said are being kept in prison because of secret evidence.

Amendment supporters argued that the use of secret evidence was inherently contradictory in the American system of justice. "It's an outrage that we have a body of law that allows this to happen in the United States," Bonior said. "It may sound like Franz Kafka, but it happens here in the United States."

Ron Paul, R-Texas, warned that if it can be done to immigrants, it could happen to citizens. "This is the way liberty is lost, by degrees, by inches, incrementally," agreed Maurice D. Hinchey, D-N.Y.

Lamar Smith, R-Texas, chairman of the Judiciary Subcommittee on Immigration and Claims, opposed the amendment and called the secret evidence provision "a rare but vital law enforcement tool" that would be dangerous to abolish. Anthony Weiner, D-N.Y., agreed. The amendment "undermines our ability to fight terrorism," he said. The administration, noted Weiner, also opposed the amendment.

Other Amendments

In other action, the House:

- Adopted by voice vote an amendment by Jim McGovern, D-Mass., that would add $4.5 million to the Small Business Administration's women's business centers, for a total of $13 million.
- Rejected, 145-223, an amendment by Howard Coble, R-N.C., to increase funding for the Patent and Trademark Office by $134 million to a total of $784 million. The amendment was offset by cuts to Commerce economic and statistical analyses, census statis-

tics and cultural and education programs at the State Department. *(Vote 321, p. H-104)*

• Rejected, 103-288, an amendment by Thomas M. Davis III, R-Va., to strip language from the bill that would prohibit the Justice Department from paying its attorneys for overtime. *(Vote 320, p. H-104)*

• Rejected, 156-254, an amendment by Diana DeGette, D-Colo., that would have stripped from the bill language prohibiting federal funds from being spent on abortions. It was an attempt by many House women to make it easier for women in federal prisons to obtain abortions. *(Vote 318, p. H-102)*

• Rejected by voice vote an amendment by Serrano to add $11.8 million in proposed funding for civil rights enforcement.

House-Passed Bill Allows Gun Deal, Retains Cuts in U.N. Peacekeeping

JULY 1 — The House ignored a veto threat June 26 and passed a fiscal 2001 spending bill for the departments of Commerce, Justice and State (CJS) by a vote of 214-195. The next stop for the measure (HR 4690) is the Senate CJS Appropriations Subcommittee, which has not yet scheduled a markup. *(Vote 326, p. H-104)*

The bill would appropriate $37.4 billion for fiscal 2001, about $2.2 billion less than President Clinton requested. Of that, $20.4 billion would go to the Justice Department, $4.4 billion would go to Commerce, and $6.4 billion would go to the State Department and broadcast agencies.

The House rewrote language in the bill to allow the Clinton administration to pursue its lawsuit against major tobacco companies — eliminating one of the White House's major complaints about the legislation.

And members boosted funding for the Legal Services Corporation from the $141 million approved by the Appropriations Committee to $275 million. That is still $30 million less than current funding and $65 million less than Clinton requested.

But proposed cuts in programs from U.N. peacekeeping to ocean protection remained, leaving the administration's veto threat in place.

In action June 26, the House rebuffed an attempt to add funds to the bill for international peacekeeping and rejected a plan that would have blocked part of the administration's gun safety deal with Smith & Wesson, a major gun manufacturer.

Gun Agreement

The House rejected, 196-201, an amendment by John Hostettler, R-Ind., that would have prohibited the Justice Department from using funds in the bill to enforce provisions of the gun agreement. Fifty Republicans opposed the amendment; 39 Democrats supported it. *(Vote 324, p. H-104)*

In a deal reached March 17, Smith & Wesson agreed to take certain actions demanded by the administration, such as offering safety locks with all handguns and working on "smart gun" technology. It also agreed to sell its products only to dealers who comply with certain requirements, such as mandatory background checks on all weapons they sell.

In return, the gun manufacturer has been dropped from a series of lawsuits filed against gun manufacturers by cities and localities seeking compensation for costs incurred from gun crimes. The federal government also agreed not to sue Smith & Wesson. And the cities are to give preference to Smith & Wesson in purchasing weapons for their law enforcement officers.

The vote followed two similar battles the week of June 19 on the fiscal 2001 appropriations bill (HR 4635) for veterans and housing.

On that bill, the House narrowly adopted an amendment that would block more cities from joining the Smith & Wesson agreement, but rejected an amendment that would have prohibited the Department of Housing and Urban Development (HUD) from spending money to enforce the agreement.

Hostettler argued that the deal between the administration and Smith & Wesson amounted to "backdoor gun control through coercion and through the threat of litigation." What is taking place, he said, "is incremental gun control by actions of the executive branch."

Jose E. Serrano, D-N.Y., ranking Democrat on the CJS Appropriations Subcommittee, objected that Hostettler's amendment would "destroy the agreement." Said Carolyn McCarthy, D-N.Y.: "This is not gun control; this is called gun safety."

Peacekeeping Funds

The House did not vote on one of the most contentious issues in the bill — $498 million for U.S. contributions to international peacekeeping by the United Nations.

The administration requested $739 million for fiscal 2001, and Democrats offered an amendment, sponsored by Jesse L. Jackson Jr. of Illinois, to increase funding by $241 million to match the request.

But CJS Subcommittee Chairman Harold Rogers, R-Ky., raised a successful point of order against the amendment, saying it violated budget rules because it did not include offsets for the additional spending. If the amendment had been adopted, it would have pushed the bill's total spending over the allocated amount. Democrats did not challenge the ruling, though they criticized the Republican stance on providing funds for peacekeeping.

Donald M. Payne, D-N.J., former chairman of the Congressional Black Caucus, noted that the bill would not provide funds for a series of peacekeeping missions in Africa. "This is a disgrace; it is a shame," he said.

One Republican, Frank R. Wolf of Virginia, spoke in favor of the Jackson amendment. After describing the horrors experienced by innocent people caught in the middle of fighting in Sierra Leone, which he said he had seen in a recent visit, Wolf said the additional funding for peacekeeping was the least the United States could do.

He said it would help create a situation where "moms and dads can raise their children in some semblance of peace."

"We are foolish if we do not fund our fair share," agreed Steny H. Hoyer, D-Md., pointing out that Clinton's request reflects the U.S. share of peacekeeping assessed by the United Nations.

Rogers said the money was not included for many of the African projects "because these missions are not quite ready yet." He urged members not to send U.N. peacekeepers into unsettled regions. "Do not expect the U.N. peacekeeping mission to be able to go in and fight a war," he said.

An attempt to allow the $498 million to be used for the Africa peacekeeping missions was blocked on procedural grounds.

Other Amendments

In other action, the House:

- Rejected, 86-312, an amendment by Mark Sanford, R-S.C., to strip the $8 million included in the bill for the Asia Foundation, a quasi-private, nonprofit organization designed to assist the development of democracy in Asia. *(Vote 322, p. H-104)*
- Adopted by voice vote an amendment by Cliff Stearns, R-Fla., that would limit to $640,000 the amount the Federal Communications Commission (FCC) could spend on its Office of Media Relations. The bill would appropriate $208 million for FCC salaries and expenses. The original bill did not include a specific amount for the media relations office. Stearns said the agency was bloated with workers.
- Adopted an amendment by David Vitter, R-La., that would prohibit the State Department from approving the purchase of property in Arlington, Va., by Xinhua News Agency, the government-affiliated news agency of China. Members said the site was too close to the Pentagon for their comfort. The vote was 367-34. *(Vote 325, p. H-104)*

Senate Panel Reins In Spending For Peacekeeping, Tobacco Suit

JULY 22 — The Senate Appropriations Committee picked battles with the Clinton administration over U.N. peacekeeping and tobacco lawsuits in its $36.7 billion version of the fiscal 2001 appropriations bill for the departments of Commerce, Justice and State (CJS).

The committee approved the bill (HR 4690), 28-0, on July 18. It would appropriate $3 billion less than the president's request and about $700 million less than the House-passed version. The bill would provide $18.7 billion for the Justice Department, $4.8 billion for Commerce, $4.2 billion for the federal judiciary and $6.6 billion for the State Department and broadcast agencies.

Senators sided with the House and against President Clinton in a heated fight over peacekeeping money. They included $500 million for that portion of U.S. payments to the United Nations — $239 million less than the administration wants. The House bill would provide $498 million. The proposed peacekeeping level was a major reason Clinton threatened to veto the House-passed bill, and the Senate version is likely to draw the same reaction. The House passed its $37.4 billion bill June 26.

The Senate bill would prohibit other departments from helping to pay for the Justice Department's lawsuit against major tobacco companies, a provision strongly opposed by the administration. The House changed its bill during floor debate to permit Justice to receive funds from other departments.

The Senate committee defeated, 14-14, an amendment by ranking Democrat Ernest F. Hollings of South Carolina to provide $20.5 million for the Justice Department to prosecute the case. "It's not about trial lawyers making money," Hollings said. "It's about getting our money back." The suit seeks to recover the $20 billion the government spends each year on health care for people who become ill because of smoking.

Mitch McConnell, R-Ky., said the lawsuit amounted to "taxation through litigation." He acknowledged that tobacco companies were unpopular now, but warned that they could become just the first in a line of similar attacks. "What's next, beer? Fast food?" he asked.

The Senate bill also includes a controversial change in immigration policy that would make it easier for people to stay in the United States while they are seeking to become permanent legal residents, rather than being required to return home. Several House members, including Lamar Smith, R-Texas, chairman of the Judiciary Subcommittee on Immigration and Claims, vehemently oppose the provision.

The Senate bill would cut funding for some popular programs, such as Byrne crime-fighting grants to states. CJS Appropriations Subcommittee Chairman Judd Gregg, R-N.H., indicated at the markup that in final negotiations, funding for these programs would increase. "Right now those numbers are low," he said.

The bill next goes to the floor of the Senate, which may not have time to consider it before the August recess.

Immigration Proposal

As approved by the committee, the bill would restore an immigration program known as 245(i). Under that program, which Congress allowed to expire in 1997, an illegal immigrant who was in line for permanent residency (a green card) through a family or employer sponsor could be processed in the United States after paying a $1,000 fee. The person would not have to return home while being processed. *(1997 Almanac, p. 9-11)*

As part of the fiscal 1998 CJS spending bill (PL 105-119), Congress agreed that while most future green cards would be issued only in an immigrant's home country, people who had submitted an application by Jan. 14, 1998, could get one in the United States. For employer-sponsored immigrants, the rules were a bit more relaxed.

Immigration advocates and the Clinton administration argue that because of a provision in the 1996 immigration overhaul (PL 104-208), the lapse of 245(i) left many immigrants in an impossible situation. The 1996 law imposed a penalty on those who had been in the United States illegally, left and attempted to return. Depending on how long they had been in the country illegally, they could be barred from reentry for up to 10 years.

The provision in the appropriations bill would "allow some flexibility in an overly rigid, harsh law," said Judith E. Golub, a lobbyist for the American Immigration Lawyers Association. It would allow immigrants to "stay with their families and keep their jobs."

The change will encounter stiff resistance in the House. Smith, for example, is opposed.

"245(i) is like a bad nickel, it just keeps turning up," Smith said July 20. "It's a bad idea that increases illegal immigration, and it's making its annual cameo appearance on the Hill."

GOP presidential candidate

George W. Bush has taken a more moderate line on immigration than Smith and many conservatives — and Republicans have been trying to avoid fights that highlight party splits on immigration.

Differing Priorities

Senators had different priorities than the House in funding a variety of programs.

The Senate bill, for example, would appropriate $2.3 billion for the Office of Justice programs, which include grants for state and local law enforcement and juvenile justice programs. The House bill included nearly $3.5 billion.

The biggest funding differences in those programs would be in state and local law enforcement grants. The Byrne crime-fighting formula grants would get $400 million under the Senate bill, $100 million less than in the House version. And the juvenile justice grants would get $100 million, $150 million less than the House appropriated.

The Senate bill would appropriate $76 million for grants to states for prison construction, compared with $687 million in the House bill. The Senate cut funding to the State Criminal Alien Assistance Program, which reimburses states for the cost of incarcerating illegal immigrants who have committed a crime. The Senate bill would provide $50 million for the program, $370 million less than the House.

At the markup, Dianne Feinstein, D-Calif., said she was disappointed with the low level for state reimbursement. She said the cost to California of housing criminal aliens is $568 million a year.

Other agencies and departments that would get less than the president wanted in the House version had better luck with the Senate. The Senate bill would appropriate $2.7 billion for the National Oceanic and Atmospheric Administration, an increase of $457 million over the House bill and close to the administration request.

The Senate bill would provide nearly $600 million for the National Institute of Standards and Technology — less than the $713 million requested by the president but $174 million more than the House bill. The Senate bill would provide $300 million for the Legal Services Corporation, $25 million more than the House version.

Senate Initiatives

The Senate bill includes several initiatives that cross departmental or agency lines.

The bill includes nearly $414 million in emergency spending for the Immigration and Naturalization Service (INS), the Justice Department and the Drug Enforcement Administration (DEA) for law enforcement along the Southwest border.

"The tidal wave of humanity crashing across the Southwest border poses a law enforcement challenge that demands the strongest and most closely coordinated response possible," said the draft report accompanying the bill.

Said Gregg: "Somehow, we have to get some control here."

The plan calls for transferring more staff to the border, upgrading Border Patrol facilities and transferring judiciary funds from administrative accounts to courts along the border, which now account for 26 percent of all criminal court filings in the United States.

The committee also would require that the DEA, FBI and INS set up their offices side by side along the border in California, Arizona, New Mexico and Texas.

The Senate committee took a broader approach than the House to challenges that the Internet poses to law enforcement. The bill would appropriate nearly $160 million for the Federal Trade Commission, $25 million more than the House bill, to crack down on Internet fraud, particularly when aimed at the elderly.

The committee included nearly $490 million for the Securities and Exchange Commission, $97 million more than the House. Gregg said the additional funds were intended to help the agency crack down on Internet stock fraud.

The bill includes $13 million for the National Center for Missing and Exploited Children, in part for a study to determine how the Internet is used to victimize children.

The DEA would get additional funding to crack down on the production of methamphetamine, known as speed. The Senate bill includes $77.7 million for improved law enforcement regarding the drug, $32 million more than the House bill. Of that amount, $21.7 million would go to state and local law enforcement to help them shut down and clean up speed labs. The chemicals used to make speed are highly combustible, and cleanup can frequently lead to fires and explosions.

According to the DEA, federal, state and local governments seized more than 7,000 such labs in 1999, up from about 3,327 in 1997.

Other Provisions

• **Handgun safety.** The bill includes a $15 million earmark for the National Shooting Sports Foundation to help it distribute gun safety kits. The organization, a trade group for gun manufacturers, has developed a package, including a gun locking device, that it wants to send to gun owners. So far, according to the foundation, more than 500 municipalities and counties have signed up for the program.

The foundation gives the safety packages to local governments for distribution. The group has given out 250,000 kits so far and wants to increase that to 500,000 by the end of the year. The provision was included in the bill at the request of full Appropriations Committee Chairman Ted Stevens, R-Alaska.

• **Foreign companies.** The bill includes a provision that would prohibit the Federal Communications Commission (FCC) from granting a license or operating authority to any company in which a "foreign entity" has more than 25 percent direct or indirect ownership. The provision, inserted into the bill at Hollings' request, is directed at Deutsche Telekom AG, a German telecommunications company that is trying to acquire VoiceStream Wireless Corp., an American company. Current law contains this prohibition, but the FCC has waived it for smaller deals.

• **COLA for judges.** The bill includes $8.8 million for a cost of living adjustment (COLA) for federal judges. For the judges to get a COLA, two things must happen: the annual COLA for members of Congress must go through unimpeded, and a provision prohibiting raises for federal judges must be waived. The bill would waive the provision. The congressional raise is usually debated on the Treasury-Postal Service spending bill.

• **Anti-trust law.** The bill includes

provisions to raise the financial threshold for merger reviews and would set up a new fee structure. The provisions are similar to legislation (S 1854) approved by the Senate Judiciary Committee in April. The House Judiciary Committee approved a similar bill (HR 4194) on July 11.

CJS Spending Bill to Bypass Senate Floor

SEPTEMBER 23 — Most senators will not get to debate the contents of the fiscal 2001 appropriations bill for the departments of Commerce, Justice, State and the judiciary (HR 4690) until the measure has been hashed out with House appropriators.

Senate leaders acknowledged the week of Sept. 18 that the $36.7 billion measure would not be considered on the floor in their chamber. Senate Republican Policy Committee Chairman Larry E. Craig of Idaho said, "I think it will go to conference" without floor action.

Republicans said the maneuver was necessary because Democrats wanted to bog down the process with unnecessary amendments that would consume valuable time in the remaining days of the 106th Congress.

Democrats countered that Republicans were eager to keep the bill from the floor to protect their members in tight re-election races from having to cast politically sensitive votes on issues relevant to the spending bill, such as gun control and immigration.

Whatever the reason, the measure now is in an informal conference, where negotiators must work out the myriad differences between the version approved July 18 by the Senate Appropriations Committee and the House bill, passed June 26. Then they must try to find common ground with the Clinton administration, which had threatened to veto the House bill.

Congressional leaders also must decide which other appropriations bill will carry the contentious CJS measure in the end. The plan is to add the final version to another spending measure already in an actual conference so the two bills can move in tandem.

The two versions of the CJS bill have significant differences, both in policy and in funding. The Senate version is $704 million less than the House's $37.4 billion bill. The Senate measure includes $414 million in emergency appropriations for a variety of projects designed to help judges and law enforcement along the Southwest border deal with immigration problems; the House bill does not.

The Senate bill contains $562 million more for the Commerce Department than the House-passed bill; $456 million of the increase is for the National Oceanic and Atmospheric Administration.

But the House measure would appropriate $1.3 billion more than the Senate for state and local law enforcement block grants. The Senate bill would appropriate $76 million for state prison construction, $610.5 million less than the House. And the State Criminal Alien Assistance Program, which helps states pay for incarceration of illegal immigrants, would get $50 million in the Senate bill, $370 million less than the House bill and $550 million less than the Clinton administration requested.

Conferees also will have to deal with the issue of peacekeeping. The House bill would appropriate $498 million and the Senate measure includes $500 million. But the Clinton administration has requested $739 million, the amount the administration expects the United Nations to charge the United States for its share of the costs of force deployments.

On policy questions, the Senate bill would create a new deputy attorney general for combating domestic terrorism; the House bill would not. The House bill would allow the Justice Department to get funding from other agencies to pay for its lawsuit against the major tobacco companies; the Senate bill would not.

The Senate bill includes a provision that would prohibit the Federal Communications Commission from approving a broadcast license for any company in which a "foreign entity" has a 25 percent ownership interest. It is aimed at the proposed acquisition of VoiceStream Wireless Corp., a U.S. company, by Deutsche Telekom AG, a German telecommunications company. The House bill does not have a similar provision.

The Senate bill would allow federal judges to collect honoraria in addition to their salaries. Currently, members, top staff of both the legislative and executive branches and judges are barred from keeping honoraria.

Democrats Aim to Add Immigration Proposals to Packed CJS Bill

SEPTEMBER 30 — Democrats are trying to load more cargo onto the already unwieldy fiscal 2001 appropriations bill for the departments of Commerce, Justice and State (HR 4690). Their effort seems likely to further complicate negotiations on the measure, which includes so many controversial provisions that the GOP leadership has declined to bring it to the Senate floor.

"Frankly, I think that will be one of the last bills and the most difficult bills to resolve," Majority Leader Trent Lott, R-Miss., said Sept. 26.

After losing a Senate fight to attach a package of immigration provisions to legislation that would increase the number of temporary visas for highly skilled workers (S 2045), Democrats are now setting their sights on the CJS bill.

At issue is a set of proposals, dubbed the Latino and Immigrant Fairness Act (S 2912), that would grant amnesty to illegal immigrants who have lived in the United States since 1986, make it easier for some immigrants to stay in the country while their residency application is pending and make it easier for some Central American, Liberian and Eastern European immigrants to apply for residency.

Democrats sent a letter Sept. 21 to President Clinton informing him that they would sustain any veto of a CJS bill that did not include the immigration package. "As Democrats, we believe the [bill] is a measured and just recognition of the important contributions these individuals have made to our country. We know you share our beliefs, and we look forward to working with you to accomplish this important goal," the letter said.

While Lott declined to endorse the package, he did say the CJS bill was the proper place to debate it. "I'm not saying that I would support that [Latino bill]. But that, you know, is a place where it could conceivably be considered."

Dealing with immigration issues on the CJS bill at the end of the session has been a fairly common strategy since Republicans won control of Congress in 1994.

Hitching a Ride

Staff on both sides of the Capitol have been trying to work out the differences between the $37.4 billion House-passed version of the appropriations bill and the $36.7 billion measure approved by the Senate Appropriations Committee.

But House CJS Appropriations Subcommittee Chairman Harold Rogers, R-Ky., said Sept. 26 that he did not believe the negotiations could be completed until at least the week of Oct. 2, and perhaps later.

In addition to working out dozens of contentious issues — from funding for the State Department security operation to research at the National Oceanic and Atmospheric Administration — Rogers said the GOP leadership also must find another vehicle to carry the bill, which has never gone to the Senate floor.

"We're looking for a good mule to ride through the mud," he said.

On at least one issue, Lott has asked his Senate colleagues to back off from their initial position. The Senate Appropriations Committee included language in its version of the bill that would prohibit the Federal Communications Commission from issuing a license to any company in which a "foreign entity" has ownership of 25 percent or more.

Inserted at the behest of Ernest F. Hollings of South Carolina, ranking Democrat on the CJS subcommittee, the provision is aimed at blocking the proposed takeover of the U.S. company VoiceStream Wireless Corp. by Deutsche Telekom, a company partially owned by the German government.

While Lott said he agreed with the idea behind the provision, he said it would be wrong for the United States to take the action unilaterally. "I would urge the conferees to drop that particular language," he said Sept. 26.

Conferees Haggle Over Tobacco, Peacekeeping

OCTOBER 7 — Negotiators of the appropriations bill for the Commerce, Justice and State departments inched closer on some funding disputes and settled a major policy question the week of Oct. 2.

The tough policy issue resolved: Conferees dropped a provision in the Senate version of the fiscal 2001 bill that would have allowed judges to take some honoraria for speeches, House CJS Subcommittee Chairman Harold Rogers of Kentucky confirmed.

The two chambers also got closer to agreement on the spending levels for the three departments covered by the bill.

But the bill (HR 4690) remains one of the most troubled. When House Rules Committee Chairman David Dreier, R-Calif., announced the House schedule for the week of Oct. 9, CJS was not even mentioned on the ambitious to-do list for appropriations.

Because the bill never passed the Senate, negotiations on its final form are informal, allowing staff and members to haggle over the measure in private, without the press or other members being privy to the discussions.

The ramifications of such closed-door bargaining are just starting to be felt. The bill is becoming a legislative magnet, attracting a wide variety of provisions from all corners of the Capitol. A nasty debate over funding for coastal protection and conservation in the Interior appropriations bill, for example, was settled in part by a promise to attach money to the CJS measure.

Five days into the new fiscal year, the staff of the Senate CJS Appropriations Subcommittee met for the first time with budget staff from the Clinton administration in order to see what the "parameters" of negotiations would be, according to subcommittee Chairman Judd Gregg, R-N.H.

But no one thinks final resolution on the bill will be easy or come soon.

While the members of the CJS subcommittees in the House and Senate have agreed on some subjects, many of the bigger issues have yet to be resolved, even among Republicans.

Rogers said Oct. 4 that some of the big-picture funding questions are close to resolution, and he said the final total for the bill would exceed the $37.4 billion in the version passed by the House June 26.

There are several policy questions that also are likely to prove difficult to resolve, such as whether to include money to pay for the federal government's lawsuit against the tobacco industry and whether to prohibit foreign ownership of U.S. telecommunications companies.

More Money

Going into the conference, spending priorities differed significantly between the House bill and the $36.7 billion measure reported by the Senate Appropriations Committee. The full Senate never considered the bill.

After about a week of negotiations, Rogers said funding for the Justice Department in the final bill would be closer to the $20.2 billion in the House-passed bill than the $18.7 billion in the Senate Appropriations version.

He said the House moved closer to the Senate's $2.7 billion for the National Oceanic and Atmospheric Administration than the $2.2 billion level in the House measure.

Rogers also said the Senate had agreed to move closer to the $1 billion requested by the administration for funding for worldwide embassy security upgrades. The Senate had cut that by some $280 million.

However, all sides remain far apart on the question of funding for international peacekeeping, Rogers said. The White House requested $739 million for the U.S. assessment from the United Nations on international peacekeeping. But the House version includes only $498 million for the account and would restrict funding for certain peacekeeping activities in Africa. The Senate bill includes $500 million for U.N. peacekeeping, though it does not include the Africa restrictions.

Even as members add more money to resolve spending differences in the bill itself, the leadership is planning to add still more money to address problems with at least one other appropriations measure, the Interior bill.

Sen. Mary L. Landrieu, D-La., and others had threatened to attach a massive $45 billion, 15-year lands conservation bill (HR 701) known as the Conservation and Reinvestment Act to the Interior bill. To appease them and keep the Interior bill on track, Senate Majority Leader Trent Lott, R-Miss., agreed to add millions to the CJS bill for conservation projects in coastal states. An as-yet-undetermined amount also likely will be included for state wildlife programs.

"We're working very hard to get the coastal impact piece and the wildlife piece into [the CJS] bill . . . and then we can come back next year and do the rest," Landrieu said.

When asked if coastal funding will be added to CJS, Gregg responded, "I presume so."

Tobacco Troubles

There is likely to be a lengthy battle over money and policy when it comes to the Justice Department's lawsuit against the major tobacco companies, seeking billions of dollars in damages.

On Sept. 28, a federal court ruled that the Justice Department could not recover federal health care costs incurred because of smoking-related illnesses. But the court ruled that the lawsuit could proceed with other charges filed by the Justice Department alleging "unlawful activity" under the Racketeer Influenced and Corrupt Organizations Act.

Neither version of the CJS bill includes money to pursue the tobacco lawsuit, though the House bill would allow the Justice Department to recoup legal costs from other federal agencies.

Both bills would require the Justice Department to ask Congress for a "reprogramming" of other funds for the tobacco suit.

"We are at a critical juncture today in this litigation," Attorney General Janet Reno said at her regular briefing on Oct. 5. "It is time to move forward with preparation for trial. In order to do so in a manner that does justice to the interest of the American people, I call on Congress to fund the Justice Department at the levels necessary to continue our efforts in this litigation."

She estimated that her department would need $23 million in fiscal 2001 for the lawsuit.

David W. Ogden, assistant attorney general, said the reprogramming requirement, which would send the Justice Department back to congressional committees regularly to request money, would be problematic. "We would need specific permission case-by-case for such a reprogramming and for such a use of the funds. And the consequence of that is that it injects the political process into funding decisions of litigation and potentially creates a roadblock to funding this case or, potentially, other cases."

Rogers, for example, who is from the tobacco state of Kentucky and has been skeptical of the lawsuit from the start, could block the reprogramming request.

"We'll get the money in there," said Sen. Ernest F. Hollings, D-S.C., the ranking Democrat on the CJS Appropriations Subcommittee. He said Reno might recommend a veto of the bill if the funds are not included.

Hollings also said his amendment limiting foreign ownership of telecommunications companies is still alive. The Senate Appropriations Committee version of the bill includes his amendment, designed to prevent the takeover of a U.S. company, VoiceStream Wireless Corp., by Deutsche Telekom AG, a business partially owned by the German government.

The provision would prohibit the Federal Communications Commission from granting a broadcast license to companies in which a "foreign entity" has a 25 percent ownership interest.

While Lott had indicated on Sept. 26 that he thought the provision should be dropped, Hollings said Oct. 5 it was still in the bill and vowed to keep it. Lott had been supportive of the provision but said the United States should not take any action unilaterally.

It is unclear what, if anything, the CJS bill will do about another FCC issue: NextWave Telecom. In 1996, NextWave agreed to pay $4.7 billion for airwave licenses that would allow the wireless phone company to operate. But after paying a $500 million down payment, the company sought bankruptcy protection. The FCC then moved to reclaim the frequencies, and the U.S. Court of Appeals for the 2nd Circuit recently ruled in the agency's favor. The FCC plans to re-auction the frequencies, which could now be worth as much as $10 billion, on Dec. 12. NextWave has been furiously lobbying the issue, but they seem to be coming up short.

The Senate bill sides with the FCC and would explicitly give the agency top priority in reclaiming assets, such as the licenses, in such cases.

Immigration Additions

Democrats in Congress and the White House have vowed to make the CJS bill the vehicle for a package of immigration changes that were blocked from being included in the H-1B visa bill (S 2045) cleared Oct. 3.

The fight is likely to be made easier by the fact that one of the three major elements of that package already is included in the Senate version of the bill. Called 245(i), the provision would allow immigrants who had applied for permanent residency to stay in the United States to complete the process, even if they had overstayed their visas. Each would pay a $1,000 fee, so the provision is a revenue-raiser, which has helped it pick up support among appropriators.

The two other major elements of the package, which taken together are called the Latino and Immigrant Fairness Act, would grant amnesty to longtime illegal immigrants who have been in the country since 1986 and would make it easier for some Central Americans, Liberians and Eastern Europeans to become permanent legal residents.

The Latino and Immigrant Fairness provisions have been a priority of Clinton and the Democrats, who are eagerly courting Hispanic votes this year.

Meanwhile, some agricultural interests are trying to revive a proposal to overhaul the visa program that governs migrant farm workers.

The House Judiciary Committee approved a bill (HR 4548) on Sept. 20 that would create a three-year pilot program that would allow growers to pay farm workers lower wages and that would remove the requirement in current law that the grower provide housing for the workers.

While the House GOP leadership has backed off its plan to bring the bill up on the floor, lobbyists are still looking for a way to get something into law.

Hispanic groups intensely oppose the farm worker bill.

Conference Continues Behind Closed Doors

OCTOBER 14 — Though they were moving closer to agreement on spending totals, negotiators continued to face a raft of contentious policy issues as they met behind closed doors the week of Oct. 9 on the fiscal 2001 spending bill for the departments of Commerce, Justice and State (HR 4690).

The most difficult issue is likely to be how far to go, if at all, in accommodating demands by the Clinton administration and congressional Democrats to add several immigration provisions, including amnesty for immigrants in the United States since 1986.

"The president is adamant about it, and we're adamant about it," House Minority Leader Richard A. Gephardt, D-Mo., said Oct. 12.

Lamar Smith, R-Texas, and other immigration critics called on GOP leaders to hold firm in opposition to the proposals. "Amnesty is a bad policy," said Smith, who chairs the House Judiciary Immigration Subcommittee. "It rewards lawbreakers, is unfair to law-abiding legal immigrants, makes a mockery of our laws and encourages new waves of illegal immigration."

Republicans sent a counter-offer to the White House on Oct. 13, which would allow illegal immigrants to apply for residency if they had been unable to do so because of the way the 1986 immigration law (PL 99-603) was implemented. The GOP plan would create a new kind of visa for spouses and children of permanent legal residents, making it easier for a family to stay together during the application period.

Conferees were unwilling to sign off on spending totals until all the policy issues were resolved, but it seemed likely that the final bill would exceed the $37.4 billion version passed by the House in June. Democratic staff sources indicated that the White House was ready to accept the funding. President Clinton had requested about $39.6 billion for the bill.

Clinton seems likely to get his full request of $739 million for the fiscal 2001 U.S. contribution to international peacekeeping, an increase of $241 million over the House-passed bill.

Members also may include additional funding for coastal conservation and wildlife programs that was in neither the House-passed nor the Senate committee-approved version of the bill.

Even with an agreement on much of the spending, however, the road ahead appears difficult. In addition to immigration, at least five significant policy issues must be resolved.

Policy Disputes

A proposal that would broaden federal hate crimes to include those committed because of a victim's gender, sexual orientation or disability, which was dropped from the fiscal 2001 defense authorization (HR 4205) on Oct. 5, reappeared as a potential amendment to the CJS bill the week of Oct. 9.

Members also must decide whether to fund the federal government's lawsuit against the tobacco companies. Neither version of the bill would directly fund the lawsuit. Instead, the Justice Department would have to come back to Congress to get approval to reprogram the money from another account.

The fate of two Federal Communications Commission (FCC) provisions is also unresolved. One, supported by Sen. Ernest F. Hollings, D-S.C., would prohibit the FCC from giving a broadcast license to companies in which a "foreign entity" has at least a 25 percent ownership. The provision, strongly opposed by the administration, is aimed at barring the takeover of the U.S. company VoiceStream Wireless Corp. by Deutsche Telekom AG, a firm partially owned by the German government. It seems likely to be dropped, though Hollings has yet to agree.

Members are also wrestling over a proposed FCC rule that would allow the licensing of low-power radio stations used by non-commercial groups to reach local audiences. It is opposed by radio broadcasters, and many in the Senate, including Commerce, Justice, State Appropriations Subcommittee Chairman Judd Gregg, R-N.H., would like to block it.

Members also must decide how to treat coastal funding. Sen. Mary L. Landrieu, D-La., and others want to earmark the money for coastal impact assistance — and not leave it to the discretion of appropriators, as was done in the Interior spending bill (HR 4578).

Immigration Battle

At issue in the immigration dispute are proposals that would grant amnesty to illegal immigrants who have been in the United States since 1986, allow some immigrants to stay in the country while their applications for residency are pending, and make it easier for some illegal aliens from Central America and Liberia to become residents.

In an unusually direct comment, the Office of Management and Budget said in an Oct. 6 policy statement: "The president will insist that these provisions be included before the bill is signed into law."

"The big stumbling block is amnesty," said House Judiciary Committee Chairman Henry J. Hyde, R-Ill. "We all remember the [1986 immigration] bill. It didn't work as it was supposed to." The 1986 bill included a large amnesty program. *(1986 Almanac, p. 61)*

Smith released a draft report Oct. 12 prepared by the Immigration and Naturalization Service, showing that, as of January 1997, there were 5.1 million illegal immigrants in the United States, almost the same level, Smith said, as before the 1986 amnesty.

Smith was joined at the press conference by Dana Rohrabacher, R-Calif., Tom Tancredo, R-Colo., Virgil H. Goode Jr., I-Va., and Nathan Deal, R-Ga. Rohrabacher said members had been promised that the 1986 amnesty would be a one-time deal.

Senate Clears Bill For Clinton, Who Promises a Veto

OCTOBER 28 — Though Republicans have given President Clinton nearly everything he requested in fiscal 2001 funding for the departments of Commerce, Justice and State, the bill remained under threat of a veto.

The total for the bill, which was attached to the final version of the fiscal 2001 District of Columbia appropriations bill (HR 4942), is nearly $40 billion.

The main complaint for Clinton and congressional Democrats is what is *not* in the bill — the package of immigration changes they call the Latino and Immigrant Fairness Act. Instead, the bill includes a narrower immigration package crafted by the GOP as an alternative.

In an Oct. 26 letter, Clinton said he would veto the bill because of the immigration provisions. His letter also highlighted several other measures left out of the bill, including provisions to broaden federal hate crime laws and money to fund the government's lawsuit against the tobacco companies.

At the end of the week of Oct. 23, Republicans appeared to have rolled the dice. Senate Majority Leader Trent Lott, R-Miss., said they planned to send the bill to the president and hope he will not veto it until negotiations on the spending bill for the departments of Labor and Health and Human Services are complete. The GOP hopes it can accommodate enough of Clinton's concerns in the appropriations bill for Labor-HHS to make CJS signable.

But Lott acknowledged there was no agreement with the administration, and Sen. Ernest F. Hollings, D-S.C., said he believed Clinton would veto the CJS bill as soon as he got it.

Clinton and Democrats also vociferously objected to a provision that Republicans said was designed to protect Social Security numbers from being sold for profit. Democrats charged that the section as it is drafted would offer little protection because it covers only the sale of such personal information by banks and credit bureaus to individuals, not companies.

Another sticky question was settled when the conferees agreed to add $420 million to the bill for conservation and coastal environment grant programs. After a long fight, appropriators also included language desired by the environmental authorizing committees earmarking large portions of the additional funding.

By Oct. 27, both chambers had passed the bill. But Clinton issued a very clear veto threat, and the margins of victory in both chambers were narrow enough to guarantee that his veto would be sustained.

The House passed the bill Oct. 26, by a vote of 206-198; the Senate cleared the measure for the president the next day by a vote of 48-43. *(House vote 562, p. H-178; Senate vote 289, p. S-52)*

Immigration Battle

At the heart of the fight was immigration. Democrats first drafted the Latino package as an amendment to the bill that increased the number of H-1B visas for highly skilled workers (PL 106-313).

The package has three major provisions. It would grant amnesty to illegal immigrants who have been in the country since 1986. It would make it easier for some Central American aliens, especially those from Honduras and Guatemala, to become permanent residents. And it would allow those who have applied for residency, but whose visa has expired, to pay a $1,000 fee to stay in the country while their application is pending, a provision called 245i, which used to be law but lapsed in 1997.

Once Democrats were foiled in their attempt to attach the package to the H-1B measure, they turned their attention to the CJS bill.

In October, the White House's statement of administration policy on the CJS appropriations bill made clear that Clinton expected the Democrats' immigration plan to be included, or he would not sign it.

Despite this and other equally direct comments, Republicans held out hope that they could avoid a veto.

"I don't think the president will veto the bill," Senate Judiciary Committee Chairman Orrin G. Hatch, R-Utah, one of the authors of the GOP's immigration package, said Oct. 25.

Told that Clinton had already said he would do so, Sen. Phil Gramm, R-Texas, a sponsor of the GOP plan, responded: "You can't believe everything the president said."

Republicans drafted an immigration package that would allow illegal aliens who have been battling the Immigration and Naturalization Service over the implementation of the 1986 amnesty program to take their case to court.

The GOP plan also would create a new kind of visitors visa that would allow spouses and children of people who are legal permanent residents to live in the United States while their applications for residency are pending.

Judith E. Golub, a lobbyist for the American Immigration Lawyers Association, called the GOP proposal "interesting, but not enough." And Oscar Chacon of the Salvadoran-American National Network said "it's really designed to divide and conquer" the immigration community.

Lott said, "We've gone as far as we can go . . . In this process, the president doesn't get everything he wants, and neither do we."

For many Republicans, amnesty seems to be the biggest issue. Senate Republicans included a reauthorization of 245i in their version of the CJS bill, and there seems to be some sympathy for Central American immigrants.

Some Republicans also suggest there could be political advantage in forcing Clinton to veto a bill that funds a number of popular programs because he wants to reward illegal immigrants. "Amnesty does not sell," said John P. Feehery, press secretary to House Speaker J. Dennis Hastert, R-Ill.

Spending Set

All the major funding controversies in the bill were solved largely by allocating more money for most programs than had been included in either the House or Senate versions of the bill.

The Justice Department would get $21.1 billion, a $2.4 billion increase over fiscal 2000. That includes $1.03 billion for one of Clinton's signature programs, Community Oriented Policing Service, which provides grants to state and local communities to hire police and beef up technology.

While the level is about $300 million less than Clinton requested, it is significantly higher than the fiscal 2000 level of $482 million. Of that, $140 million is set aside for a technology program, and the report lists dozens of programs — over 11 pages worth — that should get the money.

The bill includes $569 million for Byrne crime-fighting grants to the states, and $686.5 million in prison construction grants that are available to states that have passed truth-in-sentencing laws. Those laws generally require a criminal to serve at least 85 percent of his or her sentence.

The bill includes $250 million in juvenile justice block grants and another $279 million for juvenile justice programs (with six pages of earmarks for the money). States would get $565 million in federal assistance to help defer the costs of incarcerating aliens.

Grant programs under the 1994 Violence Against Women Act would get $288.7 million. Congress reauthorized the grant programs earlier this month.

The bill would provide at least two parts of the Clinton administration's gun enforcement plan. The bill would appropriate $100 million for the community prosecutors program, for increasing the prosecution of gun crimes. The bill also includes $8 million for research into "smart gun" technology designed to make it difficult for the wrong person to use the weapon.

It does not include any money for the tobacco lawsuit, though there is no provision preventing the department from conducting the suit, something that had been considered by Republicans in Congress.

The bill does not include a Senate provision that would have created a deputy attorney general in charge of anti-terrorism planning. A Senate plan to set aside $414 million in emergency spending for a Southwest border initiative also was rejected. The conference report notes that much of the spending called for in that initiative is included as non-emergency spending for the Justice Department.

The bill would authorize the creation of 10 new district court judge positions: one each in Arizona, Florida, Kentucky, Nevada, New Mexico, South Carolina, Virginia and Wisconsin, and two in Texas. It also contains a provision that would allow federal judges to get a cost-of-living increase in fiscal 2001 if members of Congress get one. The Senate bill included a provision that would have allowed judges to take honoraria for speaking engagements, a practice that is banned. The conference report strips that provision.

International Affairs

The bill would more than fully fund the president's fiscal 2001 request for international peacekeeping. The president requested $739 million; the bill would appropriate $846 million, with the proviso that up to 15 percent of that total can remain available until the end of fiscal 2002.

The bill would prohibit the peacekeeping money from being used in Western Sahara, but does not include other restrictions on Africa deployments included by the House.

The measure includes $1.1 billion to fully fund the president's security upgrade for embassies around the world and would create a new position, deputy secretary of state for management and resources.

And it includes $5 million to reimburse the city of Seattle, Wash., for costs incurred during the riots at last year's world trade talks.

Miscellaneous

The bill also includes:

- $330 million for the Legal Services Corp.; $1 billion for the Patent and Trademark Office; $441 million for international broadcasting programs; $303.9 million for the Equal Employment Opportunity Commission; $230 million for the Federal Communications Commission; $422.8 million for the Securities and Exchange Commission, and $40 million to help implement the Pacific Salmon Treaty.
- A new, $1.25 billion loan guarantee program designed to help companies that build the infrastructure needed to help rural areas get local television stations. The provision is similar to a bill (S 2097) passed by the Senate on March 30.
- A provision blocking a rule proposed by the Federal Communications Commission that would allow low-powered radio stations to be set up by community groups. The bill would require the FCC to study possible signal interference from the additional stations in some areas before they could proceed.
- A provision that would raise the threshold for mergers that are subject to review by the Federal Trade Commission. It would set the threshold at mergers of $50 million or more, significantly higher than the current level of $15 million. It also would create a sliding scale for fees, based on the size of the business. It is similar to legislation (S 1854) passed by the Senate Oct. 19.
- A ban on money in the bill being used to implement the Kyoto Treaty on global warming.
- A ban on money in the bill being used by the State Department to help the Chinese Xinhua News Agency buy property in Arlington, Va.

Central American Immigration Is Sticking Point In Negotiations

NOVEMBER 4 — A bitter debate during the 1980s over which Central American governments the United States should support has re-emerged in recent weeks as an obstacle to settling immigration issues currently slowing Congress' effort to adjourn for the year.

Even as the Clinton administration took a step toward the Republican position on one immigration issue involving amnesty for illegal aliens, the battle over a provision for Central Americans in the Democrats' "Latino and Immigrant Fairness Act" intensified during the week of Oct. 30.

Immigration is one of the final issues to be decided in the 106th Congress. Senate Majority Leader Trent Lott, R-Miss., cited lack of progress on it as one of the major reasons Republicans decided to take a "time out" from negotiations and send their members home for the elections Nov. 7.

President Clinton has said he will veto the fiscal 2001 spending bill for the departments of Commerce, Justice and State (HR 4942) if Republicans do not include the Democrats' immigration package. Republicans included an alternative immigration package in the CJS bill, which Clinton and congressional Democrats said would not go far enough. The $39.9 billion CJS bill, which the Senate cleared on Oct. 27, will not be sent to the White House until a final deal is reached on all spending bills.

At issue are three proposed changes to immigration law. One would provide amnesty to all illegal immigrants who have lived continuously in the United States since 1986. Another would allow those who fled Central America in the 1980s to apply for legal residency, and the third — called 245(i) — would restore a provision of law that makes it easier for some immigrants to stay in the country after their visa has expired if a residency application is pending.

While the provision for Central Americans came under increased fire, there were signs that the two sides could be moving toward a deal on other issues, including the Democrats' 1986 amnesty proposal, which Republicans considered far too broad.

White House Chief of Staff John D. Podesta offered in an Oct. 27 letter to Senate Judiciary Committee Chairman Orrin G. Hatch, R-Utah, to limit the proposal to one class of illegal immigrants: those who were unfairly denied the opportunity to apply for amnesty under the 1986 immigration overhaul. (PL 99-603) *(1986 Almanac, p. 61)*

The 1986 law granted amnesty to thousands of illegal immigrants who could prove they had been living continuously in the United States since 1981. But the regulations used to implement the law were seen by many as too restrictive. Immigration advocates, supported by several court decisions, argue that the Immigration and Naturalization Service denied amnesty to many who were eligible.

In 1996, a crackdown on illegal immigration (PL 104-208) stripped the courts of their power to adjudicate these cases unless aliens could show they had tried to apply for amnesty and were rebuffed by the government. *(1996 Almanac, p. 5-3)*

To settle the issue, Clinton proposed the amnesty. Hatch and others wrote an alternative, which was included in the final version of the CJS bill, that would make all participants in two massive class action lawsuits against the INS eligible to apply for amnesty. And it would restore the ability of federal courts to act on the cases.

In his letter, Podesta sought to broaden the GOP proposal. His response would allow illegal immigrants in the United States continuously since 1981 to apply for amnesty, whether or not they are party to a class action suit.

While Hatch did not accept the counter-offer, it did narrow the differences between the two sides considerably. And Hatch, in his response to Podesta's letter, did not reiterate his objections to 245(i), a sign, according to some immigration supporters, that the GOP might be willing to include it in a final package.

Reagan Redux

Even as negotiators took small steps toward compromise, positions appeared to harden on the third part of the Democrats' immigration bill, the Central Americans provision.

Hundreds of thousands of people came to the United States in the 1980s from Central America — most illegally — to escape oppressive regimes and civil wars. In Congress, Democrats and Republicans clashed over the foreign policy of President Ronald Reagan, who supported regimes that opposed communism, even if the governments themselves were repressive.

The 1996 immigration overhaul would have subjected many of those refugees to deportation. In 1997, Congress allowed Nicaraguans and Cubans to apply for legal residency (PL 105-100), and made it easier for Salvadorans and Guatemalans to avoid deportation. It provided no relief for Hondurans. *(1997 Almanac, p. 5-11)*

The Democrats' proposal would make all Central American refugees eligible to apply for residency, a proposal that could affect 415,000 people according to supporters. Opponents said the number could reach 1.5 million.

Republicans, led by Lamar Smith, R-Texas, chairman of the House Judiciary Immigration and Claims Subcommittee and author of the 1996 immigration law, defended their decision to treat the refugees differently.

Smith said Honduras did not have a civil war and has had a democratically elected government since 1982. But the country was at the heart of the struggle for dominance in the region — many of the anti-government forces funded by the United States against Nicaragua were located in Honduras. And for much of the early 1980s, the military retained a strong influence over the government.

Immigration Deal Clears Way For CJS Bill

DECEMBER 16 — A deal to make it easier for an estimated 1 million legal and illegal immigrants to stay in the United States freed the long-held fiscal 2001 spending bill for the departments of Commerce, Justice and State, and the federal judiciary.

Immigration was one of the last sticking points of the lame-duck session. The immigration deal, struck late Dec. 14, was included in the conference report on the fiscal 2001 omnibus spending bill (HR 4577) that the House adopted, 292-60, on Dec. 15. The Senate cleared it by voice vote. *(House vote 603, p. H-190)*

Under the agreement, some immigrant families will be allowed to remain together in the United States as they wait for permanent residency. It also would allow some illegal immigrants to apply for permanent residency while in the United States instead of having to return to their homelands.

It does not contain the more far-reaching — and more controversial — proposals espoused by the two sides in the immigration debate. Many Democrats had wanted a broad amnesty program for illegal immigrants; Republicans were pushing changes to the migrant farmworker program.

The Senate had cleared the CJS bill Oct. 27 as a part of the District of Columbia appropriations conference report (HR 4942). Republicans never sent it to the White House because President Clinton had threatened to veto it, since it did not contain the immigration provisions Democrats wanted.

Because the District's spending bill then was sent to the president in another bill (PL 106-522), the omnibus bill contains language effectively stripping the D.C. bill from HR 4942. In the end, that bill will have just the CJS spending provisions.

Also in the omnibus bill are provisions stripping from the CJS measure language that was designed to prevent the sale of Social Security numbers. That language proved so controversial that supporters decided to pull it and try again next year.

Two other programs were also attached to the CJS bill: a new $1.25 billion loan guarantee program to encourage companies to build the infrastructure necessary to help rural areas get local television signals, and a provision to block implementation of a proposed rule by the Federal Communication Commission that would have allowed local community groups to set up low-power radio stations.

CJS Spending Highlights

Where the Money Goes

HR 4942 — Conference report: H Rept 106-1005

Spending Synopsis

The fiscal 2001 appropriations bill for the departments of Commerce, Justice and State and related agencies provided $39.9 billion, $267 million more than the total enacted in fiscal 2000. The agreement was $11 billion less than President Clinton requested, but that difference was the result of advance appropriations the White House had included. Though the bill was cleared Oct. 27, it was not signed until Dec. 21, delayed by negotiations over immigration provisions. The compromise on immigration was included in the year-end omnibus spending bill (HR 4577).

● **Justice Department**

More than half the spending — $21.1 billion — would go to the Justice Department, which includes the FBI, federal prisons, the Immigration and Naturalization Service, the Drug Enforcement Administration and the handling of federal criminal prosecutions and civil lawsuits. The agreement is $576 million less than Clinton's fiscal 2001 request, but is more than either the House or Senate originally approved.

● **Commerce Department**

The conference agreement would provide $5.2 billion for the Commerce Department and related agencies. Of that, about $3 billion would go to the National Oceanic and Atmospheric Administration, which is a third of what Clinton requested, but it is $816.5 million more than the House version and $360 million more than was in the Senate bill.

● **State Department**

The conference agreement would provide $6.6 billion for the State Department, nearly $500 million more than either the House or Senate versions, but significantly below the $9.8 billion request of the administration, which included $3.35 billion in advance appropriations.

Hot-Button Issues

Δ **Peacekeeping.** The House proposed cutting $241 million from Clinton's request for U.S. contributions to international peacekeeping, which Clinton called "devastating." The conference report would spend $846 million, $107 million more than requested.

Δ **COPS.** The conference report would provide $1.03 billion for Community Oriented Policing Services, more than $300 million below Clinton's request. The House bill had offered $595 million, the same level as fiscal 2000. The Senate committee version would have appropriated $812 million.

Δ **Tobacco.** The conference agreement included no money for the Justice Department to pursue its case against tobacco companies for the federal cost of smoking-related illness. But it also eliminated a provision in the House version that effectively would have prohibited the Justice Department from continuing the suit.

Δ **Immigration.** The conference report includes a GOP alternative to the Latino Immigrant Fairness Act supported by the White House. The GOP plan would let illegal immigrants in disputes with the Immigration and Naturalization Service over a 1986 amnesty program to take their cases to court. The Latino Act would offer blanket amnesty to illegal aliens in the United States since 1986.

Δ **Conservation.** The agreement includes $420 million for conservation and coastal land grants left out of the Interior appropriations. (PL 106-291)

(figures are in thousands of dollars of new budget authority)

	Fiscal 2000 Appropriation	Fiscal 2001 Clinton Request	House Bill	Senate Bill	Conference Report
Department of Justice	$18,646,502	$21,651,347	$20,237,327	$18,726,613	$21,075,745
Commerce and Related Agencies	8,719,438	12,138,939	4,353,430	4,915,549	5,241,756
The Judiciary	3,959,292	4,421,987	4,207,691	4,236,991	4,263,525
Department of State	5,880,344	9,865,260	6,110,014	6,117,265	6,609,667
Related Agencies	2,038,370	2,417,163	2,055,664	2,248,831	2,201,917
Other*	421,774	448,272	438,135	878,531	441,424
Rescissions	-64,753	-10,000	-7,644	-433,825	-15,644
GRAND TOTAL	**$39,600,967**	**$50,932,968****	**$37,394,617**	**$36,689,955**	**$39,868,390**
Total adjusted for scorekeeping	**($38,220,346)**	**($38,250,619)**	**($35,424,219)**	**($34,058,327)**	**($38,101,711)**

* For international broadcasting; Senate number also incudes southwest border initiative. ** Includes $11.3 billion in advance appropriations.

TABLE: House and Senate Appropriations committees

Immigration Changes

The final immigration deal consists of two parts: a section included in HR 4942, and the new provisions included in the omnibus bill.

Those in HR 4942 would create a new type of temporary visa for spouses and children of permanent legal residents and spouses of U.S. citizens, allowing them to come to the United States and remain in the country until they become permanent residents.

It also would allow plaintiffs in two class-action lawsuits against the government who argue they were unfairly denied amnesty under the 1986 immigration overhaul (PL 99-603) to apply for permanent residency.

Language added to the omnibus bill would broaden that to members of three specific class-action cases, which members said would cover some 400,000 people.

The omnibus bill also would reinstate a provision of law — known as 245(i) — which applies to a broader category of immigrants. The law makes it easier for certain immigrants, who came to the country legally but have overstayed their visas while in the residency application process, to stay in the country while the process is under way. Current law requires them to return to their home countries once their visas expire. To qualify for the new 245(i), the immigrant would have to have a family member legally in the United States or be sponsored by an employer.

However, the agreement would only reinstate 245(i) for four months, meaning those immigrants who qualify would have to apply for residency within that time frame. Democrats wanted the law reinstated permanently.

Democrats Cry Foul

"The agreement takes care of about 1 million people," said Senate Judiciary Chairman Orrin G. Hatch, R-Utah, who added that remaining immigration issues could be examined next year. But members of the congressional Hispanic Caucus railed against White House officials for giving in on the broader amnesty for illegal aliens.

"I am deeply troubled to learn that your administration will accept a disappointingly insufficient and deeply flawed Republican proposal," Rep. Luis V. Gutierrez, D-Ill., said in a letter sent to Clinton on Dec. 14.

Clinton had threatened to veto the CJS bill if it did not include amnesty for those Central Americans, Haitians and Liberians who did not receive amnesty under the 1997 Nicaraguan Adjustment and Central American Relief Act (PL 105-100) ◆

Lawmakers Camouflage Some Defense Funds As "Emergency" Spending

BoxScore 2001 Fiscal Year
Defense

- **Bill:** HR 4576 — PL 106-259
- **Legislative action: House** passed HR 4576 (H Rept 106-644), 367-58, June 7.

Senate passed HR 4576, 95-3, on June 13, after substituting the text of S 2593 (S Rept 106-298).

House adopted the conference report on HR 4576 (H Rept 106-754), 367-58, on July 19.

Senate cleared the bill, 91-9, on July 27.

President signed HR 4576 on Aug. 9.

SUMMARY

Congress cleared a $289.6 billion defense spending bill for fiscal 2001, $5.1 billion more than President Clinton requested. To avoid breaking spending limits set by the annual budget resolution, conferees designated $1.8 billion of the increase as fiscal 2000 emergency spending.

Though projected budget surpluses were ballooning by the time Congress got down to drafting the annual defense funding bill, Republican defense hawks found themselves in a political bind.

Both Clinton and GOP congressional leaders had ruled out using the growing Social Security surplus for discretionary spending. That left the defense appropriations subcommittees competing with other domestic priorities for a more limited supply of extra funds. A relatively small but deeply committed band of fiscal conservatives threatened to torpedo any proposal that sacrificed tax cuts to fund defense increases.

In March, leaders of the House Armed Services Committee cited a list of unfunded needs drawn up by the Joint Chiefs of Staff to support their call for adding $12 billion to $15 billion to Clinton's request.

In the end, the practical effect of the budget process was to allow the House and Senate Appropriations committees to exceed by less than $4 billion Clinton's request for defense, which does not include separately funded military construction or defense-related programs of the Energy Department. *(Military construction, p. 2-123; Energy and water, p. 2-59)*

The decision by House and Senate conferees to designate almost a third of the increased spending as fiscal 2000 emergency appropriations was a thinly disguised ruse: The bill was cleared with about two months left in fiscal 2000, and the "emergency" spending included routine maintenance costs and operations in Bosnia, Kosovo and the Persian Gulf that had been going on for some time.

As usual, the bill was studded with projects of special interest to influential lawmakers. The largest was the addition of $460 million for components of a helicopter carrier to be built by Litton Industries in Pascagoula, Miss., hometown of Senate Majority Leader Trent Lott. The Pentagon had not planned to request most of the money for the $1.5 billion ship until 2005, but the contractor and the Navy insisted that earlier funding would save hundreds of millions of dollars.

The bill also added $400 million to Clinton's request to continue producing F-15 fighters at the Boeing Co.'s plant in St. Louis, a priority for Republican Sen. Christopher S. Bond, an Appropriations Committee member, and Democratic House Minority Leader Richard A. Gephardt, both of Missouri.

Most of the added funding was for hundreds of relatively small projects — so many that conferees included language to trim 0.7 percent from each procurement and research program, saving $705 million.

The bill funded the 3.7 percent military pay raise the president requested and added $200 million to cover the cost of a program in the companion defense authorization bill (HR 4205) that would give most military retirees access to low-cost prescription drugs.

The bill nearly doubled — to $1.6 billion — what Clinton requested for the Army's long-term effort to make its combat units lighter and thus easier to deploy overseas.

It provided the $3.9 billion Clinton requested to continue flight testing the Air Force's F-22 fighter and to buy 10 more of the planes built by Lockheed Martin.

House Panel Targets Army Mobility, Joint Strike Fighter

MAY 13 — The House Defense Appropriations Subcommittee swiftly approved a $288.6 billion fiscal 2001 defense spending bill May 11 that would increase spending for a lighter and more mobile Army and would require more testing of the military's Joint Strike Fighter before production could begin.

The subcommittee approved the unnumbered draft bill by voice vote in a closed-door session. The full Appropriations Committee is expected to consider the bill by May 25.

The measure covers Pentagon spending except for military construction, which is handled in a separate appropriation.

The subcommittee said the bill would provide about $4 billion more than President Clinton requested, $19.6 billion more than the fiscal 2000 appropriation (PL 106-79) and about $200 million more than the full committee allocated for defense.

The bill would provide about $1.8 billion, or $1.1 billion more than Clinton requested, to develop and buy lighter vehicles and weapons as part of the Army's effort to transform itself into a more mobile force.

The legislation would put restrictions on the Joint Strike Fighter (JSF) similar to those adopted by the House and Senate Armed Services committees in their fiscal 2001 authorization bills (HR 4205, S 2481))

The bill would cut $300 million from Clinton's $595 million request for the plane to enter its next phase of engineering and manufacturing development. But it would add $150 million to a program that assesses whether the plane's technology is progressing enough to merit moving into full-scale development.

Subcommittee Chairman Jerry Lewis, R-Calif., said the funding reduction and shift would result in a three-month delay, from March 2001 to June 2001, before the Air Force decides to award the contract to begin full-scale development. The nation's two largest defense contractors — The Boeing Co. and Lockheed Martin Corp. — are competing for the contract, but committee members predicted the Pentagon would split the contract between two or more companies.

"It is highly likely that the Department of Defense will soon announce a revised acquisition strategy for the JSF, from the current 'winner-take-all' to one involving a team of contractors," the subcommittee said in a statement. "The subcommittee believes that this will almost certainly change the program's schedule and costs."

The Joint Strike Fighter program, estimated to cost $200 billion, is designed to replace several aging models of fighters, including F-16s and F-18s. "We can afford to slip a little" with the JSF's schedule, Lewis said.

F-22 Redux

The Joint Strike Fighter provisions are similar to language Lewis and his subcommittee inserted in last year's appropriations bill in an attempt to delay another advanced fighter, Lockheed Martin's F-22.

The subcommittee last year cited cost increases and production problems to argue that it would be premature to commit to full-scale production of the F-22. Conferees eventually agreed on a compromise allowing the Air Force to begin building up to six F-22s, but with the planes designated to conduct additional tests

This year's bill would require that the F-22 continue to meet certain testing requirements before production could begin. If the testing goals are met, the Air Force could spend $2.1 billion to buy 10 planes.

The spending bill would provide about $375 million for the Air Force to buy five F-15 fighters — a victory for Missouri lawmakers who have been fighting to keep production lines open at the Boeing plant in St. Louis. The administration did not request money for F-15s.

In recent months, the Defense Department's director for operational test and evaluation, Philip E. Coyle, has warned that not enough testing has been done to know for certain whether the F-22 has flaws.

The bill also would provide $150 million more than Clinton sought to enhance the security of Defense Department computers.

Lewis said the bill would provide almost $2 billion more than the president's request for activities aimed at improving the "quality of life" for military personnel. It would pay for enhanced pharmacy benefits, a 3.7 percent pay raise beginning in January 2001, and increased housing allowances for members who live off-base.

Senate Committee OKs Bill, Adding $4.1 Billion for Overseas Missions

MAY 20 — Senate Appropriators want to avoid wrestling with a supplemental spending bill next year to finance military operations overseas, so they included $4.1 billion for those operations in a fiscal 2001 defense spending measure that it approved May 18.

The bill (S 2593), approved 27-0, would appropriate $287.4 billion for the Pentagon. That is $3.1 billion more than President Clinton requested, but $1.2 billion less than a draft spending bill moving through the House Appropriations Committee.

Military construction and defense programs in the Energy Department are handled in other appropriations bills.

The Senate is expected to consider the appropriations bill in June after finishing the fiscal 2001 defense authorization bill (S 2549). The House Appropriations Committee is expected to take up its version the week of May 22.

The Senate appropriations bill would fully fund many provisions of the the committee version of the Senate defense authorization bill (S 2549) aimed at improving the quality of life of military members. It would pay for a 3.7 percent pay raise, recruitment and retention bonuses, increased off-base housing allowances and prescription drug coverage for military retirees.

Senate Appropriations Committee Chairman Ted Stevens, R-Alaska, who also is chairman of the defense subcommittee, said lawmakers included the $4.1 billion for overseas contingency operations to prevent a repeat of controversies over supplemental bills.

The House passed a fiscal 2000 supplemental spending bill (HR 3908) on March 30 largely to restore military accounts depleted by peacekeeping operations in Kosovo and other areas, but Senate Majority Leader Trent Lott, R-Miss., refused to consider it. Instead, extra spending for this year has been parceled out to three fiscal 2001 appropriations measures in the Senate.

"We fully funded what we think will be the demand to stay" in those deployments, Stevens said before the Defense Subcommittee approved the bill by voice vote May 17. "There should not be a need for an emergency supplemental for the contingency operations in the year 2001."

The Clinton administration has angered Stevens and other Republicans with annual requests for supplementals to pay for military peacekeeping efforts. Although Clinton will leave office next year, Stevens said members want to discourage a new president from the practice of asking for money after deciding to deploy troops.

When that happens, "the supplementals become the *cause célèbre*, rather than the deployments," Stevens said.

During Senate floor debate May 17 about limiting troop withdrawals from Kosovo, Lott echoed Stevens' reluctance to continue deployments without budgeting for them in advance. "We cannot put men, our women, our ships, our planes in every corner of this world indefinitely with no plan," Lott said.

Joint Strike

Like the House and Senate defense authorization bills and the House defense spending bill, the Senate appropriations measure calls for the Defense Department to slow down its program for the Joint Strike Fighter (JSF), the most advanced of three air-superiority warplanes the Pentagon wants to buy.

The Navy, Marine Corps and Air Force plan to buy different versions of the plane beginning in 2008 to replace various planes of Vietnam War-era design. Current plans call for spending about $200 billion to develop and buy 3,000 planes.

The Senate appropriations bill would add $20 million to extend through June 2001 a program to assess whether the plane's technology is progressing enough to merit moving into full-scale development.

Unlike the other defense bills, though, the Senate spending legislation makes clear the preference of appropriators to have just one company build the fighter.

Many lawmakers are worried about the pace of technology development by The Boeing Co. and Lockheed Martin Corp., the two aerospace giants competing for a lucrative contract next year for engineering and manufacturing development of the fighter. Some of the lawmakers, including House appropriators, recently predicted that the Pentagon will split the contract between two or more companies. They say such a change will almost certainly affect the program's schedule and costs.

The draft Senate Appropriations committee report on the bill said the panel "is aware of no justification for changing the JSF acquisition strategy." It directs the Defense Department to use appropriated funds to continue proceeding with a "winner take all" contracting arrangement.

Stevens downplayed the notion that his committee is in conflict with the House over the contracting issue.

"We don't see the necessity to start determining what happens to the entity that loses," he told reporters. "I don't see this ought to be a situation where [Pentagon officials] sit down and say, 'Well, you've got the semi-best and you've got the near-best, so you get 55 percent and you get 45 percent.' Let's get a fighter we all like . . . and then we decide how much of that is going to be built by the entity that did not come up with the best plan."

Major Transport

On another aircraft-related issue, the Senate bill includes a provision to create a separate, servicewide program for long-range airlift cargo planes, mostly the C-17 wide-body jet.

The measure would provide $2.2 billion to buy 12 C-17s in fiscal 2001 and put that money in a new Pentagon fund to ensure that the services do not use it for other high-priced procurement programs, such as the Joint Strike Fighter or the F-22.

The proposed expansion of the account into a servicewide program is similar to the consolidation of missile defense programs under the Pentagon's Ballistic Missile Defense Organization. It also comes on the heels of a request by the service chiefs several years ago for a separate account for planes that can take off from and land on aircraft carriers.

"We just moved [the account] over, so it doesn't compete [with other programs], and we're going to keep that transportation line going on a departmental basis," Stevens said. "We believe the chiefs were right in asking us to create a sealift fund, and now we want them to create an airlift fund."

Funding for the C-17 would be placed under a new account.

Among the additions in the Senate spending bill are an extra $118 million to buy nine UH-60/CH-60 helicopters, $183 million for six F-16 fighters, $74.6 million for a KC-130J Marine Corps air refueling tanker and $90 million for one EC-130J special operations cargo plane.

Unlike the House bill, the Senate measure contains no money to purchase five new F-15 fighters. Missouri's congressional delegation has aggressively fought for money for planes to keep production lines open at Boeing's St. Louis plant.

Stevens, however, predicted, "We'll end up closer to the House figure when we come out of conference. . . . I believe there'll be some F-15s."

Mississippi Ship

The Senate bill would add $460 million in advance procurement for a $1.2 billion helicopter carrier to be built by Litton Industries in Pascagoula, Miss., Lott's hometown. The ship is designed to carry 1,800 marines and their helicopters.

A provision in the Senate version of the fiscal 2001 military construction appropriations bill (S 2521) would make the money for the carrier available in fiscal 2000, speeding up construction.

The defense appropriations bill would defer spending on two LPD-17-class cargo ships designed to carry Marine amphibious landing forces. Senators have been troubled by cost overruns and schedule delays.

The Senate bill would include $268 million to cover the overruns and $200 million in advance procurement for two ships in fiscal 2002.

The Appropriations Committee broke with the Clinton administration by restoring a proposed $92.4 million cut in the Air Force's program to build an anti-missile laser into a converted Boeing 747 airliner. The bill would provide $241 million for the program in fiscal 2001. The House version of the defense authorization bill (HR 4205) would transfer this program to the Ballistic Missile Defense Organization.

Air Force officials had said the proposed cut would defer from 2003 to 2005 the first effort to shoot down a large, ballistic missile with a prototype airborne laser. Sen. Pete V. Domenici, R-N.M., called the administration's requested cut "irresponsible."

The Senate spending bill also would add $250 million for the Army's $1 billion modernization effort. Through 2014, the Army plans to spend about $75 billion on modernization, two-thirds of which would go to new technology forces and $25 billion to upgrades of existing heavy forces.

The Senate bill would provide increases of $148.2 million for Army National Guard operations and maintenance and $150 million for Guard and Reserve equipment.

House Panel OKs Bill, Avoids Policy Confrontations

MAY 27 — House appropriators quickly approved a fiscal 2001 defense spending bill May 25 that steers clear of major policy disputes. The bill would provide nearly $4 billion more than President Clinton sought to replace aging Army equipment, protect Pentagon computers and accommodate lawmakers' pet projects.

The Appropriations Committee approved the unnumbered bill by voice vote after less than an hour of debate. At the request of Committee Chairman C.W. Bill Young, R-Fla., members proposed no changes to the measure, although several said they plan to offer amendments when the bill reaches the House floor, possibly in early June.

The measure would appropriate $288.5 billion for the Pentagon. That amount is $22.4 billion more than the fiscal 2000 level.

The bill does not include funding for construction of military facilities and housing or for defense-related programs of the Energy Department, which are funded in separate appropriations measures. *(Military construction, p. 2-123; energy and water, p. 2-59)*

The House defense bill contains $883 million more than the version (S 2593) approved May 17 by the Senate Appropriations Committee — extra funds that could increase the House's bargaining power in conference. Senate Majority Leader Trent Lott, R-Miss., attempted to call up the Senate appropriations bill May 25, but Minority Leader Tom Daschle, D-S.D., objected, blocking debate.

"I feel very, very comfortable that we've begun down a pathway to rebuild our national security," said House Defense Appropriations Subcommittee Chairman Jerry Lewis, R-Calif. His subcommittee had approved the bill on May 11.

But David R. Obey of Wisconsin, the Appropriations Committee's ranking Democrat, sharply questioned the $4 billion in add-ons to the president's $284.5 billion budget request. Obey described the additions as "a little case of one-upsmanship."

Obey said the blame rests not with the work of Lewis's subcommittee, but with the Republican-crafted budget resolution (H Con Res 290 — H Rept 106-577) and the Appropriations Committee's subsequent 302(b) spending allocation. The relatively large amount set aside for defense in those two measures "sucks out most of the increases in the other [spending] bills," Obey said.

"If we were operating in a limitless world, a world of unlimited resources, I would have no objections to this bill," he said.

The House and Senate appropriations bills would fund a 3.7 percent pay raise for military personnel that Clinton requested. They also would pay for recruiting and retention bonuses and increased off-base housing allowances.

House appropriators joined the Senate committee in including $4.1 billion for military contingency operations overseas in fiscal 2001. Appropriators are hoping to avoid having to pass a supplemental spending bill next year to finance ongoing peacekeeping operations in Kosovo and other areas.

In response to lawmakers' lingering concerns about military readiness, House appropriators added $1.3 billion for a variety of readiness-related shortfalls, including an extra $830 million for property maintenance, $343 million for depot maintenance and $110 million for training.

The House bill would add $281 million to Clinton's defense budget request to implement health care enhancements included in the House version of the fiscal 2001 defense authorization bill (HR 4205 — H Rept 106-616), including increased prescription drug coverage for military retirees.

Fighter Wings

In stark contrast to last year, House appropriators did not interfere with the Air Force's plans to continue developing the controversial Lockheed Martin F-22 fighter. The fiscal 2001 spending bill would provide $2.1 billion to buy 10 planes — the number sought by the Pentagon — as long as the Air Force met certain testing requirements before production began.

Lewis, who challenged the F-22 last year as unnecessarily expensive and sophisticated, has said he was optimistic the testing goals can be met. However, the Defense Department's director of operational testing and evaluation, Philip E. Coyle, has warned that not enough testing has been done yet to know for certain whether the F-22 has flaws.

Obey cited Coyle's warning, as well as information from Appropriations Committee investigators and the General Accounting Office, in questioning whether the committee should accede to the administration's request for 10 planes.

"I think we've still got some serious problems with the F-22," Obey said.

In response to a recommendation from Coyle, the Appropriations Committee did propose to replace the existing statutory budget limit on F-22 development with a single cap for the entire program. A committee report said the cap on development has led the Air Force to reduce or delay funding for testing in order to handle the rising costs of the aircraft's development.

On another controversial new tactical aircraft program, the Joint Strike Fighter, the committee added restrictions similar to those adopted by the House and Senate Armed Services committees in their fiscal 2001 authorization bills (HR 4205, S 2481).

Some lawmakers have raised concerns about moving too quickly on the Joint Strike Fighter program — estimated to cost upwards of $200 billion — before more testing of its technology. The plane, expected to enter service in 2008, would be built in versions for the Air Force, Navy and Marine Corps.

The House bill would cut $300 million from Clinton's $595.5 million request for full-scale engineering and manufacturing development of the plane. But it would add $150 million to a program that assesses whether the plane's technology is progressing enough to move to that next phase.

Although Lockheed Martin Corp. and Boeing Co. have competing designs for the plane, some lawmakers expect the Pentagon to change its "winner-take-all" arrangement to allow the contract to be split between two or more companies. The House spending measure would require the Pentagon to outline, within 60 days of the bill's enactment, what changes were being contemplated in the plane's acquisition.

At the urging of Missouri lawmakers, the committee added $400 million to buy five F-15 fighters, which are manufactured at the Boeing plant in St. Louis.

The administration did not request money for new F-15s. Although the Senate defense spending bill also does not have money for new F-15s, Senate Appropriations Committee Chairman

Ted Stevens, R-Alaska, has said he expects that money for at least several planes will be agreed to in conference.

Army Diet

The administration's fiscal 2001 budget request marked the first installment of an ambitious, 12- to 15-year, $70 billion effort to transform the Army from a Cold War-era force to a lighter, more mobile and more versatile branch.

The House defense spending bill includes $1.87 billion for the Army effort, an increase of $1.1 billion over Clinton's budget request.

House appropriators added $150 million for development and $133 million for procurement to completely test, equip and field a 4,000-person "Interim Brigade Combat Team" that is intended to bridge the gap between traditional heavy forces and lighter units. It also included an extra $800 million to equip and field a second team.

In addition, the committee added $46 million to the administration's request of $105 million to develop the radical new type of combat vehicle the Army is seeking.

Although Lewis expressed satisfaction with the Army's plan to reshape itself, he complained that the Defense Department's response to the interim brigade concept "has only been slightly more than lukewarm."

To prod the Pentagon, the committee report says it "expects and directs the [Defense Department] to include adequate funding in next year's budget request to meet the recommended pace of converting two brigades a year."

The report would prohibit obligating funds for the second interim brigade unless the Defense secretary certified that the budget request for fiscal 2002 and the budget plan for succeeding years would fully fund two additional brigades.

Another area that the Pentagon is seeking to modernize is its communications infrastructure. The House bill would add $150 million to address the Pentagon's most serious information technology problems. Although the committee report praised officials for making progress in protecting against computer attacks, it warned that "much more needs to be done."

Of the money added, $36 million would be for hardware and software to monitor computer networks to deter attacks. Another $35 million would be used for secure digital phones and $20 million to ensure that cell phones remain secure.

Missile Defense

To pay for ballistic missile defense programs, the appropriations bill includes $4.6 billion, an increase of $739 million over the current level and $168 million above the administration's request. The Senate spending bill contains $4.8 billion for missile defense programs.

Obey questioned the decision to add money for missile defense. He said the debate has focused on whether the system being developed by the Pentagon will function properly and has ignored "broader questions."

Among those questions, Obey said, is whether an anti-missile system would motivate China to build more nuclear weapons or provoke "a global arms race for anti-satellite weapons." He also said lawmakers have not assessed the potential damage to relations with European countries that have criticized the U.S. effort to deploy an anti-missile shield.

The missile defense issue surfaced in the presidential campaign May 23, when Texas Gov. George W. Bush, the expected Republican nominee, reiterated his desire to deploy a system if he is elected president. Russia has strongly objected to a U.S. anti-missile defense.

House-Passed Bill Adds $4 Billion To Clinton Request

JUNE 10 — House members have demonstrated their strong desire to avoid disputes over Pentagon spending by swiftly passing a $288.5 billion defense appropriations bill for fiscal 2001.

The 367-58 margin by which the bill (HR 4576) passed on June 7 showed how a profusion of money can pave over policy differences. The bill would provide $4 billion more than President Clinton requested and $22.4 billion more than was appropriated for fiscal 2000. *(Vote 241, p. H-78)*

While liberal Democrats cast most of the votes against passage, Democrats overall backed the bill by nearly 3-to-1.

"There is still a huge consensus in this Congress, at least 325 members, who are strongly committed [to more defense spending], and it is very bipartisan," said Democrat Norm Dicks of Washington, a member of the House Defense Appropriations Subcommittee, during debate on the measure.

The Senate, taking a break the next day from work on a defense authorization measure (S 2549 — S Rept 106-292), began debate on its own Pentagon spending bill (S 2593).

The Senate is expected to complete action on its measure during the week of June 12. That bill would provide about $1 billion less than the House version, but lawmakers are predicting few problems in conference.

For example, Senate Appropriations Committee Chairman Ted Stevens, R-Alaska, has said he expects the final bill to match the House's addition of $400 million to buy five F-15 fighters not included in the Senate measure or in the president's request. The planes are a priority for Missouri lawmakers, including House Minority Leader Richard A. Gephardt, eager to keep the production lines going at the Boeing Co.'s F-15 plant in St. Louis.

The White House is not happy with the extra spending in the House measure. An Office of Management and Budget statement of administration policy issued June 6 complained that it would "reduce resources for non-defense programs that are also critical to our nation's future." But the statement did not threaten a veto.

Some lawmakers, particularly Democrats, used the House debate on the defense bill to ratchet up the pressure on House and Senate leaders to expedite passage of $4.7 billion in fiscal 2000 supplemental defense spending.

The money is included in the Senate version of the fiscal 2001 military construction appropriations bill (HR 4425 — H Rept 106-614, S Rept 106-290), passed in May and awaiting a House-Senate conference. Most of the supplemental spending — $4.1 billion — is for Kosovo peacekeeping expenses, other overseas defense operations, defense health programs, unexpected fuel cost increases, nuclear weapons readiness and infrastructure improvements, and storm damage repairs.

"While there is significant money in this bill for 2001, our troops face a crisis . . . beginning in about a month, because of the inability of this Congress to fund what has already happened in Bosnia and Kosovo," said Rep. Martin Frost, D-Texas.

Fighter Programs

Unlike last year, when the House Appropriations Committee's attempt to cancel the controversial F-22 fighter provoked a months-long dispute, lawmakers appear determined to wrap up their work quickly in a critical election year.

Still, the F-22 accounted for a sizeable part of the floor debate. The House defeated, by voice vote, an amendment by Peter A. DeFazio, D-Ore., that would have sliced $930 million from the $2.1 billion that the administration requested and that the House bill would provide for F-22 procurement in fiscal 2001.

DeFazio and other Democrats said the plane's technology has still not been proven to a point that would justify starting up the F-22 production line to build the 10 planes that Clinton requested. "I think that is just one example of the choices which this Congress is not making that it should be making if it is going to impose much deeper restrictions and a much tighter squeeze on the rest of the budget," said David R. Obey of Wisconsin, the Appropriations Committee's ranking Democrat.

The bill would require the F-22 to meet certain testing requirements before the Air Force could buy the 10 planes. It also would provide $396 million for advance procurement of 16 more F-22s in fiscal 2002 and would provide the $1.4 billion Clinton requested for research, development, testing and evaluation.

The House bill would counter the administration by slowing down development of the more advanced Joint Strike Fighter, which also has been beset with technical problems.

The measure reflects a concern by the House Appropriations Committee that the Pentagon is moving too quickly to select one of two competing designs for the plane — by Boeing and Lockheed Martin Corp. — and then begin gearing up for its production. To allow for more testing of the designs, the bill would add $150 million to the $261 million requested for that phase of the project. It also would delay selection of the winner until next June, about three months later than currently planned. And it would cut $300 million from the $595.5 million Clinton requested to begin building prototypes of the chosen design.

All told, the bill would provide $707 million for the Joint Strike Fighter, $150 million less than was requested. In its June 6 statement, OMB said the restrictions could disrupt the program, costing time and money.

Missile Defense

The debate over the House bill also saw lawmakers revisit longstanding concerns over a national anti-missile defense system, for which the bill would appropriate the $1.8 billion the administration requested.

Copley News Service, quoting from documents in a whistleblower's lawsuit, reported June 2 that a Pentagon criminal investigation has found that the current design of an interceptor to knock down incoming warheads cannot distinguish them from decoys.

House members defeated, by voice vote, an amendment by John F. Tierney, D-Mass., that would have cut $75 million set aside to begin constructing the system. The amendment would have used that money instead to help pay for a prescription drug benefit for military retirees that would be created by the House version of the defense authorization bill (HR 4205). OMB has predicted that the drug benefit would cost nearly $200 million, instead of the $94 million already included in the appropriations bill.

Clinton is not scheduled to decide until later this year whether to begin building the missile defense system for an anticipated 2005 deployment date. But he requested the initial procurement money to meet the target date if necessary.

Several Democratic lawmakers argued that the proposed missile defense system is too costly and not technologically sound and would violate international arms control agreements.

"To start down the path of spending on procurement is premature and inappropriate," Tierney said.

But Republican Curt Weldon of Pennsylvania, one of Congress' staunchest advocates of a national missile defense, countered that passage of Tierney's amendment would kill the program. "We are making progress," Weldon said. "Have we solved all the problems? No. But it is a challenge that the scientists who are dealing with these issues feel that we can meet."

The House also rejected by voice vote an amendment by Dennis J. Kucinich, D-Ohio, that would have cut $174 million, or 10 percent, from the missile defense appropriation and added it to the $12.1 billion the bill would provide for the military health care system.

Besides complaining in general that the bill would increase defense spending at the expense of domestic programs, OMB also objected to some of the ways the bill would allocate money.

One administration target is the bill's single most expensive initiative: the addition of more than $1 billion to accelerate the conversion of some Army combat units to "medium-weight" forces that would have more staying power than lightly armed airborne units but could be deployed more quickly than armored forces equipped with 70-ton tanks.

In its report, the Appropriations Committee blasted the Pentagon's civilian leaders for underfunding the Army's "transformation," which, the panel insisted, could be completed in half the time if the service was given more money. OMB said the $751 million requested in Clinton's budget was enough for the Army to begin the shift.

More White House Objections

OMB also objected specifically to the bill's addition to the president's request of:

- $119 million for 11 Blackhawk helicopters, built in Connecticut by United Technologies' Sikorsky Division and used by the Army as troop carriers.
- $15 million for two Cessna Citations — small business jets built in Kansas and used by the services to carry personnel and cargo.
- $76 million for a C-130 cargo

plane adapted for use by the Marine Corps to refuel other planes and helicopters in midair.

The administration also objected to some of the cuts the bill would make in the budget request.

For instance, the bill would provide $433 million of the $458 million requested for the so-called Nunn-Lugar program, intended to help Russia and other former Soviet states dispose of nuclear, chemical and biological weapons and the missiles that could launch them. But along with some modest additions for some projects, that total reflected the elimination of all $35 million requested to continue building a factory to neutralize the huge stockpile of chemical weapons located near Shchuch'ye, in south central Russia.

The administration objected that the weapons the factory was intended to eliminate posed a serious threat to the United States, since many of them are small, modern nerve gas weapons that could easily be smuggled out of Russia by terrorists or agents of a radical government.

OMB also objected to the bill's $8 million reduction in the $65 million requested for military forces to conduct unanticipated humanitarian and disaster relief missions. Some critics have contended that these funds are used for purposes more appropriately paid for out of the foreign aid budget. But OMB insisted that such emergency assistance is a valuable tool for U.S. commanders abroad trying to build working relationships and win access rights in countries in their regions.

The administration also objected to language in the House report that would require prior approval by the House and Senate Appropriations and Armed Services committees before the Pentagon could transfer funds to the Justice Department to help pay for the federal government's litigation against the tobacco industry.

"The Defense Department spends hundreds of millions of dollars each year to treat tobacco-related illnesses and has provided a modest level of support to the litigation effort, relative to the potentially significant recoveries," OMB said. "The Department of Defense funding is making a critical contribution to the government's tobacco litigation effort."

Senate-Passed Defense Bill Differs Little From House Bill

JUNE 17 — The Senate has followed the lead of the House and overwhelmingly passed a $287.6 billion defense appropriations bill for fiscal 2001 that would increase Pentagon spending by $3.1 billion above what President Clinton requested.

The Senate approved the measure (HR 4576), 95-3, on June 13 after substituting the text of its own bill (S 2593). What totaled three days of desultory Senate debate began June 8, the day after the House passed its version of the legislation. *(Vote 127, p. S-24)*

There are few major disagreements between the two versions of the bill, though House and Senate conferees will have to reconcile many small differences on procurement programs, personnel and local projects. A compromise may be delayed by the politics of passing other, more difficult spending bills.

Jerry Lewis, R-Calif., chairman of the House Defense Appropriations Subcommittee, said June 14 that he does not want to start the conference on the defense bill until the much smaller fiscal 2001 spending bill for military construction (HR 4425) is sent to Clinton. The Senate version of the military construction bill has become the vehicle for $4.7 billion in fiscal 2000 supplemental spending for U.S. peacekeeping operations in Kosovo and other places, counterdrug activities in the Caribbean and other defense programs, including nuclear weapons laboratories.

Lewis said that enacting the supplemental spending "is the first step that's very important" before the conference.

The House and Senate versions of the defense appropriations bill include a 3.7 percent pay raise for military personnel that Clinton requested, as well as increases in recruiting and retention benefits, additional funds for ballistic missile defense programs and an expanded pharmacy benefit for military retirees.

The absence of controversy over the bill in the Senate owed partly to the determination of appropriators to keep out extraneous amendments by invoking a rule that bars authorization language on spending bills.

As a result, some of the amendments that senators tried to offer to the spending bill will instead be directed at the more controversial fiscal 2001 defense authorization bill (S 2549) that the Senate has been dealing with off and on for nearly two weeks.

In addition, the relatively large pot of money available for the military this year left all sides able to avoid disputes on the largest of the 13 annual appropriations bills in terms of discretionary spending. The defense bill would increase spending by $21.5 billion above the fiscal 2000 level.

Though the appropriations bill generally follows the direction of the authorization measure, it does not include spending for military construction or for the defense programs of the Energy Department, which are handled separately.

No Blank Check

Despite the increase, the defense bill "does not provide a blank check to the Pentagon," said Daniel K. Inouye of Hawaii, ranking Democrat on the Senate Defense Appropriations Subcommittee. "It includes some tough reductions to programs that are being scheduled, over budget or simply not ready to proceed at this time."

Inouye cited language cutting funding for the Joint Strike Fighter, which is slated for production beginning late in this decade to replace several 1970s-vintage jets used by the Navy, Marine Corps and Air Force. Lawmakers have complained that the program is being rushed into production and have called for a slowdown.

However, in what has become an annual ritual, Armed Services Committee member John McCain, R-Ariz., the Senate's most persistent critic of what he considers wasteful spending, took to the floor before passage to deride some of the projects that lawmakers added.

In particular, McCain singled out extra money Inouye sought and received for two Hawaii projects: $24 million added to a $300 million administration request for a shipyard at

Pearl Harbor and $15 million added to a $4 million administration request for an asteroid-tracking system in Maui.

McCain also questioned the addition of $9.5 million for the National Guard in West Virginia, home state of ranking Appropriations Committee Democrat Robert C. Byrd.

Although McCain noted that the defense authorization bill includes numerous additions the Pentagon has not requested, he said the Armed Services Committee — on which he serves — more closely followed the Pentagon's list of unfunded priorities in drawing up its bill. Appropriators "seem to have missed the idea," McCain said. Nonetheless, he voted in favor of the spending bill.

The White House Office of Management and Budget echoed some of McCain's concerns. The OMB said in a June 8 statement that "much of the additional funding in the committee bill is for unrequested procurement and [research and development] programs, funding that comes at the expense of more urgent needs." But the agency did not threaten to recommend a veto.

Executive Jets

The Senate did take up several controversial amendments to the spending bill. On a 65-32 vote, the Senate tabled, or killed, an amendment by Democrats Barbara Boxer of California and Tom Harkin of Iowa that would have removed permission for the Navy, Marine Corps and Army to each lease three executive jets to transport top-level officials. *(Vote 125, p. S-24)*

Harkin and Boxer have tried to limit the military's leasing of such aircraft, which they said is unnecessarily lavish. "This is about luxury," Boxer said. "What the military should be about is mission."

But Senate Appropriations Committee Chairman Ted Stevens, R-Alaska, who also chairs the Defense Subcommittee, said the services need the flexibility to decide if it is more efficient and cost-effective to lease or buy the jets.

Boxer did win approval, 84-14, for an amendment she sponsored with Democrat Harry Reid of Nevada to bar the use of funds for the application of dangerous pesticides to areas owned or managed by the Defense Department that may be used by children. *(Vote 124, p. S-24)*

Senators also voted, 83-15, to table an amendment by Paul Wellstone, D-Minn., that would have deleted $1 billion of the bill's $58 billion allocation for procurement and transferred the money to education programs for poor and disadvantaged children. *(Vote 126, p. S-24)*

The Senate adopted, by voice vote, two packages of amendments that would make minor changes, most in the research, development and procurement of defense-related items.

One amendment, by Armed Services Committee Chairman John W. Warner, R-Va., would add $3.7 million for five additional National Guard teams trained to handle domestic terrorist attacks involving nuclear, chemical or biological weapons. The teams would be authorized by the companion defense bill.

Another of the amendments approved en bloc could be the first public skirmish in a battle between aerospace giants Lockheed Martin and Boeing over Air Force cargo plane contracts.

The amendment would restore $48 million the Appropriations Committee cut from a program to develop more reliable electronics for the oldest of the giant C-5 cargo jets built by Lockheed Martin. Joint Chiefs of Staff Chairman Gen. Henry H. Shelton testified before the Defense Appropriations Subcommittee in April that the Pentagon may soon recommend retiring the 76 oldest C-5s — "A" model planes built in the 1970s — and replacing them with Boeing C-17 cargo jets, buying more than the 134 planes currently planned.

Stevens accepted the amendment by Delaware Sens. William V. Roth Jr., a Republican, and Joseph R. Biden Jr., a Democrat, that would restore the C-5A modification money. Dover Air Force Base, in Delaware's capital city, is the East Coast hub for C-5 operations and home to 36 of the planes, including 10 "A" model craft.

Following are some issues that will have to be resolved in the Senate-House conference on the authorization bill:

Personnel and Operations

The most significant personnel issue to be worked out is funding for a new program that would subsidize prescription drugs for military retirees. Clinton has publicly welcomed this initiative, versions of which are contained in the Senate and House authorization bills (S 2549, HR 4205).

The House appropriations bill would provide $94 million and the Senate bill $137 million for this program. However, OMB, in its statement of administration views on each bill, said that the pharmacy program would cost nearly $200 million in 2001, and it urged that the cost be fully covered.

In addition to approving the military pay raise, both bills would add money to Clinton's request for bonuses to encourage enlistment and re-enlistment in essential and hard-to-fill job specialties. The House bill would add $166 million, the Senate bill $156 million.

The Senate bill would fund the administration's plan to begin increasing the housing allowance paid to military personnel, with the aim of covering all housing costs by 2005. The House bill would add $64 million to accelerate the plan.

The Senate bill would cut $9 million and the House bill $8 million from the $65 million Clinton requested to cover the cost of sending U.S. forces on disaster relief and humanitarian missions abroad. The Senate Appropriations Committee justified its proposed reduction by noting that the administration's budget request would cause this account to increase at a faster rate than the budget accounts that pay for combat training. In addition, some critics have complained that the account uses Pentagon funds to pay for some costs that properly should be covered by the foreign aid budget.

The administration is pressing for full funding, contending that the humanitarian missions help top U.S. commanders overseas cultivate good working relations with foreign governments. In addition, OMB said in its policy statement that the missions provide useful training for U.S. troops.

The Senate bill would provide the $458 million requested for the so-called Nunn-Lugar program, intended to help Russia and other former Soviet states dispose of nuclear, chemical and biological weapons. The House bill would cut $25 million from the request, a net reduction that reflects increased funding for some projects more than offset by the denial of $35 million requested to continue building a facility in the Russian city of Shchuch'ye to dismantle a stockpile of chemical weapons at that site.

This tracks the position taken by the House Armed Services Committee, which eliminated the chemical weapons project from the defense authorization bill (HR 4205). The committee said that other countries were not contributing enough to build and operate the facility and that Russia could not afford to run it if it was built.

But the administration justifies the Shchuch'ye project by contending that many of the chemical weapons stored there are lethal nerve gas weapons, bombs and shells small enough to be easily smuggled out of Russia and into the United States.

The Senate bill would add a total of $65 million to the defense budget to maintain the entire fleet of 94 B-52 long-range bombers. In recent years, Senate Appropriations Committee member Byron L. Dorgan, D-N.D., has repeatedly thwarted Pentagon plans to mothball some of the big planes, about half of which are based at Minot Air Force Base in North Dakota.

Ground Combat

Both bills would increase spending on the Army's plan to transform itself into a lighter, more mobile, yet just as lethal fighting force. The key to the plan is fielding combat vehicles that weigh much less than the 70-ton M-1 tanks and the 30-ton Bradley troop carriers currently in use.

While a new generation of high-tech, lightweight equipment is developed, the Army wants to deploy interim brigades of about 4,000 troops equipped with lightweight combat vehicles currently in production for U.S. and other forces.

Clinton's budget request included $537 million to begin equipping the first of these brigades, and the Senate bill would add $100 million to that amount. But the House bill is more generous, adding $283 million to complete the equipping of the first brigade, plus $800 million to equip a second one.

The House bill would also add $46 million to the $105 million Clinton requested to develop a new generation medium-weight tank, ready for service by 2012.

The Senate bill would slice $155 million from the $355 million the administration requested to continue developing the Crusader mobile cannon. To make the big gun easier to deploy, the Army has decided to redesign it, hoping to cut its weight from 55 tons to 40. But the Senate Appropriations Committee told the Army to go back to the drawing board and come up with a more easily transported artillery piece that would better fit the transformation plan's goal of a more mobile force.

Navy Ships

The Senate bill would add $460 million to Clinton's budget request to continue work on a helicopter carrier that would be built by Litton Industries in Pascagoula, Miss., hometown of Senate Majority Leader Trent Lott.

While the House bill includes no funds for the ship, it is nearly a foregone conclusion that the conference report will include the funding, which is ardently supported by Lott and fellow Mississippi Sen. Thad Cochran, a member of the Appropriations Committee.

The Senate bill would cut $1 billion from the $1.5 billion requested for the fifth and sixth of a new class of 12 amphibious transport ships (designated LPDs), which carry Marines, tanks and cargo to landing sites. Noting that prices were rising and schedules slipping for the first four ships of the class, the Senate committee insisted that the Navy slow the program down until it nails down the details of the design and the construction schedule.

OMB protested that the administration's budget request took account of the delays and cost hikes and warned that further delays would force the Navy to keep operating older, more expensive vessels that date from the early 1960s.

The Senate bill denied a request for $263 million to cover cost overruns on various ships funded in earlier budgets. Instead, the bill would authorize the Pentagon to shift a total of $300 million appropriated for other programs to cover the unanticipated shipbuilding costs. OMB contends that additional funds are needed for the overruns because taking the money from existing programs would disrupt them.

The Senate bill would add $8 million to the $305 million requested to continue designing a new class of destroyer, the first of which is scheduled for funding in fiscal 2005. The ship, designated DD-21, is intended to be harder to detect by radar than current designs and cheaper to operate, since it is to have a much smaller crew.

The House cut $48 million from the request, and, in its report, the House Appropriations panel challenged several facets of the Navy's plan for buying the new class. Two competing teams of contractors have been given a free hand to design a ship that would meet some key performance requirements set by the Navy. The House committee complained that this "total package" approach might freeze out of the program small businesses that otherwise could propose to the Navy innovative technologies for certain components of the ship.

The committee also objected to the possibility that one or both contractor teams might include in their bids a proposal to perform all maintenance on the new destroyers during their service life, freezing other commercial and government-owned shipyards out of that business.

Aerial Combat

Of the $857 million the administration requested to continue developing the Joint Strike Fighter, the House bill would provide $707 million and the Senate bill $653 million, amounts which OMB warned would disrupt the program.

Both appropriations committees insisted that the Pentagon slow down its timetable for choosing between two competing designs.

In addition, the Senate committee objected to the possibility that the Pentagon might drop its plans to conduct the competition on a "winner take all" basis.

Pentagon officials have acknowledged that they are considering splitting production of the winning design between the two competing teams of companies, lest the losing team drop out of the jet fighter business.

Defense Conferees Withhold Details Of Agreement Pending Trims

JULY 15 — Senate-House conferees agreed July 13 on a compromise defense appropriations bill for fiscal 2001, but deferred announcing details of the measure until July 17, while aides looked for ways to reduce the bill's price tag so it will fit under congressional spending limits.

Senate Appropriations Committee Chairman Ted Stevens, R-Alaska, and House Defense Appropriations Subcommittee Chairman Jerry Lewis, R-Calif., said the bill (HR 4576) would appropriate just over $288 billion, close to the $288.5 billion House bill and the $287.6 billion Senate version. The level is nearly $4 billion more than Clinton requested and about $19.8 billion more than the fiscal 2000 level.

The conference report would also add about $1.5 billion in fiscal 2000 emergency defense spending. Stevens said much of the supplemental defense money would go toward various health care benefits and readiness accounts, but he would not go into further detail.

"We're a little bit over our allocation," Stevens acknowledged. One way the conferees hoped to pare the total cost of the bill was by asking the Pentagon to recommend where to cut about $1 billion out of the roughly $100 billion the conference report would provide for weapons procurement and research. "I don't think they're going to be able to spend all that money in one year," Stevens said.

But to protect lawmakers' pet projects from taking the brunt of that reduction, the amount that could be cut from any one program would be strictly limited.

Conferees did not have any major disputes to settle this year. Last year's conference had to resolve a conflict over procurement of the F-22 advanced fighter jet. To the Pentagon's chagrin, the agreement largely reflects decisions by both chambers to reduce funding for the Joint Strike Fighter (JSF) program and delay the construction of prototype airplanes.

Lewis and Stevens said the conference agreement would include money to purchase five F-15 fighters, which the administration did not request but which are important to Missouri lawmakers trying to keep production going at a Boeing Co. plant in St. Louis. Stevens said the funding level in the bill for the F-15s may be adjusted in the coming days.

The agreement would also include several hundred million dollars to accelerate the Army's plan to equip some of its units with lighter combat vehicles that could be deployed more easily than the heavily armored tanks and troop carriers currently in use.

Lewis said the conference agreement would provide about $1.5 billion to help the Army begin converting to lighter, more mobile units. That is more than the Senate version. In addition to buying the new equipment for one 4,000-member brigade, as the budget requested, it would pay much of the cost of modernizing a second brigade.

House Adopts Conference Report

JULY 22 — In fashioning the annual Pentagon spending bill that could reach the president's desk the week of July 24, Congress was eager to spend a great deal more money on defense but not eager to brag about how much that might cost other federal programs.

The bill (HR 4576) would give the Defense Department $5.1 billion more than President Clinton requested, which is a larger increase than anticipated by the congressional budget resolution (H Con Res 290). Rather than openly flout the budget caps in that document, House and Senate conferees — including some of the Pentagon's most powerful political allies — camouflaged more than a third of the increase to exempt it from the budget limits.

Compared with Clinton's request for $284.5 billion, the bill would provide $289.6 billion in new budget authority, including $287.8 billion for fiscal 2001.

The remaining $1.8 billion is designated as emergency supplemental funding for fiscal 2000. That is a double ruse, however. Because fiscal 2000 will end in a little more than two months, there is little chance that any significant amount of the fiscal 2000 money will be spent before the new year begins. Although the money was declared "emergency" spending exempt from the budget caps, it is intended to pay for routine maintenance and for ongoing military operations in Bosnia, Kosovo and the Persian Gulf.

The House adopted the conference report July 19 by a vote of 367-58. *(Vote 413, p. H-128)*

The Senate was expected to adopt the report and clear the bill the week of July 24.

As usual, the bill is studded with hundreds of add-ons sponsored by House and Senate members. Some of these are substantial, such as the $400 million pushed by members from Missouri to buy more F-15 fighters and thus keep the Boeing Co.'s St. Louis production line open.

But most items added by the conference committee are more modest, such as the $30 million obtained by Senate Appropriations Committee Chairman Ted Stevens, R-Alaska, for a university supercomputer in Fairbanks, or the $1.5 million won by House Appropriations Committee member Norm Dicks, D-Wash., to create a research center for underwater robots at a naval base on Puget Sound.

The conferees accommodated more members' initiatives for procurement and research and development programs than they could fit into the total spending, even with creative accounting. So they added a provision that would reduce the amount available to each of the special programs by seven-tenths of one percent, cutting the cost of the bill by $705 million.

Following are some highlights of the defense appropriations conference report.

Military Personnel

By far the most significant change the conferees made in the personnel budget was the addition of $200 million to subsidize prescription drugs for military retirees over 65. The program is expected to be created by the final version of the companion defense authorization bill (HR 4205 — H Rept 106-616; S Rept 106-292).

The House bill included $94 million for the new benefit and the Senate bill $137 million. While applauding the initiative, the administration warned that it probably would cost $200 million. In response, the conferees appropriated $100 million for the pharmacy benefit outright and provided another $100 million as an emergency fiscal 2000 appropriation, which could be spent if the president requests it.

For overall military personnel costs in fiscal 2001, the conference report would provide $75.8 billion, $46 million more than Clinton requested. But that paper increase is more than offset by another provision of the bill that would cut the personnel accounts by $392 million because of currency fluctuations overseas.

Both the House and Senate versions of the bill had approved the administration's proposed 3.7 percent military pay raise for fiscal 2001.

The conferees added $50 million to the Navy's recruitment and retention budget for fiscal 2000. The Navy, like most of the services, has lost many highly trained technical personnel to the booming civilian economy.

The conferees cut $244 million from Clinton's personnel funding request on grounds that the services would start the fiscal year with about 3,500 fewer members than the budget request assumed. But that reduction was offset by several additions, including $82 million for re-enlistment bonuses, $31 million for housing cost allowances, and a total of $160 million, divided between the personnel and operations accounts, to keep units in service that the administration wanted to abolish.

The lion's share of this "force structure" increase — $65 million — would compel the Air Force to retain all 94 B-52 bombers that are still intact. The service has tried for several years to mothball part of the fleet, but has been blocked by the senators from North Dakota, where about half of the big planes are based at Minot.

Operations and Maintenance

On paper, the conference version of the bill would provide $96.9 billion for operations and maintenance, $610 million more than Clinton requested. But the total does not include $529 million in fiscal 2000 supplemental funds added to pay for equipment overhauls, facilities maintenance and spare parts.

On the other hand, other sections of the conference report would cut $1.6 billion from the amount the bill appears to appropriate for operations and maintenance.

Taking all those adjustments into account, the conference report would give the Pentagon $450 million less than Clinton requested for operations and maintenance.

The conferees' cuts totaling $1.6 billion come from several sources that are routinely tapped by congressional budgeters prowling for cash to pay for members' initiatives or to meet spending caps. Committees contend that these traditional sources can safely be trimmed without significantly affecting military operations.

In this case, the conference report would cut:

- $893 million to be offset by drawing the same amount out of other Pentagon budget accounts that contain surplus cash.
- $443.8 million to account for foreign currency fluctuations.
- $71 million to force the Defense Department to hire fewer consultants.
- $159 million from headquarters and administrative costs.

In a statement of administration policy issued before the defense bill conference formally met, the Office of Management and Budget (OMB) objected strenuously to a provision in the House version of the bill that would cut $244 million — half again as much as the conferees called for — from headquarters and administrative costs.

"While there may be some superficial appeal to the notion of reducing headquarters to increase combat capability," the OMB statement read, "headquarters are heavily involved in the conduct of complex military operations . . . and strategic planning."

Overseas Operations

The conference report includes $3.9 billion to pay for military operations in the Balkans and the Persian Gulf, $162 million less than Clinton requested. Of the amount approved, $1.1 billion was converted into fiscal 2000 emergency supplemental spending that would not count against the budget caps for fiscal 2001.

The conference version of the bill includes $443 million of the $458 million Clinton requested for the so-called Nunn-Lugar program to help Russia and other former Soviet republics dispose of nuclear, chemical and biological weapons.

But that relatively minor reduction in funds obscures a major challenge to administration policy: Following the lead of the House, the conferees denied the $35 million Clinton requested to continue building a chemical weapons destruction plant near the Russian city of Schuch'ye.

The administration insists that the proposed facility would eliminate a large stockpile of small, easily smuggled nerve gas weapons stored at the site. But the House Armed Services Committee has blocked Nunn-Lugar spending for the project, arguing that other countries were not contributing enough to the project and that Russia could not afford to operate the facility even if it were built.

Conferees also added $25 million to Clinton's budget request to scrap aging Russian nuclear-powered submarines.

The conferees brushed aside the administration's request for $65 million to pay for sending U.S. forces on disaster relief and humanitarian missions overseas. Like the Senate version of the bill, the conference report cut $9 million from the White House request, while the House bill would have cut $8 million.

OMB insisted that such operations pay off in both diplomatic good will and useful training for U.S. forces. Critics complain that funding for these missions has risen faster than funding for regular combat training.

Ground Combat

Following the lead of the House, the conferees roughly doubled — to $1.6 billion — the amount that would be appropriated for the Army's plan to make its forces lighter and thus more easily deployable to distant trouble spots.

The key is developing a new type of tank that would weigh about one-third as much as the 70-ton M-1. The Army wants to have it by about 2012. As an interim step, Chief of Staff Gen. Eric K. Shinseki wants to equip several 4,000-person brigades with lightweight combat vehicles currently in production for U.S. and foreign forces.

Clinton requested $537 million to begin equipping the first of these brigades. The conference report added $320 million to finish equipping that first brigade, $500 million to begin equipping a second brigade and $46 million to accelerate development of the new, light-weight combat vehicle.

The latter increase is more than offset by the conference report's elimination of $69 million Clinton requested for a joint U.S.-British project to develop a lightweight, high-tech reconnaissance vehicle.

The conferees approved the $355 million requested by the Army to continue developing the Crusader self-propelled cannon.

The Army is trying to reduce the Crusader's weight from 55 tons to 40 tons. But the Senate version of the bill had cut $155 million from the administration request and ordered the Army to develop a more easily transportable cannon that would better fit the plan for a lighter, more easily deployable force.

While approving the amount requested for the Crusader, the conferees ordered the Army to conduct a study of how the weapons would fit into the planned lightweight Army forces of the future.

Shipbuilding

As was generally expected, the conferees followed the Senate's lead and added $460 million to Clinton's request to continue work on a helicopter carrier that would be built by Litton Industries in Pascagoula, hometown of Senate Majority Leader Trent Lott, R-Miss.

The Pentagon had not planned to request the bulk of the funds for this $1.5 billion ship until 2005. However, the Navy and the contractor insisted that earlier funding would reduce the cost by hundreds of millions of dollars.

The conference report cut nearly $1 billion from the $1.5 billion the administration requested to build two other ships intended to carry Marine amphibious forces. The Senate Appropriations Committee had slashed the request, complaining that prices had risen and delivery dates had slipped for previously funded ships of this type (the LPD-17 class).

Although the administration protested that the problems had been sorted out, the conferees approved only $561 million for the program, which the Navy can use to buy components of the two ships.

The conferees also followed the Senate's lead in eliminating $263 million from the bill that Clinton requested for unexpected increases in the cost of ships funded in previous years. Instead, the conference version of the bill includes a provision allowing the secretary of the Navy to transfer up to $300 million from other budget accounts to cover such increases. The administration protested in vain that the transfer provision was an inadequate substitute and would disrupt programs from which funds were taken.

The final bill would provide $292 million of the $305 million Clinton requested to continue designing the DD-21 class of destroyers, the first of which is slated for funding in fiscal 2005. The House had cut $48 million from the request.

Aircraft

Both the House and Senate had agreed to slow the Pentagon's timetable for choosing between two competing designs for the so-called Joint Strike Fighter, intended to enter service late in this decade as a replacement for several 1970s-vintage jets used by the Navy, Air Force and Marine Corps.

Not even a last minute appeal by the Pentagon shook conferees from their conviction that the program was likely to slip by at least three months, enough to warrant a reduction of $170 million from the amount Clinton requested. The conference version of the bill would provide $689 million for the project.

Both the House and Senate had approved the $3.9 billion Clinton requested to continue testing and initial production of the Air Force's F-22 fighter, including funds for 10 planes.

The conferees approved nearly all the $2.8 billion the administration requested to continue production of the C-17 cargo jet.

However, they followed the Senate's lead and removed the C-17 funds from the Air Force procurement account and put them in a separate revolving fund for long-range airlift. This was intended to make it harder for Air Force leaders to raid the C-17 budget to shore up the accounts for fighter jets.

With several other aircraft programs, the conference report illustrated the special arithmetic at work in a conference committee which dictates that when the Senate adds money for one program and the House adds money for another, the compromise frequently adds money for both:

- Clinton did not request funds to buy either fighter currently in Air Force squadrons — F-15s built by Boeing in St. Louis and F-16s built by Lockheed Martin in Fort Worth, Texas. The House added $400 million to buy five more F-15s in the hometown of Minority Leader Richard A. Gephardt, D-Mo., and the Senate added $183 million to buy six F-16s. The conference report added $400 million for F-15s and $122 million for F-16s.
- The administration requested $363 million for four of Lockheed Martin's cargo workhorses, the Georgia-built C-130 cargo plane configured for various missions. The House and Senate each funded five of the planes, and the conference report included $528 million for six.
- The administration requested $495 million for 25 H-60 helicopters built in Connecticut by the Sikorsky division of United Technologies, different versions of which are used by the Army and Navy. The House added funds to buy more of the Army's troop-carrier version while the Senate added funds to buy more of the types used by both services. The upshot was that the conference report provided $710 million for 41 H-60s of various models.

Senate Clears Project-Laden Defense Bill

JULY 29 — The Senate cleared the fiscal 2001 defense appropriations bill July 27 after a week's delay in which two Republican senators complained that their colleagues had stuffed too many special projects into the measure.

The Senate voted 91-9 to adopt the conference report on the $287.8 billion bill (HR 4576). The House adopted the report July 19. *(Vote 230, p. S-41)*

The bill would give the Defense

Defense Spending Highlights

Where the Money Goes

HR 4576 — Conference report: H Rept 106-754

Spending Synopsis

The conference report for the fiscal 2001 defense appropriations bill that the House adopted July 19 and the Senate cleared July 27 grew to $287.8 billion in final negotiations. That total does not include $1.8 billion in supplemental fiscal 2000 spending the conferees added for overseas contingency operations, general operations and maintenance and health care. The conferees came up with $1.1 billion for the supplemental by converting fiscal 2001 overseas contingency funds into fiscal 2000 spending. The supplemental funds come on top of $11.2 billion in fiscal 2000 spending that Congress tacked onto the fiscal 2001 military construction appropriations bill (PL 106-246), much of it for the Defense Department and its overseas peacekeeping. The bottom line is $21.7 billion more defense spending for fiscal 2001 than Congress appropriated for fiscal 2000 — more than the entire foreign aid budget, in fact — and $5.1 billion more than President Clinton requested. *(Military construction spending, p. 2-123)*

- **Personnel**

Conferees agreed to fund a 3.7 percent military pay raise that Clinton requested. The conferees also added $50 million in supplemental fiscal 2000 spending to help the Navy recruit and train personnel, as well as a general provision cutting $392 million from the personnel appropriation because of favorable foreign currency shifts.

- **Operations and maintenance**

On paper, operations and maintenance would have $609.7 million more than Clinton requested, but conferees also included $529 million in fiscal 2000 spending for depot maintenance, real property maintenance and spare parts. The operations and maintenance total also does not include $1.6 billion in cuts that conferees spelled out in general provisions. The final bill would cut $9 million of the $64.9 million Clinton requested for overseas disaster relief and humanitarian missions and $15 million from the $458.4 million he requested for nuclear threat reduction programs in the former Soviet Union.

- **Procurement**

The final bill would nearly double — to $1.6 billion — the amount Clinton requested to begin transforming the Army into a lighter, more mobile force. A modest increase in procurement funds is masked by the transfer of all $2.8 billion for buying C-17 transport planes into a new air transport revolving fund.

Hot-Button Issues

△ **Joint Strike Fighter.** The conferees went along with both appropriators and authorizers in calling for the Defense Department to slow down development of the most advanced of three new air-superiority fighters. Some experts say the program is outrunning available technology. The idea is for the Air Force, Navy and Marine Corps to have versions of the fighter starting in 2008.

△ **Retirees' pharmacy.** The House, Senate and the Office of Management and Budget had differed over how much it would cost in fiscal 2001 to provide prescription drug coverage to military retirees. The House estimated $94 million, the Senate $137 million and OMB $200 million. The conferees essentially accepted the OMB estimate, but by the back door — the bill includes $100 million for fiscal 2001 and another $100 million in fiscal 2000 funds.

(figures are in thousands of dollars of new budget authority)

	Fiscal 2000 Appropriation	Fiscal 2000 Clinton Request	House Bill	Senate Bill	Conference
Military personnel	$73,894,693	$75,801,666	$75,904,216	$75,817,487	$75,847,740
Operation and maintenance	92,234,779	96,280,113	97,507,228	96,720,882	96,889,774
Procurement	52,980,714	59,236,234	61,558,679	57,896,122	59,232,846
Research and development	37,605,560	37,873,184	40,170,230	39,597,489	41,359,605
Other Defense Department programs	13,168,961	13,587,774	14,029,874	14,190,824	14,114,424
Miscellaneous and rescissions	– 3,776,921*	1,722,015	– 657,427	3,407,696	361,665
GRAND TOTAL	**$266,107,786**	**$284,500,986**	**$288,512,800**	**$287,630,500**	**$287,806,054**
Fiscal 2000 emergency supplemental					**$1,779,000**

*Includes $1.8 billion in advance appropriations from fiscal 1999 for a fiscal 2000 pay increase, the net result of budget additions and cuts required by a fiscal 2000 omnibus spending bill (PL 106-113) and a $2.6 billion scorekeeping reduction for a radio spectrum sale that has not taken place.

TABLE: House and Senate Appropriations committees

Department an additional $1.8 billion, which is designated as emergency funding for fiscal 2000, and thus exempt from budget caps.

All told, for fiscal 2001 the bill would add $5.1 billion to the $284.5 billion President Clinton requested. Although the administration had objected to the increase, Clinton is expected to sign the measure.

Sens. Phil Gramm, R-Texas, and John McCain, R-Ariz., objected that House and Senate conferees added $7 billion for projects not included in the Pentagon's budget request.

Gramm was particularly critical of accounting gimmicks that conferees used to circumvent congressional spending limits, such as designating some of the money in the bill as emergency funding for fiscal 2000. He lamented that members could not resist spending the rapidly rising federal budget surplus. "The surplus is burning a hole in our pockets," he said.

McCain blasted the bill as "a disgrace" for spending what was ostensibly Pentagon money on non-defense projects while the armed services, he said, remained overworked and under-equipped. "It has millions and millions and millions of dollars devoted to projects that have nothing to do with national defense," McCain said.

The two senators singled out some relatively large budget additions, such as a $60 million transport plane for the commander of U.S. forces in the Pacific. But most of their complaints were aimed at numerous but much smaller projects. Dozens of these initiatives are earmarked for medical research projects at specific institutions.

"The distinction between the defense bill and the [Department of] Health and Human Services bill gets lost when you see $8.5 million for the Gallo Center for Alcoholism Research and $4 million for the Gallo Cancer Center," McCain said.

The alcoholism research institute, part of the University of California San Francisco, is located just west of Oakland and is named in honor of wine entrepreneur Ernest Gallo. The cancer center, a part of the New Jersey state medical school in Newark, is named in honor of former House Appropriations Committee member Dean A. Gallo, R-N.J. (1985-94).

Aside from the controversial members' initiatives, the bill would make few significant cuts in the administration's budget request, while providing some important increases.

For instance, in addition to funding a requested 3.7 percent military pay raise, the bill would add $200 million to subsidize prescription drugs for military retirees over 65.

It also would provide $1.6 billion — a net increase of $866 million over the administration request — to accelerate the Army's plan to make its combat units lighter and easier to deploy. ◆

A Pairing With the CJS Bill And a Social Policy Fight Delay D.C. Spending Bill

SUMMARY

President Clinton signed the fiscal 2001 District of Columbia appropriations bill Nov. 22.

Conferees softened a House-passed provision dealing with the District's needle exchange program for drug addicts, paving the way to relatively easy final passage of the smallest of the 13 appropriations bills. It nevertheless became a veto target when lawmakers attached the fiscal 2001 spending bill for the departments of Commerce, Justice and State, which contained an immigration package unacceptable to Clinton. After intense lobbying by city officials, who warned that vital programs could be endangered if the measure continued to languish, Congress split off the D.C. spending bill (HR 5633) and cleared it Nov. 14.

Rep. Todd Tiahrt, R-Kan., had sought to block the needle program from operating within 1,000 feet of any areas where children gather, but conferees eventually agreed to ban it only within 1,000 feet of city schools. Another controversial provision, which would have blocked a D.C. Council measure requiring employer sponsored health plans to cover contraception, died quietly after District Mayor Anthony Williams pocket-vetoed the city bill.

In addition to providing $445 million in federal funds to the city, the bill approved the city's own $6.7 billion budget. It also appropriated $25 million to help build a new Metrorail station at New York Avenue and $17 million for a college tuition program for city residents.

House Panel Debates Riders

JULY 15 — The first public sighting of the fiscal 2001 District of Columbia spending bill portends a partisan battle over policy riders — including one dealing with insurance payments for birth control — that is likely to prove just as tumultuous as in previous years.

Democrats predicted that the bill, which the House Appropriations D.C. Subcommittee approved by voice vote July 13, will never become law unless some of the riders aimed at controlling District initiatives are removed. The measure would appropriate $414 million, while the Clinton administration requested $445 million.

"Obviously, it wouldn't be signed by the president," said Democrat Eleanor Holmes Norton, the District's non-voting delegate. Clinton vetoed two fiscal 2000 D.C. appropriations bills before signing a third that was the vehicle for an omnibus budget package (PL 106-113).

David R. Obey of Wisconsin, ranking Democrat on the House Appropriations Committee, criticized subcommittee Chairman Ernest Istook Jr., R-Okla., for his penchant for social policy riders, which last year included a provision aimed at preventing the District from spending federal funds on needle exchange programs. The same rider appears in the fiscal 2001 draft.

"Mr. Mayor or Your Majesty or whatever the appropriate title is, I guess my reaction is, surely you jest," Obey told Istook. He added that the measure in its current form is about as close to a bipartisan bill "as white is to black."

Despite the partisan sparring, the panel moved toward resolution on a high-profile issue involving a D.C. City Council measure, approved July 11, that would require health insurers in the District to offer coverage for contraceptives. Istook included language in the spending bill that would block the law unless it contained an exemption for employers and insurers because of their religious convictions.

Ranking subcommittee Democrat James P. Moran of Virginia said he would try to resolve the issue by drafting an amendment that would allow the council measure to become law if D.C. added a "conscience clause" defining the kinds of religious institutions that could be exempted.

Istook surprised panel members by including another provision that would have exempted residents in "any other state" from having to pay state taxes on income they earned in Washington unless the District had negotiated a tax compact with officials from that state that included a reciprocal payment for D.C.

Julian C. Dixon, D-Calif., pointed out that the wording of Istook's provision could inadvertently exempt members of Congress from paying state taxes and offered an amendment, approved by unanimous consent, that stripped it from the spending bill.

Box Score — **2001 Fiscal Year**

District of Columbia

- **Bill:** HR 5633 — PL 106-522
- **Legislative action: House** passed HR 4942 (H Rept 106-786), 217-207, on Sept. 14.

Senate passed HR 4942 by voice vote Sept. 27, after substituting the text of S 3041 (S Rept 106-409).

House adopted the conference report (H Rept 106-1005), 206-198, on Oct. 26.

Senate cleared HR 4942, 48-43, on Oct. 27.

House passed HR 5633 by voice vote Nov. 14

Senate cleared HR 5633 by voice vote Nov. 14.

President signed the bill Nov. 22.

House Committee Approves Bill; Concerns Remain About Riders

JULY 22 — The House Appropriations Committee approved the usually contentious District of Columbia spending bill by voice vote June 20, with Republicans appearing eager to produce a stand-alone measure, something that has not happened since 1997.

Lawmakers expect to face a string of controversial policy riders related to the District's insurance requirements for contraceptive coverage and its needle exchange program when the House considers the $414 million fiscal 2001 appropriations bill the week of July 24. Still, the outlook for a relatively quick debate is strong following a markup that annoyed but did not outrage Democrats.

"I think we can work with this one," said District of Columbia Subcommittee ranking Democrat James P. Moran of Virginia. "As long as the social riders don't get more extreme, we can get a signable bill."

Appropriations Committee Chairman C.W. Bill Young, R-Fla., predicted that the House will pass the measure — which falls more than $30 million below President Clinton's $445 million request — before the August recess.

In 1998 and 1999, the District spending bill moved easily through committee markups, only to run into trouble later. The fiscal 2000 bill was vetoed twice before it was wrapped into a catch-all spending bill (PL 106-113) at the session's end.

This year, Republicans seem anxious to produce a clean fiscal 2001 measure — the last of the 13 annual spending measures to win committee approval — before the end of the session to lessen the chances that Clinton will veto it.

Much of the debate during markup centered on two of the measure's most controversial policy riders: insurance coverage for contraception and needle exchanges for drug addicts.

Lawmakers want to revise a D.C. City Council measure passed July 11 that would require health insurers in the District to offer coverage for contraceptives. The version of the spending bill approved July 13 by the House Appropriations D.C. Subcommittee included provisions by Chairman Ernest Istook, R-Okla., to block the requirements from taking effect.

Istook introduced an alternative amendment July 20, approved by voice vote, that would allow the policy if city officials drafted a "conscience clause" allowing an exemption for employers on religious or moral grounds. The committee rejected, 19-24, a rival amendment by Moran that would have allowed an exemption only for religious reasons. Democrats vowed to revive the battle in the floor debate.

The Needles Debate

The committee adopted language on needle exchange programs that differs only slightly from last year's final version. The fiscal 2000 bill banned the use of federal funds for the city's needle exchange program but allowed it to use private funds if the city documented expenditures.

An amendment by Julian C. Dixon, D-Calif., to strike a similar rider in the fiscal 2001 bill was adopted, 28-25, with support from six GOP lawmakers. Republicans later protested that they had misunderstood the amendment and believed they were supporting only the use of private funds for needle exchange centers.

Dixon then offered a second amendment that is nearly identical to the fiscal 2000 rider forbidding the use of federal funds for needle exchanges. That amendment, adopted by unanimous consent, does not include the record-keeping requirement.

Later, the committee rejected, 25-26, an amendment by Todd Tiahrt, R-Kan., that would have banned the distribution of needles within 1,000 feet of areas that attract children — including day care centers, schools, parks, video arcades and youth centers — or near any event sponsored by such facilities.

Moran said the District's small size meant there would be "virtually no place" for the centers to operate under Tiahrt's amendment. "This is a backdoor way of precluding the program from operating at all," Moran said.

Tiahrt said he may reoffer the amendment on the floor.

The committee also approved by voice vote:

• An amendment by Istook to increase by $1 million, to $14 million, funding for a program launched last year that lets D.C. students attend colleges in other states at in-state tuition rates. The provision also would add $4 million for a new Metrorail subway station at New York Avenue NE for a total of $7 million in appropriated funds. Istook said the added money for the station would be offset by funds from a drug treatment program for parolees and probationers.

• An amendment by Moran to speed up payments for court-appointed attorneys.

After Long Delay, House Passes Bill By Narrow Margin

SEPTEMBER 16 — House Republicans, under pressure to move the last of their fiscal 2001 spending bills to the Senate, passed the long-stalled $414 million District of Columbia measure (HR 4942) on Sept. 14.

The 217-207 vote came a day after the Senate Appropriations Committee approved a $441 million measure (S 3041) that is much closer to President Clinton's $445 million request and policy objectives and skirts most of the controversial social issues that conservatives tacked on to the House version. *(Vote 474, p. H-148)*

"We'd be satisfied with the Senate bill," said James P. Moran of Virginia, ranking Democrat on the D.C. Appropriations Subcommittee. "Over here, it's just too ideological, but we'll end up with something like the Senate position."

The measure is likely to be wrapped up in an omnibus spending bill as the session ends. Congress has not passed a stand-alone D.C. spending bill since 1997 because social conservatives have used the measure to add policy riders on such hot-button issues as abortion, the medical use of marijuana and domestic partnership benefit programs.

This year, the House riders include:

• An amendment by Brian P. Bilbray, R-Calif., adopted 265-155, that would make it a crime for D.C. youths under the age of 18 to possess tobacco. Penalties would range from fines to suspending the violator's driver's license. *(Vote 472, p. H-148)*

• An amendment by Mark Souder, R-Ind., adopted, 239-181, that would prohibit the District from using local or federal funds to support the city's needle exchange program for drug addicts. *(Vote 473, p. H-148)*

• A much-discussed provision by Todd Tiahrt, R-Kan., adopted by voice vote, that would prevent needle exchange programs from operating within 1,000 feet of sites that attract children, including video arcades, schools and day care centers. Tiahrt estimated that more than half of the city's needle exchange centers would be affected.

Tiahrt elevated the political risk of voting against his amendment by presenting it as a choice between protecting children and protecting drug addicts. Democrats decided not to press for a roll call vote "because it was going to pass anyway," Moran said.

A Quiet Resolution

The controversy over a D.C. Council-passed bill on insurance coverage for contraceptives — which previously had provoked several hot exchanges between Democrat Eleanor Holmes Norton, the District's non-voting delegate, and D.C. Subcommittee Chairman Ernest Istook, R-Okla. — ended quietly.

The D.C. Council measure would have required employer-sponsored health plans to cover contraceptives, but conservatives protested because it did not exempt employers who objected on religious or moral grounds.

Istook had included a ban in the spending bill to block the council measure from taking effect unless a "conscience clause" was added to exempt such employers. Norton argued the ban became moot when D.C. Mayor Anthony Williams pocket-vetoed the measure and offered an amendment, adopted by voice vote, to remove it.

Istook's acceptance of Norton's amendment was the only bipartisan gesture during debate on the spending measure. Earlier in the week, Moran unsuccessfully tried to float a compromise offering Democratic support if Istook withdrew the Tiahrt amendment and beefed up funding for a Metrorail station on New York Avenue, a tuition program to help District residents attend out-of-state colleges and "brownfields" cleanup efforts near the Anacostia River.

As passed, the House bill would directly appropriate $7 million for the rail station and $14 million for tuition assistance, but it would provide no funds for the cleanup.

The measure approved 27-1 by the Senate Appropriations Committee contains the administration's full request of $25 million for the Metro station and $17 million for the college tuition program.

Richard J. Durbin of Illinois, the ranking Democrat on the Senate D.C. Appropriations Subcommittee, applauded the collaborative spirit of Chairman Kay Bailey Hutchison, R-Texas, who eliminated many of last year's riders, saying they were outdated or unnecessary.

The Senate bill still includes provisions to ban the use of federal or city funds for the needle exchange program.

Durbin's only specific criticism was the continuation of the hourly cap on fees for lawyers representing children with special education needs. Durbin said the cap undermined the quality of representation, but Hutchison said it allows more children to be served.

Senate Passes Bill; Conferees Still Face Riders Dispute

SEPTEMBER 30 — The Senate passed the District of Columbia fiscal 2001 spending bill (HR 4942) by voice vote and without debate Sept. 27. The measure now moves to conference, where members hope to finalize a report as early as the week of Oct. 2, if they can resolve disputes on several social policy riders.

According to House and Senate negotiators, who have already started discussing provisions in the bill informally, the final measure will probably come closer to the $448.4 million Senate bill than the $414 million House version.

James P. Moran of Virginia, ranking Democrat on the House D.C. Appropriations Subcommittee, predicted Sept. 27 that most of the differences will be easily reconciled, with conferees accepting many Senate provisions. Subcommittee Chairman Ernest Istook, R-Okla., said he "always" expected funding to be increased. Now, he added, "it appears that will happen."

The bill's funding levels are expected to approach President Clinton's request for $445 million. The Senate bill, passed as a manager's amendment, boosted the overall funding from the Appropriations Committee-approved level of $441 million to $448.4 million.

The Senate included $3.5 million for environmental cleanup efforts at Poplar Point near the Anacostia River. Neither the original Senate bill nor the House-passed version contained funds for the project, for which Clinton had requested $10 million.

Needle Exchange Debate

Negotiators still must resolve several conservative-backed amendments if they are to pass the first stand-alone D.C. spending bill since 1997. Among them is a House-passed amendment that would limit areas where the District's needle exchange program could operate.

The provision, by Todd Tiahrt, R-Kan., would restrict the program from operating within 1,000 feet of schools, arcades, swimming pools and other areas that attract children.

"If pushers and users are allowed to use those areas to swap drug needles, it invites the very influences we are trying to keep away from kids," said Istook. However critics, particularly Democrats, say such restrictions would severely hinder the program's ability to provide services to drug addicts.

Negotiators also must decide whether to retain a House amendment by Brian P. Bilbray, R-Calif., that would make it a federal crime for D.C. youths under the age of 18 to possess tobacco. Penalties would range from fines to suspension of the violator's driver's license.

Funding levels for a new Metrorail station at New York Avenue and a college tuition assistance program also will have to be settled.

The Senate bill meets the administration's requests of $25 million for the new station and $17 million for the tuition program, but the House version would appropriate $7 million for the rail station and $14 million for tuition assistance. Negotiators in both chambers say they expect the final bill to match the administration's numbers.

Conferees Reach Accord on Needle Exchange Issue

OCTOBER 14 — After extensive haggling over the District of Columbia's needle exchange program for drug addicts, House and Senate conferees reached agreement on a $445 million fiscal 2001 D.C. spending bill (HR 4942) on Oct. 11 that meets most of President Clinton's funding requests.

Conferees expect to file their report early the week of Oct. 16 unless the bill becomes a vehicle for other legislation. Congress has not passed a stand-alone D.C. spending bill since 1997 because social conservatives have added policy riders on such hot-button issues as abortion and the medical use of marijuana.

"We have reached a very good compromise," said Richard J. Durbin of Illinois, ranking Democrat on the Senate D.C. Appropriations Subcommittee.

The final agreement softened a House-passed restriction on the District's needle exchange program, which House D.C. Appropriations Subcommittee ranking Democrat James P. Moran of Virginia had called "the most problematic situation on this bill."

The original needle provision, by Todd Tiahrt, R-Kan., would have barred exchanges within 1,000 feet of schools, swimming pools, arcades, daycare centers and other places where children gather. After prolonged wrangling, conferees agreed to ban needle exchanges only within 1,000 feet of schools. The compromise would force four needle exchange sites to relocate but leave six others unaffected.

Many other disputes were resolved before conferees met publicly. Moran said that took "much of the oomph out of my opening statement."

Conferees would provide about $445 million in federal payments to the District; the House bill had called for $414 million and the Senate version for $448 million. A total D.C. budget of $6.7 billion was also approved.

The report includes full funding of the District's requests for $25 million to help build a Metrorail station on New York Avenue and $17 million for a college tuition program.

Senate D.C. Appropriations Subcommittee Chairman Kay Bailey Hutchison, R-Texas, also agreed to accept an omnibus amendment by House conferees, even though she complained about the "latecoming . . . basketload of requests." The amendment includes:

- $500,000 for Children's National Medical Center to expand clinics.
- $500,000, requested by House Majority Whip Tom DeLay, R-Texas, for the Child Advocacy Center's Safe Shores program for at-risk children.

D.C. Spending Highlights

Where the Money Goes

HR 4942 — Conference report: H Rept 106-1005

Spending Synopsis:

The conference report on the fiscal 2001 District of Columbia spending bill — the smallest of the 13 regular appropriations measures — was adopted by the House on Oct. 26 and cleared by the Senate the following day. Lawmakers attached the fiscal 2001 appropriations bill for the departments of Commerce, Justice and State, prompting a veto threat from President Clinton over immigration language in that measure.

The D.C. spending bill would provide $445 million in federal funds to the city, $31 million more than the House-passed version but $3 million below the Senate measure. The bill would also approve the $6.7 billion local D.C. budget.

The measure includes $3.5 million for environmental cleanup efforts at Poplar Point near the Anacostia River, for which Clinton had sought $10 million, and $6 million for the 2001 presidential inauguration.

Hot-Button Issues

△ **Needle exchange program.** Negotiators agreed to prevent needle exchange programs for drug addicts from operating within 1,000 feet of schools, softening language by Rep. Todd Tiahrt, R-Kan., that would have restricted such programs from operating within 1,000 feet of schools and many other sites that attract children.

△ **Metrorail expansion.** The bill would provide $25 million for a Metrorail station on New York Avenue N.E. The House-passed version contained $7.1 million for the station, to be built near the future headquarters of the Bureau of Alcohol, Tobacco and Firearms.

△ **Tobacco penalty.** Conferees altered language by Brian P. Bilbray, R-Calif., that would have made it a federal crime for D.C. youths under 18 to possess tobacco. Instead, the city would get $100,000 for enforcement contingent on the District passing a law banning tobacco possession by minors.

△ **Tuition program.** The measure would appropriate $17 million for the college Resident Tuition Support program, which allows city residents to attend out- of-state schools at in-state tuition rates. The House-passed version contained $14 million for the program.

(figures are in thousands of dollars of new budget authority)

Federal Funds	Fiscal 2000 Appropriation	Fiscal 2001 Clinton Request	House Bill	Senate Bill	Conference Report
D.C. courts	($99,714)	($103,000)	($99,500)	($109,080)	($105,000)
Corrections Trustee operations	($176,000)	($134,300)	($134,300)	($134,200)	($134,200)
Court Defender Services	($33,336)	($38,387)	($34,387)	($38,387)	($34,387)
Court Services and Offender Supervision	($93,800)	($103,527)	($115,572)	(112,527)	($112,527)
Metrorail construction	______	($25,000)	($7,100)	($25,000)	($25,000)
Tuition support	($17,000)	($17,000)	($14,000)	($17,000)	($17,000)
Inauguration	______	($6,211)	($5,291)	($6,211)	($5,961)
Total federal funds	**$436,800**	**$445,425**	**$414,000**	**$448,355**	**$444,975**
TOTAL D.C. Budget	**$6,778,433**	**$6,691,932**	**$6,659,271**	**$6,666,531**	**$6,667,571**

TABLE: House, Senate Appropriations committees

• $1 million to help St. Coletta of Greater Washington, a non-sectarian school in Alexandria, Va., create a day-care program for mentally handicapped teens and adults.

The amendment also drove up the total for cleanup of an abandoned industrial site near the Anacostia River to the Senate allocation of $3.5 million. The House did not include any funds for the cleanup, while Clinton had requested $10 million.

D.C. Bill Cleared After Split From CJS Measure

NOVEMBER 18 — After intense lobbying by District of Columbia officials, Congress split off the fiscal 2001 District of Columbia spending bill (HR 5633) from the Commerce-Justice-State appropriations measure (HR 4942) on Nov. 14 and passed it by voice vote in both chambers.

Negotiators brokered a conference agreement on the $445 million D.C. measure in mid-October, but Republicans postponed final action so they could use it as a vehicle to carry the $39.9 billion CJS spending bill, which President Clinton has threatened to veto over immigration provisions. *(Commerce-Justice-State, p. 2-23)*

In private meetings with GOP leaders, Mayor Anthony Williams and the District's non-voting delegate, Democrat Eleanor Holmes Norton, insisted that critical city programs would be harmed if the spending bill was held up until December's lame-duck session.

They said further delays would have imperiled their efforts to save financially troubled D.C. General Hospital and its eight primary care clinics, which have run up a $109 million deficit over the past three years. The D.C. bill contains a provision that would allow the District to shift as much as $90 million to the hospital from other accounts.

If Congress had not acted, the hospital could have been forced to close early next year, Norton said. "Further delay imperiled ongoing action to save the hospital," she told reporters Nov. 14.

Williams praised congressional leaders "for working in an unprecedented, bipartisan way" to help the District. "None of [our] priorities were possible until Congress passed our budget," he said in a Nov. 14 statement.

The quiet, end-of-session passage of the spending bill — which also approved a total D.C. budget of $6.7 billion — marked the first time that Congress has cleared a stand-alone D.C. spending bill since 1997. Social conservatives have used the measure to add policy riders on such issues as abortion and the medical use of marijuana.

Perhaps the most contentious rider offered this year was an amendment by Todd Tiahrt, R-Kan., that would have banned the District's needle exchange program from operating within 1,000 feet of sites that attract children. House-Senate conferees softened that language to apply the restrictions only to schools.

The bill also contains a rider that would give the city an additional $100,000 if it enacts legislation to discourage children under 18 from possessing tobacco products. Such legislation would have to impose a $100 fine for the second offense and revoke an offender's driving privileges for 90 days following a third violation.

Clinton is expected to sign the measure, which reflects many of his priorities, including $25 million to help fund a new Metrorail station on New York Avenue and $17 million for a college tuition program for D.C. students.

The bill also appropriates almost $3.5 million for environmental cleanup efforts at Poplar Point near the Anacostia River. ◆

Congress Rewrites Energy-Water Bill After Missouri River Dispute Draws Veto

SUMMARY

After President Clinton vetoed a $23.6 billion fiscal 2001 energy and water appropriations bill (HR 4733) because of language dealing with federal management of the Missouri River, Congress drafted a new spending bill (HR 5483) without the provision and incorporated it by reference in the appropriations measure for the departments of Veterans Affairs and Housing and Urban Development (HR 4635). That bill was cleared and signed into law.

The Missouri River issue plunged the normally non-controversial energy and water bill into presidential election-year politics. Clinton opposed the language, added by the Senate, because it would have blocked the Army Corps of Engineers from revising its water management plan for the river in order to emphasize wildlife at the potential expense of barge traffic. The new plan, recommended by the Fish and Wildlife Service, was to release more water from upstream dams in the spring and less in the summer, providing additional habitat for endangered species. Environmentalists and lawmakers who favored the change said that barge traffic on the river had declined dramatically in recent decades, anyway.

Lawmakers from downstream states, led by Sen. Christopher S. Bond, R-Mo., argued that the bill language was necessary because changing the river's flow in spring could increase the risk of flooding.

In vetoing the bill, Clinton called the Missouri River language "an unacceptable rider" and complained that the measure omitted funding for CALFED, a massive California water program, but included nearly $700 million for more than 300 projects that his administration did not request.

Although the House voted to override the veto, Senate Majority Leader Trent Lott, R-Miss., acknowledged that he lacked the necessary two-thirds majority to follow suit. Missouri lawmakers predicted that Vice President Al Gore would suffer in their swing state in the Nov. 7 presidential election because of Clinton's veto. Gore did lose the state.

House Panel Approves Energy-Water Bill

JUNE 17 — A House Appropriations subcommittee has approved a $21.7 billion spending bill for energy and water programs in fiscal 2001 that is almost $1 billion below President Clinton's budget request.

Some members of the House Energy and Water Development Appropriations Subcommittee are optimistic, however, that the full committee will give them more money to work with.

House Republican leaders last year allocated an additional $1.1 billion to the fiscal 2000 version after committee members argued that the bill passed by the House was so low that a conference with the Senate was impossible.

"My sense is that in the end, there will be an increase in the allocation this year," said Peter J. Visclosky of Indiana, the Energy and Water Subcommittee's ranking Democrat.

The unnumbered fiscal 2001 bill, approved by voice vote, is $546 million above what Congress enacted for fiscal 2000 but $951.8 million below Clinton's request. The full committee is scheduled to consider the bill June 20.

In the House, the energy and water bill traditionally has emphasized river, lake and coastal projects popular with lawmakers. This year, though, Energy and Water Chairman Ron Packard, R-Calif., said that budget constraints forced him to deny funds to any projects not ongoing.

BoxScore — **2001** Fiscal Year

Energy and Water

- **Bill:** HR 5483, incorporated by reference in HR 4635 — PL 106-377
- **Legislative action: House** passed HR 4733 (H Rept 106-693), 407-19, June 28.

Senate passed HR 4733, amended, 93-1, on Sept. 7.

House adopted the conference report (H Rept 106-907), 301-118, on Sept. 28.

Senate cleared HR 4733, 57-37, on Oct. 2.

President vetoed HR 4733 on Oct. 7.

House voted 315-98 to override veto Oct. 11.

Senate passed HR 4635, incorporating new version of energy and water spending bill (HR 5483), 87-8, on Oct. 12.

House adopted the conference report on HR 4635 (H Rept 106-988), 386-24, on Oct. 19.

Senate cleared HR 4635, 85-8, on Oct. 19.

President signed HR 4635 on Oct. 27.

Hitting Home

Packard said the limitation even applied to a project in his home state — a partnership with the state to study and restore the estuary at the junction of San Francisco Bay and the Sacramento and San Joaquin rivers. Authorization for the project, which was started in 1994, expires in this fiscal year. The project is not in Packard's district.

"In order for me to be fair to all members and fund the ongoing projects, I had no choice," Packard said. "We're hoping we can help some more members in conference."

The House subcommittee bill would provide $4.1 billion for Army Corps of Engineers programs such as flood control, shoreline protection and navigation. The subcommittee recommendation is $59.9 million above the president's budget request and

$2.9 million less than Congress enacted for fiscal 2000.

Unlike the House, the Senate's energy and water bill usually focuses on the Energy Department's nuclear weapons programs, which are a pet concern of Pete V. Domenici, R-N.M., the Senate Appropriations subcommittee chairman. His state includes two of the department's weapons laboratories, Los Alamos and Sandia.

The Senate Appropriations Committee is expected to take up its version of the bill later this month.

The House subcommittee bill would provide the Energy Department with $17.3 billion, a $686.5 million increase above the level enacted for fiscal 2000 but $852.8 million below the president's request.

Packard said that at the request of Republican House leaders, the bill does not include language from last year's bill designed to speed up permits for construction in wetlands. The White House had threatened to veto the bill last year if those provisions were included.

House Committee OKs Bill, Hopes For More Funds In Conference

JUNE 24 — Even as they approved a $21.7 billion fiscal 2001 energy-water spending bill June 20, House appropriators were looking ahead to conference, where they hope the Republican leadership will find a way to give them more money.

The amount allocated for the House measure (HR 4733) did not allow for a single new district water project — usually a popular way to bring money home, especially in an election year.

"I've got hints that there might be some more money, but I don't know yet," Ron Packard, R-Calif., chairman of the Appropriations Subcommittee on Energy and Water, said in an interview. Still, he added, "it won't be enough to reach anywhere near the president's budget request."

The bill funds the Energy Department, the Army Corps of Engineers and Interior Department reclamation projects. As it now stands, the House measure would provide $546 million more than the fiscal 2000 level, but $952 million less than President Clinton has requested. Last year's final energy-water bill (PL 106-60) was $303 million below the president's request.

The House bill contains no funding for new projects, including those authorized through a $6.3 billion water resources development law passed last August (PL 106-53). The projects were denied funding for fiscal 2000 as well.

Gasoline Price Debate

Before approving the bill by voice vote, Appropriations Committee members clashed over the recent spike in gasoline prices, which some said had gone up by as much as 35 cents per gallon in the previous week.

The bill would reauthorize the Strategic Petroleum Reserve through Sept. 30, 2001, restoring the president's authority to release oil from the reserve.

But Democrats also wanted to restore $106 million cut from the president's request for solar and renewable energy programs, bringing the total to $457 million. The amendment, by Marcy Kaptur, D-Ohio, was rejected, 21-32.

Kaptur said the reductions in the bill would prolong U.S. dependence on oil imports, leaving the nation vulnerable to the whims of foreign producers.

"This Congress has continually cut back on funding for energy research, which has left us without the necessary tools to fight oil and gas prices," added David R. Obey of Wisconsin, ranking Democrat on the full committee and a cosponsor of the amendment.

Packard and other Republicans said some of the funds requested by Clinton were for programs, including solar energy, that have been around long enough to be left to the private sector.

Packard indicated that Republicans might try to increase spending for renewable energy on the House floor, and that unlike Kaptur's proposal, the amendment would contain offsets. His own stance, he said, would depend on "where the offsets are going to be."

The subcommittee's report on the bill drew the ire of Democrats for forbidding the use of funds for "implementing, or in contemplation of preparing to implement, the Kyoto protocol" on global warming. A Democratic amendment to change the language was rejected, 27-28.

The committee adopted an amendment that would require the U.S. Army Corps of Engineers to publish on its Web site all "findings, rulings and decisions" rendered under its appeal process.

Cuts Displease Both Parties

Democrats and Republicans alike expressed unhappiness over the bill's tight spending constraints.

The Corps of Engineers would get $4.1 billion — $60 million more than requested but $3 million below fiscal 2000 levels. The Energy Department would receive $17.3 billion — $687 million more than fiscal year 2000, but $853 million less than requested. The department's atomic energy defense programs would be funded at $12.8 billion, an increase of $850 million, but $190 million less than Clinton sought.

Funding would be increased for research on the Yucca Mountain nuclear waste repository. The Nuclear Waste Disposal Fund would receive $413 million, which is $61.8 million more than last year, but $24.5 million less than the president's package.

"I think this bill is a close call," said Obey. Packard replied that if more money is not found, Obey will not be the only one with doubts.

The Senate has allocated $727 million more than the House for the bill, and Packard's Senate counterpart, Pete V. Domenici, R-N.M., is certain to increase spending for Energy Department nuclear weapons programs, which are crucial for two laboratories in his state, Los Alamos and Sandia.

"If we don't get more money, it's going to be a hard conference," said Packard.

House Passes Bill That Addresses Soaring Fuel Prices

JULY 1 — With no money available for the annual addition of new water projects across the country, House debate on the fiscal 2001 energy and water appropriations bill focused instead on rising gasoline prices.

The House passed the $21.7 billion measure (HR 4733), 407-19, on June 28, after adding provisions aimed at lowering the cost of gas, which has climbed to over $2 a gallon in some parts of the Midwest. *(Vote 342, p. H-108)*

After debate on security at the nation's nuclear weapons laboratories, the House adopted, 239-187, an amendment designed to prevent Energy Department executives from also holding key jobs within a new nuclear agency. *(Vote 340, p. H-108)*

Most other amendments were relatively non-controversial. However, one that would reauthorize the Strategic Petroleum Reserve for three years faces an uncertain future in the Senate because of language on a home heating oil reserve in the Northeast and marginal oil wells.

The House energy and water bill would provide $546 million more than in fiscal 2000 but $952 million less than President Clinton requested. A statement by the White House Office of Management and Budget said the legislation would "significantly reduce vital programs" in science, energy research and other activities, but it did not threaten a veto.

Ron Packard, R-Calif., chairman of the House Appropriations Energy and Water Development Subcommittee, said he hopes to receive more money from Republican leaders before the bill heads to conference, but he could not say how much.

The energy and water bill funds operations at the Energy Department, U.S. Army Corps of Engineers and some Interior Department programs.

Because of a lack of available funds, subcommittee members took a hard-line stance this year and refused to fund any new or unauthorized water projects. Republican Kenny Hulshof of Missouri offered an amendment on the House floor seeking $2 million for Corps of Engineers work on the upper Mississippi River, but the proposal was defeated, 165-262, after Packard spoke against it. *(Vote 334, p. H-106)*

"We have not even funded all of the ongoing projects in the bill this year, those that are already under construction," Packard said. "And to fund a new project and not have the funds to complete existing projects, I think, would be irresponsible."

Petroleum Reserves

House members adopted, 393-33, an amendment by Donald L. Sherwood, R-Pa., that would reauthorize the Strategic Petroleum Reserve for three years, rather than one year as the committee version called for. *(Vote 339, p. H-108)*

The current authorization for the reserve — an emergency stockpile of 575 million barrels of crude oil stored in caverns on the Gulf Coast — expired March 31. Sherwood's amendment was identical to a bill (HR 2884 — H Rept 106-359) the House passed in April. It would also allow the government to buy oil from small or marginal wells — generally those that produce fewer than 15 barrels a day — when the price falls below $15 a barrel. At the behest of Northeastern lawmakers, it would authorize a new regional home heating oil reserve in case oil prices rose sharply in winter.

Many senators have opposed a regional reserve and questioned the idea of buying oil from marginal wells.

House members also adopted, by voice vote, amendments by Jack Kingston, R-Ga., that would direct the Energy Department's inspector general to study the economic basis of recent gasoline prices and require the department to report on how the executive branch is addressing high gas prices and energy in general.

Lawmakers adopted, by voice vote, an amendment by Matt Salmon, R-Ariz., that would increase funding for solar and renewable-energy technology programs by $40 million — from $351 million in the committee version to $391 million.

Lawmakers sided with the nuclear power industry in rejecting, 71-356, an amendment by Mark Foley, R-Fla., that sought to increase funding for renewable energy research by $19 million while canceling the $22.5 million in the bill for research grants to laboratories, universities and industries to study the future of nuclear energy. *(Vote 337, p. H-108)*

On another issue, the House adopted, by voice vote, an amendment by Sherwood Boehlert, R-N.Y., that struck provisions in the bill designed to speed up federal permits for wetlands development. Environmentalists had opposed the provisions.

Senate Panel Boosts Funds for Defense Programs, Nuclear Security

JULY 15 — A Senate Appropriations subcommittee has approved a $22.5 billion energy and water spending bill for fiscal 2001 that would dramatically increase funds for defense-related activities at the Energy Department, including security at nuclear weapons laboratories.

Members of the Energy and Water Subcommittee approved the unnumbered draft bill by voice vote July 13. The full Appropriations Committee is expected to take up the legislation July 18. The House passed its version (HR 4733) on June 28.

The energy and water bill funds operations at the Energy Department, Army Corps of Engineers and some Interior Department programs. It would give the Energy Department a security budget of $336 million, a $213 million increase from fiscal 2000 and an amount roughly in line with the Clinton administration's request.

Overall defense-related spending in the bill totals $13.5 billion, a $400 million increase over the administration's request and nearly $1.4 billion more than in fiscal 2000.

Part of the security money — $56 million — would be used to fund the department's Nuclear Emergency Search Team (NEST) and Accident Response Group programs. NEST members at Los Alamos National Laboratory recently spent more than a month searching for — and eventually finding — two computer hard drives containing nuclear weapons data, an embarrassing gaffe that has touched off protracted congressional criticism of Energy Secretary Bill Richardson.

The Senate bill also would increase spending for security by hundreds of millions of dollars throughout various programs in the Energy Department's National Nuclear Security Administration. The new agency, created by Congress, functions semi-autonomously within the department and is intended to address past security lapses at Los Alamos and other weapons labs.

"Clearly, there is plenty of money for energy security. . . . There can be no complaints back," said Pete V. Domenici, R-N.M., chairman of the Energy and Water Development Appropriations Subcommittee.

Stockpile Stewardship

As he has done in previous years, Domenici included hefty increases in the department's stockpile stewardship program, which uses computers to assess the reliability and safety of nuclear weapons without actual explosions. Much of the work is conducted at the Los Alamos and Sandia National laboratories in Domenici's home state.

At the same time, the bill would slash spending for non-defense programs, including water projects that are popular with many lawmakers. Non-defense spending in the bill is $9 billion, $73 million below this fiscal year's level and $603 million below the president's request.

The discrepancy between the defense and non-defense portions of the bill led Domenici to call for more money to be added as the legislation moves through the appropriations process.

In approving its $21.7 billion energy and water bill last month, the House provided $546 million more than in fiscal 2000 but $952 million less than President Clinton requested. The Clinton administration has criticized the House version for significantly reducing programs in science, energy research and other areas but has not threatened a veto.

Domenici, who also is chairman of the Senate Budget Committee, predicted the administration would be displeased with the non-defense funding levels in the Senate version.

"I think the president's going to come down on a few bills saying the allocation is too low, and this one looks like a cinch," he said. "I think we will get some additional money. I don't know if it'll be as high as I want, but we'll get some."

Like the House bill, the Senate measure contains no funds for new or unauthorized water projects. The matter has been a concern to many lawmakers, and Domenici joked at the markup that he needed a basket just to accommodate the requests he received for "hundreds and hundreds of water projects."

Despite the proposed reductions in non-defense spending, the Senate bill would not cut solar and renewable energy programs. At the behest of Nevada's Harry Reid, the subcommittee's ranking Democrat, the bill would increase funding for those programs from $360 million this year to $445 million. The administration sought $450 million.

"Clean, renewable energy sources such as the sun, wind, biomass and geothermal heat are healthy alternatives to America's debilitating reliance on fossil fuels," Reid said.

Senate Panel Approves Bill, But Angry Democrats Shackle It

JULY 22 — The Senate's $22.5 billion version of the energy and water spending bill for fiscal 2001 was sent into legislative limbo July 21 after Democrats blocked debate in a dispute over Corps of Engineers management of the Missouri River.

The furor over the bill (HR 4733) erupted three days after several Appropriations Committee members complained that the measure spends too little on water projects. The committee approved the House version of the bill, 28-0, on July 18 after substituting the text of its own draft measure.

The energy and water bill funds operations at the Energy Department, Corps of Engineers and some Interior Department programs. Because it provides money for hundreds of water projects in lawmakers' districts, as well as nuclear activities deemed vital to national security, the measure usually passes both chambers and is signed into law with little controversy.

This year, however, Minority Leader Tom Daschle, D-S.D., objected to floor debate on the measure unless Republicans removed language that would prohibit the Corps from revising its management plan for the Missouri River specifying when water from heavy spring rains is released into the river from upstream dams. The amount and timing of water releases affect commerce as well as fish and wildlife.

Daschle said the Corps has spent the past year seeking ways to more accurately reflect the importance of fish and wildlife instead of favoring commercial navigation. The plan "is written in a way that only recognizes the navigational issues, because that's all there was in 1944 when this was written," he said. "But what this provision in the bill says is that they can't even consider it."

Daschle's refusal to allow the bill to be brought up for debate drew strong objections from Christopher S. Bond, R-Mo. He said the language has been accepted in previous years and that if it is omitted, it could threaten commerce and transportation on the Missouri as well as the Mississippi River.

Bond called on Daschle to offer a motion to strike the language after allowing the legislation to come up for debate. "Let us bring the bill up because there is too much of importance in it to have it be held hostage by an effort to say what can be in a bill," Bond said.

Daschle said the Missouri River issue requires more debate time than Republicans are willing to allow if they continue to insist that work on the energy and water bill be completed by July 24. He also said that President Clinton will veto the bill if the language is included.

As a way to break the stalemate, Daschle proposed a conference with the House on the Missouri River language alone. Aides were trying to reach an agreement satisfactory to both sides.

Fusion Refusal

Earlier in the week, the energy and water bill spawned a rare public spat between two other Democratic senators. Dianne Feinstein of California and Harry Reid of Nevada are at odds over funding for the National Ignition Facility, a powerful fusion laser under construction at California's Lawrence Livermore National Laboratory. It would enable scientists to work on advanced weapons designs and test them by simulation.

The ignition facility has been plagued by construction problems and delays. Although it was initially expected to cost $1.1 billion, the Energy Department has predicted that amount could double.

Despite a recent department request to reallocate $135 million to cover the increases, the Senate bill would provide $74.1 million, the amount of the administration's initial request. At the Senate committee markup, Feinstein said the proposed funding level is inadequate and could lead to layoffs.

In an unusually stinging rebuke to Feinstein, Reid said the project was fortunate to receive any money whatsoever. He called the facility "a boondoggle" and said project officials "lied to me" in presenting overly optimistic cost projections.

Reid, the Energy and Water Appropriations Subcommittee's ranking Democrat, said his request to eliminate funding for the facility was opposed by Chairman Pete V. Domenici, R-N.M., who wants to keep the project running.

Financial Limits

When the Appropriations Committee approved the energy and water spending bill, senators seeking more for water projects said they recognized the financial constraints placed on Domenici and Reid in allocating money this year for non-defense programs.

Feinstein and others said they hoped that Appropriations Committee Chairman Ted Stevens, R-Alaska, would find additional money before the bill emerges from conference. New projections for the budget surplus could improve the chances of that happening.

Domenici told Stevens during the markup that he could use as much as $500 million extra. At present, the bill is $1.3 billion above the fiscal 2001 energy and water appropriation but $234 million below the Clinton administration's request.

"We cannot do justice to the nondefense side of the bill without additional money," Reid said.

Reid and Domenici said they were forced to follow the lead of the House and not fund any new or unauthorized water projects.

Domenici described the spending levels for water programs as a "serious shortfall."

The bill includes $1.4 billion for Corps of Engineers construction for flood control, erosion control, storm drainage, channel dredging and other water projects. That amount would be $15.5 million more than the administration sought but $23.6 million below the fiscal 2000 level.

An Appropriations Committee report on the bill said lawmakers tried to focus spending on projects where the Corps has contractual commitments, but it still had to reduce some funding.

Feinstein said it is critical for California to receive $60 million sought by Clinton — but deleted from the bill — to continue a partnership with the state government to restore estuaries at the junction of San Francisco Bay and the Sacramento and San Joaquin rivers. The project is part of a program to improve water management and water quality in the region.

Authorization for the California Bay-Delta Ecosystem Restoration project, which was started in 1995, expires this fiscal year, although the committee report said there appears to be enough money in the pipeline to allow activities to continue through fiscal 2001.

Although appropriators cut funding for water projects, they added money in another politically popular area for some areas of the country — solar and renewable energy programs — to avoid what Reid said could have become a potential floor fight.

The bill would increase funding for those programs from $362 million to $444 million. The administration sought $455 million.

The bill also includes a rider by Domenici to address an environmental controversy in his home state. The amendment would prohibit the Interior Department from using money in the bill to force the release of water into the Rio Grande River in New Mexico to protect the endangered Rio Grande silvery minnow.

The Endangered Species Coalition, made up of grass-roots organizations involved in wildlife issues, said the lower water levels would lead to the extinction of the fish this summer.

Domenici, however, said the forced release of water would harm thousands of farmers who depend on it for irrigation and would set a damaging precedent.

Nuclear Weapons

Although water issues consumed most of the attention of Appropriations Committee members at the markup, the bill includes $13.5 billion for defense-related work, a $400 million increase over the administration's request and nearly $1.4 billion more than in fiscal 2000.

Of that amount, $4.9 billion is for the Energy Department's nuclear weapons programs, a $244 million increase over Clinton's budget request and $456 million over the current level. The money funds the department's stockpile stewardship program, which uses computer simulations and high-powered lasers to assess the reliability and safety of nuclear weapons without requiring actual explosions.

For years, Domenici has made stockpile stewardship funding a top priority. Much of the work is done at two weapons laboratories in his home state — Sandia and Los Alamos — as well as at Lawrence Livermore.

In justifying an increase this year, Domenici cited testimony from scientists and other experts during last year's debate on the Comprehensive Test Ban Treaty (Treaty Doc 105-28) that the program is underfunded and not yet functioning properly. Former Defense Secretary James R. Schlesinger told senators the results of the program will not be significant for another decade.

The Senate failed to ratify the treaty last October.

"Our national laboratories are among the crown jewels of the United States' overall national security apparatus," Domenici said. "But they are not without their problems, and the funding I've outlined in this bill reflects that fact. For too long, we've not given enough attention to the security or infrastructure needs of the labs."

However, Tri-Valley Communities Against a Radioactive Environment, a group that monitors Lawrence Livermore, released a study July 17 that suggested the program could be operated more efficiently and for billions of dollars less each year.

The study was written by Robert Civiak, a former program and budget examiner for the White House Office of Management and Budget. His study compared five different strategies, including the current stockpile stewardship program and a return to nuclear testing under which the department would conduct up to four underground explosions each year.

Civiak concluded that the "curatorship option," in which the department would rely on surveillance and non-nuclear testing to assess when repairs should be made to nuclear weapons, was the only one that could be judged "good" or "superior" under his five criteria for satisfactorily maintaining the stockpile.

That option would cost $2.7 billion annually, compared with the $4.9 billion for the current program.

The current program received a "poor" rating in the arms control category. Civiak said the program to modernize and refurbish the stockpile "is inconsistent with U.S. commitments" under the Nuclear Non-Proliferation Treaty to end a nuclear arms race. He also said the program — which involves "subcritical" testing that involves a release of radiation but does not sustain a nuclear chain reaction — "is counter to the purpose" of the test ban treaty, which would ban underground tests worldwide.

"Stockpile stewardship is primarily a jobs program for nuclear weapons scientists that costs at least $2 billion more than is necessary for adequately maintaining weapons," Civiak said at a July 20 news conference.

Domenici has defended the current stockpile program, but aides said he plans to hold hearings this fall to examine it in depth.

Senate Passes Bill Without Resolving Missouri River Water-Release Issue

SEPTEMBER 9 — The Senate easily passed a $22.9 billion energy and water appropriations bill for fiscal 2001 on Sept. 7 without resolving a controversy over the Missouri River that could complicate the bill's further progress.

The energy and water bill funds operations at the Energy Department, Corps of Engineers and some Interior Department programs. It passed the Senate 93-1 after three days of off-and-on debate. *(Vote 237, p. S-42)*

As in previous years, the Senate bill includes hefty increases in funding for the Energy Department's nuclear weapons programs, while the House version tilts extra spending toward flood-control projects and other water programs popular with lawmakers. The House bill contains $635 million less than the Senate version for weapons programs at the Energy Department's national laboratories — a chief area of concern for Senate Energy and Water Appropriations Subcommittee Chairman Pete V. Domenici, R-N.M., whose state is home to two of the three weapons labs, Los Alamos and Sandia.

The Missouri River issue, however, has been at the center of this year's debate. Senate Democrats, led by Minority Leader Tom Daschle of South Dakota, called on Republicans to remove language in the bill that would prohibit the Corps from revising its management plan for the river to give greater emphasis to wildlife and less to commerce.

Environmental groups oppose the Senate language, and President Clinton has threatened to veto the bill if it is included.

The Corps is on the verge of approving a new plan to govern when water is released from upstream dams on the Missouri. Daschle has endorsed a Fish and Wildlife Service proposal to provide more water in spring through a "spring rise" while reducing river flows in the summer, a move that would provide additional habitat for endangered species in his state.

Daschle said removing the Senate language would bring the river plan into line with the current realities of water management. He noted that when the water plan was written four decades ago, the anticipated amount of barge traffic on the Missouri was 12 million tons; today it is about 1.5 million tons.

"It is time to get real," Daschle said. "It is time to allow the process to go forward. It is time to allow those agencies of the federal government, whose responsibility it is to manage the river, to do it without intervention."

Threat to Barges

Republicans representing states downstream, however, responded that they feared that any proposed change in the river's flow could increase the risk of flooding in riverside communities and on agricultural land. They also said it would end barge traffic on the Missouri.

"I don't think the Fish and Wildlife Service and the people supporting this just want to flood out the people downstream in the spring," said Christopher S. Bond, R-Mo. "I think there is a greater objective — getting rid of barge transportation altogether."

Daschle's amendment to strike the Missouri River language failed, 45-52, with senators voting largely along party lines. Democrat Blanche Lincoln of Arkansas joined Republicans in opposing it, while Republicans Lincoln Chafee of Rhode Island and William V. Roth Jr. of Delaware — both of whom are in tight re-election races this year — supported it. *(Vote 232, p. S-42)*

Just before final passage of the spending bill, Democrat Richard J. Durbin of Illinois tried to offer a compromise amendment that would have removed the Missouri River provision, but he backed down after Bond objected. Durbin did, however, win a pledge from Bond to try to negotiate a deal in conference.

In other areas, Republicans were able to head off a lengthy and divisive debate over a controversial laser facility at California's Lawrence Livermore National Laboratory that has suffered cost overruns.

The National Ignition Facility, being built to simulate nuclear weapon physics, had an original price tag of $1.1 billion. The Energy Department, however, acknowledges that the project will cost about $3.3 billion, and the General Accounting Office said in a report last month that the actual cost will be closer to $4 billion.

Senators approved, by voice vote, an amendment by Tom Harkin, D-Iowa, that calls for the National Academy of Sciences to review the facility within a year and assess whether it is necessary in order to maintain the safety and reliability of the nuclear weapons stockpile.

Harkin offered the amendment in place of another provision that would have eliminated funding for the program. He called the project "one of the big boondoggles of all time."

House Adopts Conference Report; Veto Appears Likely

SEPTEMBER 30 — A $23.6 billion energy and water appropriations bill for fiscal 2001 appears headed for a veto primarily because of a provision the Clinton administration says would favor barge traffic on the Missouri River at the expense of endangered wildlife.

Republicans said they hoped that support for the provision from downstream Missouri, a battleground state in the presidential campaign, would persuade President Clinton to sign the measure (HR 4733). It sailed through conference after lawmakers added nearly $1 billion in extra spending, most of it for water projects.

The House voted to adopt the conference report, 301-118, Sept. 28. The Senate is expected to clear the legislation the week of Oct. 2. *(Vote 501, p. H-158)*

The energy and water bill funds operations at the Energy Department, Army Corps of Engineers and some Interior Department programs. It has long been popular with lawmakers because it finances flood and erosion-control projects, river and harbor dredging and other water programs in numerous districts.

Because of its popularity, House Republican leaders initially tried to use the conference report as a tow truck for two stalled spending bills — one that funds the departments of Veterans Affairs and Housing and Urban Development (HR 4635) and the other for the District of Columbia (HR 4942). They dropped the idea after Senate Democrats indicated they would object.

In a move similar to last year's, energy and water conferees balanced competing interests in water projects and nuclear weapons programs by adding money to both areas. The conference agreement is $1.9 billion more than the House bill, $935 million more than the Senate version and $920 million more than Clinton requested.

Negotiators brought funding for the Energy Department's nuclear weapons and environmental restoration activities in line with the Senate bill by providing $13.5 billion. At the same time, they raised spending for the Corps of Engineers nearly $400 million over the House level.

"We had to reach a balance between meeting our nuclear defense needs and the overwhelming demand for non-defense funding for water and other projects," said Senate Energy and Water Appropriations Subcommittee Chairman Pete V. Domenici, R-N.M.

Some Democrats, however, said Republicans subverted the appropriations process by adding money at the last minute at the expense of programs in other spending bills that Congress has not yet completed.

"I'm not willing to vote for that added money in this bill if it is going to be squeezed out of education, health or out of worker protection programs," said David R. Obey of Wisconsin, the House Appropriations Committee's ranking Democrat. Obey called the conference agreement "a product of the total and utter collapse of the budget process."

Missouri Breaks

The Missouri River issue has dominated this year's debate over the energy and water bill. Senate Democrats, led by Minority Leader Tom Daschle of South Dakota, have criticized language that would prohibit the Corps from revising its management plan for the river to give greater emphasis to wildlife and less to commerce.

The Corps is on the verge of approving a plan to govern when water is released from upstream dams on the Missouri. Daschle has endorsed a Fish and Wildlife Service proposal to provide more water in spring, through a "spring rise," while reducing river flows in the summer, a move that would provide additional habitat for endangered species in his state. Daschle and environmentalists also said the Corps plan addresses the reality of the Missouri — barge traffic has dropped significantly since the river management plan was written four decades ago.

In its statement of policy on the Senate bill issued July 21, the administration wrote that the existing river plan "simply does not provide an appropriate balance among the competing interests, both commercial and recreational, of the many people who seek to use this great American river."

As the energy and water conference began Sept. 26, White House Chief of Staff John D. Podesta sent conferees a letter reiterating the president's intention to veto the bill unless the Missouri River language was dropped or substantially changed.

"This provision would prevent the Corps from carrying out a necessary element of any reasonable and prudent alternative to avoid jeopardizing the continued existence of the endangered least tern and pallid sturgeon and the threatened piping plover," Podesta wrote.

Republicans representing states downstream have maintained that any proposed change in the river's flow during the spring could increase the risk of flooding in riverside communities and agricultural land. They also said it would all but end barge traffic on the Missouri.

Several Republicans have questioned whether Clinton would veto the bill at a time when Vice President Al Gore is locked in a tight race in Missouri with Texas Gov. George W. Bush. They said numerous Democrats in the state oppose changing the Missouri River plan, including Gov. Mel Carnahan, who is challenging Republican Sen. John Ashcroft.

"I do not think the president will ignore the strong voices of the flood control associations, the bipartisan, strong opposition of the Democratic government of Missouri, the Democratic governor and mayors of Kansas City and St. Louis, who would be subjected to the dangers of flooding from a spring rise," said Sen. Christopher S. Bond, R-Mo.

Oil and Water

The issue of oil prices also created controversy for the energy and water bill. Conferees deleted language the House had added to the spending bill that would have reauthorized the Strategic Petroleum Reserve for three years.

The current authorization for the reserve — a 60-day supply stored in salt domes along the Gulf of Mexico coast — expired March 31. Republicans said the language did not belong in the spending bill.

Northeastern Democrats bitterly complained because the provision also would have authorized a home heating oil reserve designed to cushion their region from sudden price increases. Clinton created a reserve for the Northeast by executive order on July 10, but he cannot withdraw oil from it until Congress acts.

"This bill is severely deficient, lacking the authority to protect American consumers from these skyrocketing, outrageous energy prices," said Rep. Edward J. Markey, D-Mass.

The efforts of Senate Energy and Natural Resources Committee Chairman Frank H. Murkowski, R-Alaska, to move a separate petroleum reserve reauthorization bill (HR 2884) the week of Sept. 18 were stalled by a dispute over proposed changes in the formula for royalties that oil companies pay the government for drilling on federal land.

In the House, the oil issue was only becoming more political. House Republicans launched a new line of attack on Clinton's decision Sept. 22 to release 30 million barrels of crude from the reserve to help drive down gasoline prices.

Joe L. Barton, R-Texas, chairman of the Commerce Subcommittee on Energy and Power, said he could find no statute that permitted Clinton to take the action.

Officials at the Energy Department said the president has emergency authority to make limited swaps of oil from the reserve to deal with specific, short-term supply problems. Under a swap, oil companies purchasing oil from the reserve agree to return a comparable amount on a specific date. Without an authorization, the administration cannot order any straight sale of oil from the reserve.

California Cleaning

On the energy and water spending bill, Republicans resolved another controversy by making a last-minute addition of $25 million for an unauthorized project in southern California to clean up ground water by removing a chemical used in rocket fuel.

The provision was sought by House Rules Committee Chairman David Dreier, R-Calif., who wanted funding to go along with a House-passed bill (HR 910) on the cleanup of perchlorate contamination in the San Gabriel Basin area of his district. House aides said Dreier threatened to use his position to prevent floor consideration of the conference report if it did not include the language. Dreier denied the charge.

Conferees left another California project high and dry, dropping any funds for CALFED, a massive state-federal water management program that supplies two-thirds of the state's residents with water for drinking and irrigation.

Appropriators had decided not to include funding in the original spending bills because the project's authorization expires this year. The House Resources Committee approved a $60 million authorization (HR 5130) earlier this month.

Domenici and his House counterpart, Ron Packard, R-Calif., said they could not provide $60 million and offered $20 million on a take-it-or-leave-it basis. When supporters objected, the project ended up unfunded.

House Resources Water and Power Subcommittee Chairman John T. Doolittle, R-Calif., vowed to seek another legislative vehicle to provide funding for CALFED.

Domenici's Domain

As in previous years, the energy and water bill bore Domenici's imprint with billions of dollars for various Energy Department programs in his state.

The conference agreement includes $5 billion for the department's nuclear weapons activities, a $376 million increase over Clinton's request. That money finances the department's stockpile stewardship program, which assesses the safety and reliability of warheads without conducting explosive tests. Much of the work is done at New Mexico's Los Alamos and Sandia national laboratories.

To address morale problems at the Los Alamos lab, which has been beset by accusations of lax security, Domenici added language giving the lab's director more discretion to fund research. He exempted scientific travel for such research from congressionally imposed restrictions on other department travel.

The agreement also includes $215 million in contingent emergency funds for Los Alamos to use if needed to cover costs associated with recovering from devastating wildfires in May.

Domenici and other conferees also added money at the behest of powerful senators in other states, including:

- $10 million for the operation and maintenance of a harbor in Pascagoula, Miss., home of Senate Majority Leader Trent Lott.
- $12.5 million for repairs and maintenance of Gray's Harbor, Wash., in the home state of Republican Slade Gorton, chairman of the Senate Interior Appropriations Subcommittee, and in the district of Norm Dicks, ranking Democrat on the House Interior Appropriations Subcommittee.
- $4 million for sewer projects in several rural areas in Nevada, home of ranking Senate Energy and Water Appropriations Subcommittee Democrat Harry Reid.

Senate Clears Bill; Both Parties View Promised Veto as Political Leverage

OCTOBER 7 — President Clinton was poised to veto an Energy and Water appropriations bill in a dispute over federal management of the Missouri River, a move that has gotten the normally uncontroversial measure tangled up in election year presidential politics.

Clinton opposes the measure (HR 4733) because it would block the Army Corps of Engineers from revising its water management plan for the Missouri in order to emphasize wildlife at the potential expense of barge traffic on the river. Critics of Clinton's position say it also might lead to floods.

Republicans were confident they could use the issue against Vice President Al Gore in downstream swing states such as Missouri. Democrats hope a veto of the bill will reinforce Gore's environmental credentials.

Voting largely along party lines, the Senate cleared the bill, 57-37, on Oct. 2. The result was short of the two-thirds majority needed for any veto override. *(Vote 261, p. S-47)*

Many Senate Democrats voted

Energy-Water Spending Highlights

Where the Money Goes

HR 4733 — Conference report: H Rept 106-907

Spending Synopsis:

House and Senate conferees fattened the fiscal 2001 energy and water appropriations bill with dozens of extra water and energy projects popular with lawmakers across the country, then dared President Clinton to veto it over language that would have prohibited the Corps of Engineers from changing the way it manages the Missouri River. The bill, which cleared Oct. 2, was vetoed three days later. Lawmakers then cleared a virtually identical bill, minus the Missouri River provisions, by reference in the VA-HUD spending bill (HR 4635) on Oct. 8. The final bill provided $1.9 billion more than the House bill, $935 million more than Senate version and $920 million more than Clinton requested, most of it in Corps of Engineers projects that the committees reluctantly had denied earlier. The bill provided $2.4 billion more than Congress appropriated in fiscal 2000. Conferees shifted from fiscal 2000 to fiscal 2001 the $203 million the Senate included in contingent emergency supplemental spending to cover the cost of fighting the Cerro Grande fire in Los Alamos, N.M., in May.

- **Army Corps of Engineers**

The final version of the bill provided $4.5 billion for the Corps and its water projects, nearly $400 million more than either the House or Senate passed or than Congress appropriated for fiscal 2000. The extra funds enabled conferees to add more than 100 projects, including $10 million for the harbor in Pascagoula, Miss., hometown of Senate Majority Leader Trent Lott; $25 million for a groundwater project in the California district of House Rules Committee Chairman David Dreier; and $57 million for river projects in the Kentucky district of Harold Rogers, a senior member of the House Appropriations Committee.

- **Interior Department**

The bill included $816 million for conservation and reclamation projects, $23 million more than the Senate version and $46 million more than the House version.

- **Energy Department**

The final bill provided $18.3 billion for the department, $479 million more than the Senate version — the higher of the two — and $1.7 billion more than Congress appropriated in fiscal 2000. The bill included $5 billion for nuclear weapons activities, $376 million more than Clinton requested and $588 million more than was appropriated for fiscal 2000.

Hot-Button Issues

Δ **Missouri River.** The Clinton administration wants the Corps of Engineers to adopt a new plan for managing the flow of water from dams on the Missouri, releasing more water during spring rains to improve the habitat of fish and birds and cutting back in the summer. Downstream senators, most of them Republicans, complained that the new plan would limit barge traffic and could cause spring floods. They inserted language to block the new management plan. They hoped pressure from Missouri in an election year would keep Clinton from vetoing the bill.

Δ **Nuclear waste.** The final bill included $316 million for nuclear waste management, $30 million below Clinton's request. The administration had said that the Senate version, which cut $86.3 million from Clinton's request, would have delayed work on the proposed Yucca Mountain waste storage site in Nevada.

(figures are in thousands of dollars of new budget authority)

	Fiscal 2000 Appropriation	Fiscal 2001 Clinton Request	House Bill	Senate Bill	Conference Report
Army Corps of Engineers (DOD)	$4,126,560	$4,063,700	$4,123,607	$4,109,589	$4,522,427
Interior Department	805,802	840,973	770,468	793,107	816,365
Energy Department	16,606,924	18,064,720	17,202,425	17,863,045	18,341,776
Atomic Energy Defense Activities	(11,970,562)	(13,042,170)	(12,775,000)	(13,410,379)	(13,497,490)
Independent Agencies	128,510	177,166	107,500	162,700	171,852
Rescissions	– 20,749				
Emergency supplemental				203,460	214,460
GRAND TOTAL	**$21,647,047**	**$23,146,559**	**$22,204,000**	**$23,131,901**	**$24,066,880**
Total adjusted for scorekeeping	**($21,196,969)**	**($22,698,321)**	**($21,737,000)**	**($26,722,203)**	**(23,587,880)**

TABLE: House and Senate Appropriations committees

against the conference report at the behest of Minority Leader Tom Daschle, D-S.D., who has led the opposition to the Missouri River language that triggered the veto threat.

The $23.6 billion energy and water bill funds operations at the Energy Department and Army Corps of Engineers as well as some Interior Department programs. Daschle and the White House have criticized a provision that would bar the Corps from revising its management plan for the Missouri to give greater emphasis to wildlife — particularly three endangered species — and less to commerce.

Daschle has said that barge traffic on the Missouri has tailed off drastically in recent years.

In reiterating his intention to veto the bill, Clinton said in an Oct. 2 statement that the "deeply flawed" measure "threatens major environmental harm by blocking our efforts to modernize operations on the Missouri River." The president also said the bill "funds scores of special projects for special interests."

The Corps is on the verge of approving a plan to govern when water is released from upstream dams on the river. Daschle has endorsed a Fish and Wildlife Service proposal to provide more water in spring, through a "spring rise," while reducing river flows in the summer, a move that would provide additional habitat for endangered species.

A Veto With Ramifications?

Republicans representing states downstream, however, have maintained that any proposed change in the river's flow during springtime could increase the risk of flooding.

"If the Gore campaign believes it's in their interest to veto this, this will have ramifications," said Christopher S. Bond, R-Mo., after the Senate vote. "And I'm going to ramificate."

Within three days of the vote, a coalition of Missouri farming and flood control organizations began airing radio spots in Missouri and Iowa urging listeners to telephone Gore about the issue. "Don't let them strip away our flood protection," the commercial said, according to a transcript.

Aides for Bond also released copies of letters from Missouri Democratic Gov. Mel Carnahan and other local elected officials supporting their position. To underscore the bipartisan opposition to the veto, the letters were stamped "DEMOCRAT" beside each politician's signature.

Daschle said he preferred that Clinton not veto the bill. Daschle's House counterpart, Minority Leader Richard A. Gephardt, D-Mo., is among the lawmakers siding with Bond.

"I have indicated that procedurally as well as substantively, I'm open to compromise," Daschle said, such as putting the Missouri River provision in separate legislation.

Barring such a deal, however, Daschle saw a potential political advantage for Gore. "I would think it's going to hurt the Republicans with all the environmental groups that are concerned about this," he said.

Appropriators said the Missouri River language would be removed if the bill was vetoed. It was unclear, however, how the legislation would be returned to the president.

House Energy and Water Appropriations Subcommittee Chairman Ron Packard, R-Calif., said he would like to add several new provisions, including funding for CALFED, a huge California water program. Appropriators left $20 million in requested funds out of the bill after being unable to reach a compromise in conference.

If that did not happen, aides said the bill might be attached to another spending measure, such as the one funding the department of Veterans Affairs and Housing and Urban Development (HR 4635).

Senate Passes Revised Bill After Removing Missouri River Provisions

OCTOBER 14 — The Senate has passed energy and water development appropriations for fiscal 2001 after removing restrictions on the management of the Missouri River that had led President Clinton to veto the original legislation.

The $23.6 billion in energy and water spending, including more than a hundred projects on rivers, lakes and harbors across the country, was incorporated in a fiscal 2001 veterans and housing appropriations bill (HR 4635) the Senate passed, 87-8, Oct. 12. *(Vote 272, p. S-49; VA-HUD, p. 2-148)*

The House is expected to take up the amended legislation the week of Oct. 16.

Clinton on Oct. 7 vetoed the earlier version of the energy and water bill (HR 4733 — Conference report: H Rept 106-907) because a provision added by the Senate would have prevented the Army Corps of Engineers from revising its water management plan for the Missouri in order to emphasize wildlife at the potential expense of barge traffic. *(Text, p. D-98)*

Republicans contended that Clinton's plan for the Missouri also might increase the danger of flooding in the spring, and they hoped that Clinton's veto would hurt Vice President Al Gore's campaign in downstream swing states such as Missouri. Democrats said they did not think it would have any political consequences.

The House voted 315-98 on Oct. 11 to override the veto. Senate Republican leaders, realizing they lacked the votes to follow suit, instead removed the Missouri River language before adding the bill to the VA-HUD measure. *(House vote 523, p. H-166)*

'Unacceptable Rider'

Clinton, in his veto message, called the Missouri River language "an unacceptable rider" that would have prevented the Corps from revising its operating manual for the river across much of the upper Midwest from Montana to St. Louis.

The Corps is close to approving a revised plan for when water is released from upstream dams. The Fish and Wildlife Service has urged the Corps to release more water in spring and reduce flows in summer, which would provide more habitat for endangered species.

Environmentalists and lawmakers who favor the changes say that barge traffic has declined dramatically on the Missouri in recent decades.

"In its current form, the manual simply does not provide an appropriate balance among the competing interests, both commercial and recreational, of the many people who seek to use this great American river," Clinton said in his veto message.

Some House members said that language blocking the Corps plan had been included in four previous appropriations bills without Clinton objecting. They also said the Corps will not be ready to implement its revised manual until spring 2003.

"Therefore, this issue really is not an issue," said House Energy and Water Appropriations Subcommittee Chairman Ron Packard, R-Calif.

Senate Stalemate

Senate Majority Leader Trent Lott, R-Miss., acknowledged that he lacked the votes to override Clinton's veto. The Senate on Sept. 7 originally cleared the measure, 57-37, well short of a two-thirds majority.

Missouri lawmakers said they would settle for seeing Gore suffer politically. "If Missourians want to avoid being flooded, we're going to have to have the Nov. 7 remedy," said Sen. Christopher S. Bond, R-Mo., referring to the race between Gore and Texas Gov. George W. Bush.

Rep. Roy Blunt, R-Mo., predicted that the Missouri River issue "has the potential to move between 1 and 2 percentage points of the total vote" in his state.

Senate Minority Leader Tom Daschle, D-S.D., who led the opposition to the river provision, dismissed talk of political fallout. "There are so many more issues that I think have far greater importance," Daschle said. "This is important to the barge industry in Missouri, and that's about it."

In his veto message, Clinton cited other objections to the bill, including its omission of funding for CALFED, a huge California water program, and its lack of money to restore endangered salmon in the Pacific Northwest.

Appropriators said they did not anticipate making changes in those areas. They did, however, add $21.5 million at the last minute for water projects, including $17 million sought by Sen. Richard C. Shelby, R-Ala., for two levees in his state, as well as for projects in Missouri, Kentucky and Tennessee. ◆

Lawmakers Grant President's Foreign Aid Request, Yield On Family Planning Issue

Box Score — 2001 Fiscal Year

Foreign Operations

- **Bill:** HR 4811 — PL 106-429
- **Legislative action: Senate** passed S 2522 (S Rept 106-291), 95-4, on June 22.

House passed HR 4811 (H Rept 106-720), 239-185, on July 13.

House adopted conference report on HR 4811 (H Rept 106-977), 307-101, on Oct. 25.

Senate cleared HR 4811, 65-27, on Oct. 25.

President signed HR 4811 on Nov. 6.

SUMMARY

Eager to avoid an election-year confrontation with President Clinton, congressional Republicans yielded to his demands on key issues and cleared a fiscal 2001 foreign aid spending bill that provided debt relief for the world's poorest nations and lifted abortion restrictions on international family planning aid. Clinton signed the measure Nov. 6.

Although both the House and Senate had approved their versions of the foreign aid spending bill by July, GOP congressional leaders held off working out a compromise bill, hoping to use the measure as leverage in broader budget negotiations with the White House. But as the congressional session ground toward the Nov. 7 election, GOP leaders suddenly shifted their strategy, largely agreeing to Clinton's budget demands. The final $14.9 billion bill provided $1.8 billion more than the House version and $1.4 billion more than the version passed by the Senate. It fell $235 million below what Clinton requested.

In the most controversial spending item, Congress agreed to fund Clinton's $435 million request for Third World debt relief and included language allowing the International Monetary Fund to use up to $800 million from a revaluation of its gold reserves for additional debt forgiveness.

The final measure also increased funds for Russia and other former Soviet republics, international efforts to combat HIV/AIDS, and the Global Environmental Facility, a multilateral program which provides grants to developing countries for environmental initiatives. In an effort to help Serbia's new government, the bill provided as much as $100 million in aid to Serbia if officials there cooperate with an international war crimes tribunal and respect human rights.

But the Republicans' largest, albeit grudging, concession was on family planning aid, more a matter of policy than funding. House GOP leaders had wanted to extend abortion-related restrictions contained in the fiscal 2000 foreign aid bill (PL 106-113), but Clinton threatened to veto legislation that included any such restrictions. The conferees eventually backed down and increased family planning funds from the $385 million appropriated in fiscal 2000 to $425 million for fiscal 2001. However, the final bill prohibits spending the money until Feb. 15, one month after Clinton leaves office.

Senate Committee Slashes Clinton's Request for Colombia Aid

MAY 13 — President Clinton's billion-dollar effort to prop up the embattled government of Colombian president Andres Pastrana is in trouble in the Senate.

The Senate Appropriations Committee on May 9 approved a fiscal 2001 foreign operations spending bill (S 2522), that includes $934 million in fiscal 2000 funds for anti-drug efforts in South America, primarily in Colombia. The money is intended to help the Colombian military take on left-wing guerrillas and right-wing paramilitary groups that are protecting cocaine and heroin traffickers.

The money falls considerably short of the $1.7 billion included in a supplemental spending bill (HR 3908) that the House passed on March 30 and that Senate leaders have refused to act on. The Senate funds also come laden with conditions and still are likely to face a tough fight on the Senate floor from an unusual coalition of GOP budget hawks and liberal Democrats.

Many senators fear that the administration's efforts in Colombia are only the beginning of a costly and ineffective U.S. commitment. Some worry that the United States will be drawn into the conflict directly.

Clinton administration officials, concerned that the funds could be seriously delayed or denied outright, sharply criticized the Senate committee's action.

"The delay in the Congress has hurt our efforts to help Colombia deal with its problems," Undersecretary of State for Political Affairs Thomas R. Pickering, the administration's point man on Colombia, told reporters May 10. He was about to leave for Bogota to meet with Colombian officials.

"There appear to be some members who lack understanding of the urgency of the situation and the costs of this delay," Pickering said. "Already we have had to curtail helicopter-pilot training, and our spraying operations against coca and poppy cultivation are down 50 percent. This will degrade our ability to support Colombia's counternarcotics efforts, if our Congress is not able to act quickly to provide the adequate resources."

White House Press Secretary Joe Lockhart also warned May 10 that the committee's action would make it more difficult to round up additional funds from the European Union and Japan.

The overall foreign operations spending bill approved by the Senate committee would provide $13.4 billion in fiscal 2001 and about $1 billion in new spending for fiscal 2000. Almost all of the fiscal 2000 funds would be dedicated to anti-drug efforts in South America.

The total funds for fiscal 2001 would be about $1.9 billion less than Congress appropriated for the current fiscal year, and about $1.7 billion less than President Clinton requested. The fiscal 2000 appropriation included $1.8 billion in emergency funds that Clinton requested to help Israel, Jordan and the Palestinian Authority implement the Wye River peace accords.

The Senate bill would cut Clinton's requests for aid to Mozambique, devastated by floods this spring, and for debt relief for the world's poorest countries. It also would place conditions on aid to Kosovo and Haiti.

But it is the aid to Colombia that has stirred the most debate. Worried about the growing U.S. involvement in the conflict between Pastrana's government, guerrillas and drug traffickers, the appropriations committee added a number of provisions to the legislation.

The committee inserted language that would limit the number of U.S. military advisers who could be stationed on Colombian soil to 250, in an attempt to preclude a Vietnam-style escalation, when advisers became combatants. The House Armed Services Committee took a similar step in marking up a fiscal 2001 defense authorization bill (HR 4205), adopting language that would limit U.S. military personnel in Colombia to 500.

In a bow to the human rights concerns of Patrick J. Leahy of Vermont, ranking Democrat on the Foreign Operations Subcommittee, the Appropriations Committee's bill would condition aid on an assurance that Colombian military officers accused of human rights violations are tried in civilian courts, instead of by more lenient military tribunals.

The measure also would increase funds for prosecutors and others involved in human rights work. And it contains a provision Leahy wrote several years ago that would require that any military units trained by the United States be screened for human rights abusers.

Other provisions in the Senate committee bill would shift funds away from providing Colombia with sophisticated Blackhawk military helicopters, that Clinton requested and some leading House members, including Speaker J. Dennis Hastert, R-Ill., have demanded. The Senate bill would shift nearly a quarter of the proposed funds to neighboring countries and provide for less sophisticated military helicopters.

Growing Unease

The committee approved, by voice vote, an amendment by ranking Democrat Robert C. Byrd of West Virginia that would require Congress to pass authorizing legislation before any fiscal 2001 funds could be sent to Colombia.

That was not enough for Slade Gorton, R-Wash., who tried to further tie the administration's hands with an amendment that would have restricted current-year spending for the Andean region, including Colombia, to $100 million unless Congress passed legislation authorizing more.

"This is something we ought to decide and analyze before we spend a billion dollars," Gorton said.

His position was supported by some GOP conservatives and liberal Democrats but was defeated, 11-15.

The vote highlighted the considerable unease many senators feel over the proposal — discontent that could cause problems on the Senate floor, according to Appropriations Committee Chairman Ted Stevens, R-Alaska.

At the markup, Leahy warned Stevens that he intends to raise a point of order under Senate budget rules questioning the designation of the Colombian aid as emergency spending, which would exempt it from spending caps specified in the fiscal 2001 budget resolution (H Con Res 290).

Stevens told reporters after the markup that he is not confident he can muster the 60 votes that would be necessary to waive Leahy's point of order. If he were not successful, any new spending for Colombia would have to be offset by cuts in other programs.

"That would be hard to find," Stevens said. "I don't know how we find a billion and a half dollars."

The funds also are likely to be challenged by Sen. Arlen Specter, R-Pa., who said he intends to offer an amendment to reallocate half of the Colombia funds to domestic drug treatment programs.

The Senate's caution stands in stark contrast to the House where, under Hastert's prodding, members voted to spend more fiscal 2000 funds than Clinton had requested.

Clinton had called for spending an additional $1.3 billion over two years on top of $300 million the administration is already planning to spend this fiscal year. The House Appropriations Committee is not scheduled to mark up its fiscal 2001 foreign aid spending bill until June.

Debt and Flood Relief

The Senate committee also slashed the administration's request for debt relief for the world's poorest countries. Much of the money would go to a multilateral trust fund that would write off debt to the World Bank and other international organizations.

Clinton had requested a total of $435 million over two years, but the panel approved spending only $75 million in fiscal 2001.

Senate Foreign Operations Appropriations Subcommittee Chairman Mitch McConnell, R-Ky., said that he wanted authorizing committees to address the issue first. House appropriators also did not include fiscal 2000 funds for debt relief in the supplemental bill, pending action by authorizing panels.

In the Senate, the Foreign Relations Committee on March 23 approved a bill (S 2382 — S Rept 106-257) that would authorize the funds for debt relief, as well as allow the International Monetary Fund (IMF) to provide debt relief by profiting — to the tune of nearly $3 billion — from the difference between the current market price of gold (about $300 an ounce) and its value on the IMF books (about $47 an ounce). The gold was provided by IMF members.

But the bill has yet to be taken up by the full Senate because the Banking Committee has yet to act on the legislation. Chairman Phil Gramm, R-Texas, wants to attach conditions requiring reforms at international financial institutions such as the IMF.

In terms of fiscal 2000 spending, the Senate measure also fell far short of Clinton's request for flood-ravaged Mozambique. The panel approved

$25 million in direct aid and $38 million to reimburse the Pentagon for emergency supplies it provided the African nation.

In the fiscal 2001 portion of the legislation, Leahy won approval of $651 million in global health initiatives, including funds dedicated to combating AIDS, tuberculosis and malaria.

McConnell, widely known for specifying aid for specific countries, remained true to form in drafting the bill.

In Eastern Europe, the committee bill would provide $635 million in aid to the Balkans, with specific amounts reserved for Bosnia ($75 million), Montenegro ($89 million) — which is locked in an uneasy confederation with Slobodan Milosevic's Serbia — and Croatia ($60 million), regarded as a Balkan success story because of its turn toward multiparty democracy and economic reform.

Kosovo Conditions

The measure also would condition any economic aid to Kosovo on a certification that America's NATO allies were picking up at least 85 percent of the tab for economic recovery and reconstruction efforts. A similar provision was approved last year. The Senate committee attempted to limit U.S. participation in the Kosovo peacekeeping on a fiscal 2001 military construction bill.

The successor states of the Soviet Union would receive $775 million in the foreign operations bill, with specific totals awarded for Ukraine ($175 million), Georgia ($94 million) and Armenia ($89 million).

Once again, McConnell included tough conditions on aid to Russia, including a requirement that the Kremlin cooperate with international efforts to investigate human rights violations and provide humanitarian help in Chechnya, on top of withholding half of government-to-government aid unless the Kremlin cuts off its help to Iran's missile and weapons programs. McConnell had previously warned of such a step.

Aid to Haiti would be conditioned on Haiti holding parliamentary elections and seating a new legislature — a step it has put off for several years. U.S. lawmakers have grown weary of the delay.

The Middle East would continue to be the largest recipient of U.S. assistance, with Israel receiving about $2 billion in military aid and $840 million in economic aid and Egypt receiving $1.3 million in military aid and $695 million in economic aid. Stevens said he is likely to support allowing Egypt a benefit only Israel has received in the past: receiving all of its aid dollars at the beginning of the fiscal year so it can profit from the interest earnings.

Senate Passes Bill; House Markup Begins with Clash Over Israel Funds

JUNE 24 — Fearing that its passage was going to be delayed beyond the July Fourth recess, Senate GOP leaders have ended several months of procedural squabbles over emergency spending. That should allow drug-fighting aid to flow to Colombia and other South American countries this summer.

The Senate voted overwhelmingly to include nearly $1 billion in additional fiscal 2000 drug-fighting aid in its fiscal 2001 foreign operations appropriations bill (S 2522). The Senate passed the spending bill, 95-4, on June 22. *(Vote 141, p. S-27)*

As soon as the Senate finished voting, key aides said negotiators on the fiscal 2001 military construction appropriations bill (HR 4425), which is already in conference, have settled on $1.3 billion in fiscal 2000 emergency funding to fight drugs. That bill will be the vehicle for a total of $12 billion in emergency fiscal 2000 spending.

The House, prodded by House Speaker J. Dennis Hastert, R-Ill., had approved $1.7 billion in aid to Colombia and its neighbors as part of a broad fiscal 2000 supplemental spending bill (HR 3908) that passed March 30. That was more than President Clinton requested for current-year spending to combat drugs in the Andes.

However, Senate Majority Leader Trent Lott, R-Miss., prevented the House's supplemental measure from being considered by the Senate, saying it was too costly. He insisted that all fiscal 2000 emergency funds be considered in fiscal 2001 spending bills.

Then a tussle between Lott and Minority Leader Tom Daschle, D-S.D., delayed consideration of the foreign operations bill, despite pleas from Hastert and the Clinton administration to move quickly on the Colombia funds.

The White House and supportive lawmakers have been concerned about the fate of Colombian President Andres Pastrana, whose government is under siege from left-wing guerrillas and right-wing paramilitaries who profit from and protect drug traffickers.

"This is a guy . . . that is the real deal," Delaware Sen. Joseph R. Biden Jr., ranking Democrat on the Foreign Relations Committee, said June 21, urging senators to help Pastrana. "This is a guy who's risking his life . . . because he understands what the stake is for his country."

Lott, speaking on the Senate floor June 21, said the funds were needed to slow the flow of drugs to the United States. Colombia is the predominant source of cocaine smuggled into the United States. "The drugs coming out of Colombia are coming right into the United States [and] poisoning our children," Lott said.

He was backed by Mike DeWine, R-Ohio, who bemoaned the Clinton administration's past shift to a greater emphasis on domestic law enforcement, treatment and prevention rather than eradication and interdiction.

DeWine said the new funds would "restore the balance" in funding that prevailed under previous administrations.

But Patrick J. Leahy of Vermont, ranking Democrat on the Foreign Operations Appropriations Subcommittee, derided U.S. help to "Plan Colombia."

"This is only the first billion-dollar installment of a multi-year, open-ended commitment of many more billions of dollars," Leahy said June 20. "Nobody can say what they expect this to cost, what we can expect to achieve, in what period of time, how intensifying a war that cannot be won will lead to peace, or what the risks are to hundreds of American military and civilian personnel in Colombia."

Agreeing, Paul Wellstone, D-Minn., introduced an amendment that sought to transfer $225 million of the

$934 million slated for anti-drug efforts in South America to U.S. drug treatment programs. The funds would come out of programs to train two additional anti-drug battalions in Colombia's military and provide supporting equipment.

Wellstone complained that Colombia's military is too tied to right-wing paramilitary groups that have been accused of massive human rights violations, and said that boosting U.S. aid would only serve to aggravate the problem.

"Do we back a military escalation that may worsen a civil war?" Wellstone asked. "More weapons and more soldiers have not and cannot defeat the source of illegal" narcotics.

His amendment found little backing, however, with Biden and other Democrats speaking in support of the full anti-drug package. Wellstone's amendment was tabled, or killed, 89-11. *(Vote 138, p. S-26)*

Slade Gorton, R-Wash., then took a shot at the package from the right, attempting to cut the aid to $200 million and direct the savings to reducing the federal debt. Gorton said Congress was being asked to approve funds before the administration had proved the likely effectiveness of U.S. support.

"We lack even a clue as to whether or not it will have any positive impact on drug trafficking between Colombia and the United States," Gorton said.

" 'Let's spend a billion dollars, and after it's spent, let's ask the president for a justification.' . . . That's absolutely, completely, dangerously backwards."

He was joined by some liberal opponents of the measure, such as Russell D. Feingold, D-Wis., who also questioned the decision to classify the aid as emergency spending, thus freeing it from budget caps.

Feingold said that, by contrast, the bill shortchanged true emergencies such as aid to help Mozambique and Southern Africa recover from devastating flooding earlier this year. The Senate bill would provide only $25 million in emergency aid to Mozambique, compared with $200 million requested by the White House.

But Christopher J. Dodd, D-Conn., said the situation in Colombia was urgent. "This package may not be perfect, but our delay in responding to a neighbor's call for help is getting too long," Dodd said. "Every day means lives lost."

Gorton's amendment was defeated, 19-79. *(Vote 139, p. S-27)*

White House Dissatisfied

While claiming victory on the Colombia funds, the administration is still dissatisfied with several elements of the Senate's bill: its funding levels overall, especially for peacekeeping in the Balkans and for debt relief for impoverished nations, as well as conditions the Senate would impose on aid to Kosovo and Russia.

The bill's $13.4 billion total for fiscal 2001 is about $1.7 billion less than Clinton requested and about $1.9 billion less than Congress appropriated for foreign aid in fiscal 2000. The fiscal 2000 appropriation, however, included a one-time emergency appropriation of $1.8 billion to help seal the Wye River peace accords between Israel and the Palestinian Authority.

House appropriators began moving their fiscal 2001 foreign aid spending bill June 20, with the Foreign Operations Subcommittee approving a draft that would provide $13.3 billion.

During the markup, members of the House panel engaged in a fierce clash that pitted Congress' traditional support for Israel against concerns that Tel Aviv's planned $250 million sale of a sophisticated "Phalcon" airborne radar system to China could harm U.S. national security interests.

In an effort to retaliate for Israel's plan to sell its version of the U.S. AWACS surveillance plane to Beijing, panel Chairman Sonny Callahan, R-Ala., drafted a provision that would dispense with a unique perk that Israel has traditionally received — getting all of its foreign and military aid (a total of more than $2.8 billion) on Oct. 1, the start of the fiscal year, or 30 days after the date of enactment of the annual foreign aid bill. The provision, which was included in the Senate-passed bill, allows Israel to earn almost half a billion dollars in extra interest income each year.

Callahan, who called the proposed radar sale "a serious breach of our friendship," said that he would be inclined to restore the early disbursement provision later. But first, he said, he wanted to give U.S. negotiators leverage to help persuade their Israeli counterparts to drop the sale.

"We need this hammer over the head of Israeli negotiators," Callahan said.

Callahan, who has shown an unusual willingness to take on the powerful pro-Israel lobby, accused his fellow appropriators of caving in to pressure from the American Israel Public Affairs Committee.

"They have convinced this Congress that Israel ought not to have to stand up to the same scrutiny as other countries," Callahan said. "It's the wisdom of the Congress" to vote this way, "but it's still stupid foreign policy."

The ranking Democrat on the full Appropriations panel, David R. Obey of Wisconsin, who cosponsored an amendment to restore the early disbursal of funds for Israel, bridled at Callahan's characterization. He pointed out that he had been willing to clash with AIPAC and Israel on many occasions and shared Callahan's anger at Israel's proposed radar sale.

But he attributed the action to an earlier, hawkish Israeli government and said that delaying the U.S. aid payments would undermine the current, dovish Israeli government of Prime Minister Ehud Barak as it is trying to strike a final peace deal with the Palestinians and restart peace negotiations with Syria.

"It is not a question if we should deliver this message, the question is how, the question is when," Obey said, urging that penalties be exacted only if the sale goes through.

Appropriations Committee Chairman C.W. Bill Young, R-Fla., disagreed. "Once they get the technology in their hands, once the sale is made, it's too late," Young said.

But Young and Callahan were in the minority as the Obey amendment passed on a voice vote.

The panel first voted down, 6-9, a Callahan second-degree amendment, which would have allowed Israel to receive the bulk of its funds in a lump sum as usual but set aside $250 million — equivalent to the value of the radar sale — unless the sale was canceled or Defense Secretary William S. Cohen could certify it did not threaten U.S. national security.

Jesse L. Jackson Jr., D-Ill., crossed party lines to vote with Callahan, noting that China could use the Israeli technology to target U.S. pilots defending Taiwan. "This technology has the ability to come home to roost in Taiwan," Jackson said, adding rhetorically, "Who is China identifying with this technology? Who are we putting at risk?"

Nita M. Lowey, D-N.Y., spoke for the majority: "I think we deal with our allies with negotiations, rather than threats."

Callahan said he will raise the issue again at the full committee and on the House floor.

Provision Intended to Help Egypt

Callahan and Young also pressed a provision that would allow Egypt to enjoy a scaled-down version of the benefits Israel receives, but without an impact on the federal budget.

Under the provision, adopted by voice vote, Egypt would be allowed to receive all of the previously appropriated military aid it had been slated to receive in fiscal 2001 (estimated at $1.09 billion) in one chunk before the end of 2000, instead of receiving it in four equal chunks throughout the fiscal year. That would allow Egypt to earn at least $25 million in extra interest, which it could apply to further military purchases.

"If we are going to do it for one country, we ought to do it for another," Callahan said, noting that he was responding to a request from Clinton and Egyptian President Hosni Mubarak. The Senate by unanimous consent adopted a similar amendment offered by Appropriations Committee Chairman Ted Stevens, R-Alaska.

Callahan was successful on another fight that will be carried to the House floor — and beyond. This time, Lowey was the loser.

In drafting the bill, Callahan had carried over restrictions on family planning aid from the fiscal 2000 omnibus spending law (PL 106-113). At the last moment in last year's budget negotiations, Clinton reluctantly agreed to the restrictions on a one-year basis in order to win congressional support for repaying nearly $1 billion in U.S. dues to the United Nations.

The compromise provision barred any of the $385 million in current U.S. international family planning assistance from flowing to groups that lobby to overturn abortion laws, even if they use their own funds for the purpose. Clinton then took advantage of a provision in the law to waive those restrictions.

The administration suffered a penalty for using the waiver — the fiscal 2001 bill would shift 3 percent, or $12.5 million, from family planning efforts to child survival and disease prevention.

Callahan argued that the current law "hasn't had any detrimental effect on these organizations. . . . I see no reason to change anything."

But Lowey replied that she "thought it was outrageous" that last year's compromise was reached in the first place, and she offered an amendment to strike the restriction from the fiscal 2001 bill.

Lowey's amendment was rejected, 7-8, largely along party lines. She and ranking Democrat Nancy Pelosi of California pledged to fight the provision as it progresses through the House.

The Senate bill does not include these restrictions, and the issue is likely to be resolved in a House-Senate conference.

House Panel's Bill Retains Provisions Opposed by Clinton

JULY 1 — Holding out for an end-of-session deal with the White House on foreign aid spending, the House Appropriations Committee approved a fiscal 2001 foreign operations appropriations bill June 27 that the White House has said President Clinton probably would veto.

Committee Republicans defeated, largely along party lines, a number of attempts by Democrats to alter some of the provisions most offensive to Clinton, including sharp cuts in funds to relieve international debts of some of the world's poorest countries and abortion restrictions on international family planning aid.

The bill was approved by voice vote.

Under heavy pressure from pro-Israel lobbyists, the committee followed the lead of its Foreign Operations Subcommittee and defeated, by voice vote, an amendment that would have held up some aid to Israel because of Tel Aviv's planned sale of an airborne radar system to China.

Clinton said in a June 28 news conference that he has discussed the sale "extensively" with Israeli Prime Minister Ehud Barak.

Democrats hoping to change the foreign aid bill planned to carry their fight to the House floor and, if necessary, to a House-Senate conference likely to be one of the last of the session. An anticipated increase in the budget allocation for foreign aid could help grease any compromise.

David R. Obey of Wisconsin, ranking Democrat on the Appropriations panel, mocked Republicans for sticking to foreign aid totals that even their leaders said were insufficient.

Obey, referring to the "Star Trek" television series, said, "I feel like I'm on the Holodeck of the Starship Enterprise dealing with fictional directions on a fictional unit. Sooner or later the result is going to have to be made clear. We aren't bringing bills to the floor that we're serious about."

Only two significant changes were made during the full Appropriations Committee's consideration of the bill, despite lingering strains on many major issues.

One amendment by Jim Kolbe, R-Ariz., would hold back 10 percent of U.S. contributions to international financial institutions until they undertake several measures aimed at stemming corruption in countries that receive aid. The amendment is similar to a provision included in the Senate-passed bill (S 2522) and legislation (HR 4697) approved by the House International Relations Committee on June 29. The Appropriations panel approved the amendment by voice vote.

The other amendment, by Nancy Pelosi of California, ranking Democrat on the Foreign Operations Appropriations Subcommittee, would effectively continue aid to Armenia by reinstating a provision allowing the president to waive a congressional prohibition on aid to a former Soviet republic if it occupies the territory of another former Soviet state. Armenia has occupied Nagorno-Karabakh, a disputed enclave within neighboring Azerbaijan, since 1994.

Clinton has routinely signed a waiver allowing Armenia to receive

U.S. aid — more than $100 million in fiscal 2000. The Armenian-American community in the United States is politically influential. Pelosi's amendment was adopted by voice vote.

Radar Planes

Alabama Republican Sonny Callahan, chairman of the Foreign Operations Subcommittee, lost a second attempt to punish Israel for its plan to sell a sophisticated airborne radar system, similar to the U.S. AWACS, to China for $250 million.

Callahan's plan would have restricted a unique perk that Israel receives: getting all of its aid — a total of more than $2.8 billion — on Oct. 1, the start of the fiscal year, or 30 days after the enactment of the annual foreign aid bill. The provision allows Israel to earn almost half a billion dollars in extra interest income each year.

In retaliation for the proposed radar sale, Callahan suggested excluding $250 million of Israel's aid from this special treatment.

He was supported by a number of Republicans, including full committee Chairman C.W. Bill Young of Florida, and Rep. Randy "Duke" Cunningham of California, a decorated fighter pilot in the Vietnam War.

Cunningham noted that Israel's Phalcon system would allow China to detect U.S. pilots flying over the Taiwan Strait.

"They will know what kind of airplanes we have, what kinds of weapons," Cunningham said. "This defense is critical to the security of our country."

Jerry Lewis, R-Calif, chairman of the Defense Appropriations Subcommittee, said the proposed sale had spurred Pentagon officials to question the wisdom of continuing much of the joint defense research with Israel.

Callahan fretted that he would be unsuccessful with the proposal because of heavy lobbying by the American Israel Public Affairs Committee.

Obey chafed at Callahan's remarks, reciting what he said was his own long record of disagreeing with AIPAC.

"There's no member of this Congress that's told AIPAC to go to hell more often than I have," Obey said. But he said that slowing the aid would only harm the Middle East peace process by dealing a blow to the Barak government.

Obey and others said that American and Israeli negotiators should first be given time to work out a compromise on the radar sale. Obey pledged that if those negotiations did not succeed in blocking the sale, he would support a total cutoff in aid to Tel Aviv.

Searching for an alternative means of expressing displeasure, Pelosi and Norm Dicks, D-Wash., introduced a sense-of-Congress resolution as a substitute. Callahan dismissed that as "a back door slip-out" and a "cop out." But it was adopted on a voice vote.

Debtor Nations

Pelosi had less success in trying to win committee approval for increasing U.S. contributions to a multilateral fund to write off the debts that some poor nations owe international financial institutions such as the World Bank.

Describing the debts as a "crushing burden on the poorest people of the world," Pelosi offered an amendment that would have increased funds for debt relief by $210 million in fiscal 2001 and termed them emergency spending — exempt from budget limitations.

As approved by the subcommittee, the bill included only $82.4 million for debt relief: $69.4 million in contributions to the international Highly Indebted Poor Countries (HIPC) donors fund, and $13 million in U.S. write-downs under a program that allows countries to pay off some of their debt by investing in improving their environment.

The Clinton administration had requested $210 million for fiscal 2000 and $225 million for fiscal 2001 for debt relief.

Callahan opposed the aid, particularly on an emergency basis. He said it was essential that new loans be bound by conditions he had included in the subcommittee draft, imposing a temporary moratorium on new loans to countries that receive debt relief to prevent them, Callahan said, from squandering the money on corruption and profligacy. The recipients would still be eligible for grants, although these tend to be far more limited because of political resistance in donor nations.

"We would deny some of these leaders the opportunity to go right back into debt," Callahan said.

In support of his point of view, Callahan noted that soon after Uganda had been forgiven $1.3 billion in debts, its president, Yoweri Musevini, spent $35 million on a Gulfstream luxury jet.

Pelosi snapped back, "You've gotten more mileage out of the Gulfstream than the president of Uganda. Should the poor people of Africa suffer from the poor judgment of their president?" Still, her amendment was defeated, 21-32.

Similarly, members defeated a Pelosi amendment that would have cut $30 million from foreign military aid and spent it on combatting HIV/AIDS.

Pelosi noted that the Clinton administration has declared the disease, particularly in sub-Saharan Africa, a "national security threat."

Callahan said that with nearly all of the $3.5 billion in military aid dedicated to the Middle East, only $125 million was available for the rest of the world, including efforts to develop the peacekeeping ability of African nations.

Responding, Pelosi suggested that oil and gas producers like Kazakhstan, Turkmenistan and Ukraine could foot their own military bills. But her amendment was defeated, 22-29.

Democrats also failed to overturn existing abortion restrictions on international family planning aid that Clinton agreed to last year on a one-year basis in order to free up funds for the United Nations. An amendment by Nita M. Lowey, D-N.Y., to lift the restrictions, was defeated, 26-34.

House Passes Foreign Aid Bill With Increase For Debt Relief

JULY 15 — House Democrats shook up the Republican strategy for a budget showdown with the White House this fall by winning adoption of several foreign aid bill amendments, including one that would increase spending for debt relief for poor countries.

The House went on to pass the

$13.3 billion fiscal 2001 foreign operations appropriations bill (HR 4811) by a 239-185 vote. *(Vote 400, p. H-124)*

Administration officials have said they would recommend President Clinton veto the House committee version of the bill, if it was sent to him, because of policy disputes, and because it is $1.8 billion below the president's request. The measure also is about $100 million less than the corresponding Senate bill (S 2522).

Yet, during the debate, Democrats managed to pass several amendments that may leave the White House in a somewhat better negotiating position this fall.

Most significantly, in a drawn-out, dramatic vote of 216-211, Democrats won adoption of an amendment by Maxine Waters, D-Calif., to increase the U.S. contribution to a multilateral fund that will forgive some of the debts that poor countries owe to international financial institutions. *(Vote 397, p. H-124)*

Republican leaders have held off granting funds for debt relief, hoping to use the issue as leverage to force reforms at international financial institutions and as a bargaining chip in end-of-session budget negotiations.

Waters' amendment would increase debt relief by $156 million, bringing total funding for the multilateral debt relief effort in fiscal 2001 up to Clinton's request of $225 million. Clinton also requested $210 million in supplemental spending for debt relief for fiscal 2000, but the funds were not included in the supplemental measure (PL 106-246) Clinton signed July 13.

The vote on the Waters amendment came only after an extended tug-of-war between party leaders. With Waters and her supporters — including 26 Republicans — initially leading in the vote tally, GOP leaders held the vote open for an extra quarter-hour, as Majority Whip Tom DeLay of Texas urged wavering Republicans such as Ernie Fletcher of Kentucky and Tom Coburn and Steve Largent of Oklahoma to oppose the amendment.

Just as DeLay appeared on the verge of victory by one vote, four Democrats and one Republican switched their votes in favor of the amendment: David R. Obey of Wisconsin, ranking Democrat on the Appropriations Committee; Sander M. Levin, D-Mich.; David Wu, D-Ore.; Leonard L. Boswell, D-Iowa, and Tom Latham, R-Iowa.

In an interview afterward, Levin said he changed his vote to improve the administration's negotiating posture, despite his concern that the additional debt relief would come at the expense of military aid to Jordan as well as Export-Import Bank loans.

"On balance," Levin said, "it was better for getting a breakthrough on debt relief."

Deal on Debt

Administration officials have been concerned that Congress' unwillingness to provide debt relief would unravel a $27 billion agreement by Clinton and the leaders of other prosperous countries at a summit in Cologne, Germany, in June 1999.

Congress reluctantly provided $123 million in debt relief in the fiscal 2000 foreign operations spending bill, which was incorporated in the omnibus spending bill (PL 106-113).

Treasury Secretary Lawrence H. Summers pressed for more funds at a Capitol Hill news conference July 12. "It is imperative for our country economically, morally and diplomatically to provide this debt relief," he said.

As it emerged from the Appropriations Committee, the House bill would have provided only $82.4 million for debt relief — $69.4 million in contributions to the international Highly Indebted Poor Countries donors fund, and $13 million for reducing the U.S. debts of countries that invest in environmental improvement. The Senate version of the bill (S 2522) includes $75 million for debt relief.

Moreover, Senate Banking Committee Chairman Phil Gramm, R-Texas, has prevented legislation from moving forward that would allow the International Monetary Fund to help write off nearly $1 billion in loans.

Nancy Pelosi of California, ranking Democrat on the House Foreign Operations Appropriations panel, had sought to overcome some of these hurdles by adding $210 million in fiscal 2000 emergency spending and $179.6 million in fiscal 2001 emergency spending for debt relief. But her amendment was blocked on procedural grounds.

Pelosi was ardently supported by members of the Congressional Black Caucus, and the debate at times took on a racial character.

Foreign Operations Appropriations Subcommittee Chairman Sonny Callahan, R-Ala., opposed the Pelosi amendment, saying the debt relief plan "is going to bail out banks who have made bad loans" to corrupt leaders.

Waters called the remarks "condescending," and added, "This is Africa. Somehow it is less deserving . . . not worthy of debt relief or support."

"I sort of resent you saying that I am condescending and implying that it is racist, because it is not," Callahan replied. He said he agrees with efforts to raise the standard of living in poor countries, but disagrees with writing off loans made through international financial institutions.

In a July 13 interview, Waters called the vote on her amendment "a very big victory" and said it was part of a deliberate strategy: "The Congressional Black Caucus made a conscious decision that we were going to take charge" of the bill.

In addition to Waters' amendment, the black caucus scored another victory when the House approved, 267-156, a proposal by Barbara Lee, D-Calif., that would shift $42 million from other accounts toward programs to combat HIV/AIDS, primarily in Africa. That brought total AIDS funding in the bill up to Clinton's request of $244 million. The House, by voice vote, also adopted an amendment by Brad Sherman, D-Calif., to shift $10 million into AIDS prevention and research. *(Vote 398, p. H-124)*

GOP Victories

Republicans succeeded in including some provisions opposed by most Democrats, including anti-abortion language that either will cause Clinton to veto the measure or be worked out in autumn negotiations.

The House, by a vote of 206-221, turned down an amendment by James C. Greenwood, R-Pa., that would have removed abortion-related restrictions on international family planning aid. *(Vote 396, p. H-124)*

Clinton agreed to those restrictions last year on a one-year basis in return for congressional approval of funds to pay U.S. debts to the United Nations, but administration officials have threatened a veto if they are included again. The Senate bill does not include a similar provision.

Republicans also took aim at the Clinton administration's effort to improve relations with North Korea, as the House adopted, 298-125, an amendment by Doug Bereuter, R-Neb., that would bar the federal government from indemnifying U.S. companies that supplied parts for nuclear power plants built in North Korea. The same provision has been included in the fiscal 2001 defense authorization bill (HR 4205). *(Vote 399, p. H-124)*

Foreign Aid Conferees Named

JULY 22 — A House-Senate conference committee on the fiscal 2001 foreign operations appropriations bill (HR 4811 — H Rept 106-720, S Rept 106-291) is expected to meet the week of July 24 to hash out contentious issues such as debt relief, abortion and aid to Russia — all under the threat of a presidential veto.

The Senate appointed conferees July 18. The House is expected to follow suit after it acts on a Democratic motion to instruct conferees to retain or strike certain provisions.

Senate Appropriations Committee Chairman Ted Stevens, R-Alaska, predicted that a compromise could be reached before the August congressional recess.

To ease a compromise and placate the White House, Stevens said he would "absolutely" support the higher level of spending in the House version of the foreign aid bill to help relieve debts that the world's poorest countries owe the World Bank and other multilateral development banks.

The House on July 13 narrowly approved an amendment that would bring total funding for the multilateral debt relief initiative in fiscal 2001 up to President Clinton's request of $225 million.

The Senate agreed to provide $75 million for such debt relief in its version of the bill passed June 22.

Clinton also requested $210 million in fiscal 2000 supplemental spending for debt relief, but the money was not included in the supplemental package tacked on to the fiscal 2001 military construction appropriations bill (PL 106-246) that Clinton signed July 13. A year ago, he had pledged that the United States would contribute $600 million as part of a $27 billion international effort.

As congressional appropriators sought a deal on the funds, the World Bank and the International Monetary Fund announced July 18 that the African nation of Benin had become the ninth country eligible for the debt relief program. The announcement came just before a July 21-23 summit of the world's richest countries in Okinawa, Japan, at which debt relief was expected to be high on the agenda.

Without the U.S. contribution, World Bank officials warned July 18, the institutions will be unable to meet their commitments to several Latin American countries: Bolivia, Honduras, Nicaragua and Guyana.

In addition to the debt relief question, conferees will have to tackle the perennial issue of abortion-related restrictions on family planning funds.

Clinton reluctantly agreed to some restrictions last year as part of a broader compromise, but administration officials are urging a veto if they are included in the pending bill. The Senate version of the bill does not include the restrictions.

And conferees will have to find a way to make up $200 million in military aid funds the House cut in its effort to boost debt relief. Otherwise, some of the funds might come out of aid to Israel, Jordan and Egypt, despite Clinton's efforts at Camp David to broker a Middle East peace.

Foreign Aid Bill May Hit Snag Over Call to Boost Funds to Colombia

SEPTEMBER 16 — Two months after Congress approved a supplemental $1.3 billion aid package for Colombia, some lawmakers are seeking to alter the new U.S. policy of greater help for Colombia's military by increasing funds for the South American nation's police.

But there is resistance to reopening the carefully balanced compromise that led to the spending for Colombia.

The debate is taking place behind the scenes as House and Senate appropriators gear up to reconcile their versions of the fiscal 2001 foreign operations appropriations bill (HR 4811) and strike a deal with the White House on overseas aid.

They already face a daunting task: a budget allotment for foreign aid that is $2 billion less than the $15.4 billion President Clinton requested, and deep disputes over such issues as abortion restrictions on international family planning aid and debt relief for poor countries.

But the prospect of more spending for Colombia, as well as proposals to provide extra funds for Israel and to combat the international spread of HIV/AIDS, have added more complexity to what many observers believe will be the last appropriations bill settled before Congress adjourns.

Senate Appropriations Committee Chairman Ted Stevens, R-Alaska, expressed the frustration of many appropriators when interviewed Sept. 12 about attempts to reopen the Colombia debate.

"No one's said anything to me" about such a prospect, Stevens said. "I hope you're not trying to start something — that's a bad rumor."

Friends of the Police

Unfortunately for Stevens, House International Relations Committee Chairman Benjamin A. Gilman, R-N.Y., and Government Reform Committee Chairman Dan Burton, R-Ind., kicked off efforts to reopen the foreign aid bill with a July letter to House Speaker J. Dennis Hastert, R-Ill.

They pleaded for additional money for Colombia's national police, a longtime U.S. ally in the drug war. Gilman and Burton have developed a deep respect for a police force that has lost thousands of its members battling drug traffickers, and they have a warm relationship with the recently retired police commander, Gen. Jose Serrano, whom they view as a hero.

"I believe that Gen. Serrano saved countless American families from the nightmare of drug addiction. For this, we owe him a debt of gratitude," Gilman said upon Serrano's retirement.

Serrano, Gilman said, had made the Colombian police "the model of Latin American police agencies."

Gilman and Burton argue that the Colombia package included in the fiscal 2000 supplemental spending bill (PL 106-246) that Clinton signed July 13 should have given more money to the Colombian police, rather than the Colombian army. The remedy, they told Hastert, would be to include an additional $99.5 million in aid for the Colombian police in the foreign operations bill. The money would allow the police to buy more aircraft, ammunition and protective equipment.

Versions of the bill passed by the House and Senate would yield an estimated $50 million to $100 million in additional anti-narcotics aid to Colombia. Exact figures are not possible because spending for anti-drug programs covers a broader area than Colombia, though much of the money will be focused there.

The Colombian government is expected to benefit from between $100 million and $150 million in the fiscal 2001 defense appropriations bill (PL 106-259). Again, the money is for broader anti-drug programs.

"We have unwisely put almost all our eggs in the Colombian army's basket," Burton and Gilman wrote in The Washington Times on Sept. 13. "As matters stand, the Colombian army lacks the pilots, mechanics and infrastructure to support a substantial number of helicopters. Eradication and interdiction are law enforcement problems, and the Colombian National Police is tested, proven and effective in resolving these problems."

Hastert has agreed to study the chairmen's request, but leadership aides and other lawmakers involved in writing the supplemental spending bill said they were reluctant to tamper with the compromise that had been worked out.

For example, Patrick J. Leahy of Vermont, ranking Democrat on the Senate Foreign Operations Appropriations Subcommittee, has indicated that he would take steps to tighten human rights restrictions on aid to Colombia if the compromise is reopened.

Human Rights

Leahy had objected to Clinton's decision last month to waive human rights restrictions on fiscal 2000 aid to Bogota on the eve of Clinton's trip to Colombia to meet with President Andres Pastrana.

Leahy and other Senate Democrats have insisted that Clinton take a tougher line this fall when he considers whether to certify for another year that Colombia is complying with human rights requirements for U.S. aid. He must make such a certification before Bogota can receive the fiscal 2001 portion of the supplemental funds, administration officials have concluded.

Not wanting to undo the compromise, Leahy has stopped short of legislative attempts to force Colombia to adhere to additional human rights conditions.

Sen. Joseph R. Biden Jr. of Delaware, ranking Democrat on the Foreign Relations Committee, has pressed Pastrana to uphold the human rights conditions, but said he hoped the compromise would stand through the end of the congressional session.

And fellow Foreign Relations Committee member Paul Wellstone, D-Minn., noted that the supplemental package already included $115 million in aid for the police. "Is it too much to ask that we see the impact of the additional assistance package before we throw more money into the military strategy?" said Wellstone.

Clinton and congressional leaders also have indicated that they would like to see the enactment of trade legislation that would benefit Colombia and other Andean countries.

That bill (S 2823) is aimed at helping the economies of Colombia, Ecuador, Peru and Bolivia by giving them a one-year exemption from U.S. quotas and tariffs on apparel assembled or cut from yarn or fabric made in the United States.

In May, Congress passed and Clinton signed legislation (PL 106-200) giving similar trade preferences to 75 nations in sub-Saharan Africa, Central America and the Caribbean, putting the Andean nations at a disadvantage.

Some lawmakers also want to reopen the Colombian aid package to win support for particular aircraft produced in their states.

World Issues

Beyond the debate over Colombia, conferees on the foreign aid bill must find ways to bridge differences over issues such as abortion, debt relief and the cuts lawmakers have made in Clinton's request for aid to countries ranging from Russia to Mozambique.

At the same time, administration officials and lawmakers are discussing informal White House requests to consider additional aid for Israel and Lebanon and to combat HIV/AIDS.

The aid to Israel and Lebanon would serve to reward both countries for Israel's withdrawal of troops from south Lebanon earlier this year.

Lebanon is expected to receive $18 million in U.S. aid in fiscal 2001, but Michigan Reps. John D. Dingell, ranking Democrat on the House Commerce Committee, and Joe Knollenberg, a Republican member of the Foreign Operations Appropriations Subcommittee, have called for more — a six-year $300 million package for the Middle Eastern nation.

"A stable Lebanon is necessary in order to have a peaceful Middle East," they and other backers wrote in an Aug. 29 letter to Clinton.

They claimed the new aid could be fully financed by using a portion of the savings from a 1998 agreement between the United States, Israel and Egypt that reduces economic aid to those countries by more than $100 million annually until 2008.

Yet, aides said administration officials are now discussing additional military aid to Israel on top of the $2 billion in annual military help it already receives. The new aid would compensate Israel for having to establish new defenses along its northern border after its pullout from Lebanon.

It also comes as administration officials and Israel are talking about steps to maintain Israel's qualitative edge in weaponry over potential Middle East rivals. Steps might include greater intelligence sharing and looser controls of U.S. military exports.

U.S. officials first want to strike a deal with Israel on rules governing its export of defense technology. Israel's plans to sell a sophisticated airborne radar system to China roiled Congress and U.S.-Israel relations earlier this year.

Fighting AIDS

Some lawmakers, including Rep. Nancy Pelosi of California, ranking

Democrat on the Foreign Operations Appropriations Subcommittee, are seeking additional funds in the appropriations bill to combat the growing epidemic of HIV/AIDS overseas.

After a lengthy debate July 13, the House, 267-156, agreed to meet Clinton's initial budget request for $244 million for international HIV/AIDS programs. But that total is still well below the $300 million in annual bilateral aid for fiscal 2001 and 2002 authorized in legislation (PL 106-264) that Clinton signed into law Aug. 19.

That new law included a $60 million annual donation to two public/private partnerships supported by Microsoft founder Bill Gates to promote vaccines and immunization for developing countries.

In addition, the new law authorizes the Treasury Department to work with the World Bank on the creation of a trust fund to raise money to fight HIV/AIDS and help educate children orphaned by the disease. Once the trust fund is established, the measure authorizes the United States to contribute $150 million a year in fiscal 2001 and 2002.

During an August 19 address marking the signing of the legislation, Clinton called on Congress to approve a proposal he outlined in his State of the Union address to create a vaccine tax credit, which is designed to make some vaccines more accessible to developing nations.

Such legislation (S 2132) has been sponsored by Senate Foreign Relations Committee members John Kerry, D-Mass., and Bill Frist, R-Tenn., chairman of the panel's African Affairs subcommittee, but has not been considered by Congress.

Conferees Make Progress, Remain Divided Over Abortion Limits

OCTOBER 14 — House and Senate negotiators have agreed to increase foreign aid to $14.9 billion for fiscal 2001 — close to President Clinton's request — but stumbling blocks remain on contentious issues such as family planning assistance, according to lawmakers and congressional aides.

"We are very close," Mitch McConnell, R-Ky., chairman of the Senate Foreign Operations Appropriations Subcommittee, said in an Oct. 11 interview.

The final foreign operations appropriations bill (HR 4811) would provide significantly more money in fiscal 2001 spending than bills that the House ($13.2 billion) and the Senate ($13.7 billion) passed. Clinton asked for $15.2 billion.

Extra money is expected to flow to a variety of programs, including support for refugees and international efforts to combat HIV/AIDS.

The bill could include seed money for a World Bank trust fund to fight AIDS and help educate children orphaned by the disease. Such a fund was authorized in legislation (PL 106-264) Clinton signed earlier this year.

Negotiators have essentially agreed to meet Clinton's request for $435 million in a multilateral effort to help the World Bank and other international development banks relieve the debts of some of the world's poorest countries. Many religious groups and lawmakers from both parties, along with Vice President Al Gore and Texas Gov. George W. Bush, support the effort.

Appropriators had wanted to hold off on most of the aid until Treasury Secretary Lawrence H. Summers reached a deal with Senate Banking Committee Chairman Phil Gramm, R-Texas, and House Majority Leader Dick Armey, R-Texas, who want broad changes in the way the International Monetary Fund and similar institutions do business. They have called, for example, for the IMF to phase out long-term loans to concentrate on short-term lending.

Running out of patience, appropriators decided to accept the president's full request whether or not Gramm and Armey reach a deal with Summers.

The two Texas Republicans will still have considerable leverage on the debt relief question, since Clinton needs congressional approval to allow the IMF to revalue its gold reserves as a way to free up about $1 billion for debt relief.

The Most Difficult Issue

Once those issues are settled, negotiators must deal with a perennial headache — abortion-related restrictions on family planning.

House Republican leaders have been pressing the White House to continue a compromise they reached in high-pressure negotiations on the fiscal 2000 foreign aid bill (PL 106-113), when Clinton agreed to some restrictions for one year in order to persuade Republican congressional leaders to pay U.S. debts to the United Nations. *(1999 Almanac, p. 2-62)*

Clinton and Secretary of State Madeleine K. Albright have vowed not to continue the restrictions, and the issue has taken on particular significance as groups on both sides of the abortion debate mobilize for next month's elections.

Under last year's compromise, none of the $385 million in fiscal 2000 family planning funds could be used by organizations that perform abortions — except in cases of rape, incest, or where the life of the woman is in danger — or that lobby to change abortion policies in other countries.

Clinton could waive the restrictions, but with financial penalties.

Family planning groups said at an Oct. 12 news conference that the law has had a "chilling effect" and that proposed funding in the fiscal 2001 bill for population control was inadequate.

Balkan Response

Appropriators are receiving conflicting signals from colleagues on how to approach Yugoslavia's new government.

House and Senate versions of the foreign operations bill would ban aid to Serbia and effectively require the United States to oppose loans from international financial institutions as long as Yugoslavia harbors former President Slobodan Milosevic.

Clinton said he would like to join European leaders in lifting sanctions on Yugoslavia. On Oct. 12, he lifted an oil embargo and a flight ban and said he would review restrictions on Serbia's ability to get loans.

"We have a strong interest in supporting Yugoslavia's newly elected leaders as they work to build a truly democratic society," Clinton said.

Sen. George V. Voinovich, R-Ohio, who is partly of Serbian descent, said the United States has a "wonderful opportunity" now that Vojislav Kostunica has taken power.

Joseph R. Biden Jr. of Delaware, ranking Democrat on the Senate Foreign Relations Committee, said in an Oct. 12 interview that the foreign aid bill "should be silent" on Yugoslavia, leaving Clinton with more discretion.

But most lawmakers want to wait and see how Kostunica deals with Milosevic and his allies. They said they are willing to let the European Union take the lead.

"We can't make grand pronouncements about war crimes and taking people to justice at [the international war crimes tribunal in] the Hague, and then forget about it when it's convenient," said Gordon H. Smith, R-Ore., chairman of the European Affairs Subcommittee of the Senate Foreign Relations Committee.

John McCain, R-Ariz., a senior member of the Senate Armed Services Committee, said he favors gradually easing sanctions and providing aid, but only after further progress in Belgrade.

"This should be at the top of our agenda next year," McCain said.

Senate Clears Bill, Giving Clinton Requested Funds For Debt Relief

OCTOBER 28 — President Clinton is expected to sign a $14.9 billion foreign aid bill for fiscal 2001 after congressional negotiators agreed to lift restrictions on family planning assistance and provide the international debt relief Clinton asked for to help some of the world's poorest countries.

In an attempt to encourage Yugoslavia's new government, the bill (HR 4811) would provide as much as $100 million in aid to Serbia if officials there cooperate with an international war crimes tribunal and respect human rights.

The House adopted the conference report, 307-101, on Oct. 25, and the Senate cleared the bill, 65-27, a few hours later. *(House vote 546, p. H-174; Senate vote 280, p. S-51)*

The final foreign aid bill would provide $1.8 billion more than the House version and $1.4 billion more than the version the Senate passed. The spending still would be $235 million less than the administration sought, however.

"This is not a bill I would have written, but it is a bill I can support, because, while I would have liked more [money], the priorities are definitely in order," said Nancy Pelosi of California, ranking Democrat on the House Appropriations Foreign Operations Subcommittee.

At the insistence of Senate Republican appropriators, conferees agreed to include language raising the fiscal 2001 cap on overall discretionary spending established in the fiscal 1997 budget agreement (PL 105-33) from $541 billion to as much as $640 billion. *(1997 Almanac, p. 2-18)*

Family Planning

Each year since 1997, the major stumbling block to a deal on the foreign operations bill has been abortion-related restrictions on family planning aid. This year, conferees essentially gave abortion-rights advocates what they sought — but only for as long as Clinton remains in office.

House GOP leaders wanted to extend abortion-related restrictions in the fiscal 2000 foreign aid bill (PL 106-113). Clinton had agreed to the restrictions in order to persuade Republicans to pay U.S. debts to the United Nations. *(1999 Almanac, p. 2-62)*

The fiscal 2000 law provided $385 million for international family planning, but not for organizations that perform abortions — except in cases of rape, incest or where the life of the woman is in danger — or that lobby to change abortion policies in other countries. Clinton could, and did, waive the prohibition, but the funds were then reduced by $1.25 million.

The White House said it would not agree to extend the restrictions and said Clinton would veto any bill that sought to do so. House Republicans eventually agreed to drop the language and increase family planning funds in fiscal 2001 to $425 million.

The decision to end the restrictions "is a tremendous victory for the health of families around the world," said Kate Michelman, president of the National Abortion and Reproductive Rights Action League.

However, conferees blocked the administration from spending the money until Feb. 15, one month after Clinton leaves office. Pelosi said the prohibition is not objectionable because "there's money in the pipeline" for the groups to use until then.

Christopher H. Smith, R-N.J., a leader among anti-abortion House Republicans, expressed hope that Texas Gov. George W. Bush will be elected president and will decide not to spend any of the money.

"We're going to try to make the best of it," Smith said. "This is a Pyrrhic victory for Clinton. The real outcome will be decided on Nov. 7."

Debt Relief

Conferees agreed to fund Clinton's $435 million request for Third World debt relief and included language allowing the International Monetary Fund (IMF) to use up to $800 million from a revaluation of its gold reserves for additional debt forgiveness.

Debt-relief supporters attributed the increased funding to a persistent campaign that included Irish singer Bono of the rock group U2 and Pope John Paul II. Some religious groups consider debt forgiveness a part of the Year of Jubilee called for in the Bible every 50 years.

House Budget Committee Chairman John R. Kasich, R-Ohio, who helped Bono navigate Capitol Hill during his trips to visit lawmakers, described the provision as "a breakthrough, a historic precedent, an effort to really bring about great change in the world."

Several other Republicans, however, expressed doubt that the debt relief plan would work because it does not call for changes in the way governments in such countries are run. "We know they are going to come back, because we are not requiring economic reform in these countries," said Rep. Joe Scarborough, R-Fla. "It is a lesson we should have learned over and over again."

Senate Banking Committee Chairman Phil Gramm, R-Texas, said the measure did not go far enough in making the IMF and other international organizations overhaul their policies to prevent poor nations from sinking further into debt. "It looks as if the presi-

Foreign Aid Spending Highlights

Where the Money Goes

HR 4811 — Conference report: H Rept 106-997

Spending Synopsis

After months of delay over debt relief, family planning and aid to Russia, congressional negotiators got down to business in October — three months after the original versions of the bill were passed — and gave President Clinton most of what he asked for. The $14.9 billion measure is $1.7 billion less than Congress enacted for fiscal 2000 — the earlier measure included a last-minute $1.8 billion to help implement the Wye River peace accords — and $235 million less than Clinton requested for fiscal 2001. The House version of the foreign aid bill would have provided $2 billion less than Clinton asked. For accounting reasons, the conferees designated $468 million of the budget as contingent emergency spending — money available if the administration needs it but exempt from even the new budget caps. Most of that would be for debt relief, disaster aid and the Middle East.

- **Export and investment assistance**

Conferees basically split the difference with Clinton on funding for the Export-Import Bank, which helps finance U.S. exports with loans, guarantees and insurance, adding more than $100 million to the earlier versions of the bill. Overall spending would be $142 million less than in fiscal 2000 and $104 million less than Clinton requested.

- **Bilateral assistance**

Conferees increased aid to Russia and other states of the former Soviet Union to $810 million, still $20 million less than Clinton requested and $29 million less than for fiscal 2000, but $70 million more than where things started in the House version. Refugee assistance was raised to $700 million, $42 million more than Clinton requested.

- **Multilateral assistance**

Clinton scored significant gains in funding for the World Bank and other international financial institutions, notably unpopular in Congress and particularly in the House. The final bill includes $893 million for the World Bank — $134 million less than Clinton requested but $78 million more than in fiscal 2000 — and more than doubles what the House and Senate voted to spend on the Global Environment facility, which provides grants to developing countries for environmental initiatives.

Hot-Button Issues

△ **Abortion.** The final bill would provide $425 million for international family planning programs — in fiscal 2000 it was $385 million — and would remove any abortion-related restrictions on the money, as Clinton has wanted. Conferees specified, however, that the funds cannot be spent until Feb. 15, 2001, a month after Clinton leaves office. Republicans are gambling that Texas Gov. George W. Bush will be elected president in the meantime and will slap new restrictions on the use of the money.

△ **Debt relief.** Clinton got what he wanted in debt relief for the world's poorest countries. Conferees agreed to provide $225 million that he had requested for fiscal 2001, plus another $210 million in contingent emergency appropriations, the amount Clinton had requested for fiscal 2000 supplemental spending. The bill also would allow the International Monetary Fund to revalue its gold reserve, a way of providing another roughly $1 billion for debt relief.

(figures are in thousands of dollars of new budget authority)

	Fiscal 2000 Appropriation	Fiscal 2001 Clinton Request	House Bill	Senate Bill	Conference Bill
Export and investment assistance	$599,000	$845,000	$606,500	$636,000	$741,000
Bilateral economic assistance	9,564,417	8,896,441	8,150,484	7,841,739	8,672,589
Military assistance	4,992,000	3,727,200	3,433,150	3,659,000	3,727,000
Multilateral assistance	1,298,018	1,707,916	996,179	1,315,879	1,332,879
Contingent emergency appropriations					467,700
GRAND TOTAL	**$16,453,435**	**$15,829,432***	**$13,346,313***	**$14,807,818***	**$14,941,168**
Total adjusted for scorekeeping	**($16,694,435)**	**($15,176,557)**	**($13,186,313)**	**($13,492,618)**	**($14,941,168)**

*Includes fiscal 2000 emergency supplemental money. Clinton requested extra funds for disaster assistance, debt relief and the Balkans; the House included extra funds only for disaster aid; the Senate primarily for drug fighting and Colombia. Fiscal 2000 disaster assistance and anti-drug spending was consolidated in the fiscal 2001 military construction appropriations bill (HR 4425 — PL 106-246).

TABLE: House and Senate Appropriations committees

Aid for Russia

OCTOBER 28 — The final foreign operations spending bill includes more aid to former Soviet states — $810 million — than the House and Senate versions. But it imposes some detailed conditions and instructions for how the money is to be spent. For instance:

• **Russia.** The largest of the states would receive about $202 million, excluding nuclear safety programs. Russia could lose 60 percent of the aid if it sends weapons technology to Iran or blocks a war crimes investigation in Chechnya, and could lose all of the aid if it discriminates against religious groups. The Russian Far East would be guaranteed $20 million, with an extra $3 million to expand a program run there by the University of Alaska.

• **Georgia.** The Caucasus republic would receive $92 million. If the Agency for International Development sets up an absorptive capacity fund in Georgia, it is urged to consider Fort Valley State University, in the state of Georgia, and the University of Louisville to participate.

• **Ukraine.** Russia's neighbor in Europe would receive $170 million. Another $3 million is for programs run by the Center for Economic Initiatives in Cincinnati and the National Telephone Cooperative Association.

dent is more concerned with the appearance of helping poor people than actually helping those poor people," Gramm told reporters.

Gramm wanted the IMF banned from extending debt relief or any new loans to countries that violate human rights or that close their markets to foreign goods. The conferees rejected his request.

House and Senate negotiators did agree to a 24-month moratorium on some loans made by international banks from a fund for heavily indebted poor countries that the United States contributes to. The House version had called for a 30-month moratorium.

Republican Sonny Callahan of Alabama, chairman of the House Foreign Operations Appropriations Subcommittee, said he remains "skeptical but hopeful" that the debt-relief program will succeed.

Yugoslavia

Conferees agreed to give Serbia $100 million in aid, but only if the president certifies that the new Yugoslav government is cooperating in bringing accused war criminals such as former President Slobodan Milosevic before the International Criminal Tribunal at the Hague.

The final version of the bill also would require the new government to implement policies respecting human and minority rights and the rule of law. Conferees did agree to suspend those provisions until March "in order to give the new democratic government in Serbia time to consolidate its gains," Callahan said.

The House and Senate versions of the foreign operations bill, written before Milosevic was overthrown, called for banning aid to Serbia and effectively requiring the United States to oppose loans from international financial institutions as long as Yugoslavia harbored Milosevic. Clinton, however, has said he would like to join European leaders in lifting sanctions on Yugoslavia.

Conferees agreed to provide $4 million to the Arabian Peninsula country of Yemen to spend on counterterrorism training and investigations. The bill would require that the money be withheld until the FBI reports to Congress that Yemen's government is fully cooperating with the investigation of the Oct. 12 bombing of the destroyer USS *Cole*.

Fighting AIDS

The conference agreement contained sizable increases for children's health programs, including $963 million for child survival and disease programs. It also included $315 million to combat HIV and AIDS infection and $60 million to combat tuberculosis.

The agreement included $5.2 million for AmeriCares, a Connecticut-based relief group that operates as a private contractor for the U.S. Agency for International Development (AID). Former first lady Barbara Bush serves as the group's "ambassador-at-large." The money would be used for building and operating health care facilities in several Central American countries.

Patrick J. Leahy of Vermont, ranking Democrat on the Senate Foreign Operations Appropriations Subcommittee, complained that allocating money for a specific group — instead of giving AID discretion in spending it — was unprecedented and unwise. He predicted that scores of other private groups would begin lobbying aggressively for special attention.

Callahan, who is leaving the Foreign Operations subcommittee chairmanship after this year, said he included the funding because he said AID had not kept a promise to fund such programs. "This is sort of a going-away present from me," he said.

Senate Appropriations Committee Chairman Ted Stevens, R-Alaska, said he was unconcerned that including funding for the group would lead other groups to inundate appropriators with requests.

"We don't do it that often in that bill," Stevens said. ◆

Congress Clears Interior Bill With Big, Bipartisan Increase For Public Lands

SUMMARY

After lengthy negotiations over the level of spending on public lands programs, Congress cleared the $18.8 billion Interior Department fiscal 2001 spending bill Oct. 5, and President Clinton signed it Oct. 11. The administration scored clear victories, removing or watering down several GOP policy riders and securing funding increases for its highest environmental priorities.

Weeks of politicized negotiations between appropriators and the White House led to the creation of a protected six-year, $12 billion discretionary fund devoted to land conservation, preservation and maintenance. That opened the door to bipartisan agreement on a bill that provided twice as much for environmental programs in fiscal 2001 as was appropriated in fiscal 2000. The overall bill appropriates $3.8 billion more than the House-passed version, and $3 billion more than the Senate measure. It will provide $3.9 billion more than was enacted for fiscal 2000, and $2.4 billion more than Clinton had requested.

Much of the heavy lifting on the measure occurred during a lengthy conference that saw the addition of some $3 billion, including $1.2 billion for land conservation and $1.6 billion in emergency spending for firefighting and prevention in the wake of a devastating wildfire season. *(See CARA, p. 10-6)*

Although it is typically a magnet for partisan environmental policy disagreements, the Interior bill emerged from the House and Senate floors relatively free of riders. Democrats in both chambers defeated GOP attempts to attach language limiting Clinton's ability to declare national monuments. Republicans also backed down from riders that would have blocked administration regulations curbing recreation and road-building on public lands.

The White House fought off a renewed wave of policy riders during conference, including language by Senate Interior Appropriations Subcommittee Chairman Slade Gorton, R-Wash., that would have barred the administration from studying whether to breach dams on the lower Snake River.

Democrats also negotiated intensely with Republicans to craft language ensuring that a new fire prevention program for clearing flammable forest undergrowth does not lead to a resurgence of logging in national forests.

Ironically, the bill faced its most serious obstacle in the Senate not over policy disputes, but over a parochial objection from Peter G. Fitzgerald, R-Ill., who insisted that the construction of a Springfield, Ill., library be subject to federal procurement law. Backers of the Conservation and Reinvestment Act (HR 701) — legislation that would have created a mandatory 15-year, $45 billion fund for land conservation from federal gas and oil royalties — also threatened to hold up the bill, arguing that the discretionary lands fund devised by appropriators was an inadequate substitute. They dropped their threat to filibuster, and Fitzgerald released his grip on the bill after some 10 hours of stalling.

The final bill included a host of increases sought by the administration, including the first major boost since 1992 for the National Endowment for the Arts, which received $98 million, and an additional $7 million earmarked for arts education and outreach. It also responded to administration calls for more funding for American Indian programs, providing $2.1 billion for Interior's Bureau of Indian Affairs and $2.6 billion for the Department of Health and Human Service's Indian Health Service.

Box Score — **Interior** — **2001** Fiscal Year

- **Bill:** HR 4578 — PL 106-291
- **Legislative action: House** passed HR 4578 (H Rept 106-646), 204-172, on June 16.

Senate passed HR 4578, amended (S Rept 106-312), 97-2, on July 18.

House adopted the conference report (H Rept 106-914), 348-69, on Oct. 3.

Senate cleared the bill, 83-13, on Oct. 5.

President signed HR 4578 on Oct. 11.

House Panel OKs Bill With String Of Riders, Cuts in Clinton Requests

MAY 20 — With a veto threat already looming, the House Appropriations Interior Subcommittee approved a $14.6 billion fiscal 2001 spending bill for the Interior Department on May 17 by voice vote.

The unnumbered draft would cut Interior Department spending by $302 million below fiscal 2000 and fall $1.7 billion short of President Clinton's request. It would also chop the administration's $600 million request for the Land and Water Conservation Fund, including its prized Lands Legacy program — designed to buy environmentally sensitive land threatened by development — by more than 70 percent, to $164 million.

"I guarantee the president would not sign this bill into law unless the level [for Lands Legacy] were significantly raised," said ranking subcommittee Democrat Norm Dicks of Washington.

GOP 'Riders' Criticized

Dicks and other Democrats on the panel also criticized GOP-backed policy "riders" that would bar funding for other major Clinton administration land and resource conservation initiatives. "We all know that these riders have gotten this bill into trouble in recent years," Dicks said. "I hope, as the process goes forward, things will get better."

That is not likely. The Interior spending bill has traditionally been a magnet for policy prescriptions in both chambers on such controversial environmental issues as timber rights, mining and grazing on public lands — not to mention arts funding.

Th fiscal 2001 measure is expected to attract more riders as it moves through the legislative process. Democrats declined to offer amendments during the subcommittee markup and said they would wait until the full committee session.

Tight discretionary spending allocations forced the Interior panel to hold most accounts to fiscal 2000 levels, with notable cuts for the U.S. Forest Service, which would get $97 million less than this year's amount; new construction, which would be reduced by $80 million; and land acquisition, which would be cut by $101 million.

Interior Subcommittee Chairman Ralph Regula, R-Ohio, said major land acquisition and new construction would have to take a back seat to maintenance of existing operations and "keeping the doors open" at the Interior Department.

"We're not going to do any nice-to-do's because we don't have the money," he said. "We're going to do the must-do's and a few of the need-to-do's."

The bill would give special attention to the National Park Service, which would see its funding increased by $62 million to $1.4 billion. "That was our highest priority," Regula said.

Other substantial increases would go to the accounts of the Bureau of Land Management (BLM), which would be raised by $30 million to $1.3 billion; and national wildlife refuges, which would grow by $22 million to $345 million.

Some $350 million would be appropriated to the BLM and the Forest Service on an emergency basis — available upon the bill's enactment and without counting against the agencies' fiscal 2001 appropriations. The money would help cover the cost of battling a forest fire that began May 4 and threatened the government's Los Alamos, N.M., nuclear weapons facility.

The bill would fund federally backed cultural programs, a favorite target of Republicans in recent years, at fiscal 2000 levels: $115.2 million for the National Endowment for the Humanities and $98 million for the National Endowment for the Arts.

Limiting Monuments

The measure also contains a funding limitation, sponsored by James V. Hansen, R-Utah, that would stop federal agencies from developing management plans for land designated by Clinton as national monuments after 1999.

Clinton's monuments program — which began in September 1996 when he designated some 1.7 million acres of southern Utah as the Grand Staircase-Escalante National Monument — has angered Republicans, especially lawmakers from Western states, who say it shuts local authorities out of the process. *(1997 CQ Almanac, p. 4-16)*

Another provision, sponsored by George Nethercutt, R-Wash., would prevent federal agencies from undertaking a massive plan for managing watersheds and forests in the Columbia River basin in eastern Oregon, eastern Washington, and parts of Idaho and Montana until they assess its impact on neighboring communities. The government began studying the project in 1993 and had planned to begin implementing it this fall.

House Committee Approves Bill; Veto Threat Looms

MAY 27 — Setting the stage for a partisan showdown on the floor, the House Appropriations Committee approved, 31-22, a $14.6 billion fiscal 2001 Interior spending bill that would bar funding for key Clinton administration environmental priorities.

Before the May 25 vote, White House officials warned appropriators that several GOP-backed policy riders and the draft bill's low funding level — which would fall about $300 million below fiscal 2000 and $1.7 billion short of the president's request — would prompt a veto.

"The subcommittee's failure to fund key programs sufficiently and its inclusion of damaging riders lead the president's senior advisors to recommend a veto if the bill were presented to [him] in its current form," Office of Management and Budget Director Jack Lew wrote in a letter to appropriators.

Uneasy Riders

Still, Democrats did not attempt to strip the policy riders from the bill during the markup, holding their fire until the measure reaches the House floor. Between now and then, they must calculate whether they can appeal to enough moderate Republicans to strip the funding restrictions — or to defeat the bill.

"If we think we have enough Republican votes to defeat the bill, we'll leave [the riders] in," said a key Democrat who asked not to be named. "If not, we'll try to get them out."

Interior Appropriations Subcommittee Chairman Ralph Regula, R-Ohio, said the full House should have the opportunity to debate the funding limitations since "they go to the basic constitutional question of what is the role of Congress in setting these policies, as opposed to the executive branch."

That question lies at the heart of three GOP efforts in the Interior measure that seek to block or delay Clinton administration policy by restricting how appropriated funds can be spent.

One provision that is particularly offensive to Democrats would stop federal agencies from developing management plans for lands designated by the president as national monuments after 1999.

Ranking Appropriations Committee Democrat David R. Obey of Wisconsin called the proposed limitation "a congressional abuse of power" aimed squarely at President Clinton. "This attack on this president's prerogative goes beyond substance," Obey said.

Floor battles may also lie ahead for two riders included in the fiscal 2000 Interior bill that have resurfaced in the committee's fiscal 2001 version. One would prohibit federal agencies from implementing the Kyoto Protocol to regulate greenhouse gas emissions, which has yet to be ratified by Congress. The other would automatically extend livestock grazing permits scheduled to expire during fiscal 2001, regardless of whether federal environmental reviews of each lease had been conducted.

Despite their reluctance to address GOP riders during the markup, Democrats attempted to boost funding for two small but controversial agencies — the National Endowment for the Humanities (NEH) and the National Endowment for the Arts (NEA). The agencies have long drawn fire from conservatives for supporting what they say are elitist — and often offensive — cultural projects and programs.

The fiscal 2001 appropriations bill currently sets NEH spending at $115.3 million and NEA funding at $98 million. The Clinton administration requested $150 million for each agency for fiscal 2001.

Norm Dicks of Washington, ranking Democrat on the Interior Appropriations panel, offered an amendment that would have set funding for the NEH and NEA at $125 million for each agency. The proposal was rejected, 25-33, along party lines.

The panel also rejected, 27-31, a Dicks amendment that would have given each agency $115.3 million.

'Big Fight' Promised

Democrats argued the programs have changed and deserve more funding. "We're going to go into a big fight on the floor and make it a very controversial issue," said James P. Moran, D-Va., a cosponsor of the amendment.

Dicks and other Democrats also criticized what they said are the measure's larger funding inadequacies — such as money included for Clinton's prized Lands Legacy Initiative to protect environmentally sensitive lands from development. Dicks said the bill has enough problems to be "in serious trouble."

Regula said he hopes for a greater infusion of funds down the line and defended the panel's work thus far. He said that tight discretionary spending allocations were holding most programs to fiscal 2000 levels, forcing the panel to steer money toward maintaining existing resources rather than buying or building new ones.

Increases would go to National Park Service operations, which would be raised $62 million to $1.4 billion, and to the Bureau of Land Management (BLM), which would see a $30 million increase to $1.3 billion.

"We start out on the premise that we'll take care of what we have, and then as the opportunity comes along, we'll add to it," Regula said.

That opportunity was evidently not there for the Lands Legacy program. The administration requested $600 million for land acquisition from the Land and Water Conservation Fund, but the bill would provide only $164 million.

"It would be shortsighted not to provide adequate support for the important Lands Legacy Initiative, given the bipartisan recognition of the need . . . to protect open spaces and preserve America's great places," Lew wrote in his letter.

'Work With What We Have'

Regula said administration officials "aren't telling us anything that we didn't know, except that we have to work with what we have."

The bill also would cut U.S. Forest Service funds $96.6 million below fiscal 2000 levels, to $2.7 billion, and construction money for land management agencies would be trimmed by about $80 million, to $203 million.

Included in the measure is $350 million in emergency wildland firefighting funds for the BLM and the U.S. Forest Service in the wake of recent fires in New Mexico that threatened the nuclear weapons facility at Los Alamos.

The panel also gave voice vote approval to several minor amendments, including a measure by Joe Skeen, R-N.M., that would require the Agriculture and Interior departments to provide states and localities with maps of hazardous fuels and areas vulnerable to wildfires.

Report language sponsored by Obey and approved by voice vote would express concern that some Indian tribes are violating the spirit of their trust relationships by putting gaming facilities on property far removed from their reservations and direct the Interior secretary to review the situation.

Obey had sought to attach an amendment that would have required nearby municipalities to approve new casinos, but withdrew it in favor of language requesting a study.

House Passes Interior Bill After Deleting Limits On Monuments

JUNE 17 — After debate that spanned two days and was filled with near misses and fleeting victories for both parties, the House on June 16 passed the $14.6 billion fiscal 2001 Interior appropriations bill (HR 4578) by a vote of 204-172. *(Vote 274, p. H-88)*

Republicans — who had more members available to vote in the early morning hours of June 16 — beat back Democratic attempts to secure a funding increase for the arts and to remove a restriction that would stop completion of a resource management program in the Pacific Northwest.

Democrats were able to strip a key environmental policy provision dealing with monument lands that had drawn a veto threat from the Clinton administration, but were clearly upset by the Republicans' parliamentary maneuvering.

"It was doing by deception what you can't do by votes," a Democratic staff aide said June 16. "They undid everything we did."

The measure's funding level, which is $302 million below the fiscal 2000 Interior spending bill and $1.7 billion less than the president's request, is almost certain to increase when the Senate Interior Appropriations Subcommittee takes up its version of the bill the week of June 19.

"The Senate usually prevails on money issues, so I would expect that we'll see an increase when we get to conference," House Interior Appropriations Subcommittee Chairman Ralph Regula, R-Ohio, said in a June 15 interview. The Senate allocation for the Interior bill, which surpasses the House level by some $800 million, falls roughly $1 billion below what President Clinton has requested.

Lawmakers said it is unlikely either chamber will restore funding for Clinton's prized Lands Legacy program — which is designed to purchase and protect environmentally sensitive land — until the president gets involved personally in endgame spending negotiations. The House Interior spending measure would provide $184 million for land acquisition, compared to the $600 million the president has requested for Lands Legacy.

Critics of the funding level for land acquisition said it was out of step with House passage May 11 of the Conservation and Reinvestment Act, or CARA (HR 701). That broad bipartisan measure would set aside $2.8 billion annually from offshore oil-drilling revenues — including $900 million in land acquisition funds — for land purchases and other conservation measures.

Republicans "very much know that CARA has passed, they very much know that it has the support of a vast majority of the House," George Miller, D-Calif., the ranking member of the House Resources Committee, said June 15. "Their approach is to make the president ask for it at the end of the session, and he will do that."

Scaling Monuments

While a wide gulf remains between House Republicans and the White House on lands funding, Democrats succeeded in eliminating a provision that would have stopped federal agencies from developing management plans for lands designated by Clinton after 1999 as national monuments.

The House adopted, 243-177, an amendment by Norm Dicks of Washington, ranking Democrat on the Interior Appropriations Subcommittee, to remove the restriction. *(Vote 281, p. H-90)*

The vote followed a long and heated debate over the federal government's role in land use decisions. Western Republicans have reacted angrily to Clinton's monument designations, the latest of which were announced the week of June 12, saying they usurp local control.

"What is happening now in the West and all over America is for political purposes," said James V. Hansen, R-Utah, chairman of the House Resources National Parks and Public Lands Subcommittee and sponsor of the funding limitation. "I do not know of one president who has abused his power more than [Clinton] has."

Democrats argued that the GOP "rider" would interfere with a presidential prerogative and force federal land agencies to abandon management of existing national monuments.

"This is categorically wrong-headed," said Earl Blumenauer, D-Ore. "It is an example of an environmental extremism that we hear so often about on the [Republican] side of the aisle."

An amendment by Hansen to reinstate the monuments funding limitation was rejected 187-234. *(Vote 280, p. H-90)*

Columbia River Basin

Democrats also came close to ridding the bill of a restriction that would delay completion of a large management plan for resources in the Columbia River Basin until the agencies involved assess its effect on local communities.

Many Republicans from Western states argued that the Interior Columbia Basin Ecosystem Management Project — which would manage forests, watersheds, and fish and wildlife habitats in eastern Oregon, eastern Washington and, parts of Idaho and Montana — is a prime example of the administration overreaching on a project that has already gone on for seven years and cost some $56 million.

Republicans accused the Clinton administration of ignoring the wishes of local officials and communities in developing the plan. They invoked the 1996 Small Business Regulatory Enforcement Fairness Act (PL 104-121) — which requires agencies to assess the economic impact of their regulations on small businesses — to delay the project.

"It's no wonder the people in this region feel like there's a war being declared on them," said Republican Rick Hill, of Montana.

The funding limitation was removed as part of the Dicks amendment, and the House later rejected, 206-221, an amendment by George Nethercutt, R-Wash., that would have reinstated it. *(Vote 279, p. H-88)*

Then late at night on June 15, after many House members — more Democrats than Republicans — had left for the evening, Nethercutt offered a second amendment to the funding limitation. The amendment was adopted, 197-180. *(Vote 288, p. H-92)*

Arts Increase Defeated

In a particularly bitter defeat for Democrats, the House rejected, 184-188, a motion to recommit that would have increased funding for the National Endowment for the Arts (NEA) by $15 million, given the National Endowment for the Humanities (NEH) a $5 million boost, and added $2 million for the Institute for Museum and Library Services. *(Vote 290, p. H-92)*

The motion to recommit was a desperation move by Democrats, who tried to increase the programs' funding by steering the money from another account but were outmaneuvered by Republicans.

Arts supporters argued that the NEA, which has implemented congressionally mandated policy changes and has a new, popular leader in Chairman William J. Ivey, deserves a break this year.

"It's unbecoming for this Congress every year to debate this subject the way we do," said Louise M. Slaughter, D-N.Y., who sponsored an amendment — adopted in a nail-biting 207-204 vote with the support of 25 Republicans — to defer an additional $22 million in funding for the Energy Department's Clean Coal Technology program to set it aside for the arts and humanities increase. *(Vote 283, p. H-90)*

Before Slaughter had a chance to propose the increase, Nethercutt offered an amendment to take the $22 million for another underfunded — and more popular — program: the Indian Health Service. Democrats cried foul, accusing Republicans of manipulating the process in order to pose an impossible choice between Native American health and support for the arts.

"I don't think this amendment was meant to help the Indians," Slaughter said. "I think this amendment was meant to use them."

Republicans argued that their move to divert money to the Indian Health Service was simply a question of priorities. "There are differences on both sides as to where the priorities should be in terms of the funding," said Jim Kolbe, R-Ariz. "It is a matter of simply establishing priorities."

In the end, Democrats allowed the Indian Health Service amendment, which would raise the account's total to $2.1 billion, to be adopted by voice vote, but they did so ruefully.

"After you have done this tonight, do not go home and brag to your folks about how much you care about the arts," said David R. Obey of Wisconsin, ranking Democrat on the Appropriations Committee, "because it is clearly transparent that you would do anything possible to deny us the ability to raise the amount of funds for that purpose."

All the sound and fury over arts funding may end up signifying nothing: The Senate is expected to provide at least a modest boost for the cultural institutions, making an increase likely during conference.

Doing Deals

In the course of debate June 14 and 15, Republicans and Democrats did manage to reach compromises on other legislative provisions that had drawn White House opposition.

Under an agreement between Regula and Jay Inslee, D-Wash., a provision that would have required land management agencies to renew grazing permits pending environmental reviews was altered to give the Interior secretary the discretion — but not a mandate — to renew the leases.

Another agreement among Doug Ose, R-Calif., Regula and Dicks led to the removal of a funding limitation that would have prohibited the Fish and Wildlife Service from establishing a refuge in California's Yolo Bypass. The provision was eliminated in favor of negotiations between Fish and Wildlife officials and Ose to address the issue of flood control in the Sacramento area.

After Hansen successfully challenged a provision in the spending bill that would have allowed the secretary of the Interior to have a voice in determining water distribution as part of an Everglades restoration project, the House adopted, by voice vote, an amendment by Democrat Maurice D. Hinchey of New York that would add $9 million to the National Park Service construction budget to ensure that the funds go to the Everglades project.

Small Boosts

The House rejected several Democratic attempts to move funding from programs they oppose to ones they believe are neglected, but approved by voice vote an amendment by Bernard Sanders, I-Vt., that would shift $45 million from fossil fuel research and development to energy efficiency programs.

Regula, who has emphasized operations and maintenance funding in the bill, steered additional increases to the National Park Service during floor consideration of the measure. Under two amendments adopted by voice vote, $66 million was added to address a backlog of Park Service projects, and $20 million was added to the agency's land acquisition account.

The House also adopted, 214-211, an amendment offered by John E. Sununu, R-N.H., that would move $126.5 million in funding for diesel fuel research to debt repayment, steer $20 million to the Forest Service and Park Service for maintenance, and give $10 million each to the states' Land and Water Conservation Fund and to the Payment in Lieu of Taxes account. *(Vote 274, p. H-88)*

Senate Committee Easily Approves Interior Spending Measure

JUNE 24 — Bracing for a contentious floor debate over President Clinton's environmental policies, the Senate Appropriations Committee gave unanimous approval June 22 to a $15.5 billion fiscal 2001 Interior spending measure (HR 4578).

The vote represented a rare moment of bipartisan support for a bill that already contains provisions that would block Clinton administration environmental initiatives and is expected to gain more controversial policy prescriptions offered by Western senators when it comes before the full Senate.

The legislation would provide some $751 million more than the House bill for the Interior Department and related agencies and considerably narrow the funding gap between Congress and the administration. Still, it falls $955 million below the president's request and is likely to draw a veto threat. The Senate bill would provide $628 million more than Congress appropriated in fiscal 2000, while the House-passed measure would spend $302 million less.

Senate Interior Appropriations Subcommittee Chairman Slade Gorton, R-Wash., has said he wants to avoid the kind of legislative riders that have plagued the Interior spending bill in past years, but he supported two such provisions when his panel approved the measure, by voice vote, June 20.

"I'm not going to back away from reasonable amendments," Gorton told the full committee June 22. "But I'm not going to let the bill get hung up on any one of them when it can be relatively easily left to the next administration."

The Road to Riders

While amendments adopted during subcommittee markup of the measure would punch small holes in Clinton administration policies, Larry E. Craig, R-Idaho, announced plans June 22 to launch an all-out assault on the initiatives on the Senate floor.

Craig said he will take aim at an administration proposal that would ban new road-building on more than 43 million acres of roadless national forest land. He plans to offer an amendment that would wall off funds for implementing the ban until an advisory committee completes a review of the plan and drafts an environmental impact statement.

"This is the kind of work that has not been done by this administration," Craig said, calling the proposed road-building ban an example of "slipshod rule-making procedures."

"It is time for this Congress to step in and speak out about its rightful place in appropriate public policy," he said.

Also in Craig's sights is a recent National Park Service decision to ban the use of snowmobiles in parks.

"If you want to see an issue that angers Western members, it is the fear that this administration will progressively disallow human activities on public lands," he said June 22.

The issue inspires bitter feelings among Westerners, who say the government is steadily depriving individuals of the right to use public lands — first by limiting or banning such extraction activities as gas and oil drilling, mining and logging, and most recently by trying to curb recreation.

The land-use restrictions face a lively lobbying campaign by groups such as Americans for Responsible Recreational Access, a coalition of recreational organizations that was launched June 21 at a Capitol Hill news conference attended by Craig and other lawmakers.

Narrow Exemptions

As approved by the Appropriations panel, the Interior bill is free of the kind of broad riders Craig envisions. Still, during the swift subcommittee markup of the measure, the panel adopted, by voice vote, two amendments that could stand as indicators of the disputes to come.

Judd Gregg, R-N.H., offered an amendment that would effectively exempt the White Mountain National Forest in his state from the road-building ban.

The White Mountain forest is currently undergoing a land-use review that includes input from commercial and recreational users and environmental groups. Gregg said his provision would ensure that the road-building ban "will take second seat to the fact that this process is going forward."

Gregg said he was following "the directive of the vice president of the United States and this administration" in requesting the exemption. Gregg noted that Al Gore, the presumptive Democratic presidential nominee, praised the planning process under way in the White Mountain Forest during a Jan. 5 debate with rival Bill Bradley, saying it would continue if the road-building ban were implemented.

Also adopted during the subcommittee markup was an amendment by Ben Nighthorse Campbell, R-Colo., that would require the U.S. Forest Service to report on the economic impact of a proposed plan restricting recreational activities in Colorado's White River National Forest.

"We ought to know what the impact is going to be on people who make a living around that area," said Campbell, who estimated that the plan could result in a $1.6-billion decrease in revenue for nearby businesses.

Bolstered Funding

While environmental policy disputes are sure to complicate debate on the Interior measure, the Senate version of the bill comes much closer than the House-passed bill to fulfilling stated administration priorities.

The bill approved by the Appropriations Committee made no changes to the subcommittee measure. It would increase funding slightly for the nation's cultural agencies, providing $105 million for the National Endowment for the Arts (NEA) — a boost of $7 million over the House bill — and $120 million for the National Endowment for the Humanities, an increase of $5 million. The funding increase for the once controversial NEA is due in large part to the politicking of its chairman, William J. Ivey, who has steered his agency to a safer middle ground.

The measure also would come close to funding the administration's request for Indian schools. It would provide a total increase of $144 million for construction and repair, bringing funding for completing six schools to $121 million and money for repairs to $152 million.

The measure would appropriate $221 million from the Land and Water Conservation Fund for land acquisition, $37 million more than the House measure but $380 million less than Clinton requested.

Like the House legislation, the Senate bill places an emphasis on existing programs in the land management agencies, increasing their operations funding by a total of $259 million.

That includes total increases over fiscal 2000 of $40.5 million for the U.S. Fish and Wildlife Service, bringing it to $916 million; $64.8 million for the Bureau of Land Management, which would receive $1.3 billion; and $165 million for the Forest Service, bringing it to just under $3 billion.

Senators Move Swiftly Through Long List Of Amendments

JULY 15 — In an unexpectedly short and restrained debate on the fiscal 2001 Interior appropriations bill the week of July 10, the Senate pared a list of more than 100 proposed amendments down to less than 20 and steered clear of two major GOP policy riders that would have guaranteed a veto.

The debate may run truer to form the week of July 17, when the Senate hopes to complete the usually controversial measure, because of a Republican amendment that would prevent President Clinton from designating more national monuments in the waning months of his administration.

The $15.5 billion Interior spending bill is $603 million above the fiscal 2000 level. It is $905 million more than the measure (HR 4578 — H Rept 106-646) passed 204-172 by the House on June 16, but $806 million less than Clinton requested.

As debate began, White House officials warned July 10 that the measure's funding level "fails to address the critical needs of the American people." Most lawmakers expect the bill will be vetoed and then renegotiated with Clinton. Two potential roadblocks were removed July 12 when Western senators backed down on anticipated amendments labeled by the administration as "highly objectionable riders."

Larry E. Craig, R-Idaho, who offered an amendment that would have delayed a controversial Forest Service proposal to ban road-building on up to 60 million acres of roadless federal forest land, allowed it to be replaced with a bipartisan forest management proposal. Craig and Craig Thomas, R-Wyo., also decided not to offer an amendment to block a new National Park Service policy that would ban the use of snowmobiles in most of the nation's parks.

Still, the amendment to block Clinton's monuments program, sponsored by Assistant Majority Leader Don Nickles, R-Okla., is sure to cause heated partisan debate when the Senate resumes consideration of the spending measure. Clinton's monument program — which began in September 1996, when he designated some 1.7 million acres of southern Utah as the Grand Staircase-Escalante National Monument — angers Western Republicans, who say it usurps local control of lands.

Craig's decision to drop his amendment on the so-called roadless initiative was hardly designed to accommodate the administration. He made it after consulting with plaintiffs — including Idaho paper products giant Boise Cascade — in two pending court cases that seek to halt the road-building ban. Craig said he would delay any action until after the court's decision, which is expected the week of Aug. 7, but vowed to resurrect the issue later this year if the court does not toss out the ban.

"We really want a clean ruling on this, unencumbered by congressional influence," Craig said in a July 12 interview. An aide estimated Craig would have had about 56 votes in support of his amendment — enough to get the provision adopted but well short of the 67 votes needed to override a certain presidential veto.

"Knowing that my effort would probably be vetoed," Craig said, he partnered with Pete V. Domenici, R-N.M., to sponsor a substitute amendment that would appropriate $120 million each to the Bureau of Land Management (BLM) and the Forest Service to clear the accumulated underbrush that experts estimate has put 39 million acres of the nation's forests at considerable risk of catastrophic fire.

Adopted by voice vote, the amendment would require the Forest Service to finalize a cohesive fire prevention and protection plan and explain how the plan would affect other pending rules, such as the road-ban proposal.

"Time is running out for a strategy to successfully avert high-cost, high-loss consequences," said Dianne Feinstein, D-Calif., a cosponsor of the amendment.

Grazing Provision Remains

The Senate roundly rejected, 38-62, an amendment by Richard J. Durbin, D-Ill., that would have struck a section of the spending bill allowing expired grazing permits to remain in effect while the BLM completes environmental reviews. *(Vote 175, p. S-32)*

Domenici, who has attached the provision to past Interior spending bills, said it was needed to ensure that ranches are not held "hostage" while the bureau clears its large backlog of expired permits. The administration says the provision could allow polluters to obtain automatic permit renewals.

The Senate also rejected, 27-73, an amendment by James M. Inhofe, R-Okla., that would have shifted a $7.4 million increase for the National Endowment for the Arts to diabetes treatment, prevention and research within the Indian Health Service. *(Vote 176, p. S-32)*

Senate Passes Bill Without Several Disputed Riders

JULY 22 — Resisting the urge to attach a series of GOP environmental policy riders certain to sink the measure, the Senate passed a $15.5 billion fiscal 2001 Interior appropriations bill (HR 4578) July 18.

"I don't intend to send a bill to the president that we don't believe he ought to sign," said Interior Appropriations Subcommittee Chairman Slade Gorton, R-Wash., in arguing for the measure's passage.

The appropriations bill, passed by a 97-2 vote, is $603 million above the fiscal 2000 level. It is $905 million more than the version (HR 4578) passed 204-172 by the House on June 16 and $806 million less than President Clinton requested. *(Vote 211, p. S-38)*

Among the rejected provisions was one regarded by the administration and environmental groups as the biggest threat to the bill. Lawmakers defeated, 49-50, an amendment by Assistant Majority Leader Don Nickles, R-Okla., that would have prevented Clinton from designating any new national monuments without congressional approval. *(Vote 208, p. S-38)*

Conferees will have to resolve the difference in funding levels between the House and Senate bills, but those negotiations probably will pale in comparison to the bargaining that must occur with the administration — which has threatened a veto over remaining riders and spending — before Clinton will sign the measure.

Chief among the programs the White House says the bill neglects is Clinton's Lands Legacy Initiative, which funds government purchases of environmentally sensitive acreage. The administration requested $600 million for the land acquisition portion of the program; the Senate bill would provide some $220 million.

Six Republicans crossed party lines to oppose Nickles' amendment: Mike DeWine of Ohio, Lincoln Chafee of Rhode Island, Peter G. Fitzgerald of Illinois, James M. Jeffords of Vermont, Richard G. Lugar of Indiana and William V. Roth Jr. of Delaware. Only one Democrat, Robert C. Byrd of West Virginia, bucked his party to support it.

Western Republicans pulled back on an amendment that would have blocked administration rules to ban new road-building in roadless national forests, allowing it to be replaced with a non-controversial forest health provision. Larry E. Craig, R-Idaho, is awaiting a verdict in two pending court cases that seek to halt the road-building ban before he decides whether to revisit the issue in conference.

The bill still contains provisions — mentioned in Clinton's veto threat — that would exempt New Hampshire's White Mountain National Forest from the road-building ban and require the U.S. Forest Service to report on the economic impact of proposed recreational curbs in Colorado's White River National Forest.

Gorton, while supportive of the proposed restrictions on administration environmental initiatives, stressed that his priority is to deliver a bill the White House will have trouble vetoing in an election year.

"I know perfectly well that if this amendment is in the bill that goes to the president, the president will veto the bill," Gorton said of Nickles' monument amendment.

Nickles said the administration has been abusing its power to declare monuments for election-year advantage, citing Clinton's first and perhaps most controversial designation — a 1996 action to preserve 1.7 million acres in Utah as the Grand Staircase-Escalante National Monument.

"We had a massive land grab, power grab, mineral grab — you name it — by the president of the United States for a photo op for election purposes," Nickles said. "That is the purpose of the amendment, to make sure this type of thing does not continue without at least some input from other local officials."

The Snowmobile Ban

Craig Thomas, R-Wyo., also emphasized local control in advocating an amendment he offered — and later withdrew — on July 17 to halt a National Park Service ban on snowmobiles in many U.S. parks until an Interior study on their use could be completed.

Instead of trying to change the way snowmobiles are used or managed, Thomas said, "This administration has simply said, 'We are going to bring about a regulation unilaterally that will eliminate the use of snow machines in the parks of the United States'."

Democrats countered that the vehicles cause noise and air pollution. "Damage is being done to national parks, not some time in the future, but right now," said Minority Whip Harry Reid, D-Nev.

Thomas requested, and received, assurances from the GOP leadership that the issue will be revisited before final action on the bill. "I support the cause to which [Thomas] has spoken," Gorton said. "If there is a way to get at least part of that adopted, I will try and find it."

Forests and Parks

While policy riders provoked lively debate, partisan rifts also surfaced as the Senate considered provisions that would affect forest and park management.

The Senate rejected, 45-54, an amendment by Richard H. Bryan, D-Nev., that would have cut $30 million from the Forest Service timber sales program — which many environmentalists and Democrats view as a subsidy for logging in national forests — and shifted $15 million to the agency's fire prevention account. *(Vote 207, p. S-37)*

Bryan called timber sales "a money-losing program" and said logging worsens the risk of fires. "It is widely recognized in the scientific community that past commercial logging and associated road-building activities are the prime culprits for the severity of many of our wildfires," he said.

Craig protested that Bryan's amendment was overkill. Craig, who teamed with Pete V. Domenici, R-N.M., on an amendment — adopted July 12 by voice vote — that would spend $240 million to clear underbrush in the nation's forests, said Democrats had devastated the timber industry over the past eight years.

"If you want to do something about fires, or the safety of the forests, or the health of the forests, what you do is maintain a healthy harvest situation," said Conrad Burns, R-Mont., who also argued against Bryan's amendment. "You have to harvest those trees."

Christopher S. Bond, R-Mo., succeeded in defeating an amendment by Barbara Boxer, D-Calif., that would have barred the use of possible cancer-causing pesticides in national parks where children might be present. Bond's language would ban the use on federal lands of pesticides not approved by the EPA.

Boxer's amendment "circumvents the science-based process at EPA," Bond said. The Senate adopted his substitute, 99-0. Boxer called the provision a "sham" but voted for it because she views it as harmless. *(Vote 209, p. S-38)*

Lawmakers then voted, 41-58, to reject Boxer's original language. *(Vote 210, p. S-38)*

Richard J. Durbin, D-Ill., won adoption July 17 of language in a manager's amendment to modify a rider — opposed by the administration — that would have stopped the establishment of a wildlife refuge in Illinois' Kankakee River basin. The amendment was approved by voice vote.

Under Durbin's revision, the refuge can go forward if the U.S. Fish and Wildlife Service continues to collaborate on the project with the Army Corps of Engineers and obtains approval from the House and Senate Appropriations committees.

Another provision, inserted into the manager's amendment by Michael D. Crapo, R-Idaho, would prevent federal land management agencies from closing down back-country airstrips.

Western lawmakers have complained the airstrips are often shut down without local participation and say the closures make it more difficult to access federal lands for such purposes as fighting forest fires.

Boosts and Compromises

The Interior bill steers nearly half of its major increases toward existing programs in the four land management agencies. It would:

- Boost resource management funding for the Fish and Wildlife Service by $43.9 million over fiscal 2000, bringing it to $758 million.
- Increase by $80 million the budget for Park Service operations, which would total $1.4 billion.
- Raise the Bureau of Land Management's management account $49 million, bringing it to $693 million.
- Boost the Forest Service's operating budget by $85.9 million to $1.2 billion.

The Bureau of Indian Affairs would receive an increase of $58.3 million, to $121 million, to build six new schools.

An increase of $7.4 million over the fiscal 2000 level would go to the National Endowment for the Arts (NEA), bringing it to $105 million.

Several senators have vowed to fight for the hike — which would mark the first sizeable increase for the controversial arts agency in nine years — in the upcoming conference. Republicans were successful in blocking an increase in the House-passed bill.

Before passing the bill, senators also adopted several minor provisions by voice vote, including:

- Amendments sponsored by Paul Wellstone, D-Minn., and Rod Grams, R-Minn., that would appropriate $7.2 million in emergency funding and $4.1 million in fiscal 2001 funding to address the damage from a 1999 storm that devastated forests in their state.
- An amendment by Thomas that would increase by $3 million, to $148 million, funding for a program designed to compensate states for lost property taxes where the federal government owns significant amounts of public land.
- An amendment sponsored by Maine Republicans Susan Collins and Olympia J. Snowe that would provide $5 million in emergency funding for Atlantic salmon conservation and restoration in anticipation of the species being classified by the Fish and Wildlife Service as endangered.
- An amendment by Joseph I. Lieberman, D-Conn., that would set aside $4 million for the Northeast Home Heating Oil Reserve established by Clinton on July 11.
- An amendment sponsored by Jack Reed, D-R.I., that would increase spending for programs to improve insulation and ventilation in low-income housing by $8 million.

One proposal that met with some controversy but was ultimately adopted by voice vote was an amendment offered July 12 by Jeff Sessions, R-Ala., to halt new rules allowing the secretary of Interior to intervene in tribal-state negotiations over the issuance of Indian casino gaming permits.

Sessions said Interior Secretary

Bruce Babbitt should wait until a court rules on a challenge to the regulations brought by the Florida and Alabama attorneys general before finalizing the rules.

Babbitt "is not elected. He is not answerable to anybody. Yet he thinks he has the power to tell them what they have to do and dramatically change the nature of that town and the lives of the people who live there," Sessions said.

Advocates of American Indians — both Republican and Democrat — opposed the amendment, saying it would halt important rules that give tribes leverage to deal with the states.

"The current state of the law gives states what is in reality a veto over tribes," Ben Nighthorse Campbell, R-Colo., said. "That is unacceptable."

President Submits Forest-Fire Plan To Congress

SEPTEMBER 16 — The debate between congressional Republicans and the Clinton administration over forest management policy has muted somewhat as both sides turn to the serious and time-sensitive task of funding following the disastrous 2000 fire season.

Lawmakers active on land policy issues said they are ready to move quickly on the fire plan submitted Sept. 9 to President Clinton by the Forest Service and the Interior Department. It includes a fiscal 2001 request of $2.8 billion — including an emergency increase of $1.6 billion — for wildland fire programs and emphasizes restoring damaged lands, thinning dangerously overgrown tree stands and bolstering federal firefighting capabilities.

"We do not have the luxury of time," said Republican Larry E. Craig of Idaho, who chairs the Senate Energy Subcommittee on Forests and Public Land Management, at a Sept. 15 hearing.

Craig is working with the administration, other appropriators and Western lawmakers to include the package in the fiscal 2001 Interior spending bill (HR 4578), which is slated to go to a House-Senate conference the week of Sept. 18. Westerners will likely push for additional targeted relief for their states, but Craig expects the package to emerge from the negotiations intact. "Our goal is to have it done and out [of conference] by the end of next week," he said.

Quick action on the package will not end the ongoing debate over federal forest policy, however.

"While we are pleased that this proposal has finally been put forth, some of my colleagues and I remain skeptical that it will be implemented," said George P. Radanovich, R-Calif., chairman of the House Budget Committee Task Force on Natural Resources and the Environment, at a Sept. 13 hearing on the fires.

Administration officials have enjoyed some degree of success in recent weeks in their efforts to shift the debate over this year's catastrophic fires away from the politically charged issue of logging toward a balanced approach of removing the small-diameter trees and underbrush that most experts view as the real culprits in the spread of wildland fires. "I hate to see it turn into a logging, no-logging debate," Forest Service Deputy Chief Randle Phillips told the Budget task force Sept. 13.

Craig, a champion of the forest industry, agreed. "Shame on any . . . public interest group that wants to start that kind of argument again," he said Sept. 15. "The issue of forest health is much more complex than that."

Broad Outlines

Aside from $770 million to replenish fire suppression accounts, the bulk of the administration's proposed spending is earmarked for fire preparedness and prevention. The report calls for more than tripling the fire operations budgets of the Forest Service and the Bureau of Land Management from $324 million in fiscal 2000 to $1 billion in fiscal 2001. It would also spend some $385 million to remove underbrush through thinning and prescribed burns.

Environmentalists fear that the agencies' proposed solutions are a dangerous opening for timber interests to step up tree harvests in federal forests, while some Western lawmakers continue to argue that the Clinton administration's broader land management policies — including banning roads in large swaths of roadless forests and purchasing environmentally fragile acreage — place too many restrictions on land use.

"They just want to go ahead with the Lands Legacy [land acquisition initiative] and stopping road-building, and I think that the fires ought to make them stop and re-evaluate somewhat what they're doing," said Craig Thomas, R-Wyo., in a Sept. 12 interview.

In the report and at hearings the week of Sept. 11, the administration pointedly rejected assertions that its land management policies — including curbing timber harvests and trying to stop road-building in forests — are to blame for the current fire crisis.

"The administration's wildland fire policy does not rely on commercial logging or new road building to reduce fire risks and can be implemented under its current forest and land management policies," the report states.

Lawmakers who have been critical of the policies remained unconvinced. "I don't understand how you can continue to support your roadless policy in the forests as a consequence of your experience this year," Senate Energy and Natural Resources Committee Chairman Frank H. Murkowski, R-Alaska, told administration officials Sept. 15.

Craig said Forest Service statistics showing that 64 percent of the acres that burned this summer were in wilderness or roadless areas demonstrated the imprudence of administration policies. But forestry officials said the numbers simply reflected their decision to concentrate on fighting fires near populated areas this summer.

Unconvinced, Craig said, "There is a very intense hint of rhetoric trying to justify a policy that this administration is aggressively pushing through."

Imminent Deal On Lands Proposal Could Clear Interior Conference Report

SEPTEMBER 23 — Republican and Democratic appropriators and the White House are nearing agreement on sweeping new public lands legislation that could pave the way for clearing the conference report on the fiscal

2001 Interior spending bill (HR 4578) the week of Sept. 25.

The agreement would likely spell defeat for efforts this year to enact the Conservation and Reinvestment Act (HR 701), a more ambitious measure that would dedicate $3 billion annually in offshore oil and gas drilling revenues to an array of conservation programs.

Still, a series of GOP environmental policy riders — several of them hastily tacked onto the measure Sept. 20 and 21 — remain formidable roadblocks to producing a bill that President Clinton will sign.

"I vetoed bills before because they contained [anti-environmental riders], and if I have to, I'll do it again," Clinton said Sept. 21 during a Rose Garden news conference where he called for enactment of the Conservation and Reinvestment Act, known as CARA.

Partisan fights over the riders could jeopardize agreements reached by conferees thus far, including an emergency appropriation of $1.8 billion to address this year's disastrous rash of Western fires and pay for future fire prevention efforts.

Senate Interior Appropriations Subcommittee Chairman Slade Gorton, R-Wash., expressed confidence that the new lands proposal — which some observers are calling "CARA Lite" — can bridge the gulf between the White House and congressional Republicans on the Interior bill.

It "has the promise of getting us a bill that can get through both houses of Congress and get signed," Gorton said.

Republicans and the administration are still reviewing a Democratic proposal to boost fiscal 2001 funding dramatically — to $921 million — for Clinton's prized Lands Legacy Initiative, creating a six-year trust fund that would set aside $1.4 billion annually for acquisition and critical maintenance of environmentally sensitive acreage.

Ranking House Interior Appropriations Subcommittee Democrat Norm Dicks of Washington presented the proposal as a middle ground between the $421 million conferees had agreed to devote to land acquisition in fiscal 2001 and the nearly $3 billion that would be guaranteed annually for a wide array of environmental programs over the next 15 years under CARA.

Appropriators have objected to CARA because they feel it would automatically fund conservation programs rather than allow Congress to determine annual spending goals. CARA passed the House May 11 by a lopsided, 315-102 vote and was approved overwhelmingly by a Senate committee July 25.

The proposal now being discussed by conferees would create a "Lands Legacy Trust Fund" that would last through fiscal 2006. Appropriators would decide each year whether and where to spend the funds.

"I think the virtue of this proposal is that it recognizes a priority need while at the same time not giving up our institutional prerogatives to determine in the end what level is provided and for what projects," said Ranking House Appropriations Committee Democrat David R. Obey of Wisconsin.

CARA's supporters, who have fretted for weeks that the ambitious measure would ultimately be scaled back, expressed alarm about the Lands Legacy proposal.

Many of the environmental groups that have led the charge for the bill say they will pressure Clinton not to accept a non-permanent solution.

"A one-time appropriation a legacy does not make," Jane Danowitz, executive director of Americans for Our Heritage and Recreation, said Sept. 20.

Rider Fever

Democrats and White House negotiators are still trying to rid the bill of provisions that would restrict federal environmental initiatives.

A Sept. 21 rider by Gorton to prevent the administration from studying or implementing salmon recovery efforts — including breaching the Snake River Dam — is high on Clinton's hit list. So is language added by Republican Rep. George Nethercutt of Washington that would block a comprehensive plan to manage resources in the Interior Columbia Basin until the president gives Congress a report detailing the effects of this year's fire season and federal fire prevention efforts.

Fights also loom on riders dealing with mining and grazing on federal lands, and Republican efforts to block administration curbs on roadbuilding and recreation in specific national forests.

Deal Reached On Lands Fund, Policy Riders

SEPTEMBER 30 — After a week of intense negotiations between the White House and congressional conferees, appropriators filed a conference report for the $18.8 billion fiscal 2001 Interior spending bill (HR 4578) Sept. 29 just before Congress recessed for the week.

The House could vote on the report as early as Oct. 2, and administration officials say President Clinton is likely to sign it.

"If the bill is what we think it is, we're delighted with the result," George Frampton, chairman of the Council on Environmental Quality, said during a Sept. 29 conference call.

The breakthrough came when negotiators were able to agree on a bipartisan deal that would create a fund devoted to land acquisition, conservation and maintenance. The fund would begin at $1.6 billion in fiscal 2001, increasing to $2.4 billion by fiscal 2006. The administration also succeeded in ridding the bill of several environmental riders added by GOP appropriators.

"This is the largest increase in conservation programs funding ever approved by Congress," ranking House Interior Appropriations Subcommittee Democrat Norm Dicks of Washington said in a Sept. 28 statement. He declared the initiative "a major victory for the Clinton-Gore administration."

The conference report would authorize some $3 billion more than the Senate-passed version, $3.8 billion above the House-passed measure and $2.4 billion more than Clinton had requested.

Breakthrough on Lands

The hard-fought compromise emerged after appropriators were finally able to determine which programs should receive funding from the new conservation fund and finalized spending levels for each. Complicating the process was pressure from backers of the popular Conservation and Reinvestment Act (HR 701) — known as CARA — who wanted earmarks for specific programs included in their original legislation, which would have created a 15-year guarantee of $3 billion annually for more than a dozen conservation accounts.

The final Interior agreement would create a fund through fiscal 2006 exclusively for land conservation, preservation and management efforts. Appropriators could allocate funds for federal and state land acquisition, conservation programs, urban and historic preservation, backlogged maintenance and the Payment in Lieu of Taxes program, which compensates states for lost property tax revenues.

Coastal and fisheries programs, which are mainly funded through the Commerce-Justice-State appropriations bill, would receive $400 million in fiscal 2001 from the new program, increasing in $40-million increments through fiscal 2006. The fund also contains an account for other conservation and management programs to be chosen by appropriators. It would receive $120 million in fiscal 2002, increasing $120 million each year.

Agreement on the lands package all but dooms prospects for passage of CARA this session, although the bill's supporters say a fund that allows appropriators to choose which conservation programs are funded each year is no substitute for their measure.

"CARA would have been the greatest investment ever in recreation and conservation," Senate Energy and Natural Resources Committee Chairman Frank H. Murkowski, R-Alaska, said in a Sept. 29 statement. "Unfortunately [the appropriators'] proposal falls woefully short."

Policy Provisions Dropped

Appropriators were persuaded to abandon several policy riders the administration had vowed to oppose. Among them were:

- A provision by Senate Interior Appropriations Subcommittee Chairman Slade Gorton, R-Wash., to stop federal agencies from considering breaching dams on the lower Snake River.
- Language by Sen. Ben Nighthorse Campbell, R-Colo., to block recreational curbs in Colorado's White River National Forest, and by Sen. Judd Gregg, R-N.H., to exempt New Hampshire's White Mountain National Forest from an administration policy that would ban road-building on more than 43 million acres of roadless national forest.

At least two potential problems remain. A rider by Sen. Pete V. Domenici, R-N.M., that would require grazing permits on federal lands to be renewed automatically pending their environmental reviews, could remain a sticking point with the administration.

Also, Sen. Peter G. Fitzgerald, R-Ill., has vowed to filibuster the conference report because GOP leaders would not allow him to add language requiring competitive bidding for the construction of a library in Springfield, Ill.

House Adopts Conference Report; Senate Clears Bill

OCTOBER 7 — After months of disagreement over how much the federal government should spend for environmental programs, Congress reached a landmark deal the week of Oct. 2 to double funding for land conservation when the House and Senate adopted the $18.8 billion fiscal 2001 Interior appropriations conference report (HR 4578).

The House adopted the conference report, 348-69, on Oct. 3, and the Senate cleared it, 83-13, on Oct 5. *(House vote 507, p. H-160; Senate vote 266, p. S-47)*

The measure would provide $1.2 billion in fiscal 2001 — nearly double the amount spent in fiscal 2000 — for such activities as land acquisition, wildlife conservation, backlogged maintenance in federal parks and forests and historic preservation, and would create a six-year, $12 billion fund for the programs.

"This is one of those times when this institution has produced something which will move the country forward," said ranking House Appropriations Committee Democrat David R. Obey of Wisconsin. He called the conference report "one of the truly finest chapters of this session of Congress."

The overall bill, which surpasses President Clinton's request by $2.4 billion, would spend $3.8 billion more than the House-passed measure and $3 billion more than the Senate-passed version, allowing lawmakers from both parties to claim credit during this election year for a historic commitment to environmental programs. Much of the opposition came from conservatives, disturbed that the Interior bill surpassed the fiscal 2000 measure by some $3.9 billion, a boost of more than 25 percent.

Backers of more sweeping legislation, the Conservation and Reinvestment Act (CARA), fought unsuccessfully to include their legislation in the Interior package. The bill (HR 701) would have guaranteed $45 billion over 15 years for similar programs. Still, many CARA supporters eventually went along with the Interior bill when it became obvious the bill was dead, and Senate Majority Leader Trent Lott, R-Miss., assured them that he will push for more money for coastal states in the Commerce-Justice-State (CJS) spending measure (HR 4690). *(CJS, 2-23)*

The White House and appropriators from both parties hailed the conservation agreement as a compromise they can support.

"By doubling our investment next year in land and water conservation, and guaranteeing even more funding in the years ahead, this agreement is a major step toward ensuring communities the resources they need to protect their most precious lands," the White House said in an Oct. 3 statement.

Interior appropriators "have brought us . . . a bill that we can all support and that we can all go home and brag about — if members feel like bragging — because this is a good bill," said House Appropriations Committee Chairman C.W. Bill Young, R-Fla.

Ultimately, White House negotiators earned bragging rights. They succeeded in removing or drastically weakening several riders opposed by environmentalists and won increased funding for the often embattled National Endowment for the Arts and for American Indian programs.

Formidable Hurdles

House and Senate leaders had to overcome a number of procedural and policy obstacles in order to shepherd the Interior measure through their chambers.

Early in the week, House CARA supporters, who feared that the new lands initiative included in the confer-

Interior Spending Highlights

Where the Money Goes

HR 4578 — Conference report: H Rept 106-914

Spending Synopsis:

The $18.8 billion conference report, adopted by the House on Oct. 3 and cleared by the Senate on Oct. 5, would appropriate $3.8 billion more than the House bill, $3 billion more than the Senate version and $2.4 billion more than President Clinton requested. The report would also appropriate $1.2 billion in fiscal 2001 for a fund devoted to land acquisition, maintenance and conservation and increases the annual authorization for such funding to $2.4 billion by fiscal 2006. The lands fund represents a compromise between the White House and appropriators and a defeat for supporters of the Conservation and Reinvestment Act (HR 701), which would have set aside $3 billion annually from federal oil royalties for land conservation programs for the next 15 years.

The package also provides a total of $2.9 billion — including an emergency increase of $1.6 billion requested by Clinton in September — for fire fighting and prevention following this year's severe fires across several Western states.

- **Interior Department**

The agreement would appropriate $8.4 billion for Interior Department agencies, $983 million more than the House bill, $634 million more than Senate version and $1 billion more than in fiscal 2000.

- **Forest Service**

Conferees agreed to provide $3.6 billion for the Agriculture Department's Forest Service, $873 million more than the House bill, $622 million more than the Senate version and $502 million more than Clinton requested.

- **Indian Affairs**

The agreement would provide $2.1 billion for the Bureau of Indian Affairs — $260 million more than the House bill and $55 million more than the Senate version. Clinton had requested an additional $60 million.

Hot-Button Issues

∆ **Grazing permits.** One of the few riders the administration did not manage to eliminate during conference negotiations is language attached by Sen. Pete V. Domenici, R-N.M., requiring the Bureau of Land Management to renew grazing permits pending environmental reviews. While the White House included the provision in a July veto threat and Senate Democrats attempted to remove it from the bill on the floor, it survived the House-Senate conference.

∆ **'Roadless' policy and recreational curbs.** During floor debate, Western senators backed down from threats to attach language that would have prevented the Forest Service from implementing an administration policy to bar road-building on more than 40 million acres of roadless forest land, and to block a National Park Service ban on the use of snowmobiles in most national parks. During the conference, White House negotiators managed to rid the bill of two related riders: a provision exempting New Hampshire's White Mountain National Forest from the roadless policy and language delaying recreational curbs in Colorado's White River National Forest.

∆ **National Endowment for the Arts.** The controversy-plagued agency, which conservatives have attacked for years as elitist and once tried to eliminate, would get $98 million, the same amount it received in fiscal 2000. It would receive another $7 million for a new fund that must be used for arts education and outreach in rural and underserved areas.

(figures are in thousands of dollars of new budget authority)

	Fiscal 2000 Appropriation	Fiscal 2001 Clinton Request	House Bill	Senate Bill	Conference Report
Interior Department	$7,320,690	$8,405,904	$7,375,652	$7,724,531	$8,358,782
(Bureau of Land Management)	(1,231,402)	(1,358,955)	(1,267,120)	(1,295,239)	(1,672,673)
(National Park Service)	(1,803,847)	(2,042,285)	(1,808,424)	(1,813,181)	(1,937,612)
Forest Service	2,819,933	3,110,053	2,739,351	2,990,750	3,612,361
Energy Department	1,226,393	1,161,070	1,188,471	1,361,275	1,456,868
Other related agencies	3,279,114	3,642,745	3,305,946	3,455,486	4,279,576
Supplemental appropriations			350,000	240,300	1,060,530
GRAND TOTAL	**$14,911,630**	**$16,319,772**	**$14,609,420**	**$15,765,093**	**$18,768,117**

TABLE: House, Senate Appropriations committees

ence report would undermine their bill, threatened to block the measure by defeating the rule (H Res 603) governing floor debate.

"I am not asking that we kill the conference report, but I am asking that the conference report not be allowed to kill CARA," said California's George Miller, ranking Democrat on the House Resources Committee, in an Oct. 2 statement.

Lott made it clear that CARA could not come to the Senate floor as a stand-alone bill, however, and most House supporters of the more ambitious proposal eventually supported the procedural motion to consider the Interior bill. It was adopted by a vote of 354-65. *(Vote 506, p. H-160)*

Lott stepped in again Oct. 4 to defuse filibuster threats from Sen. Mary L. Landrieu, D-La., a leading CARA proponent. Lott, a champion of CARA — which would have assured Mississippi $83 million annually — agreed to push for more money for coastal and state wildlife programs within the 2001 CJS appropriations bill. The Interior bill authorizes $400 million in fiscal 2001 for coastal programs, to be appropriated in the CJS measure, while CARA would have guaranteed more than $800 million.

"While this could potentially be a beginning, it is not nearly where we need to be in terms of delivering a real legacy for this nation," Landrieu said.

Landrieu and Lott's deal bridged major policy and funding differences blocking the bill, but a nearly 10-hour filibuster by Peter G. Fitzgerald, R-Ill., that began Oct. 4 and ran into the next day's session threw up another roadblock.

Fitzgerald complained that $50 million provided in the conference report for construction of the Abraham Lincoln Interpretive Center in Springfield, Ill., did not include his requirement that the project follow federal procurement law.

Fitzgerald argued that Illinois' procurement statute has weak competitive bidding requirements and charged that Republican Gov. George Ryan — a political foe — would use the library project to enrich his friends and donors. House Speaker J. Dennis Hastert, R-Ill., had refused to accept language subjecting the project to federal procurement rules, saying it would slow down construction and cost more.

Fitzgerald finally relented Oct. 5, allowing a motion by Lott to end debate and vote on the Interior bill.

"I think our point has been made [and] our filibuster achieved the illumination that we were looking for," Fitzgerald said in an interview a few hours before the motion passed, 89-8. *(Vote 265, p. S-47)*

The Divide on Lands

The painstaking work of appropriators and White House negotiators to create a new fund for public lands programs — widely hailed as the centerpiece of the Interior deal — has left a great deal of bitterness in its wake.

The provision would create a fund dedicated to land conservation, preservation and maintenance that appropriators could tap each year for the next six years for specific programs. It would grow from $1.6 billion in fiscal 2001 to $2.4 billion by fiscal 2006, with the increased funds made available to appropriators each year to use for whatever eligible programs they chose.

CARA supporters had pushed for a program similar to their original legislation, which would have guaranteed $3 billion annually over 15 years for more than a dozen conservation programs. Appropriators hatched the lands program that ultimately passed as a way to resist CARA — which would largely have circumvented congressional spending committees — yet still respond to Clinton's call for a $1 billion Lands Legacy initiative to fund purchases of environmentally fragile lands.

The proposal was an acknowledgement that the widespread public and political support for land conservation and preservation could not go unaddressed.

"This will deliver the goods without putting Congress in a procedural straitjacket," Obey said Oct. 3.

What appropriators view as a straitjacket was what CARA supporters saw as the virtue of their legislation: guaranteed funding.

The Interior lands compromise presented CARA supporters with a cruel irony. After they spent years cobbling together a broad and unlikely coalition of supporters — united only in their quest for guaranteed conservation dollars — the coastal lawmakers who conceived of CARA as a way to be compensated for offshore oil and gas drilling saw the core of their bill dissipate.

Programs that had been included in CARA mainly to attract supporters were folded into the compromise deal, while coastal programs received significantly less than they would have under CARA — all with no guarantees.

"The main purpose for which this bill started is gone — it's out of here," W. J. Billy Tauzin, R-La., told the House Rules Committee on Oct. 2.

While coastal states will likely get more money in the CJS spending bill, CARA's original supporters were unable to convince colleagues that the measure was greater than the sum of its parts.

"I ask that we not be lulled . . . into thinking that this is anything more than a minor down payment on the debt we owe to our children," Landrieu said Oct. 5.

GOP Riders Stripped

In a clear victory for the administration, the conference report excludes several riders that Republicans proposed during the conference, as well as some policy provisions in the House- and Senate-passed versions of the bill. These include:

- Language by Sen. Judd Gregg, R-N.H., that would have exempted New Hampshire's White Mountain National Forest from an administration-proposed ban on road-building in roadless national forests.
- A provision by Sen. Ben Nighthorse Campbell, R-Colo., that would have delayed imposition of recreational curbs in Colorado's White River National Forest.
- Language by Sen. Jeff Sessions, R-Ala., to halt new rules allowing the Interior secretary to intervene in tribal-state negotiations over the issuance of Indian casino gaming permits.

One rider opposed by the administration, by Sen. Pete V. Domenici, R-N.M., remains in the final bill. It would require grazing permits to be renewed automatically pending their environmental reviews.

Truce on Funding

The final Interior agreement would provide some $7.2 billion for the nation's three land management agencies — the Bureau of Land Management, the National Park Service and the Forest Service — about $700 million more than Clinton requested. It also would provide $4.8 billion to American Indian programs — just $55 million below the administration's request — and a long-sought increase for the National Endowment for the Arts from $98 million in fiscal 2000 to $105 million, with $7 million earmarked for educational and outreach programs for underserved areas.

It also calls for a $1.6 billion emergency increase for this year's firefighting efforts in the nation's forests and for future prevention, bringing the total fiscal 2001 fire budget to $2.9 billion.

After days of haggling between Republicans seeking accountability for past fires and latitude for tree-thinning efforts to prevent future ones, and Democrats worried about opening federal lands to logging, negotiators agreed to a new initiative for clearing flammable underbrush and small trees in forests adjacent to settled areas.

The agreement steers $240 million to a "hazardous fuels reduction" program that would allow the Bureau of Land Management and the Forest Service to bypass federal procurement laws and expedite environmental reviews. However, it specifies — in language central to the bipartisan deal — that no environmental laws can be overridden.

The provision would also require the agencies to give Congress extensive reports on how the money is to be spent and what work will be done. ◆

Labor-HHS-Education Bill Becomes Vehicle for 11th-Hour Omnibus Package

SUMMARY

Once again, a deal on funding for the departments of Labor, Health and Human Services, and Education eluded lawmakers until the bitter end, pushing the measure to the center of end-of-session battles with the administration. Although Republicans managed to resist some of President Clinton's growing spending demands, the final deal still included a record $6.5 billion increase for education, $2 billion more than Clinton had originally sought.

The largest of the 13 appropriations bills began with a relatively modest increase for health, education and job training programs. The House bill (HR 4577) called for $97.2 billion in discretionary spending, compared to $96.8 billion in fiscal 2000, while the Senate bill (S 2553) proposed $98.1 billion. (Counting mandatory spending, both bills came in at about $352 billion.)

That fell far short of Clinton's request of $106.1 billion in discretionary spending. The House bill had such modest increases across the board that Republicans were barely able to hold together enough members to vote for it. The Senate version, with slightly larger increases, had an easier time. Eventually, however, Republicans decided they could not afford to let Clinton outbid them on education spending, especially in an era of growing budget surpluses. In a conference report finished in July but never filed, Republicans agreed to increase discretionary spending to the full amount Clinton requested.

Disagreements continued, however, over how and where to spend the money. Clinton and congressional Democrats wanted targeted spending for emergency school repairs, smaller class sizes and other specific purposes. Republicans wanted more money for special education; they offered to provide the money Democrats wanted for school repairs and class size reduction, but insisted it be labeled as a block grant so states and school districts could spend it on other things.

Another major stumbling block was a GOP a rider, added with strong support from business groups, to block the Occupational Safety and Health Administration (OSHA) from finalizing rules that would require 1.6 million employers to set up programs to prevent repetitive motion injuries.

On Oct. 30, White House and GOP appropriators reached a tentative deal to fatten the bill to $113.8 billion in discretionary spending — including a $7.5 billion increase for the Education Department, more than twice as much as the previous record increase. They split the difference on education policies, agreeing to target $1.3 billion for school repairs and $1.75 billion to reduce class size while letting states spend 25 percent of the money on other needs in both instances. GOP leaders scotched the deal, however, saying the ergonomics compromise — allowing OSHA to publish the final rule but delaying enforcement until June 2001, after a new president was in office — would not actually accomplish its goal. They also worried that spending had risen out of control and hinted they might cut it back.

Republican leaders put off further negotiations until after the elections. In the meantime, OSHA published the final ergonomics rule, effectively taking that issue off the table but fanning partisan flames.

When negotiations resumed, conservative House Republicans vowed that Clinton would have to settle for less money. Eventually, Clinton accepted some reductions from the earlier deal, but the cuts were spread so evenly they were barely noticeable. School repair funding dropped to $1.2 billion and class size funding dipped to $1.62 billion, but they remained dedicated to the same purposes. Medical research received a $2.5 billion funding boost.

Box Score 2001 Fiscal Year

Labor-HHS-Education

- **Bill:** HR 4577 — PL 106-554
- **Legislative action: House** passed HR 4577 (H Rept 106-645), 217-214, on June 14.

Senate passed HR 4577, 52-43, on June 30, after substituting the text of S 2553 (S Rept 106-293).

House adopted the conference report on HR 4577 (H Rept 106-1033), 292-60, on Dec. 15.

Senate cleared the bill by voice vote Dec. 15.

President signed the bill Dec. 21.

Labor-HHS Bills Bolt Out of the Starting Gates In Both Chambers

MAY 13 — The appropriations bill that usually encounters the biggest problems got an early start the week of May 8, as Senate and House panels marked up their versions of the fiscal 2001 Labor, Health and Human Services (HHS) and Education spending bill. President Clinton promptly threatened to veto both of them.

In a May 11 statement, Clinton said he would veto both bills if no changes were made, saying they would not provide enough money for critical education, health care and job training programs.

The early action may help Congress get past a veto and move on to the next act — negotiations between Republican leaders and the White House to produce a compromise bill — more quickly than in recent years. It also laid the markers for fights over education and health care priorities that could drag on throughout the year.

The Senate Appropriations Committee approved its draft bill by voice vote May 11, a day after the Labor-HHS-Education Subcommittee endorsed the measure, also by voice vote.

In the House, the Labor-HHS-Education Subcommittee approved its version May 10 in a party-line vote of 8-6. The draft is expected to be marked up by the full committee May 24.

"This is not a real bill," said David R. Obey of Wisconsin, ranking Democrat on the House Appropriations Committee. "It is at least $6 billion short of where it needs to be to get a presidential signature," he said in a May 10 interview. "I don't want to have a train wreck, but if we have to have it, it would be a lot better to have it now when there's still time to do something about it."

The Senate draft is more generous than the House version, with increases for a variety of education and health care programs, from special education to school construction to the National Institutes of Health (NIH). But it does so, in part, by cutting initiatives — such as the State Children's Health Insurance Program for uninsured children — that are so strongly defended it is not clear the cuts can survive in the final bill.

A Fatter Senate Bill

Overall, the Senate came up with a fatter bill — $104.5 billion in discretionary spending for the three departments, and $241.2 billion in mandatory spending, most of it for big-ticket health care items such as Medicaid grants to the states. The House bill contains $99.9 billion in discretionary spending and $242.3 billion in mandatory funds.

In both cases, the subcommittee chairmen said they did the best they could under the tight discretionary spending allocations they received from the full committees May 4. Both chairmen found ways to spend just a little more than they were allocated.

Chairman Ted Stevens, R-Alaska, during the Senate full committee markup May 11, said the draft bill was "very skillfully crafted."

The political tone in the two subcommittees was markedly different as they debated the measure. In the Senate, bipartisanship ruled. Subcommittee Chairman Arlen Specter, R-Pa., and Tom Harkin of Iowa, the ranking Democrat, worked for weeks to hash out a compromise and closed ranks to defend the bill as soon as it was ready to move.

Harkin brushed off the veto threat from his own party's president May 11, saying it was "ill-advised" and that Clinton should have "at least waited until the ink was dry."

There was no such spirit in the House, where the Labor-HHS appropriations process is usually bitterly partisan. Obey said the bill was so bad it should go straight to the House floor to get the Clinton veto over with as soon as possible, and made it clear Republicans will have to pass it without any Democratic votes.

House subcommittee Chairman John Edward Porter, R-Ill., made little effort May 11 to defend the bill's spending levels or the leadership strategy of passing a Republican-only measure, which he said was "counterproductive" and "puts the president in the position of being able to dictate the terms of our bill." Still, he said, the House is starting out right by producing the bill early in the year rather than later.

No freestanding Labor-HHS bill has been signed into law since 1997, and Republicans are trying to avoid letting the anticipated post-veto negotiations drag on past the end of the fiscal year, as they did in 1998 and 1999 — an outcome that allowed Clinton to squeeze out concessions such as funding for a class-size reduction initiative most Republicans oppose.

In the Senate, Specter is banking on the bill's spending increases in many areas, and what he says is "acknowledgment" of Clinton's priorities in critical education areas, to make the process run more smoothly.

On education, for example, the Senate bill would increase spending even more than Clinton wanted. It includes a $4.6 billion increase in discretionary funding for the Department of Education, boosting the department's budget to $40.2 billion — besting Clinton's request by $100 million. The House bill would increase the department's budget by $1.6 billion, nearly $3 billion less than Clinton requested.

In a key nod to Clinton's education priorities, Specter added $1.3 billion to cover school construction and modernization costs, the same amount Clinton proposed for grants and loans to help states fix up their oldest schools and build new ones. The House bill contains no school construction funds.

To avoid violating Republican principles on local control by dictating how states should use the money, Specter added the funds to the Title VI block grant under the 1965 Elementary and Secondary Education Act — essentially telling states that the money is there if they want to spend it on school construction, but that it can be used for other things if they have more pressing needs.

Harkin, who has been pushing the school modernization issue in the Senate, accepted the compromise for now. He said the additional funding was "a significant step forward," but that the money should be targeted to the neediest school districts, not spread around so wealthy districts can tap into it at poor communities' expense.

The compromise was not good enough for Clinton, who criticized the bill for not guaranteeing that the money would be used to build new schools or modernize existing ones.

Education and Health Care

Another flashpoint will be the failure of both versions of the bill to guarantee funding for Clinton's initiative to reduce class sizes by hiring 100,000 new teachers by 2005. The program has been funded in fiscal years 1999 and 2000, and Clinton asked for a third year of funding for 2001.

Republicans have resisted the program, saying it is often more important to find better teachers than to hire new ones. This year, both measures combine the class-size funding with teacher quality initiatives — $1.4 billion in the Senate, $1.8 billion in the House. Clinton criticized both bills for not guaranteeing that the money would be used to hire new teachers.

Both subcommittees made a dent in a key Republican education priority — more money for special education under the Individuals with Disabilities Education Act (PL 94-142) — but neither found enough money to cover the $2 billion increase sought in a House-passed bill (HR 4055) that would authorize 40 percent of states' IDEA costs within 10 years.

The Senate bill would come closer, boosting IDEA funding by $1.3 billion — $1 billion more than Clinton requested. The House settled for a $500 million increase. The program would receive a total of $7.3 billion under the Senate bill, $6.3 billion under the House bill.

More Money for NIH

For health care, the biggest appropriations battle will be the continuing drive to double the NIH's fiscal 1998 budget by 2003. To do that, as Specter, Porter and Harkin all want, the final Labor-HHS bill must increase the NIH budget by $2.7 billion, for a total of $20.5 billion.

The Senate bill would do that, but the House draft includes only enough money for a $1 billion increase — the amount requested by Clinton. The administration has not adopted the goal of doubling federal funding for biomedical research. Porter said he was disappointed he could not find the entire $2.7 billion and hoped appropriators could come up with more later on.

The Senate panel could pay for bigger increases than the House, partly because it started with a bigger discretionary spending allocation, roughly $1.5 billion more than the House had to work with. But it also found savings in critical health care and social services programs that the House did not make, cuts that the Senate appropriators are now getting blasted for.

In the biggest change, the Senate bill would knock out $1.9 billion in funding for the State Children's Health Insurance Program (S-CHIP), which offers federal matching funds to help the states provide health coverage to the nation's 11 million uninsured children. Subcommittee aides said the money represents federal funds that will not be used by the states this year; instead, they are promising to restore the money in fiscal 2003.

That proposal drew fire from Clinton, who criticized the Senate bill for "shifting money from children's health insurance." The nation's governors are warning that such a shift would threaten their ability to cover uninsured children, since they could never again count on the federal matching funds they had been promised.

Under the terms of the program, which Congress created in the Balanced Budget Act of 1997 (PL 105-33), states have three years to spend the matching funds they receive in any given fiscal year. If they do not spend the money, it is redistributed to the states that have spent all of their federal funds, since they are assumed to be the ones with the greatest numbers of uninsured children.

"This jeopardizes the integrity of the program," Cherilyn Cepriano, a legislative associate at the National Governors' Association, said in a May 11 interview. "The promise of funding two years from now is not a good one. If there's a recession, we're not going to see the money."

In another controversial move, the Senate bill would cut most of the funding for the Title XX Social Services Block Grant, which helps states pay for social programs ranging from Meals on Wheels for elderly people to foster care, day care, family planning, protective services for abused children and services for people with disabilities.

The Senate bill would cut nearly $1.2 billion from the block grant, shrinking it from $1.8 billion in fiscal 2000 to $600 million in fiscal 2001.

Clinton criticized the bill for "bankrupting" the grant, and the NGA warned in a May 11 letter to Stevens that "such a drastic reduction . . . will cause a dramatic disruption in the delivery of the most critical human services."

In a May 10 letter to Stevens, Specter and Harkin, Senate Finance Committee Chairman William V. Roth Jr., R-Del., and Sen. Daniel Patrick Moynihan of New York, the ranking Democrat, criticized the proposed S-CHIP and Social Services Block Grant cutbacks on other than policy grounds. "Policy changes affecting programs in the Finance Committee's jurisdiction," they wrote, "should be made by the Finance Committee."

House Panel OKs Bill; Both Parties Vow to Fight For More Money

MAY 27 — With a notable lack of enthusiasm, the House Appropriations Committee approved the fiscal 2001 Labor, Health and Human Services, and Education appropriations bill May 24. The draft bill's author, John Edward Porter, R-Ill., held Republicans together chiefly by promising to fight for bigger spending increases once the bill gets out of the House.

The largest of the 13 spending bills — and usually the toughest to pass — was approved on a party-line vote of 29-22 after Democrats tried unsuccessfully to add funds for a variety of education, health care and job training programs. It is expected to reach the House floor in mid-June.

Republicans generally resisted the temptation to add the kinds of policy riders that have bogged the bill down in the past. They did add a provision that would block the Occupational Safety and Health Administration (OSHA) from enforcing a proposed ergonomics rule dealing with repetitive-motion injuries in the workplace.

The panel's ranking Democrat, David R. Obey of Wisconsin, criticized the amendment, which could create even more problems for a bill that already faces a veto threat over spending priorities.

The only workplace injuries that afflict members of Congress, Obey said, are "the injuries they receive from genuflecting to big business interests."

Setting Priorities

Porter, chairman of the Labor-HHS subcommittee, gamely defended the bill from Democratic criticisms that vital programs would not get enough money. "We have had to choose priorities," Porter said. "We have to operate within a budget resolution that is real."

Porter also made it clear that he will look for more money for priority items such as biomedical research and special education funding once the measure goes to conference with the Senate.

That strategy did not sit well with Obey, who called the package a "let's pretend bill." He predicted that virtually all of the Democratic spending increases would end up in the final Labor-HHS bill — most likely after the same arduous negotiations the measure has required the past two years. *(1998 Almanac, p. 2-64)*

President Clinton has threatened to veto the bill, which would provide $97.2 billion in discretionary spending to more than 300 education, health care, workplace safety and job training programs.

"I am frankly amazed that we keep going up the same hill and down the same hill again," Obey said. Ramming a spending bill through with promises to fix it later, he said, "bleeds the last bit of credibility out of the appropriations process."

Like its Senate counterpart (S 2553), the House Labor-HHS bill would put most of its spending increases into education and health care. The increases would be larger than those in the Senate bill, which includes controversial cuts in children's health insurance and social services programs.

The Department of Education would get $37.2 billion in discretionary funding under the House bill, a $1.6 billion increase over the fiscal 2000 funding level. The Department of Health and Human Services would receive $43.9 billion, a $2.1 billion increase. The Department of Labor would receive $10.7 billion in discretionary funding, $526 million less than it received for fiscal 2000.

The education spending increases would include an additional $500 million for special-education grants to the states, $716.3 million for Pell grants to help low-income students attend college (raising the maximum grant from $3,300 to $3,500), and $400 million for the Head Start program, which provides health, social and educational services to disadvantaged students.

The biggest increases for health care would include a $1 billion boost for the National Institutes of Health; a $326.4 million increase for the Centers for Disease Control and Prevention; an additional $130.5 million for grants to community-based AIDS programs, and another $81.3 million for community health centers to provide better access in medically underserved areas.

The Agency for Healthcare Research and Quality would get an extra $24.9 million, including $20 million for research on preventing medical errors.

More Money

The House bill falls short of Clinton's budget request, which seeks $106.1 billion in discretionary spending for Labor-HHS programs. Democrats offered several amendments to raise the bill's spending levels, arguing that doing so would increase the measure's chance of being signed into law.

In one instance, some Republicans agreed with the goals of a Democratic amendment and still killed it. Rosa DeLauro, D-Conn., offered an amendment that would have added $1.5 billion in funding for special education grants to the states under the Individuals with Disabilities Education Act (IDEA) — bringing the bill's total increase to $2 billion.

DeLauro said she agreed with GOP lawmakers that Congress has not lived up to its promise of reimbursing 40 percent of the states' special education costs. She said IDEA is "grossly underfunded" and that Congress would be "putting an unfunded mandate on our communities."

Porter said he agreed with the goal of providing a larger increase for IDEA in the spending bill and assured GOP panel members he would work to "do better in the final product." His promise helped defeat the DeLauro amendment, 20-28.

The committee also rejected several other Democratic amendments, including:

- An amendment by Nita M. Lowey of New York that would have added $1.3 billion for grants and loans to pay for emergency school repairs, defeated 21-29.
- An amendment by Steny H. Hoyer of Maryland that would have added $1.8 billion for Title I programs for disadvantaged students, after-school programs, Head Start and child care, defeated 23-30.
- An amendment by Nancy Pelosi of California that would have added $1.7 billion in funding for the National Institutes of Health (NIH), defeated 23-29.
- A Lowey amendment that would have increased the maximum Pell grant by another $300, defeated 18-30.

Obey tried unsuccessfully to reserve $1.8 billion to pay for a third year of Clinton's class-size reduction program, which aims to help school districts hire 100,000 new teachers. His amendment was defeated, 22-31. The House bill would combine class-size and teacher quality funds, in keeping with the House-passed Teacher Empowerment Act (HR 1995).

The Clinton administration opposes lumping the two efforts together, and Obey said funding for smaller class sizes must be guaranteed and not become part of a block grant. "First you take everything and put it in the block grant, then you cut the block grant because then you can't be tagged with any of the specific reductions," Obey said.

In the most significant change to the bill, the committee approved, 32-22, an amendment by Anne M. Northup, R-Ky., that would prevent OSHA from doing any more work on a proposed ergonomics rule that would require about 1.6 million employers to come up with basic programs to prevent repetitive motion injuries.

Republican lawmakers have been looking for a vehicle to block the rule, which business groups say would be too open-ended and far more expensive than OSHA has predicted. The proposed rule, issued last November, would require employers to train workers to avoid ergonomic injuries. Workers who suffered an injury would be reassigned to lighter duties or put on paid leave for up to six months.

Rule 'Isn't Feasible'

Northup said the proposed rule would be too expensive for businesses, does a poor job of defining what injuries qualify and "simply isn't feasible." Everyone gets repetitive motion injuries in and out of the workplace, she said, and the proposed rule would make it easy for workers to take any ache or pain and call it an ergonomics injury.

Obey noted that the rule is still in draft stage and predicted that "significant adjustments are going to be made" before the final rule is issued.

The committee also approved, by voice vote, two amendments by Ernest Istook, R-Okla., that are contained in a bill (HR 4141) approved by the House Education and the Workforce Committee in April.

One of the Istook amendments would ban the use of federal funds to develop national skills tests, a carryover from the 1997 controversy over a Clinton proposal to give voluntary national tests to fourth-graders in reading and eighth-graders in math. The other amendment would require that any school buying computers with federal education technology funds install filters protecting children from obscene material or child pornography on the Internet. *(1997 CQ Almanac, p. 9-50)*

Throughout the markup, Porter was a reluctant spokesman for the bill, defending program spending levels as the best he could do with an allocation he thought was too tight. He is no fan of the GOP leadership's plan to rely only on Republican votes to pass the bill. In a May 24 interview, he said the measure will probably have enough votes to pass the House, but that the Republican-only strategy was "a decision of the leadership with which I disagree."

Still, Porter fought back the Democratic amendments by pleading with committee members to stay within the allocation and noting that Democrats never offered offsetting cuts to pay for their proposed spending increases.

"It's very easy to say that the other party isn't spending enough on this account or that account when you don't have that responsibility," he said.

Some of the bill's biggest cuts are aimed at Labor Department job training programs for laid-off workers and youths in impoverished communities.

The Dislocated Workers Assistance program would get $1.4 billion, $207 million less than it received in fiscal 2000; adult skills training funds to the states would be set at $857 million, $93 million less than the fiscal 2000 funding level. Youth Opportunity Grants would receive $175 million, $75 million less than they got in fiscal 2000.

Committee Republicans say the strong economy and low unemployment make these programs the least painful places to cut to stay within their tight allocation for Labor-HHS. "We think the money is adequate, and it was the proper place to make modest cuts," Porter said.

Democrats called that argument shortsighted, saying the economic expansion will not last if people do not have the skills they need to get good jobs. Jesse L. Jackson Jr., D-Ill., offered an amendment to increase funding by $1.3 billion for various job training programs, including the dislocated workers and youth grant initiatives. It was defeated, 19-30.

There was one exception to the job training cuts: The Job Corps program would receive $1.4 billion, a $42.2 million increase. Republicans like the program because it takes at-risk youths out of bad neighborhoods and puts them into supervised dormitories. They also back the increase because, according to the report language, the program "is particularly well-suited to help meet the needs of large, multistate employers for skilled entry-level workers."

Amendments Slow House Action as Leaders Scramble For Support

JUNE 10 — The Labor, Health and Human Services, and Education appropriations bill once again turned into a drawn-out and tortured affair June 8, as House Republicans scrambled to hold their conservatives and moderates together while trying to keep Democrats from slowing the process with a long list of amendments.

The fiscal 2001 spending bill (HR 4577) is scheduled to return to the floor the week of June 12 for more debate, which could include an effort by Tom Coburn, R-Okla., to declare a $500.6 million public health fund as regular spending rather than emergency spending. If successful, the move effectively would add $500.6 million to the bill's spending total and force appropriators to make offsetting cuts throughout the $351.8 billion bill.

In the long run, the specific fights will matter little, since President Clinton has vowed to veto the bill and House GOP leaders already are looking ahead to negotiations between Capitol Hill and the White House that will produce the final measure. In the meantime, the leadership has to get the original bill through the House — and is having a hard time doing it.

So far, the bill has sparked a mini-rebellion by conservative Republicans over what they consider spending gimmicks, the filing of 175 Democratic amendments to guarantee debate time they wanted and a botched attempt by James A. Traficant Jr., D-Ohio, to knock out a controversial ergonomics provision. The Traficant amendment, which failed 203-220, would have stripped out a provision by Anne M. Northup, R-Ky., to block a proposed ergonomics rule by the Occupational Safety and Health Administration (OSHA). *(Vote 250, p. H-80)*

The long-delayed rule would require about 1.6 million employers to set up programs to prevent repetitive motion injuries — a priority for labor unions but a nightmare for business groups, who say it would be far more expensive than OSHA has predicted.

Democrats had not wanted to make such a move against the ergonomics language, knowing they would probably lose the vote. They circulated a letter from the AFL-CIO declaring that labor did not support the Traficant amendment because the timing did not provide "an appropriate opportunity to work in behalf of its passage."

"I don't give a damn what the AFL-CIO says," Traficant told his Democratic colleagues on the House floor, inviting them to "shove that AFL-CIO letter right up your keister."

Moderate Republicans, meanwhile, are worried that the bill would shortchange critical education, health care and labor programs. Fred Upton, R-Mich., said some of them would "hold our noses and jump" in the hopes that the final bill will include higher spending levels close to those in the Senate bill (S 2553). Others, including Jack Quinn, R-N.Y., said they are unlikely to vote for the bill.

The ergonomics amendment was one of just two provisions the House managed to vote on. It also rejected, by voice vote, an amendment by Charles Bass, R-N.H., that would have added $1 billion in special education funding, raising that total to $6.5 billion, by making offsetting cuts in health care and other social programs.

Slow Progress

House Republicans let Democrats debate their amendments to increase social spending, but then raised points of order against them because they did not include offsetting cuts to pay for the increases. Through the points of order, they blocked two Democratic amendments — one by Jesse L. Jackson Jr., D-Ill., to increase job training funds by $1.3 billion, and one by David R. Obey, D-Wis., to add $97 million in Labor Department funds to fight child labor overseas.

Obey has nine other amendments pending, all of which would increase spending on such Democratic priorities as class size reduction, school modernization and biomedical research.

To keep debates on those provisions from consuming too much time, John Edward Porter, R-Ill., chairman of the Labor-HHS Appropriations Subcommittee, worked out a unanimous consent agreement to give Obey a half hour of debate for each, then automatically withdraw each amendment after Democrats make their points.

That agreement came only after Obey forced the Republicans' hand by filing 175 other amendments — each of which would have increased spending in individual accounts throughout the bill by $1,000. The point, staff aides said, was to have a fallback measure to make sure Democrats would get debate time for their issues one way or another. Under House rules, Republicans would have had to let Democrats debate those amendments for five minutes each.

Speaker J. Dennis Hastert, R-Ill., said in a June 8 interview that Democrats were trying to "stall this as long as possible and end up with a huge bill." The Democrats, however, may have been the least of his problems.

Several members of the House GOP Conservative Action Team threatened to bolt, complaining that the bill's $19.8 billion in advance discretionary appropriations — money that would be appropriated in fiscal 2001 but could not be spent until fiscal 2002 — was too high and put Congress at risk of exceeding the budget resolution's (H Con Res 290) overall limit of $23.5 billion in advance discretionary appropriations for all 13 spending bills. The conservatives say advance appropriations are a gimmick that lets Congress get around spending caps.

To win their support, GOP leaders agreed to rewrite the rule (H Res 518) to allow a Porter amendment that would automatically cut funds to the Child Care and Development Block Grant by whatever amount is necessary to keep overall advance appropriations under $23.5 billion. The block grant funding would not be reduced to less than the current $1.2 billion.

It was a questionable public relations move. Although the change satisfied conservative Republicans and allowed the rule to pass on a 218-204 vote, taking the money out of child care gave Democrats an opening to accuse them of being heartless — and lost the vote of Constance A. Morella, R-Md., who had been pushing for more child care funds. *(Vote 247, p. H-80)*

A House Appropriations Committee aide said the child care block grant was picked because it had the biggest increase in advance appropriations.

House Passes Labor-HHS Bill By Narrow Margin

JUNE 17 — It should have been a victory for House Republicans, but Democrats were the ones cheering after the GOP pushed the fiscal 2001 Labor, Health and Human Services, and Education spending bill through the chamber on June 14 by a narrow, 217-214, party-line vote. *(Vote 273, p. H-88)*

Democrats are convinced that GOP leaders made a major tactical error by forcing their rank and file to vote for a spending bill (HR 4577) that did not fund President Clinton's education, health care and job training requests. During attacks on the House floor — likely to be repeated in campaign advertisements — Democrats charged that at a time of growing surpluses, Republicans were more intent on cutting taxes for the well-off than protecting or expanding social programs.

"These guys are running in the same districts we are, and they're hearing the same things we are about the investments that need to be made," Harold E. Ford Jr., D-Tenn., said in a June 13 interview. "The magnitude of their tax cuts is unsustainable and, quite frankly, not supported by their own members."

Although some conservatives worried that the $351.8 billion bill would increase spending too much, the bigger political concern was shortfalls in some programs. John Edward Porter, R-Ill., chairman of the Appropriations Labor-HHS Subcommittee, persuaded moderates such as Jack Quinn, R-N.Y., to vote for the bill only after promising to fight for more education and job training money in conference with the Senate.

Not everyone was swayed by that assurance. The Republicans' problem was personified by Rick Lazio, R-N.Y., who is battling first lady Hillary Rodham Clinton for a Senate seat. Lazio, who has cast himself as a moderate in the campaign, voted against the bill because it did not include enough money for education and child care.

Republicans complained that Democrats were playing politics. Funding for Pell Grants for poor college students, special education and biomedical research has increased dramatically since the GOP took control of Congress in 1995, they said.

"We have been the champions in each of those areas; [Democrats] have been the followers," Porter said June 13. "These amendments, all of them, are false propaganda."

The final bill probably will look more like the Senate Labor-HHS version (S 2553), which could reach the Senate floor the week of June 19. The Senate bill contains an additional $5 billion for education, health care and job training programs — increases House Republican appropriators hope to match when the final bill emerges.

Rocky Road

Despite the House GOP leadership's best efforts to hold their conservatives and moderates together, the vote margin was so tight that they had to delay final passage by a day. Several Republicans were at home for primary elections June 13, and with just a six-seat House majority, the GOP leadership could not afford to lose anyone.

When the final vote was tallied June 14, seven Republicans voted no — a defection that would have been fatal if three Democrats had not broken with their own party's leaders and voted for it.

Porter also faced repeated challenges from both parties to provide a bigger funding boost for special education under the Individuals with Disabilities Education Act (PL 94-142). The bill calls for a $500 million increase, which is far short of the $2 billion increase the House authorized in May (HR 4055) to relieve what many see as an unfunded mandate on the states.

Democrats said Republicans had boxed themselves in with their budget resolution (H Con Res 290) by dedicating too much money — $150 billion over five years — to tax cuts and not enough for the investments the Labor-HHS bill is supposed to provide.

"It is clear that this bill is going nowhere," David R. Obey of Wisconsin, the ranking Democrat on the Appropriations Committee, said during the June 13 floor debate.

The Senate bill has its own problems. Like the House bill, it faces a White House veto threat. It would spend more on education than the

House, provide a bigger boost for the National Institutes of Health (NIH) and avoid the cuts the House would make in job training programs, but its other cuts and accounting mechanisms have been questioned.

A bipartisan coalition of senators, including Finance Committee Chair William V. Roth, Jr., R-Del. and Sen. Edward M. Kennedy, D-Mass., promised a fight over the bill's proposed cuts in children's health insurance and social services. In a June 16 letter, they called the cuts "incredibly short-sighted" and promised to "exert every effort" to have them removed.

A $500 Million Problem

In one change that could cause trouble for other appropriations bills, the House Labor-HHS bill ended up $500.6 million over its discretionary spending allocation after Tom Coburn, R-Okla., raised a point of order against an emergency spending designation for the Public Health and Social Services Emergency Fund.

Coburn argued that the fund — which is used for a grab bag of spending items that includes bioterrorism research and relief for such diseases as AIDS and hemophilia — has existed for years and is not for emergencies. Had he not prevailed, the spending would have been included in the bill but would not have counted against the spending allocation.

If House appropriators want to keep Coburn and other conservative Republicans happy, they will have to take $500.6 million out of another appropriations bill to avoid violating the overall spending cap. House Appropriations Committee Chairman C.W. Bill Young, R-Fla., tried to trim the Labor-HHS bill by offering an across-the-board cut of 0.6 percent, but his amendment was defeated, 186-236. *(Vote 269, p. H-86)*

While most of the debate focused on education, the House added two health care provisions, including an amendment to limit drug prices — a proposal that could dovetail with the election-year push to make prescription drugs more affordable for senior citizens by adding new coverage under Medicare.

The amendment by Bernard Sanders, I-Vt., approved 313-109, would require drug companies that receive federal support for their research to sell their products at "reasonable" prices. Sanders said the provision is needed to keep pharmaceutical firms from gouging consumers for drugs that have been developed with taxpayer support. *(Vote 268, p. H-86)*

The other health care amendment, offered by Ron Paul, R-Texas, would continue to prohibit the Department of Health and Human Services (HHS) from developing a "unique health identifier" for patients — an identifying code HHS was ordered to develop under the 1996 health insurance portability law (PL 104-191). The amendment was adopted by voice vote. The ban has been included in the last two years' spending bills. *(1998 Almanac, p. 2-64)*

The 1996 law called for HHS to develop identifiers for patients, employers, health plans and health care providers to make it easier to process claims electronically. Since then, privacy advocates have warned that a patient's unique code could also become available to employers, banks and public health officials.

Porter and the GOP leadership found themselves defending social programs such as after-school initiatives, the Job Corps and the Even Start family literacy program as rank-and-file Republicans tried to cut them to pay for bigger special education increases.

Those Republicans, including Bob Schaffer of Colorado and Paul D. Ryan of Wisconsin, said the House should live up to its May commitment to provide more special education funds to help states and school districts shoulder the burden. Porter argued that while special education is a priority, the programs that would have been cut are also important.

Conflicting Priorities

At Porter's urging, the House defeated:

- A Ryan amendment to take $300 million out of after-school programs and give it to special education, 124-293. *(Vote 260, p. H-84)*
- An amendment by Charles Bass, R-N.H., that would have boosted special education funding by $200 million by cutting college preparation programs for low-income students, 98-319. *(Vote 259, p. H-84)*
- An amendment by Gary G. Miller, R-Calif., that would have increased special education funding by $16 million, taking the money from the Ready to Learn television program, which provides educational programming to public television stations, 150-267. *(Vote 261, p. H-84)*
- A Schaffer amendment that would have cut education research by $10.4 million and given it to special education, 132-287. *(Vote 262, p. H-84)*

Republicans who voted against the bill included Constance A. Morella of Maryland, a moderate who was dissatisfied with the bill's social spending levels, and conservatives such as Schaffer, who was disgruntled over the defeat of the special education amendments.

Senate Debate Turns Into Forum For Political Power Plays

JUNE 24 — The Senate turned the fiscal 2001 Labor, Health and Human Services, and Education appropriations bill into a staging ground for the fall elections June 22, as Democrats forced a vote on Medicare prescription drug coverage in retaliation for a GOP amendment that would block new workplace safety rules.

Senate Republicans won the vote on a major GOP priority, pushing through an amendment to the Labor-HHS bill (HR 4577) that would stop the Occupational Safety and Health Administration (OSHA) from finalizing a proposed ergonomics rule that is strongly supported by labor unions. The ergonomics amendment, which is also included in the House version of the bill, was adopted by a 57-41 vote. *(Vote 143, p. S-27)*

The Democrats' amendment to establish a Medicare prescription drug benefit was rejected, 44-53. *(Vote 144, p. S-27)*

Republicans are likely to face more fallout from the votes even though they prevailed on both. The ergonomics rule — which would require some 1.6 million employers to set up programs to prevent repetitive motion injuries — is opposed mainly by business groups, while a Medicare drug benefit is a priority for millions of seniors.

Still, centrists from both parties took Democrats to task for turning a common-ground proposal into another weapon in the ongoing partisan warfare that has dominated Congress this session.

"It is clear from this procedural motion that there is no intention to work together to fashion a bipartisan compromise," Lincoln Chafee of Rhode Island, a cosponsor of the drug plan and one of two Republicans who voted with the Democrats, said in a June 22 statement.

"It's good politics, but it's bad policy," John B. Breaux, D-La., told reporters after the vote.

The dueling votes only added to Republicans' frustration at being forced constantly to vote in fiscal 2001 appropriations bills on what they consider Democratic priorities, including managed care, gun control and hate crimes.

"Really, what the minority is saying is, 'Hey, let's vote on all of our issues, but let's not vote on anything that's relevant,' " Assistant Majority Leader Don Nickles, R-Okla., said early in the debate when Democrats threatened to filibuster the ergonomics amendment.

Power Struggle

Both proposals vividly illustrate the legislative dynamics of a presidential election year. The prescription drug amendment offered a test vote on the critical issue in the Senate, where Republicans are less anxious to pass legislation than their politically endangered counterparts in the House. The ergonomics amendment deals more with who will control the White House in 2001.

Democrats and other supporters of the ergonomics rule — a coalition of labor unions, public health officials and women's groups — want the final rule to come out before President Clinton leaves office. They say opponents of the proposed rule are counting on Texas Gov. George W. Bush, the likely GOP nominee, to win the White House and are trying to stall the rule until he can take office and scrap it.

"Their strategy is clearly to delay it. Our goal is to get workers protected," Peg Seminario, director of safety and health at the AFL-CIO, the nation's largest labor organization, said in a June 22 interview.

Republicans say OSHA rushed to put out the final rule without giving enough consideration to its costs.

The agency estimates that the rule would cost employers $4.2 billion a year, but Nickles cited a Small Business Administration estimate that it would cost $40 billion to $60 billion annually. His office also distributed a four-page summary of various employers' cost estimates compiled by the U.S. Chamber of Commerce.

Republican Michael B. Enzi of Wyoming said OSHA seemed to be "blinded by the drive to get this rule done during this administration." Added Nickles: "Maybe we should let the next administration deal with it."

Overshadowed by the showdowns over the drug benefit and ergonomics amendments were the issues that are expected to define the Senate Labor-HHS debate when it resumes the week of June 26.

Democrats are planning to use the $352.2 billion bill as a vehicle for many of the education proposals they tried to advance during the aborted Senate debate on a bill (S 2) to reauthorize the 1965 Elementary and Secondary Education Act.

Majority Leader Trent Lott, R-Miss., pulled the bill from the floor in early May under the threat of a Democratic gun control amendment, and it has not reappeared.

The main Democratic proposals will include an amendment by Patty Murray, D-Wash., that would guarantee $1.8 billion for a third year of Clinton's initiative to reduce class sizes in the early grades by hiring 100,000 new teachers, and an amendment by Tom Harkin, D-Iowa, and Charles S. Robb, D-Va., that would dedicate $1.3 billion to grants and loans for emergency school repairs.

The Senate Labor-HHS bill includes $1.4 billion for class size reduction and $1.3 billion for school modernization, but they would be part of a block grant and could be spent on other things.

Clinton has threatened to veto the bill — partly because it does not dedicate funds specifically to smaller class sizes and school repairs, and partly because he believes it shortchanges health care and job training priorities.

Resolving Controversies

The biggest controversies on health care and social spending, however, may be resolved without a fight. Finance Committee Chairman William V. Roth Jr., R-Del., said June 22 that he had secured an agreement from Appropriations Committee Chairman Ted Stevens, R-Alaska, to eliminate the Senate bill's funding cuts for children's health insurance, welfare programs and social services when the bill goes to conference with the House.

Roth had been prepared to raise a point of order against a provision that would make $1.9 billion in federal funds for the State Children's Health Insurance Program unavailable until fiscal 2003. In a June 16 letter, Roth, Edward M. Kennedy, D-Mass., and several other senators said such a move would disrupt the momentum states have built up in their efforts to provide health coverage to the nation's 11 million uninsured children.

In addition, senators from both parties were prepared to fight a proposed $240 million cut in Temporary Assistance for Needy Families and a nearly $1.2 billion reduction in the Title XX Social Services Block Grant, which helps states pay for such programs as day care and services for people with disabilities.

Forcing a Vote

The prescription drug vote was the end result of a complicated series of procedural maneuvers that both parties employed to yank the debate back and forth between Medicare and the ergonomics rule.

Enzi proposed an amendment that would prevent OSHA from putting out a final rule by the end of the year, and Tim Hutchinson, R-Ark., immediately followed with a virtually identical second-degree amendment. The idea was to fill up the "amendment tree" with ergonomics measures so Democrats could not bring up their own amendments.

They missed a branch, allowing Robb to file a rarely used "motion to commit" that would have sent the bill back to the Appropriations Committee with instructions to add a Medicare prescription drug benefit for all seniors. Minority Whip Harry Reid, D-Nev., then filed a cloture motion to force a vote on Robb's motion.

The prescription drug amendment Robb proposed was a modified version of a bill unveiled two days earlier by Bob Graham, D-Fla., Chafee and several moderate Democrats.

The measure — which Graham called "a life-and-blood issue for millions of Americans" — would have created a voluntary prescription drug benefit under Medicare that would give the most generous coverage to seniors with the greatest health care needs. Democrats estimated that it would have cost $50 billion over five years and $240 billion over 10 years.

To win the support of Minority Leader Tom Daschle of South Dakota and other Democrats, Robb dropped a provision that would have added a means test to make wealthy seniors pay a greater share of the cost of their coverage.

Lott tried to turn the subject back to OSHA by filing the ergonomics amendment as both first-degree and second-degree amendments to Robb's motion and suggested that he would attempt to table it. Eventually, however, Lott and Daschle agreed to have a straight, up-or-down vote on both the ergonomics and drug amendments and be done with them.

Once that happened, the prescription drug debate was brief, taking on the air of a not-quite-ready opening act. Robb insisted that "we need to act on prescription drugs now; we need to do it in a bipartisan way, and this is the way."

Republicans said they had barely had time to read the amendment and that Congress should not enact such a potentially costly program so quickly.

"We shouldn't use our procedures and our processes in this perverted way," said Budget Committee Chairman Pete V. Domenici, R-N.M.

Senate Passes Labor-HHS Bill With Grab Bag Of Provisions

JULY 1 — The Senate passed the fiscal 2001 Labor, Health and Human Services (HHS), and Education appropriations bill relatively early this year, just as the Republican leadership had promised. By most accounts, however, the $354.6 billion measure is a mess. It is laden with an entire managed-care overhaul bill, not to mention competing provisions on a Medicare "lockbox" and genetic testing.

The measure (HR 4577), passed June 30 by a 52-43 vote, would spend about 8 percent more than the fiscal 2000 bill, according to Labor-HHS Appropriations Subcommittee Chairman Arlen Specter, R-Pa. That alone could be too large an increase for conservatives to swallow when the bill goes to conference with the House, although the leadership has hinted that it might try to tap the nation's record budget surplus for more money. *(Vote 171, p. S-31)*

"We are seeing spending increases at levels that have not been approached since Lyndon Johnson was president of the United States," Phil Gramm, R-Texas, complained during debate June 28.

Nobody expects the Labor-HHS bill to go smoothly — it is the stage for the big education, health care and social spending battles every lawmaker fights during an election year. It is unusual, however, when the political point-scoring veers out of control as badly as it did this year.

Republicans — anxious for political ammunition in the fall campaigns — attached a 223-page managed-care plan that contains everything they have produced in a House-Senate conference that is struggling to find a compromise on separate overhaul legislation (HR 2990).

Rival 'Lockbox' Provisions

There are also similar Medicare "lockbox" provisions — one by Democrats, adopted 60-37, and one by Republicans, adopted 54-43 — that would take the Medicare trust fund surplus out of the federal budget to ensure it is only spent on medical care for the elderly. *(Votes 162, 163, p. S-30)*

The clutter and political maneuvering enveloping the Senate debate — which lasted seven days — means lawmakers will have a hard time focusing on spending priorities for education, health care and job training as they prepare for the conference that will try to produce a bill that can satisfy both chambers.

It will not be easy. Just like the bill that squeaked through the House on June 14, the Senate Labor-HHS bill became a vehicle for Democratic arguments that Republicans would not spend enough money on education — the top concern of most Americans — and too much on tax cuts. Both bills face a Clinton veto threat, largely because they do not include the education spending proposals he and congressional Democrats have been pushing.

"I think most of us on this side of the aisle believe that [education] is a higher priority than having a tax cut," said Edward M. Kennedy, D-Mass., who was a thorn in Republicans' side throughout the education debate.

Republicans responded that they had included several spending increases for federal aid for special education, Pell grants to help low-income students go to college and block grants that states can spend on anything from school repairs to hiring more teachers.

"Whatever the amount of money we put in, somebody is going to offer an amendment for more money," said Specter.

Gramm nearly derailed the bill by raising a budgetary point of order against what he called a "phony pay shift" that would have saved $2.4 billion by sending out Supplemental Security Income checks on Sept. 29 rather than Oct. 2 — moving the expense from fiscal 2001 to fiscal 2000. Anxious to pass the measure before the July Fourth recess, Majority Leader Trent Lott, R-Miss., decided to accept Gramm's point of order, which adds $2.4 billion to the Senate measure.

That means appropriators will either have to scale back the entire Senate Labor-HHS bill by $2.4 billion when it gets to conference, in order to bring it back down to its spending allocation, or take $2.4 billion out of another spending bill to stay within the overall allocation for the 13 fiscal 2001 appropriations bills.

The Next Round

The Gramm episode illustrates the balancing act Republican appropriators will face when they take the House and Senate Labor-HHS bills into conference. Spend too little, and they face a veto from Clinton, who wants $106.1 billion in discretionary spending. Spend too much, and the conference report might be rejected by the House because conservative Republicans would not support it.

"You've got to ask yourself where the votes are coming from," John Edward Porter, R-Ill., chairman of the House Labor-HHS Appropriations Subcommittee, said in a June 28 interview. Before the conferees can do any work, he said, House and Senate GOP leaders will have to decide what the spending target is — and that means deciding whether they will rely on Republican votes or try to win votes from both parties.

The leadership will also have to decide whether to invite the Clinton administration into the negotiations soon and work out a compromise bill that can be signed into law, or take a veto and work out a deal later in the year.

Specter and House Appropriations Committee Chairman C.W. Bill Young, R-Fla., did not sound eager to bring in the administration. "The last time I read the Constitution, the Congress has the appropriations responsibility," Specter said on the Senate floor June 28.

Porter took a different view. "You have to ask yourself," he said, "if there's any point in sending up a bill that's going to be vetoed."

Finding more money may not be a problem if GOP leaders decide they want it. New estimates from the Office of Management and Budget put the on-budget surplus for fiscal 2001 at $79 billion. Young said in a June 27 interview that the leadership might decide to make some of that money available for the Labor-HHS bill when it goes to conference.

The budget caps in the 1997 Balanced Budget Act (PL 105-33) may not be a problem either. The conference report on the fiscal 2001 military construction spending bill (HR 4425) includes a provision that — while not technically removing the caps — would allow appropriators to spend beyond them. *(1997 Almanac, p. 2-47)*

That is how conferees may solve a problem that has dogged the Senate bill all along: opposition from some in both parties to the bill's deferral of $1.9 billion from the State Children's Health Insurance Program. Opponents say the money is supposed to be redistributed to high-need states, not taken away. Critics also target cuts of $1.2 billion from the Social Services Block Grant and $240 million from Temporary Assistance for Needy Families until 2003.

Senate Appropriations Committee Chairman Ted Stevens, R-Alaska, said June 27 that those deferrals and cuts never were intended to become law but were included to keep the bill within its allocation until appropriators were free to spend more. "Everybody knew what we were doing," he told reporters.

The Education Debate

The Democrats resurrected most of the education proposals they had planned to offer in May during the aborted debate over a Republican bill (S 2) that would have reauthorized the 1965 Elementary and Secondary Education Act.

With that bill apparently dead in the water, Democrats shifted their attention to the Labor-HHS measure. "This may be our only chance to do something about it," said Christopher J. Dodd, D-Conn., during a debate over funding for after-school programs. Specter replied that the bill already did the best it could for education with the money available to the committee.

The Senate defeated most of the Democratic education amendments by refusing to waive the congressional budget act (PL 93-344), which bans any spending that exceeds a committee's discretionary spending allocation. The Democrats would have needed 60 votes to waive the act.

The casualties included:

- An amendment by Patty Murray, D-Wash., that would have guaranteed $1.8 billion for a third year of funding to reduce class sizes in the early grades by hiring 100,000 new teachers, defeated 44-55. *(Vote 148, p. S-28)*
- An amendment by Jeff Bingaman, D-N.M., that would have dedicated $250 million to programs that help turn around failing schools, defeated 49-50. *(Vote 147, p. S-28)*
- A Kennedy amendment that would have given an extra $202 million to grants for teacher training and recruitment, defeated 51-48. *(Vote 153, p. S-29)*
- An amendment offered by Dodd that would have guaranteed an additional $400 million for after-school programs to reduce crime among youths, defeated 48-51. *(Vote 154, p. S-29)*

The Senate did approve by voice vote an amendment by George V. Voinovich, R-Ohio, that would allow states to defray their special education costs by spending funds from a $2.7 billion block grant originally intended for school construction and class-size reduction on special-needs students.

House Republicans, meanwhile, are sensing political power in the school construction issue and have readied their own proposal to take into negotiations with Clinton.

The bill (HR 4766), introduced June 27 by Education and the Workforce Committee Chairman Bill Goodling, R-Pa., a former school superintendent, would authorize $1.5 billion per year for five years to help states meet such federally mandated school modernization costs as modifying facilities to meet the needs of students with disabilities.

Johnny Isakson, R-Ga., one of the bill's authors, said such a limited approach to school modernization makes more sense than the Democratic proposals because it would help states cover specific costs — those that are required by federal laws — without raising false expectations that the federal government is ready to take on all of the nation's school construction needs.

GOP Conferees Agree to Spending Levels, But Will Contest Priorities

JULY 29 — Republicans have decided not to fight President Clinton over how much money to spend on education and health care, but they are ready to battle over how to spend it.

Even as they announced a deal July 28 on a compromise Labor, Health and Human Services and Education appropriations bill for fiscal 2001, GOP lawmakers braced for another end-of-year showdown with Clinton — not just over differing spending priorities, but over deep policy differences on educating children and protecting workers.

GOP members of the conference committee gave Clinton all the money he asked for — $106.2 billion in discretionary spending on education, health care and job training programs.

That is about $6 billion more than the House version of the bill (HR 4577).

Republicans believe their decision effectively takes away Clinton's ability to argue that they do not spend enough on the nation's domestic priorities.

"I think we can carry this bill in a national debate with the president," Sen. Arlen Specter, R-Pa., the conference committee chairman, said at a July 28 press conference. "We think we have the high ground."

The conferees did not put the money in the places Clinton wanted, however, and the policy differences between Republicans and the White House may actually have gotten worse. The agreement does not dedicate funding to school repairs and reducing public school class sizes in the way Clinton wants; moreover, it would pick a new fight by exempting construction contractors from paying a region's "prevailing wage," as required under the Davis-Bacon Act, for school construction.

The disagreements mean that the conference report, which will not be filed until Congress returns in September, may become exactly what Republicans had hoped to avoid: a prelude to yet another round of last-minute, post-veto negotiations with Clinton.

Any possibility of a bipartisan compromise broke down when Republicans, angered by a 19-page list of policy requests from the White House and claiming that top administration officials had refused to meet with them, decided to reach an agreement among themselves.

David R. Obey of Wisconsin, the top Democrat on the House Appropriations Committee, declared the exercise a waste of time. Even Sen. Tom Harkin, D-Iowa, who worked with Specter throughout the process and downplayed their disagreements, declined to sign the conference report.

"I cannot support the bill that came out of conference yesterday and the president would not sign this bill," Harkin said at the press conference with Specter.

Still, Harkin said the two sides have "narrowed our differences." Both he and Specter promised to keep working to satisfy both sides when they cut the real deal this fall.

One factor that may be complicating GOP efforts to reach out to Harkin is public speculation that Vice President Al Gore, the presumptive Democratic presidential nominee, may tap him as his running mate.

Closing the Gaps

A look at the outstanding issues shows why the coming fight will be about more than just spending.

• **Education.** Clinton and the Democrats have been pushing for $1.3 billion in guaranteed funding for emergency school repairs and $1.8 billion for a third year of funding for Clinton's seven-year program to hire 100,000 teachers and reduce class sizes in the early grades.

Instead, the conference agreement takes the approach used in the Senate bill: It would provide $1.3 billion for school repairs and $1.4 billion for class size reduction through block grants that states could spend on other things if they believe their needs lie elsewhere.

The administration rejected that approach in a July 17 memo by Office of Management and Budget Director Jack Lew. Even so, the decision at least to make the money available was a concession by House Republicans.

To get the House to agree, Specter accepted the Davis-Bacon rider by Rep. Roger Wicker, R-Miss. Harkin, who opposed the rider, said it was "unacceptable" to Clinton and senators.

• **Health care research.** In one difference Specter hopes to highlight, the conference agreement includes a $2.7 billion increase for the National Institutes of Health, a boost that would keep Congress on track toward Specter and Harkin's goal of doubling NIH's fiscal 1998 budget by 2003. Clinton, who does not share that goal, proposed a $1 billion increase. Specter, however, said biomedical research that can lead to new cures and preventions for diseases is a higher priority than many of Clinton's other proposed spending increases.

"If the president wants to have his programs and cut NIH, let him say so," Specter said.

• **Ergonomics.** The agreement includes a rider that was in both the House and Senate bills to block a proposed Occupational Safety and Health Administration rule requiring employers to set up repetitive-motion injury prevention programs. In a July 21 letter to Speaker J. Dennis Hastert, R-Ill., White House Chief of Staff John Podesta said the bill must be rid of such "objectionable legislative riders" to be signed.

• **Managed care.** The conferees rejected the administration's request to use the Labor-HHS bill as a vehicle to work out a managed care overhaul agreement. They dropped an amendment attached to the Senate bill that included tentative agreements by GOP conferees who have been working on stalled managed care legislation (HR 2990).

"It seems to us we've been talking about this for weeks and months. We know what the issues are," White House health policy adviser Chris Jennings said July 24. Specter said appropriators did not have authority to work out such an agreement.

Tempers Flare as Democrats Push For More Education Funding

OCTOBER 21 — Always the most difficult spending measure to complete, the fiscal 2001 Labor, Health and Human Services, and Education appropriations bill is struggling under the weight of the high-volume election-year battle over education — a conflict neither party is trying especially hard to resolve.

Republicans say the Labor-HHS bill (HR 4577) is already at President Clinton's proposed discretionary spending level of $106.2 billion. That figure does not count advance appropriations for special education and other school programs. When they are added, the Congressional Budget Office says the total discretionary spending level is actually $108.9 billion.

The bill is likely to grow even fatter. Clinton and congressional Democrats have their sights set on adding another $4.9 billion to the bill — including $3 billion for the Department of Education — and are waging a public-relations war against Republicans every day the money is not added. House Republicans already have offered to add $3.2 billion, a figure Democrats have rejected as inadequate.

"Republicans like to say we should

leave no child behind," Senate Minority Leader Tom Daschle, D-S.D., said at an Oct. 19 Democratic rally with Clinton, quoting a favorite catchphrase of GOP presidential nominee Texas Gov. George W. Bush. "The truth is, under their tax cuts, they'll leave no tycoon behind."

The crucial showdown is likely to come the week of Oct. 23. The current continuing resolution will expire Oct. 25, and Clinton vowed Oct. 19 not to sign any more that last longer than a day. That threat could give the Republican leadership an incentive to get more involved in talks between the appropriators and the White House budget team when they resume Oct. 23.

For now, however, Clinton's statement has irked Republican appropriators, who say Clinton and congressional Democrats have been unwilling to budge until they get everything they want. "The president of the United States just came here and demanded 100 percent of what he asked for, but we don't know what it is," fumed Senate Appropriations Committee Chairman Ted Stevens, R-Alaska.

White House officials and Democrats have reduced their spending requests, but only slightly. Early in the week, they were demanding $6 billion in additional spending — a combination of administration and congressional requests. By Oct. 19, they had reduced their price to $4.9 billion.

Specter's Last Stand?

The low point of the week came Oct. 19 when Arlen Specter, R-Pa., chairman of the Senate Labor-HHS Appropriations Subcommittee, received the new offer from the White House budget team and Democratic appropriators. Specter told them he would not add any more money to the bill or change the bill's language on school construction and class size reduction, the two biggest education flashpoints.

At that point, tempers flared. David R. Obey of Wisconsin, the ranking Democrat on the House Appropriations Committee, said he asked to talk to "someone who can make some constructive decisions before New Year's."

The bad feelings spilled into the hallway outside the meeting room, as Specter asked Obey, in front of a dozen reporters, if he would be available to meet again Oct. 20. "With you? What good does it do to meet with you?" Obey shot back and stormed off.

"We're prepared to bargain. We need someone to bargain with," Office of Management and Budget Director Jack Lew told reporters.

The bitter session highlighted a split within the Republican ranks. Unlike House GOP appropriators, Specter wants the $106.2 billion report that conferees agreed to in July but did not file to be the final offer.

He says Clinton has gained too much power since the 1995-96 government shutdown and that Congress needs to return to the constitutional role of writing its own spending bills. *(1995 Almanac p. 2-3; 1996 Almanac, p. 2-3)*

"We ought not to cave in to the president," Specter told reporters Oct. 17. "We've met his spending figure. We have different priorities, and we ought to stick by them."

It is not clear whether Specter is on the same page as Stevens, who has resisted the idea of sending the current bill to Clinton and letting him veto it.

The issue is not just how much money is in the bill. Negotiators must also decide whether Clinton and the Democrats get the dedicated money they want for such programs as school construction and class size reduction or, as Republicans insist, states and school districts are given the freedom to spend the money on other things if they have more pressing needs.

The bill includes $1.3 billion in funding for emergency school repairs, as Democrats have requested, and $1.4 billion to fund a third year of Clinton's initiative to hire 100,000 new teachers — slightly short of the $1.75 billion Clinton is seeking. Before Democrats agree to those levels, they want more ironclad language guaranteeing that the money will be spent only for those purposes.

Although the two parties have compromised on the class size dispute twice before, the inevitable compromise is taking longer to materialize this year. Tom Harkin of Iowa, the ranking Democrat on the Senate Labor-HHS Appropriations Subcommittee, said Specter rejected language similar to last year's compromise, which allowed 25 percent of class size reduction funds to be spent on testing and professional development for current teachers rather than for hiring new ones.

Stalled Measure Appears Likely Candidate for Omnibus Package

NOVEMBER 4 — The fiscal 2001 appropriations bill for the departments of Labor, Health and Human Services, and Education — the largest domestic spending bill — is shaping up as the likely omnibus package that will not only pull dozens of other bills, but could also rescue several other major year-end legislative packages from presidential vetoes by including language to fix their problems.

The troubled Labor-HHS bill (HR 4577), stalled by disputes over hot-button education issues, has become the last spending bill to be resolved by Republicans and the White House. As such, the Clinton administration and Democrats are eyeing it as a vehicle to resurrect other legislative priorities, including the centerpiece of their education agenda: tax credits to help states build new schools.

"This issue is at the heart of what's different between us and the Republicans in this budget battle," House Minority Leader Richard A. Gephardt, D-Mo., told reporters Oct. 27.

Republicans agree but say the real issue is flexibility. "We simply want to help schools get the money they need to improve education without so many Washington strings," House Speaker J. Dennis Hastert, R-Ill., said at an Oct. 24 news conference.

That is not the only legislation whose fate hinges on a successful Labor-HHS bill, however. Democrats want to add immigration policy changes that were not included in the Commerce-Justice-State spending bill (HR 4942), which faces a veto threat from President Clinton.

Then there is the annual clamor for last-minute additions to the final legislative train. Appropriators had to sift through a list of 221 proposals that lawmakers from both parties wanted to add to Labor-HHS. Most were projects for individual states and districts, but there were also more substantial measures, including a ban on Internet gambling and policy changes to help more rural hospitals receive higher Medicaid payments.

The prospect of a major omnibus package built around Labor-HHS is "not out of the realm of possibility," Senate Minority Leader Tom Daschle, D-S.D., said Oct. 27.

Before that happens, the underlying Labor-HHS bill must be massaged into a version that Clinton will sign. Those negotiations dragged on at a painfully slow pace the week of Oct. 23, as White House and Republican negotiators argued over education policies and how much money to add to the bill's $108.9 billion in discretionary spending.

By the weekend, they had made some progress. The negotiators reached a tentative agreement on new money for the bill Oct. 27; the total amount will depend on official cost estimates for the policies, but will likely fall in a range between $4.3 billion and $4.5 billion in additional spending, based on the offers Republicans and Democrats traded during the day.

Meanwhile, House Education and the Workforce Committee Chairman Bill Goodling, R-Pa., worked out a tentative agreement with appropriators that basically would repeat last year's compromise on class size reduction. The Labor-HHS bill would set aside about $1.4 billion to reduce class sizes in the early grades by hiring new teachers, but would allow states to spend 25 percent of the money on professional development.

The budget negotiators still were discussing such questions as whether to target $1.3 billion for emergency school repairs or leave the decision to the states. And they must decide whether to eliminate a Republican-backed provision, opposed by the White House, that would delay the Occupational Safety and Health Administration from issuing a final ergonomics rule requiring businesses to set up programs to prevent repetitive-motion injuries.

The School Construction Battle

The school construction issue may be the biggest obstacle of all. Because of it, the fate of the Labor-HHS bill has become entwined with a massive GOP tax package (HR 2614) that Clinton has threatened to veto.

The two sides were deadlocked over the issue of tax credits for school construction bonds and whether they should be part of the spending bill or the tax package. The school construction fight is being driven by political philosophy — Republicans would give states more flexibility in spending bond proceeds than Democrats — and by the conflicting priorities of strong lobbying groups. Business and construction groups are backing the GOP approach, while labor unions are supporting the Democrats.

The Republican proposal, now part of the tax bill, would allow as much as $5 billion a year in bonds to be issued from fiscal 2001 through 2003 for school construction. Democrats prefer a bill (HR 4094) by Charles B. Rangel of New York, ranking Democrat on the Ways and Means Committee, and Nancy L. Johnson, R-Conn., that would issue tax credits to pay the interest on $24.8 billion in school modernization bonds over two years.

The National Center for Education Statistics estimates that states need to spend some $127 billion to bring crumbling and overcrowded schools into decent condition.

Republicans tacked their bond language onto the conference report of the tax bill, arguing that Labor-HHS was an inappropriate vehicle for a tax-based school construction measure, and let it ride on the fortunes of the broader tax package. Although the package was adopted by the House 237-174 and drew 33 Democratic votes, it was an easy vote for those Democrats to cast because President Clinton had already threatened to veto it. *(Vote 555, p. H-176)*

"The bipartisan Rangel-Johnson proposal . . . is, quite frankly, the very least we should do, given the magnitude of this problem," Clinton said in an Oct. 26 letter to Senate Majority Leader Trent Lott, R-Miss.

It was unclear whether Republicans would agree to add school construction language to the Labor-HHS bill, but Lott said Oct. 27 he might agree to remove it from the tax bill to satisfy Clinton's objections.

In essence, Republicans offered to spend the same amount of money as Clinton, but on different and more flexible school construction initiatives. Democrats said the GOP language would create about a third as much school construction for the same amount of money.

None of the Republican proposals would require construction contractors working on bond-financed projects to pay the local "prevailing wage" mandated by the Davis-Bacon Act of 1931. The Rangel-Johnson bill would apply the Davis-Bacon requirements — a feature that has infuriated business and construction groups but has won the crucial backing of organized labor.

Building Schools

The two school construction proposals have major differences, but they are not totally incompatible. Part of the Republican proposal would expand a mechanism called Qualified Zone Academy Bonds, created under the 1997 tax relief law (PL 105-34), which states can issue for school renovations and other purposes in impoverished areas where businesses have promised to contribute to the schools. Rangel says his bill is similar to that approach. *(1997 Almanac, p. 2-39)*

Republicans also would allow up to $5 billion a year in bonds to be issued over the next three years for public school construction.

Other provisions, however, are more problematic. Republicans would allow school districts to take four years, rather than two years, to spend bond proceeds for school construction. Clinton said the so-called "arbitrage" provision "encourages delay in urgently needed school construction and would disproportionately help wealthy school districts."

With school construction, much of the fight is about whether the proposal will apply the Davis-Bacon "prevailing wage" requirement. Business groups and building contractors do not want Republicans to write a proposal with Davis-Bacon language — which usually means union-scale wages — and the unions are equally determined not to let the Democrats write one without it.

Republican leaders are well aware of the lobbying battle over "prevailing wages." When Hastert announced the GOP school construction offer, he promised Republicans would handle the issue "in a way that keeps Washington mandates from adding on unnecessary costs to this construction" — a thinly veiled slap at Davis-Bacon.

The Associated Builders and Contractors, a group that primarily represents nonresidential construction contractors and heads the Coalition to Repeal Davis-Bacon, has been arguing that it inflates public construction costs by an average of 15 percent.

"Our members don't want a new federal program for school construction, and they particularly don't want it when there's new mandates that would inflate the project costs and hurt school construction efforts," Jennifer Boucher Jameson, the group's director of legislative affairs, said Oct. 24.

Labor unions, however, say any school construction program that does not apply Davis-Bacon could weaken local wages.

In an Oct. 24 statement supporting the Johnson-Rangel bill, AFL-CIO President John J. Sweeney said that proposal should become law in part because it would "ensure that workers on federally funded school facilities projects are paid local prevailing wages, so that this construction does not undermine community wage standards."

The ergonomics fight, meanwhile, has been going on since the early 1990s. Labor groups have pushed for regulation to reduce the growing number of repetitive-motion injuries, while business groups have questioned whether enough scientific evidence exists to establish a link between job conditions and workplace injuries.

Most of the arguments made by business groups such as the U.S. Chamber of Commerce end up in the GOP talking points as well. They say the ergonomics rule is vague, would be nearly impossible to comply with and would give OSHA inspectors ample opportunities to slap expensive fines on well-meaning employers.

Labor officials, however, say workers need the protection and that businesses are simply trying to stall the rule in the hope that Republican Texas Gov. George W. Bush will win the presidential election and kill it.

Dispute Over Labor Standard Could Imperil Education Funds

NOVEMBER 4 — Thanks to a fat budget surplus and election-year pressures, the emerging fiscal 2001 Labor, Health and Human Services, and Education appropriations bill (HR 4577) could produce the biggest funding increase the Department of Education has ever received.

The $7.5 billion increase will only happen, however, if the bill is not rewritten in the aftermath of the pre-election war that broke out between Republicans and President Clinton shortly after an agreement was hammered out in the early morning hours Oct. 30.

Less than a day after the deal was reached, House Republican leaders rejected a proposed compromise on a controversial ergonomics rider, and Clinton and Democrats accused them of reneging on the agreement. The bill also could get bogged down by such issues as school construction tax credits and amnesty for illegal immigrants.

"We'll negotiate, but we're not going to capitulate," Senate Majority Leader Trent Lott, R-Miss., told reporters Oct. 31. "There are some principles that we're just not going to give up on."

The biggest unknown is whether the massive education increase will survive in a lame-duck session. That uncertainty is adding fuel to last-minute Democratic attacks as they try to raise fears among voters that Republicans will undo the spending increases after the elections. That charge began to gain credence as House GOP leaders grew increasingly reluctant at week's end to rule out such a move. Education groups, meanwhile, plan to step up their lobbying efforts in the days ahead to make sure their gains do not evaporate.

Will It Last?

Clinton and Democrats wasted no time playing up the idea that the GOP will try to cut the education spending increase back after the election because conservatives will not back the agreement.

"Unless we keep fighting, there will be no funds for school construction, no more progress toward cutting class size by hiring 100,000 new qualified teachers, no new investment in teacher quality," Clinton said at a Nov. 2 press conference.

David R. Obey of Wisconsin, the ranking Democrat on the House Appropriations Committee, told reporters Nov. 2 he expected members of the House GOP Conservative Action Team to demand "major surgery" on the bill and suggested they did not want to vote before the election because they wanted to avoid an embarrassing fight.

Majority Whip Tom DeLay, R-Texas, one of the bill's most vocal critics, would not rule out changes to the spending levels after the elections.

"This bill never closed. . . . That was not an agreement made by leadership," he told reporters Nov. 2. The lame-duck session, he said, "unravels everything."

House Speaker J. Dennis Hastert, R-Ill., appeared to be wavering under pressure from GOP conservatives. On Nov. 1, he told reporters it is "not my intention" to try to reduce the education spending levels after the elections. By Nov. 3, however, he had opened the door a little wider. "I don't really see changing much in that bill," Hastert told reporters, but "it'll be after the election and I can't promise that nothing will happen."

Tom Coburn, R-Okla., a Conservative Action Team member, said in a Nov. 2 interview that he would not vote for the bill as proposed because "it spends too much in all the wrong places." As a group, however, he said the CATs probably could not defeat the bill at its current spending levels because the leadership will "twist enough arms."

The Numbers

If the tentative agreement on the core of the bill holds, Congress would pump up the Department of Education's budget by $7.5 billion, a 21 percent increase over last year. That would be the largest rise in funding since the department was created in 1979, easily surpassing the $3.6 billion increase in the fiscal 1997 Labor-HHS bill. That

Deal Falls Through on Ergonomics Rules

NOVEMBER 4 — A long struggle between business and labor over Washington's role in preventing repetitive stress injuries is nearing what may be its ultimate climax — but not until after Election Day. In the campaign's closing hours, both sides are using the issue as part of their elaborate and well-financed drives to get their voters to the polls.

The fight over the proposed federal regulation of ergonomics, while invisible to most voters, is so important to corporate America and congressional Republicans, on one side, and the unions and Democrats on the other, that the long-running standoff is a main reason the 106th Congress will be reconvening the week of Nov. 13 for a lame-duck session.

Since the Bush administration, the Occupational Safety and Health Administration (OSHA) has been at work on regulations to limit injuries or disabilities from performing repetitive tasks. Earlier attempts by the Clinton administration to finalize the rules were blocked by the GOP majority in Congress, but the Republicans have so far been unable to stop the proposed rules OSHA published last November.

They would require that 1.6 million employers set up programs to limit the repetitive motion injuries of about 27 million workers — from airport cargo handlers to automobile assembly line workers, and from grocery checkout clerks to textile mill weavers. Another 300,000 businesses each year would have to act the first time a worker suffered a job-related repetitive stress disorder that required medical treatment, reassignment to light duty or time off.

If the Republicans are unable to stop OSHA this fall, the agency will be able to follow through on its plans to finalize the rules by the end of the year. They could be halted or even repealed in the future, but that is seen by the Republicans and their business allies as a far more politically difficult task. Suing in federal court is another option.

"This is the first year the regulation has actually been out, and people are taking a look at it and saying, 'Wow, this thing is bad, and it's coming down on us like a 100-ton locomotive,' " Randel Johnson, vice president for labor and employee benefits for the U.S. Chamber of Commerce, said in an interview Nov. 2.

Chamber members are a mainstay of the Business-Industry Political Action Committee (BIPAC), which is working with employers and local chambers of commerce to encourage their loyalists to go to the polls on Nov. 7 in a bid to counterbalance the AFL-CIO get-out-the-vote effort. The National Association of Manufacturers, another BIPAC member, has been running radio advertising in some pivotal House districts warning that the new rules would lead to layoffs.

The stakes are high for both sides, not only for energizing core voters but in the costs of doing business.

Business groups say the pending rules' breadth and vagueness would drive up their cost of compliance — their estimates range from $14 billion to $80 billion a year — and would wrongly cut into business productivity and profitability. OSHA and Labor Department officials, meanwhile, say the rule is intended to be flexible and would not require most companies to act. While costing employers $4.2 billion annually, they say, the rule would also save them $9 billion a year in lost productivity. This is the argument embraced by labor as well.

Failed Deal With White House

At 1:30 a.m. Oct. 30, appropriators and White House negotiators sealed a deal on ergonomics that they thought settled one of the last remaining disputes on the fiscal 2001 appropriations bill (HR 4577) for the departments of Labor, Health and Human Services, and Education — itself one of the last remaining bills in dispute for the year.

Under the deal, OSHA would have been allowed to issue its final rule on schedule, but the next president would have had the option until June 1 of stopping the rule from taking effect.

By the end of the day, House Republican leaders had spiked the deal, arguing that the legislative language — which was drafted by the Office of Management and Budget — would not accomplish the intended goal, because federal health and safety rules are more bureaucratically difficult to stop. David R. Obey of Wisconsin, the ranking Democrat on the House Appropriations Committee, countered that no legislative drafting error had occurred and charged that the GOP leaders' true motivation was to spare their nominee, Gov. George W. Bush of Texas, the potential pain of crossing organized labor early in his administration. (Vice President Al Gore, the Democratic nominee, supports OSHA's rule.) House Majority Whip Tom DeLay, R-Texas, denied Obey's contention.

The contretemps soon made its way into campaign speeches."We thought we had a good faith agreement with honorable compromises on both sides," President Clinton said as he left the White House on Oct. 31 to stump in Louisville. "That was before the special interests weighed in with the Republican leadership, and when they did, the Republican leadership killed the education bill."

House Speaker J. Dennis Hastert, R-Ill, retorted: "The president blames our interest groups. The president clearly is playing to his special interests, and that's the labor unions."

No matter which side is to blame, said Peg Seminario, the AFL-CIO's director of occupational safety and health programs: "The one thing that won't change is that there are hundreds of thousands of workers being hurt every year."

increase also came during an election year. *(1996 Almanac, p. 10-59)*

The new proposal, which would bring the Department of Education's discretionary funding up to about $43 billion, is the highlight of the Labor-HHS deal that congressional appropriators and the White House budget team thought they had worked out.

Negotiators agreed to add approximately $4.4 billion to the bill, bringing the discretionary spending total to about $113.8 billion. The fiscal 2000 bill contained approximately $97.2 billion in discretionary spending.

"This definitely shows a stronger commitment to education than we've ever seen," Edward R. Kealy, executive director of the Committee for Education Funding, a coalition of education groups that lobby for higher federal spending, said in an Oct. 30 interview.

The White House and congressional negotiators settled several funding questions — agreeing to provide $1.75 billion for class size reduction, the amount Clinton wanted — and other policy disputes.

In a compromise on school modernization, $1.3 billion would be dedicated to emergency school repairs, as Clinton asked, but school districts could spend 25 percent of it on special education or school technology, as Republicans wanted.

Among the other highlights:

• A $1.6 billion increase for special education funds under the Individuals with Disabilities Education Act (IDEA) (PL 94-142). Republicans had proposed a $1.3 billion increase in July.

The increase still falls short of the $2 billion that Republicans and some Democrats wanted in order to "fully fund" IDEA to reimburse 40 percent of states' and school districts' special education expenses within 10 years. Currently, the federal government only matches 12 percent of their expenses; Democrats say this year's extra money would raise that to 15 percent.

• A $1.4 billion increase in funding for Pell Grants for low-income college students, raising the maximum annual grant from $3,300 to $3,800.

• An extra $547 million for after-school programs, providing a total of $1 billion for educational and recreational opportunities to keep children active during the late-afternoon hours.

• A $792 million package of "teacher quality initiatives" to train and recruit good teachers. The Clinton administration had sought $1 billion; a July GOP proposal would have provided $598 million.

• A $250 million "accountability fund" for the Title I program, which aids schools with poor and disadvantaged students.

Education Funding Spared in Final Labor-HHS Bill

DECEMBER 16 — When the ax finally fell, it was not the fatal blow the education community had feared.

The final version of the fiscal 2001 Labor, Health and Human Services, and Education bill (HR 4577) salvaged most of the education spending increases that had been approved by budget negotiators in October — allowing both parties to claim credit for a record increase in federal education spending even as they pared away slices from the scuttled October agreement.

The measure, cleared Dec. 15, will boost federal education spending by $6.5 billion, a 17 percent increase over fiscal 2000. Though that is less than the increase called for in the October agreement, the hike represents the largest increase in federal education spending since the Department of Education was created in 1979. It is also roughly $2 billion more than President Clinton had originally requested.

The Labor-HHS measure (HR 4577) became the vehicle for the much-anticipated omnibus bill wrapping up the year's legislative work.

"I think we can take considerable satisfaction in the knowledge that this bill will help a lot of people whose voices don't get heard very often," Rep. David R. Obey, D-Wis., told reporters Dec. 15.

To avoid a revolt by conservative Republicans, who thought the Labor-HHS bill had grown too fat, GOP leaders forced Clinton and Democrats to scale it back to $108.9 billion in discretionary spending — down from the $112.5 billion the budget negotiators were eyeing in the scuttled October agreement. (Including advance appropriations — money that is available but cannot be spent until the following year — the October deal would have spent $113.8 billion on discretionary programs.)

That meant the proposed $7.5 billion increase in federal education spending had to be tossed out the window. What lawmakers ended up with, however, was still a massive increase.

"I think this is an indication that Republicans and Democrats in the House and Senate have come together behind a strong and improved education system," House Appropriations Committee Chairman C.W. Bill Young, R-Fla., said in a Dec. 15 interview.

"Even with the election being over, many members heard from their constituents that they wanted a major increase for education," Edward R. Kealy, executive director of the Committee for Education Funding, a coalition of education groups that lobby for greater spending, said in a Dec. 13 interview.

One major issue that did not get addressed in the package was school construction. The Republican leadership declined to include a bill (HR 4094) by Reps. Nancy L. Johnson, R-Conn., and Charles B. Rangel, D-N.Y., to provide tax credits to pay the interest on $24.8 billion in school construction bonds over two years.

The Johnson-Rangel measure was backed by the White House and was similar to a proposal in Clinton's fiscal 2001 budget.

Republican leaders never liked the bill, however, because it contradicted their view that education money should be sent directly to states and school districts without being earmarked for specific purposes.

It was also hurt by the opposition of business and construction groups, who fought the measure because the school construction projects would have had to pay the "prevailing wage" mandated by the Davis-Bacon Act of 1931.

Thin Slices

As it turned out, appropriators took so many thin slices out of every major education program that no single initiative suffered greatly.

For example, Clinton won a third year of funding for his program to re-

Labor-HHS-Education Spending

Where the Money Goes

HR 4577 — Conference report: H Rept 106-1033

Spending Synopsis

The measure, which cleared both chambers Dec. 15 and was signed by President Clinton on Dec. 21, became the vehicle for the omnibus bill that wrapped up the fiscal 2001 appropriations process. It provides $358.3 billion in fiscal 2001 for more than 300 social programs and initiatives ranging from biomedical research to workplace safety.

Most of the money goes to mandatory programs such as Medicare coverage of doctors' services and Medicaid grants. Discretionary spending totals $108.9 billion, scaled back from the $112.5 billion target budget negotiators were aiming at in October but some $2 billion more than Clinton originally requested. The final bill allowed both parties to take credit for increasing federal spending on education even as they pared back the mammoth measure to appease fiscal conservatives.

The final package boosts federal education spending by a record $6.5 billion — a 17 percent increase over last year's funding levels and the largest gain since the Department of Education was created in 1979. It also includes $50 million to help the Agency for Healthcare Research and Quality study ways to prevent medical errors. Some of the individual programs and agencies funded by the bill include:

- $1.8 billion for community-based AIDS programs, an increase of $213 million over fiscal 2000.
- $130 million to establish the National Center for Minority Health and Health Disparities within the National Institutes of Health.
- $10.7 billion for student financial assistance, an increase of $1.3 billion over fiscal 2000.
- $846 million for after-school programs, more than $453 billion above the fiscal 2000 level.

Hot-Button Issues

Δ **School renovation.** The bill includes $1.2 billion for grants and loans to help school districts pay for emergency school repairs, but up to 25 percent of the money can be spent on special education or technology upgrades instead. The language was a compromise between Clinton, who wanted dedicated funding for school repairs, and Republicans, who wanted to give the districts discretion.

Δ **Class size/teacher quality.** Clinton got the $1.62 billion he wanted to fund a third year of his proposed seven-year effort to help states reduce class sizes in the early grades by hiring 100,000 new teachers. The language allows school districts to spend up to 25 percent of the money on professional development — a trade-off between Democrats, who argued that overcrowded classrooms are a serious problem, and Republicans, who believe teacher quality is the bigger issue.

Δ **Ergonomics.** The measure omits a proposal that would have blocked the Occupational Safety and Health Administration from finalizing a rule requiring 1.6 million employers to set up programs to prevent repetitive motion injuries. The proposal became moot when OSHA published the rule after GOP negotiators rejected a White House offer to delay its enforcement until the next president took office.

Δ **Biomedical research funding.** The measure includes a $2.5 billion increase for the National Institutes of Health (NIH), just shy of the $2.7 billion Republicans sought to make good on their goal of doubling the institutes' fiscal 1998 budget by fiscal 2003.

Δ **Children's health insurance.** The final package omits a provision in the Senate version that would have deferred until 2003 $1.9 billion for the State Children's Health Insurance Program for uninsured children. The money represented matching funds, which were expected to go largely unused, in 37 states.

Δ **Social Services Block Grant.** Negotiators deleted a Senate proposal to slash this program, which helps states pay for services such as child protection, from $1.8 billion in fiscal 2000 to $600 million. The two controversial offsets became unnecessary once appropriators were able to lift their overall spending caps.

(figures are in thousands of dollars of new budget authority)

	Fiscal 2000 Appropriation	Fiscal 2001 Clinton Request	House Bill	Senate Bill	Conference Report
Department of Labor	$13,090,684	$14,329,276	$12,626,598	$13,409,013	$13,816,022
Department of Health and Human Services	241,031,247	258,864,945	259,396,591	256,029,528	259,579,394
Department of Education	37,944,687	42,494,646	39,542,049	42,674,645	44,491,439
Related Agencies	38,259,094	40,434,735	40,152,492	40,224,324	40,383,031
GRAND TOTAL	**$330,325,712**	**$356,123,602**	**$351,717,730**	**$352,337,510**	**$358,269,886**
Total adjusted for scorekeeping	($316,345,923)	($348,388,826)	($341,802,954)	($341,690,518)	($351,186,573)
Trust Funds	($9,717,615)	($10,245,563)	($9,947,711)	($9,954,227)	($10,332,331)

TABLES: House, Senate Appropriations committees

duce class sizes in the early grades by hiring 100,000 new teachers, just as the October agreement called for. But the program will be funded at $1.62 billion, rather than the $1.75 billion Clinton asked for and received in the October agreement.

Likewise, the money that Clinton and congressional Democrats won for emergency school repairs shrank from the $1.3 billion in the October agreement to $1.2 billion in the omnibus package. To satisfy Republican requests for state and local flexibility in how the money can be spent, $300 million can be used for special education or technology instead of school repairs.

IDEA Trimmed

Special education funding, a major priority for Republicans and some Democrats, was scaled back as well. The final agreement calls for a $1.4 billion increase in grants to the states under the Individuals with Disabilities Education Act (IDEA), down from the $1.6 billion increase it would have received under the October deal.

Although the increase is significant, it falls well short of the goal of a House-passed bill (HR 4055) calling for $2 billion a year in IDEA increases over 10 years. That is the amount needed for the federal government to reimburse 40 percent of states' special education costs, the target set under the 1975 law (PL 94-142).

Other key education programs received less than they would have under the October deal, but still came away with major increases.

After-school programs received $846 million, down from the $1 billion in the October agreement but well above the $453 million they received in fiscal 2000.

Higher education programs also fared well. Pell Grants for low-income college students will receive $8.8 billion in funding, enough to raise the maximum annual grant to $3,750. That is $450 more than recipients now get, and just $50 less than they would have gotten under the October agreement. ◆

Legislative Branch Bill's Tortuous Path Ends With Its Inclusion in Omnibus Package

SUMMARY

The legislative branch appropriations bill proved more contentious than in years past, with House and Senate members at odds over funding levels. GOP leaders attached to it the controversial Treasury-Postal Service appropriations bill and a repeal of a telephone excise tax. It took a defeat in the Senate and two aborted attempts at House votes before a deal was made. The bill finally cleared, only to be vetoed by President Clinton, who said he would not sign it until other spending bills were completed. The measure, which pays congressional expenses such as staff salaries and committee expenses, was finally cleared as part of the omnibus spending bill. *(Omnibus appropriations, p. 2-3)*

The House Appropriations committee initially approved a bill that would have slashed funding by $105 million from the fiscal 2000 level, and although it did not yet include Senate expenses, the House cutback would have cost up to 1,700 jobs in the House and related agencies. Senators and many House members attacked the plan as "draconian," and House leaders added $96 million. After sailing through a conference between the House and Senate on July 25, the spending bill quickly hit more roadblocks.

Republican leaders decided to make it the vehicle to pass their repeal of the telephone tax, as well as the Treasury-Postal appropriations bill, which faced strong Democratic opposition. The package was pulled twice from House floor consideration during the summer after GOP conservatives complained that the spending levels in the Treasury-Postal portion were too high. The package then was defeated in the Senate, 28-69, after Democrats said the spending was too low; senators also complained that the Treasury-Postal portion had never come to the floor as a stand-alone bill. Negotiators eventually struck a deal on the Treasury-Postal spending without touching the legislative branch funding levels. *(For stories on combined Treasury-Postal Service and legislative branch bill, see Treasury-Postal Service, p. 2-138)*

The final bill provides $2.5 billion for congressional operations, $40 million more than in fiscal 2000, but $199 million less than the president's request. The bill includes $103.9 million for the Capitol Police Department, $19 million more than in fiscal 2000. The Library of Congress and the General Accounting Office also received boosts over the previous year's funding levels.

Box Score — 2001 Fiscal Year

Legislative Branch

- **Bill:** HR 4577 — PL 106-554
- **Legislative action: House** passed HR 4516 (H Rept 103-635), 373-50, June 22.

Senate passed HR 4516 by voice vote, after adding provisions from S 2603 (S Rept 106-304), on July 17.

House adopted the conference report (H Rept 106-796), 212-209, on Sept. 14.

Senate rejected the conference report, 28-69, on Sept. 20.

Senate cleared the bill, 58-37 on Oct. 12.

President vetoed HR 4516 on Oct. 30.

House adopted the conference report on HR 4577 (H Rept 1033), 292-60, on Dec. 15.

Senate cleared the bill by voice vote Dec. 15.

President signed the bill Dec. 21.

House Panel Votes To Cut Hundreds From Legislative Branch Payroll

MAY 6 — House appropriators are expected to quickly approve a fiscal 2001 legislative branch spending measure May 9 that would eliminate more than 700 jobs from the General Accounting Office (GAO), more than 100 jobs from the Architect of the Capitol's Office and more than 400 positions from the Capitol Police.

The House Legislative Branch Appropriations Subcommittee approved the unnumbered bill in a 6-3 party-line vote May 3. Panel Republicans unanimously voted for the measure in order to move it along but agreed with Democratic opponents that the bill's spending levels were too low.

"I very much regret this," said Zach Wamp, R-Tenn. "The allocation is not enough to meet the priorities."

Members of both parties said they hoped funding would be increased before a bill is sent to the president. Republicans also said some tough cuts may be unpleasant but were needed to meet budget restraints.

"We didn't balance the budget by continuing to spend every cent we've got," said full committee Chairman C.W. Bill Young, R-Fla. "Nobody said this job was going to be easy."

Subcommittee Chairman Charles H. Taylor, R-N.C., added that Congress should set the example for belt-tightening. "It's important to show that we have determination here," he said.

The overall allocation for the measure is set at $2.4 billion, $120 million less than in fiscal 2000. The House's portion of the bill, to be marked up in full committee May 9, totals $1.8 billion — a 5.5 percent decrease from fiscal 2000. The House measure includes spending for staff and committee expenses as well as for related congressional agencies such as the Library of Congress, Congressional Budget Office and Government Printing Office.

The Senate is tentatively set to mark up its spending bill the week of May 15.

House Democrats called the measure a "misbegotten creature" and charged that it would critically damage basic House operations. "We're not going to be able to keep this place clean," Rep. Steny H. Hoyer, D-Md., said of proposed cuts in custodial staff for the Capitol. "It undermines the security of this Capitol complex and returns us to where we were on July 24, 1998."

On that date, two Capitol Police officers were killed by a gunman who went on a shooting rampage in the Capitol. Following the incident, Congress provided funds to expand the police force by 260 positions. Of those, 230 are now targeted to be eliminated in the fiscal 2001 bill, as well as another 193 police positions to be dissolved through attrition and layoffs. That would leave the department with about 1,100 positions. *(1998 Almanac, p. 2-75)*

Taylor said $14.5 million will likely be added later this year to improve fire safety in the Capitol complex, and $1.8 million will be added for security at the Library of Congress. The House approved funding for those projects earlier this year in the fiscal 2000 supplemental spending bill (HR 3908), which Senate Majority Leader Trent Lott, R-Miss., quashed in April.

Democrats did not introduce amendments in subcommittee, saying it would be a waste of time, because if spending levels do not rise, the House is unlikely to have the votes to pass the bill. "Why amend something that's not real?" said David R. Obey of Wisconsin, top Democrat on the full Appropriations Committee. "This is just a place holder. I don't believe in huffing and puffing to blow down a bill that doesn't exist." Obey said Democrats would not offer amendments at the full committee markup, either.

Hoyer said that if House funding did not increase in the final bill, he would urge President Clinton to veto it.

Spending Cuts

Hardest hit in the House measure would be the Government Printing Office, which is the target of a 25.3 percent cut to $77 million in fiscal 2001.

Next is the Architect of the Capitol, which faces a 17.7 percent cut to $133.1 million, despite its request for an increase to address fire safety concerns. Those cuts would be made by eliminating 112 custodial and maintenance positions. Another 44 positions may be cut, or six days of furloughs for all 1,850 workers may be required.

Other proposed cuts include elimination of the annual cost-of-living increase for House staff and legislative branch agencies, and reduction of budgets for House committees and members' offices. The last action could result in the loss of 42 committee positions and 61 personal staff cuts. The bill contains no funding for new member orientation or office moves that result from this fall's elections.

House Committee Votes to Cut Staffing, Hoping For Senate Refusal

MAY 13 — House appropriators are looking to their Senate counterparts to dig them out of a financial hole. On May 9, the House Appropriations Committee approved a fiscal 2001 spending bill for the legislative branch that calls for cuts of up to 1,700 jobs in the House and related agencies.

The unnumbered bill would allot a total of $2.4 billion for congressional spending, $120 million less than in fiscal 2000. The House's portion of the bill adds up to $1.8 billion — a $105 million cut from fiscal 2000.

The committee approved the bill in a party-line vote, 31-23. Members of both parties, however, said they hoped the Senate would provide more money. The Senate Appropriations Committee is scheduled to mark up its version of the bill May 18. It is already starting at a slightly higher overall allocation — $2.5 billion.

"This is just the second round of a 10-round fight," said Rep. Charles H. Taylor, R-N.C., chairman of the Legislative Branch Appropriations Subcommittee. "We expect it to change as we go to the full House, the Senate and conference."

Robert F. Bennett, R-Utah, Taylor's counterpart on the Senate Appropriations Committee, has indicated that he would not be as heavy-handed in cutting congressional spending.

Taylor said he had no choice but to come up with the cuts to stay within the spending allocations given to his panel by the full Appropriations Committee.

House Democrats, however, said it was irresponsible to rely on the Senate and accused the GOP leadership of self-flagellation to score political points.

Hill Security

Among the departments hardest hit in the House bill would be the Capitol Police, which could lose more than 400 positions; the General Accounting Office, which could lose 707 employees; and the Congressional Research Service, which could lose 114 positions.

"We're cutting our own throats," said Rep. James T. Walsh, R-N.Y. "We can't just single-handedly disarm the legislative branch of the government and still maintain co-equal power with the judicial and executive branches."

Although Walsh, a former chairman of the subcommittee, voted for the bill in order to "move it forward," he said he hoped more money would be allocated before a final bill is sent to the president.

Democrats charged that Republicans were slashing spending to save money for a politically popular tax cut. Republicans said budget cuts were painful but necessary to balance the budget. "This is a draconian approach, but in order to reach overall allocations, we had no choice," Taylor said.

Steny H. Hoyer, D-Md., and other committee members expressed the most concern about cuts in the Capitol Police Department.

Hoyer referred to the Capitol shooting in July 1998 in which two officers were killed. After the shooting, Congress approved funding for an additional 260 police positions, bringing the force to about 1,500. The fiscal 2001 spending bill would eliminate most of those new posts plus others, and deny a department request for another 100 positions. *(1998 Almanac, p. 2-75)*

The department said it needed the extra positions to staff each door in the Capitol and nearby office buildings with two officers.

"It's the security issue . . . that I'm scared about," said Ed Pastor of Arizona, the top Democrat on the subcommittee. "This will greatly diminish the security in the Capitol and House buildings."

But Taylor said security is not necessarily improved by manpower. He

Members Queasy About COLAs Again

MAY 20 — In an era of dot-com billionaires and millionaire lobbyists, one might think that members of Congress would have no trouble accepting an annual inflation-related pay raise.

Congressional pay has largely become a non-issue in congressional campaigns. The political parties have declared a non-aggression pact on the matter. Still, congressional pay raises make lawmakers so antsy that they have not taken one in an election year since 1992. This year's outlook appears cloudy at best.

Members accepted a $4,600 pay raise last year — without much controversy — for only the second time since Republicans took over Congress. The cost of living adjustment (COLA) brought their salaries to $141,300 a year. If they could get over the hump this year, the issue might fade away, say wishful lawmakers.

"If I can go two years in a row with this being a non-issue, we may have moved beyond it," said Rep. Jim Kolbe, R-Ariz. Kolbe heads the Treasury-Postal Service Appropriations Subcommittee which, for reasons dating to an obscure 1994 imbroglio, writes the bill that usually carries language to block the pay raise.

This year, a pay raise has quickly hit a major snag — House Republicans' handling of the legislative branch appropriations bill. Budget-related pressures prompted appropriators to block COLAs for Capitol Hill employees. The draft bill also would force layoffs of hundreds of Capitol police officers and other support staff. The proposed cuts have prompted an outcry among members and unusually heavy media attention to the normally low-profile spending bill.

The result is that the battle for the annual COLA may have been lost before it is even joined. "I'm not for members getting COLAs if our employees don't get COLAs," said Rep. Steny H. Hoyer, D-Md., a strong supporter of congressional pay raises. "That's absurd."

Never Easy

Under a 1989 law (PL 101-194) that raised members' pay but barred House members from taking honoraria for speeches to outside groups, lawmakers also won the automatic COLA. Among the chief benefits of the law was that it relieved members from having to cast politically difficult votes to raise their own salaries. *(1989 Almanac, p. 51)*

But it has not worked out as planned. Instead, whether to accept the COLA has bedeviled congressional leaders. For five of the past seven years, members have voted to deny themselves the raise, and the few times they have maneuvered to accept it, it has required behind-the-scenes efforts by congressional leaders of both parties. It was among the few issues upon which former Speaker Newt Gingrich, R-Ga. (1979-99), and Minority Leader Richard A. Gephardt, D-Mo., collaborated.

Hoyer played a central role in the 1994 debacle that unraveled Congress' carefully crafted pay system.

The first glitch came in 1993, when lawmakers squeezed federal workers' pay raises as part of President Clinton's landmark deficit-reduction package (PL 103-66). Because they curbed federal workers' salaries, lawmakers voted a one-year pause in their own COLAs. *(1993 Almanac, p. 12)*

Members were poised to quietly accept a return to normalcy in 1994. But Hoyer, whose district in the Washington, D.C., suburbs contains many federal workers, inserted a provision in that year's Treasury-Postal Service appropriations bill (PL 103-329) to raise federal employees' pay by more than Clinton had proposed. Accompanying the provision was language to block the congressional COLA, inserted to deflect criticism that the federal pay raise would have triggered a higher COLA for Congress. Hoyer headed the Treasury-Postal Service Subcommittee at the time.

Clinton subsequently issued a presidential order embracing the higher pay increase, and Hoyer sought to drop the entire provision in conference — both the federal workers' pay raise and the language blocking the congressional COLA.

Not so fast, said Rep. Jim Ross Lightfoot of Iowa (1985-97), the committee's ranking Republican. Lightfoot threatened to force a floor vote on the issue, and COLA advocates quickly caved in. *(1994 Almanac, p. 536)*

Accepting the COLA in the wake of the 1995 GOP takeover was unthinkable to junior GOP conservatives. In 1997, however, after a behind-the-scenes struggle, members finally got that year's COLA. Last year's effort to accept the COLA went relatively smoothly. *(1997 Almanac, p. 9-71)*

This year, Gephardt and Speaker J. Dennis Hastert, R-Ill., have yet to discuss the matter, aides said.

said Congress should rely more heavily on technology — such as placing surveillance cameras at building entrances — to keep the Capitol safe.

House Funding

Other areas targeted for cuts include salaries for House staff members. The bill does not provide any money for cost of living adjustments (COLAs) for House and legislative agency workers.

Taylor said the lack of a staff pay raise could ultimately make it difficult for members of Congress to accept an increase for themselves.

Members automatically get a cost of living increase unless they vote to deny themselves the raise, a step they frequently have taken in recent years. They accepted the pay raise in 1999, however. The money is in the spending bill that funds the Treasury Department and Postal Service.

"I don't see how there could possibly be a pay raise [for members] if this bill gives no COLA for our staffers," Taylor said.

Senate Panel Votes To Raise Spending As House Leaders Rethink Cuts

MAY 20 — Senate appropriators thumbed their noses at their House counterparts May 18 when they approved a fiscal 2001 legislative branch spending bill that would boost funding and stave off deep cuts in the Capitol police force.

The move came as House leaders scrambled to add money to their barebones measure to avoid an embarrassing floor defeat. "The bill, as is, will not pass on the House floor," said a top House leadership aide. "There's not enough money, and we're going to fix it."

The House Appropriations Committee approved a draft bill May 9 that would cut spending by almost 5 percent, compared with fiscal 2000.

Senate appropriators boasted that they added money to "every single component" for fiscal 2001.

"Sometimes it's only one-tenth of 1 percent over last year, but they are increases," said Sen. Robert F. Bennett, R-Utah, chairman of the Legislative Branch Appropriations Subcommittee. The full committee approved the bill, 27-0.

The overall allocation for the measure is set at $2.5 billion, a 1.8 percent increase over fiscal 2000. The Senate's portion of the bill is $1.7 billion, a 3.7 percent increase over fiscal 2000.

The Senate measure, which does not address funding for House offices, includes spending for Senate staff and committee expenses as well as for related congressional agencies such as the Capitol Police, the Architect of the Capitol and the Congressional Research Service.

Capitol Police

Senate appropriators from both sides of the aisle chastised the House for what they charged were "egregious" and "draconian" cuts in proposed congressional spending.

They particularly attacked the House's proposed 12 percent cut in Capitol Police funding, which would eliminate more than 400 officers.

In contrast, the Senate bill would raise the police budget to $109.6 million, a 26 percent increase over fiscal 2000. The increase is expected to allow the hiring of more than 100 new officers.

"It is penny-wise and pound-foolish to make cuts in security personnel . . . when we're talking about the Capitol of the United States," said Sen. Robert C. Byrd of West Virginia, the ranking Democrat on the full committee. "This is the most important board of directors in the world. How could anyone be so shortsighted?"

Bennett pointed to a May 17 incident in which a man broke a glass bottle and threatened to kill himself in front of lawmakers during a House Agriculture Committee hearing. Capitol Police in attendance grabbed the man and wrestled him to the floor.

"In the last 48 hours [there has been] an attack on members of Congress by some deranged individual," Bennett said. "The suggestion that we can save money by taking police out of hearings is demonstrably a bad idea."

Along with adding money to the Capitol Police, the Senate bill calls for consolidating the police forces for the Capitol, Library of Congress and Government Printing Office. Bennett said a unified force could provide better and more cost-effective security.

Other congressional agencies that would receive a boost under the Senate bill include the Congressional Budget Office, which would get a 3.8 percent increase to $27 million; the Library of Congress, which would get a 1.2 percent increase to $399 million; and the General Accounting Office, a 1.9 percent increase to $384.9 million.

House Maneuvering

Meanwhile, House leaders are looking for ways to rewrite their version of the bill to provide more money.

House Democrats and Republicans have attacked the bill as recklessly slashing spending to such an extent that about 1,700 jobs would be lost and a cost of living adjustment (COLA) would not be allowed for House and legislative agency workers.

Although the House bill was approved May 9, it has yet to be filed with the House clerk or given a bill number. The bill could be sent back to the Appropriations Committee for a new allocation, or money could be added by the Rules Committee or through a floor amendment. A new spending allocation would require an adjustment in the other 12 appropriations bills to keep overall spending at the same level of $600.4 billion.

Appropriations Chairman C. W. Bill Young, R-Fla., said he would prefer that money be added through his committee or on the floor, rather than giving the Rules Committee such authority over spending.

Procedural Feud Postpones Senate Vote on Legislative Branch Bill

MAY 27 — Congress' effort to craft a fiscal 2001 spending bill for its own operations is running aground in a spat between the chambers over a House GOP plan to cut spending in nearly every office and legislative branch agency.

The Senate completed debate on its $2.5 billion version of the bill (S 2603) May 24-25, but it stopped short of voting for final passage while Republican and Democratic leaders work out a procedural feud that is affecting much of the Senate schedule.

But senators were in general agreement on the scope of their bill and were poised to easily pass the measure upon their return from a weeklong Memorial Day recess.

House GOP leaders, meanwhile, failed to get the House version (HR 4516) to the floor before the recess. And it is far from certain when the House will be able to move it. As reported out of the House Appropriations Committee on May 9, the $2.4 billion measure would slash $105 million from the fiscal 2000 level of House spending. It called for eliminating 1,700 positions and did not provide funding for a cost of living adjustment (COLA) for congressional and other legislative branch staff.

Members from both sides of the aisle attacked the cuts, and House leaders scrambled to add more money in order to win enough votes for passage. Republicans have not yet settled on a final dollar figure, but sources say as much as $85 million could be added.

But during the week of May 22, GOP leaders could not reach any agreement on where to find the additional funds or how to allocate them. Any additional money would have to come from cuts in other appropriations bills.

The Senate did not seem concerned with the House's dilemma, as it overwhelmingly approved an amendment May 25 calling on the House to restore funding for the Capitol Police, congressional staff and support agencies.

The non-binding Senate language — approved on a 100-0 vote — said "the operation of the Capitol and the legislative process are dependent on the professionalism and hard work of those who work here." *(Vote 113, p. S-22)*

Sen. Barbara A. Mikulski, D-Md., who introduced the amendment, was more blunt in her comments on the floor. "Shame on [House members] for what they were doing. Our staff is on our side so we can be on the people's side."

In particular, Mikulski and other senators condemned the House for its 12 percent cut in the Capitol Police Department, which would result in the loss of more than 400 positions.

Unlike the House bill, the Senate language would increase funding for all legislative agencies, including a 26 percent rise for the Capitol Police.

"In a world where the number of threats seems to be growing . . . we're all better off with a strong, professional and well-trained Capitol Police," said Sen. Patty Murray, D-Wash. "Don't let the House Republican budget slap them in the face."

The Senate also approved, by voice vote, language to establish a new Center for Russian Leadership Development, which would use private funds to grant fellowships to Russian officials to visit America and learn about the free market system.

House Passes Bill After Rescinding Severe Cuts

JUNE 24 — The House on June 22 easily passed its fiscal 2001 legislative branch appropriations bill, but only after leaders restored millions of dollars for staff pay increases and Capitol security, among other things.

The spending measure (HR 4516), which would provide $1.9 billion for the House and related agencies, passed by a vote of 373-50. *(Vote 313, p. H-100)*

That represents a $96 million increase over what was approved by the House Appropriations Committee on May 9, but is still a $9.7 million cut from fiscal 2000 and $185.4 million less than the president's request. The House's overall allocation for itself, the Senate and related agencies is $2.47 billion.

The Senate, which has already completed debate on legislative branch spending, is expected to give final approval to its $1.7 billion measure (S 2603) the week of June 26. Its total allocation is $2.50 billion.

The original House version of the bill called for cuts of up to 1,700 jobs in the House and related agencies. It did not provide any money for cost of living adjustments (COLAs) for House and legislative agency workers, and it allotted no money for office moves that result from the fall elections or for orientation programs for newly elected House members.

House members from both parties attacked the low funding levels as "draconian" — as did some senators — and warned that they would severely harm congressional operations.

In the wake of the criticism, House leaders conceded that the bill would not pass without more money.

During floor consideration June 22, Charles H. Taylor, R-N.C., chairman of the Legislative Branch Appropriations Subcommittee, offered an amendment to increase the House spending level by $96 million. It was approved by voice vote. Taylor said the amendment would "avoid unwise and counterproductive layoffs."

Additional Funds

The biggest portion of the added money — $22.6 million — would be used to enhance the Capitol Police Department's $76.7 million budget. The department had been targeted for cuts of more than 400 positions under the original bill.

The extra money would allow the police force to maintain its current number of positions — about 1,360 — and add 48 officers this summer.

"Our Capitol police deserve our appreciation," said Zack Wamp, R-Tenn., a subcommittee member. "It's important we appreciate them. It's important we fund them adequately."

Also benefiting from the extra money would be the Congressional Research Service (CRS), which was originally targeted to lose 114 positions under a $66.2 million budget. Under Taylor's amendment, CRS would receive an additional $5 million to retain staff positions and $2.6 million for pay increases.

The Architect of the Capitol had $5.6 million added to its $114.8 million budget, allowing it to avoid work force reductions. Another $750,000 was restored to pay for office moves following the fall election. The Government Printing Office and the General Accounting Office also received additional funds to avoid layoffs.

Taylor's amendment added $11.5 million for COLAs for House employees and $275,000 for the orientation program for newly elected members.

"The average senator can pay $20,000 more for [staffers] than we do," David R. Obey of Wisconsin, ranking Democrat on the full Appropriations Committee, said of efforts to cut House funding levels. "We're being advised literally by kiddie corps. . . . This Congress would be less amateurish, it would be more professional, if we had many more experienced staffers than we do."

Debt Reduction

Two amendments were aimed at putting money back into the U.S. Treasury for debt reduction.

The first, offered by Dave Camp, R-Mich., and Tim Roemer, D-Ind., would mandate that any money not spent by members from their personal office accounts be returned to the Treasury. It was adopted by voice vote.

The second amendment, however, sparked a heated floor debate between House appropriators and budget hawks.

Offered by Paul D. Ryan, R-Wis., it called for a "lockbox" to prohibit money cut from appropriations bills by floor amendments from being transferred to other programs in different spending bills. Instead, spending cuts would be sent to the Treasury for debt reduction.

But C.W. Bill Young, R-Fla., chairman of the Appropriations Committee, opposed the proposal, saying it would put "the House at a terrible disadvantage with the Senate." The amendment was defeated, 184-235. *(Vote 312, p. H-100)*

Senate Passes Bill, Which Must Be Reconciled With House Cuts

JULY 22 — Congressional appropriators say they will try to send the fiscal 2001 legislative branch spending bill to the president's desk before Congress adjourns for its August recess.

"That's our goal; we're working hard to get there," said Charles H. Taylor, R-N.C., chairman of the House Legislative Branch Appropriations Subcommittee. The president has not voiced objections to the measure and is expected to sign it.

The Senate passed HR 4516 by voice vote July 17 after substituting provisions of its own bill (S 2603). The bill would provide $1.7 billion to fund Senate operations and related agencies. The Senate allocation for overall congressional spending — including the House — is $2.5 billion.

Before passing the bill, the Senate adopted by voice vote an amendment by Barbara Boxer, D-Calif., that would prohibit the routine use of highly toxic pesticides on U.S. Capitol grounds. Currently, some pesticides containing known or probable carcinogens are used for preventive spraying. Boxer's amendment would allow pesticide use in emergencies, such as a sudden outbreak of plant disease.

Immediately after passage, the Senate named conferees to resolve what some appropriators say are minor differences with the House's version of the bill. Conferees are Republicans Robert F. Bennett of Utah, Ted Stevens of Alaska, Larry E. Craig of Idaho and Thad Cochran of Mississippi, and Democrats Dianne Feinstein of California, Richard J. Durbin of Illinois and Robert C. Byrd of West Virginia.

The Senate completed debate on the bill in May, but, because of a procedural dispute between party leaders, held off final passage until the House completed action. The House version, passed June 22, would provide $1.9 billion for the House and related agencies, and $2.47 billion overall, including the Senate.

The biggest difference is in funding for congressional agencies such as the General Accounting Office, which would get $369 million under the House bill and $385 million under the Senate's. The House would cut overall legislative funding by $9.7 million from fiscal 2000. The Senate would increase spending over fiscal 2000 in every area under its jurisdiction.

The House had originally called for even greater spending cuts, but after members from both sides of the aisle threatened to defeat the measure on the floor, House leaders added $96 million to the bill.

Still, the House bill would increase police funding by $14.4 million over fiscal 2000, compared with a $24.6 million increase in the Senate version. Overall, the Senate would fund the force at $110 million, the House at $99 million.

During floor debate in May, the Senate adopted an amendment calling on conferees to "maintain the Senate position on funding" for the police and all legislative branch employees.

Conference Report Held Up By House Leaders' Add-Ons

JULY 29 — The House delayed action July 27 on the conference agreement on a $2.53 billion measure funding its own operations after the bill became embroiled in a partisan battle over broader political and spending issues.

The fiscal 2001 legislative branch appropriations bill (HR 4516) sailed through a one hour conference between House and Senate negotiators July 25, winning unanimous support from conferees.

House leaders, however, later added to the conference report the fiscal 2001 Treasury-Postal Service spending measure and a repeal of the telephone excise tax. *(Treasury-Postal Service, p. 2-138)*

Leaders then tried to bring the massive package to the House floor, sparking heated debate. House members ultimately approved a rule July 27 governing debate on the package. The vote was 214-210. Later in the day, leaders pulled the bill from floor consideration. *(Vote 448, p. H-138)*

The omnibus package is expected to be dismantled when Congress returns in September, and the legislative spending measure is expected to clear as a free-standing bill. The president is expected to sign it.

The $2.53 billion in legislative branch spending approved by conferees eclipsed both the $2.5 billion version of the measure passed by the Senate on July 17, and the $2.47 billion House version passed June 22.

Conferees approved one add-on not related to congressional spending: $40 million in "emergency" funding to cover a shortfall in the Federal Housing Administration's multifamily loan subsidy program.

Conferees also added an extra $250,000 for the Senate Sergeant at Arms office and $141,300 for the widow of Sen. Paul Coverdell, R-Ga., who died of a cerebral hemorrhage July 18. It is Senate tradition that a year's salary be granted to the spouses of deceased senators.

The total legislative appropriations bill — which funds both chambers, along with related agencies such as the Government Printing Office and the Library of Congress — would be funded at $55 million above the fiscal 2000 level.

Congressional Operations

The conference agreement sets funding for House and Senate offices at about the same levels approved by appropriators in each chamber: $769.8 million for the House and $506.8 million for the Senate.

In funding congressional agencies, however, conferees generally either split the difference between the two chambers or accepted Senate funding levels, which were generally higher than House levels.

The General Accounting Office would receive $384.9 million under the conference agreement, the exact amount agreed to in the Senate and a $7.3 million increase over fiscal 2000. The House originally voted to cut the GAO by $8.7 million.

The conference report funds the Government Printing Office (GPO) at $99.4 million, a $3.8 million cut from

Legislative Branch Spending Highlights

Where the Money Goes

HR 4577 — Conference report: H Rept 106-1033

Spending Synopsis

The fiscal 2001 legislative branch spending bill was cleared Dec. 15 as part of the year-end omnibus appropriations package (HR 4577). A nearly identical version (HR 4516), which also carried the Treasury-Postal spending bill and a repeal of the telephone excise tax, had been vetoed Oct. 30. The bill would provide $2.5 billion for the legislative branch — $40 million or 2 percent more than the fiscal 2000 level, but $199 million less than was requested. The total includes $1.8 billion for congressional operations and $771 million for activities that do not provide primary support to Congress, such as the Library of Congress and the General Accounting Office. The conference report also includes $40 million in a fiscal 2000 emergency supplemental for a variety of accounts. The report's total for legislative branch spending is $613 million more than the House bill and $3 million more than the Senate bill. The most significant increase over the House bill is for the Capitol police.

- **Payroll and staffing**

The House committee bill sought to eliminate about 1,700 full-time positions in the House and related agencies, but funding for all those positions had been restored when the bill reached the floor. The conference report's staffing total of $769.8 million exceeds the House-passed funding level of $769.6 million, so no layoffs will be needed.

- **Other agencies**

The House committee bill also would have cut the GAO by $8.7 million, but the conference report includes funding at the level passed in the Senate, $384.9 million. That total is a $7.3 million increase over the fiscal 2000 amount. The conference report funds both the Library of Congress and the Congressional Budget Office at levels higher than either received in the individual chambers. The library received $338.7 million and the CBO got $28.5 million.

Hot-Button Issues

△ **Funding differences.** After chastising House appropriators for low spending levels, Senate conferees won additional money for nearly all congressional agencies, including the Library of Congress and the GAO. The conferees either split the difference between the two chambers or accepted the Senate's higher funding levels. The final $2.53 billion conference report eclipsed both the $2.5 billion version originally passed by the Senate and the $2.47 billion the House allocated to both chambers and related agencies.

△ **Capitol police.** One major disparity between the House and Senate was in funding for the Capitol Police Department. The House originally cut the department by 12 percent, but later was forced to increase the police budget after lawmakers threatened to defeat the bill. The Senate called for a 29 percent increase in department spending. The conference report increases funding by $19 million, a 22 percent boost over fiscal 2000. Conferees also called for "sufficient resources" to implement a "two-officers-per-door" policy across the congressional complex. House appropriators originally argued that high-tech security systems could take the place of officers. Conferees rejected Senate language that called for the consolidation of the police forces for the Capitol, Library of Congress and Government Printing Office.

(figures are in thousands of dollars of new budget authority)

	Fiscal 2000 Appropriation	Fiscal 2001 Clinton Request	House Bill	Senate Bill	Conference Report
House of Representatives	$757,993	$800,738	$769,551	$769,551	$769,766
Senate	487,370	558,823	—	506,406	506,797
Capitol Police	84,907	116,030	99,318	109,584	103,914
Other joint items	15,947	18,048	13,311	15,237	14,981
Architect of the Capitol	213,474	226,927	121,352	185,996	185,190
Library of Congress	323,380	352,447	323,903	325,632	338,729
General Accounting Office	377,561	399,918	368,896	384,867	384,867
Other	225,550	252,673	217,360	226,105	222,619
GRAND TOTAL	**$2,486,182**	**$2,725,604**	**$1,913,691**	**$2,523,378**	**$2,526,863**

TABLE: House and Senate Appropriations committees

fiscal 2000, but $4 million more than the House had originally approved. The Senate had funded the GPO at $103.6 million.

The Library of Congress and the Congressional Budget Office (CBO) both ended up with more money than either chamber originally approved.

The library is funded at $412.3 million, a $17.9 million increase over fiscal 2000. The House version had called for $397.7 million, the Senate version for $399 million.

CBO would receive $28.5 million under the conference report, compared with the $27.4 million originally approved by the House and $27 million approved by the Senate.

The Capitol Police Department is funded at $103.9 million, a $17.1 million increase over fiscal 2000.

The House had come under widespread criticism in May after the Appropriations Committee voted to cut the police department's funding by 12 percent. After lawmakers threatened to defeat the bill, the House quickly added $22.6 million to the department's budget, increasing it to $99.3 million. The Senate approved $109.6 million for the department.

While the Senate generally won its funding priorities in conference, several non-fiscal provisions approved by the Senate were dropped.

Conferees rejected Senate language that would have merged the police forces of the GPO and Library of Congress with the Capitol Police. They also dropped Senate language to ban the routine use of toxic pesticides on U.S. Capitol grounds. ◆

Military Construction Bill Is First Finished, Includes Kosovo Peacekeeping Funds

Box Score — **2001** Fiscal Year

Military Construction

- **Bill:** HR 4425 — PL 106-246
- **Legislative action: House** passed HR 4425 (H Rept 106-614), 386-22, on May 16.

Senate passed HR 4425, 96-4, on May 18, after substituting the text of S 2521 (S Rept 106-290).

House adopted the conference report (H Rept 106-710), 306-110, on June 29.

Senate cleared the bill by voice vote June 30.

President signed the bill on July 13.

SUMMARY

President Clinton signed the military construction appropriations bill, HR 4425, on July 13, making it the first fiscal 2001 spending bill to become law.

The bill provided $8.8 billion for construction of barracks, family housing and other facilities on military bases — $800 million more than Clinton requested and $459.9 million, or 5.5 percent, more than the fiscal 2000 level. Funding for military family housing, which is in dismal shape at many bases, was $5.7 million less than in fiscal 2000 but $124.7 million more than the administration requested.

The bill became the vehicle for $11.2 billion in fiscal 2000 supplemental spending, mostly to cover the cost of peacekeeping operations in Kosovo, anti-drug aid to Colombia and disaster assistance at home and abroad. The emergency appropriations were not subject to budget limits. *(Supplemental, p. 2-162)*

House Panel Approves Bill With First Steps In Missile Defense

MAY 6 — The House Military Construction Appropriations Subcommittee approved an $8.6 billion spending bill May 2 that includes $65 million to begin building radar sites in Alaska for a national anti-missile defense system.

President Clinton is not expected to decide until later this year whether such a system should be deployed, if tests this summer show it is feasible. For that reason, the subcommittee cut $20 million from Clinton's $85 million request for major construction on the radar sites.

Because defense specialists believe that North Korea is further along than any other unfriendly nation in developing missiles that could reach the United States, the first anti-missile site would be built in Alaska.

Meanwhile, the House Armed Services Subcommittee on Military Installations and Facilities approved Clinton's entire anti-missile construction request in its portion of a fiscal 2001 defense authorization bill (HR 4205).

The military construction spending bill, almost always the first appropriations measure out of the box, was approved by voice vote after less than eight minutes of debate. The full House Appropriations Committee is expected to mark up the bill May 9.

The subcommittee version would provide about $260 million more than the fiscal 2000 measure (PL 106-52) and about $600 million more than Clinton requested for fiscal 2001.

But the administration's request included a $502 million increase for the costs of base realignment and closure, resulting in slight cuts for general construction and family housing.

The House subcommittee's appropriations bill is about even with the House Appropriations Committee's spending allocations, known as 302(b)s.

The subcommittee bill would appropriate nearly $200 million more than the Military Installations Subcommittee would authorize for general military construction and housing. Committee aides said Clinton's military construction budget request included $170 million for fiscal 2001 that Congress had already authorized in this year's defense bill (PL 106-65). The Military Construction Subcommittee still had to appropriate the money this year, so the spending and authorization bills are only about $30 million apart.

Missile Defense

Members of the appropriations subcommittee balked at agreeing to Clinton's entire request for construction related to the national missile defense system because it still is undergoing development and testing, and a key test has been put off until June.

"The committee is concerned about the major construction request . . . due to the fact that a decision to go forward with this program has not been made, a site has not been selected and specific project justification is not available," the subcommittee report noted.

The missile defense funding is expected to move through both chambers, but members will consider the potential impact of building a complex, expensive system that could violate the 1972 Anti-Ballistic Missile Treaty with Russia.

"I recognize the reduction you're making, which I think is appropriate," Appropriations Committee ranking Democrat David R. Obey of Wisconsin told subcommittee Chairman David L. Hobson, R-Ohio, at the markup.

"But I would nonetheless like to express my misgivings about funding anything at all until we actually know that the technology is apace with our desires," Obey said.

As is the case nearly every year, appropriators complained that they did not have enough money to repair and build military barracks and family housing, given the nearly 20 percent increase in the number of married soldiers in the services in the past four decades. But they said the bill would provide the maximum possible, given competing defense spending needs.

"These kids go through an awful lot," said Republican C.W. Bill Young of Florida, chairman of the House Appropriations Committee. "They deserve a better quality of life than they're getting today."

The measure would provide about $3.7 billion for general construction, which is some $286 million less than current levels but $534 million more than the administration requested. Included would be $759 million for barracks and $43 million for child development centers.

The bill would appropriate $3.6 billion for family housing, about $53 million less than current spending levels, and $178 million, or $97 million more than current spending, for the NATO Security Investment Program.

Effort to End Kosovo Mission Adds Drama To Senate Debate

MAY 13 — Key senators from both parties are using the otherwise innocuous military construction spending bill to pick a fight with the White House over its policy on Kosovo.

The fiscal 2000 construction bill (S 2521), which includes money for military facilities, barracks, family housing, base closings and NATO construction, moves separately from defense appropriations and is usually the first spending measure Congress clears.

This year could be different, with an amendment broadly supported in the Senate Appropriations Committee to end the deployment of U.S. troops as peacekeepers in Kosovo on July 1, 2001, unless the president requests and Congress authorizes an extension.

The bill became the vehicle for the dispute after Senate Majority Leader Trent Lott, R-Miss., last month blocked Senate consideration of a House-passed fiscal 2000 supplemental spending bill (HR 3908) that included money President Clinton requested to pay for the Kosovo mission.

Appropriations Committee Chairman Ted Stevens, R-Alaska, eager to have the Senate act quickly on the $4.7 billion in supplemental defense spending, added the money to the military construction measure, including funds to repay the Pentagon for the Kosovo mission and drug interdiction efforts in the Caribbean. Critics of the Kosovo mission jumped at the opportunity to limit the deployment.

Without the fiscal 2000 funds, the Senate military construction bill is quite similar to a bill (HR 4425) approved May 9 by the House Appropriations Committee. Each calls for $8.6 billion in fiscal 2001 spending.

But it is the Kosovo amendment that has alarmed the White House, the Pentagon and some Senate Democrats.

White House Press Secretary Joe Lockhart said May 10 that the legislation "potentially sends the wrong message to enemies of what we did [in Kosovo]. It is a mess, and it is time for the Senate Republicans to show some leadership."

Senate Minority Leader Tom Daschle, D-S.D., told reporters before the Senate began debate on the bill May 11 that he found the changes "disconcerting" and "troubling." The Senate was not expected to finish the bill until at least May 16.

Carl M. Levin of Michigan, ranking Democrat on the Armed Services Committee, said he hoped to gather the signatures of at least 33 other senators on a letter supporting a presidential veto of the legislation. That would be enough votes to sustain a veto.

The measure approved by the Senate committee includes $1.85 billion to repay the Pentagon for the cost of the Kosovo operation, about $200 million less than the House-passed supplemental bill. Military commanders had warned that without the appropriation, training programs and exercises would have to be cut back this summer.

Balkan Trouble

The amendment on Kosovo was offered by ranking Democrat Robert C. Byrd of West Virginia, with the support of Stevens and Armed Services Committee Chairman John W. Warner, R-Va. It was adopted, 23-3, by Republicans and Democrats weary of U.S. deployments to the Balkans.

The amendment would cut off the U.S. presence in Kosovo unless the president seeks and receives congressional authorization for such a deployment. In the meantime, it calls on the administration to develop a plan for turning over the operation to America's NATO allies.

It also would condition a quarter of the fiscal 2000 funds on a presidential certification that European countries are assuming at least a third of the reconstruction costs in Kosovo.

In a floor speech May 11, Warner said U.S. troops should be replaced by Europeans. The deployment would end in 14 months, Warner said, plenty of time for the administration to develop an exit plan or for Congress to authorize the mission.

"That is not cut-and-run," Warner said. "That is not undermining NATO. That is not sending a signal to [Yugoslavia President Slobodan] Milosevic that the United States is turning its back."

During an hour and a half of debate in committee, Frank R. Lautenberg, D-N.J., led opposition to the amendment. He argued that the U.S. presence in Kosovo was too important to jeopardize and said the president needs the flexibility to send troops to hot spots without waiting for congressional approval.

"We got into it because we couldn't stand the scenes of horror," Lautenberg said. "What do we do if we see another population displaced?"

But Byrd countered that the Constitution demands that Congress debate such expenditures. He said the amendment is not designed to pull the United States out of Kosovo, but to force the White House to involve Congress in the decision.

While supporting the fiscal 2000 funds as an interim step to repay the Pentagon for money it has already spent, Stevens said he has grown tired of having the White House routinely divert spending from Congress' intended purposes to such missions. He said that passing the amendment would offer a new administration and Congress the opportunity to take a fresh look at the wisdom of deploying U.S. troops to the Balkans.

In addition to the Kosovo funds, the Senate bill includes nearly $1 billion in fiscal 2000 spending to compensate the Pentagon for higher fuel costs, $700 million in supplemental spending for military health programs and $573 million for counternarcotics programs.

Construction Boosts

Both the House and Senate bills would increase fiscal 2001 spending for military construction by $293 million over fiscal 2000 levels (PL 106-52) and by $600 million more than Clinton requested.

House and Senate appropriators, with little debate, included preliminary funds for radar sites in Alaska that would be needed for a national anti-missile defense system. The Senate committee provided the $85 million Clinton sought; the House committee included $65 million.

The House measure would provide $502 million more than current spending for cleanup costs associated with the latest round of base closings. Because of this increase and the new missile defense money, most branches of the military would receive less money for other construction projects.

The House committee recommended reductions in military construction from current levels for the Army ($172 million), the Air Force ($73 million) and the reserves ($273 million).

But except for the Army, these accounts would receive much more money under the bill than Clinton requested.

The bill also would appropriate $3.6 billion for family housing, slightly less than current spending but $78 million more than Clinton asked for.

Both Chambers Pass Military Construction Bills

MAY 20 — The House and Senate passed fiscal 2001 military construction spending bills the week of May 15, after Senate action had been stalled for several days by an unrelated debate over gun control and an amendment that would have limited U.S. peacekeeping in Kosovo.

The two bills have an identical, $8.6 billion bottom line for fiscal 2001, though the Senate version (S 2521) also includes $4.7 billion in fiscal 2000 supplemental spending for the Kosovo mission, other defense projects and drug interdiction. Rather than take up a supplemental bill (HR 3908) that the House passed March 30, the Senate is dividing fiscal 2000 funds among three bills.

The Senate passed its bill, 96-4, on May 18, after agreeing, 53-47, to strike the Kosovo language. The House passed its version (HR 4425), 386-22, on May 16. *(Senate votes 105, 106, p. S-21; House vote 184, p. H-60)*

The Clinton administration had warned that if the Kosovo amendment were not removed, the president's senior advisers would recommend a veto.

The bills would provide $260 million more for military construction, family housing and base closures than Congress appropriated for fiscal 2000 (PL 106-52) and $600 million more than President Clinton requested.

"All in all, I think we are on the road to improving the quality of life for our military families," said John W. Olver of Massachusetts, ranking Democrat on the House Military Construction Appropriations Subcommittee.

Taking Care of Home

Although appropriators have complained they do not have enough money to address critical family housing needs in the armed forces, they found enough for an array of projects that the administration did not request.

The Clinton administration criticized what it said were 90 projects that the White House had not requested, including some that were not even in the Pentagon's five-year budget plan.

In the House, states with members on the Military Construction panel would receive some of the largest increases over the amount requested. The bill includes $65 million for projects in Ohio, home of subcommittee Chairman David L. Hobson, a Republican, and $20 million for Massachusetts, Olver's home. Clinton requested $24 million for Ohio and no money for Massachusetts.

The House and Senate Appropriations panels added a total of $42 million for 297 housing units at two Navy bases in Mississippi, the home state of Republican Trent Lott, the Senate majority leader. The Senate panel added $24 million for new housing at the Army's Fort Wainwright in Alaska, home state of Republican Ted Stevens, the Appropriations Committee chairman.

One provision deep in the bill would allow the Litton Industries shipyard in Lott's hometown of Pascagoula to almost immediately begin building a helicopter carrier that the Navy did not plan to request until fiscal 2004. Congress has previously approved some funding for the ship and more is expected in the fiscal 2001 defense spending bill. The military construction provision would move any such funding back to fiscal 2000.

Senate Clears Conference Report; Clinton Signature Expected

JULY 1 — After weeks of negotiations and a last-minute compromise, the Senate on June 30 cleared a fiscal 2001 military construction appropriations bill (HR 4425), which was carrying the added political burden of an $11.2 billion fiscal 2000 supplemental spending package.

The House adopted the conference report, 306-110, on June 29, and the Senate cleared the bill by voice vote before the July 4th recess. *(House vote 362, p. H-114)*

President Clinton is expected to sign the measure. The supplemental funds — designated emergency spending to avoid budget limits — are primarily for military peacekeeping costs, drug-fighting aid to Colombia, and disaster assistance, both in the United States and abroad.

The military construction measure, which would fund the construction of barracks, family housing and other facilities on military bases, is typically the first and least divisive of the 13 annual spending bills to become law.

The bill was headed for early enactment after both chambers passed their versions the week of May 15. However, when Republican leaders decided to make it the vehicle for supplemental funds, progress slowed to a crawl.

The House adopted the conference agreement easily, before most members even had time to study the details. Senate critics of the supplemental package threatened to delay a vote until they were promised that several provisions

Military Construction Highlights

Where the Money Goes

HR 4425 — Conference report: H Rept 106-710

Spending Synopsis

House and Senate appropriators say the Pentagon is not planning to invest enough in upkeep and construction of military facilities, but they have been hard-pressed to come up with additional spending. The fiscal 2001 military construction bill the Senate cleared June 30 would provide $8.8 billion, which is $459.9 million more then enacted for fiscal 2000 — a 5.5 percent increase — and $800 million more than President Clinton requested. Spending for military family housing, which is in dismal shape at many bases, would be $5.7 million less than in fiscal 2000, though it would be $124.7 million more than the administration requested. House and Senate conferees increased the bill's overall bottom line by nearly $200 million, half of it through the simple expedient of rescinding $100 million from previous but unspecified appropriations measures. The military construction bill, traditionally the first and one of the easiest spending measures to pass, this year became the vehicle for $11.2 billion in fiscal 2000 supplemental spending, which Congress declared emergency appropriations not subject to any budget limits.

• Supplemental spending

The supplemental spending, though sprinkled with special earmarked projects for individual lawmakers, was generally for the cost of peacekeeping operations in Kosovo, anti-drug aid to Colombia and disaster assistance at home and abroad. The $11.2 billion total does not include $3.9 billion in scorekeeping adjustments, because appropriators have promised to reverse them later this year.

• Military construction

The final bill would provide $4.2 billion for general construction, $205.5 million more than was enacted for fiscal 2000 and $1 billion more than Clinton requested. The measure includes Clinton's request for $85 million to begin construction related to a national missile defense system, though the White House has not decided whether such a system, still in development, should be deployed. The bill includes $90 million more than Clinton requested for building and modernizing military barracks, including several projects the House and Senate specified. The conferees added $11.9 million to Clinton's request for classroom additions at overseas bases to lower pupil-teacher ratios and increase the number of full-day kindergartens. The bill also would increase, from $17 million to $43 million, the administration's request for building and improving day care centers. With the percentage of married military personnel rising, the Defense Department now runs 800 child care centers.

• Family housing

The bill would provide $3.6 billion, a figure substantially the same as the past two fiscal years and $124.7 million more than Clinton requested. Most of the extra funds are for new housing; the bill would fund the president's request for operating and maintaining existing housing. Congress has encouraged the Pentagon to experiment with privatizing military housing, but the conferees said the Army is spending "excessive amounts" to support contractors developing such proposals. The conferees want quarterly reports on such spending.

(figures are in thousands of dollars of new budget authority)

	Fiscal 2000 Appropriation	Fiscal 2001 Clinton Request	Senate Bill	House Bill	Conference Bill
Military construction	$4,009,798	$3,189,058	$3,811,329	$3,723,941	$4,215,321
NATO infrastructure	81,000	190,000	175,000	177,500	172,000
Family housing	3,610,891	3,480,481	3,546,809	3,558,190	3,605,218
Base closure and realignment	672,311	1,174,369	1,174,369	1,174,369	1,024,369
Rescissions			– 73,507		– 100,000
GRAND TOTAL	**$8,374,000 ***	**$8,033,908**	**$8,634,000**	**$8,634,000**	**$8,833,908**
Fiscal 2000 emergency supplemental			**$4,702,097**		**$11,229,822**

* Does not include $33 million rescinded by the fiscal 2000 omnibus appropriations bill (PL 106-113).

SOURCE: House and Senate Appropriations committees.

the critics considered budget gimmicks would ultimately be reversed.

Similar Spending

The military construction figure in both the House and Senate versions of the bill was the same — $8.6 billion — though there was a $1.5 billion difference in how the money would be allocated. Conferees solved that problem by adding $200 million to the overall spending level.

The conference report would provide $8.83 billion, which is $800 million more than Clinton requested and about $460 million more than Congress appropriated for fiscal 2000 (PL 106-52).

Conferees added about $214 million to the Senate-passed bill and about $299 million to the House-passed version for general construction projects. David L. Hobson, R-Ohio, chairman of the House Appropriations Military Construction Subcommittee, said conferees increased funding for projects at U.S. military facilities along the border between North and South Korea.

"Everyone will tell you the housing in Korea is not near a standard that it should be," Hobson said. At the same time, he said that more should be done to improve housing throughout the military. "We don't have near enough money in this bill to take care of all the problems that are out there," Hobson said.

Conferees also favored projects for the National Guard and reserves, which have taken an increased role in peacekeeping missions in Bosnia and Kosovo. Guard and reserve spending would total $693 million, compared with $458 million in the House-passed bill and $581 million in the Senate version.

The bill would increase spending for family housing by about $40 million over the House and Senate versions, but it would provide about $150 million less than Clinton requested for the cost of closing military bases, most of it environmental cleanup.

Missile Defense

Conferees disagreed on how much should be spent to start building radar facilities for a possible national anti-missile defense system.

John W. Olver of Massachusetts, ranking Democrat on Hobson's subcommittee, expressed disappointment that the House agreed to the Senate's plan to spend $85 million on radar sites on one of the Aleutian Islands off Alaska.

The House version would have appropriated $65 million in major construction for the system, $20 million less than Clinton requested. Several countries, including Russia and China, have urged the United States not to proceed with the limited system, designed to defend the United States from a small number of incoming missiles.

Hobson said in a June 28 interview that it was "extremely important to the Senate" to include the full spending level for missile defense construction.

A statement in May from the Office of Management and Budget on the House-passed bill urged full funding for missile defense construction, even though Clinton may not decide until this fall whether to actually build a missile defense system.

He may leave the final decision to the next president. ◆

Transportation Bill Increases Construction Funds, Sets Standard for Drunken Driving

SUMMARY

Congress cleared a $58 billion fiscal 2001 Transportation spending bill Oct. 6 that significantly increased funding for highways and airport construction — including hundreds of last-minute projects — and struck compromises on several highway safety issues. President Clinton signed the measure into law Oct. 23, praising its new national 0.08 blood alcohol content standard for drunken driving.

The final outcome was never seriously in doubt, given the popularity of highway and airport spending. But the conference on the bill concluded only after several deals were negotiated on safety issues the Clinton administration had made a priority. Conferees waited for weeks after the August recess to meet, as congressional leaders adjusted and readjusted their overall appropriations strategy.

The final bill provided $30.7 billion for highways, plus $720 million in emergency spending; $6.3 billion for mass transit; $12.6 billion for aviation, including a record $3.2 billion for airport construction; and $6.5 billion for Federal Aviation Administration (FAA) operations. It allocated $4.5 billion for the Coast Guard. Amtrak received $521 million, the amount Clinton requested.

The House began with a $55.2 billion measure that matched funding levels for highways and aviation required by the 1998 surface transportation law (PL 105-178) and this year's aviation authorization bill (HR 1000 — PL 106-181). The legislation contained slightly lower funding for FAA operations than the administration requested, causing concern about the impact on the air traffic control system in an era of increasing passenger delays.

The bill steered clear of most policy issues, but it did contain a rider that would have blocked the government from studying updated fuel economy standards for cars and trucks.

The Senate passed a $54.8 billion version that added a number of policy issues to the mix.

Frank R. Lautenberg, D-N.J., included the proposed national 0.08 blood alcohol content drunken driving standard. The trucking industry prevailed on Transportation Appropriations Subcommittee Chairman Richard C. Shelby, R-Ala., to add language blocking the Clinton administration from proceeding on new rest regulations for truck and bus drivers. Shelby also added language requested by the auto industry to block federal rollover ratings of new vehicles. Senators rebuffed an attempt by George V. Voinovich, R-Ohio, to give states flexibility to shift some federal highway funds to passenger rail. That idea was strongly opposed by the highway construction industry.

When conferees met in October, they reached compromises on drunken driving, truck safety and the rollover tests — averting a Clinton administration veto threat.

They agreed to delay any drunken driving sanctions until 2004. The Transportation Department was barred from issuing a final trucking rule in fiscal 2001, giving industry opponents more time to make their case. And Shelby agreed to allow the rollover testing program to move forward while the National Academy of Sciences studied the issue.

Conferees also adopted a Senate compromise on the fuel economy issue that barred the Transportation Department from acting for another year but directed the National Academy of Sciences to study the impact of fuel economy standards. The bill's final passage was eased by nearly $3 billion in last-minute funding and hundreds of individually earmarked projects.

Box Score — Transportation — 2001 Fiscal Year

- **Bill:** HR 4475 — PL 106-346
- **Legislative action: House** passed HR 4475 (H Rept 106-622), 395-13, May 19.

Senate passed HR 4475, 99-0, on June 15, after substituting the text of S 2720 (S Rept 106-309).

House adopted the conference report (H Rept 106-940), 344-50, on Oct. 6

Senate cleared HR 4475, 78-10, on Oct. 6.

President signed the bill Oct. 23.

House Panel's Bill Would Block Funds for Houston Light Rail System

MAY 13 — House Majority Whip Tom DeLay, R-Texas, is known in Washington as "The Hammer." The folks back home learned why when DeLay single-handedly blocked federal funds for Houston's proposed transit system.

At a May 8 markup, the House Appropriations Transportation Subcommittee approved, by voice vote, a draft fiscal 2001 bill that includes a provision to prevent federal funding "for planning, design or construction of a light rail system in Houston."

DeLay, who hails from Sugar Land, a Houston suburb, said he would keep the ban in place until residents of the Houston metropolitan area have a chance to vote on the project.

Houston suffers some of the most severe traffic congestion in the country, and some of the worst air quality. The Metropolitan Transit Authority of Harris County has pushed light rail as a partial solution to these problems. The first segment proposed for construction would stretch 7.5 miles from the downtown business district to the Astrodome, including stops at Rice University, the Texas Medical

Center and some museums. That segment, with a price tag of $300 million, is within the districts of Democrats Sheila Jackson-Lee and Ken Bentsen — both of whom support the project.

After more than 100 public meetings, the authority's board unanimously recommended proceeding with construction of the first segment, which would generate more than $470 million in economic activity, according to an authority report.

But DeLay said the authority had not made its case on light rail and how it would fit into efforts to ease congestion for the region. The project could divert money from other important transportation projects, including suburban bus service, he said.

DeLay's move took Houston officials by surprise. Metro Chairman Robert D. Miller called it "surprising and drastic." After meeting with DeLay on May 10, Miller said: "I am convinced there is absolutely nothing Metro or the people of this region can do to convince him that we need this rail line."

Aside from the Texas controversy, there appear to be few pitfalls for the Transportation spending bill in the House. The full Appropriations Committee is expected to mark it up on May 16.

The Numbers

The $55.2 billion measure includes healthy increases over fiscal 2000 levels for nearly every major category, including a $2 billion increase for aviation programs that reflects the recently enacted FAA authorization law (PL 106-181).

The bill contains $15 billion in new discretionary budget authority and more than $40 billion in mandatory spending, mostly transfers from the highway and aviation trust fund accounts to highway, transit and airport programs.

Highway Trust Fund receipts are running about $3 billion higher than projected under the 1998 surface transportation law (PL 105-178). Spending on state highway construction grants would increase from $27.6 billion in fiscal 2000 to $29.7 billion, a 7.5 percent increase. *(1998 Almanac, p. 24-3)*

The Federal Transit Administration would receive $6.3 billion, compared with $5.8 billion in fiscal 2000, an 8.3 percent increase.

The subcommittee rebuffed Clinton administration efforts to redirect $741 million of the higher-than-expected gas tax revenues. The president's budget called for a new federal-state high-speed rail program and several other initiatives.

In an effort to rein in spending on Boston's "Big Dig" highway and tunnel project, the measure would prohibit federal officials from approving "advanced construction grants," under which state officials have spent funds based on projected federal appropriations.

The measure would enact the huge funding increases envisioned in the FAA authorization, including an increase of $1.3 billion in the Airport Improvement Program, to $3.2 billion. FAA's facilities and equipment account, which is also protected by funding guarantees, would increase from $2.1 billion to $2.7 billion. The FAA operations account, which includes all of the nation's air traffic control system, also would increase, from $5.9 billion to $6.5 billion, although this figure is $48 million below the administration's request.

The subcommittee's generous allocation enabled it to avoid cuts in the two other major programs unprotected by any spending guarantees: The Coast Guard would receive $4.6 billion, up from $4 billion this year; Amtrak would receive the $521 million the administration requested.

Stepped-Up Funding Abounds In House-Passed Transportation Bill

MAY 20 — In the first test of a Republican leadership effort to discourage policy riders on appropriations bills, the House passed May 19 a generous Transportation spending measure for fiscal 2001.

The bill was a good showcase for Republican leaders' plans because House Transportation and Infrastructure Committee Chairman Bud Shuster, R-Pa., has made it a practice over the years to wash spending bills clean of any provisions that might impinge on the authority of his committee.

The $55.2 billion appropriations bill (HR 4475), which includes increases in almost every major category, passed 395-13. *(Vote 210, p. H-68)*

But the vote masks trouble ahead. Before clearing, the bill could face spending cuts due to competition from other, more difficult spending bills for a shrinking pot of discretionary funds.

The transportation debate was the first under a rule designed to halt the time-honored practice of piggybacking legislation onto appropriations bills. The practice has become even more popular — some say necessary — as fights over social issues have stalled some authorization bills.

On May 17, the House Republican Conference adopted a resolution opposing legislative riders on spending bills. Republican Deborah Pryce of Ohio, the author of the resolution, said the Rules Committee will help enforce the policy by refusing to protect such provisions from point-of-order floor challenges.

The resolution, however, does not apply to measures that attempt to influence policy by withholding federal funding, such as a provision in the transportation bill strongly supported by Republicans and some Democrats that would prevent the administration from studying an update of car and truck fuel economy standards. Such measures are legitimate debates over spending, Pryce said.

Environmentalists argue that the Department of Transportation needs to look at the issue, especially in the face of energy policy questions spurred by high oil prices.

Kori E. Hardin, a spokeswoman for the Appropriations Committee's ranking Democrat, David R. Obey of Wisconsin, insisted that it was nonsensical to view such measures like any other spending decision. "These are riders," Hardin said May 18. "They are policy decisions."

Points of Order

Shuster successfully eliminated several provisions from the bill by raising points of order during the May 19 debate. In each case, the chair sustained his point or the pending amendment was withdrawn.

Among the victims was Transportation Appropriations Subcommittee Chairman Frank R. Wolf, R-Va., who lost language that would have allowed states with unallocated highway funds to use the money to improve railroad grade crossings. Shuster said the Wolf language would enable some states to fund such projects entirely with federal funds and evade a requirement that states pay at least 10 percent.

Shuster also succeeded in removing language that would have allowed some money from the Highway Trust Fund to be spent on rail projects.

But he withdrew his challenge to a provision that would fine the agency $100,000 a day if it did not submit a detailed capital spending plan for the Coast Guard and the Federal Aviation Administration (FAA) when it submitted its next budget request. Wolf said the capital plans were needed for appropriators to write their bill. Shuster agreed with Wolf on the need for the provision.

Sheila Jackson-Lee and Ken Bentsen, both Houston Democrats, attempted to strike language in the bill inserted by Majority Whip Tom DeLay, a Republican from suburban Houston, that would prevent the federal government from spending any money on Houston's light rail system.

Jackson-Lee and Bentsen argued that DeLay's provision undercut a project that had overwhelming public, government and business support in the city. After a debate, they withdrew their motion.

Generous Allocations

The bill would provide a total of $12.6 billion for the FAA, including $3.2 billion from the Airport and Airway Trust Fund for airport construction.

The bill would provide $30.7 billion for road projects, all of it from the Highway Trust Fund. The Federal Transit Administration would receive a total of $6.3 billion, $5 billion from the Highway Trust Fund.

The Coast Guard would receive $4.6 billion, up from $4 billion in fiscal 2000. Amtrak would receive the $521 million the administration requested, $49.5 million less than in fiscal 2000.

Senate Bill Likely to Block Implementation of Truck Safety Plan

JUNE 10 — The fiscal 2001 transportation appropriations bill could become the vehicle that halts a controversial Clinton administration truck safety initiative.

The draft spending bill, which is due to be marked up June 13 by the Senate Transportation Appropriations Subcommittee, is expected to include language that would block the administration from spending money to implement a proposed rule that would adjust how long truck and bus drivers can drive and how much they must rest.

Both the trucking industry and traffic safety groups have made a top priority of updating the 60-year-old hours-of-service rule, though they disagree on the details. Neither side is happy with the Transportation Department's proposal. Trucking companies question the science behind the department's proposed increase in the rest period — from eight hours after a 10-hour driving shift, to a minimum of 10 hours.

Trucking interests also strongly object to a proposal to require "black box" data recorders on board trucks to track compliance with the rule. Most observers of the industry say the current compliance system — truck drivers keeping track of their hours driven on paper logs — is widely abused. But the industry views the black-box requirement as intrusive and too costly.

Safety advocates also opposed the department's proposal. They have focused on the possibility that, under the new rule, truck drivers could drive longer shifts, up to 12 hours at a stretch. The extra rest required under the proposal would not be enough to offset the safety risks of a 12-hour driving shift, they argue.

With so much controversy over the proposed rule, it would be easy for the Senate to agree to the language blocking it. The proposal still could survive in conference. House Transportation Appropriations Subcommittee Chairman Frank R. Wolf, R-Va., has been one of the foremost critics of the trucking industry's safety record. He may be reluctant to stop a Transportation Department safety initiative after only one public hearing.

Highway Funding

The spending bill also could become a battleground for the dispute over whether highway money should be used for intercity rail projects, such as increased Amtrak service.

George V. Voinovich, R-Ohio, chairman of the Senate Environment and Public Works Subcommittee on Transportation and Infrastructure, is looking for a way to enact legislation (S 1144) that would give states flexibility on highway spending. The full committee approved the measure last fall, but it has languished since then.

Voinovich is expected to offer the measure as an amendment during floor debate on the appropriations bill. If he does, it will reprise an effort fought and lost by state governors during consideration of the 1998 surface transportation authorization law (PL 105-178), when highway-building interests fought hard to dedicate federal gasoline taxes to highway spending. *(1998 Almanac, p. 24-3)*

Voinovich and backers such as Frank R. Lautenberg, D-N.J., say states need the flexibility the bill would provide. Those that want to spend all the funds on highways would be able to do so, they said.

Others argue that rail projects would shortchange highway accounts and set a precedent for other types of incursions on the Highway Trust Fund.

Christopher S. Bond, R-Mo., backed by the formidable road-building lobby, is expected to lead the charge against the amendment.

In the House floor debate, Transportation and Infrastructure Chairman Bud Shuster, R-Pa., struck similar language out of the bill (HR 4475) on a point of order.

Voinovich would be subject to a similar point of order under Senate Rule XVI, which prohibits legislative language on an appropriations bill.

CAFE Standards

Environmentalists, the auto industry and their allies in the Senate are gearing up for a repeat of last year's debate on fuel economy standards.

At a June 8 news conference, Slade Gorton, R-Wa., Dianne Feinstein, D-Calif., and Richard H. Bryan, D-Nev., vowed to offer an amendment aimed at lifting a ban on the Transportation Department studying an update of corporate average fuel economy (CAFE) standards.

Gorton is backing the amendment even though Senate GOP leaders would like to avoid the controversial vote. A similar amendment was withdrawn during House debate under pressure from leaders in both parties.

In a May 19 statement, the Office of Management and Budget said the administration opposes the CAFE freeze, but it did not threaten a veto.

Spending Levels

The Senate bill will have lower funding levels than the measure passed by the House on May 19. The Senate's 302(b) allocation of $13.3 billion for discretionary budget authority is much tighter than the $15 billion figure the House used.

That will not matter much on the $30.7 billion for highway programs guaranteed by the 1998 transportation law. Similarly, some aviation capital accounts, such as the $3.2 billion Airport Improvement Program, are guaranteed by this year's Federal Aviation Administration authorization law (PL 106-181).

The budget guarantees are likely to reduce funds for the FAA's operations accounts, which include the air-traffic control system, and the Coast Guard, which is under strain after several years of tight budget allocations.

Senate Passes Lean Bill, Expecting It To Bulk Up In Conference

JUNE 17 — The Senate rushed through consideration of the fiscal 2001 Transportation spending bill (HR 4475) the week of June 12, advancing a politically popular measure that even supporters acknowledged would underfund air traffic control and the Coast Guard.

The bill, which passed 99-0 on June 15, now goes to conference, where some senators hope it will emerge closer to the more generous House version. *(Vote 132, S-25)*

The bill sailed through a subcommittee markup the morning of June 13 and full committee that afternoon. Less than 24 hours later, before the committee report had been printed, it was on the Senate floor. That reflected, in part, GOP leaders' sense of urgency to get the 13 annual spending bills moving wherever they can. The transportation bill is traditionally one of the most popular, loaded with local construction projects.

The $54.8 billion Senate measure includes $29.7 billion in highway spending, matching the level in the House bill. The Federal Aviation Administration (FAA) would receive $12.4 billion, a $2.3 billion increase over fiscal 2000. That includes $3.2 billion for the Airport Improvement Program and $2.7 billion for FAA facilities and equipment — spending levels guaranteed by an aviation authorization bill (PL 106-181).

Scrimping on Essentials

Senate appropriators were working with $1.7 billion less in budget authority than their House counterparts. With huge portions of the bill fenced off by authorizing legislation, senators resorted to cutting two essential public safety accounts: air traffic control and the Coast Guard. In both cases, supporters of the bill expressed confidence that the spending levels would be increased in conference. Aides said that most of the rest of the $1.7 billion Senate shortfall was the result of scoring differences with the House.

The Federal Aviation Administration would receive $6.4 billion for operations, $242 million below the administration budget request. The House bill was $48 million below the administration request. The FAA received $5.9 billion for operations in fiscal 2000.

The implications for air traffic control drew the harshest response from the Clinton administration. Speaking to reporters at the White House on June 13, Federal Aviation Administrator Jane F. Garvey stopped just short of threatening a veto.

"This reduction could create substantial delays in a system already strained to meet the demands arising from the rapid growth in air travel," Garvey said.

She also criticized the Senate for failing to move a House-passed supplemental spending measure (HR 3908 — H Rept 106-521) that includes $77 million for the FAA. Without the supplemental, Garvey said, the agency will have to forgo 170 safety inspectors and medical certification staff, resulting in 10,000 fewer inspections than last year.

Senators addressed some of these concerns at the full committee markup, voting to reprogram $173 million of Airport Improvement Program money for air traffic control. For accounting purposes, the funds still count against the $3.2 billion total for the airport construction fund.

The cuts to the Coast Guard also concerned many senators. The Senate's Coast Guard funding level of $4.4 billion is $257 million below the House bill and $249 million less than the administration's budget request.

This proposed funding reduction comes at a time when the Coast Guard has begun to cut back routine drug-interdiction and immigration patrols because of a fiscal 2000 funding squeeze. The cutbacks prompted the Senate to include $262 million of emergency funding in the fiscal 2001 military construction bill passed by the Senate (S 2521). Another $543 million was included in that measure for Coast Guard ship acquisition.

CAFE Conundrum

As was the case last year, the issue of whether to update fuel economy standards for cars and light trucks was hotly contested during floor debate. Amid a second dramatic rise in gasoline prices this year, the Senate reached a compromise on a procedural motion instructing conferees to accept House language that would continue to bar the Transportation Department from adjusting fuel economy standards. However, the Senate insisted on a study of the standards conducted by the Transportation Department and the National Academy of Sciences. Once the study is completed in June 2001, the department could propose adjusting the standards.

Corporate average fuel economy (CAFE) standards have remained virtually unchanged since 1985, even though engine technology has greatly advanced. Sponsors of the motion, Slade Gorton, R-Wash., Dianne Feinstein, D-Calif., and Richard H. Bryan, D-Nev., argued that a gradual increase in the standard would be the single greatest step in reducing U.S. dependence on foreign oil. Motor vehicles consume two-thirds of the oil used in the United States.

"The real question is not whether Americans want and need larger, 4-wheel drive vehicles, but whether these vehicles can be made more fuel-efficient," Bryan said.

But opponents of the motion were backed by an aggressive lobbying campaign by the auto industry. They said a CAFE update would result in automakers being forced to make lighter, less safe cars that American consumers do not want to buy. Labor unions generally backed the industry stance, leading some Democrats to also support the ban.

Spencer Abraham, R-Mich., said that consumers would be buying more small cars today if they were truly demanding fuel efficiency. "It's supply and demand," he said.

Feinstein rejected such arguments. She noted that American automakers resisted new engine technologies in the 1970s, and Japanese auto companies quickly began to produce better cars. "I thought those days were behind us," she said.

A similar amendment was withdrawn during House debate under pressure from leaders in both parties.

In a May 19 statement, the Office of Management and Budget stated its opposition to the CAFE freeze but stopped short of issuing a veto threat.

On another auto industry issue, the Senate bill included language to stop the National Highway Traffic Safety Administration from implementing a proposed regulation on how to test sport utility vehicles for rollover dangers. The auto industry opposed the new rule.

The Senate bill would prohibit the safety administration from proceeding until the National Academy of Sciences completes a study on whether the proposed test is a "scientifically valid measurement and provides practical, useful information to the public." The study also will examine the "validity" of the safety administration's proposal to make the rollover information available on a sticker at automobile showrooms, compared with making the information available on the World Wide Web.

The Senate bill also would prohibit the Transportation Department from implementing its proposal to revise hours-of-service regulations for truck and bus drivers.

Rail Flexibility Revisited

George V. Voinovich, R-Ohio, offered an amendment that would have allowed states to spend some highway money on intercity rail projects. The amendment failed on a procedural vote, 46-52, when Robert C. Smith, R-N.H., invoked Senate Rule XVI against amendments not germane to a spending bill. Before the vote, senators held a long debate about states' rights and the integrity of the Highway Trust Fund. *(Vote 130, p. S-25)*

Voinovich argued that states needed the flexibility to use other options to meet their transportation needs. The amendment mirrored a section of legislation (S 1144) approved by the Senate Environment and Public Works Committee last fall.

"As states are more able to turn towards passenger rail service as a safe, reliable and efficient mode of transportation, we will relieve congestion on our nation's highways," Voinovich said.

But opponents, led by Christopher S. Bond, R-Mo., argued that the Voinovich proposal would drain essential funds from the highway account. Bond said it would break a promise made during consideration of the six-year surface transportation authorization bill (PL 105-178) in 1998, that gas taxes would be used to bring highways back into good repair. *(1998 Almanac, p. 24-3)*

"We told the people of America we would put trust back in the trust fund," Bond said. "This is an issue about keeping our commitment to the taxpaying citizens of our states and of this country."

Drunken Driving Standard

Frank R. Lautenberg of New Jersey, ranking Democrat on the Senate Transportation Appropriations Subcommittee, incorporated in the bill language he has long pursued on a nationwide standard for drunken driving. States that did not choose to adopt the stricter new standard would be denied federal highway funds.

Eighteen states and the District of Columbia currently abide by the proposed blood-alcohol content standard of 0.08 percent. Most other states have a 0.10 percent standard.

Lautenberg and his supporters argued that drivers with 0.10 percent blood alcohol content were 29 times more likely to have a fatal accident than a non-drinking driver, while drivers under the 0.08 percent standard were 11 times more likely to be in a fatal accident.

Opponents, including some senators from states that observe the 0.08 percent standard, argued that the provision was an infringement on states' rights.

"I don't believe it is the responsibility of the federal government to set these standards," said Larry E. Craig, R-Idaho, during the committee markup.

In 1998, as part of the surface transportation authorization, Congress adopted incentives for states to use the .08 percent standard, but supporters of the national standard argued that this voluntary approach has failed. Only two states have moved to the tougher standard since 1998.

Lautenberg predicted that most states would move to adopt the new national standard. "It helps when it hurts," he said.

Administration Rebuffed

The Senate bill, like its House counterpart, ignored several administration initiatives.

The Senate passed over an administration plan to divert a $741 million portion of $3.1 billion in extra gas tax revenue toward an array of programs the White House favors, including a $468 million high-speed rail program. Instead, the Senate proposed that all $3.1 billion be returned to the states as extra highway grants.

As it did in fiscal 2000, the Senate proposed to alter the surface transportation authorization formula by increasing state grants at the expense of federally administered programs such as intelligent transportation systems and road building on American Indian lands.

The Senate rejected an array of aviation and Coast Guard user fees. The Senate-passed bill also includes language to require future administration budgets to spell out which programs would be cut if Congress refused to go along with user fee proposals.

Conferees Debate National Drunken Driving Standard, Truckers' Hours

AUGUST 5 — Two highway safety issues — a national standard for drunken driving and the number of hours truckers spend behind the wheel — are the focus of a House-Senate conference on the fiscal 2001 transportation appropriations bill.

Both were added to the Senate version of the bill (HR 4475 — S Rept 106-309), and the debate is being driven by opposing interest groups.

The conference is expected to wind up in September. Both versions of the bill would provide $30.7 billion for federal highway programs. The House bill includes $15.8 billion for federal aviation, rail, maritime and safety programs; the Senate version, $15.3 billion.

The national standard for drunken driving is a favorite of Sen. Frank R. Lautenberg, D-N.J., who is retiring from Congress as ranking Democrat on the Transportation Appropriations Subcommittee. The Senate language would penalize states that fail to adopt a 0.08 percent blood alcohol content standard for drunken driving by taking away 5 percent to 10 percent of their federal highway grants.

Eighteen states and the District of Columbia have adopted the 0.08 percent standard for drunken driving. Nearly all other states have a 0.10 percent blood alcohol standard.

Lautenberg is backed by a coalition of safety groups, including Mothers Against Drunk Driving, Advocates for Highway and Auto Safety, Public Citizen and the National PTA.

The Clinton administration also has embraced the proposal.

The issue arose during debate over the 1998 surface transportation bill (PL 105-178). After lobbying by groups such as the National Beer Wholesalers Association, the National Restaurant Association and the Distilled Spirits Council, Congress adopted a compromise giving states incentives to move to the stricter standard, rather than threatening their highway funds. Only two states have adopted tougher standards since then. *(1998 Almanac, p. 24-3)*

Other opponents of Lautenberg's proposal include local and state government groups, highway contractors, and the American Automobile Association.

In a joint letter to lawmakers, the National Governors' Association, the National Conference of State Legislatures, the Council of State Governments, the National League of Cities and the National Association of Counties argued: "States and localities are on the cutting edge in the fight against drunk driving and do not feel that a one-size-fits-all approach can work to fight the drunk driving problem."

"Work zone safety is a serious problem for us, but we don't want highway funds used as a stick," said Peter Loughlin, a lobbyist for the Associated General Contractors of America.

Alcohol Industry Contributes

According to the Center for Responsive Politics, the alcohol industry has contributed $6 million in soft money, political action committee and individual contributions to candidates for Congress in the current election cycle, up one-third from the 1995-96 cycle. Anheuser-Busch Companies Inc. contributed more than $1 million of the total.

House Republican leaders have not stated a position on the issue. Speaker J. Dennis Hastert, R-Ill., received the fourth-highest total of campaign cash from the restaurant industry, according to the Center for Responsive Politics. House Transportation Appropriations Subcommittee Chairman Frank R. Wolf, R-Va. — an aggressive advocate of traffic safety — supports the Senate language.

Wolf's traffic safety work has put him in the forefront of debate on the other hot issue in the transportation conference: hours of service for truck drivers.

The Senate version of the bill would block the administration from promulgating regulations that would require longer rest periods for drivers but allow longer shifts at the wheel.

The death toll from truck accidents rose to a peak of 5,398 in 1997, but has eased slightly since then.

Last year, Congress passed legislation (PL 106-69) creating a Federal Motor Carrier Safety Administration within the Transportation Department — there had been a unit in the Federal Highway Administration — with the hope of bolstering government oversight.

But Congress sidestepped the question of how long truckers should be on the road. Safety advocates claim that fatigue is a factor in up to 30 percent of the fatal accidents involving trucks. The trucking industry says the figure is much lower, and that many fatal accidents are caused by reckless auto drivers.

Neither side likes the Transportation Department's proposal. Safety groups say it would allow truckers to drive up to 12 hours at a time, up from 10 under current rules. The trucking industry had been hoping for 14-hour shifts.

The industry also objects to the department's proposal to require "black box" data recorders that would monitor compliance with the rule, saying the boxes cost too much — about $500 a truck — and would be intrusive.

Trucking groups say they favor a negotiated rule-making process on hours of service. This is opposed by the safety groups, who say they do not have the financial resources to match the industry's legal firepower.

Advocates for Highway and Auto Safety vice president Jackie Gillan said a Transportation Department consultant determined the parties are too far apart for an effective negotiated rule-making. The level of public interest in the department's proposal indicates that the process is working the way it is intended, she said.

Administration Threatens Veto If Truck Safety Rule Is Stalled

SEPTEMBER 2 — The Clinton administration has abandoned hope of completing action on a controversial truck safety regulation before the president leaves office, even as officials step up efforts to block a bill that would delay the new rule for at least a year.

At a briefing for reporters Aug. 24, Transportation Secretary Rodney Slater said the department would not be able to issue a final regulation to adjust the length of truck driving shifts and rest periods before the next president assumes office in January. On Aug. 9, the department had announced that it would extend the public comment period until Dec. 15.

"The process is what's critical here . . . [It's not] our resolve to cram down our thinking or our own proposal," Slater said. "That's why thwarting the process would be so unfortunate."

Still, Slater said he will recommend that President Clinton veto a fiscal 2001 transportation appropriations bill (HR 4475) if conferees decide to retain Senate-passed language that would block the truck rulemaking process for at least a year.

The Transportation Department has logged more than 50,000 public comments since issuing its draft rule on April 25. Due to the overwhelming response and intense interest among members of Congress, the department extended its comment period once before Slater's most recent announcement.

Transportation department officials say privately that regardless of who moves into the White House next year, it could be mid-2002 before a rule becomes final.

That would represent a victory of sorts for the trucking industry, which has vigorously lobbied against the hours-of-service proposal since it was unveiled April 25.

Truck safety has been a hot topic in Congress since last year, when growing concern over the rising death toll in truck-related traffic accidents led to passage of legislation (PL 106-69) to create the Federal Motor Carrier Safety Administration.

In that law, Congress sidestepped the hours-of-service issue, which for years has been the most contentious trucking safety question. Revising the rules has been a top priority of the trucking industry, auto insurers and consumer highway safety groups.

In 1995, Congress mandated that the Transportation Department come up with a new standard by March 1, 1999. In creating the new motor carrier safety agency, Congress criticized the Transportation Department for failing to make progress on "significant safety rulemaking proceedings," including hours of service. It urged the new agency to speed up its deliberations on the rules.

Rule and Reaction

The Transportation Department's tentative regulation would permit drivers to remain behind the wheel for as long as 12 hours at a stretch, up from the current 10. But it would also require longer rest periods, 10 consecutive hours and 12 hours per day, up from the current 8-hour requirement.

Reaction to the proposal in Congress has been harsh, mirroring the intense opposition by the trucking industry.

Trucking interests are calling for longer work shifts, up to 14 hours of driving per day. Highway safety groups strongly oppose any effort to lengthen driver work shifts.

A number of consumer, law enforcement and insurance groups are urging the administration to issue a final rule before Clinton leaves office.

"If the department does not act before the end of the year, we're going to continue to read about preventable deaths," said David Snyder, general counsel for the American Insurance Association.

Whether to require a delay in the rulemaking is certain to be one of the most contentious issues for transportation appropriations conferees to resolve.

House Appropriations Transportation Subcommittee Chairman Frank R. Wolf, R-Va., opposes the Senate language. A strong advocate for highway safety, Wolf worked for years to raise public awareness about truck safety issues. He was the chief advocate in Congress for stripping the Federal Highway Administration of trucking oversight after he concluded that the agency's regulators were too cozy with the trucking industry.

Truckers have launched an intensive lobbying campaign to persuade House members to support the Senate ban. More than 100 lawmakers have signed a letter supporting the industry position.

Trucking companies argue that longer rest periods would require the hiring of tens of thousands of new drivers at a time when there is already a severe shortage of qualified drivers. More trucks and inexperienced drivers could actually make the highways more dangerous, industry officials say. They also contend that added trucking costs could spur inflation, since delivery costs are factored into nearly every consumer product.

The new Dec. 15 deadline will enable the Federal Motor Carrier Safety Administration to conduct a series of "roundtable discussions" with industry, labor and safety groups to air their concerns.

Because of the overwhelming number of comments, Slater said the department will issue a revised rule, with another public comment period, before moving to a final rule. That will take the process well into the next administration.

While a Gore administration could be expected to stay the course on the current policy-making efforts, Republican George W. Bush would most likely proceed differently. The GOP platform calls for loosening the regulatory burden on the trucking industry. It describes the administration hours-of-service rule as crippling.

Senate Clears Bill, Which Sets Standard for Drunken Driving

OCTOBER 7 — A $58 billion Transportation spending bill (HR 4475) for fiscal 2001 lurched through Congress on Oct. 6, laden with $3 billion in last-minute projects and three carefully crafted compromises on highway safety issues.

The measure would set a nationwide 0.08 percent blood alcohol standard for drunken driving, allow new rules on how long truckers may stay behind the wheel and permit at least a study of higher fuel economy standards.

The House approved a conference report on the measure, 344-50, on Oct. 6, and the Senate cleared the bill, 78-10, the same day. Most lawmakers had not even seen the final version when they voted on it, let alone had a chance to read it in detail. *(House vote 516, p. H-164; Senate vote 267, p. S-48)*

The bill would provide $31.4 billion in highway funding, a $720 million increase over the House- and Senate-passed versions, and $2.6 billion more than was appropriated for fiscal 2000. The bill would allocate $30.7 billion from the Highway Trust Fund, matching the level called for under the 1998 surface transportation law (PL 105-178). But lawmakers padded that total with nearly $2 billion in highway projects that would be paid for from general funds.

Aviation programs would also be increased, matching the minimum levels required by this year's aviation authorization bill (PL 106-181). The Airport Improvement Program would soar to $3.2 billion from this year's level of $1.9 billion. Overall, the Federal Aviation Administration (FAA) would receive $12 billion, a $2 billion increase over current funding.

Amtrak would receive $521 million. The Federal Railroad Administration would receive $726 million, a $9 million decrease from fiscal 2000. Conferees rejected both a $468 million high-speed rail corridor building program and a set of user fees, proposed by the administration, designed to generate $103 million in revenue.

The Federal Transit Administration would receive $6.3 billion, $50 million below the administration's request but $486 million above the fiscal 2000 funding level.

The bill would mean a $158 million decrease in Coast Guard funding, at $4.5 billion. The administration requested $4.6 billion.

The National Highway Traffic Safety Administration would receive $404 million, up from $368 million. The new Federal Motor Carrier Safety Administration would receive $269 million.

Greasing the Way

The adoption of the conference report was greased by last-minute additions costing billions of dollars, including $600 million for the Woodrow Wilson Bridge spanning the Potomac River on Washington's Capital Beltway.

Conferees added about $1.3 billion to previous versions of the bill for major programs such as the FAA and the Coast Guard, according to a House aide.

The conferees also added about $2 billion for last-minute highway projects, including the Wilson Bridge.

Late additions included more than $800 million for improving Chicago rail stations, a cash infusion that was arranged by House Speaker J. Dennis Hastert, R-Ill. The extra spending ranged from $100 million for an Appalachian highway project in West Virginia to $1 million to help start a tourist railroad in Virginia's Shenandoah Valley.

There also was a promise of $50 million for the Dulles corridor project in the district of Frank R. Wolf, R-Va. Meanwhile, Senate Transportation Appropriations Subcommittee Chairman Richard C. Shelby, R-Ala., engineered $5 million for rail improvements at Muscle Shoals, Tuscumbia and Sheffield, Alabama.

Hurry and Wait

The conference report came to the floor after weeks of delays, mostly unrelated to the content of the legislation. Conferees were repeatedly told to wait as House and Senate leaders revised their overall strategy on appropriations bills. Even though most issues had been resolved for weeks or even months, legislative language was not available to anyone but members of the Appropriations Committee until nearly midnight before the vote early on the morning of Oct. 6. Several members were seen looking in vain for the legislative language in the Speaker's Lobby as the vote drew near.

"I am not pleased by the process, nor the overall policy, so I will be a 'no' vote," said J.D. Hayworth, R-Ariz.

If members had seen the bill, they might not have recognized it as even a distant cousin of the measure the House voted on months ago.

Those with concerns about fiscal discipline would have had a hard time sorting through hundreds of individual highway, transit, intelligent-vehicle and airport projects. Rep. David R. Obey, D-Wis., said the process ensured that no more than a few dozen members and staff knew the content of the spending bills.

"Right now, the bills that we pass on the floor have nothing to do with the final products that we enact into law," said Scott Lilly, minority staff director for the House Appropriations Committee.

Airport Earmarks

The mandatory increases in airport and FAA capital accounts had caused concern about whether there would be enough money left over to fund air traffic control. Conferees scraped together $6.5 billion for FAA operations, including $5.2 billion for administration of the air traffic control system, $48 million and $10 million, respectively, below the administration's request. Those levels were expected to be close enough for the president to sign the bill.

But the measure for the first time specifies money for 162 airport projects that the senior Democrat on the House Transportation and Infrastructure Committee decried as a detriment to the overall safety of the aviation system.

James L. Oberstar of Minnesota, said the earmarks set a dangerous precedent by limiting the discretion of the FAA to prioritize spending from the Airport Improvement Program. The FAA currently sets priorities based on safety improvements and the need to add capacity to the national aviation system.

"If next year we experience the same kind of delays we experienced this year, travelers might not feel so comfortable traveling in an aviation system designed by Congress," Oberstar said.

Oberstar said the intent of the FAA authorization bill, with its huge increase in funding for the airport program, was to address the bottlenecks that have resulted in record air travel delays in the past two years.

"They came in and made a gold rush raid on the increased dollar amount," Oberstar said.

Drunken Driving Dust-Up

Traffic safety groups squared off against alcohol and restaurant lobbyists and local government organizations, including the National Governors' Association, in an intense battle over drunken driving standards in the conference agreement.

Conferees agreed to a national 0.08 percent blood alcohol standard, but they delayed sanctions against states that do not abide by it.

States that fail to comply with the national standard would lose 2 percent of their federal highway grants starting

Transportation Spending Highlights

Where the Money Goes

HR 4475 — Conference report: H Rept 106-940

The fiscal 2001 transportation spending bill (HR 4475), cleared for the president Oct. 6, would provide $58 billion for federal highways, airports, mass transit and other programs — $3.2 billion more than the Senate-passed bill and $2.7 billion above the House-passed total. The increase would come entirely from general funds — $18.5 billion, compared with $15.3 billion in the Senate bill and $15.8 billion in the House version. The remainder — $39.5 billion — is from trust funds. Under the 1998 surface transportation law (PL 105-178) and the 2000 FAA reauthorization (PL 106-181), the bulk of the bill's funding, particularly for highway and aviation programs, is already committed. *(Background, 1998 Almanac, p. 24-3)*

• Federal Aviation Administration

The conference report would provide a total of $12.6 billion for the FAA, $2.5 billion more than in fiscal 2000 and $1.4 billion more than President Clinton requested. The total includes $3.2 billion in construction grants guaranteed from the Airport and Airway Trust Fund. It includes $6.5 billion for operations, including air traffic control, the same as the House bill and $194 million more than the Senate measure. The amount exceeds fiscal 2000 spending by $644 million but is still $48 million less than requested.

• Federal Highway Administration

Conferees agreed on $30.7 billion for highway programs, the same as in both the House and Senate bills, but they added another $720 million in emergency spending for a backlog of requests to repair damage caused by hurricanes and other recent natural disasters. The total includes a $29.7 billion limit on obligational authority from the highway trust fund, most of it for state highway grants, and $1 billion in obligations for projects exempt from the limits under prior authorization bills.

• Federal Transit Administration

Like the House and Senate bills, the conference report includes $6.3 billion, $486 million more than in fiscal 2000 but $50 million less than Clinton requested. The limit on obligational authority for public transit from the Highway Trust Fund would be $5 billion, $373 million more than in fiscal 2000 but $50 million less than Clinton requested.

Hot-Button Issues

Δ **CAFE standards.** Like the Senate bill, the conference report would block any efforts to update Corporate Average Fuel Economy standards for cars and light trucks but would direct the National Academy of Sciences to complete a study of the issue.

Δ **Hours of Service.** The conference report would allow the Transportation Department to proceed with developing regulations on the length of truck drivers' work shifts, but bar the adoption of new rules during fiscal 2001.

Δ **Drunken Driving.** Conferees agreed to a national 0.08 percent blood alcohol content standard for drunken driving, as the Senate wanted, but delayed sanctions against states that do not abide by it. The provision was the focus of intense lobbying by alcohol and restaurant lobbyists, as well as by traffic safety groups.

Δ **Auto safety.** Conferees adopted provisions that would require motor vehicle and tire manufacturers to "review and consider" overseas problems and evaluate whether vehicles or equipment in the U.S. have a defect, and that would allow the Transportation Department to proceed with a new method of testing sport utility vehicles for rollover dangers while the National Academy of Sciences studies the government's rollover test and alternative approaches.

(figures are in thousands of dollars of new budget authority)

	Fiscal 2000 Appropriation	Fiscal 2001 Clinton Request	House Bill	Senate Bill	Conference Report
Federal Aviation Administration	$8,131,495	$9,271,601	$9,385,366	$9,190,358	$9,388,000
Federal Highway Administration*	0	0	0	0	0
Federal Railroad Administration	734,952	587,687	689,263	705,015	725,618
Federal Transit Administration	1,159,000	1,254,400	1,254,400	1,254,400	1,254,400
Coast Guard	4,023,653	4,608,591	4,616,506	4,359,099	4,518,895
NHTSA	89,400	144,475	109,876	109,876	118,876
Secretary of Transportation	76,152	88,070	78,449	75,669	87,285
GRAND TOTAL	**$15,084,976**	**$16,146,737**	**$15,773,944**	**$15,295,300**	**$18,492,649**
Total adjusted for scorekeeping	($14,980,057)	($16,153,737)	($15,766,944)	($15,314,300)	($18,505,649)
Limits on obligations and exempt obligations	*($35,702,583)*	*($38,477,176)*	*($39,472,176)*	*($39,471,748)*	*($39,472,176)*

* Receives no general funds; all money comes from trust funds.

TABLE: House and Senate Appropriations committees

in fiscal 2004. That penalty would rise to 4 percent in fiscal 2005, 6 percent in fiscal 2006 and 8 percent in fiscal 2007. The agreement would allow any state that adopted the 0.08 standard by 2007 to recover previously lost highway funds.

Conferees rejected two amendments that would have altered the drunken driving provision.

One, by Rep. Martin Olav Sabo, D-Minn., would have doubled incentive grants for states that voluntarily adopt the 0.08 standard. It was rejected, 6-10, on a roll call of House conferees. Sabo argued that the decision about how to define drunken driving was a right of the states under the Constitution. Sabo served in the Minnesota State Legislature for 18 years, including a stint as the state Senate president.

Proponents of the 0.08 standard argued that the incentive grant approach, as embodied in the 1998 surface transportation law (PL 105-178), had failed. Only two states have adopted the standard since then. *(1998 Almanac, p. 24-3)*

Currently, 18 states and the District of Columbia define drunken driving at 0.08 blood alcohol content. Most other states have a 0.10 standard.

An amendment by Obey to apply the same financial sanctions to an array of other drunken driving programs failed on a voice vote.

Obey, who said his grandfather had been killed by a drunk driver and that he himself had been knocked off a bicycle at the age of 12 by a drunk driver, contended that it was unfair to penalize his state for having a higher blood alcohol standard when it has other restrictions to cut drunken driving.

"To me, if you're serious about drunk driving . . . you will look for the fairest, most effective way to deal with the problem," Obey said.

But Sen. Frank R. Lautenberg, D-N.J., who worked with Mothers Against Drunk Driving to promote the new standard, said: "It's a stick we wanted to introduce, a stick to move things along. We've had years of incentives. They hardly ever work."

Highway Safety

Conferees adopted a new provision by Shelby that would require motor vehicle and tire manufacturers to "review and consider" whether problems with their products overseas could affect domestic products. The provision does not require that federal officials be notified of overseas problems.

Both the House and Senate are considering similar, though much broader, bills on vehicle safety.

Conferees compromised on whether to allow the Transportation Department to publish statistics on the probability that individual vehicles will roll over in accidents. The new rating system would have been blocked by language in the Senate bill.

The conference report would let the National Highway Traffic Safety Administration proceed with its rollover rating program. At the same time, the National Academy of Sciences will study the government's rollover test and alternative approaches.

"People have a right to expect that information the government provides is accurate, sound and unbiased," said Shelby.

Conferees reached a similar agreement on another contentious safety issue — agreeing to allow the Transportation Department to proceed with developing regulations on the duration of truck drivers' work shifts and mandatory rest periods. But it would prevent final action on the regulation during fiscal 2001.

Conferees adopted a Senate agreement on fuel economy standards with a few minor modifications.

The final language prevents the Department of Transportation from doing anything to revise standards during fiscal 2001. But it would permit the National Academy of Sciences, in consultation with the Transportation Department, to complete a study by July 1, 2001, on the effect of raising the standards.

The agreement pleased environmentalists, who think the study will back their case that stronger new standards would reduce air pollution, slow global warming and help reduce dependence on foreign oil. The auto industry was pleased that the study will take into account the impact on motor vehicle safety as well as employment in the auto industry. Industry efforts to require an even broader study were rebuffed. ◆

Treasury-Postal Bill Clears After First Version Falls To Presidential Veto

Congress cleared a $30.4 billion fiscal 2001 spending bill for the Treasury Department, Postal Service and other agencies as part of the final omnibus appropriations package. The bill was virtually the same as an earlier version that President Clinton had vetoed. *(Omnibus appropriations, p. 2-3)*.

SUMMARY

The bill got off to a quick start, passing the House in July (HR 4871), with Senate appropriators already having approved their version (S 2900). But several tough battles loomed. The House unexpectedly adopted controversial floor amendments aimed at loosening enforcement of trade sanctions against Cuba. The White House insisted on more funds for the IRS and counter-terrorism programs. And in the Senate, Democrats promised a floor fight over gun control, an issue addressed in the Senate committee bill.

Hoping to avoid difficult votes and speed up the process, GOP leaders decided to add a negotiated version of the bill to the conference report on the legislative branch spending bill (HR 4516), thereby avoiding Senate debate on a stand-alone Treasury-Postal measure. They also added a third item, a repeal of the 3 percent excise tax on telephone service. The move backfired in the House just before the August recess, where angry Democrats, joined by some Republicans, threatened to sink the bill, forcing GOP leaders to pull it from the floor. The House narrowly adopted the conference report after the recess, but the Senate rejected it, infuriated over the lack of opportunity for debate on issues such as gun control and the absence of language to block a congressional pay raise. The Senate finally cleared the bill Oct. 12, after reaching a bipartisan compromise on additional funding.

The key was a $348 million package of additional spending, incorporated in the fiscal 2001 Transportation appropriations bill (HR 4475) that included an extra $216 million for improving customer service and enforcement at the IRS — the administration said the money was essential to meet a mandate for improving customer service under a 1998 IRS overhaul (PL 105-206) — and $37 million for fighting terrorism. It also included funding for two other administration priorities: $8 million for a new program to encourage low-income families to save money in "first accounts" in banks, and $2.5 million to fund voter education programs in Puerto Rico. The bill did not include the Cuba language, was silent on a congressional pay raise and maintained existing law requiring federal employee health plans to cover contraceptives while barring them from covering abortions.

Clinton surprised many Republicans by vetoing the bill anyway, saying funding for Congress and the White House, also covered by the bill, should not go forward when much of the rest of the appropriations process was deadlocked.

Box Score — 2001 Fiscal Year

Treasury-Postal Service

- **Bill:** HR 4577 — PL 106-554
- **Legislative action: House** passed HR 4871 (H Rept 106-756), 216-202, July 20.

House adopted the conference report (H Rept 107-796) on HR 4516, 212-209, on Sept. 14.

Senate rejected the conference report, 28-69, on Sept. 20.

Senate cleared HR 4516, 58-37, on Oct. 12.

President vetoed the bill Oct. 30.

House adopted the conference report on HR 4577 (H Rept 106-1033), 262-90, on Dec. 15.

Senate cleared the bill by voice vote Dec. 15.

President signed the bill Dec.

Democrats Decry Low IRS Funds In Bill Approved By House Panel

JULY 15 — A House subcommittee approved a fiscal 2001 appropriations bill for the Treasury Department, Postal Service and other government agencies July 11 that would provide more money to enforce gun control laws. It also would require first lady Hillary Rodham Clinton to report to Congress on the use of Air Force planes for her Senate campaign in New York.

The subcommittee approved the unnumbered bill by voice vote, setting the stage for full committee action July 18.

Democrats said they would oppose the measure because it does not contain sufficient funding for the Internal Revenue Service (IRS). They also criticized as a political attack the Republican proposal to require the first lady to account for use of Air Force planes. Despite those objections, the bill appears to be headed toward quick action in the full committee and the floor later this month.

"We have a long road ahead of us, but we are starting early. In my opinion this mark is not, as Regis Philbin says, our final answer," said Treasury, Postal Service and General Government Appropriations Subcommittee Chairman Jim Kolbe, R-Ariz. "But, until we are given a few lifelines this is the best we can do."

The bill would provide more than $29 billion in budget authority, about $2 billion less than President Clinton's request. Of that amount, more than $14 billion is for discretionary programs.

The biggest chunk of money is for the Treasury Department, which collects federal taxes and performs a variety of law enforcement tasks. The measure would fund a Clinton gun enforcement initiative, allowing Treasury's Bureau of Alcohol, Tobacco and Firearms (ATF) to hire 600 new employees.

Kolbe said he expects the bill to have strong support in full committee, but added that key issues would have to be resolved later in the process. Among them was a shortfall of about $175 million in the amount needed to allow agencies covered by the bill to maintain their current level of services.

The legislation would provide $8.5 billion for the IRS, more than $466 million less than the administration requested. Democrats charged that the Republican plan would prevent the agency from keeping up with its workload and hiring new employees to improve service and tax law enforcement.

Kolbe acknowledged that the IRS needed more money, but said he could not squeeze it under the overall budget allocation provided for the measure.

The bill was silent on another perennially touchy issue — congressional pay raises. House members have in past years used the markup as a forum on whether to permit an automatic cost-of-living increase to take effect. Under a 1989 law (PL 101-194), members get a raise unless they vote to prevent it. *(1989 Almanac, p. 51)*

This year, there has been little public debate on the pay raise. Members are expected to get an increase of 2.7 percent, or about $3,800, in their current $141,300 pay.

Lawmakers of both parties agreed last month to allow the pay raise — after coming up with extra money to ward off a possible reduction in salaries for congressional staff aides.

"There was agreement [between the parties]. You have to be sure that neither side will use it politically," said Steny. H. Hoyer of Maryland, the ranking Democrat on the subcommittee.

Another battle is emerging over construction of new federal courthouses. The House bill would fund none of the 17 courthouse projects on a list submitted by the General Services Administration. The projects' total cost would be $711.7 million; the administration had requested $488 million to fund seven of them, including courthouses in California, Washington and Virginia.

Senate Treasury and General Government Appropriations Subcommittee Chairman Ben Nighthorse Campbell, R-Colo., said finding money for the courthouses would be a top priority as his panel prepared to mark up its draft of the bill. "We think we have found the money for three," he said in an interview. "But a number of senators are interested in these projects, and they are trying to find more money."

First Lady Fracas

During the House markup, lawmakers clashed over language in the bill and the accompanying report on the first lady's Senate campaign-related travel expenses.

The bill would require her campaign to file monthly reports to the House Appropriations Committee on expenses from her use of Air Force planes on campaign trips. The campaign currently files such data with the Federal Election Commission, which requires quarterly reports.

Committee Republicans released a summary of Mrs. Clinton's travel expenses from June 1999 through May 2000. The handout, based on information provided by the White House, showed that her campaign had reimbursed the government $112,000 for those trips, while the total cost to the government was $698,000. Republicans said that taxpayers had absorbed the $586,000 difference.

Some Democrats questioned whether it was fair to impose reporting requirements on the first lady that did not have to be met by other candidates. The Clinton campaign said that the reimbursement was standard practice, based on the equivalent cost of a first-class airline ticket for each trip.

Hoyer insisted on an amendment, adopted by voice vote, that included language stating that the first lady's actions were "consistent with all current laws and regulations governing First Family travel."

The amendment also struck language referring to trips that were subsidized or "taken at taxpayer expense."

Hoyer said he agreed with the overall intent of provisions that would require disclosure of travel expenses.

Kolbe said he agreed with the thrust of Hoyer's amendment. "We don't have evidence that laws were violated," he said.

Another partisan battle flared briefly over an amendment offered by Jo Ann Emerson, R-Mo., that would require federal agencies to give companies and other interested parties an opportunity to correct inaccurate information placed on government Internet sites.

Emerson said the proposal was a response to concerns about online information posted by the Environmental Protection Agency on the issue of global warming.

David E. Price, D-N.C., said the amendment would be hard to put into practice. Kolbe said questions about the amendment, which would require the Office of Management and Budget to develop a rule on appealing the accuracy of online information, would have to be resolved, or it would probably be deleted in a House-Senate conference committee.

Other issues proved less contentious. There was little debate on a provision that would continue a current ban on abortion coverage by federal employees' health benefit plans. The bill would also preserve a requirement that those health plans cover contraceptives.

On another issue, the panel approved 7-6 an amendment by Hoyer that would erase a 0.5 percent increase in contributions by federal employees to their pension plans. The 1997 balanced budget law (PL 105-33) required the increase. *(1997 Almanac, p. 2-59)*

Hoyer said lawmakers had promised to repeal the increase once the budget was balanced, calling the move a "fundamental issue of fairness."

Gun Agreement

During the markup, Virgil H. Goode Jr., I-Va., won voice vote approval of a proposal to prevent Treasury Department law enforcement agencies from giving special preference to Smith & Wesson when purchasing firearms.

The company reached an agreement with the Clinton administration in March that resolved legal battles between it and cities and counties over its liability for gun violence. Smith & Wesson agreed to put child safety locks on its guns. It also agreed to make digital images of shell casings for every gun the company produces and to allow the ATF to match those images with casings found at crime scenes.

Goode said other gun makers were concerned that the agreement might put pressure on law enforcement agencies to use Smith & Wesson for gun purchases. The administration has not formally required such a preference, but has encouraged cities and counties to join a Communities for Safer Guns Coalition and give consideration to Smith & Wesson when police agencies buy guns.

Democrats had a mixed response to the Goode amendment. Some said it was unnecessary, but Hoyer said Goode had a valid point. A rival of Smith & Wesson, Beretta USA, has a factory in Accokeek, Md., in Hoyer's district.

"All things being equal, it might not be a good idea to require agencies to give preference to one company over another," Hoyer said.

Hoyer said he would consider offering gun-related amendments at the full committee markup. He has been considering a proposal that would require background checks of customers who make purchases at gun shows. Such checks are currently required at gun stores, but not at exhibitions.

Internal Revenue Service

Democrats strongly objected to the bill's funding level for the IRS. They said the total was well short of the amount needed to carry out a 1998 IRS overhaul (PL 105-206). That law directed the agency to take care of the needs of customers and to protect taxpayers. *(1998 Almanac, p. 21-3)*

"We asked them to provide better service, but we are not giving them the money to do it," Hoyer said.

Kolbe replied that there was simply not enough money in the subcommittee allocation to meet the administration's request. He was hopeful more could be found in the Senate.

The White House is expected to insist on funding to modernize IRS computers, allow employees to receive more returns electronically and provide better telephone service to consumers.

Committee Republicans stood by a decision to impose what amounts to a temporary ban on new funding for construction by the General Services Administration.

Kolbe said there was not enough money to cover three proposals: a new ATF headquarters; a consolidation of Maryland offices of the Food and Drug Administration; and renovation of the National Archives.

"Let me be perfectly up front about this — this mark has a moratorium on all new construction," Kolbe said.

It appeared unlikely, however, that the moratorium would stick.

In the Senate, Campbell said senators were searching for more money to pay for 17 courthouses on a GSA list of projects. The projects are ranked in priority based on assessments by federal judges of their needs for new courtrooms and improved security.

Campbell said senators had found funding for the top three on the list, located in Los Angeles, Seattle and Richmond, Va.

He said senators were continuing to search for money for more. The fourth-ranked project, a courthouse in Gulfport, Miss., that would cost nearly $43 million, is a top goal for Senate Majority Leader Trent Lott, R-Miss.

Senate Budget Committee Chairman Pete V. Domenici, R-N.M., has strongly supported efforts to fully fund virtually all of the projects on the list. He particularly wants money for a courthouse in Las Cruces, N.M.

Kolbe questioned how much spending was needed. "The administration asked for only seven of them," he said.

While House appropriators banned new buildings, they did find money for an item sought by both the administration and industry: a new computer system to help keep track of increased exports and imports through the nation's ports and airports.

The House bill would provide about $161 million for the project. The money would come from general revenues rather than a user fee, as had been proposed by the administration.

The Customs Service has complained that its current computer system suffers breakdowns and is too slow. Kolbe said the system was "antiquated" and has to be replaced.

The bill would provide more than $24.2 million to pay for protection of candidates during the presidential campaign; about $3 million for Treasury Department initiatives to halt money laundering; and more than $5.9 million for the National Archives to process Clinton administration records.

The bill includes nearly $2 million to support the Secret Service's national threat assessment center, which would provide advice to schools, hospitals and businesses on how to prevent gun violence by upgrading security systems.

The panel approved by voice vote an amendment by Republican Frank R. Wolf of Virginia to bar the import of diamonds from a half-dozen African nations. The measure was aimed at halting diamond sales used to support rebels in Sierra Leone. Diamonds could be brought from Sierra Leone if they had a certificate of origin. The amendment is in line with a United Nations policy.

Sierra Leone's government said July 14 that it had banned diamond exports until a proper certification program was in place.

House-Passed Bill Would Block Some Cuba Sanctions

JULY 22 — A tough battle over Cuba trade sanctions looms during the week of July 24, as the full Senate takes up its version of the fiscal 2001 appropriations bill funding the Treasury Department, Postal Service and other federal agencies.

After House and Senate committee markups of the legislation (HR 4871, S 2900) during the week of July 17, as well as a House floor vote, lawmakers seem to have settled one issue, however: They will receive a 2.7 percent pay raise next year, an increase of $3,800 over their current $141,300 salary.

Under existing law, members are automatically entitled to an annual pay increase, unless they vote to block it. The Treasury-Postal bill has, in the past, been the vehicle for amendments to bar the raise. Such efforts this year have been unsuccessful.

The House approved its version of the $29.1 billion Treasury-Postal bill on July 20, 216-202. The vote came after unexpected adoption of two floor amendments aimed at loosening enforcement of existing sanctions against Cuba. The amendments prevailed despite strong opposition by Republican leaders, who charged that they would prop up Cuba's communist regime and put U.S. consumers in the position of subsidizing Fidel Castro. *(Vote 428, p. H-132)*

"Nobody can paint me as a communist," said Mark Sanford, R-S.C., sponsor of one of the amendments. "It is just time for a change in our trade policy. We need to engage Cuba, not isolate it."

The House voted 232-186 to adopt Sanford's proposal to block funding for enforcing restrictions on travel to Cuba. *(Vote 425, p. H-132)*

Lawmakers also voted 301-116 to adopt an amendment by Jerry Moran, R-Kan., that would block funding to enforce current restrictions on the export of medicine and food to Cuba. *(Vote 426, p. H-132)*

President John F. Kennedy declared a trade embargo against Cuba in February 1962. The Cuba sanctions law of 1996 (PL 104-114) codified the embargo, prohibiting normal trade while Castro remains in power. *(1992 Almanac, p. 557; 1996 Almanac, p. 9-6)*

Opponents vowed to fight attempts to offer sanction-lifting amendments to the Senate version of the bill. They said they would try to delete the Cuba provisions in a House-Senate conference committee.

"This is not the end of it. We are counting on our allies to help us, including Senate Majority Leader Trent Lott [R-Miss.]. We do not want these amendments to be in the final bill," said Ileana Ros-Lehtinen, R-Fla., a Cuban-American who helped lead the unsuccessful fight against the amendments on the House floor.

The House voted 174-241 to defeat a third amendment, offered by Charles B. Rangel, D-N.Y., that would have ended enforcement of any trade sanctions against Cuba. *(Vote 424, p. H-132)*

Cuba sanctions are likely to be an issue in the presidential election. Candidates from both parties are hoping to woo Cuban-American voters who are critics of Castro. Texas Gov. George W. Bush, the presumptive GOP nominee, has opposed lifting sanctions. Vice President Al Gore has called for improved ties with Cuba, but has been cool to ending sanctions.

Rep. George Nethercutt, R-Wash., said the votes would add momentum to his own efforts to enact a provision, as part of another spending bill (HR 4461), worked out with House GOP leaders, to lift restrictions on the export of food and medicine to Cuba and four other countries: Libya, Sudan, Iran and North Korea. The drive is being propelled by a coalition that includes wheat farmers and businesses hoping to expand trade and tourism.

The Senate Appropriations Committee approved its bill by a 27-0 vote, just hours before the House floor vote. Like the House version, the Senate bill would provide about $29.1 billion in budget authority, including $14.4 billion in discretionary funding in fiscal 2001. Both bills would provide about $2 billion less than Clinton's budget proposal, and about $824.6 million more than the fiscal 2000 spending law.

Apart from the impending battle on Cuba, appropriators said their biggest hurdle in working out a final compromise bill will be funding.

"The problem is money. Everything seems to need more money. We're going to deal with the budget caps eventually. In the meantime we're going to work on this bill and others and try to finish them," Senate Appropriations Committee Chairman Ted Stevens, R-Alaska said July 19.

House Treasury, Postal Service and General Government Appropriations Subcommittee Chairman Jim Kolbe, R-Ariz., said one key issue would be to find additional funds for the Internal Revenue Service. "If we can find money for the IRS, I think the president will sign it," Kolbe said on July 18.

Both bills would provide $8.5 billion for the IRS, more than $400 million below the administration's request. The agency has estimated that the lower funding level would force cuts of more than 2,000 full-time staff positions.

Negotiators have to work out other differences in addition to the IRS issue. The House bill would slap a moratorium on new construction sought by the General Services Administration. The Senate bill would provide $374.3 million in advance funding for fiscal 2002 construction projects, including new courthouses in Los Angeles, Seattle, Richmond, Va., and Gulfport, Miss., as well as a consolidation of Food and Drug Administration offices in Maryland.

The Senate bill would provide virtually no money for a top priority of House appropriators, a new Customs Service computer system to keep track of imports and exports at ports and airports. The House would provide about $161 million for the project.

Smith & Wesson

Battle lines were also forming for an expected skirmish over gun control policy on the Senate floor.

Several Democrats, including Dianne Feinstein of California, said during the July 20 Senate Appropriations Committee markup that they would oppose language to prevent Treasury Department from giving special preference to Smith & Wesson when purchasing firearms.

The company resolved legal disputes with cities and counties over liability for gun violence earlier this year when it reached an agreement with the Clinton administration to put child safety locks on its guns and to help trace guns used by criminals. Richard C. Shelby, R-Ala., said agencies should purchase weapons without giving priority to any company. The administration has not specifically directed federal agencies to give preference but has urged cities and counties to give consideration to Smith & Wesson.

"There is going to be a fight on the Smith & Wesson language on the floor. Some members feel very strongly about this," said Sen. Byron L. Dorgan of North Dakota, ranking Democrat on the Treasury and General Government Appropriations Subcommittee.

During House floor debate on July 20, lawmakers defeated, 204-214, an amendment by John Hostettler, R-Ind., that would block funding to implement, enforce or administer provisions of the agreement. The deal called for the agency to develop a new system for matching images of shell casings at crime scenes with ballistics tests for new guns sold by Smith & Wesson. *(Vote 427, p. H-132)*

Senate Treasury and General Government Chairman Ben Nighthorse Campbell, R-Colo., said he hoped the battle over gun control would be resolved quickly. Both he and Kolbe said there was strong support for another key part of both bills: virtually full funding for the administration's request to hire 600 more Bureau of Alcohol, Tobacco and Firearms employees to bolster gun law enforcement.

In other action, the House on July 20 voted 228-190 to adopt an amendment by Thomas M. Davis III, R-Va., that would delay implementation of proposed Clinton administration rules for requiring federal contracts to meet standards for "integrity and business ethics" until the General Accounting Office has conducted a study of the issue. *(Vote 423, p. H-132)*

The House also turned back an effort by budget hawks, led by Ernie Fletcher, R-Ky., to change the rule for considering the bill in order to allow an amendment to block the congressional pay raise. A motion to close off debate and prevent further amendments passed, 250-173. *(Vote 419, p. H-130)*

Critics said the pay raise was not needed and expressed concern that it could become a political target.

The House bill would also retain a 0.5 percent increase in contributions by members of Congress and other federal employees to their pension plans. The 1997 balanced-budget law (PL 105-33) required the increase, which now amounts to about $700 a year.

Failed Bid to Bypass Senate Debate Could Set Stage For Deal in Fall

JULY 29 — Republican leaders tried unsuccessfully during the week of July 26 to sidestep Senate debate on a stand-alone fiscal 2001 spending bill (S 2900) for the Treasury Department and Postal Service and instead move a gerryrigged conference report to the floors of both chambers.

Although it failed, the GOP effort may have laid the groundwork for a deal in September on a final Treasury-Postal bill providing more money than either the Senate-drafted or House-passed (HR 4871) versions.

Top Republicans made it clear, however, that they want any final compromise measure to eliminate provisions added on the House floor July 24 to end the enforcement of some longstanding trade sanctions against Cuba. They also are eager to head off amendments by Senate Democrats for tougher gun control restrictions.

Senate Treasury and General Government Appropriations Subcommittee Chairman Ben Nighthorse Campbell, R-Colo., defended the unusual effort.

"We came up with the best compromise we could in the time that we had," he said. "I just hope everybody will kind of cool off and settle down, and we can get back to it."

Campbell said the compromise bill should have had strong appeal because of its emphasis on law enforcement. Under the draft, the Bureau of Alcohol, Tobacco and Firearms (ATF) would get virtually full funding to hire 600 new employees and toughen gun law enforcement.

Democrats, including Rep. Steny H. Hoyer of Maryland, said that while they objected to the GOP effort, their plan could serve as a blueprint for an agreement after the August recess. "The differences are not great," Hoyer said.

The Senate began action by voting, 97-0, on July 26 to invoke cloture and begin debate. The consensus quickly dissolved into a bitter partisan battle. *(Vote 227, p. S-41)*

The target of Democrats' wrath was an effort by Republicans to broker a bicameral deal under which the Senate would not debate its version of the bill. Instead the House and Senate would vote on a compromise that combined the Senate committee-approved and the House-passed versions of the legislation. The compromise Treasury-Postal language was inserted into the conference report on a fiscal 2001 legislative branch spending bill (HR 4516).

House leaders pulled the package, after two procedural votes. The Senate never took it up.

Republicans argued that the compromise Treasury-Postal package would provide much of what Democrats wanted: namely $30.3 billion in spending, about $1.2 billion more than the House-passed version. Of that, $15.6 billion would be discretionary.

Democrats said the bill was nearly $900 million below President Clinton's request, though it exceeded the fiscal 2000 level by more than $2 billion.

One point of contention was funding for the Internal Revenue Service. The compromise would provide about $8.6 billion for the IRS, about $400 million more than current levels but about $300 million less than the administration's request.

Campbell said he expected the White House to insist on full funding. The agency has argued that it needs the money to comply with a 1998 IRS overhaul (PL 105-206). *(1998 Almanac, p. 21-3)*

Pay Raise Would Go Through

Another sweetener was something the compromise did not contain: There was no provision to block a 2.7 percent pay raise for lawmakers. Lawmakers automatically receive an annual cost of living increase unless they vote to block it, usually in the Treasury-Postal bill. The raise is worth $3,800 over lawmakers' current $141,300 salary.

The GOP compromise also would give a break on a key paycheck deduction: rolling back a 0.5 percent increase in contributions by members of Congress and other federal employees to their pension plans. The difference amounts to about $700 a year per member.

Democratic Rep. David R. Obey of Wisconsin charged July 27 that the compromise bill was filled with questionable provisions, singling out one inserted at the behest of Budget Committee Chairman Pete V. Domenici, R-N.M., to give $2.5 million to the General Services Administration (GSA) to build a road in his state.

The proposal also would provide $472 million for federal construction projects including courthouses in Los Angeles; Seattle; Richmond, Va.; and Biloxi-Gulfport, Miss.; a consolidation of Food and Drug Administration offices; and a new headquarters for the ATF. It would provide $276 million in fiscal 2002 for a courthouse annex in Washington, D.C., and three courthouses in Miami; Springfield, Mass.; and Buffalo, N.Y.

It would provide $130 million, about $80 million less than the administration's request, for a computer system for the Customs Service to track trade shipments through ports and airports. And it would provide $7.1 million for presidential transition costs next year.

Democrats strongly objected to language to prevent federal law enforcement agencies from giving preference for firearms purchases to Smith & Wesson, which reached an agreement with the administration on gun standards including mandatory child safety locks.

House Adopts Conference Report On Combined Spending Package

SEPTEMBER 16 — The House narrowly passed a $33 billion spending package for congressional operations, the Treasury Department, the Postal Service and other agencies Sept. 14, setting the stage for a likely presidential veto.

Brushing aside White House concerns about the lack of a broader deal on taxes and spending, the House voted 212-209 to adopt the conference report on the so-called mini-omnibus bill (HR 4516), which combined the fiscal 2001 legislative branch and Treasury-Postal Service appropriations bills. The Senate is set to vote the week of Sept. 19. *(Vote 476, p. H-148)*

Leaders of both parties were in accord on the portion of the conference report that would provide $2.5 billion for legislative operations, about $40 million more than the current level, but $199 million less than the administration's request. Democrats and Republicans had also narrowed their differences on the second part of the bill, to provide $30.4 billion to the Treasury Department, Postal Service and other agencies. That is about $2.3 billion above fiscal 2000 levels, but $1.4 million less than the president's request.

Negotiations got tangled up, however, in broader wrangling over a GOP plan to reserve 90 percent of the fiscal 2001 budget surplus to pay down the federal debt.

Democrats also questioned a section of the conference report that would repeal a 3 percent federal telephone excise tax. The repeal, which would cost $19.9 billion over five years, was similar to a bill (HR 3916) that passed the House 420-2 on May 25.

"This dog has three tails and no legs," said ranking Appropriations Committee Democrat David R. Obey of Wisconsin.

Despite Democratic demands for concessions on tax cuts and spending, the GOP leadership decided to try to muscle the bill through the House. Supporters worked to line up balking Republicans, many of whom were concerned about the overall spending increase in the bill. The complaints of budget hawks, who portrayed the bill as a budget buster, were muted on the floor, however.

"It's clear that Democrats are blocking our bills. Thanks to their opposition, our members are unified," said David Dreier, R-Calif.

Pay Raise and Pensions

There was little debate on a sensitive subject: an automatic pay raise for lawmakers. The cost of living adjustment takes effect each year, under a 1989 law (PL 101-194), unless members vote to prevent it. In past years, the Treasury-Postal bill has been the vehicle to block a pay increase. The lack of such language in the bill virtually ensures that lawmakers will get a raise. Lawmakers' annual salary of $141,300 is expected to increase by 2.7 percent, or about $3,800. House and Senate leaders make more.

Senate Treasury and General Government Appropriations Subcommittee Chairman Ben Nighthorse Campbell, R-Colo., said he expected the conference report to win support in the Senate, but added that some members may vote "no" because of concerns about the pay raise.

Senate Majority Leader Trent Lott, R-Miss., said he did not expect such concerns to hinder the bill's passage. "We will have our vote. And we'll go from there," he said.

Members of the House GOP Conservative Action Team raised questions about another sensitive issue: The bill would repeal a scheduled 0.5 percent increase in mandatory contributions by members of Congress and other federal employees to their pension plans. A 1997 budget law (PL 105-33) required an annual increase of about $700 a year. The original House version of the bill would have required members of Congress to make the higher contribution. Senate Appropriations Committee Chairman Ted Stevens, R-Alaska, put the repeal for lawmakers back in the conference report.

"I'm tired of it," Stevens said Sept. 13. "A couple of guys over there [in the House] think this will hurt them, and they are objecting. I don't agree."

Following the vote, lawmakers turned their attention to efforts to resolve disputes with the White House.

House Treasury, Postal Service and General Government Appropriations Subcommittee Chairman Jim Kolbe, R-Ariz., said a recent Republican offer, later withdrawn, called for a $243.6 million increase in the measure's overall funding. It included another $171 million for the IRS.

The administration wants more money to meet customer service and enforcement goals under a 1998 IRS overhaul (PL 105-206).

The Democrats had been pushing for a bigger package of spending additions to the bill, totaling about $270 million.

Senate Rejects 'Mini-Omnibus,' Heartens Foes Of Pay Raise

SEPTEMBER 23 — The Senate's overwhelming rejection of a catchall bill to fund the legislative branch, Treasury Department, Postal Service and other agencies in fiscal 2001 could force Republicans to give in to White House demands for higher spending — and possibly imperil a planned congressional pay raise.

By a 28-69 vote, the Senate on Sept. 20 rejected the conference report (HR 4516), despite warnings by GOP leaders that a "no" vote could force Congress into a post-election session to deal with a backlog of spending bills. *(Vote 253, p. S-45)*

Democrats — united in voting against the measure — were angry that GOP leaders had never brought a stand-alone Treasury-Postal bill (S 2900) to the Senate floor, instead going straight from committee to conference with the House. Further, there was bipartisan concern that, in an election year, the leadership did not allow for a vote on language blocking an annual pay raise for congressmen.

Paul Wellstone, D-Minn., said

GOP maneuvers denied him a chance to "knock out our salary increase."

Senate Majority Leader Trent Lott, R-Miss., said he had no immediate plans to make more concessions in order to cut a deal with the White House, which had threatened a veto of earlier versions of the bill. "I'm going to let them stew in their own mess for a little while," he said, referring to Democrats. "It [the bill] will be frozen in place. And we'll look at other options."

Lott left the door open to scheduling another vote on the bill or inserting parts of the measure in other legislation. He said he would press the White House to back off some of its demands, including its request for more funding for the Internal Revenue Service (IRS) to improve service.

Lott said he was committed to moving a provision, which was in the defeated package, to repeal a 3 percent federal telephone excise tax. "We're going to do it before we leave town. Period," he said.

The conference report would provide $2.5 billion for legislative operations in fiscal 2001, about $40 million more than the current level, but $199 million less than President Clinton proposed. It would provide $30.4 billion for the Treasury Department, Postal Service and other agencies, about $2.3 billion more than the current budget, but $1.4 billion less than Clinton's request.

Byrd's Crucial Role

Democrats complained that Republicans had headed off contentious amendments by presenting the Treasury-Postal bill as part of the conference report on legislative branch spending, which is not open for floor revision.

GOP leaders elected not to bring the Treasury-Postal bill to the floor out of concern that it would be subject to a lengthy debate. Another worry was that it could open the door to gun-control amendments, because it contained a provision that would bar preferential government contracts for gun maker Smith & Wesson in return for its voluntary agreement to install child safety locks on new handguns. That provision was deleted in the conference report.

Ranking Appropriations Committee Democrat Robert C. Byrd of West Virginia argued that the bill violated a Senate tradition of open debate on appropriations bills.

"I was ready to vote for the bill. But Sen. Byrd opposed it. . . . Then we all voted no," said Ernest F. Hollings, D-S.C.

Lott disagreed with Byrd. "Is it a new idea to combine bills before the end of a session? No," Lott said. "Was this the way to do this? Absolutely."

Lott faced defections in his own ranks. John McCain, R-Ariz., argued the bill was laden with too much extra spending, including $14.8 million for communications infrastructure for the 2002 Salt Lake City Winter Olympics.

The Treasury-Postal bill has been the customary vehicle for blocking an annual cost of living adjustment (COLA) for legislators, which takes effect unless Congress acts to prevent it. The fiscal 2001 bill, however, was silent on the issue, paving the way for a scheduled increase of 2.7 percent, or $3,800, in the base salary of $141,300.

Congress last blocked a pay raise in 1998. *(1998 Almanac, p. 2-95)*

The measure also would repeal an increase in pension contributions by members, a move that is beginning to spark a public backlash.

Further, the bill has become ensnared in a broader debate over a GOP plan to reserve 90 percent of the fiscal 2001 budget surplus to pay down the federal debt, leaving the remaining 10 percent to be divided between spending and tax cuts.

Negotiators Reach Deal, Add Money For Anti-Terrorism Efforts, IRS

OCTOBER 7 — Congressional negotiators worked out a bipartisan deal to provide $348 million in extra funds for the Internal Revenue Service, counter-terrorism and other programs in fiscal 2001, clearing the way for Senate action on a broader "mini-omnibus" bill to fund the legislative branch, Treasury Department, Postal Service and related agencies.

The Oct. 3 agreement was designed to resolve administration objections that Congress had not provided sufficient funding. It set the stage for Senate floor action the week of Oct. 9.

The omnibus bill (HR 4516) has been in limbo since it was defeated by the Senate, 28-69, on Sept 20. Before that vote, Democrats complained that the Treasury-Postal appropriations bill (S 2900) attached to the legislative package had never been brought to the Senate floor for debate as a stand-alone measure. Instead it had gone directly from the Senate Appropriations Committee to conference with the House.

The new deal does not address that concern. Nor does it answer complaints by rank and file in both parties about the lack of a floor vote on a pending congressional pay raise. Lawmakers automatically receive an annual cost of living increase unless Congress acts to block it. The Treasury-Postal bill has been the traditional vehicle for language barring a salary increase, but this year's measure is silent on the issue. Unless such language is added, lawmakers will get a 2.7 percent, or $3,800, increase in their base salary of $141,300.

For now, it does not appear that there will be a Senate floor vote on the issue. Top lawmakers on both sides of the aisle said they supported the raise and would not back an effort to block it.

The new funding for the IRS, counter-terrorism efforts and other programs was included in the conference report for the fiscal 2001 Transportation appropriations bill (HR 4475)

The package would include another $216 million for the IRS to improve enforcement and customer service, in addition to an increase of more than $400 million from fiscal 2000; and $37 million for anti-terrorism programs.

It would provide $30 million for a new law enforcement training center in the Washington area; $25 million for the General Services Administration for computer technology and operations; $6.6 million for renovation of the John F. Kennedy Library in Boston, and $8 million for the administration's "first accounts" program to encourage low-income families to open savings accounts.

IRS Funding Dispute

While supporting the overall package, Senate Majority Leader Trent Lott, R-Miss., said the White House was using the end-of-session rush to press its demands for more funding. "This is typical of what we're being hit with," he said Oct. 3. "The White House is demanding more money for the IRS. How many people do you think agree with that?"

He brushed aside the agency's argument that it needs more workers to comply with requirements of the 1998 overhaul (PL 105-106) to improve customer service.

"Listen, the IRS is wasting a lot of money, abusing a lot of people," Lott said. Nonetheless, he said he would embrace the agreement "if that's what it takes to move bigger bills through."

Key Democrats appeared willing to support the broader bill as well, now that the major funding disputes are resolved. Senate Minority Leader Tom Daschle of South Dakota said he would not insist, for now, on a floor debate on a stand-alone Treasury-Postal Service bill. Lott had avoided bringing that bill to the floor, in part, to avoid a possible fight on gun-control amendments.

"We'll be flexible," Daschle said.

Soon after the deal was unveiled, it seemed to be in danger of coming apart when Lott questioned a small provision that was one of the White House's top demands: $2.5 million in funding for voter education programs in Puerto Rico aimed at increasing awareness of possible changes in the island's status.

Puerto Rico has been a U.S. territory since the end of the Spanish-American War. Although they are American citizens, the residents of Puerto Rico do not pay U.S. taxes and do not take part in national elections.

Lott questioned the need for funding voter education programs just two years after a 1998 plebiscite in which a majority of Puerto Rico's voters rejected a list of options that included statehood and independence.

Lott and some other Republicans expressed concern that funding could be diverted to help parties and candidates. The question is touchy because of a legal dispute over whether residents of Puerto Rico will be allowed to vote in the presidential election.

A federal judge, in deciding a lawsuit by a group of potential Puerto Rican voters, ruled in August that voting is a fundamental right of citizenship. In its appeal, the Justice Department argued that electoral votes belong to the states and that voting rights should be awarded by Congress, not the courts.

Lott agreed not to block the voter education funding after appropriators agreed to delay its release until March 31, 2001.

Another pivotal agreement was the $37 million for deterring and detecting terrorists, about half the amount in the administration's budget request.

Rep. Jim Kolbe, R-Ariz., chairman of the House Appropriations Subcommittee on Treasury, Postal Service and General Government, said the funding was needed to prevent attacks during major events such as the 2002 Winter Olympics in Salt Lake City.

"We have a lot of events coming up. We have to be focused," he said.

Senate Clears Treasury-Postal Bill as Part Of 'Mini-Omnibus'

OCTOBER 14 — The Senate has cleared a $33 billion "mini-omnibus" bill (HR 4516) that would provide funding for the legislative branch, Treasury Department, Postal Service and other agencies in fiscal 2001, after reaching a bipartisan compromise on funding for the Internal Revenue Service (IRS) and efforts to combat terrorism.

The bill also includes a provision to repeal a telephone excise tax originally levied during the Spanish-American War.

The Senate voted, 58-37, on Oct. 12 to send the bill to President Clinton, who is expected to sign it later this month. Final passage came after lawmakers reached agreement on a $348 million spending package that would provide additional funding for programs covered by the Treasury-Postal measure. *(Vote 273, p. S-49)*

The compromise, which included $216 million for improving customer service and enforcement at the IRS, did not pass as part of the Treasury-Postal package. Instead it was added to the fiscal 2001 Transportation appropriations conference report (HR 4475) cleared by the Senate Oct. 6.

Passage of the transportation measure, including enough funding to hire more than 1,000 new IRS employees, addressed concerns of the White House and many Democrats, clearing the way for the combined legislative branch and Treasury-Postal bill.

Senate Minority Leader Tom Daschle, D-S.D., said the Treasury-Postal measure would be signed by Clinton and held it up as a model for settling partisan disputes. He said he hoped Republicans "will take that as a lesson and do the right thing on the remaining appropriations bills."

Under the combined bill, the legislative branch would receive $2.5 billion, $40 million more than current funding. The Treasury Department, Postal Service and other agencies would receive $30.4 billion, about $2.3 billion more than current funding. Repeal of the 3 percent federal telephone excise tax would cost more than $19.9 billion over five years.

The Senate vote followed several concessions by GOP leaders aimed at mollifying rank-and-file lawmakers who, on Sept. 20, had rejected the combined bill, 28-69.

Congressional Pay Raise

The compromise did not deal with complaints by some members about the lack of a vote on a pending cost-of-living adjustment that will raise the average congressional salary by 2.7 percent, or $3,800, to $141,300. The Treasury-Postal bill is the customary vehicle for language to freeze salaries. The final bill was silent on the raise.

The overall deal did resolve a related concern about possible fallout from a provision of the Treasury-Postal bill that would repeal a scheduled 0.5 percent increase in mandatory contributions to pension plans by federal employees, including members of Congress. The provision was estimated to save lawmakers about $700 a year.

The effect of the language was neutralized by a provision inserted into the transportation appropriations bill requiring lawmakers to make the higher pension payments until they are phased out, as previously scheduled, in 2002.

Treasury-Postal Spending Highlights

Where the Money Goes

HR 4577 — Conference Report: H Rept 106-1033

Spending Synopsis:
The $30.3 billion fiscal 2001 Treasury-Postal Service spending bill cleared Dec. 15 as part of the end-of-session omnibus appropriations package. A nearly identical version (HR 4516), cleared as part of a "mini-omnibus" that also included the legislative branch spending bill and a repeal of the telephone excise tax, had been vetoed Oct. 30. The total in the final bill was more than either the version (HR 4871) passed by the House on July 20 or a variant (S 2900) approved by the Senate Appropriations Committee the same day. That version of the Senate bill went straight to conference, bypassing the Senate floor. The final bill was about $2.1 billion above the fiscal 2000 level, and $900 million below President Clinton's request.

- **Treasury Department**

The conference report would provide $13.6 billion for the Treasury Department, including $8.6 billion for the IRS and $2.3 billion for the Customs Service. The Customs Service funding includes $258 million to update the agency's computer system, $25 million more than the House bill and twice that recommended by Senate appropriators. The bill also would provide increases for the Bureau of Alcohol, Tobacco and Firearms (ATF) and the Secret Service.

- **Postal Service**

Although the Postal Service funds its own operations, the conference report includes $96 million, the amount requested, most of it to cover free mailing for the blind and for overseas voters.

- **Independent Agencies**

Conferees agreed to provide $16 billion for independent agencies covered by the bill, $14.6 billion of it for the Office of Personnel Management. Smaller independent agencies funded under the bill include the Federal Election Commission, the General Services Administration and the National Archives.

Hot-Button Issues

Δ **Cuba.** The conference report eliminated House-passed amendments to end the enforcement of restrictions on travel to Cuba and on the export of medicine and food to the island. Amendment supporters were furious, but top GOP leaders want to ensure that the provisions are dropped from the final bill.

Δ **IRS.** The conference report moved slightly toward the White House on IRS funding, calling for $8.6 billion — more than in either chamber's bill and about $400 million more than current levels. But the amount is still $300 million less than the administration sought. The IRS insists it needs full funding to comply with a 1998 overhaul (PL 105-206); the White House agrees.

Δ **ATF.** As part of their emphasis on improving enforcement of existing gun laws rather than enacting new ones, Republicans are agreed for the first time in recent years to a major funding increase for the ATF. The agency would get $769 million, more than in either chamber's bill and $204 million above fiscal 2000.

Δ **Courthouses.** The conference report included $472 million for new courthouses and other federal construction projects. House appropriators had included no money for new courthouses.

Δ **Pay Raise.** Like the House and Senate bills, the conference report did not include language to block an annual, automatic cost-of-living pay raise for members of Congress, effectively ensuring lawmakers would get the increase.

(figures are in thousands of dollars of new budget authority)

	Fiscal 2000 Appropriation	Fiscal 2001 Clinton Request	House Bill	Senate Bill	Conference Report
Treasury Department	$12,352,437	$14,098,443	$13,200,949	$13,161,407	$13,597,742
Customs Service	(1,809,915)	(2,386,141)	(2,184,543)	(2,064,315)	(2,258,393)
IRS	(8,216,489)	(8,943,674)	(8,452,998)	(8,535,069)	(8,639,493)
Postal Service	93,056	96,093	96,093	67,093	96,093
Executive Office of the President	654,422	702,245	681,499	594,758	691,315
Federal Election Commission	38,008	40,500	40,240	39,755	40,500
General Services Administration	137,059	870,988	152,471	167,557	632,211
Other Independent Agencies	14,794,080	15,526,308	14,931,001	15,403,014	15,313,667
GRAND TOTAL	**$28,069,062**	**$31,756,826**	**$29,102,263**	**$29,433,584**	**$30,371,258**
Total adjusted for scorekeeping	**(28,257,047)**	**(31,208,436)**	**(29,081,606)**	**(29,180,582)**	**(30,309,471)**

TABLE: House and Senate Appropriations committees

"Some members thought it looked really bad. Here's a cost of living increase, and here you are also rolling back pension payments for members. We decided not to apply the change in payments to members," said House Treasury, Postal Service and General Government Appropriations Subcommittee Chairman Jim Kolbe, R-Ariz.

In a bow to Senate Appropriations Committee ranking Democrat Robert C. Byrd of West Virginia, senators considered but rejected by voice vote a proposal that would have merged provisions of the Treasury-Postal bill with another unrelated spending bill (HR 4635) to fund the departments of Veterans Affairs and Housing and Urban Development.

The procedural feint resolved Byrd's complaint that a freestanding Treasury-Postal bill had never been debated on the Senate floor.

In the final compromise, lawmakers provided $37 million to beef up efforts by the U.S. Customs Service to fight terrorism. More than a third of the money would go to joint task forces of federal and local law enforcement officials.

Kolbe and Rep. Steny H. Hoyer, D-Md., said appropriators declined the administration's request for additional funding to use airplane surveillance.

Hoyer said the bill would provide $30 million for a law enforcement training facility in the Washington area, possibly in his district near Andrews Air Force Base.

He added that no siting decision had been made.

Treasury-Postal Bill in Play Following Veto

NOVEMBER 4 — President Clinton's veto of a $33 billion spending bill for the legislative branch, Treasury Department, Postal Service and other agencies triggered a new round of political skirmishing on Capitol Hill and opened the door to changes in the legislation.

In an Oct. 30 veto message, Clinton cited his disappointment at failing to reach a deal with Republicans on unrelated legislation to provide tax breaks for school construction and to implement proposed work safety rules aimed at reducing repetitive stress injuries.

Clinton cited no problems with the spending bill itself (HR 4516), which was cleared by the Senate, 58-37, on Oct. 12. *(Text, p. D-99)*

"The bill provides funds for the legislative branch and the White House at a time when the business of the American people remains unfinished," Clinton said. He added that he would sign the Treasury-Postal bill only as part "of a budget that puts the interests of the American people before self-interest or special interests."

The measure would provide $2.5 billion for the legislative branch, $40 million more than current funding; and $30.4 billion for the Treasury Department, Postal Service and other agencies, about $2.3 billion more than current spending. It would also repeal a 3 percent federal telephone excise tax, at an estimated cost of more than $19.9 billion over five years.

The administration had insisted for weeks that it would support the repeal of the telephone tax only as part of a broader deal on tax policy. But the timing of the veto and the wording of Clinton's message had an incendiary effect on Capitol Hill, where frustration has been mounting over the lack of a final deal on budget and policy issues that would allow lawmakers to go home.

The reference to self-interest triggered a firestorm among Republicans, who read it as a veiled attack on the lack of language in the bill to block an automatic, annual cost of living congressional pay raise. The Treasury-Postal bill is the traditional vehicle for language blocking such a raise. Without action to prevent it, the base congressional salary of $141,300 will rise by 2.7 percent, or $3,800.

Despite Clinton's criticism of Congress and its self-interest, Senate Appropriations Committee Chairman Ted Stevens, R-Alaska, said there was no plan to insert language dealing with the pay raise in any revised measure.

Republicans accused Clinton of playing politics with a bill that had bipartisan support. The veto was viewed by Republicans as yet more evidence of a White House strategy aimed at hanging a "do-nothing" label on the GOP-controlled Congress.

House Majority Whip Tom DeLay, R-Texas, hinted at possible cuts if the bill is reopened. "The political atmosphere here has been so poisoned by their actions," he said. "And I have got to tell you that this bill is back into play."

Some Republicans were uneasy with the bill's size, especially its generous funding for the Internal Revenue Service: $8.6 billion, $423 million more than current levels. The agency would receive another $220 million under the fiscal 2001 Transportation spending law (PL 106-346) signed by Clinton on Oct. 23.

Stevens, however, predicted no cuts and said the bill would move without changes as part of the conference report for fiscal 2001 Labor, Health and Human Services, and Education spending bill (HR 4577). "It's in there," he said. *(Labor-HHS, p. 2-97)*

While spending levels may not change, the telephone tax could. The administration has argued that the repeal should be handled in tandem with a broader deal on a tax bill (HR 2614). Appropriators said GOP leaders would have to decide after the election whether to put the telephone tax into another must-pass spending bill. ◆

More Than 1,000 Earmarks Adorn VA-HUD Bill; Housing Gets Big Boost

SUMMARY

The spending bill for the departments of Veterans Affairs (VA) and Housing and Urban Development (HUD) and 20 federal agencies, including the EPA and NASA, was enacted only after negotiators from the White House and Congress blunted several House Republican policy proposals and agreed to a substantial spending increase, giving President Clinton almost all of what he sought.

At $107.3 billion, the bill was the third most expensive of the fiscal 2001 appropriations measures. It increased spending 8 percent above the fiscal 2000 level overall, with a 12 percent increase in discretionary spending, to $82.6 billion. Overall spending was 98 percent of what the president sought. The bill provided $47 billion for the VA, the 6 percent increase marking the department's largest ever; $30.6 billion for HUD, an 18 percent increase; $14.3 billion for NASA, a 5 percent increase; and $7.8 billion for the EPA, also a 5 percent increase. Spread through the conference report were 1,183 earmarked economic development, university research and water and sewer construction projects worth more than $1 billion.

The bill was not nearly so generous at the outset, when Republican leaders were hewing to self-imposed discretionary spending caps. The version the House passed in June would have increased spending 2 percent over fiscal 2000 levels.

Clinton threatened a veto on the grounds that the bill would have shut off funds for AmeriCorps, the volunteer service program he pushed to enactment in 1993 (PL 103-82), and provided too little for housing, environmental protection, space and National Science Foundation (NSF) accounts.

The president also cited several Republican riders to restrict policies of HUD, the EPA and the VA.

Senate appropriators declined to mark up their version of the bill until their leadership allowed them to allocate more to discretionary accounts, which did not happen until September. At that point, they marked up a bill that would have appropriated more than the House version for HUD, NASA, EPA, NSF, the Federal Emergency Management Agency and AmeriCorps. Still, the administration said it had "serious problems" with the priorities in the bill.

Republican leaders never put that bill before the Senate, fearing it would become a magnet for Democratic amendments on top-tier election-year topics. Instead, House and Senate appropriators and administration officials negotiated for three weeks on a compromise version. They agreed to spend $453 million in unspent fiscal 2000 low-income housing to provide 79,000 new Section 8 housing subsidy vouchers, the third straight annual increase; to give AmeriCorps a 21 percent increase to $434 million; and to limit the duration of restrictions, proposed in the House bill, on the EPA's enforcement of interim water pollution standards for arsenic, dredging of waterways to remove hazardous wastes and enforcement of new air pollution standards for ozone.

The Senate voted overwhelmingly to pass a bill embodying the compromise, after which a formal conference committee was convened to issue a report spelling out the deal — including each of the $430 million in earmarks requested by senators and the $622 million for House members.

The conference report also carried a revised version of the fiscal 2001 energy and water appropriations bill, shorn of a Missouri River management provision that had prompted Clinton to veto the initial version on Oct. 7.

Box Score — **2001** Fiscal Year

VA-HUD

- **Bill:** HR 4635 – PL 106-377
- **Legislative action: House** passed HR 4635 (H Rept 106-674), 256-169, June 21.

Senate Appropriations Committee approved its version of HR 4635 (S Rept 106-410), 27-1, on Sept. 13.

Senate passed HR 4635, 87-8, on Oct. 12 after substituting the text of an agreement negotiated between the administration and appropriators.

House adopted the conference report (H Rept 106-988), 386-24, on Oct. 19.

Senate cleared HR 4635, 85-8, on Oct. 19.

President signed the bill Oct. 27.

House VA-HUD Panel Cuts Several Clinton Initiatives

MAY 27 — Chafing at tight funding levels imposed by Republican leaders, the House VA-HUD Appropriations Subcommittee took its frustrations out on President Clinton on May 23 by cutting or even eliminating several administration initiatives from its fiscal 2001 spending bill.

The panel approved, by voice vote, a $101.1 billion draft bill for the department of Veterans Affairs (VA) and Housing and Urban Development (HUD) and independent agencies that include the Environmental Protection Agency and NASA. That is an $8.2 billion increase in new spending authority over fiscal 2000 spending levels, according to the House Appropriations Committee.

As was the case last year, the bill includes another $4.2 billion in "advance appropriations" for HUD rental subsidies for fiscal 2002.

The bill would provide about $76.5

billion in discretionary draft authority, about $400 million less than the "freeze levels" needed to maintain programs included in the bill at their current level.

Members of the subcommittee complained that the full committee had cut back their discretionary allocation even though the overall amount of discretionary money available for the 13 appropriations bills increased by $20 billion over fiscal 2000.

"A larger allocation would have made our jobs much easier," said subcommittee Chairman James T. Walsh, R-N.Y. "This bill, as it now stands, represents Congress' imprint, but not [VA-HUD Subcommittee] member priorities."

"The pain has been equally spread, or the lack of opportunity has been equally spread," added Alan B. Mollohan of West Virginia, the ranking Democrat on the panel. "This Congress has the capability to meet the increasing needs of this nation. To produce bills at the current freeze levels, in their current form, is wrong."

Appropriations Chairman C.W. Bill Young, R-Fla., said the bill would provide an extra $5 billion for mandatory spending.

"There are members of other subcommittees who would have loved to have received a $5 billion increase over last year," he told members of the subcommittee.

David R. Obey of Wisconsin, the ranking Democrat on the full Appropriations Committee, called the draft a "reasonable bill by a reasonable man," referring to Walsh, and "an attempt to deal with an entirely unreasonable situation, and that is the budget."

"I wish I could vote for this bill, but I cannot," Obey said, later comparing the allocation levels to "telling someone you're going to have to go to church fully clothed, and then telling them they can only wear half a suit."

"This bill's going to have a tough time getting through the gantlet," Obey said. "I think this bill is a status quo bill that does not attack any problems. In some cases, I think it makes it worse."

Americorps War

The VA-HUD panel initiated another tug of war with the White House on one of Clinton's pet programs, the Corporation for National and Community Service, known as Americorps. As it did last year, the subcommittee bill would eliminate all funding for Clinton's community service initiative, which ultimately received $353 million in fiscal 2000.

This year Clinton is seeking $534 million for Americorps, and Walsh acknowledged that the bill eventually must provide funding for the program to win the president's signature.

Housing programs will be another area of contention between the Republicans and the administration. In a statement released before the May 23 markup, Walsh said the panel would provide $13.3 billion for HUD's Section 8 low-income rental subsidy program, an increase of $1.9 billion over last year. But within that amount, the bill specifies only $60 million for 10,000 new housing vouchers, far short of the $690 million Clinton requested for 120,000 additional vouchers.

Walsh said he could not accommodate the president's request because public housing authorities had failed to take advantage of $1.4 billion in "recaptured" Section 8 assistance. He said that money, if used, would have provided vouchers for an additional 237,000 families.

The subcommittee bill would provide $30 billion in new budget authority for HUD programs and operations, $4.1 billion more than the 2000 spending level, but $2.5 billion less than the administration requested. HUD's appropriation would include $4.2 billion in "advance appropriations" from the 2000 bill and $3.1 billion for public housing, as well as the $13.3 billion for the Section 8 program.

The bill would also keep funding for elderly housing ($710 million), homeless assistance grants ($1.02 billion), Housing Opportunities for People with AIDS ($232 million) and Native American block grants ($620 million) at fiscal 2000 levels.

VA, NASA, Science Protected

As it has typically done, the subcommittee sought to protect major programs for veterans, space and scientific research. The Department of Veterans Affairs would receive $46.8 billion, a $2.6 billion increase over fiscal 2000 funding levels.

The bill would provide the Veterans Benefits Administration $1.2 billion more than fiscal 2000 levels to speed claims processing, bringing total funding for that agency to $22.8 billion. It would also provide $107 million, a $10 million increase, to fund current and new cemetery operations.

NASA would receive $13.7 billion, a $112.8 million increase over fiscal 2000 funding levels, but $322 million less than Clinton had sought.

The National Science Foundation, a favorite of the House panel, would receive $4.1 billion, a $167 million increase over fiscal 2000.

Environmental programs fared less well with the House panel. The Environmental Protection Agency would receive $7.2 billion, a $441 million decrease in funding from fiscal 2000 levels. Subcommittee members hinted that spending for environmental and housing programs will find even less favor with them as the bill moves through the negotiation process with the Senate.

The Federal Emergency Management Agency would receive $877 million, including $300 million for disaster relief. Clinton had requested $3.6 billion; appropriators ignored a request from the president to designate $2.6 billion as "emergency spending," exempt from discretionary spending caps.

Subcommittee members complained that they had little room to set their own funding priorities, and they identified several programs that they would like to boost if extra money becomes available in House-Senate conference negotiations. The panel approved language by:

- Tom DeLay, R-Texas, to encourage the full committee to restore up to $290 million in budget authority for NASA's Alternative Access program, which will explore new alternatives for space travel. Robert E. "Bud" Cramer, an Alabama Democrat whose district includes the NASA Marshall Space Flight Center in Huntsville, agreed that the agency's work needs to be protected. "It's very important that we not interrupt what NASA has started," Cramer said.
- Anne M. Northup, R-Ky., to encourage the Consumer Product Safety Commission, which would receive $51 million in the bill, to study the safety of small appliances if more funds become available. "I don't think that we can order a new study without making

funds available," she said.

• David E. Price, D-N.C., to encourage the EPA to work with academic research laboratories to help them dispose of hazardous waste. The intent, Price said, would be to find ways of disposing of "relatively small amounts of hazardous waste" without having to follow disposal guidelines established for commercial enterprises or manufacturers who produce much larger amounts of waste.

• Virgil H. Goode Jr., I-Va., to recognize the merits of the Smart Air Transport System, part of NASA's Earth Science Enterprise, which develops and commercializes new aerospace technologies. Clinton had requested $9 million for the Smart Air program, but appropriators eliminated funding.

Mollohan modified Goode's amendment to say that the full committee would evaluate the program if money became available.

The subcommittee report language states that the program should be run by the Federal Aviation Administration. "I don't want us to say that it's going to be better in the FAA or better in NASA," Goode said. "I just want the funds for the program to go forward without focusing on which entity funds it."

Goode also said he hoped the bill could include some extra funding for economic development programs at HUD, but added, "We'll just have to wait and see what the numbers are in the conference."

Other members indicated that they would offer amendments when the bill goes to the full Appropriations Committee after the Memorial Day recess. Marcy Kaptur, D-Ohio, said she would offer an amendment to extend the responsibility of community development financial institutions, which provide grants, loans and technical assistance. Kaptur said her amendment would extend their operations in low-income communities.

Carrie P. Meek, D-Fla., said she might offer an amendment to add funding to repair damage caused by a March fire at a Miami-area VA hospital.

HUD Language Stricken

Meek won subcommittee approval to remove language in the draft bill that would have prohibited HUD from hiring outside contractors known as "community builders" for department staff positions.

Rodney Frelinghuysen, R-N.J., said he was not opposed to Meek's amendment but felt Congress needed to keep an eye on the program. Last fall, HUD Inspector General Susan Gaffney said the HUD community builders "do little to address HUD's mission," and they take resources away from improving department programs. David L. Hobson, R-Ohio, noted that the lowest salary for a community builder was $91,000 a year.

Congress and the White House reached an agreement last year to phase out the community builders program by the end of fiscal 2000. "This was agreed to with [White House budget director] Jack Lew last year," Walsh said. "HUD didn't want to do it, but there was a strong feeling in the House and Senate over this."

What bothers congressional Republicans, Walsh said, is "the political connotations of [HUD] bringing in individuals who are political activists and paying them $91,000 a year to build a political agenda."

Joe Knollenberg, R-Mich., said he would like to add report language at the full committee level dealing with the Fair Housing Initiatives Program, which provides support to government agencies and nonprofit organizations to eliminate or prevent housing discrimination.

Knollenberg highlighted two housing discrimination cases involving insurance companies and said he would like to clarify fair housing requirements for property insurance companies.

House Committee Approves Frugal VA-HUD Bill

JUNE 10 — A fiscal 2001 VA-HUD appropriations bill, made lean by the absence of the customary lawmaker earmarks, is ready for debate by the House. But even that self-sacrifice has not been enough to avoid a veto threat from President Clinton.

Despite annoyance at the measure's current discretionary spending limit — but with an expectation that more money will become available later this year — the House Appropriations Committee approved by voice vote June 7 a $101.3 billion draft version of legislation to fund veterans, housing, space, environmental, disaster relief and scientific research programs. The measure's nickname comes from the acronyms for the two departments that lay claim to three-quarters of its funding: Veterans Affairs and Housing and Urban Development.

The House measure's spending total would be 2.1 percent more than is occurring this year. Taking into account scorekeeping adjustments that, on paper, drive down the cost of the fiscal 2000 VA-HUD law (PL 106-74), the spending increase would be 8.8 percent.

The measure approved by the committee, which the House is set to debate the week of June 12, is nearly identical to the bill approved by the VA-HUD Subcommittee May 23. To hold down the bill's price tag, that panel included no earmarks for spending on the types of parochial pet projects that normally marble the measure. And the bill would provide for only a handful of the policy initiatives proposed by Clinton.

As a result, Office of Management and Budget Director Jack Lew threatened a veto even before the full committee markup. "This bill fails to address the critical needs of the American people," he said in a June 6 letter to Appropriations Committee Chairman C.W. Bill Young, R-Fla.

The bill's discretionary spending total of $76.5 billion is $6.5 billion less than the president requested. Beyond that, Lew complained that the bill would provide no funding for AmeriCorps — the national service program that was a signature achievement of Clinton's first year in office — and would cut his funding requests for HUD, NASA, the EPA, the National Science Foundation (NSF) and the Federal Emergency Management Agency. Among the big government agencies covered by the bill, only the VA would get almost what the president requested.

The panel defeated, most on party-line votes, eight amendments that sought to increase funding for domestic programs. The committee approved six amendments, none of which increased spending levels.

"This bill, as it now stands, reflects a congressional imprint on the president's budget request," said James T. Walsh, R-N.Y., chairman of the VA-HUD Subcommittee. While the measure makes no mention of special projects for members, he said he expected the bill would "address many member priorities before the process is over."

Republican appropriators also signaled that they would make at least one move to appease Clinton: inclusion of some money for AmeriCorps. He seems certain, though, not to receive the 51 percent boost in spending he sought, to $539 million.

"The best that can be said is that this budget spreads the pain equally across all levels, except, of course for Americorps," said Alan B. Mollohan of West Virginia, the VA-HUD panel's top Democrat. "The leadership has decided instead to earmark this surplus for a tax cut that will probably never be enacted. It was the wrong thing to do last year, and it's the wrong thing now."

'There Are Always Adjustments'

House Republicans continue to press ahead with plans to use part of the budget surplus to cut taxes, but the most expensive of these appear likely to be stopped either by the Senate or by Clinton's veto pen.

Once that happens, more of the surplus might be allocated to spending. "This is the same strategy we used last year," Walsh said in an interview June 7, referring to the extra spending that fueled enactment of the fiscal 2000 VA-HUD law that was made available after Clinton vetoed a tax cut bill (HR 2488) last fall.

At a break in the markup, Young indicated that more money for the VA-HUD bill was on the way, although he did not specify when.

"After the House passes the bills, there are adjustments when they go to conference with the Senate, and there are adjustments when we send the bills to the president. It doesn't make any difference who controls Congress or who's in the White House. There are always those adjustments, and that's nothing new. That's the system."

Mollohan also anticipates having more money to spend on the bill. "I think the endgame is that we get more money," he said. "If we didn't have more money in the bill after conference, then the conference report might be looked at differently enough to make its passage not assured."

That did little to placate some Democrats, who said they were impatient to write the final bill.

"I'm tired of hearing for the fourth year in a row that it's the best we can do because our hands are tied on the budget resolution," ranking Democrat David R. Obey of Wisconsin said at the markup, and he again vowed to oppose the bill on the floor. "It's going to need major repair, like most of the bills that go through this committee. Sooner or later, we're going to have to get real."

Carrie P. Meek, D-Fla., lamented that appropriators' authority was being undermined by GOP leaders. "We seem to be at the bottom of the triangle," she said in an interview after the markup.

At first blush, the big winner under the bill would appear to be HUD, which would receive $30 billion — an increase of $4.1 billion, or 16 percent, from the current appropriation. But more than half of the increase would be devoted to paying for the renewal of expiring Section 8 contracts, which provide housing subsidies to low-income families. And $2.2 billion would come from Section 8 money not being spent this year.

The bill's total also includes $4.2 billion in "advance appropriations" for fiscal 2002 Section 8 expenditures. That would perpetuate an accounting gimmick begun a year ago when — in order to stay technically within the statutory spending limits for fiscal 2000 set in the 1997 budget-balancing law (PL 105-33) — appropriators shifted an equivalent $4.2 billion into fiscal 2001.

VA Pay Date Shift

To stay under the bill's spending ceiling this time, appropriators have come up with a new accounting trick. The bill would repeal a section of that 1997 law ordering that certain VA compensation and pension payouts occur in fiscal 2001. The bill would shift those payments back to fiscal 2000, freeing up $1.8 billion.

While rental subsidies were boosted, other HUD programs were cut. The Community Development Fund, which includes Community Development Block Grants, would be reduced by 6 percent, to $4.5 billion. The Public Housing Capital Fund, which funds construction and revitalization of public housing, would be cut by 3.5 percent, to $2.8 billion.The HOPE VI program for refurbishing dilapidated housing would be cut by 2 percent, to $565 million.

Veterans Affairs, on the other hand, would receive $46.8 billion, an increase of 6 percent, much of it in line with Clinton's request. Some strings were attached, however: The bill would limit the amount of spending on overhead at VA facilities — one-quarter of its medical care budget is now being spent on upkeep, according to the General Accounting Office — and would order the VA to determine how many empty nursing home beds it has and come up with a plan for converting them to new uses.

Despite a series of recent space probe failures and cost overruns, the bill would provide NASA with $13.7 billion — essentially the same amount it has received since fiscal 1999. The figure is $322 million less than the administration's request, however. The bill would provide all $5.5 billion NASA sought for human space flight programs, including the international space station and the space shuttle. But the bill would prohibit NASA from spending any money on joint research ventures within the Air Force.

Among the bill's more contentious riders are provisions that would continue to block the EPA from spending money to carry out the 1997 Kyoto Protocol on global warming or to finalize a rule on water pollution standards.

New Section 8 Changes

The bill also contains a rider that would allow HUD to increase the face value of Section 8 vouchers in places it determines have especially high housing costs or low vacancy rates. Vouchers are worth 110 percent of the median monthly rental rate in a community, but under the bill, HUD could raise that figure in those designated communities. The aim, said Walsh, is to spend some of the Section 8 funds that are now untapped because the value of a voucher is covering fewer and fewer rental bills.

But while ensuring that more Section 8 money is spent — the committee has not estimated how much — the provision could reduce the number of vouchers available to the poor by increasing their value, a point not lost on low-income housing advocates.

While not opposed to the intent of the rider, the Banking Committee — which has authority over housing policy — did not learn of the provision until the subcommittee markup. Rick A. Lazio, chairman of the panel's Housing Subcommittee and the GOP nominee for the Senate in New York, said June 7 that he was not aware of the provision.

'Emergency Aid' Request Rejected

These were the amendments to boost spending rejected at the markup:

- By Allen Boyd, D-Fla., to grant Clinton's request for $2.9 billion in "emergency" aid, which is not counted toward discretionary spending limits, for disasters that have not yet occurred. The bill would provide just $300 million. Republicans said additional disaster funding could be provided later through supplemental appropriations. The amendment was defeated, 22-29.
- By David E. Price, D-N.C., and Joe Knollenberg, R-Mich., to add $23 million in funding for medical and prosthetic research at VA facilities by shutting down the Selective Service System, which registers young men for the draft. It was defeated, 19-36.
- By Mollohan, to grant Clinton his entire request for NASA by adding $322.7 million to study the sun's impact on Earth, develop a new generation of space vehicles, improve air traffic control and develop new technology for small airports and aircraft. It was defeated, 22-23.
- By Mollohan, to add $1.8 billion for 10 housing and community programs. It was defeated, 20-29.
- By Meek, to transfer $2 million to the Fair Housing Initiative program from the Fair Housing Assistance program. Both combat discrimination in housing. It was defeated 26-27.
- By Obey, to appropriate an additional $508 million for the NSF to bring the total in line with Clinton's $4.6 billion request. It was defeated, 21-25.
- By Obey, to add $107 million for housing programs for the homeless, elderly, disabled and people with AIDS. It was defeated, 20-27.
- By Marcy Kaptur, D-Ohio, to give Clinton the $27 million he sought for a rural housing assistance program. It was defeated by voice vote.

House Sets Rule For Floor Debate On VA-HUD Bill

JUNE 17 — The fiscal 2001 spending bill for housing and veterans affairs, expected to get its turn on the House floor June 19, already faces a list of more than 30 amendments, as well as a renewed veto threat.

The $101.3 billion measure (HR 4635 — H Rept 106-674) funds the departments of Veterans Affairs (VA) and Housing and Urban Development (HUD), along with a variety of independent agencies such as NASA and the Federal Emergency Management Agency, which provides federal help to victims of natural disasters.

Amendments are likely to include multiple efforts to reshape the bill's spending priorities and an attempt to strike language that would bar use of VA funds for Justice Department anti-tobacco litigation.

A statement issued by the White House on June 13 lambasted the bill's overall funding level, saying it fell $6 billion short of the president's request. The White House specifically criticized the proposed zeroing out of funds for the president's AmeriCorps community service program.

The bill also contains no money for the New Markets Initiative, the five-year, $5 billion program President Clinton hopes will revitalize areas lagging in the current economic expansion. Clinton reached an agreement with Speaker J. Dennis Hastert, R-Ill., on the program last month, but authorizing legislation (HR 815) remains stuck in four House committees.

The House got as far as adopting, 232-182, a rule for floor debate on the VA-HUD bill June 15, but further action was delayed by lengthy debates on the spending bills for Labor, Health and Human Services and Education (HR 4577) and for the Interior Department (HR 4578). *(Vote 278, p. H-88)*

Meanwhile, timing on the bill slipped in the Senate, where a scheduled June 15 Appropriations Committee markup was postponed until after the July Fourth recess.

House Passes Bill With Tobacco, Gun Provisions

JUNE 24 — The House staked out positions on an array of Clinton administration policies the week of June 19 — from its lawsuit against tobacco makers and gun safety initiatives to its air quality standards and space exploration priorities — before passing a $101.3 billion VA-HUD appropriations package for fiscal 2001.

The outcome of the debate on more than 40 amendments to the legislation (HR 4635) was somewhat of a split decision, with Clinton winning affirmation for a handful of his policies and the Republican majority rebuffing many more of his proposals and spending priorities. Still, the vote to pass the measure June 21 was a solid 265-169, with 43 Democrats and all but five Republicans voting in favor. *(Vote 309, p. H-100)*

That majority would not be sufficient to overcome a threatened veto. The White House issued a detailed statement June 19 decrying the bill's funding levels for environmental protection, community development and housing aid and singling out for special criticism the absence of any money for AmeriCorps, the program created during Clinton's first year in office to reward community service with college tuition help. *(1993 Almanac, p. 400)*

But more money seems certain to be added by the time the Senate Appropriations Committee drafts its version of the bill in July. James T. Walsh, R-N.Y., chairman of the House VA-HUD Appropriations Subcommittee, said June 21 that he expected to begin a round of preliminary negotiations even before then with his panel's top Democrat, Alan B. Mollohan of West Virginia, and their Senate counterparts, Christopher S. Bond, R-Mo., and Barbara A. Mikulski, D-Md.

Bond declined a request to discuss his thinking on the bill. Mikulski, in an interview June 20, said she would not begin to consider her subcommittee's policy questions in earnest until more discretionary spending was allocated to the VA-HUD bill.

"Until there's a way to get us back to what we had last year, and even with the caps, we're not going to be moving that quickly," she said. "We don't have enough money to move a bill."

In addition to getting more money to enhance spending overall, the Appropriations subcommittee leaders are under pressure to make room for the bill's customary roster of lawmakers' pet projects. The House-passed bill makes no mention of such parochial priorities; the Senate seems unlikely to take the same approach. And if senators plump up their measure with such targeted spending, the House will be hard-pressed not to follow suit in conference.

House Appropriations Committee Chairman C.W. Bill Young, R-Fla., insisted following the final vote that, by that time, a higher discretionary spending ceiling will be assigned to the bill. "It'll be resolved. Neither side may be totally satisfied," he said.

The House bill would spend 2 percent more than has been appropriated for fiscal 2000 but about 6 percent less than Clinton requested.

Gun Debate

The third most expensive of the 13 appropriations measures, the VA-HUD bill's jurisdiction ranges from politically popular programs — those of the Department of Veterans Affairs (VA) and the National Science Foundation, for example — to others far less popular with the Republican majority, including the Department of Housing and Urban Development (HUD) and the EPA.

Debate during four days of floor consideration ranged over almost every program. Some amendments were hardy perennials, but others — including tobacco and gun control — were new to the bill and seemed designed to become fodder for the campaign trail.

The House split June 21 on the two gun control amendments, both by John Hostettler, R-Ind., handing the president a narrow defeat on the first one and an equally narrow victory on the second.

First, the House voted to block HUD from adding more cities to its Communities for Safer Guns Coalition. That is the network of 411 local and state governments that have agreed, since an out-of-court settlement between HUD and gun manufacturer Smith & Wesson, to give firearms by that manufacturer — or any gun maker signing on to the settlement in the future — priority when purchasing new weapons for their police. The vote was 218-207. *(Vote 306, p. H-98)*

A few minutes later, however, the House rejected, 206-219, an amendment that would have blocked HUD from spending money to enforce the settlement with Smith & Wesson. In the March agreement, the gunmaker promised to install trigger locks and use "smart gun" technology within three years. *(Vote 308, p. H-98)*

HUD Secretary Andrew M. Cuomo derided the first vote as putting the House "firmly in the hip holster of gun lobby extremists."

During debate, Democrats insisted the riders signaled that the GOP — having succeeded in bottling up a gun control package (HR 1501) — were eager to thwart gun control efforts off Capitol Hill as well.

Republicans said the amendments were designed to stop HUD from going around Congress to set policies which, especially in the case of police weapons purchases, should be made free of pressure from Washington. "We should not allow HUD to legislate through litigation," Hostettler said in promoting his proposals.

"This amendment says that communities cannot come together to stop gun violence," replied Carolyn McCarthy, D-N.Y.

Walsh argued, successfully, for defeat of the second amendment, which he contended was frivolous because HUD had no plans to spend money to carry out its accord with Smith & Wesson.

Postponing EPA Air Quality Rules

In another defeat for the administration, the House voted to block the EPA from adding to the list of metropolitan areas that fail to meet new air quality standards issued by the agency three years ago. The amendment, by Mac Collins, R-Ga., was adopted, 226-199. *(Vote 305, p. H-98)*

The language was designed to postpone enforcement of these new rules to combat smog until the Supreme Court rules, in its 2000-01 term, on whether the EPA must consider the cost of compliance, not just the potential health benefits, in setting such regulations. The sponsors of the House amendment said that it would be prohibitively expensive to meet the new standards, designed to reduce pollution from factory and automobile emissions.

But earlier, the House approved an amendment by John W. Olver, D-Mass., designed to minimize the consequences of the bill's prohibition on the Clinton administration carrying out the 1997 Kyoto Protocol on global warming. Olver's language, adopted 314-108, specifies that the restrictions on activities related to the treaty would not prevent the EPA from doing anything else authorized by law. *(Vote 301, p. H-96)*

Democrats feared that the language barring EPA from carrying out the Kyoto Protocol would also gag the agency from carrying out other laws. "We are not compelled to act by the Kyoto treaty; we are compelled to act by common sense," said Jay Inslee, D-Wash.

The administration lost a second environmental policy battle when the House narrowly rejected an amendment by Maurice D. Hinchey, D-N.Y., His proposal, defeated 208-216, would have deleted language that would prevent the EPA from enforcing its interim water standards for arsenic and from encouraging the use of dredging to remove hazardous materials from waterways. *(Vote 304, p. H-98)*

Tobacco Suit Bolstered

Earlier in the week, the debate focused on whether the VA would be allowed to deliver $4 million to the Justice Department to help finance the lawsuit filed in September against tobacco companies. The administration is seeking to recover billions of dollars in expenses for treating smoking-related illnesses of people whose medical bills are paid for by federal programs.

The bill initially barred the VA from making that contribution, and on June 20 the House defeated, 197-207, an amendment by Henry A. Waxman, D-Calif., that would have allowed the money to be taken from the VA's medical care budget. *(Vote 293, p. H-94)*

Appropriators said they objected to

the siphoning of money from the medical care account, while some tobacco-state lawmakers signaled an eagerness to bar funding for the government litigation.

But the next day, on voice vote and with minimal debate, the House shifted course and approved a second Waxman amendment, this one allowing the transfer of $4 million only if the money came from the VA's administrative budget. That allowed Republican appropriators to achieve their goal of protecting funds for veterans' medical care and Democrats to deliver money they sought to keep the lawsuit alive.

"This shows what we can accomplish when we put the public interest ahead of special interests, the public interest ahead of partisan disputes," Clinton said June 22 in hailing the outcome of the tobacco debate on the VA-HUD bill. He urged the House to act in a similar vein when debating the appropriations bill (HR 4690) covering spending on the tobacco litigation by the Justice Department itself. The House did so the next day. *(Commerce-Justice-State, p. 2-23)*

"Without these critical funds, we will have no choice but to seek to dismiss this litigation," Attorney General Janet Reno said at a Capitol news conference June 19. Justice wants the VA, Defense Department, and Department of Health and Human Services to help defray the $20 million cost of the suit in the next year. In return, they would share in any settlement funds.

Hinchey, who had sought to assist the EPA, proposed an amendment to hamstring the VA. It would have prevented the department from continuing development of a new system for disbursing funds among regional VA medical care networks in a manner designed to account for the shift of the veteran population, generally out of the Northeast and Midwest and toward the Sunbelt. It was rejected, 145-277. *(Vote 303, p. H-96)*

Other Amendments

Members of both parties pushed amendments to increase funding for housing, space, science and other programs covered by the bill; most were either defeated or ruled out of order because they were not accompanied by offsetting spending cuts from other sections of the measure. One proposal struck down for lack of offsets, by Mollohan, sought to add $323 million, mostly for NASA research on the next generation of space travel vehicles.

The House rejected, 98-325, an amendment by Tim Roemer, D-Ind., to take $1.8 billion designated for the international space station, spend $1 billion on other programs in the bill and dedicate the rest of the money to debt reduction. *(Vote 302, p. H-96)*

Roemer has been leading a campaign to kill the space station since coming to Congress in 1991, but his effort has steadily been losing steam. A year ago, his amendment garnered 121 votes. Roemer said in an interview that he would work with Sen. John McCain, R-Ariz., a fellow NASA critic, to win language in conference that would cap space station and related mission expenses at $39.6 billion and terminate all space station contracts with Russia.

A few amendments to reorder spending within the bill were adopted. By voice vote, the House agreed to Walsh's request to add $60 million for VA medical research and extended-care facilities and offset it with cuts in space flight and EPA overhead accounts. Also by voice vote, the House adopted a proposal by Jerrold Nadler, D-N.Y., to redirect $18 million in the bill from National Science Foundation polar research to a housing program for people with AIDS. And the House voted 250-170 to transfer $1 million from HUD salaries and expenses to the department's Section 8 housing subsidies for low-income families *(Vote 299, p. H-96)*

But the House voted 138-256 to reject a Nadler amendment that would have taken $344 million from the space station and used it to pay for 60,000 additional Section 8 rental vouchers. Several lawmakers said they could back additional spending on the program, but not at NASA's expense. *(Vote 307, p. H-98)*

Overall, HUD would receive an increase of $4.1 billion, 16 percent more than in the the current fiscal year. But much of the increase would come from a carrying forward of Section 8 money not being spent this year and from $4.2 billion in "advance appropriations" under the fiscal 2000 law (PL 106-74).

FEMA Spending Protected

When debate began, the biggest threat to the bill was posed by GOP conservatives, who vowed to win deletion of the "emergency" designation from the $300 million in the bill that would cover Federal Emergency Management Agency (FEMA) disaster aid. Such a move could have forced appropriators to come up with an equivalent amount of cuts to stay under the VA-HUD bill's discretionary spending ceiling. But, as debate resumed June 20, the House Appropriations Committee voted to add another $300 million for the bill, defusing the potential problem.

Allen Boyd, D-Fla., proposed an amendment to add $2.6 billion for FEMA using the "emergency" designation — a figure that would bring FEMA's ability to pay for unforeseen disasters in the next year in line with what was set aside for fiscal 2000. The president said the figure is the rolling five-year average for disaster aid payments. But the amendment was ruled out of order, because it would have pushed overall federal spending above the limit in the budget resolution (H Con Res 290).

Senate Committee's Measure Yields To Most Demands Of White House

SEPTEMBER 16 — Signaling their eagerness to bring this year's spending battle to an end, Senate appropriators have written a package that would give in to President Clinton on almost all the major sticking points in the appropriations bill for veterans, housing, space and environmental programs.

To make that happen, the Senate Appropriations Committee will spend $4.4 billion more on the VA-HUD bill for fiscal 2001 than would the House, which passed its $101.3 billion version of the legislation (HR 4635) in June. The Senate appropriators have wanted to spend more than the House all along, but until this month they have been prevented from doing so by Republicans eager to hew to their budget's discretionary spending ceilings.

At a total of $105.7 billion, the Senate version would still spend 2 percent less than the $108 billion that Clinton sought, but it would acquiesce to the president on issues ranging from volunteer service to disaster relief and space exploration. The president has threatened to veto the House version because he did not get what he wanted in those areas.

The measure was endorsed on a voice vote in the VA-HUD Appropriations Subcommittee on Sept. 13, and a few hours later the full committee approved it, 27-1. At both markups, senators said the additional spending would come — but only for the time being — from the transportation appropriations legislation (HR 4475), which is now being negotiated in conference.

GOP leaders have tentatively decided to try to quickly merge the transportation conference agreement with a compromise VA-HUD measure, even though House and Senate appropriators say that they have not done any preliminary negotiations. This marks a continuation of the new GOP strategy of crafting "mini-omnibus" bills — combining an appropriations conference report with a second spending bill that has passed the House but not the Senate — in an effort to speed the spending debate by keeping some of the remaining fiscal 2001 bills from being subject to amendment on the Senate floor.

In the interim, Republican leaders have made clear that they will take the procedural steps necessary to breech both the $541 billion overall discretionary spending cap set for fiscal 2001 in the budget-balancing law of 1997 (PL 105-33) and the $600.3 billion cap set in the budget resolution (H Con Res 290) for fiscal 2001. They have not signaled just how they will make those changes, although slipping a few lines deep in one of the appropriations measures would be a plausible way to break the caps with a minimum of notice.

"I can move these allocations around, knowing that there is not enough money," Senate Appropriations Committee Chairman Ted Stevens, R-Alaska, said of the temporary maneuver to borrow from the transportation measure and give to VA-HUD. "We know that bill will have that much, and more, when it comes out of conference."

Republican Targets

"It is still a tight allocation, but, I believe, a fair allocation," said Christopher S. Bond, R-Mo., chairman of the Senate VA-HUD Appropriations Subcommittee, of the money reallocated to the bill.

The third most expensive of the 13 appropriations measures, the package combines programs with broad bipartisan appeal — those of the Department of Veterans Affairs (VA), NASA and the National Science Foundation (NSF), for example — with others that have been targeted by Republicans during their years in control of Congress. First among those are the Department of Housing and Urban Development (HUD), the EPA and AmeriCorps, the national service program (PL 103-82) whose creation was one of Clinton's first domestic policy victories. *(1993 Almanac, p. 400)*

The House once again moved a bill that would provide nothing to operate the program. But the Senate bill, exceeding the administration's expectations, would provide the program with a 9 percent increase, boosting its budget to $388.5 million. Clinton wanted $534 million.

The Senate bill also does not include the House version's riders staking out GOP positions on guns, air quality standards and the federal lawsuit against tobacco companies. Some of those were among the reasons cited by administration officials in threatening a veto of the House bill.

The Office of Management and Budget said it would have no formal statement on the Senate's version of the bill before the week of Sept. 18.

The measure was revived on the Senate side after hanging in limbo for nearly three months, during which both Bond and the VA-HUD Subcommittee's top Democrat, Barbara A. Mikulski of Maryland — declined to move a bill unless they were provided more money to spend.

When the additional money was made available to them, they devoted $110 million of it to several dozen small earmarks for senators' pet environmental protection projects and another $130 million for their favored economic development projects. The most expensive, at $6 million, would go to a pair of water projects in St. Louis and Kansas City, the two biggest cities in the subcommittee chairman's home state.

Still, the degree of earmarking appeared unusually small, given that the bill in the past has often been used to direct spending to a much broader array of parochial projects, not only through the EPA but also for housing and VA construction and scientific research at specified universities.

The House bill eschewed all such earmarks, although it is widely expected that in negotiations on a final deal the House VA-HUD Appropriations Subcommittee Chairman, James T. Walsh, R-N.Y., and the panel's top Democrat, Alan B. Mollohan of West Virginia, will present a list of earmarks to match those in the Senate bill.

An Increase for Vets

The Senate bill would provide $47 billion for veterans' programs, besting the House bill by $56 million and Clinton's own request by $17 million. The measure would meet the administration's requests for veterans benefits ($22.8 billion), medical care ($20.3 billion) and readjustment benefits such as the Montgomery GI Bill ($1.6 billion).

It would give HUD $30.6 billion, which would be 18 percent more than is being spent in fiscal 2000 and 2 percent more than in the House bill — but still 6 percent below the Clinton request. Much of the increase, though, would come from carrying forward unspent money from the Section 8 program for subsidized rental assistance and $4.2 billion in "advance appropriations" under the fiscal 2000 law (PL 106-74) designed not to count against budgetary spending caps imposed three years ago.

The Senate would allocate $13.2 billion for Section 8, with $4.2 billion considered "advance appropriations" for fiscal 2002 and therefore exempt from the spending caps. The House bill included a similar provision in order to save money, at least on paper.

The committee would fund the public housing capital fund at $3 billion and the public housing operating fund at $3.2 billion, matching Clinton's requests. The Senate measure would fund the community development block grant program at $4.8 billion, essentially the same as Clinton's request and a virtual match to what is being spent in this fiscal year. And it would retain at the current level of $232 million spending on the program that provides housing assistance for people with AIDS.

The committee said it would push HUD to spend its excess Section 8 housing funds from fiscal 2000 — on the creation of a new block grant for new construction or to preserve existing low-income housing. Bond said he would seek to have a bill to that end (S 3033) added to the final VA-HUD measure. Under his proposal, state housing finance agencies would be eligible for money on a per-capita basis for new construction, provided they put up a 75 percent match.

The bill would provide just over $1 billion for homeless programs, the same as currently. But the committee, as promised, required HUD to collect information on homelessness and the effectiveness of programs that have been established to help the homeless, a requirement that arose from a dust-up between Bond and HUD Secretary Andrew M. Cuomo over HUD's seizure of $60 million in homeless funding from the city of New York.

While expressing satisfaction with those figures, Mikulski urged other lawmakers to resist the temptation to make any moves to shave money from HUD to expand other programs under the bill. "If we can't keep providing affordable housing, this will be a very hollow victory," she said.

Frank R. Lautenberg, D-N.J., criticized his colleagues on the panel for including language, in the report accompanying the bill, criticizing as "unneeded and inappropriate" a HUD program that directs local public housing authorities to operate programs to buy back guns. But that was as far as the Senate bill went toward picking a gun-control fight. By contrast, the House bill would prevent HUD from expanding a group of local and state governments it has assembled to give purchasing preference to firearms made by Smith & Wesson — a reward for that company's out-of-court settlement of a lawsuit in which HUD tried to recoup from gun makers the costs of gun violence in public housing.

Winners and Losers

These are some of the highlights of how the Senate bill would treat other agencies under its purview.

• **NASA.** Despite sustaining scrutiny for cost overruns and criticism over several highly publicized space probe failures last year, the space agency survived unscathed. It would receive a 1 percent increase in funding over fiscal 2000, to $13.8 billion; the House bill would essentially freeze NASA spending.

The Senate bill would restore $290 million for a program to develop a new generation of space launch vehicles. But it would provide $5.4 billion, $111 million less than in fiscal 2000 , for human space flight programs, including upgrades to the space shuttle and the development of the international space station.

• **FEMA.** The Federal Emergency Management Agency would receive $3.5 billion, an 8 percent decrease, although $2.6 billion would be labeled a "contingency" fund for spending on future disasters, as Clinton requested. The House devoted only $300 million to this idea.

• **NSF.** The agency, which conducts basic science research, would receive $4.3 billion, a 10 percent increase but 6 percent below Clinton's request.

• **EPA.** The agency would receive $7.5 billion, essentially a freeze at the current level. The agency would also receive $1.4 billion for superfund programs, 11 percent above fiscal 2000.

Western Republicans Pete V. Domenici of New Mexico and Larry E. Craig of Idaho expressed concern about EPA proposals to tighten water standards on arsenic and other contaminants. If EPA changes the rules, Craig warned, it "will cost thousands of small water systems across our country, whose systems have met all requirements, hundreds of millions of dollars."

Deal Meets Most Clinton Priorities, Keeps Some GOP Policy Riders

OCTOBER 7 — Appropriators and the Clinton administration reached an agreement Oct. 5 on a fiscal 2001 spending measure for veterans, housing, space, science and environmental programs. The deal would give President Clinton most of what he sought — including additional funding for the EPA and for AmeriCorps, the volunteer service program he pushed to creation in 1993.

The package is likely to come to the Senate floor as a freestanding measure as soon as Oct. 11. However, C.W. Bill Young, R-Fla., the chairman of the House Appropriations Committee, said that if the bill (HR 4635) got bogged down in a series of Senate amendments, it could instead be combined with a separate conference report on a spending proposal to speed its passage.

The compromise would provide the Department of Veterans Affairs (VA) at least the $46.9 billion Clinton requested, and perhaps a bit more. Spending is also likely to approach the $32.5 billion White House target for the Department of Housing and Urban Development (HUD).

Negotiators said the bill's grand total would be close to the $107.9 billion Clinton had requested. In contrast, the bill passed by the House in June (H Rept 106-674) would have appropriated $101.3 billion; the version approved by the Senate Appropriations Committee Sept. 13 (S Rept 106-410) would have provided $105.7 billion.

Separately, House and Senate appropriators reached an agreement on a list of special research, community development and environmental quality earmarks that the House wanted to include. The Senate bill included $360 million for such projects. James T. Walsh, R-N.Y., chairman of the House Appropriations VA-HUD Subcommittee, said the Senate list would be pared to make room for the House requests.

Several environmental policy riders pressed by Republicans and opposed by the administration remain in the agreement. Further, some of the $1.8 billion in unused fiscal 2000 Section 8 low-income rental subsidy funds would be allocated for housing vouchers in 2001. The administration had called for spreading the unused funds throughout the bill, while Republicans wanted to reduce the measure's overall price tag by counting the leftover 2000 funds as a budget savings.

The Senate did not debate the committee-approved version of the VA-HUD bill as a stand-alone measure, instead taking it straight from committee to conference with the House.

Housing Program Fails

One expensive casualty in the negotiations was a proposal to boost affordable housing stock pushed by Christopher S. Bond, R-Mo., chairman of the Senate VA-HUD Subcommittee, and endorsed by Clinton. The plan died after running into opposition from Senate Banking, Housing and Urban Affairs Committee Chairman Phil Gramm, R-Texas, and Wayne Allard, R-Colo., chairman of the panel's Housing and Transportation Subcommittee.

The two complained in an Oct. 2 letter to Majority Leader Trent Lott, R-Miss., that there had been "virtually no consultation" on the idea, which would have diverted up to $1 billion of unspent Section 8 funds to state agencies for construction and revitalization of low- and moderate-income housing.

The agreement did provide 79,000 of the 120,000 Section 8 vouchers Clinton had requested. Neither the House nor the Senate bill would have provided new vouchers.

While the EPA would receive a $262 million increase to $7.7 billion, several EPA policy riders remain in the report, including one to stop the agency from enforcing new water standards for arsenic, and another to block it from putting into effect new air quality rules — at least until the Supreme Court decides whether the EPA should have taken the cost of compliance into account when drafting them.

Another rider would bar the EPA from encouraging the use of dredging as a method of removing hazardous wastes from waterways until the National Academy of Sciences completes a study of the issue. Such dredging has been supported along the Hudson River, where residents want the removal of polychlorinated biphenyls, or PCBs, dumped decades ago by the General Electric Co.

While the House voted to eliminate spending on AmeriCorps, negotiators decided to spend at least $434 million — $100 million less than Clinton wanted but $45 million more than the Senate provided. Clinton's case was aided when 49 governors, including GOP presidential nominee George W. Bush of Texas, asked Congress Sept. 20 to reauthorize the program for another five years. Bills have been introduced in the House (HR 4740) and Senate (S 2764) to reauthorize the program.

Senate leaders would clearly prefer to move a freestanding VA-HUD bill. Senate Minority Leader Tom Daschle, D-S.D., and Robert C. Byrd of West Virginia, the top Democrat on the Appropriations Committee, have blocked other GOP efforts to move spending bills by pairing an appropriations measure in conference with one that has never been taken up in the Senate.

With pressure building to bring the 106th Congress to an end, Barbara A. Mikulski of Maryland, the top Democrat on the Senate VA-HUD Subcommittee, had asked Daschle and Byrd to relent. On Oct. 3, Daschle appeared to give in.

"I'd be inclined to do so," he told reporters. "It's violating virtually every Senate rule and it's terrible precedent, but if we've got to get the work done we want to get done and as messy and as ugly as the process is, we may have to accept it."

Senate Passes Compromise VA-HUD Bill

OCTOBER 14 — A $107.3 billion spending package covering veterans, housing, space, environmental protection, science research and disaster aid programs has won the promise of President Clinton's signature. If Congress is able to steer the legislation (HR 4635) through a complicated procedural thicket the week of Oct. 16, it will have dispatched the third-most expensive of the fiscal 2001 appropriations bills.

The VA-HUD bill, which the Senate voted 87-8 to pass on Oct. 12, embodied a deal worked out the previous week between the White House and appropriators from both the House and Senate. *(Vote 272, p. S-49)*

Although negotiations are essentially complete, the bill will likely be sent to a formal House-Senate conference committee. That would enable appropriators to produce a conference report detailing the agreement — particularly earmarks parceled out to lawmakers. But it also would mean additional votes by both the House and the Senate to finish the deliberations. The alternative is for the House to clear the Senate-passed bill.

No additional spending will be added in conference, James T. Walsh, R-N.Y., chairman of the House VA-HUD Appropriations Subcommittee, promised Oct. 13. "We're not going to accept anything else," he said.

The bill also included the energy and water appropriations bill, stripped of the Missouri River management provision that had prompted Clinton to veto the initial version (HR 4733).

Under the deal, the VA-HUD spending grand total would be 8 percent more than in fiscal 2000 and 4 percent ($4.2 billion) more than the version the House passed in June, something that may give GOP fiscal conservatives pause when the measure is put before the House. They also may blanch at the $82.6 billion total for discretionary spending, which would be 8 percent ($6.4 billion) more than what both House and Senate appropriators initially said they intended to spend.

The bill's bottom line would be 2 percent ($2.4 billion) less than the president requested. Still, Clinton said in an Oct. 12 statement, the package "is clear proof of the progress we can achieve when we work together to address the nation's priorities."

Clinton pointed particularly to the administration's spending victories for economic development programs, emergency food and shelter aid and basic science research, including research on fuel efficiency technologies. But perhaps the sweetest victory for the president is that the measure would deliver a 21 percent increase, to $433.5 million, to AmeriCorps, the national service program (PL 103-82) that he pushed to enactment during his first year in office. *(1993 Almanac, p. 400)*

It has been a magnet for Republican criticism ever since, but efforts to cut off funding have never succeeded, and now GOP presidential nominee George W. Bush has endorsed it. "So it turns out that this idea that was just sort of an applause line in my '92 campaign speech, it was a pretty good idea after all," Clinton said in a speech to AmeriCorps volunteers in Philadelphia the day before the Senate vote.

'The Earmarking Has Exploded'

The price tag for the VA-HUD bill has grown in part as lawmakers have hewed to the tradition of using it to pay for a host of parochial projects. The version approved by Senate Appropriations had at least $360 million in such earmarks. The House, which passed a bill without any, won inclusion of its own list in the informal negotiations. No one was willing to disclose the final list any sooner than necessary.

Sen. John McCain, R-Ariz., who is striving to use the attention from his recent presidential candidacy to raise public interest in his longtime crusade against "pork barrel" politics, decried the process that yielded the bill, calling it a "highly questionable" method that empowered appropriators at the expense of senators. "Just because it's late in the game doesn't mean it's right to avoid the appropriations process," he said. "We are abrogating our responsibility to the taxpayers by voting on bills that we've neither seen nor read."

Sen. Jon Kyl, R-Ariz., took special aim at the election-year rewards for his colleagues. Pointing to the portion of the bill meting out economic development money, he said: "The earmarking has exploded. We have not seen the final list, but we know it is up to at least $292 million, up from $123 million in the committee-passed bill and $240 million from last year. That is too much. We have funding in here for everything from renovating theaters to restoring carousels. This is not something the federal government needs to be doing."

But most of the debate centered on the bill's inclusion of three riders to direct actions at the EPA, which Barbara Boxer, D-Calif., tried unsuccessfully to eliminate or alter. Each is a modified version of Republican language in the House-passed bill, and each was deemed acceptable by the administration.

"You may think we wimped out," Barbara A. Mikulski of Maryland, the top Democrat on the Senate VA-HUD Appropriations Subcommittee, told Boxer. "We think we had a victory."

One provision would block the EPA from carrying out stricter new air quality rules issued three years ago — under which a new list of metropolitan areas would be deemed to have excessive smog — but only until the Supreme Court decides whether those rules should have been drafted with the cost of compliance in mind or June 15, whichever comes first. The House bill would have imposed the restriction until June 15, no matter what.

Another provision would forbid the EPA from enforcing interim standards on arsenic in water until June, or earlier if the agency was ready to issue permanent arsenic standards. The House bill would have forced the EPA to finalize the standard before enforcing it.

Boxer's amendment to remove both of those provisions was tabled, or killed, 63-32. *(Vote 270, p. S-48)*

The third provision at issue would block the agency from using dredging to remove soil contaminated with hazardous materials from waterways. The compromise would allow the ban to stay in place until June 30, and it would allow the EPA to dredge anyway if it determines there is a public health threat, and it would not affect dredging permits already issued. As a result, it would not stop efforts to clean up most of the 28 superfund hazardous waste sites involved, including along the Hudson River. A Boxer amendment to express the sense of Congress that the EPA should move more quickly was tabled, or killed, 56-39. *(Vote 271, p. S-48)*

Housing for the Poor, Elderly

The largest monetary increase under the bill would go to the Department of Housing and Urban Development (HUD), which stands to receive $30.6 billion, an 18 percent increase over fiscal 2000. The extra money would go to several of the department's core programs. Elderly housing would receive a $69 million increase, to $779 million. Housing for the disabled would receive an extra $16 million, to $217 million. Housing for people with AIDS would get an extra $26 million, to $258 million. Community development block grants would get a 5 percent increase, to $5.1 billion. But the biggest winner would be the Housing Certificate Fund, the main source of federal aid for low-income housing and rental subsidies, which would get a 23 percent increase, to $13.9 billion.

Despite the scuttling during negotiations of a proposed $1 billion housing production program by Senate VA-HUD Appropriations Subcommittee Chairman Christopher S. Bond, R-Mo., appropriators earmarked $453 million to support an additional 79,000 low-income housing vouchers. That is two-thirds the additional vouchers Clinton sought, but it would nonetheless mark the third consecutive year of increases in the number of vouchers. The number of vouchers was frozen between fiscal 1994 and fiscal 1998. The extra vouchers would be paid for with unspent fiscal 2000 Section 8 funds.

The Department of Veterans Affairs, a perennial favorite of Congress, would receive just over $47 billion, a 6 percent increase and $55 million more than Clinton requested.

NASA would receive a 5 percent increase, to $14.3 billion, for its space programs. The bill would restore $290 million cut by the House for a program to develop a new generation of space launch vehicles. The space agency — which would be reauthorized under a bill (HR 1654) the Senate cleared Oct. 13 — would receive $5.5 billion, a cut of less than 1 percent, for human space flight programs, including upgrades to the space shuttle fleet and continued development of the international space station.

The Federal Emergency Management Agency would receive $2.2 billion, three-fifths of its fiscal 2000 appropriation. The agency's operating budget would be boosted by 8 percent, to $937 million. Almost all of the reduction would be to an "emergency" fund for disaster relief that would not count against the spending caps imposed by the 1997 balanced budget law (PL 105-33). The bill would allocate $1.3 billion, a middle ground between the Senate's initial $2.6 billion and the House's zero.

The EPA would receive $7.8 billion, an increase of 5 percent. Its funding for superfund cleanup and programs would remain at $1.2 billion, the same as in fiscal 2000. The National Science Foundation, which conducts basic science research, would receive $4.4 billion, a 13 percent increase but 3 percent below Clinton's request.

Before it was passed, the bill served as the vehicle for an unusual parliamentary maneuver, born after Senate Democrats insisted that they be allowed to consider each appropriations bill. Robert C. Byrd, D-W.Va., tried to add the Senate Appropriations Committee's Treasury-Postal bill (S 2900) to the VA-HUD bill, knowing the request would be rejected on a voice vote.

Senate Clears Project-Laden VA-HUD Measure

OCTOBER 21 — Congress cleared a $107.3 billion veterans, housing, space, science and environmental protection spending bill on Oct. 19 — the final fiscal 2001 appropriations measure finished before the whirlwind of budgetary dealmaking that will end in the adjournment of the 106th Congress.

The House voted 386-24 to adopt the conference report, and the Senate voted 85-8 to clear the bill a few hours later. *(House vote 536, p. H-172; Senate vote 278, p. S-50)*

The VA-HUD bill (HR 4635) was hailed by President Clinton as a model of bipartisanship "that will open the doors of opportunity in America for those who need it most, improve veterans' medical care, build on our agenda for national energy security and strengthen our commitment to the environment."

Those did not appear to be the only reasons the bill received such a warm embrace at the Capitol. Written into the conference report were 1,183 earmarks for the university research, water and sewer construction, and local economic development initiatives promoted by members of Congress. The combined value of the pet projects is just under $1.1 billion, a few million dollars more than the bill would provide for assisting the homeless.

"This is one of the few times that the committee has funded everything," Carrie P. Meek, a Miami Democrat on the VA-HUD Appropriations Subcommittee, said during the House debate. Among the community and economic development earmarks is $215,000 for Shake-A-Leg Miami Inc., for "recreation facilities serving people with disabilities and at-risk youth."

When the conference report was debated on the other side of the Capitol, however, a rare note of dissent was sounded by another Florida Democrat, Sen. Bob Graham. "We are in the midst of an orgy of spending," he said, "which threatens the fiscal discipline that many members of this Congress and the administration have worked so hard to achieve."

But in a week when the president and congressional Democrats were deriding the glacial pace toward the end of the year's budget debate, the payoff was that the GOP could boast that it had finished the third biggest of the 13 appropriations bills, and had dispatched another one in the process. The VA-HUD bill also carried a $23.6 billion package of energy and water development appropriations, trimmed of the Missouri River management provision that had prompted Clinton to veto the original version of the bill (HR 4733) this month.

About three-quarters of the spending in the VA-HUD bill is discretionary; virtually all the mandatory spending is for the benefits programs administered by the Department of Veterans Affairs (VA). The measure would increase both mandatory and discretionary spending by 8 percent from fiscal 2000 levels, but it would allocate 2 percent, or $2.4 billion, less than Clinton's request. The totals nonetheless delighted the Democrats.

"After being lost in wonderland territory for over eight months, the committee is finally being allowed to be realistic," David R. Obey of Wisconsin, the ranking Democrat on the Appropriations Committee, said during the House debate.

The $103.1 billion bill the House passed in June made no mention of parochial rewards. But the Senate Appropriations Committee put at least 378 special projects in its bill, at a cost of $430 million, in September. That measure was never debated by the Senate. Instead, appropriators from both sides of the Capitol and the White House met for several days behind closed doors and reached an informal conference agreement in which at least $622 million in House largess was added. The Senate passed a version of the VA-HUD bill embodying the deal Oct. 12, but the depth and breadth of the earmarking was not available for public review until a few hours before the House took up the bill Oct. 19.

18 Percent Increase for HUD

The Department of Housing and Urban Development (HUD), a frequent target of frequent Republican congressional animus, would nonetheless get the biggest monetary increase under the bill — $4.7 billion, or 18 percent. "With this budget, we have the most resources we've had in 20 years to meet the needs of America's families," HUD Secretary Andrew M. Cuomo said Oct. 19.

Much of the extra money would be directed to several core programs. The Housing Certificate Fund, the main source of federal aid for low-income housing and rental subsidies, would get a 23 percent increase to $13.9 billion — in part by continuing to carry forward $4.2 billion in "advance appropriations" begun in fiscal 2000. Spending for community development block grants would grow 5 percent, to $5.1 billion. Funding for the HOME Investment Partnerships program, which gives money to state and local governments to increase affordable housing, would increase 13 percent, to $1.8 billion. Funding for programs to help the homeless would stay nearly the same at $1 billion, 15 percent below Clinton's request.

Nothing would be provided for the proposals crafted by Clinton and House Speaker J. Dennis Hastert, R-Ill., to boost investment in low-income communities, but conferees promised money next year if a bill (HR 4923, S 3152) is enacted, which it may be as part of a year-end tax package.

Programs that are perennial favorites of Congress did especially well, while those expected to face deep cuts at the GOP's hands emerged with increases or only minor cuts.

Clinton's national service program, AmeriCorps, was targeted for elimination under the House bill. Under the compromise, it would receive a 21 percent increase, to $434 million.

NASA, which has had a rocky relationship with Congress in the past, would get a 5 percent increase to $14.3 billion for its space programs, as $290 million cut by the House from the development of a new generation of space launch vehicles was revived in conference. The agency would receive $5.5 billion, a cut of less than 1 percent, for human space flight programs, including continued development of the international space station and upgrades to the space shuttle fleet.

The Federal Emergency Management Agency's operating budget would increase 8 percent to $937 million. But the agency's reserve fund for providing

VA-HUD Spending Highlights

Where the Money Goes

HR 4635 — Conference Report: H Rept 106-988

Spending Synopsis

The House voted 386-24 to adopt the VA-HUD conference report, and the Senate cleared it, 85-8, Oct. 19. Conferees met for only 15 minutes Oct. 18 to formally seal the deal, which was informally finished Oct. 5. (The Senate passed a version of the bill embodying the agreement Oct. 12.) At $107.3 billion, the bill would spend 8 percent more in fiscal 2001 than was spent in fiscal 2000 but 2 percent less than Clinton requested. Discretionary spending accounts for about three-quarters of the bill's total. The bill also served as a vehicle for a revised $23.6 billion energy and water development appropriations bill, shorn of a Missouri River management provision that had prompted Clinton's veto of the original bill (HR 4733).

• Department of Veterans Affairs (VA)

The VA would receive a 7 percent increase in discretionary spending, its largest ever, mostly for health care delivery. The bill allocates $55 million more than Clinton sought, with extra money for extended-care facilities and medical research.

• Department of Housing and Urban Development (HUD)

HUD would receive 18 percent more than in fiscal 2000, with money for 79,000 new Section 8 vouchers for low-income renters. Community development block grants, the fund for public housing and empowerment zones would get increases.

• NASA

The space agency would get a 5 percent increase, and 2 percent more than Clinton requested, including most of what the president wanted for the space station and $290 million to help develop a new generation of space launch vehicles.

• Environmental Protection Agency

The EPA's key fund for environmental programs and management would get a 10 percent increase over last year. The Senate originally increased its allocation by 5 percent, while the House essentially froze funding at fiscal 2000 levels.

• Federal Emergency Management Agency

The report gave Clinton $2.2 billion to help with disasters in the next year, including $1.3 billion in a "contingency" fund. The Senate gave Clinton the $2.6 billion he sought, while the House originally ignored his request.

Hot-Button Issues

Δ **Pet projects.** The measure is greased with 1,183 earmarks worth almost $1.1 billion — the lion's share going to appropriators and members of the leadership. The roster of pet projects is three times longer than in the bill produced by the Senate Appropriations Committee (worth $430 million) because the House, which initially passed a bill without any earmarks, decided to to take its cut in conference.

Δ **AmeriCorps.** At the GOP's behest, the House bill would have shut down the volunteer service program; in the face of a veto threat, negotiators instead settled on a 21 percent increase, to $434 million.

Δ **Environmental policy.** Curbs on the EPA sought by the House were softened. It must wait until June 15, or a Supreme Court ruling, to enforce new air quality standards, and until June 30 to enforce new arsenic standards in water and to resume dredging of hazardous materials from waterways.

Δ **Tobacco lawsuit.** The bill retains House language allowing the VA to spend administrative money, but not health care funds, to help press the government's lawsuit against tobacco companies.

Δ **Guns.** Conferees dropped a House provision that would prohibit HUD from expanding a coalition of local governments aimed at preventing gun violence as part of the settlement of a lawsuit against Smith & Wesson.

(figures are in thousands of dollars of new budget authority)

	Fiscal 2000 Appropriation	Fiscal 2001 Clinton Request	House Bill	Senate Committee Bill [1]	Conference Report
Department of Veterans Affairs	$44,255,165	$46,948,405	$46,909,667	$46,965,583	$47,003,083
Department of Housing and Urban Development	25,923,683	32,465,550	29,980,030	30,633,726	30,620,607
NASA	13,652,700	14,035,300	13,658,600	13,844,000	14,285,300
Environmental Protection Agency	7,461,659	7,164,072	7,143,888	7,534,190	7,827,851
National Science Foundation	3,912,050	4,572,400	4,046,300	4,297,184	4,426,122
Federal Emergency Management Agency	3,838,421	3,580,477	876,730	3,515,977	2,236,757
Other independent agencies	707,167	1,016,895	486,621	717,293	938,597
GRAND TOTAL	**$99,736,845**	**$109,783,099** [2]	**$103,101,836** [2]	**$107,507,953** [2]	**$107,341,317** [2]
Total adjusted for scorekeeping	($95,274,918)	($109,392,099)	($102,928,836)	($105,304,953)	($107,138,317)

NOTES: (1) The Appropriations Committee bill was not considered by the Senate. (2) Assumes shift of $1.8 billion in VA compensation and pension payments to fiscal 2000.

TABLE: House and Senate Appropriations committees

disaster relief would be cut to $1.3 billion, from $3 billion in fiscal 2000.

The National Science Foundation, which conducts basic research, would receive $4.4 billion, a 13 percent increase, but 3 percent below Clinton's request. The president hailed the bill's funding for research in nano-technology — the manipulation of matter at the molecular and atomic level — and in technologies to increase fuel efficiency.

The EPA would receive $7.8 billion, an increase of 5 percent. Its funding for superfund cleanup and programs would be frozen at $1.2 billion. Riders designed by Republicans to check agency policies — on urban air quality, arsenic in water and dredging of contaminated soil — were each limited in conference enough to win favor from Clinton.

The Community Development Financial Institutions Fund — which provides mortgages and economic development lending in poor areas — would get $118 million, a 24 percent increase. The Consumer Product Safety Commission would get $53 million, a 7 percent increase. The Selective Service System, which registers young men for possible drafting into the military, was held to $25 million, a 2 percent increase — one of the few increases under the bill that would not keep up with inflation. ◆

Emergency Spending Bill Beefs Up Military Readiness, Disaster Aid, Drug War Funds

SUMMARY

Congress cleared an $11.2 billion assortment of supplemental fiscal 2000 appropriations June 30, when fiscal 2000 was three-quarters complete. The package — mostly for the military, disaster aid and a new initiative to stem Colombia's narcotics trade — was added to the conference report on the military construction spending bill for fiscal 2001, the first of the 13 regular appropriations measures to clear. The unusual method for advancing the supplemental was insisted on by Majority Leader Trent Lott, R-Miss., who refused to let the Senate consider a stand-alone measure.

When President Clinton sent his fiscal 2001 budget request to Capitol Hill on Feb. 7, it included a request for about $4.4 billion in supplemental budget authority for fiscal 2000. Almost half the request was to replenish Pentagon accounts tapped to pay for U.S. soldiers in the NATO peacekeeping force in Kosovo. The second-biggest request was to begin delivering aid to the Colombian government to combat drug barons and the leftist guerrillas who aid them, a cause embraced by both Clinton and House Speaker J. Dennis Hastert, R-Ill. Clinton added to his request several times in the ensuing weeks, bringing it to a total of $5.5 billion.

The price tag escalated quickly after that. The bill (HR 3908) approved by the House Appropriations Committee on March 9 had a $9.1 billion bottom line. When the House passed it three weeks later, the total was $13.2 billion. Most of the increase — $4 billion — was added to bolster Pentagon arms procurement, maintenance and health programs.

The supplemental was halted in the Senate, where Lott refused to bring up a stand-alone bill. He said he did not want to devote scarce floor time to a debate that could last for weeks, and he feared the bill's price tag would balloon further in such a debate. Instead, he pressed Senate appropriators to spread about $8 billion in supplemental spending among the first three fiscal 2001 appropriations measures they marked up — agriculture, foreign operations and military construction — hoping that would spur those bills to early completion.

As work on the three bills proceeded, however, Lott's strategy was increasingly viewed as backfiring. While he had said his aim was to produce a "quick and clean" supplemental, the delay meant many "emergency" needs went unmet for months, caused the package to attract a host of special projects, and allowed time for congressional skepticism about the Colombia initiative to grow. Lott relented at a meeting of GOP leaders June 22. By that point, the Defense Department was saying that, if its share of the supplemental was not guaranteed for delivery by month's end, it would be forced to cancel training exercises and maintenance projects, the accounts that had been tapped to finance the Kosovo mission.

The final package was assembled with speed and unusual secrecy, mostly by the top four members of the Appropriations committees. The biggest items were $2 billion to replenish the accounts used for the Kosovo mission; $1.6 billion to pay higher than expected military fuel bills; $1.3 billion for unfunded military health programs; $1.3 billion to battle drug smugglers in Colombia and other South American countries, $1 billion in disaster aid, and $700 million for the Coast Guard, mostly for new equipment. GOP leaders limited the appropriators to allocating $200 million in overt earmarks, most of it going to senior lawmakers. Most legislative riders were kept out of the package.

The measure voided more than $4 billion in scorekeeping adjustments that had artificially deflated overall fiscal 2000 spending by shifting the spending into fiscal 2001. By abandoning that gimmickry, appropriators were able to free up more money for the fiscal 2001 cycle. A handful of conservatives charged that the accounting maneuver effectively allowed the money to count toward the total for neither fiscal year, but their attempts to alter that outcome fell through the cracks as the budget wars dragged into the fall.

For the first time since Republicans took over Congress, the party's conservatives did not press for offsetting cuts to help finance the supplemental. With the surplus surging, this was no longer a political requirement.

Box Score — 2000 Fiscal Year

Fiscal 2000 Supplemental

- **Bill:** HR 4425 — PL 106-246
- **Legislative action: House** passed HR 3908 (H Rept 106-521), 263-146, on March 30.

House adopted the conference report on HR 4425 (H Rept 106-710), 306-110, on June 29.

Senate cleared HR 4425 by voice vote June 30.

President signed the bill July 13.

Clinton Seeks Extra $4.4 Billion To Fight Drugs, Keep Peace

FEBRUARY 12 — Looking for extra money to combat drug traffickers in Colombia and maintain peace in the Balkans, among other initiatives, President Clinton on Feb. 7 asked Congress for $4.4 billion in supplemental budget authority for the current fiscal year.

Clinton said he would offset about $400 million of the new spending by cutting current programs, including some in the departments of Energy and Housing and Urban Development, as well as by eliminating a proposed increase in White House staff. Most of the supplemental funds — about $4 billion — would be designated emergency spending, eliminating the need under budget laws to balance the increase with offsetting cuts.

Clinton's proposed supplemental would actually spend almost twice as much money this year — $8.4 billion in outlays — than its budget authority. That is because the administration also wants to use the supplemental to reverse some accounting tricks employed last year to help Congress stay close to discretionary spending limits.

Last year, for instance, Congress authorized delaying the Pentagon's final fiscal 2000 payday by one day, shifting an estimated $3.6 billion in outlays into fiscal 2001. Clinton now has proposed moving that last paycheck back before Oct. 1.

The administration also proposed reversing a decision to delay payments to defense contractors, which had resulted in another $1.25 billion in fiscal 2000 outlays being pushed into fiscal 2001.

Balkan Peace

The proposed supplemental received little immediate reaction on Capitol Hill, but Congress has been generally supportive of the major elements in the package, which were announced in advance.

Just under half the extra budget authority, or about $2.2 billion, would go to the Pentagon to pay for the 6,200 U.S. soldiers in the NATO peacekeeping force in Kosovo, 1,000 support personnel in neighboring countries, and enforcement of international sanctions against the former Yugoslavia.

Members of the Armed Services and Defense Appropriations panels have previously supported these plans, partly to ensure that the Pentagon would not have to plunder training and other military accounts to pay for operations in the Balkans.

However, Senate Armed Services Committee Chairman John W. Warner, R-Va., has said that he might not allow the funds to be released until America's European allies pay their promised share of the costs of rebuilding Kosovo and protecting its civilians.

The State Department and the Agency for International Development (AID) would receive $618 million for their efforts in the Balkans.

The State Department would receive $263 million, most of it for building a diplomatic mission in Kosovo and upgrading security at embassies in neighboring countries.

Clinton requested that $107 million be provided to the United Nations for peacekeeping activities, particularly in Kosovo and East Timor.

The remaining funds would largely be provided to AID for economic aid to the Balkans.

Fighting Drugs

Another $955 million in supplemental budget authority would go to the State and Defense departments for the drug war.

The funds are the first major installment of a two-year package of $1.3 billion in new economic and military aid to Colombia that President Clinton announced last month. Colombia's government is under attack by drug traffickers and leftist guerrillas.

Congressional Republicans, particularly House Speaker J. Dennis Hastert, R-Ill., have long been pushing for the aid.

So despite opposition from some leading Democrats, such as Sen. Patrick J. Leahy, D-Vt., the Colombia aid piece of the package is likely to move forward, according to Sen. Mike DeWine, R-Ohio, a leading proponent of the aid.

The State Department and AID would receive $818 million in supplemental budget authority, including money to buy dozens of U.S. made helicopters, interdict drug shipments, and bolster crop substitution and alternative development in Colombia and the Andean region.

The Defense Department would receive $98 million to train two additional counterdrug battalions, assist an ongoing program to eliminate corruption and human rights violations and enhance Colombian Army air bases to accommodate additional helicopters.

In addition, the supplemental request would provide $39 million toward construction of a "forward operating location" in Manta, Ecuador, intended as a substitute take-off point for U.S. anti-drug flights. U.S. planes needed a new airfield in the region because they can no longer use former U.S. facilities in Panama that were turned over to the Panamanian government last year along with the Panama Canal.

Debt Relief

Clinton also requested that Congress further ease the debt burden of the world's poorest countries, as announced by Treasury Secretary Lawrence H. Summers on Feb. 1. The supplemental proposal includes a request for an additional $210 million in budget authority in fiscal 2000 for debt relief programs.

Senate Banking Committee Chairman Phil Gramm has said that the proposal, and other funds already slated to be released this year, will be carefully scrutinized by his panel.

Senate's Unease Over Kosovo, Colombia Policy Imperils Proposal

FEBRUARY 26 — President Clinton's proposal for $4.4 billion in supplemental budget authority for fiscal 2000, which only weeks ago seemed assured of passage, is running into growing opposition on Capitol Hill.

Most surprising, the administration's request for $955 million in emergency aid to Colombia has drawn fire, despite support from House Speaker J. Dennis Hastert, R-Ill., and Senate Majority Leader Trent Lott, R-Miss. Critics worry that U.S. plans are inadequate to help Colombia deal with guerrillas and drug traffickers and that the United States will be drawn into the conflict.

"We have some very, very serious problems to resolve in this committee if we expect this supplemental to survive on the floor," warned Senate Appropriations Committee Chairman Ted Stevens, R-Alaska, at a Feb. 24 subcommittee hearing.

The House has been more receptive to Clinton's proposal. The Appropriations Committee is scheduled to mark up its version of the supplemental bill the week of March 7, and it could be on the floor the following week.

Clinton's supplemental request,

submitted Feb. 7, would provide the first installment in a two-year, $1.6 billion aid package for Colombia.

It also includes $2.2 billion for the U.S. share of the NATO peacekeeping force in Kosovo and $618 million for diplomacy and economic aid in the Balkans. And it includes $210 million to further ease the foreign debt burden of the world's poorest countries.

Those aid requests have run into opposition.

Senate Banking Committee Chairman Phil Gramm, R-Texas, has said he will scrutinize the request for additional debt relief.

Senate Armed Services Committee Chairman John W. Warner, R-Va., has expressed concern about the Kosovo request, given what he says are inadequate contributions from the European Union to help police and rebuild the war-torn region.

On Feb. 24, Warner told reporters he would add an amendment to the supplemental bill requiring the administration to spell out other countries' commitments to the Balkans.

"Those nations that haven't fulfilled their commitment in terms of police, dollars for infrastructure and so forth, we should know about it here in Congress," Warner said.

Growing Tension

His concerns were heightened by the deteriorating security situation in the mining town of Mitrovica, where NATO troops have become embroiled in violence between Serbs and ethnic Albanians. On Feb. 23, NATO's supreme commander, U.S. Army Gen. Wesley K. Clark, appealed for reinforcements.

Warner said, "I'm gravely concerned about the risks, the increasing risks to the men and women of our armed forces and the other armed forces. I'll support the additional funds for our military in Kosovo, but we're going to have to have a very clear procedure in place so as to tell the president that Congress wants a voice in this matter."

But it was the proposal for stepped-up aid to Colombia that ran into a barrage of criticism at the Feb. 24 hearing.

Stevens, who counted himself among the supporters of the administration's plans, offered some of the harshest criticism.

He said that a planned 3,000-member counternarcotics brigade, which the U.S. would train for the Colombian army would be ineffective against tens of thousands of guerrilla fighters.

And Stevens warned Army Gen. Charles Wilhelm, commander of U.S. forces in Latin America, that his forces would ultimately be called upon to rescue their Colombian allies.

"Who's going to go in if this blows up?" Stevens challenged Wilhelm. "Tell me this is not Vietnam."

"This is not Vietnam," replied Wilhelm, who served in that war. "When I go to Colombia, I do not feel a quagmire sucking at my boots."

Sen. Patrick J. Leahy of Vermont, the ranking Democrat on the Foreign Operations Appropriations Subcommittee, said he was skeptical of the plan.

"It looks like we're embarking on an open-ended, multibillion [dollar] commitment without any benchmarks to know if we're successful," Leahy said.

Leahy put into the fiscal 1999 foreign operations spending bill, which was included in an omnibus appropriations law (PL 105-277), a requirement that Colombian military units trained by U.S. forces be vetted for human rights abusers.

Relying on a Feb. 23 report by the independent monitoring group Human Rights Watch, Leahy said the military has not done enough to sever its ties to right-wing paramilitary groups blamed for thousands of human rights violations. "We may have some down there who give lip service, but when they are pushed, they don't do anything," Leahy said.

The Human Rights Watch report linked half of Colombia's 18 brigade-level army units to paramilitary activity.

Leahy said he believed that any supplemental bill should require Colombian President Andres Pastrana to first order that Colombian troops accused of human rights abuses be tried by civilian courts rather than what Leahy said were more lenient military tribunals.

Mitch McConnell, R-Ky., chairman of the Foreign Operations Subcommittee, said he is considering including such a condition in the supplemental bill. Undersecretary of State for Political Affairs Thomas Pickering said the administration would oppose this requirement, preferring that the matter be handled diplomatically.

McConnell also called for a broader attack on Colombia's problems and increasing aid to neighboring countries such as Bolivia, Peru and Ecuador.

Congress Balks at Aid to Colombia In Supplemental Spending Bill

MARCH 4 — President Clinton's proposal for $5.2 billion in supplemental budget authority for fiscal 2000, already under fire in the Senate, is facing growing opposition in the House, largely because of its stepped up aid to Colombia.

"In the beginning, when I was faced with this request, I didn't think there was going to be much of a problem," said Rep. Sonny Callahan, R-Ala., chairman of the Foreign Operations Appropriations Subcommittee, which is responsible for much of the aid. "But now I'm hearing a lot of questions."

"If we were to bring it up before the House today," Callahan said at a Feb. 29 hearing, "it would not pass."

His concerns echoed those from the Senate, where Appropriations Committee Chairman Ted Stevens, R-Alaska, told reporters Feb. 29 that he no longer expected to take up the bill before a Senate recess the week of March 13. Members of Stevens' committee had expressed strong reservations about the legislation.

Trouble over the supplemental was another sign that GOP hopes for a smooth budget year were on the rocks.

Clinton on Feb. 7 asked Congress for $4.4 billion in additional budget authority for fiscal 2000, and on Feb. 25 he added about $876 million to the request, including $600 million to help low-income residents of the Northeast cope with high heating-oil prices.

The supplemental package includes $955 million to help the Colombian government fight drug traffickers and insurgents, the first installment of a proposed two-year $1.6 billion aid package.

The budget request also includes $2 billion for the U.S. share of the NATO peacekeeping operation in

Kosovo; $618 million for diplomacy and economic aid in the Balkans; $210 million to further ease the foreign debt burden of the world's poorest countries; and an additional $107 million for the U.S. share of United Nations peacekeeping operations.

But it was the Colombia request that drew the most fire at a Feb. 29 House hearing. Callahan, along with the subcommittee's ranking Democrat, Nancy Pelosi of California, and David R. Obey of Wisconsin, ranking Democrat on the full Appropriations Committee, expressed concerns.

Only Appropriations Committee Chairman C.W. Bill Young, R-Fla., expressed strong support for the proposal, which enjoys the enthusiastic backing of House Speaker J. Dennis Hastert, R-Ill.

"This reminds me very much of Vietnam," Obey commented. "I have minimal faith in the ability of the political elite in that society to change the conditions on the ground that must be changed if any U.S. policy is to have a snowball's chance in you know where of succeeding."

Critics described the Colombian government's $7.5 billion plan to counter drug lords and guerrillas as unfocused, incomplete, and incapable of being implemented.

Pelosi asked where Colombia, given its stagnant economy, was going to get the $4 billion it is supposed to contribute to the program. She and Callahan, who recently traveled to Colombia, said that a two-year funding plan is unrealistically short. The director of the Office of National Drug Control Policy, retired Army Gen. Barry McCaffrey, acknowledged that the effort to control Colombia's drug production would take at least five years.

Some critics of the Colombia plan also said the money could be better spent on domestic anti-drug efforts, particularly drug treatment programs. "We are fooling ourselves if we think we are ridding ourselves of drugs by eradicating coca leaf," Pelosi said.

Kosovo Tension

As Pelosi and her colleagues debated Colombia policy with the administration, other lawmakers were questioning aspects of the U.S. military mission in the Balkan province of Kosovo.

Congress is under intense pressure to approve extra spending for the Kosovo deployment because the money has already been borrowed and spent from military training budgets. If Congress does not come through, some training exercises will have to be canceled.

Nevertheless, congressional frustration with the Kosovo mission is rising. A bloc of Republicans had been skeptical of the operation from the outset. But even some of the mission's supporters have decried in recent weeks the failure of European allies to fulfill their pledges to provide police officers to keep order in the province and to provide funds for economic reconstruction.

Widespread congressional anger at the Europeans' performance was exacerbated in February when NATO commanders had to shift peacekeeping forces from six countries stationed in other parts of Kosovo into the city of Mitrovica after the French peacekeeping contingent in that town proved too small to keep a lid on ethnic violence between Serbs and Albanians. Among the forces moved to Mitrovica were 350 U.S. paratroopers.

The crisis underscored two issues on which Defense Secretary William S. Cohen and top-ranking Army officers have publicly lambasted the other governments involved in the Kosovo operation:

• The U.N.-led police force in the province is too small to keep order, because too many countries have not produced the number of officers they had promised.

• The NATO-led military force that is occupying the province has shrunk from an initial strength of about 50,000 to a current level of about 37,000 because participating countries have decided, on their own, to reduce their contingents.

At the request of U.S. Army Gen. Wesley K. Clark, NATO's senior military commander, France agreed Feb. 23 to reinforce its two battalions in Kosovo with a third.

Burden Sharing

On March 1, Cohen told the House Defense Appropriations Subcommittee that while the commander of the peacekeeping force needed — and had — authority to move his troops around to meet unforeseen crises, the Pentagon was demanding that U.S. troops not routinely be moved out of their assigned areas.

"We have to look to the Europeans to do their part," Cohen told the House subcommittee. "We are doing our part, and we want to see them do more when it's required."

Ernest Istook, R-Okla., asked what proportion of the operation's cost was being paid by the United States.

Pentagon Comptroller William J. Lynn III replied that the United States had paid about 60 percent of the cost of the 78-day bombing campaign against Serbia last spring that preceded the occupation of Kosovo. Lynn said the United States was paying about one-third of the cost of the peacekeeping deployment and 20 to 25 percent of the cost of economic reconstruction.

During a Feb. 29 Senate Armed Services Committee hearing with NATO commander Clark as a witness, panel members expressed a similar frustration about "the failure of the allies to pull on the oars as hard as we are," in the words of Chairman John W. Warner, R-Va.

"We're not going to do anything that would jerk the rug or cut and run," Warner said, "but it's an enormous disappointment."

Warner reiterated his determination to insert into the supplemental budget request some kind of a provision designed to turn up the heat on allied governments to pull harder.

"I'm going forward, guns blazing, on this amendment," he declared.

House Committee OKs Draft; Leaders Postpone Floor Action

MARCH 11 — A swelling fiscal 2000 supplemental spending bill is lumbering toward trouble, as members of both parties grow uneasy with its cost and its ambitious policy goals.

Meanwhile, Republican leaders in both chambers plan to mark up fiscal 2001 budget resolutions within the next two weeks after reaching a tentative agreement to spend $596.5 billion in discretionary funds next year. But the deal faces strong opposition from key Senate budget hawks.

The House Appropriations Committee voted 33-13 on March 9 to approve a $9 billion unnumbered draft supplemental bill with "emergency" funding for disaster relief, the anti-drug campaign in South America and Kosovo peacekeeping. But the next day, House GOP leaders set aside plans to put the measure on the House floor the week of March 13. And the Senate's version will not begin to move until the week of March 20 at the earliest, after senators return from a weeklong recess.

The size of the House bill presents a dilemma for Republicans because it nearly doubles the $5.2 billion package requested by President Clinton at a time when the GOP is attacking Clinton as a spendthrift. The fact that the plan has grown substantially from Clinton's proposal, and is expected to grow bigger still in the Senate and in conference, has some conservative Republicans worried.

"We're trying to manage it the best we can to keep that thing from getting out of control," House GOP Conference Chairman J.C. Watts Jr. of Oklahoma said March 9. "It's making a lot of folks nervous."

The rift influenced the already complicated dynamics surrounding the minimum wage and tax cut package (HR 3081) that the House passed March 9. As the day began, a band of GOP conservatives threatened to vote against the rule setting the parameters of the debate — and thereby keep the bill off the floor — because it allowed an amendment to be offered that most Republicans opposed. To gather enough votes to push the rule through, GOP leaders promised these conservatives that their views would receive greater consideration on other matters this year, including the supplemental spending plan.

"We have a concern about policy being driven by people who do not share the views of the majority of the Republican Party," said Budget Committee member Wally Herger, R-Calif., one of the potential rebels. "There was a very strong message sent and received by the leadership of a [need for] greater involvement by the conservative Republican point of view."

Said John Feehery, spokesman for House Speaker J. Dennis Hastert, R-Ill.: "They got our attention."

Still, Democrats expect the midyear spending bill to grow more expensive after it leaves the House, said Kori E. Hardin, a spokesman for David R. Obey of Wisconsin, the Appropriations Committee's ranking Democrat. Hardin said Democrats have nicknamed it the "10-20-30" bill — predicting a price tag of nearly $10 billion in the House, perhaps $20 billion in the Senate, and approaching $30 billion by the time it emerges from conference.

Pressure to load up the bill will be particularly intense because this is an election year, former Congressional Budget Office (CBO) director Robert D. Reischauer said in a March 10 interview. "Members see this as a vehicle which can carry a load that doesn't get full scrutiny," he said. "It's an express train, so to speak."

There was little evidence of concern for the bottom line at the Appropriations Committee markup. No amendments were offered to cut spending, while amendments worth about $2 billion in additional spending were proposed by members of both parties. However, only about $28 million was added for disaster relief and other items. The unsuccessful amendments included requests for struggling New England lobstermen, domestic drug programs and Navy ship repairs.

Randy "Duke" Cunningham of California and Todd Tiahrt of Kansas cast the only GOP votes against the bill; they were joined by 10 Democrats and one independent.

In addition to substantially boosting the administration's defense request, the committee heavily padded Clinton's proposal by spreading additional money around the nation for highway repairs and agriculture assistance.

Overall, the bill would spend:

- $5 billion for Kosovo peacekeeping and other Defense Department activities, including $1.6 billion for unexpected increases in fuel costs. Clinton sought $2.8 billion for Kosovo and other security needs.
- $2.2 billion for natural disaster assistance, particularly for damage caused by Hurricane Floyd. Clinton sought $1 billion in disaster assistance.
- $1.7 billion for counternarcotics efforts in Colombia and neighboring areas. Clinton sought $1.3 billion.

Anti-drug efforts in Colombia are strongly backed by Clinton and Hastert, but some in both parties are concerned about how the money will be spent and whether the United States is getting too deeply involved. Senate Appropriations Committee Chairman Ted Stevens, R-Alaska, also has deep concerns about the funds for anti-drug efforts in South America.

Jump Start on 2001

The committee used the bill to ease the strain on next year's budget by covering some of Clinton's fiscal 2001 requests this year, including $282.5 million for improvements in domestic electronic surveillance of drug activities. Also, of the money allocated for anti-drug efforts in Colombia, $318.4 million would be a prepayment on administration fiscal 2001 requests.

The bill would also reverse some of the gimmicks employed last fall to help appropriators stay under the fiscal 2000 statutory spending caps, at least technically. Then, Congress moved one military pay date into fiscal 2001 and delayed some contractor payments past Oct. 1. The supplemental would undo those maneuvers by moving the spending back into fiscal 2000 — a shift of about $6 billion in outlays. This accounting move is separate from the supplemental's proposed increase in budget authority for defense programs.

By budgeting for some fiscal 2001 expenses this year, and moving the defense outlays back to the dates where the money more accurately belongs, Congress makes budgeting easier for itself in two respects, Reischauer said: It puts those expenses out of the way in fiscal 2001, making room for other spending, and it increases the fiscal 2000 baseline from which appropriators will work.

Budget Feuds Continue

Meanwhile, Republican leaders announced March 10 that they had reached a deal on overall fiscal 2001 discretionary spending levels, a development they hope will help them reach their oft-stated goal of completing work on a budget resolution by late March. The deal calls for $596.5 billion in discretionary spending, of which $306.8 billion would be for defense. The April 15 statutory deadline for completing a budget resolution has been met only four times since it was set in 1974 (PL 93-344).

The deal also calls for $10 billion in tax cuts in fiscal 2001, and a total of $150 billion in tax cuts over five years. House Budget Chairman John R. Kasich, R-Ohio, said the tax cuts could end up being even bigger, particularly if the Congressional Budget Office revises its surplus projections upward later this year. The deal has the support of Hastert and Senate Majority Leader Trent Lott, R-Miss., Kasich said.

The deal immediately came under fire from Senate Budget Committee member Phil Gramm, R-Texas, who wants to spend about the same amount as last year — $586 billion in discretionary spending. Less than an hour after Kasich and Senate Budget Chairman Pete V. Domenici, R-N.M., announced the budget deal, Gramm released a statement blasting the two chairmen by name.

"If this budget is adopted, we will have found a sure-fire way to stop the Democrats from spending the surplus – have Republicans spend it first," Gramm stated. "This proposal takes the most egregious abuses of last year's budget process, allows even more spending, and then has the audacity to call that 'honest budgeting.' "

The Senate Budget Committee will mark up a budget resolution March 22 and 23, Domenici said. Domenici on March 9 said the markup date was "firm," implying that he was ready to press ahead whether he had agreement among the Republicans on his committee or not. Among those holding out for less discretionary spending was Majority Whip Don Nickles, R-Okla.; an aide said March 10 that Nickles knew nothing about the deal announced by Kasich and Domenici.

Clinton's budget outlined $614.3 billion in discretionary spending in fiscal 2001. However, CBO disagrees with some of the administration's accounting methods, according to a CBO analysis of the president's budget released March 9. CBO calculates that Clinton's discretionary proposals actually add up to $625 billion. That means the administration's budget would break its own proposed fiscal 2001 spending cap by more than $10 billion, according to the CBO.

House-Passed Bill Sets Costly Example For Senate's Supplemental

APRIL 1 — A solid House vote for spending an extra $13.2 billion this year is adding pressure on the Senate to move a fiscal 2000 supplemental appropriations bill as well.

Majority Leader Trent Lott, R-Miss., opposes such a measure but could have his hands full trying to hold off the groundswell. In an open break with Lott, Appropriations Committee Chairman Ted Stevens, R-Alaska, plans to push ahead with a markup of his own midyear spending package, tentatively set for April 4. His bill's total will be in the range of $7 billion to $8 billion, an aide said March 31.

The bill the House passed (HR 3908) on March 30 would allocate money principally to finance the peacekeeping mission in Kosovo, replenish an array of other Defense Department accounts, underwrite an anti-drug campaign in Colombia and provide domestic disaster aid. The vote was 263-146, with 64 percent of Republicans and 56 percent of Democrats voting in favor. *(Vote 95, p. H-34)*

"Passage of this bill affects every school, hospital, courtroom , neighborhood," International Relations Committee Chairman Benjamin A. Gilman, R-N.Y., declared on the House floor March 29. In addition, he said, "Colombia's survival as a democracy and our own national security interests are at stake."

The White House has raised several objections to the House bill — including strings it would attach to the Kosovo aid and its denial of certain administration requests. Still, the Office of Management and Budget issued a statement March 29 urging Congress to clear a bill quickly.

"This legislation is time-sensitive," it said. "For example, if the bill is not enacted soon, the Department of Defense will have to make irreversible decisions to curtail training and maintenance activities essential to readiness, [and] victims of Hurricane Floyd may have to spend a second winter in temporary shelters."

Meanwhile, Lott and House Speaker J. Dennis Hastert, R-Ill., made little progress in talks aimed at sorting out their disagreement over the need for such a bill. Hastert — the main congressional proponent of the anti-drug efforts in South America — wants the supplemental but would say little about his talks with Lott. "We've discussed it," he said March 29. "We'll do what we have to do." That same day Lott said his message to Hastert was, "You do what you have to, and I'll do what I have to."

The situation was complicated by confusion over whether Lott had promised Sen. Phil Gramm that there would be no supplemental bill in order to win the Texas Republican's support for the GOP leadership's fiscal 2001 budget. Gramm delivered a pivotal "yes" vote when the Senate Budget Committee approved its budget resolution March 30, enhancing Republican hopes that they can meet their budgetary timetable.

Hours after the House passed its bill, however, Lott's opposition to doing likewise sounded tenuous. "I've never said, 'No, never under any circumstances,' " he said. "It depends on what it is."

House Appropriations Committee Chairman C.W. Bill Young, R-Fla., said passage of his bill could kick-start progress in the Senate. "We need to get it down to the other body so that then our friend and colleague, Sen. Stevens, can work his magic," he said on the House floor March 29.

Lott has said one of his chief objections to the supplemental is that such bills tend to grow at every stage in the process, and this year provides evidence to support that. Clinton originally asked for $4.4 billion, but soon raised his own request to $5.2 billion. The package emerged from the House Appropriations Committee with a $9.1 billion price tag. It grew to $13.2 billion during two days of debate and amendment by the House, although the bill includes $421 million in offsets for some of the non-emergency items.

The support of Democrats — 119 of them voted for the bill — allowed Republican leaders to disregard attacks on the bill by some GOP fiscal conservatives. The bill "threatens the fiscal discipline Republicans should represent," said a March 30 statement from

John Shadegg of Arizona, chairman of the Conservative Action Team and one of 61 Republicans to vote against the bill.

Mark Sanford, R-S.C., offered an amendment with $1.6 billion in trims from the bill, items ranging from about $300 million in Drug Enforcement Administration expenses to $16 million for a "uranium enrichment decontamination and decommissioning fund." It was rejected, 108-315. *(Vote 82, p. H-30)*

The amendment also would have removed the word "emergency" from the bill, a provision that would have required Congress to find billions in offsetting cuts to fund the supplemental. Under the 1997 budget-balancing law (PL 105-33), non-emergency spending is subject to budget caps, and expenditures that exceed those caps must be offset. *(1997 Almanac, p. 2-48)*

The Defense Debate

In pushing the supplemental, Young urged his colleagues to put aside their views on whether the U.S. mission in Kosovo was appropriate.

"The Kosovo experience is not going to be a positive one for the United States, and I hate to say that, because our troops do such a good job," Young said. "But the problem with Kosovo is that the money is already being spent . . . . If we do not replace this money, whether we like it or not, the fourth-quarter training exercises of the United States military will have to stand down."

By 200-219, the House rejected an amendment by Budget Committee Chairman John R. Kasich, R-Ohio, that would have withheld half of the $2.1 billion in funding for the military in Kosovo until Europe did more to assist in the mission. Opponents said that such a move would be tantamount to a U.S. withdrawal from the area. *(Vote 89, p. H-32)*

Senate Armed Services Committee Chairman John W. Warner, R-Va., said March 30 that he plans to offer a similar amendment if a supplemental is debated by the Senate.

The most costly amendment to the bill was offered by Defense Appropriations Subcommittee Chairman Jerry Lewis, R-Calif. It added another $4 billion for Defense Department accounts, including $1.2 billion for new weapons procurement, another $1.2 billion for operation and maintenance, and $750 million for health programs. The vote to add the spending was a resounding 289-130. *(Vote 85, p. H-32)*

"It simply makes room in next year's budget for $4 billion worth of other items, including a lot of congressional projects and pork," said David R. Obey of Wisconsin, the top Democrat on the Appropriations Committee, adding the money also could imperil passage of the supplemental bill by the Senate, a sentiment echoed by the administration.

The House bill would also reverse some of the devices used to keep fiscal 2000 appropriations — at least technically — under the statutory spending caps: the shift of one military pay date into fiscal 2001, for example, and delays of some contractor payments. Making the items fiscal 2000 spending again would add about $6 billion in outlays for this year. This is separate from the measure's proposed increase in budget authority for defense programs.

Gramm's Demands

The House's add-ons are sure to fuel the arguments of Senate opponents such as Lott and Gramm. The majority leader favors delivering supplemental fiscal 2000 spending through the normal fiscal 2001 appropriations process as a way of restraining midyear spending. Critics say this approach would put the money in abeyance too long, because it could not be released until the bill to which it was attached was signed, which could be in the fall.

Gramm has been creating headaches for proponents of both the supplemental and the budget resolution. For four weeks, he held out against the GOP budget plan because he said its level for discretionary spending was too high, and as a member of the Budget Committee's 12-10 Republican majority, his concerns were impossible for Republican leaders to ignore.

On March 28, Gramm announced that he was dropping his opposition to the budget resolution in return for assurances from Lott and Budget Committee Chairman Pete V. Domenici, R-N.M., that there would be no fiscal 2000 supplemental in the Senate. Gramm also said he won a guarantee that when spending caps are revised, they will be reset at a level that does not exceed the spending total in the budget resolution. He also won addition of language to the resolution to require a 60-vote Senate majority for emergency designations, pay date shifts, and other sorts of budgetary gimmicks like those used in fiscal 2000 to mask the amount of federal spending — and which would be reversed under the House bill.

But Domenici's first order of business at the start of the markup that afternoon was to declare Gramm's announcement erroneous. "We have no such agreement," Domenici said. "There's nothing in [the resolution] saying we're not going to have a supplemental."

Gramm did not dispute Domenici's statement, but he added that he was confident he had a promise from Lott that there would be no supplemental.

Sen. Frank R. Lautenberg, D-N.J., said the conflicting statements left him confused about the Republican plans. "I believe there's going to be a supplemental, at least an attempt for a supplemental," he said.

Gramm has tried to play the spoiler against supplemental spending bills before. For a month in 1987, for example, he delayed a measure (PL 100-71) that included funding for farm programs, federal employee pay raises and pension benefits. Gramm sought repeatedly to scale back that bill, complaining that it violated budget rules and included funding for items that were not emergencies.

But that law has been followed by 21 other supplemental spending statutes in the past 13 fiscal years.

Joseph R. Biden Jr. of Delaware, the top Democrat on the Senate Foreign Relations Committee, said March 29 that a Senate GOP leadership decision not to move a supplemental spending bill for fiscal 2000 would be irresponsible, especially because of the situation in Kosovo. "We've been pushing the Europeans to move more quickly, and now we're not going to do anything?" he said.

Debt Relief Debated

The more fiscally conservative members of the GOP demanded to be heard in the House as well. By 420-0, the House amended the supplemental with a provision by Patrick J. Toomey, R-Pa., that would set aside $4 billion of the on-budget surplus for fiscal 2000 — the surplus not derived from excess Social Security receipts — for paying down the national debt. *(Vote 83, p. H-32)*

Toomey, a member of the Budget Committee, had won a promise of support from the House GOP leadership for his debt amendment the previous week when he agreed to back off his demand for a provision in the fiscal 2001 budget resolution that would have all but doomed a fiscal 2000 supplemental. It would have added procedural hurdles to House passage of a supplemental bill without offsetting cuts.

Obey mocked Toomey's debt amendment as an empty gesture, because any surplus not spent before the end of the fiscal year Sept. 30 will go to debt reduction even without such a requirement. "Only in Washington would this transaction be considered real," Obey said. "I do not care how members vote on this amendment. This amendment is a big nothing." He and two others voted "present."

Obey said he believed the GOP had a tactical motive in Toomey's amendment that was made obvious by its dollar amount: The $4 billion is the same amount as was added for defense under the Lewis amendment.

Colombia Concerns

Members of both parties expressed concerns about expanding U.S. involvement in the efforts to control narcotics exports from Colombia.

But the House nonetheless defeated, 186-239, an amendment by Obey to cut $552 million from the anti-drug allocation of $1.7 billion in the bill. *(Vote 84, p. H-32)*

Obey has warned that the United States could be entering a quagmire in Colombia, and some in the GOP agreed. "It will cost billions and billions of dollars, all without a full hearing and all without a full national debate," Roger Wicker, R-Miss., said March 29. Wicker, who voted for Obey's amendment, added, "The American people ought to be fully informed before we embark on a course of action which will last for decades . . . with doubtful results."

Obey and other Democrats also complained bitterly that Republicans had refused to allow Nancy Pelosi, D-Calif., to offer an amendment that would add funds for domestic drug treatment to the supplemental.

Hastert said the police force in Colombia are credible partners in the fight against drugs, but do not have the resources to do the job. "We have a responsibility to stop drugs in Colombia, to stop them in transit, to stop them at our border, to stop them in our streets and in our schools," the Speaker said. He also noted that the United States had helped curb drug production in Peru without getting into a protracted affair involving U.S. troops.

Lott Stalls Action On Supplemental, Leaving Host Of Sticky Issues

APRIL 8 — Senate Majority Leader Trent Lott's decision to quash the fiscal 2000 supplemental spending bill could have policy and political ramifications in areas from military readiness to disaster aid to low-income fuel assistance.

The Mississippi Republican is gambling that he can contain any fallout from his move by adding needed funds to fiscal 2001 appropriations measures and moving them on an expedited schedule. The House passed legislation (HR 3908) March 30 with $13.2 billion in midyear appropriations.

House GOP leaders and Clinton administration officials are skeptical about prospects for quick action on next year's bills. They also are having a hard time finding much in the House bill to classify as extraneous.

"The Senate should be under no illusion that the levels we have voted will be easily conceded," a bipartisan groups of five senior House members influential on defense policy said in an April 5 letter to Lott. Ten governors whose states have been hit by natural disasters wrote to Lott and Senate Minority Leader Tom Daschle, D-S.D., pleading for action on the bill.

Defense Secretary William S. Cohen has warned that if new spending is not approved by the end of April, military commanders will have to curtail training and maintenance. The Pentagon has been diverting money from training accounts in order to maintain U.S. forces in Kosovo and compensate for rising fuel prices that have increased normal operating costs.

The House bill included $4.7 billion that President Clinton requested for the Pentagon and $4 billion more for an array of defense needs, including procurement and medical care.

Anti-drug efforts are another question. Pentagon and civilian administration officials testifying before the Senate Armed Services Committee on April 4 expressed concern about delaying $1.7 billion in the House measure for Colombia. That nation is battling left-wing guerrillas and right-wing paramilitary groups, funded partly through profits from narcotics trafficking. The House vote for aid was a major step toward increasing U.S. involvement.

Small but Troublesome

Defense and Colombia make up the bulk of the bill, but smaller, politically important items may be hung up — or used by the White House to try to hang Lott up politically.

Because of rising fuel costs, the administration has already exhausted the Low Income Home Energy Assistance Program's emergency funding reserve. The House bill included $600 million extra for the program, which helps pay heating and cooling bills for the poor.

The administration also said that a delay in funding could harm Federal Aviation Administration safety and air-traffic control efforts. The National Transportation Safety Board's attempts to determine the causes of the recent Egypt Air and Alaska Air crashes also would be hampered if the supplemental, which includes $24.7 million for the investigations, remains stalled.

In a statement issued March 29, the Office of Management and Budget also declared that without a supplemental, the government will not be able to cover the first-year cost of popular legislation (HR 5) to partly repeal the Social Security earnings limit, which cleared Congress on March 28 and which the president signed April 7. Clinton wants $35 million in preliminary funding, but his request came too late to be included in the House supplemental.

Some of the issues cut close to home. Young is desperate to combat citrus canker, a disease that is devastating orange and lime groves in his home state. The House bill included $40 million for the effort.

Lott's Stance on Emergency Funding Upsets House, President

MAY 13 — Senate Majority Leader Trent Lott, R-Miss., tried to make it sound easy: Instead of funding a variety of midyear emergency spending needs in one large fiscal 2000 supplemental package, as the House tried to do in March, why not attach them to related fiscal 2001 appropriations bills?

Supplemental spending bills tend to become bloated, slow-moving targets for legislators looking to find homes for their pet projects. Lott said his piecemeal approach would be a cleaner, more fiscally responsible way to encourage prompt action on next year's spending while limiting this year's extras.

But the appropriations process is rarely easy or predictable. As Lott's game plan was first put to the test the week of May 8 — when an estimated $8 billion in midyear aid was attached to the first three fiscal 2001 spending bills marked up by the Senate Appropriations Committee — House members and staff from both parties complained that the approach is leading to a dead end.

"I don't see how this . . . works," House Appropriations Committee Staff Director James W. Dyer groused about the senatorial strategy.

"I don't know what they are doing," David R. Obey of Wisconsin, the top Democrat on the House Appropriations Committee, said of Republicans. "I don't think they do either."

Lott pointed to the House's $13.2 billion supplemental spending package (HR 3908) — three times larger than President Clinton's original midyear request — as ample evidence that Congress needs help to control its appetite. Under Lott's plan, the emergency spending for fiscal 2000 would be released as soon as each fiscal 2001 spending bill to which it is attached were signed into law.

"The additional money will be provided through the regular appropriations process," the majority leader said of federal disaster relief April 14. "It will be there, and it shouldn't become a political issue. . . . We are committed to make sure that it is going to be there."

The White House disagrees. "The situation's gotten out of control, and it's a mess," White House spokesman Joe Lockhart said May 10. "And often the best way, when you've dug a hole, is to stop digging, and to figure out a way to get it done in a way that meets the country's needs."

Disaster Aid on Hold

Each of the three Senate bills carrying supplemental funding faces problems of its own, meaning all three of the biggest programs needing midyear help could have to wait for months.

• Disaster assistance. Supplemental disaster aid, including help for victims of Hurricane Floyd, is attached to the Senate agriculture appropriations bill (S 2536), which faces trouble on the floor because of a provision to lift restrictions on the sale of food and medicine to certain countries, including Cuba. Even if the bill is passed in the Senate, it will face similar obstacles in the House, which may take up its still unnumbered draft the week of May 15.

And there is no way for the bill to be a successful vehicle for supplemental spending unless it is passed in both chambers and makes it to conference, where the Senate's disaster assistance would be added.

• **Anti-drug money.** Facing even more serious problems are supplemental funds to help Colombia and other South American countries fight drug trafficking. The funding is a priority for House Speaker J. Dennis Hastert, R-Ill. Clinton and Lott also support it.

The Senate's fiscal 2001 foreign operations spending bill (S 2522) would allocate $934 million for the effort. Although the Senate Appropriations Committee approved the measure May 9 and floor action could follow soon, it is likely to be one of the last appropriations bills to move in the House.

In addition, the foreign operations bill traditionally is one of the most difficult for Congress, particularly in the House, with the White House and congressional Republicans battling over foreign aid levels, population control and other provisions. Last year, the initial version of the bill was vetoed and a new version became law (PL 106-113) only as part of the omnibus appropriations package that ended the legislative year in late November.

Still, Lott is so confident his strategy will work that on April 12 he assured Colombian President Andres Pastrana in a meeting that the counter-narcotics money will be approved by early June.

• **Defense spending.** Even the normally well-greased military construction bill — the Senate version of which (S 2521) is currently the home for $4.7 billion in fiscal 2000 supplemental defense spending — could be in trouble this year as a result of an amendment added in committee that would end the deployment of U.S. troops as peacekeepers in Kosovo on July 1, 2001, unless Congress authorizes an extension.

Although the White House has not yet issued an explicit veto threat, the administration has made clear its opposition to the provision. The Senate began its debate May 11; the House version (HR 4425) is expected to be on the floor the week of May 15.

Advocates say the defense money is needed because the Pentagon has dipped into its training funds to help pay for U.S. operations in Kosovo. Military leaders have stressed that unless Congress clears the supplemental funds within the next few weeks, they will have to cancel some training exercises scheduled for this summer.

Conference Difficulties Predicted

Robert C. Byrd, D.-W.Va., who wrote the amendment that would place restrictions on the Kosovo deployment, complained May 9 that Lott's supplemental strategy imperils passage of important emergency funds. "This procedure . . . will greatly complicate the committee's work when it convenes a conference with the House on these bills," he said.

Sonny Callahan, R-Ala., chairman of the House Appropriations Subcommittee on Foreign Operations, expressed frustration over the uncertainty surrounding the Colombia supplemental spending. Callahan said he was not sure what an alternative plan might be, although he said he had heard a "rumor" that the money could be shifted again — to the military construction bill.

"I'm OK with that," Callahan said May 11. "I'd rather do it myself, I'd rather do it on my regular bill, but they have a different strategy planned. I wasn't in on the strategy session."

House Appropriations Chairman C.W. Bill Young, R-Fla., endorsed the idea of adding the Colombia money to the military construction bill. "I would like to just put the whole supplemental on a bill," namely, the military construction bill, Young said. "I don't think Sen. Lott is going to let that happen."

Noting a lack of enthusiasm among Senate appropriators for funding anti-drug efforts in Colombia, Dyer added, "The whole question of what you can do in the Senate on 'Plan Colombia' is pretty much up in the air."

The disaster assistance and Colombia funding face an additional — and brand new — hurdle in the Senate. The fiscal 2001 budget resolution (H Con Res 290) created a point of order allowing any senator to object to any bill's designation of "emergency" non-defense spending. Those wanting to retain that designation would need to come up with 60 votes, and Senate Appropriations Committee Chairman Ted Stevens, R-Alaska, told reporters May 9 that he is not confident he can muster such a supermajority for either the Colombia or disaster aid designations.

If a stand-alone fiscal 2000 supplemental does not clear this year, it will be the first time in decades that a midyear spending bill has not been enacted.

Stanley E. Collender, senior managing director of Fleishman-Hillard's Federal Budget Consulting Group, said in a May 12 interview that the White House has leverage it is not fully using yet: It could crank up the intensity of its criticism of congressional Republicans by accusing them of failing to support the troops. "This is one where the White House has a lot more control than you might think," Collender said.

While the Pentagon clearly wants the money, however, there is political advantage in an election year for the White House to let Congress founder and appear to be accomplishing nothing, Collender said.

Budget Picture Brightens

Election year politics also could play a role in how the two parties respond to a May 12 report from the Congressional Budget Office (CBO), which estimates the total budget surplus for this fiscal year will exceed $200 billion. Of that amount, more than $40 billion is projected to be "on-budget" surplus, which excludes surplus Social Security revenue. As recently as March 9, CBO projected a surplus of $179 billion, of which $26 billion was on budget.

The new CBO report also suggests that further upward revisions in fiscal 2000 surplus estimates are likely as the economy continues to exceed expected growth levels.

The new estimates should please House Budget Committee Chairman John R. Kasich, R-Ohio, who has been counting on CBO to ratchet up its on-budget surplus estimates to underwrite his efforts to boost the size of the proposed GOP tax cuts. Although the fiscal 2001 budget resolution specifies a five-year, $150 billion package of tax cuts, it allows the size of the tax cuts to grow if sufficient surplus revenue is available.

Lott's Strategy Sparks Senate Feud; Bill Stalls

MAY 27 — Lawmakers left for the Memorial Day recess without any breakthrough on "emergency" legislation to provide supplemental funding for disaster relief, drug interdiction and Pentagon peacekeeping efforts.

Pressure to break the logjam will only build when they return the week of June 5.

A $13.2 billion fiscal 2000 supplemental spending package (HR 3908) passed by the House in March remains in limbo, awaiting companion legislation from the Senate. Majority Leader Trent Lott, R-Miss., continues to insist that the supplemental spending be broken up and attached to regular fiscal 2001 appropriations bills — it is now being carried by the Senate agriculture, foreign operations and military construction bills — rather than moving forward in a stand-alone measure.

Lott's strategy appears to have backfired. None of those bills will emerge from conference until after the recess; only one, for military construction, has passed both chambers.

Pentagon leaders have said they need to know for certain by early June whether they will get supplemental defense funds to replace money already spent on peacekeeping operations. Otherwise, they say they will have to start canceling summer training exercises. The earliest that bill could be cleared is the week of June 5.

Democratic Sen. John Edwards of North Carolina, whose state is in line for emergency funds to cover hurricane damage, said he supports the position of Minority Leader Tom Daschle, D-S.D., who has vowed to slow Senate progress across the board unless Lott agrees to be more flexible in allowing Democrats to press their agenda on the floor.

But Sen. Connie Mack, R-Fla., whose home state is waiting for disaster funding in the agriculture bill to compensate for a citrus canker problem hurting some Florida harvests, blasted Democrats for "playing games with the lives of farmers."

In his feud with Lott, Daschle is insisting that the Senate honor a long-ignored rule prohibiting it from taking up appropriations bills until they are passed in the House. During the week of May 22, Daschle briefly softened to allow debate on the fiscal 2001 spending bill for the legislative branch (S 2603).

He said May 23, however, that that was an exception. "We're not going to allow that for any other legislation for the foreseeable future," Daschle said. To show he meant business, he refused to allow the Senate to take a final vote on the legislative spending bill until the full House acts on its version.

Even if the bills start moving after the recess, Lott will be hard-pressed to support his claim that his tactics have kept supplemental spending focused on true emergencies. The list of special favors and funds attached to the supplemental portions of the bills stretches from Hawaii to Alaska to Maine.

The list includes money for the 2002 Winter Olympics in Utah, hospital construction in Montana and salmon research in Maine.

Lott Under Pressure

Appropriations Committee Chairman Ted Stevens, R-Alaska, whose attempts to move a separate supplemental bill in the Senate were rebuffed by Lott, declined to comment directly on the majority leader's strategy. However, he fretted that the combination of presidential election-year politics and this year's compressed legislative calendar will make it increasingly difficult to get anything done. "It's going to be a very difficult year," Stevens said. "I am very disturbed about the process."

Stevens said the appropriations bills are already weeks behind schedule. The extent of his frustration was evident when he suggested a far-fetched scenario in which negotiations break down so hopelessly that Congress ends up passing a long-term continuing resolution that would stretch into the spring of 2001, when a new president and a new Congress could work out a new spending plan.

Senate Budget Committee staff director G. William Hoagland said he could not recall Congress ever attempting to deal with its major midyear spending needs in Lott's piecemeal fashion. If there still appears to be little movement on the supplemental spending after the Memorial Day break, substantial pressure will build to find another way to get it through, Hoagland said.

One alternative strategy floated by several Republicans who are hoping to move the emergency funds would be to attach all of the Senate's supplemental spending to the military construction bill in conference, since it is the only one of the three regular bills with supplemental spending to pass in both chambers. "As an outside observer, I see this as a clear possibility," Hoagland said.

Stalled Bills

The Senate's fiscal 2001 agriculture spending bill (S 2536) carries about $2.2 billion in supplemental spending, most of it emergency funds for disaster recovery and other needs. The House version (HR 3908) is stalled over a controversial provision that would lift restrictions on the sale of food and medicine to certain countries, including Cuba.

House leaders pulled the rule for the bill from the floor May 25. Unless Daschle relents, the hold-up in the House leaves the Senate bill stalled as well. The Cuba issue could also cause problems for the Senate bill.

The picture for the bill was further clouded by a bicameral deal that cleared a separate crop insurance bill (HR 2559) on May 25. That measure includes $5.5 billion in fiscal 2000 payments to farmers. The money is covered under the fiscal 2001 budget resolution (H Con Res 290), and its disbursement does not require action by appropriators, Hoagland said.

Although the money in the crop insurance bill is separate, the fact that it has cleared could raise serious questions about whether the additional emergency money for crop failure in the agricultural appropriations bill is still needed, Hoagland said.

The core purpose of the emergency supplemental spending, at least in theory, is to pay for damage done to crops, housing or other facilities by Hurricane Floyd and other disasters. It would also provide crop assistance to compensate for damage done by certain pests.

But the supplemental portion of the bill also carries a variety of special projects, many of them dealing with issues not related to agriculture.

Another $4.7 billion in fiscal 2000 supplemental spending is attached to the Senate's fiscal 2001 bill (S 2522) for military construction projects. Most of the supplemental money is for Kosovo contingency expenses, other overseas defense operations, defense health programs, unexpected fuel cost increases, nuclear weapons readiness and infrastructure improvements, and storm damage repairs. The military construction bill also carries its share of unrelated projects and policy directives, including:

• $8 million in funding for communications and other logistical support for the 2002 Olympics.

• Instructions that at least $1 million in previously appropriated funds be available for the design of an elementary school for military dependents at the submarine base in Bangor, Wash.

• A "National Guard Challenge Program" for civilian youth. This provision would allow the secretary of Defense to spend up to $50 million annually for the National Guard to provide military-based training, including supervised work experience in community service and conservation projects, to civilian high school dropouts.

The bill that funds foreign operations (S 2522) carries the most straightforward of the three supplemental requests, and contains no direct, substantial home-state funds or favors. It contains about $1 billion in fiscal 2000 funds, mostly for counternarcotics efforts in Colombia and surrounding countries.

However, it will also be the most difficult of the three bills to pass — which may help explain members' lack of interest in attaching unrelated funding requests to it. Senate leaders are ready to charge ahead on the bill, but House leaders say it will be one of the last to move in their chamber.

If Lott sticks to his guns, there is no way to move the supplemental Colombia money until the House passes the foreign operations spending bill, because the supplemental money would have to be negotiated in conference.

The money for Colombia is a high priority for House Speaker J. Dennis Hastert, R-Ill., but conservative Republicans have said they do not want the bill to come up until later this summer. The foreign operations bill traditionally is one of the most difficult for Congress to move, with the White House and congressional Republicans battling over foreign aid levels, population control and other provisions.

Last year, the initial version of the bill was vetoed, and a new version became law (PL 106-113) only as part of the omnibus appropriations package that ended the legislative year in late November.

Supplementals Could Grow

Robert Bixby, executive director of the Concord Coalition, a bipartisan budget watchdog group, said that if the appropriations bills start advancing, there is little reason to hope Lott's strategy will restrain supplemental spending. Members will use whatever vehicle is available and moving for the projects they want funded, Bixby said, and when spending bills go to conference, Congress usually "compromises up."

Bixby said Lott's supplemental strategy has a "stealth quality" that could make it increasingly difficult to keep track of extra spending that gets tacked on to the three separate bills. "The big House bill was much easier to follow," Bixby said. "One of the advantages of a big bill is that it gets a lot of scrutiny."

The problem with supplementals is Congress' ability to stretch the definition of an "emergency," not the vehicle used to move the money, according to Bixby. Even the core purposes of this year's supplementals — such as the funds for Colombia and military maintenance — do not fit the definition of an "emergency" and should be debated as policy choices in the regular appropriations process, Bixby said.

The Concord Coalition supported a provision in a budget process overhaul bill (HR 853) that was defeated May 16 in the House. The provision called for Congress to abandon its current emergency spending strategy, which results in annual supplementals with no structural restraints. Instead, it would have established a budgeted pot of money for emergencies.

Bixby warned that taxpayers could be hit up for more money either on the existing supplementals or on a subsequent one, depending on whether there are more storms or other major events. "Sometime over the summer, there will be real emergencies," Bixby said. "The year's not done. This is only supplemental No. 1." Indeed, Congress on several occasions has passed more than one supplemental.

Leaders Continue To Weigh Options As Prospects Fade For Single Package

JUNE 17 — A House-Senate proposal intended to kick-start stalled fiscal 2000 emergency funds for defense needs, disaster aid and Colombia drug interdiction collapsed before it got off the ground the week of June 12, after several senators complained that the strategy would deny them an opportunity for full debate.

"There's a lot of different options that need to be vetted, that need to be voted, that need to be dealt with," said Senate Assistant Majority Leader Don Nickles, R-Okla.

Meanwhile, White House and Pentagon officials were sounding increasingly dire warnings that U.S. military readiness and drug-fighting efforts were beginning to suffer during the delay in approving supplemental aid.

The House in March passed a $13.2 billion stand-alone bill that wrapped fiscal 2000 supplemental funds into one package. Senate Majority Leader Trent Lott, R-Miss., initially opposed that approach, insisting instead on the unconventional strategy of attaching the funds to three fiscal 2001 appropriations bills.

Lott also had opposed an alternative pushed by some GOP House leaders to add all the supplemental funds to a fiscal 2001 military construction appropriations bill (HR 4425, S 2521) that has passed the House and Senate, but not yet been considered by a conference committee. On June 12 he indicated a new openness to that approach.

"I'm hoping maybe we can find a way that we can agree on the substance and find a number that could possibly be added to the military construction bill," he said.

Lott said his main concern was holding down the cost of the supplemental, indicating he favored a number closer to President Clinton's $5.5 billion request than the House's $13.2 billion package.

Dollar totals are only one of Lott's problems. Senators from both parties worry that a dramatic increase in aid to Colombia could draw the United States into a quagmire with a government of questionable stability. Even some senators who support the idea of a partnership with Colombia were nervous about Lott's willingness to attach the money to a conference report on an unrelated bill, which would prohibit amendments and limit debate.

Sen. Mitch McConnell, R-Ky., said he supports the Colombia money, but said it should be part of the fiscal 2001 foreign operations bill, as planned.

"That's where it belongs, and that's where I think it ought to stay," said McConnell, who heads the Foreign Operations Appropriations Subcommittee. "I don't think there's any need to strip that out and pass it earlier by dropping it in some other conference."

The Senate's fiscal 2001 foreign operations bill contains about $1 billion in emergency fiscal 2000 funds for counternarcotics efforts in South America. The Appropriations Committee approved the bill May 9.

The House supplemental bill included about $1.7 billion for counternarcotics efforts.

White House Criticism

The administration has bashed Congress for failing to move the supplemental, and military leaders have begun planning for cutbacks. Pentagon officials say money is needed to replace funds already spent on Kosovo peacekeeping operations. A top Army budget official recently wrote to the heads of major command posts asking for lists of construction projects, supply purchases and maintenance procedures that could be curtailed if the supplemental did not emerge quickly.

"Though it is possible that Congress and the administration will come to quick agreement . . . military prudence dictates we must plan now for the worst case — receipt of a supplemental late in the fiscal year," the letter said.

GOP leaders continued to speak optimistically about wrapping up the 13 fiscal 2001 appropriations bills quickly. The Senate passed two appropriations bills and the House passed two the week of June 12, the most productive week so far this year.

The Senate passed bills funding defense (HR 4576) and transportation (HR 4475), while the House passed the bill that funds the departments of Labor, Health and Human Services, and Education (HR 4577), and Interior (HR 4578).

That brings the grand total to three appropriations bills approved by the Senate and five by the House. No appropriations bills have emerged from conference.

House Majority Leader Dick Armey, R-Texas, had predicted 12 appropriations bills would pass the House before the July Fourth recess. With only two weeks left before the break, the House would have to approve seven appropriations bills over the next two weeks to meet Armey's goal.

That would seem wildly optimistic, given what has occurred so far. The Labor-HHS bill required four days of debate, and was pulled from the floor twice at various times as Republican leaders struggled to hold together a coalition to pass the measure.

House leaders have another appropriations problem to solve: finding offsets for a $500.6 million overrun in the allocation for the Labor-HHS bill. Appropriators originally had designated a public health fund as an "emergency" expenditure, meaning it would not be subject to spending caps specified in the budget resolution (H Con Res 290).

Tom Coburn, R-Okla., successfully raised a point of order against the "emergency" designation, saying the fund has existed for years. Thus, House leaders will have to find offsetting cuts to avoid violating the spending limits.

"If we squeeze the balloon in one place, it comes out in another," said John Edward Porter, R-Ill., chairman of the Labor-HHS Appropriations Subcommittee.

Urgency, Secrecy Carry the Day As Congress Clears Supplemental

JULY 1 — It was, in the words of one of its own House Republican negotiators, a classic legislative "cram down" — one of those must-pass but unamendable bills pressed upon lawmakers with no time left before a deadline.

But with jet fumes in their nostrils and record budget surpluses at their backs, a handful of leaders have assembled and quickly pushed through Congress an $11.2 billion package of midyear fiscal 2000 appropriations, adding billions of dollars to the Pentagon budget and financing a new initiative to combat the drug barons of Colombia.

Less than an hour after the conference agreement was formally filed, the House adopted it, 306-110, the night of June 29. *(House vote 362, p. H-114)*

The Senate cleared the bill by voice vote the next afternoon, after a pair of last-minute protests were defused. Both Phil Gramm, R-Texas, and John McCain, R-Ariz., threatened to block the final vote — or at least delay it into the weekend — until they received assurances that provisions in the measure that they view as "budget gimmicks" would ultimately be reversed.

Once that contretemps subsided, the Capitol quickly emptied for the start of the cherished July Fourth recess. Clinton, whose request for supplemental fiscal 2000 funds was $5.5 billion, indicated that he would promptly sign the bill.

Members of the rank and file had little choice but to accept the package, negotiated in secrecy unusual even for the appropriations barons who dominate spending decisions at the Capitol. But after four months of false starts and delay, Congress was under extraordinary pressure to replenish the military readiness accounts that have been tapped to finance U.S. peacekeeping operations in Kosovo. The politically untenable alternative would have been to risk severe cutbacks in Defense Department training and maintenance activities, which the Pentagon said would have been required had their additional money been delayed any longer.

The final obstacle to the agreement was a last-ditch effort by House Speaker J. Dennis Hastert, R-Ill., to use the supplemental package as a vehicle for enacting a compromise — worked out among warring House GOP factions — to partially lift trade sanctions on Cuba and other "rogue" nations such as Libya. But the idea of including that provision prompted filibuster threats from Senate Democrats. A daylong standoff between the Speaker and Sen. Ted Stevens ended in the favor of the crusty Alaska Republican, who heads the Senate Appropriations Committee.

Hastert will now seek to add the language to the conference report to settle differences between the chambers' versions of the agriculture spending bill (HR 4461, S 2536) for fiscal 2001.

The supplemental package was included in the final version of an $8.8 billion military construction measure (HR 4425), the first regular fiscal 2001 appropriations legislation to clear Congress.

A Spring Ritual of Wrangling

The unusual method of advancing the supplemental package came at the insistence of Majority Leader Trent Lott, R-Miss., who refused to let the Senate consider a stand-alone measure.

The package contains $1.3 billion to battle drug smugglers in Colombia and other South American countries, $2 billion to replenish Pentagon accounts used for the Kosovo mission, and $361 million in long-delayed disaster aid for victims of Hurricane Floyd and other calamities.

Urgency to clear the package and get it signed fostered a freewheeling conference in which Clinton had ample leverage to prevent many legislative "riders" from being forced on him.

For example, an attempt by Senate Republicans to prevent the Justice Department from receiving money from other agencies to press its lawsuit against tobacco companies was dropped, as was an effort to block an Interior Department environmental ruling that would limit hard-rock mining waste sites on public lands.

An effort by Sen. Judd Gregg, R-N.H., to win extension of a biotechnology drug patent held by Columbia University, his alma mater, that nets the school up to $100 million a year was also rebuffed, as was an attempt to allow New Jersey-based Schering-Plough Corp. to seek a three-year extension of its patent on the popular but expensive allergy drug Claritin.

When he signs the measure, Clinton will be compelled to accept its provisions to delay his administration's new rules on groundwater runoff.

The bill would void more than $4 billion in scorekeeping legerdemain that was used a year ago to boost this year's spending — in effect, borrowing from 2001 to pay for Clinton add-ons without dipping into projected Social Security surpluses. But with higher surpluses, appropriators had sought to dump the gimmicks and free up money for this year's appropriations cycle. This was the provision that drew the wrath of McCain and Gramm, who backed down only after Stevens promised to use an upcoming spending bill to reverse course — and thereby restore the current accounting gimmickry.

Tempting Vehicle

Virtually every spring, Congress clears at least one bill to augment the current fiscal year's spending, often fueled by a need to deliver funds to provide relief for fall hurricanes, winter ice storms or spring floods. In each year of GOP control, Clinton and Congress have wrangled over a midyear bill to finance peacekeeping operations. But these measures have also provided tempting vehicles for lawmakers seeking to attach legislation to something that Clinton appeared sure to sign. They also have been attractive opportunities for old-fashioned parochial projects.

In assembling this year's version, Hastert and Lott limited their appropriators to allocating a total of $200 mil-

Midyear Spending Highlights

ISSUE	DESCRIPTION
Defense Department	$6.4 billion, including $2 billion to replenish accounts tapped for U.S. participation in the international peacekeeping force in Kosovo; $1.6 billion to pay higher military fuel bills; $1.3 billion for unfunded military health programs; $358 million for military personnel; $504 million to enhance readiness; $148 million for disaster-related repairs to U.S. bases; and $125 million for Patriot missile tests.
Anti-drug initiative	$1.3 billion, including $185 million to equip Colombian Army battalions; $129 million for drug interdiction; $391 million to seek control of drug-producing regions of Southern Colombia; $116 million for the Colombian National Police; $180 million for anti-drug efforts in other countries, particularly Bolivia; and $203 million for economic development and democracy-building initiatives.
Disaster aid	$1 billion, including $661 million for claims and damages resulting from New Mexico wildfires and $361 million for victims of Hurricane Floyd and other natural disasters.
Coast Guard	$700 million, including $468 million for six C-130 cargo planes, $110 million for an icebreaker for the Great Lakes; and $45 million for a private jet for the Coast Guard commandant.
Utility bill subsidies	$600 million for the Low Income Heating and Energy Assistance Program, which helps pay heating and air conditioning bills of the poor.
Wildfire fighting	$350 million for Interior Department and National Forest Service firefighting efforts.
Energy Department	$192.5 million to aid nuclear weapons and environmental cleanup, including $66.5 million for nuclear weapons plant infrastructure improvements; $45 million for cyber-security; and $58 million for decontamination activities.
Surveillance	$181 million for drug enforcement agents for wiretapping and court-authorized surveillance of digital communications systems.
Federal Aviation Administration	$75 million for inspectors and medical certification personnel.
Social Security Administration	$35 million to finance additional staff work resulting from the recent repeal (PL 106-182) of the Social Security earnings limit.
White House	$8 million for restoring lost electronic mail messages.
Member projects	$25 million for a Customs Service firearms training facility in West Virginia; $25 million for a convention center in Youngstown, Ohio; $11 million for the 2002 Olympics in Salt Lake City; $3 million for the New York City subway; $12 million for hospital improvements and economic development grants for Libby, Mont.; $14 million for Northeastern lobstermen; $5 million to protect sea turtles in Hawaii; $2 million to buy a southern Maryland Civil War site; permission to begin building a new Wilson Bridge near Washington, D.C., in the absence of matching funds from Maryland and Virginia.

lion in overt earmarks. Most went to senior lawmakers, but renegade House Democrat James A. Traficant Jr. of Ohio was awarded $25 million for a community center.

The most overt battle over bringing money back home pitted the Texas delegation against Connecticut's over which type of helicopter would be given to Colombia to use in thwarting drug traffickers and the Marxist guerrillas who protect them. The president, Hastert and Sen. Christopher J. Dodd, D-Conn., favored top-of-the-line Blackhawks built in Connecticut; Stevens and the powerful Texas delegation favored Vietnam-era Hueys that would be refurbished in Texas. In the end, Clinton won 18 of the 30 powerful Blackhawks he requested.

While past midyear spending requests have invariably advanced as stand-alone bills, this year Lott insisted for weeks that the fiscal 2000 version be split up and carried by three fiscal 2001 spending bills — military construction, agriculture and foreign operations (S 2522). He said he wanted to neither tie up Senate time debating a compressive package nor watch the bill's price tag balloon during such a debate.

Appropriators protested that the maneuver would fail to produce the "quick and clean" result that the majority leader sought. It is impossible to know whether the final package ended up much different than it would have had it proceeded under normal procedures, but Lott's move at the very least delayed final action by perhaps a month.

While the deal's final bottom line is more than double what Clinton requested, it is less than the $13.2 billion price tag on the supplemental spending bill (HR 3908) the House passed in March. In addition, the measure cleared June 30 will appropriate money on top of the $5.5 billion emergency relief package for farmers hurt by low commodity prices, which was attached to a crop insurance subsidy law (HR 2559 — PL 106-224) Clinton signed in June.

Even before the tenuous climactic moment on the Senate floor, the supplemental's tumultuous legislative journey had tested many relationships, including that of Lott and Stevens, over which of them would dominate this year's appropriations process.

Hastert feuded with Sen. Mitch McConnell, R-Ky., who heads the Foreign Operations Appropriations Subcommittee, over whether the Speaker's cherished Colombian initiative would be included. McConnell wanted the administration-backed package in his panel's fiscal 2001 bill as an incentive for easing its always-difficult path.

At the same time, longtime Senate GOP friends Stevens and Pete V. Domenici butted heads over the New Mexican's demands that ample emergency funds be delivered to his wildfire-ravaged state. Domenici won $660 million to rebuild some 400 homes and repair other damage cause by the recent fires, which were started after an ill-conceived National Park Service controlled burn. But Domenici was rebuffed in a bid to create a multimillion-dollar timber salvage program to clear ultra-flammable materials near populated areas.

Minimal Meeting

The appropriations process is often secretive, particularly during the negotiations leading to a compromise between House and Senate versions of a spending bill. Conferences on supplemental measures are among the most difficult and typically require at least a couple of public meetings, during which House and Senate negotiators publicly announce their agreements and articulate their differences. Those opposing attempts to slip in previously unconsidered provisions are able to mount a public battle against such moves in these proceedings.

This year's supplemental had none of that, only a brief June 27 meeting where conferees on the military construction bill announced accord on their non-controversial bill. Having fulfilled the requirement for at least one public meeting, negotiators retired behind closed doors. There, the final package was assembled chiefly by the chairmen and top Democrats on the two Appropriations committees.

For the first time since Republicans took over Congress, the party's conservatives did not press for offsetting cuts to existing spending to at least help to finance the supplemental. The federal budget is running surpluses unthinkable when the fiscal purists in the GOP held their biggest sway over the Capitol five years ago, so the annual ritual of finding offsets — often paper savings with no effect on the deficit — was no longer a political requirement.

The military stands to get big increases under the fiscal 2001 budget cycle, but defense hawks such as Jerry Lewis, R-Calif., chairman of the House Defense Appropriations Subcommittee, used the supplemental to give the uniformed services even more. Some of the largess raised eyebrows among those on the lookout for potential "pork." For example, the Coast Guard would receive six new Lockheed C-130 transport planes, a private jet to be put in the service of its commandant and a new icebreaker for the Great Lakes. Skeptics suggested that none of this equipment was readily deserving of the "emergency" designation that is officially required to make spending on it exempt from budget limits.

"A lot of this was unnecessary. The defense guys in the House, Jerry Lewis, are just absolutely out of control," said one aide to a Senate Appropriations subcommittee chairman. "What this has become is an instrument for pulling through a lot of unnecessary and unreviewed . . . spending." ◆

CQ

Chapter 3

ABORTION

Supreme Court Decision On 'Partial Birth' Ban Stops Senate Action on Bill

Box Score

- **Bill:** HR 3660
- **Legislative action: House** passed HR 3660, 287-141, on April 5.

SUMMARY

Following the lead set by the Senate in 1999, the House passed a bill to outlaw a procedure that abortion foes call "partial birth" abortion. However, no further action was taken on the bill after the Supreme Court in June struck down a Nebraska state law banning such abortions.

The House bill would have allowed the procedure only in instances where it might save a woman's life. Those who performed it for other reasons would have been subject to two years in prison. The woman would not have been criminally liable. Opponents of the bill argued that the procedure also should be allowed to protect a woman's health.

Congress had cleared similar legislation twice before, in 1996 and 1997; both times President Clinton vetoed the bill for failing to include provisions protecting the woman's health. The House voted to override both vetoes, while the Senate sustained them. In the 106th Congress, bill supporters secured a veto-proof majority for passage in the House but not in the Senate.

The Supreme Court made further work on the bill irrelevant when it ruled, 5-4, on June 28 that the Nebraska law was unconstitutional because it imposed an undue burden on a woman's decision to end her pregnancy by failing to include language protecting a woman's health. The court also said the Nebraska law was too vague, possibly threatening women's access to abortions for non-viable fetuses.

House Judiciary Sends Bill to Floor Over Objections

APRIL 1 — The scheduled April 5 House floor vote on legislation (HR 3660) that would ban a procedure opponents refer to as "partial birth" abortion likely will be a repeat of the battle that has raged since Republicans took control of the chamber in 1995.

The House is expected to pass the measure for a third time. And President Clinton is just as likely to veto it, as he did in 1996 and 1997, when he said the legislation did not provide adequate exceptions to protect women's health.

The House voted to override both of Clinton's vetoes, but the Senate sustained them on each occasion.

The abortion issue will be debated in a different arena April 25 when the Supreme Court is scheduled to consider the constitutionality of a Nebraska law banning the abortion procedure.

Hyde's Decision

The House Judiciary Committee was scheduled to mark up the abortion bill March 30. Chairman Henry J. Hyde, R-Ill., decided instead to send the bill directly to the House floor for a vote. "Leadership wants it up fairly soon," Hyde said. The full Judiciary panel has twice debated and voted on the issue.

Hyde's action angered panel Democrats and abortion rights advocates, but he dismissed their complaints, saying that there would be "lots of amendments and lots of passionate debate" on the House floor.

In a March 30 letter to Hyde, Judiciary Democrats said that previous floor debates were run "under the most stringent and narrow terms permitted by House rules," with debate times "severely circumscribed" and no amendments other than a procedural motion to recommit allowed.

Once floor debate begins, the arguments will most likely reflect those made in earlier years. Backers of the measure say it would stop a gruesome, unnecessary procedure. Abortion rights supporters will argue that the bill is too vaguely worded and would weaken *Roe v. Wade*, the Supreme Court's 1973 decision establishing a constitutional right to abortion.

As described by the bill, the procedure is one where the physician performing the abortion "deliberately and intentionally vaginally delivers some portion of an intact living fetus until the fetus is partially outside the body of the mother, for the purpose of performing an overt act that the person knows will kill the fetus while the fetus is partially outside the body of the mother" and commits the act that kills the fetus while it is "partially outside the body of the mother."

The bill would allow the procedure only to save the woman's life and would subject those who perform the procedure for other reasons to two years in prison; the woman having the abortion would not be criminally liable.

Full House Votes To Ban 'Partial Birth' Procedure

APRIL 8 — As Congress has debated legislation to ban a procedure opponents call "partial birth" abortion, activists pushing the bill have known exactly what strategy they wanted to take: Move the gut-wrenching tactics of their longtime street protests inside the House and Senate chambers.

They have succeeded. Since 1995, lawmakers have engaged in protracted, graphic debates about specific abortion procedures, replete with pictures of what look like full-term fetuses being pulled out of the birth canal and having scissors stuck in their skulls.

"It's opened [members'] eyes to the violence of abortion," said Rep. Christopher H. Smith, R-N.J., an outspoken opponent of abortion rights. Once lawmakers hear the details of one procedure, Smith said, they wonder, "how violent are the other methods?"

Abortion rights supporters have not been as consistent — and arguably not as effective — in their fight against legislation (HR 3660) that would outlaw the procedure.

The House on April 5 passed the bill, 287-141. Congress has cleared similar legislation twice before, but been unable to override vetoes by President Clinton. The president has threatened to veto the House bill in its current form. *(Vote 104, p. H-38)*

The Senate in October voted 63-34 to approve legislation (S 1692) similar to Canady's measure. Added to the bill was a non-binding amendment stating that a Supreme Court decision legalizing abortion was "appropriate" and should not be overturned. It was adopted 51-47.

When Democrats controlled Congress, the debate over abortion focused more on general questions about a woman's right to choose and whether the government should provide Medicaid funding for the procedure for poor women. Now that the debate has shifted to specifics, abortion rights supporters have been thrown off balance.

At first, they argued that the partial- birth procedure was performed infrequently and only in dire circumstances, such as to save the woman's life. Those statements lost credibility, however, when a member of the abortion rights movement said in 1997 that the procedure was performed far more frequently than previously thought.

Facts and Emotion

Ron Fitzsimmons, then executive director of the National Coalition of Abortion Providers, told the American Medical News that the procedure was performed 3,000 to 5,000 times per year, rather than 500 to 600 times annually, as some abortion rights groups had said. Fitzsimmons also said the procedure was performed in both the second and third trimesters of pregnancy, not just in the final months, and that it was done for reasons other than to protect the mother's health. *(1997 Almanac, p. 6-12)*

Douglas Johnson, legislative director of the National Right to Life Committee, said Fitzsimmons' admission gave momentum to abortion rights opponents. "It was an important demarcation in the evolution of this debate," he said April 5.

Under attack, abortion rights supporters began looking for firmer ground on which to defend their stance. They believe they have found it. They emphasize that the legislative language in the bill the House passed April 5 is so loosely worded that it could apply to any abortion procedure, a claim proponents of the bill reject.

Abortion rights groups claim that if the bill became law — which is unlikely since Clinton has threatened to veto it — it would be ruled unconstitutional, in part because it does not deal with the issue of viability.

The landmark 1973 Supreme Court decision *Roe v. Wade* gave women the legal right to have an abortion before viability, the point at which a fetus can live outside the womb. The ruling and also a 1992 ruling, Planned Parenthood vs. Casey, said that after viability, Congress and state legislatures can restrict abortions as long as exceptions are made to protect a woman's life and health.

According to the Alan Guttmacher Institute, a nonprofit reproductive health research organization that favors abortion rights, as of February 2000 a dozen states had laws partially or fully in effect to ban the partial-birth procedure, while 18 state bans have been blocked by state or federal courts.

The issue will take the national stage April 25 when the Supreme Court is scheduled to consider the constitutionality of a Nebraska law banning partial-birth abortions.

Abortion rights proponents say that while debate has shifted, the basic issue remains the same — women and their physicians, rather than politicians, should decide whether an abortion is necessary.

"I think from the very beginning, pro-choice organizations should have stayed absolutely focused on the issue of who should make the decision," said Kate Michelman, president of the National Abortion and Reproductive Rights Action League (NARAL). "Our initial discussion about procedures and numbers was a reaction to the moment."

Rep. Nita M. Lowey, D-N.Y., said it is inappropriate for Congress to discuss the specifics of any medical procedure, especially one as personal as abortion. "Who are we to be making these decisions?" said Lowey, a staunch defender of abortion rights.

But Rep. Charles T. Canady, R-Fla., the chief sponsor of the House bill, said March 30 that abortion groups intentionally avoid discussing the procedure outlined in the bill because "they're embarrassed to come forth with a defense of partial-birth abortion."

Defining the Issue

As defined in Canady's bill, the procedure, also known as dilation and extraction, is one where the person performing the abortion "deliberately and intentionally vaginally delivers some portion of an intact living fetus until the fetus is partially outside the body of the mother" and commits the act that kills the fetus while it is partially outside the body of the woman.

The bill would allow the procedure only to save the woman's life and would subject those who perform the procedure for other reasons to two years in prison. The woman having the abortion would not be criminally liable. Opponents of the measure have said the procedure should also be permitted to protect a woman's health.

A motion to recommit Canady's bill and add language to protect the health of the woman failed, 140-289, on April 5. Clinton has previously insisted such language must be included for the bill to receive his signature. *(Vote 103, p. H-36)*

Some public opinion polls have shown that Americans who favor abortion rights oppose the particular procedure defined in Canady's bill. For example, a Gallup Poll conducted last April found that while 48 percent of those surveyed said they favored abortion rights, nearly two-thirds of the respondents said they would oppose the procedure that Canady and others define as partial-birth abortion.

Planned Parenthood Federation of America President Gloria Feldt said the graphic descriptions that Canady and others present in floor debate may initially sway voters toward legislation to ban such a procedure. She added that once those arguments are rebutted on grounds such as constitutionality and concerns that the measure is a first step toward outlawing all forms of abortion, people often end up opposing such bills.

"Whenever we have the opportunity to lay out all the facts, people get it," Feldt said. As evidence, she cited referendums in 1998 and 1999 in Washington, Colorado and Maine, where voters defeated measures that would have banned specific abortion procedures.

But Johnson of the Right to Life group said the yearly debate that has occurred on abortion since Republicans took control of the chamber in 1995 has helped abortion rights opponents win more public support.

"It educates people on how extreme the abortion situation is in this country," he said. "When people learn of it, they are more willing to have changes in the law."

Johnson said the defeat of state measures that would ban the procedure are a result of the abortion rights movement's deep pockets. "A group with enough money can go on television and say this is going to ban all abortions" whether the claim is true or not.

House Floor Debate

The April 5 floor debate was, as expected, passionate, rancorous and graphic.

House Judiciary Committee Chairman Henry J. Hyde, R-Ill., said House members could not "hide from the ugly reality of partial-birth infanticide. . . . The torture of partial-birth abortion takes only the time it takes to stab the little baby in the back of the neck. . . ."

Majority Leader Dick Armey, R-Texas, urged members not to shy away from discussing the issue. "Our discomfort here is nothing compared to the discomfort of that baby," he said.

Tom Coburn, R-Okla., a physician who has delivered more than 3,500 babies, said the procedure described in the bill was never necessary to protect a woman's health or fertility as abortion rights supporters say.

"It's the last procedure I would ever do to help a woman eliminate a nonviable child," Coburn said.

Jerrold Nadler, D-N.Y., said the legislation was "deceptive, extreme and unconstitutional. . . . Do not be fooled. This is nothing less than an attempt to outlaw all abortions."

In an interview April 5, Lowey said the GOP's motives in supporting the bill were "purely political."

As evidence, she cited the Republican leadership's decision to bring the abortion bill to the floor without allowing Hyde's committee to mark it up as scheduled March 30, a move with which Hyde concurred.

Lowey also pointed to the closed rule that prohibited any amendments from being offered. "If that's the case, and they know the president is going to veto the bill, why are we having the vote?" Lowey said.

Canady's bill passed with a veto-proof margin in the House, but prospects for a reaching a two-thirds majority of those present and voting are less certain in the Senate, where members failed both in 1996 and 1997 to garner enough votes to override a veto.

Supporters of the House measure remain optimistic that their chances of overcoming Clinton in the Senate will increase in coming weeks.

"We're giving this our best shot. We understand it's an uphill battle in the Senate and it's an uphill battle with the president," said Canady.

Supreme Court Hears Nebraska 'Partial Birth' Case

APRIL 29 — A skeptical Supreme Court heard arguments April 25 on the constitutionality of a Nebraska law banning a procedure known to abortion foes as "partial birth" abortion. A majority of justices seemed doubtful that the law met the constitutional tests the court had set out in previous decisions to allow a state to restrict a woman's access to abortion.

The court's decision on the state law's constitutionality, expected this summer, could have a widespread impact on the national abortion debate: Most of the 29 other state laws prohibiting the procedure use nearly identical language, as do bills (HR 3660, S 1692) passed by the House and Senate.

The procedure in question is generally performed in the the second trimester of pregnancy. Most abortions are performed in the first trimester using methods that are not at issue in the case.

The effort to ban a specific abortion procedure is a relatively new tack for anti-abortion activists. The emphasis has shifted in recent years from a broad, frontal attack on the legality of abortion, first employed after the landmark 1973 Supreme Court decision in *Roe v. Wade*. That ruling effectively gave women the right to have an abortion before the fetus becomes viable after 21 to 24 weeks.

Roe and a 1992 case, *Planned Parenthood of Southeastern Pennsylvania v. Casey*, set limits on government's ability to restrict access to abortion. *Casey* allows states to regulate abortion as long as laws do not impose an "undue burden" on a woman's right to an abortion. *(1992 Almanac, p. 398)*

Congress has twice cleared legislation to ban the controversial "partial birth" procedure; President Clinton vetoed it both times and is expected to veto this year's legislation. *(1997 Almanac, p. 6-12, 1996 Almanac, p. 6-43)*

Graphic Debate

Questions asked by a majority of justices during oral arguments in the Nebraska case, *Stenberg v. Carhart*, seemed to indicate that they found flaws in the language of that state's law that could render it unconstitutional.

In a debate that became quite graphic, Justice Antonin Scalia provided the most vociferous defense of the law. "The state is worried about rendering society callous to infanticide," he said. "Why is that not a valid state interest?"

But of the three justices seen as swing votes in abortion debates, two — Sandra Day O'Connor and David H. Souter — seemed uncomfortable with the broad definition of the procedure and the law's lack of exceptions to protect a woman's health.

The Nebraska law, enacted in 1997, defines the abortion procedure in question as "partially deliver[ing] vaginally a living unborn child before killing the unborn child and completing the delivery."

The law goes on to prohibit "deliberately and intentionally delivering into the vagina a living unborn child or a substantial portion thereof, for the purpose of performing a procedure that the person performing such procedure knows will kill the unborn child and does kill the unborn child."

Violation of the law can result in up to 25 years in prison and a fine of up to $25,000. A Nebraska doctor, LeRoy H. Carhart, filed suit against the law, arguing that it imposes an undue burden on women seeking abortions. Court papers say Carhart is the only physician in Nebraska who performs second-trimester abortions.

The 8th U.S. Circuit Court of Appeals, based in St. Louis, struck down the Nebraska law in September, ruling that it was so broad it could prohibit other abortion procedures and impose an undue burden. But in October, the 7th U.S. appeals court upheld similar laws in Illinois and Wisconsin.

The Supreme Court agreed to take the case to resolve differences between the two circuits.

The first question the high court is reviewing is whether the Nebraska statute can be interpreted in a way that is consistent with the Constitution. Previous court decisions have held that if a court can find a law constitutional, it should do so.

How Many Procedures Banned?

The court must decide whether the Nebraska law prohibits one abortion procedure, as supporters argue, or several procedures, as argued by opponents. If the court finds that the language prohibits more than one procedure, it is likely to find that it imposes an "undue burden," fails the *Casey* test and cannot be interpreted as constitutional.

Supporters argue that the definition included in the law is intended to outlaw only one procedure, known as intact dilation and extraction, or D and X. In that procedure, the fetus is delivered feet-first until the head reaches the cervix, then the skull is crushed or the contents of the skull are evacuated before the fetus is removed.

Nebraska Attorney General Don Stenberg argued for the law before the court. "Clearly a state can ban some abortion procedures," he said. The Nebraska law is "drawing a bright line between infanticide and abortion."

But opponents of the law argue that the language also would prohibit doctors from performing another kind of abortion, known as dilation and evacuation (D and E). It is similar to D and X, but the fetus is dismembered as it is pulled from the uterus. It is the primary procedure used in second-trimester abortions.

Scalia said the state has an interest in preventing D-and-X abortions. "It can coarsen public perception to other forms of killing children outside the womb," he said.

But O'Connor said "it is difficult to read this statute" as applying only to the D-and-X method. "I am not certain the statute might not prohibit the D-and-E procedure as well."

The Woman's Health

The court is also exploring whether the law is out of bounds because it does not include an exception that would permit the procedure to protect the health of the woman.

Justice Stephen G. Breyer, noting that there is contradictory medical evidence on whether the method in question is ever medically necessary, asked Stenberg, "What are we supposed to do when medical opinion seems, at least, divided?"

Replied Stenberg: "Defer to the judgment of the legislative branch." He added that the medical community had testified that other abortion options would not risk the woman's health.

But Souter said that without an exception to protect the woman's health, doctors would not be allowed to perform the procedure that they judged to be the most conducive to her health. "You can't allow the legislature to ignore those cases," he said.

High Court Rules Nebraska Ban is Unconstitutional

JULY 1 — The Supreme Court's June 28 decision striking down a late-term abortion ban in Nebraska appears to make it very difficult for the Republican majority in Congress to continue its battle to outlaw the procedure that opponents call "partial birth abortion."

In a 5-4 decision, the court ruled that the Nebraska law was unconstitutional because it did not include an exception to protect the health of the woman and because the language defining the procedure was too broad. It presented the woman seeking to end her pregnancy with an "undue burden" on her right to choose abortion, the majority said.

Congress has twice cleared legislation to outlaw the procedure; both times President Clinton vetoed it. The House and Senate have passed similar versions of the ban this Congress (HR 3660, S 1692). *(1997 Almanac, p. 6-12; 1996 Almanac, p. 6-43)*

While the language in the House and Senate bills defining the controversial procedure is far more specific than the Nebraska law, neither bill includes an exception for the health of the woman — an exception its supporters say would gut the bill.

Clinton said again on June 28 that he would sign the bill if it contained a health exception.

Though anti-abortion lawmakers roundly criticized the ruling in *Stenberg v. Carhart*, none articulated any way that Congress could get around the health issue. Rep. Charles T. Canady, R-Fla., and Sen. Rick Santorum, R-Pa., sponsors of the two bills, were slated to meet to discuss their options, according to a staff aide.

The only solution to their problem might be the one advocated by House GOP Conference Chairman J.C. Watts Jr., R-Okla. — a new Supreme Court. The issue is being debated in the presidential race.

"I look forward to the day when a Republican president will replace retiring liberals with justices who will truthfully interpret the Constitution rather than impose their activist views against states and the people," Watts said in a statement.

The *Casey* Case

The majority and minority opinions in *Stenberg* relied on their interpretation of the court's 1992 abortion decision, *Planned Parenthood of Southeastern Pennsylvania v. Casey*.

In that case, also settled by a narrow 5-4 majority, the court held that the 1973 Supreme Court decision, *Roe v. Wade* — which effectively gave women the right to have an abortion before the fetus becomes viable after 21 to 24 weeks — did not prohibit states from regulating abortions.

But, under *Casey*, the state could only do so if the regulation did not impose an "undue burden" on women seeking to have an abortion before fetal viability. As for later abortions, the court held the state could ban them, except when it was "necessary, in appropriate medical judgement, for the preservation of the life or health of the mother." *(1992 Almanac, p. 398)*

At issue in the Stenberg decision was a 1997 Nebraska law that defined the abortion procedure in question as "partially deliver[ing] vaginally a living unborn child before killing the unborn child and completing the delivery."

The law prohibited "deliberately and intentionally delivering into the vagina a living unborn child or a substantial portion thereof, for the purpose of performing a procedure that the person performing such procedure knows will kill the unborn child and does kill the unborn child."

LeRoy H. Carhart, a Nebraska doctor who performs third-trimester abortions, sued, and the 8th U.S. Circuit Court of Appeals, based in St. Louis, Mo., struck down the Nebraska law.

The Supreme Court, in an opinion written by the newest member of the court, Stephen G. Breyer, held that *Casey* required a health exception. "[T]his court has made it clear that a state may promote but not endanger a woman's health when it regulates the methods of abortion. . . . A risk to a woman's health is the same whether it happens to arise from regulating a particular method of abortion, or from barring abortion entirely," he wrote.

The court also found the description of the abortion procedure in the Nebraska law to be too vague. The majority found that because it did not specify the one kind of abortion opponents said they were trying to ban — the dilation and extraction, or D-and-X method — it could also ban another, far more common kind of abortion for pre-viable fetuses, called a D-and-E, or dilation and evacuation.

"All those who perform abortion procedures using that [D-and-E] method must fear prosecution, conviction, and imprisonment. The result is an undue burden upon a woman's right to make an abortion decision," Breyer wrote.

Joining Breyer in the majority were Justices John Paul Stevens, Sandra Day O'Connor, David H. Souter and Ruth Bader Ginsburg. Dissenting were Chief Justice William H. Rehnquist and Justices Antonin Scalia, Anthony M. Kennedy and Clarence Thomas.

"Ignoring substantial medical and ethical opinion, the court substitutes its own judgement for the judgement of Nebraska and some 30 other states and sweeps the law away," Kennedy wrote in his own dissent. "The court's holding stems from misunderstanding the record, misinterpretation of Casey, outright refusal to respect the law of a state and statutory construction in conflict with settled rules."

Thomas, writing for the other three dissenters, argued that the decision, rather than resting on the *Casey* decision, obliterated the *Casey* decision: "The rule set forth by the majority . . . dramatically expands our prior abortion cases and threatens to undo *any* state regulation of abortion procedures." ◆

CQ

Chapter 4

AGRICULTURE

Farm Aid Bill Clears With Higher Subsidies To Offset Low Crop Prices

SUMMARY

President Clinton signed legislation June 20 aimed at encouraging farmers to purchase crop insurance by having the government subsidize a greater share of the premium. The bill also included $7.1 billion in emergency spending for farmers hit by low prices — on top of $15 billion in aid enacted since fiscal 1999.

Under the bill, the government's share of insurance premiums increased to a range of 38 percent to 67 percent. The government previously paid 13 percent to 57 percent. The House passed its version of the bill (H Rept 106-300, Parts 1 and 2) in 1999.

While saying they wanted to wean farmers from emergency aid by making it easier for them to buy crop insurance, lawmakers also used the bill to dole out $5.5 billion in supplemental fiscal 2000 payments to make up for low prices on such staple crops as wheat, cotton and corn. Livestock also were covered for the first time. The remaining $1.6 billion will be provided in fiscal 2001 for producers of specialty crops not covered by current programs.

The bill included about $50 million in special interest provisions, including $14 million for a plant to make the gasoline additive ethanol in the home state of House Speaker J. Dennis Hastert, R-Ill., and special payments to tobacco growers hit by falling sales.

Democrats argued that the need for yet another insurance package proved Congress should take another look at the impact of the 1996 Freedom to Farm law (PL 104-127), which replaced farm subsidies with a seven-year schedule of fixed payments to move agriculture away from government subsidies and toward the market. They also complained that the lists of agricultural producers eligible for relief are outdated and favor large agribusiness over family farms. Republicans said those arguments were overshadowed by a spate of droughts and other natural disasters.

Box Score

- **Bill:** HR 2559 — PL 106-224
- **Legislative action: Senate** passed HR 2559, 95-5, on March 23 after substituting the text of S 2251 (S Rept 106-247).

House adopted the conference report (H Rept 106-639) by voice vote May 25.

Senate cleared the bill, 91-4, on May 25.

President signed HR 2559 on June 22.

Senate Agriculture Panel Approves Narrow Crop Insurance Bill

MARCH 4 — Driven by a group of unified and determined senators from the Great Plains, the Senate Agriculture, Nutrition and Forestry Committee on March 2 approved by voice vote a long-delayed crop insurance bill that would substantially lower farmers' premiums.

In approving the unnumbered bill — which is almost a replica of S 1580, sponsored by Pat Roberts, R-Kan., and Bob Kerrey, D-Neb. — the committee turned its back on a competing bill by Chairman Richard G. Lugar, R-Ind.

The key moment in the markup came when the committee adopted the Roberts-Kerrey version as a substitute for Lugar's. The vote was 10-8.

"I supported the Kerrey-Roberts substitute amendment because it will help make crop insurance . . . more affordable to farmers in need of protection," said Sen. Tom Harkin, D-Iowa.

The most important feature of the Roberts-Kerrey bill is a requirement that the federal government pay a higher share of the annual crop insurance premium than under the present program. The bill would make the government responsible for 45 percent to 60 percent of the premium. The current range is 13 percent to 57 percent.

The committee also accepted, without debate, an amendment by Harkin requiring farmers to "develop and carry out" conservation measures on highly erodable land as a condition of qualifying for crop insurance.

The Roberts-Kerrey bill has the backing of major farm groups, which insist that lower premiums will induce more growers to participate. It is similar to a bill (HR 2559) that the House passed by voice vote Sept. 29.

Mary Kay Thatcher, a lobbyist for the American Farm Bureau Federation, said her organization and other farm groups will press for a quick vote on the Senate floor.

The reason is that the $6 billion allocated in the fiscal 1999 budget agreement for crop insurance between fiscal 2001 and 2004 could be taken away if Congress creates a new budget blueprint for fiscal 2001. Thatcher fears that the money will be a tempting target unless a crop insurance bill is passed quickly and taken off the table.

"There is $6 billion sitting out there, and we're afraid someone is going to nab it," Thatcher said.

Farm organizations as well as the administration have said that increased participation in crop insurance would be one of the best ways to help farmers avoid financial ruin caused by bad weather or low prices. But farmers have balked at buying it because many believe the premiums are too costly.

Lugar, who had stalled consideration of crop insurance to improve prospects for his bill (S 1666), proposed a broader risk-management initiative that would have provided a direct government payment to any farmer who agreed to use any two of 12 risk-management practices each year. Among the choices were: purchasing crop insurance at the current, less subsidized rate; diversifying production to lessen chances that a failure of one crop would cause financial ruin; eliminating debt; and attending a seminar on risk management.

Faced with unyielding opposition, Lugar sought to mark up a hybrid bill that basically combined his language with the Roberts-Kerrey bill. Under that plan, farmers would have been able to choose either approach. But farm groups and a majority of the committee said the payments in Lugar's plan were too small and that participation would not increase.

Lugar's proposal, Roberts said, "has too many unanswered questions to risk spending several billion dollars on."

In a concession to Lugar, however, the Roberts-Kerrey bill includes a pilot risk-management program that would cover previously uncovered specialty and regional crops and nursery and greenhouse crops. That change was sufficient to swing the support of Rick Santorum, R-Pa., the only senator from a state east of the Mississippi River to vote for the Roberts-Kerrey bill.

Regional Split

When the vote came, it broke along predictable lines, with members from the Great Plains — which suffer from a high rate of drought and severe weather — voting for the bill, and senators from the South and Northeast opposing it. Farmers in those areas are more likely to grow such regional specialty crops as apples or cranberries, which are not covered by crop insurance.

Lugar had delayed the markup for a week in hopes that compromise could be found during discussions that had been going on for months.

That proved impossible.

"Working on crop insurance has been a long and more difficult trail ride than any of us expected," Roberts said.

Lugar would not predict when the bill might come to the floor. He also declined to say whether he would support the bill when the full Senate votes.

Senate Passes Bill After Adding Aid For Northeast

MARCH 25 — After sweetening the pot for Northeastern farmers by $126 million, the Senate easily passed crop insurance legislation March 23. The bill would increase the federal share of crop insurance premiums in hopes of encouraging farmers to buy disaster insurance.

Supporters say a more robust crop insurance program will save money in the long run, because it will lessen the need for Congress to enact expensive and often poorly targeted emergency aid bills in times of agricultural crisis.

The measure (HR 2559) passed by a vote of 95-5 and now heads for a conference with the House that all sides expect to be largely free of snags. *(Vote 45, p. S-12)*

"I don't see any major real differences" between the two versions, said Pat Roberts, R-Kan., a member of the Agriculture, Nutrition and Forestry Committee, who wrote the Senate bill with Bob Kerrey, D-Neb.

"I think we're all very much aware that this is something we should have done four years ago, so I think there should be expeditious handling and approval by the president," Roberts said.

The White House endorsed the broad reach of the bill, but it has objected to language that would modify the composition of the board of directors overseeing the program. The administration also wants to link crop insurance to participation in other federal farm benefit programs.

While Kerrey acknowledged those concerns, he believes they will not stall progress. "I think it will move rather quickly," he said in an interview March 23. "I think the White House is happy with 90 percent of it."

The version adopted by the Senate closely parallels the bill approved by the House on Sept. 29 by voice vote.

Both bills call for mandatory spending of an additional $1.5 billion annually to subsidize premiums for calendar years 2001 to 2004. The Roberts-Kerrey bill would make the government responsible for 45 percent to 60 percent of the premium. The House bill, sponsored by Agriculture Committee Chairman Larry Combest, R-Texas, calls for a range of 31 percent to 67 percent. The government currently pays 13 percent to 57 percent.

Both versions also would offer insurance for the first time to ranchers and other livestock producers, as well as growers of fruits, nuts, vegetables and other specialty crops.

Congress approved $15.3 billion in disaster payments to farmers in 1998 and 1999 and is under increasing pressure to provide another package this year. While no bill has yet been written, lawmakers and agriculture lobbyists expect the government to provide between $2 billion and $6 billion in aid to farmers, who are again suffering from low commodity prices and poor weather.

"I don't think there is going to be the hue and cry virtually every year to have a disaster program [if the insurance measure passes]," Roberts said March 23.

"What this does is give that farmer and his lender and his crop insurance agent the means where he takes control of those bad years in much better fashion. So it ought to lessen the need for these annual disaster bills, which are a disaster to pass and a disaster to implement because they're never entirely fair, and there's always somebody who gets left out."

The Senate moved quickly to pass the Roberts-Kerrey bill after money was added to help producers in the Northeast who raise specialty crops such as fruits, nuts and nursery plants. Sen. Robert G. Torricelli, D-N.J., placed a brief hold on the bill until changes were made to eliminate what he called a "geographic bias" favoring the Midwest and South.

"The simplistic assumption that New Jersey and other states in the Northeast are completely industrialized — so we don't need farm aid — took root as an institutionalized bias that denied our farmers help when they were struck by natural disasters," Torricelli said March 22.

As is the case on many agriculture issues, the vote followed regional rather than partisan lines. All five votes cast against the measure came from Republicans who represent areas that traditionally do not benefit from crop insurance. The five were: Majority Leader Trent Lott and Thad Cochran of Mississippi, Judd Gregg of New Hampshire and John McCain and Jon Kyl of Arizona.

Charles E. Grassley, R-Iowa, a champion of agricultural interests, praised the bill. "This legislation . . . will accomplish many of the most important goals requested by my constituency," he said. "The high levels of coverage will help to support family farmers in poor years and alleviate some of the need for what is becoming an annual economic relief payment."

Senate Clears Bill To Help Farmers With Insurance Premiums

MAY 27 — Taking up its third major farm aid bill in as many years, Congress May 25 cleared legislation that would encourage growers to buy crop insurance by subsidizing a greater share of the annual premium. The bill (HR 2559) also included $7.1 billion in economic assistance to farmers hit by low prices, on top of about $15 billion in aid approved since fiscal 1999.

The House adopted the conference report on the measure by voice vote, while the Senate tally was 91-4, underscoring the political clout of the farm community, despite its dwindling numbers. President Clinton is expected to quickly sign it into law. *(Senate vote 115, p. S-22)*

"We have the opportunity to strengthen farmers' ability to manage the risk the future may bring and to provide them the financial assistance that they badly need to cope with their immediate financial crisis," said House Agriculture Committee Chairman Larry Combest, R-Texas.

The final bill included about $50 million in special interest provisions, such as $14 million for an ethanol plant in the home state of House Speaker J. Dennis Hastert, R-Ill., and special payments to tobacco growers hit by falling sales. A provision backed by Senate Minority Leader Tom Daschle, D-S.D., directs the Army Corps of Engineers to accelerate the buyout of flooded homes in his state.

Lawmakers also tacked on legislation by Senate Agriculture, Nutrition and Forestry Committee Chairman Richard G. Lugar, R-Ind., that would authorize $49 million annually during the next six years for research on biofuels — alternative fuels produced from plants. Lugar's legislation (S 935) passed the Senate by voice vote Feb. 29, but was never considered by the House.

Sen. Tom Harkin, D-Iowa, and other Democrats said the need for yet another assistance package proves Congress should take another look at the impact of the 1996 "Freedom to Farm" law (PL 104-127). That law replaced farm subsidies with a seven-year schedule of fixed payments to move agriculture away from government subsidies and toward the market.

"Every year we keep doing the same thing over and over, and we expect some different result, and we do not get a different result," Harkin said before the Senate adopted the report.

No More Bailouts

The crop insurance package is intended to encourage farmers to indemnify themselves against losses from bad weather and natural disasters. In the process, lawmakers hope to end the ritual of massive emergency payments.

The conference report would authorize $8.2 billion over five years for crop insurance. The government now subsidizes anywhere from 13 percent to 57 percent of the premium. The bill would increase those subsidies to a range of 38 percent to 67 percent.

For example, a farmer who bought a policy covering 50 percent of the average yield of his crops at 100 percent of the cost would have to pay only 33 percent of the premium, compared with 43 percent under current law.

In addition, the conference report includes a new procedure to help farmers whose coverage is limited because their crops have been wiped out by a few bad years of natural disasters.

The bill would let growers plug in a higher crop yield number — 60 percent of the county's long-term average yield — for any year that was so bad it would ruin their overall production history.

The parallel aid package in the bill would direct more money to farmers, $5.5 billion in fiscal 2000 and $1.6 billion in fiscal 2001, to protect against low prices. Rep. Charles W. Stenholm, D-Texas, complained that Congress was moving too quickly, arguing that the true extent of need would not be known until later in this growing season.

The $5.5 billion would come in the form of higher Agricultural Market Transition Act (AMTA) payments — part of the fixed schedule of payments set under the 1996 law to ease farmers gradually off federal subsidies. Farmers would receive their scheduled 2000 AMTA payments, plus an extra payment equal to the amount they were initially scheduled to receive in 1999.

The $1.6 billion would go to various producers who would not benefit from the AMTA payments. It would include $500 million for oilseed producers; $200 million for specialty crops such as black-eyed peas, cranberries and melons; $100 million for cottonseed crops; and $340 million for tobacco growers.

The AMTA payments are controversial, with critics saying they go to corporate rather than family farms. Harkin said the payments are "not an effective mechanism in targeting aid to those who need it." Republicans said they are the most practical way to get fast relief to suffering farmers. As one House GOP Agriculture Committee aide put it, they are "the only way the Agriculture Department knows how to get a payment out the door quickly." ◆

Chapter 5

BANKING & FINANCE

Bankruptcy Overhaul Bill Cleared at Eleventh Hour; Ends In Pocket Veto

SUMMARY

President Clinton pocket-vetoed a major overhaul of the nation's bankruptcy laws Dec. 19. Congress had cleared the measure, a top priority for the credit industry, Dec. 7. The bill would have required debtors who could repay at least $10,000 or 25 percent of their debts (down to a minimum of $6,000) over five years to file under the stricter terms of Chapter 13, instead of Chapter 7.

The House and Senate each passed versions of the bill — the House in 1999 and the Senate in February 2000. The main thrust in both cases was to limit use of Chapter 7 of the bankruptcy code, which allows cancellation of debts beyond those that can be repaid after non-essential assets are liquidated. Debtors who exceeded a specific means test would have been required to file, instead, under Chapter 13, which requires repayment of debts over three to five years.

The Senate version quickly ran into trouble, because it also included an increase in the minimum wage and a package of tax sweeteners for business. That made it vulnerable to a challenge from the House, which is charged with writing tax bills under the Constitution, and made a conference on the bill impossible. *(Minimum wage, p. 14-3)*

Unable to hold a formal conference on the measure (HR 833), GOP negotiators ultimately shed the minimum wage increase and tax cuts and produced a conference report on the bankruptcy provisions, using the shell of a discarded House bill (HR 2415) as the vehicle.

The White House warned that the president would veto the bill, citing the deletion of language sponsored by Charles E. Schumer, D-N.Y., that would have barred violent anti-abortion protesters from seeking bankruptcy to avoid fines and court judgments. It also criticized as too lenient a proposed cap of $100,000 on the amount of the home equity that could be shielded from creditors. The cap only applied to homes bought within two years of a bankruptcy filing.

The House adopted the conference report Oct. 12, and the Senate cleared it Dec. 7.

To protect farmers in case the broader bill did not become law, the House on Oct. 31 passed a bill (HR 5540) by voice vote that would extend the Chapter 12 farm bankruptcy program, which expired in June, until June 1, 2001, but the measure died in the Senate.

Box Score

- **Bill:** HR 2415
- **Legislative action: Senate** passed HR 833, 83-14, Feb. 2, after substituting the text of S 625 (S Rept 106-49)

House adopted the conference report on HR 2415 (H Rept 106-970), by voice vote, Oct. 12.

Senate cleared HR 2415, 70-28, Dec. 7.

President pocket-vetoed the bill Dec. 19.

Senate Passes Bankruptcy Bill; White House Opposition Certain

FEBRUARY 5 — A plan to rewrite the nation's bankruptcy laws won an overwhelming show of support in the Senate after months of maneuvering, but several provisions added during debate left the bill's future more uncertain than ever.

Senators easily passed the measure (HR 833) Feb. 2, 83-14, after Republicans backed away from a confrontation over an abortion-related provision and defeated an attempt to prevent gun manufacturers from using bankruptcy to get rid of debts arising from lawsuits against them. *(Vote 5, p. S-4)*

The catch is that the Senate-passed bill is also the vehicle for controversial provisions that would raise the minimum wage over three years to $6.15 and provide $18.4 billion in tax cuts over five years. Neither proposal is in the companion House-passed version of HR 833, and both are opposed by the White House. Administration officials say that the tax breaks are unnecessary and that the wage increase should take effect over two years, not three.

The underlying bill would force more debtors to file under Chapter 13 of the bankruptcy code, which requires some repayment of debt, and limit access to Chapter 7, which erases debt beyond the amount that can be paid off by liquidating the debtors' assets.

It would also put a $100,000 limit on the amount of housing equity that could be exempted from seizure, and it includes new consumer protections, such as a requirement that credit card issuers warn customers of the costs of making only minimum payments.

Lawmakers' Tangle

The Senate's core bankruptcy provisions are generally less restrictive than those in the House version, but the real tangle is over what to do about the minimum wage and tax proposals.

"We don't think the actual rise in the minimum wage goes up quickly enough," White House spokesman Joe Lockhart said Feb. 2. "I think we've made very clear . . . that that's not the kind of legislation the president can sign with the minimum wage provision in it."

Many Republicans in Congress insist that any minimum wage increase passed this year will have to be paired with tax cuts, especially breaks for businesses to help offset their higher labor costs.

"I don't see those being separated,"

Senate Banking Committee Chairman Phil Gramm, R-Texas, said Feb. 2. "I think if the president wants an increase in the minimum wage, he's going to have to sign a bill that has some tax cuts in it."

Iowa Republican Charles E. Grassley, chief sponsor of the Senate bankruptcy bill, said he was confident that House and Senate leaders would eventually cut a deal with Democrats.

"The Republican leadership of the House thinks that, before they get out in October, that there will have to be a minimum wage bill passed. . . . That dictates that things will be worked out," Grassley said Feb. 1.

But the question is how? Split the minimum wage increase off now and put it into a separate bill? With or without the tax breaks? Or take the two versions of the bankruptcy bill to conference and sort it out there?

Under one scenario, House Ways and Means Committee Chairman Bill Archer, R-Texas, could "blue slip" the bill — return it to the Senate on the grounds that it violates the House's constitutional prerogative to initiate tax legislation. "I want to look at the specifics," Archer said of the Senate bill Feb. 2. By week's end, staffers said he had still not decided.

Such an objection by Archer could force the Senate to remove the tax provisions and wait for the House to take them up first, or risk having the bankruptcy bill die. Alternatively, the Senate could hold back sending the bill to the House. In either case, the conference would be delayed.

Another scenario has House Democrats blue-slipping the bill over the tax and minimum wage provisions. They could then try to pass language from a bill (HR 325), sponsored by Minority Whip David E. Bonior, D-Mich., that would phase in the $1 wage increase over two years and offer approximately $8 billion in tax breaks over five years.

Bonior's bill has been stalled in the House Education and the Workforce Committee for nearly a year. Bonior has 164 of the 218 signatures needed on a discharge petition to force the bill to the floor.

Under a third scenario, House GOP leaders could take up a stand-alone bill (HR 3081) that would provide $30.2 billion worth of tax breaks and "sweeteners" over five years while phasing in the $1 minimum wage increase over three years.

That bipartisan bill, sponsored by Republicans Rick A. Lazio of New York and John Shimkus of Illinois and Democrats Gary A. Condit of California and Robert E. "Bud" Cramer of Alabama, was approved, 23-14, by the Ways and Means Committee on Nov. 9. It would also reduce estate taxes and increase deductions for health care costs of self-employed persons.

Business lobbyists and supporters of the bankruptcy bill are urging lawmakers to split off the minimum wage increase and tax cuts, saying that would increase the likelihood that the bill would be cleared and signed. But for many Democrats, the minimum wage increase is crucial to their support of a bill that some believe is too favorable to creditors.

Senate Action

Senate passage of the bankruptcy bill came after Republicans averted a showdown with Democrats, including Vice President Al Gore, over an amendment by Charles E. Schumer, D-N.Y., to prevent those convicted of violence at abortion clinics from avoiding debts related to the violence.

Republicans initially sought to defeat the Schumer amendment but found that some in their party wanted to cast a vote against abortion clinic violence. The chances for defections increased when the National Right To Life Committee, a group that opposes abortion, announced that it would not include the vote in scorecards of lawmakers to determine whether they should receive political support.

Breaking away from his campaign for the Democratic presidential nomination, Gore appeared at the Capitol minutes before the vote with supporters of the amendment, including Schumer and Minority Leader Tom Daschle of South Dakota.

"This issue is totally important. I'm not going to take a chance to see it fail," Gore said.

As Gore presided over the chamber, ready to break a tie vote, GOP leaders abruptly changed strategy and urged Republican senators to vote for the amendment. The proposal was adopted 80-17, although key lawmakers, including Judiciary Committee Chairman Orrin G. Hatch, R-Utah, pledged to "correct the amendment" in conference. *(Vote 2, p. S-4)*

Lott said he was not willing to hand Gore a chance to make political points. "We'll never let him cast another tie-breaking vote again," Lott told The Associated Press on Feb. 2.

Last May, Gore cast the deciding vote to adopt an amendment to a juvenile crime bill (S 254) requiring criminal background checks on all firearm sales at gun shows. It was the fourth tie-breaking vote of his vice presidency.

Republicans argued that the amendment was not needed. They considered but did not offer an alternative measure to restrict the discharge of debts by persons convicted of violence at any venue. Democrats contended that the alternative would be filled with loopholes.

Another potential obstacle was cleared away when the Senate voted, 29-68, to defeat an amendment sponsored by Democrat Carl Levin of Michigan to deny bankruptcy protection to gun manufacturers for firearm-related debts arising from lawsuits filed by cities and other localities alleging fraud, negligence or product liability. *(Vote 4, p. S-4)*

In other action, the Senate tabled, or killed, 54-43, an amendment by Russell D. Feingold, D-Wis., to protect debtors from eviction during bankruptcy proceedings. *(Vote 3, p. S-4)*

An amendment by Paul Wellstone, D-Minn., to prevent lenders who charge annual interest rates of more than 100 percent from collecting debts in bankruptcy proceedings was tabled, 53-44. *(Vote 1, p. S-4)*

The Senate approved by voice vote a Schumer amendment aimed at aiding larger families. It would expand a provision in the bill to exempt a debtor from the means test for Chapter 7 bankruptcy filing if his family's income was below the greater of the median family income for the nation or for his state. For families with more than four members, the amendment would raise the income limit by $583 for each additional family member.

Bankruptcy Issues

With the floor fight over the Schumer amendment finished, Grassley said he would work with Democrats, including Robert G. Torricelli of New Jersey, to hold together bipartisan support for the bill.

Grassley predicted that House-Senate differences over the bankruptcy provisions would be resolved relatively quickly.

George W. Gekas, R-Pa., chief sponsor of the House bill, agreed. He said Clinton will be under pressure to sign the bill if controversial riders are removed, or he is likely to face a veto override. The House passed its version, 313-108, on May 5.

"We should send the president a slim, mean and clean bankruptcy bill," Gekas said.

Both the House and Senate versions would establish criteria to be used by judges to determine whether debtors should be excused from some debts under Chapter 7, or required to repay all their debts over time under Chapter 13.

Business lobbyists clearly prefer some provisions in the House version, including a more stringent means test.

The House bill would require cases to be handled under Chapter 13 if debtors earned enough to pay back $6,000 of their debts over five years. The Senate bill would require cases to be handled under Chapter 13 if debtors earned enough to pay back the lesser of $15,000 or 25 percent of their debt over five years.

Of the 1.3 million bankruptcy filings last year, about 70 percent were filed under Chapter 7. The credit card industry argues that a means test could substantially reduce the number of Chapter 7 filings.

But consumer groups and some researchers disagree. A 1998 study by the American Bankruptcy Institute, a non-profit research group, found that 97 percent of debtors who filed for bankruptcy under Chapter 7 had too little income to repay 20 percent of their debts over five years. The study found that only 3 percent had sufficient earnings to exceed that income threshold, if it were used to screen out bankruptcy filings under Chapter 7.

Despite such findings, supporters of the legislation argue that the mere existence of income limits for Chapter 7 filings and increased efforts by courts to encourage debt counseling would help to reduce filings across the board.

Grassley said the Senate would favor a higher income limit but was likely to lean toward House language on homestead exemptions, which shield a debtor's home equity from creditors.

The Senate bill would cap the exemption at $100,000. The House bill would cap it at $250,000, but it would allow states to opt out and set their own limits.

"There will be some give by the Senate on that," Grassley said. The opt-out provision may be essential to win support from senators from the five states that place no cap on the homestead exemption: Texas, Florida, Kansas, South Dakota and Iowa.

The 14 senators who voted against the bill included four from states with no cap: Republicans Sam Brownback of Kansas and Kay Bailey Hutchison of Texas, and Democrats Bob Graham of Florida and Tom Harkin of Iowa.

In addition to defenders of the homestead exemption, the primary opposition to the bill came from a small group of Democrats who argued that the bill was biased against consumers. They joined consumer advocacy groups such as the Consumer Federation of America in pointing out that the bankruptcy filings declined last year for the first time in recent years.

For example, Sen. Edward M. Kennedy, D-Mass., said the bill fails to take steps to prevent banks and other credit card issuers from trying to "hook unsuspecting citizens" on high-interest credit cards. He suggested that credit-card companies would become more careful in marketing credit cards if bad loans continued to mount. "Leading economists believe that the bankruptcy crisis is self-correcting," he said.

Minimum Wage

Despite the recent decline in bankruptcy filings, bill cosponsor Torricelli said he believed legislation was required to protect not only lenders but consumers who must foot the bill for the bad debts of those who file for bankruptcy. He said the legislation would attract strong bipartisan support if disputes about the minimum wage could be resolved.

That remains the key obstacle in any conference. Democrats want the increase to be phased in over two years and are backing a narrower $9.5 billion reduction in taxes.

"The bill cannot come back from conference with the same minimum wage provision. If it does, it will fail," Democratic Sen. John Kerry of Massachusetts said on Feb. 2.

Kerry was one of 45 Democrats who signed a letter saying tax cuts in the bill — including a proposal to raise the maximum annual limit on contributions to 401(k) retirement plans from $10,500 in 2000 to $15,000 in 2005 — were "skewed disproportionately to upper-income people."

Negotiators Closer After Grassley Pulls Unpopular Pension Provision

MAY 6 — Prospects for agreement on a compromise bankruptcy bill (HR 833) improved the week of May 1, after Republican Sen. Charles E. Grassley of Iowa dropped a provision that would have given creditors broad authority to tap into individuals' pension funds to collect outstanding debt. The provision was adamantly opposed by many lawmakers and consumer groups.

"We'll get a bill done," Senate Banking, Housing and Urban Affairs Committee Chairman Phil Gramm, R-Texas, said May 3.

Despite the progress, a number of thorny issues still must be resolved. The biggest problem, as it has been for weeks, is that the bill cannot formally be sent to a conference committee.

Going to conference would subject the measure to an objection by House members that it contains Senate-originated tax provisions — namely $103 billion in business tax breaks over 10 years — in violation of the constitutional requirement that the House act first on revenue issues.

Further complicating matters, the Senate bill would also increase the minimum wage by $1 an hour over three years. The House bill would not.

Senate Majority Leader Trent Lott, R-Miss., expressed frustration May 2 at Democrats' unwillingness to separate the minimum wage increase from the bankruptcy provisions. "I got an alternative, if they like it. Let them [minimum wage and bankruptcy] both sit out there," he said.

If lawmakers can work out the bankruptcy provisions, that could provide the momentum to cut a deal clearing away the procedural roadblocks.

Grassley has been leading informal negotiations in lieu of a conference. Lott originally set an early April deadline for completing work on bankruptcy. Grassley said no new deadline had been set but that negotiators hoped to finish quickly.

After angry protests and a hearing in the Senate Health, Education, Labor and Pensions Committee, Grassley backed down from the provision he had quietly inserted in the Senate version of the bill that would have allowed debtors to waive bankruptcy protection for retirement savings.

Pension Controversy

The provision was intended to ensure that wealthy individuals did not shift funds to their pensions to avoid paying off their debts. Opponents said its actual reach would have been much greater, however. It was opposed by Senate Judiciary Committee Chairman Orrin G. Hatch, R-Utah, and Finance Committee Chairman William V. Roth Jr., R-Del.

Hatch in a May 1 letter took credit for deleting the measure from the Senate's offer to House negotiators. "I have vehemently opposed any attempts to erode the protection of pension plans in bankruptcy," Hatch said.

The next day, Grassley said he would work with Republican Sen. Jeff Sessions of Alabama to promote a substitute amendment. Their revised plan would set a cap, based on age, on the amount of retirement funds that a debtor could shelter from creditors. The cap would rise from $250,000 at age 21, by $17,045 a year, to a maximum of about $1 million at age 65.

House and Senate negotiators also reached some other tentative agreements. One compromise would bar debtors who were financially able to repay $10,000 or more over five years from filing for bankruptcy under Chapter 7 of the bankruptcy code, which erases debt beyond the amount that can be paid by liquidating a debtor's assets. Such individuals, instead, would file under Chapter 13, which requires some repayment.

Senators may try to get a bankruptcy deal to the floor by inserting it in another bill. There is precedent. In a 1996 maneuver, an unrelated provision was attached to an aviation conference report (PL 104-264). *(1996 Almanac, p. 3-34)*

Republicans Settle Their Differences; Democrats Seek Further Changes

MAY 20 — House and Senate Republican leaders settled on the main elements of a compromise bill to overhaul bankruptcy law (HR 833), laying the groundwork for possible floor action the week of May 22.

After an hours-long meeting in his office with GOP lawmakers on May 18, Senate Majority Leader Trent Lott, R-Miss., said a "conceptual agreement" had been reached on key provisions in the bill, adding he was hopeful that final details could be hammered out rapidly. While the accord resolves intraparty Republican disputes, some Democrats are unhappy with the outlines of the proposal.

"Language has got to be written down," Lott said. "Everybody's got to have a chance to get a final look at it."

The linchpin of the deal was a decision to limit to $100,000 the amount of home equity that a debtor could shield from creditors. Negotiators were continuing to discuss whether to allow states to opt out of that cap.

House Majority Leader Dick Armey and fellow Texas Republican Majority Whip Tom DeLay have argued in favor of the House's opt-out provision. Texas is one of five states that have no limit on the so-called homestead exemption. The others are Florida, Iowa, Kansas and South Dakota.

Sen. Jeff Sessions, R-Ala., argued that a cap was needed to prevent debtors from moving to one of the five states to buy a home and shield assets from creditors. In response, negotiators were trying to work out a provision that would bar a new state resident from claiming the exemption unless he had owned the home for more than three years before filing for bankruptcy.

The compromise would also set a $1 million cap on the amount of funds that would be off-limits to creditors in an individual retirement account.

It would preserve a Senate provision, sponsored by Harry Reid, D-Nev., to prevent credit card companies from terminating consumers' accounts simply because they paid their bills immediately, rather than letting debt and interest accrue.

Negotiators decided not to add a proposal pushed by Senate Judiciary Committee Chairman Orrin G. Hatch, R-Utah that would have allowed NextWave Telecom Inc. to reopen a deal under which it was purchasing wireless licenses from the Federal Communications Commission (FCC). The FCC reclaimed the licenses after the company went into bankruptcy proceedings and plans to auction them off.

Sen. Judd Gregg, R-N.H., strongly criticized efforts to help NextWave, arguing that the company's original agreement to buy the licenses for more than $4 billion was far less than the FCC could get for them in an open auction. "This is a fleecing of taxpayers," Gregg said.

Moving the Bill

Now, Republicans hope to work out a bipartisan deal with Democrats on final language and figure out a way to get the bankruptcy provisions to the House and Senate floors.

The overall bankruptcy legislation is intended to force more debtors to file under Chapter 13 of the bankruptcy code, which requires some repayment of debt, and to limit access to Chapter 7, which erases debt beyond the amount that can be paid off by liquidating a debtor's assets.

Opponents question the need for the bill, saying it would help banks and credit card companies at the expense of consumers. Supporters, pointing to a growing number of bankruptcies in recent years, say action is needed.

Some Democrats, including Reid and Sen. Robert G. Torricelli, D-N.J., said they were optimistic a bipartisan deal could be reached but were waiting to review the draft bill. Other longstanding critics of the bill, such as Edward M. Kennedy, D-Mass., said they would continue to oppose it.

"It's a bad bill. It doesn't matter if

you tie a bow on it," Kennedy said.

The administration, which monitored the talks, praised Republicans for making some concessions but complained that the bill would not give bankruptcy judges enough discretion to grant exceptions to a proposed means test that would prevent debtors from filing under Chapter 7 if they could repay $10,000 or more over five years.

The administration has threatened to veto the Senate version of the bill because it includes language to increase the minimum wage by $1 an hour over three years and to provide $103 billion in business tax breaks. The White House wants the minimum wage increase to take effect in two years

Republicans plan to separate the minimum wage and tax provisions from bankruptcy and move the measures down separate tracks. Lott may attach the bankruptcy provisions to a bill (S 761) to authorize the use of electronic signatures to seal business contracts, though other alternatives are being considered.

Leaders Work Behind Scenes To Get Stalled Bill Moving Again

MAY 27 — Democrats and Republicans worked during the week of May 22 to salvage a long-stalled bankruptcy overhaul (HR 833) and appeared close to a deal that would clear the way for floor action.

Senate Majority Leader Trent Lott, R-Miss., and Minority Leader Tom Daschle, D-S.D., labored to try to resolve a handful of remaining Democratic objections holding up a final bill.

Republican leaders in the Senate and House reached a tentative pact on the bankruptcy overhaul on May 18. At a May 23 news conference, Daschle charged that Democrats had been "completely locked out of any meaningful discussion."

His views were echoed by others.

"Republicans are taking the temperature of Democrats. They want to know if we will stick together on this," Sen. Edward M. Kennedy, D-Mass., a staunch critic of the bill, said in an interview May 24.

Eager to move the measure, which has lingered in limbo for months, the two parties stepped up behind-the-scenes efforts to break the impasse.

"Key Republicans and Democrats will have to be satisfied, or we won't have a conference report," said Sen. Charles E. Grassley, R-Iowa, who led talks to resolve outstanding issues.

Sen. Patrick J. Leahy, D-Vt., listed a half-dozen objections to the Republican proposal on May 23, and he and other Democrats hinted that they would fight the legislation if changes were not made. By May 25, their concerns had been narrowed to two primary issues.

Leahy was insisting on deleting a provision, backed by Senate Judiciary Committee Chairman Orrin G. Hatch, R-Utah, that would limit the ability of certain debtors to collect attorney fees in lawsuits accusing debt collectors of harassment under a fair debt collection law (PL 104-208).

"I am not aware of any other Democrat or Republican that supports this measure," Leahy said May 25.

Hatch argued that the provision was a key part of the GOP compromise. He said he had already watered down a proposal that would have given debt collectors more leeway to force debtors to make good on bad checks.

Abortion an Issue

On the second big issue, Democrats led by Sen. Charles E. Schumer of New York insisted on hewing close to the language in the Senate-passed bill (S 625) that would limit bankruptcy protection for persons fined for convictions of violent acts at abortion clinics.

Republicans wanted language that would apply to violent crimes anywhere and certain other offenses including "willful and malicious" threats.

"The Republican proposal is not acceptable," Schumer said May 24.

Schumer and other Democrats said the GOP language could result in a rash of lawsuits that called for determining the intent of persons who made threats.

Negotiations were expected to continue after the Memorial Day recess. Even if they are successful, Republicans still face a daunting procedural task: finding a suitable bill to serve as the vehicle for moving the bankruptcy provisions that would be acceptable to both parties and industry groups.

The Republican compromise does not include controversial Senate language to raise the minimum wage by $1 an hour over three years — rather than the two-year period favored by President Clinton — and to provide $103 billion over 10 years in business tax breaks.

For process reasons, lawmakers want to divorce the bankruptcy bill from the minimum wage and tax increases, and bring it to the floor wedded to another, unrelated measure.

Republicans had been considering a plan to put the bankruptcy overhaul on a crop insurance conference report (HR 2559).

Farm-state lawmakers, however, argued that the bankruptcy measure should be kept separate unless a bipartisan agreement was reached. The crop insurance bill cleared Congress on May 25 without bankruptcy.

High-tech companies quietly objected to a plan to insert bankruptcy in a bill to allow so-called electronic signatures to complete Internet transactions (S 761).

"Put one bauble on the Christmas tree, and everybody else has a bauble they want to put on. Then the tree falls over," said a high-tech lobbyist.

Another, more difficult option is a stand-alone bill.

"We're almost there. There are just a few issues that are left. We are very close," said Democratic Sen. Robert G. Torricelli of New Jersey

Divided Democrats

For Daschle, the bankruptcy bill is a political problem because it has deeply divided his caucus. Some Democrats, including Kennedy and Paul Wellstone of Minnesota, are staunch critics of the bill. Others, including Daschle, support its main thrust, but oppose amendments attached in GOP negotiations.

The measure is important to one of Daschle's constituents: Citigroup Inc. operates a large credit-card processing unit in South Dakota that is one of the state's biggest employers.

Opponents began gearing up a campaign to portray the bill as a biased attempt to help credit card companies collect debts at the expense of consumers. Wellstone and Kennedy said disputes over procedural issues and the minimum wage had obscured the bill's deeper flaws. They called the measure a major setback for consumers.

"I will do everything in my power to try to stop this bill. It is a bad bill. It does not matter what legislation it is attached to," Wellstone said.

Concern about a rising tide of unpaid debts in the 1990s — when Americans filed for bankruptcy at eight times the rate of the economically depressed 1930s — has propelled the push to tighten bankruptcy laws. Credit card companies, banks and retailers that support the bill argue that the increase in bankruptcies is due to legal loopholes. Consumer groups counter that lenders are to blame for hawking credit cards and encouraging consumers to run up interest charges.

Industry groups have lobbied heavily for legislation. A study by Common Cause, a public watchdog group, found that the industry contributed $7.5 million in donations to candidates and political parties in 1999, with about 60 percent going to Republicans.

Gary Klein, a spokesman for the National Consumer Law Center, a non-profit research group, said opponents were not optimistic about their chances of blocking the measure. "This bill has a lot of support, unfortunately. We think it will be bad for consumers," he said.

Lawmakers of both parties agree with the bill's main goal of prodding more debtors to file under Chapter 13 of the bankruptcy code, which requires repayment of some debt, rather than Chapter 7, which eliminates debts beyond the amount that can be paid by selling a debtor's assets. Of the 1.3 million bankruptcy filings last year, about 70 percent were filed under Chapter 7. *(1997 Almanac, p. 2-81)*

Wellstone and Kennedy say other measures should have been added to the bill to cushion its possible effect on consumers, who will be faced with tougher requirements to pay off debts instead of having them canceled.

They and other critics charge that lawmakers missed a chance to establish a "safe harbor" exemption to a means test in the bill. As it currently stands, the bill would require debtors to file under Chapter 13 if they were able to repay at least $10,000 or 25 percent of their debts over five years.

Democrats wanted to exempt families earning less than the national median income of about $39,000 a year from having to comply with the means test, on the grounds they would be forced to pay expensive attorney fees and back debt they could not afford.

House Judiciary Committee Chairman Henry J. Hyde, R-Ill., was a champion of efforts to exempt low-income families from the means test. He did not prevail in negotiations between House and Senate Republican leaders.

Democrats also complain that Republican negotiators eliminated consumer protection provisions that had bipartisan support in the Senate.

One deleted Senate provision, backed by Robert C. Byrd, D-W.Va., would have required online applications for new credit card accounts to include a link to an electronic version of a pamphlet by the Federal Trade Commission explaining the types of consumer credit.

Democrats cut a deal to revise a provision by Senate Banking, Housing and Urban Affairs Committee Chairman Phil Gramm of Texas. The compromise would require the Federal Reserve to help small banks, with less than $250 million in assets, by setting up toll-free numbers that consumers could call to get information about the amount of time it would take to pay off their balance.

Homestead Exemption

Even while working out revisions with Democrats, Republicans were putting the final touches on parts of their draft conference report.

On May 24, lawmakers agreed on a compromise to cap at $100,000 the amount of home equity that debtors could protect from creditors. The cap would apply only to homes purchased within the previous two years.

Stories about prominent people, such as actor Burt Reynolds, who declared bankruptcy but got to keep expensive homes helped contribute to the initial outrage that led to the bill.

A previous draft would have applied the cap to homes purchased within the previous three years and would not have applied to five states that have an unlimited homestead exemption: Texas, Kansas, South Dakota, Florida and Iowa. Some senators, including Jeff Sessions, R-Ala., insisted that all states should be subject to a cap.

Sen. Kay Bailey Hutchison, R-Texas, who wanted to exempt the five states, said the deal would give states most of what they wanted — flexibility to let debtors protect homes owned longer than two years.

Dispute Over Abortion Protesters Keeps Bankruptcy Bill in Limbo

OCTOBER 7 — Hopes are fading for approval of long-stalled bankruptcy overhaul legislation in the face of a seemingly intractable dispute over a provision that would limit financial protections for abortion protesters.

Senate Majority Leader Trent Lott, R-Miss., said Oct 3. there was still a "50-50 chance" of a deal with the White House on the measure (HR 833, S 3046). He added, however, that chances for final passage were fading as legislators instead focused on completing must-pass spending bills for fiscal 2001 so they can adjourn for the year.

Privately, lawmakers in both parties were gloomy about the prospects for cutting a deal. They said it was unlikely that a bankruptcy compromise could be added as a rider to an appropriations bill because of the expectation it would trigger a veto by President Clinton.

The bleak prognosis came despite signs of progress on several disputes that have blocked a final bill. Supporters say the overhaul would help to curb rampant bankruptcy filings and force more debtors to pay their bills. But consumer groups argue that the measure would force debtors to choose between creditors and family needs.

The House passed its version of bankruptcy on May 5, 1999, and the Senate acted Feb. 2. The GOP draft conference report would require those who were able to pay $10,000 or 25 percent of their consumer debts, whichever is less, to file for bankruptcy under Chapter 13 of the bankruptcy code, which requires some repayment. They would not be allowed to file under Chapter 7, which erases debts beyond those that can be repaid by liquidating a debtor's assets.

GOP leaders agreed to drop a provision in the draft conference report that would have set a $100,000 cap on the amount of home equity that debtors could shield from creditors. Some homeowners would have been allowed to opt out of the cap, however.

Instead, Republicans offered a "hard cap" of $500,000 on the so-called homestead exemption.

Republicans also have agreed to drop a provision, backed by Senate Judiciary Committee Chairman Orrin G. Hatch, R-Utah, that would have denied payment of attorney fees to some writers of bad checks who sued debt collectors for using unfair practices.

The White House praised lawmakers for seeking to find a compromise. But administration officials objected to a Republican decision to delete Senate language that would prevent abortion protesters convicted of violent crimes from seeking bankruptcy protection to avoid paying hefty legal penalties.

Some of the main Senate negotiators, including Lott and Charles E. Grassley, R-Iowa, cited the disagreement on the abortion provision as the main stumbling point.

Searching for a Vehicle

Lott said Republicans were not sure whether Clinton would follow through on this threat to veto the bill over the abortion dispute. For their part, Republicans were unwilling to give ground on the issue because of strong pressure from House Judiciary Committee Chairman Henry J. Hyde, R-Ill., a staunch abortion opponent.

Lott introduced a pared down version of the bankruptcy bill (S 3046) on Sept. 14 that included the abortion clinic language. But Republicans could not find a formulation that would satisfy both the White House, which wanted specific language on clinic violence, and Hyde.

Frustrated Republicans charged that Clinton was only a lukewarm supporter of the bill and was happy to let it die without reaching his desk.

"I think he's under orders from John Podesta and Hillary not to sign this bill," Lott said, referring to the White House chief of staff and First Lady Hillary Rodham Clinton, a candidate for Senate in New York.

Lott also contended that Democrats were holding up the bill because of opposition by influential party constituents including labor unions and consumer groups.

A White House spokesman declined comment. Senate Minority Leader Tom Daschle, D-S.D., said he strongly disagreed with allegations that Democrats were trying to scuttle the bill. He blamed Republicans for waiting too long to make major concessions. "There is a chance for this bill, but it is diminishing," Daschle said.

In a Sept. 22 letter to Lott, Gene Sperling, Clinton's national economic adviser, said the administration believed the bill's provisions would place "unnecessary barriers before those who genuinely need bankruptcy protection when faced with the most difficult obstacles life has to offer."

In a short-lived attempt to force a floor vote, Republicans briefly considered a plan for merging the bankruptcy bill with a reauthorization (HR 1248) of the 1994 Violence Against Women Act (PL 103-322). However, supporters of the latter law insisted on keeping the two bills separate. The House overwhelmingly passed the reauthorization, 415-3, Sept. 26.

Assistant Majority Leader Don Nickles, R-Okla., said one of the last remaining hopes for supporters of the bankruptcy measure would be to attach it to a draft proposal that would raise the current minimum wage by $1 to $6.15 an hour and provide tax breaks to small business.

"This is one way to break the stalemate," he said.

Democrats were doubtful. The minimum wage issue derailed the Senate version of the bankruptcy bill (HR 833), after Republicans agreed to a compromise that included tax breaks for small business. That amendment blocked a formal conference because the House refused to accept a bill that did not comply with the constitutional requirement that revenue-raising measures start in the House.

House Adopts Conference Report By Voice Vote

OCTOBER 14 — House approval of a compromise bankruptcy overhaul bill (HR 2415) set the stage for a Senate floor fight during the week of Oct. 16 and a virtually certain presidential veto.

After months of fruitless negotiations with the White House, GOP leaders on Oct. 12 forced a showdown with President Clinton by bringing the conference report to the House floor, where it was adopted by voice vote. The president has strongly opposed the compromise legislation because it omits Senate-approved language that would have limited bankruptcy law protection for protesters convicted of violent crimes at abortion clinics.

In the Senate, Assistant Majority Leader Don Nickles, R-Okla., said a vote on an expected cloture motion to limit debate on the conference report would likely come toward the end of the week of Oct. 16. "Once we get 60 votes," he said, referring to the minimum number needed to invoke cloture, "I think we'll get a large vote in favor of cloture. If we get to a final vote, we'll pass it."

Senate Minority Leader Tom Daschle, D-S.D., said he would likely favor moving toward a vote so that the bill could travel to the White House for Clinton's expected veto. "I'd be inclined to support cloture and allow the [final passage] vote. The president says he will veto it," Daschle said.

A longtime supporter of revising federal bankruptcy laws, Daschle has criticized Republicans for not giving ground to satisfy the administration.

With no opposition from Democratic leaders, the bill now appears to be poised for final passage. While supporters prepared for a floor vote, however, opponents said they would continue efforts to block the bill.

"There is going to be as much delay and discussion as possible," said Paul Wellstone, D-Minn.

"I'm going to do everything I can to defeat this bill," said Charles E. Schumer, D-N.Y.

With time running out on the session, lawmakers on both sides of the issue said the bill's future was doubtful. Clinton would likely be able to make a veto stick, because there would be little time to vote on an override, they said.

John D. Podesta, the White House chief of staff, told House Speaker J. Dennis Hastert, R-Ill., in an Oct. 12 letter that Clinton would veto the bill because it "gets the balance wrong" between the needs of creditors and debtors.

Homestead Exemption

In attacking the bill, Podesta criticized the lack of language on abortion clinic protesters and argued that the bill was too lenient with debtors who buy homes in any of five states that have unlimited homestead exemptions allowing debtors keep their home equity even after filing for bankruptcy. Those states are: Texas, Kansas, South Dakota, Florida and Iowa.

The conference report that was considered by the House would set a $100,000 homestead cap. However, the limit would apply only to homes purchased within two years of a bankruptcy filing. Moreover, the cap would not apply to proceeds from a home sold by a debtor if they were invested in a new home in the same state as the debtor's old residence.

House and Senate GOP leaders dropped a concession previously worked out with the White House: a "hard cap" of $500,000 on the amount of home equity that any debtor could shield from creditors. Podesta complained that the bill would leave open a "loophole for the wealthy."

There is bipartisan support for the bill's main focus — forcing more debtors to file for bankruptcy under Chapter 13 of the code, which requires some repayment of debts, rather than Chapter 7, which allows debts to be erased beyond those repaid by selling a debtor's assets.

The compromise measure would require debtors, if they were financially able, to repay over a five-year period at least 25 percent of their debts (if that percentage totaled at least $6,000), or $10,000, whichever was less. Debtors would be exempt if their annual income equaled or fell below the median income for their home state.

The bill would make permanent Chapter 12 bankruptcy protections for family farmers.

Senate and House leaders on Oct. 11 unveiled a novel strategy for moving the bill to get around procedural roadblocks. They took a long-dormant bill dealing with embassy security (HR 2415) that had been passed, in different forms, by both the Senate and House, deleted its text and inserted the provisions of the bankruptcy bill.

A formal conference was not possible on the original bill (HR 833) because the House objected to Senate business tax breaks on grounds that they violated a constitutional mandate that revenue bills originate in the House.

Senate Approves Motion to Proceed To Conference Report

OCTOBER 21 — Final passage of legislation to toughen the nation's bankruptcy code is tantalizingly close, but the chances of the bill — a priority of the credit industry — becoming law are still just out of reach.

Senate adoption of the conference report on bankruptcy overhaul (HR 2415) appears likely during the week of Oct. 23. The industry's victory looks to be short-lived, however, because President Clinton has vowed to veto the bill. Consumer, women's and labor groups oppose the measure, arguing it would impose a harsh financial burden on low-income families.

The Senate voted 89-0 on Oct. 19 to approve a motion to proceed to the conference report. That sets the stage during the week of Oct. 23 for a vote on a cloture motion to limit debate on the measure, and possibly, for final Senate floor action. *(Vote 279, p. S-50)*

In a letter to lawmakers on Oct. 12, just hours before the House approved the measure by voice vote, John Podesta, the White House chief of staff, said Clinton opposed the final measure because of the deletion of Senate-approved language that would have limited bankruptcy protection for protesters convicted of violent crimes at abortion clinics.

Podesta said Clinton also objected to language in the bill that would allow five states — Texas, Kansas, South Dakota, Florida and Iowa — to keep laws on their books that allow many debtors to protect home equity from creditors. The bill would cap the so-called homestead exemption at $100,000, but would only apply to homes purchased within two years of a bankruptcy filing.

The conference report, expected to have bipartisan support, would force more debtors to file under Chapter 13 of the bankruptcy code, which requires debtors to repay debts over three to five years, instead of the more lenient Chapter 7, which allows cancellation of debts beyond those that can be repaid after non-essential assets are liquidated.

Debtors who could repay at least $10,000 or 25 percent of their debts, whichever is less, would be required to file under Chapter 13. Debtors who earned sums less than or equal to their state's median income would be exempted.

Senate Prospects

As part of a proposal discussed by Senate GOP leaders, a cloture vote would be held Oct. 25. Republican leaders are hopeful that senators will agree to allow unrelated spending bills to be taken up during breaks in the bankruptcy debate.

Democratic Sen. Paul Wellstone of Minnesota, an opponent of the bankruptcy bill, said he would insist on a full debate. "We want to burn as much time as possible," he said. He added that he did not want to tie up the floor completely and block action on appropriations bills.

The Republican decision to defer a vote on the bankruptcy conference report was essential for getting cooperation from Democrats. For Democrats, many of whom oppose the measure, the strategy makes it likely that Clinton will have the last word on the issue by minimizing the chances of a veto override vote.

"The bankruptcy bill is probably going to have to be the last bill that we bring up, because we have other work to finish," Charles E. Grassley, R-Iowa, said Oct. 18.

Grassley, a sponsor of the original Senate version, and Assistant Majority Leader Don Nickles, R-Okla., said they were confident senators would clear procedural hurdles and get to a final vote. "We'll get it done," Grassley said.

Republicans were divided on the question of an override vote. "Sure, we should vote to override, if we have the votes," said Phil Gramm, R-Texas. But Grassley said he doubted lawmakers would want to wait around for Clinton to veto the bill.

"We'll be gone by then," he said. Democrats said they would strongly oppose any effort to override a veto. "If this is vetoed, it will not be overridden," said Sen. Patrick J. Leahy, D-Vt.

While the Senate prepared for final action, some supporters of the measure sought to salvage key provisions. House Judiciary Committee Chairman Henry J. Hyde, R-Ill., told appropriators in an Oct. 17 letter that it was "unclear whether there is sufficient time in which to enact the bankruptcy reform legislation." He urged them to insert a a provision of the bankruptcy conference report into the fiscal 2001 foreign operations spending bill (HR 4811) now moving through Congress.

That provision would permit investors in Lloyd's of London, the British insurance market, to file suit in U.S. courts to recoup damages for fraud that allegedly took place from the late 1970s to late 1980s. Investors want the courts to determine liability for losses on pollution and asbestos claims. Appropriators said they would try to craft a bipartisan deal to implement Hyde's request.

Senate Girds for Final Showdown On Bankruptcy Overhaul Measure

OCTOBER 28 — Faced with a presidential veto threat, supporters of the conference report on a pending bankruptcy overhaul (HR 2415) prepared for a showdown vote on the Senate floor set for the week of Oct. 30. At the same time, they worked on plans to salvage some other key changes in bankruptcy law by passing them as stand-alone measures.

The Senate voted 87-1 on Oct. 27 to approve a motion to proceed to the bankruptcy conference report, clearing the way for a vote on a cloture motion to limit debate, and possibly, final Senate floor action.

The lone "nay" vote was cast by Herb Kohl, D-Wis., who echoed White House concerns that the bankruptcy bill contained loopholes for wealthy debtors.

Clinton administration officials have threatened a veto on the grounds that the bill puts too much pressure on low-income families to repay their debts.

The administration also opposes language intended to limit state laws that now permit debtors to shield home equity from creditors, calling it too narrow. The bill would cap the equity that could be protected at $100,000. The limit would only apply, however, to homes purchased within two years of a bankruptcy filing.

Clinton has further criticized the bill for omitting Senate-approved language to limit bankruptcy law protection for protesters convicted of violent crimes at abortion clinics.

The House adopted the conference report by voice vote Oct. 12. Senate action has been delayed since then as lawmakers have focused on first trying to complete must-pass spending bills.

Senate Majority Leader Trent Lott, R-Miss., said Oct. 27 that he hoped to file for cloture early in the week of Oct. 30. "This is very important legislation. It needs to get enacted into law," he said.

Key Democrats said they would back procedural moves to get to a final vote. Senate Minority Leader Tom Daschle, D-S.D., said he would support a limit on debate, though he said it was a "close call" on whether he would vote for the conference report.

Democratic Splits

Patrick J. Kennedy, D-R.I., the top House Democratic fundraiser, wrote a letter to the White House earlier this month stressing his support for the bill. He was joined by Reps. Martin Frost, D-Texas, and Robert Menendez, D-N.J. The letter is emblematic of a schism in the Democratic Party: Kennedy's father, Sen. Edward M. Kennedy of Massachusetts, opposes the measure.

Some Democrats are concerned that a presidential veto could cripple efforts to raise campaign money from the credit industry. But White House officials said privately that Clinton was firm in his intent to veto the bill.

While the Senate prepared for final action on the conference report, lawmakers worked on separate efforts to move other bankruptcy law changes.

The House passed by voice vote Oct. 24 a bill (HR 1161) that would simplify efforts by Wall Street executives to untangle complex business deals and recoup money from business partners who file for protection under federal bankruptcy law.

Wall Street investment firms now face delays in trying to collect money from bankrupt business partners in financial deals known as derivative swaps. In such transactions, investment firms and their partners take opposing market positions on derivatives, financial instruments that track changes in the value of underlying commodities, foreign currencies, stocks or other securities.

Currently, a business must first pay any outstanding balance in a derivative deal to the estate of a bankrupt partner before it can file a claim to collect any money it may itself be owed from the estate. The legislation would allow the business partners to tally up and settle all outstanding debts at once.

Federal Reserve Chairman Alan Greenspan and Treasury Secretary Lawrence H. Summers told Speaker J. Dennis Hastert, R-Ill., in an Oct. 20 letter that the so-called contract netting bill could reduce the chance of market incidents such as the near collapse of a big hedge fund, Long-Term Capital Management, in September 1998. Such incidents could pose a "broader threat to our financial system" they said.

Senate Banking, Housing and Urban Affairs Committee Chairman Phil Gramm, R-Texas, said he would support the measure.

Another draft measure was being readied to extend Chapter 12 of the bankruptcy code, which expired at the end of June. That section of the law is designed to help farmers avoid foreclosures while they seek protection from creditors in bankruptcy court. Action was expected as a stand-alone bill or an appropriations rider.

Senate Cloture Vote Fails To Limit Debate

NOVEMBER 4 — The bankruptcy overhaul hit a speed bump when the Senate declined to limit debate on a conference report for the bill the week of Oct. 30. Still, Senate leaders hoped to schedule a vote on final passage during a special, lame-duck session that will begin the week of Nov. 14. Even if they succeed, however, the measure faces a likely veto.

With the bankruptcy overhaul in doubt, the House passed by voice vote on Oct. 31 a bill (HR 5540) to extend Chapter 12 of the federal bankruptcy code until June 1, 2001. Chapter 12, which expired at the end of June, is intended to protect farmers from foreclosures when they reorganize their debts. That measure now heads to the Senate.

The Senate on Nov. 1 rejected a cloture motion to limit debate on the conference report for the bankruptcy overhaul (HR 2415) 53-30, seven votes short of the required 60. *(Vote 294, p. S-52)*

Majority Leader Trent Lott, R-Miss., said the bill would be one of three priorities after the election, along with spending bills and a deal on tax cuts. He said he would bring the bill up "as soon as we have the votes."

Clinton has threatened to veto the bill because it lacks Senate-passed language to bar bankruptcy protection for protesters convicted of violent crimes at abortion clinics.

If Republicans keep control of Congress and win the White House, GOP aides envision a scenario where Clinton might back off his veto threat and sign the bill in order to head off a measure next year that would be less favorable to debtors. But key Democrats say a veto is virtually certain.

For his part, Lott was hopeful Clinton would sign the bill.

The bill would require debtors able to repay $10,000 or 25 percent of their debts over five years to develop repayment plans instead of seeking to discharge debts in bankruptcy court.

The cloture motion failed because of 16 absentee senators.

Senate Clears Bankruptcy Bill By Strong Margin

DECEMBER 9 — A bill to revamp the nation's bankruptcy laws, the top priority for the credit industry, won eleventh-hour passage from the Senate on Dec. 7 — and headed for a certain presidential veto and a possible veto override showdown.

The 70-28 vote was well above the two-thirds needed to override the president. *(Vote 297, p. S-53)*

With the 106th Congress nearing an end, a veto override appears to be a long shot. But supporters were organizing a strong grass-roots lobbying campaign aimed at mobilizing local banks, credit unions and retailers to lobby 17 Democrats who voted yes on the bill.

Congress sent the measure to the White House immediately after the vote to get the clock started. President Clinton has 10 days, not counting Sundays, or until Dec. 19, to sign or veto it.

Charles E. Grassley, R-Iowa, said both chambers could technically remain in session so that members could be summoned back to Washington for a veto override vote. "If we are in session for six or seven legislative days, there is a chance for a veto override," Grassley said. "With 70 votes, we've got a chance."

Until the final vote, opponents of the bill (HR 2415) — a coalition of consumer groups, labor unions and women's organizations — appeared to have the advantage, with the promise of a veto and time dwindling on the 106th Congress. But their efforts and a late bid by Clinton to rally wavering Democrats with personal telephone calls were overwhelmed by a business lobbying blitz in the final days.

Jake Siewert, a White House spokesman, said Dec. 7 that Clinton continued to oppose the bill. "We believe that bill is still deeply flawed, and the president has no choice but to veto it," he said. Clinton has argued that the bill would put a heavy burden on low-income families while containing loopholes that would let some abortion protesters and wealthy homeowners escape financial obligations.

The heavy business lobbying campaign was fueled in part by fears that Congress would have difficulty dealing with complex legislation in the 107th because of the evenly divided Senate. Lobbyists said they believed their best chance for enactment may be now, before lawmakers adjourn for the year.

"In this crazy political environment, most of us believe a bird in the hand is what you want to go for, " said Edward L. Yingling, chief lobbyist for the American Bankers Association.

The hard-fought battle ended with more than a dozen business lobbyists cheering just outside the Senate chamber, and some of them confidently predicting that they will be able to defeat Clinton if he vetoes the bill.

Whether or not the bill becomes law this year, its backers appear to have a solid base of support to win similar legislation in the 107th. And, should Texas Gov. George W. Bush prevail in the election, the industry would have an ally in the White House.

But after the strong Senate vote, business lobbyists were not inclined to take a chance on waiting until next year, after spending months of trying to navigate through a frustrating thicket of procedural delays. Key lawmakers acknowledged that the measure would face a tough road next year. "The 50-50 split in the Senate makes it a little more difficult," said Grassley, the bill's chief proponent.

Of the 70 senators who voted for the bill, nine will not be back. Of those nine, seven will be replaced by Democrats, most of whom have not formally taken a position on the measure. One of them, however, Sen.-elect Debbie Stabenow of Michigan, voted for an earlier version (HR 833) in the House.

In the days leading up to the Dec. 7 vote, opponents were hopeful of blocking the bill this year and mobilizing strong opposition in the next Congress with the help of new allies on Capitol Hill, including Sen.-elect Hillary Rodham Clinton, D-N.Y., a staunch critic of the bill.

"It doesn't happen very often, but sometimes David beats Goliath," said former Sen. Howard M. Metzenbaum, D-Ohio (1974, 1976-95), chairman of the Consumer Federation of America, a nonprofit watchdog group.

But Goliath, the credit industry, quietly mobilized its forces before the vote. The industry's stake in the bill is huge. It estimates that debtors walk away from $35 billion in unsecured debt each year — leading to direct losses for lenders and other businesses that are passed along to consumers in the form of higher interest rates.

The bill would force more debtors to file for bankruptcy under Chapter 13 of the code, which requires some repayment of debts, rather than Chapter 7, which allows debts to be erased beyond those that can be repaid by selling a debtor's non-essential assets.

Individuals with the resources after basic expenses to repay at least $10,000 or 25 percent of their debts, whichever was less (down to a minimum of $6,000), over five years would be required to file under the more stringent Chapter 13. The bill would also speed up deadlines in business bankruptcy cases and allow sellers to recoup the full retail value of cars, not just the fair market value.

The bill was cleared after weeks of failed negotiations with the White House. If Congress adjourns soon, Clinton could simply hold the bill and not sign it for 10 days — a pocket veto. "We won't be around to deal with it," warned Senate Banking, Housing and Urban Affairs Committee Chairman Phil Gramm, R-Texas.

But Grassley said Senate leaders were considering a plan for staying in session on a pro forma basis if other legislation is finished the week of Dec. 11.

Privately, Democrats attributed the strong vote in favor of the bill to the sentiment that Clinton would veto it and the belief that time would run out before a veto took effect.

Grassley said he had expected to win support from six or seven Democrats, and was shocked when the final tally showed 17 Democrats voting yes. Said Charles E. Schumer, D-N.Y., an ardent foe of the bill: "I've got to talk to people to find out what happened."

"The conventional wisdom was that the clock would run out and there would be no override. But the conventional wisdom changed 24 hours ago," Yingling said Dec. 8. He said he doubted that opponents would be able to mount a grass-roots lobbying campaign to match the one being organized by business. "You cannot just push a button and make it happen," he said.

The outcome of a veto override vote would depend on whether at least enough Democrats can be persuaded to sustain a veto, including the 28 Democrats who voted no.

One vote could be supplied by Mary L. Landrieu, D-La., who did not vote. At least 66 votes would probably be required for an override — one less than usual — because Democrat Peter G. Fitzgerald of Illinois has been voting present on the legislation, citing his ownership of a large block of Bank of Montreal stock.

Some key Democrats were leery of taking sides on an override. "I'll cross that bridge when I come to it," said Kent Conrad of North Dakota. Jeff Bingaman, D-N.M., who spoke with Clinton by telephone before voting yes, said simply, "I don't know."

Lobbyists were expected to focus on four Democratic supporters of the bill who voted no Dec. 5 when the Senate adopted, 67-31, a motion to limit debate: Conrad, Byron L. Dorgan of North Dakota, Ernest F. Hollings of South Carolina and Richard H. Bryan of Nevada. *(Vote 296, p. S-53)*

Another key Democratic supporter, Blanche Lincoln of Arkansas, said she was undecided about a veto override.

Grassley and other supporters said they hoped to persuade Clinton to sign the bill. Grassley said he would be under pressure from the industry to construct a bill more favorable to creditors next year, and that Clinton may prefer to enact the bill as it stands.

But some Democrats argued that Clinton would have a motive for holding fast and could count on strong opposition in the Senate next year. "This bill will have a tough time next year," said Paul S. Sarbanes, D-Md.

"Some people believe that this bill will not come back in its current form because it's going to be harder to get things done in a 50-50 Senate," said Sam Gerdano, executive director of the American Bankruptcy Institute, a nonprofit research group.

On the floor, critics such as Patrick J. Leahy, D-Vt., praised the bill's thrust but complained of being frozen out of negotiations. "It is being shoved down our throats," said Democrat Richard J. Durbin of Illinois, who had previously supported bankruptcy overhaul.

Supporters said a rewrite of bankruptcy statutes was long overdue and accused Democrats of trying to have it both ways — supporting the bill to secure campaign contributions from business, but doing little to stop Clinton from killing it.

"Democrats say they are for a bankruptcy bill," said Gramm. "But really, they aren't. It isn't good for them politically. A lot of liberal groups and unions are opposed."

Jeff Sessions, R-Ala., charged that the bill was delayed by election-year politics. "Trial lawyers in the bankruptcy bar were afraid this would lead to fewer filings," he said. "And the White House was set on running against the 'do-nothing' Congress."

What Happened

Opponents of the legislation began the 106th Congress facing an uphill battle. Congress had come close to completing work on a similar measure in the 105th Congress. A conference report was adopted by the House in 1998 but died in the Senate. *(1998 Almanac, p. 5-24)*

The credit industry — with backing from leaders of both parties, including Clinton — seized on a sharp rise in personal bankruptcy filings and made a strong case for promoting similar legislation in the 106th Congress. Filings nearly tripled from 500,000 in 1986 to a peak of 1.4 million in 1998.

For much of the year, key Democrats, including Senate Minority Leader Tom Daschle of South Dakota, straddled the issue. Daschle finally voted against the measure after a conversation with Clinton.

In an Oct. 12 letter to Speaker J. Dennis Hastert, R-Ill., the White House opposed language intended to limit state laws that allow debtors to protect home equity from creditors.

The bill would cap the so-called homestead exemption at $100,000, but the limit would apply only to homes purchased within two years of a bankruptcy filing. Most states already cap the exemption at $50,000 or less.

The White House also objected that the compromise omitted an amendment by Schumer to the Senate-passed version of the bill that would have prevented violent anti-abortion protesters from seeking bankruptcy to avoid fines and court judgments.

Though Schumer denied that his amendment was intended as a "poison pill," it sparked a bitter battle between Republicans, including House Judiciary Chairman Henry J. Hyde of Illinois, who insisted on its deletion, and Democrats who staunchly defended the language.

"It was an early knockdown," said Rep. George W. Gekas, R-Pa. Some Republicans were ready to accept Schumer's amendment in order to salvage the bill, but Hyde, a strong opponent of abortion, refused. ◆

Complex Effort to Revamp Commodities Law Realized As Part of Year-End Wrapup

SUMMARY

A wide-ranging rewrite of the commodities laws that govern financial markets was attached to the fiscal 2001 omnibus spending bill at the end of the session after negotiators reached a deal with Senate Banking, Housing and Urban Affairs Committee Chairman Phil Gramm, R-Texas. Gramm wanted the bill to spell out more clearly the legal status of a category of unregulated, privately negotiated investments known as swaps. In the end, the bill was reworked to limit oversight of such investments by the Commodity Futures Trading Commission (CFTC).

Key lawmakers in the House and Senate, backed by Treasury Secretary Lawrence H. Summers and Federal Reserve Chairman Alan Greenspan, strongly urged passage of legislation that would set new ground rules for the trading of financial derivatives — a category of investment that is tied to an underlying asset. Once used by farmers to lock in prices for corn, sugar and other commodities, derivatives have evolved into sophisticated financial instruments tied to currency exchange rates, interest rates and other economic indicators. The global market for derivatives was estimated at $88.2 trillion in 1999 by the Bank for International Settlements in Switzerland. U.S. commodities exchanges, such as the Chicago Board of Trade and Chicago Mercantile Exchange, complained that uncertainty over the legal status of derivatives under U.S. law was driving business overseas, mostly to European financial exchanges.

The legislative effort was so complex that the House Agriculture, Banking and Commerce committees each held hearings and produced their own versions of the bill. After weeks of deliberation, committee chairmen agreed to blend the bills into a compromise that resembled the original Agriculture panel version written by Thomas W. Ewing, R-Ill. The bill dealt with two separate issues. Lawmakers wanted to ensure that the CFTC, the Securities and Exchange Commission (SEC) or other regulatory bodies could not exert primacy over swaps. Doing so could have thrown the legality of these forward contracts in doubt, potentially allowing participants to walk away from billions of dollars in commitments and leading to a possible market meltdown.

Lawmakers legalized the trading of futures contracts based on single stocks — a top priority of the Chicago commodity exchanges. The move overturns a 1982 ban on trading the instruments that was enacted due to a regulatory turf fight between the CFTC and SEC. Compromise language included in HR 4541 split jurisdiction over the futures between the two regulatory bodies, recognizing that the investments share characteristics of both stocks and futures.

Box Score

- **Bill:** HR 4577 — PL 106-554
- **Legislative action: House** passed HR 4541 (H Rept. 106-711, Parts 1-3), 377-4, Oct. 19.

House adopted the conference report on HR 4577 (H Rept 106-1033), 292-60, on Dec. 15.

Senate cleared the bill by voice vote Dec. 15.

President signed bill Dec. 21.

House Panel Approves CEA Reauthorization

JUNE 24 — Concerned that U.S. commodity exchanges are losing ground to overseas rivals, House and Senate panels took up bills the week of June 19 that would rewrite the nation's commodities laws and overhaul the market for stock futures, derivatives and other complicated investments.

The House Agriculture Risk Management, Research and Specialty Crops Subcommittee on June 22 approved by voice vote bipartisan legislation (HR 4541) that would reauthorize the Commodity Exchange Act for five years and clarify the way the government regulates derivatives — financial products tied to an underlying asset.

The measure also would lift the ban on trading potentially volatile single-stock futures that has been in place for 18 years because the Securities and Exchange Commission (SEC) and the Commodity Futures Trading Commission (CFTC) cannot agree on how to regulate them.

'A Strong Signal'

The House Agriculture Committee is slated to mark up the bill June 27, a schedule that "sends the message we're pretty united on both sides of the aisle," said subcommittee Chairman Thomas W. Ewing, R-Ill. "This sends a strong signal that we want to move quickly on legislation that really modernizes the financial industry."

Senate Agriculture Committee

Chairman Richard G. Lugar, R-Ind., said his panel would try to mark up its bill (S 2697) before the July Fourth recess.

The interest by both panels reflects lawmakers' concerns that U.S. commodity exchanges such as the Chicago Board of Trade and the Chicago Mercantile Exchange are losing business to overseas futures markets that trade unregulated over-the-counter (OTC) derivatives contracts. The value of goods and services underlying trades in the OTC market worldwide totaled $88.2 trillion at the end of 1999, according to the Bank for International Settlements in Switzerland.

At a joint hearing June 21 of the Senate Agriculture and Banking committees on a companion measure, Federal Reserve Chairman Alan Greenspan and Treasury Secretary Lawrence H. Summers urged lawmakers to pass a reauthorization bill this year and endorsed most portions of the Senate measure.

Designing new controls to deal with the scope and complexity of commodities trading presents challenges that recall last year's arduous overhaul of financial service laws (PL 106-102).

Among those with major stakes in the debate are banks, bond traders, stock exchanges and derivatives traders. Lawmakers said they will have to juggle the needs of those interests while drafting rules that protect investors but do not overregulate fast-growing financial markets.

"We have to separate out those concerns that are just about money and control from those legitimate concerns . . . [involving] risk to investors and so forth," Bob Kerrey, D-Neb., said at the Senate hearing.

The Commodity Exchange Act, which expires Sept. 30, governs the CFTC, which oversees the U.S. futures industry. The measure was drafted in 1936, a time when farmers and food processors traded physical commodities — such as wheat, pork bellies and sugar — and entered into futures contracts to lock in favorable prices and avoid market fluctuations.

Dramatic Chance

The futures industry has changed dramatically since then and now centers on swaps of complicated financial instruments such as international currency exchange rates and interest rates. Newer risk-shifting products that have emerged include privately negotiated OTC derivatives that are based on an underlying product such as a stock index.

At the urging of the Treasury Department, Congress created the CFTC in 1974 (PL93-463) to address the changing futures market. *(1974 Almanac, p. 215)*

Congress last reauthorized the CFTC in 1992 (PL 102-546) after nearly four years of deliberations. A 1995 effort to update the law failed, in part due to disputes between the two major Chicago exchanges. That prompted lawmakers to extend the existing law for another five years. *(1995 Almanac, p. 3-39; 1992 Almanac, p. 127)*

The bill passed by the House panel would clearly exempt OTC derivatives from federal regulation — a move designed to ease concerns in the financial industry about the government asserting control over the currently unregulated market. Many derivatives traders fear such a move could invalidate some existing OTC contracts and drive business overseas.

The bill also would exempt transactions between "sophisticated" investors — a corporation, partnership or other entity with assets exceeding $10 million — from most regulatory scrutiny.

Perhaps the most controversial provision in the bill is the proposed lifting of the 1982 regulatory ban on trading futures contracts based on single stocks. Currently, the only stock-based futures contracts traded in the United States are based on broad indices such as the Standard & Poor's 500 stock index.

An 18-Year Spat

The prohibition on single-stock futures, embodied in a pact known as the Shad-Johnson Accord, has been the object of continual wrangling between the SEC and CFTC since 1982.

The House bill envisions splitting enforcement authority, with the CFTC getting substantial oversight over the trading of contracts and the SEC policing fraud and other wrongdoing.

Greenspan told the joint Senate hearing that congressional repeal of Shad-Johnson this year is essential to prevent European markets from building a huge lead in single-stock futures.

"If we don't resolve the issue, Shad-Johnson will get resolved, but not in a manner that would be desirable by any of us," Greenspan said.

Representatives of the SEC and CFTC indicated at the hearing that they still disagree on how to split jurisdiction over the contracts. CFTC Chairman William J. Rainer said his agency was concerned about SEC proposals to define futures contracts based on single stocks as "securities" and apply "the panoply of both securities and commodities regulation to these products, [which] could result in overly burdensome regulation."

SEC Chairman Arthur Levitt responded that single-stock futures could change the investing landscape, requiring the SEC to have direct authority over the market and its participants, which could include small investors.

"While extremely complex derivative products might not attract retail customers, a simple future on a share of a blue chip stock is the type of product that is sure to do so," Levitt said. "Accordingly, legislation must maintain the SEC's ability to protect investors and to maintain integrity of the markets on which they trade."

Lugar said the two agencies' disagreement would not deter lawmakers from moving quickly and prescribing their own solution.

"Already, the United States has lost its leadership role in the exchange-traded futures market to Europe, and the over-the-counter market may not be far behind," Lugar said. "Congress has a good opportunity to reverse this tide by enacting sound legislation this year."

Not all lawmakers are as optimistic about quick passage. Sen. Charles E. Schumer, D-N.Y., said the legislation would create different requirements for margins — the deposits investors put up when buying or selling securities or contracts. He noted that the margin requirement for a stock is 50 percent while the requirement for a futures contract is 5 percent.

"I'm not opposed to single-stock futures. But the regulatory framework has to be right," said Schumer, whose New York constituency includes stock exchanges worried that the introduction of single-stock futures will increase speculation on individual issues.

Jurisdictional issues may also hinder

progress. The House bill would have to be referred to the Banking and Commerce committees if it is passed by the full agriculture panel and Ewing indicated those panels could seek changes in the measure's language. One focus might be a provision that makes oversight of commodities futures clearinghouses optional.

House, Senate Panels Approve Bills to Ease Rules On Futures Trading

JULY 1 — Continuing a rapid effort to overhaul U.S. commodities laws, the House and Senate Agriculture committees each moved bills the week of June 26 that would deregulate portions of the financial derivatives market and commodity futures exchanges.

But an end-of-the-session push to enact legislation could be complicated by the need for hearings in other committees that have jurisdiction over the bills. Lingering disagreements among financial regulators over how to regulate certain financial instruments also cloud prospects for action this year.

The Senate Agriculture Committee on June 29 approved, by voice vote, legislation (S 2697) to reauthorize the Commodity Exchange Act for five years. The act, which expires Sept. 30, sets standards for the Commodities Futures Trading Commission (CFTC), which, in turn, regulates U.S. futures trading.

The House Agriculture Committee on June 27 approved, by voice vote, a companion bill (HR 4541) after clarifying the definition of commercial participants in the trading of futures contracts and making other technical changes. The changes were contained in an en bloc amendment by Chairman Larry Combest, R-Texas, that was accepted by voice vote.

Lawmakers on both committees stressed the need to pass legislation this year to prevent U.S. commodities exchanges from losing business to foreign futures markets that trade over-the-counter (OTC) derivatives — financial products that are tied to an underlying asset.

"The time is ripe, and the world is passing us by," said Charles W. Stenholm of Texas, ranking Democrat on the House committee. "If parts of our financial industry have to wait another year for us to resolve this . . . parts of our financial industry will be gone."

While the overhaul effort has enthusiastic support on the agriculture panels, its prospects are less certain in other committees with jurisdiction over the issue. The House bill will be referred to the Commerce and the Banking and Financial Services committees, which have not yet scheduled hearings.

Combest said he would prefer giving the committees 30 days to take action, noting that the tight legislative calendar limits how much work can be accomplished before the end of the current session.

"They haven't been overly involved [in discussions]," Combest said, referring to the other House committees. "A 30-day referral . . . would enforce this in a timely fashion and still give them ample time."

The effort is more coordinated in the Senate, where the Agriculture and Banking, Housing and Urban Affairs committees held a joint hearing on futures and derivatives markets June 21.

However, Senate Agriculture Committee Chairman Richard G. Lugar, R-Ind., and Banking Chairman Phil Gramm, R-Texas, remain divided over some issues, such as whether the Securities and Exchange Commission (SEC) can regulate swaps of derivatives.

Gramm favors limiting the SEC's ability to claim jurisdiction over the market. The Senate bill leaves the issue unresolved and directs regulators to study it further, a situation Lugar said that Gramm did not completely agree with.

Both bills would lift an 18-year ban on the trading of futures contracts based on individual stocks. The potentially volatile investments have been the object of a long-running feud between the CFTC and the SEC over which is better equipped to police the market.

The SEC is opposed to lifting the ban without getting direct authority over the market, which had a worldwide value of $88.2 trillion at the end of 1999. The commission argues that the futures contracts should be legally treated like securities, offering more protection to small investors from fraud or market manipulation. The commodities commission argues that such criteria could result in overly burdensome regulation.

The Senate committee tried to address the issue in its legislation, allowing each agency to take its own enforcement action with regard to single-stock futures without having to get the other's permission.

Both the House and Senate bills would exempt OTC derivatives from federal regulation — a move that some lawmakers say will ease concerns in the financial industry about potential government control over what is now an unregulated market.

Derivatives traders worry that such a move could invalidate some existing OTC contracts and drive business away from the United States.

Another House Subcommittee OKs Rewrite of Commodities Law

JULY 22 — The House Commerce Finance Subcommittee gave voice-vote approval July 20 to a major rewrite of commodities laws that would overhaul the market for stock futures, derivatives and other complicated investments.

The legislation (HR 4541) would reauthorize the Commodities Exchange Act for five years. The act, which expires Sept. 30, sets standards for the Commodity Futures Trading Commission (CFTC). The measure still must weather revision by the House Commerce and Banking panels before it is ready for floor action. The House and Senate Agriculture Committees approved the measure the week of June 26.

"It is rare to see deliberation of a bill of such magnitude in such a tight time schedule," said Commerce Chairman Thomas J. Bliley Jr., R-Va., whose committee is expected to mark up the measure the week of July 24.

The bill would lift a ban against trading single-stock futures that has been the object of an 18-year spat between the CFTC and the Securities and Exchange Commission (SEC), which regulates securities, over how potentially volatile single-stock futures should be controlled. Such futures set a specific price at which holders must buy or sell an underlying asset based on a single stock.

Before the subcommittee approved the measure, it adopted by voice vote a bipartisan substitute amendment that would clarify the SEC's role in regulating single-stock futures. The provision would give the agency the power to:

- Monitor futures exchanges to guard against insider trading.
- Adopt margin requirements for single-stock futures that match those governing options.
- Require the National Futures Association, in consultation with the SEC, to develop suitability and sales practice rules for single-stock futures similar to those that govern equity exchanges.

The Finance subcommittee's race to move the measure prevented lawmakers from focusing on the issue of whether and how over-the-counter (OTC) derivatives should be regulated. The bills approved by the Senate and House Agriculture committees would exempt OTC derivatives from federal regulation, a provision Finance Chairman Michael G. Oxley, R-Ohio, said "can be improved further."

Commodities Exchange Bills Emerge From Two House Panels

JULY 29 — An accelerated effort to overhaul the nation's commodities laws cleared two more hurdles the week of July 24, as the House Banking and Financial Services and Commerce committees approved separate versions of legislation (HR 4541) to reauthorize the Commodity Exchange Act. The current authorization is due to expire Sept. 30.

Significant differences between the two bills, combined with changes each panel made to the language approved by the House Agriculture Committee on June 27, could cloud prospects for enactment of any measure this year.

The House Rules Committee will have to reconcile the three versions after Congress returns from its August recess. Even if the committee reaches consensus, the short legislative year and pending Senate consideration of a companion bill (S 2697) will make final passage difficult.

"Of all the laws [on] the books, the most out-of-step law in finance is the Commodity Exchange Act," said Banking Committee Chairman Jim Leach, R-Iowa. He predicted that lawmakers will have to accept what he terms an imperfect bill to pass legislation this year.

The bill would reauthorize the Commodity Exchange Act, which sets standards for the Commodities Futures Trading Commission (CFTC), the regulatory body that oversees the U.S. futures industry. It would also clarify rules for the trading of stock futures, derivatives and other complicated investments whose values are tied to an underlying asset. All three versions would lift an 18-year ban on trading futures contracts based on single stocks.

The changes made by the Banking and Commerce panels generally would give the Securities and Exchange Commission (SEC) more jurisdiction over the fast-growing derivatives market, particularly in regulating single-stock futures. Lawmakers say this will ensure consumer protection against fraud.

By contrast, the agriculture panel would give more power to the CFTC, which traditionally has regulated such agriculture-based products as contracts on pork bellies, sugar and coffee. The CFTC and the SEC have spent nearly two decades bickering over how to treat derivatives.

Complicating the debate, some Illinois lawmakers want provisions ensuring that large futures exchanges such as the Chicago Board of Trade and Chicago Mercantile Exchange would be allowed to trade single-stock futures.

"This will have a dramatic effect on the Chicago exchanges, which for generations provided hundreds of thousands of jobs and were a big help to commodities markets," said Jan Schakowsky, D-Ill., a member of the Banking Committee who represents the north side of Chicago and some suburban areas.

The Banking Committee approved its version by voice vote July 27 after accepting, by voice vote, a manager's amendment offered by Leach and ranking Democrat John J. LaFalce of New York. The amendment includes language declaring swaps — transactions where investors take opposing market positions based on derivatives — to be banking products. Rules for trading swaps would be developed by the Federal Reserve and Treasury Department. The legislation approved by the Agriculture panel would give the CFTC oversight of swaps trading.

Swaps are used by corporations and other large institutions as a hedge against interest rate swings and other market risks. If the Banking Committee-approved language becomes law, banks and other financial institutions could sell swaps to ordinary consumers.

The House Commerce Committee approved its changes to the reauthorization language July 26, accepting by voice vote an amendment in the nature of a substitute by John Shimkus, R-Ill.

His amendment would give the SEC the authority to regulate single-stock futures listed on futures and securities exchanges. The Agriculture Committee-approved version would give primary regulatory responsibility to the CFTC.

Lawmakers on the Commerce and Banking panels complained about the short time they had to consider the complicated legislation and said the Agriculture Committee measure did not contain enough consumer protections.

Commerce Committee Chairman Thomas J. Bliley Jr., R-Va., said the bill his committee reported was "significantly better than what came to us."

Officials, Industry Push Congress to Finish Rewriting Commodities Law

AUGUST 12 — Before he was elected to Congress in 1998, Rep. Patrick J. Toomey, R-Pa., spent seven years as an investment banker, trading futures contracts, swaps and other sophisticated, and often volatile, financial instruments. So the first-term lawmaker had a strong sense of déjà vu as he and colleagues on the Banking and Financial Services Committee marked up legislation the week of July 24 to rewrite the laws that govern how such investments — collectively known as derivatives — are traded.

"There it was, all over again," Toomey said in an Aug. 7 interview. "Most people understand stocks and bonds, but they know less about these instruments, which are an equally important aspect of capital markets. It's a vital industry that . . . is not well understood."

Toomey is likely to find himself explaining the world of derivatives to colleagues in the coming weeks. Reauthorization of the Commodity Exchange Act has evolved into one of the most complicated and heavily lobbied issues Congress is facing this year, with securities dealers, investment bankers, commodities exchanges, the Treasury Department and Federal Reserve Chairman Alan Greenspan all seeking specific changes.

The law dates to 1936, when it was enacted to address market manipulation that led to a grain price collapse. It has been rewritten numerous times since, as the agricultural futures market evolved into a home for increasingly sophisticated financial instruments. The last major rewrite (PL 102-546) was in 1992 and involved nearly four years of debate before it was passed. The current version of the act expires Sept. 30. *(1992 Almanac, p. 127)*

Reauthorization involves so many overlapping jurisdictions that the House bill (HR 4541) was referred to the Agriculture, Commerce and Banking committees, which approved three considerably different versions of the legislation before the August recess.

The House Rules Committee and leadership will have to reconcile the bills quickly after lawmakers return if the legislation is to have any chance of passing this session. The Senate Agriculture Committee approved a companion bill (S 2697) on June 29, but more changes are likely when Phil Gramm, R-Texas, chairman of the Banking, Housing and Urban Affairs Committee weighs in.

"There's still obviously a lot of heavy lifting to be done," John Vogt, executive vice president of the Bond Market Association, told reporters Aug. 9. "It's easy to be pessimistic [about passage] because it's a comprehensive rewrite in an election year . . . and an incredibly arcane issue. But stranger things have happened."

The bond association is involved because bill language may clarify how derivatives based on bonds are treated under securities and futures laws.

The global market in derivatives — financial contracts tied to an underlying asset — has an estimated face value of $88.2 trillion and grew at an 8 percent clip during the second half of 1999, according to the most recent figures compiled by the Bank for International Settlements in Basle, Switzerland.

Institutions with a stake in the outcome read like a who's who of financial powerhouses and have contributed at least $6.7 million to federal candidates, the Democratic and Republican parties and lawmakers' political action committees during the current campaign cycle, according to Federal Election Commission data released Aug. 1. Of that amount, $3.33 million went to congressional candidates.

The players include the politically influential Chicago Board of Trade and Chicago Mercantile Exchange, the Chicago Board Options Exchange and the New York Stock Exchange as well as numerous investment banks and securities dealers.

"Reauthorizing the act would be the best thing that happened to Chicago since Sammy Sosa came to the Cubs [in 1994]," Sen. Peter G. Fitzgerald, R-Ill., said in a July 25 interview, noting that 200,000 Chicago-area jobs depend on the futures industry. "Those attempting to derail the legislation do a disservice to investors and the nation's financial exchanges."

The high stakes surrounding the legislation, combined with the multiple venues for debate, have led to some unusual lobbying tactics. A group of investment banks, said to include Merrill Lynch & Co., Citigroup and Credit Suisse First Boston Grp., hired several lobbyists who usually represent growers and processors of sugar, corn and other commodities to help press their case for regulatory relief before the House and Senate Agriculture committees.

The House panel is a particular focus because Thomas W. Ewing, R-Ill., who wrote most of the committee's draft reauthorization bill, is a confidant of Speaker J. Dennis Hastert, R-Ill., with a friendship that dates to their days in the Illinois legislature. "The Speaker is paying attention [to the reauthorization] in a way that he may not have otherwise," said one financial industry lobbyist.

Deliberations have an added sense of urgency because of the tight congressional calendar and the strong urging of Greenspan and Treasury Secretary Lawrence H. Summers to deliver legislation to President Clinton before the end of his term. Failure to do so would return the various players to the starting line with a new administration next year.

Greenspan and Summers believe Congress must provide legal backing to all the customized derivatives that have been developed in recent years. If lawmakers do not act, the two fear business will shift from the United States to such foreign financial exchanges as Eurex, a fast-growing electronic market created in Germany two years ago that already is the world's largest derivatives exchange.

Establishing a legal framework has been complicated by a long-running dispute between the Securities and Exchange Commission (SEC), which regulates securities products, and the Commodities Futures Trading Commission (CFTC), which is authorized by the Commodity Exchange Act and oversees the futures markets.

To satisfy the various financial and political players, any bill that emerges this year will probably have to clarify which derivatives products are subject to regulation and lift a prohibition on writing futures contracts based on individual stocks and bonds.

The ban on so-called single-stock futures was written into the 1982 reauthorization of the Commodity Exchange Act (PL 97-444) because the SEC and CFTC could not solve their jurisdictional spat. The law only allows futures contracts on such broad market indices as the Standard & Poor's 500 stock index. *(1982 Almanac, p. 365)*

The task of clearing up rules for derivatives trading presents vexing problems legislatively because of the complex nature of the financial instruments involved.

For example, futures contracts were originally created to ensure that farmers and food processors received a given price on a given date for delivery of a commodity. In recent years, they have become highly sophisticated investments tied to such financial yardsticks as stock indices, interest rates and currency exchange rates. Futures contracts are currently traded only on commodity exchanges regulated by the CFTC.

Another sophisticated financial instrument — currently unregulated — is the swap, a privately negotiated contract sometimes referred to as an over-the-counter, or OTC, derivative. Large institutions typically use swaps to hedge against market risk. A corporation might use a swap with a bank to lock in the interest rate on a loan, much the way homeowners lock in rates on their mortgages.

Current law treats interest-rate swaps as legal because the CFTC exempts them from oversight. If the agency were to reverse its position, swaps contracts would become regulated — and thus invalid. Participants could walk away from billions of dollars in commitments, creating the potential for a market meltdown.

Financial institutions also have worked around the ban on trading single-stock futures by developing equity swaps tied to the price of single shares of a company. These contracts work the same way as a futures contract but are not legally defined as a future.

All that leaves Congress pondering whether it should clarify what a future is. So far, most lawmakers have sidestepped the issue by refusing to include such definitions in any of their reauthorization bills. Investment banks that deal heavily in swaps, particularly J.P. Morgan & Co., are pressing for legislation and may have a sympathetic ear in Gramm, who is insisting on legal certainty for OTC derivatives. He also would end the ban on single-stock futures but limit the SEC's jurisdiction over them.

Too Much Tinkering?

All sides worry that excessive tinkering with the bill's language could derail the reauthorization. Toomey, the former derivatives trader, offered an amendment during markup by the House Banking Committee on July 27 that would define futures as forward contracts for the sale of commodities under sole jurisdiction of the CFTC. He withdrew it after Chairman Jim Leach, R-Iowa, said the amendment would make the panel's bill diverge too far from versions approved by the Agriculture and Commerce committees.

The Banking Committee nonetheless added a new twist to the legal certainty debate when it adopted, by voice vote, a manager's amendment by Leach and ranking Democrat John J. LaFalce of New York declaring swaps to be banking products that could be traded subject to rules developed by the Federal Reserve and the Treasury Department. That upset a consensus among the House Agriculture and Commerce panels and the Senate Agriculture Committee that swaps would remain subject to CFTC jurisdiction but exempt from regulation.

"The CFTC is very appropriate for regulating exchanges, but not very appropriate as a consumer product regulator," Leach said July 27.

The Political Debate

While the legal certainty debate hinges on semantic distinctions and technicalities in existing laws, lifting the ban on trading single-stock futures is more of a political fight, pitting Chicago-area lawmakers against securities exchanges, most notably the New York Stock Exchange, some broker-dealers, the Chicago Board Options Exchange and the SEC.

The Chicago commodity exchanges, worried about business slipping to overseas exchanges, have joined forces in lobbying to lift the ban and contributed $863,250 to congressional and presidential candidates, parties and leadership PACs during the current election cycle.

Fitzgerald and the Chicago commodity exchanges argue that the trading of single-stock futures would allow investors to hedge against price declines in stocks they own by purchasing a futures contract on the issues. The securities industry, however, worries that single-stock futures would siphon business away from its exchanges and inject a new element of volatility into the markets.

The industry and such supporters as Sen. Charles E. Schumer, D-N.Y., a member of the Banking panel, point out that the legislation, as written, would maintain different requirements for margins — the deposits investors have to put up when buying or selling securities or contracts.

"As long as there's a level and rigorous playing field, we can go with it," Schumer said in a July 25 interview. "Those who want single-stock futures should agree that there's got to be that playing field. So far, they have not, and that's holding it up."

The securities industry also has been donating heavily to federal candidates and PACs to get its point across. The Securities Industry Association contributed $487,931 during the current campaign cycle, while the Chicago Board Options Exchange gave $221,500 and the New York Stock Exchange gave $162,186.

The industry's arguments are reinforced by the SEC, which wants legislation giving it a strong hand to police fraud and manipulation in any new market for single-stock futures. However, it is again bumping heads with the CFTC, which wants primary jurisdiction over the new instruments because they are futures. Having three House bills complicates the issue: The Agriculture Committee would give the CFTC primary responsibility for policing trading of the new securities, while the Commerce and Banking committees would give the SEC more jurisdiction.

At the urging of Treasury Department officials and others, the SEC and CFTC have continued to hold discussions in the hope of finding a compromise. Doing so would relieve lawmakers of having to referee their turf battle and enhance the chances of passing comprehensive legislation this year.

If the two agencies cannot agree, or if lawmakers decide not to lift the ban on single-stock futures, the Chicago exchanges could bring pressure on lawmakers to kill the legal certainty provisions in the bill. Sources familiar with the issue say the Chicago exchanges might settle for a compromise that would allow them to trade futures on small numbers of stocks in a particular industry.

Lawmakers also could decide to confer legal certainty on OTC derivatives without addressing single-stock futures, but they appear reluctant to uncouple the issues just yet. Senate Agriculture Committee Chairman Richard G. Lugar, R-Ind., said in a July 25 interview that he hoped the SEC and CFTC could reach an agreement on single-stock futures, eliminating the need to narrow the bill.

CFTC, SEC Agree To Share Oversight

SEPTEMBER 16 — The push to pass sweeping legislation overhauling the nation's commodities laws gained momentum Sept. 14 when the Commodity Futures Trading Commission (CFTC) and Securities and Exchange Commission (SEC) announced they had settled a long-running feud over how to trade futures contracts based on individual stocks.

The two regulatory agencies agreed to share oversight of the products, with the CFTC given primary jurisdiction. The SEC would be responsible for policing security brokers and markets.

The issue threatened to hold up broader deliberations over House and Senate bills (HR 4541, S 2697) that would reauthorize the Commodity Exchange Act and devise ground rules for the trading of complicated financial instruments known as derivatives.

Senate Agriculture Committee Chairman Richard G. Lugar, R-Ind., said the agreement increased the likelihood of passage of legislation this year, but major hurdles remain, including clarifying the legal status of a variety of derivative known as a swap. Commodities exchanges say failure to clear up this issue will cause them to lose more business to foreign financial exchanges.

House Passes Bill To Reauthorize Commodity Exchange Act

OCTOBER 21 — The House breathed new life into an effort to rewrite laws that govern commodities markets, overwhelmingly passing legislation (HR 4541) to reauthorize the Commodity Exchange Act.

The 377-4 vote on Oct. 19 puts pressure on the Senate to enact its version of a reauthorization bill before the end of the session. Prospects in that chamber remain uncertain due to the insistence of Banking, Housing and Urban Affairs Committee Chairman Phil Gramm, R-Texas., on language that would exempt from regulation a category of privately negotiated investments known as swaps — used by big corporations and financial institutions to hedge market risk. *(Vote 540, p. H-172)*

"It's important that we sent a strong signal to the Senate because they, as a body, haven't focused on the issue as much," Thomas W. Ewing, R-Ill., author of the reauthorization bill, said in an Oct. 19 interview. "Sen. Gramm promised to look at the bill closely, and there still is time."

Other lawmakers are not so sure.

"It is dubious whether Congress can produce a public law this session," John J. LaFalce of New York, ranking Democrat on the House Banking and Financial Services Committee, said during floor debate. "Even if we cannot, passage of today's bill will at least set down a marker for . . . next year."

Gramm, speaking to reporters Oct. 18, repeated his concerns about provisions in the House bill dealing with "legal certainty" of swaps, but said he would work hard to pass legislation this year. If the Senate passes a significantly different version of the bill, however, that would leave little time for a conference to iron out differences and send a final version to President Clinton before adjournment.

New Ground Rules

The complicated legislation would set new ground rules for the trading of financial derivatives — a variety of investment that is tied to an underlying asset. Once used by farmers to lock in prices for corn, sugar and other commodities, derivatives have evolved into sophisticated financial instruments tied to currency exchange rates, interest rates and other economic benchmarks. The global market in derivatives was estimated at $88.2 trillion in 1999, according to the Bank for International Settlements in Switzerland.

House passage came after weeks of intense negotiations between the Agriculture, Banking and Financial Services and Commerce committees, which share jurisdiction over the issue. Differences in the way derivatives are taxed also required the participation of the Ways and Means Committee to ensure that no market had a competitive trading advantage. Most of the tax questions concerned options — the right to buy or sell shares of stock within a stated period at a predetermined price — and futures, which are forward contracts based on stocks and bonds.

Under the bill, forward contracts traded on exchanges such as the Chicago Mercantile Exchange and Chicago Board of Trade would continue to be regulated by the Commodity Futures Trading Commission (CFTC).

The bill also would lift an 18-year ban on trading futures contracts based on single stocks. The CFTC and Securities and Exchange Commission (SEC) would share oversight because the products share characteristics of both stocks and futures. The language allowing single-stock futures was a priority of the major Chicago commodities exchanges, which complained they are losing business to European rivals. The ban was enacted in 1982 after the CFTC and SEC could not agree on how to regulate the market.

Stock exchanges that opposed single-stock futures over fears they would lose business softened their stance after Ways and Means devised language directing the U.S. Treasury to issue regulations spelling out the kinds of profits to be treated as long-term capital gains, which are taxed at a lower rate.

Negotiators on the three House committees with jurisdiction over the bill also ironed out disputes dealing with differences over margin requirements — the amount of money investors must put down to purchase a stock or option.

"While the tax issue was perhaps the most significant of our outstanding concerns with the bill, there are other issues which we believe require further attention," a group of stock exchanges wrote to House Speaker J. Dennis Hastert, R-Ill., prior to the vote. "Despite these enumerated concerns . . . we do not object to passage [of the bill] as drafted."

The bill would exempt swaps from oversight, addressing fears that the government might choose to regulate them. Such a move would throw their legal status into question, which could allow participants to walk away from billions of dollars in commitments and create the potential for a market meltdown.

Industry Seeks Deal To Keep Commodities Law Rewrite Alive

DECEMBER 9 — A deal to revive legislation (HR 4541) that would rewrite the nation's commodities laws appeared to be in the works after meetings the week of Dec. 4 between representatives of Chicago's big commodities exchanges and the senator who has been blocking the bill. *(See omnibus appropriations, p. 2-3)*

Representatives of the Chicago Board of Trade and Chicago Mercantile Exchange reached tentative agreement with Sen. Phil Gramm, R-Texas, chairman of the Banking, Housing and Urban Affairs Committee, on compromise language that would reauthorize the Commodity Exchange Act and set new ground rules for the trading of a complicated class of investments known as derivatives, congressional aides said.

The language was being reviewed by aides to the House Agriculture, Banking and Commerce committees, each of which had a hand in drafting the original bill, as well as by the Treasury Department. If there are no objections, the language could be attached to the still-pending fiscal 2001 appropriations bill (HR 4577) for the departments of Labor-HHS-Education.

The original commodities bill passed the House, 377-4, on Oct. 19.

However, Gramm has blocked the measure because of concerns over how it would affect the legal status of a type of privately negotiated contracts known as swaps. Swaps, which are used by large corporations to hedge market risk, account for a global market worth nearly $90 trillion, according to the Bank for International Settlements in Switzerland.

The legislation would keep swaps unregulated. It would also give the commodities exchanges a boost by authorizing the trading of futures contracts based on single stocks.

Trading such investments on U.S. exchanges is currently prohibited because the Commodity Futures Trading Commission and the Securities and Exchange Commission previously were unable to agree on who would regulate the instruments. The legislation would give both agencies regulatory oversight. ◆

Chapter 6

BUDGET

Delivering a Budget Without Breaking It: Clinton's Numbers Look Suprisingly Similar to the GOP's

FEBRUARY 12 — Republicans had tried to grab the voters' attention in this year's budget debate even before Congress reconvened last month, calling for more domestic spending for education and health care. Now President Clinton has responded, unveiling a fiscal 2001 budget that dares the GOP to make good on its latest promises. As a result, the president now has a platform that could make him a surprisingly influential lame duck.

The $1.84 trillion budget that Clinton unveiled on Feb. 7 embodies the clichéd response of Clint Eastwood's "Dirty Harry" character: "Go ahead, make my day." It dares the GOP to deliver the largest increase in discretionary spending in the Education Department's history, to create a new entitlement in the form of prescription drug coverage for Medicare beneficiaries, and to give up on the appropriations caps that the party struggled and failed to live within last year. Administration officials also chided Congress to budget "more realistically" this year, even though the White House itself participated in the gimmickry that stalled — but ultimately greased — the fiscal 2000 spending battles.

Republicans have long complained that Clinton has a penchant for touting GOP touchstones and making them his own. And indeed, Clinton this year has appropriated the "lockbox" terminology that the GOP coined last year as a mantra for fiscal discipline: The budget proposes to prohibit the use of Social Security surpluses for boosting domestic spending or deeply cutting taxes; at the same time, it heeds the GOP call for some tax cuts, including those to limit the "marriage penalty" quirk in the income tax code and to spur investments in areas left behind during the economic boom.

Republicans were trying to outflank the president even before the budget books were delivered to the Capitol. With potentially huge federal surpluses on the horizon for the coming decade and party leaders nervous about retaining control of Congress this fall, GOP leaders have apparently decided that the electorate is no longer in the mood to hear talk about cutting spending and curtailing the federal government's role — the very talk that helped to propel the Republican takeover of Congress five years ago.

Instead, the Republicans borrowed a page from their nemesis and promised a bit of everything, and in some cases a bit more than Clinton. When the president signaled that he would call for an increase in defense spending, the Republican hierarchy responded by promising to send the Pentagon even more. And before Clinton unveiled his laundry list of proposals in his final State of the Union address Jan. 27, the GOP had professed a new love for more education spending, improved access to medical care and other enhancements to the federal social safety net.

But the difficulty of trying to seize control of the spending agenda was illustrated Feb. 7, when Senate Budget Committee Chairman Pete V. Domenici, R-N.M., appeared for his annual news conference to rail against the levels of spending and the number of new programs in the Clinton budget. "We think we'll put in more money than the president is going to put in education," he boasted at one point.

A few minutes later, after a senior aide whispered in Domenici's ear that the Clinton budget — at least by one accounting — would increase discretionary education spending by 37 percent, the senator returned to the microphone to back away from his earlier claim. "Now this is some kind of game. There can't be any question about it. Maybe it's a mistake. I mean, it sounds so absolutely wild," Domenici said of the president's line items.

Arguing Over the Details

The GOP could find it difficult to out-maneuver the White House on domestic issues. Still, Republicans are eager to avoid being labeled "the anti-environment, anti-education, anti-family party," said Robert D. Reischauer, president of the Urban Institute and a former director of the Congressional Budget Office (CBO).

"This is a president who will have influence up until inauguration day simply because of his energy and his ability to command the media," he said in a Feb. 11 interview.

For all the one-upmanship on the details, the president and the majority in Congress are unusually close on a broad array of the biggest budgetary issues — perhaps the closest they have been since the Republicans took control of Congress after the 1994 election. While they disagree on the details, the president and most congressional Republicans agree that:

- The law's caps on discretionary spending for the next two years should be increased.
- All excess revenue being collected in the Social Security trust funds should be used to pay down the publicly held federal debt.
- Some of the "on-budget" surplus should be used to fund a new drug benefit under Medicare, the federal medical insurance for the elderly and disabled.
- The marriage penalty should be limited.

One might think that Clinton and Congress could wrap up their work in a few months and get an early start on the campaign trail. But elections are all about staking out positions, defining differences and attacking the opponent, so it is the squabbling over the details that will keep this year lively — and may yet assure that no deals on any of the big issues are hatched.

At a speech unveiling his budget, Clinton poked fun at his own reputa-

The President's Budget Totals

(fiscal years, in billions of dollars)

	Estimated 2000	2001	2002	Proposed 2003	2004	2005
Budget authority	$1,801.1	$1,885.4	$1,926.8	$1,987.9	$2,064.9	$2,144.5
Outlays	1,789.6	1,835.0	1,895.3	1,962.9	2,041.1	2,125.5
Revenues	1,956.3	2,019.0	2,081.2	2,147.5	2,236.1	2,340.9
Off-budget surplus	148.0	175.0	185.0	184.0	195.0	214.0
On-budget surplus	19.0	9.0	1.0	*	*	2.0

** Less than $500 million*

SOURCE: Office of Management and Budget

tion as a "policy wonk," but he also stressed repeatedly that the details matter, and he urged his staff to fight for them. "Specific decisions do matter, and that's what this budget is all about," he said.

Republicans are harping on the spending levels and the number of new initiatives in the Clinton budget, but they have yet to offer any specific counterproposals. Despite their goal of getting their budgetary work done early — the end of March is their self-imposed deadline for completion of a fiscal 2001 budget resolution — GOP senators emerged from a caucus Feb. 9 saying that they were not close to settling on overall spending targets yet. No firm numbers are likely to emerge from Republicans before the week of Feb. 28, the next time the Senate and House will be in session after back-to-back recesses.

The biggest partisan fight so far is over the size and timing of tax cuts. Republicans won House passage Feb. 10 of their legislation (HR 6) to reduce the marriage penalty by $182 billion in the next decade with the help of almost one-quarter of the chamber's Democrats. But by that time, House Democratic leaders and the White House had united behind a new demand: that a framework be established to pay down the debt, shore up the Social Security retirement income system and bolster Medicare before any tax cut is enacted.

Republicans, meanwhile, pressed ahead with their plans to move a series of additional bills embodying deeper tax cuts than Clinton wants, and they complained about the tax increases in Clinton's plan. The president called for cutting taxes by $350.3 billion over 10 years, with his plan for fixing the marriage penalty accounting for $44 billion of that. Another $40 billion would be used to adjust the alternative minimum tax and reduce its impact on middle-income families with children. And a series of offsetting tax increases and closures in loopholes would create a net 10-year tax cut of $168.6 billion.

Senate Minority Leader Tom Daschle, D-S.D., said Feb. 9 that unless Republicans dramatically reduce the size of their marriage penalty tax cut, Senate Democrats will insist on attaching a Medicare prescription drug benefit to the measure. "We support addressing the marriage penalty," he told reporters, but the GOP bill would cost "vastly more money, 10 times more money, than we should be spending, perhaps."

Even if Democrats follow through on Daschle's threat, however, that by itself would not necessarily create gridlock for the year, because Republicans embraced the idea of a Medicare prescription benefit even before Clinton outlined it.

However, in perhaps the best example of his "right back at you" approach to GOP attempts to take control of the budget agenda, Clinton threw a late-breaking curve into his prescription drug proposal: a $35 billion program to cover "catastrophic drug costs" incurred by Medicare recipients.

"This is something that I did not talk about in the State of the Union, because I did not know for sure that we would have this money," he said in explaining the unexpected addition.

The Office of Management and Budget (OMB) projected the catastrophic drug benefit would cost $35 billion over five years, starting in fiscal 2006. The administration has provided few specifics on how the program would work. In fact, it is not actually listed as an expenditure in the budget, but rather is a "memorandum" — in essence no more than a suggestion for future presidents. The money actually is counted for debt reduction in the budget.

Allocating the Surplus

The unveiling of the budget signaled the start of the eighth and final fiscal policy confrontation between Clinton and Congress, and allowed the president to make one final stab at putting his imprint on government spending priorities — this time by dedicating billions to a range of educational environmental, scientific, foreign policy and military endeavors.

"This budget, in short, makes really strong and significant steps toward achieving the great goals that I believe America should pursue in this new century," Clinton said.

For a second straight year, OMB published its annual collection of budget books with stark black and white covers, a reminder that both proposals conclude with "black ink" on the bottom lines. Overall, the new budget proposes spending only 91 percent of the $2.02 trillion in anticipated fiscal 2001 revenue, yielding a surplus of $184 billion. *(Chart, this page)*

Republicans and Democrats are jockeying furiously to position themselves as saviors of the budget surpluses, even though both parties are staking out positions that eat into them. Administration aides and congressional Democrats relentlessly defended the president's spending proposals, while Republicans demanded bigger tax cuts.

At a Feb. 8 House Budget Committee hearing, Christopher Shays, R-Conn., asked OMB Director Jack Lew how many new programs were in the administration's budget. "I haven't done a count," Lew replied.

Chairman John R. Kasich, R-Ohio, also blasted the administration for failing to propose any long-term changes to Social Security and Medicare that would limit the costs of those programs in order to guarantee their long-term solvency. Kasich pointedly asked Lew why the administration had not moved to spend any of its final-year political capital to promote such politically risky limitations on those entitlements. "How could you punt on Social Security and Medicare?" asked Kasich, who is retiring this fall at the end of his sixth and final year at the helm of the panel. "Every day you wait, you get yourself deeper and deeper in a hole."

Lew responded that the administration had proposed structural changes and savings initiatives that — combined with debt reduction — would extend the solvency of Medicare to 2025, a decade beyond its current estimated life span. The budget calls for $62.1 billion in savings over 10 years by reducing improper Medicare payments and other measures.

At the same time, it proposes spending $168.2 billion on the drug benefit — beneficiaries would split the cost of prescriptions with the government, up to a limit of $5,000 when the program is fully phased in by 2009 — and allowing displaced workers between the ages of 55 and 65 to buy into Medicare.

Semantics and Scenarios

Republicans picked both policy and semantic fights with the administration officials who flocked to Capitol Hill to explain and defend the budget.

At the House Budget hearing, they hammered Lew for refusing to describe an administration proposal on tobacco excise taxes — one that is certain to be ignored from now on — as a tax increase. The administration proposed generating $65.9 billion in additional revenue over 10 years from "a youth smoking assessment on tobacco manufacturers," in lay terms a 30-cent increase in the price of a pack of cigarettes. Lew insisted that this was not a tax increase, but a penalty on companies that market to underage smokers and a device to deter young people from buying cigarettes.

Overall, administration officials maintained that they had drafted a fiscally cautious budget that would restrain spending even more than Congress has in recent years. The president proposed increasing discretionary spending by 3.9 percent above the cur-

Clinton's Tax Proposals

FEBRUARY 12 — President Clinton's fiscal 2001 budget details proposals that would cut taxes by $350.3 billion in the next 10 years. But he would partially offset that lost revenue with $95.9 billion generated by shutting down corporate tax shelters and increasing taxes on life insurance, and by raising $85.8 billion with miscellaneous tax increases. Among his proposals are those to:

- **Retirement savings.** Allow employers or financial institutions that matched a taxpayer's contribution to a 401(k) or Individual Retirement Account to receive an equal credit on their taxes, within limits. **Cost: $77.3 billion.**

- **Family incentives.** Limit the "marriage penalty" by making the standard deduction for two-earner couples who file jointly twice what it is for single filers, and by increasing the standard deduction for married couples by $500 and for singles by $250; increase, expand and make refundable the child and dependent care tax credit, allowing taxpayers with one dependent a credit as high as $1,200, up from $720, and with two or more dependents a credit as high as $2,400, up from $1,440. **Cost: $75.7 billion.**

- **Poverty relief.** Increase and expand the earned-income tax credit, which enhances tax refunds for the working poor; increase the low-income housing tax credit, which encourages construction of affordable housing; create a "new markets" tax credit for investments in low-income rural and urban communities; create a trio of tax credits for businesses that increase the availability of computers and computer literacy in low-income areas. **Cost: $45 billion.**

- **Health care.** Provide a $3,000 tax credit for those who are disabled or have other long-term care needs, or who care for a dependent with such needs; allow a credit worth 25 percent of a taxpayer's costs for health insurance premiums under COBRA, a post-employment health plan, and for buying into Medicare. **Cost: $41.5 billion.**

- **Education.** Increase and expand the "lifetime learning" tax credit, allowing a credit of as much as 28 percent, up from 20 percent, for tuition and other college expenses; continue to cap eligible expenses — at $5,000 until 2002, then $10,000 — but make people with higher incomes eligible; allow deductions of college expenses from taxes, rather than permit a claim for credit, which would help non-itemizers; create new bonds to modernize public schools; expand and extend qualified zone academy bonds, which finance school construction and equipment. **Cost: $39.3 billion.**

- **Miscellaneous cuts.** Allow those subject to the alternative minimum tax to claim the standard deduction and personal exemptions; allow non-itemizers to deduct 50 percent of their charitable contributions in excess of $1,000 for singles and $2,000 for joint filers; provide several tax credits for using energy-efficient technology and alternative energy sources. **Cost: $72.1 billion.**

- **Corporate loopholes.** Establish new disclosure requirements for corporate tax transactions that might indicate sheltering; increase penalties to 40 percent from 20 percent for substantially understating corporate taxes related to shelters; make more parties subject to tax consequences if a corporate tax shelter proves illegal; increase taxes on corporate life insurance. **Revenue: $95.9 billion.**

- **Miscellaneous increases.** Raise excise taxes on all tobacco, including an increase to 64 cents from 34 cents on each pack of 20 cigarettes; reinstate excise taxes on crude oil, petroleum products and hazardous chemicals to replenish the superfund trust fund. **Revenue: $85.8 billion.**

rent level — which would be slightly more than 1 percentage point above the expected rate of inflation. The fiscal 1999 appropriations laws raised discretionary spending by 7 percent above fiscal 1998 levels; the fiscal 2000 laws raised the figure another 3.5 percent.

By tying growth in discretionary spending to the expected pace of inflation, the administration proposed raising the caps on statutory spending enacted in the 1997 budget-balancing law (PL 105-33) from $542 billion to $614.3 billion in budget authority in fiscal 2001, and from $551.1 billion to $625.5 billion in fiscal 2002. There are no caps written into law after the end of fiscal 2002.

"What we've proposed is to put in place a new set of limits that Congress and we can work with, and that can be enforceable over 10 years," Lew said.

The administration expects that such a change in those spending limits is politically plausible because the projection for cumulative black ink after a decade — the sum of each year's on-budget and Social Security surpluses — will be $2.9 trillion if current services are maintained by allowing programs to grow with modest inflation. Enacting Clinton's entire budget would limit that unified cumulative surplus to $2.5 trillion, OMB calculates.

Those projections are close to those released last month by the Congressional Budget Office. Assuming that discretionary spending grows with inflation, CBO forecast a $3.15 trillion surplus by 2010, with just $860 billion on-budget and the rest in the Social Security trust fund. The comparable OMB projection comes up with a $746 billion on-budget cumulative surplus by 2010. The agencies based their projections on similar economic assumptions.

CBO also said that a 10-year cumulative surplus of $4.2 trillion is conceivable, but only if the budget caps hold through fiscal 2002 or else discretionary spending is frozen at this year's level, either of which would require program cuts.

"We should be wary of a new rosy scenario . . . in which people pretend there's over a trillion dollars larger surplus — not by inflating the growth numbers but by assuming completely unimaginable and unrealistic cuts in domestic programs from education to veterans to agriculture," Gene Sperling, chairman of the president's National Economic Council, told reporters Feb. 7. "If you're assuming a $1.9 trillion [on-budget] surplus based on the assumption that you're going to cut 30 or 40 or 50 percent of key programs in the future, that is unrealistic, and that essentially creates a rosy scenario surplus that we should reject."

Lew said: "If you start with realistic, honest numbers and make the tough decisions within that framework, we can get to paying off the debt by 2013. But we can't pretend. We can't go to numbers that no one really believes."

Republicans and Democrats generally agree that last year's budget made a mockery of the spending caps by, for example, declaring the funds needed to conduct the census an "emergency" exempt from being counted toward the limit. CBO pegged the excess for this year at more than $30 billion.

"Starting work on this year's budget was an extraordinarily complicated task because it took us several weeks to figure where things ended up last year," Lew said. "Budgets had reached a level of complexity that taxed even the most technically expert. . . . We try to put all the spending back where it belongs . . . so that we've reversed and corrected the gimmicks that, frankly, made the budget impossible to understand."

The budget was accompanied by a $4.4 billion request for supplemental spending for this fiscal year, which ends Sept. 30, primarily for peacekeeping. The major elements in the package had been announced in advance, and the proposal stirred minimal reaction at the Capitol.

Administration's View Is Slightly More Positive

FEBRUARY 12 — Like virtually everyone else, White House forecasters have consistently underestimated the recently sizzling performance of the economy. But now, with the economy growing by more than 4 percent in each of the previous four years, President Clinton's economic team has become ever-so-slightly more optimistic.

While drafting the administration's budget proposal for fiscal 2001, Clinton advisers assumed slightly less vigorous growth of the gross domestic product (GDP), continued low inflation, continued low unemployment and stable interest rates — in short, a nearly perfect economy. In earlier times, such a prognostication might have been attacked with the label of "rosy scenario," but the economy has bested the consensus expectations of analysts throughout Clinton's time in office.)

In fact, previously cautious economic projections by both the White House Office of Management and Budget (OMB) and the Congressional Budget Office (CBO) are the principal reason that the surplus projections from both agencies have been skyrocketing.

Now, OMB projects that the economy will grow 2.9 percent in fiscal 2000 and another 2.6 percent in fiscal 2001, then hover between 2.5 and 3.0 percent a year during the rest of the decade. This is an especially benign rendering of what, in economics parlance, could become a "soft landing," a gradual slowing of the economy without a slide into recession.

Those predictions are for more robust growth than was foreseen in prior Clinton budgets, which had typically forecast near-term growth in the GDP — the sum of the value of all the goods and services produced by the U.S. economy — at about 2 percent a year. Long-term forecasts are educated guesses at best, but the upward revision appears to reflect growing faith that the economy's remarkable run will have lasting effects, even after it inevitably slows. Big increases in productivity and stunning advances in communications and information technology have fostered a "new economy" that will exhibit better long-term growth than had been believed possible, some government economists say.

As the president's fiscal 2001 budget was unveiled Feb. 7, Martin N. Baily, chairman of Clinton's Council of Economic Advisers, told reporters that while the economy could yet again exceed expectations, it would be prudent to err on the low side. "The administration's economic team does not believe that real GDP growth of just under 3 percent a year going for-

Economy's Effect on the Budget

(fiscal years, in billions of dollars)

	2000	2001	2002	2003	2004	2005
Previous Economic Forecast						
Receipts	$1,899.3	$1,947.5	$2,004.1	$2,076.2	$2,166.4	$2,259.3
Outlays	1,793.6	1,835.7	1,893.1	1,960.3	2,041.3	2,128.8
Surplus	105.7	111.8	111.0	116.0	125.1	130.5
Changes Due to New Economic Assumptions						
Receipts	$57.0	$71.5	$77.1	$71.3	$69.7	$81.6
Outlays						
Inflation	−1.8	−0.9	0.3	2.0	3.7	5.8
Unemployment	−7.8	−7.7	−3.5	−0.7	−0.9	−1.1
Interest rates	6.9	12.2	13.2	12.5	11.5	9.9
Reduced borrowing	−1.4	−4.4	−7.8	−11.2	−14.4	−17.9
Increase in surplus	61.0	72.2	74.9	68.7	69.9	85.0
Revised Economic Forecast						
Receipts	$1,956.3	$2,019.0	$2,081.2	$2,147.5	$2,236.1	$2,340.9
Outlays	1,789.6	1,835.0	1,895.3	1,962.9	2,041.1	2,125.5
Surplus	166.7	184.0	185.9	184.6	195.0	215.4

This table shows the effects of changed economic assumptions between President Clinton's fiscal 2000 and fiscal 2001 budget requests. Some numbers may not add due to rounding.

The changes in economic assumptions from year to year are primarily due to more favorable results in fiscal 1999 and the first part of fiscal 2000 than anticipated; economic growth was stronger, and inflation and unemployment were lower. As a result, the annual averages for fiscal 2000 for unemployment and inflation have been reduced slightly. Interest rates are again assumed to decline in the long run, but the decline is smaller in percentage terms because the surplus has increased so much faster than expected.

The greatest of the net effects of these modifications is higher receipts from 2000-2005 due to higher projected taxable incomes. In all years through 2005, there are higher outlays for interest as a result of the expected increases in interest rates, plus higher outlays for cost of living adjustments for most federal programs due to higher rates of inflation.

SOURCE: President's fiscal 2001 budget

ward is necessarily the best that this economy can do," he said.

"Growth could indeed be stronger than we are projecting," Baily said, and the budget's economic assumptions are "a realistic — maybe even a little conservative — view of the future, one appropriate for budget analysis."

While the White House and CBO have the same forecast for growth this year, CBO takes a slightly more optimistic view of the next three years. One widely cited consensus view of private economists, that of Aspen Publishers' "Blue Chip" group, is different: 3.6 percent growth this year dipping to 3.0 percent next year.

The chief reason for the optimistic forecasts is that worker productivity has increased in recent years, approaching 3 percent annually, roughly double the levels of the prior two decades. The productivity gain is a major reason the economy has grown so much without triggering inflation. Also, more people than expected have joined the work force.

"What we've seen by CBO and the administration and among private-sector forecasts is a gradual acceptance of higher productivity growth in the future," said Robert D. Reischauer, a former CBO director who is president of the Urban Institute, a nonpartisan think tank.

The White House and CBO also share similarly optimistic views about inflation and unemployment. In the next decade, both predict, the Consumer Price Index will grow no more than 2.6 percent and the annual jobless rate never will top 5.2 percent.

Of a period of economic growth that in February entered a record 107th uninterrupted month, the budget declares: "There is every reason to believe that this expansion will continue for many more years."

A recession-proof economy "would be remarkable," said economist Ray Stone of Stone & McCarthy Research Associates in Princeton, N.J. "But on the other hand, what we have seen is remarkable as well." He said that in the absence of some external shock, such as a huge run-up in oil prices, a stock market collapse or an overzealous tightening of Federal Reserve monetary policy, there is no reason to doubt that growth can be sustained. Still, the economy shrugged off concerns of about a year ago that fallout from the Asian economic crisis would harm the U.S. expansion.

Forecasting Bipartisanship

With OMB and CBO consistently underestimating the performance of the economy and the ensuing budget surplus, a chief consequence has been that partisan wrangling over the competing estimates has melted away.

Over the years, there has been considerable tension sparked by differences between the forecasts of the two offices and the presumed tendency of the president's economic team to devise economic projections that would suit his political needs. Democrats for years railed at the "rosy scenarios" undergirding Ronald Reagan's budgets, which used extraordinarily optimistic economic assumptions to minimize the estimates of budget deficits. When the Republicans took over Congress in 1995, they insisted on using "honest CBO numbers" as the yardstick by which any potential budget-balancing deal with Clinton would be measured.

The experience of the past few years has highlighted the uncertainty inher-

(Continued on p. 6-12)

Administration Economic Assumptions

(Calendar years; dollar amounts in billions) [1]

	Actual	Projections						
	1998	1999	2000	2001	2002	2003	2004	2005
Gross Domestic Product (GDP)								
Dollar levels:								
Current dollars	$8,760	$9,232	$9,685	$10,156	$10,621	$11,105	$11,644	$12,236
Real, chained (1996) dollars	8,516	8,850	9,142	9,393	9,629	9,870	10,146	10,451
Chained price index (1996 = 100), Annual average	102.9	104.3	105.9	108.1	110.3	112.5	114.8	117.1
Percent change, fourth quarter over fourth quarter:								
Current dollars	5.9	5.2	4.8	4.6	4.6	4.5	5.0	5.1
Real, chained (1996) dollars	4.6	3.8	2.9	2.6	2.5	2.5	3.0	3.0
Chained price index (1996 = 100)	1.1	1.4	1.9	2.0	2.0	2.0	2.0	2.0
Percent change, year over year:								
Current dollars	5.5	5.4	4.9	4.9	4.6	4.6	4.9	5.1
Real, chained (1996) dollars	4.3	3.9	3.3	2.7	2.5	2.5	2.8	3.0
Chained price index (1996 = 100)	1.2	1.4	1.6	2.0	2.0	2.0	2.0	2.0
Incomes, current dollars:								
Corporate profits before tax	782	845	842	828	827	824	852	892
Wages and salaries	4,186	4,470	4,711	4,942	5,161	5,388	5,629	5,892
Other taxable income [2]	1,990	2,088	2,161	2,231	2,293	2,356	2,431	2,518
Consumer Price Index (all urban): [3]								
Level (1982-84 = 100), annual average	163.1	166.7	171.0	175.1	179.6	184.3	189.1	194.0
Percent change, fourth quarter over fourth quarter	1.5	2.7	2.3	2.5	2.6	2.6	2.6	2.6
Percent change, year over year	1.6	2.2	2.6	2.4	2.6	2.6	2.6	2.6
Unemployment rate, civilian, percent:								
Fourth quarter level	4.4	4.1	4.3	4.7	5.1	5.2	5.2	5.2
Annual average	4.5	4.2	4.2	4.5	5.0	5.2	5.2	5.2
Federal pay raises, January, percent:								
Military [4]	2.8	3.6	4.8	3.7	3.7	3.2	3.2	3.2
Civilian [5]	2.8	3.6	4.8	3.7	3.7	3.2	3.2	3.2
Interest rates, percent:								
91-day Treasury bills [6]	4.8	4.7	5.2	5.2	5.2	5.2	5.2	5.2
10-year Treasury notes	5.3	5.6	6.1	6.1	6.1	6.1	6.1	6.1

[1] Based on information available as of late November 1999.

[2] Rent, interest, dividend and proprietor's components of personal income.

[3] Seasonally adjusted CPI for all urban consumers.

[4] Beginning with the 1999 increase, percentages apply to basic pay only; adjustments for housing and subsistence allowances will be determined by the secretary of Defense.

[5] Overall average increase, including locality pay adjustments.

[6] Average rate (bank discount basis) on new issues within period.

SOURCE: President's fiscal 2001 budget

Budget Authority, Outlays by Agency

(fiscal years, in millions of dollars)

	BUDGET AUTHORITY			OUTLAYS		
Agency	1999 Actual	2000* Estimate	2001 Proposed	1999 Actual	2000* Estimate	2001 Proposed
Legislative Branch	$2,961	$2,797	$3,082	$2,609	$3,197	$3,022
The Judiciary	3,808	4,093	4,577	3,790	4,378	4,555
Executive Office of the President	428	274	288	417	267	288
Agriculture	67,729	72,311	66,362	62,834	71,096	64,940
Commerce	5,449	8,688	5,467	5,036	8,134	5,407
Defense-Military	278,398	279,924	291,087	261,380	277,476	277,484
Defense-Civil	32,106	33,120	34,073	32,014	33,008	33,970
Education	33,684	32,739	43,462	32,436	36,444	38,155
Energy	16,546	15,383	16,948	16,048	15,269	16,365
Health and Human Services	365,297	394,827	427,470	359,701	387,339	421,395
Housing and Urban Development	26,344	16,290	34,249	32,734	30,076	32,277
Interior	8,129	8,238	9,103	7,815	8,397	8,496
Justice	19,412	19,504	21,211	18,317	18,536	22,368
Labor	35,240	31,747	39,710	32,461	33,986	38,604
State	8,816	8,403	8,162	6,456	8,402	8,831
Transportation	50,834	53,121	58,277	41,829	45,925	49,042
Treasury	388,840	389,402	390,382	386,698	388,412	388,374
Veterans Affairs	44,113	47,329	46,129	43,168	46,723	46,442
Corps of Engineers	4,054	4,150	3,053	4,191	4,498	2,901
Environmental Protection Agency	7,260	7,277	7,171	6,750	7,040	7,453
FEMA	2,761	3,192	3,308	4,039	3,198	2,222
General Services Administration	529	118	894	-46	525	475
International Assistance Programs	27,426	12,025	12,317	10,059	10,498	12,207
NASA	13,655	13,602	14,036	13,664	13,447	13,676
National Science Foundation	3,739	3,972	4,639	3,283	3,596	3,972
Office of Personnel Management	48,706	50,766	53,260	47,515	49,352	51,829
Small Business Administration	342	452	988	57	107	675
Social Security Administration	420,608	440,822	456,852	419,788	439,465	455,595
(On-budget)	(40,340)	(44,473)	(39,702)	(40,575)	(44,518)	(39,707)
(Off-budget)	(380,268)	(396,349)	(417,150)	(379,213)	(394,947)	(415,888)
Other Independent Agencies	18,377	20,586	18,173	7,075	14,001	14,214,
(On-budget)	(12,770)	(15070)	(16,598)	(6,054)	(12,503)	(13,767)
(Off-budget)	(5,607)	(5,516)	(1,575)	(1,021)	(1,498)	(447)
Allowances	—	—	-161	—	843	-993
Undistributed offsetting receipts	-159,078	-174,073	-189,208	-159,078	-174,073	-189,208
(On-budget)	(-99,622)	(-106,557)	(-113,129)	(-99,622)	(-106,557)	(-113,129)
(Off-budget)	(-59,456)	(-67,516)	(-76,079)	(-59,456)	(-67,516)	(-76,079)
TOTAL	$1,776,513	$1,801,079	$1,885,361	$1,703,040	$1,789,562	$1,835,033
(On-budget)	(1,450,094)	(1,466,730)	(1,542,715)	(1,382,262)	(1,460,633)	(1,494,777)
(Off-budget)	(326,419)	(334,349)	(342,646)	(320,778)	(328,929)	(340,256)

* Includes president's request for supplemental spending.
Figures may not add due to rounding
SOURCE: President's fiscal 2001 budget

Clinton's Fiscal 2001 Proposal . . .

(fiscal years, in millions of dollars; figures may not add due to rounding)

	BUDGET AUTHORITY			OUTLAYS		
	1999	2000*	2001	1999	2000*	2001
NATIONAL DEFENSE						
Military Defense	$278,398	$279,924	$291,087	$261,380	$277,476	$277,484
Atomic energy defense activities	12,600	12,157	13,084	12,358	11,947	12,515
Defense-related activities	1,149	1,202	1,250	1,135	1,213	1,203
Total, National defense	292,147	293,283	305,421	274,873	290,636	291,202
INTERNATIONAL AFFAIRS						
International development and humanitarian assistance	8,975	8,014	8,087	5,654	7,281	7,379
International security assistance	5,869	7,634	5,846	5,531	5,354	6,678
Conduct of foreign affairs	5,891	5,877	6,103	4,162	5,960	6,508
Foreign information and exchange activities	1,210	670	735	1,227	821	733
International financial programs	15,930	-1,592	726	-1,331	-2,338	-1,691
Total, International affairs	37,875	20,603	21,497	15,243	17,078	19,607
GENERAL SCIENCE, SPACE AND TECHNOLOGY						
General science and basic research	6,397	6,697	7,727	5,679	6,260	6,905
Space flight, research, and supporting activities	12,460	12,570	13,100	12,446	12,593	12,733
Total, General science, space and technology	18,857	19,267	20,827	18,125	18,853	19,638
ENERGY						
Energy supply	-36	-2,926	-2,158	-118	-2,694	-1,769
Energy conservation	619	745	850	586	690	767
Emergency energy preparedness	160	146	151	225	164	158
Energy information, policy, and regulation	238	205	201	219	200	193
Total, Energy	981	-1,830	-956	912	-1,640	-651
NATURAL RESOURCES AND ENVIRONMENT						
Water resources	4,713	4,810	3,735	4,728	5,562	3,652
Conservation and land management	5,674	5,116	7,269	5,679	5,082	6,611
Recreational resources	3,460	3,733	3,987	3,498	3,611	3,771
Pollution control and abatement	7,429	7,438	7,346	6,898	7,202	7,630
Other natural resources	3,152	3,234	3,617	3,165	3,022	3,309
Total, Natural resources and environment	24,428	24,331	25,954	23,968	24,479	24,973
AGRICULTURE						
Farm income stabilization	21,029	28,757	19,072	20,020	28,748	19,011
Agricultural research and services	3,061	3,198	3,501	2,991	3,240	3,403
Total, Agriculture	24,090	31,955	22,573	23,011	31,988	22,414
COMMERCE AND HOUSING CREDIT						
Mortgage credit	792	-6,211	1,446	364	-4,464	-3,662
Postal Service (On-budget)	29	100	93	29	100	93
Postal Service (Off-budget)	5,607	5,516	1,575	1,021	1,498	447
Deposit insurance	1	2	-95	-5,280	-1,378	-1,589
Other advancement of commerce	7,924	10,751	7,736	6,513	9,842	7,656
Total, Commerce and housing credit	14,353	10,158	10,755	2,647	5,598	2,945
(On-budget)	(8,746)	(4,642)	(9,180)	(1,626)	(4,100)	(2,498)
(Off-budget)	(5,607)	(5,516)	(1,575)	(1,021)	(1,498)	(447)
TRANSPORTATION						
Ground transportation	35,856	38,614	42,222	28,052	31,639	33,829
Air transportation	11,368	11,026	12,178	10,720	10,600	11,523
Water transportation	4,139	3,854	4,090	3,544	4,208	3,974
Other transportation	223	231	230	215	262	206
Total, Transportation	51,586	53,725	58,720	42,531	46,709	49,532
COMMUNITY AND REGIONAL DEVELOPMENT						
Community development	5,486	5,366	5,772	5,116	5,396	5,434
Area and regional development	2,705	2,607	3,130	2,327	2,527	2,434
Disaster relief and insurance	3,102	3,246	3,342	4,427	3,192	2,309
Total, Community and regional development	11,293	11,219	12,244	11,870	11,115	10,177
EDUCATION, TRAINING, EMPLOYMENT, AND SOCIAL SERVICES						
Elementary, secondary, and vocational education	16,859	17,177	26,817	17,589	21,313	22,479
Higher education	13,680	12,377	13,468	11,783	11,653	12,408
Research and general education aids	2,588	2,649	2,914	2,318	2,752	2,778
Training and employment	8,727	4,779	8,054	6,781	8,214	8,450
Other labor services	1,133	1,248	1,509	1,078	1,185	1,461
Social services	17,413	17,408	20,916	16,853	18,280	19,968
Total, Educ., training, employ., and social services	60,400	55,638	73,678	56,402	63,397	67,544

. . . Budget Authority, Outlays by Function

	BUDGET AUTHORITY			OUTLAYS		
	1999	2000*	2001	1999	2000*	2001
HEALTH						
Health care services	123,664	137,740	148,900	124,526	135,371	146,086
Health research and training	16,305	18,537	19,668	14,382	16,501	18,512
Consumer and occupational health and safety	2,230	2,370	2,077	2,171	2,355	2,088
Total, Health	142,199	158,647	170,645	141,079	154,227	166,686
MEDICARE	190,625	206,304	220,204	190,447	202,513	220,515
INCOME SECURITY						
General retirement and disability insurance	2,635	6,193	6,336	1,940	5,042	4,831
Federal employee retirement and disability	76,783	79,428	82,584	75,146	77,710	80,960
Unemployment compensation	23,725	24,119	27,024	23,631	24,095	27,024
Housing assistance	20,402	17,134	27,269	27,677	29,221	30,676
Food and nutrition assistance	35,552	35,891	36,970	33,147	34,174	36,216
Other income security	79,483	80,802	81,435	76,166	81,044	80,017
Total, Income security	238,580	243,567	261,618	237,707	251,286	259,724
SOCIAL SECURITY	391,110	408,027	427,000	390,041	406,625	425,738
(On-budget)	(10,842)	(11,678)	(9,850)	(10,828)	(11,678)	(9,850)
(Off-budget)	(380,268)	(396,349)	(417,150)	(379,213)	(394,947)	(415,888)
VETERANS BENEFITS AND SERVICES						
Income security	22,934	24,536	22,481	22,153	25,052	22,508
Education, training and rehabilitation	989	1,216	1,396	1,273	1,255	1,449
Hospital and medical care	18,032	19,594	20,602	18,168	18,627	20,899
Housing	1,087	783	333	560	610	249
Other benefits and services	1,115	1,281	1,343	1,058	1,252	1,344
Total, Veterans benefits and services	44,157	47,410	46,155	43,212	46,796	46,449
ADMINISTRATION OF JUSTICE						
Federal law enforcement activities	11,404	11,390	12,974	11,005	11,477	12,366
Federal litigative and judicial activities	7,445	7,804	8,648	7,427	7,945	8,459
Federal correctional activities	3,299	3,669	4,408	3,204	3,558	4,066
Criminal justice assistance	5,244	4,586	4,379	4,288	3,791	6,517
Total, Administration of justice	27,392	27,449	30,409	25,924	26,771	31,408
GENERAL GOVERNMENT						
Legislative functions	2,344	2,211	2,433	2,093	2,349	2,512
Executive direction and management	670	645	749	604	550	684
Central fiscal operations	9,814	8,616	9,477	9,479	8,826	9,261
General property and records management	772	336	1,180	175	709	730
Central personnel management	154	162	177	156	157	172
General purpose fiscal assistance	2,033	2,004	1,929	1,958	2,077	1,928
Other general government	2,332	1,201	1,236	2,264	1,467	1,241
Deductions for offsetting receipts	-971	-1,100	-1,099	-971	-1,100	-1,099
Total, General government	17,148	14,075	16,082	15,758	15,035	15,429
NET INTEREST						
Interest on the public debt	353,504	359,045	359,982	353,504	359,045	359,982
Interest received by on-budget trust funds	-66,561	-71,356	-74,112	-66,561	-71,356	-74,112
Interest received by off-budget trust funds	-52,071	-59,656	-68,138	-52,071	-59,656	-68,138
Other interest	-5,135	-7,721	-9,420	-5,137	-7,719	-9,420
Total, Net interest	229,737	220,312	208,312	229,735	220,314	208,312
(On-budget)	(281,808)	(279,968)	(276,450)	(281,806)	(279,970)	(276,450)
(Off-budget)	(-52,071)	(-59,656)	(-68,138)	(-52,071)	(-59,656)	(-68,138)
ALLOWANCES	—	—	-161	—	843	-993
UNDISTRIBUTED OFFSETTING RECEIPTS	-40,445	-43,061	-45,616	-40,445	-43,061	-45,616
(On-budget)	(-33,060)	(-35,201)	(-37,675)	(-33,060)	(-35,201)	(-37,675)
(Off-budget)	(-7,385)	(-7,860)	(-7,941)	(-7,385)	(-7,860)	(-7,941)
TOTAL	$1,776,513	$1,801,079	$1,885,361	$1,703,040	$1,789,562	$1,835,033
(On-budget)	(1,450,094)	(1,466,730)	(1,542,715)	(1,382,262)	(1,460,633)	(1,494,777)
(Off-budget)	(326,419)	(334,349)	(342,646)	(320,778)	(328,929)	(340,256)

**Includes president's request for supplemental spending*

SOURCE: President's fiscal 2001 budget

(Continued from p. 6-7)

ent in long-term projections. For budgeting purposes, small changes in economic variables can produce big differences in receipts and spending. For example, according to White House models, if the economy grows just 1 percentage point less in 2000 than predicted, the cumulative surplus by fiscal 2005 would be $169 billion less than the OMB now forecasts.

In its January budget and economic forecast, CBO devoted an entire chapter to "The Uncertainties of Budget Projections," and the different surplus figures that would flow from alternatives to its current projections are eye-popping. Under an optimistic scenario — in which economic growth declines slowly and hovers at just above 3 percent over the long term — CBO's estimate of the surplus doubles, provided discretionary spending grows at the rate of inflation. Under a more pessimistic view of the economy — one in line with more traditionally cautious CBO projections — the surplus could disappear.

The CBO report highlights the central, and unanswered, question involving the economy: Is increased productivity permanent, or a short-term departure from historic patterns? Absent an answer, CBO notes, "projecting the economy and the budget under those circumstances is more uncertain than usual." ◆

Lawmakers Unable to Live Within Tight Limits Set In Budget Resolution

Box Score

- **Bill:** H Con Res 290
- **Legislative action: House** adopted H Con Res 290 (H Rept 106-530), 211-207, on March 24.

Senate adopted H Con Res 290, 51-45, on April 7, after substituting the text of S Con Res 101 (S Rept 106-251).

House adopted the conference report on H Con Res 290 (H Rept 106-577), 220-208, on April 13.

Senate adopted the conference report, 50-48, on April 13.

SUMMARY

Republicans pushed though Congress a fiscal 2001 budget resolution with a discretionary spending limit that exceeded the statutory caps yet was still so tight that even some GOP lawmakers warned that the party was setting itself up for failure. By fall, it was clear just how far from reality the budget had been: Fiscal 2001 appropriations bills overshot the $600.3 billion discretionary ceiling by a cumulative $34.2 billion. The pressure to spend came from President Clinton, congressional Democratic leaders and members of both parties pushing parochial interests. And the growing surplus was a new force weakening fiscal restraint on Capitol Hill.

Congress never expected to make the drastic spending cuts necessary to meet the $541 billion discretionary spending limit for fiscal 2001 specified in the 1997 law (PL 105-33) designed to assure a balanced budget by fiscal 2002. Additional tax receipts in a surging economy had erased the deficit in fiscal 1998 well ahead of schedule, and estimates of the new surplus only grew more optimistic as the year went on. The $1.86 trillion budget request Clinton sent to Congress on Feb. 7 projected that — if discretionary spending were to grow at the rate of inflation — the cumulative surplus for fiscal 2001-10 would total $2.9 trillion. In July, the White House's Office of Management and Budget raised the cumulative projection to $4.2 trillion and estimated the fiscal 2001 "on-budget" surplus, which excludes the Social Security trust fund surpluses, would be $79 billion.

The budget resolution's $600.3 billion limit on discretionary spending was $14.3 billion above a freeze at the fiscal 2000 level and $6.7 billion less than required to account for the rate of inflation, according to the Congressional Budget Office (CBO). Clinton's initial budget, by CBO's calculus, would have spent $625 billion.

The budget was adopted on nearly straight, party-line votes, and by the statutory April 15 deadline for the second straight year. It did not require the president's signature. Some Republicans who voted for it, particularly the appropriators, warned that the ceiling was so low that it was bound to snarl the appropriations process. As a practical matter, the spending limit was being disregarded by the time Congress returned from its summer recess.

The GOP tax cut provided for in the budget fared no better. The resolution provided for two reconciliation bills to implement no more than $150 billion in tax cuts over five years. Clinton vetoed the first bill (HR 4810), to cut taxes for married couples by $90 billion over five years, and the House sustained the veto. Retirement savings incentives at the heart of the second reconciliation bill (HR 5203) were included in a wrapup tax package (HR 2614) worth $240.4 billion over 10 years that died in the Senate. *(Taxes, pp. 18-3, 18-32)*

Rebellion of a Few Could Stymie GOP Leaders' Budget Plans

MARCH 18 — Republican leaders trying to advance their fiscal 2001 budget blueprint on both sides of the Capitol the week of March 20 will find themselves in an ideological vise — between the conservative members of their own party, who are pushing for less spending, and the Democrats who want to spend more and are united in opposition to the GOP plan.

Fiscally conservative Republicans have been firing warning shots for weeks, urging and sometimes threatening the leadership to limit domestic spending to display election year adherence to the core GOP principle of smaller government. The leaders resisted and agreed among themselves on an overall spending level designed to appeal to the broadest number of GOP rank and file, most of whom want to avoid casting election year votes to cut popular programs.

Now, twin showdowns may be at hand. On both the House floor and in the Senate Budget Committee, narrow GOP majorities mean that a few dissatisfied Republicans have the power to combine with unified Democrats to stop the budget in its tracks.

By March 23, the House is expected to vote on a budget resolution that calls for no more than $596.5 billion in discretionary spending in the fiscal year beginning Oct. 1. The Senate Budget Committee is scheduled to mark up a budget resolution with that same bottom line beginning March 22. The rift on the committee could be so wide that the GOP leadership is hinting that it may bypass the committee and put the resolution directly on the Senate floor.

The measure the House will debate was approved, 23-18, by the Budget Committee on March 15. According to the Congressional Budget Office (CBO), its discretionary spending total is the exact midpoint between a freeze in spending at the levels enacted for fiscal 2000 and an increase to account for the rate of inflation. President Clinton has proposed spending $614.3 billion.

All 17 Democrats present voted against the measure. Mac Collins of Georgia, the only Republican to vote "no," said he wanted to send a signal to the GOP leadership that the party is not doing enough to restrain spending. In an interview March 16, he said he likely will have more allies when the the measure comes up on the floor. "I think it spends too much," Collins said. "I think there are several of us in the Congress who feel that way."

Michele Davis, spokeswoman for House Majority Leader Dick Armey, R-Texas, acknowledged that GOP leaders have been hearing complaints from conservatives in their caucus. Conservatives have also been grumbling about the $9 billion price of the fiscal 2000 supplemental appropriations bill (HR 3908 — H Rept 106-521), which is nearly double what Clinton requested for anti-drug efforts in Colombia, peacekeeping in Kosovo and domestic disaster aid. The discontent has prompted GOP leaders to keep the supplemental bill off the House floor at least until the budget resolution has been adopted.

The uneasy fate for both packages could be a sign that the GOP is on track to repeat its budget difficulties of last year, when a small band of fiscal conservatives snarled progress on appropriations by pressing for cuts in many of the 13 regular spending bills. Although their efforts were largely unsuccessful, they cranked up the level of partisanship in the House and helped keep Congress in town almost until Thanksgiving.

The GOP schism on spending will create serious obstacles to House adoption of the budget resolution, and Republican leaders will be unable to find help across the aisle, said Stanley E. Collender, senior managing director of Fleishman-Hillard's Federal Budget Consulting Group. "The Democrats are not going to play on this one," he said in a March 13 interview.

Clinton Assails Plan

Clinton said March 16 that the Republican budget would cut domestic spending too deeply, and that its level of anticipated tax cuts would endanger debt reduction efforts and the long-term fiscal health of Social Security. "The risks it poses are unconscionable. It is as risky and costly as the budget they proposed last year that I vetoed," he told reporters.

"The only way they can meet their spending priorities with this tax cut is to go back to huge deficits," Clinton continued. "I ask the leadership to change course, to go back and write a budget that maintains our fiscal discipline and meets our most pressing priorities."

The budget resolution outlines a fiscal policy blueprint for Congress to follow and is not presented to the president. But it does set the parameters for the drafting of tax cut and appropriations legislation. Last fall, Clinton vetoed a $792 billion, 10-year tax cut (HR 2488) provided for by the fiscal 2000 budget resolution (H Con Res 68). He also vetoed four spending bills and threatened to veto a fifth.

This year, differences between Clinton and the GOP are largely over items other than defense. The president has requested $306.3 billion in budget authority for defense, a 4.1 percent increase. The GOP budget resolution sets aside a symbolic $1 billion more. Discretionary spending on non-defense programs is limited to $289.2 billion under the GOP plan. Thus, it appears certain that a two-year trend will be reversed, and for the first time since fiscal 1998 defense spending will consume more of the discretionary budget than all other discretionary programs combined.

The House budget resolution also hews closely to the administration's proposed discretionary spending levels for energy, natural resources, agriculture, transportation, science, technology, veterans and health programs. It also proposes setting aside $40 billion during the next five years to shore up the finances of Medicare, the federal medical insurance for the elderly and disabled, and pay for a prescription drug benefit package. Democrats complained, however, that the GOP plan does not specifically call for creation of a prescription drug program. Clinton has proposed creating a Medicare prescription drug cost-sharing program beginning in fiscal 2002 that the administration projects would cost $60.5 billion over five years.

Republicans have proposed cutting the president's request for $61.5 billion in discretionary spending on education, training and social services to $56.8 billion. Still, both figures would represent a significant increase from the $44.5 billion appropriated for this year. Republicans also want to cut the president's proposed $22.8 billion budget for international affairs by about $3 billion.

The House GOP plan would trim about $6 billion from Clinton's $41.3 billion request for discretionary spending in the "income security" category of programs, which includes food stamps and special nutrition assistance programs for women and children. The resolution is not more specific.

At the eight-hour markup, the panel adopted a handful of relatively non-controversial Democratic amendments

— such as an $11.5 million, five-year proposal to enhance Alzheimer's research — but none involved amounts of money big enough to alter the spending bottom line or the GOP imprint on the underlying policies. Almost always on party-line votes, the panel rejected about two dozen Democratic amendments to recast the budget to their liking.

Bush Tax Cut Debated

In an effort to undermine the fiscal policy credibility of George W. Bush, the presumptive Republican presidential nominee, Budget Committee Democrats unveiled an analysis of how Bush's proposed five-year tax cut of $483 billion would square with the GOP budget. They concluded that enacting his proposals would yield an on-budget deficit of $73.4 billion over five years and $244.8 billion over 10 years — and thus some of the Social Security surplus would need to be allocated to cover the lost revenue.

The House resolution instructs the Ways and Means Committee to draft no more than $150 billion in tax cuts during the next five years. House Budget Committee Chairman John R. Kasich, R-Ohio, said that was the ceiling insisted upon by his Senate counterpart, Pete V. Domenici, R-N.M., before the two unveiled the outlines of their joint budget proposal March 10.

But Kasich sketched out a way to push the figure to $250 billion. Another $60 billion in the on-budget — or non-Social Security — surplus would be set aside under the budget for paying down the national debt in the next five years, but Kasich said that, too, could be assigned to tax cuts. And more optimistic economic assumptions expected from CBO this summer could create, at least on paper, an additional $40 billion in on-budget surplus that could be converted to tax cuts. Kasich said that devoting all that money to tax cuts would allow Republicans to follow "at least the spirit" of their presidential candidate's tax platform.

Democrats attempted to take the debate a step further. Jim McDermott, D-Wash., offered an amendment to require the Ways and Means Committee to produce a bill to implement the Bush tax cut — a package that CBO almost certainly would have concluded would eat into Social Security revenues. Republicans sidestepped a direct vote on the Bush tax plan by amending McDermott's amendment with language stating that money derived from efforts to root out government waste be used for debt relief or tax cuts. It was adopted by voice vote.

Even the most ardent GOP tax-cutters have drawn a line against anything that would consume more than the on-budget surplus. Each party is poised to hammer the other over any tax cut or spending proposal that would eat into the Social Security trust fund surplus. This line has become the new de facto spending cap in this year's budget debate, as both parties have chosen to ignore the spending caps imposed by the budget-balancing law (PL 105-33) of 1997. Although the caps remain on the books, it appears certain Congress will vote on raising them this year. So far, however, GOP leaders have not said when that debate will occur or what the legislative vehicle will be.

Senate Struggles

Before the Senate budget resolution can advance far, Domenici most likely will have to repair his relationship with several conservative Republicans on his committee. The chairman negotiated at length with these senators over the resolution's discretionary spending total. Domenici wanted $600 billion or a little more; the others wanted to spend about $15 billion less. Several senators involved in the talks said March 9 that they were progressing toward a deal but had not reached one yet. But the next day, Domenici and Kasich announced the outlines of their agreement — endorsed by House Speaker J. Dennis Hastert, R-Ill., and Senate Majority Leader Trent Lott, R-Miss. — to set the $596.5 billion discretionary spending total.

The deal immediately came under fire from Senate Budget Committee member Phil Gramm, R-Texas, who was among those pushing for a lower amount. Gramm spokesman Larry Neal said March 13 that Domenici's office made no attempt to inform Gramm ahead of time that the announcement of a deal was at hand. Instead, Neal said, Gramm's office learned of the deal when members of the media started calling about it the morning of March 10.

Another Republican holding out with Gramm for less spending, Rod Grams of Minnesota, also said he was not informed of the deal before the announcement. Spokesmen for the other holdouts — Majority Whip Don Nickles of Oklahoma and Judd Gregg of New Hampshire — said the senators had not announced their positions on the deal.

Any serious GOP discontent on the committee could spell trouble for the budget resolution. It is unlikely that any of the 10 Democrats on the panel would vote for the GOP plan because it would call for cuts in non-defense discretionary programs, according to a senior Democratic aide who works on budget issues. This means that if just one of the 12 Republicans on the committee refuses to go along, the committee could not adopt the GOP budget resolution.

The discord is so great that the Senate leadership is refusing to rule out the unusual and potentially controversial option of bypassing the committee and taking a budget resolution directly to the floor. "We're going to have that budget on the floor in short order," Lott spokesman John Czwartacki said March 16. When asked about the difficulties of getting it through committee, he added, "There's more than one way to skin a cat."

Supplemental Stalls

Similar conservative annoyance is what has stalled the fiscal 2000 supplemental spending bill since its approval by the House Appropriations Committee on March 9. House GOP conservatives are particularly concerned about the widespread expectation that the bill — which has grown from a $5.2 billion Clinton request to a $9 billion House package — will get more expensive in the Senate and more expensive again in conference. After a GOP Conference meeting March 15, Appropriations Committee Chairman C.W. Bill Young, R-Fla., said the leadership had decided not to bring the supplemental bill to the floor until after the House has adopted its budget resolution.

The next day, Young threatened to vote against the budget unless the House drops a provision that would set up a roadblock to tapping the surplus to pay for the supplemental bill. The point of order — which would require that added fiscal 2000 spending be offset by cuts in other accounts — was a last-minute addition to the resolution to appease freshman committee member Patrick J. Toomey, R-Pa.

The supplemental measure faces different problems in the Senate, where Lott has concluded that the additional spending should be allocated through fiscal 2001 appropriations bills. Under the plan, the money could be released during fiscal 2000 only if fiscal 2001 spending measures were enacted in time. This could pose a particular problem for the Pentagon, which has served notice that it will need to cancel big training exercises this summer if supplemental spending is not delivered soon. That is because money for the training was recently redirected to underwrite peacekeeping operations.

But handling the bill Lott's way would help limit spending, because supplementals "have this uncanny ability to get, shall we say, obese," Czwartacki said.

House Passes GOP Budget Plan By Narrow Margin

MARCH 25 — After surviving a near-death experience in the House, the Republican budget is facing an equally problematic path in the Senate, where party leaders have been unable to jump-start the measure because of an intraparty schism between spenders and savers.

Negotiators appeared to be making progress toward agreement among Senate Republicans late in the week of March 20, however, and party leaders were hopeful that they could put a budget resolution to a vote on the Senate floor by early April.

In the House, GOP leaders skated a razor-thin margin for error to win adoption of their budget resolution (H Con Res 290) for fiscal 2001 on a nearly party-line vote. The tally early in the morning of March 24 was 211-207. *(Vote 75, p. H-28)*

At both ends of the Capitol, the difficulty for members of the Republican hierarchy was the same: They are pushing spending levels that are barely big enough to keep appropriators happy, but these same numbers are not small enough to avoid alienating a potentially pivotal number of the most fiscally conservative GOP members. Beyond that dilemma, the budget proposes spending that is too low — and tax cuts that are too high — to skirt another election year confrontation with President Clinton.

The House GOP budget is "fundamentally flawed and fails to provide a balanced and workable economic plan," Office of Management and Budget Director Jack Lew wrote to congressional leaders March 23. "The resolution creates room for the tax cut through an unrealistic assumption that Congress will be able to pass deep cuts in domestic discretionary spending. . . . It would reverse much of the fiscal progress of recent years and could endanger our hard-won budget surplus."

So far, the White House has seen only the House version. The Senate Budget Committee postponed a markup scheduled for March 22 after Republicans on the panel were unable to settle their differences. The markup is rescheduled for March 28, giving Chairman Pete V. Domenici, R-N.M., more time to get all the Republicans on his panel to sign on to a blueprint calling for $596.5 billion in discretionary spending — a 1.8 percent increase from the current year's appropriations and the same grand total as in the House budget resolution for the fiscal year that opens Oct. 1.

Republican Phil Gramm of Texas remained a key holdout. He has sought a freeze in spending at the fiscal 2000 level of about $586 billion, but his spokesman, Larry Neal, indicated March 24 that Gramm and Domenici were making progress in closing the gap. "The negotiations are under way," Neal said. "They are still amicable."

Weeks of behind-closed-doors negotiating have done little so far to satisfy Gramm and the three other GOP committee members who have been insisting on less spending: Majority Whip Don Nickles of Oklahoma, Rod Grams of Minnesota and Judd Gregg of New Hampshire. The others have not announced firm positions. Republicans have only a 12-10 majority on the panel, so the adoption of the resolution could be blocked if just one GOP senator joins the Democrats, each of whom is expected to vote against Domenici's resolution.

Dealing With Defectors

House Republican leaders had a little more breathing room, but not much. During 14 hours of debate that stretched from the morning of March 23 until after midnight, they had to scrape for every vote they could get. But in the end, days of delicate negotiations and deal-cutting paid off, and their resolution was adopted with only five GOP "no" votes.

The defectors came from both ends of the party's fiscal policy spectrum. Sonny Callahan of Alabama, chairman of the Appropriations Subcommittee on Foreign Operations, said he opposed the resolution because it would allow too little in discretionary spending. The same reason was given by Constance A. Morella of Maryland. But two members of the "revolutionary" Class of 1994 — John Hostettler of Indiana and Mark Sanford of South Carolina, who is retiring this year — joined Ron Paul of Texas in opposing the measure on the grounds that it would spend too much.

Among the key pickups for the leadership was Mac Collins of Georgia. When he broke GOP ranks to oppose the resolution in the Budget Committee, he said he had done so to send a signal to the leadership that the party was not doing enough to restrain spending.

Only two Democrats — Gary A. Condit of California and Ralph M. Hall of Texas — voted for the budget. Had they not done so, the resolution could have been defeated on a 209-209 tie, at least in theory. But a GOP budget aide said he was confident that Majority Whip Tom DeLay, R-Texas, could then have brought enough wayward Republicans back on board to ensure adoption.

Leaders limited defections by meticulously balancing the demands of party moderates and appropriators, who generally favor higher spending levels, and GOP conservatives, who advocate cuts in non-defense programs. For example, at the urging of Appropriations Committee members, the leaders arranged to drop a procedural provision — added to win the support of Patrick J. Toomey, R-Pa., in the Budget Committee — that would likely have made it more difficult to win House passage of the fiscal 2000 supplemental appropriations bill (HR 3908 — H Rept 106-521). To avoid losing the support of Toomey and his allies on the House floor, Republican leaders promised to back future debt buy-down efforts that Toomey plans to propose.

Republican leaders even agreed to protect millions of dollars in federal funding for the replacement of the Woodrow Wilson Bridge, the dominant public works project in the Virginia district of Thomas M. Davis III, the chairman of the National Republican Congressional Committee, which raises money for House candidates.

Davis was concerned that a point of order that would be created under the resolution — another piece of language added at the last minute to appease fiscal conservatives — would have endangered federal funding for the bridge, which carries Interstate 95 across the Potomac River just south of Washington.

The point of order would limit the use of "forward funding," an accounting mechanism used to commit money to projects in one year while spreading the budgetary impact of that spending into the subsequent year. Conservatives say the device is frequently used to mask congressional commitments to spending. But Davis complained that the point of order could jeopardize his ability to win the next installment of funding. "We don't want to preclude any avenue for getting that bridge through," he said in a March 23 interview.

Davis lifted his threat to vote against the budget when Rules Committee Chairman David Dreier, R-Calif., told him in a colloquy on the floor that the point of order would not apply to funding for the bridge.

While fiscal conservatives complained that the budget would allow too much spending — and contained insufficiently tough language to prevent Congress from finding ways to spend even more — the appropriators were complaining that the budget leaves them too little leeway to produce the 13 spending bills to allocate all fiscal 2001 discretionary spending.

"It's not a realistic budget," said Appropriations Committee Chairman C.W. Bill Young, R-Fla., who voted for the plan nonetheless.

All Alternatives Defeated

As is customary, the leadership allowed several factions in the House to offer alternative budgets. Each was soundly rejected.

Democrats touted their principal alternative as a middle-of-the-road plan that would reserve more of the surplus to pay down the debt while avoiding cuts to social programs. The plan, by John M. Spratt Jr. of South Carolina, the ranking member of the Budget Committee, would accomplish that by proposing a $50 billion, five-year tax cut — just one-quarter of what the GOP resolution would allow. It was rejected, 184-233. *(Vote 74, p. H-28)*

Republicans "put massive tax cuts ahead of paying down the debt," said Melvin Watt, D-N.C., priorities that he said ignored the advice of Federal Reserve Chairman Alan Greenspan, who has said that debt reduction is the best use for surpluses.

Spratt's plan called for $615.7 billion in discretionary spending, slightly more than the $614.3 in Clinton's budget and $19.2 billion more than the Republicans' budget. Under the Spratt plan, discretionary budget authority would increase to $667.2 billion in fiscal 2005, which would be $31.6 billion more than under the plan the House adopted. Spratt's blueprint called for the same amount of defense spending as the administration, $306.3 billion, which is $1 billion less than in the Republican plan. It outlined $309.4 billion for non-defense spending, $20.2 billion more than the GOP plan.

Two plans focused on boosting funding for a variety of social programs and would have called for cuts in Pentagon spending. The version advanced by the Congressional Black Caucus was rejected, 70-348; the budget of the Progressive Caucus was rejected, 61-351. *(Votes 70, 71, p. H-28)*

The plan of the "Blue Dogs," the coalition of mostly Southern fiscally conservative Democrats, was endorsed by the nonpartisan Concord Coalition as the most responsible budget offered in the debate. It called for smaller tax cuts and a greater focus on debt reduction than either the main Democratic alternative or the Republican budget plans, and higher levels of defense spending than either of them. It was rejected, 171-243. *(Vote 72, p. H-28)*

The Conservative Action Team, a group of the most fiscally hard-line GOP members, called in their budget for $270 billion in tax cuts over five years, including a repeal of the 4.3-cents-a-gallon increase in the federal gasoline tax enacted in 1993 and less in non-defense discretionary spending than the GOP plan that was adopted. It was rejected, 78-339. *(Vote 73, p. H-28)*

Senate Floor Fight

The adoption of the GOP leadership's budget resolution in the House focuses the undivided attention of budget watchers on the Senate, increasing the pressure on the GOP leadership to make something happen. The week of March 27 could be Domenici's last shot at moving the resolution through his committee. The precedents of the Senate allow the budget resolution to go directly to the floor if the Budget Committee fails to act by April 1, and Majority Leader Trent Lott, R-Miss., is hinting that this is a prerogative he is prepared to exercise.

The impasse on the committee was serious enough that Domenici postponed the markup set to begin March 22. The day before, panel spokesman Bob Stevenson had said the debate would open on schedule "unless there's a flood and pestilence."

Apparently, Gramm's opposition was deemed sufficient to meet that definition. In a March 23 interview, Gramm said the markup was canceled because the leadership "just felt it wouldn't do any good." Gramm added, "We're working and praying. The problem is we're praying to the same God but for different things."

Domenici said he would prefer to work out a deal in committee, but he would support going straight to the floor if that was the only way to get it done. "I have a responsibility to get a budget through," he said.

Minority Leader Tom Daschle, D-S.D., said he also would support moving the budget directly to the floor — at least procedurally. "If this will accelerate our opportunities to ensure that we meet the deadlines and have a good debate, we'd be for it," he said March 22.

But Gramm sounded like he was prepared for all-out war if Republican leaders try to bypass him. "I'm going to defeat this budget if we can't work out an agreement in committee," he said.

Supplemental Spending Next?

Their success at pushing their budget through the House means that Republican leaders in that chamber may concentrate the week of March 27 on their next big challenge: winning passage of the fiscal 2000 supplemental spending bill.

Its $9 billion bottom line has also made some fiscal conservatives in the GOP queasy, especially given that Clinton requested $5.2 billion. The package is primarily aimed at anti-drug efforts in Colombia — a cause of Speaker J. Dennis Hastert, R-Ill. — peacekeeping in Kosovo and domestic disaster aid.

For now, the two chambers are taking different approaches to the supplemental, imperiling it further. Advocates for the measure in the House say the Pentagon is in dire need of a cash infusion because Kosovo operations have drained its accounts. In a March 22 letter to Hastert, Defense Secretary William S. Cohen warned that unless more money is guaranteed soon, the Defense Department will begin canceling training programs and maintenance projects to keep the forces in Kosovo deployed.

"Major delays, underfunding or restrictions would hurt the readiness of America's armed forces and undermine NATO efforts to foster stability in this critical and dangerous region," he wrote.

But Lott has concluded that the additional spending should be allocated through fiscal 2001 spending bills — principally as a way to limit the number of requests for midyear money. Under Lott's plan, supplemental spending could occur during fiscal 2000 only if the fiscal 2001 measure in which it was contained were enacted in time.

House GOP Appropriations aides have scoffed at the feasibility of handling the midyear requests that way. Senate Appropriations Committee Chairman Ted Stevens, R-Alaska, said March 21 that he would prefer to move a stand-alone bill after the House acts but is deferring to Lott's plan.

New Powers for Chairmen

The era of budget surpluses appears to be boosting the power of the Budget Committee chairmen, who could be granted new unilateral power to revise the budget resolution after adoption.

The House resolution would give Budget Committee Chairman John R. Kasich, R-Ohio, the power to approve a new grand total for tax cuts over and above those specified in the resolution. The measure would direct the Ways and Means Committee to produce four bills between May and September dictating tax cuts of as much as $150 billion over five years. However, it also would give Kasich authority to sign off on another $50 billion in tax cuts if Ways and Means were so inclined.

But Kasich's new authority would not end there. The Congressional Budget Office will release revised revenue estimates this summer. If the agency estimates of the fiscal 2000 on-budget surplus are bigger than is now forecast, Kasich would be given authority — by himself — to turn the additional revenue over to the Ways and Means Committee for tax cuts.

Democrats said the provisions were intended to conceal, at least for now, the size of the cuts the GOP plans to enact. House Minority Leader Richard A. Gephardt, D-Mo., said the language was for use "after the smoke clears" over the budget.

Since Kasich is likely to use his authority to push for the biggest tax cuts possible, Spratt said, the provisions mean Republicans "just wiped out the surplus" that is on-budget, meaning the funds have not been derived from a surge in Social Security trust fund revenue.

"I think it's unusual," Spratt said. "There are no conditions, no criteria. It's carte blanche authority."

But House Budget spokesman Terry Holt said the provisions make sense because "we can't write a new budget resolution with every revision in CBO forecasts." He also noted that the fiscal 2000 budget resolution (H Con Res 68) contained similar provisions giving the Budget Committee chairmen in both chambers the ability to revise some figures.

Stanley E. Collender, senior managing director of Fleishman-Hilliard's Federal Budget Consulting Group, noted that until the past few years Congress has not had to worry about what to do with surpluses, or midyear increases in surplus estimates, because budgets had been bleeding red ink for decades.

Senate Budget Panel Approves Draft Resolution

APRIL 1 — Republicans are turning their attention to the difficult task of dividing up the fiscal 2001 spending pot after making substantial headway on a budget that would greatly increase defense spending but squeeze many other accounts.

The Senate Budget Committee's 12-10 vote along party lines March 30 to approve a draft budget resolution capped two weeks of balky but steady progress for the GOP, and puts Congress on track to accomplish a rare feat — adoption of a budget resolution by the April 15 deadline set in law. But the amount of discretionary spending that it seems certain to allow — $596.5 billion, or $17.8 billion less than President Clinton has requested — would force GOP leaders to make tough election year decisions that will almost certainly annoy members in both parties.

"There will be some problems," House Appropriations Committee Chairman C.W. Bill Young, R-Fla., said March 29. "There will be some disappointment."

His panel's staff director, James W. Dyer, said March 30 that he plans to distribute to the 13 subcommittee chairmen the proposed limits on their discretionary spending — the so-called 302(b) allocations — by the end of the week of April 3.

The full Senate is expected to have adopted its budget resolution by that time, leaving one week before the spring recess, and the legal deadline, for adoption of a conference report. The House adopted its budget (H Con Res 290) on March 24.

Both budgets provide for tax cuts of at least $150 billion during the next five years; each resolution also gives the Budget Committee chairmen authority to instruct the House Ways and Means and Senate Finance committees to draft deeper tax cuts, particularly if the Congressional Budget Office boosts its revenue estimates for fiscal 2000 this summer, as expected.

Republicans are already moving ahead with various tax cut bills, most recently with the Finance Committee's approval of a bill to alleviate the "marriage penalty" by $69.8 billion over five years.

The Senate budget provides for the repeal of the 4.3-cent-a-gallon increase in federal gasoline taxes of 1993, unlikely given the problems facing a bill (S 2285) to roll back the gas tax through year's end.

Last-Minute Deal

The Senate Budget markup convened just hours after Chairman Pete V. Domenici, R-N.M., and committee Republican Phil Gramm of Texas reached a deal that paved the way for GOP conservatives to endorse a budget they had spurned for much of the past month.

After that, the three-day debate proved anticlimactic, with amendments proposed by Democrats rejected on party-line votes.

An exception came when, on a voice vote, the panel voted not only to double the amount in the budget resolution set aside through fiscal 2005 for a new Medicare prescription drug benefit — to $40 billion — but also to allow half the total to be used even if the benefit is not created as part of an overhaul of Medicare. Such an overhaul of the federal medical insurance for the elderly and disabled will not advance this election year, but a drug benefit bill still may.

Democrats sought to embarrass Republicans with an amendment to accommodate the $483 billion, five-year cost of the tax plan of George W. Bush, the presumptive GOP presidential nominee. Combined with current spending levels, Bush's tax cut most likely would consume all the on-budget surplus and eat into the projected Social Security surpluses as well, although GOP senators argued that as president, Bush could effect spending cuts deep enough to make room for his tax cut. Still, to avoid a vote on Bush's plan, Domenici offered a substitute declaring that deeper tax cuts than those in the budget resolution could be achieved by reducing wasteful spending. It was adopted, 12-10.

In retaliation, Gramm offered an amendment proposing an increase of $3 a gallon in the federal gas tax, saying it would follow a plan that Vice President Al Gore, the presumptive Democratic presidential nominee, advanced in his environmentalist tome, "Earth in the Balance." Democrats countered that unlike Bush's tax cut, Gore's book was neither a presidential platform nor a concrete legislative proposal. A motion by Barbara Boxer, D-Calif., to table, or kill, the amendment was agreed to, 22-0.

By 10-12, the committee rejected an alternative Democratic budget that generally tracked Clinton's request. It called for tax cuts of $59 billion during the next five years and total discretionary spending in fiscal 2001 of $614 billion.

Senate Adopts Its Version of Budget Resolution

APRIL 8 — Congress likely will finalize its fiscal 2001 budget resolution the week of April 10, an event that would mark both a rare achievement and a challenge for Republicans. It would allow the GOP to boast of meeting the deadline for adopting a budget resolution on time for only the third time in 10 years, but it would leave them with a spending plan that key members of the party complain is so tightfisted it will snarl the appropriations process.

Conference sessions are scheduled to begin as early as April 11 to sort out differences between the two chambers' versions of the budget resolution, and work already is under way behind closed doors to speed an agreement. GOP leaders say a conference report will be placed on a fast track to floor votes in both chambers by the end of the week. The resolution does not require the president's signature.

The Senate adopted its version of the budget resolution (H Con Res 290) on April 7 by a vote of 51-45. It called for approximately $601 billion in fiscal 2000 discretionary spending, about $4 billion more than the House plan. Republicans Lincoln Chafee of Rhode Island and George V. Voinovich of Ohio voted against the resolution; they were the only senators to cross party lines. *(Vote 79, p. S-30)*

The House narrowly adopted its budget resolution for fiscal 2001 on a nearly party-line vote March 24.

Democrats and some Republican appropriators have complained that the non-defense allocations in the budget resolution are so low that appropriators will find it difficult or impossible to move several of the non-defense spending bills.

That battle was presaged in a dispute among Senate Republicans in the Budget Committee and on the floor over the inclusion of procedural hurdles aimed at limiting appropriators' control over spending.

Fiscal conservatives led by Phil Gramm, R-Texas, had insisted on several provisions that would require 60-vote supermajorities in the Senate to exceed the resolution's discretionary spending limits.

Gramm used his leverage in the committee, where Republicans have a narrow 12-10 majority, to insist that the provisions be included.

But when the bill reached the floor, Appropriations Committee Chairman Ted Stevens, R-Alaska, balked and prepared to offer floor amendments that would have deleted the restraints. Had he succeeded, Gramm and perhaps others would have opposed the budget resolution, imperiling floor adoption. While the measure was being debated on the floor, Stevens, Gramm and Budget Committee Chairman Pete V. Domenici, R-N.M., negotiated at length behind closed doors.

A compromise reached the evening of April 6 pleased Gramm and Domenici, but left Stevens visibly annoyed. Although the 60-vote requirements remained, they were relaxed somewhat to apply primarily to non-defense spending.

Stevens said on the floor April 6 that the points of order would make passing the appropriations bills "extremely difficult," but he went along with the deal because appropriators need a budget resolution to get started on their work. "I have no alternative," Stevens said.

The agreement included an additional $4.1 billion for defense spending, which was originally proposed by Armed Services Committee Chairman John W. Warner, R-Va., but was later added to the deal on enforcement mechanisms as a sweetener for Stevens.

The additional defense spending was not designated for specific programs; it corresponds with a $4 billion amendment to a House fiscal 2000 supplemental bill offered by Defense Appropriations Subcommittee Chairman Jerry Lewis, R-Calif. Although the amendment was approved and the House passed the supplemental, Senate leaders remain adamantly opposed to taking up that spending bill.

Priorities Debated

In addition to providing a spending blueprint for the year, the budget resolution provides an annual forum for debating and forcing votes on a raft of controversial but non-binding policy statements. Senators offered "sense of the Senate" amendments on issues ranging from gun violence to oil drilling. Many were adopted on voice votes; others were defeated or ducked with the offering of less controversial substitutes. Domenici complained bitterly that senators on both sides of the aisle were wasting valuable time on the non-binding language.

Still, the Senate was able to finish work on its resolution the afternoon of April 7 after a week of debate, putting Congress on track to meet the April 15 deadline for completing a budget resolution. The deadline was set at May 15 in the Budget Act (PL 93-344) of 1974, and amended to April 15 in the 1985 Gramm-Rudman budget law (PL 99-177).

The resolution heads to conference without one unpopular provision — a suggested 4.3 cents-per-gallon cut in the federal gas tax. The proposed tax cut came under withering assault from members of both parties who were eager to protect a source of funds for transportation projects across the nation. *(Vote 57, p. S-13)*

However, another controversial proposal — to open the Arctic National Wildlife Refuge (ANWR) to oil drilling — narrowly survived, 51-49. Republicans and Democrats sparred over whether opening the reserve would help ease U.S. dependence on foreign oil, and whether drilling there would be ecologically harmful. *(Vote 58, p. S-13)*

Both the gas tax and the ANWR provisions, which are not in the House version, would require separate legislation to enact. Still, the GOP might strip the controversial ANWR language in conference negotiations so centrist Republicans will not have to align themselves with it in an election year.

Negotiators should face a fairly easy task in reconciling the House and Senate versions of the resolution. The two blueprints differ on the details but match up closely on the major points. Both call for trimming President Clinton's $614.3 billion spending proposal substantially. The House version calls for $596.5 billion in discretionary spending. Although the Senate bill would provide an additional $4 billion, the extra money would be allocated to defense, which should make it relatively easy for the two chambers to reach a compromise.

Both also call for tax cuts of about $150 billion over five years, and perhaps even more. Both chambers would also set aside about $40 billion over five years to fund a new Medicare prescription drug benefit.

Medicare Squabble Continues

Democrats claimed victory on an attempt to speed implementation of a proposed Medicare prescription drug benefit, even though they lost on the amendment.

Six Republicans voted with all 45 Democrats in support of an amendment offered by Charles S. Robb, D-Va., that called for delaying the GOP's tax cuts — including its high-priority "marriage penalty" fix — until prescription drug coverage has been added to Medicare.

However, the Robb amendment failed despite the 51-49 vote in favor of it; because it was not germane to the budget resolution, Senate rules required that it have 60 votes to prevail. *(Vote 52, p. S-13)*

Democrats complained that the budget resolution contained no guarantee that a Medicare prescription drug benefit would be enacted. "If we have hundreds of billions of dollars in the next several years to spend on tax reductions that will primarily benefit the wealthiest Americans . . . then we should certainly enact a meaningful Medicare outpatient drug benefit first," John D. Rockefeller IV, D-W.Va., said on the floor April 5. "We have the resources, if we don't fritter them away by picking favored constituencies for special tax breaks."

But Bill Frist, R-Tenn., who is a physician, said creation of a new Medicare drug benefit should be linked with a structural overhaul of Medicare to ensure the program's long-term solvency, not with tax cuts. "We should not be pitting the health of our nation's Medicare beneficiaries against tax relief," Frist said. "It is unfair and it is irresponsible."

Four of the six Republicans voting for the amendment — Spencer Abraham of Michigan, Conrad Burns of Montana, Chafee and Mike DeWine of Ohio — are up for re-election this fall. The other two were Peter G. Fitzgerald of Illinois and Arlen Specter of Pennsylvania.

After the tally, Robb and other Democratic senators said the majority vote for the Robb amendment proves that there is sufficient support to move ahead with a Medicare drug program if the GOP leadership would allow such a measure to reach the floor.

Just a day after the Senate vote on prescription drug coverage for seniors, House Speaker J. Dennis Hastert of Illinois said he planned to have a drug proposal on the House floor "early this summer." Pete Jeffries, a Hastert spokesman, said House GOP leaders hope to introduce the basic points of their prescription drug legislation by the end of next week so that members "are armed and ready" to meet constituents who may want to discuss the issue during the spring recess.

Republicans tend to favor prescription drug proposals that would provide assistance to low-income elderly and seniors with high drug costs. Many Democrats believe that any subsidies must be provided to all qualified Americans.

House Minority Leader Richard A. Gephardt, D-Mo., said April 6 that he hoped Republicans would introduce legislation on the drug issue. "I wish we could get a consensus behind something to get it done," Gephardt said.

Daschle said a Democratic version of the legislation, which is likely to resemble Clinton's plan, may be ready next week. Clinton has proposed dedicating a portion of expected budget surpluses over the next 10 years to shore up Medicare and include a prescription drug benefit.

"I realize that there are a lot of different ideas, but I think the one that unites Democrats most effectively is the one offered by the administration," Daschle told reporters.

After meeting with Senate Democrats, including Daschle and Robb, on April 4, Clinton reiterated his interest in passing prescription drug legislation this year. Clinton said Robb's amendment would have insisted "that we do first things first, and modernize Medicare with an affordable, accessible and voluntary Medicare prescription drug benefit for all seniors."

Bush Tax Cut Draws Fire

As they did in the Senate Budget Committee and in the House, Democrats sought to embarrass Republicans on the floor by forcing a vote on GOP presidential candidate George W. Bush's five year, $483 billion tax cut proposal.

Richard J. Durbin, D-Ill., offered an amendment April 5 to insert the Texas governor's tax cut in the budget resolution, and then called for its rejection. "We establish our positions by our votes," Durbin said. "I hope they don't continue to duck this vote. . . . If you disagree with his position, at least have the courage to go on the record and say so."

Durbin said he believed Republicans did not want to go on the record endorsing the Bush tax cut because they know it is so large that it would consume all of the on-budget surplus and eat into the off-budget Social Security surplus.

Republicans said that they agreed there was no way to offer substantial tax relief with what they regard as a free-spending Democrat in the White House but that a GOP administration would be able to find room for the Bush tax cut. Republicans sidestepped a direct vote on Bush's plan by offering a motion to table, or kill, the Durbin amendment. The motion was approved, 99-0. *(Vote 59, p. S-14)*

In retaliation for the Democratic ploy, Gramm offered a sense of the Senate resolution that called for rejecting Al Gore's proposal to eliminate the internal-combustion engine as outlined in the vice president's book, "Earth in the Balance." Phasing out the internal combustion engine would require a dramatic increase in the gas tax, Gramm said. His amendment was approved, 99-0. *(Vote 60, p. S-14)*

Other Amendments

- The Senate approved, 51-49, on April 7 an amendment by Edward M. Kennedy, D-Mass., to reduce the Republican's proposed five-year tax cut by about $2.7 billion to provide a corresponding increase in the Pell grant program. Pell grants are offered to lower-income college students to help fund education expenses. *(Vote 69, p. S-15)*
- The Senate rejected, 44-56, an amendment offered April 7 by Voinovich to strip the tax cuts from the resolution in order to dedicate more money for debt relief. Four Republicans voted for the measure, as did all but six Democrats. *(Vote 68, p. S-15)*
- The Senate voted, 45-55, on April 7 to reject a Democratic alternative to the Republican budget. The Democratic plan closely tracked Clinton's proposed budget. *(Vote 71, p. S-15)*
- Kennedy offered a sense of the Senate amendment urging the adoption of a $1 increase in the minimum wage over two years. Republicans have pushed an alternative calling for a $1 increase over three years coupled with business tax breaks. The GOP avoided a vote on the Kennedy language by adopting, 51-49, a substitute sense of the Senate amendment affirming support of the Republican minimum wage plan. *(Vote 75, p. S-16)*

But Kennedy vowed to keep offering his plan in slightly different versions until Republicans agreed to vote on it. Eventually he was able force a vote, and his non-binding amendment was approved, 51-48. *(Vote 76, p. S-16)*

Measure Passes Both Chambers After Speedy Conference Action

APRIL 15 — Republicans eager to enact tax cuts will return from their spring recess armed with new tools for knocking down obstructions erected by Democrats in the Senate. But the congressional majority still appears to be lacking a strategy for averting a presidential veto, the fate that doomed the GOP tax cut of last year.

The hand of Senate Republicans was strengthened — at least procedurally — with the adoption of a compromise fiscal 2001 budget resolution (H Con Res 290) by both chambers on April 13. The measure calls for two tax cut bills to be drafted this summer outlining as much as $150 billion in tax cuts during the next five years. Such bills produced under the authority of reconciliation instructions in the budget resolution have unique procedural protections that are particularly important in the Senate, where they trump filibuster rights.

A likely candidate would be provisions to alleviate the tax code's "marriage penalty," one of the signature Republican tax-cutting aspirations. Such legislation (HR 6) was thwarted by a Democratic filibuster the week of April 10. Reviving the language in a reconciliation measure would eliminate the need for the 60-vote supermajority the GOP has so far been unable to obtain.

The House vote for the budget resolution conference report was 220-208, with five Republicans who voted against the measure offset by six Democrats who voted for it. The Senate vote several hours later was an even narrower 50-48, as four Republicans joined a united Democratic front in opposition. *(House vote 125, p. H-44; Senate vote 85, p. S-17)*

The measure calls for a limit of $600.3 billion in discretionary budget authority, less than required to keep pace with inflation. Of the tax cuts it allows, $11.6 billion could be delivered in the budget year beginning Oct. 1. The resolution also targets an additional $25 billion for tax cuts — and perhaps even more if revenue receipt forecasts are revised upward later this year — so long as the cuts do not eat into the Social Security surplus. It instructs the House Ways and Means Committee and the Senate Finance Committee each to produce one tax bill by July 14 and a second by Sept. 13.

The Senate's version of the budget called for one reconciliation bill, while the House's plan outlined four. House Budget Committee Chairman John R. Kasich, R-Ohio, told reporters April 13 that there was no specific strategy yet for how to use the two tax reconciliation measures, and no specific reason other than compromise for settling on two. "We wanted four, but the Senate didn't want the pressure of doing more than two," he said.

Although a reconciliation bill is shielded from filibuster, debate on one generally consumes about a week of Senate floor time, a precious commodity in an election year when the GOP wants to adjourn the 106th Congress early to leave time for campaigning.

The House has already passed two tax bills this year — its marriage penalty measure and a package that combines business tax cuts (HR 3081) with a minimum wage increase.

The fiscal 2000 budget resolution (H Con Res 68) called for only one tax bill, and the GOP used it to produce a $792 billion package that Clinton vetoed last September. Republicans then gave up on tax cuts for the year rather than face the daunting task of moving a new bill without the procedural protections afforded by reconciliation. Noting last year's events, Kasich indicated that having two shots at tax cuts would give Congress the flexibility to pass measures that Clinton might be more hard-pressed to veto.

Stanley E. Collender, senior managing director of Fleishman-Hilliard's Federal Budget Consulting Group, said in an April 12 interview that so far this year the Republicans have been muddling through their tax cut agenda without an overall strategy. He also questioned the legitimacy of the GOP spending blueprint, and said he has no doubt its discretionary spending total will be exceeded.

In his last year, Clinton has little motive to compromise, Collender said, so "if Congress wants to go home and campaign, they're going to have to give the president what he wants. . . . They're speaking loudly and carrying a small stick."

More Spending Approved

The House budget called for $596.5 billion in discretionary spending; the Senate started from that figure but during floor debate added about $4 billion more for defense and $1.6 billion for the National Institutes of Health (NIH). Conferees, who met briefly in public April 11 but did most of their work in private, generally accepted the increase in defense spending but dropped the extra allocation for the NIH.

The author of the NIH amendment, Arlen Specter, R-Pa., was among the four Senate GOP floor votes against the conference report. The others were Lincoln Chafee of Rhode Island, who said the budget did not ensure enough debt relief; John McCain of Arizona, who said the tax cuts were too deep, debt reduction was insufficient and entitlement changes were nonexistent; and James M. Jeffords of Vermont.

The budget sets aside as much as $40 billion in the next five years to finance an as-yet nonexistent Medicare prescription drug benefit. Democrats complained that the budget resolution does not specifically demand that Congress move such legislation, but Republicans replied that they have every intention of doing so.

The votes to adopt the conference report heralded the second straight year Congress has met the April 15 deadline for settling on a budget. GOP leaders hope that making that deadline will give them a running start on their main obligation for the rest of the year — moving the 13 required annual appropriations bills. To that end, John Czwartacki, a spokesman for Senate Majority Leader Trent Lott, R-Miss., said April 13 that the Senate would become "the appropriations express" starting in May.

In the House, aides on the Appropriations Committee have already drafted proposed allocations to the 13 subcommittees, and some of the numbers could spell trouble for the GOP's hopes of a speedy spending season. Although defense and education spending would be allowed to rise sharply under the plan, other programs would face outright cuts or increases below the inflation rate.

John M. Spratt Jr. of South Carolina., the top Democrat on the House Budget Committee, said the GOP was setting itself up for another end-of-session "train wreck" in which it would be unable to pass several of the more weakly funded appropriations measures.

Budget Resolution in Brief

Discretionary spending: $600.3 billion in fiscal 2001 — $310.8 billion for defense and $289.5 billion for non-defense programs.

Tax cuts: $150 billion over five years — $11.6 billion of it in fiscal 2001 — plus a $25 billion reserve fund that could be used for additional tax cuts. In addition, any upward revisions in the non-Social Security surplus projected by the Congressional Budget Office could be used for tax reduction, at the discretion of the Budget committee chairmen.

Medicare: In the House, a $40 billion reserve fund over five years to pay for a Medicare overhaul and a prescription drug benefit. In the Senate, a $40 billion reserve fund over five years for a prescription drug benefit, $20 billion of it contingent on legislation to improve Medicare solvency.

Reconciliation: Two reconciliation bills to be reported by Senate Finance and House Ways and Means to implement the $150 billion, five-year tax cut. Bills are to be reported by July 14 and Sept. 13.

Debt reduction: Two separate bills to reduce the level of debt held by the public, to be reported by House Ways and Means. The first, due July 14, would reduce the debt by $7.5 billion; the second, due Sept. 13, would increase the amount for debt reduction to $19.1 billion.

Enforcement: In the House, points of order allowed until Jan. 1 against spending bills that contain "directed scoring" or that would provide advance discretionary spending in excess of $23.5 billion. In the Senate, a 60-vote point of order allowed until Sept. 30, 2002, against advance discretionary spending in excess of $23.5 billion; a permanent 60-vote point of order against "emergency" non-defense spending; and a "firewall" in fiscal 2001 to prevent the use of defense discretionary spending for non-defense programs and vice versa.

Supplemental's Stall

At the same time, the fiscal 2000 supplemental appropriations bill remained moribund the week of April 10, despite new pleas from the Clinton administration and the Pentagon. The House passed a $13.2 billion supplemental (HR 3908) March 30 primarily to replenish defense accounts drained by the Kosovo peacekeeping mission, fund defense procurement and maintenance, provide funds for counter-narcotics operations in Colombia and provide domestic disaster relief.

The cost of the bill had grown steadily from Clinton's original $4.4 billion request, as the administration and House Republicans tacked on additional spending. Lott, the primary opponent of the midyear package, said April 11 that he feared the bill would have continued to swell if he had agreed to bring it to the Senate floor. "It looked to me like that bill was headed toward $15 [billion] to $17 billion," Lott said.

Lott met with Colombian President Andres Pastrana on April 12 and assured Pastrana that Congress will provide fiscal 2000 funds to help Colombia fight drug trafficking. Lott said he believes emergency funds can be approved through the regular appropriations process by the end of May or early June.

Secretary of State Madeleine K. Albright told reporters April 11 that Lott's strategy was inadequate.

Senate Appropriations Committee Chairman Ted Stevens, R-Alaska, reported that Army Gen. Henry H. Shelton, the Joint Chiefs of Staff chairman, told him April 11 that the military needs at least $2 billion by June 1 in order to avoid curtailing training exercises, money for which has been diverted to cover Kosovo costs. ◆

House Passes Multiple Bills Aimed at Debt Reduction; Senate Does Not Follow Suit

Box Score

- **Bills:** HR 3859, HR 4601, HR 4866, HR 5173, HR 5203
- **Legislative action: House** passed HR 4601 (H Rept 106-673, Part 1), 419-5, on June 20.

House passed HR 3859, 420-2, on June 20

House passed HR 4866, 422-1, on July 18.

House passed HR 5173 (H Rept 106-862, Part 1), 381-3, on Sept. 18.

House passed HR 5203, 401-20, on Sept. 19.

SUMMARY

Five times during the session, House Republicans won passage of measures to commit slices of the federal surplus to debt reduction. Democrats called the bills meaningless but voted for them anyway. The Senate ignored all five bills.

The year began with both the Republicans and President Clinton applying the term "lockbox" to their proposals to retire the publicly held portion of the national debt, which then stood at $3.6 trillion. Clinton's fiscal 2001 budget aimed to retire the debt by 2013. House Republicans promised to pursue policies that would at least match that timetable.

The first GOP effort (HR 4601) was the most modest. Passed in June, it would have allocated to debt reduction any portion of the fiscal 2000 "on-budget," or non-Social Security, surplus above $24.4 billion. A second bill (HR 3859), passed the same day, would have reserved Social Security and Medicare trust fund surpluses for debt reduction as well. A month later, the House passed a bill (HR 4866) to allocate $25 billion of the fiscal 2001 surplus to debt relief.

When these measures failed to draw much public notice, and with the GOP searching for a way to gain the upper hand against Clinton in their annual appropriations tussle, Republicans unveiled their so-called "90-10" plan, which pledged 90 percent of the fiscal 2001 surplus to debt reduction. GOP leaders never put it in writing, but they said their intent was to split the remainder — about $28 billion — between tax cuts and additional discretionary spending. The GOP passed the measure first as a stand-alone bill (HR 5173) and then as the second reconciliation bill of the year (HR 5203), which combined it with a set of provisions to expand tax breaks for retirement savings. *(Taxes, p. 18-32)*

Although a large majority of members voted for each of these bills, Democrats derided the measures as pointless, saying that the Treasury would use surplus funds to service the debt even without a law instructing it to do so.

House Panel Votes To Use Surplus To Pay Debt

JUNE 10 — The House Ways and Means Committee on June 8 agreed to sock away any unexpected budget surpluses to pay down the public debt and remove the temptation to use the money for a last-minute spending spree. Democrats offered little opposition to the Republican measure (HR 4601), and the committee approved it, 32-3.

The bill would allocate to debt reduction any fiscal 2000 non-Social Security, or "on-budget," surpluses in excess of the Congressional Budget Office's March estimate of $24.4 billion. It would create a "Public Debt Reduction Payment Account" at the Treasury Department; if the Congressional Budget Office increases its surplus projection for fiscal 2000 by several billion dollars, as it is expected to do this summer, that additional amount would be directed to the new account.

Republicans have been promising all year to move legislation that would lead to paying off the publicly held federal debt. They said this bill's enactment would ensure that future on-budget surpluses generated by the surging economy would go for such debt relief instead of being spent.

"Debt relief should be a top priority, and not simply an afterthought," Ways and Means Chairman Bill Archer, R-Texas, said in unveiling the bill at a June 7 news conference. "It's time to repair the roof when the sun is shining," added fellow Republican Ernie Fletcher of Kentucky.

Democrats called the measure meaningless. "It's hard to vote against a bill that does so little," ranking Ways and Means Democrat Charles B. Rangel of New York said at the markup.

While the bill would be effective only for fiscal 2000, which ends Sept. 30, its backers said it would serve as a model for future legislation to cover subsequent years.

Under current law, surplus federal revenue is already put in the service of the debt, so "the change here is a change in attitude," in the words of Jim Nussle, R-Iowa, a member of the Budget and Ways and Means panels. GOP staffers conceded that there is nothing in the legislation that would stop Congress from spending as much as it wants in fiscal 2001, regardless of how much on-budget surplus money is available.

Budget Committee Chairman John R. Kasich, R-Ohio, maintained that the bill is more than a symbolic gesture. Since the money in the debt account would be off-limits, spending more than the current on-budget surplus would amount to raiding Social Security, which has become politically untenable, Kasich said.

Asked whether his support for the bill suggested that debt relief had supplanted his itch for deep tax cuts, Kasich was quick to reiterate his preference for tax cuts, saying that he and Archer will unveil a plan for a major restructuring of the tax code later this year.

Kasich also was asked whether funds for the debt relief account would have to be allocated by the appropriators. "Are you kidding? This is what you call a bypass operation," he said.

House Passes Pair Of Bills Aimed at Guarding Surplus

JUNE 24 — Ernie Fletcher of Kentucky is among the most vulnerable House Republicans this fall, so the party's top brass came to his aid the week of June 19, working overtime to champion his relatively benign debt-reduction bill even though it faced minimal opposition.

The House voted 419-5 on June 20 to pass the measure (HR 4601), which would reserve a portion of the burgeoning fiscal 2000 surplus for debt reduction. *(Vote 296, p. H-94)*

The bill would create a new "Public Debt Reduction Payment Account." If the Congressional Budget Office boosts its fiscal 2000 surplus projections, as expected later this summer, the increase would be dedicated to the new account.

Before debate began, Speaker J. Dennis Hastert, R-Ill., and Majority Leader Dick Armey, R-Texas, joined Fletcher at a news conference to tout his legislation. "Thanks to Ernie Fletcher, today we're standing up and doing the right thing," Armey said.

Eager to speed passage after the bill's markup in the Ways and Means, Republican leaders bypassed the Budget Committee, which shares jurisdiction over the measure, with the blessing of Budget Chairman John R. Kasich, R-Ohio.

Fletcher's measure was one of two the GOP put before the House on June 20 to demonstrate their zeal for guarding excess revenue. The vote was 420-2 to pass the second (HR 3859), intended to reserve Social Security and Medicare surpluses for debt reduction. *(Vote 297, p. H-94)*

Democrats derided both bills as pointless posturing. The Budget Committee's top Democrat, John M. Spratt Jr. of South Carolina, also complained that in their eagerness to rush HR 3859 to the floor, Republicans had written flawed legislation: The bill would require the annual budget resolution to report the Social Security surplus amount, for example, but would leave in place current law, which prohibits the inclusion of the figure in that document.

Democrats also insisted that the Medicare bill is a pale imitation of a proposal put forward on the Democratic presidential campaign trail this month by Vice President Al Gore.

Republicans denied that electoral concerns affected the bills' timing or substance. Still, Chief Deputy Majority Whip Roy Blunt, R-Mo., said June 21 interview that GOP leaders are eager to help Fletcher — and that giving him top-billing on a high-profile issue is one of them. "He's in a district where this kind of common sense is exactly in line with the people he represents, and he's in a tough re-election effort," Blunt said. "There are lots of reasons to ask a guy like Ernie Fletcher to do this."

Fletcher is the top recipient of GOP leadership political action committee contributions, having taken in more than $90,000 so far from Republican colleagues, according to the latest Federal Election Commission data.

Fletcher's Democratic opponent, former Rep. Scotty Baesler (1993-99), said in a telephone interview June 21 that GOP leaders are trying to bolster Fletcher's résumé. "He's going down, and they're trying to prop him up," Baesler said. "Scotty is just crying sour grapes, because when he was here, he did nothing," Fletcher replied June 23.

Senate Dead End?

During the debate, Ways and Means Committee member Jim McDermott, D-Wash., alleged that the Fletcher bill was drafted to cover only fiscal 2000 surpluses because the GOP wants to use future years' surpluses for tax cuts. "When you come here and vote for tax cut after tax cut after tax cut and then say, 'We want to reduce the debt,' you simply are not making any sense," McDermott said. He also predicted that the bill "will die in the Senate from laughter," in part because the Treasury will use surpluses to service the national debt regardless of the fate of Fletcher's bill.

However, the Senate has twice voted for a proposal by Wayne Allard, R-Colo., to set aside $12.2 billion in fiscal 2000 surplus funds for debt relief. It was added by voice vote June 13 to the fiscal 2001 defense appropriations bill (HR 4576), and two days later senators voted 95-3 to add it to the transportation spending bill (HR 4475). *(Vote 131, p. S-25)*

Senate Appropriations Chairman

Ted Stevens, R-Alaska, reluctantly supported the provision but said he was worried that if money is taken off-budget for a debt-reduction account, some emergency or an unexpected cost increase in a mandatory program beyond appropriators' control could push the federal government into a deficit for fiscal 2000.

That would hand Democrats a potent political weapon, and appropriators would take the heat, Stevens said in an interview June 15. "There'll be a deficit, and they'll blame us," Stevens said.

House Passes Bill To Allocate Funds For Debt Reduction

JULY 22 — Democrats continue to complain that the Republicans are needlessly wasting the House's time with debt-reduction measures that would have no effect other than to make a symbolic election-year gesture.

"It is Howdy Doody time again," Jim McDermott, D-Wash., said July 18 as the debate began on the third bill the House has considered this year that would dedicate different slices of the surplus to debt relief.

But while the Democrats say they are convinced that these bills are a joke, they have nonetheless been helping to deliver the punch line. The vote to pass the bill (HR 4866) was 422-1. *(Vote 409, p. H-128)*

The measure would allocate $25 billion in on-budget fiscal 2001 surplus funds for debt reduction, among other provisions. A month ago, the House passed a similar bill (HR 4601), dedicating some on-budget fiscal 2000 surplus funds for debt relief, and a bill (HR 3859) to reserve both the Medicare hospital trust fund surplus, which is technically on-budget, and the off-budget Social Security surpluses for debt reduction.

Republicans say their aim with all the legislation is to make sure that Congress votes to lock away the initial windfalls promised by the latest round of surplus forecasts — and does so before it votes on an array of proposals to spend the money.

Democrats say surplus funds are automatically used for debt reduction without any such legislation, and that Republicans should scale back the size of their tax cuts if they are worried about debt relief.

"It is a waste of people's time to do this," said Charles B. Rangel, D-N.Y. "We need people to do this by action, not just by statement."

Budget Committee member Jim Nussle, R-Iowa, derided Democrats for blasting the bill and then voting for it in droves. "They rush here, down to the floor. And they say, 'Oh, what a bad bill. Oh, it is just theater' . . . and then they vote for it," Nussle said. "Boy, that is courage."

None of the bills has been scheduled for action in the Senate.

House Panel OKs Bill to Dedicate 90% of FY 2001 Surplus to Pay Debt

SEPTEMBER 16 — The Republican budget proposal unveiled the week of Sept. 11 presents perhaps the starkest example yet of how radically the exploding budget surplus projections have changed the politics of spending on Capitol Hill. The latest GOP plan would ignore the party's own budget blueprint and allow spending to grow well beyond the pace of inflation next year — yet party leaders tout it as a way to ensure frugality in the campaign season whirl of appropriations.

Republican leaders outlined the proposal to President Clinton on Sept. 12. It took the form of legislation (HR 5173) that would dedicate 90 percent of the cumulative fiscal 2001 surplus to paying down the publicly held debt, now $3.1 trillion. The Ways and Means Committee approved the bill, 33-0, on Sept. 14. The House debate is scheduled for Sept. 18.

"We are dedicated to using the surplus to pay off the debt that hangs around the neck of every American family like an unpaid credit card bill," Majority Whip Tom DeLay, R-Texas, said at a Sept. 13 news conference.

Democrats glibly endorsed the measure, saying it should be read as repudiation of the Republicans' push for deep tax cuts. "This has to be a pretty embarrassing day for my Republican friends," said Charles B. Rangel of New York, the top Democrat on Ways and Means.

Democrats also criticized the GOP for advancing a plan that would emphasize debt relief for only one year, leaving the door open to embracing the tax cuts proposed by the Republican presidential candidate, Texas Gov. George W. Bush.

The bill would create points of order against using the surpluses in the Social Security and Medicare Hospital Insurance (Part A) trust funds for anything other than servicing the debt. It would also set aside $42 billion of the remaining "on-budget" surplus for debt reduction, although it would not create points of order to protect those funds. The dedicated funds would be placed in a new debt reduction account at the Treasury Department.

Senate Republicans endorsed the idea but would not commit to moving the legislation. A Senate Budget Committee spokesman said GOP senators view the plan more as a guide for the coming spate of deal-cutting than as a legislative vehicle. A spokesman for Majority Leader Trent Lott, R-Miss., was noncommittal when asked Sept. 13 whether Lott would call up the bill if the House passed it.

The House has already voted three times this summer on similar GOP debt reduction measures; each (HR 4866, HR 4601, HR 3859) passed overwhelmingly despite their being labeled meaningless by the Democrats.

Spending Shift

The Republicans have countered that each of their debt reduction measures is an exercise in fiscal discipline. But a close examination of the most recent proposal shows that the GOP is willing to increase discretionary spending by about 7 percent in fiscal 2001 — essentially the price it is willing to pay to minimize another round of election-year conflict with the president.

Excluding Social Security and Medicare, the fiscal 2001 surplus will be about $70 billion, the Congressional Budget Office (CBO) estimates. If $42 billion were set aside for debt reduction, about $28 billion would remain. Although no firm plan for that money has yet been declared, Republican leaders have signaled that they would split it between tax cuts and spending.

The same CBO surplus estimate, however, assumes that discretionary spending will keep up with inflation next year, meaning it would grow from $608 billion to $638 billion in outlays. If an additional $14 billion were added on top of that, spending would total $652 billion. That is $27 billion more in outlays than allowed under the GOP-drafted budget resolution (H Con Res 290) for fiscal 2001.

House Appropriations Committee Chairman C.W. Bill Young, R-Fla., who for months has pleaded with party leaders to abandon the budget resolution and provide the funds needed to get bills cleared and signed by Clinton, appeared pleased with the debt-reduction plan. Young said in a Sept. 13 interview that he believes it would give him the extra money he needs to get his work done.

Young also endorsed another idea making the rounds among GOP leaders — divvying up the debt relief and having each unfinished appropriations bill carry a piece of it in the form of a debt reduction rider. GOP leaders hope that would make the remaining spending bills more appealing to the the party's most fiscally conservative members.

The focus on debt reduction appeared to have the desired effect of getting spending bills moving again in the House, even though none of the measures have yet been equipped with a debt rider. On Sept. 14, the House was able to finish two appropriations tasks that had been on its agenda since before the summer recess, narrowly passing the measure (HR 4942) that funds the District of Columbia and adopting a conference report (HR 4516) that combines the Treasury-Postal Service and legislative branch bills and would repeal the telephone excise tax.

Two more such "mini-omnibus" packages are in the works. One would combine the conference report on the energy and water development bill (HR 4733) with provisions of the Commerce-Justice-State measure (HR 4690), which the House passed but the Senate has never voted on. The other would merge the transportation bill (HR 4475) conference agreement with versions of the VA-HUD measure (HR 4635) passed by the House and approved by the Senate Appropriations Committee on Sept. 13.

It appears, however, that trouble may lie ahead for this newly formed tactic, which was designed to advance the spending agenda by essentially denying senators a chance to amend the bills. "I will resist it," said Pete V. Domenici, R-N.M., chairman of the Senate Energy and Water Development Subcommittee. "I have enough trouble doing my own" bill. ◆

House Rejects Overhaul Of Annual Budget Process, Retains Deficit-Era Rules

Box Score

- **Bill:** HR 853
- **Legislative action: House** defeated HR 853 (H Rept 106-198, Parts 1-3), 166-250, on May 16.

SUMMARY

The House defeated a proposal, two years in the making, to revamp the congressional budget process. Only 12 Democrats supported the measure, while 63 Republicans opposed the bill. The White House also objected to the bill.

Critics of the current system say Congress spends too much time and energy on budgeting and appropriations and too little effort on program oversight and authorization. They also have complained about the growth of emergency and supplemental spending measures. The bill sparked a territorial war between its sponsors and the appropriators, who saw it as an assault on their authority.

The bill would have created an annual reserve fund for emergencies, designed to limit non-budgeted supplemental spending. The annual budget resolution would have been changed from a concurrent resolution, which does not require the president's signature, to a joint resolution, which has the force of law upon enactment. It would have eased pay-as-you-go budget rules to allow surpluses not generated by Social Security to be used for tax cuts or new entitlement spending, and weakened the Senate rule that requires 60 votes to amend budget-reconciliation bills with non-germane provisions.

In an attempt to overcome objections by appropriators, Republican leaders put before the House a somewhat narrow bill, without some of the proposals that had engendered the most opposition. The rules for floor debate allowed these provisions to be considered as amendments.

The two most controversial amendments were rejected. One would have created automatic continuing resolutions, the stopgap spending measures that keep the government running whenever the appropriations process is not completed by the start of a new fiscal year. The other, backed by GOP leaders and President Clinton, would have created a two-year budget cycle, with passage of a budget resolution and appropriations bills in the first year of each Congress, and the election year reserved for program authorization and oversight.

House Defeats Bill That Would Have Updated Process

MAY 20 — An overhaul of the budget process is likely dead for the year, despite near universal agreement in Congress that changes are sorely needed.

Budget Law: A Brief History

MAY 20 — The federal government did not operate under a budget in its first 130 years, as each agency pressed its own spending request upon Congress. Five major laws to revamp the budget process have been enacted since.

1921. The president was given the statutory responsibility to send Congress an annual budget. The Bureau of the Budget — later renamed the Office of Management and Budget — was created as a clearinghouse for agency budget requests, and the General Accounting Office was formed as Congress' first attempt to strengthen its oversight of spending.

1946. Congress was required to approve a concurrent resolution setting an annual ceiling on spending, and a Joint Budget Committee — the entire House Appropriations and Ways and Means and Senate Appropriations and Finance committees — was created to prepare the resolution. The process was abandoned as unwieldy three years later.

1974. The main tenets for the current budget process were set under a law (PL 93-344) creating the Congressional Budget Office and the House and Senate Budget committees. Those panels were directed to review the impact of legislation on federal expenditures and to draft two concurrent budget resolutions, in the spring and fall. The fall resolution was informally dropped in the early 1980s. The law also set the ground rules for reconciliation, the process by which tax laws and spending programs are changed to reach targets set by the budget resolution.

1985. The Gramm-Rudman-Hollings Act (PL 99-177) created an automatic deficit reduction tool called sequestration — across-the-board spending cuts — to be triggered when Congress and the president failed to meet an annual deficit target. The law also mandated that any increase in spending be offset with either spending cuts or revenue increases.

1990. A deficit reduction law (PL 101-508) set annual caps for three fiscal years on discretionary appropriations for domestic, defense and international programs. It also subjected taxes and entitlements to pay-as-you-go procedures, which required all tax cuts, new entitlement programs or expansions of existing entitlements to be offset either by additional taxes or by cuts in existing entitlement programs.

Advocates of changing the way congressional fiscal policy is set generally agree that less time should be devoted to budgeting and appropriations and more time should be devoted to program oversight. But they have been outmuscled by the appropriators, who viewed some of the key provisions in the latest package as attempts to shackle their power. Other opponents said they feared some of the changes would have transferred too much power to the executive branch.

The result is that Congress, while awash in surplus revenue, likely will be stuck with an aging set of budget rules designed in an era of deficit spending. These now seem sure to stay in place until at least 2003, when surpluses are expected to hit perhaps $250 billion or more and the federal government will likely be in the black for the sixth straight year.

Many House members expressed enthusiasm for various portions of a bill (HR 853) to alter the budget process that was brought to the House floor May 16, or for some of the amendments proposed for the measure. "We have got to change the system," said Bob Clement, D-Tenn., a Budget Committee member. "We are going to be fighting over surpluses and priorities rather than fighting over deficits in the past."

But even after rejecting several of the more controversial proposed amendments, the House resoundingly defeated the legislation, 166-250. *(Vote 189, p. H-62)*

Only 12 Democrats supported the measure, while 63 Republicans opposed the bill, which also drew an array of objections from the White House. The vote was the surest sign yet that those who want to change the way Congress sets fiscal policy have yet to divine the combination of provisions needed to put a head of steam behind their effort. In the Senate, the Governmental Affairs Committee approved a budget overhaul bill (S 92) last year, but Senate leaders have shown no inclination to schedule floor time for it.

With both chambers now focused on the fiscal 2001 appropriations bills and narrowing their other priorities to a handful — so that adjournment can come in plenty of time for the fall campaign — any change to the budget process has effectively been deferred to the 107th Congress. Even if a deal were struck early next year, however, budget analysts say that any significant package of changes could not be implemented until the following Congress.

Patrick J. Toomey, R-Pa., who supported the House bill, was not disheartened. He said overhauling the budget process probably would require multiple attempts, and just getting something to the floor represented progress. "I think it's helpful for our cause for the American public to hear this debate," he said May 16.

But Joe Moakley of Massachusetts, the top Democrat on the Rules Committee, said he would have preferred that the House debate bills to boost patients' rights, alter the campaign finance system or other priorities than spend floor time on a doomed effort. "I don't know why this thing came up," he said. "That's just the way the game goes."

Even Republican leaders who supported the bill seemed nonchalant about its fate, and there was little evident GOP arm-twisting on the bill's behalf. During the vote, retiring Budget Committee Chairman John R. Kasich, R-Ohio, a cosponsor, demonstrated his golf swing for a small gathering of colleagues on the floor, as the number of "no" votes on the tally board surpassed 200 and kept climbing.

The effort was spearheaded by Jim Nussle, R-Iowa, who hopes to succeed Kasich as chairman.

The bill had two main provisions. In a bid to constrain unbudgeted midyear "supplemental" spending, it proposed to establish a budgeted — and therefore limited — annual reserve fund for emergencies to replace the current "emergency" spending measures that have no budgetary or other structural ceilings.

In a bid to put more teeth in the budget Congress drafts for each fiscal year, it would have turned that document into a joint resolution, which has the force of law upon enactment. The budget now moves as a concurrent resolution, legislative vehicles generally reserved for matters affecting internal congressional operations that are not sent to the president for signature. As such, critics of the budget process see the annual resolution as a paper tiger — and one that Congress routinely ignores.

Supporters say making the budget an annual law would force Congress and the White House to settle their fiscal disputes early in the year and avoid end-of-session showdowns. Opponents said it would give the president too much power over Congress' ability to influence the budget and national priorities.

Sonny Callahan, R-Ala., chairman of the House Appropriations Foreign Operations Subcommittee, had been expected to try to strike this provision, but he did not do so. Callahan disliked the entire bill, and other Republicans suggested he abandon his amendment as a strategic move, believing that leaving the provision in the bill would help ensure the measure's defeat.

Appropriators Unite

Although some Appropriations Committee members supported pieces of the budget overhaul effort, they generally viewed the bill as an assault on their authority. Of the 60 panel members, only nine Republicans voted for passage; no Democrats did so.

Appropriators were particularly opposed to an amendment calling for automatic continuing resolutions, the stopgap spending measures that keep the government running whenever Congress and the president fail to wrap up the annual appropriations process by the Oct. 1 start of the new fiscal year. It was rejected, 173-236. *(Vote 187, p. H-62)*

Opponents said the amendment was a serious threat to congressional authority. Appropriations Committee member James T. Walsh, R-N.Y., compared it with the line-item veto law (PL 104-130) struck down two years ago. *(1998 Almanac, p. 6-17)*

"The Supreme Court said, 'Do not do that, you idiots. Do not give the that power to the president,' " Walsh said. "They gave it back to us, thank God. Now we are going to yield more power to the president by putting the government out on automatic pilot."

Budget Committee member Ken Bentsen, D-Texas, added, "If we pass this, we might as well shut the place down, go home . . . and let the bureaucrats run the operation."

George W. Gekas, R-Pa., who offered the amendment, and other supporters said the proposal would prevent government shutdowns and reduce partisan budget brinkmanship. Supporters of the amendment, and of the bill in general, shied away from directly accusing the appropriators of fighting a turf war, but the sentiment was evident nonetheless. Nussle complained that some foes of the budget overhaul were motivated by "personal and individual power, committee jurisdiction [and] prerogative."

Biennial Budgeting

Rules Committee Chairman David Dreier, R-Calif., offered an amendment calling for a two-year budget cycle, saying that change would give Congress more time to spend on program oversight and reauthorization. It was defeated, 201-217. *(Vote 186, p. H-60)*

Although the White House supported the amendment, a coalition led by ranking Budget Committee Democrat John M. Spratt Jr. of South Carolina opposed it. "Members of Congress would write appropriations bills only in the early months of a term and would be fiscal lame ducks thereafter, with significantly less leverage in getting agencies to change their policies or practices," Spratt's group wrote in a May 15 letter to all House Democrats.

Under the amendment, the first year of each Congress would be devoted to a budget resolution and appropriations bills; the next would be devoted to program authorization and oversight.

The Senate bill similarly called for biennial budgeting, and the idea has been endorsed by Senate Majority Leader Trent Lott, R-Miss., and House Speaker J. Dennis Hastert, R-Ill.

Two amendments by Paul D. Ryan, R-Wis., were approved on voice votes. One would direct that funds cut from appropriations bills could not be spent elsewhere. The other would allow on-budget surpluses to be used for tax relief or new mandatory spending programs. Under current law, such items are subject to rules requiring offsetting revenue increases or spending cuts. Ryan said the provisions would help Congress do its budget work better in an era of surpluses. The White House had threatened vetoes over both items. ◆

CQ

Chapter 7

CONGRESSIONAL AFFAIRS

Action on Campaign Finance Reform Limited to Closing Tax Loophole on '527' PACs

SUMMARY

Congress passed, and the president signed on July 1, the first change in federal election law in two decades. The new law closed the loophole on so-called 527 political action committees, but Congress failed to pass broader bills pushed by advocates of overhauling the nation's campaign finance system.

For years, Congress had failed to pass any sweeping changes in the way political elections are funded. Measures often were approved in the House, but eventually fell victim to Senate filibusters.

In June, Sen. John McCain, R-Ariz., Congress' leading proponent of campaign finance overhaul, decided to take a more targeted approach and pushed for a narrow bill that would crack down on "527" political action committees. The secret fundraising groups, organized under Section 527 of the tax code, spent millions of dollars on elections but were not required to disclose their donors or expenditures as long as they did not expressly advocate the election or defeat of a candidate.

McCain had been the target of such a group, Republicans for Clean Air, which ran more than $2 million in television ads attacking the senator in his race for the GOP presidential nomination against Texas Gov. George W. Bush.

McCain, along with Sens. Russell D. Feingold, D-Wis., and Joseph I. Lieberman, D-Conn., on June 8 offered an amendment to the defense authorization bill (S 2549) requiring full public disclosure of "527" groups. The amendment required the groups to register with the IRS and file publicly available tax returns. The groups also were required to specify annual expenditures of more than $500 to any individual, and to report the names and addresses of those who contribute more than $200 a year.

Despite strong opposition from GOP leaders, the Senate adopted the amendment by voice vote, after a procedural attempt to block the vote failed, 42-57.

Senate action prompted some House members to push their leaders to take up the disclosure language. House GOP leaders, generally opposed to changing campaign finance laws, wrote their own legislation, which proponents of overhaul attacked as overly broad and weighted with controversial measures that seemed likely to doom it. They also said it was possibly unconstitutional. The Ways and Means Committee approved the leadership bill (HR 4717 — H Rept 106-702) on a 23-14 party-line vote June 22.

House leaders, however, quickly bowed to pressure from their members and from outside groups that opposed HR 4717 and instead brought to the floor a straightforward "527" disclosure bill. The House easily passed the measure, which the Senate cleared less than 36 hours later.

Box Score

- **Bill:** HR 4762 — PL 106-230
- **Legislative action: House** passed HR 4762, 385-39, on June 28.

Senate cleared HR 4762, 92-6, on June 29.

President signed the bill July 1.

Senate Adopts Measure That Requires Full Disclosure of '527s'

JUNE 10 — The wide-eyed grin on Arizona Sen. John McCain's face was an image as distant as the February snow in New Hampshire, where he rocked the political establishment with a presidential primary win — until the dramatic events on the Senate floor June 8.

Months after McCain dropped out of a presidential campaign that he had built on a call for an overhaul of campaign finance laws, the senator launched an attack on his rivals in the Senate leadership, winning adoption of an amendment that would require full disclosure of contributors and spending by a growing number of secret political groups.

McCain was targeted by one of the groups, called "527s" after the section of the tax code that governs their existence, when Republicans for Clean Air ran TV ads attacking the senator shortly before his March primaries against Texas Gov. George W. Bush. The groups span the political and ideological spectrum, from the Sierra Club's organization to the Club for Growth, which advocates limited government and lower taxes.

McCain's Senate victory was the first evidence that the popularity he gained through his presidential bid could give him greater power to push his agenda on Capitol Hill. The Senate's voice vote approval of McCain's amendment, which took place after the chamber voted, 42-57, against a point of order that would have blocked the vote, was the first time since 1993 that the chamber had voted for a major campaign finance change. *(Vote 122, p. S-23; 1993 Almanac, p. 37)*

"Now that we've won, it will become law one way or another because we'll just keep forcing votes," said a jubilant McCain, standing beside his longtime partner in the campaign finance debate, Russell D. Feingold, D-Wis., and a newcomer to the fight, Joseph I. Lieberman, D-Conn., who last month introduced legislation (S 2583) to crack down on 527s.

McCain's words could prove true in the House, as well, where Republican moderates forced the leadership to agree to bring up some disclosure legislation before the July Fourth recess.

"It's getting harder and harder to hold people in line," said Rep. Michael N. Castle, R-Del., who introduced a

Amendment Highlights

JUNE 10 — The campaign finance amendment sponsored by Sens. John McCain, R-Ariz., Russell D. Feingold, D-Wis., and Joseph I. Lieberman, D-Conn., would impose certain requirements on so-called 527 organizations, which are named after Section 527 of the tax code.

527s are political groups formed to influence elections. Individuals, corporations and unions can donate unlimited amounts of money to these organizations. The groups do not have to report their contributions or spending to the Federal Election Commission, as long as they do not expressly call for the election or defeat of specific candidates. They generally are involved in issue advocacy.

Section 527 was written in 1975 after the Watergate scandal to set tax rules for political groups.

The amendment would:

- Require 527 groups to disclose their existence to the IRS and file publicly available tax returns. Disclosure would include the group's name and address, e-mail address, purpose, and names and addresses of officers and highly paid employees. A list of 527s would be posted on the Internet and be available through the IRS.
- Require 527 groups to file reports specifying annual expenditures of more than $500 to any individual, including the person's name, address and occupation. The IRS would be required to make the reports available to the public.
- Mandate that the names and addresses of those who contribute more than $200 a year to 527 groups be disclosed.

bill (HR 4621) on June 9 to require public disclosure by groups that sponsor political ads during an election. The morning after McCain's victory, Castle walked unannounced into the office of Speaker J. Dennis Hastert, R-Ill., with Amo Houghton, R-N.Y., to say several colleagues were considering a procedural motion to force a vote on the issue. "The McCain legislation really galvanized this big-time," Castle told reporters June 9.

After a brief, heated exchange on the floor June 9, the House defeated a procedural motion on the estate tax bill (HR 8) that would have forced a vote on a proposal by Lloyd Doggett, D-Texas, to require all political organizations to disclose their contributors. The 202-216 tally was largely partisan, but the GOP leadership agreed to allow a disclosure proposal to be brought to the floor before the recess. *(Vote 253, p. H-82)*

For advocates of campaign finance disclosure laws, the possibility that something could pass was a strange sensation. "This has been a year of dark storm clouds on the subject of money and politics. This is the first silver lining I've seen," said Larry Makinson, executive director of the Center for Responsive Politics, which monitors campaign contributions.

McCain and Feingold predicted that their victory — a precision attack on a single area of the law — could pressure colleagues to support their broader campaign finance goal: a complete ban on "soft money," the unlimited, unregulated cash that flows from corporations and labor unions to political parties. Senate Majority Leader Trent Lott, R-Miss., and National Republican Senatorial Committee Chairman Mitch McConnell, R-Ky., opposed the June 8 effort, just as they have fought McCain and Feingold on other campaign finance proposals.

"The significance of this is not just about this very important [provision]," Feingold told reporters minutes after the vote. "It's about banning soft money, and it's about momentum. This is really quite striking. [The leadership] vigorously opposed it. Sen. McConnell did what he could; Sen. Lott did what he could."

A New Dynamic

McCain said the idea for his sneak attack on stealth groups struck him in the middle of the night June 5: Why not change the nature of the campaign finance battle by seizing on one, easily definable area to fix? With several senators in tight re-election fights, McCain wanted to force their hand. Of the 13 Republicans who voted with him, eight are up for re-election in November.

For years, opponents of McCain's broader legislation (S 1593) have argued that one requirement — full public disclosure of contributions and expenditures — was the only necessary solution. In essence, McCain took their rhetoric and ran with it. "I thought, 'How could they vote against disclosure?' " McCain said shortly after the vote. "I thought we could change the dynamic."

On June 6, he called Feingold to his office and suggested they offer Lieberman's proposal as an amendment to an unrelated Defense Department authorization bill (S 2549). Under pressure from Democrats looking for ways to push their agenda, Lott had announced that he would allow amendments to that bill.

On the evening of June 7, GOP leaders agreed to schedule a vote on the McCain amendment for the next day. When the debate erupted June 8, it seemed McConnell and Lott expected to have the votes to block McCain. Lott and Armed Services Committee Chairman John W. Warner, R-Va., warned that the measure would kill the underlying defense bill because it would be rejected by the House for violating the constitutional requirement that changes in tax law originate in the House.

What resulted was an unusually open debate on the idea that the bill would be "blue-slipped" by the House. (The term arises because a House resolution to reject a Senate bill on constitutional grounds is printed on blue paper.)

The debate was replete with irony. Lawmakers who last year attached a five-year, $18.4 billion tax cut for small businesses to the Senate bankruptcy bill (S 625) as part of a proposal to raise the minimum wage, now fretted about whether McCain's amendment would, as Warner put it, "torpedo" the Pentagon budget bill and "send it to the bottom of the sea."

In fact, what often happens when a

bill is "blue-slipped" — especially one with such strong support — is that the Senate agrees to strip the objectionable language and send it back to the House. That occurred in 1994, when the House blue-slipped an appropriations bill because of a tax provision. *(1994 Almanac, p. 536)*

But it was not even clear that McCain's proposal would have qualified for such a fate. While the House zealously guards its right to originate tax bills, McCain's provision, in the view of several senior Senate aides in both parties, probably did not rise to the standard for a blue slip because its objective was to force disclosure, and any impact on revenue would be incidental. Still, the argument could give candidates some cover at election time.

Lott and others also attacked McCain's proposal as unfairly narrow, arguing that it would not curb the power of labor unions and other Democratic-leaning political groups. Sen. Rick Santorum, R-Pa., facing a tough re-election challenge, said on the floor: "Let's be honest with the public. We are rifle-shooting here and killing the political process by picking winners and losers."

McCain countered that 527s are used by both sides, noting the Sierra Club as a prime example of a left-leaning group that uses the law to obscure its activities. As for the charge that clouding the defense bill with unrelated measures could threaten the Pentagon, McCain charged: "This [opposition] is not about the defense of our nation; it's about the defense of a corrupt system."

Earlier in the day, McCain sent an e-mail to 200,000 supporters urging them to contact senators and pressure them to support the disclosure amendment. When the victory was complete, he e-mailed a thank you note: "I am pleased to inform you that your voices were heard. Today, and with your help, the Senate passed my amendment.

Republicans voting with McCain were Spencer Abraham of Michigan, Conrad Burns of Montana, Lincoln Chafee of Rhode Island, Susan Collins of Maine, Mike DeWine of Ohio, Chuck Hagel of Nebraska, Kay Bailey Hutchison of Texas, James M. Jeffords of Vermont, Richard G. Lugar of Indiana, Olympia J. Snowe of Maine, Gordon H. Smith of Oregon, Arlen Specter of Pennsylvania and Fred Thompson of Tennessee.

McCain agreed to negotiate an agreement with Lott to possibly broaden the disclosure law to include other political organizations that are not 527 groups but are not required to fully disclose donors and expenditures. "I'm not averse to full disclosure on any organization that's in American political campaigns, but we need to make sure it's balanced," McCain said. He also was gleeful about his win. "It's like New Hampshire," he said, chatting with reporters in the Senate press gallery. "Where's the confetti?"

Support Grows for Curbing Secrecy Of '527' Groups

JUNE 17 — A surprise drive to require some of the most secretive organizations involved in U.S. politics to disclose their spending and contributors gained momentum the week of June 12.

Just days after GOP leaders failed to defeat a plan to require such confidential political groups to reveal their activities, Mitch McConnell, R-Ky., the leading Senate opponent of that effort, turned around and embraced a bill that included it — provided labor unions and business groups also would be forced to disclose more about their political activities.

The fledgling election-year move to correct what campaign finance overhaul advocates such as Sen. John McCain, R-Ariz., consider the system's worst abuses also picked up behind-the-scenes momentum in the House. There, advocates of changing campaign finance laws worked toward a promised vote by July Fourth on bipartisan legislation to require greater openness from politically active tax-exempt groups, including those that run issue ads financed by unregulated "soft money" donations.

"We believe the public — at a bare minimum — has the right to know who is spending money on advertising that seeks to influence elections, be it corporations, labor unions, wealthy individuals or foreign nationals," Reps. Christopher Shays, R-Conn., Martin T. Meehan, D-Mass., and several others said in a June 15 "Dear Colleague" letter.

The burgeoning effort on both sides of Capitol Hill comes on the heels of a Senate vote June 8 to require groups governed by Section 527 of the tax code, which currently do not have to disclose information on their political operations, to do so.

The controversial "527s" are the latest cause célèbre among advocates of tightening campaign finance laws. Such 527s include groups organized by House GOP Whip Tom DeLay of Texas to sway close House races, and an organization called Republicans for Clean Air, which ran television ads financed by wealthy Texas businessmen supporting presumptive GOP presidential nominee George W. Bush in his tough primary campaign against McCain.

Nobody says that the renewed drive on campaign finance is a sure bet to become law this year. The bitterness engulfing campaign finance issues is difficult to overstate, and efforts to expand disclosure requirements beyond 527 organizations are sure to draw powerful opposition from interest groups, including unions and business associations such as the U.S. Chamber of Commerce.

"They've decided that they're not fighting the 527 disclosure movement," Sen. Joseph I. Lieberman, D-Conn., said of Senate GOP leaders. "We want to make sure that they don't love it to death."

Driving the effort to overhaul laws on campaign finance is the potential for abuse by 527s, which can secretly accept unlimited amounts of money from unidentified contributors and spend it on political activities such as running attack ads, registering voters or distributing voter guides. Organizations across the political spectrum, from the Sierra Club to the Christian Coalition, have organized 527s. Increasingly, however, such political arms are being established by congressional leaders such as DeLay to collect large contributions. DeLay's Republican Majority Issues Committee aims to spend $25 million to elect Republicans this year.

Many Proposals

It is unclear just how the latest campaign overhaul effort will proceed and whether GOP leaders in either chamber can control it. House leaders — who last year unsuccessfully resisted a bill (HR 417) by Shays and Meehan to rein in soft money and make other campaign finance changes — have promised a vote by July Fourth on the issue. GOP leaders tried to quash the 527 effort, led by partisan Democrat Lloyd Doggett of Texas, but bowed to pressure from their own ranks to schedule a vote after Republican overhaul advocates threatened to vote with Democrats to bring Doggett's proposal to the floor over GOP leaders' objections.

The task of developing the House measure was assigned to moderate Amo Houghton, R-N.Y., chairman of the Ways and Means Subcommittee on Oversight, which will hold a hearing June 20. Houghton pledged to develop a bipartisan consensus, but he has to weigh the desires of overhaul advocates against the demands of GOP leaders such as DeLay, whose political activities would be affected by the drive.

"We want something we can argue is real reform and then try to get DeLay to be neutral on it," said an aide to a House GOP moderate. "We don't expect him to endorse anything."

Houghton supports disclosure requirements for 527 organizations, but wants to extend such disclosure to unions, nonprofit groups and trade associations that spend more than $10,000 on political activities such as television and radio ads, phone banks and mass mailings. His proposal would also require such groups to disclose any money they funnel to 527s, and to file quarterly reports with the IRS on their lobbying and political activities.

Shays and Meehan's approach is somewhat different. They are pushing for disclosure mandates on 527 groups, coupled with a plan modeled on an amendment by Sens. Olympia J. Snowe, R-Maine, and James M. Jeffords, R-Vt., to require disclosure of fundraising and spending by all groups that spend $10,000 per year or more on electioneering ads that mention any federal candidate. It would not apply to other political activities, such as get-out-the-vote drives. The Snowe-Jeffords plan garnered a narrow majority in the Senate in 1998 but died in a McConnell-led filibuster. *(1998 Almanac, p. 18-3)*

The measure would give nonprofits an incentive to segregate their political spending from general revenues.

GOP leaders and the campaign finance overhaul wing of the party have a longstanding antagonistic history. But given the June 8 Senate vote and the upcoming House vote, it may be impossible to put the genie back in the bottle. "If a balanced bill comes out, it may be tough for anyone to stop it," said Paul Leonard, chief of staff for Rep. Michael N. Castle, R-Del.

Constitutional Muster

The latest Senate bill (S 2742), sponsored by Gordon H. Smith, R-Ore., with the blessing of GOP leaders such as Majority Leader Trent Lott of Mississippi, appears to be an effort to wrest control of the debate from McCain and allies Lieberman and Russell D. Feingold, D-Wis. McCain dealt Lott an embarrassing loss June 8 when he succeeded in attaching a 527 disclosure measure to the fiscal 2001 defense authorization bill (S 2549).

McCain cautiously embraced the Senate GOP leadership effort even though it contained elements that he regards as "poison pills," such as a broad requirement that unions and business trade associations disclose spending not just on advertising but also on grassroots political and lobbying efforts. McConnell's foes accuse him of a vendetta against labor unions, a key Democratic ally in campaigns.

"It's clear when you read the language that what [McConnell] is trying to do is go after a lot of internal union communications and in-kind contributions," said a Senate aide to a McConnell critic.

McCain also criticized a provision in the Smith-McConnell bill that would invalidate the entire measure if any piece of it was declared unconstitutional. The effect of such a "nonseverability" clause would be to invalidate disclosure requirements on 527 groups, which would be constitutional, if greater disclosure requirements on other groups were found to be unconstitutional.

Among the main legal issues is whether requiring groups to list donors of political money would violate a 1958 Supreme Court decision in *NAACP v. Alabama*. The justices held that private organizations cannot be forced to divulge their membership. Another is whether it would violate the 1976 decision in *Buckley v. Valeo* that said the government cannot require disclosure of issue advocacy activities, including election-related activities that do not expressly call for the defeat or election of a particular candidate.

McConnell said he expects anything that might pass to be challenged in the courts. He acknowledged that he thinks the bill he supports may be unconstitutional.

"I think requiring disclosure of issue advocacy is of dubious constitutionality," McConnell said at a June 15 news conference. "However, the Senate last week decided it wanted to go down this road. And so my view is, if the majority of the Senate wants to go down this path, let's make sure it's broad and effective."

The Smith-McConnell bill came in the wake of a major battle over McCain and Lieberman's more narrowly targeted effort on 527 disclosure. During debate on that measure, several Republicans embraced requiring 527s to disclose their activities, but said other groups should do so as well.

S 2742 covers trade and business associations and unions, including Democratic-tilting groups such as the Association of Trial Lawyers of America. But it would not apply to nonprofit civic and social welfare groups, such as the National Right to Life Committee, the AARP or the National Rifle Association. McConnell said such groups would unite to topple the effort if they were included.

Hagel's Bill

The developments on disclosure came as McConnell canceled a June 14 Rules and Administration Committee markup of a bill (S 1816) by Chuck Hagel, R-Neb., to increase limits on "hard money" contributions to candidates from $1,000 per election to $3,000 and to limit "soft money" giving to national party committees. The bill had a smattering of support among Democrats but is opposed by McCain and his allies.

McConnell said he called off the markup because he did not want to force panel Republicans, whose roster is dominated by senior senators such as Lott and GOP Whip Don Nickles of Oklahoma, to sit through a lengthy markup. The chance of Hagel's bill making it to the floor was remote at best, and it worsened as prospects for a disclosure-related measure brightened.

House Ways and Means Approves Campaign Finance Measure

JUNE 24 — A popular effort to close a loophole in federal campaign finance law that permits secret organizations to pump millions of dollars in untraceable money into political campaigns has become ensnared in bitter partisanship.

The bill (HR 4717) is scheduled for a House vote the week of June 26 after the Ways and Means Committee approved it, 23-14, in a party-line vote June 22.

Its prospects on the floor are poor. A coalition of Republican and Democratic advocates of tighter campaign finance laws oppose it out of concern that it would infringe on constitutional rights of free association. Traditional GOP allies such as the National Right to Life Committee and the Christian Coalition strongly oppose the prospect of having to disclose their donors and activities. The bill was sponsored by moderate Amo Houghton, R-N.Y., but bears the fingerprints of House GOP Whip Tom DeLay of Texas, Republican aides said.

What started as an attempt to force often-secretive political groups organized under Section 527 of the tax code to disclose their political activities and funding sources was broadened to apply to the politicking of virtually all tax-exempt organizations, including labor unions, trade associations and issue-oriented nonprofits such as the National Rifle Association and the Sierra Club.

"527s," as they have been dubbed by Washington insiders, are increasingly the weapon of choice of those who seek to use largely unregulated "soft money" to influence elections.

Recent examples of controversial 527s include a group linked to DeLay that financed advertisements linking Republican-turned-Democrat Rep. Michael P. Forbes of New York to former Speaker Newt Gingrich, R-Ga. (1979-99). Another 527, called Republicans for Clean Air, ran more than $2 million in television ads supporting presumptive GOP presidential nominee George W. Bush in his hard-fought primary against Sen. John McCain, R-Ariz., a top supporter of tighter campaign finance laws. McCain and Joseph I. Lieberman, D-Conn., won a big Senate vote June 8 to require 527s to disclose information on their activities to the public.

House Republicans opted instead to broaden new disclosure rules beyond the activities of 527s.

"Disclosure of political activities by tax- exempt organizations — all tax-exempt organizations — is good for our system," said Ways and Means Chairman Bill Archer, R-Texas. "Voters have a right to know what groups are running ads or writing letters and who is paying for them."

Democrats on the often-partisan Ways and Means panel protested that the bill was drafted so broadly that it would apply to non-political activities by nonprofits and would almost certainly be declared unconstitutional by the Supreme Court, which has held that groups that do not specifically call for a vote for or against a candidate do not have to reveal their activities or who pays for them. The court, ruling in the 1976 case of *Buckley v. Valeo*, held that only political activity to "expressly advocate the election or defeat" of a candidate must be disclosed. This standard leaves room for "issue advocacy" ads financed by soft money contributions to support or attack candidates. *(1976 Almanac, p. 461)*

The House GOP bill is sweeping in scope. It would require any tax-exempt group that spends $10,000 or more per year on political activity to disclose to the IRS any actions that seek to influence the selection or election of any federal, state or local public official. The names of those who contributed $1,000 or more per year to the organization would also have to be disclosed. Only veterans' groups would be exempt.

In addition, the groups would have to disclose all mass media communications — including mailings, ads, phone banks and e-mail alerts — that mentioned any federal officeholder or candidate. Democrats complained that this requirement would cover many non-political activities by nonprofits, which would then have to disclose many of their members.

"This will have a chilling effect" on nonprofits, said California Democrat Robert T. Matsui. "This is such overkill."

The alternative offered by Democrats, however, also had potential constitutional problems. That plan, defeated on a 14-23 party-line vote, combined a 527 disclosure requirement with a provision to require virtually all groups or individuals who ran political ads within 90 days of a federal general election to disclose their spending and the names of anyone who gave more than $1,000 for such electioneering. The plan mirrored elements of a proposal by Sens. Olympia J. Snowe, R-Maine, and James M. Jeffords, R-Vt., that the Senate narrowly endorsed in 1998. *(1998 Almanac, p. 18-3)*

The Democratic plan, offered by top 527 critic Lloyd Doggett, D-Texas, was based on a proposal by House campaign finance overhaul advocates Michael N. Castle, R-Del., Christopher Shays, R-Conn., and Martin T. Meehan, D-Mass., that was outlined in a June 15 letter to Houghton. Negotiations with Houghton had a positive tone, members and staff aides said, but Houghton could not persuade GOP leaders to make any substantive changes. "Amo was very unhappy with what happened. . . . He really wanted a truly bipartisan bill," said a senior Ways and Means Democrat.

A federal appeals court ruling in *Vermont Right to Life Committee, Inc. v. Sorrell*, issued a week before the markup, held that the Snowe-Jeffords approach endorsed by Democrats and some GOP moderates was "unconstitutional on its face" because it would apply to issue-related speech specifically protected under the *Buckley* decision.

Compounding the constitutional questions surrounding efforts to require disclosure of those who finance political ads is the fact that lawyers advising 527s and other politically active nonprofits could probably find ways to avert any new disclosure requirements passed by Congress. For example, a 527 nonprofit could be converted into a for-profit shell corporation devoted to the same political purposes.

"If the McCain bill passed, I and other election lawyers in town could get around it in 24 hours," said a Senate GOP staff aide.

Senate Majority Leader Trent Lott, R-Miss., said June 22 that he hoped to bring a bill to the floor soon. But Lott may have difficulty controlling the outcome. A bill (S 2742) by Gordon H. Smith, R-Ore., and Mitch McConnell, R-Ky., which would require 527s as well as unions and trade associations to disclose their spending and contributors, has come under attack from McCain — who prevailed June 8.

Senate Clears Bill After GOP Drops Effort to Include Labor Unions

JULY 1 — Calling its passage "a big deal," President Clinton said he will sign a bill that is intended to shed light on a new breed of secretive nonprofit political organizations. But some political analysts said the measure would have a negligible effect on the campaign finance system and this year's elections.

The bill (HR 4762) would close a loophole in election law and require so-called 527s to disclose their political activities and who pays for them. It won a surprisingly swift and decisive victory: The Senate voted 92-6 on June 29 to clear the bill, less than 36 hours after the House voted, 385-39, to pass it in the wee hours of June 28. *(Senate vote 160, p. S-29; House vote 341, p. H-108)*

"This bill will not solve what is wrong with our campaign finance system. It will not do away with the millions of soft-money dollars that are polluting our elections," said Sen. John McCain, R-Ariz., referring to the largely unregulated contributions that flow to political parties.

"But it will give the public information regarding one especially pernicious weapon that is being used in modern campaigns, an egregious and outrageous insult to the principles of how democracies function."

"Getting the disclosure of these secret committees is a big deal," Clinton said at a June 28 Democratic fundraising event. "It could ratify a principle that we all in both parties say we believe in, which is full disclosure."

The bill would require that any 527 group that raises at least $25,000 annually report to the IRS each donor of $200 or more and any spending of more than $500.

McCain sparked the boomlet three weeks ago when he unexpectedly won a vote to require disclosure by the under-the-radar political groups organized under section 527 of the tax code.

One such group, Republicans for Clean Air, ran about $2.5 million worth of television ads supporting Texas Gov. George W. Bush against McCain during their tough GOP presidential primary campaign. But the bill would not affect the activities of nonprofit groups such as the National Right to Life Committee, which also worked against McCain.

In the end, Republican leaders in both the House and Senate moved with remarkable speed to get out of the way of the McCain steamroller.

"I do not think this is a spear worth falling on . . . four months in advance of an election," said Mitch McConnell of Kentucky, chairman of the National Republican Senatorial Committee, who is a sometimes bitter foe of McCain and his campaign finance crusade.

But McConnell and others said the measure may end up having a negligible impact on people who are determined to secretly finance campaign ads and other political activities. In fact, even before the bill's passage, lawmakers and aides said several organizations had devised ways to reorganize and get around the looming law.

"These groups could just disband and reconstitute themselves," said McConnell spokesman Robert Steurer. For example, they could convert themselves into a for-profit shell corporation but avoid any tax penalty by ensuring that they always operate at a loss.

Among those pushing hardest for a quick vote was McConnell, who said Republicans will not be harmed in the fall.

Both House and Senate GOP leaders shelved plans to try to advance alternatives to broaden the measure to cover Democratic-tilting groups such as labor unions along with Republican allies on the conservative side of the political spectrum.

GOP leaders instead accepted a move by advocates of overhauling campaign finance laws to return to an approach that would affect only 527 groups. Such groups — which are not currently required to disclose their activities and donors if they do not specifically call for election or defeat of a candidate — are increasingly the weapon of choice for those seeking to use soft money to influence elections.

House Was Focus

When the week of June 26 began, the focus was on the House, where GOP leaders officially stood behind a sweeping bill (HR 4717) approved by the House Ways and Means Committee only a few days before.

That bill had immediately come under withering fire from nonprofit groups across the political spectrum. From the GOP-tilting National Rifle Association (NRA) to Democratic-friendly unions, a wave of nonprofit organizations went nuclear in their efforts to kill the bill.

The Ways and Means bill, sponsored by Amo Houghton, R-N.Y., included 527 disclosure requirements similar to those that ultimately passed, but it also would have covered a huge number of politically potent tax-exempt groups that engage in "issue advocacy" activities that aim to sway lawmakers or affect their prospects at the polls.

Opponents vigorously argued that the Ways and Means bill would have deprived their members of their right to free association and to participate in legislative and political advocacy without having to name their members and subject them to possible harassment from the government or their rivals.

Republican-friendly groups such as the NRA, the National Right to Life Committee and the Christian Coalition denounced the bill as an unconstitutional infringement on the right of free association. They also said the Ways and Means bill was drafted so broadly that even routine grassroots advocacy would trigger reporting requirements.

"We do not believe that the Constitution permits our elected representatives to demand that groups of citizens, organized to promote a cause, must report to government bureaucrats every instance in which they dare to utter the name of a federal politician," said National Right to Life Committee Executive Director David N. O'Steen and Legislative Director Douglas Johnson, in a June 23 letter to Congress.

Among those pushing to broaden the bill to cover more groups than 527s was Majority Whip Tom DeLay, R-Texas, who organized his own 527, the Republican Majority Issues Committee, which aims to spend $25 million to help elect Republicans in the fall.

DeLay's critics suggested he was working to broaden the bill so that it would topple of its own weight. DeLay aide Tony Rudy, however, insisted his boss played no role in writing Houghton's bill.

Houghton's broad approach was clearly doomed. But House GOP leaders had promised Republican advocates of overhauling campaign finance laws a vote prior to the July Fourth recess. As the week of June 26 began, the question was how to fulfill that promise.

Moderates saw a plot aimed at ensuring failure on the floor. Indeed, the Houghton bill, which almost certainly would fail to garner a majority, was first tentatively slated for consideration under House rules that require a two-thirds vote for passage.

Reps. Michael N. Castle, R-Del., and Christopher Shays, R-Conn., immediately protested and sought the chance to offer a bipartisan alternative. They focused on an approach that would have combined 527 disclosure requirements with a measure that would have required disclosure by virtually every outside organization — unions, nonprofits, trade associations and corporations — that spends more than $25,000 on political activity such as running ads, organizing phone banks or doing mass mailings shortly before an election.

Efforts to produce such an alternative failed to come together — and might have failed on the floor anyway. Still, it was clear that Speaker J. Dennis Hastert, R-Ill., wanted the issue out of his hair, so GOP leaders turned to what they knew could pass — a straightforward 527 disclosure bill.

"It needed to happen. It needed to get done," Hastert said the morning after the vote. "They were out there trying to tag that on to every bill we wanted to pass. That's just not acceptable."

Movement Began June 8

The runaway legislative locomotive began June 8, when McCain, Russell D. Feingold, D-Wis., and Joseph I. Lieberman, D-Conn., won a big Senate vote to attach their 527 disclosure bill to the fiscal 2001 defense authorization bill (S 2549) over the strong objections of Majority Leader Trent Lott, R-Miss., and McConnell. The vote was a 57-42 endorsement of the measure, but it understated the depth of support because it came on a procedural maneuver.

The impact of the legislation on this year's campaigns is expected to be modest.

Election law attorneys have already started devising ways to circumvent the disclosure requirements, which have an effective date of June 30. A Senate aide said even before the vote, one such 527, which the aide declined to identify, already had dropped its 527 status and reorganized its operations.

The measure may not be challenged in the courts if existing 527s decide it is less expensive to reorganize than to mount a lawsuit challenging the law as unconstitutional.

The constitutional argument is based on the view that private citizens seeking to express their views should not have to reveal who they are to the government. ◆

House Ends Three-Year Shuster Ethics Case With Grant of Immunity

SUMMARY

There was little public action on congressional ethics cases in 2000. The House Committee on Standards of Official Conduct publicly resolved two cases, while the Senate ethics panel concluded none. The House completed its three-year probe into powerful Transportation and Infrastructure Committee Chairman Bud Shuster, R-Pa., while setting what some called a questionable precedent by granting Shuster limited immunity in the investigation.

Baucus Sued By His Former Chief of Staff

OCTOBER 21 — Sen. Max Baucus' former chief of staff, who earlier this year declined to sue the Montana Democrat for alleged sexual harassment, has instead filed a lawsuit claiming employment discrimination.

In an Oct. 18 complaint, the former staff aide, Christine M. Niedermeier, alleged that Baucus has retaliated against her since she filed a harassment complaint in September 1999 by thwarting her efforts to find a job. "Sen. Baucus has told others that he would not give me a positive reference because I filed a sexual harassment complaint against him," Niedermeier said in a statement through her attorney.

Baucus, who is up for re-election in 2002, fired Niedermeier in August of last year. Baucus' spokesman, Michael Siegel, called Niedermeier's charge that Baucus and his staff have sought to "blackball" her efforts to find a job "completely and absolutely 100 percent false."

"I am unaware of a single prospective employer that has called Sen. Baucus or his staff looking for a reference for Ms. Niedermeier," Siegel added.

Niedermeier's original complaint, released Sept. 23, 1999, alleged a "continuous course of conduct of sexual harassment," which included "requesting more of my personal time and presence than the job warranted." Niedermeier also claimed she was fired after complaining of harassment. *(1999 Almanac, p. 8-17)*

Niedermeier declined to follow up her complaint, lodged under the Congressional Accountability Act (PL 104-1), with a lawsuit.

The suit for employment discrimination seeks $300,000 in damages because Niedermeier's "personal life, her financial security and her professional career have been devastated."

Baucus has consistently denied the allegations and has stated that he fired Niedermeier because she had behaved abusively toward other staff aides as well as constituents.

Brown Probe Ends; No Ethics Violations Found

SEPTEMBER 23 — The House ethics committee Sept. 20 wrapped up its 15-month investigation of Rep. Corrine Brown, D-Fla., saying it could not find sufficient evidence to prove improper conduct, but criticized her dealings with a wealthy African businessman.

The committee, formally called the Committee on Standards of Official Conduct, concluded that Brown's relationship with West African businessman Foutanga Dit Babani Sissoko "raised concerns" and "demonstrated, at the least, poor judgement."

The committee first launched its investigation of the lawmaker in June 1999 after Sissoko provided Brown lodging in his luxury Miami condominium. Sissoko's chief financial officer also gave Brown's daughter a $50,000 Lexus automobile. *(1999 Almanac, p. 8-17)*

The gifts were first reported by the St. Petersburg Times newspaper. The Lexus was given to Brown's daughter Shantrel just weeks after the lawmaker aggressively lobbied the Clinton administration to have Sissoko released from a U.S. prison where he was serving time in a bribery case.

In a written statement, the committee said the dearth of evidence against Brown "was due in large part to the fact that key witnesses who had actual knowledge of the events . . . were beyond the reach of the committee's subpoena power and could not be compelled to give testimony."

Sissoko and his financial officer are both in Africa, where they are not subject to U.S. subpoenas.

The statement added that the committee believes Brown's "actions and associations . . . created substantial concerns regarding both the appearance of impropriety and the reputation of the House of Representatives."

Brown, who denied any wrongdoing, released a statement Sept. 21 saying she was pleased to have "this matter behind me."

"For more than a year I have looked forward to the day when this matter would be put to rest and I am grateful that this day has finally come."

Shuster Receives Letter of Reproval For Misconduct, Rules Violations

OCTOBER 7 — A three-year ethics investigation of Rep. Bud Shuster, R-Pa., concluded Oct. 4 with a formal Letter of Reproval saying the chairman of the Transportation and Infrastructure Committee "engaged in serious official misconduct" and "committed substantial violations" of House rules.

The letter was part of a negotiated settlement to end the inquiry into a variety of charges that centered on Shuster's business conduct with his former chief of staff, Ann Eppard.

The panel, formally called the Committee on Standards of Official Conduct, also faulted Shuster for improperly accepting gifts and for spending campaign contributions on travel and meals at fancy restaurants.

The rebuke was approved unanimously by the committee and does not require action by the full House.

In accepting the committee's decision, Shuster admitted that his actions created the "appearance of impropriety," and he waived the right to separate hearings on the charges and the penalty. But in an Oct. 5 speech on the House floor after the ethics committee released its findings, Shuster defended his behavior and said he accepted the negotiated settlement in order to "stop the hemorrhaging of legal fees" and to "put this behind us."

Following his speech, Rep. James L. Oberstar of Minnesota, the top Democrat on Shuster's committee, expressed his support for Shuster and said the chairman had led the committee "with dignity and effectiveness."

Other lawmakers on the House floor then applauded and lined up to shake Shuster's hand. Shuster faces no further sanctions, but will step down as chairman at the end of this session because of term limits set by the Republican leadership.

Shuster submitted a 30-page response to the committee's findings, describing the settlement as a "negotiated armistice" and calling the Letter of Reproval "overkill for the charge of causing misguided public perceptions . . . contrary to the objective truth."

Shuster said he "complied with the law, and with his understanding of what was right." He also said "there is not a single instance" when he "took legislative action to benefit private interests instead of the public good."

The ethics committee, however, attacked Shuster's declarations of innocence, saying his written response was "rife with patently inaccurate and misleading statements."

"The Committee is disturbed not only by the content of your response but by its tone," the letter of reproval said. "It is one of blame-shifting about and trivializing of misconduct to which you have admitted and which this Committee does not and can not characterize as de minimis or technical, either in whole or in part."

The Charges

The ethics committee launched its investigation of Shuster in November

1997 in response to a complaint filed by the Congressional Accountability Project, a watchdog group associated with Ralph Nader.

The original complaint focused on Shuster's relationship with Eppard, who served as Shuster's chief of staff for 22 years and later became a transportation lobbyist representing clients with business before Shuster's committee. House rules prohibit staff members from lobbying their former bosses for one year after leaving.

During the course of the investigation, the committee issued more than 150 subpoenas, interviewed approximately 75 people, and deposed 33 witnesses. It eventually expanded its investigation into Shuster's campaign committee.

The ethics panel ruled that Shuster violated House rules by:

- "Engaging in a pattern and practice" of contact with Eppard in an official capacity during the 12 months following her resignation from his office. Shuster's interaction with Eppard "created the appearance that your official decisions might have been improperly affected," the committee said.
- Accepting lodging for himself and his family during a trip to Puerto Rico. "The American people should not be made to question whether, through gifts or favors, the public interest has been subordinated to those with business before the House," the panel said.
- Accepting scheduling and advisory services from Eppard on official matters for 18 months after she left Shuster's office.
- Allowing congressional employees to work for Shuster's political campaign committee while in his congressional office "to the apparent detriment of the time they were required to spend" on congressional business.
- Spending hundreds of thousands of dollars in campaign contributions between 1993 and 1998 that "may not have been attributable to bona fide campaign or political purposes." The panel said Shuster could not prove the expenses were campaign-related.

Last November, Eppard pleaded guilty to a single federal misdemeanor charge that she took $15,000 in cash and a $30,000 interest-free loan from a transportation lobbyist in exchange for helping two of the lobbyist's clients while she was working for Shuster.

House Panel Grants Shuster Limited Immunity

OCTOBER 14 — The House ethics committee's decision to grant limited immunity to Rep. Bud Shuster, R-Pa., does not necessarily protect him from prosecution based on charges outlined in the panel's case against the chairman of the Transportation and Infrastructure Committee, according to legal experts.

The committee, formally known as the Committee on Standards of Official Conduct, issued Shuster a letter of reproval on Oct. 4, in which the panel strongly denounced the way the lawmaker had conducted business, saying, "By your actions you have brought discredit to the House of Representatives."

The letter marked the end of a three-year investigation of Shuster that began with questions about his relationship with former staffer-turned-lobbyist Ann Eppard, but was broadened to include questionable campaign expenses and his acceptance of gifts.

Shuster demanded and received limited immunity before he would provide complete copies of his 1995 and 1996 calendars, which he previously had sent the committee after redacting portions. His attorneys claimed the redacted sections were protected from committee inspection because they dealt with national security concerns, personal issues or attorney-client privilege.

It is believed to be the first time a sitting member of Congress has received immunity from the ethics committee. But despite its precedent-setting nature, the limited type of immunity granted and the apparent lack of significant information the evidence provided could make the immunity of little practical consequence.

It also is unclear whether federal prosecutors, who previously declined to prosecute Shuster, would now attempt to pursue criminal charges.

Stanley Brand, former House counsel, said that while other members may be "more likely to use that defense now that somebody has successfully raised it," the peculiar nature of Shuster's case means the immunity precedent established by the committee is very narrow.

Although an Investigations Subcommittee began work on the Shuster case in late 1997, the case was effectively on hold for much of 1998 while the Justice Department conducted a criminal probe of related allegations.

That investigation led Eppard to plead guilty to a federal misdemeanor charge last November. She admitted that while working for Shuster she accepted $15,000 in cash and a $30,000 interest-free loan from a lobbyist in exchange for helping two of the lobbyists' clients. *(1999 Almanac, p. 8-17)*

After the Eppard case ended, House committee investigators decided they needed to review Shuster's 1995 and 1996 calendars in order to complete their ethics probe. On Feb. 17, the panel sent Shuster a letter requesting unredacted copies of the two calendars. Shuster's lawyers advised him not to comply with the request unless he was given "act of production immunity."

The ethics committee unanimously agreed to provide the requested immunity on March 15, and on March 17, the U.S. District Court for the District of Columbia granted the request. According to the committee, the Justice Department did not object.

The "act of production immunity" is limited to evidence prosecutors could not have found without the redacted portion of those calendars, a distinction that leaves open the potential for criminal prosecution if evidence of wrongdoing found in the calendars can also be found elsewhere, experts said.

Few References to Calendars

The findings in the committee's report are backed by 125 citations to documentary evidence collected during the investigation, but the calendars accounted for only five of those citations. Experts say this suggests the calendars may not offer pivotal evidence to a potential criminal case. Three of the five calendar citations relate to a committee finding that is of no legal consequence at all — that Shuster "created the appearance that (his) official decisions might have been improperly affected."

The Violations

Legal experts said that of the five violations of House rules outlined by the ethics committee, three also may be considered violations of federal law. But the calendars provided only a small portion of the evidence against Shuster in one of those three, and none in the other two.

The calendars figure most prominently in the House ethics committee's finding that Shuster engaged in significant contact with Eppard in the year after she left his staff. Top staffers are barred by federal law from lobbying their former colleagues for one year after leaving office. Shuster could face criminal charges that through this contact he aided or abetted Eppard.

In addition, the panel charged, "While under your supervision and control, employees of your congressional office performed services for your campaign in your congressional office." According to one ethics source, that could lead to a criminal charge that Shuster "misused" money appropriated to his congressional office.

The committee also found Shuster violated House gift rules by accepting a trip to Puerto Rico for him and his family from a lobbyist. A legal expert said the trip could be grounds for a criminal charge of accepting a bribe if it was determined that Shuster helped those who paid for the trip, although the committee offered no such conclusion.

The calendars were not cited in either the use of office staff for campaign purposes or the Puerto Rico trip.

The calendars were cited by the committee to criticize Shuster for allowing Eppard to act as a member of his staff after she had resigned. But legal experts said such activity would not be the basis for criminal charges. ◆

CQ

Chapter 8

DEFENSE

Congress Adds Little To Defense Request Despite Criticism of Clinton Policies

SUMMARY

Deadlocked for weeks, the $309.9 billion fiscal 2001 defense authorization bill was cleared only after an agreement was reached to include expanded medical care for military retirees and a compensation program for nuclear weapons workers exposed to radioactive and other toxic substances. The final bill added $4.6 billion to President Clinton's budget request for the Pentagon and defense-related programs of the Energy Department.

Defense hawks of both parties contend that Clinton has undermined combat readiness with defense budgets that are too small and a military workload that is too ambitious. However, as it had in the five previous years of Republican control on Capitol Hill, Congress exceeded Clinton's defense budget request only modestly — about 1.5 percent, much of it spread over dozens of smaller programs.

The bill allocated about $2.6 billion of the additional funds to procurement and development, including nearly $800 million more for the Army's effort to transform itself into a lighter force, able to move overseas more quickly.

As work on the bill was wrapping up in late September, rising estimates of the federal budget surplus for fiscal 2001 and beyond emboldened conferees to create a new, permanent retiree health entitlement. The program will allow military retirees to remain covered by the Pentagon's health insurance program for life, rather than having to rely on the more restrictive coverage provided by Medicare. The initiative is expected to cost $60 billion over the first 10 years.

Also added to the bill was a provision to allow most retirees to obtain low-cost prescriptions through a Pentagon-sponsored pharmacy network or by mail order.

The health care provision is rooted in the argument by retirees that they were promised lifetime care for themselves and their dependents in return for a full career — at least 20 years — on active duty.

In other areas, conferees included several provisions intended to assert more congressional control over how U.S. nuclear secrets are protected, including expanded polygraph testing of Energy Department workers in sensitive jobs. The provision could add 5,000 workers to the estimated 15,000 already being tested.

Conferees added $349 million to the $4.9 billion Clinton requested to develop anti-missile defenses, including $135 million more than the $1.8 billion requested to develop a limited national missile defense system. The bill did not include provisions that would accelerate or beef up Clinton's missile defense program, even though many Republicans condemn it as dilatory and anemic.

Among the bill's additions for ongoing programs were:

- $460 million for components to be used in a $1.5 billion helicopter carrier to be built by Litton Industries in Pascagoula, Miss., hometown of Senate Majority Leader Trent Lott, a Republican.
- $209 million for 16 H-60 helicopters, in addition to the $495 million requested for 25 of the craft, which are built in Connecticut by United Technologies' Sikorsky division.
- $165 million for two Lockheed Martin C-130 cargo planes, in addition to the $363 million requested for four of them.
- $150 million for two Boeing F-15 jet fighters, built in St. Louis, Mo.
- $52 million for two Lockheed Martin F-16 fighters, built in Fort Worth, Texas.

The only major reduction in the bill was a cut of $168 million — to $689 million — for the Joint Strike Fighter. The Armed Services committees thought the development program was moving too fast.

Box Score

- **Bill:** HR 4205 — PL 106-398
- **Legislative action: House** passed HR 4205 (H Rept 106-616), 353-63, on May 18.

Senate passed HR 4205, 97-3, on July 13, after substituting the text of S 2549 (S Rept 106-292), as amended.

House adopted the conference report on HR 4205 (H Rept 106-945), 382-31, on Oct. 11.

Senate cleared the bill, 90-3, on Oct. 12.

President signed the bill Oct. 30.

Lawmakers Likely To Add Funds To President's Pentagon Budget

FEBRUARY 12 — President Clinton has taken steps in his $291.1 billion fiscal 2001 defense budget to address the Pentagon's most pressing problems — aging weapons and an exodus of experienced personnel — but the House and Senate Armed Services committees likely will try to add billions more. And in these heady days of budget surpluses, the odds are in their favor.

The administration has proposed raising military pay and housing allowances and spending $60 billion for new equipment, a goal set by the Joint Chiefs of Staff in 1995.

But there is growing pressure for Congress to also improve medical care for military retirees, something likely to cost billions a year.

And Clinton's budget omits money for some weapons programs with influential congressional patrons — the Boeing F-15 fighter built in St. Louis, the Lockheed Martin F-16 fighter built in Fort Worth, Texas, and a Navy helicopter carrier built by Litton Industries in Pascagoula, Miss., the hometown of Senate Majority Leader Trent Lott, R-Miss.

Beyond such pressures, some outside experts warn that Clinton's budget is simply too small to replace the military's huge inventory of weapons dating from the Reagan administration at the rate they are wearing out. According to the Center for Strategic and International Studies (CSIS), a centrist Washington think tank, Clinton's projected budgets for future years fall short of what would be needed by a $100 billion a year.

"That is not a matter of opinion. That is a matter of simple arithmetic," former Defense Secretary James R. Schlesinger warned the House Armed Services Committee on Feb. 8.

Defense Secretary William S. Cohen and others say the CSIS projection is exaggerated. But Cohen himself warns that procurement funding will have to be significantly increased by the end of this decade in order to manufacture high-tech weapons now under development.

At a Feb. 10 hearing of the House Armed Services Committee, top officers of the Army, Navy, Air Force and Marine Corps said Clinton's fiscal 2001 budget is $16 billion short of their most pressing requirements.

Liberal critics, however, objected that even Clinton's request was excessive in light of pressing domestic needs and the absence of a major military threat to U.S. interests. "We rank No. 1 [among nations] in military spending, by a wide margin, yet we rank 10th in education spending per student," Council for a Livable World President John Isaacs said during a Feb. 7 news conference. "This makes no sense."

But liberals such as Isaacs will have to wage that fight alone this year, without much help from fiscally conservative Republicans who helped restrain defense spending in the past.

House Budget Committee Chairman John R. Kasich, R-Ohio, a leading deficit hawk, told reporters Feb. 7, "We're going to have to put more money in the Pentagon."

Military Personnel Issues

Clinton's proposed 3.7 percent military pay raise meets a requirement Congress wrote into the fiscal 2000 defense authorization bill (PL 106-65) for a raise one-half percentage point higher than the predicted increase in civilian wages as measured by a government index. The requirement was in response to the widespread view of military personnel that their pay raises have lagged behind those for civilians for several years.

Since the cost of living as measured by the Consumer Price Index is expected to rise by only 2.4 percent between 2000 and 2001, Clinton's proposed military pay raise also would provide an increase in real purchasing power.

The budget includes $160 million to increase the housing allowances paid to service members who do not live in government-provided housing. This would reduce from 19 percent to 15 percent the average proportion of military pay spent on housing. The Pentagon plans to continue increasing the allowance until the cost of all off-base housing is covered by 2005.

Clinton's budget incorporates a more generous military retirement program enacted as part of last year's authorization bill. Although that legislation gave the administration discretion to propose a voluntary savings investment plan for military personnel, similar to the popular 401(k) plans available to many private-sector employees, no such plan was proposed in the budget. The reason is that, because savings deposited in such accounts would be tax exempt, congressional budget rules would have required the Pentagon to propose offsetting cuts in other areas to make up the lost tax revenue.

"We simply didn't have the money to do it," Cohen told the House Armed Services Committee on Feb. 9. "We'll have to look for it in the future."

Medical Care

The most contentious personnel issue in this year's budget fight is likely to be an effort to streamline and expand the range of medical services provided to service members, their families and retirees.

The budget includes $80 million to eliminate some irritants from the Pentagon's TRICARE medical insurance program, such as the co-payments required from active-duty military families. But some members of Congress, with the ardent support of the Joint Chiefs of Staff, are pressing for a more radical — and more expensive — expansion of medical care for retirees, particularly those over 65.

The laws and administrative rules governing eligibility for medical care are complex and have changed frequently in the past four decades. In general, however, retirees who served at least 20 years on active duty and their dependents are eligible for medical care in military hospitals and clinics, if the facilities can accommodate them in addition to the active-duty personnel and dependents who are accorded higher priority.

Such "space-available" medical care has become harder for retirees to obtain because so many military bases have been closed since the end of the Cold War. The result has been a firestorm of complaints that the Pentagon is reneging on its promise of lifetime medical care for veterans.

The issue also might further hinder recruiting, as House Armed Services Committee member Gene Taylor, D-Miss., pointed out during a Feb. 9 hearing. "In south Mississippi alone, I've got about 14,000 military retirees who, on a daily basis, are telling kids not to join the service because they feel like they have been given the short stick when it comes to their health care," Taylor told Cohen and Joint Chiefs of Staff Chairman Gen. Henry H. Shelton.

Shelton said the administration, in its budget, had turned down two medical care initiatives for retirees that the chiefs had proposed: a mail-order pharmacy ($420 million) and the "medigap" insurance currently available to civilian federal employees that covers the difference between the cost of medical treatment and what Medicare will pay ($1.8 billion).

Bills with broad, bipartisan sponsorship in both the Senate and House (S 2003, HR 3573) would include military retirees in the federal civilian retirees' health care plan at a cost that may run as high as $10 billion a year. "So what?" demanded Rep. Charlie Norwood, R-Ga., a chief sponsor of the House bill: "We gave our word."

Cohen and Shelton both insisted that they will come up with a plan to improve health care for retirees as well as active duty personnel. "It's a moral obligation that we will take care of," Cohen assured the House committee. "But there's going to be a big cost."

Combat Readiness

The administration's $109.3 billion budget for operations and maintenance would continue a trend of steady increases, adjusted for the size of the force. But evidence strongly suggests that the combat-readiness of many units has declined despite these increases in spending.

Administration officials say it costs more to run the military because of the increasing expense of quality-of-life programs such as medical care, and because it costs more to maintain an aging inventory of ships, planes and ground vehicles, most of which were fielded in the 1980s.

Clinton's conservative critics argue that the administration has compounded these problems by sending the smaller, post-Cold War military on too many missions, building up a backlog of deferred maintenance and training.

The fiscal 2001 budget would allow the services' major combat units to train at the desired pace. For instance, Air Force fighter pilots would be able to fly an average of 17.1 hours per month.

The budget also includes $4.2 billion to pay for operations during fiscal 2001 in Kosovo ($1.7 billion), Bosnia ($1.4 billion) and the region around Iraq ($1.1 billion). In addition, the supplemental appropriations requested for fiscal 2000 include more than $2 billion for operations in Kosovo since Oct. 1. If those funds are not approved, planned training and maintenance would have to be canceled to free up the money needed to pay for the overseas operations. That prospect has partly stymied most past attempts by congressional critics to end unpopular deployments by denying them funds.

Among the services' most significant efforts to bolster combat readiness are organizational changes, which the budget would support, intended to make overseas deployments more predictable and less disruptive both to the lives of military personnel and their families and to the training and maintenance schedules of their units. They include:

- By the end of fiscal 2000, the Army plans to have filled every job in its 10 combat divisions, some of which currently have as many as 15 percent of their billets vacant. By the end of 2001, all those jobs are expected to be filled by personnel of the appropriate rank and job specialty. When undermanned units have been sent overseas, critical vacancies have been filled by personnel pulled out of other units on short notice.
- The Air Force continues to organize most of its combat, tanker and cargo planes into 10 "expeditionary forces," two of which will be on call at any time for overseas missions. The Air Force budget also includes a total of $2.8 billion for nearly 300 projects intended to reduce the maintenance burden of existing planes by improving the reliability of their engines and electronic components.
- The Navy has convinced Pentagon leaders that it has too few active-duty ships for the missions it is assigned. Accordingly, the carrier *John F. Kennedy*, relegated to training duty and crewed partly by reservists since fiscal 1996, is being returned to active duty and will be deployed to the Mediterranean this year. Similarly, the Navy now plans to refuel several nuclear-powered submarines that were scheduled for retirement within the next few years.

Army 'Transformation'

The Army's budget request includes $1 billion to begin fielding "medium-weight" combat units that would be easier to transport to distant trouble spots than today's heavily armored tank battalions but would be more heavily armed than current air-mobile forces. Of that amount, $400 million would be offset by canceling or scaling back planned purchases of heavily armored equipment.

The goal, set by Army chief of staff Gen. Eric K. Shinseki, is to be able to put a brigade of about 3,000 troops anywhere in the world in four days, a division of 15,000 within five days and a corps of five divisions within a month.

As an initial step, the budget includes $537 million to begin equipping two brigades at Fort Lewis, Wash., with medium-weight vehicles selected from models in production by U.S. and foreign manufacturers. Unveiled by Shinseki last October, less than four months after he became the Army's top-ranking officer, the schedule calls for signing the first production contract by September, less than a year after the project's announcement.

"That's about lightning speed in the [Pentagon] procurement process," one Army official observed.

By 2012, Shinseki's plan aims to field a 20-ton combat vehicle to supplant 70-ton M-1 tanks and 30-ton Bradley troop carriers in some units.

One offset for all this will be the Crusader long-range, mobile cannon, which proponents tout for its promised combat versatility, but which critics have faulted for its weight. The budget request includes $355 million to continue developing the Crusader. But the Army plans to cut its weight from 55 tons to 40, delay its deployment by two years, until 2007, and buy 480 of them — fewer than half the number originally planned.

The budget would continue upgrading existing M-1 tanks ($513 million) and Bradley troop carriers ($379 million) with improved night-vision electronics and digital communications links. But it would cancel production of two other heavily armored combat vehicles based on lessons learned from the 1991 war with Iraq. One of them is designed to plow through minefields and tank traps, the other would carry a 25-yard-long portable bridge.

Not affected by the budget shuffle is continued development of the Comanche armed scout helicopter ($614 million) and the addition to existing Apache attack helicopters of Longbow target-finding radar ($745 million).

Naval Forces

The Navy's budget includes more than $800 million to develop new-technology warships for construction later this decade. But it also would fund continued production of current ship classes, including $4 billion for the 10th *Nimitz*-class nuclear-powered carrier and $2.7 billion for three additional destroyers equipped with the Aegis anti-aircraft system.

The first of the new generation of ships would be a new class of destroyers, designated DD-21, the first of which is slated for inclusion in the 2005 budget. Two teams of shipyards are competing to design the ship, which may have the aspect of a Civil

War ironclad, with inward-sloping sides making it harder for radar to detect.

The budget includes $555 million to develop DD-21 and its components, the most radical of which would be a drive system linking the ship's turbine engines to the propellers by electrical cables and motors rather than by long shafts and heavy gears.

In addition to being lighter and quieter, the electrical system would require less maintenance, contributing to the goal of greatly reducing the cost of operating the ship by running it with about 100 sailors — fewer than one-third the number on a current destroyer. Moreover, the powerplant would be designed to shunt electrical energy on demand from the propeller motors to radar or powerful lasers with which — someday — it might be armed.

The administration also has requested $296 million to develop the next generation aircraft carrier, expected to include such features as a smaller crew and electromagnetic catapults, instead of the heavy steam launchers currently used to hurl 30-ton combat jets into the air.

The budget includes $1.2 billion for a nuclear-powered submarine, $508 million for components to be used in new subs funded in future budgets and $283 million to refuel nuclear subs already in service.

Also requested is $728 million to refuel nuclear-powered carriers.

Air Combat

The budget would continue, essentially unchanged, the services' plans to buy three new types of combat jets. It requests:

- $1.4 billion to continue developing the Air Force's F-22, and $2.5 billion for 10 of the planes. The House last year tried unsuccessfully to kill the air-superiority fighter.
- $2.9 billion for 42 additional F/A-18 E and F model planes, used by the Navy chiefly to attack ground targets.
- $857 million to continue developing the Joint Strike Fighter, which the Navy, Marine Corps and Air Force plan to buy in different versions beginning late in this decade to replace various planes of Vietnam War-era design.

The major additions to the air combat budget that reflect the lessons of last spring's air war against Serbia are:

- $261 million to buy a 15th Joint Stars radar plane, built to find small ground targets at great distance.
- $203 million to begin organizing a ninth squadron of Prowler radar-jamming planes, using existing aircraft.

The budget also includes $1.4 billion to develop and purchase various types of precision-guided "smart" bombs and ground-attack missiles.

It further includes $296 million to develop and buy various types of remotely piloted drone aircraft equipped with TV cameras, night-vision gear and radar to find ground targets.

Air and Sea Transport

The budget seeks 12 C-17, wide-body intercontinental cargo jets ($2.2 billion) instead of the 15 planes projected a year ago. This is to make room in Boeing's production run for three planes the British government may acquire.

It requests $363 million for four Lockheed C-130 cargo planes, two of them equipped as midair refueling tankers for the Marine Corps. The Air Force had not planned to begin buying new models of this venerable design until 2005, but Pentagon officials insisted that keeping the production line going between now and then would save the government $600 million.

In the case of the helicopter carrier that would be built in Mississippi, Congress has added about $400 million to previous defense funding bills for advance components. The Navy does not plan to ask for the remaining $1 billion until 2005.

Pentagon's Wish List Heavy On Traditional Spending

FEBRUARY 26 — Despite all the talk of high-tech weapons and revolutionizing the nation's armed forces, the wish lists of additional defense spending that military leaders have sent Congress for fiscal 2001 are heavy with housing construction, maintenance and weapons designed during the Cold War.

The prioritized lists that service chiefs submitted would add a total of $15.5 billion to President Clinton's $291.1 billion Pentagon budget. They do not include proposals to improve military and retiree health plans, which could run to more than $5 billion and which the administration turned down.

These lists have become an annual feature since 1995, when Republicans, newly in control of Congress and convinced that Clinton's request was too stingy, asked the services to outline how they would like Congress to allocate additional funds. *(1995 Almanac, p. 9-3)*

Although the Armed Services and Appropriations committees have not confined additional spending to the lists, they have given them great weight.

As in earlier years, most of the top priorities for each service are personnel, maintenance, construction or training, rather than weapons. And most of the weapons requests would add money to programs already included in Clinton's budget.

One notable exception is the largest single item on any of the four lists: The Navy's $1.2 billion request for a helicopter carrier to be built by Litton Industries in Pascagoula, Miss., hometown of Senate Majority Leader Trent Lott. Critics say its inclusion is an effort to curry favor with a powerful Republican politician. But Navy Secretary Richard Danzig told reporters Feb. 23 that, since the ship is slated for the fiscal 2005 budget anyway, buying it sooner would be a reasonable decision if the money is available. "It can be bought significantly less expensively, if we accelerate it . . . since we already have a production line running," Danzig said.

Army: Light but Heavy

Although Army Chief of Staff Gen. Eric K. Shinseki has launched an effort to reduce the weight but increase the firepower of ground forces, making them easier to transport but just as lethal, his $5.5 billion wish list of 144 items would allocate far more money to continue upgrading the current heavy forces than it would to develop lighter equipment.

The 11th item on Shinseki's list is $46 million more to speed development of a 20-ton combat vehicle, less than one-third the weight of today's main battle tanks and more maneuverable. It would enter service in 2012.

But among the items that account for the first $1 billion of additional spending on the Army list are $330 million in heavy tank programs, including:

• $145 million to outfit another 20 M-1 tanks, in addition to the 80 proposed in Clinton's budget, with improved night-vision equipment and digital communications. General Dynamics Corp. modifies the tanks in the same Sterling Heights, Mich., plant where the company built them.

• $77 million to begin buying the Wolverine, an M-1 tank chassis with a portable bridge that can carry a tank across a 25-yard ditch. This also is built at the Sterling Heights plant.

• $108 million to continue buying the Grizzly, a modified M-1 chassis designed to plow through minefields with a bulldozer blade and rip open obstacles with a backhoe. It is built in York, Pa., by United Defense, General Dynamics' only domestic competitor in heavily armored combat equipment.

To pay for developing Shinseki's new technology, the Army had proposed reducing, but not eliminating, funds for the Wolverine and the Grizzly as well as for the Crusader, a mobile artillery piece being developed by United Defense that supporters tout for its rapid rate of fire and agility, but which critics fault as too heavy (55 tons) to be easily deployed to distant trouble spots.

The Pentagon accepted the plan to scale back the Crusader's budget — and to slice its weight to 40 tons — but insisted on killing outright the other two programs. While proposing to resuscitate the Wolverine and Grizzly, the Army's list would not add any funds to the $355 million requested for the Crusader.

From the Army's perspective, the wish list is consistent with Shinseki's "transformation" plan. The 2001 budget already includes $1 billion for that effort, and Shinseki himself has emphasized that the service will keep its heavyweight "legacy" force up to date while lighter equipment is perfected and put into the field. Through 2014, the Army plans to spend about $75 billion on modernization, two-thirds of which would go to the new technology forces and $25 billion to upgrade the existing heavy forces.

All told, the Army's $5.5 billion list of proposed budget additions includes about $1.5 billion for major items of equipment currently in service, including:

• $272 million to upgrade United Defense's Paladin mobile cannon, which the Crusader is intended to supplant.

• $280 million to equip Apache attack helicopters with Longbow target-finding radar, a joint project of Lockheed Martin Corp. and Northrop Grumman Corp.

• $196 million for Blackhawk troop-carrying helicopters built by United Technologies Corp. in Stratford, Conn.

• $171 million for long-range rocket launchers built by Lockheed Martin.

Although traditional hardware accounts for most of the list, the Army, like the other services, has personnel and maintenance priorities: $250 million for facilities maintenance, $51 million to improve the readiness of reserve and National Guard units, $109 million for information technology, and $102 million for the service's research and development infrastructure.

Navy: Spare Parts

The $1.2 billion helicopter carrier and a total of $1.4 billion for 41 aircraft of 11 different types account for less than half the $5.7 billion on the Navy's priority list. Most of the 114 items would provide small increases to the amounts in Clinton's budget to buy or upgrade various weapons and other types of equipment.

The Navy's top seven priorities, which would cost a total of more than $700 million, would increase funding for recruiting ($77 million), spare parts for aircraft ($174 million), ship overhauls ($214 million), real property maintenance ($137 million) and the bonus paid to sailors on sea duty ($119 million).

Next in priority are requests totaling $119 million for various types of precision-guided "smart" bombs. Then come requests for $1 billion worth of aircraft, among which are:

• $172 million for three Boeing F/A-18 E and F model attack planes, built in St. Louis, in addition to the 42 planes in Clinton's budget.

• $229 million for nine Seahawk helicopters, in addition to funds in the budget that would buy 19 of these seagoing versions of the Army's Blackhawk.

• $166 million for two Boeing V-22 Ospreys — airplane/helicopter hybrids used by the Marines as troop carriers. The budget includes $1.6 billion for 20 of the craft, including four that the Air Force plans to use to retrieve downed pilots from behind enemy lines.

• $153 million for two C-130 cargo planes equipped as midair refueling tankers for Marine aircraft. The budget includes $363 million for four C-130s, two of which would be tankers.

The 50th item on the Navy's list is an addition of $55 million to the $296 million in Clinton's budget to design a new class of aircraft carriers that would need fewer crew members than current ships.

Also on the Navy's list is $289 million for construction of facilities and family housing and $84 million for additional personnel incentives.

Air Force: Better Ready

In the Air Force wish list of 62 items, personnel and readiness not only have the highest priority but account for the lion's share of the $3.5 billion requested.

The four items that lead the list would add funds to the amounts in the budget for recruiting and retention ($61 million), day-to-day base operations ($145 million), information technology infrastructure ($30 million) and training munitions ($125 million). Also high on the Air Force priority list are funds for facilities maintenance ($438 million) and construction ($728 million).

The only major weapons program that would get a big boost out of the Air Force list is the Lockheed Martin F-16 fighter-bomber, built in Fort Worth, Texas. The 20th item in priority is $336 million to buy 12 of the planes, in a version equipped to attack anti-aircraft defenses. Clinton's budget would buy no F-16s in 2001, but the Pentagon plans to purchase 20 of the planes in the next few years.

The list also includes $92 million to reverse a budget-driven slowdown in developing an anti-missile laser carried by a 747 jetliner. The proposed addition would put the project back on track for a test in 2003, the Air Force said.

Other items on the Air Force list would fix problems highlighted by the air war against Serbia last spring, such as requests for $86 million to develop a long-range, air-launched cruise missile, $86 million to perfect a smaller "smart" bomb and $50 million for simulators to train more crews for surveillance planes.

Marines: Bricks and Mortar

Since the Navy pays for the ships and aircraft the Marine Corps uses, nearly half its $755 million wish list is for construction ($189 million) and operations and maintenance ($174 million).

The largest amount requested for hardware is $55 million to buy more "Humvee" light trucks. Also on the list is $28 million to beef up development of General Dynamics' amphibious troop carrier designed to haul Marines from transport ships to the beach at 25 mph — three times the speed of current craft.

The total does not include $159 million that would be needed to buy port facilities at Blount Island, Fla., near Jacksonville, which currently are leased as a base for 13 cargo ships that carry weapons and supplies for Marine units flown to distant trouble spots. Marine Corps Commandant Gen. James L. Jones cites acquisition of the leased facility as a priority.

Appropriators Are Hard-Pressed To Pump Up Pentagon Budget

MARCH 11 — During a House Republican leadership meeting early in March, Defense Appropriations Subcommittee Chairman Jerry Lewis of California insisted that he be allowed to draft a military spending bill that at least would equal President Clinton's request.

"I cannot take a bill to the full committee or to the floor that provides less money than the president's budget," Lewis declared in a March 8 interview.

As it turns out, a tentative deal on a fiscal 2001 budget resolution would allow Congress to add just $1.4 billion to Clinton's request for $305 billion for the military and defense-related programs of the Energy Department.

That is a blow to the Pentagon and its political allies who have been accustomed to a modest but reliable flow of extra money since Republicans took control of Congress in 1995.

Early in February, conservative commentator William Kristol, editor of "The Weekly Standard," criticized Republicans for not building public support for higher defense budgets.

"Through the Clinton years, congressional Republicans have been complicit in the neglect that is sapping American military strength," he wrote in the magazine's Feb. 7 edition.

House Republican Conference Chairman J.C. Watts Jr. of Oklahoma challenged Kristol's argument in a Feb. 11 letter to the editor that summarized GOP initiatives that had bolstered Clinton's earlier budgets. "We will get our troops needed resources for training, improved readiness levels, more quality family housing, and continued research and testing on a national missile defense system and other important priorities," Watts wrote.

But with Republicans and Clinton promising not to touch the Social Security surplus, there is no sign that Congress could grant anything approaching the roughly $6 billion that, on average, the Republican-led Congress has added in each of the past five years.

Frustrated defense hawks can take solace in the fact that the budget resolution is not the last word on fiscal 2001 appropriations: Before the year is out, Congress easily could use budgeting gimmicks or supplemental appropriations to bulk up the Pentagon's coffers. But the current state of the debate highlights the obstacles that proponents of a higher defense increase face.

Unlikely Scenario

On its face, the scenario seems improbable. The budget surplus is ballooning, and Republicans regularly bash Clinton for not giving the armed forces enough money to do their job.

Influential defense experts in both parties agree that Clinton's fiscal 2001 request falls short of what is needed. A study by the Center for Strategic and International Studies (CSIS), a centrist Washington think tank, warns that projected defense budgets over the next five years average $100 billion below what is needed to carry out the Clinton administration's strategy of being able to win two major regional wars almost simultaneously.

That study has been criticized as politically unrealistic and methodologically flawed. But William J. Perry, who was Clinton's Defense secretary in 1994-97, told a House Armed Services subcommittee hearing Feb. 8 that the $60 billion procurement piece of Clinton's defense request probably should be $10 billion to $20 billion higher. Perry added that as much as half of that increase could be paid for by making the Pentagon's purchasing system more efficient.

Deputy Defense Secretary John J. Hamre, who is leaving the Pentagon to become president of CSIS, offered a bottom line similar to Perry's during a Senate Defense Appropriations Subcommittee hearing March 6. A $60 billion procurement budget would not make up for equipment shortfalls caused by the low procurement spending of the late 1980s and '90s, Hamre said.

"I don't believe it's $100 billion a year to do that," he said, "but I think it's in the range of $10 billion to $15 billion more a year for procurement in order to start getting out of that hole."

As has become routine since the Republicans took over Congress, the uniformed chiefs of the Army, Navy, Air Force and Marine Corps sent lawmakers a list of their spending priorities that were left off the administration's budget — a total of $15.5 billion.

Not everyone, of course, thinks Clinton is denying the military necessary resources. The Center for Defense Information, a think tank skeptical of the Pentagon's budget demands, notes that U.S. defense spending dwarfs the combined budgets of all conceivable adversaries — at least five times the size of Russia's and nearly 20 times the combined budgets of Cuba, Iraq, Iran, Libya, North Korea, Sudan and Syria — the radical regimes most often cited as the U.S. military's prospective foes.

The counterargument is that the United States expects its military to serve a much broader set of purposes and geography than do other countries.

"Most of our allies have regional interests," Marine Corps Commandant Gen. James L. Jones Jr. told the Senate Armed Services Committee on March 1. "We alone, at the end of the 20th Century, have global responsibilities."

But the U.S. defense budget, which was at least 5 percent of the gross national product during most of the Cold War, has declined to about 3 percent — not much larger a share of the national wealth than regional allies such as Britain and France spend on their militaries, Jones noted. "My judgment is that the American people like that global leadership and those conditions we enjoy as the sole remaining superpower," he told the panel, adding, "It doesn't come cheaply."

Hawks in a Trap

Nevertheless, congressional defense hawks are caught in a seemingly unbreakable snare woven of financial necessity.

Clinton and Republican leaders have taken off the table tens of billions of dollars of the projected Social Security surplus in fiscal 2001. Clinton first used this pledge in order to shoot down Republican hopes of parlaying the projected surplus into a large tax cut. Their own top priority thus stymied, Republicans used the same promise on Social Security to sharply reduce the amount Clinton could use to fund new initiatives.

Clinton, meanwhile, submitted a fiscal 2001 defense budget request that is several billion dollars larger than the administration projected a year ago. This reduced the amount of the "on budget" surplus — the amount not derived from Social Security — from which any congressional defense increase would have to come.

GOP defense leaders brand this a cynical ploy to bolster Vice President Al Gore's presidential bid, after seven years in which, they say, the U.S. military has been underfunded and overused by the Clinton team.

"The president knew what he had to do politically," said House Armed Services Committee member Curt Weldon, R-Pa. "In the last year of his presidency, he increased defense, after criticizing us" for having added to his earlier budget requests.

Whatever Clinton's motivation, his proposed budget is nearly $15 billion larger than the amount Congress appropriated for defense in fiscal 2000 and is his first defense budget request that would provide an inflation-adjusted increase in purchasing power. Thus, the case for a congressional increase is harder to make.

Hawk vs. Hawk

The decisive factor in the political equation driving the defense budget, however, is that a significant group of congressional Republicans place a higher priority on holding down federal spending and cutting taxes than they do on increasing funds for defense.

Within the GOP aviary, these deficit hawks probably are outnumbered by defense hawks. However, since the budget resolution has become a purely partisan debate, a small but committed group of fiscal conservatives can threaten to torpedo any budget that subordinates their priorities to defense — particularly in the House, where House Speaker J. Dennis Hastert, R-Ill., leads a very narrow Republican majority.

"We've got other pressing issues which, when we've got a margin of six votes, we've got to take care of," Weldon conceded. "Denny's doing the best he can to hold the coalition together."

A more jaundiced view is expressed by the Project for a New American Century, a group of conservative internationalists led by Kristol. "The congressional Republican Party has inverted the political priorities of Ronald Reagan," said Thomas Donnelly, the organization's deputy director. "He was willing to run deficits in order to finance the military buildup that won the Cold War; they will allow the erosion of that force and jeopardize the fruits of that victory in order to cut taxes and 'save Social Security.' "

House Defense Appropriations Chairman Lewis, for one, has not given up the fight for a higher congressional defense increase.

"It's time for us to recognize that we've got a commitment to national defense," Lewis said, "and we've got a highly credible list of shortfalls from the chiefs."

House Armed Services Chairman Floyd D. Spence, R-S.C., invoked the chief's list as the justification for his recommendation that the House Budget Committee allow a $15.5 billion addition to Clinton's defense request. Senior Armed Services Democrat Ike Skelton of Missouri called for a $12 billion increase.

However, Senate Armed Services Chairman John W. Warner, R-Va., asked the Senate Budget Committee to allow an increase of slightly more than $3 billion, still double the eventual number.

Some Democratic defense hawks, such as John P. Murtha of Pennsylvania, the senior minority member of House Defense Appropriations, profess confidence that, one way or another, Congress will wind up adding funds to Clinton's request.

"They can't not find more money," he told a reporter March. 8.

Armed Services Panels in Both Chambers Approve Defense Budgets

MAY 13 — The House and Senate Armed Services committees approved fiscal 2001 defense authorization bills the week of May 8 that are likely to win broad support, thanks to an increase of about $4.5 billion above President Clinton's defense budget request, a 3.7 percent military pay raise and a chance for uniformed personnel to invest in a 401(k)-style retirement savings plan.

But the path of the legislation (HR 4205, S 2481) could be complicated by language the Senate panel added that would curtail Energy Secretary Bill Richardson's authority over a nuclear weapons agency Congress created last year.

Senate Armed Services Committee Chairman John W. Warner, R-Va., predicted as much in an interview May 10, the day after his committee approved its authorization bill in a closed-door markup. House Armed Services followed suit by approving its version, 56-1.

"That's going to be a holy war," Warner said of the language, which deals with the National Nuclear Security Administration. The agency was created to improve the security and accountability of the Energy Department's nuclear weapons programs.

The most urgent military debate this year may take place on the normally peaceful military construction Appropriations bill (S 2521). Senate appropriators, including Warner, are trying to set a July 1, 2001, limit on U.S. participation in the Kosovo peacekeeping operation. The Senate is expected to continue debating the bill the week of May 15.

The House and Senate are expected to take up their defense bills the same week. The Senate bill would authorize $309.8 billion for fiscal 2001 for the Defense Department and the Energy Department's atomic energy defense activities. The House version would authorize $309.9 billion.

Members of the House and Senate committees expressed satisfaction that the bills would help reverse a decade of declining defense budgets while giving the military another pay increase and improving medical care for military retirees.

Both committee bills would allow military personnel to participate in the government's Thrift Savings Plan. The bills also include an expansion of pharmacy benefits for military retirees.

Warner said he recognized that military retiree organizations have sought broader changes, but he said the committee was limited by what it could spend. Without offering specifics, he said he anticipates further action on the issue when the bill reaches the Senate floor.

"We must recognize that each time we add, something must be subtracted from the overall defense budget," Warner said.

Other lawmakers said the increases in spending authorized for fiscal 2001 would not solve critical funding shortfalls that have hampered other areas of the military.

Members of House Armed Services Military Procurement Subcommittee lamented that there was not more money to modernize military equipment. Pentagon officials and defense analysts estimate that the procurement shortfall over the next several years will range from $15 billion to $100 billion.

"We are still vastly short," said Subcommittee Chairman Duncan Hunter, R-Calif. "In the meantime, I think we've presented a pretty good holding action."

Going Nuclear

The language on the nuclear security administration could trigger a repeat of last year's showdown between Republicans and Richardson over the new agency. Richardson fought attempts to create it as a remedy for apparent security lapses that may have allowed China to obtain secret material from weapons labs. Richardson argued that the semi-independent agency Congress wanted to create would undermine his authority. Lawmakers succeeded in getting the proposal into the fiscal 2000 defense authorization law (PL 106-65).

In the fiscal 2001 defense bill, Senate Republicans added provisions that would:

- Prohibit paying a salary to anyone serving in the same position in the Energy Department and in the nuclear agency — a procedure known as "dual-hatting." Richardson has said that about 18 of the new agency's 2,000 employees are dual-hatted, mainly senior-level officials overseeing such critical functions as security and counterintelligence.
- Remove the Energy secretary's authority under the Department of Energy Organization Act (PL 95-91) to make any organizational changes to the new agency. *(1977 Almanac, p. 609)*

Senate Republicans contend that the changes are necessary because Richardson did not follow their intentions in submitting an implementation plan for the nuclear administration earlier this year. Richardson said through a spokeswoman that the Senate language "will only hamper the effectiveness" of the new weapons agency.

"I will oppose petty actions like these that only divert attention from what should be our shared goal of keeping our nuclear secrets safe," Richardson said. "The department has been diligently working for months to implement poorly drafted legislation in a way that increases accountability, not reduces it."

Choice of Weapons

The bills contain other issues for the House and Senate to argue about in floor debate and conference.

The Senate included no money to buy F-15 or F-16 fighters, a priority for many House members. The House committee bill includes $149.8 million for two F-15Es and $51.7 million for three F-16Cs.

The House Defense Appropriations Subcommittee approved a spending bill May 11 that includes money for five F-15s, although it did not fund any new F-16s.

In addressing another congressional concern, the dwindling number of Navy ships, neither committee added to Clinton's request for money to build eight ships in fiscal 2001. Some Navy officials and the shipbuilding industry have called for Congress to authorize at least 10 new ships a year if the Navy is to have at least 300 ships in the decades ahead.

But both committees gave the secretary of the Navy authority for a "block buy" of up to five *Virginia*-class attack submarines over the next several years. The arrangement would give the Navy authority to acquire materials in larger-than-usual quantities to achieve greater savings, but does not commit the government to buy the submarines.

The committees also authorized extending and modifying a multiyear procurement contract for the DDG-51 class of guided-missile destroyers to support the procurement of up to three ships in each fiscal year through 2005.

The Senate bill includes $460 million in advance procurement for a $1.2 billion helicopter carrier to be built by Litton Industries in Pascagoula, Miss., the hometown of Senate Majority Leader Trent Lott, R-Miss. The ship is designed to carry 1,800 marines and their helicopters.

The House committee approved, 31-21, an amendment by Roscoe G. Bartlett, R-Md., to bar the Navy from spending any money to assign women to its submarines. Senate Armed Services Seapower Subcommittee Chairman Olympia J. Snowe, R-Maine, said she will oppose any such proposal. The issue, she said, should be left for the Navy to decide.

Bartlett's amendment came in response to a recent recommendation by the Defense Advisory Committee on Women in the Services that the Navy commit to integrating women into the submarine force. The Navy says it does not assign women to submarines because of the limited living space.

Joint Strikes

On most areas, there were relatively few differences between the House and Senate committee bills. Spending increases were authorized for ballistic missile defense and chemical and biological defense programs.

Both committees spoke with one voice on Congress' strong desire for the Pentagon to slow down its plans for developing the Joint Strike Fighter.

The Navy, Marine Corps and Air Force plan to buy different versions of the plane beginning in 2008 to replace various planes of Vietnam War-era design. Current plans for the program call for spending about $200 billion to develop and buy 3,000 planes.

The Joint Strike Fighter is the most advanced of three air-superiority warplanes the Pentagon wants to buy. The others are the F-22, which some House appropriators tried to block last year, and the F/A-18 E and F, the closest to production.

The Defense Department has awarded contracts of more than $2 billion each to The Boeing Co. and Lockheed Martin Corp. to develop concept planes for the Joint Strike Fighter. The department has planned to award a contract for engineering and manufacturing development to one of the companies by April 2001.

But some lawmakers are worried about the pace of technology development by the competing contractors.

An official from the General Accounting Office (GAO), Louis J. Rodrigues, told the House Government Reform Subcommittee on National Security on May 10 that neither company will have critical technology ready in time to support the plane's next phase of engineering and manufacturing development. The GAO recommended that the Defense Department consider allowing the technology to catch up.

After meeting with Defense Secretary William S. Cohen on May 9, members of the Senate Armed Services Committee said they would delete authority for $595.5 million that the administration had requested for the plane's next phase and add $424 million to the development account. But they also said the department would retain the option of asking the Armed Services and Appropriations committees for the money to be shifted back if it determined that the Joint Strike Fighter is ready for the next stage.

"There's a lot of technological risk in the program, [and] we don't want it to feel rushed," said Sen. Joseph I. Lieberman of Connecticut, ranking Democrat on Armed Services Airland Forces Subcommittee. "If [the Pentagon] feels they can make the case that they're ready, we can reprogram the money. It's a good result. We certainly don't mean it to be negative."

Despite the continued congressional support for the Joint Strike Fighter, some lawmakers expressed unease about the price at the same time the Pentagon is pursuing the F/A-18E and F and the F-22.

"We need to address the whole issue of funding [tactical aircraft]," said Curt Weldon, R-Pa., chairman of the House Armed Services Subcommittee on Military Research and Development. "If we have to keep funding the whole [Joint Strike Fighter] program . . . something's got to give. There's not enough to fund all three programs."

Meanwhile, other House members objected to the Armed Services Committee's decision to shift $206 million in authorization for the Navy's F/A-18E and F to an account to authorize buying two Air Force F-15 fighters at $75 million apiece and perform a $56 million study on the earlier F-15 C and D models.

"This takes robbing Peter to pay Paul to a whole new level," said Rep. Norman Sisisky of Virginia, ranking Democrat on the Armed Services Subcommittee on Military Procurement.

Unsettling Vieques

Conferees are likely to have to settle differences in the House and Senate bills over several overseas issues. One is language the House committee added regarding the Puerto Rican island of Vieques, where the Navy recently resumed training exercises after Justice Department agents removed about 220 protesters May 4 and 5.

The Navy suspended all training exercises for about a year after a Viequen security guard working for the Navy was killed by an errant bomb April 19, 1999. That event became a lightening rod for protests against noise, environmental destruction and health concerns caused by the bombing.

Clinton is trying to implement an agreement reached Jan. 31 with Puerto Rican Gov. Pedro Rossello on the status of the island. Although the proposal appears to have Senate support, it faces challenges from House members.

That agreement would provide $40 million in immediate economic and development assistance to the island and require a referendum conducted by the federal government to give the residents of the island a choice of whether the Navy should stay or go.

If the residents vote the Navy out, the service would have to leave by May 2003; but if it is allowed to stay, the federal government would give the island an additional $50 million and ensure that live-fire training occurs for no more than 90 days each year. The Navy has used its property on both ends of the island for amphibious assault training since World War II.

While the Senate bill essentially would authorize the president's request, the House bill would not require a referendum and would authorize the initial $40 million payment to Vieques only if the president certified that the Navy would resume all training, including live bombing, "without interference."

Tillie Fowler, R-Fla., expected to be named a House conferee, acknowledged that the island needs more economic support, but she has reservations about setting a precedent of allowing residents to decide whether the Navy can use the island for training.

Foreign Involvement

On another issue, the House committee adopted, by voice vote, an amendment by Mississippi Democrat Gene Taylor that would limit the number of U.S. troops serving in Colombia to no more than 500 at a time. The amendment would allow the Pentagon to break the limit during times of natural disasters or to rescue U.S. troops.

The Senate Appropriations Committee on May 9 approved as part of its fiscal 2001 foreign operations spending bill (S 2522) a $934 million package of fiscal 2000 funds to help Colombia's military fight guerrillas and drug traffickers.

Taylor said he was concerned that at the same time Congress is considering giving Colombia $1 billion in aid, that country is cutting its defense budget. "I don't want to see us stumble into armed conflict with Colombia," he said.

For the second straight year, defense authorizers in both chambers included language that would prohibit any money from being used to plan, design or build a chemical weapons destruction plant near Shchuch'ye in Russia's Ural Mountains.

The administration has been pushing funds for the plant as part of an initiative, enacted in 1991 (PL 102-228) to help Russia safeguard and destroy its nuclear, chemical and other weapons. But some Republicans have said the money should be going to enhance security at weapons sites in Russia.

The Senate bill would prohibit the construction of the plant unless Russia provides $25 million for the program, and unless the Defense Department ensures that the plant would be used to destroy nerve agent stockpiles in Russia and that the international community commits to helping fund the plant over several years.

The House committee defeated two amendments during its markup that would have loosened restrictions on abortions for female military personnel or family members. Both expect to emerge again on the House floor, but neither is expected to become law this year.

One proposal, offered by California Democrat Loretta Sanchez, was rejected 20-31. It would have allowed women to obtain abortions at overseas military hospitals if they were paid for with private funds. Current law prohibits abortions at military facilities unless the life of the mother is at risk, in which case the Defense Department's health care plan pays for the abortion.

The panel also rejected, 26-29, an amendment by Hawaii Democrat Neil Abercrombie that would have allowed women to obtain abortions, funded by the Defense Department, if the pregnancy were the result of rape or incest. The House committee adopted similar language in last year's authorization bill, but it was deleted in conference.

House Passes Bill That Includes Retiree Benefits, Kosovo Conditions

MAY 20 — The House passed a $309.98 billion defense authorization bill for fiscal 2001 on May 18 after adding amendments that could shorten the U.S. peacekeeping mission to Kosovo, speed up the export of high-performance computers and improve benefits for military retirees.

At the same time, the House adopted a key component of President Clinton's plan to settle the dispute over Navy bombing on the Puerto Rican island of Vieques. The bill would authorize the transfer of a portion of Navy-owned land on the western end of the island to the Puerto Rican government.

The House passed the defense measure (HR 4205) by a vote of 353-63 after two days of debate. *(Vote 208, p. H-66)*

On May 17, the House adopted, 264-153, an amendment by Budget Committee Chairman John R. Kasich, R-Ohio, that could force the withdrawal of U.S. forces from Kosovo by next summer if NATO allies do not fulfill their promise to aid the province. *(Vote 191, p. H-62)*

The following day, as the House wound up work on its bill, the Senate voted to remove an amendment to its fiscal 2001 military construction appropriations bill (S 2521) that would have required a pullout by July 1, 2001, unless Congress authorized the mission.

The Senate is expected to take up its defense authorization bill (S 2549) in June.

Although the Senate bill is expected to win passage, Energy Secretary Bill Richardson has objected to provisions aimed at curtailing his authority over a nuclear weapons security agency created by Congress last year. The House measure contains no similar language.

Raising the Ante

The House defense bill would authorize $4.6 billion more than Clinton requested and $21.1 billion more than the fiscal 2000 authorization for the armed forces, military construction and defense programs of the Energy Department. Many lawmakers repeated their concern that the Pentagon needs even more money for such critical programs as modernization and procurement.

"A serious mismatch between requirements, forces and resources continues to exist," House Armed Services Committee Chairman Floyd D. Spence, R-S.C., said during the debate.

A May 17 statement by the Office of Management and Budget said the funding level in the House bill "would reduce resources from non-defense programs that are critical to our nation's future." The administration did not threaten to veto the measure.

One of the most popular floor amendments, offered by Rules Committee Chairman David Dreier, R-Calif., would shorten the period for congressional review of high-performance computer exports from 180 days to 60. The change is strongly backed by technology companies that contend the six-month review period is costing them business.

The six-month time frame was established in the fiscal 1998 defense authorization law (PL 105-85). It allows for congressional review of administration changes to regulations governing computer exports to countries that pose the greatest risk to U.S. national security. *(1997 Almanac, p. 8-3)*

Dreier and other lawmakers would prefer a 30-day waiting period — the same as for such military exports as tanks — but compromised with Spence and those who want more time.

Senate Banking, Housing and Urban Affairs Committee Chairman Phil Gramm, R-Texas, supports a 60-day period as part of a broader measure (S 1712) that would reauthorize the Export Administration Act for controlling "dual use" exports of technology that has both military and commercial uses. That bill has been stalled for months because of objections from four Senate committee chairmen with national security and jurisdictional concerns.

Caring for Retirees

On a lopsided, 406-10 vote May 18, the House adopted an amendment by Gene Taylor, D-Miss., that would allow retirees over age 65 to obtain health care at military hospitals and clinics, with Medicare reimbursing the Defense Department for 95 percent of the cost. *(Vote 207, p. H-66)*

Military retirees who reach 65 now must switch from the Defense Department's HMO-style health plan, called Tricare, to Medicare, where they lose some benefits such as prescription drug coverage.

The House bill would allow older retirees to participate in the Tricare mail-order drug program and pharmacy network.

Taylor's proposal would broaden to the entire nation what is now a limited pilot program for Medicare subvention, in which Medicare reimburses the military for treating retirees over 65.

"This is the biggest issue in my district," Taylor said. "They're the only Americans getting shortchanged on health care, and they're the most deserving Americans."

But Steve Buyer, R-Ind., chairman of the House Armed Services Subcommittee on Military Personnel, said Medicare subvention is too expensive and needs to be tested further, along with other demonstration programs, before Congress commits to a long-term plan.

A substitute proposal by Buyer that would have expanded the program but reauthorized it only through 2003, failed 95-323. *(Vote 206, p. H-66)*

Island in the Sun

In dealing with Vieques, lawmakers narrowly backed Clinton's proposal for the land transfer by a 218-201 vote on an amendment by House Armed Services ranking Democrat Ike Skelton of Missouri. *(Vote 202, p. H-66)*

According to a deal Clinton brokered in January with Puerto Rican Gov. Pedro Rossello, the Navy would transfer land at the western end of the island — the land is not used for bombing — and provide $40 million in assistance up front before the residents of Vieques hold a referendum sometime in the next two years on whether to allow the Navy to remain on its land on the eastern end of the island.

If residents vote the Navy out, the service would have to leave by May 2003. If the Navy is permitted to stay, it may resume bombing, but the federal government would provide an additional $50 million in assistance to the island.

Skelton said his amendment "is the only way we can get back the range at Vieques permanently." Opponents said the deal sets a precedent of allowing residents near the other 33 U.S.-based live-fire training facilities to demand compensation and determine how much training can occur.

On another contentious issue, the House defeated, 204-214, an amendment by Joe Moakley, D-Mass., that would have closed the U.S. Army School of the Americas. The school, at Fort Benning, Ga., the Army's main infantry training base, receives about $15 million a year from the federal government to train Latin American military officers. Critics say that some of its graduates have violated human rights at home. *(Vote 204, p. H-66)*

The defense bill would rename the school the "Defense Institute for Hemispheric Security Cooperation" and require a curriculum based on human rights, the rule of law and respect for democratic values.

Moakley said the changes "don't amount to much more than a new coat of paint." His amendment would have created a congressional commission to oversee the school.

The House last year voted to cut off the foreign aid portion of funding for the school, but House leaders backed down when Senate appropriators threatened to shift all funding for the school to the Defense budget.

The House also rejected, 195-221, an amendment by Loretta Sanchez, D-Calif., that would have allowed women in the military and dependents to obtain abortions at overseas military hospitals if they used private funds. *(Vote 203, p. H-66)*

Following are other highlights of the defense bill:

Military Personnel

In addition to approving the 3.7 percent military pay raise that Clinton proposed, the bill would accelerate the administration's plan to increase housing allowances. As a first step toward covering all off-base housing costs by 2005, Clinton requested $160 million to reduce the average proportion of military pay spent on housing from 19 percent to 15 percent in 2001. The bill would authorize $30 million more.

The bill also would allow uniformed personnel to participate in the government's 401(k) style retirement savings plan by depositing up to 5 percent of their pre-tax basic pay in the tax-deferred program.

Conditional authorization for this program was among many provisions of the fiscal 2000 defense authorization bill (PL 106-65) that were intended to make the military retirement system more attractive in order to retain talented personnel. To conform with last year's congressional budget resolution, that bill authorized service members' participation in the savings plan only if Congress offset the resulting loss of tax revenue — which it did not do. This year, the defense bill could simply authorize the savings plan with no strings attached because the budget resolution for 2001 (H Con Res 290) allowed for the revenue loss.

The bill also would add $218 million to the budget request for initiatives intended to improve recruiting and retention. Nearly three-quarters of the increase would go to bonuses for those who enlist or re-enlist in critical or hard-to-fill job specialties.

Operations and Maintenance

For operations and maintenance, the largest part of the Pentagon budget, the bill would authorize nearly $111 billion, only $668 million more than Clinton requested.

Among the largest readiness-related additions to the budget are:

- $660 million for the maintenance and repair of facilities.
- $461 million for major overhauls of ships, aircraft, vehicles and their components.
- $153 million to modernize the equipment and facilities at training ranges.

Among the offsetting reductions are several hardy perennials that Congress insists every year can be cut without harming military effectiveness:

- $440 million because the dollar's strength against various foreign currency reduces the cost in dollars of goods and services purchased locally by U.S. forces stationed abroad.
- $145 million that is not needed be-

cause the Pentagon has fewer people on its military and civilian payrolls than the budget assumed.

• $72 million to force the Pentagon to comply with previously mandated reductions in the number of personnel assigned to headquarters units.

Anti-Missile Defense

The bill would authorize $5.2 billion to develop and field anti-ballistic missile defenses, which is $283 million more than Clinton requested.

The total includes $2.2 billion for national missile defense, the administration's controversial plan to deploy a system in Alaska to defend U.S. territory against a small number of missiles from North Korea.

In addition to continuing development and testing of the anti-missile system, the $2.2 billion includes $75 million for procurement and $104 million for initial construction of facilities, including a radar on remote Shemya Island in the Aleutians.

The bill would authorize $85 million more than Clinton requested for the national missile defense system. It also would incorporate into that program $241 million to develop a missile detection satellite that is a key element of the nationwide defense but that has been funded in the Air Force budget.

The House Armed Services Committee said the Air Force was subordinating the anti-missile mission to other jobs in designing the satellite, which is designated SBIRS Low (Space-Based Infra-Red System, Low-altitude).

The bill also would shift from the Air Force to the anti-missile program the development of a Boeing 747 armed with an anti-missile laser. The Air Force was short-changing the project to fund other programs, the panel said. The bill would authorize $231 million for this airborne laser, $87 million more than requested.

Weapons Modernization

The bill would authorize a total of $3.5 billion more than the $98 billion the administration requested to develop and purchase military hardware. But in drafting the bill, the Armed Services Committee followed the priorities set by the chiefs of the military services, who want most of the increase to upgrade weapons already in service, or to buy more of them.

In addition to the blessing of Pentagon chiefs, programs already in production typically have the political advantage of a larger and more dispersed work force than a program still under development.

• **Ground combat.** For example, Army Chief of Staff Gen. Eric K. Shinseki has launched an effort to make his combat force weigh less, so it can be transported more easily, without sacrificing firepower. The bill would authorize $537 million, as budgeted, to jump-start this transformation by equipping some units with currently available lightweight combat vehicles. And, as Shinseki requested, it would authorize $194 million — $46 million more than Clinton requested — to develop the radically new type of combat vehicle the Army is looking for.

But the bill would add more for the current heavyweight force — built around the 70-ton M-1 tank — than it would add to accelerate development of the lighter force. For instance, the bill would authorize $72 million for a portable bridge, carried on an M-1 chassis, on which a tank could cross a 25-yard ditch, and $80 million for another M-1 variant, equipped to plow through minefields with a bulldozer blade and rip apart obstacles with a backhoe.

Senior Pentagon civilians had told the Army to cancel both those programs to pay for the transformation effort.

• **Air combat.** The bill would make only minor changes in the budget request for three new types of fighter jets in the early stages of production or still under development, authorizing:

• $3.9 billion, as requested, to develop and build the Air Force's F-22.

• $872 million — $15 million more than requested — to continue developing the Joint Strike Fighter, three versions of which are slated to enter service at the end of the decade.

• $2.6 billion to buy 39 F/A-18 E and F model Super Hornets for the Navy and Marine Corps, a reduction of three planes ($206 million) from the budget request.

But the bill also would authorize funds not requested to build more of the planes that the F-22 and Joint Strike Fighter are slated to replace:

• $150 million for two F-15Es, built in St. Louis by the Boeing Co.

• $52 million for three F-16s, built in Fort Worth, Texas, by Lockheed Martin Corp.

• **Ships.** The Navy's shipbuilding plan, largely authorized as requested, would continue buying current models while radical new vessels are being designed. The bill would authorize one more of the big Nimitz-class carriers that have been built for three decades ($4.1 billion) and funds to design a new carrier, with a much smaller crew ($258 million). It would fund three Aegis destroyers ($3.1 billion) while designing a new type of surface warship ($544 million — $6 million less than requested).

The only major ship for which the bill would add funds to the budget is a $1.2 billion helicopter carrier. HR 4205 would add only $10 million. But since the vessel would be built by Litton Industries in Pascagoula, Miss., the hometown of Senate Majority Leader Trent Lott, it is generally expected that Congress ultimately will approve a much larger amount.

Senate Bill Leans On Military To Speed Pace Of Change

JUNE 3 — The Senate Armed Services Committee is using its $309.8 billion defense authorization bill for fiscal 2001 to challenge some of the armed services' modernization plans and to goad the Pentagon into a more active transformation of forces to better meet the threats of the post-Cold War world.

"The military dimensions of the next century are likely to be so different from those on which the current force was built that an evolutionary approach — based on correcting near-term deficiencies — will not be sufficient," the committee said in its report accompanying S 2549, which was approved May 9.

"We must ensure that our ongoing efforts to maintain current advantages . . . are complemented with bold action that can effect the true transformation required for the 21st century force."

So, for instance, the bill would accelerate to 2002 the Defense Department's timetable for launching in 2004 a series of large-scale, realistic, multiservice (or "joint") war games that are to be used as the basis for testing new war-fighting concepts and choosing among competing ways of accomplishing the same mission. The committee directs the chairman of the Joint Chiefs of Staff to report on the advisability of creating a national training center at which to conduct such joint experimentation.

Like everything else on the Senate's legislative agenda, the defense bill is bogged down in a partisan quagmire. But, one way or another, the influential Armed Services panel is likely to get the authorization provisions enacted into law.

In general, the committee's bill supports the services' attempts to craft new types of forces while maintaining the combat-readiness of units currently in the field. But on some key issues, the Senate panel has weighed in with its own views. For example:

- The authorization bill would approve, in general, the Army's plan to develop "medium-weight" combat units that would have more staying power than lightly armed airborne units but could be deployed more quickly than armored forces equipped with 70-ton tanks.

However, the committee ordered the Army to concentrate its money and effort on developing and testing radically new lightweight combat vehicles that could enter service in about a dozen years, while focusing less on a planned "interim" force to be equipped with medium-weight combat vehicles currently available.

- Despite strong objections from top Pentagon leaders, the committee ordered a slowdown in development of the Joint Strike Fighter, different versions of which are slated to enter service with the Navy, Air Force and Marine Corps toward the end of the decade. While affirming its support for the program, the panel complained that the fighter was being rushed to production without adequate testing.
- At the insistence of committee Chairman John W. Warner, R-Va., the panel set very ambitious goals — backed up by a $200 million authorization — for introducing into the U.S. arsenal remotely controlled tanks and bombers to minimize the number of U.S. personnel put at risk on particularly dangerous missions.

"Casualty aversion limits the flexibility of foreign policy," the committee said in its report accompanying the bill. "Taking advantage of advances in technology will allow future administrations greater flexibility and, at the same time, reduce exposure of U.S. personnel."

Bolstering Enlistment

Like the companion measure passed May 18 by the House (HR 4205), the Senate bill would approve a 3.7 percent military pay raise requested by President Clinton and liberalized medical benefits for military personnel and retirees. Those steps are an effort to bolster sagging enlistment and re-enlistment rates. S 2549 would also authorize some pilot projects to test new Army recruiting strategies, including sponsoring motor sports competitions and an Army racing team to drum up interest among potential recruits.

The Senate bill would authorize $4.5 billion more than the $305.3 billion Clinton requested for defense programs in fiscal 2001. It would approve $21 billion more than Congress authorized for fiscal 2000, which was the first defense budget in 14 years to provide a "real" increase in purchasing power, after allowing for the cost of inflation. S 2549 would authorize an inflation-adjusted increase in purchasing power of 4.4 percent.

In addition to funds authorized for the Defense Department, the bill's total includes $12.8 billion for defense-related nuclear programs conducted by the Energy Department.

Potentially much more significant than the relatively small amounts of money the committee shuffled around are those provisions intended to make top Pentagon leaders focus on long-term defense needs and challenge the services' deeply rooted assumptions about how to win a war.

Ground Combat Forces

Last fall, Army Chief of Staff Gen. Eric K. Shinseki launched the quest for a lighter, but no less lethal, force with a warning to his fellow soldiers that heavily armed Army units will have to be more quickly deployable over long distances if the service is to remain "strategically relevant." There had been widespread complaints that it took too long for Army units to reach the Balkans during the Kosovo crisis in mid-1999 and that once the units arrived, some of their equipment was too unwieldy to operate in the mountainous terrain.

The linchpin of Shinseki's planned medium-weight force is to be a combat vehicle incorporating new types of armor, automotive systems and weapons, ready for service by 2012. Intended to be as lethal as the M-1 tank and as safe on the battlefield, it would weigh no more than 20 tons — less than one-third the weight of the tank, and small enough to be carried by the Air Force's ubiquitous C-130 cargo planes.

The Senate bill would strongly endorse moving toward that "objective" force, authorizing not only the $148 million requested to develop this so-called future combat system, but also an additional $46 million to speed up the program. That addition was included in a wish list of additional spending that the Army sent Congress. The committee also added $6 million to develop composite materials for the new vehicles that would combine light weight with great strength.

The committee added $75 million for Warner's proposal to develop unmanned combat vehicles as part of this project. In its report accompanying the bill, the Senate panel sets a goal of having remotely operated vehicles make up one-third of the Army's force within 15 years.

In addition to lighter fighting vehicles, a more agile Army would also need to reduce its logistical "tail" — the vast amounts of diesel fuel and spare parts that have to be shipped along with the combat units. The committee authorized additional funds along those lines, adding $8 million to develop portable machines to fabricate on the spot various types of spare parts and $4 million to continue work on fuel cells that would require less fuel than current types of generators to provide electrical power for units in the field.

On the other hand, the committee qualified its support for Shinseki's plan to jump-start the transformation by quickly equipping at least two 4,000-member brigades with lightweight

Defense Bills Compared

JUNE 3 — Here are the chief categories in the fiscal 2001 defense authorization bills as passed by the House (HR 4205 — H Rept 106-616) and approved by the Senate Armed Services Committee (S 2549 — S Rept 106-292), compared with President Clinton's request:

(in billions of dollars of new budget authority)

	Clinton	House	Senate
Procurement	$60.27	$62.30	$63.28
Research/Development	37.86	39.31	39.33
Operation/Maintenance	109.31	109.98	109.19
Revolving/Management Funds	0.94	1.28	0.94
Personnel	75.80	75.80	75.63
Military Construction	4.55	4.87	4.92
Family Housing	3.48	3.56	3.54
Other	(1.22)	(1.22)	1.04
Atomic Energy	13.08	12.80	12.76
Related Activities	1.25	1.20	1.20
TOTAL *	**$305.33**	**$309.89**	**$309.84**

* Numbers may not add to totals due to rounding

SOURCE: House and Senate Armed Services committees

combat vehicles currently available. While the Army pursues the technological breakthroughs needed for the new fighting vehicles, these so-called "interim" units are intended to experiment with tactics and organization for the forces to come. But they would also be available for deployment on peacekeeping missions.

The bill would authorize the $537 million requested to begin equipping this interim force. In keeping with the committee's insistence that the Army focus on the new-technology, future force, however, the panel told the Army to make the interim force as cheap as possible. In particular, the committee insisted that, if the service decides to equip the interim force with vehicles not currently in the Army's inventory, it must conduct a field test comparing the effectiveness of a unit equipped with existing Army equipment and one equipped with the new gear, and it must give Congress a detailed justification of the new equipment's cost.

That could tilt the fierce competition among armored vehicle manufacturers for the contract to equip the interim brigades. General Motors Corp. is offering several versions of a wheeled armored car it sold the Marine Corps in the mid-1980s. But United Defense insists that it could equip the units more cheaply by upgrading some of the 17,000 M-113 troop carriers, which move on tank-like caterpillar tracks, that the Army already owns.

At the Army's request, the committee added to the bill authorization to continue buying two combat vehicles that are modifications of the M-1 tank: $77 million for a portable bridge carrier and $108 million for an armored demolition bulldozer. Top Pentagon officials had insisted that the two projects be killed to free up funds for developing the new, lighter forces. But the Army put both near the top of its wish list of things it wants Congress to cover with any addition to Clinton's defense budget.

On the other hand, the committee seemed ambivalent about the place in the future Army of one other heavyweight system: the Crusader mobile cannon. The bill would authorize the $355 million requested to continue developing the big gun, and the panel lauded, in principle, the Army's decision to cut its weight from 55 tons to 40 tons. But since the necessary redesign would delay production until late in the decade, the committee told the Army to explain how the big cannon would fit into the medium-weight units slated to be coming on-line at about that time.

In the companion defense appropriations bill (S 2593), the Senate Appropriations Committee took a harder line on the Crusader, slicing $155 million from the request and ordering the Army to make the gun more compatible with the readily deployable, 20-ton combat vehicles being developed.

The authorization bill would approve the $614 million requested to continue developing the Comanche scout helicopter. To upgrade the existing fleet of missile-armed Apache helicopters, the bill would authorize $903 million, instead of the $745 million requested. The additional $158 million is for specialized radios and other improvements based on lessons drawn from the operations against Serbia during the 1999 conflict over Kosovo.

Air Combat

Clinton's budget included $857 million to continue developing the Joint Strike Fighter, three versions of which are slated for production beginning late in the decade to replace several 1970s-vintage jets currently used by the Navy, Air Force and Marine Corps. More than two-thirds of that amount was to gear up for production after the Pentagon chooses between two competing designs.

The committee expressed strong support for the joint fighter program, but complained that the Pentagon was rushing it into production, without adequately testing the competing designs, particularly for the vertical-takeoff version intended for the Marines. The bill would cut $171 million from the request, authorizing $685 million, which it designated for additional test flights to be conducted before the winning design is chosen.

Deputy Defense Secretary Rudy de Leon has warned that a delay could leave the Air Force short of fighters if aging F-16s wear out before its version of the new joint fighter comes off the production line.

The bill would also authorize $125 million for Warner's initiative to accelerate development of remotely controlled airplanes equipped to attack heavily defended ground targets. The bill would set a goal of having unmanned aircraft make up one-third of that part of the force designed to attack ground targets far behind enemy lines, partly in hopes of palliating the growing demand by politicians and the public for casualty-free combat.

The bill would authorize the amounts requested for the Air Force's new F-22 fighter: $2.2 billion for 10 planes, $396 million for components to be used in 16 planes to be funded in the next budget, and $1.4 billion to continue developing the craft. It would also increase by 1 percent a cap Congress had set by law on the total amount that could be spent on developing and testing for the plane. While insisting that the cap had imposed a useful discipline on the project, the committee accepted the Pentagon's request for a slight increase in the testing budget.

As requested, the bill would authorize $2.9 billion for 42 of the Navy's F/A-18E and F model jets.

Unlike the House-passed version, the Senate bill would not add to the budget authorization for F-15 fighters, built by The Boeing Co. in St. Louis, or F-16s, built by Lockheed Martin Corp. in Fort Worth, Texas.

Several other committee initiatives in the bill reflect lessons drawn from the 1999 air war over Kosovo, particularly how valuable surveillance aircraft are and how few of them are in the Pentagon's inventory. The bill would approve the $261 million requested for a 15th JSTARS radar plane — a jetliner equipped to detect tanks and trucks hundreds of miles away. It would also authorize an additional $46 million for components to be used in another JSTARS, should it be requested in the next budget.

The committee also ordered the Air Force to spend $18 million to test whether a ground surveillance radar could be carried by a high-altitude robot plane being designed for photo reconnaissance.

The bill also would authorize, in addition to the budget request:

- $86 million to design a long-range, air-launched cruise missile. The Air Force stockpile of such weapons has been depleted over the past decade by unanticipated use in the Balkans and Iraq.
- $46 million, in addition to the $32 million requested, for decoys to be towed behind U.S. fighters to lead astray radar-guided missiles homing in on the planes.

Naval Combat

While backing the Navy's plans to design new types of warships, the Senate panel focused most of its shipbuilding initiatives on building a case for spending more money to buy ships and buying more of the types currently being built — some of them by shipyards in committee members' home states.

The committee warned that the annual shipbuilding budgets projected in future years fall short of the $10 billion to $12 billion that would be needed to sustain the Navy's current fleet of more than 300 ships. While calling for larger budgets, the committee also told the Navy to consider changing its budgeting rules in hopes of getting more ships for the dollar. For example, it urged the Navy to make greater use of multi-year contracts, which have saved an estimated $1.4 billion in the construction of Aegis destroyers.

The committee also recommended more frequent use of "incremental" funding, with the Navy requesting in a given fiscal year only the amount that would be spent on a particular ship during that year. To prevent the Pentagon from seducing Congress into high-priced procurements with very small initial outlays, Congress insists that the Navy request "full funding" for the entire cost of a ship in one lump sum, except for certain components that need to be purchased ahead of time. But the Navy and shipbuilding companies insist that incremental funding has shaved hundreds of millions of dollars from the price of an aircraft carrier and a helicopter carrier, by allowing contractors to plan for a more steady flow of work.

As requested, the bill would authorize $4.1 billion for a nuclear-powered carrier slated to enter service in 2008, when it would replace the *Kitty Hawk*, then 47 years old. That would be the 10th ship of the *Nimitz* class, which the Navy has been buying for three decades.

In addition to approving the $2.7 billion requested for three destroyers equipped with the Aegis anti-aircraft system, the bill would authorize $500 million for "long lead time" components to be used in similar ships to be funded in future budgets — an increase of $143 million over the request, which would buy enough components to continue building the ships at the rate of three per year, with production split between a General Dynamics Corp. yard in Bath, Maine, and a Litton Industries yard in Pascagoula, Miss. The committee complained that the Navy's plan to begin in 2002 buying only two destroyers a year would drive up the cost of each ship and might force one of the two shipyards to drop out of the program.

The committee approved the $1.2 billion requested for a nuclear-powered submarine and the $508 million requested for long-lead-time components. While not adding to the budget the funds that would be needed to step up the submarine building rate, however, the committee ordered the Navy to report on how much it would save if it bought two subs annually instead of one, as projected.

The bill would authorize the $236 million requested to design a new class of aircraft carrier, with a smaller crew and lower operating costs than the *Nimitz* class. Also approved is $22 million for components to be used in the first of the new ships, slated to begin construction in 2006 and enter service in 2013, when it would replace the 52-year-old *Enterprise*.

The committee objected to the Navy's decision to delay from 2004 to 2005 the start of construction of the first of a new class of destroyers intended to save money by having a crew of only 95 — about one-third the number on existing destroyers. But the panel approved in the bill only the $550 million requested to continue designing the new ship, without adding the funds that would be needed to speed up the program.

The bill would slice $18 million from the Navy's $48 million request for the "smart ship" programs, touted as efforts to use automation and information technology to reduce the size of ships' crews, which account for the greater part of operating costs over the long haul. The committee complained that no savings had materialized in five years because of delays and software problems.

On the other hand, the bill would authorize an additional $2 million to let the Navy test cruise ship food service technologies to see whether they could reduce the large number of sailors tied up in food service operations on warships.

Sea and Air Transport

The bill's largest addition to the budget request for a single project is $460 million to continue incrementally funding a $1.2 billion helicopter carrier designed to carry nearly 2,000 Marines and the helicopters and landing barges to haul them ashore. The ship will be built by Litton Industries in Pascagoula, hometown of Senate Majority Leader Trent Lott, R-Miss.

While Lott's avid support ensured that funding was begun before the Navy decided to build the ship, the Navy, Litton and the Senate committee now all agree that, assuming the ship will be bought, incremental funding would save at least $500 million, compared with the cost of deferring most of the appropriation until 2005, as the Pentagon had planned.

As requested, the bill would also authorize $1.5 billion for two other ships intended to carry Marine units and their equipment.

The $2.2 billion requested for 12 C-17, wide-body, long-range cargo jets would be authorized by the bill, as would $267 million requested for components to be used in future production.

The bill would authorize hefty additions to the amounts requested for two other types of aircraft:

• $165 million for two C-130s, one equipped as a midair refueling tanker for the Marine Corps, and one equipped as a flying radio and TV station for psychological warfare. The budget requested $363 million for four C-130s — two plain cargo carriers and two tankers.

• $355 million for 26 H-60 helicopters, built in Stratford, Conn., by the Sikorsky Division of United Technologies and used by the Army as troop carriers and by the Navy as submarine hunters and cargo haulers. Clinton requested $465 million for 25 H-60s.

Senate Debates Amendments, Blocks Nuclear Cuts by President

JUNE 10 — Senate Republicans, unwilling to give President Clinton any leeway to strike an arms deal with Russia during his final months in office, blocked an amendment to a fiscal 2001 defense authorization bill that would have allowed the chief executive to cut the nation's nuclear arsenal below 6,000 warheads.

After a spirited debate, the Senate on June 7 voted 51-47, largely along party lines, to allow the president to make unilateral arms reductions only after the Pentagon completes a review of nuclear weapons status, which is unlikely until late next year after Clinton leaves office. *(Vote 119, p. S-23)*

The provision, offered by Senate Armed Services Committee Chairman John W. Warner, R-Va., replaced an amendment by Bob Kerrey, D-Neb., that would have given Clinton a free hand on nuclear arms reductions by removing an existing limit.

Carl Levin of Michigan, ranking Democrat on the Armed Services panel, said the final amendment would "hobble this president . . . I think it is a mistake in terms of precedent and in terms of what we should be doing as a body."

After four days of debate, the Senate is expected to continue work on the $309.8 billion defense authorization bill (S 2549) sometime this month after Democratic and Republican leaders work with their caucuses to winnow down the list of nearly 200 proposed amendments.

Meanwhile, the Senate began debate June 8 on a fiscal 2001 defense spending measure (HR 4576) that passed the House on June 7.

Work on the authorization bill has been slowed by debate on amendments unrelated to defense, including campaign finance and patients' rights in managed health care plans. Scheduled votes on those issues helped break a protracted stalemate over the right of Democrats to offer amendments to pending legislation, an impasse that had virtually paralyzed the Senate.

Senators voted 96-1 to accept a Warner amendment that would allow military retirees 65 and older to participate in two health care plans for retirees and their dependents. *(Vote 117, p. S-23)*

But the Senate refused to waive a budget point of order against a Democratic proposal — an amendment by Tim Johnson of South Dakota — to further expand retirees' health care options to the same plan as civilian federal workers. The 52-46 vote was eight short of the required three-fifths majority. *(Vote 118, p. S-23)*

Among amendments that may be debated when the Senate returns to the authorization bill is a proposal by Richard J. Durbin, D-Ill., to require the Pentagon to conduct more extensive tests of a proposed national anti-missile defense system. Critics of the program have argued that tests so far have not been realistic and that the interceptors being developed cannot distinguish between incoming warheads and decoys.

Other amendments that may be debated would:

• Increase funding for a program that tries to foster technology-based industries in areas of the former Soviet Union that have been home to nuclear weapons complexes.

• Eliminate language Republicans added to restrict the authority of the Energy secretary over a new agency that runs the nation's nuclear weapons laboratories.

• Prohibit the leasing of executive jet planes for high-level Pentagon officials.

Warner said he would wait until a conference with the House to offer an amendment that would place restrictions on the continued deployment of U.S. troops in Kosovo. The House included a similar proposal in its version of the authorization bill.

The Kosovo proposal, which has drawn objections from the administration, would require the president to certify by April 2001 that European allies are paying a fair share of peacekeeping costs or face the potential withdrawal of U.S. troops.

Nuclear Weapons

Warner's amendment dealing with nuclear weapons reductions marked the first Senate vote on a high-profile nuclear issue since the Senate resoundingly rejected the Comprehensive Test Ban Treaty (Treaty Doc 105-28) last Oct. 13, dealing a blow to Clinton's quest for more arms control.

Because of the high cost of maintaining their nuclear arsenal at Cold War levels, Russian leaders have expressed a desire to reduce arms below the levels in the START II agreement that the lower house of the Russian parliament, the Duma, ratified in April. The treaty — ratified by the U.S. Senate in 1996 — calls for slashing the number of long-range U.S. and Russian nuclear weapons to no more than 3,500 weapons each. *(1996 Almanac, p. 8-17)*

The two sides have held preliminary discussions about the framework for a possible START III pact. But the Clinton administration has resisted the idea and linked START III talks to Russian acceptance of a limited U.S. national missile defense system — something Russia has strongly objected to because it would violate the 1972 Anti-Ballistic Missile (ABM) Treaty.

For the past four years, the Armed Services Committee has included a provision in its authorization bill preventing the Pentagon from reducing the number of nuclear warheads deployed on long-range missiles and bombers. The language initially was added in hopes of pressuring Russia to ratify START II.

Kerrey said the Russian parliament's recent action means that the language no longer is necessary.

"The remaining argument [for its inclusion] is, 'We don't trust Bill Clinton,' " he said. "That's a very dangerous thing to make a part of our foreign policy, if we're going to allow one president to do one thing that we're not going to allow another president to do."

Kerrey's amendment would have immediately eliminated the congressionally imposed restriction and permitted the president to reduce nuclear force levels below the levels in the START I arms-control agreement, around 6,000 weapons.

Kerrey offered a similar amendment to the fiscal 2000 defense authorization bill, only to have it tabled (killed) 56-44.

This year, Kerrey and other Democrats argued that Warner's language would hamstring not only Clinton but the presumptive GOP presidential nominee, Texas Gov. George W. Bush, if he is elected to succeed Clinton.

Bush, who is expected to face Vice President Al Gore in the November elections said at a May 23 news conference that "it should be possible" to reduce the number of weapons below the numbers agreed to under START II "without compromising our security in any way."

Warner's amendment "is not just a slap in the face of our president — although it is surely that," said Joseph R. Biden Jr. of Delaware, the Senate Foreign Relations Committee's ranking Democrat. "It is also a slap in the face of the likely Republican nominee for president, Gov. Bush of Texas."

Pointing to Bush's recent speech indicating his willingness to seek further nuclear arms cuts, Biden said: "Imagine our new president negotiating with President Putin of Russia in 2001. Putin says, 'Let's do START III.' President Bush — or President Gore — replies, 'Heck, my Senate won't even let me go under START I. Come back next year.' "

Warner responded that his amendment would not preclude Clinton from continuing to negotiate with Russia, or from exercising his authority as commander in chief.

Warner argued that the Russian Duma attached conditions to the START II treaty knowing that they would be unacceptable to the Senate. Russia has said its acceptance of all agreements limiting offensive nuclear forces is conditioned on retaining the ABM Treaty's restrictions on missile defense systems.

The treaty prohibits any truly national missile defense system by allowing only a small number of interceptors in one fixed site. The idea was that neither the United States nor the Soviet Union would launch a first strike because they would be defenseless against the other's missiles — the theory of "mutual assured destruction."

"Had [the Duma's] ratification been in accordance with the way this chamber ratified it, I would say it is time to let the statute go," Warner said. "But they did not do it. They put protocols on that treaty which pose a great problem to the next president — indeed, to this president — as he saw when he went to the summit."

All Senate Republicans voted for Warner's amendment except for James M. Jeffords of Vermont, Gordon H. Smith of Oregon and Lincoln Chafee of Rhode Island. Jeffords and Smith voted in favor of Kerrey's amendment last year, as did Chafee's father, former Sen. John Chafee (1976-99). North Dakota's Kent Conrad was the only Democratic senator to support Warner's amendment.

On health care, the Senate agreed with Warner's proposal that military retirees reaching 65 should be allowed to remain in the Defense Department's CHAMPUS or Tricare health plans for retirees and their dependents rather than having to switch to Medicare.

Competing Plans

Although the defense authorization bill already contained a number of provisions to expand health care coverage for military retirees, Warner has been criticized by some veterans' groups for not doing more. Noting the politics surrounding the subject, Warner said he was "absolutely confident that this issue of retiree health care will be injected into the presidential campaign."

Johnson's amendment that the Senate turned away would have allowed military retirees to join the Federal Employees Health Benefits Program.

The Congressional Budget Office estimated that Johnson's plan would have cost $92 billion over 10 years, while Warner's is estimated to cost $40 billion over the same period.

"The difference between the two approaches is very significant in terms of dollars," Warner said. He said he scaled back his proposal because he "wanted to make sure we got started on some major series of benefits for retirees."

Johnson's amendment fell victim to a point of order raised by Phil Gramm, R-Texas.

On another health-related issue, the Senate, by voice vote, agreed to an amendment by Harry Reid, D-Nev., that would permit retirees with service-connected disabilities to receive military retired pay concurrently with veterans' disability compensation.

For the second straight year, senators rejected, 35-63, an attempt by Levin and John McCain, R-Ariz., to authorize additional base closures — in this case two new rounds the Pentagon says would save money. *(Vote 120, p. S-23)*

Since many Republicans contend that Clinton improperly manipulated the last round of base closures in 1995 in order to save jobs in California and Texas, two key electoral states. McCain and Levin noted that their amendment would not begin a new round until 2003, after Clinton leaves office.

Warner and other senators, however, responded that they should not tie the hands of the next president by forcing him to have to close military bases.

On a 93-0 vote, McCain won approval of another amendment that would create a $180-a-month allowance for armed forces enlisted personnel who are eligible for food stamps. *(Vote 116, p. S-23)*

An estimated 6,300 to 13,500 enlisted personnel rely on food stamps. McCain's proposal, based on separate legislation (S 2322), would cost about $6 million a year.

Changing Payday

Taking a step toward eliminating one of the budgetary gimmicks Congress used last fall to reduce fiscal 2000 spending, the Senate adopted, by voice vote, an amendment by Warner repealing a law that would have deferred the last federal pay day of fiscal 2000 until Oct. 1, the first day of fiscal 2001.

The law, enacted as part of the omnibus appropriations bill (PL 106-113), would have pushed more than $2 billion in outlays into fiscal 2001. The House-passed version of the authorization bill includes a similar provision.

Among the other amendments agreed to by voice vote:

• A proposal by Jeff Bingaman, D-N.M., and other senators representing states with nuclear weapons laboratories to provide compensation to Energy Department employees and private contractors who suffered health problems as a result of building bombs during the Cold War.

"We spend billions of dollars every year cleaning up the contamination left behind, yet we have all but ignored the human legacy," Bingaman said.

• A proposal by Joseph I. Lieberman, D-Conn., to establish a commission to assess the future of the U.S. aerospace industry and make recommendations for action by Congress and the White House.

• A proposal by Max Cleland, D-Ga., to extend educational benefits under the Montgomery GI Bill to family members of military veterans.

The House in May passed a separate proposal (S 1402) that would increase the amount of educational benefits for military veterans.

Cleland's bill would expand access to benefits and would allow military personnel to transfer their GI bill benefits to immediate family members.

• A proposal by Charles S. Robb, D-Va., to have the Pentagon submit a report on the Defense Travel System and limit the use of funds for the system.

Senate Expected To Vote to Curb Energy Secretary's Authority

JUNE 17 — The disappearance for more than a month of two top-secret computer hard drives at the Los Alamos National Laboratory angered members of Congress already upset over spying allegations and appeared to ensure that Senate Republicans would be able to curtail Energy Secretary Bill Richardson's authority over a new nuclear weapons agency.

Richardson has strongly objected to language in the Senate version of the fiscal 2001 defense authorization bill (S 2549) on the management of the National Nuclear Security Administration. He said the provisions would hamper the effectiveness of the new agency.

Senate Democrats planned to offer an amendment to remove the provisions when the Senate returns to debate on the defense bill June 19. But Democrats said June 14 that they would abandon those plans amid congressional outrage over the latest Los Alamos incident.

The uproar also cleared the way June 14 for the 97-0 Senate confirmation of retired Air Force Gen. John A. Gordon to head the nuclear administration. Lawmakers are anxious to see if Gordon, now the deputy director of Central Intelligence, can give the public and Congress more confidence in security at the weapons labs. *(Vote 128, p. S-25)*

"Clearly, the [Energy Department] and the labs have not been under control," Senate Energy and Natural Resources Committee Chairman Frank H. Murkowski, R-Alaska, said after the vote. "I hope that now we have cleared the nomination . . . that process can get under way."

The hard drives turned up June 16 within the same general secured area in which they had been stored, indicating they may have been misplaced. Richardson said the FBI was evaluating the authenticity of the storage disks and conducting an "intensive investigation" of the disappearance, which House Intelligence Committee Chairman Porter J. Goss, R-Fla., had called "a potentially devastating compromise of information that directly affects U.S. national interests."

Marking Time

During three days of work on the defense authorization bill, the Senate dealt with dozens of non-controversial amendments — including, for instance, authority to spend $2.8 million to weatherproof buildings at Keesler Air Force Base in Mississippi, home state of Senate Majority Leader Trent Lott.

Most of the debate, however, has been on amendments unrelated to the military, such as campaign finance and managed-care medical plans.

The Senate also has paused to take up other legislation, including a fiscal 2001 defense appropriations bill (HR 4576).

When authorization debate resumes June 19, the Senate is expected to take up two competing amendments on hate crimes — one by Judiciary Committee Chairman Orrin G. Hatch, R-Utah, and one from Edward M. Kennedy, D-Mass.

On June 20, the Senate is expected to consider a contentious amendment by Christopher J. Dodd, D-Conn., that would establish a bipartisan commission to examine U.S.-Cuba relations.

The commission would examine whether Cuba still poses a security risk to the United States and assess the Cuban government's role in international terrorism and drug trafficking. It also would evaluate the impact of the U.S. trade embargo against Cuba.

A growing number of lawmakers favor lifting sanctions on the sale of food and medicine to Cuba.

Another amendment likely to spark heavy debate if it is offered is an attempt by Patty Murray, D-Wash., to allow military women and dependents stationed overseas to obtain abortions at military hospitals if they pay for the procedure themselves.

Senate Republicans, meanwhile, may seek to offer an amendment that would bar U.S. cooperation with a proposed International Criminal Court, unless the United States signs and the Senate ratifies the treaty that would create the court.

Nuclear Insecurity

The nuclear security administration has been a continuing source of friction over the defense bill. Republicans created the agency in the fiscal 2000 defense authorization law (PL 106-65) to improve security and accountability in the nuclear weapons program after allegations in a special committee report that China obtained secret data from the weapons labs.

The nuclear security administration functions semi-autonomously within the Energy Department and is independent of normal departmental bureaucracy and procedures.

Republican lawmakers said the changes this year were necessary because Richardson did not follow their intentions in submitting an implementation plan for the new administration.

The new provisions would:

• Prohibit paying a salary to anyone serving in the same position in the Energy Department and in the nuclear agency — a procedure known as "dual-hatting." Richardson has said that about 18 of the new agency's 2,000 employees are dual-hatted, mainly senior-level officials overseeing such functions as security and counterintelligence.

• Remove the Energy secretary's authority under the Department of Energy Organizational Act (PL 95-91) to make any structural changes to the new agency. *(1977 Almanac, p. 609)*

In the wake of news reports from Los Alamos, Sen. Richard H. Bryan, D-Nev., agreed June 13 to lift his legislative "hold" on Gordon's nomination in exchange for a vote on an amendment to the defense bill to remove the provisions relating to the nuclear administration. Bryan said he had placed the hold in response to the GOP language.

Given the depth of dissatisfaction with the department's handling of the Los Alamos incident, however, Bryan later acknowledged that he probably would have to settle for trying to rewrite the language in conference — something Republicans are unwilling to do.

Gordon, a retired Air Force general who has held the second-ranking intelligence post since 1997, has drawn enthusiastic praise from lawmakers. He said in a statement that the new administration faces "many challenges and difficult problems.

Carl Levin of Michigan, the Senate Armed Services Committee's ranking Democrat, said the provisions in the defense bill "will make Gen. Gordon's job harder and not easier."

Hunting the Missing Disks

Although employees at the Los Alamos lab discovered hard disks missing May 7 from their storage place in a heavily guarded vault at the New Mexico facility, they waited more than three weeks to notify top lab officials. During much of that time, the lab was evacuated because of a nearby forest fire.

As the search continued, Richardson announced that former Sen. Howard H. Baker Jr., R-Tenn. (1967-85) and former Rep. Lee H. Hamilton, D-Ind. (1965-99) would conduct an independent assessment of the incident. The move did little to pacify lawmakers, who rebuked Richardson for declaring earlier this year that security at the three labs was under control.

The appointment of Baker and Hamilton "is a political way to deal with a catastrophe," said William M. "Mac" Thornberry, R-Texas.

Other lawmakers demanded immediate disciplinary action. Los Alamos executives placed six employees on leave and began administering polygraph tests to scientists with access to the secrets.

"It's disgusting," fumed Curt Weldon, R-Pa., at a June 14 House Armed Services hearing on the incident. "Somebody ought to be fired for this."

Weldon's anger was shared by Democrats across the Capitol. Bryan, ranking Democrat on the Senate Intelligence Committee, told Energy Department officials at a separate June 14 hearing that the lab's policy of allowing 26 unescorted employees access to nuclear data without being required to sign out for them "sounds like a real bonehead security procedure to me."

Some Republicans said the incident underscored the conclusions of the President's Foreign Intelligence Advisory Board, which last year found "organizational disarray, managerial neglect and a culture of arrogance" at the Energy Department.

Republicans also used the security incident to score political points against Richardson, who has campaigned on behalf of Vice President Al Gore's bid for the White House and has been mentioned as a possible running mate. Richardson turned down an invitation to testify.

"Perhaps if the secretary would spend more time ensuring the safety of our nation's nuclear treasures and less time trying to get the vice president elected president, we would not be here today," Richard C. Shelby, R-Ala., said.

Senate Armed Services Committee Chairman John W. Warner, R-Va., said Richardson has agreed to appear at a June 21 committee hearing.

Senate Continues Debate, Focuses On Testing Of Missile System

JUNE 24 — The Senate may vote the week of June 26 on an amendment to the defense authorization bill (S 2549) that would highlight alleged flaws in President Clinton's plan for a limited, nationwide anti-missile defense.

The amendment, by Richard J. Durbin, D-Ill., would require the Pentagon to test the system against countermeasures that an adversary might use to thwart it, such as surrounding an attacking warhead with a flock of decoys. Critics, led by Massachusetts Institute of Technology professor Theodore Postol, contend that the planned system could be defeated by a variety of such simple techniques.

Pentagon officials reject that claim, but insist that a detailed rebuttal would tip off adversaries how to design more effective countermeasures.

Durbin's proposal is one of more than 100 potential amendments to the defense bill, which the Senate has had under desultory consideration since June 6. Agreement on a timetable to wrap up work on the measure has been prevented by a political deadlock over a proposed amendment on campaign finance.

The Senate could finesse this problem by completing action on all amendments except campaign finance and then — while the defense bill technically remains before the Senate — holding an informal conference with the House to hammer out a compromise on the authorization measure.

In addition to adopting several non-controversial amendments during the week of June 19, the Senate tabled (killed), 50-49, an amendment by Patty Murray, D-Wash., and Olympia J. Snowe, R-Maine, that would have allowed servicewomen stationed overseas and female dependents to obtain abortions in U.S. military hospitals, provided they pay for the procedure. *(Vote 134, p. S-26)*

The administration's missile defense program is aimed at fielding by 2005 a defense that could fend off a small number of warheads launched at U.S. territory from North Korea.

The claim that the system could easily be flummoxed by decoys has become a central theme in critics' efforts to kill or slow the program. However, opponents also cite other developments to support their case.

The Russian government has flatly rejected administration proposals to make even modest changes in the 1972 treaty limiting anti-ballistic missile (ABM) defenses, which would be necessary to make the treaty compatible with the planned U.S. system. Rather than a limited shield against North Korean missiles, Russian officials have condemned it as the first step toward a more robust anti-missile system intended to neutralize the thousands of missiles on which Russia relies to deter a U.S. attack.

But Rep. Curt Weldon, R-Pa., and other anti-missile proponents contend that Russian President Vladimir Putin has undermined that argument by proposing to cooperate with the United States and Europe on anti-missile defenses that would deal with the very threats the U.S. program is designed to combat.

Anti-missile opponents also argue that the prospect of a rapprochement between North Korea and South Korea could remove the urgency driving the missile defense timetable. Administration officials counter that the two Koreas have a long way to go and insist that potential threats are multiplying.

Meanwhile, the administration is downplaying the significance of events earlier presented as turning points for the anti-missile program:

- Because the system missed its target in one of two earlier tests, there had been speculation that a third test, scheduled for July 7, would be crucial in determining whether the program was technically feasible. But Pentagon officials now say their evaluation will turn on many factors, and that they might recommend a "go" even if the next test misses its target.
- The Pentagon remains adamant that, if the system is to be in operation by 2005, work must begin next spring on a radar in Shemya, Alaska. Administration officials now are weighing contending legal opinions as to how much work can be done at that site before it would violate the ABM Treaty.
- A "go" decision by Clinton this fall now is presented as only the first of several decisions that would have to be made before the country was irreversibly committed to deploying a missile defense system.

Even in terms of domestic politics, Clinton's decision may be dwindling in significance. On June 22, Senate Majority Leader Trent Lott, R-Miss., joined other GOP heavyweights in saying Clinton could defer to the next president any decision on whether to deploy the planned system.

Senate Passes Bill; Conferees Must Reconcile Kosovo Differences

JULY 15 — A forthcoming conference on the fiscal 2001 defense authorization bill is expected to focus on sharp differences between Democrats and Republicans over language that could restrict the continued deployment of U.S. troops in Kosovo.

After more than a month of intermittent debate, the Senate on July 13 overwhelmingly passed the defense bill (HR 4205), 97-3, after substituting the text of the Senate version (S 2549). The $309.8 billion measure authorizes funds for Pentagon operations, military construction and family housing. *(Vote 179, p. S-33)*

The House version of the bill contains a provision that would require the president to certify by April 2001 that European allies are paying a fair share of peacekeeping costs in Kosovo, or U.S. troops potentially could be withdrawn from the Serbian province.

In May, Senate Republicans tried to include an even more stringent Kosovo proposal in its version of the fiscal 2001 military construction appropriations bill (S 2521). That provision would have set a 14-month limit on U.S. participation in the NATO peacekeeping mission without congressional authority. That amendment was removed after extensive lobbying by the Clinton administration and criticism from Texas Gov. George W. Bush, the presumed Republican presidential nominee.

Senate Armed Services Committee Chairman John W. Warner, R-Va., a leading critic of the Kosovo deployment, said he expects the House-passed provision on Kosovo to be in the final conference agreement on the defense bill.

Warner and other critics of the Kosovo mission argue that the United States did its share when it led an 11-week air war against Serbia last year to force Serb troops out of the province. They say European allies need to pick up a larger portion of the financial burden.

"Just look at the situation over there," Warner said in an interview. "There's still a lot of need for the allies to come in there and allocate their funding."

Democrats on the Armed Services Committee, however, are pledging to ensure that any language dealing with Kosovo in the final bill does not lead to a forced troop withdrawal.

"This conference should be one of the more manageable . . . we've had in recent years, but [the Kosovo provision] will be a point of contention," said Sen. Joseph I. Lieberman, D-Conn. "I think it is problematic."

Army Mobility

Another issue that Lieberman and other lawmakers said is likely to consume much of their attention in conference is language dealing with the Army's effort to transform itself into a lighter, more mobile force.

The Senate version of the bill approves, in general, the Army's plan to develop "medium-weight" combat units that could be deployed quickly. But the committee ordered the Army to concentrate its money and effort on developing and testing radically new lightweight combat vehicles that could enter service in a dozen years and focus less on a planned "interim" force to be equipped with currently available, medium-weight vehicles.

At Warner's insistence, the Senate bill also would authorize $200 million for introducing more remote-controlled tanks and bombers to minimize the risk to U.S. personnel.

Warner said he plans to meet with Army Chief of Staff Eric K. Shinseki to discuss the Pentagon's concerns over the modernization provisions.

The ease with which this year's defense bill sailed through the Senate Armed Services Committee reflected the relatively large amount of money available, as well as the inclusion of a 3.7 percent military pay raise sought by President Clinton and liberalized medical benefits for military personnel and retirees.

The broad support for the legislation also illustrated the success of Warner and other Republicans in keeping the legislation largely free of controversial amendments.

A few hotly debated amendments did make it through. One of them, sponsored by John McCain, R-Ariz., to require disclosure by political groups organized under section 527 of the tax code, ceased to be a contentious issue in the defense conference after the House passed a stand-alone bill containing similar language, with the Senate following suit.

Still in the Senate defense bill, however, is a provision sponsored by Edward M. Kennedy, D-Mass., that would expand the definition of federal hate crimes to include those committed because of the victim's gender, sexual orientation or disability.

House Armed Services Committee Chairman Floyd D. Spence, R-S.C., predicted that the addition of such amendments will mean the authorization conference "is going to take more time than usual." Spence and other lawmakers do not expect to complete their negotiations before the August recess.

In the Senate, most other controversial Democratic amendments offered to the bill were defeated. Shortly before final passage, the Senate tabled, or killed, 52-48, an amendment by Richard J. Durbin, D-Ill., that called for additional testing of a proposed national missile defense system to ensure that it would work against decoys and other countermeasures. *(Vote 178, p. S-33)*

The Senate also voted, 81-18, to table an amendment by Russell D. Feingold, D-Wis., that would have terminated the Trident II submarine-launched missile. *(Vote 177, p. S-32)*

The Senate on July 12 did follow the lead of the House in adopting, 86-11, an amendment that would shorten the period for congressional review of export rules for high-performance computers from 180 days to 60. The amendment, offered by Robert F. Bennett, R-Utah, and Harry Reid, D-Nev., is strongly backed by technology companies that contend the six-month review period is costing them business. *(Vote 174, p. S-32)*

The six-month time frame was established in the fiscal 1998 defense authorization law (PL 105-85) and allows for congressional review of administration changes to regulations governing computer exports to countries that pose the greatest risk to U.S. national security. *(1997 Almanac, p. 8-3)*

The Senate also adopted more than 100 relatively non-controversial amendments to the defense bill by voice vote. Those adopted during the week of July 10 included an amendment by Robert C. Byrd, D-W.Va., to require an annual report to Congress on the national security implications of U.S.-China trade.

Also adopted was an amendment by Fred Thompson, R-Tenn., and Lieberman that mirrored legislation (S 1993) they introduced last year to secure federal government computer systems against hacker attacks. The proposal would require agencies to develop information security programs and submit those programs to annual audits.

Conferees File Report With Expanded Benefits For Retirees

OCTOBER 7 — Brushing aside congressional budget limits, conferees on the fiscal 2001 defense authorization bill have added expanded medical benefits for retired military personnel and their dependents that could cost nearly $60 billion over the next 10 years.

The House and Senate are expected to vote on the conference report the week of Oct. 9.

The health care initiative would allow retirees to remain in the Pentagon's medical care and insurance system for life rather than having to rely on the more restricted coverage provided by Medicare after they turn 65.

It also would allow most retirees to obtain low-cost prescriptions through a Pentagon-sponsored mail-order system.

The new programs would be available only to those who have retired after serving at least 20 years on active duty. They would not apply to the much larger population of veterans who served shorter stints.

Although large majorities of the House and Senate Armed Services committees strongly supported the concept of providing lifetime medical care to military retirees, disagreements over how far to push the effort this year made this one of the last issues to be settled in the conference negotiations.

"You're talking about men and women who've served a minimum of 20 years," said Senate Armed Services Chairman John W. Warner, R-Va. "At the time they joined, and later, representations were made to them by senior civilian and military officials that, 'You'll be cared for for life.' "

The conference report filed Oct. 6 also:

- Dropped a House provision that could have led to the withdrawal of U.S. peacekeeping forces from Kosovo.
- Created a program to compensate thousands of Energy Department workers exposed to dangerous levels of radiation and other toxic substances

Deal Reached on Radiation Exposure

OCTOBER 7 — Despite widespread support for compensating Energy Department workers exposed to radiation and toxic materials at nuclear weapons plants during the Cold War, House and Senate negotiators struggled until Oct. 5 to reach a compromise acceptable to the Clinton administration and congressional Republicans, who worried about the cost of creating a new federal entitlement.

In many respects, the proposed compensation package included in the conference report was close to the original Senate plan written by Fred Thompson, R-Tenn., and Jeff Bingaman, D-N.M. Negotiators estimated that the agreement would cost about $1.8 billion over five years.

The original proposal by Thompson and Bingaman, which was estimated to cost about $1 billion, would have given injured workers a choice between receiving lost wages and medical care or a lump sum payment of $200,000 and medical care.

The compromise dropped the lost-wages alternative and would offer all workers a $150,000 payment and medical care. Existing payments for Navajo uranium miners exposed to radiation would be increased from $100,000 to $150,000, and they would be offered medical care.

"If you're going to proceed, everyone's got to be treated equally," said Rep. Edward Whitfield, R-Ky.

The original Thompson-Bingaman proposal also called for the Health and Human Services Department to develop a process to determine whether illnesses were related to a worker's employment at an Energy Department facility. The compromise ceded all responsibility to the president to determine which agency should be involved.

The compensation agreement came as a new Energy Department report revealed that current and former employees of the agency's uranium enrichment plant in Paducah, Ky., were unknowingly exposed to dangerously high levels of radiation in processing nuclear materials. Recent news reports have highlighted health risks to workers at other nuclear weapons facilities.

Richardson Victory

The inclusion of the compensation language in the defense bill was a rare victory for Energy Secretary Bill Richardson, under fire in recent months for his agency's handling of security at nuclear weapons labs and the Clinton administration's oil policies. Richardson lobbied extensively for keeping the provision in the conference agreement.

"Nuclear workers' compensation is a national debt long overdue to our Cold War veterans who have paid the highest possible prices for their service," Richardson said.

House Republican leaders originally sought to pull the compensation provision from the bill, calling it a costly entitlement that could drain other spending. They relented after a bipartisan group of lawmakers objected.

House Republicans proposed to spend less money, but senators from several states with Energy workers who had become sickened by exposure to beryllium dust, radiation and other toxic materials made it clear they wanted to stick closely to the original agreement.

"I don't think we should settle for half a loaf," said Sen. George V. Voinovich, R-Ohio.

At the same time, the White House also made it clear that it would not accept a watered-down alternative.

"Congress should not delay action by imposing future study requirements or requiring the enactment of subsequent implementing legislation," White House Chief of Staff John D. Podesta said in an Oct. 4 letter to House Armed Services Committee Chairman Floyd D. Spence, R-S.C. "Forcing these workers to endure further delays would be a profound injustice."

during the Cold War.

• Dropped a Senate provision that would have expanded the scope of federal laws against hate crimes to include attacks based on the sexual orientation of the victim.

The conference report would authorize $310 billion in discretionary spending for defense-related programs in fiscal 2001. This is $4.5 billion more than President Clinton requested, but within the ceiling on discretionary spending set earlier this year by the congressional budget resolution (H Con Res 290).

However, the total does not include the cost of the proposed health care expansion, which would create new entitlement programs requiring mandatory annual funding not subject to the appropriations process.

Entitled to Care

Making the retirees' benefit a mandatory spending program would buffer the program from any future pressure to cut the budget. The staunchly pro-defense majorities on the Senate and House Armed Services committees favored this approach because it would mean that retirees' health benefits would not compete against such things as new weapons programs or combat training in the Pentagon's annual budget process.

The version of the defense bill passed by the Senate in July would have provided expanded medical coverage for retirees but only for two years, during which it would be subject to the annual appropriations process. This was because Senate Armed Services leaders wanted to avoid a challenge to the congressionally mandated spending caps.

But in September, with budget discipline deeply eroded by ballooning estimates of the federal surplus, Republican Steve Buyer of Indiana, who chairs the House Armed Services Subcommittee on Military Personnel, publicly floated the idea of making expanded health coverage for retirees an entitlement.

Warner balked at the proposal on tactical grounds. If the conference report created an expensive new entitlement program, he warned, it might be killed by a budgetary point of order under the rules of the Senate. This would doom the Senate's two-year plan, which — Warner maintained — would give proponents a foot in the door toward subsequent enactment of a permanent entitlement.

As late as Oct. 4, Warner was concerned that he might not be able to muster the 60 votes needed to waive a point of order against a new entitlement for retirees. One of his concerns was that a point of order might be supported, not only by senators concerned about the long-term budget implications of the health care plan, but also by some who simply were disgruntled because provisions they supported — such as the expanded definition of hate crimes — had been dropped from the final version of the defense bill.

By Oct. 5, Warner and senior Armed Services Democrat Carl Levin of Michigan predicted that they could muster the 60 votes, because the retirees' health care proposals are widely supported.

Congress mandated medical care for military retirees in a 1956 law that entitled them to treatment in the Pentagon's network of hospitals and clinics. Their access was contingent on the ability of the facilities to accommodate retirees and their dependents in addition to the active-duty personnel and their dependents, who had a higher priority.

Since Medicare was created in the mid-1960s, the policy has been to provide retirees with medical care until they became eligible for Medicare at age 65, either in Pentagon facilities on a "space available" basis or through private health care providers reimbursed by the Pentagon.

Over the past decade, as the size of the military has been cut by one-third and a number of bases and base hospitals have been closed, "space available" treatment in military medical facilities has become less available. At the same time, the number of Medicare-eligible retirees and dependents has grown to nearly 1.4 million.

Military retiree associations have insisted that, whatever the government's precise legal obligation may be, the promise made to millions of service personnel by generations of recruiters was that they and their families would get free medical care for life, in return for a 20-year career. Thus, they contend, the government has a moral obligation to meet that commitment. Moreover, they insist that their years of service at relatively low pay entitles them to better treatment than they would get if they were forced to rely on Medicare.

By Oct. 5, Warner said he believed that argument would carry the day if the conference report were challenged on budgetary grounds.

Defense Bill Clears After Debate Tinged By Mideast Crises

OCTOBER 14 — Against a backdrop of growing violence in the Middle East, Congress cleared a $310 billion defense authorization bill for fiscal 2001 that would add $4.5 billion to President Clinton's budget request.

The House adopted the conference report on the bill (HR 4205) Oct. 11 by a vote of 382-31. *(Vote 522, p. H-166)*

The Senate cleared the bill the following day by a vote of 90-3, hours after the U.S. Navy destroyer *Cole* was severely damaged by a suicide bombing attack in the port of Aden, in the Arabian Peninsula nation of Yemen. As many as 17 of the ship's 350-member crew were feared dead. *(Vote 275, p. S-49)*

In addition to expressing condolences to the victims' families, lawmakers said the incident illustrated the broad range of threats that U.S. forces confront. "This is a most dangerous world," said Senate Armed Services Committee Chairman John W. Warner, R-Va.

For some lawmakers, the *Cole* incident underscored their contention that Clinton has undermined military effectiveness by sending troops and ships on far-flung peacekeeping and humanitarian missions even as he has cut the size of the military by nearly one-third and reduced its budget accordingly.

"Either we accept our role as the sole global superpower and . . . provide our military with the . . . necessary resources, or we decline this difficult responsibility and start to walk away," said House Armed Services Committee Chairman Floyd D. Spence, R-S.C. "Continuing to attempt to fulfill our superpower responsibilities on the cheap is simply no longer an option."

Retirees vs. Budget Caps

In clearing the defense bill, the Senate brushed aside a budgetary challenge to provisions in the conference report that would create new health care entitlements for military retirees and their dependents at an estimated cost of $60 billion over the next 10 years.

Since those costs would exceed the amount allowed for mandatory spending in the congressional budget resolution (H Con Res 290), it was subject to a point of order, which was raised by Bob Kerrey, D-Neb. However, by a vote of 84-9, the Senate adopted a motion by Warner to waive the point of order. *(Vote 274, p. S-49)*

The health care initiative would allow retirees — those who serve at least 20 years on active duty — to remain in the Pentagon's medical care and insurance system for life rather than having to rely on the more restrictive coverage provided by Medicare after they turn 65. It also would allow most retirees to buy prescription drugs at low cost by mail order or from retail pharmacies participating in a Pentagon-sponsored network.

Organizations of retirees and active-duty personnel have lobbied vigorously for such changes, contending that they were promised lifetime medical care in return for serving a full career in the service. The hardships and low pay they accepted as conditions of military life, they insist, entitle them to better treatment than they would get if they had to rely on Medicare.

Kerrey, who lost a leg in combat during the Vietnam War and was awarded the Medal of Honor, was the only member of either chamber to publicly challenge the proposed new medical benefits.

He objected to the argument that former service members were entitled to a higher quality of medical care than the average citizen, who relies on Medicare. "I didn't volunteer for the U.S. Navy in return for anything," Kerrey said. "I have heard an awful lot of rhetoric here that implies that I am a mercenary. . . . I did it as a consequence of believing that it was my duty."

Kerrey also complained that the provisions would provide free or low-cost benefits to many who were relatively well-off. "I didn't see an awful lot of military retirees out there foraging in the alleys for food," he said.

But Warner countered that the benefit was limited, in most cases, to those who had spent at least 20 years on active duty. (Kerrey is an exception to this generality: While his service as a Navy SEAL lasted only three years, he was retired on medical grounds because of his wounds.)

The government has a moral obligation to provide health care to those people, Warner insisted, because Pentagon recruiters and recruiting literature had promised for decades that a career would earn lifetime medical care for themselves and their families. He buttressed the point by displaying a poster-sized blow up of an Army recruiting pamphlet making that very statement.

"On that basis, my government owes me a lot of travel," Kerrey quipped. "They promised me I'd see the world, but all I saw was Vietnam."

Aside from the merits of the health care provisions, Kerrey, Phil Gramm, R-Texas, and Budget Committee Chairman Pete V. Domenici, R-N.M., all warned that waiving the budget caps to allow the new entitlement would open the floodgates for more big-ticket initiatives.

"The Budget Act . . . has created the fiscal discipline that enabled us to get to where we are today," Kerrey said. "[It] allowed us to turn to our citizens and say, 'We have got to be disciplined.' "

But there was no stopping the new initiative, propelled both by pressure from retirees and by the insistence of top service leaders that the promise of lifetime medical care was a key element of keeping a quality force.

"Expert recruiters and the chairman of the Joint Chiefs of Staff tell us it's an important recruiting and retention tool," said Carl Levin, D-Mich., the senior Armed Services Committee Democrat.

Final Defense Bill Authorizes $309.9 Billion For Fiscal 2001

OCTOBER 21 — Members of the House and Senate Armed Services committees have called for greater spending to modernize the nation's military and have accused President Clinton of wearing out the armed forces with overseas missions. But for fiscal 2001, Congress has added relatively little to Clinton's defense budget request and dispersed much of that among dozens of projects and programs.

A conspicuous exception is nearly $800 million in the defense authorization bill (HR 4205) to help the Army transform itself into a lighter force able to move overseas more quickly. The concept has become popular on Capitol Hill.

Overall, the $309.9 billion authorization bill that Congress cleared Oct. 12 would add $4.6 billion to Clinton's defense budget, about a 1.5 percent increase. That is not nearly enough to make the sort of improvements many lawmakers have said are necessary if the military is to continue its current pace of operations. Some lawmakers say the armed forces are spread too thin.

In hopes of stimulating a debate that might generate support for more defense spending in the future, the authorization bill would require the Pentagon to draw up several long-range plans, including:

• A plan to sustain U.S. nuclear forces as the current force of missiles, bombers and missile-launching submarines reach the end of their useful life.

• An analysis of the military airlift fleet, a study likely to conclude that more planes are needed.

• A study of aerial reconnaissance, which likely will conclude that more radar picket planes and electronic eavesdroppers are necessary.

While such reports do not guarantee more funding, they would provide defense hawks with concrete goals at which to aim in future budget fights.

Completion of the defense bill conference was delayed for several weeks by disagreements over medical benefits for military retirees and compensation for civilians formerly employed in nuclear weapons production who were exposed to hazardous materials. The final version of the bill includes both expanded retiree medical benefits and a compensation program for nuclear weapons workers.

Buying Goods

Of the $4.6 billion Congress would authorize above what Clinton requested for fiscal 2001, $2.6 billion is for procurement, much of it for a handful of projects:

• $600 million to buy new, lighter equipment for the Army's "transformation." Another $196 million was added to the Army's research and development account for this program.

• $460 million as a down payment toward the $1.5 billion cost of a helicopter carrier to be built by Litton Industries in Pascagoula, Miss., the hometown of Senate Majority Leader Trent Lott.

• $209 million for 16 H-60 helicopters, in addition to the $495 million Clinton requested for 25 of the craft, which are built in Connecticut by United Technologies' Sikorsky division.

• $165 million for two Lockheed Martin C-130s, built in Marietta, Ga., in addition to the $363 million requested for four of the planes.

• $150 million for two Boeing F-15 fighters, built in St. Louis, Mo.

• $52 million for two Lockheed Martin F-16s, built in Fort Worth, Texas.

Other highlights of the conference report on HR 4205 include the following:

Ground and Air Combat

All told, the bill would authorize about $1.8 billion for the Army's effort to field a new, medium-weight force. While strongly endorsing that goal, however, the conference report (H Rept 106-945) raised questions about the Army's plan to jump-start its transformation by equipping some brigades in the near term with off-the-shelf armored vehicles while it pursues the technological break-

Bill Mandates Widespread Polygraphing At Nuclear Laboratories

OCTOBER 21 — Congress included several provisions in the fiscal 2001 defense authorization bill intended to assert more control over how U.S. nuclear secrets are protected, including expanded polygraph testing of Energy Department workers in sensitive jobs.

Opponents said the testing would be an undue burden on thousands of employees at the nation's nuclear weapons labs and could drive some to seek other jobs.

The Senate Judiciary Committee, meanwhile, could not come up with a quorum for an Oct. 19 meeting to consider whether it should subpoena Energy Secretary Bill Richardson to testify on the Wen Ho Lee investigation that originally set off security alarms on Capitol Hill.

Lee, a former scientist at the Los Alamos National Laboratory in New Mexico, was suspected of giving nuclear weapons data to China, though he was not charged with espionage. He recently pleaded guilty to one felony count of mishandling classified information and is out of jail.

Judiciary Committee member Arlen Specter, R-Pa., said Richardson has turned down other invitations to testify. Specter said he wants to know if Richardson gave Lee's name to the news media; if Lee's polygraph test was mishandled, and why Lee was allowed to keep his security clearance while he was under investigation.

In what could be a warning to the Energy Department, Specter said the committee may already have authority to compel Richardson to produce relevant documents and testify under a broad subpoena approved by the committee in November 1999.

More Polygraphs

The defense authorization bill (HR 4205) Congress cleared Oct. 12 would require the department to polygraph all employees with access to "sensitive compartmented information" — the highly classified intelligence data produced under the CIA's supervision. The data includes material intercepted from foreign electronic communications.

Republicans have argued for widespread polygraphing to send a message to lab workers that further security lapses will not be tolerated. Energy Department officials, however, said the new provision is unnecessarily burdensome and goes beyond what is required at the State Department and Pentagon.

"This is outright punishment," said Edward Curran, a former FBI official who serves as the department's counterintelligence chief.

Curran said the provision would require polygraphing 5,000 additional employees. However, congressional sources said the actual number could be lower because an undetermined number of those employees already are required to undergo polygraphs. In the fiscal 2000 defense bill, Congress required that more employees undergo polygraph testing, raising the number to an estimated 15,000.

Defense conferees this year added language that would allow the secretary of Energy to waive polygraph requirements for employees on a one-time basis. However, the secretary could not grant a waiver on the grounds that polygraphing would hurt science at any of the labs.

Lawmakers are still dismayed over revelations of lax security at the department's nuclear weapons laboratories. Last year, in the fiscal 2000 defense authorization law (PL 106-65) Congress created a semi-autonomous nuclear weapons agency within the department. *(1999 Almanac, p. 9-26)*

Members of Congress renewed their criticism of security after two computer hard drives containing weapons data were found missing in May at New Mexico's Los Alamos National Laboratory. The hard drives later turned up behind a photo copying machine in the same secure area in which they had vanished.

Harmful to Morale?

Pete V. Domenici, R-N.M., chairman of the Senate Energy and Water Appropriations Subcommittee, complained that the provisions would hurt morale at the weapons labs. Domenici and other lawmakers have said they fear that widespread polygraphing could lead many scientists to quit, and that it might harm the non-defense scientific work at the labs.

"I believe these provisions will only make a bad situation worse," Domenici said. "Security will be a moot point if our national laboratories fail to achieve scientific advances worth protecting."

Domenici's Senate colleague from New Mexico, Democrat Jeff Bingaman, said that "using polygraphs as a prescreening device makes no sense."

"I support them where a person's under suspicion of criminal activity," he said, "but this provision was obviously misguided, and we need to make every effort to get it deleted."

Besides requiring that more people be tested, defense conferees added to the scope of polygraph questions. They included a requirement that employees be asked if they had caused "deliberate damage to or malicious misuse of" a government information system.

The defense bill also contains language that would prohibit Energy Secretary Bill Richardson and his employees from serving in the same positions in both the Energy Department and the new National Nuclear Security Administration. The provision would bar "dual-hatting," a practice that Richardson has argued is useful in some areas, but that lawmakers have criticized as contrary to their intentions.

throughs needed to build a 20-ton light tank that could do the job of today's 70-ton M-1.

If the Army selected an "interim armored vehicle" other than an upgraded version of United Defense's M-113 troop carrier, some 17,000 of which the service already owns, the bill would require the Army to give Congress a comparison of the cost and operational effectiveness of the new vehicle and the one already in service. The bill would also require the new interim units to be tested in mock combat against armored tank units.

The conference report would authorize $25 million to develop robot ground combat vehicles and $75 million to develop robot airplanes to attack especially dangerous targets. The Senate version of the bill included an initiative by Senate Armed Services Chairman John W. Warner, R-Va., that would have authorized twice as much to work on the air and ground robots.

The bill would authorize $2.5 billion to continue production of the Air Force's new Lockheed Martin F-22 fighter, as Clinton requested, and $2.9 billion — slightly more than Clinton asked for — to continue building the Navy's Boeing F/A-18 E and F model fighters.

Confirming a decision incorporated in both the House and Senate versions of the bill, the conferees agreed to authorize $689 million — $168 million less than Clinton requested — to continue developing the Joint Strike Fighter, which would be built in versions for use by the Navy, Air Force and Marine Corps. Top Pentagon leaders had objected to the cut, but both Armed Services panels insisted that the Defense Department was pushing the program too fast.

The conference report would authorize a total of $118 million above Clinton's request to develop long-range, precision-guided "smart" bombs and cruise missiles. About two-thirds of that amount is for an effort to capitalize on the fact that satellite-guided bombs now in service are so accurate that they carry much more explosive power than is needed to destroy many types of targets. If the weapons could be made smaller, one plane could carry more bombs and thus could hit more targets.

Naval Forces and Airlift

The bill would basically authorize the amounts the administration requested for new warships: $4 billion for a Nimitz-class carrier, $2.7 billion for three destroyers equipped with the Aegis anti-aircraft system, and $1.2 billion for a nuclear-powered submarine.

The bill would authorize the $274 million Clinton requested to continue designing a new carrier that would be included in the 2006 budget, and $540 million — $10 million less than Clinton requested — to continue designing a new destroyer slated for the 2005 budget. Both new classes are expected to be cheaper to operate because they will have smaller crews.

In addition to the $460 million included for a helicopter carrier, the bill would authorize the $1.5 billion Clinton requested for two other ships also intended to carry Marine Corps combat units to their landing sites. The companion defense appropriations bill (PL 106-259) provides only $561 million to begin work on these two ships (designated LPD-17s).

The authorization bill would require the Navy to give Congress 30 days' notice before assigning women to duty on submarines or beginning any design work or ship modifications intended to accommodate women as members of sub crews. The House version of the bill would have required a 120-day waiting period after notification.

Currently, submarines are the only class of major Navy ships to which women are not assigned, an exception based on the difficulty of assuring privacy in the cramped accommodations of a sub.

House Armed Services Committee member Roscoe G. Bartlett, R-Md., sponsored the House-passed version of the restriction after Navy Secretary Richard Danzig made a speech criticizing the "men only" policy for submarines.

Anti-Missile Defenses

The administration requested $4.5 billion for the Pentagon's anti-missile defense organization and an additional $390 million for anti-missile projects run by the Air Force. The conference report would add $349 million to these requests, authorizing more than $5.2 billion for missile defense.

Clinton's request included $1.8 billion to continue developing a system that would be deployed in Alaska to protect U.S. territory from a small number of attacking missiles. Clinton had been expected to decide this fall whether to begin building the project. In September, he deferred the decision for his successor, contending that test failures had left too many questions unanswered for him to make a decision before he leaves office. The final defense bill would add $135 million to Clinton's request for his national missile defense project.

The bill would also authorize $80 million more than the $383 million Clinton requested to continue developing a long-range anti-missile system based on ships. Some Republicans contend that this Navy Theater-Wide system could be upgraded relatively quickly and cheaply to a limited national missile defense shield. Critics say it would take much longer and cost much more.

The defense bill would transfer from the Air Force to the Ballistic Missile Defense Organization in 2002 the Space-Based Infra-Red System, Low-altitude (SBIRS-Low), a program to develop satellites that could track missile warheads as they speed through space. The conference report would authorize $241 million for the program in fiscal 2001, as the White House requested.

The House version of the defense bill would have transferred from the Air Force to the missile defense organization the program to mount an anti-missile laser in the nose of a wide-body jet transport. Supporters of this airborne laser complained that, like SBIRS-Low, the program was getting shortchanged by Air Force leaders more interested in funding the F-22 fighter.

Defense conferees left the airborne laser in the Air Force budget but required the service to obtain the consent of the missile defense organization before making any changes in the project's budget, schedule or specifications.

The conference report also would authorize $85 million more than the $149 million Clinton requested for the laser program, thus reversing an Air Force decision to slow the program for budget reasons. The resulting authorization — $234 million — would

Coalition of Interests, Budget Surplus Won New Benefits for Military Retirees

OCTOBER 28 — The expansion of medical benefits for military retirees — a new entitlement expected to cost $60 billion over 10 years — is a politically popular policy highlight of the 106th Congress.

It cannot be claimed as a victory solely by Republicans, for it was pushed into law by a formidable coalition that included retirees, the Joint Chiefs of Staff and members of both parties. And it would not have happened without forecasts of a growing budget surplus.

The health care initiative was cleared as part of the fiscal 2001 defense authorization bill (HR 4205). It will allow military retirees — those who serve at least 20 years on active duty — and their dependents to remain in the Pentagon's medical care and insurance system for life, rather than having to rely on Medicare after they turn 65. It also would allow most retirees to buy prescription drugs through a military system.

Medical care for retirees was authorized by law in 1956, but the government's legal obligation became defined as allowing retirees to use military hospitals and clinics on a space-available basis or else to obtain care from private health care providers who would accept reimbursement from a Pentagon-run insurance program. Once they turned 65, the retirees were to rely on Medicare.

Retirees complained for years that recruiters promised that career service members and their dependents would get free medical care for life. Their grumbling got louder during the 1990s, as many military bases and their hospitals were closed, making access more difficult for retirees even as health care costs were climbing and the number of Medicare-eligible retirees and dependents was growing to a current total of nearly 1.4 million.

By 1997, leaders of the armed services were warning that the issue of medical care was affecting recruitment and retention. That year, Congress authorized several pilot programs to test ways of offering retirees more satisfactory medical care options. But they were not enough.

President Clinton's fiscal 2001 budget request included $80 million to address some problems in the Pentagon's medical insurance program. But the administration turned down proposals by the Joint Chiefs of Staff to offer retirees mail-order pharmacy service and "medi-gap" insurance already available to civilian federal employees to cover the difference between the cost of medical treatment and what Medicare pays.

By February, it was clear that the House and Senate Armed Services committees, supported by many members not on those panels, would join the retirees' associations and the Joint Chiefs in trying to improve retirees' medical care.)

House Speaker J. Dennis Hastert, R-Ill., helped House Armed Services members ensure that the budget resolution (H Con Res 290) included enough funds to pay for a mail-order pharmacy benefit. The committee then wrote the pharmacy benefit into its version of the defense authorization bill, along with other provisions that would expand the existing pilot health care programs.

Projections of a growing surplus allowed the Senate Armed Services panel to write its version of the authorization bill with a grant to retirees of permanent, lifetime access to the Pentagon's medical insurance coverage. But Senate rules permit a point of order to block any bill that spends more than the budget caps allow, unless the point is waived by a 60-vote majority. Leery of that risk, Armed Services Chairman John W. Warner, R-Va., amended the bill on the floor to limit the program to two years' duration.

In conference, House Armed Services personnel subcommittee Chairman Steve Buyer, R-Ind., argued that a permanent entitlement had gathered enough political steam to roll over any opposition. Armed Services member Tillie Fowler, R-Fla., vice chairman of the GOP Conference, had secured Hastert's personal support.

Buyer likened the situation to a rare astronomical phenomenon: "We have a syzygy. . . . All the planets are aligned."

Breaking with the longstanding Armed Services tradition of keeping conference negotiations confidential, Buyer briefed several retirees' organizations and reporters on his proposal in hopes of putting pressure on the Senate. During a Sept. 27 hearing, he got the Joint Chiefs to endorse his proposal.

In a letter written the same day, Warner outlined to Senate Majority Leader Trent Lott, R-Miss., his concern that the House proposal risked losing a point of order that could jeopardize the whole defense bill. At a meeting in Lott's office a few days later, Hastert made a strong pitch for Buyer's proposal, saying that in return he would accept a Senate proposal for compensating nuclear weapons workers who had been exposed to hazardous substances.

Lott assured Warner he would help him round up the 60 votes needed to fend off a challenge from deficit hawks. Warner promptly accepted the House proposal and, in a news conference with senior Armed Services Democrat Carl Levin, D-Mich., predicted the budget challenge would fail.

The Senate took up the conference report on Oct. 12, hours after a terrorist bomb attack on the destroyer USS *Cole* killed 17 sailors. Warner, lauding the medical care provisions as a promise kept to America's military, offered a motion to waive the budget point of order.

It was agreed to, 84-9. *(Vote 274, p. S-49)*

keep the project on schedule to try to shoot down a target missile in 2003.

Weapons of Mass Destruction

For the Nunn-Lugar program to help former Soviet republics dispose of nuclear, chemical and biological weapons and the missiles and bombers that could deliver them, the bill would authorize $443 million, which is $15 million less than Clinton requested.

While the bill would allow slightly more than requested for some Nunn-Lugar projects, conferees rejected $35 million Clinton requested to continue construction of a facility designed to destroy chemical weapons.

The Defense and Energy Departments would be authorized to study methods of destroying stockpiles of nuclear, chemical and biological weapons buried deep underground. Anti-nuclear activists warn that this is a foot in the door for future efforts to develop and test very small nuclear weapons intended to destroy such targets, thus derailing efforts to secure a global ban on nuclear weapons tests. *(Test ban treaty background, 1999 Almanac, p. 9-40)*

The bill also includes several provisions intended to help the government respond to terrorist acts on U.S. territory. It would authorize $16 million more than Clinton requested to increase from 27 to 32 the number of National Guard teams trained to help local police, fire and emergency medical personnel deal with suspected nuclear, chemical or biological weapons attacks.

It also would require the secretary of Defense to designate one assistant as his principal adviser on counterterrorism, responsible for coordinating the Defense Department's preparation to deal with terrorism.

The bill would establish a commission of outside experts to examine the vulnerability of the U.S. electronic infrastructure to electromagnetic pulses — powerful radio waves that could be caused by a high-altitude nuclear explosion. Rep. Bartlett has warned for some time that a hostile country with only a handful of long-range, nuclear-armed missiles might get the most leverage out of them by trying to cripple U.S. communications and electronics by such an attack.

The bill would require the president to prepare a report on the country's preparedness to deal with the threat of biological terrorism. It also would require the secretary of Defense and the director of Central Intelligence to prepare an intelligence estimate assessing that threat.

Personnel and Readiness

The defense bill would authorize the 3.7 percent military pay raise Clinton requested, effective Jan. 1, 2001. The raise is one half of 1 percent more than the average increase in private-sector pay, as measured by a government index.

The bill would also authorize higher raises for senior sergeants and petty officers, at a cost of $88 million.

It would authorize the Pentagon to increase the housing allowance for personnel who do not live in government quarters, with the aim of covering all housing costs by 2005. As a step in that direction, the bill would authorize $25 million more than the administration requested for housing allowances.

To assist personnel who qualify for food stamps, the bill would authorize additional pay of up to $500 a month.

For recruiting and retention, the bill would authorize $105 million more than Clinton requested, $84 million of which is for enlistment and re-enlistment bonuses. It would also authorize a $50 increase in the $200 monthly stipend paid to senior ROTC cadets, in hopes of making that program more attractive to college students. It would also authorize adding $14 million to the amount Clinton requested for high school ROTC, which the services regard as a valuable recruiting tool.

Other Provisions

The bill would convert the Army's controversial School of the Americas into the Defense Institute for Hemispheric Security Cooperation. A board of overseers would include representatives from religious organizations and human rights groups that have complained that the institution's curriculum did not sufficiently emphasize to military officers from Latin American countries the importance of civilian control and the rule of law.

The bill would also:

- Name the anti-missile test range on Kwajalein Atoll in the Pacific for former President Ronald Reagan.
- Codify an agreement between the Pentagon and the governor of Puerto Rico over how to settle the future of the Navy bombing range on the island of Vieques, which many Puerto Ricans want to see closed. The bill would authorize $40 million in economic assistance to Vieques with the provision that an additional $50 million would be turned over if the island's residents approve, in a referendum, the continued use of live ammunition on the firing range.
- Authorize — with conditions — a $6.9 billion contract to privatize all Navy and Marine Corps communications, including telephone, video and computer services. Eventually, Electronic Data Services, which won the contract, would replace about 200 in-house networks that are currently maintained by nearly 2,000 Navy civilians. After a first phase of the contract was completed, covering about 45,000 work stations (15 percent of the total network), the bill would require a complete evaluation of how well the contract was working before more jobs were converted. The bill would also bar privatizing communications networks at Navy shipyards and aircraft repair depots and at Marine Corps installations during 2001.
- Reduce from 9,500 to 4,750 the number of jobs in Pentagon management that would have to be eliminated by the end of fiscal 2002. Congress mandated the larger reduction in the fiscal 2000 defense authorization bill (PL 106-65), but the Pentagon will have eliminated only 3,000 by the end of 2001, leaving an impossibly large number of jobs — nearly 7,000 — to be eliminated in 2002.
- Express the sense of Congress that three officers held responsible for disasters that befell U.S. forces during World War II were, in fact, innocent. The bill would call for the exoneration of Capt. Charles McVay III, captain of the cruiser *Indianapolis*, sunk by a Japanese submarine in July 1945. It also would call for posthumously restoring the ranks of the Navy and Army commanders in charge of defending Hawaii when Japanese forces attacked Pearl Harbor — Adm. Husband E. Kimmel and Lt. Gen. Walter C. Short — who were demoted after the attack. ◆

CQ

Chapter 9

EDUCATION

Lawmakers Extend Some ESEA Programs as Part of Omnibus Spending Package

SUMMARY

For the first time in the law's 35-year history, Congress failed to reauthorize the Elementary and Secondary Education Act (ESEA), the Great Society-era legislation that is the main source of federal aid to public schools. Instead, lawmakers ended up funding ESEA programs for an additional year in the omnibus spending package, which included the fiscal 2001 Labor, Health and Human Services, and Education appropriations bill (HR 4577). The task of giving the programs a longer lease on life, and possibly restructuring them along the way, was left for the 107th Congress.

The Senate ESEA reauthorization bill (S 2) reached the floor May 1, but became bogged down in ideological disputes. Republicans tried to use it as a vehicle to give state and local authorities more control over the use of federal education dollars, while Democrats fought to retain the targeting of federal funds to address specific needs. Another factor that doomed the bill was a long list of riders, including a Democratic gun control amendment, that Republicans wanted to avoid. Majority Leader Trent Lott, R-Miss., pulled the bill May 9, and it never returned.

S 2 would have created a "Straight A's" pilot program in 15 states, allowing federal funds to be used for any educational purpose permitted under state law in exchange for better academic results. Another pilot program would have created "portability" for Title I funds, which are supposed to improve education for children in low-income neighborhoods, by letting parents in 10 states and 20 school districts take the funds out of failing schools and buy public or private educational services.

The two pilot programs — added by Sen. Judd Gregg of New Hampshire and other GOP conservatives during the Senate Health, Education, Labor, and Pensions Committee markup — were the major flexibility initiatives in the bill. The measure also would have created a block grant combining the Eisenhower Professional Development Program for teacher training with President Clinton's initiative to reduce class sizes in the early grades by hiring 100,000 new teachers.

In the House, the legislation was broken into seven bills aimed at reauthorizing and revising separate titles of the 1965 law. Four passed the House in 1999; two more passed in 2000, while a third never made it to the House floor.

In the end, three of the bills became law. They were:

- **"Ed-flex."** The so-called ed-flex bill (PL 106-25), signed in 1999, allows states to apply for waivers from federal regulations to experiment with innovative approaches to education. *(1999 Almanac, p. 10-3)*
- **"Impact Aid."** The Impact Aid Reauthorization Act (HR 3616) renews a program that gives extra funds to school districts that have trouble raising property taxes because they contain tax-exempt zones, such as military bases and American Indian reservations. The three-year reauthorization was signed into law as part of the fiscal 2001 defense authorization bill (HR 4205 — PL 106-398). The legislation reworks the Impact Aid funding formula to prevent federal payments from becoming too skewed toward urban school districts. It also will provide extra funds more quickly for the neediest school districts and create school modernization grants for districts that are too poor to issue their own bonds.
- **"Even Start."** The Literacy Involves Families Together Act (HR 3222) reauthorizes the Even Start family literacy program with more funding and structural changes to make it more effective. The five-year reauthorization bill became a rider to the year-end omnibus spending package (HR 4577). The structural changes include more state oversight and better training for instructors. A "charitable choice" provision to allow faith-based literacy programs to receive federal funds was dropped from the final version.

Three bills died for lack of a Senate counterpart once that chamber failed in its all-at-once reauthorization effort:

- HR 2, the Student Results Act, would have reauthorized and expanded the Title I program while giving states more flexibility on bilingual education.
- HR 1995, the Teacher Empowerment Act, would have combined the Eisenhower training program, Goals 2000, which offers grants to improve education quality, and Clinton's class size reduction initiative into block grants to improve teacher quality.
- HR 2300, the "Straight A's Act," would have set up a 10-state pilot program similar to the one in the Senate bill.

The last bill, the Education Opportunities to Protect and Invest in Our Nation's Students Act (HR 4141) did not reach the House floor. It would

Box Score

- **Bills:** S 2; HR 2; HR 1995; HR 2300, HR 3616, HR 3222, HR 4141
- **Legislative action: House** Education and Workforce Committee approved HR 4141 (H Rept 106-608), 25-21, April 13.

Senate began debate on S 2 (S Rept 106-261) on May 1; it was pulled from floor May 9.

House passed HR 3616 (H Rept 106-504) by voice vote May 15.

House passed HR 3222 (H Rept 106-503) by voice vote Sept. 12.

House adopted the conference report on HR 4205 (H Rept 106-945), 382-31, Oct. 11.

Senate cleared the bill, 90-3, Oct. 12.

President signed the bill Oct. 30.

have reauthorized the Safe and Drug-Free Schools title of ESEA while allowing states to transfer federal funds between programs to suit their needs. The bill contained so many divisive provisions — one would have banned the Department of Education from funding classes that teach the prevention of hate crimes — and struggled through such a bitter markup in the Education and Workforce Committee that it sank out of sight afterward.

Senate Markup Off to a Rancorous Start Over Issue Of Block Grants

MARCH 4 — Any illusions that the Senate Health, Education, Labor and Pensions Committee would reach a quick compromise on legislation to reauthorize the nation's main federal education law were shattered March 1 when members began what looks to be a protracted — and cantankerous — markup.

The committee was scheduled to embark on its first round of amendments to a draft bill (S 2) to extend the 1965 Elementary and Secondary Education Act for five years. Reauthorization of the act, which will expire at the end of the current fiscal year, is a priority for both parties as they vie to claim the education issue as their own.

The House has already begun moving its rewrite as a series of smaller bills. Senate Committee Chairman James M. Jeffords, R-Vt., floated a reauthorization plan last fall that would have established new early childhood education programs and expanded longstanding aid such as Title I, which directs $8 billion a year to disadvantaged children.

Conservative Republicans raised concerns about that draft. At the markup, Jeffords laid down a revised bill that eliminated the child care plan and included a proposal that would allow states to roll a number of categorical aid programs, including teacher quality, enrichment activities and some portions of Title I, into block grants.

The House passed a watered-down version of the block grant proposal (HR 2300) by a 213-208 vote Oct. 21. That bill would create a 10-state pilot program allowing officials to combine funds from federal education programs. To qualify, states would have to meet a series of academic improvement goals set by the Department of Education.

Jeffords' new bill still does not go as far as conservatives want. Although Jeffords adjourned the markup before any votes were cast, citing floor action on a separate Republican bill to create education savings accounts (S 1134), Democrats had enough time to make it clear that they did not like the bill, either.

Democrats panned the block grant proposal, in part they said because it lacked adequate accountability and could siphon money away from needy students.

"I'm disappointed with the product we're starting out with," said Paul Wellstone, D-Minn. "I just don't want to go to straight block grants. . . .That's the philosophical divide here."

In response to the bill, Democrats drafted an avalanche of amendments, ranging from proposals to kill the block grant section outright to adding new initiatives for school construction, smaller class sizes and better access to technology. Committee aides said between 60 and 70 Democrat amendments were expected.

Ranking Democrat Edward M. Kennedy of Massachusetts introduced the first amendment, a comprehensive, $2 billion, teacher-quality program that would be exempt from the block grant proposal.

Republicans, who are pushing for more local control of federal funds, railed against current federal programs. They charged that the $185 billion spent in the past 35 years under the 1965 act has largely been wasted.

"The [law] has provided very little in the way of positive effects on society," said Judd Gregg, R-N.H. Gregg said he may offer amendments to make Title I grants "portable," with the funds following each eligible student rather than being allocated to schools. He may also push a choice proposal, under which students could change public schools if their home school was labeled by the state as failing.

Overall, the draft bill would authorize $19.7 billion in fiscal 2001 for federal elementary and secondary education programs, compared with about $15 billion allocated in fiscal 2000. The committee is expected to resume action the week of March 6.

Senate Panel's ESEA Rewrite Allows Vouchers, Block Grants

MARCH 11 — Senate Republicans sparked an election-year fight over public schools March 9 when the Health, Education, Labor and Pensions Committee approved legislation (S 2) to rewrite the landmark 1965 Elementary and Secondary Education Act (ESEA). The GOP plan includes state block grants and a limited program of private school vouchers.

Education Secretary Richard W. Riley promised that President Clinton would veto the bill, approved by the committee on a 10-8 party-line vote. Senate Democrats, who offered a series of unsuccessful amendments to increase funding for school construction, reduce class size and improve teacher training, vowed an all-out battle on the chamber floor.

"They turned their backs on the progress that has been made in setting and implementing high standards for all children," said Edward M. Kennedy of Massachusetts, the committee's ranking Democrat.

"The Republican bill is the wrong direction for education and the wrong direction for the nation. We will do all we can to enact a bill that will make a real difference in helping the nation's public schools and improving the education of every child," he said.

Republicans countered that Democratic efforts to maintain tight federal regulations would stymie state attempts to improve academic performance. They pointed out that the test scores of low-income children had improved little in the 35 years since the ESEA became law, despite federal spending to the tune of $185 billion.

"This [committee bill] is the most flexible of all current federal education programs, permitting local schools to undertake the activities most likely to improve their schools and enhance the performance of their students," said committee Chairman James M. Jeffords, R-Vt.

"These funds are put to work where the need is greatest, be it technology or library books or teacher training," he said.

Still, Jeffords, who is more moderate than his fellow committee Republicans, voted "present" on two successful amendments by Judd Gregg, R-N.H., that would rewrite the $8 billion-a-year Title I program for disadvantaged students, the foundation of the ESEA.

The first amendment would turn some Title I funds into vouchers that could be used to purchase educational services from private or religious schools. Another would let states roll Title I and most other federal programs into block grants.

Philosophy and Politics

As approved, the committee bill goes further in reshaping Title I than a House measure (HR 2) passed in October. The House bill would keep the basic structure of Title I intact, while setting more stringent academic standards and increasing funding.

Jeffords opened debate on the Senate bill March 1, offering a draft that would have authorized roughly $19.7 billion a year for the myriad programs in the ESEA, including Title I, bilingual education, and safe and drug-free schools. It also includes the Impact Aid program for local districts that are burdened by having non-taxable federal installations within their boundaries.

Jeffords' draft moved existing teacher development programs and Clinton's plan to hire 100,000 teachers into a new $2 billion annual block grant for teacher training. Like the House bill, it would require tougher state standards to ensure that students served by Title I were showing academic improvement.

Democrats roundly rejected Jeffords' proposal, particularly the block grant portion, as giving a blank check to state governors. Some of Jeffords' fellow Republicans argued that his plan did not deviate enough from 35 years of federal intervention.

Most of the GOP complaints were directed at Title I, which provides funds to schools specifically to raise the academic performance of disadvantaged students.

Schools where 50 percent of the student population is economically disadvantaged can use Title I money to implement school-wide programs. Schools with smaller populations of low-income students focus on using the funds to help individuals.

During debate, the committee adopted by voice vote an amendment by Bill Frist, R-Tenn., that would allow schools with 40 percent of students in poverty to set up school-wide Title I programs, down from the current 50 percent threshold.

The Jeffords bill originally would have maintained separate funding streams for Title I funds. That changed with the Gregg amendments.

One of the Gregg proposals adopted by the committee would establish a 15-

Senate Bill Highlights

APRIL 29 — Following are highlights of S 2 as approved March 9 by the Senate Health, Education, Labor and Pensions Committee. The bill would reauthorize the Elementary and Secondary Education Act (ESEA) of 1965, including Title I programs for disadvantaged children.

ISSUE	DESCRIPTION
"Straight A's"	A new pilot program would allow 15 states to combine funds from various federal programs for any educational purpose allowed under state law in exchange for better academic results.
Education Performance Partnerships	All states would be able to combine federal funds to improve student achievement. Similar to "Straight A's," but the Department of Education would have a greater say in setting student performance goals, and the targeting of Title I funds for low-income school districts would be protected.
Portability	Another pilot program would allow parents in 10 states and 20 school districts to take Title I funds out of failing schools and use them to pay for public or private educational services for children.
Teacher empowerment	The Eisenhower Professional Development Program for teachers would be combined with the Class Size Reduction initiative, the Clinton administration program aimed at hiring 100,000 new teachers by the end of fiscal year 2005.
Rural flexibility	Rural school districts with fewer than 600 students would be allowed to pool federal funds. The bill would add a supplemental grant to ensure that each district has at least $20,000 to support efforts to improve student achievement.
After-school programs	Funding authorized for after-school programs would increase from $453 million in fiscal 2000 to $500 million in fiscal 2001.
Safe and Drug-Free Schools	The bill would reauthorize the law (PL 103-382), enacted in 1994 to discourage violence and substance abuse in schools. The law requires a one-year expulsion for any student who brings a gun to school.
Technology education	The bill would authorize $815 million in grants for fiscal 2001 to help schools work educational technology into the classroom and ensure that every child is able to use computers by the end of the eighth grade.

state pilot program under which governors could elect to receive nearly all federal education funding, including parts of Title I, as a block grant. The proposal was based on one of the GOP leadership's primary education priorities, the so-called Straight A's bill.

In exchange for the greater flexibility, states would have to enter a five-year agreement with the Department of Education that would include student performance goals. States would have to establish, and show progress in reaching, student performance standards or risk losing their flexibility.

"If you accept that flexibility, you also have to accept the responsibility of teaching these children how to read and write," Gregg said. His amendment was adopted, 9-8.

The House passed legislation (HR 2300) by 213-208 on Oct. 21 that would allow 10 states to participate in a similar block grant pilot.

"Passage of the Straight A's is a signal that this Congress intends to turn its back on over 15 years of bipartisan effort to raise achievement levels through standards-based reform," Riley said in a March 9 statement. "I will certainly recommend that the president veto this unfocused and undemanding piece of legislation."

Gregg shepherded two other major amendments through the panel.

One would allow 10 states to turn Title I into a "portable" program. Under his plan, pupils from low-income families who received Title I funds would receive a voucher instead. The funds would move with the students if they transferred to another public school and could be used to purchase services from private schools. That passed 9-8.

A second amendment approved by voice vote would allow students in Title I schools classified as failing to transfer to other public schools. More than 7,000 schools receiving Title I funds have been classified as failing. If a school did not improve its performance after four years, the district would have to pay the transportation costs to move students to another school.

Republicans based many of their arguments for change on the belief that the ESEA has been a massive failure. States and local school districts are in a better position to determine their own needs and priorities, they said, and should not follow Washington dictates.

"It is my hope that additional improvements will be made on the floor and in conference that will provide even greater local control over education dollars and programs," said Tim Hutchinson, R-Ark.

Democrats countered that states could use their own funds to make the kinds of improvements Republicans claimed were priorities. Federal money accounts for 7 percent of education, and states and local governments provide the remaining 93 percent. Democrats also said the federal government does a far better job than states of directing aid to low-income students.

Targeted Aid

"The whole reason the federal government got involved was because states were not targeting money to disadvantaged students," said Joel Packer of the National Education Association (NEA), a labor union that counts about 2.3 million education workers in its membership.

Democrats offered dozens of amendments, including an effort by Kennedy to specify that the $2 billion teacher training block grant in the bill would have to be spent in specific areas.

Patty Murray, D-Wash., proposed an amendment that would have authorized $1.75 billion for the third year of Clinton's seven-year plan to hire 100,000 new teachers and reduce average class size to 18 in early grades. Like the Kennedy amendment, Murray's proposal was rejected on party lines.

Republicans, outnumbering Democrats 10-8 on the committee, voted cohesively throughout most deliberations. Five GOP members joined Democrats, however, to soundly reject an amendment offered by Jeff Sessions, R-Ala., that would have prohibited the Department of Education from using funds to develop publications on hate crimes. Sessions said hate crimes were too difficult to define.

All Republicans joined Democrats to raise the authorization for Title I in fiscal 2001 to $15 billion from the $10 billion Jeffords had suggested. The Clinton administration's fiscal 2001 budget calls for $8.4 billion for Title I. Funding would be determined by a separate appropriations bill.

Any hint of bipartisan cooperation that surfaced in committee is likely to be short-lived, as election-year politics intensify the debate on an issue both parties want to claim as their own.

"The bill as it's now written is beyond repair," the NEA's Packer said.

During markup, the committee also:

• Adopted by voice vote an amendment by Barbara A. Mikulski, D-Md., that would establish as a national goal having all students computer literate by the eighth grade.

• Adopted, 9-8, a Sessions amendment that would incorporate several provisions from a juvenile justice bill (S 254), such as violence-prevention programs and the transfer of records of expelled students to new schools.

• Rejected, 8-10, an amendment by Tom Harkin, D-Iowa, that would have authorized $1.3 billion for school construction grants and loans.

• Rejected, 8-10, an amendment by Jack Reed, D-R.I., that would have dedicated funding for school library collections.

• Rejected, 8-10, a Reed amendment that would require states to publish names of schools that were considered failing.

Senate Debates Dozens of Amendments

MAY 6 — The Senate began plodding through a series of amendments to a bill reauthorizing the 1965 Elementary and Secondary Education Act the week of May 1, a long and seemingly endless process that could peak with a showdown vote over a gun control amendment the Democrats may offer as early as the week of May 8.

The first week of debate illustrated how hard it will be for Majority Leader Trent Lott, R-Miss., to keep the number of amendments under control or hold senators to a brief dialogue on even the most minor changes to the education bill (S 2).

By the end of the week, the Senate had voted on only five amendments — defeating a Democratic substitute, adopting two Republican proposals and killing two Democratic amendments — out of dozens that have been proposed by both parties.

The debate dragged on as both sides hammered away at their competing ideas for fixing America's schools: shifting control to states and school districts, as Republicans would do in their bill, or making a greater national effort to address specific problems, as the Democrats would do via their amendments.

Republicans seek to use the ESEA rewrite as a vehicle to loosen the strings on federal funding for public education. The bill includes a "Straight A's" pilot program, which would allow 15 states to combine funds from several federal programs in exchange for promising better academic results. These goals would be defined by the states.

GOP lawmakers said their bill would hold states accountable for better academic results in exchange for added flexibility and that the Democratic proposals would merely pump more money into a failed system.

"We've been functioning for the past 35 years under a system that was developed by a Democratic Congress. What has it delivered? It has delivered generations of children who haven't been able to read or write," said Judd Gregg, R-N.H., author of the "Straight A's" proposal.

"What they are proposing is not reform. It is a retreat," Senate Minority Leader Tom Daschle, D-S.D., said at a May 3 news conference.

The White House issued its most detailed veto threat to date on May 1, saying the bill would weaken accountability for schools that receive federal funds and hurt programs to address national education priorities by turning them into "unfocused block grants."

Democratic Substitute Defeated

The most significant vote of the week came when the Senate defeated a Democratic substitute May 3, on a party-line vote of 45-54. The Democrats' proposal would have replaced the Republican rewrite of ESEA with a collection of programs that reflect their own priorities: school construction, class size reduction, after-school programs, and funds to help schools recruit and train teachers. All of those elements are expected to return as individual Democratic amendments. *(Vote 90, p. S-18)*

The turning point could come soon, when Democrats offer a gun control amendment that is certain to be opposed by most Republicans. At that point, Lott will have to decide whether to file a cloture motion or even pull the bill from the floor if he does not get the 60 votes needed to cut off debate.

"If it does come up, I would encourage him to do exactly that," Gregg said in a May 4 interview.

Lott has not said he will go that far, and Daschle told reporters May 4 that it would be unrealistic for Lott to give up on the bill because "obviously ESEA needs to be reauthorized."

Still, Lott's press secretary, John Czwartacki, said May 5 that the majority leader will attempt to stop "extraneous amendments from either side" in order to keep the debate focused on education.

The Senate on May 4 defeated, 44-53, one of the Democrats' main amendments, a proposal by Patty Murray of Washington that would have authorized funds for the remaining five years of President Clinton's program to provide funds to hire 100,000 new teachers. *(Vote 93, p. S-19)*

In other education votes, the Senate:

- Adopted, 54-42, an amendment by Spencer Abraham, R-Mich., and Connie Mack, R-Fla., that would let states use federal funds under Title II of ESEA to test teachers on the subjects they teach and give merit pay increases to the best instructors. *(Vote 92, p. S-19)*
- Rejected, 43-54, a second-degree amendment by Democrat Edward M. Kennedy of Massachusetts that would have eliminated the teacher testing language and allowed merit pay for all teachers in schools that improved student achievement, rather than just individual teachers. *(Vote 91, p. S-18)*
- Adopted, 98-0, an amendment by Slade Gorton, R-Wash., intended to ensure that the bill does not create a new right to use federal funds for school vouchers. Democrats charged that a proposed demonstration program allowing parents to use federal funds for private educational services would open the door to vouchers for private schools, ultimately draining funds from the public schools. *(Vote 89, p. S-18)*

A key upcoming amendment will be a proposal by Democrat Tom Harkin, of Iowa, that would authorize $1.3 billion in grants and loans for emergency school repairs and renovations. Democrats are making school repairs a major issue this year, saying one-third of all public schools need extensive fixes.

ESEA Pulled From Senate Floor To Make Way For Spending Bills

MAY 13 — The biggest education bill of the year was on life support in the Senate the week of May 8, pulled from the floor in what Republicans said was a sign the measure may never come to a final vote.

Majority Leader Trent Lott, R-Miss., told reporters May 9 that the bill (S 2) reauthorizing and rewriting the 1965 Elementary and Secondary Education Act (ESEA) was shelved temporarily to make way for appropriations bills and other measures. Democrats did not buy that explanation, and by May 11 key Republicans were saying the bill is probably dead in this Congress.

"The ESEA bill is probably going to be wrapped up in the wheels of appropriations bills, to be honest with you," Judd Gregg, R-N.H., said May 11 during the Senate Appropriations Committee markup of the Labor, Health and Human Services, and Education spending bill for fiscal 2001. Gregg is the author of the bill's most ambitious and controversial proposals.

Arlen Specter, R-Pa., was even more blunt: "The bill is not likely to come to fruition."

Even if the bill returns to the floor the week of May 15 as scheduled — after the Senate completes work on the military construction appropriations bill (S 2521) — lawmakers are increasingly doubtful that it will lead to anything. Lott said the bill could move on and off the floor as other appropriations bills are debated. But Democrats said that strategy is mostly a dodge to avoid a gun control amendment that Frank R. Lautenberg, D-

N.J., wants to offer.

"I don't think that [ESEA] has a real bright future," Lautenberg told reporters May 11. Barbara Boxer, D-Calif., called that analysis "an understatement."

The dire predictions capped a week in which the Senate inched along in a partisan and largely repetitive debate on the ESEA bill, consuming hours of debate and voting on only two amendments before Lott shelved it.

If the ESEA reauthorization dies, either officially or unofficially, that would not spell the end of the education debate in this Congress. More likely, the arena for the biggest battles would simply shift from ESEA to the Labor-HHS-Education appropriations bill that Congress must pass before it can adjourn.

Indeed, there are already signs that the ESEA debate is morphing into the appropriations debate. The Senate and House Labor-HHS bills call for flexibility and consolidation of some programs — the Republican education goals — while Democrats are likely to try to add targeted programs for school construction and class size reduction, their biggest priorities.

Still, a collapse of the ESEA bill would rob Republicans of their education agenda's biggest showcase: greater flexibility for states and school districts to improve education in whatever ways achieve the best results. That would happen at a time when the presumptive Republican presidential nominee, Texas Gov. George W. Bush, is getting traction with a similar education agenda in his race against Vice President Al Gore, the likely Democratic nominee.

Gun Politics

The one factor that has overshadowed the entire education debate, even more than the ideological differences over who can do the best job fixing the schools, is the stalemate over the shifting politics of gun control.

For nearly a year, the juvenile crime bill (S 254), which passed the Senate last May with several far-reaching gun provisions, has been stuck in a conference committee with a House measure that does not include the gun restrictions (HR 1501). The conferees have met only once, and Democrats such as Lautenberg, the author of the Senate provision that would require background checks for everyone who buys firearms at gun shows, have been looking for ways to get the gun measures out of limbo.

Democrats thought they would have their chance with the education bill the week of May 8, and wanted to squeeze in a gun control amendment before the May 14 "Million Mom March" on the National Mall, a gathering designed to step up pressure for Congress to pass new gun control laws.

When Lott pulled the education bill off the floor May 9, that chance disappeared. The best Lautenberg could manage was a non-binding resolution (S Res 305), which he brought to the Senate floor May 11, praising the marchers and calling on Congress to adopt a conference report on the juvenile justice bill with all of the gun control provisions before the Memorial Day recess.

The resolution failed; Lautenberg tried to get the Senate to adopt it by unanimous consent, but Wayne Allard, R-Colo., objected. Lautenberg and Boxer told reporters they would continue to push the gun control issue every chance they get, whether it is on the education bill or other legislation moving through the Senate.

Democrats and the Million Moms were not the only ones ratcheting up the pressure. The National Education Association (NEA) waged its own campaign for "common-sense gun laws" with a full-page ad in The Washington Post and a May 9 press conference with Andy Pope, a world history and geography teacher who was shot in the chest by a 13-year-old middle school student in Chadron, Neb., in February 1995.

"We do not believe that we can simply shrug our shoulders and say, 'School violence is a societal problem, not a school problem,' and walk away," said NEA President Bob Chase.

The amendment Lautenberg wants to offer would include gun show background checks and all of the other gun measures in the Senate juvenile justice bill, including a ban on importing high-capacity ammunition clips and a requirement that all handguns be sold with child safety trigger locks or safety storage boxes.

To avoid a repeat of the juvenile justice showdown last year, when the gun show provision squeaked through in a tie vote that was broken by Gore, Lott would have to file a cloture motion to cut off debate and round up 60 votes to approve it. At the moment, he does not have them.

Avoiding a Rehash

Lott and other Republicans, including Gregg, have tried to avoid a rehash of last year's gun control debate by arguing that the education bill should not stray into "extraneous" issues. Lautenberg and his Democratic colleagues have insisted just as strongly that school safety is a valid education issue and that gun restrictions are the key to avoiding more school shootings such as the massacre at Columbine High School in Littleton, Colo., in April 1999.

Lott's other problem, even if he could find a way to hold off the gun amendment, is that Democrats and Republicans keep lining up with new education amendments to offer, and each one consumes hours and hours of debate time on the floor. Democrats want to offer amendments that would add targeted funds for school construction and teacher training. Republicans have their own priorities, including an amendment Jeff Sessions, R-Ala., wants to offer that would allow teachers to discipline special-education students in the same ways that other children are punished for violent or disruptive behavior.

On May 9, Lott suggested an on-again, off-again scenario in which the Senate could set aside ESEA every time an appropriations bill became available, pass the appropriations bill, return to the education bill, then set it aside again when the next spending bill is ready for floor action.

The "dual track" strategy, as Lott called it, is not unusual in the Senate, where the must-pass appropriations bills have the highest priority and often bump other bills off the agenda. But with all the amendments the Senate still has to plow through, such a strategy could force the education debate to drag on for weeks — if it does not simply fade away.

"No one wants to be blamed for killing ESEA," NEA lobbyist Joel Packer said in a May 11 interview. "This way, [Lott] can keep saying,

'Well, we'll get back to it, we'll get back to it.' "

Before the bill was set aside, the Senate on May 9 rejected, 13-84, a substitute by Sen. Joseph I. Lieberman, D-Conn., and other centrist Democrats that would have moved toward the Republican proposals by condensing the more than 50 ESEA programs into five grants aimed at achieving general goals. *(Vote 95, p. S-19)*

The proposal drew praise from some Republicans, but no GOP votes. Republicans said it did not offer as much flexibility as their bill would give to states and local school districts. Democratic critics said it would have diluted the effectiveness of such important programs as after-school initiatives and the Safe and Drug-Free Schools program by folding them into grants.

The Senate did adopt, 97-0, a Lott-Gregg amendment that would establish what they called a "Teachers Bill of Rights" — liability protections for teachers who take "reasonable actions" to discipline unruly students. The measure would limit the non-economic damages teachers would have to pay in any lawsuit and would shield them from punitive damages unless they showed a "conscious, flagrant indifference" to the student's rights or safety. *(Vote 94, p. S-19)*

House Panel OKs Impact Aid and Literacy Measures

FEBRUARY 19 — The House Education and the Workforce Committee approved two more pieces of the 1965 Elementary and Secondary Education Act on Feb. 16 by voice vote. One measure (HR 3222) would reauthorize the Even Start program on literacy, while the other (HR 3616) would reauthorize impact aid for school districts that have small tax bases because of a large federal presence.

The literacy program grew out of a program that the bill's author, Committee Chairman Bill Goodling, R-Pa., wrote when he was a school superintendent in Pennsylvania. The measure would increase funding from $118 million to $500 million for Even Start (PL 103-382), which authorizes grants to states for programs that help adults and their children learn to read. *(1994 Almanac, p. 383)*

The impact aid bill would authorize $910.5 million for fiscal 2001, the same level as fiscal 2000. The measure would allow schools to apply for construction funds, with priority given to districts with deteriorating facilities.

House ESEA Markup Becomes Showdown Over Partisan Issues

APRIL 8 — The last of a series of House bills to reauthorize the 1965 Elementary and Secondary Education Act is becoming the most partisan exercise of the entire package, as the House Education and the Workforce Committee began a markup the week of April 3 that strayed into such political minefields as gun control and hate crimes.

The bill (HR 4141) has turned into a predictable election year showcase for the Republican education agenda, based on flexibility for states and school districts, and the competing Democratic agenda of fixing aging schools and making classes smaller by hiring 100,000 new teachers.

The flexibility agenda nearly sank in the House last fall when the GOP "Straight A's" proposal (HR 2300), which would have let states turn most elementary and secondary education programs into block grants, ran into trouble with moderate Republicans. It was whittled down to a 10-state pilot program.

The core of the new bill — crafted by Chairman Bill Goodling, R-Pa., to secure the support of all committee Republicans — is a narrower take on flexibility that would let school districts transfer more federal money from one program to another, as long as the funds are still spent for the programs' original purposes.

For example, districts would be able to shift funds between programs involving teacher training, technology, substance abuse, violence prevention and education for immigrants, as well as the Title VI block grant that funds local education reform efforts.

That provision alone has created a chasm between Republicans — who say school districts should be able to decide which of their needs are most pressing and use the funds accordingly — and Democrats, who say there would be no standards for making sure federal funds are being used wisely.

On the big-ticket education items, Republicans voted down Democratic efforts to add such Clinton administration priorities as school construction and class size reduction programs, calling them halfhearted efforts that would never come close to fixing the problems they were supposed to solve.

An effort by William L. Clay, D-Mo., to add $1.3 billion in school repair grants and loans was defeated 19-23. And a Clay amendment that would have authorized five years of funding for President Clinton's class size reduction program was rejected, 19-27.

In the long run, the partisan bickering may be little more than a warmup for the real showdown this fall.

In an April 5 statement, Education Secretary Richard W. Riley said he would recommend that Clinton veto the bill, largely because of the funding flexibility proposal and other provisions that would consolidate existing programs into block grants. Consolidation, he said, would undermine any effort to set national education goals.

Back to Appropriations

A veto would mean that federal education programs would still be funded by annual appropriations, but major changes would be difficult to enact. In recent years, the Labor-HHS spending bill, which funds education programs, has been hammered out in negotiations between Republicans and White House officials — which is how Clinton got the funds for the first two years of the class size reduction effort. *(1998 Almanac, p. 2-64)*

In the meantime, the latest ESEA bill, which would reauthorize such education programs as drug and violence prevention and technology in the classrooms, has become a magnet for fights over all kinds of socially divisive issues.

Democrats forced Republicans to cast politically embarrassing votes against such gun control measures as trigger locks and background checks at gun shows — votes that Goodling tried to head off with repeated scoldings that the measure "is not a gun bill."

Still, the committee Republicans will face other gun votes when the markup resumes April 11. And they may face a Democratic move to strike a provision that would bar federal education funds from being used to teach the prevention of "hate crimes."

Even if Republicans prevail on the remaining gun votes and can avoid a rehash when the bill reaches the House floor, their Senate colleagues are bracing for a similar round of votes when the Senate is expected to take up its ESEA reauthorization bill (S 2) in May. Jim Manley, a spokesman for Edward M. Kennedy, D-Mass., said Senate Democrats are considering offering gun safety amendments to that bill.

The main House champion of the gun amendments is Carolyn McCarthy, D-N.Y., whose husband was killed in a December 1993 shooting on a Long Island Rail Road commuter train. Goodling fought her gun safety measures by watering one down and turning the other into a mere procedural vote, arguing that it belonged in the Judiciary Committee.

The procedural vote came on the main McCarthy amendment, which would have required gun show organizers to run criminal background checks on potential gun buyers and required handguns to be sold with trigger locks.

Goodling said he supports the gun-show provision and will vote for it "when it comes through the proper channels." But he ruled that the amendment was not germane to the education bill. McCarthy appealed the ruling, but her appeal was tabled 28-17.

Later, through a second-degree amendment, Goodling scaled back a McCarthy proposal that would have made school districts with a high rate of expulsions spend part of their violence prevention funds to promote child safety locks on guns. McCarthy's proposal, as amended, was approved 26-21. It would allow — not require — those school districts to study whether safety lock promotions are effective.

House Panel Approves Bill Giving Districts Broad Discretion

APRIL 15 — After a grueling and often bitter five-day markup, the House Education and the Workforce Committee approved on April 13 the last of a series of bills to reauthorize the 1965 Elementary and Secondary Education Act (ESEA) with streamlined programs and more local control over federal funds.

The bill (HR 4141) turned out to be the most difficult piece of the House ESEA reauthorization effort, as Republicans rejected one Democratic attempt after another to restore existing education programs or create new ones. The measure ultimately was approved 25-21, with all Republicans present except Ron Paul of Texas supporting the measure, and all Democrats present voting against it.

By the time it was over, the committee had plowed through 68 amendments, mostly Democratic measures that were killed off on party-line votes. Republicans said they produced a measure that would end the status quo of piling on one federal program after another; Democrats said they simply caved in to the demands of their most hard-line conservative backers.

"I have never seen anything like this in my 32 years in Congress," William L. Clay, D-Mo., the ranking Democrat on the committee, said in an April 13 interview. "If they want to lose the majority in the House of Representatives, let them go to the floor with this piece of junk and see how the American people respond."

Chairman Bill Goodling, R-Pa., said the measure provides a needed challenge to the status quo — a long history of federal programs that he said have failed children because there is no evidence they have improved academic achievement or accomplished their other goals.

"The cry has always been, 'If we have more money, we will cover more children,' " Goodling told reporters after the vote. "You're covering them with mediocrity. . . . We have done nothing to close the achievement gap."

The bill's centerpiece is a GOP-crafted provision that would let local school districts shift funds from one program to another — transferring money between teacher training, technology, substance abuse and other areas — to meet their needs.

The legislation would address other Republican priorities by consolidating eight education technology programs into one, $731 million block grant. It also would combine the Safe and Drug-Free Schools program and the 21st Century Community Learning Centers initiative for after-school programs. Republicans say that would be more efficient because 75 percent of the funds requested in 1997 for after-school programs went to anti-drug efforts, anyway.

Republicans stuck together on those themes, but the markup also showed how divided they have become on the issue of school vouchers — or anything resembling them. An amendment by Peter Hoekstra, R-Mich., that would have let states use federal funds for public and private school choice programs was defeated, 22-23, when four moderate Republicans joined with the Democrats to kill the measure.

Hoekstra said his amendment was not a voucher proposal because it did not involve a fixed amount of money, and he called it a "scholarship" that would be considered aid to the student, not the school. But Clay and other Democrats said anything that takes federal money from public schools and gives it to private or parochial schools would hurt public education.

Shaky Future

In the short run, the ESEA bill probably has enough GOP support to pass the House. Conservative and moderate Republicans said it is balanced enough to hold them together, thanks to months of negotiations between Goodling and the other committee Republicans.

The Clinton administration has threatened a veto, and Goodling said it is likely to change once the House goes into conference with the Senate, which will attempt to pass its ESEA reauthorization bill (S 2) in early May. Unlike the Senate, which will attempt

Other House ESEA Bills

BILL	DESCRIPTION	STATUS
HR 800 — PL 106-25, Education Flexibility Partnership Act (H Rept 106-43)	The law allows states to opt out of some federal regulations to experiment with innovative approaches to education.	Signed into law on April 29, 1999.
HR 2, Student Results Act (H Rept 106-394)	The bill would reauthorize and expand Title I, the elementary and secondary education program for disadvantaged students, and give states more latitude in spending federal funds earmarked for bilingual education.	House passed, 358-67, on Oct. 21, 1999. To be taken into conference with the Senate.
HR 1995, Teacher Empowerment Act (H Rept 106-232, part I)	The bill would consolidate three programs — the Eisenhower Professional Development program for teacher training, the Goals 2000 grants for improving education quality, and President Clinton's class size reduction initiative — into block grants to help improve teacher quality.	House passed, 239-185, on July 20, 1999. To be taken into conference with the Senate. Clinton administration has threatened a veto.
HR 2300, Academic Achievement for All Act ("Straight A's" Act) (H Rept 106-386)	The bill would set up a 10-state pilot program allowing states to mix funds from different federal programs if they can produce better academic results.	House passed, 213-208, on Oct. 21, 1999. To be taken into conference with the Senate. Clinton administration has threatened a veto.
HR 3616, Impact Aid Reauthorization Act (H Rept 106-504)	The bill would reauthorize the program that compensates school districts that lose potential tax revenues because they contain federal property.	Approved by House Education and the Workforce Committee on Feb. 16 by voice vote.
HR 3222, Literacy Involves Families Together Act (H Rept 106-503)	The bill would reauthorize Even Start, the program that supports local family literacy initiatives.	Approved by House Education and the Workforce Committee on Feb. 16 by voice vote.

its rewrite of the education law in one package, the House has split its effort into seven bills that focus on different parts of ESEA.

HR 4141 would continue the GOP theme of flexibility for states and school districts. It also strayed into such social issues as hate crimes and religious freedom — issues Goodling felt he had to include to win the support of conservative Republicans, but at the cost of even more bruising attacks from Democrats.

For example, the bill would eliminate the Department of Education's authority to fund classes that teach the prevention of hate crimes. Robert C. Scott, D-Va., tried to restore those programs, but his amendment failed, 23-24.

The hate crimes language sparked some of the most bitter debate of the session. Donald M. Payne, D-N.J., said schools should reach out to children to end the nation's "climate of intolerance"; Goodling countered that the bill "shouldn't be fostering any political correctness issues."

Scott also tried unsuccessfully to apply the employment discrimination protections of the Civil Rights Act of 1964 to religious organizations that receive Safe and Drug-Free Schools funds; his amendment failed, 18-28. Clay later accused Republicans of allowing religious discrimination in hiring, but Mark Souder, R-Ind., said the amendment would have forced religious organizations to change their character.

Even though moderate Republicans ultimately supported the bill, some of the social issues made them nervous. Michael N. Castle, R-Del., who voted for the Scott amendment to restore the hate crimes program, said in an April 11 interview that the GOP's hate crimes language and other provisions were needed to bring conservatives on board, though admitting that "any one of them could screw the bill up" when it gets to the House floor.

Goodling did take the steam out of one Democratic issue by accepting two relatively mild gun control amendments: a measure by Carolyn McCarthy of New York that would allow school districts to promote child safety locks on guns, and another McCarthy amendment that would require the National Center for Education Statistics to collect data on the common characteristics of school shootings. Both were approved by voice vote.

The Democrats lost a series of battles to preserve existing programs that they believe are working. A McCarthy amendment to preserve the 21st Century Community Learning Centers program was defeated, 21-25, and an attempt by Ron Kind of Wisconsin to restore the Technology Literacy Challenge Fund to help schools work computer technology into their classes was defeated, 21-27.

Democrats also lost whenever they tried to add new programs. An amendment by Lynn Woolsey of California to create a $50 million "Go Girl" program, which would support efforts to draw more girls into math and science classes, was rejected, 21-22. And an effort by Patsy T. Mink of Hawaii to authorize $14 billion over five years to help schools hire 100,000 new counselors was defeated, 20-25.

House Passes Bill That Would Revise Funding Of Impact Aid

MAY 20 — A bill that would change the funding formula of the impact aid program, which helps school districts with large amounts of tax-exempt federal property, passed the House by voice vote May 15.

The easy passage of HR 3616 reflects the House's piecemeal strategy for reauthorizing the 1965 Elementary and Secondary Education Act. The outlook for the program is less clear in the Senate, because its vehicle for reauthorizing impact aid is the ESEA package (S 2), which has been stalled since the week of May 8 and may never come to a final vote.

If the Senate measure dies, impact aid and all other ESEA programs would be funded for an extra year through the fiscal 2001 Labor, Health and Human Services and Education appropriations bill. That would keep impact aid running, but most likely without the changes that the House reauthorization bill would create.

'A Federal Responsibility'

Unlike other education programs — where Republicans and Democrats are arguing over whether the federal government or states and school districts should play the dominant role — "impact aid is truly a federal responsibility," Education and the Workforce Committee Chairman Bill Goodling, R-Pa., said May 15 before the bill's passage.

The impact aid program, Title VIII of ESEA, provides $906.5 million in federal aid to local education agencies that have trouble financing their schools because they contain federal facilities, such as military bases and Native American reservations, that are exempt from property taxes.

The five-year, $4.8 billion reauthorization bill, which breezed through the House with bipartisan support, would rework the funding formula to prevent federal payments from becoming skewed toward urban school districts.

It also would provide extra funds more quickly for the neediest districts, and it would create school modernization grants for districts that are too poor to issue their own bonds — or where the schools are so decrepit that they endanger students' health or safety.

The legislation would authorize $3 million for the modernization grants in fiscal 2000, along with $7 million for school construction assistance already offered under the program. The Congressional Budget Office estimated that the bill would provide $53 million for the two initiatives between 2001 and 2005.

In a May 16 interview, Goodling said the Senate's lack of progress on its ESEA package, which would reauthorize all of the programs at once, does not necessarily spell trouble for impact aid. The Senate could take the House bill and pass it as a separate vehicle, he said, or it could break out its own impact aid piece from S 2 and pass it as a stand-alone bill to have something to take into a conference committee with the House.

Impact aid itself has never been controversial in the Senate. In general, however, Senate Republicans have been reluctant to reauthorize ESEA in separate pieces, as the House is doing, because they cannot control the number of amendments for each piece — just as they have been unable to control the number of amendments to the overall bill.

House Passes Bill To Reauthorize 'Even Start' Literacy Program

SEPTEMBER 16 — House Education and the Workforce Chairman Bill Goodling wanted to leave a legacy before he retires: a literacy program that finally has a real impact on the reading skills of low-income families. Election-year politics will probably prevent that from happening, however.

By voice vote, the House on Sept. 12 passed Goodling's bill (HR 3222) to reauthorize the Even Start program, which funds more than 900 local projects nationwide that combine early childhood education, parenting instruction and adult education to help families improve their literacy.

Goodling's measure would authorize $250 million for the program in fiscal 2001, an increase of $100 million over fiscal 2000. It also has several new strings attached, including more state oversight, better training for instructors and a "charitable choice" provision that would allow religious groups to vie for Even Start funds.

"It has been a successful program, but we want to make sure it is even more successful," said the Pennsylvania Republican, a former school superintendent, who is leaving Congress next year after 26 years. As a tribute, Lindsey Graham, R-S.C., added a provision, approved during committee markup, to rename Even Start for Goodling.

By any name, the measure faces grim prospects in the Senate — not because anybody objects to it, but because election year politics and the dynamics of the Senate may make it impossible to pass any education bill this year.

Even Start (PL 103-382) is part of the broader Senate bill (S 2) to reauthorize the 1965 Elementary and Secondary Education Act (ESEA), the Great Society law that governs most federal aid to public schools.

That bill has languished since May, when Majority Leader Trent Lott, R-Miss., pulled it from the floor because both parties were eager to attach amendments designed to highlight their election year differences on education policy. Republicans especially wanted to avoid a Democratic gun control provision.

If any education bill comes to the Senate floor now — even one as limited as Even Start — Republicans fear it would become a magnet for all of those amendments. Unlike the House, the Senate cannot write a tight rule that would restrict the debate to Even Start. If one title of ESEA is up for debate, anything goes.

"Any education vehicle would be vulnerable to the same problems that ESEA has faced," Joe Karpinski, a spokesman for Health, Education, Labor and Pensions Committee Chairman James M. Jeffords, R-Vt., said in a Sept. 13 interview.

The most likely outcome this year will be more money for Even Start — without the policy changes Goodling wants. The conference report for the fiscal 2001 Labor, Health and Human Services, and Education appropriations bill (HR 4577), which has not yet been filed, includes $250 million for Even Start, and that figure is unlikely to drop when appropriators negotiate the final package with the White House.

Money was the one issue that had threatened House passage of the Goodling bill. The original measure called for $500 million for fiscal 2001, but conservative House Republicans said they would not support such a large increase in a government program.

Goodling wanted the extra funds to ensure that local literacy projects are successful. His bill would require local literacy projects to demonstrate progress in meeting the program's literacy goals and base their strategies on the latest techniques. States would also be able to use the federal funds to train and assist instructors.

Head Start Complaints

Those changes were prompted by Goodling's longtime complaints about Head Start (PL 89-253), the early childhood development program for low-income, preschool children. Goodling was the driving force behind a 1998 overhaul of the program that set tougher quality standards and required a greater share of funds to be spent on higher salaries and better teacher training. *(1998 Almanac, p. 9-23)*

Goodling believes the program has not lived up to its potential because there has not been an effort to determine how well it works and he said he did not want Even Start to fall into the same trap.

"It was not working because no one was paying any attention to whether there were quality programs or not, so it became a poverty jobs program, it became a babysitting program," Goodling said.

The Even Start bill is the latest in a series of "charitable choice" measures to pass the House. Similar proposals to fund faith-based social services are included in the anti-poverty legislation (HR 4923) that passed in July and the child support bill (HR 4678) passed Sept. 7.

Impact Aid for Schools Enacted As Part of Defense Reauthorization

NOVEMBER 4 — While Congress continues to bicker over education, the impact aid program, which gives federal assistance to school districts that have trouble raising enough property taxes to meet their funding needs, has won a new lease on life.

The program was reauthorized through fiscal 2003 as part of the fiscal 2001 defense authorization bill. (HR 4205)

The conference agreement on the defense bill was adopted by the House on Oct. 11 and cleared by the Senate on Oct. 12.

President Clinton signed the measure into law Oct. 30 (PL 106-398).

"Without this program, many districts would be without the full complement of resources they need for providing high quality education for their students," House Education and the Workforce Committee Chairman Bill Goodling, R-Pa., said in a Nov. 1 statement.

The impact aid reauthorization effort had been stalled since May, when the House passed a stand-alone bill (HR 3616) to renew the program.

The Senate included its version in the reauthorization bill (S 2) for the 1965 Elementary and Secondary Education Act. Republicans pulled that measure from the floor the week of May 8 over fears that Democrats would try to add a gun control amendment.

Sen. Judd Gregg, R-N.H., said at the time that ESEA would probably "be wrapped up in the wheels of appropriations bills," and impact aid ended up in the defense authorization bill. The only way House Republicans felt they could get the program through was as a rider to another measure.

Defense bill conferees agreed to accept the impact aid language because the program helps school districts that contain military bases, which are exempt from property taxes. It also aids districts with American Indian reservations. ◆

Senate Passes Legislation That Would Allow Annual, Tax-Free Accounts

Box Score

- **Bills:** S 1134, HR 7
- **Legislative action: Senate** passed S 1134 (S Rept 106-54), 61-37, on March 2.

House Ways and Means Committee approved HR 7 (H Rept 106-546), 21-16, on March 22.

SUMMARY

The Senate passed a bill (S 1134) March 2 that would have allowed families to set aside up to $2,000 per child annually in tax-free accounts for a broad range of education expenses. It also would have made permanent a tax exemption for employee-provided education assistance.

A similar bill (HR 7) won committee approval in the House, but floor action was blocked by a dispute over a school construction amendment.

As one of the centerpieces of their tax-cutting agenda, congressional Republicans attempted to pass legislation aimed at expanding so-called Education IRAs.

Both House and Senate versions of the legislation would have raised the annual limit on the amount that could be contributed to such an account to $2,000 per child, up from $500 under current law. The funds could have been used for pre-kindergarten through 12th-grade education expenses, including private school tuition. Currently, the accounts are restricted to higher education expenses.

President Clinton vetoed a similar bill in 1998 and threatened to do the same to S 1134. He and other Democratic critics argued that expanding the accounts would do little to benefit low- and middle-income families. They also said use of the accounts should be more limited. Republicans argued that the accounts would encourage personal savings and that no money would be diverted from public schools. *(1998 Almanac, p. 9-14)*

In the Senate, Republicans managed to fend off several Democratic amendments, passing S 1134 on March 2 with the help of nine crossovers, including Joseph I. Lieberman of Connecticut, who later became the Democratic vice presidential nominee.

However, the 61-37 vote was still short of the two-thirds majority that would have been needed to override a veto.

The House version of the bill (HR 7) was derailed when a group of Republican moderates, led by Nancy L. Johnson of Connecticut, threw their weight behind a plan to attach a school construction initiative being pushed by the White House. That led the House leadership to pull the bill from the floor.

Senate Passes Bill To Expand Use Of Education Savings Accounts

MARCH 4 — After turning back a series of Democratic amendments, the Senate on March 2 passed legislation (S 1134) that would let families deposit up to $2,000 per year in tax-preferred savings accounts for elementary and secondary education expenses, including private school tuition and tutoring.

The 61-37 vote was short of the two-thirds margin needed to override President Clinton's threatened veto.

In a Feb. 24 statement, the Office of Management and Budget said the bill's tax benefits were too heavily weighted toward affluent families and would do little to help lower-income and middle-class parents. Clinton vetoed a similar measure in 1998. Still, nine Democrats voted for the measure, sponsored by Paul Coverdell, R-Ga., and Robert G. Torricelli, D-N.J. *(Vote 33, p. S-9)*

Supporters said the bill would give parents more ability to finance their children's education, without taking funds away from public schools.

"Not a dollar of public money is diverted from the public schools," Torricelli said. "It does allow . . . a family at the birth of a child, to establish these savings accounts and then call upon grandparents, parents, cousins, churches, synagogues, labor unions and corporations to contribute moneys into these funds."

The bill has been a priority of Republican leaders, who are acutely aware of public opinion polls ranking school quality as the No. 1 concern of voters. The House Ways and Means Committee may mark up a companion bill the week of March 6.

During the debate, Democrats offered amendments that would have shifted federal funds designated to pay for the savings accounts to other priorities such as teacher training, education of the disabled, school construction and college Pell grants for low-income students.

Coverdell said Democrats had raised "an apple-pie goal" as a tactic to "neuter" the savings accounts.

The underlying bill builds on a law (PL 105-34) that lets parents set aside up to $500 per year in tax-preferred accounts for college education. Interest and principal on the accounts are tax-free when the funds are used for education expenses. *(1997 Almanac, p. 2-30)*

Expands Existing Accounts

The new bill would expand the accounts to let families put away up to $2,000 annually per child for elementary and secondary expenses as well as higher education.

As approved by the committee, the bill would have allowed individuals with adjusted gross annual incomes of up to $95,000 and couples with incomes of up to $150,000 to realize the full tax benefits of the accounts. Eligibility for the accounts would have been phased out as individuals reached an overall income limit of $110,000 and joint filers hit a $160,000 limit. The Senate adopted an amendment that would raise the income limit for joint filers to $190,000, phasing out at $220,000. *(Vote 22, p. S-8)*

On March 2, the Senate adopted, 59-40, a substitute amendment by Finance Committee Chairman William V. Roth Jr., R-Del., that made important changes. *(Vote 24, p. S-8)*

The amendment would make the accounts permanent, by deleting a provision that would have ended them after 2003. It eliminated an estimated $5.5 billion worth of revenue-raising provisions that had been designed to help cover the 10-year cost of the measure. Roth said the bill should be funded out of the federal budget surplus.

Another provision in his substitute would make permanent an exclusion from taxable income for employer-provided educational assistance for undergraduate education and extend the provision to graduate studies. Clinton last year signed legislation (PL 106-170) that temporarily extended that provision.

While it turned back a number of Democratic amendments, the Senate did adopt some key changes, including a proposal by Richard J. Durbin, D-Ill., to authorize $7 million for fiscal 2001 and more for succeeding years for violence prevention programs in elementary and secondary schools.

The proposal, adopted 91-7, was spurred by the Feb. 29 shooting of a first-grader by her 6-year-old classmate in a school near Flint, Mich. *(Vote 32, p. S-9)*

The Senate also adopted an amendment by Susan Collins, R-Maine, to let teachers deduct the cost of school supplies and related expenses from their taxes. The National Education Association has estimated that teachers spend an average of $408 of their own money on supplies each year. *(Vote 16, p. S-7)*

It also adopted an amendment by Spencer Abraham, R-Mich., to extend from two years to three the age of computers that companies could donate to schools for a tax deduction. *(Vote 18, p. S-7)*

GOP Leaders To Promote Bill Approved by House Committee

MARCH 25 — Facing a probable veto from President Clinton, Republicans will try to push an education savings accounts bill (HR 7) through the House the week of March 27 as part of an education agenda that they believe is starting to catch fire with voters.

The proposal would increase the amount parents can put into tax-preferred savings accounts for their children's education expenses from $500 to $2,000 a year. It also would allow them to use the money for private school tuition and tutoring. The bill would build on a law (PL 105-34) that set up the accounts for college expenses. *(1997 Almanac, p. 2-30)*

The $11.6 billion measure is similar to a bill (S 1134) passed by the Senate earlier this month. The House Ways and Means Committee approved HR 7 on March 22 on a mostly party-line vote of 21-16. The lone GOP defector was Nancy L. Johnson of Connecticut. Johnson teamed with Charles B. Rangel, D-N.Y., on an unsuccessful attempt to kill the education savings account expansion and replace it with a school modernization proposal that has won the Clinton administration's endorsement.

The Johnson-Rangel proposal would set up a tax credit to pay the interest on $24.8 billion in school modernization bonds. That would help states and school districts "do what they really want to do," said Rangel, while education savings accounts would just be "tax gimmicks."

The proposal would help states and school districts offer $22 billion in bonds, with 60 percent going to states and 40 percent going to the school districts with the highest number of low-income students. The rest of the federal aid would go to Bureau of Indian Affairs schools and an expansion of the Qualified Zone Academy Bond program, which helps schools in low-income neighborhoods.

The amendment was defeated by voice vote, but Democrats are still trying to woo Republican supporters and could push for a floor vote on it when the House takes up the bill.

Republicans, meanwhile, are framing the education savings accounts bill as part of a broader education agenda they think will set them apart from the Democrats: local control, greater flexibility in the use of federal dollars and more choices for parents who need help paying for their children's education expenses.

Their agenda includes the so-called Straight A's proposal, which would allow states to transform most federal elementary and secondary education aid programs into block grants as long as they come up with detailed plans for achieving better results.

The House passed a 10-state pilot program in October (HR 2300) that was pared back to satisfy moderate Republicans. The Senate will consider a 15-state pilot program when it debates its Elementary and Secondary Education Act reauthorization bill (S 2) next month.

Plunging Ahead

What is driving the agenda, in the face of veto threats and skittishness among moderate Republicans, is a set of internal polling numbers that has convinced GOP leaders they can reverse a long history of lagging behind the Democrats on education issues.

At the House GOP retreat at Williamsburg, Va., in January, rank-and-file Republicans were briefed on the poll results. On education, they were told, Democrats started out with a double-digit advantage. Then people were asked on a sample ballot whether they preferred a Republican candidate who would give states and communities more flexibility to hire new teachers, buy computers or repair classrooms, or a Democratic candidate who would hire 100,000 new teachers, as Clinton has proposed. The Republican won, 56 percent to 32 percent.

Ways and Means Democrats, meanwhile, charged that Republicans were plunging headlong into a certain veto to make a campaign issue out of education savings accounts. The Clinton administration has threatened to veto the Senate savings accounts bill, saying it would mostly help wealthy families and would become a recordkeeping nightmare, since participants would have to prove they spent their money properly to avoid being taxed on withdrawals. Clinton vetoed a similar bill in 1998.

The debate in Congress is already on a parallel track with the presidential campaign. Texas Gov. George W. Bush, the presumptive GOP nominee, is calling for an increase in the limit on education savings accounts to $5,000.

Vice President Al Gore, the likely Democratic standard-bearer, has already lined up with opponents. Shortly before the Ways and Means markup, he issued a statement endorsing the Johnson-Rangel proposal.

House Leaders Pull Savings Account Bill

APRIL 1 — A group of moderate Republicans may have changed the course of their party's education agenda the week of March 27 when they threw their weight behind a school construction initiative being pushed by the White House — causing the House leadership to pull an education savings account bill (HR 7) from the floor.

The moderates, led by Rep. Nancy L. Johnson, R-Conn., are demanding a floor vote on a bipartisan plan that would subsidize $24.8 billion in bonds to build or renovate public schools as a substitute for the savings account bill.

Most Republicans oppose the construction plan. But with virtually all House Democrats in their camp, the moderates appeared to have enough votes to win on a planned motion to recommit the savings account bill to the Ways and Means Committee.

Rather than face that outcome, Republican leaders postponed debate indefinitely, and the bill's backers went to work trying to craft a rule that would give Johnson a vote on school construction without endangering the education savings accounts, possibly by allowing votes on two separate bills.

The two sides are likely to keep talking into the week of April 3. But the House may not get to take another crack at education savings accounts until after the spring recess April 17-28. Michele Davis, a spokeswoman for House Majority Leader Dick Armey, R-Texas, said March 30 the chances are "not real good right now" that the bill will return before the recess; she said too many other bills are already lined up.

Whose Agenda?

The situation is turning into a political nightmare for House Republicans, as the education agenda shifts from their priorities to President Clinton's — thanks to Johnson and the other moderates.

Clinton vetoed a similar education savings account bill (HR 2646) in 1998 and has already promised to do the same to the version the Senate passed March 2 (S 1134). He has made school construction a priority; his budget includes a school modernization bond measure, and Education Secretary Richard W. Riley has endorsed the Johnson version. *(1998 Almanac, p. 9-14)*

Like its Senate counterpart, the GOP House bill would expand education savings accounts, created under a 1997 tax overhaul law (PL 105-34), by allowing parents to save up to $2,000 tax-free and use it to pay for elementary and secondary education expenses at public or private schools. Right now, they can save $500 a year, and it can be used only for higher education expenses. *(1997 Almanac, p. 2-30)*

Johnson, who sees school construction as a higher priority, has teamed up with Charles B. Rangel, D-N.Y., on a proposal to help states and school districts renovate rundown schools by offering tax credits to pay the interest on $24.8 billion in modernization bonds. The measure would cost $1.74 billion over five years.

The duo had offered their plan as an amendment during the Ways and Means markup of the education savings account bill March 22, but were voted down. This time, they wanted to offer a motion on the floor to recommit the education savings account bill to committee with instructions to strip out the savings account provisions and replace them with the school bond measure.

Johnson's aides estimated that a dozen moderate Republicans were ready to vote for the motion; a Rangel aide predicted that they could have pulled as many as 15. With the GOP holding only a six-seat majority — and less than that in real terms, since several key Republicans were out for various reasons — that prospect was enough to persuade the leadership to hit the abort switch.

"As we speak, they do not have the votes to defeat the motion," Fred Upton, R-Mich., said March 30.

Republican leadership aides insisted the danger was less serious than it appeared. "There's no question we were going to have to work it," Davis said, but "had the time been available, we could have pulled it off."

The House breakdown may have looked like a clear-cut disagreement between savings account supporters on one side and school construction advocates on the other, but the reality was more complicated.

There were Republicans who, like most Democrats, were uneasy with the idea that parents could use tax-free savings to send their kids to private schools. "I fail to see how denying resources to public schools improves public education," said Sherwood Boehlert, R-N.Y.

Why Not Both Bills?

And then there were Republicans like Upton, who liked both the education savings accounts and the school modernization bill. "I'd rather make it an add-on," Upton said of the school bond legislation, rather than a replacement for savings accounts.

Some Democrats might have crossed over and voted for savings accounts, as they did in the Senate. The problem for GOP leaders was that they could not count on those Democrats to vote against a motion to recommit.

Republicans are considering the possibility of having votes on two separate education savings account and school construction bills, and then merging them after they pass. That could produce a measure with something for each party to hate, however — a savings account bill that Clinton is likely to veto, and a school construction bill that goes too far for many Republicans.

Sound familiar? Ask lawmakers who put together the House's managed-care reform package (HR 2990). They got it through the House using a similar strategy. As it turns out, that was the easy part. The bill has yet to move out of conference. ◆

CQ

Chapter 10

ENERGY & ENVIRONMENT

Clinton Rejects Legislation To Establish Temporary Nuclear Waste Dump Site

SUMMARY

While awaiting the go-ahead for permanent storage of nuclear waste at Yucca Mountain in Nevada, Congress cleared legislation (S 1287) to facilitate short-term storage by the utilities that generate it. As promised, President Clinton vetoed the bill; a Senate attempt to override the veto failed.

In 1987, Congress designated Yucca Mountain as the likely permanent burial site for high-level nuclear waste from nuclear power plants in 34 states. But the project, which has been slowed by questions about safety and feasibility, is not expected to begin receiving waste before 2010. In the meantime, congressional Republicans have tried without success to win enactment of legislation that would allow temporary storage above ground near Yucca Mountain.

The new legislation (S 1287) took a different tack and would have authorized the Energy Department to offer utilities a combination of money and storage casks for short-term spent fuel storage in settlement negotiations over what to do with the waste. The bill also included a provision to transfer the authority to set radiation protection standards for Yucca Mountain from the EPA to the Nuclear Regulatory Commission (NRC). The provision was offered in response to GOP fears that the EPA's proposed standards would prove impossible to meet, effectively killing permanent storage at Yucca Mountain. The Clinton administration, backed by congressional Democrats, vowed to veto the proposal, arguing that it was improper to take the power from an agency that had wielded it for three decades. *(1999 Almanac, p. 12-3)*

The legislation languished until early 2000, when the Senate passed a heavily reworked version that would have allowed the EPA to establish radiation standards before June 1, 2001, only after consulting with the National Academy of Sciences and the NRC. The House cleared the bill, but since supporters in both chambers were unable to secure a two-thirds majority for passage, it was clear that a veto would stand. The Senate tried but failed to override it on May 2.

Senators Seek Compromise On Nuclear Dump

FEBRUARY 12 — With the Senate scheduled to consider long-delayed nuclear waste legislation the week of Feb. 7, Republicans and Democrats were struggling to work out a compromise acceptable to senators from states eager to be rid of high-level waste and to senators who want to preserve strict environmental protection.

The Senate is expected to take up the bill (S 1287 — S Rept 106-98) on Feb. 8. Republicans postponed a scheduled Feb. 2 cloture vote in order to give the two sides more time to strike a deal.

Once considered a priority of House and Senate GOP leaders, the legislation has languished since the Senate Energy and Natural Resources Committee approved it last June.

The bill incorporates a suggestion from Energy Secretary Bill Richardson to have his department take title and assume management responsibility for high-level spent fuel accumulating at nuclear power plants in 34 states.

But the measure has drawn a veto threat from President Clinton, largely because it would transfer authority for setting radiation protection standards at Nevada's Yucca Mountain, the proposed permanent U.S. nuclear waste burial site, from the Environmental Protection Agency (EPA) to the Nuclear Regulatory Commission (NRC).

Box Score

- **Bill:** S 1287
- **Legislative action: Senate** passed S 1287 (S Rept 106-98), 64-34, on Feb. 10.

House cleared S 1287, 253-167, on March 22.

President vetoed the bill April 25.

Senate failed to override the veto, 64-35, (two-thirds needed) on May 2.

Republican backers of the legislation have feared that EPA's proposed radiation standard is too stringent and would prove impossible to meet, thus effectively killing permanent storage at Yucca Mountain. The remote site, which is now under study to assess its suitability, is 100 miles northwest of Las Vegas.

Nevertheless, in what would be a significant concession to Democrats, Republicans were trying to draft a manager's amendment that would require the NRC and National Academy of Sciences to consult with the EPA before issuing the standards by June 2001.

"We're saying we may look at giving EPA some input, as long as the primary findings are established by the NRC and [the academy of sciences]," said Senate Republican Policy Committee Chairman Larry E. Craig, R-Idaho.

But that approach could draw objections from Democrats who would prefer to see the EPA continue to set the standards. They have noted that the agency has had that authority since its creation in 1970, and its standards were used for a separate burial site for defense wastes — New Mexico's Waste Isolation Pilot Plant.

"I'm much more comfortable with the EPA," Senate Minority Leader Tom Daschle, D-S.D., said Feb. 3. "I think they're in a position to do it. They have done it, in my view, admirably in the past."

The White House Office of Management and Budget issued a statement Feb. 2 warning that any legislation "that undermines the EPA's current role in setting standards . . . is unacceptable."

Seeking Storage

Jeff Bingaman of New Mexico, the Energy Committee's ranking Democrat, has pointed to other problems with the Senate committee-approved legislation.

In particular, Bingaman has cited language in the bill that would require the Energy Department to enter into contracts to store spent fuel for commercial utilities that run out of storage space. Bingaman also has said the bill would not solve problems at a Minnesota power plant that will run out of storage space in 2006.

The inclusion of the June 2001 deadline for standards also could prove troublesome in any compromise. Some Democrats note that the EPA is expected to finalize its proposed standards this year, before a new presidential administration takes office.

At the same time, the legislation could run into trouble from lawmakers who want to quickly move nuclear waste out of their states and into temporary above-ground storage at the Nevada Test Site near Yucca Mountain. The House Commerce Committee approved a bill (HR 45) last April calling for temporary storage there by 2003.

But proponents of temporary storage in Nevada have been unable to muster the 67 Senate votes necessary to override a presidential veto. *(1998 Almanac, p. 11-4)*

House Clears Bill For President, Who Promises to Veto

MARCH 25 — The inability of the House to pass a nuclear waste storage bill by a veto-proof margin March 22 all but ensures that the controversial issue will carry over into the next presidential administration.

The House voted 253-167 to clear the bill (S 1287) for President Clinton, who has vowed to veto the measure. The vote was 27 votes shy of a two-thirds majority required to override a veto. *(Vote 63, p. H-26)*

Clinton's objection centers on a provision that would modify the authority of the Environmental Protection Agency (EPA) to set radiation protection standards at Nevada's Yucca Mountain, located 100 miles northwest of Las Vegas. Yucca Mountain is under study as the possible permanent burial site for high-level spent fuel from commercial nuclear power plants and military reactors.

The bill would allow the EPA to establish standards before June 1, 2001, only after consulting with the National Academy of Sciences and Nuclear Regulatory Commission. In a March 21 letter to House Minority Leader Richard A. Gephardt, D-Mo., White House Chief of Staff John D. Podesta said the language "undermines the EPA's current role in setting these standards."

Unlike earlier nuclear waste bills, the legislation would not provide for temporary above-ground storage near Yucca Mountain until the permanent site is ready. Instead, it would give the Energy Department authority to offer utilities a combination of money and storage casks for short-term spent fuel storage during negotiations over what to do with the waste.

Without Delay

The House vote came six weeks after the Senate passed the measure but fell short of a veto-proof margin. House leaders brought up the Senate bill, instead of a version approved last year by the House Commerce Committee (HR 45 — H Rept 106-155), in order to get the bill to Clinton without a conference, which could have led to more delays by opponents in the Senate. But the move angered several key lawmakers who preferred the House measure, which would establish short-term storage in Nevada. They also complained that the floor rule for the bill did not allow amendments, which could have required Senate agreement and likely more delays.

"This is a bad bill; this is a bad procedure," John D. Dingell of Michigan, the Commerce Committee's ranking Democrat, said before the vote. "What we find ourselves confronting is a bill which will be vetoed, a bill which does not have a chance of getting a veto-proof majority."

In a sign of dissatisfaction with the legislation, the House voted by a narrow 206-205 to consider the bill despite a point of order against it as a violation of budget law. Rep. Jim Gibbons, R-Nev., who raised the point of order, argued that the measure would impose an unfunded mandate on some states by freezing payments that customers of nuclear utilities make, through their electric bills, to a fund to pay for permanent storage. *(Vote 61, p. H-24)*

Although Senate supporters are expected to lobby colleagues who opposed the bill to change their minds on a veto override, opponents are confident they can prevent any switches.

"The die is cast — this is a piece of legislation that will never become law," said Sen. Richard H. Bryan, D-Nev., one of the bill's staunchest opponents.

Nevada's other Democratic senator, Minority Whip Harry Reid, said the only reason the House voted at all on the measure was "to fulfill the financial commitments the nuclear power industry has given to House members."

The Senate presumably would need to pick up two additional votes for an override. Although the vote was 64-34 when the measure passed in February, one of the two senators absent was John McCain, R-Ariz., who has supported the legislation in the past. The other absent member was Edward M. Kennedy, D-Mass., an opponent.

Rep. Fred Upton, R-Mich., who sponsored the House's nuclear waste bill, held out hope that two other senators could be persuaded to change their minds. "If they [senators] vote to override, we've got a whole different picture here," Upton said.

But several senators who opposed the bill and who have been the targets of past lobbying indicated they would not alter their position. Sen. Ben Nighthorse Campbell, R-Colo., said he remains troubled by the prospect of waste shipments through busy urban areas of his state.

Another senator who voted against the bill, Democrat John Edwards of North Carolina, said he would look at supporting the legislation only if changes can be made to it. He did not specify what changes.

Even some Republicans who want to see a nuclear waste bill become law acknowledged they are looking to see if Texas Gov. George W. Bush can help them deal with the issue in the 107th Congress if he is elected president.

"If Gov. Bush becomes President

Bush [then] next year we've got to solve the problem," said Joe L. Barton, R-Texas, chairman of the House Commerce Subcommittee on Energy and Power.

Barton joined 17 other House Republicans in voting against the Senate bill. He said the legislation would not address the long-term funding needs for a permanent repository and includes "cumbersome" training for emergency personnel in states where waste would be transported. He predicted it would lead to litigation and appeals by governors.

Bush's likely Democratic opponent in November, Vice President Al Gore, has joined Clinton in adamantly opposing short-term storage in Nevada. Because nuclear waste is such a volatile political issue there, some Democrats have suggested the vice president's stance could make the difference in reaping the state's four electoral votes.

Gibbons, who has endorsed Bush, said the Texas governor "has promised me an open-door policy" to discuss the nuclear waste issue. But Barton said he is certain that Bush favors some type of short-term storage solution.

Even with a new administration, another bill governing the short-term disposal of commercial nuclear waste may not emerge. In the 107th Congress, the focus is expected to shift to whether Yucca Mountain should be the permanent burial site.

Under the project's current schedule, the secretary of Energy must decide in 2001 whether to recommend Yucca Mountain as a permanent repository. The president, in turn, will decide whether to submit that recommendation to Congress. If lawmakers agree and the site is designated, the Energy Department will ask the Nuclear Regulatory Commission for a license to operate it.

The earliest that Yucca Mountain is expected to be ready is 2010, although many observers predict the date will slip. In the meantime, many lawmakers are eager to deal with the growing backlog of waste accumulating at commercial power plant sites. Utilities have filed numerous lawsuits against the federal government stemming from its inability to meet a 1998 deadline to take control of the waste. *(1998 Almanac, p. 11-3)*

Clinton's Veto Appears Likely To Be Sustained

APRIL 29 — A nuclear waste storage bill appears dead for this year because supporters are unlikely to pick up the two votes that would be necessary to override President Clinton's April 25 veto.

The bill (S 1287) would set in motion a process for storing high-level spent fuel from commercial nuclear power plants in 34 states at Nevada's Yucca Mountain, 100 miles northwest of Las Vegas.

The bill failed to clear the House or Senate by the two-thirds majority needed to override a veto. The Senate passed the bill 64-34 on Feb. 10, while the House cleared it, 253-167, on March 22.

Senate Majority Leader Trent Lott, R-Miss., scheduled a May 2 vote to attempt to overturn the veto. But Lott and other supporters acknowledged that they would have to persuade two senators to switch their votes. House sponsors have said their strategy rests on a successful Senate override.

Nevada Democratic Sens. Harry Reid and Richard H. Bryan remained confident that they could prevent any defections. Both have sought to turn the issue to their party's political advantage in Nevada, where voters overwhelmingly oppose waste storage.

In a sign of the issue's potential importance in the November presidential election, Vice President Al Gore released a statement along with Clinton's veto message lauding the chief executive's action.

Clinton's objection to the bill centers on a provision that would modify the authority of the Environmental Protection Agency (EPA) to set radiation protection standards for Yucca Mountain. The bill would allow the EPA to establish standards before June 2001 only after consulting with the National Academy of Sciences and the Nuclear Regulatory Commission.

Clinton said "there is no scientific reason" to delay the standards. The EPA hopes to issue final standards by the summer. *(Veto message, p. D-15)*

Senate is One Vote Short of Override

MAY 6 — Senate supporters of legislation for storing nuclear waste in Nevada's Yucca Mountain fell one vote short May 2 of overturning President Clinton's veto. Although a parliamentary maneuver by Senate Majority Leader Trent Lott, R-Miss., kept the bill alive, opponents expressed confidence that they can block it again later in the year.

The bill (S 1287) would set in motion a process for storing high-level spent fuel from commercial nuclear power plants in 34 states at Yucca Mountain, 100 miles northwest of Las Vegas, as early as 2007.

Clinton vetoed the bill April 25, saying it would encroach on the authority of the Environmental Protection Agency (EPA) to set radiation protection standards for the storage site. The bill would allow the EPA to establish standards before June 2001 only after consulting with the National Academy of Sciences and the Nuclear Regulatory Commission.

The 64-35 vote on whether to override the veto was technically two votes short of the two-thirds majority needed. But Lott switched his vote from "yes" to "no" in a procedural move that would allow him to call for another vote in the future. *(Vote 88, p. S-18)*

The tactic has been used before. In 1995, then-Senate Majority Leader Bob Dole, R-Kan. (1969-96), changed his vote on a constitutional balanced-budget amendment so he could call for another vote the following year. It failed both times. *(1996 Almanac, p. 2-32; 1995 Almanac, p. 2-34)*

Lott promised to bring up the nuclear waste bill again if proponents can persuade one senator to switch and support the measure. "This is achievable," he said, "and I look forward to the opportunity to revisit this issue."

If all senators are present and voting, it would take 67 votes to override Clinton's veto. William V. Roth Jr., R-Del., was absent from the May 2 vote, but he voted for the bill when it passed Feb. 10. That gives supporters 66 votes, or one shy of an override.

When the House cleared the bill March 22, supporters were 27 votes short of what they would need to override a veto.

Nevada Democratic Sens. Harry Reid and Richard H. Bryan said they have no doubt they can defeat the bill and keep high-level nuclear waste out of Nevada. "We'll always have 34 votes, no matter what they do," said Reid, the Senate minority whip.

Although 13 Democrats voted to override Clinton's veto, Reid said some of those Democrats would have sided with him if their support was needed.

John Edwards, D-N.C., was the only senator to switch his vote from when the Senate voted to pass the bill in February. But Edwards was the last senator to cast his vote in favor of the override — a sign that he wanted to ensure that there were enough votes to sustain Clinton's veto.

Supporters of nuclear waste legislation hope that if Texas Gov. George W. Bush is elected president, he can help them enact the legislation in the 107th Congress.

Rep. Fred Upton, R-Mich., who sponsored the House's nuclear waste bill (HR 45), said he plans to reintroduce it next year. "We probably have to look to the next administration" for action on waste storage, Upton said. ◆

Conservation Bill Stalls In the Senate as Opponents Fan Fears of 'Land Grabs'

Box Score

- **Bill:** HR 701
- **Legislative action: House** passed HR 701 (H Rept 106-499, Part 1), 315-102, on May 11.

Senate Energy and Natural Resources Committee approved HR 701 (S Rept 106-413) by voice vote July 25.

SUMMARY

The Conservation and Reinvestment Act (CARA), a bipartisan measure that would have guaranteed about $3 billion annually in offshore drilling revenues to a host of federal and state conservation programs, died at the close of the 106th Congress as part of an end-of-session compromise between congressional appropriators and the White House on a smaller conservation measure subject to annual appropriations.

After years spent cobbling together a broad and often unlikely coalition of supporters, CARA backers saw their original goal of assuring a mandatory stream of spending for conservation programs dissipate with enactment of the fiscal 2001 Interior appropriations bill (PL 106-291), which created a six-year, $12 billion discretionary fund for public land programs. *(Appropriations, p. 2-83)*

CARA aimed to provide steady, predictable funding for recreation and conservation programs by setting aside a portion of offshore oil and gas royalties exclusively for that purpose over 15 years. It included full funding of $900 million a year for the Land and Water Conservation Fund (PL 88-578), which was established in 1965 to pay for federal land purchases, as well as $1 billion annually for coastal states and $350 million for state wildlife programs.

The measure grew out of an effort by officials and legislators from coastal states such as Louisiana and Alaska to capture some of the windfall from oil and gas drilling off their shores and "reinvest" it to mitigate the punishing effects of these activities on their coastlines. It began gaining steam when coastal state representatives such as House Resources Committee Chairman Don Young, R-Alaska — rarely accused of being "green" — partnered with environmentalists such as ranking Resources Democrat George Miller of California to produce a mammoth environmental bill.

Scores of lawmakers came on board at the prospect of guaranteed funding for their states, and hundreds of grass-roots and national environmental groups joined the effort in hopes of winning coveted earmarks for their programs.

However, a small but powerful group of appropriators joined by a determined bloc of Western lawmakers vowed to prevent the measure from coming to the Senate floor. Appropriators and budget hawks portrayed the bill as an end-run around the appropriations committees, while Westerners railed against more federal land purchases.

President Clinton swore to make passage of CARA a priority in final budget negotiations, but resistance to making conservation funding an entitlement — which would have deprived appropriators of politically advantageous sway over where the money should be spent — proved too strong. In the end, a legacy-conscious White House, which had proposed a discretionary "Lands Legacy" fund to pay for conservation programs, pushed for the more-achievable six-year program, an approach put forth by House Democratic appropriators Norm Dicks of Washington and David R. Obey of Wisconsin.

Through the tenacious efforts of CARA proponents — including Sen. Mary L. Landrieu, D-La., and Senate Majority Leader Trent Lott, R-Miss. — programs that would have been assured funding under CARA did secure a fiscal 2001 boost through the appropriations process and the possibility of more during the next five years.

House Passes Extensive Environmental Bill

MAY 13 — Jack Caldwell has watched the Houma Navigation Canal swallow 10 square miles of Louisiana wetlands since it was carved out of the Mississippi River Delta in 1964. The canal, built to allow offshore drilling rigs manufactured nearby to be barged to the Gulf of Mexico, has swallowed once lush marshes and destroyed fragile habitat — one reason coastal wetlands are disappearing faster in the Pelican State than anywhere in the nation.

Caldwell, secretary of Louisiana's Department of Natural Resources, may finally have the money he needs to address the damage wrought by the 25 mile-long canal if the Conservation and Reinvestment Act (HR 701) becomes law. That measure, known as CARA, passed the House 315-102 on May 11. *(Vote 179, p. H-58)*

"Today that canal would not have a chance of getting dug. At that time people did not realize how fragile or valuable the marsh was," said Caldwell, who has been working on the issue for years. "It took a while to get things going."

During the time it took to "get things going," a metamorphosis took place in Congress. What started as a comparatively limited proposal to use royalties that the federal government receives from offshore oil and gas drilling to mitigate the damages caused by those activities broadened into the wide-ranging House-passed bill to guarantee nearly $3 billion a year to expand parks, buy fragile land, preserve wildlife, protect farms from urban encroachment, and restore historic buildings and sites in all 50 states.

"This is the largest environmental bill for the conservation of American resources in the past 36 years," said Rep. George Miller, D-Calif., a chief sponsor of the measure.

The question is whether the bill's transformation will ensure its passage or guarantee its defeat. As the measure has grown, it has become a top priority of the nation's governors, thousands of state legislators and a slew of organizations from the Camp Fire Girls to the Wilderness Society. Within Congress, however, the bill has drawn intense opposition from private property advocates, who call it a massive federal land grab and complain that Congress has not provided enough money to maintain the existing network of national parks and forests. There is an estimated $5 billion maintenance backlog on federal lands.

Powerful appropriators are fighting the bill because its funding would be mandatory, rather than subject to yearly votes by Congress. They consider the measure one in a series of attempted end-runs around their committees, which are responsible for writing annual spending bills.

Despite having more than 300 cosponsors, the bill came to the floor only after a series of impassioned meetings between conservatives and House Republican leaders. When the measure was finally brought up, opponents peppered it with more than 20 amendments.

Although the Senate version (S 2123) is cosponsored by Majority Leader Trent Lott, R-Miss., whose coastal state would reap major benefits, Western conservatives such as Larry E. Craig, an Idaho Republican, are threatening a filibuster.

"What the House said yesterday is that they will put land acquisition over health care and education" by making it a mandatory program, Craig said May 12. "Congress and the administration have this habit of thinking it is good to purchase land, but they don't look back and see how the land they have acquired is maintained."

A Closet Environmentalist?

The House bill is a joint effort by Resources Committee Chairman Don Young, R-Alaska, and Miller, the committee's top-ranking Democrat. The combination is unusual because Young and Miller disagree on many land use and conservation issues and rarely work together. The committee approved the bill by a 37-12 vote on Nov. 10.

Western conservatives feel especially betrayed by Young, usually their ally. The Alaska Republican, who is stepping down as chairman of the Resources Committee at the end of this Congress due to a six-year chairmanship term limit imposed by the GOP, has had to defend himself against charges that he has sold out to environmentalists.

Under the Young-Miller measure, about $2.8 billion a year in royalties that the federal government receives from oil and gas drilling on federal lands would be set aside annually for the next 15 years to purchase environmentally sensitive land and other conservation programs. Currently, all of the royalties are deposited in the federal Treasury. *(Highlights, p. 10-8)*

The bill would mandate $1 billion annually for a coastal conservation fund, $900 million for the Land and Water Conservation Fund (PL 88-578), and $350 million for wildlife conservation and education programs. It would also provide annual payments of $575 million for everything from urban parks to Indian land restoration to historic preservation.

In the Senate, Energy and Natural Resources Committee Chairman Frank H. Murkowski, R-Alaska, and Mary L. Landrieu, D-La., are leading the effort to pass the legislation.

After introducing a CARA measure (S 25) at the beginning of the 106th Congress, Landrieu introduced a bill (S 2123) in February 2000 that is a replica of HR 701 in hopes of accelerating passage.

The administration supports the intent of the House-passed measure, while seeking a series of changes.

House Floor Shuffle

The tensions over the bill played out in House debate. Young and Miller, along with W.J. "Billy" Tauzin, R-La., and John D. Dingell, D-Mich., who are also strong supporters of the bill, fended off all but a handful of amendments that were proposed on the House floor. Among those were efforts to provide additional protections for private landowners and limit the scope of the measure.

"It seems to be a piece of a larger puzzle to extend the federal government's control over more of our land base," said Idaho Republican Helen Chenoweth-Hage.

"This is America's new Trail of Tears," she added, in reference to the federal government driving the Cherokee Indians off their land in the early 1800s. "Whether it's Native American Indians or Native American white people, the government has to be respectful of their rights."

The federal government owns a vast amount of acreage across the nation, most of that in the West. For example, about 242 million acres in Alaska alone are federal property.

Bill supporters said they had tried to take concerns such as Chenoweth-

Conservation Bill Highlights

MAY 13 — The following are highlights of the Conservation and Reinvestment Act (HR 701) passed by the House on May 11. The bill would create a permanent, automatic funding mechanism that would channel royalties from offshore drilling to numerous federal and state resource and land conservation programs.

ISSUE	DESCRIPTION
Conservation and Reinvestment Act Fund	The bill would require the Treasury to deposit up to $2.8 billion a year in royalties from oil and gas drilling on the Outer Continental Shelf into a new conservation fund that would provide money to federal and state programs. Most of the spending from the fund, about $2.4 billion a year, would be mandatory and thus not subject to annual appropriations.
Coastal conservation	$1 billion a year from the fund would go to a new Interior Department program to help coastal states manage the effects of offshore drilling. Eligible states would be those bordering on the Atlantic and Pacific oceans, the Gulf of Mexico and the Great Lakes.
Land and water conservation	$900 million a year would be guaranteed for the Land and Water Conservation Fund, the main federal fund providing money to acquire land for recreation and conservation. The money would be equally divided between state and federal programs. The fund is currently authorized to spend about $900 million annually, but actual appropriations have averaged less than one-third of that amount.
Wildlife conservation	$350 million a year would be dedicated to an existing wildlife conservation and restoration program that provides formula-based grants to states.
Farmland protection	$100 million would flow to an Agriculture Department program of matching grants aimed at protecting prime farm, ranch and forest lands by limiting non-agricultural uses.
Other programs	Other guaranteed funding would include: $125 million a year for matching grants for urban parks and recreation, $100 million a year for the Historic Preservation Fund, $200 million a year to protect and restore Indian lands, and $50 million a year to provide incentives for landowners to aid in the recovery of endangered and threatened species.

Hage's into consideration.

One provision of the bill would institute tougher prohibitions against the taking of private property without just compensation. Another would place tougher restrictions on the use of federal funds for land acquisition.

The House did approve an amendment by Republican John Shadegg of Arizona, 216-208, late on May 10. The amendment would prohibit the Treasury Department from transferring oil royalty revenue for the conservation program unless certain conditions were met. *(Vote 163, p. H-54)*

Among the requirements of the amendment was that Congress be on track to eliminate all publicly held debt by 2013. A second provision would require Congress to certify that Social Security and Medicare were not going to run a deficit in the next five years.

On May 11, as part of a procedural motion to recommit the bill, the House agreed to a less stringent proposal by bill sponsors that would prohibit funds from being spent under the bill if they would diminish benefit obligations to several trust funds, including those for federal disability insurance and supplemental medical insurance. The motion was approved 413-3. *(Vote 178, p. H-58)*

"Imitation is the sincerest form of flattery," Shadegg said. "And what they've done is imitate what we did last night. It is clearly not as strong in protecting Social Security as our language. This language is absolutely meaningless. But their goal was to give themselves political cover."

The House defeated, 126-291, an amendment by William M. "Mac" Thornberry, R-Texas, that combined several proposals sought by private property owners and appropriators. The amendment would have required that the maintenance backlog in national parks be decreased by 5 percent a year before the federal government could purchase additional land. For the first five years, funding under the bill would not have been mandatory — meaning that appropriators would decide how much to spend. *(Vote 177, p. H-58)*

Clinton Land Grab

Despite CARA's success in the House, Murkowski said he expects to have a tough time getting the bill through the Senate. He has scheduled a June 14 markup on the measure in his committee.

Supporters say they have been undercut by President Clinton's recent actions, including issuing a federal order on May 9 to bar roads in 43 million acres of federal forests and, earlier this spring, declaring some Western lands to be national monuments off limits to development.

Murkowski and other supporters of the bill met with Clinton at the White House on April 12 and told him he was jeopardizing the measure.

"I said this to his face, and what did he do? A few days later he created (a national monument). I think that attitude jeopardizes this legislation," Murkowski said May 11.

The bill is expected to continue to be dogged by opposition from Western lawmakers, property rights advocates and budget writers.

Although Murkowski said he believes he can mollify Western lawmakers with a provision that would guarantee no net loss of private land, he does not know how he will satisfy the concerns of the budget hawks and appropriators.

Down-Home Impact

Louisiana's Caldwell has been working on the legislation since 1996. He and other public officials from states that are home to offshore drilling operations were spurred to action by what they describe as unequal treatment.

Under current law, when drilling for oil and natural gas takes place on federal land, 50 percent of the royalties that are paid to the federal government come back to the local community, but when drilling takes place offshore in federal waters, all the royalties go into the federal Treasury.

The initial version of a bill that Caldwell and other state and local officials drafted in 1996 sought to address only this inequity. It consisted solely of the first title of the current measure, which now has eight titles. The draft plan would have created a revenue-sharing and coastal conservation fund for coastal states and eligible local governments to mitigate the damage caused by activities related to offshore drilling, and it also authorized funds for the conservation of coastal areas.

Although under HR 701 coastal states such as Louisiana, Alaska and Texas would receive the lion's share of the funding, Rocky Mountain and Midwestern states, along with urban areas, would also receive money.

By the time legislation was introduced in 1998, it also included provisions to ensure funding for the Land and Water Conservation Fund and authorize funding for wildlife conservation and restoration. Bills introduced in the 105th Congress by Young and Landrieu (HR 4717, S 2566) died in committee.

By the time the bill passed May 11, it was a mammoth conservation measure that enjoyed the support of legislators who represent districts thousands of miles from the nearest offshore drilling rig.

"All of these disparate groups have come together, and now we have the greatest conservation bill ever," Caldwell said.

Western Senators Attack Bill During Markup

JULY 22 — Bitter opposition by Western senators slowed action on a sweeping land conservation measure to a crawl the week of July 17, as the Senate Energy and Natural Resources Committee beat back — perhaps only temporarily — attempts to kill the measure through a series of amendments.

As the panel began consideration July 19 of the Conservation and Reinvestment Act (HR 701), critics said the bill, known as CARA, will have to overcome determined opposition in the coming weeks. The bill would steer $3 billion a year in offshore oil and gas drilling revenues to land purchases and conservation programs.

"It's going to require 60 votes several times to get this bill through the Senate," said Interior Appropriations Subcommittee Chairman Slade Gorton, R-Wash., referring to the number of votes needed to break a filibuster.

It might not even get that far. The most significant test for the bill will take place not on the Senate floor — where the millions of dollars each state would receive under the measure are likely to sway a majority of senators — but in the committee itself, where a coalition of GOP Westerners opposed to more federal land acquisition is determined to sink it.

The panel is slated to continue action on the bill, including a series of amendments designed to alter it drastically, the week of July 24.

Assistant Majority Leader Don Nickles, R-Okla., repeatedly threw up parliamentary roadblocks to the ongoing markup — forcing the panel to meet in two-hour chunks to consider a few amendments at a time — in an effort to run out the clock as the legislative session winds down.

"No one wants to carve the tombstone just yet, but there is clearly a problem with the clock," said John Czwartacki, a spokesman for Majority Leader Trent Lott, R-Miss., who supports the bill.

Energy Committee Chairman Frank H. Murkowski, R-Alaska, said July 21 that he will not allow delays to lock up the bill much longer. He plans to close the measure to amendments July 25 and move to report it to the Senate.

The Philosophical Divide

While the bill began as an effort to assist coastal states affected by drilling on the Outer Continental Shelf, it has ballooned to include $900 million a year for federal and state acquisition of fragile land, $350 million a year for wildlife conservation, and $325 million annually for a program that compensates states for lost property taxes where the federal government owns large tracts of land.

Murkowski, who spent weeks forging a compromise with ranking Democrat Jeff Bingaman of New Mexico, called it "the most significant commitment of resources ever."

The measure calls for royalties from drilling on the Outer Continental Shelf for oil and gas — depletable resources — to be used for conservation programs that sustain such renewable resources as land and wildlife.

"You either accept it on that or you reject it," Murkowski said.

Most Western senators rejected it, arguing that more government land purchases are not the way to protect resources. "I believe that the great American legacy . . . is the right to own private land," said Larry E. Craig, R-Idaho. "Somehow, we've been sold the idea that the best way to manage the land is to lock it up."

Other Republicans focused their ire on the bill's intricate funding mechanism. While the version that the House passed 315-102 on May 11 would make most of the $3 billion mandatory spending — rather than having it subject to annual congressional appropriations — the Murkowski-Bingaman compromise would trigger the release of the funds only after Congress voted to spend the $450 million included for federal land acquisition.

Budget Committee Chairman Pete V. Domenici, R-N.M., and Gorton said the funding scheme is a disingenuous way of prioritizing environmental programs over all other federally funded accounts.

"Previously, this bill was an ill-advised but honest entitlement; now it's an ill-advised and dishonest entitlement," Gorton said.

The Senate panel voted on several amendments, including:

• A Domenici amendment, rejected 8-11 on July 20, to make the entire amount subject to appropriations.

• A Gorton amendment, rejected 7-12 on July 21, that would have removed the trigger mechanism.

• An amendment offered by Republican Jim Bunning of Kentucky, and adopted by voice vote July 21, to require guarantees that the bill would not prevent the government from paying off the public debt by 2013 or maintaining the solvency of Medicare and Social Security.

Senate Panel Votes To Spend Royalties On Conservation

JULY 29 — A broad and tenacious bipartisan coalition in the Senate Energy and Natural Resources Committee won voice-vote approval July 25 of the Conservation and Reinvestment Act (HR 701). A small and equally determined group of GOP conservatives is vowing to delay the bill to death.

"We will work to use all of the tactics we can to prevent the bill from coming to the floor," said Larry E. Craig, R-Idaho, one of a handful of Western senators who view the legislation as a federal land-grab.

That may be the only way to defeat the measure, known as CARA, which which would steer $3 billion a year from offshore oil and gas drilling royalties to federal and state land acquisition and conservation programs for the life of its 15-year authorization. The measure enjoys the support of 4,500 interest groups around the country.

Battles Ahead

Supporters agreed only that victory at the committee level assures a bigger fight, in the thick of end-of-the-session scrambling, to see CARA enacted. "This fight is not over," John B. Breaux, D-La., said at a July 25 news conference. "In fact, it has just begun."

Majority Leader Trent Lott, R-Miss., one of CARA's most ardent supporters, admitted that time is his enemy in seeking to schedule debate on the measure, which would give his state $83 million annually.

"Our biggest problem now is . . . finding the time to do anything other than the appropriations bills and other must-pass business," Lott told reporters July 25. Still, should negotiations with the bill's opponents fail, Lott said he is willing to engage in a parliamentary war to move it. "If you have to go the cloture route [to limit debate], you do that," he said.

He may end up warring with a member of his own leadership team, Assistant Majority Leader Don Nickles, R-Okla., who offered three amendments during the markup — all rejected — designed to radically change the measure.

Nickles was particularly critical of the bill's unusual funding arrangement, which would essentially create an entitlement for conservation and land preservation programs but allow it to be spent only after Congress voted to appropriate the $450 million authorized in the bill for federal land acquisition. The mechanism is designed to mollify critics who said an automatic appropriation would limit congressional oversight.

"I think it's a major shift, and I don't know of any other authorizing committee that's trying to act as appropriators," Nickles said in a July 25 interview. "I think it's very unusual, and it's not likely to happen."

Likely or not, the commitment embodied in CARA is unprecedented. Under the bill, the 35-year-old Land and Water Conservation Fund — a chronically underfunded account used to pay for state and federal purchase and protection of fragile land — would receive $900 million a year. Another $350 million a year would go to wildlife conservation and $325 million annually would go to a program that compensates states for the property taxes lost where the federal government owns large tracts of land.

The funding mechanism was worked out during weeks of negotiations between Energy Chairman Frank H. Murkowski, R-Alaska, and ranking Democrat Jeff Bingaman of New Mexico. It gives appropriators a powerful incentive to spend the $450 million designated for federal land purchases.

"Long term, if we're going to make it a priority, we need to lock it in," Bingaman said July 20, the second day of the five-day markup.

End Run Around Appropriators

Budget hawks have portrayed the bill as an end run around appropriators. "You have done an ingenious thing in this bill . . . it is an automatic expenditure of $3 billion a year," Budget Committee Chairman Pete V. Domenici, R-N.M., said July 19 as the panel took up the bill.

"Are we all prepared to say that this is the most important priority on the appropriations side of the ledger?" he added later.

The Senate Energy Committee rejected several amendments offered by budget hardliners that would have altered the funding method, including:

• An amendment offered by Nickles and Domenici, rejected 8-11 on July 20, to make the entire bill subject to annual appropriations.

• An amendment by Interior Appropriations Subcommittee Chairman Slade Gorton, R-Wash., rejected 7-12 on July 21, to remove the trigger mechanism.

• A Gorton amendment, tabled 11-9 on July 25, that sought to prevent CARA funds from being spent until the maintenance backlog in national parks was eliminated.

• An amendment by Domenici, rejected 7-13 on July 25, to require biennial authorizations of CARA.

• A Nickles amendment, rejected 9-11 on July 25, that would have sunset the bill after five years.

Other Energy panel opponents focused on the measure's land acquisition funding.

"There is a constant, continuous gain of federal [land] ownership — no question about that," Craig Thomas, R-Wyo., said in arguing for his "no net loss" amendment, which would have required the federal government to sell a parcel of land of equal value if it wanted to buy more than 100 acres in a state where more than 25 percent of the land was federally owned.

"This is sort of a recognition in the Congress of the difference between public land states and non-public land states," Thomas said before his amendment was rejected, 9-11, on July 25.

The bill's supporters said Thomas' amendment would have given state authorities veto power over federal land purchases. They agreed to adopt, by voice vote, an amendment offered July 20 by Conrad Burns, R-Mont., that would require federal officials to consult with state authorities on which lands to purchase.

Willing Sellers

Western senators played to the fears and concerns of many in their region by arguing that CARA would give the government the ability to kick landowners off their property.

Nickles offered an amendment, rejected, 8-12 on July 25, that would have eliminated Congress' ability to authorize federal land acquisitions unless the property owner was a "willing seller."

By negotiating language on land sales, proponents managed to win the support of one Western Republican who had opposed the legislation.

Gordon H. Smith, R-Ore., decided to back the Murkowski-Bingaman compromise after the sponsors agreed to include language that would require the government to find willing sellers wherever possible and to avoid removing land owners from their property by force.

"However real or imagined this problem is, it is certainly an imagined feeling in rural Oregon, and I think we should address it," Smith said July 20.

Opponents Vow To Keep CARA From Senate Floor

AUGUST 5 — About a week before a Senate committee was slated to begin voting on the Conservation and Reinvestment Act (CARA), which would guarantee some $3 billion annually for environmental programs through 2015, Boise Mayor H. Brent Coles came knocking on the door of his senior senator, fellow Republican Larry E. Craig.

Coles, who also heads the U.S. Conference of Mayors, had come July 12 to plead with Craig to support the measure (HR 701), which would bring Idaho an estimated $45 million a year for land conservation and urban park restoration.

"I've got the mayor of my biggest city . . . saying, 'Larry!' And I say, 'I understand, Brent, but step outside the city of Boise and the world changes,' " said Craig, who adamantly opposes the measure even though he admits it would "bring money into areas where, quite frankly, I'd like some."

Stiffened Resistance

Two decades after the "Sagebrush Rebellion" — a revolt against government controls on public lands — swept the West, the region and its political representatives are deeply divided over land policy. Urban growth and suburban sprawl have expanded the constituency that supports conservation and protection of open spaces, but the resistance among rural landowners to government stewardship has stiffened. *(Sagebrush Rebellion, 1979 Almanac, p. 604)*

Despite some polls that peg voter support for CARA at 75 percent to 88 percent, Craig and other Westerners argue it is their job to protect the minority of rural landowners who have been affected by such Clinton administration environmental policies as restricting mining, grazing and timber harvesting on public lands; attempting to ban road-building in national forests and snowmobiling in national parks, and designating millions of acres as national monuments without local input.

"It's interesting politics for me in a state that is very frustrated and angry with this administration for the way they've treated general public land issues," Craig said July 28. "The West is so frustrated and angry at [Clinton] for disallowing a level of participation, stiffing . . . the governors and all the interested parties, that part of that spillover is spilling onto CARA right now."

Craig is leading a band of Senate budget hawks and Westerners who have vowed to prevent the bill from reaching the floor after the Energy and Natural Resources Committee approved it by voice vote July 25.

Opponents argue that CARA — widely seen as the only major environmental legislation with a chance for passage this year — encourages the kind of federal "land grabs" they say President Clinton has perpetrated for years. They face a strong bipartisan coalition supporting the bill, including House Resources Committee Chairman Don Young and Senate Energy and Natural Resources Committee Chairman Frank H. Murkowski. The two Alaska Republicans are eager for the $164 million annual windfall the bill would give their state. The House passed CARA by a lopsided vote of 315-102 on May 11.

Most of the money from CARA, which would come from offshore oil and gas royalties, is slated for such coastal states as Mississippi and Louisiana, where the federal government owns less than 5 percent of the land. Many Western states, which are more than 50 percent federally owned, would see proportionately less benefit. The measure has the support of Senate Majority Leader Trent Lott, R-Miss., whose coastal state would receive an estimated $83 million a year, and of Minority Leader Tom Daschle, D-S.D., whose landlocked state would get $20 million.

Two Opposing Arguments

Western senators' main quarrel with the measure is its authorization of $900 million annually for federal and state purchases of environmentally sensitive land.

They say that would lock in funding and allow the government to continue the Clinton administration practice of acquiring large parcels of public land and restricting grazing and other uses.

Powerful budget writers and appropriators, who guard their turf jealously, complain that CARA would allow environmental programs to escape congressional scrutiny.

They were not mollified by Murkowski's July 19 assertion that the bill "fully preserved the rights and prerogatives of the Congress and the House and Senate Appropriations Committees."

"To ask the Senate to ignore [budget rules] in this fashion has an impact that goes far beyond CARA," Senate Interior Appropriations Subcommittee Chairman Slade Gorton, R-Wash., said July 21. Gorton has said he would rather boost the funding for Clinton's Lands Legacy Initiative — which also would steer hundreds of millions to land acquisition — than see CARA enacted.

While the $3 billion is not an automatic appropriation, the bill's practical effect would be to create a quasi-entitlement for conservation programs. In order to retain lawmakers' oversight of land purchases, the legislation would not allow Congress to release the money until it voted the annual appropriation of $450 million authorized in the bill for federal land acquisition.

"Whatever you've added is not enough to convince me that we ought to do this," Budget Committee Chairman Pete V. Domenici, R-N.M., said July 19. "People are going to say, 'Spend it, because it's a gravy train.' "

After annual endgame spending negotiations with the White House, Murkowski said Congress has appropriated an average of more than $400 million annually for land purchases the past five years. He told his Energy panel colleagues there is a $12 billion backlog of authorized land purchases and that his committee has authorized another $300 million this session.

One of the bill's staunch supporters agrees that institutional sentiments could determine CARA's fate.

"It is true that parts of this bill interfere with the prerogatives of committees and all sort of entrenched interests within Congress," said Jim Souby, executive director of the Western Governors Association, in a July 18 interview.

"The institution of the Senate has to protect its own interests," he said. "Its ability to have influence on the administration and in negotiations with the House is part of that."

A Plethora of Polls

How does CARA play with voters? Well, according to most — but not all — polls.

The House passed CARA just one week after a survey by Republican pollster Frank Luntz found that 88 percent of 1,200 respondents support protecting national parks, historic areas, wilderness areas and coasts.

"Conservation of land, water and open spaces presents a winning issue to political leaders who want to connect with the broadest spectrum of Americans," Luntz wrote in a May 5 news release. "This set of issues is a perfect opportunity for the Congress to address public priorities and build credibility."

A June 23 poll conducted by the GOP polling firm The Tarrance Group for the environmental groups Americans for Our Heritage and Recreation and the Wilderness Society had similar findings. It found that 75 percent of the 1,001 people surveyed favor creating a permanent trust fund to protect natural resources. Support was particularly strong among such voting blocs as working women, mothers, people under 45 and Hispanics.

The survey also found that 68 percent of voters would be more likely to support a candidate for the House or Senate who was in favor of creating such a trust fund. That percentage rose to 77 percent among voters in open-seat congressional districts.

A Marked Shift

Such findings show a marked political shift from the public land furor 20 years ago and are bolstered by a strong grassroots coalition of local agencies and recreation and conservation groups — numbering nearly 5,000 and including many Western organizations — that have been lobbying actively for CARA's enactment.

"We have been building the political will for this issue slowly but steadily over the last several years," Sen. Mary L. Landrieu, D-La., a cosponsor, said July 25. "The senators feel this when they go home to their districts, and that's the best lobbying you can have."

When supporters cite the polls illustrating the widespread consensus on creating a trust fund for environmental programs, opponents refer to another May study that found respondents conflicted on the bill.

In a survey conducted by Vox Populi Communications Inc. — which one anti-CARA lobbyist said was sponsored by House Majority Whip Tom DeLay, R-Texas — market researchers asked 400 subjects to weigh their support for land conservation against such issues as Social Security, reduction of the national debt and the $8 billion maintenance backlog in the nation's parks.

Some 45 percent of respondents said they favored CARA's general premise of government land purchases to create more parks and wilderness areas. Their support fell to 13 percent when they were asked to weigh CARA against Social Security and debt buydown and to 12 percent against park maintenance.

The poll's findings bolster opponents' argument that steering offshore energy royalties to environmental programs — instead of depositing them in the general Treasury fund, as is currently done — would reduce the funding available to pay for other priorities.

"I do not believe that the bill is popular; I believe what they've tried to sell is popular," said Myron Ebell, director of environment and trade policy at the conservative Competitive Enterprise Institute, in an Aug. 1 interview. "When you then start talking about what's really in the bill . . . then the poll numbers switch. Overwhelmingly, majorities say no."

Changing the Debate

Max Peterson, who served as chief of the U.S. Forest Service from 1979 to 1987 and now runs the non-profit International Association of Fish and Wildlife Agencies, says economics have changed the debate over public lands.

"The reason this type of conservation bill is even feasible is the fact that the federal budget is in this kind of shape," Peterson said in a July 18 interview. "The public mood right now, as I read it, is we have enough money now so that we can spend it to do something for conservation."

Critics of the measure agree while reaching different conclusions. "It's very doubtful that this bill would have even been considered three years ago," Gorton said at the Energy markup on July 20. "Now that we've got a surplus, boy is that money burning a hole in our pockets — we can't spend it fast enough."

CARA was first envisioned by Alaska's Young, its sponsor, and Democrat Rep. George Miller of California, sponsor of a similar measure, as a way of steering revenues from offshore oil and gas drilling to the coastal states where most of those activities take place.

Since the House Resources Committee approved it in November 1999, however, CARA has become a vehicle for creating an annual funding stream for all sorts of environmental programs. To garner widespread support for a bill that would direct the lion's share of its benefits to coastal states, sponsors made sure interior states would also receive millions for land acquisition, wildlife programs, urban parks and historic preservation.

To some critics, that smells an awful lot like buying support.

"The impetus behind the bill is a very unusual coalition of a lot of people who want financial gain — who want pork," said Ebell. "This is really an old-fashioned pork barrel bill. . . . They essentially bought everybody off."

"The supporters of this bill have somewhat been blinded by the idea of dollars — free dollars — coming to their respective states," said Conrad Burns, R-Mont., July 19 as the Senate Energy Committee took up CARA. "Land ownership is a cornerstone of individual freedom that most Americans hold very dear."

Assistant Majority Leader Don Nickles, R-Okla., who unsuccessfully attempted to stall markup of the legislation until the August recess, said the bill represents all that is wrong with Clinton's environmental policies.

"It shows an attitude that, 'Frankly, we don't care what people think in the local areas.' This administration has gone way too far," Nickles said July 20. He cited Clinton's national monument designations as examples of his affinity for grabbing land without any regard for local opinion.

"To give this kind of control to the government without going through appropriations to me is a mistake," he said.

Clinton began his monuments program in 1996 when he used the 1906 Antiquities Act to designate some 1.7 million acres of southern Utah as the Grand Staircase-Escalante National Monument. Since then he has designated eight more tracts as monuments. *(1997 Almanac, p. 4-16)*

Murkowski has attempted to steer the discussion away from the administration's land policies, saying CARA is not intended "to rectify the authority of the president over antiquities."

Emotion vs. Logic

Such arguments are not likely to play well in the West, where emotion often trumps logic when it comes to land issues.

"It appears to the person living out there that someone that they don't even know — who lives inside the Beltway — is making decisions that affect their livelihoods," said Peterson. He compares Westerners' feelings to those of revolutionaries protesting "taxation without representation" in 1776. "That really causes emotional upheaval," he said.

Supporters and critics acknowledge that few voters thoroughly understand the issues surrounding CARA.

"While [it] is wildly popular in Oregon, I doubt that many Oregonians know the effect of these things," Gordon H. Smith, R-Ore., said as the Senate Energy Committee took up the bill July 19. "I don't want to go home and explain why I empowered a federal government that has besieged them — why I gave them the power to do more of the same."

Smith ended up voting for the compromise after reaching an agreement with the architects of the bipartisan measure, Murkowski and ranking Energy Committee Democrat Jeff Bingaman of New Mexico, on language ensuring that the bill would not allow the federal government to acquire land from unwilling sellers.

While the voters may not fully grasp the impact of CARA now, opponents of the measure say Smith's decision is one that could haunt him politically when he is up for re-election in 2002.

Facing Vote's Consequences

"He will face the repercussions of this in Eastern rural Oregon for the rest of his career; they will never forget this," Ebell said. "He's going to have a really hard time motivating his base in four years because this vote is not going to be forgotten."

Ebell says Smith is not the only Republican who will have problems with voters for supporting CARA. "The long-term implications for Republicans in this bill are disastrous [because] they win in districts that have suburban areas with rural hinterland," Ebell said.

Most Western governors disagree. "The governors certainly believe . . . this bill and the funding, of course, that it will provide will be a godsend," Souby said.

He believes support for CARA goes beyond public officials to property owners who believe the measure would help protect the environment and their pocketbooks.

"There's a growing number of landowners who agree with this, and who are willing to stand up and say, 'We need this,' " Souby said. "These are deeply held values on their part. They would like to see this resolved too, but not at the expense of their families." ◆

Everglades Revival Bill Clears As Shuster Wins Promise To Restore Slashed Projects

SUMMARY

Legislation authorizing the first $1.4 billion of a $7.8 billion federal-state project to restore Florida's Everglades made it through Congress just before Election Day, as the broader water projects bill that carried it faltered in conference due to House-Senate disagreements over environmental infrastructure projects.

Widespread bipartisan support for the Everglades restoration project, along with election-year pressures, kept the measure alive even as the water resources bill met with several near-death experiences.

Senate Environment and Public Works Committee Chairman Robert C. Smith, R-N.H., vowed in a January 2000 visit to the Everglades to make the restoration plan the top priority in his first term leading that panel. As the year wore on and Florida emerged as a key battleground in the presidential elections, the state's delegation made herculean efforts to push the bill through before Election Day.

The bill — which codified a bipartisan 1999 agreement between the Clinton administration, Florida officials, environmental and agricultural groups and tribal leaders — divides the cost of the 35-year restoration effort equally between state and federal sources. It also authorizes the first 10 water projects and four pilot programs in the plan at a cost of some $1.4 billion. The initiative is designed to undo a 1948 Army Corps of Engineers flood-control project that has had the effect of flushing more than 1.5 billion gallons of water a day into the Atlantic Ocean and the Gulf of Mexico, drying out vast portions of the Everglades, polluting others with runoff and creating water supply problems in South Florida.

House Transportation and Infrastructure Committee Chairman Bud Shuster, R-Pa., stalled the bill, using the popular Everglades portion as a bargaining chip to secure an alternative vehicle for some $400 million worth of water supply and sewerage projects that Smith refused to carry in the water measure. Just five days before Election Day, House Appropriations Committee Chairman C.W. Bill Young, R-Fla., and Speaker J. Dennis Hastert, R-Ill., promised Shuster they would fund his projects if he would free the Everglades bill. *(See omnibus appropriations, p. 2-3)*

Box Score

- **Bill:** S 2796 — PL 106-541
- **Legislative action: Senate** passed S 2796 (S Rept 106-362), 85-1, on Sept. 25.

House passed S 2796, amended, 394-14, on Oct. 19.

Senate adopted the conference report (H Rept 106-1020) by voice vote Oct. 31.

House cleared the bill, 312-2 on Nov. 3.

President signed S 2796 on Dec. 11.

Senate Panel OKs Everglades Bill Despite Concern About Costs

JULY 1 — Despite foes' complaints that it would produce decades of uncontrolled spending, the Senate Environment and Public Works Committee approved legislation June 28 to begin a $7.8 billion project aimed at restoring the Florida Everglades.

The measure (S 2797) would authorize some $1.4 billion to begin 10 specific projects, start four pilot projects and conduct additional planning to replenish the vast South Florida ecosystem, which encompasses some 2.4 million acres.

After the measure was approved 16-1, panel Chairman Robert C. Smith, R-N.H., the bill's sponsor, sought to boost the Everglades legislation's chances of swift Senate passage by offering it as an amendment to a popular water resources bill (S 2796) that would fund an array of flood control, navigation and water projects. His amendment was approved unanimously.

Still, the Everglades bill faces tough opposition from senators who oppose a provision that would require the federal government to pay half the operations and maintenance costs for the sweeping Army Corps of Engineers project, which is slated to last until 2036.

John W. Warner, R-Va., warned that a federal commitment to pay half the costs is one "that we cannot afford to make. It is . . . unfair to other communities who are financing [all operations and maintenance] costs for projects of equal merit."

Warner offered an amendment that would have removed the cost-sharing provisions from the bill and retained provisions in the 1996 water resources law (PL 104-303) that require states to pay all operations and maintenance costs for corps projects. *(1996 Almanac, p. 4-17)* The amendment was rejected, 8-10, prompting Warner to try to offer a second amendment that would have shifted the federal share from the Defense Department to the Interior Department.

Warner was ruled out of order, but he vowed to resurrect the issue if the legislation reaches the Senate floor. "This will not be lost. Someday you'll see that again," he said.

Reversing a 1948 Project

The Everglades plan, which has been characterized as the largest and most expensive ecosystem restoration project ever, would reverse the effects of a 1948 Army Corps of Engineers project designed to control flooding and supply water to South Florida. The network of waterways and dams built by the corps has had the unintended consequence of draining

1.7 billion gallons of water a day from the Everglades into the Atlantic Ocean.

The bill calls for restoring the natural water flow to the Everglades and providing flood control and potable water to South Florida. Supporters say the federal government's role in the initial damage, coupled with its interest in the entire ecosystem justifies its participation in the restoration.

"The federal government was a willing partner. . . . They destroyed the Everglades ecosystem," Smith said. "We are now coming back to undo that damage."

The measure aims to control federal costs and ensure congressional oversight by prohibiting projects from exceeding their authorizations by more than 20 percent, requiring that Congress authorize any future Everglades projects and mandating that House and Senate panels approve implementation reports before any of the 10 authorized projects could receive funding.

Warner and James M. Inhofe,R-Okla., the only panel member to vote against the legislation, said the plan could still commit the government to decades of out-of-control spending. "This project is going to be a giant sucking machine," Warner complained.

Who Doles Out Water?

The legislation also would settle the question of who decides how water recaptured by the project is distributed. The Clinton administration proposed in April that the federal government reallocate water with the state in a consultative role, while Smith's bill would require the secretary of the Interior and Florida's governor to share responsibility for distribution.

The issue also concerns House lawmakers. "The question is, who gets what in terms of the water?" said Bud Shuster, R-Pa., chairman of the Transportation and Infrastructure Committee, which has jurisdiction over water projects.

Shuster said June 28 that he is working with Republicans and Democrats on his panel to craft a two-pronged Everglades package, encompassing both water policy and a project authorization, that he hopes to mark up before the August recess.

Senators Debate Cost-Sharing Plan

SEPTEMBER 23 — After defeating attempts to shift more of the project's costs to the state of Florida, the Senate is poised to pass legislation that would require the federal government to pay for half of a 35-year, $7.8 billion venture to restore the Everglades.

The measure came to the Senate floor Sept. 21 as part of a bill (S 2796) that would authorize $5.6 billion worth of Army Corps of Engineers flood control, navigation and water projects, including $1.4 billion to fund the first 10 water projects and four pilot projects in the Everglades restoration.

Those projects would begin the process of reconstructing the rich South Florida ecosystem — which has shrunk by almost half since a federal flood control project interrupted its natural water flows in 1948 — while supplying water to agricultural and urban areas and threatened estuaries, improving water quality and providing flood protection.

"The Everglades are very special; it's a very environmentally sensitive region of the country, and it clearly is a treasure," said bill sponsor Robert C. Smith, R-N.H., who in January pegged Everglades restoration as his top priority as chairman of the Environment and Public Works Committee.

"We are saying that if we don't do something to save the Everglades, we will lose the Everglades — so we have to try," Smith said.

An agreement among federal and Florida officials, Indian tribal leaders, agricultural groups and environmentalists — who have been struggling in recent months to determine how Everglades water will be distributed — paved the way for the bill's consideration. They agreed that water captured through the various projects would go first to environmental uses. Any remaining water would be distributed according to Florida's permit process.

"This restoration program will be the most significant and the most expensive environmental restoration project ever attempted anywhere in the world," said Bob Graham, D-Fla. "This is going to be a world laboratory for how we will restore damaged environmental systems."

A Fine Distinction

During debate, several senators took issue with the plan's cost-sharing element, which envisions the federal government footing 50 percent of the bill for operations and maintenance. In most water projects the costs are covered by the individual states.

The Senate roundly rejected, 24-71, an amendment by Republican John W. Warner of Virginia that would have required Florida to pay all operations and maintenance costs during the Everglades restoration program. *(Vote 254, p. S-45)*

"All I am trying to do is preserve equity and fairness — equity and fairness for what has been done in the past and what shall be done in the future," said Warner. "Fine — clean up the water, but do it like every other municipality: Have the states pay for it."

Warner's amendment would have required the legislation to be consistent with a 1996 water projects law (PL 104-303) that requires non-federal sources to take responsibility for operations and maintenance costs. *(1996 Almanac, p. 4-16)*

Supporters of the Everglades measure argued that the project — which would restore an ecosystem jointly managed by Florida and the federal government — warrants splitting the costs. "Both the state and federal government have a vital interest in the restoration of the Everglades," said Connie Mack, R-Fla. "If the project is not operated properly — if the water is not right — these important federal holdings in South Florida will continue to suffer."

George V. Voinovich, R-Ohio, joined Warner in opposing the cost-sharing arrangement. He argued that the federal government would actually be paying for 65 percent of the project because it would ultimately improve the output from Florida's municipal water supply systems.

Proponents said the federal government usually pays for 65 percent of construction costs on federal-state environmental projects, so splitting the cost of the Everglades reclamation would really save money.

"I see no distinction," Warner insisted. "Water is water. Cleanup is cleanup. The question is who is going to pay for it."

Supporters of the federal commitment to the Everglades project acknowledged during the debate that much remains to be learned about how to handle the many needs of the troubled ecosystem.

A provision in the bill known as "adaptive management" would provide for changes to be made to the restoration plan as the Army Corps of Engineers and the state of Florida learn which strategies work and which need modification.

"This is a risk; this is not a sure thing," conceded Smith, adding, "We take risks all the time."

Senate Passes Bill To Fund Everglades Restoration

SEPTEMBER 30 — The Senate overwhelmingly passed water projects legislation Sept. 25 that would authorize the first phase of an unprecedented $7.8 billion, 35-year state-federal project to restore Florida's Everglades.

The elation that accompanied the 85-1 passage of the $6.7 billion measure (S 2796) was tempered by uncertainty over the bill's murky future in the House, where lawmakers have reached an impasse in their efforts to craft similar legislation. *(Vote 255, p. S-46)*

"I expect you to hand-carry it down the hall and get it passed," Senate Environment and Public Works Committee Chairman Robert C. Smith, R-N.H., told Rep. E. Clay Shaw Jr., R-Fla., handing him the thick bill at a news conference following the vote.

Smith, who had made the Everglades project a priority, said the bill's passage proved politicians can look beyond the next election "to the next generation."

"With this vote," Smith said, "our grandchildren and their children will enjoy alligators and wading birds and the river of grass once again."

While he has received no assurances from House GOP leaders that they will make the Everglades project a priority, Shaw, who is in a tight re-election race, said he might try to move it as a stand-alone measure if the House Transportation and Infrastructure Committee — which has been hung up over a labor-related provision in the larger water projects bill — fails to break its logjam.

The 'Goofy Season'

"We're in the goofy season," Shaw said, referring to the end-of-session scramble as congressional leaders negotiate with the White House to complete appropriations bills. If the House water resources bill remains stalled, he suggested, the Everglades restoration could also join the ranks of measures tacked on to fiscal 2001 spending bills in endgame negotiations.

Environmental Protection Agency Administrator Carol M. Browner, in a Sept. 25 statement, called the Everglades initiative "a top environmental priority of the Clinton-Gore administration."

The Everglades portion of the water projects measure would approve a blueprint for a 35-year restoration plan that many experts have called the largest ecosystem cleanup effort ever. It would authorize the first 10 projects, four pilot projects and additional work on currently authorized restoration efforts, at a cost of about $1.4 billion.

Under the plan, the state of Florida and the federal government would split the costs of operating and maintaining the restoration projects. The Senate rejected an amendment, offered by Republican John W. Warner of Virginia on Sept. 21, that would have required Florida to cover all of those costs.

George V. Voinovich, R-Ohio, chairman of the Environment and Public Works Subcommittee on Transportation and Infrastructure, called the legislation "an important legacy for our country and for our future."

James M. Inhofe, R-Okla., the lone senator who voted "no," said a dangerous precedent was being set. "All of us support protecting the environment and preserving the Everglades," he said. "But this bill is not sound stewardship of federal policy and public resources. This is an open-ended commitment which will end up costing the taxpayers a tremendous amount of money."

Tough Conference Lies Ahead for House-Passed Bill

OCTOBER 21 — The House overwhelmingly passed a massive water projects bill (S 2796) that includes the first phase of a 35-year, $7.8 billion project to restore Florida's Everglades.

The 394-14 vote Oct. 19 all but assured that the Florida project will be enacted this year, but the underlying $6.9 billion water bill now heads to a difficult conference the week of Oct. 23, where it could be jeopardized by substantial differences between the House and Senate versions. *(Vote 534, p. H-170)*

"They have a lot of work to do, and they don't have a lot of time to do it," said Michael L. Davis, deputy assistant secretary of the Army, in an Oct. 19 interview. The Army Corps of Engineers constructs water projects authorized by Congress.

The Senate easily passed a $6.7 billion version of the bill on Sept. 25.

Environmentalists complained that the House added provisions unrelated to the Everglades project that threaten the bill. However, proponents of the popular project — whose cost would be shared equally by the federal government and the state of Florida — said they will not allow it to fall victim to end-of-session disagreements on the larger water measure.

"Our hope and expectation is that we can reach agreement with the Senate and move forward with the bill," Sherwood Boehlert, R-N.Y., chairman of the House Transportation and Infrastructure Subcommittee on Water Resources and Environment, said in an interview Oct. 19. "But if there is a breakdown in negotiations, we should not sacrifice one of the most important environmental issues of our time."

House Appropriations Committee Chairman C.W. Bill Young, R-Fla., is expected to rescue the bipartisan Everglades initiative by attaching the language to a spending bill if the water resources measure gets stuck in conference.

"He's going to be holding on to a number of important bills that he has to complete before we close up shop here," E. Clay Shaw Jr., R-Fla., told reporters Oct. 19. "We're not going to leave town without it," said Shaw, who needs passage of the bill to help his tight re-election race.

Historic Restoration Effort

Administration officials and lawmakers hailed the Everglades project, with Environmental Protection Agency Administrator Carol M. Browner calling it "the most aggressive . . . forward-thinking restoration plan ever — period."

The water resources bill would authorize a blueprint agreed upon last year by federal and state officials, American Indian tribal leaders and agricultural interests to restore the Everglades' natural water flows, which were interrupted by a 1948 Corps of Engineers project designed to prevent flooding.

The re-engineering of the sprawling ecosystem — which is home to four national parks, 16 national wildlife refuges and one national marine sanctuary — had the unintended consequence of drying out large portions of the Everglades by flushing some 1.7 billion gallons of water a day into the Atlantic Ocean and the Gulf of Mexico. It also polluted bodies of water in South Florida with agricultural runoff.

The bill would authorize some $1.4 billion for the first 10 construction projects and four pilot projects and require an assessment and monitoring program to ensure that the restoration measures are working and allow changes where necessary.

Carefully crafted provisions governing the distribution of the water captured by the restoration projects were instrumental in building broad support among agricultural and environmental groups, state and federal officials, and Republicans and Democrats.

The bill would require the president and Florida's governor to make a binding agreement under which the state would reserve water captured by the various projects for the ecosystem before re-allocating it for other uses. The Army also would have to issue rules within two years — acceptable to both Florida's governor and the Interior Department — setting out the goals of the restoration plan and requiring that all the projects be in line with those goals.

Conservatives complained that the water resources bill is loaded with expensive projects designed to appeal to members, such as a $15 million navigation initiative in False Pass, Alaska. It also includes $85 million for groundwater improvements in California's San Gabriel Basin and would allow the Corps to participate in a massive California estuary rehabilitation project known as CALFED.

"To me, this bill is simply nothing more than a feeding frenzy," Mark Sanford, R-S.C., said Oct. 19.

Natural resources groups complained the House version added several provisions that could harm the environment, including language that they said would lead to an increase in dredging in the nation's harbors by contributing more federal money for such projects.

Negotiators Revive Bill by Diverting Disputed Provisions To Other Bills

OCTOBER 28 — House and Senate negotiators narrowly saved a major water resources bill from dying in conference the week of Oct. 23, agreeing to move several environmental infrastructure projects and policy provisions that senators opposed to another measure.

The agreement appears to assure passage of the measure, including a much-touted Everglades restoration project expected to cost $7.8 billion over 35 years. The larger water bill (S 2796) would authorize more than $6.5 billion for Army Corps of Engineers projects.

Progress on the Everglades project — generally considered to be the largest ecosystem restoration project ever — came with a high price: House Transportation and Infrastructure Committee Chairman Bud Shuster, R-Pa., threatened not to sign a final agreement on the conference report until he secures a commitment to attach water supply, wastewater treatment and sewage projects the Senate resisted to the measure (HR 4577) funding the departments of Labor, Health and Human Services and Education for fiscal 2001.

"It was dead last night, and we got some gravediggers to come along and dig up the corpse," Shuster said of the water resources conference report Oct. 26. "I think there's a way to do [the water resources bill] without those things that the Senate objects to, and to take care of those someplace else."

The fate of the Everglades provisions was never truly in doubt. House and Senate leaders and appropriators had vowed to resurrect the South Florida project by tacking it onto a spending bill if the water resources development bill crumbled.

Instead, conferees brought the water resources bill back to life after Shuster tore a page from the Florida delegation's plans and suggested keeping the water resources bill whole while including the environmental infrastructure projects, which fall outside the corps' traditional mission, in endgame spending negotiations.

Senate Environment and Public Works Committee Chairman Robert C. Smith, R-N.H., who led the opposition to the infrastructure projects, said he had done all he could do keeping the provisions off his bill. "Do they have other, more sinister things on their mind? Probably," Smith said of House conferees Oct. 27. "But I had to stand firm that those projects could not go on my bill."

Environmental Infrastructure

The Shuster-Smith standoff over the water resources bill centered on at least $385 million in the House version for wastewater treatment and water supply projects usually funded through local sponsors or the Environmental Protection Agency (EPA).

The corps already has a backlog of close to $30 billion in water resources projects it is responsible for, including navigation, flood control and beach restoration.

"We are very firm that the environmental infrastructure should not be on that bill," Smith had said in an Oct. 24 interview. "I intend to hang tough on it, because I think we need to reform that process."

Projects funded by EPA grants must pass agency environmental reviews, while corps projects are not subject to the same accountability or selection requirements.

Observers said Smith's firm stance on the projects energized Shuster, who is finishing his last term as Transportation chairman, to find another vehicle for them. "That was basically taking a square shot at Bud Shuster's legacy," said Steve Ellis, who handles water resources issues for the watchdog group Taxpayers for Common Sense, in an Oct. 27 interview.

Down to the Wire

By mid-week, Florida lawmakers feared that passage of the top-priority Everglades provision — which would authorize the first 10 construction projects and four pilot projects in the federal-state plan, at a cost of $1.4 billion — was no longer a certainty.

The water resources bill "is done. It's cooked. That toilet is leaking, and it isn't going to be fixed," Mark Foley, R-Fla., said in an Oct. 25 interview, adding, "I'm not talking to Shuster on Everglades any more."

Shuster, however, used the popularity of the South Florida plan to his advantage, keeping negotiations on the full water resources bill alive even as House Appropriations Committee Chairman C.W. Bill Young, R-Fla., said he would allow Everglades language to be attached to the last spending bill of the year, the Labor-HHS-Education measure.

That is the likely vehicle for Shuster's infrastructure provisions, but conferees were not expected to sign an agreement until details of the Labor-HHS-Education measure are finalized.

House Clears Everglades Bill

NOVEMBER 4 — Powered by widespread bipartisan support for a massive Everglades restoration project, the House on Nov. 3 cleared a sweeping water projects bill (S 2796) totaling some $7 billion.

The House adopted the conference report on the measure, 312-2, after Transportation and Infrastructure Committee Chairman Bud Shuster, R-Pa., received assurances from the leadership that more than $400 million in local wastewater, sewerage and water supply projects removed during negotiations would be added to one of the remaining fiscal 2001 spending bills. *(Vote 594, p. H-188)*

The Senate had adopted the conference report by voice vote Oct. 31.

Despite the popularity of the Everglades plan — a $7.8-billion, 35-year project that would receive its first $1.4 billion under the legislation — Shuster had refused to move the water bill until a home was found for his projects.

"Important as it is, I do not see how I could call up the [water] conference report until I have assurances that the full package will be enacted," Shuster told the Rules Committee on Nov. 1.

He got that commitment Nov. 2, when Speaker J. Dennis Hastert, R-Ill., and Appropriations Committee Chairman C.W. Bill Young, R-Fla., promised to include the projects in the final agreement on the fiscal 2001 spending measure for the departments of Labor, Health and Human Services, and Education (HR 4577). "That was the agreement," Hastert confirmed in a Nov. 3 interview.

The Labor-HHS bill is expected to be finalized when Congress reconvenes the week of Nov. 13.

"I am pleased with the assurances we received that it will be included when we wrap up our appropriations legislation," Shuster said shortly before the House vote. The Senate adopted the conference report by voice vote on Oct. 31.

With a lame-duck session looming, GOP leaders made an intense push to move the water bill before Election Day. They hoped to help Rep. E. Clay Shaw Jr., R-Fla., who is locked in a tight race against state Rep. Elaine Bloom. Shaw has tried to make political capital out of the Everglades restoration plan, which was hammered out by Florida's Republican Gov. Jeb Bush, local officials and the administration.

"If [Democrats] were counting on this as an issue, it's gone," Shaw said.

Shuster said he is "confident" House leaders will keep their word to include his projects — which include 52 "environmental infrastructure" projects typically funded by local sources or EPA grants. However, the projects could face opposition from House budget hawks and in the Senate.

Senate Environment and Public Works Committee Chairman Robert C. Smith, R-N.H., had refused to include the sewage and water projects in the water resources bill — which funds navigation, flood and beach erosion control and environmental restoration projects — saying he wants to reform the way such projects are handled. ◆

Congress Unable to Satisfy Gas Industry and Farmers Over Possible Ban of MTBE

SUMMARY

Legislation to ban the clean-burning gasoline additive methyl tertiary butyl ether (MTBE) — which was found to be leaking from underground storage tanks in some 30 states and is a suspected carcinogen — died at the end of the 106th Congress, after lawmakers failed to forge a compromise that could satisfy both the agriculture and petroleum industries. Senate Environment and Public Works Committee Chairman Robert C. Smith, R-N.H., plans to resurrect the issue during the 107th Congress.

The measure (S 2962) would have phased out MTBE over four years while still requiring states to achieve the clean air standards for which the additive was developed. It also would have authorized $200 million to clean up MTBE contamination and required that a growing portion of the nation's fuel market be composed of non-petroleum, "clean alternative fuels" such as fuel cells or a corn-derived MTBE alternative known as ethanol.

Oil refiners began using MTBE in the 1990s after Congress mandated (PL 101-549) that cities with serious air pollution sell gasoline containing 2 percent oxygen, which makes a cleaner-burning fuel. After MTBE contamination became widespread, agriculture groups pushed for a straight ban, recognizing that the 1990 oxygenate mandate would then force refiners to use ethanol, the only other commercially developed, clean-burning fuel additive. Oil refiners said that approach would be too expensive and restrictive and pressed Congress to get rid of the oxygen requirement altogether.

After months of unsuccessful negotiations, Smith introduced a compromise bill that would allow states to waive the oxygenate requirement but still require them to achieve the toxic emissions reductions they reached under the mandate.

The petroleum industry said the bill was a "de facto ethanol mandate" that would exacerbate the problem of skyrocketing fuel prices by tying the hands of refiners already struggling to address supply shortages. Agriculture groups and farm-state lawmakers said the measure did not go far enough to ensure that air quality benefits would be maintained.

Box Score

- **Bill:** S 2962
- **Legislative action: Senate** Environment and Public Works Committee approved S 2962 (S Rept 106-426), 11-6, on Sept. 7.

GOP, EPA Concur On Banning Gasoline Additive

MARCH 25 — The Clinton administration, in a decision embraced by environmental groups and even some anti-regulation Republicans, proposed March 20 to ban a popular gasoline additive that has yielded cleaner air but fouled drinking water supplies nationwide.

The proposal to ban methyl tertiary butyl ether (MTBE) was generally well received, but making it happen will require that two often-incompatible interests — Congress and the EPA — join hands.

Given the strained relations between the two since the GOP won control of Congress in 1995, such a collaboration may prove difficult. Indeed, some lawmakers have already expressed concern over the fine print in the EPA's plan.

"I think we're going to do it, yes. It won't be easy," Republican Sen. Robert C. Smith of New Hampshire, chairman of the Environment and Public Works Committee, said in a March 21 interview. "There are some real roadblocks, but we're going to try. We need to do it because [MTBE is] clearly a problem."

Smith was not pleased with the route chosen by EPA Administrator Carol M. Browner. Instead of simply banning MTBE, Browner called for replacing the chemical additive with one made from renewable resources. Ethanol, which is made from corn, is the only commercially developed substitute.

"I agree with what she's said in spirit. The problem is, she's put in a new regulation," Smith said, referring to the mandate for the renewable additive.

Sen. James M. Inhofe, R-Okla., chairman of the committee's Clean Air Subcommittee, was also unhappy.

"Now is not the time to rush into a new fuels mandate, while we're facing an energy crisis," Inhofe said. "The last time EPA and Congress joined together on a fuels requirement like this, we ended up with MTBE."

As outlined by Browner, the effort relies heavily on Congress to eliminate a provision of the 1990 Clean Air Act amendments (PL 101-549) that requires gasoline sold in cities with acute air pollution to be spiked with at least 2 percent more oxygen, which produces a cleaner-burning fuel. Most refiners choose MTBE because it works, is relatively cheap and is readily available. *(1990 Almanac, p. 229)*

Using such reformulated gasoline has led to dramatic reductions in air pollution in 17 states and the District of Columbia. But that improvement has come at a high cost. MTBE is a suspected carcinogen that has leaked from storage tanks and has polluted groundwater in almost every state. California, for example, has at least 10,000 contaminated sites.

The problems with MTBE have become so acute that Congress has responded with eight bills designed to resolve the problems.

California lawmakers have been particularly active. Democrat Dianne Feinstein is cosponsor of a bill (S 1886) with Republicans Smith and Inhofe that would allow the governor of a state to waive the requirement for reformulated gasoline. The bill would require the state to continue meeting clean air standards even if the fuel standard were waived.

"Problem Must Be Addressed"

"MTBE is a problem that must be addressed," Browner said in announcing the proposed ban March 20. "If we delay too long, the problem will become worse. The time has come to take action. Americans deserve both clean air and clean water and never one at the expense of the other."

But in acknowledging the agency's strained relationship with Congress, she said the EPA will be moving on a parallel — but more time-consuming — path to force the change though regulation.

"We want to be very clear," Browner said. "The best solution to preserve clean water, clean air and . . . a clean fuels program is for Congress to act. No one should make any mistake about that. But in the meantime, we have explored every legal authority available to us."

Farmers Pleased

Regardless of whether the ban of MTBE comes through regulation or Congress, corn growers will be the big beneficiaries, since ethanol is the only alternative.

Farm-state lawmakers hailed the administration's decision to seek a ban. "The announcement is great news for farmers, clean air, clean water and efforts to reduce our dependence on foreign oil," said Senate Minority Leader Tom Daschle, D-S.D. "Under the administration's proposed framework, we can more than triple the use of ethanol over the next decade."

The EPA's proposal could increase the price of corn by as much as 10 cents a bushel, according to the Department of Agriculture's chief economist, Keith Collins. Corn sold for $1.88 a bushel last year, compared with $3.55 in 1996.

The companies that manufacture MTBE say a ban would create a host of new problems. John Kneiss, director of science, policy and research for the industry's trade association, the Oxygenated Fuels Association, said in a March 21 interview that ethanol production would not be sufficient to replace MTBE. The result, Kneiss said, would be dirtier air, higher gas prices and disruptions in the supply of gasoline.

A better choice, he said, would be for the EPA to vigorously enforce safety standards for storage tanks to reduce leaks and spills.

"We plan to make everybody very aware of the impact of this to consumers and to the public," Kneiss said.

The American Petroleum Institute (API), a major voice for the industry, also raised concerns. "API strongly opposes replacing the federal oxygenate mandate with a renewables mandate that would increase the cost of gasoline and is completely unnecessary to improving air quality," the group said in a statement.

"That's replacing one mistake with another."

Senate Panel Votes to Ban Gasoline Additive

SEPTEMBER 9 — Determined to put his panel on the record supporting a ban on MTBE, a gasoline additive now thought to be a water contaminant, Senate Environment and Public Works Committee Chairman Robert C. Smith, R-N.H., succeeded Sept. 7 in winning his panel's approval, 11-6, of legislation (S 2962) to phase it out.

Approval of the measure, which would terminate over four years the use of methyl tertiary butyl ether — a clean-burning fuel additive — answers few questions about its future. With only five weeks left in the legislative session, no House action on the subject and a sizable group of opponents, the bill faces little chance of enactment this year.

"The question is whether or not we have a bill that can pass the Senate, and I don't know the answer to that," Smith said before the vote.

Smith began a late push to move the legislation July 27 when he introduced the bill as a "compromise" designed to bridge the divide between agricultural and oil interests, as well as regional differences, that have frustrated progress on the MTBE issue.

A Mandate or a Market?

Oil refiners began using MTBE a decade ago in response to a congressionally imposed mandate — tacked onto the 1990 Clean Air Act (PL 101-549) — that requires cities with serious air pollution to sell gasoline containing 2 percent oxygen, which makes a cleaner-burning fuel.

While it helped improve air quality, MTBE, which has a strong taste and odor and is a suspected carcinogen, has been found to be leaking from thousands of underground storage tanks across the country, contaminating drinking water in some 30 states. The bill would authorize $200 million to clean up MTBE contamination.

Smith's measure would allow states to waive the oxygenate requirement, but require them to live up to the toxic emission reductions they achieved under the mandate. To do so, states would rely in large part on the corn-based oxygenate ethanol, the only commercially developed MTBE alternative.

A provision in the bill that Smith called a "market-based incentive program" — included to appease oil interests that say a straight ethanol mandate would be too expensive — would establish a portion of the gasoline market to be comprised of "clean alternative fuels," which could include premium gasoline blends or fuel cell technology in addition to ethanol.

Still, oil refiners and lawmakers who represent them said the bill is a "de facto ethanol mandate" that will exacerbate the problem of skyrocketing fuel prices by tying the hands of refiners already struggling to address shortages in supply.

"No matter how you try to disguise this thing, it is a huge ethanol mandate . . . no region of the country will escape [it]," said Marc Meteyer of the American Petroleum Institute.

Smith acknowledged that in his zeal for compromise he may have gone too far in guaranteeing the use of ethanol. "I moved over toward ethanol further than I actually wanted to," he said following the vote.

Agriculture groups and farm-state lawmakers — who estimate an ethanol mandate could increase the demand for corn by 600 million bushels a year — also criticized the measure. In particular, they say the bill does not go far enough to ensure that air quality benefits are maintained without the oxygenate requirement.

Floor Fight

The panel rejected, by voice vote, an amendment by Republican James M. Inhofe of Oklahoma to protect oil companies that manufacture or handle MTBE from liability for injury or damage associated with it. An amendment by Kay Bailey Hutchison, R-Texas, to establish a federal fund for oil companies that invested in MTBE to modify or refit their facilities to accommodate substitutes, was also rejected by voice vote.

While no amendments were adopted during the markup, opponents signaled plans to offer their own provisions should the bill reach the floor. Amendments that were withdrawn but could resurface include:

- An amendment by Inhofe that would require the Environmental Protection Agency (EPA) to study the effects of the bill's renewable fuels requirements on fuel supply, the economy, human health and the environment before allowing them to take effect.
- An Inhofe amendment that would eliminate a provision allowing the EPA to make new regulations on performance standards for fuel and additives.
- A substitute amendment by Christopher S. Bond, R-Mo., that would ban MTBE but retain the oxygenate requirement. ◆

Lawmakers, White House Spend Much of the Year Wrangling Over Oil Reserves

Box Score

- **Bill:** HR 2884 — PL 106-469
- **Legislative action: House** passed HR 2884 (H Rept 106-359), 416-8, April 12.

Senate passed HR 2884, amended, by voice vote, Oct. 19.

House cleared HR 2884, by voice vote, Oct. 24.

President signed the bill Nov. 9.

SUMMARY

After failing several times to move a broader energy package in a year of rising fuel prices, Congress sent President Clinton legislation to reauthorize the Strategic Petroleum Reserve and create a home heating oil reserve in the Northeast.

There was little controversy over the central element of the bill: reauthorizing the Strategic Petroleum Reserve for three years. But the legislation was bogged down for almost a year by side issues and policy differences, such as when oil could be sold from the reserve.

Democrats charged that the failure to pass the legislation before the reserve's authorization expired March 31 put the country at risk. The Clinton administration said it had emergency power to swap small quantities of oil from the reserve, and did so Sept. 22 to bolster the supply of home heating oil. Republicans criticized the move and some even questioned its legality.

The final obstacle to the bill was a dispute over language the Senate added that would have allowed oil companies to pay their government royalties in oil instead of cash. Barbara Boxer, D-Calif., charged that the provision would undermine a new Interior Department regulation intended to increase royalties. Supporters of the provision relented and dropped it after a five-week standoff.

The bill would authorize a home heating oil reserve in the Northeast, where prices were expected to soar over the winter. As the House prepared to debate the measure in April, Democrats made the heating oil reserve their top priority. The idea of another petroleum reserve was more controversial in the Senate, where some Western Republicans strongly opposed the idea.

Clinton created a home heating oil reserve by executive order on July 10 but could not release oil from it without congressional authorization. The Senate added language that will clarify under what circumstances oil can be released from the heating oil reserve.

Lott Promotes 'Gas-Tax Holiday'

APRIL 1 — Even before OPEC oil producers decided March 28 to increase their output, which should eventually ease prices, Republicans in Congress were planning to keep the oil issue alive for months to come.

"The search is on for a villain for high oil prices," Sen. Jeff Bingaman, D-N.M., commented dryly. "Some would like the villain to be at the other end of Pennsylvania Avenue."

Senate Republicans opened a new front on the issue by raising national security concerns about the country's heavy reliance on foreign oil. They accused President Clinton of ignoring a Commerce Department report about the possible danger.

Senate Majority Leader Trent Lott, R-Miss., meanwhile, pushed to the floor a "gas-tax holiday" bill (S 2285) that aimed to give consumers short-term relief from soaring fuel prices. The measure, which would suspend all or part of the federal gasoline tax, depending on prices at the pump, was never marked up by committee.

"Something needs to be done now," Lott said.

The Senate GOP also was putting the finishing touches on a wide-ranging energy plan that party leaders said would revive the ailing domestic oil industry. Republicans in both the House and Senate complained that Clinton lacked such a plan.

"Today's escalating prices at the pump are a direct result of a failed Clinton-Gore energy policy that leaves America with no domestic energy alternatives and puts this great nation at the mercy of OPEC," said House Majority Whip Tom DeLay, R-Texas.

Clinton, at a March 29 news conference, responded, "I think it is ironic that they would say that since for years now I have been pleading with them to give us some more tools to promote the development of alternative fuels and to promote both the manufacture and the purchase of energy-saving technologies."

Energy self-reliance, Clinton said, will result from greater efficiency and alternative fuels, not from more domestic drilling.

The administration breathed a sigh of relief after members of the Organization of Petroleum Exporting Countries (OPEC) announced that they would increase combined oil production by 1.7 million barrels per day. Since several members already were exceeding the limit, the net increase was estimated at about 1 million barrels a day.

While the increase fell short of the 2 million-barrel target the administration pushed for, Energy Secretary Bill Richardson expressed confidence that additional production from Mexico and Norway, neither of which are in OPEC, would help fill the gap.

Richardson said it would take four to six weeks for the OPEC crude oil to make it to refineries, so consumers were facing high gas prices for several more months. But he predicted a price drop of 11 cents a gallon by September.

Richardson's high-pressure diplomatic efforts tried the patience of at least two U.S. allies in OPEC — Saudi Arabia and Kuwait — and offended Iran, which refused to endorse the production increase at the alliance's meeting in Vienna.

That may have achieved an unstated U.S. goal: breaking up the détente that Saudi Arabia and Iran have been developing. Cooperation between OPEC's two largest producers had helped restore the unity that made OPEC a world player again.

Republicans expressed frustration over the OPEC deliberations and U.S. dependence on the outcome, and they blamed Clinton for the increasing imports of oil during his two terms.

"I cannot understand why this great nation would allow its destiny to be determined by a small group of nations in the most unstable part of the world," said Sen. Larry E. Craig, R-Idaho. "It's time to put our domestic supply and our national security together."

The United States imported 37 percent of its oil in 1975 and 47.2 percent in 1990. It imports 52.7 percent today, according to the Energy Department. The decline in U.S. production began when the international price of oil collapsed in 1985.

Republicans also criticized the administration for proposing on March 21 that the United Nations allow Iraq to double the money it can spend on spare parts for its oil industry.

Iraq's allowable oil exports under the U.N.'s "oil for food" program have gradually increased. Republicans charged that the increased exports at the current high price would give Saddam Hussein more funds to build weapons of mass destruction.

Senate Armed Services Chairman John W. Warner, R-Va., said high oil prices are "driving up the costs of operating military equipment worldwide. It is having an effect on the defense budget and on readiness accounts."

Republicans said the administration dragged its feet in responding to a November 1999 Commerce Department report that U.S. dependence on foreign oil weakened national security. The White House took no apparent notice of the report until March.

Lott, Warner, Senate Energy Committee Chairman Frank H. Murkowski, R-Alaska, and Senate Foreign Relations Committee Chairman Jesse Helms, R-N.C., wrote Clinton on March 21: "The actions taken by the administration since that time have only served to aggravate the situation. Your administration has repeatedly taken actions to limit access to domestic oil and gas supplies from exploration through production and even to transportation."

In a March 24 memo to Commerce Secretary William M. Daley, Clinton agreed with Daley's recommendations to continue policies to promote renewable energy sources, conservation and tax credits for oil producers.

Clinton did not address access to public lands or lower oil and gas royalties — two key priorities for the oil and gas industry.

Short-Term Relief

Senate Republican leaders were moving quickly on their proposed gas-tax holiday despite the misgivings of some lawmakers.

The legislation would suspend 4.3 cents of the 18.4 cents-a-gallon federal gasoline tax between April 15 and Dec. 31, 2000. If the average price of unleaded regular gasoline reached $2 a gallon, the remainder of the tax would be suspended through Dec. 31. The plan calls for using the budget surplus to replace revenue lost from the Highway Trust Fund.

But despite a strong push from the Senate leadership, many Republicans opposed the plan.

Lobbying by road builders strengthened opponents of the plan, including Warner and Sen. George V. Voinovich, R-Ohio. Senators representing states that received large increases in road construction funds from the 1998 surface transportation law (PL 105-178) also lined up against the plan. It was opposed by the National Governors' Association, the American Association of State and Local Highway and Transportation Officials, and the American Automobile Association. *(1998 Almanac, p. 24-3)*

Voinovich, a former Ohio governor who lobbied for the highway and transit funding guarantees in the 1998 law, said governors did not want to fight the surface transportation battle over again. Voinovich said states would end up fighting over the budget surplus with those who want to pay down the national debt, shore up Social Security and help Medicare beneficiaries buy prescription drugs.

Democrats said they doubted that the surplus could accommodate the estimated $150 billion in proposed tax cuts outlined in the House version of the fiscal 2001 budget resolution (H Con Res 290) and the gas tax rollback.

By week's end, at least nine Senate Republicans indicated that they were against the gas-tax rollback. Democrats were embracing the chance to debate the bill, confident they had the votes to defeat it.

Diminishing Returns

Though the tax cut might lower gasoline prices, it could encourage more consumption and work against the goal of reducing the U.S. dependence on imported oil, said David M. Nemtzow, president of the nonprofit Alliance to Save Energy.

Congress has blocked the Department of Transportation from studying whether to update fuel efficiency standards each year since 1995.

If fuel economy does not improve, American cars and trucks will consume 1.7 million barrels of oil a day more by the end of the next decade — the exact amount of the OPEC production increase, Nemtzow said. "OPEC is back in the driver's seat, and Congress gave them the keys," he said.

Republicans, meanwhile, were putting the finishing touches on their long-term energy plan, focusing on policies that would encourage the expansion of the domestic oil drilling industry.

Because of the relatively high costs of producing oil in this country, U.S. oil production dropped from a peak of 9.6 million barrels per day in 1970 to 6.3 million barrels per day in 1998.

The extremely low $10-per-barrel prices that American consumers enjoyed in 1998 and 1999 took their toll on American oil producers. Many marginal wells were plugged, and oil producers say those reserves are lost forever.

The high price of crude oil now will make domestic sources more attractive, but drilling is a risky proposition, producers say. The volatility of oil prices makes lenders hesitant to fund oil projects.

The GOP energy plan would seek to address the problem that oil producers have in raising capital by giving them tax incentives that could offset losses in times of low oil prices. The plan aims to boost domestic oil production by 1.5 million barrels a day.

In the short term, the plan would open some public lands for oil exploration, specifically in the Rocky Mountains.

The plan also would encourage more drilling in the Outer Continental Shelf. In the long-term, it would encourage exploration in the Arctic National Wildlife Refuge (ANWR), which Clinton has strongly opposed.

House Votes to Reauthorize Reserve

APRIL 15 — Republicans in Congress have run into more problems trying to capitalize on consumer frustration with high oil prices.

An effort by Senate leaders to roll back at least part of the federal gasoline tax collapsed April 11 in the face of bipartisan opposition.

Although the House on April 12 passed a bill (HR 2884), 416-8, that would reauthorize the Strategic Petroleum Reserve, prospects for a quick conference with the Senate, which passed similar legislation (S 1051) last Sept. 29, are dim. The current authorization expired March 31. *(Vote 122, p. H-42)*

Meanwhile, policy differences among Republicans have delayed release of a Senate GOP energy package that is likely to include incentives designed to increase domestic oil production.

Senate leaders pulled the gas tax bill (S 2285) after a vote on April 11 to limit debate failed, 43-56, 17 votes short of the 60 necessary. *(Vote 80, p. S-17)*

Even though oil prices already had begun falling after a decision by oil producing nations to increase supplies, Majority Leader Trent Lott, R-Miss., the bill's author, vowed to return to the issue.

The public, Lott said, overwhelmingly backs the gas tax rollback. "If not this, what? If not now, when?" Lott told reporters April 11. "This issue will not go away."

"We're still going to be 55 percent dependent on foreign oil," Lott said. "One of these days, [foreign producers are] going to turn off the spigot and [this] economy will be on its knees."

Republican Frank H. Murkowski of Alaska, chairman of the Senate Energy and Natural Resources Committee, said that one of President Clinton's solutions to high prices is to import more oil from Iraq.

"How in the world can we justify being at war with Saddam Hussein, increasing our dependence to 700,000 barrels a day?" Murkowski asked. "We are really taking his oil, putting it into our airplanes, and going over and bombing. . . . Is that the kind of policy we have on energy?"

But Lott had trouble holding some Republicans who support his efforts to fashion an overall energy policy. Twelve Republicans defected on the April 11 cloture vote.

Lott's promise that the tax rollback would not harm highway construction programs that depend on the revenue failed to win over key Republicans, including George V. Voinovich of Ohio and John W. Warner of Virginia, two supporters of the 1998 surface transportation law (PL 105-178), which tied highway spending levels to gasoline tax receipts in the Highway Trust Fund. *(1998 Almanac, p. 24-3)*

Voinovich was chairman of the National Governors' Association when the 1998 law was written and now is chairman of the Environment and Public Works Subcommittee on Transportation and Infrastructure. He said that rolling back the gas tax would break a vow made to the states to ensure a steady revenue stream for highway and transit projects.

Warner, who was chairman of the Transportation and Infrastructure Subcommittee in 1998, said the surface transportation law was only now beginning to fulfill its promise.

The American people "see this cancer of the transportation system slowly devouring their lifestyle," Warner said. "Stability in this program is essential because these modernization programs cannot be done overnight."

Reviving the Reserve

The House ended its stalemate over the future of the Strategic Petroleum Reserve by passing a reauthorization that also would allow the government to buy oil from marginal wells — those that produce fewer than 15 barrels a day — when the price falls below $15 a barrel.

Joe L. Barton, R-Texas, argued that the provision would save money, because the reserve had been filled with oil at $27 per barrel, on average. He also said the government purchases would help keep the marginal wells, which often lose money when the price of oil drops, in production.

Critics say it is potentially expensive to truck oil from thousands of small wells to the reserve sites along the Gulf Coast. The usual method of getting oil there now is by pipeline. Barton said the transportation infrastructure is already in place. "That oil is already going somewhere," he said.

Sen. Kay Bailey Hutchison, R-Texas, has introduced legislation (S 2265) aimed at propping up small oil producers when prices drop. That measure would rely on a tax credit phased in when oil prices fall below $17 a barrel.

A coalition of northeastern lawmakers, including Reps. Edward J. Markey, D-Mass., and Vito J. Fossella,

R-N.Y., had language included in the oil reserve bill that would create a two-million-barrel home heating oil reserve to help their region in case oil prices again rose sharply in winter.

Rather than establish a regional oil reserve, the Senate version of the legislation, like an earlier administration proposal, would repeal the government's authority to establish regional reserves.

Testifying on the issue last Sept. 22, Robert W. Gee, the Department of Energy's assistant secretary for fossil energy, said there was no foreseeable need for a regional reserve.

After pressure from northeastern lawmakers, however, the Clinton administration changed its policy. A House Democratic aide said the Northeast reserve provisions added to HR 2884 were close to a proposal Clinton made in a March 18 radio address.

Plan Lacks Energy

A Senate Republican task force led by Murkowski continued to refine the elements of an energy package the week of April 10. But the panel has had difficulty in arriving at a consensus about what to include and what to emphasize in the plan.

The package is expected to stake out a markedly different energy policy than the Clinton administration has pursued. For example, it will emphasize oil drilling efforts that the administration has discouraged for environmental reasons.

Lott noted the administration's threat to veto a nuclear waste storage bill (S 1287), attempts by the EPA to limit the use of coal and the lack of incentives for natural gas production, and he asked: "What do they propose?"

But supporters of the administration say Republicans have downplayed the environmental problems while overselling the potential of their proposals, especially in oil production. A main factor in the decline of the American oil industry is the high cost of recovering its dwindling reserves. It is simply cheaper to produce oil elsewhere, they say.

"In a global economy, they will produce energy where it is least expensive to produce. You can bring up oil under the sands in the Persian Gulf for a fraction of the cost of bringing up oil in the United States," said Sen. Byron L. Dorgan, D-N.D.

Senate Passes Bill To Reauthorize Strategic Reserve

OCTOBER 21 — The Senate passed legislation that would reauthorize the Strategic Petroleum Reserve and stockpile home heating oil for the Northeast, after dropping a provision on federal oil royalties that had upset some conservationists.

The Senate passed the measure (HR 2884) Oct. 19 by voice vote, and it now returns to the House for final approval or a conference.

The bill, which languished for seven months in the House and five in the Senate, was blocked in September by Democratic Sen. Barbara Boxer of California. She contended that a last-minute provision added by Energy and Natural Resources Committee Chairman Frank H. Murkowski, R-Alaska, could have allowed oil companies to avoid paying higher royalties for drilling on public lands. The royalties go to the Interior Department's land and water conservation fund.

Murkowski dropped his royalties provision the week of Oct. 16. He added a requirement that the Defense secretary assess and report whether any future draw-down of oil from the petroleum reserve would harm national security. Republicans have criticized President Clinton for trading some oil from the reserve to buffer a recent spike in fuel prices.

The authorization for the reserve expired March 31, but the president has authority to swap small quantities to deal with minor supply problems. The bill would reauthorize the reserve for three years.

The legislation also would authorize a new home heating oil reserve in the Northeast and clarify the conditions under which the president could draw down the oil.

Murkowski's provision would have allowed oil companies to pay their government royalties with oil instead of cash. Boxer said that might undermine a new federal rule designed to increase royalties by basing them on the market price of oil, rather than on company estimates.

House Clears Narrowed Version Of Oil Bill

OCTOBER 28 — Congress cleared a narrowly targeted energy bill Oct. 24 that would reauthorize the Strategic Petroleum Reserve and create a home heating oil reserve in the Northeast.

Congress failed to move more comprehensive energy legislation despite wide-ranging concern about high energy prices and rising dependence on foreign oil. Lawmakers remained widely divided on issues such as increased drilling on public lands and tighter fuel economy standards for cars and trucks.

The House agreed to Senate amendments and cleared the more modest reserves bill (HR 2884), by voice vote, on Oct. 24. President Clinton is expected to sign it.

There was little controversy over the central element: reauthorizing the nearly 570 million-barrel Strategic Petroleum Reserve for three years. Side issues such as marginal oil wells and oil royalties had delayed the bill for more than a year.

Authorization for the petroleum reserve expired March 31, and Democrats said that Congress' failure to extend it had placed the country at risk. The administration said it had emergency power to make small-scale swaps from the reserve, but Republicans criticized Clinton's Sept. 22 decision to release 30 million barrels of oil to cushion a home heating oil price increase.

Sen. Frank H. Murkowski, R-Alaska, added a provision that would require the Defense secretary to assess and report whether future releases from the reserve would affect national security.

The legislation would authorize a home heating oil reserve in the Northeast, a key sweetener for lawmakers from that region. Clinton created such a reserve by executive order on July 10, but the administration can not actually release oil from it without authorization.

The Senate added language that would clarify under what circumstances oil can be released from the heating oil reserve. ◆

Chapter 11

FOREIGN POLICY

Helms Gets Most of What He Wants by Dividing Foreign Aid Bill Into Parts

SUMMARY

When his foreign aid authorization bill (S 2382) ran aground in the Senate Banking, Housing and Urban Affairs Committee, Foreign Relations Committee Chairman Jesse Helms, R-N.C., successfully moved parts of it as separate legislation. The pieces included bills for overseas military assistance, loans for "microenterprises" and a World Bank trust fund to combat HIV/AIDS.

Other parts of the original bill were incorporated in the final version of the fiscal 2001 foreign operations appropriations bill (PL 106-429). A bill to promote democracy in Serbia stalled.

Because of declining congressional support for foreign aid and bitter disagreements over policy, Congress has not fully authorized the program since 1985 (PL 99-83). As a result, members of the House and Senate foreign affairs committees have lost much of their influence to appropriators who fashion the annual foreign operations spending bills.

This year, in an effort to reclaim territory, Helms and ranking Democrat Joseph R. Biden Jr. of Delaware introduced legislation (S 2382) that would have authorized the bulk of foreign aid spending while avoiding such politically vulnerable programs as basic development assistance and aid to Russia.

Helms was unable to move the measure to the Senate floor because of opposition from Banking Committee Chairman Phil Gramm, R-Texas, who claimed jurisdiction and insisted that the Clinton administration first agree to changes in the operation of the International Monetary Fund and other international financial institutions.

Helms had better luck moving some components of his legislation.

• The largest bill (HR 4919) authorized $3.6 billion per year in fiscal 2001 and 2002 for foreign military aid and military training, anti-terrorism, non-proliferation and export control assistance. The legislation took steps to make it easier to export defense-related technology to friendly countries and for U.S. companies to launch satellites from several former Soviet republics.

The bill also met one of Helms' key goals by increasing military aid to countries other than Israel, Egypt and Jordan.

• **AIDS.** Congress also cleared legislation (HR 3519) authorizing $300 million in annual bilateral aid for programs to combat the spread of HIV/AIDS in fiscal 2001 and 2002. The new law also authorized the Treasury Department to work with the World Bank on the creation of a trust fund to raise money to help fight HIV/AIDS and educate children orphaned by the disease. Once the trust fund is established, the United States is authorized to contribute $150 million a year in fiscal 2001 and 2002.

• **"Microenterprises."** Helms scored another victory when Congress cleared legislation (HR 1143) authorizing $155 million in fiscal 2001 and 2002 for small loans for "microenterprises" — businesses with 10 or fewer employees — in developing countries.

• **U.S.-Serbia Relations.** Legislation (HR 1064) aimed at promoting a democratic transition in Serbia ground to a halt in the Senate when some lawmakers, led by Republican Policy Committee Chairman Larry E. Craig of Idaho, objected that by writing some existing sanctions into law, the bill might make it too difficult for the White House to eventually lift sanctions on a new government after the departure of former Yugoslav President Slobodan Milosevic, ousted in a peaceful revolt in early October.

Box Score

• **Bills:** S 2382; HR 4919 — PL 106-280; HR 1143 — PL 106-309; HR 3519— PL 106-264; HR 1064

• **Legislative action: Senate** Foreign Relations Committee approved S 2382 (S Rept 106-257) by voice vote March 23.

House passed HR 4919 by voice vote July 24.

Senate passed HR 4919, after substituting the text of S 2901 (S Rept 106-351), by voice vote Sept. 7.

House adopted the conference report on HR 4919 (H Rept 106-868), 396-17, on Sept. 21.

Senate cleared HR 4919 by voice vote Sept. 22.

President signed HR 4919 on Oct. 6.

Senate passed HR 1143 by voice vote Oct. 3.

House cleared the bill by voice vote Oct. 5.

President signed HR 1143 Oct. 17.

House passed HR 3519 (H Rept 106-548) by voice vote May 15.

Senate passed HR 3519, amended, by voice vote July 26.

House cleared HR 3519 by voice vote July 27.

President signed HR 3519 Aug. 19.

Foreign Aid Bill Returns Reins To Senate Panel

MARCH 25 — Attempting to reassert control over foreign aid spending that it has ceded to appropriators since the mid-1980s, the Senate Foreign Relations Committee on March 23 approved a limited authorization bill.

The draft measure, approved on a voice vote, touches on subjects ranging from lifting restrictions on the sale of food and medicine abroad to debt relief for the world's poorest countries. But it steers clear of some basic development programs that lack strong political constituencies.

Congress has not cleared a comprehensive foreign aid authorization bill since 1985 (PL 99-83). The last sustained attempt was in 1993, when the House passed a measure that the Senate failed to consider. A House committee bill in 1997 was swallowed by a State Department authorization measure drafted by House leaders. *(1985 Almanac, p. 41; 1993 Almanac, p. 502; 1997 Almanac, p. 8-32)*

Although the committee made several significant changes at the March 23 markup, the most important aspects of the legislation had been worked out in months of closed-door negotiations between Chairman Jesse Helms, R-N.C., ranking Democrat Joseph R. Biden Jr. of Delaware and other committee members.

They include:

- Further debt relief for the world's poorest countries, a key Clinton administration goal. The measure would authorize a total of $600 million in fiscal years 2000-03 for a multilateral debt relief fund administered by the World Bank.

The draft also would let the International Monetary Fund (IMF) set new, higher values for the gold its members have on deposit, freeing up new funds that would allow the international organization to forgive some debts owed by poor countries.

In return, the measure calls for the Treasury Department to show that the World Bank and the IMF are adopting new polices to spur reform, fight corruption, operate with more openness and restrict their missions to core functions, such as grants to the poorest countries for the World Bank and short-term lending by the IMF. But the draft bill stops short of more drastic restrictions on the two organizations urged by House Majority Leader Dick Armey, R-Texas, and an independent congressionally appointed commission earlier this month.

- An effective end to U.S. sanctions on food and medicine. The provision would allow sales of such products to countries, such as Cuba, that are on the State Department's list of terrorist nations. The language is essentially identical to a provision the Senate approved last year in the fiscal 2000 agriculture appropriations bill (S 1233) but later dropped in conference after opposition from House conservatives led by Majority Whip Tom DeLay, R-Texas.

- A modified version of legislation (S 1453) the Senate passed last year designed to help end a civil war in Sudan.

The measure calls for an administration report on the means that the Sudanese government is using to finance oil field development. The bill would grant the president authority to assist groups that have not come under Sudanese control and ensure that food gets to southern Sudan if Khartoum prohibits U.N. relief flights.

- Legislation that Helms included in the fiscal 2000 omnibus spending bill (PL 106-113) to give financial support to a democratic opposition to Yugoslav President Slobodan Milosevic.

- Authority for $310 million in "microenterprise" loans over two years and the creation of new funds and programs to provide the loans. Such loans, usually only several hundred dollars apiece, are designed to help poor people in developing countries start their own businesses.

- Denying U.S. funds for 10 years to any international family planning organization that violates the Helms amendment to the 1973 foreign aid authorization law (PL 93-189) that prohibits the use of U.S. funds to perform abortions overseas. *(1973 Almanac, p. 816)*

Attacking AIDS

By voice vote, the committee also approved a Helms amendment that would significantly increase authorized funds to attack AIDS and other diseases, particularly in Africa — a key administration priority.

The measure would authorize $300 million in new funds in fiscal 2001 for U.S.-run AIDS prevention programs. It would authorize donating $60 million to two public/private partnerships supported by Microsoft founder Bill Gates to promote vaccines and immunization for developing countries.

And the bill includes a provision, similar to legislation (HR 3519) approved March 15 by the House Banking and Financial Services Committee, that would endorse creating a World Bank trust fund to provide grants to fight the spread of AIDS worldwide.

The most controversial issue during the markup was an attempt by GOP Sen. Richard G. Lugar of Indiana to win inclusion of legislation (S 757) he has championed for several years, with support from business organizations, to make it more difficult for Congress to impose unilateral trade sanctions. His measure would require that Congress weigh the costs and benefits of proposed sanctions, and it would automatically end those Congress did not renew.

"The effect of unilateral sanctions in almost every instance is that they did not work," Lugar said.

But he was opposed by both Helms and Biden, and his amendment was defeated, 8-10.

Helms said the measure "needlessly bureaucratizes the process of enacting sanctions." Biden said a more reasonable approach would be to give the president more authority to waive sanctions.

Helms also blocked an amendment by Democrat Paul S. Sarbanes of Maryland that would have eliminated a provision exempting U.S. intelligence activities from a ban on U.S. aid to the government of Azerbaijan, a former Soviet republic on the shores of the Caspian Sea. Sarbanes' amendment failed on a tie 9-9 vote.

But Helms lost a close vote as the committee agreed, 10-8, to an amendment by Democrat Christopher J. Dodd of Connecticut, to restore funding for the 30-year-old Inter-American Foundation.

The panel also approved, by voice vote, an amendment by Republican John Ashcroft of Missouri incorporating his legislation (S 2106) to assist developing countries with regulatory systems that can review the benefits and potential risks of biotechnology based on objective scientific principles.

The safety of biologically engineered agricultural products has become a major trade issue for the United States.

IMF Dispute Holds Up Foreign Aid Bill

MAY 27 — A dispute between the Clinton administration and Senate Banking Committee Chairman Phil Gramm, R-Texas, over the International Monetary Fund (IMF) continues to delay major foreign aid legislation that includes debt relief for the world's poorest nations.

Gramm last month asserted his prerogative to have his committee examine the foreign aid authorization measure (S 2382 — S Rept 106-257), approved by the Senate Foreign Relations Committee on March 23, before it comes to the Senate floor.

Gramm, a critic of the IMF, then insisted that the administration agree to major changes in the way the IMF does business before he would allow the authorization to go forward.

But the Texas Republican, who said he had hoped his panel would take up the legislation May 24, said those issues are far from being worked out.

The dispute has prevented Senate consideration of a provision in the legislation that would allow the IMF to provide debt relief by profiting — to the tune of nearly $1 billion — from the difference between the current market price of gold (about $300 an ounce) and its value on the IMF books (about $47 an ounce). The gold is held in reserve by the IMF as a guarantee on its loans.

Senate appropriators also are waiting for Gramm's go-ahead before they agree to provide most of the funds that the Clinton administration has requested for debt relief.

A fiscal 2001 foreign operations appropriations bill (S 2522 — S Rept 106-291), approved by the Appropriations Committee on May 9, includes $75 million of the $472 million that President Clinton requested for debt relief in fiscal years 2000 and 2001.

"We've tried to see if we could work out something with the administration," Gramm said in a May 23 interview, "but we're far apart" on such issues as whether the IMF should be restricted to short-term lending.

"No reform, no bill," Gramm said.

House Passes Tough Curbs on Military Exports

JULY 29 — The House has passed legislation that would set strict conditions on the ability of U.S. companies to sell military equipment and technology to friendly nations without export licenses.

The restrictions are part of an otherwise routine bill (HR 4919) authorizing security assistance to other countries and transferring surplus naval vessels. The bill, introduced by International Relations Committee Chairman Benjamin A. Gilman, R-N.Y., passed the House on July 24 by voice vote.

The chairmen and ranking Democrats on the House and Senate foreign affairs committees have been concerned for some time about new administration rules urged by the Defense Department that would allow close U.S. allies, such as Britain and Australia, to buy defense goods without the cumbersome licensing process for munitions. The State Department had opposed the plan.

Under Gilman's bill, foreign countries could be exempt from licensing only if they had signed a bilateral agreement with the United States to adopt an export control regime, including written U.S. approval of third country transfers and monitoring where the equipment eventually winds up.

In May, the administration threatened to end Canada's 60-year exemption from military export licensing after U.S. equipment sold to Canada was found in Iran and China. Canada said the hardware was outdated.

The United States and Canada signed an agreement in June to restore about 80 percent of the exemption after Canada agreed to change its export control laws.

The bill also would allow the export of commercial communications satellites to all NATO countries, Australia, Japan, New Zealand, Russia and Ukraine without congressional review. The State Department now must allow Congress 30 days to review such exports.

Senate Passes Military Aid Measure

SEPTEMBER 9 — Blocked earlier this year from moving a broad foreign aid authorization bill (S 2382), Senate Foreign Relations Committee Chairman Jesse Helms, R-N.C., is gaining ground in his strategy of moving parts of the measure by themselves.

On Sept. 7, the Senate passed, by unanimous consent and without debate, its version of legislation (HR 4919) that would authorize $3.9 billion for military aid and counterproliferation programs for fiscal 2001, $119 million more than President Clinton requested. Lawmakers said they added the extra funds because 98 percent of Clinton's request was dedicated to Israel, Egypt and Jordan to support the Middle East peace process.

The Foreign Relations Committee expressed concern in its report on the bill that "a steadily increasing number of countries are pursuing a relationship with the United States which is funded by a steadily decreasing amount of money."

In addition to military aid, the bill would authorize $19 million extra for initiatives designed to curb the spread of nuclear weapons.

The measure must now be reconciled with the House version of the military aid bill that would impose new restrictions on the export of military equipment and technology to friendly nations. A conference is expected the week of Sept. 11.

Meanwhile, the House International Relations Committee on Sept. 7 approved, by voice vote, legislation (HR 1064) that would authorize $105 million to support the democratic opposition to Yugoslav President Slobodan Milosevic. The measure originally was included in Helms' foreign aid bill.

Helms' aides said details of the legislation already had been worked out between the House and Senate so that when the measure is passed by the House, an identical measure can be quickly passed by the Senate.

However, at the urging of the State Department, the House is not expected to take up the bill until after elections Sept. 24 in Milosevic's homeland of Serbia.

Tough Going

Two other parts of Helms' package face higher hurdles.

Administration officials and Senate aides still must resolve disputes over funding levels in a measure (S 2844) that would authorize a program of small loans to budding entrepreneurs in developing countries.

The biggest holdup is on the most controversial bill: draft legislation that would authorize the forgiveness of debts that poor countries owe to international financial institutions.

The same issue also has dogged the fiscal 2001 foreign operations appropriations bill (HR 4811), and most aides on Capitol Hill and in the executive branch expect that it will only be resolved as part of endgame budget negotiations, and then just in the spending bill.

Senate Banking Committee Chairman Phil Gramm, R-Texas, had held up Helms' original measure in order to force changes on the debt relief provisions. In a Sept. 5 interview, however, Gramm said that he had reached an "agreement on principles" with Treasury Secretary Lawrence H. Summers.

Military Aid Bill Clears Quickly After Negotiators Work Out Deal

SEPTEMBER 23 — Standing alone amid the clutter of an earlier meeting, House International Relations Committee Chairman Benjamin A. Gilman, R-N.Y., opened and moments later adjourned the formal conference on a bill that would authorize some foreign aid — military assistance in this case — for the first time in 15 years.

Working behind closed doors, House and Senate negotiators had ironed out the final details of a fiscal 2001-02 foreign military aid bill (HR 4919) before Gilman's lone meeting Sept. 19.

The House adopted the conference report, 396-17, on Sept. 21. The Senate cleared the bill by unanimous consent on Sept. 22. *(House vote 485, p. H-152)*

The measure would authorize $3.8 billion in fiscal 2001 and $3.9 billion in fiscal 2002 for foreign military financing and military training, antiterrorism, non-proliferation and export control assistance.

Congress has not fully authorized these programs since 1985, the last time it passed a free-standing foreign aid bill (PL 99-83). Instead, the programs have been funded through the annual appropriations bills.

This year, Foreign Relations Committee Chairman Jesse Helms, R-N.C., has made a determined push to revive the power of the foreign affairs committees. He has met some success by steering clear of the most politically vulnerable programs — those that provide basic development assistance, for example, or aid to Russia. When his broad foreign aid bill (S 2382) was blocked in the Senate Banking Committee, he started moving it in installments.

The military aid measure meets one of Helms' key goals by increasing aid and U.S. military training for countries outside the Middle East — $99 million more in fiscal 2002 for countries other than Israel, Egypt and Jordan. The three now receive 98 percent of U.S. military assistance, according to committee reports on the bill.

The measure would specify $30.3 million in fiscal 2001 and $35 million in fiscal 2002 for military aid to new NATO members Poland, Hungary and the Czech Republic. It also would set aside significant military aid and training funds for NATO aspirants such as Romania, Bulgaria, and Estonia.

Middle East Players

Israel and Egypt were hardly slighted in the conference report. It would codify a 1998 agreement under which Israel agreed to phase out U.S. economic assistance over 10 years in return for receiving half the funds in increased military aid. In fiscal 2001, the bill would authorize about $2 billion in military aid and $840 million in economic assistance to Israel.

Israel would still be allowed to spend about one-quarter of its military aid on Israeli-made weapons. Other recipients have to buy U.S. made products. Israel also would still receive all of its aid near the start of the fiscal year in order to benefit from the interest earnings.

Egypt won a similar though less lucrative early disbursement option.

The bill also authorized for the first time a number of counterproliferation programs, including anti-terrorist efforts and programs to prevent the spread of advanced weapons and technology from the former Soviet Union.

The legislation also calls for assessing the effectiveness of training programs for foreign military personnel — such as the Army's School of the Americas — by tracking the performance of graduates, including any human rights abuses or criminal activity.

Controlling Exports

Conferees took some steps to make it easier to export defense-related technology to friendly countries, primarily NATO members. In the most controversial step, they agreed to an administration plan to open negotiations with such allies as Australia and Britain to largely bypass U.S. export control laws, provided those nations sign binding accords that violations of U.S. export controls would be treated as violations of their domestic laws.

Negotiators agreed to a House effort to make it easier for U.S. companies to launch satellites from countries other than China, shortening the congressional review period for satellite exports to such countries as Russia, Ukraine and Kazakhstan from 30 to 15 days.

But they stopped short of endorsing an effort by Sam Gejdenson of Connecticut, ranking Democrat on the International Relations Committee, to shift jurisdiction over such exports back to the Commerce Department from the State Department, saying such a change should be deferred. Differences over the issue have prevented passage of legislation (S 1712) this year that would reauthorize the Export Administration Act.

Helms Splits Foreign Aid Bill Into Four

JULY 1 — Frustrated by a rival chairman's decision to hold up a foreign aid authorization bill (S 2382), Senate Foreign Relations Committee Chairman Jesse Helms, R-N.C., on June 28 split the measure into four bills that he will try to advance separately to the Senate floor.

Helms' action was endorsed by the rest of the Foreign Relations Committee, which approved the bills and a broader slate of legislation and ambassadorial nominations by a single voice vote.

The new, so far unnumbered bills would relieve the debts of some of the world's poorest countries; authorize more money to combat HIV/AIDS, tuberculosis and other diseases; authorize an increase in U.S. military assistance overseas; and authorize a program of small loans to budding entrepreneurs in developing countries.

While most of the measures enjoy broad support, forgiving debts that poor countries owe to international financial institutions has become a major sticking point between congressional Republicans and the Clinton administration. The issue is part of the debate over the fiscal 2001 foreign operations appropriations bills (S 2522, unnumbered House bill).

In the Senate, appropriators held off providing most of the money the administration requested for debt relief, saying they first wanted the funds authorized. In marking up the original foreign aid authorization bill, the Foreign Relations Committee largely met the administration's goal, conditioning the payment on internal changes at the International Monetary Fund and other international financial institutions.

Yet Helms was unable to advance that bill to the Senate floor because Banking Committee Chairman Phil Gramm, R-Texas, demanded that his committee consider it.

Gramm wants to force more drastic changes at the financial institutions than Helms agreed to in negotiations with the Treasury Department. Gramm has been unable to persuade a majority of his committee to support the tougher restrictions.

In an interview after the June 28 markup, Helms said he hoped Gramm would release his bill. "I don't understand why they don't go along and do it, because it's an important piece of legislation," he said.

Helms has offered as a compromise to introduce jointly with Gramm an amendment on the Senate floor calling for broader changes at the international financial institutions, aides said.

Other lawmakers, however, said that Gramm had another motive for holding up the debt relief legislation: forcing Helms to side with him on a proposed reauthorization of the Export Administration Act (S 1712 — S Rept 106-180).

That bill has been held up for months by a dispute among the chairmen of four Senate committees over which Cabinet department — Commerce, Defense or State — should have the most control over the export of "dual use" products and technology — those with both military and civilian applications. Helms and Gramm, traditional allies, have found themselves on opposite sides of the issue.

In a June 28 interview, Chuck Hagel, R-Neb., who serves on both the Foreign Relations and Banking committees and supports both of the controversial bills, said that Gramm had linked the fate of the two measures. "He's saying that since they've taken our bill hostage, we're going to hold up theirs," Hagel said. "There doesn't seem to be any way to get beyond that at this point."

Banking Committee spokeswoman Christi Harlan denied a link. "I think Sen. Hagel needs to listen more closely when Chairman Gramm speaks at committee hearings on his commitment to reform of the IMF," Harlan said.

Other measures approved by the Foreign Relations Committee are less likely to ignite controversy. The military aid measure is nearly identical to an unnumbered bill approved by the House International Relations Committee on June 29.

The Senate committee also approved a host of nominations, including that of Owen James Sheaks to the new arms control position of assistant secretary of State for verification and compliance, and 13 ambassadors. But it has held up several other ambassadorial nominees accused of violating diplomatic security rules.

Aides said many of the minor violators are being held up in order to pressure the State Department to change its personnel policies and put greater stress on security in selecting which career diplomats are nominated as ambassadors. A number of recent scandals have prompted Secretary of State Madeleine K. Albright to vow to tighten security in the department.

Senate Passes Increase in AIDS Funds

JULY 29 — In an effort to bolster the global fight against AIDS, the House has cleared legislation that would authorize more U.S. spending to combat the disease and begin negotiations with the World Bank for an international AIDS trust fund.

The Senate passed the bill (HR 3519) by voice vote on July 26, and the House on July 27 agreed to the Senate amendments, also by voice vote. The House passed the bill by voice vote on May 15.

The Senate version largely incorporates legislation (S 2845) introduced by Senate Foreign Relations Committee Chairman Jesse Helms, R-N.C.

The bill would require the Treasury secretary to negotiate with the World Bank for an AIDS trust fund that the bank would administer through its International Bank for Reconstruction and Development.

Money from the fund would be used for education, prevention and treatment programs to combat the spread of HIV and AIDS.

The bill also would authorize $150 million a year for fiscal 2001 and 2002 for the trust fund. The House-passed version of the bill would authorize $100 million a year for fiscal 2001 to 2005.

If the trust fund performs as expected, Congress may decide later to make more money available, Helms said.

The bill would authorize approximately $300 million a year in fiscal 2001 and 2002 for ongoing HIV/AIDS programs worldwide. Of that amount, 65 percent would be specifically authorized for non-governmental organizations, including religious groups.

Also, 20 percent of the U.S. bilateral funding would be set aside for helping orphans in Africa, including the growing number of AIDS orphans.

The bill also would authorize a total of $120 million for fiscal 2001 and 2002 for tuberculosis prevention and treatment.

Helms called the bill one of the most important pieces of international humanitarian legislation that Congress has passed in years.

Congress Backs Clinton's Push For Milosevic To Step Down

SEPTEMBER 30 — Sensing a chance to bring U.S. troops home from the Balkans, members of Congress closed ranks behind President Clinton's efforts to get Yugoslav President Slobodan Milosevic to step down after he apparently lost a Sept. 24 election.

On Sept. 25, the House passed legislation (HR 1064) by voice vote designed to strengthen groups opposed to Milosevic, codify sanctions against his regime and lay the groundwork for a change of power in Belgrade. The Senate was expected to follow suit.

"Milosevic should respect the wishes of the Serbian people and step down," said International Relations Committee Democrat Earl Pomeroy of North Dakota during House debate.

Senate Foreign Relations Committee Chairman Jesse Helms, R-N.C., chimed in from the floor Sept. 26: "The people of Yugoslavia clearly have voted for democratic change, and the time has come for Yugoslavia's brutal dictator, Slobodan Milosevic, to have the decency to accept the will of his people and leave office gracefully."

Meanwhile, conferees on a fiscal 2001 defense authorization bill (HR 4205) were expected to water down or remove a House-passed provision that could limit U.S. participation in a peacekeeping force in Kosovo.

In Belgrade, Milosevic claimed that although official results showed him running behind Vojislav Kostunica, his opponent had not managed to win an outright majority, forcing a second-round runoff Oct. 8.

Kostunica, on the other hand, claimed to have won far more than 50 percent of the vote, an assessment shared by Clinton.

"The government's official election commission has no credibility whatever," Clinton said. "It certainly appears from a distance that they had a free election and somebody's trying to take it away from them."

Clinton held out the promise that Serbia without Milosevic would also be free of economic sanctions.

"If the will of the people is respected, the doors to Europe and the world will be open again to Serbia," he said. "We will take steps with our allies to lift economic sanctions, and the people of Serbia, who have suffered so much, finally will have a chance to lead normal lives. I hope that day is arriving."

U.S. lawmakers said the bill they were moving would be useful regardless of whether a second round of voting was held or if Milosevic heeded the calls to step down.

Ranking Senate Foreign Relations Committee Democrat Joseph R. Biden Jr. of Delaware said in a floor speech Sept. 26 that the bill "offers the president ample flexibility in dealing with Serbia."

"If Milosevic should succeed in frustrating the will of the Serbian people by stealing this election, the act will give the President of the United States a complete kit of peaceful tools to continue to try to undermine his oppressive regime," Biden said.

Among the provisions:

- $50 million in aid to Serbian opposition groups.
- $55 million in aid to Montenegro, the junior member of the Yugoslav federation, which has bristled under Milosevic's control.
- Continued U.S. participation in sanctions on Serbia until a number of conditions are met, including Milosevic's trial as a war criminal by a tribunal in the Hague.
- Stepped-up television and radio broadcasting aimed at undermining Milosevic's regime.

Helms noted that the measure also would authorize aid to an appropriate new government, and he pledged, "When the Serbian people finally gain a government in Belgrade that they voted for this weekend — a government based on freedom, democracy, and rule of law — I will lead an effort to ensure that the United States in Congress provides them with substantial support to assist their nation's democracy transition."

Key Tests

Biden cautioned that it was not yet clear if a Kostunica government would meet key tests laid out in the legislation for ending sanctions and receive U.S. aid. In particular, he said that cooperation with the war crimes tribunal and full implementation of the 1995 Dayton peace accord, which brought an end to the war in Bosnia, were prerequisites to receiving U.S. aid. *(1995 Almanac, p. 10-23)*

"To be blunt: respect for Dayton and cooperation with the Hague tribunal must be litmus tests for any democratic government in Serbia," Biden said.

Still, the bill's House sponsor, Rep. Christopher H. Smith, R-N.J., chairman of the International Relations subcommittee on international operations and human rights, noted that both opponents and supporters of U.S. troop deployments to Bosnia and Kosovo had backed the legislation. With lukewarm congressional support, the Clinton administration had dispatched U.S. troops to those regions as part of NATO peacekeeping forces. Both were part of Yugoslavia when Milosevic took power in 1987, and he waged wars to bring them under Serbian control.

"We may differ in our positions regarding the decision to use American forces in the Balkans either for peacekeeping or peacemaking," Smith said. "Nothing, however, could better create the conditions for regional stability which would allow our forces to come home with their mission accomplished than a Serbia on the road to democratic recovery."

Lawmakers Split On Economic Aid For Yugoslavia

OCTOBER 7 — President Clinton called for a new approach to events in Yugoslavia, where Slobodan Milosevic relinquished power Oct. 6 after a popular revolt. Key members of Congress have not yet been able to agree on a fresh policy, beyond relief that Milosevic had departed.

Clinton, speaking to reporters at the White House Oct. 6, said it was time to bring Yugoslavia "out of isolation." He pledged to lift economic sanctions and provide the new government of opposition leader Vojislav

Kostunica with economic aid.

"The United States and our European allies, having done so much in Bosnia and Kosovo, having supported the institutions of a free election in this last process in Serbia, we owe it to those people now to reward the decision they have made," Clinton said.

Milosevic went on Serbian television to concede defeat.

Lawmakers and aides indicated that they would support Clinton's call to lift sanctions once Kostunica took power, but they were split over Clinton's call for economic aid to Yugoslavia and its neighbors.

Sen. Joseph R. Biden Jr. of Delaware, ranking Democrat on the Foreign Relations Committee, said on the Senate floor Sept. 26 that cooperation with an international war crimes tribunal and full implementation of the 1995 Dayton peace accord, which brought an end to the war in Bosnia, must be prerequisites to Yugoslavia receiving U.S. aid. *(1995 Almanac, p. 10-23)*

That is a position shared to some degree by leading congressional Republicans but likely to be disputed by other lawmakers. Aides said that Republican leaders are not inclined to loosen the purse strings on aid to Yugoslavia until the nature of a new government becomes clear.

But Sen. George V. Voinovich, R-Ohio, who is part Serbian and has been a critic of Clinton administration policy toward Serbia, said in an Oct. 3 interview that he was looking to provide some tangible support for Yugoslavia in the pending conference report on the fiscal 2001 foreign operations appropriations bill (HR 4811).

Lightning Revolt

The apparently peaceful, lightning- fast revolt in the streets of Belgrade that drove Milosevic from power caught the world by surprise and Congress in the midst of trying to resolve disputes over Yugoslavia legislation.

The bill (HR 1064), designed to encourage opposition to Milosevic and reward his successors, was part of a package of measures that originally formed a foreign aid authorization bill (S 2382) by Senate Foreign Relations Committee Chairman Jesse Helms, R-N.C. The overall bill has been held for months in the Senate Banking, Housing and Urban Affairs Committee in a dispute over international financial institutions.

Another part of the Helms package — a bill (HR 1143) authorizing limited loans for very small businesses in other countries — was passed by the Senate, on a voice vote, Oct. 3. The House agreed to the Senate version Oct. 5, clearing the measure for the president.

The Balkan bill was aimed at strengthening opposition to Milosevic in Serbia, which along with Montenegro makes up what is left of Yugoslavia. The bill would have codified sanctions against the Milosevic regime and expressed U.S. support for a change of power, including the prospect of U.S. aid and an end to sanctions.

The House had passed the measure by voice vote on Sept. 25, and Helms had picked up the support of potential Senate opponents such as Voinovich. The Senate had passed similar legislation (S 720) last November.

But a few senators, originally led by Republican Policy Committee Chairman Larry E. Craig of Idaho, held up the legislation.

Craig said the bill "wasn't going anywhere" because of tensions within the Serbian-American community, which he said was "very divided about this bill and what to do," particularly on the issue of sanctions and whether the legislation should condition aid on Milosevic being turned over to a war crimes tribunal in the Hague, which has indicted him.

Craig said before the Belgrade revolt that congressional passage of such a measure might backfire by painting Kostunica, who received the most votes in the election, as a U.S. puppet.

Kostunica has criticized the United States for repeatedly saying that Milosevic, indicted for alleged atrocities in the separatist Serbian province of Kosovo, must be tried by the international tribunal.

In addition, Craig earlier expressed concern that Kostunica could be politically damaged if Congress wrote the sanctions into law, rather than leaving them as executive orders.

The bill would have allowed the president to waive many of the sanctions for a post-Milosevic government. ◆

Lawmakers Seek to Curb Russian Involvement In Iran's Weapons Program

Box Score

- **Bills:** HR 1883 — PL 106-178; HR 4811 — PL 106-429; HR 4118; HR 4022
- **Legislative action: Senate** passed HR 1883, amended, 98-0, on Feb. 24.

House cleared HR 1883, 420-0, on March 1.

President signed HR 1883 on March 14.

House passed HR 4118 (H Rept 106-668), 275-146, July 19.

House passed HR 4022 (H Rept 106-667) by voice vote on Oct 3.

President signed HR 4811 on Nov 6.

SUMMARY

Republicans made several attempts to put new conditions on U.S. aid to Russia. Successes came in the fiscal 2001 foreign aid bill and in legislation to punish Russian companies or labs that transfer major weapons technology to Iran.

In an effort to diminish Vice President Al Gore's foreign policy reputation, congressional Republicans turned a critical eye toward the administration's policy toward Russia, an area where Gore had been active. They also advanced a number of bills aimed at Russia.

Early in the year, a bill (PL 106-78) intended to curb the transfer of Russian missile technology to Iran cleared with bipartisan support. The bill provided for economic sanctions against any country, company or individual that knowingly transferred items, information or sensitive technology that Iran could use to develop weapons of mass destruction. It also allowed the president to withhold subsidies to Russia for its share of the International Space Station, unless Russia showed a commitment to non-proliferation.

Clinton had vetoed a similar bill in 1998, saying it would make it harder to work with Russia on many issues, including nuclear non-proliferation. This time, the bill included language added by the Senate to clarify that the president would be authorized, but not required, to impose the sanctions.

The fiscal 2001 foreign aid spending bill (PL 106-429) includes a provision cutting aid to Russia by 60 percent if it sends weapons technology to Iran, blocks a war crimes investigation in Chechnya or violates a treaty on conventional forces in Europe. *(Appropriations, p. 2-70)*

Other measures passed the House but did not come up in the Senate, including a bill (HR 4022) to tie any rescheduling or cancellation of Russia's debts to its halting the sale of SSN-22 Moskit anti-ship missiles to China, and another (HR 4118) to forbid the debt restructuring unless Russia closed its intelligence facility at Lourdes, Cuba.

Senate Passes Bill Targeting Russia's Aid to Iran

FEBRUARY 26 — Overwhelming support in Congress for legislation designed to punish Russia and other countries that assist Iran's weapons program has raised hopes among supporters that it can be a model for curbing the spread of major weapons.

The Senate passed the bill (HR 1883), 98-0, on Feb. 24, five months after the House passed it on a similarly decisive 419-0 vote. *(Senate vote 12, p. S-6)*

Although the Clinton administration threatened to veto the House version, Senate sponsors adopted a manager's amendment with modest changes that eased the concerns of both Democrats and the administration.

The House is expected to clear the bill for President Clinton as early as Feb. 29, and he is expected to sign it.

"I would say that this can be a model, to state the policy [and] give the president the power to punish those who are assisting our enemies," said Sen. Joseph I. Lieberman, D-Conn., a leading supporter of the measure.

Henry Sokolski, the Pentagon's deputy director of non-proliferation policy in the Bush administration and now executive director of the Nonproliferation Policy Education Center, a Washington-based nuclear weapons group, said the bill "sets a critical precedent." He expressed hope it would lead to similar measures to deter other countries from sharing technology with countries considered hostile to U.S. interests, such as Iran, Iraq and Libya.

The bill was sparked by concerns about Iran's growing capability, with the help of Russian scientists, to launch ballistic missiles that could reach Israel, the Arabian peninsula and Europe. Although the administration contends that Moscow is making progress in controlling proliferation, Senate Majority Leader Trent Lott, R-Miss., said the situation has "probably gotten worse. . . . It is a clear message to Russia that they must do more."

The bill would require the president to inform Congress every six months of any countries, groups or individuals it believes are transferring sensitive items or information that could help Iran develop medium- or long-range missiles. The president either could impose sanctions or inform Congress why he did not.

Similar legislation that passed both chambers in 1998 but was vetoed by Clinton would have required the president to impose sanctions but allowed him to waive them on national security grounds. The new bill would authorize sanctions. It also would allow those threatened with sanctions to respond before the penalties took effect. *(1998 Almanac, p. 16-16)*

The legislation is broader than the

previous bill because it applies not only to transfers of missile technology, but to anything that could contribute to developing nuclear, chemical, biological and advanced conventional weapons.

The new bill would withhold subsidies to Russia for the International Space Station, a joint scientific venture among the United States, Russia and other nations, unless Moscow shows a "sustained commitment" to non-proliferation.

NASA officials have expressed concerns over using the space station as a diplomatic tool. But Lieberman said the legislation serves notice to the administration "that as important as good relations with Russia are, they are not more important than our national security."

At the same time, Lieberman said, Russia's presidential election in March should not affect the timing of U.S. actions on proliferation. "Our first concern has to be not what happens in Russia, but what we can do to protect the security of the American people," he said.

Winds of Change

Senate passage of the bill came on the heels of a substantial reformist victory in Iran's parliamentary elections the week of Feb. 14. Lott said the bill should strengthen the reformers while warning Iran's Islamic fundamentalists that the United States remains concerned about the country's quest for long-range missiles.

Other lawmakers expressed hope that the election can lead to improved U.S.-Iranian relations. For two decades, the United States has maintained an almost total ban on trade and financial dealings with Iran, originally because of its 1979 seizure of the U.S. embassy in Tehran and later due to its support of international terrorism. *(1980 Almanac, p. 352)*

Several senators expressed hope the State Department can lift travel restrictions. Appropriations Committee Chairman Ted Stevens, R-Alaska, and other lawmakers have wanted to make good-will trips to Iran.

"We cannot be in a position of negotiating anything, but we certainly could be in a position of opening up a door," Sen. Pat Roberts, R-Kan., told reporters Feb. 24.

House Clears Sanctions on Iran Arms Aid

MARCH 4 — The House on March 1 cleared for President Clinton's expected signature legislation that would allow the president to punish Russia and other countries that help Iran develop weapons of mass destruction.

The 420-0 vote nearly duplicated the 419-0 House floor vote on the bill (HR 1883) this past September. *(Vote 28, p. H-12)*

House members took about 45 minutes to praise the legislation and condemn Iran, despite the victory of moderates in recent Iranian elections.

Iranian officials have called for improved relations with the United States. The two countries have been in a cold war since militant Islamists took over Iran in 1979 and occupied the U.S. embassy.

Though strongly supported in Congress, the legislation long was opposed by the administration, which said it would complicate relations with Russia and efforts to control the spread of Russian military technology.

Responding to those reservations, the Senate adopted a series of amendments last week to clarify that the bill would authorize, but not require, the president to impose economic sanctions on any country, company or individual that knowingly transferred items, information or sensitive technology that Iran could use to develop weapons of mass destruction.

Republican Benjamin A. Gilman of New York, chairman of the House International Relations Committee, said March 1 that the Senate amendments made "no major substantive changes" and assured his colleagues that the original bill would have made the sanctions discretionary, not mandatory.

The latest version would allow any entities threatened with sanctions to address the allegations before the sanctions would be put in place. It also would allow the president to withhold subsidies to Russia for its share of the International Space Station unless Russia showed a commitment to non-proliferation.

House Bill Would Tie Russia's Debt To Missile Sale

APRIL 15 — Concerned that China's purchases of sophisticated military hardware could upset the strategic balance with Taiwan, members of Congress are threatening to punish third countries that supply such arms to China.

On April 13, the House International Relations Committee approved, by voice vote, legislation (HR 4022) that would authorize the president to prevent any rescheduling or cancellation of Russia's debt with the United States unless Moscow canceled a sale of Moskit anti-ship missiles to China. Democrats gave the president flexibility on whether to implement the restrictions, with an amendment, adopted 20-16, that was also supported by Republicans Doug Bereuter of Nebraska and Matt Salmon of Arizona.

If other nations follow the U.S. lead, House aides said the bill could prohibit $14 billion in debt relief Russia has requested from the Paris Club of official creditors, which includes the United States.

Dana Rohrabacher, R-Calif., who sponsored the bill, said that by the end of April, China is expected to purchase the first eight Moskit missiles, which travel at supersonic speeds and can evade advanced countermeasures. The missiles would be mounted on a Sovremenny-class destroyer that Russia already has sold to China. The missiles "were developed for one purpose and one purpose only, and that is to destroy American warships," Rohrabacher said.

Meanwhile, House Foreign Operations Appropriations Committee Chairman Sonny Callahan, R-Ala., has threatened to block $250 million in military aid to Israel if it follows through with a planned sale of an advanced airborne radar system to China.

Israeli officials, hosting Chinese President Jiang Zemin for an unprecedented visit, refused to cancel the planned deal but said they would consider not going forward with future sales.

Russians Say Missile Defense Unneeded Now

MAY 6 — An unusual meeting of Russian and American lawmakers on May 2 laid bare their differences over the threat of missile attack by smaller countries and whether treaties that limit anti-missile defense systems are necessary.

In the meeting, sponsored by the conservative Free Congress Foundation, three experts on foreign policy in the lower house of the Russian legislature, the Duma, challenged the assessment of some U.S. officials that unfriendly nations such as North Korea, Iran and Iraq will soon have nuclear-armed missiles capable of reaching the United States.

Konstantin Kosachev, deputy chairman of the Duma's Foreign Relations Committee and a member of the centrist Motherland party, said the United States and Russia should conduct a joint assessment of the threat.

"The American side exaggerates this threat too much," Kosachev said.

But Sen. Jon Kyl, R-Ariz., a leading proponent of anti-missile defenses, said, "Over the five years that it will take to build a [missile defense] system, the threat will have evolved to the point where it will be important to the United States to defend against it."

Gordon H. Smith, R-Ore., chairman of the Senate Foreign Relations Subcommittee on European Affairs, told the Russians that Kyl's view was increasingly shared by his Senate colleagues.

Smith said that not all senators agreed with Foreign Relations Committee Chairman Jesse Helms, R-N.C., who said in an April 26 floor speech that any accord limiting anti-missile defenses would be "dead on arrival" in his committee.

But Smith said that any bilateral negotiations aimed at revising the 1972 Anti-Ballistic Missile (ABM) Treaty would be best left to the next administration.

"President Clinton does not enjoy the trust of the United States Senate when it comes to arms control or military matters," Smith said.

Under the ABM Treaty, the United States and the Soviet Union, and now Russia, have agreed to remain defenseless against each other's nuclear arsenals, in effect holding each other hostage to "mutually assured destruction." *(1972 Almanac, p. 589)*

Deploying Defenses

Congress last year passed and Clinton signed a law (PL 106-38) declaring U.S. policy to deploy a limited, national anti-missile defense as soon as "technologically possible."

Russian lawmakers, however, said the United States should hold off on deploying any anti-missile defense, should one prove feasible, before an agreement can be reached on revising the ABM Treaty. Otherwise, they warned, the whole structure of arms control between the two countries could unravel.

"We will have to get out of all the talks we've been negotiating for the past 30 years," said Alexander Shabanov, a Communist who serves as deputy chairman of the Duma's Foreign Relations Committee. "That would be the reaction to this anxious and too quick attempt by the United States."

At a breakfast meeting with reporters May 3, several prominent arms control activists criticized Clinton's desire to decide by this summer whether to deploy an anti-missile defense.

"It's politics that's driving this system forward, not the threat or the technology," said Joseph Cirincione, who heads the non-proliferation project at the Carnegie Endowment for International Peace.

Cirincione and other activists are skeptical that Clinton will reach any agreement on arms control with Russian President Vladimir V. Putin at a June 4-5 summit in Moscow.

Joseph R. Biden Jr. of Delaware, the Senate Foreign Relations Committee's ranking Democrat, said he hopes an agreement between Clinton and Putin can be reached and that a way can be found to surmount Helms' "very inappropriate" decision to block any potential deal.

"I'm more worried about the relationship between the White House and the Senate than I am about the relationship at this moment on arms control between the president and the Russians," Biden told reporters May 3.

GOP Targets Gore In Attacks On Russia Policy

JULY 29 — Hoping to weaken public opinion of Vice President Al Gore's foreign policy credentials going into the fall campaign against Texas Gov. George W. Bush, congressional Republicans are conducting a sustained attack on his overseas specialty: U.S. relations with Russia.

In recent months, GOP leaders have drafted and moved several bills that would punish Russia for a range of behavior Republicans consider inimical to U.S. interests — the war in Chechnya, the sale of arms to China and loans to Yugoslav President Slobodan Milosevic.

Republican lawmakers such as Senate Foreign Relations Committee Chairman Jesse Helms of North Carolina have placed much of the blame for Russia's behavior on the White House, which they say has been too cozy with the Kremlin. Helms for a month blocked Senate action on 13 ambassadorial nominees his committee already had approved, seeking to force the administration to take a tougher line toward Russian President Vladimir V. Putin's government.

Helms said July 26 that he was lifting his hold after administration assurances that its support for Russia's efforts to write off old Soviet-era debts would be tied to steps for a peaceful solution in Chechnya and a cutoff of Moscow's support for Milosevic.

Now Republicans are attempting to zero in on Gore, whose foreign policy portfolio includes co-chairing a binational commission on U.S.-Russian relations with a series of Russian prime ministers.

In September, House Republican leaders are planning to release a report sharply criticizing Gore's actions. The report has been drafted by House Republican Policy Committee Chairman Christopher Cox of California at the behest of Speaker J. Dennis Hastert, R-Ill. It follows several months of closed hearings by Hastert's Task Force on Russia and is being circulated among the chairmen of five committees. A copy was reviewed by CQ Weekly.

It focuses on the economic shortcomings of Russia's transition from a communist dictatorship to democracy. It says the Clinton administration failed to grasp a window of opportunity after the collapse of the Soviet Union in 1991, and accuses the White House of actually worsening the situation by steering money and attention to Russia's central government.

The report calls for a greater emphasis on helping economic reform in Russia, but largely without contributing significant amounts of money. The report recommends tying Russia's debt restructuring to its behavior in Chechnya and its control of weapons transfers to potential U.S. adversaries such as China. And it suggests that the United States make a renewed push for a free trade agreement with Moscow and allowing Russia to join the World Trade Organization.

Compare and Contrast

Cox denied that the report is merely an election-year document, but he acknowledges that its fundamental purpose is to offer a contrast between Republican policies and the perceived failures of President Clinton and Gore.

Cox said the task force has received input from the Bush campaign and said that many of his foreign policy advisers also work for Bush, including Condoleeza Rice, Bush's senior foreign policy adviser.

"This is a bookend, contrasting the administration's position with our own policies," Cox said.

Indeed, the panel's position jibes closely with the views offered by Rice in a recent interview. She portrayed the modern global economy as a train that Russia needs to climb aboard.

"They can be the roadkill of history or get on the train," Rice said last month. "The rules of what it means to be a modern country, a developed country, are increasingly clear to everybody."

Otherwise, she said, Russia could drift in a nationalist direction reminiscent of European fascism in the 1930s.

Leon Fuerth, Gore's national security adviser, defended the administration's record on Russia in remarks July 25 at the Woodrow Wilson Center for International Scholars. He called the GOP attacks a "vehement brand of political partisanship."

"We can surely claim that we have laid down the foundation for constructive development," Fuerth said of Gore's work with Russia. "Because we chose to engage Russia — vigorously and creatively — we have succeeded in locking-in important, practically irreversible progress that serves U.S. national interest."

"We were determined to achieve concrete results — not photo-ops and paperwork — for the American people and the Russian people," Fuerth added. "The practical benefits of the commission included reduced trade barriers, improved public health, heightened attention to the environment, improved safety of nuclear plants, tighter protection for fissionable materials, efficient cooperation in the demilitarization of Russian nuclear weapons, cooperation in commercial space launch, work with Russia's regional government to improve investment and trade flows."

Russian Debt

The Republican report comes as recent polls, such as July 25 surveys for CBS News and the New York Times and for the Washington Post and ABC News, indicate that the public trusts Bush and Gore almost equally to handle foreign affairs, with Gore seen as the more knowledgeable on global issues.

In an effort to dampen Gore's standing and exploit what they see as flaws in the administration's policy toward Russia, Republicans are advancing legislation Clinton is almost certain to veto if it is not watered down to largely symbolic rhetoric.

For example, lawmakers have moved to attach foreign policy conditions to Russia's attempts to reschedule about $485 million in Soviet-era debt to the United States, some of which dates back to the Lend-Lease payments of World War II. *(1945 Almanac, p. 147)*

One measure (HR 4022), approved by the House International Relations Committee April 13, but not yet considered by the full House, would tie any rescheduling or cancelation of Russia's debt to the ending of sales of SSN-22 Moskit anti-ship missiles to China.

The House on July 19 approved another proposal (HR 4118), 275-146, that would forbid the debt restructuring unless Russia closes its intelligence facility at Lourdes, Cuba. The president could waive the requirement under certain conditions. *(Vote 414, H-128)*

Arguing against the legislation, administration officials said Russia needed the facilities to monitor U.S. compliance with arms control accords. They said questioning Russia's right to the site could undermine the Kremlin's willingness to permit the United States to conduct similar monitoring.

House Intelligence Committee Chairman Porter J. Goss, R-Fla., attacked that logic during debate in an explicit reference to Gore.

Goss questioned why such a facility was needed when "the Clinton-Gore administration, and in particular, Vice President Gore, who spearheaded administration policy toward Russia through the Gore-Chernomyrdin Commission, has repeatedly claimed that it had achieved a special relationship of trust with Russia, referring to them as partners. . . .

"I encourage my colleagues to send a very strong signal to the Clinton-Gore administration that the American people will no longer stand for their culture of disdain for security," Goss said.

Foreign Aid

The Senate attached other conditions to the rescheduling of the Soviet-era debt when it approved its version of the fiscal 2001 foreign operations appropriations bill (HR 4811) on June 22.

The Senate adopted a Helms amendment that would preclude any debt forgiveness or rescheduling, trade financing or loans from international financial institutions to Russia until the Kremlin stops providing aid to the Milosevic government. The amendment also would cut aid to Russia by an amount equal to that which the Kremlin has loaned to the Milosevic government.

The president could waive the restrictions on the grounds of national interest.

In addition, a provision included in the legislation by Mitch McConnell, R-Ky., chairman of the Foreign Operations Appropriations Subcommittee, would make aid to Russia conditional on Kremlin cooperation with international efforts to investigate alleged human rights violations and to provide humanitarian help in war-torn Chechnya.

The House version of the foreign

aid bill includes tough language tying aid to Russia to its movement of troops out of areas flanking Chechnya, which the House said violates the 1990 Conventional Forces in Europe treaty, which was amended in 1997. *(1997 Almanac, 8-28; 1990 Almanac, p. 696)*

Both the House and Senate bills would continue a current provision that makes nearly half of government-to-government assistance to Russia conditional on an end to the Kremlin's cooperation with Iran's ballistic missile program.

On July 18, before a summit meeting of wealthy nations in Okinawa, Japan, Senate Majority Leader Trent Lott, R-Miss., and Senate Armed Services Committee Chairman John W. Warner, R-Va., along with McConnell and Helms, wrote Clinton asking him not to join any agreement to restructure Russia's debts unless certain conditions were met.

"Debt relief is not an entitlement or a political gift," the Republican senators wrote to the president.

At the Okinawa summit, the Clinton administration attempted unsuccessfully to tie any debt restructuring to two conditions: Russia would have to prove it had met International Monetary Fund criteria for the loans, and then would have to prove that it really needed the money, despite indications to the contrary, such as its soaring oil revenues, its apparent ability to wage a costly war in Chechnya, and the loan to Milosevic.

House-Passed Bill Ties Russian Debt To Missile Sales

OCTOBER 7 — By voice vote Oct. 3, the House passed legislation (HR 4022) that would prevent the president from rescheduling Russia's U.S. debts unless Moscow stops selling SSN-22 Moskit anti-ship missiles to China.

Republican Dana Rohrabacher of California, who sponsored the legislation, said on the House floor that the missile sales "allow the Communist Chinese to endanger the lives of thousands of American service personnel. . . . It is the most dangerous anti-ship missile the Russians and now the Communist Chinese have in their fleet."

The bill would allow the president to waive the proposed restrictions on national security grounds.

The legislation is part of a broader attack by congressional Republicans on the Clinton administration's and particularly Vice President Al Gore's handling of U.S. policy towards Russia. House GOP leaders released a long-expected report critical of that policy Sept. 20. ◆

Senate Ratifies Pact That Seeks to Protect Children In International Adoptions

SUMMARY

The Senate ratified an international treaty on adoptions after Congress reached agreement on legislation to implement the pact in the United States, including giving the State Department primary authority. President Clinton signed the legislation Oct. 6.

The Hague Convention on Protection of Children and Cooperation in Respect of Intercountry Adoption (Treaty Doc 105-51) aims to ensure that international adoptions take place in the best interests of the child, that countries cooperate to prevent child abductions and trafficking and that adoptions adhere to basic standards. Senate Foreign Relations Committee Chairman Jesse Helms, R-N.C., one of the key movers in ratifying the treaty, had held it up in 1999 to ensure that the State Department would be the lead U.S. agency in implementing the pact. The bill was further delayed by social conservatives in the House who worried that it might supersede laws restricting adoptions by gay adults. The Senate included language allowing foreign countries to review "home studies" that screen potential adoptive parents.

Box Score

- **Bill:** HR 2909 — PL 106-279
- **Legislative action: House** passed HR 2909 (H Rept 106-691, Part 1), by voice vote, July 18.

Senate passed HR 2909, amended, by voice vote, July 27.

House further amended HR 2909, by voice vote, Sept. 18.

Senate cleared HR 2909 and ratified the Hague convention on adoptions, both by voice vote on Sept. 20.

President signed HR 2909 on Oct. 6.

Senate Committee Approves Treaty On Adoption

APRIL 15 — The Senate Foreign Relations Committee has approved a treaty and implementing legislation designed to regulate the international adoption of children, after reaching agreement with a House panel that the State Department should control the process.

The Foreign Relations Committee on April 13 approved, by voice vote, the Hague Convention on Protection of Children and Cooperation in Respect of Intercountry Adoption (Treaty Doc 105-51) and legislation (S 682) necessary for the treaty's operation in the United States.

The committee in March reached agreement with the House International Relations Committee over which federal agency should have primary jurisdiction over the program. The disagreement had slowed action on the bill.

Senate committee Chairman Jesse Helms, R-N.C, who sponsored the bill along with Mary L. Landrieu, D-La., said the State Department should be the lead agency because it is better placed to monitor adoption agencies overseas. The House committee said the Department of Health and Human Services, experienced in adoptions, should have the main responsibility.

The House panel gave in to Helms and Landrieu and approved its version of the legislation (HR 2909), 28-0, on March 22. The measure still must be considered by the Judiciary and Education and the Workforce committees in the House.

Some members of the Senate committee had reservations about the treaty and legislation. Sam Brownback, R-Kan., who has adopted two foreign children, said he was concerned the treaty would add "unnecessary cost and bureaucracy to the process."

Brownback noted that U.S. adoptions of foreign children have doubled in the last five years. "I don't think the system's broken," he said.

Paul S. Sarbanes, D-Md., however, said the pact was needed because a number of countries have said they will not allow children to be adopted by people in countries that have not ratified the treaty.

State Department officials agreed, noting that some countries are worried about the U.S. practice of state-licensed adoption agencies. They prefer to deal with a single national system of accreditation.

Bill sponsors also say the treaty would combat the kidnapping of children for adoption, falsification of medical records to make children seem healthier, and charging of excessive fees for adoption services.

The panel approved the treaty and implementing measure, along with a slate of other legislation and nominations, on a single voice vote.

Other Nations

Other measures approved by the panel include:

- A House-passed bill (HR 3707) that would authorize $75 million to construct new offices for the American Institute in Taipei, the unofficial U.S. embassy in Taiwan.
- A non-binding resolution (S. Res. 289) expressing support for efforts by the United States to condemn Cuba's human rights practices at the U.N. Human Rights Convention in Geneva.
- A non-binding resolution (S. Res. 287) by Helms, Edward Kennedy, D-Mass., and Frank R. Lautenberg, D-N.J., calling for the United States to maintain a hard line with Libya.

The Clinton Administration has been exploring some means of improving its bitter relations with Libya since the government of Muammar el-Qaddafi agreed last year to surrender two suspects in the 1988 bombing of Pan Am Flight 103 over Lockerbie, Scotland.

But the resolution states that some of the steps being explored — such as easing a ban on travel by U.S. citizens to Libya — should not be considered until after the Libyan government takes responsibility for the bombing and other acts of international terrorism.

The conservative Helms noted the unusual alliance he had formed on the issue with the liberal Kennedy.

"When Helms and Kennedy get together on an issue, that covers the world," Helms said. Kennedy helped tighten U.S. sanctions (PL 104-172) on Libya four years ago. *(1996 Almanac, p. 9-5)*

House Passes Bill To Implement Adoption Treaty

JULY 22 — Congress has come one step closer to ratifying a treaty designed to regulate the international adoption of children — but only after the House included language in implementing legislation that social conservatives believe will reduce the number of adoptions they find inappropriate, such as those by gays.

On July 18, the House passed, by voice vote, legislation (HR 2909) designed to guide federal agencies in implementing the treaty. The Senate Foreign Relations Committee in April approved both the treaty — called the Hague Convention on Protection of Children and Cooperation in Respect of Intercountry Adoption (Treaty Doc 105-51) — and its version of implementing legislation (S 682).

According to aides, the Senate is expected to consider the treaty and implementing legislation the week of July 24, where it is likely to face little opposition.

The House bill had been held up since March by demands from social conservatives led by Republican Christopher H. Smith of New Jersey, chairman of the House International Relations Subcommittee on International Operations and Human Rights. Smith feared that the treaty and implementing legislation were not strict enough in determining which parents could adopt and which agencies could be involved in the process.

In particular, they fear that the implementing legislation could undermine state and foreign laws governing the potential pool of adoptive parents. Some countries such as China, Romania and Bulgaria, and many U.S. states, prohibit or restrict the rights of gay adults to adopt.

"I have been concerned that the new regulatory scheme not facilitate 'end runs' around legitimate laws and policies of states and foreign countries designed to protect the best interests of children," Smith said on the House floor.

After prodding by Republican leaders, Smith eventually agreed to a compromise that would beef up provisions governing "home studies" that screen potential adoptive parents, to effectively continue such restrictions. The amended bill would call for foreign countries to be given the results of the home studies before they signed off on adoptions. That would allow them to prevent "placing children in inappropriate settings." Adoption services that did not carry out sufficiently rigorous studies could be punished by being banned or suspended from the program.

During the brief House debate, some lawmakers who have adopted children from overseas testified to the importance of approving the implementing legislation.

Bill Delahunt, D-Mass., whose adopted daughter, Kara, was born in Vietnam, said the treaty would help remedy some problems such as exorbitant fees, kidnapping, baby smuggling, a lack of information about the child's medical and psychological conditions, and even the forcing of women to give up their children for adoption.

Delahunt said those problems have caused a number of countries, including Russia, Romania and Guatemala, to suspend overseas adoptions until safeguards can be put in place.

Americans adopt four out of five children placed through international adoption, Delahunt said.

Senate Passes Bill; Quick Conference Expected

JULY 29 — The Senate is waiting until September and final action on implementing legislation before ratifying a treaty designed to regulate international adoptions.

The Senate on July 27 amended and passed, by voice vote, the bill (HR 2909)to set up U.S. procedures for joining the Hague Convention on Protection of Children and Cooperation in Respect of Intercountry Adoption (Treaty Doc 105-51).

The treaty, which was not brought up on the floor, aims to make sure that international adoptions take place in the best interests of the child, that countries cooperate to prevent child abductions and trafficking, and that adoptions adhere to basic standards.

The measure calls for the secretary of State to oversee the accreditation process for adoption agencies abroad.

The bill would require that adoption papers include the child's medical records in English, said Senate Foreign Relations Committee Chairman Jesse Helms, R-N.C.

Some lawmakers have said they worry the bill does not protect the confidentiality of personal information about parents and the children they adopt. The bill would leave it to the states to address those issues.

The measure now heads to conference, which is expected to be swift once Congress returns because Helms and House International Relations Committee Chairman Benjamin A. Gilman, R-N.Y., have already begun to negotiate.

During the bill's House consideration, Democratic Rep. Bill Delahunt, of Massachusetts said the bill would put an end to practices such as kidnapping children for adoptions, falsifying medical records to make children seem more attractive to adoptive parents, and charging exorbitant fees for adoption services.

The House passed the legislation July 18 by voice vote. It had languished until language was added that social conservatives believe will reduce the number of adoptions they find inappropriate, such as those by gays.

Senate Ratifies International Adoption Pact

SEPTEMBER 23 — The Senate on Sept. 20 ratified a treaty designed to regulate international adoptions and cleared legislation to bring U.S. laws into compliance.

The Hague Convention on Protection of Children and Cooperation in Respect of Intercountry Adoption (Treaty Doc 105-51) was ratified by unanimous consent. The House passed the accompanying bill (HR 2909) by voice vote Sept. 18, after an exchange of amendments with the Senate, which then cleared the measure by voice vote.

The treaty aims to ensure that international adoptions take place in the best interests of the child, that countries cooperate to prevent child abductions and trafficking, and that adoptions adhere to basic standards.

Foreign Relations Committee Chairman Jesse Helms, R-N.C., one of the key movers in ratifying the treaty, said on the Senate floor Sept. 21 that he hoped the accord would "encourage more intercountry adoptions, while protecting all those involved in the process."

Families in Western Europe, North America, Israel and Australia have adopted 20,000 children from developing countries and Eastern Europe since the early 1980s. In some cases, however, the adoptions have produced a backlash, including accusations of exorbitant fees, kidnapping, baby smuggling, and a lack of information about the children's medical and psychological conditions. Supporters of the bill say this has led a number of countries, including Russia, Romania and Guatemala, to suspend overseas adoptions until safeguards can be put in place.

The legislation, Helms said, "is intended to build some accountability into agencies that provide intercountry adoption services in the United States, while strengthening the hand of the secretary of State in ensuring that U.S. adoption agencies engage in an ethical manner to find homes for children."

Last year, Helms held up the legislation in a successful effort to ensure that the State Department was the lead agency in implementing the treaty.

The bill was further delayed by social conservatives in the House, led by Christopher H. Smith, R-N.J., chairman of the International Relations Subcommittee on International Operations and Human Rights.

Smith feared that the treaty and implementing legislation were not strict enough in setting rules on who could adopt and which agencies could be involved in the process. In particular, he worried that the bill could undermine state and foreign laws governing the potential pool of adoptive parents. Some countries, such as China, Romania and Bulgaria, and many U.S. states, prohibit or restrict adoptions by gay adults.

The Senate took these concerns into account when it passed the measure July 27 by allowing foreign countries to review the result of the "home studies" that screen potential adoptive parents.

The House made further changes before sending the bill back for final passage by the Senate, including a provision that would allow U.S. adoption officials to take into account whether a child's biological parents are seeking to immigrate to the United States at the same time. ◆

Lawmakers Clear Amended Intelligence Bill After First Attempt Draws Clinton Veto

SUMMARY

Congress cleared a revised intelligence authorization bill Dec. 11, after President Clinton vetoed an earlier version because it contained provisions establishing criminal penalties for leaking classified information. Clinton signed the new bill Dec. 27.

Total spending for intelligence activities is classified, although published reports put the figure in the range of $30 billion for fiscal 2000.

The issue of information leaks entangled the normally noncontroversial intelligence bill, which covers the Central Intelligence Agency and other intelligence-gathering agencies. The provision would have made almost all unauthorized and willful disclosures of classified information, whether or not they jeopardized national security, a felony punishable by up to three years in prison.

Supporters said the language was narrowly drawn and had the backing of the Justice Department. Critics, including many Democrats and news organizations, said it would silence whistleblowers and undermine the First Amendment.

In vetoing the initial bill (HR 4392) on Nov. 4, Clinton said the provision was "badly flawed and "overbroad" and "may unnecessarily chill legitimate activities that are at the heart of a democracy." The House responded by stripping out the provision and passing an otherwise identical authorization bill (HR 5630). *(Veto text, p. D-100)*

Before passing the new bill, the Senate adopted an amendment to restrict some activities of the super-secret National Reconnaissance Office, which operates the nation's spy satellites. That sent the measure back to the House, where angry Select Intelligence Committee Republicans initially refused to let the bill clear by unanimous consent. They reluctantly relented, clearing the bill.

Senate Intelligence Markup Gives NSA Increase

APRIL 29 — The Senate Intelligence Committee has taken a step toward addressing congressional alarm over the quality of information derived from satellites and other sources that intercept, process and analyze communications, telemetry and other electronic signals.

In a closed-door markup April 27, the committee approved an intelligence authorization bill for fiscal 2001 that panel members said includes a significant increase for the National Security Agency (NSA), the super-secret eavesdropping arm of the intelligence community.

The overall level of spending for intelligence activities is classified, although several published reports have put the figure in the range of $30 billion for fiscal 2000. The last time the Clinton administration made spending figures public for intelligence and security-related activities was 1998, when it announced that the fiscal 1998 budget was $26.7 billion. It had made public the fiscal 1997 total of $26.6 billion in response to a successful lawsuit by the Federation of American Scientists.

The unnumbered bill covers the intelligence-gathering activities of 11 agencies, including the Central Intelligence Agency and operations in the State, Defense and Energy departments.

Committee members said this year's bill places special emphasis on the NSA, which is responsible for so-called signals intelligence. Published reports say NSA has an annual budget of about $3.6 billion.

An advisory group to the Senate Intelligence Committee has concluded that the NSA is in dire need of modernizing its technology infrastructure.

"It's obligatory on our part, the Senate and House, to properly fund NSA," Intelligence Committee Chairman Richard C. Shelby, R-Ala., said in an April 26 interview. "Otherwise it will go deaf. It will be totally irrelevant in the future, when technology advances."

The NSA has recently been the subject of worldwide news media reports that have accused the agency of spying on U.S. citizens and providing intelligence data to U.S. companies, among other things. Director of Central Intelligence George J. Tenet and NSA's director, Air Force Lt. Gen. Michael V. Hayden, strongly denied the allegations April 12 at a rare public hearing of the House Intelligence Committee.

Manpower Needs

Shelby also said the fiscal 2001 intelligence authorization bill emphasizes the intelligence community's need to recruit, employ and retain more skilled agents. Tenet has made recruitment a priority, conducting what he has described as the CIA's

Box Score

- **Bill:** HR 5630 — PL 106-567
- **Legislative action: House** passed HR 4392 (H Rept 106-620) by voice vote on May 23.

Senate passed HR 4392 by voice vote Oct. 2, after substituting the text of S 2507.

Senate adopted the conference report on HR 4392 (H Rept 106-969) by voice vote Oct. 12.

House cleared HR 4392 by voice vote Oct. 12.

President vetoed the bill Nov. 4.

House passed HR 5630 by voice vote on Nov. 13.

Senate passed HR 5630, amended, by voice vote Dec. 6.

House cleared HR 5630 by voice vote Dec. 11.

President signed the bill Dec. 27.

largest recruiting drive since the end of the Cold War.

The committee adopted an amendment by Carl Levin, D-Mich., that aides said they would not discuss in detail until the bill was filed.

Levin said before the markup that he would seek to revise language in the fiscal 2000 authorization bill (PL 106-120) that imposes sanctions on alleged drug kingpins.

Levin and other lawmakers have raised concerns that the drug kingpin language would allow officials to take property from those suspected of drug trafficking without due process of law.

House Panel Approves Increase For Spy Agency

MAY 13 — The House Intelligence Committee has joined its Senate counterpart in authorizing more money to improve the government's electronic eavesdropping capabilities.

In a closed-door markup May 10, the House committee approved a fiscal 2001 intelligence authorization bill (HR 4392) that members said would substantially exceed President Clinton's request for modernization at the National Security Agency (NSA), the super-secret arm of the intelligence community that uses satellites and other equipment to intercept, process and analyze electronic signals.

The Senate Intelligence Committee authorized a sizable spending increase for the NSA when it marked up its bill (S 2507) last month, Senate committee members said.

The NSA has come under heavy criticism from lawmakers for its inability to keep up with the rapid technological changes in signals intelligence. Published reports say the agency has an annual budget of about $3.6 billion.

Overall intelligence spending in the House bill is "very close" to Clinton's request, said House Intelligence Committee Chairman Porter J. Goss, R-Fla.

The committee's ranking Democrat, Julian C. Dixon of California, said Clinton proposed "a substantial increase" for intelligence activities. But Goss said a growing number of diverse international threats warranted an even larger increase.

"I am sorry we did not get a bigger number from the president," Goss said.

Spending for intelligence activities is classified, although several published reports have put the figure in the range of $30 billion for fiscal 2000. The only time the Clinton administration made spending figures public for intelligence and security-related activities was 1998, when it announced that the fiscal 1998 budget was $26.7 billion.

The bills cover the intelligence-gathering activities of 11 agencies, including the CIA and operations in the State, Defense and Energy departments.

An Intelligence Committee statement said the House bill would make "major new investments" in the National Imagery and Mapping Agency's development of a system to use new imagery satellites in the next decade.

The statement said the legislation also would put additional money into operations, training and technical capabilities of the CIA's overseas spying arm, the Directorate of Operations.

In response to recent disappearances of laptop computers at the State Department, the statement said the bill "severely restricts" the department's ability to use money for its Bureau of Intelligence and Research until the director of Central Intelligence certifies that the department is meeting standards for protecting classified information.

Goss said the House bill contains no language revising a provision in the fiscal 2000 authorization bill (PL 106-120) that imposed sanctions against alleged drug kingpins.

Some members of the Senate Intelligence Committee have raised concerns that the drug kingpin language would allow officials to take property, without due process of law, from those suspected of drug trafficking.

House Debates Bill Giving NSA Means To Modernize

MAY 20 — The House on May 19 began debating a fiscal 2001 authorization bill for intelligence activities that lawmakers said would raise spending significantly — 6.6 percent above the current level.

The legislation (HR 4392) covers the intelligence-gathering activities of 11 agencies, including the CIA and operations in the State, Defense and Energy departments. Spending for intelligence activities is classified, although several published reports have put the figure for fiscal 2000 in the range of $30 billion.

The House is expected to vote on the bill during the week of May 22 after considering an amendment by Tim Roemer, D-Ind., that would require public disclosure of the amount authorized for intelligence the previous fiscal year. The only time the Clinton administration made spending figures public for intelligence and security-related activities was 1998, when it announced that the fiscal 1998 budget was $26.7 billion.

House Select Intelligence Committee Chairman Porter J. Goss, R-Fla., said the level of spending on intelligence should be dramatically increased to address the growing number of diverse international threats.

"We've tried to address all the critical problems," Goss said during floor debate. "We can't go all the way, but at least we go in the proper direction."

Upgrading the NSA

Much of the additional spending authorized in the bill would be used to modernize equipment at the National Security Agency (NSA), the super-secret arm of the intelligence community that uses satellites and other equipment to intercept, process and analyze electronic signals.

The Intelligence Committee's report on the bill said lagging funding levels for signals intelligence is the security community's most pressing problem. Committee member Sanford D. Bishop Jr., D-Ga., said the rapid pace of technology and communications growth "appears as a whirlwind, with NSA following in its wake."

In addition to money, the bill calls for NSA to restructure its operations to better handle the rapid technological changes in signals intelligence. The committee report said the agency "cannot remain split into multiple, separate collection 'stovepipes.' " Instead, it said, the agency "must be organized and operated as a single, cohesive enterprise."

The report calls for the intelligence

community to develop by Nov. 1 a plan for review, approval and continued monitoring of NSA's integrated modernization program.

In another management move, the committee report calls for the director of central intelligence to create a new position of "intelligence community communications architect." The position would help address lawmakers' frustrations about a continued lack of coordination in how the different intelligence agencies communicate with each other.

In response to the recent disappearances of laptop computers at the State Department, the authorization bill asks that the director of central intelligence certify to the committee that the department is complying with standards for protecting classified information. It also would authorize a study of whether a new security office should be set up at State to manage intelligence information security.

CIA Absolved in Drug Probe

The House debate on the intelligence authorization bill came a week after the Intelligence Committee released the results of an investigation that found no evidence to support allegations that the CIA was involved in drug trafficking in the 1980s to assist Nicaraguan contras.

The investigation began after a 1996 series of articles in the San Jose Mercury News fueled suspicions among some lawmakers and others that there was a government conspiracy to addict young urban blacks to crack cocaine. But the Intelligence Committee reached conclusions similar to those of the CIA's inspector general, the Justice Department and the Los Angeles County Sheriff's Department that there was no evidence of any drug trafficking by the CIA or any other intelligence agencies.

"I am satisfied that we chased down all relevant leads and covered the necessary ground, and that the findings of this report are fully supported by the facts," Goss said in a statement. "Bottom line, the allegations were false."

Earlier this year, Rep. Maxine Waters, D-Calif., accused the committee of not conducting an in-depth investigation. But the panel's ranking Democrat, Julian C. Dixon of California, concurred with Goss that the allegations were "thoroughly examined."

House Passes Intelligence Authorization

MAY 27 — The House on May 23 easily passed legislation authorizing a spending increase for intelligence activities in fiscal 2001, but the measure could face a bumpier road in the Senate.

The House bill (HR 4392), passed by voice vote, would increase spending 6.6 percent over the fiscal 2000 level, which is classified. The measure covers the intelligence-gathering activities of 11 agencies, including the Central Intelligence Agency and operations in the State, Defense and Energy departments.

Some lawmakers remain concerned with language in a version of the authorization bill (S 2507) approved by the Senate Intelligence Committee on April 27 designed to clarify a provision in last year's intelligence authorization law (PL 106-120) that imposed financial sanctions on international drug kingpins.

The drug kingpin provision allows U.S. officials to freeze the assets of individuals who have been found to play a significant role in international drug trafficking. Some senators, led by Carl Levin, D-Mich., worry that the language allows officials to take property without due process of law.

At Levin's behest, this year's Senate bill would amend the drug kingpin law to say that U.S. citizens would still have the power to challenge a decision to have their property seized. Other lawmakers say they do not want to make legislative changes until a commission set up in last year's law completes its work of reviewing the legal authority under which the government can block assets.

Sen. Paul Coverdell, R-Ga., said he has been working with Senate Intelligence Committee Chairman Richard C. Shelby, R-Ala., to resolve the issue.

NSA Increase

Much of the increased spending in the House bill would cover modernization of the National Security Agency (NSA), the super-secret arm of the intelligence community that analyzes electronic signals. The legislation also would call on the NSA to restructure and consolidate its operations to keep pace with technological change.

By a 175-225 vote, House members rejected an amendment by Tim Roemer, D-Ind., that would have required declassifying the costs of intelligence-gathering activities for the previous fiscal year. *(Vote 214, p. H-68)*

The only time the White House has voluntarily made intelligence budget figures public was 1998, when it said the fiscal 1998 budget was $26.7 billion. Published reports have put this year's budget at about $30 billion.

Roemer said his amendment would have provided "one ray of sunshine" to help the public assess spending for intelligence. But opponents of the amendment, led by House Intelligence Committee Chairman Porter J. Goss, R-Fla., said Congress should not give terrorists or hostile nations any information that might prove useful.

The House adopted two amendments by James A. Traficant Jr., D-Ohio. One, adopted 404-8, would require the CIA to submit a report to the House Intelligence Committee on whether China's government poses a threat to U.S. security. The other, adopted 407-1, would require the CIA to report to Congress on the effects of espionage against the United States. *(Votes 215, p. H-68; 216, p. H-70)*

Senate Passes Bill, Proposes Sanctions For Drug Cases

OCTOBER 7 — The ability of U.S. citizens to challenge federal agencies that freeze their property in some international drug cases will be a focus of a House-Senate conference on the fiscal 2001 intelligence authorization bill the week of Oct. 9.

The Senate passed the bill (HR 4392) by voice vote Oct. 2 after substituting the text of its own measure (S 2507). The measure covers the intelligence-gathering activities of 11 agencies, including the Central Intelligence Agency and operations in the State, Defense and Energy departments.

Although many of the agencies already have received funding through the fiscal 2001 defense appropriations law (PL 106-259), the authorizing committees want a say in how intelligence-gathering funds are spent.

The Senate bill would authorize increased spending for modernizing the National Security Agency (NSA), the super-secret arm of the intelligence community that analyzes electronic signals.

The overall level of spending for intelligence activities is classified, although published reports have put the figure in the range of $30 billion for fiscal 2000.

The Clinton administration said it generally supported the Senate bill, but warned that it would oppose any efforts by Congress to dictate procedures for handling diplomatic telecommunications. Lawmakers apparently have expressed concern about the security of such communications.

Matter of Assets

The Senate vote came five months after the Senate Intelligence Committee approved the measure. Majority Leader Trent Lott, R-Miss., blamed the delay on senators who suspected it might be attached to a stalled bankruptcy overhaul measure (S 625). Lott said such a procedural move "was never intended."

The bill also was held up by lawmakers concerned about language designed to clarify a provision in the fiscal 2000 intelligence authorization law (PL 106-120) that imposed financial sanctions on international drug kingpins. *(1999 Almanac, p. 14-13)*

The provision allows U.S. officials to freeze the assets of individuals who have been found to play a significant role in international drug trafficking. Some senators, led by Carl Levin, D-Mich., worry that the language would allow officials to take property without due process of law.

At Levin's behest, the Intelligence Committee sought to amend the drug kingpin law in the fiscal 2001 bill to say that U.S. citizens would still have the power to challenge a decision blocking them from using property.

Some House members, however, say they do not want to make any legislative changes until a commission set up in last year's law completes a review of the legal authority under which the government can sieze assets.

"We had an understanding last year to set up a commission. We should let the commission do its job," House Intelligence Chairman Porter J. Goss, R-Fla., said in an interview. He said he expects to receive the commission's findings by December.

Classified Information a Concern

Conferees also are expected to address a Senate provision that would criminalize leaks of classified information. Defense Secretary William S. Cohen said in an Oct. 2 speech that he has been surprised by how much classified material is given to reporters.

"I find not only highly classified materials, I find internal memos that have just been typed that go to the media before they even come to me," Cohen said. "I think it's something that should be of concern."

Goss said he will "take a close look" at the Senate language on leaks. "My own thought is that it may be helpful, if it's worded properly," he said.

The Senate adopted several amendments to the authorization bill by voice vote. One offered by Arlen Specter, R-Pa., would modify procedures for surveillance and searches for foreign spies based on legislation (S 2089) that Specter introduced separately.

Another amendment, by Daniel Patrick Moynihan, D-N.Y., would establish a new advisory board on declassifying government data.

Jon Kyl, R-Ariz., had hoped to offer an amendment to improve counterterrorism programs, including language that would make it easier for local law enforcement agencies to share information with intelligence agencies. He backed off after civil rights groups and the Justice Department joined Democrats in saying the provision could violate the constitutional separation of local law enforcement and national intelligence.

Bill Clears Despite Provisions About Classified Leaks

OCTOBER 14 — President Clinton is expected to sign a fiscal 2001 intelligence authorization bill that Congress passed over the objections of some House members troubled by language that would make it a crime to leak classified information.

The Senate adopted the conference report on the bill (HR 4392) by voice vote Oct. 12 without discussion. The House cleared the bill less than two hours later, after an unusually heated debate on whether the classified-information language would silence whistleblowers and undermine the First Amendment.

The provision was in the Senate version of the intelligence bill (S 2507), which covers the Central Intelligence Agency and 10 other intelligence-gathering agencies in the State, Defense and Energy departments. Conferees agreed Oct. 10 to keep the provision in the final version of the bill.

Lawmakers have become increasingly concerned in recent years over the amount of classified information leaked to the news media. Under current law, government employees face felony charges if they release material that harms national security.

The new provision would make almost all other unauthorized and willful disclosures of classified information a felony punishable by up to three years in prison.

Debating Secrets

House Intelligence Committee Chairman Porter J. Goss, R-Fla., said the provision was "narrowly crafted" and had the backing of the Justice Department. He quoted Director of Central Intelligence George J. Tenet as saying the Clinton administration "leaks like a sieve."

Several Intelligence Committee Democrats, however, blasted the provision for giving the government far too much power to punish suspected leakers.

"Congress is foolish . . . to give a blank check to the executive branch for prosecutions in this important area," said Nancy Pelosi, D-Calif.

Georgia Republican Bob Barr said the provision amounted to "an official secrets act" and "would silence whistleblowers in a way that has never come before this body."

John Conyers Jr. of Michigan, the House Judiciary Committee's ranking Democrat, also criticized the Intelligence committees for failing to give his panel a chance to review the issue and hold hearings.

Judiciary Committee member Asa Hutchinson, R-Ark., said whistleblowers would remain fully protected under current law. He said the issue had been adequately considered in the Senate.

Intelligence conferees dropped a provision in the Senate bill designed to clarify the fiscal 2000 intelligence authorization law (PL 106-120) that imposed financial sanctions on international drug kingpins. House members said they preferred to wait for the findings of a commission set up to review the issue. *(1999 Almanac, p. 14-13)*

Veto Urged Over New Penalties For Leaking Classified Data

NOVEMBER 4 — Administration officials were divided over whether President Clinton should sign or veto legislation that would make it a crime to leak classified information. Clinton had until Nov. 4 to decide.

News organizations and some lawmakers mounted a last-minute lobbying campaign against the language, included in the fiscal 2001 intelligence authorization bill (HR 4392). They said it would undermine the First Amendment and silence whistleblowers.

Some critics suggested a compromise — a one-year delay in implementing the provision to give Congress time to assess its implications.

Supporters of the provision said concerns over its effects on press freedom were unjustified. They said it should become law immediately to curtail what they described as a growing flood of government secrets leaked to the news media.

Under current law, government employees risk felony charges if they release material that could harm national security. The new provision would make almost all unauthorized and willful disclosures of classified information a felony punishable by up to three years in prison.

The provision was initially included in the Senate version of the intelligence bill (S 2507 — S Rept 106-279), which authorizes activities of the Central Intelligence Agency and 10 other intelligence-gathering agencies in the State, Defense and Energy departments.

Conferees agreed last month to keep the provision in the final version of the bill (H Rept 106-969).

The administration did not object to the provision when it was first included in the intelligence bill. White House officials, however, became increasingly concerned about its implications after the legislation cleared Congress.

House Intelligence Committee Chairman Porter J. Goss, R-Fla., said he has urged the administration to sign the bill, noting that the provision on leaked material has had the backing of the Justice Department. Goss said that "damage has been done" to national security in recent years as a result of leaks.

Defense Secretary William S. Cohen has said he was startled by how much classified material is given to reporters, including Pentagon memos that have been leaked before he has had a chance to read them.

Attorney General Janet Reno told reporters Nov. 2 that the provision would fill "a very narrow gap" in existing law and would cover material that did not involve national security but that could still harm U.S. interests. "It is not going to result in many new prosecutions," she said.

Julian C. Dixon of California, ranking Democrat on the House Intelligence Committee, said he offered an amendment in conference to narrow the definition of leaks to ensure that only "leaks of information of substantial sensitivity" would be subject to penalties. Dixon said House conferees approved his proposal, but Senate negotiators rejected it.

Goss acknowledged that he would have preferred to pass more narrowly drafted legislation. "I agree it's not perfect, but very little in life is," he said.

False Security?

Lawmakers critical of the provision on classified information contended that it is so broad it would threaten the freedom of journalists to publish important information.

"We should never forget that one of the core purposes of the First Amendment was to prohibit government from suppressing embarrassing information, not criminalizing its release," said Sen. Charles E. Schumer, D-N.Y., a member of the Judiciary Committee. "This legislation attempts to protect our national security at the expense of an informed public, and, in the end, that's no real security at all."

Although the Senate Intelligence Committee held hearings on the proposal that included testimony from outside witnesses, the hearings were conducted in closed session. Schumer said open hearings in the House and Senate Judiciary committees are required to examine the issue.

"This is a good example of why the process in Congress ought to be rather slow and certainly rather open," he told reporters Nov. 1.

Schumer joined two other Judiciary Committee members — Democrat Patrick J. Leahy of Vermont and Republican Charles E. Grassley of Iowa — in arguing that the provision would conflict with existing laws protecting government whistleblowers.

The three senators wrote Senate Appropriations Committee Chairman Ted Stevens, R-Alaska, and ranking Appropriations Democrat Robert C. Byrd of West Virginia on Oct. 27 urging them to include language in a spending bill that would delay the provision for a year.

The current provision, they wrote, "appears to be incompatible" with a law (PL 101-12) beefing up job protections for federal workers who report incidents of government waste, fraud and abuse. *(1989 Almanac, p. 353)*

If the provision becomes law, they wrote, "would-be whistleblowers who believe that certain information should be disclosed would be required to check with their superiors about the status of the information."

Goss said he would be amenable to a delay. Several Senate aides, however, said there was resistance among Republicans who believe the news media have exaggerated the harm the provision would cause.

In an Oct. 30 letter to White House Chief of Staff John D. Podesta, more than 20 organizations — including the American Society of Newspaper Editors, the American Library Association, the Society of Professional Journalists and the Federation of American Scientists — wrote that the provision "creates multiple strikes against the public's right to know."

In particular, the groups said that it would discourage anonymous disclosures of government misconduct, create opportunities for officials to cover up misconduct by destroying classified information, and encourage an overclassification of information.

"If such a provision had been law, the public might never have seen or known about the Pentagon Papers, evidence exposing human rights violations such as the My Lai massacre, false statements concealing leaks of radiation and other toxic substances on workers and into the environment [and] sloppy security creating vulnerability to terrorist attack at defense and national energy facilities," the letter said.

Executives from several leading news organizations, including The New York Times, The Washington Post and Cable News Network, also urged Clinton to veto the legislation.

House Passes New Bill Without Controversial Leaks Provision

NOVEMBER 18 — Lawmakers hope that public hearings next year can generate a compromise on a controversial proposal that would make it a crime to leak classified government information.

After President Clinton vetoed an intelligence authorization bill (HR 4392) that included such a provision, the House removed the language and passed a fresh intelligence bill (HR 5630) on Nov. 13 by voice vote.

Aides to Senate Select Intelligence Committee Chairman Richard C. Shelby, R-Ala., said he has not decided whether to have the Senate take up the new bill. Some observers said the swift House action makes it likely Congress will defer the leaks issue until next year.

Clinton sided with some lawmakers, news media organizations and other critics who said the language would silence whistle-blowers and undermine the First Amendment.

House Judiciary Committee member Bob Barr, R-Ga., said lawmakers need to carefully examine the matter. Barr was among those who criticized the language, which was the subject of closed-door hearings in the Senate Select Intelligence Committee but received no similar scrutiny in the House.

"Hopefully we'll have some hearings on it in a proper venue," Barr said. "Maybe we can come up with something that's much more carefully tailored."

The vetoed provision would have made almost all unauthorized and willful disclosures of classified information a felony punishable by up to three years in prison. Under current law, government employees risk felony charges if they release material that could harm national security.

"The blunderbuss solution that was proposed was overkill," said House Judiciary Chairman Henry J. Hyde, R-Ill. "Hearings might help us."

The provision was backed by the CIA and the Justice Department, and the White House did not object when it was first included in the bill.

Spies in the Sky

Action on the House bill came as a bipartisan commission set up by Congress concluded that bureaucratic changes are needed at the intelligence agency charged with operating the nation's spy satellites.

The National Commission for the Review of the National Reconnaissance Office (NRO) recommended in a report in November that an Office of Space Reconnaissance be established as a semi-autonomous agency within the reconnaissance office.

The report noted that the NRO historically has benefited from the personal attention of the president, close relations between the director of Central Intelligence and the secretary of Defense and "a strong cloak of secrecy" surrounding its activities. It said, however, that such advantages have eroded and more information about the agency has been made public.

The commission was established in the fiscal 2000 intelligence authorization law (PL 106-120). It was chaired by House Select Intelligence Committee Chairman Porter J. Goss, R-Fla., and Sen. Bob Kerrey, D-Neb. *(1999 Almanac, p. 14-13)*

Senate Passes Bill But Raises Ire of House GOP Over Satellite Provision

DECEMBER 9 — A new impasse between House and Senate members has stalled a revised fiscal 2001 intelligence authorization bill, leaving its fate deeper in doubt in the lame-duck session.

The Senate passed the revamped measure (HR 5630) on Dec. 6 by voice vote. The legislation would authorize activities of the Central Intelligence Agency and 10 other intelligence-gathering agencies in the State, Defense and Energy departments.

The vote came three weeks after the House passed the measure in response to President Clinton's veto of the original authorization bill (HR 4392) over a provision that would make it a crime to leak classified information. The new House bill was identical to the original version but omitted the language on leaks.

The Senate, however, adopted an amendment to the new bill by Wayne Allard, R-Colo., to restrict some activities of the super-secret National Reconnaissance Office (NRO), the agency responsible for operating the nation's spy satellites. The amendment sent the measure back to the House, where angry Intelligence Committee Republicans refused to let the bill clear by unanimous consent.

Allard's amendment, approved by voice vote, deleted a section of the House bill that would allow the NRO to enter into contracts for satellite launches without involving the Air Force. Allard originally sought to have the language removed in conference, but his proposal was voted down.

Allard was among the members of a recent bipartisan commission set up by Congress to study the NRO's operations. Allard aides said the senator is not necessarily opposed to allowing the NRO to launch satellites without Air Force involvement, but that he viewed it as a dramatic shift from current practice and wanted more time to study the idea.

However, Michael N. Castle, R-

Del., chairman of the House Subcommittee on Technical and Tactical Intelligence, said the NRO language belongs in the bill and that he would seek to have it reinstated.

Castle said he and Intelligence Committee Chairman Porter J. Goss, R-Fla., agreed that the NRO provision would greatly help streamline the satellite launch process. Castle noted that since 1998, six rocket launch failures have destroyed or damaged military communications and intelligence satellites.

"A series of meetings, hearings and briefings on the severity of these problems has made it obvious that our failures and problems were rooted in the morass of contracts used in the launch program and exacerbated by a tangle of bureaucratic turf concerns," Castle said.

"The Senate's refusal to acknowledge that these reforms are needed is shortsighted and risks more problems in the satellite launch program."

Negotiations ensued, and House Intelligence Committee aides said there was a chance the House would consider the bill on Friday, Dec. 8. But no action was taken as most of the day's session was devoted to speeches paying tribute to the panel's ranking Democrat, Julian C. Dixon of California, who died of an apparent heart attack.

Stalemate on Classified Leaks

Before the Senate passed the new authorization bill, Republicans on the Senate Intelligence Committee had hoped to include compromise language on penalties for leaking classified information, but they were unable to reach agreement with the Clinton administration.

"They were unwilling to scale it back," said a Senate Republican aide.

Although the provision to criminalize leaks had the backing of the Justice Department before the original version of the bill was vetoed, White House Chief of Staff John D. Podesta was among its chief critics.

The provision would have made almost all unauthorized and willful disclosures of classified information a felony punishable by up to three years in prison. Under current law, government employees risk felony charges if they release material that could harm national security.

Supporters of the provision said it was needed to control the proliferation of sensitive material leaked to the news media in recent years. Defense Secretary William S. Cohen said he has been startled by how much classified material is given to reporters, including Pentagon memos that have been leaked before he has had a chance to read them.

However, Podesta and other critics of the secrecy provision — including lawmakers and many prominent media organizations — contended that the language would silence whistleblowers and undermine the First Amendment.

In vetoing the bill Nov. 4, Clinton criticized the provisions as "badly flawed" and "overbroad," and said it "may unnecessarily chill legitimate activities that are at the heart of a democracy."

The president also noted the provision had not been discussed at public hearings before being included in the Senate version of the bill (S 2507 — S Rept 106-279).

Several House Judiciary Committee members who criticized the provision said they expect hearings to be held next year to try to find an acceptable compromise.

'Dire Consequences'

The president's veto led Senate Intelligence Committee Chairman Richard C. Shelby, R-Ala., to angrily accuse opponents of the provision of mischaracterizing what it would do and overstating the harm it could cause.

"Media organizations and others have conjured up a parade of dire consequences that would ensue if [the provision] had become law," Shelby said in a floor speech before the vote on the revised bill.

"Yet this carefully drafted provision would not have silenced whistleblowers, who would continue to enjoy current statutory protections, including those governing the disclosure of classified information to appropriate congressional oversight committees."

Shelby insisted the provision would not have eroded First Amendment rights.

"Even under existing statutes, the Department of Justice rarely seeks to interview or subpoena journalists when investigating leaks," he said.

In addition, Shelby said, an existing executive order on classification already addresses critics' fears that the provision would lead the federal government to overclassify information.

The order "not only provides a procedure for government employees to challenge a classification determination they believe to be improper, but encourages them to do so," he said.

House Clears Bill After Dropping Provision on Launch Contracts

DECEMBER 16 — The House cleared a fiscal 2001 intelligence authorization bill Dec. 11 after agreeing to drop a provision that would have allowed the National Reconnaissance Office (NRO) to negotiate and manage its own contracts for launching spy satellites without help from the Air Force.

The House Intelligence Committee is expected to move quickly next year to try to enact the provision.

The NRO has lost several satellites in launch failures. Michael N. Castle, R-Del., chairman of the House Intelligence Subcommittee on Technical and Tactical Intelligence, said many of the problems with launches could be improved by streamlining the contracting process and eliminating "bureaucratic turf concerns."

Although the House provision had been agreed to in a conference on an earlier version (HR 4392) of the intelligence bill — which President Clinton vetoed for other reasons — the Senate adopted an amendment by Wayne Allard, R-Colo., to the second version (HR 5630) striking the satellite language.

Allard aides said the senator viewed the provision as a dramatic shift from current practice and wanted more time to study the idea.

House Intelligence Committee Chairman Porter J. Goss, R-Fla., called Allard's move "unjustified and inexplicable."

However, Goss said he did not want to hold up the entire bill over the issue. "I am planning to make NRO launch issues, including all aspects of Air Force support for this activity, a top priority . . . in the 107th Congress," he said.

The House agreed to the Senate amendment and cleared the bill by voice vote. Clinton is expected to sign the legislation.

Goss and Allard recently served on a bipartisan commission set up by Congress to study the NRO's operations. The commission was established in the wake of several rocket launch failures that have destroyed or damaged military communications and intelligence satellites.

Commission members noted that at the same time the NRO is proceeding with new satellite acquisition programs, the Air Force is shifting its launch program to a newly developed class of rockets that the commission said "carry a significantly increased risk" of causing further problems.

"The commission is alarmed that there appears to be no comprehensive strategy to address the increased risks presented by simultaneously developing new reconnaissance satellites and launch vehicles," the panel said in its November report. "This contributes to an already uncertain situation where new satellites will be launched on new boosters."

Clinton vetoed the earlier version of the bill over a provision that would have made it a crime to leak classified information. ◆

CQ

Chapter 12

HEALTH

Despite Lengthy Conference, Lawmakers Cannot Agree On Managed Care

SUMMARY

A House-Senate conference was unable to resolve differences between the two chambers' versions of a managed-care bill, and Senate Democrats lacked the votes to pass the House bill, which called for broader federal regulations of health-care insurers than the Senate measure. The issue is likely to resurface in the 107th Congress.

Trying to merge two extremely different managed-care measures — in a conference loaded with GOP members who disagreed with key elements of the House-passed bill — was a Herculean task. Guiding the talks were two politically entrenched senators: conference chairman Don Nickles, R-Okla., who opposed any sweeping, new federal regulations, and conferee Edward M. Kennedy, D-Mass., who pushed for them. Early in the negotiations, Kennedy made it clear he saw the House bill as the "right benchmark against which to measure any conference report." Nickles was just as adamant about the Senate plan. *(Background, 1999 Almanac, p. 16-3)*

Liability was a key stumbling block. The House measure would have allowed patients to sue their health plans for damages in state courts, a departure from current law, which allows such suits only in federal courts and, generally, only to recover the cost of denied care. The Senate bill would not have expanded health plans' liability but would have levied large fines on plans that did not follow an external reviewer's recommendations on medical care.

When both House Majority Leader Dick Armey, R-Texas, and Senate Majority Leader Trent Lott, R-Miss., signaled early in the year that Republicans likely would have to accept some expansion of liability for health insurers, hopes rose for a quick deal that would settle the issue and remove it from the fall elections. House Speaker J. Dennis Hastert, R-Ill., who favored expanded liability, made securing a managed-care deal one of his top legislative priorities for the year. Nickles, however, feared that expanding insurers' liability would lead to lawsuits against employers who provide health insurance to millions of workers.

Nickles said he wanted conferees to reach agreement before the April recess, but little progress was made. Lawmakers squabbled over both liability and scope — which groups of Americans would be covered by the legislation. The House bill would have applied to all 191 million people with private health insurance. The Senate bill would have parceled out its protections, with some provisions covering the approximately 56 million Americans in plans that are exempt from state regulations, and some applying to the 131 million Americans whose health plans are subject to state and federal regulations. Conferees also disagreed over how to structure an external appeals process.

The talks were essentially over by early June. Kennedy tried unsuccessfully to attach the House managed-care measure to the fiscal 2001 defense authorization bill, saying the floor maneuver would help conferees produce a managed-care proposal acceptable to both parties. Nickles called Kennedy's move "political theater." Kennedy's tactics reinforced GOP suspicions that Democrats did not want an agreement and preferred to campaign on managed care.

From that point on, Nickles and other GOP members worked only with Republicans to draft a managed-care agreement, even bringing Charlie Norwood, R-Ga., a cosponsor of the House bill loathed by many Republicans, into the talks. The strategy produced no new legislation, mainly because House and Senate Republicans still could not agree on how to structure a bill. Norwood tried on his own to bring Republicans together, a strategy Nickles rejected.

When Senate Democrats tried unsuccessfully for the third time to embarrass Republicans with a vote on managed care, the GOP fought back with a major concession. On June 29, for the first time, Senate Republicans went on record in favor of expanding patients' rights, under limited circumstances, to sue managed-care plans that deny or delay needed medical care. Four Republicans — Lincoln Chafee of Rhode Island, Peter G. Fitzgerald of Illinois, John McCain of Arizona and Arlen Specter of Pennsylvania — broke ranks to vote with Democrats.

As summer turned to fall, Kennedy and other Senate Democrats boasted that GOP support for the House approach was growing — especially from vulnerable Republicans running for re-election — and predicted they would have enough votes to pass the House bill before adjournment. That prediction never came true. Instead, federal regulation of managed-care plans turned out to be an issue for the fall presidential and congressional campaigns rather than a focus of floor action in either chamber.

Box Score

- **Bill:** HR 2990
- **Legislative action: Senate** voted, 51-48, on June 8 to table (kill) an amendment that would have attached the House managed-care bill to the fiscal 2001 defense authorization measure (S 2549).

Senate voted, 51-47, on June 29, in favor of limited expansion of patients' rights to sue managed-care plans for damages if they deny or delay needed medical care.

For Conferees, Insurer Liability Is Among Obstacles

FEBRUARY 5 — Health plan liability has been such a focus of the managed care debate that when GOP leaders recently expressed their willingness to

Managed Care Bills Compared

FEBRUARY 5 — Key differences between the House (HR 2990) and Senate (S 1344) managed care bills:

Scope: While the House bill would apply to all 161 million Americans in private insurance plans, some protections in the Senate plan would apply only to the 48 million people in plans exempt from state regulations. Some provisions in the Senate bill would cover 124 million Americans in employer-sponsored plans, while others would affect everyone in a private plan.

Liability: The House bill would permit patients to sue their health plans for damages in state courts. The Senate bill would not. Both plans also call for large penalties against health plans that do not follow the decision of an external review panel. For example, the Senate bill would allow penalties up to $10,000 if a health plan ignored a reviewer's decision. The House bill has penalties as well, including a $1,000 fine per day if a plan doesn't abide by a reviewer's decision.

Purchasing Groups: The House bill would allow the creation of so-called HealthMarts and association health plans, which backers say would help consumers form purchasing groups that would make insurance more affordable. The Senate bill does not contain these provisions.

Both bills share a series of tax provisions, such as allowing a 100 percent tax deduction for health care insurance premiums for the self-employed and for long-term care premiums. Both measures also would expand a current pilot program for medical savings accounts, which are tax-exempt and are used to pay medical expenses. Democrats have said they view many of the tax provisions as "poison pills" they want stripped from the legislation.

give patients the right to sue their health plans, many thought Congress would quickly send a bill to President Clinton before the fall campaigns.

But lurking behind the high-profile liability issue are differences both large and small, technical and political that could cause House and Senate conferees to stumble as they reconcile the two chambers' managed care bills (HR 2990 and S 1344).

"There's far more dangerous aspects than just the right to sue," said conferee Rep. John A. Boehner, R-Ohio.

One potential obstacle is scope. Provisions of the House-passed bill apply to all 161 million Americans in private insurance plans, while the Senate bill parcels out its protections.

For example, the Senate provisions governing emergency care apply only to the 48 million Americans in plans that are exempt from state regulations. Other sections, including those detailing appeals processes, apply to the 124 million Americans who are covered under employer-sponsored plans subject to both state and federal regulation.

Still other parts of the Senate bill, such as a provision dealing with mastectomy care, would affect all 161 million Americans in private plans.

While these divisions have caused some confusion, they are crucial to GOP senators who do not want to interfere with individual state laws on managed care. Democrats have repeatedly attacked the Senate bill for its limitations, saying they render the bill meaningless for millions of Americans.

The question of external appeals may also create more trouble for conferees. Critics of the House bill say it would allow a reviewer to order a health plan to provide services not covered in a patient's policy, which could prove costly to insurers. On the other hand, critics of the Senate bill say it takes too long for patients to get through the appeals process and would not allow them to opt out — as the House bill would — and head directly to court for a resolution.

Furthermore, conferees must slog through differences in provisions dealing with emergency care, and access to clinical trials and specialists, among others. The lawmakers are also expected to include provisions of legislation (HR 2824) — in particular its liability sections — that House GOP leaders backed last year, even though that bill failed to pass.

How to handle legislation dealing with medical mistakes is another area where negotiations could break down. Several Republicans want the issue folded into the managed care bill, while Democrats argue against that approach. Senate conferee Bill Frist, R-Tenn., said the medical errors issue would only be added if there is consensus between the parties on how to proceed.

Some GOP members also want the final bill to make public a database that lists physicians who have been sued for malpractice, a proposal the American Medical Association opposes.

Conferee Deliberations

House and Senate conferees are scheduled to begin work Feb. 10. Republican conferees met without Democrats on Feb. 3 but were tight-lipped as they left the office of Assistant Senate Majority Leader Don Nickles, R-Okla., the conference chairman.

Frist said the GOP conferees needed to learn more specifics before returning to their deliberations.

"It's clear that senators don't know what's in the House bill and they don't know what's in our bill. . . . Now we've got to make a concerted effort to learn what's in the bills," said Frist, a heart-lung transplant surgeon.

Although many conferees have yet to talk publicly about what provisions they want to see in the conference report, Boehner has launched a full-scale attack against the House-passed bill, which was cosponsored by Charlie Norwood, R-Ga., and John D. Dingell, D-Mich.

In remarks made Jan. 31 to the American Hospital Association, Boehner, the former House GOP conference chairman, said lawmakers and the public need to look beyond the liability provisions of the Norwood-Dingell bill to see its other flaws.

Boehner said the measure would give far too much power to the Department of Labor to decide issues such as the adequacy of a health plan's provider network. He believes the bill would place more than 400 new requirements on insurers that would be monitored by the Labor Department, the Department of Health and Human Services and, in some cases, the Internal Revenue Service.

Giving the federal government that large a role in overseeing health care would reduce coverage and cut jobs, he said. Those charges are echoed by the insurance and business groups, of which Boehner is a key ally.

"You're asking for a whole lot of trouble," said Boehner, who is chairman of the House Education and the Workforce Employer-Employee Relations Subcommittee.

Liability Concerns

Despite Boehner's pleas that lawmakers focus on other aspects of the managed care debate, liability continues to be a main topic of discussion.

Senate Majority Leader Trent Lott, R-Miss., said Feb. 1 that while he predicts the conference package will give patients the right to sue in "egregious cases," he does not want managed care legislation to become "just a lawyers' bill of rights. We don't want it just to become an invitation for an avalanche of lawsuits."

The announcement Feb. 1 that Nickles would serve as conference chairman seemed to signal that the GOP would take a hard line against expanding health plans' liability. "I'm sending a message that we are not going to cave to the House position, which is a trial lawyer's dream. . . . I have faith that Don Nickles will not allow that to happen," Lott said.

Yet it is clear that the final package must make some movement toward making health plans more legally liable for the decisions they make about health care coverage for patients.

Sixty-eight House Republicans voted with Democrats on Oct. 7 for the Norwood-Dingell bill, which would allow patients to sue their health plans in state courts. The Senate bill would not permit such suits, but would assess fees as high as $10,000 for offenses such as ignoring a reviewer's decision on patient care. The House bill also assesses fines, including a $1,000 per day penalty if a plan does not abide by a reviewer's decision.

The 1974 Employee Retirement Income Security Act (PL 93-406), known as ERISA, permits health plans to be sued only in federal courts and generally limits damages to the cost of denied care. *(1974 Almanac, p. 244)*

A middle ground that could please lawmakers may lie in a House GOP bill that was cosponsored by Republicans Porter J. Goss of Florida, Tom Coburn of Oklahoma and John Shadegg of Arizona. That measure would permit patients to sue their health plans in federal courts after exhausting a series of appeals and would also allow suits in state courts if state laws permitted them.

Even if Congress does not resolve the liability issue this year, states and the courts are taking steps to make health plans more legally liable for the decisions they make. Texas and California, for example, have already passed laws allowing patients to sue health plans in state courts.

In addition, lawyers are filing class action suits against health insurers. The managed care industry is currently facing at least 16 class action suits, including some filed by Lott's brother-in-law, Pascagoula, Miss. lawyer Richard Scruggs, who has won multimillion-dollar awards against the tobacco industry. Attorneys general for Connecticut and Missouri also have filed suits against managed care insurers.

Political Wrangling

With the fall elections looming, many Republicans are eager to get managed care off the table as an issue for Democrats, who are more than willing to keep it alive.

The political wrangling that lies ahead became clear Feb. 1 when House Democrats sought to shape the conference negotiations with a nonbinding "motion to instruct." *(Vote 6, p. H-4)*

The proposal, sponsored by Rep. Marion Berry, D-Ark., urged conferees to meet quickly and, when they did meet, to disregard the so-called access provisions of the House bill, which includes tax breaks that supporters say would help more people afford insurance coverage.

House Ways and Means Health Subcommittee Chairman Bill Thomas, R-Calif., said the motion was "a clear indication that somebody wants political game-playing rather than a solution." Many Republicans have long said that Democrats are interested in managed care as a political issue rather than an area where they want to find compromise with Republicans.

Dingell said he was "distressed" at Thomas' accusations.

"It is simply orderly business of the House provided for in the rules," said Dingell. "It is a resolution that is going to expedite the process. There is no politics here."

While the Democrats won the vote on Berry's motion, 207-175, 28 members — most of them Republicans who voted for the Norwood-Dingell bill last year — voted "present" rather than offend House and Senate Republican leaders who have said they want to take action on managed care before the spring recess.

Norwood voted "present" and chided Democrats for their action.

"People who have been our hard-core opponents are now offering an olive branch," Norwood said. "We need to take it and make the best of it that we possibly can make."

Conferees Begin Work With High Hopes, Tight Schedule

MARCH 4 — Managed-care conferees began deliberations March 2 with hopes of striking a deal by the end of the month. But members of both parties admitted that the substantive and political differences between the two bills (S 1344 and HR 2990) will complicate that goal.

For example, many of the Senate bill's protections would apply to limited groups of people, while the House measure would apply to all 161 million Americans who have health insurance.

Another key point of disagreement is that the House bill would allow lawsuits in state courts against health insurers, but the Senate bill would not.

Despite such obstacles, Assistant Senate Majority Leader Don Nickles,

R-Okla., who was selected to head the conference, told conferees March 2 that he expects them to work "real hard" to conclude their discussions by the end of March. Nickles also said he wanted to have a final package pass both houses by the Easter/Passover recess.

"It will take a lot of work and a lot of cooperation," Nickles said. "I think we have a much better chance of passing good legislation . . . if we work sooner rather than later."

Moving the legislation quickly would also remove the contentious issue from the fall elections, where Democrats would be sure to make it prominent in their campaigns.

Areas of Difference

It is unclear, however, whether Nickles can obtain his objectives. Staff discussions have yet to iron out differences even in areas where the two bills are similar, such as the degree of emergency medical treatment and allowing patients to seek care directly from a gynecologist rather than first seeking authorization from an insurer. On March 3, however, staff aides agreed — subject to members' approval — to allow pediatricians to be primary care providers.

While Democratic and Republican conferees pledged to work together, members of both sides peppered their opening remarks with partisan jabs that hinted at difficulties to come.

Rep. Thomas J. Bliley Jr., R-Va., said provisions in the House measure that would create purchasing groups to help consumers buy insurance — which Democrats adamantly oppose — should be in the final package. And Sen. James M. Jeffords, R-Vt., said the Senate bill would avoid costly mandates that would increase health insurance premiums.

Sen. Edward M. Kennedy, D-Mass., said the House-passed bill should be the "right benchmark against which to measure any conference report." And just hours before conferees met, President Clinton said at a White House news conference that Congress must send him a "strong, enforceable" measure in order to avoid a veto.

Rep. Charlie Norwood, R-Ga., a main sponsor of the House-passed bill, was clearly irritated at the lack of progress. "They've got to get down to the damn nitty-gritty," he said after the March 2 conference concluded. Although Norwood is not an official conferee, his support of any deal is critical for it to win House passage.

Nickles said he hoped staff discussions would produce several areas of agreement before conferees meet again March 9.

Areas where compromise may be found, Nickles said, are in providing timely access to specialists, giving patients the ability to participate in clinical trials and requiring health plans to cover prescription drugs not included in a health plan's pre-approved list.

Once those issues are resolved, however, conferees will have to tackle more serious obstacles.

Liability remains a key stumbling block. Nickles and other GOP conferees do not favor expanding patients' ability to sue their health plans. But some key House and Senate Republican leaders have expressed a willingness to do so. In a March 2 interview, House Speaker J. Dennis Hastert, R-Ill., said "We couldn't pass a bill without some form of liability."

The 1974 Employee Retirement Income Security Act (PL 93-406), known as ERISA, permits health plans to be sued only in federal courts and generally limits damages to the cost of denied care. *(1974 Almanac, p. 244)*

Another main point of contention is the scope of the Senate bill. For example, provisions governing emergency care would apply only to the 55 million Americans in plans that are exempt from state regulations. Sections dealing with how to appeal an insurer's decision would apply only to the 128 million Americans who are covered under employer-sponsored plans subject to both state and federal regulations. Still other parts of the Senate legislation, such as a provision dealing with mastectomy care, would apply to all 161 million Americans who have health insurance.

Those distinctions irritate Democrats, who say that any bill ought to cover all Americans. "The Senate bill is riddled with loopholes and flaws," said Rep. Frank Pallone Jr., D-N.J.

Scheduling Problems

While conferees are to meet again March 9, scheduling subsequent sessions may be a problem, since the Senate is in recess the following week. Other legislative business, such as passing a budget resolution, may also take conferees' attention away from the deliberations over managed care.

And even if a deal is reached, congressional action could stall if it is not endorsed by groups representing doctors, hospitals and other health care providers, as well as by patients groups. Business and insurance organizations also present formidable opposition; they dislike many provisions of both the House and Senate bills and are unlikely to accept any final deal.

"I don't underestimate the difficulty of our task," Jeffords said.

Republicans Look To Nickles To Deliver on Patients' Rights

MARCH 11 — Don Nickles is in a bind. He has spent the better part of his four-year tenure as Senate GOP whip trying to beat Edward M. Kennedy like a mule. So why should anyone believe that Nickles, a deeply conservative Oklahoma Republican, can — or even wants to — cut a deal with the liberal icon from Massachusetts on a bitterly fought bill to give patients more clout with their health care providers?

Maybe he cannot. After all, he has spent almost two decades in the Senate battling costly regulations on business. And it is clear that any approach to the legislation (HR 2990, S 1344) that would be acceptable to Kennedy — and to President Clinton — would give the government a sweeping new role in overseeing health care. That would be anathema to Nickles.

Nickles is not naive. But to hear him talk about the unfolding House-Senate conference on HR 2990, which he chairs, you would think he believes that in this fiercely partisan Congress, he and Kennedy and legendary House Democrat John D. Dingell of Michigan can roll up their sleeves and hash things out like policy wonks. "I hope everybody lowers the decibels a little bit and just see — we'll just see — if we have the possibility of working out these issues," he said.

Nickles' greatest strength as a whip has been his ability to rally moderate and conservative Republicans around a unified position. But what he has yet to demonstrate, particularly on an issue of the political magnitude of the "patients' bill of rights," is an ability to negotiate with Democrats.

Democrats clearly have the political edge, having driven the issue to the congressional stage, spurred by horror stories of patients being denied care by their health maintenance organizations (HMOs). Nickles faces intense pressure to substantially compromise from the narrowly drawn Senate bill, which he took the lead in crafting. It would give the 56 million people whose health insurance plans are exempt from state laws a series of new protections, such as guaranteed payment for emergency room visits. The House bill, written by Dingell and Charlie Norwood, R-Ga. — and passed with 68 GOP votes — would cover everyone with private health insurance. It contains a hotly contested provision that would give patients broad rights to sue their health plans over denial of care.

With Democrats and Clinton playing hardball, any viable bill would have to move toward the House position, winning the blessing of Norwood and a critical bloc of House Republicans who feel strongly about the need for more sweeping protections than the Senate's, which Democrats and the White House have dismissed as a "charade." But Nickles feels strongly that the House measure is a "bad bill" that would increase health care costs and prompt companies to drop coverage for their workers.

The pressure on Nickles does not come from Democrats alone. It comes from fellow Republicans, especially in the House, who see their cherished GOP majority in peril if they fail to deliver a patients' bill of rights. They are desperate to find a solution and rid themselves of a political albatross.

Moreover, managed health care is perhaps the hottest issue before the public. GOP presidential front-runner George W. Bush backs the idea of a patients' bill of rights, and vulnerable Senate Republicans, such as Spencer Abraham of Michigan, are said to be pushing for a bill.

So Nickles has to choose between deeply held policy beliefs on one hand and his party's political needs on the other. He admits that the conference may have little chance of producing a bill that could become law. But he says he wants to try.

"Maybe there's some ways around some of the obstructions if people lay aside some of the political rhetoric and say, 'Hey, can we adopt patient protections that will improve health care without dramatically increasing cost?' " Nickles said in an interview March 7. "I think so. I am optimistic. But it's going to be a difficult conference."

Said Ron Pollack, executive director of the Families USA Foundation, which supports the House bill: "Nickles is the 500-pound gorilla on the patients' bill of rights. He is the one person who will make or break whether legislation gets adopted. . . . So Nickles needs to make a judgment whether he wants to follow his own ideology or whether he wants to be politically more practical."

Unifying Republicans

Nickles was the obvious choice to run the conference. He led a GOP task force on the issue that met for 18 months before Senate Majority Leader Trent Lott, R-Miss. — in response to pressure from Democrats — brought the bill up for a vote last July. Working with disparate wings of the GOP conference, Nickles fashioned a bill that won the support of all but two Republicans. Moderates such as James M. Jeffords, R-Vt., and Susan Collins, R-Maine — who might have otherwise forged coalitions with Democrats — were kept in the fold during a week of partisan fighting on the Senate floor.

"His work on the patients' bill of rights is probably the best leadership I've seen since I've been in the Senate," said Phil Gramm, R-Texas, a conservative ally of Nickles. "He did it by working hard at it, by getting people involved early, by everybody going through a joint education process, and so what we have is a bill that Jim Jeffords is as strong for as I am." Added Collins: "One reason we stuck together is because he had been so inclusive."

The managed health care issue is but one of several that Lott has handed off to Nickles. Another example is the recent Senate floor fight over raising the minimum wage, in which Nickles fashioned an amendment — offered by Pete V. Domenici, R-N.M. — to raise the wage by $1 over three years, accompanied by a five-year, $18 billion package of business-related tax cuts. The Nickles-Domenici proposal passed in February as part of a bill (HR 833) to overhaul federal bankruptcy laws. Nickles outmaneuvered Kennedy, who lost a bid to impose the wage increase over two years.

Nickles' role in crafting GOP policy is a natural outgrowth of his role as the Senate's second-ranking Republican. He considered running against Lott for majority leader in 1996 but ultimately opted for the No. 2 job after negotiating with Lott for more staff members and a plum office just off the Senate floor. His title is "assistant majority leader" instead of whip.

"I think what they've worked out with the whip position . . . is that Nickles is not merely a vote counter. He is a consensus builder," said Nickles' former chief of staff Doug Badger, a principal at Washington Counsel, a lobbying firm. "And so, he'll actually take a raw issue on which there is substantial disagreement and forge consensus. And the votes are there."

But Nickles has not done as well with Democrats. "I can't remember a time when he was asked to negotiate from the right to the center," said a longtime adversary. It is unclear whether Nickles can effectively make the moves toward the House position required to get a bill that the House could pass.

"I have a very high regard for his positive political skills, especially in closed-door and small group dynamics," said Rep. Bill Thomas, R-Calif., who added that Nickles' proven ability to forge consensus among Republicans could be applied as well to his dealings with Democrats. "Just appreciate the fact that Republicans in the House and Senate sometimes have a gulf as large if not larger than some Republicans and Democrats."

Added a senior Senate GOP leadership aide: "Can he move the various people into configuration where you can get the conference report through? I don't know. I don't know if anyone can do that."

The Right Moves

So far at least, Nickles has tried to make all the right moves. He has taken pains to try to create a "real" conference, in which members of both parties and chambers hash out differences over policy among themselves without taking dictation from the leadership. To try to keep the issue out of the campaign season, Nickles set an ambitious deadline of March 31 to seal an agreement, though virtually no one believes the deadline can be met.

Nickles also has reached out to Democrats such as Kennedy and Dingell, who credit him with establishing a fair and open conference process. The way Nickles sees it, the long-shot chance for a successful conference is to build momentum by agreeing on smaller issues and hope that it grows into agreement on the bigger issues, such as determining how many people to protect.

"It would be very easy for a pundit on the outside to say, 'There's no way you're going to do that because there's just too big a difference. Nickles is not giving on scope, and liability is just impossible, so you're not going to have a bill,' " Nickles said. "But I almost think that I can see a way. . . . It's a long shot, it's not a high probability to even have a successful conference, but it's still my hope."

Democrats are, to say the least, skeptical. "Nickles is, as a matter of strategy, and it's pretty apparent, trying to set this up that if there's agreement on the narrower issues . . . he wants to be able to say, 'Well, we've agreed on 90 percent and why don't we just go with that?' " said an aide to a top Democratic conferee. "That's not going to happen."

But to the extent there is a chance for a successful conference, say those following the process closely, it may depend to a great degree on the natural instincts of Democrats Kennedy and Dingell to produce legislation. "Kennedy and Dingell are people I think who genuinely want a bill," said a labor union lobbyist. "If there was any way that they could cut a deal on this, they would."

Added a senior Nickles staff aide: "We're sitting across the table from one institutionalist . . . Ted Kennedy. And across the rotunda, is another, a man who's been here since 1955, John Dingell. These are the people who can make something happen if we all choose to reject the 1990s models of bitter partisanship and try to work it out with good will, good faith and a good, firm handshake."

Kennedy and Nickles, however, are renowned for their intense floor tussles. And ever since Kennedy successfully led Senate Democrats in a 1996 bid to raise the minimum wage, Nickles and Lott seem to have gone out of their way to make sure Kennedy takes his lumps on the floor. *(1996 Almanac, p. 7-3)*

Two years after Kennedy teamed up with Nancy Landon Kassebaum, R-Kan. (1978-97), to enact a popular law (PL 104-191) aimed at ensuring that workers who change their jobs or get sick could keep their health insurance, Nickles stripped money to help enforce the law from a 1998 supplemental appropriations bill (PL 105-174) and moved to kill a Kennedy bid to restore some of the funding. Nickles' motion passed, 51-49. *(1998 Almanac, p. 2-121)*

A Kennedy staff aide said that his boss and Nickles nonetheless have a "pretty friendly relationship." Asked about the conference, Kennedy said, "We've been at this now for over three and a half years. The president wants a bill. I want a bill. We all want a bill. And it's really going to be dependent upon whether we come out with something that's closer to the House than the Senate."

Kennedy pointed out that 47 senators, including two Republicans, have announced they support the House bill, and other likely supporters have not announced positions yet. "I think we have a majority of the Senate now," he said.

While Kennedy and other Democratic conferees are taking pains to be diplomatic, other Democrats barely bother to hide their disdain for Nickles, who they think undercuts Lott and destroys deals. "I don't trust him as far as I could throw him," said a senior Senate Democrat, who called Nickles an unprintable epithet.

Moving Nickles

House Republicans eager for a bill have yet to detect enough flexibility on Nickles' part to produce an agreement. "Is it possible? Yes," said Rep. W.J. "Billy" Tauzin, R-La. "Probable yet? No."

The key to moving Nickles, said a senior House GOP leadership aide, is for vulnerable senators up for re-election such as Abraham, John Ashcroft, R-Mo., and Rick Santorum, R-Pa., to press Nickles and Lott to move toward the House. "We need to get those senators who are vulnerable engaged, and they are. That's our strategy," the aide said.

Olympia J. Snowe, R-Maine, a moderate member of Nickles' whip operation who is up for re-election, said she pushed Nickles to move. "I want to be able to give assurances to people that we're going to resolve this issue once and for all," Snowe said.

It is no secret that Democrats believe they hold a politically strong hand and are perfectly willing to use the issue to club Republicans.

"For us, it's a win-win. We win if we don't get a bill, politically," said Senate Minority Leader Tom Daschle, D-S.D. "We win politically and legislatively if we do get a bill."

While Democrats such as Kennedy are happy to participate in the talks, their leverage comes from turning up the heat. Their plan seems to be to make Republicans crumble under pressure from the public and other Republicans. But Nickles says he does not "succumb to pressure very easily," adding, "I want to pass a good bill. I will not pass a bad bill. . . . I think I can stop a bad bill from passing."

If Nickles' conference collapses, or if Republicans send a bill to the White House that Clinton vetoes, it will not end there. "There is no such thing as killing this issue," said a lobbyist opposed to the bill.

The prospect of Republicans sending a bill to the White House for a Clinton veto prompted this response from Sen. Christopher J. Dodd, D-Conn.: "If they come out of [conference] and they call that a patients' bill of rights and [Clinton] looks into the camera and says that 'this is anything but, and I can't leave as one of my final acts as president of the United States to sign something that so violates what the American people want,' they're cooked. That's the worst scenario for them."

But the idea that Nickles and Clinton could agree on this issue and appear in a Rose Garden signing ceremony is difficult for many members to wrap their minds around. "It's hard to believe that could happen," said conservative Sen. Robert C. Smith, R-N.H. "But stranger things have happened."

Target Date Slips As Conferees Wrangle Over Scope, Liability

APRIL 1 — A March 31 deadline that managed-care conference chairman Sen. Don Nickles, R-Okla., set for conferees passed with no announcement, a missed benchmark that could illustrate the rough road ahead as legislators try to reach consensus on the politically sensitive issue.

The GOP would like to pass a bill in order to remove the issue from the Democrats' arsenal in the fall election campaigns. Republican and Democratic conferees said that while they have made progress toward melding the two managed-care measures (HR 2990, S 1344) into one bill — more agreements may be announced at an April 5 meeting — substantial disputes remain. Areas of dissent include how to structure the external appeals process, whom the bill would cover and whether to expand health plans' liability in disputes over medical care.

"I'm increasingly concerned now that time is moving on and we have great obstacles ahead," conferee Sen. Edward M. Kennedy, D-Mass., said March 29.

House conferee John D. Dingell, D-Mich., said if the group does not reach a deal by the April 17 spring recess, additional pressure may be necessary. "It gives a fine opportunity to those who want a bill to beat on those standing in the way," he said March 29.

Republican conferees were upbeat about the progress of negotiations, and some said a conference deal may not be that far away. "This is time well-spent," said Rep. Porter J. Goss, R-Fla. Sen. James M. Jeffords, R-Vt., said March 29 he was "encouraged" a bipartisan deal could come soon.

Steady Progress

Although there have been no public conferee meetings since a March 9 session where Nickles announced agreement on coverage for emergency medical care, pediatric coverage and professional licensing, members and their staffs have continued negotiating on such issues as whether to allow direct access to obstetrical and gynecological care and ensuring individuals more timely access to specialists and to clinical trials.

Most recently, discussions have focused on internal and external appeals processes, which Nickles termed "the most important part of the bill." He and other backers of the Senate measure believe that a strong appeals process is more important for consumers than expanding their ability to sue their health plans. The 1974 Employee Retirement Income Security Act (PL 93-406), known as ERISA, usually permits health plans to be sued only in federal courts and generally limits damages to the cost of denied care. *(1974 Almanac, p. 244)*

"We've made good progress [on the appeals discussions]," Nickles said March 28. But Dingell said he was "not convinced" that a deal was near.

Despite missing his March 31 deadline, Nickles said it was still "very much my objective" to have both chambers vote on a conferee managed-care agreement by the recess.

Before that can occur, however, Republicans "have to get on the same page," said Sen. Judd Gregg, R-N.H.

For example, Republicans differ on the issue of coverage limits. In the Senate measure, provisions such as emergency medical care would apply only to the 56 million Americans in self-insured health plans. But appeals provisions would apply to the 131 million individuals covered under employer-sponsored plans that are subject to both state and federal regulation. Provisions dealing with mastectomy care and genetic testing would apply to the 191 million Americans covered under private health insurance plans.

All provisions of the House bill would apply to the 191 million individuals with private health insurance.

The coverage figures are based on the latest Labor Department estimates.

Gregg and other Senate GOP conferees believe that maintaining the narrower scope of the Senate bill is critical. They say that Congress should not interfere with states' authority to pass their own medical mandate laws.

Many House Republicans, however, see it differently. Last October, 68 Republicans supported the House managed-care bill sponsored by Dingell and Charlie Norwood, R-Ga., which would cover all people in private insurance plans. If conferees do not keep its provisions intact, they can expect a barrage of criticism not only from Democrats, who have argued loudly that everyone must be covered under any managed-care bill, but from Republicans as well.

Other Influences

So far, Senate Majority Leader Trent Lott, R-Miss., and House Speaker J. Dennis Hastert, R-Ill., have steered clear of the managed-care conference. Lott said March 29 he has "a lot of confidence in the people involved in these negotiations" — Nickles in particular — adding that "if . . . they need the Speaker and I to become involved, we would."

Pressure from interest groups could also alter the conference dynamic. On March 28, the American Association of Health Plans, which represents managed-care providers, announced a $200,000 ad campaign to encourage conferees and other lawmakers to broaden the debate to include the issue of medical errors. An Institute of Medicine report released last year said that medical errors kill as many as 98,000 people annually.

The insurance group's 30-second television spot urges lawmakers to "get patients the care they need instead of getting lawyers the clients they need."

Hospital groups, which oppose the mandatory reporting of medical errors, were quick to criticize the ad campaign. It is "nothing more than a thinly veiled attempt to divert attention away from critical good faith negotiations currently occurring between Republicans and Democrats in Congress," said Dick Davidson, president of the American Hospital Association.

Conferees Struggle For Consensus On External Review Process

APRIL 8 — Despite intense negotiations, House and Senate managed-care conferees were unable to agree the week of April 3 on how to structure a provision that would allow patients to appeal a health insurer's decision to an independent review panel.

The issue is one of the most critical disputes among conferees trying to merge two managed-care measures (HR 2990, S 1344) into one bill. Central to the debate over so-called external appeals is whether physicians or insurers would make the final decision on what care is medically necessary.

Republicans generally do not want to establish a precedent that would undermine contractual agreements between health plans and patients, while many Democrats argue that an outside reviewer should be able to recommend care that is medically necessary but may not be explicitly covered under a patient's health plan.

"Precision is so important here," said House conferee Robert E. Andrews, D-N.J. "That's why the members have been working with the actual drafts of actual legislative language. . . . We understand the way something is precisely phrased is very consequential."

Optimism on Appeals

Andrews and others who attended the April 6 closed-door session in the office of conference chairman Sen. Don Nickles, R-Okla., are optimistic a deal can be reached on external appeals, and they said discussions would resume April 11. Issues at play in the negotiations include what constitutes an independent reviewer, what claims should be eligible for external review and how to select members of a review panel.

Nickles and other GOP conferees believe a strong external appeals provision would eliminate the need to expand health plans' liability, a provision that Democrats insist is key to any final deal on managed care. Resolving external appeals also could help clear the way for conferees to reach agreement on whom the bill would cover, another key difference between the House and Senate bills.

As conferees continued their deliberations, watchdog groups released reports showing how the managed-care industry is spending heavily to help stop Congress from passing any managed-care legislation this year.

An April 5 report from the consumer advocacy group Public Citizen said that managed-care interests had given $21 million in federal campaign contributions to Republicans and Democrats since 1995, with Republicans receiving nearly $16 million. Almost 40 percent of the contributions were "soft money" donations — which are unlimited and unregulated — to Republican Party committees.

A report issued April 4 by the nonpartisan Center for Responsive Politics found that members of the Health Benefits Coalition, which represents insurers and employer groups opposed to new mandates, accounted for at least $3.9 million in soft money, political action committee and individual contributions to federal parties and candidates in 1999. Nearly $1 million of that went to Republicans, an increase of nearly 40 percent since 1995, the opening year of the last presidential election cycle.

Insurers also spent heavily on lobbying members of Congress and the Clinton administration in 1999, the center said. For example, Aetna spent $2.1 million in 1999, a 15 percent increase over 1998, and Cigna Corp. spent nearly $1.6 million last year, an increase of 20 percent over 1998. The American Association of Health Plans (AAHP), which represents managed-care providers, spent nearly $2.5 million on lobbying expenditures last year — an increase of nearly $500,000 over 1998.

The AAHP also drew attention for a series of television advertisements designed to encourage managed-care conferees and other lawmakers to broaden the ongoing debate to include the issue of medical errors. An Institute of Medicine report released last year said medical errors kill as many as 98,000 people annually.

$200,000 Ad Campaign

Supporters of the House managed-care bill urged the group April 5 to pull the spots, which are part of a two-week, $200,000 advertising campaign that began March 28. The 30-second spot encourages lawmakers to "get patients the care they need instead of getting lawyers the clients they need."

Managed-care conferee Rep. Frank Pallone Jr., D-N.J., said at an April 5 press conference that the commercials were designed to "muck up the conference" by trying to force a discussion of medical errors. Fellow conferee Rep. John D. Dingell, D-Mich., agreed. "Managed-care reform is not about medical errors," he said.

Added Martin Frost of Texas, chairman of the House Democratic Caucus: The AAHP "know[s] better than to try to fight this battle on the merits."

The American Medical Association, the American Nurses Association and the American Hospital Association wrote to AAHP President and Chief Executive Officer Karen M. Ignagni on March 31 asking her to pull the ads. "Stop the rapid erosion of your organization's credibility by the immediate withdrawal of your media campaign on medical errors," the groups said.

The campaign even caused Premier Inc., a buying consortium for hospitals, to resign March 31 from the Health Benefits Coalition, of which AAHP is also a member.

But Ignagni said she has no intention of pulling the ads.

"To the extent that our current television advertising campaign has helped spark a broader awareness that the true path to patient protection is not built on more litigation, that's a step forward," she said April 5.

Conferees Agree On Principles For Appeals; Key Details Unresolved

APRIL 15 — After three weeks of negotiations, House and Senate managed-care conferees tentatively agreed April 13 to a list of "principles" that would allow patients to appeal an insurer's decision to an independent oversight panel.

Appeals could be made if a benefit denial exceeded an undefined "significant threshold" or if a patient's "life, health or development" were in jeopardy, according to an outline of the agreement. Plans could charge $50 for an appeal, but would have to refund it if the patient's appeal were successful. The fee would be waived for low-income individuals.

Conferees still have not settled several key issues involving so-called external appeals — including how many patients would be covered. In the House managed-care bill (HR 2990) that passed in October, all 191 million

Americans with private health insurance would be able to make an external appeal. Under the Senate bill (S 1344), which passed in July, only 131 million Americans would be eligible.

Conferees also have not yet spelled out a time frame for insurers to act on appeals, nor have they said what action a patient could take if an insurer ignored an appeal board's decision, even though such a decision is binding on the health plan.

Big Differences Remain

Conferees are still far from reaching accord on many of the larger differences separating the two bills. Lawmakers must decide who will be covered by any final deal and whether or not to broaden health plans' liability for decisions they make about patient care. House conferee John D. Dingell, D-Mich., said April 13 that resolving those two areas is critical to any final deal.

Still, Dingell joined conference Chairman Sen. Don Nickles, R-Okla., in praising the agreement on external appeals. "One key issue is that the reviewer, not the HMO, will decide what can be appealed," Dingell said.

Nickles said the review process "is the most important way for patients to have a remedy." He had described the external review as the "guts of the bill."

House conferee John A. Boehner, R-Ohio, said the tentative agreement on external appeals made him "more optimistic than ever that a responsible, meaningful health reform measure will be enacted" this year.

Nickles had hoped to have conferees reach agreement on a managed-care package before the spring recess, which began April 14. But as conferees' discussions continued on the external appeals issue, it became clear that deadline would not be met.

Senate and House staff aides will spend the recess attempting to flesh out the external appeals agreement. But these details have already been agreed to by both parties:

- A patient could appeal an insurer's decision that a procedure either is not medically necessary, or is experimental or investigational.
- Patients could appeal for coverage of a benefit they believe is within their contract, even if the health plan disagrees.
- Patients could not appeal to receive a benefit that their health insurance plan explicitly does not cover.
- An appeals board could decide that a claim does not warrant a review.

Karen Ignagni, president and chief executive officer of the American Association of Health Plans, a managed-care trade group, said the tentative agreement recognizes "that patients should receive care based on scientific evidence and best practices."

The appeals process can be costly for health plans, with estimates ranging from $500 to $1,000 or more to conduct an individual review. With such a large price tag, conferees want to take steps to guard against frivolous appeals. Yet they do not want to exclude any deserving patient from such a process.

In addition to the larger questions of scope and liability, conferees have yet to announce agreement on other differences between the Senate and House bills, such as coverage of clinical trials, access to specialty care and whether patients in special medical circumstances — such as pregnancy — would be covered if they continued to see a physician who had left an insurer's network after treatment had begun.

Just as conferees struggled with how to structure the external appeals process, they will likely face lengthy debate over "access" provisions that Republicans believe would give more people affordable coverage. The provisions include an expansion of the current pilot program for medical savings accounts, which are tax-exempt accounts used for medical expenses, and the creation of purchasing groups that backers say will allow people to get coverage at more affordable rates.

Democrats have widely criticized medical savings accounts as a tax gimmick that would benefit the healthiest and wealthiest individuals by removing them from the insurance risk pool, causing premiums to increase for those left behind. Democrats also want any new purchasing groups subject to state regulation, a demand many Republicans say is unnecessary and would simply drive up costs.

Outside Influences

Should managed-care deliberations start to stumble again, lawmakers could look beyond Capitol Hill to see how the courts, state agencies and private insurers are resolving disputes.

In Texas, for example, insurer Aetna U.S. Healthcare on April 11 settled a lawsuit with the Texas attorney general by promising to give doctors more power to determine medical treatments and to remove financial incentives for them to limit care.

Under the settlement, Aetna is prohibited from fining doctors who exceed treatment spending caps and from giving them bonuses for staying within limits, according to The Associated Press.

Conferees Remain Sharply Divided on Employer Liability

MAY 27 — Democratic managed-care conferees said May 25 that discussions to merge House and Senate bills (HR 2990, S 1344) have reached an impasse that may be beyond repair.

"Patients continue to suffer while these talks continue to struggle on," Sen. Edward M. Kennedy, D-Mass., told reporters after conferees met behind closed doors. "For all intents and purposes, these talks are stalled."

Republican conferees were more optimistic, saying that talks were accelerating and that they had shown some movement in key areas.

"If there's anybody moving, anybody having any flexibility, it's been on our side," conference chairman Sen. Don Nickles, R-Okla., told reporters.

The vastly different interpretations of the conference's progress — or lack of it — illustrate how hard it is for conferees to combine two very different pieces of legislation into a bill that can pass both chambers and be signed by President Clinton.

Enacting legislation this year is more critical for House Republicans — who are feeling election-year pressure for a managed-care compromise that could help them retain control of the chamber — than for the handful of Senate Republicans who face tough reelection campaigns.

Liability Showdown

Whether to expand patients' ability to sue their health plans for damages has been a key sticking point not only among House and Senate Republicans but between the GOP and Democrats.

The issue — when and how employers might be liable for an insurer's decision about medical care — dominated much of the May 25 meeting, conferees said. No conclusions were reached.

Nickles said the fact that Senate Republicans were willing to discuss expanding health plans' liability, even though the Senate bill would not do that, was a sign of progress. "We have discussed liability. Liability is not in the Senate [bill]," Nickles said.

In a May 23 offer to Republicans, Democrats said they were willing to modify bill language dealing with when employers could be sued.

Some Republicans and business groups have said the House bill could expose employers to liability, even if they do not make specific decisions about coverage. Democrats said they were willing to limit employers' liability to cases in which they make a decision denying a specific claim for benefits and that decision results in a patient's injury or death.

House Ways and Means Health Subcommittee Chairman Bill Thomas, R-Calif., said the Democrats' offer did not advance discussions. "As a document to remind you where the Democrats are coming from, it was useful," he said.

Republicans did not submit a counteroffer, which Democrats said was another sign that the negotiations were in trouble. "We don't know what they do like. We know what they don't like," said House conferee Robert E. Andrews, D-N.J.

Sen. James M. Jeffords, R-Vt., said Republicans had made movement in the area of scope, which deals with what groups of patients would be covered by the legislation. Jeffords said House and Senate Republicans had agreed that "everybody will be covered" by either a new federal law or an existing state law, which had been a point of contention among Republicans in the two chambers.

Jeffords did not say how state and federal regulations dealing with the same area, such as emergency medical care, would be administered so they would not conflict.

Nickles cautioned that blending state and federal regulations can be difficult. "If you have a federal [emergency medical care] provision, does the state provision have to be identical to it? Can it be similar to it? . . . That's what we're wrestling with."

Democrats sent a letter to Nickles on May 23 urging "prompt action" on managed care if legislation is to be enacted this year. Republicans and Democrats alike said that there may not be enough time for a deal to be reached before Congress' scheduled adjournment in October.

"We're not going to foreclose our options on this issue . . . by having a conference that is incomplete," Kennedy said, adding that could mean forcing floor action on managed-care legislation.

Nickles had hoped that conferees would reach agreement by March 31. When that date passed, he pushed for a deal by the spring recess, which has come and gone. Memorial Day was the new deadline, but now Nickles is hoping for a deal before the two parties' presidential nominating conventions in August.

A Plea for Patience

Nickles said he urged conferees to have "a little more patience" with the negotiations. "Some people are closer to walking away from the conference than others," he said. "We're in the process of making changes for every single health plan in America, with enormous cost if we do it wrong."

House Speaker J. Dennis Hastert, R-Ill., continues to push hard for legislation and met with Nickles on May 24 to convey that point. Hastert had hoped to have the House vote on a conference report by Memorial Day and is now pressing for a deal before the July 4 recess.

Charlie Norwood, R-Ga., who cosponsored the House legislation but was not appointed to the conference committee, said legislators should "move past the conference" if conferees do not reach a deal immediately after they return from the Memorial Day recess.

"I'm here to say time's up on the conference committee," Norwood said at a May 25 news conference. "We've waited eight months for this committee to approve a compromise bill."

Pre-Election Deal Seems Unlikely As Fight Spills Onto Senate Floor

JUNE 10 — Senate managed-care conferees made their private disputes public June 8 in a partisan, often rancorous, floor debate that may destroy already fragile discussions to merge House (HR 2990) and Senate (S 1344) bills, pushing the issue to the forefront of the November elections.

Edward M. Kennedy, D-Mass., tried to attach the House managed-care bill — minus several provisions Democrats dislike — to the fiscal 2001 defense authorization measure (S 2549). His efforts failed when the managed-care conference chairman, Don Nickles, R-Okla., moved to table the amendment and won on a 51-48 vote.

Republicans — who said they offered compromises on several issues June 4 after staff worked through the weekend — labeled Kennedy's actions pure political chicanery that did little to help resolve deep differences between the two parties. Kennedy contended the Senate action could add new momentum to the managed-care talks, which have been going on since February but have yet to produce legislation.

Republicans Lincoln Chafee of Rhode Island, Peter G. Fitzgerald of Illinois, Arlen Specter of Pennsylvania and John McCain of Arizona joined Democrats to support Kennedy. McCain and Specter voted with Republicans last July when their managed-care bill passed the Senate, 53-47. The late John H. Chafee, R-R.I., voted with Democrats last summer, just as his son did June 8. Sen. Kent Conrad, D-N.D., was absent but would have likely voted with his fellow Democrats.

"This is the clearest message we're going to get a bill this year, and a worthy one," Kennedy said June 8 at a news conference after the Senate vote. "This has moved the process and moved the bill."

Nickles was decidedly downbeat, calling Kennedy's actions "regrettable" and "political theater." Conferee Sen.

Phil Gramm, R-Texas, said Republicans may focus their efforts on House GOP lawmakers rather than Senate Democrats to forge a compromise on managed care. "I don't think we can count on [Democrats'] help to get the job done. . . . I'm pessimistic about bipartisanship," Gramm said at a June 8 GOP news conference.

Last October, 68 House Republicans joined Democrats to pass the managed-care bill (HR 2723) sponsored by Charlie Norwood, R-Ga., and John D. Dingell, D-Mich. The Norwood-Dingell measure was then combined with separate House-passed legislation (HR 2990) that featured so-called "access" provisions, which many Republicans believe would give more people affordable coverage.

Those provisions include an expansion of the current pilot program for medical savings accounts, which are tax-exempt accounts used for medical expenses; and the creation of insurance-purchasing groups, which backers say will allow people to get coverage at more affordable rates. Many Democrats have said that they doubt the ideas would help reduce the ranks of the uninsured.

Gaining the support of those Republicans is key to passing any managed-care legislation in the House, so the GOP leadership must include elements of the Norwood-Dingell bill — such as expanding the power of consumers to sue their health plans for damages — if it is to have any hope of passing legislation this year.

Taking Democrats out of the equation guarantees a veto from President Clinton, which would give Democrats and Vice President Al Gore, the party's presumptive presidential nominee, more clout to tout managed-care legislation as a defining issue between the parties as they fight for control of the White House and the House.

Clinton and Democrats have consistently made managed-care legislation a top political priority, and the president summoned conferees to the White House on May 11 to urge them to strike a deal. Clinton continued the pressure with a letter written June 8 aboard Air Force One. The missive, sent to Senate Minority Leader Tom Daschle, D-S.D., expressed "strong support" for Democrats' efforts to push for a Senate vote on managed care.

Clinton said the move was necessary because some conferees "have reluctantly concluded that the likelihood of an acceptable bill emerging from the conference is remote."

GOP Pressure

Republican pressure for a managed-care deal may prove to be just as strong. House Speaker J. Dennis Hastert, R-Ill., is eager for a compromise bill that House Republicans can vote on before the elections, and Senate Republicans in tough re-election races may feel the same heat.

Texas Gov. George W. Bush, the presumptive GOP nominee, who touts his state's managed-care law — which includes the right to sue — on his Web site, may push GOP leaders to pass legislation that would remove the issue from the fall campaigns.

Nickles and other Republican conferees said that their June 4 offer to Democrats, with concessions in the key areas of scope — who would be covered by the bill — and liability was an earnest attempt to bridge differences between the two sides.

For the first time, Senate Republicans proposed to give patients some new rights to sue their health insurers for limited damages when a coverage denial results in harm. Under the 1974 Employee Retirement Income Security Act, known as ERISA (PL 93-406), most courts have held that patients can sue their insurers only in federal courts for the cost of the denied treatment and some court costs.

The House-passed measure would permit patients to sue in state courts for damages. Plans would be protected from punitive damages if they followed an external review.

The June 4 Republican liability offer also would:

- Allow patients to sue for economic damages, some pain-and-suffering damages and limited punitive damages.
- Exempt employers from being sued.
- Require patients to exhaust all administrative remedies before they could sue their plans.
- Place "reasonable monetary limitations" on non-economic damages.
- Allow punitive damages "with reasonable monetary limitations under limited circumstances," with some percentage of the award distributed to a health care improvement fund.
- Forbid class action lawsuits.

On the scope issue, Republicans tried to broaden the number of Americans covered by their plan but not take too much power away from states that might have similar laws in place.

Democrats offered in May to modify language concerning employer liability and other areas, but GOP members said the proposal did little to advance discussions.

Most provisions in the Senate bill cover only the 56 million patients in plans exempt from state regulation, although the external and internal review provisions would apply to all 131 million people in group plans. The House bill would cover all 191 million privately insured Americans.

The Senate GOP offer would give state governors wide latitude to decide if they wanted to accept or reject any new federal health insurance requirement. Governors could certify that their laws already included such a requirement or that their state legislatures planned to pass a law mandating such a benefit. Governors also could reject federal benefit mandates on the basis that they would drive up insurance premiums.

Senate Majority Leader Trent Lott, R-Miss., defended the GOP proposal as a "major serious breakthrough effort" to accelerate action in the conference. Nickles said the proposal was a "significant move both on scope and liability."

Liability Showdown

The June 8 Senate debate was the first public showdown over managed care since the House voted last fall. Senators on both sides of the managed-care issue hammered away at familiar themes during the two-hour debate. Republicans said allowing patients to sue their health plans for damages at any time, without restrictions, could expose employers to costly litigation that would cause the number of uninsured to rise rapidly.

"You'll have a lot of employers who say, 'I don't have to offer health care,' " Nickles said, citing letters from Ford Motor Co., Wal-Mart Stores Inc. and IBM expressing concern about broadening their liability for employee health benefits. Bill Frist, R-Tenn., said the Democrats' measure could cause a million people to lose their health insurance.

Democrats accused Republicans of showing more concern for insurance companies than for their constituents and said the delay in passing managed-care legislation has caused serious problems for the public.

"Yes, people die while Congress fiddles," said Byron L. Dorgan, D-N.D. To stress his point that HMOs are unpopular, Kennedy displayed a still from the movie "As Good as It Gets" in which a mother chastises an HMO for giving her son poor medical treatment.

Kennedy and most other Democrats believe employers should be held liable only if they participate in a decision that results in a patient's injury or death. They are unlikely to back away from giving patients the right to sue their health plan at any time, rather than forcing them first to follow a series of steps, as Republicans advocate.

"The Patients' Bill of Rights means nothing unless those rights are enforceable," said John Edwards, D-N.C.

Supreme Court Bounces Liability Issue Back To Congress

JUNE 17 — A U.S. Supreme Court ruling on patients' right to sue did little to resolve differences over managed-care overhaul.

Broadening patients' limited rights to sue their health plans is one of several sticking points that have stymied House and Senate conferees trying to reconcile two different managed-care bills (HR 2990) and (S 1344). Senate GOP leaders nevertheless insist they will reach a conference agreement this year — with or without Democratic support.

The court ruled June 12 in *Pegram v. Herdrich* that a patient cannot sue their health plan under ERISA, the 1974 Employee Retirement Income Security Act (PL 93-406), for offering bonuses to physicians to hold down costs.

The justices said a decision in the patient's favor would have undermined the fundamental structure of the managed-care system. They emphasized that Congress, not the courts, must set guidelines for insurers and patients.

"The federal judiciary would be acting contrary to the Congressional policy of allowing [health maintenance] organizations if it were to entertain [a] claim portending wholesale attacks on existing HMOs solely because of their structure," wrote Justice David H. Souter.

Nickles 'Still Committed'

"I'm still very committed to seeing if we can't put out a package," Senate Assistant Majority Leader and managed-care conference Chairman Don Nickles, R-Okla., told reporters June 13. "We'll be working more with our Republican colleagues."

The same day, Sen. Edward M. Kennedy, D-Mass., and several other Democratic conferees wrote to Nickles requesting that he end closed-door negotiations on managed care and meet only in open sessions.

In more than two months of discussions, they wrote, "We have fully resolved only two out of 22 patient protection issues before the conference." They also claimed that a GOP staff memo ignored several of their proposals to break the conference impasse.

For its part, the GOP leadership is still fuming over an unsuccessful attempt by Kennedy to attach the House managed-care bill — without several provisions Democrats dislike — to the fiscal 2001 defense authorization bill (S 2549) on June 8.

The floor maneuvering "certainly didn't help the cause of getting a good bipartisan bill," Nickles said. Many Republican lawmakers acknowledge, however, that they will probably have to agree to expand consumers' rights to sue their health plans — a Democratic priority — if they have any hope of passing legislation that will remove health care as an issue from the fall election campaigns.

Rep. Charlie Norwood, R-Ga., cosponsor of the original House managed-care legislation, said June 12 that the court's opinion was "screaming for a legislative remedy" to silence criticism of the nation's managed-care system, which covered just 4 percent of Americans in 1977 but was treating 86 percent by 1998, the latest year for which statistics are available.

Congress endorsed the concept of managed care's cost-cutting practices through a 1973 law (PL 93-222) that encouraged the growth of health plans and through the 1997 Balanced Budget Act (PL 105-33), which supported their participation in such federal programs as Medicare. (*1973 Almanac, p. 999*)

Today, the managed-care industry is under a number of legal assaults stemming from complaints that insurers are withholding care to reduce costs. *Pegram v. Herdrich* was the first case to reach the Supreme Court.

The lawsuit grew out of a claim by Cynthia Herdrich of Bloomington, Ill., that her physician, Lori Pegram, compromised her treatment in 1991 after she complained of abdominal pain. Instead of sending Herdrich immediately for a diagnostic ultrasound at a nearby clinic, Pegram scheduled the test eight days later at a less expensive clinic 50 miles away. During the delay, Herdrich's appendix burst.

In oral arguments before the court in February, her attorney tried to persuade the high court that it should expand the right to sue under ERISA by allowing Herdrich to claim Pegram failed to meet her duties as a "fiduciary," a trustee who controlled her health plan's administration of benefits.

ERISA's Aim

ERISA was enacted mainly to protect workers' pension rights but it has long been considered a liability shield for health insurers. Most courts have held that an individual injured by an ERISA denial can only sue in federal court, and then only to recover the cost of a denied benefit and some court costs.

Attorney James P. Ginzkey claimed Pegram neglected her legal duties under ERISA because she received bonuses for limiting her physician-owned health plan's expenses. The court ruled that because Pegram was making a medical decision as well as an administrative one when she postponed treatment, Herdrich was not entitled to sue in federal court under ERISA.

To rule otherwise, Souter wrote, would result in "nothing less than elimination of the for-profit HMO."

All managed-care plans routinely use cost-saving mechanisms, he wrote, adding that "for over 27 years, the Congress of the United States has promoted the formation of HMO practices."

The court left open the possibility of other legal avenues for patients to explore. The justices suggested, in a lengthy footnote, that health plans may have a duty to disclose details about coverage to their participants. That could influence a host of class action suits nationwide claiming plans breached their ERISA responsibilities by failing to tell patients about their financial structure.

GOP Concession On Patients' Right To Sue Is Unlikely To End Impasse

JULY 1 — For the first time, Senate Republicans on June 29 went on record in favor of expanding patients' rights, under limited circumstances, to sue managed-care plans for damages if they deny or delay needed medical care.

The vote — on an amendment to the fiscal 2001 Labor, Health and Human Services, and Education appropriations bill (HR 4577) — may not be enough, however, to revive House-Senate negotiations on a managed-care overhaul bill (HR 2990). If anything, the partisan punching and counterpunching left both sides more bitter than ever.

The lead GOP sponsor of the House-passed managed-care bill — Charlie Norwood of Georgia — declared the conference committee officially dead. "This vote on this bill brings that disaster to a merciful end," he said in a statement after the vote.

The GOP managed-care amendment was rushed to the floor in response to the second Democratic effort in three weeks to embarrass Republicans by forcing a vote on the issue. Democrats were offering an amendment that would require any managed-care bill that passes Congress to cover all 193 million Americans with private health insurance.

The Republican amendment, by Majority Whip Don Nickles, R-Okla., was adopted 51-47, with four Republicans — Lincoln Chafee of Rhode Island, Peter G. Fitzgerald of Illinois, John McCain of Arizona, and Arlen Specter of Pennsylvania — breaking ranks and voting with the Democrats. *(Vote 166, p. S-30)*

The Democratic amendment then fell, 47-51. *(Vote 167, p. S-30)*

The GOP proposal broke new ground by endorsing a limited right to sue managed-care plans for damages, something Senate Republicans had resisted fiercely when the Senate passed its first managed-care bill in July 1999.

The 223-page amendment approved June 29 went beyond a limited liability proposal Senate Republicans had included in a June 4 offer to the Democratic conferees. The new package would allow lawsuits against managed-care plans under two conditions: unreasonable delays in medical care and a failure to cover treatment that an independent physician said the plan should cover.

In addition, the new Senate proposal fleshed out the details on the kind of damages injured patients could recover. They could not win punitive damages, but they could recover unlimited economic damages and up to $350,000 for noneconomic damages such as pain and suffering.

That in itself, however, is not enough for Democrats and the House Republicans who voted for the Norwood bill. They want the lawsuits to be handled in state courts, not federal courts, and oppose limits on noneconomic damages.

Dispute Over Coverage

The bigger disagreement is over who should be covered by the new managed-care rules. Like the Senate bill passed last year, the new proposal would limit most of its protections to the 56 million Americans in self-insured health plans that are beyond the reach of state patient protection laws. Democrats, and the House Republicans who support the Norwood bill, say all privately insured Americans should be covered.

"It seems to me that if you don't want a patients' bill of rights . . . just say so," Byron L. Dorgan, D-N.D., the sponsor of the Democratic managed-care amendment, said during the Senate floor debate.

"They're interested in press conferences. . . . They're not interested in helping patients," Nickles shot back. "We're going to give people substance on which to vote."

In effect, the Democrats smoked out the Republicans by forcing them to go to the Senate floor with everything produced to date by the House-Senate conference committee.

The GOP package is a work in progress. If GOP conferees from both chambers continue their own negotiations, as lawmakers and aides said they would, a newer version is likely to emerge and the one that is now part of the Senate Labor-HHS bill could be dropped when that bill goes to conference.

The big question is who, if anyone, would be willing to negotiate in the aftermath of the Senate vote.

Republican conferees already stopped negotiating with their Democratic counterparts after the first forced vote June 8, when Sen. Edward M. Kennedy, D-Mass., tried to attach the House managed-care bill — which would cover all privately insured Americans and includes a broad right to sue in state courts — to the fiscal 2001 defense authorization bill (S 2549). That effort failed, 51-48. *(Vote 121, p. S-23)*

"I believe the Democrats have poisoned the conference to the point where it's going to take a lot of work to reconstruct a good faith effort on everybody's part," Sen. Bill Frist of Tennessee, a GOP conferee, said in an interview after the June 29 vote.

House Republicans, however, may want to keep talking to their Senate counterparts to produce a more mutually acceptable deal. More than a dozen House Republicans, including Norwood, insisted June 29 they would never support anything that does not include a strong right to sue and apply to all privately insured Americans.

As for the Democrats, they claim they are doing exactly what they need to do to get a strong managed-care overhaul. "The only way they'll do the right thing is if we continue to pressure them," Dorgan said of Senate Republicans after the vote. "They'll never do it on their own." ◆

House-Passed Bill Looks To Insurers for Drug Plans; No Parallel Bill in the Senate

House Republicans won passage of a bill calling on insurance companies to develop and sell prescription drug policies to Medicare recipients, but the Senate did not act on it. President Clinton, who along with many congressional Democrats favored adding prescription drug coverage to Medicare, threatened to veto the measure if it ever reached his desk. With no consensus, GOP leaders looked to the 107th Congress to make the issue part of overhauling the 35-year-old Medicare program.

In June, after months of closed-door deliberations, House Republicans unveiled a prescription drug proposal that relied on the private insurance market to develop coverage; the bill included subsidies to help insurers cover the cost. But the insurers surprised their longtime GOP allies by opposing the plan as unworkable. Industry officials said they could not develop or keep such policies at affordable rates, knowing that many of the purchasers would be seniors who would have the highest drug bills. Insurers also feared that regulators would not allow them to raise premiums if drug costs continued to climb.

The industry's opposition was a powerful blow, as was the lukewarm reception from AARP, the lobbying group representing millions of senior citizens. AARP said none of the pending proposals would help seniors afford prescription drugs because they would require both co-payments and monthly premiums that many elderly patients could not afford.

Democrats labeled the Republican drug plan a sham, and many of them streamed down the Capitol steps carrying yellow umbrellas emblazoned with the word "shame" to protest the GOP's refusal to give them a straight up-or-down vote on their plan for the government to create a standard package for all beneficiaries. House Republicans also were damaged by the perception that they were more interested in political cover in the fall campaigns than in producing a workable prescription plan for the elderly. A GOP pollster, in an assessment obtained by the media, advised Republican lawmakers that passing some plan — any plan — was a "political imperative" for the party.

The Republican drug plan squeaked through the House on June 28 on a 217-214 vote, nowhere near enough to override Clinton's promised veto. The Senate did little with the prescription drug issue, though there were numerous plans from Republicans and Democrats alike that the chamber could have considered. Senate Republican leaders said they preferred to add a prescription drug benefit in the context of a broad Medicare overhaul, which could not be accomplished in the final months of the 106th Congress.

SUMMARY

Box Score

- **Bill:** HR 4680
- **Legislative action: Senate** defeated, 44-53, on June 22 a Democratic amendment to the fiscal 2001 Labor, Health and Human Services, and Education appropriations bill (HR 4577) that would have added a prescription drug benefit to Medicare and required the federal government to pay at least half the cost of premiums.

House passed HR 4680 (H Rept 106-703, Part 1), 217-214, on June 28.

GOP Told Its Prescription Drug Bill Is a 'Political Imperative'

JUNE 17 — Speaker J. Dennis Hastert is determined to push legislation through the House in the next few weeks that would, for the first time, cover prescription drug bills for tens of millions of seniors enrolled in Medicare.

The Illinois Republican's sense of urgency is not based on any likelihood that legislation will become law this year. Efforts to add drug coverage to Medicare have failed since President Lyndon Johnson created the program in 1965 as part of his Great Society. President Clinton and Democrats have sharply condemned the new House GOP plan, prescription drug coverage is not a legislative priority for Senate Republicans and House conservatives are balking at its $40 billion price tag.

Instead, as the speaker's staff readily admits, the planned floor vote is preventive medicine for House Republicans who are guarding a slight six-vote majority and see health care emerging as an issue in the districts of vulnerable members.

Legislation to give consumers greater rights in managed-care plans, which the GOP had hoped could be a banner health care issue, is bogged down in a conference with the Senate. And new voter surveys give Democratic candidates a slight edge in the November election — a Gallup poll taken June 6-7 among likely voters in House races shows Democrats leading Republicans 48 percent to 46 percent.

So it is not surprising that GOP pollster Glen Bolger told the House Republican Conference June 8 that it is a "political imperative" that they pass a prescription drug bill this year.

"You can't stop something that is as politically enticing as providing prescription drugs for seniors," conservative Rep. Mark Sanford, R-S.C., said in a June 13 interview. "Politics always come first around this place."

Two months after Hastert and other House Republican leaders unveiled a set of principles for Medicare prescription drug coverage, details of that proposal were made public the week of June 13. The Ways and Means Committee is tentatively scheduled to mark up the bill June 21, and the House could vote on it the week of June 26.

Among its provisions, the GOP proposal would offer voluntary drug coverage to all seniors beginning in fiscal 2003, provide subsidies to help low-income seniors afford monthly premiums and deductibles, and pick up all medication costs for seniors whose annual drug bills were $6,000 or higher. The plan would look to the private sector to develop the benefits policies and mandate that seniors have at least two different choices for coverage. If private insurers did not offer coverage in a particular area, the federal government would.

Democrats, pollster Bolger said, see the issue as part of their "four corner" strategy to win back the House, along with health care, education and Social Security, and they are perceived as the party best able to provide drugs to seniors.

Bolger, of the firm Public Opinion Strategies, told House Republicans they could gain ground simply by saying they have a plan. "It is more important to communicate that you have a plan than it is to communicate what is in the plan," reads a document that was prepared by Bolger's firm and obtained by CQ.

Hastert spokesman John P. Feehery acknowledged that politics is playing a large role in the timing of the prescription drug legislation.

"The quicker we get this done, the less chance it has to become embroiled in end-of-the-year politics," Feehery said in a June 14 interview. "It's important for our members to point to this as an accomplishment."

Since the beginning of the year, the GOP strategy has been to stay "on the offensive," Feehery said, "moving issues that are important to our voters, on our terms."

Part of that strategy has been to take up a series of small, targeted tax bills this year, in contrast to past years, when Republicans brought out one broad tax package that never garnered enough bipartisan support for passage.

Among the small bills that the House has been able to pass this year are measures to eliminate the "marriage penalty" (HR 6), estate and gift taxes (HR 8) and the Social Security earnings test, and to impose a five-year moratorium on Internet-specific taxes (HR 3709).

Though the prescription drugs measure may not pass in the Senate, House Republicans say they can capitalize politically from their own action.

'A Good Start for Next Year'

"I don't think the president will sign a [drug] bill we come up with," Charlie Norwood, R-Ga., cosponsor of the managed-care bill (HR 2990) that passed the House in October, said in a June 14 interview. "But it will give a good start for next year when we can really do it."

He added that House Republicans must act this year for political reasons. "If we don't pass something, [Democrats] will say we hate senior citizens and that we don't want them to have medication. I can hear it all now."

The White House is already drumming up opposition to the Republican bill. It held three media events on prescription drugs the week of June 12 and used each occasion to blast the GOP plan.

"We have grave concerns because the Republican plan relies on a trickle-down scheme that would provide a subsidy for insurers and not a single dollar of direct premium assistance for middle-class seniors," President Clinton said June 14.

With Senate Republican leaders hesitant to move on the drug issue, passing a House bill may be the only political cover House Republicans have on health care this year. Senate Republican leaders have said they prefer to add prescription drugs in the context of an overhaul of the 35-year-old Medicare program rather than consider a stand-alone measure.

There were some signs of Senate movement during the week of June 12 — such as a Health, Education, Labor and Pensions Committee hearing June 13 on drug safety and pricing and a private meeting June 15 of Senate Finance Committee members to discuss Medicare modernization and prescription drugs — but it is unclear whether they will produce legislation.

Some Republican senators whose fall election opponents are making prescription drugs a key issue, such as Spencer Abraham of Michigan and Conrad Burns of Montana, may only be able to cosponsor a measure rather than cast votes for one.

Assistant Senate Majority Leader Don Nickles, R-Okla., who has had trouble finding consensus in the managed-care conference he heads, told reporters June 13 that Senate Republicans were "working on" a prescription drug plan, but he gave no details. Senate Republican Policy Committee Chairman Larry E. Craig of Idaho said in a June 13 interview that the party has not yet developed a strategy on the prescription drug issue, and it may take time to do so. "My guess is we won't get that consensus right away," Craig said.

Testifying before the full Ways and Means panel June 13, Health Subcommittee Chairman Bill Thomas, R-Calif., the chief GOP proponent of the drug plan, stressed repeatedly that the proposal was a bipartisan one because it had garnered the support of two Democrats — Collin C. Peterson of Minnesota and Ralph M. Hall of Texas.

Hall and Peterson are hardly typical Democrats. In a 1999 CQ study, Hall voted against his party's position 70 percent of the time, including three "yes" votes on four impeachment articles against Clinton. The same study found that Peterson voted against the Democratic position 49 percent of the time. At a June 13 news conference, Hall said presumptive GOP presidential nominee George W. Bush might be more open to signing a prescription drug benefit into law. "Maybe in late January, we'll have a president that . . . I can talk to," Hall said. *(Vote studies, 1999 Almanac, p. B-6)*

Looking to the Private Sector

The House GOP plan would look to the private sector to create drug policies for seniors and would provide "subsidies" to encourage insurers to participate, although industry officials have said it would be difficult to offer affordable policies. Federal reimbursements to insurers would increase on a sliding scale. The government would pay insurers 30 percent for drug costs between $1,250 and $1,350, rising to 90 percent once a beneficiary's yearly bill reached $6,000 or more.

Seniors would be required to pay the first $250 of drug costs each year, then half of their expenses would be covered up to $2,100. Medicare re-

Drug Benefit Programs Compared

JUNE 17 — In 1996, the latest year for which statistics are available, nearly one-third of Medicare beneficiaries — more than 11 million people — lacked prescription drug coverage. President Clinton and House Republicans are offering competing plans to close that gap by proposing a Medicare prescription drug benefit for the elderly. Though their plans differ, both sides cite these statistics to make their point:

- The elderly make up 13 percent of the population but account for more than one-third of the nation's annual drug expenditures — estimated to reach $112 billion in 2000.
- In 1968, seniors spent an average of $64 annually on prescription drugs. By 1998, average expenditures had risen to $848.
- The average amount Medicare beneficiaries spent on drugs increased from 2.4 percent of their income in 1968 to 4.1 percent in 1998.
- In 1999, about half of Medicare beneficiaries spent less than $500 annually for drugs; 45 percent spent $500 to $3,000 and 6 percent spent $3,000 or more.

Issue	House GOP plan would:	President's plan would:
Premiums and Deductibles	Charge $40 in monthly premiums on average in fiscal 2003, the first year of the plan. Require beneficiaries to pay the first $250 in yearly drug costs, then cover half of prescription drug costs up to $2,100.	Assess monthly premiums of about $24 in fiscal 2003, rising to about $51 by fiscal 2010. Cover half of beneficiaries' yearly drug costs up to $2,000 in fiscal 2003, rising to half of $5,000 in fiscal 2009. There would be no yearly deductible.
Choice of Plans	Offer Medicare beneficiaries a choice of at least two plans for drug coverage. The federal government would only offer coverage in areas where private insurers did not. Beneficiary participation would be voluntary.	Cover all fee-for-service Medicare beneficiaries under the same plan. Medicare+Choice plans could continue to offer different packages. Beneficiary participation would be voluntary.
Catastrophic Coverage	Offer catastrophic coverage, beginning in fiscal 2003, once seniors' annual out-of-pocket drug costs reach $6,000. At that point, the government would pay 90 percent and the insurer 10 percent.	Set aside another $35 billion of the federal budget surplus from fiscal 2006 through fiscal 2010 to help cover catastrophic drug costs. No details have been released.
Effective Date	Begin in fiscal 2003.	Begin in fiscal 2003, excluding catastrophic coverage.
Cost	Approximately $40 billion over five years, including catastrophic coverage.	Approximately $38 billion over five years, excluding catastrophic coverage.
Method of Implementation	Be run by a new agency — the Medicare Benefits Administration — within the Department of Health and Human Services. Participating plans could use pharmaceutical benefit managers — companies that specialize in running insurers' drug benefit programs.	Be run by pharmaceutical benefits managers and supervised by the Health Care Financing Administration.

SOURCES: Medicare Payment Advisory Commission June 2000 report to Congress, Congressional Budget Office, Health Care Financing Administration, Kaiser Family Foundation, House Republican plan.

cipients whose drug bills were higher than $2,350 would be responsible for that amount until their annual out-of-pocket costs reached $6,000. At that point, so-called catastrophic coverage would begin, with insurers and the federal government paying all costs.

Under the GOP plan, catastrophic coverage begins in fiscal 2003. In Clinton's prescription drug proposal, it would not begin until fiscal 2006, and White House officials have provided few details. Thomas and other supporters stress this distinction as a key one, and it will be used to offset another difference between the two plans.

The GOP bill requires that beneficiaries, except those who qualify for low-income subsidies, pay monthly premiums — which would likely average $40 a month — plus a $250 deductible for a total of $730 in fiscal 2003. Clinton's plan would cost beneficiaries $288 in premiums with no deductible.

Thomas told the Ways and Means Committee on June 13 that the bill would include a "lockbox" that would return any Medicare-generated surpluses to the program rather than to the general treasury, which is the current practice. The provision was discussed again at a June 15 briefing for reporters but was not included in the drug bill's legislative language.

Rather, the Medicare "lockbox" may move as a separate piece of legislation. If approved, it would allow lawmakers to use Medicare savings to increase payments to doctors, hospitals, managed-care plans and other Medicare providers, which were cut in the 1997 balanced-budget law (PL 105-33).

Although Congress passed legislation (PL 106-113) last year to give those providers an additional $16 billion, they say that was not enough and are pressing for more money this year.

"Members should view Medicare as pork — it's just as important as a highway or an appropriations bill," said Fred Graefe, a health care lobbyist representing hospitals and manufacturers. "It's important for members to show that in an era of surplus they can return Medicare dollars to their districts, which benefits both beneficiaries and providers."

Karen Ignagni, president and chief executive officer of the American Association of Health Plans, which represents managed-care companies, said that since her members provide prescription drug coverage to millions of seniors, it is critical for Congress to give managed-care plans more money.

"Building on that success . . . is the first significant step we can make to answering the Medicare prescription drug challenge," Ignagni said June 13 in testimony before the Ways and Means Committee.

Thomas predicted that his plan will receive strong Democratic backing on the House floor even if it emerges from Ways and Means with only Republican support.

"That will be more than enough evidence that this bill is bipartisan," Thomas said at the hearing.

Ways and Means Democrats and other critics of the Thomas plan said its reliance on private insurers could hurt seniors if the plans decided to alter benefits or leave a particular market. Allowing a variety of insurers to negotiate with drug companies would also divide the Medicare beneficiary pool into many segments, weakening the ability to get deep discounts based on volume, critics say.

'A Complicated Scheme'

Charles B. Rangel, the panel's ranking Democrat, said at the Ways and Means hearing that the GOP plan was "not a true Medicare prescription drug benefit, but a complicated scheme designed to sell expensive, inadequate private insurance plans."

Ways and Means member Sander M. Levin, D-Mich., said few Democrats would sign on: "There may be some Democratic votes on the floor — a small minority — but it won't become law."

Thomas' plan must overcome more than just the ire of Democrats and Clinton. Insurance industry representatives have said they do not want to write the policies because they cannot make a profit doing so. Seniors with high drug bills would sign up in large numbers for the policies and file claims, which would drive up costs, increase premiums and make coverage unaffordable, insurers say.

"The pressures of ever-increasing drug costs, the predictability of drug expenses and the likelihood that the people most likely to purchase this coverage will be the people anticipating the highest drug claims would make drug-only coverage virtually impossible for insurers to offer at an affordable premium," Health Insurance Association of America President Chip Kahn said in a statement issued June 13.

Thomas believes there would be plenty of private insurers who would offer drug benefits to seniors.

"When you tell somebody you don't need them and, in fact, it's going to succeed without them, you'll be amazed at how some people will come around the back door and want to be part of it," Thomas told reporters June 13.

Peterson was confident that insurers would participate. "If you don't believe in the marketplace, you don't believe in this plan," he told reporters June 15.

A $2.5 Billion Criticism

Democrats also criticized Thomas' proposal to give roughly $2.5 billion of the $40 billion drug package to managed-care plans over the next five years and provide additional incentives to lure managed care to rural areas.

Such funding may persuade plans to stay in Medicare+Choice, which was created in the 1997 balanced-budget law (PL 105-33) to encourage more managed-care insurers to offer coverage to beneficiaries. In each of the past two years, 99 plans have reduced services or left the program altogether. More plans are expected to announce by July 3, the federal deadline for plans to apply for participation in Medicare+Choice next year, that they will not be back.

"Why would we prop up [Medicare+Choice plans] . . . when they are continually pulling out of these counties?" said Ways and Means member Karen L. Thurman, D-Fla.

While the prescription drug debate is being fought mostly in the political arena, policy implications loom large for any benefit that becomes law.

The Republican proposal and the president's plan focus on providing a drug benefit for the short term, but if either became law, drug coverage would likely become a permanent part of Medicare. That would make lawmakers reluctant to scale back or eliminate drug coverage for the elderly, even if the current era of bountiful budget surpluses fades.

The Boomer Problem

Rep. Sanford said expanding Medicare to cover prescription drugs is "starting a new program which requires annual cuttings, which there won't be," because lawmakers will be reluctant to do something that could hurt them politically. Medicare is expected to be further taxed when millions of Baby Boomers begin to qualify for Medicare beginning in 2010.

Richard M. Burr of North Carolina, one of the plan's GOP cosponsors, said that the legislation would give Congress "a vision of where we need to be 15 to 20 years down the road," with Medicare, rather than creating more problems for the program.

There are no guarantees that any prescription plan that passes the House will become law, but Sanford is not so sure it will be added to the Senate's casualty list.

"It's like the boy in Holland who put his finger in the dike. One senator may be able to do it for a while, but over time the water comes over the dam," Sanford said.

Senate Rejects Democrats' Ploy; House GOP Plans Vote Before Recess

JUNE 24 — The wrangling over a Medicare prescription drug benefit, which has crept toward center stage for weeks, took a leading role on Capitol Hill the week of June 19 with both parties pushing bills on an issue they view as critical to capturing seniors' votes in the November elections.

Senate Democrats on June 20 introduced a "bipartisan" measure to give Medicare beneficiaries drug coverage. Backers said the measure could be the basis for a compromise on prescription drugs this year, but two days later they tried to force Republicans to fold it into the fiscal 2001 Labor, Health and Human Services, and Education appropriations bill (HR 4577).

Richard J. Durbin, D-Ill., said the vote on prescription drugs would "really define the difference in values between the two parties." A few moments later, Phil Gramm, R-Texas, called the Democrats' maneuvering "politics at its worst." The Democrats' amendment eventually was rejected, 44 to 53. *(Vote 144, p. S-27; Labor-HHS-Education, p. 2-97)*

House GOP leaders, meanwhile, pushed ahead with plans to vote on their drug bill (HR 4680) before the July Fourth recess, concerned that allowing the $39.7 billion package to linger longer would weaken chances for passage, especially since President Clinton and Democrats continue to describe it as a "false promise" that would benefit insurers and drug manufacturers more than seniors.

The Ways and Means Committee approved the GOP bill June 21 along party lines, 23-14. The action came after Democrats failed, on a 14-23 vote, to substitute their own measure, which would have given drug coverage to seniors and added some $21 billion for payments to hospitals, nursing homes and other Medicare providers who say they are still hurting from spending cuts made in the 1997 budget law (PL 105-33). *(1997 Almanac, p. 2-47)*

Dubious Prospects

Despite the push by both parties the week of June 19, prospects are slim for enactment of any prescription drug legislation this year. Vast differences between the two parties' measures have kept a bipartisan consensus from emerging, and the number of days in the legislative calendar is dwindling.

"I don't think there's enough time to do it this year," said Martin Corry, director of federal affairs for AARP, the lobbying group for seniors.

Sen. John B. Breaux, D-La., said the Senate skirmish all but guarantees that prescription drug legislation is dead for the year. "We're going to end up with nothing come the end of this year but an issue," he told reporters after the vote.

Still, even if no new drug benefit is created, the debate lays the groundwork for action when the 107th Congress and a new administration take office next year. Once the elections are over, lawmakers may find it easier to find common ground on the tough questions that must be answered before the 35-year-old entitlement program can be expanded to include prescription drugs. Among them: Should benefits be determined by the federal government or private sector, and when should so-called catastrophic coverage begin for beneficiaries with high drug bills?

Seniors Lobbyists Pleased

Despite the partisan rancor heard during the debate, advocates for the elderly are pleased with the ongoing discussion. "This debate is now over how, not whether," to add prescription drugs to Medicare, said Corry.

While the prescription drug issue has been a top legislative priority for months for House Republicans, Senate GOP leaders have moved more slowly. "The prescription drug proposal can explode in costs if isn't done carefully," Senate Majority Whip Don Nickles, R-Okla., told reporters June 20.

Senate Finance Committee members have recently begun meeting privately to try to develop a legislative compromise on prescription drugs. On June 20, several members of that panel, including Democrats Bob Graham of Florida and Charles S. Robb of Virginia, came forward with their own drug plan, which tried to find the middle ground between the House Republican bill and Clinton's prescription drug proposal.

The Graham plan would offer coverage beginning in fiscal 2003, with beneficiaries paying premiums on an income-related scale. Most beneficiaries would pay 50 percent of the premium's cost; wealthier seniors would pay up to 75 percent. After meeting a $250 deductible, seniors would pay half their drug costs up to $3,500 and Medicare would pay the remainder. For costs between $3,500 and $4,000, beneficiaries would pay 25 percent and Medicare 75 percent. Medicare would pay all expenses above $4,000.

Both the House GOP bill and Clinton's plan would initially pay half of beneficiaries' expenses, up to $2,100 and $2,000, respectively, and increase over the life of both bills. In the House Republican plan, catastrophic coverage would begin in fiscal 2003 when beneficiaries' expenses reached $6,000. Clinton has proposed setting aside $35 billion of the federal budget surplus to begin catastrophic coverage in fiscal 2006.

Democrats said Graham's proposal, which Robb offered June 22 as an amendment to the Labor-HHS bill, should be approved because Republicans had nothing to offer. "We've waited for years for your prescription drug benefit. But there's nothing for us to consider from the Republican side," Durbin said.

Senate Republicans complained that Democrats were trying to rush to the floor a proposal that few members had read, that had not been reviewed by the committees of jurisdiction and that would increase Medicare spending by billions of dollars. "The last thing we need to do is put our Medicare program at greater risk," said Finance Committee Chairman William V. Roth Jr., R-Del.

Exchanges between Ways and Means Republicans and Democrats were just as combative as those on the Senate floor when the committee met June 21 to mark up legislation sponsored by Health Subcommittee Chairman Bill Thomas, R-Calif.

His package would look to the private insurance market to create drug benefit packages that would be available to all beneficiaries, an approach that Democrats and insurers have criticized. The Health Insurance Association of America has said its members would not write such policies because they would be too expensive.

A Different View

At least one company has embraced the Thomas plan. Per G.H. Lofberg, the chairman of Merck-Medco Managed Care, a division of the drug manufacturer Merck & Co., told Thomas in a June 21 letter that his company would be willing to develop a drug plan for seniors and participate in "what we expect will be a highly competitive market." Thomas said the letter was evidence that the private market would offer drug policies to seniors.

Charles B. Rangel of New York, the panel's ranking Democrat, said the GOP bill would privatize the Medicare program "and give the money not to the people but to the insurance companies." Pete Stark, D-Calif., called the Republican plan "a prescription for failure" because it would not give the government enough power to ensure that beneficiaries received comprehensive drug coverage at affordable rates.

Benjamin L. Cardin, D-Md., offered an amendment that would have allowed the government to create a standard package of drug benefits available to all Medicare beneficiaries. It failed on a 14-22 party-line vote.

Ways and Means Democrats, led by Stark, later offered a substitute drug package that, like Clinton's, would pay up to half of beneficiaries' costs, up to $2,000 in 2003 and 2004, rising to half of $5,000 in 2009. Unlike Clinton's plan, it would begin catastrophic coverage in 2003 once a senior's out-of-pocket costs reached $4,000.

Stark said his proposal, which failed on a party-line vote, 14-23, would "provide a defined benefit on which [seniors] can depend for uniform benefits across this country." Thomas faulted it for relying too heavily on future budget surpluses for funding.

Thomas and House Speaker J. Dennis Hastert, R-Ill., said June 21 that House Republicans would work to give Medicare providers more money later this year, most likely after the widely anticipated Congressional Budget Office mid-session review, which could add $40 billion to the budget surplus.

Thomas said he was confident House Republicans would support his drug plan even without any additional "givebacks" for Medicare providers.

"That wouldn't affect the vote one way or the other," said Thomas. "You can't spend money you don't have."

Should Thomas' bill fail, Republicans may be able to find more Medicare money via "lockbox" legislation (HR 3859) the House passed June 20 by a vote of 420-2. That measure would require any Medicare surpluses to be used only for the Medicare program. That could include giving more money to hospitals, nursing homes, managed-care plans and other Medicare providers. *(Vote 297, p. H-94)*

The "lockbox" legislation was dropped from the GOP drug bill to showcase it on the House floor. "This was so important it should stand on its own," said Wally Herger, R-Calif.

House Passes GOP Drug Plan; Democrats to Take Case to Voters

JULY 1 — In the 24 hours preceding the June 28 House vote on the GOP proposal to provide prescription drug benefits to seniors (HR 4680), Democrats ran a "war room" where members conducted around-the-clock rallies in their effort to defeat the bill.

To pump themselves up, they watched a scene from the movie "Gladiator" where actor Russell Crowe huddles with several of his cohorts who are about to be slaughtered and tells them they will win if they remain united. Two days earlier, they had viewed a clip from the film "Apollo 13" in which a central character declares, "Failure is not an option."

Despite Democrats' search for inspiration, they could not muster enough votes to defeat the measure, and it squeaked through the House, 217-214. *(Vote 358, p. H-112)*

The GOP leadership may not be able to savor its triumph for long, however. The Democrats — who stalled floor action for hours in protest that they were not allowed to offer their drug plan as an alternative to the Republican bill — will continue to push their approach with voters as the parties struggle for control over one of the most volatile political issues Congress has considered this year. Prospects for Senate action remain unclear.

President Clinton said June 29 that he would not sign the GOP bill should it reach his desk, in part because the proposal relies on the private insurance market.

"The bill that they passed is an empty promise to most of our seniors," Clinton said. "The insurance companies themselves have said . . . this will not work, these policies will not be affordable [and] most seniors will not be able to take advantage of this bill."

Both the GOP and Democratic plans would expand Medicare, the federal health insurance program for nearly 40 million elderly and disabled Americans, to include prescription drugs. Both also would help low-income seniors pay for coverage.

The Republican drug plan would look to the private insurance market to develop coverage, providing subsidies to help insurers with the cost. Clinton and congressional Democrats would look to the government to create one standard package for all beneficiaries.

Participation in both plans would be voluntary, but seniors would face penalties if they did not enroll within specific time periods. Coverage would not begin until fiscal 2003.

Under the GOP plan, the policies offered would likely require beneficiaries to pay monthly premiums of between $35 and $40 and require a $250 deductible. While individual policies could vary, the Republican plan would cover half of prescription drug costs up to $2,100 per year. Catastrophic coverage would kick in once a beneficiary's out-of-pocket costs hit $6,000.

Under Clinton's proposal, premiums would be about $24 a month, rising to $51 by fiscal 2010. There would be no deductibles and half of seniors' drug costs would be covered up to $2,000 in fiscal 2003, rising to half of $5,000 in fiscal 2009.

House and Senate Democrats have advocated similar approaches but would begin catastrophic coverage in fiscal 2003, while Clinton would start it in fiscal 2006. Coverage in the Democrats' plans would kick in when beneficiaries' expenses reached $4,000.

AARP's Assessment

AARP, the lobbying group representing millions of senior citizens, cautions that none of the proposals may actually help more seniors afford prescription drugs.

"For millions of older persons — middle-income singles and couples — the monthly premiums, coupled with 50 percent co-insurance, may prove too high a cost," wrote AARP Executive Director Horace B. Deets in a June 27 letter to Speaker J. Dennis Hastert, R-Ill. "As a result, many beneficiaries may elect not to participate."

Deets also warned lawmakers on both sides of the aisle to stop partisan posturing and work together. "We also know that a solution that can stand the test of time will require true bipartisanship," he wrote.

Any bipartisanship this year on the prescription drug issue is unlikely, however.

While Clinton may want to strike a deal in order to add another health care accomplishment to his legacy, that would undercut Democrats who have focused on prescription drugs in their quest to regain control of Congress. Forging a compromise with Republicans would take the issue out of the November elections.

At a packed news conference on June 28, Democratic Congressional Campaign Committee Chairman Patrick J. Kennedy of Rhode Island shook an empty prescription bottle in front of the television cameras.

"Every time seniors choose between drugs and food, they are going to remember this vote. They are going to remember this vote in November," he warned.

In the Senate, the drug issue is just as partisan. Republican leaders have said they are hesitant to add drug coverage to Medicare without first overhauling the entire program.

Democrats tried, but failed June 22 to offer their prescription drug plan as an amendment to the fiscal 2001 Labor, Health and Human Services and Education bill (HR 4577).

While that effort did not succeed, Senate Democrats intend to keep pushing the issue and force Republicans to respond, said Minority Leader Tom Daschle, D-S.D.

"I think the heat is going to continue to rise," Daschle told reporters June 28. "Ultimately, we're going to get this legislation passed."

Sens. John B. Breaux, D-La., and Republican Bill Frist of Tennessee, the chamber's only physician, offered another alternative June 28 when they introduced a bill that would, like the House GOP plan, look to the private market to develop prescription drug plans for seniors.

"We think we have something that is workable. We think it is doable, and we think it is politically feasible," Breaux told reporters. "This will break the logjam."

Both parties understand the need to include prescription drugs for Medicare beneficiaries, nearly one-third of whom have no drug coverage. Lawmakers agree that if the entitlement program — which was created in 1965 — were assembled today, it would include prescription drugs because physicians have a greater arsenal of medications that are effective in treating illness and reducing medical costs.

Long-Term Price Tag

Both Democrats and Republicans are also keenly aware that the cost of providing such a benefit — especially as drug expenditures continue to climb — creates a long-term price tag that is impossible to predict. Another complication is opposition from drug makers and insurers to aspects of each drug proposal.

The pharmaceutical industry, for example, opposes the government-run approach of Clinton's plan, arguing that it would result in price controls that would stifle the research and development of new drugs. Insurers say the House GOP's proposal is unworkable because they would not be able to develop and sell such policies at rates that seniors could afford.

Nearly 12 hours of House floor debate on prescription drugs included several procedural votes on matters such as motions to adjourn and whether or not lawmakers should be allowed to use charts during floor remarks.

Democrats orchestrated the votes because they were not permitted to offer their drug proposal as an alternative to the GOP plan. They were only allowed a motion to recommit with instructions, which would have sent the bill back to the committees of jurisdiction for further consideration. It failed, 204-222. *(Vote 356, p. H-112)*

Just as the House floor debate began, Democrats left the floor en masse and marched onto the Capitol's East Front steps. Sporting yellow umbrellas emblazoned with the word "shame," they chastised Republicans for not allowing a clean up-or-down vote on their plan.

At a news conference just minutes later, Republican Conference Chairman J.C. Watts Jr., R-Okla., said that the Democrats' walkout proved they did not want prescription drug legislation to pass this year.

"They didn't walk out on the members up here," he said. "They walked out on seniors."

GOP Meets Roth's Drug Plan With Reserve; Clinton Expresses Interest

JULY 15 — Prospects for passage this year of legislation to provide prescription drug benefits to seniors grew murkier when Senate Finance Committee Chairman William V. Roth Jr., R-Del., unveiled the outline of a measure July 12 that critics said could create more problems than it would solve.

Roth's proposal would develop a new, optional drug benefit for Medicare beneficiaries that would be administered by private pharmaceutical benefit managers, companies that specialize in administering drug benefit programs.

Beneficiaries who select the new option would have to meet a deductible — possibly $500 — before benefits would start. Once drug expenditures hit a still-unspecified level, so-called catastrophic coverage would begin, with the government picking up 80 percent of subsequent costs, according to GOP staff aides.

President Clinton welcomed Roth's proposal, saying July 12 he was "pleased there is growing momentum on Capitol Hill to provide a real Medicare prescription drug benefit, not a flawed insurance model." Clinton's plan, like Roth's, features a government-defined benefit that would be administered by pharmaceutical benefit managers.

Both the Roth and Clinton proposals differ drastically from legislation (HR 4680) the House passed June 28 that would look to the private insurance market to provide policies for seniors and subsidize insurers to help finance the benefit.

While several senators praised Roth's effort to produce a Medicare drug benefit, they said they could not support it in its current form.

Bill Frist, R-Tenn. — a surgeon whose views on health care issues are widely respected — called Roth's measure "too Clintonesque" in a July 12 interview and said it would not "involve competition to a degree that [would] adequately restrain [drug] costs in the future." Frist and Finance Committee member John B. Breaux, D-La., are backing legislation (S 2807) that, like the House bill, would look to the private sector to develop prescription drug policies for seniors.

Breaux told reporters July 12 that because Roth's plan would not require all Medicare recipients to participate, only beneficiaries with high drug expenses would enroll, driving up its cost.

Changing Political Equation

For months, Senate Republican leaders have resisted the idea of expanding Medicare to include prescription drugs without first overhauling the 1965 program — whose enrollment is expected to double in the next 15 to 20 years — but that reluctance now appears to be softening.

On July 11, Senate Majority Leader Trent Lott, R-Miss., told reporters that House and Senate Republicans feel the drug issue was "a need to be addressed" this year. Charles E. Grassley, R-Iowa, added that the chamber must act on the drug issue — the sooner the better. If Republicans delay, "it's not going to look to the public that we're serious about a bill," he said.

Those pronouncements do not mean Roth's proposal will win over many GOP colleagues — but it could help him at home, where he is locked in a tight re-election race with Delaware Gov. Thomas R. Carper, a Democrat.

Democrats have also tried to capture the drug issue. They walked off the House floor June 28 to protest Republicans' refusal to let them offer their own drug plan as a free-standing alternative to the House bill, and they tried to force a prescription drug vote in the Senate July 13 as the chamber debated legislation to repeal the estate tax (HR 8).

The Roth Plan

Among its many provisions, Roth's plan would:

• Combine the existing $776 deductible for Part A of Medicare, which deals with hospital costs, and the $100 deductible for Part B, which deals with doctors' visits and other outpatient services, into one lower, still unspecified number for Medicare beneficiaries. Once met, all hospital services would be covered for the year.

• Require Medicare beneficiaries who enrolled in the drug plan to pay a new co-payment of around 20 percent for some Part B services, including home health care, an element that may cause concern among seniors worried about increasing out-of-pocket expenditures.

• Provide subsidies for beneficiaries with incomes of up to 150 percent of the poverty level — $12,525 for individuals — to help them meet co-payments and deductibles.

Specific premiums and deductibles will be set once the Congressional Budget Office completes its analysis of the plan, but aides said the Roth proposal would fit within the $40 billion allowed by the Senate budget resolution to finance a prescription drug benefit this year.

Chip Kahn, president of the Health Insurance Association of America, said in a July 13 interview that Roth's proposal is "a useful contribution to the process" because it "raises the right issues," including restructuring Medicare and trying to help seniors get coverage for the prescription drugs they need. Kahn did not endorse Roth's plan, however, and he and other industry executives are cool to the House GOP plan because they feel writing drug benefit policies would not be profitable.

Roth Offers New Medicare Drug Proposal

JULY 29 — Senate Finance Committee Chairman William V. Roth Jr., R-Del., offered panel members a new set of Medicare prescription drug proposals July 27, including a targeted plan for low-income beneficiaries that is likely to win the backing of Majority Leader Trent Lott, R-Miss.

Lott had complained that an earlier Roth plan, which would offer drug coverage to all Medicare recipients, would be too costly.

Sen. John B. Breaux, D-La, a member of the Finance panel, said Roth's revised proposal would still leave millions of seniors without coverage.

"I think that everybody else who works hard and pays taxes feels like they ought to be part of any kind of overall assistance program as well," Breaux said.

Roth's low-income plan would:

• Offer coverage as of Oct. 1, 2000.

• Provide matching funds for states that already have prescription drug programs for elderly individuals with annual incomes of up to 200 percent of the poverty level, or $16,700.

• Require the federal government to provide benefits if a state did not.

• Sunset in four years or sooner if Congress passed legislation to overhaul Medicare.

Roth revamped the plan he released July 12 to permit private insurers to offer Medicare recipients prescription drug coverage. He also asked Finance panel members to review a bill (S 2807) from Bill Frist, R-Tenn., and Breaux that would look to the private sector to offer drug coverage.

The House passed legislation (HR 4680) in June that would subsidize private insurers to help them offer prescription drug coverage to Medicare recipients.

Roth has asked the Congressional Budget Office to score his new package and hopes to present the data to Finance members after the August recess.

Insurers' Queasiness About Costs Helps Sink Republican Prescription Bill

OCTOBER 28 — Encouraging the private sector to do more so government can do less is a deeply held Republican ideal.

In practice, however, the philosophy has not always worked. Dozens of managed-care companies, which were supposed to move Medicare toward the open market, have left the program, citing low payments and burdensome rules. And few insurers offer tax-exempt medical savings accounts, even though many Republicans and some Democrats believe such accounts could reduce the ranks of the uninsured.

Despite that spotty record, House Republicans this year looked once again to the private sector on the politically charged issue of whether to add prescription drug coverage to Medicare. The GOP developed legislation that called on private insurers to set up drug-only policies for Medicare recipients. The party figured that insurers, longtime GOP allies, would come to the table to help derail President Clinton's government-run prescription drug plan.

They didn't. Nor did the AARP, the powerful seniors' lobbying group, due to fears that the monthly premiums for the proposed coverage would be too costly for many elderly.

"We were stepping off a cliff but we didn't have everyone together when we were jumping," said Rep. Mark Foley, R-Fla.

Perhaps most damaging to the GOP's prescription drug quest was the perception that the party was moving legislation solely for political cover. A GOP pollster, in an assessment later obtained by the press, asserted that passing some plan — any plan — was a "political imperative" for the party. "It is more important to communicate that you have a plan as it is to communicate what is in the plan," read the document presented to the House Republican Conference.

Clinton and Democrats honed in on what they perceived to be the weaknesses of the House initiative and pounced quickly to kill any momentum. On June 29, one day after the House legislation (HR 4680) squeaked through on a 217-214 vote, Clinton announced he would veto the bill should it reach his desk.

"The insurance companies themselves have said . . . this will not work, these policies will not be affordable [and] most seniors will not be able to take advantage of this bill," Clinton said.

Rep. Pete Stark of California, the ranking Democrat on the Ways and Means Health Subcommittee, called the GOP plan "a political placebo, not a real prescription drug benefit."

Ways and Means Health Subcommittee Chairman Bill Thomas, R-Calif., the chief architect of the GOP drug plan, dismissed such comments as "hogwash." But the criticisms stuck. House passage achieved Speaker J. Dennis Hastert's (R-Ill.) goal of acting on a drug bill, but was not a solution for getting a measure to Clinton's desk.

The Senate took no action, not even a committee markup, despite the fact that Finance Committee Chairman William V. Roth Jr., R-Del., facing a tight re-election race, proposed two different plans.

With little chance for enactment, the issue quickly became a political dividing line in the fall elections, with Republicans sticking to a private-market approach and Democrats preferring government oversight.

Industry Opposition

The strongest attack on the House Republican plan came from Chip Kahn, president of the Health Insurance Association of America, the powerful insurers group.

Kahn, a former Ways and Means Health Subcommittee staffer, had worked closely with Thomas on issues such as the 1997 balanced-budget act (PL 105-33), which made some of the most significant changes to Medicare and Medicaid since they were created in 1965.

This time, however, Kahn sided with his membership, insurers who feared the policies Thomas envisioned would be too costly to maintain.

"The pressures of ever-increasing drug costs, the predictability of drug expenses, and the likelihood that the people most likely to purchase this coverage will be the people anticipating the highest drug claims would make drug-only coverage virtually impossible for insurers to offer at an affordable premium," Kahn said in a statement issued June 13.

While the House Republican plan would have helped insurers pay the drug bills of higher-cost beneficiaries, insurers fretted over the smaller, yet steadier, expenses of millions of seniors who take drugs on a daily basis. As those costs increased, insurers would want to raise premiums, but lawmakers, eager to keep Medicare expenses under control, would probably try to limit such premium hikes.

Thomas said that if his plan became law, plenty of insurers would step up. "When you tell somebody you don't need them and, in fact, it's going to succeed without them, you'll be amazed at how some people will come around the back door and want to be part of it," Thomas said.

Although the House GOP plan did not become law, some lawmakers viewed it as a foundation for action in the 107th Congress.

"I don't think the president will sign a [drug] bill we come up with," Rep. Charlie Norwood, R-Ga., said in June. "But it will give a good start for next year when we can really do it." ◆

'Givebacks' to Medicare Providers Will Rise to Double Previous Year's Level

Box Score

- **Bill:** HR 4577 — PL 106-554
- **Legislative action: House** adopted the conference report on HR 2614 (H Rept 106-1004), 237-174, on Oct. 26.

House adopted the conference report on HR 4577 (H Rept 106-1033), 292-60, on Dec. 15.

Senate cleared the bill by voice vote on Dec. 15.

President signed the bill Dec.

SUMMARY

Congress cleared a bill to restore funding cut in 1997 after providers complained vigorously for months that the lower reimbursements were hurting seniors. The GOP leadership, fearing that a measure aimed at reversing more of the Medicare cuts enacted in the 1997 Balanced Budget Act (PL 105-33) might die, attached it to a larger tax bill (HR 2614). The House passed that bill Oct. 26, with only six Republicans opposing it. The Senate did not clear the bill and President Clinton threatened to veto it if it reached his desk. So lawmakers pulled the Medicare changes out of the bill and combined them with outstanding appropriations measures that cleared as one omnibus package (HR 4577) on Dec. 15. *(GOP tax bill, p. 18-32; 1997 Almanac, p. 2-52)*

At the beginning of the year, one of the few health care bills lawmakers considered a sure thing was a measure to restore some of the $112 billion, five-year Medicare spending cuts made in 1997. Lawmakers in both parties were eager to heed the health industry's pleas for more money. But by fall, the measure had become consumed in partisan debate. Republicans, shunning Democrats' input, reconciled three Medicare "giveback" bills: HR 5291, S 3165 and an unnumbered measure approved by the House Ways and Means Health Subcommittee.

Although Clinton had signed a similar bill (PL 106-113) in 1999 — estimated to cost about $17 billion billion over five years — he threatened to veto this year's measure. He said it made no sense to reward Medicare+Choice managed-care plans — which have abandoned the insurance program for seniors in droves since their creation in 1997 — with more money unless the insurers agreed to maintain benefits for more than one year. *(1999 Almanac, p. 16-31)*

Lobbyists for the managed-care plans replied that insurers have little choice but to leave the system, arguing that Medicare is over-regulated and pays too little to providers. In January, 115 plans are expected to leave Medicare, forcing 934,000 seniors to find an alternative. Most Republicans believe that giving the plans more money may convince them to stay in the system and draw new insurers.

According to staff estimates, the Medicare package would cost about $35 billion over five years. About $11 billion would be channeled to managed-care insurance plans that serve Medicare patients, while another $14 billion would go to hospitals. The provision also would provide about $1.7 billion to home health agencies, while skilled nursing homes would get about $1.6 billion over five years.

House Committee OKs Bill Restoring $21 Billion in Medicare Cuts

SEPTEMBER 30 — Of all the bills the 106th Congress has considered to aid patients, the only one that is almost certain to be enacted is one that would help Medicare beneficiaries by making sure their providers are paid more.

On Sept. 26, the House Commerce Committee approved a $21 billion, five-year measure (HR 5291) that would tap the budget surplus to restore some of the funds that were cut in the 1997 Balanced Budget Act (PL 105-33).

The Ways and Means Committee, which shares jurisdiction over Medicare, must produce a counterpart measure, which could be marked up the week of Oct. 2. The two bills then will have to be merged into a comprehensive package — acceptable to the Senate — to restore or delay funding cuts to managed-care plans, hospitals, skilled nursing homes, home health agencies and other providers.

It would be the second major attempt to reverse some of the Medicare payment reductions Congress approved in 1997. Last year, President Clinton signed a measure in the omnibus spending bill (PL 106-113) that contained a "giveback" of more than $16 billion over five years.

The Commerce bill already would use up the entire $21 billion that Clinton and congressional lawmakers set as the informal spending limit, but providers hope the final package will exceed that figure — just as last year's package ended up roughly twice as large as it started.

"I don't mean to minimize this package," Karen M. Ignagni, president and chief executive officer of the American Association of Health Plans, said in a Sept. 26 interview. "But if you're asking, 'Is this enough? Does it meet the test of rescuing the system?' Sadly, the answer is that this is not there yet."

This year's Medicare reimbursements bill is partly an exercise in helping patients, mainly those Medicare beneficiaries whose managed-care plans are withdrawing from the program and blaming the 1997 funding cuts for their decisions. It is also a statement about the political power of the health care industry and the effectiveness of its lobbyists.

When Congress approved the funding reductions in 1997, the federal government still was running deficits, and lawmakers believed the reductions were needed to get Medicare spending under control. *(1997 Almanac, p. 2-52)*

Now, with the budget surplus growing, health care lobbyists have convinced lawmakers that the payment reductions went too far, jeopardizing their ability to provide health care to seniors.

Since the 1997 budget law was enacted, some 3,000 home health care agencies have stopped participating in Medicare because of the reductions, estimates an industry official. A number of managed-care plans that joined Medicare+Choice — created in the budget act to attract them to the program — are also leaving the system.

By January 2001, according to the Health Care Financing Administration (HCFA), withdrawals will have forced about 934,000 seniors to search for other plans that will accept them or return to traditional Medicare coverage, which does not cover many expenses — in particular, costly prescription drugs.

Virtually every member of Congress has heard complaints from voters and providers about the Medicare cuts. "This is one of those issues that affects all of us and our constituents," committee member Michael G. Oxley, R-Ohio, said at the markup.

Lawmakers said the arm-twisting by lobbyists has been hard to ignore. Broad-scale media campaigns with television and radio advertising, coupled with grass-roots pressure, are forcing members to pay attention.

"I know the kind of pressure that you've been under," committee member Brian P. Bilbray, R-Calif., told Chairman Thomas J. Bliley, Jr., R-Va. during the markup.

Preliminary figures are available for some parts of the bill. The biggest chunk so far — about $6 billion — would go to managed-care providers through a bigger payment increase in fiscal 2001 for some plans and increases in the minimum payments they would get for each beneficiary. For example, the minimum payment would increase from $415 to $475 per month for beneficiaries in rural areas.

Home health care agencies would receive about $1.3 billion, primarily through the delay of a scheduled 15 percent payment cut — already postponed twice — until October 2002.

Neither provision would restore enough money to please industry groups. Ignagni called it "a good start," but said she would prefer $15 billion for managed-care plans.

Home health care agency representatives said they would rather see the 15 percent payment cut killed altogether, not just delayed year after year.

"These changes aren't restorations. They simply prevent future cuts," Theresa M. Forster, vice president for policy at the National Association for Home Care, said in a Sept. 27 interview.

About $3.2 billion would go to hospitals that care for a disproportionately large number of low-income beneficiaries, and another $300 million would compensate hospitals for a greater share of the debts that Medicare patients leave unpaid.

The bill also includes $300 million to buy another year's delay in imposing payment caps on rehabilitation therapy and $600 million to pay for additional coverage of drugs needed after organ transplants.

House Panel Approves Bill That Sets Groundwork For Givebacks

OCTOBER 7 — As health care and business lobbyists clogged the hearing room, the House Ways and Means Health Subcommittee approved an unnumbered bill Oct. 3 that could form the template for a measure to provide as much as $30 billion over five years to rescind Medicare cuts set in the 1997 Balanced-Budget Act.

That was the only public progress on so-called Medicare givebacks the week of Oct. 2 — even though lawmakers are anxious to court the generous health care lobby and eager to demonstrate concern for seniors, who constitute a key voting bloc in presidential and congressional races this election year.

Lawmakers are working behind the scenes to reconcile three measures: a package (HR 5291) approved by the House Commerce Committee Sept. 26 now estimated at $18.2 billion; the draft approved by the Ways and Means Health Subcommittee, and a measure (S 3165) introduced Oct. 5 by Senate Finance Committee Chairman William V. Roth Jr., R-Del, that would cost an estimated $28 billion.

'More than $21 Billion'

The final measure "will be more than $21 billion, but it won't be [the] $36 billion" in the first Ways and Means estimate, said Senate Majority Leader Trent Lott, R-Miss., in an Oct. 5 interview. "There are issues of unfairness that members of all sides want to see addressed."

His fellow Senate Republicans have declined to mark up Roth's measure, because Democrats have warned they will try to add language providing a prescription drug benefit for Medicare. Still, it is likely that a unified position can be forged the week of Oct. 9, even though Democrats grumbled because they were not included in the congressional bartering.

Most Democrats acknowledged they will support the final product no matter what shape it takes. "When it comes down to it, I have to take the money for my people," said Sen. John D. Rockefeller IV, D-W.Va, in an Oct. 4 interview.

Members of both parties are calling for at least $30 billion over five years in additional spending, tapping the budget surplus to help such Medicare providers as hospitals, home health agencies, skilled nursing homes and managed-care plans. Last year's givebacks, included in a session-end spending law (PL 106-113), restored $16 billion over five years.

The two provider groups poised to get the most relief are hospitals and managed-care plans.

Hospitals have lobbied hard on the issue and plan to spend $30 million for media ads by the end of 2001.

Even though no bill has yet been passed, the hospitals are pleased by what they have seen thus far. The Ways and Means Health Subcommittee draft — which some experts believe comes closest to what is likely to be the bill's final form — would provide roughly $5.5 billion for hospitals, according to preliminary estimates. The bill also includes payments to rural hospitals, acute-care facilities and medical education costs at teaching hospitals.

"There are a lot of things for hospitals to be happy about," said Thomas A. Scully, president of the Federation of American Hospitals, in an Oct. 3 interview.

Daniel Patrick Moynihan of New York, ranking Democrat on the Senate Finance Committee, is backing sizable increases for teaching hospitals — including several institutions in New York, where first lady Hillary Rodham Clinton is running against Rep. Rick A. Lazio, R-N.Y., for the seat Moynihan is vacating.

Possible Stumbling Block

One of the stumbling blocks in the way of any agreement with the White House centers on funding for Medicare+Choice managed-care plans, which give beneficiaries some prescription drug benefits.

According to the Health Care Financing Administration, by January 2001, some 934,000 seniors enrolled in Medicare+Choice will be forced either to search for other plans or return to traditional Medicare coverage because their insurers have dropped out of the program, citing low payments and high administrative costs. Only about 6 million of Medicare's 40 million beneficiaries rely on Medicare+Choice plans.

President Clinton has proposed a $21 billion, five-year package that would give the plans only about $1 billion in indirect payments linked to any rise in fee-for-service payments. The Ways and Means subcommittee draft would give the plans nearly $9 billion directly and as much as $4 billion in fee-for-service payments. It would also increase the monthly minimum payments for some managed-care providers from $415 per month to $450 per month in fiscal 2001.

The White House says managed-care plans would get too much money.

"This bloated package with extravagant, unnecessary managed-care dollars . . . drains money away from other worthy providers," said a senior administration official in an Oct. 4 interview. "To the extent that more money is given, we will insist on more accountability."

Both the Ways and Means draft and the Commerce Committee measure would give home health care agencies about $1.3 billion, primarily by delaying a scheduled 15 percent payment cut until October 2002. The cut already has been postponed twice.

Other providers, including skilled nursing homes, hospices and medical device manufacturers, would also benefit, but the amount of the payments they would receive is still unclear.

Clinton Wants In On Talks to Rescind Medicare Cuts

OCTOBER 14 — Raising the stakes surrounding an issue that has enjoyed broad bipartisan support, President Clinton warned congressional Republicans Oct. 11 that the White House must be involved in final negotiations on legislation to rescind some of the Medicare cuts set in the 1997 Balanced Budget Act.

The president and lawmakers agree on the need to provide funds for hospitals, Medicare+Choice managed-care plans, skilled nursing facilities, home health agencies, medical device manufacturers and other providers that have lobbied for relief all year.

They disagree on how to allot the money, however. Clinton says GOP lawmakers want to return too much money to the managed-care industry — a target of Democrats in this year's presidential and congressional elections.

"It appears that instead of passing patient protections, legislation intended to restore reductions in the Medicare program is unduly tilted toward the HMOs who killed the patients' bill of rights," Clinton said at a news conference.

Speaker J. Dennis Hastert, R-Ill., responded he was "disappointed that the president has chosen partisanship over progress when it comes to the issue of health care for our nation's seniors."

Democrats Shut Out

Republicans have irritated Clinton and congressional Democrats by shutting them out of talks to finalize a measure that would reconcile three giveback bills — HR 5291, S 3165 and unnumbered legislation approved by the House Ways and Means Health Subcommittee.

In an Oct. 11 letter to Hastert, Minority Leader Richard A. Gephardt, D-Mo., and more than 100 Democrats said they were "very concerned that the House will be asked to vote quickly on a final bill which we have not seen or been involved with."

They also argued they should be given the opportunity to offer an amendment adding a Medicare drug benefit. "Adequate and open floor debate is essential, because this is the last chance for this Congress to consider adding a real prescription drug program to Medicare," the Democrats wrote.

In its current form, the unnumbered Republican bill — which was basically completed the week of Oct. 9 but not released — would cost $26 billion to $28 billion over five years. The measure could come to the House floor the week of Oct. 16, either as a stand-alone measure or attached to a fiscal 2001 appropriations bill, said Ways and Means Health Subcommittee Chairman Bill Thomas, R-Calif.

Hospitals — which account for the majority of Medicare spending — would get about $9 billion, according to a preliminary draft. Medicare+Choice plans — which give beneficiaries some prescription drug benefits — would get at least $7 billion and as much as another $4 billion for automatic payments tied to fee-for-service increases.

Home health agencies would receive about $1.3 billion, largely through a one-year delay of a 15 percent cut previously scheduled for Oct. 2001, lawmakers said. Skilled nursing homes would get $1 billion to $3 billion over five years.

Clinton has proposed a $21 billion, five-year plan that would give Medicare+Choice plans about $1 billion in indirect payments linked to rises in fee-for-service payments.

"Managed care reform in the 106th Congress should focus on patient protections, not on excessive payments to [Medicare] managed care plans," Clinton wrote in an Oct. 10 letter to GOP leaders.

When Medicare+Choice managed-care plans were created in the 1997 budget law (PL 105-33), Republicans expected them to gradually become a strong, market-based alternative to traditional, fee-for-service Medicare. *(1997 Almanac, p. 2-52)*

However, the number of seniors who belong to Medicare+Choice plans is about the same as it was three years ago — some 16 percent of Medicare's nearly 40 million beneficiaries. That is because an increasing number of plans have dropped out of Medicare+Choice, saying that payments are too low and the administrative burdens are too high. In January, the expected exodus of more than 115 plans will force about 934,000 seniors to search for other plans or return to traditional Medicare.

Clinton argued in his letter that higher payments "provide no guarantee that Medicare HMOs will stop dropping benefits or abandoning seniors' communities altogether." Democrats would like health plans to certify that they would remain in the program for at least two years, but Republicans have rejected that proposal.

Providers' Position

The managed-care industry argues that Congress should make a strong financial commitment to shore up the program.

Karen M. Ignagni, president and chief executive officer of the American Association of Health Plans, said seniors should be able to choose additional benefits — such as prescription drug coverage — that traditional Medicare does not offer.

"The resources" in the givebacks bill "are aimed at restoring an extraordinary safety net for seniors," Ignagni said in an Oct. 11 interview. "Members of Congress are doing it for the seniors, not for the Medicare+Choice plans."

Clinton would prefer that more funds go to what he said in his letter were other "critically important health care priorities" such as teaching hospitals, home health agencies and skilled nursing facilities.

Last year's givebacks were part of a session-ending spending law (PL 106-113) that restored $16 billion over five years. *(1999 Almanac, p. 16-31)*

White House Objects Strongly To HMO Totals In House Bill

OCTOBER 21 — The House is likely to approve a GOP plan to provide approximately $28 billion over five years in additional payments to hospitals, nursing homes and other Medicare providers despite complaints from Democrats and the Clinton administration that the proposal is too generous to managed-care plans.

The unnumbered package, which is scheduled for floor action the week of Oct. 23, is unlikely to change significantly, said staff aides. Both parties are eager to adjourn and campaign, and providers have been lobbying lawmakers for months not to leave town without giving them more money to help care for Medicare's nearly 40 million elderly and disabled beneficiaries.

If President Clinton were to veto the proposal, "there is a good chance there won't be any time" this year for another try, House Commerce Committee Chairman Thomas J. Bliley Jr., R-Va., told reporters Oct. 19 when the plan was unveiled.

Ways and Means member Karen L. Thurman, D-Fla., said both parties are eager to pass a Medicare "giveback" bill. "I don't think [Republicans] can go home . . . without this," Thurman said in an interview Oct. 19.

Passage could give Republicans additional cover on one of the year's most politically potent issues — adding a prescription drug benefit to Medicare — because Medicare+Choice plans, which offer some drug coverage, would receive a large share of the givebacks.

Chris Jennings, Clinton's top health policy adviser, told reporters Oct. 19 that the GOP bill "represents a misguided sense of priorities." Jennings and other administration officials met Oct. 20 with Ways and Means Health Subcommittee Chairman Bill Thomas, R-Calif.; the panel's ranking Democrat, Pete Stark of California; and House and Senate committee aides to discuss the Medicare package.

"This was not a negotiating session; this was a discussion session," Thomas said later. Stark said Republicans realize many Democrats will vote against the measure and, if necessary, sustain a Clinton veto.

The Republican measure would give hospitals about $8.4 billion over the next five years, including an adjustment in fiscal 2001 for inflationary increases on goods and services they purchase. Managed-care insurers would receive $6.2 billion plus about $4 billion of additional payments from expanded benefits in Medicare's traditional fee-for-service program, according to House and Senate aides.

Home health agencies would receive about $1.3 billion, primarily from an additional one-year delay in a scheduled 15 percent across-the-board rollback in Medicare payments. Nursing homes would receive another $1.6 billion in additional payment. The facilities could use the money to pay higher wages to nursing staff, but would not be required to do so.

Beneficiaries would receive some new benefits, such as glaucoma screenings and lower co-payments for outpatient hospital visits. They also would get more power to appeal a denial of care.

"This package makes Medicare stronger than it ever has been. We lower out-of-pocket costs, put more doctors in emergency rooms, more ambulances in rural areas, and more health aides in seniors' homes," Thomas said in an Oct. 19 news release.

The Medicare legislation is the second consecutive package of givebacks Congress has contemplated since passing legislation (PL 105-33) in 1997 that trimmed Medicare spending by $112 billion over five years. *(1997 Almanac, p. 2-52)*

Last year, lawmakers gave providers an additional $16 billion over five years (PL 106-113), but hospitals, managed-care companies and others continued to complain that the 1997 law had cut their reimbursements too deeply. *(1999 Almanac, p. 16-31)*

Dozens of managed-care companies have left Medicare, citing inadequate reimbursement, although experts from the General Accounting Office say the plans actually are overpaid. In January, the expected exodus of more than 115 plans will force some 934,000 seniors to search for other insurers or return to traditional fee-for-service Medicare coverage.

Managed-Care Conflict

Even before Thomas and other GOP leaders unveiled their Medicare package, administration officials and congressional Democrats were blasting the plan because they said it was too generous to the managed-care industry.

In an Oct. 17 letter to House Speaker J. Dennis Hastert, R-Ill., Health and Human Services Secretary Donna E. Shalala and Office of Management and Budget Director Jacob

Lew said they would recommend that Clinton veto the Medicare package if it contained "untargeted, excessive and unaccountable HMO payment increases without meaningful investments in beneficiary and health care provider policies."

Speaking to the National Press Club on Oct. 17, White House Chief of Staff John D. Podesta said that Congress was "on the verge of giving billions of dollars more of Medicare money to the same HMOs that have fought tooth and nail to defeat patient protections."

Key House Democrats from the Ways and Means and Commerce panels — who had backed committee bills that would give a similar amount of money to Medicare+Choice — urged colleagues to support the administration's veto threat so that money could be redirected to hospitals, home health agencies and other Medicare providers. "It is time to say no," they wrote in an Oct. 17 letter.

Eighteen provider groups that stand to benefit from the Republican Medicare giveback bill, including the Federation of American Hospitals and the National Multiple Sclerosis Society, endorsed it Oct. 19. Not surprisingly, that pits them against the American Medical Association (AMA), which has pushed hard for patients' rights legislation this year.

AMA Runs Anti-HMO Ads

The AMA ran newspaper ads Oct. 13 proclaiming that Congress was poised to "give big HMOs billions of dollars in Balanced Budget Act relief while giving individual patients nothing."

Medicare+Choice was created in the 1997 balanced-budget law to encourage insurers to expand Medicare coverage. Allowing it to fail would undercut the GOP strategy of turning to the private sector for help in controlling growing health care costs and providing new Medicare benefits such as prescription drugs. Medicare managed-care plans provide benefits not included in fee-for-service Medicare, such as prescription drugs, dental care and routine physicals.

Ways and Means member Jim McCrery, R-La., said Medicare+Choice payments were increased to help beneficiaries who had lost their health coverage. "I've heard from hundreds of people . . . 'I've lost my Medicare HMO and I want to get it back.' That's what real people out there are clamoring for," he told reporters Oct. 19.

The GOP plan would raise the minimum payments for managed-care plans in rural and urban areas and guarantee that all plans receive at least a 3 percent payment hike in fiscal 2001. Insurers who went into an area with no Medicare managed-care provider would get a 5 percent bonus.

Clinton Denounces House-Passed Bill As Too Generous To Managed Care

OCTOBER 28 — President Clinton has threatened to veto a Republican-crafted Medicare funding bill, charging that it is a "massive giveaway" to managed-care companies at the expense of hospitals, nursing homes and other health care providers.

GOP leaders urged the president on Oct. 27 to sign the Medicare bill, which was folded into a package (HR 2614) that includes tax and pension provisions and an increase in the minimum wage. The measure passed the House, 237-174, Oct. 26, with just six Republicans voting against it. *(Vote 555, p. H-176)*

Republicans gladly would blame Clinton for any damage his veto might cause to Medicare providers. Democrats probably would attempt to turn a veto to their advantage by accusing Republicans of not only acceding to the HMOs but working with them to defeat patients' rights legislation, which would expand consumers' ability to sue their health plans.

Providers — even those who feel shortchanged by the bill — fear all their lobbying for a Medicare package will go to waste should it become demonized over managed-care funding.

The approximately $30 billion Medicare package would give managed-care companies about $11 billion in new payments over the next five years to offset payments cuts made in the 1997 balanced-budget act (PL 105-33). Hospitals also would receive more than $11 billion.

Other funding provisions in the Medicare bill include about $1.6 billion for home health agencies, primarily from an additional one-year deal in a scheduled 15 percent across-the-board rollback in Medicare payments. Nursing homes also would receive $1.6 billion in additional payments.

"Everybody loses if this thing goes down," said Thomas A. Scully, president and chief executive officer of the Federation of American Hospitals, a trade organization of for-profit hospitals that supports the GOP bill.

"The problem is Republicans will not come back to pass a second Medicare provider bill," Scully said.

Aching HMOs?

Managed-care industry officials have complained that Medicare payments have been insufficient, forcing them to scale back services or leave the program. However, some government officials charge the plans are actually overpaid. William J. Scanlon of the General Accounting Office told a House panel July 19 that Medicare payments to managed-care plans "well exceeded what Medicare would have paid had these individuals remained in the traditional fee-for-service program."

Scanlon cited a California study showing that aggregate payments to managed-care plans exceeded enrollees' estimated fee-for-service costs by more than an estimated $1 billion in 1995.

Nearly 100 managed-care companies have either reduced services or left Medicare in the last two years, forcing 725,000 seniors to seek coverage from other managed-care providers or return to Medicare's traditional fee-for-service program. Another 115 plans are expected to depart in January, leaving an additional 934,000 seniors to find an alternative.

For months, Democrats and Republicans alike have lamented the pullouts and urged Congress to take action to stem further erosion. While some Democrats dislike Medicare HMOs, they have had to deal with complaints from seniors, many of whom like managed care and are upset when a plan leaves town.

"HMOs are pulling out of Democrats' districts, not just mine," Rep. Mark Foley, R-Fla., said in an interview Oct. 25.

Rep. Jim McDermott, D-Wash., said

the HMO funding in the Medicare bill was simply "a political payoff." Republicans are unwilling to compromise with Clinton because of political concerns, not policy differences, he said in an Oct. 26 interview.

"This is unique in that it's a presidential election and they're trying not to give the president a victory in anything," McDermott said. By his assessment, 33 Democrats helped Republicans toward that goal by voting for the Medicare bill.

"There isn't a member in here who can't go home without something," said McDermott, a veteran of end-of-session gamesmanship. "I've been here for 30 years. This is just the same old game. This is all a game of chicken now."

House Ways and Means Health Subcommittee Chairman Bill Thomas, R-Calif., said Democrats should be mollified by administration language in the Medicare bill that would require managed-care companies to spend the givebacks on beneficiaries — either through reduced premiums or additional benefits — not to plump up their bottom lines.

The tax package is likely to pass the Senate along party lines but faces opposition from Democrats, who are upset with some of its provisions. For example, Ron Wyden, D-Ore., is angry that a measure banning physician-assisted suicide — which is legal only in his state — was included in the bill at the request of Assistant Majority Leader Don Nickles, R-Okla.

The additional funding for Medicare managed-care plans in the Republican bill would raise the minimum payments for plans in rural and urban areas and guarantee that all plans would receive at least a 3 percent payment hike in fiscal 2001. Skeptics argue that the payment increases will not be enough to lure managed-care plans to areas where they do not currently exist.

The measure also would call for a slower phase-in of a so-called "risk adjuster," which is supposed to give managed-care plans treating the sickest beneficiaries more money.

Attacking managed care makes sense politically for Clinton and Democrats, who are eager to keep the White House and regain control of Congress. The industry has spent millions trying to block patients' rights legislation — a point that Democratic presidential nominee Vice President Al Gore has made repeatedly. So Democrats see no reason to reward managed care with billions of dollars in Medicare money.

"It makes great sense in an election year to say the Republican party is the party of HMOs," Scully said in an Oct. 27 interview.

Robert D. Reischauer, president of the Urban Institute, a Washington think tank, said that Democrats "have become quite skillful at playing two contradictory themes" on managed care. When the plans pull out of an area or scale back benefits, Democrats chastise them. "But when managed-care companies are wearing the white hat — providing extra benefits — Democrats want to be their defenders," Reischauer said in an Oct. 27 interview.

Democrats and Clinton also are angry that Republicans developed the Medicare "givebacks" package without their input. The two sides did not talk face-to-face until Oct. 20, well after Republicans had written the bill. Discussions continued via telephone and fax during the week of Oct. 23 but Democrats were still angry at not being included from the beginning.

"This will probably pass the Senate but the problem is that it was written in a closet with no windows," Sen. John B. Breaux, D-La., said in a Oct. 26 interview. "Had they let us help them write this, it could have become law with no problems."

In a letter he sent Oct. 26 to GOP leaders, Clinton said he would veto the bill should it reach his desk.

The measure "continues to fail to attach accountability provisions to excessive payment increases to health maintenance organizations while rejecting critical investments in beneficiaries and vulnerable health care providers," Clinton wrote.

Clinton also said the bill excluded such bipartisan policies as funding health insurance for children with disabilities and for legal aliens who are pregnant. He reiterated those concerns during an Oct. 27 news conference at the White House.

Like Professional Wrestling

Thomas said Clinton's veto threat reminded him of a staged professional wrestling match.

"It's theater," Thomas told reporters Oct. 26. "I don't think he's serious." Thomas has said he does not understand why Clinton would veto a measure that has so many new benefits for beneficiaries, especially when nearly 50 provider groups have endorsed the bill.

Clinton and Gore want health maintenance organizations (HMOs) to remain in Medicare for at least two years, double the current requirement. They say that would protect the thousands of seniors who are left without coverage, including prescription drug benefits, when a managed-care plan departs.

Managed-care companies are reluctant to make a two-year commitment. "You can't lock in to an overregulated, underfunded program," said Karen M. Ignagni, president and chief executive officer of the American Association of Health Plans, which represents managed-care plans.

Democrats trashed the bill in House floor debate Oct. 26. Minority Whip David Bonior, D-Mich., called the deal "a huge, enormous, gargantuan handout to the HMOs" at the expense of other providers who care for seniors.

Rep. Sherrod Brown, D-Ohio, said the money that HMOs would receive over the next five years demonstrated that "the power the managed-care industry has over this chamber is astounding."

During negotiations with the White House Republicans added approximately $2.7 billion in so-called "disproportionate share" payments to hospitals that serve large numbers of poor people.

The Medicare bill also would authorize $475 million in fiscal 2001 for a federal program for hemophiliacs infected with the HIV virus. The money would be in addition to HIV-AIDS funding in the fiscal 2001 Labor, Health and Human Services, and Education appropriations bill.

The bill also would delay by one year a proposed change in Medicaid "upper payment limit" regulations to stop abuses that have resulted in higher Medicaid payments to a handful of states, including New York and Illinois.

According to the administration, officials in those states have been overcharging Medicaid for care provided to poor people in hospitals and nursing homes run by counties, cities and local governments, and using the money for other purposes.

The Senate Finance Committee said Oct. 25 that requiring the Health Care Financing Administration to finalize its proposed regulation on upper payment limits by the end of this year would save the government more than $20 billion over the next five years. However, committee Chairman William V. Roth Jr., R-Del., said the bill "makes too many special accommodations to those states that have abused the system."

Campaign Help

The Medicaid payment change delay could help the campaign of First Lady Hillary Rodham Clinton, who is challenging Rep. Rick Lazio, R-N.Y., to fill the seat of Sen. Daniel Patrick Moynihan, D-N.Y., who is retiring. The change also benefits Illinois, which pleased House Speaker J. Dennis Hastert, R-Ill.

The more than $11 billion for hospitals includes a full inflation adjustment in fiscal 2001 to cover increases on goods and services. Managed-care insurers would receive $6.2 billion in direct payments and $4.8 billion of additional payments from expanded benefits in Medicare's traditional fee-for-service.

Hill, White House Grapple Over How to Boost Provider Payments

DECEMBER 9— Republicans, Democrats and President Clinton battled throughout the week of Dec. 4 over how — not whether — to give hospitals, nursing homes, managed-care insurers and other Medicare providers approximately $31.5 billion more in payments over the next five years. Floor action could come the week of Dec. 11.

Bipartisan consensus emerged quickly to strip the "giveback" measure from the doomed GOP tax package (HR 2614). But lawmakers and administration officials remained undecided on whether to pass it as a stand-alone measure, as part of the fiscal 2001 Labor, Health and Human Services, and Education appropriations bill (HR 4577), or in separate, catch-all legislation that would allow the 106th Congress to adjourn.

Medicare providers kept up the pressure for a deal, testifying at a Dec. 6 Washington forum that the nation's hospitals, nursing homes and home health agencies would continue to crumble unless Congress takes action immediately to restore the Medicare payment cuts made in the 1997 Balanced Budget Act (PL 105-33).

"As I cut costs further, I'm affecting the quality [of medical care]. Unless I see some . . . relief we won't be viable . . . I don't know where to turn right now," said Carl Fischer, executive vice president for corporate functions at the VCU Health System Authority in Richmond, Va.

Republican and Democratic lawmakers attending the forum also urged Congress and Clinton to reach a Medicare deal as soon as possible.

Sen. Edward M. Kennedy, D-Mass., said that since the 1997 law went into effect, 20 home health care agencies and 43 nursing homes have closed in his state, and one of every four nursing homes still operating has declared bankruptcy.

"Virtually every community in the nation faces a worsening crisis. Hospitals, nursing homes, hospices, home health agencies and community health centers across the country are struggling to provide essential services to their patients," Kennedy said.

States with large rural areas, such as Maine, have been particularly hard-hit by Medicare cuts, said Sen. Olympia J. Snowe, R-Maine. "We are so close here to providing some relief that we should do it," Snowe said in a Dec. 5 interview.

The Medicare measure is likely to include additional funding for Medicaid, the federal health insurance program for the poor, and for the Children's Health Insurance Program, a federal-state program created in the 1997 law.

The Medicaid language would also delay by one year a proposed change in the program's "upper payment limit" regulations to close a loophole that allows states to pay county-owned health care institutions the highest possible reimbursement rate. The institutions then return part of the money to the states, some of which have been using the money for purposes other than health care, such as tax cuts.

Illinois alone would receive an additional $500 million a year in Medicaid funding due to the delay, said Sen. Richard J. Durbin, D-Ill.

Should the 106th approve Medicare givebacks, it would mark the second time in as many years that Congress has moved to increase provider payments since the 1997 balanced-budget law was enacted.

While some lobbyists are already dreaming of another package next year — dubbed BBA III — lawmakers such as House Ways and Means Health Subcommittee Chairman Bill Thomas, R-Calif., have said the Medicare giveback deal should give Congress enough of a financial cushion to focus on other Medicare priorities. Chief among them would be a comprehensive overhaul of the 35-year-old program, which could include expanding coverage to include prescription drugs. The topic of Medicare drug benefits was one of the hot-button issues in the 2000 presidential and congressional campaigns.

Striking a Deal

Republican leaders signaled early the week of Dec. 4 that they were eager for a deal on the Medicare givebacks package. "I think we all agree that we are going to address the Medicare adjustments one way or another," Senate Majority Leader Trent Lott, R-Miss., told reporters Dec. 5.

The White House seemed amenable to reaching agreement. "We think that there's ample room to work on this legislation, and that we ought to wrap the work up pretty quickly," White House spokesman Jake Siewert told reporters Dec. 7.

Lott was part of a bipartisan congressional delegation that met with Clinton Dec. 4 and Dec. 7 to try to cut a deal. Negotiators agreed during the second session to add $1.7 billion in funding for hospitals, hospice centers and home health providers.

Other additions could come the week of Dec. 11. The White House, for example, wants the giveback bill to contain about $5 billion in new Medicaid benefits, including legislation (S 2274) sponsored by Kennedy and Sen. Charles E. Grassley, R-Iowa, that would increase coverage for children with disabilities. Some conservatives, however, oppose such a provision because they say it is too broad an expansion of Medicaid.

The administration is also offering to increase payments to Medicare managed-care plans that promise to stay in the program for two years. Plans can leave now after one year, if they choose.

Clinton has said the medicare give-back bill (HR 2614) that Republicans pushed through the House on Oct. 26 would give too much money to Medicare HMOs — about $11 billion of the approximately $31.5 billion package — without requiring them to make any significant changes to their business practices.

Nearly 100 managed-care companies have either reduced services or left Medicare in the last two years, and another 115 plans are expected to depart in January. The insurers cite low reimbursement rates and too much federal regulation as their reasons for quitting the program.

The current comity between the White House and GOP Republicans may fade if discussions linger too long. A Dec. 5 prediction by Sen. Phil Gramm, R-Texas, that "They're going to basically have to take the bill we've got" may prove to be the GOP's bottom line. In addition, dozens of provider groups have thrown their support behind the GOP bill and would accept it without any changes.

Consequences Ahead

As Republicans, Democrats and Clinton negotiated, provider groups took to the airwaves and Capitol Hill to push Congress for action this year, rather than wait until the beginning of the 107th Congress.

The Coalition to Protect America's Health Care, which represents hospitals, launched a nationwide television advertising campaign featuring a nurse who urges Congress to take action before it adjourns. The ad is part of the group's $30 million campaign — most of it spent in the 2000 elections — to highlight what the groups says is a critical need for more hospital funding.

Hospital, nursing home and home health industry executives testifying at the Dec. 6 Medicare forum implored lawmakers to move as fast as possible to pass the Medicare bill.

Cuts from private and public insurance programs have forced health care facilities to cut back or shut down services such as pain clinics, nurse midwife programs and burn units, the executives said.

Dr. Peter Levine of the University of Massachusetts Memorial Health-Care in Worcester, told the hushed hearing room about one male patient who suffered a heart attack but was refused by five different emergency rooms because they were already full. The man was ultimately treated and survived, but only after going into cardiac arrest, Levine said.

The Medicare cuts have also caused facilities to consider whether they should still participate in the program.

Lynn Collins O'Connor, president and chief executive officer of The Washington Home and Hospice of Washington, said in many cases her facility has lost $200 to $300 per day per Medicare patient since 1997.

"With 33 Medicare patients, seven days a week, you can see how this adds up and creates a $3 million loss for . . . every year since BBA's enactment," she said.

Lawmakers Agree To Provide $35 Billion More For Medicare

DECEMBER 16 — After months of negotiations, Congress and the White House agreed to give about $35 billion more to hospitals, managed-care plans, nursing homes and other Medicare providers over the next five years.

The proposal nearly fell victim to a prolonged legislative session singed by post-election partisanship. In the end, however, Democrats, Republicans and President Clinton agreed for a second consecutive year to restore cuts in Medicare made by the 1997 Balanced Budget Act (PL 105-33). *(1999 Almanac, p. 16-31)*

"This plan will help every Medicare beneficiary in every corner of America," House Ways and Means Health Subcommittee Chairman Bill Thomas, R-Calif., said in a Dec. 15 statement.

The deal was part of an omnibus package (HR4577) that cleared Dec. 15 and also included four outstanding appropriations bills.

This year's "givebacks" for Medicare, the federal insurance program for the elderly and disabled, more than double the $16 billion package passed last year.

According to staff estimates, hospitals will receive about $14 billion and managed-care companies will get $11 billion. Nursing homes will get about $1.6 billion and home-health agencies will receive about $1.7 billion. Direct benefits for beneficiaries total about $7 billion.

Providers, citing lower-than-expected Medicare spending, had pressed Congress vigorously for months to pass a second "giveback" measure.

'A Major Step'

"This is a major step toward the full-scale rescue mission for Medicare+ Choice, and it provides the building blocks for saving Medicare," said Karen M. Ignagni, president and chief executive officer of the American Association of Health Plans, which represents managed-care companies.

Many of the group's members have left Medicare+Choice — which gives beneficiaries some prescription drug benefits — in the last two years, citing low reimbursements and too much regulation.

Striking a Deal

During the week of Dec. 11, negotiators also agreed to language boosting funding for Medicaid, the federal health insurance program for the poor. They added $700 million to extend Medicaid benefits by one year for welfare recipients who enter the work force.

However, language to broaden Medicaid eligibility requirements for children with disabilities did not survive negotiations.

The measure also provides $300 million to help increase enrollment in the federal-state Children's Health Insurance Program, which was created in the 1997 budget law.

A $300 million provision was

added that will make patients with Lou Gehrig's disease immediately eligible for Medicare. The current waiting period for people afflicted with the fatal neuromuscular disease is 24 months.

Other language in the Medicare deal includes broader coverage for diagnostic tests such as glaucoma and colon cancer screenings, and lifetime coverage of immunosuppressive drugs, which are given to transplant recipients to prevent organ rejection.

Negotiators failed to reach agreement on language sought by Clinton and Democratic lawmakers that would have required managed-care insurers to remain in Medicare for more than one year. Democrats complained that Republicans wanted to give insurers too much money without forcing them to change their business practices to cut costs.

To ease those concerns, the final bill will levy a $100,000 fine against managed-care companies that leave a region without the government's permission before their annual contract expires.

Stark's Complaint

Rep. Pete Stark, D-Calif., complained that the bill includes a "$200 million gift" to drug makers. He cited a provision that would prevent federal officials from reducing Medicare payments to drug makers but would allow the government to reimburse them at higher rates.

In a Dec. 15 statement, Stark said the provision was "undoubtedly a payoff for the industry's massive, $80 million contribution to the Republicans and [Texas Gov. George W.] Bush," now the GOP president-elect.

While the official price tag for the entire giveback package is about $35 billion, an accounting gimmick could trim health-care spending in the long run.

Language dealing with Medicaid reimbursements will delay by one year — and as much as six years in some cases — the closing of a loophole that allows states to pay county-owned health care institutions the highest possible reimbursement rate.

The loophole permits the institutions to return part of the money to the states, some of which have been using it for purposes other than health care, including tax cuts.

An Oct. 26 Congressional Budget Office scoring of the giveback bill estimates that closing the loophole eventually will save $21.5 billion over five years and $76.7 billion over 10 years, significantly reducing the final price tag of the package. ◆

Congress Makes Attempt To Tackle Medical Privacy, Although No Laws Result

Box Score

- **Bills:** HR 4585, HR 4577
- **Legislative action: House** Banking Committee approved HR 4585, 26-14, on June 29.

Senate adopted privacy amendment to HR 4577, 58-40, on June 29.

SUMMARY

Congress made a first attempt to grapple with the growing issue of medical privacy, though no legislation made it into law in 2000.

The profusion of medical websites and online pharmacies that collect personal information raised questions about who has access to individuals' medical histories and whether that information could be used to deny employment or health insurance. Those concerns were heightened in late June when the Clinton administration joined scientists to announce that a working draft of the human genome had been completed.

The announcement sparked a flurry of activity by lawmakers. On June 27, Senate Banking, Housing and Urban Affairs Committee Chairman Phil Gramm, R-Texas, announced he was considering a narrow amendment to one of several pending banking bills that would protect the privacy of medical records. On June 29, the Senate adopted an amendment to the appropriations bill for the departments of Labor, Health and Human Services and Education (HR 4577) that would have prohibited health insurers from discriminating against patients on the basis of genetic information or testing. The amendment was offered by James M. Jeffords, R-Vt.

Also on June 29, the House Banking and Financial Services Committee approved a bill (HR 4585 — H Rept 106-773, Part 1) that would have required insurance companies and banks to get consumers' consent before sharing their medical records with affiliated companies and third parties. Backed by committee Chairman Jim Leach, R-Iowa, the measure also would have allowed consumers to file suit against financial institutions for disclosing personal medical information without their consent.

The amended Senate banking bill never materialized, however, and HR 4585 became bottled up in the Commerce Committee, which shared jurisdiction over it. Top Republican leaders remained unpersuaded about the need for medical privacy legislation, and the health care industry strongly opposed the House bill, arguing that it would require multiple consents and high compliance costs.

The Senate Labor-HHS bill provision was dropped in final negotiations.

House Panel Approves Medical Privacy Bill

JULY 1 — The House Banking and Financial Services Committee approved a bill (HR 4585) June 29 that would require insurance companies and banks to get consumers' consent before sharing their medical records with third parties or affiliated companies, setting the stage for a contentious battle in both chambers.

The committee voted 26-14 to approve the bill, sponsored by Chairman Jim Leach, R-Iowa. President Clinton has recommended a similar but broader plan, building on provisions in last year's banking overhaul (PL 106-102).

The measure now goes to the Commerce Committee, where it faces an uncertain fate because of strong opposition by industry and some Republicans.

Senate prospects are beginning to appear a bit more hopeful, however. Banking, Housing and Urban Affairs Committee Chairman Sen. Phil Gramm, R-Texas, had opposed expanding privacy protection measures until fledgling privacy provisions in last year's banking law could be evaluated.

Gramm confirmed a shift of position on June 27, when he confirmed that he was actively considering a narrow amendment to one of several pending banking bills that would protect the privacy of medical records. It would be an alternative to a broader measure being considered by Richard C. Shelby, R-Ala.

Last year's financial services overhaul required financial services companies to give consumers a chance to opt out before their personal financial information is shared with unaffiliated third parties.

Clinton asked Congress for legislation (HR 4380) that would require consumer consent for sharing of medical and personal spending records by both affiliated and unaffiliated companies.

The House Banking bill would provide safeguards for medical records similar to those requested by Clinton, but it does not include expanded protection sought by the administration to prevent the sharing of financial records by affiliated companies without customer consent.

Prior to final approval, the Banking Committee adopted, by voice vote, a Democratic amendment by John J. LaFalce of New York that would permit consumers to sue financial institutions for disclosing personal medical information without their consent.

GOP critics of the original bill charged that the LaFalce provision would lead to frivolous lawsuits.

"That was the straw that broke some backs," Leach said, referring to the 14 Republicans who voted against the bill. Only four Republicans voted yea. "We'll have to see what happens."

Marge Roukema, R-N.J., one of the Republicans to support the measure, predicted a stalemate unless action was taken to eliminate or narrow the LaFalce language. "It will have to be fixed," she said.

Industry Opposition

The bill was strongly opposed by several financial services trade groups, including the American Bankers Association (ABA). The groups argued that the bill would be burdensome because it would require "multiple express consents" by consumers for the sharing of some types of medical information. A June 29 letter by the ABA said the bill would impose new costs by requiring companies to search records for medical information if requested by consumers, even though lenders generally do not keep or use such information.

The industry has argued that voluntary guidelines used by companies and existing state and federal regulations are sufficient to protect health data.

Lawmakers have been struggling throughout the 106th Congress to deal with the issue of medical privacy. The stakes of the debate have been rising due to developments in biotechnology that increase the likelihood that doctors soon will have the ability to use genetic testing to diagnose illnesses.

On June 26, Clinton was joined at the White House by representatives of two rival groups of scientists who announced jointly that they had compiled working drafts of the human genome, or genetic code. The announcement generated ripples of concern on Capitol Hill, where lawmakers already had been considering legislation to restrict disclosure of genetic information and prevent bias based on genetic traits.

Leach said the White House announcement helped build momentum for moving the bill in his committee. "The import of this kind of legislation is underscored by the extraordinary new breakthroughs," he said.

Leach's medical-record privacy protection bill includes a key amendment that would require financial institutions to obtain a consumer's consent before disclosing any personal genetic information. The provision, sponsored by Ken Bentsen, D-Texas, was approved by voice vote in the June 29 markup.

In the Senate, Minority Leader Tom Daschle, D-S.D., a longtime advocate of medical-record privacy, said June 29 there was growing concern by the public that deciphering the genetic code would "work to their detriment" by providing information that could be used against them by employers, insurers and lenders. "We need to reduce that level of fear and concern about their privacy and their own genetic character," he said.

The Senate addressed concerns about the use of genetic information on the same day. It approved, 58-40, an amendment to a Labor, Health and Human Services, and Education spending bill (HR 4577) that would prohibit health insurers from discriminating against customers based on genetic information. The amendment was sponsored by Health, Education, Labor and Pensions Committee Chairman James M. Jeffords, R-Vt. *(Vote 165, p. S-54)*

The amendment was similar to language in a Senate-passed bill to regulate the managed care industry, which has stalled in a bipartisan conference committee, though Senate Republicans brought a new version of the bill to the floor on June 29. With the ultimate fate of managed care in doubt, Jeffords said it was important to attach a measure similar to the initial Senate provisions to another legislative vehicle.

"The pace of change is rapid," Jeffords said. "Everyone in this chamber and outside of it agrees we need to guard genetic privacy and guard against genetic discrimination." His amendment barred health insurers from using predictive genetic information to raise premiums or to deny coverage.

Daschle argued for broader language to bar discrimination by both health insurers and employers based on predictive genetic information. His amendment was defeated, 44-54. *(Vote 164, p. S-30)*

Republicans argued that job discrimination was already outlawed by the Americans with Disabilities Act (PL 101-336). *(1990 Almanac, p. 447)*

Rep. Louise M. Slaughter, D-N.Y., has sponsored stand-alone legislation (HR 2457) similar to the Daschle amendment, but it has been stalled in the House Commerce Committee. Slaughter has collected 174 of the 218 signatures required on a discharge petition to bring the bill directly to the House floor.

Is Legislation Needed?

Top Republicans, including Senate Majority Leader Trent Lott, R-Miss., said they were still uncertain of the need for specific legislation on medical-record privacy. Some Republicans complained that Democrats were trying to gain political advantage for November by promoting broad legislation on which there is no political consensus.

"Medical-records privacy has become a hot issue. I'm still not convinced that we will see final passage of legislation or that we need it. Democrats are desperate to seize this as a political issue," said Thomas M. Davis III, R-Va., the top House Republican fundraiser.

For months, lawmakers have been clearly divided on key issues such as whether patients should have to give their consent every time a firm wants to disclose information from their medical files to outsiders, including health plans and researchers, or whether a "blanket" consent would be sufficient. The health insurance industry has argued that information should not be kept so private that health care companies cannot use it to diagnose patients and provide needed services.

Unlike Shelby, who wants to expand protections for both financial and medical records, Gramm wants to focus on medical records. "My proposal would basically prevent the financial services industry from using people's medical records without their permission," Gramm said.

With Gramm and Shelby continuing to discuss a possible deal, other lawmakers of both parties have been backing legislation to put off a decision.

The House Government Reform Committee by voice vote on June 29 approved a bill (HR 4049) that would establish a commission to conduct an 18-month study of the need for privacy protection and make recommendations to Congress.

Republican bill sponsor Asa Hutchinson of Arkansas said he believed the measure would have broad bipartisan support and likely would come to a House floor vote after the July Fourth recess. "This will not preclude other legislation on privacy. It will just ensure we take some action," Hutchinson said.

The 1996 Health Insurance Portability and Accountability Act (PL 104-191) directed Congress to pass legislation to protect medical records by August 1999. *(1996 Almanac, p. 6-28)*

Lawmakers could not reach consensus last year and have instead punted the issue to the Department of Health and Human Services. The agency is expected to complete regulations to ensure the privacy of personal medical records later this year. ◆

Congress Tries Two Paths To Bypass Administration's New Organ Allocation Rules

SUMMARY

House and Senate lawmakers were unable to agree on legislation to overhaul the current system for distributing hearts, lungs, livers and other organs for transplant.

Since 1998, the United Network for Organ Sharing (UNOS), a private contractor that administers the nation's organ allocation system, has been fighting efforts by the Department of Health and Human Services (HHS) to make medical urgency the primary requirement in deciding who receives an organ for transplant.

UNOS operates under a system that distributes organs geographically. Local recipients — those who live nearest a donor and are the best potential match — get preference, followed by those on regional and national waiting lists.

In April, the House passed a bill (HR 2418), backed by Thomas J. Bliley Jr., R-Va., chairman of the House Commerce Committee, that would have overturned the proposed HHS regulation and kept allocation power with UNOS. UNOS is located in Bliley's district.

The White House said President Clinton would veto the bill.

Also in April in the Senate, Republican Bill Frist of Tennessee and Democrat Edward M. Kennedy of Massachusetts wrote a compromise bill (S 2366) that sought to balance power more equally between HHS officials and UNOS.

The bill won unanimous approval from the Senate Health, Education, Labor and Pensions Committee, but Wisconsin's Democratic senators, Herb Kohl and Russell D. Feingold, blocked the measure from floor consideration over concerns that it would take organs away from their state's procurement and transplant programs.

Bliley, Frist and Kennedy were unable to merge their approaches into a bill that could be passed by both chambers. UNOS and HHS signed an agreement in September that included many of the provisions of the HHS regulation. Bliley is retiring, but other lawmakers may move during the 107th Congress to intervene in the UNOS-HHS deal out of concern that the pact could hurt their states or districts.

Box Score

- **Bills:** HR 2418, S 2366
- **Legislative action: House** passed HR 2418 (H Rept 106-429), 245-147, on April 4.

Senate Health, Education, Labor and Pensions Committee approved S 2366, 18-0, on April 12.

House Passes Bill To Shift Organ Allocations to Private Network

APRIL 8 — Congress' struggle to regulate how hearts and other organs are distributed to transplant patients grew more complicated the week of April 3 as House and Senate members backed vastly different proposals in an effort to circumvent new administration regulations.

The administration's rules call for allocating organs nationally, with medical necessity rather than geography determining which patient receives an organ. Currently, local recipients get priority, followed by regional and national patients.

The House voted 245-147 on April 4 to pass legislation (HR 2418) that would give the United Network for Organ Sharing (UNOS) — the Richmond, Va.-based private contractor that runs the nation's organ network — the power to dictate how organs are distributed. On a voice vote, House members also adopted an amendment to the bill, sponsored by Michael Bilirakis, R-Fla., that would overturn the administration's new regulations. *(Vote 101, p. H-36)*

The White House said President Clinton would veto the bill.

In the Senate, Bill Frist, R-Tenn., introduced legislation (S 2366) on April 5 that would create a board comprised of medical experts and patients to establish organ transplant and allocation policies. A private contractor would administer the policies, and the Department of Health and Human Services (HHS) would review and enforce them. The Senate Health, Education, Labor and Pensions Committee is scheduled to mark up the bill April 12.

Frist, a physician who performed heart and lung transplants before he was elected to the Senate, and other opponents of the administration regulations say they give HHS too much power over transplant policy. HHS officials say that while they want organ allocation decisions made on a nationwide basis, the specifics of how to accomplish that goal are being left to UNOS.

Both Bilirakis' and Frist's proposals would overhaul the 1984 Organ Procurement and Transplantation Act (PL 98-507), which established the present allocation system and is also known as the National Organ Transplant Act. Both bills also would seek to improve public education about the need to increase the number of organ donors, a problem all parties in the debate agree must be addressed.

Avoidable Deaths?

HHS proposed the organ allocation change in April 1998, saying many patients die each year because they either do not live near a transplant facility that has the organ they need or cannot afford to travel to one that does.

The new HHS regulations not only highlight the philosophical differences between the agency and UNOS, it pits small and midsize regional transplant centers against their larger urban counterparts.

The regional centers say they have worked hard to establish organ donor programs and claim the HHS plan would force them to ship organs out of state. The larger urban programs often have long waiting lists and believe their patients — as well as those from smaller centers — would benefit from a national system based on medical need.

Lawmakers such as Senate Majority Leader Trent Lott, R-Miss., who want to protect local transplant programs, placed riders on fiscal 1999 and fiscal 2000 appropriations measures to block the HHS proposal. Those riders expired March 16 when the new administration regulations took effect. UNOS is currently developing proposals to meet HHS' goal of a nationwide organ allocation system.

Under Frist's bill, HHS would review organ allocation proposals developed by the policy-making board and suggest changes. If the board and HHS disagreed, the dispute would be settled by a commission composed of members appointed by the board, HHS and the Institute of Medicine, a division of the National Academy of Sciences.

Frist said he wants medical professionals rather than federal bureaucrats or Congress to decide how organs should be distributed.

Frist introduced his bill April 5 without the support of Sen. Edward M. Kennedy, D-Mass., with whom he has worked for months to broker a compromise on the organ issue. The two disagree over how much oversight authority HHS should have, and Kennedy is also concerned that Frist's approach may not result in an equitable distribution of organs. But Kennedy pledged to keep working with him to resolve concerns.

Like Frist, Bilirakis said his bill would put the decision for organ policy where it belongs — with medical experts. "They and not [HHS] Secretary [Donna E.] Shalala know best when it comes to transplant policy," Bilirakis said in floor debate April 4.

Senate Committee Approves Compromise Bill

APRIL 15 — After months of wrangling, Sens. Bill Frist, R-Tenn., and Edward M. Kennedy, D-Mass., have reached agreement on a proposal they believe would more equitably distribute the nation's scant supply of hearts, kidneys and other organs to the thousands of patients awaiting transplants.

The Senate Health, Education, Labor and Pensions Committee, approved their plan — offered as an amendment to S 2366, which would change the nation's organ allocation system — 18-0 during an April 12 markup.

Frist's amendment would create a board of medical experts and patients to establish organ transplant and allocation policies. A private contractor would administer the policies, and the Department of Health and Human Services (HHS) would review and enforce them. Disputes between HHS and the policy board would be settled by an appeals panel comprising members appointed by the board, HHS and the Institute of Medicine, a division of the National Academy of Sciences.

The policy board would also be charged with eliminating disparities among "socioeconomic status, race, ethnicity, geographic area or region of residence or transplantation." Those changes would address HHS concerns that the current system, which distributes organs on a local, then regional, then national basis, is unfair.

The dispute over how to allocate organs has been brewing since April 1998, when HHS proposed regulations that would base organ allocation more on medical urgency than geography. In proposing the rules, which took effect March 16, the Clinton administration said many patients die each year because they do not live near a transplant center that has an available organ and cannot afford the travel expenses involved in putting themselves on several centers' waiting lists.

The debate has caused dissent not only between lawmakers and HHS but among the transplant centers themselves. Those with strong procurement programs feel that other centers that have not worked hard enough to find donors simply want to take organs away from them. But other centers say all transplant patients and facilities would benefit from a national distribution system that put a greater emphasis on medical need than on geography.

The amended measure drew immediate criticism from a group of transplant surgeons, who said it would give HHS too large a role in deciding how organs are allocated.

"The majority of large centers don't want this [and] the majority of small centers don't want this," said Dr. Anthony M. D'Alessandro, a Wisconsin surgeon and spokesman for the Coalition of Major Transplant Centers, a group of 20 hospitals that perform one-quarter of the 5,000 transplants done annually nationwide.

Responding to those concerns, Russell D. Feingold, D-Wis., placed a hold on the legislation, which blocked Frist and Kennedy's efforts to get their measure passed on voice vote before the Senate adjourned for the spring recess. "I have significant concerns about the changes made," Feingold said in an April 12 statement.

Language Changes

The Kennedy-Frist compromise changed some elements of a bill that Frist introduced April 5 in an attempt to supersede the Clinton administration regulations. Kennedy did not back Frist's bill when it was introduced because he was concerned it would not distribute organs equitably or give HHS enough oversight.

But Frist, Kennedy and HHS Secretary Donna E. Shalala reached a compromise the week of April 10 that would increase the appeals panel from 15 to 21 members and give the HHS secretary more say in its composition.

If the HHS secretary disagreed with the policy board's allocation policies, the appeals board would have the final say.

Frist — himself a heart and lung transplant surgeon — said the compromise bill was carefully crafted to address concerns of doctors, patients and transplant centers fearful that the new HHS regulations would cause them undue harm. The measure, he said, was "very good news for all the transplant candidates, recipients, doctors and families that are counting on us."

Kennedy said the revised bill would mean that patients waiting for an organ will be treated equitably. "I think this legislation improves the status quo," he said.

But D'Alessandro said allowing HHS to pick the members of the appeals panel would give the agency an unfair advantage in disputes. He also said that transplant centers and surgeons are committed to giving organs to patients most in need, but "a lot of those decisions of who is sickest and neediest are medical" and should be made by doctors, not bureaucrats.

At the April 12 Senate markup, the panel, on voice vote, approved an amendment from Republican Mike DeWine of Ohio and Democrat Patty Murray of Washington that would require HHS to study the costs of transplant-related anti-rejection drugs for children and whether health insurers are paying for them.

The committee also adopted on voice vote an amendment from Susan Collins, R-Maine, and Christopher J. Dodd, D-Conn., that would require HHS to change by 2002 how it certifies organ procurement organizations.

Competing Measures

Should the Frist-Kennedy bill pass the Senate, it will face off in conference with a radically different measure (HR 2418) the House passed 245-147 on April 4. That legislation, which is sponsored by Rep. Michael Bilirakis, R-Fla., would overturn the administration's new regulations and give the United Network for Organ Sharing (UNOS) — the Richmond, Va.-based private contractor that runs the nation's organ network — the power to dictate how organs are distributed.

The White House has said President Clinton would veto the House bill, but backers believe it may have enough support to allow them to override a veto.

The Frist-Kennedy bill also may get some competition from legislation (S 2398) introduced April 11 by Sens. Peter G. Fitzgerald, R-Ill., and Charles E. Schumer, D-N.Y., that would give more power to HHS to decide how organs are distributed. It also would block state laws that require organs procured in a state to go to patients at that state's facilities.

All of the measures would overhaul the 1984 Organ Procurement and Transplantation Act (PL 98-507), which established the present allocation system. That law is also known as the National Organ Transplant Act. ◆

House Votes for Change In Antitrust Law to Allow Doctors to Unionize

Box Score

- **Bill:** HR 1304
- **Legislative action: House** passed HR 1304 (H Rept 106-625), 276-136, on June 30.

SUMMARY

After a months-long effort by sponsor Tom Campbell, R-Calif., to force a vote, the House passed a bill to allow doctors to bargain collectively with insurers. However, the measure went no further.

The bill would have changed antitrust laws to give health care professionals the right to bargain collectively with insurers over treatments and fee schedules, though doctors would not have been allowed to strike. The measure would have expired in three years, to allow analysis of its economic effects. The Congressional Budget Office estimated the total cost to insurers at $4.3 billion over five years. The measure included an amendment by Tom Coburn, R-Okla., to bar discussions of abortion coverage during collective bargaining negotiations.

Supporters argued that the limited exemption would give doctors greater leverage to fight for higher quality treatments, needed drugs and longer hospital stays for patients. Critics said the bill would result in increased health costs and fewer insured patients. House consideration was originally scheduled in May but was abruptly postponed, leading Campbell to charge that lawmakers were delaying the vote so they could continue receiving campaign contributions from both doctors, who backed the bill, and insurers, who did not.

With fierce opposition from employers and the insurance industry, there was little support for the measure in the Senate, which did not take it up.

House Judiciary Approves Doctor Unionization Bill

APRIL 1 — Doctors and unions praised the House Judiciary Committee's 26-2 vote March 30 approving legislation (HR 1304) that would allow physicians and other health care professionals in private practice who contract with insurance plans to bargain collectively. But insurers warned of price fixing, work slowdowns and rising health insurance premiums that could hurt consumers.

The American Medical Association (AMA), a key proponent of the bill, said it would "level the playing field between enormous health plans and individual patients and physicians."

The Healthcare Leadership Council, an association of chief executive officers of health care companies, countered the bill would permit "cartels" that would do for health care what OPEC has done for gasoline costs: create an upward price spiral that is difficult to control.

Quick Floor Vote Predicted

Tom Campbell, R-Calif., who cosponsored the measure with John Conyers Jr., of Michigan, the Judiciary panel's ranking Democrat, predicted a floor vote within the next two weeks.

It is unclear, however, whether the bill will become law this year. While the strong bipartisan vote in the Judiciary Committee may signal widespread support, jurisdictional battles could slow the timetable for floor action.

Three House committees — Commerce, Education and the Workforce, and Ways and Means — all want to review the bill, even though the Judiciary panel took steps to prevent them from doing so.

Campbell is still looking for a Senate sponsor, but Democrats may be reluctant to embrace the measure, since he is the GOP challenger for the seat held by Sen. Dianne Feinstein, D-Calif.

The bill also faces opposition from the Department of Justice and the Federal Trade Commission (FTC), which, like insurers, fear it will lead to price fixing.

Campbell, however, remained upbeat. "This is a very important step toward improving the quality of health care for all Americans, and I look forward to its passage on the House floor," he said March 30.

Campbell has said his bill would level the playing field between health insurance plans and physicians, who argue that insurers have too much power to dictate contract terms. But some observers say the measure is also a way for House Republicans to smooth rocky relations with the AMA after the doctors group backed a managed care bill (HR 2990) last year that GOP leaders did not support.

The Judiciary Committee made some key changes in the bill that proponents said would improve its prospects for House passage.

When the panel began considering the bill March 16, it strengthened the measure's language so it would not create any new right to strike, although opponents have said work stoppages could occur if the bill became law. The committee also stripped out references to the federal Medicare and Medicaid programs to block other House committees' consideration.

Conyers took that a step further March 30, when he offered an amendment that would remove any references to federal health care from the bill. The amendment was approved by voice vote.

Conyers' amendment also would have the General Accounting Office, rather than the Federal Trade Commission (FTC), conduct a study of the bill's impact on the quality of patient care when the measure expires three years after enactment. The Commerce panel has oversight of the FTC.

Rep. Ed Pease, R-Ind., introduced, then withdrew, an amendment that would have required groups covered by the bill to first seek approval from the FTC or Justice Department before they could engage in collective bargaining with health plans.

Democrats argued that no other unions have to seek such permission, and neither should physicians. Democrats also argued that since both agencies oppose the bill, they should not be charged with overseeing it.

Robert W. Goodlatte, R-Va., offered an amendment to Pease's that would have exempted groups with less than 20 percent market share in their specialty area from needing pre-approval to bargain collectively. Goodlatte said the amendment would exempt most physicians from the requirements of Pease's amendment.

Rep. Howard L. Berman, D-Calif., said Goodlatte's amendment did not go far enough to modify the damage of Pease's proposal. Goodlatte's amendment, said Berman, would say, in essence, "[because] you are weak enough to not have any power, we will allow you to negotiate."

Goodlatte's amendment was adopted on a 17-13 vote but became void when Pease withdrew his amendment.

House Set to Vote On Giving Doctors Collective Bargaining Rights

MAY 20 — Legislation (HR 1304) that would allow physicians and other health care professionals in private practice to engage in collective bargaining is scheduled for a House floor vote the week of May 22.

The bill, sponsored by Tom Campbell, R-Calif., would offer a limited antitrust exemption that would permit doctors who contract with health plans to bargain collectively.

Opponents of the bill, which include a wide range of employer and insurance groups, say the legislation may drive up health plan costs and insurance premiums. The bill's critics argue that employers faced with higher premiums might drop health care coverage for workers.

The Justice Department and the Federal Trade Commission oppose the bill over fears that it will lead to price fixing.

Proponents, including the American Medical Association (AMA), believe the bill would give physicians more leverage with health insurance plans.

The bill would "level the playing field between enormous health plans and individual patients and physicians," the AMA said March 30 after the House Judiciary Committee approved Campbell's bill 26-2.

Hastert Abruptly Delays House Vote But Promises Another Chance

MAY 27 — The sudden postponement May 25 of House floor action on legislation (HR 1304) that would permit some physicians to bargain collectively has drawn the ire of the American Medical Association and other supporters, who accused Speaker J. Dennis Hastert, R-Ill., of backing away from his promise the bill would get a floor vote.

Although Hastert said he intends to allow a vote this year, the measure's legislative future remains uncertain. "We're not going to forge a compromise on a bill that no one really likes very much," John P. Feehery, a spokesman for Hastert, said May 25.

Even if the House were to pass the bill, the measure does not have a Senate sponsor, and GOP leaders are unlikely to be very interested in bringing it to the floor. Some Senate Democrats support the bill, but they will not embrace it because that could help the chief House backer, Tom Campbell, R-Calif., who is challenging Sen. Dianne Feinstein, D-Calif.

At a May 26 news conference, Campbell said Hastert assured him the House would vote on his bill in June. Campbell also said that other lawmakers told him they wanted the vote delayed so they could receive campaign contributions from physicians, who want the measure to pass, and insurers, who do not.

'Milk Both Cows'

"In what members told me individually, the most common expression was, 'Don't force me to choose between two potential contributors — doctors and insurers. . . . Just delay it so we can milk both cows,' " Campbell said.

His bill would create a limited antitrust exemption permitting doctors in private practice and other health care professionals who contract with health plans to bargain collectively. Campbell and other supporters of the measure argue it is needed to even the playing field between health insurance plans and physicians.

Hastert told reporters May 25 the House vote was delayed because "it was late at night, the votes weren't there to move [the bill], and we didn't want to lose it in committee."

House Rules Committee spokesman Rich Mills said that Republican members of the panel decided to postpone the vote because "there wasn't a comfort level in the [GOP] conference about moving forward with the bill."

During a House Republican Conference meeting on May 24, Anne M. Northup of Kentucky offered a resolution to postpone action until the House can vote on legislation that would expand consumers' clout with their health insurers. Conferees are currently trying to reconcile differences between the House and Senate versions of the legislation (HR 2990, S 1344).

Northup's resolution did not receive the necessary two-thirds vote for approval, but it did spark members' concerns about the bill's possible consequences. Opponents, who launched an advertising blitz in the days preceding the scheduled vote, say Campbell's bill would allow physicians to create "cartels" that would fix prices and drive up health insurance costs.

The Justice Department and Federal Trade Commission also oppose the bill, because they fear it would lead to price fixing.

Supporters of the legislation said it was pulled from the floor because business and insurance groups that oppose it want the vote delayed indefinitely. Some even linked the action to last-minute pressure lobbyists placed on GOP leaders who attended a May 24 party fundraiser in Washington, noting that the Rules Committee action occurred later that evening.

"It is no secret that last night the

insurance industry dumped millions of dollars into fundraisers here in Washington," Greg Ganske, R-Iowa, said May 25 on the House floor.

Feehery and Mills said there was no connection between the two events.

Unionization Bill Passes House But Lacks Sponsor in Senate

JULY 1 — After a months-long effort by sponsor Tom Campbell, R-Calif., to force a vote, the House easily passed legislation (HR 1304) June 30 that would give physicians the right to bargain collectively with insurers.

The House passed the bill 276-136, but that may mark its high point. The measure faces fierce opposition from employers and the insurance industry, and Campbell has been unable to find a Republican sponsor in the Senate, where many GOP leaders oppose it. *(Vote 372, p. H-116)*

The House vote, said Campbell, was "in favor of patients, if you believe they are not being adequately taken care of under today's medical care system because there is not a balance between doctors and the HMOs."

Karen Ignagni, president of the American Association of Health Plans, called the bill "one of the the most anti-consumer proposals ever approved by any Congress" in a June 30 statement. She cited industry studies claiming it would drive up health care premiums by nearly 9 percent and force 3 million Americans to drop their coverage.

Despite opposition by the health care industry, the measure's passage could give Campbell some much-needed political ammunition with voters in his race against Sen. Dianne Feinstein, D-Calif.

It could also allow Republicans to heal tensions with the nation's doctors, who are disappointed that many GOP lawmakers did not back the broad patients' protection bill (HR 2990) the House passed in October.

Supporters say the limited antitrust exemption would give physicians and other health care professionals greater leverage to fight for higher quality treatments, the use of needed drugs and longer hospital stays for patients.

Cosponsor John D. Dingell of Michigan, ranking Democrat on the Commerce Committee, said it "shifts the balance back to the point where it is fair. It is simple justice."

Opponents say regardless of its intent, the bill would increase costs and kick more patients into the ranks of the uninsured — an estimated 44 million Americans have no health coverage. The Federal Trade Commission (FTC) and the Justice Department oppose the measure because of concerns over price fixing.

Campbell's legislation was passed a few hours after Senate Republicans voted 51-47 to add an amendment to the fiscal 2001 Labor, Health and Human Services, and Education appropriations bill (HR 4577) that would expand the right of patients to sue managed-care plans for damages. *(Vote 166, p. S-30)*

Fulfilling a Promise

The vote on Campbell's bill fulfilled a promise made by Speaker J. Dennis Hastert, R-Ill., last year to bring it to the floor. Hastert had scheduled a vote on May 25 but yanked the bill abruptly, prompting Campbell to accuse fellow lawmakers of pushing for a delay so they could "milk" campaign contributions from both physicians and the health care industry.

A Hastert aide made it clear that the Speaker was allowing a vote on the bill only to honor a commitment. "The Speaker is none too fond of the bill," said his spokesman, John P. Feehery, in a June 29 interview. Hastert voted for the rule but also supported several amendments that would have undermined the bill.

Lawmakers debated the measure for nearly five hours before they voted. The bill would change antitrust laws to give health care professionals the right to negotiate with insurance plans over treatments and fee schedules but they would not be permitted to strike. The law would expire in three years so its economic effects could be analyzed. The Congressional Budget Office estimates the bill's total cost to insurers at $4.3 billion over five years.

The measure includes an amendment, offered by Tom Coburn, R-Okla., that would bar discussions of abortion coverage during collective bargaining negotiations. It was approved 213-202. *(Vote 371, p. H-116)*

The House killed four other amendments:

- A provision by Cass Ballenger, R-N.C., to tighten the bill's antitrust exemption so physicians could not negotiate on fees or charge patients for the amount of a bill not reimbursed by insurers, 71-345. *(Vote 367, p. H-116)*
- A provision by Cliff Stearns, R-Fla., to require doctors to get Justice Department or FTC certification that any negotiations would promote competition and enhance health care quality, 94-320. *(Vote 368, p. H-116)*
- A provision by Lee Terry, R-Neb., to ban doctors from negotiating fees, 78-338. *(Vote 370, p. H-116)*
- A provision by Christopher Cox, R-Calif., to clarify that insurers could not force doctors to join a union, 201-214. *(Vote 369, p. H-116)* ◆

Lawmakers Clear Package Of Initiatives Aimed at Improving Children's Health

SUMMARY

A children's health bill that covered programs for physical and mental health, substance abuse and day care was enacted into law Oct. 17.

The package included children's health provisions (S 2868), a substance abuse and mental health measure (S 976), a day care bill (S 2236), and provisions increasing penalties for manufacturing the illegal drugs methamphetamine and Ecstasy. *(Methamphetamine, p. 15-44)*

The legislation won quick passage in the House in May, once members gave up attempts to use it as a vehicle for dozens of health amendments, some of them highly controversial.

In the Senate, sponsors Bill Frist, R-Tenn., and Edward M. Kennedy, D-Mass., negotiated a compromise version with House sponsors before bringing the bill to the floor in September. The Senate-passed version then was ratified quickly by the House, clearing it for the president.

The children's health provisions reauthorized an array of programs with a focus on injury prevention, maternal and infant health, public education and new pediatric research at the National Institutes of Health. It included House-passed provisions that target specific conditions, including autism, Fragile X mental retardation syndrome, arthritis, diabetes and asthma. The bill also reauthorized the Substance Abuse and Mental Health Services Administration, giving states new flexibility in using funds but requiring reports to track accountability. The measure expanded services under the Healthy Start program to help low-income mothers receive prenatal care and child care guidance, and it provided for state grants to improve safety in day-care facilities.

Religious organizations can receive some funds resulting from grants in the bill.

House Passes Children's Health Act After Barrage Of Amendments

MAY 13 — The Children's Health Act of 2000 was supposed to breeze through the House — the kind of motherhood-and-apple-pie legislation that members rush to rally behind in an election year.

The measure (HR 4365) would authorize unspecified levels of funding for five years for childhood health research and disease-prevention projects, goals few lawmakers would disparage.

The House passed the bill, 419-2, on May 9. Before it did, however, the measure became a magnet for controversy, underscoring how difficult it is to shepherd even a seemingly simple children's health bill through Congress in an election year. *(Vote 152, p. H-50)*

Almost Sunk

"There never was a problem with the merits of the bill," said Sherrod Brown of Ohio, ranking Democrat on the Commerce Subcommittee on Health and Environment, in a May 10 interview. "But there is so much left undone on health care in this Congress that any time you have a health vehicle moving through the House, people want to use it to forward their agendas," he said. "Once one [controversial] issue was put on the table, then it was Katie-bar-the-door. That's what almost sunk the bill."

The problems started, say members of both parties, in early April when Commerce Committee Chairman Thomas J. Bliley Jr., R-Va., suggested that language be added to the original bill (HR 3301) encouraging health clinic counselors to advise pregnant women that adoption is a viable alternative to abortion.

Democrats bristled at the thought of introducing the sensitive topic and threatened to attach amendments dealing with the regulation of nicotine as a drug and access to pediatric managed-care services to the measure.

By April 13, the planned date of the subcommittee markup, both parties were seeking a home for dozens of health amendments. So they agreed to move a new, narrowly focused children's health bill (HR 4365) directly to the House floor under expedited procedures.

Members suspended the rules, which ban amendments from the floor, limit debate and require a two-thirds vote for passage.

Health and Environment Subcommittee Chairman Michael Bilirakis, R-Fla., Brown, Bliley and others pushed for consensus. No anti-smoking language was attached, but lawmakers on both sides of the abortion debate hammered out a provision that would provide grants to train counselors at federally funded family planning clinics to give general adoption information.

In the end, only Ron Paul, R-Texas, and Mark Sanford, R-S.C., voted against the measure.

"It didn't have to be this way," said Greg Ganske, R-Iowa, in a May 9 interview. "The problem, quite frankly, is that sometimes my party has not reached out and tried to do things in a bipartisan manner."

Some Republicans, however, labeled Democrats as the agents of politicization. Bliley urged Democrat-

Box Score

- **Bill:** HR 4365 — PL 106-310
- **Legislative action: House** passed HR 4365, 419-2, May 9.

Senate passed HR 4365, amended, by voice vote, Sept. 22.

House cleared the bill, 394-25, on Sept. 27.

President signed the bill Oct. 17.

ic senators May 9 "to reject the efforts of Rep. [John D.] Dingell and others to clutter this consensus bill with controversy." Dingell, of Michigan, is the Commerce Committee's ranking Democrat.

The original bill formed the core of the final measure, which is a smorgasbord of provisions to improve children's health. Diseases or medical problems targeted by the legislation for increased research and education funding include autism, asthma, birth defects, diabetes, epilepsy, Fragile X syndrome — a genetic cause of mental retardation — hearing loss, hepatitis C, lead poisoning, multiple sclerosis, oral diseases, organ transplantation complications, skeletal malignancies and traumatic brain injury.

Better Pediatric Drug Trials

The measure includes a provision calling for the development of better clinical trials for children's pharmaceuticals.

"We've found that unless you tailor research to children specifically, you end up with a product that is maladapted for kids," said James C. Greenwood, R-Pa., in a May 9 interview.

Additionally, the bill would create a pediatric research initiative within the National Institutes of Health (NIH) to coordinate children's research projects, and NIH officials would be directed to seek more grant money for research at medical school pediatric departments.

The measure also would reauthorize the Healthy Start program, which is aimed at reducing infant mortality and low birth weights in high-risk populations. Grants would go to community groups that help women in targeted communities participate in prenatal and nutritional programs to increase the percentage of healthier live births.

When the Senate takes up the measure, Bill Frist, R-Tenn., and Edward M. Kennedy, D-Mass. — two of the chamber's leaders on health care issues — want to construct a bipartisan bill that will sidestep the political land mines that stalled the House legislation.

Senate Passes Health Programs

SEPTEMBER 23 — By voice vote, the Senate on Sept. 22 passed a comprehensive bill (HR 4365) to reauthorize and revise health programs for children, drug abuse prevention and treatment programs, and funding for child care facilities.

Sponsors Bill Frist, R-Tenn. and Edward M. Kennedy, D-Mass., have already negotiated an agreement on the measure with House sponsors and expect quick action in that chamber.

The package includes: a children's health bill (S 2868); a substance abuse and mental health measure (S 976); and a day care measure (S 2236). Sponsors also folded in provisions to increase penalties for manufacturing two illegal drugs — methamphetamine and Ecstasy.

The package would reauthorize the Substance Abuse and Mental Health Services Administration, giving states new flexibility in using funds but requiring reports to track accountability. It would increase the emphasis on youth drug and mental health programs, authorizing grants of $100 million to public entities to help cities fight youth violence and another $50 million to research psychiatric disorders among children who have witnessed domestic or community violence.

Religious organizations would be allowed to receive some funds originating from federal grants in the bill.

The children's health provisions would reauthorize an array of programs, with a particular focus on injury prevention, maternal and infant health, public education, and new pediatric research efforts at the National Institutes of Health. The measure includes House-passed provisions that target specific conditions including autism, asthma and muscular dystrophy. Frist added provisions to authorize research on childhood obesity.

The measure would expand services allowed under the Healthy Start program, which began as a demonstration program in 1991 to help mothers from disadvantaged neighborhoods receive prenatal care and child care guidance.

The Senate-passed measure would allow the Department of Health and Human Services to provide state grants to improve the safety of children in day care facilities.

House Clears Health Programs

SEPTEMBER 30 — Hoping to avoid the partisan battles that have stalled other health care measures, the House cleared a bipartisan catchall bill (HR 4365) that would revise and reauthorize several programs affecting children's health, mental health, substance abuse and day care. The measure passed 394-25 on Sept. 27. *(Vote 496, p. H-156)*

The Senate passed the measure by voice vote Sept. 22.

President Clinton is expected to sign the measure, which contains provisions to:

- Reauthorize and, in some instances, revise federal health programs related to autism, Fragile X mental retardation syndrome, arthritis, diabetes, asthma, birth defects, hearing loss, epilepsy, maternal health, prenatal care, poisoning, hepatitis C and other conditions.
- Require the federal government to support programs to improve the health of children in day care.
- Reauthorize the Substance Abuse and Mental Health Services Administration, giving states new flexibility in using funds but requiring reports to track accountability.

The measure would authorize the agency to make grants of $100 million to help cities fight youth violence and $50 million for research into psychiatric disorders among children who have witnessed violence. It calls for another $70 million for substance abuse programs — including those aimed at preventing the use of methamphetamines and the drug "Ecstasy" — $40 million to help offenders released from juvenile justice facilities, $25 million for programs to prevent underage drinking and $75 million for suicide prevention. ◆

Congress Clears Bill to Help Women With Cancer; No Progress on Medical Errors

SUMMARY

In other action on health care legislation, lawmakers cleared a bill to help low-income women with breast or cervical cancer. Legislation to reduce medical errors was introduced but saw no action.

Female Cancers:

A bill aimed at encouraging states to provide treatment for low-income women diagnosed with breast or cervical cancer was signed into law Oct. 24 (PL 106-354).

The measure allows states to provide Medicaid coverage for eligible women diagnosed under the Centers for Disease Control and Prevention (CDC) early detection program. The states are to be reimbursed for between 65 percent and 68 percent of the costs.

Previously, poor women could receive the screening, but if they were diagnosed as having cancer, federal health care programs did not automatically pay for treatment. Treatment was paid for only if the woman was pregnant, receiving assistance under the Temporary Assistance for Needy Families program, or receiving Supplemental Security Income payments for disability.

The House passed a version of the bill, 421-1, on May 9 that proposed a federal payment of 75 percent. Also, the bill would have required condom packages to carry warning labels stating that condoms do not protect against the HPV virus, a leading cause of cervical cancer. *(Vote 151, p. H-50)*

The Senate passed a revised version by voice vote Oct. 4, after substituting the text of a Senate bill (S 662 — S Rept 106-323). The Senate bill had the 65 percent to 68 percent reimbursement language and dropped the condom labeling.

The House agreed to the changes Oct. 12, clearing the bill by voice vote.

Medical Errors

Although President Clinton and members of both parties called for efforts to reduce medical errors, the issue was overshadowed by more politically potent priorities, such as expanding patients' rights to sue their insurers and adding a prescription drug benefit to Medicare. As a result, Congress took only minimal action.

The Institute of Medicine reported in November 1999 that as many as 98,000 Americans die every year because of medical mistakes. It recommended that Congress create a mandatory, public national reporting system for all errors that lead to severe injury or death. The agency proposed a voluntary, confidential reporting system for less serious incidents.

Several senators, including James M. Jeffords, R-Vt., chairman of the Health, Education, Labor and Pensions Committee, and ranking committee Democrat Edward M. Kennedy of Massachusetts, introduced bills to establish error-reporting guidelines, but discussions bogged down over the level of accountability.

Health care providers — fearing that either mandatory or voluntary public disclosure would increase their legal liability — also did their best to sidetrack the proposals, telling lawmakers that their first priority should be restoring the Medicare cuts enacted in the 1997 Balanced Budget Act (PL 105-33).

The only action taken was inclusion of $50 million to study ways to prevent medical errors cleared as part of the fiscal 2001 Labor, Health and Human Services, and Education appropriations bill (PL 106-354). The language called for studying both voluntary and mandatory reporting of errors as well as confidential and public notification. ◆

Chapter 13

INDUSTRY & REGULATION

Power Politics: Lawmakers Fail in Effort to Deregulate Electricity, Spur Competition

Box Score

- **Bills:** HR 2944, S 2071
- **Legislative action: Senate** passed S 2071 (S Rept 106-324) by voice vote June 30.

SUMMARY

Lacking consensus in either chamber, legislation to foster competition in the electric power industry foundered in the second consecutive Congress. Unable to agree on a broad bill, the Senate on June 30 passed a measure (S 2071) designed to bolster reliability of the nation's antiquated and overtaxed electric grid by creating more federal oversight of its use by utilities. The House did not take up the bill.

The generation, transmission and marketing of electricity is the last major regulated monopoly in the nation; at $217 billion in sales, it also is the country's eighth biggest business. Republicans have been advocating deregulation since they took control of Congress, but they never have reached accord on the myriad issues in the debate.

In 1999, the House Commerce Energy and Power Subcommittee approved a bill (HR 2944) that would have given states much of the power to restructure their electric markets. The White House and Commerce Committee Chairman Thomas J. Bliley Jr., R-Va., advocated federal oversight instead. A July 13 markup by the full committee was adjourned when Bliley realized he lacked the votes to amend the bill to his liking.

After the Senate Energy Committee failed to forge a compromise at two markups on a bill (S 2098) in May, its leaders tried to cut a deal themselves. Their talks collapsed over two issues. The first was how much oversight to give the Federal Energy Regulatory Commission — Chairman Frank H. Murkowski, R-Alaska, wanted less while ranking Democrat Jeff Bingaman of New Mexico wanted more — and the second was Bingaman's insistence that at least 7.5 percent of electric production come from renewable sources.

All sides agree that two laws should be repealed: the Public Utility Holding Company Act of 1935, which limits utilities to defined "service areas" and keeps them out of other markets, and the Public Utility Regulatory Policies Act of 1978, which forces utilities to get some power from renewable sources. There is also consensus to scrap the idea, at the heart of the 105th Congress' debate, of imposing a deadline on the states for deregulation.

Senate Panel Focus Is on Reliability, Efficiency

MAY 20 — Members of the Senate Energy and Natural Resources Committee appear to agree that even if they produce a comprehensive bill to restructure the electric power industry, it is unlikely to become law in the 106th Congress. As their effort to mark up such a measure began May 17, however, most committee members vowed to press more limited legislation to address issues of power supply.

After the three-hour session — at which no votes were taken but most panel members sketched their views — Chairman Frank H. Murkowski, R-Alaska, said he was surprised by the number of issues on which senators appeared to have a consensus. "I don't expect to finish next week, but we're off to a pretty good start," Murkowski said. "In fact, I got a little bit further than I expected."

The committee formally took up Murkowski's bill (S 2098) to move the $220 billion electric market to a "more competitive and efficient" system, but it also deliberated proposals put forth by the Clinton administration and several other senators. Panel members sounded agreement that regional transmission organizations should be created to distribute electricity in a deregulated — and therefore competitive — environment, and they seemed to concur that a bill to maintain reliability of the nation's electricity supply would be their top priority if a more sweeping measure foundered this year.

The push for comprehensive legislation continued in the House, however, as Commerce Committee Chairman Thomas J. Bliley Jr., R-Va., scheduled a June 14 markup for a bill (HR 2944) approved by a subcommittee in October. "It's not, by any means, too late to move legislation," Bliley said at a news conference May 19, although he said he would not attempt to impose a solution of his own on the committee for resolving its members' various disputes.

When the Senate markup resumes May 24, Murkowski said he would push to begin voting on specific proposals; he did not say how much longer he would allow the deliberations to go on.

The panel must decide whether to allow utilities to recover "stranded costs" — investments in generating plants, now normally recouped by raising electric rates, that would be harder to recover if competition drives down power prices; whether to allow groups of retail consumers to form groups to buy power; how to provide consumer protections for the poor; whether to require that some electricity be generated from renewable sources; and whether the Tennessee Valley Authority and other power marketing associations should be forced to compete with investor-owned utilities in a deregulated market.

Best Prices

Under Murkowski's bill, states would be encouraged — but not compelled — to deregulate their electricity markets, with local utilities continuing to transmit and distribute electricity and consumers free to shop for the best price from a national array of generating concerns. For that to happen, Congress would need to repeal the Public Utility Holding Company Act (PUHCA) of 1935, which limits the area that each investor-owned utility may serve. Murkowski's bill also would alter a 1978 law (PL 95-617) that enhanced state power to regulate electric rates. *(1978 Almanac, p. 639)*

In recent weeks, federal and state regulators have called for reduced consumption in a bid to stave off problems caused by the overloading of the electric grid. In the past two summers, heat waves combined with seasonal generating plant repairs and maintenance caused wholesale power availability to drop — and prices to soar — causing brownouts in the East and Midwest and prompting utilities in those regions to raise retail prices. Five Senate bills aim to assure a steady electric supply, but no consensus has emerged. Jeff Bingaman of New Mexico, the panel's top Democrat, led the chorus at the May 17 markup saying that enacting an agreement on this provision should be the committee's main effort.

Slade Gorton, R-Wash., said he would back PUHCA repeal only if public power producers were allowed to opt out of the current system, under which they may sell tax-exempt bonds to build generating plants but are limited in how much power they may produce — a restriction that would curb their ability to compete in deregulated markets.

Byron L. Dorgan, D-N.D., suggested that rural states such as his would not benefit from deregulation, because few companies would want to compete for their sparse customer base. In contrast, Ron Wyden, D-Ore., expressed concerns that his constituents, who now pay less than those in some other states for power, would see their prices go up under deregulation. "I would need some ironclad guarantees that the folks I represent wouldn't be picking up the rest of the country's electric bills," he said.

3rd Senate Markup Scheduled to Settle Jurisdictional Issues

MAY 27 — After setting aside more than 30 amendments and failing to reach agreement on several key sticking points, the Senate Energy and Natural Resources Committee on May 24 scheduled a third markup on a bill (S 2098) to deregulate the $220 billion U.S. electricity market.

By the time it reconvenes June 7, the committee hopes to have a plan on how to proceed with the amendments. The two most difficult issues — raising money to decommission nuclear plants and giving states the power to block utilities from coming into their states — involve jurisdictional questions of whether the states or the federal government should have primary authority in a restructured electric utility market.

So far, the committee has made little progress in two markups. Energy Chairman Frank H. Murkowski, R-Alaska, said he will not give up. "I think we need a comprehensive bill, and I'm going to work toward a comprehensive bill, and I'm not going to be the one to kill a comprehensive bill," he said.

But by scheduling a third markup after the Memorial Day recess, Murkowski puts the committee agenda right in the middle of the Senate's appropriations season, when annual spending bills must get priority attention.

The House, meanwhile, faces a similarly bottled-up schedule for electricity deregulation. House Commerce Chairman Thomas J. Bliley Jr., R-Va., announced May 19 that his committee would mark up a deregulation bill (HR 2944) approved in a Commerce subcommittee last October.

On the Senate side, Murkowski will need cooperation from a committee already skeptical of its chances of getting any deregulation bill signed into law by the end of the 106th Congress. Murkowski seemed to realize that difficulty, alluding to unnamed "other alternatives" that the committee would explore if progress became more difficult.

The toughest issue to resolve in the markup process was how utilities would raise money in a deregulated market to decommission, or take out of operation, nuclear power plants no longer suitable for use. Murkowski and ranking Democrat Jeff Bingaman of New Mexico could not agree how to accomplish that goal.

Murkowski's bill would give the Nuclear Regulatory Commission the authority to determine if a utility had adequate funds for nuclear decommissioning and to direct a utility to increase collections if necessary. Murkowski also suggested letting a utility apply to the Federal Energy Regulatory Commission for a "wires charge" on consumers to pay decommissioning costs.

Bingaman objected, saying such a charge ultimately would spread decommissioning costs to ratepayers in areas not served by the utility that needed the money for decommissioning. Those customers, Bingaman said, shouldn't be forced to pay for cleaning up nuclear plants "that benefit them not one iota." Bingaman said he would offer an amendment striking that portion of the bill.

Murkowski said Bingaman's amendment would make states responsible for ensuring that utilities raised money for decommissioning, a task he said he doubted states would follow through on. "We need to enforce and have the assurance that we're going to have enough money for decommissioning," Murkowski said.

The issue of giving deregulated states the power to block utilities in regulated states from entering their jurisdictions — known as "retail reciprocity" — has struck federalist chords on the committee. Murkowski and his supporters believe that state utility commissions should have jurisdiction to act on behalf of their consumers and utilities, protecting them from possible abuses by utilities based in states that chose not to deregulate.

Opponents of Murkowski's approach believe the national electric grid is interstate in nature, and thus the federal government should have the right to regulate electric transmission.

Renewable Energy

Slade Gorton, R-Wash., said he will offer an amendment to increase the amount of electric generation from "renewable" sources such as solar, wind or biomass. And Peter G. Fitzgerald, R-Ill., said he would offer an amendment requiring federal agencies to buy at least 3 percent of their electricity from renewable sources.

Committee members also tentatively agreed on a Clinton administration proposal to create a $6 billion "public benefits fund" to educate consumers and provide services for low-income consumers. But Craig Thomas, R-Wyo., expressed concern about the fund's activities. "If we're going to talk about universal service, that's one thing. If you're talking about setting environmental standards, that's entirely something else."

Senate Panel OKs Scaled-Back Bill

JUNE 24 — The Senate Energy Committee has officially abandoned its efforts to craft a comprehensive restructuring of the $220 billion electric utility industry, instead giving its blessing to a fallback election-year measure designed only to bolster the reliability of the national electric grid.

After two markups in May failed to yield a consensus on key components of the comprehensive bill (S 2098), Chairman Frank H. Murkowski, R-Alaska, and ranking Democrat Jeff Bingaman of New Mexico spent several weeks trying to cut a deal to spur federal incentives to deregulate electricity — an idea that has foundered for four years amid intense lobbying from several quarters.

But they could not agree on how much jurisdiction to give the Federal Energy Regulatory Commission (FERC), how to prevent significant differences between wholesale and retail service, or whether to include federal requirements designed to increase the generation of electricity from renewable sources.

Instead, the committee approved by voice vote June 21 the narrower measure (S 2071) by Republican Slade Gorton of Washington.

Murkowski said he would try to win a unanimous consent agreement that would lead to Senate passage, probably in July. That means the bill could not become law in time to have an effect on the power supply this summer. But its path in Congress still may be aided by a campaign season during which voter attention is increasingly focused on energy, not only soaring gas prices but also uncertainty in the electricity supply. Increased demand caused by a growing population, a booming economy and heat waves — combined with a shortage of new generating capacity — has led to spikes in the prices of wholesale electricity as well as brownouts and blackouts, including one during record heat in California's Silicon Valley this month.

Gorton's bill would replace the North American Electric Reliability Council, a group in which utility participation is voluntary, with an Electric Reliability Organization, charged with setting reliability standards for utilities. Any utility or power marketer that used the national network of interconnected power lines and generators to move electricity would be required to participate in the organization, which would fall under FERC jurisdiction. The organization would be allowed to set rules governing the emergency supply of power that is kept on the grid — which utilities may tap to cover peak needs — and could penalize those that did not donate their fair share or took from the reserve inappropriately.

The measure would not repeal the Public Utility Holding Company Act of 1935 (PUHCA). Proponents say repeal would both spur competition and enhance reliability, because it would mean utilities could sell electricity outside their prescribed service areas.

"I do not want anyone to think that I have abandoned my belief that eventually we will have to tackle the issues in a more comprehensive bill," Murkowski said in a statement, but "we are late in the Senate session and we need to take action on the more limited, although still very important, provisions on reliability."

Left for the Next President

Groups representing rural electric cooperatives, municipal utilities and independent power producers all hailed the decision to move the scaled-back bill. But the Electric Power Supply Association, which represents independent producers, said only comprehensive restructuring would create "an efficient, seamless and truly competitive nationwide marketplace for electricity."

That sentiment was echoed by Energy Secretary Bill Richardson. Despite Murkowski's declaration that a sweeping measure is off the Senate's agenda until the 107th Congress, Richardson urged the House to press ahead with its efforts to advance a comprehensive bill.

Senior members from both parties on the House Commerce Committee, where a comprehensive restructuring bill (HR 2944) has not moved beyond a subcommittee markup, said they would have trouble moving even a narrow bill like Gorton's in the remaining weeks of the 106th Congress.

"I am not optimistic about anything happening, even on a narrow basis, this summer," Joe L. Barton, R-Texas, chairman of the Energy and Power Subcommittee, said in an interview June 21.

John D. Dingell of Michigan, the full committee's top Democrat, said that no legislation passed this year could address long-term questions about reliability because of a lack of provisions to encourage the development of new electric generation.

Barton said Murkowski's failed attempt to produce a comprehensive bill had nonetheless "moved the bill forward a lot" and provided a good foundation for the future. He vowed to revive negotiations with electric producers, utilities and consumer groups in the hope of moving a bill that could give the next president a victory early in his tenure.

Senate Passes Power Grid Reliability Measure

JULY 1 — With another summer of power shortages at hand and the election five months away, the Senate has passed legislation (S 2071) designed to encourage greater reliability standards for companies that use the nation's electric power grid.

Since negotiations on a broad restructuring of the electric utility industry have foundered, the new bill, passed by voice vote, may be the only chance for action this year.

The measure, sponsored by Slade Gorton, R-Wash., would replace the North American Electric Reliability Council, a group in which utility participation is voluntary, with an Electric Reliability Organization responsible for setting and enforcing reliability standards. Any utility or power marketer using the network of power lines and generators to move electricity would be required to participate in the organization. It would be under the jurisdiction of the Federal Electric Regulatory Commission. The organization would be allowed to set rules governing the emergency supply of power on the grid — which utilities may tap to cover peak electric needs — and could penalize

House Committee's Electricity Bill Short-Circuits

JULY 15 — The House Commerce Committee on July 13 delayed an impending public meltdown over comprehensive legislation (HR 2944) to encourage greater competition in the nation's $220 billion-a-year electric power industry.

Afterward, few saw any reason to believe that postponing the committee markup would create time for crafting a deal to revive the measure, which has languished in a series of disagreements since it was approved by a subcommittee almost nine months ago.

The Senate gave up on its effort to produce a comprehensive bill (S 2098) last month.

Had the markup proceeded, Chairman Thomas J. Bliley Jr., R-Va., faced a lopsided defeat at the hands of his chief Republican rival on the issue, Joe L. Barton of Texas, chairman of the Energy and Power Subcommittee.

Barton acknowledged after the markup was postponed that passing a comprehensive deregulation bill was "barely possible" this year.

After a round of negotiations early in the week of July 10 failed to yield a deal, Bliley was ready to offer an amendment that would have given much of the oversight of electric transmission in a deregulated era to the Federal Energy Regulatory Commission (FERC), in effect stripping language in the bill — language backed by Barton — that would give that oversight to the states.

That is the chief disagreement between the two. They also differ on whether municipal utilities should continue to receive tax breaks for generation facilities they built.

Disputes over electric transmission regulatory authority and whether renewable power sources should be required for electric power generators also stymied senators. They eventually passed legislation (S 2071) June 30 confined to encouraging increased standards for ensuring the reliability of the nation's electric power grid. Barton has said he is not optimistic about that measure's passage by the House.

Money and Power: Lobbying Groups Spend Freely

AUGUST 12 — Ask Alan H. Richardson, Washington's chief advocate for municipal electric utilities, about the money fueling the electricity deregulation debate, and he offers this: So much has been spent to woo Congress that a colleague has labeled this the "two-Lexus bill."

The allusion is not only to the number of luxury sedans this lobbyist sees himself affording with the fees he has collected from his clients. It could just as well be a tart reminder of the number of cars he may wear out before the debate yields a law.

The generation, transmission and marketing of electric power remains the last major regulated monopoly in the United States. With $217 billion in sales last year, according to the Energy Department, it was also the nation's eighth biggest business. Eight years ago, Congress ordered the deregulation of wholesale electricity transmission, setting the stage for half the states to take steps to spur retail competition as well. To foster such competition nationally, Congress must, at a minimum, remove one impediment — a law enacted 65 years ago that bars utilities from selling to customers outside their regions.

So far, change has been easier to advocate than to enact. Despite the predictions of some Republican leaders, the debate got nowhere in the 105th Congress. With top players on the issue unable to reach agreement, consumers more worried about rising gas prices and the election-year congressional agenda already trimmed to the bare bones, it is nearly certain that the 106th Congress will not produce a comprehensive measure, either.

More broadly, there have not been widespread interruptions in the nation's flow of power that would trigger public calls for action. And despite what experts say, most consumers do not realize that they could save money in a deregulated world. "I don't see great political gain for most members of Congress to go back home and say, 'Look, I passed an energy restructuring bill,' " said Richardson, the executive director of the American Public Power Association.

Blackouts early this summer in Detroit and Silicon Valley spurred the Senate to pass a limited measure to enhance the reliability of the nation's antiquated power transmission grid. That effort appeared to have died in the House as the summer recess began July 28, although it may be revived if the most recent power shortages and price spikes across California catch the electorate's attention on the issue.

Plenty of positioning and horse-trading on a broad measure have nonetheless occurred behind the scenes, much of it this summer. Negotiations among senior lawmakers and various advocates, while failing to hatch a sweeping compromise, at least narrowed the areas of disagreement, giving rise to some claims of optimism that 2001 will be the issue's year, no matter which parties control the White House and the Capitol.

"There's a time when the process matures," said Rep. W. J. "Billy" Tauzin, R-La. "That moment's close, and if this moment doesn't happen this year, it will happen early next year."

The vigorous lobbying campaign also is illustrative of a classic Washington phenomenon: A proposal to revamp an important slice of American business is trapped — neither advancing nor dying in the sort of blaze of congressional acrimony that might be felt on the campaign trail. Those with high-stakes interests in the debate keep pouring money in anyway, hoping to ensure that they will be as well positioned as their adversaries when — and if — Congress gets serious about legislating.

It is "one of those rare moments here in Washington, where you see so many players fighting among themselves," said Holly Bailey, a researcher with the Center for Responsive Politics, a campaign finance research group in Washington. "There are so many people pulling in so many directions that the bill essentially gets stuck."

The consumer advocacy group Public Citizen sees a more sinister motive emanating from Washington's lobbying core. "Both sides of the debate are giving Congress large amounts of money, which is why we haven't seen a bill go anywhere," said Wenonah Hauter, director of the group's energy and environment arm. That way, lawmakers "can keep the money-raising going. There's no benefit to passing a bill now. . . . They have to make it appear that there's enough movement to allow the K Street crowd to keep billing their clients."

The recent history of Congress contains several other examples of the big-money disputes that take years to resolve: the ongoing debates over regulating managed health care insurance and making prescription drug coverage a part of Medicare, and the struggles that spanned several Congresses before enactment of laws to overhaul the regulation of telecommunications (PL 104-104) four years ago and the regulation of financial services (PL 106-102) last year. *(1996 Almanac, p. 3-43)*

Lobbying Forefront

Much of the most visible lobbying, both the buttonholing of lawmakers and the waging of advertising campaigns, has been undertaken by seven groups, including four trade associations representing municipal, investor-owned and rural utilities and independent power producers. Combined, the seven spent $50 million lobbying Congress in the past three years, according to their own reports to Congress, which are widely viewed as extremely conservative estimates of the range of their advocacy efforts.

Each utility association is seeking different sets of provisions to ensure that its members can thrive in a deregulated environment. A coalition representing large-scale electricity consumers — mostly retailers and manufacturers — is pushing for quick congressional action because its members see themselves saving billions of dollars each year if they can shop for power. Their effort is being spearheaded by former Rep. Bill Paxon, R-N.Y. (1989-99).

The remaining two high-profile groups are both campaigning for Congress to dictate a hands-off federal approach to a restructured industry, with any oversight power given to the states. One, Citizens for State Power, is a coalition of conservative policy groups. The other, the Electric Utility Shareholders Alliance, has some funding from the electrical workers' union. Neither was willing to describe its financial underpinnings in detail, but The Washington Post reported in May that both "stealth" groups' efforts are being paid for primarily by the same nine investor-owned utilities.

The newspaper said the utilities had spent $17 million on the effort since 1997 in a bid to stop deregulation — which would end their monopolies to sell power in parts of Illinois, Texas, Florida, Ohio, Michigan, Missouri and the Carolinas — or at least assure that state regulators were put in charge of setting the ground rules. Much of that money has financed advertising campaigns with messages implying that the two groups have little in common.

"Certain investor-owned utilities don't want any legislation," said Thomas J. Bliley Jr., R-Va., who sought to make a sweeping bill the hallmark of his final year as chairman of the House Commerce Committee. "They've spent a lot of money trying to block a bill, and they've been successful so far."

Clinton's Plan Faded Early

The seed of the debate was planted eight years ago, with the enactment of a sweeping energy law (PL 102-486) in the closing days of the 102nd Congress. It set the stage for the current debate over nationalizing electricity restructuring when it allowed utilities and independent producers to compete in the wholesale power market by ensuring them access to one another's utility lines. Since then, 24 states and the District of Columbia have moved to create retail competition for electricity. *(1992 Almanac, p. 231)*

During his second term, President Clinton has been pushing Congress to take the next step. He has proposed a bill (S 1047) that would open the market to retail competition by 2003, give the Federal Energy Regulatory Commission (FERC) oversight and set up a $3 billion federal fund for energy conservation and low-income energy assistance.

In his July 1 radio address, the president said his plan would save consumers $20 billion a year. In theory, retail restructuring would allow competition that would give homeowners choices among power sellers, driving down prices and making service more reliable.

But the administration's campaign for the plan has gained little notice — and has received even less attention as consumers have become preoccupied with a more palpable energy concern, the sudden surge in heating oil and gasoline prices earlier this year.

When months of negotiations failed to produce deals on comprehensive legislation in either the House (HR 2944) or the Senate (S 2098), senators settled for the grid reliability bill, although it was clear that measure (S 2071) could not be enacted in time to have an effect this summer. Key House members signaled before the August recess that they would not embrace the Senate bill this fall, apparently concluding that there was no urgency to move the bill — and thereby take away a "sweetener" that might ease passage of a comprehensive bill in the next Congress.

Repealing PUHCA

All players in the debate agree on one threshold point: In order for robust, comprehensive, nationwide competition in the electric power market to get under way, Congress must make one sweeping deregulatory move: repeal the 1935 law universally known by the acronym PUHCA, which stands for the Public Utility Holding Company Act. The statute, enacted to prevent the nation's power supply from being held in only a few corporate hands, restricts the growth and business activities of the biggest, multistate corporate utilities, barring them from doing business outside their areas. While repeal would take away the monopolies the big utilities have in their geographic area, it would allow them to expand their reach, with the ensuing competition presumably lowering monthly utility bills for consumers.

Beyond that, it is hard to find an issue on which all sides agree. And the roster of issues that have yielded major disagreements continues to change. In the 105th Congress, the core dispute that scuttled a bill was over whether Congress should set a federal deadline, or "date certain," for states to open their electric markets to competition. When Bliley unilaterally eliminated that option in March, the focus shifted.

The key question now is who should be responsible for oversight of the flow of electricity in a nationally restructured market: state legislators and utility commissioners, or FERC.

In Congress, supporters of a strong federal hand include Bliley and key Democrats in the debate, including House Commerce's Edward J. Markey of Massachusetts and Jeff Bingaman of New Mexico, the ranking minority member on the Senate Energy panel. All of them see the issue as federal regulation of interstate commerce.

The associations representing investor-owned and municipal utilities, and the coalition of big-volume electrical consumers, have all endorsed putting FERC in charge, believing they would benefit from the application of a uniform set of rules nationwide.

Joe L. Barton, R-Texas, chairman of the House Commerce Energy and Power Subcommittee, and Senate Energy Committee Chairman Frank H. Murkowski, R-Alaska, are the leading congressional proponents of giving the states most decision-making power. State governments are better equipped to deal with local conditions, they say, and restructuring should allow states to take innovative approaches rather than deal with a "one size fits all" framework set in Washington.

The rural cooperatives group is the lone utility trade association in this camp, although it is joined by the two shadow coalitions. The investor-owned companies participating in those coalitions have concluded that they will get their best treatment from state legislators and public utility commissioners.

Associated issues are whether Congress should create "regional transmission organizations," or RTOs, to operate and maintain the infrastructure handling electricity transmission; whether utility participation should be compulsory or voluntary; and whether RTO oversight should be handled by the states or the federal government.

As proposed in several of the pending bills, an RTO would ensure that all producers of electricity had an equal opportunity to place power on the grid when it was needed. It could also safeguard against "market power" abuses, in which a utility has enough control of the transmission and distribution to shut out competition — not only in setting prices but also in physically restricting a rival's transmission. An RTO also could ensure cheaper electricity by allowing transmission of electric power across competing utility grids without added transmission charges being tacked on.

What About Nonprofits?

While a federal deadline for state action has been taken off the table, Congress is considering proposals that would set the pace for restructuring.

Big electricity consumers want competition to arrive as soon as possible so they may begin shopping for better prices. Their drive is joined by independent power suppliers such as Enron Corp. and Calpine Corp., municipal utilities and those investor-owned utilities who believe they could make the most profits by offering the best prices — all groups that stand to succeed in a nationally deregulated market.

Investor-owned utilities advocating a go-slow approach are those that have to pay more to generate their power, most likely because of costly efforts to develop nuclear power in the 1970s. They are worried that they could become targets for takeover or closure if they cannot compete with the more financially healthy utilities.

Absent a deadline, each state may decide when — or if — it should restructure its electric market.

Among the thorniest issues is how restructuring should affect those utilities that are not out to make a profit for their shareholders — municipal electric systems, cooperatives and federal power agencies like the Tennessee Valley Authority (TVA) and the Bonneville Power Administration, which together account for about one-fifth of the national electric market. They are now exempt from FERC oversight, unlike investor-owned utilities, which have their electric rates and power charges for sale and transmission established by the agency.

The question is whether that for-profit/not-for-profit distinction — and some others involving tax differences between municipal utilities, cooperatives and investor-owned utilities — should continue to exist or be modified in some form.

Municipal utilities, which are nonprofit organizations, are allowed to use tax-exempt bonds to finance the construction of new generation plants; investor-owned utilities may not. Cooperatives may derive no more than 15 percent of their profit from "wholesale wheeling" of electric power, or allowing its lines to be used as the conduits for another utility's electricity. Federal power agencies such as the TVA, meanwhile, sell federally subsidized electricity, and a key issue is how they should be included in a restructured market without giving them an automatic advantage over investor-owned utilities.

Investor-owned utilities all maintain that municipals, cooperatives and the federal power agencies should be treated as they are. Municipal utilities and cooperatives say their members would be different enough, even in a reconstructed market, that their current competitive advantages should remain.

Legislation (S 2967, HR 4971) by Murkowski and Rep. J.D. Hayworth, R-Ariz., would make some changes to the tax structure that both public power and investor-owned utility representatives have agreed to. This narrow deal would set new rules for the use of tax-exempt bonds by public utilities and provide tax relief for utilities that sold transmission facilities or connected new generation facilities to the electric grid. The bills are not expected to move except as part of a larger package.

More Rough Spots

Other issues could prove less contentious, but no less difficult for Congress to navigate. These include:

- **Aggregation.** Consumer groups worry that lowering barriers to electric competition would benefit only the largest consumers. As a result, they have proposed allowing smaller customers — neighborhoods, clusters of small businesses — to form groups that might have more leverage to purchase at better prices, a process known as "aggregation."
- **Renewable energy.** Some groups — which lament the environmental consequences of coal-fired and nuclear plants and want to combat rising oil prices — hope to use a restructuring

bill as the vehicle to increase reliance on renewable sources. Some have proposed creation of a "renewable portfolio standard" under which utilities would be required to produce a certain amount of electricity from wind, solar or other renewable sources. In the Senate, debate over this standard, which Bingaman sought and Murkowski opposed, helped doom chances for a comprehensive restructuring bill.

• **Public benefits fund.** Some fear that a deregulated market could wind up depriving consumers of service, force poorer customers to prepay for electric service or accept service that could be turned off in times of peak demand. Markey advocates creation of a fund — which could be financed with nuclear plant decommissioning charges, appropriations or an electricity surcharge — to subsidize the poor.

• **Stranded costs.** These are the monetary differences between the costs that a regulated utility may charge to cover its operation and profits, and the prices it would likely face in a competitive market. These costs are highest for those with investments in nuclear plants. While Congress has for now chosen to let the states decide how much of these expenses their utilities may pass along to consumers, the issue could return to Congress if it were to give the federal government jurisdiction over a deregulated market.

Next year, a new president and a reconfigured Congress — with at least one new chairman in a position of influence over the issue — could help to create new momentum for the long-sought legislation. But the lawmakers say that they cannot do it alone.

"The outside groups have got to realize that they're not going to get everything they want," Barton said. "Congressman C has to realize that you have to get Outside Interest Group A and Outside Interest Group B to recognize there's going to be a compromise." ◆

Chapter 14

LABOR & EMPLOYMENT

Minimum Wage Increase Falters Due to Procedural Obstacles, Timing Dispute

SUMMARY

The House and Senate both passed bills to increase the federal minimum wage by $1, to $6.15 per hour, but leaders were unable to iron out the differences — most notably between the two-year phase-in passed by the House and the three-year time frame agreed to in the Senate. The minimum wage increase also was caught up in a procedural thicket for much of the session, with the Senate version attached to a bill to overhaul personal bankruptcy law. The Senate finally disentangled the minimum wage and bankruptcy measures, clearing the bankruptcy bill but setting the minimum wage aside. The House tried adding its two-year increase to a package of tax breaks, but that proposal died in the Senate in the face of a presidential veto.

After nearly two years of effort by President Clinton and both parties in Congress to raise the minimum wage, the Senate in February passed an overhaul of personal bankruptcy laws (HR 833) that included a three-year minimum wage increase, to $6.15 an hour. The bill also included $103 billion in tax breaks over 10 years as a sweetener to businesses. Those provisions, however, made the bill vulnerable to a parliamentary challenge from the House, which is required under the Constitution to initiate tax legislation. *(Bankruptcy, p. 5-3)*

A month later, on March 9, the House gave lopsided support to a bill (HR 3846) that sought to increase the minimum wage by $1 over two years. Under the rule for floor debate, the measure was then automatically added to legislation (HR 3081) that would have provided $122.7 billion in tax breaks over the next decade.

In late August, Clinton and Speaker J. Dennis Hastert, R-Ill., agreed in principle on a plan to provide a two-year minimum wage increase and $76 billion in tax breaks over 10 years. Democrats worried both about the amount of business tax breaks and about proposals to exclude funeral directors and telemarketers from the wage increase and to allow employers to include bonuses in calculating workers' salaries. The latter provision, they said, would enable employers to effectively drive salaries down by offering large bonuses.

Ultimately, the wage increase — minus those provisions but including $36 billion in tax relief over the next decade — was added to a package of tax breaks totaling $240.4 billion over 10 years (HR 2614). The House adopted the conference report on the bill in late October, but the Senate held off in the wake of a threatened veto. With the minimum wage not emerging as a major campaign issue for Democrats, and other tax provisions not at the top of the GOP agenda, the issue did not come up again in the lame duck session. *(Taxes, p. 18-3)*

Box Score

- **Bills:** HR 833, HR 2614, HR 3081
- **Legislative action: Senate** passed HR 833, 83-14, on Feb. 2, after substituting the text of S 625 (S Rept 106-49).

House passed HR 3081 (H Rept 106-467), 257-169, on March 9.

House adopted the conference report on HR 2614 (H Rept 106-1004), 237-174, on Oct. 26.

GOP Leaders Agree in Theory To Wage Increase

FEBRUARY 12 — Republican congressional leaders signaled the week of Feb. 7 that they were eager to allow a $1 increase in the minimum wage to become law with a minimum of parliamentary fuss or political fallout. They also made clear that they had not agreed how to do that.

And the parties are still at odds about how quickly to increase the hourly minimum to $6.15. Republicans are willing to do so over three years, and only if paired with tax breaks for small businesses, which argue they would be most adversely affected by the higher wage. Democrats want the increase phased in over two years and support fewer tax breaks.

House Majority Leader Dick Armey, R-Texas, said Feb. 8 that negotiations with Senate leaders on a unified GOP strategy for the issue are under way, even though support among House Republicans has not coalesced.

"I find myself in the ridiculous position of trying to find a possible way of doing the wrong thing," said Armey, who opposes a higher minimum wage but is searching for a way to move legislation quickly, and with the least political pain for the GOP.

Complicating that search, he said, is the near certainty that any attempt by the House to begin conference negotiations on the combined minimum wage, tax break and bankruptcy overhaul bill (HR 833) that the Senate passed Feb. 2 would be thwarted by a "blue slip." That is the parliamentary nickname for a privileged motion against a tax bill that originates in the Senate; the Constitution requires tax provisions to originate in the House and "that's a tradition that's very jealously protected by" the Ways and Means Committee, Armey said.

As an alternative, House leaders are considering a procedure in which the tax and wage provisions in a bill (HR 3081) Ways and Means endorsed in November would be put before the House separately, then rejoined and sent to the Senate for a conference if both components were passed. A similar procedure was used to advance the last minimum wage increase (PL 104-188) four years ago. *(1996 Almanac, p. C-39)*

John Shimkus, R-Ill., a sponsor of HR 3081, said he expects the minimum wage debate to reach the House floor the week of March 6.

But even though the bankruptcy bill is ardently sought by business interests, President Clinton has threatened to veto it over the $18.4 billion in tax cuts included with the minimum wage provisions. And on Feb. 9, Senate Minority Leader Tom Daschle, D-S.D., said he had the votes to sustain such a veto.

House-Passed Bill Heads Toward Another Thicket

MARCH 11 — Reacting to conflicting rebellions, Republican leaders were able to manage House passage March 9 of legislation they both adore and despise — to cut business taxes on the one hand and raise the minimum wage on the other. But, having emerged from one morass, their next round of political and procedural troubles has only just begun.

By a lopsided 282-143, the House passed legislation (HR 3846) to raise the federally guaranteed minimum wage by $1, to $6.15 an hour, over two years. *(Vote 45, p. H-18)*

The measure was then automatically added to legislation (HR 3081) that the House had voted 257-169 to pass, earlier in the day. It would offer tax reductions to benefit businesses, their owners, pensioners and those receiving inheritances by $122.7 billion in the next decade. *(Vote 41, p. H-18)*

Not only does the dual-edged package face a veto threat from President Clinton, but leaders on both sides of the Capitol also will have to perform procedural gymnastics just to get a bill to the White House. Ultimately, they will have to reconcile the House provisions with an even more cumbersome package in the Senate: legislation (HR 833) passed in February that would raise the minimum wage, although less rapidly than the House, would give out somewhat more limited tax cuts than the House and would rewrite the personal bankruptcy law.

While Sen. Charles E. Grassley, R-Iowa, the sponsor of the bankruptcy provisions, has not been told of any official leadership decision, an aide said March 9, the widespread expectation is that Majority Leader Trent Lott, R-Miss., will press the Senate to separate the minimum wage and tax language from the bankruptcy language in a bid to open up two distinct conference negotiations with the House, which passed its version of the bankruptcy bill last year.

That would be good for the advocates of the bankruptcy bill, who have been at work since 1997 trying to make it more difficult for overextended consumers to escape their debt.

But House Ways and Means Committee Chairman Bill Archer, R-Texas, said GOP leaders may instead decide to keep all three issues together in a single bill, with distinct sets of members negotiating each issue.

"I don't think we've decided on that," John P. Feehery, chief spokesman for House Speaker J. Dennis Hastert, R-Ill., said when asked about the next step March 10. "We haven't figured it all out."

The same day, however, Clinton and Democratic leaders served notice that their strategy was in place. Clinton called the House package "a dead letter" that would impermissibly drain surpluses that might otherwise shore up Social Security for the disproportionate benefit of the rich.

Minority Leader Tom Daschle, D-S.D., said Senate Democrats would provide more than enough votes to sustain a veto that the president pegged to excessive tax cuts. The Senate bill would cut taxes $103 billion in a decade.

"The American people question why Congress can't do something as simple as raising the minimum wage without loading it up with special favors, and I think it's a good question," Clinton told reporters. "The right answer is to send me a clean bill, a bill simple and clear that could fit on [one] side of one piece of paper."

Reacting to an earlier veto threat, Lott said March 9: "If the president wants to veto a minimum wage increase because of small-business tax considerations, go ahead. I don't think he can get away with that one. Now he gets away with an awful lot, but that will be a hard sell."

Complicating matters further is the Senate bill, which is procedurally anathema to the House because it would affect revenue; under the Constitution, such measures must originate in the House. This parliamentary hurdle can be used by both sides to complicate conference negotiations.

The minimum wage was raised to its current $5.15 an hour in September 1997 under a 1996 law (PL 104-188) that also offset the raise requirements with tax breaks for businesses, which say the cost of paying the higher wage cuts too deeply into their profits. The wage has been increased 18 other times since the first hourly minimum, 25 cents, was set with enactment of the Fair Labor Standards Act in 1938.

Protecting a Fragile Majority

Throughout the 106th Congress, another change in the wage has seemed likely. After the Senate voted last fall to raise the hourly minimum by $1 over three years, Clinton used the word "implore" in his State of the Union speech to press Congress to send him a bill. At that point, one Republican supporter, Jack Quinn of New York, sensed an increase would be "one of the first things going" in the new year.

While the House is led by pro-business GOP conservatives, their ideology against the wage is more than offset by their desire to protect, if not enhance, their narrow majority of House control in November. To that end, they signaled last year that they were intent on keeping a potentially explosive issue out of the Democrats' hands in an election year. By again pairing the wage hike and the tax breaks, they hoped to replicate their success of four years ago, when they were able to neutralize the issue on the campaign trail and also help a small but essential bloc of moderate Republicans like Quinn, who hail from districts where organized labor is a significant presence.

But in recent weeks the concept appeared to be losing ground fast. Democrats and rank-and-file Republicans alike were unwilling to accept what the GOP leadership initially offered. Democrats pushed their own plan to cut business taxes $12.7 billion over five years and add $1 to the minimum wage over two years; Republicans pushed an earlier version of HR 3081, with $30.2 billion in tax breaks over five years and the minimum wage raised over three years.

GOP leaders served notice that they would bring the dispute to a head and push some sort of compromise to a vote the week of March 6, but it was not until the afternoon of March 9 that they settled on their final strategy. In the interim, they alternately agreed with, then rebuffed, the conservatives' call to disallow any vote on a two-year wage hike. And they arranged for, then abandoned, a vote on a proposal by conservatives led by Jim DeMint, R-S.C., to allow states to opt out of the minimum wage increase when they could find other ways to improve worker benefits.

The leaders' hand was forced in part when Quinn announced March 8 that at least two dozen fellow GOP moderates were insisting on the chance to vote for adding the $1 to the minimum wage in just two years.

That prompted a counter rebellion by the conservatives. The morning of March 9, with debate set to begin, they threatened to provide the margin of defeat for the rule setting the parameters for debate on both the tax and wage measures — a rule that Democrats were sure to oppose as a protest against the size of the tax cuts. After an hour venting their grievances to Hastert in a closed-door meeting — and hearing the Speaker's appeal for party unity in reply — the conservatives backed down. They said they had been promised a more receptive ear in the future.

Among those allowed to address the group was iconoclastic Democrat James A. Traficant Jr. of Ohio, who reportedly argued to the Republicans that their opposition to a speedy rise in the minimum wage could cost them the House in November.

The Debate

With loyalties divided and tensions high, the rule was adopted, 214-211. *(Vote 39, p. H-16)*

The proposed wage increase in the Republican bill — $1 an hour, phased in over a three-year period — was estimated by the Congressional Budget Office last year to cost businesses $13.3 billion over five years. The GOP tax package would cost the Treasury $45.8 billion in lost revenue over the same period, by the Joint Committee on Taxation's calculation. Those numbers were not lost on Democrats, who argued on the House floor that Republicans were trying to pass a portion of the $792 billion tax (HR 2488) bill Clinton vetoed last year. Their attempted to recommit the bill with instructions to replace it with a Democratic tax package was defeated, 207-218. *(Vote 40, p. H-16)*

GOP leaders initially considered allowing one of several embattled party moderates to propose the faster-rising wage amendment as a means of shoring up one of their chances for reelection. But under lobbying from business groups — which objected to that symbolism of putting a GOP stamp on the idea — the authorship of that amendment was put in the hands of two Democrats to whom it could do minimal political good: Traficant, who had won a hot primary contest for renomination March 7, and Matthew G. Martinez of California, who was defeated for renomination the same day.

"The last minimum wage increase spurred an economic boom for the following simple reason: Poor people do not have enough money to save. Poor people spend their money, put their money on the streets, and they grow the economy," Traficant said. "When someone waters the tree . . . do they water the leaves, or do they water the roots?"

With 42 Republicans — or 19 percent of GOP members — voting in favor if it, and just five Democrats voting against it, the amendment was adopted, 246-179. *(Vote 43, p. H-18)*

Priciest Tax Provisions

Though some moderates worry that the tax package had grown too large, Republicans argued little over the measure. But the House GOP may find a greater challenge when negotiating a settlement between its bill and the Senate version.

The House bill's most costly component — and the chief reason for the opposition of Clinton and the Democrats — is a package of reductions in taxes on estates, gifts and other bequests. The Senate's most expensive provision centers on allowing workers whose employers pay less than 50 percent of their health and long-term-care insurance to deduct those costs from their taxes.

Though cutting estate taxes has been a priority for many Republicans in the House and the Senate, GOP leaders also are looking to counter Democratic efforts on health care this year.

And Hastert is considering bringing tax measures to the floor in coming months that would allow deductibility of long-term care insurance, in addition to providing some more tax incentives for retirement savings. How such plans would fit together with the minimum wage tax bill — a significant portion of which focuses on pension overhaul in both chambers' versions — is a key question.

Because it is unclear how and when the bill will go to conference, and because the precise nature of what Clinton would actually veto is open to question, some business lobbyists said that they would work to find other potential vehicles for their provisions.

Many lobbyists said that if Republicans had a plan for how to proceed on the minimum wage-tax package, they could not decipher it.

Regardless of the fate of the minimum wage, Archer still intends to push for a tax bill that would include cuts for businesses and across-the-board reductions in income tax rates. And, he signaled his strong support for changing the tax code to fully comply with a recent World Trade Organization ruling against a U.S. tax provision that cuts taxes for some exporters. Such a proposal may carry some tax cuts.

His plans will be subject to the amount of revenue decreases allowed under the fiscal 2001 budget resolution. The GOP chairmen of the two Budget committees, Rep. John R. Kasich of Ohio and Sen. Pete V. Domenici of New Mexico, announced March 10 that they would propose a budget making room for $150 billion in tax cuts over five years. They said Hastert and Lott had endorsed that figure.

Though some, including Senate Banking Committee Chairman Phil Gramm, R-Texas, want to set aside enough of the budget surplus to shepherd through Congress the $1 trillion, 10-year tax cut of Texas Gov. George W. Bush — who all but sealed the GOP presidential nomination the week of March 6 — many other Republicans hesitated to support that idea, largely because they said Bush's plan was based on different revenue projections.

Mollifying Businesses

Though many business lobbyists said that they were happy with the provisions in the tax bill, one pivotal group — the National Restaurant Association, whose members employ a large percentage of the minimum wage work force and who held a convention in Washington the week of March 6 —

lobbied for a longer extension of the Work Opportunity Tax Credit. Extended through Dec. 31, 2001, by a measure (PL 106-170) enacted last year, it gives employers a credit of as much as $2,400 for each worker hired from eight groups of people who generally have trouble getting jobs, including the disabled, ex-felons and inner-city youth.

Restaurant officials, many of whom hire workers from the specified groups, wanted to extend the provision for another two and a half years, putting it on par with a five-year extension given a credit for business research and development last year.

While House leaders appeared to support the extension, Archer said that the credit should not be extended until Congress has had a chance to consider merging it with a similar credit for hiring workers off welfare rolls. "It will not be extended in this Congress," he said.

National Restaurant Association lobbyist Lee Culpepper said March 9 that his group believed it still had a good chance of getting the extension in a final bill, since the Senate tax plan included a further extension.

Education and the Workforce Committee Chairman Bill Goodling, R-Pa., said after the bill was passed on March 9 that he thought the tax breaks and retention of Fair Labor Standards Act standards in the tax package made the minimum wage "palatable" and that Clinton should reconsider his vows for the bill. "If he gets his two-year business, he'd have to think" before vetoing the bill, he said.

Leaders Will Try To Disentangle Bankruptcy, Taxes, Minimum Wage

MARCH 18 — House and Senate Republican leaders are expected to meet during the week of March 20 to try to make a path out of the legislative maze that has trapped legislation to tighten the laws governing personal bankruptcy.

David Hoppe, chief of staff to Senate Majority Leader Trent Lott, R-Miss., said March 17 that the aim would be to devise a way to separate the bankruptcy debate from the issues with which it has become procedurally intertwined — to raise the minimum wage and create business tax breaks.

The House passed legislation (HR 3081) on March 9 that would raise the federally guaranteed minimum hourly wage by $1, to $6.15, over two years but also would cut taxes by $122.7 billion in the next decade. Last year, the House passed a bill (HR 833) to rewrite bankruptcy law. The Senate took up that measure and passed it in February — but only after substituting its own bankruptcy provisions, a three-year minimum wage hike and $103 billion in tax breaks over 10 years.

Republicans want to set aside the more nettlesome wage and tax proposals, at least for now, and move forward with a bankruptcy conference. But Democrats are unlikely to consent to any procedural move that would endanger ultimate enactment of a minimum wage increase.

While the Senate and House bankruptcy versions are different, both are designed to make it more difficult for overextended consumers to make their debts disappear by seeking protection under the federal bankruptcy code.

To complicate matters, lobbyists for the nation's restaurants and retailers signaled the week of March 13 that they viewed the tax breaks Congress has drafted as insufficient to win their acquiescence in raising the minimum wage. They and other business groups had sought the breaks as a form of compensation for the wage increase — if that was the price required to clear a bankruptcy bill. In general, business groups object less to the Senate's three-year timetable for raising the wage, but they also prefer the House's more generous tax package.

"We believe an increase is bad policy, and we're going to try to work to defeat an increase," Lee Culpepper, the National Restaurant Association senior vice president of government affairs and public policy, said of the minimum wage in an interview March 15. "I appreciate the attempts at tying this to tax relief, but at this point that tax relief does not outweigh the negative of an increase."

Katherine Graham, the senior director of government relations for the National Retail Federation, said her association agrees. "This is definitely the fact for us, too," she said.

Many Scenarios for Compromise

There appear to be several scenarios for trying to negotiate compromises on all three issues, but none of them appears flawless — either procedurally or politically.

As a matter of constitutional prerogative, the Senate-passed bill is unacceptable to the House because it originated revenue provisions. Because the Constitution says such bills must start in the House, any attempt to call it up there would be met with the procedural stop-work order known as a "blue slip." To avoid that problem, lawmakers could try to negotiate a new, stand-alone bankruptcy bill. There were reports that some Republicans were hoping this measure could somehow be packaged as a conference report — because these cannot be amended on the floor — and then put before the House and Senate.

Senate Minority Leader Tom Daschle, D-S.D., is also willing to separate the wage and tax package from the bankruptcy bill, but only if he concludes that the minimum wage would be raised this year by some other bill.

"We need to work that out, but I think it's doable, and we're going to move forward on that," House Speaker J. Dennis Hastert, R-Ill., said when asked March 15 about the prospects for keeping the three measures alive. He was not more specific.

"We ought to be able to complete that conference, either separately or in fact integrating the whole package as the Senate has it, standing together," House Majority Leader Dick Armey, R-Texas, said March 14.

But House Ways and Means Committee Chairman Bill Archer, R-Texas, also has said the leadership might decide to resolve the three issues together and set up a conference in which separate sets of members were named to negotiate each of the three issues.

If GOP leaders do not show their hand soon, Lott could find himself tangling with Senate Democrats over a two-year increase they are seeking. Sen. Edward M. Kennedy, D-Mass., is expected to introduce a stand-alone minimum wage bill on March 22 and is considering other bills to which he might try to amend with similar legislation, his office said March 16. ◆

Senate Puts Brakes on Bill To Restructure Pensions For Railroad Retirees

BoxScore

- **Bill:** HR 4844
- **Legislative action: House** passed HR 4844 (H Rept 106-777, Parts 1 and 2), 391-25, on Sept. 7.

Senate Finance Committee approved HR 4484 (S Rept 106-475) by voice vote Sept. 28.

SUMMARY

The House passed legislation to bolster the long-term solvency of the federally guaranteed pensions for nearly 1 million railroad workers, retirees and their families. The bill died in the Senate, where it ran into opposition to its cost.

After many railroad bankruptcies in the Depression, the government assumed responsibility for workers' pensions, financed with a special payroll tax paid by both rail concerns and their employees. (Rail workers do not qualify for Social Security). The system is now $40 billion short of what would be required to pay benefits to all the workers who have yet to retire, and their survivors.

The bill has broader policy implications, because it would emulate what some propose to do with Social Security: $15 billion now held by the Treasury for railroad retirees would go to a new board that would invest in stocks and bonds. Assuming those investments were profitable, the bill would reduce the percentage of each covered worker's salary that the railroads must pay to the system. It also would allow survivors to claim all of a deceased worker's pension, whereas only a partial claim is now allowed, and the vesting time of an employee would be halved, to five years.

As a matter of congressional scorekeeping, transferring the funds to the new board would count as $15 billion in lost revenue in the first year. That caused fiscally conservative Senate Republicans to balk, killing the bill.

Shuster Balks at Tax Cut Added To Railroad Bill

JULY 29 — A seemingly innocuous attempt to increase benefits to railroad retirees was sidetracked July 25 by a dispute between two powerful House chairmen over tax-cutting strategy.

The railroad retirement bill (HR 4844) would codify a painstakingly negotiated agreement between labor unions and the railroad industry. In approving the measure July 19 (H Rept 106-777, Part 1), members of the House Transportation and Infrastructure Committee said they were not offering amendments because they did not want to jeopardize a deal that was the result of years of talks between the parties.

Transportation and Infrastructure Chairman Bud Shuster, R-Pa., expected the Ways and Means Committee to mark up an identical bill. Instead, the tax-writing panel added a new title that would repeal a 4.3 cents-per-gallon tax on diesel fuel paid by freight railroads and inland barges (H Rept 106-777, Part 2).

Although Shuster and the railroad industry support the diesel tax repeal, they are vehemently against adding it to the retirement proposal. Shuster fears that the tax provision would open the bill up to other potentially controversial tax proposals once it arrived in the Senate, said spokesman Scott Brenner.

In a letter to Republican Bill Archer of Texas, the chairman of Ways and Means, the Association of American Railroads urged that the two issues be separated.

"We cannot support repeal [of the tax] as part of railroad retirement reform," wrote association President and CEO Edward R. Hamberger. "Adding that provision . . . has serious unintended consequences."

The diesel tax on railroads and barges was enacted as part of the 1993 balanced-budget law (PL 103-66). In 1998, Congress transferred other budget-balancing fuel taxes into transportation trust funds, but the railroad and barge diesel tax continued to go into general funds. The railroad industry opposes taxes that are not linked to an infrastructure trust fund.

The underlying bill would grant railroad retirees or their widows full annuities instead of the 50 percent maximum for which they are currently eligible. It also would lower railroad workers' payroll taxes. Railroad companies would receive a set of tax breaks.

House GOP leaders had hoped to forge a compromise between Shuster and Archer and pass the retirement measure before the August recess. But as the House departed, there was no sign either chairman was ready to back down.

House Passes Rail Pension Bill Minus Fuel Tax Repeal

The House easily passed legislation (HR 4844) Sept. 7 to overhaul the pension system for railroad workers after Transportation and Infrastructure Committee Chairman Bud Shuster, R-Pa., forced the removal of an amendment that would have repealed the federal tax on diesel fuel.

The tax repeal is now unlikely to pass independently or as part of other legislation, said supporter Kenny Hulshof, R-Mo., whose district includes heavy barge traffic on the Missouri and Mississippi rivers.

The Ways and Means Committee had tacked the amendment — which would have repealed the 4.3 cent-per-gallon tax on diesel fuel used by trains and barges — onto the pension bill in July. Shuster supports the tax repeal, but demanded it be pulled from the pension bill because he feared it would open the measure to more controversial tax cut proposals when it reached the Senate.

Ways and Means Chairman Bill Archer, R-Texas, at the urging of the GOP leadership, pulled the tax provision Sept. 7, and the House easily passed the bill, 391-25. The pension measure would increase payments to beneficiaries and reduce the vesting requirement from 10 years to five years. *(Vote 459, p. H-142)*

Senate Panel OKs Bill to Restructure Rail Pensions

SEPTEMBER 30 — A long-running effort by railroads and railroad workers to revamp their ailing pension system was approved by voice vote by the Senate Finance Committee Sept. 28. But further progress on the bill (HR 4844), which the House had passed overwhelmingly three weeks earlier, may be derailed by this fall's congressional commitment to debt reduction.

The bill aims to address a relatively obscure federal problem — the long-term insolvency of the federally guaranteed pensions of nearly 1 million railroad workers, retirees and their families — but it has broader policy implications. Although on a much smaller scale, it would imitate what some propose to do with Social Security by transferring $15 billion now held by the Treasury for railroad retirees to a new board that would invest the money in stocks and bonds.

After many railroads went bankrupt in the Depression, the government assumed responsibility for workers' pensions. Under the current system, rail concerns and their employees pay a special payroll tax to finance these pensions. The tax is separate from the one that finances Social Security, for which rail workers do not qualify.

Investment of the pension funds would be welcomed by both the railroads and rail unions, which say they are confident the move would boost workers' retirement security. The system is now $40 billion short of what would be required to pay benefits to all the workers who have yet to retire, and their survivors.

Confidence of reaping profits from the markets is high enough that the bill would reduce, to as low as 13.1 percent from 16.1 percent, the percentage of each covered worker's compensation that the railroads must pay to the system. The bill also would allow survivors to claim all of a deceased worker's pension, whereas only a partial claim is now allowed, and the time an employee must work to become fully vested in the plan would be halved, to five years.

As a matter of congressional scorekeeping, transferring the funds to the new board would count as $15 billion in lost revenue in fiscal 2001. That creates difficulty for those who support both the bill and the GOP promise to refrain from using more than 10 percent, or about $28 billion, of the projected fiscal 2001 surplus for anything other than debt service.

At the markup, Majority Whip Don Nickles, R-Okla., proposed postponing the bill's effective date until fiscal 2002, beyond the scope of the GOP debt reduction bill (HR 5173). Chairman William V. Roth Jr., R-Del., balked, because the delay would also mean postponing a provision to allow workers to retire at age 60, instead of the current 62, and still qualify for full benefits.

When Daniel Patrick Moynihan, D-N.Y., proposed postponing the date of the financial transfer, Nickles and Phil Gramm, R-Texas, objected, saying it would be fiscally irresponsible to implement the new benefits ahead of the mechanism intended to pay for them.

Both amendments were withdrawn. Some suggested a compromise under which the effective date would be tied to increased surplus projections. Additional talks to determine how to delay the measure's official cost will be required for the bill to advance further.

A host of other amendments were rejected. One, by Republican Charles E. Grassley of Iowa, would have expanded Medicaid to cover disabled children with middle-income parents. By 7-10, the panel voted against overriding Roth's ruling that the proposal was not germane. ◆

CQ

Chapter 15

LAW & JUDICIARY

Lawmakers Grant Request Of Business to Increase Numbers of H-1B Visas

SUMMARY

After an intense push from the business community, Congress agreed to dramatically increase the number of non-immigrant visas available for highly skilled workers. The bill authorized 195,000 H-1B visas each year for fiscal years 2001, 2002 and 2003. Congress also cleared a second, smaller bill to raise the fee paid by businesses for such visas to $1,000. President Clinton signed both bills Oct. 17.

Getting Congress to increase the number of H-1B visas was one of the high-tech community's top priorities for the year. Under a 1998 law (PL 105-277), H-1B visas had increased from 65,000 annually to 115,000 in fiscal 2000. But the level was slated to drop back to 107,500 in fiscal 2001 and 65,000 after that. Heavy demand for tech workers in the roaring economy had consumed the 2000 allotment of H-1B visas by March. The visas allow individuals to come to the United States for three years and can be renewed once, for an additional three years. It is the only non-immigrant visa that allows the alien to apply for permanent residency.

Lawmakers began working on the issue early in the year. On March 9, the Senate Judiciary Committee approved a bill (S 2045), introduced by Chairman Orrin G. Hatch, R-Utah, to set H-1B visa levels at 195,000 for three years. The bill exempted from the overall cap H-1B visas issued to those who had just obtained a master's degree or doctorate from a U.S. institution, and to those who worked for a nonprofit, a government entity or a university-affiliated research facility.

In the House, the process was controlled, at least at the committee level, by Judiciary Immigration and Claims Subcommittee Chairman Lamar Smith, R-Texas. Smith drafted several versions of the H-1B legislation, all of which included provisions designed to protect U.S. technology workers from layoffs or unfair competition from foreign workers. Although the high-tech community disliked those provisions and opposed the bill (HR 4227 — H Rept 106-692), it was approved by the Judiciary Committee on May 17.

While House Republicans were reluctant to bring Smith's bill to the floor, their Senate counterparts resisted bringing their version up for fear that Democrats would offer a package of immigration-related amendments. The Democrats' package, dubbed the Latino and Immigrant Fairness Act, sought to grant amnesty to illegal immigrants who had been in the United States since 1986, make it easier for some Central American and Liberian aliens to become residents, and allow some immigrants to pay a fee and stay in the country while their residency application was pending. GOP leaders in both chambers, but particularly the Senate, were loath to expose their members to politically sensitive immigration votes during an election year, and talk grew of including H-1B visa provisions in a wrapup spending bill at the end of the Congress.

But the business community continued to push for a separate bill, fearing it would lose control of the provisions if they were inserted in a huge omnibus bill. Senate Majority Leader Trent Lott, R-Miss., finally decided to bring the bill up in September and used a series of parliamentary maneuvers to block amendments. Democrats were able to force a debate on their immigration package, but they did not get a clear vote on it. Once that argument was over, the Senate passed the bill (S 2045) without any immigration provisions by a vote of 96-1 on Oct. 3. Building on the Senate momentum, the House cleared the bill hours later with little debate.

Because the bill had originated in the Senate, it did not increase the fees businesses paid for H-1B visas. (Revenue-raising bills must start in the House under the Constitution.) On Oct. 6, the House passed by voice vote legislation (HR 5362) to increase the fee from $500 to $1,000 per visa. The Senate cleared the change for the president by voice vote on Oct. 10.

Box Score

- **Bills:** S 2045 — PL 106-313; HR 5362 — PL 106-311
- **Legislative action: Senate** passed S 2045 (S Rept 106-260), 96-1, on Oct. 3.

House cleared S 2045 by voice vote Oct. 3.

President signed S 2045 on Oct. 17.

Congress Appears Set to Allow More Foreign Workers In High-Tech Jobs

FEBRUARY 19 — Less than two years after persuading lawmakers to nearly double the number of highly skilled foreign workers allowed temporarily into the country, the high-tech industry is back, asking for more. And it looks like Congress is willing to go along, with perhaps some additional training or protections for U.S. workers added to the mix.

The Clinton administration, which was skeptical of the need for more foreign workers during the last debate, has been silent on the issue thus far. But the technology community's strong ties to Vice President Al Gore may soften any administration resistance. According to the Center for Responsive Politics, the computer industry contributed more than $330,000 to Gore's presidential campaign last year, placing it among his 20 top industry donors.

Increasing the numbers of temporary, H-1B visas for high-tech workers is one of the top legislative goals for the technology community. Trade groups say there are not enough skilled

U.S. workers to fill the thousands of jobs created by their thriving industry. And they warn that without a new infusion of workers, the high-tech sector, which has helped to fuel the current economic boom, could falter.

In 1998, Congress increased the number of H-1B visas, from 65,000 that year to 115,000 a year in fiscal 1999 and 2000. Under the bill, enacted as part of the fiscal 1999 omnibus spending measure (PL 105-277), H-1Bs will decline to 107,500 in 2001 and to 65,000 after that. The visas allow workers to come to the United States for three years and usually can be renewed once, for an additional three years. All of the 1999 visas were used by June 15. *(1998 Almanac, p. 17-3)*

Now the industry is pleading to increase the numbers further and has thrown its weight behind legislation (S 2045) introduced Feb. 9 by Senate Judiciary Committee Chairman Orrin G. Hatch, R-Utah, and Immigration Subcommittee Chairman Spencer Abraham, R-Mich. The bill would increase the number of H-1Bs to 195,000 annually in fiscal 2000 though 2002.

Senate Majority Leader Trent Lott of Mississippi and Assistant Majority Leader Don Nickles of Oklahoma have signed on to Hatch's bill. In the House, Majority Whip Tom DeLay, R-Texas, lent his support Feb. 10, saying, "We need to recruit as many of the great brains of the world to work and become Americans as we can."

The technology industry also may benefit from organized labor's relatively low-key response to the new push for H-1Bs. Organized labor is not well-represented in most high technology workplaces. And the intense battle over granting permanent normal trading relations to China is likely to leave labor with little time or political capital to spend on the H-1B visa fight.

Democrats "will feel less pressure on this" from labor because of China, said Rep. Barney Frank, D-Mass., who said he believes the industry has shown it needs the workers.

High-tech companies large and small argue that, given the tight job market, they simply cannot get the skilled workers they need at home.

Julie Holdren is president of Olympus Group, a technology company in Alexandria, Va., that designs Web sites and database management systems for other businesses, such as AT&T Wireless. She has 75 employees and openings for another 30.

Like many high-tech entrepreneurs, Holdren has been creative in designing a benefits package, in the hopes of attracting and retaining workers. Olympus Group employees get stock options, seated massages and free lunch on Fridays. And the company is picking up the tab this month for a group Caribbean cruise that includes each employee and a significant other.

"Anything we can do" to persuade people to work for Olympus is considered, she said in a Feb. 14 interview.

Her company employs at least six H-1B visa holders and is actively looking to hire more.

The use of special incentives is not confined to small companies. Ali Cleveland, manager of labor policy for the U.S. Chamber of Commerce, said Texas Instruments is giving $1,500 bonuses to current employees who help locate hot prospects. The employees also get their name entered into a drawing for a new Ford Explorer.

"There's literally full employment" in the technology sector, said Thom Stohler, director of human resources policy for the American Electronics Association, the largest high-tech trade group. Businesses "have to scramble to fill those jobs."

Stohler cites Cisco Systems as an example of the phenomenal growth in the technology sector. Cisco, which provides the infrastructure that undergirds much of Internet, has gone from 254 employees in 1990 to some 26,140 currently. Companies are "just screaming for people," Stohler says.

Natural Market Forces

"There's no shortage," counters Norman Matloff, computer science professor at the University of California at Davis. Employers, he argues, are simply "extremely picky in terms of who they hire."

Matloff says many technology companies hire less than 3 percent of those who apply for jobs and most do not consider applications from older workers. "These are people who claim to be desperate; that's not desperate," he said in an interview Feb. 11.

Dan Stein, executive director of the Federation for American Immigration Reform, a group that largely opposes increased immigration, says the influx of foreign labor has distorted the market and led to the shortage. "We need natural market forces," to push up wages and create demand for American workers, he said Feb. 9.

Bringing in foreign high-tech workers, Stein says, is "the modern-day equivalent of bringing in 'coolie' labor for the railroads." He adds, "All Congress will be doing with this law is expanding the industry's dependence on foreign labor and creating calls for future increases down the line."

But Stein calls the momentum behind the increase "a freight train," and fully expects Congress to pass some kind of increase in skilled-worker visas.

Legislative Options

Hatch says he wants to mark up his bill before the middle of March. In addition to raising the annual cap on H-1B visas to 195,000, the bill would exempt a number of foreign workers from counting toward the total.

Foreign workers employed by universities, colleges or research facilities associated with universities or colleges would not be counted. Foreign nationals who have received advanced degrees from American universities or colleges within six months of their employment would also be exempt.

The bill would continue the $500-per-visa application fee for H-1Bs, which was first included in the 1998 law. According to Hatch, that would raise a total of $150 million for scholarships and training for U.S. workers.

The bill does not include any specific provisions for offering worker training, something that troubles Sen. Dianne Feinstein, D-Calif., a cosponsor. She says she is working with Hatch and others to develop some help for the U.S. work force.

Another bill, S 1645, introduced by Charles S. Robb, D-Va., focuses more on the training issue. It would create a new category — a "T" visa — that would allow firms to hire foreign workers who get advanced degrees in the United States. It would only apply to jobs that pay $60,000 or more a year.

Each T visa application would cost $1,000, money that would be used for partnerships between elementary and secondary schools and businesses to improve science and math education.

Zoe Lofgren, D-Calif., has introduced a similar measure (HR 2687) in the House.

But the technology industry says these bills would not meet their urgent needs, and neither one seems to have swung significant support from Hatch's industry-supported measure in the Senate. In fact, one of Robb's five cosponsors, Joseph I. Lieberman, D-Conn., also signed on to Hatch's bill.

In the House, the industry is working with several members, including Lamar Smith, R-Texas, chairman of the Judiciary Committee's Immigration Subcommittee. Smith says he is "committed" to moving an H-1B bill this year. But, he cautioned, "there needs to be a balance between meeting the legitimate needs of the high-tech community and the legitimate needs of American workers."

Smith is looking at a variety of options for helping workers. In the 1998 law, for example, certain companies were required to show they had made a good faith effort to hire a U.S. worker for the job, and they could not hire H-1B workers to replace laid-off workers.

In 1998, Smith sought to apply those conditions to all companies applying for H-1B visas, but in the final compromise they applied only to businesses that rely on H-1B employees for more than 15 percent of their work force or that have violated the program at some time.

Smith is considering whether to again try to extend the conditions to all businesses using H-1B workers.

He also may seek to require companies that get H-1B visas to show they are thriving — meaning they are not on the edge, looking for cheap labor. This could be done by comparing average salaries or the number of U.S. workers from one year to the next.

Finally, he is looking at a proposal to require a certain minimum wage, $50,000 or more, for a position to qualify for an H-1B worker. This would address another concern of opponents: that not all H-1Bs go to well-paid high-tech workers.

Geri Palast, assistant secretary of Labor for congressional and intergovernmental affairs, said Feb. 14 that the key to the 1998 deal was finding the middle ground. She said that while the Clinton administration has no official position on the H-1B visa legislation, its goal is to "make sure the education of American workers is happening."

Palast said the $500 visa fee enacted in 1998 has just started generating funds for worker training. The Labor Department gave out $12.4 million in grants earlier this month to help about 3,000 workers, and expects to give out another $40 million. Palast cautions that it is still too soon to know how the training is working. "Let's see what progress is being made before we rush to judgment on this issue," she said.

High-Tech Visa Debate Shifts To House Panel

MARCH 4 — A leading House member has declined to go as far as industry wanted to increase special visas for highly skilled foreign workers.

Republican Lamar Smith of Texas, chairman of the House Judiciary Subcommittee on Immigration and Claims, introduced a bill (HR 3814) on March 1 that would authorize the additional visas, known as H-1Bs, but that falls far short of the increase sought by the high-tech industry.

Smith's move sets the stage for debate on the number of temporary workers allowed into the United States and on what protections to include for U.S. workers. Congress increased H-1B visa levels in 1998.

Smith's bill, cosponsored by GOP Reps. Tom Campbell of California, Christopher B. Cannon of Utah and Robert W. Goodlatte of Virginia, would increase the number of visas for highly skilled workers from 115,000 to 160,000 for fiscal 2000. The number would then drop to 107,500 in fiscal 2001. An H-1B visa allows workers to stay in the United States for three years, with one renewal, for a total of six years.

The industry supports Senate legislation (S 2045), sponsored by Judiciary Committee Chairman Orrin G. Hatch, R-Utah, that would increase the number of H-1B visas to 195,000 for each of three years.

The Senate bill also would exempt several categories of workers, such as government or university researchers, from the H-1B cap, thus allowing even more people to get visas. The Senate Judiciary Committee may consider its bill the week of March 6.

Smith said his subcommittee was likely to mark up his bill in early April.

Cautious Approach

Smith called his approach "a reasonable and measured response to the concerns of the high-tech industry." Smith's bill would permit the increase in visas only after the administration shows that it is enforcing provisions in the 1998 immigration law (PL 105-277) aimed at preventing companies from abusing the program at the expense of U.S. workers. *(1998 Almanac, p. 17-3)*

Those provisions required a business to show that it tried to recruit domestic employees and did not use H-1B visa holders to replace laid-off workers. They applied only to companies that either relied on visa holders for more than 15 percent of their work force or that violated program rules at some point.

Smith's bill would require employers to show that they had hired more full-time U.S. workers than in the previous year and had increased both the average and total wages paid to U.S. workers.

Those conditions aim to answer critics of the H-1B program who argue that the influx of foreign workers keeps high-tech wages artificially low.

Only businesses with gross assets of at least $5 million would be eligible for the program, though that restriction would not apply to government employers seeking H-1B employees.

The bill would require H-1B visa holders to work full time and to have a bachelor's degree or the equivalent. The State Department would monitor the provisions.

It would double, to $1,000 per visa, the basic fee for H-1Bs, and use the money for scholarships, administered by the National Science Foundation, for U.S. graduate or undergraduate science students. Currently, the funds go to job training programs at the Labor Department. Companies also would pay $100 per visa application — on top of basic fees — to be used to root out fraud.

The bill would set up a "fast track" H-1B visa program for certain businesses. For an additional $250 per application, a company in good standing with the program, in business for five years and with gross receipts of at least $100 million for each of the past two years, would be able to get applications acted on within 30 days.

The Immigration and Naturalization Service (INS) runs the H-1B program and is responsible for keeping tabs on how many visas are given out and what kinds of jobs are filled. Critics have charged that INS statistics are unreliable. The Smith bill would transfer record-keeping to the State Department.

Senate Committee Approves Bill, Rejects Attempts To Limit Visas

MARCH 11 — A plan to dramatically increase the number of temporary foreign workers permitted into the country won easy approval from the Senate Judiciary Committee on March 9.

The bill (S 2045), approved 16-2, would allow the Immigration and Naturalization Service (INS) to issue 195,000 H-1B visas each year for the next three years, to help alleviate labor shortages in the technology industry.

Introduced last month by Committee Chairman Orrin G. Hatch, R-Utah, the measure has the strong support of the business community, which favors it over a narrower bill (HR 3814) introduced in the House by Lamar Smith, R-Texas.

"Common sense tells us that we must allow American high-tech companies to fill their labor needs in the U.S., or they will be forced to take these opportunities of growth abroad," Hatch said.

The House bill would raise the cap on H-1Bs to 160,000 for fiscal 2000 only and would make that increase contingent on certain fraud-reduction efforts within the visa program.

Though a date has not yet been set, committee staff say they expect the Senate measure to go to the floor soon. HR 3814 is not likely to see House subcommittee action until early next month.

H-1B visas allow skilled workers into the United States for a three-year period. They can be renewed once, for a total of six years.

Congress in 1998 raised the ceiling on the visas from 65,000 to the current 115,000, under a law (PL 105-277) that calls for the allotment to drop to 107,500 in fiscal 2001 and back to 65,000 thereafter. *(1998 Almanac, p. 17-3)*

But technology companies argue that the visas did not provide enough workers and point out that last year the visas were all used up by June 15. They say they expect similar problems this year.

Sen. Edward M. Kennedy, D-Mass., who unsuccessfully tried to reduce the number of visas offered under the bill, cited the INS as saying that as of Feb. 15, 2000, 67,000 H-1B visa applications had been approved and another 44,000 were in the pipeline.

The Senate bill also would exempt from the cap foreigners employed by universities or research organizations. That could allow as many as 20,000 additional foreign workers to enter the United States, according to Senate aides.

Some Democrats expressed concern that the measure would not adequately protect and promote U.S. workers and students, but the committee turned back their efforts to rewrite the bill.

Amendments Rejected

The panel defeated, 8-10, a Kennedy substitute that would have increased the number of visas to 145,000 per year through fiscal 2002. His amendment won the support of all committee Democrats except Dianne Feinstein of California and attracted one Republican supporter, Charles E. Grassley of Iowa.

Kennedy's amendment also would have increased the current $500-per-visa fee paid by businesses to between $1,000 and $3,000, with the higher fees levied on businesses with more employees. Most of the revenue would have gone to U.S. worker training, and the rest to high-tech college scholarships and computers for low-income areas.

Kennedy also included a provision aimed at making sure that temporary foreign workers do not displace Americans. His substitute would have required employers with a large number of H-1B visa-holders to attest that no U.S. worker will be laid off six months before or six months after the employer petitions for a visa.

The House bill includes similar protections aimed at making sure the high-tech industry does not use H-1B visa workers as a cheap substitute for domestic labor.

But Hatch, Feinstein and others said protections were already in place, and that stricter ones were unjustified. They also objected to the increased visa fees, saying the high-tech industry already pours billions of dollars into training and scholarships for U.S. students and workers.

Kennedy called the proposed increases modest. "We charge $1,000 to immigrant families now to obtain green cards," he said. "Certainly multi-million dollar companies can pay such fees."

The committee did adopt, 12-6, an amendment by Feinstein that would reallocate the visa fee revenues. Her amendment would direct more money to computer training programs for elementary and secondary schools and to scholarships for low-income students.

Currently, much of the money raised by the fee program goes to worker-training programs.

Despite her opposition to Kennedy's fee increase, Feinstein said she is willing to work with panel members on providing more money for training.

House Panel OKs Visa Bill; Tech Firms Object To Restrictions

APRIL 15 — At first glance, it would seem to be a proposal that businesses would love: lift the cap for three years on the number of highly skilled foreign workers allowed to come to the United States. These workers, who are given H-1B visas, are mainly sought by high-technology companies.

Nevertheless, Lamar Smith, R-Texas, discovered April 12 that the fine print in his H-1B visa proposal (HR 4227) — in which Smith proposed restrictions aimed at protecting American workers — proved distasteful to high-tech companies. "It's purportedly uncapped, but with the conditions put on it, the numbers may be unusable," said Sandra J. Boyd, a lobbyist for the National Association of Manufacturers.

Smith chairs the Judiciary Subcommittee on Immigration and Claims, which approved the bill by voice vote April 12. The next step is unclear.

The business community has made an increase in the annual number of H-1B visas a top goal, arguing that foreign workers are essential to the technology industry. The Clinton administration and many Democrats now seem to agree. The remaining questions are how large an increase to allow, what restrictions to place on employers and what else to include in the rapidly moving bill.

A 1998 law (PL 105-277) increased the number of visas from 65,000 to 115,000 in fiscal 2000. That figure is set to drop to 107,500 in fiscal 2001 and then back to 65,000. *(1998 Almanac, p. 17-3)*

Demand for the visas, which allow people to work in the United States for up to six years, is intense. The Immigration and Naturalization Service (INS) announced March 21 that it was no longer accepting applications for fiscal 2000 because the 115,000 slots would be filled by pending applications.

The Senate Judiciary Committee approved legislation (S 2045) on March 9 that would increase the cap to 195,000 workers for three years. It has none of the conditions in Smith's bill.

A second House bill (HR 3983), introduced by Rules Committee Chairman David Dreier, R-Calif., and Zoe Lofgren, D-Calif., would increase the H-1B level to 200,000 for three years. It has few restrictions on eligibility. Industry strongly supports S 2045 and the Dreier-Lofgren bill.

During the markup a move by Lofgren to amend Smith's bill raised another potential problem: Democrats may try to attach an amnesty for certain illegal immigrants.

At issue are the roughly 500,000 illegal immigrants who have been in the United States since 1986 but who were left out of the amnesty program in the 1986 immigration overhaul (PL 99-603). The Clinton administration has proposed granting amnesty, allowing the immigrants to become legal residents. Lofgren included amnesty in her amendment, which she then withdrew on a technicality. She is likely to offer it again at the full committee markup. *(1986 Almanac, p. 61)*

Smith's Move

Smith remains unconvinced that more foreign workers are needed. "Today there is still no objective, credible study that documents a shortage of American high-tech workers," he said.

Smith had introduced a bill (HR 3814) on March 1 to increase H-1B visas to 160,000 for one year and take steps to protect American workers. But that bill went nowhere. One business lobbyist said Smith introduced the second bill to get back into the debate.

Smith's new bill would require that the Clinton administration implement regulations in the 1998 law before any fiscal 2001 or 2002 visas were issued beyond the levels in that law. The regulations require businesses in which more than 15 percent of the work force is made up of H-1B workers to recruit U.S. workers and refrain from laying off Americans if they want to remain eligible for visas. No final regulation has been promulgated by the Labor Department. Also in fiscal 2001 and 2002, a company would have to show that compared with the previous year, it had increased both the number of U.S. employees and their compensation.

Smith's bill generally would allow H-1Bs to go only to full-time workers making at least $40,000 a year. Information on each H-1B employee, including name, job title and salary, would be given to the Labor Department, which would post it on the Internet. Some members raised privacy concerns over that provision. The bill also would institute a $100 visa fee to combat fraud and would transfer responsibility from the INS to the State Department for keeping track of the number of visas issued.

The panel adopted by voice vote an amendment by Elton Gallegly, R-Calif., to require anyone seeking an H-1B visa to work as a physical therapist to have a master's degree. U.S. physical therapists say there is a glut of domestic professionals and no need for foreign workers.

House Committee Set to Approve H-1B Visa Bill

MAY 13 — The House Judiciary Committee is expected to give final approval the week of May 15 to a bill (HR 4227) to dramatically increase the number of foreign workers allowed to temporarily come into the United States.

The committee began work May 9, and Lamar Smith, R-Texas, chairman of the Judiciary Subcommittee on Immigration and Claims, and sponsor of the bill, said all the panel had left to do was vote on approval.

The measure would remove a cap, for three years, on the number of H-1B visas (the current cap is 115,000), but it includes provisions designed to protect American workers that the high-tech community and its allies in Congress oppose. Foreign workers who obtain H-1B visas can work in the United States for up to six years.

During the markup, Smith offered an amendment, adopted 24-7, that stripped some worker protections from the bill in an attempt to broaden support. The amendment eliminated a requirement that the number of U.S. workers increase from one year to the next for a firm to use the program, and that a company show that, compared to the previous year, total salaries for their American workers had increased.

But it left in place several provisions opposed by industry. Under the bill, a prospective H-1B employee would have to be paid at least $40,000 a year. Further, a company's median wage for U.S. workers would have to increase from one year to the next in order for it to be eligible to hire an H-1B worker.

The bill would not lift a cap in the employment-based immigration program on the number of workers permitted from specific countries, a provision strongly sought by technology companies because it would allow more Chinese and South Asian workers to be hired.

After the panel acts, all eyes will turn to the Rules Committee, whose chairman, David Dreier, R-Calif., has a competing, industry-backed bill (HR 3983) to increase the cap to 200,000 for three years with fewer strings.

Panel OKs Bill With Provisions That Are Opposed By Businesses

MAY 20 — The House Republican leadership faces a dilemma on the issue of temporary foreign workers: how to get a bill favored by industry groups and most members to the floor without stripping authority from a key subcommittee chairman.

Leaders also must decide whether to include a proposal from President Clinton, pushed by Democrats, that would grant amnesty to thousands of illegal immigrants and relief to some Central American and Haitian immigrants.

On May 17, the House Judiciary Committee approved legislation (HR 4227) that would lift the cap on the number of special visas, called H-1Bs, issued to highly skilled foreign workers — many of whom work for high-tech companies. The vote was 18-11. But the bill, sponsored by Immigration Subcommittee Chairman Lamar Smith, R-Texas, contains restrictions on employers that the business community loathes.

Zoe Lofgren, D-Calif., cosponsor with Rules Chairman David Dreier, R-Calif., of alternative legislation (HR 3983) that has strong industry support, said after the markup, "CEOs have told me they would prefer nothing — they would prefer no bill to [Smith's] bill."

The Dreier-Lofgren bill would raise the cap on H-1B visas from 115,000 in fiscal 2000 to 200,000 per year from fiscal 2001 through 2003. It would impose no new conditions on employers to obtain visas. Smith's bill would require businesses to show, among other things, that they had increased the median wage paid to U.S. workers from year to year. Employees with H-1B visas can work in the United States for up to six years.

The Senate Judiciary Committee approved its version of H-1B legislation (S 2045) on March 9.

The House bills are now headed for the Rules Committee, which may consider them the week of May 22. Dreier could either make his bill the primary bill for House action or make it a substitute to the Smith bill. He has declined to discuss his strategy.

The Rules Committee is expected to meld into the package a bill (HR 4402) approved May 10 by the Education and the Workforce Committee that would reauthorize job training and education programs for U.S. workers. The Rules panel also must decide whether to allow the Democratic amendment on amnesty.

Amnesty and Residency

The amnesty amendment is part of a Clinton proposal that Lofgren wants added to the bipartisan bill — although Dreier has seemed skeptical. Much of the business community is staying on the sidelines in the amnesty battle. As business lobbyist Sandra J. Boyd said, industry wants more visas. "I don't think we have a good sense of what the impact of the other immigration legislation would be," she said.

The coalition backing the amnesty recently gained the support of two conservatives, former Rep. Jack F. Kemp, R-N.Y. (1971-89) and Americans for Tax Reform President Grover Norquist, adding momentum to the proposal.

One provision would make it easier for Guatemalans, Hondurans and Salvadorans who have been in the United States since the 1980s to get permanent residency. Thousands of Central Americans fled oppressive regimes or civil wars in the 1980s, frequently coming to the United States illegally. Similarly, Haitians came in the 1990s.

A 1997 law (PL 105-100) allowed immigrants from Nicaragua and Cuba who had fled leftist regimes and who had been in the United States since the 1980s to apply for permanent residency. *(1997 Almanac, p. 5-11)*

Guatemalans and Salvadorans who had fled right-wing dictatorships were allowed to apply for suspension of deportation, which allowed them to stay, but in an ambiguous position. The 1997 law did not grant relief to Hondurans or Haitians. In 1998, Congress made it easier for some Haitians to get residency (PL 105-277), but Hondurans were still left out. The provision would grant permanent residency to all the groups.

The other issue is known as "legal amnesty." In the 1986 immigration overhaul (PL 99-603), Congress granted amnesty to thousands of illegal immigrants if they had been in the United States since 1981. *(1986 Almanac, p. 61)*

But Immigration and Naturalization Service (INS) regulations implementing the law led to years of litigation. Courts generally have held that the INS misapplied the law, and have provided some relief to aliens who missed the application deadline. The 1996 immigration law (PL 104-208) stripped the courts of jurisdiction, however, unless immigrants could show they had tried to apply for amnesty but had been rebuffed. *(1996 Almanac, p. 5-3)*

The Democratic amendment seeks to make eligible for residency anyone who has been in the United States since 1986 and is of "good moral character."

Lawmakers Juggle Business' Agenda, With Immigrants' Interests

SEPTEMBER 23 — It should have been a slam dunk. Virtually every major business group, the vast majority of both Republicans and Democrats in Congress, and the Clinton administration all agreed earlier this year to support proposals for increasing visas for temporary, highly skilled workers coming to the United States to help feed the high-tech community's voracious need for more workers.

Even organized labor has not opposed the visa increases this time, though it fought them bitterly in 1998.

But by mid-September, H-1B visa bills in both the House and the Senate were stalled (HR 4227, HR 3983, S 2045), not so much because of controversy over the bills, but over a host of other immigration issues advocates want added to the popular measures.

Several proposals are in play as additions to H-1B, including a bill that would make it easier for immigrants in the United States to become permanent residents. And some Republicans are pushing to change the agriculture guest-worker program, which could force the party to choose between satisfying business interests and alienating voting blocs like Hispanics who have grown to critical importance in states such as Florida and California.

"Immigration issues are white hot," said Judith Golub, a lobbyist for the American Immigration Lawyers Association. "They are important for the election."

No one believes the H-1B visa issue will be allowed to die. Even though few immigration issues have been formally considered by Congress, pressure from outside groups is building, and Democrats and the White House seem likely to get some of their issues in a final package that carries business' top priority: H-1B visas. Some form of that proposal is almost certain to travel on a year-end spending bill, the new way for immigration issues to become law.

Indeed, in what has become an annual tradition since Republicans won control of Congress in 1994, many of the most serious immigration issues likely to become law will be added quietly to an end-of-session bill, with little or no floor debate in either chamber.

It wasn't always this way. Republicans passed a stand-alone bill cracking down on illegal immigration in 1996 (PL 104-208) and included provisions restricting immigrant access to government benefits in the welfare overhaul that year (PL 104-193). *(1996 Almanac, pp. 5-3, 6-3)*

But those measures proved tremendously problematic for Republicans, opening fissures within the party and generating a backlash, especially from the Hispanic community. Many of the most dramatic revisions have since been reversed; the fixes tucked into year-end spending bills.

This year, the piecemeal strategy continues as Republicans try to accommodate the wishes of business leaders without giving ground on immigration issues important to Hispanics. In fact, with the presidential campaign of GOP Texas Gov. George W. Bush reaching out to Hispanic voters, there is pressure on congressional Republicans not to rock the boat with Latinos.

High-tech lobbyists want to see their visa bill stand for a floor vote, and the Hispanic community hopes to take advantage of the political atmosphere to push proposals that would make it easier for some immigrants to become permanent legal residents.

"The community is watching very closely," said Cecilia Muñoz, vice president of the office of research, advocacy and legislation for the National Council of La Raza, a civil rights group. "This is where the rubber meets the road."

One measure the Hispanic community does not want to see enacted is the bill (HR 4548) that would lower minimum wages for temporary farm workers and ease other hiring rules. "It's poison for all of us," said Muñoz.

With the bill, Republicans are "planting the seeds for national Latino opposition to the Republican Party," said Howard L. Berman, D-Calif.

Senate Shuffle

The H-1B proposal is at the heart of the debate. The intense lobbying campaign by the computer industry and other high-tech sectors for the additional workers has made the visa increase a must-pass this Congress. No one wants to be blamed for its failure.

The visas allow highly skilled foreign workers to come to the United States for up to six years. While the majority of the visas are used by the high-tech community, others go to a variety of occupations including nurses and physical therapists.

Neither chamber has debated the proposals on the floor. The Senate on Sept. 19 voted 97-1 to proceed to the bill (S 2045) that had been approved by the Judiciary Committee on March 9. *(Vote 252, p. S-45)*

The House Judiciary Committee approved a vastly different measure (HR 4227) on May 17.

Under a 1998 law (PL 105-277), the number of H-1B visas authorized to be issued will drop to 107,500 in fiscal 2001, which begins Oct. 1. In fiscal 2000, 115,000 visas were permitted, but the supply was exhausted by the end of March. *(1998 Almanac, p. 17-3)*

The Senate version would increase the visa allocation to 195,000 each year for three years, but the cap excludes a large number of visas for those graduating from or working for universities.

Republicans argue that Democrats have blocked the bill by demanding votes on unrelated immigration issues. Democrats respond that the GOP is afraid to cast votes on politically touchy issues.

The Sept. 19 vote served two purposes for Republicans. It removed one procedural obstacle, and, more importantly, gave a strong signal to the increasingly nervous high-tech community that senators support the bill.

"We are pleased that both Republican and Democratic leaders in the Senate have acknowledged the need to act on the H-1B visa bill before Congress adjourns this year and applaud today's action," said Sandra Boyd, who chairs an umbrella group of businesses known as the American Businesses for Legal Immigration.

An H-1B increase "is very important to our country, to the need for high-tech workers," Senate Majority Leader Trent Lott, R-Miss., said Sept. 19. "And this is not just a large corporation issue; small businesses, businesses all across America need these additional high-tech workers."

Democrats want to offer amendments that would make it easier for longtime illegal immigrants to gain permanent legal residency, extend deadlines for residency applications for immigrants from some Central American countries, and restore a law that allowed immigrants to stay in the country beyond their visa if an application for residency was pending.

At their luncheon before the cloture vote on Sept. 19, Senate Democrats were briefed by members of the House Hispanic Caucus on the value of those proposals. Vice Chairman of the House Democratic Caucus Robert Menendez, of New Jersey, said the issue is fairness for Hispanics. He said if Republicans block the Democrats' amendment package, the GOP will be telling Hispanics "we'll do immigration issues for businesses, but we won't do immigration issues for families who want to be reunited."

The Senate may hold another cloture vote Sept. 26, this time to limit debate, but it is not clear whether Democrats will support this second motion. Democrats expect their amendments to be ruled out of order as non-germane if the Senate ever considers the H-1B bill, though that will not end the battle. "We're not going to give up on them just because we can't get a vote," said a top Democratic staffer.

House Problems

The difficulties in the House are similar but more extensive. House leaders have been reluctant to bring an H-1B visa bill to the floor because of concerns about the immigration provisions Democrats want to debate. Though House rules would allow the GOP to preclude amendments, Democrats could use parliamentary tools to get symbolic votes.

In addition, Republicans have not decided which version of the H-1B bill to bring to the floor.

The House Judiciary Committee approved a bill (HR 4227) in May that was largely authored by Immigration and Claims Subcommittee Chairman Lamar Smith, R-Texas. Though it would remove any cap on H-1B visas for three years, the business community intensely dislikes a provision that would require companies seeking H-1B workers to pay them at least $40,000 a year. Those companies would have to show an increase in the median wage paid to U.S. workers from year to year.

House Rules Committee Chairman David Dreier, R-Calif., and Zoe Lofgren, D-Calif., introduced legislation (HR 3983) far more to the industry's liking. It would raise the cap to 200,000 annually for three years, with no new conditions for employers.

Lobbyists thought the House leadership was planning to bring the Dreier-Lofgren bill to the floor in place of the Smith bill, but the two sponsors appear to have had a falling out over Lofgren's support of the other immigration proposals, and theirs has gone nowhere.

Agriculture Workers

A bill that might reach the House floor is the one (HR 4548) most strongly opposed by Hispanics, that was approved 16-11 by the House Judiciary Committee on Sept. 20.

The bill would create a three-year pilot program that would require all U.S. farm workers to be listed in a state registry to make them easier for employers to locate. It also would allow growers to pay lower wages and in some cases give workers a housing stipend instead of housing.

The measure was pushed through the committee at the behest of House Speaker J. Dennis Hastert, R-Ill., according to Judiciary Committee Chairman Henry J. Hyde, R-Ill. Hyde voted against the measure, calling it "a bad bill . . . I thought it was unfair to workers."

John P. Feehery, a spokesman for Hastert, said the bill was intended to ease a farm-worker shortage. "We need to help our farmers," he said.

The measure could be on the floor as soon as the week of Sept. 25.

Hispanic groups have vowed all-out war against the bill, even if it is packaged with the other immigration provisions they want. "[I]f anyone in Congress is flirting with the notion of adding the farm worker bill as the 'price' for other immigration legislation, I would like to state, clearly and unequivocally, that the National Council of La Raza will never agree to sacrifice our farm worker brothers and sisters for the sake of any legislation," La Raza president and chief executive officer Raul Yzaguirre said in a statement Sept. 12.

Democrats said Clinton likely would veto the bill, but some groups were clearly uneasy that it had gone as far as being marked up. "We're nervous," said Bruce Goldstein, a lobbyist for the Farmworker Justice Fund.

Much of the debate during the two days of the committee markup centered on wages and housing for farmworkers. Under current law, an employer must provide housing for temporary workers.

The bill as approved by the Immigration and Claims Subcommittee would have allowed employers to charge farmworkers for maintenance and utilities and collect a security deposit. It also would have let employers pay workers a "reasonable housing allowance," in lieu of actually providing housing.

Democrats attacked the idea that farmworkers could compete for apartments in such a tight housing market with a relatively small allowance. Berman did some calculations, based on an annual average salary for most workers of $7,500, and said: "If you think that a weekly allowance of $27 is going to get somebody an apartment . . . you're dreaming."

Republicans responded that their plan would take some of the burden off employers. "This is more than fair, considering this is in addition to the wages they are being paid," Smith said. "It's not fair to make them landlords."

The issue was the subject of two competing amendments during the markup. On Sept. 19, the committee adopted, 14-13, an amendment by Sheila Jackson-Lee, D-Texas, that stripped the new housing provision and replaced it with current law.

The vote succeeded, in part, because three Republicans, Hyde, F. James Sensenbrenner Jr., Wis., and Elton Gallegly, Calif., joined the Democrats.

But just before the committee concluded its work for the day on Sept. 19, Gallegly said he had changed his mind and called for a revote on the amendment. Democrats managed to postpone it until the next morning.

By that time, Gallegly had changed his plan. Instead of re-voting on the first amendment, he offered a second provision. That amendment, adopted 17-14 on Sept. 20 after an equally intense debate, would allow growers to pay workers a subsidy for housing if the governor of the state certified that housing was available.

Democrats did win on another Jackson-Lee amendment. The committee adopted, 15-13, her provision that would restore something called the "three-quarters" rule.

Under current law, employers are required to pay workers for at least three-quarters of the time for which they were promised work (barring an Act of God such as weather). So, if a grower promised eight weeks of work, he must pay at least six weeks wages.

The bill would have lifted that requirement. Smith argued that it had "long been a burdensome requirement" on employers. He said workers "know going into the program they will have work only as long as there is work to do."

Jackson-Lee responded, "It's not unfair to simply ask [employers] to keep their word."

The committee rejected, by voice vote, an amendment by Berman that would have limited the number of foreign guest workers allowed into the country to 100,000 per year.

Smith argued that the cap was "not nearly enough to meet demand — estimated at nearly one million."

In the Senate, Republican Policy Chairman Larry E. Craig of Idaho has been pushing similar legislation and has said for months he wanted to attach it to the H-1B bill. But he acknowledged Sept. 19 that a deal seemed unlikely and H-1B visas are too important to risk.

"I will offer it if we can get to a compromise," he said. "We may not get there this year."

Senate Passage Of High-Tech Worker Visa Bill Appears Likely

SEPTEMBER 30 — The Senate appears poised to pass legislation (S 2045), strongly backed by the high-tech industry, to increase the number of highly skilled temporary foreign workers allowed into the United States. A vote on passage is scheduled for Oct. 3. However, the measure faces an uncertain reception in the House, where a competing bill, despised by business, has won committee approval.

"This is a painful way to get there," Sandra J. Boyd, top lobbyist for the coalition of business groups supporting the H-1B increase, said of the often-bitter Senate debate. "There's a lot of confusion" about what comes next, she said.

Senate Republicans proceeded carefully the week of Sept. 25, bringing the bill up but using complicated parliamentary tools to protect their members from difficult votes on other immigration issues that Democrats sought to attach to the measure.

Democrats wanted to add provisions that would make it easier for a variety of groups to become permanent legal residents and grant amnesty to some longtime illegal immigrants. The proposals are supported by the Hispanic community and the Clinton administration.

While they were never formally permitted to vote on the amendment, Democrats did use several hours of debate time during the parliamentary wrangling to make their point. And they forced some Republicans to debate the issues around their proposals.

The bill itself would allow the Immigration and Naturalization Service to issue 195,000 H-1B visas annually over three years, up from the 107,500 such visas currently authorized for fiscal 2001.

Exempt from that cap would be foreign workers who sign up to work for government or nonprofit research organizations and those who recently obtained a master's degree or higher at a U.S. college or university.

The bill also would make it easier for individuals from countries that quickly reach their H-1B cap, such as India and China, to qualify for unused visas at the end of each quarter.

With the booming economy, businesses, especially in the high-tech community, have lobbied heavily for more H-1B visas. While they are pleased to see the bill moving after such a long delay — the Senate Judiciary Committee approved it in March — some lobbyists worry that it is hardly a done deal.

The House Judiciary Committee approved its own H-1B visa bill (HR 4227) in May. But that legislation, sponsored by Lamar Smith, R-Texas, is rejected by the business community because it would add significantly to the requirements that businesses must meet to participate in the H-1B program.

Majority Leader Dick Armey, R-Texas, has said the House could take up the Senate bill, but it is unlikely the leadership would prevent Smith from getting a vote on his measure in the House.

Given the often nasty tenor of the Senate debate, House leaders may be reluctant to bring the bill up at all so close to such an important election.

Democrats, for their part, have not given up on their immigration package, but they have changed their target: They are now agitating to attach the provisions to the already troubled fiscal 2001 appropriations bill for the departments of Commerce, Justice, State and the federal judiciary (HR 4690).

Immigration Debate

Very little of the Senate debate on the H-1B bill actually focused on the issue of temporary worker visas. Instead, Democrats succeeded in changing the subject and forcing the GOP to debate their package of immigration changes.

At issue are several provisions that would make it easier for certain Central Americans, Eastern Europeans and Liberians to become legal residents; grant amnesty to illegal immigrants who have been in the United States since 1986; and make it easier for some immigrants to stay in the country while their applications for residency are being processed.

Democrats billed the debate as one of fairness — helping the poorest of the immigrants at the same time the Senate was acting to help the wealthy tech community and its largely well-paid work force. They also emphasized how important these proposals are to a significant voting bloc in the fall elections: Hispanics.

"It is clear that Republican support for the Latino community is all talk and no action. When it's time to pass legislation of importance to the Latino community, the Republican leadership is nowhere to be found," said Sen. Edward M. Kennedy, D-Mass.

"There is a stark disagreement between our parties on the issue of fairness to immigrants," agreed Senate Minority Leader Tom Daschle, D-S.D.

Republicans angrily responded that all Democrats wanted to do was reward illegal immigration and make political hay out of the issue.

Judd Gregg, R-N.H., accused Daschle of crying "crocodile tears" for the immigrants. Judiciary Committee Chairman Orrin G. Hatch, R-Utah, called the Democrats' charges "absolutely shameless."

"We all know what is going on: This is a doggone political game," Hatch said angrily. "The bottom line is that the Senate is not and should not be prepared to consider this bill at this time. It raises far-reaching questions concerning immigration policy, whose consequences have never been addressed by proponents." He put the cost of the package at $1.4 billion over 10 years.

Larry E. Craig, R-Idaho, said immigration laws, which Democrats argued were too complicated, were designed to be that way. "We want it to be complicated," he said. "We do not want all of the world at our doorstep."

Democrats also decried the way Majority Leader Trent Lott, R-Miss., brought up the H-1B bill. Once the Senate had invoked cloture, limiting debate on the bill, Lott blocked Democrats from offering germane amendments by putting forward a series of minor amendments of his own, thereby "filling the amendment tree" and leav-

H-1B Bill Highlights

OCTOBER 7 — The following are highlights of the H-1B visa bill (S 2045) that Congress cleared Oct. 3. The bill would increase the number of highly skilled workers temporarily permitted into the United States for specialized jobs, responding to what the high-tech business community has called an urgent need caused by economic growth.

ISSUE	DESCRIPTION
The H-1B Cap	The bill would set the limit on H-1B visas for highly skilled workers brought into the U.S. for specialized jobs at 195,000 each year for fiscal years 2001, 2002 and 2003, up from 115,000 in fiscal 2000.
Exemptions	Workers hired at institutions of higher education and their affiliated offices, and workers employed by government and nonprofit research organizations, would not count against the new H-1B quota.
Portability	Workers holding an H-1B visa could change jobs by having their new employer file a petition with INS, assuming the employee was properly employed under the program.
Application Fee	Despite agreement by lawmakers and the business community to raise the application fee charged companies for each H-1B visa from $500 to $1,000, the change was not included in the cleared bill. A separate bill is being pushed through Congress to fix the measure.
Training for U.S. Workers	Money generated by the visa application fee would be used to fund a variety of training programs for U.S. workers. Fifty-five percent of the training money would go toward technical training programs operated by the Department of Labor. Smaller portions would go to programs in such agencies as the National Science Foundation.
Raising Previous Year Caps	The bill would protect the fiscal 2001 supply of visas from being consumed by a backlog of H-1B applications for workers who were approved in fiscal year 1999 or on or before Sept. 1, 2000, after those two years' caps had been reached. The bill would raise the caps for those two years to cover all workers already approved.
INS Processing	The bill would require the INS to provide to Congress within 90 days of enactment a plan to improve the average processing time of all immigration cases, which now stands at 180 days. The bill also would require the INS to provide annual reports on its progress, and would create a funding account for such improvements.

ing no room for Democratic proposals.

Democrats failed in an effort to waive germaneness rules and allow consideration of their amendment. The vote was 43-55. All but two Democrats — Paul Wellstone of Minnesota and Ernest F. Hollings of South Carolina — voted for an amendment that was virtually identical to the underlying bill, showing its strong bipartisan support. That vote was 94-3. *(Votes 257, 258, p. S-46)*

Supporters still plan to make several changes to the bill before the Senate votes on it. For example, as approved by committee, the bill would apply to fiscal years 2000 through 2002. As fiscal 2000 will end before the bill becomes law, they want to change it to apply to fiscal 2001-2003.

Other issues will be left for later negotiations. The Senate bill's fee structure for H-1B applications differs from competing House proposals. Also, the House bill would transfer some of the education and worker training programs from the Labor Department to the Education Department, a proposal strongly disliked by some senators.

House Clears Bill; Well-Timed Push Gives Businesses All They Asked

OCTOBER 7 — Rep. Zoe Lofgren, D-Calif., has been a leader in the battle to increase the number of foreign high-tech workers allowed into the country temporarily. But even she was caught unaware when the House took up the H-1B visa bill Oct. 3.

Lofgren raced back from the Best Buy in Crystal City, Va., where she was shopping for a home computer, so she could reach the floor in time to praise passage of the legislation (S 2045) she had worked so hard to get through.

"I am a little bit surprised that we are standing here tonight," she said from the floor. "I was glad I was able to get into the car pool lanes and get here in time to talk about why this bill deserves our support."

Lofgren was not the only member who had not expected such rapid final action on the H-1B bill. Only hours after the Senate passed it by an overwhelming vote of 96-1, the House dropped its own versions of the bill, took up the Senate measure under expedited procedures and passed it by voice vote, long after members had been told there would be no more votes for the day. Though they grumbled about the sudden change in schedule, most members seemed relieved that the H-1B battle could be behind them. *(Senate vote 262, p. S-47)*

The Senate's action that morning had opened a window for the House GOP leadership to swiftly clear a bill that was near the top of the business community's agenda.

"We saw an opportunity to run it

through, and we ran it through," said John P. Feehery, press secretary for House Speaker J. Dennis Hastert, R-Ill. He said the House leadership had watched the Senate GOP grapple with politically sensitive side issues surrounding the H-1B bill and wanted to avoid a similar battle in the House.

"The best way to take the politics out of it was to do it," he said.

"We couldn't be happier," said Sandra J. Boyd, top lobbyist for American Businesses for Legal Immigration, an umbrella group that has led the efforts to pass the H-1B bill. "There was never any doubt about the outcome. There was doubt about the process."

The bill now goes to the White House, where President Clinton is expected to sign it.

The rapid conclusion to the visa battle was an unusual, almost anticlimactic end to a fight that had been lengthy and increasingly nasty. While virtually no one opposed the core of the bill, which would increase H-1B visas to at least 195,000 each year for three years, there was considerable debate about what other immigration issues should be addressed by the bill.

In the end, the only major additions to the measure were designed to speed the processing of immigration petitions by the Immigration and Naturalization Service.

Other provisions that would have granted amnesty to some illegal immigrants, allowed other immigrants to stay in the United States while their residency petition was pending, and lengthen the time for some Central American and Liberian immigrants to apply for residency, were not included.

Democrats have vowed that they will attach those measures, known as the Latino Fairness and Immigrant Act (S 2912), to the final version of the fiscal 2001 appropriations bill for the departments of Commerce, Justice and State (HR 4690), or they will encourage Clinton to veto the bill.

The Campaign Started Early

Companies began their campaign on the H-1B visas early this year. Arguing that they needed more temporary, highly skilled workers to keep up with the booming economy, especially in the technology sector, they persuaded leading members of both parties early on to take up their cause.

At first, the bills moved rapidly. The Senate measure (S 2045) introduced Feb. 9 by Judiciary Committee Chairman Orrin G. Hatch, R-Utah, and Immigration Subcommittee Chairman Spencer Abraham, R-Mich., was approved March 9 by the Judiciary Committee, a very quick timetable.

In March, House Judiciary Immigration and Claims Subcommittee Chairman Lamar Smith, R-Texas, introduced his first H-1B bill (HR 3814), and by April 12, his subcommittee had approved a second version. The full House Judiciary Committee approved that measure (HR 4227) on May 17.

The business community disliked the House Judiciary Committee bill because it included a variety of new conditions Smith had sought for employers wanting to hire workers through the H-1B program. But top members of the House GOP reassured lobbyists that the alternative House bill they supported, HR 3983, sponsored by Rules Committee Chairman David Dreier, R-Calif., and Lofgren, would be the bill that passed the House.

And then the action stopped. Neither chamber made any progress in bringing a bill to the floor. Talk grew of skipping floor debate entirely and including H-1B provisions in an end-of-the-year spending bill, which unnerved the tech companies and their allies.

Republicans argue that progress stalled because Democrats demanded that other immigration issues be attached to the H-1B bill. Discussion of those measures surfaced in May.

"They have tried to make this into a political brouhaha, which it doesn't deserve," said Hatch.

Democrats responded that they only wanted to offer the amendments for an up-or-down vote, and countered that Republicans control the process.

Visa-Waiver Program Extended

President Clinton signed a bill Oct. 30 (HR 3767 — PL 106-396) reauthorizing the visa waiver program that allows travel between the United States and 29 other countries without requiring visas.

The Senate passed the bill by voice vote Oct. 3, and the House cleared it Oct. 10. The program had expired in April, but the Clinton administration, with the support of Congress, continued to operate it without authorization.

The waivers allow people to travel between the United States and the other countries for both business and tourism without having to obtain visas. Foreigners covered by the program can stay in the United States for up to 90 days; the time U.S. travelers can spend abroad varies by country.

The visa waiver system was created as a pilot program in the 1986 immigration overhaul (PL 99-603) and has been reauthorized several times. The House passed its first version of the bill April 11. The Senate Judiciary Committee approved its bill (S 2367) on April 13.

The final bill, an amended version of the original House bill, made the program permanent. It required that all countries participating in the program on May 1, 2000, certify that by 2003 they will have an automated passport system. By Oct. 1, 2007, visitors to the United States covered by the program would be required to have machine-readable passports.

While the bill itself was noncontroversial, it was held up several times by members seeking to use it as a vehicle for amendments.

Sen. Charles E. Schumer, D-N.Y., for example, briefly stalled the bill in an attempt to win adoption of an amendment to make it easier for some Syrian Jews already in the United States to become citizens. Schumer backed off, and the bill does not include that provision.

The bill does include a provision, not in earlier versions, giving travelers on private jets the same access to the visa waiver as those using commercial airlines.

Bill Provides Immigration Relief

Pro-immigration groups, with the aid of Democrats and the Clinton administration, managed to win approval of a small portion of their plan to provide immigration relief for several specific groups.

Included in the end-of-session omnibus spending bill (HR 4577 — PL 106-554), the provisions made it easier for some illegal immigrants who feel they were unfairly denied a chance to apply for amnesty under the 1986 immigration overhaul (PL 99-603) to have their claims reviewed.

It opened a four-month window for those who came to the country legally but whose visas have expired and who are are waiting for their residency to be decided, to finish the process in the United States. But the bill did not provide the large-scale amnesty for illegal immigrants the Clinton administration and Democrats had sought, nor did it provide relief for some illegal aliens from Central America who were hoping to be able to stay in the country as legal residents.

The immigration issue arose as Congress considered increasing the number of temporary, H-1B visas that allow highly skilled foreign workers to come to the United States. Immigration groups argued that if Congress was going to help the better-off group of would-be immigrants, it should also address some imbalances in other immigration programs.

In the Senate, Democrats tried to attach their broad immigration proposal to the H-1B bill (S 2045), but Senate Majority Leader Trent Lott, R-Miss., structured the debate to preclude their amendment. *(See H-1B visas, p. 15-3)*

Democrats then turned to another must-pass piece of legislation, the fiscal 2001 appropriations bill for the departments of Commerce, Justice, State and the federal judiciary (HR 4942). With Democrats assuring Clinton they had the votes to sustain him, the White House said flatly that the president would veto the spending bill if it did not contain the immigration provisions. *(Commerce-Justice-State appropriations, p. 2-23)*

The Republican leadership cleared the CJS bill without the provisions, but did not send it to the White House until the modest immigration package was cleared as part of the omnibus bill.

"During this long stretch of inactivity, it has often appeared that the Republican majority has been more interested in gaining partisan advantage from a delay than in actually making this bill law," said Patrick J. Leahy, D-Vt., ranking Democrat on the Senate Judiciary Committee.

Tech companies turned up the heat. Executives of top companies made the rounds and made it clear they did not want the issue dealt with in an omnibus spending bill. Lawmakers were warned that even procedural votes would be scrutinized, because they were necessary to prevent amendments to the Senate bill. High-tech industry executives particularly feared the provisions Smith wanted, which would have prevented foreign workers from being hired in the wake of a layoff and would have set a minimum salary of $40,000 a year for each H-1B employee. They argued that Smith's proposals would mean a virtual hiring freeze, and insisted that the H-1B bill be dealt with on its own.

High-Tech Generosity

The intensified lobbying was paired with generous check-writing. For many lawmakers, Silicon Valley has been a valuable campaign stop, but since June 1, technology PACs have been especially active, giving congressional candidates at least $467,884, according to Federal Election Commission data. In June alone, those PACs doled out $326,818, the highest monthly total so far this year.

The tech companies seemed to increase their donations to the majority party during the same period. For the entire cycle (since Jan. 1, 1999), tech PACs have given Republican candidates $1,028,219, compared with $706,477 to Democrats. Since June, $300,670 went to Republicans, while $167,214 went to Democrats.

It took until late September, but the Senate finally brought its bill to the floor. Senate Majority Leader Trent Lott, R-Miss., moved to prevent Democrats from offering amendments, and after more than a week of frequently bitter debate, the Senate voted. The House took action later the same day.

Not everyone was pleased with the outcome. "This legislation is nothing more than a betrayal of American working people," said Rep. Dana Rohrabacher, R-Calif.

And Smith, whose provisions never got floor consideration, said he was "disappointed that there were no safeguards for American workers," in the final bill.

For all the complicated maneuvering, the version of the legislation cleared by Congress is perhaps the one most generous to the high-tech community. It is the "best possible product" for businesses, acknowledged Boyd.

At a minimum, the bill would authorize 195,000 H-1B visas each year in fiscal years 2001-03. But the total number of H-1B workers in the United States for those years could be much higher, because the bill would not count toward the cap those who work for the government, nonprofits or colleges and universities and their affiliated groups.

In addition, the bill would not count all the visas that were awarded after the cap was reached in the last two fiscal years. This provision would clear out the backlog of visas from previous years so that the current and future-year quotas are not used up by pending applications.

The bill would make it a little easier for an H-1B employee to change jobs without losing his or her visa, and it would allow H-1B visa-holders who have applied for residency to stay in the country under the H-1B status until their application is decided, even if their six-year time limit is up.

The bill would continue the requirement of the 1998 H-1B visa law (PL 105-277) that employers attest that they have tried to find U.S. workers to fill the jobs for which they now seek H-1B visa workers. *(1998 Almanac, p. 17-3)*

The bill does not include an expected increase in the fee paid by the employer for each H-1B visa. Because the bill originated in the Senate, it could not include an increase in revenue without running afoul of the House Ways and Means Committee.

On Oct. 6, the House passed by voice vote a bill (HR 5362) that would raise the H-1B visa fee from $500 to $1,000, a figure that business lobbyists and members have agreed upon.

Education and Training

The additional money from the increase in fees as well as visas would go to a variety of education and training programs for American workers. If all the H-1B visas were given out at a $1,000 fee, there would be $195 million available to spend on these kinds of programs (though about 8 percent of the total would go to enforcement and administrative costs).

More than half of the money raised by the fee would go to the Labor Department for grant programs designed to provide technical skills training. The vast majority of those grants would go to training for high-tech jobs in areas such as information services and biotechnology. Some money would go to scholarships for low-income students attending colleges or universities.

The bill also includes a provision requiring INS to develop a plan to erase a backlog of applications for residency or non-immigrant visas.

But it was the heart of the bill that was celebrated by business advocates, such as Rhett B. Dawson, president of the Information Technology Industry Council, representing more than 25 high-tech companies.

"We are grateful that the Senate realized the national importance of this legislation," he said, "and refused to let it fall victim to end-of-the-year partisan politics." ◆

Juvenile Justice Bill Gets Hung Up on Dispute Over Gun Control

Box Score

- **Bills:** HR 1501, HR 4051
- **Legislative action: House** passed, HR 4051, 358-60, on April 11.

House voted, 406-22, on April 11 to instruct conferees on the juvenile justice bill (HR 1501) to back the Senate gun provisions.

Senate adopted, 50-49, on May 17 a sense-of-the-Senate amendment urging Congress to adopt a conference report on HR 1501, including the Senate-passed gun amendments.

SUMMARY

An effort by Democrats to tighten gun laws ended the year as it began: attached to a juvenile justice bill that remained stuck in a House-Senate conference.

Largely as a result of the impasse over gun control, conferees did not even meet during the year on the juvenile justice bill (HR 1501), which died at session's end.

The House did pass a bill (HR 4051) in April, designed to encourage states to toughen their enforcement of gun laws, but the measure was never considered in the Senate. Also in April, the House voted overwhelmingly to instruct conferees on the juvenile justice bill to accept a package of gun control provisions that was included in the Senate version of HR 1501.

In May, the Senate adopted a sense-of-the-Senate amendment offered by Minority Leader Tom Daschle, D-S.D., to express support for the juvenile justice bill and the Senate's gun provisions. *(Background, 1999 Almanac, p. 18-3)*

The Senate had added its fairly limited gun control package to the bill in 1999, with Vice President Al Gore casting the tie-breaking vote. The measure would have required background checks on purchases at gun shows, banned ammunition clips holding more than 10 rounds and prohibited anyone convicted of a violent offense while a teenager from ever being allowed to own a gun.

The House rejected a separate gun control bill (HR 2122), and passed its version of the juvenile justice bill without gun control language. Conferees met once in 1999, but could not reach agreement.

House Passes Bill To Encourage Tougher Penalties For Gun Crimes

APRIL 15 — Jockeying on gun issues intensified in the House as the first anniversary of the April 20 massacre at Columbine High School approached.

On April 11, the House passed GOP-crafted legislation (HR 4051) that aims to encourage states to toughen their sentencing laws for crimes committed with guns. The vote was 358-60. *(Vote 115, p. H-40)*

That same day, the House endorsed, 406-22, a non-binding motion by Democrats to instruct conferees on the moribund House-Senate juvenile justice bill (HR 1501) to meet and send the bill back to the House with additional gun law enforcement and safety provisions. *(Vote 118, p. H-42)*

The action came as both sides prepared to go home April 14 for the spring recess for a flurry of meetings with constituents.

Despite months of battling over gun laws, advocates of gun control do not have much to show for their efforts. The gun-control provisions included in the Senate-passed version of the juvenile justice bill remain stuck in conference with no apparent way out of the logjam. The provisions would mandate child safety trigger locks on all handguns, ban the import of high capacity ammunition clips capable of holding more than 10 rounds, prohibit anyone convicted of a serious crime as a juvenile from ever owning a gun and prohibit juveniles from owning assault weapons. There is widespread agreement on those provisions.

There is less agreement on how rigorously to make background checks on gun purchasers at gun shows, specifically on how much time the seller would have to wait. Currently, no check is required at most gun shows. The Senate bill would apply background checks to purchasers of guns at shows at which 50 or more firearms are for sale, and would provide three business days to conduct the check.

House Judiciary Committee Chairman Henry J. Hyde, R-Ill., on April 12 sent a letter to President Clinton offering alternative language, though it seemed unlikely to break the impasse.

Hyde last year offered a compromise that would require a 24-hour background check. If that turned up an unresolved arrest that would disqualify the buyer from purchasing a gun, law enforcement officials would be given three business days to check out the buyer.

Hyde staff aides said that when Clinton called Hyde and others to the White House in March in an effort to get the conference moving, the president raised the issue of other kinds of problems that might arise regarding a purchaser's background, such as mental illness or allegations of domestic violence. In his April 12 offer, Hyde broadened the three-day provision to cover "purchasers who have red flags for other disqualifying offenses, like unlawful drug use, mental incapacity, dishonorable discharge, domestic violence or stalking."

Said Sam Stratman, a spokesman for Hyde: "Every issue raised by the president in the summit a month ago has been resolved." Hyde charged in the letter to Clinton that Democrats want gun control for use as a campaign issue more than they want a deal.

Project Exile

For their part, Democrats cried foul when Republicans brought up the so-called Project Exile bill (HR 4051) on April 11. The Judiciary Subcommittee on Crime held a hearing on it April 6, but the bill then moved directly to the floor, with no consideration by either the subcommittee or the full Judiciary panel.

The bill would authorize $100 million in grants over five years to states with tough gun sentencing laws, including a five-year mandatory minimum sentence for using a gun while committing a violent or serious drug-trafficking crime. Of that, $10 million would be available in the first year. So far, just six states would qualify.

The bill is modeled after the federal Project Exile pilot program in Richmond, Va., which mandates a five-year sentence for gun crimes. While many Democrats and judges oppose mandatory sentences as too inflexible, Republicans and others laud them as a way to get proven criminals off the streets for longer periods.

"In states and cities around the country where aggressive prosecution of gun crimes has been coupled with tough prison sentences, violent crime has gone down," said bill sponsor Bill McCollum, R-Fla., a candidate for the GOP nomination for the Senate seat to be vacated by Connie Mack, R-Fla., who is retiring.

John Conyers Jr. of Michigan, ranking Democrat on the Judiciary Committee, objected to the process. "I think it is a kind of way of getting political cover for us not taking action on the gun safety measures that are before us, because here the Republican leadership has aborted the normal legislative process."

Gun Control Vote Provokes Clash Over Management Of the Senate

MAY 20 — A long-simmering battle between Senate Democrats and Majority Leader Trent Lott, R-Miss., over GOP efforts to block votes on Democratic issues boiled over the week of May 15, halting work in the Senate and threatening to destroy comity for the year.

The latest round started May 16 when Minority Leader Tom Daschle, D-S.D., offered a non-binding, "sense of the Senate" amendment on gun control to a spending bill (S 2521) for military construction, the first fiscal 2001 appropriations bill to reach the floor. *(Military construction, p. 2-123)*

The move sparked an unusual display of parliamentary gymnastics as Lott tried unsuccessfully to spare his GOP colleagues from having to cast a politically difficult vote against gun control provisions.

Daschle ultimately prevailed, but only after Lott employed strong-arm parliamentary tactics May 17 that will allow him to block any future sense-of-the-Senate amendments on appropriations bills. That move, in turn, sparked an unusually heated exchange between Lott and Daschle over the way the Senate is being run.

"No majority leader in history has attempted to constrain Senate debate as aggressively as Sen. Lott has chosen to do," Daschle said. "I defy anybody to come to the floor to challenge that statement."

The infighting promises to have ramifications far beyond the substance of Daschle's amendment, which applauded the May 14 Million Mom March in Washington in support of gun control and called for inclusion of gun provisions and swift approval of HR 1501, a juvenile crime bill that is stalled in conference.

The vote affirmed Senate support for requiring new background checks at gun shows, a difficult vote for endangered Republicans such as Spencer Abraham, R-Mich. The Senate adopted the amendment, 50-49, with seven Republicans joining 43 Democrats in support. *(Vote 104, p. S-20)*

Daschle vowed to block Lott from taking up any spending bill until the Senate receives it from the House, a longstanding tradition. In recent years, the Senate often has gone first on some of the bills. Daschle's move threatens to bog down this year's appropriations cycle. But any such hardball tactics by Daschle could prompt Republicans to retaliate by refusing to vote on presidential nominees for federal judgeships.

Lott and Daschle have been wrangling over the minority party's ability to offer amendments that are unrelated to the subject at hand. Senate rules permit any member to offer any amendment to any bill except spending bills. The freewheeling rules have frustrated leaders for years.

So as soon as a bill hits the floor, Lott often moves to invoke cloture, which limits debate and bars non-germane amendments. Daschle invariably denies cloture, which requires 60 votes, by holding all 45 Democrats in line.

Another Lott tactic, especially on bills favored by Democrats, is to negotiate with Democrats to allow a limited roster of amendments or none at all. Democrats sometimes accept the limits as the cost of getting anything done.

Lott says he is merely trying to move the Senate along. "What it is really about is getting the work of the Senate done, dealing with real bills and real issues, not playing games," Lott said. "Somebody has to be charged with the responsibility of trying to get the process to move forward."

But many GOP senators and aides concede that Lott is taking extraordinary procedural steps to keep vulnerable Republicans from having to vote on difficult issues such as gun control or the minimum wage. "He is trying to protect his members," Daschle said.

Daschle said Lott would be less infuriating if he would allow Democratic amendments and then make non-debatable motions to table, or kill, them. Lott would prevail if he could hold 51 senators.

Parliamentary Maneuvering

When Daschle offered the gun control amendment May 16, Lott tried unsuccessfully to have the Senate declare it non-germane. But Daschle threatened Lott with a filibuster of the underlying spending bill, so Lott reluctantly agreed to a vote the next day.

The next day Lott stoked the battle with a procedural move that will prevent Democrats from offering other sense-of-the-Senate amendments to spending bills, broadening the existing rule that bans legislative amendments on such bills.

Lott tried to have his own gun amendment ruled out of order, and then forced a vote to reverse the parliamentarian's ruling that it was in order. The 45-54 vote rejected the ruling, thus establishing the precedent that sense-of-the-Senate amendments are not germane to spending bills. Lott's non-binding amendment to enforce gun laws was then adopted, 69-30. *(Votes 102, 103, p. S-20)*

Dispute Over Gun Provisions Brings Juvenile Justice Bill To a Standstill

JULY 15 — Pieces of a huge bill that would overhaul the juvenile justice system are breaking free and moving separately, a sure sign that members are abandoning hope that the underlying bill (HR 1501) will be enacted this year.

For example, the House passed legislation (HR 894) by voice vote July 11 that aims to punish states that do not give murderers, rapists and child molesters lengthy prison sentences. A measure (HR 2031) regulating the sale of alcohol on the Internet has passed the House, and its counterpart (S 577) is ready for Senate consideration. And a provision creating new federal judgeships has already become law. All of these were included in the mammoth juvenile justice bill in at least one chamber.

Many of the breakaway measures were separate bills initially that hitched a ride on the juvenile justice bill last year when it appeared to be moving fast. Now sponsors are seeking another way to get their measures to the president's desk.

"It's kind of like the crazy aunt in the attic that nobody wants to talk about," said Rep. Matt Salmon, R-Ariz. "Everybody knows that juvenile justice is not going anywhere."

The juvenile justice bill has been stuck in a House-Senate conference for more than a year. Conferees met only once, last August. Both the House and Senate versions of the bill would toughen penalties for teens who break the law, make it easier to try some juveniles as adults and provide state grants for prevention programs. None of those core provisions is moving separately.

Conference is the furthest the bill has gone in several attempts in recent years. In the 105th Congress, juvenile justice legislation passed the House but never made it to the Senate floor. *(1998 Almanac, p. 17-15)*

This year the measure is hung up over a set of gun restrictions that the Senate added to its version (S 254) following the April 1999 shooting at Colorado's Columbine High School, in which 15 people died.

The Senate bill would ban imports of magazines or clips that hold more than 10 bullets, require that all guns be sold with a child safety lock or storage device, bar juveniles who have been convicted of a violent crime from owning a handgun and broaden federal regulation of sales at gun shows.

It is the last provision that has proved to be the most intractable. As passed by the Senate, the provision would require a background check on anyone who wants to buy a weapon at a gun show where more than 50 firearms are for sale. It would allow three business days for such a check.

Opponents, including the National Rifle Association, have argued that three days is too long, in part because many gun shows last for only a weekend. Gun control supporters have said they will not accept any change to the Senate-passed language.

Asked if the juvenile justice bill was dead for the year, Senate Republican Policy Committee Chairman Larry E. Craig, R-Idaho, responded "sadly enough, it probably is." Craig strongly supported the juvenile justice provisions, though he fought hard to defeat the gun control language.

Aimee's Law

Salmon is the sponsor of HR 894, which he dubbed Aimee's Law.

Aimee Willard, a 22-year-old student at George Mason University in Virginia, was raped and killed in 1996 by a convicted murderer who had served 12 years of a life sentence before being released from jail in Nevada.

"Aimee Willard's death is not an isolated incident but part of a totally preventable crime epidemic, recidivist attacks by released convicted murderers, rapists and child molesters," said Salmon, who said about 14,000 such crimes occur annually.

As passed by the House, the bill would stipulate that states would be reimbursed for the cost of catching, prosecuting and incarcerating someone accused of murder, rape or child molestation if that person had been convicted in another state of a similar crime.

Under the bill, the attorney general would take the money from federal crime-fighting funds intended for the state that originally convicted the criminal and give it to the second state.

States would not be penalized if they had passed truth-in-sentencing laws, which require prisoners to serve at least 85 percent of their sentence, and if the sentence imposed for the crime was 10 percent more than the national average for that crime and the prisoner in question had served 85 percent or more of the sentence.

The measure also calls for a Justice Department report to Congress by March 1, 2001, on the annual scope of recidivism for rapists, murderers and child molesters.

While the bill has the strong support of victims' groups, such as Kids Safe and Childhelp USA, the National Governors Association and the National Conference of State Legislatures (NCSL) vehemently oppose it.

"Aimee's Law is worse than an unfunded mandate. Its retroactive application will pit one state against another and turn already limited law enforcement assistance funds into a superfund of sorts for clever state budget balancers," said Mike Lawlor, an NCSL vice chairman, in testimony May 11 to the House Judiciary Subcommittee on Crime.

Robert C. Scott, D-Va., one of two members to speak against the bill, said it would "simply allow members of Congress to take credit for passing a good sound bite and continue to avoid doing all of what the experts say will actually reduce crime, and that is investing in prevention and early intervention programs."

Scott also said the exemption for truth-in-sentencing states would protect about 30 states from losing their federal crime-fighting funds.

"The states that are doing a poor job keeping violent rapists, murderers and molesters off the streets, they will be affected," responded Salmon. "And, of course, their bureaucrats do not like that. They do not want to have any kind of comeuppance. They do not want to be responsible. At the end of the day, though, we have a responsibility to protect our neighborhoods."

The House passed the bill by voice vote. When the House added Aimee's Law to the juvenile justice bill last year, the amendment was adopted, 412-15. The Senate amendment was adopted, 81-17.

It is not clear when, or if, Salmon's bill will come up on the crowded Senate calendar. Though it passed overwhelmingly, some senators said they had concerns about the details that had to be worked out.

The Justice Department also has concerns. In a May 10 letter to Scott, Assistant Attorney General Robert Raben wrote that, while the bill is "well intended, the Department has numerous concerns . . . [including] significant enforcement challenges."

Salmon, who took a term-limits pledge and is retiring at the end of this Congress, knows that this is his last chance. He is working hard to see the bill through.

Internet, Alcohol and Judges

Another bill looking for room on the Senate calendar is a measure (S 577), sponsored by Judiciary Chairman Orrin G. Hatch, R-Utah, to help states regulate the sale of alcohol on the Internet. It also was part of the Senate-passed juvenile justice bill.

The Senate Judiciary Committee approved the alcohol bill by voice vote March 2. It would allow states to seek federal injunctions to enforce state liquor laws.

Many states limit or ban direct shipment of alcohol across their borders, forcing alcohol producers to go through wholesalers who then sell to retailers. But the advent of the Internet has allowed some smaller alcohol producers to get around state laws by selling directly to customers. The House passed a similar measure (HR 2031) last year.

Hatch and ranking Judiciary panel Democrat Patrick J. Leahy of Vermont joined together to offer an Internet filtering amendment — virtually identical to a provision in the Senate juvenile justice bill — to the fiscal 2001 appropriations bill (HR 4577) for the departments of Labor, Health and Human Services and Education. *(Labor-HHS-Education, p. 2-97)*

The amendment, which would require Internet service providers to offer their customers access to filtering or screening software, was adopted by voice vote.

Another provision of the juvenile justice bill has already become law. Language creating nine new district court judgeships — three for Arizona, four for Florida and two for Nevada — was included in the fiscal 2000 omnibus appropriations bill (PL 106-113).

Other provisions from the juvenile justice measure are being readied for House consideration.

Rep. Mark Green, R-Wis., for example, introduced legislation (HR 4047) in March that would require a sentence of life in prison for repeat child molesters. Rep. Randy "Duke" Cunningham, R-Calif., has introduced a bill (HR 4045) that would require enhanced penalties and allow the FBI to get involved if a crime involved a child under 13.

GOP Senate candidate Rep. Bill McCollum, R-Fla., held a hearing on both measures in his Crime Subcommittee on May 11. ◆

Anti-Crime Package Seeks To Protect Women and Children From Violence

Box Score

- **Bill:** HR 3244 — PL 106-386
- **Legislative action: House** adopted the conference report on HR 3244 (H Rept 106-939), 371-1, on Oct. 6.

Senate cleared the bill, 95-0, on Oct. 11.

President signed the bill Oct. 28.

SUMMARY

An anti-crime package assembled late in the session and signed into law Oct. 28 reauthorized the popular Violence Against Women Act and launched a new effort to combat international slavery and sex trafficking.

The anti-crime legislation bundled a series of five bills into the conference report on HR 3244. In addition to the Violence Against Women Act (HR 1248) and the underlying sex trafficking act (HR 3244), the package included a bill on sexual predators (HR 894), tighter limits on the sale of alcohol over the Internet (HR 2031), and a measure to aid victims of international terrorism (HR 3485).

• **Sex trafficking.** This bill, which had been passed in slightly different forms by the House on May 9 and the Senate on July 27, authorized nearly $94.5 million over two years to combat trafficking and aid its victims.

The bill created a new federal crime for trafficking in persons, doubled the punishment to 20 years imprisonment for selling someone into slavery, and extended the penalty to related crimes.

The bill also created a new, non-immigrant "T" visa for up to 5,000 victims of trafficking per year. Victims who agree to cooperate with law enforcement and who face severe retribution in their home country are eligible. Under certain circumstances, victims could apply for permanent residency several years after receiving the T visa.

An estimated 50,000 people are brought into the United States each year hoping for a legitimate job only to become de facto slaves to their employers through prostitution or forced labor. Up to 2 million people around the world are victimized in this way each year.

• **Violence against women.** Reauthorization of the 1994 law (PL 103-322) had broad support. The House passed its version of the bill, 415-3, on Sept. 26 with strong backing from President Clinton.

The final bill authorized nearly $3.3 billion for a variety of grant programs designed to address domestic violence, date rape, stalking, and other crimes directed largely at women.

The authorization included $185 million a year for five years for a state grant program that coordinates the work of victim advocates, police and prosecutors in fighting domestic violence.

It also included $175 million a year for five years for grants to support shelters for battered women and children, and more than $15 million annually to aid victims of child abuse.

The bill also made changes to the underlying act, including making it easier for women to get enforcement of protective orders, and for battered immigrant women to call police and get help from government agencies without fear of deportation.

Several new grant programs were authorized, including a $40 million program to provide legal assistance to battered women, and $25 million for a one-year, transitional housing assistance program for women seeking to reconstruct their lives after leaving a shelter.

• **"Aimee's law."** This bill, the most controversial part of the package, was named after a George Mason University student who was raped and murdered in 1996 by a convicted killer who had been released from a Nevada prison. It was originally attached to the stalled juvenile justice measure (HR 1501).

Under the bill, states that fail to ensure that murderers, rapists or others convicted of "dangerous sexual offenses" serve stiff sentences can have their federal crime-fighting grants cut if a criminal commits an offense in another state after being released. The money would go to reimburse the second state for the cost of catching, prosecuting and incarcerating the criminal. (*Also see gun control, p. 15-15*)

Sen. Fred Thompson, R-Tenn., tried but failed to strip the provisions from the conference report, arguing that they were unconstitutional. Lawmakers reluctant to include Aimee's law warned that it violates states' rights and would likely be struck down by courts.

• **Internet alcohol sales.** These hard-fought provisions were designed to allow states to better enforce laws that ban interstate alcohol shipments in the face of growing Internet sales. The bill, originally incorporated in the juvenile justice bill, allows states to seek federal injunctions to enforce state liquor laws. However, it does not provide for civil or criminal penalties, or allow the awarding of attorneys' fees.

• **Aid to victims of terrorism.** The final piece of the package was designed to give the president greater authority to help victims of terrorism collect on court-won judgments against the sponsoring government. A 1996 anti-terrorism law (PL 104-132) enabled U.S. victims of state-sponsored terrorism to sue the government they believe responsible for damages.

Since then, victims have won judgments in court against governments such as those of Iran and Cuba, but they have not been able to collect, because any assets those countries have in the United States are controlled or frozen by the federal government. The bill allows the president to review each case independently and decide whether to pay the court judgments out of the blocked assets.

House Panel OKs Bill to Punish Human Trafficking, Assist Victims

APRIL 8 — The House Judiciary Committee approved legislation by voice vote April 4 that aims to crack down on the illegal trafficking of humans across international borders.

The International Relations Committee approved the bill (HR 3244) on Nov. 9, and the Banking and Financial Services panel has until April 14 to act on sections under its jurisdiction.

According to sponsor Christopher H. Smith, R-N.J., international trafficking in humans, for forced labor or the sex trade, is a growing problem. "Especially tragic is the fact that traffickers often escape severe punishment," Smith has said. "Existing law does not reflect the gravity of the offenses involved, and even the most brutal crimes are punished under laws that apply to far less serious crimes — if they are punished at all."

According to Smith, about 1 million people around the world cross national lines each year with the expectation of honest employment only to find themselves de facto slaves to their employers, usually working as prostitutes or in hard labor. Smith estimates that about 50,000 such people are brought into the United States each year.

The portion of the bill under Judiciary's jurisdiction would enhance penalties for trafficking crimes and create a special visa for victims of trafficking. The bill would double the maximum penalty — to 20 years — for those convicted of selling others into involuntary servitude or other trafficking crimes.

The visa, called a "T" visa, would be given to victims if they agreed to cooperate with law enforcement and faced a well-founded fear of retribution if they returned to their native country. Up to 5,000 T visas could be granted each year. After living in the United States for three years on this visa, the victim would be eligible for permanent residency status.

The committee approved by voice vote an amendment by Immigration Subcommittee Chairman Lamar Smith, R-Texas, and Charles T. Canady, R-Fla., to modify the standards for qualifying for a visa.

As approved, the bill would make anyone who was a victim of sex trafficking or involuntary servitude, and who was afraid of retribution, eligible for the visa. Children under 15 would qualify if they showed they were victims of trafficking. That is broader than the version approved by the subcommittee March 8. Under that version, only those who were 16 and younger and the victims of sex trafficking would have been eligible.

The committee rejected several amendments by Democrats that sought to broaden the categories of people eligible for the visas and the number of such visas to be given out each year.

The committee rejected, 14-16, an amendment by ranking Democrat John Conyers Jr. of Michigan that would have allowed the attorney general to lift the cap on T visas for humanitarian reasons. The committee also rejected, 14-16, an amendment by Sheila Jackson-Lee, D-Texas, that would have made it easier for victims' families to come to the United States.

House Passes Sanctions on Sex Trafficking

MAY 13 — Legislation that aims to combat international sex trafficking won House passage by voice vote May 9. An estimated 50,000 people are brought into the United States each year hoping for a legitimate job only to find themselves de facto slaves to their employers, either through prostitution or forced labor. Up to 2 million people are victimized by this trade around the world each year.

The bill (HR 3244) will now go to the Senate, where two similar bills (S 2414, S 2449) have been referred to the Foreign Relations Committee.

As passed by the House, HR 3244 would strengthen laws that prohibit trafficking in people and would create a "T" visa that would allow victims in particularly egregious cases who are brought into the United States to stay in the country instead of being deported.

"We cannot wait one more day to begin saving these millions of women and children who are forced every day to submit to the most atrocious offenses against their persons and against their dignity as human beings," said bill sponsor Christopher H. Smith, R-N.J.

The Clinton administration supports many provisions of the bill, but it opposes a section that would require a cutoff of non-humanitarian aid to countries that did not adopt procedures laid out in the bill to reduce trafficking by fiscal 2002.

Though the bill would allow the president to waive the cutoff for national security reasons, the administration argues that it would "have a debilitating effect on the fight against trafficking," according to a May 9 statement.

Republicans defended the provision as a tool to change the behavior of countries, particularly those in Southeast Asia and the former Soviet Union. "This threat should provide a powerful incentive to nations with a trafficking problem to meet the minimum standards," said Benjamin A. Gilman, R-N.Y., chairman of the House International Relations Committee.

The administration also objects that the conditions that victims of trafficking would have to meet to qualify for a T visa are too restrictive.

Victims would have to show that they were in the country as a direct result of trafficking, that they did not agree to their servitude, and that they had a "well-founded fear of retribution" if they were forced to leave the United States. Up to 5,000 of these T visas could be issued annually. The Justice Department also would be authorized to give visas to the victim's immediate family, parents if the victim was under 21, or spouse and children. After three years, visa holders would be eligible for permanent residency.

The restrictions on the visa were included at the request of Judiciary Committee members, who feared that earlier versions of the visa would have invited fraud.

The bill would double to up to 20 years the penalty for various sex trafficking crimes, such as selling a person into involuntary servitude. It would make the sex trafficking of children a federal crime, punishable by life in prison.

The bill would authorize $95 million over two years for programs to combat trafficking, treat and counsel victims, and monitor the situation.

House Panel Votes To Reauthorize Grant Programs To Protect Women

MAY 13 — The House Judiciary Subcommittee on Crime approved legislation by voice vote May 11 that would reauthorize federal grant programs designed to combat violence against women.

The bill (HR 1248), by Constance A. Morella, R-Md., would reauthorize a section of the 1994 omnibus anti-crime bill (PL 103-322) known as the Violence Against Women Act. The act made federal crimes of interstate stalking and interstate domestic abuse, and strengthened penalties for repeat sex offenders.

The law also created grant programs, administered by the Justice Department's Violence Against Women Office, that provide funds to state and local entities for shelters for battered women, rape crisis centers and related programs.

Morella is not a member of the Judiciary panel but was permitted to speak at the markup. "My presence here is just to emphasize that the Violence Against Women Act . . . has made a tremendous difference" for abused women and children, she said.

As an example, she cited a hotline for domestic violence, created by the 1994 law, that gets about 13,000 calls a month. Operators can answer questions in dozens of languages.

The committee approved by voice vote an amendment by Anthony Weiner, D-N.Y., and Steve Chabot, R-Ohio, that would require some funds to be used to hire nurses with specialized training in how to treat evidence collected from victims of rape and other sexual assaults. The nurses would be available in hospitals 24 hours a day. Weiner said that evidence collected improperly can weaken a case against an alleged rapist.

Under the 1994 bill, states seeking to qualify for funds were required to pay for medical exams for rape victims and to stop requiring victims of domestic violence to pay court fees for filing charges.

According to testimony last fall by Bonnie J. Campbell, director of the Violence Against Women Office, all 50 states and the District of Columbia now pay for the medical exams and mandate HIV testing for convicted sex offenders.

Subcommittee Chairman Bill McCollum, R-Fla., noted that since 1994, Congress has appropriated $700 million for all grant programs in the act, including $270 million for fiscal 2000.

The bill, which has 178 cosponsors, would authorize $1 billion over five years for family violence prevention programs, including shelters for battered women. It also would authorize $185 million a year in fiscal 2001 through 2003 and $195 million in fiscal 2004 for grants for law enforcement and prosecution.

Not under consideration is a section of the 1994 law now under scrutiny by the Supreme Court, which heard arguments in January about a provision that allows victims of gender-motivated crimes to sue their attackers in federal court to recover damages. The question is whether the provision is constitutional under Congress' authority to regulate interstate commerce. It is permanent law and does not need to be reauthorized.

High Court Rules Against Portion of Violence Against Women Act

MAY 20 — The Supreme Court's May 15 decision striking down part of the 1994 Violence Against Women Act continues a pattern by the court's conservative majority of drawing sharp, new limits on congressional power.

The court, ruling 5-4 in *United States v. Morrison*, held that Congress exceeded its authority in a section of the law that allowed women who were victims of gender-motivated violence, such as rape, to sue their attackers in federal court. The court said the law intruded on states' power to regulate crime.

Congress included the provision in a broader initiative to curb violence against women. Other provisions of the law (PL 103-322), including an anti-stalking statute, were not affected by the court's ruling. *(1994 Almanac, p. 273)*

The decision was a victory for the court's federalist majority — although dozens of states had sent briefs to the court in support of the law.

Lawmakers blasted the ruling, but most said they recognized that the broadly written decision precluded them from redrafting the provision to pass muster. Legislation (HR 1248) to reauthorize Violence Against Women grant programs is moving through Congress and could have provided a vehicle.

Sen. Joseph R. Biden Jr., D-Del., a prime sponsor of the 1994 act, said the decision shows that "the Supreme Court has become bolder and bolder in stripping the federal government of the ability to make decisions on behalf of the American people."

Biden said he could not figure out a way to rewrite the law to allow rape victims to circumvent the ruling. Asked by The Associated Press if there were any changes that could be made to make federal rape lawsuits legal, he replied: "Yes, two new justices."

The decision could provide ammunition for Democrats who are trying to use the court's makeup as an issue in the fall's presidential election. Three justices have been mentioned as potential near-term retirees: conservative Antonin Scalia, liberal John Paul Stevens and Sandra Day O'Connor, a moderate who tends to side with conservatives on federalism issues. Any new justice appointed by a new president could shift the balance on defining the boundaries of congressional power.

Defining Commerce

In writing the law, Congress relied on its constitutional authority to regulate interstate commerce and its 14th Amendment power to provide equal protection under the law. Writing for the majority, Chief Justice William H. Rehnquist held that Congress does not have the power under the commerce clause to regulate non-economic activity. "Gender-motivated crimes of violence are not, in any sense of the phrase, economic activity," he wrote.

The case involved Christy Brzonkala, who as a freshman at Virginia Polytechnic Institute in 1994 alleged that she was raped by two students, Antonio Morrison and James Crawford. Although the school determined that there was sufficient evidence to punish Morrison, it did not do so.

Brzonkala sued under the 1994 law. The 4th U.S. Circuit Court of Appeals, based in Richmond, threw out the lawsuit, arguing that the law exceeded congressional powers.

While Rehnquist was sensitive to the situation that had brought the case before the court, he said the victim needed to look closer to home for a solution. "If the allegations here are true, no civilized system of justice could fail to provide her a remedy. . . . But under our federal system that remedy must be provided by the Commonwealth of Virginia," he wrote.

Though Congress had assembled what dissenting Justice David H. Souter called a "mountain of data" about the interstate economic effects of violence against women, Rehnquist said the congressional finding was not persuasive. Quoting a previous decision, he wrote that "simply because Congress may conclude that a particular activity substantially affects interstate commerce does not necessarily make it so."

The quote was from a 1995 case, *United States v. Lopez*, in which the court, again by a 5-4 majority, struck down a federal law prohibiting possession of a gun within 1,000 feet of a school. *(1995 Almanac, p. 6-40)*

Rehnquist relied heavily on the court's reasoning in *Lopez* in the *Morrison* ruling. "The Constitution requires a distinction between what is truly national and what is truly local," he wrote. "The concern we expressed in *Lopez* that Congress might use the Commerce Clause to completely obliterate the Constitution's distinction between national and local authority seems well founded."

Rehnquist also found that Congress could not rely on its authority under the 14th Amendment because that protection applies only to states or "state actors," not to private individuals.

Joining Rehnquist in the majority were Justices O'Connor, Scalia, Anthony M. Kennedy and Clarence Thomas. Souter wrote the dissent, joined by Justices Stevens, Ruth Bader Ginsburg and Stephen G. Breyer.

Souter found that Congress had provided more than enough testimony and evidence, over four years of hearings, to justify finding an economic interstate interest in combating violence against women. "The fact of such a substantial effect is not an issue for the courts in the first instance, but for the Congress, whose institutional capacity for gathering evidence and taking testimony far exceeds ours," he wrote. "The sufficiency of the evidence before Congress to provide a rational basis for the finding cannot seriously be questioned."

He closed with a shot at the majority opinion: "All of this convinces me that today's ebb of the commerce power rests on error, and at the same time leads me to doubt that the majority's view will prove to be enduring law."

House Panel Backs Aid for Women Victims

JUNE 24 — The House Judiciary Committee voted June 21 to create a legal assistance program for female victims of violence to help them obtain protective orders and other help.

The committee approved the program by voice vote as an amendment to legislation (HR 1248) that would reauthorize grant programs under the 1994 Violence Against Women Act (PL 103-322). The Crime Subcommittee approved the bill May 11, and the Senate Judiciary Committee expects to consider its draft version of the measure the week of June 26. *(1994 Almanac, p. 273)*

The House Judiciary Committee did not complete work on HR 1248. Panel Chairman Henry J. Hyde, R-Ill., said the markup would continue June 27.

The bill would reauthorize the grant programs in the 1994 law, including grants to state and local governments to expand prosecution of violent crimes against women and money for shelters for battered women and children.

The bill would authorize more than $3 billion over five years, more than double the authorization in the original bill. The House Appropriations Committee included $284 million for such programs in its fiscal 2001 spending bill (HR 4690) for the departments of Commerce, Justice and State. *(CJS, p. 2-23)*

The legal aid amendment, offered by Asa Hutchinson, R-Ark., would authorize $225 million over five years. The money, to be given as grants to nonprofits and other groups, could be used to help women obtain protective orders or deal with immigration or housing problems. The funds could not be used to help a woman obtain an abortion. The committee rejected attempts by Democrats to delete or narrow this restriction.

The committee also approved by voice vote an amendment by Crime panel Chairman Bill McCollum, R-Fla., to establish a $30 million, two-year pilot program aimed at protecting children during visits with a parent who has been accused of domestic violence.

Reauthorization Bills Ready for Floor Action

JULY 1 — Bills that would reauthorize the grant programs of the Violence Against Women Act of 1994 (PL 103-322) stand ready for floor action in both chambers.

Democrats and Republicans are eager to reauthorize the popular programs, which provide grants to states and private organizations to target crimes against women, from beefing up law enforcement to expanding shelter space available for women fleeing abusers.

Members tout the grant programs as one of the true success stories of the 1994 omnibus anti-crime law. *(1994 Almanac, p. 273)*

Funding for the grants has provided shelter space for more than 300,000 women and children each year, according to Senate Judiciary Committee Chairman Orrin G. Hatch, R-Utah. And the Justice Department estimates that violence against women committed by intimate partners has decreased by 21 percent since passage of the law.

The House and Senate Judiciary committees approved five-year reauthorizations the week of June 26. The

House panel approved its bill (HR 1248) by voice vote June 27. The Senate committee voted 17-0 for its bill (S 2787) on June 29.

Both measures would authorize more than $3 billion over five years for the grant programs. They would create a new temporary housing grant program that would provide funding to help women move out of shelters and into their own homes.

The bills also would authorize a new grant program for legal assistance to women who have been victims of violence, to help in obtaining protective orders, for example. And both bills prohibit any of those funds from being used in lawsuits involving abortion.

The one major difference between the two bills deals with immigration. The Senate bill would make it easier for battered immigrant women to leave their abusers and help in their prosecution, without fear of deportation. The House bill does not include similar provisions.

The Senate Judiciary Committee markup saw virtually no debate and no amendments. Hatch and the panel's ranking Democrat, Patrick J. Leahy of Vermont, had told their members not to offer amendments to speed committee consideration of the bill. Instead, they were urged to save changes for the floor.

Jon Kyl, R-Ariz., reluctantly agreed to hold an amendment he wanted to offer that would require states to inform colleges, along with local police, when a convicted sex offender moved into a neighborhood. "Too much of our work is done behind closed doors," he said about the agreement not to offer amendments.

The House markup of the bill lasted two days, spread over two weeks, and it was more contentious. The Judiciary panel rejected attempts by Democrats to broaden the bill's scope and establish new federal crimes.

The committee rejected, 8-13, an amendment by ranking Democrat John Conyers Jr. of Michigan that would have required states seeking the bill's funds to pass laws allowing victims of gender-motivated violence to sue for damages in state court.

It was an attempt by Democrats to get around a recent Supreme Court decision, *United States v. Morrison*, that struck down the portion of the 1994 law that allowed victims to sue their attackers for damages in federal court. The court ruled that Congress did not have the authority to open federal courts to these kinds of suits.

Conyers said it was one way of "fixing" the law to comply with the Supreme Court decision, which said that state courts were the proper forum for the lawsuits.

Bill McCollum, R-Fla., chairman of the House Judiciary Subcommittee on Crime, said he agreed with the thrust of the amendment but was concerned that it conditioned too many of the grants on a change in state law. Conyers agreed but said, "It was the only way we could think of to highly motivate the states."

Republicans used a parliamentary move to block Democrats from offering an amendment to broaden the definition of hate crimes to include those based on gender, sexual orientation or disability. The Senate on June 20 adopted similar language as an amendment to the fiscal 2001 defense authorization bill (S 2549).

The House committee adopted several amendments to allow grant funds to be used to aid specific populations or meet needs not anticipated in the 1994 law.

It adopted by voice vote an amendment by Tammy Baldwin, D-Wis., that would authorize grants aimed at helping disabled women who are victims of violence. The amendment would authorize $10 million a year for such grants. A similar provision is included in the Senate bill.

The committee also adopted by voice vote an amendment by Conyers that would allow states to use grants to improve reporting of domestic violence incidents to the National Instant Criminal Background Check System. People convicted of domestic abuse are prohibited from owning guns. The check system is supposed to alert gun sellers that a potential buyer is not eligible.

Senate Passes Bill To Combat Sex Trafficking

JULY 29 — The Senate on July 27 passed a bipartisan bill aimed at combating international sex trafficking. The measure (HR 3244), passed by voice vote, must now be reconciled with a version passed by the House on May 9.

About 50,000 women and children are brought illegally into the United States each year, with many forced into the sex trade or other jobs under the threat of deportation or retribution from their traffickers.

Like the House version, the Senate bill would create a "T" visa for trafficking victims who agreed to cooperate with law enforcement, and for those who faced a well-founded fear of retribution if they returned to their native country. The attorney general could adjust the immigration status to allow victims to stay in the United States permanently.

The bill would strengthen existing criminal penalties and criminalize all forms of trafficking in persons. It calls for life imprisonment for cases resulting in death or involving kidnapping, aggravated sexual abuse, or an attempt to kill, as well as for sex trafficking in victims younger than 14 years old.

The measure would require expanded reporting on trafficking, including a separate list in the annual State Department human rights report showing countries that are not meeting minimum standards for eliminating the practice. The president would be authorized, but not required, to suspend assistance to the worst violators.

Both the House and Senate versions would authorize $94.5 million over two years.

House Passes Bill Reauthorizing Programs to Help Battered Women

SEPTEMBER 30 — Programs to aid battered women and to prosecute their tormentors would be authorized for five more years under legislation passed overwhelmingly by the House on Sept. 26. *(Vote 491, p. H-154)*

The measure (HR 1248) would reauthorize grant programs under the 1994 Violence Against Women Act (PL 103-322). The legislation would extend funding through fiscal 2005 and create several programs designed to curb violence against women.

President Clinton has urged the bill's passage, which is seen to have critical political importance in the upcoming elections.

A companion measure (S 2787) has been approved by the Senate Judiciary Committee but has not reached the floor. A key difference between the House and Senate versions is that the Senate bill contains a provision making it easier for battered immigrant women to report abuse without fear of deportation; the House bill does not.

Advocates for the reauthorization say a compromise is likely to be attached to a spending bill.

The House measure would reauthorize several programs to help battered women, support investigations of criminals who cross state lines to commit domestic violence and provide hotline services for women.

The bill would authorize $185 million annually for fiscal 2001 through fiscal 2003 and $195 million for fiscal 2004 and 2005. Money would be divided among law enforcement, prosecutors, victim services and court grants. Nine months into each fiscal year, unused money from other areas would be transferred to victim services programs.

Domestic violence "continues to be a serious national problem that takes various forms, including domestic battery, stalking, rape and murder," said House Judiciary Committee Chairman Henry J. Hyde, R-Ill. "This legislation strengthens the ability of local communities to respond effectively to such crimes."

The House bill focuses on strengthening state court programs, improving training of forensic nurse examiners who deal with victims of domestic violence, and awarding grants to coordinate victim services between states.

The bill excludes a provision that would allow rape victims to sue their attackers in federal court. Last May, the Supreme Court struck down that provision in the 1994 law, saying the issue belonged in state rather than federal jurisdiction. *(1994 Almanac, p. 273)*

States would be allowed to use the grants to improve their reporting of domestic violence records to the National Instant Criminal Background Check System, which is designed to keep guns out of the hands of those who are not allowed to own them.

Constance A. Morella, R-Md., the bill's sponsor, said the federal government has an important role in helping to pay for local programs aimed at protecting women.

House Adopts Conference Report On Anti-Crime Package

OCTOBER 7 — The House endorsed legislation Oct. 6 that would reauthorize the popular Violence Against Women Act and launch a new effort to combat international slavery and sex trafficking. The Senate may take up the bill the week of Oct. 9.

The conference report (HR 3244) debated by the House was really a series of five bills bundled together, including "Aimee's Law," regarding sexual predators; a ban on the sale of alcohol over the Internet; and a measure to aid victims of international terrorism. The House passed the measure 371-1. *(Vote 518, p. H-164)*

President Clinton was expected to sign the conference report, if the Senate clears it, despite earlier objections to the victims of terrorism measure.

Carolyn B. Maloney, D-N.Y., praised the domestic violence provision, saying it "has been and must remain a powerful tool in the fight against domestic violence, stalking and sexual assault."

The underlying bill aims to end the trafficking of persons (mostly women and children) into the international sex trade, slavery and forced labor.

"This will be a giant, landmark, sweeping win for victims," said Rep. Christopher H. Smith, R-N.J. "This will help so many women. It doesn't come a moment too soon."

Smith, who sponsored the trafficking bill, had been eager to marry his measure with legislation (HR 1248) already passed by the House that would fund programs to aid battered women.

The domestic violence bill, which would reauthorize grant programs under the 1994 Violence Against Women Act (PL 103-322), passed the House on Sept. 26 with only three dissenting votes. But a companion measure (S 2787) never passed the Senate.

Clinton used the Oct. 2 proclamation of October as National Domestic Violence Awareness Month to urge passage of the Violence Against Women Act, "so we may continue to build on the progress we have made in combating domestic violence in our nation."

The measure would authorize more than $3 billion over the next five years for programs to combat violence against women, including battered women's shelters and services, sexual assault prevention programs, and education and training for judges.

The sex trafficking provisions of the conference report would authorize $94.5 million over two years to work with other countries to stop international sex trafficking.

It would also establish a new "T" visa for victims of trafficking who agreed to cooperate with law enforcement. And it would make victims of sex trafficking or involuntary servitude who were afraid of retribution in their home country eligible for the visa.

The measure would place an annual cap of 5,000 on the number of T visa holders who would be eligible to adjust their status to lawful permanent residence. The measure would also limit the number of non-immigrant visas to 5,000 a year.

According to Smith, many people are smuggled into the United States and forced into the sex trade or other jobs under the threat of deportation or retribution from their traffickers.

The conference agreement would require the State Department to submit to Congress an annual report on the status of international trafficking. Beginning in fiscal 2003, the president would have to withhold non-humanitarian and non-trade related U.S. foreign assistance to governments that failed to meet certain standards and failed to make significant efforts to comply. The president would be able to waive the requirement in cases of national security.

Also included in the conference agreement is legislation that would grant state attorneys general authority to use federal courts to make other states enforce their own laws on Internet alcohol sales when the alcohol was shipped across state lines.

The provision is similar to House-passed legislation (HR 2031), and to provisions in the Senate's version of the juvenile justice bill (HR 1501). Many states limit or ban direct shipment of alcohol across their borders, forcing alcohol producers to go through wholesalers. The proposal targets small alcohol producers who violate these laws by shipping directly to consumers, primarily through the Internet.

In addition, the conference report includes language similar to a House-passed bill (HR 894) under which any state that prematurely released a convicted murderer, rapist or child molester from prison would be required to pay the cost of apprehending, prosecuting and jailing him if he later committed the same crime in another state. The measure is dubbed "Aimee's Law" after a 22-year-old woman who was raped and murdered in Philadelphia by a convicted killer released from a Nevada prison.

Finally, the conference agreement includes provisions to allow victims of terrorism, or their families in the United States, to recover judgements against countries listed by the State Department as sponsors of terrorism.

Under the legislation (HR 3485), federal courts could allow damages to terrorist victims and their families, using the frozen assets of countries suspected of supporting terrorism.

Senate Clears Package Of Anti-Crime Initiatives

OCTOBER 14 — Congress completed action the week of Oct. 9 on an election year staple — a crime bill.

Using traditional end-of-the-session horse trading, members of the judiciary committees in both chambers fashioned a bill carrying anti-crime provisions previously included in five other measures. Most had passed the House in some form, and many had seen action on the Senate floor.

But the final bill, which the Senate cleared on Oct. 11 by an overwhelming vote of 95-0 and which is expected to be signed by President Clinton, is not without controversy. *(Vote 269, p. S-48)*

One of the bill's chief elements — which is known as "Aimee's law" and would make states "accountable" for the sentences they had imposed if violent criminals who had been released committed new crimes in other states — is considered likely to face tough constitutional questions.

Still, the overall bill (HR 3244) has been hailed for its provisions on sex trafficking and the reauthorization of the 1994 Violence Against Women Act (PL 103-322).

Sen. Joseph R. Biden Jr., D-Del., a sponsor of the 1994 law that authorized grant money to prevent domestic crime, said he saw an opportunity to get the reauthorization of those programs through Congress when the sex trafficking bill emerged from a House-Senate conference. He blocked that conference report from proceeding without the anti-violence grant bill, with the support of most Democrats and some Republicans.

Senate Judiciary Committee Chairman Orrin G. Hatch, R-Utah, said Rick Santorum, R-Pa., had then insisted that Aimee's law be included in the package, a move Rep. Matt Salmon, R-Ariz., also had been pushing. At the same time, Hatch was leading the fight to include a law that would allow states to use federal courts to enforce state laws on alcohol sales, while Sen. Connie Mack, R-Fla., and Rep. Bill McCollum, R-Fla., pushed to add a measure that would make it easier for the victims of international terrorism to sue for damages.

In the end, Hatch said the combination represented an "end-of-session accommodation" for all the interested parties. The House adopted the conference report by an overwhelming 371-1 vote on Oct. 6.

Violence Against Women

"We're changing the attitudes of America about what constitutes proper behavior," Biden said of the violence against women law, noting that violent crime against women had dropped significantly since the 1994 bill passed.

The new bill, which Clinton has touted, would authorize nearly $3.3 billion for a variety of grant programs that are designed to address domestic violence and other crimes directed largely at women. The bill would authorize $185 million a year for five years for a state grant program designed to coordinate the work of victim advocates, police and prosecutors in the fight against domestic violence.

It also would authorize $175 million a year through fiscal 2005 for grants to communities to support shelters for battered women and children. Several grant programs to aid victims of child abuse would be authorized at more than $15 million annually.

The bill also would make several changes to the underlying act, including making it easier for women to get enforcement of protective orders, even when the order was issued in a state different from the one where it would be enforced.

Additionally, it would make it easier for battered immigrant women to call police and get help from government agencies without fear of deportation. The bill also would authorize new programs designed to reach out to older women and women with disabilities who are the victims of violence.

The bill would require states to honor one another's court orders on child support and child custody, as well. It also would broaden the definition of stalking to include "cyber-stalking," harassment done through e-mail or other electronic means.

The bill would broaden the circumstances for using some of the grant money, allowing it to be used for crimes such as date rape as well as domestic violence.

Several new grant programs would be authorized. They include a $40 million annual program to provide legal assistance to battered women, and a $25 million, one-year, transitional housing assistance program for women seeking to re-establish their lives after leaving a shelter.

Sex Trafficking

The other major part of the bill would create a new federal crime for trafficking in persons. While current law already prohibits slavery and the sale of persons into slavery, the bill would extend that prohibition to a variety of activities that make up "trafficking." Those include the forced transportation of persons across a country's borders or coercing or threatening others into service.

The bill would authorize nearly $94.5 million over two years to combat trafficking and aid its victims.

According to Sen. Sam Brownback, R-Kansas, one of the bill's sponsors, more than 700,000 women and children annually are transported across borders and forced into prostitution.

"Trafficking is the new slavery of the world," he said. "Worldwide, trafficking nets at least $7 billion per year, exceeded only by the international drug and arms trade."

The bill would double to 20 years imprisonment the punishment for selling someone into slavery, as well as for other similar crimes.

It also would create a new, non-immigrant, "T" visa for up to 5,000 victims of trafficking per year. To be eligible for the visa, victims would have to show they would suffer extreme hardship involving unusual or severe harm. If the victims could meet certain criteria, they could be eligible to adjust their status and apply for permanent residency several years after receiving the "T" visa.

The bill also would require the president, in some limited circumstances, to withhold non-humanitarian foreign aid to any country that was the origin of much of the human trafficking, and which the State Department decided had not met minimum standards for combating the trafficking. But it also contains several waivers of this provision, including a waiver the president could exercise for national security reasons.

Aimee's Law

The most controversial addition to the package was Aimee's law, named after Aimee Willard, a 22-year-old student at George Mason University in Virginia, who was raped and killed in 1996 by a convicted murderer who had served 12 years of a life sentence before being released from jail in Nevada.

Brownback said the provisions would "hold states accountable" for their decisions about when to release violent criminals.

States that did not ensure that murderers, rapists or others convicted of "dangerous sexual offenses" served stiff sentences could find their federal crime-fighting grants cut if a criminal committed an offense in another state after being released. The money would go to reimburse the second state for the cost of catching, prosecuting and incarcerating the criminal.

Salmon has said about 14,000 such crimes occur annually.

States would be penalized if the criminal did not serve at least 85 percent of the sentence, or if the average sentence for the crime in the state was below the national average.

The U.S. attorney general would take the money from federal crime-fighting funds intended for the state that originally convicted the criminal, and give it to the second state.

Two organizations that represent states vehemently opposed these provisions. "This is what we call feel-good, bad legislation," said Susan Parnas Frederick of the National Conference of State Legislatures. She said it was the first step in "the federalization of criminal law."

Sen. Fred Thompson, R-Tenn., tried to strip Aimee's law from the conference report. His motion failed, 90-5. *(Vote 268, p. S-48)*

"Everyone is scared to vote against it," said Frank Shafroth of the National Governors' Association.

He said he was told by members and staff not to waste too much time trying to defeat Aimee's law, because it had too much momentum.

"This is so unworkable and likely unconstitutional, we should just let it go, and let it get struck down by the courts," Shafroth said he was told.

The provisions of the bill would be retroactive, and would apply to any criminals a state had ever released, if they committed another crime. That could easily run afoul of the prohibition in the Constitution on retroactive punishment.

"I think the governors will find that they will have a fairly good chance" at winning that case, said Biden. Both Biden and Hatch said they questioned the provision's constitutionality, but Hatch said keeping Aimee's law in the final package was necessary to get the other portions through the Senate.

Liquor and Terrorism

The bill also includes hard-fought provisions designed to allow states to better enforce their laws on interstate alcohol shipments.

The rising popularity of the Internet has made it increasingly difficult for states that prohibit direct shipment of alcohol to consumers to enforce those laws. Although there is a 1935 federal law that prohibits the interstate shipment of alcohol in violation of state law, that law has no means of enforcement.

The bill would allow state attorneys general to go to federal court for an injunction to stop the shipments, if they had good reason to believe their state laws were being violated. But the new law would allow only injunctive relief — and the traditional threat of court sanction for violating the injunction. But the bill does not provide for penalties, either civil or criminal, or allow the awarding of attorneys' fees.

Hatch said that because of some of the provisions included in the final version of the bill, both the Wine Institute and the American Vintners Association no longer oppose it.

Finally, the bill includes language that is designed to give the president greater authority to help victims of state-sponsored terrorism collect on court-won judgments against the sponsoring government.

In the 1996 anti-terrorism law (PL 104-132), Congress gave American citizens or their families killed or injured by state-sponsored terrorism the ability to sue the government they believe responsible for damages.

Since then, a variety of cases have been brought against the governments of Iran and Cuba. And while the victims have won judgments in court, they have not been able to collect because any assets those countries have in the United States are controlled or frozen by the federal government.

The bill would allow the president to review each case independently and decide whether to pay the court judgments out of the blocked assets. And the language of the report makes it clear that Congress intends for the president to do so unless he seriously believes it will hurt national security. ◆

After Standoff, Conferees Cut Hate Crimes Provisions From Defense Authorization

SUMMARY

The Senate attempted for the second straight year to expand federal hate crimes law to include sexual orientation, gender and disability, but the initiative was dropped in conference. The Senate language, attached to the defense authorization bill, would have expanded both the definition of federal hate crimes and the government's jurisdiction to prosecute them.

In June, the Senate adopted an amendment by Edward M. Kennedy, D-Mass., to its version of the defense authorization bill (S 2549) that would have broadened the definition of hate crimes to include those committed because of the victim's gender, sexual orientation or disability. It also would have allowed prosecution of hate crimes even if no federally protected activities were involved. Currently, hate crimes are defined under a 1968 law (PL 90-284) as those motivated by the race, color, religion or national origin of the victim. The federal government is allowed to intervene and prosecute such crimes only if they occur on federal property or during specific protected activities, such as voting.

While the House did not vote on separate hate crimes legislation, members voted on Sept. 13 to instruct House conferees on the defense bill to accept the Senate language. The motion, while non-binding, expressed strong support in the House for an expansion of hate crimes law. President Clinton, who had sought such an expansion for some time, made enactment of the hate crimes language a top priority in the final days of his term. After a lengthy standoff, however, conferees dropped the provisions from the final version of the defense bill. In a last-ditch attempt, supporters tried to include the language in the fiscal 2001 Commerce Justice State spending bill but were unsuccessful.

Senate Votes To Expand Federal Hate Crimes

JUNE 24 — A House-Senate showdown on whether to expand the definition of federal hate crimes is expected later this year after the Senate adopted an amendment that would broaden such crimes to include those committed because of the victim's gender, sexual orientation or disability.

The Senate adopted the amendment June 20 by the surprisingly large margin of 57-42. *(Vote 136, p. S-26)*

Civil rights groups — especially gay rights groups — cheered the outcome, but the provision's fate is unclear. It is attached to the Senate's fiscal 2001 defense authorization bill (S 2549), which is bogged down on the floor. GOP leaders have repeatedly pushed it aside to allow the Senate to take up fiscal 2001 appropriations bills. *(Defense, p. 8-3)*

Besides adding to categories considered hate crimes — acts motivated by racial, religious or ethnic bias already are covered — the amendment would expand the federal government's jurisdiction to prosecute such crimes.

The House GOP leadership is unlikely to allow a similar vote in that chamber, so the fight over hate crimes will take place later this year in the conference on the defense bill. President Clinton supports the amendment and is expected to fight to keep it in the bill.

It is the second year in a row that the Senate has acted to expand federal hate crimes. Last year, members attached a similar amendment to the fiscal 2000 appropriations bill for the departments of Commerce, Justice and State, but it was dropped in conference.

"We are talking about what our country is really about, what steps we are prepared to take to make America America," said amendment sponsor Edward M. Kennedy, D-Mass. "Crimes based upon hatred and bigotry wound not only the individual, but they also wound and scar an entire community."

Republicans argued that there was no need for the amendment because hate crimes are not going unpunished.

"Before we make all hate crimes federal offenses, I believe we should provide assistance to the states and analyze whether our assumptions about what the states are doing, or are not doing, are valid," said Judiciary Committee Chairman Orrin G. Hatch, R-Utah.

Hatch sponsored a competing amendment that would not expand hate crimes but would authorize $5 million for grants to states and local governments to help cover the cost of prosecuting hate crimes and would mandate a federal study of the prevalence of hate crimes. It was adopted 50-49. *(Vote 135, p. S-26)*

One-Sided Debate

The outcome was sufficiently in doubt at midday June 20 that Democrats asked Vice President Al Gore to be on hand in case he was needed to break a tie. Gore canceled a planned presidential campaign stop in Iowa, flew to Washington and was in the chair to read the final tally on the Kennedy amendment. Key to victory was support from 13 Republicans. One Democrat, Robert C. Byrd of West Virginia, voted against the measure.

Gordon H. Smith, R-Ore., an amendment cosponsor, strongly urged Republican colleagues to overcome their objections to homosexuality. "Put down the stone and cast a vote

Box Score

- **Bills:** S 2549, HR 4205
- **Legislative action: Senate** on June 20 adopted, 57-42, a hate crimes amendment to its version of the defense authorization bill (S 2549).

House on Sept. 13 agreed, 232-192, to a motion to instruct conferees on the defense bill (HR 4205) to accept the Senate hate crimes amendment.

based on love. . . . Many will say that to legislate favorably towards a gay man is to legitimize homosexuality for our society," Smith said. "I used to have that feeling myself, but I do not any longer. I truly believe it is possible to object to gay marriage and yet come to the defense of a gay person when it comes to violence."

Several of the 13 Republicans who supported the amendment are in close re-election races, including William V. Roth Jr. of Delaware and Lincoln Chafee of Rhode Island. Conrad Burns of Montana switched votes on the floor to support the amendment. Burns is favored to win his race, and Chafee's seat leans Republican, according to Congressional Quarterly risk rankings. Roth's race has no clear favorite.

Although many Republicans were uncomfortable with the amendment, few except Hatch spoke against it. Forty-one voted against it. Republican Policy Committee Chairman Larry E. Craig of Idaho said many senators decided not to voice their objections because of the issue's sensitivity. "I think all of us are extremely concerned that we don't appear to be racist or prejudiced, because none of us are," he said.

Senate Majority Leader Trent Lott, R-Miss., ducked questions about why he opposed the amendment, finally saying: "I would prefer we not rush in here and start taking over state functions." States' rights was one argument against the plan. Some Republicans, as well as Byrd, also said it was unconstitutional.

The current federal hate crime law (PL 90-284), passed in 1968, allows federal prosecution of crimes that are based on the victim's race, color, religion or national origin. But the federal government can get involved only if the act occurs while the victim is on federal property or engaged in one of six federally protected activities, such as voting.

Kennedy's plan would broaden federal jurisdiction to cover most existing hate crimes by stipulating that the 13th Amendment, which eliminated slavery, allows the federal government to protect people from such crimes. The measure also would create a federal hate crime for acts of violence based on prejudice toward the victim's gender, sexual orientation or disability. It bases that federal right on the Constitution's commerce clause, which allows Congress to regulate interstate commerce.

However, the Supreme Court ruled in May in *United States v. Morrison* that there must be a substantial economic interest at stake for Congress to rely on commerce clause authority. Amendment supporters argued that because the provision would require that a link to interstate commerce be established for each case, it would pass constitutional muster.

House Vote for Hate Crimes Rider May Back Leaders Into Corner

SEPTEMBER 16 — A House vote in support of expanding federal hate crimes law may have been largely symbolic but could put Republican congressional leaders in a very real political bind.

The House voted 232-192 on Sept. 13 to instruct conferees on a fiscal 2001 defense authorization bill (S 2549) to accept an amendment, added in the Senate, that would broaden the federal hate crimes statute to include illegal acts committed because of a victim's gender, sexual orientation or disability. The motion is non-binding. By sending a clear signal of House support, however, the vote put additional pressure on conferees. *(Vote 471, p. H-146)*

"We understand that no act of Congress can ever outlaw bigoted thoughts," said House Minority Whip David E. Bonior, D-Mich. "But we also understand that, when hateful thoughts turn into hateful deeds, the Congress must act, and act decisively."

The Senate adopted the amendment by a strong vote of 57-42 on June 20. Conferees have yet to reach agreement on it and other issues in the underlying authorization measure.

House Majority Leader Dick Armey, R-Texas, indicated before the House vote that he thought the hate crimes language would be stripped from any final bill.

"I expect we'll drop that," he said. Armey and the rest of the House GOP leadership oppose the amendment, arguing that it is not needed because all crimes are hate crimes.

Many Republicans who supported the motion are in tight re-election races or swing districts and could face 30-second political ads saying they switched their position if they support a final defense bill without the hate crimes language.

Among Republicans who voted for the motion were Brian P. Bilbray and Steven T. Kuykendall of California and Charles Bass of New Hampshire, all in tough re-election races. Florida GOP Senate candidate Bill McCollum, chairman of the House Judiciary Crime Subcommittee, who is in a close fight with Democratic insurance commissioner Bill Nelson, also voted for it.

Pointing to opinion polls in favor of strengthening hate crimes laws, David M. Smith, communications director for the Human Rights Campaign, a gay and lesbian lobbying group, warned that the vote could resonate.

"If [the amendment is] thwarted by a few members of the GOP leadership, that will be a significant political issue," he said. The Human Rights Campaign political action committee has contributed nearly $1.7 million to congressional campaigns so far this cycle, with $1.4 million going to Democrats.

Double-Edged Issue

The issue is a double-edged sword for some lawmakers. While gay rights groups, growing in political clout, strongly support it, conservative organizations are adamantly opposed.

"We are issuing a warning to those who voted for this legislation: We will notify our 43,000 churches about your vote today, and Christians will remember this on Election Day," said Andrea Lafferty, executive director of the Traditional Values Coalition in a Sept. 12 statement.

The group has already gone after McCollum, who had announced before the vote that he would support expanding the hate crimes law.

House Armed Services Committee Chairman Floyd D. Spence, R-S.C., said he did not know whether the provision would be dropped and acknowledged the intense pressure on his colleagues. "I don't think the vote reflects the true feeling of people on the matter," he said. "A lot of people are worried about it politically."

President Clinton has made enactment of the hate crimes bill a top priority in the final days of his term. The same day the House voted to support the amendment, Clinton announced a new report on the frequency of hate crimes, which found that they may be seriously under-reported. He directed Attorney General Janet Reno to come up with a plan in the next four months to improve reporting.

"I don't think any of us believe we can ever root it out just by punishing people," Clinton said. "The most important thing is that we do have the tools we need to take a strong stand before these things spread even wider."

Federal vs. State

Currently, hate crimes are defined under a 1968 law (PL 90-284) as those motivated by the race, color, religion or national origin of the victim. The federal government is allowed to intervene and prosecute such crimes only if they occur on federal property or during one of six specific protected activities, such as voting.

Several recent murders, including the vicious beating death of gay college student Matthew Shepard in Wyoming, have ignited calls to broaden the law to protect other vulnerable groups.

As passed by the Senate, the hate crimes provision would add gender, sexual orientation and disability to the categories of groups already protected. It also would make it easier for the federal government to get involved in the prosecution of such crimes.

Republicans seized on the broadened jurisdiction as one reason they opposed the amendment.

"The question we need to ask as a member of Congress is, do we trust our states to deal with situations where people are assaulted in general and specifically where race, religion or sexual orientation is involved?" said Lindsey Graham, R-S.C. "If we do, we do not need this legislation."

Lawmakers who supported the motion said there was plenty of evidence to show that hate crimes are a national problem. They said the federal authority was intended to provide a backstop for state and local law enforcement, giving added help in prosecuting crimes that can be hard to prove.

Defense Bill Stalls Over Hate Crimes, Worker Payments

SEPTEMBER 23 — Conference negotiations on the fiscal 2001 defense authorization bill (HR 4205) remained stalled the week of Sept. 18 over such issues as compensation for nuclear weapons plant workers injured during the Cold War and an amendment that would expand federal hate crimes law.

Lawmakers hoped to finish the conference and vote on the report the week of Sept. 25. But conferees were unable to decide whether the hate crimes provision should remain in the legislation.

House Armed Services Committee Chairman Floyd D. Spence, R-S.C., predicted the issue would not stop Congress from sending an authorization bill to the president. The urgency for the measure has slowed since Clinton signed the defense appropriations bill (PL 106-259) into law.

"All of the sudden, hate crimes gets to be the biggest thing in the defense bill," Spence said.

The language would broaden the federal hate crimes statute to include illegal acts committed because of a victim's gender, sexual orientation or disability. The Senate adopted the provision as an amendment to its version of the bill. President Clinton has made expansion of the hate crimes law a priority. House Republican leaders oppose the amendment, but the House voted 232-192 on Sept. 13 for a nonbinding resolution to instruct conferees to accept the Senate language.

Spence and Senate Armed Services Committee Chairman John W. Warner, R-Va., said conferees also are struggling to resolve a handful of other issues, including an Energy Department proposal to compensate workers who were exposed to radiation and toxic chemicals during the Cold War.

Although there is widespread support in the House for compensation, its version of the defense bill contains no such provision. At a House Judiciary Subcommittee on Immigration and Claims hearing on the issue Sept. 21, Energy Secretary Bill Richardson joined eight lawmakers in urging the Judiciary Committee not to block action on the compensation provision.

"I just think it's very important that this becomes law this year," Richardson told reporters.

Conferees Drop Hate Crimes From Defense Bill

OCTOBER 7 — Efforts to broaden federal hate crimes laws to cover homosexuals and the disabled failed Oct. 5 when, after a lengthy standoff, conferees on the fiscal 2001 defense authorization (HR 4205) dropped the provision from the final version of their bill.

Supporters still held out hope it might be included in another bill during end-of-the-year negotiations with the White House, which strongly backs the hate crime provisions.

"I will continue to fight the Republican leadership in Congress to make sure that this important work gets done this year," President Clinton said in an Oct. 5 statement.

But the defense authorization bill was the most likely place for the provision to become law. The language was attached to the Senate bill by a bipartisan vote of 57-42 on June 20. While the GOP leadership in the House never allowed a vote on the legislation, that chamber voted 232-190 on Sept. 13 to instruct House conferees on the defense bill to accept the Senate language.

Republican leaders oppose the measure and said the vote was purely symbolic since motions to instruct are non-binding. Now that they have won the difficult fight to strip the provision from the defense authorization bill, according to a GOP leadership aide, it is very unlikely they will agree to add it to any other legislation.

Federal law (PL 90-284) defines a hate crime as one motivated by the victim's race, color, religion or national origin. The provision would have broadened that to include the victim's sexual orientation, disability or gender.

Winnie Stachelberg, political director of the Human Rights Campaign, the largest gay and lesbian lobbying group, warned, "This is not only bad policy, it is bad politics, and their irresponsible actions may cost the party in November." ◆

Bill to Federalize Asbestos Cases Pits GOP, Industry Against Democrats, Lawyers

SUMMARY

A hotly contested bill that would have federalized the compensation process for people exposed to asbestos was narrowly approved by the House Judiciary Committee in March but saw no further action.

With billions of settlement dollars at stake, neither side in the asbestos fight pulled punches during two weeks of Judiciary Committee consideration in March. Bill supporters, led by Republican Chairman Henry J. Hyde of Illinois, argued that trial lawyers were flooding the courts with claims for people who were not really sick, making it harder for those who had become ill from asbestos to get compensation.

Opponents of the bill called it a gift to asbestos companies, which spent millions lobbying for the bill's passage.

As approved by the committee, the bill would have required anyone who sought compensation from an asbestos company to first obtain a certificate from a new federal agency verifying that they suffered from one of a specific set of illnesses outlined in the bill. With the certificate, a person could choose an arbitration process or go to state or federal court.

The issue took on political overtones after a series of articles in the Seattle Post-Intelligencer detailed the suffering of people in the small mining town of Libby, Mont., population 2,700, where at least 192 people had died of asbestos-related illnesses and some 375 were sick.

Republican Sen. Conrad Burns of Montana, a cosponsor of the Senate bill, dropped his support after the Libby exposé. Despite the Judiciary Committee approval, House Republican leaders chose not to bring the bill to the floor and force their members to cast what could have been politically dangerous votes.

Both Chambers To Consider Rules For Asbestos Compensation

FEBRUARY 6 — The charges flying in a fight over a bill to rewrite the rules governing compensation for people exposed to asbestos may soon make the raucous presidential primaries look like a gentleman's debating society.

The bill (HR 1283), sponsored by House Judiciary Committee Chairman Henry J. Hyde, R-Ill., and set for a markup the week of Feb. 28, would federalize thousands of asbestos lawsuits filed against manufacturers and builders during the past 30 years. A companion Senate bill (S 758) was introduced by John Ashcroft, R-Mo. With billions of settlement dollars at issue, neither side is pulling any punches in attempting to sway lawmakers.

The legislation would set deadlines that aimed to speed up the processing of claims. It also caps punitive damages in asbestos cases and makes it harder to file lawsuits.

Bill supporters — mostly asbestos companies — argue that people who have become sick from exposure to asbestos are being held hostage by trial lawyers who improperly solicit cases and file fraudulent claims.

Trial lawyers disagree. "There have been millions of people who have become sick and died because of asbestos poisoning," said Carlton Carl, a spokesman for the Association of Trial Lawyers of America. He said companies "knowingly killed" people by withholding critical information about the dangers of asbestos.

The congressional fight is breaking down largely along party lines, with Republicans supporting efforts to consolidate asbestos litigation and most Democrats opposed.

The House Judiciary Committee is likely to approve the bill and send it to the House floor. But the prospects in the Senate are less clear, and Democrats are confident that President Clinton would react as he has to other attempts to rewrite civil litigation laws — with a veto threat.

The industry has fought hard to bring the bill before Congress. A recent series in the Seattle Post-Intelligencer on people suffering from asbestos exposure in a small Montana mining town has raised the issue's profile and strengthened lawyers' opposition to the measure. That series and a story in the Boston Globe led the Consumer Product Safety Commission to announce Feb. 16 that it was opening a nationwide investigation of asbestos in consumer products.

Deadly Fiber

Asbestos is a fibrous mineral that has been used in insulation and other products for nearly a century. It was a popular choice in shipyards, buildings and mines because it is nearly indestructible. But that virtue makes asbestos a killer. The fibers, once inhaled, lodge in the lungs and scar them, leading to several illnesses.

The most virulent is malignant mesothelioma, a cancer of the lining of the lung or abdomen. Doctors say almost all cases of the disease are caused by asbestos. Rep. Bruce F. Vento, D-Minn., announced Feb. 2 that he was retiring from Congress at the end of this session because he is suffering from the disease.

The fibers also cause asbestosis, a severe scarring of the lungs, and are suspects in diseases such as lung cancer and cancer of the larynx and stomach. Millions of workers have been exposed to asbestos over the years, resulting in decades of litigation with more to

Box Score

- **Bills:** HR 1283, S 758
- **Legislative action: House** Judiciary Committee approved HR 1283 (H Rept 106-782), 18-15, on March 16.

come: It can take up to 40 years for an illness to appear. There have been about 300,000 settlements, with 200,000 cases pending, industry officials said at a hearing in October. Trial lawyers say both figures are too low.

A key dispute between the lawyers and the companies revolves around people who have been exposed to asbestos and show signs of lung damage but no impairment so far. Lawyers argue that the impairment is a sign of impending disease and that victims must sue now to avoid statutes of limitations and to get restitution while the companies can still pay.

Asbestos companies and bill sponsors say that by winning awards for people who are not yet sick, lawyers are taking money away from those already suffering. They add that many people exposed to asbestos never develop a serious ailment.

Despite the acrimony, the two sides nearly reached a deal in 1997. Some asbestos companies established a fund of more than $1 billion to pay claimants and settle thousands of lawsuits. But in 1997 the Supreme Court, in *Amchem Products Inc. v. Windsor*, threw out the settlement on a technicality. In that case and in a 1999 case, *Ortiz v. Fibreboard*, the court called on Congress to craft a national solution. The "elephantine mass of asbestos cases . . . defies customary judicial administration and calls for national legislation," Associate Justice David H. Souter wrote for the majority.

Hyde's Bill

Hyde's original bill, introduced in 1999, met with strong opposition from trial lawyers, labor unions and consumer groups, who argued that it cut the risk for asbestos companies while making it more difficult for asbestos victims to make their case. On Feb. 14, Hyde unveiled a substitute, which supporters say answers many of those criticisms. The bill includes key changes but did not win over its critics.

The revised bill would create a large government clearinghouse, the Office of Asbestos Compensation, within the Justice Department. Its leader would be appointed by the president for a 10-year term, subject to Senate confirmation.

The office would be a required stop for anyone seeking restitution for an asbestos-related ailment. The office would issue a certificate to claimants who proved they had an ailment, verifying that the person was suffering from specific diseases related to asbestos exposure. Claimants could not proceed without the certificate.

The revised bill includes specific medical criteria for granting a certificate, and would limit claims by those not yet impaired to reimbursement of up to 80 percent for testing.

Once they got a certificate, claimants could choose between filing a lawsuit in state or federal court, or going through a settlement process created under the bill.

The bill would set deadlines that seek to speed up the process. And it addresses a concern of many asbestos victims: It would prohibit any state's statute of limitations from applying to asbestos-related diseases, because of the long latency period. It also would retain joint and several liability for asbestos companies, the legal doctrine that holds that all defendants in a suit are liable for all damages awarded.

The substitute bill still has many provisions to which trial lawyers object. A claimant could not pursue a case if no defendant was solvent, for example. Also, government doctors would certify the claimant's medical condition, but an asbestos company could fight the determination in court.

The revised bill would allow claimants to sue for punitive damages, as they can under current law, but it would cap punitive damages at three times the award for economic and non-economic damages. They are now uncapped.

The bill would authorize up to $250 million for the office for the first year and up to $150 million a year after that. It also would authorize $200 million annually to reimburse the cost of medical testing for some people exposed to asbestos but not yet suffering from a specific disease.

Full-Court Press

After the Amchem settlement fell apart, the industry looked to Congress for help. GAF Corp., based in Wayne, N.J., and other major asbestos companies have spent millions lobbying Congress. According to the Center for Responsive Politics, which monitors campaign funding and lobbying efforts, GAF spent $1.5 million on lobbying in 1998, the year that company officials helped write the bill. The company hired 29 lobbyists from five Washington firms to press its cause, the center said.

The campaign seemed to work. Hyde and Ashcroft introduced legislation, and Hyde got 77 cosponsors, including House Majority Leader Dick Armey, R-Texas, and Majority Whip Tom DeLay, R-Texas. Ashcroft's bill won the support of Senate Majority Leader Trent Lott, R-Miss., and Majority Whip Don Nickles, R-Okla. Several Democrats signed on to the bill, including Senate Judiciary members Charles E. Schumer of New York and Robert G. Torricelli of New Jersey.

A coalition of asbestos companies, led by GAF, formed the Coalition for Asbestos Resolution, which has deluged Capitol Hill publications with ads.

A two-page ad Feb. 10 in the Capitol Hill newspaper Roll Call put the case this way: "In order to assure themselves of a never ending supply of asbestos cases, asbestos lawyers engage in improper practices with regard to the solicitation and filing of hundreds of thousands of non-sick cases, collaborating with corrupt mass screening companies and doctors to generate fraudulent medical test results to 'support' these filings."

Bill supporters also arranged a letter-writing campaign to members —and to avoid a stack of letters that all looked the same, the group came up with several letters in different type faces.

But wrenching stories in the Seattle Post-Intelligencer, beginning Nov. 18, may have pushed the bill off the fast track. The stories detailed suffering in Libby, Mont., a town of 2,700 in the northwest corner of the state. The newspaper's investigation found that at least 192 people had died of asbestos-related diseases and that 375 were sick. It turned out that as part of operations at a mine three miles east of town, workers had dug up tremolite asbestos, a particularly hazardous form of the mineral. The mine closed in 1990, but with the potential 40-year latency period, the people of Libby may feel repercussions in 2030.

More recently, the Boston Globe discovered that Zolonite Attic Insulation, a type of insulation widely used in houses, came from the Libby mine and contained tremolite asbestos. The Environmental Protection Agency recently warned homeowners not to handle the insulation.

The fallout from the stories has put pressure on some members. Sen. Conrad Burns, R-Mont., who is up for reelection this year and is favored to win, signed on to Ashcroft's bill before the Libby series.

Since the revelations, the group Montanans for Common Sense Mining Laws has launched a television ad campaign against Burns, attacking his support for the bill. A spokesman for Burns said the senator generally supports the Hyde revisions but wants to be sure the bill would help the people of Libby. Meanwhile, one of Burns' Democratic opponents, farmer-rancher Brian Schweitzer, has been hitting him hard on the asbestos issue.

There are signs that some companies want to work things out on their own. Owens Corning, based in Toledo, Ohio, has reached a settlement deal with more than 80 law firms, covering about 215,000 claims. The company will pay out about $2.5 billion over the next five years, in addition to the $2.7 billion already paid to asbestos victims.

In a statement to the House Judiciary Committee last July, Owens Corning Senior Vice President Maura J. Abeln said the legislation before Congress would not get to the heart of the problem as a settlement would. "The real problem faced by asbestos victims and companies alike is that there is not enough money available today to pay all of the pending and future claims unless there are cash flow and cash management tools negotiated by the parties," she said.

Asbestos Bill's Racial Aspect Halts Progress

MARCH 11 — Personal and political attacks — including charges of "racial profiling" — dominated the first day of committee action March 9 on a broad bill (HR 1283) to revamp the way people are compensated for injuries resulting from exposure to asbestos. They foreshadowed a difficult future for the controversial measure.

After more than an hour of bickering between House Judiciary Committee Chairman Henry J. Hyde, R-Ill., and ranking panel Democrat John Conyers Jr. of Michigan, the committee adjourned until March 14 to resume consideration of the bill.

Dozens of amendments — some aides estimated close to 100 — are expected to be offered during the markup, which could take as long as a week, aides said.

The bill, sponsored by Hyde, aims to speed up the processing of lawsuits filed by hundreds of thousands of people who claim they have been been harmed by exposure to asbestos. The measure, supported mostly by Republicans and asbestos companies, would create a government agency to certify that claimants were harmed by exposure. Victims could then choose between filing a lawsuit in state or federal court, or going through a settlement process that would be created under the bill.

During the opening day of committee action, Conyers called the bill "mean-spirited" and said its medical criteria for claims would deny compensation to tens of thousands of victims. He said the bill would "once again demonstrate the difference between our two parties."

Conyers focused his attacks on what he described as "racial profiling" in the bill. He said the bill contains references to medical studies that say African-Americans generally have lower lung capacity than whites. If such medical criteria were used in determining lung damage from asbestos, blacks would "face a higher bar" in winning their legal claims for compensation, Conyers said. "I thought this type of discriminatory thinking went out in the 1960s," he said.

Hyde said his bill did not contain racial references, and attacked Conyers for raising the issue in such a public forum. Hyde said Democratic and Republican staff members had held 20 meetings in recent months to hammer out compromise bill language, and he criticized Conyers for not raising the race issue during those behind-the-scenes negotiations.

Although the bill does not explicitly refer to racial lung differences as part of the medical criteria, it does refer to standards outlined in a 1994 American Thoracic Society study. That study in turn refers to an earlier study that outlines racial differences in lung function.

Hyde denied that the references would result in racial profiling but offered an amendment stating that "race should not be considered as a factor in any medical determination."

Conyers and other Democrats objected, saying it was not adequate. Democrats said they would later offer amendments stripping all references to the medical race studies.

Amid the partisan attacks, committee Democrat Barney Frank of Massachusetts commended Hyde for making a "good faith effort" to settle asbestos suits, but said the bill did not adequately address victims' claims. He urged lawmakers to put politics aside and "start fresh" in drafting a new bill.

House Panel Approves Bill, But Floor Action Is Unlikely

MARCH 18 — A controversial measure to set up a federal system to compensate asbestos victims may have reached its high-water mark March 16 when the House Judiciary Committee approved it, 18-15. It seems unlikely that the bill (HR 1283) will be brought up on the House floor, and the companion Senate bill (S 758) has not been set for a markup.

The committee approved a substitute version of the bill after three days of debate stretching over two weeks. At stake are billions of dollars in awards to the hundreds of thousands of people who have been exposed to asbestos, a largely indestructible substance that can cause cancer and has been linked to other diseases.

The Clinton administration opposes the measure. A March 8 letter from Assistant Attorney General Robert Raben to committee Chairman Henry J. Hyde, R-Ill., said the administration believes the bill "would delay and worsen, rather than accelerate and improve, compensation to the sick."

Bill supporters, including Hyde and a coalition of asbestos companies, argue that thousands of pending asbestos lawsuits are overwhelming the courts. They also say that awards are going to people who have been exposed to asbestos but are not yet sick, which could take money away from those who are ill now.

"You've got to get the people who have been impaired to the front of the line," said Hyde, the bill's sponsor. "We cannot allow the system to remain clogged."

Most Democrats oppose the bill, as does the Association of Trial Lawyers of America. They say the bill would provide unwarranted protection to companies that manufactured or distributed asbestos, many of which knowingly exposed workers to the deadly substance. They also say the bill would exclude from compensation thousands of people who have been hurt by asbestos.

"These companies face enormous liability because they ought to," said Anthony Weiner, D-N.Y., whose grandfather suffered from asbestos-related diseases after working in the Brooklyn Naval Yard. "They've done harm to people."

As approved by the committee, the bill would require people who claim they were harmed by exposure to asbestos to obtain a certificate from a new federal agency, the Office of Asbestos Compensation, proving that they are impaired.

Without the certificate, which would be given only to those who met strict medical criteria specified in the bill, claimants could not recover damages from asbestos companies. Those who obtained certificates could choose to pursue their case in state or federal court or through a federally negotiated settlement process.

Hundreds of thousands of cases are pending in the courts, but relatively few are tried each year. For example, 55 cases went to trial in 1998. About 9,600 people have died from asbestosis, one of several diseases linked to exposure, since 1986.

Two Republicans — Joe Scarborough of Florida and Lindsey Graham of South Carolina — voted against the bill. Both said they were told after the markup that the bill would probably not go to the House floor because Senate Majority Leader Trent Lott, R-Miss., had signaled that it would not be considered in his chamber during an election year.

One senator, Conrad Burns, R-Mont., already has been singed by the controversy. Burns recently dropped his cosponsorship of the Senate bill following newspaper revelations of how people in the small mining town of Libby, Mont., have suffered from asbestos-related illnesses.

But a spokeswoman for House Majority Leader Dick Armey, R-Texas, said Armey was committed to bringing the measure up for a House vote.

Scarborough said he voted against the measure because he "didn't think it was an especially bright bill for the Republicans to support."

Narrow Margin

In the committee room during the markup, lobbyists frequently outnumbered House members. Lobbyists for the trial lawyers huddled with Democrats and helped craft their amendments while representatives of asbestos companies and some insurance agencies watched carefully as members debated a bill that they helped to write.

Neutral parties included a lobbyist for the American Insurance Association, a trade group whose membership is divided on the bill.

Democrats initially threatened to bog down the process by offering as many as 100 amendments, but they changed tactics and settled for offering amendments to the provisions they found most troubling. The committee considered 13 amendments and approved four.

Although the final vote for the bill was 18-15, the true margin was one vote. At the last minute, when the tally was 17-16, Robert C. Scott, D-Va., changed his vote to "yea" as a parliamentary maneuver aimed at forcing a second vote on the bill. Weiner and Maxine Waters, D-Calif., were absent at the time, and Democrats hoped if they could delay the proceedings long enough for one of them to get to the markup, they could defeat the bill.

But Republicans rallied and tabled, or killed, Scott's motion for a second vote, 17-16.

Democrats Rebuffed

During the markup, the committee rejected a series of amendments offered by Democrats that would have stripped the bill's medical provisions, delayed its effective date and made the new procedures voluntary.

The medical criteria provoked the strongest debate. Members agreed by voice vote to an amendment by Hyde, Scott and ranking Democrat John Conyers Jr. of Michigan that would make it clear that race would play no part in the medical evaluation.

In a markup session March 9, Conyers had said the bill referred to medical studies saying that African-Americans have lower lung capacity than whites, something Conyers said could make it harder for blacks to prove they were hurt by asbestos.

But agreement ended when the discussion turned to the section of the bill on medical qualifications. The legislation includes more than five pages of detailed medical provisions and definitions to be used to determine whether someone is eligible for compensation.

For example, the bill says someone "whose chest X-ray shows either small irregular opacities of ILO Grade 1/0 or bilateral pleural thickening of ILO Grade b/2" would be eligible to be reimbursed for medical tests.

Members defeated, 10-10, an amendment by Scott that sought to delete the medical standards and leave the determination of those standards to the attorney general and the National Institute for Occupational Safety and Health, a division of the Centers for Disease Control and Prevention.

"I am not trained to do this kind of assessment," said Melvin Watt, D-N.C., noting that one group told him the provisions were fair and another said they were not. "I have, as a member of Congress, not one iota of ability to tell me which group is telling me the truth."

Hyde said the medical criteria were drawn from a large-scale settlement in Louisiana and are the "most favorable known criteria for asbestos victims." He said Congress has a responsibility to set up a fair system, including medical criteria, and it "shouldn't try to duck that responsibility."

The committee also rejected, 12-17, an amendment by Scott that sought to delay the bill's effective date until the new asbestos office was up and running with appropriated funds.

And the panel rejected, 11-18, an amendment by Conyers that would have made the new process voluntary.

The committee approved by voice vote an amendment by Weiner that aimed to make sure taxpayers were not left paying for the claims of asbestos victims.

The original bill would have allowed the administrator for the compensation program to collect funds from asbestos companies to pay for the program's administrative costs.

Weiner's amendment would broaden that authority to allow the administrator to devise a plan to obtain payment for all costs from the asbestos companies. His amendment clarifies that the administrator would have the authority to take the companies to federal court to get the money.

Exemptions

The committee first adopted, then rejected, an amendment by Ed Pease, R-Ind., to allow states to pass legislation to exempt claims within a state from the federal process. The committee initially voted 15-14 for the amendment, which Hyde said would "gut" the bill. Then Christopher B. Cannon, R-Utah, switched his vote and the amendment was defeated, 14-15.

The committee approved by voice vote an amendment by Asa Hutchinson, R-Ark., that would protect existing large settlements from the new process.

In recent years there have been several large-scale settlements between asbestos companies and plaintiffs, including payouts over several years.

Hutchinson said he particularly wanted to protect a settlement reached by Owens Corning last year. The company, based in Toledo, Ohio, has agreed to pay $2.5 billion over the next five years, settling about 215,000 claims. Hutchinson said Owens Corning has two plants in his district.

His amendment would extend from five years to seven the time that companies could pay claims under previously negotiated agreements without being affected by the bill.

And his amendment removed from the bill a requirement that settlements must have been approved before July 1, 1999, to qualify for the exemption. ◆

Oregon Senator Blocks Vote On Legislation to Ban Doctor-Assisted Suicide

SUMMARY

An effort to make the use of federally controlled drugs in physician-assisted suicide illegal failed in the 106th Congress when supporters could not muster enough support to overcome a filibuster in the Senate.

Ever since Oregon approved a voter referendum permitting physician-assisted suicide in 1994, congressional Republicans have sought to overturn it.

In 1998, Attorney General Janet Reno ruled that the Oregon law did not run afoul of federal drug control laws. That year, both the House and Senate Judiciary committees approved legislation to block the Oregon law, but neither measure went further.

In 1999, the House passed a similar bill (HR 2260 — H Rept 106-378) that would have barred doctors from helping patients kill themselves with prescription drugs but would have permitted them to prescribe controlled substances to alleviate pain. The Senate Judiciary Committee approved a slightly different version in April 2000. But Democrat Ron Wyden, Oregon's senior senator, vowed to filibuster the bill. *(1999 Almanac, p. 18-35)*

The bill was a top priority for Senate Assistant Majority Leader Don Nickles, R-Okla., and he won inclusion of the Senate version in the conference report on a year-end, catch-all tax bill (HR 2614).

The tax bill conference report was adopted by the House on Oct. 26, but when it reached the Senate floor, Wyden began his threatened filibuster.

In the end, Republican leaders decided to abandon the tax bill (which also faced a veto threat), and with it the assisted suicide measure. *(Also see Medicare reimbursements, p. 12-25; tax package, p. 18-3)*

Box Score

- **Bills:** HR 2260, HR 2614
- **Legislative action: Senate** Judiciary Committee approved HR 2260 (S Rept 106-299), 10-8, on April 27.

House adopted the conference report on HR 2614 (H Rept 106-1004), 237-174, on Oct. 26.

Senate Panel OKs Bill to Outlaw Assisted Suicide

APRIL 29 — After weeks of delay, the Senate Judiciary Committee on April 27 approved an amended version of a House-passed bill (HR 2260) that would make it a federal crime for any doctor to assist in a suicide. The largely party-line vote was 10-8. The measure would effectively stop Oregon from implementing its physician-assisted suicide law.

The bill is a top priority of Senate Majority Whip Don Nickles, R-Okla., but faces determined opposition from Oregon's senior senator, Democrat Ron Wyden. Wyden previously forced the committee to delay consideration of the bill and has vowed to prevent the Senate from passing it.

"If nothing else, this vote should give the Senate leadership an unmistakable sign that walking all over Oregon will be no stroll in the park," Wyden said in a statement. "They should pack up this bad bill and start focusing on solutions that will actually help those in pain, like helping seniors pay for their prescription drugs."

Countered committee Chairman Orrin G. Hatch, R-Utah: "By accepting assisted suicide, we are, in essence, telling terminally ill patients that we are unwilling to help them alleviate their suffering, that they should give up because society has given up on them." He added: "This bill promotes improved knowledge of palliative care and pain management and . . . prevents assisted suicide from becoming a legally sanctioned medical practice."

Dianne Feinstein of California, one of seven Democrats to oppose the bill, predicted that the legislation would "increase suicide, not decrease it." She said provisions that would make it a crime for a doctor to prescribe a controlled substance with the intent of assisting a suicide would deter physicians from prescribing large doses for people in extreme pain. And without relief, she said, those patients might choose suicide.

Republicans have been determined to block the Oregon statute since Attorney General Janet Reno ruled in 1998 that doctors could obey the state law without running afoul of federal drug control laws. Oregon citizens first passed the assisted suicide law, known as the Death with Dignity Act, in 1994, but it was immediately blocked by a lawsuit. In 1997, Oregon voters rejected a ballot initiative that would have repealed the 1994 law, and it went into effect soon thereafter.

In 1998, the first full year the law was in effect, 15 people used it to obtain drugs and commit suicide, according to a report by the Oregon Health Division. In 1998, the House and Senate Judiciary committees approved legislation to block the Oregon law, but neither measure advanced further in the 105th Congress. *(1998 Almanac, p. 17-18)*

The bill has divided the medical community. The American Medical Association has said it opposes legalizing physician-assisted suicide, and eventually endorsed both the House-passed bill and the Senate version. But several state medical associations have opposed various forms of the bill.

Committee Action

The committee adopted by voice vote a substitute version of the bill written by Hatch, in which he tried to alleviate the major concern of health care groups — that the bill would have a chilling effect on doctors prescribing pain relief for the terminally ill.

Hatch said the amended version would create a "safe haven" for doctors who prescribe drugs that unintentionally cause a patient's death when they were intended to relieve intense pain.

All committee Democrats except Joseph R. Biden Jr. of Delaware voted against the bill. All committee Republicans except Arlen Specter of Pennsylvania voted for it.

The bill would not strike down the Oregon law, but it would prohibit doctors from using controlled substances for assisted suicide, thus making it nearly impossible for Oregon doctors to assist in suicides in what they would call a humane fashion.

Hatch's substitute also would raise the bar for the attorney general to prove that a doctor had intended to aid in a suicide, requiring "clear and convincing" evidence rather than the lower "preponderance of the evidence" standard. Hatch said his substitute states that a doctor can knowingly prescribe a dose of medication for pain that may lead to death, as long as the doctor's intent is not to kill the patient.

The bill would authorize unspecified grants to schools, hospices and other groups to provide training and education on pain management.

Wyden Filibusters To Block Passage Of Suicide Rider Added to Tax Bill

OCTOBER 28 — Sen. Ron Wyden, D-Ore., began a filibuster on Oct. 27 over a provision quietly added to the omnibus tax bill that would effectively overturn an Oregon law that permits physician-assisted suicide.

The underlying tax bill (HR 2614), which faces a veto threat from President Clinton, passed the House on Oct. 26 but stalled in the Senate the next day.

Senate Assistant Majority Leader Don Nickles, R-Okla., added a provision that would reverse a federal decision to not pursue drug violations when prescriptions are used for physician-assisted suicides under Oregon's law.

"These drugs can't be used for assisted suicide," Nickles said on Oct. 27. "Oregon can't change federal law."

Responded Wyden: "What [Nickles'] legislation does is take away from all states what has traditionally been their prerogative — to decide appropriate medical practice."

Oregon was the first state in the nation with such a law, but it could soon be joined by Maine, which has a physician-assisted suicide initiative on its ballot this fall.

Oregon residents first passed the assisted suicide law in 1994, but it was immediately blocked by a lawsuit. In 1997, Oregon voters rejected a ballot initiative that would have repealed the law, and it went into effect soon after.

U.S. Attorney General Janet Reno ruled in 1998 that doctors could obey the state law without running afoul of federal drug control laws.

That year, the first full year the law was in effect, 15 people used it to obtain drugs and commit suicide, according to a report by the Oregon Health Division. Also, the House and Senate Judiciary committees approved legislation to block the Oregon law, but neither measure advanced further in the 105th Congress. *(1998 Almanac, p. 17-18)*

Overturning Reno's decision, and with it, the Oregon law, has been a top priority for Nickles, who says it violates laws controlling dangerous drugs. ◆

Lawmakers Make Changes To Laws Governing Seizure Of Assets in Criminal Cases

SUMMARY

President Clinton and members of Congress agreed to rein in one of the most powerful tools in law enforcement's arsenal: the ability to seize private property allegedly linked to a crime. The bill, signed April 25, makes a variety of changes to seizure laws, with the aim of making it more difficult for the government to seize some property, while granting more authority to seize assets once criminal charges have been proved.

The bill represents the culmination of years of effort, especially by House Judiciary Committee Chairman Henry J. Hyde, R-Ill., who introduced his first overhaul of civil asset forfeiture laws in 1993. Hyde and others were concerned that law enforcement abused its authority to seize property, and that too few protections existed for innocent property owners.

The bill shifts the burden of proof to the government, which must now prove property was used in the commission of a crime before it can be seized. Previously, the burden was on the property owner to show that the property was not used in a crime. The bill also repealed a portion of forfeiture law that had required those seeking to reclaim their property to post a bond. At the same time, it gives law enforcement greater ability to seize property once a person is convicted.

The bill makes it easier, under some circumstances, for property owners to get free legal help. It establishes a uniform, innocent-owner defense that allows people to show, by the preponderance of the evidence, that their property was not used in a crime. It also makes it easier for an individual to reclaim some property, such as a home, while the court decides the government's claim.

The House had overwhelmingly passed a version of the bill (H Rept 106-192) in 1999, giving impetus to negotiations with the Clinton administration. After a compromise was reached March 22, the revised legislation sailed through, passing the Senate by voice vote March 27 and clearing the House on April 11. *(1999 Almanac, p. 18-44)*

Box Score

- **Bill:** HR 1658 — PL 106-185
- **Legislative action: Senate** passed HR 1658, amended, by voice vote on March 27.

House cleared HR 1658, by voice vote April 11.

President signed HR 1658 on April 25.

Senate Panel Backs Limits on Power To Seize Property Used in Crimes

MARCH 25 — Congressional negotiators and the Clinton administration reached an agreement March 22 on legislation that would overhaul laws governing law-enforcement seizure of personal assets, paving the way for quick action on the bill.

A day later, the Senate Judiciary Committee approved the measure (HR 1658) by voice vote. The committee also adopted by voice vote a substitute amendment that incorporated provisions from the agreement.

Panel Chairman Orrin G. Hatch, R-Utah, said he expects the bill, which would make it more difficult for federal agencies to seize and keep private property used in a crime, to move to the Senate floor soon. "I don't want it to sit around and simmer," he said.

Shaking hands on the agreement were Hatch, ranking committee Democrat Patrick J. Leahy of Vermont, Attorney General Janet Reno and House Judiciary Chairman Henry J. Hyde, R-Ill., among others. "Everyone walked away pretty happy," said Sen. Charles E. Schumer, D-N.Y., a key negotiator.

Leahy said in a statement: "This is a significant improvement over the current system and should go a long way toward stemming the abuses that have so offended Americans across the country and the political spectrum."

The House originally passed the bill June 24 and will have to vote again to incorporate the changes from the March 22 agreement.

At issue is a formidable law enforcement weapon: the broad power of the government to seize property allegedly used in a crime. Virtually all state and local governments and the federal government use this power extensively. The Justice Department took in $450 million from such seizures in 1998.

But critics charge that the deck is stacked against people whose property is seized, many of whom are poor and lacking legal representation, making it too easy for the government to take property.

Hyde has led the campaign to overhaul the laws. The House-passed version of the bill was far more favorable to property owners than the final agreement. But a Hyde staff aide said of the deal that the chairman "likes it a lot."

Burden of Proof

The biggest change proposed in the bill is also the most basic: shifting the burden of proof from the property owner to the government. Under current law, once the government seizes property the owner must prove it was not used in the commission of a crime to get it back.

The bill approved by the Senate panel would shift the burden to the government to prove by "preponderance of the evidence" that an asset had been used in a crime. The original Hyde bill would have required the government to meet an even more difficult "clear and convincing evidence" threshold.

The bill also would eliminate a requirement that the person trying to retrieve property post a "cost bond," usually 10 percent of the value of the asset. The owner must post the bond in cash at the start of a legal challenge, which the government says helps deter frivolous cases.

But Hyde and others successfully argued that it made the process far too burdensome on property owners.

Instead, to prevent bad-faith attempts to regain property, the bill would permit a judge to levy a fine on someone whose claim was found to be without merit.

Hyde's most controversial provision would have provided legal representation to all property owners who could not afford to hire a lawyer. The final version allows appointment of a lawyer only if a person is being prosecuted criminally and has already qualified for a court-appointed attorney or in cases in which an indigent person's primary residence has been seized.

The bill also would provide an "innocent owner" defense to allow certain people, such as a child or a spouse, whose property was used in a crime to regain it if they can show that they did not know about the crime or that when they found out about it, they did all they could to prevent it.

The bill would expand the Justice Department's ability to use criminal forfeiture, in which the department first proves that a crime occurred then seizes the property.

The bill also includes a provision by Sen. Jeff Sessions, R-Ala., that would allow a judge to dismiss a complaint if the property owner was a fugitive outside the country and refused to come back for fear of arrest.

It also would make it easier for other countries to seize assets in the United States in connection with civil cases in that country.

Senate Passes Asset Seizure Overhaul Bill

APRIL 1 — Legislation that would overhaul federal asset-forfeiture laws sailed through the Senate on March 27, passing by voice vote with little debate.

The bill (HR 1658) is expected to win easy approval in the House, as early as the week of April 3, and be signed into law by President Clinton.

The ease of the final action belies the years of intense battling over asset forfeiture, a crime-fighting tool that has added millions of dollars to the budgets of federal, state and local law enforcement agencies. The House passed its original version of HR 1658 on June 24.

The bill is backed by a diverse group of outside organizations, including the American Civil Liberties Union, the National Rifle Association and the American Bankers Association.

Bill supporters, led by Henry J. Hyde, R-Ill., chairman of the House Judiciary Committee, have argued for years that the current system is stacked against property owners.

But law enforcement agencies had resisted change. The two sides finally reached agreement in face-to-face negotiations the week of March 20 and put forth compromise legislation.

"While civil forfeiture is a valuable law enforcement tool, it has become increasingly clear that some reform of civil forfeiture law is necessary, given the numerous controversial seizures of property in the last decade," Senate Judiciary Committee Chairman Orrin G. Hatch, R-Utah, said March 27.

Questionable Seizures

Sen. Patrick J. Leahy of Vermont, ranking Democrat on the Judiciary Committee, said there have been several instances in Vermont of questionable government actions. In 1989, for example, federal prosecutors moved to seize a house and 49 surrounding acres that had been in one family for years, he said.

The husband had pleaded guilty to growing six marijuana plants without his wife's knowledge and had been sentenced to 50 hours of community service. A year later, the federal government moved to seize the property but backed down after a widely publicized protest.

The bill passed by the Senate would give something to both sides in the debate. The bill would flip the burden of proof for seizing property, requiring the government to show "by preponderance of the evidence" that the asset had been used in a crime — rather than requiring the owner to prove it had not been so used.

And the bill would make it easier for property owners to sue to get their property back by deleting a provision of current law that requires them to post a bond before trial.

For indigent defendants whose primary residence is the subject of seizure, the bill calls on the Legal Services Corporation to provide representation. The bill originally passed by the House would have provided legal representation to virtually all poor defendants.

The bill would also expand the Justice Department's ability to use criminal forfeiture, in which the department first proves a defendant's guilt, then seizes the property.

House Sends Asset Seizure Bill to Clinton

APRIL 15 — Legislation that would make it more difficult for federal agents to confiscate property that police believe is linked to a crime was cleared by a voice vote in the House April 11.

The measure (HR 1658 — H Rept 106-192) now goes to President Clinton, who is expected to sign it. The bill would change civil asset forfeiture law in part by making the government prove the property was associated with the crime — rather than requiring the owner to prove it was not. *(Provisions, p. 15-38)*

The bill is the culmination of seven years' work by House Judiciary Committee Chairman Henry J. Hyde, R-Ill., who first introduced legislation to overhaul civil asset forfeiture laws in 1993 because of what he saw as abuses in the system. Existing law allows prosecutors to seize property such as homes, cars and boats for "probable cause," the same standard used for search warrants. Forfeiture laws, enacted in the 1970s to combat drug trafficking and terrorism, allow the government to seize property before a trial begins.

The final bill is the product of lengthy negotiations among Hyde, his Senate counterpart Orrin G. Hatch,

Bill Requires Government to Show Seized Property Was Used in Crime

APRIL 15 — The House cleared a bill (HR 1658) by voice vote April 11 that would make it more difficult for federal agents to seize property allegedly linked to crime. It generally would take effect 120 days after enactment. Here are key provisions:

Burden of Proof. The bill would switch the burden of proof from the owner to the government. It would require the government to show, by a "preponderance of the evidence," that the asset was used in a crime. Current law requires the owner to prove that the asset was not used in a crime.

Cost Bond. The bill would repeal a law requiring the property owner to post a cost bond before challenging the government's seizure. Cost bonds were set at 10 percent of the value of the asset or $5,000, whichever was less, with a minimum of $250. Instead, the bill would allow a judge to fine a property owner for filing a frivolous complaint, using the same calculations previously used to determine the amount of the cost bond. Property owners found to have filed three frivolous complaints while in prison would be prohibited from filing further complaints unless they could show "extraordinary and exceptional circumstances."

Attorney Fees/Representation. The bill would require the government to reimburse the property owner for "reasonable" attorney fees in cases in which the owner substantially prevailed in a challenge to a seizure. Currently, few property owners are repaid their legal costs. The bill would require the appointment of counsel by the Legal Services Corp. for a property owner whose home was subject to forfeiture and who could not afford an attorney. It would also require appointment of counsel for indigents already represented in a criminal case.

Innocent Owners. The measure would establish a uniform, innocent-owner defense in civil asset forfeiture cases for people who could show, by a preponderance of the evidence, that they were not connected to a crime. To be considered innocent, an owner either could not have known the illegal activity was occurring or, once aware of it, would have had to do "all that reasonably could be expected" to stop the use of the property. Owners would have to show that they notified law enforcement about the situation and tried to take back the asset in question. These requirements would be waived if the owner reasonably believed that meeting them would subject someone to physical harm. Owners who bought tainted property would have to show they did not know it was connected to a crime.

Release of Property. The bill would require the government to release property to the owner pending a decision on the seizure if the owner had strong community ties and could show that government possession of the asset would cause "substantial hardship." Examples of hardship include leaving someone homeless or making it difficult for a person to run a business. The owner would have to show that the asset was unlikely to be disposed of or destroyed while out of government custody.

Damage Claims. The measure would allow property owners who prevailed in a forfeiture case to recoup some costs for damages to their assets incurred while the government held them. Under current law, the government is immune from liability for damages.

Criminal Assets. The bill would expand federal agents' ability to seize assets after the owner was convicted of a crime. It would broaden criminal forfeiture laws to mirror civil forfeiture laws.

Statute of Limitations. The bill would give the government more time to lay claims against assets. Under current law, claims must be made within five years of the date of the crime. The bill would set the limit at five years or two years after the discovery that the asset was used in the crime, whichever was later.

Foreign Enforcement. The bill would make it easier for foreign governments that have signed agreements with the United States to get help from a U.S. court in enforcing an asset forfeiture decision. The court could decline to enforce the judgment if it found that the process in the other country was unfair to the property owner.

Fugitive Forfeiture. The bill would allow a judge to deny a claim by a property owner if the owner left the country to avoid arrest and refused to return, unless the owner was in custody elsewhere.

Banking Records. The bill would allow a judge to sanction a property owner, up to dismissing a claim, if the owner refused to supply foreign banking records that could be material to the case.

Civil Restraining Orders. The bill would allow the government to take steps, such as appointing a conservator, to protect property it had decided to seize if there was a substantial probability that the government would win the case and that the asset would be destroyed before being turned over.

Reports. The bill would require the attorney general to send Congress an annual report on assets the government seized during the year, broken down by state and other parameters.

R-Utah, top congressional Democrats and the administration. The Senate passed the compromise March 27. Besides making seizures more difficult, the bill would expand the government's ability to confiscate property after convictions.

"This bill is one we can all be proud of," Hyde said. "It returns civil asset forfeiture to the ranks of respected law enforcement tools that can be used without risk to the civil liberties and property rights of American citizens."

Forfeiture is a widely used law enforcement tool. In 1998, the Justice Department got the proceeds from about $450 million in seized property.

The Congressional Budget Office estimates that the bill could cost about $115 million in lost seizures annually, beginning in fiscal 2001. The bill also would cost about $14 million in annual fees to lawyers for the indigent. ◆

Democratic Opposition Stops GOP Plans to Rewrite Rules Governing Class Action Suits

Box Score

- **Bills:** S 353, HR 1875
- **Legislative action: Senate** Judiciary approved S 353 (S Rept 106-420), 11-7, on June 29.

SUMMARY

Republican efforts to overhaul the class action litigation system died in the Senate in the face of a Democratic filibuster threat.

The Senate Judiciary Committee gave near party-line approval in June to a bill (S 353) that would have given federal courts more authority to hear class action lawsuits. The measure had strong backing from the business community, whose leaders believed it would be easier to block class action lawsuits in federal, as opposed to state, courts.

Supporters also said the legislation could make it more difficult for attorneys to go "jury shopping" — bringing suits in states such as Alabama, where enormous damages had been awarded.

Trial lawyers, consumer groups and Democrats strongly opposed the bill, saying it would make it too difficult for ordinary people to hold corporations accountable for their actions. Committee Democrats warned they would engage in an extended debate on the bill if it came to the floor. It never did.

The bill would have allowed a case involving at least $2 million in potential damages and more than 100 members of an affected class to be moved to federal court if parties to the suit were from more than one state.

The House had passed its version of the legislation (HR 1875 — H Rept 106-320) in 1999. *(1999 Almanac, p. 18-46)*

Senate Panel Approves Bill; Filibuster Likely

JULY 1 — Congressional Republicans are moving closer to a showdown with the Clinton administration over legislation that would overhaul the class action litigation system by pushing more cases into federal court.

The Senate Judiciary Committee on June 29 approved class action legislation (S 353) by a nearly party-line vote of 11-7. Herb Kohl of Wisconsin was the lone Democrat to vote for it.

The bill now heads to the floor. Senate Majority Leader Trent Lott, R-Miss., has said this is the one litigation bill likely to be considered by his chamber this year.

The House passed its version of the bill (HR 1875) on Sept. 23, 1999, by 222-207.

The legislation has strong backing from the business community, whose leaders believe it would be easier to block class action lawsuits in federal courts. The change in venue could also help firms avoid some of the huge jury awards given out in state courts in recent years. For example, it might make it harder for attorneys to go "jury shopping" — bringing suits in states such as Alabama that have been more likely to recommend enormous awards.

Trial lawyers, consumer groups and Democrats strongly oppose the bills, arguing they would make it too difficult for average people to hold corporations accountable for their actions. Class action suits have been filed against tobacco companies, auto and gun manufacturers and health maintenance organizations, for example.

Committee Democrats warned June 29 that floor consideration of the bill would be lengthy. Joseph R. Biden Jr., D-Del., said when the bill comes up he will "enlighten my colleagues to my thinking on this issue for a long time."

Ranking Democrat Patrick J. Leahy, D-Vt., said he intended to talk about the "225 years of jurisprudence in Vermont," and any other state history he felt needed to be discussed.

Even if the bill survived a filibuster, the White House has promised a veto, which would almost certainly be sustained.

"We're trying to get it ready for when [Texas Gov.] George W. Bush is president," said Charles E. Grassley, R-Iowa, sponsor of the Senate bill. Bush, the presumptive GOP presidential nominee, has promised to overhaul the litigation system if he wins in November.

Lawsuit Lottery

Grassley said the bill was aimed at curtailing abuses by attorneys who get huge awards for themselves and very little for the victims. "We've heard about settlement after settlement where class members got coupons or nothing, but the lawyers got millions of dollars in fees," he said. "Is this fair?"

The committee approved, by voice vote, a manager's amendment that would tighten the criteria for removing lawsuits from state court, as compared with the bill as introduced. The changes were made to try to win over skeptics of the measure. Under the amendment, to qualify for federal court, a suit would have to involve at least $2 million in potential damages and more than 100 members of an affected class.

If those requirements were met, the lawsuit could be moved to federal court if any of the parties to the lawsuit were from differing states, including the defending company or companies.

The manager's amendment removed a controversial section of the bill that would have mandated sanctions for lawyers who employ tactics designed to harass, delay or increase the cost of the litigation at hand.

It also removed a provision that would have limited attorneys' fees, based on a formula. Instead, the bill calls for a study of fees and asks the Judicial Conference, the administrative body of the federal courts, for recommendations about how to rein in large awards to lawyers.

During the markup, the committee turned back a series of Democratic amendments designed to carve out types of lawsuits that would not be covered by the new class action law.

Leahy offered an amendment, defeated 7-10, that would have exempted tobacco lawsuits. "I can almost see the headlines all over the nation: 'Congress Protects Tobacco Again,' " he said.

The committee rejected, 7-10, amendments by Robert G. Torricelli, D-N.J., to exempt suits against gunmakers, and by Leahy, to exempt environmental lawsuits.

Russell D. Feingold, D-Wis., offered an amendment to allow lawsuits filed under a state's consumer protection laws to proceed in state court, noting, "There is little or no federal interest in these cases." It was defeated, 7-10.

Leahy offered an amendment on behalf of Dianne Feinstein, D-Calif., to add eight permanent judges to federal district courts along the Southwestern border. It fell, 7-10. ◆

Senate Vote Falls Short, Killing Flag Amendment For 106th Congress

Box Score

- **Bills:** S J Res 14, H J Res 33
- **Legislative action: Senate** rejected S J Res 14 (S Rept 106-246), 63-37 on March 29.

SUMMARY

Senate supporters fell four votes shy of the 67 they needed to pass a constitutional amendment that would give Congress the authority to ban desecration of the American flag.

The House had passed an identical measure (H J Res 33) in the first session of the 106th Congress. *(1999 Almanac, p. 18-39)*

Flag desecration became a national issue after a 1989 Supreme Court ruling in *Texas v. Johnson*. In that case, the court held that state laws prohibiting flag desecration violated speech protections guaranteed under the First Amendment.

The court used the same rationale in 1990 to strike down a federal law (PL 101-131) against flag desecration.

Congress had tried to overturn the court's decisions twice before, in 1990 and 1995.

In 1990, supporters fell 34 votes short in the House and nine votes short in the Senate. In 1995, the House adopted the resolution, but the Senate was three votes short. *(1995 Almanac, p. 6-22; 1990 Almanac, p. 524)*

Senate Backers Fail to Muster Needed Majority

APRIL 1 — Senate supporters of a constitutional amendment that would give Congress the authority to ban flag desecration won no additional converts and lost some previous supporters of their cause March 29, leaving the issue dead for the year.

The Senate voted 63-37 for the resolution (S J Res 14), four votes short of the two-thirds necessary to pass a constitutional amendment. The House passed its amendment (H J Res 33) on June 24, 1999, by a vote of 305-124 — 19 votes more than needed. *(Senate vote 48, p. S-12)*

A dozen Senate Democrats voted for the amendment, and four Republicans voted against it. Supporters lost the backing of Sens. Robert C. Byrd, D-W.Va., and Richard H. Bryan, D-Nev. Byrd said that since 1995, the last time the Senate voted on such a measure, he had changed his mind about the need for it. "Flag burning, though loathsome, is hardly pervasive enough to warrant amending the Constitution of the United States," he said. More than 10,000 amendments have been proposed over the years, but only 27 have been adopted.

To amend the Constitution, a resolution must pass with a two-thirds majority in both chambers, then be ratified by three-quarters of the states. Similar flag resolutions have easily passed the House several times, but they have never won a big enough Senate majority to go to the states for ratification.

The March 29 vote ended the effort to pass the amendment this Congress, but supporters said the issue will not go away. "This is going to pass. Whether it does today or tomorrow or next year, it's going to pass," said Judiciary Committee Chairman Orrin G. Hatch, R-Utah, sponsor of S J Res 14. He spoke at a March 28 rally for the resolution that featured more than 200 military veterans and Miss America, Heather French.

"We will not surrender," said Alan G. Lance, national commander of the American Legion, whose group formed the Citizens Flag Alliance Inc. to lobby for the resolution. He said senators should understand that "we did not send them here to vote their conscience, we sent them here to vote the will of their constituents."

The Senate rejected, 36-64, an amendment by Mitch McConnell, R-Ky., that would have changed the measure from a constitutional amendment to a regular bill to prohibit some kinds of flag desecration. *(Vote 45, p. S-12)*

The Senate also voted, 67-33, to table, or kill, an amendment by Ernest F. Hollings, D-S.C., that would have added language to the resolution permitting Congress to regulate campaign spending. The Supreme Court has held that campaign spending is a form of free speech that Congress cannot regulate under the Constitution. *(Vote 46, p. S-12)*

Actions or Speech

Flag desecration became a national issue after the 1989 Supreme Court ruling *Texas v. Johnson*, which held that state laws prohibiting flag desecration violated First Amendment free speech protections. The ruling split the justices, 5-4. The court used the same rationale in 1990 to strike down a federal law (PL 101-131) against flag desecration. *(1990 Almanac, p. 524)*

An effort in 1990 to pass a constitutional amendment to protect the flag fell 34 votes short in the House and nine votes short in the Senate. In 1995, the House adopted the resolution, but the Senate was three votes short. *(1995 Almanac, p. 6-22)*

Debate on the amendment the week of March 27 centered on whether burning or defacing a flag should be considered a crime or a form of protected speech.

"The American people understand the difference between freedom of speech and 'anything goes,' " said Chuck Hagel, R-Neb., a Vietnam War veteran. "Let them protest, let them write to their newspaper, let them organize, let them march, let them shout to the rooftops — but we should not let them burn the flag. Too many have died defending the flag for us to allow it to be used in any way that does not honor their sacrifice."

But Charles S. Robb, D-Va., another Vietnam veteran, opposed the amendment. "It is precisely because the act of flag burning sends a message that elicits such a visceral and powerful response that it is undeniably speech. Vulgar, crude, infantile, repulsive, ungrateful speech, but undeniably speech. . . . And when we seek to punish those who express views we don't share, then we — not the flag burners — we begin to erode the very values, the very freedoms that make America the greatest democracy the world has ever known." ◆

Longstanding Judicial Vacancies Revive 'Smaller Is Better' Crusade

SUMMARY

The Senate confirmed 39 federal judges in 2000, bringing the total for the 106th Congress to 73. Among those confirmed in 2000 were four to the U.S. Circuit Court of Appeals for the 9th District, a court that most Republicans believe is too liberal. A total of 377 judges were confirmed during the eight years of the Clinton administration; 40 nominations were left pending at the end of the session.

The battle between the Clinton administration and Senate Republicans over confirmation of federal judges intensified in 2000. Late in 1999, Sen. James M. Inhofe, R-Okla., vowed to block all future judicial nominations because of several recess appointments made by President Clinton. But after a protracted battle, Senate Majority Leader Trent Lott, R-Miss., kept a promise he had made at the end of the first session to hold a vote on several long-delayed appointments, particularly those of Richard A. Paez and Marcia L. Berzon, both to lifetime seats on the 9th Circuit. After some impassioned debate, the Senate confirmed Paez by a vote of 59-29 on March 9. The same day, Berzon was confirmed, 64-34. Despite these successes, Democrats were deeply frustrated that more Clinton appointees were not considered, and Senate Minority Leader Tom Daschle, D-S.D., complained bitterly about the process.

Judicial Conference Deems Vacancies Emergencies

MARCH 11 — Other judges may be complaining about their workloads, but J. Harvie Wilkinson III does not believe a federal appeals court has to be big to be effective. He has argued against filling the vacancies on the bench of the Richmond-based 4th U.S. Circuit Court of Appeals, where he has been the chief judge since February 1996.

"Courts weren't meant to be that big," Wilkinson, first named to the federal bench in 1984 by President Ronald Reagan, said in a Feb. 25 interview.

His circuit has four vacancies and 11 active judges, which he thinks is sufficient to manage its caseload.

Not everyone agrees.

The Judicial Conference of the United States has designated two of the four vacancies as emergencies, meaning the circuit — which includes Virginia, Maryland, North and South Carolina, and West Virginia — has a caseload in excess of 500 filings. The median time for disposition of a case by the 4th Circuit is 8.9 months, compared with a national median for appeals courts of 12 months.

Patrick J. Leahy of Vermont, the ranking Democrat on the Senate Judiciary Committee, said March 3 that the vacancies in the 4th Circuit and elsewhere mean that "prosecutors have to plea bargain cases they don't want to" or else run afoul of speedy-trial rules. For years, Leahy and other Democrats have accused Senate Republicans of political foot-dragging on President Clinton's judicial nominations in hopes of winning back the White House in 2001.

On the other side of the country, the 9th U.S. Circuit Court of Appeals — by far the biggest circuit — has four vacancies among its 28 authorized judges, with two just filled. The Senate voted March 9 to confirm Richard A. Paez and Marsha L. Berzon as appellate judges. All four openings have been designated emergencies.

Of those four, one has existed since the seat was created in 1990. Another has existed since 1994, and two others opened in 1999.

The 9th Circuit's median disposition time is 14.2 months per case.

Conservative critics have charged that the 9th Circuit is a liberal behemoth, a huge court out of touch with the people it serves. Its jurisdiction includes more than 50 million people in states from Alaska to Nevada to Hawaii. That has led some, including Senate Judiciary Committee Chairman Orrin G. Hatch, R-Utah, to endorse legislation that would split the massive circuit.

Vacancies are only one of several issues that members of Congress are looking at more closely these days, given the increasing importance of the circuit courts. As the Supreme Court hears fewer and fewer cases, "the courts of appeals have become our regional Supreme Courts," said Sheldon Goldman, a political science professor at the University of Massachusetts at Amherst.

The 'Liberal' Circuit

"I think the 9th Circuit is a circuit that is very much out of touch with mainstream America," Senate Majority Leader Trent Lott, R-Miss., said March 7, explaining in part why he would vote against Paez and Berzon. "[It has] been overruled in something over 80 out of the last 100 cases that have been appealed to the Supreme Court."

Based in San Francisco, the 9th Circuit includes Alaska, Arizona, California, Hawaii, Idaho, Montana, Nevada, Oregon, Washington, Guam and the Northern Mariana Islands.

There have been efforts over the years to carve the circuit into smaller units. In 1997, an attempt by the Senate to cut the court into two sections eventually was scaled back to a provision in the fiscal 1998 appropriations bill for the departments of Commerce, Justice and State (PL 105-119) creating a commission to study the structure of the circuits. *(1997 Almanac, p. 5-18)*

That commission, headed by former Supreme Court Justice Byron R. White, recommended that the 9th Circuit be divided into three sections for administrative purposes, but it did not go as far as Republicans had wanted. The commission did not call for a split of the circuit itself. Congress has not acted on the recommendation.

The debates over Paez and Berzon have resurrected the issue for the GOP. Alaska Republican Sen. Frank H. Murkowski on March 7 introduced legislation (S 2184) that would halve the court. Hatch cosponsored the bill.

The smaller 9th Circuit would include Arizona, California and Nevada. A new 12th Circuit would get the other states: Alaska, Hawaii, Idaho, Montana, Oregon, Washington, Guam and the Northern Mariana Islands.

Murkowski said the population served by the current circuit court is expected to grow to 63 million by 2010 — a 26 percent increase.

But it is not clear whether subdividing the court would really get at the heart of the complaint of many Republicans — what they perceive as the liberal nature of the court. "It is the furthest-left circuit in the American judiciary, and there is no doubt about it," said Sen. Jeff Sessions, R-Ala.

"The 9th Circuit is notorious for its anti-law enforcement record, its frequent creation of new rights for criminals and defendants, often in the face of clearly established law," said Robert C. Smith, R-N.H.

Many Republicans point to the numerous times the Supreme Court has overruled the 9th Circuit as evidence of the court's liberal activism. Most recently, on March 6 the Supreme Court unanimously overruled a 9th Circuit decision upholding a Washington state law that imposed stricter regulations on oil tankers than federal law. The court held that the federal government's power to regulate maritime law trumps state power.

The 'Conservative' Bench

Meanwhile, the 4th Circuit is gaining a reputation for its conservative rulings. A recent series of decisions by the court, appealed to the Supreme Court, have given the high court the opportunity to re-examine the scope of some federal laws.

For example, the justices are reviewing a decision by the 4th Circuit that limited the Miranda warning given to criminal suspects, and they seemed sympathetic to the 4th Circuit's reasoning when it threw out part of the 1994 Violence Against Women Act (PL 103-322). *(1994 Almanac, p. 273)*

The 4th Circuit — which now has six GOP appointees and five named by Democratic presidents — has never had a black judge. President Clinton has nominated two African-Americans, at different times, for one of the open seats, but neither has had a hearing. That is because the Senate confirmation process defers to home-state senators.

According to tradition, both senators from the nominee's state are supposed to turn in a form to the Judiciary Committee before its hearing, noting whether they support the nominee.

Sen. Jesse Helms, R-N.C., has never returned the slips for the nominated blacks on the 4th Circuit, and the vacancy is one that is supposed to be filled by a North Carolinian. That means Clinton's most recent nominee, James A. Wynn Jr., is unlikely to even get a chance to testify.

Helms argues that the court is doing well without any additional judges. And he has the support of the court's chief judge. "My view is that we're doing a fine job with the personnel that we have," Wilkinson said. "We're on top of our docket."

The court is certainly a busy one. The docket of oral arguments for the first week in March listed 74 cases. Each case is argued before a three-judge panel — for most of the March arguments, four panels were to meet simultaneously.

Judges are required to be familiar with a vast range of issues, from copyright infringement to National Labor Relations Board decisions to the regulations regarding railroad crossings.

The court heard a variety of criminal cases, including one in which it was asked to determine whether a juvenile who had helped rob a bank with a sawed-off shotgun should be tried in federal, not state, court.

The courtroom is an interesting mix of the formal and the familiar. Lawyers approach the bench and introduce themselves with, "May it please the court," just as is done at the Supreme Court. Also as at the high court, each argument is carefully timed — most only get 10 minutes per side, though some cases, involving black-lung disease, for example, get 15 minutes.

But at the end of each case, the senior judge gavels down the case, and the judges come down from the dais, shake hands and chat with the lawyers.

Each panel must have three judges in order to conduct business. With only 11 active judges on the 4th Circuit, the panel led by Wilkinson included an African-American district court judge, who was "sitting by designation" to help the appellate court hear its cases.

Confirmations End Years of Impasse

MARCH 11 — After years of delay and controversy — including charges that Republicans opposed some judicial nominees based on their race and ethnicity — the Senate on March 9 voted to confirm Richard A. Paez and Marsha L. Berzon to lifetime seats on the 9th U.S. Circuit Court of Appeals.

The vote for Paez was 59-29; the vote for Berzon was 64-34. *(Votes 38 and 40, p. S-10)*

Opposition to Paez and Berzon stemmed both from their backgrounds and from the fact that they were appointed to serve on the massive 9th Circuit, a court that conservatives say is too liberal and out of touch with its constituents.

On March 7, the Senate confirmed, 93-0, Julio M. Fuentes to be a judge on the 3rd U.S. Circuit Court of Appeals, which hears cases from New Jersey, Pennsylvania, Delaware and the U.S. Virgin Islands. *(Vote 34, p. S-10)*

Fuentes will be the first Hispanic on that court. He was confirmed just one day short of the first anniversary of his nomination.

The Senate has confirmed seven judicial nominees this year. Another two have been approved by the Judiciary Committee and await floor action, while 33 are pending before the committee.

Thirty-nine vacancies have no nominee named.

Paez's Problems

President Clinton decided in 1996 to elevate Paez, 52, a U.S. District Court judge in central California. Clinton resubmitted the nomination at the start of the 106th Congress. The Senate Judiciary Committee approved his nomination, 10-8, on July 29, 1999.

Berzon, 54, a labor lawyer, was first nominated in January 1998. Clinton renominated her in early 1999, and the Judiciary Committee reported out her nomination on July 1, 1999.

But the nominations lingered on the calendar until Senate Majority Leader Trent Lott, R-Miss., agreed last year to bring the pair up for a vote before March 15 in order to end a Democratic hold on a nominee to the Tennessee Valley Authority who was supported by Lott.

According to Democrats, Paez spent longer waiting for confirmation than any previous nominee. The seat he will fill has been vacant since January 1996.

Vice President Al Gore, who rushed to Washington from the presidential campaign trail in case he was needed to break a tie vote, urged the Senate to act more rapidly on future nominations. "When it comes to our judiciary, justice delayed is still justice denied. So today I say to the Senate majority once again, stop holding our justice system hostage," Gore said.

"It has been a tortured path to this day," said Democratic Sen. Barbara Boxer of California, a key supporter of Paez and Berzon. "Thank goodness that Richard and Marsha hung in there."

Republicans had raised objections to Paez on several fronts, including his handling of a trial dealing with abortion protesters and his ruling in a case dealing with human rights in Burma.

Most recently, Republican Sen. Jeff Sessions of Alabama — who lost a bid for a federal judgeship in 1986 when the Judiciary Committee rejected him — raised questions about Paez's sentencing of John Huang, a key figure in the campaign fundraising scandal that grew out of the Clinton-Gore 1996 re-election campaign.

Based on the recommendation made and evidence presented by the Justice Department, Paez sentenced Huang to no jail time.

"We ought not to be doing this," Sessions said March 8. "We ought not to be shoving this thing through."

A motion by Sessions to delay consideration of Paez's nomination indefinitely failed, 31-67. *(Vote 39, p. S-10)*

Lott said he opposed Paez because of "highly questionable rulings and political statements while sitting on the bench. . . . You should assume the bench and keep your mouth shut."

But Paez won the support of Judiciary Committee Chairman Orrin G. Hatch, R-Utah, and 13 other Republicans crossed party lines to vote for him.

Berzon's Record

Berzon, a San Francisco lawyer, has specialized in employment discrimination cases and has prepared many briefs for the Supreme Court, including four she personally argued before the justices.

Berzon seemed to be more a victim of the GOP's antipathy toward the 9th Circuit than anything specific she had done. While many Republicans included her with Paez, the objections generally had to do with Paez's statements or rulings.

For example, Jim Bunning, R-Ky., said on March 8 that he opposed Berzon's nomination because "looking at her past and the causes which she has pushed show that, if confirmed, she is not going to help steer the 9th Circuit toward the judicial mainstream."

Lott was even more oblique: "When you look at her position on many issues that will come before the court, there's high doubt about the basis of her confirmation."

But even more Republicans defected in favor of Berzon. Nineteen Republicans crossed party lines to support her confirmation.

Gordon H. Smith, R-Ore., summed up his reason for supporting Paez's nomination this way: "I didn't find anything that disqualified him, so I voted yes." ◆

Congress Creates Tougher Penalties for Distribution, Manufacture of 'Speed'

Box Score

- **Bill:** HR 4365 — PL 106-310
- **Legislative action: House** passed HR 4365, 419-2, on May 9.

Senate passed HR 4365, amended, by voice vote Sept. 22.

House cleared the bill, 394-25, on Sept. 27.

President signed the bill Oct. 17.

SUMMARY

Legislation to increase penalties for manufacturing methamphetamine and amphetamine was enacted as part of a package of children's health legislation.

Both chambers had worked on legislation aimed at curbing the the growing use of methamphetamine, a drug that provides a temporary high but can lead to both mental and physical ailments. The Senate passed a similar bill (S 486) in 1999. The House Judiciary Committee approved its version (HR 2987) on July 26, 2000, after removing several controversial provisions, including language that would have made it a crime to distribute information on how to manufacture the drug, including via the Internet. Another provision stripped from the bill would have expanded law enforcement's ability to search property without immediately notifying the owners.

Those provisions were not included in the children's health package. In addition to creating tougher penalties for those who manufacture and distribute methamphetamine and the similar drug amphetamine, the final bill authorized extra funding to assist local and federal drug enforcement agencies and to increase research, training and prevention efforts. *(Children's health, p. 12-41)*

House Panel OKs Crackdown on Methamphetamine

JULY 29 — A comprehensive measure to toughen penalties for the manufacture or sale of methamphetamine and related drugs is headed to the House floor, but changes made by the Judiciary Committee will likely produce a lively conference with the Senate.

Committee members approved the bill (HR 2987) by voice vote July 25. It is likely to pass the House in early September under expedited procedures, since the panel removed provisions that some House members found controversial. Those provisions remain in the Senate-passed bill (S 486).

Both measures would authorize more money for law enforcement agencies and for drug prevention and treatment programs. They also would stiffen penalties for making and selling methamphetamine (known as "speed") as well as amphetamine. The House bill would stiffen penalties for certain "club drugs," including ecstasy.

The House bill ran into problems in committee over provisions that some panel members said would infringe on free speech and other rights.

In a surprise development, the committee adopted an amendment, 15-12, to remove a provision that would have made it a crime to teach others how to make drugs — including by posting recipes on the Internet. The Senate bill contains that language.

The amendment, a rare example of teamwork between Tammy Baldwin, D-Wis., and Bob Barr, R-Ga., won support from five Republicans and opposition from three Democrats. Barr said the language would for the first time "codify a restriction on free speech."

Asa Hutchinson, R-Ark., disagreed, saying a similar law already makes it illegal to teach bomb-making techniques. "It's frustrating," Hutchinson said after the language was removed. "There's no way we can stop information from going out to teach people how to do meth labs, even if it's with the intent to commit a federal crime."

The panel adopted by voice vote a substitute by Bill McCollum, R-Fla., that dropped a controversial provision that would expand law enforcement's ability to search property without immediately notifying the owner. It also dropped language mandating specific increases in penalties for operating a methamphetamine lab. Instead, the U.S. Sentencing Commission would decide whether increases were necessary.

Republicans also agreed to cut a controversial section holding Internet service providers liable if they failed to dump Web sites that promoted crimes related to methamphetamine. The Senate bill includes these provisions.

Democrats pushed hard but failed to remove from the bill language they said would create new mandatory minimum sentences. They argued that such sentences are ineffective and limit judges' discretion.

The bill would direct the Sentencing Commission to increase penalties for making amphetamine, bringing them in line with penalties for making methamphetamine. The two drugs are similar in composition and effect, yet penalties for amphetamine are currently less severe, said a committee aide. McCollum's substitute would add a similar provision to increase penalties for making or selling ecstasy and other drugs.

Hutchinson argued that these provisions would not create mandatory minimums and that judges would be able to lower sentences on a case-by-case basis.

But most Democrats were not convinced. The panel gave voice vote approval to an amendment by ranking Democrat John Conyers Jr. of Michigan, stipulating that the bill would not create new mandatory minimum sentences.

Conyers also added language to allow federal judges to apply alternative sentences — such as house arrest, substance abuse treatment and electronic monitoring — in certain drug cases.

Hutchinson secured $10 million in additional funds to reimburse states for cleaning up the residue left by closed-down methamphetamine labs. States have run out of money for those cleanups this year, an issue lawmakers have raised repeatedly.

His amendment, adopted by voice vote, also would authorize $20 million for cleanups in fiscal 2001. The House-passed appropriations bill for the departments of Commerce, Justice and State (HR 4690) currently includes $20 million for fiscal 2001 but no funding to reimburse the states for fiscal 2000. *(CJS appropriations, 2-23)*

While most illegal drugs are manufactured outside U.S. borders and smuggled in, methamphetamine presents a unique problem because it is mainly produced in the United States and can be made with readily available over-the-counter medications.

Ecstasy is also a growing problem. On July 26, law enforcement authorities seized more than 2 million tablets of the dance-party drug in Los Angeles. ◆

Congress Clears Bill To Protect Religious Groups In Land-Use Disputes

Box Score

- **Bill:** S 2869 — PL 106-274
- **Legislative action: Senate** passed S 2869 by voice vote July 27.

House cleared the bill by voice vote July 27.

President signed the bill Sept. 22.

SEPTEMBER 2 — Congress has cleared legislation that would give federal protection to religious groups in some of their battles with state and local governments.

The bill (S 2869) would make it harder for local governments to enforce zoning or other land-use regulations against religious groups. It also would make it easier for prisoners or others confined in state-run institutions to practice their faith, even if they need special treatment to do so.

The Senate passed the bill by unanimous consent on July 27. The House passed it by voice vote later the same day, clearing the measure for President Clinton, who is expected to sign it.

It was an unexpectedly quick resolution to a thorny issue Congress has been working on for three years. In 1997, the Supreme Court struck down a much broader law that was designed to protect virtually all religious expression from state and local interference.

The current version of the bill is far more limited, offering protection to religious groups only in land-use disputes such as zoning issues. That change hastened its voyage through Congress. No committee marked up the bill before it was enacted, though committees have held hearings on the issue.

Because the bill was so narrowly crafted, the Leadership Conference on Civil Rights, which had opposed previous versions, endorsed it. Bipartisan support for the bill was evidenced by its backers: It was introduced by Senate Judiciary Committee Chairman Orrin G. Hatch, R-Utah, with veteran liberal Sen. Edward M. Kennedy, D-Mass., as a cosponsor.

"Our goal in passing this legislation is to reach a reasonable and constitutionally sound balance between respecting the compelling interests of government and protecting the ability of people to freely exercise their religion," Kennedy said in a statement issued the day the bill cleared.

Still, not everyone supported the effort, and it remains to be seen whether the courts will allow Congress to assert this authority. A coalition of state and local municipal groups opposed the measure, arguing it would essentially exempt religious organizations from critical local land regulation.

"The law is designed to create a special standard for religious institutions," said Stephanie Osborn, associate legislative director at the National Association of Counties.

Strict Scrutiny

In fact, creating a special standard for religious groups is exactly what leaders in Congress are trying to accomplish. Or, more precisely, what they are trying to return to.

The Supreme Court started this particular fight with its 1990 ruling in *Employment Division, Department of Human Resources v. Smith*. In that case, the court upheld, 5-4, an Oregon law that barred the use of peyote, a hallucinogen used by some American Indians in religious ceremonies.

The court found that because the Oregon law applied to everyone and did not single out a particular religion, it was constitutionally sound. The decision marked an important departure from tradition for the court, which had previously rejected all government regulations that impinged upon religious practices unless the government could prove a "compelling" public interest for the rule. *(1990 Almanac, p. 514)*

Congress responded in 1993 with the Religious Freedom Restoration Act (PL 103-141). That law restored the "compelling interest" or strict scrutiny test for all government actions that could affect the practice of religion. *(1993 Almanac, p. 315)*

But the Supreme Court struck down much of that law in 1997, in *City of Boerne v. Flores*. By a vote of 6-3, the court ruled that Congress had exceeded its authority in applying the law to state and local governments (portions of the law which applied to the federal government were upheld.) *(1997 Almanac, p. 5-23)*

New Attempt

In one sense, the new bill is an attempt by Congress to reassert its authority on constitutional rights. The bill would require that when land use regulations impose a significant burden on a religious institution the government must show that its rules serve a compelling state interest and are the least restrictive means of doing so.

The bill also would require all governments to allow those who were institutionalized in a state facility to practice their faith, unless the government could show it had a compelling interest in blocking such activity. That standard would apply to prisons, state hospitals, nursing homes and similar institutions.

In addition to narrowing the bill's focus, drafters of the current measure aim to get around the 1997 ruling by tying its authority to federal purse strings. The bill would apply to any organization that received federal money, including the vast majority of state and local prisons that get federal construction and maintenance funds.

The bill also would apply when a conflict over religious practices was in any way linked to interstate commerce. Bill sponsors said that because construction materials are shipped between states, the bill would cover construction or renovation of buildings owned by religious organizations.

But the Supreme Court has been skeptical of Commerce Clause claims: In May it struck down part of the 1994 Violence Against Women Act (PL 103-322) partly because of what the court considered Congress' overly broad application of its Commerce Clause power.

Finally, the bill would apply when a government had formal or informal procedures by which it made individual assessments of the proposed use of property, a description that would fit most local zoning plans. ◆

Sponsors of Victims' Rights Amendment Pull Bill In Face of Senate Opposition

Box Score

- **Bills:** S J Res 3, H J Res 64
- **Legislative action: Senate** voted to limit debate on a motion to proceed to S J Res 3, 82-12, on April 25.

Senate debated the motion until the bill was pulled from the floor April 27.

APRIL 29 —After a week of debate, the Senate on April 27 shelved a proposed constitutional amendment to guarantee rights to crime victims. It seemed unlikely to return to the floor this year.

The resolution (S J Res 3) would grant nine specific constitutional rights to victims of violent crime, including the rights to be notified of and to attend all public proceedings related to the crime.

"Not enough is being done to protect the rights of . . . victims," said Jon Kyl, R-Ariz., sponsor of the amendment. Defendants' rights, on the other hand, are spelled out in the Constitution, he said. "It is time to level the playing field, to balance the scales of justice, and provide some rights for the victims of crime."

But the unwieldy and frequently changing nature of the proposal, combined with members' general reluctance to amend the Constitution, left supporters far short of the two-thirds majority needed for approval of such an amendment. Supporters acknowledged that they did not even have the 60 votes needed to invoke cloture to limit debate on the proposal. The Senate invoked cloture on a motion to proceed to the proposal, 82-12, on April 25. *(Vote 86, p. S-18)*

Many Democrats and some Republicans said they would rather protect victims through passage of a law, turning to a constitutional amendment only if the law proved inadequate.

Kyl said April 27 that resolution sponsors had decided to pull the measure without an up-or-down vote. "We recognize that to proceed would result in a vote that would not be successful," he said. "I don't understand why there is such a visceral negative reaction to what we are trying to do."

Kyl added: "That merely means a timeout in our efforts to secure passage of this constitutional amendment." Dianne Feinstein, D-Calif., the lead cosponsor of the amendment, agreed: "We will come back, and we will fight again another day."

Further Along

Despite its ending, the Senate floor debate was the furthest supporters had been able to push the proposal in more than four years. Kyl and Feinstein began their joint effort in 1996, introducing victims' rights amendments in the 104th and 105th Congresses. The Judiciary Committee approved a resolution in 1998 but it never saw floor action.

According to the committee, 32 states have adopted some version of a victims' rights amendment to their constitutions.

Dozens of groups lobbied for the measure, forming an umbrella coalition called the National Victims' Constitutional Amendment Network. It includes such organizations as Mothers Against Drunk Driving, the National Governors' Association, and the National Center for Missing and Exploited Children.

The amendment also picked up some high-profile detractors, such as conservative columnist George Will. The Judicial Conference, the administrative organ of the federal judicial system, also opposed the amendment and urged Congress to pass a statute instead.

The nine specific rights for victims of violent crimes that would be added to the Constitution under the Senate resolution are:

- To be notified of proceedings in the case.
- To attend important proceedings,

such as a trial or plea bargain.

- To be heard at five points in the process: at plea bargain, bail or release hearings, sentencing, parole hearings and pardon or commutation decisions.
- To be notified of a proposed pardon and to be heard on the proposal.
- To be notified of escape or release.
- To be considered in decisions regarding delay of trial.
- To be allowed to recover restitution for the crime.
- To have their safety considered.
- To be notified of these rights.

Constitutional Need

From the beginning of the debate, the toughest argument Kyl and Feinstein faced came from those who agreed that victims' rights deserved protection but thought that a law would suffice.

"One should only debate constitutional amendments when there is no other way to go. We should not mess with the Constitution. We should not tamper with the Constitution," said Charles E. Schumer, D-N.Y. Over the years, more than 11,000 constitutional amendments have been proposed, but only 27 have been adopted. "What is called for here is a statute," Schumer said.

But Feinstein said: "The reason a federal statute will not work is that it has not worked before."

In 1997, Congress passed a law (PL 105-6) to make sure that the victims of the 1995 Oklahoma City bombing and their families could attend the trials of the two men accused of the crime. The law allowed victims who intended to speak during the penalty phase to attend the trial itself, and prohibited federal judges from barring them from the courtroom. *(1997 Almanac, p. 5-16)*

Previously, judges were allowed to bar the victims if the judge thought their testimony could be tainted by watching the proceedings. The judge in the Oklahoma case, Richard Matsch, had ruled that victims who wanted to testify at the penalty phase would be barred from watching the trial.

After Congress passed the 1997 law, Matsch reversed himself and allowed the victims to watch the trial. He then required them to undergo questioning by lawyers in the case to ensure that their testimony had not been influenced by what they had seen at the trial. According to prosecutors, no victim who wanted to testify was prevented from doing so.

Feinstein and Kyl argued that victims' rights were not adequately protected by the process, yet government attorneys testified that most victims felt they had been treated fairly. Some Oklahoma victims support the proposed constitutional amendment; some do not.

The process on the Senate floor the week of April 24 also made many members uncomfortable. Kyl said his proposal had gone through 63 drafts in four years and that negotiations with the White House were ongoing.

"The fact that so many changes were made over the years indicates to me that the subject matter would be better dealt with by legislation than by a federal constitutional amendment," said Robert C. Byrd, D-W.Va. "To me, it suggests a less than serious — dare I say — a frivolous view of a constitutional amendment."

Adding to that problem was what critics said was the bulky nature of the proposal — comprising more than two pages of text, compared with the leaner, less specific language of other constitutional amendments. ◆

CQ

Chapter 16

SCIENCE

NASA's 1st Reauthorization Since 1992 Includes Curb On Space Station's Cost

SUMMARY

Congress finished work on a $42.4 billion, three-year reauthorization for NASA, the first time since 1992 that the space agency has had its own authorizing legislation. The bill was signed into law Oct. 30.

After the House and Senate passed separate reauthorization bills in 1999, conferees spent the first half of 2000 in on-and-off talks to solve lingering differences. Key points of contention included the cost and scope of the International Space Station and the $75 million Triana satellite, a project championed by Vice President Al Gore to beam images of Earth to the Internet. *(1999 Almanac, p. 19-3)*

The final bill capped space station development costs at $25 billion over three years and limited the amount of money that can be spent flying the space shuttle on assembly missions to $17.7 billion. In exchange for the cost caps, Republicans dropped a provision in the House bill that would have blocked funding for the earth-imaging satellite. The conference report also contained language instructing NASA to obtain assurances from Russia that it places completion of the space station ahead of keeping its aging Mir space station in orbit.

While the reauthorization reasserted the House Science Committee's oversight of NASA, much of the agency's future operations will be influenced by funding decisions in the VA-HUD spending bill (HR 4635).

Box Score

- **Bill:** HR 1654 — PL 106-391
- **Legislative action: House** adopted the conference report on HR 1654 (H Rept 106-843), 399-17, on Sept. 14.

Senate cleared the bill by voice vote Oct. 13.

President signed the bill Oct. 30.

Lawmakers Want NASA to Solve Its Ongoing Troubles

MARCH 25 — NASA's self-styled "faster, better, cheaper" approach to management came under sharp congressional criticism the week of March 20 as lawmakers renewed questions about whether the space agency suffers from pervasive problems and is getting inaccurate cost estimates from its contractors.

The criticisms, aired at a March 22 hearing of the Senate Commerce Science, Technology and Space Subcommittee, are testing the political skills of NASA Administrator Daniel S. Goldin. They come as the agency is seeking a budget increase and awaiting a much-anticipated investigative report into last December's disappearance of the Mars Polar Lander space probe. A team led by former Lockheed Martin Corp. executive Thomas Young is preparing the report, which is scheduled to be released on March 28.

The congressional concern could affect NASA's fiscal 2001 funding. Senate Commerce Committee Chairman John McCain, R-Ariz., indicated that he may seek to add riders to the spending bill for the departments of Veterans Affairs (VA) and Housing and Urban Development (HUD) and independent agencies — which funds NASA — placing strict spending caps on such high-profile efforts as the International Space Station, unmanned missions to Mars and development of a reusable launch vehicle to replace the space shuttle. McCain said failures and delays arising from those three programs have already cost about $10.4 billion.

McCain Reiterates Concern

"Over the past year, I have continually been amazed by the reports coming out of NASA about the mission failures and program delays," McCain said at the hearing. "For years now, I have expressed concern regarding NASA's management, and I repeat that concern at this time."

Science Subcommittee Chairman Bill Frist, R-Tenn., echoed those sentiments. "Regardless of whether NASA's mantra is 'faster, better, cheaper,' 'mission success first' or some other phrase, 'back to basics' should be . . . an integral part of the agency's infrastructure," he said. "We need to confirm that proper management is in place and functioning as it should be."

A string of high-profile problems — from the loss of the Mars Polar Lander and Mars Climate Orbiter, to space station delays and cost overruns, to production problems with the X-33 prototype reusable space launch vehicle — have put NASA in an unusually harsh spotlight. Lawmakers on the House Science Committee castigated NASA on Feb. 16 for relying on Russia to build a critical space station module.

More broadly, lawmakers in both the House and Senate have questioned whether Goldin moved too hastily to push the agency away from what critics in the 1980s called a bloated bureaucracy.

Goldin said NASA's administrators continue to review the findings of several investigative reports into prior mishaps. He acknowledged that NASA, in some cases, suffered from a lack of communication in its ranks, and he added that turnover and budget cuts left the agency with an insufficient number of senior scientists and engineers at a time when it was flying more missions.

"Did we do things too fast? In some cases, yes," Goldin told reporters after the March 22 hearing. "We can't hide from our problems and failures. We are going to look and surgically fix the problems."

But the glitches continue to cause friction between NASA and the congressional committees that oversee the agency. For example, Frist's subcommittee last September asked NASA for a cost estimate for a key U.S. propulsion module for the space station. Frist pointedly told Goldin at the hearing that he had not yet received an answer. An embarrassed Goldin had to admit the agency was having difficulties getting reliable cost estimates from its prime contractor, Boeing Co., saying the contractor was "good" but "not outstanding."

"If we can't answer it, and you can't answer it, and your contractor can't answer it . . . something is wrong," Frist replied.

Used to Criticism

It is not the first time that the politically skilled Goldin has had to contend with congressional criticism. Last year, he persuaded House appropriators to restore some funding after warning that budget cuts could result in the closing of between one and three space centers and significant layoffs.

This year, however, NASA is seeking a budget increase after a steady decline in funding for seven years. President Clinton, in his fiscal 2001 budget, requested $13.7 billion for the space agency, a $229 million increase over estimated fiscal 2000 levels.

Members of the House Appropriations VA, HUD and Independent Agencies Subcommittee told Goldin on March 15 that while they want to help the agency, they may not be able to accommodate the budget increase because of competing spending priorities and tight budget caps.

Space Station Debate Delays Reauthorization

JULY 1 — A House-Senate conference attempting to reauthorize NASA for the first time since 1992 remains stalled after Republicans and Democrats failed June 27 to resolve lingering differences over the cost and scope of the troubled International Space Station being built with Russia.

House Republicans offered to drop language they inserted in the bill (HR 1654) that would kill Vice President Al Gore's Triana satellite project in exchange for Democrats' agreeing to cap the space station's costs. However, House Democrats insisted that their GOP colleagues first consider a series of legislative proposals they submitted June 23.

After a series of testy exchanges, Rep. F. James Sensenbrenner Jr., R-Wis., chairman of the conference, told conferees to adjourn until after the July Fourth recess while staff aides try to resolve the most contentious issues.

Committed to an Agreement

Both parties said they remain committed to producing an agreement this year. "Nobody gets everything they wanted, but I am willing to meet folks in the middle," said Sensenbrenner, who is chairman of the House Science Committee.

Ralph M. Hall of Texas, ranking Democrat on the House Science Committee, held out his own olive branch to Republicans. "The compromise proposal we presented . . . would add words that soften the situation," he said.

The reauthorization measure would provide $41 billion for the space agency through fiscal 2002. The House and Senate passed separate versions last year and have spent the past six months in on-and-off negotiations. Because of the lack of an authorization bill, funding and policy decisions for the space agency have been made as part of the VA-HUD spending bill since the 102nd Congress.

GOP conferees said they were making a major concession in dropping House-passed language that would cancel the Triana Earth-observation satellite, charging that its cost has more than tripled, to as much as $221 million. Triana, named for the sailor on Christopher Columbus' flagship who legend says was the first European to sight the New World, is designed to study global climate and solar energy patterns. It would also transmit full-color images of the sunlit side of Earth to the Internet.

Republicans have derided the project as an expensive "screen saver," while Democrats say the GOP is focusing on it to take political shots at their likely 2000 presidential nominee.

When GOP lawmakers sought to cap space station spending in exchange for the concession on Triana, House Democrats complained that Republicans had not responded to several proposals they submitted on June 23 regarding spending for the station and other NASA programs.

Sensenbrenner said the proposals arrived too late — as lawmakers were preparing to return to their districts for the weekend.

Arguments over the space station had been expected because of continued delays and overruns associated with the project, whose final cost could reach $60 billion, according to some estimates.

Sensenbrenner and Senate Commerce Committee Chairman John McCain, R-Ariz., also a conferee, support the project but are concerned about Russia's failure to deliver a key service module as well as NASA's management of program costs.

The two lawmakers asked the General Accounting Office (GAO) on June 21 to investigate development of a U.S. module designed as a backup to the Russian unit. The U.S. module, which consists of a propulsion segment and short-term crew quarters, has encountered design difficulties and may be as much as $200 million over budget. The Russian module consists of a propulsion unit and permanent crew quarters.

The lawmakers contend that U.S. dependence on Russian performance in the space station program has cost taxpayers an estimated $5 billion and delayed the program by three years.

Republican conferees want language in the authorization bill instructing NASA to recover $1.3 billion from Russia in goods and services the space agency had to purchase due to production delays.

The GOP lawmakers also insist on capping space station costs at $25 billion — about $1 billion more than administration estimates — which they say will ensure that NASA does not overspend to complete the project.

"In a sense, Congress is committing to a reserve for the program that will reverse NASA's history of putting off solving problems due to a lack of reserves," said GOP Rep. Dana Rohrabacher of California, chairman of the Science Subcommittee on Space and Aeronautics.

Deflating TransHab

Republicans also insist on keeping a restriction in the House-passed bill that would prevent spending money on the TransHab, an inflatable, reinforced fabric module that could serve as a home for space station astronauts. Rohrabacher said developing TransHab would lead to a redesign of the station, further delaying the project and driving up costs.

NASA has objected to the cost caps and the restriction on TransHab, though it is unclear whether either provision would prompt a veto from President Clinton.

House Democrats, while echoing concerns about Russian involvement in the program, said they want to allow spending exemptions to improve space shuttle safety and reliability. They also want language in the bill that would allow NASA to cooperate on a commercially developed TransHab module.

Congress Votes To Reauthorize Space Agency

SEPTEMBER 16 — The House overwhelmingly backed legislation (HR 1654) reauthorizing NASA through 2002, marking the first time since 1992 that the space agency has been authorized by either chamber.

Lawmakers voted 399-17 to adopt a conference report (H Rept 106-843) on Sept. 14 that calls for spending $42.4 billion over three years and places caps on development costs of the International Space Station, which has been plagued by delays and billions of dollars in overruns. *(Vote 475, p. H-148)*

[The Senate cleared the bill by voice vote Oct. 13.]

"This is an important bill because it helps put a congressional imprimatur on the civil space program," said House Space and Aeronautics Subcommittee Chairman Dana Rohrabacher, R-Calif. The bill includes $14.2 billion for NASA in fiscal 2001 and $14.6 billion in fiscal 2002 — more than the Clinton administration had requested.

The vote represented a victory of sorts for the panel, which oversees NASA but has seen funding and policy decisions for the agency made by House and Senate appropriators since the 102nd Congress as part of the annual VA-HUD appropriations bill. Appropriators still will have the final say on all funding levels.

The filing of the conference report Sept. 12 came after months of behind-the-scenes wrangling between Republicans and Democrats over the cost and scope of the space station and such related issues as development of TransHab, an inflatable module designed to serve as its crew quarters.

The two sides also sparred over the Triana earth-observation satellite — a pet project of Vice President Al Gore's designed to provide high-definition views of the Earth on television and the Internet. Republicans complained that the satellite's cost had quadrupled to more than $220 million, while Democrats said the GOP was focusing on the project to embarrass Gore, their presidential candidate.

Republicans dropped a provision in the original House bill blocking funding for Triana — which they once derided as an expensive computer "screen saver" — in exchange for new cost controls on the space station. The conference report caps development costs for the station at $25 billion and limits the amount of money that can be spent flying the space shuttle on assembly missions to $17.7 billion, or $380 million per launch.

The report also contains language instructing NASA to obtain assurances from Russia that it places completion of the station ahead of keeping its own aging Mir space station in orbit. The provision reflects congressional frustration at Russia's decision earlier this year to divert three spacecraft intended for the international station to Mir.

Conferees, including Sens. John McCain, R-Ariz., and Bill Frist, R-Tenn., contend that problems associated with Russian involvement in the space station have resulted in cost overruns of $5 billion and at least three years of delays. The biggest problem centered on a critical Russian-built service module that was finally placed into orbit this summer.

The TransHab Debate

The report contains language advocated by House Science Committee Chairman F. James Sensenbrenner Jr., R-Wis., and Rohrabacher that would bar any federal money from being used to buy or design the three-level TransHab module. Opponents believe including TransHab will dramatically alter the station's design and drive up costs. However, the report allows NASA to lease a privately developed TransHab. Conferees gave NASA until April 1, 2001, to assess its options.

The TransHab provision did not sit well with lawmakers from the greater Houston area, where the structure is being developed at the Johnson Space Center. Nick Lampson, D-Texas, said he would introduce legislation allowing NASA to jointly develop the module with private industry. Sheila Jackson-Lee, D-Texas, said she would back Lampson's effort.

The report also:

• Establishes contingency funds of $5 billion for the space station and $3.5 billion for the shuttle to address "any urgent situation" on the station that could endanger the crew.

• Contains language modeled on a provision in the fiscal 2000 defense authorization law (PL 106-65) stipulating that any joint ventures between NASA and the People's Republic of China not indirectly help Chinese efforts to develop new commercial launch vehicles or ballistic missile capabilities.

• Includes Senate language prohibiting "obtrusive space advertising" that can be viewed by the naked eye. The prohibition does not apply to such advertising practices as placing logos on commercial space launch vehicles and satellites. ◆

CQ

Chapter 17

SOCIAL POLICY

Clinton Lauds Earnings-Limit Repeal as First Step Toward Social Security Overhaul

SUMMARY

Congress cleared legislation that removes the limit on how much outside income retirees age 65 through 69 may earn and still collect full Social Security benefits. The president signed the bill April 7.

The Social Security "earnings test" was created during the Depression in an effort to discourage senior citizens from holding onto their jobs in a period of high unemployment. Under that law, senior citizens age 65 through 69 lost $1 in benefits for every $3 they received in wages above an annual limit ($17,000 in 2000, rising to $30,000 by 2002).

Those who lost benefits in this way received higher monthly checks to compensate for the loss later on. There were no earnings limits for recipients age 70 and older. According to the Social Security Administration, 800,000 people had some benefits deferred because they exceeded the earnings limit in 1999.

The bill repealed the test for people above the age required to reap full Social Security benefits, which is scheduled to increase gradually from 65 in 2000 to 67 by 2027. It did not repeal the earnings test for retirees age 62 through 64 or for individuals who receive Social Security disability insurance.

Enactment of the earnings repeal was the end result of 27 months of discussion on overhauling Social Security that began with Clinton's 1998 State of the Union address. Despite several attempts by the White House and various members of Congress to revamp the Social Security system, the politically popular earnings repeal was the only Social Security bill enacted.

Ending the earnings test should have no long-term budgetary impact, since working seniors eventually got the money back under the old system. Still, it is expected to deplete the Social Security trust fund by $8.2 billion in fiscal 2001 and by $22.7 billion in the next decade. That is because Social Security will continue to pay higher monthly benefits to people who had their benefits deferred while the earnings test was in effect, and at the same time begin paying full benefits to those previously subject to the limit.

Bipartisan Support Propels House Social Security Bill

FEBRUARY 19 — Having played Charlie Brown to President Clinton's Lucy on so many political footballs that have emerged in the past three years from the House Ways and Means Committee, it appeared the week of Feb. 14 as though Republicans were finally ready to kick one through the uprights.

Legislation (HR 5) to lift the limit on how much outside income retirees ages 65 through 69 may earn and still collect their full Social Security benefits looks to be headed for quick enactment. That would mark the first substantive change to tax or entitlement law since 1997, when twin reconciliation measures were enacted to carry out the budget-balancing and tax cut deal between Clinton and the GOP.

"This is going to be one of the happiest days . . . which all of us are going to remember for doing the right thing," Republican E. Clay Shaw Jr. of Florida, chairman of the Ways and Means Social Security Subcommittee, declared as the Feb. 16 markup began. Ten minutes later, the bill to repeal the "earnings test" had been approved by voice vote.

Robert T. Matsui of California, the panel's ranking Democrat, used the markup to highlight other Democratic priorities — helping impoverished women and disabled people on Social Security. But he did not offer a disparaging remark about the bill, which did not specifically help those groups. "You make a better friend than an enemy," Shaw told Matsui, referring to the acrimonious debates that have engulfed Ways and Means in recent years.

Some of that ire has already surfaced this year, on legislation (HR 6) the House passed Feb. 10 to change the tax treatment for most married couples. Though Democrats and Clinton share the Republican goal of reducing penalties in the tax code for married couples, they have a host of objections to the GOP bill; their chief argument is that such an expensive tax cut — $182 billion in the next decade — should wait until Social Security and Medicare are made solvent and the national debt is paid down.

The "marriage penalty" and earnings test measures are among the few stand-alone bills advanced by Ways and Means in recent years. Although the Social Security legislation is not a tax cut bill per se — as are most of the stand-alone GOP measures going before the panel this year — many Social Security recipients would view it as one, because they describe the current earnings limit as essentially a tax on their income.

People ages 65 through 69 now lose $1 in Social Security benefits for each $3 they earn above an annual limit — $17,000 this year, rising to $30,000 in two years. Those 62 through 64 lose $1 for every $2 in excess earnings. But all who lose benefits in this way receive higher monthly checks to compensate for the loss later on. There are no earnings limits for recipients age 70 and older.

In an interview with CNN on Feb. 14, Clinton said he was "thrilled" with

Box Score

- **Bill:** HR 5 — PL 106-182
- **Legislative action: House** passed HR 5 (H Rept 106-507), 422-0, on March 1.

Senate passed HR 5, amended, 100-0, on March 22.

House cleared HR 5, 419-0, on March 28.

President signed the bill April 7.

the proposal. "If they will send me a bill," he said, that "doesn't have a lot of other things unrelated to that littered to it, I will be happy to sign it."

Clinton added that he hoped Congress would still consider broader Social Security overhaul, an unlikely proposition this year. At a Feb. 15 Ways and Means hearing on the earnings limit, Lloyd Doggett, D-Texas, said, "Congress should be grappling with the tough choices about how to extend the solvency of Social Security for all," not just considering an "eat dessert first" bill. But he did not oppose the measure at the markup the next day.

Keeping the bill clean, as Clinton wants, could be easy under the rules of the House, which may consider the measure as soon as March 2. Keeping the measure narrow in scope could be far more tricky under the rules governing the other side of the Capitol. The Senate was in recess the week of Feb. 14, but lobbyists speculated that a number of senators might see the bill as an opportunity to carry favored provisions to the White House. Such efforts could slow action on the bill, but few senators in either party are likely to oppose the underlying measure.

Bipartisan enthusiasm for the legislation was made easier by the endorsement of the AARP, voiced at a Social Security Subcommittee hearing Feb. 15. "Given the increased longevity and generally improved health of many retirees, the prospect of an aging society, and a slower-growing work force, it is critical that we find ways to better tap the valuable and underutilized skills of older workers," said Jane Baumgarten, a board member of the association.

Republicans have long attacked the limit as unwise and unfair. A proposal to reduce it was in the "Contract With America," the House GOP candidates' platform that helped propel the party's takeover of Congress in 1994. An increase in the limit (PL 104-121) was enacted two years later, and last year Clinton proposed a further relaxation.

How Far to Go?

In order to avoid controversy, Shaw and bill sponsor Sam Johnson, R-Texas, decided against proposing a repeal of the penalty for those workers who begin collecting Social Security benefits before turning 65. About three of every five workers begin taking benefits at age 62, the earliest opportunity; in exchange, their monthly benefits are forever reduced. Benefits are further reduced — by $1 for every $2 earned above $10,080 annually — for those ages 62, 63 and 64 who continue to work. Those lost Social Security earnings are replenished when workers turn 65 through what are known as delayed-retirement credits.

At the Feb. 15 hearing, Social Security Commissioner Kenneth S. Apfel said that ending the earnings test for early retirees could exacerbate elderly poverty. That is because, he said, the move might make it more attractive for workers to retire early, even though they — and perhaps their surviving spouses — could receive benefits so reduced as to make them insufficient to live on without additional income.

Repealing the earnings limit for retirees ages 65 through 69 did not raise such questions and enjoyed the added benefit of being less costly.

The bill would deplete the Social Security trust fund by $8.2 billion in fiscal 2001 and by $22.7 billion in the next decade. That is because Social Security would continue to be paying higher monthly benefits to people who lost aid while the earnings test was in effect, and at the same would be required to begin paying full benefits to those who have earned income that is above the previous penalty-free limit. Once both the limits and the corresponding credits are removed, the proposed repeal would be cost-neutral in the long term.

Under the bill, the earnings limit would be repealed for people older than the age required to reap full Social Security benefits, which is scheduled to increase gradually to 67 by 2027.

Some subcommittee Democrats said they also would like to repeal the earnings limit for the blind, $1,170 a month this year. Republicans said that would be unfair without also repealing a $700 monthly cap on earnings by other disabled people. Both groups can qualify for Social Security before retirement age if they do not partake in "substantial gainful activity" above those limits. Members decided not to tackle the changes because they would have increased the bill's costs and possibly jeopardized a smooth ride through Congress.

House Votes Unanimously for Social Security Bill

MARCH 4 — Spurred on by a rare signal of unanimity from the House, Republican and Democratic leaders in the Senate are working together to clear legislation the week of March 6 that would allow senior citizens to earn as much as they want without sacrificing any Social Security benefits.

Aides to Majority Leader Trent Lott, R-Miss., and Minority Leader Tom Daschle, D-S.D., say they are working to win the unanimous consent of senators to call up the bill (HR 5) that the House passed on March 1 and put it to a vote without any amendments. They appear confident that a vote to clear the measure would be overwhelming, if not unanimous, and President Clinton has pledged to sign it if it arrives on his desk free of unrelated provisions.

The bill won a voice-vote endorsement from the Ways and Means Committee on Feb. 29. The House vote was 422-0 to pass the legislation the next day. *(Vote 27, p. H-12)*

The measure is popular with two important constituencies — the elderly, who are already receiving benefits from the retirement income system, and Baby Boomers, whose retirements are looming. The bill would do away with a rule under which senior citizens ages 65 through 69 lose $1 in benefits for every $3 they receive in wages beyond an annual limit, which is $17,000 this year. The Social Security Administration says 800,000 people sacrificed some benefits by exceeding the earnings limit in 1999.

Senators — especially those in the minority party — typically resist efforts to curtail their cherished right to try to amend high-profile legislation on the floor. But they appear likely to do so in this case, because controversial amendments could be portrayed as obstructionist on the campaign trail and could jeopardize one of the more high-profile entitlement changes in three years.

Hours after the House passed the earnings test bill, Lott signaled in an interview that he might seek to amend it with language to alleviate the tax code's "marriage penalty," which would be accomplished under a bill (HR 6) the House passed Feb. 10. Democrats had also considered trying to use it as a vehicle for some of their policy initiatives.

But such talk had faded by the evening of March 2, after a huddle on the Senate floor among Lott and a half-dozen other Republicans. Two of them, Finance Committee Chairman William V. Roth Jr. of Delaware and Republican Policy Committee Chairman Larry E. Craig of Idaho, said afterward that the GOP leaders had concluded it would be best to try to clear the House bill without alteration.

Broader Changes Urged

In a letter Feb. 29, Clinton urged Daschle to support enactment of "a clean, straightforward bill." In prior years, the president had conditioned support for altering the earnings test on a more comprehensive overhaul to ensure Social Security's long-term financial viability. Despite the strong economy, serious potential funding shortfalls lie ahead, particularly if life expectancy increases as fast as predicted.

Social Security paid out $257 billion to more than 31 million retirees and their families last year. The trust fund keeping that money will exhaust its assets by 2034, when payroll taxes will cover only 71 percent of benefits, the president's fiscal 2001 budget estimates.

Ending the earnings test would have no long-term impact on the balance sheet of the Social Security system. But it would take away an important political sweetener from those in Congress who would like to enact sweeping changes to entitlements such as Social Security. Shoring up the program's finances might require benefit cuts or further increases in the eligibility age, and some members were hoping that doing away with the earnings test could help such bitter medicine go down.

"We should have spent the last year working on a comprehensive plan to strengthen Social Security that would restore solvency, reduce unfunded liabilities, give workers greater control of their retirement income, improve the safety net, and reward work," Charles W. Stenholm, D-Texas, said during the House debate. "But we, both the president and Congress, have ignored our opportunity to deal with the long-term challenges facing Social Security."

Jim Kolbe, R-Ariz., also urged that the earnings limit repeal be used as the opening move toward a more comprehensive rewrite of Social Security. "Election year or not . . . this nation must address the financial crisis that looms over Social Security," he said. "The longer we wait, the tougher the choices are going to be."

But the concerns of Kolbe and Stenholm were among the few discordant notes during the House debate, in which dozens took the microphones to sing the measure's praises.

"Seniors should be free to work without penalty and treated fairly by a program they paid into all of their lives," said Ways and Means Committee Chairman Bill Archer, R-Texas.

Partisan Sniping

The earnings test was created during the Depression, when it was intended to discourage senior citizens from holding on to their jobs during a period of high unemployment.

Despite the united show of support for repeal in the House, the vote was not taken without some partisan wrangling. There were reports that the National Republican Congressional Committee, the House GOP campaign arm, had urged Republican congressional challengers to consider criticizing Democratic incumbents who are now supporting an idea they opposed as recently as 1998.

For many years, the debate over efforts to increase the earnings test fell along party lines. The ceiling on penalty-free income was last raised under a law (PL 104-121) enacted in 1996.

"The $80 billion tax cut considered by the House in the fall of 1998 that included repeal of the Social Security earnings limit would have been funded entirely out of the Social Security surplus," Stenholm said.

The legislation would have neutral budget impact in the long run, because working seniors who see their benefits reduced under the earnings limit eventually get their lost benefits back in the form of higher Social Security payments after they turn 70. Still, the measure would cost $22.7 billion over the next decade, because Social Security would begin paying higher monthly benefits to those previously subject to the limit while still paying out credits to those who lost benefits under the program in previous years.

Although eliminating the earnings test would not change the tax code, the provision is often described by critics as a 33 percent income tax on many senior citizens. As such, the GOP portrays the repeal as part of its package of election-year tax breaks. The others include the marriage penalty proposal and the bill (S 1134) passed by the Senate on March 2, that would allow parents to set aside $2,000 per child per year in tax-sheltered savings accounts for education expenses. But the other two bills have nowhere near the same Democratic support as the Social Security bill.

Senate Decisively Votes to Repeal Social Security Earnings Limit

MARCH 25 — By a lopsided vote, the Senate passed a popular measure March 22 to repeal the Social Security earnings limit for people over age 65 — and effectively shut the door on two years of talk about a possible overhaul of the program.

Nobody declared the overhaul effort dead in so many words. Even as the Senate was preparing to pass the one politically attractive slice of all the Social Security proposals, senators declared that they should not stop here and that more needed to be done.

"Without question, there is still much to do on Social Security reform," said Senate Finance Committee Chairman William V. Roth Jr., R-Del.

"This is just the first step," said Sen. John McCain, R-Ariz., fresh from the presidential campaign trail.

For now, though, it is the only step.

The earnings limit repeal (HR 5) passed the Senate 100-0, with one technical correction added by a Roth amendment that would keep 64-year-olds from hitting a lower income limit than they would under current law. *(Vote 42, p. S-11)*

All that is left is House passage of the corrected version, expected the week of March 27. Then it goes to President Clinton, who said March 22 that he will sign it.

The legislation would end the practice of deferring Social Security benefits for people ages 65 through 69 if they continue to work and earn more than a certain amount each year. Although they get it back after they turn 70, they currently lose $1 in benefits for every $3 they earn over $17,000; that is scheduled to go up to $30,000 in two years.

In a statement after the Senate vote, Clinton said the earnings limit repeal is "an important first step in undertaking comprehensive Social Security reform this year."

But virtually nobody in Congress expects that to happen. Clinton asked lawmakers to follow up by passing his plan to use the Social Security surplus to pay down the debt, then using the savings on interest payments to extend the life of the Social Security trust fund. The plan has gotten no traction with congressional Republicans, who say it is nothing more than a gimmick.

A high-profile Republican plan to create private savings accounts, proposed by House Ways and Means Committee Chairman Bill Archer, R-Texas, and Social Security Subcommittee Chairman E. Clay Shaw Jr., R-Fla., went nowhere.

A bipartisan group of Senate centrists, including Judd Gregg, R-N.H., and Bob Kerrey, D-Neb., tried to shop a similar overhaul plan around but got no takers.

"This is it. This is the last hurrah for Social Security reform in this Congress," said Robert Bixby, executive director of the Concord Coalition, a watchdog group that pushes for entitlement reforms.

A Clean Bill

Eager to get the earnings limit repeal to Clinton's desk quickly, the Senate rejected a Kerrey amendment that would have rewritten the Social Security Act of 1935 to use the phrase "eligibility for old-age benefits" instead of "retirement." Kerrey wanted to make that change as a symbolic gesture to make people quit thinking of Social Security as a program for retirees, but the amendment was killed, 55-44. *(Vote 42, p. S-11)*

Gregg, meanwhile, was ready to offer an amendment that would have required the Social Security Administration to report a wide range of information to Congress on the true state of the program's finances, such as the deficits it is expected to run and the shrinking lifetime benefits it would be able to pay out under current revenue projections.

But he backed off under pressure from lawmakers from both parties, who did not want any changes that could have forced a House-Senate conference — an event that could have opened the door to other changes and threatened the bill's future. Instead, Gregg settled for a promise from Roth to try to find some other vehicle for the reporting requirements. And both Gregg and Kerrey used their floor time to talk about the dangers of doing nothing to fix the program's underlying problems.

Social Security is facing a huge strain in the coming years on several fronts. The nation's 76 million Baby Boomers are beginning to retire, older people are living longer and fewer young people are around to pay into the system.

By 2014, Social Security is expected to start paying out more than it takes in, according to the fund's trustees. By 2034, its reserves are expected to run out.

Congressional leaders say they are still determined to enact a long-term overhaul. "We have to do it in the next couple of years," said Senate Majority Leader Trent Lott, R-Miss.

But that is a far cry from the early days of 1998, when Clinton laid out a plan for a series of "town hall" meetings on Social Security, followed by a White House conference on the subject, and finally a serious bargaining session with the bipartisan leadership in 1999 that was supposed to lead to a solution. For most of the next two years, leaders of both parties routinely talked about Social Security restructuring as if it were just around the corner.

Slow Death

So what happened?

You can take your pick of the causes of death. Republicans say it died of a lack of leadership from Clinton. Centrists from both parties say it died because nobody was willing to face the traditional choices, such as cutting benefits or raising the Social Security payroll tax or considering new options such as individual investment accounts.

"It was dropped because no one picked it up," John B. Breaux, D-La., a cosponsor of the Senate centrist plan, said of the reform effort.

Still, the landscape is not totally unchanged. Both parties did start considering private investment options for the first time. But that led to a new dividing line between the parties, according to Wendell Primus of the Center on Budget and Policy Priorities, a research group that monitors programs for low-income people. Democrats wanted to go for collective investments, such as public pension plans, to earn a higher rate of return, while Republicans preferred to push for individual savings accounts.

"There's just too much of a gulf between the right and the left," Primus said in a March 20 interview.

Bixby said the "high water mark" for the Social Security debate came during the summer of 1998, when Clinton appeared with Senate Budget Committee Chairman Pete V. Domenici, R-N.M., at the last of the three town hall meetings.

Their speeches were full of promises of bipartisanship. "If we are going to do this next year," Domenici told Clinton, "it's got to have Republicans and Democrats in the House and Senate joining you to do what's best for our people."

But 1998 was also the year of Monica Lewinsky. By the fall, the momentum for change had started to slow.

Clinton went ahead with a White House conference on Social Security Dec. 9 — but "there was an air of unreality to the discussion," said Robert D. Reischauer, president of the Urban Institute and one of the experts chosen to brief the lawmakers. Ten days later, Clinton was impeached by the House. That vote, Bixby said, "poisoned the atmosphere for Social Security reform." *(1998 Almanac, p. 12-3)*

Other problems, overhaul advocates say, involve the actual plans that Clinton and the Republicans later proposed. Both sides were criticized for avoiding hard choices by simply proposing to dump general revenues into the Social Security fund, rather than making structural changes such as raising Social Security taxes or cutting benefits.

The original plan Clinton proposed in January 1999 would have used 60 percent of the projected budget surpluses over the next 15 years to prop up the Social Security trust fund. His 2001 budget included a revised version. It would use the entire Social Security surplus to pay down the national debt and then use the projected interest savings to extend the life of the Social Security trust fund until 2050.

Critics said that approach would simply put off the day of reckoning a while longer, and would rely on guesses about future budget surpluses — guesses that could be wrong.

Then, in April 1999, Archer and Shaw proposed their own plan. It called for creating private investment accounts, funded by a tax credit that would come from general revenues, as a partial replacement for regular Social Security benefits.

Seniors would get monthly payments from their accounts when they retired, with Social Security making up the difference if their investment accounts could not pay the full amount of current-law Social Security benefits.

But their plan never got past the hearing stage. The Republican leadership never endorsed it, and their conspicuous silence left Archer and Shaw open to tough questions from Democrats and outside critics. The Concord Coalition said the plan relied on a "risky game of financial arbitrage," and the Center on Budget and Policy Priorities said it would put a huge strain on the budget and probably require tax increases or program cuts.

Other types of personal savings accounts showed up in two bipartisan centrist proposals: the Gregg-Kerrey-Breaux plan in the Senate (S 1383) and a similar plan (HR 1793) by Jim Kolbe, R-Ariz., and Charles W. Stenholm, D-Texas, in the House. Neither one got out of committee.

There was one piece of the Archer-Shaw plan, however, that looked politically attractive to everyone — the repeal of the earnings limit. By February, it was the only Social Security bill that was moving through Congress.

"We're taking dessert before the rest of the dinner," warned Breaux. But he voted for it. So did everybody else.

House Clears Bill to Repeal Social Security Earnings Limit

APRIL 1 — The House passed, 419-0, an ever-so-slightly amended version of the Social Security earnings limit repeal (HR 5) on March 28. That clears the popular bill for President Clinton's signature in a ceremony that could take place the week of April 3. *(Vote 79, p. H-30)*

Now Congress has to find a way to pay for the repeal's start-up costs.

Clinton has asked Congress to add $35 million to the fiscal 2000 supplemental appropriations bill (HR 3908) for the one-time administrative costs of the repeal, such as processing new claims, handling extra telephone calls and reprogramming the computers of the Social Security Administration (SSA). But that bill faces a big fight in the Senate, where Majority Leader Trent Lott, R-Miss., has vowed not to bring up a separate supplemental spending bill.

The March 28 House vote on the repeal was necessary to approve a technical amendment added by the Senate March 22 to keep 64-year-olds from hitting a stricter earnings limit than they would have experienced under current law.

The legislation would end a Depression-era policy that defers some Social Security benefits for working seniors between the ages of 65 and 69. According to the SSA, the legislation would restore benefits to approximately 800,000 beneficiaries or their dependents this year.

Another 100,000 Americans are expected to apply for benefits in 2000 who would not have applied under the old policy because they work or are dependents.

The SSA expects to pay an additional $6 billion in benefits this year and puts the overall cost of the repeal at about $22 billion over the next 10 years.

But it is not expected to have any long-term cost, because seniors would have gotten the benefits back, anyway, after they turn 70.

Trustees Release Optimistic New Solvency Figures For Entitlements

APRIL 1 — The latest bill of health for Social Security and Medicare is only adding heat to the partisan disagreements over long-term overhaul of the programs — making it more likely than ever that new benefits for both programs are the only changes Congress will pass this year.

On March 30, the trustees for the federal government's two biggest entitlement programs announced that the booming economy has brought eight more years of expected life to the Medicare trust fund and three more years to the Social Security trust fund.

In their annual report, the trustees predicted that the Medicare Hospital Insurance trust fund, known as Part A, which pays for inpatient hospital care and related expenses, will be solvent through 2023. Last year, they had predicted the trust fund reserves would run dry in 2015.

The trustees also said they expect the Social Security trust fund to be solvent through 2037 rather than 2034.

In both cases, though, the programs will start running deficits — paying out more money in benefits than they collect in payroll taxes — long before they become insolvent. With Social Security, that is now expected to happen in 2015, only one year later than the trustees predicted last year. Medicare is now expected to resort to deficit spending in 2010; that is a better picture than the trustees painted last year, when they said the cash flow problems would begin immediately.

The release of the annual report by the trustees has become a ritual in recent years in which the predicted insolvency dates for Social Security and Medicare are moved back a few years, policy-makers hail the new estimates and praise the strong economy that made it possible, and everyone agrees that the programs still need to be overhauled — later.

The report should give Democrats new ammunition with which to reject Republican calls for a long-term

Medicare overhaul to hold down its costs. That leaves prescription drug coverage as the only Medicare proposal with enough support to move through Congress this year, assuming the two parties can work out the details.

"We don't need to radically change Medicare," said Rep. Charles B. Rangel of New York, the top Democrat on the Ways and Means Committee, which oversees Medicare.

Health and Human Services Secretary Donna E. Shalala, one of the trustees, criticized Republicans for not supporting the Clinton administration's proposal to transfer some of the budget surpluses to the Social Security and Medicare trust funds. But Republicans say the Clinton proposals would not solve the long-term problems of either program.

House Ways and Means Committee Chairman Bill Archer, R-Texas, and Social Security Subcommittee Chairman E. Clay Shaw Jr., R-Fla., renewed their call for personal investment accounts to supplement Social Security, while Health Subcommittee Chairman Bill Thomas, R-Calif., said prescription drug coverage should be added only as part of "a stronger and more modern Medicare system."

The reports have been used both as a call to action and an unspoken reason to put it off.

Every year, the trustees — three Cabinet secretaries, the Social Security commissioner and two public members named by the president and confirmed by the Senate — use a set of complex economic and demographic assumptions to look 75 years into the future of Social Security and Medicare.

Last year, the trustees moved the Social Security insolvency date back two years, from 2032 to 2034, and the Medicare date back seven years, from 2008 to 2015.

Those are not looming crisis dates. But in 1995, when the Medicare trustees said the trust fund would be out of funds in 2002, Republicans used the report to justify Medicare changes they were trying to push through Congress. President Clinton vetoed their package that year, but the pressure of the looming bankruptcy eventually led to the cuts in Medicare growth that became law in 1997 (PL 105-33). *(1995 CQ Almanac, p. 7-3; 1997 CQ Almanac, p. 2-47)*

This year, lawmakers from both parties said the good news should not become an excuse to avoid curbing the long-range costs of Social Security and Medicare. Their statements had none of the urgency of the earlier Medicare debate, and experts say the crisis dates are too remote to put any real pressure on Congress.

Both parties say they want to add a prescription drug benefit to Medicare, giving seniors drug coverage for the first time since the program was created in 1965 (PL 89-97). But they have big disagreements over how to reshape the underlying program.

Some Republicans lean toward a "competitive premium" plan, touted by Sens. John B. Breaux, D-La., and Bill Frist, R-Tenn., in which the government would subsidize seniors and let them choose from a range of private and public plans — but steer them toward the cheaper plans by making them pay more for the expensive ones. Clinton came out against a similar plan in 1999, saying it would not do enough to extend the life of the Medicare trust fund.

The Social Security debate, meanwhile, is deadlocked. That leaves the repeal of the so-called "earnings limit" — restoring benefits that would have been deferred for many seniors between the ages of 65 and 69 who have other income — as the only Social Security measure that is on track to become law. The House gave its final approval to the measure March 28.

The short-term picture for both programs may have improved, but some lawmakers warned that the long-term picture for Social Security is actually getting worse.

Rep. Jim Kolbe, R-Ariz., noted in a March 30 statement that the cash-flow deficits over the next 75 years are now estimated to reach $20.6 trillion — $1 trillion more than the trustees predicted last year.

Why? Because, he said, there is a down side to the strong economy. Social Security benefits are based on the wages people earn. So when people earn bigger salaries, as they do now, Social Security will owe them more later in life than it would have otherwise.

The trustees did throw in some warnings about the long-term outlook. By 2037, the year the Social Security trust fund reserves would be exhausted, payroll tax revenues coming into the program would be able to pay for only 72 percent of the benefits seniors will be owed, according to the report.

In addition, a second Medicare trust fund, known as Medicare Part B, which pays for doctors' bills and other outpatient care, is solvent only because spending is set each year to meet the following year's expected costs. Since medical costs are rising every year, the price increases "make finding solutions to Medicare's financing problems more difficult than for Social Security," the report warned.

Social Security paid benefits to 44.5 million Americans last year, while Medicare covered about 39 million beneficiaries.

With Baby Boomers retiring and fewer people coming behind them to pay for their benefits, the trustees said the strain on both programs is about to grow dramatically.

Next year, they said, there will be 3.4 workers for every retiree receiving Social Security benefits. They project there will be only two by 2030. The outlook for Medicare is about the same. ◆

Anti-Poverty Initiative Catches a Ride on Omnibus Spending Bill

SUMMARY

Based on a November 1999 agreement negotiated by President Clinton and House Speaker J. Dennis Hastert, R-Ill., Congress cleared a package of anti-poverty initiatives as part of the final omnibus bill. President Clinton signed the measure Dec. 21.

The anti-poverty package was a hybrid of Democratic and Republican ideas, balanced nearly 50-50, on how to stimulate the economies of poor inner-city and rural communities. As proposed by Clinton, the resulting bill included a "new markets" tax credit intended to lure investors to low-income neighborhoods by letting them claim up to $15 billion in credits for investments over seven years. It also included an expansion of "empowerment zones," which provide wage credits and other tax incentives to attract businesses, by extending the life of 31 zones and creating nine new ones.

In line with proposals by Hastert and other Republicans, it included the creation of 40 "renewal communities," similar to empowerment zones but with the addition of regulatory relief and an exemption from capital gains taxes on profits from the sale of businesses or assets held for more than five years. Another GOP provision aimed to expand "charitable choice" options by allowing the use of federal funds to support faith-based substance abuse programs.

To avoid hangups in committee, House Republicans brought the entire package to the floor under suspension of the rules, which protected it from amendments but required a two-thirds majority to pass. It achieved that threshold easily, passing 394-27.

The wheels nearly came off in the Senate, however, when Finance Committee members, sensing an opportunity to attach pet projects to must-pass legislation, tried to add dozens of unrelated tax breaks and other provisions. Chairman William V. Roth, Jr., R-Del., accepted many of the proposals but gave up trying to move the bill through the normal committee markup process when the costs threatened to escalate out of control. Instead, he introduced his chairman's mark as a stand-alone bill (S 3152).

As the year drew to a close, Republicans worked out a final community renewal package with the White House — but dealt it a near fatal blow by attaching it to a tax bill (HR 2614) that Clinton threatened to veto. The rescue came during the post-election budget talks, as Clinton asked Republicans to add the community renewal package and other White House priorities to the omnibus spending package. Many of the other White House priorities got shelved, but the antipoverty package survived.

Box Score

- **Bill:** HR 4577 — PL 106-554
- **Legislative action: House** passed HR 4923, 394-27, on July 25.

House adopted the conference report on HR 2614 (H Rept 106-1004), 237-174, on Oct. 26.

House adopted the conference on HR 4577 (H Rept 106-1033), 292-60, on Dec. 15.

Senate cleared the bill by voice vote Dec. 15.

President signed the bill Dec. 21.

'New Markets' Deal Stymied by Differences Over Poverty Relief

APRIL 15 — Five months after President Clinton and House Speaker J. Dennis Hastert, R-Ill., announced that they would blend their community development proposals into a bipartisan, anti-poverty package, a deal has yet to come together — and the road ahead is looking pretty bumpy, even if they do pull one off.

The idea is to merge Clinton's "New Markets" initiative — including a tax credit and other incentives to attract capital to low-income areas — with a House Republican proposal called the American Community Renewal Act (HR 815), which would give tax and regulatory relief to economically distressed areas and help poor families set up subsidized savings accounts.

Ever since Clinton and Hastert announced the effort at a November 1999 joint appearance in Chicago, it has taken on the aura of a done deal.

Every week, aides on both sides say the agreement could come through any day. Committee chairmen and ranking members have been expected to fall in line, pass their respective pieces of the two proposals and have everything ready to move in Congress when the big guys finish working out the package.

Lawmakers are discovering, however, that the problem is not just how to reconcile different legislative provisions, but different philosophies of how best to help the poor.

Republicans see the Clinton-Hastert drive as a chance to get capital gains tax and regulatory relief, and bolster the use of faith-based organizations, to help the poor help themselves. Democrats have traditionally opposed those approaches and are moving more in the direction of subsidies for private investment — an approach that to some Republicans smacks of central government planning.

That tension was clear April 12 when the House Banking and Financial Services Committee approved, 33-14, a key piece of Clinton's New Markets plan that would encourage large business developments in low-income communities. Rather than providing momentum, the panel's grudging support for the bill (HR 2764) served to underscore the political uncertainty surrounding the Clinton-Hastert talks.

Banking Committee Chairman Jim Leach, R-Iowa, acknowledged that Republicans had "no great enthusiasm" for the measure. It would give subsidies to for-profit investment companies — which would be called America's Private Investment Companies (APICs) — to make equity and credit investments designed to bring shopping centers and other large commercial projects to economically distressed neighborhoods.

Leach said that since Clinton and the Democrats wanted it, the panel acted on the legislation to "get as much consensus as possible" and fill in the details in case a broader agreement can be reached.

But Rep. Paul D. Ryan, R-Wis., tried to derail the bill with a substitute that called for the General Accounting Office to study the best ways of helping low-income communities. He said the administration proposal would get the federal government involved in picking "winners and losers."

"I don't care if there's a deal. It's coming through our committee," Ryan said.

Ryan's substitute failed, 15-31, but not before other Republican committee members joined the protest and said they were being asked to rubber-stamp a Clinton proposal they hated.

"Doesn't he know there's a deal here?" Rep. Ed Royce, R-Calif., said in Ryan's defense. "What does he think this is, a legislature?"

Symbolism Is Not Success

For all of the symbolic power of a Democratic president and a Republican Speaker working together to help impoverished communities, they are still working with two very different proposals. The sticking points may not be insurmountable, but for the moment, they have been big enough to stall the deal.

On the surface, there is a lot of common ground. Clinton wants to extend the life of the 31 existing "empowerment zones," which give tax incentives and performance grants and loans to businesses that set up in economically depressed neighborhoods, and authorize 10 new ones.

The Republican bill, HR 814, sponsored by House GOP Conference Chairman J.C. Watts Jr., R-Okla., and House Small Business Committee Chairman James M. Talent, R-Mo., would offer similar incentives in so-called renewal communities.

In both cases, community businesses would get a tax credit to subsidize workers' wages, could write off an additional $35,000 of expenses and could deduct the costs of environmental cleanup in those neighborhoods.

Republicans say the approach does not go far enough. They say businesses need greater tax relief and a reprieve from state and local regulations. The Watts-Talent bill proposes a capital gains tax exemption for the assets that would be held in the renewal communities, and state and local governments would have to agree to cut back on business regulation before any area could be designated as a renewal community.

Moreover, the bill would allow the use of federal funds to pay for drug counseling and rehabilitation by religious organizations. "If there's a faith-based organization out there with a better solution to any problem, we want to empower them," said a Watts spokesman.

At the moment, the capital gains tax exemption appears to be the biggest hang-up in the Clinton-Hastert talks.

The administration opposes the capital gains exemption, saying investors are unlikely to be lured by a tax break that would not help them until their assets were sold. But in an April 6 interview, Talent said the capital gains exemption is the "heart of the bill" and is "really not negotiable for me."

Nor is it negotiable for other key Republicans, who believe a capital gains tax exemption would be more useful to businesses than most of the White House initiatives.

In addition, both sides have proposed ways to let low-income workers save money in government-subsidized savings accounts. But the administration says the Republican version would set a bad precedent because it contains too many tax deductions.

And the deregulation in the Republican plan rubs Democrats the wrong way. "It is ironic that the same Republicans who push 'devolution' and local control when it comes to federal regulations they don't like, turn around and deprive local communities of the capacity to protect their own citizens as they see fit," Charles B. Rangel of New York, ranking Democrat on the Ways and Means Committee, wrote in a March critique of the Watts-Talent bill.

Even if the two sides work out those differences, they may have trouble winning over powerful committee chairmen — not to mention the rest of the committee members, who are growing increasingly resentful that the deal is being worked out without them.

House Ways and Means Committee Chairman Bill Archer, R-Texas, says he is wary of the tax credit proposals because he does not want to use the tax code to achieve social goals. That could spell trouble for a proposal in Clinton's New Markets plan that would give investors a 25 percent tax credit if they invest in community development banks that serve low-income communities.

The tax credit is a critical part of the Clinton proposal. Since high-technology and service firms tend to locate in areas that already have plenty of similar operations, not low-income areas where there is little economic development, the administration wants to use the tax credit to lure the big companies to neighborhoods that need an economic jump-start.

Archer said in an April 13 interview that he is trying to persuade the administration to make the credit a tax deduction instead. That would help investors reduce their tax liability, he said, while a tax credit often "becomes a spending program" that should be handled in an appropriations bill.

Meanwhile, some committee members are grumbling about their lack of involvement in the talks. Rangel says he might set up parallel discussions at the committee level to cut a separate deal.

"I keep hearing that Clinton and Hastert are working together. No one's working with me," he said in an April 6 interview.

It is not clear how high the New Markets talks are on the priority list of either side. Discussions have been taking place at the staff level, with the National Economic Council heading the negotiations for the White House. But with issues like trade relations with China and the push for a prescription drug benefit for Medicare dominating the political agenda, Talent said, the New Markets talks may have to take a back seat for a while.

Uncertain Future

White House officials remain publicly hopeful that they can get an initiative through Congress this year, pointing to the Banking Committee action as a positive, if limited, first step.

In an April 12 statement, Clinton said the committee's approval of the bill represented "some progress" on the promise he made with Hastert and that he looked forward to working with Congress toward a comprehensive community renewal package this year.

The administration predicts that companies could invest as much as $1.5 billion in economically distressed neighborhoods if the legislation became law. They would be licensed by the Department of Housing and Urban Development (HUD), which would issue loan guarantees to help the companies with their investments.

Before it can come to the floor, Clinton's full New Markets package (HR 2848) must also be approved by the House Ways and Means and Small Business committees, which share jurisdiction over its provisions.

The measure approved by the Banking Committee represents a compromise carefully worked out between such Republicans as Leach and Rick A. Lazio of New York, and Democrats such as John J. LaFalce of New York.

Some Republicans were concerned that businesses would not use the federal aid for the right purposes and wary of putting HUD in charge of loan guarantees they do not think it can handle.

To address those issues, a manager's amendment, approved by voice vote, gave Republicans a number of concessions. Under the amendment, there would be annual audits of each company and HUD would have to report to Congress every year on the companies' activities. In addition, the HUD inspector general would keep a close watch on the program.

As an added safety measure, the committee approved an amendment that drew protests from Democrats — a provision that would end the program five years after the first company was licensed. The amendment, offered by Richard H. Baker, R-La., was approved 24-23.

LaFalce complained that such a move would be like closing a business after five years if it was not doing well. But Baker said it was necessary to hold the companies accountable for the government aid they would receive.

"You're going to have to demonstrate that you're making these work," he said.

Should Clinton and Hastert reach a deal, Leach said April 12, the APICs legislation could move through the House as a stand-alone bill or could be merged with one of the year-end spending measures.

If there is no deal between the president and the Speaker, Leach said, "it would be hard to bring this to the floor" because its support is so weak among Republicans.

Clinton, Hastert Clinch Deal On Community Development

MAY 27 — Acting quickly to settle differences that had lingered for months, President Clinton and House Speaker J. Dennis Hastert, R-Ill., announced agreement May 23 on a community development package that would use tax incentives and other market tools to try to revitalize the nation's inner cities and impoverished rural areas.

If the package of measures is enacted, it will represent a rare bipartisan agreement on economic development — spurred by government but not dictated by it — as the key to fighting poverty in struggling communities where other social programs have failed.

"We may be wrong, but we actually believe that we can bring the benefits of free enterprise to poor people," Clinton said as he and Hastert announced their agreement at the White House.

The pieces of the package — expected to cost $5 billion over five years — are already moving through House committees. GOP staff aides said the separate bills will likely be merged into one package by the House Rules Committee before the legislation reaches the floor. Hastert wants the House to vote on the package by mid-June and is pushing the committees of jurisdiction to have their bills ready by then.

The White House ceremony was a surprising leap forward in a bipartisan effort that Clinton and Hastert launched in November 1999, then saw drag along in staff talks for months as aides tried to reconcile the basic philosophical differences between Clinton's "New Markets" initiative and a proposal by House GOP Conference Chairman J.C. Watts Jr., R-Okla., and House Small Business Committee Chairman James M. Talent, R-Mo.

The deal came together May 22, two days before the House was to vote on giving permanent normal trading relations (NTR) status to China. Commerce Secretary William M. Daley told the U.S. Chamber of Commerce May 23 that the New Markets deal was needed to win crucial votes from wavering lawmakers, including members of the Congressional Black Caucus.

Hastert all but acknowledged the connection at the May 23 ceremony when he and Clinton announced the agreement. "I think we'd be remiss, now that we can accomplish a lot of things that help people abroad, if we can't do something extra to help our folks at home, especially folks that need it the most," Hastert said.

The solution to their lingering disagreements, Clinton and Hastert found, was not to split the difference between their ideas but to splice them together — and throw in something for everybody to brag about.

Clinton got most of the main pieces of his New Markets proposal, including the centerpiece — a tax credit that would lure private investors to economically deprived neighborhoods by giving them credit for more than 30 percent of their investment.

He also won a commitment from Republicans to support his other proposals, including the New Markets venture capital program, which would provide loans and technical assistance grants to help small businesses get started in low-income areas. The House Small Business Committee moved quickly on the venture capital firms legislation (HR 4530), approving the bill by voice vote May 25.

Republicans, meanwhile, won a big concession from Clinton: support for a capital gains tax exclusion to lure private investors into "renewal communities" — low-income neighborhoods that would offer tax and regulatory relief to attract new businesses. In a nod to Watts, Clinton agreed to allow faith-based organizations to receive federal funds to provide substance-abuse treatment services.

Such partnerships between government and religious organizations are tricky; at a May 23 briefing, National Economic Council Chairman Gene Sperling said the Justice Department had researched the proposal's language to make sure it would meet the constitutional test of separation of church and state. The proposal won praise from Congressional Black Caucus Chairman James E. Clyburn, D-S.C., who said it was an opportunity to bring new resources to churches that play an important role in providing drug counseling and child care services in African-American communities.

The deal also strikes a compromise between the "empowerment zones" favored by Clinton, which give tax breaks and performance-based grants and loans to businesses that locate in impoverished neighborhoods, and the similar GOP proposal for "renewal communities" — there will be 40 of each.

Clinton won nine new "empowerment zones" and extended the life of the 31 existing ones, a victory that was important to Democrats such as Rep. Charles B. Rangel of New York, whose Harlem district contains one of the zones. In return, Republicans won 40 renewal communities, which would offer similar tax incentives and add the capital gains exclusion and regulatory relief.

"To me, this is the biggest anti-drug, anti-crime, anti-poverty bill we've ever had," Rangel gushed May 23.

Prospects in the Senate are uncertain. Majority Leader Trent Lott, R-Miss., has put Rick Santorum, R-Pa., and Spencer Abraham, R-Mich., in charge of assembling a counterpart package, but he has not set a timetable for moving it. Lott sounded less than sold on the Clinton-Hastert package May 23, noting that empowerment zones have not worked well in rural communities.

One key area where Clinton and Hastert could not reach agreement involved competing proposals for subsidized savings accounts for poor people. Santorum said May 23 that his package will include a saving accounts provision, and Talent said May 25 he hoped that will increase the odds that some form of savings accounts will be in the final package.

House Passes Bill To Help Revive Inner Cities, Rural Economies

JULY 29 — In a rare show of election-year bipartisanship, the House overwhelmingly passed an economic development bill July 25 aimed at reviving some of the nation's impoverished inner cities and rural areas. The only issue that could derail the Community Renewal and New Markets Act (HR 4923) is the growing debate over a provision that would subsidize faith-based drug and alcohol treatment programs.

The measure is based on an agreement President Clinton and House Speaker J. Dennis Hastert, R-Ill., announced in May. It would combine tax incentives, regulatory relief, loan guarantees, housing assistance and new drug treatment options to launch a multilayered assault on the economic and social ills of the poorest communities.

To get the bill to the floor, House Republican leaders bypassed the Ways and Means Committee, where Chairman Bill Archer, R-Texas, was holding out for a no-amendment pledge from Democrats. They took the package to the floor under a suspension of the rules, which protected it from amendments but required a two-thirds majority for passage. It cleared that hurdle easily: The vote was 394-27. *(Vote 430, p. H-134)*

"This is the most significant anti-poverty program to come out of Washington in decades," House Small Business Committee Chairman James M. Talent, R-Mo., said at a news conference after the vote. "I think it's going to have a major, day-to-day impact on the lives of the most vulnerable people in this country."

Clinton affirmed his support in a statement after the vote. "At a time of unprecedented prosperity, too many Americans in our cities and rural areas still do not have access to investment capital and economic opportunity," he said. "I look forward to working with members of both parties in the House and the Senate this year to enact this historic and innovative legislation."

The package would cost $5.8 billion over five years, according to the Joint Committee on Taxation. It has no offsets, which are required under the 1990 Omnibus Budget Reconciliation Act (PL 101-508); the administration promised to work with Congress to fix that problem.

Bragging Rights

While the package could give an economic shot in the arm to some impoverished neighborhoods, it also contains major bragging points for both parties to take to their conventions.

Republicans will be able to talk up their "renewal communities," areas where tax and regulatory relief — including an exemption from capital gains taxes — could help poor people through a free-market approach. Democrats will be able to point to their proposals for using government as a tool to help the private sector: tax credits, loan guarantees, venture capital and technical assistance for small businesses.

Both parties will be able to say they did something for the poor, assuming the so-called charitable choice provision to aid faith-based groups can be worked out with the Senate. It was the only issue that raised concerns in the House debate, where opponents said the measure could lead to taxpayer-subsidized employment discrimination because faith-based groups do not have to comply with federal anti-discrimination laws.

"I frankly do not care how much money might come to my community. I am not going to turn the clock back on fundamental civil and constitutional rights," Robert C. Scott, D-Va., who led the opposition to the House bill, said during floor debate.

Supporters of charitable choice — including Republican Conference Chairman J.C. Watts Jr. of Oklahoma, who sponsored the House bill — say faith-based groups often have more success than other programs in treating substance abusers and should not be barred from federal aid because they are religious.

The controversy was not strong enough to endanger the bill in the House, but it could complicate the picture in the Senate, where a community development measure (S 2779) offered by Rick Santorum, R-Pa., contains broader language that would let faith-based groups provide any service that the government contracts out to private organizations.

Charles S. Robb, D-Va., who is locked in a tight re-election race against George Allen Jr., the former Republican governor of Virginia, announced July 26 that he will sponsor a community renewal bill as an alternative to the Santorum legislation. Robb's measure (S 2936) would require faith-based organizations to obey federal anti-discrimination laws if they receive federal money.

The administration signaled its support by sending White House Chief of Staff John D. Podesta and National Economic Council Chairman Gene Sperling to appear with Robb at a July 26 press conference.

The version cosponsored by Santorum and Joseph I. Lieberman, D-Conn., is supported by the GOP leadership, which put Santorum in charge of the community renewal issue in the Senate. Both sides, however, promised to work to design a mutually acceptable bill.

Santorum said he and Lieberman are revising their bill to broaden its support and are open to including language from Robb's measure. "We'll look at what he's got and see if we can work with it," he said in a July 26 interview.

Court Challenge

As Congress pondered the new charitable choice proposals, the groundbreaking version that was included in the welfare overhaul of 1996 (PL 104-193) faced its first known constitutional challenge. *(1996 Almanac, p. 6-13)*

A lawsuit filed July 24 in Texas charges that the Jobs Partnership of Washington County, a Christian job training program in the central Texas city of Brenham, uses public funds to "promote religious doctrine [and] subsidize religious discrimination" in violation of the First Amendment. It was filed by the American Jewish Congress and the Texas Civil Rights Project.

Chris Traylor, a spokesman for the Texas Department of Human Services, said the state's contracts forbid sectarian worship or proselytizing by faith-based groups that receive welfare-to-work funds. "We've had no complaints from any of the participants in the Brenham program," he said in a July 26 interview.

In addition, Traylor said, Texas' charitable choice program provides a secular option for anyone who is uncomfortable participating in a welfare-to-work program with a religious message, a safety valve that also is included in the community renewal bill passed by the House.

Other Provisions

The House-passed bill includes individual provisions that had been approved by the Small Business Committee (HR 4530) and the Banking and Financial Services Committee (HR 2764), as well as the tax-related provisions that Archer had been unable to move through his committee.

In addition to 40 renewal communities, a Republican proposal, the package would create nine new empowerment zones and extend the life of the 31 existing ones, a Democratic priority. Empowerment zones provide tax incentives, grants and loans to lure businesses to low-income areas.

The House measure attempts to tackle the shortage of affordable housing by allowing states to issue more tax credits to property owners who rent to low-income people. It would also require the Department of Housing and Urban Development to give its vacant, substandard single-family properties to local governments or nonprofits.

According to the Center for Housing Policy, a nonprofit research group, 13.7 million families have "critical housing needs," meaning they spend more than half their income on housing or live in substandard houses or apartments.

Renewal Package Buckles Under Weight of Scores Of Senate Add-Ons

SEPTEMBER 30 — An anti-poverty package launched by President Clinton and House Speaker J. Dennis Hastert, R-Ill., no longer looks unstoppable.

Two months after the Community Renewal and New Markets Act (HR 4923) to provide tax breaks and other incentives to impoverished areas easily passed the House, its Senate counterpart melted down in the Finance Committee the week of Sept. 25. Unable to hold off a barrage of incoming amendments or control a ballooning price tag, committee Chairman William V. Roth Jr., R-Del., gave up trying to mark up a package Sept. 28 and announced that he would simply introduce a new bill to take into negotiations with the House.

The economic development package swelled in size and cost as senators clamored to attach 72 amendments, mostly tax breaks and pet projects that had little to do with the measure's original goal of helping poor people. The House bill was estimated to cost $21 billion over 10 years, according to House GOP staff aides. The Senate version started at $28.8 billion over 10 years and began growing as lawmakers added amendments.

By the time Roth tried — for the fourth time — to mark up the package Sept. 28, it had reached $38.8 billion, according to the Joint Committee on Taxation. The measure included 41 amendments on everything from tax-deductible savings accounts for farmers to a new oil and gas production tax credit to a tax deduction for whale hunting by native Alaskans.

When Roth offered the revised package as a take-it-or-leave-it deal, senators were angry. "We didn't sign on to be potted plants," Democrat Bob Graham of Florida complained to reporters Sept. 27.

In a statement, Roth said he gave up on moving the bill through the committee because "going forward would have opened the bill up to become a grab-bag of special interest provisions" — notwithstanding all the provisions he had already added in the failed effort to get senators on board.

The most expensive rider was one by Roth himself: a provision to let Amtrak issue $10 billion in tax credit bonds, at a cost to the federal government of $3.3 billion over 10 years, to expand and improve its high-speed rail lines in the Northeast. Roth is locked in a tight re-election race, and his Delaware constituents rely heavily on Amtrak for quick access to major cities along the East Coast.

Not Dead Yet

The bill is not necessarily dead, however. Lawmakers and community development lobbyists are already looking to an end-of-year omnibus spending measure, not yet planned by Republican leaders but expected by virtually everyone else, as a vehicle for the package of tax incentives and regulatory relief intended to revive the poorest neighborhoods.

"If the president wants it and the Speaker wants it, it will happen," Sen. Connie Mack, R-Fla., told reporters Sept. 27.

The measure's problems served as a reminder of how difficult it is to reach agreement on most tax bills — even a measure that has the backing of the president and the House Speaker.

To the House, it was a bill to help poor people. It had tax breaks, but only to achieve the goal of stimulating investment in impoverished inner cities and rural areas.

To the Senate, however, it became the last train likely to leave the station in this session. Thus it attracted virtually all of the tax breaks senators had been trying to move throughout the year.

"When they see a tax bill, it brings out the worst in them," Charles B. Rangel of New York, the ranking Democrat on the House Ways and Means Committee and a key negotiator of the original anti-poverty package, said in a Sept. 26 interview.

The GOP leadership did not have much luck moving other tax bills either, including measures to expand tax benefits for retirement savings (HR 1102) and packages of business tax breaks attached to proposals (HR 833, HR 3081) that would raise the minimum wage by $1 an hour.

House Majority Leader Dick Armey, R-Texas, and Treasury Secretary Lawrence H. Summers hoped to advance the process when they met for 90 minutes the evening of Sept. 28 to discuss tax policy. Armey termed it "a very good beginning."

The community renewal bill was no ordinary tax bill, however, thanks to Clinton and Hastert's backing. "You always want to leave one train that's heavy enough to carry all of their cats and dogs," said one Senate Democratic aide. "It's been held in abeyance just for that reason."

What Emerged

The revised chairman's mark that Roth unveiled Sept. 27 — and is expected to introduce as a bill the week of Oct. 2 — is similar to the House bill but includes a slightly different mix of tax incentives to help poor areas.

Like the House bill, the Roth proposal includes Democrat-favored empowerment zones — designated areas where businesses receive tax breaks to locate in poor neighborhoods — and GOP-favored "renewal communities," which would offer both tax breaks and regulatory relief.

Unlike the House bill, however, the Roth proposal would not create nine new empowerment zones. It would simply extend the life of the 31 existing ones and make sure they all get the same tax breaks. The current zones get different sets of incentives.

In addition, the Roth proposal would create only 30 renewal communities, rather than the 40 called for in the House bill.

The anti-poverty efforts are only some of the tax provisions that ended up in Roth's package. There are also provisions calling for $2.4 billion worth of tax breaks for farmers, $1.5 billion in energy tax breaks and $1.8 billion in conservation proposals, including an expanded tax credit for electricity produced by biomass or poultry waste facilities.

Majority Leader Trent Lott, R-Miss., filed amendments to repeal the "marriage penalty" and estate taxes — which Clinton had already vetoed as stand-alone bills. Lott never seriously pursued them, however, and acknowledged Sept. 26 that "those issues are dead for this year."

In addition, Republican Charles E. Grassley of Iowa wanted to attach a bill (S 2274), cosponsored by Edward M. Kennedy, D-Mass., that would let states allow the parents of children with disabilities to buy Medicaid coverage.

The biggest problem, however, was not all the added proposals, but the fact that the Senate was never involved in the negotiations that led to the original Clinton-Hastert deal — and therefore never had a real stake in making sure the package becomes law.

A One-Sided Deal

When Clinton wrote to Hastert in October 1999, inviting him privately to begin talking about a bipartisan effort to revive the inner cities and rural communities, it was a letter aimed squarely at the House.

Clinton wanted to merge his "New Markets" proposal, a package of tax incentives and loan guarantees to stimulate investment in poor areas, with a more expansive proposal (HR 815) by Republican Conference Chairman J.C. Watts Jr. of Oklahoma and Small Business Committee Chairman James M. Talent, R-Mo. The Watts-Talent bill included not only tax incentives but also regulatory relief, subsidized savings accounts and aid to faith-based drug treatment programs.

With no comparable Senate Republican bill, however, Clinton confined his invitation to the House. He did not try to pull Lott into the talks — though that may be partly because Lott did not ask to be invited. "There are other Republicans who are more interested in this than we are," a top aide to Lott said Sept. 26.

Instead, Lott asked Republicans Rick Santorum of Pennsylvania and Spencer Abraham of Michigan to monitor the talks. Both senators are in close re-election races, and while they kept abreast of the Clinton-Hastert talks, they did not participate.

The arm's-length treatment of the Senate came at a price. As the Clinton-Hastert bill came together, high-ranking House members of both parties were included in the process and therefore had an incentive to lean on the rank and file not to amend the package. The Senate leaders never had a big enough interest in the outcome to persuade lawmakers to leave the package alone.

As Democrat Kent Conrad of North Dakota put it Sept. 27: "If others are going to offer amendments, then I insist on offering mine."

GOP Leaders Tie Development Bill to Tax Relief Package

OCTOBER 28 — Having survived a brush with death by amendment in the Senate, an anti-poverty package proposed by President Clinton and House Speaker J. Dennis Hastert, R-Ill., seemed once again near oblivion.

Republican leaders wrapped the community renewal bill into a broader tax relief package (HR 2614) during the week of Oct. 23 that the White House threatened to veto. Supporters feared unless it is resurrected in an omnibus package, the tactic may have doomed the anti-poverty agreement worked out in months of negotiations between Clinton and Hastert. *(Tax package, p. 18-32)*

Unlike the War on Poverty programs championed by former President Lyndon B. Johnson that pumped billions of dollars into social programs — many later dismissed by Republicans as failed "handouts" — the new proposal would be limited to tax incentives and other economic development measures. They would be less expensive and have a lighter, free-market touch.

Still, the original proposal (HR 4923) had been a model of bipartisan cooperation, a marriage of Republican and Democratic ideas on how to revitalize poor neighborhoods. Clinton and Hastert rolled out the proposal in a joint news conference flanked by members of both parties. The package was crafted to achieve a near 50-50 split in spending on GOP and Democratic initiatives.

By Oct. 26, that bipartisan spirit was gone. Democrats complained that Republicans wrote the tax bill without their input. Republicans charged that Clinton and the Democrats wanted their way on everything. Community renewal was all but lost in the sniping.

"I don't care who was consulted. I don't care whether the regular protocols were followed. This bill means real things to real, vulnerable people," House Small Business Committee Chairman James M. Talent, R-Mo., one of the cosponsors of the GOP community renewal proposals, said during floor debate.

To Rep. Danny K. Davis of Illinois, a Democrat who had cosponsored a Talent anti-poverty bill (HR 815) that helped inspire the Clinton-Hastert package, the tax bill was bad enough to overwhelm the good in the community renewal provisions. "It's like a wagon that's been overloaded. . . . This vehicle is stuck in the mud," he said.

Hastert would not admit the community renewal bill had slipped away. "I can't believe there's enough petulance on the other end of Pennsylvania Avenue to veto this bill. I just don't see why he would do it," Hastert said Oct. 26.

Even House Ways and Means Committee Chairman Bill Archer, R-Texas, who voted against the tax bill, said Clinton would be vetoing "his own, negotiated community renewal package."

The Package

In its final form, the community renewal package more closely resembled the House bill than the Senate version (S 3152), which became loaded down with extraneous tax breaks. Senate Finance Committee Chairman William V. Roth, Jr., R-Del., introduced the bill as a stand-alone vehicle after the committee markup threatened to run amok.

The community renewal section in the broader tax bill would cost $25.2 billion over 10 years, according to the Joint Committee on Taxation.

Among the highlights:

• **Renewal communities and empowerment zones.** Like the House bill, the tax package would strike a balance between Republican and Democratic ideas by creating 40 new "renewal communities" — a GOP proposal to revive depressed areas through tax and regulatory relief — and expand the number of Democratic-favored "empowerment zones" to 40. The Senate bill would have created 30 renewal communities.

The bill would extend the life of the 31 existing empowerment zones, which provide wage credits and other tax incentives to lure businesses, while creating nine new ones. Renewal communities would be similar, except that they also would provide regulatory relief by requiring state and local governments to cut rules and red tape. In addition, business owners would pay no capital gains taxes on the sale of businesses or assets held for more than five years.

• **New Markets tax credit.** This Clinton proposal would lure investors to low-income areas by letting them claim up to $15 billion of investments over seven years for investing in community development entities.

• **Low-income housing tax credit.** The provision would allow more of a credit to be issued to property owners who rent to low-income people by raising the per capita state limits from $1.25 to $1.75 by 2002.

• **Private activity bond volume caps.** The bill would help state and local governments issue more of these bonds, the interest on which is exempt from federal income taxes, by raising the limits to $75 for each state resident or $225 million in 2002, whichever is greater. The bonds can be used for such infrastructure projects as low-income housing, and small manufacturing facilities.

• **Charitable choice.** Sponsored by House GOP Conference Chairman J.C. Watts Jr., R-Okla., this provision would allow faith-based substance abuse treatment programs to receive federal funds. Watts and other supporters say the provision is needed to bolster religion-based drug treatment programs, which they say can be more effective than conventional initiatives.

In one major departure from the Senate bill, Republicans dropped a plan for individual development accounts – special matched savings accounts that would help low-income workers save enough money to buy a home, go to college or start a business by giving banks tax credits to match their contributions.

The provision, sponsored by Sen. Rick Santorum, R-Pa., ran into opposition from Archer, who opposes adding new credits to the tax code. ◆

Congress Reauthorizes Older Americans Act In States-vs.-Nonprofits Deal

The Older Americans Act was reauthorized for the first time since 1995 in a bill enacted Nov. 13. **SUMMARY** The measure covers a number of programs for seniors including Meals on Wheels, home assistance, supplemental nutrition, legal aid, job placement and caregiver assistance.

The bill is similar to a bipartisan Senate measure (S 1536) approved July 21 by the Health, Education, Labor and Pensions Committee. The House and Senate worked out the final version of the bill, making a conference unnecessary. The five-year reauthorization of the Older Americans Act (PL 89-73) establishes a new National Family Caregiver Support Program to help families care for elderly people at home by subsidizing such services as caregiver training, respite care, counseling and support groups, and providing information on where to get other services. Funds are to be distributed on the basis of a state's population over the age of 70 and targeted to low-income seniors.

The bill had been stalled in the House since 1999 over a GOP push to shift community service job programs from nonprofit seniors' groups to the states. For years, senior advocacy groups such as AARP, Green Thumb and the National Council of Senior Citizens received 78 percent of the funds, leaving only 22 percent for states. *(1999 Almanac, p. 20-3)*

The compromise guarantees that no advocacy group or state will receive less money than it did in fiscal 2000. Lawmakers agreed to give 75 percent of the first $35 million in additional funds to states, and 25 percent to the nonprofits. The rest will be split 50-50. In addition, nonprofit seniors groups will have to meet new performance criteria to continue receiving federal funds.

The bill also allows states to impose cost-sharing charges on seniors for respite care and homemaker services, though other services, such as ombudsman services and legal assistance, are exempted from the cost-sharing charges. The charges will be based on the beneficiary's income in order to protect the poorest seniors.

Senate Panel OKs Rewrite of Older Americans Act

JULY 22 — The Senate Health Education, Labor and Pensions Committee approved legislation (S 1536) to reauthorize the long-stalled Older Americans Act by voice vote July 21.

The 1965 law — which governs the popular Meals on Wheels program and several seniors job programs — has not been reauthorized since 1995, but advocates hope they can work out differences with the House and clear a bill this session.

"We have here a very strong bipartisan agreement on the Older Americans Act," said Barbara A. Mikulski of Maryland, ranking Democrat on the Aging Subcommittee.

Health Committee Chairman James M. Jeffords, R-Vt., urged the bill's passage, saying it would authorize "a range of needed services."

Most senior advocacy groups support the measure and hope a new authorization will lead to higher spending levels as Baby Boomers age over the next decade. A coalition of seniors groups sent a letter to the panel July 18 praising the "[committee] leadership for developing a bipartisan bill."

A vote in the Senate could come as early as the week of July 24 but is more likely after Congress returns from its August recess. Prospects are more uncertain in the House, where a different measure (HR 782) stalled last fall over GOP efforts to shift funds for a job-training program to state control.

Box Score

- **Bill:** HR 782 — PL 106-501
- **Legislative action: House** passed HR 782 (H Rept 106-343), 405-2, Oct. 25.

Senate cleared HR 782, 94-0, on Oct 26.

President signed the bill Nov. 13.

House Education and the Workforce Committee Chairman Bill Goodling, R-Pa., said in a July 19 interview that he feels strongly about retaining some House provisions, but above all would like to present a bill to President Clinton this year.

"It's a tragedy it hasn't been reauthorized already," Goodling said.

Job Training Dispute

The House bill has been mired for the most part in a dispute over proposed changes to a part-time job training program, run by senior advocacy groups such as Green Thumb, AARP and the National Council of Senior Citizens, that provides about 60,000 minimum wage jobs annually.

For years, appropriators directed 78 percent of funds for the program to the advocacy groups and 22 percent to the states. Last year, House Republicans tried to shift that balance toward the states in their reauthorization draft, prompting seniors groups to launch a campaign against the measure after it was scheduled for a floor vote. The bill has not moved since, but appropriations have continued.

The training formula approved by the Senate Health Committee would guarantee that each state and advocacy group receives sufficient funding to maintain fiscal 2000 levels of operation. It also would increase performance and accountability standards for groups receiving the funds.

If appropriators provided more money than needed to maintain current efforts, additional funds up to $35 million would be split between the seniors' groups and the states: The groups would get 25 percent and the states would get 75 percent. Any funds beyond $35 million would be divided equally. That formula won the blessing of nearly all Senate committee members and 30 major advocacy groups.

If the House accepts the formula or a close alternative, the bill still faces some hurdles. House Republicans are likely to insist on additional help for seniors in rural areas, Rep. Howard P. "Buck" McKeon, R-Calif., chairman of the Subcommittee on Postsecondary Education, Training and Life-Long Learning, said July 19.

Republicans also want more flexibility for local groups to transfer money between the Meals on Wheels program for homebound seniors and other initiatives for group meals.

Cost-Sharing Complaints

Some advocacy groups are concerned about a provision in the Senate bill that would allow states to impose cost-sharing requirements on seniors for such federally supported services as respite care, home care and transportation. Cost-sharing would be determined on a sliding scale based on self-reported income and the cost of delivering services.

The measure would exempt seniors who earn less than the federal poverty level of $8,350 for individuals and would not allow agencies to deny services to seniors who fail to pay.

The bill also contains a provision that would establish the National Family Caregiver Support Program to help people care for frail relatives. The measure would provide grants to states for services such as counseling, respite care and information assistance. The grants also could be used to aid grandparents who were helping to raise their grandchildren.

Senate Clears Reauthorization

OCTOBER 28 — After five years of squaring off with the powerful seniors' lobby, Congress is giving the 1965 Older Americans Act a new lease on life — and backing away from a face-off that had threatened to bring the whole effort down.

By a resounding 94-0 vote, the Senate cleared a compromise bill (HR 782) on Oct. 26 to reauthorize the law (PL 89-73) for the first time since 1995. The House passed the measure 405-2 on Oct. 25. The act supports nutrition programs for elderly people, such as Meals on Wheels, and support services, such as community service jobs. *(House vote 547, p. H-174; Senate vote 285, p. S-51)*

The bill is similar to a bipartisan Senate measure (S 1536) approved by the Health, Education, Labor and Pensions Committee on July 21. Because the two chambers have worked out the final version in advance, no House-Senate conference was necessary. President Clinton is expected to sign the measure.

Republican Sen. Mike DeWine of Ohio, one of the main Senate negotiators, said the compromise bill will create a "modern and streamlined" act and result in "the most substantial reforms . . . since its creation."

Appropriators have funded the seniors' programs, despite the absence of an authorization, since 1995. Republicans fought a losing battle to turn the community service jobs programs over to the states — and halt what they saw as a never-ending political handout to a few liberal, nonprofit groups. The GOP eventually settled for a bipartisan bill that would strike more of a balance between the states and the nonprofits. *(1995 Almanac, p. 7-54)*

"It's good to get it done," a weary Republican Rep. Howard P. "Buck" McKeon of California said Oct 24. He has been working on the reauthorization since last year as chairman of the House Education and the Workforce Subcommittee on Postsecondary Education, Training and Lifelong Learning.

The five-year reauthorization would toughen the community service jobs program, which funnels millions of dollars to nonprofit seniors' groups, by creating new performance measures the groups must meet to continue to receive federal funds.

In addition, the legislation would create a new, $125 million National Family Caregiver Support Program to help families care for elderly people at home by subsidizing such services as respite care, counseling and support groups, and information on where to get other services.

Passing the Bucks

The community service jobs program, which provides part-time jobs to elderly Americans, has turned into a lifeline of federal support over the years for a handful of groups such as AARP, Green Thumb and the National Council of Senior Citizens.

During Senate debate, Judd Gregg, R-N.H., claiming the National Council of Senior Citizens had misused funds in the past, offered an amendment to require states and nonprofits to pass "responsibility tests" before they could receive grants. It failed, 25-69. *(Vote 284, p. S-51)*

Although the law originally called for a balance of funds between states and the nonprofit groups, in practice the annual appropriations bills have steered 78 percent of the funds to the advocacy groups and left only 22 percent for the states.

The idea was to restore the original balance, Republicans said, but the effort took on more ideological overtones as GOP lawmakers fought for funding restrictions on the groups, which they believed were aligned too closely with Democrats.

To soften the blow, lawmakers added a "hold harmless" provision guaranteeing that no advocacy group or state would receive less money than it did in fiscal 2000.

That alone did not settle the fight, however; the lawmakers had to figure out what to do with the extra money. After months of negotiations with the seniors' groups, they struck a compromise: Seventy-five percent of the first $35 million in additional funds will be given to the states, and 25 percent to the nonprofits. The rest will be split 50-50.

A bigger goal, however, was to add performance measures and competition to the program to make sure the nonprofit groups were effective. "From day one, the groups have just kind of received the money" and little has been expected in return, McKeon said.

One provision that the seniors' groups had to swallow, despite their vigorous objections, would allow states to impose cost-sharing charges on seniors for respite care and homemaker services.

The language was softened by exempting other services from the cost-sharing charges, including ombudsman services and legal assistance, and basing the charges on the beneficiary's income to protect the poorest seniors. ◆

Lawmakers Clear Legislation Aimed at Helping More Families Afford Housing

SUMMARY

Concerned that the thriving economy was making housing too expensive for poor and moderate-income families, lawmakers cleared legislation (HR 5640) designed to make home ownership easier for millions. The bill also included a revised system for regulating manufactured housing.

The House in April overwhelmingly passed a bill by Rick A. Lazio, R-N.Y., to establish or modify numerous programs for low- and moderate-income families. It sought to allow some beneficiaries of the Section 8 rent-subsidy program to use their vouchers for down payments on homes; expand a federal program to help localities lower regulatory barriers to the development of affordable housing; and revise rules governing reverse mortgages by waiving mortgage insurance premiums for senior citizens who used part of the money to cover long-term health care. Reverse mortgages allow seniors to borrow against the equity in their homes, with the loans repaid when the house is sold.

The bill also proposed expanding a program that allows teachers, law enforcement officers and corrections officers to purchase federally owned homes for half their market value, and starting a program to enable some public employees to buy homes with as little as 1 percent up front and some police officers to buy homes in high-crime areas with no money down.

When the Senate had not acted on the measure by October, the House took key provisions and added them to a separate Senate-passed bill (S 1452) on manufactured housing, passing it on Oct. 24. The Senate bill proposed creating a committee, split between industry and consumer representatives, to revise federal construction and safety provisions for mobile and prefabricated homes.

Senators, including Banking Committee Chairman Phil Gramm, R-Texas, balked at the provisions for police and other public employees. With the session nearing an end, the House dropped those provisions and passed a clean bill (HR 5640) on Dec. 5. The Senate cleared it two days later.

House Panel Approves Home Ownership Bill

FEBRUARY 19 — Multifaceted legislation designed to expand home ownership has won an important, initial bipartisan show of support, even though it still contains provisions that have elicited concern from the Clinton administration and lobbying groups for the elderly and residents of low-income housing.

The bill (HR 1776), approved on a voice vote Feb. 15 by the House Banking Subcommittee on Housing and Community Opportunity, has emerged as the main vehicle for housing legislation in the 106th Congress. And it incorporates some proposals that fell by the wayside when public housing law was overhauled (PL 105-276) two years ago.

Sponsors say their main aim is to increase the percentage of people who own their own homes. The bill would do this in part by encouraging local governments to reduce regulatory barriers to home ownership and the purchase of affordable housing. The bill would raise the maximum income allowed to be eligible to borrow from loan pools — money that people may borrow to buy houses — funded by the HOME Investment Partnerships Program, which helps residents refurbish dilapidated housing, and the Community Development Block Grant (CDBG), which local governments often use to revitalize economically distressed areas.

Box Score

- **Bill:** HR 5640 — PL 106-569
- **Legislative action: House** passed HR 1776 (H Rept 106-553), 417-8, April 6.

Senate passed S 1452 (S Rept 106-274) by voice vote on May 4.

House passed S 1452, amended, by voice vote Oct. 24.

House passed HR 5640 by voice vote Dec. 5.

Senate cleared HR 5640 by voice vote Dec. 7.

President signed the bill Dec. 27.

Both programs would be reauthorized through fiscal 2005. For fiscal 2001, the authorized limits would be $4.8 billion for CDBG and $1.7 billion for the HOME program. Those amounts match the requests in the budget President Clinton submitted Feb. 7 and are essentially the same as what is being spent in fiscal 2000, which ends Sept. 30.

The measure would extend and expand a provision in the 1998 housing overhaul that allows recipients of Section 8 rental subsidies to use them for down payments on homes.

The bill also incorporates language from a measure (HR 3617) to create stronger anti-fraud protections in the 203(k) home acquisition and rehabilitation program offered by HUD, which allows home buyers to finance home purchases and rehabilitations in a single mortgage; from a bill (HR 2860) to expand homeownership opportunities for the disabled; and from legislation (HR 2931) to encourage law enforcement officers to buy housing in high-crime neighborhoods.

For and Against

The measure has been endorsed by lobbying groups representing home builders, mortgage brokers and the disabled, while the AARP and the National Low-Income Housing Coalition have withheld their backing.

AARP complains that the bill lacks consumer protections for mobile-home owners, and lobbyist Roy Green of the association said Feb. 15 that his group would seek language to standardize warranties and installation requirements for this so-called manufactured housing. While AARP agrees with makers of mobile homes that new federal standards for their construction are needed, the association maintains that a 25-member committee that would be created under the bill to propose the new standards would give manufacturers and retailers too much say.

The subcommittee deferred action on manufactured housing. Chairman Rick A. Lazio, R-N.Y., said the issue would be engaged when the bill is marked up by the full Banking Committee, probably in March.

Low-income housing advocates and HUD say they are concerned that the bill would divert money away from low-income families to give more housing opportunities to middle-income people.

Formally, neither HUD nor the White House has taken a position on the bill. But in testimony before the Housing Subcommittee on Sept. 15, William Apgar, the head of HUD's Federal Housing Administration, said he opposes a provision that appears to require HUD to offer its vacant or substandard housing to local governments or community development corporations for carrying costs like property taxes and maintenance. That provision, Apgar said, would have cost $3.25 billion in 1998, based on HUD's single-family home sales then.

In addition, Apgar has criticized the bill's proposal to increase income limits for receiving HOME and CDBG money to 115 percent of area median income, up from the current 80 percent.

But the subcommittee's ranking Democrat, Barney Frank of Massachusetts, said in an interview Feb. 15 that he has endorsed the bill's provisions to raise income levels for those receiving federal housing help. "We're more likely to get more money to increase eligibility levels than to target the low-income," he said.

In his final year as subcommittee chairman, Lazio is attempting to complete an agenda he set for the panel in 1995. In 1998, he was the main sponsor of the public housing law, which turned block grants and decision-making over to local public housing authorities. In addition to HR 1776, he has set out to move five other housing-related bills. These include a bill (HR 1073) to overhaul homeless programs that is similar to a bill that did not make it beyond the Banking Committee in the 105th Congress; a measure (HR 21) offering a federal reinsurance program to government and private insurers; and a bill (HR 202) to expand options for senior citizens and disabled residents in affordable housing.

Senate Banking Committee OKs Bill to Regulate Prefab Housing

MARCH 11 — Legislation (S 1452) to change the way government sets regulations for "manufactured housing" — prefabricated and mobile homes — was endorsed on a voice vote March 8 by the Senate Banking Committee.

Similar language is expected to be offered at a House Banking Committee markup of a housing bill (HR 1776) on March 14. Manufactured housing provisions were set aside during a subcommittee markup of that bill in February, in hopes of winning the support of the AARP and other consumer groups. The groups signaled that the bill now moving in the Senate was a step in the right direction.

The Senate bill, sponsored by Richard C. Shelby, R-Ala., and John D. Rockefeller IV, D-W.Va., would create a 26-member independent panel to recommend safety regulations for building, operating and installing manufactured houses.

The panel's proposals would become federal regulation unless the Department of Housing and Urban Development (HUD) rejected them within one year. The measure would allow HUD to impose small fees on home manufacturers to cover safety inspection costs and pay the panel's expenses.

Since federal safety regulation of manufactured homes was first enacted in 1974 (PL 93-383), the department's staff to assess and modify the rules has been cut to eight from 34.

Multipurpose Housing Bill Wins Approval of House Committee

MARCH 18 — A multifaceted measure designed to ease barriers to home ownership was approved on a voice vote March 14 by the House Banking and Financial Services Committee. Chairman Jim Leach, R-Iowa, said he hoped for a summer House vote on the bill (HR 1776), which incorporates many proposals left out of the 1998 public housing law (PL 105-276) and has become the main vehicle for housing policy in the 106th Congress.

"What this bill is is a considerable approach to trying to do as many things, without breaking the bank, to provide home ownership to as many Americans as possible," Leach said.

The measure would encourage municipalities to reduce regulatory barriers to the purchase of affordable housing by low-income residents.

It would raise the income ceiling for people who want to borrow from loan pools — money people may borrow for home purchases — funded through the HOME Investment Partnerships Program, which helps residents refurbish dilapidated housing, and Community Development Block Grants (CDBG), often used to revitalize economically distressed areas. The National Low-Income Housing Coalition says it continues to have concerns with this provision.

The measure would allow cities to use CDBG and HOME grants to help teachers, police officers, firefighters and sanitation workers with closing costs, down payments, counseling and subsidized mortgage rates on homes inside their city's limits

The bill also would create a test program under which families with disabled members could use their Section 8 rental vouchers for house down payments.

The bill would reauthorize both community development grants and HOME through fiscal 2005. In fiscal 2001, the authorized limits would be $4.8 billion for CDBG and $1.7 billion for HOME — the same amounts sought by President Clinton in his fiscal 2001 budget, and nearly the same amounts appropriated for the current fiscal year, which ends Sept. 30.

The bill had already been endorsed by lobbying groups for home builders, mortgage brokers and the disabled. It won the backing of the AARP after provisions it sought were added at the markup. They would create a new board — with membership balanced between industry and consumers — to set safety standards for prefabricated or mobile homes. The language is similar to a bill (S 1452) approved by the Senate Banking Committee on March 8.

The committee rejected two prefab housing amendments by Barney Frank, D-Mass. One, defeated 19-23, would have let states inspect such homes as they were being manufactured, in addition to at their point of sale. The second, defeated 11-28, would have given consumers greater access to information about manufactured housing defects.

By voice vote, the committee approved these amendments:

- By Dave Weldon, R-Fla., to require municipal workers qualifying for the new type of assistance to pay back what they borrowed in full if they sold their home within seven years — and to limit their aid to a single year.
- By Michael E. Capuano, D-Mass., to create a down payment assistance program under HOME and the community development program for buyers of two- and three-family homes.
- By Jan Schakowsky, D-Ill., to strike language that would have made it more difficult for disabled home buyers under the pilot program to requalify for Section 8 rental subsidies after a default.

House Passes Home Ownership Bill After Adding Ohio Project

APRIL 8 — A wide-ranging bill designed to expand home ownership among low-income Americans passed overwhelmingly in the House on April 6 after it was amended to make churches eligible for housing grants and to provide a $35 million grant for a community center in the district of a Democrat being wooed by Republicans.

The bill (HR 1776), incorporating proposals not included in a 1998 law (PL 105-276) to overhaul public housing programs, passed on a 417-8 vote. *(Vote 110, p. H-38)*

Sponsored by Rick A. Lazio, R-N.Y., the bill would make changes in home ownership programs offered through the Department of Housing and Urban Development (HUD) and city and local governments. The changes include giving local governments greater flexibility to design low-income home ownership programs while encouraging those governments to reduce regulatory barriers to home buyers.

The House Banking Committee estimates the bill would help 125,000 teachers, police officers, firefighters, municipal employees, corrections officers and persons with disabilities become homeowners in the next five years. It would do so through numerous programs, including one that offers 1 percent down payments for Federal Housing Administration home mortgages for qualifying teachers and some municipal employees.

But the broad support for the bill may not help it in the Senate, or with the Clinton administration. A spokesman for the Senate Banking, Housing and Urban Affairs Committee on April 7 said its Housing Subcommittee would probably want to look at the bill this summer. The administration supports the bill but has reservations about several provisions, including one establishing a "consensus committee" to revise manufactured housing standards.

Meanwhile, a spokesman for subcommittee Chairman Wayne Allard, R-Colo., on April 7 said Allard plans to introduce a broad housing bill in about a month.

A related bill (S 1452), approved March 8 by the Senate Banking Committee, would revise federal construction and safety provisions for manufactured homes. It may become a vehicle for negotiations with the House over the broader provisions of HR 1776.

One of the more controversial amendments added to the House bill was a $35 million allocation of Community Development Block Grant (CDBG) money for a convocation and community center in Youngstown, Ohio, the home city of Democratic Rep. James A. Traficant Jr. The measure comes as both parties are fighting for majority control of the House next year, and as Traficant has begun hinting that he might vote with Republicans in selecting a Speaker next year.

The amendment marked the second time in a month Traficant played a highly visible role on a bill. Last month, he cosponsored an amendment to increase the federal minimum wage by $1 over two years, encouraging Republicans to support the measure with a similar hint of winning his vote for a GOP Speaker.

The House ultimately approved the Ohio grant on a raucous, 225-201 roll call vote, with 129 Republicans and 96 Democrats voting "aye." Democrats and Republicans alike were shouting their votes in the chamber as time ended. *(Vote 108, p. H-38)*

"The Republican and Democratic leadership are bidding for him," said Barney Frank, D-Mass., likening the vote to an auction for Traficant's allegiance. "We temporarily became [Web site] eBay, which I think is a very grave error."

Meeting the Mortgage

The bill comes at a period of record American home ownership. Nearly two-thirds of all U.S. households — roughly 70 million — own their homes. But households with annual incomes of less than $25,000 still face significant barriers to buying a home or meeting the monthly mortgage payments, despite low interest rates and a healthy economy.

To reduce barriers to home ownership, the bill would set up numerous programs aimed at low- and moderate-income families. The bill contains a provision to allow disabled recipients of HUD's Section 8 rent-subsidy program to use their vouchers for down payments on homes. It also would expand the use of so-called reverse mortgages to let senior citizens include long-term health care expenses in the cost of buying a home.

The consensus committee, with representation balanced among consumers, government officials and industry experts, would advise HUD on safety standards and regulations for manufactured housing.

In addition, the bill would reauthorize two HUD programs through fiscal year 2005, allocating up to $4.9 billion for the CDBG program in fiscal 2001 and $1.65 billion for the HOME program. Local governments use both programs to provide affordable housing.

Low-income housing advocates and some members were concerned that the bill would leave less money for the poor because it raised income limits for the CDBG and HOME municipal employee home-ownership programs.

A provision added to the bill in subcommittee by Michael E. Capuano, D-Mass., would have allowed teachers and "uniformed municipal employees" such as police officers and firefighters earning less than 150 percent of the area median income to buy homes through the HOME and CDBG programs. But that income cutoff was later revised to 115 percent, with the proviso that the HUD secretary can designate "high cost" areas to use the 150 percent income limit.

A group of Democratic representatives from poor urban districts, including Carrie P. Meek of Florida, Stephanie Tubbs Jones of Ohio and Maxine Waters of California, sought to keep income guidelines at 80 percent, but the House rejected Waters' amendment, 60-367. *(Vote 107, p. H-38)*

A more controversial amendment came from Mark Souder, R-Ind., to make religious organizations eligible to compete for CDBG money. The issue is expected to resurface in the 2000 presidential campaign, since presumptive Republican candidate Texas Gov. George W. Bush has advanced the involvement of "faith-based organizations" in finding solutions to social problems.

Chet Edwards, D-Texas, argued that Souder's language contradicted legal precedents restricting the flow of public money to religious organizations. The amendment was adopted, 299-124, after Souder modified it on the floor to prevent organizations from discriminating against participants who did not belong to that denomination or did not practice a religion. *(Vote 109, p. H-38)*

In other floor action, the House approved by voice vote an amendment by Christopher Shays, R-Conn., Jerrold Nadler, D-N.Y., Constance A. Morella, R-Md., and Joseph Crowley, D-N.Y., to increase the funding authorization level for Housing Opportunities for Persons With AIDS (HOPWA) from $260 million to $275 million for fiscal year 2001. Congress appropriated $232 million for the HOPWA program in fiscal 2000.

House-Passed Housing Bill Stalls In the Senate

OCTOBER 28 — Legislation designed to expand home ownership opportunities for millions of Americans was passed by voice vote in the House on Oct. 24. But the multifaceted measure (S 1452) stalled in the Senate, where Republicans said it went too far and Democrats tried to weigh it down with additional provisions that could find no other legislative vehicle as the 106th Congress moved toward its conclusion.

"I think it's a little late in the game to expect that package to pass," Housing and Urban Development (HUD) Secretary Andrew M. Cuomo told reporters Oct. 26. He declined to endorse the bill, although it would have expanded some department programs, including one under which HUD-owned homes are sold to teachers and law enforcement officers at a 50 percent discount.

As initially passed by the Senate on May 4, the bill was designed to create a new board — its membership balanced between industry and consumers — to rewrite federal standards for mobile and prefabricated homes, a priority of the AARP. The House amended that measure with parts of seven other housing and banking bills — including several sections of a home-ownership measure (HR 1776) the House passed April 6.

By Oct. 27, the broader bill had been abandoned. Instead, senators readied a deal under which the Senate would amend the bill again — retaining only the mobile home language and housing aid for American Indians and native Hawaiians — then send the measure back to the House.

That decision spelled the end of proposals to allow poor people to apply their Section 8 federal rental subsidies to down payments on home purchases and to authorize $15 million annually through fiscal 2005 to help localities lower regulatory barriers to the development of affordable housing. Also dropped was language to change a 1998 law (PL 105-216) to clarify homeowners' rights to cancel their private mortgage insurance — even on adjustable-rate mortgages — once they have enough equity in the property, usually 20 percent.

The bill the House passed Oct. 24 also would have modified the rules for cash-poor senior citizens to refinance "reverse mortgages," which effectively enable them to borrow against the equity in their homes in order to pay their living expenses. Under the bill, seniors could have their up-front premiums waived for mortgages that included the cost of long-term care insurance.

The new House bill had already dropped several provisions of the package passed in the spring, including language to allow churches to compete for Community Development Block Grants with other nonprofit groups.

Timing of Package Curious

The new package was put before the House the same week that HUD announced that 67.7 percent of U.S. households owned their homes — a record high. Still, members pointed out the need to expand home ownership opportunities for those who have seen a robust economy push their rents and housing costs higher.

"Affordable housing is increasingly out of the reach of many Americans," said Banking Committee Chairman Jim Leach, R-Iowa. "A strong economy has created a situation where, in many parts of the country, the price of housing is simply going up faster than income."

Leach said more than 3 million working households, including those of approximately 220,000 teachers and public safety officers, spend more than half their income on housing.

The bill was negotiated with Senate Republicans, including Wayne Allard, R-Colo., chairman of the Banking Housing Subcommittee. But after the House passed it, he initially put his staff to work on possible additional compromises with Democrats. Paul Wellstone of Minnesota, for example, was said to want to add parts of a bill (S 2733) to create grants for the preservation of affordable housing. Richard H. Bryan, D-Nev., sought to add banking customer privacy protections — language he tried unsuccessfully to include in the law overhauling the financial services industry (PL 106-102) enacted last year. (1999 *Almanac*, p. 5-3)

Progress was also blocked by Banking Committee Chairman Phil Gramm, R-Texas, who said he could not support provisions offering teachers and public safety officers low-interest loans and 1 percent down payments on Federal Housing Administration mortgages. "I don't understand a bill that says that the people who work for us get treated better than we do," he said Oct. 25.

The bill's demise was a setback for Rick A. Lazio, R-N.Y., chairman of House Banking's Housing Subcommittee, who pushed HR 1776 and is making his housing record a key part of his Senate campaign. Lazio was also denied the spotlight Oct. 24, when President Clinton decided against holding a ceremony to sign a measure Lazio promoted (HR 4386 — PL 106-354) to help poor women with breast or cervical cancer.

Senate Clears Bill After Deleting Provisions to Help Public Employees

DECEMBER 9 — A measure aimed at promoting home ownership among elderly, disabled and low-income Americans cleared Congress the week of Dec. 4 after several sections objectionable to Senate Republicans were removed.

The House passed the bill (HR 5640) by voice vote Dec. 5, and the Senate cleared it by voice vote Dec. 7. The measure actually contains parts of seven bills, including a widely supported home ownership measure (HR 1776) and a manufactured-housing bill (S 1452).

The home ownership portion, passed by the House in April, would create several new programs and change housing laws to make it easier for low-income people to purchases homes, including a proposal that would allow the use of Section 8 federal rental subsidies to make a down payment.

The manufactured housing bill, originally passed by the Senate on May 4, was designed to create a new board — its membership balanced between industry and consumers — to rewrite federal standards for mobile and prefabricated homes.

In October, the House amended it by attaching portions of seven banking and housing bills, including the home ownership measure, and passed it on a voice vote.

But senators, including Banking Committee Chairman Phil Gramm, R-Texas, balked at provisions that would have allowed police officers to buy homes in high-crime areas with no down payment, and allowed public employees to purchase homes in low-income neighborhoods with a 1 percent down payment.

The sections objectionable to Gramm were removed after he and House Banking Committee Chairman Jim Leach, R-Iowa, met Dec. 4. Gramm and Paul S. Sarbanes, D-Md., the ranking member of the Senate Banking Committee, also ironed out partisan differences on the bill to allow its passage.

House members vowed to continue fighting for low down-payment programs for public employees. "Be assured, the House will be back again next year fighting for its enactment," John J. LaFalce of New York, the ranking Democrat on the Banking Committee, said Dec. 5.

"I am hopeful in the next Congress we can move forward with that kind of provision," Leach responded.

The bill would authorize $15 million annually through fiscal 2005 to help local governments lower regulatory barriers to the development of affordable housing. It would clarify a 1998 law (PL 105-216) ensuring the right of home owners, even those with adjustable-rate mortgages, to cancel their private mortgage insurance once they have enough equity in their property, usually 20 percent.

The bill also would make FHA "reverse mortgages" more affordable for seniors who use the money for long-term health care insurance. Such mortgages generally allow seniors to borrow against the equity in their home for living expenses, with the loans repaid from the proceeds when the house is sold. Mortgage insurance premiums would be waived for those using the funds for long-term care insurance.

The bill contains no new housing production program, a priority several members believe the 107th Congress should address. Although home ownership rates now are at 67.7 percent, a housing affordability crisis looms in part because the economy has pushed up rents and housing costs. "It is time for us to get back in the business of increasing housing production," Rep. Barney Frank, D-Mass., said during floor debate Dec. 5.

Negotiations between appropriators and the White House in October on the fiscal 2001 VA-HUD appropriations bill (HR 4635 — PL 106-377) nearly added a one-year housing production program using $1 billion of unspent Section 8 money, but it was eliminated after Gramm and Sen. Wayne Allard, R-Colo., objected.

The bill also would reinstate a requirement that the chairman of the Federal Reserve appear twice yearly before Congress in so-called Humphrey-Hawkings hearings to discuss monetary policy and economic performance. In a slight change, the hearings would alternate between House and Senate Banking committees. Salaries for the Fed chairman and board of governors would be increased.

The bill is the last housing measure for Rep. Rick A. Lazio, R-N.Y., chairman of the Banking Committee's Housing and Community Opportunity Subcommittee. Lazio made his housing record, including the 1998 bill overhauling public housing (PL 105-276), a key part of his unsuccessful New York Senate campaign, and has been mentioned as a possible nominee for secretary of the Department of Housing and Urban Development (HUD) if Texas Gov. George W. Bush wins the presidency. ◆

House-Passed Bill to Help Families Keep Child Support Payments Dies in the Senate

Box Score

- **Bill:** HR 4678
- **Legislative action: House** passed HR 4678 (H Rept 106-793, Part 1), 405-18, on Sept. 7.

SUMMARY

Breaking with a longstanding assumption that single mothers should receive either child support or welfare benefits but not both, the House passed legislation Sept. 7 to allow poor families to keep more of the child-support payments the states collect for them. In addition, the legislation would have provided $140 million in grants over four years for job training, parenting classes, and other programs to get low-income fathers more involved in their families' lives.

With no action in the Senate, however, the legislation died at the end of the session.

The legislation got off to a shaky start, with Republican Rep. Nancy L. Johnson of Connecticut floating a draft that included a controversial provision to give private child-support firms access to sensitive information — including Social Security numbers, earnings histories and addresses — that state child-support agencies collect on newly hired workers. The fight over that provision, which critics called a threat to privacy, nearly overshadowed the policy changes that were supposed to be the focus of the bill: streamlined child-support distribution rules and grants for fatherhood programs.

To avoid dragging down the entire bill, Johnson scaled back the privatization section to a pilot program, then eliminated it entirely and settled for a General Accounting Office study that would collect information on private collection companies' practices.

With the one divisive issue out of the way, the bill sailed through the Ways and Means Committee and the full House with bipartisan support.

According to a Ways and Means Committee report, there is a $55 million pool, nation-wide, of uncollected child-support payments.

House Committee OKs Bill to Direct More Child Support To Poor Families

JULY 1 — A bitter debate over the privatization of child-support collection threatens the future of a bill approved by a House Ways and Means subcommittee June 27 that would give more child support to poor families leaving welfare. The measure would also revive a House-passed bill aimed at getting low-income fathers more involved in their families' lives.

The bill (HR 4678), approved 7-6 by the Human Resources Subcommittee, would allow poor families to keep more of any child support collected by state agencies.

It would also set up demonstration programs giving private collection agencies access to government data to track down debtors. Some lawmakers say that provision could doom the bill.

"It takes a positive step forward . . . but then takes a giant step backward" by including the privatization proposal, said Benjamin L. Cardin of Maryland, ranking Democrat on the subcommittee.

Democrats, some Republicans on the panel and consumer groups are uneasy about giving private companies access to sensitive information — including Social Security numbers, earnings and addresses — that state child-support agencies collect on newly hired workers.

That raises huge privacy concerns, privatization opponents say, and is too risky at a time when some collection agencies are under fire for allegedly using threats and harassment to collect support, usually from fathers, and charging mothers excessive fees for their services.

Subcommittee Chairwoman Nancy L. Johnson, R-Conn., the bill's author, acknowledged that some child-support companies have been "scandalously bad," but said some have proven more effective than the state child-support agencies.

That debate is diverting attention from Johnson's main goal: putting more child support — by some estimates as much as $3.5 billion over five years — in the hands of low-income, working mothers by simplifying the complicated rules that determine how much they receive and how much is kept by the states once they leave welfare.

Under the bill — which would makes changes to the sweeping welfare overhaul (PL 104-193) enacted in 1996 — states would have to pass on any overdue child support that a family should have received before or after it was on welfare. States would keep any child support owed a family while it was on welfare, as they do now. The difference lies in who would be repaid first: As the states collected overdue support, they would have to repay a family in full before they could keep anything for themselves. *(Welfare overhaul, 1996 Almanac, p. 7-35)*

Lawmakers from both parties say it is important to make sure families get the support they are owed — especially since welfare restructuring has sent many single mothers into the work force, struggling to make ends meet. According to a Ways and Means Committee report:

- There is a $55 million pool nationwide of uncollected child support, and four in five families have not received anything from state agencies.
- Of some 11.5 million single-parent families nationwide, only 6.2 million (54 percent) had awards or agreements for child support.

Fewer Poor Children

A March report by the Urban Institute, a social policy think tank, estimates that child support reduces the number of children living in poverty nationwide by half a million and lessens income inequality among children eligible to receive it. The institute also reported that about 70 percent of poor children eligible for child support were not getting it in 1996.

All those numbers should add up to private collection agencies playing a bigger role, according to Johnson, because shrinking welfare caseloads are making it harder for federal and state governments to cover their costs.

The problem is how best to use private collection agencies. Johnson whittled her original proposal down to a pilot program that would allow three demonstration projects by private collection agencies, require written agreements between the states and the federal government to guarantee privacy, and have the General Accounting Office report to Congress on how the companies are using their expanded powers.

Cardin, however, said the idea cannot be salvaged because the privacy concerns are too urgent. That also could doom the House "Fathers Count" bill (HR 3073), which would provide funds for parenting classes and make it easier for low-income fathers to get job training under a federal welfare-to-work program. The legislation, passed Nov. 10, would authorize $140 million in grants over six years.

House Panel Approves Child Support Bill

JULY 22 — The House Ways and Means Committee on July 19 easily approved a bill to simplify the nation's child-support laws, after removing a controversial provision that would have set up demonstration programs to strengthen the role of private child-support collection agencies.

Private contracting was the one provision that threatened to derail the entire bill (HR 4678), which would help poor families by letting them keep more of the overdue child support collected by state agencies.

Bill sponsor Nancy L. Johnson, R-Conn., chairman of the Human Resources Subcommittee, dropped the private collection demonstration programs in a substitute the committee approved by voice vote. With that change out of the way, the committee approved the revised legislation by voice vote.

The change is likely to improve the bill's prospects dramatically once it goes to the House floor. Johnson said in a July 20 interview that she hopes to get the House to pass it as a suspension bill, possibly the week of July 24.

"This will get significantly more money in the hands of families rather than in the hands of states," Vicki Turetsky, a senior staff attorney at the Center for Law and Social Policy, a research and advocacy group, said in a July 20 interview.

The bill would streamline the complicated rules that govern how much child support poor families can keep and put as much as $3.5 billion in their hands over five years, according to committee estimates, by letting them keep more of what states collect.

The measure includes a revised version of the House-passed "Fathers Count" legislation (HR 3073), which would authorize $140 million in grants over six years to get low-income fathers more involved with their families. The grants would pay for parenting classes and make it easier for the fathers to receive job training.

Most of the bill's major provisions were overshadowed by the controversy surrounding Johnson's plan to give a bigger role to private collection agencies. Her bill, as originally approved by the subcommittee, would have set up three demonstration projects giving private agencies access to government data so they could track down debtors. It also called for a General Accounting Office (GAO) study of how private collection agencies operate.

Democrats and advocacy groups for low-income families complained that some private collection agencies use questionable tactics to collect overdue support, including threats and harassment. They said it would be unwise to give private agencies sensitive information collected by state child-support agencies, including Social Security numbers, earnings and addresses.

"I think it's sort of absurd not to even look into this," Johnson said, but added that she understood critics' concerns about proceeding with the demonstrations before the GAO study was completed. The study remains in the bill.

The bill would allow public demonstration projects that make child-support agency information available to court-run programs and other government collection initiatives. At least three states — Florida, Texas and Arizona — have such programs, according to the Human Resources Subcommittee.

House Passes Bill Amid Growing Reservations About 'Charitable Choice'

SEPTEMBER 9 — The House overwhelmingly passed a bill Sept. 7 to let poor families keep more of the child-support payments collected by the states — but the lack of any similar effort in the Senate may threaten the future of the initiative to help struggling single parents.

The 405-18 vote for the bill (HR 4678) sponsored by Nancy L. Johnson, R-Conn., highlighted the broad bipartisan support for changing existing rules that allow states and the federal government to keep, on average, half the support they collected for families on welfare. *(Vote 457, p. H-142)*

Johnson said the change could put an extra $3.5 billion in families' hands over the next five years.

"Welfare reform has put us on the right track, but many single mothers and children are struggling with low incomes," Johnson, who chairs the Ways and Means Subcommittee on Human Resources, said during the floor debate. "We are coming forward with this proposal to ensure that these mothers get the help that they deserve."

A Strong Uprising

The vote followed a surprisingly strong uprising against a provision that would allow faith-based organizations to receive federal support for programs to help low-income fathers get more involved in their families' lives. The provision was part of a section of the bill that would provide $140 million in grants over four years to help these fathers through parenting classes, marriage counseling and job training.

The House defeated, 175-249, a motion by Robert C. Scott, D-Va., to recommit the bill to the Ways and Means Committee with instructions to ban faith-based organizations from practicing religious discrimination in their hiring.

Scott wanted to ensure that a religious-based fatherhood program that accepted federal funds would have to consider job applicants who did not share its religious beliefs. *(Vote 456, p. H-142)*

Lawmakers also defeated, 163-257, a broader Scott amendment that would have banned not only hiring discrimination but any efforts by employees and volunteers in faith-based programs to make clients participate in religious worship or instruction. *(Vote 455, p. H-140)*

Although the motion and the amendment both failed, the votes were far stronger than previous efforts to defeat so-called charitable-choice provisions that would allow federal funds to flow to religious groups. When the House passed a community development bill (HR 4923) in July with similar charitable-choice language, only 27 lawmakers voted against it because of concerns about religious discrimination.

Critics said the charitable-choice language ran the risk of encouraging what Scott called "religious bigotry." According to Johnson and other supporters, however, the limits Scott proposed would have had a chilling effect, scaring religious groups away from the fatherhood programs because they no longer would be able to give hiring preference to people who share their faith.

"Are we now going to say that in order to participate in any federal program, churches cannot be churches?" Mark Souder, R-Ind., asked during the floor debate.

No Momentum In Senate

House members lined up in droves to endorse the child support and fatherhood provisions that make up the core of the bill. However, the Senate has no clear plan for dealing with Johnson's bill in the short time remaining in the session and has taken little action on two comparable measures sponsored by Herb Kohl, D-Wis., and Evan Bayh, D-Ind.

Kohl has tried to promote a measure (S 1036) with provisions similar to Johnson's bill but has made little progress. Bayh is sponsoring a measure (S 1364) that would let states use child-support collections to fund fatherhood programs. The Finance Subcommittee on Social Security and Family Policy held a hearing on Bayh's bill July 25.

Chairman William V. Roth Jr., R-Del., has not scheduled a markup on Bayh's measure, and with appropriations bills and trade relations dominating the Senate agenda, Republican and Democratic aides say child support is not high on the list at the moment.

"If Roth said he wanted to do something, we could go work something out with the House in a week," said one Democratic aide.

Johnson said she hoped the strong House vote would make child support a more urgent issue for the Senate. It could just take the House measure straight to the floor, Johnson said, but she added that was unlikely because the Senate probably would prefer to act on its own bills. ◆

Funding of Faith-Based Groups Spurs New Civil Rights Debate

JUNE 10 — If House GOP Conference Chairman J.C. Watts Jr. of Oklahoma has his way, Congress may offer federal funds to Freddie Garcia, the "Junkie Preacher."

Garcia is the ex-addict-turned-pastor who founded Victory Fellowship — a Christian substance abuse program in San Antonio that puts addicts through a three-month, total-immersion program of chapel services and Bible studies. Its stated goal is to help clients kick their bad habits and establish "a personal relationship with Jesus Christ."

Garcia's church has opened 65 centers throughout Texas, New Mexico and California and in five foreign countries — and has caught the eye of Watts and other Republicans. Victory Fellowship, Watts said in a June 5 interview, is a perfect model for the kinds of faith-based drug treatment programs that ought to qualify for federal support because their spiritual approach can be more complete and effective than traditional substance abuse efforts.

"They take a much more comprehensive approach to healing. They try to deal with the mental and physical and spiritual person," said Watts.

The faith-based approach has been gaining currency since the welfare overhaul of 1996 (PL 104-193), and President Clinton has accepted it as part of the "New Markets" anti-poverty package he worked out last month with House Speaker J. Dennis Hastert, R-Ill. If the House Ways and Means Committee marks up its provisions the week of June 12, as expected, the package could be on the House floor by the end of the month

The approach's popularity is raising new concerns. Some lawmakers fear that giving taxpayers' money to the nation's churches, synagogues and mosques raises serious civil rights issues. They warn that religious organizations are already free to discriminate in their hiring practices because of an exemption in the Civil Rights Act of 1964 — and that Congress could end up knocking another hole in the wall between church and state.

"The meaning is clear: It would not be illegal to practice religious bigotry," Rep. Robert C. Scott, D-Va., said in a June 6 interview.

"This is, I think, a hugely important issue that has been ignored by many members of Congress," Rep. Chet Edwards, D-Texas, said in a June 6 interview. "For the first time in this country's history, we would be saying that faith-based organizations could receive federal funds and then put up a sign saying no Jews, Catholics or Methodists need apply for a federally funded job."

Running on Faith

The debate could resonate on both Capitol Hill and the presidential campaign trail, as leaders of both parties abandon a longstanding resistance to public support for social services in a religious setting.

Both Texas Gov. George W. Bush, the presumptive Republican nominee, and Vice President Al Gore, the likely Democratic nominee, have called for new partnerships between government and faith-based organizations to attack social problems that government alone has been unable to solve.

Such partnerships are raising concerns that even their supporters say are legitimate: Should the government allow churches to hire and serve only those who agree with their religious views? Should the needy be required to attend prayer breakfasts or take communion to get the help they need? How many strings can be attached to government aid before sectarian groups will lose interest?

To Watts and other supporters, there are important practical benefits to the faith-based drug treatment efforts, and they believe the problems can be worked out. They say these programs — by treating drug addiction in part as a spiritual problem and not just as a physical or mental illness — have achieved a strong record of success and should not be disqualified from federal support simply because of their religious character.

The Victory Fellowship says its success rate in treating substance abusers runs from 60 to 80 percent.

"The wall of separation between church and state becomes too high when it's impossible to provide any encouragement or support to any of the positive activities the churches are doing," Jim Wallis, leader of Call to Renewal, an alliance of churches and faith-based organizations that fight poverty, said in a June 6 interview.

Charitable Choice

The debate marks an important turning point in the history of "charitable choice" — giving government funds not just to groups with a religious affiliation, such as Catholic Charities, to provide social services, but to the houses of worship themselves.

The idea is to let them take public funds without having to strip out the religious art, icons and scriptures that are crucial to their sectarian character. That was never a problem with Catholic Charities, which receives federal funds to provide housing services and other social services but does not give clients an overtly religious message. It is a problem, however, for groups like Victory Fellowship, where the religious message is the whole point of the social services they provide.

The welfare overhaul of 1996 allowed faith-based groups to receive federal funds for welfare-to-work programs. *(1996 Almanac, p. 6-3)*

Congress added a similar provision to the Community Services Block Grant when it reauthorized the program in 1998 (PL 105-285), opening the door to other faith-based anti-poverty efforts. *(1998 Almanac, p. 9-23)*

Now, several bills in Congress, including the anti-poverty package, would expand "charitable choice" to include everything from school violence prevention to literacy to assistance for low-income fathers.

To critics such as Scott and Edwards, the potential consequences of charitable choice have never received a full airing because it has always been a side issue.

So far, the welfare bill has not resulted in a huge shift of public funds to faith-based organizations. The exact figures are anybody's guess because states are not required to report charitable choice expenditures to the federal government.

However, a nine-state study by the Center for Public Justice, a Christian policy research organization based in Annapolis, Md., found a "modest, though notable" impact — 84 new financial relationships between government and social service providers since 1996, as well as 41 new collaborations that did not involve the use of public funds.

Stanley W. Carlson-Thies, the center's director of social policy studies, said the welfare bill's charitable choice program has been slow to take hold. If charitable choice is expanded to drug treatment programs, however, there could be "a fairly immediate takeup by some sophisticated organizations," he said in a June 6 interview.

The Civil Rights Problem

Critics' concerns go beyond the traditional arguments about the separation of church and state. Under most charitable choice proposals, including the original language of the American Community Renewal Act (HR 815) — the Watts bill that served as the model for the New Markets drug treatment provision — faith-based organizations would be able to require employees to adhere to their religious beliefs and practices.

That would expand their exemption from Title VII of the Civil Rights Act, which bans public and private employers from discriminating on the basis of race, color, religion, sex or national origin. Critics say such discrimination should not be federally funded.

The exemption already has allowed some faith-based organizations to set hiring and firing standards that would draw lawsuits in the private and nonprofit sectors.

According to the Congressional Research Service, courts have protected a Christian college that refused to hire a Jewish professor; a Catholic university that refused to hire a professor because it did not agree with her views on abortion; a Baptist university that would not allow a professor to teach because his theological views conflicted with the dean's views; and a Christian retirement home that fired a Muslim receptionist who insisted on wearing a head covering.

There have been no such legal challenges to religious groups that have gotten charitable choice funds under the welfare law. However, critics are watching a federal lawsuit in Kentucky they say raises the same issue of publicly funded discrimination. The Kentucky Baptist Homes for Children, a child-care agency that receives state funds, is being sued for firing a lesbian employee because her "lifestyle" was "inconsistent with [the ministry's] religious beliefs."

The ministry does not deny firing

the employee because of her homosexuality, but insists that it was not a religious issue. "We just felt that it was not in the best interests of our children to be promoting that kind of lifestyle," Vickie Grassman, a spokeswoman for the Louisville-based ministry, said in a June 6 interview.

Watts said employment discrimination is "a legitimate concern," but he argued that zealots are likely to be screened out because they would have to win state certification before they could receive federal funds.

The issue is troubling enough to split members of the Congressional Black Caucus. Some, including Chairman James E. Clyburn, D-S.C., are drawn to the charitable choice proposal because church-based drug treatment programs have played an important role in African-American communities. Others, including Scott and Rep. John Lewis, D-Ga., the former Freedom Rider and civil rights leader, oppose it.

"It is not the role of our government to subsidize the spread of God's word," Lewis said in a June 1999 debate on the American Community Renewal Act on the House floor.

Some supporters of charitable choice do not pretend there is no danger of discrimination. They simply do not believe it is realistic to expect faith-based organizations to deny their religious preferences in order to qualify for federal funds.

"They shouldn't be barred from federal funds because they're a Christian organization and they like to hire Christians," Call to Renewal's Wallis said. "If they discriminate against hiring black people, that's a different case." ◆

CQ

Chapter 18

TAXES

Partisanship Proves Too Big An Obstacle in the Effort To End 'Marriage Penalty'

SUMMARY

Republicans were unswerving in their push to cut taxes for married couples, but their unwillingness to negotiate the details with President Clinton or congressional Democrats meant the proposal served only as a campaign issue. Clinton vetoed the GOP bill, and the House sustained the veto. *(Veto text, p. D-61)*

Both parties began the year with a fix for the so-called marriage penalty at the top of their "to do" lists. Clinton proposed a plan in his fiscal 2001 budget that would have cost $44 billion over 10 years to alleviate the penalty, a quirk in the federal income tax code that causes most married couples to pay more in income taxes than they would as two single people. Republicans favored a pricier package that would not only have reduced the tax burden for the estimated 24.8 million couples who pay the penalty — generally those in which the husband and wife have similar incomes — but also given tax breaks to another group of about 21 million couples who were paying less in federal taxes than they would as two single people. These were mainly couples with one stay-at-home spouse, or in which one person earned much more than the other.

Though congressional leaders and Clinton agreed on the need for legislation at a Feb. 1 meeting, House GOP leaders moved the next day to mark up a bill (HR 6) in the Ways and Means Committee that no Democrat supported. Democrats said the measure, estimated to cost $182 billion over 10 years, should not move before an overall budget blueprint passed the House, and that too much of the relief was for couples already receiving a marriage bonus. Administration officials also made it more difficult to achieve consensus on tax matters by insisting, after the markup, that Clinton would not sign any tax bill until a framework was established to pay down the debt and shore up the long-term solvency of Social Security and Medicare.

GOP hopes were buoyed, however, when 48 Democrats joined them in voting to pass the bill in the House. If congressional Democrats moved en masse to support the bill, GOP officials believed, Clinton could be persuaded to sign it, as he had the 1996 welfare overhaul measure (PL 104-193).

But House leaders underestimated the difficulty of getting such a bill through the Senate. When the Finance Committee took up the measure, Chairman William V. Roth Jr., R-Del., who was launching a tough reelection campaign and was under pressure from Senate leaders to make a big splash, ballooned the bill to $248 billion by adding a provision that would have expanded the 28 percent tax bracket for married couples. Republican leaders tried to bring the bill to the floor but three times fell short of the 60 votes needed to overcome a filibuster.

Two months later, GOP leaders tried to revive the proposal by designating it as the first of two tax bills given expedited consideration under the reconciliation instructions in the fiscal 2001 budget resolution (H Con Res 290). Clinton offered to sign the bill (HR 4810) if Republicans would adopt his plan to have Medicare cover senior citizens' prescription drug costs, but the GOP rejected the trade.

With the new protection, the marriage penalty bill moved through both chambers relatively easily. As he had vowed to do, Clinton vetoed the bill, citing its cost and saying it would disproportionately benefit wealthier couples.

The final compromise would have cost $90 billion over five years, but $292 billion if kept on the books for 10 years. It would have allowed married couples filing jointly to claim a standard deduction twice that of singles.

Box Score

- **Bills:** HR 4810, HR 6
- **Legislative action: House** passed HR 6 (H Rept 106-493), 268-158, on Feb. 10.

House passed HR 4810, 269-159, July 12.

Senate passed HR 4810, 61-38, on July 18 after substituting the text of S 2839 (S Rept 106-329).

House adopted the conference report on HR 4810 (H Rept 106-765), 271-156, on July 20.

Senate cleared HR 4810, 60-34, on July 21.

President vetoed the bill Aug. 5.

House sustained the veto, 270-158, on Sept. 13 (16 votes short of the two-thirds majority required).

The lowest 15 percent income tax bracket for married couples would have been expanded to twice the corresponding bracket for singles. Married couples filing jointly could have continued using certain non-refundable tax credits to offset their tax liability even if they were subject to the alternative minimum tax, the system designed to prevent the wealthy from avoiding all tax liability. And lower-income couples would have been allowed to earn up to $2,000 more annually while still qualifying for the earned-income tax credit, which enhances or provides refunds for the working poor.

Quick Fix for 'Marriage Penalty' Held Up by Partisan Jostling

FEBRUARY 5 — When congressional leaders from both parties emerged from a meeting with President Clinton on Feb. 1, they proclaimed surprise at how much potential had appeared for agreement on major issues. But as soon as they left the White House, they built partisan roadblocks against action on a key election-year topic — tax relief, particularly for married couples — on which both Clinton and the GOP say they want accomplishment.

The next day, the House Ways and Means Committee approved a measure (HR 6) that would cut taxes for married couples by an estimated $182 billion over 10 years, although the 23-13 vote was exactly along party lines. Republican leaders say they will put the bill before the House the week of Feb. 7.

Panel members expressed frustration that the parties could not signal an early agreement on a fix for the so-called marriage penalty, a quirk of the income tax code that causes an estimated 24.8 million married couples to pay more in taxes than they would if they remained single.

Democrats and Republicans alike have proposed marriage penalty relief, and in general their plans are not dissimilar. But Democrats said they would not support the GOP measure for two reasons. It was being moved through the House weeks before even the initial consideration of a fiscal 2001 budget resolution, which will lay out congressional spending, entitlement and revenue priorities for the next year. And in their view the bill would direct too much relief to the 21 million couples, mostly with only one wage-earner, who already receive tax bonuses for being married. Republicans had precipitated the procedural opposition by not consulting Democrats on the drafting of the bill. They defended their effort to increase bonuses for stay-at-home parents, however, saying those people should be rewarded for sacrificing a salary to care for their children.

At the markup, some members urged their colleagues to set differences aside. "If both parties are happy to support the marriage penalty" limitation, said Jennifer Dunn, R-Wash., "let's get with it, let's pass something."

But Benjamin L. Cardin, D-Md., spoke for many in his party when he said, "We think there should be relief from the marriage penalty, but the way you're doing it in this bill is wrong."

As part of the tax package Clinton sketched out in his Jan. 27 State of the Union message, the administration is ready to send Congress a fiscal 2001 budget request on Feb. 7 that would alleviate the marriage penalty by a cumulative $45 billion in the next decade. Already, the administration has signaled that it is unlikely to cut Republicans much slack on their bill. In a Feb. 1 letter to Charles B. Rangel of New York, the top Democrat on Ways and Means, Treasury Secretary Lawrence H. Summers said that he and Clinton's other senior advisers would "not recommend that the president sign a bill of this magnitude until a proper framework for paying down the debt, strengthening Social Security and Medicare, and funding critical initiatives has been established."

The letter came just a few hours after Senate and House leaders from both parties and chambers met with Clinton and discussed paying down the debt, addressing health care issues and expanding international trade. Leaders from both sides called the meeting productive, and Senate Minority Leader Tom Daschle, D-S.D., said it was "unusual that we find ourselves at that level of agreement."

But Rangel said the congressional leaders and the president had not discussed taxes, and the lack of agreement on the topic between the parties — and even between the majorities on each side of the Capitol — showed throughout the week.

On Jan. 31, Ways and Means Committee Chairman Bill Archer, R-Texas, announced his marriage penalty plan and predicted that it would be cleared quickly. "I can't believe that any individual senator will hold it up," he declared. But the next day, Senate Majority Leader Trent Lott, R-Miss., expressed concern that Archer's proposal might not do enough to help married couples at all income levels, and Daschle said Democrats would not give the unanimous consent necessary to bring up a stand-alone tax bill outside the budget reconciliation process.

In addition, Republican senators on the tax-writing Finance Committee continued to differ on how and whether to proceed with tax cuts at all this year. Charles E. Grassley of Iowa, the second most senior GOP panel member, said he would not favor moving any tax bill this year. Phil Gramm of Texas said Congress should move a comprehensive bill similar to the $792 billion, 10-year tax cut legislation (HR 2488) Clinton vetoed last year. Chairman William V. Roth Jr., R-Del., has said he will also push a marriage penalty bill this year, but he has remained vague on his plans for any other tax bills.

GOP senators were expected to caucus the week of Feb. 7 to search for a united front on tax policy for the year.

Finance Committee Democrat John B. Breaux of Louisiana said he expected that the Senate will consider a marriage penalty bill once the budget resolution has cleared, which GOP leaders want to do by the end of next month.

Broader Tax Strategy

If the Senate will not take up any in the series of GOP tax bills expected to move through the House — and Daschle answered a blunt "no" when asked if Democrats would grant unanimous consent to bring up such measures — it appears that the chambers will proceed down different paths this year.

Speaker J. Dennis Hastert, R-Ill., has already announced that the House will debate at least three tax bills: to alleviate the marriage penalty; to expand Individual Retirement Accounts for education to cover primary and secondary school expenses, including private school tuition; and to provide tax and regulatory incentives for investing in low-income urban and rural communities.

In addition, his chief spokesman, John Feehery, said Feb. 2 that there is a "distinct possibility" that two more stand-alone bills may come to the floor from the Ways and Means Committee. One would address the estate tax, which many Republicans and some Democrats want repealed or at least reduced. The other would increase the amount of outside income Social Security recipients could earn and still keep their full benefits. Both of those proposals — like the three bills to which Hastert already has committed — have been included in other legislation, all but the Social Security earnings limit most recently in the vetoed 1999 tax bill.

Rangel and House Minority Leader Richard A. Gephardt, D-Mo., said it appeared to them that the GOP wants to resurrect last year's bill piece by piece. At the Groundhog Day markup, Rangel said that strategy would not work; he also likened it to the 1993 movie named after that folksy holiday, in which the protagonist played by Bill Murray "did the same dumb thing every day, day after day."

Republicans countered that Democrats, by opposing the bill, were reviving a strategy of blocking legislation in order to paint the GOP as a "do nothing" party. But Rangel said that he would not attempt to slow action because, if he did so, voters might not distinguish between the parties. "They may vote against all of us because we haven't done anything," he said.

Moving stand-alone bills has two practical benefits for House Republicans: It will win kudos from Christian conservatives and others who have long wanted up-or-down votes on "pro-family" tax policy, and it bulks up the legislative agenda at an often slow season of the year. Still, Hastert has said he does not rule out considering a more comprehensive tax measure later in the year. Archer has also signaled that he wants to again push a broader tax cut.

'Marriage Penalty' Markup

Although there is no fiscal 2001 budget resolution to follow, Archer said the markup could be conducted with an eye to the fiscal 2000 resolution (H Con Res 68), because the $792 billion earmarked for tax cuts in that document were never committed.

The committee replaced the original text of HR 6 — a marriage penalty relief bill by Jerry Weller, R-Ill., cosponsored by 235 lawmakers, 25 of them Democrats — with a new, three-pronged approach by Archer. Beginning in 2001, it would increase the standard deduction for married couples to double that of single individuals; it is now 60 percent higher.

It would also expand the limit on couples' income taxed at the lowest marginal rate — 15 percent — to eventually be twice that for individuals. The change would be phased in from 2003 to 2008. On returns for 2000, the lowest bracket will apply to the first $43,850 of a married couple's taxable income and the first $26,250 of a single person's taxable income. Bracket limits are adjusted each year for inflation.

Finally, it would increase by $2,000 the income levels by which married couples qualified for at least some earned-income tax credit, a program that enhances tax refunds for the working poor.

Democrats opposed increasing the 15 percent bracket — a proposal they said would benefit the top 25 percent of taxpayers because more of their income would be taxed at a lower rate. But Weller and other Republicans said that without the provision, the bill would have nothing for taxpaying couples who chose to itemize their tax deductions, including those who own homes.

Democrats also argued that the bill would do too much to help taxpayers who already receive a marriage bonus, because the tax relief is not tailored to the two-earner couples who generally pay a penalty. Clinton's plan would help two-earner couples who do not itemize more than other couples and singles.

But Dunn and Nancy L. Johnson of Connecticut, the two GOP women on the panel, defended giving extra help to families with a stay-at-home spouse. "It is very hard to stay at home and take care of kids in today's world," Johnson said, adding that there is "a crying need to better reward those young couples where they're making the sacrifices."

Members on both sides of the aisle spent much of the markup trying to understand the tax ramifications of the bill, especially how it might bump some taxpayers into the Alternative Minimum Tax (AMT), a parallel tax system that aims to prevent wealthy individuals and corporations from wiping out their entire tax liability by using credits and deductions.

Because taxpayers are subject to the AMT if their taxes would be higher under it than under the regular system, reducing regular taxes puts some taxpayers at risk of being moved into the AMT. Archer included a provision to tweak AMT calculations to ensure that no one would owe more taxes as a result of the bill, but Democrats said the bill would contribute to the growing number of families subject to the AMT. The Treasury Department estimates that 45 percent of all families with two children will be subject to the tax by 2010; committee Democrats said that under Archer's bill the figure would be above 50 percent. Less than 10 percent of such families currently pay the AMT.

House Passes Bill To Eliminate 'Marriage Penalty'

FEBRUARY 12 — Hopes for bipartisan agreement on taxes this year dimmed significantly the week of Feb. 7, as Democrats ganged up against the Republican plan for alleviating the "marriage penalty," and President Clinton's advisers distanced themselves from cooperation with Congress as soon as they had laid out the administration's more limited fiscal 2001 tax plan.

The confluence of events frustrated those who had once seen fertile ground for compromise on politically popular tax cuts, first and foremost to minimize the tax disadvantage facing a plurality of married couples.

At a Senate Finance Committee hearing Feb. 8, Chairman William V. Roth Jr., R-Del., took Treasury Secretary Lawrence H. Summers and the Clinton administration to task for "moving the goal posts after the kickoff" by asserting that Clinton would not sign any tax bill until a framework is established to pay down the debt and shore up the long-term solvencies of Social Security and Medicare.

By "laying down conditions that you have to recognize are not going to be realized," Roth said, the White House is essentially ruling out enactment of the GOP marriage penalty measure (HR 6) or any other election-year tax cut.

Summers replied that a marriage penalty bill "can be done, but it needs to be done in the right way and at the right time." Office of Management and Budget Director Jack Lew repeated a similar mantra as he made a round of appearances before congressional committees to discuss Clinton's fiscal 2001 budget, submitted to Congress on Feb. 7.

That budget called for a more limited tax cut for married couples facing penalties and focused proposed tax relief in other directions: toward middle-income and poor people faced with paying college tuition or caring for a disabled relative and toward businesses willing to invest in environmental technology or low-income areas. Many of the proposals had been included in past budget submissions. Together, they would cut taxes by $350.3 billion over the next decade. Clinton also would raise $181.7 billion in revenue over the same period by closing corporate income tax loopholes, increasing taxes on life insurance and increasing the excise tax on a pack of cigarettes to 64 cents. It is 34 cents now, but will rise by a nickel in 2002.

But House GOP Conference Chairman J.C. Watts Jr. of Oklahoma said the president's plan has "tax increases that Republicans in Congress could never support," and Summers acknowledged at a Feb. 7 news conference that he did not know "what the prospects for their passage would be."

First Things First?

Three days later, when the House took up the GOP marriage tax measure, Democrats took up the administration's drumbeat that Social Security, Medicare and the national debt should be addressed before tax cuts.

"You have the cart before the horse," said Sander M. Levin, D-Mich., adding, "the president is going to veto this with red ink," a reference to the GOP's desire to pass the bill before Valentine's Day.

But Republicans responded that there is no need to wait to enact relief for the 24.8 million married couples who pay more in income taxes than they would if they had remained single, or to give additional tax incentives to the 21 million couples, mostly with one wage-earner, who pay less tax than they did as single people. The GOP plan would dole out $182 billion in relief during the next 10 years.

The vote for the bill was 268-158. Although few Democrats spoke in favor of it on the floor, 48 of them — or 23 percent of their caucus — voted for the measure. Most are from marginally Democratic districts or are running for higher office, among them Senate aspirant Debbie Stabenow of Michigan and gubernatorial candidate Bob Wise of West Virginia. No Republican voted against the bill. *(Vote 15, p. H-6)*

The Ways and Means Committee's ranking Democrat, Charles B. Rangel of New York, offered an alternative that would have provided $95 billion in marriage penalty relief in the coming decade. But it also would have conditioned the start of the cut on administration certification that steps had been taken to ensure Social Security would be solvent through 2050, Medicare's trust fund would be in balance until 2030 and the public debt would be eliminated by 2013. It was rejected, 192-233. *(Vote 13, p. H-6)*

Republicans predicted the proposal would not serve Democrats well in their quest to retake the House this fall. "It sounds like a lot of excuses," Jim Nussle, R-Iowa, said of the substitute's contingencies. "It's high time that you came up with a bill that did something."

In an attempt to turn up the heat under the Democrats, Jerry Weller, R-Ill., stood up after each Democratic opponent spoke in the debate and announced how many couples in that member's district — according to a study by the conservative Heritage Foundation — would receive tax relief under the GOP bill, which Weller sponsored.

In a strategy designed to "triangulate" congressional Democrats and prompt a presidential signature, Republicans described what they said was a distinction on tax policy between House Democrats and Clinton. After Nussle criticized House Democrats, he pointed out that he was not castigating Clinton. "At least he's trying," Nussle said, in reference to the $44 billion of marriage tax relief in Clinton's budget.

Clinton's senior advisers are recommending that he not sign the House bill. But the bill must first make it through the Senate, where its prospects are far less certain.

Majority Leader Trent Lott, R-Miss., intends to attempt to bring the House measure before the Senate in the first few weeks of March, according to his spokesman. But — because that will still be before a fiscal 2001 budget resolution might give a tax bill special procedural protections — the GOP would have to come up with 60 votes to overcome a filibuster. And Senate Democrats are just as intent as were their House colleagues on changing the bill. At a press briefing Feb. 9, Minority Leader Tom Daschle, D-S.D., said Democrats would offer a substitute that would reduce taxes by a lesser amount and commit the leftovers to provide Medicare coverage of prescription drugs.

The 'Marriage Penalty'

Though most moderate and liberal House Democrats opposed the GOP bill, they were quick to note that they did not support charging married couples more taxes than they would pay if they were simply living together.

The so-called marriage penalty is a quirk of the income tax code created with President Richard M. Nixon's signature on a law (PL 91-172) to ensure that tax rates for single people would be no more than 20 percent higher than those for married taxpayers with the same income. This affected few married couples at the time the bill took effect, in 1971, because most families then had only one wage earner. But as more women joined the work force, the marriage penalty began to balloon. The penalty generally falls on couples in which one person earns 70 percent or less of the income, and the other earns 30 percent or more.

According to the Treasury Department, on tax returns for 1999 — due April 15 — 48 percent of married couples will see a penalty, averaging $1,141, while 41 percent will see a bonus, averaging $1,274. The other 11 percent of married couples will see no difference.

To alleviate the marriage penalty, the bill would make the standard deduction for married couples filing jointly twice what it is for single people; the differential is now 60 percent. Because that change would benefit only taxpayer couples who did not itemize their deductions, Republicans also would increase the limits on income subject to the lowest tax bracket — 15 percent — to double the limits for single taxpayers. The change would be phased in between 2003 to 2008. On returns for income in 2000, the lowest bracket will apply to the first $43,850 of a married couple's taxable income and the first $26,250 of a single person's taxable income. Bracket limits are adjusted each year for inflation.

The bill would also increase by $2,000 the limits by which married couples may qualify for the earned-income tax credit (EITC), a program that enhances tax refunds for the working poor.

The Democratic substitute would also have made the standard deduction for married couples double that of singles, and it would have increased the limit for qualifying for the EITC by

$2,000 for a married couple in 2001, by $2,500 in 2002 and adjusted for inflation thereafter.

Clinton's plan would differentiate between couples who generally are penalized and those who receive a bonus. The standard deduction would be made twice that of single taxpayers only for two-earner couples, and the change would be phased in over five years. Additional relief for all married couples would come in 2005, when the standard deduction would be increased by $500. At that time, the deduction for single heads of households would increase by $350 and for singles by $250.

The President's Budget

While the week of Feb. 7 ended with debate on the marriage penalty, it began with the president's budget release.

The revenue provisions in that budget, and a subsequent Treasury Department release of a 221-page book detailing the proposals, provided a glimpse at the increasing federal revenue that has made much of the tax debate possible.

But Treasury officials said that more and more corporations are improperly sheltering their income from taxes, a problem that the president's budget aims to address both by requiring greater disclosure of possible shelters and by increasing penalties for substantially understating taxes.

Clinton had proposed taking similar steps last year but with considerably lower estimates of how much revenue they would generate. The Treasury Department says such plans would provide about $14.5 billion in revenue in the next decade, about double last year's estimate. Roth pledged to hold hearings on the issue. The Ways and Means Committee heard testimony on the issue last year, when the Treasury Department released a detailed study of corporate tax shelters.

The Clinton budget also proposed to raise taxes on many corporate life insurance products, a plan that has often been proposed in presidential budgets but has not been implemented.

Phil Anderson, vice president for federal affairs at the American Council of Life Insurers, distributed letters from three Senate Democrats — Christopher J. Dodd and Joseph I. Lieberman, both of Connecticut, and Kent Conrad of North Dakota — who opposed the plans. Anderson predicted the proposal would "receive no traction among Republican or Democratic members of Congress."

While the president was outlining his proposals, Republicans in the House continued to move ahead with plans to advance a series of stand-alone measures, many of them revivals of proposals that Clinton has thwarted in the five years of GOP control of Congress. The next bill expected to reach the floor, perhaps in early March, will repeal the earnings limit for Social Security recipients. A Ways and Means markup of the measure was scheduled for Feb. 16.

Though such a measure is not a tax bill as such, it has some negative revenue implications in early years. But the chairman of the panel's Social Security Subcommittee, E. Clay Shaw Jr., R-Fla., said Feb. 10 that in the out years, the bill he is drafting is revenue neutral, because forecasters predict that removing the limit would enable more beneficiaries to retire later, thus putting off the date by which they need full Social Security payments.

Senate Panel Votes For Tax Relief Bill

APRIL 1 — Senate Republicans are advancing an ambitious bill to give tax relief to married couples, but their most recent efforts appear to be aimed more at embarrassing Democrats as tax day looms than at genuinely passing something into law.

The Finance Committee on March 30 approved, by an 11-9, party-line vote, a $248 billion draft bill to ease the so-called marriage tax penalty. Majority Leader Trent Lott, R-Miss., had already announced that he will call the measure to the floor the week of April 10.

Minority Leader Tom Daschle, D-S.D., just as promptly announced that Republicans will not be able to win over enough Democrats to reach the 60 votes needed to break a filibuster.

Any filibuster would push the bill up against the April 17 deadline for filing tax returns. In this thrust-and-parry election year on Capitol Hill, the prospect of seeing Democrats kill a marriage penalty bill just before the deadline has Republicans smiling.

"Oh, we can spend all week talking about this," said a Senate GOP aide. "It's tax day week after next, isn't it?"

But that scenario does nothing to clarify the ultimate outcome of this election year debate on taxes. Only a few weeks ago, Senate Republicans had balked at the idea of advancing a stand-alone tax bill to ease the marriage penalty precisely because it would be vulnerable to a filibuster. The alternative was to wait for the budget process to unfold, or to wait and move the provisions as part of a larger tax bill protected by the budget resolution.

The Senate Budget Committee on March 30 approved a draft fiscal 2001 budget resolution that calls for $150 billion in tax cuts over the next five years, including marriage penalty relief, to be incorporated into a budget "reconciliation" bill. That would allow any such tax provision to advance under filibuster-proof conditions that apply to such bills.

The Republican Divide

Even though all factions in Congress say they want to fix the deceptively complicated pieces of the tax code that make many couples pay higher taxes than if they filed as singles, the parties remain divided over key details.

The House on Feb. 10 passed a $182 billion version of the marriage tax penalty relief bill (HR 6) with a bevy of Democratic votes — and glowing media coverage. That prompted Senate Republicans to reconsider their options and decide to go ahead with the stand-alone approach.

Even so, Senate Republicans remain divided over whether they want to make a serious bid to cut taxes this year or wait until President Clinton is out of the picture.

"We've started with, and continue to have, a divide amongst members on our side as to whether we should try to enact tax cuts this year," said an aide to a member of the Senate GOP leadership. "Some people want to save money for the next president and cut taxes the right way. Some people think it's better to have the issue than to have a bill."

For the moment, however, Senate Republicans have outdone their House counterparts. The bill that the Finance Committee approved is bigger and broader than the House measure — and was developed without Democratic support — and thus appears sure to fail on the Senate floor.

Senate Finance Chairman William V. Roth Jr., R-Del., called the measure the "centerpiece of our effort to reduce the tax overpayment by America's working families. Not only does it reduce families' tax burden, it eliminates some of the most egregious examples of unfairness and complexity in the tax code today."

Following the House

The Senate Finance bill generally follows the lead of the House measure. Both bills would:

• Increase the standard deduction for married couples to double that of single people; the deduction is now only 60 percent higher. The 10-year cost would be $66 billion.

• Tax a steadily increasing portion of married couples' income now taxed at the lowest 15 percent rate, up to twice that for individuals. (Cost: $105 billion.) The Senate bill would broaden the 28 percent bracket, giving additional tax relief to couples at the higher end of the income scale. (Cost: More than $5 billion.)

• Make more married couples eligible for tax rebates under the earned-income tax credit for the working poor, by increasing by $2,000-2,500 the income levels at which the EITC begins to phase out. (Cost: $11-14 billion.)

The Senate measure went further to provide $45 billion in relief over the next decade to taxpayers who pay the alternative minimum tax (AMT), a provision in the tax code that seeks to make sure higher bracket taxpayers pay a certain amount of their income in taxes regardless of the number of deductions they claim. As incomes have risen, more and more taxpayers have been hit by the AMT and have lost deductions such as the $500-per-child tax credit.

Democrats countered with a less costly alternative that, as its centerpiece, would have allowed married couples to file as if they were two single taxpayers. This was the approach that Roth favored when crafting the original Senate version of last year's vetoed $792 billion tax bill.

The Democratic alternative, which would have been phased in slowly over 2002-10, would have cost $151 billion over 10 years, but only $20 billion over five years. The proposal would have reduced the marriage penalty for those now hit by it but would not have provided a greater marriage bonus to other married couples. It failed by a 9-11, party-line vote.

Republicans will need five Democrats to break ranks to overcome a filibuster. Some of the most likely candidates, however, including moderate John B. Breaux, D-La., sit on Finance and voted against the measure there. Roth had earlier promised to try to forge a bipartisan measure in committee. But several Finance Democrats said in interviews they believed Roth instead gave in to pressure by panel conservatives and outside groups, such as the Christian Coalition, to produce a much bigger bill than Democrats could support.

"This has much more to do with the Christian Coalition's agenda than it has to do with eliminating the marriage penalty," said Richard H. Bryan, D-Nev., a member of Finance. "I think that the chairman always operates on a short tether."

Democrats support the idea of easing the marriage penalty, but they say the GOP goes way too far, claiming budget surplus money that Democrats would like to target for education or health care programs such as a prescription drug benefit for senior citizens.

Democrats seem confident of blocking Roth's measure on the floor. "We're not going to lose any Democrats on the Republican marriage penalty bill," said Daschle. "They made it easier to oppose, by far" by drafting a bill more costly than the House measure.

Conservatives successfully pressed not only to erase the marriage tax penalty paid by two-earner couples, but also to add to the marriage "bonus," which benefits many other couples, especially traditional single wage-earner households. "Family values" advocates lobbied hard for tax relief for families with stay-at-home mothers. "If you're going to fix the marriage penalty in the tax code, don't create a new one," said Lori Cole, executive director of the conservative Eagle Forum, founded by Phyllis Schlafly. "Do a bill that is fair to all married couples."

The Treasury Department says that the Senate bill would provide more than half of its benefits to taxpayers who do not suffer from the marriage penalty. And committee Democrats charged that, even though the bill would alleviate the marriage penalty relative to the existing code, it would create an entirely new marriage penalty by also increasing the marriage bonus.

Republicans were unfazed. "I am not offended that we're going beyond" addressing the marriage penalty, said panel member Paul Coverdell of Georgia. "It is meaningful relief to people who need it."

Driving the process, senators and staff aides said, were GOP leaders, especially Lott and Assistant Majority Leader Don Nickles of Oklahoma.

Said a staff aide to a senior Finance Committee Republican: "We promised long ago to make every effort we could to try to do as much as possible on the marriage tax penalty for people who have been in our corner for years, and for whom we haven't done that much. I hope we get the votes, but the fate of the bill is in Democrats' hands."

That Roth and others did not cultivate Democratic support was taken as a sign that Republicans had political motives.

"[Republicans] almost had to work at it to produce a partisan marriage penalty bill," said a senior Daschle staff aide.

Bill Stalled By Senate Leaders' Impasse Over Amendments

APRIL 15 — Senate Republicans could easily have scored a huge political victory the week of April 10 by passing a quarter-trillion-dollar tax cut for married couples.

Instead, the bill (S 2346) fell victim to procedural infighting between a majority leader seeking to protect his members from having to cast a few difficult votes and a minority leader trying to protect his colleagues' rights to offer amendments in the freewheeling fashion of Senates of the past.

The impasse between Majority

Leader Trent Lott, R-Miss., and Minority Leader Tom Daschle, D-S.D., over what type of amendments could be offered to the "marriage penalty" relief bill produced twin, 53-45 votes April 13 when Lott tried to invoke cloture, or limit debate on the measure. Sixty votes are needed. *(Votes 82, 83, p. S-17)*

When the Senate returns from its spring recess April 25, Lott has to choose whether to allow Democrats to obtain votes on some of their amendments or to continue the deadlock with Daschle. The first option would permit Republicans to pass a huge tax bill through the Senate without having to rely on special filibuster-free budget "reconciliation" rules — which would be extraordinary in today's partisan times. The second course is also attractive: Republicans could portray Democrats as blocking relief from the marriage penalty, and revisit the issue later during reconciliation.

The sparring on the floor over procedure was far more dramatic than debate on the underlying bill, which would cut taxes for married people by $248 billion over the next decade.

At one point on April 11, Minority Whip Harry Reid, D-Nev., temporarily stopped Republicans from even debating the bill, in response to a move by Lott to prevent Democrats from being allowed to offer their amendments. The usually unflappable Reid snapped at Lott: "My friend, the majority leader, is treating us as if we are in the House" — where the GOP-dominated Rules Committee dictates the terms of floor debate. "He is the Rules Committee — the one-man Rules Committee. . . . We are tired of playing make-believe senators."

Democrats have long chafed at Lott's attempts to deny them the opportunity to offer unrelated amendments to bills that come to the floor, a right afforded to every senator under the rules. Instead, Lott almost always tries to invoke cloture — which permits only germane amendments — or negotiates with Daschle to sharply limit the number and scope of amendments.

Republicans cast the Democrats' objections as simple attempts to derail the marriage penalty relief effort. "It's going to be clear who's for marriage penalty relief and who's not," Lott said.

Impasse

Lott has slated another cloture vote for April 25, but it seems clear that Democrats genuinely have their backs up over the way he is running the Senate and that vote will almost surely fail.

"I'm very confident we can hold our position as long as they are intransigent" about denying Democrats opportunities to change the measure with off-topic amendments, Daschle said.

Lott said he would continue negotiations with Daschle toward a way out of the impasse.

If the deadlock continues, the marriage penalty issue could be revisited when and if Republicans advance budget-reconciliation bills as permitted under the fiscal 2001 budget resolution (H Con Res 290), adopted by both House and Senate on April 13. That non-binding measure calls for up to $175 billion in tax cuts over the next five years and would permit two filibuster-free tax bills to get rolling. Any such effort, labeled a reconciliation bill because it would reconcile tax laws with the non-binding budget resolution, would provide Senate Democrats with numerous opportunities for amendment.

The so-called marriage tax penalty affects many married couples who pay more income tax than they would if they filed as singles. On the other hand, the tax code provides a marriage "bonus" to many other couples, especially traditional single-earner families with a stay-at-home parent.

Both congressional Republicans and Democrats, as well as President Clinton, want to ease or erase the marriage penalty, though they have very different approaches on how to do so. The Senate Republican plan, which is very close to the version (HR 6) passed by the House in February, would provide a tax cut to virtually all married couples, those hit by the marriage penalty but also those who already get a marriage bonus.

Democrats charge that the GOP plan is far too costly and would provide more than half its tax relief to couples unaffected by the marriage penalty. Many Democrats support a 10-year, $151 billion alternative that, as its centerpiece, would permit married couples to file their tax returns as if they were single. The Democratic plan would help those hit by the marriage penalty but not those who get a marriage bonus. When fully implemented, however, the Democratic alternative would be more costly than the Republican plan.

An administration position paper said April 11 that Clinton's "senior advisers would not recommend that he sign" the bill, a somewhat nebulous position that falls short of an explicit veto threat.

Stand-Alone Bills

The decision to advance HR 6 in the Senate is part of a broader GOP strategy, advocated most vociferously by House Speaker J. Dennis Hastert, R-Ill., to break up last year's vetoed $792 billion tax bill (HR 2488) and pass some of its most popular pieces as stand-alone bills. That approach is far easier to pursue in the House, and many Senate Republicans were initially reluctant to follow it because Senate rules give Democrats the right to filibuster and offer politically challenging amendments.

But prospects for passing a free-standing marriage penalty bill brightened after Lott shepherded through the Senate bills to establish tax-free education savings accounts (S 1134) and to permit some Social Security recipients to earn outside income without deferring a portion of their federal benefits (HR 5). Democrats agreed not to offer off-topic amendments to these bills.

"The Social Security earnings test elimination worked so smoothly and so easily . . . I thought, 'Well, if it's really good, if it's really powerful, and if we really need to do it, we might agree on these things,' " Lott said in an April 12 interview. As for the marriage penalty effort, Lott said, "It's working better than I thought it would."

In fact, some Democrats were nervous about simply killing the GOP bill outright, even if they believe it is far too costly. That was one of the reasons Daschle was willing to agree to let the measure pass with a simple majority vote, provided his side could offer amendments.

"It is fair to say that there are people within our caucus who believe that just killing the marriage penalty [bill] outright would be perceived by some as opposing attempts to fix it, and I want to be sensitive to that," Daschle said.

After the April 11 floor scuffle between Lott and Reid, Daschle and Lott agreed to try to work it out. The next day, Daschle provided Lott with a roster of 10 amendments on topics such as low-cost imports of prescription drugs, college tuition tax credits and allowing victims of natural disasters to deduct disaster-related costs on their tax returns.

Daschle dissuaded Democrats from seeking to offer amendments on "poison pill" topics, such as gun control or raising the minimum wage, and, according to Daschle, Lott initially seemed to think the winnowed list "was a pretty good deal."

But Lott ultimately balked at Daschle's offer: "Why should I ask my people to walk the plank on issues that they may even be for?"

Added a GOP leadership staff aide: "We have some of our guys in [an election] cycle who say, 'Look, I've voted enough' " on politically sensitive topics.

Republicans were content to let the opportunity to pass the bill slide. They said pressure from the public would likely cause Democrats to ease their demands on amendments.

Democrats counter that they are not in a mood to budge and appear, at least so far, to be choosing to take a stand to defend their rights.

"I think that the Senate has gone downhill in recent years. I think that it is far too partisan. I have seen bills called up, and immediately cloture is filed on them to end debate on them, when there has not even been a debate," Robert C. Byrd, D-W. Va., a former majority leader and expert on the Senate rules, said in an April 13 floor speech. "I will not support the erosion of minority rights in the Senate simply to advance a politically popular initiative."

Even as Democrats complained about the way Lott runs the Senate, the fact remains that they have often gone along, especially when they support the underlying bill. The alternative is to let legislation die.

"We have been forced to do certain things," Reid acknowledged. "It is the only way we can get legislation to move forward, and we're sick of it."

Third Senate Cloture Vote Fails

APRIL 29 — Efforts to move a generous tax cut for married couples through the Senate were thwarted for a third time April 27. On a 51-44 vote, supporters failed to muster the 60 votes necessary to limit debate on an amendment containing the Senate version (S 2346) of legislation (HR 6) passed by the House to reduce the tax code's "marriage penalty." *(Vote 87, p. S-18)*

Two earlier cloture votes on the proposal came up short the week of April 10, after the leaders of the two parties came to an impasse on amendments.

The most recent vote likely heralded an end to Republican attempts to move a variety of tax cuts to President Clinton's desk as separate bills. Particularly in the House, Republican leaders had hoped that Clinton, who vetoed the $792 billion tax cut of 1999 (HR 2488), would find it difficult during an election year to veto incremental tax cuts.

Majority Leader Trent Lott, R-Miss., said he would urge Finance Committee Chairman William V. Roth Jr., R-Del., to use one of the reconciliation bills provided for in the fiscal 2001 budget resolution (H Con Res 290) to bring the marriage penalty bill back before the Senate. The second reconciliation bill, Lott said, could be a vehicle for a package of House-passed initiatives, including education savings account legislation, community development proposals and debt reduction. The budget provides for at least $150 billion in tax cuts over five years, and reconciliation makes it procedurally easier to move tax cuts through the Senate.

GOP Tax Strategy Streamlines the Path for 'Marriage Penalty' Relief Bill

JUNE 17 — After spending much of the year on divergent tracks, House and Senate Republican leaders began developing a comprehensive tax strategy the week of June 12.

GOP aides said leaders agreed that the first tax bill to be given protection from amendment and open-ended debate under the fiscal 2001 budget resolution (H Con Res 290) will be a measure to reduce taxes for most married couples. It is scheduled to move through Congress in July and will not include other provisions.

It was not clear whether that would be the leaders' final decision, or if the two chambers would move the same bill. The House passed a $182 billion measure (HR 6) Feb. 10, and the Senate Finance Committee approved a $248 billion measure March 30, but Senate leaders failed in several attempts to stem debate and bring it to the floor. Both cost estimates cover 10 years.

The two chambers' versions both aim to eliminate a quirk of the tax code known as the "marriage penalty." It causes some couples to pay more in income taxes when they marry than they would if they remained single. But both bills also would help those families who already earn a "bonus" from the code for marrying. In general, two-earner couples with similar incomes are hit by penalties that average $1,141, while one-earner couples often receive bonuses averaging $1,274. Eleven percent of couples see no tax difference.

Both bills would take much the same tack in addressing the issue — making the standard deduction for married couples filing jointly twice the deduction for single people; increasing the limits on income subject to the lowest tax bracket (15 percent) to double the limits for single taxpayers; and increasing by at least $2,000 the limits by which married couples may qualify for the earned-income tax credit, which enhances tax refunds and rebates for the working poor.

The Senate bill also would broaden the second income tax bracket — 28 percent — for married couples. It would also provide $45 billion in relief for taxpayers subject to the Alternative Minimum Tax, a parallel tax system designed to ensure that taxpayers with many deductions and credits still pay some tax.

Democrats and the Clinton administration believe that the Republican bills do too much to help couples already receiving a bonus.

In their own proposals, which were defeated on the floor, House Democrats sought to increase the standard deduction for married couples and raise the eligibility levels for the earned-income tax credit. Senate Democrats had proposed simply changing tax laws to allow married couples to file as if they were two single taxpayers.

Because both parties in Congress and the White House agree that something should be done to alleviate the marriage penalty, some members say it will be possible to work out a bipartisan deal on the issue, perhaps in a conference committee. It seems more likely, however, that Republican leaders will focus on making a political issue of the president's probable refusal to sign their bill.

In addition to the marriage penalty, both committees are scheduled to mark up another tax reconciliation measure in September, as called for in the budget resolution. That bill likely will be of broader scope and could include a number of stand-alone measures the House has passed. A prime candidate would appear to be a bill (HR 8) passed resoundingly on June 9 to phase out estate, gift and generation-skipping taxes by 2010

But Senate Majority Leader Trent Lott, R-Miss., who met with Finance Committee Chairman William V. Roth Jr., R-Del., on June 14 to set a tax markup schedule, said the estate tax repeal could be brought up as a stand-alone measure containing some campaign finance provisions that Democrats and some Republicans have been advocating.

Senate Committee Revives 'Marriage Penalty' as First Reconciliation Bill

JULY 1 — An unexpected offer by President Clinton, to sign a Republican bill to cut taxes for married couples if the GOP would follow his lead on enhancing Medicare with a prescription drug benefit, did little the week of June 26 to sooth partisan passions in Congress on either issue.

Republican leaders quickly responded that they were not interested in horse-trading. The Senate Finance Committee drove the point home June 28, dividing along party lines in approving, 10-5, draft reconciliation legislation to alleviate the so-called marriage penalty — quirks in the tax code that cause some couples to owe more income taxes if they marry than they do if they remain single.

The measure is Congress' initial response to the provision in the budget resolution (H Con Res 290) for fiscal 2001 that calls for the Finance and House Ways and Means committees to write two tax cutting reconciliation bills this year. Reconciliation legislation may be debated for no more than 20 hours in the Senate, and as a result, GOP leaders will be able to force a straightforward vote on their marriage penalty proposal. An almost identical measure (S 2346) was marked up by Finance in March, but it was never put to a vote on the floor because the GOP did not have the votes to thwart a filibuster by Democrats, who wanted to use the bill as a vehicle for a variety of amendments.

Majority Leader Trent Lott, R-Miss., said he planned to put the new version on the floor July 13, a Thursday, and would insist on a vote on passage before senators could leave for the weekend. It is not clear whether Ways and Means will mark up a similar bill when it returns from the July Fourth recess, or whether such a measure will go directly to the House floor. The House passed its first version of a marriage penalty bill (HR 6) in February.

Republicans have long sought to make alleviating the marriage penalty — and increasing bonuses for those, mostly one-earner couples, who already reap advantages under the tax code — a centerpiece of their agenda. Finance Committee Chairman William V. Roth Jr., R-Del., said June 28 that Clinton's proposed compromise should not "change the focus of this markup."

Democrats readied a dozen amendments to tie prescription coverage for Medicare recipients to the marriage penalty bill — as Clinton had proposed. They did not offer them, because Roth pledged at the start of the markup that Finance would take up a drug benefit measure after the recess and would work with Democrats to craft the bill.

Some Senate Finance members said political forces will have completely overtaken the issue by then. "Are we going to have a better chance of a compromise after the July Fourth weekend? I very much doubt it," said John D. Rockefeller IV, D-W.Va.

Several hours later, the House narrowly passed a GOP prescription drug bill (HR 4680) amid bitter partisan acrimony.

Clinton sounded unfazed that Congress was not quickly embracing his offer. "I haven't given up, and we're still working," he told reporters June 29.

Floating Compromises

Clinton offered his swap when he announced the White House forecast that an additional $1.1 trillion in on-budget surpluses will be available in the next decade.

He made clear that he still views GOP marriage penalty relief as "too big and not targeted toward those who need it most." But, he said, if Republicans could accept his prescription drug proposal, estimated to cost about $250 billion over 10 years, and would agree to separate the Medicare trust fund from the rest of the federal budget, he would agree to sign a tax cut for married couples. The Senate version has been estimated to cost $248 billion over 10 years.

The bill put before the Finance Committee June 28 was estimated to cost $55.6 billion over five years, however, because it included a provision to sunset its own changes to the tax code at the end of 2004. That was an effort to get around the Senate's so-called Byrd rule, which requires a supermajority of 60 votes for budget reconciliation proposals that would not be offset entirely by spending cuts or revenue increases. The budget resolution only dedicates $150 billion of the surplus to tax cuts over the next five years.

The bill is otherwise the same as the version marked up in March. It would:

- Increase the standard deduction for married couples to twice that of single taxpayers, beginning in 2001. The deduction is now roughly 60 percent. The provision is estimated to cost $25 billion over five years.
- Increase by $2,500 the limit for qualifying for the earned-income tax credit (EITC) for married couples, beginning in 2001. The program pro-

vides or enhances tax refunds for the working poor. Currently, the credit is phased out for couples with two or more children with earned income above $12,690; they become ineligible when their income is above $31,152. Both those figures would increase by $2,500 under the bill. Couples with one child and no children have lower qualification thresholds, which also would increase by $2,500. The provision is estimated to cost $6.3 billion over five years.

• Make the 15 percent and 28 percent personal income tax brackets for married couples twice the size of those for single taxpayers. The brackets are the lowest two in the five-rate income tax hierarchy. Republicans say it is important to include the provision, because it ensures some tax relief for those who itemize and so do not take the standard deduction. Phasing in of the provision would begin in 2002 and be complete in 2007. Because of the bill's sunset language, this provision would need to be extended by a subsequent Congress before it could be fully implemented. The estimated cost of the provision is $17.5 billion through 2004.

• Permanently allow taxpayers — regardless of marital status — to claim personal tax credits, such as the $500-per-child credit, against their alternative minimum tax. Those whose deductions and credits surpass their total tax liability are now subject to an alternative calculation of taxes that generally precludes counting such credits.

Committee Debate

A number of Finance Committee Democrats continued to insist that the GOP's bill was not fair, because it would give extra tax breaks to the 21 million couples who already receive a bonus, while alleviating the penalty for 24.8 million couples. "You're giving breaks to people who already get a marital bonus," said Democrat Kent Conrad of North Dakota.

Phil Gramm, R-Texas, urged the Democrats to accept the Republican marriage penalty bill. "You're for love and we're for marriage, and this bill gives us more of both," he said.

Ranking Democrat Daniel Patrick Moynihan of New York offered a substitute amendment to allow married couples with earnings of less than $100,000 to choose whether to file singly, but on the same tax form, or jointly. The benefit would be phased out for couples with incomes between $100,000 and $150,000. The amendment was defeated, 9-11, along party lines.

Conrad and Max Baucus, D-Mont., offered an amendment to move the Medicare trust fund off-budget, as Clinton proposed June 26, and to establish additional points of order against spending either Social Security or Medicare funds. Roth ruled the plan was under the Budget Committee's jurisdiction and so the amendment was not in order; the panel voted 6-11 along party lines against overturning that ruling. Republican leaders said they would work with Conrad to pass such a "lockbox" for Medicare as a separate bill.

House Passes Marriage Tax Cut; Senate Gets Set For Debate

JULY 15 — Congressional Republicans likely will be able to cross at least one big "to do" item off their pre-convention legislative list the week of July 17: Send President Clinton a politically dicey bill to cut taxes for married couples.

The Senate is expected to pass its version of the year's first reconciliation bill (HR 4810) by July 18, after disposing of dozens of amendments. With the support of four dozen Democrats, the House voted, 269-159, to pass its version of the bill July 12. *(Vote 392, p. H-122)*

If negotiations are called for — some think the House may instead vote to clear the Senate bill — the talks will be quick enough that the compromise version will be sent to Clinton by July 21, GOP aides said.

"Now, no one is going to delay us from passing this bill," Finance Committee Chairman William V. Roth Jr., R-Del., said as Senate debate began July 14. He recalled how nearly identical legislation passed the House in February but was bottled up in a Senate filibuster thereafter because it was not given the special procedural protections of reconciliation.

Clinton's aides continue to insist that they will recommend a veto, now that the GOP has rejected the president's offer to sign a "marriage penalty" relief measure if Republicans back his plan to create a Medicare prescription drug benefit. A Democratic attempt to attach such a compromise to the House bill was defeated, 197-230. *(Vote 391, p. H-122)*

A statement by the Office of Management and Budget on July 11 said the House bill would provide "too small a share of benefits to lower- and middle-income taxpayers, and too large a share devoted to couples who do not suffer marriage penalties."

The marriage penalty is a quirk of the federal income tax code under which 24.8 million married couples pay more taxes than they would as two singles. Most affected by the penalty are couples in which the husband and wife have similar incomes. Couples in which only one person has earned income, or in which one person earns much more than the other, tend to receive more favorable tax treatment than they would if they were single. About 21 million couples receive such a marriage bonus.

The House and Senate versions of the bill would take the same tack, cutting taxes for married couples regardless of whether they currently receive a bonus or a penalty.

Democrats in both chambers said that, as a result, the legislation is too costly. The Treasury would lose $55.6 billion in revenue in the next five years under the Senate bill and $50.7 billion under the version passed by the House.

The GOP plan "spends much more than we need to to deal with the issue," said Rep. Benjamin L. Cardin, D-Md.

House Minority Leader Richard A. Gephardt, D-Mo., warned that the bill was so expensive that other tax cuts and priorities would fall by the wayside. He urged Republicans to compromise with Democrats instead of daring Clinton to veto the bill. "If you're suffering from the marriage penalty, you want relief now, this year, not next year," he said.

But many House Republicans said they believed Clinton would sign the bill in the end. "Don't be left holding the bag here on the floor," David M.

McIntosh, R-Ind., told Democrats. "We all know the president has changed his mind before," added Jerry Weller, R-Ill., a main patron of the bill, referring to Clinton's decision to sign the welfare overhaul bill (PL 104-193) after vetoing a previous version. *(1996 Almanac, p. 6-3)*

The Senate's debate followed the rhetorical patterns set in the House, although the period set aside for speechmaking was sparsely attended. Most senators left the Capitol for the weekend soon after the vote July 14 that cleared another expensive GOP tax proposal: a bill (HR 8) to end the federal estate tax.

Edward M. Kennedy, D-Mass., ran through an extensive list of social programs that he sees as more deserving of the surplus than a tax cut. Kay Bailey Hutchison, R-Texas, sponsor of the original Senate marriage penalty measure (S 12), said her intent was to use the surplus to help a group of taxpayers wronged by the IRS code get some of their money back.

Once Clinton receives the bill he will have 10 days to sign or veto it, meaning he will have to address it before the conclusion of the Republican National Convention, in Philadelphia the week of July 31.

Republicans are anxious to show that their presidential candidate, Texas Gov. George W. Bush, would sign such measures, and to paint his Democratic opponent, Vice President Al Gore, as a Clinton acolyte who would stand in the way of tax cuts.

Bill Details

The version the Senate is expected to pass, based on a bill (S 2839) approved by the Finance Committee June 28, is more generous than the House-passed bill.

Both would increase the standard deduction — claimed by those who who do not itemize — for married couples filing jointly to twice the deduction for singles. Currently, the deduction for a married couple is only 60 percent more than that for a single taxpayer. Both would also increase the income ceilings for people who want to claim the earned-income tax credit, which provides or supplements tax refunds for the working poor: The increase would be $2,500 under the Senate bill, $500 more than the House bill. Both have language to allow taxpayers subject to the alternative minimum tax to claim some additional personal tax credits, although the Senate bill would go further than the House.

The Senate bill would expand the ceiling on income taxed at both the 15 percent and 28 percent rates for married couples; the House measure would only expand the 15 percent bracket.

To avoid challenges under the Senate rules for reconciliation bills, which require 60 votes for proposals that would exceed the parameters of the budget resolution (H Con Res 290) without accompanying offsets, the Senate bill would sunset on Dec. 31, 2004. That dramatically reduces its price tag. The cost of a nearly identical bill approved in March by the Finance Committee (S 2346 — S Rept 106-253) would have swelled to $248 billion over the next decade, more than quadruple its five-year cost.

Senate Consideration

Although the Senate took up the measure under the restrictive rules of budget reconciliation, which allow only 20 hours of debate and prohibit consideration of non-germane amendments, members were attempting to attach dozens of proposals to the bill. Some will likely be quashed by budget points of order.

Amendments that could be considered range from a provision by Ted Stevens, R-Alaska, to increase tax deductions for whaling captains to a plan by Richard J. Durbin, D-Ill., to allow self-employed persons to deduct 100 percent of their health care insurance costs from their taxes. (They are already set to get that deduction by 2003.)

The House allowed debate on only one amendment to its bill.

It was a Democratic substitute, by Ways and Means Committee ranking Democrat Charles B. Rangel of New York, that would have increased the standard deduction for married couples to double that of singles, increased by $2,500 the limits to qualify for the earned-income tax credit, and ensured that the changes would not have forced more couples to pay the alternative minimum tax, the parallel tax system designed to ensure taxpayers do not wipe out all tax liability through their large claims for credits and deductions. It was defeated, 198-228. *(Vote 390, p. H-122)*

Divide-and-Conquer Strategy Pays Off For GOP as Senate Clears Tax Bill

JULY 22 — Republicans, who got no political traction from their tax cut package of a year ago, appear to have turned the corner — convincing voters that the series of targeted tax bills they are moving through Congress this election year are populist measures that benefit almost everyone.

Democrats, meanwhile, are struggling to make the political case that the bills will mainly benefit the rich, draining forecast surplus funds they say should be used for Medicare, Social Security and education.

The wave of bills moving through the Capitol this summer, under a plan crafted by House Speaker J. Dennis Hastert, R-Ill., would cut taxes for married couples, end the taxation of estates, and cut taxes on both retirement savings and Social Security benefits. Whether any of them becomes law in the 106th Congress will depend on which party can best press its argument at the national political conventions and in town hall meetings during the August recess.

The stage may have been set for the climax of the battle July 21, when Congress sent President Clinton legislation that seems more likely than any high-profile measure since the welfare overhaul to elicit squirms from the famously fluid chief executive.

The bill (HR 4810) — to cut income taxes for almost all married couples by nearly $90 billion over the next five years, and by $292 billion if kept on the books for a decade — has made many Democrats on Capitol Hill squeamish all year. Many of them supported early GOP calls to rid the tax code of the so-called "marriage penalty," a quirk that forces many two-earner couples to pay more in taxes than they would if they had remained single. But many say that the bill Republicans wrote would focus too much relief on other married people —

members of traditional, one-earner couples who already receive a "marriage bonus."

Nonetheless, unusually large numbers of Democrats voted for the final version of the tax cuts. Seven Democrats (16 percent) were in the majority when the Senate voted 60-34 to clear the bill July 21. Fifty-one Democrats (24 percent) voted for the conference report when the House adopted it, 271-156, the day before. And eight Democrats were in the 61-38 majority that passed the Senate's initial version of the bill on July 18. *(House vote 418, p. H-130; Senate vote 215, p. S-39)*

"They're a little gun shy" about voting against tax cuts, Sen. Max Baucus of Montana said of his fellow Democrats. He heeded the entreaties of Minority Leader Tom Daschle, D-S.D., and voted "no" both times.

The votes illustrate that "Democrats want to cut people's taxes," House Minority Leader Richard A. Gephardt, D-Mo., declared at a July 20 news conference. After alternatives sponsored by the minority party have failed, he said, some members of his caucus have voted for GOP tax legislation under the following rationale: "I tried to fix it but I wanted to go the next step."

Gephardt, Daschle and Treasury Secretary Lawrence H. Summers nonetheless labored throughout the week of July 18 to bolster the case against the GOP tax agenda in the eyes of the public — and to enlist more of their fellow Democrats in their class war fight.

The Treasury Department released a study July 17 of 11 of the most expensive tax cut provisions that have been advanced by the 106th Congress. It concluded that the richest 1 percent of families would garner an average annual tax cut of $17,074, while the 60 percent of families in the middle would get tax cuts averaging between $77 and $380 a year.

"The Republican Party is up to its same old tricks," Gephardt declared at a Capitol news conference the next day. "Their base is that rich 2 percent, our base is the rest," Daschle said of the GOP. "That will be the fight."

Despite Daschle's insistence that Democrats looked forward to voting against the marriage penalty bill again — during a possible attempt this fall to override a Clinton veto — party aides and some members said that Democrats were nervous that their party was not reacting effectively to the Republican tax-cut offensive.

At a House Democratic Caucus meeting July 20, leaders stressed the importance of denying any of the bills in the GOP tax arsenal a veto-proof majority. They argued that if they could hold firm against the tax-cut tide, Republicans might relax their attacks after their presidential nominating convention. "We're in the second quarter of the ball game," said Jim McDermott, D-Wash.

And despite the solid votes for the marriage tax bill, the majorities were at least six short in the Senate, and 20 short in the House, of what would be required to enact the measure with a veto override.

Some Democrats hoped that the Republicans and Clinton would meet to strike a climactic tax deal in September, thereby muting any GOP attack on congressional Democrats during the pivotal weeks of the campaign season. But Republicans showed no sign of making peace on the issue with the president, who has already offered to sign a $250 billion tax cut for married couples in the next decade if Congress would embrace his plan to create a Medicare prescription drug benefit.

"The day of reckoning is here," Senate Majority Leader Trent Lott, R-Miss., told reporters July 18. "You can complicate it with a lot of arguments . . . [but] do you actually want to eliminate the marriage penalty . . . or not?"

Shifting Ground

Last year, Democrats relied on the arguments that their leaders are trying to revive this summer: The GOP tax bills are too focused on the rich and would take too much of the newly forecast budget surplus. Their united front gave Clinton comfort when he vetoed a measure (HR 2488) to cut taxes by $792 billion over 10 years.

When Clinton's veto generated little public consternation, Hastert took the House GOP leadership back to the drawing board and crafted a deceptively simple plan: Move the key components from the 1999 measure through Congress again — one at a time, in steady succession.

The House passed an initial version of the marriage tax bill (HR 6) in February, vying for headlines with the president's budget submission, and since then the House Republicans have advanced their plan with discipline and dispatch. They have been spurred on by polls showing that the sustained strength of the economy has revived interest in tax reduction. They have been aided by Democrats, who are vying to retake the House and so leery of opposing popular proposals. And they have been buoyed by a surplus that keeps growing. The most recent estimate, by the Congressional Budget Office (CBO), forecasts a cumulative "on-budget" surplus — what would be left over after Social Security trust fund balances are set aside — of $2.2 trillion between fiscal 2001 and fiscal 2010.

Only one bill, to repeal the Social Security earnings test, has been sent to the White House, where Clinton made good on his promise and signed it (PL 106-182) in April. But the outlook is murkier for the rest of the items on the GOP tax roster.

As part of their strategy of moving the bills separately, Republican leaders say they will wait until September to deliver to the White House their bill (HR 8) to cut estate, gift and trust fund taxes. That way, Clinton may not veto it and the marriage bill simultaneously.

Clinton likely will be forced to accept or reject the marriage measure before the Aug. 3 finale of the Republican National Convention. Most congressional Democrats say they are certain of a veto. Still, many are wary of the president at such times; four summers ago, for example, he signed the welfare overhaul bill (PL 104-193) after vetoing an earlier version. *(1996 Almanac, p. 6-3)*

The Office of Management and Budget (OMB) statements of administration policy on the marriage bill have left Clinton with some wiggle room. They say the president's top advisers would recommend a veto — short of the explicit declaration that he "would veto" the bill, the wording used in the estate tax statement.

Congressional Democrats in tight races are trying to find a middle ground. Rep. Debbie Stabenow — whose challenge in Michigan to Republican incumbent Spencer Abraham is among the Democrats' best prospects for picking up a Senate seat — voted for the couples tax cut, she said, after concluding that it would benefit many of her state's working families. She voted against the estate tax bill because she was not persuaded it would be of similar benefit to her constituents. Abraham voted for both. "It's a matter of balance," she said.

Strategy Gives Campaign Focus

The Republican strategy "helps take away the Democratic message of a do-nothing Congress, and it gives a fiscal focus to the campaign," said Glen Bolger, partner in the GOP polling firm Public Opinion Strategies. "Whenever a campaign is focused on taxes or other fiscal matters, it helps Republicans."

But daring Clinton to sign bills crafted with little Democratic input carries its own risk for the Republicans: If the president rejects the measures, the GOP will have fewer tangible accomplishments to tout on the campaign trail.

Ways and Means Committee Chairman Bill Archer, R-Texas, said July 20 that, no matter the outcome, the 106th Congress had done enough to address the tax code to deserve a "can-do" label. At a press briefing the same day, Gephardt said the legislative action would mean little if it did not yield a tax law: "At the end of the day, voters are going to ask themselves, what has this Congress done for me?"

Mark Mellman, a Democratic pollster and strategist, predicted that his party would be able to turn the issue to its advantage if Clinton made use of the bully pulpit to explain his veto rationale — and to trumpet the alternative Democratic uses for the revenue.

"Tax cuts are a preference but not a priority," he said of public opinion. "Republicans are really walking into a big trap here. They're voting against things that people want even more," he said, listing proposals to spend more on education and health care coverage.

A Different Dynamic

During the six years that Republicans have controlled Congress, they have been the lawmakers who most frequently have had trouble selling their arguments in favor of tax cuts, while the Democrats have had little difficulty getting the public to agree that the GOP tax proposals were skewed to the rich. That dynamic has, at least temporarily, turned around.

House and Senate Democrats propounded a list of reasons for voting against the GOP tax agenda the week of July 17: The bills collectively were too expensive; they would not accomplish what their titles suggested; they should be considered in the context of other national priorities, such as prescription drug coverage for Medicare recipients; and in some cases, they threatened to harm taxpayers in unintended ways.

The most united Democratic front was presented on the newest legislation on the Republican list, to cut taxes on the Social Security benefits of the wealthiest elderly people. All but one Democrat voted against the measure (HR 4865) when it was approved by the House Ways and Means Committee July 19.

By contrast, six out of seven Democrats in the House spurned their leadership and voted June 19 to pass legislation (HR 1102) that would increase the levels of tax-deductible contributions to individual retirement accounts and pension plans.

The next day, the 51 Democrats who voted for the marriage penalty conference report exceeded by three the number of Democratic votes for the proposals in July and February. Changing their votes to "yes" from "no" were Neil Abercrombie of Hawaii, Marcy Kaptur of Ohio, Tim Holden of Pennsylvania and Rick Boucher of Virginia. Mark Udall of

Highlights of HR 4810

ISSUE	DESCRIPTION
Total cost	$89.8 billion over five years, according to the Joint Tax Committee.
Effective dates	Jan. 1, 2000, through Dec. 31, 2004. Without the five-year sunset provision, the bill would violate Senate budget rules that bar consideration of a reconciliation bill that exceeds the parameters of the budget resolution without accompanying offsets.
Standard deduction	The bill would allow married couples filing jointly to claim a standard deduction twice that for singles. In 2000, the deduction for married couples would be $8,800, rather than $7,350. Estimated cost: $30.7 billion.
Bracket expansion	The lowest, 15 percent income tax bracket for married couples would be expanded to twice the corresponding bracket for singles. In 2000, the 15 percent rate covers up to $26,500 in taxable income for individuals, $43,850 for married couples. When fully phased in in 2004, the change would allow up to $52,500 of a couples' income to be taxed at 15 percent. Estimated cost: $44.1 billion.
Alternative Minimum Tax (AMT)	Married couples filing jointly could continue using certain nonrefundable tax credits to offset their tax liability even if they fell under the AMT, a parallel tax system designed to prevent wealthy taxpayers from avoiding all tax liability. Under current law, in 2000 and 2001 individuals and married couples can use certain credits, such as child, education and adoption tax credits, whether or not they qualify for the AMT. The bill would extend this practice for married couples for years 2002 through 2004. Estimated cost: $8.5 billion.
Earned-income tax credit	Lower-income couples could earn up to $2,000 more each year than under current law ($12,460 for a family of four in 1999) and still be able to claim the full earned-income tax credit, which provides or enhances rebates for the working poor. Refunds would also be larger for some married couples who receive the credit. Estimated cost: $6.3 billion.

Colorado voted "no" after having voted "yes" in the past.

Abercrombie, also a leading Democratic proponent of the estate tax repeal, said he decided to vote for the conference report because it was "as good as we're going to get." He said he agreed with his party leadership's arguments that the bill would do too much to help single-earner couples who already receive a marriage bonus, but he concluded that criticism should not outweigh the need to help couples facing a marriage penalty.

Kaptur said she switched to send a message "that there ought to be something done in the area of tax equity . . . not that this is the perfect bill."

Party leaders do not appear to be threatening retaliation for "yes" votes, however. In an interview July 20, Gephardt said he believed Democrats were doing a sufficient job in avoiding veto-proof majorities on the tax bills.

Since assuming the role of minority leader in 1995, Gephardt has been widely credited with uniting his disparate caucus of inner-city liberals, suburban moderates and rural conservatives. Part of the way he has done that has been by making room in the party for different points of view.

In contrast, Republicans, under the leadership of Hastert and Majority Whip Tom DeLay of Texas, have maintained a tight rein on their narrow majority — at least on tax bills this year.

Anticipating Excuses

Republican leaders attempted to make the marriage penalty bill harder for Clinton to reject, and for congressional Democrats to assail, when they met July 19 to craft a compromise between the House and Senate versions. *(Highlights, p. 18-15)*

Concerned about Democratic arguments that the bill was too weighted to the rich, Hastert successfully pressed for the inclusion of a House provision to expand the amount of income on couples' tax returns subject to the 15 percent income tax rate. The Senate version would have expanded the 28 percent bracket as well.

"We are taking the last excuse off the table" with that decision, Kay Bailey Hutchison, R-Texas, sponsor of the original Senate bill, said at a news conference July 20.

Leaders opted, however, to also take the less generous provisions for working poor couples. Under the House version, which leaders chose, couples could make $2,000 more annually and qualify for the earned-income tax credit, which enhances or provides refunds for those with low incomes. The Senate would have increased the limits by $2,500.

With the new CBO surplus forecasts freshly delivered, however, the leadership decided to begin phasing in the tax cuts one year faster — on returns for 2000 income, due next April 15. That would add significantly to the measure's cost. The House version would have cost an estimated $50.7 billion in revenue over five years and the Senate bill $55.6 billion; the bill as cleared would cost $89.8 billion.

To keep within the parameters of the budget resolution (H Con Res 290), the bill would sunset at the end of 2004. But Democrats cited the bill's 10-year cost of $292 billion as a truer measure of its price tag, especially given Lott's prediction that, "Once this is signed into law, there's no way this Congress, this president, or any future Congress or president would ever put it back into place."

Formally, the deal was to have been cut by six conferees — two senior Republicans and one senior Democrat from each side of the Capitol. But Rep. Charles B. Rangel, D-N.Y., of the Ways and Means Committee said that neither he nor Sen. Daniel Patrick Moynihan, D-N.Y., of the Finance Committee, the other Democratic conferee, were ever informed of or invited to participate in negotiations.

"We have to recognize that there is no Republican, or Democratic, party way to do this. The only way we can give effective tax relief is by working together," Rangel said.

Archer called Democratic assertions that the bill should be considered in a broader context "the same siren song. There's always a higher priority than helping families, giving families tax relief," he said.

Rangel countered that Republicans were counting on Clinton's veto almost as much as the Democrats were, because that was the only way they could continue moving bill after bill. Had all the bills been signed, he noted, the projected lost revenues would already have exceeded the funding set aside under the budget for tax cuts.

Earlier Version

The speedy conference accord came just one day after the Senate passed its bill, after considering dozens of amendments. But, as had been the case in the Senate estate tax debate July 14, the few amendments adopted were wiped from the bill by a Lott motion. The Senate voted 54-45 July 18 to send the marriage bill back to committee and immediately return it to the floor with all amendments removed. *(Votes 196, 214; pp. S-36, S-39)*

That nullified language to allow self-employed taxpayers to deduct 100 percent of their health care premiums, retroactive to the end of 1999. Under current law, such a deduction would be allowed in 2003. The amendment, endorsed by voice vote July 17, was the work of Richard J. Durbin, D-Ill., and Christopher S. Bond, R-Mo..

The chamber had also agreed by voice vote to a package of amendments assembled by Finance Committee Chairman William V. Roth Jr., R-Del. These included proposals by Max Cleland, D-Ga., to withhold income taxes on U.S. savings bonds cashed out to pay for long-term care; by Jack Reed, D-R.I., and Robert G. Torricelli, D-N.J., to allow Medicaid to cover more lead poisoning screening for poor children; and by Torricelli to waive a waiting period for Medicare for individuals with amyotrophic lateral sclerosis, also known as Lou Gehrig's disease.

Senators voted 99-0 for an amendment by Conrad Burns, R-Mont., to repeal a provision in a 1999 law (PL 106-170) requiring businesses such as architects, who use the accrual accounting method, to pay capital gains in the first year even, if they sold their firm over a longer period. *(Vote 212, p. S-38)*

The Senate also rejected a host of politically charged amendments on July 17, including these:

- A Democratic alternative by Moynihan, rejected 46-50, to allow married couples to file their taxes jointly or singly on the same return. This would remove the marriage penalty by allowing couples to choose whichever system was more advantageous. *(Vote 200, p. S-36)*
- A plan by Russell G. Feingold, D-Wis., rejected 45-49, to return the bill to committee with the requirement that it be rewritten to include some plan to ex-

tend the solvency of Social Security and Medicare. *(Vote 198, p. S-36)*

- Another Feingold proposal, rejected 40-56, to strike the bracket expansions in the bill and increase the standard deduction for singles and single heads of household instead. The amendment would have retained the bill provision making the standard deduction for married couples double that of singles. *(Vote 201, p. S-36)*

Clinton Vetoes Bill; House Attempt To Override Fails

SEPTEMBER 16 — While Republican leaders were struggling the week of Sept. 11 to assemble the year's second budget reconciliation bill, they sent the first such bill to its foreordained death on the House floor.

The bill (HR 4810) was by far the most expensive on the broad menu of tax cuts pushed by the GOP this year. While it was labeled as an effort to help the 24.8 million couples who are subject to a "marriage penalty" under the tax code, the legislation would have cut taxes not only for them but also for the 21 million couples whose marriage helps reduce their tax liability. As a result, the measure's cost would have been $292 billion if kept on the books for the next decade.

President Clinton cited the price tag as the main reason he vetoed the bill in August. By 270-158, the House sustained the veto on Sept. 13. Sixteen more votes were needed to meet the two-thirds majority required for an override. *(Vote 466, p. H-146)*

The level of support for the bill has essentially stayed static in the House throughout the year: 268 lawmakers voted to pass the first version (HR 6) in February, 269 backed initial House passage of the the reconciliation bill in July, and 271 supported the version cleared later that month. Senate support was also well short of a two-thirds majority.

GOP leaders, eager to end the 106th Congress quickly, are signaling that they are not willing to play out any additional veto fights this fall, so the vote Sept. 13 should stand as the final attempt to override a Clinton veto. The penultimate such effort came a week before, when the House came up 14 votes short of overriding his veto of legislation (HR 8) to phase out estate taxes in the next decade at a cost of $104 billion.

Only twice has a measure that Clinton rejected been enacted anyway.

A scaled-down package to limit the marriage penalty could find new life in year-end negotiations, some in both parties insisted after the veto vote, perhaps as part of the second reconciliation bill. Clinton has not backed away from his offer to sign a $250 billion tax cut for married couples during the next decade if Congress embraces his plan to create a Medicare prescription drug benefit.

But many Republicans, who say they are convinced that the measure's demise will work to their advantage as they campaign for re-election, appear inclined to hold firm against any such deal.

Campaign rhetoric peppered both sides of the override debate. "Instead of dedicating the surplus to more spending ideas and bigger government plans, we should return some of it to the American people who earned it," said Republican Joe Knollenberg of Michigan.

"President Clinton's latest veto leaves a Clinton-Gore legacy of denying 25 million married couples relief from the marriage tax penalty," added Ways and Means Committee Chairman Bill Archer, R-Texas. "They will have to vote for new leadership in the White House if they want justice and fairness in the tax code."

GOP leaders also used the debate to focus attention on their colleague Anne M. Northup of Kentucky, who faces a tough re-election challenge in the Democratic-leaning, Louisville-based 3rd District from state Rep. Eleanor Jordan. Northup was invited to join the leadership at a news conference after the vote, where GOP Conference Chairman J.C. Watts Jr. of Oklahoma lavishly praised her devotion to improving the lives of families.

Grim Outlook for Compromise

Some Democrats lamented the GOP's apparent lack of interest in a middle ground. "We should eliminate the marriage tax penalty, but it does not require $292 billion of the projected surplus," said Charles W. Stenholm of Texas. "It takes $82 billion." Scolded Charles B. Rangel of New York, the ranking Democrat on Ways and Means, "You do not want to pass laws, you want to pass bills that are going to be vetoed."

Ways and Means member Jim McDermott, D-Wash., said on the floor that he was all but certain that a compromise would be enacted in the swirl of year-end deal cutting. But Archer called that "wishful thinking," and a spokesman for Speaker J. Dennis Hastert, R-Ill., gave a similar assessment on Sept. 13 shortly after the override vote.

However, Majority Whip Tom DeLay, R-Texas, left the door open for a deal. "We'd be glad to talk to them," he said of the Democrats after the vote, but he also offered that he could foresee no means for dramatically decreasing the cost of the tax cut while still providing the range of relief promised by the vetoed bill. ◆

Inheritance Tax Repeal Hits Dead End Even as Its Constituency Grows

SUMMARY

The Republican bid to repeal the combined tax on estates and gifts advanced rapidly once farmers, minority business owners and other constituency groups persuaded three out of every 10 House Democrats to support the cause. As a result, even traditional liberals backed some cut in the tax, although not an outright repeal. With bill sponsors refusing to accept anything less, President Clinton vetoed the measure and the House failed to override his decision. *(Veto text, p. D-93)*

The estate tax was enacted in 1916 to help finance World War I and to stem the consolidation of wealth in the families of the "robber barons." The top rate then was 10 percent. It climbed to 77 percent in 1941, before dropping to 50 percent under President Ronald Reagan and bumping up to 55 percent under Clinton. A 5 percent surcharge on some estates could bring the top rate to 60 percent. In 2000, the first $675,000 of an estate's value is exempt from taxation; the figure is set to rise to $1 million in 2006.

Since Republicans took control of Congress in 1995, business and farm groups had been pressing to repeal the tax, although at the outset many of their members viewed the idea as only a pipe dream. But by 2000, the time seemed right to launch a full-scale attack on the tax: Baby Boomers were inheriting ever-more-valuable estates, more farmers and business owners found themselves paying for estate planning, and a surging stock market led many people to believe that their own estates — or those they might inherit — were worth more than ever.

In addition to phasing out the estate tax over 10 years, the legislation would have eliminated a tax on gifts worth more than $10,000 and rid the code of the generation-skipping tax, a levy imposed on trust funds and other gifts generally set up for grandchildren. In exchange for this relief, the bill would have raised capital gains taxes on some who sold an inherited asset. The bill's cost would have been $104 billion in the first decade, when the repeal would have been complete, and $75 billion a year after that.

Critics pointed to studies concluding that half the cost would benefit about 3,000 people a year. But the campaign in favor was joined not only by business and farm groups, but by a number of minority business associations, who said the tax inhibited capital growth in their communities.

Their work paid off. The bill moved easily through the Ways and Means Committee, where it was sponsored by Jennifer Dunn, R-Wash., and John Tanner, D-Tenn., and won by such a broad margin on the House floor that even supporters were surprised: 65 Democrats and all Republicans present voted for it. The House defeated an alternative by Democrats Charles B. Rangel, N.Y., Charles W. Stenholm, Texas, and Benjamin L. Cardin, Md., to cut rates and exempt more small farmers and business owners from the tax.

Despite the strong House vote, the Senate was reluctant to include the repeal in the first tax bill given reconciliation protection under the fiscal 2001 budget resolution (H Con Res 290). GOP leaders waited for more than a month to take up the bill, and when they did, consideration was overtly political. During two days of debate, the Senate considered dozens of amendments on nearly every hot-button election-year issue. A handful were adopted but were struck when Majority Leader Trent Lott, R-Miss., won a motion to recommit the bill to the Finance Committee and then return it immediately to the floor absent any amendments.

While Republicans pressured Clinton to sign the bill, he had never given any indication he would. His veto message described the bill as "a very expensive tax break for the best-off Americans" but said he would have signed something akin to what House Democrats proposed.

After the House sustained the veto, a group of moderate House Democrats, known as the Blue Dogs, tried unsuccessfully to forge a compromise between Clinton and the GOP.

Box Score

- **Bill:** HR 8
- **Legislative action: House** passed HR 8 (H Rept 106-651), 279-136, on June 9.

Senate cleared HR 8, 59-39, on July 14.

President vetoed the bill Aug. 31.

House voted 274-157 on Sept. 7 to override the veto (14 votes short of the two-thirds majority needed).

GOP Whips Up House Enthusiasm For Repealing Inheritance Tax

MAY 27 — House Republicans advanced one of their most popular and expensive tax-cutting proposals May 25, riding a wave of support from small-business owners and family farmers who want relief from the federal estate tax.

Although little has changed to indicate President Clinton might drop his past opposition, the repeal of the inheritance tax has managed to attract growing support in the House. The bill (HR 8) has 241 cosponsors, including 45 Democrats. Even some liberals have signed on.

Surrounded by small-business owners preparing to fan out on Capitol Hill at the May 23 "Death Tax Summit," Jennifer Dunn, R-Wash., said the debate had moved beyond the argument that the tax cut was a windfall for the rich. "That debate faded a long time ago. This is about fairness."

Two vastly different portraits of fairness were presented as the House Ways and Means Committee approved the bill, 24-11, on May 25.

Republicans described a tax that has become a heavy burden on family-owned farms and businesses. They said business owners are spending billions of dollars each year on estate planning costs, money that could be better spent on expanding their businesses, hiring new employees or providing benefits such as health insurance. In the case of a sudden death of a principal owner, they said, heirs are often forced to sell the business to pay the tax.

Oprah-Archer Connection

Ways and Means Committee Chairman Bill Archer, R-Texas, said the tax sent exactly the wrong message by discouraging savings. "Every dollar taken out in death taxes takes a dollar out of private invested capital savings," Archer said.

He noted that even TV talk show host Oprah Winfrey has spoken against the tax, saying the government should not get 55 percent of her money after her death when it has already taxed 50 percent of her income while she is alive. "When Oprah . . . and Bill Archer agree on something, it just might be time to do something about it," Archer said.

But for all the enthusiasm and confident talk of a bipartisan coalition, the measure seems to have little chance of becoming law. The committee-approved legislation differs little from the measure that became part of a $792 billion, multi-year tax cut package Clinton vetoed last year (HR 2488).

Ranking committee Democrat Charles B. Rangel of New York said the measure was not truly bipartisan because sponsors had not bothered to negotiate with their Democratic opponents.

"Here we go again," Rangel said. "Bipartisan means we have gotten together and worked with the White House to come up with legislation that won't be vetoed."

"Oprah is not your ranking member. I am," Rangel told Archer.

A Democratic Alternative

While Republicans on the panel decried the inherent unfairness of imposing a tax on families who are grieving, Democrats refused to buy their portrayal of estate taxpayers as common folk.

Lindy L. Paull, chief of staff for the Joint Committee on Taxation, confirmed for lawmakers that, under current law, the estate tax applies to fewer than 2 percent of all estates. About 58,000 estates pay the tax each year.

Under questioning from Democrats, Paull said 90 percent of the estates affected were valued at less than $5 million. The 10 percent of estates worth more than $5 million generated about half the $30 billion raised by estate and gift taxes each year, she added.

Jonathan Talisman, the Treasury Department's deputy assistant secretary for tax policy, estimated that of the 58,000 payers of the estate tax, about 6 percent had inherited farms and 3 percent small businesses.

Robert T. Matsui, D-Calif., warned of huge costs during the out-years of the tax-cut measure. The bill is expected to cost $28.3 billion over its first five years. But when fully incorporated in 2010, the measure would result in $50 billion of lost revenue each year, Matsui said. "It creates cataclysmic results for the budget, especially Social Security," he said.

Rangel and Benjamin L. Cardin, D-Md., offered a substitute amendment they said would be acceptable to the White House. Instead of an outright repeal, the Democratic substitute would raise the threshold for qualifying for the tax, to $4 million from the current $650,000 (which is already scheduled to increase to $1.3 million). It would decrease the tax rates by 20 percent.

The Joint Committee on Taxation estimated the Democratic substitute would cost $15 billion over 10 years.

Republicans dismissed the Democratic substitute as insufficient, since it would leave the basic tax structure in place.

"Why take baby steps when you can support the bipartisan proposal and get the whole job done?" said Bill Thomas, R-Calif.

The panel rejected the Democratic substitute, 12-21, largely along party lines.

The Growing Business Coalition

The estate tax repeal has been gathering steam, fueled by the efforts of an expanding coalition of trade groups. The groups gathered for a show of force May 23, standing beside lawmakers from both parties to decry the tax. As many as 200 trade groups are lobbying on the effort, joined together by three separate umbrella organizations.

At the news conference, owners of companies ranging from newspapers to grocery stores talked about the costs of carrying insurance and attorneys to plan for the tax. They argued that the tax puts an added pressure on heirs trying to hold a business together in its most vulnerable, transitional period.

"The death tax hovers over us like a dark cloud," said Barbara Vidmar, an auto dealer from Pueblo, Colo. "It's unfair to [our employees] and their families that a federal tax could put them out of a job."

Democrats Aboard

The small-business focus has also attracted a number of liberals to the issue. New women- and minority-owned businesses are among the hardest hit by the tax, because they are least likely to have the resources for sophisticated estate planning, supporters say.

John Tanner, D-Tenn., a cosponsor of HR 8, is among the Democrats who have been convinced of the need for a repeal. "We think there is a societal value in family-owned businesses," Tanner said. "This tax only applies to people, not corporations. Corporations don't die, people do."

Neil Abercrombie, D-Hawaii, a loyal member of the Progressive Caucus, has been won over on the measure because of the importance of small businesses in his state's economy. In a statement, Abercrombie said Hawaii was dependent on small specialty and niche farms, and that it was vital to keep them in business. "The middle class in Hawaii has developed from small-business origins," he said. "I want to help preserve and develop those elements in Hawaii and the U.S. economy and society that generate hundreds of thousands and millions of jobs."

But as broad as the small-business coalition has become, and all the inroads it has made in the House, it has not yet made a dent in the Clinton administration's opposition to repeal. In a letter released as the Ways and Means Committee met, the administration repeated its "strong opposition" to HR 8.

"While the administration supports appropriately targeted estate tax relief for small business and family farms, most of the tax relief provided under this measure does not accrue to these important sectors of our economy," wrote Treasury Secretary Lawrence H. Summers and White House Chief of Staff John D. Podesta.

The estate tax dates back to 1916, when Congress enacted it, in part, to raise money to fight World War I. The memory of the robber barons was still fresh, and the law's drafters aimed at preventing the concentration of wealth in a few families. The top rate of 10 percent was applied to estates worth more than $5 million.

In 1917, as World War I approached, the top rate was increased to 25 percent for estates greater than $10 million. That top rate continued to climb during the Great Depression, reaching 77 percent in 1941.

The estate tax was overhauled in 1976 (PL 94-455). That act combined estate taxes and gift taxes and added a benefit to heirs known as "stepped-up basis." This saved heirs money by revaluing property, vastly reducing capital gains taxes.

In 1981, President Ronald Reagan's Economic Recovery Act (PL 97-34) reduced the top estate and gift tax rate from 70 percent to 50 percent; it has since gone back up to 55 percent. It also increased the estate and gift tax credit to $192,800 from $47,000.

House Votes To Kill Estate Tax

JUNE 10 — The House has voted resoundingly to repeal the taxes on estates, gifts and trust funds during the next decade — sending that measure, like several other stand-alone tax bills it has passed this year, to legislative limbo in the Senate.

Although the main sponsors of the legislation, Jennifer Dunn, R-Wash., and John Tanner, D-Tenn., huddled after the 279-136 vote June 9 to come up with a game plan for moving their measure (HR 8) through the Senate, the bill's prospects are tangled. *(Vote 254, p. H-82)*

Since taking control of Congress five years ago, Republicans have rarely been able to craft a bicameral tax strategy. This year, House and Senate differences have been highlighted by the desire of House Speaker J. Dennis Hastert, R-Ill., to pass single-issue tax measures, despite the Senate's well-known difficulty in moving any tax bill other than as one part of a sweeping budget reconciliation package. When Senate GOP leaders attempted in April to take up legislation (S 2346) to cut taxes for most married couples — similar to one of the stand-alone measures passed by the House (HR 6) — they were soon thwarted by their inability to limit debate.

House advocates of the estate tax repeal said that they believe the healthy show of support for passage will prompt the Senate to take a closer look. No Republican opposed the bill, and 65 Democrats — 31 percent of their House caucus — voted for it. There were two more votes than needed to form a two-thirds majority, the percentage that would be required to override the veto threatened by President Clinton, although a score of members were absent.

Some supportive senators said they thought such a big House vote might at least prompt their leaders to consider bringing the bill up. But many others in the Senate seemed content to wait.

A number of senators interviewed the week of June 5 said the bill's best chance for consideration by their chamber would be as part of a larger tax package given protection from amendments and excessive debate under the fiscal 2001 budget resolution (H Con Res 290). The budget provides for at least $150 billion in tax cuts over five years and allows for two tax reconciliation bills, one of which would be reported from committee in July, the other to be moved in September.

Senate Majority Leader Trent Lott, R-Miss., has said he believes the first reconciliation bill should include the so-called marriage penalty bill. With the 148-margin for the estate taxes repeal, it appeared that House Republican leaders might push Lott to include those provisions in the first bill as well.

The second reconciliation bill would likely focus on a broader array of tax cuts, including lower-profile changes in the tax code sought by businesses. Hastert said in an interview June 7 that he and other leaders had not decided which bill might include the estate tax.

Double Trouble?

Hastert said that Congress would move two reconciliation bills this year, as the budget permits, instead of the traditional one. A number of lobbyists and lawmakers from both chambers doubted that, however. They said they found it hard to imagine that the GOP leadership would take up precious legislative time in the waning weeks of the 106th Congress to craft and move two tax bills, especially if they continue to have little hope of winning Clinton signatures.

"You want to have two root canals instead of one? If I had a choice, I know which I'd pick," said longtime tax lobbyist Clint Stretch, director of tax policy for the accounting firm Deloitte & Touche.

The decisions on how many bills to move and what to include in them will not likely be made until leaders know whether the Congressional Budget Office (CBO) will significantly increase its estimates of the budget surplus.

The office is likely to revise its budget projections before Congress leaves for its summer recess, and members are expecting a significant bump — perhaps as much as a gross $1 trillion more in surplus during the next decade. The CBO has already given signals that its new numbers will be significantly higher than past projections. Last month, officials said the total budget surplus for fiscal 2000, not including Social Security, would be $40 billion — which would be 54 percent higher than the February projection.

GOP leaders must be able to point to an increase in anticipated revenues if they intend to pay for the tax cuts that have already passed through one chamber or the other or have been approved by various committees.

The combined estimated cost of the measures to repeal the estate tax, cut taxes for married couples and small businesses (HR 3081, HR 833), repeal an excise tax on telephone calls (HR 3916) and allow parents greater tax-free savings for their children's education (S 1134, HR 7) comes to more than $600 billion over the next 10 years — in excess of $500 billion if duplicated provisions are not counted twice. And Republicans plan to bring up still other revenue measures in the coming weeks, including a bill to restructure pension laws and increase limits on tax-preferred contributions to Individual Retirement Accounts and a measure to provide tax incentives to those who invest in struggling urban and rural communities.

It is unlikely that a sizable increase in the CBO surplus projections could pay for all that legislation, although additional revenue could be dedicated to tax cuts under the budget resolution. A bill (HR 4601) the House is to debate the week of June 12, to dedicate fiscal 2000 surpluses to debt reduction, would have no practical effect on the GOP's tax cutting aspirations.

Still, some members see possibility for compromise between Republicans and the White House on smaller steps toward the larger GOP goal.

Senate Republican Policy Committee Chairman Larry E. Craig of Idaho said he expects the two parties could come together on the bill to alleviate the penalties some couples pay under a quirk of the tax code when they marry. Clinton, congressional Democrats and Republicans all favor abolishing this quirk, but Republicans also want to ensure that the traditional single-earner families who already receive a bonus from the tax code for marrying receive greater relief. Democrats object to that.

Richard H. Bryan, D-Nev., a member of the Senate Finance Committee, said the marriage penalty appears to be the best hope for compromise. But he predicted that a tax bill will not come together until the congressional leadership and Clinton meet at the end of the session to resolve spending and other differences: "Everybody swallows hard and we head on into the campaign this fall."

Other Strategies

On other issues, including estate taxes, Senate Republicans seem ready to hold off on any heavy lifting this year, content to place their bets on Texas Gov. George W. Bush's prospects of winning the presidency in November. "Many of us are of the growing belief that we may have the White House next year," Craig said, so members were not anxious to get into a "place and show" contest with Clinton this year. Bush supports a repeal of the estate tax.

Craig was not alone in wondering if Republicans would not just be better off waiting for a new president.

Organizations pushing for the repeal, such as the National Federation of Independent Business, showed little interest in compromising by endorsing only a reduction in the tax. That sentiment was not universal, although most of the more than 100 groups advocating the repeal appeared to be hesitant to settle for anything less than their ultimate goal. Even when the GOP took control of Congress in 1995, few tax opponents would have wagered that the House would pass an estate tax repeal.

The tax, created in 1916 to finance World War I and to stem the consolidation of giant fortunes in a few families, had long been a thorn in the side of some businesses and families. Though the tax took only 10 percent of an estate when first enacted, the rate rose to as high as 77 percent in 1941. In 1976, Congress cut the top rate to 70 percent (PL 94-455), and in 1981 it voted to cut the top rate to 50 percent over four years (PL 97-34). Subsequent Congresses delayed that cut, however, and in 1993 created a 55 percent top rate (PL 103-66). *(1981 Almanac, p. 91; 1993 Almanac, p. 124)*

Congress increased the threshold for estates subject to taxation four years later: Under the biggest tax cut to become law during GOP control (PL 105-34), the $600,000 threshold would be increased gradually to $1 million by 2006. Another provision gave an additional exemption to family farms and closely held family businesses. Both groups would not be subject to the tax until their estates topped $1.3 million. *(1997 Almanac, p. 2-39)*

Republicans have pushed a repeal and have begun moving legislation to that effect in the past two years. A repeal with provisions similar to those the House passed June 9 were in the tax bill (HR 2488) Clinton vetoed last year.

Opponents of a repeal say that the estate, gift and generation-skipping taxes help make the tax code more progressive by increasing the taxes the wealthiest pay.

But the coalitions that oppose the tax maintain that owners of small businesses and farmers are the ones who really suffer under the tax, either because they must dole out tens of thousands of dollars for life insurance premiums and other estate planning or because they are caught off guard in cases of unexpected deaths. The wealthiest families, those whose estates are worth more than $20 million, have an easier time structuring their assets to avoid the tax, repeal proponents say.

In response to such arguments, Ways and Means Committee ranking Democrat Charles B. Rangel of New York, panel member Benjamin L. Cardin, D-Md., and Agriculture Committee ranking Democrat Charles W. Stenholm of Texas crafted an alternative. It sought to lower estate tax rates and increase from $1.3 million to $4 million the worth of an estate that would be exempted from taxes if it was part of a family farm or a closely held family business and a surviving spouse could inherit it.

Although on June 9 the House defeated the amendment, 196-222, its supporters predicted that the language was more likely than an outright repeal to become law. *(Vote 252, p. H-82)*

Clinton gave them a boost June 8, sending a letter to Hastert saying that he recognized that "some small businesses and family farms struggle with the estate tax" and that he was "supportive of targeted, fiscally responsible legislation to make the estate tax fairer, simpler and more efficient." Clinton touted the Democratic substitute and said he wanted to work with congressional leaders of both parties to forge a compromise.

Rangel expressed frustration that Republicans had not discussed HR 8 with him. "We could have worked this darn thing out," he said. "That's what almost makes me angry."

But not all Democrats were left out of the process. Tanner joined Dunn as the chief sponsor, and several members of the party, including liberal Neil Abercrombie of Hawaii, spoke at events to promote the bill.

The issue created interesting splits within the party. While the bill was backed by Tanner and many of his counterparts in the "Blue Dog" coalition, the most fiscally conservative wing of Democrats, Stenholm — perhaps the most fiscally conservative House Democrat — stood strongly against it. Some coalition members sided with him, saying that the repeal should occur only in a broader budget and tax overhaul framework.

In addition, a few Congressional Black Caucus members voted for the bill, in part because of the efforts of the National Black Chamber of Commerce and other minority business groups, which believe the tax is a barrier to building wealth in their communities.

While some Democrats called the bill a sop to the richest families, proponents appeared to have come a long way from earlier days. Rangel said repeal was "a good concept" and that the tax was not fair, but he also said that Congress could not afford the measure's $104 billion cost over 10 years. His alternative would cost $22 billion over the same period.

In addition to increasing exemptions for family farmers and family-owned businesses, Rangel's amendment would have reduced estate and gift tax rates by one-fifth. The highest rate, 55 percent, would have been reduced to 44 percent, for instance. It would have increased the threshold to pay estate taxes from $675,000 in 2000 to $1.1 million. (The threshold is currently scheduled to increase to $1 million in 2006.) It also included several provisions to offset the cost, including one that would have barred taxpayers from offsetting their federal estate taxes with the amount of state inheritance and estate taxes they had paid.

Democrats also attempted to send the bill back to committee with instructions that it include a provision barring people from making tax-exempt gifts to politically active organizations, known as "527s" for their section in the tax code, unless those groups disclose their contributions and spending. It was defeated, 202-216. *(Vote 253, p. H-82)*

Senate Clears Bill Despite Veto Threat

JULY 15 — Despite growing public sentiment against the federal taxation of estates, the move by Congress to repeal all such taxes appears to have gotten as far as it is going to this year.

President Clinton is remaining steadfast in his promise to veto the legislation (HR 8) that Congress cleared on July 14, which would do away with all federal taxes on estates, gifts and trusts during the coming decade at a cost of $104 billion. And the Senate's 59-39 vote for the measure, while somewhat bipartisan, was in effect seven votes short of the two-thirds majority that would be required to enact the bill in response to such a veto. *(Vote 197, p. S-36)*

Assailing the bill as "costly, irresponsible and regressive" in a statement after the Senate vote, Clinton said he would not sign the measure because its benefits would go "to the most well-off Americans at the expense of working families." He cited estimates that the bill would cost the Treasury $75 billion annually when fully phased in, with half the money left in the hands of about 3,000 people a year.

Some Republican leaders already have signaled that they are unlikely to bring the bill back for an override attempt because of the seemingly insurmountable odds against success. The House majority to pass the bill last month skated just two votes beyond two-thirds, but in the Senate, Minority Leader Tom Daschle, D-S.D., declared July 13, "We have the votes to sustain the veto. This isn't going anywhere."

Fifty Republicans and these nine Democrats voted for the measure: John B. Breaux of Louisiana, Max Cleland of Georgia, Dianne Feinstein of California, Mary L. Landrieu of Louisiana, Blanche Lincoln of Arkansas, Patty Murray of Washington, Charles S. Robb of Virginia, Robert G. Torricelli of New Jersey and Ron Wyden of Oregon. Thirty-five Democrats and these four Republicans voted against it: Lincoln Chafee of Rhode Island, James M. Jeffords of Vermont, Arlen Specter of Pennsylvania and George V. Voinovich of Ohio.

Had all senators answered the roll call, the vote would have been 60-40. Absent were two who were traveling to attend the weddings of their sons: Daschle, an opponent, and Tim Hutchinson, R-Ark., a supporter.

The Senate then began debating another top Republican tax-cutting objective — to alleviate the "marriage penalty" in the tax code (HR 4810) — as the first of two reconciliation bills that may move this year. It is likely to be sent to Clinton for another veto the week of July 17.

Lobbyists said it seemed increasingly unlikely that repeal of the estate tax would become the heart of the second reconciliation measure, as Republican leaders had discussed, now that Congress had cleared such a repeal as a stand-alone bill.

As an alternative, one lobbyist expressed hope that the leadership might include a provision, now in a package of tax cuts (HR 3081) the House passed in March that would cut the tax rates on estates, gifts and trust funds over five years, at an estimated cost of $78.7 billion over a decade. That bill is politically and procedurally entangled with proposals to raise the minimum wage and revamp consumer bankruptcy law.

Opponents Still Pleased

Estate tax opponents still found plenty to celebrate in the quick congressional embrace of a repeal.

Associations that lobby on behalf of small businesses, manufacturing concerns and farmers, all of which had stepped up pressure on senators back home during the July Fourth break, said the fact that the Senate had considered, much less endorsed, repeal legislation was a monumental advance. Even among its supporters, the effort had been given little chance of success at its inception five years ago, when it became part of the tax-cut aspirations of the new Republican congressional majority.

"It's just amazing really, considering where this issue came from," said Dorothy Coleman, director of tax policy for the National Association of Manufacturers.

Coupled with the strong House vote, when three in 10 Democrats voted "yes," repeal supporters said they increasingly believed that they would some day see their bill become law.

While Coleman's group, the National Federation of Independent Business and the American Farm Bureau all put pressure on the Senate to take up the House-passed bill, some of the new congressional support for reducing the tax also likely grew out of opinion polls showing a strong belief that it is unfair to tax an estate that a person has worked a lifetime to build. Public opinion may have had particular sway in this campaign season: Of the 35 House Democrats identified by Congressional Quarterly as being in competitive reelection races, 20 of them, or 57 percent, voted for the bill.

The surging stock market means

that many people now are creating for their children — or are expecting to inherit themselves — portfolios of a size they may have never imagined, although perhaps still not worth enough to meet the existing $675,000 floor for estates subject to taxation. While no group with a strong lobbying presence on Capitol Hill has been representing them, a desire to court this new generation of "paper millionaires" may also have enhanced the bill's support. Of the 68 wealthiest House districts, where the median family income is at least 30 percent more than the national average, 26 are represented by Democrats; a dozen, almost half, voted "yes."

"The attempt to demagogue this, to appeal to class warfare . . . doesn't work with the American people," Jon Kyl, R-Ariz., sponsor of a Senate version (S 1128) of the repeal, said at a news conference after the July 14 vote.

But Democratic opponents countered with IRS statistics showing that only the top 2 percent of estates are subject to the tax. Daschle dismissed the belief that many heirs are forced to liquidate their parents' property or sell their parents' businesses because they cannot afford to pay the taxes on them, calling that "one of the biggest myths that exists in the country today."

The bill would phase out the combined tax on gifts and estates over a 10-year period but would change capital gains laws to require heirs to pay more tax on the appreciated value if they sold family assets.

Another reconciliation measure, so called because it reconciles revenue cuts with targets set in the fiscal 2001 budget resolution (H Con Res 290), is due out of the Finance and Ways and Means committees in September. Members, staff and lobbyists said it remained unclear the week of July 10 what would go into that bill, although some of the GOP amendments offered to the estate tax bill in the Senate — to repeal the century-old telephone excise tax and to temporarily abate 18.4 cents a gallon of the federal gasoline tax — would be likely candidates.

The Senate considered 19 amendments to the estate tax measure but all were either defeated, held out of order under budget rules or wiped away by an unusual motion by Majority Leader Trent Lott, R-Miss., which returned the bill to the Finance Committee and then returned it immediately to the Senate floor absent any amendments. The motion was adopted July 14, 53-45. *(Vote 196, p. S-36)*

Finance Committee Chairman William V. Roth Jr., R-Del., said the procedure was necessary to expedite the measure's delivery to the White House. Otherwise, the few amendments would have required another vote by the House, or conference committee negotiations. Those delays likely would have kept the bill off Clinton's desk until after the Republican National Convention. Now, it appears the president will have to make good on his vows to veto both the estate tax and marriage penalty bills before the delegates leave Philadelphia — timing the GOP hopes works to its electoral advantage.

The party sees advocacy of tax cuts as a strong position for its presidential candidate, Texas Gov. George W. Bush, who has called for an estate tax repeal as part of his plan to cut taxes $483 billion over five years. "The only thing that stands in the way of death tax relief . . . that stands in the way of marriage penalty relief, is the president of the United States," Sen. Sam Brownback, R-Kan., said July 14.

Vice President Al Gore, the presumed Democratic nominee, also favors addressing the estate tax and marriage penalty, but he says shoring up Social Security and Medicare and providing prescription drug coverage for senior citizens should take priority as a use for at least part of the soaring budget surplus.

An Election Year Special

In most years, it would have taken the Senate, notorious for the snail's pace at its legislative debates, days to consider a proposal as weighty as repealing the 84-year-old tax on estates. Under an unusual arrangement embraced by both parties, the Senate considered the bill for less than two days — and made time along the way to cast a steady stream of votes on hot-button issues for the campaign trail.

"They seem to get some kind of sadistic excitement by making us walk the plank on these votes," Lott said of the Democrats.

"It's message stuff," Bob Kerrey, D-Neb., said of the GOP drive.

"It's just a political exercise," Jeffords said. "Everything between now and the election is for political gain."

Democrats were defeated when they offered amendments to provide tax breaks for college tuition and school construction and to create prescription drug coverage for Medicare recipients. Only five amendments, all by Republicans, were endorsed, and all were struck by Lott's motion to recommit. They were:

- By Orrin G. Hatch, R-Utah, to make permanent a tax credit for businesses that conduct research. The provision would mostly benefit high-technology, biotechnology and manufacturing firms. A bill (PL 106-170) enacted last year extended the credit through 2004. The amendment was adopted, 98-1, July 13. *(Vote 181, p. S-33)*
- By Roth, to repeal a tax on telephone service in effect since the Spanish-American War. The amendment was the same as a bill (HR 3916) the Finance Committee endorsed in June. The House passed its version in May. The amendment was adopted, 97-3, on July 13. *(Vote 185, p. S-34)*
- By Charles E. Grassley, R-Iowa, to allow farmers and commercial fishermen to set aside, tax free, as much as 20 percent of their taxable income in a new type of savings account they could tap in hard times. It also would allow businesses that use the accrual method of accounting, such as architects and other service providers, to pay capital gains over a period of years if they sold their businesses in installments. It was adopted by voice vote July 13.
- By Rod Grams, R-Minn., to cut to 50 percent from 85 percent the amount of taxable Social Security benefits. The amendment would have reversed the 1993 tax law (PL 103-66), which increased the amount for upper-income retirees. It was adopted, 58-41, July 13. *(Vote 188, p. S-34)*
- By Roth, to change a number of pension and retirement laws, including increasing the contribution limit on Individual Retirement Accounts from $2,000 to $5,000 by 2003. It was adopted by voice vote July 14. A version of pension and retirement savings law changes (HR 4843) was approved by the House Ways and Means Committee the day before.

Some of the defeated amendments had strong political appeal. Responding to consumer anger over a surge in retail fuel prices, Spencer Abraham of Michigan, one of the most vulnerable GOP senators seeking re-election this year, proposed suspending 18.4 cents of the federal gas tax for 150 days. But he was defeated, 40-59, when he tried to waive a Democratic point of order that the amendment should not be allowed because its cut in revenue would not be offset. *(Vote 183, p. S-33)*

Bob Graham, D-Fla., was defeated, 46-53, when he tried to overcome a similar budget point of order July 13 against his amendment to double the amount of budget surplus set aside for Medicare, making $80 billion over five years available to create a prescription benefit in the health care program for the elderly. *(Vote 186, p. S-34)*

Joseph. I. Lieberman, D-Conn., and Rick Santorum, R-Pa., pushed an amendment to provide incentives to invest in low income rural and urban communities. The vote July 14 was 57-40 to waive the budget point of order raised against the proposal, but a 60-vote majority was required. *(Vote 190, p. S-35)*

The Senate voted, 14-84, on July 14 against waiving a budget point of order on an amendment by Lott to increase the annual allowable contribution to education savings accounts from $500 to $2,000, provide a tax deduction for college tuition of up to $12,000, and grant a tax credit of up to $1,500 for student loan interest. *(Vote 194, p. S-35)*

The Senate defeated, 46-53, the Democratic alternative July 13. It would have increased to $2 million by 2009 the value of estates that would be exempted from estate tax and increase from $1.3 million to $3.38 million by 2009 the exemption from the tax for family-owned farms and businesses. *(Vote 180, p. S-33)*

House Sustains Clinton's Veto

SEPTEMBER 9 — The small businesses, manufacturers and agricultural groups that have been pressing for a repeal of the estate tax came much closer to their goal this year than most of them thought possible when their quest began six years ago. In the end, however, they did not get close enough, and their next chance is unlikely to come before the arrival of the next president.

On Sept. 7, the House fell 14 votes short of the two-thirds majority needed to overturn President Clinton's Aug. 31 veto of legislation (HR 8) to phase out federal taxes on estates, gifts and trust funds by 2010. The vote was 274-157 in favor of the override, with four members not voting. *(Vote 458, p. H-142)*

The fact that 65 Democrats voted for the bill in June raised the hopes of repeal proponents, but they lost ground over the summer. Thirteen of those lawmakers voted to sustain the veto. Some said that, while they viewed the estate tax as too onerous, they had supported the initial bill only in the hope that it would lead to a compromise on something less than a repeal.

Democratic leaders, who lost sizable blocs of votes on several bills in the GOP tax agenda this year, worked hard to keep their troops in line. They arranged a party caucus with Treasury Secretary Lawrence H. Summers a few hours before the override vote, and party whips stayed in close contact with colleagues who they believed might vote either way.

Two months before Election Day, each party aimed to use the debate on the override to define the other for the voters. Republicans portrayed Democrats as defenders of a tax that unfairly takes from children some of the hard-earned (and sometimes taxed once already) inheritance left by their parents. Democrats portrayed the GOP as willing to give an estimated $104 billion of the budget surpluses in the next decade to those who inherit only the most valuable 2 percent of estates.

"These are pure raw politics. We can go back to our base and say we tried," said Ray LaHood, R-Ill.

At a news conference, Majority Whip Tom DeLay, R-Texas, read the names of the 13 Democrats who abandoned their support for the bill and urged voters "to focus on [them] when they express their outrage." Only two — Joe Baca of California and Mark Udall of Colorado — are in competitive races for re-election.

No Deal Likely

The partisan jabbing made it all the more unlikely that an end-of-the session compromise might be reached. Clinton has endorsed a proposal by Charles B. Rangel, D-N.Y., and Charles W. Stenholm, D-Texas, to cut estate tax rates and exempt family farms and businesses worth up to $4 million from the tax. Farms and closely held family businesses worth $1.3 million are now exempt under certain conditions. Other estates are exempt until they reach $675,000 in worth, and the exemption is to rise to $1 million in 2006 under the tax cut act (PL 105-34) of 1997. Tax experts say that, with some planning, most estates worth less than $3 million can be shielded from the tax.

Republican leaders and most business lobbyists are not interested in anything less than repeal, especially since one of their allies is Gov. George W. Bush of Texas, the GOP presidential nominee. "We've carried it as far as we can this year," Majority Leader Dick Armey, R-Texas, told reporters Sept. 7. "If we don't have it now, we'll have it within the first six months of the Bush presidency."

"Repeal is our goal," said Dorothy B. Coleman, director of tax policy for the National Association of Manufacturers. "A lot of the fixes they [Democrats] talk about really aren't acceptable to us."

Some high-ranking Republicans, including Rep. Thomas M. Davis III of Virginia, the head of the House GOP campaign committee, held out the prospect of compromise. "Everything is on the table toward the end of the game," he said.

While Democrats criticized the GOP for not responding to the veto with calls for compromise, the override vote was a step beyond where most vetoed GOP measures have gone. Clinton has rejected 33 bills since the Republicans took over Congress in 1995, and 21 of them were never put to an override vote — among them the $792 billion tax cut (HR 2488) of last year.

As part of their election year tax strategy, House Republicans have arranged to follow the failed estate tax override vote with a vote the week of Sept. 11 on overriding Clinton's veto of the reconciliation bill (HR 4810) to alleviate the tax code's "marriage penalty." It, too, will apparently come to naught; the conference report garnered 271 votes, 19 shy of the majority needed to assure an override. ◆

Law Overhauls Taxes On Income Earned Abroad In Response to EU Complaint

SUMMARY

The U.S. system for taxing income earned abroad was revamped under a bill signed late in the year. But the European Union (EU), whose complaint to the World Trade Organization (WTO) spurred the change, was not fully satisfied.

Under pressure from the White House and leaders of the nation's largest corporations to avert a trade war with Europe, Congress cleared a measure to repeal a tax break for exporters that ran counter to WTO rules. In its place, the bill created a new tax regime that exempts from U.S. taxes much of the income earned from sales overseas. The change was estimated to cost $4.5 billion over 10 years.

The measure came in response to a February decision by a WTO appellate body, which upheld a 1999 ruling that existing U.S. law provided an unfair subsidy to exporting companies. Under that law, exporters were able to reduce their taxes by routing their sales overseas through entities known as foreign sales corporations. The WTO set an Oct. 1 deadline for action.

After waiting until Deputy Treasury Secretary Stuart E. Eizenstat and congressional staff could draft a change to the law, the House passed the bill in September and urged the Senate to act quickly. The Senate Finance Committee, however, voted to amend the House-passed bill, removing a provision that would have given U.S. companies a tax deduction on dividends from foreign subsidiaries. The provision's main beneficiary would have been the Illinois-based machinery maker Caterpillar Inc. With the bill mired in election-year Senate wrangling, and with time running out, the EU agreed to extend the WTO deadline until Nov. 1.

GOP leaders tried to break the gridlock by wrapping the measure into a broader tax package (HR 2614), but that bill also bogged down in the Senate. With businesses in a frenzy and the EU threatening to move ahead with retaliation, the Senate passed the stand-alone measure. House leaders resisted, saying they wanted the bigger tax package to move, but they relented upon returning for the lame-duck session, clearing the Senate version. *(GOP tax package, p. 18-32)*

WTO Rules Tax Shelter Is Unfair

FEBRUARY 26 — The World Trade Organization (WTO) handed Congress and the Clinton administration a new trade dilemma Feb. 24, ruling that a federal tax shelter important to U.S. exporters is an unfair trade practice.

The United States has until Oct. 1 to comply with the decision that the special tax law for Foreign Sales Corporations (PL 97-290) is an illegal trade subsidy, as the European Union claims. After that, Europe could retaliate with trade sanctions.

The law allows U.S. companies to set up subsidiaries in the Virgin Islands, Barbados and Guam and exempt 15-30 percent of the export earnings from federal income tax as long as the products are at least 50 percent American-made. Loss of the tax break would cost U.S. companies $4.1 billion in fiscal 2001 and $25 billion over the next five years, the White House estimated.

The Clinton administration vowed to try to negotiate a settlement with the European Union. If that fails, Congress would need to change its tax law to comply with the ruling. But that could be politically problematic, especially in a year when Congress is likely to vote on whether to drop out of the WTO, the 135-nation body that regulates global trade.

"The WTO is wrong, and those who suggest that we withdraw from the WTO are wrong," said Senate Minority Leader Tom Daschle, D-S.D. "We can't take all of our marbles and go home just because we disagree with one decision out of the WTO."

Charles E. Grassley, R-Iowa, chairman of the Senate Finance Subcommittee on International Trade, urged Clinton to make the issue a top priority when the leaders of the eight industrial powers meet this summer in Japan. House Ways and Means Committee Chairman Bill Archer, R-Texas, said he would soon convene a hearing to discuss options. Archer has previously said he would like to rewrite the corporate tax code to make it more like the European system.

That idea has gained support among U.S. business leaders, said Kimberly J. Pinter, an international tax expert at the National Association of Manufacturers.

Some trade experts have suggested that Europe will make concessions in exchange for more lenient treatment in beef and banana disputes that Europe recently lost to the United States.

House Panel OKs Taxation Measure

JULY 29 — Under an admonition from world trade regulators and in the face of a looming tariff war with Europe,

Box Score

- **Bill:** HR 4986 — PL 106-519
- **Legislative action: House** passed HR 4986 (H Rept 106-845), 315-109, on Sept. 13.

Senate Finance approved HR 4986, amended (S Rept 106-416), by voice vote Sept. 19.

House adopted the conference report on HR 2614 (H Rept 106-1004), 237-174, on Oct. 26.

Senate passed HR 4986, amended, by voice vote on Nov. 1.

House cleared HR 4986, 316-72, on Nov. 14.

President signed the bill Nov. 15.

Congress and the Clinton administration have launched a joint effort to repeal a tax break for several thousand U.S. companies that set up export subsidiaries in offshore tax havens.

But it is unclear if the proposal will satisfy the Word Trade Organization (WTO) and the European Union (EU), or if action on the legislation will do no more than postpone tariff retaliation, which could drive up the European prices for U.S. products by billions of dollars.

The bill (HR 4986), which the House Ways and Means Committee approved, 34-1, on July 27, would exempt most income earned abroad from federal taxation and would repeal portions of the 1984 law (PL 98-369) that created a tax shelter for companies whose export operations are run by offshore offices known as foreign sales corporations, or FSCs.

By simply exempting much income earned abroad from federal taxation, the bill aims to overcome the EU argument, endorsed in February by the WTO, that FSCs amount to an unfair subsidy by giving a tax break only to exporters. As a result, foreign companies with U.S. offices could also take advantage of the proposed new system, along with U.S. companies that export or have overseas units.

Some of the rules that applied to FSCs would remain, however, such as a provision requiring goods sold abroad to be made of at least 50 percent U.S. components to qualify.

Because it would apply to a broader range of businesses and individuals, the measure would cost the Treasury $1.5 billion more between 2001 and 2005 than would retaining the FSC system. According to Jonathan Talisman, deputy assistant Treasury secretary for tax policy, FSCs have allowed U.S. exporters to shield about $4 billion annually.

Pete Stark, D-Calif., cast the only "no" vote in the committee markup, saying the measure would do nothing more than help "wealthy businesses that already get subsidies."

Ways and Means Committee Chairman Bill Archer, R-Texas, called the bill "critical for the continued U.S. competitiveness in the global marketplace."

If Congress doesn't change the law by the Oct. 1 deadline the WTO set, the EU would be entitled to retaliate by imposing higher tariffs on goods from the United States to counterbalance the perceived trade benefit of the tax shelters to U.S. corporations. European officials did not immediately take a position on the bill, saying July 27 that it needed more time to review the legislation.

Even if Europe declares that the measure would not mark a significant improvement, passage of a bill designed to comply with the WTO ruling would delay the imposition of European retaliation. Under the WTO system, both sides have several opportunities to object and appeal at each stage in a dispute like this.

Such a tit-for-tat could lead to the same sort of gridlock that has gripped parts of U.S.-European trade for several years. Despite WTO rulings to the contrary, Europeans have refused to give their supermarkets greater access to hormone-treated beef from U.S. ranches and bananas sold by U.S. companies. U.S. trade officials believe their EU counterparts filed the FSC complaint in a bid to show that Europe also could also win a trade dispute at the WTO.

Taxing Systems

The 15 nations in the EU tend to rely more on value-added taxes and other duties to tap government revenue from their businesses' receipts. Most European nations, for instance, impose no income tax on their companies' earnings abroad.

The United States has relied on a broader-based tax system, under which more earnings are considered taxable unless offset by credits, deductions or other shelters, such as that available from the creation of an FSC.

Business lobbyists and congressional tax policy aides said enacting HR 4986 would move the United States closer to the European system.

Stark and Lloyd Doggett, D-Texas, offered several amendments to limit the bill by adding to the list of half a dozen industries — oil and gas and unprocessed softwood timber among them — that do not benefit from creating FSCs and would also be exempt from the benefits under HR 4986. All were defeated by voice vote. One would have taxed income earned overseas on tobacco sales. Another would have denied the bill's benefits to pharmaceutical companies that sold drugs abroad for more than 5 percent below U.S. prices.

Doggett also offered an amendment to allow defense contractors to shield half their qualifying foreign-source income from taxation, as is allowed under the FSC law. Stark offered an amendment to Doggett's proposal that would have kept all defense contractor income outside of tax shelters. The proposal was defeated by voice vote.

House Passes Bill To Exempt Income Earned Abroad From U.S. Taxes

SEPTEMBER 16 — Hoping at least to delay billions of dollars in sanctions that could be imposed on American exports before the end of the year and perhaps by Election Day, a bipartisan House majority passed legislation Sept. 13 that would change the way the United States taxes income earned abroad.

The Clinton administration and leaders of both parties acted in the face of an Oct. 1 deadline set by the World Trade Organization (WTO), which has ruled that current U.S. law on foreign earnings amounts to an unfair government subsidy because it gives tax breaks only to exporters.

The relatively united front in the House — the vote was 315-109 to pass the legislation (HR 4986) — does not guarantee that the Senate will go along. *(Vote 467, p. H-146)*

Administration officials, led by Deputy Treasury Secretary Stuart E. Eizenstat, have appealed to Congress to clear the bill quickly and without attaching other provisions.

Asked whether senators would heed that request, Minority Leader Tom Daschle, D-S.D., said Sept. 12 that it remains "very hard to get 99 other senators to say, 'We'll leave it' " alone.

The Finance Committee is expected to mark up the bill the week of Sept. 18. Daschle's comments indicate — and some lobbyists and other lawmakers maintain — that the measure might not make it through the Senate unless it is attached to the retirement savings measure (HR 1102) given protection from excessive amendment and debate under the reconciliation provisions of the budget resolution (H Con Res 290) for fiscal 2001.

Even if the provisions were enacted, it is not clear they would mollify the WTO. "There's some controversy about whether or not it accomplishes what we need to do," Charles E. Grassley, R-Iowa, the chairman of Finance's Trade Subcommittee, said in a Sept. 12 interview.

The WTO ruling came in response to a complaint by the European Union (EU) over a U.S. law (PL 98-369) that provides a tax credit to a relatively small group of companies that set up offshore offices, known as foreign sales corporations, usually in tax havens such as Bermuda or the Virgin Islands, to manage their export business.

The EU claims that the credit amounts to an unfair subsidy because it gives tax breaks only to exporters. The credit allows an estimated 7,100 exporters to save approximately $4 billion in federal taxes annually.

The House-passed bill would replace that system with a much broader exemption for all foreign-source income, both from exports and from goods manufactured abroad, so long as a majority of the value of the product or service was derived from U.S. components or labor. The exemption would save eligible individuals and corporations an additional $1.5 billion in taxes between 2001 and 2005.

The EU maintains that the measure would not change the U.S. tax system sufficiently because it would still provide a tax break specifically aimed at exporters.

House Ways and Means Committee Chairman Bill Archer, R-Texas, said that the administration was nonetheless "very confident that this bill will pass muster with the WTO."

And, after a meeting among European officials the week of Sept. 4, it appears that the EU may be willing to at least extend the Oct. 1 deadline, after which sanctions could be imposed under the WTO's rules.

Subsidy or Necessity?

During the House's 40-minute debate on the bill — it was taken up under suspension of the rules, an expedited procedure generally reserved for non-controversial legislation — leaders of both parties stressed the bill's virtues.

Minority Leader Richard A. Gephardt of Missouri, Ways and Means ranking member Charles B. Rangel of New York and Trade Subcommittee ranking member Sander M. Levin of Michigan sent a letter to other Democrats urging a "yes" vote.

A handful of liberal Democrats decried the bill as corporate welfare. Pete Stark, D-Calif., said the proposal "has a new name and a new face, but it's the same old subsidy." Archer retorted that many U.S. corporations were at "a gigantic disadvantage against their foreign competitors," because, he said, many other countries do not tax income earned abroad. The EU contends, however, that many of its members' tax rates on corporations are higher overall than those faced by U.S. companies.

Stark and Democrats such as Henry A. Waxman of California and Lloyd Doggett of Texas argued that the bill's benefits should be denied to tobacco concerns, defense contractors and some pharmaceutical companies. Stark had offered amendments to exclude such industries when the Ways and Means Committee approved the bill July 27, but they were defeated.

Senate Panel Races to Beat WTO Clock

SEPTEMBER 23 — With the deadline fast approaching to answer an international trade complaint against the United States, the Senate Finance Committee approved a bill Sept. 19 that would eliminate a tax break for certain U.S. exporters.

The bill (HR 4986), approved by voice vote, would repeal a provision of U.S. law (PL 98-369) that the World Trade Organization (WTO) has ruled constitutes an unfair subsidy because it is available only to a small group of U.S. exporters.

The House easily passed the bill Sept. 13, and the administration is eager to have it enacted by Oct. 1, the deadline set by the WTO, to avoid potential sanctions.

But the Senate Finance Committee added a new wrinkle, dropping a separate provision in the House bill that would preserve a tax break for overseas dividends. Charles E. Grassley, R-Iowa, said including the break in the bill would further antagonize the European Union (EU), which brought the complaint to the WTO in the first place. The change could require further negotiations, slowing the measure.

U.S. vs. Europe

The WTO ruling came in 1999 in response to an EU complaint that the United States was giving its exporters an unfair advantage. Under current law, U.S. companies are taxed on income they earn abroad, but exporters that set up offshore offices, or "foreign sales corporations," are eligible for a credit that reduces their tax bill. That break enables U.S. exporters to save about $4 billion a year.

In February, an appellate panel upheld the ruling that this amounts to a subsidy for U.S. exporters disallowed under the WTO's rules for free trade.

If President Clinton does not offer a plan to comply with the ruling by Oct. 1, Europe will be eligible to apply at least $4 billion in sanctions to U.S.-made products sold there.

The remedy proposed in the bill would give U.S. companies a much broader tax break. The bill would simply eliminate taxes on income that is earned overseas, whether by a subsidiary of a U.S. company or by a foreign company with a U.S. presence, as long as a majority of the value of the product or service came from U.S. components or labor. Tax credits for foreign sales corporations would no longer exist. The change would save companies an extra $1.5 billion in taxes over five years, according to the Joint Committee on Taxation.

During the Finance markup, Grassley persuaded Chairman William V. Roth Jr., R-Del., to drop the House provision, which would retain a law that allows U.S. companies a tax deduction on dividends from foreign subsidiaries.

Grassley said that the dividends deduction "sticks out very much like a sore thumb" in U.S. efforts to end the dispute. European negotiators mentioned it in arguing against the current U.S. export tax credit, he said after the markup, so leaving it in is "just like ignoring the WTO ruling."

One of the main business lobbyists on the issue, Kenneth Kies, a partner in the accounting firm PriceWaterhouseCoopers' Washington International Tax Service, termed Grassley's provision a "relatively minor change" and predicted that members and staff would come up with a way to exclude dividends from taxation that would not offend the Europeans.

Deputy Treasury Secretary Stuart E. Eizenstat, who attended the markup, said afterward that "given how close the bills are, I hope there could be found ways to resolve" differences over the dividends provision.

Majority Leader Trent Lott, R-Miss., said Sept. 19 that he may try to win unanimous consent to bring the bill up on the Senate floor; otherwise, he may be forced to look for other vehicles. Either way, he said, "we will get it done."

Other Concerns

In addition to Grassley's change, panel member Richard H. Bryan, D-Nev., had readied amendments to prevent the bill's tax preferences from going to pharmaceutical concerns that charge U.S. consumers more than they do foreigners for an identical product.

Bryan, who said a cholesterol-fighting drug he takes is 190 percent more expensive in the United States than in Canada, was "deeply troubled by conferring a tax benefit on an industry that is highly profitable." But he did not offer his amendments, heeding Roth's request to allow speedy action on the bill.

In addition, several unions and advocacy groups passed out literature decrying all or part of the bill. One coalition of environmental, labor, family farm, consumer and religious advocates known as the Citizens' Trade Campaign charged that the measure "expands corporate welfare for the largest multinational corporations."

Among the estimated 7,100 companies that currently take advantage of tax breaks on overseas income are such giants as Boeing and Microsoft.

EU Willingness To Talk About Exporters' Tax Reduces Urgency

SEPTEMBER 30 — Congressional indecision has caused the United States to miss an Oct. 1 deadline for repealing a piece of the tax code that runs counter to world trade rules.

But neither the Republican leadership nor the Clinton administration appears worried by the delay. The European Union, the U.S. nemesis on the issue, is unlikely to take advantage of its right under World Trade Organization (WTO) rules to begin leveling billions of dollars in new tariffs on U.S. goods exported to the continent. It did, however, request an Oct. 19 WTO meeting to authorize sanctions if the United States has not acted by then.

Fear of such retaliation initially drove the administration to push hard to move legislation through Congress quickly this fall. The bill (HR 4986) would repeal a tax break now used by an estimated 7,100 exporters and replace it with a system under which most income earned overseas would not be taxed. Under a 1984 law (PL 98-369), U.S. companies and individuals are taxed on income they earn abroad, but exporters that set up offshore units, or "foreign sales corporations," are eligible for a credit that reduces their tax bill.

The House passed the measure Sept. 13; the Senate Finance Committee approved its version Sept. 19.

Majority Leader Trent Lott, R-Miss., attempted to call up the bill and have the Senate immediately pass it on a voice vote the evening of Sept. 28, but Minority Whip Harry Reid, D-Nev., blocked the maneuver. Several senators wanted to offer amendments that would restrict from the bill's benefits tobacco, pharmaceutical and defense companies.

The leaders of both parties and the White House are eager to clear the bill with a minimum of changes, in an effort to limit the time needed to resolve differences between the two chambers.

Even had Lott succeeded, the bill still would have required more consideration by Congress, because the House and Senate versions already differ. In the Finance Committee, Charles E. Grassley, R-Iowa, won removal of a House provision that would retain a tax deduction for U.S. companies on dividends from their foreign subsidiaries.

That language was inserted by Ways and Means Committee Chairman Bill Archer, R-Texas, between the time his panel approved the bill in July and when the House took it up in September. The provision would allow companies with overseas subsidiaries to claim some tax breaks for their international sales.

Among those that would be adversely affected if Archer's provision were dropped is Caterpillar Inc., the world's largest manufacturer of construction and mining equipment and one of the top U.S. exporters.

Archer said Sept. 26 that removing the provision would be unfair, and that the House should not just accept a Senate bill that included Grassley's amendment. The change, he said, would "deny one company from receiving the benefits that other companies get" just because of the way it is structured.

The legislation is likeliest to become part of a large, end-of-session measure or an obscure but sure-to-become-law vehicle. Still, Lott has not ruled out trying to call up the bill again if he can get agreement to debate only a few amendments.

Tit for Tat?

In 1999, a WTO panel agreed with the European Union's complaint that the current foreign sales corporation system constitutes an unfair government subsidy to certain U.S. exporters. An appellate body upheld that decision in February.

Under WTO rules, President Clinton had to announce how he planned to comply by Oct. 1, or the European Union could then announce what sanctions it would place on U.S. goods entering its 15 nations. European officials began to signal in September that they were unlikely to immediately hold feet to the fire if the deadline was missed. Some breathing room came the week of Sept. 25, when European officials met in Brussels to discuss a timeline for action after the proposed new U.S. law was enacted and submitted to the WTO for review.

House Majority Leader Dick Armey, R-Texas, told reporters Sept. 28 that he was confident the bill would be enacted by the 106th Congress and that he didn't "see any concern that alarms will go off around the globe" on Oct. 1.

For some of the bill's critics, the lack of recrimination for failing to meet the deadline confirmed what they had long expected — that Oct. 1 had ceased to be a hard deadline.

They believe the relaxed attitude can be attributed to Clinton's decision, in another trade dispute, to delay releasing a new list of European imports on which the United States will impose 100 percent tariffs. Though that move was widely reported to be a response to British Prime Minister Tony Blair's concerns about tariffs on cashmere, some believe Clinton's delay was designed to lessen chances that the Europeans would prove unyielding in the tax dispute.

The U.S. tariffs on European imports come in response to Europe's failure to change its laws after the WTO ruled that Europe was improperly blocking U.S. companies from selling bananas and beef in Europe. The first round of tariffs was imposed in 1999, but most were on relatively low-export items, such as soups and broths from Germany and France.

Those in Congress with constituents affected by Europe's continued intransigence on the banana and beef dispute wanted tougher punishment. At the urging of Chiquita Inc., congressional leaders inserted a provision in a trade bill (PL 106-200) for African, Central American and Caribbean countries to require the U.S. trade representative to rotate the roster of goods subject to punitive tariffs. They hoped the new "carousel retaliation" system would touch on more sensitive European imports, such as pork and cashmere.

Senate Passes Version of Bill

NOVEMBER 4 — In their continued effort to avoid politically risky tax and budget negotiations with President Clinton, House Republican leaders have inserted themselves into an international dispute, raising the already high economic stakes.

Despite strong pressure not only from their regular allies in corporate America but also from their usual Democratic opponents, the leadership refused to clear legislation (HR 4986) that would restructure U.S. taxes on income earned abroad in an effort to comply with world trading rules. That decision left the proposal in limbo at least until the 106th Congress convenes for its lame-duck session the week of Nov. 13 — a delay during which U.S.-European trade tensions may escalate.

The Senate, after six weeks of delay at the hands of a few opponents, passed its version of the measure by voice vote Nov. 1. The desire to avoid or at least stall billions of dollars in tariffs on U.S. goods sold in Europe was the impetus, said Daniel Patrick Moynihan of New York, the ranking Democrat on the Finance Committee.

"Not every morning do we avoid a trade war," Moynihan said after he steered a bill to passage for perhaps the last time before his retirement. "This morning we did."

Lobbyists for some of the largest U.S. corporations and members of Congress from both parties said that the Senate's action alone would not accomplish that end. They said Congress needed to send a bill to Clinton's desk no later than Nov. 1 if Europeans were to remain bound to abide by their delayed schedule for imposing retaliatory tariffs on U.S. products.

"I am extremely disappointed with the way the House leadership has played politics with this vital legislation," said Don Reed, the chairman of a group of more than 85 companies known as the European-American Business Council.

In a Nov. 2 statement, House Speaker J. Dennis Hastert, R-Ill., said that while proponents of the foreign tax bill "make a compelling case" for speedy action on their proposal, their arguments were no more persuasive than those who are pushing for a $1-an-hour increase in the minimum wage, a tax cut for small businesses or plans to free up more funding for school construction.

Those proposals and the foreign sales measure are all part of a multifaceted policy and tax package (HR 2614) written into a conference report that the House adopted Oct. 26. The bill, which would cost $240.4 billion over the next 10 years, also included plans to spur private retirement savings and to remove tax and regulatory hurdles to investing in low-income communities. Unrelated legislation to reimburse some health providers who accept Medicare payments (HR 5291) and to ban physician-assisted suicides (HR 2260) also caught rides on the tax package.

Republican leaders were fearful that Clinton would attempt to load up the tax bill with provisions they did not like or to block some of their favored provisions, so they did not directly negotiate with the administration on the bill. Instead, they cobbled together pieces of legislation that they said they thought he would be willing to sign and gave administration officials the details in telephone calls and letters. Clinton responded with suggestions, but when they fell on deaf ears, he threatened to veto the tax package.

Hastert wanted Senate Majority Leader Trent Lott, R-Miss., to push the broader bill through his chamber, but Lott faces challenges in doing so. Most Democrats have lined up against it, and Oregon Democrat Ron Wyden is filibustering the bill to protest the assisted-suicide provision, which would have the effect of overturning his state's law permitting such medically supervised deaths.

'It's Still Alive'

Lott said Nov. 1 that he still intends for the Senate to return to the catchall bill after the election. "It's still alive; we intend to do it. And we hope that the president will sign it," he said.

The bill's fortunes will turn on the results Nov. 7, although only a few of the possible outcomes would seem likely to lead all sides to agree on the pending collection of tax cuts as the right prescription for the IRS code this fall.

If Republican Gov. George W. Bush of Texas is elected president and Republicans retain control of Congress, they will probably be content to wait until next year to push a much broader tax cut, one that includes many more of their top priorities.

If Democratic Vice President Al Gore wins and Democrats retake at least one chamber of Congress, those victories will likely throw cold water on the current Republican tax plan.

Perhaps the best-case scenario for

those pushing the current package is that the election maintains the status quo: Gore holds the White House for the Democrats and Republicans retain Congress. That would do little to patch up the poor relations between the administration and Congress, however.

A number of lobbyists and aides from both parties and chambers said, however, that they did not think that a lame-duck Congress would have much reason to move a tax package.

"There's no real leverage to pass a $240 billion tax bill when the elections have already happened. It's all about something to take home to the voters," said Mark Garay, associate director of tax policy for the accounting firm Deloitte & Touche.

International Ramifications

Though the omnibus package appears to face an uphill climb, the foreign tax bill still seems more likely than not to become law during the lame-duck session. Majority Whip Tom DeLay, R-Texas, indicated Nov. 2 that the House would "get it done" but would not be rushed. "There's not going to be a trade war in two weeks," he said.

At the end of September, U.S. and European negotiators agreed on Nov. 1 as the deadline by which the United States was to have passed a law repealing a provision of its tax code that the World Trade Organization (WTO) found objectionable. The law (PL 98-369) gives exporters that set up offshore offices known as foreign sales corporations tax breaks on income earned abroad.

The European Union (EU) filed a complaint against the provision with the WTO, alleging that the tax break gave U.S. companies an unfair trading advantage. A WTO panel ruled in Europe's favor in 1999, and an appellate body upheld the ruling in February.

As a result, the EU would be entitled to place tariffs equal to the worth of the tax break — about $4 billion a year — on goods imported from the United States. Congressional staff members believe Europeans would impose the tariffs on such high-profile American exports as aircraft, wine, food and computer hardware and software.

Because the United States has missed the deadline, the EU, as the aggrieved party in the original complaint, could begin making plans to place tariffs on U.S. imports. But it will not likely obtain WTO authority to take the next step until a Nov. 17 meeting.

In the pact reached in September that set the deadline, the Europeans agreed to withhold application of the tariffs until the WTO rules on the validity of the new U.S. law. In addition to repealing the foreign sales corporation provision, the bill would exempt most income earned abroad from U.S. taxation, giving a larger group of companies and individuals the tax benefits once reserved for exporters.

U.S. officials say the bill is modeled after the European tax system, but the measure includes some provisions the EU maintains will not stand up in a WTO dispute. One would require that goods sold abroad be made of at least 50 percent U.S. components in order for the proceeds from their sale to be tax exempt.

Though EU Trade Commissioner Pascal Lamy was in Washington the week of Oct. 30, he and other officials from the 15-nation bloc remained relatively quiet on the issue. Lamy simply reminded Congress Nov. 2 that it "should be aware of the consequences if it does not act," Reuters reported.

It has never been clear that the Europeans prefer retaliation to a negotiated settlement. U.S. officials have long viewed the the EU's foreign sales tax complaint as a retort to U.S. objections to European laws that have kept U.S. bananas and beef out of EU markets. WTO panels ruled in favor of the United States on the two issues. As a result, the Clinton administration has imposed about $300 million in tariffs on European goods.

Mutual Suspicion

The subtleties of the trade disagreements between the United States and Europe have sometimes appeared to be lost on House leaders.

Democrats charged that their inability to clear the foreign tax measure — a bill on which the leaders of both parties and the president agreed — showed that the Republicans are unworthy stewards of Congress.

"There's no more dangerous example of Republican inaction," Senate Minority Leader Tom Daschle, D-S.D., told reporters Nov. 2.

In response, House leaders pointed to their distrust of the president. They signaled their suspicion that, if they worked to clear the measure, Clinton would veto it and use the incident to chide the Republicans for attending to the needs of corporations before helping average Americans.

They have long since given up trying to build a legislative dealmaking relationship with Clinton, and the breakdown of talks over spending measures earlier in the week of Oct. 30 heightened their mistrust of the president. Clinton's veto of legislation (HR 4516) to fund the Treasury Department, Postal Service and legislative branch during fiscal 2001 was particularly irksome to GOP leaders, who said they had been led to believe he would sign the bill. The measure also included legislation (HR 3916) to repeal the 3 percent excise tax on telephone service.

U.S. Trade Representative Charlene Barshefsky, in a telephone news conference Nov. 2, signaled that Clinton would sign the income-earned-abroad bill. "Congress has been assured by the administration that their fears are entirely unfounded," she said. "This is a piece of legislation that concerns the broad interests of the United States as well as our trade relationship with the European Union. This is not a small matter."

The loudest advocate for the bill in the House GOP hierarchy was Bill Archer of Texas, until his retirement at year's end the Ways and Means Committee chairman. But while Archer and several corporate groups pressed the leadership to move the measure independently of the catchall tax package, the leaders were under pressure from other business interests determined to keep the package together.

The National Federation of Independent Business is pushing House leaders to hold firm. It believes that if the foreign tax measure moves as a stand-alone "emergency" bill, then so too should a portion of HR 2614 that would repeal a 1999 law (PL 106-170) requiring small business owners to pay, within one year, capital gains taxes on business assets sold over a number of years. *(1999 Almanac, p. 21-3)*

A lobbyist for the group said that if the 1999 law was not repealed, many small businesses would go bankrupt.

That drove home Hastert's point that all the provisions in the tax bill were important to someone, and underscored how difficult it would be to pass a pared-down measure that included more than the foreign tax measure. The minute a second provision was added, lobbyists and staff said, the line would form for another dozen riders.

Exporters' Tax Repeal Grants Broad Exemptions To Corporations

NOVEMBER 18 — In an effort to remove itself — at least temporarily — from a growing international dispute, Congress used the start of its lame-duck session to clear a bill designed to bring the federal tax code into compliance with the rules of global commerce.

The issue may nonetheless reappear in the 107th Congress, because the new law is likely to be challenged by Europe as a violation of World Trade Organization (WTO) rules.

President Clinton, whose senior aides helped to draft the legislation (HR 4986), signed it Nov. 15 while attending a summit of Pacific Rim nations in Brunei. The House had voted 316-72 to clear the bill the day before. *(Vote 597, p. H-188)*

The new law repeals a 16-year-old statute (PL 98-369) that created a tax break for U.S. exporters that set up offshore offices, known as foreign sales corporations, in tax havens such as the U.S. Virgin Islands. In an attempt to keep taxes low for the thousands of large corporations that had benefited from that provision, the new law exempts much of the income earned abroad from U.S. taxes. The law applies not only to American firms doing business overseas but also to foreign companies with operations in the United States.

The new law is estimated to cost the Treasury $4.5 billion over the next decade. During the next five years, that would be about $1.5 billion more than retaining the old system — at an annual cost of about $4 billion — according to the Treasury Department.

The decision by House Republican leaders to move the legislation was a reversal. Before Election Day, they said they would not to take up the bill because that would reduce the motivation for both Congress and Clinton to embrace a multifaceted tax cut, Medicare and minimum wage bill (HR 2614) that also included the language on income earned abroad. When the muddled election results failed to spur any interest in clearing that package, however, the GOP decided to clear the overseas income bill, find a legislative home elsewhere for the language to boost reimbursements to Medicare providers and shelve almost all of the rest of the package.

Not Over Yet

U.S. officials said they are confident that the new law will meet the standards of the WTO, which ruled in 1999 and again in February that the system then in effect was conferring unfair subsidies to exporters. U.S. Trade Representative Charlene Barshefsky said in a statement Nov. 14 that the new tax regime "should put an end to this matter."

Leaders from the European Union (EU) disagreed, saying that the new law still inappropriately benefits exporters. One section requires that at least half the value of goods sold abroad be attributable to U.S. components and direct labor for the proceeds of their sale to be exempt from taxation.

The EU will likely request that a WTO panel examine the new U.S. law.

The 15-nation bloc also made sure it would not forfeit its ability to retaliate against the United States for the unfair subsidies under the old tax system. At a WTO meeting Nov. 17, European officials submitted a proposal to impose $4 billion a year in tariffs on 45 categories of U.S. imports, ranging from nuclear reactors to cereal to leather handbags.

Ambassador Rita Hayes immediately announced that the U.S. would object to that level of retaliation and formally requested that a WTO arbitration panel consider whether the sanctions are proper. That will launch what is expected to be a long line of challenges, both on the permissible value of the tariffs and on the suitability of the new U.S. law. If the WTO says the new law does not comply with its rules and the United States appeals, any European retaliation would not likely be authorized before next summer.

"We will be back here as soon as the WTO considers and rejects this bill, doing this all over again," Lloyd Doggett, D-Texas, an opponent of the measure, predicted in the debate Nov. 14.

If the next president is forced to seek yet another change in the tax code to comply with WTO rules, a number of members may use the moment to press for a broad overhaul of the way the United States taxes income earned outside its borders. It seems unlikely, however, that a Congress as closely divided as the 107th will be able to push through a tax measure to benefit the wealthiest corporations and individuals. A Bush administration would likely attempt to move a tax bill focusing on domestic tax cuts. They key votes on it could be expected to come in the summer.

Competing Concerns

In the debate, some Democrats argued that the new tax system amounts to welfare for the nation's largest businesses, including Boeing Co. and Microsoft Corp. "It is the silliest kind of gift to the people who need it the least," said Pete Stark, D-Calif.

Stark and Doggett wanted the bill's benefits withheld from tobacco companies, defense contractors and those pharmaceutical firms that charge more for their drugs in the United States than in other countries. The bill does exempt sellers of petroleum, some timber products and a handful of other products from reaping tax benefits from overseas sales. Such sales had also been exempt from benefits under the old law.

Some Republicans argued complying with WTO rulings ceded too much power to international organizations. Delegates from the Virgin Islands and Guam worried the measure would shut down business in their territories.

In the end, only six Republicans and 65 Democrats voted "no," however.

The House originally passed the bill Sept. 13, but the measure's progress was slowed when Sen. Charles E. Grassley, R-Iowa, persuaded the Finance Committee to remove a provision that would have given U.S. companies a tax deduction on dividends from foreign subsidiaries. Instead, the new law includes provisions to help companies adversely affected, such as manufacturing giant Caterpillar Inc., restructure themselves. ◆

Clinton's Vetoes Force Republicans to Scale Back Their Tax-Cut Package

SUMMARY

A $240.4 billion 10-year tax cut package, assembled by Republicans after it was clear their top priority tax bills would not win enactment, died an uneventful death as the 106th Congress limped to a close.

With their main tax proposals — a tax cut for married couples and repeal of the estate tax — stopped by presidential vetoes, Republicans fell back on an assemblage of other tax bills, many of which had garnered bipartisan support earlier in the year.

The package (HR 2614) included bills to: increase tax incentives for retirement savings (HR 1102); establish new tax breaks for investing in struggling urban and rural communities (HR 4923, S 3152); increase the minimum wage by $1 an hour over two years and provide tax breaks to the retailers, restaurateurs and others most likely to have to pay the increased wage (HR 833; HR 3081); and repeal a tax break for exporters that ran counter to World Trade Organization rules (HR 4986). *(Community development, p. 17-9; minimum wage, p. 14-3; income earned abroad, p. 18-25)*

For a time, the retirement savings bill had seemed a likely candidate to carry the tax package, but it became bogged down by repeated makeovers. As passed by the House on July 19, it contained provisions to increase contribution limits for tax-preferred individual retirement accounts and tax-deferred 401(k) pension plans, expand eligibility for IRAs and make pensions more portable. The Senate Finance Committee approved a revised version Sept. 7, giving the bill special protection from amendment in the Senate by making it the second of two budget-reconciliation bills allowed under the fiscal 2001 budget resolution.

By then, House leaders were stressing the party's interest in debt reduction in the wake of Clinton's vetoes of their main tax bills, and were hesitant to make retirement savings the exclusive focus of the second reconciliation bill. On Sept. 19, the House passed its own reconciliation bill (HR 5203), combining HR 1102 with a proposal to dedicate 90 percent of the fiscal 2001 budget surplus to debt reduction. *("Lockbox," p. 6-22)*

Meanwhile, Clinton was insisting on tax breaks for school construction and repairs as the price for any tax bill. GOP leaders agreed to expand an existing school bond program to help in school construction, but the administration had little formal input into the discussions.

Despite a veto threat, the House on Oct. 26 adopted the conference report on a relatively obscure small business bill (HR 2614) that had been selected to carry the tax package, along with a two-year increase in the minimum wage. The measure also included a plan to add about $30 billion over five years to reimbursements for some Medicare health providers, and a bill that would have overturned an Oregon law permitting doctor-assisted suicide, two proposals that Clinton and many congressional Democrats rejected. *(Medicare reimbursements, p. 12-25; assisted suicide, p. 15-34)*

With most Democrats lined up against the bill, and Sen. Ron Wyden, D-Ore., filibustering to protest the assisted-suicide provision, Senate Majority Leader Trent Lott, R-Miss., postponed consideration of the conference report until after the Nov. 7 election.

Instead, the Senate passed a separate bill (HR 4986) to restructure taxes on income earned abroad, in hopes of satisfying the WTO. House leaders resisted, hoping to use the tax code fix, a high priority for U.S. businesses, to drive the broader tax bill to enactment. When they finally relented Nov. 14, clearing the separate bill on foreign income, it signaled the death knell for the catch-all bill, which did not come up again in the lame duck session.

Box Score

- **Bill:** HR 2614
- **Legislative action: House** passed HR 1102 (H Rept 106-331, Part 1), 401-25, July 19.

House passed HR 5203, 401-20, Sept. 19

House adopted the conference report on HR 2614 (H Rept 106-1004), 237-174, on Oct. 26.

House Panel OKs Bill to Encourage Retirement Savings

JULY 15 — A package of pension and retirement savings incentives has been put on the fast track in the House and appears to enjoy some bipartisan support. But the legislation (HR 4843) has met with a cool reception at the White House and criticism from some Democrats, who describe it as the latest in a series of Republican bills that would benefit the wealthiest but do little for those with midrange or low incomes.

Still, five Democrats joined all 22 voting Republicans to form the majority when the House Ways and Means Committee approved the bill, 27-9, on July 13. It is scheduled for House debate July 19. If the bill stalls after that, GOP leaders on tax policy say it may be resurrected as part of the year's second reconciliation bill, which is expected to begin moving after Labor Day.

Since President Clinton vetoed a similar retirement savings package as part of last year's $792 billion tax cut (HR 2488), the sponsors have been saying they would prefer to move their package as a stand-alone bill.

The measure that was marked up was based on a bill (HR 1102) by Rob Portman, R-Ohio, and Benjamin L. Cardin, D-Md., that counted 90 Democrats among its 181 cosponsors. Supporters said the proposals would enable workers to better provide for their retirement at a time when Americans' rate of personal savings is at an all-time low.

"Pension coverage and retirement savings today is wholly inadequate at a time when it is badly needed," said Portman. He said the measure was essential to address the needs of the Baby Boom generation, 76 million of whom will reach retirement age in the next 15 years, and the half of the national work force, or 70 million people, who now have no pension coverage.

Congressional restrictions on pension plans contributed to a decline in the number of businesses offering traditional plans to 45,000 in 1997, down from 114,000 a decade earlier, Portman said.

Sponsors say the time is also ripe for increasing the tax benefits of retirement savings accounts, which have been reduced or held unchanged in recent years as a means of increasing federal revenue. The bill would cost the Treasury $16.1 billion in lost revenue over five years and, according to committee staff, $52.2 billion over a decade.

The bill would increase the annual contribution limit to a tax-free individual retirement account (IRA) from $2,000 to $5,000 by 2003, with an annual $500 increase in the limit after that. It would increase the annual limit on salary reduction contributions to tax-deferred 401(k) pension plans from $10,500 to $15,000 by 2005.

To help those close to retirement age and those, such as stay-at-home mothers who have been out of the work force for any period of time, the bill includes "catch-up" provisions. Those older than 50 could contribute $5,000 to IRAs beginning in 2001 and could add another $5,000 to their contribution to a 401(k) plan.

The bill would allow workers to take their pension benefits with them when changing jobs and allow workers to become vested in their pension plans in three years, rather than the current five.

Benefit for the Wealthy?

At the markup, opponents charged that the bill would not do enough to help low-income workers and that its benefits would be reaped mostly by those who already can most afford to save for retirement. Some Democrats also worried that boosting the attractiveness of IRAs and pension plans might induce more businesses to drop traditional retirement plans.

Jonathan Talisman, the Treasury Department's acting assistant secretary for tax policy, said the administration shared these concerns but might support the changes if they were balanced with employee protections.

The Office of Management and Budget has not issued a formal policy statement on the bill. But the administration is expected to push for its alternative, under which employers or financial institutions that match an individual's contribution to an IRA or a 401(k) could receive an equal credit on their taxes, within limits.

An amendment by William J. Jefferson, D-La., aimed at shoring up benefits for the lowest-paid workers, was rejected, 13-22, along party lines.

"I am not offended that high income individuals will benefit so much from your bill," Jefferson said. "But have we really done our job in this area if we alone encourage some who are already saving to have more, while neglecting to provide incentives to encourage savings for those who now save nothing or little at all?"

The Democratic plan called for a refundable tax credit of up to 50 percent of annual contributions to an IRA or 401(k) plan, phased out for individuals with adjusted gross incomes above $80,000, plus tax relief for small businesses that set up pension plans. Republicans said it would cost too much.

House Decisively Passes Pension Bill Despite Clinton Objections

JULY 22 — Republicans moved a big step toward issuing another one of their election-year tax dares to President Clinton on July 19, when the House overwhelmingly endorsed a package of pension and retirement savings incentives that the administration says would benefit wealthier Americans and hurt lower-income workers.

The vote to pass the legislation (HR 1102) was 401-25. Only 23 members of the Democratic Caucus, or 11 percent, voted "no." *(Vote 412, p. H-128)*

Finance Committee Chairman William V. Roth Jr., R-Del., told reporters July 19 that the Senate will probably take up the measure after Labor Day, perhaps as part of the second reconciliation measure of the year. Roth's panel is supposed to draft its version by Sept. 13 under the terms of the budget resolution (H Con Res 290) for fiscal 2001. Such a vehicle is insulated from a filibuster and is more difficult to amend.

Clinton vetoed a similar retirement savings package as part of the 10-year, $792 billion tax cut reconciliation bill (HR 2488) he was sent last year. This year, House Republicans are pursuing a strategy of moving many of the components of the 1999 package separately, hoping to raise the profile of each proposal and build sufficient public support to win over moderate congressional Democrats and — ultimately — the president.

Richard E. Neal, D-Mass., who led opposition to the retirement savings bill on the House floor, said that Treasury Secretary Lawrence H. Summers had promised, in a telephone conversation with Neal, to urge the president to veto the bill. Republicans say they believe that Clinton would not reject a measure with such widespread support.

In a July 19 statement, the Office of Management and Budget said the administration "strongly opposes" the bill, but it made no veto threat.

"Legislation to expand retirement savings must address the fundamental problem that 75 million Americans are not covered by any employer-sponsored retirement plan," the statement said, and should be considered "in a fiscal framework" that takes into account the president's other priorities for the surplus, such as school construction and prescription drug coverage for Medicare recipients.

Higher IRA Limits

The bill would cost the Treasury an estimated $16.1 billion in lost revenue during the next five years and $52.2 billion over a decade.

It would increase the annual contribution limit to a tax-free individual retirement account (IRA) from $2,000 to $5,000 by 2003, with an increase in the limit of at least $500 a year after that. The change would apply to both Roth IRAs, in which contributions are taxed but withdrawals are generally tax-free, and traditional IRAs, in which taxes are deferred until funds are withdrawn.

The bill would also increase the annual limit on contributions to tax-deferred 401(k) pension plans from $10,500 to $15,000 by 2005.

To help those close to retirement age and those, such as stay-at-home mothers, who have been out of the work force for a time, the bill includes "catch-up" provisions. Those older than 50 could contribute an additional $5,000 to IRAs each year beginning in 2001 and could add another $5,000 each year to their contribution to a 401(k) plan.

The bill would make it easier for workers to take their pension benefits with them when changing jobs and allow workers to become vested in their pension plans in three years, rather than the current five.

Supporters of the measure, sponsored by Rob Portman, R-Ohio, and Benjamin L. Cardin, D-Md., said it would enable workers to better provide for their retirements at a time when their rates of personal savings are at an all-time low.

The bill was backed by the Wall Street interests that administer retirement plans and stand to benefit from increased levels of savings for retirement in professionally managed accounts.

On a nearly party-line vote of 200-221, the House rejected a Democratic alternative that would have included the core provisions of the bill and added a refundable tax credit for lower-income workers who contribute to an IRA or employer-sponsored pension plan. *(Vote 410, p. H-128)*

J.D. Hayworth, R-Ariz., said the Democratic plan would cost nearly $250 billion over 10 years and invite fraud. "We have a simple, straightforward plan," Hayworth said. "We do not need to set up a Rube Goldbergesque machination of entitlement."

In arguing that the GOP bill would do too little for low-income workers, Democrats and the administration noted that it would weaken rules that restrict businesses from making their pension plans too "top heavy," with the preponderance of the benefits going to the best-paid employees. Some Democrats also worried that boosting the attractiveness of IRAs might give some businesses an excuse to drop their defined benefit pension plans.

Reconciliation Bill: Last Chance For Republican Tax Victory?

SEPTEMBER 9 — The most ambitious Republican tax cuts — those to benefit heirs and married couples — are tanking yet again. So in the final weeks before the 106th Congress ends, the party is turning to those few proposals that are less flashy but more likely to be enacted before Election Day arrives.

GOP leaders on both sides of the Capitol deliberated the week of Sept. 4 on how to revise and narrow their tax cut aspirations for the remainder of the year. They announced no strategy, but two proposals emerged as the leading contenders to carry forward the GOP effort to shield some of the budget surplus from being devoted to government programs. One would give taxpayers new incentives to save for retirement. The other would try to commit the government to paying down the $3.2 trillion publicly held national debt.

Those are not the only revenue measures still in play. Congress and the administration are anxious to enact legislation that would change the way income earned abroad is taxed, both for individuals and corporations, in response to a World Trade Organization (WTO) ruling against a current U.S. tax break.

And the recent overture by House Speaker J. Dennis Hastert, R-Ill., to President Clinton on increasing the minimum wage by $1 raises the possibility that some business tax breaks, attached to wage increase bills that have passed the House and Senate (HR 833, HR 3081), could become law this fall.

Whatever tax proposals are agreed to in the coming weeks are certain to be a far cry — both in financial terms and in the breadth of the subjects covered — from the $792 billion, 10-year tax cut package (HR 2488) that Congress cleared and Clinton vetoed last fall. Still, lawmakers and lobbyists said the number of measures being considered illustrates that some accomplishments with bipartisan support are possible.

House Majority Whip Tom DeLay, R-Texas, said Sept. 7 that there will be tax relief this year, "albeit very small tax relief."

In addition to the bills already in play, lobbyists are hoping to find room in any end-of-the-session omnibus fiscal 2001 appropriations package for less contentious tax proposals that might not have a place on another vehicle.

Pieces of the Puzzle

The easiest way to move a tax proposal through Congress is to shield it from excessive Senate debate or amendment by using a special provision of budget law. The fiscal 2001 budget resolution (H Con Res 290) specified that the tax-writing committees could give this "reconciliation" protection — so-called because it is designed to speed bills that reconcile federal revenues with the budget — to two measures this year. The budget said the pair could not cost more than $150 billion in the next five years.

A $90 billion measure (HR 4810) to cut taxes for married couples was the first bill given such protection. The week of Sept. 11, the House is expected to come up well short of the two-thirds majority needed to override Clinton's veto of that legislation.

That fate has already befallen the other marquee GOP tax cut of the year, a repeal of taxes on estates, gifts and trusts. The House failed to override Clinton's veto of that bill (HR 8) on Sept 7.

The same day, the Senate Finance Committee approved, 16-0, its version of what it believes should be the second of the year's reconciliation bills. The measure (HR 1102) would make a host of changes to pension and retirement laws, including increasing from $2,000 to $5,000 the amount taxpayers could set aside in tax-preferred Individual Retirement Accounts (IRAs). The bill would cost

$42.3 billion over 10 years, even though it would be crafted to sunset after 2004, a provision included to help it advance under the special budget protections. The five-year cost is estimated at $26.7 billion.

Critics say a future Congress would be loath to repeal such a tax break, and thus the sunset should not be included in realistic estimates of its cost. The Treasury Department estimates that the government would lose $100 billion in revenue in the next 10 years if the bill did not expire. The administration does not like either chamber's version but has not explicitly threatened a veto.

Chairman William V. Roth Jr., R-Del., who is locked in a tough re-election race, was clearly confident that the bill would make a good campaign season statement. He smiled broadly when the panel approved, by voice vote, an amendment by ranking Democrat Daniel Patrick Moynihan of New York to name a beefed-up retirement program that the bill would create the "Roth 401(k)."

Roth's name has been publicly linked to retirement issues since he wrote a provision in the 1997 tax law (PL 105-34) that created an IRA under which taxes are due when taxpayers contribute, but not when they withdraw, funds. *(1997 Almanac, p. 2-30)*

Similarly, the Roth 401(k) would allow workers to set aside contributions on which they would be taxed, but withdrawals would be tax-free.

In a bid to increase retirement savings, the bill would reduce barriers that prevent many workers from contributing more to tax-preferred accounts. Employees could become eligible for retirement plans quicker, and the bill would ease workers' ability to take their retirement funds with them when they switch jobs.

The bill sailed through the markup in part because Roth had added proposals by many panel members to the version the House passed in July.

The only overt criticism at the Senate markup was offered by Don Nickles, R-Okla., the assistant majority leader, who opposed inclusion of an $8.3 billion tax credit for lower-income individuals who contributed to an IRA or other retirement plan and a $5.4 billion tax credit for small businesses that set up retirement accounts for as many as 100 workers. The credit would cover 50 percent of the administrative and educational costs of setting up the accounts in the first three years.

"I think that's too much," Nickles said, describing the House version as "a very good package."

Others on the panel indicated that they may offer amendments when the bill reaches the Senate floor. Orrin G. Hatch, R-Utah, offered but withdrew an amendment to provide an income tax credit to businesses and individuals who purchase vehicles run by alternative fuels, such as compressed natural gas, and to take other steps to alleviate high energy costs. James M. Jeffords, R-Vt., said he intends to offer amendments on the floor relating to the Employee Retirement Income Security Act (PL 93-406). *(1974 Almanac, p. 244)*

Some liberal advocacy groups opposed the bill, saying it focused too much on helping higher-income workers contribute more and too little on providing pensions for the 53 percent of workers who, according to the General Accounting Office, do not have them. A provision to set up disclosure rules for companies switching from traditional defined-benefit to so-called cash balance plans drew particular opposition. Switches to cash balance plans often catch older workers in a bind just as their pensions are set to mature.

Karen D. Friedman of the Pension Rights Center, a group that works to expand and preserve pensions, said in a Sept. 6 letter to Roth that the provisions "would legitimize a practice that has robbed tens of thousands of employees of millions of dollars in expected pensions."

A Bit of Debt Reduction?

While House leaders also intend to use pension provisions as a centerpiece of the reconciliation bill that the Ways and Means Committee may mark up the week of Sept. 11, some were as adamant that the bill also focus on debt reduction.

At a news conference Sept. 7, DeLay said the bill should include $245 billion to pay down the debt and "what other taxes that we can actually get through."

Some members and lobbyists are still holding out hope that it might include some smaller items as well, such as the alteration of a 1999 law (HR 1180 — PL 106-170) that could force some businesses to pay additional capital gains taxes if they sell their companies on installment.

Ways and Means Chairman Bill Archer, R-Texas, met with Hastert and Majority Leader Dick Armey, R-Texas, throughout the day Sept. 7, but the trio did not reach a conclusion on what the reconciliation bill should include. A decision seems likely Sept. 12, after Republicans go to the White House to talk to Clinton. While that meeting is ostensibly about appropriations, it is likely to include talk of other year-end horse trades, such as Hastert's Aug. 28 minimum wage offer.

The Speaker proposed raising the federal hourly wage floor to $6.15 as of January 2002 — a timetable the GOP had previously rejected as too fast — in exchange for a package of tax breaks worth $76 billion over 10 years. That is significantly smaller than the $122.7 billion in breaks the House endorsed along with a minimum wage increase in March. The proposal bogged down in the Senate when it was tied up with a bill to revamp personal bankruptcy law.

Rep. Jack Quinn of New York, a key GOP supporter of a higher minimum wage, warned of "sticking points, especially on the tax side," but predicted in a Sept. 6 interview that a deal will be hatched by month's end.

Senate Minority Leader Tom Daschle, D-S.D., also sounded optimistic, although he said the $76 billion total for the tax breaks was too high. He urged dropping a provision to increase the deductibility of business meals, which he derided as $30 billion in breaks for "the three-martini lunch."

One Seems Certain

While leaders have a long way to go before reaching agreement on that deal, there appears to be rock-solid support for the legislation (HR 4986) to rewrite a part of the tax code to appease the WTO. The bill would exempt much income earned abroad from federal taxation in an effort to replace the provision in question — a tax break for companies whose export operations are run by offshore offices, known as foreign sales corporations.

Numerous large corporations, including Boeing Co. and Microsoft Corp., save millions in taxes by setting up such offices.

"We're moving ahead with complete cooperation with both the minority and the administration," Archer said after a Sept. 7 meeting with Ways and Means members and Deputy Treasury Secretary Stuart E. Eizenstat.

The House is scheduled to take up the bill Sept. 12 under suspension of the rules, an expedited procedure reserved for non-controversial measures.

Eizenstat appealed to members to move a bill by Oct. 1 — when the president must declare to the WTO how he intends to address their ruling — and without riders that could make advancing it difficult. Trade Subcommittee Chairman Philip M. Crane, R-Ill., said the GOP would agree to those terms.

Despite high hopes for moving the bill in a bipartisan fashion, it appears that the United States may face tough sledding in trying to convince the WTO that the new system is an acceptable substitute. The European Union, which filed the complaint against the existing law, says the bill also appears to violate trade rules by providing a subsidy. Lawmakers say they believe the WTO will side with them, however.

House Passes Debt Reduction, IRA Bills

SEPTEMBER 23 — The House passed the GOP debt reduction proposal twice during the week of Sept. 18. The second time, Republicans coupled the measure with their retirement savings package and passed that bill for the second time this summer, too. The repetitive motions seemed designed to prompt Senate action on those initiatives, but progress there did not appear forthcoming on either — or on any other revenue bill.

Senate attention to tax policy was diverted by the implosion of the Republican strategy for finishing must-pass fiscal 2001 appropriations bills. Senate Finance Committee leaders twice postponed marking up a House-passed bill (HR 4923) to create tax incentives for investing in poor rural and urban communities, after members threatened to offer more than 70 amendments. The bill embodies a rare deal between President Clinton and House Speaker J. Dennis Hastert, R-Ill.

The House is largely hamstrung until senators take steps on several fronts. "All eyes are fixed on them," Ways and Means Committee spokesman Trent Duffy said Sept. 21.

The picture may clear up the week of Sept. 25, which Majority Leader Trent Lott, R-Miss., has mentioned as a likely time for floor consideration of the Senate version of the measure (HR 1102) to expand tax incentives for retirement savings. Lott may also attempt to bring up a separate measure (HR 4986) to bring U.S. tax law into compliance with world trade rules, or he may attempt to attach it to the retirement bill.

When the House passed its first retirement bill July 19, it was not designated a reconciliation measure, which would give it special protection from amendment and extended debate in the Senate. At its Sept. 7 markup, however, the Finance panel gave its version such preferred status — one of two tax cut bills allowed the designation under the budget resolution (H Con Res 290) for fiscal 2001.

While the House measure did not bear the reconciliation label, negotiators could work out a conference agreement blending it with a Senate-passed version. House leaders, however, have become less enamored of the idea of making retirement savings the exclusive focus of the year's second such bill. The House sustained President Clinton's veto of the first (HR 4810), the "marriage penalty" tax cut, Sept. 13.

Now the GOP leadership is stressing the party's interest in using 90 percent of the surplus, at least in fiscal 2001, for debt reduction. The House voted 381-3 to pass a bill to that end (HR 5173) on Sept. 18, and gave it a form of reconciliation protection. *(Vote 477, p. H-150)*

The vote was 401-20 the next day for the legislation (HR 5203) combining the debt and pension bills, which carries the designation as the House's second permitted tax cut reconciliation measure. Republicans said the move was made to ensure that Senate Democrats cannot block Senate Republicans from attaching a debt bill to the tax reconciliation measure, something for which Senate GOP leaders have shown little overt enthusiasm. *(Vote 479, p. H-150)*

Wage Increase and Business Taxes

Negotiations between Congress and the White House continued on a plan to merge an increase in the minimum wage — to $6.15 an hour in 50-cent increments at the beginning of next year and 2002 — with a package of tax cuts mostly to benefit small businesses over two year. Progress remained elusive, however, although all sides sounded optimistic that a deal would be enacted this fall. Sen. Edward M. Kennedy, D-Mass., and House Minority Whip David E. Bonior, D-Mich., indicated in a Sept. 21 briefing that the parties were not far apart, but that the cost of the GOP sweeteners would need to be reduced.

Those include a provision to exempt bonuses from the calculation of base pay — which could reduce the overtime rate for 73 million workers — and a deduction allowing those who pay a majority of their health insurance premiums to deduct 100 percent of their medical expenses without itemizing. The cost of that change would be $48 billion over 10 years.

The overall cost of the proposed package of tax breaks is also an issue. The GOP wish list would reduce revenue $76 billion over 10 years. Democrats favor a package worth between $28 billion and $46 billion over a decade.

Fate of Tax Cut Package Tied To Education and Health Issues

OCTOBER 21 — For any tax cut to become law this year, Republican leaders and President Clinton likely will need to forge agreement in the next several days on the hot-button election year issues of education and health care.

Administration officials are insisting that bipartisan legislation (HR 4094) that aims to provide tax credits for school repair and construction bonds be included in any tax measure. At the same time, House Speaker J. Dennis Hastert, R-Ill., continues to insist on language to allow workers to deduct medical insurance costs from their income taxes if their employers pay no more than half of their plan's premiums.

Republicans reiterated the week of Oct. 16 that they intended to clear a tax bill before adjournment that Clinton would sign.

However, some lobbyists questioned how hard the GOP would push a bill that embodies few of their top priorities and cuts taxes by $260 billion to $300 billion over the next 10 years — 38 percent of the tax cut (HR 2488) Clinton vetoed last year. The GOP's main proposals — repeal of the estate tax (HR 8) and a tax cut for married couples (HR 4810) — were stopped by Clinton vetoes this year. *(Background, 1999 Almanac, p. 21-7)*

Republicans attempted to involve the administration in discussions on the developing measure. Hastert said he and the president discussed their priorities in a telephone call the night of Oct. 18. Some GOP lawmakers talked with high-level Treasury Department officials about potential pieces of the package, including a measure (HR 1102) that would increase the amount of retirement savings taxpayers could set aside before paying taxes.

With formal negotiations still in the offing, it was unclear precisely where Clinton stood.

Spokesman Jake Siewert said Oct. 19 that the president was waiting to see the entire GOP tax package before making a decision whether to accept any one piece. As a result, Clinton has not acted on a bill (HR 4516) combining fiscal 2001 appropriations for the legislative branch, the Treasury and Postal Service with repeal of the 3 percent excise tax on telephone service.

Union Jobs at Stake?

At a raucous rally with congressional Democrats in the Cannon House Office Building on Oct. 19, Clinton did not comment on any pieces of the tax package except to repeat his demand for the school construction provision.

While Democrats are united behind it, the proposal splits the House GOP. Conservatives generally oppose it, but 27 of the measure's 227 cosponsors are Republicans.

Ways and Means Committee Chairman Bill Archer, R-Texas, after waxing nostalgic Oct. 19 at what was billed as his final news conference before his retirement, pledged to hold the line against more tax credits, including the school bond credit. "You open to one, and you've got a line of about 20-30 waiting," he said.

Some members, including Randy "Duke" Cunningham, R-Calif., took to the House floor to denounce the school bonds provision as a sop to unions. The bill would not waive the 1931 Davis-Bacon Act, which requires contractors on federally funded projects to pay their workers prevailing wages.

Nancy L. Johnson, R-Conn., who sponsored the school construction measure with Charles B. Rangel, D-N.Y., took issue with the Davis-Bacon arguments. In a letter to all House GOP members Oct. 18, she said such requirements were "nothing new. My bill is not a new mandate on states."

Johnson and other moderates hoped to pressure GOP leaders to accept the bill with the Davis-Bacon requirement intact. It is supported not only by education groups, but by the unions whose workers would build the schools.

Jack Quinn, R-N.Y., said that with the construction bill, Hastert's health care proposal and other measures being discussed, "There's enough for a deal. I think all they need to do is sit down and talk."

Pressure also comes from the calendar. Clinton has promised to support only one-day stopgap spending bills after the current one (H J Res 114) lapses Oct. 25, a move designed to force agreements on the last four fiscal 2001 spending bills and allow Congress to depart.

Tit for Tat?

The health insurance provision Hastert is touting was included in the Senate version of a bill (HR 833) to increase the minimum wage. At the insistence of Democrats and some Republicans, Hastert has endorsed raising the wage by $1 an hour, to $6.15, over two years: That provision likely will be included in the tax package.

Clinton's and Hastert's favored proposals share important attributes. Both would be helpful election-year measures with little downside. And, neither has much of a cost in fiscal 2001, when $11 billion to $14 billion is projected to be available for tax cuts.

The school construction bill would cost $6.8 billion over 10 years, by Democratic estimates. The Senate-passed health care provision would not take effect until 2002 and would cost $9.7 billion over the same period, according to the Joint Committee on Taxation.

The bulk of the tax bill's cost would come from items long designated for inclusion: the retirement measure, a bill (HR 4986) to replace a tax break for exporters with a system exempting much income earned abroad from U.S. taxes, and a measure (HR 4923, S 3152) to lower tax and regulatory burdens for investors in low-income communities.

The package will also likely include other proposals that would benefit specific industries or businesses, though it is not clear what those might be.

House Passes Tax Bill After GOP Adds Disputed Policy Riders

OCTOBER 28 — Republicans have combined a collection of tax breaks and an increase in the minimum wage with several more controversial election-year riders, and are pushing it through Congress despite a veto threat from President Clinton. As a result, the 106th Congress may well end with the tax cutting aspirations of the GOP majority almost entirely unfulfilled.

The House voted 237-174 for the package (HR 2614) on Oct. 26, with 33 Democrats in favor and just six Republicans opposed. *(Vote 560, p. H-178)*

A blizzard of oppositional rhetoric descended on the bill when it arrived in the Senate, where Democrats delayed the vote to clear the measure until the week of Oct. 30.

At the same time, however, some GOP leaders and the White House sent signals that they would be open to embracing another, probably more limited measure to replace the doomed Republican package. The president told reporters Oct. 27 that his main interest was in being invited to join in the negotiations, from which he said he had been excluded. "The fix to this bill is a relatively minor one," added a White House spokesman, Jake Siewert.

Senate Majority Leader Trent Lott, R-Miss., and Finance Committee Chairman William V. Roth Jr., R-Del., signaled a willingness to revive some tax provisions in the session's closing days.

The package produced by the Republicans the week of Oct. 23 would cut federal taxes by a net $240.4 billion during the next 10 years, with the biggest benefits going to constituencies with broad bipartisan support: small businesses, people who are saving for their retirement, and those paying their own medical insurance premiums. The bill would also raise the minimum wage by $1, to $6.15 an hour by 2002. But the measure also included portions of a plan to add about $30 billion in the next five years to the reimbursements of some health providers that accept Medicare payments (HR 5291) and the crux of a bill (HR 2260) to ban physician-assisted suicides — two of the proposals that the president and many congressional Democrats would not accept.

The provisions were added to the conference report on an otherwise obscure bill to expand a Small Business Administration loan program. The deal was cut in a crush of work by a relatively tight circle of Republicans and their aides that ended early the morning of Oct. 26. By then, the tower of typewritten pages, some annotated in hard-to-decipher handwriting, stood 960 pages tall.

As they had signaled they would do all fall, the leaders included major sections from four measures that had stalled in recent months, even though they had drawn broad-based support at the Capitol: A bill (HR 1102) to create tax incentives for contributing to pension plans and retirement savings accounts; bills (HR 833, HR 3081) to increase the minimum wage while cutting taxes on businesses that pay those wages; a bill (HR 4986) to exempt much income earned abroad from U.S. taxation; and bills (HR 4923, S 3152) to lower taxes and regulatory burdens on those who invest in low-income urban and rural communities.

Clinton spurned the package in a letter to GOP leaders as the House debate got under way. "Without any consultation with me or congressional Democrats, you chose to put forward a partisan legislative package that ignores our key concerns on school construction, health care and pensions policy," he wrote.

Saying he had received no response from GOP leaders to several offers of compromise and explanations of his priorities, the president said in the Rose Garden Oct. 27: "I will not bend over backwards to be run over."

Republicans initially countered with the same confrontational tone that has served as the death knell for so many other GOP tax bills. "The American people understand this is a political season and tempers get a little short, people get a little desperate in their actions," said Lott, "but the American people are going to know who did what needed to be done and who vetoed it."

Before the measure could get to the White House, however, it would have to overcome the anger of Democrats and some moderate Republicans, who wanted more tax breaks to build schools and stronger language to assure that union workers would build them. Some conservative Republicans also lamented that the measure did not contain enough straightforward tax cuts of the type that the GOP has been pushing throughout its six years in control of Congress.

As a result, many Republicans saw little reason for enthusiasm for the hodgepodge of tax provisions — or had any willingness to work in the season's waning hours on another iteration. Instead, some preferred to bank on the prospect that in the 107th Congress a more sweeping package would be signed by Republican George W. Bush.

"This is really a spending bill much more than a tax bill," Sen. Phil Gramm, R-Texas, complained Oct. 25. "I would prefer to wait until next year, until we have a president who's for tax cuts."

Democrats, meanwhile, joined the current president in complaining that they had not seen the package with enough time before the votes to confirm for themselves what was really in it.

White House Role Limited

Although some Treasury Department officials had been consulted on the provisions that would provide greater tax incentives for retirement savings, White House officials were not invited to join the Republicans who settled on the package's final form. The administration's input appeared to have been limited to a Sept. 28 meeting between Treasury Secretary Lawrence H. Summers and House Majority Leader Dick Armey, R-Texas; an Oct. 18 telephone conversation between Clinton and House Speaker J. Dennis Hastert, R-Ill., and a few exchanges of correspondence between the two.

Republican negotiators had signed off on the main provisions in the bill by the time Hastert received a letter Oct. 25 in which Clinton outlined his priorities, including a bill (HR 4094) to create a new tax credit for school construction bonds and a proposal to give tax breaks to those who research new vaccines.

Republican leaders made no apparent effort at that point to tack the provisions on. Instead, they initially said they were confident that Clinton would sign the legislation because it included two of the priorities he had listed for his final year in office: increasing the minimum wage, which has not gone up since September 1997, and enacting his "New Markets" initiative for investing in areas that have not benefited from the economic boom.

In the haste of the drafting process, however, the bill was written so that its enactment would do away with the minimum wage altogether until the end of the year. The bill says the current minimum wage of $5.15 an hour should last only until June 30, 2000; and a minimum wage of $5.65 should take effect on Jan. 1, 2001; it would rise by another 50 cents on Jan. 1, 2002.

The GOP's take-it-or-leave-it approach was a return to a strategy that has led to minimal tax lawmaking in the past six years. Hoping for better results this year, Hastert had led Republicans on the opposite tack through the summer, promoting the production of a series of narrower tax bills that might pique the public's attention and win Clinton's election year signature. But that tactic, too, won limited results.

International Repercussions

The death of HR 2614 would have more than political consequences; it also could intensify trade tensions between the United States and Europe. The one provision in the measure labeled "must pass" by both the administration and congressional leaders would repeal a tax break for exporters that violates World Trade Organization (WTO) rules. In its place, the bill would create a broader provision to exempt much income earned abroad from U.S. taxation.

If the United States does not move toward repealing its current law — known by the acronym FSC, for foreign sales corporation — by Nov. 1, the European Union, which filed the complaint against the current tax break, can begin preparing to place billions of dollars in tariffs on U.S. products sold in the 15-nation bloc. Having already extended the deadline once — it originally was Oct. 1 — European officials showed no interest in cutting Congress more slack.

Several tax writers, including Sen. Bob Kerrey, D-Neb., and Rep. Benjamin L. Cardin, D-Md., said they were confident the foreign tax provision would be enacted, probably as part of the Labor-HHS-Education spending bill (HR 4577).

Lott said Oct. 27 that he was "not going to cry crocodile tears" if the provision died. But House Ways and Means Committee Chairman Bill Archer, R-Texas, said he would push to enact it. "The danger in not doing so is too great."

Killing the measure is "a huge economic risk," said Rep. Robert T. Matsui, D-Calif., a key administration ally on trade. "It's a question of do we get blamed or do they get blamed if it doesn't become law."

A Modest Yet Complicated Bill

For much of the week, it was unclear how much time and energy the GOP was willing to expend to see the package enacted. It had few enthusiastic backers in the party, because so few top-tier Republican priorities were at issue. The bill promised less than one-third of the tax cuts contained in the $792 billion package (HR 2488) that Clinton vetoed last year. *(1999 Almanac, p. 21-7)*

(Continued on p. 40)

Tax Package Highlights

ISSUE	DESCRIPTION
Health insurance deductibility	A law allowing the self-employed to deduct 100 percent of their medical insurance costs by 2003 would be accelerated to 2001 and be extended to those choosing not to join an employer-provided plan. Taxpayers whose employers pay less than half their health care costs could deduct 25 percent of their premiums in 2001 and 100 percent by 2006. Cost: $88.3 billion over 10 years.
Retirement and pension plan savings	Contribution limits for traditional and Roth Individual Retirement Accounts (IRAs) would be increased from $2,000 to $5,000 by 2003 and indexed for inflation thereafter. Workers 50 and older could contribute $1,500 more by 2003. Contribution limits for 401(k)s and other defined contribution plans would increase from $10,000 to $15,000 by 2005 and would be indexed for inflation thereafter. Companies would have to notify workers if they planned to significantly reduce pension coverage. Cost: $63.8 billion over 10 years.
Minimum wage increase and offsetting tax cuts	The $5.15-an-hour minimum wage would increase by $1 by 2002. Businesses that most often pay the wage — retailers, restaurants and small companies — would benefit most from tax breaks in the bill. Businesses could deduct 70 percent of business meal costs, up from 50 percent, and could deduct a maximum of $35,000, up from $20,000, for purchases of property. Timber companies would be able to claim tax credits of $25,000, up from $10,000, for the cost of planting new trees. Cost: $35.9 billion over 10 years.
Community renewal	Forty renewal communities, 12 of them rural, would be created; investors would receive benefits such as a 15 percent tax credit on the first $10,000 of wages paid, higher deductions for purchases of business property, and no capital gains taxes for qualifying assets held for more than five years. Nine new empowerment zones would be created, a New Markets tax credit would be established and the Low-Income Housing Tax Credit would be expanded. Cost: $25.2 billion over 10 years.
School construction	Tax credits for purchasing Qualified Zone Academy Bonds, which now cover renovation, staffing and other school costs, would be extended to cover construction. Local officials could invest bond proceeds at higher interest rates than the borrowing level for four years, up from two years. Cost: $7.8 billion over 10 years.
Income earned abroad	A tax break for exporters that set up off-shore branches, known as foreign sales corporations, would be repealed, to comply with World Trade Organization (WTO) rules. Instead, most income earned abroad would be exempt from U.S. taxation. The measure does not include a House-passed tax break for corporations such as Caterpillar Inc. that receive dividends from foreign subsidiaries. Language was inserted, however, that would remove some tax barriers to converting foreign subsidiaries to domestic companies. Cost: $4.5 billion over 10 years.
Other major provisions	The bill also includes: Provisions of a bill (HR 5291) to restore cuts to Medicare providers, a measure (HR 2260) to ban physician-assisted suicide and a plan to give investors tax credits for purchasing bonds that fund Amtrak and Alaska Railroad lines.

COST ESTIMATES: Joint Committee on Taxation

This session's wrap-up package also lacked the popular resonance of the tax measures pushed through Congress earlier in the year: a repeal of estate taxes (HR 8), costing $104 billion over a decade, and a tax cut for married couples (HR 4810) that would have cost $90 billion. The House sustained Clinton vetoes of each.

Neither did the package have much of the usual resonance with businesses. While it had a number of policy changes designed to help certain industries or regions, it contained neither a sweeping cut in corporate taxes nor a bevy of "rifle shots" — provisions written to lift tax burdens on a single business or a narrowly defined industry.

Most of the debate centered on education, which far exceeds tax cuts on the roster of voter concerns this year. But the main provision at issue — to aid school construction — seemed to please no one but GOP leaders. Clinton, congressional Democrats and moderate Republicans said it would not do enough, while conservatives in the GOP thought the issue should not have been addressed at all.

Hastert had attempted to blunt the issue by proposing a compromise designed to spur school construction without a new tax credit. Such provisions are generally anathema to conservatives because they complicate the already esoteric tax code and put the IRS in a position of implementing social policy programs. Archer is particularly opposed to tax credits and was determined not to allow any more on the final tax bill written before his retirement.

The proposal would expand the use of so-called Qualified Zone Academy Bonds to pay for school construction. It would also allow local officials to increase the funds available for school projects by taking proceeds from bond sales and investing them at higher rates of interest than the borrowing rate. Such arbitrage could occur for as long as four years before construction, as opposed to the two years allowed under current law.

Democrats charged that the bill would not spur enough school construction. The plan they backed would provide an estimated $24.8 billion over the next two years by creating a new bond program specifically to give tax credits to investors in bonds designated for school construction. That bill would also require that construction workers under the program be paid the prevailing wage as designated by the 1931 Davis-Bacon Act. The final tax package would allow each school district to decide whether to pay that rate.

Archer nonetheless cast one of the six GOP votes against the bill, citing its minimum wage increase, the school construction package and some expansions of tax credits, including a credit for investors who purchase bonds to help Amtrak and the Alaska Railroad build more lines.

Few Rifle Shots, Lots of Riders

That credit was a priority for Roth, who is in a tight re-election race. Had the provision not been included, Roth would not have had much of his handiwork to point to in the bill. Two high-profile items in his version of the retirement savings bill were left out: a tax credit for low-income and middle-income people who contributed to retirement accounts and a plan to give tax breaks to businesses that started retirement plans for 100 or fewer employees.

Roth's version of the bill for community investment fared better. Some of the narrow tax breaks that Finance Committee members had attached to it also made their way into the final package. Among them was a plan by Charles E. Grassley, R-Iowa, to allow farmers and fishermen to defer taxes on funds set aside in savings accounts to be used during financial crises.

Another, pushed by computer maker Gateway Inc., would extend through 2003 a tax write-off for computers donated to public schools and expand the program to include businesses' donations to public libraries — and of machines as old as three years. The bill also included a provision that would require banks to pay interest on the checking accounts of businesses, a provision pushed by the National Federation of Independent Business.

Despite the inclusion of such provisions, members said they had been bombarded by requests for dozens more.

Republican Rep. Rob Portman of Ohio said leaders had agreed to include "items we all agree are helpful."

While Wrapup Tax Bill Falters, Medicare Boost Likely to Survive

NOVEMBER 18 — The chances that most individuals and businesses would receive even a modest tax cut from the 106th Congress continued to dwindle the week of Nov. 13 .

Attempting to tamp down a trade dispute with Europe, the House GOP leadership reversed course and cleared stand-alone legislation (HR 4986) Nov. 14 to replace the system for taxing income earned abroad. That appears to have taken what little wind remained out of the sails of a catch-all bill (HR 2614) that included the overseas income provision.

Absent the need to move the overseas taxation language — and with the election yielding no clear political signal for either party to act on other tax matters this fall — the Senate showed no interest in resuming its debate on the measure when the lame-duck session of Congress convenes.

At a cost of $240.4 billion over 10 years, the bill — in the form of a conference report (H Rept 106-1004) adopted by the House on Oct. 26 — would provide tax incentives for saving for retirement, investing in low-income communities, purchasing health insurance and buying school construction bonds. It also would increase the minimum wage by $1 an hour, to $6.15 over two years.

Proponents of certain provisions turned their efforts to peeling off their favorite pieces and trying to attach them to the principal measure (HR 4577) that must still be finished by the 106th Congress, to fund the Labor, Education and Health and Human Services departments in fiscal 2001.

The element most likely to become a part of the the Labor-HHS measure is a version of legislation (HR 5291) to boost by $31.5 billion in the next five years reimbursements to Medicare providers, who have been chafing under cuts set in the budget-balancing act (PL 105-33) of 1997.

Health care lobbyists have launched another wave in their campaign for the money, using advertising, Capitol Hill visits by industry leaders and attempts at applying grass-roots pressure. An alliance of hospitals, the Coalition to Protect America's Health Care, planned to spend more than $700,000 during the week of Nov. 13 on a new television, radio and print campaign.

Details Not Settled Yet

The legislation would provide millions to hospitals, home health care agencies, skilled nursing homes, Medicare+Choice health plans, medical device manufacturers and others who are paid by the federal medical insurance program for the elderly and disabled. As a result, there are important advocates for the package from both parties in both the House and Senate. GOP leaders and the Clinton administration disagree about some provisions in the measure, however.

Administration officials have suggested that President Clinton would sign the measure if a handful of his priorities were added. Republicans have been reluctant to reopen the bill.

"We're not going to open it up again," Finance Committee member Phil Gramm, R-Texas, said Nov. 14. Bill Thomas, R-Calif., chairman of the Ways and Means Health Subcommittee, said Nov. 15 that he is only willing to make "tweaks, not wholesale adjustments."

Sixteen major health care groups—which have competed much of the fall for funds in the package — urged House and Senate leaders of both parties to set aside their differences. "We have foregone any disagreements to join hands to strongly encourage action this year," they said in a Nov. 14 letter. "Relief cannot wait."

House Ways and Means Committee Chairman Bill Archer, R-Texas, said Nov. 14 he still hoped to find room elsewhere for at least two other tax bill provisions. One would reverse a 1999 law (PL 106-170) and allow owners of some companies to pay capital gains in installments if they sell their businesses in installments. The other would adjust entitlement checks, tax schedules and other government programs affected by an error that kept the Consumer Price Index too low in 1999. The change would cost an estimated $40 million in lost revenue in the next 10 years but would add $5.8 billion to government spending.

Some members said they thought the GOP might move the tax package if Vice President Al Gore was declared president. Archer disagreed. "Irrespective of who goes into the White House, it seems to me that there's a reason not to do it," he said.

Lawmakers Clear Modest Tax Deal

DECEMBER 16 — In the end, the antipoverty initiative promoted by President Clinton and House Speaker J. Dennis Hastert, R-Ill., survived because it was one of the few trophies the Republicans could stand to let Clinton walk away with.

Negotiators agreed Dec. 11 to rescue the community renewal package from otherwise moribund tax legislation (HR 2614). They attached it to the conference report for the fiscal 2001 Labor, Health and Human Services and Education appropriations bill, which became the vehicle for almost all of the deals cut in the lame-duck session that is ending the 106th Congress. The House voted 292-60 on Dec. 15 to adopt the package (HR 4577); the Senate cleared it on a voice vote later the same day. *(Vote 603, p. H-190)*

At a cost of $25.9 billion in the next 10 years, the delicately balanced collection of tax credits, regulatory relief and other economic development measures seeks to breathe new life into urban and rural areas left behind in the economic boom.

Clinton's signature would make the "community renewal" package the only significant year-end tax measure of 2000. The only other major tax provision in the wrapup was a two-year extension of a demonstration program under which the self-employed and small-business employees may create tax-free accounts to pay medical bills. The provision, which gives new life to a pilot program created in 1996 (PL 104-191), was a priority of House Ways and Means Committee Chairman Bill Archer, R-Texas. The bill names the program for Archer, who is retiring. *(1996 CQ Almanac, p. 6-28)*

In another victory for Archer, the lawmakers left out a proposal to expand tax credits for investors in bonds that finance Amtrak improvements, a priority of Republican William V. Roth Jr. of Delaware, whose election defeat ends his tenure as Senate Finance Committee chairman.

Other tax proposals that had survived until the final round of deal-cutting for the year were left out, among them a repeal of the federal excise tax on telephone service at a cost of $51 billion over a decade. The repeal was in an appropriations bill (HR 4516) Clinton vetoed Oct. 30.

Republicans' interest in negotiating more tax cuts with Clinton quickly dissipated once they became confident that George W. Bush would prevail in the disputed presidential election. "We'll do the tax package next year and do a better job of it," Senate Majority Whip Don Nickles, R-Okla., told reporters Dec. 5.

The survival of the community renewal package was motivated in part by Clinton's desire to bolster his legacy and in part by Hastert's gentle prodding. Because it had the politically symbolic advantage of being a joint venture of a Democratic president and a Republican Speaker, it survived in the year-end process of elimination.

At a Dec. 11 meeting at the White House, Clinton appealed to GOP leaders to include in the year's final bill the community renewal measure, a $1 increase in the minimum wage and expansions of Medicaid, including a Senate bill (S 2774) by Charles E. Grassley, R-Iowa, and Edward M. Kennedy, D-Mass., to let the parents of children with disabilities buy coverage. The congressional leaders in essence told Clinton to pick his favorite. "Republicans are willing to give him a sugar plum, but not three sugar plums," a GOP leadership aide familiar with the talks said at the time.

The minimum wage increase was never a strong possibility, because most Republican leaders oppose it and their acquiescence in it would have angered business leaders. The Grassley and Kennedy bill's chances were hurt by cost estimates from the Congressional Budget Office — $3.9 billion over five years, later reduced to $2.1 billion. Republicans also balked at expanding an entitlement program. The antipoverty package was the only option left.

The package was essentially unchanged from the version endorsed by the House in October. It would extend the life of 31 existing "empowerment zones," which provide wage credits and other tax incentives to lure businesses, while creating nine new ones; create 40 "renewal communities," a Republican idea that expands on the empowerment zones favored by Democrats by adding regulatory relief and an exemption from capital gains taxes on some assets held for longer than five years; establish a New Markets tax credit worth $15 billion during the next seven years, to lure private investors to low-income areas; expand the Low-Income Housing Tax Credit; and allow state and local governments to issue more private activity bonds, which can be used for construction projects such as low-income housing.

Other Provisions

Ten other, mostly technical tax provisions are also in HR 4577. One would allow federal agencies to use a corrected 1999 figure for the Consumer Price Index, raising entitlement checks and altering some tax schedules. The Bureau of Labor Statistics admitted it made the mistake but has not corrected it.

Another provision would allow parents of kidnapped children to continue counting them as dependents on their returns and to claim the $500 child tax credit for them. The House passed the proposal in September as a measure (HR 5117) by Jim Ramstad, R-Minn.

The bill also would exempt some international tax information at the IRS from being disclosed through the Freedom of Information Act. The newsletter Tax Notes had filed such a request and a number of business groups had opposed it, fearing that the disclosure would make public proprietary business practices.

The House by voice vote Dec. 14 passed one additional tax provision, a bill (HR 3594) to repeal a 1999 law (PL 106-170) that required business owners who sold their company in installments to pay all capital gains within the first year of the sale. The National Federation of Independent Business and other groups had pushed vociferously for the repeal. ◆

Move to Ban New Internet Fees Stalls After States Seek Ways to Collect Sales Taxes

Box Score

- **Bills:** HR 3709, S 1611, S 2255, S 2775
- **Legislative action: House** passed HR 3709 (H Rept 106-609), 352-75, May 10.

SUMMARY

Lawmakers of both parties supported an extension of a current moratorium (PL 105-277) on new, Internet-specific taxes, but efforts to move legislation stalled after governors requested broader authority to collect current sales taxes from online vendors. The moratorium, created in 1998, is set to end in October 2001. The House passed legislation to provide a five year-extension, but the measure died in the Senate.

Extending the moratorium was a top goal of Internet-related business officials, who argued it would encourage the growth of electronic commerce. The existing moratorium bars new access charges and e-mail tariffs, but does not cover existing state sales taxes.

Initially, key lawmakers including Senate Commerce, Science and Transportation Committee Chairman John McCain, R-Ariz., backed a plan (S 1611) to make the moratorium permanent. But governors urged Congress not to extend the moratorium unless it addressed an inequity between Main Street retailers, who must pay sales taxes, and online vendors, who often do not. Current law allows states to collect sales taxes only from businesses with a physical presence in their borders. Many of the governors asked lawmakers to endorse a plan to simplify state sales taxes and allow them to be collected from online vendors in other states.

Congress got less help than it had hoped from a 19-member Advisory Commission on Electronic Commerce, created by Congress to study online taxation. The commission issued a report in April that called for a five-year extension of the moratorium, but the report was supported by just 11 members, two short of the two-thirds majority needed to make formal recommendations to Congress.

Despite the divided views on the panel, the House passed a five-year extension of the moratorium (HR 3709) on May 10. McCain introduced a similar bill (S 2255) in the Senate, but it stalled in his committee when lawmakers disagreed on whether to expand state sales tax collection powers. Byron L. Dorgan, D-N.D., offered a compromise (S 2775) that would have extended the current moratorium for four years, but he was unable to cut a deal on language to let states develop a national system for collecting state sales taxes.

Governors Advise Against Ban On Internet Taxes

MARCH 4 — The nation's governors implored senators to oppose legislation that would permanently bar state sales taxes on online purchases during a first-ever summit meeting Feb. 29. They received sympathy but no final assurances.

The chief executives made their case for protecting state authority over sales taxes, and they opposed any new unfunded federal mandates for education, health care and environmental protection, during a special meeting between the National Governors' Association (NGA) and the Senate in the Russell Caucus Room.

The broad, bipartisan gathering marked what several participants said they hoped would be the beginning of a new tradition. In the past, there have been smaller, intraparty meetings between lawmakers and select governors.

Democratic Gov. Parris N. Glendening of Maryland, the NGA's vice chairman, said cooperation was vital to set rules of the road for the Internet regarding issues such as taxation and privacy. "We are trying to deal with the 21st century economy with laws for the 20th century," he said. "If we don't work together, we are going to have an economy that becomes absolutely straitjacketed and less competitive."

At the top of the list of issues that straddle federal and state jurisdiction is the question of how to apply taxes to the Internet.

President Clinton, who met with the governors a day earlier, said he would oppose a ban on taxes based on the value of goods purchased on the Internet. Some lawmakers, such as House Majority Leader Dick Armey, R-Texas, have said they would support such a ban, which is contained in a bill (HR 3252) sponsored by House Budget Committee Chairman John R. Kasich, R-Ohio.

Senate Commerce, Science and Transportation Committee Chairman John McCain of Arizona, whose panel oversees the issue, has vowed to push a proposal (S 1611) similar to the Kasich bill. McCain, who is battling Texas Gov. George W. Bush for the Republican presidential nomination, has made a ban on Internet taxation a chief element of his platform. Neither Bush nor McCain attended the summit.

Moratorium to Expire

As part of an omnibus spending law (PL 105-277), Congress in 1998 imposed a three-year moratorium on new Internet-specific taxes, such as special levies added to access fees. The moratorium, which will expire in October 2001, does not apply to sales taxes owed by customers on purchases from companies with a physical presence in their state. *(Background, 1998 Almanac, p. 21-19)*

Although sales taxes are not restricted by the moratorium, states have difficulty collecting them because they do not keep track of online sales. A study by Forrester Research, a marketing research firm, estimates that uncollected sales taxes on online retail sales cost the states $525 million in 1999.

The study predicted that losses will mount as online sales increase from $13 billion last year to $184 billion forecast in 2004.

While states wrestle with the sales tax dilemma, support appears to be growing for extension of the current moratorium on other Internet fees beyond 2001, and perhaps indefinitely. Senate Majority Leader Trent Lott, R-Miss., said Feb. 29 that he would support an extension of the moratorium.

Sen. Ron Wyden, D-Ore., has sponsored a bill (S 2028) to make permanent the temporary ban on Internet-related taxes. Rep. Christopher Cox, R-Calif., has introduced a companion bill (HR 3709).

No action is expected by Congress until after it receives the report of a special commission it created two years ago to recommend a proper policy on Internet taxation.

The Advisory Commission on Electronic Commerce, which will hold its last meeting March 20, has been divided on the sales tax issue and has yet to take a position on extending the tax moratorium.

McCain Seeks Longer Hiatus For Web Taxes

APRIL 8 — Congress will formally reenter the battle over taxation of the Internet April 13 when Senate Commerce, Science and Transportation Committee Chairman John McCain plans to mark up a measure that would extend the life of a current moratorium on Internet-specific taxes from 2001 to 2006.

The Arizona Republican, who made Internet taxation a main issue in his unsuccessful bid for the GOP presidential nomination, has taken the lead in trying to develop a compromise bill (S 2255) aimed at extending, and perhaps broadening, the current three-year moratorium (PL 105-277) enacted in 1998. *(1998 Almanac, p. 21-19)*

"This is an important issue. And I think the extension of the moratorium will be supported by members of both parties," McCain said.

McCain and Ron Wyden, D-Ore., a cosponsor of the bill, are discussing with other members possible amendments that could be offered in the markup, including a proposal to make any tax ban permanent.

Congress faces two issues regarding Internet taxation. One is Internet-specific taxes, such as possible access fees for services. The second is whether the federal government should step in, as McCain and some other lawmakers have advocated, to ban collection of sales taxes on the value of goods and services sold over the Internet. The current moratorium bars Internet-specific taxes but does not bar states from collecting sales tax on goods sold over the Internet, if companies have brick-and-mortar facilities in their state.

A five-year extension of the current moratorium appears to have strong support from key lawmakers, including House Speaker J. Dennis Hastert, R-Ill., who plans to give a speech on the issue on April 10, and Republican Texas Gov. George W. Bush. The proposal could run into opposition in the full Senate.

Senate Minority Leader Tom Daschle, D-S.D., has argued for keeping the moratorium's current 2001 expiration date in order to keep pressure on Congress, the states and industry to reach a compromise on the issue of whether to ban Internet sales taxes.

As Senate and House lawmakers develop legislation, a special Advisory Commission on Electronic Commerce is preparing to deliver its final report to Congress the week of April 10. McCain's committee will hold a hearing on the commission report April 12.

Virginia Gov. James S. Gilmore III, the chairman of the 19-member panel created by Congress to study taxation on the Internet, summarized the report at a hearing of the House Commerce Committee on April 6.

The panel's recommendations include proposals to extend the moratorium on Internet-specific taxes for five years and to make permanent the ban on Internet access taxes. While those proposals have broad support, the overall report has been mired in controversy because it was approved by only 11 members, two short of the two-thirds majority required to make recommendations to Congress.

One of the report's proposals — opposed by eight of the commission members — was a request to Congress to create a "bright line" codification of activities that would determine whether a business had a presence, or nexus, in a state and was liable to pay sales taxes. Currently, businesses do not remit sales taxes if they have no presence, such as an office, in a buyer's home state.

In the House, the Judiciary Committee is preparing to mark up a bill (HR 3709) sponsored by Christopher Cox, R-Calif., to permanently ban Internet-specific taxes. Cox is expected to revise the bill to provide a five-year extension of the moratorium. Democrats are expected to push for a shorter extension of about three years.

Hastert met with Judiciary Committee Chairman Henry J. Hyde, R-Ill., and Commerce Committee Chairman Thomas J. Bliley Jr., R-Va., on April 6 to discuss strategy for dealing with the Cox bill. The committees share jurisdiction over the measure. Hyde said his panel would deal with the Cox bill in the near future. Bliley echoed his comments: "We want to move as quickly on it as we can." Bliley added that the Cox bill probably would not be broadened to deal with the liability of businesses to remit state sales taxes.

House Panel Approves Bill To Extend Internet Tax Moratorium

MAY 6 — The House could vote as early as May 10 on legislation (HR 3709) that would extend a current moratorium on new Internet-specific taxes until Oct. 21, 2006. The Judiciary Committee swiftly approved the measure on May 4.

"The Internet is fueling our economy like no other sector," Robert W. Goodlatte, R-Va., said at the markup. Goodlatte is co-chairman of the bipartisan Congressional Internet Caucus.

The legislation, approved by a vote of 29-8, would not go as far as many members had sought. The original bill, introduced by Christopher Cox, R-Calif., would have imposed a permanent ban on Internet taxes, such as access charges to hook up to the Web.

Instead, the committee approved a Goodlatte amendment that would provide a five-year extension of the moratorium, set by Congress in 1998 (PL 105-277).

The bill does not address the issue of whether to strengthen states' authority to collect sales taxes on online purchases.

"The larger tax issue for states and localities is clearly that of whether and how they should be able to require sales and use taxes to be collected on sales that occur using the Internet," said Judiciary Chairman Henry J. Hyde, R-Ill., who said the committee would explore the question further.

A use tax, often called a remote tax, is the tax that a consumer owes to his state when he makes a catalogue, phone or Internet purchase from a business in another state.

States can now levy sales taxes only on sellers that have a physical presence, such as a store, inside their boundaries. That leaves it to consumers to report their remote purchases on their state tax forms, a system that states say consumers rarely use.

The National Governors' Association has been trying to work out a system that would make it easier to keep track of online purchases, fearing the loss of billions of dollars in needed revenue as more and more individuals move to Web retailers and away from "brick and mortar" stores. Most governors want Congress to expand states' ability to collect sales taxes.

Some lawmakers, especially Democrats, were frustrated that the bill was marked up without any hearings. But GOP leaders decided to move it quickly as part of a push to pass a handful of high-tech bills this month.

A special bipartisan Advisory Commission on Electronic Commerce, created by Congress to examine issues relating to the Internet economy, recommended placing limits on states' ability to collect sales taxes. The commission report, however, did not receive support from the mandatory two-thirds majority of its members.

Leaders from both parties have been reaching out to the high-technology community and have made legislation such as the Internet tax moratorium and so-called e-signatures bill high priorities.

Getting such measures passed, however, has proved to be problematic.

Senate Commerce, Science and Transportation Committee Chairman John McCain, R-Ariz., had to postpone a planned markup of a parallel measure (S 2255) to extend the moratorium the week of April 10 after running into opposition from governors and traditional retailers.

House Votes To Continue Ban On Internet Taxes

MAY 13 — The House on May 10 moved to extend a current moratorium on Internet-specific taxes for another five years, increasing pressure on a reluctant Senate to act.

Brushing aside protests from state governors — who want expanded authority to collect sales taxes on Internet sales — and bricks-and-mortar retailers, the House by 352-75 passed a bill (HR 3709) that would continue until October 21, 2006, a ban on taxation of data transmission, e-mail and other Internet services. *(Vote 159, p. H-52)*

The current moratorium, enacted in 1998 (PL 105-277), expires in October 2001. The House-passed bill also would erase a grandfather clause in the original, three-year Internet tax moratorium that had permitted states to retain existing taxes on Internet access. Currently, 11 states, including Texas and Ohio, collect an estimated $55 million a year in taxes on Internet access.

The House vote — and a May 10 Commerce Committee markup of a related bill (HR 1291) to prevent the Federal Communications Commission (FCC) from imposing new Internet fees to subsidize universal telephone service — are all part of a concerted push by GOP leaders to reach out to the burgeoning high-tech industry.

Hours before the floor vote, House Majority Leader Dick Armey, R-Texas, unveiled a new House Republican agenda for the new economy.

"Instead of recognizing Internet sales as a wonderful convenience for consumers, big-government bureaucrats see it as another opportunity to levy a tax. Government at every level takes enough of your money," he said.

Armey said the moratorium was the first of three Internet-related tax measures that will be taken up by the House this month. Also on the agenda are the access fee bill and a measure (HR 3916) to repeal a 3 percent federal excise tax on telephone service levied in 1898 to help finance the Spanish-American War.

Democrats accused the GOP of trying to rush legislation through the chamber in a craven effort to build support in the high-tech industry.

"We have passage first, hearings afterwards," said Ralph M. Hall, D-Texas.

High-Speed Committee Approval

The House Commerce Committee made quick work of the access fee measure, approving it by voice vote on May 10. The bill, introduced by Rep. Fred Upton, R-Mich., is expected to come to the House floor the week of May 15.

The panel's speedy action on the access bill disguised growing opposition.

As approved by the committee, the bill would prevent the FCC from levying so-called access charges on monthly Internet service bills to pay for a federal universal service program that subsidizes rural telephone service.

Currently, long-distance carriers are required to pay access charges to local telephone companies at the beginning and finish of each long-distance telephone call. The charges are designed to help local telephone companies cover their costs and to provide funding for the universal service program.

Voice telephone calls carried over the Internet via local telephone lines are not currently subject to access charges. Governors warn that if the market for Internet telephone calls grows, the volume of regular long-distance telephone calls might decline, and local telephone companies could see a drop in revenues from access charges that they need for new equipment and repairs of existing lines.

The Baby Bells and long-distance companies worry that the proposed ban on Internet access fees could put them at a competitive disadvantage.

Upton's measure was tailored to leave open the question of whether access charges — beside those used to pay for universal service — could be imposed on Internet service providers to help local telephone companies recover costs.

A manager's amendment, approved by voice vote, made clear that the FCC would be able to make its own decision on whether to impose any access charges on long-distance voice communications carried over the Internet that compete with long-distance telephone calls.

Upton said the bill was needed in part to help lawmakers respond to a flood of e-mail from constituents who were worried about possible legislation to create access charges on Internet service bills. He said his measure would reassure consumers that such legislation was not being contemplated.

The panel defeated, 8-31, an amendment by Edward J. Markey, D-Mass., that would have encouraged Internet telephone firms to bill customers at a fixed rate, rather than a fee based on per-minute charges.

Commerce Committee Chairman Thomas J. Bliley Jr., R-Va., acknowledged that lawmakers were having trouble reaching agreement on the bill. "A consensus has not developed on what the scope of this legislation should be," he said.

Afterward he said he expected that the bill would nonetheless have strong support when it came to the floor. "I think it will pass easily," he said.

The measure is certain to face heavy opposition in the Senate, where lawmakers such as Ted Stevens, R-Alaska, chairman of the Appropriations Committee, are strong defenders of the universal service program.

Moratorium Opposition

The outlook for enacting a five-year extension of the moratorium on Internet-specific taxes is also dicey.

The key opposition is from states and several trade groups representing bricks-and-mortar retailers, such as the e-Fairness Coalition, which includes Wal-Mart and Target Inc. They argue that the bill does not provide stronger authority sought by states to collect taxes on online purchases.

The bill would not affect sales taxes owed on online purchases. Although states currently are able to collect such taxes, they argue that they are losing revenue because they lack the ability to monitor transactions and cannot force vendors outside their borders to collect the tax.

A recent University of Tennessee study estimated that the 45 states that levy sales taxes, along with local governments across the nation, by 2003 would lose $20 billion annually in uncollected sales taxes on online purchases.

"Merely extending the moratorium while failing to deal with this underlying problem, I think, would be irresponsible," said Spencer Bachus, R-Ala., during the May 10 House debate.

An amendment to shorten the length of the extension from five years to two years was narrowly defeated, 208-219. *(Vote 156, p. H-52)*

Barney Frank, D-Mass., called the vote a choice between a "moratorium or a less-atorium."

States found they could muster support only for a non-binding amendment putting Congress on record that states should move forward to develop a simplified system for collecting "states taxes" on electronic commerce. The amendment was approved, 289-138. *(Vote 157, p. H-52)*

Ernest Istook, R-Okla., the amendment's sponsor, said the measure would provide important support for states' efforts to collect sales taxes on online purchases.

Many lawmakers and governors worry that by 2006, the moratorium will have become too entrenched to be repealed and will lay the groundwork for a ban on collecting sales taxes on the Internet — a development they contend would provide an unfair advantage to online retailers, hurt main-street retailers and cost states billions of dollars in lost revenues.

A plan for simplifying the collection of taxes and creating a compact of states has been developed by the National Governors' Association (NGA). States created the proposal in response to a Supreme Court ruling, in *Quill Corp. v. North Dakota,* in 1992 that found vendors do not have to collect sales taxes if purchasers do not live in states where the companies have a physical presence, such as an office.

Utah Republican Gov. Michael O. Leavitt, who is chairman of the NGA, has warned that the states need federal legislation to authorize the implementation of the plan and stave off the loss of revenue that will come if consumers migrate from shopping malls that pay sales taxes to online outlets that do not.

The NGA is continuing talks with lawmakers of both parties about legislation to implement the plan. The proposal faces strong opposition.

The dispute has stalled the Senate version of the moratorium (S 2255). Commerce, Science and Transportation Committee Chairman John McCain, R-Ariz., has joined Texas Gov. George W. Bush, the presumptive GOP presidential nominee, in supporting an extension of at least five years. On the other side, a two-year extension is backed by some lawmakers of both parties and by the Clinton administration.

On May 9, Senate Majority Leader Trent Lott, R-Miss., suggested splitting the difference between the Bush-backed five-year proposal and the Clinton-backed two-year proposal by providing for "maybe a three-year" extension of the moratorium.

Senate aides of both parties predicted a strong push to resolve the issue in McCain's committee, and if necessary, to attach the measure as a rider to a fiscal 2001 appropriations bill at the end of the session, much like the original 1998 legislation (PL 105-277) that created the moratorium. *(1998 Almanac, p. 2-112)*

But many other lawmakers of both parties appear willing to put off the debate on sales taxes until later in the session or until the 107th Congress.

"We will have hearings on the issue of sales taxes, but I am doubtful that it will result in legislation," said Rep. Robert W. Goodlatte, R-Va., a sponsor of the bill.

House Passes Bill To Keep FCC From Charging Fees For Internet Access

MAY 20 — House Republican leaders pressed forward with their election year drive to ensure minimal regulation in the telecommunications market.

On May 16, the House passed by voice vote a bill (HR 1291) that would prevent the Federal Communications Commission (FCC) from imposing per-minute access charges on monthly Internet service bills if such fees were used to support the federal Universal Service Fund. The fund subsidizes telephone services to rural and high-cost areas and Internet connections at schools and libraries.

The FCC had no plans to levy such charges, and no bill has been introduced to do so. The House mounted a pre-emptive strike, spurred by an Internet-fueled rumor about impending new fees that prompted a flood of e-mail from constituents to members' offices.

John D. Dingell of Michigan, ranking Democrat on the House Commerce Committee, called the vote "Kafkaesque" because it was a counterattack to a fictitious bill.

Still, the votes bolstered an agenda that supporters have touted as a way of encouraging further growth of the Internet and related technologies while narrowing the "digital divide" by getting poorer Americans connected to the World Wide Web. The House voted May 10 to extend the current moratorium on Internet-specific taxes for another five years.

Components of the agenda that remain unresolved include electronic signatures legislation (S 761) and proposals (HR 3615, S 2097) that would create a government loan program to enhance television reception in rural areas.

The measure generated some partisan friction, though it is supported by many Republicans and Democrats. Some members objected to the bill's failure to provide protections against taxing voice transmissions over the Internet.

A corresponding measure (S 2330) has been introduced in the Senate by William V. Roth Jr., R-Del., and John B. Breaux, D-La.

Some Democrats ridiculed the bill because it was prompted by a hoax. Dingell and Edward J. Markey, D-Mass., also accused Republicans of using the measure to help Internet providers avoid paying into the Universal Service Fund. ◆

Effort to Repeal Century-Old Phone Tax Fizzles Out At End of 106th Congress

SUMMARY

One of the Republicans' last hopes for cutting taxes — legislation to repeal the 3 percent federal excise tax on telephones — died as the session came to a close.

The tax, first enacted in 1898 to help finance the Spanish-American War, was widely regarded as archaic and regressive. The House voted overwhelmingly May 25 (HR 3916) to phase the levy over three years, at an estimated cost of $19.9 billion over five years. Democrats and Republicans said the levy was a burden on the poor that could widen the so-called digital divide, limiting disadvantaged people's access to the Internet. The Senate Fi-

Box Score

- **Bills:** HR 3916, HR 4516
- **Legislative action: House** passed HR 3916 (H Rept 106-631), 420-2, May 25.

House adopted the conference report on HR 4516 (H Rept 106-796), 212-209, on Sept. 14.

Senate cleared HR 4516, 58-37, on Oct. 12.

President vetoed HR 4516 on Oct. 30.

nance Committee approved an amended version of the bill (S Rept 106-328) on June 14, proposing to repeal the tax in full on all phone bills after Aug. 31 at an estimated cost of $24.2 billion over five years.

The White House was lukewarm to the idea, saying a repeal should not be put before other budget priorities, such as shoring up Medicare and Social Security. The administration also said it wanted to see the entire Republican tax package for the year before deciding whether to accept any one piece.

Uncertain about the fate of their other tax proposals, GOP leaders folded the three-year phase-out into the conference report on (HR 4516) the fiscal 2001 Treasury-Postal Service and legislative branch appropriations bills. President Clinton vetoed that package Oct. 30. *(Treasury-Postal Service appropriations, p. 2-138)*

The original 1 percent phone tax had been imposed on long-distance service at a time when telephones were a luxury. Congress repealed it in 1902 but brought it back to help pay for World War I. The tax was repealed again in 1924 but resurrected in 1932 during the Great Depression. In 1941, it was extended to general local service to help pay for World War II. The tax was increased to 3 percent in 1982 and made permanent in 1990 as part of balanced-budget efforts.

House Panel OKs Bill to Repeal Telephone Tax

MAY 20 — The House Ways and Means Committee approved by voice vote May 17 a bill (HR 3916) that would repeal the 3 percent federal excise tax on telephone service. The tax was enacted in 1898 to finance the Spanish-American War when there were just 1,376 telephones in the United States.

"It's a classic example of a tax that, once it is imposed by Washington, just never seems to die," said Republican Rob Portman of Ohio, a cosponsor of the measure offered by Robert T. Matsui, D-Calif.

The bill has wide support from telecommunications companies and small-business and minority groups, and is expected to move to the House floor the week of May 22. Its future is uncertain, however, because the Clinton administration has offered only a lukewarm endorsement. That has raised the prospect that a tax repeal could become the focus of a budgetary showdown between Republican congressional leaders and President Clinton.

Portman and Matsui argued that the tax is regressive and unnecessary during a time of federal budget surpluses.

Under an amendment offered by Ways and Means Chairman Bill Archer, R-Texas, and adopted by voice vote, the tax would be phased out by October 2002. The budgetary impact is estimated at $19.9 billion over five years.

Treasury Secretary Lawrence H. Summers, in a May 17 letter to Archer, said repeal of the tax, while worthy in principle, must be balanced against the need to extend the solvency of Social Security and Medicare and pay down the national debt.

But House Speaker J. Dennis Hastert, R-Ill., said in a May 17 statement, "If the president cannot support the repeal of this ridiculous tax, where will he agree to bring tax fairness to the American people?"

House Passes Phone-Tax Repeal

MAY 27 — The legislative campaign to scrap the 3 percent federal excise tax on telephones took another step forward May 25 when the House overwhelmingly passed legislation (HR 3916) to repeal it by a vote of 420-2. *(Vote 233, p. H-74)*

The move followed House Ways and Means Committee approval of the bill May 17.

The stage is now set for possible Senate action later this year. A similar, though not identical, bill (S 2330) was introduced in March by William V. Roth Jr., R-Del., and John B. Breaux, D-La.

Many Senate Republicans and Democrats view the tax as a burden on the poor and elderly that could widen the so-called digital divide, limiting disadvantaged people's access to the Internet.

"The tax on talking poses an unfair burden on low-income families, seniors on fixed incomes and small businesses struggling to make ends meet," Breaux said in a statement May 25.

Passage of the House bill, sponsored by Rob Portman, R-Ohio, and Robert T. Matsui, D-Calif., came after Democrats unsuccessfully offered a motion to send the bill back to Ways and Means with instructions to include an amendment that would have required certain tax-exempt organizations to reveal the identities of their donors. The motion to recommit was rejected, 208-214. *(Vote 232, p. H-74)*

The telephone excise tax was enacted by Congress to finance the Spanish-American War more than 100 years ago.

Republicans made much of the vote, holding a rally outside the Capitol featuring a Theodore Roosevelt impersonator and Spanish-American War re-enactors.

"Getting tax relief through Congress is often a rough ride and a tough ride," said Speaker J. Dennis Hastert, R-Ill. "The Spanish-American War tax ought to be history as well."

The budgetary impact of the repeal is estimated at $19.9 billion over five years. Portman said current budget surpluses and economic prosperity make it a good time to strike the tax.

The White House remains lukewarm to the idea. Treasury Secretary Lawrence H. Summers, in a May 17 letter to Ways and Means Chairman Bill Archer, R-Texas, said repeal of the tax, while a worthy policy objective, should not be placed before other budget priorities, such as shoring up Medicare and Social Security.

Senate Committee Approves Bill By Voice Vote

JUNE 17 — Legislation to repeal the federal excise tax on telephones continued its fast ride June 14, when the Senate Finance Committee approved its version of a House-passed bill (HR 3916) to scrap the 3 percent charge.

Lawmakers, by voice vote, agreed to an amendment, in the nature of a substitute, offered by Chairman William V. Roth Jr., R-Del., that would repeal the tax in full on all phone bills after Aug. 31. The repeal would reduce government revenues by an estimated $24.2 billion over five years.

"For too long, while America is listening to a dial tone, Washington has been hearing a dollar tone," Roth said. "Let us hang up the phone tax once and for all."

The vote sets the stage for Senate floor action and a House-Senate conference to resolve rival versions of the legislation. The bill that passed the House on May 25 by a vote of 420-2 would phase out the tax over three years. The budgetary impact has been estimated at $19.9 billion over five years.

Roth said the tax, first enacted in 1898 to help finance the Spanish-American War, creates hardships for low-income families and should be eliminated.

Committee Democrats, who generally support the repeal, warned that it should not be placed ahead of other priorities for the budget surplus, such as bolstering the Social Security and Medicare trust funds.

Bob Graham, D-Fla., offered an amendment with Charles S. Robb, D-Va., and Richard H. Bryan, D-Nev., to delay repeal of the tax until after Congress passes legislation extending the solvency of the Social Security trust funds to 2075 and the Medicare trust funds to 2025. The amendment was rejected, 9-11, along party lines.

"In government, as in our private lives, we should have some sense of priorities," Graham said. "I would not place repeal of the 3 percent phone tax as a very high national priority."

The Clinton administration has voiced similar misgivings about the phone tax repeal, especially when viewed with separate proposals to gradually eliminate inheritance taxes. The House voted 279-136 on June 9 to repeal the tax on estates, gifts and trust funds over the next 10 years.

Most Republican and Democratic lawmakers view the phone tax as archaic and regressive and want to use passage of the measure to bolster their parties' election-year, technology-friendly agendas.

The original 1 percent phone tax was imposed on long-distance service at a time when telephones were a luxury. Congress repealed it in 1902 but brought it back to help pay for World War I. The tax was repealed again in 1924 but resurrected in 1932 during the Great Depression. In 1941, it was extended to general local service to help pay for World War II. The tax was increased to 3 percent in 1982; in 1990, Congress made it permanent as part of efforts to reduce the federal budget deficit. ◆

Chapter 19

TELECOMMUNICATIONS

Bipartisan Compromise Reached to Allow Electronic Signatures in Business Deals

SUMMARY

On June 30, President Clinton signed into law a bill authorizing the use of electronic signatures to close business deals over the Internet. The final bill, a hard-fought bipartisan compromise, was hailed by both parties as a milestone that would spur much wider use of the Internet while also protecting consumers from fraud.

The House and Senate had produced significantly different versions of the bill in the first session, setting the stage for a contentious conference in 2000. Conferees remained stalemated for weeks, largely over issues that went beyond the electronic signature provisions in both bills.

The House bill, backed by a wide range of business groups, offered companies the option of providing loan terms and other consumer protection information electronically to consumers who preferred to receive it that way. It also sought to pre-empt state laws that required companies to keep original paper records of transactions. Financial services companies, in particular, hoped that reducing paperwork would produce major savings in paper handling and storage costs. The Senate measure, which would have given states wide leeway to continue requiring paper records, had the support of consumer groups and state governors, who worried that a rush to electronic commerce could outstrip anti-fraud laws designed for a paper-based society.

A compromise finally was reached June 8, after Sen. Phil Gramm, R-Texas, a champion of the financial services companies, agreed to concessions on consumer protections offered by House Commerce Committee Chairman Thomas J. Bliley Jr., R-Va., to assuage key Democrats.

The final bill gives deals signed electronically the same legal standing as paper contracts. Consumers can open bank accounts, transfer money and buy big-ticket items such as automobiles without having to sign any paper. But the bill also requires companies to verify that customers have the necessary technology to receive electronic records before they waive their right to receive paper copies. Customers must consent in a manner that "reasonably demonstrates" they can open the electronic files, and they can opt out of the agreement at any time. Some sensitive documents, such as wills, court orders, eviction notices and product recalls, still will be provided on paper. The bill also requires that new regulations be developed to ensure that electronic data is stored in a way that prevents tampering.

BoxScore

- **Bill:** S 761 — PL 106-229
- **Legislative action: House** passed S 761, amended by voice vote Feb. 16.

House adopted the conference report on S 761 (H Rept 106-661), 426-4, on June 14.

Senate cleared the bill, 87-0, on June 16.

President signed S 761 on June 30.

Conferees Work To Satisfy Demand For Safeguards

MAY 20 — House and Senate negotiators have narrowed their differences on a bill (S 761) to authorize the use of electronic signatures to seal business and legal transactions via the Internet, leaving GOP leaders hopeful of quickly clinching a deal.

After conferees finished their first formal gathering May 18, Senate Majority Leader Trent Lott, R-Miss., said that he would host a follow-up meeting of GOP leaders early in the week of May 22 to resolve remaining differences. Republican negotiators have agreed among themselves on a draft bill, but disagree about how far to go in making revisions to satisfy Democrats. "We're going to have to have a meeting on that Monday or Tuesday of next week," Lott said. "I understand there may be a couple of unresolved issues."

There is broad, bipartisan support in Congress for allowing business deals to be started and completed on the Internet by authorizing the use of electronic signatures such as a name written on a touch-sensitive computer screen or electronic coding.

There is disagreement, however, on two main points. Democrats want tougher safeguards than the GOP has recommended to ensure that consumers can actually receive online documents.

Further, Democrats want federal and state agencies to have the continued power to require the use of paper, rather than electronic, documents if they deem it necessary to prevent fraud, or if agencies need more time to develop the ability to receive electronic communications.

Some states have adopted a model law that would authorize the use of electronic signatures, and governors have questioned the wisdom of broad federal legislation. But supporters of the bill argue there is a need for a uniform national standard that gives businesses leeway, without intervention by state or federal agencies.

Democrats have complained that they were largely left out of GOP negotiations that produced the draft bill. Ranking House Commerce Committee Democrat John D. Dingell, of Michigan, charged that "after nearly two months of negotiations among themselves" Republicans had produced a bill that was biased against consumers.

Silicon Valley companies, worried that the electronic signatures bill could get bogged down, have been quietly urging Republican lawmakers to address Democrats' concerns.

The sharp differences between the parties began to soften a bit during bipartisan staff meetings that began May 17. Clinton administration officials joined in the discussions.

By the time the conferees met on May 18, there were signs that both sides might be willing to give ground. House Commerce Committee Chairman Thomas J. Bliley Jr., R-Va., chairman of the conference, wants the negotiators to send a bill to the White House before Memorial Day.

"We are very close to a final agreement," Bliley said during the meeting.

Electronic Records

Bliley said he believed progress was being made on the main sticking point: a requirement that consumers be able to receive electronic documents from businesses, such as automobile recall notices or summaries of loan terms.

Democrats have insisted that any final bill include language to require consumers to demonstrate they can receive electronic versions of important documents before they waive their right to obtain written copies.

In a 13-page critique of the Republicans' draft bill, however, Democrats backed away from tough provisions they had been advocating that would guarantee consumers received electronic documents by requiring them to give their consent to receive electronic records in the same e-mail format that would be used to send the documents.

New, proposed Democratic language would require consumers to give their consent instead by some electronic means such as e-mail or clicking on a pop-up box on an Internet Web site. The electronic consent would have to be provided "in a manner that reasonably confirms the capacity of the consumer to access information in the electronic form that will be used to provide the information."

Bliley was hopeful of working out an agreement. He and some other GOP negotiators have been privately sympathetic to the Democratic call for tougher consumer safeguards.

Sen. Paul S. Sarbanes, D-Md., said the need for verification language was proven by the fact that staff aides, themselves, had difficulty circulating the draft bill via e-mail because it was written in a format incompatible with some computers in Congress.

Another key issue is a dispute over the authority of federal agencies to implement the law and set terms for use of electronic records in business deals and government-related activities.

The draft bill would not allow agencies to impose "any requirement that a record be in a tangible printed or paper form." Democrats argue that agencies should be allowed to require the use of paper if they think it is necessary.

"We don't want agencies to have so much authority that it guts the bill," said one industry lobbyist.

Some Republicans, including Senate Banking, Housing and Urban Affairs Committee Phil Gramm, R-Texas, are reluctant to make further compromises. Gramm argued that the draft bill was already likely to win strong bipartisan support and questioned whether critics would vote against a bill that is a top priority of the high-tech industry.

"Don't take a hostage unless you're willing to shoot it," Gramm said. "They've taken a hostage here that they're not willing to shoot."

Still, top negotiators said progress was being made.

Bliley Makes Deal With Democrats, But Gramm Says He Went Too Far

MAY 27 — House Commerce Committee Chairman Thomas J. Bliley Jr., R-Va., held out an olive branch to Democrats by making major concessions in a draft conference report on a bill (S 761) to authorize the use of electronic signatures to seal contracts on the Internet.

Industry and top Republicans balked at some of the revisions, however, and lawmakers expect more negotiations after the Memorial Day recess.

Capping weeks of effort, Bliley on May 23 worked out a compromise on the bill with key Democrats, including Sens. Patrick J. Leahy of Vermont and Ron Wyden of Oregon. The legislation would let consumers seal online contracts or business deals with electronic signatures, such as a chain of computer code.

"It's a solid and reasonable consensus bill," Leahy said. He and other senators signed the conference report May 25. Democratic Reps. John D. Dingell of Michigan and Edward J. Markey of Massachusetts were prepared to sign a similar document. Bliley was continuing to review the text.

Lawmakers' efforts to craft a final bill had been hung up for weeks on the issue of how far to go to pre-empt state consumer protection laws that require paper copies of documents.

Further, there was disagreement about how or whether companies should be required to guarantee delivery of electronic notices, such as product recall warnings and summaries of loan terms, to consumers who agree to accept e-mail or posted messages on an Internet site.

Bliley and key lawmakers satisfied the concerns of consumer groups by agreeing to language that would require companies to verify that customers had the necessary technology to receive electronic records before waiving their right to receive paper copies. In addition, Bliley decided to give states leeway to craft their own version of legislation on electronic signatures and records.

News of the deal, which is also supported by Senate Commerce, Science and Transportation Committee Chairman John McCain, R-Ariz., triggered a flurry of behind-the-scenes meetings to try to assuage the concerns of some other pivotal lawmakers, including Senate Banking, Housing and Urban Affairs Committee Chairman Phil Gramm, R-Texas.

Gramm criticized the negotiators' language as too broad and said it would put time-consuming demands on companies to verify that consumers could receive electronic messages.

The Texas Republican has been a champion of financial services companies that want to remove restrictions that they fear would prevent or discourage consumers from using e-mail instead of paper to communicate with companies.

Elimination of paper is considered vital to companies that are hoping to market loans, credit cards and insurance policies over the Internet and to provide customer service electronically instead of at a bank teller's counter or by telephone.

Hours after the bipartisan agreement was reached, Gramm made his case to House and Senate Republican leaders in the office of Senate Majority Leader Trent Lott, R-Miss., on May 24.

Lott has been seeking a quick deal on the legislation, which he calls the "electronic commerce bill." He knows the measure is important to the high-technology community, and also hopes it can become a vehicle for moving to the floor other legislation including the bankruptcy overhaul (HR 833). *(Bankruptcy, p. 5-3)*

Gramm Is Insistent

Staff aides tried to resolve two key issues May 25, but did not satisfy all the objections of critics.

Gramm is insisting on revisions in language that would set new standards to determine whether consumers have given their consent to receive electronic records instead of paper documents.

Gramm said May 24 he was determined to fight for changes in the bill and expressed strong support for an idea floated by House Majority Leader Dick Armey, R-Texas, to eliminate, or sunset, the consumer consent provisions after four years. The idea was rejected by other negotiators.

"I don't think it's good for America," Gramm said. "There would be more hoops to jump through for e-commerce than for paper commerce. That's a bad precedent to set."

Democrats won a key round May 24 when a number of House and Senate negotiators agreed to language that would require consumers to give their consent, or to confirm they have given consent, by an electronic means that "reasonably demonstrates that the consumer can access the information" sent in an electronic record. Consumer groups fear that e-mail documents could be sent in a format incompatible with a consumer's computer, which would render them unreadable

In addition to the issue of language to ensure companies verify that consumers can receive electronic records, financial services companies were focusing on a section of the bill that would trump most state laws that require the use of paper and would ensure companies could provide electronic records in place of written documents.

Industry was concerned that the bill, while pre-empting existing state laws that require the use of paper, would allow states to enact a model law that could require the use of paper.

Financial services companies circulated a letter May 25, signed by more than 20 firms and trade groups, urging broader language to ensure that paper requirements set by states would be pre-empted by the proposed law.

But Bliley and other supporters of the compromise said they were confident their deal would stand.

"We're getting closer," Bliley said May 24. "I think we're almost there."

Progress Slows On Internet Bills Despite Pressure From Industry

JUNE 10 — While high-tech industry executives pressed their case on Capitol Hill the week of June 5, Congressional leaders met behind the scenes to try to work out deals on Silicon Valley initiatives ranging from extending a moratorium on Internet-specific taxes to a bill authorizing the use of electronic signatures to seal online contracts.

The industry's agenda sits atop the must-do lists of both parties as they race to raise campaign donations for the November election. Even with the industry's growing clout, it has been a struggle to craft compromises on several technology-related issues.

So far, lawmakers have proved more adept at collecting contributions than in moving their legislative agenda.

"We will work these things out," Senate Majority Leader Trent Lott, R-Miss, said on June 6. "But it's going to take some time."

In renewed talks during the week, a conference report on a bill (S 761, H Rept 106-661) to authorize the use of electronic versions of written signatures and documents was completed. Senate Banking, Housing and Urban Affairs Committee Chairman Phil Gramm, R-Texas, who had demanded that House and Senate negotiators grant additional concessions to the financial services industry, said he would vote for the final deal.

A second bill, to increase the number of skilled foreign workers temporarily allowed into United States (S 2045), continued to languish off the Senate floor, with opponents announcing a stepped-up ad campaign criticizing bill supporters. *(H-1B visas, p. 15-3)*

There was a glimmer of good news for governors, who want the Senate to add provisions to any extension of the moratorium on new Internet taxes (S 2255) giving them greater power to collect existing sales taxes on online purchases.

In testimony to the Joint Economic Committee on June 6, Intel Corp. Chairman Andrew S. Grove broke ranks with other business leaders who oppose the governors' proposal. Grove gave explicit support to the states' battle and backed efforts by lawmakers to set minimum standards for consumer privacy protection on the Internet.

In response to a question from Sen. Ted Stevens, R-Alaska, Grove said he had intentionally avoided mentioning the privacy and Internet tax issues in his opening statement.

"I'm kind of in a minority position. And I'm afraid of being hit by my colleagues from the back," Grove said.

"My feeling is that our industry, or those parts of our industry that are asking for a tax-advantaged treatment of commerce on the Internet, are ill-advised," he said. He called for developing "a fair and legally appropriate system for collecting taxes" on online goods.

Other executives, including Microsoft Corp. Chairman Bill Gates and Hewlett-Packard Co. President and CEO Carleton S. Fiorina, focused on broad issues such as education and China trade while making their rounds on Capitol Hill.

Gates underscored the industry's importance to the economy, while avoiding mention of specific bills or a Justice Department antitrust case against his company. A federal judge on June 7 handed down an order that, if upheld on appeal, would split Microsoft into two firms.

"This is a time of unprecedented prosperity and growth, a good deal of it generated by the high-tech industry," Gates said. "The United States has been fortunate to lead the way, but we cannot rest on present laurels or past achievements."

Sealing the Deal

Lawmakers and lobbyists cut a deal on an industry-backed bill to authorize the use of electronic signatures to seal legal contracts or other business transactions.

Under the bill, consumers would have to give their consent to receive documents electronically, and companies would have to verify that they were able, technologically, to receive them. Further, consumers could chose to stop receiving electronic documents.

Another provision would allow such sensitive documents as eviction notices, court orders, gas or water cancellations, or product recalls to be issued on paper.

Gramm had pushed in behalf of banks for revisions in a deal that Commerce Committee Chairman Thomas J. Bliley Jr., R-Va., chairman of the conference committee on the bill, cut with Democrats on May 23.

Bliley agreed to revise his May 23 agreement, adding new concessions aimed at winning support from business groups. The revisions would bar states from favoring any specific technology for transmitting or receiving electronic signatures and records.

Bliley also agreed to a deadline of March 1, 2001 — seven months earlier than originally proposed — for federal and state agencies to complete rules that would specify how they would maintain required records for auditing purposes.

One major concern has been that it would be easier for individuals to tamper with documents stored electronically than with existing paper files. States and the Justice Department wanted more time to develop such rules. They fear that a move toward a paperless society could hinder efforts at law enforcement.

Financial services companies have made reduction of paperwork a priority. The firms are hoping for major cost savings in paper handling and storage costs by converting written documents to computer files.

In a June 9 statement, Gramm said that he could support the final compromise agreement.

"The electronic signature bill is an important step into the future that establishes legal footing for electronic commerce, which, over time, will be parallel to the existing paper-based commerce," Gramm said.

Gramm praised changes in the final bill that would close what he called a loophole that would have allowed some states to use both paper and electronic notification, but said he was still concerned that there would be a delay in the ability of financial services to use electronic commerce.

With Gramm's backing and the support of other Republicans , including Sen. Spencer Abraham, R-Mich., House and Senate aides were optimistic about possible House floor action the week of June 12.

"On the whole, this is very good legislation, it is superior to existing law," Abraham said June 8.

Taxes Also Undone

While negotiations continued on the electronic signatures legislation, a stalemate continued on a bill to extend the current moratorium on Internet-specific taxes, such as charges on e-mail or monthly Internet service bills. The legislation would extend the current online tax moratorium to Dec. 31, 2006, from October 2001.

Senate Commerce, Science and Transportation Committee Chairman John McCain, R-Ariz., said he was continuing to consider a compromise sponsored by Byron L. Dorgan, D-N.D., on behalf of the National Governors' Association, to broaden the authority of states to collect sales taxes on the Internet.

McCain said June 6 that he had discussed the need for equity in sales taxes paid by online businesses and brick-and-mortar stores with Intel's Grove about two weeks ago. He had not decided whether to deal with the issue of sales tax equity in legislation.

Dorgan's draft proposal would give any state that agreed to set a uniform sales tax rate for its residents the authority to collect that tax on remote sellers of goods and services.

Lott said June 6 he did not plan to move a similar House-passed bill (HR 3709) to the floor "unless the decision is made that's the only way to go." Lott was optimistic that the Senate would move quickly on other parts of the high-tech agenda, including legislation (HR 4444) to promote trade with China.

Senate Clears Bill As Gramm Gives In on Consumer Protections

JUNE 17 — The Senate cleared a bill (S 761) June 16 to authorize the use of electronic signatures to close business deals over the Internet, laying the groundwork for a new generation of digital contracts displayed on computer screens and sealed with the touch of a mouse or scrawled moniker on an electronic sketchpad.

The final conference report, produced after a hard-fought bipartisan compromise was reached on June 8, was hailed by both parties as a milestone that would encourage much wider use of the Internet

Under the measure, deals signed electronically would have the same legal standing as paper contracts. Consumers would be able to open bank accounts, transfer money and buy big-ticket items such as automobiles without having to sign any paper.

"We are saving time. We are saving frustration. We are saving trees," said House Majority Leader Dick Armey, R-Texas. House Commerce Committee Chairman Thomas J. Bliley, Jr., R-Va., who was also chairman of the conference committee, called the bill "the most important high-technology vote" of the year.

The House passed the bill by an overwhelming 426-4 vote on June 14. The Senate cleared the bill, 87-0. *(House vote 271, p. H-86; Senate vote 133, S-26)*

President Clinton, who was expected to sign the bill in a White House ceremony, called it an important legal cornerstone that would encourage use of the Internet, while also protecting purchasers from fraud. The White House played a key role in including strong consumer protections.

"It will encourage the information technology revolution that has helped lower inflation, raise productivity and spur new research and development," Clinton said on June 14. "By marrying one of our oldest values — our commitment to consumer protection — with the newest technologies, we can achieve the full measure of the benefits that e-commerce has to offer."

Consumers would have to give consent to receive electronic documents and could opt out of agreements at any time. Some sensitive documents, such as wills, court orders, product recalls and eviction notices, still would be provided on paper.

Businesses expect to save millions of dollars by speeding up transactions and storing data electronically, rather than on paper. However, the legislation requires the development of new regulations to ensure that electronic data is stored in a way that prevents tampering.

E-Signature Bill Highlights

ISSUE	DESCRIPTION
Legal Standing	The bill (S 761, H Rept 106-661) would generally give online legal or financial agreements, signed with a digital signature or chain of electronic code, the same legal standing as traditional paper documents. It would not, however, eliminate requirements that sensitive documents such as wills, eviction notices, court orders or suspension of utilities, product recalls or documents pertaining to hazardous materials be issued and retained on paper.
Consumer Protections	Consumers would have to give prior consent to receive online documents and could opt out at any time to again receive agreements on paper. Firms would have to reasonably demonstrate that individuals had the necessary software or other equipment to receive documents electronically. If the hardware or software used to transmit data changed substantially, firms would have to provide updated information to clients. Companies would have to tell consumers of their right to receive information in non-electronic form.
Record Retention	The law would take effect Oct. 1, 2000, except for provisions requiring entities to detail how they will store electronic records in a way that prevents tampering. That would kick in March 1, 2001.

Possible Privacy Precedent

While lawmakers of both parties declared victory, wrangling over the meaning of a key consumer consent provision in the measure continued until the final floor votes. The interpretation was considered crucial for clarifying the responsibilities of consumers and businesses in holding up their respective ends of online business deals.

The final bill would require companies to get explicit consent from consumers before they provide electronic versions of important written documents via e-mail. Consumers would be required to provide consent in a manner that "reasonably demonstrates" they can open electronic files.

Financial service industry lobbyists, and their champion, Senate Banking, Housing and Urban Affairs Committee Chairman Phil Gramm, R-Texas, fought unsuccessfully to delete that provision in conference and, later, to add a provision sunsetting the requirement.

Gramm finally backed down and bowed to the language worked out in late May by Senate Commerce, Science and Transportation Committee Chairman John McCain, R-Ariz., Bliley and key Democrats, including Rep. John D. Dingell of Michigan and Sens. Ron Wyden of Oregon and Patrick J. Leahy of Vermont.

Gramm and other critics were still concerned, however, that the language would lead to lawsuits over the question of what it means for a consumer to reasonably demonstrate that he can open an e-mail attachment. Gramm hinted that the fight could continue in the next Congress. "We will probably go back and do a cleanup with respect to our jurisdiction," he said June 15.

In a colloquy on the House floor with Rep. Edward J. Markey, D-Mass., Bliley said companies could fulfill their consent obligation by sending a sample message to a consumer in an e-mail attachment. The recipient then would have to send an e-mail to the company stating that he had received, opened and read the attachment.

The language and the colloquy could have a ripple effect on other legislation. McCain said the e-signatures bill could set a precedent for developing legislation to ensure protection of consumer privacy on the Internet.

McCain has been considering proposals to require companies to get a consumer's agreement before they can share or resell personal information they collect. A key question has been that of how consumers could provide that consent. An e-mail message could be one means. *(Internet privacy, p. 19-15)*

Businesses have argued for much more lenient self-regulation that would encourage companies to post privacy policies and would not require written consent from consumers.

"It could become a model for discussion," McCain said of the e-signatures bill on June 15.

State Pre-Emption

Businesses were hopeful that another part of the bill would set a precedent: broad, federal pre-emption of state and federal regulations that now require the retention of paper financial records. Businesses want to establish federal standards for doing business on the Internet, in order to head off a patchwork of possibly contradictory state laws.

The bill would establish a uniform March 1 deadline after which the electronic record-keeping provisions in the bill, allowing businesses to store most data on computers, take effect. Federal agencies initially argued for a later effective date, saying they needed more time to develop regulations and standards.

State and federal agencies would not be able to implement new electronic record-keeping standards before March 1. If they were not finished writing new rules by that date, they would have until June 1 to complete the work.

The American Council of Life Insurers said the uniform March 1 deadline would ensure businesses were on an even footing.

"Earlier versions would have allowed regulators of any business to speed up the starting date. The problem for the insurance industry in this connection is that those industries with a single regulator stood a very good chance of getting permission to enter the paperless era before insurers, who are regulated by 50 different states and the District of Columbia," the group said in a press release.

The conference report was something that both parties and a wide range of business and consumer groups could praise after months of hard negotiation that began in February.

Bliley, on the House floor, seemed relieved that the acrimony had ended. It is much better to negotiate, he said, than to "stand on opposite sides of the room and throw rhetorical grenades at each other." ◆

Congress Acts to Help Provide Better Television Access for Rural Areas

SUMMARY

Congress agreed to create a loan guarantee program to help rural satellite and cable systems deliver local broadcast stations to viewers who do not have access to local television channels. The measure was enacted as part of the fiscal 2000 Commerce-Justice-State appropriations bill.

During the 1999 appropriations process, Senate leaders agreed to delete the loan guarantee program from a broader bill aimed at allowing satellite services to transmit local stations. Republican Phil Gramm of Texas, chairman of Senate Banking, Housing, and Urban Affairs Committee, objected that the loan guarantee program had not been examined by his committee. The compromise, reached as part of clearing an omnibus spending measure (PL 106-113), required that Congress begin debate on the program by March 30, 2000. *(1999 Almanac, p. 22-3)*

Proponents of the loan guarantees argued they would insure that rural residents could receive local broadcast signals. Residents in rural areas often cannot receive the broadcast signals of the major networks from the nearest metropolitan area.

Satellite and cable systems argue that they do not have the money or the broadcast spectrum to expand their coverage to include these signals.

The Senate passed a bill (S 2097) in March that sought to authorize a $1.25 billion loan program and guarantee up to 80 percent of each loan.

The similar House bill (HR 3615), passed in April, also called for a $1.25 billion program, with loans guaranteed up to a limit of 80 percent. The measure was a compromise between a $1 billion program with an 80 percent limit on loan guarantees approved by the Commerce Committee, and a $1.25 billion program with guarantees of up to 100 percent approved by the Agriculture Committee. The bill called for the loans to be administered by the Rural Utilities Service (RUS), a Department of Agriculture agency that oversees a $42 billion loan portfolio supporting rural telecommunications, electric and water projects.

Lawmakers voiced some concern over two audits that questioned the effectiveness of the RUS and over the bill's cost. Congressional Budget Office Director Dan L. Crippen estimated that it would translate into a taxpayer subsidy of $350 million.

After months of negotiations over the details, House and Senate negotiators agreed to a $1.25 billion loan program and an 80 percent loan guarantee, with loans available to cable companies only for use in providing service to areas that are currently unserved. The compromise was included in the appropriations bill for the departments of Commerce, Justice, State and the federal judiciary (HR 4942), which was cleared Oct. 27. *(CJS appropriations, p. 2-23)*

Box Score

- **Bill:** HR 4942 — PL 106-553
- **Legislative action: Senate** passed S 2097 (S Rept 106-243), 97-0, on March 30.

House passed HR 3615, (H Rept 106-508, Parts 1,2), amended, 375-37, on April 13.

House adopted the conference report on HR 4942 (H Rept 106-1005), 206-198, on Oct. 26.

Senate cleared the bill, 48-43, on Oct. 27.

House adopted the conference on HR 4577 (H Rept 106-1033), 292-60, on Dec. 15.

Senate cleared the bill by voice vote Dec. 15.

President signed the bill Dec. 21.

House Agriculture Committee Approves Satellite TV Loan Bill

FEBRUARY 19 — The House Agriculture Committee approved, by a 41-0 vote, legislation Feb. 16 that would provide loan guarantees to help underwrite satellite transmission of local TV stations in rural areas.

The measure (HR 3615) would authorize the Agriculture Department's Rural Utilities Service to guarantee up to $1.25 billion in loans to businesses and organizations to build infrastructure for delivering satellite service to sparsely populated areas.

Rep. Robert W. Goodlatte, R-Va., the bill's author, expects easy passage in the House. He said without the guarantees, more than 50 percent of the nation's 6 million-plus satellite subscribers could not get local signals.

The debate now moves to the Senate, where the Banking, Housing and Urban Affairs Committee must produce legislation by March 30 under a deal struck in November. At that time, Senate leaders agreed to fold a bill allowing satellite services to carry local signals into the omnibus spending bill (PL 106-113) while stripping out the loan guarantees so they could be considered separately. Chairman Phil Gramm, R-Texas, expects to produce a bill by the end of February.

Meanwhile, the Congressional Budget Office released a report Feb. 9 that says the government would have to pay an additional $350 million to provide local signals to 3 million homes.

Senators Unveil Satellite TV Subsidy Bill

FEBRUARY 26 — Moving quickly on an issue that has bipartisan support, Senate Banking, Housing and Urban Affairs Chairman Phil Gramm, R-Texas, and Sen. Conrad Burns, R-Mont., introduced legislation Feb. 24 that would establish a loan guarantee program to underwrite transmission of local television stations in rural areas.

The measure addresses an issue that was left hanging last year during deliberations over a sweeping satellite television bill (S 1948). The new bill comes despite warnings from the Congressional Budget Office (CBO) that government-backed loans for rural TV service could be financially risky and leave taxpayers bearing the cost of unprofitable ventures.

The bill is the product of a series of hearings Gramm held in the Banking Committee in February that highlighted the scattershot nature of television reception in rural states. Republican and Democratic lawmakers from such states as Montana, Wyoming and Arkansas complained that constituents who rely on satellite dishes for TV reception cannot receive signals from their nearest broadcast market and must watch less useful news originating from such faraway cities as New York or Los Angeles.

The House Agriculture Committee on Feb. 16 approved, 41-0, a similar bill (HR 3615) authored by Rep. Robert W. Goodlatte, R-Va.

House Republican leaders have not determined whether the legislation should also be referred to the House Commerce Committee before it goes to the House floor for a vote. Gramm said the Senate measure he is cosponsoring with Burns is scheduled for markup in the Banking Committee on March 3, adding that he would try to move it quickly to the Senate floor.

Both the Senate and House bills would authorize $1.25 billion in loan guarantees that would be used to finance the technology needed to deliver local TV signals to remote areas, either by satellite transmission or cable TV lines. All the money would have to be provided through appropriations bills.

A three-member board would review all loan applications and decide on the size and number of the loans. Board members would consist of the secretary of the Treasury, the secretary of Agriculture and the chairman of the Federal Reserve Board, or their appointees. The loans would be administered by the Rural Utilities Service, a Department of Agriculture agency that now oversees a $42 billion loan portfolio supporting telecommunications, electric and water projects in rural America.

"We want to minimize the taxpayers' risk and maximize the chances of getting this done," Gramm said at a Feb. 24 news conference. "Every American should have the ability to get their local TV station."

The focus on rural reception came out of deliberations surrounding last year's satellite bill. Satellite TV companies such as DirecTV and EchoStar won the right to transmit local programming to their more than 6 million subscribers as part of legislation incorporated into an omnibus spending measure (PL 106-113). However, the companies say they only have enough capacity to deliver local signals in 30 to 40 of the nation's 210 television markets.

Gramm Sets Deadline

Lawmakers from rural areas attached the loan guarantee program to the broader legislation in an effort to ensure that their home districts would not be shut out. However, Gramm prevailed on Senate leaders to strip out the loan guarantee language, insisting that any program come out of his committee. Under terms of an agreement struck with Republican leaders, Gramm promised to produce legislation by the end of March.

The proposed loan program has drawn concern from the CBO, which says millions of households would have to pay a premium to receive local TV signals to make the government-backed ventures profitable. CBO Director Dan L. Crippen, in Feb. 9 testimony before Gramm's Banking panel, estimated that a $1.25 billion loan program would translate into a taxpayer subsidy of $350 million.

Gramm said the bill he introduced with Burns addresses the concerns, noting that the government would back only up to 70 percent of the loans used to provide local TV signals.

Senate Panel OKs Rural TV Bill With Loan Enhancements

MARCH 11 — A last-minute deal between Senate Banking, Housing and Urban Affairs Committee Chairman Phil Gramm, R-Texas, and panel Democrats March 8 broke the logjam on legislation (S 2097) that would create a $1.25 billion loan guarantee program to improve television service in rural areas.

The committee approved the bill by a 19-0 vote after Gramm, ranking Democrat Paul S. Sarbanes of Maryland and Tim Johnson, D-S.D., added language that increased the percentage of the loans the government would guarantee from 70 percent to 80 percent. Their amendment also would allow the approval of individual loans up to $20 million to organizations such as direct-broadcast satellite services, cable TV operators or rural phone cooperatives.

Both provisions addressed Democrats' eagerness to ensure that smaller entities such as rural utilities receive adequate government backing to beam local TV programming to underserved areas.

Democrats had indicated that without such provisions, they might have voted against the bill.

Sarbanes, in remarks March 8, said the last-minute talks with Gramm moved the two sides closer on issues "that separated us significantly" just days earlier.

While the bill enjoys wide support among rural states' lawmakers, it is unclear whether it alone can address the lack of local TV signals in outlying areas. The satellite industry contends it cannot squeeze more signals into its services to reach the most sparsely populated states unless Congress persuades the Federal Communications Commission to allocate more broadcast spectrum.

It also is unclear whether the committee-passed bill will fare as well on the Senate floor, in light of recent Congressional Budget Office warnings that bankrolling rural TV enhancement could expose taxpayers to losses from unprofitable ventures.

Gramm said the language represented a "fairly comprehensive compromise" that would require loan applicants to put up significant collateral, reducing the chance of dummy corporations winning government guarantees. Some sticking points over loans remain, however.

Johnson and Sarbanes criticized a provision that would require loan applicants to be backed by Federal Deposit Insurance Corporation-approved lenders, which may not offer the lowest rates. They said the issue could be addressed during Senate floor debate, which is expected to begin before April.

The House Agriculture Committee approved a companion bill (HR 3615) on Feb. 16 that would guarantee 100 percent of eligible loans.

Lawmakers have described the bills as "technologically neutral," but most observers believe direct-broadcast satellite services are the best way to provide local signals to hard-to-reach areas.

Cable systems are required to retransmit local broadcasts, but say they lack the money to extend their lines over wider areas.

House Panel Includes Loan Guarantees In Rural TV Bill

MARCH 25 — Supporters of legislation (HR 3615) that would establish a loan guarantee program to improve rural television reception fought off a passel of amendments designed to gut the bill at a House Commerce Telecommunications, Trade and Consumer Protection Subcommittee markup March 23.

Fiscal conservatives opposed to the bill, sponsored by Robert W. Goodlatte, R-Va., and Rick Boucher, D-Va., succeeded in reducing the size of the loan program from $1.25 billion to $1 billion and placing an 80 percent cap on the amount of a loan guaranteed by the government. Goodlatte's original proposal would have guaranteed 100 percent of the loan.

But opponents, led by Steve Largent, R-Okla., and Christopher Cox, R-Calif., failed to get support for amendments that would have phased out the program in 2004 and prevented loans from being used to improve reception in midsize cities and suburban areas.

The measure that emerged resembles a rural TV bill that was approved, 19-0, by the Senate Banking, Housing and Urban Affairs Committee on March 8.

The full House Commerce Committee is expected to mark up the legislation the week of March 27. The Goodlatte-Boucher House bill was approved, 41-0, by the House Agriculture Committee on Feb. 16.

Most criticisms of the bill came from opponents who said the loans could go to companies that would use the money to provide local TV signals in areas that already get them by antenna or cable TV.

Some opponents also expressed displeasure with the Rural Utilities Service (RUS), the Department of Agriculture branch that would administer the loans. Those concerns stemmed from recent reports by the Agriculture Department's inspector general that some recipients of RUS loans for telephone and electric projects had significant financial reserves and made few investments that could be classified as rural development

"The underlying notion that we should expand the charter of the Rural Utilities Service is exceptional," Cox said. "We would be rewarding failure with an expanded mandate."

Boucher defended the RUS, saying it had never experienced a loan default. He said the loan package could extend direct-broadcast satellite service to approximately 160 TV markets that currently do not have the option.

Cox offered an amendment, adopted by voice vote, that would exempt loan recipients from rules that require them to retransmit all local TV stations to subscribers. The amendment would require recipients to broadcast only stations with an average of 21 hours a week of local news, sports and weather.

Bills Advance In Both Chambers

APRIL 1 — Legislation that would establish a federal loan guarantee program to improve local television reception in rural areas inched closer to final resolution the week of March 27.

After rejecting a series of amendments, the House Commerce Committee March 29 approved by voice vote a measure (HR 3615) that would provide $1 billion in loan guarantees to encourage companies and organizations to provide local broadcast signals via satellite or cable transmission where home-owners do not have access.

The following day, the Senate passed, 97-0, legislation (S 2097) calling for $1.25 billion in loans after adopting an amendment by Tim Johnson, D-S.D., and Craig Thomas, R-Wyo., that would allow lending institutions not covered by the Federal Deposit Insurance Corporation to participate in the program. *(Votes 49, 50, p. S-12)*

The Senate bill would guarantee up to 80 percent of each loan and contains an amendment, adopted by voice vote, that would give preference to loan applicants who propose to offer rural areas such additional services as high-speed Internet and National

Weather Service alerts.

House lawmakers could consider the House Commerce bill — which calls for $1 billion in loans and would guarantee up to 80 percent of each loan — or a version approved earlier by the House Agriculture Committee that would guarantee the entire amount of each loan and calls for $1.25 billion for the program. They also could decide to draft a compromise bill.

Gramm Confident

Senate Banking, Housing and Urban Affairs Committee Chairman Phil Gramm, R-Texas, said March 30 the differing dollar amounts created prospects for a difficult conference but said he was confident that both chambers will pass a reconciled measure by a wide margin.

Each of the bills would designate the Department of Agriculture's Rural Utilities Service (RUS) to administer the loans. The RUS, which oversees a $42 billion loan portfolio supporting rural development projects, has come under criticism because it issues loans without specific spending requirements.

All three measures would also allow the loan guarantees to be used for providing direct-broadcast satellite services in markets that only have cable. Supporters say this would encourage competition that could lead to lower rates for consumers.

"It's about whether Americans are going to receive local broadcast stations in a competitive package," said Republican Rep. W. J. "Billy" Tauzin, of Louisiana, chairman of the House Commerce Subcommittee on Telecommunications, Trade and Consumer Protection.

Tauzin said he expects a compromise version of the House bill to pass easily when it goes to the floor sometime next month. However, fiscal conservatives and other critics of the legislation are expected to offer amendments that propose shrinking the size of the loan program or reducing the percentage of each loan the government agrees to guarantee.

House Passes Compromise Rural TV Bill

APRIL 15 — The House on April 13 overwhelmingly passed legislation (HR 3615) that would establish a loan guarantee program to improve rural television reception after lawmakers reconciled rival versions of the bill approved by the House Commerce and Agriculture committees.

The 375-37 vote sets the stage for a House-Senate conference soon after Congress returns from the spring recess. *(Vote 128, p. H-44)*

The House package resembles a $1.25 billion Senate measure (S 2097) that passed by a 97-0 vote March 30.

Robert W. Goodlatte, R-Va., chief sponsor of the House-approved package, said the loans would enable telecommunications providers to serve more than 30 million households that currently cannot obtain over-the-air TV reception or direct-broadcast satellite services. Goodlatte said the reception is crucial for Americans who rely on local television as a lifeline in times of bad weather or natural disasters. "This bill not only will benefit consumers, it will save lives," Goodlatte said.

However, some lawmakers questioned whether the legislation is too broadly written and would provide government-subsidized TV to areas already served by cable systems. Opponents said the bill, as written, would put the Department of Agriculture's Rural Utilities Service (RUS) — the proposed program administrator — in the role of a high-tech venture capitalist, picking one technology to serve a TV market at a competitive advantage. The RUS currently oversees a $42 billion loan portfolio supporting telecommunications, electric and water projects.

"Don't be fooled into thinking this is not a controversial issue," Steve Largent, R-Okla., warned colleagues during floor debate. "We will be subsidizing businesses with loan guarantees so they can compete against people in the private sector."

The House bill would prevent cable TV system owners from applying for government loans to extend their existing franchises. It also would exempt direct-broadcast satellite providers from "must carry" provisions of satellite legislation (PL 106-113) passed last year, meaning they would have to carry only the number of local broadcast stations that the largest regional cable outlet offers.

The final House version struck a compromise between a bill approved March 29 by the Commerce Committee — which authorized a $1 billion loan program — and an Agriculture Committee version, approved Feb. 16, that authorized a $1.25 billion program. While the compromise opted for the higher amount, it included a Commerce Committee provision that would limit the portion of each loan guaranteed by the government to 80 percent.

The House-passed measure also included a provision by Rep. Edward J. Markey, D-Mass., that would prevent companies from using the loan guarantees to bid for more space on broadcast satellites.

The rural TV loans were originally included in last year's satellite bill, but they were broken out into stand-alone legislation at the behest of Senate Banking, Housing and Urban Affairs Committee Chairman Phil Gramm, R-Texas, who contended that his committee should have jurisdiction over loan guarantees. ◆

States Gain Power to Limit Online Liquor Sales; Bill to Curb Internet Gambling Dies

Box Score

- **Bills:** HR 3244 — PL 106-386; HR 3125.
- **Legislative action: House** failed, 245-159, to pass HR 3125 (H Rept 106-655) under suspension of the rules July 17 (two-thirds vote required).

House adopted the conference report on HR 3244 (H Rept 106-939), 371-1, on Oct. 6.

Senate cleared the bill, 95-0, on Oct. 11.

President signed the bill Oct. 28.

SUMMARY

States got new power to halt interstate sales of alcohol via the Internet as part of an anti-crime package (HR 3244) enacted Oct. 28. Attempts to ban gambling on the Internet did not fare as well. The Senate passed an Internet gambling bill in the first session, but the House did not act and the measure died. *(Anti-crime package, p. 15-19)*

Liquor wholesalers successfully teamed up with proponents of restricting liquor sales to minors to pass legislation giving states new power to limit sales of alcohol over the Internet. Added to the conference report on HR 3244, the provisions allow state attorneys general to file federal suits for injunctive relief against alcohol distributors who sell directly to consumers in states where such sales are banned.

Supporters, led by Sen. Orrin G. Hatch, R-Utah, said the change would help enforce the laws of at least 19 states and, while no proof-of-age requirements are in place for Internet alcohol sales, would help curb liquor sales to minors. Opponents, including the Wine Institute, representing California wineries, argued that Web alcohol sales are important for smaller wineries and breweries that are unable to secure limited shelf space in retail stores for their products. The provisions were similar to a bill (HR 2031) passed by the House in the first session and to language in the Senate-passed version of a juvenile crime bill (HR 1501).

Attempts to outlaw Internet casinos folded in July, when the House failed to muster enough votes to overcome opposition from an unlikely alliance made up of the Clinton administration, state lottery advocates and social conservatives. The bill (HR 3125) was defeated under suspension of the rules, a procedure that requires a two-thirds majority for passage and usually is reserved for non-controversial measures. The bill would have banned many forms of online wagering, but would have allowed state-sanctioned, closed-circuit networks for dog, horse and jai alai betting in an attempt to satisfy lawmakers from states such as Florida and Kentucky where such betting is legal.

Social conservatives teamed up with the Clinton administration to lobby against the exemptions. State lottery interests also opposed the bill, saying it would ban lottery ticket sales to consumers in their homes via the Internet.

House Judiciary Approves Ban on Internet Gambling

APRIL 8 — The House Judiciary Committee on April 6 approved a bill (HR 3125) to ban Internet gambling, after adopting changes needed to resolve a turf battle with Resources Committee Chairman Don Young, R-Alaska.

Young had been demanding that the bill be referred to his panel until Robert W. Goodlatte, R-Va., and Speaker J. Dennis Hastert, R-Ill., brokered a deal regarding gambling on Indian reservations.

The Judiciary Committee on April 5 approved, 19-5, an amendment that incorporated changes demanded by Young, including a provision that would allow Indian casinos to operate so-called reservation-to-reservation Internet gambling networks. The language would allow bettors to place wagers on the Internet if they were on Indian reservations.

Similar language is included in a Senate-passed bill (S 692).

The committee, 24-11, adopted an amendment by Ed Pease, R-Ind., to narrow provisions in the bill that had largely exempted state lotteries from the proposed Internet gambling ban. The Pease amendment would limit that exemption by barring the sale of state lottery tickets via the Internet to customers in their homes — meaning the revised bill would permit the sale of lottery tickets via the Internet only in public places.

The Pease amendment was opposed by the National Governors' Association as an intrusion on state sovereignty.

In an April 4 letter to Judiciary Committee Chairman Henry J. Hyde, R-Ill., Democratic South Carolina Gov. Jim Hodges said states were "best positioned to decide for themselves" the scope of state lotteries.

The committee on April 6 approved the bill, 21-8, setting the stage for floor action after the spring recess. Goodlatte, the bill's sponsor, said he was confident it would have strong bipartisan support. He predicted agreement could quickly be reached on the minor differences between the House and Senate versions of the bill.

Second House Panel OKs Online Gambling Curbs

JULY 1 — Legislation that would ban gambling businesses from accepting checks or credit card bets over the Internet was approved by the House

Banking and Financial Services Committee on June 28. Violators could be liable to five years in prison.

Committee Chairman Jim Leach, R-Iowa, said the bill (HR 4419), which he sponsored, would put a brake on the growth of Internet casinos and predicted it would have bipartisan support. "The bill will totally shut down offshore gambling. That is a huge plus," he said.

The measure, approved by voice vote, is backed by the financial services industry, which wants to limit liability for gambling losses.

The panel adopted, by voice vote, an amendment by John E. Sweeney, R-N.Y., that would limit the restrictions to gambling already illegal under state or federal law. It would not apply to legal bets in states that permit gambling. Sweeney's district includes the Saratoga Springs horse racing track.

The House Judiciary Committee, which shares jurisdiction over the measure, has already approved a separate bill (HR 3125) that would ban online gambling outright, but that bill has stalled. Crime Subcommittee Chairman Bill McCollum, R-Fla., said he has no target date for marking up HR 4419.

Social conservative advocacy groups, including the Eagle Forum and the Traditional Values Coalition, have objected to HR 3125. W.J. "Billy" Tauzin, R-La., chairman of the Commerce Subcommittee on Telecommunications, Trade and Consumer Protection, has been negotiating with the groups and said he is working on a draft that would narrow language that allows states to permit online betting on horse and dog racing and jai alai.

Rev. Lou Sheldon, chairman of the Traditional Values Coalition, said the bill had been "hijacked by the gambling lobby." But he said Tauzin had assured him in a June 22 meeting that he would try to work out a compromise.

"If they make the changes they have agreed to, I will be pushing the bill like crazy," Sheldon said June 27.

Backers of the proposed online gambling ban said they were doubtful about prospects for merging the two bills. "We will look at it. But there may be complications to putting an amendment on our bill," said Robert W. Goodlatte, R-Va., the bill's sponsor.

Goodlatte said one key problem was that there was no legislation similar to the credit card bill in the Senate. He said he wanted to clear the way for a floor vote for his own bill, and for eventual negotiations with the Senate, which passed its version of the online gambling ban (S 692) last year.

States' Rights Remain a Concern As House Edges Toward Vote

JULY 15 — The House is poised to vote on an Internet gambling ban (HR 3125) during the week of July 17, despite expected opposition from state lottery advocates and some conservative groups.

Supporters predicted that compromise language developed the week of July 10 would clear the way for passage.

"I think the bill has overwhelming bipartisan support. We will try to bring it up under a suspension of the rules," sponsor Robert W. Goodlatte, R-Va., said in a July 14 interview. Bills under suspension cannot be amended, but require a two-thirds majority to pass.

The legislation would ban many gambling businesses from taking wagers online. The fledgling Internet gambling industry already takes in about $1 billion a year, with more than 700 sites.

The compromise worked out by Goodlatte would make it clear that states still have power to allow for electronic wagering if they use closed-loop, subscriber-based systems rather than the open Internet.

While the measure was being prepared for floor action, opponents made plans to try to block it and, if necessary, to seek revisions in a conference committee. The Senate has already passed its version of the bill (S 692).

Potential opponents include Patrick J. Kennedy of Rhode Island, the House Democrats' top fundraiser, who has raised questions about the bill on behalf of a home-state constituent, GTECH Holdings Corp., the nation's largest operator of online lottery systems.

The company is concerned about a House amendment adopted by the Judiciary Committee on April 5. The language, sponsored by Ed Pease, R-Ind., would permit online sales of state lottery tickets only in public places, not in private homes.

Governors, including Republican Jeb Bush of Florida, have charged that the bill would intrude on states' rights by effectively preventing officials from going online to sell lottery tickets to consumers via home computers. Such concerns remain a primary hurdle to final passage.

Working With Conservatives

Commerce Telecommunications, Trade and Consumer Protection Subcommittee Chairman W.J. "Billy" Tauzin, R-La., said other issues previously raised by social conservatives had been addressed by the compromise language on state authority worked out with Goodlatte. He stressed that the bill would not expand existing laws.

"When finally approved, this bill will be a victory for American families and traditional values," Tauzin said July 11.

Not all social conservatives were satisfied. Some complained that the measure would do nothing to narrow existing state laws that allow online betting on horse and dog races and jai alai.

Rev. Louis P. Sheldon, chairman of the Traditional Values Coalition, a political advocacy group, said Tauzin's changes failed to resolve his group's concerns. Sheldon repeated his complaints in a private meeting with House Majority Whip Tom DeLay, R-Texas, on July 13.

"I told him I strongly opposed the bill. All they have done is move chairs around on the deck of the Titanic," Sheldon said.

Ken Johnson, a Tauzin aide, said GOP lawmakers were expected to give the bill strong support. He said Tauzin had been asked by a number of Republicans to broker a deal and that most were now pleased with the changes.

Goodlatte pointed out that a number of social conservative groups, including the Christian Coalition and Rev. Jerry Falwell, had expressed strong support for the bill for "holding the line on a new form of gambling."

The Justice Department has argued that online betting on horse and dog races may already be banned under a 1961 law (PL 87-216) that barred the transmission of wagers or gambling information across telephone wires. *(1961 Almanac, p. 383)*

The administration has predicted that enforcement will be difficult because many online gambling operations are offshore.

Strong Resistance Stops House Effort To Ban Gambling On the Internet

JULY 22 — Legislation (HR 3125) to ban Internet casinos faces a doubtful future after running into strong opposition on the House floor July 17 from an unlikely alliance of conservative Republicans, the Clinton administration and state lottery advocates.

GOP leaders had hoped to speed the bill through the House on the suspension calendar, a procedure that limits debate and bars amendments but requires a two-thirds majority for passage. The House, on a 245-159 vote, fell short of the supermajority needed. *(Vote 404, p. H-126)*

Robert W. Goodlatte, R-Va., a leading sponsor of the bill, said he would push for another vote during the week of July 24 under a yet-to-be-drafted rule that would allow for certain amendments. "We're going to move ahead," he said.

Although the bill received a majority vote, its fate is in doubt because opponents are likely to offer amendments to close what they call loopholes in the bill that would allow state-sanctioned, closed-circuit networks for betting on dog and horse races and jai alai.

"Carve-outs are essential to this bill. Without them, there is no bill," said a Republican aide familiar with negotiations on the legislation. He said the exemptions were needed to satisfy lawmakers from states such as Kentucky and Florida that allow betting on dog and horse racing and jai alai.

The White House in a July 17 statement argued that the bill "appears to be designed to protect certain forms of Internet gambling that currently are illegal, while potentially opening the floodgates for other forms of illegal gambling." It said the provisions on dog and horse racing and jai alai could give individuals unlimited, unsupervised ability to bet from their homes.

The stalemate came after weeks of efforts by Goodlatte and W.J. "Billy" Tauzin, R-La. The two tried to develop a bill that would mollify legal gambling interests as well as social conservatives. They succeeded in winning support from a number of prominent social conservatives, including the Christian Coalition and the Rev. Jerry Falwell, who argued that the bill would help curb the spread of gaming. The measure would bar many gambling businesses from accepting bets online.

Some key Republicans, however, questioned whether the bill was worth supporting because of continued opposition from other social conservatives, who want a tougher ban, and from libertarians, who want to keep the Internet free of regulation.

Members voting "no" included Majority Whip Tom DeLay, R-Texas, and Thomas M. Davis III, R-Va., the Republicans' top fundraiser. DeLay's opposition came after he had a private meeting on July 13 with the Rev. Louis P. Sheldon, head of the Traditional Values Coalition. Sheldon argued that the bill did not go far enough in trumping state laws and preventing all types of online betting.

Gambling interests have been major contributors to both the Democratic and Republican parties. Casino interests in Nevada support the bill because it would limit competition from Internet outfits. Online gambling already accounts for more than $1 billion in annual revenues.

Goodlatte argued that the bill would only allow closed-circuit gambling networks for horse and dog races and jai alai in states where they are already legal.

"We certainly do not expand gambling. We attack the multibillion-dollar industry that is growing on the Internet, the 700 cyber-casinos, the sports betting, the threat of sales of lottery tickets in peoples' homes," he said.

Some critics argued that the bill's overall restrictions would be ineffective because casinos could move offshore and bettors could use technology to mask their geographic location. They said the bill was well-meaning but ineffective regulation of the Internet that would set a bad precedent.

Christopher B. Cannon, R-Utah, said the online gambling ban was "ultimately unenforceable."

Other opponents, including Patrick J. Kennedy of Rhode Island, the Democrats' head fundraiser, took up the cause of state lotteries. The legislation would ban lottery ticket sales to consumers in their homes via the Internet.

Kennedy argued that revenues from state lotteries provided needed support for education and other programs and deserved special treatment.

"The real rub," Kennedy said, "is that, while [horse racing and jai alai] have exceptions, state lotteries do not." A Rhode Island-based company, GTECH Holdings Inc., is the nation's largest lottery system operator.

The Clinton administration also has stressed concerns about potential inconsistencies between the bill and a current prohibition on betting over telephone lines. ◆

No Consensus on Hill For Bill to Protect Privacy Of Online Consumers

SUMMARY

Despite pressure from consumer rights advocates and the Clinton administration, neither chamber passed legislation aimed at protecting the confidentiality of individuals' personal information from release on the Internet.

Top lawmakers from both parties tended to side with Internet companies' demands for self-regulation. As a result, there was little movement on numerous proposals aimed at strengthening an individual's right to prevent personal information from being distributed by off-line and Internet companies.

The lack of consensus was evident in early October when the House failed to pass legislation (HR 4049) establishing a commission to study privacy issues, and Senate Judiciary Committee Chairman Orrin G. Hatch, R-Utah, agreed to pull provisions from a bill to combat electronic crime (S 2448) that would have required the posting of privacy policies on websites.

Similarly failing to make much headway was a package of electronic surveillance and privacy protections supported by the Clinton administration that included safeguards for personal financial and medical information (HR 4380). The Clinton-backed proposals were introduced amidst revelations that market researcher DoubleClick Inc. was doing in-depth tracking of Internet user data and that the FBI was using the controversial Carnivore e-mail "wiretap" system.

The one piece of privacy-related legislation to receive serious consideration was a provision in the fiscal 2001 Commerce, Justice and State (CJS) appropriations bill (HR 4942) that would have barred acquisition of a person's Social Security number with the intent to do harm. The proposal was intended to keep Social Security numbers from being sold over the Internet, but critics said changes made during negotiations with the financial services industry had left loopholes that could actually weaken personal information protection. The provision was in the bill as cleared Oct. 27, but was removed during negotiations in December before the measure was sent to the president.

Box Score

- **Bills:** HR 4049, HR 4380, HR 4942, S 2448
- **Legislative action: House** failed to pass HR 4049, under suspension of the rules, 250-146, (two-thirds vote required), on Oct. 2.

Senate Judiciary Committee approved S 2448, 15-1, on Oct. 5, after striking privacy provisions.

House adopted the conference report on HR 4942 (H Rept 106-1005), 206-198, on Oct. 26.

Senate cleared HR 4942, 48-43, on Oct. 27.

FTC Asks for Expanded Authority To Protect Internet Privacy

MAY 27 — The Federal Trade Commission is taking a harder line on protecting the privacy of Internet users, urging Congress to impose tough new regulations on online businesses. Lawmakers and the White House appear unwilling to go as far as the agency recommends, despite growing public concern.

In a move that signaled the end of a long honeymoon between the agency and online companies, the FTC requested broad new power from Congress during the week of May 22 to protect the privacy of Internet consumers.

FTC Chairman Robert Pitofsky told a Senate panel May 25 that self-regulation was not enough to ensure adequate privacy protection; legislation was required.

"Without such protections, electronic commerce will not reach its full potential," he told the Senate Committee on Commerce, Science and Transportation.

Committee Chairman John McCain, R-Ariz., said after Pitofsky's testimony that he was considering several legislative proposals, including a narrower measure than the FTC plan, developed by Sen. John Kerry, D-Mass., but had not decided whether to act.

"I don't know yet if I'm going to do a bill. We're going to discuss all these issues with a lot of people. I do have concerns about privacy," McCain said.

Other lawmakers were even more skeptical about Congress' ability to act this year.

"In an election year, I think it's unlikely that Congress will adopt broad legislation that imposes new privacy protection requirements," said House Commerce Telecommunications, Trade and Consumer Protection Subcommittee Chairman W.J. "Billy" Tauzin, R-La.

The FTC's request went well beyond privacy protection measures sought by President Clinton. The White House has supported more targeted legislation (HR 4380) that would increase requirements on financial services companies to get consent from consumers before sharing information about their records or personal spending habits with affiliated companies.

The White House pointedly did not comment on the FTC plan.

By a split 3-2 vote of its commissioners on May 19, the FTC proposed legislation that would require online companies to protect the security of any information they collected and to give consumers three other basic rights: notice of any corporate privacy protection policy, a choice of whether to participate in any information-sharing program, and the ability to view and correct errors in personal files compiled by companies.

Support in Principle

Those four principles have broad support in Congress, but there is little consensus about the role the FTC should play and how far to go to turn the generalities into legislation.

The issue is further complicated by the fact that leaders of both parties this election year are trying to raise campaign donations from high-tech companies that strongly oppose government regulation of the Internet.

Senate Minority Whip Harry Reid, D-Nev., questioned giving the FTC broad authority to police privacy on the Internet.

"I am concerned that the FTC's proposal would stifle innovation and would hurt the continued growth of electronic commerce and the Internet," Reid said.

Some lawmakers have expressed concern that privacy protection measures would hurt online businesses that rely on income from advertising and from exchanging personal information they compile about their customers with other companies. The information — which includes data provided voluntarily by consumers and information about their spending habits — can be used to tailor advertising messages on Internet sites and in e-mail.

Sens. John D. Rockefeller IV, D-W.Va., and Ernest F. Hollings, D-S.C., both back draft legislation that would provide the full authority the FTC wants.

A number of lawmakers in both parties say that would be too broad, however, and are proposing tighter bills. The Kerry draft bill, and a similar measure (S 2448) sponsored by Judiciary Committee Chairman Orrin G. Hatch, R-Utah, would focus on only one of the four elements cited by the FTC: requiring companies to disclose online privacy protection practices on their Internet sites.

Hatch held a hearing on privacy protection and computer crimes in his committee May 25 and said he was determined to push forward with his bill.

Hatch, who is preparing to mark up legislation in June, said his bill would provide "privacy protection without imposing a burdensome regulatory framework."

The FTC appears to have little better odds of getting what it wants from the House Commerce Committee.

Tauzin said he would not support the FTC-proposed legislation, but would consider offering his own bill to give companies incentives, such as tax benefits or protection from certain consumer lawsuits, if they participate in voluntary "seal of approval" programs to guarantee privacy protections.

The FTC's harder line came after its officials reviewed the agency's new survey of 335 Internet sites.

The study found that only 20 percent of the sites complied with all fair practice guidelines that have been developed by the industry and the FTC. Those guidelines require companies to divulge plans for sharing personal information and let consumers opt out.

The percentage of complying sites doubled since last year, but was still far too low for some FTC members. Further, only 8 percent of the sites surveyed had seals of approval from outside watchdog groups.

House Panel Seeks Internet Privacy Study

JUNE 17 — Months of rhetoric about the need to better protect consumer privacy in the Internet age has resulted in a House panel's approval of a bill to create a commission to study the issue.

The House Government Reform Subcommittee on Government Management, Information and Technology approved the measure (HR 4049) by voice vote June 14. The full committee could take up the bill the week of June 19.

The House panel gave voice vote approval to an amendment that would authorize $5 million in funding, require 10 field hearings and provide subpoena power to the commission. The group would have 18 months to make its recommendations.

Subcommittee Chairman Steve Horn, R-Calif., said he expected the bill would have strong support in full committee and, eventually, on the House floor.

But the measure could face obstacles; opponents say creating the commission would reduce pressure on Congress to act this year on privacy protection legislation.

"The public doesn't want another study. It wants action," said Richard C. Shelby, R-Ala.

A May 18 letter signed by representatives of a handful of privacy protection advocacy groups, including the Electronic Privacy Information Center, argued that the commission bill would "likely retard the progress of legislation that would result in meaningful legal protections for Americans."

A similar Senate bill (S 1901), sponsored by Herb Kohl, D-Wis., has been bottled up in the Judiciary Committee.

Judiciary Committee Chairman Orrin G. Hatch, R-Utah, said he still hopes to move privacy protection measures, especially those in a bill (S 2448) he has sponsored. Among other steps, it would require online businesses to post privacy protection policies on their World Wide Web sites, and it would broaden the Justice Department's authority to investigate computer crimes.

But Hatch's bill has been opposed by online businesses that favor industry self-policing programs, including one that awards seals of approval to companies that meet minimum standards for privacy protection.

Hatch said he was still trying to build support for his own bill but may eventually hold a markup for Kohl's proposal. "I would not rule anything out. I am still looking at the Kohl bill," Hatch said June 15.

Rallying Point

Rep. James P. Moran, D-Va., a cosponsor of the commission bill, said he believed both parties would rally around the proposal, particularly if it becomes clear that no consensus can be reached on privacy legislation this year.

The administration has been seeking broader legislation to restrict the sharing of financial and medical records among affiliated financial services companies, including insurers. Last month, John T. Spotila, administrator of the office of information and regulatory affairs in the Office of Management and Budget, told Horn's subcommittee that the administration has "significant concerns that the study commission might be used by some as an excuse for delaying" needed action.

But Moran said he believed the administration would not block the study. "They could live with it," he said.

While that measure heads to full committee, House Banking and Financial Services Committee Chairman Jim Leach, R-Iowa, is trying to build support for his own proposal (HR 4585) aimed at preventing financial services companies from sharing medical records without the consent of consumers.

Leach said June 14 that consensus was developing among key players in government on the need for "a legislative approach to medical privacy" similar to his bill. It would require a financial services company to get a customer's consent before disclosing individually identifiable health information from medical records to an affiliate or another company.

Leach hopes to mark up the bill this month, and he would like to persuade Senate Banking Committee Chairman Phil Gramm, R-Texas, to support similar legislation in the Senate.

Bill Appears Dead For the Year

OCTOBER 7 — Major legislation aimed at protecting the privacy of consumers on the internet died during the week of Oct. 2.

"We won't do a big privacy bill this year. There is no consensus," said Senate Commerce, Science and Transportation Committee Chairman John McCain, R-Ariz.

The final blow may have come when the House failed to muster a needed two-thirds majority for legislation (HR 4049) that would have created a commission to study the issue of privacy on the Internet. The House voted 250-146 for the bill, well short of the supermajority required for legislation considered under suspension of the rules. *(Vote 503, p. H-160)*

"Congress should deal with this issue, not a commission," said Rep. Robert W. Goodlatte, R-Va.

Meanwhile Senate Judiciary Committee Chairman Orrin G. Hatch, R-Utah, agreed on Oct. 5 to strike online privacy protection provisions from a bill (S 2448) that would authorize $100 million in fiscal 2001 for the Federal Bureau of Investigation to establish a National Cyber Crime Technical Support Center and 10 regional forensic support labs. Hatch's panel approved a substitute version of the bill by a 15-1 vote. Floor action is expected the week of Oct. 9. ◆

CQ

Chapter 20

TRADE

Lawmakers Hand Clinton Big Victory in Granting China Permanent Trade Status

BoxScore

- **Bill:** HR 4444 — PL 106-286
- **Legislative action: House** passed HR 4444 (H Rept 106-632), 237-197, on May 24.

Senate cleared HR 4444, 83-15, on Sept. 19.

President signed the bill Oct. 10.

SUMMARY

Business leaders, particularly those in the high-tech and agriculture sectors, helped push a skeptical House and a generally gridlocked Senate to pass legislation to permanently apply the same low tariff rates to Chinese imports as those already applied to goods from all but a handful of countries. President Clinton made the bill a top priority during his final year in office. Enactment capped his efforts to expand trade opportunities for U.S. businesses that began in 1993 with the enactment of a law (PL 103-182) to implement the North American Free Trade Agreement (NAFTA). The measure also put the U.S. imprimatur on China's bid to join the World Trade Organization (WTO), the body that governs global commerce.

Goods from China had won reduced tariff rates annually since 1980, after President Jimmy Carter re-established trade ties with Beijing. Under the Jackson-Vanik amendment to the 1974 Trade Act (PL 93-618), the president was required to annually review the trade status of certain communist nations such as China.

China's efforts to join the WTO conflicted with that law. WTO rules require member nations to grant one another's products "permanent normal trade relations status," unless they are willing to forgo the benefits of more open trade with a particular country.

In November 1999, U.S. Trade Representative Charlene Barshefsky and Chinese Premier Zhu Rongji reached an agreement to drastically cut tariffs, quotas and other trade barriers on U.S. exports to China. In return, the administration agreed to support China's entry into the WTO.

That required Congress to vote to remove China from the list of communist countries subject to Jackson-Vanik. The administration knew the issue would embolden opponents of close U.S.-China trade relations, such as labor unions and environmental groups, and critics of China's social policies, including human rights activists and social conservatives, at a particularly uncomfortable time for Democrats. Facing their best chance in six years to retake the House, Democrats were wary of embracing the China bill and, thereby, offending the very constituencies they were courting in the campaign.

As a result, the White House approached the issue gingerly at first. Republicans pressured the president to become more involved in the fight, as he had done with NAFTA. In March, Clinton submitted his formal proposal to Congress, which became the heart of the bill that was debated. The submission prompted the onset of one of the most intense lobbying campaigns of the 106th Congress. House Minority Whip David E. Bonior, D-Mich., led the opposition and predicted the vote would be close enough that one or two members could make the difference. At the same time, business leaders initiated a multimillion-dollar advertising campaign.

A few House centrists began to look for an option other than "yes" or "no." Sander M. Levin, D-Mich., and Doug Bereuter, R-Neb., explored ways to hold China accountable for its actions on human rights, compliance with trade rules and other issues. As the vote drew near, they came together with a proposal to establish a joint congressional-executive branch commission to monitor China's actions and report to Congress. When GOP leaders agreed to attach the plan to the China bill, their success was assured. Whips said the Levin-Bereuter package had won over as many as 30 votes. The China bill passed by a 40-vote margin.

Passage by the more internationalist Senate was never in doubt, and both sides expected an expeditious vote there. But Fred Thompson, R-Tenn., and Robert G. Torricelli, D-N.J., pressed leaders to allow a vote on their proposal to require the president to impose sanctions if China was found to be contributing to the spread of weapons of mass destruction. Their proposal, popular with many conservatives, threatened to force the bill back to the House if it was attached to the measure. Majority Leader Trent Lott, R-Miss., took four months to bring the bill to the floor. When he did, senators agreed, 65-32, to kill the Thompson-Torricelli amendment, and voted overwhelmingly to clear the bill.

Supporters Deploy Celebrities to Woo House's Undecided

MAY 13 — Cajoling, pleading, arm-twisting and some old-fashioned legislative log-rolling may well come in the final hours. But a fortnight before the most politically dicey and economically important vote of the 106th Congress — on whether to permanently grant China normal trading status with the United States — supporters and opponents relied on star power to woo the pivotal undecided of the House.

President Clinton arranged a White House ceremony May 9 to tout his proposal alongside former Presidents Gerald R. Ford and Jimmy Carter and a host of other dignitaries, from Minnesota's Independent Gov. Jesse Ventura to former Secretary of State Henry A. Kissinger. Officials released a letter in which Federal Reserve Chairman Alan Greenspan, custodian of much of the current economic prosperity, declared that the proposal would "create new opportunities for American businesses and farmers." The top four House Republican leaders appeared together May 11 to extol the benefits of an expanded and stable trade relationship with the world's most populous nation.

Opponents offered their own star-studded counteroffensives. House Minority Whip David E. Bonior, D-Mich., held a May 9 news conference at which actress Goldie Hawn denounced the bill; he also met with Chinese dissidents who oppose the proposal. Republican opponents, led by Bob Ney of Ohio and Charlie Norwood of Georgia, initiated classified briefings for undecided colleagues at which the Central Intelligence Agency laid bare the details of China's military strength.

But all that competing information was doing little to lighten the particularly weighty policy and political load for wavering lawmakers such as David L. Hobson.

Asked when and how he will decide his vote on the China bill, Hobson — a generally unflappable Republican who has represented the factories and farms of west-central Ohio for a decade — said simply, "I don't know."

In the House, which is scheduled to vote on the issue the week of May 22, more than 100 members remain officially uncommitted. Members and lobbyists working on both sides of the issue say the truly undecided, those such as Hobson, whose vote could go either way, number fewer than three dozen. The rest, they say, have already tipped their hand in some way or seem nearly ready to announce their position.

The ranks of the undeclared shrank the week of May 8. Among those who announced they would vote "no" were Democrats Bob Clement of Tennessee, Juanita Millender-McDonald of California, Nick Lampson of Texas, Robert Menendez of New Jersey and David Phelps of Illinois. Among those who announced they would vote "yes" were Republican Gil Gutknecht of Minnesota and Democrats Gary L. Ackerman of New York, Tom Allen of Maine, Ken Bentsen of Texas and Ken Lucas of Kentucky.

Many of those not quite ready to make such an announcement were, like Hobson, struggling to come to terms with their decision. Hobson says he fears that making permanent the normal trade relations (NTR) status that China now holds for only one year at a time could lead Beijing to crack down on human rights. If it did, Congress would have lost its main public relations tool for trying to combat mistreatment of Chinese dissidents — an annual vote on revoking China's NTR with the United States. Hobson also worries that the vote could hurt Taiwan, even though its newly elected president favors the proposal before Congress. China considers Taiwan a renegade province.

"I don't come to this easily. I have a lot of concern about what effect this will have," Hobson said of his pending decision in a May 10 interview.

Others in the truly undecided column have different agendas. James L. Oberstar, D-Minn., said May 11 that he would vote for the bill if he received two assurances from the leadership: that workers in his blue-collar district would get government help to pay for retraining programs should they lose their jobs as a result of trade, and that negotiators would address the concerns of the taconite industry, centered in Northeastern Minnesota and the Upper Peninsula of Michigan, in future trade agreements. Taconite is a low-grade iron ore used to make steel.

Still others just wanted the barrage of pressure to stop so they could take a moment to gather their thoughts. Sherwood Boehlert, R-N.Y., said he is asking "all comers" to give him some space, telling them, "I've heard all the arguments from all viewpoints. Now, give me the luxury to consider all of them."

But the push to pick a side — from Clinton, GOP leaders and business lobbyists pushing for a "yes" vote, and from the Democratic leaders, labor unions and some religious groups advocating a "no" vote — will only intensify as the proposal faces its first formal legislative test. On May 17, the Senate Finance Committee will mark up its version of Clinton's proposal (S 2277) and the House Ways and Means Committee will take up an as-yet unnumbered measure.

For wavering members on the Ways and Means — including Democrats Charles B. Rangel of New York, the ranking member, Benjamin L. Cardin of Maryland, Xavier Becerra of California, Karen L. Thurman of Florida and Lloyd Doggett of Texas — it will be time to decide.

For others, the markup may provide pertinent information for their decision. If the panel addresses human rights, labor and other concerns with legislative language, some of the undecideds would find it easier to vote for the China bill.

Parallel Ideas

For months, the ranking Democrat on the Ways and Means Trade Subcommittee, Sander M. Levin of Michigan, has been pushing a set of proposals designed to mitigate some members' concerns that the bill could have a negative effect on human and worker rights in China, and that a trade agreement U.S. and Chinese negotiators reached in November would not be enforced.

On May 9, Levin and Doug Bereuter, R-Neb., released a written "framework" of their proposal. It would codify certain safeguards against import surges included in the November agreement; enhance the executive branch staff needed to monitor the agreement; offer China technical assistance in developing commercial and labor laws; set up an interagency task force to monitor and promote enforcement of laws prohibiting the import of goods made with forced or prison labor; and establish a congressional-executive branch panel on human rights in China, modeled after the Helsinki Commission.

By the end of the week, the Clinton administration and Levin had written the proposal into draft legislation and were circulating it to key GOP supporters, such as Ways and Means Trade Subcommittee Chairman Philip M. Crane, R-Ill., Republican leaders and some Democrats.

While Bereuter said May 11 that he thought the Ways and Means and International Relations committees should mark up portions of the proposal in their jurisdiction, other members said the language would fare better if it bypassed the panels. International Relations Committee Chairman Benjamin A. Gilman, R-N.Y., opposes the China bill, and the proposals could be picked apart in both committees.

Members strongly pushing the China bill said the first formal debate on the Levin-Bereuter proposal should come in the Rules Committee, chaired by David Dreier of California, one of the the measure's leading Republican proponents. In such a scenario, the panel likely would attach the plan to the China bill through a self-enacting rule — a procedure that automatically amends a bill as it arrives on the floor — or otherwise ensure that the proposal would become part of the underlying legislation.

While some members were mapping a legislative strategy for the proposal and some undecideds were carefully watching their progress, Majority Leader Dick Armey, R-Texas, and Majority Whip Tom DeLay, R-Texas, expressed hesitance about integrating the Levin-Bereuter proposal into the debate. While Armey suggested that the proposal might not be needed to guarantee passage of the NTR legislation, DeLay said it might drain too much badly needed support away. A small but potentially crucial bloc of lawmakers support the bill but do not like all the Levin-Bereuter provisions.

"We're not closing the door on parallel legislation," DeLay said at a May 10 news briefing, "but at the same time it's got to be a very well-written piece of legislation that doesn't cost us votes, and I don't know how they do it."

The whip also said that he does not not foresee the need for legislation unveiled May 9 by Christopher Cox, R-Calif., to retain the opportunity for Congress to vote annually on China's behavior. The proposal, dubbed "Jackson-Vanik II" after the 1974 Trade Act (PL 93-618) amendment that has led to the annual votes on China's trade status, would condition federal aid to U.S. businesses in China on improving human rights and other issues.

Though Cox's proposal was intriguing for some undecided members — among them John Baldacci, D-Maine, who described it as having more "teeth" than the Levin-Bereuter plan — it gained little support from GOP leaders or the Clinton administration.

Bereuter said that, while he would keep an open mind on including some of Cox's proposals in any parallel legislation, the language appeared likely to cost the China bill more votes than it would attract, largely because members may not want to cast the two votes it could annually require on U.S.-China policy.

Cox, who headed a congressional panel last year that issued a report condemning China for spying and other security breaches, is likely to vote against the China bill if his measure is not at least considered.

Hammers and Nails

Debate over how to handle so-called parallel legislation grew in importance as DeLay and Commerce Secretary William M. Daley indicated that securing a guaranteed majority of 218 lawmakers for the China measure remained problematic.

DeLay said that a whip count May 9 had shown that "we have a very tough assignment ahead of us," in which the White House would need to produce between 85 and 90 Democratic votes — leaving the GOP with the task of producing as many as 133 votes. The 70 to 80 votes that Democratic whips have estimated they will be able to obtain are "not enough," DeLay said.

In an interview May 12, Daley said that he believed DeLay's assessment of the GOP vote situation. Democrats, he conceded, were straining to reach their goal of 70. But, he said, Republican leaders would make the task of passing the bill exponentially more difficult if they did not allow Levin-Bereuter or some similar plan to go through.

"If there isn't some version of this that addresses the concerns of members like Levin and Bereuter . . . we would probably see a substantial downslide," Daley said, in which only 30 to 40 of the 211 House Democrats would vote "yes." If that happened, Republicans would have to come up with 180 to 190 votes, which "we know is impossible," the secretary said. (The House's two independents are expected to vote "no.")

Daley's estimates played into the hands of some GOP opponents. Ney and Norwood both maintained that the number of Democrats willing to support the bill has been exaggerated; Ney said that he was certain at least 50 Republicans would vote "no," which would preclude passage if only 30 Democrats voted "yes."

Norwood said 160 Republicans were still "in play," but he said the vote could change if Clinton begins horse-trading for votes. "None of the bridges have been given out yet," he said.

Members and administration officials said few of the undeclared have sought to condition their "yes" vote on the promise of support for a parochial concern. Those who have, such as Oberstar, are seeking trade concessions. Many undecided members said they had not made any request to the administration or GOP leaders, in part because a lawmaker reported to have "sold" his vote on such a weighty foreign policy issue in return for a new road or bridge could be portrayed on the campaign trail as neither committed nor intelligent. Members on all sides anticipated that such deals might still come.

In an interview May 9, U.S. Trade Representative Charlene Barshefsky, who has met with hundreds of members to tout the benefits of permanent NTR for China, said, "The vast majority of members know this is absolutely the right thing for us to do," although that "doesn't necessarily mean . . . they will vote affirmatively."

Weighing a History-Making Step

Martin T. Meehan D-Mass., sees both sides of the issue. He is convinced the bill would help the burgeoning high-technology industry in his district, northwest of Boston, but he is not so certain that voting for permanent normal trade relations is the right thing to do, when China has a well-documented record of human rights abuses and intellectual property violations.

While "trying to get through the minutiae" of the foreign and trade policy implications of the vote, however, Meehan said one thing has become clear to him: The claims both sides are making about the dire consequences of the coming vote "are a little overblown."

Echoing Meehan's comments about the immense amount of information being pressed on wavering lawmakers, Baldacci said: "I've gotten my college course on China in two weeks. It's been truly an educational process. And it's an important decision that requires that."

With the exception of Congressional Research Service briefers, Baldacci's teachers are proponents of one position or the other. He has spoken by telephone with Clinton, met with

Barshefsky and chatted with Defense Secretary William S. Cohen about national security. He has also discussed the bill with union leaders.

Baldacci's decision may be made easier if leaders allow the Levin-Bereuter or Cox proposals to be attached. Still, that — and all the lobbying and endorsements — will probably not influence Baldacci much in the end, he said. Instead, he will have had to work out in his mind which is more likely to help China and the United States — more engagement or a pulling back. "I just have to feel comfortable about it," he said.

Cardin, another undecided, finds himself in a similar position. He would find it easier to vote for the bill if leaders promised him stepped up protections for the domestic steel industry against cheap imports dumped on the U.S. market. But, he said, the decision will have to be about the bigger picture.

"My ultimate judgment will be whether on balance this is in the best interest of the country."

Senate, House Panels Approve Bills to Normalize Trade With China

MAY 20 — Embrace of a new Sino-American economic era, which now seems increasingly likely, would be described by both sides in the hard-fought debate as a hallmark of the 106th Congress. On the cusp of the determinative vote by the House, however, these adversaries bluntly disagree on the consequence — either a colossal blunder or a great step forward in the relationship between the most powerful nation and the most populous nation in the world.

Unions, human rights activists, veterans groups, environmentalists and some religious organizations predict the former, believing that a congressional decision to grant China permanent status as a normal U.S. trading partner would not only culminate a decade of errant trade policy, in which thousands of quality U.S. jobs were lost, but also would nullify the ability of the United States to pressure China on labor, human rights and national security issues.

Businesses, farmers and some academics predict the latter, believing that enactment of the bill would open wide China's economy, and thereby its society, to a breadth of foreign ideas and individuals never known before.

The momentum behind that second view grew May 17, when President Clinton's proposal resoundingly prevailed on its first two test votes in Congress. The Senate Finance Committee voted 18-1 to approve the bill (S 2277), and a few hours later the House Ways and Means Committee voted 34-4 to approve its version (HR 4444).

Despite those lopsided votes — and the unveiling of a package of legislative sweeteners in the House — some suspense remained. The outcome of the vote that the House is scheduled to take May 24 has always been more in question than the outcome in the Senate. The White House and its Democratic allies continued to work to line up between 70 and 80 Democratic "yes" votes, the number they have deemed necessary to secure — in combination with a solid majority of Republicans — the 218 votes required to guarantee passage. Republicans who oppose the bill, meanwhile, appeared to have persuaded 60 of the 222 members of the House GOP to buck their leadership and vote against the bill.

Nonetheless, Speaker J. Dennis Hastert, R-Ill., told the U.S. Chamber of Commerce on May 18, "I think we're set." House Rules Committee Chairman David Dreier, R-Calif., added: "It's obvious to me that we're going to win this."

In contrast, the bill's chief opponents, Minority Leader Richard A. Gephardt, D-Mo., and Minority Whip David E. Bonior, D-Mich., insisted that their side could still prevail. "I'm not going to concede that we are going to lose this vote," Bonior said at a May 18 news conference. "It could go one way or the other with just a handful, a few votes," Gephardt said.

Announcements the week of May 15 that a dozen previously uncommitted members would vote for the bill helped buoy the hopes of Clinton and his staff, who were meeting at the White House almost nonstop with undeclared Democrats. Word of "yes" decisions by two senior members — Charles B. Rangel of New York, the top Democrat on the Ways and Means Committee, and Henry J. Hyde of Illinois, the Republican chairman of the Judiciary Committee — was seen as particularly important because of the respect each commands from other wavering members.

Left to make the case to lower-profile lawmakers, opponents warned that a decision against them would not be forgotten on the campaign trail.

Those less secure in their districts continued to worry that a "yes" vote might hurt their bids for re-election. As a result, some lobbyists for the bill said that a number of members had served notice that they would vote "yes" only if their vote was absolutely necessary to create a majority for the measure. "I've had too many members say they want it to pass by one vote," said former Rep. Dave McCurdy, D-Okla. (1981-95), president of the Electronics Industries Alliance, part of a coalition of high-tech concerns pressing for expanded and stabilized trade with China.

Doug Bereuter, R-Neb., who with Sander M. Levin, D-Mich., unveiled the additional legislation that appeared to enhance the bill's prospects, said he expected the majority to be paper-thin, perhaps 222. But he said such a narrow vote would belie greater support for the proposal. "Members on both sides of the aisle will find it more convenient not to vote 'aye' if they think it's going to pass. They will stand in reserve," he said in a May 18 interview.

Arrangements to give some members in politically tenuous positions a "bye" on the legislation — and to do so just five months before a hotly contested election — could challenge efforts to hold together a coalition on trade run by a Democratic president and a Republican Speaker. And members working for passage insisted they were not hearing such requests.

Senate Outlook

With House passage looking more likely by the day — and with the the vast majority of lobbying effort focused there — Senate Majority Leader Trent Lott, R-Miss., served notice at the Finance Committee's markup that his side of the Capitol also needed suffi-

House Diplomacy

May 20 — If the House passes its bill to permanently normalize trade relations with China, credit for bringing the crucial bloc of lawmakers on board will go largely to two low-key intellectuals of the House.

Sander M. Levin, D-Mich., and Doug Bereuter, R-Neb., spent months crafting language to address concerns about enhancing the trade status of a nation with a record for human rights violations, labor abuses and military posturing. When they unveiled it May 19, high-ranking Republicans announced that they intended to make the proposal part of the China bill (HR 4444) that the House will consider the week of May 22. Several wavering lawmakers said that move would secure their "yes" votes.

"It makes the vote substantially easier," declared Chief Deputy Majority Whip Roy Blunt, R-Mo.

Bill supporters, particularly Democrats, long had said such provisions would ease passage by securing as many as 40 votes and shoring up others whose support was only tentative. And at the news conference, two previously undeclared members — Diana DeGette, D-Colo., and John J. LaFalce, D-N.Y. — said they now would vote "yes." Jim DeMint, R-S.C., suggested he would do so as well. Tom Sawyer, D-Ohio, and Asa Hutchinson, R-Ark., said the language had eased their decisions to vote "yes."

Chairman David Dreier, R-Calif., declined to say how the Rules Committee would handle the language when it meets May 23 to craft a rule to govern the floor debate. But he said "a compelling argument can be made" for a procedure under which a House vote to adopt the rule would automatically amend the China bill to include the Levin-Bereuter package. Such a procedure would avoid a direct vote exclusively on the merits of the Levin-Bereuter proposal.

Language by the two lawmakers to deal with surges of Chinese imports had already been added to the bill by the Ways and Means Committee.

The additional proposals — which the two principals refined the week of May 15 to address concerns of GOP leaders and others, would:

- Create a 23-member panel with a full-time staff to monitor human rights in China, including labor standards and religious freedom. It would report to Congress and the president at least once a year. The House International Relations Committee would be required to hold a hearing on the findings within 30 days of receiving them and could mark up legislation to follow up on the panel's recommendations no later than 60 days after receiving the report.
- Require the U.S. trade representative to push the World Trade Organization (WTO) to annually review China's record of compliance with trade agreements.
- Establish an interagency task force to monitor the import of products made with forced or prison labor and to take steps to enforce U.S. laws on the issue.
- Add administrative staff to monitor China's compliance with U.S. trade agreements.
- Provide technical assistance to China on the development of its commercial and labor laws.
- Express the sense of Congress that the WTO should accept Taiwan as a member at the same meeting at which China joins.

Opponents insisted, as they had for months, that the plan was no more than a "fig leaf" that would affect no change in China. "That is a feel-good amendment, that is a let's-get-a-couple-more-votes amendment," said Bob Ney, R-Ohio.

Minority Leader David E. Bonior, D-Mich., also pointed to recent cases in which Congress ignored the recommendations of commissions it created, most recently a panel on religious persecution and human rights that recommended against permanent trade status for China. That, Bonior said, was a sign that Congress also would ignore the panel Levin and Bereuter would create.

cient attention paid. "I don't think any member's vote should be taken for granted. There may be a little more hidden problem out there than we recognize," he said.

Two other panel members, Majority Whip Don Nickles, R-Okla., and Bob Kerrey, D-Neb., both said the Senate was likely to pass its bill. What Lott was referring to, they said, was the difficulty the leadership could face in moving the measure quickly — debate is expected to begin the week of June 5, just after the Memorial Day recess — if senators seek to use delaying tactics or try to make the bill a vehicle for amendments.

Those most vehemently opposed are among the most vocal and dogged senators, including Democrats Ernest F. Hollings of South Carolina and Paul Wellstone of Minnesota. Even some bill supporters could offer amendments. Fred Thompson, R-Tenn., may propose conditioning some technology transfers to China on Beijing's reduction of its role in the proliferation of nuclear weapons. Leaders may try to persuade Thompson to use legislation (S 1712) to speed high-technology exports as the vehicle for his proposal. Thompson is among the senators who have bottled up that measure. A spokeswoman said May 18 that the senator had not yet decided how he would proceed.

In addition to watching developments in their own chamber, Senate leaders were monitoring the evolution of the China bill in the House.

The measure approved by Ways and Means included a provision by Levin and Bereuter that aims to stem the negative effects on specific U.S. industries of a potential surge of Chinese imports, by allowing the president to raise tariffs and quotas on the excess volume of goods. The provision would codify language in the agreement U.S. Trade Representative Charlene Barshefsky and Chinese Premier Zhu Rongji negotiated in November. Under that pact, the administration vowed to ask Congress to make permanent the normal trade relations (NTR) status now granted to China only one year at a time.

The Finance Committee bill has no "anti-surge" provision. Lott made clear that he would prefer the provision disappear, but he also said, "I think we shouldn't jump to conclusions before we see what they do" in the House.

Leaders fear that a successful move to alter the bill in the House could make it harder to fight amendments in the Senate, but Kerrey said the anti-surge language would ease passage there. Industries including steelmakers and farmers, whose bottom lines often are closely linked to the price of imports, could benefit from the ability to raise tariffs and quotas on large volumes of Chinese imports. Finance Committee members Max Baucus, a Democrat from the agricultural state of Montana, and Orrin G. Hatch, a Republican from steel-producing Utah, sent a letter to colleagues May 16 seeking support for the language should it reach the Senate.

While Senate leaders might not like the House approach, a senior Senate GOP aide indicated that leaders were anxious to avoid conference negotiations, which could take away attention from other legislative priorities this summer, and so might push for the Senate to clear the House bill.

Both measures have the same core provision: To amend a 1974 trade law (PL 93-618) requiring the president to annually renew NTR — meaning preferential tariff treatment — with certain communist nations.

Under both bills, the president could make NTR with China permanent once the World Trade Organization (WTO), the 135-nation group that oversees international commerce, accepts China as a member and the president certified that the terms of China's WTO entry did nothing to undermine the U.S. position under the deal that Barshefsky and Zhu reached last year.

'Yes' from the Once Uncommitted

In the last full week before the House vote, a number of previously uncommitted lawmakers took sides, and most went in the "yes" column. Besides Hyde, these included Republicans Tillie Fowler of Florida and Rick Hill of Montana and six Democrats on the Ways and Means Committee: Rangel, Benjamin L. Cardin of Maryland, Richard E. Neal of Massachusetts, Xavier Becerra of California, Karen L. Thurman of Florida and Lloyd Doggett of Texas.

Previously undecided members who put themselves in the "no" column included Democrats Carolyn McCarthy of New York, Karen McCarthy of Missouri, Rush D. Holt of New Jersey, Carrie P. Meek of Florida and Bart Gordon of Tennessee.

Bereuter said he thought the focus on winning over the undecided with the package he and Levin produced May 19 had limited the amount of parochial horse-trading to win votes.

Still, some members discussed proposals for their districts in the same meetings at which administration officials appealed for their votes.

Among the projects being discussed were a federal weather station for the tornado-prone Alabama district of undecided Democrat Robert E. "Bud" Cramer, and completion of an oil pipeline across southern Texas advocated by two undecided Democrats from that region, Rubén Hinojosa and Silvestre Reyes. But any promises of the pipeline could cost the administration the support of Doggett, who is troubled by the environmental ramifications of the project.

Members working to pass the China measure said the newly secured support of key members and the leadership's embrace of the Levin-Bereuter provisions were more important to House passage than random deals the White House or GOP leaders might make to win over individual members. Rob Portman, R-Ohio, called Rangel's announcement "the single most important pro-permanent NTR event of the last month."

Its impact was likely to be felt most in the New York delegation, where several lawmakers in each party remain undeclared, in the Congressional Black Caucus and among Ways and Means Committee Democrats. Almost immediately after Rangel's May 16 announcement, fellow New York Democrat Nita M. Lowey issued a statement that she had decided to vote for the bill. Rangel's support also was credited with swaying several of the undecided Democrats on his committee. Additionally, black caucus members including Gregory W. Meeks, D-N.Y., Chaka Fattah, D-Pa., and Sheila Jackson-Lee, D-Texas, remained in play.

At a news conference, Rangel noted that he had not been a fan of the Chinese since he suffered shrapnel wounds in a 1950 Korean War battle between his Army unit and Chinese soldiers. He said that he had decided to support the bill because "no one can challenge the fact that this is a tremendous market" to open.

Still, he expressed frustration both with the Clinton administration, for bringing up a divisive bill in a year in which the Democrats have their best chance in three elections to regain control of the House, which they lost in 1994, and with unions, for making a vote against the bill a "litmus test" for labor's support.

Rangel wryly noted that his reward from the administration was "a free plane ride up to Albany so I can endorse the president's wife. Big deal." New York Democrats endorsed Hillary Rodham Clinton as their Senate nominee at a convention May 16.

Busy Week for White House

The administration had a busy week, as it sought to win over the 20 to 30 remaining members it viewed as sincerely undecided. In the span of an hour on May 16, the president — joined by his chief legislative lobbyist, Charles Brain, and White House Deputy Chief of Staff Steve Ricchetti — met separately at the White House with Doggett, Jackson-Lee, Neal and two other Democrats, John Baldacci of Maine and Max Sandlin of Texas. Sandlin said it was the third time he had traveled down Pennsylvania Avenue to hear the president's pitch that the bill would strengthen the U.S. economy and lead to change in China.

Clinton prepared a five-minute Oval Office speech to the nation May 21. Three days before, he brought to the White House Federal Reserve Chairman Alan Greenspan, who said the vote "will have profound implications for the free world's trading system

How Russian Jews Molded U.S.-China Trade

MAY 20 — The longstanding congressional practice of holding an annual debate on the Sino-American trade relationship was born a quarter-century ago in a statute crafted without China much in mind.

The law (PL 93-618) allowed the president to liberalize trade with communist countries so long as they allowed free emigration. It was the first time Congress had made trade decisions contingent on a human rights consideration — and in this case, the principal intended beneficiaries were Jews being prevented from leaving the Soviet Union.

Then, as now, the president wanted unfettered authority to negotiate trade agreements and resented what he considered congressional meddling.

Then, as now, Congress demanded a periodic review of trade accords with a competing world power it neither liked nor trusted.

Between 1951 and the law's enactment in January 1975 — the peak of the Cold War — the United States imposed discriminatory tariffs and denied trade credits to the Soviet Union, nearly all of its satellites, China and the parts of Asia under communist control. Cuba was added to the list in 1962. Only Yugoslavia and, after 1960, Poland were exempt.

In 1972, as part of their policy of détente with the Soviet Union, President Richard M. Nixon and Secretary of State Henry A. Kissinger negotiated a trade deal with Moscow that was contingent on the United States extending it "most favored nation" (MFN) tariff treatment. In essence, the Soviet Union would be accorded the same customs duties and trade credits as most U.S. trading partners.

In 1973, when Nixon asked Congress to renew his trade negotiating authority for a round of international talks in Tokyo, he also asked for the power to lift discriminatory tariffs on selected communist countries, referred to in subsequent legislation as "non-market" economies. *(1973 Almanac, p. 833)*

Congress was willing to agree up to a point, and that point was the Soviet Union. The world was tense in 1973 after the OPEC oil embargo and the Yom Kippur War. Newspapers had been full of stories of Soviet Jews, "refuseniks," who had been prevented from emigrating to Israel. Their plight became a cause on Capitol Hill and a serious problem for Nixon and Kissinger.

When the House Ways and Means Committee marked up the trade bill, Ohio Democrat Charles A. Vanik (1955-81), an unabashed liberal from the ethnic neighborhoods of Cleveland, attached an amendment stating that the president could give the Soviet Union MFN trade status only if he certified that Jews were being allowed to freely leave the country.

In 1974, when the Senate gathered itself to move a trade bill, Henry M. Jackson (1953-83), a defense hawk Democrat from Washington state, attached an amendment similar to Vanik's. Jackson, who had run for the Democratic presidential nomination in 1972, distrusted the whole strategy of détente with the Soviet Union and regularly criticized Kissinger. The two would savage each other before the trade bill was finally signed by President Gerald R. Ford. *(1974 Almanac, p. 553)*

The law authorizes the president to grant MFN trade status to communist countries if he certifies that they allow free emigration. Or he may waive the restrictions for one year at a time if he finds that a country's policies are leading toward free emigration. The law also gives Congress 60 days to use expedited procedures to pass a concurrent resolution nullifying his decision.

How It's Worked

The Soviet Union, in a fit of pique over the restrictions, abrogated the 1972 trade deal with Nixon. Over the next decade, waivers were granted only sparingly. That changed with the collapse of the Soviet Bloc; beginning in 1989, annual or permanent waivers became common.

The waiver for China, first granted in 1980, did not become controversial until Beijing crushed a fledgling pro-democracy movement in Tiananmen Square in 1989. Since then, the renewal of China's tariff treatment has been the source of annual springtime debate in Congress, primarily over China's human rights record.

After his inauguration in 1993, President Clinton even specified new human rights conditions for the renewal of China's trade status, but he rescinded them in 1994.

Today, only a handful of countries are denied what Congress has renamed normal trade relations: Afghanistan, Cuba, Laos, North Korea, Vietnam, Serbia and Montenegro.

Despite the heated debate over the past 11 years, Congress has never come close to overturning the president's decision on trade with China. The Senate has never even voted directly on the question.

and the long-term growth potential of the American economy."

The vote formally disappeared from the list of possible presidential campaign issues. Although he has not been as outspoken as supporters hoped, Vice President Al Gore, the presumed Democratic nominee, backs the bill. Gov. George W. Bush of Texas, the presumed GOP nominee, endorsed it May 17, saying permanent NTR for China would aid the domestic economy and, for the Chinese, hold out "the hope of more open contact with the world of freedom."

The Business Roundtable, a group of corporate executives, launched a new television advertisement suggesting permanent trade relations would improve living conditions in China, while some business organizations continued to fly in manufacturing officials and others to press lawmakers to vote for the bill.

Opponents continued to work the undecided, too. Bonior held several news conferences, often more than one a day, that featured Chinese dissidents or others who opposed the measure.

In a May 18 news conference, Gephardt said, "I talk to members all the time about the vote."

When he announced his opposition to the bill April 19, business leaders and others who support the bill said that Gephardt had given assurances that he would not press his Democratic troops to vote against the bill as well. He said May 18 that he had continued to leave such whipping duties to Bonior, but that he had met with many members who sought his counsel on the issue. "I've been actively involved in this," Gephardt said, but he told reporters not to overestimate his influence. "Nobody can call a member, including the president, and command their vote on this issue," he said.

A senior aide said that Gephardt has urged undecided Democrats to take a position and announce it as soon as possible, in order to avoid the perception during a razor-thin roll call that one last-minute decision had sealed the measure's fate either way. Just such a perception helped to doom the career of Rep. Marjorie Margolies-Mezvinsky, D-Pa. (1993-95), who cast a decisive 1993 vote to pass a controversial budget bill.

Markup Action

Approval of the China bill was not particularly suspenseful in either the Finance or the Ways and Means committee. Both panels enjoy sole jurisdiction over trade in their chambers, and both tend to be far more attentive to the needs of commerce than most other committees are.

The most nerve-wracking aspect of either panel's consideration was whether Ways and Means would be able to keep a quorum to report the bill May 17. With several committee members planning to be on a chartered flight to attend the funeral that evening of a son of Bart Stupak, D-Mich., Chairman Bill Archer, R-Texas, encouraged his colleagues to shorten their speeches and allow amendments to pass or die on voice votes. But they did not always heed his request, and the panel's vote of approval came just minutes before some had to leave.

The most dramatic moment in the debate the week of May 15 came as three top administration officials were testifying for the bill to the House Agriculture Committee. An observer — identified by the Capitol Police as Daniel Chagashvili, 49, a Georgian native holding an Australian passport — stood and smashed together two soda-filled glass bottles, held one of them to his neck and threatened suicide. He was later charged with disrupting Congress and assaulting an officer.

In another twist, the legislative number assigned at random to the House measure, formally introduced May 16, was four consecutive fours, and four is the unluckiest number in Chinese numerology.

The Ways and Means Committee considered four amendments to the bill. One, by Archer to incorporate the anti-surge language of the Levin-Bereuter proposal, was approved by voice vote.

Another, by Cardin, aimed to strengthen U.S. trade law to make it easier for manufacturers such as steelmakers to prove that foreign products had been dumped on the U.S. market, and called on the administration to raise tariffs and quotas on imported products. It was ruled non-germane.

Two by Pete Stark, D-Calif., were defeated. The vote was 10-28 against one, to preclude the president from granting permanent NTR to China unless Taiwan was allowed into the WTO before or at the same time as China. The vote was 6-16 against the other, which would have required China and the United States to reach an agreement on banning the import of AK-47s and similar weapons made in China. Administration officials said the provision was unnecessary, because Clinton had already signed an executive order banning such imports, and the China agreement would not nullify it.

Mac Collins, R-Ga., refrained from offering an amendment once Archer promised to work with him to bring it before the Rules Committee, which will propose the terms for the floor debate. It would require the government to review the effect of the Barshefsky-Zhu agreement on the U.S. textile industry and commit Congress to resuming an annual renewal of China's trade status, if permanent NTR is ever revoked.

Finance Welcomes Roth Back

At the Finance markup, where no amendments were considered, the most notable aspect of the markup, other than the lopsided vote, was the return of Chairman William V. Roth Jr., R-Del., who had back surgery April 12. Most on the panel could not let the occasion pass without commenting on how healthy the tanned Roth looked; all but a few took time to share their views on the historic nature of the vote before them, or to explain how they came to a decision on the bill.

Phil Gramm, R-Texas, said that a chance to vote on such a measure, which could bring China "back from the dark side," was something senators lived for when they were kissing babies, shaking hands and considering legislation over which they were "bored to tears" much of the rest of their careers.

A senator whose vote had been more in question — John D. Rockefeller IV, D-W.Va. — said he decided to support the bill because the status quo of annual renewal of China's trade status, and past trade agreements in general, "have not worked for my state." He said there was little question that "virtually all" the provisions in the November trade agreement "are to our advantage and not theirs."

The "no" vote was cast by James M. Jeffords, R-Vt., after an emotional description of his efforts to help a Tibetan who once attended Middlebury College in Vermont and is now in a Chinese prison for attempting to record Tibetan songs and dances during a trip to China. Jeffords said that he had sent money to the man's mother in an attempt to help her visit her son in jail, as is permissible under Chinese law, but that authorities had blocked her from doing so.

"If China cannot obey its own laws in this case, how can we expect it to follow the far more burdensome rules of the WTO?" Jeffords asked.

Finance member Connie Mack, R-Fla., predicted that almost all senators have heard of similar problems with the Chinese government from constituents. At the Ways and Means markup, E. Clay Shaw Jr., R-Fla., mentioned the plight of a constituent who had lost $10 million to a Chinese government-run company and had tried unsuccessfully for a decade to get it back. Still, such experiences were not the deciding factors cited by other members who have declared their positions in recent days.

The Bigger Picture

Members on both sides say they had bigger pictures in mind, both how their vote would affect the often complex Sino-American relationship and how it might shape future trade policy.

For lawmakers such as Roth and the Finance Committee's retiring ranking Democrat, Daniel Patrick Moynihan of New York, the lopsided vote for the measure was evidence that the United States was back on track to open markets. The tally "sent an unequivocal message that we are committed to breaking down barriers to American exports," Roth declared at a news conference.

For those such as Rep. Sherrod Brown, D-Ohio, a leading opponent of the measure, the difficulty bill supporters were having in coming up with the decisive votes was evidence that the bill, and momentum for future trade agreements, still could be quashed. "If we beat China, it does really show," he said, "that Congress really does care about human rights, labor standards and the environment."

And for former members, a number of whom attended the Ways and Means markup — some as lobbyists — it was a time to reflect on a truly important vote. "I wanted to witness history," the previous chairman of the committee, Sam M. Gibbons, D-Fla. (1963-97), said as he sat in the front row of spectators with his wife, Martha, at his side.

Despite Decisive House Passage, Smooth Road Ahead Not Assured

MAY 27 — An unexpectedly strong House vote to usher China into the new global economy is evidence that a bipartisan coalition can be formed in Congress to endorse trade expansion — but only when the benefits are overwhelmingly embraced by American business, and only if the concerns of detractors and skeptics are addressed head-on.

Such was the case as President Clinton worked with Speaker J. Dennis Hastert, R-Ill. and his tenacious majority whip, Tom DeLay, R-Texas, to secure House passage on May 24 of the legislation (HR 4444) that would make permanent China's standing as a regular trading partner of the United States, ensuring that U.S. goods and services reap the full benefits of a market-opening deal that the administration reached with Beijing last year.

The vote was 237-197, the majority formed when better than one-third of the chamber's Democrats joined nearly three-quarters of its Republicans. *(Vote 228, p. H-74)*

That 30-vote margin was the result of patient negotiations, all-out lobbying by business coalitions and not-so-subtle dealmaking by the White House. It was also a step toward a broader approach to trade policy, which the administration was criticized for pushing in the most recent round of talks by the World Trade Organization (WTO) — one that recognizes human rights, labor standards and other issues as relevant in charting economic relations between nations.

But those very provisions, crafted to win over perhaps 30 House members and guarantee victory, may well lead to delays in the Senate. Majority Leader Trent Lott, R-Miss., would prefer to pass a bill without the addons and says he is inclined to send the House bill to committee instead of directly to the Senate floor after the Memorial Day recess.

There is little chance such a delay would dampen Senate enthusiasm for the proposal; at least 70 senators are said to be committed to voting "yes." Forestalling the vote until the time of the Independence Day recess, however, would make supporters anxious, and they seem certain to pressure Lott to rethink his statements and to quickly clear the House bill. If the Senate passes its own, more straightforward bill (S 2277) or amends the House's legislation, the issue will have to return to the House for reconsideration.

"Another vote over here is not something everybody's looking forward to," said Thomas J. Donohue, president of the U.S. Chamber of Commerce, which made House passage of the bill the object of an intense and expensive campaign.

Clinton and House Republican leaders said they intended to press the Senate to take up the House bill. "I am confident it too will act swiftly to advance these interests," Clinton said May 24. "I will be speaking with many senators in the days ahead to ensure that we continue to move ahead to get this done as promptly as possible."

By abandoning an annual renewal of China's normal trade relations (NTR) status, both bills would pave the way for that nation to join the WTO and allow the United States to join in fostering a new economy in the most populous nation on Earth. The House bill also includes provisions designed to protect domestic industries harmed by surges in Chinese imports and to monitor Chinese human rights and labor abuses, the key concerns of those opposed to expanding trade with Beijing. *(Highlights, p. 20-12)*

If the Senate were to make only slight changes to that package, a conference to work out differences between the two chambers could be finished quickly, members said, and the House would probably be able to clear the bill.

Such movement would cement what history may view as Clinton's most significant achievement — bolstering the U.S. economy and advancing long-term foreign policy goals through international commerce. The pivotal decisions would have come at the bookends of his presidency. Congress cleared the North American Free Trade Agreement (NAFTA) at Clinton's urging in 1993. Along with the overhaul of the welfare system, the balancing of the federal budget and the saga of impeachment, the advancement of market-opening policies would likely rate at the top of the Clinton legacy.

A Host of Pressures

But the more circuitous the route the Senate takes, and the more skeptical senators are of the changes the House crafted to keep the proposal alive, the more trouble that could come from a legislative body that not only was designed to thoroughly vet

Highlights of the House Bill

MAY 27 — The heart of the measure (HR 4444) that the House passed, 237-197, on May 24 was the legislative language President Clinton unveiled March 8 for making permanent the favorable trade treatment the United States now affords China one year at a time. Additional provisions were added in the week before the vote in a bid to secure the support of blocs of wavering lawmakers.

ISSUE	DESCRIPTION
Normal Trade Relations	The bill would authorize the president to exempt China from the Jackson-Vanik amendment to the 1974 Trade Act (PL 93-618), and to extend permanent, non-discriminatory treatment to Chinese goods once China is accepted into the World Trade Organization (WTO). Under Jackson-Vanik, normal, non-discriminatory trade status — currently known as normal trade relations (NTR) — can only be extended to some communist countries for one year at a time.
Presidential Certification	Before granting permanent NTR, the president would have to certify to Congress that the terms for China's entry into the WTO are as rigorous as those agreed to between the U.S. and Beijing in 1999.
Anti-Surge Safeguards	The president could increase tariffs and quotas to provide relief to specific domestic industries and workers in response to instances when the U.S. International Trade Commission found that a surge of Chinese imports threatened to disrupt the U.S. market.
Human Rights and Labor Commission	A 23-member commission, its members appointed by Congress and the president, would be created to monitor human rights and labor issues in China. The commission would submit an annual report of its findings on internationally recognized freedoms, such as freedom from torture and from being jailed for political views or advocacy of human rights; freedom from arbitrary arrest, detention or exile; the right to a fair public trial by an independent tribunal; freedom of choice in employment; and freedom of religion.
World Trade Organization Compliance	The Office of the U.S. Trade Representative would be required to issue an annual report on China's compliance with multilateral and bilateral trade agreements. The WTO would be urged to cary out an annual review of China's compliance.
Forced Labor	An interagency task force, headed by the Treasury Department, would be created to monitor imports and promote effective enforcement of U.S. laws barring goods made with forced or prison labor.
Trade Pact Enforcement	Federal agencies would receive additional resources to monitor and enforce trade agreements with China and other nations.
Technical Assistance	The Commerce, State and Labor departments would be directed to provide training and technical assistance to help China develop its labor and commercial laws.
Taiwan	The bill would express the sense of Congress that the WTO should accept Taiwan as a member at the same time China joins.
Radio Free Asia, Voice of America	The bill would authorize $99 million in fiscal 2001 for Radio Free Asia and the Voice of America to expand broadcasts to China and neighboring countries.

contentious proposals, but also is in the throes of a particularly nasty period of partisan ill will.

"I don't anticipate a jurisdictional roadblock being erected to our being able to do this in a timely fashion, but anything is possible in this place," said Joseph R. Biden Jr. of Delaware, the ranking Democrat on the Foreign Relations Committee, which is likely to hold hearings on the House bill.

Though Lott and Minority Leader Tom Daschle, D-S.D., both support the China measure, they will have to work together to keep members from fatally amending it. While most of those amendments likely would be tabled — or thwarted in advance with a successful vote to invoke cloture, or limit debate — a roster of contentious amendments could drag out Senate debate for more than a week.

Ideas being floated as amendments include an overhaul of campaign finance law. Lobbying on the China bill, which has included thousands of dollars in campaign contributions from both businesses and unions, would provide opponents of the current system with ample evidence to damn it. John McCain of Arizona, who made changing the way money influences politics the centerpiece of his Republican presidential campaign, said May 24 that he reserves the right to try to offer his bill (S 1593) as an amendment. If that happens, Lott said that he would hold McCain responsible for killing the China legislation.

At the same time, Robert G. Torricelli, D-N.J., and Fred Thompson, R-Tenn., held a news conference May 25 to announce that they were introducing a bill (S 2645) to set up an annual presidential review of China's record in supplying nuclear weapons and technology to nations that may not be friendly to the United States, and to require the president to take action if he determines that such transfers are taking place. They said they may attempt to attach that measure to the trade bill as an amendment, though they could be persuaded to move it as a parallel measure just before or after the Senate takes up the China bill. Still, both Torricelli and Thompson would probably vote for the China bill even if their measure were not considered.

Senators more hostile to the bill — generally the most liberal and the most conservative lawmakers — also were readying amendments.

Paul Wellstone, D-Minn., will focus his efforts on monitoring human rights, labor rights and the environment in China and will also touch on agriculture policy, according to his spokesman, Jim Farrell. He said the senator's aim is not to stall the bill but to foster a comprehensive debate.

Foreign Relations Committee Chairman Jesse Helms, R-N.C., enunciated the same goal. In a statement May 24, he predicted "robust" Senate deliberations that would delve into prison labor, religious persecution, human rights abuses, proliferation of nuclear weapons, and military threats to Taiwan. "We are going to have a debate, Mr. Clinton. And we are going to have votes, perhaps uncomfortable votes, on a range of issues relating to China," Helms said.

While Lott said in a floor speech May 25 that he did not want to move to limit amendments — a tactic that has increasingly infuriated Democrats — Daschle told reporters May 24 that he would try to quell any attempts by Democrats to offer amendments on some of their main legislative priorities, such as gun control and prescription drug coverage for Medicare beneficiaries.

In addition to the threatened amendments, Lott faces a rapidly dwindling legislative session. When Congress returns the week of June 5, only 11 legislative weeks will remain before Oct. 6, the target adjournment date for the 106th Congress. And the Senate has passed just one fiscal 2001 appropriations bill.

Appropriations Committee Chairman Ted Stevens, R-Alaska, said May 23 that he would push for the Senate to complete action on all 13 spending measures before the China bill is taken up. "Why should we take it up when we can't get other things done?" Stevens asked.

Mitch McConnell, R-Ky., also espoused such a view. The China bill "ought to be the last thing we do after the president signs the last appropriations bill" or "the first thing President Bush will do," he said, referring to Texas Gov. George W. Bush, the presumed GOP nominee.

While such comments indicated some GOP belief that holding up Clinton's capstone legislative achievement might give them some advantages — either in the perennial fight over government funding or perhaps in the campaign — some lobbyists sensed that the Senate, which has received scant attention or campaign largess on the China bill, wants to ensure that it does not pass the measure without receiving some of the political benefits House members garnered.

"There are too many strong supporters over there for this to get derailed, but they certainly want to leverage it as much as they possibly can," said former Rep. Dave McCurdy, D-Okla. (1981-95), president of the Electronics Industries Alliance, a high-tech group pushing for expanded trade with China.

Pivotal Promises

The House had been considered the main battleground for the bill since U.S. Trade Representative Charlene Barshefsky and Chinese Premier Zhu Rongji reached agreement in November on a trade pact. China promised to greatly cut its tariffs and other barriers to U.S. imports and investments, while the Clinton administration promised to press for the removal of China from the dwindling list of nations subject to only short-term standing as a regular U.S. trade partner. Under the 1974 trade law (PL 93-618), the president is required to annually review tariff and quota treatment for some communist nations, including China, and to base renewal decisions on whether the country allows free immigration, a throwback to the days of the Soviet Union.

Because Clinton will not be able to permanently normalize China's trade treatment until the legislation is enacted and China joins the WTO — both of which are not likely to occur before China's current NTR status expires July 3 — during the first week of June the president is expected to announce that he will renew the country's status for another year. It is not clear, however, whether the House will vote on a joint resolution disapproving of the president's decision. Such a measure has been put to a vote annually, although never successfully, for the past decade.

Many members had long expressed frustration that the annual U.S. review of Beijing's policies did not spur much democratization in China — even in years such as 1992, when the House twice voted to place conditions on China's trade standing because of its human rights record. *(1992 Almanac, p. 157)*

But when confronted this year with the proposal to permanently extend NTR, a status that greatly reduces Chinese tariffs on imports, a number of those lawmakers said they would just as soon keep the annual review as a potential cudgel.

Businesses joined together to fight that inclination tooth and nail, and they spent millions of dollars — on both sides of the partisan aisle — in their efforts. The Business Roundtable, a group of executives from large corporations, estimates it will spend $10 million on advertisements, lobbying and other expenses by the time the bill is enacted. At the same time, labor unions, religious groups, veterans organizations, human rights advocates and environmentalists also countered with an intense, though less costly, campaign.

As a result, the pivotal bloc of undecided lawmakers described themselves as feeling under siege — not only from lobbyists on both sides, but also from the president and his Cabinet and from some impassioned constituents.

Two in the eye of the storm were Democrats Gregory W. Meeks of New York and Rubén Hinojosa of Texas. They were ultimately the only two wavering lawmakers who took the administration up on its offer of a trip to China this spring to assess its behavior, and its market potential, firsthand. The factors they said they considered in weighing their decisions were a microcosm of what House members as a whole faced.

Meeks' district includes John F. Kennedy International Airport, which stands to gain from increased commerce with China, but it is also home to a strong contingent of unionized workers concerned that jobs like theirs could be exported.

Hinojosa's Rio Grande Valley district, one of the poorest in the nation, is desperate to find jobs and new outlets for its small businesses and manufacturing efforts. Its constituents also have some concerns that the NAFTA law (PL 103-182), which lowered U.S.-Mexican trade barriers in 1993, also shifted some production to lower-wage Mexico and brought environmental problems across the border. Critics cite NAFTA as an ominous precedent for what may happen in China, where workers are paid even less and environmental conditions are already some of the worst in the world.

At a May 23 news conference where they announced their intention to vote "yes," Meeks and Hinojosa said that the biggest impression left by their trip was of the Chinese people. "I came away with the feeling that they were just like the average American citizen," Meeks said.

The trip alone was not convincing enough. In the end, their decisions were eased by progress on an unrelated bill. Clinton and Hastert agreed May 22 on a package of legislation to help impoverished inner cities and rural areas through tax cuts and other development incentives.

Commerce Secretary William M. Daley acknowledged in a press briefing May 23 that the timing of that deal was no coincidence. He said there was a strong desire "by a number of members, especially minority members, that as we move forward with trade, we address some of the difficult areas of our nation."

In addition, Hinojosa was influenced by an administration promise that the EPA would quickly complete its required review before a gas pipeline across southern Texas may open. That also swayed previously undecided Silvestre Reyes, D-Texas, and secured what had been tenuous support from Solomon P. Ortiz, D-Texas.

Other local matters were also addressed by the administration. Democrat Robert E. "Bud" Cramer voted "yes" after the Commerce Department vowed to reconsider a plan to close a national weather station in his tornado-prone Alabama district. Democratic Caucus Chairman Martin Frost voted "yes" after the Northrop Grumman Corp. signaled, in an internal memorandum, that it would stay put in Dallas after reaching agreements with the Navy and the city.

Meeks' decision was eased by senior New York Democrat Charles B. Rangel's announcement May 16 that he would vote for the bill. Clinton, Republican leaders and House Democrats in favor of the China bill cited Rangel's influence in securing "yes" votes. Tim Roemer, D-Ind., a Democratic whip for the bill, referred often to "Rangel coattails."

The three groups with which Rangel is most influential split on the bill: eight of 19 New York Democrats voted "yes," nine of the 36 Congressional Black Caucus members did so, and so did 11 of the 16 Democrats on the Ways and Means Committee, of which Rangel is the ranking member.

The bill split various other blocs of votes, as well. Rural representatives voted overwhelmingly for it but urban and suburban lawmakers did not, for example. Electoral considerations appeared to have little influence on members' votes: Republicans and Democrats with narrow holds on their seats — as well as those with certain prospects for re-election — voted for and against the bill in percentages that echoed the House as a whole.

The vote, and the six hours of floor debate beforehand, were somewhat anti-climactic. Nine minutes into the 15-minute period for voting, the "yes" votes surpassed 218 — the absolute majority of the House — and applause broke out on the floor. No members entered the well at the last moment to change their votes once passage of the bill was assured.

Legislating From the Center

The prospects of passage appeared to solidify with the decision by the House GOP leadership to embrace the proposals of Sander M. Levin, D-Mich. After receiving encouragement from senior Ways and Means Committee Republican Bill Thomas of California and others, Levin worked for months to craft a proposal that would address the China-specific concerns of human rights advocates, labor leaders and those who feared that China would never follow through on its trade promises.

As the vote drew near, Levin joined forces with Doug Bereuter, R-Neb., who had been putting together a similar proposal. Working with Trade Subcommittee Chairman Philip M. Crane, R-Ill., and others, their package was credited with winning over as many as 30 members, many of them Democrats. In the end, the bill passed with 19 votes to spare.

The Ways and Means Committee attached the anti-surge portion of the Levin-Bereuter proposal to its bill at its May 17 markup. The Rules Committee agreed May 23 to a procedure under which the rest of the proposal was automatically attached to the bill when the resolution setting the rules for floor debate (H Res 510) was adopted by the House. That same procedure amended the bill with a list of specific human rights abuses that would have to be addressed by the commission the bill would create, and it added a $99 million authorization for news broadcasts into China, a priority of undecided John Edward Porter, R-Ill., who then announced support for the bill.

The vote to adopt the rule was 294-136. *(Vote 225, p. H-72)*

While applauding the House endorsement of permanent NTR, top Chinese government officials May 25 denounced as an unwarranted intrusion the provision in the bill calling for a new commission to monitor Chinese labor and human rights. Their statements signaled that, while the bill could herald a new era in Sino-American relations, deep divisions between the two nations will not soon disappear.

Presidential Effort

The deep partisan divisions in Washington, however, were put on hold in the days surrounding the House debate. Majority Leader Dick Armey, R-Texas, who normally prizes his role as a Clinton nemesis, said at a May 24 news conference that he was "proud of the effort the president made."

At the start of the year, proponents of the trade initiative feared that Clinton would back away from the bill to aid Vice President Al Gore, who was caught between his loyalty to the administration and his desire for union support in his bid for the presidency. Instead, Clinton made much of his time available to win over undecided Democrats. Robert T. Matsui of California, the main Democratic vote-counter for the bill in the House, said that many to whom Clinton paid the most attention voted for the bill.

In the House, Clinton relied not only on Matsui but also on Roemer, Cal Dooley of California and James P. Moran of Virginia, leaders of the centrist New Democratic coalition. For them, winning one-third of Democrats to their side on a trade issue in a highly contested election year was something to crow about. "It showed that when we put our minds to it, we can govern from the center out," Moran said.

Roemer identified 50 of those in his party who voted "yes" as New Democrats — somewhat of a consolation prize for unions. While they lost the vote, they were still able to muster their core constituency of Democrats to vote against the bill. And of the 46 Democrats who hail from five of the states seen as pivotal to a presidential victory this year — New Jersey, Pennsylvania, Illinois, Ohio and Michigan — only Levin and Tom Sawyer of Ohio cast votes in favor of the bill.

The Down Side

Such factors did little to lift the spirits of the main opponents who had worked vociferously against the bill. Some union officials threatened to refrain from helping to re-elect Democrats who crossed them on the vote.

At a news conference after the bill passed, Bonior and Nancy Pelosi, D-Calif., who had to wait through more than an hour of celebratory comments from Hastert's and Matsui's groups before they could face reporters in the House Radio-TV studio, found it difficult to conceal their frustration and exhaustion. "The burden is now on members of Congress who voted for this legislation and on the president of the United States to produce some results," Pelosi said.

Bonior was more upbeat, saying that the "no" vote from 45 percent of the House meant that concern about globalization would not go away.

"We will win this" in the long run, he said. "There's a real good feeling I have about what we did today."

Opponents attempted to make passage of the bill more difficult by offering a motion to recommit the bill to Ways and Means with the requirement that it add language saying China's permanent normal trade status would be revoked if it attacked or blockaded Taiwan. China regards Taiwan as a renegade province, and it has threatened military action against it in the recent past. The proposal was designed to make the China vote more difficult for Republicans, but it was defeated, 176-258. *(Vote 227, p. H-72)*

Consideration of the bill had proved divisive for both parties, but it was Democrats who were most split. Some likened the Democratic division over trade, in its fervor and import, to the GOP split over abortion. And many Democrats expressed frustration that Clinton — who pushed NAFTA to enactment one year before Democrats lost control of the House — would push another trade measure just months before Democrats have a chance to win back the majority.

The 237 votes for the China bill were three more than the number who voted in the House for NAFTA. Members such as Matsui said that the president was more engaged and focused on the China debate than he had been on the first trade debate of his presidency, although in that case 102 Democrats took his side, 29 more than did so on May 24.

Shortly after the vote, Democrats began trying to rally around the party. Levin said he agreed with bill opponents that the next president would have to address labor and environmental standards before he would win fast-track trading authority. That authority, which requires Congress to vote up or down on trade agreements the president negotiates, expired in 1994, and Clinton has been unable to win it back. *(1998 Almanac, p. 23-3)*

The day after the vote, Clinton called Minority Leader Richard A. Gephardt, D-Mo., who had opposed the bill, and Bonior to the White House to discuss prescription drugs for Medicare recipients, a proposal Democrats are firmly behind.

Business leaders responded to union threats by offering to cross the country to personally thank the Democrats who sided with them. Still, Donohue noted, the Chamber of Commerce would not be endorsing or contributing to Democratic supporters, who may have a history of voting against the business group 80 percent of the time. That could leave some Democrats in a difficult position.

But Levin, whose district is home to Teamsters President James P. Hoffa and a host of union members, said he was not worried. "When voters look at issues in 2000, they're going to look at all of the issues, at the whole person," he said.

Lott Says Senate Won't Rush Into China NTR Vote

JUNE 17 — Majority Leader Trent Lott, R-Miss., insisted the week of June 12 that the Senate would not rush consideration of legislation to make permanent the normal trade relationship between China and the United States.

Lott said he was attempting to negotiate on possible amendments to the hard-fought, House-passed measure (HR 4444), before bringing it to the floor.

"Senators have strong feelings on all sides, and some of them are going to insist on offering amendments. And I just think if we rush to it we could . . . take something that probably is going to pass overwhelmingly and get it tangled up in a way that would be counterproductive," Lott told reporters June 12.

White House officials, business leaders and others who worked to push the measure through the House in May do not want senators to alter the bill, because that would require the House to consider it a second time. They hope Lott will overrule the desires of Appropriations Committee Chairman Ted Stevens, R-Alaska, and Mitch McConnell, R-Ky., to delay consideration of the China bill until President Clinton has signed appropriations measures.

Joe Lockhart, Clinton's spokesman, said at a press briefing June 13 that Lott would be "making a huge mistake if he decided to use an issue of this importance to play politics."

Senate Minority Leader Tom Daschle, D-S.D., said June 12 that "there's an urgency" to moving the bill as soon as possible so unforeseen international events don't derail it.

Another impetus for moving the bill before the August recess: Commerce Secretary William M. Daley, who has spearheaded administration efforts on the China bill, is resigning July 15 to take a top spot in Vice President Al Gore's presidential campaign.

While bill opponents Paul Wellstone, D-Minn., and Foreign Relations Committee Chairman Jesse Helms, R-N.C., plan to offer amendments on human rights, the most dangerous to leaders' plans for a "clean" measure is a proposal (S 2645) by Fred Thompson, R-Tenn., and Robert G. Torricelli, D-N.J. It would initiate an annual presidential review of China's record in supplying nuclear weapons and technology to nations unfriendly to the United States and would require the president to take action, including suspending exports to individual Chinese arms dealers and withholding foreign aid to the Chinese government, if he determines that such transfers are taking place.

Thompson reiterated June 13 that he would attempt to attach his bill to the China measure if leaders did not allow him to move it as a stand-alone measure. "The Constitution doesn't say anything about our requirement to have a clean bill, [but] it does require us to take care of matters of national security," he told reporters. "I'm determined to have a vote."

While Lott and other Republicans appear to favor S 2645, Thompson said that some Democrats oppose it, and that those senators would be pivotal in determining whether the nuclear proliferation measure was allowed to come up for a free-standing vote. When such a vote could be taken was as unclear as the schedule for the China bill itself.

While more than a dozen GOP senators sent a letter to Lott on June 16 calling on him to move the bill before the July 4 recess, Lott continued to insist that his priority was progress on appropriations. Ten moderate Democrats had also sent Lott a letter the week of June 5 pledging to refrain from introducing amendments to the bill or voting for any offered.

Lott said a "large number" of senators did not want to see the China bill amended. He said he would continue to see if Thompson's provision could be addressed separately, perhaps with debate on a Monday with a vote on the measure the following day.

Senate Will Not Vote Until After July Recess

JUNE 24 — Despite stepped-up efforts by the administration and business groups, President Clinton and Senate Majority Leader Trent Lott, R-Miss., concurred June 22 that the Senate will not vote before the July Fourth recess on whether to permanently normalize U.S.-China trade relations.

"We're working together, and I look forward to a successful conclusion of this in July," Clinton told reporters.

Lott said he was continuing to work to address issues raised by potential amendments to the legislation (HR 4444) that the House passed May 24. Supporters of enhanced China trade are not eager to force another vote in the House, which would be required if senators amended the measure.

Lott and Fred Thompson, R-Tenn., the sponsor with Robert G. Torricelli, D-N.J., of a potential amendment to punish China if it sells nuclear weapons to nations unfriendly to the United States, met separately with national security adviser Samuel R. Berger on June 20 to discuss the proposal. An administration spokesman said Berger sees some of the standards for imposing sanctions in the Thompson-Torricelli proposal (S 2645) as too low.

A Democratic aide said that GOP leaders would attempt to move S 2645 as a stand-alone bill and were circulating a unanimous consent agreement to bring it to the floor July 10. Presumably, the China bill would be taken up soon after. Thompson has said he is amenable to taking up the bill on its own as long as it is done before the China trade measure comes up.

Minority Leader Tom Daschle, D-S.D., warned that if consideration slips to later in the year, "We really raise the possibility that it won't happen at all" because of election-year politics and changing world events.

U.S. Trade Representative Charlene Barshefsky, testifying before the Senate Finance Trade Subcommittee on June 20, said that "every day of delay damages fundamental interests of the United States."

Business groups also sought to push the Senate, through direct lobbying and by encouraging members close to them to back a quick vote. "We're trying to send the message that we want the bill moved as soon as possible, immediately, yesterday," said Rob Nichols, spokesman for the Electronics Industry Alliance, an organization of technology companies.

White House, Senate at Odds Over Arms Proliferation

JULY 15 — Senators concerned about China's role in supplying weapons of mass destruction failed to reach a deal with the White House the week of July 10, casting renewed doubt on the Senate timetable for voting to clear legislation permanently normalizing China's standing as a U.S. trade partner.

Fred Thompson, R-Tenn., and other senators said July 14 that talks had broken down between their staffs and Clinton administration officials on legislation (S 2645) by Thompson and Robert G. Torricelli, D-N.J., to require the president to punish the Chinese government or individual Chinese companies found to be supplying weapons or components to other nations.

The White House, led in negotiations by Deputy Chief of Staff Stephen Ricchetti, wanted the bill expanded to cover other nations known to trade in nuclear weapons. The administration also wanted to lower some thresholds for actions against countries found to be engaging in such activities. Thompson said he would draft an amendment to address administration concerns, but others involved in the talks said they were skeptical a compromise would be reached.

Majority Leader Trent Lott, R-Miss., said he might move to invoke cloture, or limit debate, on the bill the week of July 17. Consideration of that measure is increasingly seen as a politically necessary precursor for debating the China trade bill (HR 4444).

Before the breakdown was announced July 14, Minority Leader Tom Daschle, D-S.D., and the chairman of the Finance Committee's trade panel, Charles E. Grassley, R-Iowa, were predicting that Lott would arrange for votes on both Thompson's bill and the China trade measure before the start of the summer recess on July 28. But earlier in the week, Lott and other Republican senators suggested that the trade bill would not come up before September, a potential delay that caused great worry for the business leaders and members of Congress who were instrumental in pushing the bill through the more trade-hesitant House in May.

Putting the China measure before the Senate so close to the election "would be a terrible mistake," U.S. Chamber of Commerce President Tom Donohue warned at a July 10 press briefing. "The risk of screwing this bill up is serious."

By attempting to brush aside the Thompson-Torricelli measure, Republicans said, it was the White House that was endangering the China measure.

Lott and Thompson chided the administration, which does not support the nuclear proliferation bill, for seeming to advocate that bill's consideration as an amendment to the China measure. More than 70 senators support the China trade bill, and many would be likely to oppose amendments — even those with which they agree — because they do not want the bill forced back to the House for a second vote due to alterations made in the Senate.

Backers of the China bill say the outcome of a second House vote would be in doubt, especially if anti-trade protesters disrupt the GOP and Democratic conventions, as some members fear.

Majority Whip Don Nickles, R-Okla., said that strategy was "playing with fire," because many senators would be hard pressed to vote against language that could bolster U.S. national security.

Foreign Relations Committee Chairman Jesse Helms, R-N.C., and Paul Wellstone, D-Minn., also are expected to offer amendments to the China trade bill, but the Thompson-Torricelli proposal is the most likely to be adopted if offered as an amendment. Torricelli said that the negotiations had pressed home the point to the administration "that the Senate is not going to pass the China bill without some non-proliferation action."

Next House Vote July 18

The House is scheduled to cast its next vote on China on July 18, when it will debate a measure (H J Res 103) by Dana Rohrabacher, R-Calif., disapproving of Clinton's extension of normal trade relations with China for another year.

With no debate, the House Ways and Means Committee voted July 13 to recommend the House defeat the resolution, which seems certain. Under the 1974 trade law (PL 93-618), the president must yearly certify that communist nations are allowing free emigration before they can receive the lowest tariffs on their exports to the United States. Because the bill to make China's status permanent has not been enacted, Clinton needed to make his annual declaration, or the status would have expired this month.

Later this month, the House also likely will consider another Rohrabacher measure (H J Res 99) that would disapprove of the president's decision to continue help for U.S. companies doing business in Vietnam. Congress may also be called on to vote on legislation to implement the trade expansion agreement that Clinton and Vietnam's leaders announced July 13.

Senate Debate Scheduled, but Further Delay On Vote Likely

JULY 22 — One of the few bills that President Clinton, the GOP leadership and the business community all have labeled "must pass" this year — to make permanent the normal U.S.-China trade relationship — is likely to come before the Senate on July 26, but the final vote will be after Labor Day.

Majority Leader Trent Lott, R-Miss., who has been under pressure to move the measure, outlined a schedule July 18 under which the Senate would devote three days to debate on trade with China before the start of the summer recess, but only if it first passes three more appropriations bills.

If all goes as planned, Lott said, he will move to limit debate on whether the China legislation (HR 4444) should be formally put before the Senate; senators would take that test vote before the recess. If Lott wins the 60 votes he needs to cut off a filibuster, debate and a vote to clear the measure will occur soon after Labor Day. Though consideration would be bifurcated, Lott told senators, his plan should "show clearly that we intend to go to this legislation."

Minority Leader Tom Daschle, D-S.D., who also backs the bill, praised Lott for "approaching the issue in that way."

Proponents of China trade expansion in the House — which passed the bill with a 40-vote margin in May — objected to what they termed a tardy debate and a risky scenario. Jim Kolbe, R-Ariz., called the delay until fall "a terrible mistake," adding that "if, God forbid, permanent normal trade relations [NTR] is lost, the blame will be placed on Republicans — and rightly so."

The challenge for Lott and Daschle will be to move the measure without amendment. Supporters do not want the Senate to alter the bill and thereby force its return to the House, where it would be challenged once again by unions, environmentalists, human rights advocates and other groups that maintain that permanent NTR would lower working standards and add to pollution worldwide.

In the Senate, Fred Thompson, R-Tenn., and Robert G. Torricelli, D-N.J., are pushing for Congress to debate legislation to address China's role in the spread of weapons of mass destruction concurrently with the debate on enhancing trade. Their bill (S 2645) would require the president to punish China if its leaders or business officials were found, through a new annual review, to be furnishing weapons or weapons components to other nations.

Democrats argued the week of July 17 that taking up the Thompson-Torricelli bill should not be a precursor to considering the China trade measure. Nonetheless, Lott announced July 21 that he wants the nuclear weapons bill considered as an amendment to the fiscal 2001 intelligence authorization measure (S 2507), set to go before the Senate July 24.

If that move is thwarted somehow, Lott could try and arrange consideration of the Thompson-Torricelli legislation in the evenings, after debate on the trade bill had subsided.

Lott is a cosponsor of the anti-proliferation bill and has worked for months to move it separately, saying that he believes it probably would be adopted as an amendment to the trade legislation. The administration, which opposes the Thompson-Torricelli bill, appears to believe it would be easier to defeat as an amendment. A number of the 70 senators said to be committed to voting for the trade bill have said they do not want that measure returned to the House and so would oppose amendments.

NTR Extended for Now

Under the 1974 trade law (PL 93-618), the president may grant NTR status, which brings with it the most favorable U.S. tariff treatment, to some communist nations only one year at a time, and only after he declares that the nations in question have policies leading toward free emigration. HR 4444 would allow the president to drop China from that list of communist nations once it joins the World Trade Organization on terms at least as favorable to the United States as those set in a November agreement between Beijing and Washington. That is expected to happen this fall.

While the bill awaited debate in the Senate, Clinton on June 2 declared the most recent one-year extension of NTR status for Beijing, creating for House critics of China another opportunity to take a legislative stand. On July 18, the House rejected, 147-281, a resolution (H J Res 103) to overturn Clinton's decision. *(Vote 405, p. H-126)*

House members showed little desire to reconsider the China issue, having so recently been compelled to take sides in what will likely be remembered as the most contentious congressional debate ever on trade with China. As a result, 164 Republicans voted to defeat the resolution, the same number as voted for the permanent NTR bill. However, 117 Democrats voted against the resolution, 44 more than voted for the permanent NTR bill.

Thompson Eyes China Trade Bill As Vehicle for Arms Provisions

JULY 29 — Fred Thompson has returned to a familiar position. For the second time in three years, Tennessee's senior Republican senator is squarely in the middle of a dispute involving China, with money at the core and the White House and most congressional Democrats on the other side.

Thompson's prospects for prevailing in this year's showdown became more tenuous the week of July 24. Democrats were able to forestall his efforts to get a Senate vote on his legislation (S 2645) that would require the president to punish the Chinese government or individual Chinese companies if they were found to be supplying weapons of mass destruction or components to other nations.

With the backing of Majority Leader Trent Lott, R-Miss., Thompson wanted to offer his proposal as an amendment to the intelligence authorization bill (S 2507) for fiscal 2001. The Senate voted 96-1 July 26 to limit debate to 30 hours on a motion to call up that bill. After that, however, Democrats showed no interest in allowing the process to move any faster, and Lott went on to other business. *(Vote 228, p. S-41)*

Thompson now must wait until fall, when he will face at least as difficult a legislative task — trying to make his bill an amendment to the bill (HR 4444) that would grant permanent normal trade relations (PNTR) to China.

Supporters of that measure — leaders of both parties in the Senate, the administration and the business community — are anxious to keep the proliferation proposal at bay, because any amendment would return the bill to the House. The House passed the measure handily in May after a hard-fought battle, but some fear the outcome would be hard to predict on a second vote closer to the election.

The Senate voted 86-12 on July 27 to limit debate on a motion to proceed to the China trade measure, setting up what will likely be at least a week of debate starting Sept. 5, when the Senate's summer recess ends. *(Vote 231, p. S-41)*

Lott vowed to refrain from making an early move to cut off debate on the bill itself. He plans, however, to have the Senate debate fiscal 2001 spending bills in the evenings during the trade debate.

"There will be no rush to judgment," Lott said, "but I do think the responsible thing to do is to begin making progress toward an eventual judgment."

Senators will likely be called on to vote on several amendments by two opponents of normalized trade with China — Jesse Helms, R-N.C., and Paul Wellstone, D-Minn. — but none is considered as likely to be adopted as Thompson's proposal.

Thompson's Determination

In an effort to head off that possibility, Lott worked for weeks to arrange for the proliferation bill to move on its own or as an amendment to another measure. The procedural wrangling proved irritating to Thompson. A former Watergate prosecutor, he is known for being impatient with such tactical maneuvering — a peeve that surfaced three years ago when, as chairman of the Governmental Affairs Committee, he directed a yearlong probe of alleged campaign fundraising improprieties that centered on Chinese donations to the Democratic Party. *(1997 Almanac, p. 1-20)*

"At a time of monumental change in our relationship with Beijing," he said in a July 25 floor speech, "is it asking too much for a fellow permanent member of the U.N. Security Council to obey international rules and norms with regard to the proliferation of weapons of mass destruction?"

In some ways, Thompson said, his experience with this legislation parallels his committee's campaign finance inquiry. Although he has had Democratic cooperation in this case, he said he still must confront a White House that, in his view, has not been suitably cautious about China. "In both cases, the administration has been apologists for the Chinese," he said.

Opponents of Thompson's measure, including some Republicans and many business and trade groups, maintain it should not be considered in the context of Sino-American trade. Thompson says his legislation's detractors have left him with little alternative. His bill's critics "can't say, 'We're worried about this with regard to PNTR,' and yet we're being forced to either go home or put it on that," Thompson said in a July 27 interview. "I ain't going home. This is something that's going to be with us for a while."

If his proposal is offered as an amendment to the China trade measure, Democrats are expected to offer alternatives that could create a committee to oversee China's proliferation activities or take other less drastic steps.

"The concept of an alternative is just going to grow," said former Rep. Dave McCurdy, D-Okla. (1981-95), president of the Electronic Industries Alliance, a major lobbying force for expanded China trade.

Thompson and co-sponsor Robert G. Torricelli, D-N.J., have modified their legislation in a so-far unsuccessful bid to accommodate the White House. The new version would apply to all key suppliers of weapons instead of just China, while making sanctions against those countries discretionary rather than mandatory.

Critics still contend the proposal is being rushed and requires more discussion. "You can't expect 100 members of the Senate to understand something this complicated," said Chuck Hagel, R-Neb.

In response, Thompson said the bill already has provoked a debate about China's role in the spread of arms that might not have otherwise occurred at the Capitol this year. "I realize it's an uphill battle in terms of 51 votes or 60," he said. "But even if I lose, it doesn't mean this is going away. . . . We've had a good debate."

China Trade Bill Nears Its Finale As Senators Spurn Amendments

SEPTEMBER 9 — Business interests pushing eagerly for the bill to boost trade opportunities with China spent a long, antsy summer wringing their hands about delays in getting the measure on the Senate floor. But as the Senate took up the bill the week of Sept. 4, it appeared that there had been little reason for their fretting. A smooth path to enactment seemed assured after a bipartisan, pro-trade bloc decisively swatted away the first cluster of amendments that might have imperiled the legislation.

The measure (HR 4444) would make permanent the normal trade relations status now extended to China only one year at a time. That would ease the way for Beijing to become a member of the World Trade Organization (WTO) and assure a relaxation of Chinese barriers to the importation of all manner of goods and services from the United States. The bill is among the top priorities of President Clinton in his last year in office. Most Republicans and a bevy of Democrats support the proposal as well, especially those from states with large export-oriented agricultural and high-tech sectors.

With about three-fourths of the Senate prepared to vote for the bill, the only suspense as the debate got under way was whether any effort to amend the legislation — and thereby require that it be sent back for more deliberations by the House — might succeed.

But a pact among bill supporters to try to block any and all attempts to change the measure appeared to be holding strong, as the Senate voted by wide margins against amendments by opponents Paul Wellstone, D-Minn., Ernest F. Hollings, D-S.C., and Robert C. Byrd, D-W.Va.

Even as he offered an amendment aimed at spurring the use of "clean coal" technology in China, Byrd conceded that he was "utterly wasting my time" since so many senators had taken a "blood oath" to reject even amendments that they might otherwise support — all in the name of averting another vote by the House. The amendment was rejected, 32-64. *(Vote 235, p. S-42)*

Byrd's speech Sept. 7 provided a good measure of the drama surrounding the debate during the week, as he tore into his colleagues for abandoning their cherished right to amend legislation sent to them by the House. "What is the Senate coming to when the Senate engages in that kind of charade?" Byrd asked. "Senators ought to bow their heads in shame."

The House passed the bill by a 40-vote margin just before Memorial Day, but only after an arduous lobbying campaign led by Clinton, the GOP leadership and a broad array of business leaders. None of them want to repeat that exercise again less than two months before Election Day — especially Democrats, who are eager to mend their fences with labor unions, which have led the opposition.

Rep. Robert T. Matsui, D-Calif., a top proponent of the China trade bill, said he could not guarantee a comparable level of Democratic support on a second House vote. (The bill drew 73 Democratic votes in May.)

Matsui added that he was optimistic that the issue would not hurt Democrats in November. "I don't want to say they've gotten over it, but they know the stakes are so high now," he said of labor unions in a Sept. 6 interview. "They can't afford now to slow down the momentum. And they really want the House."

In the Senate, Finance Committee Chairman William V. Roth Jr., R-Del., agreed with Matsui on the risks associated with returning the bill to the House. "Bluntly, a vote to amend is a vote to kill this bill and, with it, any chance that U.S. workers, farmers and businesses will benefit from China's accession to the WTO."

Minority Leader Tom Daschle, D-S.D., said he would probably support a move by Majority Leader Trent Lott, R-Miss., the week of Sept. 11 to invoke cloture and limit debate and amendments to the bill. Lott wants to clear the measure by the end of the week.

Supporters of the legislation say the final vote should be characterized as the most important ballot that senators cast this year, given the huge economic consequences of expanding trade with the most populous nation in the world.

Opponents, too, see the vote as historic, viewing the bill's enactment as tantamount to giving Beijing a free pass for any labor, human rights and environmental misdeeds.

For an issue in which the stakes are so high, however, the debate had a going-through-the-motions feel. On the first day, Sept. 5, speechmaking on the measure often took a back seat as senators took to the floor to discuss parochial concerns or hot-button political issues such as raising the minimum wage, adding a prescription drug benefit to the Medicare program or giving a "patients' bill of rights" to those whose health care is provided by health maintenance organizations.

"There was never any thought on our side that there would be any difficulty getting it done," said Jade West, staff director of the Republican Policy

Committee. "The only question was when to get it done and whether or not to let it precede appropriations bills. We always figured it would be an almost autopilot process once it hit the floor."

Senate debates tend to be less passionate than those in the House, but the lack of "buzz" was notable. Senate anterooms were mostly bereft of union and business lobbyists, who had swarmed the other side of the Capitol this spring.

Opponents such as Jesse Helms, R-N.C., lambasted China's human rights record, its hostility towards Taiwan and its record on the proliferation of nuclear weapons technology. In his speech, Helms sought to call attention to the State Department's 1999 assessment of China's human rights record, which said: "The Chinese government's poor human rights record deteriorated markedly throughout the past year, as the government intensified efforts to suppress dissent."

The next speaker, Larry E. Craig, R-Idaho, turned the discussion to the wildfires in the West this summer.

Some supporters remained unnerved by lingering talk in GOP circles that the scheduling of a vote on the China bill — perhaps the Clinton legislative priority with the best chance of enactment in the closing days of the 106th Congress — might be used as leverage to obtain his signature on the 11 fiscal 2001 appropriations bills that still need to be completed before adjournment.

"There are those in leadership and others who feel that [the China bill] should be . . . used for political leverage," lamented Pat Roberts, R-Kan. "And I think that's more prevalent today than it was a month ago."

But several senators and senior GOP aides dismissed the notion that the China bill might be held hostage. Hostage-taking only works when one is willing to shoot the captive, something Republicans seem unwilling to do to the China trade initiative.

The Final Hurdle

By weeks' end, the only potential roadblock involved a bid by Fred Thompson, R-Tenn., and Robert G. Torricelli, D-N.J., to use the bill as a vehicle to carry their bill (S 2645) to require the government to impose sanctions on the Chinese government or individual Chinese companies if they were found to be supplying weapons of mass destruction or their components to other countries.

Thompson and Torricelli have been frustrated at almost every turn in their push for that idea. Their original proposal called for sanctions against China if it was found to be sending weapons of mass destruction to other nations. In an unsuccessful bid to accommodate the White House, the senators reworked the legislation this summer to make it apply to all key suppliers of weapons as well, while making sanctions against those countries discretionary rather than mandatory.

With even that proposal unlikely to win a majority, Thompson said he may offer a second amendment that would limit it further, by adding weapons of mass destruction to the list of congressional concerns about China included in the House-passed bill.

As the duo continued to water down their plan in a bid to win votes, they nonetheless appeared shy of a majority in the face of the "no amendment" pact by bill supporters. Lott added a wrinkle when he said he would vote for Thompson and Torricelli's plan, although a senior Lott aide predicted the amendment would fail anyway, as did supporters of the bill.

Efforts to bring Thompson and Torricelli's amendment to the floor as a separate bill continued but remained fruitless by week's end; opponents of the China trade measure blocked the idea because it would smooth out the remaining obstacle to passage of the underlying legislation, a senior Democratic staff aide said.

On Sept. 7, the Senate voted 92-5 to take up the bill. *(Vote 233, p. S-42)*

But a more accurate barometer of the bill's momentum came later that day on the first spate of amendments. Wellstone and Helms proposed to delay the awarding of permanent normal trade relations status until the president certifies that China has made substantial strides towards permitting greater religious freedom. It was defeated, 30-67. Hollings proposed a requirement for annual reviews of China's trade status, as called for under current law. It was rejected 13-81. *(Votes 234, 236, p. S-42)*

China Trade Bill Remains Intact As Senate Rejects Arms Sanctions

SEPTEMBER 16 — With the surprisingly resounding rejection of a proposal aimed at checking China's national security threat to the United States, the Senate is poised to overwhelmingly approve legislation Sept. 19 that would establish permanent normal trade relations with China.

At least 70 senators are expected to vote to clear the bill (HR 4444), a final vote of confidence for an initiative that has been at the center of one of the most hard-fought lobbying campaigns in recent years.

By making permanent China's standing as a normal U.S. trading partner, the measure would seal a sweeping agreement under which the world's most populous nation will open its markets to American goods and services. The prospect of those benefits led the Clinton administration to team up with the business community against unions, environmentalists, human right advocates and defense hawks, who maintain that some of China's behavior might be worsened given the reward of a trade deal.

The White House and business lobby successfully opposed all amendments to address those concerns, out of fear that altering the measure and forcing its return to the House could doom it so late in the 106th Congress. The House passed the bill in May.

Proponents heaved a huge sigh of relief Sept. 13 after the defeat of the marquee amendment — a move by Sens. Fred Thompson, R-Tenn., and Robert G. Torricelli, D-N.J., to impose sanctions on Chinese companies if they were caught exporting nuclear, chemical or biological weapons. Buffeted by procedural setbacks and bipartisan criticism, their amendment was tabled, or killed, 65-32. *(Vote 242, p. S-43)*

"I was hoping we could get into the 40s rather than the 30s," Thompson said afterward, tacitly acknowledging that his proposal never posed a true threat to the China bill. "Clearly, the no-amendment strategy is working for them."

Torricelli agreed: "The pressure from the White House and business community was intense and could not be resisted."

Several Republicans who had endorsed the proposal voted to table the amendment because, they said, it did not belong in the trade bill. Max Baucus, D-Mont., a leading proponent of the China bill, attributed the amendment's large margin of defeat to the realization of about a dozen senators that the measure "probably caused more problems than it was going to solve."

Supporters of enhanced trade with China professed not to be bothered by the Senate's prolonged deliberations on the bill, which stretched over 10 days. Some, however, expressed frustration with Majority Leader Trent Lott, R-Miss., for waiting so long to move on a bill that so many senators would seek to amend.

"A major tactical error," said Rep. Robert T. Matsui, D-Calif., the administration's point man on the measure. "A bill like that should never be brought up in the last month of Congress."

Others faulted Lott for allowing consideration of amendments they said could send the wrong signal internationally were they adopted, or wondered if his tactics were designed to gain leverage on year-end negotiations with the president on other issues.

"I don't understand the strategy or the position of Sen. Lott on this," said Joseph R. Biden Jr. of Delaware, the Foreign Relations Committee's ranking Democrat. "At this point, to turn down China has enormous foreign policy consequences, as far as I'm concerned."

Lott offered no apologies for his handling of the trade issue. He noted that he supported efforts in July to offer an earlier version of the Thompson-Torricelli proposal (S 2645) to the fiscal 2001 intelligence authorization bill (S 2507), but that he was met with objections from Democrats.

Lott was among the 23 Republicans who joined nine Democrats in supporting the amendment.

Security vs. Commerce

The failure of the Thompson-Torricelli amendment underscored how difficult it has been for Republicans worried about China's danger to U.S. national security to make their voices heard over those more concerned with promoting commerce. Although senior GOP lawmakers have condemned the administration for using the term "strategic partnership" to characterize U.S.-Chinese relations, they also have heeded the warning of the party's business allies not to stir up any anti-China sentiment.

Thompson pointed to recent intelligence reports of increasing Chinese export of weapons of mass destruction as evidence Congress should hold the government in Beijing accountable.

The amendment, as weakened in recent weeks in an effort to draw more support, would have required the president to review China's proliferation activities each year and cut off technology exports as well as government loans and credits if he determined any weapons or components were leaving the country. The president would have been allowed to waive the sanctions in the name of national security.

Opponents questioned whether unilateral sanctions would prove effective against China and said few other nations were likely to follow the U.S. lead in punishing the country, so the effect could be to put American companies at a competitive disadvantage.

Even before the amendment was defeated, Thompson vowed to continue working on the issue. Other supporters of reining in proliferation welcomed having more time. "It needs to be modified, it needs to be debated, the Commerce, State and Defense departments need to weigh in, industry needs to weigh in," said Larry M. Wortzel, director of the Asian Studies Center at the Heritage Foundation, a conservative think tank.

Coincidentally, the vote came the same day that former Los Alamos National Laboratory scientist Wen Ho Lee was freed after striking a deal with federal prosecutors to plead guilty to a single felony charge in the 59-count indictment against him. Lee's release was an embarrassing setback for the Clinton administration, which had accused the Taiwan-born physicist of giving highly sensitive nuclear secrets to China.

Republicans have sought to make a political issue of Chinese espionage. In the Senate alone, five committees have held more than 20 hearings on the subject, and angry GOP senators promised more hearings on the Justice Department's handling of the Lee case.

Democrats, however, said Republicans did not acknowledge the possibility that congressional overreaction played any role in shaping events on the case. They said the GOP misplayed its hand by appearing so partisan on China. "Whether it is trade, whether it is human rights, whether it is the environment, whether it is Wen Ho Lee, there's a legitimate cause to look at all these things," Biden said. "I'm of the opinion they were looked at through the prism of politics at the front end. It was viewed through the wrong prism."

Other Amendments

The Senate rebuffed 17 other amendments, all primarily on the grounds that their inclusion could delay or perhaps destroy the measure's chances for enactment. Among them were proposals:

- By Jesse Helms, R-N.C., to require the president to certify that China had made strides on improving a range of human rights issues, including dismantling labor camps, opening access to Tibet and reviewing prison sentences and releasing those imprisoned for religious or political reasons. Defeated 32-63 on Sept. 12. *(Vote 239, p. S-43)*
- By Robert C. Smith, R-N.H., who offered three proposals to require the congressional-executive branch commission created under the bill to monitor China's cooperation with U.S. goals on human rights issues, such as reducing the harvesting of organs from prisoners. That one was defeated, 29-66, on Sept. 13. *(Vote 241, p. S-43)*
- By Paul Wellstone, D-Minn., to require the president to certify that China is not exporting goods made with prison labor before he grants the country permanent normal trade status. Defeated, 29-68, on Sept. 12. *(Vote 238, p. S-43)*
- By Robert C. Byrd, D-W.Va., to require that China disclose information on how it will reduce reliance on state-owned businesses and other government intervention in commerce. Defeated by voice vote Sept. 12.
- By Helms, to require the Commerce secretary to establish a voluntary code of conduct for U.S. business-

es operating in China. Defeated, 23-73, on Sept. 13. *(Vote 244, p. S-43)*

• By Ernest F. Hollings, D-S.C., to restrict eligibility for assistance from the Export-Import Bank or Overseas Private Investment Corp. to those with no recent advanced technology transfers to China or to those who had not recently moved production plants to China. Defeated by voice vote Sept. 14.

Support for Trade Expansion Strong As Senate Clears China Trade Bill

SEPTEMBER 23 — The overwhelming Senate vote to make permanent China's standing as a normal trading partner of the United States is more than a historic milestone in Sino-American relations and the finale in one of the most consequential debates of the 106th Congress. It also is a dramatic illustration of the breadth of support that trade expansion is capable of generating.

The 83-15 vote on Sept. 19 to clear the China trade legislation (HR 4444) is no guarantee, however, that the next Congress and the next president will face easy sledding when it comes to trade expansion. *(Vote 251, p. S-45)*

The questions on their collective trade plate during the next two years are wide-ranging: Whether to revive an expedited process for congressional debate of trade pacts; whether to embrace a bilateral trade deal with Vietnam reached this summer and another one about to be sealed with Jordan; what weight to give attempts to chip away at sanctions on countries unfriendly to the United States, especially Cuba and Iran; and how to tackle public concerns about international commerce, namely its effects on labor rights and environmental degradation.

Outside Congress, U.S. negotiators will continue to push trade expansion forward, by attempting to reduce trade barriers world-wide through the World Trade Organization (WTO) and trying to facilitate trade throughout the Western Hemisphere.

Debates on the benefits of most of those actions will not be as easy to sell to Congress — and the public — as the virtues of enhanced and stable trade with the world's most populous nation. The sales pitch for that bill was eased by the sheer number of cuts to tariffs, quotas and other trade barriers that the Chinese committed to make last fall in return for one change to U.S. law: ending the annual rite of the president and Congress reviewing China's behavior before granting its imports another year of low tariffs.

The bill's enactment promises that billions of dollars in economic benefits will come to American business. They will come despite continued complaints that a country with a poor labor and human rights history is not worthy of the same low-tariff treatment most other countries get. Still, the issue has received scant debate outside Washington or on the campaign trail.

Both Vice President Al Gore, the Democratic nominee, and Gov. George W. Bush of Texas, the Republican nominee, supported the bill. Both also espouse the importance of continuing the expansion of trade — particularly within the Western Hemisphere — that has been one of the foreign policy hallmarks of the Clinton administration.

The candidates' similar views, and the splits trade creates in both major political parties, has forced trade expansion into the background on the campaign trail. When it does come up, it is usually in the stump speeches of the two most prominent minor party candidates — Reform nominee Pat Buchanan and Green nominee Ralph Nader. Although from the right and left edges of the American political spectrum, they share an opposition to trade expansion, contending that it is wrong to give potential boosts to corporate profits priority over national security, in Buchanan's view, or the well-being of people worldwide, in Nader's.

A similar political pattern was evident in the Senate's vote Sept. 19, in which the smaller-than-expected minority was formed by five of the more liberal Democrats, five of the most conservative Republicans, three GOP senators with pro-union leanings and two Democrats from import sensitive states in voting against the bill. (The Senate's 83 percent show of support dwarfed the 54 percent House majority that passed the bill May 24.)

Fast Track Authority

If either Bush or Gore is to achieve his goal of expanding trade, the path would be eased by the renewal of "fast track" trade negotiating authority, granted to each president since Gerald R. Ford but allowed to lapse at the end of 1994. The procedure allows the administration to negotiate a trade agreement without fear that Congress will amend the pact. Instead, when a president submits a bill to Congress to implement a trade agreement, Congress has 90 days to endorse it or reject it, but may not alter it.

Two years ago, the House defeated Clinton's request to revive this procedure. *(1998 Almanac, p. 23-3)*

The next president will be under great pressure, particularly if Democrats control all or part of Congress, to alter the fast track procedure of the past to ensure that trade's effects on laborers' rights and environmental degradation are taken into account.

That debate could be joined on some trade agreements that will be put before the 107th Congress, including those with Vietnam and Jordan. The pending deal with Jordan will contain language on labor and the environment, according to U.S. Trade Representative Charlene Barshefsky, and could serve as a test case for tackling such concerns overall.

Bush would likely seek to revive the previous fast track terms, and would probably get his wish if Republicans retain control of Congress. If Democrats take back the House their insistence on addressing labor and environmental matters could polarize the debate anew, straining trade's longstanding tradition — so clearly echoed in the Senate vote — of being a non-partisan issue.

Gore has already said that if elected he would ensure that future trade pacts address labor rights and environmental quality. How strongly he would push would be paramount to his success in winning concessions in those areas, on which many nations say the United States has no business butting in. So his promise could bog down progress on trade expansion.

It is also not clear that Gore would seek to revive fast track. Barshefsky, in a Sept. 20 interview, said that Congress' growing involvement in trade matters may make the need for fast track obsolete.

"We need to think very carefully about whether to pursue fast track," said Barshefsky, whose views are likely to carry weight even though she is unlikely to be a part of a Gore administration. "The question has to be considered anew in a very dispassionate way and not blinded by old thinking."

Scaling the Great Wall

Those on both sides of the trade debate agree on one thing: Making permanent the U.S. trade relationship with China — and making possible billions of dollars in projected benefits for U.S. industries — was a much easier sell than a somewhat fuzzy trade procedure such as fast track will be.

As part of its effort to join the WTO later this year, China committed in November to significant cuts in tariffs and other trade barriers on U.S.-made products. The United States has similarly cut tariffs on Chinese-made products since 1980, a year after leaders in Beijing signed a trade pact with President Jimmy Carter. Since 1989, Congress has annually voted to uphold that trade status. *(1980 Almanac, p. 356)*

Big business poured millions into lobbying for a permanent trade relationship with China, and smaller organizations, such as farm groups, put grass-roots pressure on lawmakers. The high-technology industry cut its fledgling lobbying teeth on the bill.

Enactment of the bill had also been one of the few top-tier priorities for Clinton during his last year in the White House. His signature will provide the coda on a presidency that will be marked as one under which international trade was greatly expanded. He opened his first term by pushing through a hesitant Congress the North American Free Trade Agreement (PL 103-182), which had been negotiated by his predecessor, George Bush. The next year, just before his fast-track power lapsed, he pushed Congress to send him a measure (PL 103-465) to implement a new General Agreement on Tariffs and Trade, the sweeping changes to the world trade system under which the WTO was created. *(1993 Almanac, p. 171; 1994 Almanac p. 123)*

"The China debate became a debate on the overall course of the China relationship," said Myron A. Brilliant, a lobbyist for the U.S. Chamber of Commerce, which has led lobbying campaigns for trade expansion. "On trade agreements and on fast track, it centers much more on the role of labor and environmental issues."

Daniel A. Seligman, director of the Sierra Club's Responsible Trade Campaign, said that "if the debate is around a country, the issue often gets reduced to whether or not you like that particular country. Having a debate around a trade agreement or trade negotiating authority, then it's easier to conduct the debate on a level of principle."

The principles Seligman would like debated focus on preventing world trade rules from tying the hands of governments that want to set their own environmental and labor laws. Environmentalists say that in the name of creating a level playing field for businesses, the WTO has essentially overridden local regulations.

Some in Congress see the China debate as an example of how they might deal with some constituent worries about the global marketplace.

Despite months of ardent lobbying, success for the China bill was not assured until a week before the House vote, when its supporters agreed to add on creation of an executive branch-congressional commission to review China's record on labor and human rights, the environment and other issues. Any legislation it recommended would receive expedited consideration in Congress.

"If fast track did take into consideration those issues on the same basis the China trade bill does, it would be a worthy compromise," Charles E. Grassley, R-Iowa, chairman of the Senate Finance International Trade Subcommittee, told reporters Sept. 19.

"In my judgment, there's no choice but to tackle these issues; they won't go away," said Rep. Sander M. Levin, D-Mich., a sponsor of the additional language, which has been derided by unions and other opponents of the China bill as no more than a "fig leaf" to cover Congress' failure to take steps guaranteeing that the Chinese will see their lives improved along with expanded trade.

Some pro-trade Democrats such as Rep. Robert T. Matsui of California, who led the administration's campaign for passage of the China bill, say it will be necessary in future deals to take such steps. Without them, said Rep. Sherrod Brown, D-Ohio, a leading opponent of recent trade expansion legislation, fast track will remain a dead letter. "If Bill Clinton couldn't do it . . . no president will be able to do it," he said in an interview Sept. 19.

Some of the most pro-trade members in both parties, however, see such steps as unnecessary. Congress would "build the support we need for fast track," Sen. Phil Gramm, R-Texas, said in an interview Sept. 19, if there was "a president that we trust." Former Rep. David K. McCurdy, D-Okla., (1981-95), president of the pro-trade Electronics Industries Alliance, said, "There's no reason to qualify it [fast track] right now."

The Long Term

For the loose coalition of environmental, labor, religious, consumer and other groups that lost the hard-fought battle over China trade, the last year has still presented some bright spots. They pressed their cause to the forefront of national awareness with their protests at the WTO session in Seattle last year, and they see the lingering attention as offering hope for future success.

While she termed the China loss "a pretty big blow," Thea Lee, the AFL-CIO's assistant director of public policy, said that "there's a long-term struggle that we have made progress on."

Seligman was less circumspect. "I think Seattle knocked Humpty Dumpty off the wall in a way that the victory on China will not be able to put him back together," he said.

While some believe the China vote showed that the anti-globalization forces are not as strong as thought, it is increasingly unlikely that Seligman's group and others will be shut out of the arenas in which trade policy is made.

Much of their focus in coming years will not be on Congress. A dialogue with the nations of Latin America, initiated in the Reagan and Bush administrations and known as the Free Trade Area of the Americas, is considered a prime spot to address trade's affects on environment and culture. The talks have a 2005 deadline, although Barshefsky said a new president could speed their conclusion. While Congress would not have a vote on the process until a trade agreement was completed, members have provided input to U.S. negotiators and are expected to be consulted more often as the process zeroes in on controversial issues.

This proposal would essentially extend NAFTA throughout the Western Hemisphere, but the next president may aim to give some nations a head start. For instance, GOP nominee Bush's father promised to work for Chile's inclusion in 1992. (The Clinton administration has done little to advance that proposal.) In addition, some Republicans, such as Gramm, want to see Great Britain admitted to NAFTA. And members will also push for a one-year exemption from some textile quotas for Colombia, Ecuador, Peru and Bolivia, if that proposal does not find its way into an end-of-the-session bill this year.

Separate negotiations will also probably be ongoing within the WTO on a new round of talks to reduce trade barriers across a spectrum of industries.

Although the Seattle meeting failed to launch a new round as had been anticipated, some observers believe the election of a new U.S. president may jump start world-wide trade talks. Such discussions usually take three to five years to be completed.

Because Clinton, as a lame duck, could not see through any negotiations he launched, his status has been an obstacle to beginning new trade projects. Many in Congress look forward to returning to full strength next year.

"It may be on the back burner in the campaign — all foreign policy issues seem to be — but it will very much be on the front burner" in 2001, Levin said. ◆

African-Caribbean Initiative Lowers Tariffs, Quotas on Some Foreign-Made Apparel

Box Score

- **Bill:** HR 434 — PL 106-200
- **Legislative action: House** adopted the conference report (H Rept 106-606), 309-110, on May 4.

Senate cleared the bill, 77-19, on May 11.

President signed HR 434 on May 18.

SUMMARY

Congress cleared legislation to lower import tariffs and remove quotas on certain goods — mainly apparel made from U.S. cloth and yarn — from sub-Saharan Africa, Central America and the Caribbean. It was the first major legislation in six years to expand U.S. trade.

President Clinton pushed Congress vigorously to clear HR 434, which had stalled at the end of 1999, partly in an effort to create a pro-trade environment for the more crucial vote on legislation that would make permanent the normalized trade relations between the United States and China. *(Background, 1999 Almanac, p. 23-11, 1998 Almanac, p. 23-10)*

The bill was originally envisioned as a way to stimulate the economies of some of the world's poorest nations through trade, rather than aid and loans. The final bill, however, was restricted primarily to supporting the apparel industry in the Caribbean and Central America and to stimulating the development of such an industry in the 48 nations of sub-Saharan Africa.

The bill allowed countries from both regions to export apparel made from U.S. yarns and fabric to the United States free of duties or quotas. Other clothing was allowed to enter duty-free under limited conditions. For example, a small amount of clothing made in African countries using African yarn can enter without duties. U.S. textile manufacturers pushed hard for those limits.

The bill was complicated by several provisions with little connection to the core purpose of boosting commerce in the Third World. Language to step up retaliation against the European Union for discriminating against bananas grown in Central America and beef raised on U.S. ranches was added during negotiations. The bill also lowered tariffs on high-quality wool, a provision backed by U.S. suit manufacturers. U.S. pharmaceutical companies successfully fought off a proposal that would have allowed Africans to bypass U.S. patent protections and buy AIDS-fighting drugs more cheaply.

Negotiators Make Progress on Bill To Expand Trade In Africa, Caribbean

MARCH 25— Members of Congress and business lobbyists hoping to expand access to the U.S. market for goods coming from the Caribbean, Central America and sub-Saharan Africa appeared to be narrowing their differences the week of March 20 and preparing for an agreement before the spring recess begins April 14.

"I think that deals are ready to be made," said Julia K. Hughes, vice president of international trade and government relations for the U.S. Association of Importers of Textiles and Apparel. Ronald J. Sorini, a lobbyist for underwear-maker Fruit of the Loom Inc., said officials are optimistic that an agreement will be reached, although there are "still many problems to overcome."

Plans to expand trade with the 24 countries of the Caribbean Basin and the 48 nations of sub-Saharan Africa have been in the works since the North American Free Trade Agreement was implemented (PL 103-182) in 1993. If the measure (HR 434) now under consideration clears Congress, it would be the first big trade bill to reach the president since the 1994 law

(PL 103-465) to implement the General Agreement on Tariffs and Trade. *(1993 Almanac, p. 171; 1994 Almanac, p. 123)*

But the House and Senate still have significant hurdles to overcome, namely the concerns of textile-state members who believe that industry has already been hurt too much by cheap imports.

The House bill would generally place few conditions on products being imported, while the Senate would insist that apparel be made from U.S. components if it is to be imported free of duties or quotas. The Senate bill covers African and Caribbean components, while the House bill covers only Africa, but the Ways and Means Committee also approved a Caribbean bill (HR 984) last year.

Senate Majority Leader Trent Lott, R-Miss., met March 21 with senior members from both parties on the Senate Finance and House Ways and Means committees to discuss the legislation, according to Charles B. Rangel of New York, the ranking Democrat on Ways and Means. The chairman of the panel's Trade Subcommittee, Philip M. Crane, R-Ill., a staunch supporter of the House bills, did not attend because he is seeking treatment for alcoholism.

Meanwhile, lobbyists interested in the bills were busy floating potential compromises. Among them was a plan that Sara Lee Corp., which sells underwear under the Hanes label, and the now-bankrupt Fruit of the Loom discussed in a meeting with Lott the week of March 13. The plan would give apparelmakers in the Caribbean and Central America duty-free and tariff-free treatment for products made with fabric manufactured in the Caribbean Basin region from U.S.-made yarn.

While that would be beneficial for the yarn spinners, cotton growers and manufacturers of synthetic fibers, it would leave out many other segments of the textile industry. As a result, some lobbyists were trying to expand the compromise.

Still, the plan appeared relatively firm and shifted focus away from the Caribbean Basin component and to the African provisions.

Only a handful of African countries have the infrastructure and investment necessary to ship substantial amounts of goods to the U.S. market. Because of that, many in Congress and U.S. retail and apparel companies say that fewer restrictions should be placed on those countries than on the Caribbean Basin, where many U.S. apparel-makers already have set up shop. But some U.S. textilemakers are concerned that Africa would become a conduit for Asian nations seeking to avoid U.S. quotas. They doubt that promises to step up federal enforcement to combat such "transshipment" would be kept.

Also, lobbyists said proposals have been floated to bar the nations with the highest gross domestic product — South Africa, Botswana and Mauritius — from most of the bill's benefits.

Settlement of Textile Dispute Clears Way For Final Deal

APRIL 15 — House and Senate leaders agreed April 13 on the basics of a compromise bill to expand access to the U.S. market for goods from the 72 countries of sub-Saharan Africa, the Caribbean and Central America. The breakthrough came under pressure from the White House, which wants an agreement in order to set a positive tone for congressional consideration of a bill to permanently normalize trade relations with China.

Aides were directed to work out the details during the spring recess. A spokesman said April 13 that Speaker J. Dennis Hastert, R-Ill., wants the conference report on the bill (HR 434) ready for a House vote the week of May 1.

Most members involved in closing the gap between the House and Senate versions, passed last year, shied away from saying they had a deal, in part because some dicey issues — including how to confront international child labor and the spread of AIDS in Africa — remained unresolved. And, with the House yet to officially appoint conferees on the bill, several steps in the process remain.

Still, it was clear that Senate Majority Leader Trent Lott, R-Miss., and four House members — Hastert, Ways and Means Committee Chairman Bill Archer, R-Texas, ranking panel Democrat Charles B. Rangel of New York and Trade Subcommittee Chairman Philip M. Crane, R-Ill. — had reached a relatively firm framework on how much apparel made in Africa and the Caribbean Basin would be allowed into the United States duty-free.

Long the biggest stumbling block, the apparel debate pitted textile-state legislators, who want to guarantee a market for their region's products against high-profile national retailers, and others, who want to remove U.S. barriers to foreign-made clothing. To cut a deal to the liking of trade critics such as Sen. Jesse Helms, R-N.C., Lott wanted more limits on imported goods. House negotiators sought to open the U.S. market as wide as possible.

The compromise would allow apparel made in both regions from U.S. fabrics or yarns into the United States free of duties and quotas.

Apparel made from African components that could be imported duty-free would be capped for eight years — at 1.5 percent of total U.S. apparel imports initially, rising to about 3.5 percent. For four years, apparel from the poorest African nations would be free of duties if made from fabric manufactured outside the United States and sub-Saharan Africa.

For Caribbean nations, there would be no duties on the first 25 million square meters of imported clothing made with regional fabric — except for T-shirts, which could be imported duty-free until the volume of imports reached current levels.

In addition, negotiators agreed to retain a Senate provision — attached as a floor amendment by Mike DeWine, R-Ohio — to require the U.S. trade representative to vary the types of foreign goods sanctioned as retaliation in trade disputes. This "carousel retaliation" aims to more greatly hurt nations with which the United States has trade disputes, including the European Union, with whom the United States has disputes over U.S.-grown beef treated with hormones and bananas sold by Cincinnati-based Chiquita Brands International.

While the Clinton administration

had put pressure on Congress to move the bill, negotiators also faced significant demands from large U.S. corporations — including Fruit of the Loom Inc. and Sara Lee Corp. — that have operations in Central America or the Caribbean and want to be able to import their wares at lower costs. In addition, African diplomats and a handful of House members who have long wanted to develop a trade relationship with the African continent held a news conference April 13, before the framework was reached, to call on the Senate to agree to scale back its limits on African products given duty- and quota-free treatment.

House Wins Softer Limits on Apparel Imports, Adopts Conference Report

MAY 6 — For weeks, it appeared that House negotiators would take a beating as they tried to breach textile-state opposition in the Senate in order to win trade concessions in the final version of legislation (HR 434) to expand imports from sub-Saharan African, Caribbean and Central American nations.

But — thanks to a concerted bipartisan effort by Republican leaders, the Clinton administration and House Ways and Means Committee ranking Democrat Charles B. Rangel of New York — the deal was written more to the House's liking than once thought possible, as negotiators succeeded in muting some of the Senate-backed limits on apparel imports.

The result was a resounding, 309-110 House vote May 4 to adopt the conference report. *(Vote 145, p. H-28)*

With greater consternation, the Senate will likely take up the measure the week of May 8. Several senators are unhappy, for different reasons. John B. Breaux, D-La., is upset that a sugar provision he pushed was kept out when it was ruled non-germane. Dianne Feinstein, D-Calif., is "appalled" that language she advocated to allow Africans to buy AIDS medicine more cheaply was dropped. And, textile-state senators, particularly the ever-vigilant Ernest F. Hollings, D-S.C., are expected to generally lambaste the bill.

However, support is expected to come from both Majority Leader Trent Lott, R-Miss. — who was deeply involved in forging the compromise — and Minority Leader Tom Daschle, D-S.D. Finance Committee member Max Baucus, D-Mont., predicted that opponents would be "nowhere close" to rounding up the 41 votes they need to block action on the conference report.

Many senators, it seemed, would take the tack of House members such as Ed Royce, R-Calif., chairman of the International Relations Subcommittee on Africa, who said during debate that he would have liked something less cumbersome, but that "this conference report is a clear and important step in the right direction."

The Deal's Provisions

The competing bills passed last year were quite far apart on the main provision — the treatment of apparel and textile imports. The House would have imposed relatively few restrictions; the Senate would have given duty- and quota-free treatment only to apparel made from U.S. fabrics and yarns. The final version, a complex combination of the two, would allow countries from both regions to send apparel to the United States without duties or quotas so long as the goods were made from U.S. yarns and fabric.

For Africa, the bill would:

- Suspend quotas and duties on clothing made from African-made fabrics of African-made yarns, so long as the amount sent to the United States did not initially exceed 1.5 percent of all U.S. imported apparel and 3.5 percent of the national total during the eight-year life of the bill.
- Suspend duties and quotas on clothing made of fabric made outside Africa or the United States for four years, so long as the originating nation's per capita income did not exceed $1,500 annually.
- Allow imports of many sweaters, including those made from silk, cashmere and merino wool, without duties or quotas.
- Extend through 2008 the General System of Preferences (GSP), a program that removes most trade barriers for low-income countries, and — with some stipulations — remove quotas on products from Kenya and Mauritius, which do not qualify for the GSP. Countries eligible for the GSP would be required to implement an international convention banning the worst forms of child labor.
- Take several steps to protect U.S. industries hurt by increased imports and ensure that non-African countries do not use that continent as a conduit to ship clothing to the United States and avoid quotas.

For the Caribbean, the bill would:

- Allow knit apparel made with Caribbean basin fabric to enter the United States duty-free until imports reached the equivalent of 250 million square meters the first year. The cap would be increased by 16 percent in each of the next three years.
- Duty-free imports of outerwear T-shirts would be limited to 4.2 million dozen in the first year, though the cap would also grow by 16 percent a year for three years.
- Brassieres, many of which are made in Central America, could also be imported without duties or quotas if the manufacturer purchased 75 percent of its cloth from the United States.

Senate Clears Bill, Thus Ending Years Of Policy Debate

MAY 13 — Those seeking to use federal law to boost U.S. trade declared the end of a six-year dry spell May 11, when the Senate voted overwhelmingly to clear legislation to lower import tariffs and remove quotas on certain goods made in sub-Saharan Africa, Central America and the Caribbean.

The bill (HR 434) will be signed by President Clinton, who pushed hard for a final agreement this spring partly in an effort to create momentum for the next — and more pivotal — trade vote of the 106th Congress: on legislation that would make permanent the normalized trade relations between the United States and China. That measure (S 2277) will likely come to the Senate floor in June, after the House votes on its not-yet-introduced version the week of May 22.

The 77-19 Senate vote for the

Africa and Caribbean basin bill sends "a message to the rest of the world that American trade policy is alive and it's well," said Charles E. Grassley, R-Iowa, chairman of the Senate Finance Subcommittee on International Trade. *(Vote 98, p. S-20)*

By its lopsidedness, the Senate vote brought to a somewhat anti-climactic end more than five years of sporadically heated debate over how to enhance the trade benefits for two of the world's poorest regions. "You wonder why all the huffing and puffing," Majority Leader Trent Lott, R-Miss., said after the vote.

The measure would remove duties and quotas on some goods manufactured in the 75 covered nations, including clothing made from U.S. fabrics and yarns. But it would retain quotas on the number of garments made from other types of fabric that could enter the United States free of duties. It also includes several provisions, most unrelated to the bill's core purpose of boosting commerce in the Third World, that were pushed by influential U.S. business interests.

Two of the better-known are provisions for stepped-up retaliation against the European Union, which has been resisting efforts to put U.S. bananas and beef in European supermarkets, and a lowering of wool tariffs to help U.S. suit makers. But the bill also has language to ensure that duties and quotas remain on imports of clothing made in the Caribbean basin with non-American "elastomeric" fabric. The main U.S. version is Lycra spandex made by E.I. du Pont de Nemours and Co.

The conference agreement was finalized May 4 and pushed through the House that day, before several such last-minute additions were widely understood. But several more days did little to engender new grounds for senatorial opposition, and only a few tried to block the bill's final progress. The Senate voted 90-6 on May 10 and 76-18 the next day to invoke cloture, or curtail debate. *(Votes 96 and 97, p. S-19)*

Voicing Concerns

Senators against the bill generally fell into three groups: those such as Ernest F. Hollings, D-S.C., and Jesse Helms, R-N.C., fearful that more imports will cost textile jobs in their states; those such as Edward M. Kennedy, D-Mass., and Patrick J. Leahy, D-Vt., responding to union concerns that the bill would do too little to protect workers in the affected countries from exploitation by big corporations; and those such as Russell D. Feingold, D-Wis., and Dianne Feinstein, D-Calif., angry that the bill lacked a provision to make AIDS-fighting drugs more cheaply available in Africa.

Only a handful of the opponents spoke during the debate, Feinstein and Feingold principal among them. Before the Senate passed its initial bill in November, they had won an amendment that would have allowed African countries to make generic versions of AIDS drugs themselves or to purchase them from low-cost foreign manufacturers without violating patent laws. Conferees dropped the provision, a decision Feinstein decried. But her ire was soothed by the administration, which announced May 10 that Clinton will implement many of the amendment's provisions through an executive order.

White House spokesman Joe Lockhart said that executive order was an attempt to "balance between protecting intellectual property rights and also promoting accessibility of the drugs" by allowing countries to make generic versions as long as they faced health emergencies and otherwise adhered to an international intellectual property agreement. ◆

Lawmakers Extend Regulations on 'Dual-Use' Exports for One Year

Box Score

- **Bill:** HR 5239 — PL 106-508
- **Legislative action: House** passed HR 5239 by voice vote Sept. 25.

Senate passed HR 5239, amended, by voice vote Oct. 11.

House cleared the bill by voice vote Oct. 30.

President signed the bill Nov. 13.

SUMMARY

With Congress at an impasse over legislation regulating high-technology exports, lawmakers cleared a stopgap bill to govern the export of products with military as well as commercial applications for one year. President Clinton signed the bill into law Nov. 13.

The most recent version of the Export Administration Act (PL 96-72) expired in 1994. Since then, Clinton has regulated exports of sensitive "dual-use" technology — including such things as supercomputers — through executive orders and waivers. Interest in reauthorizing the act was revived after allegations in 1998 that China had improved its long-range missiles with technology gleaned from launching U.S. commercial satellites.

The Senate Banking, Housing and Urban Affairs Committee approved a comprehensive bill (S 1712) in 1999, but several Senate committee chairmen blocked floor action, citing national security and jurisdictional concerns. Commerce Department officials, however, said a formal extension of the act was needed because its expiration left the department in a precarious position in defending against lawsuits.

As passed by the House in September, HR 5239 would have continued certain export controls under the 1977 International Emergency Economic Powers Act (PL 95-223), with stiffer civil penalties. When the Senate took up the bill, it substituted a one-year extension of the Export Administration Act. Banking Committee members said they wanted to keep the enhanced penalty language for another comprehensive bill they plan to introduce in 2001.

Senate Committees Argue Over Jurisdiction

FEBRUARY 26 — Supporters of Senate legislation to regulate "dual-use" exports — those with both military and commercial uses — struggled during the week of Feb. 21 to reach a compromise acceptable to four influential committee chairmen who have raised jurisdictional and national security concerns.

A spokesman for the Senate Banking, Housing and Urban Affairs Committee, which is handling the bill, said enough progress had been made on the reauthorization of the Export Administration Act (S 1712 — S Rept 106-180) that it could come to the Senate floor the week of Feb. 28.

The Banking Committee has a two-day hearing in New York on Feb. 28 and 29, leaving March 1 as the earliest floor debate could start.

The export bill, which the Banking Committee approved 20-0 in September, would reduce the number of products restricted for trade abroad while raising penalties for violations.

The debate has centered on which federal department — Commerce, Defense or State — will have the most control of export licensing.

Senate Majority Leader Trent Lott, R-Miss., met Feb. 22 with Banking committee members and the chairmen of four committees — Armed Services, Foreign Relations, Governmental Affairs and Intelligence — who had implored him not to bring up the bill until their concerns had been addressed.

After the meeting, one of the chairmen, Armed Services' John W. Warner, R-Va., said he considered it "highly possible that we can bridge our differences."

Warner had scheduled a Feb. 24 hearing on export controls, but canceled it when one witness became ill.

In the days following the senators' meeting, talks among the committee staffs became bogged down. An industry source said Feb. 23 that what the committees proposed would "substantially undercut" the bill by "turning back the clock on the kinds of technology that would be subject to strict export licensing."

Two days later, however, Banking committee spokeswoman Christi Harlan, said, "We think most of the concerns have been laid to rest, or at least allayed."

Banking committee Chairman Phil Gramm, R-Texas, said he was trying to strike a "proper balance" between national security and commerce. He said Lott might bring up the bill without all concerns being fully addressed.

Edgy Industry

Industry officials were nervous that changes or floor amendments could tilt the balance too far toward defense. "I haven't seen anything [from the staff discussions] that's an improvement over what's in the bill," said Jason M. Mahler, vice president and general counsel for the Computer and Communications Industry Association.

But Mahler supported one change under discussion to shorten the congressional review period for supercomputer exports, currently 180 days. The bill would reduce it to 60 days, and some Democrats want to cut it to 30.

As the Senate committees sought a compromise, officials in the Commerce and Defense departments negotiated an exemption that would retain stricter export controls on some defense-related items.

William A. Reinsch, undersecretary of Commerce for export administration, said in a Feb. 24 interview that the two agencies were close to a deal. Although Reinsch declined to provide details, he said it was "pretty much the language that [Defense] wanted; there may be some more tweaks."

A new complication was criticism of the bill from the American Israel Public Affairs Committee. The lobby group sent Foreign Relations Chairman Jesse Helms, R-N.C., a letter Feb. 18 saying that the bill does not recognize Israel's adherence to missile technology controls under an agreement with the United States.

Lott Says Export Bill Must Move To Senate Floor

MARCH 4 — The Senate is expected to take up legislation the week of March 6 to regulate exports with both military and commercial uses despite signs that a compromise might not be reached between the bill's supporters and critics.

The stubborn impasse over reauthorizing the Export Administration Act (S 1712 — S Rept 106-180) prompted Senate Majority Leader Trent Lott, R-Miss., to warn that he was prepared to file for cloture on the bill whether or not there was a deal.

Members of the Senate Banking, Housing and Urban Affairs Committee were trying to reach agreement with four other committees that have raised national security and jurisdictional concerns. The debate has centered on which federal department — Commerce, Defense or State — will have the most control over export licensing.

If no deal can be struck, "I'm going to call it up and let the fur fly," Lott said in a March 1 interview.

The bill's supporters have warned that if no action is taken this month, the issue is unlikely to be resolved this year because of the tight legislative calendar and a change in administrations.

The chairman of one of the committees, Armed Services' John W. Warner, R-Va., said at a Feb. 28 hearing that the bill must address three major concerns: the need to protect militarily sensitive technology, such as encryption; the need to enhance the role of the secretary of Defense and the intelligence community in export licensing; and the need to ensure that officials understand the national security impact of any proposed loosening of controls.

Rewrite Stalls As Senate Panels Squabble

MARCH 11 — Prospects for Senate legislation regulating the export of goods that have both military and commercial uses appear to have faded in the face of unrelenting objections from a group of Republican committee chairmen.

Debate on a bill (S 1712 — S Rept 106-180) reauthorizing the Export Administration Act had been under way for only a few minutes on March 8 when sponsors abruptly pulled it from the floor, citing the inability of Senate Republicans to reach an understanding on the proper balance between the interests of commerce and national security. Similar debates have dogged the issue for six years.

The next day, Majority Leader Trent Lott, R-Miss., said he remains interested in bringing the bill back to the floor, but only if a deal can be struck among members of the Senate Banking, Housing and Urban Affairs Committee and four other committees that have raised national security and jurisdictional concerns.

"If they could come to some acceptable agreement, I would like to go forward with it," Lott said in an interview. "We could have a window of a day or two [of floor time] that I don't know about."

Lott has warned, however, that the bill risks being crowded out of the Senate schedule as the budget and appropriations season gets under way this spring.

At least one industry official who has been pressing for action on the export measure refused to abandon hope that a bill could emerge from the Senate following its recess the week of March 13.

"I don't think [the delay] is fatal at all," said Edmund Rice, president of the Committee for Employment through Exports. "This is early March. There's not exactly a lot of heavy stuff on the Senate's agenda."

But Banking Committee Chairman Phil Gramm, R-Texas, sounded considerably less optimistic that all sides could resolve their differences after weeks of negotiating.

"We'll have to see," Gramm told reporters March 9. "Obviously, we're a long way from the starting line."

Given such an uncertain climate, some lawmakers may try to break off parts of the bill that are likely to pass on their own.

In particular, Senate Minority Whip Harry Reid, D-Nev., is eager to pass an amendment he offered to the legislation that would reduce the time Congress has to review administration changes to computer export controls from the 60 days in the bill to 30 days. Under the fiscal 1998 defense authorization act (PL 105-85), Congress now has 180 days to review such changes.

Dueling Uses

The legislation represents the latest attempt to rewrite Cold War-era laws governing "dual use" products, many of which use advanced technology. Since the most recent export control law (PL 103-10) expired in 1994, President Clinton has regulated such trade through executive orders and individual waivers, with little congressional oversight or intervention.

Gramm and other supporters of reauthorization had hoped that their efforts would gain momentum from a special House panel headed by Rep. Christopher Cox, R-Calif. The panel concluded last year that weak export laws contributed to China's apparent success in stealing technology from U.S. satellite, missile, telecommunications and machine tool companies.

The bill that resulted from months of talks among Banking Committee members, industry and Clinton administration officials was approved by the committee 20-0 last September. But the chairmen of the Armed Services, Foreign Relations, Intelligence and Governmental Affairs committees have remained concerned that the bill gives the Commerce Department too much of a central role in regulating exports. They say the Defense and State departments should have a greater say.

Although Banking Committee members believed they had addressed those concerns before going to the floor, Gramm said staff members were unable to translate what members agreed on into legislation that would satisfy everyone involved.

"Agreeing in principle is not agreeing to the details," Gramm said shortly before pulling the bill from the floor.

Although he took part in talks to resolve differences over the bill, Governmental Affairs Committee Chairman Fred Thompson, R-Tenn., said he eventually concluded that there was no way Gramm could accommodate all of his concerns.

Thompson noted that even proposed language allowing the president to deny the transfer of some sensitive items for national security reasons would still require the president to "jump through some hoops" to protect national security. He said he plans to oppose the bill if it comes to the floor and will offer a series of amendments.

"I think we ought to be tightening [export controls], and they think we ought to be loosening, and never the twain will meet," Thompson said.

Thompson's stance drew an unusually harsh rebuke from Lott. "I frankly think that what has been done here is very irresponsible by the opponents," the majority leader said. "I am extremely disappointed in the conduct of some of the Republican senators on this matter."

Even if the Senate eventually passes a bill, the legislation faces a similarly rough road in the House. Many Republicans share Thompson's concerns about the national security implications.

"The Export Administration Act is always a tough one for us," said Rep. Duncan Hunter, R-Calif., chairman of the House Armed Services Subcommittee on Military Procurement.

House Passes Stiffer Penalties For Dual-Use Export Violations

SEPTEMBER 30 — The House on Sept. 25 passed by voice vote a bill that would increase penalties for companies and individuals that violate rules on the export of high-technology equipment with both military and commercial uses.

The bill (HR 5239) is the latest attempt by Congress to incrementally change laws on "dual-use" exports. A comprehensive bill (S 1712) to reauthorize the Export Administration Act (PL 96-72) has stalled in the Senate, with action unlikely this year.

The House and Senate have separately adopted amendments to the fiscal 2001 defense authorization bill (HR 4205) that would shorten the period for congressional review of high-performance computer exports from 180 days to 60.

The chief proponent of the Senate export reauthorization bill, Republican Michael B. Enzi of Wyoming, objects to moving further provisions individually. "This is not the time of year to be doing things piecemeal," Enzi spokesman Coy Knobel said.

The House-passed bill would increase fines for violations of the act by companies from $50,000 to $500,000 or five times the value of the exports. For individuals, the fines would be $250,000 or five times the value of the exports.

Since the Export Administration Act expired in 1994, the president has had authority to administer export controls through executive orders and waivers. However, House International Relations Committee Chairman Benjamin A. Gilman, R-N.Y., said that in some key areas, the president has less authority to penalize violators than under the original act.

"Even these penalties are too low, having been eroded by inflation over the past 20 years," Gilman said.

Senate Votes To Revive Expired High-Tech Export Law for a Year

OCTOBER 14 — The Senate on Oct. 11 voted to revive for a year a law governing high-technology exports that expired in 1994. Congress has been unable to reach a consensus on updating the law, and President Clinton has administered export controls through executive orders and waivers.

The House had passed legislation (HR 5239) on Sept. 25 that would have increased penalties for companies and individuals who violate the expired statute, the Export Administration Act (PL 96-72).

When the Senate took up the bill, it substituted a one-year extension of the earlier law and sent the measure back to the House.

Republican Sens. Phil Gramm of Texas and Michael B. Enzi of Wyoming, who want to keep the penalty language in negotiations over a comprehensive export administration bill (S 1712) that has stalled in the Senate, offered the amendment for a simple extension of the law.

The amendment was adopted and the bill was passed by voice vote.

"This solution is only temporary," Enzi said. "Our country needs comprehensive reform of its export control system."

William A. Reinsch, undersecretary of Commerce for export administration, said the formal extension of the act is needed because its expiration has left the department in a precarious position in defending itself against lawsuits.

He said companies have argued they are not subject to the act because it has expired.

The Senate's action sent the bill to conference. However, Reinsch said he hopes the House will simply pass the version amended by the Senate. House International Relations Committee Chairman Benjamin A. Gilman, R-N.Y., said he did not yet know how the House would handle the issue.

House Clears Extension of Law To Regulate 'Dual Use' Exports

NOVEMBER 4 — With Congress at an impasse over legislation regulating high-technology exports, the House cleared a stopgap bill that would govern the export of products with military as well as commercial applications for one year.

The House on Oct. 30 agreed, by voice vote, to a Senate amendment to legislation (HR 5239) that would extend the Export Administration Act until August 2001. The most recent version of the act (PL 96-72) expired in 1994, and President Clinton has regulated "dual use" exports since then through executive orders and waivers.

Lawmakers have been unable to reach a consensus on a broad rewrite of the export law. The chairmen of several Senate committees have blocked action on a comprehensive bill (S 1712), citing national security and jurisdictional concerns.

Commerce Department officials, however, said a formal extension of the act was needed because its expiration has left the department in a precarious position in defending against lawsuits.

Officials at Commerce's Bureau of Export Administration said two recent court cases have called into question the department's ability to protect the confidentiality of information provided by exporters. The officials said they feared businesses would not be as likely to trust the government with information if the agency could not ensure that it would be kept secret.

"We have got to pass this law to make sure that they can keep the information confidential so that the exporters will fully use the Commerce Department's assistance in exporting our products," said House International Relations Committee member Barbara Lee, D-Calif., before the vote.

The export act establishes licensing policy for nearly 2,400 dual-use items, including high-performance computers and software. It includes penalties for companies and individuals who violate the act.

The original version of HR 5239 that the House passed Sept. 25 would only have increased penalties for violating the Export Administration Act. When the Senate took up the bill, it substituted a one-year extension of the earlier law.

Michael B. Enzi, R-Wyo., chairman of the Senate Banking, Housing and Urban Affairs subcommittee on trade and finance, said he wanted to keep the enhanced penalty language in a comprehensive export control bill he plans to introduce next year.

The bill being sent to Clinton "is just for one year, so it keeps the pressure on" to enact a broader measure, Enzi said.

Interest in reauthorizing the Export Administration Act was revived after allegations in 1998 that China had improved its long-range missiles with technology gleaned from launching U.S. commercial satellites.

A bipartisan House commission headed by Christopher Cox, R-Calif., concluded that weak U.S. export laws contributed to China's success. ◆

CQ

Chapter 21

TRANSPORTATION & INFRASTRUCTURE

Shuster-Driven Bill Funds Billions in Upgrades for Airports, Air-Traffic Control

Box Score

- **Bill:** HR 1000 — PL 106-181
- **Legislative action: Senate** adopted the conference report (H Rept 106-513), 82-17, on March 8.

House cleared the bill, 319-101, on March 15.

President signed HR 1000 on April 5.

SUMMARY

Congress cleared a three-year, $40 billion bill reauthorizing the Federal Aviation Administration (FAA) and guaranteeing a huge spending increase for airport construction. The measure, signed into law April 5, included a controversial mechanism to ensure that all revenue credited each year to the aviation trust fund is spent on aviation programs. It also allowed airports to increase the local fee on airline tickets, and eased flight restrictions at some of the nation's most congested airports.

Conferees had begun meeting in late 1999 to reconcile significantly different versions of the bill passed by the House and Senate earlier in the year, but they made little progress. They resumed work almost as soon as the second session opened in January, but it took another three months to reach a compromise. *(1999 Almanac, p. 24-3)*

Much of the controversy focused on a proposal by House Transportation and Infrastructure Committee Chairman Bud Shuster, R-Pa., to make spending on aviation programs mandatory, largely exempting it from the appropriations process. Opponents, especially the appropriators, objected that a spending guarantee for aviation programs would leave too little money for other transportation needs. The six-month deadlock finally ended March 1, with an agreement brokered by Senate Majority Leader Trent Lott, R-Miss.

In a significant victory for Shuster and the airports, the bill provided that all of the receipts and interest in the Airport and Airway Trust Fund — a projected total of $33 billion — would be appropriated for the next three years for aviation programs, with a priority on capital accounts. Legislation that does not comply was made subject to a point of order. Shuster agreed to drop a provision that would have prevented the House and Senate from waiving the points of order.

Shuster lost on one key demand — guaranteed spending for aviation from the general fund. The final bill authorized an additional $20.8 billion over three years for aviation programs, but the money was subject to the normal appropriations process. That left the FAA to fight for its highest priorities — operations and safety programs such as air traffic control — in the annual transportation spending bill.

The bill increased the maximum per-segment fee paid to local airports by each passenger from $3 per airport to $4.50, giving airports a further boost for construction spending. It also eliminated existing restrictions on the number of takeoff and landing slots at New York's John F. Kennedy and LaGuardia international airports by Jan. 1, 2007, and Chicago's O'Hare International by July 1, 2002. Flights also were increased at Ronald Reagan Washington National Airport.

Deal on Trust Fund Clears Way For 3-Year FAA Reauthorization

MARCH 4 — The key antagonists over funding for aviation programs reached tentative agreement March 1, ending a yearlong dispute over a three-year, $40 billion measure (HR 1000 — H Rept 106-167, Parts 1 and 2) to reauthorize the Federal Aviation Administration (FAA) and guarantee a spending increase for airport construction.

One immediate effect of the deal would be to increase the maximum passenger facility charge from $3 to $4.50 for each leg of travel. Airports can levy the charge for their own use.

Airlines have opposed any increase in the fee. The House wanted to raise the limit to $6; the Senate said nothing, and negotiators split the difference.

Negotiators reached agreement to begin eliminating restrictions on the number of takeoffs and landings at three of the nation's most congested airports: Chicago's O'Hare International by March 1, 2002, and New York's John F. Kennedy and LaGuardia international airports by Jan. 1, 2007. All three would be opened to regional jet service without limits this spring.

At Ronald Reagan Washington National Airport, 24 more daily flights would be allowed, including 12 outside a 1,250-mile "perimeter."

That would permit America West, based in Phoenix to fly directly to National. John McCain, R-Ariz., chairman of the Senate Commerce, Science and Transportation Committee, had insisted on the additional flights in negotiations with the House.

The spending agreement between Senate Majority Leader Trent Lott, R-Miss., Senate Budget Chairman Pete V. Domenici, R-N.M., and House Transportation and Infrastructure Chairman Bud Shuster, R-Pa., would put in place a new method of financing the nation's aviation programs.

As lawmakers worked out details of the package at week's end, aides predicted the conference report could be considered by the Senate the week of March 6 and by the House the week of March 13, if procedural hurdles can be overcome. President Clinton has not indicated whether he would sign the measure.

The budget agreement resolved a standoff between Shuster, one of the Hill's most feared negotiators, and several determined Senate budget hawks.

The agreement calls for a guarantee that all of the receipts and interest in the Airport and Airway Trust Fund will be appropriated for the next three years for aviation programs — a projected total of $33 billion. The money comes mainly from airline ticket taxes.

The measure would authorize an additional $6.7 billion for aviation programs, but that money would be subject to the normal appropriations process.

All told, the bill would authorize $12.7 billion for aviation programs in fiscal 2001, a $2.7 billion increase.

The House-passed version was a more wide-ranging, five-year plan. It would have taken aviation programs "off-budget," meaning that their funding would have been guaranteed and would not have counted against the federal surplus. The House bill also would have included a fixed contribution from the general treasury for aviation.

As a fallback, Shuster pushed for funding guarantees for aviation programs along the lines of the firewalls he won for highway and transit spending in the 1998 surface transportation authorization (PL 105-178). That law requires that road and transit programs be funded at certain levels, based on the balance in the Highway Trust Fund, but the money is counted as part of the overall budget. *(1998 Almanac, p. 24-3)*

Senate conferees, led by Domenici, Appropriations Committee Chairman Ted Stevens, R-Alaska, and Slade Gorton, R-Wash., chairman of the Commerce, Science and Transportation Subcommittee on Aviation, were intent on making a stand against another transportation entitlement program. They argued that the highway and transit firewalls have put a squeeze on other transportation programs.

A Senate aide said the deal was acceptable to the senators because the spending guarantees would only apply to money in the aviation trust fund, which historically has lagged behind the needs of aviation. Since there will be no guaranteed windfall for aviation programs, the bill should not further strain other transportation needs.

"This is a package we can live with," Stevens said March 1.

Shuster Loses a Battle

Shuster lost on a key demand — guaranteed general fund spending. The House chairman pulled out of conference negotiations over the issue Nov. 10.

The March 1 deal gives no assurances that general fund money will be appropriated. "The final agreement permits the use of general funds for aviation programs subject to the normal appropriations process," Domenici said.

But Shuster won a significant concession on the Airport Improvement Program and the FAA's facilities and equipment account. The two capital programs are key concerns for Shuster and his legislative ally, the airports. The programs would be funded out of the trust fund first.

The Airport Improvement Program would receive a significant authorization increase, from $1.9 billion in fiscal 2000 to $3.2 billion in fiscal 2001, $3.3 billion in fiscal 2002 and $3.4 billion in fiscal 2003. The program provides construction grants to airports.

That would leave the burden on the FAA to fight for its highest priorities — operations and safety programs such as air traffic control — through the regular appropriations process.

In a sign of administration concern on this point, Transportation Secretary Rodney Slater said it was "most important that any final legislation fully fund Federal Aviation Administration operations at the level requested in the president's budget for fiscal year 2001."

Senate Adopts Report Despite Concerns About Funding Disparities

MARCH 11 — Compromise legislation to reauthorize the Federal Aviation Administration (FAA) is expected to clear the House the week of March 13, despite the opposition of key lawmakers upset by spending guarantees in the bill.

The Senate adopted the conference report to the fiscal 2000-03 aviation bill (HR 1000), 82-17, on March 8. *(Vote 35, p. S-10)*

On March 6, House Appropriations Committee Chairman C.W. Bill Young, R-Fla., outlined "serious reservations" with the aviation bill, noting that it would require a $2.7 billion funding increase for fiscal 2001, $1.5 billion above President Clinton's budget request.

Young and allies such as Budget Committee Chairman John R. Kasich, R-Ohio, and Majority Whip Tom DeLay, R-Texas, are expected to argue that the House should not go along with guarantees for aviation programs at the possible expense of other domestic needs.

But Bud Shuster, R-Pa., chairman of the Transportation and Infrastructure Committee, won a nasty fight over the bill on the House floor last June — DeLay at one point called the bill "irresponsible" — and the conference agreement moderates the funding and budget guarantees of the original House bill.

"We're in a better position than we were," said Rep. John E. Sweeney, R-N.Y., a strong supporter of the bill.

If the Senate vote is any indication, House opponents have a tough job. Opposition to the bill's most contentious issues — budget protections, increased spending and more flights at some congested airports — had been much stronger in the Senate.

Smooth Flight

All the controversies that had dogged the aviation bill for more than two years faded into the background by the time the Senate began debate on the conference report March 8.

John D. Rockefeller IV, D-W.Va., noted that the FAA has operated under a half-dozen temporary extensions since 1998, a period in which airline traffic has grown to historic levels.

"It's been an extraordinary but frustrating process, but a successful one," Rockefeller said.

Slade Gorton, R-Wash., chairman of the Senate Commerce Subcommittee on Aviation and one of several fiscal conservatives who opposed broad guarantees of aviation spending, praised the final bill as "a reasonable balance with the needs of that [aviation] system and our limited federal resources."

But the prospect of guaranteeing $33 billion for aviation over the next three years, on top of the spending guarantees for highways and transit adopted in the 1998 surface transportation authorization (PL 105-178), was too much for Frank R. Lautenberg of New Jersey, the senior Democrat on the Senate Transportation Appropriations Subcommittee. Lautenberg said prospects for deep cuts in funding for Amtrak, the Coast Guard and other transportation programs were now very real. *(1998 Almanac, p. 24-3)*

"You can't ignore the needs of one mode of transportation in favor of another," Lautenberg said. "Are we less concerned about those at sea than those in the air?"

Despite the Senate vote, controversy remained over easing restrictions on the number of takeoff and landing slots at some of the nation's most congested airports in order to give newer airlines a shot at more markets, and to open more service to smaller, regional airports.

"The phase-out of the slot rule . . . will open a new era of aviation," said Charles E. Grassley, R-Iowa. "It should give smaller airports a better chance at a piece of the economic pie."

Increasing the number of flights was fiercely opposed by lawmakers whose constituents would have to bear the increased noise. The compromise was to gradually eliminate restrictions at Chicago's O'Hare Airport and New York's John F. Kennedy and LaGuardia airports, and to add two dozen more slots a day at Ronald Reagan Washington National Airport.

Most of the opponents had been won over through negotiations last year. But Peter G. Fitzgerald, R-Ill., Charles S. Robb, D-Va., and Daniel Patrick Moynihan, D-N.Y., voted against the final measure.

The lone no-show on the vote was the Senate sponsor, Commerce, Science and Transportation Committee Chairman John McCain, R-Ariz., who had pushed for more slots at Reagan National, which would benefit Phoenix-based America West Airlines.

McCain, who was barely mentioned in the floor debate, was in Arizona deciding the future of his presidential campaign.

Administration officials seemed pleased with the final legislation. Transportation Secretary Rodney Slater, who was at the Capitol for the vote along with FAA Administrator Jane F. Garvey, said that the bill embodied 95 percent of the administration's goals for safety, airport security, modernizing air- traffic control, adding capacity and increasing airline competition.

"We put it on the table, and the Congress responded," Slater said. "It's a good day for us."

Airports Hit the Jackpot

Airports emerged as the measure's biggest winners, getting the largest spending increases and the strongest guarantees for that spending. Funding for the Airport Improvement Program would increase from $1.9 billion appropriated this year to $3.4 billion by fiscal 2003 — all ensured by points of order against changes on the floor.

The legislation says it would not be in order for the House or Senate to consider appropriations that do not allocate all trust fund revenue for aviation and do not match authorization levels for airport construction and FAA capital programs.

Under pressure from Senate Appropriations Committee Chairman Ted Stevens, R-Alaska, Shuster dropped a section that would have prevented the House and Senate from waiving the points of order.

Every airport with construction would see an increase — part of the real selling power of the legislation. The basic construction grant would double, from a minimum of $500,000 to $1 million. Bill sponsors hope the money will help ensure that airports can add capacity as air travel continues to increase — from current levels of 650 million passengers a year to more than 1 billion by 2007.

Airports also would be able to finance their own construction projects through a higher personal facility charge paid by each passenger — the maximum fee would increase $3 per airport to $4.50.

The legislation contains scores of other policy initiatives, including:

• Creation of a chief operating officer at the FAA in charge of the air-traffic control system.

• Continuation of a grant program for small communities and a study of airline marketing practices that raise their ticket prices.

• All airport security personnel would

Highlights of the FAA Deal

MARCH 11— The conference agreement on HR 1000 (H Rept 106-513) would authorize $40 billion for FAA activities in fiscal 2001-03, including $12.7 billion in fiscal 2001 — a $2.7 billion increase over what Congress appropriated for fiscal 2000. Among the highlights:

Aviation Trust Fund

All the revenue and interest from the Airport and Airway Trust Fund the next three years — an estimated $33 billion — would have to be spent on aviation. Another $6.7 billion would be authorized from general funds.

Airport Construction

Authorized spending for the Airport Improvement Program would increase from the $1.9 billion appropriated this year to $3.2 billion in fiscal 2001, then to $3.4 billion by fiscal 2003.

Slot Restrictions

The measure would phase out restrictions on the number of flights at three congested airports: Chicago's O'Hare by 2002, New York's Kennedy and LaGuardia by 2007. Two dozen more flights a day would be allowed at Northern Virginia's Reagan National starting this year.

Passenger Facility Charge

Airports would be allowed to increase the local fee on airline tickets from $3 to $4.50. Not all airports use the charge. The typical passenger with two connecting flights on a round trip could pay $18, rather than $12.

be subjected to background checks.

• Families of airline crash victims could collect compensation for accidents within 12 miles of the U.S. coast, rather than the current three miles. The boundary would be retroactive to the crash of TWA Flight 800 off New York in 1996.

• New and increased penalties for customer service violations. The Transportation Department's inspector general could monitor airline service agreements.

But financing all of the new programs will be a challenge. The deal funds FAA operations at the level of the fiscal 2001 Clinton budget request — a promise that removed administration objections to the bill. But funding in future years could be hard to come by, as appropriators find themselves squeezed by airport and capital funding guarantees.

A Concrete Legacy

With the likely adoption of the conference report by the House, Shuster will have ensured a second huge transportation building program largely exempt from the appropriations process.

The 1998 surface transportation bill dedicates all revenue collected by the Highway Trust Fund for highway and transit programs. Shuster hoped to duplicate the feat in aviation, frequently warning that the country was "hurtling toward gridlock in the skies."

The struggle over "unlocking" the Airport and Airway Trust Fund, which is largely financed by airline ticket taxes, was the central issue that took two years to resolve. Shuster got much less than he asked for, and probably less than he expected.

In the end, he was helped immeasurably by a meeting of the minds with Senate Majority Leader Trent Lott, R-Miss., who was convinced that the big spending increases were justified and who was eager to move the bill before budget season closed its window of opportunity.

A March 1 agreement Lott brokered ended a six-month deadlock on how to guarantee spending from the aviation trust fund while protecting oversight. Under pressure from Lott, Senate Budget Chairman Pete V. Domenici, R-N.M., and Stevens went along with the compromise.

House Clears FAA Reauthorization

MARCH 18 — Pennsylvania's Bud Shuster finally achieved for the aviation industry what he did for highways and transit in 1998 — a guaranteed source of funding for airports, runways and air-traffic technology.

Any criticism of Shuster's plan or his tactics was drowned out when the House, on a 319-101 vote, cleared a sweeping, three-year aviation authorization bill (HR 1000) and sent the measure to President Clinton for his expected signature. *(Vote 48, p. H-20)*

The bill has the potential to reshape the nation's aviation system, speed an airport construction boom, boost airline competition and service to small cities, and spur a new effort to modernize the air-traffic control system. It would pay for those efforts by earmarking funds raised through aviation excise taxes.

"This legislation will go a long way in relieving our overburdened aviation system without raising taxes," said Shuster, R-Pa., chairman of the House Transportation and Infrastructure Committee.

The vote capped a two-year test of wills between two powerful blocs in Congress. One side featured Shuster and his public works allies, who advocated massive, guaranteed infrastructure investments to meet growing aviation traffic. On the other side were fiscal conservatives in both chambers, who warned that the effort to give aviation special status would shortchange other urgent domestic priorities, and appropriators, who are used to having wide discretion in doling out aviation trust funds.

"This is one of the worst bills I've seen go through Congress," said Martin Olav Sabo, Minn., ranking Democrat on the Appropriations Transportation Subcommittee. "It says the top priorities are concrete, and the lowest priorities are people."

The decisive vote for Shuster and his capital investment program ended a two-year stalemate in which Congress could manage only a series of short-term extensions that kept the aviation system on life support, while passenger traffic continued to surge.

Transportation Secretary Rodney Slater hailed the bill's passage and indicated that Clinton would sign the measure. "I look forward to this new era in American aviation history," he said.

Airport Improvements

Nowhere will the effect of the bill be more apparent than at the nation's airports. The bill fences off funding for a massive building program that aims to keep up with growing passenger traffic.

There were 640 million commercial passengers in 1998, according to the Air Transport Association, more than double the number in 1980. And growth is projected well into the future — more than 1 billion passengers a year by 2010.

To keep pace, airport officials argued, they need to build. And given the long construction period required for most airport projects, which must go through numerous planning and environmental reviews, it could take seven years or more to see new projects to fruition.

"You've got to invest today in much larger dollars to meet tomorrow's needs," said Todd Hauptli, a lobbyist for the American Association of Airport Executives.

The bill would make those investments in airports in a big way: The Airport Improvement Program, which funds construction projects such as terminals, runways and baggage handling systems, would grow from its current funding of about $1.9 billion to $3.2 billion in fiscal 2001 and $3.4 billion in fiscal 2003, a 79 percent increase.

Airports will also benefit from an increase in the "passenger facility charge," a $3-per-airport fee assessed on passengers. Under the bill, airports could raise the fee to $4.50 per airport, generating about $700 million nationwide.

Airport officials say that will go a long way toward closing a funding gap that has persisted over the past several years. The legislation will accelerate a backlog of expansion projects already approved by the FAA but delayed for lack of funding, including runways in Northern states with a short construction season. A report from state aviation officials warning of the possibility of losing another entire year of construction in the North was one factor that pressured conferees to come to an agreement.

Most of all, airport officials said it

will allow them to start making new plans for construction in a way that has not been possible for the past two years of legislative gridlock.

For the second time in three years, Shuster was able to engineer a massive transportation construction bill through a Congress dominated by fiscal conservatives and appropriators. This time, he capitalized on growing consumer frustration over delays and limited choices in airlines and flights. Further, every lawmaker either has an airport in his district or has constituents who use a nearby airport.

The House debate reprised a spirited floor fight last year, when a coalition of the House's most powerful chairmen argued that Shuster's bill would put aviation funding ahead of all other domestic priorities.

The bill would authorize a total of $40 billion for aviation programs for fiscal 2001-03. Most of that funding, $33 billion, will come from the revenues of the Airport and Airway Trust Fund and is locked into place by HR 1000.

Indeed, the bill dictates that all of the revenues from the trust fund be directed to aviation programs, with airport construction and FAA capital accounts getting priority. Appropriators would thus have to overcome some difficult procedural hurdles to change these priorities; Shuster would be able to raise points of order against any spending bill that does not follow HR 1000's priorities. And Shuster received assurances from House Speaker J. Dennis Hastert, R-Ill., and Rules Committee Chairman David Dreier, R-Calif., that they would back his points of order.

Appropriators will still set the overall funding level for aviation programs up to the $40 billion ceiling — a key concession for several senators who fought Shuster in conference committee. But the limited amount of flexibility for the spending panels led House appropriators to charge that the bill would create a new category of mandatory spending.

"Every time we create a new entitlement program, we are taking each member of this Congress a little more out of the process," said Appropriations Chairman C.W. Bill Young, R-Fla.

David R. Obey of Wisconsin, the senior Democrat on Appropriations, said the aviation bill was another broken promise by the GOP-controlled House to maintain fiscal responsibility. "This bill throws that promise out the window," said Obey.

Obey argued that the measure put airports ahead of all other domestic priorities.

"I don't want anyone who votes [for the bill] to say they were for making more room for cancer research, for education or for defense," Obey told his colleagues during floor debate.

But James L. Oberstar of Minnesota, ranking Democrat on the Transportation Committee, defended the conference agreement as a way to ensure that airline passengers will see a return on their ticket taxes. He said the spending guarantees in the bill were warranted, because passengers have been told they are paying taxes into a trust fund for aviation, while the money actually has been used for other purposes.

"What the appropriators argue is they should be allowed to hoard those dollars," he said. "That doesn't keep the faith with the travelling public."

Slots and Competition

Lawmakers embraced the idea that expanded competition could help solve some passenger woes. Many small cities are served by only one airline, and many "hub" cities have service dominated by a single airline. In these markets, passengers often face high fares.

The bill's sponsors hope to alleviate the problem with greater use of lower-cost regional jets and by opening up access to four key airports: Chicago's O'Hare International, New York's John F. Kennedy and LaGuardia international airports, and Ronald Reagan Washington National Airport.

The bill would completely eliminate slot restrictions at O'Hare by July 2002, and at New York's airports by January 2007. It would allow unlimited, regional jet service into those airports beginning this spring. At National, 24 new flights would be permitted each day, including 12 long-distance flights beyond a federally imposed 1,250-mile "perimeter."

The efforts to relax slot restrictions drew rebukes on the House floor, especially from lawmakers from Chicago, New York and Northern Virginia representing constituents in the affected flight paths. Opponents to the new flights cited safety concerns and the environmental impact of the traffic.

"There will come a day when the chickens come home to roost on this bill," said Henry J. Hyde, R-Ill.

But lawmakers from areas with high ticket prices and limited airline service welcomed the elimination of slots.

"This is a day of hope for my region," said John E. Sweeney, R-N.Y. Upstate New York has seen some of the highest ticket prices in the country as airlines have pulled out of markets like Albany, Buffalo and Rochester.

Sweeney's upstate colleague, Democrat Louise M. Slaughter, noted that JetBlue, a new airline serving Buffalo and Ft. Lauderdale, Fla., from JFK Airport, now would be able to expand and connect her constituents in the Rochester area to New York City.

The number of lawmakers from underserved areas turned out to be far greater than those representing areas that will suffer the effects of more flights. But the defeat left many lawmakers from Illinois and Virginia bitter about what they said were the federal government's "broken promises" to limit the impact of the airports. "They want to stuff as many airplanes as they can, from wherever they can," said Frank R. Wolf, R-Va.

Controlling the Traffic

Airlines clearly hope the bill will have an impact on the strained air-traffic control system.

Passengers were frustrated by a record number of delays in 1999. Airlines blamed most of the delays on management problems at the FAA. The effort to modernize the air-traffic control system has been under way since 1981, and it has been plagued by numerous setbacks and cost overruns. Some of the computer systems designed to take over air-traffic control were deemed obsolete before they were even deployed.

The bill would create a new chief operating officer for air-traffic control at FAA. This new executive would enable the FAA administrator to act more like a chief executive officer, setting the overall policy and tone for the agency.

Among the goals for the legislation are facilitating a new scheme to fit more planes into the national airspace; employing modern global positioning satellite technology on a large scale; and authorizing "free flight," a new system that gives pilots more route flexi-

Transportation Trust Funds

MARCH 18 — The federal government has 14 trust funds financed by excise taxes to accomplish specific jobs in transportation, nature conservation, environmental cleanup and health compensation. Each has a dedicated source of revenue. Four of the funds deal with roads, aviation or waterways:

Highway Trust Fund (1956 — PL 84-627)

The fund uses excise taxes on motor fuels, heavy trucks, trailers and tires for the maintenance and construction of federal-aid highways and bridges, mass transit projects, highway safety programs and development of alternative forms of transportation. *(1956 Almanac, p. 398)*

Airport and Airway Trust Fund (1970 — PL 91-258)

The fund uses excise taxes on airline tickets, international departures, domestic air cargo and fuel used in general aviation for airport improvement grants, air-traffic control modernization, research and development, and a portion of the cost of Federal Aviation Administration operations. *(1970 Almanac, p. 168)*

The Inland Waterways Trust Fund (1978 — PL 95-502)

Excise taxes on fuel for inland and intracoastal waterway transportation vessels, such as towboats, are used to pay up to half the cost of inland waterway navigation projects. *(1978 Almanac, p. 513)*

The Harbor Maintenance Trust Fund (1986 — PL 99-662)

The fund uses excise taxes on cargo and cruise ship passengers and a portion of St. Lawrence Seaway tolls for the operation and maintenance of the seaway and a portion of the cost of harbor maintenance and operations. *(1986 Almanac, p. 127)*

SOURCE: Congressional Research Service

bility. The bill would enable the FAA to collaborate closely with the airline industry on traffic control issues.

"The [current] system is safe, but it is old and inefficient," said David Fuscus of the Air Transport Association. "It can't handle the traffic out there. It was designed to control the traffic flows of 20 years ago."

But several lawmakers on the House floor said the bill's emphasis on construction could put air-traffic control in a tight spending environment. Young noted that Republicans were preparing a tight fiscal 2001 budget resolution even as the House was debating the FAA bill.

"The electronics and concrete companies are going to like this bill. I have no problem with them," said Young. "I'm concerned about the people who run the system, who ensure safety."

The Clinton administration also voiced concern over operations funding levels, but it backed the agreement when conferees increased authorization levels to match the president's fiscal 2001 budget request.

Shuster and Oberstar said they received assurances from House leaders that the transportation appropriations spending allocation would allow for growth in aviation without cutting into programs like the Coast Guard or Amtrak. But many observers think appropriators will be hard-pressed to fund those programs as soon as fiscal 2002.

The bill also seeks to monitor the airlines' self-imposed "customer service commitments," which they created last year to fend off a burgeoning "passengers' rights" movement in Congress.

The customer service plans cover such areas as making the lowest fares available to consumers on their telephone reservation systems, notifying passengers of delays and allowing reservations to be held for 24 hours.

The aviation bill would require each airline to file its customer service plan with the Department of Transportation. It would enable the department's inspector general to monitor those agreements and report back to Congress by Dec. 31.

Help for Small Communities

Besides encouraging new regional jet services, the bill bolsters the Essential Air Service program, which subsidizes airline service to underserved communities. The program currently is funded through a permanent, $50 million fund; the bill would add another $15 million each year.

John J. "Jimmy" Duncan Jr., R-Tenn., chairman of the Transportation Subcommittee on Aviation, concentrated his efforts on bolstering small cities such as those in his home state.

"This bill does more for medium and small airports than any bill ever passed by Congress," he said.

The legislation would also establish a three-year pilot program to communities that are underserved by airlines. Under the bill, that would include cities not covered by the Essential Air Service Program that have limited service or unreasonably high fares.

The bill would also require airlines that control more than 60 percent of the flights at an airport to share their facilities with other airlines. ◆

FAA Reauthorization Provisions

MAY 27 — The sweeping reauthorization of the Federal Aviation Administration (HR 1000 — PL 106-181) cleared by Congress on March 15 promises to reshape the nation's aviation infrastructure for years to come.

The law marked the end of a two-year struggle by House Transportation and Infrastructure Committee Chairman Bud Shuster, R-Pa., to guarantee that all receipts of the Airport and Airway Trust Fund are spent on aviation programs. Shuster argued that travelers paying user fees, primarily on airline ticket taxes, should see those fees invested in better airports and air-traffic control.

The Senate agreed, adopting the conference report 82-17 on March 8. The House cleared the report, 319-101, on March 15, and President Clinton signed the measure into law April 5. The law is retroactive to Oct. 1, 1999.

Just as with the 1998 surface transportation law (PL 105-178), which protects Highway Trust Fund revenue for road building, Shuster was able to overcome the objections of appropriators, who said the dedicated funding plans would greatly restrict their ability to rein in government spending.

A compromise was struck to satisfy Senate critics, such as Appropriations Chairman Ted Stevens, R-Alaska, and Budget Chairman Pete V. Domenici, R-N.M. It will allow every penny of the trust fund and its earned interest to be dedicated to aviation, while appropriators will retain oversight of the overall aviation funding level — several billion dollars beyond what the trust fund brings in.

In a bid to keep up with booming airline traffic, the law will accelerate airport construction. The Airport Improvement Program funding level will rise from $1.9 billion in fiscal 2000 to $3.4 billion by fiscal 2003 — levels protected by parliamentary points of order.

The measure's sponsors hope that the airport construction spree also will spur competition among airlines — with benefits to consumers — by adding gates that are more accessible to low-cost airlines. To further foster competition, lawmakers set forth a plan to remove restrictions on the number of flights at busy airports in Chicago and New York. When that process is complete, Ronald Reagan Washington National Airport will be the only airport in the country with "slot" restrictions.

Many lawmakers from small- and medium-size cities welcomed these provisions and hope airlines will move to serve their markets with the new flights. The law also places special emphasis on rural markets by expanding the Essential Air Service program and approving several pilot programs aimed at drawing airlines into smaller markets.

The law also addresses what the airline industry considers the greatest threat to its future: the air-traffic control system. Airlines blame many of their delays, which reached a peak last summer, on the FAA's inability to modernize the system. The aviation law will create a chief operating officer at the FAA in charge of traffic control, who will operate with a great deal of autonomy and will be held accountable for reaching "measurable goals."

Finally, the law attempts to address consumer frustration by giving the Department of Transportation's inspector general authority to monitor the airline industry's voluntary plans to improve customer service. The industry plans were the major reason Congress backed off legislating a "bill of rights" for airline passengers. If the inspector general reports that the plans don't work, Congress will have an opening to reconsider the issue.

What follows is a provision-by-provision breakdown of the new aviation law. The law:

Spending Levels and Guarantees

Authorizes $40 billion in total aviation spending over three years, fiscal 2001 through fiscal 2003. Authorizes $12.7 billion for fiscal 2001, a $2.6 billion increase over fiscal 2000 spending levels. Authorizes $13.3 billion in fiscal 2002 and $13.7 billion in fiscal 2003.

Guarantees $33 billion of the spending through parliamentary points of order that can be brought against appropriations bills that do not spend all of the receipts and interest generated by the Airport and Airway Trust Fund each year.

- **Airport Improvement Program.** Authorizes $14.8 billion in spending over five years, including $2.4 billion retroactively authorized for fiscal 1999 and $2.5 billion in fiscal 2000, $3.2 billion in fiscal 2001, $3.3 billion in fiscal 2002 and $3.4 billion in fiscal 2003.
- **FAA Operations.** Authorizes $20.8 billion over three years for Federal Aviation Administration operations, including $6.6 billion in fiscal 2001, $6.9 billion in fiscal 2002 and $7.4 billion in fiscal 2003. Also authorizes funds as needed for fiscal 2000.

Continues to authorize special work rules and procurement procedures for FAA.

- **FAA Facilities and Equipment.** Authorizes $8.6 billion over three years, with $2.7 billion in fiscal 2001, $2.9 billion in fiscal 2002 and $3 billion in fiscal 2003. Also retroactively authorizes $2.1 billion for fiscal 1999 and $2.7 billion for fiscal 2000.
- **FAA Research and Development.** Retroactively authorizes $224 million in fiscal 2000 and authorizes $237 million for fiscal 2001 and $249 million for fiscal 2002. Makes no authorization for fiscal 2003.
- **Spending guarantees.** Establishes a parliamentary mechanism to ensure that all revenues deposited each year in the Airport and Airway Trust Fund, and all interest earned on the fund's balances, be spent on aviation programs administered by the Federal Aviation Administration. A senator or House member can bring a point of order against any spending bill that does not appropriate all such revenues in a given year.

Makes a priority of using trust fund money to finance the Airport Improvement Program and the FAA's facilities and equipment modernization program. Allows for general taxpayer revenue to be spent on aviation, but that money is subject to the checks and balances of the annual appropriations process. These priorities are also protected by parliamentary points of order.

If appropriators choose to spend less on the FAA's Facilities and Equipment program than the amount authorized, the extra funds can be shifted to the Airport Improvement Program, but only there. The law protects spending with a point of order.

- **Airport and Airway Trust Fund.** Extends the federal government's authority to collect for and distribute money from the Airport and Airway Trust Fund until Oct. 1, 2003.

Airport and Airway Improvements

• **Airport Improvement Program Formula Changes.** Doubles most basic airport entitlement grants. Raises the minimum entitlement grant for a "primary" airport (those serving more than 10,000 passengers a year) from $500,000 to $650,000. In years in which at least $3.2 billion is provided for the Airport Improvement Program — the amount authorized for fiscal 2001 — the law increases the minimum grant for a primary airport to $1 million and the maximum grant from $22 million to $26 million. Allows the Transportation secretary to keep a grant for a primary airport at the previous year's level if passenger traffic drops below 10,000 a year because of a labor dispute or natural disaster.

For cargo airports, increases the overall entitlement from 2.5 percent to 3 percent of Airport Improvement Program funds — the money is distributed to airports based on the proportion of cargo they handle out of the nationwide total. In years in which the airport program receives $3.2 billion or more, the 8 percent limit on amount any single airport may receive is lifted.

In years in which the airport program receives $3.2 billion or more, the law increases the state entitlement for general aviation airports from 18.5 percent to 20 percent of available program funds. A general aviation airport will be eligible for one-fifth of its five-year cost estimate for infrastructure needs — as identified in the FAA's national airport system plan — up to a maximum of $150,000 a year.

Gives the FAA flexibility to use an airport's Airport Improvement Program entitlement grant for discretionary grants at other airports if the original recipient does not plan to use the funds in a given fiscal year. Requires funds to be restored to the original recipient at a later date.

Increases the set-aside for noise abatement projects from 31 percent to 34 percent of all discretionary grants. Allows the FAA to make Airport Improvement Program grants for noise abatement even if the noise is primarily caused by military aircraft.

Sets aside $15 million, or 20 percent — whichever is less — of the portion of the small airport fund designated for non-hub portion of the small airport fund, which helps small airports meet new small airport safety certification standards. Authorizes set-aside for five years, but gives FAA authority to end program sooner if all airports have met the new standards.

Continues the existing 4 percent set-aside for airports with a significant military presence. Expands, from 12 to 15, the number of airports that may participate in the program. One of the additional airports may be a general aviation airport.

Establishes a new set-aside for "reliever" airports, those with at least 75,000 flights per year and near airports with 20,000 hours or more in delays in commercial passenger takeoffs and landings each year. The set-aside would be equal to 0.75 percent of discretionary Airport Improvement Program funds, if AIP funding totals $3.2 billion or more.

Expands allowable uses of AIP funds. Permits airports to use funds for wind shear protection devices, in-pavement lighting systems, emergency call boxes and certain enhanced-vision technologies. Permits airports to use AIP funds for constructing intermodal connectors at airports — for instance with highways and mass transit — and for purchasing capital equipment for intermodal connectors.

Allows some general aviation and small commercial airports to use AIP funds for routine maintenance work on runways, taxiways and aprons.

• **Passenger Facility Charges.** Gives airports authority to impose a surcharge of $4 or $4.50 on each paying passenger boarding an aircraft at the airport, if the money generated is used for projects to improve air safety or security, increase airline competition, reduce congestion or reduce noise. The airports must demonstrate that the projects could not be paid for with Airport Improvement Program funding and a passenger fee of $3 or less.

An airport may use fees higher than $3 for road, transit or non-aviation terminal improvements only if it has taken care of aviation needs such as runways, taxiways and gates.

Reduces Airport Improvement Program grants for airports that charge the fee: by up to 50 percent for airports charging $3 or less, and by up to 75 percent for airports charging more than $3.

• **Airline Competition Plans.** Requires major airports that wish to impose a passenger facility fee to develop plans to ensure that all air carriers have reasonable access to the airport's facilities. Beginning in fiscal 2001, the FAA may not approve the fees for airports without such a plan.

Creates a $5 million airport security program in which the Transportation secretary evaluates and funds innovative airport security systems.

Conveys certain properties made available from the military base-closing process to public airports.

Requires the Transportation secretary to study federal environmental requirements for airport improvement projects and report to Congress within one year on the level of coordination between federal agencies, the role of public involvement in the process, staff and resource requirements for the reviews, and the time the reviews take.

• **FAA Operations.** Allows the FAA to use operations funds to: hire additional inspectors for cargo security programs; develop and improve training programs for airport security; implement measures to prevent birds and other wildlife from colliding with aircraft; implement a plan to reduce runway incursions; develop bad-weather approach procedures that enable helicopters to transport trauma patients to hospitals; modify air-traffic control procedures to accommodate tilt-rotor aircraft; and support development of general aviation and helicopter industry infrastructure.

• **Facilities and Equipment.** Allows the FAA to use its Facilities and Equipment account to upgrade the FAA's automated surface weather observing system. Allows the FAA to use the account for the Alaska National Air Space Interfacility Communications system, an agency communications network in that state.

Air-Traffic Control

• **Chief Operating Officer.** Creates a chief operating officer for the air-traffic control system at FAA. The chief operating officer will be appointed by the FAA administrator, with the approval of the Aviation Management Advisory Council, for a five-year term.

The chief operating officer will report directly to the FAA administrator and will have a salary equal to the administrator's. A bonus of up to 30 percent of the annual salary is authorized for successfully meeting the goals of an annual performance agreement. The chief operating officer must produce an annual performance report for Congress and the Transportation secretary.

• **Air Traffic Demonstration Program.** Creates a program to permit non-federal partners, such as airport authorities and airlines, to share costs on air-traffic control modernization projects. Examples could include air-traffic control facilities located at airports, automation tools and radar and other flight tracking equipment.

Creates an experimental program to allow airports covered by the federal essential air service program to contract for private air-traffic control services.

Allows the Transportation secretary to approve 20 development projects at small airports using "innovative financing techniques."

• **Aviation Management Advisory Council.** Adds six new members to the 10-member council, made up of representatives of aviation interests who advise the FAA.

One of the six new members must be an air-traffic control employee union leader. The other five new members must be private citizens who are not in the aviation industry but have experience in one of the following areas: management, procurement, customer service, information technology, organizational development or labor relations.

Creates an Air Traffic Services Subcommittee to oversee the administration, management, conduct, direction and supervision of the air-traffic control system. Requires the panel to: review strategic plans for system; approve methods of accelerating the modernization and improvement of the system; approve procurements of $100 million or more; review operational plans and management, including the appointment of a chief operating officer; and review and approve the administration's annual budget request. Allows subcommittee to hire staff as necessary.

Requires the subcommittee to submit an annual report to Congress. Requires an additional report if the panel finds that the air traffic control system is failing to carry out its mission. Requires the FAA administrator, in the event of such a finding, to respond within 60 days, to adopt the subcommittee's recommendations or to report to Congress on the reasons for failing to do so.

Requires the FAA comptroller general to report to Congress by April 30, 2003, on the performance of the subcommittee in improving the air-traffic control system.

• **Airline Service Quality Performance Reports.** Establishes a task force within 90 days of enactment to modify regulations so that the FAA will disclose more fully the nature and source of delays and cancellations air travelers experience. Requires the task force to include members from the FAA, airlines and consumers.

Airline Competition

• **"Slot" Restrictions.** Completely eliminates federally imposed restrictions on the number of daily flights permitted at Chicago O'Hare International Airport by July 1, 2002. Eliminates restrictions on the number of daily flights at New York's John F. Kennedy and LaGuardia airports by Jan. 1, 2007. Allows 24 additional daily flights at Ronald Reagan Washington National Airport.

Permits the Transportation Department to immediately allow an unlimited number of flights for regional jets with 70 or fewer seats at O'Hare, John F. Kennedy and LaGuardia, if the planes fly to small hub airports or those that are not hubs. Also permits the Transportation Department to allow "slot" exemptions for airlines that have 20 or fewer slots or that currently do not fly to the three airports.

At O'Hare, beginning July 1, 2001, slot restrictions will apply only between 2:45 p.m. and 8:15 p.m. each day.

At Ronald Reagan Washington National Airport, half the 24 new daily flights can be to or from destinations of more than 1,250 miles, an exception to the so-called perimeter rule. Four of these 12 long-distance flights must be to small-hub or non-hub airports, and eight must be to medium, small or non-hub airports. All of the new flights must be between 7 a.m. and 10 p.m. each day, and no more than two new flights per hour are permitted. Requires 10 percent of the airport's Airport Improvement Program entitlement grant to be used for noise mitigation activities.

Requires the Transportation Department to conduct a study comparing noise levels around the four slot-controlled airports in fiscal 2001 to noise levels at the four airports before 1991.

Airline Service Improvements

• **Essential Air Service program.** Authorizes an additional $15 million per year for subsidizing airline service to underserved communities covered by the Essential Air Service program, which is currently funded through a permanent $50 million federal fund. Nullifies all Transportation Department orders since Sept. 30, 1999, that have established, modified or revoked Essential Air Service subsidies and requires the department to re-evaluate them. (The program was established when airlines were deregulated in 1978 to ensure that small towns that had scheduled air service could keep a minimum level of service. The program subsidizes commuter airline service to about 100 communities, many of them in the West.)

Adds language to the Essential Air Service program law: "ensuring that consumers in all regions of the United States, including those in small communities and rural and remote areas, have access to affordable, regularly scheduled air service." Waives local contribution requirement for communities approved for service between Oct. 1, 1991, and Dec. 31, 1997.

• **Underserved airports.** Establishes a new, three-year pilot program for improving air service to small, underserved airports. Qualifying airports are defined as non-hub or small-hub facilities not served by the existing Essential Air Service program.

Allows the Transportation secretary to designate up to 40 communities to participate in the program, not more than four from a single state. Gives priority to communities that provide a local share of the cost and establish public-private partnerships to improve air service. Any direct subsidies to airlines would be limited to three years. The measure authorizes $20 million in fiscal 2001 and $28 million each in fiscal 2002 and fiscal 2003.

Authorizes the Transportation Department to require that any airline controlling 60 percent or more of the flights at a major airport must share its facilities with airlines that provide essential air services to underserved communities, or take other steps to help them.

• **Regional Service Incentives.** Permits the FAA to provide financial assistance to regional commuter air carriers for purchasing regional jets to provide passenger service to underserved markets in small- and medium-size communities. The assistance can be in the form of federal loans, loan guarantees or lines of credit. Authorizes such sums as necessary for this purpose.

Requires medium- and large-hub airports dominated by one or two airlines to file "competition plans" with FAA in order to receive federal airport grants or to obtain approval for a passenger facility charge. The plans must explain the availability of airport gates and related facilities; state whether the airport is planning to build or redistribute gates that could be shared among airlines; and compare average airfares with those of comparably sized airports.

Requires the FAA to study whether airline marketing practices inhibit the availability and affordability of service to small and medium-size communities. Permits the FAA to study code-sharing arrangements between airlines, computer reservation system partnerships, and exclusive deals and gate arrangements. If the FAA finds that airlines inhibit service or affordability, the agency is authorized to issue regulations to correct the problem.

Customer Service and Passenger Rights

• **Customer Service Agreements.** Requires the Transportation Department to monitor the airline industry's voluntary customer service agreements, in which they promised to offer the lowest available fares to customers over telephone reservation systems, to notify passengers in advance of delays and to allow reservations to be held free of charge for 24 hours.

Requires airlines to file copies of their customer service plans with the Transportation Department's inspector general. Requires the inspector general to evaluate plans and report to Congress on their implementation, issue an interim report by June 15 and final report by Dec. 21.

Raises fines for violations of aviation consumer protection laws from $1,100 to $2,500. Requires airlines to notify passengers of the date their electronic tickets for airline service expire.

Requires the Transportation Department to issue regulations increasing airline financial responsibility for lost luggage.

Authorizes $8 million over three years for the department's consumer office to enforce airline consumer protection laws and regulations.

• **Ticket-splitting study.** Requires the General Accounting Office to study the potential impact of allowing airline passengers to use only a portion of their roundtrip or multistop airline tickets, a practice currently prohibited by most airlines.

• **Travel agent study.** Establishes a nine-member National Commission to Ensure Consumer Information and Choice in the Airline Industry. Requires the commission to examine and report to Congress on whether the travel agent industry is deteriorating financially, and whether the airline industry is erecting impediments to sharing airline schedule and fare information.

Family Assistance

Modifies the Aviation Disaster Family Assistance Act (PL 104-264), which requires the National Transportation Safety Board and airlines to more quickly notify the families of those involved in air crashes and to handle the news with proper sensitivity. *(1996 Almanac, p. 3-41)*

Lengthens, from 30 days to 45 days after a crash, the moratorium on lawyers contacting families of airline crash victims. Extends the moratorium to associates, agents and employees of lawyers. Extends the moratorium to cover crashes involving foreign airlines that occur in the United States.

Allows out-of-state Red Cross mental health workers to provide assistance at accident sites for up to 60 days (currently, mental health workers must be licensed in the state where a crash occurs). Extends family assistance services to families of foreign airline employees and others aboard a flight even if they did not pay for a seat on the plane. Requires airlines to improve employee training on meeting the needs of families. Requires airlines, if requested, to inform families whether their loved ones had a reservation on a flight that crashed.

• **Death on the High Seas.** Allows the family members of those killed in airline crashes up to 12 miles off the U.S. coast to sue for punitive damages. The former limit was three miles. (A 1996 Supreme Court ruling limited families of offshore airline crash victims to the recovery of lost income allowed by the 1920 Death on the High Seas Act, passed to protect the families of merchant seamen.)

Allows families of victims of crashes beyond the 12-mile perimeter to seek additional compensation for loss of care, comfort or companionship, but not punitive damages.

Makes the effective date of new standards July 16, 1996, which allows it to apply to victims of the TWA Flight 800 crash off the coast of Long Island.

Safety

• **Whistleblower Protections.** Prohibits airlines from firing or retaliating against employees who report safety problems. Allows employees who feel they have been retaliated against to file a complaint with the Labor Department, which must investigate and make a finding if a settlement has not been reached. The secretary of Labor can order restitution and compensatory damages. Permits fines of up to $1,000 for frivolous complaints. Allows appeals of Labor Department decisions to the U.S. Court of Appeals.

• **Small Airport Certification.** Requires the FAA, within 60 days of enactment, to issue a proposed rule allowing small passenger airports that upgrade their operations and facilities to receive federal certification. Requires a final rule one year after the comment period for proposed rule.

• **Occupational Injuries.** Requires the FAA administrator to conduct a study to determine the number of airport workers who are injured or killed by moving vehicles, the seriousness of such injuries and whether protective vests or other requirements would enhance safety.

• **Emergency Locator Transmitters.** Requires private and business jet aircraft, as well as certain charter and air taxi aircraft, to be equipped with emergency locator beacons. The requirement would take effect Jan. 1, 2002, unless the FAA administrator deems a delay necessary to promote a safe and orderly transition.

• **Counterfeit Parts.** Prohibits the certification by the FAA or hiring by aircraft parts companies of individuals or companies convicted of making or selling counterfeit aircraft parts. Establishes civil and criminal penalties for persons who sell or manufacture aircraft or spacecraft parts that they fraudulently claim are of aviation quality.

• **Disposal of Worn Parts.** Requires the FAA to propose a rule on the disposal of aircraft parts that have a limited useful life, to ensure they are not used on other aircraft.

• **Unruly Passengers.** Establishes fines of up to $25,000 for unruly passengers who interfere with an airline flight crew or endanger the safety of an aircraft, passengers or crew. Allows for deputizing of state and local law enforcement officers as deputy United States marshals to help enforce security on board aircraft, particularly as relates to unruly passengers.

• **Collision Avoidance Systems.** Requires most cargo aircraft to have collision avoidance systems — similar to those required on passenger airliners — installed by the end of 2002.

• **Flying Without a License.** Sets criminal fines and prison terms of up to three years for pilots who fly without a valid license and for companies that hire such pilots. Establishes a prison term of up to five years if the pilot is aiding or facilitating a drug-related crime.

• **Security Personnel.** Authorizes the FAA to permit criminal background checks for airport security employees, including those responsible for screening baggage and passengers.

• **Landfills.** Prohibits the building of new landfills within six miles of a small airport, due to concerns about birds that could pose a safety hazard to small aircraft. Alaska is exempted.

National Parks Air Tour Management

Provides a framework for regulating sightseeing flights over national parks, except the Grand Canyon, which is subject to a separate law (PL 100-91). Allows air tour operators to negotiate individual agreements at each national park. *(1988 Almanac, p. 297)*

• **Overflight Plans.** Requires the FAA to work with the National Park Service on an air tour flight management plan at each national park. Plans would be negotiated between the two federal agencies, tour operators, any American Indian tribes affected by the flights and the general public. Requires at least one public hearing for each flight management plan. Requires air tour operators to be certified by the FAA. Requires the FAA and the National Park Service to establish an advisory group to provide continuing advice and counsel regarding commercial air tours over and near national parks. Requires the FAA to report within 180 days of enactment on the impact of fees on commercial air tour operators, the viability of tax credits for operators to offset the fees and the financial impact of the fees on the FAA's budget and appropriations. Requires the FAA to report to Congress on quiet aircraft technology within two years of enactment.

• **Grand Canyon.** Requires the FAA to establish quiet aircraft standards for the Grand Canyon within one year of enactment. Requires the FAA to designate routes and corridors for commercial air tours in the Grand Canyon for airplanes and helicopters using such quiet aircraft technology. The quiet aircraft would not be subject to existing limits on Grand Canyon flights.

• **Rocky Mountain National Park.** Prohibits any commercial air tours over the Rocky Mountain National Park in Colorado.

Aeronautical Charting Activity

Transfers the Office of Aeronautical Charting and Cartography of the National Oceanic and Atmospheric Administration and all of its employees from the Department of Commerce to the Federal Aviation Administration. Allows the sale of such charts and maps. Requires the FAA to consider procuring map and chart services from the private sector, if that would further the mission of the FAA and be cost-effective.

Research and Development

Authorizes $224 million for FAA research and development in fiscal 2000, including:

- $17 million for system development and infrastructure.
- $33 million for capacity and air-traffic management technology.
- $11 million for communications, navigation and surveillance.
- $19 million for weather technology.
- $7 million for airport technology.
- $44 million for aircraft safety technology.
- $53 million for system security.
- $26 million for human factors and aviation medicine research.
- $3 million for environment and energy research.
- $2 million for innovative or cooperative research projects and activities.

Authorizes $237 million for fiscal 2001 and $249 million for fiscal 2002.

• **Integrated National Aviation Research Plan.** Requires the FAA administrator and the administrator of the National Aeronautics and Space Administration (NASA) to prepare jointly an integrated civil aviation research and development plan. Requires plan to address the research requirements, roles and responsibilities for the FAA and NASA; formal mechanisms for the two agencies to share information; and procedures for increased communications and coordination between them.

• **Internet Availability.** Requires the FAA to make available on the Internet abstracts relating to research grants and awards.

• **Airfield Pavement.** Requires the FAA administrator to consider awards to nonprofit concrete pavement research foundations to study improved design, construction, rehabilitation and repair of rigid concrete airfield pavements.

Miscellaneous Provisions

• **War Risk Insurance.** Reauthorizes through Dec. 31, 2003, the war risk insurance program, allowing the federal government to provide insurance to commercial airlines flying into high-risk areas, such as war zones, for U.S. foreign policy and national security purposes and when cost-effective commercial insurance is not available.

• **Aircraft Noise.** Requires the FAA to work toward a new standard for quieter aircraft, known as "Stage 4" aircraft. Requires the FAA to submit annual reports to Congress on efforts to apply new technologies to reduce aircraft noise levels.

Makes foreign airlines eligible for FAA waivers from a requirement they operate only Stage 3 aircraft after Dec. 31, 1999. Requires the FAA to permit Stage 2 aircraft to be brought into U.S. airspace without passengers for certain purposes — including maintenance needs, upgrades to Stage 3 standards and the disposal, sale or leasing of aircraft to be used outside the United States.

Requires the General Accounting Office to conduct a study of airport noise in the United States — including the impact of aircraft noise on local communities and schools, the threshold at which noise begins to threaten human health, and the effectiveness of noise abatement programs at U.S. airports.

• **Airport Security.** Authorizes $5 million for the FAA to carry out at least one program to test and evaluate innovative security systems and related technology. Authorizes $9 million over three years for a university consortium to develop an air safety and security certificate management program.

• **Smoking Ban.** Extends the current ban on smoking on all domestic flights to those segments of international flights that take off from or land in the United States. Applies the ban to both U.S. and foreign airlines. In cases in which a foreign government objects, requires the Transportation Department to negotiate a bilateral agreement to ban smoking on flights between the two nations.

• **U.S.-British Aviation Agreement.** Requires the Transportation secretary to consider several trade actions in response to Great Britain's refusal to agree to a new bilateral aviation agreement. Finds that the current aviation agreement significantly favors British airlines. Finds that Britain has refused to accept reasonable proposals for a new bilateral agreement. Lists actions for the secretary to consider: revoking the current noise exemption that allows British carriers to operate the Concorde supersonic aircraft in the United States; revoking all slots and slot exemptions held by British carriers at U.S. slot-controlled airports; rescinding the current permits and prohibiting flights by British carriers into the United States; and renouncing the current bilateral agreement.

• **D.C. Airports Authority.** Extends from 2001 to 2004 the time limit for Congress to reauthorize the Metropolitan Washington Airport Authority, which operates Dulles International Airport and Ronald Reagan Washington National Airport, both in Virginia. Eliminates the requirement that federal appointees to the authority's board be confirmed before the airport authority may receive federal AIP grants or be authorized to impose new passenger facility fees.

• **License Revocations.** Establishes a procedure under which pilots, mechanics, air carriers and others licensed by FAA whose licenses are revoked on an emergency basis may request an expedited appeal of the revocation by the National Transportation Safety Board, instead of by a federal appeals court.

• **Discrimination.** Explicitly prohibits airlines from discriminating against individuals because of race, color, religion, national origin, sex or a physical disability. Prohibits a state or local government from restricting the use of a private airport by individuals because of race, color, religion, national origin, sex or a physical disability.

Establishes civil penalties for discrimination against handicapped individuals. Requires the Transportation secretary to investigate complaints against airlines for acts of discrimination against passengers with physical disabilities. Requires the Transportation secretary to work with other governments and international organizations to bring about a higher standard for accommodating physically disabled passengers.

• **Pets on Airplanes.** Requires airlines to submit monthly reports to the Department of Transportation about any incidents involving the loss, injury or death of animals during transport by that airline. Requires the department to publish such data. Requires the department to work with airlines to improve employee training on how to carry animals. Requires airlines to inform passengers that animals may be carried in compartments that are not air-conditioned.

• **Pilot Records.** Exempts the military from providing records under the Pilot Records Improvement Act, passed as part of the 1996 FAA reauthorization law (PL 104-264), except for an airman's name, address and ratings held. Makes the exemption effective 120 days after enactment. The 1996 law requires airlines to check the backgrounds of prospective pilots. The new law allows airlines to hire pilots previously employed by foreign airlines without receiving a pilot's records if the airline has made a good-faith effort to obtain such records. *(1996 Almanac, p. 3-42)*

• **Foreign Reservation Systems.** Authorizes the Transportation Department to take action against foreign airline reservation systems that discriminate against U.S. systems.

• **Air Taxi Industry.** Requires the FAA to study the air taxi industry to increase government understanding of the size and nature of the industry, including types of aircraft used, hours flown, airports served and the industry's safety record.

• **Equal Employment Opportunity Complaints.** Authorizes $2 million for the Transportation Department to hire additional employees or contract personnel to investigate equal employment opportunity complaints. ◆

Outcry Over Tire Recall Results in Stricter Penalties, Broader Data Requirements

Box Score

- **Bill:** HR 5164 — PL 106-414
- **Legislative action: House** passed HR 5164 (H Rept 106-954), by voice vote, Oct. 11.

Senate cleared HR 5164, by voice vote, Oct. 11.

President signed the bill Nov. 1.

SUMMARY

Riding a crest of consumer concern over a huge Firestone tire recall, Congress cleared auto safety legislation that required manufacturers to give federal regulators a broad range of data on possible product defects and increased the penalties for those that withhold information. The bill also broke a stalemate on whether the government should test and rate vehicles on rollover dangers, and it set the stage for revising federal tire standards for the first time since 1968. President Clinton signed the bill into law on Nov. 1.

Congress returned from its August recess following weeks of intense news coverage and public concern about the Aug. 9 Bridgestone/Firestone Inc. recall of 6.5 million tires on sport utility vehicles. Tread separation was linked to accidents that claimed 101 lives, most when Ford Explorers rolled over. In several congressional hearings, executives from Bridgestone/Firestone and Ford Motor Co. acknowledged they had not told the government that some tires had been recalled overseas. The government, in turn, ignored tips from someone at State Farm Insurance Co. about a pattern of tire-related claims.

Senate Commerce, Science and Transportation Committee Chairman John McCain, R-Ariz., along with House Commerce Committee members W.J. "Billy" Tauzin, R-La., and Fred Upton, R-Mich., planned to try to close loopholes in federal regulations, but they wound up going much further, reaching a compromise on criminal penalties that had been anathema to industry.

McCain began the process with a hard-edged bill (S 3059 — S Rept 106-423) that the industry found totally unacceptable, warning that it would criminalize ordinary business decisions. McCain's efforts to bring his bill to the floor were blocked on several occasions by senators exercising anonymous "holds." The House bill mollified the industry with "safe harbor" language providing amnesty to employees who eventually admit to their criminal violations. With strong bipartisan backing as well as partial support from both business and consumer groups, the measure sailed easily through both chambers.

The final bill included a provision by Rep. Edward J. Markey, D-Mass., requiring the government to devise a crash test for rollovers and offer the results to consumers. Before the Firestone recall, the auto industry had fought off the rollover tests for years.

McCain and Ernest F. Hollings of South Carolina, the ranking Democrat on Commerce, vowed to revisit auto safety issues next year.

Tire Hearings Will Likely Put Highway Bill on Fast Track

SEPTEMBER 16 — After three high-profile hearings on the Firestone tire recall and the prospect of at least two more, Congress is moving rapidly to address what lawmakers perceive as gaping holes in the highway safety regulatory structure.

Key lawmakers in the House and Senate predict that legislation on the issue will clear this year — an extraordinary timetable given that lawmakers had their first hearing on the matter Sept. 6 and congressional leaders are hoping to meet an Oct. 6 adjournment target.

It was the latest sign that Congress is trying to stay ahead of mushrooming public concern over one of the largest consumer recalls in the nation's history. So far, the federal government has linked at least 88 U.S. deaths and more than 250 injuries to the failure of Firestone tires on Ford Explorer sport utility vehicles.

Fred Upton, R-Mich., and W.J. "Billy" Tauzin, R-La., two House Commerce subcommittee chairmen, unveiled a measure Sept. 13 (HR 5164) that focuses on broader reporting requirements for auto and tire manufacturers and increased penalties for failing to notify government officials on safety matters.

Tauzin and Upton presided over a 10-hour grilling of Clinton administration officials and executives of Bridgestone/Firestone Inc. and Ford Motor Co. on Sept. 6. They plan another joint hearing, this time on tire testing, Sept. 21. Later that day, Tauzin will preside over a hearing on the bill.

The legislation would give the National Highway Traffic Safety Administration (NHTSA) new powers to collect information on overseas recalls, and it would require companies to share with the government data on deaths, injuries and property damage related to tire and automobile failures.

NHTSA officials have testified that they did not pursue early tips about Firestone tire failures because the problems did not seem statistically significant. The officials said that if they had seen more company data on warranty adjustments, the evidence of a pattern would have been clearer.

"As I look into this, and into the documents in this case, Firestone didn't do the right thing," said Heather A. Wilson, R-N.M., a cosponsor of the Tauzin-Upton bill. "They were looking at profitability and liability. And what they forgot is responsibility."

The legislation would require the traffic safety administration to update tire safety standards last adjusted in 1968, when most cars and trucks still used bias-ply rather than radial-ply tires.

Tauzin said that House Commerce Committee Chairman Thomas J. Bliley, Jr., R-Va., and House Speaker J. Dennis Hastert, R-Ill., had assured him that they would do what they could to make sure the measure moved before the end of the session.

More Revelations

Senate Commerce Committee Chairman John McCain, R-Ariz., said he also would mark up legislation the week of Sept. 18 along the lines of the Tauzin-Upton bill. "People are in agreement on a number of the issues," McCain said in an interview.

"I think Americans would like some action," McCain added. "I think we might have difficulty explaining why we didn't act."

McCain and Tauzin both said they expect to return to the issue next year.

A Sept. 12 Senate Commerce Committee hearing produced more evidence that executives from Bridgestone/Firestone and Ford knew for years of overseas problems with the ATX and Wilderness AT tires on the Explorer without notifying the Transportation Department.

"I find my level of disbelief only increasing," said Olympia J. Snowe, R-Maine. "How is it we ever got to this point? How is it so many warning signs went undetected? How is it the companies involved and the federal regulators failed to notice?"

Tauzin said he expected more crucial evidence to turn up Sept. 15, the deadline House investigators imposed on Ford and Firestone to turn over their testing data on the tires used on the Explorer at an inflation pressure of 26 pounds per square inch (psi).

In the days after its Aug. 9 tire recall, Firestone recommended that Explorer owners increase tire pressure to 30 psi to lessen the likelihood of tread separation. Ford adjusted its recommendations to Explorer owners, saying a range from 26 psi to 30 psi was acceptable.

Some consumer advocates have charged that Ford earlier had recommended a lower tire pressure to reduce the likelihood of a vehicle rollover and to give a smoother ride. But lower tire pressures make tires more likely to blow out if heavy SUVs are overloaded with people and cargo, experts say. Underinflated tires can also run hotter at high speeds, increasing the likelihood of tread separation.

Level of Support

In the congressional hearings, administration officials were repeatedly asked whether they needed greater authority and resources to deal with manufacturers' reluctance to share data about potentially faulty products.

McCain pressed Transportation Secretary Rodney Slater about whether Congress had ever fallen short on an administration request for NHTSA resources. Slater said that Congress had not.

NHTSA's budget was sharply reduced in fiscal 1981 and 1982, the first two years of the Reagan administration, and has remained relatively flat since then in inflation-adjusted terms. In recent years, including fiscal 2001, Congress has matched President Clinton's budget requests for NHTSA. That has resulted in modest budget increases since 1996.

But Clinton's fiscal 2001 budget request to redirect $70 million in higher-than-expected gasoline tax revenues toward NHTSA went nowhere in Congress.

Slater said Sept. 12 that the Transportation Department would redirect $1.8 million from other NHTSA programs to its defects investigators. He asked that Congress shift another $9 million during final negotiations on the fiscal 2001 transportation appropriations bill (HR 4475).

The Tauzin-Upton bill would earmark an additional $500,000 for the defects unit.

While Congress has provided the funding the administration requested for NHTSA, it has not embraced efforts to strengthen the agency's powers.

Legislation that would have enhanced the government's ability to collect fines from companies that knowingly sell defective products went ignored in March. Slater sent it to the Commerce committee chairmen, but the measure languished without a sponsor.

Tauzin and Upton, in a Sept. 13 interview, said that they had never been approached by the Clinton administration on the proposed bill.

An Effective Watchdog?

Tauzin denied that Republican efforts during and after the Reagan administration to reduce government regulation of business had harmed NHTSA. The GOP, he said, was trying to eliminate red tape and "regulations that didn't make sense."

"We never proposed dismantling NHTSA," Tauzin said. He said Republican efforts at deregulation have focused on opening up industries to competition.

"Should we have strong safety regulations? You're doggone right. Democrats and Republicans will agree upon that," Tauzin added.

Consumer safety groups say that NHTSA had become too close to the auto industry over the last several years.

Testifying before the Senate Commerce Committee on Sept. 12, Joan Claybrook, president of the consumer group Public Citizen, said NHTSA has rarely used its subpoena power over the last 20 years and has seldom imposed even the limited penalties it is allowed.

"NHTSA was caught flatfooted in this case because it rarely pushes companies to obey the law," said Claybrook, who headed NHTSA during the Carter administration. "Auto manufacturers roll the dice in attempts to avoid mandatory recalls, and usually win."

Clarence Ditlow, executive director of the Center for Auto Safety, testified that auto companies cover up defects because, even if they are caught by NHTSA, delayed recalls save millions of dollars. Delayed recalls always have a lower completion rate and are therefore less expensive, he said.

Ditlow recounted several major company violations over the years. Mitsubishi was recently caught concealing consumer complaints through a double record-keeping system. Toyota concealed fuel tank defects. Honda did not report seat belt warranty claims. And General Motors hid problems with side-saddle gas tanks on pickup trucks from 1973 through 1987.

"All manufacturers conceal information from NHTSA and the public," Ditlow said.

Slater said Sept. 12 that the traffic safety agency had concentrated, with some success, on cooperative efforts with the auto industry on initiatives to promote seat-belt use and discourage drunken driving.

Slater also cited the public-private "Partnership for a New Generation of

Vehicles" research program as a successful way of improving fuel-efficiency technology.

Rollover Ratings

The continuing tire debate could affect another provision in the Senate version of the fiscal 2001 Transportation appropriations bill — a requirement that NHTSA delay a consumer information program on the rollover risk of new vehicles, particularly SUVs.

NHTSA proposed the program in May as a complement to the agency's other well-known consumer information program, which rates new cars and trucks from one to five stars based on their performance in crash tests.

McCain and Ernest F. Hollings of South Carolina, ranking Democrat on the Commerce Committee, sent a letter to appropriators urging them to drop a rider in the spending bill that would delay NHTSA's rollover ratings for at least a year while the National Academy of Sciences studied the proposed system and its usefulness for consumers. NHTSA has been working on the rollover rating system since the mid-1980s.

McCain called the provision "a classic example of inappropriate legislation on an appropriations bill" and "a classic example of special interests" at work.

At the Sept. 12 hearing, McCain asked Ford President and CEO Jacques A. Nasser to commit to supporting a rollover ratings system without the delay of a study. Nasser said he would.

Panels in Both Chambers Consider Criminal Penalties

SEPTEMBER 23 — Tough-minded legislation aimed at creating a stronger highway safety watchdog agency began moving through Congress the week of Sept. 18 in the aftermath of the Firestone tire recall.

Working against a deadline of weeks until Congress adjourns, lawmakers are contemplating powers and punishments unthinkable just a few months ago.

Both the House and the Senate are considering steeper sanctions — including criminal penalties — for companies and executives who fail to report a new range of safety information to the government.

They are also considering requiring manufacturers and insurers to share a wide variety of safety data with the National Highway Traffic Safety Administration (NHTSA), an agency of the Transportation Department.

And lawmakers are moving toward allowing NHTSA to add rollover ratings to its tests of cars, light trucks and SUVs, something the Senate has tried to block. NHTSA proposed the ratings in May.

John McCain, R-Ariz., chairman of the Senate Commerce, Science and Transportation Committee, steered a hastily drafted bill (S 3059) through a markup on Sept. 20.

Just before the session, McCain noted that the government had revised its casualty figures: 101 U.S. deaths and more than 400 injuries related to the failure of Firestone tires. Most occurred when treads separated on Ford Explorer sport utility vehicles that then rolled over.

"The continuing saga of Ford and Firestone should serve as a reminder that we must attempt to address the problems demonstrated by the recent recall before we adjourn," McCain said. He sponsored the bill along with ranking Democrat Ernest F. Hollings of South Carolina.

The Commerce Committee approved the bill on a voice vote, and the measure could come to the floor as early as the week of Sept. 25. The House Commerce Subcommittee on Telecommunications, Trade and Consumer Protection began marking up a similar measure (HR 5164) on Sept. 21, and it is expected to approve the bill Sept. 27.

Question of Criminality

McCain said his legislation would focus on areas where there is broad agreement, to ensure that it could be cleared before adjournment. But already there are elements of the bill that the auto industry is resisting, none more than the Senate's proposed criminal penalties.

Highway safety advocates say the Firestone case has demonstrated that civil penalties alone are not sufficient to force corporations to share vital safety information with the government.

The auto industry, backed by the broader business community, is fighting the McCain legislation.

"We support measures that will enhance auto safety," said Josephine S. Cooper of the Alliance of Automobile Manufacturers. "But in the haste to further protect consumers from potential safety defects, Congress should be wary of producing legislation with defects."

The alliance says the bill does not clearly define what would be a criminal action, leaving the possibility that executives could be charged based on their subjective engineering judgments. Industry officials said, for example, there is no clear definition of "defect" in the Senate bill.

The U.S. Chamber of Commerce sent a letter to all senators on Sept. 20 outlining its opposition to the bill. The chamber said the bill would have a chilling effect because executives would fear criminal penalties.

"The legislation creates a strong incentive for willful ignorance," wrote R. Bruce Josten, the group's executive vice president for government affairs.

The House bill, sponsored by W.J. "Billy" Tauzin, R-La., and Fred Upton, R-Mich., includes a more modest increase in NHTSA's power in order to punish companies that withhold highway safety information.

The House bill as currently drafted steers clear of criminal penalties. But Tauzin spokesman Ken Johnson said the House bill would eventually contain some language on criminal penalties.

Transportation Secretary Rodney Slater said the Clinton administration supports criminal penalties, but only as part of a package of other regulatory tools.

Slater said legislation should include increased civil penalties — both fines that the department could levy and those for courts to decide. He also said there should be criminal penalties for "egregious and knowing" safety violations.

"At the end of the day, we're going to have a good bill with auto industry support as well," he said.

Both measures would significantly increase the civil penalties available to federal regulators, a change that is not being fought as much by the industry.

The Senate bill would increase the maximum civil penalty from the current level of $800,000 to $15 million.

A House substitute offered by

Tauzin on Sept. 21 would increase the maximum civil penalty for a company that failed to report defects or other safety problems from $925,000 to $4 million.

The $4 million limit would match an administration proposal from March, but the Transportation Department has since drafted a plan calling for the discretion to levy unlimited fines in some cases.

Much of the testimony in congressional hearings on the Firestone recall focused on the inability of NHTSA to spot the trend of fatal accidents involving tire tread separations on Ford Explorers, partially because Firestone and Ford did not share information with federal regulators on accidents and property damage claims in the United States and overseas.

Data Gap

NHTSA Administrator Sue Bailey told lawmakers that the agency did not follow up tips from State Farm Insurance Co. about problems with Firestone tread separations because they did not seem statistically significant. But government investigators would have spotted the trend, she said, if they had been supplied with information about consumers' tire warranty claims.

With the two bills, Congress is moving to fill in that data gap with a slew of new reporting requirements for auto and tire makers as well as insurers.

Both bills would require automobile and tire companies to notify the Transportation Department about overseas consumer recalls. They also would require auto and tire manufacturers to report regularly to NHTSA about deaths, injuries and vehicle fires.

The Senate bill for the first time would require insurers to provide aggregate data about claims, with an eye to giving the government a better data base from which to spot trends that could uncover a product defect.

The auto industry describes the reporting requirements as onerous, and they maintain that useful insights about safety trends would be buried in the resulting "mountains of paper."

Rollover Resolution

The House Commerce subcommittee's ranking Democrat, Edward J. Markey of Massachusetts, said he intends to offer an amendment the week of Sept. 25 that would require NHTSA to develop a new test to determine how easily motor vehicles roll over. If that provision became law, NHTSA would have to develop a more comprehensive rollover rating system than the one currently proposed and blocked in the Senate version of the fiscal 2001 Transportation appropriations bill (HR 4475).

Slater said that a rollover rating for new vehicles was an administration priority, and that he would recommend that President Clinton veto the spending bill if it blocked the ratings.

The auto industry strongly opposes the ratings, arguing that they would not take into account safety features such as air bags that can reduce the likelihood of injury in a rollover.

After a heavy lobbying campaign, the Senate version of the appropriations bill included language that would block NHTSA from adding rollover tests until the National Academy of Sciences completed a nine-month study on whether the government test was "a scientifically valid measurement" that presents "practical, useful information to the public."

In the wake of the Firestone tire recall, however, the industry has been in retreat on the issue.

Senate Transportation Appropriations Subcommittee Chairman Richard C. Shelby, R-Ala., said on Sept. 20 that he would drop the prohibition from the Senate bill, and that the government could go ahead with plans to publish the ratings.

But conferees reportedly have agreed to a compromise that would allow the ratings while still ordering the National Academy of Sciences study.

House Panel Approves Penalties For Nondisclosure Of Safety Data

SEPTEMBER 30 — Despite heavy opposition from business groups, legislation that could impose criminal penalties on those who mislead the government about the safety of motor vehicles and equipment appears headed for swift passage.

One bill (HR 5164) was approved Sept. 27 by the House Commerce Subcommittee on Telecommunications, Trade and Consumer Protection and is scheduled for a full committee markup the week of Oct. 2. Subcommittee Chairman W.J. "Billy" Tauzin, R-La., predicted that it will clear Congress this year, despite the dwindling number of legislative days available.

The legislation stemmed from a massive recall of Firestone tires on sport utility vehicles, primarily Ford Explorers. The government has linked the tire problems to accidents in the United States that resulted in 101 deaths and more than 400 injuries.

"We need to avoid these things in the future. It's not just because people are getting hurt and dying on the highways. It's because the credibility of the industry is at stake," Tauzin said.

The Senate Commerce, Science and Transportation Committee approved a similar measure (S 3059) on Sept. 20. That bill could come to the Senate floor the week of Oct. 2.

Industry lobbying, including a letter from the U.S. Chamber of Commerce, has failed to slow down the legislation, which would extend an existing fraud law to anyone who misleads the government on vehicle safety information.

Company documents and congressional testimony showed that corporate executives failed to tell government highway safety officials that the tires had been recalled in some countries overseas and that the number of warranty claims about the tires was mounting.

The idea behind the criminal penalties is to ensure compliance with requirements in the bill that companies share a broad range of product data with government regulators.

The criminal liability issue was at the core of industry objections to the measure. The Alliance of Automobile Manufacturers, the Chamber of Commerce and the National Association of Manufacturers told lawmakers they thought the bill was being written so quickly that drafting errors were likely to criminalize ordinary business decisions.

"The inclusion of significant criminal penalties . . . could result in severe jail time for individuals who are unintentionally swept up in the subcommittee's rush to markup," the chamber wrote Commerce Committee Chairman Thomas J. Bliley Jr., R-Va.

Tauzin was unmoved. "All of them ought to embrace this bill," he said of the business groups. "They ought to endorse it. It's the right thing to do."

Indeed, both Bliley and ranking Commerce Committee Democrat John D. Dingell of Michigan, a strong supporter of the auto industry, voted in favor of the criminal penalties, which were included on a 23-0 vote.

The subcommittee did try to offer a more precise definition of what would constitute criminal behavior — penalties of up to $100,000 and up to 15 years in prison for lying to or misleading the government about motor vehicle or equipment defects that lead to death or grievous injury. The provision builds on current federal fraud and false-statement statutes.

Workers and lower-level executives who knew about violations and reported them to the government in a reasonable time would be protected from prosecution.

Reporting and Rollovers

The subcommittee also adopted, by voice vote, new language on industry reporting requirements. The amendment would result in new requirements for auto and auto equipment companies to report on warranty and claims data. The amendment also required the Transportation Department to specify how the information will be reviewed and used.

Tauzin said the provision would enable the National Highway Traffic Safety Administration to develop a framework for analyzing information as it came in.

"So much information was available, and yet it was not used properly," Tauzin said of the months leading up to the Firestone recall.

Ranking Democrat Edward J. Markey of Massachusetts tried unsuccessfully, for the second week in a row, to offer an amendment that would require a new consumer information program on the rollover risk of new vehicles.

Markey withdrew the amendment when Republicans Paul E. Gillmor of Ohio and Robert L. Ehrlich Jr. of Maryland strongly objected that the language would subject auto dealers to criminal liability for failing to give consumers rollover information.

Auto Safety Bill Heads to House Floor But Faces Holds in Senate

OCTOBER 7 — Despite the furor over the massive recall of Firestone tires, time may be running out for legislation aimed at stricter government oversight of auto safety.

House sponsors hoped to bring their version of the bill to the floor on Oct. 10, but attempts to set a vote on its Senate counterpart got blocked Oct. 6.

"The fix is in," complained Senate Commerce, Science and Transportation Committee Chairman John McCain, R-Ariz., after his attempts to bring his bill (S 3059) to the floor were repeatedly blocked by objections from other senators. McCain blamed intense lobbying by automakers and their allies.

McCain initially stalled consideration of the conference report on the fiscal 2001 transportation appropriations bill (HR 4475) to try to get his bill scheduled. He relented when majority Leader Trent Lott, R-Miss., agreed to work to ensure that the safety measure could come to the floor the week of Oct. 9. But each of McCain's subsequent procedural motions, which required unanimous consent, drew an objection.

One of those who objected, Jeff Sessions, R-Ala., complained that the measure could blur the lines between criminal and civil liabilities and had not been considered by the Judiciary committee, on which he serves.

George V. Voinovich, R-Ohio, said he would block the bill until it was rewritten to address concerns about criminal penalties and whether some of the details spelled out in the bill could be left to the National Highway Traffic Safety Administration (NHTSA) to decide through rulemaking.

Voinovich said he had no objections to the underlying legislation if his concerns were addressed. "I'm interested in good legislation that does make a difference, he said. "I think my concerns should be addressed responsibly. If they are, then I'd be supportive."

If the opponents prevent action this year, McCain said, "then they'll have the American people to answer to."

Civil, Criminal Penalties

The House bill (HR 5164) would require the auto and tire industries to share with the government a broader range of data on possible defects in their products. To ensure compliance, the bill would increase civil penalties for companies that violate the rules to a maximum of $15 million. It would also create criminal consequences — up to 15 years of prison and $100,000 in fines — for employees who withheld critical defect information.

The House Commerce Committee, which approved the bill, 42-0, on Oct. 5, added a provision by Edward J. Markey, D-Mass., that would require the government to develop rollover tests for cars and light trucks. NHTSA would decide how to distribute the results to consumers.

Both the House and Senate bills are a response to documents and testimony indicating that executives at Ford Motor Co. and Bridgestone/Firestone Inc. failed to tell government highway safety officials that defective Firestone tires had been recalled in other countries and that warranty claims were increasing.

"This bill represents solutions to problems with our process," said W.J. "Billy" Tauzin, R-La., chairman of the House Commerce Subcommittee on Telecommunications, Trade and Consumer Protection. "It will ensure we not just get information. It will ensure the federal government pays attention to that information."

The committee rejected, 14-30, an amendment by Henry A. Waxman, D-Calif., that would have allowed NHTSA to assess civil penalties without first consulting the Justice Department.

The amendment was patterned on power that the Clean Air Act (PL 101-549) has given the Environmental Protection Agency. Tauzin said the issue had not come up during the Firestone hearings, and other members said the administration had not asked for such expanded authority.

The committee adopted, by voice vote, another Markey amendment that would require NHTSA to establish guidelines for motor vehicles to have tire pressure gauges installed.

Behind the scenes, business groups kept up a campaign to soften the legislation, especially in areas that would create new criminal penalties. The U.S. Chamber of Commerce urged greater protection for companies' proprietary information, while the auto industry was looking for assurances that normal business practices could not be criminalized.

"Our goal is to be constructive and make sure whatever comes out deals with safety and produces as few unintended consequences as possible," said Mike Stanton, chief lobbyist of the Alliance of Automobile Manufacturers.

But the industry efforts failed to stop the bill's momentum in the House, especially after many lawmakers were visited during the week of Oct. 2 by victims of Firestone-related accidents.

Hill Clears Auto Safety Bill With Some Concessions To Industry

OCTOBER 14 — Congress sent landmark auto safety legislation to President Clinton on Oct. 11, having overcome strong objections from business groups. The bill would require the auto industry to share with the government a broad range of data on possible defects in their products. Those who hide information or mislead regulators could get 15 years in prison.

The Senate cleared the bill (HR 5164) Oct. 11 after the House passed it early the same day, both by voice vote. The Senate had been considering similar legislation (S 3059). Clinton is expected to sign the bill.

The legislation, a direct response to this summer's recall of 6.5 million Firestone tires, promises to alter the political landscape for the auto industry in Washington. After years of blocking increases in fuel economy standards, more stringent air bag tests and public disclosure of the risk that vehicles might roll over, the industry now will be more closely monitored by the National Highway Traffic Safety Administration (NHTSA) and a coalition of consumer groups energized by the Firestone case.

During a flurry of hearings in the weeks following the August recess, lawmakers heard repeated testimony that Bridgestone/Firestone Inc. and Ford Motor Co. had extensive knowledge of tread separation on Firestone's ATX and Wilderness AT tires causing Ford Explorer sport utility vehicles to spin out of control. Federal investigators are looking into 101 deaths and more than 400 injuries linked to the tires. Almost all of the accidents occurred on the Explorer, the country's best-selling SUV.

Final passage of the auto safety bill came barely one month after the first hearings on the tire issue.

"The last time there was such a massive tire recall was in the '70s, and Congress did nothing to fix the problem," said Fred Upton, R-Mich., sponsor of the House bill. "As a result, our tire standards haven't been updated in some 30 years. Tonight we changed that trend."

Many of those involved in highway safety issues hailed the bill as much more than the minimum Congress could have done after hearings exposed gaping holes in the system for reporting auto safety problems.

Instead of settling on a simple bill to close one or two loopholes, Upton and W.J. "Billy" Tauzin, R-La., wrote a comprehensive measure that will result in broad new data collection efforts and fines of up to $15 million and possible prison terms for those who try to evade the requirements.

Rating Risks

The bill also broke a logjam on other contentious auto safety issues. For instance, it would require new tests to determine the propensity of cars and light trucks to roll over. Rollover accidents account for more than 9,000 deaths annually, but efforts to create a government rollover test and ratings have been stymied for years. A much more modest government proposal on rollover tests had been blocked most of this year on the fiscal 2001 transportation appropriations bill (HR 4475) until conferees removed the provision the week of Oct. 2.

The auto safety bill would also update a 30-year-old safety standard for tires, requiring a low-tire-pressure warning system for new cars, and launch a program that aims to improve children's car seats.

"This is some of the best work we have ever seen Congress do," said David Snyder of the American Insurance Association. "It usually takes years to get these things done."

Before the measure cleared, it was in danger of falling victim to complex Senate procedures. Commerce Committee Chairman John McCain, R-Ariz., was blocked several times in trying to bring up his own auto safety bill (S 3059) and the House bill with amendments. In most cases, a fellow senator exercised an anonymous "hold" on the legislation.

The delay made McCain apoplectic. But his scoldings on the Senate floor did little to sway opponents of his bill, which contained stiffer criminal penalties than the House measure and was strongly opposed by the auto industry and business groups.

"I will tell you, in straight talk, what this is all about," McCain said. "Trial lawyers do not want it because . . . they want to be able to sue anybody for anything under any circumstances. And the automotive industry wants this thing killed, figuring that the publicity surrounding these accidents and these tragedies that are taking place will die out and they will be able to kill off this legislation next year."

McCain settled for moving the House bill without any amendments. That measure had drawn support from the Alliance of Automobile Manufacturers and the U.S. Chamber of Commerce.

"The reality we face in the remaining days of Congress because of these tactics is that we pass the House bill or we pass nothing," McCain complained.

Judiciary Committee Chairman Orrin G. Hatch, R-Utah, said earlier on Oct. 11 that he was concerned about the speed with which the measure was being considered. He also said his committee should have had a hand in writing the Senate bill's criminal penalties but had not been contacted.

"These are very difficult issues," Hatch said. "We don't want to play politics. I don't think enough hearings have been held."

Unresolved Issues

When Congress returns next year, it will be looking to fine-tune the auto safety initiatives. The authorization for NHTSA is scheduled to expire, and the reauthorization bill could become a new battleground for the controversies McCain was seeking to debate. McCain's Commerce, Science and Transportation Committee will have jurisdiction over that bill.

Sen. Ernest F. Hollings, D-S.C., wants to look at whether the auto industry should have to supply the government with more information about warranty claims and warranty lawsuits, according to Hollings spokesman Andy Davis. The industry has been unwilling to take that step.

Consumer groups vowed to return to fight what they described as loopholes created by the House bill, another concern of Hollings'.

Public Citizen, an interest group founded by Green Party presidential candidate Ralph Nader, criticized concessions made to the industry on keeping vast portions of the new collected data secret. Auto companies had lobbied hard on this issue, claiming it was necessary to protect proprietary information.

Under the bill, the new data will be made public only if the Transportation secretary deems it in the public interest. Currently, NHTSA information is made public unless the secretary makes an affirmative decision to block the release, after industry states a specific objection. Consumer groups fear that the new restrictions will curtail the flow of information.

Auto lobbyists said that the relevant information will still be available under the Freedom of Information Act, but that it will not be as easy for consumer groups and others to fish for auto information.

Public Citizen had also urged lawmakers to strengthen penalty provisions and place more limitations on an escape clause, or "safe harbor," that would allow those who know of safety problems to avoid criminal penalties by coming clean and eventually reporting them.

"No one will be prosecuted under this bill," said Laura MacCleery, a lawyer with the group.

Consumer groups also will continue pushing for safety standards not included in the legislation, such as a manufacturing standard for preventing rollovers and a stronger standard for roofs to protect passengers in rollover crashes. Automakers have resisted these measures. ◆

Chapter 22

VETERANS AFFAIRS

Congress Clears Compromise Bill to Increase Health and Education Benefits for Vets

SUMMARY

President Clinton signed into law on Nov. 1, a bill to increase veterans' benefits under the Montgomery GI bill, improve certain health benefits and boost pay for Department of Veterans Affairs (VA) nurses and dentists.

The legislation, a compromise that incorporated provisions from several veterans bills, increased education assistance under the GI bill from $552 per month to $650 per month for three years of service. It guaranteed VA nurses the same annual pay increase that federal employees receive, increased pay for dentists and allowed VA hospitals to hire physician assistants. It authorized the VA to furnish temporary lodging for veterans getting treatment or other services, and expanded health benefits to a number of specific groups.

As passed by the Senate in 1999, S 1402 focused on veterans' education benefits. The House took the measure up in May, substituting its own veterans education bill (HR 4268).

On Sept. 21, each chamber passed a version of veterans health care legislation. The House bill (HR 5109) contained a controversial provision by Dave Weldon, R-Fla., which would have allowed veterans to receive health care funded by the Department of Veterans Affairs at non-VA hospitals. The Senate-passed version (S 1810) had no comparable language. The pilot program was supported by some of the largest veterans associations, including the American Legion and the Veterans of Foreign Wars. Other veterans groups, such as the Disabled American Veterans, the Paralyzed Veterans of America and the Blinded Veterans Association, lobbied against it, arguing that it would begin a process that would eventually close the VA health care system by making it more convenient for veterans to seek care at local hospitals.

Working behind the scenes, House and Senate negotiators blended the bills into a single package, dropping Weldon's pilot program. The Senate passed the compromise Oct. 12 as a substitute to S 1402; the House cleared it Oct. 17.

House Panel Reins In Rise in Stipends

MAY 13 — A Democratic attempt to boost monthly education stipends for veterans beyond the increase envisioned by the House Veterans' Affairs Committee was blocked by budget realities at a May 11 markup.

The amendment, offered by Bob Filner, D-Calif., failed on a 6-15 vote. The bill (HR 4268) eventually was approved, 21-0.

The legislation would substantially increase monthly reimbursement rates for veterans' educational expenses. Full-time students now receive $536 a month. That would increase to $600 a month on Oct. 1, 2000, then to $720 a month on Oct. 1, 2002. Part-time students' monthly reimbursements would increase from $429 to $487 on Oct. 1, 2000, then to $585 on Oct. 1, 2002.

Supporters from both parties said the increases are needed to keep up with increasing educational costs.

Filner wanted an even larger increase for full-time students to $975 a month in fiscal 2001. He also wanted the rate to increase in subsequent years to reflect changes in the cost of living.

Filner argued that limiting the increase to $720 a month does not cover today's educational costs, and that the committee should fight to include as much money as possible in the legislation even if it could not find offsets.

"Our small steps are going to be eaten up by inflation before we even begin," he said.

But Jack Quinn, R-N.Y., said budget constraints would not allow any more money.

"Very little of what we ever do in this place is perfect," Quinn said.

Democrats said the committee should have at least tried for the higher funding level, even if it required an attempt to change House rules regarding the budget surplus.

"My position is you don't have a surplus until you pay your bills," said Corrine Brown, D-Fla.

The measure is expected to be considered on the House suspension calendar the week of May 15.

Box Score

- **Bill:** S 1402 — PL 106-419
- **Legislative action:** House passed S 1402, 417-0, on May 23, after substituting the text of HR 4268 (H Rept 106-628).

Senate passed S 1402, amended, by voice vote Oct. 12.

House cleared S 1402 by voice vote on Oct. 17.

President signed the bill Nov. 1.

House Increases Vets' Tuition Reimbursement

MAY 27 — The House on May 23 passed an amended version of a Senate bill that would increase and expand access to educational benefits for veterans.

Under the bill, veterans would see their monthly reimbursement for college tuition increase from $536 to $600 on Oct. 1, and to $720 on Oct. 1, 2002. There would be proportional increases for part-time students.

The House passed the bill (S 1402), 417-0, after substituting the text of a House measure (HR 4268). *(Vote 220, p. H-70)*

Supporters say the increases are necessary to keep up with the rising costs of higher education. Some lawmakers, however, think the measure would not go far enough.

"The best way to honor members of the armed services is to pay the full cost of a four-year state college education," said Bob Filner, D-Calif., who tried unsuccessfully to increase the stipend during the House Veterans' Affairs Committee markup on May 11.

Former Rep. G.V. "Sonny" Montgomery, D-Miss. (1967-97) was on the House floor during the debate and passage. Montgomery revived the World War II-era "GI Bill of Rights" in 1984 legislation (PL 98-525) after it had been allowed to lapse in 1976 with the end of the draft. *(1984 Almanac, p. 56)*

Both Chambers Pass Benefits Bills

JULY 29 — The House passed legislation July 25 designed to make it easier for veterans to file claims with the government. But in the Senate, similar legislation has become a vehicle for a number of veterans bills, most of them dealing with medical issues.

The House bill (HR 4864 — H Rept 106-781), passed on a 414-0 vote, would reverse a July 1999 decision by the Court of Appeals for Veterans Claims that the Department of Veterans Affairs (VA) may only help veterans obtain records relevant to filing a benefit claim if it can be proved the claim is well-grounded, which includes producing medical and other evidence. *(Vote 432, p. H-134)*

The bill would require the VA to make reasonable efforts to obtain records that would help a veteran establish entitlement to a benefit.

The Senate bill (S 1810), approved by the Veterans' Affairs Committee on July 27, was drafted by Patty Murray, D-Wash., to help veterans file claims. However, it picked up other measures, including one that would provide benefits to children born with birth defects whose mothers were Vietnam veterans.

Three Benefits Bills Clear

OCTOBER 21 — The House on Oct. 17 cleared three measures affecting military veterans. All passed by voice vote.

One of the bills (HR 4864 — H Rept 106-781) would make it easier for veterans to file claims with the Department of Veterans Affairs (VA). Bob Stump, R-Ariz., said the measure would clarify the department's duty to help claimants and "restore the balance in the VA claims system."

The House first passed the bill July 25. The Senate made technical corrections and passed it by voice vote Sept. 25.

The measure includes provisions to:

- Require the VA to make reasonable efforts to help veterans determine whether they are entitled to benefits.
- Give claimants the benefit of the doubt in cases where evidence equally supports the veteran and the government.
- Prevent the VA from denying claims to veterans who do not have a mailing address.

The second bill (HR 4850 — H Rept 106-783) would authorize cost-of-living increases for disability claimants.

The third (S 1402) would increase the rate of assistance under the Montgomery G.I. Bill and boost pay for VA nurses and dentists. ◆

Appendix A

CONGRESS AND ITS MEMBERS

Glossary of Congressional Terms

Act — The term for legislation once it has passed both chambers of Congress and has been signed by the president or passed over his veto, thus becoming law. Also used in parliamentary terminology for a bill that has been passed by one house and engrossed. *(Also see engrossed bill.)*

Adjournment sine die — Adjournment without a fixed day for reconvening — literally, "adjournment without a day." Usually used to connote the final adjournment of a session of Congress. A session can continue until noon Jan. 3 of the following year, when, under the 20th Amendment to the Constitution, it automatically terminates. Both chambers must agree to a concurrent resolution for either chamber to adjourn for more than three days.

Adjournment to a day certain — Adjournment under a motion or resolution that fixes the next time of meeting. Under the Constitution, neither chamber can adjourn for more than three days without the concurrence of the other. A session of Congress is not ended by adjournment to a day certain.

Amendment — A proposal by a member of Congress to alter the language, provisions or stipulations in a bill or in another amendment. An amendment usually is printed, debated and voted upon in the same manner as a bill.

Amendment in the nature of a substitute — Usually an amendment that seeks to replace the entire text of a bill by striking out everything after the enacting clause and inserting a new version of the bill. An amendment in the nature of a substitute can also refer to an amendment that replaces a large portion of the text of a bill.

Appeal — A member's challenge of a ruling or decision made by the presiding officer of the chamber. A senator can appeal to members of the Senate to override the decision. If carried by a majority vote, the appeal nullifies the chair's ruling. In the House, the decision of the Speaker traditionally has been final; seldom are there appeals to the members to reverse the Speaker's stand. To appeal a ruling is considered an attack on the Speaker.

Appropriations bill — A bill that gives legal authority to spend or obligate money from the Treasury. The Constitution disallows money to be drawn from the Treasury "but in Consequence of Appropriations made by Law."

By congressional custom, an appropriations bill originates in the House. It is not supposed to be considered by the full House or Senate until a related measure authorizing the funding is enacted. An appropriations bill grants the actual budget authority approved by the authorization bill, though not necessarily the full amount permissible under the authorization.

If the 13 regular appropriations bills are not enacted by the start of the fiscal year, Congress must pass a stopgap spending bill or the departments and agencies covered by the unfinished bills must shut down.

About half of all budget authority, notably that for Social Security and interest on the federal debt, does not require annual appropriations; those programs exist under permanent appropriations. *(Also see authorization bill, budget authority, budget process, supplemental appropriations bill.)*

Authorization bill — Basic, substantive legislation that establishes or continues the legal operation of a federal program or agency either indefinitely or for a specific period of time, or which sanctions a particular type of obligation or expenditure. Under the rules of both chambers, appropriations for a program or agency may not be considered until the program has been authorized, although this requirement is often waived.

An authorization sets the maximum amount of funds that can be given to a program or agency, although sometimes it merely authorizes "such sums as may be necessary." *(Also see backdoor spending authority.)*

Backdoor spending authority — Budget authority provided in legislation outside the normal appropriations process. The most common forms of backdoor spending are borrowing authority, contract authority, entitlements and loan guarantees that commit the government to payments of principal and interest on loans — such as guaranteed student loans — made by banks or other private lenders. Loan guarantees result in actual outlays only when there is a default by the borrower.

In some cases, such as interest on the public debt, a permanent appropriation is provided that becomes available without further action by Congress.

Bills — Most legislative proposals before Congress are in the form of bills and are designated according to the chamber in which they originate — HR in the House of Representatives or S in the Senate — and by a number assigned in the order in which they are introduced during the two-year period of a congressional term.

"Public bills" deal with general questions and become public laws if they are cleared by Congress and signed by the president. "Private bills" deal with individual matters, such as claims against the government, immigration and naturalization cases or land titles, and become private laws if approved and signed. *(Also see private bills, resolution.)*

Bills introduced — In both the House and Senate, any number of members may join in introducing a single bill or resolution. The first member listed is the sponsor of the bill, and all subsequent members listed are cosponsors.

Many bills are committee bills and are introduced under the name of the chairman of the committee or subcommittee. All appropriations bills fall into this category. A committee frequently holds hearings on a number of related bills and may agree to one of them or to an entirely new bill. *(Also see clean bill.)*

Bills referred — After a bill is introduced, it is referred to the committee or committees that have jurisdiction over the subject with which the bill is concerned. Under the standing rules of the House and Senate, bills are referred by the Speaker in the House and by the presiding officer in the Senate. In practice, the House and Senate parliamentarians act for these officials and refer the vast majority of bills. *(Also see discharge a committee.)*

Borrowing authority — Statutory authority that permits a federal agency to incur obligations and make payments for specified purposes with borrowed money.

Budget — The document sent to Congress by the president early each year estimating government revenue and expenditures for the ensuing fiscal year.

Budget Act — The common name for the Congressional Budget and Impoundment Control Act of 1974, which established the current budget process and created the Congressional Budget Office. The act also put limits on presidential authority to spend appropriated money. It has undergone several major revisions since 1974. *(Also see budget process, impoundments.)*

Budget authority — Authority for federal agencies to enter into obligations that result in immediate or future outlays. The basic forms of budget authority are appropriations, contract authority and borrowing authority. Budget authority may be classified by (1) the period of availability (one-year, multiple-year or without a time limitation), (2) the timing of congressional action (current or permanent) or (3) the manner of determining the amount available (definite or indefinite). *(Also see appropriations, outlays.)*

Budget process — The annual budget process was created by the Congressional Budget and Impoundment Control Act of 1974, with a timetable that was modified in 1990. Under the law, the president must submit his proposed budget by the first Monday in February. Congress is supposed to complete an annual budget resolution by April 15, setting guidelines for congressional action on spending and tax measures.

Budget rules enacted in the 1990 Budget Enforcement Act and updated in 1993 and 1997 set caps on discretionary spending through fiscal 2002. The caps can be adjusted annually to account for changes in the economy and other limited factors. In addition, pay-as-you-go (PAYGO) rules require that any tax cut, new entitlement program or expansion of existing entitlement benefits that would increase a deficit be offset by an increase in taxes or a cut in entitlement spending.

The rules hold Congress harmless for budget-deficit increases that lawmakers do not explicitly cause — for example, increases due to a recession or to an expansion in the number of beneficiaries qualifying for Medicare or food stamps. PAYGO does not apply if there is a budget surplus.

If Congress exceeds the discretionary spending caps in its appropriations bills, the law requires an across-the-board cut — known as a sequester — in non-exempt discretionary spending accounts. If Congress violates the PAYGO rules, entitlement programs are subject to a sequester. Supplemental appropriations are subject to similar controls, with the proviso that if both Congress and the president agree, spending designated as an emergency can exceed the caps.

Budget resolution — A concurrent resolution that is passed by both chambers of Congress but does not require the president's signature. The measure sets a strict ceiling on discretionary budget authority, along with non-binding recommendations about how the spending should be allocated. The budget resolution may also contain "reconciliation instructions" requiring authorizing and tax-writing committees to propose changes in existing law to meet deficit-reduction goals. The Budget Committee in each chamber then bundles those proposals into a reconciliation bill and sends it to the floor. *(Also see reconciliation.)*

By request — A phrase used when a senator or representative introduces a bill at the request of an executive agency or private organization but does not necessarily endorse the legislation.

Calendar — An agenda or list of business awaiting possible action by each chamber. The House uses six legislative calendars. They are the Consent, Corrections, Discharge, House, Private and Union calendars. *(Also see individual listings.)*

In the Senate, all legislative matters reported from committee go on one calendar. They are listed there in the order in which committees report them or the Senate places them on the calendar, but they may be called up out of order by the majority leader, either by obtaining unanimous consent of the Senate or by a motion to call up a bill. The Senate also has one non-legislative calendar, which is used for treaties and nominations. *(Also see executive calendar.)*

Call of the calendar — Senate bills that are not brought up for debate by a motion, unanimous consent or a unanimous consent agreement are brought before the Senate for action when the calendar listing them is "called." Bills must be called in the order listed. Measures considered by this method usually are non-controversial, and debate on the bill and any proposed amendments is limited to five minutes for each senator.

Chamber — The meeting place for the membership of either the House or the Senate; also the membership of the House or Senate meeting as such.

Clean bill — Frequently after a committee has finished a major revision of a bill, one of the committee members, usually the chairman, will assemble the changes and what is left of the original bill into a new measure and introduce it as a "clean bill." The revised measure, which is given a new number, is referred back to the committee, which reports it to the floor for consideration. This often is a timesaver, as committee-recommended changes in a clean bill do not have to be considered and voted on by the chamber. Reporting a clean bill also protects committee amendments that could be subject to points of order concerning germaneness.

Clerk of the House — An officer of the House of Representatives who supervises its records and legislative business. Many former administrative duties were transferred in 1992 to a new position, the director of non-legislative and financial services.

Cloture — The process by which a filibuster can be ended in the Senate other than by unanimous consent. A motion for cloture can apply to any measure before the Senate, including a proposal to change the chamber's rules. A cloture motion requires the signatures of 16 senators to be introduced. To end a filibuster, the cloture motion must obtain the votes of three-fifths of the entire Senate membership (60 if there are no vacancies), except when the filibuster is against a proposal to amend the standing rules of the Senate and a two-thirds vote of senators present and voting is required.

The cloture request is put to a roll call vote one hour after the Senate meets on the second day following introduction of the motion. If approved, cloture limits each senator to one hour of debate. The bill or amendment in question comes to a final vote after 30 hours of consideration, including debate time and the time it takes to conduct roll calls, quorum calls and other procedural motions. *(Also see filibuster.)*

Committee — A division of the House or Senate that prepares legislation for action by the parent chamber or makes investigations as directed by the parent chamber.

There are several types of committees. Most standing committees are divided into subcommittees, which study legislation, hold hearings and report bills, with or without amendments, to the full committee. Only the full committee can report legislation for action by the House or Senate. *(Also see standing, oversight, select and special committees.)*

Committee of the Whole — The working title of what is formally "The Committee of the Whole House [of Representatives] on the State of the Union." The membership is composed of all House members sitting as a committee. Any 100 members who are present on the floor of the chamber to consider legislation comprise a quorum of the committee. Any legislation, however, must first have passed through the regular legislative or appropriations committee and have been placed on the calendar.

Technically, the Committee of the Whole considers only bills directly or indirectly appropriating money, authorizing appropriations or involving taxes or charges on the public. Because the Committee of the Whole need number only 100 representatives, a quorum is more readily attained and legislative business is expedited. Before 1971, members' positions were not individually recorded on votes taken in the Committee of the Whole.

When the full House resolves itself into the Committee of the Whole, it replaces the Speaker with a "chairman." A measure is debated and amendments may be proposed, with votes on amendments as needed. *(Also see five-minute rule.)*

When the committee completes its work on the measure, it dissolves itself by "rising." The Speaker returns, and the chairman of the Committee of the Whole reports to the House that the committee's work has been completed. At this time, members may demand a roll call vote on any amendment adopted in the Committee of the Whole. The final vote is on passage of the legislation.

In 1993 and 1994, the four delegates from the territories and the resident commissioner of Puerto Rico were allowed to vote on questions before the Committee of the Whole. If their votes were decisive in the outcome, however, the matter was automatically re-voted, with the delegates and resident commissioner ineligible. They could vote on final passage of bills or on separate votes demanded after the Committee of the Whole rises. This limited voting right was rescinded in 1995.

Committee veto — A requirement added to a few statutes directing that certain policy directives by an executive department or agency be reviewed by certain congressional committees before they are implemented. Under common practice, the government department or agency and the committees involved are expected to reach a consensus before the directives are carried out. *(Also see legislative veto.)*

Concurrent resolution — A concurrent resolution, designated H Con Res or S Con Res, must be adopted by both chambers, but it is not sent to the president for approval and, therefore, does not have the force of law. A concurrent resolution, for example, is used to fix the time for adjournment of a Congress. It is also used to express the sense of Congress on a foreign policy or domestic issue. The annual budget resolution is a concurrent resolution.

Conference — A meeting between representatives of the House and the Senate to reconcile differences between the two chambers on provisions of a bill. Members of the conference committee are appointed by the Speaker and the presiding officer of the Senate.

A majority of the conferees for each chamber must agree on a compromise, reflected in a "conference report" before the final bill can go back to both chambers for approval. When the conference report goes to the floor, it is difficult to amend. If it is not approved by both chambers, the bill may go back to conference under certain situations, or a new conference may be convened. Many rules and informal practices govern the conduct of conference committees.

Bills that are passed by both chambers with only minor differences need not be sent to conference. Either chamber may "concur" with the other's amendments, completing action on the legislation. Sometimes leaders of the committees of jurisdiction work out an informal compromise instead of having a formal conference. *(Also see custody of the papers.)*

Confirmations — *(See nominations.)*

Congressional Record — The daily, printed account of proceedings in both the House and Senate chambers, showing substantially verbatim debate, statements and a record of floor action. Highlights of legislative and committee action are given in a Daily Digest section of the Record, and members are entitled to have their extraneous remarks printed in an appendix known as "Extension of Remarks." Members may edit and revise remarks made on the floor during debate, although the House in 1995 limited members to technical or grammatical changes.

The Congressional Record provides a way to distinguish remarks spoken on the floor of the House and Senate from undelivered speeches. In the Senate, all speeches, articles and other matter that members insert in the Record without actually reading them on the floor are set off by large black dots, or bullets. However, a loophole allows a member to avoid the bulleting if he or she delivers any portion of the speech in person. In the House, undelivered speeches and other material are printed in a distinctive typeface. The record is also available in electronic form. *(Also see Journal.)*

Congressional terms of office — Terms normally begin on Jan. 3 of the year following a general election. Terms are two years for representatives and six years for senators. Representatives elected in special elections are sworn in for the remainder of a term. Under most state laws, a person may be appointed to fill a Senate vacancy and serve until a successor is elected; the successor serves until the end of the term applying to the vacant seat.

Consent Calendar — Members of the House may place on this calendar most bills on the Union or House Calendar that are considered non-controversial. Bills on the Consent Calendar normally are called on the first and third Mondays of each month. On the first occasion that a bill is called in this manner, consideration may be blocked by the objection of any member. The second time, if there are three objections, the bill is stricken from the Consent Calendar. If fewer than three members object, the bill is given immediate consideration.

A member may also postpone action on the bill by asking that the measure be passed over "without prejudice." In that case, no objection is recorded against the bill and its status on the Consent Calendar remains unchanged. A bill stricken from the Consent Calendar remains on the Union or House Calendar. The Consent Calendar has seldom been used in recent years.

Continuing resolution — A joint resolution, cleared by Congress and signed by the president, to provide new budget authority for federal agencies and programs until the regular appropriations bills have been enacted. Also known as "CRs" or continuing appropriation, continuing resolutions are used to keep agencies operating when, as often happens, Congress fails to finish the regular appropriations process by the start of the new fiscal year.

The CR usually specifies a maximum rate at which an agency may incur obligations, based on the rate of the prior year, the president's budget request or an appropriations bill passed by either or both chambers of Congress but not yet enacted.

Contract authority — Budget authority contained in an authorization bill that permits the federal government to enter into contracts or other obligations for future payments from funds not yet appropriated by Congress. The assumption is that funds will be provided in a subsequent appropriations act. *(Also see budget authority.)*

Corrections Calendar, Corrections Day — A House calendar established in 1995 to speed consideration of bills aimed at eliminating burdensome or unnecessary regulations. Bills on the Corrections Calendar can be called up on the second and fourth Tuesday of each month, called Corrections Day. They are subject to one hour of debate without amendment, and require a three-fifths majority for passage. *(Also see calendar.)*

Correcting recorded votes — Rules prohibit members from changing their votes after the result has been announced. Occasionally, however, a member may announce hours, days or months after a vote has been taken that he or she was "incorrectly recorded." In the Senate, a request to change one's vote almost always receives unanimous consent, so long as it does not change the outcome. In the House, members are prohibited from changing votes if they were tallied by the electronic voting system.

Cosponsor — *(See bills introduced.)*

Current services estimates — Estimated budget authority and outlays for federal programs and operations for the forthcoming fiscal year based on continuation of existing levels of service without policy changes but with adjustments for inflation and for demographic changes that affect programs. These estimates, accompanied by the underlying economic and policy assumptions upon which they are based, are transmitted by the president to Congress when the budget is submitted.

Custody of the papers — To reconcile differences between the House and Senate versions of a bill, a conference may be arranged. The chamber with "custody of the papers" — the engrossed bill, engrossed amendments, messages of transmittal — is the only body empowered to request the conference. By custom, the chamber that asks for a conference is the last to act on the conference report.

Custody of the papers sometimes is manipulated to ensure that a particular chamber acts either first or last on the conference report. *(Also see conference.)*

Deferral — Executive branch action to defer, or delay, the spending of appropriated money. The 1974 Congressional Budget and Impoundment Control Act requires a special message from the president to Congress reporting a proposed deferral of spending. Deferrals may not extend beyond the end of the fiscal year in which the message is transmitted. A federal district court in 1986 struck down the president's authority to defer spending for policy reasons; the ruling was upheld by a federal appeals court in 1987. Congress can prohibit proposed deferrals by enacting a law doing so; most often, cancellations of proposed deferrals are included in appropriations bills. *(Also see rescission.)*

Dilatory motion — A motion made for the purpose of killing time and preventing action on a bill or amendment. House rules outlaw dilatory motions, but enforcement is largely within the discretion of the Speaker or chairman of the Committee of the Whole. The Senate does not have a rule barring dilatory motions except under cloture.

Discharge a committee — Occasionally, attempts are made to relieve a committee of jurisdiction over a bill that is before it. This is attempted more often in the House than in the Senate, and the procedure rarely is successful.

In the House, if a committee does not report a bill within 30 days after the measure is referred to it, any member may file a discharge motion. Once offered, the motion is treated as a petition needing the signatures of a majority of members (218 if there are no vacancies). After the required signatures have been obtained, there is a delay of seven days.

Thereafter, on the second and fourth Mondays of each month, except during the last six days of a session, any member who has signed the petition must be recognized, if he or she so desires, to move that the committee be discharged. Debate on the motion to discharge is limited to 20 minutes. If the motion is carried, consideration of the bill becomes a matter of high privilege.

If a resolution to consider a bill is held up in the Rules Committee for more than seven legislative days, any member may enter a motion to discharge the committee. The motion is handled like any other discharge petition in the House. Occasionally, to expedite non-controversial legislative business, a committee is discharged by unanimous consent of the House, and a petition is not required. In 1993, the signatures on pending discharge petitions — previously kept secret — were made a matter of public record. *(For Senate procedure, see discharge resolution.)*

Discharge Calendar — The House calendar to which motions to discharge committees are referred when they have the required number of signatures (218) and are awaiting floor action. *(Also see calendar.)*

Discharge petition — *(See discharge a committee.)*

Discharge resolution — In the Senate, a special motion that any senator may introduce to relieve a committee from consideration of a bill before it. The resolution can be called up for Senate approval or disapproval in the same manner as any other Senate business. *(For House procedure, see discharge a committee.)*

Discretionary spending caps — *(See budget process.)*

Division of a question for voting — A practice that is more common in the Senate but also used in the House whereby a member may demand a division of an amendment or a motion for purposes of voting. Where an amendment or motion can be divided, the individual parts are voted on separately when a member demands a division. This procedure occurs most often during the consideration of conference reports.

Enacting clause — Key phrase in bills beginning, "Be it enacted by the Senate and House of Representatives . . ." A successful motion to strike it from legislation kills the measure.

Engrossed bill — The final copy of a bill as passed by one chamber, with the text as amended by floor action and certified by the clerk of the House or the secretary of the Senate.

Enrolled bill — The final copy of a bill that has been passed in identical form by both chambers. It is certified by an officer of the chamber of origin (clerk of the House or secretary of the Senate) and then sent on for the signatures of the House Speaker, the Senate president pro tempore and the president of the United States. An enrolled bill is printed on parchment.

Entitlement program — A federal program that guarantees a certain level of benefits to people or other entities who meet requirements set by law. Examples include Social Security and unemployment benefits. Some entitlements have permanent appropriations; others are funded under annual appropriations bills. In either case, it is mandatory for Congress to provide the money.

Executive Calendar — A non-legislative calendar in the Senate that lists presidential documents such as treaties and nominations. *(Also see calendar.)*

Executive document — A document, usually a treaty, sent to the Senate by the president for consideration or approval. Executive documents are referred to committee in the same manner as other measures. Unlike legislative documents, treaties do not die at the end of a Congress but remain "live" proposals until acted on by the Senate or withdrawn by the president.

Executive session — A meeting of a Senate or House committee (or occasionally of either chamber) that only its members may attend. Witnesses regularly appear at committee meetings in executive session — for example, Defense Department officials during presentations of classified defense information. Other members of Congress may be invited, but the public and news media are not allowed to attend.

Filibuster — A time-delaying tactic associated with the Senate and used by a minority in an effort to prevent a vote on a bill or amendment that probably would pass if voted upon directly. The most common method is to take advantage of the Senate's rules permitting unlimited debate, but other forms of parliamentary maneuvering may be used.

The stricter rules of the House make filibusters more difficult, but delaying tactics are employed occasionally through various procedural devices allowed by House rules. *(Also see cloture.)*

Fiscal year — Financial operations of the government are carried out in a 12-month fiscal year, beginning on Oct. 1 and ending on Sept. 30. The fiscal year carries the date of the calendar year in which it ends. (From fiscal 1844 to fiscal 1976, the fiscal year began July 1 and ended the following June 30.)

Five-minute rule — A debate-limiting rule of the House that is invoked when the House sits as the Committee of the Whole. Under the rule, a member offering an amendment and a member opposing it are each allowed to speak for five minutes. Debate is then closed. In practice, amendments regularly are debated for more than 10 minutes, with members gaining the floor by offering pro forma amendments or obtaining unanimous consent to speak longer than five minutes. *(Also see Committee of the Whole, hour rule, strike out the last word.)*

Floor manager — A member who has the task of steering legislation through floor debate and amendment to a final vote in the House or the Senate. Floor managers usually are chairmen or ranking members of the committee that reported the bill. Managers are responsible for apportioning the debate time granted to supporters of the bill. The ranking minority member of the committee normally apportions time for the minority party's participation in the debate.

Frank — A member's facsimile signature, which is used on envelopes in lieu of stamps for the member's official outgoing mail. The "franking privilege" is the right to send mail postage-free.

Germane — Pertaining to the subject matter of the measure at hand. All House amendments must be germane to the bill being considered. The Senate requires that amendments be germane when they are proposed to general appropriations bills or to bills being considered once cloture has been adopted or, frequently, when the Senate is proceeding under a unanimous consent agreement placing a time limit on consideration of a bill. The 1974 budget act also requires that amendments to concurrent budget resolutions be germane.

In the House, floor debate must be germane, and the first three hours of debate each day in the Senate must be germane to the pending business.

Gramm-Rudman-Hollings Deficit Reduction Act — *(See sequester.)*

Grandfather clause — A provision that exempts people or other entities already engaged in an activity from rules or legislation affecting that activity.

Hearings — Committee sessions for taking testimony from witnesses. At hearings on legislation, witnesses usually include specialists, government officials and spokesmen for individuals or entities affected by the bill or bills under study. Hearings related to special investigations bring forth a variety of witnesses. Committees sometimes use their subpoena power to summon reluctant witnesses. The public and news media may attend open hearings but are barred from closed, or "executive," hearings. The vast majority of hearings are open to the public. *(Also see executive session.)*

Hold-harmless clause — A provision added to legislation to ensure that recipients of federal funds do not receive less in a future year than they did in the current year if a new formula for allocating funds authorized in the legislation would result in a reduction to the recipients. This clause has been used most often to soften the impact of sudden reductions in federal grants.

Hopper — Box on House clerk's desk into which members deposit bills and resolutions to introduce them.

Hour rule — A provision in the rules of the House that permits one hour of debate time for each member on amendments debated in the House of Representatives sitting as the House. Therefore, the House normally amends bills while sitting as the Committee of the Whole, where the five-minute rule on amendments operates.

House as in the Committee of the Whole — A procedure that can be used to expedite consideration of certain measures such as continuing resolutions and, when there is debate, private bills. The procedure can be invoked only with the unanimous consent of the House or a rule from the Rules Committee and has procedural elements of both the House sitting as the House of Representatives, such as the Speaker presiding and the previous question motion being in order, and the House sitting as the Committee of the Whole, with the five-minute rule being in order. *(See Committee of the Whole.)*

House Calendar — A listing for action by the House of public bills that do not directly or indirectly appropriate money or raise revenue. *(Also see calendar.)*

Immunity — The constitutional privilege of members of Congress to make verbal statements on the floor and in committee for which they cannot be sued or arrested for slander or libel. Also, freedom from arrest while traveling to or from sessions of Congress or on official business. Members in this status may only be arrested for treason, felonies or a breach of the peace, as defined by congressional manuals.

Joint committee — A committee composed of a specified number of members of both the House and Senate. A joint committee may be investigative or research-oriented, an example of the latter being the Joint Economic Committee. Others have housekeeping duties; examples include the joint committees on Printing and on the Library of Congress.

Joint resolution — Like a bill, a joint resolution, designated H J Res or S J Res, requires the approval of both chambers and the signature of the president, and has the force of law if approved. There is no practical difference between a bill and a joint resolution. A joint resolution generally is used to deal with a limited matter such as a single appropriation.

Joint resolutions are also used to propose amendments to the Constitution. In that case they require a two-thirds majority in both chambers. They do not require a presidential signature, but they must be ratified by three-fourths of the states to become a part of the Constitution. *(Also see concurrent resolution, resolution.)*

Journal — The official record of the proceedings of the House and Senate. The Journal records the actions taken in each chamber, but, unlike the Congressional Record, it does not include the substantially verbatim report of speeches, debates, statements and the like.

Law — An act of Congress that has been signed by the president or passed, over his veto, by Congress. Public bills, when signed, become public laws and are cited by the letters PL and a hyphenated number. The number before the hyphen corresponds to the Congress, and the one or more digits after the hyphen refer to the numerical sequence in which the president signed the bills during that Congress. Private bills, when signed, become private laws. *(Also see bills, private bills.)*

Legislative day — The "day" extending from the time either chamber meets after an adjournment until the time it next adjourns. Because the House normally adjourns from day to day, legislative days and calendar days usually coincide. But in the Senate, a legislative day may, and frequently does, extend over several calendar days. *(Also see recess.)*

Line-item veto — Presidential authority to strike individual items from appropriations bills, which presidents since Ulysses S. Grant have sought. Congress gave the president a form of the power in 1996 (PL 104-130), but this "enhanced rescission authority" was struck down by the Supreme Court in 1998 as unconstitutional because it allowed the president to change laws on his own.

Loan guarantees — Loans to third parties for which the federal government guarantees the repayment of principal or interest, in whole or in part, to the lender in the event of default.

Lobby — A group seeking to influence the passage or defeat of legislation. Originally the term referred to people frequenting the lobbies or corridors of legislative chambers to speak to lawmakers.

The definition of a lobby and the activity of lobbying is a matter of differing interpretation. By some definitions, lobbying is limited to direct attempts to influence lawmakers through personal interviews and persuasion. Under other definitions, lobbying includes attempts at indirect, or "grass-roots," influence, such as persuading members of a group to write or visit their district's representative and state's senators or attempting to create a climate of opinion favorable to a desired legislative goal.

The right to attempt to influence legislation is based on the First Amendment to the Constitution, which says Congress shall make no law abridging the right of the people "to petition the government for a redress of grievances."

Majority leader — Floor leader for the majority party in each chamber. In the Senate, in consultation with the minority leader, the majority leader directs the legislative schedule for the chamber. He or she is also his party's spokesperson and chief strategist. In the House, the majority leader is second to the Speaker in the majority party's leadership and serves as the party's legislative strategist. *(Also see Speaker, whip.)*

Manual — The official handbook in each chamber prescribing in detail its organization, procedures and operations.

Marking up a bill — Going through the contents of a piece of legislation in committee or subcommittee to, for example, consider the provisions, act on amendments to provisions and proposed revisions to the language, and insert new sections and phraseology. If the bill is extensively amended, the committee's version may be introduced as a separate (or "clean") bill, with a new number, before being considered by the full House or Senate. *(Also see clean bill.)*

Minority leader — Floor leader for the minority party in each chamber.

Morning hour — The time set aside at the beginning of each legislative day for the consideration of regular, routine business. The "hour" is of indefinite duration in the House, where it is rarely used. In the Senate, it is the first two hours of a session following an adjournment, as distinguished from a recess. The morning hour can be terminated earlier if the morning business has been completed.

Business includes such matters as messages from the president, communications from the heads of departments, messages from the House, the presentation of petitions, reports of standing and select committees and the introduction of bills and resolutions.

During the first hour of the morning hour in the Senate, no motion to proceed to the consideration of any bill on the calendar is in order except by unanimous consent. During the second hour, motions can be made but must be decided without debate. Senate committees may meet while the Senate conducts the morning hour.

Motion — In the House or Senate chamber, a request by a member to institute any one of a wide array of parliamentary actions. He or she "moves" for a certain procedure, such as the consideration of a measure. The precedence of motions, and whether they are debatable, is set forth in the House and Senate manuals.

Nominations — Presidential appointments to office subject to Senate confirmation. Although most nominations win quick Senate approval, some are controversial and become the topic of hearings and debate. Sometimes senators object to appointees for patronage reasons — for example, when a nomination to a local federal job is made without consulting the senators of the state concerned. In some situations a senator may object that the nominee is "personally obnoxious" to him. Usually other senators join in blocking such appointments out of courtesy to their colleagues. *(Also see senatorial courtesy.)*

One-minute speeches — Addresses by House members at the beginning of a legislative day. The speeches may cover any subject but are limited to one minute's duration.

Outlays — Actual spending that flows from the liquidation of budget authority. Outlays associated with appropriations bills and other legislation are estimates of future spending made by the Congressional Budget Office (CBO) and the White House's Office of Management and Budget (OMB). CBO's estimates govern bills for the purpose of congressional floor debate, while OMB's numbers govern when it comes to determining whether legislation exceeds spending caps.

Outlays in a given fiscal year may result from budget authority provided in the current year or in previous years. *(Also see budget authority, budget process.)*

Override a veto — If the president vetoes a bill and sends it back to Congress with his objections, Congress may try to override his veto and enact the bill into law. Neither chamber is required to attempt to override a veto. The override of a veto requires a recorded vote with a two-thirds majority of those present and voting in each chamber. The question put to each chamber is: "Shall the bill pass, the objections of the president to the contrary notwithstanding?" *(Also see pocket veto, veto.)*

Oversight committee — A congressional committee or designated subcommittee that is charged with general oversight of one or more federal agencies' programs and activities. Usually, the oversight panel for a particular agency is also the authorizing committee for that agency's programs and operations.

Pair — A voluntary, informal arrangement that two lawmakers, usually on opposite sides of an issue, make on recorded votes. In many cases the result is to subtract a vote from each side, with no effect on the outcome.

Pairs are not authorized in the rules of either chamber, are not counted in tabulating the final result and have no official standing. However, members pairing are identified in the Congressional Record, along with their positions on such votes, if known. A member who expects to be absent for a vote can pair with a member who plans to vote, with the latter agreeing to withhold his or her vote.

There are three types of pairs:

(1) A live pair involves a member who is present for a vote and another who is absent. The member in attendance votes and then withdraws the vote, announcing that he or she has a live pair with colleague "X" and stating how the two members would have voted, one in favor, the other opposed. A live pair may affect the outcome of a closely contested vote, since it subtracts one "yea" or one "nay" from the final tally. A live pair may cover one or several specific issues.

(2) A general pair, widely used in the House, does not entail any arrangement between two members and does not affect the vote. Members who expect to be absent notify the clerk that they wish to make a general pair. Each member then is paired with another desiring a pair, and their names are listed in the Congressional Record. The member may or may not be paired with another taking the opposite position, and no indication of how the members would have voted is given.

(3) A specific pair is similar to a general pair, except that the opposing stands of the two members are identified and printed in the Congressional Record.

Pay-as-you go (PAYGO) rules — *(See budget process.)*

Petition — A request or plea sent to one or both chambers from an organization or private citizens' group seeking support for particular legislation or favorable consideration of a matter not yet receiving congressional attention. Petitions are referred to appropriate committees. In the House, a petition signed by a majority of members (218) can discharge a bill from a committee. *(Also see discharge a committee.)*

Pocket veto — The act of the president in withholding his approval of a bill after Congress has adjourned. When Congress is in session, a bill becomes law without the president's signature if he does not act upon it within 10 days, excluding Sundays, from the time he receives it. But if Congress adjourns sine die within that 10-day period, the bill will die even if the president does not formally veto it.

The Supreme Court in 1986 agreed to decide whether the president could pocket veto a bill during recesses and between sessions of the same Congress or only between Congresses. The justices in 1987 declared the case moot, however, because the bill in question was invalid once the case reached the court. *(Also see adjournment sine die, veto.)*

Point of order — An objection raised by a member that the chamber is departing from rules governing its conduct of business. The objector cites the rule violated, with the chair sustaining his or her objection if correctly made. Order is restored by the chair's suspending proceedings of the chamber until it conforms to the prescribed "order of business."

Both chambers have procedures for overcoming a point of order, either by vote or, what is most common in the House, by including language in the rule for floor consideration that waives a point of order against a given bill. *(Also see rules.)*

President of the Senate — Under the Constitution, the vice president of the United States presides over the Senate. In his absence, the president pro tempore, or a senator designated by the president pro tempore, presides over the chamber.

President pro tempore — The chief officer of the Senate in the absence of the vice president — literally, but loosely, the president for a time. The president pro tempore is elected by his fellow senators. Recent practice has been to elect the senator of the majority party with the longest period of continuous service.

Previous question — A motion for the previous question, when carried, has the effect of cutting off all debate, preventing the offering of further amendments and forcing a vote on the pending matter. In the House, a motion for the previous question is not permitted in the Committee of the Whole, unless a rule governing debate provides otherwise. The motion for the previous question is a debate-limiting device and is not in order in the Senate.

Printed amendment — A House rule guarantees five minutes of floor debate in support and five minutes in opposition, and no other debate time, on amendments printed in the Congressional Record at least one day prior to the amendment's consideration in the Committee of the Whole.

In the Senate, while amendments may be submitted for printing, they have no parliamentary standing or status. An amendment submitted for printing in the Senate, however, may be called up by any senator.

Private bill — A bill dealing with individual matters such as claims against the government, immigration or land titles. When a private bill is before the chamber, two members may block its consideration, thereby recommitting the bill to committee. The backers still have recourse, however. The measure can be put into an "omnibus claims bill" — several private bills rolled into one. As with any bill, no part of an omnibus claims bill may be deleted without a vote. When the private bill goes back to the House floor in this form, it can be deleted from the omnibus bill only by majority vote.

Private Calendar — The House calendar for private bills. The Private Calendar must be called on the first Tuesday of each month, and the Speaker may call it on the third Tuesday of each month as well. *(Also see calendar, private bill.)*

Privileged questions — The order in which bills, motions and other legislative measures are considered on the floor of the Senate and House is governed by strict priorities. A motion to table, for instance, is more privileged than a motion to recommit. Thus, if a member moves to recommit a bill to committee for further consideration, another member can supersede the first action by moving to table it, and a vote will occur on the motion to table (or kill) before the motion to recommit. A motion to adjourn is considered "of the highest privilege" and must be considered before virtually any other motion.

Pro forma amendment — *(See strike out the last word.)*

Public Laws — *(See law.)*

Questions of privilege — These are matters affecting members of Congress individually or collectively. Matters affecting the rights, safety, dignity and integrity of proceedings of the House or Senate as a whole are questions of privilege in both chambers.

Questions involving individual members are called questions of "personal privilege." A member rising to ask a question of personal privilege is given precedence over almost all other proceedings. For instance, if a member feels that he or she has been improperly impugned in comments by another member, he or she can immediately demand to be heard on the floor on a question of personal privilege. An annotation in the House rules points out that the privilege rests primarily on the Constitution, which gives members a conditional immunity from arrest and an unconditional freedom to speak in the House.

In 1993, the House changed its rules to allow the Speaker to delay for two legislative days the floor consideration of a question of the privileges of the House unless it is offered by the majority leader or minority leader.

Quorum — The number of members whose presence is necessary for the transaction of business. In the Senate and House, it is a majority of the membership. In the Committee of the Whole House, a quorum is 100. If a point of order is made that a quorum is not present, the only business that is in order is either a motion to adjourn or a motion to direct the sergeant-at-arms to request the attendance of absentees. In practice, however, both chambers conduct much of their business without a quorum present. *(Also see Committee of the Whole House.)*

Reading of bills — Traditional parliamentary procedure required bills to be read three times before they were passed. This custom is of little modern significance. Normally a bill is considered to have its first reading when it is introduced and printed, by title, in the Congressional Record. In the House, a bill's second reading comes when floor consideration begins. (The actual reading of a bill is most likely to occur at this point, if at all.) The second reading in the Senate is supposed to occur on the legislative day after the measure is introduced, but before it is referred to committee. The third reading (again, usually by title) takes place when floor action has been completed on amendments.

Recess — A recess, as distinguished from adjournment, does not end a legislative day and therefore does not interrupt unfinished business. (The rules in each chamber set forth certain matters to be taken up and disposed of at the beginning of each legislative day.) The House usually adjourns from day to day. The Senate often recesses, thus meeting on the same legislative day for several calendar days or even weeks at a time.

Recognition — The power of recognition of a member is lodged in the Speaker of the House and the presiding officer of the Senate. The presiding officer names the member to speak first when two or more members simultaneously request recognition. The order of recognition is governed by precedents and tradition for many situations. In the Senate, for instance, the majority leader has the right to be recognized first.

Recommit to committee — A motion, made on the floor after a bill has been debated, to return it to the committee that reported it. If approved, recommittal usually is considered a death blow to the bill. In the House, the right to offer a motion to recommit is guaranteed to the minority leader or someone he or she designates.

A motion to recommit may include instructions to the committee to report the bill again with specific amendments or by a certain date. Or the instructions may direct that a particular study be made, with no definite deadline for further action.

If the recommittal motion includes instructions to "report the bill back forthwith" and the motion is adopted, floor action on the bill continues with the changes directed by the instructions automatically incorporated into the bill; the committee does not actually reconsider the legislation.

Reconciliation — The 1974 budget act created a "reconciliation" procedure for bringing existing tax and spending laws into conformity with ceilings set in the congressional budget resolution. Under the procedure, the budget resolution sets specific deficit-reduction targets and instructs tax-writing and authorizing committees to propose changes in existing law to meet those targets. Those recommendations are consolidated without change by the Budget committees into an omnibus reconciliation bill, which then must be considered and approved by both chambers of Congress.

Special rules in the Senate limit debate on a reconciliation bill to 20 hours and bar extraneous or non-germane amendments. *(Also see budget resolution, sequester.)*

Reconsider a vote — Until it is disposed of, a motion to reconsider the vote by which an action was taken has the effect of putting the action in abeyance. In the Senate, the motion can be made only by a member who voted on the prevailing side of the original question or by a member who did not vote at all. In the House, it can be made only by a member on the prevailing side.

A common practice in the Senate after close votes on an issue is a motion to reconsider, followed by a motion to table the motion to reconsider. On this motion to table, senators vote as they voted on the original question, which allows the motion to table to prevail, assuming there are no switches. That closes the matter, and further motions to reconsider are not entertained.

In the House, as a routine precaution, a motion to reconsider usually is made every time a measure is passed. Such a motion almost always is tabled immediately, thus shutting off the possibility of future reconsideration except by unanimous consent.

Motions to reconsider must be entered in the Senate within the next two days the Senate is in session after the original vote has been taken. In the House, they must be entered either on the same day or on the next succeeding day the House is in session. Sometimes on a close vote, a member will switch his or her vote to be eligible to offer a motion to reconsider.

Recorded vote — A vote upon which each member's stand is individually made known. In the Senate, this is accomplished through a roll call of the entire membership, to which each senator on the floor must answer "yea," "nay" or "present." Since January 1973, the House has used an electronic voting system for recorded votes, including yea-and-nay votes formerly taken by roll calls.

When not required by the Constitution, a recorded vote can be obtained on questions in the House on the demand of one-fifth (44 members) of a quorum or one-fourth (25) of a quorum in the Committee of the Whole. Recorded votes are required in the House for appropriations, budget and tax bills. *(Also see yeas and nays.)*

Report — Both a verb and a noun as a congressional term. A committee that has been examining a bill referred to it by the parent chamber "reports" its findings and recommendations to the chamber when it completes consideration and returns the measure. The process is called "reporting" a bill. In some cases, a bill is reported without a written report.

A "report" is the document setting forth the committee's explanation of its action. Senate and House reports are numbered separately and are designated S Rept or H Rept. When a committee report is not unanimous, the dissenting committee members may file a statement of their views, called minority or dissenting views and referred to as a minority report. Members in disagreement with some provisions of a bill may file additional or supplementary views. Sometimes a bill is reported without a committee recommendation.

Legislative committees occasionally submit adverse reports. However, when a committee is opposed to a bill, it usually fails to report the bill at all. Some laws require that committee reports — favorable or adverse — be made.

Rescission — Cancellation of budget authority that was previously appropriated but has not yet been spent.

Resolution — A "simple" resolution, designated H Res or S Res, deals with matters entirely within the prerogatives of a single chamber. It requires neither passage by the other chamber nor approval by the president, and it does not have the force of law. Most resolutions deal with the rules or procedures of one chamber. They are also used to express the sentiments of a single chamber, such as condolences to the family of a deceased member, or to comment on foreign policy or executive business. A simple resolution is the vehicle for a "rule" from the House Rules Committee. *(Also see concurrent and joint resolutions, rules.)*

Rider — An amendment, usually not germane, that its sponsor hopes to get through more easily by including it in other legislation. A rider becomes law if the bill to which it is attached is enacted. Amendments providing legislative directives in appropriations bills are examples of riders, though technically legislation is banned from appropriations bills.

The House, unlike the Senate, has a strict germaneness rule; thus, riders usually are Senate devices to get legislation enacted quickly or to bypass lengthy House consideration and, possibly, opposition.

Rules — Each chamber has a body of rules and precedents that govern the conduct of business. These rules deal with issues such as duties of officers, the order of business, admission to the floor, parliamentary procedures on handling amendments and voting, and jurisdictions of committees. They are normally changed only at the start of each Congress.

In the House, a rule may also be a resolution reported by the Rules Committee to govern the handling of a particular bill on the floor. The committee may report a rule, also called a special order, in the form of a simple resolution. If the House adopts the resolution, the temporary rule becomes as valid as any standing rule and lapses only after action has been completed on the measure to which it pertains.

The rule sets the time limit on general debate. It may also waive points of order against provisions of the bill in question such as nongermane language or against certain amendments expected on the floor. It may even forbid all amendments or all amendments except those proposed by the legislative committee that handled the bill. In this instance, it is known as a "closed" rule as opposed to an "open" rule, which puts no limitation on floor amendments, thus leaving the bill completely open to alteration by the adoption of germane amendments. *(Also see point of order.)*

Secretary of the Senate — Chief administrative officer of the Senate, responsible for overseeing the duties of Senate employees, educating Senate pages, administering oaths, overseeing the registration of lobbyists and handling other tasks necessary for the continuing operation of the Senate. *(Also see Clerk of the House.)*

Select or special committee — A committee set up for a special purpose and, usually, for a limited time by resolution of either the House or Senate. Most special committees are investigative and lack legislative authority: Legislation is not referred to them, and they cannot report bills to their parent chambers. The House in 1993 terminated its four select committees.

Senatorial courtesy — A general practice with no written rule — sometimes referred to as "the courtesy of the Senate" — applied to consideration of executive nominations. Generally, it means that nominations from a state are not to be confirmed unless they have been approved by the senators of the president's party of that state, with other senators following their colleagues' lead in the attitude they take toward consideration of such nominations. *(Also see nominations.)*

Sequester — Automatic, across-the-board spending cuts, generally triggered after the close of a session by a report issued by the Office of Management and Budget. Under the 1985 Gramm-Rudman anti-deficit law, modified in 1987, a year-end sequester was triggered if the deficit exceeded a pre-set maximum. However, the Budget Enforcement Act of 1990, updated in 1993 and 1997, effectively replaced that procedure through fiscal 2002.

Instead, if Congress exceeds an annual cap on discretionary budget authority or outlays, a sequester is triggered for all eligible discretionary spending to make up the difference. If Congress violates pay-as-you-go rules by allowing the net effect of legislated changes in mandatory spending and taxes to increase the deficit, a sequester is triggered for all non-exempt entitlement programs. Similar procedures apply to supplemental appropriations bills. *(Also see budget process.)*

Sine die — *(See adjournment sine die.)*

Speaker — The presiding officer of the House of Representatives, selected by his party caucus and formally elected by the whole House. While both parties nominate candidates, choice by the majority party is tantamount to election. In 1995, House rules were changed to limit the Speaker to four consecutive terms.

Special session — A session of Congress after it has adjourned sine die, completing its regular session. Special sessions are convened by the president.

Spending authority — The 1974 budget act defines spending authority as borrowing authority, contract authority and entitlement authority for which budget authority is not provided in advance by appropriation acts.

Sponsor — *(See bills introduced.)*

Standing committees — Committees that are permanently established by House and Senate rules. The standing committees of the House were reorganized in 1974, with some changes in jurisdictions and titles made when Republicans took control of the House in 1995. The last major realignment of Senate committees was in 1977. The standing committees are legislative committees: Legislation may be referred to them, and they may report bills and resolutions to their parent chambers.

Standing vote — A non-recorded vote used in both the House and Senate. (A standing vote is also called a division vote.) Members in favor of a proposal stand and are counted by the presiding officer. Then members opposed stand and are counted. There is no record of how individual members voted.

Statutes at large — A chronological arrangement of the laws enacted in each session of Congress. Though indexed, the laws are not arranged by subject matter, and there is no indication of how they changed previously enacted laws. *(Also see law, U.S. Code.)*

Strike from the Record — A member of the House who is offended by remarks made on the House floor may move that the offending words be "taken down" for the Speaker's cognizance and then expunged from the debate as published in the Congressional Record.

Strike out the last word — A motion whereby a House member is entitled to speak for five minutes on an amendment then being debated by the chamber. A member gains recognition from the chair by moving to "strike out the last word" of the amendment or section of the bill under consideration. The motion is pro forma, requires no vote and does not change the amendment being debated. *(Also see five-minute rule.)*

Substitute — A motion, amendment or entire bill introduced in place of the pending legislative business. Passage of the substitute kills the original measure by supplanting it. The substitute may also be amended. *(Also see amendment in the nature of a substitute.)*

Supplemental appropriations bill — Legislation appropriating funds after the regular annual appropriations bill for a federal department or agency has been enacted. Supplemental appropriations bills often arrive about halfway through the fiscal year, when needs that Congress and the president did not anticipate (or may not have wanted to fund) become pressing. In recent years, supplementals have been driven by spending to help victims of natural disasters and to carry out peacekeeping commitments.

Suspend the rules — A time-saving procedure for passing bills in the House. The wording of the motion, which may be made by any member recognized by the Speaker, is: "I move to suspend the rules and pass the bill . . ." A favorable vote by two-thirds of those present is required for passage. Debate is limited to 40 minutes, and no amendments from the floor are permitted. If a two-thirds favorable vote is not attained, the bill may be considered later under regular procedures. The suspension procedure is in order every Monday and Tuesday and is intended to be reserved for non-controversial bills.

Table a bill — Motions to table, or to "lay on the table," are used to block or kill amendments or other parliamentary questions. When approved, a tabling motion is considered the final disposition of that issue. One of the most widely used parliamentary procedures, the motion to table is not debatable, and adoption requires a simple majority vote.

In the Senate, however, different language sometimes is used. The motion may be worded to let a bill "lie on the table," perhaps for subsequent "picking up." This motion is more flexible, keeping the bill pending for later action, if desired. Tabling motions on amendments are effective debate-ending devices in the Senate.

Treaties — Executive proposals — in the form of resolutions of ratification — which must be submitted to the Senate for approval by two-thirds of the senators present. Treaties are normally sent to the Foreign Relations Committee for scrutiny before the Senate takes action. Foreign Relations has jurisdiction over all treaties, regardless of the subject matter. Treaties are read three times and debated on the floor in much the same manner as legislative proposals. After approval by the Senate, treaties are formally ratified by the president.

Trust funds — Funds collected and used by the federal government for carrying out specific purposes and programs according to terms of a trust agreement or statute such as the Social Security and unemployment compensation trust funds. Such funds are administered by the government in a fiduciary capacity and are not available for the general purposes of the government.

Unanimous consent — A procedure used to expedite floor action. Proceedings of the House or Senate and action on legislation often take place upon the unanimous consent of the chamber, whether or not a rule of the chamber is being violated. It is frequently used in a routine fashion, such as by a senator requesting the unanimous consent of the Senate to have specified members of his or her staff present on the floor during debate on a specific amendment. A single member's objection blocks a unanimous consent request.

Unanimous consent agreement — A device used in the Senate to expedite legislation. Much of the Senate's legislative business, dealing with both minor and controversial issues, is conducted through unanimous consent or unanimous consent agreements. On major legislation, such agreements usually are printed and transmitted to all senators in advance of floor debate. Once agreed to, they are binding on all members unless the Senate, by unanimous consent, agrees to modify them. An agreement may list the order in which various bills are to be considered; specify the length of time for debate on bills and contested amendments and when they are to be voted upon; and, frequently, require that all amendments introduced be germane to the bill under consideration.

In this regard, unanimous consent agreements are similar to the "rules" issued by the House Rules Committee for bills pending in the House.

Union Calendar — Bills that directly or indirectly appropriate money or raise revenue are placed on this House calendar according to the date they are reported from committee. *(Also see calendar.)*

U.S. Code — A consolidation and codification of the general and permanent laws of the United States arranged by subject under 50 titles, the first six dealing with general or political subjects, and the other 44 alphabetically arranged from agriculture to war. The U.S. Code is updated annually, and a new set of bound volumes is published every six years. *(Also see law, statutes at large.)*

Veto — Disapproval by the president of a bill or joint resolution (other than one proposing an amendment to the Constitution). When Congress is in session, the president must veto a bill within 10 days, excluding Sundays, after he has received it; otherwise, it becomes law without his signature. When the president vetoes a bill, he returns it to the chamber of origin along with a message stating his objections. *(Also see pocket veto, override a veto.)*

Voice vote — In either the House or Senate, members answer "aye" or "no" in chorus, and the presiding officer decides the result. The term is also used loosely to indicate action by unanimous consent or without objection. *(Also see yeas and nays.)*

Whip — In effect, the assistant majority or minority leader, in either the House or Senate. His or her job is to help marshal votes in support of party strategy and legislation.

Without objection — Used in lieu of a vote on non-controversial motions, amendments or bills that may be passed in either chamber if no member voices an objection.

Yeas and nays — The Constitution requires that yea-and-nay votes be taken and recorded when requested by one-fifth of the members present. In the House, the Speaker determines whether one-fifth of the members present requested a vote. In the Senate, practice requires only 11 members. The Constitution requires the yeas and nays on a veto override attempt. *(Also see recorded vote.)*

Yielding — When a member has been recognized to speak, no other member may speak unless he or she obtains permission from the member recognized. This permission is called yielding and usually is requested in the form, "Will the gentleman (or gentlelady) yield to me?" While this activity occasionally is seen in the Senate, the Senate has no rule or practice to parcel out time.

In the House, the floor manager of a bill usually apportions debate time by yielding specific amounts of time to members who have requested it. ◆

Members of the 106th Congress, 2nd Session . . .

(As of Dec. 15, 2000, when the second session of the 106th Congress adjourned sine die.)

Representatives
R 222; D 208; I 2

— A —

Abercrombie, Neil, D-Hawaii (1)
Ackerman, Gary L., D-N.Y. (5)
Aderholt, Robert B., R-Ala. (4)
Allen, Tom, D-Maine (1)
Andrews, Robert E., D-N.J. (1)
Archer, Bill, R-Texas (7)
Armey, Dick, R-Texas (26)

— B —

Baca, Joe, D-Calif. (42)
Bachus, Spencer, R-Ala. (6)
Baird, Brian, D-Wash. (3)
Baker, Richard H., R-La. (6)
Baldacci, John, D-Maine (2)
Baldwin, Tammy, D-Wis. (2)
Ballenger, Cass, R-N.C. (10)
Barcia, James A., D-Mich. (5)
Barr, Bob, R-Ga. (7)
Barrett, Bill, R-Neb. (3)
Barrett, Thomas M., D-Wis. (5)
Bartlett, Roscoe G., R-Md. (6)
Barton, Joe L., R-Texas (6)
Bass, Charles, R-N.H. (2)
Becerra, Xavier, D-Calif. (30)
Bentsen, Ken, D-Texas (25)
Bereuter, Doug, R-Neb. (1)
Berkley, Shelley, D-Nev. (1)
Berman, Howard L., D-Calif. (26)
Berry, Marion, D-Ark. (1)
Biggert, Judy, R-Ill. (13)
Bilbray, Brian P., R-Calif. (49)
Bilirakis, Michael, R-Fla. (9)
Bishop, Sanford D. Jr., D-Ga. (2)
Blagojevich, Rod R., D-Ill. (5)
Bliley, Thomas J. Jr., R-Va. (7)
Blumenauer, Earl, D-Ore. (3)
Blunt, Roy, R-Mo. (7)
Boehlert, Sherwood, R-N.Y. (23)
Boehner, John A., R-Ohio (8)
Bonilla, Henry, R-Texas (23)
Bonior, David E., D-Mich. (10)
Bono, Mary, R-Calif. (44)
Borski, Robert A., D-Pa. (3)
Boswell, Leonard L., D-Iowa (3)
Boucher, Rick, D-Va. (9)
Boyd, Allen, D-Fla. (2)
Brady, Kevin, R-Texas (8)
Brady, Robert A., D-Pa. (1)
Brown, Corrine, D-Fla. (3)
Brown, Sherrod, D-Ohio (13)
Bryant, Ed, R-Tenn. (7)
Burr, Richard M., R-N.C. (5)
Burton, Dan, R-Ind. (6)
Buyer, Steve, R-Ind. (5)

— C —

Callahan, Sonny, R-Ala. (1)
Calvert, Ken, R-Calif. (43)
Camp, Dave, R-Mich. (4)
Campbell, Tom, R-Calif. (15)
Canady, Charles T., R-Fla. (12)
Cannon, Christopher B., R-Utah (3)
Capps, Lois, D-Calif. (22)
Capuano, Michael E., D-Mass. (8)
Cardin, Benjamin L., D-Md. (3)
Carson, Julia, D-Ind. (10)
Castle, Michael N., R-Del. (AL)
Chabot, Steve, R-Ohio (1)
Chambliss, Saxby, R-Ga. (8)
Chenoweth-Hage, Helen, R-Idaho (1)
Clay, William L., D-Mo. (1)
Clayton, Eva, D-N.C. (1)
Clement, Bob, D-Tenn. (5)
Clyburn, James E., D-S.C. (6)
Coble, Howard, R-N.C. (6)
Coburn, Tom, R-Okla. (2)
Collins, Mac, R-Ga. (3)
Combest, Larry, R-Texas (19)
Condit, Gary A., D-Calif. (18)
Conyers, John Jr., D-Mich. (14)
Cook, Merrill, R-Utah (2)
Cooksey, John, R-La. (5)
Costello, Jerry F., D-Ill. (12)
Cox, Christopher, R-Calif. (47)
Coyne, William J., D-Pa. (14)
Cramer, Robert E. "Bud," D-Ala. (5)
Crane, Philip M., R-Ill. (8)
Crowley, Joseph, D-N.Y. (7)
Cubin, Barbara, R-Wyo. (AL)
Cummings, Elijah E., D-Md. (7)
Cunningham, Randy "Duke," R-Calif. (51)

— D —

Danner, Pat, D-Mo. (6)
Davis, Danny K., D-Ill. (7)
Davis, Jim, D-Fla. (11)
Davis, Thomas M. III, R-Va. (11)
Deal, Nathan, R-Ga. (9)
DeFazio, Peter A., D-Ore. (4)
DeGette, Diana, D-Colo. (1)
Delahunt, Bill, D-Mass. (10)
DeLauro, Rosa, D-Conn. (3)
DeLay, Tom, R-Texas (22)
DeMint, Jim, R-S.C. (4)
Deutsch, Peter, D-Fla. (20)
Diaz-Balart, Lincoln, R-Fla. (21)
Dickey, Jay, R-Ark. (4)
Dicks, Norm, D-Wash. (6)
Dingell, John D., D-Mich. (16)
Doggett, Lloyd, D-Texas (10)
Dooley, Cal, D-Calif. (20)
Doolittle, John T., R-Calif. (4)
Doyle, Mike, D-Pa. (18)
Dreier, David, R-Calif. (28)
Duncan, John J. "Jimmy" Jr., R-Tenn. (2)
Dunn, Jennifer, R-Wash. (8)

— E —

Edwards, Chet, D-Texas (11)
Ehlers, Vernon J., R-Mich. (3)
Ehrlich, Robert L. Jr., R-Md. (2)
Emerson, Jo Ann, R-Mo. (8)
Engel, Eliot L., D-N.Y. (17)
English, Phil, R-Pa. (21)
Eshoo, Anna G., D-Calif. (14)
Etheridge, Bob, D-N.C. (2)
Evans, Lane, D-Ill. (17)
Everett, Terry, R-Ala. (2)
Ewing, Thomas W., R-Ill. (15)

— F —

Farr, Sam, D-Calif. (17)
Fattah, Chaka, D-Pa. (2)
Filner, Bob, D-Calif. (50)
Fletcher, Ernie, R-Ky. (6)
Foley, Mark, R-Fla. (16)
Forbes, Michael P., D-N.Y. (1)
Ford, Harold E. Jr., D-Tenn. (9)
Fossella, Vito J., R-N.Y. (13)
Fowler, Tillie, R-Fla. (4)
Frank, Barney, D-Mass. (4)
Franks, Bob, R-N.J. (7)
Frelinghuysen, Rodney, R-N.J. (11)
Frost, Martin, D-Texas (24)

— G —

Gallegly, Elton, R-Calif. (23)
Ganske, Greg, R-Iowa (4)
Gejdenson, Sam, D-Conn. (2)
Gekas, George W., R-Pa. (17)
Gephardt, Richard A., D-Mo. (3)
Gibbons, Jim, R-Nev. (2)
Gilchrest, Wayne T., R-Md. (1)
Gillmor, Paul E., R-Ohio (5)
Gilman, Benjamin A., R-N.Y. (20)
Gonzalez, Charlie, D-Texas (20)
Goode, Virgil H. Jr., D-Va. (5)
Goodlatte, Robert W., R-Va. (6)
Goodling, Bill, R-Pa. (19)
Gordon, Bart, D-Tenn. (6)
Goss, Porter J., R-Fla. (14)
Graham, Lindsey, R-S.C. (3)
Granger, Kay, R-Texas (12)
Green, Gene, D-Texas (29)
Green, Mark, R-Wis. (8)
Greenwood, James C., R-Pa. (8)
Gutierrez, Luis V., D-Ill. (4)
Gutknecht, Gil, R-Minn. (1)

— H —

Hall, Ralph M., D-Texas (4)
Hall, Tony P., D-Ohio (3)
Hansen, James V., R-Utah (1)
Hastert, J. Dennis, R-Ill. (14)
Hastings, Alcee L., D-Fla. (23)
Hastings, Richard "Doc," R-Wash. (4)
Hayes, Robin, R-N.C. (8)
Hayworth, J.D., R-Ariz. (6)
Hefley, Joel, R-Colo. (5)
Herger, Wally, R-Calif. (2)
Hill, Baron P., D-Ind. (9)
Hill, Rick, R-Mont. (AL)
Hilleary, Van, R-Tenn. (4)
Hilliard, Earl F., D-Ala. (7)
Hinchey, Maurice D., D-N.Y. (26)
Hinojosa, Rubén, D-Texas (15)
Hobson, David L., R-Ohio (7)
Hoeffel, Joseph M., D-Pa. (13)
Hoekstra, Peter, R-Mich. (2)
Holden, Tim, D-Pa. (6)
Holt, Rush D., D-N.J. (12)
Hooley, Darlene, D-Ore. (5)
Horn, Steve, R-Calif. (38)
Hostettler, John, R-Ind. (8)
Houghton, Amo, R-N.Y. (31)
Hoyer, Steny H., D-Md. (5)
Hulshof, Kenny, R-Mo. (9)
Hunter, Duncan, R-Calif. (52)
Hutchinson, Asa, R-Ark. (3)
Hyde, Henry J., R-Ill. (6)

— I, J —

Inslee, Jay, D-Wash. (1)
Isakson, Johnny, R-Ga. (6)
Istook, Ernest, R-Okla. (5)
Jackson, Jesse L. Jr., D-Ill. (2)
Jackson-Lee, Sheila, D-Texas (18)
Jefferson, William J., D-La. (2)
Jenkins, Bill, R-Tenn. (1)
John, Chris, D-La. (7)
Johnson, Eddie Bernice, D-Texas (30)
Johnson, Nancy L., R-Conn. (6)
Johnson, Sam, R-Texas (3)
Jones, Walter B. Jr., R-N.C. (3)
Jones, Stephanie Tubbs, D-Ohio (11)

— K —

Kanjorski, Paul E., D-Pa. (11)
Kaptur, Marcy, D-Ohio (9)
Kasich, John R., R-Ohio (12)
Kelly, Sue W., R-N.Y. (19)
Kennedy, Patrick J., D-R.I. (1)
Kildee, Dale E., D-Mich. (9)
Kilpatrick, Carolyn Cheeks, D-Mich. (15)
Kind, Ron, D-Wis. (3)
King, Peter T., R-N.Y. (3)
Kingston, Jack, R-Ga. (1)
Kleczka, Gerald D., D-Wis. (4)
Klink, Ron, D-Pa. (4)
Knollenberg, Joe, R-Mich. (11)
Kolbe, Jim, R-Ariz. (5)
Kucinich, Dennis J., D-Ohio (10)
Kuykendall, Steven T., R-Calif. (36)

— L —

LaFalce, John J., D-N.Y. (29)
LaHood, Ray, R-Ill. (18)
Lampson, Nick, D-Texas (9)
Lantos, Tom, D-Calif. (12)
Largent, Steve, R-Okla. (1)
Larson, John B., D-Conn. (1)
Latham, Tom, R-Iowa (5)
LaTourette, Steven C., R-Ohio (19)
Lazio, Rick A., R-N.Y. (2)
Leach, Jim, R-Iowa (1)
Lee, Barbara, D-Calif. (9)
Levin, Sander M., D-Mich. (12)
Lewis, Jerry, R-Calif. (40)
Lewis, John, D-Ga. (5)
Lewis, Ron, R-Ky. (2)
Linder, John, R-Ga. (11)
Lipinski, William O., D-Ill. (3)
LoBiondo, Frank A., R-N.J. (2)
Lofgren, Zoe, D-Calif. (16)
Lowey, Nita M., D-N.Y. (18)
Lucas, Frank D., R-Okla. (6)
Lucas, Ken, D-Ky. (4)
Luther, Bill, D-Minn. (6)

— M —

Maloney, Carolyn B., D-N.Y. (14)
Maloney, Jim, D-Conn. (5)
Manzullo, Donald, R-Ill. (16)
Markey, Edward J., D-Mass. (7)
Martinez, Matthew G., R-Calif. (31)
Mascara, Frank R., D-Pa. (20)
Matsui, Robert T., D-Calif. (5)
McCarthy, Carolyn, D-N.Y. (4)
McCarthy, Karen, D-Mo. (5)
McCollum, Bill, R-Fla. (8)
McCrery, Jim, R-La. (4)
McDermott, Jim, D-Wash. (7)
McGovern, Jim, D-Mass. (3)
McHugh, John M., R-N.Y. (24)
McInnis, Scott, R-Colo. (3)
McIntosh, David M., R-Ind. (2)
McIntyre, Mike, D-N.C. (7)
McKeon, Howard P. "Buck," R-Calif. (25)
McKinney, Cynthia A., D-Ga. (4)
McNulty, Michael R., D-N.Y. (21)
Meehan, Martin T., D-Mass. (5)
Meek, Carrie P., D-Fla. (17)
Meeks, Gregory W., D-N.Y. (6)
Menendez, Robert, D-N.J. (13)
Metcalf, Jack, R-Wash. (2)
Mica, John L., R-Fla. (7)
Millender-McDonald, Juanita, D-Calif. (37)
Miller, Dan, R-Fla. (13)
Miller, Gary G., R-Calif. (41)
Miller, George, D-Calif. (7)
Minge, David, D-Minn. (2)
Mink, Patsy T., D-Hawaii (2)
Moakley, Joe, D-Mass. (9)
Mollohan, Alan B., D-W.Va. (1)
Moore, Dennis, D-Kan. (3)
Moran, James P., D-Va. (8)
Moran, Jerry, R-Kan. (1)
Morella, Constance A., R-Md. (8)
Murtha, John P., D-Pa. (12)
Myrick, Sue, R-N.C. (9)

— N —

Nadler, Jerrold, D-N.Y. (8)
Napolitano, Grace F., D-Calif. (34)
Neal, Richard E., D-Mass. (2)
Nethercutt, George, R-Wash. (5)
Ney, Bob, R-Ohio (18)
Northup, Anne M., R-Ky. (3)
Norwood, Charlie, R-Ga. (10)
Nussle, Jim, R-Iowa (2)

— O —

Oberstar, James L., D-Minn. (8)
Obey, David R., D-Wis. (7)
Olver, John W., D-Mass. (1)
Ortiz, Solomon P., D-Texas (27)
Ose, Doug, R-Calif. (3)
Owens, Major R., D-N.Y. (11)
Oxley, Michael G., R-Ohio (4)

— P —

Packard, Ron, R-Calif., (48)
Pallone, Frank Jr., D-N.J. (6)
Pascrell, Bill Jr., D-N.J. (8)
Pastor, Ed, D-Ariz. (2)
Paul, Ron, R-Texas (14)
Payne, Donald M., D-N.J. (10)
Pease, Ed, R-Ind. (7)
Pelosi, Nancy, D-Calif. (8)
Peterson, Collin C., D-Minn. (7)
Peterson, John E., R-Pa. (5)
Petri, Tom, R-Wis. (6)
Phelps, David, D-Ill. (19)
Pickering, Charles W. "Chip" Jr., R-Miss. (3)
Pickett, Owen B., D-Va. (2)
Pitts, Joseph R., R-Pa. (16)
Pombo, Richard W., R-Calif. (11)
Pomeroy, Earl, D-N.D. (AL)
Porter, John Edward, R-Ill. (10)
Portman, Rob, R-Ohio (2)

. . . Governors, Justices, Cabinet-Rank Officers

Price, David E., D-N.C. (4)
Pryce, Deborah, R-Ohio (15)

— Q, R —

Quinn, Jack, R-N.Y. (30)
Radanovich, George P., R-Calif. (19)
Rahall, Nick J. II, D-W.Va. (3)
Ramstad, Jim, R-Minn. (3)
Rangel, Charles B., D-N.Y. (15)
Regula, Ralph, R-Ohio (16)
Reyes, Silvestre, D-Texas (16)
Reynolds, Thomas M., R-N.Y. (27)
Riley, Bob, R-Ala. (3)
Rivers, Lynn, D-Mich. (13)
Rodriguez, Ciro D., D-Texas (28)
Roemer, Tim, D-Ind. (3)
Rogan, James E., R-Calif. (27)
Rogers, Harold, R-Ky. (5)
Rohrabacher, Dana, R-Calif. (45)
Ros-Lehtinen, Ileana, R-Fla. (18)
Rothman, Steven R., D-N.J. (9)
Roukema, Marge, R-N.J. (5)
Roybal-Allard, Lucille, D-Calif. (33)
Royce, Ed, R-Calif. (39)
Rush, Bobby L., D-Ill. (1)
Ryan, Paul D., R-Wis. (1)
Ryun, Jim, R-Kan. (2)

— S —

Sabo, Martin Olav, D-Minn. (5)
Salmon, Matt, R-Ariz. (1)
Sanchez, Loretta, D-Calif. (46)
Sanders, Bernard, I-Vt. (AL)
Sandlin, Max, D-Texas (1)
Sanford, Mark, R-S.C. (1)
Sawyer, Tom, D-Ohio (14)
Saxton, H. James, R-N.J. (3)
Scarborough, Joe, R-Fla. (1)
Schaffer, Bob, R-Colo. (4)
Schakowsky, Jan, D-Ill. (9)
Scott, Robert C., D-Va. (3)
Sensenbrenner, F. James Jr., R-Wis. (9)
Serrano, Jose E., D-N.Y. (16)
Sessions, Pete, R-Texas (5)
Shadegg, John, R-Ariz. (4)
Shaw, E. Clay Jr., R-Fla. (22)
Shays, Christopher, R-Conn. (4)
Sherman, Brad, D-Calif. (24)
Sherwood, Donald L., R-Pa. (10)
Shimkus, John, R-Ill. (20)
Shows, Ronnie, D-Miss. (4)
Shuster, Bud, R-Pa. (9)
Simpson, Mike, R-Idaho (2)
Sisisky, Norman, D-Va. (4)
Skeen, Joe, R-N.M. (2)
Skelton, Ike, D-Mo. (4)
Slaughter, Louise M., D-N.Y. (28)
Smith, Adam, D-Wash. (9)
Smith, Christopher H., R-N.J. (4)
Smith, Lamar, R-Texas (21)
Smith, Nick, R-Mich. (7)
Snyder, Vic, D-Ark. (2)
Souder, Mark, R-Ind. (4)
Spence, Floyd D., R-S.C. (2)
Spratt, John M. Jr., D-S.C. (5)
Stabenow, Debbie, D-Mich. (8)
Stark, Pete, D-Calif. (13)
Stearns, Cliff, R-Fla. (6)
Stenholm, Charles W., D-Texas (17)
Strickland, Ted, D-Ohio (6)
Stump, Bob, R-Ariz. (3)
Stupak, Bart, D-Mich. (1)
Sununu, John E., R-N.H. (1)
Sweeney, John E., R-N.Y. (22)

— T —

Talent, James M., R-Mo. (2)
Tancredo, Tom, R-Colo. (6)
Tanner, John, D-Tenn. (8)
Tauscher, Ellen O., D-Calif. (10)
Tauzin, W.J. "Billy," R-La. (3)
Taylor, Charles H., R-N.C. (11)
Taylor, Gene, D-Miss. (5)
Terry, Lee, R-Neb. (2)
Thomas, Bill, R-Calif. (21)
Thompson, Bennie, D-Miss. (2)
Thompson, Mike, D-Calif. (1)
Thornberry, William M. "Mac," R-Texas (13)
Thune, John, R-S.D. (AL)
Thurman, Karen L., D-Fla. (5)
Tiahrt, Todd, R-Kan. (4)
Tierney, John F., D-Mass. (6)
Toomey, Patrick J., R-Pa. (15)
Towns, Edolphus, D-N.Y. (10)
Traficant, James A. Jr., D-Ohio (17)
Turner, Jim, D-Texas (2)

— U, V —

Udall, Mark, D-Colo. (2)
Udall, Tom, D-N.M. (3)
Upton, Fred, R-Mich. (6)
Velázquez, Nydia M., D-N.Y. (12)
Visclosky, Peter J., D-Ind. (1)
Vitter, David, R-La. (1)

— W —

Walden, Greg, R-Ore. (2)
Walsh, James T., R-N.Y. (25)
Wamp, Zach, R-Tenn. (3)
Waters, Maxine, D-Calif. (35)
Watkins, Wes, R-Okla. (3)
Watt, Melvin, D-N.C. (12)
Watts, J.C. Jr., R-Okla. (4)
Waxman, Henry A., D-Calif. (29)
Weiner, Anthony, D-N.Y. (9)
Weldon, Curt, R-Pa. (7)
Weldon, Dave, R-Fla. (15)
Weller, Jerry, R-Ill. (11)
Wexler, Robert, D-Fla. (19)
Weygand, Bob, D-R.I. (2)
Whitfield, Edward, R-Ky. (1)
Wicker, Roger, R-Miss. (1)
Wilson, Heather A., R-N.M. (1)
Wise, Bob, D-W.Va. (2)
Wolf, Frank R., R-Va. (10)
Woolsey, Lynn, D-Calif. (6)
Wu, David, D-Ore. (1)
Wynn, Albert R., D-Md. (4)

— X, Y, Z —

Young, C.W. Bill, R-Fla. (10)
Young, Don, R-Alaska (AL)

Delegates

Christensen, Donna M.C., D-Virgin Is.
Faleomavaega, Eni F.H., D-Am. Samoa
Norton, Eleanor Holmes, D-D.C.
Romero-Barceló, Carlos A., D-P.R.
Underwood, Robert A., D-Guam

Senators
R 54; D 46

Abraham, Spencer, R-Mich.
Akaka, Daniel K., D-Hawaii
Allard, Wayne, R-Colo.
Ashcroft, John, R-Mo.
Baucus, Max, D-Mont.
Bayh, Evan, D-Ind.
Bennett, Robert F., R-Utah
Biden, Joseph R. Jr., D-Del.
Bingaman, Jeff, D-N.M.
Bond, Christopher S., R-Mo.
Boxer, Barbara, D-Calif.
Breaux, John B., D-La.
Brownback, Sam, R-Kan.
Bryan, Richard H., D-Nev.
Bunning, Jim, R-Ky.
Burns, Conrad, R-Mont.
Byrd, Robert C., D-W.Va.
Campbell, Ben Nighthorse, R-Colo.
Chafee, Lincoln, R-R.I.
Cleland, Max, D-Ga.
Cochran, Thad, R-Miss.
Collins, Susan, R-Maine
Conrad, Kent, D-N.D.
Craig, Larry E., R-Idaho
Crapo, Michael D., R-Idaho
Daschle, Tom, D-S.D.
DeWine, Mike, R-Ohio
Dodd, Christopher J., D-Conn.
Domenici, Pete V., R-N.M.
Dorgan, Byron L., D-N.D.
Durbin, Richard J., D-Ill.
Edwards, John, D-N.C.
Enzi, Michael B., R-Wyo.
Feingold, Russell D., D-Wis.
Feinstein, Dianne, D-Calif.
Fitzgerald, Peter G., R-Ill.
Frist, Bill, R-Tenn.
Gorton, Slade, R-Wash.
Graham, Bob, D-Fla.
Gramm, Phil, R-Texas
Grams, Rod, R-Minn.
Grassley, Charles E., R-Iowa
Gregg, Judd, R-N.H.
Hagel, Chuck, R-Neb.
Harkin, Tom, D-Iowa
Hatch, Orrin G., R-Utah
Helms, Jesse, R-N.C.
Hollings, Ernest F., D-S.C.
Hutchinson, Tim, R-Ark.
Hutchison, Kay Bailey, R-Texas
Inhofe, James M., R-Okla.
Inouye, Daniel K., D-Hawaii
Jeffords, James M., R-Vt.
Johnson, Tim, D-S.D.
Kennedy, Edward M., D-Mass.
Kerrey, Bob, D-Neb.
Kerry, John, D-Mass.
Kohl, Herb, D-Wis.
Kyl, Jon, R-Ariz.
Landrieu, Mary L., D-La.
Lautenberg, Frank R., D-N.J.
Leahy, Patrick J., D-Vt.
Levin, Carl, D-Mich.
Lieberman, Joseph I., D-Conn.
Lincoln, Blanche, D-Ark.
Lott, Trent, R-Miss.
Lugar, Richard G., R-Ind.
Mack, Connie, R-Fla.
McCain, John, R-Ariz.
McConnell, Mitch, R-Ky.
Mikulski, Barbara A., D-Md.
Miller, Zell, D-Ga.
Moynihan, Daniel Patrick, D-N.Y.
Murkowski, Frank H., R-Alaska
Murray, Patty, D-Wash.
Nickles, Don, R-Okla.
Reed, Jack, D-R.I.
Reid, Harry, D-Nev.
Robb, Charles S., D-Va.
Roberts, Pat, R-Kan.
Rockefeller, John D. IV, D-W.Va.
Roth, William V. Jr., R-Del.
Santorum, Rick, R-Pa.
Sarbanes, Paul S., D-Md.
Schumer, Charles E., D-N.Y.
Sessions, Jeff, R-Ala.
Shelby, Richard C., R-Ala.
Smith, Gordon H., R-Ore.
Smith, Robert C., R-N.H.
Snowe, Olympia J., R-Maine
Specter, Arlen, R-Pa.
Stevens, Ted, R-Alaska
Thomas, Craig, R-Wyo.
Thompson, Fred, R-Tenn.
Thurmond, Strom, R-S.C.
Torricelli, Robert G., D-N.J.
Voinovich, George V., R-Ohio
Warner, John W., R-Va.
Wellstone, Paul, D-Minn.
Wyden, Ron, D-Ore.

Governors
R 30; D 18; I 2

Ala. — Donald Siegelman, D
Alaska — Tony Knowles, D
Ariz. — Jane Dee Hull, R
Ark. — Mike Huckabee, R
Calif. — Gray Davis, D
Colo. — Bill Owens, R
Conn. — John G. Rowland, R
Del. — Thomas R. Carper, D
Fla. — Jeb Bush, R
Ga. — Roy Barnes, D
Hawaii — Benjamin J. Cayetano, D
Idaho — Dirk Kempthorne, R
Ill. — George Ryan, R
Ind. — Frank L. O'Bannon, D
Iowa — Tom Vilsack, D
Kan. — Bill Graves, R
Ky. — Paul E. Patton, D
La. — Mike Foster, R
Maine — Angus King, I
Md. — Parris N. Glendening, D
Mass. — Paul Cellucci, R
Mich. — John Engler, R
Minn. — Jesse Ventura, I
Miss. — Ronnie Musgrove, D
Mo. — Roger B. Wilson, D
Mont. — Marc Racicot, R
Neb. — Mike Johanns, R
Nev. — Kenny Guinn, R
N.H. — Jeanne Shaheen, D
N.J. — Christine Todd Whitman, R
N.M. — Gary E. Johnson, R
N.Y. — George E. Pataki, R
N.C. — James B. Hunt Jr., D
N.D. — Edward T. Schafer, R
Ohio — Bob Taft, R
Okla. — Frank Keating, R
Ore. — John Kitzhaber, D
Pa. — Tom Ridge, R
R.I. — Lincoln C. Almond, R
S.C. — Jim Hodges, D
S.D. — William J. Janklow, R
Tenn. — Don Sundquist, R
Texas — George W. Bush, R
Utah — Michael O. Leavitt, R
Vt. — Howard Dean, D
Va. — James S. Gilmore III, R
Wash. — Gary Locke, D
W.Va. — Cecil H. Underwood, R
Wis. — Tommy G. Thompson, R
Wyo. — Jim Geringer, R

Supreme Court

Rehnquist, William H. — Va., Chief Justice
Breyer, Stephen G. — Mass.
Ginsburg, Ruth Bader — N.Y.
Kennedy, Anthony M. — Calif.
O'Connor, Sandra Day — Ariz.
Scalia, Antonin — Va.
Souter, David H. — N.H.
Stevens, John Paul — Ill.
Thomas, Clarence — Ga.

Cabinet

Albright, Madeleine K. — State
Babbitt, Bruce — Interior
Cohen, William S. — Defense
Cuomo, Andrew M. — HUD
Glickman, Dan — Agriculture
Gober, Hershel — Veterans Affairs
Herman, Alexis M. — Labor
Holbrooke, Richard C. — U.N. Representative
Mineta, Norman Y. — Commerce
Reno, Janet — Attorney General
Richardson, Bill — Energy
Riley, Richard W. — Education
Shalala, Donna E. — HHS
Slater, Rodney — Transportation
Summers, Lawrence H. — Treasury

Other Executive Branch Officers

Gore, Al — Vice President
Baily, Martin N. — Chairman, Council of Economic Advisers
Barshefsky, Charlene — U.S. Trade Representative
Berger, Samuel R. — National Security Adviser
Browner, Carol M. — EPA Administrator
Lew, Jack — OMB Director
Podesta, John D. — Chief of Staff
Sperling, Gene — Chairman, National Economic Council
Tenet, George J. — Director of Central Intelligence

CQ

Appendix B

VOTE STUDIES

Clinton's Floor Vote Victories Yield Few Accomplishments, Limited to Trade, Education

On paper, President Clinton seemed to have as good a year in 2000 as any he has had since Republicans gained the majority in Congress in 1995. If floor votes were all that mattered in a president's legislative record, Clinton could dust off the "Comeback Kid" banner and leave office with a shinier gloss in the history books.

Floor votes alone, however, cannot tell the story of the final year of Clinton's presidency. He eked out a few accomplishments on trade and education, but for the most part Clinton's last months will be remembered, if at all, for a laundry list of proposals that caught brief flashes of presidential interest and then quickly sank out of sight.

In his eighth year in office, Clinton won on 55 percent of the roll call votes on which he took a clear position. That rating is essentially a tie with his best year facing a Republican Congress — the election year of 1996, when Congress supported Clinton in 55.1 percent of the votes judged by Congressional Quarterly as presidential support votes. Clinton's track record in 2000 was boosted significantly by a large number of nominations confirmed by the Senate; without them, his success rate would have been considerably lower.

Still, it was a solid recovery from 1999, when Clinton racked up a lackluster 37.8 percent success rate — the second-lowest ranking in the 48 years that CQ has been evaluating presidential success in Congress. That year's failings were blamed largely on the bitter post-impeachment climate, when Republicans' distrust of Clinton rose into the stratosphere and neither side found any real reason to compromise. *(1999 Almanac, p. B-10)*

Add a hotly contested presidential election to the mix, not to mention the battle for control of Congress, and the incentive to compromise became even weaker. Throw in the fact that Republicans expected to deal with a president from their own party in 2001 — a hope that was to become true Jan. 20 with the inauguration of President-elect George W. Bush — and the political environment only got worse.

CQ Vote Studies

Those factors made Clinton's high score in 2000 even more noteworthy.

"These have not been productive times," said George C. Edwards III, director of the Center for Presidential Studies at Texas A&M University. "The parties are so clearly divided. You don't have a center. When you combine that with a narrow Republican majority where they know how to use the majority to control the agenda, the prospects for success are not really encouraging."

The one saving grace for Clinton in 2000, as in every year since the 1995-96 government shutdown, was his skillful use of veto threats to maximize his bargaining leverage, enabling him to salvage real successes out of the appropriations process. In 2000, he persuaded Republicans to accept a 17 percent increase in education spending for fiscal 2001 — by far the largest increase in the history of the Department of Education.

The fact that Republicans talked him down from 21 percent hardly made the victory less impressive. Ultimately, Clinton got the Republicans to fund virtually all of his priorities, from school repairs to smaller class sizes and grants for improving schools in low-income communities.

"I think he did a lot better on education than we would have hoped," Sen. Jon Kyl, R-Ariz., conceded in a Dec. 21 interview. Otherwise, Kyl said, "I don't think he's had a particularly good last two years."

What He Won

While Clinton tied his 1996 success rating in his last year in office, his legislative record in the two presidential election years was quite different.

In 1996, Clinton and the Republicans were coming off a dramatic budget battle that shut the government down twice, and they felt the need to remind voters that they could get things done. In rapid succession, they struck deals on legislation to overhaul the welfare system, allow people to change jobs and still qualify for health insurance, and raise the minimum wage — all lasting changes on the social policy front. *(1996 Almanac, pp. 6-3, 7-3, 7-14)*

In 2000, Clinton chalked up one victory on a major and contentious piece of legislation: permanent status for China as a normal U.S. trading partner (PL 106-286). He could point to one moderate social policy accomplishment: a community renewal package to revitalize poor neighborhoods, largely through tax breaks (PL 106-554), that he had worked out with House Speaker J. Dennis Hastert, R-Ill.

While the huge increase in education funding is sure to have a long-term impact on spending levels, it may not translate into a lasting impact on policies. Clinton's plan to use federal money to hire 100,000 teachers, for example, has had to exist on year-to-year appropriations; there is no guar-

PRESIDENTIAL SUCCESS History

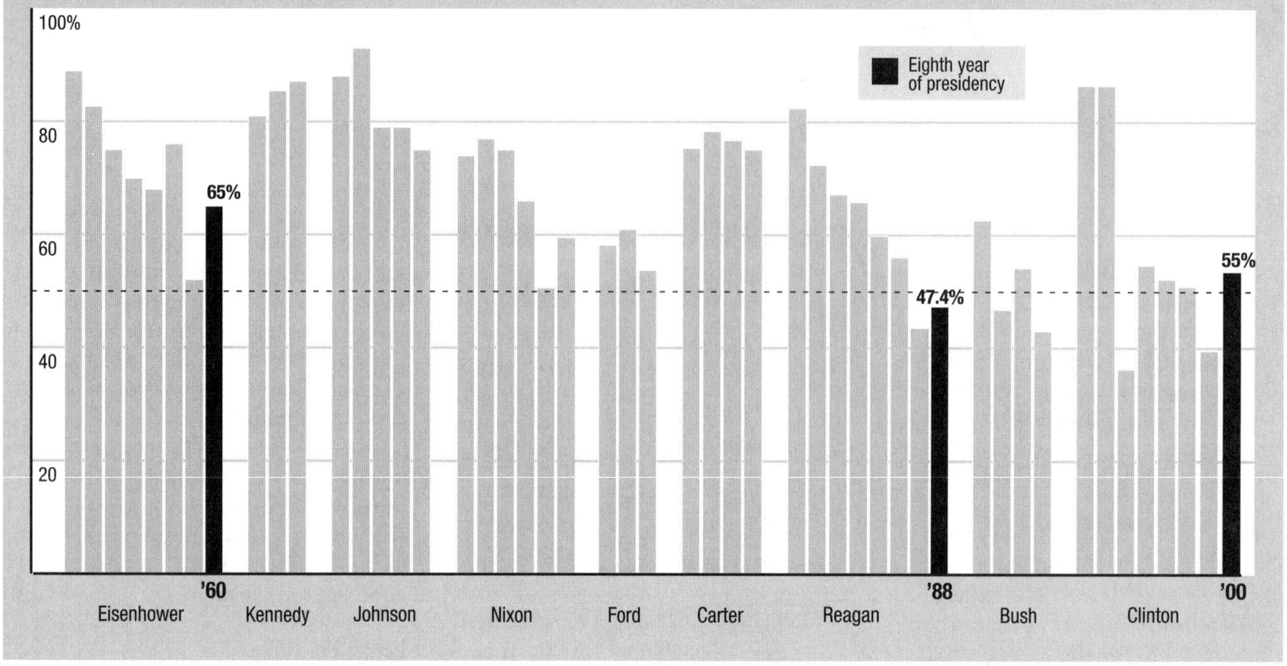

antee it will survive beyond this year.

The limits to Clinton's successes in 2000 are also evident when compared with the weighty list of proposals crammed into his State of the Union address: Prescription drug coverage for Medicare. New rules for managed-care plans. Health coverage for low-income parents as well as their kids. Gun control measures. Another increase in the minimum wage. Targeted tax cuts, and an expansion of the Earned Income Tax Credit for the working poor. Ratification of the Comprehensive Test Ban Treaty to prevent any more nuclear testing throughout the world.

"He may look successful" based on the floor votes, said Eric Schickler, an assistant professor of political science at the University of California at Berkeley, "but he's not getting a lot done."

Fewer, Easier Votes

So why did Clinton show so much improvement in his congressional success rate in 2000? Much of the explanation is in what lies behind the numbers:

• **Less challenging issues.** In 1999, Clinton mobilized members of Congress to oppose the GOP leadership on some high-profile issues, such as managed care and campaign finance. This year, there were a few uphill battles — notably on raising the minimum wage again and strengthening the penalties against "hate crimes" — but other Clinton victories took place on fairly easy issues.

On Social Security, for example, there was no showdown on a structural overhaul. Instead, the big vote was on a popular, election-year measure (PL 106-182) repealing the so-called earnings limit that deferred some Social Security benefits for seniors between the ages of 65 and 69. Clinton did not have to twist many arms on that one.

"A success on these kinds of bills is misleading, because it doesn't reflect the kind of leadership we expect of a president," said Cary R. Covington, an associate professor of political science at the University of Iowa.

• **Leadership backing on major issues.** There were certainly some tougher issues. The China trade legislation faced concern from pro-labor Democrats who feared a loss of U.S. jobs; the community renewal bill was opposed by some conservative Senate Republicans and nearly got tripped up in both chambers several times.

Still, Clinton had a built-in advantage on both: the support of the Republican leadership. The China vote "was kind of a natural alliance, because Republicans were inclined to support free trade anyway," said Schickler. And community renewal was as much Hastert's project as Clinton's. The bill received special procedural consideration that it never would have gotten if it had been Clinton's project alone.

• **More nominations.** A president's Senate success rate in the CQ rankings is padded by successful nominations. They are a legitimate measure of a president's effectiveness with

Definition

How often the president won on roll call votes on which he took a clear position.

2000 Data

Senate	26 victories 14 defeats
House	34 victories 35 defeats

Total Clinton success rate: 55%

For More Information

Individual leaders ....p. B-5
Background and data..........p. B-12
List of House votes ....p. B-13
House members' scores ......p. B-14
List of Senate votes ....p. B-16
Senators' scores ....p. B-17

Leading Scorers: Presidential Support

Support indicates those who in 2000 voted most often for President Clinton's position; **opposition** shows those who voted most often against the president's position. Scores are based on actual votes cast; members are listed alphabetically when their scores are tied. Members who missed half or more of the votes are not listed.

SENATE

Support: Republicans		Support: Democrats		Opposition: Republicans		Opposition: Democrats	
Chafee, R.I.	88%	Bryan, Nev.	100%	Smith, N.H.	72%	Byrd, W.Va.	25%
Jeffords, Vt.	75	Moynihan, N.Y.	100	Inhofe, Okla.	70	Cleland, Ga.	22
Roth, Del.	68	Bayh, Ind.	98	Helms, N.C.	69	Kohl, Wis.	21
Lugar, Ind.	65	Dodd, Conn.	98	Bunning, Ky.	67	Hollings, S.C.	18
Smith, Ore.	62	Johnson, S.D.	98	Allard, Colo.	65	Feinstein, Calif.	16
Snowe, Maine	62	Lautenberg, N.J.	98	Enzi, Wyo.	65	Kerrey, Neb.	16
Specter, Pa.	59	Schumer, N.Y.	98	Gramm, Texas	65	Lincoln, Ark.	16
Voinovich, Ohio	59	Akaka, Hawaii	97	Grams, Minn.	62	Breaux, La.	15
Collins, Maine	58	Baucus, Mont.	97	Gregg, N.H.	62	Landrieu, La.	15
Stevens, Alaska	56	Durbin, Ill.	97	Hutchinson, Ark.	62		
Hatch, Utah	55	Kerry, Mass.	97	McCain, Ariz.	62		
Bennett, Utah	52	Rockefeller, W.Va.	97	Roberts, Kan.	62		
DeWine, Ohio	52						
Warner, Va.	52						

HOUSE

Support: Republicans		Support: Democrats		Opposition: Republicans		Opposition: Democrats	
Morella, Md.	63%	Rangel, N.Y.	97%	Duncan, Tenn.	88%	Hall, Texas	78%
Boehlert, N.Y.	61	Ackerman, N.Y.	94	Cook, Utah	87	Traficant, Ohio	68
Gilman, N.Y.	58	Berman, Calif.	94	Everett, Ala.	86	Shows, Miss.	66
Houghton, N.Y.	55	Cardin, Md.	94	Hilleary, Tenn.	86	Danner, Mo.	65
Greenwood, Pa.	54	Fattah, Pa.	94	Deal, Ga.	85	Barcia, Mich.	61
Porter, Ill.	54	Hinchey, N.Y.	94	Hefley, Colo.	85	McIntyre, N.C.	60
Johnson, Conn.	51	McDermott, Wash.	94	Rohrabacher, Calif.	84	Taylor, Miss.	60
Gilchrest, Md.	50	Napolitano, Calif.	94			Lucas, Ky.	59
Castle, Del.	49	Sawyer, Ohio	93			Phelps, Ill.	57
Shays, Conn.	49					Sisisky, Va.	56

Congress, but they can also distort his successes on policy matters. In 2000, 17 of the 40 Senate presidential support votes were on nominations; all were confirmed. By contrast, there were 10 nominations in 1999 and only three in 1996.

Without the nominations, Clinton's Senate success rate for 2000 drops considerably — from 65 percent to 39.1 percent. (In the House, where nominations are not an issue, Clinton won 49.3 percent of the votes.)

The Senate score without nominations is still an improvement over Clinton's comparable rating in 1999, but it falls well short of his 1998 score. Not counting nominations, he succeeded in only 28.6 percent of the Senate votes in 1999, while he won 57.1 percent of the votes in 1998.

The confirmation votes themselves are not a complete measure of Clinton's ability to get his choices through the Senate. He did not lose on any of the 17 votes that came to the floor in 2000, but many never made it that far. Forty judicial nominations were left pending at the end of the session.

"There were a whole lot of people he wanted that he didn't get," said Kyl. "We worked a lot of those nominations so that he ended up with more moderate candidates. A lot of his early nominations were very liberal."

Votes That Never Happened

At the same time, Clinton's score may have been lowered by strategic decisions made by the Republicans — as well as a few made by Democrats.

Clinton's success rate might have been higher, for example, if the Senate had voted on a Democratic amendment to the 1965 Elementary and Secondary Education Act reauthorization bill to require background checks on anyone who buys firearms at gun shows. The same proposal had been adopted in the Senate in 1999 as an amendment to the juvenile justice bill, with Vice President Al Gore casting the tie-breaking vote. Instead, Senate Majority Leader Trent Lott, R-Miss., pulled the education bill from the floor, and the vote never took place. *(1999 Almanac, p. 18-3)*

By contrast, Clinton's piecemeal initiatives for helping the uninsured, including a proposal to expand the State Children's Health Program to cover the parents of low-income children, might have failed in the GOP-controlled Congress. But those proposals did not come up in either chamber.

The leadership's ability to avoid floor votes on a number of Democratic issues contributed to the relatively small number of presidential support votes in 2000 — 109 votes in all, 69 in the House and 40 in the Senate. In 1999, there were 127 that had clearly stated presidential positions attached to them.

Those numbers have been falling since 1996, when 138 votes had clearly stated presidential positions — and 1995, when there were 235 votes on issues on which Clinton was trying to get his way with Congress. *(1996 Almanac, p. C-3; 1995 Almanac, p. C-3)*

When Clinton did get votes on his proposals in 2000, they were not always "clean" votes. The House approved a two-year, $1 increase in the minimum wage, for example, which counted as a vote in support of Clinton. Later in the year, however, the wage increase was rolled into a tax cut conference report that Clinton threatened to veto. The House vote to approve that conference report counted against Clinton, even though he supported the minimum wage piece of it. "The biggest problem for Clinton is just getting his agenda items onto the floor for direct votes," said Schickler.

In some cases, however, Democrats brought up those proposals not so much to pass them as to embarrass Republicans, who they knew would vote against them.

When the Senate debated its version of the Labor, Health and Human Services, and Education Appropriations bill, for example, Democrats offered a series of amendments supporting Clinton's education proposals, including his 100,000 teachers initiative.

Those votes added three defeats to Clinton's presidential support rankings. Another came on a Democratic amendment stating that any managed-care overhaul would have to cover all privately insured Americans — a slap at Senate Republicans, who insisted on applying the new rules only to patients who were not already protected by state laws.

Ultimately, Clinton won most of his education funding priorities in the end-of-year budget negotiations. The managed-care overhaul bill died in conference. The fact that Clinton did not fight as hard for the managed-care bill and so many other agenda priorities may have been dictated by the constraints of an election year in which his vice president was trying to succeed him.

"If Clinton had created World War III with the Congress," said Kyl, "it would have helped Bush and hurt Gore. So he really had to hold back from confronting us . . . and let us slide into the lame-duck session. And then he lost most of his leverage."

Whatever the reasons, Clinton settled for the few victories he could get from a Republican Congress and called it a day. ◆

Votes Belie Partisan Intensity; Leaders Kept Issues Off Floor Unless Victory Seemed Certain

In a year that ended with voters and their representatives almost evenly divided along party lines, partisan voting in Congress was, in fact, at its lowest level in more than a decade.

Recorded votes that split Republicans and Democrats accounted for fewer than half of all the votes tallied in the House and Senate — the first time that has happened since 1988, according to Congressional Quarterly's annual vote analysis. The decline came despite pitched battles over issues such as Medicare drug coverage, gun control and targeted tax cuts.

A party unity vote is defined as one in which the majority of voting Republicans opposes the majority of voting Democrats. In other words, if all members were voting, 105 of the 208 Democrats at the end of the 106th Congress would have had to cross party lines and join with Republicans for the vote not to be considered a party unity vote. In all, 404 House and Senate roll call votes out of a total of 898 were categorized as party unity votes.

Political scientists say there are a number of reasons that the partisan warfare on particular issues in 2000 did not translate into a higher percentage of party-line votes.

First, the Republican majority's narrow margin in the House discouraged GOP leaders from bringing intensely partisan issues to the floor unless they were sure they had the votes for passage. An increasingly diverse House Republican Conference put pressure on Speaker J. Dennis Hastert, R-Ill., to steer a course between hard-line conservatives and an influential group of party moderates who tended to vote with Democrats on some social issues. In the end, messy intramural battles over education, health care and other hot-button issues often were settled in caucus rooms, in committees or in conference negotiations with the Senate.

"It's different from 1995, when Republicans marched in lockstep with [Speaker] Newt Gingrich [R-Ga., 1979-99] and the leadership put more partisan bills right on the floor to force showdowns over things like term limits, property rights, welfare reform and large-scale tax cuts," said Sarah Binder, assistant professor of political science at George Washington University.

Second, when bills did reach the floor of the Senate, Republican leaders often refused to allow Democratic amendments, resulting in fewer total roll call votes (298, compared with 374

PARTY UNITY Partisan Voting by Chamber

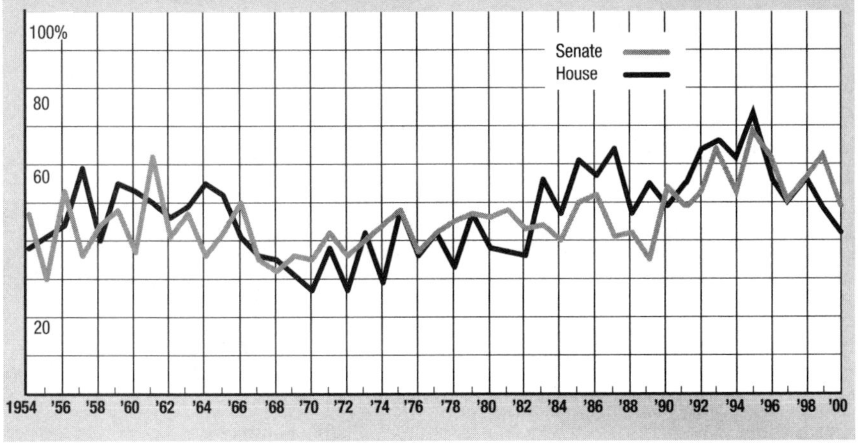

Definition

The percentage of recorded floor votes in each chamber on which a majority of one party voted against a majority of the other party.

2000 Data

	Partisan Votes	Total Votes	Percent
Senate	145	298	49
House	259	600	43

For More Information

Individual leaders....................p. B-8
Background and data..............p. B-18
List of votes..............................p. B-19
House members' scores ....p. B-20
Senators' scores......................p. B-22

in 1999). That and other procedural maneuvers — such as pulling measures that lacked the 60 votes needed to approve a cloture motion that would cut off debate — prevented divisive showdowns on such issues as gun control and the package of health-care reforms known as the patients' "bill of rights."

"It's a great contradiction — if you look at the numbers in the Senate, you would think they must be getting along. But they really have reached a low point in relations between Republicans and Democrats," said Norman J. Ornstein, resident scholar at the American Enterprise Institute.

Avoiding Showdowns

As defined by CQ, the rate of party unity voting in the House declined to 43 percent in 2000 from 47 percent in 1999 — its lowest level in 18 years. The drop-off was even more notable in the Senate, where party unity votes fell to 49 percent of all votes cast in 2000, compared with 63 percent in 1999.

Christopher Shays of Connecticut, a moderate House Republican, said the results reflect an incremental approach to legislating that discourages sweeping, ideologically driven bills.

Hastert "took bite-sized pieces to get things done," Shays said in a Dec. 12 interview. "Given that the numbers were so close — and will stay that way in the 107th Congress — they have to produce good, sensible legislation with good conservative ideas and values. They're not going to be able to ram anything through."

Unanimous voting on party unity votes generally declined in 2000, especially in the Senate. The number of times Republicans in that chamber voted unanimously fell to 19 in 2000 from 63 in 1999, as moderates such as Lincoln Chafee of Rhode Island and James M. Jeffords of Vermont regularly defied Majority Leader Trent Lott of Mississippi to join the Democrats.

While Senate Democrats presented a more unified front under Minority Leader Tom Daschle of South Dakota, they voted unanimously 52 times on party unity votes in 2000, compared with 100 times in 1999. Those most likely to break ranks included Robert C. Byrd of West Virginia and John B. Breaux of Louisiana.

House Republicans bucked the overall trend by voting unanimously on party unity votes more often in 2000 — 67 times, compared with 59 times in 1999. In contrast, House Democrats showed little unity even on the most polarizing issues, voting unanimously just once in 2000 — in support of a motion to instruct conferees on the fiscal 2001 budget resolution. The motion stipulated that tax cuts should not be reported by the House Ways and Means Committee before Congress had a chance to enact a Medicare prescription drug benefit. House Democrats voted unanimously 11 times in 1999. *(Vote 114, H-40)*

Seeking Out Moderates

CQ's analysis showed that, as in recent years, Republicans relied on a cadre of 30 conservative Democrats known as the Blue Dog Coalition to help provide the margin of victory on key party unity votes. Nine times in 2000, a majority of Blue Dogs voted against a majority of their fellow Democrats to give the Republicans victories of less than 15 votes. The votes involved restricting guns, protecting the environment and pursuing lawsuits against tobacco companies — issues that in the past have attracted overwhelming Democratic support in the House.

In June, for example, Blue Dogs sided with Republicans to kill a Democratic amendment to delete language that would prevent the Environmental Protection Agency f rom enforcing interim water standards for arsenic. The amendment, to the fiscal 2001 VA-HUD appropriations bill, also proposed striking language that would bar the agency from encouraging the use of dredging to remove hazardous materials from waterways. It was defeated, 208-216. *(Vote 304, p. H-98)*

Similarly, a majority of Blue Dogs teamed with the GOP majority to adopt, 218-207, an amendment blocking the Department of Housing and Urban Development from expanding a program that encourages communities to buy guns for their police from manufacturers that have promised to install trigger locks and use "smart gun" technology on their products within three years. *(Vote 306, p. H-98)*

However, the landscape changed for GOP leaders when their party moderates jumped ship. For example, an amendment to the fiscal 2001 agriculture appropriations bill pro-

Leading Scorers: Party Unity

Support indicates those who in 2000 voted most consistently with their party's majority against the other party; **Opposition** shows those who voted most often against their party's majority. Scores are based on votes cast; members are listed alphabetically when their scores are tied. Members who missed half or more of the votes are not listed.

SENATE

Support: Republicans		Support: Democrats		Opposition: Republicans		Opposition: Democrats	
Craig, Idaho	100%	Boxer, Calif.	100%	Chafee, R.I.	63%	Byrd, W.Va.	28%
Crapo, Idaho	100	Durbin, Ill.	99	Jeffords, Vt.	45	Breaux, La.	27
Inhofe, Okla.	100	Sarbanes, Md.	99	Specter, Pa.	33	Lincoln, Ark.	20
Kyl, Ariz.	99	Akaka, Hawaii	98	Snowe, Maine	29	Torricelli, N.J.	19
McConnell, Ky.	99	Kennedy, Mass.	98	Collins, Maine	26	Kerrey, Neb.	17
Murkowski, Alaska	99	Lautenberg, N.J.	98			Cleland, Ga.	16

HOUSE

Support: Republicans		Support: Democrats		Opposition: Republicans		Opposition: Democrats	
Armey, Texas	99%	Filner, Calif.	99%	Morella, Md.	50%	Traficant, Ohio	78%
Cannon, Utah	99	Capuano, Mass.	98	Porter, Ill.	35	Hall, Texas	65
DeLay, Texas	99	Conyers, Mich.	98	Gilman, N.Y.	33	Shows, Miss.	49
Smith, Texas	99	Coyne, Pa.,	98	Boehlert, N.Y.	32	Lucas, Ky.	46
Blunt, Mo.	98	Hinchey, N.Y.	98	Horn, Calif.	29	Taylor, Miss.	43
Burton, Ind.	98	Jones, Ohio	98	Johnson, Conn.	29	Stenholm, Texas	41
DeMint, S.C.	98	Lantos, Calif.	98	Shays, Conn.	29	Peterson, Minn.	40
Graham, S.C.	98	Markey, Mass.	98	Frelinghuysen, N.J.	27	Barcia, Mich.	39
Hastings, Wash.	98	McGovern, Mass.	98	Greenwood, Pa.	27	Danner, Mo.	39
Johnson, Texas	98	Millender-McDonald, Calif.	98	Lazio, N.Y.	27	McIntyre, N.C.	39
Pitts, Pa.	98	Owens, N.Y.	98	Leach, Iowa	27	Sisisky, Va.	39
Ryun, Kan.	98	Roybal-Allard, Calif.	98	Smith, N.J.	27		
Sessions, Texas	98	Rush, Ill.	98				
Watts, Okla.	98	Waxman, Calif.	98				
		Woolsey, Calif.	98				

hibiting the use of federal funds for testing or approving abortion-inducing drugs, such as the French-made RU-486, was defeated, 182-187, in July, when 34 moderate Republicans voted with Democrats. The restriction had passed the House in recent years when the GOP had a wider majority and could also count on picking up a number of conservative Democrats. Each time, it was later stripped out in the House-Senate conference on the bill. *(Vote 373, p. H-118)*

GOP leaders' efforts to modify bills on the House floor also failed when enough Republicans crossed party lines. Typical was the House version of the Conservation and Reinvestment Act, which had more than 300 cosponsors and would have channeled royalties from offshore drilling to federal and state resource and land conservation programs.

Conservatives peppered the bill with more than 20 amendments when it came to the floor in May, most aimed at providing additional protections for private landowners or limiting the scope of the legislation. Despite having the backing of the Republican leadership, most of the proposals were defeated.

In the Senate, a July effort by Republican leaders to prevent President Clinton from designating any new national monuments without congressional approval failed, 49-50. Six mostly moderate Republicans crossed party lines to help give Democrats the margin of victory. The amendment, to the fiscal 2001 interior appropriations bill, was considered by the administration and environmental groups as the biggest threat to the bill. *(Vote 208, p. S-38)*

Most of the same moderates joined Democrats in April to adopt, 51-49, an amendment to the fiscal 2001 budget resolution to reduce the Republicans' proposed five-year tax cut by approximately $2.7 billion and provide a corresponding increase in the Pell grant program for lower-income college students. *(Vote 69, p. S-15)*

Crossing Party Lines

The CQ analysis of party unity votes showed that many of the members who regularly broke with their parties in past years did so again in 2000.

Moderate House Republicans identified as most likely to vote with Democrats were led by Constance A. Morella of Maryland, who voted exactly half the time with her party. Others in the group included, in descending order, retiring Rep. John Edward Porter of Illinois; Benjamin A.

Gilman and Sherwood Boehlert, both of New York; Steve Horn of California; and Shays and Nancy L. Johnson of Connecticut.

Among House Democrats, maverick James A. Traficant Jr. of Ohio, who frequently feuded with his party's leadership, voted 78 percent of the time with the GOP. Others who regularly sided with the Republican majority in 2000 included Ralph M. Hall of Texas, Ronnie Shows of Mississippi, Ken Lucas of Kentucky, Gene Taylor of Mississippi, Charles W. Stenholm of Texas and Collin C. Peterson of Minnesota. All but Traficant are Blue Dogs.

Chafee led the Senate Republicans who broke most often with their party, voting with Democrats 63 percent of the time. Others included, in descending order, Jeffords; Arlen Specter of Pennsylvania; and Olympia J. Snowe and Susan Collins, both of Maine.

Among Senate Democrats, Byrd and Breaux voted with Republicans 28 and 27 percent of the time, respectively. Others who regularly broke ranks included, in descending order, Blanche Lincoln of Arkansas; Robert G. Torricelli of New Jersey; retiring Sen. Bob Kerrey of Nebraska; and Max Cleland of Georgia. ◆

Voting Rate Remains High Despite Campaign Pressures And Late End to Session

Members of the House and Senate maintained relatively high voting participation scores in 2000 — even as the second session of the 106th Congress spilled into prime campaign season. The key was careful scheduling of floor action that allowed members to campaign during extended weekends without missing roll call votes.

The overall participation rate for both chambers was 94.4 percent in 2000. That was a slight drop from the 96.6 percent registered in 1999 and a slimmer decrease from the 95.7 percent scored in 1998, the last election year.

Historically, voting participation — measured by how often members vote "yea" or "nay" on roll call votes — tended to dip in election years as members were forced to choose between campaigning and voting. Since the mid-1970s, however, voting has been considered a potential campaign issue, and members have worked diligently to balance their campaigning duties with the demand of roll call votes.

The average score for the two chambers did not rise above 90 percent until 1975, and it has not slipped below 90 percent since 1980. In the past decade, scores have generally hovered around 95 percent.

Neither the number of roll call votes nor the length of the session appears to have affected voting participation scores. The number of votes (898) was the fifth highest in the past decade; it was the second highest in an election year for the past 18 years, exceeded only by 924 votes in 1982.

In 2000, House members voted 94.1 percent of the time on yea-or-nay votes, only slightly below the 95.5 percent scored in 1998. Yet the House took 600 yea-or-nay votes in 2000, significantly more than the 533 held in 1998. The 1998 session lasted until Dec. 19 in the House because of the impeachment of President Clinton. In 2000, the House adjourned on Dec. 15, although members took a one-week break for the elections.

Senators maintained a voting participation record of 96.9 percent in 2000, compared with 97.4 percent in 1998. The Senate took 298 yea-or-nay votes in 2000; 314 in 1998. The chamber adjourned Dec. 15, 2000, far later than the Oct. 21 date recorded in 1998.

Participation as a Campaign Issue

Even those in competitive races managed to maintain high participa-

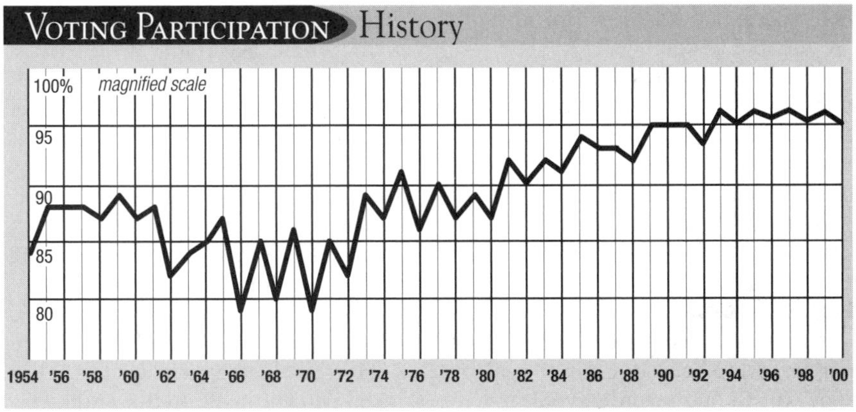

Definition

How often individual members voted "yea" or "nay" on roll call votes on the floor of the House or Senate.

2000 Data

	Recorded Votes	Percentage
Senate	298	96.9%
House	600	94.1%
Total Congress	898	94.4%

For More Information

Senators' scores....................p. B-23
House members' scores.......p. B-24

tion scores. Voting participation has become a campaign issue because members often fear their opponents will charge them with failing to fulfill their duties in their pursuit of higher office or re-election.

In 1998, Republican Alfonse M. D'Amato criticized his opponent in the New York Senate race — then-Rep. Charles E. Schumer — for missing roll call votes in the House in order to campaign for the Senate. Schumer won anyway, but incumbents take the prospect of such a challenge seriously. Of those who won their races with less than 55 percent of the vote in the November 2000 elections, the average participation score was 91 percent. For House members in competitive races, the average was 90 percent, only four percentage points lower than the overall rate. The lowest voting participation scores among House members in competitive races came not from those seeking re-election to their own seats but from members running for the offices of senator or governor.

In the 2000 New York Senate race, Republican Rep. Rick A. Lazio had only a 67 percent voting participation rate, but his Democratic opponent, Hillary Rodham Clinton, did not make Lazio's voting record an issue.

Lott's Promise

Senate Majority Leader Trent Lott, R-Miss., promised early last fall that if the session dragged into October and the campaign season, he would schedule floor action to allow vulnerable Republican incumbents to both cast votes and campaign at home. While the Senate incumbents fared poorly in the election, they did maintain high voting percentages. Spencer Abraham, R-Mich., who was locked in a tightly contested race for most of the fall, had a perfect voting record. His Democratic challenger, Rep. Debbie Stabenow, who ousted Abraham, maintained a participation rate of 97 percent.

Geographic distance did not make a big difference for those who needed to spend significant time campaigning. Slade Gorton, R-Wash., who tried unsuccessfully to defend his Senate seat, maintained a 93 percent score despite the long trip to his home state. Conrad Burns, R-Mont., had a 94 percent rate; Rod Grams, R-Minn., 91 percent; John Ashcroft, R-Mo., 96 percent; William V. Roth Jr., R-Del., 90 percent; Charles S. Robb, D-Va., 99 percent; Rick Santorum, R-Pa., 99 percent.

The two senators with the lowest scores were campaigners of another sort. John McCain, R-Ariz., had an overall voting participation record of 78 percent. He did not make any of the first 40 Senate votes before he withdrew from his race for the GOP presidential nomination on March 9. Of the 258 after that date, he voted on 232, a 90 percent rate. His voting participation score in 1999, the year he began his presidential effort, was 64 percent, a career low. In prior years, he maintained voting records of above 90 percent.

The only other senator to drop below 80 percent was Joseph I. Lieberman of Connecticut, the Democratic vice presidential nominee. In his 1988 contest to become senator, Lieberman repeatedly cited the low voting participation record of his Republican opponent, incumbent Lowell P. Weicker Jr. Weicker had accepted more than $200,000 in honoraria for speaking engagements while missing important roll call votes over the course of his term.

Before the congressional recess in August, and before he became actively involved in the presidential campaign, Lieberman voted 231 times — a 100 percent voting record. But after the recess, his record was dismal: He voted on only 4 of the 67 votes, a 3 percent rate. His overall voting participation score was 79 percent.

Throughout his Senate career, Lieberman maintained participation rates of at least 99 percent, except in 1994, the year he defended his Senate seat, when he voted on 97 percent of the roll call votes. By comparison, Vice President Al Gore had a 56 percent score as a senator in 1992 while he campaigned for the Clinton-Gore presidential ticket.

Retiring members did not take the opportunity to skip out on votes. In the House, those retiring and not running for other offices maintained an overall voting participation score of 90 percent, while their counterparts in the Senate had a score of 97 percent.

Perfect Scores

Six House members had perfect participation scores, voting "yea" or "nay" on all 600 recorded votes in the House. They were David Dreir, R-Calif; Bill Luther, D-Minn.; Jerry Moran, R-Kan.; Joe Skeen, R-N.M.; James A. Traficant Jr., D-Ohio; and Fred Upton, R-Mich. Moran has maintained a 100 percent voting participation score since 1997; Upton has held his perfect score three years in a row.

Jesse L. Jackson Jr., D-Ill., had maintained a perfect voting record since taking office in December 1995, casting a "yea" or "nay" on every recorded vote. However, on Sept. 13, 2000, he voted "present" on roll call vote 468, a resolution to revoke the federal charter of the Boy Scouts of America.

The resolution, sponsored by Lynn Woolsey, D-Calif., was brought up under suspension of the rules, which limits debate and bars amendments. Democrats charged the move was politically motivated to embarrass Woolsey. Jackson joined 49 other Democrats in voting "present" as a protest. He voted "yea" or "nay" on every other recorded vote in 2000 and had a voting participation score of 99 percent.

Eighteen senators, including several up for re-election, maintained perfect participation scores. The 18 were: Abraham; Wayne Allard, R-Colo.; Evan Bayh, D-Ind.; Robert C. Byrd, D-W.Va.; Lincoln Chafee, R-R.I.; Susan Collins, R-Maine; Mike DeWine, R-Ohio; John Edwards, D-N.C.; Russell Feingold, D-Wis.; Bob Graham, D-Fla.; Phil Gramm, R-Texas; Charles E. Grassley, R-Iowa; Carl Levin, D-Mich.; Zell Miller, D-Ga.; Pat Roberts, R-Kan.; Paul S. Sarbanes, D-Md.; Richard C. Shelby, R-Ala.; and Robert C. Smith, R-N.H. Abraham had not missed a vote during his entire term.

Grassley kept a perfect participation score for the seventh consecutive year. Grassley's streak, the longest active run in the Senate, began July 20, 1993, and now stands at 2,731 consecutive votes. Miller, who was sworn in July 27 after the death of Paul Coverdell, R-Ga., was eligible for 69 votes and maintained a voting participation score of 100 percent. Coverdell was eligible for 215 votes and had a 91 percent score before his death on July 18.

The only senators to fall below 80 percent were McCain and Lieberman.

Thirteen House members fell below the 80 percent mark. In descending order, they were: retiring Missouri Democrats Pat Danner and William L. Clay, both 75 percent; Matthew G. Martinez, R-Calif., who switched parties after losing the Democratic primary in March to Hilda Solis, 73 percent; Lazio, 67 percent; losing incumbent Merrill Cook, R-Utah, Senate candidate Bob Franks, R-N.J., and gubernatorial candidate Bob Wise, D-W.Va., all 66 percent; Senate candidate Ron Klink, D-Pa., 57 percent; Senate candidate Bill McCollum, R-Fla., 48 percent; Senate candidate Tom Campbell, R-Calif., 43 percent; David M. McIntosh, R-Ind., 39 percent; and Bruce F. Vento, D-Minn., who underwent treatment for cancer and died Oct. 10, 24 percent.

J. Dennis Hastert, R-Ill., cast 110 votes, a participation score of 18 percent. The score is consistent with past years. Historically, the Speaker votes only on symbolic issues or issues of critical importance to his party. ◆

Guide to CQ's Voting Analyses

Since 1945, Congressional Quarterly has analyzed the voting behavior of members of Congress. These studies have become references for academics, journalists, politicians and students who want information on how Congress behaves as an institution and how individual members vote.

What votes are used: CQ bases its vote studies on all roll call votes on which members were asked to vote "yea" or "nay." In 2000 there were 298 such votes in the Senate and 600 in the House. The CQ study excludes quorum calls, which require only that members vote "present." There were three quorum calls in the House in 2000, for a total of 603 roll calls.

The totals used by CQ do include votes in the House to approve the Journal (26 in 2000) and in the Senate to instruct the sergeant at arms to request members' presence in the chamber (two in 2000).

The studies on presidential support and party unity cover specific votes selected from the total according to the criteria described on pp. B-12 and B-18.

Individual scores: In the charts that follow, a member's scores are calculated based only on the votes he or she actually cast. The same method is used for leading scorers on pp. B-5 and B-8.

Overall scores: For consistency with previous years, graphs and breakdowns of chambers, parties and regions are based on all yea-or-nay votes. In those cases, absences lower scores. *(Methodology, 1987 Almanac, p. 22-C)*

Rounding: Scores are rounded to the nearest percentage point, except that rounding is not used to bring any score up to 100 percent.

Regions: Congressional Quarterly defines regions of the United States as follows: **East:** Conn., Del., Maine, Md., Mass., N.H., N.J., N.Y., Pa., R.I., Vt., W.Va. **West:** Alaska, Ariz., Calif., Colo., Hawaii, Idaho, Mont., Nev., N.M., Ore., Utah, Wash., Wyo. **South:** Ala., Ark., Fla., Ga., Ky., La., Miss., N.C., Okla., S.C., Tenn., Texas, Va. **Midwest:** Ill., Ind., Iowa, Kan., Mich., Minn., Mo., Neb., N.D., Ohio, S.D., Wis.

References to Northern Democrats and Northern Republicans include all members who do not represent the 13 Southern states, as defined by CQ.

Presidential Support Background

Presidential support votes. Congressional Quarterly selects roll call votes for this study based on statements made by the president or his authorized spokesmen.

Support shows the percentage of the time members voted in agreement with the president on these votes. **Opposition** shows the percentage of the time members voted against the president's position.

Success is the percentage of votes selected for the study on which the president prevailed. Absences lowered parties' scores. Scores for 1999 are given for comparison.

Success Scores by Issue

Following are presidential success scores by category. "Economic affairs" includes votes on trade and on omnibus and supplemental spending bills, which may fund both domestic and defense/foreign policy programs.

	Defense/Foreign Policy		Domestic		Economic Affairs		Average	
	2000	1999	2000	1999	2000	1999	2000	1999
Senate	67%	33%	33%	44%	40%	43%	65%	42%
House	40	50	49	22	55	56	49	35
Average	**46**	**46**	**44**	**31**	**52**	**52**	**55**	**38**

Average Party Scores

Support

	Republicans		Democrats	
	2000	1999	2000	1999
Senate	46%	34%	89%	84%
House	27	23	73	73

Opposition

	Republicans		Democrats	
	2000	1999	2000	1999
Senate	52%	64%	8%	14%
House	69	74	23	24

Regional Averages *

Support

	East		West		South		Midwest	
	2000	1999	2000	1999	2000	1999	2000	1999
Republicans								
Senate	57%	48%	45%	30%	42%	29%	48%	36%
House	37	32	25	22	23	20	28	24
Democrats								
Senate	89	85	88	84	87	83	90	84
House	78	76	77	78	67	68	69	72

Opposition

	East		West		South		Midwest	
	2000	1999	2000	1999	2000	1999	2000	1999
Republicans								
Senate	41%	51%	52%	66%	57%	69%	52%	63%
House	58	65	70	75	73	77	69	74
Democrats								
Senate	6	13	6	14	12	16	9	16
House	18	21	19	19	31	29	25	26

Success-Rate History

Average score for both chambers of Congress:

Eisenhower	
1953	89.0%
1954	82.8
1955	75.0
1956	70.0
1957	68.0
1958	76.0
1959	52.0
1960	65.0
Kennedy	
1961	81.0%
1962	85.4
1963	87.1
Johnson	
1964	88.0%
1965	93.0
1966	79.0
1967	79.0
1968	75.0
Nixon	
1969	74.0%
1970	77.0
1971	75.0
1972	66.0
1973	50.6
1974	59.6
Ford	
1974	58.2%
1975	61.0
1976	53.8
Carter	
1977	75.4%
1978	78.3
1979	76.8
1980	75.1
Reagan	
1981	82.4%
1982	72.4
1983	67.1
1984	65.8
1985	59.9
1986	56.1
1987	43.5
1988	47.4
Bush	
1989	62.6%
1990	46.8
1991	54.2
1992	43.0
Clinton	
1993	86.4%
1994	86.4
1995	36.2
1996	55.1
1997	53.6
1998	50.6
1999	37.8
2000	55.0

* **Regions:** Congressional Quarterly defines regions of the United States as follows: **East:** Conn., Del., Maine, Md., Mass., N.H., N.J., N.Y., Pa., R.I., Vt., W.Va. **West:** Alaska, Ariz., Calif., Colo., Hawaii, Idaho, Mont., Nev., N.M., Ore., Utah, Wash., Wyo. **South:** Ala., Ark., Fla., Ga., Ky., La., Miss., N.C., Okla., S.C., Tenn., Texas, Va. **Midwest:** Ill., Ind., Iowa, Kan., Mich., Minn., Mo., Neb., N.D., Ohio, S.D., Wis.

2000 House Presidential Position Votes

The following is a list of House votes in 2000 on which there was a clear presidential position. Votes are categorized by topic and listed by roll-call number with a brief description.

Domestic Policy

18 Victories

Vote Number	Description
27	Social Security
43	Minimum wage
139	Labor
267	OSHA
279	Environment
280	Environment
281	Environment
302	Space station
319	Tobacco
324	Guns
373	Abortion
404	Internet
427	Guns
430	Community renewal
471	Hate crimes
491	Crime
503	Privacy
518	Crime

19 Defeats

Vote Number	Description
7	Product liability
25	Product liability
55	Property rights
63	Nuclear waste
98	Organ procurement
101	Organ procurement
104	Abortion
130	Religious expression
250	OSHA
274	Environment
288	Environment
293	Tobacco
304	Environment
305	Environment
357	Prescription drugs
412	Pensions
422	Abortion
423	Federal contracts
473	Needle exchange

Defense and Foreign Policy

4 Victories

Vote Number	Description
84	Colombia
86	Colombia
89	Kosovo
202	Vieques

6 Defeats

Vote Number	Description
5	Taiwan
65	OPEC
85	Defense spending
193	Kosovo
396	Family planning
414	Russia

Economic Affairs and Trade

12 Victories

Vote Number	Description
82	Supplemental appropriations
119	Taxes
145	Africa/Caribbean trade
187	Government shutdowns
228	China trade status
310	WTO
405	China trade status
441	Vietnam trade status
458	Taxes
466	Taxes (veto override)
467	Trade
540	Commodities law

10 Defeats

Vote Number	Description
15	Taxes
41	Taxes
127	Taxes
156	Internet taxes
254	Taxes
392	Taxes
418	Taxes
450	Taxes
523	Appropriations (veto override)
560	Taxes

House Success Score

Victories	34
Defeats	35
Total	**69**
Success rate	49.3%

Presidential Support and Opposition: House

1. Presidential Support Score. Percentage of recorded votes cast in 2000 on which President Clinton took a position and on which the member voted "yea" or "nay" in agreement with the president's position. Failure to vote did not lower an individual's score.

2. Presidential Opposition Score. Percentage of recorded votes cast in 2000 on which President Clinton took a position and on which a member voted "yea" or "nay" in disagreement with the president's position. Failure to vote did not lower an individual's score.

3. Participation in Presidential Support Votes. Percentage of the 69 recorded House votes on which President Clinton took a position and on which a member was present and voted "yea" or "nay."

[1] *Julian C. Dixon, D-Calif., died Dec. 8. He was eligible for 69 presidential support votes in 2000.*

[2] *J. Dennis Hastert, R-Ill., as Speaker of the House, voted on 25 presidential support votes at his discretion in 2000.*

[3] *Bruce F. Vento, D-Minn., died Oct. 10. He was eligible for 66 presidential support votes in 2000.*

[4] *Herbert H. Bateman, R-Va., died Sept. 11. He was eligible for 59 presidential support votes in 2000.*

Key

Democrats ***Republicans***
Independents

	1	2	3
ALABAMA			
1 ***Callahan***	28	72	93
2 ***Everett***	14	86	84
3 ***Riley***	19	81	97
4 ***Aderholt***	20	80	100
5 Cramer	49	51	99
6 ***Bachus***	24	76	97
7 Hilliard	78	22	97
ALASKA			
AL ***Young***	21	79	91
ARIZONA			
1 ***Salmon***	25	75	94
2 Pastor	81	19	100
3 ***Stump***	25	75	100
4 ***Shadegg***	22	78	99
5 ***Kolbe***	39	61	97
6 ***Hayworth***	20	80	96
ARKANSAS			
1 Berry	55	45	100
2 Snyder	90	10	99
3 ***Hutchinson***	24	76	97
4 ***Dickey***	25	75	100
CALIFORNIA			
1 Thompson	81	19	100
2 ***Herger***	21	79	97
3 ***Ose***	33	67	100
4 ***Doolittle***	23	77	100
5 Matsui	91	9	99
6 Woolsey	79	21	99
7 Miller	76	24	97
8 Pelosi	79	21	99
9 Lee	82	18	99
10 Tauscher	78	22	100
11 ***Pombo***	19	81	100
12 Lantos	87	13	100
13 Stark	81	19	93
14 Eshoo	82	18	90
15 ***Campbell***	36	64	41
16 Lofgren	82	18	90
17 Farr	82	18	99
18 Condit	58	42	100
19 ***Radanovich***	22	78	94
20 Dooley	71	29	100
21 ***Thomas***	32	68	100
22 Capps	73	27	97
23 ***Gallegly***	35	65	99
24 Sherman	83	17	100
25 ***McKeon***	30	70	100
26 Berman	94	6	91
27 ***Rogan***	23	77	96
28 ***Dreier***	30	70	100
29 Waxman	87	13	91
30 Becerra	92	8	91
31 ***Martinez***	37	63	78
32 Dixon[1]	91	9	97
33 Roybal-Allard	90	10	91
34 Napolitano	94	6	99
35 Waters	85	15	94
36 ***Kuykendall***	46	54	94
37 Millender-McD.	91	9	96
38 ***Horn***	46	54	99
39 ***Royce***	25	75	97
40 ***Lewis***	36	64	97
41 ***Miller***	25	75	94
42 Baca	75	25	91
43 ***Calvert***	31	69	99
44 ***Bono***	30	70	100
45 ***Rohrabacher***	16	84	100
46 Sanchez	75	25	88
47 ***Cox***	19	81	97
48 ***Packard***	28	72	97
49 ***Bilbray***	38	62	99
50 Filner	88	12	94
51 ***Cunningham***	26	74	99
52 ***Hunter***	19	81	97
COLORADO			
1 DeGette	88	12	99
2 Udall	77	23	100
3 ***McInnis***	25	75	93
4 ***Schaffer***	20	80	96
5 ***Hefley***	15	85	99
6 ***Tancredo***	17	83	100
CONNECTICUT			
1 Larson	85	15	99
2 Gejdenson	84	16	100
3 DeLauro	87	13	100
4 ***Shays***	49	51	97
5 Maloney	62	38	99
6 ***Johnson***	51	49	100
DELAWARE			
AL ***Castle***	49	51	100
FLORIDA			
1 ***Scarborough***	26	74	94
2 Boyd	57	43	99
3 Brown	82	18	94
4 ***Fowler***	26	74	94
5 Thurman	78	22	100
6 ***Stearns***	17	83	100
7 ***Mica***	19	81	97
8 ***McCollum***	33	67	62
9 ***Bilirakis***	24	76	96
10 ***Young***	33	67	88
11 Davis	82	18	99
12 ***Canady***	22	78	97
13 ***Miller***	29	71	96
14 ***Goss***	26	74	99
15 ***Weldon***	19	81	99
16 ***Foley***	39	61	100
17 Meek	77	23	96
18 ***Ros-Lehtinen***	30	70	97
19 Wexler	79	21	97
20 Deutsch	71	29	100
21 ***Diaz-Balart***	35	65	94
22 ***Shaw***	31	69	97
23 Hastings	82	18	94
GEORGIA			
1 ***Kingston***	17	83	100
2 Bishop	55	45	96
3 ***Collins***	19	81	99
4 McKinney	72	28	99
5 Lewis	80	20	96
6 ***Isakson***	30	70	97
7 ***Barr***	18	82	99
8 ***Chambliss***	24	76	97
9 ***Deal***	15	85	97
10 ***Norwood***	17	83	94
11 ***Linder***	22	78	99
HAWAII			
1 Abercrombie	72	28	97
2 Mink	67	33	100
IDAHO			
1 ***Chenoweth-Hage***	20	80	87
2 ***Simpson***	29	71	100
ILLINOIS			
1 Rush	91	9	84
2 Jackson	83	17	100
3 Lipinski	52	48	90
4 Gutierrez	84	16	88
5 Blagojevich	74	26	94
6 ***Hyde***	35	65	99
7 Davis	88	12	97
8 ***Crane***	24	76	84
9 Schakowsky	85	15	96
10 ***Porter***	54	46	100
11 ***Weller***	41	59	96
12 Costello	52	48	97

ND Northern Democrats SD Southern Democrats

	1	2	3
13 ***Biggert***	43	57	99
14 ***Hastert*** [2]	28	72	36
15 ***Ewing***	28	72	94
16 ***Manzullo***	22	78	99
17 Evans	76	24	99
18 ***LaHood***	32	68	100
19 Phelps	43	57	100
20 ***Shimkus***	29	71	100
INDIANA			
1 Visclosky	75	25	100
2 ***McIntosh***	21	79	61
3 Roemer	52	48	94
4 ***Souder***	19	81	100
5 ***Buyer***	22	78	100
6 ***Burton***	17	83	94
7 ***Pease***	23	77	100
8 ***Hostettler***	17	83	100
9 Hill	76	24	96
10 Carson	84	16	90
IOWA			
1 ***Leach***	45	55	96
2 ***Nussle***	25	75	99
3 Boswell	60	40	94
4 ***Ganske***	39	61	97
5 ***Latham***	26	74	100
KANSAS			
1 ***Moran***	25	75	100
2 ***Ryun***	25	75	99
3 Moore	68	32	100
4 ***Tiahrt***	24	76	99
KENTUCKY			
1 ***Whitfield***	29	71	96
2 ***Lewis***	25	75	100
3 ***Northup***	32	68	99
4 Lucas	41	59	99
5 ***Rogers***	23	77	100
6 ***Fletcher***	22	78	99
LOUISIANA			
1 ***Vitter***	25	75	100
2 Jefferson	80	20	93
3 ***Tauzin***	26	74	96
4 ***McCrery***	27	73	97
5 ***Cooksey***	33	67	84
6 ***Baker***	26	74	94
7 John	49	51	100
MAINE			
1 Allen	84	16	100
2 Baldacci	79	21	96
MARYLAND			
1 ***Gilchrest***	50	50	93
2 ***Ehrlich***	29	71	99
3 Cardin	94	6	100
4 Wynn	84	16	93
5 Hoyer	90	10	100
6 ***Bartlett***	17	83	100
7 Cummings	88	12	97
8 ***Morella***	63	37	99
MASSACHUSETTS			
1 Olver	83	17	100
2 Neal	83	17	96
3 McGovern	86	14	100
4 Frank	84	16	99
5 Meehan	81	19	97
6 Tierney	81	19	99
7 Markey	88	12	93
8 Capuano	87	13	99
9 Moakley	81	19	99
10 Delahunt	80	20	94
MICHIGAN			
1 Stupak	67	33	96
2 ***Hoekstra***	23	77	100
3 ***Ehlers***	38	62	100
4 ***Camp***	24	76	99
5 Barcia	39	61	100
6 ***Upton***	39	61	100
7 ***Smith***	24	76	96
8 Stabenow	74	26	100
9 Kildee	72	28	100
10 Bonior	80	20	100
11 ***Knollenberg***	32	68	99
12 Levin	90	10	100
13 Rivers	73	27	96
14 Conyers	85	15	96
15 Kilpatrick	83	17	93
16 Dingell	81	19	99

	1	2	3
MINNESOTA			
1 ***Gutknecht***	24	76	99
2 Minge	75	25	100
3 ***Ramstad***	41	59	100
4 Vento [3]	73	27	17
5 Sabo	90	10	100
6 Luther	75	25	100
7 Peterson	49	51	100
8 Oberstar	80	20	96
MISSISSIPPI			
1 ***Wicker***	22	78	100
2 Thompson	77	23	93
3 ***Pickering***	25	75	100
4 Shows	34	66	94
5 Taylor	40	60	97
MISSOURI			
1 Clay	87	13	80
2 ***Talent***	23	77	94
3 Gephardt	83	17	96
4 Skelton	61	39	97
5 McCarthy	87	13	99
6 Danner	35	65	83
7 ***Blunt***	25	75	100
8 ***Emerson***	24	76	97
9 ***Hulshof***	19	81	99
MONTANA			
AL ***Hill***	22	78	100
NEBRASKA			
1 ***Bereuter***	32	68	99
2 ***Terry***	25	75	100
3 ***Barrett***	29	71	99
NEVADA			
1 Berkley	63	37	99
2 ***Gibbons***	29	71	100
NEW HAMPSHIRE			
1 ***Sununu***	28	72	100
2 ***Bass***	34	66	99
NEW JERSEY			
1 Andrews	75	25	99
2 ***LoBiondo***	35	65	100
3 ***Saxton***	40	60	99
4 ***Smith***	42	58	100
5 ***Roukema***	44	56	99
6 Pallone	77	23	96
7 ***Franks***	42	58	75
8 Pascrell	66	34	97
9 Rothman	80	20	94
10 Payne	86	14	93
11 ***Frelinghuysen***	48	52	100
12 Holt	67	33	100
13 Menendez	78	22	99
NEW MEXICO			
1 ***Wilson***	33	67	100
2 ***Skeen***	29	71	100
3 Udall	77	23	96
NEW YORK			
1 Forbes	53	47	93
2 ***Lazio***	48	52	75
3 ***King***	45	55	97
4 McCarthy	68	32	100
5 Ackerman	94	6	90
6 Meeks	92	8	96
7 Crowley	82	18	97
8 Nadler	84	16	97
9 Weiner	90	10	99
10 Towns	89	11	91
11 Owens	88	12	87
12 Velázquez	85	15	94
13 ***Fossella***	26	74	99
14 Maloney	82	18	99
15 Rangel	97	3	84
16 Serrano	90	10	88
17 Engel	87	13	91
18 Lowey	91	9	94
19 ***Kelly***	46	54	100
20 ***Gilman***	58	42	90
21 McNulty	75	25	93
22 ***Sweeney***	32	68	100
23 ***Boehlert***	61	39	100
24 ***McHugh***	34	66	99
25 ***Walsh***	43	57	100
26 Hinchey	94	6	97
27 ***Reynolds***	25	75	97
28 Slaughter	87	13	99
29 LaFalce	84	16	97

	1	2	3
30 ***Quinn***	43	57	87
31 ***Houghton***	55	45	94
NORTH CAROLINA			
1 Clayton	79	21	97
2 Etheridge	65	35	100
3 ***Jones***	19	81	100
4 Price	80	20	100
5 ***Burr***	22	78	97
6 ***Coble***	21	79	99
7 McIntyre	40	60	99
8 ***Hayes***	19	81	99
9 ***Myrick***	26	74	83
10 ***Ballenger***	23	77	96
11 ***Taylor***	21	79	97
12 Watt	82	18	96
NORTH DAKOTA			
AL Pomeroy	85	15	97
OHIO			
1 ***Chabot***	21	79	99
2 ***Portman***	31	69	97
3 Hall	70	30	96
4 ***Oxley***	30	70	96
5 ***Gillmor***	32	68	94
6 Strickland	67	33	97
7 ***Hobson***	33	67	100
8 ***Boehner***	30	70	97
9 Kaptur	73	27	93
10 Kucinich	76	24	96
11 Jones	89	11	90
12 ***Kasich***	30	70	97
13 Brown	81	19	91
14 Sawyer	93	7	100
15 ***Pryce***	35	65	99
16 ***Regula***	36	64	100
17 Traficant	32	68	100
18 ***Ney***	29	71	99
19 ***LaTourette***	35	65	96
OKLAHOMA			
1 ***Largent***	23	77	94
2 ***Coburn***	23	77	90
3 ***Watkins***	28	72	97
4 ***Watts***	25	75	99
5 ***Istook***	25	75	93
6 ***Lucas***	22	78	94
OREGON			
1 Wu	67	33	100
2 ***Walden***	25	75	100
3 Blumenauer	88	12	96
4 DeFazio	67	33	97
5 Hooley	67	33	97
PENNSYLVANIA			
1 Brady	86	14	94
2 Fattah	94	6	90
3 Borski	84	16	97
4 Klink	72	28	68
5 ***Peterson***	27	73	97
6 Holden	68	32	100
7 ***Weldon***	33	67	100
8 ***Greenwood***	54	46	83
9 ***Shuster***	25	75	86
10 ***Sherwood***	38	62	99
11 Kanjorski	80	20	100
12 Murtha	74	26	99
13 Hoeffel	87	13	99
14 Coyne	85	15	99
15 ***Toomey***	29	71	99
16 ***Pitts***	19	81	99
17 ***Gekas***	28	72	97
18 Doyle	70	30	97
19 ***Goodling***	21	79	96
20 Mascara	65	35	100
21 ***English***	38	62	100
RHODE ISLAND			
1 Kennedy	81	19	99
2 Weygand	77	23	94
SOUTH CAROLINA			
1 ***Sanford***	26	74	96
2 ***Spence***	19	81	90
3 ***Graham***	17	83	96
4 ***DeMint***	22	78	94
5 Spratt	59	41	91
6 Clyburn	75	25	94
SOUTH DAKOTA			
AL ***Thune***	29	71	100

	1	2	3
TENNESSEE			
1 ***Jenkins***	22	78	94
2 ***Duncan***	12	88	99
3 ***Wamp***	19	81	97
4 ***Hilleary***	14	86	96
5 Clement	57	43	97
6 Gordon	50	50	99
7 ***Bryant***	24	76	99
8 Tanner	56	44	99
9 Ford	74	26	96
TEXAS			
1 Sandlin	57	43	99
2 Turner	68	32	96
3 ***Johnson, Sam***	25	75	99
4 Hall	22	78	100
5 ***Sessions***	26	74	99
6 ***Barton***	23	77	75
7 ***Archer***	29	71	96
8 ***Brady***	24	76	97
9 Lampson	69	31	99
10 Doggett	86	14	100
11 Edwards	78	22	99
12 ***Granger***	25	75	86
13 ***Thornberry***	25	75	100
14 ***Paul***	27	73	91
15 Hinojosa	88	12	87
16 Reyes	88	12	97
17 Stenholm	52	48	100
18 Jackson-Lee	88	12	93
19 ***Combest***	22	78	100
20 Gonzalez	88	12	100
21 ***Smith***	25	75	99
22 ***DeLay***	23	77	93
23 ***Bonilla***	30	70	100
24 Frost	81	19	99
25 Bentsen	86	14	100
26 ***Armey***	23	77	100
27 Ortiz	71	29	100
28 Rodriguez	84	16	99
29 Green	69	31	97
30 Johnson	88	12	94
UTAH			
1 ***Hansen***	25	75	94
2 ***Cook***	13	87	65
3 ***Cannon***	24	76	99
VERMONT			
AL *Sanders*	78	22	100
VIRGINIA			
1 ***Bateman*** [4]	27	73	100
2 Pickett	61	39	97
3 Scott	81	19	100
4 Sisisky	44	56	99
5 *Goode*	14	86	100
6 ***Goodlatte***	22	78	99
7 ***Bliley***	27	73	90
8 Moran	77	23	96
9 Boucher	61	39	97
10 ***Wolf***	30	70	100
11 ***Davis***	36	64	97
WASHINGTON			
1 Inslee	67	33	100
2 ***Metcalf***	20	80	94
3 Baird	75	25	99
4 ***Hastings***	23	77	100
5 ***Nethercutt***	25	75	100
6 Dicks	88	12	96
7 McDermott	94	6	94
8 ***Dunn***	28	72	99
9 Smith	78	22	72
WEST VIRGINIA			
1 Mollohan	69	31	97
2 Wise	66	34	84
3 Rahall	71	29	100
WISCONSIN			
1 ***Ryan***	22	78	100
2 Baldwin	78	22	100
3 Kind	81	19	99
4 Kleczka	78	22	100
5 Barrett	79	21	99
6 ***Petri***	32	68	100
7 Obey	82	18	99
8 ***Green***	22	78	100
9 ***Sensenbrenner***	20	80	100
WYOMING			
AL ***Cubin***	24	76	99

Southern states - Ala., Ark., Fla., Ga., Ky., La., Miss., N.C., Okla., S.C., Tenn., Texas, Va.

2000 Senate Presidential Position Votes

The following is a list of Senate votes in 2000 on which there was a clear presidential position. Votes are categorized by topic and listed by roll-call number with a brief description.

Domestic Policy

5 Victories

Vote Number	Description
42	Social Security
88	Nuclear waste (veto override)
136	Hate crimes
208	National monuments
269	Crime

10 Defeats

Vote Number	Description
8	Nuclear waste
33	Education
93	Education
143	Ergonomic standards
147	Education
148	Education
154	Education
167	Health care
175	Grazing
232	Environment

Defense and Foreign Policy

2 Victories

Vote Number	Description
105	Kosovo
139	Aid to Colombia

1 Defeat

Vote Number	Description
119	Nuclear weapons

Economic Affairs and Trade

2 Victories

Vote Number	Description
98	Sub-Saharan Africa, Caribbean trade
251	China trade

3 Defeats

Vote Number	Description
197	Taxes
215	Taxes
226	Taxes

Nominations

17 Victories

Vote Number	Description
6	Alan Greenspan
10	Thomas L. Ambro
11	Joel A. Pisano
13	Kermit Bye
14	George B. Daniels
34	Julio M. Fuentes
38	Marsha L. Berzon
40	Richard A. Paez
107	Bradley A. Smith
108	Danny Lee McDonald
109	Timothy B. Dyk
110	Gerard E. Lynch
111	James J. Brady
112	Mary A. McLaughlin
128	Gen. John A. Gordon
172	Madelyn R. Creedon
263	James A. Teilborg

0 Defeats

Senate Success Score

Victories	26
Defeats	14
Total	**40**
Success rate	65%

	1	2	3
ALABAMA			
Shelby	45	55	100
Sessions	42	58	100
ALASKA			
Stevens	56	44	98
Murkowski	45	55	95
ARIZONA			
McCain	38	62	73
Kyl	41	59	98
ARKANSAS			
Hutchinson	38	62	98
Lincoln	84	16	95
CALIFORNIA			
Feinstein	84	16	93
Boxer	92	8	93
COLORADO			
Campbell	50	50	95
Allard	35	65	100
CONNECTICUT			
Dodd	98	2	100
Lieberman	94	6	90
DELAWARE			
Roth	68	32	93
Biden	91	9	83
FLORIDA			
Graham	95	5	100
Mack	51	49	98
GEORGIA			
Miller [1]	100	0	100
Cleland	78	22	100
HAWAII			
Inouye	94	6	80
Akaka	97	3	93
IDAHO			
Craig	40	60	100
Crapo	41	59	98
ILLINOIS			
Durbin	97	3	98
Fitzgerald	51	49	98
INDIANA			
Lugar	65	35	100
Bayh	98	2	100
IOWA			
Grassley	42	58	100
Harkin	92	8	98
KANSAS			
Brownback	40	60	100
Roberts	38	62	100
KENTUCKY			
McConnell	42	58	100
Bunning	33	67	98
LOUISIANA			
Breaux	85	15	100
Landrieu	85	15	100
MAINE			
Snowe	62	38	100
Collins	58	42	100
MARYLAND			
Sarbanes	95	5	100
Mikulski	92	8	98
MASSACHUSETTS			
Kennedy	94	6	90
Kerry	97	3	93
MICHIGAN			
Levin	92	8	100
Abraham	50	50	100
MINNESOTA			
Wellstone	90	10	98
Grams	38	62	100
MISSISSIPPI			
Cochran	45	55	100
Lott	45	55	100
MISSOURI			
Bond	46	54	98
Ashcroft	45	55	100
MONTANA			
Baucus	97	3	95
Burns	51	49	98
NEBRASKA			
Kerrey	84	16	95
Hagel	49	51	98
NEVADA			
Reid	92	8	100
Bryan	100	0	98
NEW HAMPSHIRE			
Smith	28	72	100
Gregg	38	62	98
NEW JERSEY			
Lautenberg	98	2	100
Torricelli	87	13	98
NEW MEXICO			
Domenici	51	49	92
Bingaman	95	5	98
NEW YORK			
Moynihan	100	0	98
Schumer	98	2	100
NORTH CAROLINA			
Helms	31	69	98
Edwards	92	8	100
NORTH DAKOTA			
Conrad	90	10	100
Dorgan	90	10	100
OHIO			
DeWine	52	48	100
Voinovich	59	41	98
OKLAHOMA			
Nickles	40	60	100
Inhofe	30	70	93
OREGON			
Wyden	95	5	100
Smith	62	38	100
PENNSYLVANIA			
Specter	59	41	98
Santorum	49	51	98
RHODE ISLAND			
Reed	95	5	95
Chafee, L.	88	12	100
SOUTH CAROLINA			
Thurmond	45	55	100
Hollings	82	18	100
SOUTH DAKOTA			
Daschle	95	5	98
Johnson	98	2	100
TENNESSEE			
Thompson	50	50	100
Frist	50	50	100
TEXAS			
Gramm	35	65	100
Hutchison	45	55	100
UTAH			
Hatch	55	45	100
Bennett	52	48	100
VERMONT			
Leahy	89	11	95
Jeffords	75	25	100
VIRGINIA			
Warner	52	48	100
Robb	90	10	100
WASHINGTON			
Gorton	48	52	100
Murray	87	13	98
WEST VIRGINIA			
Byrd	75	25	100
Rockefeller	97	3	98
WISCONSIN			
Kohl	79	21	98
Feingold	90	10	100
WYOMING			
Thomas	40	60	100
Enzi	35	65	100

ND Northern Democrats SD Southern Democrats

Southern states - Ala., Ark., Fla., Ga., Ky., La., Miss., N.C., Okla., S.C., Tenn., Texas, Va.

Key

Democrats ***Republicans***
Independents

Presidential Support and Opposition: Senate

1. Presidential Support Score. Percentage of recorded votes cast in 2000 on which President Clinton took a position and on which the senator voted "yea" or "nay" in agreement with the president's position. Failure to vote did not lower an individual's score.

2. Presidential Opposition Score. Percentage of recorded votes cast in 2000 on which President Clinton took a position and on which the senator voted "yea" or "nay" in disagreement with the president's position. Failure to vote did not lower an individual's score.

3. Participation in Presidential Support Votes. Percentage of the 40 recorded Senate votes in 2000 on which President Clinton took a position and on which the senator was present and voted "yea" or "nay."

[1] Zell Miller, D-Ga., was sworn in on July 27, replacing Paul Coverdell, R-Ga.,who died July 18. Miller was eligible for four presidential support votes in 2000. Coverdell was eligible for 35 presidential support votes; his presidential support score was 41 percent.

Party Unity Background

Party unity votes. Votes used for this study are those on which a majority of voting Democrats opposed a majority of voting Republicans.

Support is the percentage of the time that a member voted *in agreement* with a majority of his or her party on party unity votes. **Opposition** is the percentage of the time a member voted *against* a majority of his or her party on party unity votes.

Averages below show the average of members' scores by party, chamber and region.

(Party switchers are accounted for; failure to vote lowered support and opposition scores for chambers and parties.)

Average Scores by Chamber

	Republicans		Democrats	
	2000	1999	2000	1999
Support				
Senate	89%	88%	88%	89%
House	88	86	82	83

	Republicans		Democrats	
	2000	1999	2000	1999
Opposition				
Senate	9%	10%	10%	9%
House	10	12	13	14

Sectional Support, Opposition *

Senate	Support	Opposition
Northern Republicans	87%	12%
Southern Republicans	95	3
Northern Democrats	90	7
Southern Democrats	79	20

House	Support	Opposition
Northern Republicans	86%	11%
Southern Republicans	89	7
Northern Democrats	84	10
Southern Democrats	77	19

*Southern Democrats and Republicans are those from Ala., Ark., Fla., Ga., Ky., La., Miss., N.C., Okla., S.C., Tenn., Texas, Va. All others are considered Northern.

2000 Victories

	Senate	House	Total
Republicans won	114	182	296
Democrats won	31	77	108

Unanimous Voting by Parties

The number of times each party voted unanimously on party unity votes:

	Senate		House		Total	
	2000	1999	2000	1999	2000	1999
Republicans voted unanimously	19	63	67	59	86	122
Democrats voted unanimously	52	100	1	11	53	111

Party Unity Average Scores

Average score for each party in both chambers of Congress:

Year	Republicans	Democrats
1965	70%	69%
1966	67	61
1967	71	66
1968	63	57
1969	62	62
1970	59	57
1971	66	62
1972	64	57
1973	68	68
1974	62	63
1975	70	69
1976	66	65
1977	70	67
1978	67	64
1979	72	69
1980	70	68
1981	76	69
1982	71	72

Year	Republicans	Democrats
1983	74%	76%
1984	72	74
1985	75	79
1986	71	78
1987	74	81
1988	73	79
1989	73	81
1990	74	81
1991	78	81
1992	79	79
1993	84	85
1994	83	83
1995	91	80
1996	87	80
1997	88	82
1998	86	83
1999	86	84
2000	87	83

2000 Party Unity Votes

Following are the votes, by roll call number, on which a majority of Democrats voted against a majority of Republicans.

House

(259 of 600 "yea/nay" votes)

6	52	89	144	185	228	265	290	317	354	399	447	503	559
7	53	93	146	186	229	267	291	318	355	400	448	510	560
12	54	94	154	187	232	269	292	319	356	404	449	515	562
13	55	98	156	188	238	272	293	321	357	408	450	519	573
14	59	100	157	189	239	273	294	323	358	410	455	524	576
15	60	101	158	190	240	274	295	324	364	411	456	528	579
23	61	102	161	191	247	276	299	326	365	414	458	529	582
24	62	103	163	192	248	277	300	335	369	415	466	537	588
25	63	104	164	193	249	278	304	336	371	417	470	538	590
38	64	108	165	197	250	279	305	340	373	418	471	539	591
39	67	109	167	200	252	280	306	343	382	422	472	541	595
40	68	114	168	201	253	281	307	344	384	423	473	543	596
41	69	119	169	202	254	282	308	345	390	424	474	545	
42	72	124	170	203	255	283	309	346	391	425	476	548	
43	74	125	171	204	256	284	311	347	392	427	480	551	
44	75	126	172	209	260	286	312	348	394	428	481	555	
45	81	127	174	214	261	287	314	349	396	433	484	556	
50	84	129	175	225	262	288	315	350	397	442	494	557	
51	88	130	177	227	263	289	316	351	398	446	500	558	

Senate

(145 of 298 "yea/nay" votes)

1	25	46	68	79	93	121	146	164	180	193	205	226	296
3	27	48	69	80	100	122	147	165	182	195	206	232	297
4	28	52	70	82	101	125	148	166	183	196	207	253	
8	29	54	71	83	102	130	153	167	184	197	208	257	
15	30	55	72	84	103	134	154	168	186	198	210	261	
17	33	57	73	85	104	135	155	169	187	199	214	270	
19	38	58	74	87	105	136	156	170	188	200	215	271	
21	39	62	75	88	107	137	157	171	189	201	218	281	
22	40	64	76	90	110	140	159	172	190	202	220	286	
23	41	65	77	91	118	143	162	175	191	203	221	289	
24	45	67	78	92	119	144	163	178	192	204	224	294	

Proportion of Partisan Roll Calls

How often a majority of Democrats voted against a majority of Republicans:

Year	House	Senate	Year	House	Senate	Year	House	Senate	Year	House	Senate
1957	59%	36%	1968	35%	32%	1979	47%	47%	1990	49%	54%
1958	40	44	1969	31	36	1980	38	46	1991	55	49
1959	55	48	1970	27	35	1981	37	48	1992	64	53
1960	53	37	1971	38	42	1982	36	43	1993	65	67
1961	50	62	1972	27	36	1983	56	44	1994	62	52
1962	46	41	1973	42	40	1984	47	40	1995	73	69
1963	49	47	1974	29	44	1985	61	50	1996	56	62
1964	55	36	1975	48	48	1986	57	52	1997	50	50
1965	52	42	1976	36	37	1987	64	41	1998	56	56
1966	41	50	1977	42	42	1988	47	42	1999	47	63
1967	36	35	1978	33	45	1989	55	35	2000	43	49

Party Unity and Party Opposition: House

1. Party Unity. Percentage of recorded party unity votes in 2000 on which a member voted "yea" or "nay" in agreement with a majority of his or her party. (Party unity roll calls are those on which a majority of voting Democrats opposed a majority of voting Republicans.) Percentages are based on votes cast; thus, failure to vote did not lower a member's score.

2. Party Opposition. Percentage of recorded party unity votes in 2000 on which a member voted "yea" or "nay" in disagreement with a majority of his or her party. Percentages are based on votes cast; thus, failure to vote did not lower a member's score.

3. Participation in Party Unity Votes. Percentage of the 259 recorded House party unity votes in 2000 on which a member was present and voted "yea" or "nay."

[1] *Matthew G. Martinez, R-Calif., switched party affiliation from Democrat to Republican on July 26. His party unity score is based on the 53 party unity votes he was eligible for as a Republican. As a Democrat, Martinez was eligible for 207 party unity votes; his support score as a Democrat was 19 percent.*

[2] *Julian C. Dixon, D-Calif., died Dec. 8. He was eligible for 259 party unity votes in 2000.*

[3] *J. Dennis Hastert, R-Ill., as Speaker of the House, voted on 72 party unity votes at his discretion in 2000.*

[4] *Bruce F. Vento, D-Minn., died Oct. 10. He was eligible for 231 party unity votes in 2000.*

[5] *Herbert H. Bateman, R-Va., died Sept. 11. He was eligible for 216 party unity votes in 2000.*

Key

Democrats ***Republicans***
Independents

	1	2	3
ALABAMA			
1 ***Callahan***	89	11	95
2 ***Everett***	97	3	93
3 ***Riley***	95	5	97
4 ***Aderholt***	91	9	99
5 Cramer	66	34	100
6 ***Bachus***	89	11	97
7 Hilliard	91	9	95
ALASKA			
AL ***Young***	86	14	96
ARIZONA			
1 ***Salmon***	95	5	93
2 Pastor	90	10	100
3 ***Stump***	97	3	99
4 ***Shadegg***	96	4	97
5 ***Kolbe***	85	15	97
6 ***Hayworth***	96	4	98
ARKANSAS			
1 Berry	67	33	99
2 Snyder	89	11	98
3 ***Hutchinson***	94	6	98
4 ***Dickey***	95	5	94
CALIFORNIA			
1 Thompson	89	11	100
2 ***Herger***	96	4	96
3 ***Ose***	89	11	98
4 ***Doolittle***	96	4	99
5 Matsui	97	3	97
6 Woolsey	98	2	98
7 Miller	96	4	97
8 Pelosi	96	4	98
9 Lee	97	3	99
10 Tauscher	85	15	99
11 ***Pombo***	95	5	98
12 Lantos	98	2	97
13 Stark	96	4	86
14 Eshoo	89	11	94
15 ***Campbell***	78	22	43
16 Lofgren	90	10	87
17 Farr	95	5	98
18 Condit	72	28	100
19 ***Radanovich***	96	4	96
20 Dooley	82	18	95
21 ***Thomas***	92	8	97
22 Capps	89	11	97
23 ***Gallegly***	85	15	99
24 Sherman	93	7	100
25 ***McKeon***	95	5	98
26 Berman	96	4	92
27 ***Rogan***	92	8	96
28 ***Dreier***	94	6	100
29 Waxman	98	2	90
30 Becerra	95	5	89
31 ***Martinez*** [1]	100	0	85
32 Dixon [2]	95	5	93
33 Roybal-Allard	98	2	92
34 Napolitano	95	5	99
35 Waters	96	4	95
36 ***Kuykendall***	81	19	93
37 Millender-McD.	98	2	96
38 ***Horn***	71	29	98
39 ***Royce***	93	7	95
40 ***Lewis***	87	13	95
41 ***Miller***	97	3	97
42 Baca	83	17	93
43 ***Calvert***	94	6	99
44 ***Bono***	86	14	99
45 ***Rohrabacher***	94	6	99
46 Sanchez	94	6	95
47 ***Cox***	95	5	95
48 ***Packard***	92	8	97
49 ***Bilbray***	76	24	97
50 Filner	99	1	90
51 ***Cunningham***	94	6	98
52 ***Hunter***	94	6	98
COLORADO			
1 DeGette	93	7	94
2 Udall	93	7	100
3 ***McInnis***	93	7	94
4 ***Schaffer***	90	10	95
5 ***Hefley***	93	7	96
6 ***Tancredo***	93	7	99
CONNECTICUT			
1 Larson	93	7	98
2 Gejdenson	94	6	98
3 DeLauro	97	3	99
4 ***Shays***	71	29	95
5 Maloney	78	22	98
6 ***Johnson***	71	29	98
DELAWARE			
AL ***Castle***	74	26	99
FLORIDA			
1 ***Scarborough***	90	10	91
2 Boyd	68	32	96
3 Brown	92	8	92
4 ***Fowler***	93	7	93
5 Thurman	88	12	99
6 ***Stearns***	96	4	98
7 ***Mica***	96	4	97
8 ***McCollum***	91	9	54
9 ***Bilirakis***	91	9	98
10 ***Young***	90	10	92
11 Davis	85	15	97
12 ***Canady***	96	4	97
13 ***Miller***	93	7	97
14 ***Goss***	95	5	99
15 ***Weldon***	96	4	96
16 ***Foley***	81	19	99
17 Meek	92	8	90
18 ***Ros-Lehtinen***	86	14	96
19 Wexler	91	9	95
20 Deutsch	87	13	98
21 ***Diaz-Balart***	84	16	96
22 ***Shaw***	87	13	96
23 Hastings	95	5	92
GEORGIA			
1 ***Kingston***	95	5	99
2 Bishop	65	35	93
3 ***Collins***	96	4	97
4 McKinney	91	9	98
5 Lewis	96	4	97
6 ***Isakson***	91	9	99
7 ***Barr***	94	6	96
8 ***Chambliss***	95	5	98
9 ***Deal***	95	5	97
10 ***Norwood***	97	3	96
11 ***Linder***	96	4	95
HAWAII			
1 Abercrombie	86	14	97
2 Mink	89	11	99
IDAHO			
1 ***Chenoweth-Hage***	90	10	85
2 ***Simpson***	94	6	100
ILLINOIS			
1 Rush	98	2	88
2 Jackson	96	4	100
3 Lipinski	73	27	93
4 Gutierrez	96	4	90
5 Blagojevich	86	14	95
6 ***Hyde***	89	11	95
7 Davis	97	3	96
8 ***Crane***	94	6	85
9 Schakowsky	97	3	95
10 ***Porter***	65	35	95
11 ***Weller***	86	14	96
12 Costello	76	24	96

ND Northern Democrats SD Southern Democrats

	1	2	3
13 ***Biggert***	82	18	98
14 ***Hastert***[3]	100	0	28
15 ***Ewing***	92	8	91
16 ***Manzullo***	95	5	98
17 Evans	94	6	98
18 ***LaHood***	87	13	99
19 Phelps	74	26	99
20 ***Shimkus***	93	7	99
INDIANA			
1 Visclosky	92	8	97
2 ***McIntosh***	91	9	53
3 Roemer	69	31	96
4 ***Souder***	91	9	98
5 ***Buyer***	94	6	98
6 ***Burton***	98	2	94
7 ***Pease***	91	9	99
8 ***Hostettler***	92	8	100
9 Hill	81	19	98
10 Carson	96	4	95
IOWA			
1 ***Leach***	73	27	97
2 ***Nussle***	93	7	98
3 Boswell	69	31	96
4 ***Ganske***	77	23	95
5 ***Latham***	94	6	99
KANSAS			
1 ***Moran***	93	7	100
2 ***Ryun***	98	2	98
3 Moore	76	24	99
4 ***Tiahrt***	94	6	99
KENTUCKY			
1 ***Whitfield***	90	10	96
2 ***Lewis***	94	6	100
3 ***Northup***	89	11	98
4 Lucas	54	46	99
5 ***Rogers***	91	9	100
6 ***Fletcher***	92	8	98
LOUISIANA			
1 ***Vitter***	92	8	99
2 Jefferson	90	10	90
3 ***Tauzin***	92	8	97
4 ***McCrery***	90	10	98
5 ***Cooksey***	88	12	83
6 ***Baker***	90	10	97
7 John	65	35	97
MAINE			
1 Allen	94	6	98
2 Baldacci	89	11	97
MARYLAND			
1 ***Gilchrest***	79	21	97
2 ***Ehrlich***	89	11	98
3 Cardin	92	8	99
4 Wynn	95	5	91
5 Hoyer	93	7	99
6 ***Bartlett***	97	3	100
7 Cummings	97	3	97
8 ***Morella***	50	50	98
MASSACHUSETTS			
1 Olver	97	3	99
2 Neal	92	8	93
3 McGovern	98	2	99
4 Frank	94	6	96
5 Meehan	92	8	95
6 Tierney	97	3	99
7 Markey	98	2	83
8 Capuano	98	2	98
9 Moakley	92	8	97
10 Delahunt	95	5	92
MICHIGAN			
1 Stupak	83	17	88
2 ***Hoekstra***	93	7	98
3 ***Ehlers***	78	22	99
4 ***Camp***	91	9	99
5 Barcia	61	39	98
6 ***Upton***	79	21	100
7 ***Smith***	93	7	94
8 Stabenow	82	18	98
9 Kildee	87	13	100
10 Bonior	97	3	99
11 ***Knollenberg***	92	8	98
12 Levin	93	7	100
13 Rivers	91	9	99
14 Conyers	98	2	94
15 Kilpatrick	96	4	95
16 Dingell	89	11	96
MINNESOTA			
1 ***Gutknecht***	92	8	99
2 Minge	81	19	99
3 ***Ramstad***	78	22	100
4 Vento[4]	98	2	23
5 Sabo	96	4	98
6 Luther	88	12	100
7 Peterson	60	40	98
8 Oberstar	92	8	96
MISSISSIPPI			
1 ***Wicker***	93	7	98
2 Thompson	92	8	92
3 ***Pickering***	97	3	98
4 Shows	51	49	94
5 Taylor	57	43	99
MISSOURI			
1 Clay	97	3	78
2 ***Talent***	94	6	89
3 Gephardt	93	7	94
4 Skelton	70	30	95
5 McCarthy	94	6	97
6 Danner	61	39	76
7 ***Blunt***	98	2	99
8 ***Emerson***	91	9	96
9 ***Hulshof***	96	4	97
MONTANA			
AL ***Hill***	96	4	99
NEBRASKA			
1 ***Bereuter***	82	18	99
2 ***Terry***	96	4	99
3 ***Barrett***	92	8	99
NEVADA			
1 Berkley	81	19	99
2 ***Gibbons***	92	8	99
NEW HAMPSHIRE			
1 ***Sununu***	95	5	99
2 ***Bass***	85	15	99
NEW JERSEY			
1 Andrews	88	12	97
2 ***LoBiondo***	77	23	99
3 ***Saxton***	78	22	98
4 ***Smith***	73	27	99
5 ***Roukema***	82	18	97
6 Pallone	91	9	93
7 ***Franks***	77	23	74
8 Pascrell	84	16	97
9 Rothman	89	11	97
10 Payne	97	3	94
11 ***Frelinghuysen***	73	27	99
12 Holt	88	12	100
13 Menendez	91	9	98
NEW MEXICO			
1 ***Wilson***	87	13	98
2 ***Skeen***	93	7	100
3 Udall	91	9	94
NEW YORK			
1 Forbes	71	29	88
2 ***Lazio***	73	27	74
3 ***King***	77	23	96
4 McCarthy	84	16	99
5 Ackerman	96	4	87
6 Meeks	95	5	92
7 Crowley	91	9	93
8 Nadler	95	5	94
9 Weiner	94	6	95
10 Towns	97	3	93
11 Owens	98	2	86
12 Velázquez	97	3	94
13 ***Fossella***	91	9	95
14 Maloney	92	8	95
15 Rangel	93	7	83
16 Serrano	93	7	88
17 Engel	94	6	86
18 Lowey	94	6	92
19 ***Kelly***	75	25	99
20 ***Gilman***	67	33	94
21 McNulty	88	12	90
22 ***Sweeney***	89	11	98
23 ***Boehlert***	68	32	99
24 ***McHugh***	87	13	98
25 ***Walsh***	79	21	99
26 Hinchey	98	2	97
27 ***Reynolds***	93	7	97
28 Slaughter	96	4	96
29 LaFalce	89	11	95
30 ***Quinn***	76	24	92
31 ***Houghton***	76	24	93
NORTH CAROLINA			
1 Clayton	93	7	97
2 Etheridge	84	16	99
3 ***Jones***	92	8	98
4 Price	90	10	99
5 ***Burr***	92	8	97
6 ***Coble***	96	4	95
7 McIntyre	61	39	96
8 ***Hayes***	89	11	98
9 ***Myrick***	96	4	84
10 ***Ballenger***	96	4	98
11 ***Taylor***	94	6	96
12 Watt	94	6	97
NORTH DAKOTA			
AL Pomeroy	88	12	97
OHIO			
1 ***Chabot***	94	6	99
2 ***Portman***	91	9	99
3 Hall	84	16	92
4 ***Oxley***	96	4	91
5 ***Gillmor***	91	9	94
6 Strickland	85	15	95
7 ***Hobson***	90	10	98
8 ***Boehner***	95	5	97
9 Kaptur	91	9	94
10 Kucinich	89	11	99
11 Jones	98	2	89
12 ***Kasich***	92	8	92
13 Brown	97	3	91
14 Sawyer	95	5	99
15 ***Pryce***	90	10	98
16 ***Regula***	88	12	99
17 Traficant	22	78	100
18 ***Ney***	88	12	97
19 ***LaTourette***	84	16	97
OKLAHOMA			
1 ***Largent***	95	5	92
2 ***Coburn***	91	9	89
3 ***Watkins***	94	6	97
4 ***Watts***	98	2	92
5 ***Istook***	93	7	93
6 ***Lucas***	97	3	92
OREGON			
1 Wu	83	17	99
2 ***Walden***	96	4	99
3 Blumenauer	93	7	95
4 DeFazio	86	14	97
5 Hooley	85	15	95
PENNSYLVANIA			
1 Brady	95	5	94
2 Fattah	97	3	91
3 Borski	89	11	96
4 Klink	84	16	64
5 ***Peterson***	94	6	92
6 Holden	75	25	99
7 ***Weldon***	85	15	93
8 ***Greenwood***	73	27	81
9 ***Shuster***	91	9	85
10 ***Sherwood***	86	14	96
11 Kanjorski	82	18	98
12 Murtha	70	30	95
13 Hoeffel	91	9	98
14 Coyne	98	2	98
15 ***Toomey***	92	8	96
16 ***Pitts***	98	2	98
17 ***Gekas***	92	8	97
18 Doyle	79	21	97
19 ***Goodling***	92	8	97
20 Mascara	79	21	99
21 ***English***	83	17	98
RHODE ISLAND			
1 Kennedy	97	3	96
2 Weygand	88	12	93
SOUTH CAROLINA			
1 ***Sanford***	86	14	98
2 ***Spence***	95	5	93
3 ***Graham***	98	2	98
4 ***DeMint***	98	2	95
5 Spratt	82	18	91
6 Clyburn	91	9	97
SOUTH DAKOTA			
AL ***Thune***	91	9	100
TENNESSEE			
1 ***Jenkins***	94	6	94
2 ***Duncan***	89	11	98
3 ***Wamp***	93	7	96
4 ***Hilleary***	96	4	98
5 Clement	74	26	96
6 Gordon	71	29	95
7 ***Bryant***	96	4	99
8 Tanner	71	29	98
9 Ford	89	11	97
TEXAS			
1 Sandlin	75	25	99
2 Turner	75	25	96
3 ***Johnson, Sam***	98	2	98
4 Hall	35	65	100
5 ***Sessions***	98	2	99
6 ***Barton***	93	7	88
7 ***Archer***	97	3	93
8 ***Brady***	97	3	98
9 Lampson	82	18	100
10 Doggett	90	10	100
11 Edwards	84	16	98
12 ***Granger***	93	7	93
13 ***Thornberry***	97	3	100
14 ***Paul***	80	20	97
15 Hinojosa	92	8	86
16 Reyes	88	12	98
17 Stenholm	59	41	99
18 Jackson-Lee	92	8	92
19 ***Combest***	97	3	99
20 Gonzalez	93	7	100
21 ***Smith***	99	1	99
22 ***DeLay***	99	1	94
23 ***Bonilla***	92	8	98
24 Frost	87	13	98
25 Bentsen	88	12	99
26 ***Armey***	99	1	98
27 Ortiz	76	24	100
28 Rodriguez	94	6	97
29 Green	81	19	95
30 Johnson	95	5	95
UTAH			
1 ***Hansen***	95	5	93
2 ***Cook***	93	7	65
3 ***Cannon***	99	1	96
VERMONT			
AL *Sanders*	96	4	99
VIRGINIA			
1 ***Bateman***[5]	86	14	94
2 Pickett	64	36	96
3 Scott	93	7	97
4 Sisisky	61	39	97
5 *Goode*	94	6	99
6 ***Goodlatte***	97	3	95
7 ***Bliley***	94	6	92
8 Moran	83	17	95
9 Boucher	80	20	91
10 ***Wolf***	85	15	98
11 ***Davis***	87	13	98
WASHINGTON			
1 Inslee	80	20	100
2 ***Metcalf***	89	11	93
3 Baird	89	11	98
4 ***Hastings***	98	2	98
5 ***Nethercutt***	93	7	97
6 Dicks	89	11	97
7 McDermott	97	3	90
8 ***Dunn***	92	8	96
9 Smith	80	20	82
WEST VIRGINIA			
1 Mollohan	70	30	95
2 Wise	77	23	76
3 Rahall	79	21	100
WISCONSIN			
1 ***Ryan***	95	5	100
2 Baldwin	96	4	100
3 Kind	86	14	98
4 Kleczka	88	12	99
5 Barrett	93	7	99
6 ***Petri***	89	11	100
7 Obey	94	6	98
8 ***Green***	93	7	98
9 ***Sensenbrenner***	91	9	98
WYOMING			
AL ***Cubin***	97	3	97

Southern states - Ala., Ark., Fla., Ga., Ky., La., Miss., N.C., Okla., S.C., Tenn., Texas, Va.

	1	2	3
ALABAMA			
Shelby	97	3	100
Sessions	97	3	99
ALASKA			
Stevens	92	8	100
Murkowski	99	1	98
ARIZONA			
McCain	83	17	81
Kyl	99	1	100
ARKANSAS			
Hutchinson	98	2	92
Lincoln	80	20	99
CALIFORNIA			
Feinstein	88	12	94
Boxer	100	0	94
COLORADO			
Campbell	97	3	97
Allard	98	2	100
CONNECTICUT			
Dodd	95	5	92
Lieberman	88	12	93
DELAWARE			
Roth	78	22	92
Biden	88	12	97
FLORIDA			
Graham	91	9	100
Mack	94	6	99
GEORGIA			
Miller [1]	25	75	100
Cleland	84	16	100
HAWAII			
Inouye	91	9	80
Akaka	98	2	97
IDAHO			
Craig	100	0	100
Crapo	100	0	99
ILLINOIS			
Durbin	99	1	99
Fitzgerald	81	19	95
INDIANA			
Lugar	86	14	100
Bayh	92	8	100
IOWA			
Grassley	94	6	100
Harkin	97	3	99
KANSAS			
Brownback	98	2	100
Roberts	97	3	100
KENTUCKY			
McConnell	99	1	99
Bunning	98	2	96
LOUISIANA			
Breaux	73	27	99
Landrieu	88	12	99
MAINE			
Snowe	71	29	100
Collins	74	26	100
MARYLAND			
Sarbanes	99	1	100
Mikulski	97	3	99
MASSACHUSETTS			
Kennedy	98	2	97
Kerry	96	4	97
MICHIGAN			
Levin	97	3	100
Abraham	86	14	100
MINNESOTA			
Wellstone	97	3	100
Grams	96	4	95
MISSISSIPPI			
Cochran	98	2	100
Lott	98	2	100
MISSOURI			
Bond	96	4	98
Ashcroft	94	6	98
MONTANA			
Baucus	88	12	100
Burns	90	10	97
NEBRASKA			
Kerrey	83	17	99
Hagel	94	6	100
NEVADA			
Reid	94	6	99
Bryan	94	6	100
NEW HAMPSHIRE			
Smith	97	3	100
Gregg	98	2	97
NEW JERSEY			
Lautenberg	98	2	99
Torricelli	81	19	97
NEW MEXICO			
Domenici	94	6	96
Bingaman	87	13	99
NEW YORK			
Moynihan	92	8	91
Schumer	97	3	99
NORTH CAROLINA			
Helms	98	2	96
Edwards	94	6	100
NORTH DAKOTA			
Conrad	87	13	99
Dorgan	90	10	100
OHIO			
DeWine	86	14	100
Voinovich	78	22	99
OKLAHOMA			
Nickles	97	3	100
Inhofe	100	0	94
OREGON			
Wyden	97	3	99
Smith	89	11	99
PENNSYLVANIA			
Specter	67	33	97
Santorum	96	4	99
RHODE ISLAND			
Reed	97	3	100
Chafee, L.	37	63	100
SOUTH CAROLINA			
Thurmond	98	2	100
Hollings	90	10	100
SOUTH DAKOTA			
Daschle	93	7	94
Johnson	91	9	100
TENNESSEE			
Thompson	93	7	100
Frist	95	5	99
TEXAS			
Gramm	97	3	100
Hutchison	96	4	97
UTAH			
Hatch	94	6	97
Bennett	92	8	97
VERMONT			
Leahy	94	6	92
Jeffords	55	45	99
VIRGINIA			
Warner	92	8	99
Robb	93	7	100
WASHINGTON			
Gorton	93	7	97
Murray	94	6	98
WEST VIRGINIA			
Byrd	72	28	100
Rockefeller	96	4	97
WISCONSIN			
Kohl	87	13	98
Feingold	92	8	100
WYOMING			
Thomas	97	3	100
Enzi	97	3	100

Key

Democrats ***Republicans***
Independents

ND Northern Democrats SD Southern Democrats

Southern states - Ala., Ark., Fla., Ga., Ky., La., Miss., N.C., Okla., S.C., Tenn., Texas, Va.

Party Unity and Party Opposition: Senate

1. Party Unity. Percentage of recorded party unity votes in 2000 on which a senator voted "yea" or "nay" in agreement with a majority of his or her party. (Party unity roll calls are those on which a majority of voting Democrats opposed a majority of voting Republicans.) Percentages are based on votes cast; thus, failure to vote did not lower a member's score.

2. Party Opposition. Percentage of recorded party unity votes in 2000 on which a senator voted "yea" or "nay" in disagreement with a majority of his or her party. Percentages are based on votes cast; thus, failure to vote did not lower a member's score.

3. Participation in Party Unity Votes. Percentage of the 145 recorded Senate party unity votes in 2000 on which a senator was present and voted "yea" or "nay."

[1] *Zell Miller, D-Ga., was sworn in on July 27, replacing Paul Coverdell, R-Ga., who died July 18. Miller was eligible for 12 party unity votes in 2000. Coverdell was eligible for 128 party unity votes; his party unity score was 98 percent.*

	1	2
ALABAMA		
Shelby	100	100
Sessions	99	99
ALASKA		
Stevens	99	99
Murkowski	96	96
ARIZONA		
McCain	78	78
Kyl	98	98
ARKANSAS		
Hutchinson	96	96
Lincoln	99	99
CALIFORNIA		
Feinstein	85	84
Boxer	92	93
COLORADO		
Campbell	97	97
Allard	100	100
CONNECTICUT		
Dodd	95	95
Lieberman	79	79
DELAWARE		
Roth	90	90
Biden	94	95
FLORIDA		
Graham	100	100
Mack	98	98
GEORGIA		
Miller[1]	100	100
Cleland	99	99
HAWAII		
Inouye	85	85
Akaka	90	90
IDAHO		
Craig	99	99
Crapo	97	97
ILLINOIS		
Durbin	98	98
Fitzgerald	96	96
INDIANA		
Lugar	99	99
Bayh	100	100
IOWA		
Grassley	100	100
Harkin	99	99
KANSAS		
Brownback	99	99
Roberts	100	100
KENTUCKY		
McConnell	98	98
Bunning	96	96
LOUISIANA		
Breaux	99	99
Landrieu	99	99
MAINE		
Snowe	99	99
Collins	100	100
MARYLAND		
Sarbanes	100	100
Mikulski	99	99
MASSACHUSETTS		
Kennedy	92	92
Kerry	95	95
MICHIGAN		
Levin	100	100
Abraham	100	100
MINNESOTA		
Wellstone	98	98
Grams	91	91
MISSISSIPPI		
Cochran	99	99
Lott	99	99
MISSOURI		
Bond	97	97
Ashcroft	96	96
MONTANA		
Baucus	99	99
Burns	94	94
NEBRASKA		
Kerrey	98	98
Hagel	98	98
NEVADA		
Reid	99	99
Bryan	99	99
NEW HAMPSHIRE		
Smith	100	100
Gregg	96	96
NEW JERSEY		
Lautenberg	98	98
Torricelli	96	96
NEW MEXICO		
Domenici	94	94
Bingaman	99	99
NEW YORK		
Moynihan	94	94
Schumer	98	99
NORTH CAROLINA		
Helms	90	90
Edwards	100	100
NORTH DAKOTA		
Conrad	98	98
Dorgan	99	99
OHIO		
DeWine	100	100
Voinovich	99	99
OKLAHOMA		
Nickles	99	99
Inhofe	95	95
OREGON		
Wyden	99	99
Smith	99	99
PENNSYLVANIA		
Specter	96	96
Santorum	99	99
RHODE ISLAND		
Reed	99	99
Chafee, L.	100	100
SOUTH CAROLINA		
Thurmond	99	99
Hollings	98	98
SOUTH DAKOTA		
Daschle	97	97
Johnson	99	99
TENNESSEE		
Thompson	99	99
Frist	98	98
TEXAS		
Gramm	100	100
Hutchison	98	98
UTAH		
Hatch	98	98
Bennett	99	99
VERMONT		
Leahy	95	95
Jeffords	95	95
VIRGINIA		
Warner	99	99
Robb	99	99
WASHINGTON		
Gorton	93	93
Murray	97	97
WEST VIRGINIA		
Byrd	100	100
Rockefeller	95	95
WISCONSIN		
Kohl	98	98
Feingold	100	100
WYOMING		
Thomas	97	97
Enzi	99	99

Key

Democrats ***Republicans***
Independents

ND Northern Democrats SD Southern Democrats

Southern states - Ala., Ark., Fla., Ga., Ky., La., Miss., N.C., Okla., S.C., Tenn., Texas, Va.

Voting Participation: Senate

1. Voting Participation. Percentage of the 298 recorded votes in 2000 on which a senator voted "yea" or "nay."

2. Voting Participation (without motions to instruct). Percentage of 296 recorded votes in 2000 on which a senator voted "yea" or "nay." In this version of the study, two votes to instruct the sergeant at arms to request the attendance of absent senators were excluded.

Absences due to illness. *Congressional Quarterly no longer designates members who missed votes due to illness. In the past, notations to that effect were based on official statements published in the Congressional Record, but these were found to be inconsistently used.*

Rounding. *Scores are rounded to nearest percentage, except that no scores are rounded up to 100 percent. Members with a 100 percent score participated in all recorded votes for which they were eligible.*

[1] *Zell Miller, D-Ga., was sworn in July 27, replacing Paul Coverdell, R-Ga., who died July 18. Miller was eligible for 69 votes in 2000. Coverdell was eligible for 215 votes; his voting participation score was 91 percent.*

Voting Participation: House

1. Voting Participation. Percentage of 600 recorded votes in 2000 on which a representative voted "yea" or "nay."

2. Voting Participation (without Journal votes). Percentage of 574 recorded votes in 2000 on which a representative voted "yea" or "nay." In this version of the study, 26 votes on approval of the House Journal were not included.

Absences due to illness. *Congressional Quarterly no longer designates members who missed votes due to illness. In the past, notations to that effect were based on official statements published in the Congressional Record, but these were found to be inconsistently used.*

Rounding. *Scores are rounded to the nearest percentage, except that no scores are rounded up to 100 percent. Members with a 100 percent score participated in all recorded votes for which they were eligible.*

[1] *Julian C. Dixon, D-Calif., died Dec. 8. He was eligible for 601 House votes in 2000.*

[2] *J. Dennis Hastert, R-Ill., as Speaker, voted on 110 House votes at his discretion in 2000.*

[3] *Bruce F. Vento, D-Minn., died Oct. 10. He was eligible for 518 House votes in 2000.*

[4] *Herbert H. Bateman, R-Va., died Sept. 11. He was eligible for 459 House votes in 2000.*

Key

Democrats ***Republicans*** *Independents*

	1	2
ALABAMA		
1 ***Callahan***	93	93
2 ***Everett***	92	92
3 ***Riley***	95	95
4 ***Aderholt***	99	99
5 Cramer	98	98
6 ***Bachus***	98	98
7 Hilliard	93	93
ALASKA		
AL ***Young***	84	86
ARIZONA		
1 ***Salmon***	91	91
2 Pastor	99	99
3 ***Stump***	99	99
4 ***Shadegg***	95	95
5 ***Kolbe***	94	94
6 ***Hayworth***	99	98
ARKANSAS		
1 Berry	99	99
2 Snyder	97	98
3 ***Hutchinson***	94	95
4 ***Dickey***	91	92
CALIFORNIA		
1 Thompson	99	99
2 ***Herger***	96	97
3 ***Ose***	98	98
4 ***Doolittle***	97	97
5 Matsui	97	97
6 Woolsey	96	96
7 Miller	93	93
8 Pelosi	95	95
9 Lee	98	98
10 Tauscher	99	99
11 ***Pombo***	98	98
12 Lantos	93	94
13 Stark	85	86
14 Eshoo	90	90
15 ***Campbell***	43	43
16 Lofgren	90	90
17 Farr	97	97
18 Condit	99	99
19 ***Radanovich***	94	95
20 Dooley	91	92
21 ***Thomas***	97	97
22 Capps	95	95
23 ***Gallegly***	98	98
24 Sherman	99	99
25 ***McKeon***	97	97
26 Berman	92	92
27 ***Rogan***	94	94
28 ***Dreier***	100	100
29 Waxman	83	83
30 Becerra	87	87
31 ***Martinez***	73	74
32 Dixon [1]	94	94
33 Roybal-Allard	93	93
34 Napolitano	98	98
35 Waters	91	92
36 ***Kuykendall***	94	94
37 Millender-McD.	95	96
38 ***Horn***	97	97
39 ***Royce***	94	95
40 ***Lewis***	95	95
41 ***Miller***	96	96
42 Baca	94	94
43 ***Calvert***	97	97
44 ***Bono***	97	98
45 ***Rohrabacher***	99	99
46 Sanchez	93	93
47 ***Cox***	92	92
48 ***Packard***	97	97
49 ***Bilbray***	93	93
50 Filner	90	90
51 ***Cunningham***	97	97
52 ***Hunter***	96	96
COLORADO		
1 DeGette	93	93
2 Udall	99	99
3 ***McInnis***	92	93
4 ***Schaffer***	93	93
5 ***Hefley***	91	92
6 ***Tancredo***	95	98
CONNECTICUT		
1 Larson	96	96
2 Gejdenson	97	97
3 DeLauro	99	99
4 ***Shays***	92	92
5 Maloney	96	96
6 ***Johnson***	96	97
DELAWARE		
AL ***Castle***	99	99
FLORIDA		
1 ***Scarborough***	89	90
2 Boyd	97	97
3 Brown	89	89
4 ***Fowler***	89	89
5 Thurman	99	98
6 ***Stearns***	97	98
7 ***Mica***	96	96
8 ***McCollum***	48	49
9 ***Bilirakis***	98	98
10 ***Young***	91	90
11 Davis	98	98
12 ***Canady***	97	97
13 ***Miller***	94	94
14 ***Goss***	99	99
15 ***Weldon***	95	95
16 ***Foley***	99	99
17 Meek	89	90
18 ***Ros-Lehtinen***	92	92
19 Wexler	93	94
20 Deutsch	98	98
21 ***Diaz-Balart***	95	95
22 ***Shaw***	95	96
23 Hastings	90	91
GEORGIA		
1 ***Kingston***	96	96
2 Bishop	94	94
3 ***Collins***	95	95
4 McKinney	96	96
5 Lewis	96	96
6 ***Isakson***	97	97
7 ***Barr***	94	94
8 ***Chambliss***	96	96
9 ***Deal***	96	95
10 ***Norwood***	93	93
11 ***Linder***	96	96
HAWAII		
1 Abercrombie	93	93
2 Mink	97	97
IDAHO		
1 ***Chenoweth-Hage***	81	82
2 ***Simpson***	99	99
ILLINOIS		
1 Rush	85	85
2 Jackson	99	99
3 Lipinski	89	89
4 Gutierrez	86	86
5 Blagojevich	93	93
6 ***Hyde***	96	97
7 Davis	94	95
8 ***Crane***	85	86
9 Schakowsky	94	94
10 ***Porter***	94	95
11 ***Weller***	97	97
12 Costello	97	97

ND Northern Democrats SD Southern Democrats

	1	2
13 ***Biggert***	99	99
14 ***Hastert*** [2]	18	19
15 ***Ewing***	90	90
16 ***Manzullo***	97	97
17 Evans	98	98
18 ***LaHood***	99	99
19 Phelps	99	99
20 ***Shimkus***	99	99
INDIANA		
1 Visclosky	96	97
2 ***McIntosh***	39	39
3 Roemer	97	97
4 ***Souder***	93	94
5 ***Buyer***	96	96
6 ***Burton***	99	94
7 ***Pease***	99	99
8 ***Hostettler***	99	99
9 Hill	97	97
10 Carson	91	92
IOWA		
1 ***Leach***	97	98
2 ***Nussle***	98	98
3 Boswell	96	96
4 ***Ganske***	94	94
5 ***Latham***	99	99
KANSAS		
1 ***Moran***	100	100
2 ***Ryun***	97	97
3 Moore	99	99
4 ***Tiahrt***	97	97
KENTUCKY		
1 ***Whitfield***	97	97
2 ***Lewis***	99	99
3 ***Northup***	98	98
4 Lucas	99	99
5 ***Rogers***	98	99
6 ***Fletcher***	98	98
LOUISIANA		
1 ***Vitter***	98	98
2 Jefferson	90	90
3 ***Tauzin***	97	97
4 ***McCrery***	96	97
5 ***Cooksey***	85	85
6 ***Baker***	96	96
7 John	97	97
MAINE		
1 Allen	98	98
2 Baldacci	98	98
MARYLAND		
1 ***Gilchrest***	96	96
2 ***Ehrlich***	95	95
3 Cardin	99	99
4 Wynn	91	92
5 Hoyer	97	98
6 ***Bartlett***	99	99
7 Cummings	96	97
8 ***Morella***	95	96
MASSACHUSETTS		
1 Olver	99	99
2 Neal	90	90
3 McGovern	98	98
4 Frank	94	94
5 Meehan	93	93
6 Tierney	96	97
7 Markey	84	84
8 Capuano	96	96
9 Moakley	92	92
10 Delahunt	88	90
MICHIGAN		
1 Stupak	85	86
2 ***Hoekstra***	98	98
3 ***Ehlers***	99	99
4 ***Camp***	98	98
5 Barcia	98	99
6 ***Upton***	100	100
7 ***Smith***	93	93
8 Stabenow	97	98
9 Kildee	99	100
10 Bonior	98	98
11 ***Knollenberg***	99	99
12 Levin	99	99
13 Rivers	98	98
14 Conyers	90	91
15 Kilpatrick	91	92
16 Dingell	95	96

	1	2
MINNESOTA		
1 ***Gutknecht***	98	98
2 Minge	98	98
3 ***Ramstad***	99	99
4 Vento [3]	24	24
5 Sabo	98	98
6 Luther	100	100
7 Peterson	99	99
8 Oberstar	97	97
MISSISSIPPI		
1 ***Wicker***	97	97
2 Thompson	91	92
3 ***Pickering***	97	98
4 Shows	95	95
5 Taylor	96	96
MISSOURI		
1 Clay	75	76
2 ***Talent***	82	83
3 Gephardt	91	91
4 Skelton	97	97
5 McCarthy	96	97
6 Danner	75	76
7 ***Blunt***	97	98
8 ***Emerson***	95	95
9 ***Hulshof***	95	95
MONTANA		
AL ***Hill***	97	98
NEBRASKA		
1 ***Bereuter***	99	99
2 ***Terry***	99	99
3 ***Barrett***	98	98
NEVADA		
1 Berkley	99	99
2 ***Gibbons***	99	99
NEW HAMPSHIRE		
1 ***Sununu***	99	99
2 ***Bass***	99	98
NEW JERSEY		
1 Andrews	97	97
2 ***LoBiondo***	99	99
3 ***Saxton***	98	97
4 ***Smith***	99	99
5 ***Roukema***	96	95
6 Pallone	95	96
7 ***Franks***	66	67
8 Pascrell	95	95
9 Rothman	97	96
10 Payne	90	90
11 ***Frelinghuysen***	99	99
12 Holt	99	99
13 Menendez	96	97
NEW MEXICO		
1 ***Wilson***	97	97
2 ***Skeen***	100	100
3 Udall	94	94
NEW YORK		
1 Forbes	85	85
2 ***Lazio***	67	68
3 ***King***	94	94
4 McCarthy	97	97
5 Ackerman	82	82
6 Meeks	91	91
7 Crowley	93	94
8 Nadler	95	95
9 Weiner	91	91
10 Towns	92	93
11 Owens	82	82
12 Velázquez	93	93
13 ***Fossella***	93	94
14 Maloney	96	96
15 Rangel	86	86
16 Serrano	90	90
17 Engel	87	88
18 Lowey	92	93
19 ***Kelly***	99	99
20 ***Gilman***	94	94
21 McNulty	87	87
22 ***Sweeney***	94	94
23 ***Boehlert***	98	98
24 ***McHugh***	98	98
25 ***Walsh***	98	98
26 Hinchey	94	95
27 ***Reynolds***	97	97
28 Slaughter	95	95
29 LaFalce	95	96

	1	2
30 ***Quinn***	91	91
31 ***Houghton***	90	90
NORTH CAROLINA		
1 Clayton	97	97
2 Etheridge	99	99
3 ***Jones***	97	97
4 Price	97	98
5 ***Burr***	96	96
6 ***Coble***	96	96
7 McIntyre	96	96
8 ***Hayes***	99	99
9 ***Myrick***	86	86
10 ***Ballenger***	96	97
11 ***Taylor***	91	91
12 Watt	97	97
NORTH DAKOTA		
AL Pomeroy	96	96
OHIO		
1 ***Chabot***	99	99
2 ***Portman***	98	99
3 Hall	95	95
4 ***Oxley***	91	91
5 ***Gillmor***	92	92
6 Strickland	96	97
7 ***Hobson***	98	98
8 ***Boehner***	98	98
9 Kaptur	92	93
10 Kucinich	98	98
11 Jones	84	84
12 ***Kasich***	86	88
13 Brown	86	87
14 Sawyer	99	99
15 ***Pryce***	94	95
16 ***Regula***	99	99
17 Traficant	100	100
18 ***Ney***	97	97
19 ***LaTourette***	93	94
OKLAHOMA		
1 ***Largent***	91	92
2 ***Coburn***	84	84
3 ***Watkins***	94	94
4 ***Watts***	90	91
5 ***Istook***	95	95
6 ***Lucas***	90	90
OREGON		
1 Wu	99	99
2 ***Walden***	98	98
3 Blumenauer	95	96
4 DeFazio	94	94
5 Hooley	97	97
PENNSYLVANIA		
1 Brady	94	94
2 Fattah	88	89
3 Borski	95	95
4 Klink	57	58
5 ***Peterson***	90	90
6 Holden	99	99
7 ***Weldon***	94	94
8 ***Greenwood***	85	86
9 ***Shuster***	87	87
10 ***Sherwood***	97	97
11 Kanjorski	97	98
12 Murtha	94	94
13 Hoeffel	99	99
14 Coyne	96	96
15 ***Toomey***	97	97
16 ***Pitts***	97	97
17 ***Gekas***	97	97
18 Doyle	96	97
19 ***Goodling***	94	94
20 Mascara	99	99
21 ***English***	97	97
RHODE ISLAND		
1 Kennedy	93	93
2 Weygand	90	91
SOUTH CAROLINA		
1 ***Sanford***	97	97
2 ***Spence***	91	91
3 ***Graham***	93	93
4 ***DeMint***	94	94
5 Spratt	89	90
6 Clyburn	97	97
SOUTH DAKOTA		
AL ***Thune***	99	99

	1	2
TENNESSEE		
1 ***Jenkins***	94	94
2 ***Duncan***	98	98
3 ***Wamp***	97	97
4 ***Hilleary***	95	95
5 Clement	96	96
6 Gordon	95	95
7 ***Bryant***	97	97
8 Tanner	97	97
9 Ford	93	93
TEXAS		
1 Sandlin	98	98
2 Turner	94	95
3 ***Johnson, Sam***	95	96
4 Hall	99	99
5 ***Sessions***	96	97
6 ***Barton***	83	84
7 ***Archer***	90	91
8 ***Brady***	97	97
9 Lampson	98	98
10 Doggett	99	99
11 Edwards	96	97
12 ***Granger***	91	91
13 ***Thornberry***	99	99
14 ***Paul***	93	93
15 Hinojosa	88	88
16 Reyes	95	95
17 Stenholm	99	99
18 Jackson-Lee	93	93
19 ***Combest***	98	98
20 Gonzalez	99	99
21 ***Smith***	99	99
22 ***DeLay***	94	94
23 ***Bonilla***	97	97
24 Frost	97	97
25 Bentsen	99	99
26 ***Armey***	97	98
27 Ortiz	99	98
28 Rodriguez	92	92
29 Green	97	97
30 Johnson	95	95
UTAH		
1 ***Hansen***	90	90
2 ***Cook***	66	65
3 ***Cannon***	96	97
VERMONT		
AL *Sanders*	96	97
VIRGINIA		
1 ***Bateman*** [4]	91	91
2 Pickett	92	92
3 Scott	97	98
4 Sisisky	97	97
5 *Goode*	98	99
6 ***Goodlatte***	96	96
7 ***Bliley***	93	93
8 Moran	95	95
9 Boucher	90	91
10 ***Wolf***	98	99
11 ***Davis***	97	97
WASHINGTON		
1 Inslee	99	99
2 ***Metcalf***	90	91
3 Baird	97	97
4 ***Hastings***	98	97
5 ***Nethercutt***	95	95
6 Dicks	96	96
7 McDermott	93	94
8 ***Dunn***	93	94
9 Smith	83	83
WEST VIRGINIA		
1 Mollohan	90	90
2 Wise	66	67
3 Rahall	99	99
WISCONSIN		
1 ***Ryan***	99	99
2 Baldwin	99	99
3 Kind	98	98
4 Kleczka	99	99
5 Barrett	98	98
6 ***Petri***	99	99
7 Obey	98	98
8 ***Green***	98	99
9 ***Sensenbrenner***	98	99
WYOMING		
AL ***Cubin***	92	92

Southern states - Ala., Ark., Fla., Ga., Ky., La., Miss., N.C., Okla., S.C., Tenn., Texas, Va.

CQ

Appendix C

KEY VOTES

Key Votes

Individual Members' Votes

New GOP Leadership Tactics Fail to Get Bills Past Clinton

SUMMARY

Since 1945, Congressional Quarterly has selected a series of key votes on major issues of the year.

An issue is judged by the extent to which it represents:

- A matter of major controversy.
- A matter of presidential or political power.
- A matter of potentially great impact on the nation and lives of Americans.

For each group of related votes on an issue, one key vote is usually chosen — one that, in the opinion of CQ editors, was most important in determining the outcome.

Charts showing how each member of Congress voted on these issues begin on p. C-17.

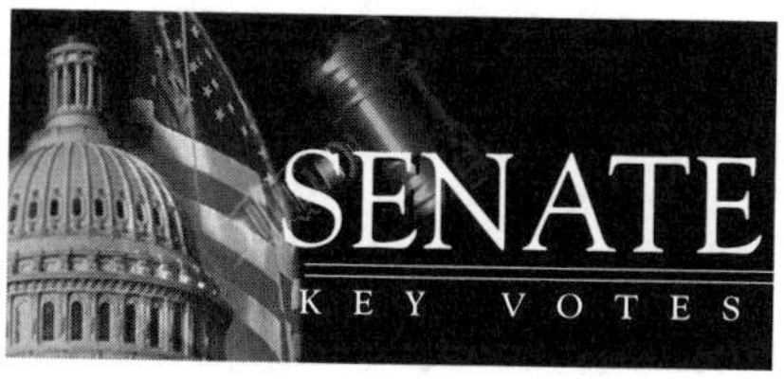

85 Fiscal 2001 Budget Resolution

A contentious fight among Senate Republicans in the spring over how much to spend in fiscal 2001 offered a preview of the budget-related turmoil within the party that would last through much of the year. Conservatives pressed for tight spending restraints, while centrists with an eye on the upcoming elections argued for spending levels high enough to boost funding for popular social programs.

The more tightfisted Senate Republicans won initially, but their victory turned out to be short-lived. The intraparty squabbling, in the end, did little to restrain fiscal 2001 spending.

A defining moment came April 13, when the Senate voted to adopt the conference report on a budget resolution (H Con Res 290) that would limit discretionary budget authority to $600.3 billion — less than an inflationary increase and about $25 billion less than President Clinton requested. The budget resolution also called for $150 billion in tax cuts during the next five years, and perhaps more depending on changes in Congressional Budget Office surplus projections. The vote was 50-48: R 50-4; D 0-44 (ND 0-36, SD 0-8). *(Key vote 1, p. C-17)*

Three Republican fiscal moderates — Arlen Specter of Pennsylvania, Lincoln Chafee of Rhode Island and James M. Jeffords of Vermont — voted against the budget deal, as did John McCain of Arizona, who said it called for excessive tax cuts that could jeopardize debt reduction efforts. Chafee also complained about the lack of emphasis on debt reduction.

Democrats warned that the GOP was setting itself up for another end-of-session "train wreck" in which Congress would be unable to pass several appropriations bills because of the tight budget constraints.

GOP moderates also worried that the budget resolution was unrealistic, but they had been forced to give ground to fiscal conservatives in the party just to get the budget to the Senate floor for a vote. A band of four Republicans on the Senate Budget Committee, led by Phil Gramm of Texas, had threatened to sink the budget unless GOP leaders agreed to a tight spending limit. Gramm and his cohorts got their way, and the budget emerged from committee on a party-line vote with a spending limit of $596.5 billion. The total was plumped on the Senate floor with an additional $4.1 billion for defense spending. The budget resolution emerged from conference at $600.3 billion.

The House adopted the budget resolution on a near party-line vote; the Senate vote cleared it later the same day. It was the second straight year Congress met the April 15 deadline for settling on a budget, and GOP leaders hoped it would give them a running start on the difficult task ahead of clearing spending bills.

But as appropriators had warned, party leaders would quickly find themselves wedged between fiscal conservatives, who insisted at least initially on living within the budget, and President Clinton, who said he would refuse to sign bills that did not fund his priorities.

The result was that by mid-September, GOP leaders had tacitly abandoned the limits of the budget resolution. They capitulated to most of Clinton's spending demands, and in some cases Republicans endorsed even more spending than Clinton requested, as special projects were heaped on to several spending bills.

88 Nuclear Waste Disposal

Legislation that would decide where the nation stores its most lethal nuclear waste fell victim to much of the same political squabbling in 2000 that has doomed previous attempts to resolve the issue.

Yucca Mountain in the remote Nevada desert is under study as the permanent disposal site, but it is not expected to be ready until 2010 at the earliest. That leaves spent fuel piling up at commercial nuclear power plants in 34 states. Until last year, Republicans had concentrated on legislation that would store the fuel temporarily at an above-ground site near Yucca Mountain, but the bills had been blocked or threatened by a presidential veto.

In an attempt to reach a compromise with nuclear utilities that are running out of storage space, Energy Secretary Bill Richardson in 1999 proposed that the Energy Department assume legal title and management of the waste, instead of sending it to Nevada. The Senate Energy and Natural Resources Committee backed the idea, incorporating it into a bill (S 1287) it approved in June 1999.

Governors of several northeastern states, however, complained that such a provision would remove Congress' incentive to develop a permanent site. Frank H. Murkowski, R-Alaska, chairman of the Senate Energy and Natural Resources Committee, sought to placate those critics by calling for the Energy Department to offer utilities a combination of money and storage casks.

However, Murkowski ended up alienating the Clinton administration and key Democrats who backed the original proposal. Murkowski also angered the White House by including language that would have allowed the Environmental Protection Agency to establish radiation standards for the permanent site at Yucca Mountain only after consulting with the National Academy of Sciences and the Nuclear Regulatory Commission. Democrats complained that the storage deadlines and milestones included throughout the bill were unrealistic.

The Senate on Feb. 10 passed the reworked storage bill, 64-34 — three votes short of the two-thirds majority required to overturn a veto. Six weeks later, on March 22, the House voted to clear the bill, 253-167 — 27 votes short of a two-thirds majority. President Clinton responded by vetoing the bill, calling it "a step backward" in developing a permanent waste storage solution. The veto prompted Murkowski and other supporters to scramble to find senators who would support an override.

In the end, however, backers of the bill came up short, thanks to a lobbying effort against the measure led by Nevada Democratic Sens. Richard H. Bryan and Harry Reid. The Senate on May 2 failed to override the veto on a 64-35 vote: R 51-3; D 13-32 (ND 5-32, SD 8-0). *(Key vote 2, p. C-17)*

The margin was actually two votes: Senate Majority Leader Trent Lott, R-Miss., switched his vote from "yes" to "no" in a procedural move that allowed him to call for another vote in the future.

Lott promised to bring up the bill again if proponents could collect more support. However, another opportunity never arose on the Senate calendar, and supporters turned their sights toward reviving the storage issue under a new presidential administration.

105 Kosovo Deployment

Republican-led opponents of the deployment of U.S. troops on peacekeeping missions in the former Yugoslavia went one more round with President Clinton on May 18. They ran into the same brick wall they have hit every time they have forced a vote since the troops went to Bosnia in late 1995.

This time, the test came on a provision in the fiscal 2001 military construction appropriations bill (S 2521). It would have required Clinton to withdraw by July 1, 2001, the 5,900 U.S. troops then serving as part of a NATO-led peacekeeping force in the Serbian province of Kosovo unless Congress authorized their continued deployment.

The language, co-sponsored by Armed Services Committee Chairman John W. Warner, R-Va., and senior Appropriations Committee Democrat Robert C. Byrd of West Virginia, had been approved by the Appropriations panel, 23-3.

Contending that Clinton had given U.S. forces too little money and too many missions, most congressional Republicans — including even some committed internationalists like Warner — opposed committing U.S. ground forces to Balkan peacekeeping for fear of overstressing both the troops and their equipment.

For Byrd and some others, the fight was one more skirmish in the quarter-century conflict over the assertion by presidents of a unilateral right to commit military forces abroad without congressional sanction.

Clinton's Senate opponents had not won even one of their several legislative challenges to the deployments in Bosnia and Kosovo. Each time, Clinton had been backed by a Democratic-led majority, some of whom supported the Balkan mission on its merits, some of whom were loath to take action that might endanger U.S. forces already deployed, and some of whom simply feared undermining U.S. diplomatic clout by what would be a futile effort to reverse a presidential fait accompli.

Indeed, the critics had never come close to forcing a U.S. troop withdrawal, since they fell short of even a simple majority in the Senate, let alone the two-thirds majority they would need to override a Clinton veto of any binding language that would force a pullout.

When the full Senate took up the Warner-Byrd language, the administration weighed in as usual: a veto threat by Clinton, extensive lobbying by administration officials — and the presence of Vice President Al Gore in the chair in case his tie-breaking vote was needed. Ultimately, all but seven Democrats aligned with the president.

However, a new element was thrown into the mix by Texas Gov. George W. Bush, who at the time was the all-but-certain Republican presidential nominee. Just as every president of both parties has done since Congress tried to assert a role in deployment decisions by passing the 1973 War Powers Resolution (PL 93-148), Bush came down squarely in favor of presidential prerogative, announcing his opposition to the Warner-Byrd language.

The key vote came on a motion by senior Armed Services Committee Democrat Carl Levin of Michigan to delete the provision from the military construction bill. The motion was agreed to, and the language was dropped, by a vote of 53-47: R 15-40; D 38-7 (ND 32-5; SD 6-2). *(Key vote 3, p. C-17)*

Warner later claimed that the key to his defeat was Bush's intervention, pointing to the 15 Republicans who voted to drop the restrictive language.

122 Campaign Finance

For years, Congress tried — and failed — to pass a broad overhaul of the nation's campaign finance system. But on June 8, a leader in those efforts, Sen. John McCain, R-Ariz., shifted tactics and successfully pushed through a narrowly written bill that opened to public review an area of private political spending.

It was the first change in federal election law in two decades. The new law requires so-called 527 organizations to publicly disclose their fundraising and spending activities. The groups were named after the section of the tax code that previously exempted them from public disclosure so long as they did not expressly call for the election or defeat of specific candidates.

For years, opponents of curbing campaign spending said the best way to improve the system was to require greater disclosure. McCain, who had been the target of attack ads by a secretly funded 527 group while he sought the GOP presidential nomination, saw an opening to do what the foes of campaign finance overhaul had long advocated. He took his rivals at their word and introduced the legislation along with Sens. Russell D. Feingold, D-Wis., and Joseph I. Lieberman, D-Conn.

McCain and his colleagues decided to offer the language as an amendment to an unrelated Defense Department authorization bill (S 2549). Majority Leader Trent Lott, R-Miss., agreed to allow the amendment, believing he had the votes to defeat it.

Lott and Armed Services Committee Chairman John W. Warner, R-Va., warned that the McCain amendment would mean the death of the underlying defense bill because it would be rejected by the House for violating the constitutional requirement that changes in tax law must originate in the House.

Debate on the amendment was replete with contradiction. Lawmakers who a year before attached an $18.4 billion tax cut for small business to the Senate bankruptcy bill (S 625) as part of a proposal to raise the minimum wage, now fretted about whether McCain's amendment would, as Warner put it, "torpedo" the Pentagon bill and "send it to the bottom of the sea."

Lott and others also attacked McCain's proposal as unfairly narrow, arguing that it did not apply to campaign spending by labor unions and other Democratic-leaning political groups. McCain countered that 527s are used by both sides, noting the Sierra Club as a prime example of a left-leaning group that used the law to obscure its activities.

The decisive vote was not on the amendment itself, but came on a point of order motion by Warner on the constitutional issue he had raised.

Warner's motion was soundly rejected, 42-57: R 41-14; D 1-43 (ND 1-35, SD 0-8). Election-year politics played into the vote. Of the 13 Republicans who sided with McCain, eight were up for re-election that November. *(Key vote 4, p. C-17)*

After defeating Warner's motion, the Senate passed McCain's amendment by voice vote.

The Senate vote broke the bottleneck of political maneuvering that for so long had blocked congressional efforts to change campaign financing. Within one month of the Senate's action, the House approved similar language (HR 4762). President Clinton signed it into law on July 1 (PL 106-230).

McCain and Feingold predicted their success would ultimately pressure colleagues to support broader campaign finance changes.

136 Hate Crimes

Although expanding the federal definition of a hate crime to include offenses against gays and the disabled has been a top goal of civil rights groups and the Clinton administration, the issue had never been debated by the Senate. In 1999, the Senate attached a hate crimes provision to a fiscal 2000 spending bill by voice vote with no debate, but it was quickly dropped during conference on the measure.

This year, the chief sponsor of the provision, Edward M. Kennedy, D-Mass., changed his target. Instead of going after a spending bill, Kennedy offered his amendment during floor consideration of the fiscal 2001 defense authorization bill (S 2549). As a member of the Senate Armed Services Committee, Kennedy was sure to be on the conference committee, where he could fight to preserve the provision.

Criminal acts motivated by racial, religious or ethnic bias already are considered hate crimes under federal law. Kennedy's amendment would add those in which victims were chosen because of sexual orientation, gender or disability. In addition to expanding the definition, the measure also would have made it easier for the federal government to prosecute hate crimes. Currently, the government may prosecute only if the crime takes place on federal property or if it occurs during one of six very specific protected activities, such as voting. The Kennedy amendment would have allowed the federal government to get involved in most prosecutions of hate crimes.

Kennedy offered his amendment on June 19, and despite the controversial nature of the language, there was little debate. While many spoke in favor of it, few voiced opposition. GOP Policy Committee Chairman Larry E. Craig, R-Idaho, said after the June 20 vote that members were concerned about how their opposition would be interpreted. "I think all of us are extremely concerned that we don't appear to be racist or prejudiced, because none of us are," he said.

Fearing a tie, Democrats called Vice President Al Gore back from the campaign trail to be on hand in case his vote was needed.

But Gore was not needed because the first-ever recorded vote by the Senate on the volatile question passed by the surprisingly strong vote of 57-42: R 13-41; D 44-1 (ND 36-1, SD 8-0). The 13 Republicans who voted for the measure ranged from moderates such as Vermont's James M. Jeffords to conservatives such as Alaska's Ted Stevens. The one Democratic opponent, Robert C. Byrd of West Virginia, argued that the provision was unconstitutional. *(Key vote 5, p. C-17)*

Hate crimes became one of the most difficult issues to be decided by the House-Senate negotiators on the defense authorization bill. During the lengthy conference, the strong Senate vote helped House supporters of the amendment pass a non-binding motion instructing conferees to accept the Kennedy amendment. It passed, 232-192, on Sept. 13.

Despite the strong votes and Kennedy's presence on the conference committee, the Republican leadership worked hard to strip the proposal from the defense bill, and on Oct. 5, conferees announced it had been dropped from the final version.

139 Colombia Drug-Fighting Aid

With strong support from President Clinton and House Speaker J. Dennis Hastert, R-Ill., Congress this year made a major new foreign policy commitment by approving $1.3 billion in emergency spending to fight drug trafficking in South America, mainly in Colombia.

Efforts to reduce the funding in the Senate version of the fiscal 2001 foreign operations bill (HR 4811 — PL 106-429) or redirect it to other programs were overwhelmingly defeated, as only a small band of liberals and a few budget conservatives opposed the massive aid program. Some say the Colombia military and police are repressive; others worry that the cost to the United States will escalate.

On the most explicit vote taken on the issue, an amendment by Slade Gorton, R-Wash., to cut the emergency counternarcotics spending from $934 million to $200 million was rejected, 19-79: R 13-41; D 6-38 (ND 6-30, SD 0-8). *(Key vote 6, p. C-17)*

The bipartisan push by Hastert and Clinton cemented support among centrists in both parties. The two leaders had expressed deep concern about the fate of Colombian President Andres Pastrana's government, which was under siege from leftist guerrillas and right-wing paramilitaries who profit from and protect drug traffickers. Hastert is the leader of a group of Republicans who had pushed for more aid to Colombia for four years before they were successful.

Supporters of the aid package also managed to mute some of the opposition from liberals by making the aid contingent on the president's certification that Colombia had met a number of human rights conditions. The president could waive the requirement in the interest of national security.

Pastrana and some of his top officials also became regular visitors to Capitol Hill, lobbying lawmakers on behalf of the aid package, a cornerstone of what Pastrana called "Plan Colombia," a multi-year effort to restore security, eliminate drug trafficking, and spur economic development in the Andean nation.

Opponents of the aid package, such as Sen. Patrick J. Leahy of Vermont, ranking Democrat on the Foreign Operations Appropriations Subcommittee, made clear that the Senate votes were only the first skirmish in an extended battle over the funds. Even the most optimistic forecasts are that Pastrana's government will need the aid for at least five years.

"This is only the first billion-dollar installment of a multi-year, open-ended commitment of many more billions of dollars," Leahy said on the Senate floor June 20. "Nobody can say what they expect this to cost; what can we expect to achieve, in what period of time; how intensifying a war that cannot be won will lead to peace, or what the risks are to hundreds of American military and civilian personnel in Colombia."

165 Genetic Information Privacy

Just three days after two teams of scientists announced that they had decoded most of the human genome — mankind's genetic blueprint — the Senate debated an amendment by James M. Jeffords, R-Vt., to the fiscal 2001 Labor-HHS-Education spending bill (HR 4577) that would prohibit health insurers from using genetic information to deny coverage or raise premiums.

The debate signaled the beginning of what promises to be a long congressional exploration of the boundaries of genetic discrimination. While deciphering the human genome has been almost universally hailed as a landmark development that may lead to cures for many diseases, it also has raised questions about whether patients' health information could be used to single out individuals prone to certain medical conditions. The concerns stem from the fact that an individual's genetic profile not only yields clues about current afflictions but may reveal whether a person or his or her offspring is more prone to certain cancers or other gene-based diseases.

The Senate's response reflected a cautious approach to potential problems. Just before the June 29 vote on Jeffords' amendment, senators rejected, 44-54, an amendment by Minority Leader Tom Daschle, D-S.D., that would have prohibited employers from using genetic information to discriminate in hiring practices or promotions. The provision, which was defeated largely along party lines, also would have prevented insurers from tying coverage or premiums to genetic tests and from requiring genetic tests as a condition of coverage. Daschle's amendment also would have allowed an individual to take genetic discrimination claims to court.

Republicans argued that the 1990 Americans With Disabilities Act (PL 101-336) already prevented workplace discrimination based on one's genetic profile and said Daschle's measure would prompt a flood of lawsuits. Democrats responded there was ample evidence that genetic discrimination exists, pointing to the case of a North Carolina woman who claimed she lost her job at an insurance company after officials there learned she had tested positive for a potentially fatal amino acid deficiency.

"We cannot take one step forward in science but two steps backward in civil rights," Daschle said. "This is an opportunity to simply say no to discrimination in the workplace."

The amendment by Jeffords, chairman of the Senate Health, Education, Labor and Pensions Committee, was similar to language in a Senate-passed bill (S 1344) to regulate the managed-care industry that had stalled in conference negotiations. Jeffords said that with the fate of the managed-care legislation in doubt, it was important to attach the language to another vehicle. "The pace of change is rapid," Jeffords said. "Everyone in this chamber and outside of it agrees we need to guard genetic privacy and guard against genetic discrimination."

The Jeffords amendment was adopted 58-40: R 55-0; D-3-40 (ND 3-32, SD 0-8) *(Key vote 7, p. C-22)*

The privacy language remained in the Labor-HHS bill during the lame-duck session. The legislation is expected to dovetail with broader medical privacy guidelines the Department of Health and Human Services is expected to release before the end of the Clinton administration that will outline who should have access to patient records and under what circumstances information can be released.

166 Managed-Care Regulation

As House and Senate negotiators stumbled in their efforts to strike a deal on managed-care legislation (HR 2990), Democrats and Republicans in both chambers grew weary of the talks. Senate Democrats took their frustration a step further in June, forcing floor showdowns to embarrass Republicans who had blocked action on the politically volatile patients' rights issue.

On June 8, for example, Edward M. Kennedy, D-Mass., tried unsuccessfully to attach the House-passed managedcare bill — stripped of several provisions that Democrats disliked — to the fiscal 2001 Defense appropriations bill (S 2549). After that attempt, Majority Whip Don Nickles, R-Okla., said Kennedy's effort "certainly didn't help the cause of getting a good bipartisan bill."

On June 29, Senate Democrats were at it again, this time trying to amend the fiscal 2001 Labor, Health and Human Services, and Education appropriations bill (HR 4577). Byron L. Dorgan, D-N.D., offered an amendment that would require any managed-care bill passed by Congress to cover all 193 million Americans who have private health insurance. Nickles and other Senate Republicans had said for months that any federal legislation should not interfere with state laws governing health benefits, while Democrats felt that any health care law coming from Washington had to apply to every state.

Dorgan's amendment was rejected, 47-51, but it sparked a strategic move from Senate Republicans, who battled back with a proposal of their own.

Nickles offered an amendment that would permit patients, under limited circumstances, to sue health insurance plans for damages if they denied or delayed needed medical care. The GOP proposal broke new ground by endorsing a limited right to sue managed-care plans for damages, something Senate Republicans had resisted fiercely when the Senate passed its first managed-care bill in July 1999.

Lawsuits would be allowed under two conditions: unreasonable delays in medical care and a failure to cover treatment that an independent physician determined the plan should cover. While patients could not win punitive damages, they could recover unlimited economic damages and up to $350,000 for non-economic damages such as pain and suffering. Democrats wanted no caps on non-economic damages and wanted the lawsuits to be handled in state courts, not federal courts.

Nickles' amendment passed, 51-47: R 51-4; D 0-43 (ND 0-35, SD 0-8). *(Key vote 8, p. C-22)*

While the vote marked a turning point in the debate, it was not enough to revive the stalled managed-care talks, which concluded with no consensus package.

178 Missile Defense

Though many Democrats are skeptical of the nationwide missile defense system being developed by the Clinton administration, their opposition was muted until a test failure in July galvanized them to try to slow the program down.

The administration's program was intended to deploy by 2005 a defense that could shoot down a handful of missiles that might be launched at U.S. territory by radical regimes in North Korea or the Middle East. Republicans, who favor developing a more robust shield, attack the Clinton program as too puny and complain that its military capability has been artificially constrained to live within limits set by the 1972 treaty limiting anti-ballistic missile (ABM) weapons.

On the other hand, many Democrats worry that even Clinton's limited anti-missile program would violate the ABM Treaty and thus spark a nuclear arms race around the globe. However, many of these critics have been loath to challenge the program head-on, especially since 1998, when North Korea tested a long-range ballistic missile.

Early in 2000, the liberal skeptics were heartened when Massachusetts Institute of Technology professor Theodore A. Postol and others launched a vigorous attack on the technical effectiveness of the current anti-missile program. Even a minor adversary could flummox the system by using decoys and other relatively simple countermeasures, Postol argued.

Then on July 8, a test was aborted by failure of a normally reliable booster rocket that was unrelated to the sophisticated "kill vehicle," designed to home in on an attacking warhead, which Postol had criticized. Nevertheless, the incident unleashed pent-up criticism of the anti-missile program — particularly of its accelerated timetable.

The vehicle was an amendment by Richard J. Durbin, D-Ill., to the annual defense authorization bill (HR 4205) that would have required more extensive tests of the system against various types of decoys and other possible countermeasures.

The amendment was tabled, or killed, on July 13 by a vote of 52-48: R 52-3; D 0-45 (ND 0-37; SD 0-8). Three Republican centrists crossed party lines: Olympia J. Snowe and Susan Collins from Maine, and Vermont's James M. Jeffords. *(Key vote 9, p. C-22)*

In September, Clinton cited the July test failure in announcing that he was deferring to his successor a decision about whether to deploy the anti-missile defense.

226 'Marriage Penalty'

Modern Congresses have tended to consider tax provisions en masse. Leaders theorize that a big package creates its own momentum, and hides in its girth controversial tax fixes for specific businesses.

In the most recent Congresses, however, such mammoth measures have become White House targets. Republican majorities in both chambers would pass them, but President Clinton would inevitably argue that — although he supported some provisions — the bills were too large. Clinton said vetoing them was necessary to prevent growth of the national debt.

As the second session of the 106th Congress began, Speaker J. Dennis Hastert, R-Ill., decided it was time for a new strategy. With input from former Minority Leader Robert H. Michel, R-Ill. (1957-95), Hastert devised a plan to move a host of smaller tax bills. That would accomplish two goals: Giving members a chance for favorable publicity when their tax bills came to the floor, and creating a campaign issue if Clinton vetoed a bill.

House Republicans knew that the first test of Hastert's strategy would come not at the White House, but in the Senate. For several years, that chamber's Republicans had refused to go along with House tax plans, saying they were either too expensive or not well conceived. And, though many Democrats had expressed interest in the proposals that would be pushed, it was unclear how many would go against their party's leaders.

The first stand-alone measure the House passed — a bill (HR 6) to cut taxes for married couples — was the one on which the Senate's intentions would become clear.

The House passed it easily in February. But Senate Majority Leader Trent Lott, R-Miss., could not move his chamber's more generous version (HR 4810) until July, when it had been given protection from endless amendment and debate under the fiscal 2001 budget resolution (H Con Res 290). In the meantime, the House had passed it again.

After the Senate cleared it, Republicans quickly worked out their differences in an attempt to put the bill on Clinton's desk by the GOP presidential nominating convention, which began in late July. Conferees removed some of the most expensive Senate provisions, settling on a $90 billion tax cut over the next five years.

They then pushed it to the Senate floor, setting up a political fight over a bill that had once held the promise of bipartisan compromise.

Republicans and Democrats had both long agreed that the tax code should be fairer for married couples, who often pay more in income taxes than they would if they had remained single individuals. Democrats generally insisted the fixes should go to the 24.8 million couples who suffered the penalty. Republicans said the 21 million couples who were not penalized, mostly single-income households, also should receive tax relief.

When Clinton said early in the year that he would not approve tax cuts before Social Security and Medicare were shored up, House Republicans moved their tax bill without Democratic input. Later, Clinton offered to sign a $250 billion-version of the "marriage penalty" bill if Republicans approved his similarly priced measure to cover prescription drugs for the elderly. Republicans quickly rejected such a trade-off.

In the days before the vote, Minority Leader Tom Daschle, D-S.D., and Treasury Secretary Lawrence H. Summers worked mightily to make a case against the bill. Daschle and House Minority Leader Richard A. Gephardt, D-Mo., held news conferences charging that Republicans were up to "the same old tricks" when Summers released data showing that the bill's benefits were heavily weighted toward the richest families.

Republicans said Democrats were not for tax cuts at all. "The day of reckoning is here," Lott said July 18. "Do you actually want to eliminate the marriage penalty . . . or not?"

In the end, seven Senate Democrats voted for the conference report, as 51 of their House counterparts had. That was enough for the measure to pass, but six votes short of the super-majority needed to override a veto. That tally — 60-34; R 53-1; D 7-33 (ND 5-27, SD 2-6) — signaled that Hastert's individual tax bills might move through Congress, but would not become law. *(Key vote 10, p. C-22)*

Clinton vetoed the bill in August, and the House failed in September to override his decision.

242 China's Nuclear Threat

The Senate's resounding rejection of a proposal aimed at stemming China's nuclear proliferation showed the difficulty U.S. officials face in addressing national security concerns while promoting commerce with the world's most populous nation.

Senior Republican lawmakers have condemned the Clinton administration for conducting U.S.-China relations under a so-called strategic partnership — a policy of openness they say does not regard Beijing with enough wariness as a potential security threat. At the same time, though, GOP leaders have heeded warnings from the party's business allies not to stir up anti-China sentiment.

The conflicts between the two competing interests came to a head in 2000 on a bill (HR 4444) that granted permanent normal trade relations to China. The House passed the trade measure in May after a hard-fought battle, but supporters expected it to coast through the Senate. *(House vote, p. C-11)*

However, Sens. Fred Thompson, R-Tenn., and Robert G. Torricelli, D-N.J., argued that the national security concerns with China deserved to be debated on par with trade. They introduced a bill (S 2645) that would have required the president to punish the Chinese government or individual Chinese companies if they were found to be supplying weapons of mass destruction or components to other nations.

With the backing of Majority Leader Trent Lott, R-Miss., Thompson sought to offer his proposal as an amendment to the fiscal 2001 intelligence authorization bill (S 2507). The Senate, however, ground to a halt in July in an impasse over judicial nominees and several Democratic legislative priorities. The delays and procedural wrangling prompted an exasperated Thompson to seek to attach his proposal to the China trade bill after lawmakers returned from the August recess.

Supporters of the trade measure — including the Clinton administration and numerous industry groups — were anxious to keep the proliferation proposal at bay because approval of the amendment would have required the return of the trade bill to the House. They successfully lobbied Republicans who endorsed Thompson's measure not to jeopardize relations with China by adopting any amendments to the trade bill.

In the end, Thompson's amendment was tabled, or killed, 65-32: R 30-23; D 35-9 (ND 27-8, SD 8-1). The 30 Republicans who joined 35 Democrats in rejecting the measure included several of the Senate's most influential GOP voices on international matters: Richard G. Lugar of Indiana, John W. Warner of Virginia and Chuck Hagel of Nebraska. *(Key vote 11, p. C-22)*

Thompson and Torricelli acknowledged that their proposal faced an uphill struggle in the context of the China trade bill, but they vowed to continue to pursue the proliferation issue.

253 'Mini-Omnibus'

Republican prospects for finishing the fiscal 2001 appropriations process before the Nov. 7 election were dealt a major setback when the Senate took the unusual step of rejecting the conference report on a combined legislative branch and Treasury-Postal spending bill (HR 4516 — H Rept 106-796).

The tactic of using the conference report on one spending bill to carry a second, unfinished measure was conceived in late summer. With only two fiscal 2001 appropriations bills cleared and the August recess and the two national political conventions looming, the leadership crafted its own $30.4 billion version of the Treasury-Postal bill — combining elements of the House-passed version with a version approved by the Senate Appropriations Committee — and inserted it into the conference report on the legislative branch spending measure. Also included was a proposal to repeal the 3 percent federal telephone excise tax, at an estimated cost of more than $19.9 billion over five years.

GOP leaders hoped to avert a lengthy and politically difficult debate over the Treasury bill on the Senate floor, where fights were expected both on House-passed provisions to broaden contacts with Cuba and on expected Democratic gun control amendments. Because it was a conference report, the combined measure was not subject to amendment.

Initial reaction in the House to the hastily assembled package was not encouraging. Democrats lambasted its secret overnight drafting; conservatives were unhappy with spending levels. Concluding they did not have the votes, GOP leaders pulled the package. When members returned after the recess, House leaders and other key supporters managed to rally enough support to win adoption of the conference report on a 212-209 vote Sept. 14.

But the combination of anger over the way the measure was brought to the Senate floor and complaints from all sides over spending — Democrats said it was too little; conservatives said it was too much — produced a dramatic showdown Sept. 20. The Senate rejected the conference report by an overwhelming vote of 28-69: R 28-26; D 0-43 (ND 0-34, SD 0-9). *(Key vote 12, p. C-22)*

Angry that GOP leaders had never brought a stand-alone Treasury-Postal bill (S 2900) to the floor, Democrats united in voting against the measure. There was also bipartisan concern that, in an election year, the leadership had not allowed for a vote to add language to the bill blocking an automatic annual pay increase for members of Congress.

To quell the opposition, GOP leaders subsequently cut a deal with the White House to provide $348 million in additional funding for the IRS and anti-terrorism programs in the Transportation spending bill (PL 106-346). The Transportation bill also included language to nullify a provision in the Treasury conference report that would have erased a temporary increase in pension payments by lawmakers under the 1997 balanced-budget law (PL 105-33). The Senate eventually cleared the Treasury-Postal conference report, 58-37, on Oct. 12.

But Republican prospects for moving the spending bills did not recover. Indeed, the Treasury-Postal-legislative branch package fell victim to the prolonged disarray. President Clinton vetoed it Oct. 30, saying he could not sign a bill for the legislative branch when "the business of the American people remains unfinished."

The Treasury-Postal bill was resolved as part of the final budget negotiations in the lame-duck session.

43 Minimum Wage

From early in the 106th Congress, Republican leaders had tried to block, or at least blunt, calls from Democrats including President Clinton for an increase in the minimum wage. They hoped to avoid the kind of defeat they suffered in 1996, when moderate Republicans joined with Democrats to pass a wage increase (PL 104-188) over the vociferous opposition of GOP leaders.

This time, the leadership sought to pre-empt the Democrats with a proposal to stretch a $1 increase to $6.15 an hour, over three years — Democrats wanted a two-year increase — and pair it with tax cuts to mollify business owners, as they had in 1996.

Though Democrats acknowledged they would have to allow some form of tax relief as the cost of a minimum wage increase, they held firm on their two-year time frame. In February, Senate Democrats tried but failed to remove a three-year minimum wage amendment added in late 1999 to a rewrite of personal bankruptcy law (HR 833) and replace it with a two-year phase-in. That appeared to kill efforts to get a two-year increase included in a bill in 2000.

But on March 9, facing a threatened Clinton veto of any minimum-wage increase longer than two years, the House broke with its Republican leadership. It voted, 246-179, to adopt an amendment offered by James A. Traficant Jr., D-Ohio, that would have raised the minimum wage by $1 over two years. Forty-two Republicans joined 203 Democrats and one independent in voting to add the language to a business tax-relief package (HR 3081); only five Democrats opposed the measure. *(Key vote 1, p. C-18)*

The vote demonstrated the strength of support among moderate Republicans and all but the most conservative Democrats for a two-year increase, settling the question for the 106th Congress. Republicans also gained support for combining the increase with business tax relief, a fallback position for business owners opposed to an increase in the minimum wage. While the 106th Congress adjourned without clearing a minimum wage increase, the vote did encourage Congress and the White House to make several attempts over the rest of the year to combine the two-year phase-in that Clinton wanted with the business tax relief sought by Republicans.

The GOP, then facing a bitter partisan battle for control of the House in the 107th Congress, also gained a possible ally by allowing Traficant to offer the amendment. Following the vote and amid other considerations he later received on a housing measure (HR 1776) and the fiscal 2000 supplemental spending bill (PL 106-246), the iconoclastic Traficant vowed to support J. Dennis Hastert, R-Ill., for a second term as Speaker when the 107th Congress convenes in January.

193 Kosovo Deployment

Opponents of deploying U.S. ground troops in the former Yugoslavia won an impressive — though largely symbolic — victory May 17 by tapping into the widespread suspicion that other NATO allies were shirking their fair share of the peacekeeping burden.

Critics of the dispatch of U.S. troops to Bosnia in 1995 and to Kosovo in 1999 contend that President Clinton was undermining U.S. military power by giving the forces too few resources and too many jobs peripheral to basic national interests. But for at least two decades before this issue arose, the demand for more equitable "burden sharing" by wealthy European allies — that is, higher European defense budgets to allow a lower Pentagon budget — had rallied some liberal Democrats and GOP conservatives alike.

Because the most immediate threat posed by the Yugoslavia conflict was that it would exacerbate ethnic tensions in neighboring countries, critics touted it as a prime opportunity for the European NATO members to take a larger role, particularly by relieving U.S. ground troops from the dangerous business of policing.

In March, House Budget Committee Chairman John R. Kasich, R-Ohio, a leading opponent of the Balkan deployments, offered an amendment to the supplemental appropriations bill for fiscal 2000 (HR 3908) that would have withheld half the $2.1 billion included in the bill for the Kosovo operation until the Europeans took on a larger role in the mission. The amendment was rejected, 200-219, with many members objecting that it would have tied the president's hands in case of a crisis.

When the House took up the annual defense authorization bill (HR 4205) several weeks later, Kasich refined his proposal to give the president more flexibility. This time, the amendment would require the president to withdraw U.S. ground troops from Kosovo unless he could certify to Congress by April 1, 2001, that European countries had actually delivered certain percentages of the police manpower and financial aid they had already pledged for the province's reconstruction. The president could waive this rule for up to six months in case of a military crisis, or if Congress approved a longer deployment.

Supporters of the deployment argued that Europeans already had taken on most of the heavy lifting, providing about 80 percent of the peacekeeping troops in Kosovo. But an overwhelming majority of Republicans joined by nearly one-third of the Democrats backed the amendment on May 17, and it passed, 264-153: R 195-18; D 67-135 (ND 49-100; SD 18-35); I 2-0. *(Key vote 2, p. C-18)*

Kasich's supporters fell 14 votes shy of the two-thirds majority they would have needed to override a certain Clinton veto, but they never faced that test. The provision was not included in the conference report on the bill.

207 Military Retirees Health Care

A long-running debate over the adequacy of health care for military retirees was resolved in 2000 in the most dramatic way possible: Congress approved a sweeping expansion of medical benefits that is expected to cost $60 billion over 10 years.

The House vote in May was seen by some observers as early evidence of a political tsunami: Congress' first open break from its self-imposed budget limits, thanks to burgeoning budget surpluses produced by a booming economy.

The issue played well on both sides of the aisle. Republicans argued that the complaints of military retirees were proving to be a detriment to the armed services, especially in recruitment and retention. At least some liberal Democrats backed the move in hopes that it would help create momentum for their effort to greatly expand the medical care entitlement currently available to all citizens over the age of 65.

Specifically at issue was the retirees' contention that they had been promised free, lifetime medical care for themselves and their dependents if they served on active duty for at least 20 years. The government's legal obligation to the retirees was much narrower than that. But for decades, most retirees could easily obtain free health care either from military hospitals, which they could use on a space-available basis, or from private health-care providers who would accept reimbursement from a Pentagon-run insurance program. However, once they turned 65, retirees were to rely on Medicare.

Retirees had complained for years about being forced to turn to Medicare and about limitations in the Pentagon-run insurance program. But the complaints became more insistent in the mid-1990s. As many military bases were closed, access to military hospitals became more difficult, even as health costs were rising and the number of Medicare-eligible retirees and dependents was growing to a current total of nearly 1.4 million. In response, Congress created in 1997 several pilot programs to test alternative medical benefits for retirees.

President Clinton's fiscal 2001 defense budget requested $80 million to fix certain problems in the existing program, but the administration turned down the Joint Chiefs' proposals to offer retirees cut-price, mail-order pharmacy service and "medi-gap" insurance to cover the difference between their expenses and what Medicare would pay.

The House Armed Services Committee added to the annual defense authorization bill (HR 4205) provisions that would expand the mail-order pharmacy benefit. When the bill came to the House floor, committee member Gene Taylor, D-Miss., offered an amendment that would have transformed one of the pilot programs into a new benefit available to all retirees under which Medicare would reimburse the military for their medical care.

Warning that this approach was untested and would cost too much, House Armed Services military personnel subcommittee Chairman Steve Buyer, R-Ind., offered an alternative amendment that would have expanded the pilot program and extended it through 2003. But Buyer's proposal was rejected, 95-323, after which the House passed Taylor's amendment by 406-10: R 207-9; D 197-1 (ND 145-1; SD 52-0); I 2-0. *(Key vote 3, p. C-18)*

The conference report on the defense bill passed in October, and it included even more generous health care entitlements for retirees.

228 China's Trade Status

Ever since China's leaders sent tanks to quell student rebellions in Tiananmen Square in 1989, that country's trade status with the United States had sparked fiery annual debates in Congress.

Every year, the president would certify that China had met the conditions for maintaining a normal trade relationship with the United States. (Under the Jackson-Vanik amendment to the 1974 Trade Act [PL 93-618], communist nations must allow free immigration in order for their imports to win the same beneficial tariffs that the goods of other nations receive.) After the president's annual certification, a member of Congress would challenge his decision and accuse the United States of forsaking human rights to make a buck. Efforts to overturn the certification inevitably failed, as the majority determined that isolation would not change China's policies.

With such a heated history, it came as no surprise that the most hard-fought vote of the 106th Congress would be the Clinton administration's bid to exempt China from the annual review and grant it permanent normal trading status. The House, where trade expansion often divides both parties, would be the main battleground. The more reliably pro-trade Senate was a lesser hurdle.

The issue had been looming since November 1999, when U.S. and Chinese officials concluded 13 years of negotiations with a sweeping trade agreement. It would provide unprecedented U.S. access to the more than 1 billion consumers of China, requiring the Asian nation to change hundreds of laws and practices. The United States would be required to take only one step: making China a permanent normal trading partner. That move would put the U.S. imprimatur on China's bid to join the World Trade Organization (WTO).

It would also make life difficult for many members of Congress, particularly House Democrats. They looked forward to their best chance in six years to retake the chamber and they did not want to risk offending their allies in organized labor, who vociferously opposed the bill.

As a result, President Clinton approached the issue gingerly. He did not release details of the agreement or send draft legislation to the Hill until March, several weeks after many Republicans worried publicly that Clinton would not engage in the debate to the extent necessary to ensure passage. They dredged up his failure in 1997 and 1998 to win fast-track trading authority from Congress as proof that he was not sufficiently committed to expanding world trade. *(1998 Almanac, p. 23-3; 1997 Almanac, p. 2-85)*

But Clinton had his own agenda. He had shepherded the North American Free Trade Agreement (PL 103-182) and the General Agreement on Tariffs and Trade (PL 103-465) through skeptical Congresses in 1993 and 1994. Success on the China bill, which would allow the president to grant permanent trade status when China joined the WTO, would cap his achievements as a president who had greatly expanded international commerce.

Through weekly meetings with wavering members at the White House, frequent calls to the Capitol and the appointment of NAFTA veteran William M. Daley to head his lobbying efforts, Clinton showed he would be in the game. Meanwhile, Clinton's usual union and environmental allies were gearing up against the measure. They were joined by human rights campaigners and groups focused on preventing abortions, which generally appealed to more conservative members.

The nation's largest businesses, particularly those in the high-technology, agricultural and manufacturing sectors, lined up on the other side. They ponied up millions for lobbying and advertising campaigns in favor of the bill.

The target for both groups was a pack of wavering members, which dwindled from almost a third of the House when the issue was first discussed to less than a dozen by the time the vote came on May 24.

Opponents of the measure, led by Minority Whip David E. Bonior, D-Mich., held news conferences to hail members they had persuaded to vote against the bill. Minority Leader Richard A. Gephardt, D-Mo., opposed the bill but refrained from lobbying against it in deference to his caucus' mixed feelings. The administration's point man — inveterate pro-trader Robert T. Matsui, D-Calif. — and Majority Whip Tom DeLay, R-Texas, joined forces to round up votes for the bill. Well known for his intense dislike of Clinton, DeLay's involvement in whipping for the president's priority was key to keeping partisan tensions at a minimum during the critical final days of debate. And proponents' ability to win endorsement from some high-ranking Democrats, led by Charles B. Rangel of New York, helped sway some new members as well.

Despite the pressure, a number of undecided members still worried that they were giving China, a country with a history of human rights violations and saber rattling, a blank check by agreeing to the bill.

Two members — Sander M. Levin, D-Mich., and Doug Bereuter, R-Neb. — provided cover to some wavering members. They wrote an amendment to create a commission whose members, chosen by Congress and the administration, would monitor China's compliance with the November trade pact and its activity on human and labor rights, and to forward legislation to Congress if the need arose.

Though opponents decried it as a "fig leaf," many wavering members said it gave them some peace of mind, and leaders eventually agreed to attach it to the measure.

When the vote finally came, the House passed it by a margin of more than 30 votes, roughly the number of members who said they were swayed by the Levin-Bereuter amendment. The tally was 237-197; R 164-57; D 73-138 (ND 43-114; SD 30-24); I 0-2. *(Key vote 4, p. C-18)*

Bill supporters breathed a sigh of relief and moved onto the Senate, which would pass it handily four months later.

254 Estate Tax

With many Americans' stock portfolios becoming more and more valuable, the business groups pushing to repeal taxes on estates, gifts and trust funds found their idea playing well in some unexpected quarters.

The main proponents of the bill were the small business, manufacturing and farm groups that had pushed a repeal since Republicans took control of Congress in 1995. They were joined by a host of other groups, including several minority chambers of commerce, who believed that the estate tax was stemming the creation of wealth in black and Hispanic communities. That prompted some of the more liberal House Democrats to sign on to the measure.

The bill (HR 8), sponsored by Jennifer Dunn, R-Wash., and John Tanner, D-Tenn., had been long praised by Republicans and farm-district Democrats. In 2000, liberal Neil Abercrombie, D-Hawaii, frequently called for its passage at press events, and a number of other liberal members, including Eva Clayton, D-N.C., and Nydia M. Velázquez, D-N.Y., joined the cause.

As a result, Republican leaders expected a strong Democratic vote when they brought the bill to the floor in June. It was one of a host of stand-alone tax measures Speaker J. Dennis Hastert, R-Ill., moved as an alternative to the usual omnibus tax package that President Clinton had consistently vetoed.

Some Democratic leaders worked to head off "yes" votes from their party mates by proposing an alternative that would substantially cut tax rates on estates, gifts and trust funds and would exempt more small farms and businesses from the estate tax altogether. The proposal, sponsored by Charles B. Rangel, D-N.Y., Charles W. Stenholm, D-Texas, and Benjamin L. Cardin, D-Md., garnered strong support, but not as much as the repeal itself.

The vote on HR 8, taken June 9, was 279-136. All 213 Republicans and 65 Democrats (ND 43-104; SD 22-31) voted for the measure. The veto-proof margin was more than even the bill's staunchest proponents had expected. *(Key vote 5, p. C-18)*

It gave the measure life in the Senate, where leaders had suggested they were not interested in taking up a stand-alone repeal bill. The measure cleared Congress on July 14, the eve of the party conventions, but President Clinton vetoed it on Aug. 31, saying its $104 billion cost over 10 years was too much.

The House subsequently failed to override his decision, as pressure from party leaders caused some Democrats, including Velázquez, to reconsider and vote against the repeal.

271 Electronic Signatures

It seemed a simple task at the start of the 106th Congress: Establish a federal standard for sealing contracts on the Internet. The legislation would lay groundwork for use of binding electronic signatures, such as a scrawled moniker on a touch-sensitive computer screen, or bits of computer code that identify a buyer and seller.

Complications began soon after high-tech companies began their effort to move the legislation, aimed at speeding up the growth of electronic commerce. A potential major obstacle emerged when the financial services industry insisted that the bill be used as a vehicle for new standards that would allow them to meet record retention requirements with computer records instead of paper. The industry also sought language that would allow customers over the Internet to fill out applications and receive disclosures that are required by law before they can open an account, get a loan and transact other financial business online.

For some Democrats, the paperwork elimination effort smacked of an attempt to skirt laws meant to ensure that consumers get important information from businesses in writing, including recall notices and foreclosure warnings.

Jay Inslee, D-Wash., resolved some of the consumer protection concerns with compromise language endorsed by a coalition of New Democrats in the House that required companies to get affirmative consent of consumers to receive records by e-mail instead of printed copies. The amendment was adopted, 418-2, on Nov. 9, 1999. And the House passed the measure (HR 1714) overwhelmingly, 356-66. *(1999 Almanac, p. 22-30)*

The Senate passed its own narrower version of the legislation (S 761) by voice vote on Nov. 19, 1999. It would have allowed the use of electronic signatures without addressing the issue of expanding use of electronic records.

In a conference committee of Senate and House negotiators, strong objections by the White House and consumer groups threatened to scuttle broader House language supported by industry. The administration and key lawmakers including Reps. John D. Dingell, D-Mich., and Edward J. Markey, D-Mass., and Sen. Patrick J. Leahy, D-Vt., insisted on language that would ensure consumers were given a chance to demonstrate they could receive important records electronically before they gave consent to receive them in lieu of paper records.

Commerce Committee Chairman Thomas J. Bliley Jr., R-Va., worked out a compromise requiring companies to confirm that customers could receive copies of disclosures and other information by e-mail before they gave formal consent to receive them in lieu of paper copies. The deal allowed for companies to meet record retention requirements with computer files in lieu of paper copies starting March 1, 2001, and required state and federal agencies to complete any new electronic record-keeping standards by June 1.

In a colloquy on the floor with Markey, Bliley said companies could fulfill their consent obligation by sending a sample message to a consumer in an e-mail attachment. The recipient would then send an e-mail to the company stating he had received, opened and read the attachment. The conversation helped clear the way for the compromise to become law.

The House voted to approve the conference report, 426-4, on June 14: R 216-3; D 208-1; (ND 155-0, SD 53-1); I 2-0. *(Key vote 6, p. C-18)*

The Senate cleared the bill, 87-0, on June 16.

280 National Monuments

The long-running battle between the Clinton administration and Republicans over federal land management policy intensified during the 106th Congress, as Western lawmakers attempted to halt President Clinton's actions protecting millions of acres by declaring them national monuments. The failed GOP efforts to block funding for the management of new monuments designated in the last months of Clinton's tenure highlighted a deep divide over the government's role in local land-use decisions.

As Republicans sat down to craft the fiscal 2001 spending bill to fund the Department of the Interior (HR 4578 — PL 106-291), Rep. James V. Hansen, R-Utah, pressed appropriators to include a provision limiting funds to manage monuments designated after 1999. Hansen had objected vigorously in 1996 when Clinton declared nearly 1.7 million acres of Southern Utah as the Grand Staircase Escalante National Monument — halting virtually all commercial development of that land — and tried unsuccessfully to change the 1906 Antiquities Act (16 U.S.C. 431), which allows presidents to take such action.

In the months leading up to consideration of the Interior bill, Clinton created four national monuments totaling more than 1.4 million acres — including an area on the north rim of the Grand Canyon, a site in Arizona containing prehistoric ruins, the 840-mile-long California coast and sequoia groves in California's Sierra Nevada. He also expanded the Pinnacles National Monument south of San Jose, Calif.

Heeding the pleas of Hansen and other Western Republicans — who characterized the designations as federal land grabs that took decisions out of the hands of local authorities — appropriators ignored a veto threat and included a policy "rider" in the Interior measure to deny funds for the management of these areas.

As the Interior measure headed to the floor, Clinton created another four national monuments totaling 540,000 acres and Norm Dicks of Washington, the ranking Democrat on the House Appropriations Interior Subcommittee, drafted an amendment to strip the monuments funding rider from the spending legislation.

Dicks and other Democrats argued that the GOP provision would interfere with a presidential prerogative and force federal land agencies to abandon management of existing monuments.

Dicks' amendment was adopted, but only after Westerners tried a last-ditch attempt to stop Clinton from following through with his legacy-building land initiatives, which they said were purely political. Right before the vote on Dicks' provision, Hansen offered an amendment that would have reinstated the restriction on monuments funding. It was rejected, 187-234: R 177-38; D 9-195 (ND 4-148, SD 5-47); I 1-1. *(Key vote 7, p. C-20)*

Following the vote, Clinton continued to exercise his right to declare monuments. He designated 11 monuments covering 4.6 million acres by the end of 2000 and repeatedly boasted — to Republicans' consternation — that he "protected more land as national monuments in the lower 48 states than any president in history."

341 Campaign Finance

House approval June 28 of the first change in federal election law in two decades came only after a surprising victory for Senate overhaul advocates less than a month earlier.

Following the Senate's passage of legislation to stiffen campaign finance disclosure laws, Republican moderates on the House side increased pressure on their leadership to take up similar legislation. Realizing they were outnumbered, GOP leaders — who generally opposed any changes to the nation's campaign finance system — agreed to move forward.

But the leaders decided to craft their own legislation rather than simply take up what the Senate had passed as an amendment to the defense authorization bill. House leaders appointed moderate GOP Rep. Amo Houghton of New York to lead the effort, but many charged that Majority Whip Tom DeLay, R-Texas — a strong opponent of changing finance laws — played a major role in drafting the bill (HR 4717).

The House legislation was much broader than the Senate language, which simply called for so-called 527 organizations to publicly disclose to the Internal Revenue Service their political fundraising and spending activities. The groups were named after the section of the tax code that exempted them from public disclosure requirements as long as they did not expressly call for the election or defeat of specific candidates.

The House bill included disclosure requirements for 527 groups, similar to the Senate language, but it expanded those rules to cover a huge number of other politically potent tax-exempt groups.

The bill immediately came under withering attack from nonprofit groups across the political spectrum, including the National Rifle Association and Democratic-friendly unions.

The groups argued that the bill would prevent them from participating in even routine grass-roots advocacy without having to name their members and subject them to possible harassment from the government or their rivals.

Opponents of the House bill also charged that it was drafted so broadly it would be declared unconstitutional for its infringement on the right of free association. Many charged that GOP leaders intentionally made the bill overly broad in hopes that it would crumble under its own weight.

It quickly became obvious the bill was doomed to failure on the House floor. But House leaders had promised overhaul-minded Republicans a vote on campaign finance, and Speaker J. Dennis Hastert, R-Ill., wanted the issue out of his hair in a tough election year. So GOP leaders turned to what they knew could pass: the straightforward 527 disclosure bill (HR 4762).

On the key vote, the House overwhelmingly passed the legislation 385-39: R 178-39; D 205-0 (ND 151-0, SD 54-0); I 2-0. *(Key vote 8, p. C-20)*

"It needed to happen. It needed to get done," Hastert said the morning after the vote. "They were out there trying to tag that on to every bill we wanted to pass. That's just not acceptable."

Less than 36 hours later, the Senate, which had begun the process by approving the 527 language as an amendment offered by Sen. John McCain, R-Ariz., voted 92-6 to clear the House's free-standing bill. President Clinton signed it into law on July 1 (PL 106-230). *(Senate vote, p. C-4)*

357 Prescription Drugs

Developing and passing legislation that would give senior citizens drug coverage became, in the words of one GOP pollster, a "political imperative" for Republicans. Removing the issue from the fall election campaigns was a top priority for House Speaker J. Dennis Hastert, R-Ill., and he looked to House Ways and Means Health Subcommittee Chairman Bill Thomas, R-Calif., to take the reins.

Thomas developed a package that looked to the private sector to develop drug-only policies that seniors could purchase. The additional coverage would be optional under Medicare, the federal health insurance program for nearly 40 million elderly and disabled Americans.

Coverage would begin in fiscal 2003. The government would provide subsidies to help low-income seniors afford monthly premiums and deductibles and pay all medication costs for seniors whose annual drug bills were $6,000 or higher. Seniors would have at least two different options for their coverage. If private insurers did not offer coverage in a particular area, the government would.

The same week the House GOP unveiled its prescription drug plan, the White House held three events to blast it. President Clinton labeled the proposal a "trickle-down scheme that would provide a subsidy for insurers and not a single dollar of direct premium assistance for middle-class seniors." House Democrats offered similar assessments. Charles B. Rangel, D-N.Y., the ranking Democrat on Ways and Means, said the proposal was "not a true Medicare prescription drug benefit." Senate Republicans, preferring to wait until they could tackle a comprehensive Medicare overhaul, did little to support their House counterparts' plan.

Insurers, usually a strong GOP ally, balked at the proposal, fearing they could not make a profit by selling such policies. They felt that seniors with the highest drug costs would be most likely to purchase coverage. And with drug prices almost certain to rise, insurers feared lawmakers would pressure them not to raise premiums.

But Thomas said that if the plan became law, plenty of insurers would offer coverage to seniors. "When you tell somebody you don't need them and, in fact, it's going to succeed without them, you'll be amazed at how some people will come around the back door and want to be part of it," he told reporters June 13.

Thomas tried to sell the proposal as a bipartisan measure, but it garnered just five Democratic votes when it squeaked through the House 217-214 on June 28: R 211-10; D 5-203 (ND 4-150, SD 1-53); I 1-1. *(Key vote 9, p. C-20)*

While the bill went nowhere after the floor vote — Senate Republicans never acted on either the House bill or a package of their own — the measure did give House Republicans cover in the fall elections and put them on record as favoring prescription drugs for Medicare recipients.

397 Debt Relief

To some, the millennial year 2000 carried with it the notion of a biblical jubilee — a time of renewal when debts are to be forgiven. A coalition that included religious leaders, President Clinton, lawmakers from both parties and even rock star Bono of the Irish group U2, set about trying to persuade Congress that the United States should contribute to an international debt relief fund for the world's poorest countries.

Supporters said these countries, most of them in sub-Saharan Africa, needed help paying off debts to international financial institutions, such as the World Bank and International Monetary Fund (IMF). The burden of debt payments is so great, they said, that the countries have precious little money left over for social programs such as health and education.

The coalition's backing put the issue on the congressional agenda. But they had not succeeded in getting most of the money they had sought until the fiscal 2001 foreign operations appropriations bill (HR 4811) was taken up by the House. Clinton had asked for $435 million in cash and permission for the IMF to revalue its gold reserves so it could provide as much as $1 billion in additional debt relief.

In the House, Foreign Operations Appropriations Subcommittee Chairman Sonny Callahan, R-Ala., and House Majority Leader Dick Armey, R-Texas, had blocked most of the funds, saying the promise of aid should be used to force changes in the way the financial institutions do business and as a bargaining chip in end-of-session budget negotiations with the White House. Callahan's Senate counterpart, Mitch McConnell, R-Ky., and Senate Banking Committee Chairman Phil Gramm, R-Texas, had agreed to hold up substantial debt relief in that chamber.

The showdown between the groups came on an amendment by Rep. Maxine Waters, D-Calif., to the foreign operations bill to increase funds for debt relief by $156 million, with offsetting cuts in other areas, essentially giving Clinton what he had asked for. The amendment was adopted, 216-211: R26-194; D 189-16 (ND 142-9, SD 47-7); I 1-1. *(Key vote 10, p. C-20)*

Waters triumphed only after an extended tug-of-war between party leaders. With Waters and her supporters — including 26 Republicans — leading in the vote tally, GOP leaders held the vote open for an extra quarter-hour, as Majority Whip Tom DeLay of Texas urged wavering members such as Ernie Fletcher of Kentucky and Tom Coburn and Steve Largent of Oklahoma to oppose the amendment as part of his overall budget strategy.

Just as DeLay appeared on the verge of victory by one vote, Democrats surprised him when they managed to get several of their own members to drop their "no" votes, convincing them that their support would both allow a breakthrough on debt relief and permit those funds that Waters cut (such as military aid to the Middle East) to be restored in a future House-Senate conference.

Their confidence proved well-founded. The final version of the foreign aid bill restored Waters' cuts and included the debt relief the coalition had favored: $435 million in cash and permission for the IMF to revalue its gold reserves in order to provide another $800 million.

430 Community Development

When the House Republican leadership decided to bring the Community Renewal and New Markets Act (HR 4923) straight to the floor, it was acknowledging that the political stakes on the bill were so high that the regular committee process could not be allowed to derail it.

The antipoverty bill was the result of months of negotiations between President Clinton and Speaker J. Dennis Hastert, R-Ill. That history alone gave the bill special status — the backing of a Democratic president and a Republican Speaker is not to be taken lightly.

It was also one of the rare occasions when top Republicans and Democrats saw eye to eye on social policy, an area that traditionally has been a philosophical chasm between the two parties. By limiting the bill to tax incentives, regulatory relief and economic development, the package struck a non-threatening balance that avoided both new government programs and all-out deregulation — the approaches that had gotten Democrats and Republicans in trouble in the past.

Most of the provisions were tax-related, which put them under the jurisdiction of the Ways and Means Committee, but its key members had trouble translating the broad Clinton-Hastert agreement, announced in May, into detailed legislation.

By the end of July, the committee still had not scheduled a markup, as Chairman Bill Archer, R-Texas, and ranking Democrat Charles B. Rangel of New York found themselves disagreeing on everything from how quickly to expand the availability of the low-income housing tax credit to which provisions should count as Republican spending and which ones should count as Democratic spending. In addition, Archer wanted a no-amendment pledge from Democrats, which Rangel was unwilling and unable to provide.

Other issues also surfaced as potential threats to the bill's passage. A key concession to Republicans was the inclusion of a "charitable choice" provision that would allow faith-based substance abuse treatment programs to receive federal funds. Robert C. Scott, D-Va., argued that the provision could lead to federally subsidized "religious bigotry" because the organizations running such programs could refuse to hire people who disagreed with their religious beliefs.

To steer past that and other land mines and get the legislation through the House before the August recess, GOP leaders decided to finish writing the bill themselves and bring it straight to the floor under suspension of the rules — which limits debate, prohibits amendments and requires a two-thirds vote to pass.

The gambit worked. Despite their concerns, few members were willing to vote against an antipoverty package with as much political momentum as this one. On July 25, the legislation passed the House, 394-27: R 214-1; D 179-25 (ND 130-23; SD 49-2); I 1-1. *(Key vote 11, p. C-20)*

The bill was central in final negotiations between the GOP and Clinton during the lame-duck session.

477 Reserving the Surplus

Using a proposal touted as a debt-reduction measure, Republican leaders got themselves out of a mid-year appropriations jam and signaled their intention to break their own budget caps by about $27 billion.

The problem the GOP was trying to solve with the debt-reduction plan began in the spring, when conservatives in both chambers successfully pushed for the adoption of a budget resolution (H Con Res 290) that would have held discretionary spending to less than an inflationary increase.

Appropriators from both parties warned that the spending limit was too tight, and they turned out to be right. It became clear relatively early in the appropriations process that Congress would have to ignore the budget resolution's spending limits for there to be any hope of passing bills that President Clinton would sign.

But by mid-year, fiscally conservative Republicans were already nervous about the budget-breaking spending totals that were working their way through the appropriations process, and they were threatening to vote against appropriations bills that were too heavily funded.

In response, GOP leaders in September rolled out a so-called "90-10" debt reduction plan, which specified that 90 percent of the cumulative fiscal 2001 surplus would go to paying down the $3.1 trillion publicly held debt. The remaining 10 percent — about $28 billion based on the most recent fiscal 2001 surplus projections available at the time — could be used for a combination of tax cuts and spending increases, and party leaders said they likely would split it evenly between the two priorities.

While Republican leaders trumpeted the debt reduction aspect of their plan, it actually amounted to a blueprint for a big increase in fiscal 2001 spending. In drafting their 90-10 plan, the GOP used an inflationary increase in the budget as its baseline. This assumption by itself amounted to an abandonment of the spending limit in the budget resolution. The plan used a Congressional Budget Office projection showing that discretionary spending would have to grow from $608 billion to $638 billion in outlays to keep pace with inflation. With an additional $14 billion on top of that, the 90-10 proposal's called-for spending would total about $652 billion — $27 billion more in outlays than allowed under the budget resolution.

Democrats said the GOP plan was a meaningless gimmick. Surplus funds are automatically used to pay down the public debt, they argued, so the way to reduce the debt was simply to not spend the money. Still, Democrats glibly endorsed the measure, saying it amounted to a symbolic repudiation of the Republicans' own large tax cuts proposed earlier in the year, since there would be insufficient room for them under the 90-10 plan.

Democrats also complained that the plan would be in effect only for fiscal 2001, leaving the door open to big, surplus-gobbling tax cuts in subsequent years if Texas Gov. George W. Bush was elected president.

The House had already voted three times previously on similar GOP debt "lockbox" measures (HR 4866, HR 4601, HR 3859), but the 90-10 plan was unique in terms of its political ramifications. It was aimed in large part at the GOP's own rank-and-file, particularly its most fiscally conservative members, who were beginning to squirm as appropriations bills with budget-breaking totals worked their way toward the House floor.

As part of their overall strategy, GOP leaders said they also would attach debt-reduction riders to the remaining appropriations bills, thereby setting aside specific amounts of surplus funds for debt relief with each corresponding spending bill approved.

The strategy worked. Conservative Republicans liked the 90-10 plan and the debt-reduction riders. The 90-10 plan passed overwhelmingly — twice. The first measure (HR 5173) passed, 381-3 on Sept. 18: R 191-0; D 188-3;(ND 139-3, SD 49-0); I 2-0. *(Key vote 12, p. C-20)*

The second measure (HR 5203), which also included a package of expanded tax breaks for retirement savings, passed, 401-20, the next day.

Senate Republicans endorsed the 90-10 idea, but never moved companion legislation. GOP senators said they viewed the plan as a guide for the coming spate of deal-cutting rather than as a legislative vehicle.

Although the proposal never neared the status of law, the House vote Sept. 18 was the first clear acknowledgement of Congress' intention to abandon the budget resolution. And it cleared the way for approval of several subsequent spending bills. In the six weeks following the Sept. 18 vote, the House passed eight of the 13 appropriations bills.

Although policy fights and presidential politics would eventually stall the appropriations process again later in the year, the fight over how much to spend was largely over. The vote for the 90-10 plan gave appropriators all the room they needed to meet Clinton's requested fiscal 2001 spending levels, if not his priorities. It also gave GOP leaders support from GOP rank-and-file, who previously had threatened to walk away from any abandonment of the budget resolution. ◆

Senate Key Votes 1, 2, 3, 4, 5, 6

	1	2	3	4	5	6
ALABAMA						
Shelby	Y	Y	N	Y	N	N
Sessions	Y	Y	N	Y	N	N
ALASKA						
Stevens	Y	Y	N	Y	Y	N
Murkowski	Y	Y	N	Y	N	N
ARIZONA						
McCain	N	Y	Y	N	N	N
Kyl	Y	Y	N	Y	N	N
ARKANSAS						
Hutchinson	Y	Y	N	Y	N	Y
Lincoln	N	Y	Y	N	Y	N
CALIFORNIA						
Feinstein	N	N	Y	N	Y	N
Boxer	N	N	Y	N	Y	Y
COLORADO						
Campbell	Y	N	N	Y	N	N
Allard	Y	Y	N	Y	N	Y
CONNECTICUT						
Dodd	N	N	Y	N	Y	N
Lieberman	N	N	Y	N	Y	N
DELAWARE						
Roth	?	?	Y	Y	Y	N
Biden	N	N	Y	N	Y	N
FLORIDA						
Graham	N	Y	Y	N	Y	N
Mack	Y	Y	Y	Y	Y	N
GEORGIA						
Coverdell	Y	Y	N	Y	N	N
Cleland	N	Y	N	N	Y	N
HAWAII						
Inouye	N	N	N	N	Y	?
Akaka	N	N	Y	N	Y	N
IDAHO						
Craig	Y	Y	N	Y	N	Y
Crapo	Y	Y	N	Y	N	Y
ILLINOIS						
Durbin	N	N	Y	N	Y	N
Fitzgerald	Y	Y	N	Y	N	Y
INDIANA						
Lugar	Y	Y	Y	N	Y	N
Bayh	N	N	Y	N	Y	N
IOWA						
Grassley	Y	Y	N	Y	N	N
Harkin	N	N	Y	N	Y	Y
KANSAS						
Brownback	Y	Y	N	Y	N	N
Roberts	Y	Y	N	Y	N	N
KENTUCKY						
McConnell	Y	Y	N	Y	N	N
Bunning	Y	Y	N	Y	N	N
LOUISIANA						
Breaux	N	Y	Y	N	Y	N
Landrieu	N	Y	Y	N	Y	N
MAINE						
Snowe	Y	Y	N	N	Y	N
Collins	Y	Y	N	N	Y	Y
MARYLAND						
Sarbanes	N	N	Y	N	Y	N
Mikulski	N	N	Y	N	Y	Y
MASSACHUSETTS						
Kennedy	N	N	Y	N	Y	N
Kerry	N	N	Y	N	Y	N
MICHIGAN						
Levin	N	Y	Y	N	Y	N
Abraham	Y	Y	Y	N	N	N
MINNESOTA						
Wellstone	N	N	Y	N	Y	N
Grams	Y	Y	N	Y	N	Y
MISSISSIPPI						
Cochran	Y	Y	Y	Y	N	N
Lott	Y	N	N	Y	N	N
MISSOURI						
Bond	Y	Y	N	Y	N	N
Ashcroft	Y	Y	N	Y	N	N
MONTANA						
Baucus	N	N	Y	N	Y	N
Burns	Y	Y	N	N	Y	N
NEBRASKA						
Kerrey	N	Y	Y	N	Y	N
Hagel	Y	Y	Y	N	N	N
NEVADA						
Reid	N	N	Y	N	Y	N
Bryan	N	N	Y	N	Y	N
NEW HAMPSHIRE						
Smith	Y	Y	N	Y	N	N
Gregg	Y	Y	N	Y	N	Y
NEW JERSEY						
Lautenberg	N	N	Y	N	Y	N
Torricelli	N	N	N	N	Y	N
NEW MEXICO						
Domenici	Y	Y	N	Y	N	?
Bingaman	N	N	Y	N	Y	N
NEW YORK						
Moynihan	?	N	Y	Y	Y	N
Schumer	N	N	Y	N	Y	N
NORTH CAROLINA						
Helms	Y	Y	N	Y	N	N
Edwards	N	Y	Y	N	Y	N
NORTH DAKOTA						
Conrad	N	N	Y	?	Y	N
Dorgan	N	N	Y	N	Y	N
OHIO						
DeWine	Y	Y	Y	N	Y	N
Voinovich	Y	Y	Y	Y	Y	N
OKLAHOMA						
Nickles	Y	Y	N	Y	N	N
Inhofe	Y	Y	N	Y	?	N
OREGON						
Wyden	N	N	Y	N	Y	N
Smith	Y	Y	Y	N	Y	N
PENNSYLVANIA						
Specter	N	Y	N	N	Y	Y
Santorum	Y	Y	N	Y	N	N
RHODE ISLAND						
Reed	N	N	Y	N	Y	N
Chafee, L.	N	N	Y	N	Y	N
SOUTH CAROLINA						
Thurmond	Y	Y	N	Y	N	N
Hollings	N	Y	N	N	Y	N
SOUTH DAKOTA						
Daschle	N	N	Y	N	Y	N
Johnson	N	N	Y	N	Y	N
TENNESSEE						
Thompson	Y	Y	Y	N	N	N
Frist	Y	Y	Y	Y	N	N
TEXAS						
Gramm	Y	Y	N	Y	N	Y
Hutchison	Y	Y	N	N	N	N
UTAH						
Hatch	Y	Y	Y	Y	N	N
Bennett	Y	Y	N	Y	N	N
VERMONT						
Leahy	N	Y	Y	N	Y	Y
Jeffords	N	Y	Y	N	Y	N
VIRGINIA						
Warner	Y	Y	N	Y	N	N
Robb	N	Y	Y	N	Y	N
WASHINGTON						
Gorton	Y	Y	N	Y	N	Y
Murray	N	Y	Y	N	Y	Y
WEST VIRGINIA						
Byrd	N	N	N	N	N	N
Rockefeller	N	N	Y	N	Y	N
WISCONSIN						
Kohl	N	Y	N	N	Y	Y
Feingold	N	N	N	N	Y	N
WYOMING						
Thomas	Y	Y	N	Y	N	Y
Enzi	Y	Y	N	Y	N	Y

ND Northern Democrats SD Southern Democrats

Southern states - Ala., Ark., Fla., Ga., Ky., La., Miss., N.C., Okla., S.C., Tenn., Texas, Va.

Key

- Y Voted for (yea).
- \# Paired for.
- \+ Announced for.
- N Voted against (nay).
- X Paired against.
- – Announced against.
- P Voted "present."
- C Voted "present" to avoid possible conflict of interest.
- ? Did not vote or otherwise make a position known.

Democrats ***Republicans***
Independents

Following are Senate votes from 2000 selected by Congressional Quarterly as key votes. Original roll call vote number is in parentheses. (Story, p. C-3)

1. H Con Res 290. Fiscal 2001 Budget Resolution/Conference Report. Adoption of the conference report on the fiscal 2001 concurrent resolution on the budget. The resolution calls for cutting taxes by $150 billion over five years and creating a "reserve fund" of $25 billion that could also be used for tax cuts. It also would establish a $40 billion reserve fund for Medicare overhaul and to provide prescription drug coverage for seniors. The plan calls for $600.3 billion in discretionary spending and allows for $310.8 billion in defense appropriations. Adopted 50-48: R 50-4; D 0-44 (ND 0-36, SD 0-8). April 13, 2000. *(Senate vote 85)*

2. S 1287. Nuclear Waste Storage/Veto Override. Passage, over President Clinton's April 25, 2000, veto, of the bill that would provide for the completion of siting and licensing activities for a permanent nuclear waste repository at Yucca Mountain, Nev., and establish a timetable for the development of the proposed site. Rejected 64-35: R 51-3; D 13-32 (ND 5-32, SD 8-0). A two-thirds majority of those present and voting (66 in this case) of both houses is required to override a veto. A "nay" was a vote in support of the president's position. May 2, 2000. *(Senate vote 88)*

3. S 2521. Fiscal 2001 Military Construction Appropriations/U.S. Troops in Kosovo. Levin, D-Mich., amendment that would strike the provision that would terminate funding for continued deployment of U.S. ground troops in Kosovo after July 1, 2001, unless Congress authorizes the deployment. The provision also would state that not more than 75 percent of the fiscal 2000 supplemental spending for Kosovo could be obligated until the president certifies that European allies are paying 33 percent of reconstruction assistance, 75 percent of humanitarian assistance, 75 percent of general administrative costs, and 75 percent of the civilian police force. Adopted 53-47: R 15-40; D 38-7 (ND 32-5, SD 6-2). A "yea" was a vote in support of the president's position. May 18, 2000. *(Senate vote 105)*

4. S 2549. Fiscal 2001 Defense Authorization/Campaign Finance Disclosures. Warner, R-Va., point of order that the McCain, R-Ariz., amendment to the Smith, R-N.H., amendment is out of order because the Constitution requires that revenue provisions must originate in the House. The McCain amendment would require section 527 organizations to disclose their existence to the IRS, file publicly available tax returns, and publicly disclose annual expenditures of more than $500 and names of contributors who gave more than $200 a year to the organization. The Smith amendment would bar granting Defense Department security clearances to certain employees or contractors. Rejected 42-57: R 41-14; D 1-43 (ND 1-35, SD 0-8). Subsequently, the McCain amendment was adopted by voice vote. June 8, 2000. *(Senate vote 122)*

5. S 2549. Fiscal 2001 Defense Authorization/Hate Crimes. Kennedy, D-Mass., amendment that would broaden hate crimes to include crimes related to gender, sexual orientation and disability and would make it easier for the federal government to get involved in the investigation and prosecution of hate crimes. Adopted 57-42: R 13-41; D 44-1 (ND 36-1, SD 8-0). A "yea" was a vote in support of the president's position. June 20, 2000. *(Senate vote 136)*

6. S 2522. Fiscal 2001 Foreign Operations/Counternarcotics Funding Reduction. Gorton, R-Wash., amendment that would reduce the $934 million for South American and Caribbean counternarcotics activities to $200 million. Rejected 19-79: R 13-41; D 6-38 (ND 6-30, SD 0-8). A "nay" was a vote in support of the president's position. June 21, 2000. *(Senate vote 139)*

Senate key votes continued on p. C-22

House Key Votes 1, 2, 3, 4, 5, 6

Following are House votes from 2000 selected by Congressional Quarterly as key votes. Original roll call vote number is in parentheses. (Story, p. C-9)

1. HR 3846. Minimum Wage/Two-Year Increase. Traficant, D-Ohio, amendment that would increase the minimum wage by $1 over two years. Adopted 246-179: R 42-173; D 203-5 (ND 155-0, SD 48-5); I 1-1. March 9, 2000. A "yea" was a vote in support of the president's position. *(House vote 43)*

2. HR 4205. Fiscal 2001 Defense Authorization/Kosovo Operations. Kasich, R-Ohio, amendment that would withhold the bill's funding authorization for Kosovo operations, unless extenuating circumstances arise, until the president certifies that European nations are meeting specific burden-sharing targets by April 1, 2001. Kosovo funds could be used only for withdrawing U.S. ground forces from Kosovo if the president failed to provide such certification. Adopted 264-153: R 195-18; D 67-135 (ND 49-100, SD 18-35); I 2-0. May 17, 2000. A "nay" was a vote in support of the president's position. *(House vote 193)*

3. HR 4205. Fiscal 2001 Defense Authorization/Retiree Health Care. Taylor, D-Miss., amendment that would expand and make permanent the Defense Department Medicare subvention demonstration program. The program would be available to all Medicare-eligible military retirees and their dependents by Jan. 1, 2006. Adopted 406-10: R 207-9; D 197-1 (ND 145-1, SD 52-0); I 2-0. May 18, 2000. *(House vote 207)*

4. HR 4444. China Trade/Passage. Passage of the bill that would make normal trade relations with the People's Republic of China permanent. The bill includes provisions to protect U.S. businesses and workers from import surges; establish a commission to monitor human rights, labor standards and religious freedom in China; require the administration to report annually on China's compliance with trade agreements; and express the sense of Congress that Taiwan should be admitted to the World Trade Organization.The measure would also authorize $99 million for Radio Free Asia and the Voice of America to expand broadcasts to China and neighboring countries. Passed 237-197: R 164-57; D 73-138 (ND 43-114, SD 30-24); I 0-2. May 24, 2000. A "yea" was a vote in support of the president's position. *(House vote 228)*

5. HR 8. Estate Tax Repeal/Passage. Passage of the bill that would amend the Internal Revenue Code of 1986 to phase out the estate and gift taxes, repealing them entirely by 2010. Passed 279-136: R 213-0; D 65-135 (ND 43-104, SD 22-31); I 1-1. June 9, 2000. A "nay" was a vote in support of the president's position. *(House vote 254)*

6. S 761. Electronic Signatures/Conference Report. Adoption of the conference report on the bill to promote electronic commerce and establish a minimum federal standard for the use and recognition of electronic signatures. The bill would ensure that electronic signatures are given the same legal validity and enforceability as written ones. Consumers would have to consent to the use of electronic records and be provided with information on how to access those records. Adopted (thus sent to the Senate) 426-4: R 216-3; D 208-1 (ND 155-0, SD 53-1); I 2-0. June 14, 2000. *(House vote 271)*

[1] *The Speaker votes only at his discretion, usually to break a tie or to emphasize the importance of a matter.*

Key

- Y Voted for (yea).
- # Paired for.
- + Announced for.
- N Voted against (nay).
- X Paired against.
- – Announced against.
- P Voted "present."
- C Voted "present" to avoid possible conflict of interest.
- ? Did not vote or otherwise make a position known.

•

Democrats ***Republicans***
Independents

	1	2	3	4	5	6
ALABAMA						
1 ***Callahan***	N	N	Y	Y	Y	Y
2 ***Everett***	N	Y	Y	Y	Y	Y
3 ***Riley***	N	Y	Y	N	Y	Y
4 ***Aderholt***	Y	Y	Y	N	Y	Y
5 Cramer	Y	N	Y	Y	Y	Y
6 ***Bachus***	N	Y	Y	Y	Y	Y
7 Hilliard	Y	N	Y	N	N	Y
ALASKA						
AL ***Young***	Y	Y	Y	N	Y	Y
ARIZONA						
1 ***Salmon***	N	Y	?	Y	Y	Y
2 Pastor	Y	N	Y	N	N	Y
3 ***Stump***	N	N	N	Y	Y	N
4 ***Shadegg***	N	Y	+	Y	Y	Y
5 ***Kolbe***	N	N	Y	Y	Y	Y
6 ***Hayworth***	N	Y	Y	N	Y	Y
ARKANSAS						
1 Berry	Y	Y	Y	Y	Y	Y
2 Snyder	Y	N	Y	Y	N	Y
3 ***Hutchinson***	N	Y	Y	Y	Y	Y
4 ***Dickey***	N	Y	Y	Y	Y	Y
CALIFORNIA						
1 Thompson	Y	Y	Y	Y	Y	Y
2 ***Herger***	N	?	Y	Y	Y	Y
3 ***Ose***	N	Y	Y	Y	Y	Y
4 ***Doolittle***	N	Y	Y	Y	Y	Y
5 Matsui	Y	N	Y	Y	N	Y
6 Woolsey	Y	Y	+	N	N	Y
7 Miller, George	Y	Y	Y	N	N	Y
8 Pelosi	Y	Y	Y	N	N	Y
9 Lee	Y	Y	Y	N	N	Y
10 Tauscher	Y	N	Y	Y	Y	Y
11 ***Pombo***	N	Y	Y	N	Y	Y
12 Lantos	Y	N	Y	N	Y	Y
13 Stark	Y	Y	N	N	N	Y
14 Eshoo	Y	Y	Y	Y	Y	Y
15 ***Campbell***	N	?	?	Y	Y	Y
16 Lofgren	Y	Y	Y	Y	Y	Y
17 Farr	Y	Y	Y	N	Y	Y
18 Condit	Y	Y	Y	N	Y	Y
19 ***Radanovich***	N	Y	Y	Y	Y	Y
20 Dooley	Y	N	Y	Y	Y	Y
21 ***Thomas***	N	Y	N	Y	Y	Y
22 Capps	Y	N	Y	Y	Y	Y
23 ***Gallegly***	N	Y	Y	Y	Y	Y
24 Sherman	Y	Y	Y	N	N	Y
25 ***McKeon***	N	Y	Y	Y	Y	Y
26 Berman	Y	N	Y	N	N	Y
27 ***Rogan***	N	Y	Y	Y	Y	Y
28 ***Dreier***	N	Y	Y	Y	Y	Y
29 Waxman	Y	N	Y	Y	N	Y
30 Becerra	Y	Y	Y	Y	N	Y
31 Martinez	Y	Y	Y	Y	Y	Y
32 Dixon	Y	N	Y	Y	N	Y
33 Roybal-Allard	Y	N	Y	N	N	Y
34 Napolitano	Y	N	Y	N	N	Y
35 Waters	Y	N	?	N	N	Y
36 ***Kuykendall***	N	Y	Y	Y	Y	Y
37 Millender-McD.	Y	N	Y	N	N	Y
38 ***Horn***	Y	Y	Y	N	Y	Y
39 ***Royce***	N	Y	Y	Y	Y	Y
40 ***Lewis***	N	N	Y	Y	Y	Y
41 ***Miller, Gary***	N	Y	Y	Y	Y	Y
42 Baca	Y	N	Y	N	Y	Y
43 ***Calvert***	N	Y	Y	Y	Y	Y
44 ***Bono***	N	Y	Y	Y	Y	Y
45 ***Rohrabacher***	N	Y	Y	N	Y	Y
46 Sanchez	Y	N	Y	N	Y	Y
47 ***Cox***	N	Y	Y	Y	Y	Y
48 ***Packard***	N	Y	N	Y	?	Y
49 ***Bilbray***	Y	Y	Y	Y	Y	Y
50 Filner	Y	N	Y	N	N	Y
51 ***Cunningham***	N	Y	Y	Y	?	Y
52 ***Hunter***	N	N	Y	N	Y	Y
COLORADO						
1 DeGette	Y	N	Y	Y	N	Y
2 Udall	Y	Y	Y	N	Y	Y
3 ***McInnis***	N	Y	Y	Y	Y	Y
4 ***Schaffer***	?	Y	Y	Y	Y	Y
5 ***Hefley***	N	Y	Y	N	Y	Y
6 ***Tancredo***	N	Y	Y	N	Y	Y
CONNECTICUT						
1 Larson	Y	N	Y	N	N	Y
2 Gejdenson	Y	N	Y	N	N	Y
3 DeLauro	Y	N	Y	N	N	Y
4 ***Shays***	Y	Y	N	Y	Y	Y
5 Maloney	Y	N	Y	N	Y	Y
6 ***Johnson***	Y	Y	Y	Y	Y	Y
DELAWARE						
AL ***Castle***	Y	Y	Y	Y	Y	Y
FLORIDA						
1 ***Scarborough***	?	Y	Y	?	Y	Y
2 Boyd	N	Y	Y	Y	Y	Y
3 Brown	Y	Y	Y	N	N	Y
4 ***Fowler***	N	Y	Y	Y	Y	Y
5 Thurman	Y	Y	Y	Y	N	Y
6 ***Stearns***	N	Y	Y	N	Y	Y
7 ***Mica***	N	Y	Y	N	Y	Y
8 ***McCollum***	–	Y	Y	Y	Y	Y
9 ***Bilirakis***	N	Y	Y	N	Y	Y
10 ***Young***	Y	Y	Y	Y	Y	Y
11 Davis	Y	N	Y	Y	N	Y
12 ***Canady***	N	Y	Y	Y	Y	Y
13 ***Miller***	N	Y	Y	Y	Y	Y
14 ***Goss***	N	Y	Y	Y	Y	Y
15 ***Weldon***	N	Y	Y	N	Y	Y
16 ***Foley***	N	Y	Y	Y	Y	Y
17 Meek	Y	Y	Y	N	N	Y
18 ***Ros-Lehtinen***	Y	Y	Y	N	Y	Y
19 Wexler	Y	N	Y	N	N	Y
20 Deutsch	Y	Y	Y	N	Y	Y
21 ***Diaz-Balart***	Y	N	Y	N	Y	Y
22 ***Shaw***	N	Y	Y	Y	Y	Y
23 Hastings	Y	N	Y	N	N	Y
GEORGIA						
1 ***Kingston***	N	Y	Y	N	Y	Y
2 Bishop	Y	Y	Y	Y	Y	Y
3 ***Collins***	N	Y	Y	N	Y	Y
4 McKinney	Y	?	Y	N	N	Y
5 Lewis	Y	N	?	N	N	Y
6 ***Isakson***	N	Y	Y	Y	Y	Y
7 ***Barr***	N	Y	Y	N	Y	Y
8 ***Chambliss***	N	Y	Y	Y	Y	Y
9 ***Deal***	N	Y	Y	N	Y	Y
10 ***Norwood***	N	Y	Y	N	Y	Y
11 ***Linder***	N	Y	Y	Y	Y	Y
HAWAII						
1 Abercrombie	Y	N	Y	N	Y	Y
2 Mink	Y	Y	Y	N	Y	Y
IDAHO						
1 ***Chenoweth-Hage***	N	Y	Y	N	Y	N
2 ***Simpson***	N	Y	Y	Y	Y	Y
ILLINOIS						
1 Rush	Y	N	Y	N	N	Y
2 Jackson	Y	Y	Y	N	N	Y
3 Lipinski	Y	Y	?	N	Y	Y
4 Gutierrez	Y	Y	Y	N	N	Y
5 Blagojevich	Y	Y	Y	N	Y	Y
6 ***Hyde***	Y	Y	Y	Y	Y	Y
7 Davis	Y	Y	Y	N	N	Y
8 ***Crane***	N	Y	Y	Y	Y	Y
9 Schakowsky	Y	N	Y	N	N	Y
10 ***Porter***	N	N	Y	Y	Y	Y
11 ***Weller***	Y	Y	Y	Y	Y	Y
12 Costello	Y	Y	Y	N	Y	Y
13 ***Biggert***	N	Y	Y	Y	Y	Y
14 ***Hastert*** [1]				Y	Y	

ND Northern Democrats SD Southern Democrats

	1	2	3	4	5	6
15 ***Ewing***	N	Y	Y	Y	Y	Y
16 ***Manzullo***	N	Y	Y	Y	Y	Y
17 Evans	Y	Y	Y	N	N	Y
18 ***LaHood***	Y	Y	Y	Y	Y	Y
19 Phelps	Y	Y	Y	N	Y	Y
20 ***Shimkus***	Y	Y	Y	Y	Y	Y
INDIANA						
1 Visclosky	Y	N	Y	N	N	Y
2 ***McIntosh***	N	?	Y	Y	Y	Y
3 Roemer	Y	Y	Y	Y	Y	Y
4 ***Souder***	N	Y	Y	N	Y	Y
5 ***Buyer***	N	Y	N	N	Y	Y
6 ***Burton***	N	Y	Y	N	Y	Y
7 ***Pease***	N	Y	Y	Y	Y	Y
8 ***Hostettler***	N	Y	Y	N	Y	Y
9 Hill	Y	N	Y	Y	N	Y
10 Carson	Y	Y	Y	Y	N	Y
IOWA						
1 ***Leach***	Y	Y	Y	Y	Y	Y
2 ***Nussle***	N	Y	Y	Y	Y	Y
3 Boswell	Y	Y	Y	Y	Y	Y
4 ***Ganske***	Y	Y	Y	Y	Y	Y
5 ***Latham***	N	Y	Y	Y	Y	Y
KANSAS						
1 ***Moran***	N	Y	Y	Y	Y	Y
2 ***Ryun***	N	Y	Y	Y	Y	Y
3 Moore	Y	Y	Y	Y	Y	Y
4 ***Tiahrt***	N	Y	Y	Y	Y	Y
KENTUCKY						
1 ***Whitfield***	N	Y	Y	Y	+	Y
2 ***Lewis***	N	Y	Y	Y	Y	Y
3 ***Northup***	N	Y	Y	Y	Y	Y
4 Lucas	N	N	Y	Y	Y	Y
5 ***Rogers***	N	Y	Y	N	Y	Y
6 ***Fletcher***	N	Y	Y	Y	Y	Y
LOUISIANA						
1 ***Vitter***	N	Y	Y	Y	Y	Y
2 Jefferson	Y	N	Y	Y	Y	Y
3 ***Tauzin***	N	Y	Y	Y	Y	Y
4 ***McCrery***	N	Y	Y	Y	Y	Y
5 ***Cooksey***	?	Y	Y	Y	Y	Y
6 ***Baker***	N	Y	Y	Y	Y	Y
7 John	Y	N	Y	Y	Y	Y
MAINE						
1 Allen	Y	N	Y	Y	N	Y
2 Baldacci	Y	–	Y	N	N	Y
MARYLAND						
1 ***Gilchrest***	Y	Y	Y	Y	Y	Y
2 ***Ehrlich***	N	Y	Y	N	Y	Y
3 Cardin	Y	N	Y	Y	N	Y
4 Wynn	Y	N	Y	N	Y	Y
5 Hoyer	Y	N	Y	Y	N	Y
6 ***Bartlett***	N	Y	Y	N	Y	Y
7 Cummings	Y	N	Y	N	N	Y
8 ***Morella***	Y	Y	Y	Y	Y	Y
MASSACHUSETTS						
1 Olver	Y	N	Y	N	N	Y
2 Neal	Y	Y	Y	Y	N	Y
3 McGovern	Y	N	Y	N	N	Y
4 Frank	Y	Y	Y	N	N	Y
5 Meehan	Y	Y	?	Y	N	Y
6 Tierney	Y	Y	Y	N	N	Y
7 Markey	Y	N	Y	N	?	Y
8 Capuano	Y	N	Y	N	N	Y
9 Moakley	Y	Y	Y	N	N	Y
10 Delahunt	Y	Y	Y	N	Y	Y
MICHIGAN						
1 Stupak	Y	?	?	N	N	Y
2 ***Hoekstra***	N	Y	Y	N	Y	Y
3 ***Ehlers***	Y	Y	Y	Y	Y	Y
4 ***Camp***	N	Y	Y	Y	Y	Y
5 Barcia	Y	Y	Y	N	Y	Y
6 ***Upton***	Y	Y	Y	Y	Y	Y
7 ***Smith***	N	Y	Y	Y	?	Y
8 Stabenow	Y	N	Y	N	N	Y
9 Kildee	Y	N	Y	N	N	Y
10 Bonior	Y	N	Y	N	N	Y
11 ***Knollenberg***	N	N	Y	Y	Y	Y
12 Levin	Y	N	Y	Y	N	Y
13 Rivers	Y	Y	Y	N	N	Y
14 Conyers	Y	N	Y	N	–	Y
15 Kilpatrick	Y	N	Y	N	N	Y
16 Dingell	Y	N	Y	N	N	Y
MINNESOTA						
1 ***Gutknecht***	N	Y	Y	Y	Y	Y
2 Minge	Y	Y	Y	Y	N	Y
3 ***Ramstad***	N	Y	Y	Y	Y	Y
4 Vento	?	N	?	N	?	?
5 Sabo	Y	N	Y	N	N	Y
6 Luther	Y	Y	Y	N	N	Y
7 Peterson	Y	Y	Y	N	Y	Y
8 Oberstar	Y	N	Y	N	N	Y
MISSISSIPPI						
1 ***Wicker***	N	Y	Y	Y	Y	Y
2 Thompson	Y	N	Y	N	N	Y
3 ***Pickering***	N	Y	Y	Y	Y	Y
4 Shows	Y	Y	Y	N	Y	Y
5 Taylor	Y	N	Y	N	N	N
MISSOURI						
1 Clay	Y	N	Y	N	?	Y
2 ***Talent***	N	Y	Y	Y	Y	Y
3 Gephardt	Y	N	Y	N	N	Y
4 Skelton	Y	N	Y	Y	Y	Y
5 McCarthy	Y	N	Y	N	N	Y
6 Danner	Y	Y	Y	N	?	?
7 ***Blunt***	N	Y	Y	Y	Y	Y
8 ***Emerson***	N	Y	Y	Y	Y	Y
9 ***Hulshof***	N	Y	Y	Y	Y	Y
MONTANA						
AL ***Hill***	N	Y	Y	Y	Y	Y
NEBRASKA						
1 ***Bereuter***	N	Y	Y	Y	Y	Y
2 ***Terry***	N	Y	Y	Y	Y	Y
3 ***Barrett***	N	Y	Y	Y	Y	Y
NEVADA						
1 Berkley	Y	N	Y	N	Y	Y
2 ***Gibbons***	Y	Y	Y	N	Y	Y
NEW HAMPSHIRE						
1 ***Sununu***	N	Y	Y	Y	Y	Y
2 ***Bass***	N	Y	Y	Y	Y	Y
NEW JERSEY						
1 Andrews	Y	N	Y	N	Y	Y
2 ***LoBiondo***	Y	Y	Y	N	Y	Y
3 ***Saxton***	Y	Y	Y	N	Y	Y
4 ***Smith***	Y	Y	Y	N	Y	Y
5 ***Roukema***	N	Y	Y	Y	Y	Y
6 Pallone	Y	N	Y	N	N	Y
7 ***Franks***	Y	Y	?	Y	Y	Y
8 Pascrell	Y	N	Y	N	Y	Y
9 Rothman	Y	N	Y	N	N	Y
10 Payne	Y	N	Y	N	N	Y
11 ***Frelinghuysen***	Y	Y	Y	Y	Y	Y
12 Holt	Y	N	Y	N	Y	Y
13 Menendez	Y	N	Y	N	N	Y
NEW MEXICO						
1 ***Wilson***	Y	Y	Y	Y	Y	Y
2 ***Skeen***	N	Y	Y	Y	Y	Y
3 Udall	Y	?	?	N	N	Y
NEW YORK						
1 Forbes	Y	N	Y	N	Y	Y
2 ***Lazio***	Y	Y	Y	Y	?	Y
3 ***King***	Y	N	Y	N	Y	Y
4 McCarthy	Y	N	Y	N	Y	Y
5 Ackerman	Y	N	?	Y	N	Y
6 Meeks	Y	N	Y	Y	N	Y
7 Crowley	Y	–	Y	N	N	Y
8 Nadler	Y	N	Y	N	N	Y
9 Weiner	Y	N	Y	Y	N	Y
10 Towns	Y	N	?	N	N	Y
11 Owens	Y	N	Y	N	N	Y
12 Velázquez	Y	N	Y	N	Y	Y
13 ***Fossella***	N	N	Y	Y	Y	Y
14 Maloney	Y	N	Y	Y	N	Y
15 Rangel	Y	N	?	Y	N	Y
16 Serrano	Y	N	Y	Y	N	Y
17 Engel	Y	N	Y	N	N	Y
18 Lowey	Y	N	Y	Y	N	Y
19 ***Kelly***	N	N	Y	Y	Y	Y
20 ***Gilman***	Y	N	Y	N	?	Y
21 McNulty	Y	N	Y	N	Y	Y
22 ***Sweeney***	N	Y	Y	Y	Y	Y
23 ***Boehlert***	Y	N	Y	Y	Y	Y
24 ***McHugh***	Y	Y	Y	Y	Y	Y
25 ***Walsh***	Y	Y	Y	Y	Y	Y
26 Hinchey	Y	N	Y	N	N	Y
27 ***Reynolds***	N	Y	Y	Y	Y	Y
28 Slaughter	Y	N	Y	N	N	Y
29 LaFalce	Y	?	Y	Y	N	Y
30 ***Quinn***	Y	Y	?	N	Y	Y
31 ***Houghton***	Y	N	N	Y	Y	Y
NORTH CAROLINA						
1 Clayton	Y	Y	Y	N	Y	Y
2 Etheridge	Y	N	Y	Y	Y	Y
3 ***Jones***	N	Y	Y	N	Y	Y
4 Price	Y	N	Y	Y	N	Y
5 ***Burr***	N	Y	Y	N	Y	Y
6 ***Coble***	N	Y	Y	N	Y	Y
7 McIntyre	Y	N	Y	N	Y	Y
8 ***Hayes***	N	Y	Y	N	Y	Y
9 ***Myrick***	N	Y	Y	Y	Y	Y
10 ***Ballenger***	N	+	Y	Y	Y	Y
11 ***Taylor***	N	Y	Y	N	Y	Y
12 Watt	Y	Y	Y	N	?	Y
NORTH DAKOTA						
AL Pomeroy	Y	N	Y	Y	N	Y
OHIO						
1 ***Chabot***	N	Y	Y	Y	Y	Y
2 ***Portman***	N	Y	Y	Y	Y	Y
3 Hall	Y	?	Y	N	N	Y
4 ***Oxley***	N	Y	Y	Y	Y	Y
5 ***Gillmor***	N	Y	Y	Y	?	Y
6 Strickland	Y	N	Y	N	N	Y
7 ***Hobson***	N	N	Y	Y	Y	Y
8 ***Boehner***	N	Y	Y	Y	?	Y
9 Kaptur	Y	N	Y	N	N	Y
10 Kucinich	Y	Y	Y	N	N	Y
11 Jones	Y	N	Y	N	N	Y
12 ***Kasich***	N	Y	Y	Y	Y	Y
13 Brown	Y	Y	Y	N	N	Y
14 Sawyer	Y	N	Y	Y	N	Y
15 ***Pryce***	N	Y	Y	Y	Y	Y
16 ***Regula***	N	Y	Y	Y	Y	Y
17 Traficant	Y	Y	Y	N	Y	Y
18 ***Ney***	Y	Y	Y	N	Y	Y
19 ***LaTourette***	N	Y	Y	N	Y	Y
OKLAHOMA						
1 ***Largent***	N	?	Y	Y	Y	Y
2 ***Coburn***	N	?	Y	N	Y	Y
3 ***Watkins***	N	Y	Y	Y	Y	Y
4 ***Watts***	N	Y	Y	Y	Y	Y
5 ***Istook***	N	Y	Y	Y	+	Y
6 ***Lucas***	N	Y	Y	Y	Y	Y
OREGON						
1 Wu	Y	Y	Y	N	N	Y
2 ***Walden***	N	Y	Y	Y	Y	Y
3 Blumenauer	Y	N	Y	Y	?	Y
4 DeFazio	Y	Y	Y	N	N	Y
5 Hooley	Y	Y	Y	Y	Y	Y
PENNSYLVANIA						
1 Brady	Y	N	Y	N	N	Y
2 Fattah	Y	N	Y	N	N	Y
3 Borski	Y	N	Y	N	N	Y
4 Klink	Y	N	Y	N	?	Y
5 ***Peterson***	N	Y	Y	Y	Y	Y
6 Holden	Y	N	Y	N	N	Y
7 ***Weldon***	Y	Y	Y	Y	Y	Y
8 ***Greenwood***	Y	Y	Y	Y	Y	Y
9 ***Shuster***	N	Y	Y	Y	Y	Y
10 ***Sherwood***	Y	Y	Y	Y	Y	Y
11 Kanjorski	Y	N	Y	N	N	Y
12 Murtha	Y	N	?	N	N	Y
13 Hoeffel	Y	N	Y	N	N	Y
14 Coyne	Y	N	Y	N	N	Y
15 ***Toomey***	N	Y	Y	Y	Y	Y
16 ***Pitts***	N	Y	Y	Y	Y	Y
17 ***Gekas***	N	Y	Y	Y	Y	Y
18 Doyle	Y	+	Y	N	N	Y
19 ***Goodling***	N	Y	Y	N	Y	Y
20 Mascara	Y	N	Y	N	N	Y
21 ***English***	Y	Y	Y	Y	Y	Y
RHODE ISLAND						
1 Kennedy	Y	N	Y	N	N	Y
2 Weygand	Y	N	Y	N	N	Y
SOUTH CAROLINA						
1 ***Sanford***	N	?	N	N	Y	Y
2 ***Spence***	?	Y	Y	N	Y	Y
3 ***Graham***	N	Y	Y	N	Y	Y
4 ***DeMint***	N	Y	Y	Y	Y	Y
5 Spratt	Y	N	Y	N	N	Y
6 Clyburn	Y	N	Y	N	N	Y
SOUTH DAKOTA						
AL ***Thune***	Y	Y	Y	Y	Y	Y
TENNESSEE						
1 ***Jenkins***	N	Y	Y	Y	Y	Y
2 ***Duncan***	N	Y	Y	N	Y	Y
3 ***Wamp***	N	?	Y	N	Y	Y
4 ***Hilleary***	N	Y	Y	Y	Y	Y
5 Clement	Y	N	Y	N	Y	Y
6 Gordon	Y	Y	Y	N	Y	Y
7 ***Bryant***	N	Y	Y	Y	Y	Y
8 Tanner	Y	Y	Y	Y	Y	Y
9 Ford	Y	Y	?	Y	Y	Y
TEXAS						
1 Sandlin	Y	N	Y	Y	Y	Y
2 Turner	Y	N	Y	Y	N	Y
3 ***Johnson, Sam***	N	Y	Y	Y	Y	Y
4 Hall	N	Y	Y	Y	Y	Y
5 ***Sessions***	N	Y	Y	Y	Y	Y
6 ***Barton***	N	Y	Y	N	Y	Y
7 ***Archer***	N	Y	N	Y	Y	Y
8 ***Brady***	N	Y	Y	Y	Y	Y
9 Lampson	Y	N	Y	N	Y	Y
10 Doggett	Y	Y	Y	Y	N	Y
11 Edwards	Y	N	Y	Y	N	Y
12 ***Granger***	?	Y	Y	Y	Y	Y
13 ***Thornberry***	N	Y	Y	Y	Y	Y
14 ***Paul***	N	Y	Y	N	Y	N
15 Hinojosa	Y	N	Y	Y	N	Y
16 Reyes	Y	N	Y	Y	N	Y
17 Stenholm	N	N	Y	Y	N	Y
18 Jackson-Lee	Y	N	Y	Y	N	Y
19 ***Combest***	N	Y	Y	Y	Y	Y
20 Gonzalez	Y	N	Y	Y	N	Y
21 ***Smith***	N	Y	Y	Y	Y	Y
22 ***DeLay***	N	Y	Y	Y	Y	Y
23 ***Bonilla***	N	N	Y	Y	Y	Y
24 Frost	Y	N	Y	Y	N	Y
25 Bentsen	Y	N	Y	Y	N	Y
26 ***Armey***	N	Y	Y	Y	Y	Y
27 Ortiz	Y	N	Y	Y	N	Y
28 Rodriguez	Y	Y	Y	N	N	Y
29 Green	Y	Y	Y	N	N	Y
30 Johnson, E.B.	?	N	Y	Y	N	Y
UTAH						
1 ***Hansen***	N	Y	Y	Y	Y	Y
2 ***Cook***	N	Y	Y	N	Y	?
3 ***Cannon***	N	Y	Y	Y	Y	Y
VERMONT						
AL *Sanders*	Y	Y	Y	N	N	Y
VIRGINIA						
1 ***Bateman***	N	Y	Y	Y	Y	Y
2 Pickett	N	N	Y	Y	N	Y
3 Scott	Y	N	Y	N	N	Y
4 Sisisky	Y	N	Y	N	Y	Y
5 *Goode*	N	Y	Y	N	Y	Y
6 ***Goodlatte***	N	Y	Y	Y	Y	Y
7 ***Bliley***	N	N	Y	Y	Y	Y
8 Moran	Y	N	Y	Y	Y	Y
9 Boucher	Y	Y	Y	N	Y	Y
10 ***Wolf***	N	N	Y	N	Y	Y
11 ***Davis, T.***	N	Y	Y	Y	Y	Y
WASHINGTON						
1 Inslee	Y	Y	Y	Y	Y	Y
2 ***Metcalf***	Y	Y	Y	N	Y	Y
3 Baird	Y	N	Y	Y	Y	Y
4 ***Hastings***	N	Y	Y	Y	Y	Y
5 ***Nethercutt***	N	Y	Y	Y	Y	Y
6 Dicks	Y	N	Y	Y	N	Y
7 McDermott	Y	N	Y	Y	–	Y
8 ***Dunn***	N	Y	Y	Y	Y	Y
9 Smith	+	N	Y	Y	+	Y
WEST VIRGINIA						
1 Mollohan	Y	N	Y	N	Y	Y
2 Wise	Y	–	Y	N	Y	Y
3 Rahall	Y	N	Y	N	Y	Y
WISCONSIN						
1 ***Ryan***	N	Y	Y	Y	Y	Y
2 Baldwin	Y	Y	Y	N	N	Y
3 Kind	Y	N	Y	Y	?	Y
4 Kleczka	Y	Y	Y	N	N	Y
5 Barrett	Y	Y	Y	N	N	Y
6 ***Petri***	N	Y	Y	Y	Y	Y
7 Obey	Y	N	Y	N	N	Y
8 ***Green***	N	Y	Y	Y	Y	Y
9 ***Sensenbrenner***	N	Y	N	N	Y	?
WYOMING						
AL ***Cubin***	N	Y	Y	Y	Y	Y

Southern states - Ala., Ark., Fla., Ga., Ky., La., Miss., N.C., Okla., S.C., Tenn., Texas, Va.

7. HR 4578. Fiscal 2001 Interior Appropriations/National Monuments. Hansen, R-Utah, amendment to the Dicks, D-Wash., amendment that would reinstate the bill's provision that would prohibit the Interior Department from using funds to design, plan or manage federal lands as national monuments that have been designated since 1999 under the Antiquities Act. Rejected 187-234: R 177-38; D 9-195 (ND 4-148, SD 5-47); I 1-1. June 15, 2000. A "nay" was a vote in support of the president's position. *(House vote 280)*

8. HR 4762. Campaign Finance Disclosure/Passage. Houghton, R-N.Y., motion to suspend the rules and pass the bill that would amend the tax code to require groups organized under section 527 of the code to disclose contribution and expenditure information to the Treasury Department. Motion agreed to 385-39: R 178-39; D 205-0 (ND 151-0, SD 54-0); I 2-0. A two-thirds majority of those present and voting (283 in this case) is required for passage under suspension of the rules. June 28, 2000. *(House vote 341)*

9. HR 4680. Prescription Drugs/Passage. Passage of the bill that would provide prescription drug coverage for Medicare beneficiaries and establish the Medicare Benefits Administration within the Department of Health and Human Services to administer the program. The benefit would be provided by private insurers with a choice between at least two plans. Passed 217-214: R 211-10; D 5-203 (ND 4-150, SD 1-53); I 1-1. June 28, 2000. A "nay" was a vote in support of the president's position. *(House vote 357)*

10. HR 4811. Fiscal 2001 Foreign Operations Appropriations/Debt Relief. Waters, D-Calif., amendment that would increase funding for the Highly Indebted Poor Countries Trust Fund by $156 million and offset it with cuts to various other programs. The fund was created to help debtor countries write off most of the money owed to multilateral agencies. Adopted 216-211: R 26-194; D 189-16 (ND 142-9, SD 47-7); I 1-1. July 13, 2000. *(House vote 397)*

11. HR 4923. Community Renewal Program/Passage. English, R-Pa., motion to suspend the rules and pass the bill that would provide tax credits and economic incentives to encourage investment and job creation in economically depressed urban and rural communities. It would authorize President Clinton's "New Markets Initiative," and designate nine new "empowerment zones" and 40 new "renewal communities." Motion agreed to 394-27: R 214-1; D 179-25 (ND 130-23, SD 49-2); I 1-1. A two-thirds majority of those present and voting (281 in this case) is required for passage under suspension of the rules. July 25, 2000. A "yea" was a vote in support of the president's position. *(House vote 430)*

12. HR 5173. Debt Reduction/Passage. Herger, R-Calif., motion to suspend the rules and pass the bill that would require all Social Security and Medicare surpluses to be used for debt reduction, pending enactment of legislation to overhaul those programs. In fiscal 2001, $42 billion of the non-Social Security and non-Medicare surplus would have to be used for debt reduction. Motion agreed to 381-3: R 191-0; D 188-3 (ND 139-3, SD 49-0); I 2-0. A two-thirds majority of those present and voting (256 in this case) is required for passage under suspension of the rules. Sept. 18, 2000. *(House vote 477)*

[1] *Rep. Matthew G. Martinez of California switched parties from Democrat to Republican on July 26, 2000. The first vote he cast as a Republican was vote 439.*

[2] *The Speaker votes only at his discretion, usually to break a tie or to emphasize the importance of a matter.*

[3] *Rep. Herbert H. Bateman, R-Va., died on Sept. 11, 2000. The last vote for which he was eligible was 459.*

Key

Y	Voted for (yea).
#	Paired for.
+	Announced for.
N	Voted against (nay).
X	Paired against.
–	Announced against.
P	Voted "present."
C	Voted "present" to avoid possible conflict of interest.
?	Did not vote or otherwise make a position known.

Democrats ***Republicans*** *Independents*

	7	8	9	10	11	12
ALABAMA						
1 ***Callahan***	Y	Y	Y	N	Y	Y
2 ***Everett***	Y	Y	Y	N	Y	Y
3 ***Riley***	Y	Y	Y	N	Y	Y
4 ***Aderholt***	Y	Y	Y	Y	Y	Y
5 Cramer	N	Y	N	N	Y	Y
6 ***Bachus***	Y	Y	Y	Y	Y	Y
7 Hilliard	N	Y	N	Y	Y	Y
ALASKA						
AL ***Young***	Y	?	Y	N	Y	Y
ARIZONA						
1 ***Salmon***	Y	Y	Y	N	Y	Y
2 Pastor	N	Y	N	Y	Y	Y
3 ***Stump***	Y	N	Y	N	Y	Y
4 ***Shadegg***	Y	Y	Y	N	Y	Y
5 ***Kolbe***	Y	Y	Y	N	Y	Y
6 ***Hayworth***	Y	N	Y	N	Y	Y
ARKANSAS						
1 Berry	N	Y	N	Y	Y	Y
2 Snyder	N	Y	N	Y	Y	Y
3 ***Hutchinson***	Y	Y	Y	N	Y	Y
4 ***Dickey***	Y	N	Y	N	Y	Y
CALIFORNIA						
1 Thompson	N	Y	N	Y	Y	Y
2 ***Herger***	Y	N	Y	N	Y	Y
3 ***Ose***	Y	Y	Y	N	Y	Y
4 ***Doolittle***	Y	N	Y	N	Y	Y
5 Matsui	N	Y	N	Y	Y	Y
6 Woolsey	N	Y	N	Y	Y	Y
7 Miller, George	N	Y	N	Y	N	Y
8 Pelosi	N	Y	N	Y	N	?
9 Lee	N	Y	N	Y	Y	Y
10 Tauscher	N	Y	N	Y	Y	Y
11 ***Pombo***	Y	N	Y	N	Y	Y
12 Lantos	N	Y	N	Y	Y	Y
13 Stark	N	Y	N	Y	N	?
14 Eshoo	N	Y	N	Y	Y	Y
15 ***Campbell***	?	Y	Y	Y	Y	?
16 Lofgren	?	Y	N	Y	N	Y
17 Farr	N	Y	N	Y	N	Y
18 Condit	N	Y	N	N	Y	Y
19 ***Radanovich***	Y	N	Y	N	Y	Y
20 Dooley	Y	Y	N	Y	Y	?
21 ***Thomas***	Y	N	Y	N	Y	Y
22 Capps	N	Y	N	Y	Y	Y
23 ***Gallegly***	Y	Y	Y	N	Y	Y
24 Sherman	N	Y	N	Y	N	Y
25 ***McKeon***	Y	Y	Y	N	Y	Y
26 Berman	N	Y	N	Y	Y	Y
27 ***Rogan***	Y	Y	Y	N	Y	?
28 ***Dreier***	Y	Y	Y	N	Y	Y
29 Waxman	N	Y	N	Y	N	?
30 Becerra	?	Y	N	Y	Y	Y
31 ***Martinez*** [1]	Y	?	Y	N	Y	Y
32 Dixon	N	Y	N	Y	Y	Y
33 Roybal-Allard	N	Y	N	Y	Y	Y
34 Napolitano	N	Y	N	Y	Y	Y
35 Waters	N	?	N	Y	N	Y
36 ***Kuykendall***	N	Y	Y	N	Y	Y
37 Millender-McD.	N	Y	N	Y	Y	Y
38 ***Horn***	N	Y	Y	Y	Y	Y
39 ***Royce***	Y	Y	Y	N	Y	Y
40 ***Lewis***	Y	N	Y	N	Y	?
41 ***Miller, Gary***	Y	Y	Y	N	Y	Y
42 Baca	N	Y	N	Y	Y	Y
43 ***Calvert***	Y	Y	Y	N	Y	Y
44 ***Bono***	Y	Y	Y	N	Y	Y
45 ***Rohrabacher***	Y	Y	Y	N	Y	Y
46 Sanchez	N	Y	N	Y	Y	Y
47 ***Cox***	Y	Y	Y	N	Y	Y
48 ***Packard***	Y	Y	Y	N	Y	Y
49 ***Bilbray***	N	Y	Y	N	Y	Y
50 Filner	N	Y	–	Y	N	Y
51 ***Cunningham***	Y	Y	Y	N	Y	Y
52 ***Hunter***	Y	Y	Y	N	Y	Y
COLORADO						
1 DeGette	N	Y	N	Y	Y	Y
2 Udall	N	Y	N	Y	Y	Y
3 ***McInnis***	N	Y	Y	N	Y	Y
4 ***Schaffer***	Y	?	N	Y	Y	Y
5 ***Hefley***	Y	N	Y	N	Y	Y
6 ***Tancredo***	Y	N	Y	N	Y	Y
CONNECTICUT						
1 Larson	N	Y	N	Y	Y	Y
2 Gejdenson	N	Y	N	Y	N	Y
3 DeLauro	N	Y	N	Y	Y	Y
4 ***Shays***	N	Y	Y	Y	Y	Y
5 Maloney	N	Y	Y	N	Y	Y
6 ***Johnson***	Y	Y	Y	N	Y	Y
DELAWARE						
AL ***Castle***	N	Y	Y	Y	Y	Y
FLORIDA						
1 ***Scarborough***	N	Y	Y	N	Y	Y
2 Boyd	N	Y	N	N	Y	Y
3 Brown	N	Y	N	Y	Y	Y
4 ***Fowler***	Y	Y	Y	N	Y	Y
5 Thurman	N	Y	N	Y	Y	?
6 ***Stearns***	Y	Y	Y	N	Y	Y
7 ***Mica***	Y	N	Y	N	Y	Y
8 ***McCollum***	?	Y	Y	N	?	?
9 ***Bilirakis***	Y	Y	Y	N	Y	Y
10 ***Young***	?	Y	Y	N	Y	Y
11 Davis	N	Y	N	Y	Y	Y
12 ***Canady***	Y	N	Y	N	Y	Y
13 ***Miller***	Y	Y	Y	N	Y	Y
14 ***Goss***	Y	Y	Y	N	Y	Y
15 ***Weldon***	Y	Y	Y	N	Y	Y
16 ***Foley***	N	Y	Y	N	Y	Y
17 Meek	N	Y	N	Y	Y	Y
18 ***Ros-Lehtinen***	Y	Y	Y	N	+	Y
19 Wexler	N	Y	N	Y	Y	Y
20 Deutsch	N	Y	N	Y	Y	Y
21 ***Diaz-Balart***	Y	Y	Y	N	Y	Y
22 ***Shaw***	Y	Y	Y	N	Y	Y
23 Hastings	N	Y	N	Y	N	Y
GEORGIA						
1 ***Kingston***	Y	N	Y	N	Y	?
2 Bishop	N	Y	N	Y	Y	Y
3 ***Collins***	Y	Y	Y	N	Y	Y
4 McKinney	N	Y	N	Y	Y	Y
5 Lewis	N	Y	N	Y	Y	?
6 ***Isakson***	Y	Y	Y	N	Y	Y
7 ***Barr***	Y	N	Y	N	Y	Y
8 ***Chambliss***	Y	Y	Y	N	Y	Y
9 ***Deal***	Y	Y	Y	N	Y	Y
10 ***Norwood***	?	Y	Y	N	Y	?
11 ***Linder***	Y	N	Y	N	Y	Y
HAWAII						
1 Abercrombie	N	Y	N	Y	Y	Y
2 Mink	N	Y	N	Y	Y	Y
IDAHO						
1 ***Chenoweth-Hage***	Y	N	N	–	Y	+
2 ***Simpson***	Y	Y	Y	N	Y	Y
ILLINOIS						
1 Rush	N	Y	N	Y	Y	Y
2 Jackson	N	Y	N	Y	N	Y
3 Lipinski	N	Y	N	Y	Y	Y
4 Gutierrez	N	Y	N	Y	N	Y
5 Blagojevich	N	Y	N	Y	Y	Y
6 ***Hyde***	Y	Y	Y	N	Y	Y
7 Davis	N	Y	N	Y	Y	Y
8 ***Crane***	Y	N	Y	N	Y	?
9 Schakowsky	N	Y	N	Y	N	Y
10 ***Porter***	N	Y	Y	Y	Y	Y
11 ***Weller***	Y	Y	Y	N	Y	Y
12 Costello	N	Y	N	Y	Y	Y
13 ***Biggert***	N	Y	Y	N	Y	Y
14 ***Hastert*** [2]		Y	Y	N	Y	Y

ND Northern Democrats SD Southern Democrats

	7	8	9	10	11	12
15 *Ewing*	Y	Y	Y	N	?	Y
16 *Manzullo*	Y	N	Y	N	Y	Y
17 Evans	N	Y	N	Y	Y	Y
18 *LaHood*	Y	Y	Y	N	Y	Y
19 Phelps	N	Y	N	Y	Y	Y
20 *Shimkus*	Y	Y	Y	N	Y	Y
INDIANA						
1 Visclosky	N	Y	N	Y	N	Y
2 *McIntosh*	Y	?	Y	?	?	?
3 Roemer	N	Y	N	N	Y	Y
4 *Souder*	Y	N	Y	N	Y	Y
5 *Buyer*	Y	Y	Y	N	Y	Y
6 *Burton*	Y	N	Y	N	Y	Y
7 *Pease*	Y	Y	Y	N	Y	Y
8 *Hostettler*	Y	N	N	N	Y	Y
9 Hill	N	Y	N	N	Y	Y
10 Carson	N	Y	N	Y	Y	Y
IOWA						
1 *Leach*	N	Y	Y	Y	Y	Y
2 *Nussle*	Y	Y	Y	Y	Y	Y
3 Boswell	N	Y	N	Y	Y	Y
4 *Ganske*	N	Y	N	Y	Y	Y
5 *Latham*	Y	Y	Y	Y	Y	Y
KANSAS						
1 *Moran*	Y	Y	Y	N	Y	Y
2 *Ryun*	Y	N	Y	N	Y	Y
3 Moore	N	Y	N	Y	Y	Y
4 *Tiahrt*	Y	N	Y	N	Y	Y
KENTUCKY						
1 *Whitfield*	Y	Y	Y	N	Y	Y
2 *Lewis*	Y	Y	Y	N	Y	Y
3 *Northup*	Y	+	Y	N	Y	Y
4 Lucas	N	Y	N	Y	Y	Y
5 *Rogers*	Y	Y	Y	N	Y	Y
6 *Fletcher*	Y	Y	Y	N	Y	Y
LOUISIANA						
1 *Vitter*	Y	Y	Y	N	Y	Y
2 Jefferson	N	Y	N	Y	Y	Y
3 *Tauzin*	Y	Y	Y	N	Y	Y
4 *McCrery*	Y	Y	Y	N	Y	Y
5 *Cooksey*	Y	N	Y	N	Y	Y
6 *Baker*	Y	Y	Y	N	Y	Y
7 John	N	Y	N	Y	Y	Y
MAINE						
1 Allen	N	Y	N	Y	Y	Y
2 Baldacci	N	Y	N	Y	Y	Y
MARYLAND						
1 *Gilchrest*	N	Y	Y	Y	Y	Y
2 *Ehrlich*	Y	Y	Y	N	Y	?
3 Cardin	N	Y	N	Y	Y	Y
4 Wynn	N	Y	N	Y	Y	Y
5 Hoyer	N	Y	N	Y	Y	Y
6 *Bartlett*	Y	Y	Y	N	Y	Y
7 Cummings	N	Y	N	+	Y	Y
8 *Morella*	N	Y	N	Y	Y	Y
MASSACHUSETTS						
1 Olver	N	Y	N	Y	N	Y
2 Neal	N	Y	N	Y	Y	?
3 McGovern	N	Y	N	Y	Y	Y
4 Frank	N	Y	N	Y	N	Y
5 Meehan	N	Y	N	Y	Y	Y
6 Tierney	N	Y	N	Y	Y	Y
7 Markey	N	?	?	Y	Y	Y
8 Capuano	N	Y	N	Y	Y	Y
9 Moakley	N	Y	N	Y	Y	?
10 Delahunt	N	Y	N	Y	Y	Y
MICHIGAN						
1 Stupak	N	Y	N	Y	Y	Y
2 *Hoekstra*	N	Y	Y	N	Y	Y
3 *Ehlers*	N	Y	Y	Y	Y	Y
4 *Camp*	Y	Y	Y	N	Y	Y
5 Barcia	N	Y	N	Y	Y	Y
6 *Upton*	N	Y	Y	N	Y	Y
7 *Smith*	Y	Y	N	N	Y	Y
8 Stabenow	N	Y	N	Y	Y	Y
9 Kildee	N	Y	N	Y	Y	Y
10 Bonior	N	Y	N	Y	Y	Y
11 *Knollenberg*	Y	Y	Y	N	Y	Y
12 Levin	N	Y	N	Y	Y	Y
13 Rivers	N	Y	N	Y	Y	Y
14 Conyers	N	Y	N	Y	N	Y
15 Kilpatrick	N	Y	N	Y	Y	Y
16 Dingell	N	Y	N	Y	Y	Y

	7	8	9	10	11	12
MINNESOTA						
1 *Gutknecht*	Y	Y	Y	N	Y	Y
2 Minge	N	Y	N	Y	Y	Y
3 *Ramstad*	N	Y	Y	Y	Y	Y
4 Vento	?	?	?	?	?	?
5 Sabo	N	Y	N	Y	N	N
6 Luther	N	Y	N	Y	Y	Y
7 Peterson	Y	Y	Y	Y	Y	Y
8 Oberstar	N	+	N	Y	Y	+
MISSISSIPPI						
1 *Wicker*	Y	Y	Y	N	Y	Y
2 Thompson	N	Y	N	Y	Y	Y
3 *Pickering*	Y	Y	Y	N	Y	Y
4 Shows	?	Y	N	N	Y	Y
5 Taylor	N	Y	N	N	Y	Y
MISSOURI						
1 Clay	N	Y	N	?	Y	Y
2 *Talent*	Y	Y	Y	N	Y	?
3 Gephardt	N	Y	N	Y	Y	Y
4 Skelton	N	Y	N	Y	Y	Y
5 McCarthy	N	#	N	Y	Y	Y
6 Danner	?	Y	N	N	?	Y
7 *Blunt*	Y	Y	Y	N	Y	?
8 *Emerson*	Y	Y	Y	N	Y	+
9 *Hulshof*	Y	Y	Y	N	Y	Y
MONTANA						
AL *Hill*	Y	Y	Y	N	Y	Y
NEBRASKA						
1 *Bereuter*	Y	Y	Y	N	Y	Y
2 *Terry*	Y	Y	Y	N	Y	Y
3 *Barrett*	Y	Y	Y	N	Y	Y
NEVADA						
1 Berkley	N	Y	N	Y	Y	Y
2 *Gibbons*	Y	Y	Y	N	Y	Y
NEW HAMPSHIRE						
1 *Sununu*	Y	Y	Y	Y	Y	Y
2 *Bass*	N	Y	Y	N	Y	Y
NEW JERSEY						
1 Andrews	N	Y	N	Y	Y	Y
2 *LoBiondo*	N	Y	Y	N	Y	Y
3 *Saxton*	N	Y	Y	N	Y	?
4 *Smith*	N	Y	Y	Y	Y	Y
5 *Roukema*	N	Y	Y	N	Y	Y
6 Pallone	N	Y	N	Y	Y	Y
7 *Franks*	?	Y	Y	N	Y	?
8 Pascrell	N	Y	N	Y	Y	?
9 Rothman	N	Y	N	Y	Y	Y
10 Payne	N	Y	N	Y	N	Y
11 *Frelinghuysen*	N	Y	Y	N	Y	Y
12 Holt	N	Y	N	Y	Y	Y
13 Menendez	N	Y	N	Y	?	Y
NEW MEXICO						
1 *Wilson*	Y	Y	Y	N	Y	Y
2 *Skeen*	Y	Y	Y	N	Y	Y
3 Udall	N	Y	N	Y	Y	Y
NEW YORK						
1 Forbes	N	Y	N	?	Y	Y
2 *Lazio*	N	Y	Y	N	Y	?
3 *King*	Y	Y	Y	N	Y	Y
4 McCarthy	N	Y	N	Y	Y	Y
5 Ackerman	N	Y	N	Y	N	Y
6 Meeks	N	Y	N	Y	Y	Y
7 Crowley	N	Y	N	Y	Y	Y
8 Nadler	N	Y	N	Y	Y	N
9 Weiner	N	Y	N	Y	Y	Y
10 Towns	N	Y	N	Y	Y	Y
11 Owens	N	Y	N	Y	Y	?
12 Velázquez	N	Y	N	Y	Y	Y
13 *Fossella*	Y	Y	Y	N	Y	Y
14 Maloney	N	Y	N	Y	Y	Y
15 Rangel	N	Y	N	Y	Y	Y
16 Serrano	N	Y	N	Y	Y	Y
17 Engel	N	Y	N	Y	Y	Y
18 Lowey	N	Y	N	Y	Y	Y
19 *Kelly*	N	Y	Y	N	Y	Y
20 *Gilman*	N	Y	Y	N	?	Y
21 McNulty	N	Y	N	?	Y	Y
22 *Sweeney*	Y	Y	Y	N	Y	?
23 *Boehlert*	N	Y	Y	Y	Y	Y
24 *McHugh*	Y	Y	Y	N	Y	Y
25 *Walsh*	N	Y	Y	N	Y	?
26 Hinchey	N	Y	N	Y	Y	?
27 *Reynolds*	N	Y	Y	N	Y	Y
28 Slaughter	N	Y	N	Y	Y	Y
29 LaFalce	N	Y	N	Y	Y	Y

	7	8	9	10	11	12
30 *Quinn*	N	Y	Y	N	Y	Y
31 *Houghton*	N	Y	Y	N	Y	Y
NORTH CAROLINA						
1 Clayton	N	Y	N	Y	Y	Y
2 Etheridge	N	Y	N	Y	Y	Y
3 *Jones*	Y	Y	Y	N	Y	+
4 Price	N	Y	N	Y	Y	Y
5 *Burr*	Y	Y	Y	N	Y	Y
6 *Coble*	Y	Y	Y	N	Y	Y
7 McIntyre	N	Y	N	N	Y	Y
8 *Hayes*	Y	Y	Y	N	Y	Y
9 *Myrick*	Y	N	Y	N	Y	Y
10 *Ballenger*	Y	Y	Y	N	Y	Y
11 *Taylor*	Y	Y	Y	N	Y	+
12 Watt	N	Y	N	Y	Y	Y
NORTH DAKOTA						
AL Pomeroy	N	Y	N	Y	Y	Y
OHIO						
1 *Chabot*	Y	Y	Y	N	Y	Y
2 *Portman*	Y	Y	Y	N	Y	Y
3 Hall	N	Y	N	Y	Y	Y
4 *Oxley*	Y	N	Y	N	Y	?
5 *Gillmor*	Y	Y	Y	N	Y	Y
6 Strickland	N	Y	N	Y	Y	Y
7 *Hobson*	N	Y	Y	N	Y	Y
8 *Boehner*	Y	Y	Y	N	Y	Y
9 Kaptur	N	Y	N	Y	Y	Y
10 Kucinich	N	Y	N	N	Y	Y
11 Jones	?	Y	N	Y	Y	Y
12 *Kasich*	N	Y	Y	Y	Y	?
13 Brown	N	Y	N	Y	Y	Y
14 Sawyer	N	Y	N	Y	Y	Y
15 *Pryce*	Y	Y	Y	N	Y	?
16 *Regula*	Y	Y	Y	N	Y	Y
17 Traficant	Y	Y	Y	Y	Y	Y
18 *Ney*	Y	Y	Y	N	Y	Y
19 *LaTourette*	Y	Y	Y	Y	Y	Y
OKLAHOMA						
1 *Largent*	Y	Y	Y	N	Y	Y
2 *Coburn*	Y	N	N	N	Y	Y
3 *Watkins*	Y	Y	Y	N	Y	Y
4 *Watts*	Y	Y	Y	N	Y	Y
5 *Istook*	Y	Y	N	N	Y	Y
6 *Lucas*	Y	Y	Y	N	Y	Y
OREGON						
1 Wu	N	Y	N	Y	Y	Y
2 *Walden*	Y	Y	Y	N	Y	Y
3 Blumenauer	N	Y	N	Y	Y	Y
4 DeFazio	N	Y	N	Y	N	Y
5 Hooley	N	Y	N	Y	Y	Y
PENNSYLVANIA						
1 Brady	N	Y	N	Y	Y	Y
2 Fattah	N	Y	N	Y	Y	?
3 Borski	N	Y	N	Y	Y	Y
4 Klink	N	Y	N	Y	Y	?
5 *Peterson*	Y	N	Y	N	Y	Y
6 Holden	N	Y	N	N	Y	Y
7 *Weldon*	N	Y	Y	N	Y	Y
8 *Greenwood*	?	Y	Y	N	Y	Y
9 *Shuster*	Y	Y	Y	N	Y	Y
10 *Sherwood*	Y	Y	Y	N	Y	Y
11 Kanjorski	N	Y	N	Y	Y	Y
12 Murtha	N	Y	N	Y	Y	Y
13 Hoeffel	N	Y	N	Y	Y	Y
14 Coyne	N	Y	N	Y	Y	Y
15 *Toomey*	Y	Y	Y	N	Y	Y
16 *Pitts*	Y	N	Y	N	Y	Y
17 *Gekas*	Y	Y	Y	N	Y	Y
18 Doyle	N	Y	N	Y	Y	Y
19 *Goodling*	Y	Y	Y	N	Y	Y
20 Mascara	N	Y	N	Y	Y	Y
21 *English*	N	Y	Y	Y	Y	Y
RHODE ISLAND						
1 Kennedy	N	Y	N	Y	Y	Y
2 Weygand	N	Y	N	Y	Y	Y
SOUTH CAROLINA						
1 *Sanford*	Y	Y	N	N	Y	Y
2 *Spence*	Y	Y	Y	N	Y	Y
3 *Graham*	Y	Y	Y	N	Y	Y
4 *DeMint*	Y	Y	Y	N	Y	Y
5 Spratt	N	Y	N	Y	Y	Y
6 Clyburn	N	Y	N	Y	Y	Y
SOUTH DAKOTA						
AL *Thune*	Y	Y	Y	N	Y	Y

	7	8	9	10	11	12
TENNESSEE						
1 *Jenkins*	Y	N	Y	N	+	Y
2 *Duncan*	Y	Y	Y	N	Y	Y
3 *Wamp*	Y	Y	Y	N	Y	?
4 *Hilleary*	Y	Y	Y	N	Y	+
5 Clement	N	Y	N	Y	Y	Y
6 Gordon	N	Y	N	Y	?	?
7 *Bryant*	Y	Y	Y	N	Y	Y
8 Tanner	N	Y	N	Y	Y	Y
9 Ford	N	Y	N	Y	Y	Y
TEXAS						
1 Sandlin	N	Y	N	Y	Y	Y
2 Turner	N	Y	N	Y	Y	Y
3 *Johnson, Sam*	Y	N	Y	N	Y	?
4 Hall	Y	Y	Y	N	Y	Y
5 *Sessions*	Y	Y	Y	N	Y	Y
6 *Barton*	Y	N	Y	N	?	Y
7 *Archer*	Y	Y	Y	N	Y	Y
8 *Brady*	Y	Y	Y	N	Y	Y
9 Lampson	N	Y	N	Y	?	Y
10 Doggett	N	Y	N	Y	Y	Y
11 Edwards	N	Y	N	Y	?	Y
12 *Granger*	Y	Y	Y	N	Y	Y
13 *Thornberry*	Y	N	Y	N	Y	Y
14 *Paul*	Y	N	N	N	N	Y
15 Hinojosa	?	Y	N	Y	Y	Y
16 Reyes	N	Y	N	Y	Y	Y
17 Stenholm	Y	Y	N	Y	Y	Y
18 Jackson-Lee	N	Y	N	Y	Y	Y
19 *Combest*	Y	N	Y	N	Y	Y
20 Gonzalez	N	Y	N	Y	Y	Y
21 *Smith*	Y	Y	Y	N	Y	Y
22 *DeLay*	Y	N	Y	N	Y	Y
23 *Bonilla*	Y	N	Y	N	Y	Y
24 Frost	N	Y	N	Y	Y	?
25 Bentsen	N	Y	N	Y	Y	Y
26 *Armey*	Y	Y	Y	N	Y	Y
27 Ortiz	Y	Y	N	Y	Y	Y
28 Rodriguez	N	Y	N	Y	Y	Y
29 Green	N	Y	N	Y	Y	Y
30 Johnson, E.B.	N	Y	N	Y	Y	Y
UTAH						
1 *Hansen*	Y	Y	Y	N	Y	Y
2 *Cook*	Y	?	?	N	Y	?
3 *Cannon*	Y	Y	Y	N	Y	Y
VERMONT						
AL *Sanders*	N	Y	N	Y	N	Y
VIRGINIA						
1 *Bateman* [3]	Y	N	Y	N	Y	
2 Pickett	Y	Y	N	N	Y	Y
3 Scott	N	Y	N	Y	N	Y
4 Sisisky	Y	Y	N	Y	Y	Y
5 *Goode*	Y	Y	Y	N	Y	Y
6 *Goodlatte*	Y	Y	Y	N	Y	Y
7 *Bliley*	Y	Y	Y	N	Y	Y
8 Moran	N	Y	N	Y	Y	Y
9 Boucher	N	Y	N	Y	Y	?
10 *Wolf*	Y	Y	Y	Y	Y	Y
11 *Davis, T.*	N	Y	Y	N	Y	Y
WASHINGTON						
1 Inslee	N	Y	N	Y	Y	Y
2 *Metcalf*	Y	Y	Y	N	Y	Y
3 Baird	N	Y	N	Y	Y	Y
4 *Hastings*	Y	Y	Y	N	Y	?
5 *Nethercutt*	Y	Y	Y	N	Y	?
6 Dicks	N	Y	N	N	Y	Y
7 McDermott	N	Y	N	Y	N	Y
8 *Dunn*	Y	Y	Y	N	Y	?
9 Smith	N	Y	N	?	?	Y
WEST VIRGINIA						
1 Mollohan	N	Y	N	Y	Y	N
2 Wise	N	Y	N	Y	Y	?
3 Rahall	N	Y	N	Y	Y	Y
WISCONSIN						
1 *Ryan*	Y	Y	Y	N	Y	Y
2 Baldwin	N	Y	N	Y	N	Y
3 Kind	N	Y	N	Y	Y	Y
4 Kleczka	N	Y	N	Y	Y	Y
5 Barrett	N	Y	N	Y	Y	Y
6 *Petri*	N	Y	Y	N	Y	Y
7 Obey	N	Y	N	Y	Y	Y
8 *Green*	Y	Y	Y	N	Y	Y
9 *Sensenbrenner*	Y	Y	Y	Y	Y	Y
WYOMING						
AL *Cubin*	Y	Y	Y	Y	Y	?

Southern states - Ala., Ark., Fla., Ga., Ky., La., Miss., N.C., Okla., S.C., Tenn., Texas, Va.

Senate Key Votes 7, 8, 9, 10, 11, 12

	7	8	9	10	11	12
ALABAMA						
Shelby	Y	Y	Y	Y	N	Y
Sessions	Y	Y	Y	Y	N	N
ALASKA						
Stevens	Y	Y	Y	Y	Y	N
Murkowski	Y	Y	Y	Y	Y	Y
ARIZONA						
McCain	Y	N	Y	Y	N	N
Kyl	Y	Y	Y	Y	N	Y
ARKANSAS						
Hutchinson	Y	Y	Y	Y	N	Y
Lincoln	N	N	N	N	Y	N
CALIFORNIA						
Feinstein	Y	N	N	Y	Y	?
Boxer	N	N	N	?	Y	N
COLORADO						
Campbell	Y	Y	Y	Y	Y	Y
Allard	Y	Y	Y	Y	Y	Y
CONNECTICUT						
Dodd	N	N	N	N	Y	N
Lieberman	Y	N	N	N	?	?
DELAWARE						
Roth	Y	Y	Y	Y	Y	N
Biden	N	N	N	Y	Y	N
FLORIDA						
Graham	N	N	N	N	Y	N
Mack	Y	Y	Y	Y	Y	Y
GEORGIA						
Coverdell/Miller[1]	Y	Y	Y		Y	N
Cleland	N	N	N	Y	Y	N
HAWAII						
Inouye	?	?	N	?	Y	N
Akaka	N	N	N	N	?	?
IDAHO						
Craig	Y	Y	Y	Y	Y	Y
Crapo	Y	Y	Y	Y	Y	Y
ILLINOIS						
Durbin	N	N	N	N	Y	N
Fitzgerald	Y	N	Y	Y	Y	Y
INDIANA						
Lugar	Y	Y	Y	Y	Y	Y
Bayh	N	N	N	N	Y	N
IOWA						
Grassley	Y	Y	Y	Y	Y	Y
Harkin	N	N	N	N	Y	N
KANSAS						
Brownback	Y	Y	Y	Y	Y	N
Roberts	Y	Y	Y	Y	Y	N
KENTUCKY						
McConnell	Y	Y	Y	Y	N	Y
Bunning	Y	Y	Y	Y	N	N
LOUISIANA						
Breaux	N	N	N	N	Y	N
Landrieu	N	N	N	Y	Y	N
MAINE						
Snowe	Y	Y	N	Y	N	N
Collins	Y	Y	N	Y	N	N
MARYLAND						
Sarbanes	N	N	N	N	N	N
Mikulski	N	N	N	N	N	N
MASSACHUSETTS						
Kennedy	N	N	N	N	Y	N
Kerry	N	N	N	?	Y	N
MICHIGAN						
Levin	N	N	N	N	Y	N
Abraham	Y	Y	Y	Y	N	N
MINNESOTA						
Wellstone	N	N	N	N	N	N
Grams	Y	Y	Y	Y	Y	N
MISSISSIPPI						
Cochran	Y	Y	Y	Y	Y	Y
Lott	Y	Y	Y	Y	N	Y
MISSOURI						
Bond	Y	Y	Y	Y	Y	Y
Ashcroft	Y	Y	Y	Y	N	N
MONTANA						
Baucus	N	N	N	N	Y	N
Burns	Y	Y	Y	Y	Y	N
NEBRASKA						
Kerrey	N	N	N	?	Y	N
Hagel	Y	Y	Y	Y	Y	Y
NEVADA						
Reid	N	N	N	N	Y	N
Bryan	N	N	N	N	Y	N
NEW HAMPSHIRE						
Smith	Y	Y	Y	Y	N	N
Gregg	Y	Y	Y	Y	N	Y
NEW JERSEY						
Lautenberg	N	N	N	N	Y	N
Torricelli	N	N	N	Y	N	N
NEW MEXICO						
Domenici	Y	Y	Y	Y	Y	Y
Bingaman	N	N	N	N	Y	N
NEW YORK						
Moynihan	N	N	N	N	Y	N
Schumer	N	N	N	N	Y	N
NORTH CAROLINA						
Helms	Y	Y	Y	Y	N	N
Edwards	N	N	N	N	Y	N
NORTH DAKOTA						
Conrad	N	N	N	N	N	N
Dorgan	N	N	N	N	Y	N
OHIO						
DeWine	Y	Y	Y	Y	N	N
Voinovich	Y	Y	Y	N	Y	N
OKLAHOMA						
Nickles	Y	Y	Y	Y	Y	Y
Inhofe	Y	Y	Y	Y	N	Y
OREGON						
Wyden	N	N	N	N	Y	N
Smith	Y	Y	Y	Y	Y	Y
PENNSYLVANIA						
Specter	Y	N	Y	Y	N	Y
Santorum	Y	Y	Y	Y	N	N
RHODE ISLAND						
Reed	N	N	N	N	Y	N
Chafee, L.	Y	N	Y	Y	Y	N
SOUTH CAROLINA						
Thurmond	Y	Y	Y	Y	N	Y
Hollings	N	N	N	N	N	N
SOUTH DAKOTA						
Daschle	N	N	N	N	Y	N
Johnson	N	N	N	N	Y	N
TENNESSEE						
Thompson	Y	Y	Y	Y	N	N
Frist	Y	Y	Y	Y	N	N
TEXAS						
Gramm	Y	Y	Y	Y	Y	N
Hutchison	Y	Y	Y	Y	N	N
UTAH						
Hatch	Y	Y	Y	Y	Y	N
Bennett	Y	Y	Y	Y	Y	Y
VERMONT						
Leahy	?	?	N	N	Y	N
Jeffords	Y	Y	N	Y	Y	N
VIRGINIA						
Warner	Y	Y	Y	Y	Y	N
Robb	N	N	N	N	Y	N
WASHINGTON						
Gorton	Y	Y	Y	Y	?	Y
Murray	N	N	N	?	Y	N
WEST VIRGINIA						
Byrd	Y	N	N	Y	N	N
Rockefeller	N	N	N	N	Y	N
WISCONSIN						
Kohl	N	N	N	Y	N	N
Feingold	N	N	N	N	N	N
WYOMING						
Thomas	Y	Y	Y	Y	Y	Y
Enzi	Y	Y	Y	Y	Y	Y

ND Northern Democrats SD Southern Democrats

Southern states - Ala., Ark., Fla., Ga., Ky., La., Miss., N.C., Okla., S.C., Tenn., Texas, Va.

Key

- Y Voted for (yea).
- \# Paired for.
- \+ Announced for.
- N Voted against (nay).
- X Paired against.
- – Announced against.
- P Voted "present."
- C Voted "present" to avoid possible conflict of interest.
- ? Did not vote or otherwise make a position known.

•

Democrats ***Republicans***
Independents

7. HR 4577. Fiscal 2001 Labor-HHS-Education Appropriations/Genetic Discrimination. Jeffords, R-Vt., amendment that would prohibit health insurers from using predictive genetic information to discriminate in the health care system. It also would prohibit insurance companies from raising rates or denying patients health coverage based on the results of genetic tests. Adopted 58-40: R 55-0; D 3-40 (ND 3-32, SD 0-8). June 29, 2000. *(Senate vote 165)*

8. HR 4577. Fiscal 2001 Labor-HHS-Education Appropriations/Managed Care. Nickles, R-Okla., amendment that would provide federal protections, such as access to emergency care, internal and external appeals, specialists and out-of-network doctors, primarily for the 56 million Americans in self-insured health plans. It also would prohibit denials based on predictive genetic information for patients in self-insured and employer plans, and allow patients to sue in federal court for harm caused by the failure to comply with the external medical review or harm caused due to delay in providing care. Adopted 51-47: R 51-4; D 0-43 (ND 0-35, SD 0-8). June 29, 2000. *(Senate vote 166)*

9. S 2549. Fiscal 2001 Defense Authorization/Missile Defense System Testing. Cochran, R-Miss., motion to table (kill) the Durbin, D-Ill., amendment that would require the Pentagon to test the national missile defense system against reasonable decoys and countermeasures that the system could encounter in a launch, and establish an independent panel to review the testing. Motion agreed to 52-48: R 52-3; D 0-45 (ND 0-37, SD 0-8). July 13, 2000. *(Senate vote 178)*

10. HR 4810. Alleviate "Marriage Penalty" Tax/Conference Report. Adoption of the conference report on the bill that would reduce taxes for married couples by approximately $89.8 billion over five years. The measure would increase the standard deduction claimed by married couples to twice the amount claimed by single taxpayers. The upper boundary of the 15 percent tax bracket would gradually increase to twice the limit for singles. The measure also would allow couples to earn an additional $2,000 before being disqualified from receiving the earned income tax credit. The bill would also allow couples to use certain tax credits without paying the alternative minimum tax. Adopted (thus cleared for the president) 60-34: R 53-1; D 7-33 (ND 5-27, SD 2-6). A "nay" was a vote in support of the president's position. July 21, 2000. *(Senate vote 226)*

11. HR 4444. China Trade/Nonproliferation of Weapons. Roth, R-Del., motion to table (kill) the Thompson, R-Tenn., amendment that would provide for sanctions against China and other countries for selling illicit weapons of mass destruction. The proposal would establish an annual review process and require the president to impose non-trade related sanctions on individuals, companies and groups found to be spreading weapons of mass destruction. The president also would be authorized to impose additional sanctions on key supplier countries. Motion agreed to 65-32: R 30-23; D 35-9 (ND 27-8, SD 8-1). Sept. 13, 2000. *(Senate vote 242)*

12. HR 4516. Fiscal 2001 Legislative Branch, Treasury-Postal Service Appropriations/Conference Report. Adoption of the conference report on the bill that would appropriate $2.5 billion in fiscal 2001 for the legislative branch; appropriate $30.4 billion for the Treasury Department, Postal Service, executive office of the president and certain independent agencies; and repeal the 3 percent federal excise tax on telecommunications services by the end of 2002. Rejected 28-69: R 28-26; D 0-43 (ND 0-34, SD 0-9). Sept. 20, 2000. *(Senate vote 253)*

[1] *Sen. Paul Coverdell, R-Ga., died July 18, 2000. The last vote for which he was eligible was 215. He was replaced by Democrat Zell Miller, who was sworn in July 27. The first vote for which Miller was eligible was 229.*

CQ

Appendix D

TEXTS

In His State of the Union Address, Clinton Calls for an American Century Of Opportunity, Responsibility, Community

Following is a transcript of President Clinton's Jan. 27 State of the Union address. Transcript provided by Federal Document Clearing House.

Mr. Speaker, Mr. Vice President, members of Congress, honored guests, my fellow Americans: We are fortunate to be alive at this moment in history.

Never before has our nation enjoyed, at once, so much prosperity and social progress with so little internal crisis and so few external threats. Never before have we had such a blessed opportunity — and, therefore, such a profound obligation — to build the more perfect union of our founders' dreams.

We begin the new century with over 20 million new jobs. The fastest economic growth in more than 30 years. The lowest unemployment rates in 30 years. The lowest poverty rates in 20 years. The lowest African-American and Hispanic unemployment on record; the first back-to-back surpluses in 42 years; and next month America will achieve the longest period of economic growth in our entire history.

We have built a new economy, and our economic revolution has been matched by a revival of the American spirit: crime down by 20 percent to its lowest level in 25 years; teen births down seven years in a row; adoptions up by 30 percent; welfare rolls cut in half to their lowest levels in 30 years.

My fellow Americans, the state of our union is the strongest it has ever been.

Reinventing America

As always, the real credit belongs to the American people. My gratitude also goes to those of you in this chamber who have worked with us to put progress over partisanship. Eight years ago, it was not so clear to most Americans there would be much to celebrate in the year 2000. Then our nation was gripped by economic distress, social decline, political gridlock. The title of a best-selling book that year asked: "America: What Went Wrong?"

In the best traditions of our nation, Americans determined to set things right. We restored the vital center, replacing outdated ideologies with a new vision anchored in basic, enduring values: opportunity for all, responsibility from all, a community of all Americans.

We reinvented government, transforming it into a catalyst for new ideas that stress both opportunity and responsibility, and give our people the tools to solve their own problems.

With the smallest federal work force in 40 years, we turned record deficits into record surpluses and doubled our investment in education. We cut crime with 100,000 community police and the Brady law, which has kept guns out of the hands of half a million criminals.

We ended welfare as we knew it, requiring work while protecting health care and nutrition for children, and investing more in child care, transportation and housing to help their parents go to work.

We've helped parents to succeed at home and at work, with family leave, which 20 million Americans have now used to care for a newborn child or a sick loved one. We have engaged 150,000 young Americans in citizen service through AmeriCorps, while helping them earn money for college.

In 1992, we just had a road map. Today, we have results.

But even more important, America again has the confidence to dream big dreams. But we must not let this confidence drift into complacency, for we, all of us, will be judged by the dreams and deeds we pass on to our children. And on that score, we will be held to a high standard indeed, because our chance to do good is so great.

21st Century Revolution

My fellow Americans, we have crossed the bridge we built to the 21st century. Now we must shape a 21st century American revolution of opportunity, responsibility and community. We must be now, as we were in the beginning, a new nation.

At the dawn of the last century, Theodore Roosevelt said, "The one characteristic more essential than any other is foresight. It should be the growing nation with a future that takes the long look ahead."

So tonight, let us take our long look ahead and set great goals for our nation. To 21st century America, let us pledge these things: Every child will begin school ready to learn and graduate ready to succeed . . . every family will be able to succeed at home and at work, and no child will be raised in poverty.

We will meet the challenge of the aging of America. We will assure quality affordable health care at last for all Americans.

We will make America the safest big country on Earth.

We will pay off our national debt for the first time since 1835.

We will bring prosperity to every American community. We will reverse the course of climate change and leave a safer, cleaner planet. America will lead the world toward shared peace and prosperity, and the far frontiers of science and technology. And we will become at last what our founders pledged us to be so long ago: one nation, under God, indivisible, with liberty and justice for all.

Great Goals

These are great goals, worthy of a great nation. We will not reach them all this year. Not even in this decade. But we will reach them.

Let us remember that the first American revolution was not won with a single shot. The continent was not settled in a single year. The lesson of our history, and the lesson of the last seven years, is that great goals are reached step by step, always building on our progress, always gaining ground. Of course, you can't gain ground if you're standing still. For too long, this Congress has been standing still on some of our most pressing national priorities. So let's begin tonight with them.

Again, I ask you to pass a real patients' bill of rights.

I ask you to pass common-sense gun-safety legislation.

I ask you to pass campaign finance reform.

I ask you to vote up or down on judicial nominations and other important appointees.

And again I ask you — I implore you — to raise the minimum wage.

Now, two years ago . . . as we reached across party lines to reach our first balanced budget, I asked that we meet our responsibility to the next generation by maintaining our fiscal discipline. Because we refused to stray from that path, we are doing something that would have seemed unimaginable seven years ago. We are actually paying down the national debt. If we stay on this path, we can pay down the debt entirely in just 13 years now and make America debt-free for the first time since Andrew Jackson was president in 1835.

In 1993, we began to put our fiscal house in order with the Deficit Reduction Act, which you'll all remember won passage in both houses by just a single vote. Your former colleague, my first secretary of the Treasury, led that effort and sparked our long boom. He's here with us tonight.

Lloyd Bentsen, you have served America well, and we thank you.

Beyond paying off the debt, we must ensure that the benefits of debt reduction go to preserving two of the most important guarantees we make to every American: Social Security and Medicare.

Tonight — tonight, I ask you to work with me to make a bipartisan down payment on Social Security reform, by crediting the interest savings from debt reduction to the Social Security trust fund so that it will be strong and sound for the next 50 years.

But this is just the start of our journey. We must also take the right steps toward reaching our great goals.

Education Goals

First and foremost, we need a 21st century revolution in education, guided by our faith that every single child can learn.

Because education is more important than ever, more than ever the key to our children's future, we must make sure all our children have that key. That means quality preschool and after-school, the best-trained teachers in the classroom and college opportunities for all our children.

For seven years now, we've worked hard to improve our schools with opportunity and responsibility, investing more but demanding more in turn. Reading, math, college entrance scores are up. Some of the most impressive gains are in schools in very poor neighborhoods.

But all successful schools have followed the same proven formula: higher standards, more accountability and extra help so children who need it can get it to reach those standards.

I have sent Congress a reform plan based on that formula. It holds states and school districts accountable for progress and rewards them for results.

Each year, our national government invests more than $15 billion in our schools. It is time to support what works and stop supporting what doesn't.

Now, as we demand more from our schools, we should also invest more in our schools.

Let's double our investment to help states and districts turn around their worst-performing schools or shut them down.

Let's double our investments in after-school and summer school programs, which boost achievement and keep people off the street and out of trouble. If — if we do this, we can give every single child in every failing school in America — everyone — the chance to meet high standards.

Since 1993, we've nearly doubled our investment in Head Start and improved its quality. Tonight, I ask you for another $1 billion for Head Start, the largest increase in the history of the program.

We know that children learn best in smaller classes with good teachers. For two years in a row, Congress has supported my plan to hire 100,000 new, qualified teachers to lower class sizes in the early grades. I thank you for that, and I ask you to make it three in a row.

And to make sure all teachers know the subjects they teach, tonight I propose a new teacher quality initiative to recruit more talented people into the classroom, reward good teachers for staying there and give all teachers the training they need.

We know charter schools provide real public school choice. When I became president, there was just one independent public charter school in all America. Today, thanks to you, there are 1,700. I ask you now to help us meet our goal of 3,000 charter schools by next year.

We know we must connect all our classrooms to the Internet. And we're getting there. In 1994, only 3 percent of our classrooms were connected. Today, with the help of the vice president's E-rate program, more than half of them are, and 90 percent of our schools have at least one Internet connection.

But we cannot finish the job when a third of all our schools are in serious disrepair.

Many of them have walls and wires so old they're too old for the Internet.

So tonight, I propose to help 5,000 schools a year make immediate and urgent repairs, and again, to help build or modernize 6,000 more to get students out of trailers and into high-tech classrooms.

I ask all of you to help me double our bipartisan GEAR-UP program, which provides mentors for disadvantaged young people. If we double it, we can provide mentors for 1.4 million of them.

Let's also offer these kids from disadvantaged backgrounds the same chance to take the same college test prep courses wealthier students use to boost their test scores. To make the American dream achievable for all, we must make college affordable for all. For seven years, on a bipartisan basis, we have taken action toward that goal: larger Pell grants, more-affordable student loans, education IRAs and our HOPE scholarships, which have already benefited 5 million young people. Now, 67 percent of high school graduates are going on to college. That's up 10 percent since 1993. Yet millions of families still strain to pay college tuition. They need help.

Tax Cuts for Education

So I propose a landmark, $30 billion college opportunity tax cut, a middle-class tax deduction for up to $10,000 in college tuition costs. The previous actions of this Congress have already made two years of college affordable for all. It's time to make four years of college affordable for all.

If we take all these steps, we will move a long way toward making sure every child starts school ready to learn and graduates ready to succeed.

We also need a 21st century revolution to reward work and strengthen families by giving every parent the tools to succeed at work and at the most important work of all: raising children.

Health Care

That means making sure every family has health care and the support to care for aging parents, the tools to bring their children up right, and that no child grows up in poverty. From my first days as president, we've worked to give families better access to better health care. In 1997, we passed the Children's Health Insurance Program, CHIP, so that workers who don't have coverage through their employers at least can get it for their children.

So far, we've enrolled 2 million children. We're well on our way to our goal of 5 million. But there are still more than 40 million of our fellow Americans without health insurance — more than there were in 1993.

Tonight, I propose that we follow Vice President Gore's suggestion to make low-income parents eligible for the insurance that covers their children.

Together with our children's initiative — think of this — together with our children's initiative, this action would enable us to cover nearly a quarter of all the uninsured people in America.

Again, I want to ask you to let people between the ages of 55 and 65, the fastest-growing group of uninsured, buy into Medicare.

And this year I propose to give them a tax credit to make that choice an affordable one. I hope you will support that as well.

When the Baby Boomers retire, Medicare will be faced with caring for twice as many of our citizens, yet it is far from ready to do so. My generation must not ask our children's generation to shoulder our burden. We simply must act now to strengthen and modernize Medicare.

My budget includes a comprehensive plan to reform Medicare, to make it more efficient and more competitive. And it dedicates nearly $400 billion of our budget surplus to keep Medicare solvent past 2025.

And at long last, it also provides funds to give every senior a voluntary choice of affordable coverage for prescription drugs.

Life-saving drugs are an indispensable part of modern medicine. No one creating a Medicare program today would even think of excluding coverage for prescription drugs. Yet more than three in five of our seniors now lack dependable drug coverage, which can lengthen and enrich their lives. The millions of older Americans who need prescription drugs the most pay the highest prices for them.

In good conscience, we cannot let another year pass without extending to all our seniors this lifeline of affordable prescription drugs.

Record numbers of Americans are providing for aging or ailing loved ones at home. It's a loving but a difficult and often very expensive choice. Last year, I proposed a $1,000 tax credit for long-term care. Frankly, it wasn't enough. This year, let's triple it to $3,000.

But this year, let's pass it. We also have to make needed investments to expand access to mental health care. I want to take a moment to thank the person who led our first White House conference on mental health last year, and who, for seven years, has led all our efforts to break down the barriers to decent treatment of people with mental illness. Thank you, Tipper Gore.

Taken together, these proposals would mark the largest investment in health care in the 35 years since Medicare was created — the largest investment in 35 years. That would be a big step toward assuring quality health care for all Americans, young and old. And I ask you to embrace them and pass them.

Earning the Tax Credit

We must also make investments that reward work and support families. Nothing does that better than the earned income tax credit, the EITC. The "E" in the "EITC" is about earning, working, taking responsibility and being rewarded for it.

In my very first address to you, I asked Congress to greatly expand this credit, and you did. As a result, in 1998 alone, the EITC helped more than 4.3 million Americans work their way out of poverty toward the middle class. That's double the number in 1993.

Tonight, I propose another major expansion of the EITC, to reduce the marriage penalty, to make sure it rewards marriage as it rewards work and also to expand the tax credit for families that have more than two children.

It punishes people with more than two children today.

Our proposal would allow families with three or more children to get up to $1,100 more in tax relief. These are working families, their children should not be in poverty. We also can't reward work and family unless men and women get equal pay for equal work.

Today — today, the female unemployment rate is the lowest it has been in 46 years. Yet women still only earn about 75 cents for every dollar men earn. We must do better by providing the resources to enforce present equal pay laws, training more women for high-paying, high-tech jobs, and passing the Paycheck Fairness Act. Many working parents spend up to a quarter, a quarter of their income on child care. Last year, we helped parents provide child care for about 2 million children. My child care initiative before you now along with funds already secured in welfare reform would make child care better, safer and more affordable for another 400,000 children. I ask you to pass that. They need it out there in America.

For hard-pressed middle-income families, we should also expand the child care tax credit. And I believe strongly we should take the next big step and make that tax credit refundable for low-income families.

For those — for people making under $30,000 a year, that could mean up to $2,400 for child care costs.

You know, we all say we're pro-work

and pro-family. Passing this proposal would prove it.

Tens of millions of Americans live from paycheck to paycheck.

As hard as they work, they still don't have the opportunity to save. Too few can make use of IRAs and 401(k) plans. We should do more to help all working families save and accumulate wealth.

That's the idea behind the individual development accounts, the IDAs. I ask you to take that idea to a new level, with new retirement savings accounts that enable every low- and moderate-income family in America to save for retirement, a first home, a medical emergency or a college education. I propose to match their contributions, however small, dollar for dollar, every year they save. And I propose to give a major new tax credit to any small business that will provide a meaningful pension to its workers. Those people ought to have retirement as well as the rest of us.

Nearly one in three American children grows up without a father. These children are five times more likely to live in poverty than children with both parents at home. Clearly, demanding and supporting responsible fatherhood is critical to lifting all our children out of poverty.

We've doubled child support collections since 1992, and I am proposing to you tough new measures to hold still more fathers responsible. But we should recognize that a lot of fathers want to do right by their children but need help to do it.

A Father's Responsibility

Carlos Rosas of St. Paul, Minn., wanted to do right by his son, and he got the help to do it. Now, he's got a good job and he supports his little boy. My budget will help 40,000 more fathers make the same choices Carlos Rosas did. And I thank him for being here tonight.

Stand up, Carlos. Thank you.

If there is any single issue on which we should be able to reach across party lines, it is in our common commitment to reward work and strengthen families. Just remember what we did last year: We came together to help people with disabilities keep their health insurance when they go to work, and I thank you for that.

Thanks to overwhelming bipartisan support from this Congress, we have improved foster care. We've helped those young people who leave it when they turn 18. And we have dramatically increased the number of foster care children going into adoptive homes. I thank all of you for all of that.

Of course, I am forever grateful to the person who has led our efforts from the beginning and who has worked so tirelessly for children and families for 30 years now, my wife Hillary. And I thank her. If we take the steps I've just discussed, we can go a long, long way toward empowering parents to succeed at home and at work and ensuring that no child is raised in poverty.

We can make these vital investments in health care, education, support for working families, and still offer tax cuts to help pay for college, for retirement, to care for aging parents, to reduce the marriage penalty.

We can do these things without forsaking the path of fiscal discipline that got us to this point here tonight.

Indeed, we must make these investments and these tax cuts in the context of a balanced budget that strengthens and extends the life of Social Security and Medicare and pays down the national debt.

Crime in America has dropped for the past seven years — that's the longest decline on record — thanks to a national consensus we helped to forge on community police, sensible gun safety and effective prevention. But nobody, nobody here, nobody in America believes we're safe enough. So again, I ask you to set a higher goal. Let's make this country the safest big country in the world.

Now, last fall, Congress supported my plan to hire, in addition to the 100,000 community police we've already funded, 50,000 more, concentrated in high-crime neighborhoods. I ask your continued support for that.

Gun Control

Soon after the Columbine tragedy, Congress considered common-sense gun legislation to require Brady background checks at the gun shows, child safety locks for new handguns, and a ban on the importation of large-capacity ammunition clips. With courage, and a tie-breaking vote by the vice president, the Senate faced down the gun lobby, stood up to the American people and passed this legislation. But the House failed to follow suit.

Now, we have all seen what happens when guns fall into the wrong hands. Daniel Mauser was only 15 years old when he was gunned down at Columbine. He was an amazing kid, a straight-A student, a good skier.

Like all parents who lose their children, his father, Tom, has borne unimaginable grief. Somehow he has found the strength to honor his son by transforming his grief into action. Earlier this month, he took a leave of absence from his job to fight for tougher gun safety laws. I pray that his courage and wisdom will at long last move this Congress to make common-sense gun legislation the very next order of business.

Tom Mauser, stand up. We thank you for being here tonight.

We must strengthen our gun laws and enforce those already on the books better.

Federal gun crime prosecutions are up 16 percent since I took office, but we must do more. I propose to hire more federal and local gun prosecutors and more ATF [Bureau of Alcohol, Tobacco and Firearms] agents to crack down on illegal gun traffickers and bad-apple dealers. And we must give them the enforcement tools that they need — tools to trace every gun and every bullet used in every gun crime in the United States. I ask you to help us do that.

Every state in this country already requires hunters and automobile drivers to have a license. I think they ought to do the same thing for handgun purchases.

Now, specifically — specifically, I propose a plan to ensure that all new handgun buyers must first have a photo license from their state showing they passed a Brady background check and a gun safety course before they get the gun. I hope you'll help me pass that in this Congress.

Listen to this. Listen to this. The accidental gun rate — the accidental gun death rate of children under 15 in the United States is nine times higher than in the other 25 industrialized countries combined.

Now, technologies now exist that

could lead to guns that can only be fired by the adults who own them. I ask Congress to fund research into smart-gun technology to save these children's lives. I ask responsible leaders in the gun industry to work with us on smart guns and other steps to keep guns out of the wrong hands to keep our children safe.

You know, every parent I know worries about the impact of violence in the media on their children. I want to begin by thanking the entertainment industry for accepting my challenge to put voluntary ratings on TV programs and video and Internet games. But frankly, the ratings are too numerous, diverse and confusing to be really useful to parents.

So tonight, I ask the industry to accept the first lady's challenge: to develop a single, voluntary rating system for all children's entertainment that is easier for parents to understand and enforce.

The steps I outline will take us well on our way to make America the safest big country in the world.

Now, to keep our historic economic expansion going — the subject of a lot of discussion in this community and others — I believe we need a 21st-century revolution to open new markets, start new businesses, hire new workers right here in America: in our inner cities, poor rural areas and Native American reservations.

Our nation's prosperity hasn't yet reached these places. Over the last six months, I have traveled to a lot of them — joined by many of you and many far-sighted business people — to shine a spotlight on the enormous potential in communities from Appalachia to the Mississippi Delta, from Watts to the Pine Ridge Reservation. Everywhere I go, I meet talented people eager for opportunity and able to work. Tonight, I ask you, let's put them to work.

I also — because empowerment zones have been creating these opportunities for five years now, I also ask you to increase incentives to invest in them and to create more of them.

A Common Goal

And let me say to all of you again, what I have tried to say at every turn. This is not a Democratic or a Republican issue. Giving people a chance to live their dreams is an American issue.

Mr. Speaker, it was a powerful moment last November when you joined the Rev. Jesse Jackson and me in your home state of Illinois and committed to working toward our common goal, by combining the best ideas from both sides of the aisle. I want to thank you again and to tell you, Mr. Speaker, I look forward to working with you. This is a worthy joint endeavor.

I also ask you to make special efforts to address the areas of our nation with the highest rates of poverty: our Native American reservations and the Mississippi Delta. My budget includes a $110 million initiative to promote economic development in the Delta and a billion dollars to increase economic opportunity, health care, education and law enforcement for our Native American communities.

We should begin this new century by honoring our historic responsibility to empower the first Americans. And I want to thank tonight the leaders and the members from both parties who have expressed to me an interest in working with us on these efforts. They are profoundly important.

Farming's Future

There's another part of our American community in trouble tonight: our family farmers. When I signed the Farm Bill in 1996, I said there was great danger it would work well in good times but not in bad. Well, droughts, floods and historically low prices have made these times very bad for the farmers. We must work together to strengthen the farm safety net, invest in land conservation, and create some new markets for them by expanding our programs for bio-based fuels and products. Please, they need help. Let's do it together.

Opportunity for all requires something else today: having access to a computer and knowing how to use it. That means we must close the digital divide between those who've got the tools and those who don't.

Now, connecting classrooms and libraries to the Internet is crucial, but it's just a start. My budget ensures that all new teachers are trained to teach 21st century skills, and it creates technology centers in 1,000 communities to serve adults.

This spring, I'll invite high-tech leaders to join me on another "new markets tour" to close the digital divide and open opportunity for our people. I want to thank the high-tech companies that already are doing so much in this area, and I hope the new tax incentives I have proposed will get all the rest of them to join us. This is a national crusade. We have got to do this and do it quickly.

Now, again I say to you, these are steps. But step by step we can go a long way toward our goal of bringing opportunity to every community.

To realize the full possibilities of this economy, we must reach beyond our own borders, to shape the revolution that is tearing down barriers and building new networks among nations and individuals, and economies and cultures: globalization.

It is the central reality of our time. Of course, change this profound is both liberating and threatening to people. But there is no turning back. And our open, creative society stands to benefit more than any other if we understand, and act on the realities of interdependence. We have to be at the center of every vital global network as a good neighbor and a good partner. We have to recognize that we cannot build our future without helping others to build theirs.

Trade Initiatives

The first thing we have got to do is to forge a new consensus on trade.

Now those of us who believe passionately in the power of open trade, we have to ensure that it lifts both our living standards and our values, never tolerating abusive child labor or a race to the bottom on the environment and worker protection.

But others must recognize that open markets and rules-based trade are the best engines we know for raising living standards, reducing global poverty and environmental destruction, and assuring the free flow of ideas. I believe as strongly as I did the first day I got here the only direction forward for America on trade, the only direction for America on trade, is to keep going forward. I ask you to help me forge that consensus. Now, we have to make developing economies our partners in prosperity. That's why I would like to ask you again to finalize our groundbreaking

African and Caribbean Basin Trade Initiatives.

But globalization is about more than economics. Our purpose must be to bring together the world around freedom and democracy and peace, and to oppose those who would tear it apart.

Here are the fundamental challenges I believe America must meet to shape the 21st century world:

World Economics

First, we must continue to encourage our former adversaries, Russia and China, to emerge as stable, prosperous, democratic nations. Both are being held back today from reaching their full potential — Russia by the legacy of communism, an economy in turmoil, a cruel and self-defeating war in Chechnya; China by the illusion that it can buy stability at the expense of freedom.

But think how much has changed in the past decade: 5,000 former Soviet nuclear weapons taken out of commission; Russian soldiers actually serving with ours in the Balkans; Russian people electing their leaders for the first time in 1,000 years; and in China, an economy more open to the world than ever before.

Of course, no one — not a single person in this chamber tonight — can know for sure what direction these great nations will take, but we do know for sure that we can choose what we do. And we should do everything in our power to increase the chance that they will choose wisely to be constructive members of our global community.

That's why we should support those Russians who are struggling for a democratic, prosperous future; continue to reduce both our nuclear arsenals; and help Russia to safeguard weapons and materials that remain. And that's why I believe Congress should support the agreement we negotiated to bring China into the WTO by passing permanent normal trade relations as soon as possible this year.

I think you ought to do it for two reasons. First of all, our markets are already open to China. This agreement will open China's markets to us.

And second, it will plainly advance the cause of peace in Asia and promote the cause of change in China. No, we don't know where it's going. All we can do is decide what we're going to do. But when all is said and done, we need to know we did everything we possibly could to maximize the chance that China will choose the right future. A second challenge we've got is to protect our own security from conflicts that pose the risk of wider war and threaten our common humanity. We can't prevent every conflict or stop every outrage, but where our interests are at stake and we can make a difference, we should be and we must be peace-makers.

We should be proud of our role in bringing the Middle East closer to a lasting peace; building peace in Northern Ireland; working for peace in East Timor and Africa; promoting reconciliation between Greece and Turkey and in Cyprus; working to defuse these crises between India and Pakistan; and defending human rights and religious freedom.

And we should be proud of the men and women of our armed forces and those of our allies who stopped the ethnic cleansing in Kosovo, enabling a million people to return to their homes.

When Slobodan Milosevic unleashed his terror on Kosovo, Capt. John Cherrey was one of the brave airmen who turned the tide. And when another American plane was shot down over Serbia, he flew into the teeth of enemy air defenses to bring his fellow pilot home.

Thanks to our armed forces' skill and bravery, we prevailed in Kosovo without losing a single American in combat.

I want to introduce Capt. Cherrey to you. We honor Capt. Cherrey and we promise you, captain, we'll finish the job you began. Stand up so we can see you.

Safe Technology

A third challenge we have is to keep this inexorable march of technology from giving terrorists and potentially hostile nations the means to undermine our defenses. Keep in mind, the same technological advances that have shrunk cell phones to fit in the palms of our hands, can also make weapons of terror easier to conceal and easier to use.

We must meet this threat by making effective agreements to restrain nuclear and missile programs in North Korea, curbing the flow of lethal technology to Iran, preventing Iraq from threatening its neighbors, increasing our preparedness against chemical and biological attack, protecting our vital computer systems from hackers and criminals, and developing a system to defend against new missile threats while working to preserve our ABM [Anti-ballistic missile] missile treaty with Russia. We must do all these things.

I predict to you, when most of us are long gone, but some time in the next 10 to 20 years, the major security threat this country will face will come from the enemies of the nation-state: the narco-traffickers, and the terrorists, and the organized criminals who will be organized together — working together with increasing access to ever more sophisticated chemical and biological weapons.

And I want to thank the Pentagon and others for doing what they're doing right now to try to help protect us and plan for that so that our defenses will be strong. I ask for your support so they can succeed.

I also want to ask you for a constructive bipartisan dialogue this year to work to build a consensus which I hope will eventually lead to the ratification of the Comprehensive Nuclear Test Ban Treaty.

I hope we can also have a constructive effort to meet the challenge that is presented to our planet by the huge gulf between rich and poor. We cannot accept a world in which part of humanity lives on the cutting edge of a new economy and the rest lives on the bare edge of survival. I think we have to do our part to change that with expanded trade, expanded aid and the expansion of freedom.

This is interesting: From Nigeria to Indonesia, more people got the right to choose their leaders in 1999 than in 1989 when the Berlin Wall fell. We've got to stand by these democracies, including and especially tonight Colombia, which is fighting narco-traffickers for its own people's lives and for our children's lives. I have proposed a strong two-year package to help Colombia win this fight. I want to thank the leaders in both parties, in both houses for listening to me and the president of Colombia about it.

We have got to pass this. I want to ask your help. A lot is riding on this. And it's so important for the long-term stability of our country and for what happens in Latin America.

I also want you to know I'm going to send you new legislation to go after what these drug barons value the most: their money. And I hope you will pass that as well. In a world where over a billion people live on less than a dollar a day, we also have got to do our part in the global endeavor to reduce the debts of the poorest countries so they can invest in education, health care and economic growth. That's what the pope and other religious leaders have urged us to do, and last year Congress made a down payment on America's share. I ask you to continue that. I thank you for what you did and ask you to stay the course.

Final Challenges and Thanks

I also want to say that America must help more nations to break the bonds of disease. Last year in Africa, 10 times as many people died from AIDS as were killed in wars. Ten times. The budget I give you invests $150 million more in the fight against this and other infectious killers. And today I propose a tax credit to speed the development of vaccines for diseases like malaria, TB and AIDS.

I ask the private sector and our partners around the world to join us in embracing this cause. We can save millions of lives together and we ought to do it.

I also want to mention our final challenge which, as always, is the most important. I ask you to pass a national security budget that keeps our military the best trained and best equipped in the world, with heightened readiness and 21st century weapons; which raises salaries for our servicemen and women; which protects our veterans; which fully funds the diplomacy that keeps our soldiers out of war; which makes good on our commitment to our U.N. dues and arrears. I ask you to pass this budget.

I also want to say something, if I might, very personal tonight.

The American people watching us at home, with the help of all the commentators, can tell from who stands and who sits and who claps and who doesn't, that there are still modest differences of opinion in this room. But I want to thank you for something, every one of you. I want to thank you for the extraordinary support you have given, Republicans and Democrats alike, to our men and women in uniform. I thank you for that.

And I also want to thank especially two people. First, I want to thank our secretary of Defense, Bill Cohen, for symbolizing our bipartisan commitment to national security. Thank you, sir. Even more, I want to thank his wife, Janet, who more than any other American citizen has tirelessly traveled this world to show the support we all feel for our troops. Thank you, Janet Cohen. I appreciate it.

These are the challenges we have to meet so that we can lead the world toward peace and freedom in an era of globalization.

Environmental Commitment

I want to tell you that I am very grateful for many things as president. But one of the things I'm grateful for is the opportunities that the vice president and I have had to finally put to rest the bogus idea that you cannot grow the economy and protect the environment at the same time.

Now, as our economy has grown, we have rid more than 500 neighborhoods of toxic waste; ensured cleaner air and water for millions of people; in the past three months alone, we've helped preserve more than 40 million acres of roadless lands in our national forests; created three new national monuments.

But as our communities grow, our commitment to conservation must continue to grow. Tonight, I propose creating a permanent conservation fund to restore our wildlife, protect coastlines, save natural treasures, from the California redwoods to the Everglades.

This Lands Legacy endowment would represent by far the most enduring investment in land preservation ever proposed in this house. I hope we can get together with all the people with different ideas and do this. This is a gift we should give to our children and our children for all time, across party lines.

We can make an agreement to do this. Last year, the vice president launched a new effort to make communities more liberal — livable.

Liberal — no. No.

(Laughter)

Wait a minute. I got a punchline now.

That's this year's agenda. Last year it was livable, right?

(Laughter)

That's what Sen. Lott's going to say in the commentary afterward.

(Laughter)

To make our communities for livable — this is big business. This is a big issue. What does that mean?

You ask anybody that lives in an unlivable community and they'll tell you. They want their kids to grow up next to parks, not parking lots. The parents don't want to have to spend all their time stalled in traffic when they could be home with their children.

Tonight I ask you to support new funding for the following things to make American communities more liberal — livable.

(Laughter)

One — I've done pretty well with this speech, but I can't say that. One, I want you to help us to do three things. We need more funding for advanced transit systems.

We need more funding for saving open spaces in places of heavy development.

And we need more funding — this ought to have bipartisan appeal — we need more funding for helping major cities around the Great Lakes protect their waterways and enhance their quality of life. We need these things, and I want you to help.

Now, the greatest environmental challenge of the new century is global warming. The scientists tell us the 1990s were the hottest decade of the entire millennium. If we fail to reduce the emission of greenhouse gases, deadly heat waves and droughts will become more frequent, coastal areas will flood and economies will be disrupted.

That is going to happen unless we act. Many people in the United States, some people in this chamber, and lots of folks around the world still believe you cannot cut greenhouse gas emissions without slowing economic growth.

In the Industrial Age that may well have been true. But in this digital economy, it is not true anymore. New technologies make it possible to cut harmful emissions and provide even more growth.

For example, just last week, automakers unveiled cars that get 70 to 80 miles a gallon, the fruits of a unique research partnership between government and industry. And before you know it, efficient production of biofuels will give us the equivalent of hundreds of miles from a gallon of gasoline.

To speed innovation in these kinds of technologies, I think we should give a major tax incentive to business for the production of clean energy, and to families for buying energy-saving homes and appliances and the next generation of super-efficient cars when they hit the showroom floor. And I also ask the auto industry to use available technologies to make all new cars more fuel efficient right away.

And I ask this Congress to do something else: Please help us make more of our clean-energy technology available to the developing world. That will create cleaner growth abroad and a lot more new jobs here in the United States of America.

Now, in this new century — in this new century innovations in science and technology will be key not only to the health of the environment but to miraculous improvements in the quality of our lives and advances in the economy.

Later this year, researchers will complete the first draft of the entire human genome: the very blueprint of life. It is important for all our fellow Americans to recognize that federal tax dollars have funded much of this research, and that this and other wise investments in science are leading to a revolution in our ability to detect, treat and prevent disease.

For example, researchers have identified genes that cause Parkinson's, diabetes and certain kinds of cancer. They are designing precision therapies that will block the harmful effect of these genes for good. Researchers already are using this new technique to target and destroy cells that cause breast cancer. Soon we may be able to use it to prevent the onset of Alzheimer's.

Scientists are also working on an artificial retina to help many blind people to see; and, listen to this, microchips that would actually directly stimulate damaged spinal cords in a way that could allow people now paralyzed to stand up and walk.

These kinds of innovations are also propelling our remarkable prosperity. Information technology only includes 8 percent of our employment, but now accounts for a third of our economic growth — along with jobs that pay, by the way, about 80 percent above the private sector average.

Again, we ought to keep in mind government-funded research brought supercomputers, the Internet and communications satellites into being.

Soon researchers will bring us devices that can translate foreign languages as fast as you can talk, materials 10 times stronger than steel at a fraction of the weight, and — this is unbelievable to me — molecular computers the size of a teardrop with the power of today's fastest supercomputers.

To accelerate the march of discovery across all these disciplines of science and technology, I ask you to support my recommendation of an unprecedented $3 billion in the 21st Century Research Fund, the largest increase in civilian research in a generation.

We owe it to our future.

Technology With Values

Now, these new breakthroughs have to be used in ways that reflect our values. First and foremost, we have to safeguard our citizens' privacy. Last year, we proposed to protect every citizen's medical records. This year, we will finalize those rules. We have also taken the first steps to protect the privacy of bank and credit card records and other financial statements. Soon I will send legislation to you to finish that job.

We must also act to prevent any genetic discrimination whatever by employers or insurers. I hope you will support that.

These steps will allow us to lead toward the far frontiers of science and technology. They will enhance our health, the environment, the economy in ways we can't even imagine today.

But we all know that at a time when science, technology and the forces of globalization are bringing so many changes into all our lives, it's more important than ever that we strengthen the bonds that root us in our local communities and in our national community.

No tie binds different people together like citizen service. There is a new spirit of service in America, a movement we have tried to support with AmeriCorps, expanded Peace Corps, unprecedented new partnerships with businesses, foundations, community groups.

Partnerships, for example, like the one that enlisted 12,000 companies which have now moved 650,000 of our fellow citizens from welfare to work. Partnerships to battle drug abuse, AIDS, teach young people to read, save America's treasures, strengthen the arts, fight teen pregnancy, prevent violence among young people, promote racial healing. The American people are working together.

But we should do more to help Americans help each other. First, we should help faith-based organizations to do more to fight poverty and drug abuse and help people get back on the right track with initiatives like Second Chance Homes that do so much to help unwed teen mothers.

Second, we should support Americans who tithe and contribute to charities but don't earn enough to claim a tax deduction for it.

Tonight, I propose new tax incentives that would allow low- and middle-income citizens who don't itemize to get that deduction. It's nothing but fair, and it will get more people to give.

We should do more — thank you.

We should do more to help new immigrants to fully participate in our community. That's why I recommend spending more to teach them civics and English. And since everybody in our community counts, we've got to make sure everyone is counted in this year's census.

Now, within 10 years, just 10 years, there will be no majority race in our largest state of California. In a little more than 50 years, there'll be no majority race in America. In a more interconnected world, this diversity can be our greatest strength. Just look around this chamber. Look around. We have members in this Congress from virtually every racial, ethnic and religious background. And I think you would agree that America is stronger because of it.

But you also have to agree that all those differences you just clapped for all too often spark hatred and division even here at home.

Just in the last couple of years, we've seen a man dragged to death in Texas just because he was black. We saw a young man murdered in Wyoming just because he was gay. Last year, we saw the shootings of African-Americans, Asian-Americans and Jewish children just because of who they were.

This is not the American way and we must draw the line.

I ask you — I ask you to draw that line by passing without delay the Hate Crimes Prevention Act and the Employment Non-Discrimination Act.

And I ask you to reauthorize the Violence Against Women Act.

Civil Rights Protection

Finally, tonight I propose the largest ever investment in our civil rights laws for enforcement, because no American should be subjected to discrimination in finding a home, getting a job, going to school or securing a loan.

Protections in law should be protections in fact.

Last February, because I thought this was so important, I created the White House Office of One America to promote racial reconciliation. That's what one of my personal heroes, Hank Aaron, has done all his life. From his days as our all-time home run king to his recent acts of healing, he has always brought people together. We should follow his example and we're honored to have him with us tonight.

Stand up, Hank Aaron.

I just want to say one more thing about this, and I want everyone of you to think about this next time you get mad at one of your colleagues on the other side of the aisle. This fall at the White House, Hillary had one of her millennium dinners, and we had a very distinguished scientist there. He was an expert in this whole work on the human genome. And he said that we are all, regardless of race, genetically 99.9 percent the same.

Now, you may find that uncomfortable when you look around here.

But it's — it is worth remembering. We can laugh about this, but you think about it. Modern science has confirmed what ancient faiths have always taught. The most important fact of life is our common humanity.

Therefore, we should do more than just tolerate our diversity. We should honor it and celebrate it.

My fellow Americans, every time I prepare for the State of the Union, I approach it with hope and expectation and excitement for our nation. But tonight is very special because we stand on the mountain top of a new millennium. Behind us we can look back and see the great expanse of American achievement, and before us we can see even greater, grander frontiers of possibility.

We should all of us be filled with gratitude and humility for our present progress and prosperity. We should be filled with awe and joy at what lies over the horizon. And we should be filled with absolute determination to make the most of it.

You know, when the framers finished crafting our Constitution in Philadelphia, Benjamin Franklin stood in Independence Hall and he reflected on the carving of the sun that was on the back of a chair he saw.

The sun was low on the horizon. So he said this: He said, "I've often wondered whether that sun was rising or setting. Today," Franklin said, "I have the happiness to know it's a rising sun."

Today, because each succeeding generation of Americans has kept the fire of freedom burning brightly, lighting those frontiers of possibility, we all still bask in the glow and the warmth of Mr. Franklin's rising sun.

After 224 years, the American Revolution continues. We remain a new nation. As long as our dreams outweigh our memories, America will be forever young. That is our destiny. And this is our moment.

Thank you, God bless you, and God bless America. ◆

Sens. Frist, Collins Stress Choice in Medical Care, Local Control of Education

Following is the Republican response to the State of the Union address, delivered Jan. 27 by Sens. Susan Collins, R-Maine, and Bill Frist, R-Tenn. Transcript provided by Federal Document Clearing House.

Collins: Good evening. I'm Susan Collins of Maine. Tonight, Sen. Bill Frist of Tennessee and I would like to talk with you about issues that are vital to all of us.

Our Republican agenda is driven by the simple but powerful truth that America will continue to lead the world as long as our government allows opportunity, initiative and freedom to flourish. Letting people create what they can dream has transformed our economy.

As we reflect on our economic health, we should never forget that America's recent success is, above all, a triumph of values. Americans will never let our country become rich in things and poor in spirit.

The achievements of the "dotcom" generation rest on the foundation built by our parents and our grandparents. They prevailed through the Depression, defeated the forces of fascism and made personal freedom the hallmark of countries around the globe.

To pay tribute to those great Americans on whose shoulders we stand, we are honor-bound to keep our promise to protect Social Security. Last year, for the first time in 39 years, the federal budget was balanced without dipping into the Social Security trust fund.

We'll do it again this year, and we'll pay down even more of the national debt. We've already paid off $150 billion in the last two years. Now, our goal is to eliminate the $3.6 trillion debt entirely in the next 15 years.

To promote job growth, we'll continue to help our small businesses. That means reducing burdens like the federal "death tax," so that when parents work their whole lives to leave their children a family business, it won't have to be sold just to pay the IRS.

Taxes, in general, are simply too high. We will continue to fight for tax relief for American families so that they can keep more of what they earn.

We'll honor our commitment to our brave men and women in uniform.

Last year, the Republican Congress approved the largest increase in military pay in more than a decade. And to protect our country from terrorist nations, we will build a shield against missile attack.

As important as all these issues are, there's something else that is vital to securing our future, and that is education. Prior to coming to the Senate, I worked at Husson College in Bangor, Maine. I know firsthand the difference that education can make.

We live in a time of unparalleled prosperity, but between Silicon Valley and Wall Street, many Americans still live in the shadows of the new prosperity. New technologies, unimagined a decade ago, provide exciting opportunities for some but pose unsettling challenges to others. As we enter the 21st century, every young American must be educated to adapt to a changing workplace, and many in our current work force must be provided with new skills to succeed in the new economy.

A good education is the ladder of opportunity. It turns dreams into reality. That's why education is at the top of the Republican agenda.

Four-Point Education Plan

Tonight, I ask the president to join with Republicans in our commitment to bring a good education to all our children. Our four-point plan for educational excellence will ensure that all children have an equal opportunity to reach their full potential.

First, we will continue to increase federal funds for elementary and secondary education. Last year, the Republicans boosted education spending by $500 million more than the president's budget, and we added funds for children with special needs.

Second, rather than Washington dictating to communities how they should run their schools, we should listen to those who know best: our parents, our teachers and local school boards.

The debate in Washington is not about money: It is about who makes the decisions. We need a change of approach — one that recognizes that local schools, not Washington offices, are the heart and home of education. We will empower states and communities to use federal education dollars in the ways children need most.

I've watched my younger brother Sam serve on the school board in our hometown of Caribou, Maine. He is motivated by the same goal as parents everywhere, to get the world's best education for their children. Doesn't it make sense to have the people who know your children's names decide how best to educate them?

Republicans want what all parents want for their children's schools: more federal help, but less federal interference. Instead of imposing a one-size-fits-all straitjacket, our plan recognizes that one community may need more math teachers, while another may need better reading programs, and still others new computers.

The point is, it should be your community's decision, not Washington's.

In return for that flexibility, the Republican plan requires real accountability — not more paperwork, but better results. Schools will be held responsible for what is truly important: improving student achievement.

Third, our plan will strengthen

teaching excellence. America's teachers need our help. About one-third of our new teachers get so discouraged that they leave the profession. Many are prevented from doing their very best because they don't have a chance to get enough training in the subject they teach.We will increase federal grants to states and communities and give them the freedom to use that money to better prepare, recruit and retain good teachers. The lessons are clear: We must encourage talented people to choose teaching as a career and keep them in the classroom.

Fourth, our plan will continue the long-time Republican support for higher education. Last year, we increased Pell Grants and student loans to open the doors to college for more low- and middle-income families. This year, we will increase the amount that families can contribute to education savings accounts to make higher education more affordable.

Education today is America's broadband to the future, a powerful conduit for achievement and success. Let us work together to ensure that all Americans have the opportunity for a bright future.

Now I'd like to call upon my friend and colleague, Dr. Bill Frist, the Senate's only physician.

Frist: Thank you, Susan.

I'm Bill Frist. I'm a senator from the state of Tennessee, but I've spent the better part of my life working in hospitals, caring for people with heart disease. I've learned a lot by listening to my patients and to the people who work in hospitals.

Earlier tonight we heard the president talk about his latest health care proposals. The last time he proposed a health plan was seven years ago, and then it amounted to a federal government takeover of our entire health system. It would have forced every American into a Washington-run HMO and denied them the right to choose their own doctor.

In the end, thank goodness, it was soundly defeated by Democrats and Republicans alike.

Now tonight, 84 months later, the president has unveiled a similar plan just as bad as the first. It makes government even bigger and more bloated, because each new proposal we heard about tonight — and there were about 11 of them in health care alone — comes with its own massive bureaucracy. And each will cost you, the taxpayer, billions more of your tax dollars: more than $1,000 for every man, woman and child.

During my surgical fellowship, I worked in England for the British National Health Service, and I saw firsthand the rationing, the lack of choice, the long waits and the denial of care for seniors. I learned that socialized medicine — whether in England or in Canada, where patients are fleeing to the U.S. for treatment — just does not work. In fact, if David Letterman had lived in Canada, he'd still be waiting for his heart surgery.

But I think we all know that America's health care system can be better. Costs are climbing. Too many people can't get insurance or breakthrough drugs. Too many heavy-handed HMOs tell doctors how to do their jobs. And yet we should remember that Americans still enjoy the best and most advanced health care in the world. That's why people from all over the globe come here for their latest treatments.

If you have diabetes, or arthritis, or high blood pressure, chances are medicines that you're taking weren't even around 10 years ago. Today we live longer and stay healthier than ever before.

So a lot is good. A lot is working. But we still have to make it even better.

As Republicans in Congress, we're determined not to be guided by bigger government, but by your freedom to choose your kind of health care and to select the doctor of your choice.

Already, because of Republican efforts, 5 million more children now have access to health care; if you change jobs, you can now take your health insurance with you; new mothers can leave the hospital when their doctor, not some bureaucrat, says they're ready; and we're doubling medical research for more and better cures.

A great start, but not enough.

As a doctor, I've cared for thousands of seniors. I know Medicare is their lifeline, their security. But this 35-year-old program, with 130,000 pages of regulations, creates waste and abuse, and leaves our seniors with confusing red tape and heartache. Worst of all, Medicare doesn't even include the mainstay of modern medicine: outpatient prescription drugs.

Medical Choice and Security

The answer is not government-dictated price controls that stop life-saving research or forcing the 65 percent of seniors who now have drug coverage to pay more or give up what they have. Instead, both Republicans and Democrats in Congress have come together with a plan to build on two simple principles: choice and security.

It lets people choose the type of medical plan that is best for them, including prescription drugs. No senior citizen, no mother, no person with a disability will ever be told by a bureaucrat what plan to pick, what doctor to see or what service they can receive.

But just last year, the president said no to this plan put forth by the National Bipartisan Medicare Commission, the very commission the president and Congress appointed to save Medicare.

However, I'm proud to say that I've asked for and received full assurances today from our majority leader, [Sen.] Trent Lott, [R-Miss.], that he is prepared to bring this needed bipartisan legislation to the Senate floor within two weeks. For this to happen, Mr. President, all we need is for you to tell the American people "yes" to this Democrat and Republican plan to fix Medicare, so that people like my fellow Tennessean, Patricia Brown, whom we honor in the gallery this evening, will have the vital prescription drug coverage she needs.

And tonight, to show you and others that we are sincere and that we mean business, Republicans take a first step toward making Medicare stronger. To guarantee that seniors can rely on Medicare forever, we will add it to the Social Security lockbox, which will lock away the surplus for both Social Security and Medicare. We will not let anyone spend your Medicare money.

We believe that neither HMOs nor the government should be practicing medicine. That's why Congress will, for the first time, send the president a real patients' bill of rights with strong patient protections. In our plan, if you're denied the treatment that you and your doctor decide is right, you'll get a quick appeal to an independent doctor.

Unlike the president, we see lawsuits as a last resort, not the first, because as every American knows, your sick child needs to see a doctor, not a lawyer.

During the Clinton years, the number of individuals without insurance has increased by 6 million people. But with the plan we announced yesterday, we will finally make it easier for low- and middle-income families to buy the coverage of their choice.

I believe we will dramatically improve medical care in America. How could anyone not be hopeful with what we've seen? Just look at our ability to correct heart defects in children, to halt the progression of osteoporosis, and to treat breast and prostate cancer. Soon we'll see revolutionary new treatments for conditions like Alzheimer's, sickle cell anemia and schizophrenia.

But all of these innovations require freedom, because progress and freedom go hand in hand.

You know, my father was a family doctor for 55 years. As a young boy making house calls with him, I remember his stethoscope, his doctor's black bag, and best of all, his wonderful and compassionate heart. But these were his only tools. Just one generation later, he would join me on my surgical rounds and he'd witness the miraculous new technologies and medicines that allowed us to transplant hearts and to give new life.

It's all possible because Americans are blessed with the spirit to dream, the freedom to explore and the work ethic to produce.

And so tonight, Mr. President, I ask you to put your trust in the American people, in their creativity, in their resourcefulness, in their ability to achieve free of government interference.

Mr. President, please, no more red tape. Instead, give us a health plan that includes choice and security. The American people deserve no less.

On behalf of Sen. Collins and myself, thank you for being with us. Goodnight and may God bless all of you in our great nation. ◆

Clinton Calls Nuclear Waste Bill 'Step Backward' That Would Halt New EPA Radiation Standards

Following is the text of President Clinton's April 25 veto message on S 1287, a bill to set in motion a process for high-level nuclear waste storage in Nevada:

TO THE SENATE:

I am returning herewith without my approval S 1287, the "Nuclear Waste Policy Amendments Act of 2000."

The overriding goal of the federal government's high-level radioactive waste management policy is the establishment of a permanent, geologic repository. This policy not only addresses commercial spent nuclear fuel but also advances our non-proliferation efforts by providing an option for disposal of surplus plutonium from nuclear weapons stockpiles and an alternative to reprocessing. It supports our national defense by allowing continuing operation of our nuclear navy, and it is essential for the cleanup of the Department of Energy's nuclear weapons complex.

Since 1993, my administration has been conducting a rigorous world-class scientific and technical program to evaluate the suitability of the Yucca Mountain, Nevada, site for use as a repository. The work being done at Yucca Mountain represents a significant scientific and technical undertaking, and public confidence in this first-of-a-kind effort is essential.

Unfortunately, the bill passed by the Congress will do nothing to advance the scientific program at Yucca Mountain or promote public confidence in the decision of whether or not to recommend the site for a repository in 2001. Instead, this bill could be a step backward in both respects. The bill would limit the Environmental Protection Agency's (EPA) authority to issue radiation standards that protect human health and the environment and would prohibit the issuance of EPA's final standards until June 2001. EPA's current intent is to issue final radiation standards this summer so that they will be in place well in advance of the Department of Energy's recommendation in 2001 on the suitability of the Yucca Mountain site.

There is no scientific reason to delay issuance of these final radiation standards beyond the last year of this administration; in fact, waiting until next year to issue these standards could have the unintended effect of delaying a recommendation on whether or not to go forward with Yucca Mountain. The process for further review of the EPA standards laid out in the bill passed by the Congress would simply create duplicative and unnecessary layers of bureaucracy by requiring additional review by the Nuclear Regulatory Commission and the National Academy of Sciences, even though both have already provided detailed comments to the EPA. This burdensome process would add time, but would do nothing to advance the state of scientific knowledge about the Yucca Mountain site.

Finally, the bill passed by the Congress does little to minimize the potential for continued claims against the federal government for damages as a result of the delay in accepting spent fuel from utilities. In particular, the bill does not include authority to take title to spent fuel at reactor sites, which my administration believes would have offered a practical near-term solution to address the contractual obligation to utilities and minimize the potential for lengthy and costly proceedings against the federal government. Instead, the bill would impose substantial new requirements on the Department of Energy without establishing sufficient funding mechanisms to meet those obligations. In effect, these requirements would create new unfunded liabilities for the Department.

My administration remains committed to resolving the complex and important issue of nuclear waste disposal in a timely and sensible manner consistent with sound science and protection of public health, safety, and the environment. We have made considerable progress in the scientific evaluation of the Yucca Mountain site and the Department of Energy is close to completing the work needed for a decision. It is critical that we develop the capability to permanently dispose of spent nuclear fuel and high-level radioactive waste, and I believe we are on a path to do that. Unfortunately, the bill passed by the Congress does not advance these basic goals.

WILLIAM J. CLINTON
THE WHITE HOUSE,
April 25, 2000

Clinton and Greenspan: Free Trade With China Enhances Security, Prosperity, Freedom

Following is a transcript of remarks made May 18 at the White House by President Clinton and Federal Reserve Board Chairman Alan Greenspan on the subject of permanent normal trading relations with China. Transcript provided by the White House.

Clinton: Good morning.

It's always good to have Chairman Greenspan back at the White House, and I'm especially pleased that he has come today to join me in voicing his support for permanent normal trade relations with China. We all know that when Chairman Greenspan talks, the world listens. I just hope that Congress is listening today.

Many members remain undecided, and we are doing everything we possibly can to round up each and every potential vote. I'm encouraged by the vote in the committees in both Houses, including both Republican and Democratic members, to overwhelmingly approve extending permanent normal trade relations with China. This legislation now goes before the full Congress.

All the former presidents support it, along with former secretaries of State, Defense, Trade, Transportation, national security advisers, chairmen of the Joint Chiefs of Staff, religious leaders, many of the courageous people in China fighting for human rights and the rule of law.

Momentum is building, but we've still got a challenging fight. I thank Chairman Greenspan for coming here today, and I'd like for him to say whatever is on his mind about this issue.

Mr. Chairman.

Greenspan: Thank you very much, Mr. President.

The outcome of the debate on permanent normal trade relations with China will have profound implications for the free world's trading system and the long-term growth potential of the American economy.

Jim Leach [R-Iowa], the chairman of the House Banking Committee, a couple of weeks ago requested that I share with his committee my perspective on PNTR for China. Let me read you my response:

"The addition of the Chinese economy to the global marketplace will result in a more efficient worldwide allocation of resources, and will raise standards of living in China and its trading partners. Should China accept the challenge of international competition embodied in World Trade Organization [WTO] membership, it will doubtless promote internal economic development, encourage the adoption of modern technologies, and contribute to lifting its citizens out of poverty.

History has demonstrated that implicit in any removal of power from central planners and broadening of market mechanisms, as would occur under WTO, is a more general spread of rights to individuals. Such a development will be a far stronger vehicle to foster other individual rights than any other alternative of which I am aware.

Further development of China's trading relationships with the United States and other industrial countries will work to strengthen the rule of law within China and to firm its commitment to economic reform.

China's citizens will come to have greater choice about their lifestyles and employment and to enjoy enhanced access to communication and information from around the globe.

As China's citizens experience economic gains, so will the American firms that trade in their expanding markets. China's progress towards prosperity and accession into the WTO will create new opportunities for American businesses and farmers. China, with a population of 1.2 billion people, has an economy that when measured — taking into account the purchasing power of alternative currencies — is larger than that of Japan, and may be approaching half the size of the American economy.

China's trade now accounts for 3 percent of world trade, and should expand further in response to WTO participation. Our markets are already generally open to China, and that will not be altered by PNTR.

Passage of PNTR, however, will facilitate a further opening of China's markets to U.S. producers. Accordingly, I believe extending PNTR to China, and full participation by China in the WTO, is in the interests of the United States.

Thank you, Mr. President, for having me here today to express my views on so vital an issue affecting our nation's future.

Clinton: Thank you very much, Mr. Chairman.

I would just like to say that, first, I believe that Chairman Greenspan has established a pretty good record for knowing what is in America's economic interest. He has once again reiterated, clearly and unambiguously, that this agreement exchanges membership rights for China in the WTO for economic opportunities for America in China — for American businesses and American workers — without the tariffs and technology transfer requirements, and production in China requirements, and other requirements which have limited our ability to benefit from their market for too long.

So, economically, the case is clear and compelling.

But I would also like to emphasize here the national security aspects of this, and the human and political rights aspects.

You've heard Chairman Greenspan address the human and political rights aspects, and make the point that increasing access to a market economy increases personal freedom in other ways. I will just cite one example, which is that China has gone from 2 million to 9 million to 20 million Internet users over the last three years. And it was exploding again this year; we do not know where it will be next year. But this is a profoundly significant thing.

That's why Martin Lee came all the way from Hong Kong. That's why people who have been, themselves, oppressed in China have pleaded with us to support this — because they know getting into a rules-based system and promoting economic competition will both enhance the march of liberty and law, and human rights.

The other point I would like to make is, there is a serious national security issue here. We do not know what China will choose to do in the future, and China will make that decision for itself.

But we know that one decision will dramatically increase the chances of a constructive relationship with China in a stable Asia, and the other will dramatically increase the chances of a less happy outcome. That's why Japan and North [sic] Korea, Thailand and the Philippines, our democratic allies in Northeast Asia, are for this.

If you want to reduce tensions along the Taiwan Strait, if you want a more stable Asia, if you want to maximize the chances of avoiding proliferation of dangerous weapons and a new arms race, a "yes" is the right vote.

Last point: As has been well-documented by those of you in our press, it is indeed ironic that the only people in China who want this vote to fail are the more reactionary elements of the military, economic and political structure, who do not want to give up control, and may need America as a continuing adversary to maintain that control and that capacity to repress liberty and human rights.

I believe the issue is profound and clear. And I am grateful for what Chairman Greenspan has said today.

Thank you very much. ◆

Clinton: 'Time Is Running Out For Congress to Meet Its Obligations To the American People. . . .'

What follows are excerpts of President Clinton's June 28 news conference. Transcript provided by the White House.

CLINTON: Good afternoon. This has been a good week for the American people: First, the landmark breakthrough in human genomic research, which promises to eradicate once incurable diseases and revolutionize health care for a very long time to come; second, the release of the Mid-session Review, which told us that the health of our economy continues its remarkable expansion. Our budget surplus this year will be the largest in history — $211 billion. Over the next 10 years, after we lock away Medicare and Social Security surpluses, the remaining surplus is expected to be almost $1.5 trillion. This progress exceeds even our own predictions just four months ago, another milestone in what is now the longest economic expansion in our history.

This is a tribute to the hard work of the American people and our commitment to fiscal discipline, expanded trade and investments in our people and our future. Now is not the time to abandon the path that has brought us here. We must use this moment of prosperity to make important investments in our most pressing priorities.

Chief among them is the need to provide affordable, reliable prescription drug coverage to our seniors. There is no question that this is a critical need. Just yesterday, a study released showed that prescription drugs shot up over 10 percent last year alone. That is too heavy a burden for our older seniors to pay and for our people with disabilities to pay.

There are some who say we can't provide affordable, accessible prescription drug coverage for all our seniors. I believe that's wrong. With millions of them without coverage, the absence of prescription drug coverage is a fatal flaw in our present health care system. Think about it: Because of breakthroughs like the Human Genome Project, in our lifetime there may be new life-saving drug treatments for many dreaded diseases. But they won't mean anything if our seniors and people with disabilities can't afford them. That's what this debate is really all about.

Today, the House is set to vote on a prescription drug plan that amounts to an empty promise for too many of our seniors. It's a private insurance plan that many seniors and people with disabilities simply won't be able to afford. Insurers, themselves, say the Republican plan won't work. The bottom line is, their plan is designed to benefit the companies who make the prescription drugs, not the older Americans who need to take them. It puts special interest above the public interest.

Let me make it specific and clear: This plan would not guarantee affordable prescription drugs to single senior citizens with incomes above $12,600 a year, or to senior couples with incomes above $16,600 a year. And we have all heard countless, countless stories of those with crushing medical burdens, that if they could get these prescription drugs, would have their lives lengthened and the quality of their lives improved.

An article in today's paper reveals that a group calling itself Citizens for Better Medicare is running — I give it points for chutzpa — Citizens for Better Medicare is running millions of dollars in ads to kill our prescription drug proposal. You'd think a group with this name would be in favor of affordable Medicare prescription drug coverage for all seniors and people with disabilities. But this is one of those mysterious interest groups whose financial backers are cloaked in secrecy.

Now, just last night, the House of Representatives voted overwhelmingly to force groups like this to open their books and disclose their fundraising sources to the American people. I applaud the House for this vote, and all those, Democrats and Republicans, who voted for it. With the vote on Medicare in the House, I call on Citizens for Better Medicare to respect the will of the Congress and reveal the sources of their support today. We should let the American people judge who is truly interested in better Medicare.

It is clear that this lobbying effort is part of a larger campaign to block real progress. In fact, the Republican leadership in Congress won't even allow our prescription plan to come up for a vote in the House — I suspect because they're afraid it would pass.

I have offered a Medicare prescription drug benefit that is voluntary and affordable. My plan puts the interest of seniors first. Whether you're on a fixed income, live in a big city or a rural area, the plan is dependable, and it is affordable. This is particularly important for rural Americans. More than half of our oldest seniors in rural communities go the entire year without any prescription drug coverage at all.

Earlier this week, in an effort to break the logjam, I offered a compromise proposal to give seniors the relief they desperately need. I said we could pass a prescription drug benefit while providing real tax relief to married couples, something the majority in Congress say they want to do. And we could do both now within the framework of fiscal responsibility.

As the vice president has proposed, the first thing we should do is to take the Medicare tax receipts we get off budget, so they are saved for Medicare alone and, meanwhile, used to pay down the debt. That will do more to protect and strengthen Medicare; it will help extend the life of the Medicare trust fund to 2023; it will put us in a position to pay down the debt completely by 2012, a year ahead of schedule. It will enable us still to set aside $500 billion to reserve for America's future, to be used after a full debate and after this year's elections to meet the country's key priorities.

Now, with less than 35 days left in the legislative year, time is running out for Congress to meet its obligations to the American people. They have to make the tough choices to get something done or continue to be dragged down by the weight of special interests.

So, again, I ask Congress, let's not waste these precious weeks. It's time to get down to business, to pass a strong patients' bill of rights; to raise the minimum wage by $1 over two years; to pass the common-sense gun legislation; to hold tobacco companies, not taxpayers, accountable for the health care costs of tobacco; to pass hate crimes legislation; to finish the jobs of giving American businesses and farmers access to a huge new market by passing permanent normal trade relations with China; to open new markets to American investors here at home; to bring prosperity to people in places who have been left behind; and, most important of all, to continue to improve our schools, to demand more of them and invest more in them, including more teachers for smaller class sizes, after-school programs for all our kids who need them, and repairing or modernizing thousands of our schools that are today literally falling apart or so over-crowded they can't contain all the kids.

We can still do a lot of this if we work together in the days ahead. That's what the American people want us to do, even in an election year.

There's been some encouraging developments in this Congress. We lifted the earnings limit on Social Security; we passed the Africa-Caribbean Basin trade bill. Apparently, the bill to aid Colombia is making good progress. And I think the China legislation will pass if we can get it up to a vote in a timely fashion. So the Congress can do a lot of things and I hope they will, and I'm looking forward to working with them.

QUESTION: Mr. President, after seven months, the Elián González case is coming to a conclusion, removing a thorn from U.S.-Cuban relations. And House Republican leaders have struck a deal to ease decades-old sanctions against Cuba. Would you accept that legislation? Is it time to normalize relations with Fidel Castro's government? What would that take?

CLINTON: Let me deal with the questions separately; first, on the question of the legislation proposed by Mr. [George] Nethercutt [R-Wash.]. If I believe that the legislation essentially allows for the sales of American food and medicine to Cuba or to other countries, but has some protection for us for extraordinary circumstances that foreign policy might require, like Sen. [Richard G.] Lugar's [R-Ind.] bill does in the Senate, then I would be inclined to sign the bill and to support it. I've always wanted to sell more food and medicine, not only to Cuba, but to other countries, as well.

I have some concerns about it, and I just have to analyze the bill as it passed and whatever legislation finally makes its way to my desk, because, as I understand it, they put some new restrictions on travel to Cuba, which might undermine our people-to-people contacts, which had been more and more extensive over the last several months and which I believe to be very important. And since no federal programs can be used to help finance these food sales, as they can be to other countries, we need an analysis of whether there actually will be more sales under the legislation. . . .

Now, the second question you ask is whether it's time to move toward normalization. . . . I don't believe that we can change that [Helms-Burton sanctions] law until there is a bipartisan majority which believes that there has been some effort on the part of the Cuban government to reach out to us, as well. I like the old law, I thought it was working well. . . .

That brings us back to the Nethercutt bill. If I think on balance, it allows the president — not just me, my successor as well — to pursue our foreign policy interest, and will, on balance, further that policy, then I would support it. . . .

Q: Mr. President, does the closeness of today's abortion vote in the Supreme Court suggest to you that abortion rights are at risk in the next court? Or does it suggest that the fact that "partial birth" abortion can survive even a conservative court say that they aren't as threatened as some believe?

CLINTON: Well, first, I think the court decision is clearly the only decision it could reach consistent with *Roe v. Wade*. So I think what you know there is that that's the vote for *Roe v. Wade*. You can't have a rule like the rule of *Roe* and then ignore it. . . .

If you remember, on this late-term abortion issue, a couple of years ago I pleaded with the Congress to adopt a broad limitation on late-term abortions, consistent with *Roe v. Wade*, but to make an exception for the life and health of the mother, as the Supreme Court decision required. They declined to do that, and so we've had a political impasse here, and then you've seen what's happened in all these states. . . .

I think that in the next four years, there will be somewhere between two and four appointments to the Supreme Court, and depending on who those appointees are, I think the rule will either be maintained or overturned. . . .

Q: Mr. President, Gov. [George W.] Bush has been critical of you and the energy policy of the administration, saying that you've failed to adequately convince OPEC to increase oil production. He also claims that if he became president, he'd be able to use personal diplomacy to persuade allies like Kuwait and Saudi Arabia to — I believe he said — turn on the spigot. Do you find that kind of claim realistic? And do you have any reaction to his criticism of you?

CLINTON: Well, first of all, I have spent an enormous amount of time on this in the last several months, and there have been two decisions by OPEC to increase production — not as much as we would like.

If you look at the allocation of the production increases against the real capacity of those countries, most countries don't have the capacity to produce much more than their latest allocation, except for the Saudis. . . .

I think that these big increases in gasoline prices in America are the result . . . first and foremost, of the unfortunate decision of OPEC several months ago to cut back production at the very time the world economy was growing. . . .

I think what we have to do now is to keep doing what we can to get production up, to let this FTC investigation proceed — I think the gas prices have dropped eight cents a gallon in the Midwest, and in the blended fuels area, 12.5 cents a gallon just since the investigation was announced. But the main thing I would say to you is, we need a long-term energy strategy to maximize conservation and maximize the development of alternative sources of energy, and also, maximize domestic sources of energy. . . .

The House has reauthorized the Strategic Petroleum Reserve. And I compliment them on that; that's a good thing. We also need a home heating oil reserve for the Northeast. . . . We ought to pass my proposal to provide tax credits to people who manufacture or buy energy-efficient homes, cars and consumer products. . . . We ought to pass my appropriations to help develop alternative sources of energy and energy conservation technologies.

Since I've been president, or since '95, anyway, the Congress has approved approximately 12 percent of my requests. And the House voted to zero our participation in the Partnership for New Generation Vehicles. This kind of research is just as important as the human genome research in terms of the role of the government in this. . . . We can be driving cars that get 80 miles to the gallon through fuel cells, through electric cars, through natural gas fuel, a lot of other options, within a matter of three or four years if we'll just get after it and treat this like it's important. . . .

Q: Mr. President, we hear increasingly from senior officials here and at the Pentagon that when it comes to national missile defense, you're inclined essentially to split the difference, authorize the contracting, but leave the decision about whether to break from the ABM Treaty to the next president. Is that a fair reflection of your thinking?

CLINTON: The most important thing I can say to you about that today is that I have not made a final decision, and that most of this speculation that is coming in the press is coming from people who have not talked to me about it. . . .

When Congress passed a law about this a couple years ago, you remember, and we had to sort of come up with some timetables, I said two things that I want to repeat today:

First of all, insofar as there might be technology available which would protect us and other people around the world from missile attacks with warheads of weapons of mass destruction, obviously, anybody would have a moral obligation to explore that technology and its potential. I believe that.

Secondly, whether I would make a decision to go forward with deployment would depend upon four things: one, the nature of the threat; two, the feasibility of the technology; three, the cost and, therefore, the relative cost of doing this as compared with something else to protect the national security; and, four, the overall impact on our national security, which includes our nuclear allies and our European alliance, our relationships with Russia, our relationships with China, what the boomerang effect might be about whatever China might do in South Asia, with the Indians and then the Pakistanis, and so on.

So what I have tried to do since then is to say as little as possible, except to explore what would have to be done in our relationships with the Europeans, our allies and with the Russians, in the first instance, to keep our options open — could we get an agreed upon modification to the ABM Treaty? . . . Everybody talked about how we didn't reach an agreement, Mr. [Vladimir] Putin and I, when I was in Russia. And that's absolutely true, we didn't. But we did get a document out of there which I think is quite important, because the Russians acknowledged that there are new and different security threats on the horizon. That is, that it's quite possible that in the next few years, countries not part of the arms control regimes of the last three decades could develop both long-range missile delivery capability and weapons of mass destruction which they could put on warheads. . . .

So they recognize, too, that we, in the new century, in the coming decades, are going to have to make adjustments. Now, what they don't say is, they don't want America unilaterally building a missile defense that they think someday can undermine their deterrent capacity. That's kind of where they are now, and we're still talking about all that. . . .

Q: Republicans in Congress are seeking to pass the spending bills early this year, in an effort to get out of Washington and go campaign in the fall. And, yet, there are significant differences between what they want to spend and what you have proposed. I'm wondering, what do you see as the major points of disagreement at this time, and do you think that we're in for the same type of prolonged budget stalemate that has been featured in the past?

CLINTON: That's entirely up to them whether we're in for the budget stalemate. . . . Look at the education budget. I mean, how many times do we have to go down this road? You know, it's still not supportive of the 100,000 teachers and the smaller classes; it's still not supportive of the dramatic expansion in after-school programs, which is critical to school performance; still has nothing in there for school construction; still is inadequate in terms of my plan that people ought to either identify these failing schools and either turn them around or shut them down — and lots of other problems with the school program.

If you look at the crime proposals — this is unbelievable. When they wouldn't adopt the common-sense gun safety legislation, all I heard was this constant barrage about how, if only the administration would enforce the gun laws on the books, everything would be wonderful, we wouldn't have any problems in America.

So what I said — look, why don't we do both? We have increased gun prosecutions under my administration, but we can do more. So please, give me some more money for people to investigate gun crimes, for people to prosecute gun crimes, to develop safe gun technology — this whole — it was nothing but a straight enforcement measure, exactly what they said they wanted, and no money for it.

Still no support for the 50,000 new police officers in the higher crime areas. And still the constant threat of these environmental riders, and underfunding of the Lands Legacy Initiative, and a number of other things.

So we still have some serious differences. Now, we've been doing this every year since 1995; we just sort of slightly change the script every year. And I'm more than happy to do it again, because, frankly, in the end, we normally wind up with an agreement that's pretty good for the American people.

But the timing in which we do it — it depends more on them than me. I'm not going to give up my commitment to education as our most important domestic priority, and what we're doing to build the future of our children. . . .

So we'll just have to see what happens. I'm kind of hopeful about it, though. It's just late June, here. This drama has several more acts before it's over. . . .

Thank you. ◆

Republicans Adopt 'Uplifting and Visionary' Party Platform

What follows is the text of the 2000 platform for the Republican Party. It was adopted by the GOP convention in Philadelphia on July 31:

Renewing America's Purpose. Together.

Preamble. We meet at a remarkable time in the life of our country. Our powerful economy gives America a unique chance to confront persistent challenges. Our country, after an era of drift, must now set itself to important tasks and higher goals. The Republican Party has the vision and leadership to address these issues.

Our platform is uplifting and visionary. It reflects the views of countless Americans all across this country who believe in prosperity with a purpose — who believe in Renewing America's Purpose. Together.

This platform makes clear that we are the party of ideas. We are the party that follows its bold words with bold deeds.

Since the election of 1860, the Republican Party has had a special calling — to advance the founding principles of freedom and limited government and the dignity and worth of every individual.

These principles form the foundation of both an agenda for America in the year 2000 and this platform for our party. They point us toward reforms in government, a restoration of timeless values and a renewal of our national purpose.

The twenty-fifth man to receive our party's nomination is equal to the challenges facing our country. After a period of bitter division in national politics, our nominee is a leader who brings people together. In a time of fierce partisanship, he calls all citizens to common goals. To longstanding problems, he brings a fresh outlook and innovative ideas — and a record of results.

Under his leadership, the Republican Party commits itself to bold reforms in education — to make every school a place of learning and achievement for every child. We will preserve local control of public schools, while demanding high standards and accountability for results.

We commit ourselves to saving and strengthening Social Security. After years of neglect and delay, we will keep this fundamental commitment to the senior citizens of today and tomorrow.

We commit ourselves to rebuilding the American military and returning to a foreign policy of strength and purpose and a renewed commitment to our allies. We will deploy defenses against ballistic missiles and develop the weapons and strategies needed to win battles in this new technological era.

We commit ourselves to tax reforms that will sustain our nation's prosperity and reflect its decency. We will reduce the burden on all Americans, especially those who struggle most.

We commit ourselves to aiding and encouraging the work of charitable and faith-based organizations, which today are making great strides in overcoming poverty and other social problems, bringing new hope into millions of lives. For every American there must be a ladder of opportunity, and for those most in need, a safety net of care.

We recommit ourselves to the values that strengthen our culture and sustain our nation: family, faith, personal responsibility and a belief in the dignity of every human life.

We offer not only a new agenda, but also a new approach — a vision of a welcoming society in which all have a place. To all Americans, particularly immigrants and minorities, we send a clear message: This is the party of freedom and progress, and it is your home.

The diversity of our nation is reflected in this platform. We ask for the support and participation of all who substantially share our agenda. In one way or another, every Republican is a dissenter. At the same time, we are not morally indifferent. In this, as in many things, Lincoln is our model. He spoke words of healing and words of conviction. We do likewise, for we are bound together in a great enterprise for our children's future.

We seek to be faithful to the best traditions of our party. We are the party that ended slavery, granted homesteads, built land grant colleges and moved control of government out of Washington back into the hands of the people. We believe in service to the common good — and that good is not common until it is shared.

We believe that from freedom comes opportunity; from opportunity comes growth; and from growth comes progress and prosperity.

Our vision is one of clear direction, new ideas, civility in public life, and leadership with honor and distinction.

This is an election with clear alternatives. The Republican Party offers America a chance to begin anew. To give purpose to our plenty. To apply enduring principles to new challenges. To extend to all citizens the full promise of American life. With confidence in our fellow Americans and great hopes for the future of our country, we respectfully submit this platform to the people of the United States. This platform is dedicated to the memory of Paul Douglas Coverdell (1939-2000), United States Senator from Georgia, practical visionary, principled unifier, proud American and our friend.

Old Truths for the New Economy

The highest hopes of the American people — a world at peace, scientific progress, a just and caring society — cannot be achieved by prosperity alone, but neither can they be fulfilled without it. Yet prosperity is not an end in itself. Rather, it is the means by which great things can be achieved for the common good. Our commitment to the nation's economic growth is an affirmation of the real riches of our country: the works of compassion that link home to home, community to community and hand to helping hand. This is the foundation of America, and that foundation is sound. Even though our economy, and that of the world to which we are now so closely tied, has been utterly transformed over the last two decades, Americans remain true to the faith of our founding fathers.

Yesterday's wildest dreams are today's realities, and there is no limit on the promise of tomorrow. The headiness of technological progress has made our society more future-oriented than ever before. But the fascination with the future means that, more than ever, we need to preserve the foundation that has served us so well. We must not overlook the practical experience of the past. To successfully chart where we should go in the years ahead, we must first look back to see how we got where we are today.

Twenty years ago, the economy was in shambles. Unemployment was at 7.1 percent, inflation at 13.5 percent and interest rates at 15.3 percent. The Democratic Party accepted that malaise as the price the nation had to pay for Big Government, and in so doing lost the confidence of the American people. Inspired by Presidents Reagan and Bush, Republicans hammered into place the framework for today's prosperity and surpluses. We cut tax rates, simplified the tax code, deregulated industries and opened world markets to American enterprise. The result was the tremendous growth in the 1980s that created the venture capital to launch the technology revolution of the 1990s.

That's the origin of what is now called the New Economy: the longest economic boom in the Twentieth Century, 40 million new jobs, the lowest inflation and unemployment in memory. The stock market, once a preserve of the well-to-do, now drives forward with the modest investments of tens of millions of households as ownership in America's economy becomes the norm rather than the exception.

The Republican Congress

We could have lost it all after the Democratic Congress passed the largest tax hike in history in 1993 that threatened to bring back the tax-and-spend follies of the bad old days. But the voters wouldn't have it and, in the next election, for the first time in forty years, they put Republican majorities in charge of both Houses of Congress. The difference that made can be put into numbers. In the four decades from 1954 to 1994, government spending increased at an average annual rate of 7.9 percent, and the public's debt increased from $224 billion to $3.4 trillion. Since 1994, with Republicans leading the House and Senate, spending has been held to an annual 3.1 percent rate of growth, and the nation's debt will be nearly $400 billion lower by the end of this year. The federal government has operated in the black for the last two years and is now projected to run a surplus of nearly $5 trillion over ten years.

That wasn't magic. It took honesty and guts from a Congress that manages the nation's purse strings. Over a five year period, as surpluses continue to grow, we will return half a trillion dollars to the taxpayers who really own it, without touching the Social Security surplus. That's what we mean by our Lock-Box: The Social Security surplus is off-limits, off budget, and will not be touched. We will not stop there, for we are also determined to protect Medicare and to pay down the national debt. Reducing that debt is both a sound policy goal and a moral imperative. Our families and most states are required to balance their budgets; it is reasonable to assume the federal government should do the same. Therefore, we reaffirm our support for a constitutional amendment to require a balanced budget.

Taxes and Budget: Render to Caesar, But Let the People Keep Their Own

"I believe our country must be prosperous, but prosperity must have a purpose . . . to make sure the American dream touches every willing heart."

— *George W. Bush*

It takes both candor and courage to say, as George W. Bush has said, that, even in times of large surpluses, the economy is far from perfect and we should not be satisfied with the status quo. Budget surpluses are the result of over-taxation of the American people. The weak link in the chain of prosperity is the tax system. It not only burdens the American people; it threatens to slow, and perhaps to reverse, the economic expansion.

The federal tax code is dysfunctional. It penalizes hard work, marriage, thrift and success — the very factors that are the foundations for lasting prosperity. Federal taxes are the highest they have ever been in peacetime.

Taxes at all levels of government absorb 36 percent of the net national product.

When the average American family has to work more than four months out of every year to fund all levels of government, it's time to change the tax system, to make it simpler, flatter and fairer for everyone. It's time for an economics of inclusion that will let people keep more of what they earn and accelerate movement up the opportunity ladder.

We therefore enthusiastically endorse the principles of Governor Bush's Tax Cut with a Purpose:

- Replace the five current tax brackets with four lower ones, ensuring all taxpayers significant tax relief while targeting it especially toward low-income workers.
- Help families by doubling the child tax credit to $1,000, making it available to more families, and eliminating the marriage penalty.
- Encourage entrepreneurship and growth by capping the top marginal rate, ending the death tax and making permanent the Research and Development credit.
- Promote charitable giving and education. Foster capital investment and savings to boost today's dangerously low personal savings rate.

This is more than just an economic program to promote growth and job creation. It is our blueprint for the kind of society we want for our children and grandchildren. It is a call to conscience, a reminder that, even in times of great prosperity, there are those who bear great burdens. That is why, with the tax cuts we propose, while every taxpayer benefits, six million families — one in five taxpaying families with children — will no longer pay any federal income tax.

It took a Republican Congress to stand up to the Internal Revenue Service by publicly exposing its abuses and enacting a Taxpayer's Bill of Rights. Within the simpler and fairer tax system proposed by Governor Bush, the IRS will be downsized and made less intrusive. IRS rules should be understandable by all, enforced by few, with low-cost compliance. We applaud the efforts of the Republican Congress to expand the use and availability of Individual Retirement Accounts.

In 1997 the Republican Congress cut the capital gains tax from 28 percent to 20 percent. As a result, capital gains for Americans doubled and federal government tax receipts from capital gains jumped from $50 billion in 1996 to $75 billion in 1997. These tax cuts produce more economic growth and often more tax revenues. We cheer their lowering of the capital gains tax rate and look forward to further reductions that will stimulate property sales and development to bring jobs and renewal to our urban neighborhoods.

To guard against future tax hikes, we support legislation requiring a super-majority vote in both houses of Congress to raise taxes. We will prohibit retroactive taxation and will not tolerate attempts by federal judges to impose taxes. Because of the vital role of religious and fraternal benevolent societies in fostering charity and patriotism, they should not be subject to taxation.

Income taxes and payroll taxes are the most obvious parts of the public's tax burden but consumers foot the bills in higher prices for most of the user fees that are nothing but under-radar taxes. Excise taxes of all kinds have snowballed, because they shift public resentment from government to the businesses that are forced to collect them. One example is the gas tax of 1993.

Another is the phone tax imposed to finance the Spanish-American War — and still in place a century later. We call for the immediate repeal of the phone tax.

Homeownership is central to the American dream, and Republicans want to make it more accessible for everyone. That starts with access to capital for entrepreneurs and access to credit for consumers. Our proposals for helping millions of low-income families move from renting to owning are detailed elsewhere in this platform as major elements in Governor Bush's program for a New Prosperity. For those families, and for all other potential homebuyers, low interest rates make mortgages affordable and open up more housing opportunities than any government program.

Affordable housing is in the national interest. That is why the mortgage interest deduction for primary residences was put into the federal tax code, and why tax reform of any kind should continue to encourage homeownership. At the same time, a balanced national housing policy must recognize that decent housing includes apartments, and addresses the needs of all citizens, including renters.

We will turn over to local communities foreclosed and abandoned HUD properties for urban homesteading, a citizen renovation effort that has been remarkably successful in revitalizing neighborhoods. We affirm our commitment to open housing, without quotas or controls, and we applaud the proactive efforts by the realty and housing industries to assure access for everyone.

In many areas, housing prices are higher than they need to be because of regulations that drive up building costs. Some regulation is of course necessary, and so is sensible zoning. But we urge states and localities to work with local builders and lenders to eliminate unnecessary burdens that price many families out of the market. We see no role for any federal regulation of homebuilding, but we do foresee a larger role for state and local governments in controlling the federally assisted housing that has been so poorly managed from Washington. We also encourage the modification of restrictions that inhibit the rehabilitation of existing distressed properties.

Small Business: Where Prosperity Starts

Small businesses are the underlying essence of our economy. Small businesses create most of the new jobs and keep this country a land of opportunity. They have been the primary engines of economic advance by American women, whose dynamic entry into small business in recent years has accounted for much of the nation's growth. Small businesses generate more than half the gross domestic product. Their willingness to give people a chance, and their ability to train individuals new to the work force, made welfare reform the success that it is. They deserve far better treatment from government than they have received. We will provide it through many of the initiatives explained elsewhere in this platform: lower tax rates, ending the death tax, cutting through red tape, legal and product liability reform and the aggressive expansion of overseas markets for their goods and services.

We will end the harassment of small businesses by federal agencies. In the case of OSHA, we will withdraw its proposed ergonomics standard, ban its bureaucracy from the homes of telecommuting workers, and change the agency from an adversary to a partner for safer productivity.

We will halt the IRS discrimination against independent contractors and, in order to guard against unwise regulation, will include the agency in the current procedures of the Small Business Regulatory Enforcement Fairness Act.

Providing health insurance is a major challenge for small-business owners. Almost 60 percent of uninsured workers are either employed by small business or are self-employed. That is compelling reason to immediately allow 100 percent deductibility of health insurance premiums and let small businesses to band together, across state lines, to purchase insurance through association health plans.

Work Place of the Future

Individual Americans, on their own initiative, are already creating the work place of the future. Employees and employers alike need to act as a team, not as adversaries, to be competitive in the world market. Republicans want to empower them to do all of that, because we believe they know what is best for their families, their earnings and their advancement in an opportunity economy. To help them reach their goals, government must replace antiquated laws that restrict opportunity, increase costs and inhibit innovation.

Trade: The Force of Economic Freedom

"The fearful build walls; the confident demolish them. I am confident in American workers, farmers and producers, and I am confident that America's best is the best in the world."

— *George W. Bush*

International trade has become the world's most powerful economic force. International trade is not the creation of the world's rulers, but of the world's peoples, who strive for a better future and break down any barriers governments may erect to it. The result is today's global economy of open markets in democratic nations. That system is poised to sweep away both the counterproductive vestiges of protectionism and the backwater remnants of Marxism. We launched this revolution during the Reagan and Bush administrations. Now we will bring it to completion: U.S. leadership of a global economy without limits to growth.

For our country, that outcome will be critical. Exports account for almost one-third of U.S. economic growth, while average wages in export-related industries are significantly higher. As for agriculture, expanding exports is key to saving the family farm. We must secure America's competitive advantage in the New Economy by preventing other countries from erecting barriers to innovation. For American producers and consumers alike, the benefits of free trade are already enormous. In the near future, they will be incalculable.

But free trade must be fair trade, within an open, rules-based international trading system. That will depend on American leadership, which has been lacking for the last eight years. The administration's failure to renew fast track (expedited legislative procedures to approve free-trade legislation) has undermined its ability to open new markets abroad for American goods and services. As a result, America's trade deficit with the rest of the world has surged to record highs. We must be at the table when trade agreements are negotiated, make the interests of American workers and farmers paramount and ensure that the drive to open new markets is successful.

The vitality of that agenda depends upon the vigorous enforcement of U.S. trade laws against unfair competition. We will not tolerate the foreign practices, rules and subsidization that put our exports on an unequal footing. It is not enough to secure signatures on a piece of paper; our trading partners must follow through on the promises they make. First and foremost, we must restore the credibility of U.S. trade leadership. We therefore propose to:

- Launch a new and ambitious round of multilateral negotiations focused solely on opening markets.
- Revitalize the World Trade Organization negotiations on agriculture and services.
- Give the next president fast-track negotiating authority.
- Negotiate reductions in tariffs on U.S. industrial goods and the elimination of other trade barriers so that our autos, heavy machinery, textiles and other products will no longer be shut out of foreign markets.
- Take action against any trading partner that uses pseudo-science to block importation of U.S. bioengineered crops.
- Advance a Free Trade Area of the Americas to take advantage of burgeoning new markets at our doorstep.
- Revise export controls to tighten control over military technology and ease restrictions on technology already available commercially.

Technology and the New Economy: The Force for Change

"Governments don't create wealth. Wealth is created by Americans – by creativity and enterprise and risk-taking. The great engine of wealth has become the human mind – creating value out of genius."

— *George W. Bush*

The innovation at the heart of our New Economy has become the greatest force for change all over the world. With information technology, people in bondage can taste freedom, and people in freedom can bond more securely with each other. People who used to work for others are now independent entrepreneurs. And citizens are drilling through layers of entrenched bureaucracy to directly access information and transact business.

Republicans have embraced this change, for it advances the central values of our party and our country: a reduced role for government, greater personal liberty, economic freedom, reliance on the market and decentralized decision-making. This revolution also suits our national character — rewarding creativity, hard work, tenacity and a willingness to take risks. It empowers. This is America's moment.

Republicans recognize that the role of government in the New Economy is to foster an environment where innovation can flourish. The Information Revolution is the product of the creative efforts and hard work of men and women in the private sector, and not of government bureaucrats. At the same time, we recognize that the magnitude and pace of change require vigilance to make the most of its opportunities and to mitigate its possible difficulties. For what we have experienced thus far is surely only the beginning of almost unimaginable growth, change, and more change. Let others be timid in the face of it, but let this country seize the opportunity.

The Republican Congress deserves great credit for what it has already done to fulfill its historic E-Contract with the American people:

- The Internet Tax Freedom Act put a three-year moratorium on new Internet taxes to ensure that electronic commerce would not be smothered in its infancy.
- An expanded visa program (H1-B) provided much of the highly skilled labor that makes rapid technological progress possible.
- The Securities Litigation Reform Act, enacted by overriding a veto, is preventing trial lawyers from preying on new cutting-edge companies. The threat of abusive lawsuits must not be allowed to cripple the capital formation that will drive the Information Revolution.
- A codified World Intellectual Property Organization (WIPO) agreement ensured that content providers are protected from foreign criminals.
- Our extended research and development tax credit allows companies to innovate, when innovation is the name of the high-tech game.
- Deregulation of telecommunications, still in its early stages, shattered monopolies and opened the door to

worldwide communication.

These initiatives are grounded in a steadfast commitment to open markets, to minimal regulations and to reducing taxes that snuff out innovation — principles at the heart of the new economy and our party.

Our latest breakthrough, enacted only weeks ago, is a landmark commercial law granting electronic signatures used in the formation of contracts online the same legal validity as pen-and-ink signatures on paper. With this single stroke, business-to-business e-commerce will explode, paperwork costs will decline, convenience will increase, and consumers rack up another major victory.

The impact of the Internet on the daily workings of government to make it more responsive and citizen-centered is considered elsewhere in this platform. But Republicans welcome the Information Revolution to the political arena too. Democracy thrives on well-informed citizens, and now the public will have unprecedented access to the workings of government, including the voting records of their Members of Congress and the written opinions of judges, whose decisions will now be reviewable in the court of public opinion.

Where do we go from here?

First, commit to global markets and free trade. Internet curtains must not take the place of the Iron Curtain through tariffs, duties, or taxes on Internet access. We call for a permanent ban on access taxes and an extension of the current moratorium on new and discriminatory taxes, which shall not prohibit a state from collecting taxes that are currently authorized by law.

Second, maintain a highly educated work force so that continued progress need not depend on imported personnel. Like Governor Bush, we have made this a vital part of our education program that is detailed elsewhere in this platform. Instead of burdening schools with red tape and narrow government programs, we will give them maximum flexibility in using federal education technology dollars to meet their specific needs — whether it be for computers, teacher training, software development or systems integration.

Third, speed up the research and innovation that drive technological progress, along the lines of our proposed tax reforms, National Institute of Health (NIH) funding, and a $20 billion increase in the research and development budget of the Defense Department.

Fourth, protect the technology industry from modern-day pirates at home and abroad: both those who violate copyrights and those who loot by litigation.

Restrain the hand of government so that it cannot smother or slow the growth of worldwide commerce and communication through the Internet.

In addition, we must encourage government at all levels to work with the private sector to ensure that the Internet must be a medium for everyone. The old liberal approach — using the threat of stifling regulations to redistribute wealth and opportunity — will work no better than it ever has, and perhaps much worse, in the new economy. The Republican Party embraces a creative, incentive-based, public/private approach and a Republican president will use the influence of his office to urge high-tech philanthropy, with such initiatives as Governor Bush's plan to create and strengthen more than 2,000 community technology centers every year — centers which provide such services as free Internet access and technology skills training.

The prosperity of our New Economy provides unprecedented opportunities for philanthropic giving.

What holds true for the Internet applies as well to other areas of scientific advance, from biotechnology to chemistry. These fields require enormous infusions of capital, as well as regulatory flexibility by government. The federal government must refocus and reinvigorate its role in promoting cutting-edge basic research, and the tax code must foster research and development.

These policies will increase the pace of technological developments by de-emphasizing the direct role of government while strengthening private-public partnerships and the role of the private sector.

In addition, the Republican Party will remain committed to America's leadership in space research and exploration. We will ensure that this Nation can expand our knowledge of the universe, and with the support of the American people, continue the exploration of Mars and the rest of the solar system. We consider space travel and space science a national priority with virtually unlimited benefits, in areas ranging from medicine to micro-machinery, for those on Earth. Development of space will give us a growing economic resource and a source of new scientific discoveries. The potential benefits of new science and technology to the American people, indeed to all humanity, are incalculable and can only be hastened by the international free market in ideas that the Information Revolution has created.

Privacy and Secure Technologies

Government also has a responsibility to protect personal privacy, which is the single greatest concern Americans now have about the Information Revolution. Citizens must have the confidence that their personal privacy will be respected in the use of technology by both business and government. That privacy is an essential part of our personal freedom and our family life, and it must not be sacrificed in the name of progress. At the same time, consumers should have the benefit of new products, services and treatments that result from the legitimate use of data with appropriate safeguards. We applaud the leadership already demonstrated in this regard by many outstanding businesses, which are ensuring individuals' privacy in various ways and promoting public education about the consumer's right to privacy.

Education and Opportunity: Leave No American Behind

A Responsibility Era. Sometimes it's important to state the obvious. This is one of those times. America is a great country. There are many reasons for this, foremost among them our long tradition of personal responsibility, the demand for high standards and clear values, and the central importance of family in social and economic progress.

In recent years, America seemed to move away from some of the qualities that make her great, but we are now relearning some important lessons. The key is to acknowledge the mistakes, fix them, learn from them and move on.

We're coming to understand that a good and civil society cannot be packaged into government programs but must originate in our homes, in our neighborhoods and in the private institutions that bring us together, in all our diversity, for the works of mercy and labors of love.

This section of our platform deals with some of America's most enduring, and seemingly intractable, challenges. We approach these challenges with compassionate conservatism, a concept that is as old as the pioneers heading West in wagon trains, in which everyone had responsibility to follow the rules, but no one would be left behind.

Real Education Reform: Strengthening Accountability and Empowering Parents

"No child in America should be segregated by low expectations . . . imprisoned by illiteracy . . . abandoned to frustration and the darkness of self-doubt."

— *George W. Bush*

The question is "Are our schools better off now than they were eight years ago?" At a time of remarkable economic growth, when a world of opportunity awaits students who are prepared for it, American colleges and universities are offering remedial courses and American businesses are unable to find enough qualified or trainable workers to meet the demand. Worst of all, so many of our children, America's most precious asset, are headed toward failure in school, and that will hold them back throughout their lives. Republicans desire a better result. We believe that every child in this land should have access to a high-quality, indeed, a world-class education, and we're determined to meet that goal.

It's long past time to debate what works in education. The verdict is in, and our Republican governors provided the key testimony: strong parental involvement, excellent teachers, safe and orderly classrooms, high academic standards and a commitment to teaching the basics — from an early start in phonics to mastery of computer technology. Federal programs that fail to support these fundamental principles are sadly out of date and, under the next president, out of time. For dramatic and swift improvement, we endorse the principles of Governor Bush's education reforms, which will:

- Raise academic standards through increased local control and accountability to parents, shrinking a multitude of federal programs into five flexible grants in exchange for real, measured progress in student achievement
- Assist states in closing the achievement gap and empower needy families to escape persistently failing schools by allowing federal dollars to follow their children to the school of their choice.
- Expand parental choice and encourage competition by providing parents with information on their child's school, increasing the number of charter schools and expanding education savings accounts for use from kindergarten through college.
- Help states ensure school safety by letting children in dangerous schools transfer to schools that are safe for learning and by forcefully prosecuting youths who carry or use guns and the adults who provide them.
- Ensure that all children learn to read by reforming Head Start and by facilitating state reading initiatives that focus on scientifically based reading research, including phonics.

Nothing is more important than literacy, and yet many children have trouble reading. This problem must be addressed at all grade levels. And as is so often the case in education, the solution is parent and child working together with teachers to help break a cycle of illiteracy that may have extended from generation to generation. We want to replace that pattern with the rich legacy of reading.

We recognize that under the American constitutional system, education is a state, local and family responsibility, not a federal obligation. Since over 90 percent of public school funding is state and local, not federal, it is obvious that state and local governments must assume most of the responsibility to improve the schools, and the role of the federal government must be progressively limited as we return control to parents, teachers and local school boards. Programs beginning the process by congressional Republicans to return power to the people, such as "Straight As" legislation and "Dollars to the Classroom," are a good step to reach this goal. The Republican Congress rightly opposed attempts by the Department of Education to establish federal testing that would set the stage for a national curriculum. We believe it's time to test the Department, and each of its programs, instead.

Over thirty years ago, the federal government assumed a special financial responsibility to advance the education of disadvantaged children through the Title I program. Today, $120 billion later, the achievement gap between those youngsters and their peers has only widened. The fiscal loss is not a good thing, but the human loss is tragic. We cannot allow another generation of kids to be written off. For dramatic and swift improvement, we endorse Governor Bush's principles of local control, with accountability, parental choice and meaningful student achievement as essential to education reform.

Qualified teachers are the vanguard of education reform. With mastery of their subjects, a contagious enthusiasm for learning and a heartfelt commitment to their students, they can make any school great. That is why we advocate merit pay for them and expanded opportunities for professional development. Today, however, many teachers face danger and disrespect in the classroom, and their efforts to maintain order are hampered by the threat of litigation. We propose special legal protection for teachers to shield them from meritless lawsuits. We advocate a zero-tolerance policy toward all students who disrupt the classroom and we reaffirm that school officials must have the right and responsibility to appropriately discipline all students, including students with disabilities, who are disruptive or violent. Toward the same end, we will encourage faith-based and community organizations to take leading roles in after-school programs that build character and improve behavior. We propose to improve teacher training and recruiting by expanding the Troops-to-Teachers program, which places retired military personnel in the classroom, and by rewarding states that enact a system for teacher accountability. We will expand teacher loan-forgiveness to encourage qualified candidates to serve in high-need schools. As a matter of fairness, we will establish a teacher tax deduction to help defray the out-of-pocket teaching expenses so many good home, private and public school teachers make to benefit their students.

Local responsibility for neighborhood schools has been the key to successful education since the days of the little red schoolhouse. We salute congressional Republicans for their continuing efforts, through Ed-Flex and other initiatives, to shift decision-making away from the federal bureaucracy and back to localities. We strongly endorse Governor Bush's proposal to consolidate cumbersome categorical programs into flexible performance grants, targeting resources to the classroom and tying them directly to student achievement. That is real reform.

In the Individuals with Disabilities Education Act (IDEA), the Congress required that every community in the country provide a free and appropriate education for all students with special needs and fund their schooling at higher levels. In return, the federal government promised to pay 40 percent of the average per pupil expenditure to cover the excess costs. During all the years the Democrats controlled Congress, that was not done. It was congressional Republicans who took the first real strides toward fulfillment of the IDEA promise. We applaud them for recognizing that federal mandates must include federal funding. We will strive to promote the early diagnosis of learning deficiencies. Preventive efforts in early childhood should reduce the demand for special education and help many youngsters move beyond the need for IDEA's protections.

In the final analysis, education remains a parental right and responsibility. We advocate choice in education, not as an abstract theory, but as the surest way for families, especially low-income families, to free their youngsters from failing or dangerous schools and put them onto the road to opportunity and success. By the same token, we defend the option for home schooling and call for vigilant enforcement of laws designed to protect family rights and privacy in education. Children should not be compelled to answer offensive or intrusive questionnaires. We will continue to work for the return of voluntary school prayer to our schools and will strongly enforce the Republican legislation that guarantees equal access to school facilities by student religious groups. We strongly support voluntary student-initiated prayer in school without governmental interference. We strongly disagree with the Supreme Court's recent ruling, backed by the current administration, against student-initiated prayer.

Higher Education: Increased Access For All

One of the most profound changes in American society in the last half-century was the opening of post-secondary education to virtually everyone. Competition among institutions has been the key to that success. What began with the GI Bill in the 1940s has now, through student loans and grants, become the best higher education system in the world. Ours is a system in which achievement can count for more than money or social status. Americans are rightly proud of that. Now the challenges we face in the technological revolution and in the global economy require us to continue to expand the extent and excellence of higher education.

That is why both Governor Bush and congressional Republicans have given priority to programs that increase access to higher education for qualified students. The centerpiece of this effort has been education savings accounts — the ideal combination of minimal red tape and maximum consumer choice. Along with that innovation, congressional Republicans passed legislation to allow tax-free distributions from state pre-paid tuition plans, enhance the tax deduction for student loans, and make it more practicable for employers to provide educational assistance to train workers. Unfortunately, that legislation was vetoed. Next year, a Republican president will sign it into law.

Meanwhile, under Republican fiscal discipline, interest rates on federally guaranteed student loans are lower than ever before so student aspirations can reach higher than ever before. Pell Grants, the doorway to learning for millions of low-income families, are greater than ever — and will become a dynamic force in math, science and technology when a Republican Congress enacts Governor Bush's proposal to:

- Target increased benefits to students taking challenging course in those fields.
- Form partnerships with colleges and universities to improve science and math education.
- Attract science, math and engineering grads to low-income schools and areas with shortages of those teachers.

Overall college costs, however, continue to climb, usually far ahead of inflation. Whatever the reasons, these costs squeeze the budgets of the middle class. Many families feel they're on a treadmill, working harder to pay tuition bills that never stop rising. We call upon campus administrators to search for ways to hold down that price spiral; and, in fairness to them, we propose a presidentially directed study on the effect of government regulation and paperwork demands.

At many institutions of higher learning, the ideal of academic freedom is threatened by intolerance. Students should not be compelled to support, through mandatory student fees, anyone's political agenda. The Republican party stands in solidarity with the dedicated faculty who are penalized for their conservatism and also with the courageous students who run independent campus newspapers to confront the powerful with the power of truth. To protect the nation's colleges and universities against intolerance, we will work with independent educators to maintain alternatives to ideological accrediting bodies. We also support a reasonable approach to Title IX that seeks to expand opportunities for women without adversely affecting men's teams.

A New Prosperity: Seats for All At the Welcome Table

"America has been successful because it offers a realistic shot at a better life. America has been successful because poverty has been a stage, not a fate. America has been successful because anyone can ascend the ladder and transcend their birth."

— *George W. Bush*

We want to expand opportunity instead of government. Governor Bush calls this "the Duty of Hope." We see it as our duty to act. But whatever we name it, the goal is the same — to give hope and real upward mobility to those who have never known either. It's clear that the old left-liberal order of social policy has collapsed in failure; and its failure was the most egregious among those whom it most professed to serve: the poor and those on the margins of society.

The time is here to act, to bring hope, to expand opportunity. Republican governors throughout the country sparked a revolution that brought about the greatest social policy change in nearly 60 years — welfare reform. Inspired by the innovative reforms of Republican governors that successfully moved families from welfare dependence to the independence of work, congressional Republicans passed landmark welfare reform legislation in 1996 that has helped millions of Americans break the cycle of welfare and gain independence for their families. Because of that legislation — turning welfare resources and decision-making back to the states, with the understanding that recipients must meet a work requirement and such assistance would be only temporary — about six million Americans are now gainfully employed, many for the first time. We salute them.

And now it's time to take more steps in the right direction by helping these families climb the opportunity ladder. It won't be easy, but welfare reform wasn't easy either, though the results were surely worth the fight. Here are our next steps:

- Reward work with tax reform that takes 6 million families off the tax rolls, cuts the rate for those who remain on the rolls, and doubles the child tax credit to $1,000.
- Implement the "American Dream Down Payment" program, which will allow a half million families who currently draw federal rental assistance to become homeowners, and allow families receiving federal rental payments to apply one year's worth of their existing assistance money toward the purchase of their own first home, thus becoming independent of any further government housing assistance. This approach builds upon our longstanding commitment to resident management of public housing and other initiatives.
- Increase the supply of affordable housing for low-income working families and rehabilitate abandoned housing that blights neighborhoods by establishing the Renewing the Dream tax credit. This investor-based tax credit will create or renovate more than 100,000 single-family housing units in distressed communities.
- Build savings and personal wealth through Individual Development Accounts, in partnership with banks, to accelerate the savings of low-income earners.

For many individuals, poverty signals more than the lack of money. It often represents obstacles that cannot be overcome with just a paycheck. These are the challenging cases, where government aid is least effective. These, too, are the situations where neighborhood and faith-based intervention has its greatest power. For this reason, the Republican Congress mandated charitable choice in the welfare reform law of 1996, allowing states to contract with faith-based providers for welfare services on the same basis as any other providers. The current administration has done its utmost to block the implementation of that provision, insisting that all symbols of religion must be removed or covered over — precisely what the 1996 provisions set out to prevent. The result is that many of the most successful service programs are essentially blacklisted because they will neither conceal nor compromise the faith that makes them so effective in changing lives. While this is unfair to faith-based organizations, it is unjust to those whom they could help conquer abuse, addiction and hopelessness.

Texas was the first state to implement charitable choice in welfare, and its governor intends to expand it to all federally-funded human services programs. We support his plans to unbar the gates of the government ghetto, inviting into the American dream those who are now in its shadows and using the dedication and expertise of faith communities to make it happen.

This is what we propose:

- Apply charitable Choice to all federal social service programs.
- Encourage an outpouring of giving by extending the current federal charity tax deduction to the 70 percent of all tax filers who do not itemize their deductions and by allowing people to make donations tax-free from their IRAs.
- Promote corporate giving by raising the cap on their charitable deductions and assuring them liability protection for their in-kind donations.

The renewal of entire communities is an awesome task and involves one human face, one human heart at a time. But the American people have a long and seasoned history of working wonders. Government does have a role to play, but as a partner, not a rival, to the armies of compassion. These forces have roots in the areas they serve, and their leaders are people to whom the disadvantaged are not statistics, but neighbors, friends and moral individuals created in the image of God. With these approaches, government becomes a partner with community and faith-based providers in supporting families and children and helping them improve their opportunities for a better life.

Children at Risk

Republicans recognize the importance of having a father and a mother in the home. The two-parent family still provides the best environment of stability, discipline, responsibility and character. Documentation shows that where the father has deserted his family, children are more likely to commit a crime, drop out of school, become violent, become teen parents, take illegal drugs, become mired in poverty or have emotional or behavioral problems. We support the courageous efforts of single-parent families to have [stable homes].

The participation of faith-based and community groups will be especially important in dealing with the twin problems of non-marital pregnancy and substance abuse. Reducing those behaviors is the surest way to end the cycle of child poverty. After-school programs should be fully open to the community and faith-based groups that know best how to reach out to our children and help them reach their true potential.

We renew our call for replacing "family planning" programs for teens with increased funding for abstinence education, which teaches abstinence until marriage as the responsible and expected standard of behavior. Abstinence from sexual activity is the only protection that is 100 percent effective against out-of-wedlock pregnancies and sexually transmitted diseases, including HIV/AIDS, when transmitted sexually. We oppose school-based clinics that provide referrals, counseling and related services for contraception and abortion. We urge the states to enforce laws against statutory rape, which accounts for an enormous portion of teen pregnancy. We support the establishment of Second Chance Maternity Homes, like the ones Governor Bush has proposed, to give young unwed mothers the opportunity to develop parenting skills, finish school and enter the work force. Because many youngsters fall into poverty as a result of divorce, we also encourage states to review their divorce laws and to support projects that strengthen marriage, promote successful parenting, bolster the stability of the home and protect the economic rights of the innocent spouse and children. Finally, because so many social ills plaguing America are fueled by the absence of fathers, we support initiatives that strengthen marriage rates and promote committed fatherhood.

The entire nation has suffered from the administration's virtual surrender in the war against drugs, but children in poor communities have paid the highest price in the threat of addiction and the daily reality of violence. Drug kingpins have turned entire neighborhoods into wastelands and ruined uncounted lives with their poison. The statistics are shocking. Since 1992, among 10th-graders, overall drug use has increased 55 percent, marijuana and hashish use has risen 91 percent, heroin use has gone up 92 percent and cocaine use has soared 133 percent. Not surprisingly, teen attitudes toward drug abuse have veered sharply away from disapproval. With abundant supplies in their deadly arsenal, drug traffickers are targeting younger children, as well as rural kids.

Still, there is no substitute for presidential leadership, whether internationally or here at home, where America's families cry out for safe, drug-free schools. A Republican president will hear those cries and work with parents to protect children. We will bring accountability to anti-drug programs, promote those that work and cease funding for those that waste resources. Equally important, in a Republican administration the Department of Justice will require all federal prosecutors to aggressively pursue drug dealers, from the kingpins to the lackeys. We renew our support for capital punishment for drug traffickers who take innocent life.

Illegal drugs and alcohol abuse are closely related to the incidence of child abuse. Government at all levels spends about $20 billion annually on a confusing array of programs to help either the children or adults in abusive or neglectful families. While the largest federal effort is the open-ended entitlements aimed at foster care and adoption, very little is allotted to preventive and family support services.

We must decrease abuse caseloads and increase accountability throughout the child protection system. We propose to restructure that system along the lines of our welfare reform success, by combining the separate and competing funding sources into a Child Protection Block Grant with guaranteed levels of funding. This will empower the states to respond more quickly, more flexibly and with greater compassion to children in peril. We call for the stringent and effective enforcement of laws against the abuse of children.

For many of those children, adoption may be the only route to a stable and loving home. Government at all levels should work with the charitable and faith-based groups that provide adoption services to remove the obstacles they sometimes encounter in their efforts to unite children in need with families who need them.

We call for state and local efforts to help the more than two million children of prisoners through pre-schools, mentoring and family rebuilding programs. These children are often the ignored victims of crime. Early intervention in their plight is essential to reduce the cycle of violence and to save a child. We should be tough on criminals but compassionate toward our children.

Renewing Family and Community

Individual rights — and the responsibilities that go with them — are the foundation of a free society. In protecting those rights, and in asserting those responsibilities, we affirm the common good, and common goals, that should unite all Americans.

We are the party of the open door, determined to strengthen the social, cultural and political ties that bind us together and make our country the greatest force for good in the world. Steadfast in our commitment to our ideals, we recognize that members of our party can have deeply held and sometimes differing views. This diversity is a source of strength, not a sign of weakness, and so we welcome into our ranks all who may hold differing positions. We commit to resolve our differences with civility, trust and mutual respect.

Family Matters

The family is society's central core of energy. That is why efforts to strengthen family life are the surest way to improve life for everyone. For this reason, congressional Republicans made adoption easier and enacted the child tax credit — and that is why Governor Bush wants to double that credit to $1,000 per child and increase the adoption credit. It's why we advocate a family-friendly tax code; why we promote comp time and flextime to accommodate family needs; and why we advocate choice in child care. We support the traditional definition of "marriage" as the legal union of one man and one woman, and we believe that federal judges and bureaucrats should not force states to recognize other living arrangements as marriages. We rely on the home, as did the founders of the American Republic, to instill the virtues that sustain democracy itself. That belief led Congress to enact the Defense of Marriage Act, which a Republican Department of Justice will energetically defend in the courts. For the same reason, we do not believe sexual preference should be given special legal protection or standing in law.

Just as environmental pollution affects our physical health, so too does the pollution of our culture affect the health of our communities. There is much to celebrate in contemporary culture, but also much to deplore: the glorification of violence, the glamorizing of drugs, the abuse of women and children, whether in music or videos, advertising, or tabloid journalism. Still, there are individuals and organizations using their power as citizens and consumers to advance a cultural renewal in all aspects of American life. We support and applaud them.

Their efforts will be critically important in the Information Age, which, with all its tremendous benefits, brings a major challenge to families. When the FBI reports that porn sites are the most frequently accessed on the Internet, it's time for parents at home — and communities through their public institutions — to take action. We endorse Republican legislation pending in the Congress to require schools and libraries to secure their computers against online porn and predators if they accept federal subsidies to connect to the Internet. This is not a question of free speech. Kids in a public library should not be victims of filth, and porn addicts should not use library facilities for their addiction. Therefore, public libraries and schools should secure their computers against online pornography.

Upholding the Rights of All

Equality of individuals before the law has always been a cornerstone of our party. We therefore oppose discrimination based on sex, race, age, religion, creed, disability, or national origin and will vigorously enforce anti-discrimination statutes. As we strive to forge a national consensus on the crucial issues of our time, we call on all Americans to reject the forces of hatred and bigotry. Accordingly, we denounce all who practice or promote racism, anti-Semitism, ethnic prejudice, or religious intolerance.

Our country was founded in faith and upon the truth that self-government is rooted in religious conviction. While the Constitution guards against the establishment of state-sponsored religion, it also honors the free exercise of religion. We believe the federal courts must respect this freedom and the original intent of the Framers. We assert the right of religious leaders to speak out on public issues and will not allow the EEOC or any other arm of government to regulate or ban religious symbols from the workplace. We condemn the desecration of places of worship and objects of religious devotion, and call upon the media to reconsider their role in fostering bias through negative stereotyping of religious citizens. We support the First Amendment right of freedom of association and stand united with private organizations, such as the Boy Scouts of America, and support their positions.

Because we treasure freedom of conscience, we oppose attempts to compel individuals or institutions to violate their moral standards in providing health-related services. We believe religious institutions and schools should not be taxed. When government funds privately operated social, welfare or educational programs, it must not discriminate against faith-based organizations, whose record in providing services to those in need far exceeds that of the public sector. Their participation should be actively encouraged, and never conditioned upon the covering or removing of religious objects or symbols.

We believe rights inhere in individuals, not in groups. We will attain our nation's goal of equal opportunity without quotas or other forms of preferential treatment. It is as simple as this: No one should be denied a job, promotion, contract, or chance at higher education because of their race or gender. Equal access, energetically offered, should guarantee every person a fair shot based on their potential and merit.

The Supreme Court's recent decision, prohibiting states from banning partial-birth abortions — a procedure denounced by a committee of the American Medical Association and rightly branded as four-fifths infanticide — shocks the conscience of the nation. As a country, we must keep our pledge to the first guarantee of the Declaration of Independence. That is why we say the unborn child has a fundamental individual right to life which cannot be infringed. We support a human life amendment to the Constitution and we endorse legislation to make clear that the Fourteenth Amendment's protections apply to unborn children. Our purpose is to have legislative and judicial protection of that right against those who perform abortions. We oppose using public revenues for abortion and will not fund organizations which advocate it. We support the appointment of judges who respect traditional family values and the sanctity of innocent human life.

Our goal is to ensure that women with problem pregnancies have the kind of support, material and otherwise, they need for themselves and for their babies, not to be punitive toward those for whose difficult situation we have only compassion. We oppose abortion, but our pro-life agenda does not include punitive action against women who have [abortions]. We salute those who provide alternatives to abortion and offer adoption services, and we commend congressional Republicans for expanding assistance to adopting families and for removing racial barriers to adoption. The impact of those measures and of our Adoption and Safe Families Act of 1997 has been spectacular. Adoptions out of foster care have jumped forty percent and the incidence of child abuse and neglect has actually declined. We second Governor Bush's call to make permanent the adoption tax credit and expand it to $7,500.

An essential part of a culture that respects life is integration and inclusion of persons with disabilities. That is the goal of Governor Bush's New Freedom Initiative, a comprehensive agenda for the breakthrough research and practical assistance that can help individuals with disabilities live independently, hold jobs and take part in the daily life of their communities. We applaud his proposal and we salute congressional Republicans for the way they have protected access to health care for individuals with disabilities against the administration's attempts to ration it. We pledge continued vigilance in that regard, especially in Medicare and Medicaid.

We oppose the non-consensual withholding of care or treatment because of disability, age, or infirmity, just as we oppose euthanasia and assisted suicide, which endanger especially the poor and those on the margins of society. We applaud congressional Republicans for their leadership against those abuses and their pioneering legislation to focus research and treatment resources on the alleviation of pain and the care of terminally ill patients.

Seeking the counsel of those who would be most affected by it, the Republican Congress enacted the new Ticket-to-Work law, empowering persons with disabilities to choose their own support services by voucher. Equally important, and with the inspiration of initiatives by some Republican governors, we have made it possible for millions of individuals with disabilities to rejoin the work force without losing their health benefits. We pledge full enforcement of these and prior enactments that have helped bring individuals with disabilities into the mainstream of a society that needs their skills and their industry.

We support their full access to the polls and to the entire political process. The promise of assistive technology, so costly but offering hope to so many, makes it all the more crucial that we maintain the expanding economy that sustains the investment necessary to make miracles happen.

We defend the constitutional right to keep and bear arms, and we affirm the individual responsibility to safely use and store firearms. Because self-defense is a basic human right, we will promote training in their safe usage, especially in federal programs for women and the elderly. A Republican administration will vigorously enforce current gun laws, neglected by the Democrats, especially by prosecuting dangerous offenders identified as felons in instant background checks. Although we support background checks to ensure that guns do not fall into the hands of criminals, we oppose federal licensing of law-abiding gun owners and national gun registration as a violation of the Second Amendment and an invasion of privacy of honest citizens. Through programs like Project Exile, we will hold criminals individually accountable for their actions by strong enforcement of federal and state firearm laws, especially when guns are used in violent or drug-related crimes. With a special emphasis upon school safety, we propose the crackdown on youth violence explained elsewhere in this platform.

We affirm the right of individuals to voluntarily participate in labor organizations and to bargain collectively. We therefore support the right of states to enact Right-to-Work laws. No one should be forced to contribute to a campaign or a candidate, so we will vigorously implement the Supreme Court's Beck decision to stop the involuntary use of union dues for political purposes. We will revoke the illegal executive order excluding millions of workers from federal contracts, and safeguard the unemployment compensation system against the diversion of its funds for political purposes.

From Many, One

Our country's ethnic diversity within a shared national culture is unique in all the world. We benefit from our differences, but we must also strengthen the ties that bind us to one another. Foremost among those is the flag. Its deliberate desecration is not "free speech" but an assault against both our proud history and our greatest hopes. We therefore support a constitutional amendment that will restore to the people, through their elected representatives, their right to safeguard Old Glory.

Another sign of our unity is the role of English as our common language. It has enabled people from every corner of the world to come together to build this nation. For newcomers, it has always been the fastest route to the mainstream of American life. English empowers. That is why fluency in English must be the goal of bilingual education programs. We support the recognition of English as the nation's common language. At the same time, mastery of other languages is important for America's competitiveness in the world market. We advocate foreign language training in our schools and the fostering of respect for other languages and cultures throughout our society.

We have reaped enormous human capital in the genius and talent and industry of those who have escaped nations captive to totalitarianism. Our country still attracts the best and brightest to invent here, create wealth here, improve the quality of life here. As a nation of immigrants, we welcome all new Americans who have entered lawfully and are prepared to follow our laws and provide for themselves and their families. In their search for a better life, they strengthen our economy, enrich our culture and defend the nation in war and in peace. To ensure fairness for those wishing to reside in this country, and to meet the manpower needs of our expanding economy, a total overhaul of the immigration system is sorely needed.

The administration's lax enforcement of our borders has led to tragic exploitation of smuggled immigrants, and untold suffering, at the hands of law-breakers. We call for harsh penalties against smugglers and those who provide fake documents. We oppose the creation of any national ID card.

Because free trade is the most powerful force for the kind of development that creates a middle class and offers opportunity at home, the long-term solution for illegal immigration is economic growth in Mexico, Central America and the Caribbean. In the short run, however, decisive action is needed. We therefore endorse the recommendations of the U.S. Commission on Immigration Reform:

- Restore credibility to enforcement by devoting more resources both to border control and to internal operations.
- Reorganize family unification preferences to give priority to spouses and children, rather than extended family members.
- Emphasize needed skills in determining eligibility for admission.
- Overhaul the failed Labor Certification Program to end the huge delays in matching qualified workers with urgent work.
- Reform the Immigration and Naturalization Service by splitting its functions into two agencies, one focusing on enforcement and one exclusively devoted to service.

The education reforms we propose elsewhere in this platform will, over time, greatly increase the number of highly qualified workers in all sectors of the American economy. To meet immediate needs, however, we support increasing the number of H-1B visas to ensure high-tech workers in specialized positions, provided such workers do not pose a national security risk; and we will expand the H-2A program for the temporary agricultural workers so important to the nation's farms.

Justice And Safety

Most Americans over the age of fifty remember a time when streets and schoolyards were safe, doors unlocked, windows unbarred. The elderly did not live in fear and the young did not die in gunfire. That world is gone, swept away in the social upheaval provoked by the welfare, drug and crime policies of the 1960s and later.

We cannot go back to that time of innocence, but we can go forward, step by difficult step, to recreate respect for law — and law that is worthy of respect. Most of that effort must come on the state and local levels, which have the primary responsibility for law enforcement. While we support community policing and other proven initiatives against crime, we strongly oppose any erosion of that responsibility by the federal government. Our Republican governors, legislators, and local leaders have taken a zero tolerance approach to crime that has led to the lowest crime and murder rates in a generation.

At the same time, we recognize the crucial leadership role the president and the Congress should play in restoring public safety. The congressional half of that team, in cooperation with governors and local officials who are the front line against crime, has been hard at work. Within proper federal jurisdiction, the Republican Congress has enacted legislation for an effective deterrent death penalty, restitution to victims, removal of criminal aliens and vigilance against terrorism. They stopped federal judges from releasing criminals because of prison overcrowding, made it harder to file lawsuits about prison conditions, and, with a truth-in-sentencing law, pushed states to make sure violent felons actually do time. They have also provided billions of dollars, in the form of block grants, for law enforcement agencies to hire police and acquire new equipment and technology.

The other part of the team — a president engaged in the fight against crime — has been ineffective for the last eight years. To the contrary, sixteen hard-core terrorists were granted clemency, sending the wrong signal to others who would use terror against the American people. The administration started out by slashing the nation's funding for drug interdiction and overseas operations against the narcotics cartel. It finishes by presiding over the near collapse of drug policy. The only bright spot has been the determination of the Republican Congress. Its Western Hemisphere Drug Elimination Act of 1998 has just begun to restore the nation's ability to strike at the source of illegal drugs. Now the Congress is taking the lead to assist Colombia against the narco-insurgents who control large parts of that country, a stone's throw from the Panama Canal.

A Republican president will advance an agenda to restore the public's safety:

- No-frills prisons, with productive work requirements, that make the threat of jail a powerful deterrent to crime.
- Increased penalties and resources to combat the dramatic rise in production and use of methamphetamine and new drugs such as ecstasy.
- An effective program of rehabilitation, where appropriate.
- Support of community-based diversion programs for first time, non-violent offenders.
- Reforming the Supreme Court's invented Exclusionary Rule, which has allowed countless criminals to get off on technicalities.
- A constitutional amendment to protect victims' rights at every stage of the criminal justice system. Reservation of two seats on the U.S. Sentencing Commission for victims of violent crimes.

We will reopen Pennsylvania Avenue in front of the White House as a symbolic expression of our confidence in the restoration of the rule of law.

Crimes against women and children demand an emphatic response. That is why the Republican Congress enacted Megan's Law, requiring local notification when sex offenders are released, and why we advocate special penalties against thugs who, in assaults against pregnant women, harm them or their unborn children. Federal obscenity and child pornography laws, especially crimes involving the Internet, must be vigorously enforced — in contrast to the current administration's failure in this area. We urge states to follow the lead of congressional Republicans by making admissible in court the prior similar criminal acts of defendants in sexual assault cases.

Millions of Americans suffer from problem or pathological gambling that can destroy families. We support legislation prohibiting gambling over the Internet or in student athletics by student athletes who are participating in competitive sports.

On both the federal and state levels, juvenile crime demands special attention, as the age of young offenders has fallen and their brutality has increased. We renew our call for a complete overhaul of the juvenile justice system that will punish juvenile offenders, open criminal proceedings to victims and the public, make conviction records more available, and enforce accountability for offenders, parents and judges.

With regard to school safety, we encourage local school systems to develop a single system of discipline for all students who commit offenses involving drugs or violence in school, not the federally imposed dual system which leaves today's teachers and students at risk from the behavior of others.

Any juvenile who commits any crime while carrying a gun should automatically be detained, not released to someone's custody. We urge localities to consider zero-tolerance for juvenile drinking and driving and early intervention to keep delinquency from escalating to crime. While recognizing the important role of both parents to the well-being of their children, we must acknowledge the critical need for positive role models to put a generation of fatherless boys on the right road to manhood. We affirm the right of public schools, court houses and other public buildings to post copies of the Ten Commandments.

Finally, continued assistance to state and local law enforcement is critical. Through research, grants and joint task forces, the federal government should encourage smarter, more effective anticrime efforts. In particular, we advocate assistance to police for their personal protection, continuing education and training, and family care.

What Is at Stake

The rule of law, the very foundation for a free society, has been under assault, not only by criminals from the ground up, but also from the top down. An administration that lives by evasion, coverup, stonewalling and duplicity has given us a totally discredited Department of Justice. The credibility of those who now manage the nation's top law enforcement agency is tragically eroded. We are fortunate to have its dedicated career work force, especially its criminal prosecutors, who have faced the unprecedented politicization of decisions regarding both personnel and investigations.

In the federal courts, scores of judges with activist backgrounds in the hard-left now have lifetime tenure. Our agenda for judicial reform is laid out elsewhere in this platform, but this is the heart of the matter: Whom do the American people trust to restore the rule of law, not just in our streets and playgrounds, not just in boardrooms and on Wall Street, but in our courts and in the Justice Department itself? The answer is clear. Governor Bush is determined to name only judges who have demonstrated respect for the Constitution and the processes of our republic.

Retirement Security and Quality Health Care

Our Pledge to America. There are those who say Americans must choose between security and freedom. They are wrong.

Security and liberty are not enemies. When properly balanced, they are kindred means for advancing individual achievement. In the century past, that balance was not always maintained. There were times when the exercise of independence left too many Americans insecure, especially in their old age. And there were more times when the governmental imposition of security smothered the freedoms that should be at the center of American life.

The Republican vision for a good society restores the balance most Americans seek, by maintaining the structures that guard against unforeseen misfortune and, at the same time, encouraging individual decision-making and personal control.

Saving Social Security: Helping Individuals Build Wealth

"Social Security is a defining American promise, and we will not turn back. This issue is a test of government's capacity to give its word and to keep it, to act in good faith and to pursue the common good."

— *George W. Bush*

"A defining American promise" — a strong phrase from a strong leader, with which we strongly agree.

The Social Security program is the touchstone by which the American people now gauge the reliability, competence and integrity of government. Unfortunately, the gauge is registering real problems. This is not breaking news to most Americans. They have known for years of the deterioration of Social Security's fiscal health but fully expected their leaders to address it. But with each passing year leading to an ever grimmer prognosis, the gauge has dropped, notch by notch, into the red zone.

Since 1992, Social Security's unfunded liability has increased from $7.4 trillion to $8.8 trillion. Its trustees project that, by the year 2015, there will not be enough cash coming in from payroll taxes to pay currently promised Social Security benefits.

The current administration has treated Social Security as a slogan rather than a priority, demanding billions for new government programs instead of attending to the stability of our most important domestic program. Even worse, their proposal to let the government buy stocks on behalf of the Social Security trust fund was an unprecedented power grab over the entire American economy.

Doing nothing is no longer an option, for it leads to three bitter choices in the near future: crippling levels of payroll taxation, significantly reduced benefits for Social Security recipients, or a crushing burden of public debt for generations to come.

We reject each of those outcomes and accept the mandate which others have abandoned: to keep faith with both the past and the future by saving Social Security. For starters, congressional Republicans stopped the annual raids on the Social Security trust funds by balancing the federal budget without that program's surplus. In addition, government agencies have improved — and should continue efforts to improve — the accuracy of economic indicators. Now a Republican president will forge a national consensus on these principles to protect this national priority.

Anyone currently receiving Social Security, or close to being eligible for it, will not be impacted by any changes. Key changes should merit bipartisan agreement so any reforms will be a win for the American people rather than a political victory for any one party. Real reform does not require, and will not include, tax increases. Personal savings accounts must be the cornerstone of restructuring. Each of today's workers should be free to direct a portion of their payroll taxes to personal investments for their retirement future. It is crucial that individuals be offered a variety of investment alternatives and that detailed information be provided to each participant to help them judge the risks and benefits of each plan.

Today's financial markets offer a variety of investment options, including some that guarantee a rate of return higher than the current Social Security system with no risk to the investor. Choice is the key. Any new options for retirement security should be voluntary, so workers can choose to remain in the current system or opt for something different. This is a challenge that demands the kind of presidential leadership the country has not seen in almost a decade. Governor Bush has shown his commitment by proposing a bold alternative to the collapse of Social Security. Along with Americans everywhere, we pledge to join him in this endeavor of a lifetime.

Security for Older Americans

For most of us, retirement holds both promise and problems. Today's elderly have far more economic security than earlier generations, and opportunities for learning, teaching and leading are greater than ever. Public policy must encourage, not inhibit, this. To that end, for half a century, the Republican Party fought to repeal the Democrats' earnings limitation on Social Security recipients, which took away a dollar for every three they earned.

That fight has finally been won, and we salute congressional Republicans for leading it. We likewise note with pride the Republican legislation that has simplified pension law and made it easier for more businesses, especially small ones, to offer pension plans.

We call for full repeal of the death tax, as proposed in Governor Bush's program, Prosperity with a Purpose, and as recently passed by congressional Republicans. Hard-working Americans should not live with the fear that the fruits of their lifetime of labor will fall into the hands of government instead of their children. The growing need for long-term care calls for long-term planning both by individuals and by government. We encourage, at all levels of government, regulatory flexibility and sensitivity to human needs in nursing homes and related facilities. In this area, as in so many other unheralded corners of American lives, heroic sacrifices are being made by millions of families to care for their mothers and fathers as their parents cared for them. We support Governor Bush's call for a 100 percent above-the-line tax deduction for premiums for long-term care insurance, recognizing and rewarding individual responsibility, and we welcome his proposal to allow an additional exemption for each elderly spouse, parent, or relative a family tends to in their own residence.

Preserving and Improving Medicare

"Our nation must reform Medicare — and in doing so, ensure that prescription drugs are affordable and available for every senior who needs them. Seniors deserve a wider scope of coverage, and they deserve to have more choices among health plans. Over the last few years, both Republicans and Democrats have embraced these goals, yet the Clinton-Gore administration has blocked bipartisan Medicare reform. When I am president, I will lead Republicans and Democrats to reform and strengthen Medicare and set it on firm financial ground."

— *George W. Bush*

Medicare, at age 35, needs a new lease on life. It's time to bring this program, so critical for 39 million seniors and individuals with disabilities, into the 21st century. It's time to modernize the benefit package to match current medical science, improve the program's financial stability, and cut back the bureaucratic jungle that is smothering it. It's time to give older Americans access to the same health insurance plan the Congress has created for itself, so that seniors will have the same choices and security as Members of Congress, including elimination of all current limitations and restrictions that prevent the establishment of medical savings accounts. To do that, we need to build on the strengths of the free market system, offer seniors real choices in coverage, give participants flexibility, and make sure there are incentives for the private sector to develop new and inexpensive drugs.

No one in their right mind would choose a physician who limited her practice to the treatments and procedures of the 1960s. By the same token, no one should be content with a Medicare program based on benefit packages and delivery models of that same era. For example, it denies coverage for necessary preventive services, like cholesterol screenings, and limits access to new life-saving technologies. This must change. Every Medicare beneficiary should have a choice of health care options. We want them to have access to the health plan that best fits their medical needs. In short: no more governmental one-size-fits-all.

Medicare also needs new measures of solvency that look at total program expenses and provide an honest reading of how we can guarantee benefits for decades to come. At the same time, we must dramatically reduce the program's administrative complexities symbolized both by its 130,000 pages of regulations and by its $13.5 billion in improper payments in 1999 alone. Some of that is due to fraud, waste and abuse, but most of it comes from the sad fact that Medicare is a creaking, bureaucratic and oppressive dinosaur in the age of MRIs. This frustrates health care providers, hospitals and patients alike. Let us be clear: We support vigorous enforcement of anti-fraud laws in cases where there is intent to commit fraud, but it is unfair to blame honest health care providers who must seek reimbursement within a minefield of confusing Medicare regulations.

For Medicare to survive — and more important, to succeed — it must become a common enterprise of government, health professionals and hospitals alike. Rather than continue the practice of recurrent and unpredictable cuts in provider payments, a reformed Medicare program will allow health care providers, particularly those helping rural and underserved populations, to adapt to changing conditions in health care by providing reimbursement at levels that will permit health care providers to continue to care for these patients. Republican leadership will reopen and broaden the door to health care by fulfilling the promise of medical research and innovation, by offering choice and protecting consumer rights, and by modernizing antiquated systems to deliver affordable care for all its beneficiaries.

Quality Health Care: A Commitment to All Americans

Americans enjoy the best health care in the world. Their system, the envy of all mankind, is the center of debate and controversy. This contradiction arises from the dynamism that is changing every aspect of American medicine. Change is seldom easy, and when it relates to the health of those we love, it can be downright scary. Still, the outcome of all this change is a world of unimagined promise in health. We must embrace that change, and master it as well.

The mapping of the human genome, identifying every gene in the human body, may, over time, translate into new treatments and cures for scourges like cancer, Alzheimer's, heart disease and HIV/AIDS, as well as diseases that affect the very young, such as muscular dystrophy and juvenile diabetes. A century ago, the average American life span was 55. Today, it is 78, and children born in this decade have the realistic prospect of living into the Twenty-Second Century. A simple blood test can now screen for prostate cancer at its earliest appearance. Biochemistry is revolutionizing the field of mental health. Millions of operations have been replaced with CAT scans. We want that progress to continue. But translating the promise of medical research into readily available treatments requires more than just money; it needs a whole new prescription for health care. That prescription is what the Republican party offers in the elections of 2000.

Let's start with the diagnosis. After eight years of pressure from the current administration, the foundations of our health care system are cracking. We can spot the fissures everywhere: There are currently 44 million uninsured Americans, an increase of one million for each of the past eight years. The institutions and the people who provide health care are at risk. Hospitals in our poorest urban and rural areas are being callously closed, by the same administration that budgets far less than was originally projected, while calling for greater coverage. The quality of health care is in jeopardy. Recent reports estimate that almost 100,000 patients die each year from medical errors. This is more than from auto accidents, murders, or AIDS.

Medicare, the bedrock of care for our elderly, is suffocating under more than 130,000 pages of federal rules, three times the size of the entire IRS code. It pays for only 53 percent of seniors' care, provides no outpatient prescription drugs, and does not cover real long-term care, and it is still headed for bankruptcy in the near future.

The doctor-patient relationship has been eroded, and in some instances replaced, by external decision-making and managed-care bureaucracy.

We intend to save this beleaguered system with a vision of health care adapted to the changing demands of a new century. It is as simple, and yet as profound, as this: All Americans should have access to high-quality and affordable health care. They should have a range of options and be able to select what is the best care for their individual and family needs. The integration of access, affordability, quality and choice into the nation's health care system is the goal that brings together all of the following proposals. In achieving that goal, we will promote a health care system that supports, not supplants, the private sector; that promotes personal responsibility in health care decision-making; and that ensures the least intrusive role for the federal government.

Affordable, Quality Health Insurance

"We will not nationalize our health care system. We will promote individual choice. We will rely on private insurance. But make no mistake: In my administration, low-income Americans will have access to high-quality health care."

— *George W. Bush*

Let's give credit where due: More than 100 million American workers and their families have sound health insurance through their places of employment. The job-creating dynamism of our free economy has thus done more to advance health care than any government program possibly could. The tie between good jobs and good insurance coverage is the single most important factor in advancing health care for those who need it.

That's why the Republican party remains determined to change federal law to give small employers the liberty to band together to purchase group insurance for their employees at reduced rates, thus providing them that important security. The tragedy is that this urgent expansion of coverage has this far been blocked by veto threats. With a Republican president, that will change.

Uninsured Americans do not have a single face. Their situations vary tremendously, with changes in family status, age and income. It makes sense to let them decide what kind of coverage best suits their needs. To give them that power of choice, we propose an unprecedented tax credit that will enable 27 million individuals and families to purchase the private health insurance that's right for them. We also support full deductibility of health insurance premiums for the self-employed.

Truly positive market forces occur when individuals have the ability to make individual marketplace decisions. We therefore strongly encourage support of the emerging concepts of defined contribution plans and medical savings accounts. Individuals should be free to manage their own health care needs through Flexible Savings Accounts (FSAs) and Medical Savings Accounts (MSAs). These initiatives make a government takeover of health care as anachronistic as surgery without anesthesia. We will make these accounts the vanguard of a new consumer rights movement in health care. Individuals should be able to roll over excess FSA dollars from one year to the next, instead of losing their unspent money at the end of each year. MSAs should be a permanent part of tax law, offered to all workers without restriction, with both employers and employees allowed to contribute.

Still, more needs to be done. A major reason why health insurance is so expensive is that many state legislatures now require all insurance policies to provide benefits and treatments which many families do not want and do not need. It is as if automakers were required by law to sell only fully equipped cars, even to buyers who didn't want or need all the extras. These mandates, extending far beyond minimum standards, increase costs for everyone, price low-income families out of the insurance market and advance the interests of specific providers. They have no place in a health care system based on consumer rights and patient choice. One area of health care that is sadly ignored is the role of primary and preventive care. This is particularly important in our inner cities and rural communities, where the emergency room may be the only avenue for assistance. People in rural and underserved areas need access to critical primary care. We will boost funding for community health centers and establish stronger public-private partnerships for safety net providers and hospitals in rural and underserved communities.

When Congressional Republicans established the State Children's Health Insurance Program (S-CHIP) program in 1997, they enabled us to secure health insurance coverage for approximately 8 million youngsters. Republicans want to ensure that children have access to quality health care, and that states have the flexibility to innovate, expand family coverage without interference from the Health Care Financing Administration, and reach out to eligible households that are currently not enrolled in a health insurance program or in Medicaid. In a Republican administration, the first order of business at the Department of

Health and Human Services will be to eliminate regulations that are stymieing the effectiveness of S-CHIP program and to stop imposing unwarranted mandates, so states can make sure children who need health care can get it. A streamlined enrollment process and energetic outreach efforts will finally fulfill the promise of S-CHIP. All it takes is caring.

Improving the Quality of Health Care

Protecting Patients' Rights. The tremendous growth of managed health care was driven by a market response to the fractured system of health care delivery that preceded it. One result of that growth has been a welcomed slowing of the rapid increases in health costs that were a regular occurrence of the 1970s and 1980s. However, this has come at the cost of patient dissatisfaction with the, at times, impersonal or insufficient health care delivery mechanism. Simply put, patients deserve more protections if we are to achieve a patient-centered system that offers high-quality, affordable care. The parents of a sick child should have access to the nearest emergency care. A patient in need of a heart specialist's expertise should be allowed to seek that opinion. A woman with breast cancer should be able to participate in a potentially life-saving clinical trial, and patients should have prompt access to independent physicians, or when appropriate, other health care professionals, to override any wrongful denial of treatment.

The traditional patient-doctor relationship must be preserved. Medical decision-making should be in the hands of physicians and their patients. In cases when a health plan denies treatment, a rapid appeals process geared toward ensuring that patients receive the right treatment without delays that might threaten a patient's health — as opposed to a lengthy trial — must be readily accessible to everyone in all health plans. We believe a quick and fair resolution to treatment disputes without going to court is the best result. However, as a last resort, we also support a patient's right to adjudicate claims in court to receive necessary medical care. In the interest of fairness to the thousands of businesses that purchase health benefits for their employees and for physicians who care for patients, employers and physicians should not be liable for the actions of the health plan and should be shielded from frivolous and unnecessary lawsuits.

Our overall philosophy is to trust state and local government to know what best suits the needs of their people. We believe the federal government should respect the states' traditional authority to regulate health insurance, health care professionals and health practice guidelines through their medical boards.

Medical Errors and Malpractice Reform. Our goal is to reduce the rate of medical errors, especially those that result in a patient's death. We will support scientific research to provide the public and health care providers with information about why these errors occur and what can be done to prevent them. We should not displace the current, very effective hospital peer review system.

Another key step will be reform of malpractice law. In its current form, it encourages health care providers to conceal even innocent mistakes, lest they be subject to vilifying publicity through the trial lawyers' system of jackpot justice. That is why a cloak of secrecy envelops operating rooms. We must open up the free flow of information concerning medical errors, both to protect patients and to reduce the cost of modern medicine. Patients who are genuinely injured should be rightly compensated, but the punitive and random aspects of today's litigation lottery cry out for reform. Just as we hold all health care personnel to the highest standards, so too must public policy respect their ethical conscience. No individual or institution should be compelled to assist in providing any medical service that violates their moral or religious convictions.

Women's Health. As Republicans, we hold dear the health and vitality of our families. Our efforts to build healthier families must begin with women — our mothers, daughters, grandmothers and grand-daughters. This nation needs far greater focus on the needs of women who have historically been underrepresented in medical research and access to the proper level of medical attention. We are reversing this historic trend.

Across this country, and at all levels of government, Republicans are at the forefront in aggressively developing health care initiatives targeted specifically at the needs of women. The enormous increases in the NIH budget brought about by the Republican Congress will make possible aggressive new research and clinical trials into diseases and health issues that disproportionately affect women as well as into conditions that affect the elderly, the majority of whom are women. And we are leading efforts to reach out to underserved and minority female populations, where disparities persist in life expectancy, infant mortality and death rates from cancer, heart disease and diabetes.

Republicans are dedicated to pursuing comprehensive women's health care initiatives that include access to state-of-the-art medical advances and technology; equality for women in the delivery of health care services; medical research that focuses specifically on women; appropriate representation of women in clinical trials; and direct access to women's health providers.

The increasing focus upon health problems of the very elderly, the great majority of whom are women, holds the promise of advances concerning osteoporosis and other ailments which should no longer be considered the inevitable price of old age. Because nutrition is intimately related to health, we advocate state flexibility in managing the various federal nutrition programs for low-income families, especially those receiving TANF assistance, most of whom are female-headed households. Their transition to jobs and independence should include nutritional improvement both for mothers and for their children.

The united efforts of Republican leaders at all levels of government and within our communities will make sure that women gain greater access to relevant care, research and education on health care issues important to them.

Children's Health. The huge strides we have already made in improving children's health must be balanced against sobering statistics. Asthma affects nearly five million children, and the incidence is dramatically increasing. Childhood obesity has jumped 100 percent in the last 15 years and can be a forerunner of the most serious illnesses later in life. Diabetes is now the second most common chronic disease in children. Youth drug abuse has more than doubled in the past eight years. Smoking rates for youth have risen alarmingly. Every year, 2,500 babies are born with fetal alcohol syndrome. So much of the suffering caused by childhood diseases can be prevented — by increasing immunization rates; by increasing resources for biomedical research, not by crippling pharmaceutical progress; by sensible strategies against teen smoking rather than the folly of prohibition; by a real war on drugs in place of the white flag policies of recent years. Our commitment is to address the emotional, behavioral and mental illnesses affecting children. With parental involvement as the critical component, we can help our youth make the healthy and the right choice in avoiding risk behaviors involving alcohol, drugs, premarital sex, tobacco and violence.

Biomedical Research. Recognizing the critical importance of research, the Republican Congress, rejecting the administration's lower figures, has already begun to fulfill its pledge to double funding for the National Institutes of Health (NIH). This is one of the few areas in which government investment yields tangible results; and those benefits can be greatest for currently underserved and minority populations, in which disparities persist in life expectancy and infant mortality, as well as death rates from heart disease, diabetes and cancer. With one out of four Americans contracting cancer, we need to increase not only research but also early detection and prevention efforts. Since Republicans took control of Congress in January 1995, our party has led in setting sound HIV/AIDS policy, including increased research funding and access to health services. We remain committed to, and place a high priority on, finding a cure for HIV/AIDS. With the enormous increase in resources for biomedical research comes accountability for its use, as well as responsibility to maintain the highest ethical standards. We applaud congressional Republicans for the steps they have taken for protection of human embryos and against human cloning, the trafficking in fetal tissue organs, and related abuses.

Academic Medical Centers. Adequate government reimbursement for medical services is critical to our nation's comprehensive academic medical centers, which serve as the primary health care resource for our poorest citizens, provide cutting-edge medical discovery, and teach and train our next generation of physicians.

Medical Privacy. The revolution in information and medical technology has created concerns about who has access to personal data — and how it might be used. Patients and their families should feel free to share all medical information with their doctor, but they will feel safe in doing so only if that information is protected. A related concern is genetic discrimination, now that genetic testing will become a routine part of medical health care. Well-conceived, thoughtful action is clearly needed, action that will protect and not harm patients. In both Congress and the Executive Branch, Republicans will work with patients, health care providers, researchers and insurers to establish new rules for dealing with these new challenges.

Safe Clinical Trials. Ensuring the safety of patients who participate in investigational clinical trials is fundamental to the future of medical innovation. The lack of oversight by the current administration in gene therapy trials put patients at risk and undermined critical research. A Republican administration will require the Food and Drug Administration and NIH to make patient protection a priority in clinical trial research.

Emerging Threats and Bioterrorism. The current administration has left our public health system inadequate to respond to the threats of emerging infectious diseases and the possibility of bioterrorism. We pledge to ensure the ability of the public health service to detect, track and prevent infectious outbreaks, whether natural or provoked by those who hate America.

Wellness. We repeat our statement that America has the finest health care delivery system that is still the envy of the world. We also recognize that an individual's health is often a reflection of the everyday choices made. While government's role is to help ensure a quality health care system, only individuals can make healthy choices.

American Partners in Conservation and Preservation: Stewardship of Our Natural Resources

"As an avid outdoorsman, I know all our prosperity as a nation will mean little if we leave future generations a world of polluted air, toxic waste, and vanished wilderness and forests."

— *George W. Bush*

Today's Republican party stands in the proud tradition of Teddy Roosevelt, the first president to stress the importance of environmental conservation. We approach both the national and individual stewardship of natural resources in the spirit of his maxim: "The nation behaves well if it treats the natural resources as assets which it must turn over to the next generation increased, and not impaired, in value." Over the past three decades, we have made progress. Air and water are cleaner. Some endangered species have made comebacks. Wetlands are being preserved. Recycling is commonplace in our homes. That progress itself has brought us to the threshold of a new era in environmental policy. The lessons we have learned over the last three decades, along with the steady advance of environmental technology, gives us the opportunity to explore better ways to achieve even higher goals.

Our way is to trust the innate good sense and decency of the American people. We will make them partners with government, rather than adversaries of it. The way current laws have been implemented has often fostered costly litigation and discouraged personal innovation in environmental conservation. We need to get back on a common track, so that both the people and their government can jointly focus on the real problems at hand. As a basis for that cooperation, we propose these principles:

- Economic prosperity and environmental protection must advance together. Prosperity gives our society the wherewithal to advance environmental protection, and a thriving natural environment enhances the quality of life that makes prosperity worthwhile. Scare tactics and scapegoating of legitimate economic interests undermine support for environmental causes and, what is worse, can discredit actual threats to health and safety.

• Environmental regulations should be based upon the best science, peer-reviewed and available for public consideration.

• We support the federal, local, state and tribal responsibilities for environmental protection.

• We believe the government's main role should be to provide market-based incentives to innovate and develop the new technologies for Americans to meet — and exceed — environmental standards. We condemn the current administration's policy of resorting to confrontation first. Instead we should work cooperatively to ensure that our environmental policy meets the particular needs of geographic regions and localities.

Environmental policy should focus on achieving results — cleaner air, water and lands — not crafting bureaucratic processes. Where environmental standards are violated, the government should take consistent enforcement.

While the very nature of environmental concerns at times requires federal intervention, the heartening progress made by many of states and localities demonstrates their unique ability to solve problems at the local level. As the laboratories of innovation, they should be given flexibility, authority and finality by the federal government. Many states have enacted environmental education and voluntary self-audit laws to encourage people to find and correct pollution; the Congress should remove disincentives for states to achieve these goals. Strong leadership by governors, legislators and local officials is the key to solving the emerging environmental issues of this new century.

For example, the reauthorization of the Safe Drinking Water Act by the Republican Congress enabled states and communities to take stronger action to ensure reliable and safe water supplies. Another example is the way states are handling the problem of brownfields. In 35 states, voluntary programs are cleaning up thousands of brownfield sites faster and more effectively, and with less litigation, than under the federal superfund program. A case in point is Texas, where, under Governor Bush, the number of brownfield sites restored to productive use climbed from zero to 451, not only improving the environment but restoring more than $200 million in property value to local tax rolls, most of it in poor communities.

We will replicate Governor Bush's success on the national level. We will use superfund resources to actually clean up places where people live and labor, rather than waste it on costly litigation. The old approach of mandate, regulate and litigate has sent potential developers away from brownfield neighborhoods. The result: no new businesses, no new jobs — only dirty and dangerous sites. Governor Bush has pledged to transform this failure into an environmental win for those communities, just as he did in Texas, and we heartily endorse his agenda for doing so.

Wherever it is environmentally responsible to do so, we will promote market-based programs that are voluntary, flexible, comprehensive and cost-effective. The Endangered Species Act (ESA), for example, is sometimes counter-productive toward its truly important goal of protecting rare species, 75 percent of which are located on private land. Its punitive approach actually encourages landowners to remove habitat to avoid federal intervention. This serves as a disincentive for private landowners to do more to restore habitat and become private stewards of wildlife. The legislation needs incentive-based cooperation among federal, state, local and tribal governments and private citizens. The result will be a more effective ESA that better protects wildlife diversity.

As environmental issues become increasingly international, progress will increasingly depend on strong and credible presidential leadership. Complex and contentious issues like global warming call for a far more realistic approach than that of the Kyoto Conference. Its deliberations were not based on the best science; its proposed agreements would be ineffective and unfair inasmuch as they do not apply to the developing world; and the current administration is still trying to implement it, without authority of law. More research is needed to understand both the cause and the impact of global warming. That is why the Kyoto treaty was repudiated in a lopsided bipartisan Senate vote. A Republican president will work with businesses and with other nations to reduce harmful emissions through new technologies without compromising America's sovereignty or competitiveness — and without forcing Americans to walk to work.

Protecting Property Rights

We link the security of private property to our environmental agenda for the best of reasons: Environmental stewardship has best advanced where property is privately held. After all, people who live on the land, work the land and own the land also love the land and protect it. As Governor Bush has said, "For the American farmer, every day is Earth Day." Conversely, the world's worst cases of environmental degradation have occurred in places where most property is under government control. For reasons both constitutional and environmental, therefore, we will safeguard private property rights by enforcing the Takings Clause of the Fifth Amendment and by providing just compensation whenever private property is needed to achieve a compelling public purpose.

Public Lands for the Public Good

Collaborative conservation represents the future for the 657 million acres of America we call the "Public Lands." Working from the grass roots up, local groups are finding solutions for the problems of the public lands in their areas. Republicans want to encourage that approach, for it holds the greatest promise of sound environmental stewardship and productive use of the nation's natural resources. We will change the operating culture of the federal agencies that manage public lands, giving a greater role to states and to their political subdivisions in order to foster a creative partnership with the American people. As a sign of that partnership, we applaud Governor Bush's intention to make all federal facilities comply with the environmental laws by which the

American people live.

If there had been any doubt that major reform is needed in the management of public lands, it was burnt away in the catastrophic wildfires of recent months. This avoidable devastation was the price innocent people and helpless communities paid for the extreme policies — and environmental arrogance — of the current administration. Greater tragedies await the people of our Western states if those policies are not changed. Republicans will employ the best techniques of forestry science to implement a national management strategy for public lands that minimizes the risk to local communities while preserving our natural heritage.

Our national parks are the crown jewels of the country's environmental heritage. They belong to all Americans and should be accessible to all. Congressional Republicans have taken the lead in reversing years of neglect and abuse of these treasures, and we will continue that proactive agenda to keep the park system healthy and accessible to all. We should make it a priority to alleviate the maintenance and operations backlog at our national parks. Rather than adding to this magnificent legacy by unilateral executive branch action, such as the administration's recent National Monument designations, we will seek to actively involve Congress, as well as affected states and local communities, in land acquisition decisions.

We support multiple use of public lands conducted in an environmentally and economically sustainable manner. We are committed to preserving high priority wilderness and wetlands. The Everglades are a crucial example of a special federal responsibility. We call for a review of lands owned by the national government — half the total territory of our Western states — to develop a comprehensive plan to better manage existing holdings. In some cases, that may mean transferring or sharing responsibility for managing those lands with state or local governments, while all levels of government should recognize existing rights to water, minerals and grazing. We reaffirm the traditional state primacy over water allocations and will continue the availability of renewable rangeland under conditions that ensure both expanded production of livestock and protection of the range environment. We also reaffirm our commitment to preserve access to public lands for multiple use.

We recognize the vital role the timber industry plays in our economy, particularly in homebuilding, and we support its efforts to improve the health of the country's forests. Because so many people in rural America rely on public forests for their livelihood, a Republican administration will promote sustainable forest management, using the best science in place of the no-growth policies that have devastated communities in the Pacific Northwest and Alaska.

American Agriculture and Rural America in the Global Economy

Agriculture is at the heart of the U.S. economy. The food and fiber sector accounts for 13 percent of the nation's economic output and employs, directly or indirectly, more than 22 million people. When agriculture is hurting, the entire country aches. In all our policies and programs, the Republican party is guided by two principles. First, to farmers and ranchers, nothing beats production and sales at a good price. As long as they have truly fair and open domestic and foreign markets, they can do for themselves far better than anything government can do for them. Second, they want to produce what makes sense on their own private property, not what official Washington thinks should be grown there. Under Republican leadership, government will never again run our family farms.

While these are not the best of times for farmers and ranchers, the hopeful promise of our Freedom to Farm Act, which finally replaced decades of controls by a federal bureaucracy, has been limited by events at home and abroad. Farmers were promised that, along with the end of governmental protection for commodities markets, there would be reforms in tax, trade and regulatory policy. Opposition from the current administration minimized progress in all three areas. As a result, American farmers were hard-pressed to deal with the challenge of increased global production and slack demand in Asia. The ineptitude of current U.S. trade policy only made it worse.

For American agriculture, prosperity depends in large measure on expansion of global markets. Our farmers already export some $54 billion in products and commodities every year. For them, for the aspirations of their families and the dreams of their children, the opening of foreign markets is essential. Governor Bush understands that. That's why he has asked for restoration of presidential fast-track negotiating authority, the key to forceful trade negotiations abroad. And it's why he's determined to open the China market for America's farmers and ranchers. It's why he's called for the United States to demand, in the next round of global trade talks, the complete elimination of agricultural export subsidies and tariffs. It's why he will fight the European Community's outrageous restrictions against imports of U.S. crops and livestock. And it's why he has pledged to exempt food exports from any new trade sanctions.

Results will take time, and so, looking toward the Farm Bill of the year 2002, we call for immediate action on a safety net that will give farmers the means to manage cyclical downturns. This year's reform of the Federal Crop Insurance Act by the Republican Congress was a good start. In its wake, we propose:

- Emergency assistance to facilitate the transition to a market-driven regime.
- A farm income savings plan: tax-deferred accounts to soften fluctuations in farm earnings.
- Total repeal of the death tax. Immediate 100 percent deductibility for health insurance costs. A one-time exemption from capital gains tax on the sale of farms.
- Regulatory relief. We reaffirm our strong support for agricultural research, including biotech and biomass research, and for a permanent research and development tax credit.

We likewise support the ethanol tax credit, which is good for both the environment and for farmers. Our program of regulatory reform has special relevance to farming, which bears an annual regulatory burden of $20 billion. Every farm family has better uses for that money. Apart from costs, there are grave questions about the impact of the 1996 Food Quality Protection Act. Its implementation must not disrupt farmers' access to safe crop protection products.

We reaffirm our support for cooperative partnerships between federal, state and local governments and private landowners for the conservation of our soil, water and biological resources on private land. The federal government should work with the states to adopt water quality standards that rely on the best science and implementation of best management practices, including addressing hypoxia and runoff issues.

We call for the elimination of outdated laws that hamper the adaptation of agriculture to the demands and opportunities of a new century. Futures trading should be deregulated. Regional restrictions on dairy products that drive up consumer prices and penalize productive farmers should be ended. We commend the livestock industry for its efforts to ensure accurate and open price reporting to ensure a competitive market.

There is much more to rural America than agriculture, ranching and forestry. The kind of economic development that generates family-sustaining jobs is critical to small towns and rural communities. We recognize the special challenges they face in working for good schools, accessible health care, decent housing, safe drinking water and waste disposal, and serviceable transportation. The federal government should be an active partner with state and local entities in that process, especially in advancing the availability of the Internet and modern telecommunications technology in rural America.

Energy

What happened? Eight years ago, the nation was energy confident. Our standing in the Middle East was at its zenith. The oil cartel was in retreat; gasoline was affordable, even as automotive progress reduced emissions from cars. Today, gas prices have skyrocketed, and oil imports are at all-time highs. Foreign oil now accounts for one-third of our total trade deficit. Meanwhile, domestic oil production has fallen 17 percent over the last eight years, as vast areas of the continental U.S. have been put off limits to energy leasing — though we depend on oil and natural gas for 65 percent of our energy supply. Additional oil reserves and deposits of low-sulfur coal may be out of reach because of unilateral designation of new national monuments.

By any reasonable standard, the Department of Energy has utterly failed in its mission to safeguard America's energy security. The Federal Energy Regulatory Commission has been no better, and the Environmental Protection Agency (EPA) has been shutting off America's energy pipeline with a regulatory blitz that has only just begun. In fact, 36 oil refineries have closed in just the last eight years, while not a single new refinery has been built in this country in the last quarter-century. EPA's patchwork of regulations has driven fuel prices higher in some areas than in others and has made energy supplies no longer fungible. What meets EPA's standards in one city may not be legally sold in another. The result has been localized shortages and sharp price spikes, as suppliers scramble to get acceptable fuels to the markets where they are needed.

Environmental concerns are not at the heart of the matter. In fact, the current administration has turned its back on the two sources that produce virtually all of the nation's emission-free power: nuclear and hydro, the sources for 30 percent of the country's electricity. Because of cumbersome federal relicensing of hydro and nuclear operations, we face the prospect of increasing emissions and dirtier air. Meanwhile, nuclear plants are choking on waste because the current administration breached its contract to remove it — and then vetoed bipartisan legislation to store it at a safe, permanent repository for which the taxpayers have already paid $7 billion. At the same time, power-producing dams are being torn down by federal edict in energy-short areas, and the Pacific Northwest is their next target. Breaching dams would not only raise electric rates but would deny western farmers irreplaceable water for irrigation and a cost-effective means of moving their crops to West Coast ports. We should develop and use technologies that will help entrance salmon runs while keeping the dams in place.

It's a man-made nightmare, but at last the public is waking up and demanding change. What is at stake, after all, is not just the price we pay to heat and cool our homes. What is at stake is the nation's New Economy, which relies heavily on electricity for its infrastructure and on petroleum for its trade. Affordable energy, the result of Republican policies in the 1980s, helped create the New Economy. If we do not carefully plan for our energy needs, the entire economy could be significantly weakened. The Republican Congress has moved to deregulate the electricity industry and empower consumers through a competitive market — but congressional Democrats are holding up the process, and the administration has provided no leadership. America needs a national energy strategy — and a Republican president will work with congressional Republicans to enact their National Energy Security Act. That strategy will:

- Increase domestic supplies of coal, oil and natural gas. Our country does have ample energy resources waiting to be developed, and there is simply no substitute for an increase in their domestic production.
- Improve federal oil and gas lease permit processing and management, including coalbed methane.
- Provide tax incentives for production.
- Promote environmentally responsible exploration and development of oil and gas reserves on federally-owned land, including the Coastal Plain of Alaska's Arctic National Wildlife Refuge.
- Offer a degree of price certainty to keep small domestic stripper producers in operation.
- Advance clean coal technology.
- Expand the tax credit for renewable energy sources to include wind and open-loop biomass facilities, and electricity produced from steel cogeneration.
- Maintain the ethanol tax credit.
- Provide a tax incentive for residential use of solar power.

This agenda will reduce America's dependence on foreign oil, help consumers by lowering energy prices, and result in lower carbon emissions than would result from the current administration's policies. To protect consumers against seasonal price spikes, that legislation also authorizes a home heating oil reserve for the Northeastern states and allows expensing of costs for its storage. It will also make low-income housing more energy-efficient. All in all, it is a dramatic reversal of the nation's present course, and that's just what America needs: a balanced portfolio of energy options that is stable, secure and affordable, with minimal impact on the environment.

A Nation on The Move

Commerce is the lifeblood of our economy, and the transportation infrastructure is its circulatory system. Without safe and efficient transport, the economy withers away. Maintaining that vital infrastructure has always been, in part, a federal responsibility, and Republicans have historically been the party of builders. From the era of the transcontinental railroad and the Panama Canal to President Eisenhower's establishment of the Interstate Highway System, we have championed investment in transportation assets as a cornerstone of the economy and, indeed, our national way of life.

More recently, the Republican-led Congress has enacted two historic pieces of legislation: the 1998 Transportation Equity Act for the Twenty-First Century, and this year's Aviation Investment and Reform Act. These landmark laws represent an unprecedented federal investment in roads, bridges, transit systems, airports and air traffic control systems — without additional taxes. They simply unlock the transportation trust funds to invest the dollars that motorists and the traveling public have already paid. Those funds had been subject to years of abuse under Democrat-controlled Congresses but are now statutorily dedicated to building and maintaining the transportation system for which our citizens pay. The same budgetary protections should be extended to other transportation trust funds.

Our national railroad network is a crucial component of our public transportation system. Railroads helped build our country, and our national passenger railroad network remains a precious resource that can play a key role in transportation and economic growth. Republicans support a healthy intercity passenger rail system, and where economically viable, the development of a national high-speed passenger railroad system as an instrument of economic development and enhanced mobility. We also support a multi-modal approach to our transportation needs.

By reducing mandates, cutting red tape and promoting regulatory common sense, congressional Republicans have given state and local officials unprecedented flexibility to set their own transportation priorities, from highways to bike trails. That will improve communities throughout the nation, and will also strengthen travel and tourism, a vital force for job creation with a positive annual trade balance to boot. But transportation policy remains inseparable from energy policy

The trucking industry, for example, is hard hit by current gas prices and would be crippled by the administration's new "hours of service" regulation. Consumers everywhere are literally paying the price both for what the administration has done and for what it has failed to do.

Republicans are going to get transportation policy back on track, both here at home through a sound, long-term energy policy, and internationally as well, by pursuing the "Open Skies" agreements, first proposed by President George Bush, to open foreign markets for American aviation services. In short, we will keep Americans moving safely and keep our country, in the words of the song, "a thoroughfare for freedom."

Government for the People

Trust, pride and respect: We pledge to restore these qualities to the way Americans view their government. It is the most important of tasks and reflects the overwhelming desire of our citizens for fundamental change in official Washington.

The templates to make this happen are readily available in the 30 states led by Republican governors. These visionary leaders have opened a new era of creative federalism, making government citizen-centered, results-oriented, and, where possible, market-based. Their sound management of public dollars has led to unprecedented surpluses. Services have improved. Waste has been reduced. Taxes have been cut.

State and local governments are also far ahead of official Washington in the creation of e-government: providing information and services to the public via the Internet. Citizens can conduct business with government by going online instead of wasting hours in line. We will e-power citizens at all levels of government. And we will require federal agencies to use savvy, online practices to buy smart — and save enormous amounts of money in procurement.

The leadership our governors have shown in these matters only strengthens our commitment to restore the force of the Tenth Amendment, the best protection the American people have against federal intrusion and bullying. We have limited the ability of Congress to impose unfunded mandates on states and on local and tribal governments. The next logical step is to address the unfunded mandates of the past in areas like education and social services. The dramatic success of welfare reform — once the states were allowed to manage their programs — is a stellar example of what happens when we give power back to the people.

Therefore, in our effort to shift power from Washington back to the states, we must acknowledge as a general matter of course that the federal government's role should be to set high standards and expectations in policies, then get out of the way and let the states implement and operate those policies as they best know how. Washington must respect that one size does not fit all states and must not overburden states with unnecessary strings and red tape attached to its policies.

In the Congress, a Republican majority has modernized our national legislature. They have set term limits for committee chairs and leadership positions, and they have, by law, required Congress to live by the same rules it imposes on others. And, at a time when the nation felt betrayed by misconduct in high office, the Republican Congress responded with gravity and high purpose. We applaud those Members who did their duty to conscience and the Constitution.

There is much to be done, but it can be done only when a Republican president works in tandem with a Republican Congress. We will work to pass legislation to make it clear that public officials who commit crimes will subsequently forfeit their pension rights. We will ensure that IRS audits are never used as a political weapon, so innocent Americans will never again fear the snooping, harassment and intimidation of recent years. And because an accurate census is essential for representative government, we will respect the Supreme Court's judgment that an actual headcount of persons is the proper way to determine the apportionment of congressional districts.

A Republican president will take the lead in proposing, and fighting for, the structural changes that are long overdue in the federal government. For starters, the twenty-five year old congressional budget process, though it has helped to make possible today's budget surpluses, has become almost unintelligible to legislators, let alone the average citizen. It has been inadequate to enforce legislated spending caps and cannot stop the phony "emergency" bills that cause the spending caps to be exceeded. It cannot control runaway spending on entitlements and "mandatory" spending; it does not even prevent our government spending $120 billion on programs whose statutory authority has expired.

Our goal is to replace the status quo with clarity, simplicity and accountability to the budget process. We will have a biennial budget that has the force of law. To end pork barrel abuses on Capitol Hill, we will:

- Eliminate the "baseline budgeting" that artificially boosts spending.
- Create a constitutionally sound line-item veto for the president, and direct the savings from items vetoed to paying down the national debt.
- Prevent government shutdowns by enacting a "Permanent Continuing Resolution" so the spending lobbies can never again extort billions from the taxpayers by blocking the regular order of appropriation bills.
- Define legislatively the conditions for "emergency" spending.

Like Congress, the Executive Branch must adapt to the challenges of the new century. There are too many departments and agencies with competing programs that waste resources and fail to deliver the goods: 342 economic development programs, 788 education programs in 40 different agencies at a cost of over $100 billion a year, 163 job training programs in 15 different agencies. Twelve agencies administer over 35 food safety laws. One agency regulates pizzas with meat; another regulates vegetarian pizzas. (Still another regulates the people who deliver them. Enough said.)

We intend to downsize this mess and make government actually do what it is supposed to, simply by ensuring that all agencies adhere to the Government Performance and Results Act, which has been neglected or ignored by the current administration. By applying its procedures to all federal programs, we can stop the loss of millions of Medicare dollars for services rendered after patients have died. We can put the brakes on an Education Department that pays out $3.3 billion on defaulted student loans, and an Energy Department that spends $10 billion on projects that are never completed. Because of its history of needless partisan litigation, we call for the Legal Services Corporation to return to its original purpose of providing legal aid to the indigent, rather than pursuing political causes and agendas. We will, as an urgent priority, restore the integrity of the nation's space program by imposing sound management and strong oversight on NASA.

A Republican president will run the federal government much as the Republican governors run state agencies. Bureaucracy will be reduced and trimmed in size at its upper echelons. If public services can be delivered more efficiently and less expensively through the private sector, they will be privatized. A Republican president will establish accountability, reward performance, put civility back into the civil service, and restore dignity and ethics to the White House.

Political Reform

The First Amendment enshrines in our Constitution and guarantees indispensable democratic freedoms of speech, press, association and the right to petition our government. The Republican party affirms that any regulation of the political process must not infringe upon the rights of the people to full participation in the political process. The principal cure for the ills of democracy is greater participation in the political process by more citizens. To that end, we have one guiding principle in the development of laws to regulate campaigns: Will any particular proposal encourage or restrict the energetic engagement of Americans in elections? Governor Bush's agenda for more honest and more open politics meets that standard. It will:

- Stop the abuses of corporate and labor "soft" money contributions to political parties.
- Enact "Paycheck Protection," ensuring that no union member is forced to contribute to anybody's campaign — and stopping an annual rip-off of $300 million from union families by Washington-based politicos.
- Preserve the right of every individual and all groups — whether for us or against us — to express their opinions and advocate their issues. We will not allow any arm of government to restrict this constitutionally guaranteed right.
- Level the playing field by forbidding incumbents to roll over their leftover campaign funds into a campaign for a different office.
- Require full and timely disclosure on the Internet of all campaign contributions — so the media and the public can immediately know who is giving how much to whom.
- Encourage all citizens to donate their time and resources to the campaigns of their choice by updating for inflation the quarter-century-old limits on individual contributions.
- Preserve access to the Internet for political speech and debate.

Gerrymandered congressional districts are an affront to democracy and an insult to the voters. We oppose that and any other attempt to rig the electoral process.

Common Sense In Regulation

Effective government requires regulation for health, safety and other concerns. By the same token, regulation requires regular review — for efficiency, economy and plain common sense. That Republican model of regulatory reform is a good fit for an Information Age economy. It will replace a bureaucratic mentality clicking along at a Morse Code pace. We will use the advance of science and information technology to:

• Target the most serious risks to health, safety and the environment, then put regulatory resources where they best serve the public, not politics.

• Make sound science, not ideological whim, the basis for regulation, with peer-reviewed risk assessments and full disclosure. Require periodic review of existing regulations to strengthen where necessary and change where obsolete.

• Require agencies to disclose the cost to consumers and small businesses of any proposed regulations.

• Let the American people know the full price they pay for government regulations, through a new regulatory budget that explains the likely cost for meeting regulatory requirements.

• Use cost-benefit analyses of regulations to develop alternatives to the outdated command-and-control attitude of recent years.

• Retrain civil servants to work with those affected by regulation rather than dictating to them.

The current administration has repeatedly evaded the normal regulatory process through executive orders, some of dubious legality. Withdrawing these orders should be a priority of a new administration dedicated to the rule of law.

We oppose and will work to end taxpayer-supported grants for projects and programs that promote religious bigotry in America.

Judicial Reform: Courts That Work, Laws That Make Sense

Americans have the right to a judicial system they can trust. There is no question that the need for reform extends to the judicial branch of government. Many judges disregard the safety, values and freedom of law-abiding citizens. At the expense of our children and families, they make up laws, invent new rights, free vicious criminals and pamper felons in prison. They have arbitrarily overturned state laws enacted by citizen referenda, utterly disregarding the right of the people and the democratic process.

The sound principle of judicial review has turned into an intolerable presumption of judicial supremacy. A Republican Congress, working with a Republican president, will restore the separation of powers and re-establish a government of law. There are different ways to achieve that goal — setting terms for federal judges, for example, or using Article III of the Constitution to limit their appellate jurisdiction — but the most important factor is the appointing power of the presidency. We applaud Governor Bush's pledge to name only judges who have demonstrated that they share his conservative beliefs and respect the Constitution.

Reform of the legal profession is an essential part of court reform. Today's litigation practices make a mockery of justice, hinder our country's competitiveness in the world market and, far worse, erode the public's trust in the entire judicial process.

Avarice among many plaintiffs' lawyers has clogged our civil courts, drastically changed the practice of medicine, and costs American companies and consumers more than $150 billion a year. Who profits? On average, more than fifty cents of every dollar paid out in tort cases goes to lawyers' fees, not to an injured party. This amounts to a tax on consumers to fatten the wallets of trial lawyers.

Let's be blunt about the effects of all that cash: Our civil justice reforms have been blocked in the Capitol and vetoed in the Oval Office. It's why federal agencies have colluded with the trial lawyer lobby in sweetheart litigation, to advance through the courts what they could not accomplish through the political process. We fully support the role of the courts in vindicating the rights of individuals and organizations, but we want to require higher standards for trial lawyers within federal jurisdiction, much as Governor Bush has already done in Texas — and as we encourage other states to do within their own legal codes. To achieve that goal, we will strengthen the federal rules of civil procedure to increase penalties for frivolous suits and impose a "Three Strikes, You're Out" rule on attorneys who repeatedly file such suits. We will limit "fishing expeditions" by amending federal discovery rules, curb the use of junk science in testimony and end the abusive use of the RICO statute. We encourage all states to consider placing caps on non-economic and punitive damages in civil cases. We also support such caps in federal causes of action. We also encourage states to examine the effects on the democratic process of advancing policies through litigation that could not be accomplished through the political process.

We will enact a Teacher Protection Act to protect educators from meritless federal lawsuits against their efforts to maintain discipline in the classroom. We will extend similar protections to nonprofit organizations — churches, civic and community groups and the volunteers who sustain them.

To reduce health care costs and keep doctors practicing in critical areas like obstetrics, we will reform medical malpractice law on the federal level and urge decisive action on the state level as well.

To encourage settlements and to discourage prolonged litigation, a Fair Settlements Rule should be enacted requiring either party in federal court who rejects a timely, reasonable and good faith pre-trial settlement offer, and who ultimately loses their case, to pay the other party's costs, including legal fees. We also encourage states to consider enacting such rules. To improve access to justice, we will make it easier for cases of national import to be heard in federal courts.

To protect clients against unscrupulous lawyers, we will enact a Clients' Bill of Rights for all federal courts, requiring attorneys to disclose both the range of their fees and their ethical obligation to charge reasonable fees and allowing those fees to be challenged in federal courts. Because private lawyers should not unreasonably profit at public expense, we will prohibit federal agencies from paying contingency fees and encourage states to do so as well. Even more important, we will require attorneys to return to the people any excessive fees they gain under contract to states or municipalities.

An integral part of legal reform is a federal product liability law. Without it, consumers face higher costs, needed products don't make it to the market, and American jobs are lost to foreign competitors. That, too, will change when the American people break the grip of the trial lawyers on our legal system.

Native Americans

The federal government has a special responsibility, ethical and legal, to make the American dream accessible to Native Americans. Unfortunately, the resources that the United States holds in trust for them, financial and otherwise, have been misused and abused. While many tribes have become energetic participants in the mainstream of American life, the serious social ills afflicting some reservations have been worsened by decades of mismanagement from Washington. In its place, we offer these guiding principles:

• Tribal governments are best situated to gauge the needs of their communities and members. Political self-determination and economic self-sufficiency are twin pillars of an effective Indian policy. Private sector initiatives, rather than public assistance, can best improve material conditions in Indian communities. High taxes and unreasonable regulations stifle new and expanded businesses and thwart the creation of job opportunities and prosperity.

• We will strengthen Native American self-determination by respecting tribal sovereignty, encouraging economic development on reservations and working with them to reorganize the Bureau of Indian Affairs and the Indian Health Service. We uphold the unique government-to-government relationship between the tribes and the United States and honor our nation's trust obligations to them.

• We support efforts to ensure equitable participation in federal programs by Native Americans, Native Alaskans and Native Hawaiians and to preserve their cultures and languages.

The Nation's Capital

The District of Columbia is a special responsibility of the federal government and should be a model for urban areas throughout the country. Its downhill slide has at least been arrested, both through its internal efforts and the active intervention of congressional Republicans, who have taken unprecedented steps to help the city recover. Their D.C. homebuyers' tax credit is helping to revitalize marginal neighborhoods; their landmark tuition assistance act has opened the doors of the nation's colleges to D.C. students.

Now, to enhance the city's economic security, reverse the movement out of the city and ensure a safe and healthy environment for families, we advocate deep reductions in the District's taxes, currently among the highest in the nation, and encourage user-friendly development policies.

We call once again for structural reform of the city's schools so that none of its children will be left behind. We strongly support both charter schools and the opportunity scholarships for poor kids who have been repeatedly blocked by the administration.

We respect the design of the Framers of the Constitution that our nation's capital has a unique status and should remain independent of any individual state.

Americans in the Territories

We welcome greater participation in all aspects of the political process by Americans residing in Guam, the Virgin Islands, American Samoa, the Northern Marianas and Puerto Rico. Since no single approach can meet the needs of those diverse communities, we emphasize respect for their wishes regarding their relationship to the rest of the Union. We affirm their right to seek the full extension of the Constitution, with all the rights and responsibilities it entails.

We support the Native American Samoans' efforts to preserve their culture and land-tenure system, which fosters self-reliance and strong extended-family values.

We support increased local self-government for the United States citizens of the Virgin Islands, and closer cooperation between the local and federal governments to promote private sector-led development and self-sufficiency.

We recognize that Guam is a strategically vital U.S. territory in the far western Pacific, an American fortress in the Asian region. We affirm our support for the patriotic U.S. citizens of Guam to achieve greater local self-government, an improved federal-territorial relationship, new economic development strategies and continued self-determination as desired with respect to political status.

We support the right of the United States citizens of Puerto Rico to be admitted to the Union as a fully sovereign state after they freely so determine. We recognize that Congress has the final authority to define the constitutionally valid options for Puerto Rico to achieve a permanent status with government by consent and full enfranchisement. As long as Puerto Rico is not a state, however, the will of its people regarding their political status should be ascertained by means of a general right of referendum or specific referenda sponsored by the United States government.

Principled American Leadership

"The duties of our day are different. But the values of our nation do not change.Let us reject the blinders of isolationism, just as we refuse the crown of empire. Let us not dominate others with our power — or betray them with our indifference. And let us have an American foreign policy that reflects American character. The modesty of true strength. The humility of real greatness. This is the strong heart of America. And this will be the spirit of my administration."

— *George W. Bush*

The Emerging Fellowship Of Freedom

The Twenty-First Century opens with unique promise for the United States. Democratic values are celebrated on every continent. The productivity and ingenuity of American business are the envy of the world. American innovation is leading the way in the information age. New technology speeds an exchange of ideas that often bear the mark of American inspiration. No other great power challenges American international pre-eminence. There is every reason for Americans to be extraordinarily optimistic about their future.

Few nations in history have been granted such a singular opportunity to shape the future. Even after World War II the United States had to reckon with a divided world and terrible dangers. Now America can help mold international ideals and institutions for decades to come. Handed the torch by generations that won great battles, our generation of Americans with its allies and friends can build a different and better world, promoting U.S. interests and principles, avoiding the economic convulsions and perilous conflicts that so scarred the century just past. Through a distinctly American internationalism, a new Republican president will build public support for a new strategy that can lead the United States of America toward a more peaceful and prosperous world for us, our children and future generations.

Almost all Americans know they cannot prosper alone in the world. They know that America is safest when more and more countries share a profound belief in political and economic liberty, human dignity, and the rule of law, when more and more nations join the United States in an emerging fellowship of freedom.

That is what happened during the twelve years of Republican presidential leadership from 1981 to 1992. The Cold War ended with the triumph of freedom. The Soviet Empire collapsed, and the Soviet Union followed it into history. The proud Atlantic community welcomed a united Germany and new friends in Central and Eastern Europe. Iraq tried the law of the jungle and was routed, its aggressive power broken. The Arab-Israeli peace process was revived. Alliances and friendships in Asia were robust and successful. Mexico joined with the United States in an unprecedented new economic partnership as peace and democracy spread through Latin America. Around the globe, the word, the ideals and the power of the United States commanded respect. The American presidency showed bright and purposeful.

In the last eight years the administration has squandered the opportunity granted to the United States by the courage and sacrifice of previous generations.

The administration has run America's defenses down over the decade through inadequate resources, promiscuous commitments and the absence of a forward-looking military strategy. The ballistic missile threat to the United States has been persistently dismissed, delaying for years the day when America will have the capability to defend itself against this growing danger. The arrogance, inconsistency and unreliability of the administration's diplomacy have undermined American alliances, alienated friends and emboldened our adversaries. World trade talks in Seattle that the current administration had sponsored collapsed in spectacular failure. Authority to negotiate new fast-track trade agreements was slapped down by the administration's own party in the Congress. An initiative to establish free trade throughout the Americas has stalled because of this lack of Presidential leadership. The problems of Mexico have been ignored, as our indispensable neighbor to the south struggled with too little American help to deal with its formidable challenges. The tide of democracy in Latin America has begun to ebb with a sharp rise in corruption and narco-trafficking. A misguided policy toward China was exemplified by President Clinton's trip to Beijing that produced an embarrassing presidential kowtow and a public insult to our longstanding ally, Japan. With weak and wavering policies toward Russia, the administration has diverted its gaze from corruption at the top of the Russian government, the slaughter of thousands of innocent civilians in Chechnya and the export of dangerous Russian technologies to Iran and elsewhere. A chorus of empty threats destroyed America's credibility in the Balkans, so that promised safe havens became killing fields.

The administration prolonged the war in Kosovo by publicly limiting America's military options — something no commander in chief should ever do. A generation of American efforts to slow proliferation of weapons of mass destruction has unraveled as first India and Pakistan set off their nuclear bombs, then Iraq defied the international community. Token air strikes against Iraq could not long mask the collapse of an inspection regime that had — until then — at least kept an ambitious, murderous tyrant from acquiring additional nuclear, biological and chemical weapons.

A humanitarian intervention in Somalia was escalated thoughtlessly into nation-building at the cost of the lives of courageous Americans. A military intervention in Haiti displayed administrative indecision and incoherence and, after billions of dollars had been spent, accomplished nothing of lasting value. Reacting belatedly to inevitable crises, the administration constantly enlarges the reach of its rhetoric — most recently in Vice President Al Gore's "new security agenda" that adds disease, climate and all the world's ethnic or religious conflicts to an undiminished set of existing American responsibilities. If there is some limit to candidate Gore's new agenda for America as global social worker, he has yet to define it.

It is time for America to regain its focus. Winston Churchill, after he had lived through other years that the "locust hath eaten," declared: "The era of procrastination, of half-measures, of soothing and baffling expedients, of delays, is coming to a close. In its place we are entering a period of consequences." As idle indulgence gives way to a new Republican president in the coming new "period of consequences," the United States can again regain the hope it lost eight years ago. We can restore our country's sense of international purpose and national honor.

A Republican president will identify and pursue vital American national interests. He will set priorities and he will stick to them. Under his leadership, the United States will build and secure the peace. Republicans know what it takes to accomplish this: robust military forces, strong alliances, expanding trade and resolute diplomacy.

Yet this new realism must be inspired by what we stand for as a nation. Republicans know that the American commitment to freedom is the true source of our nation's strength. That is why, for one example, Congressional Republicans have made political and religious liberty a cornerstone of their approach to international affairs. That commitment is the glue that binds our great alliances. It is strong precisely because it is not just an American ideal. We propose our principles; we must not impose our culture. Yet the basic values of human freedom and dignity are universal.

A Military for the 21st Century

Republicans are the party of peace through strength. A strong and well-trained American military is the world's best guarantee of peace. It is the shield of this republic's liberty, security and prosperity. Only a president, as commander in chief of the Armed Forces, can ensure that our military stands ready to defend America and triumph against new challenges.

A Republican president and a Republican Congress will transform America's defense capabilities for the Information Age, ensuring that U.S. armed forces remain paramount against emerging dangers.

They will restore the health of a defense industry weakened by a combination of neglect and misguided policies. To do all this, the United States must align its military power with the strengths of American society: our skilled people, our advanced technology and our proficiency at integrating fast-paced systems into potent networks. While we are on the crest of a new age in military technology, we will not forget that the strength of our military lies with the combat soldier, sailor, airman and Marine.

Americans are justly proud of their armed forces. But today, only nine years after the tremendous victory in the Persian Gulf War, the U.S. military faces growing problems in readiness, morale and its ability to prepare for the threats of the future. The administration has cut defense spending to its lowest percentage of gross domestic product since before Pearl Harbor. At the same time, the current administration has casually sent American armed forces on dozens of missions without clear goals, realizable objectives, favorable rules of engagement or defined exit strategies.

Over the past seven years, a shrunken American military has been run ragged by a deployment tempo that has eroded its military readiness. Many units have seen their operational requirements increased four-fold, wearing out both people and equipment. Only last fall the Army certified two of its premier combat divisions as unready for war because of underfunding, mismanagement and over-commitment to peacekeeping missions around the globe. More Army units and the other armed services report similar problems. It is a national scandal that almost one quarter of our Army's active combat strength is unfit for wartime duty.

When presidents fail to make hard choices, those who serve must make them instead. Soldiers must choose whether to stay with their families or to stay in the armed forces at all. Sending our military on vague, aimless and endless missions rapidly saps morale. Even the highest morale is eventually undermined by back-to-back deployments, poor pay, shortages of spare parts and equipment, inadequate training and rapidly declining readiness. When it comes to military health, the administration is not providing an adequate military health care system for active-duty service members and their families and for retired service members and their dependents. The nation is failing to fulfill its ethical and legal health care obligations to those who are serving or have honorably served in the Armed Forces of the United States.

It is no surprise that the all-volunteer force — the pride of America — is struggling to recruit and retain soldiers, sailors, airmen and Marines. As recruiting lags, well-trained personnel are leaving in record numbers. Those dedicated military personnel who stay in the force face a pay gap of some 13 percent relative to their civilian counterparts. Thousands of military families are forced to rely on food stamps. The Chairman of the Joint Chiefs of Staff has said that two-thirds of the nation's military housing is substandard. The calculated indifference of the administration to national defense has forced thousands of our most experienced and patriotic warriors to leave the military. We will once again make wearing the uniform an object of national pride.

The new Republican government will renew the bond of trust between the commander in chief, the American military and the American people. The military is not a civilian police force or a political referee. We believe the military must no longer be the object of social experiments. We affirm traditional military culture. We affirm that homosexuality is incompatible with military service.

The U.S. military under the leadership of a Republican President and a Republican Congress will focus on its most demanding task — fighting and winning in combat. Readiness prevents wars. Also, by being prepared for this most exacting mission with an uncommon sense of urgency, our military will know, unlike today, that its loyalty and self-sacrifice have meaning and purpose.

In a time of fluid change and uncertainty, intelligence is truly America's first line of defense. The current administration has weakened that defense by allowing a series of shocking security breaches, from blatant espionage and its virtual abandonment of national security-related export controls to sheer sloppiness at the highest levels of government. This must stop, immediately. Nor should the intelligence community be made the scapegoat for political misjudgments. A Republican administration working with the Congress will respect the needs and quiet sacrifices of these public servants as it strengthens America's intelligence and counter-intelligence capabilities and reorients them toward the dangers of the future.

A Republican president will challenge America's military leaders to envision a new architecture of American defense for decades to come. Our next president will balance the need to prepare for Information Age battles while keeping our conventional fighting skills second to none. To pay for profligate deployments, the administration's defense budgets have been eating their seed corn — slashing spending on modernization to levels not seen since before the Korean War, undermining the health of our defense industry and producing what one administration official admitted was a "death spiral" for the U.S. defense capability of the future. Even our elite combat units are scraping the bottom of the barrel to find funds for basic training.

A Republican president, working in partnership with a Republican Congress, will push beyond marginal improvements and incorporate new technologies and new strategies — spending more and investing wisely to transform our military into a true twenty-first century force. A Republican government will use this time of relative American strength in the world to prepare for a different kind of future. In the twenty-first century, U.S. forces must be agile, lethal, readily deployable and require a minimum of logistical support. They must also be fully prepared for possible enemy use of weapons of mass destruction.

To build such U.S. military forces

will require foresight and steadfast commitment. We must be willing to act now to give the next generation of Americans what they will need to protect our country. This will also require a new spirit of innovation. Republicans believe that our military leaders will welcome and meet these challenges. Moments of national opportunity are either seized or lost. America's opportunity beckons: to demonstrate that a new approach to U.S. defense can shape the future with new concepts, new strategies and new resolve.

The men and women of the National Guard and Reserve are an important part of the nation's military readiness, and we will maintain their strength in the states. Their role as citizen soldiers must continue to be a proud tradition that links every community in the country with the cause of national security. The Republican party created the all-volunteer force and opposes reinstitution of the draft, whether directly or through compulsory national service. We support the advancement of women in the military, support their exemption from ground combat units and call for implementation of the recommendations of the Kassebaum Commission, which unanimously recommended that co-ed basic training be ended. We support restoration of sound priorities in the making of personnel policies, and candid analysis of the consequences of unprecedented social changes in the military. We will put renewed emphasis on encouraging the best and brightest of our young people to join our armed forces.

As the traditional advocate of America's veterans, the Republican Party remains committed to fulfilling America's obligations to them. That is why we defeated the administration's attempt to replace veterans' health care with a national system for everybody. It is why Congressional Republicans enacted the Veterans Employment Opportunities Act of 1998, to thwart attempts to water down veterans' preference in federal civil service hiring and retention, and why they created the National Veterans Business Development Corporation to assist vets in becoming entrepreneurs. The same holds true for their Veterans Millennium Health Care and Benefits Act, a first step toward correcting the deficiencies in medical care for vets and ensuring a medical infrastructure that will better honor the nation's commitment to those who served. In a Republican administration, a true advocate for veterans will become Secretary of Veteran Affairs.

The maintenance and expansion of our national cemeteries is a solemn duty; a Republican administration will attend to it. Many of the programs designed to assist veterans cry out for modernization and reform. The American people cannot be content with the current unemployment rate of recently separated veterans, or with the significant number of veterans among the homeless. With a backlog of almost a half million cases, the Veterans Benefit Administration needs to be brought into the Information Age. The work of the Veterans Employment and Training Service needs a stronger focus on vocational education, and the nation as a whole must reconsider the ways restrictive licensing and certification rules prevent fully qualified vets from moving up the opportunity ladder.

Protecting the Fellowship Of Freedom from Weapons Of Mass Destruction

The new century will bring new threats, but America — properly led — can master them. Just as the generations of World War II and the Cold War were quick to seize the high frontier of science and craft the national defense America needed, so our country can build on its strengths and defend against unprecedented perils once again.

Ballistic missiles and weapons of mass destruction threaten the world's future. America is currently without defense against these threats. The administration's failure to guard America's nuclear secrets is allowing China to modernize its ballistic missile force, thereby increasing the threat to our country and to our allies. The theft of vital nuclear secrets by China represents one of the greatest security defeats in the history of the United States. The next Republican president will protect our nuclear secrets and aggressively implement a sweeping reorganization of our nuclear weapons program.

More than two dozen countries have ballistic missiles today. A number of them, including North Korea, will be capable of striking the United States within a few years, and with little warning. America is now unable to counter the rampant proliferation of nuclear, biological and chemical weapons and their missile delivery systems around the world.

The response of the current administration has been anachronistic and politicized. Stuck in the mindset and agreements of the Cold War and immune to fresh ideas, the administration has not developed a sensible strategy that responds to the emerging missile threat. They have no adequate plan for how they will defend America and its allies. Visionary leadership, not the present delay and prevarication, is urgently needed for America to be ready for the future. The new Republican president will deploy a national missile defense for reasons of national security, but he will also do so because there is a moral imperative involved: The American people deserve to be protected. It is the president's constitutional obligation.

America must deploy effective missile defenses based on an evaluation of the best available options, including sea-based, at the earliest possible date. These defenses must be designed to protect all 50 states, America's deployed forces overseas, and our friends and allies in the fellowship of freedom against missile attacks by outlaw states or accidental launches.

The current administration at first denied the need for a national missile defense system. Then it endlessly delayed, despite constant concern expressed by the Republican Congress. Now the administration has become hopelessly entangled in its commitment to an obsolete treaty signed in 1972 with a Soviet Union that no longer exists while it is constrained by its failure to explore vigorously the technological possibilities. In order to avoid the need for any significant revisions to the ABM Treaty, the administration supports an inadequate national missile defense design based on a single site, instead of a system based on the most effective means available. Their approach does not defend America's allies, who must be consulted as U.S. plans are developed. Their concept is a symbolic political solution designed on a cynical political timetable. It will not protect America.

We will seek a negotiated change in the Anti-Ballistic Missile (ABM) Treaty that will allow the United States to use all technologies and experiments required to deploy robust missile defenses. Republicans believe that the administration should not negotiate inadequate modifications to the ABM Treaty that would leave us with a flawed agreement that ties the hands of the next president and prevents America from defending itself. The United States must be able to select the systems that will work best, not those that answer political expediency, and we must aggressively reinvigorate the ballistic missile defense technology base necessary to ensure that these systems succeed. There are today more positive, practical ways to reassure Russia that missile defenses are a search for common security, not for unilateral advantage. If Russia refuses to make the necessary changes, a Republican president will give prompt notice that the United States will exercise the right guaranteed to us in the treaty to withdraw after six months. The president has a solemn obligation to protect the American people and our allies, not to protect arms control agreements signed almost 30 years ago.

Clear thinking about defensive systems must be accompanied by a fresh strategy for offensive ones too. The Cold War logic that led to the creation of massive stockpiles of nuclear weapons on both sides is now outdated and actually enhances the danger of weapons or nuclear material falling into the hands of America's adversaries. Russia is not the great enemy. The age of vast hostile armies in the heart of Europe deterred by the threat of U.S. nuclear response is also past. American security need no longer depend on the old nuclear balance of terror. It is time to defend against the threats of today and tomorrow, not yesterday.

It is past time that the United States should re-examine the requirements of nuclear deterrence. Working with U.S. military leaders and with the Congress, a Republican president will re-evaluate America's nuclear force posture and pursue the lowest possible number consistent with our national security. We can safely eliminate thousands more of these horrific weapons. We should do so. In the Cold War the United States rightfully worried about the danger of a conventional war in Europe and needed the nuclear counterweight. That made sense then. It does not make sense now. The premises of Cold War targeting should no longer dictate the size of the U.S. nuclear arsenal. The current administration seems not to realize that this notion, too, is old-think of the worst order. In addition, the United States should work with other nuclear nations to remove as many weapons as possible from high-alert, hair-trigger status — another unnecessary vestige of Cold War confrontation — to reduce the risks of accidental or unauthorized launch.

In 1991, the United States invited the Soviet Union to join it in removing tactical nuclear weapons from their arsenals. Huge reductions were achieved in a matter of months, quickly making the world much safer. Under a Republican president, Russia will again be invited to do the same with respect to strategic nuclear weapons. America should be prepared to lead by example, because it is in our best interest and the best interest of the world. These measures can begin a new global era of nuclear security and safety.

Republicans recognize new threats but also new opportunities. With Republican leadership, the United States has an opportunity to create a safer world, both to defend against nuclear threats and to reduce nuclear arsenals and tensions. America can build a robust missile defense, make dramatic reductions in its nuclear weapons and defuse confrontation with Russia. A Republican president will do all these things.

A comprehensive strategy for combating the new dangers posed by weapons of mass destruction must include a variety of other measures to contain and prevent the spread of such weapons. We need the cooperation of friends and allies — and should seek the cooperation of Russia and China — in developing realistic strategies using political, economic and military instruments to deter and defeat the proliferation efforts of others. We need to address threats from both rogue states and terrorist groups — whether delivered by missile, aircraft, shipping container or suitcase.

In this context, the Comprehensive Test Ban Treaty is another anachronism of obsolete strategic thinking. This treaty is not verifiable, not enforceable, and would not enable the United States to ensure the reliability of the U.S. nuclear deterrent. It also does not deal with the real dangers of nuclear proliferation, which are rogue regimes — such as Iran, Iraq and North Korea — that seek to hide their dangerous weapons programs behind weak international treaties. We can fight the spread of nuclear weapons, but we cannot wish them away with unwise agreements. Republicans in the Senate reacted accordingly and responsibly in rejecting the Comprehensive Test Ban Treaty.

A new Republican president will renew America's faltering fight against the contagious spread of nuclear, biological and chemical weapons, as well as their means of delivery. The weak leadership and neglect of the current administration have allowed America's intelligence capabilities, including space based systems, to atrophy, resulting in repeated proliferation surprises such as Iraq's renewed chemical and biological weapons programs, India's nuclear weapon test and North Korea's test of a three-stage ballistic missile. Again in a partnership with the Congress, a new Republican administration will give the intelligence community the leadership, resources and operational latitude it requires.

Seeking Enduring Prosperity

Under Republican leadership, the United States will foster an environment of economic openness to capitalize on our country's greatest asset in the information age: a vital, innovative society that welcomes creative ideas and adapts to them. American companies are once more showing the world breathtaking ways to improve productivity and redraw traditional business models. This is an extraordinary foundation on which to rebuild an effective American trade policy.

Under the policies of the present administration, many markets remain closed and U.S. trade deficits keep rising. New economic structures are needed to combine regional agreements with the development of global rules for opening the world economy. Collaborating with the Congress, a Republican administration will engage the Latin American and the Asia-Pacific nations, including a new dialogue with India, about political economy and free trade. As impoverished countries in Eurasia, the Middle East and Africa accept freer economies, they will need the incentives of more open world markets. In addition, the United States can encourage the European Union and our Asian friends and allies to open more sectors to cross-investment and competition with the aim of freer trans-oceanic trade.

Republicans are confident that the worldwide trade agenda is full of promise. From the traditional goods of agriculture to the virtual links of e-commerce, gates can swing open. Tariffs should be cut further. The United States can back private sector efforts to streamline common standards and deregulate services, from finance to filmmaking. As the one economy with truly global reach, America can set the standards and be at the center of a worldwide web of trade, finance and openness. If some nations choose to opt out, they will see how other countries accepting economic freedom will advance on their own, working together.

This is the Republican approach, and a critical dimension of a distinctly American internationalism. It goes beyond the old choice of private sector laissez-faire vs. government regulation. Instead it is a vision of private initiative encouraged, not stifled, by governments. Private parties are already fashioning new ways to exchange goods and settle disputes but national governments still struggle to define many of the underlying rules. Republicans will also go beyond the old arguments that pitted bilateral deals against global trade rules. Instead they envision a comprehensive approach to the more interdependent global economy, one that uses bilateral, regional, and global arrangements to spur reluctant states to become more open or to be left behind. At the same time, innovative and flexible global rules and structures can facilitate regional progress.

Rooted in America's political and economic ideals, this Republican blueprint promotes open markets and open societies, free trade and the free flow of information, and the development of new ideas and private sectors. These nurture the human spirit, the middle class, law and liberty.

As the Cold War ended, Republican presidents fought off protectionist pressure, eased the debt crisis then facing developing countries, signed the North American Free Trade Agreement (NAFTA), and started to enlarge free trade arrangements throughout the Western Hemisphere. They promoted the Asia-Pacific Economic Cooperation (APEC) group that could bind economic interests across the Pacific. They then used these regional initiatives to bring the global trade talks of the Uruguay Round to the edge of conclusion. Thus America began to build on victory in the Cold War to build new structures for economic liberty as well.

For nearly eight years this promising construction project has languished half-built, the old blueprint shelved and no new ones drawn.

The administration returned to the old rhetoric of managed trade — demanding government intervention from a Japanese government that needed less regulation in its sputtering economy, not more. On the verge of a foolish trade war, the administration backed down and dropped its quota demands. After failing for years to make the case for free trade, the administration finally got around to seeking fast-track trade negotiating authority, but could persuade only one-fifth of Democratic members of Congress to follow its lead.

With China, the administration sought to link normal trade relations to human rights performance. Then it flip-flopped and dropped the linkage. They tried to bring China into the World Trade Organization as the Prime Minister of China visited the United States in 1999, but the political waters got choppy. So the administration reversed course again. Finally the administration turned to Republican leadership in the Congress to enact permanent normal trade relations with China. The administration refused to fight for passage of the Caribbean Basin Initiative that was designed to extend the benefits of free trade to some of America's poorest neighbors. Congressional Republicans did the job on their own. They also enacted the Africa Growth and Opportunity Act as a companion to CBI. The failed leadership of the administration in international economics is exemplified by the humiliating debacle of the WTO meeting in Seattle — a conference the current administration first sponsored and then wrecked through its own indecision and inconsistency.

Republicans know that prosperous democracies depend upon the promise of shared economic opportunity across national borders. If the new globalized information economy provokes a fearful drift into national or regional isolation, hopes for a better world will vanish. Institutions founded in the Second World War and its aftermath built the basis for America's position today, but those institutions, like the Bretton Woods monetary system and the General Agreement on Tariffs and Trade, were partly sustained by the Cold War. In this new century, the United States should devise new mechanisms to enable the private sector to unleash productivity, innovation, and a free flow of ideas.

Communities of private groups can achieve results far beyond the reach of governments and international bureaucracies. Given America's strong and diverse private sector, the United States, with close cooperation between a Republican president and a Republican Congress, can gain from the widening global influence of American citizens, businesses, associations and norms. A Republican administration will have the opportunity to fashion, with like-minded nations, the international structures of sustainable prosperity for the next several decades.

The older international financial institutions should be overhauled but not scrapped. The International Monetary Fund and the World Bank should no longer stand for unelected elites imposing their often flawed solutions to tough problems by offering bailouts of corrupt officials and risk-taking investors. The IMF should concentrate on its original mission of promoting sound fiscal and monetary policies, advancing sound central banking practices, and easing global exchange rate adjustments. It should improve transparency and accountability, tackling corruption rather than contributing to it. The World Bank should continue to move away from counterproductive development schemes of the past to an agenda that promotes the provision of basic needs. This agenda will include support for structural reforms that will encourage self-help through efficient markets.

The United States should aggressively pursue its national interest. Unlike the current administration, Republicans do not believe multilateral agreements and international institutions are ends in themselves. The Kyoto treaty to address momentous energy and environmental issues was a case in point. Whatever the theories on global warming, a treaty that does not include China and exempts "developing" countries from necessary standards while penalizing American industry is not in the national interest. We reject the extremist call for the United Nations to create a "Stewardship Council," modeled on the Security Council, to oversee the global environment. Republicans understand that workable agreements will build on the free democratic processes of national governments, not try to bypass them with international bureaucrats.

Unlike the Democratic minority in Congress, Republicans do not believe that economic growth is always the enemy of protecting the world's common environmental heritage. Rather, the Republican vision seeks more creative international solutions. These solutions should use market mechanisms to allocate the costs of adjustment, help governments competently manage the resources they do control, and encourage application of the new technologies that offer the greatest promise to protect the global environment.

Neighborhood of the Americas

Latin America and Canada have helped shape the United States and its people. The countries of the Western Hemisphere are our neighbors. For tens of millions of Americans these neighbors are also our relatives. Latin America buys more than one-fifth of U.S. exports while Canada is America's largest trading partner. These purchases by our Latin American neighbors are rising at a rate almost twice as fast as the rate for the rest of the world. In the next decade, U.S. trade and investment in the Western Hemisphere are projected to exceed our trade and investment with either Europe or Japan. Future prospects for America's neighborhood are extraordinarily bright.

Secure in its strength and its principles, the United States wants strong, healthy neighbors. The next American century should include all of the Americas. Democracy and free markets are again under siege from narcotics traffickers, guerrillas, economic uncertainty and demographic upheaval. Poverty, inadequate education, rampant crime and corruption all tear at the fabric of several of these societies. In Peru, Ecuador, Colombia, Venezuela and other countries, democracy is faltering or under serious attack.

The next Republican president will pay serious and sustained attention to the American neighborhood. In concert with the Congress, he will work with key democracies like Argentina, Brazil, Chile and — above all — Mexico. His administration will be guided by the principles of respect for sovereignty, private initiative, multilateral action, free politics and markets, the rule of law and regard for the variety of peoples and cultures that make up the Western Hemisphere.

With Mexico, whose historic recent election we salute, the United States should continue to reduce barriers to trade and investment, including the implementation of existing commitments where the current administration has backtracked. Yet a true North American community should have a wider agenda that also includes the development of civil society. Our two countries can share ideas for improving education and public services on both sides of the border and using the federal system in both countries to promote governmental cooperation between honest officials who are close to their people.

A new Republican government committed to NAFTA can enlarge it into a vision for hemispheric free trade, drawing nations closer in business, common commercial standards, dispute resolution and education. Republicans do not want to create new trading blocs to battle rivals. They mean to encourage general political and economic reform, starting with the American neighborhood.

In Cuba, Fidel Castro continues to impose communist economic controls and absolute political repression of 11 million Cubans. His regime harasses and jails dissidents, restricts economic activity, and forces Cubans into the sea in a desperate bid for freedom. He gives refuge to fugitives from American justice, hosts a sophisticated Russian espionage facility that intercepts U.S. government and private communications, and has ordered his air force to shoot down two unarmed U.S. civilian airplanes thereby killing American citizens.

U.S. policy toward Cuba should be based upon sound, clear principles. Our economic and political relations will change when the Cuban regime frees all prisoners of conscience, legalizes peaceful protest, allows opposition political activity, permits free expression and commits to democratic elections. This policy will be strengthened by active American support for Cuban dissidents. Under no circumstances should Republicans support any subsidy of Castro's Cuba or any other terrorist state.

Republicans also support a continued effort to promote freedom and democracy by communicating objective and uncensored news and information to the Cuban people via U.S. broadcasts to the captive island. Finally, Republicans believe that the United States should adhere to the principles established by the 1966 Cuban Adjustment Act, which recognizes the rights of Cuban refugees fleeing communist tyranny.

Across the Pacific. As in every region of the world, America's foreign policy in Asia starts with its allies: Japan, the Republic of Korea, Australia, Thailand and the Philippines. Our allies are critical in building and expanding peace, security, democracy and prosperity in East Asia joined by long-standing American friends like Singapore, Indonesia, Taiwan and New Zealand.

Republican priorities in the next administration will be clear. We will strengthen our alliance with Japan. We will help to deter aggression on the Korean peninsula. We will counter the regional proliferation of weapons of mass destruction and their delivery systems and deploy, in cooperation with our allies, effective theater missile defenses. We will promote peace in the Taiwan Strait. We will reconstitute our relations with the nations of Southeast Asia. We will obtain the fullest possible accounting for our POW/MIAs from the Pacific wars. And we will promote democracy, open markets and human rights for the betterment of the people of Asia and the United States.

Japan is a key partner of the United States, and the U.S.-Japan alliance is an important foundation of peace, stability, security and prosperity in Asia. America supports an economically vibrant and open Japan that can serve as an engine of expanding prosperity and trade in the Asia-Pacific region.

The Republic of Korea is a valued democratic ally of the United States. North Korea, on the other hand, lies outside of the international system. Americans have shed their blood to stop North Korean aggression before. Fifty years after the outbreak of the Korean War, Republicans remember this "forgotten war." Americans should honor the sacrifices of the past and remain prepared to resist aggression today. Policies to protect the peace on the Korean peninsula will be developed in concert with America's allies, starting with South Korea and Japan. What must be clear is an American policy of decisive resolve. The United States will stand by its commitments and will take all necessary measures to thwart, deter, and defend itself and its allies against attack, including enemy use of weapons of mass destruction.

After fighting together in both world wars, the United States forged a formal alliance with Australia that has stood the test of fire in the Korean, Vietnam and Persian Gulf conflicts. American partnership with Australia is just as relevant to the challenges of Asia's future, as exemplified by Australia's leadership in the East Timor crisis.

American ties to the Philippines have been close for more than a hundred years. We Republicans have supported the victory of Filipino democracy and cherish our continuing friendship with this great nation and its people who have been by our side in war as in peace.

America's key challenge in Asia is the People's Republic of China. China is not a free society. The Chinese government represses political expression at home and unsettles neighbors abroad. It stifles freedom of religion and proliferates weapons of mass destruction.

Yet China is a country in transition, all the more reason for the policies of the United States to be firm and steady. America will welcome the advent of a free and prosperous China. Conflict is not inevitable, and the United States offers no threat to China. Republicans support China's accession into the World Trade Organization, but this will not be a substitute for, or lessen the resolve of, our pursuit of improved human rights and an end to proliferation of dangerous technologies by China.

China is a strategic competitor of the United States, not a strategic partner. We will deal with China without ill will — but also without illusions. A new Republican government will understand the importance of China but not place China at the center of its Asia policy.

A Republican president will honor our promises to the people of Taiwan, a longstanding friend of the United States and a genuine democracy. Only months ago the people of Taiwan chose a new president in free and fair elections. Taiwan deserves America's strong support, including the timely sale of defensive arms to enhance Taiwan's security.

In recognition of its growing importance in the global economy, we support Taiwan's accession to the World Trade Organization, as well as its participation in the World Health Organization and other multilateral institutions.

America has acknowledged the view that there is one China. Our policy is based on the principle that there must be no use of force by China against Taiwan. We deny the right of Beijing to impose its rule on the free Taiwanese people. All issues regarding Taiwan's future must be resolved peacefully and must be agreeable to the people of Taiwan. If China violates these principles and attacks Taiwan, then the United States will respond appropriately in accordance with the Taiwan Relations Act. America will help Taiwan defend itself.

This country's relations with Vietnam are still overshadowed by two grave concerns. The first is uncertainty concerning the Americans who became prisoners of war or were missing in action. A Republican president will accelerate efforts in every honorable way to obtain the fullest possible accounting for those still missing and for the repatriation of the remains of those who died in the cause of freedom. The second is continued retribution by the government of Vietnam against its ethnic minorities and others who fought alongside our forces there. The United States owes those individuals a debt of honor and will not be blind to their suffering.

Attention to the fate of East Asia should not obscure American attention to the future of South Asia. India is emerging as one of the great democracies of the twenty-first century. Soon it will be the world's most populous state. India is now redefining its identity and future strategy. The United States should engage India, respecting its great multicultural achievements and encouraging Indian choices for a more open world. Mindful of its longstanding relationship with Pakistan, the United States will place a priority on the secure, stable development of this volatile region where adversaries now face each other with nuclear arsenals.

The Republican party is committed to democracy in Burma, and to Nobel Laureate Aung San Suu Kyi and other democratic leaders whose election in 1990 was brutally suppressed and who have been arrested and imprisoned for their belief in freedom and democracy. We share with her the view that the basic principles of human freedom and dignity are universal. We are committed to working with our allies in Europe and Asia to maintain a firm and resolute opposition to the military junta in Rangoon.

Because of the strategic location and historical ties of the Pacific island nations to the United States, the next Republican administration will work closely with the countries of this region on a wide variety of issues of common concern.

Europe. As a result of the courageous and resolute leadership of Presidents Reagan and Bush, the Cold War has been won, Germany unified and, with the leadership of a Republican Senate, Poland, the Czech Republic and Hungary returned to the Euro-Atlantic Community. The security of the United States is inseparable from the security of Europe. Now in its second half-century, a strong NATO is the foundation of peace. Sustained American commitment to the security of Europe has paid off. Our allies across the Atlantic face no conventional external threats. American military deployments are a fraction of their Cold War size. But alliances are not just for crises. They are sustained by the kind of joint planning, political and economic as well as military, that defines and reinforces common interests and mutual trust.

Standing alongside our allies, we seek a NATO that is strong, cohesive, and active. The next Republican president will give consistent direction on the alliance's purpose, on Europe's need to invest more in defense capabilities, and, when necessary, on acting jointly with the United States in military conflict. The United States needs its European allies to help with key regional security problems as they arise, since America also has global responsibilities. Our goal for NATO is a strong political and security fellowship of independent nations in which consultations are mutually respected and defense burdens mutually shared.

For our allies, sharing the enormous opportunities of Eurasia also means sharing the burdens and risks of sustaining the peace. We seek greater cooperation within NATO to deal with the geopolitical problems of the Middle East and Eurasia. We will work with our European partners as we develop our plans to build effective missile defenses that can protect all of America's allies.

Republicans believe that the political objectives of Europe and America are mutually reinforcing and complementary. The next Republican president will ensure that the relationship between NATO and the European Union, particularly in the division of military responsibilities, is clear and constructive. The leaders of the European Union must resist the temptation of protectionism as we work together to build a Europe whole and free.

We are proud that America's long-standing commitment to the forward defense of democracy is being rewarded as Europe becomes whole and free. In the new era that resulted, some of America's strongest allies and friends have been the democracies of Central and Eastern Europe. In their recent histories, these nations have shown their commitment to the values shared by members of the Trans-Atlantic community. Poles, Czechs and Hungarians inspired the world, assaulting the Iron Curtain again and again until finally it crashed down forever.

As the new democracies of Central Europe chose freedom, America was ready to respond. Republicans made the enlargement of NATO part of our Contract with America. Their firm stand before the American people and in the Congress finally succeeded in bringing Poland, the Czech Republic and Hungary into the North Atlantic Alliance. Republicans recognize and applaud the tremendous achievements of the people of Albania, Bulgaria, Estonia, Lithuania, Latvia, Macedonia, Romania, Slovakia and Slovenia in reclaiming their freedom and rejoining the Trans-Atlantic community of democracies.

It is in America's interest that the new European democracies become fully integrated into the economic, political and security institutions of the Trans-Atlantic community. These countries are today making great progress toward developing the market economies and democratic political systems that are the best way to ensure both their long-term stability and their security. The enlargement of NATO to include other nations with democratic values, pluralist political systems, and free market economies should continue. Neither geographical nor historical circumstances shall dictate the future of a Europe whole and free. Russia must never be given a veto over enlargement.

The Republican party has long been the advocate of independence for the people of Lithuania, Latvia, and Estonia, even when others despaired of their emergence from foreign rule. We reaffirm our traditional ties with and strong support for the courageous Ukrainian and Armenian people who, like the people of the Baltic States, have endured both persecution and tyranny to reassert their ancient nationhood. The United States should promote reconciliation and friendship not only between the United States and Russia, but also between Russia and its neighbors.

The current administration has damaged the NATO alliance with years of insensitivity and episodic attention. In the Yugoslav war the administration bungled the diplomacy, misjudged the adversary, and ignored the advice of our military commanders. Even after NATO's operations in Bosnia and Kosovo laid bare Europe's lagging military capabilities, the administration failed to persuade the allies to enhance these capabilities. The next Republican administration will work to repair this damage.

After the many trials and errors of the current administration, the United States is contributing to NATO's peacekeeping efforts in Bosnia-Herzegovina and Kosovo. Those troops cannot stay indefinitely without jeopardizing the American ability to defend other important U.S. and allied interests. Over time European troops should take the place of American forces under the NATO umbrella as the United States and its allies work together to bring peace and democracy to the Balkans. The next Republican president will not negotiate with indicted war criminals such as Slobodan Milosevic but will seek their arrest, trial, and imprisonment.

Russia stands as another reminder that a world increasingly at peace is also a world in transition. If Russia can realize the enormous potential of its people and abundant resources, it can achieve the greatness that is currently defined solely by the reach of its weapons. Russia has the potential to be a great power and should be treated as such. With Russia, the United States needs patience, consistency and a principled reliance on democratic forces.

America's own national security is the first order of business with Russia. The United States and Russia share critical common interests. Both Russia and the United States confront the legacy of a dead ideological rivalry — thousands of nuclear weapons, which, in the case of Russia, may not be entirely secure. And together we also face an emerging threat – from rogue nations, nuclear theft and accidental launch. For its own sake and ours, Russia must stop encouraging the proliferation of weapons of mass destruction.

The development of a democratic and stable Russia is in the interest of the United States and all of Europe. But the battle for democracy is a fight that must be won by Russians. We must avoid misguided attempts to remake Russia from the outside. The current administration's quixotic efforts have only propped up corrupt elites, identified America with discredited factions and failed policies, and encouraged anti-Americanism.

The United States should show its concern about Russia's future by focusing on the structures, spirit, and reality of democracy in Russia, embodied by the rule of law. We will do this by directing our aid and attention to help the Russian people, not enriching the bank accounts of corrupt officials.

The rule of law is not consistent with state-sponsored brutality. When the Russian government attacks civilians in Chechnya — killing innocents without discrimination or accountability, neglecting orphans and refugees — it can no longer expect aid from international lending institutions. Moscow needs to operate with civilized self-restraint.

Russia should also display such self-restraint in its shipments of sensitive nuclear and military technology to Iran. As long as Iran remains an international outlaw, preventing such transfers must be a priority for U.S. policy. Americans stand ready to cooperate with Russia in sharing technology for missile defense that can promote a more stable world, but Russia must also choose lasting stability over transitory profit and support the effort against proliferation.

Republicans welcome the historic reconciliation in Northern Ireland that is slowly bringing peace and a representative local assembly to this beautiful land that means so much to Americans. We congratulate the people of Northern Ireland for their approval of the Good Friday Agreement, and we call for the full and fastest possible implementation of its terms. In the spirit of that healing document, we call for a review of issues of deportation and extradition arising prior to the accord. We applaud the work of the Patten Commission to reform the police authorities in Northern Ireland and urge complete implementation of the Commission's recommendations.

The sufferings of the people on the island of Ireland have been our sorrow too, and the new hope for peace and reconciliation is the answer to America's prayers. We continue to support this progress toward peace with justice and, accordingly, we encourage private U.S. investment in the North, with care to ensure fair employment and better opportunities for all. Though the burdens of history weigh heavily upon this land, we cheer its people for taking the lead in building for themselves and for their children a future of peace and understanding. The next president will use the prestige and influence of the United States to help the parties achieve a lasting peace. If necessary, he will appoint a special envoy to help facilitate the search for lasting peace, justice and reconciliation.

We likewise encourage a peaceful settlement for Cyprus and respect by all parties for the wishes of the Cypriot people. A fair and lasting Cyprus settlement will benefit the people of Cyprus, as well as serve the interests of America and our allies, Greece and Turkey.

The Middle East and Persian Gulf. In the Middle East, the advancement of U.S. national interests requires clear and consistent priorities as well as close cooperation with America's friends and allies. We have four priorities for the Middle East. First, we seek to promote and maintain peace throughout the region. Second, we must ensure that Israel remains safe and secure. Third, we must protect our economic interests and ensure the reliable flow of oil from the Persian Gulf. And fourth, we must reduce the threat of weapons of mass destruction in the region. Because America cannot achieve these objectives by acting alone, U.S. policy must rest on leadership that can build strong coalitions of like-minded states and hold them together to achieve common aims.

As American influence declined during the current administration, the OPEC cartel drove up the price of oil. Anti-Americanism among the Arab people redoubled. Iran continued to sponsor international terrorism, oppose the Arab-Israeli peace process and pursue nuclear, biological, chemical and missile capabilities with extensive foreign assistance. America's closest allies expanded their political and economic relations with Iran. A Republican president will work to reverse these damaging trends.

It is important for the United States to support and honor Israel, the only true democracy in the Middle East. We will ensure that Israel maintains a qualitative edge in defensive technology over any potential adversaries. We will not pick sides in Israeli elections. The United States has a moral and legal obligation to maintain its Embassy and Ambassador in Jerusalem. Immediately upon taking office, the next Republican president will begin the process of moving the U.S. Embassy from Tel Aviv to Israel's capital, Jerusalem.

The United States seeks a comprehensive and lasting peace in the Middle East. America can use its prestige to encourage discussions and negotiations. But peace must be negotiated between the parties themselves. We will not impose our view or an artificial timetable. At the heart of the peace process is the commitment to resolve all issues through negotiation. A unilateral declaration of independence by the Palestinians would be a violation of that commitment. A new Republican administration would oppose any such declaration. It will also do everything possible to promote the conclusion of a genuine peace in the Middle East. While we have hopes for the peace process, our commitment to the security of Israel is an overriding moral and strategic concern.

Perhaps nowhere has the inheritance of Republican governance been squandered so fatefully as with respect to Iraq. The anti-Iraq coalition assembled to oppose Saddam Hussein has disintegrated. The administration has pretended to support the removal of Saddam Hussein from power, but did nothing when Saddam Hussein's army smashed the democratic opposition in northern Iraq in August 1996. The administration also surrendered the diplomatic initiative to Iraq and Iraq's friends, and failed to champion the international inspectors charged with erasing Iraq's nuclear, biological, chemical and ballistic missile programs. When, in late 1998, the administration decided to take military action, it did too little, too late. Because of the administration's failures there is no coalition, no peace and no effective inspection regime to prevent Saddam's development of weapons of mass destruction.

A new Republican administration will patiently rebuild an international coalition opposed to Saddam Hussein and committed to joint action. We will insist that Iraq comply fully with its disarmament commitments. We will maintain the sanctions on the Iraqi regime while seeking to alleviate the suffering of innocent Iraqi people. We will react forcefully and unequivocally to any evidence of reconstituted Iraqi capabilities for producing weapons of mass destruction. In 1998, Congress passed and the president signed the Iraq Liberation Act, the clear purpose of which is to assist the opposition to Saddam Hussein. The administration has used an arsenal of dilatory tactics to block any serious support to the Iraqi National Congress, an umbrella organization reflecting a broad and representative group of Iraqis who wish to free their country from the scourge of Saddam Hussein's regime. We support the full implementation of the Iraq Liberation Act, which should be regarded as a starting point in a comprehensive plan for the removal of Saddam Hussein and the restoration of international inspections in collaboration with his successor. Republicans recognize that peace and stability in the Persian Gulf is impossible as long as Saddam Hussein rules Iraq.

All Americans hope that a new generation of Iranian leaders will rise to power seeking friendlier relations with the United States and a less threatening posture in the region. But Iran's record of supporting terrorism, opposing the Middle East peace process, developing weapons of mass destruction and long-range missiles, and its denial of human rights, most recently demonstrated in the trial and conviction of Iranian Jews on unfounded espionage charges, demonstrates that Tehran remains a dangerous threat to the United States and our interests in the region. The next Republican administration will form its policy toward Iran based on Iranian actions, not words. It will stop making unilateral gestures toward the Iranian government which, to date, have failed to result in a change in Iranian behavior. We will work to convince our friends and allies, most importantly the Europeans, to join us in a firm, common approach toward Iran.

Republicans endorse continued assistance and support for countries that have made peace with Israel — led by Egypt and Jordan. We appreciate the significant contributions by Jordan to our common struggle against terrorism, and will take steps to bolster relations with Amman including negotiating a U.S.-Jordan Free Trade Agreement.

The United States and its allies depend on oil from the Middle East. Republicans prefer an America that is far less dependent on foreign crude oil. A Republican president will not be so tolerant if OPEC colludes to drive up the world price of oil, as it has done this past year. Yet influence also comes from friendship. The United States should restore its underlying good and cooperative relations with the oil-exporting nations, most importantly Saudi Arabia, as well as with other moderate Arab governments.

Africa. The nations of Africa have endured tremendous burdens of war, poverty, disease and bad government. But freedom is gaining ground in South Africa, Nigeria, Niger, Mozambique and Mauritius. Democracy can help ensure that the interests of the people are elevated above the preoccupations and self-enrichment of corrupt elites.

Some of Africa's developing countries are turning to private markets, building middle classes, and evolving toward more representative forms of government that respect individual liberties. But such transformation is not simple. A Republican president and Congress will work to encourage these efforts through closer economic integration, security assistance, and support for freedom.

Republicans will replace process with outcome and rhetoric with substance.

Americans are troubled by the humanitarian catastrophes that have plagued the people of Africa including conflicts in Sierra Leone, the Great Lakes region, the Horn of Africa, and elsewhere. The risk of famine is never far away. Millions live in poverty and suffer from disease, especially AIDS and the vaccine-preventable diseases that prey on innocent children. The situation in the Sudan demands special attention, due to its employment of the slave trade and its persecution of Sudanese Christians, and we deplore the government of Zimbabwe's refusal to adhere to the rule of law. The conflict in Angola should be resolved through dialogue leading to the release of political prisoners and democratic government.

The people of Africa need economic opportunity, foreign investment, and access to markets, food, and medicine. The United States will support international organizations and nongovernmental organizations that can improve the daily lives of Africans. The United States must also work to promote democracy and sound governance in Africa, and the prevention and resolution of conflict. We will help the continent achieve its economic potential by implementing measures to reduce trade barriers. Republicans will not ignore the challenges of Africa.

International Assistance. The promotion of freedom and democracy is a critical national interest. President Reagan was a champion of this idea, establishing the National Endowment for Democracy in 1983 as an instrument of U.S. public diplomacy. The National Endowment for Democracy and other American public diplomacy institutions continue today to advance and protect American ideals and interests abroad.

The United States must commit itself to doing more to assist refugees and displaced persons. A Republican administration will improve America's longstanding practice of aiding the innocent victims of political repression, conflict, famine, and natural disasters, and we will lead other countries in responding similarly. Republicans fully recognize that the spread of AIDS is a terrible humanitarian disaster and will continue to emphasize action over rhetoric. In particular, we commend the Republican Congress for recently approving legislation to assist the victims of this disease in Africa.

The United Nations

International organizations can serve the cause of peace, but they can never serve as a substitute for, or exercise a veto over, principled American leadership. The United Nations was not designed to summon or lead armies in the field and, as a matter of U.S. sovereignty, American troops must never serve under United Nations command. Nor will they be subject to the jurisdiction of an International Criminal Court. The United Nations can provide a valuable forum for nations to peacefully resolve their differences, and it can help monitor international agreements and organize international humanitarian assistance. The United States will pay a fair, not disproportionate, share of dues to the United Nations once it has reformed its management and taken steps to eliminate waste, fraud and abuse. All funds that the United States contributes for operations, conferences, and peacekeeping should count against these dues.

The next Republican administration will use its diplomatic influence to put an end to a pattern of discrimination that persists at the United Nations in denying committee assignments to Israel. It will do likewise at the International Red Cross, which refuses to accredit the symbol of Magen David Adom, Israel's equivalent of the Red Cross. Moreover, Republicans oppose the ideological campaign against participation by the Vatican in U.N. conferences and other activities. The United Nations was created to benefit all peoples and nations, not to promote a radical agenda of social engineering. Any effort to address global social problems must be firmly placed into a context of respect for the fundamental social institutions of marriage and family. We reject any treaty or convention that would contradict these values. For that reason, we will protect the rights of families in international programs and will not fund organizations involved in abortion. This approach to foreign assistance will unify people, respect their diverse beliefs, and uphold basic human rights. It will enable us, in cooperation with other free societies around the world, to more effectively oppose religious persecution and the sex trafficking that ruins the lives of women and children.

Terrorism, International Crime, And Cyber Threats

America faces a new and rapidly evolving threat from terrorism and international crime. Meeting this threat requires not just new measures, but also consistent policies and determination from America's leaders.

Many established terrorist groups faded away in the 1990s after the Cold War ended. But the decade also witnessed a series of enormously destructive attacks against America. Increasingly, terrorists seem to be motivated by amorphous religious causes or simple hatred of America rather than by specific political aims. Terrorism crosses borders easily and frequently, including U.S. borders, and cannot easily be categorized as either domestic or international.

Republicans support a response to terrorism that is resolute but not impulsive. The most likely highly destructive terrorist attack remains a large bomb hidden in a car or truck. Yet, as with the rest of our defense posture, we must prepare for the most dangerous threats as well as the most likely ones.

Therefore the United States must be extremely vigilant about the possibility that future terrorists might use weapons of mass destruction, which are increasingly available and present an unprecedented threat to America. In many instances the military will have to rethink it traditional doctrine and begin to focus on counterterrorism, human intelligence gathering, and unconventional warfare.

Republicans endorse the four principles of U.S. counterterrorism policy that were laid down originally by Vice President George Bush's Commission on Combating Terrorism in 1985. First, we will make no concessions to terrorists. Giving in simply encourages future terrorist actions and debases America's power and moral authority. Second, we will isolate, pressure and punish the state sponsors of terrorism. Third, we will bring individual terrorists to justice. Past and potential terrorists will know that America will never stop hunting them. Fourth, we will provide assistance to other governments combating terrorism. Fighting international terrorism requires international collaboration. Once again, allies matter.

Republicans in Congress have led the way in building the domestic preparedness programs to train and equip local, state and federal response personnel to deal with terrorist dangers in America. The administration has not offered clear leadership over these programs. They remain scattered across many agencies, uncoordinated and poorly managed. We will streamline and improve the federal coordination of the domestic emergency preparedness programs.

We will ensure that federal law enforcement agencies have every lawful resource and authority they require to combat international organized crime. A Republican administration will work to improve international cooperation against all forms of cross-border criminality, especially the burgeoning threat of cyber-crime that threatens the vitality of American industries as diverse as aerospace and entertainment.

Nowhere has the administration been more timid in protecting America's national interests than in cyberspace. Americans have recently glimpsed the full vulnerability of their information systems to penetration and massive disruption by amateurs. A sophisticated terrorist or adversary government could potentially cripple a critical U.S. infrastructure, such as the electrical grid or a military logistics system, in time of crisis. A new Republican government will work closely with our international partners and the private sector to conceive and implement a viable strategy for reducing America's vulnerability to the spectrum of cyber threats, from the adolescent hacker launching a contagious computer virus to the most advanced threat of strategic information warfare.

Principled American Leadership

Americans have good reason to be optimistic about our role in world. Few nations in history have been afforded the range of possibilities to shape the future that has been presented to this generation of Americans. After the wavering and ambivalence of the current administration, Americans have a fresh chance to build on the enormous opportunities of this new era and new century. Earlier generations defended America through great trials. This generation can adapt America to thrive amid great change — change in economies, societies, technologies, and weapons.

Republicans have a strategy. It is a strategy that recalls traditional truths about power and ideals and applies them to networked marketplaces, modern diplomacy and the high-tech battlefield. A Republican administration will use power wisely, set priorities, craft needed institutions of openness and freedom and invest in the future. A Republican president and a Republican Congress can achieve the unity of national governance that has so long been absent. We see a confident America united in the fellowship of freedom with friends and allies throughout the world. We envision the restoration of a respected American leadership firmly grounded in a distinctly American internationalism. ◆

Bush, Accepting Nomination, Pledges to 'Confront Hard Issues,' 'Reclaim Essential Values'

Following are excerpts of Texas Gov. George W. Bush's Aug. 3 speech to the Republican National Convention. Transcript provided by Federal Document Clearing House:

Mr. Chairman, delegates and my fellow citizens, I proudly accept your nomination.

Thank you for this honor. Together, we will renew America's purpose.

Our founders first defined that purpose here in Philadelphia. Ben Franklin was here, Thomas Jefferson and, of course, George Washington, or, as his friends called him, George W.

I am proud to have Dick Cheney by my side. He is a man — he is a man of integrity and sound judgment who has proven that public service can be noble service. America will be proud to have a leader of such character to succeed Al Gore as vice president of the United States.

I'm grateful for Sen. John McCain. I appreciate so very much his speech two nights ago. I appreciate his friendship. I love his spirit for America. And I want to thank the other candidates who sought this office, as well. Their convictions have strengthened our party.

I'm especially grateful tonight to my family. . . . My father was the last president of a great generation, a generation of Americans who stormed beaches, liberated concentration camps and delivered us from evil. Some never came home. Those who did put their medals in drawers, went to work and built on a heroic scale highways and universities, suburbs and factories, great cities and grand alliances, the strong foundations of an American century. Now the question comes to the sons and daughters of this achievement: What is asked of us?

This is a remarkable moment in the life of our nation. Never has the promise of prosperity been so vivid. But times of plenty like times of crises are tests of American character. Prosperity can be a tool in our hands used to build and better our country, or it can be a drug in our system dulling our sense of urgency, of empathy, of duty. Our opportunities are too great, our lives too short, to waste this moment.

So tonight, we vow to our nation we will seize this moment of American promise. We will use these good times for great goals. We will confront the hard issues, threats to our national security, threats to our health and retirement security, before the challenges of our time become crises for our children.

And we will extend the promise of prosperity to every forgotten corner of this country: to every man and woman, a chance to succeed; to every child, a chance to learn; and to every family, a chance to live with dignity and hope.

For eight years, the Clinton-Gore administration has coasted through prosperity. The path of least resistance is always downhill. But America's way is the rising road. This nation is daring and decent and ready for change.

Our current president embodied the potential of a generation — so many talents, so much charm, such great skill. But in the end, to what end? So much promise to no great purpose.

Little more than a decade ago, the Cold War thawed, and with the leadership of Presidents Reagan and Bush, that wall came down.

But instead of seizing this moment, the Clinton-Gore administration has squandered it. We have seen a steady erosion of American power and an unsteady exercise of American influence. Our military is low on parts, pay and morale. If called on by the commander in chief today, two entire divisions of the Army would have to report, "Not ready for duty, sir."

This administration had its moment, they had their chance. They have not led. We will.

This generation was given the gift of the best education in American history, yet we do not share that gift with everyone. Seven of 10 fourth-graders in our highest poverty schools cannot read a simple children's book. And still this administration continues on the same old path, the same old programs, while millions are trapped in schools where violence is common and learning is rare. This administration had its chance. They have not led. We will.

America has a strong economy and a surplus. We have the public resources and the public will, even the bipartisan opportunities to strengthen Social Security and repair Medicare. But this administration, during eight years of increasing need, did nothing. They had their moment. They have not led. We will.

Our generation has a chance to reclaim some essential values, to show we have grown up before we grow old. But when the moment for leadership came, this administration did not teach our children, it disillusioned them. They had their chance. They have not led. We will.

And now they come asking for another chance, another shot. Our answer: Not this time, not this year. This is not the time for third chances; it is the time for new beginnings.

The rising generations of this country have our own appointment with greatness. It does not rise or fall with the stock market. It cannot be bought with our wealth. Greatness is found when American character and American courage overcome American challenges.

When Lewis Morris of New York was about to sign the Declaration of Independence, his brother advised against it, warning he would lose all his property. But Morris, a plain-spoken founder, responded, "Damn the consequences, give me the pen."

That is the eloquence of American action. . . . An American president must call upon that character.

Tonight in this hall, we resolve to be the party not of repose but of reform. We will write not footnotes but chapters in the American story. We will add the work of our hands to the inheritance of our fathers and mothers and leave this nation greater than we found it. . . . We know the test of leadership. The issues are joined. We will strengthen Social Security and Medicare for the greatest generation and for generations to come. Medicare does more than meet the needs of our elderly; it reflects the values of our society. We will set it on firm financial ground and make prescription drugs available and affordable for every senior who needs them. Social Security has been called the third rail of American politics, the one you're not supposed to touch because it might shock you. But if you don't touch it, you cannot fix it. And I intend to fix it.

To the seniors in this country, you earned your benefits, you made your plans, and President George W. Bush will keep the promise of Social Security, no changes, no reductions, no way. . . . Now is the time for Republicans and Democrats to end the politics of fear and save Social Security together. For younger workers, we will give you the option, your choice, to put part of your payroll taxes into sound, responsible investments. When this money is in your name, in your account, it's just not a program, it's your property. . . .

One size does not fit all when it comes to educating our children, so local people should control local schools. And those who spend your tax dollars must be held accountable. When a school district receives federal funds to teach poor children, we expect them to learn. And if they don't, parents should get the money to make a different choice.

Now is the time to make Head Start an early learning program to teach all our children to read and renew the promise of America's public schools.

Another test of leadership is tax relief. The last time taxes were this high as a percentage of our economy, there was a good reason: We were fighting World War II. Today our high taxes fund a surplus. . . . The surplus is not the government's money; the surplus is the people's money.

I will use this moment of opportunity to bring common sense and fairness to the tax code. And I will act on principle. On principle, every family, every farmer and small-business person should be free to pass on their life's work to those they love, so we will abolish the death tax.

On principle, no one in America should have to pay more than a third of their income to the federal government, so we will reduce tax rates for everyone in every bracket.

On principle, those with the greatest need should receive the greatest help, so we will lower the bottom rate from 15 percent to 10 percent and double the child credit. . . .

The world needs America's strength and leadership. And America's armed forces need better equipment, better training and better pay. We will give our military the means to keep the peace, and we will give it one thing more: a commander in chief who respects our men and women in uniform and a commander in chief who earns their respect. A generation shaped by Vietnam must remember the lessons of Vietnam: When America uses force in the world, the cause must be just, the goal must be clear, and the victory must be overwhelming.

I will work to reduce nuclear weapons and nuclear tension in the world, to turn these years of influence into decades of peace. And at the earliest possible date, my administration will deploy missile defenses to guard against attack and blackmail. Now is the time not to defend outdated treaties but to defend the American people.

A time of prosperity is a test of vision, and our nation today needs vision. That's a fact. Or as my opponent might call it, a risky truth scheme.

Every one of the proposals I've talked about tonight he's called a risky scheme over and over again. It is the sum of his message, the politics of the roadblock, the philosophy of the stop sign. . . . He now leads the party of Franklin Delano Roosevelt, but the only thing he has to offer is fear itself. That outlook is typical of many in Washington, always seeing the tunnel at the end of the light.

But I come from a different place and it has made me a different leader. In Midland, Texas, where I grew up, the town motto was, "The sky's the limit," and we believed it. There was a restless energy, a basic conviction that with hard work, anybody could succeed and everybody deserved a chance. . . .

This background leaves more than an accent, it leaves an outlook: optimistic, impatient with pretense, confident that people can chart their own course in life. That background may lack the polish of Washington. Then again, I don't have a lot of things that come with Washington. I don't have enemies to fight. I have no stake in the bitter arguments of the last few years. I want to change the tone of Washington to one of civility and respect. . . .

As governor, I've made difficult decisions and stood by them under pressure. I've been where the buck stops in business and in government. I've been a chief executive who sets an agenda, sets big goals, and rallies people to believe and achieve them. I am proud of this record, and I am prepared for the work ahead.

If you give me your trust, I will honor it. Grant me a mandate, I will use it. Give me the opportunity to lead this nation, and I will lead.

And we need a leader to seize the opportunities of this new century: the new cures of medicine, the amazing technologies that will drive our economy and keep the peace. But our new economy must never forget the old, unfinished struggle for human dignity. . . .

Big government is not the answer, but the alternative to bureaucracy is not indifference. It is to put conservative values and conservative ideas into the thick of the fight for justice and opportunity. This is what I mean by compassionate conservatism. And on this ground, we will lead our nation.

We will give low-income Americans tax credits to buy the private health insurance they need and deserve. We will transform today's housing rental program to help hundreds of thousands of low-income families find stability and dignity in a home of their own. And in the next bold step of welfare reform, we will support the heroic work of homeless shelters and hospices, food [pantries] and crisis pregnancy centers, people reclaiming their communities block by block and heart by heart. . . . My administration will give taxpayers new incentives to donate to charity, encourage after-school programs that build character, and support mentoring groups that shape and save young lives.

I will lead our nation toward a culture that values life — the life of the elderly and sick, the life of the young and the life of the unborn. Good people can disagree on this issue, but surely we can agree on ways to value life by promoting adoption, parental notification. And when Congress sends me a bill against "partial birth" abortion, I will sign it into law.

Behind every goal I've talked about tonight is a great hope for our country. A hundred years from now this must not be remembered as an age rich in possession and poor in ideals. . . . ◆

Clinton Rejects 'Marriage Tax' Bill, Saying It Would Contribute To Drain on Projected Surplus

Following is the text of President Clinton's Aug. 5 veto message on HR 4810, a bill to eliminate the "marriage penalty" and make other changes in tax law:

TO THE HOUSE OF REPRESENTATIVES:

I am returning herewith without my approval HR 4810, the "Marriage Tax Relief Reconciliation Act of 2000," because it is poorly targeted and one part of a costly and regressive tax plan that reverses the principle of fiscal responsibility that has contributed to the longest economic expansion in history.

My administration supports marriage penalty relief and has offered a targeted and fiscally responsible proposal in our fiscal year 2001 budget to provide it. However, I must oppose HR 4810. Combined with the numerous other tax bills approved by the Congress this year and supported by the congressional majority for next year, it would drain away the projected surplus that the American people have worked so hard to create. Even by the Congressional Budget Office's more optimistic projection, this tax plan would plunge America back into deficit and would leave nothing for lengthening the life of Social Security or Medicare; nothing for voluntary and affordable Medicare prescription drug benefits; nothing for education and school construction. Moreover, the congressional majority's tax plan would make it impossible for us to get America out of debt by 2012.

HR 4810 would cost more than $280 billion over 10 years if its provisions were permanent, making it significantly more expensive than either of the bills originally approved by the House and the Senate. It is poorly targeted toward delivering marriage penalty relief — only about 40 percent of the cost of HR 4810 actually would reduce marriage penalties. It also provides little tax relief to those families that need it most, while devoting a large fraction of its benefits to families with higher incomes.

Taking into account HR 4810, the fiscally irresponsible tax cuts passed by the House Ways and Means Committee this year provide about as much benefit to the top 1 percent of Americans as to the bottom 80 percent combined. Families in the top 1 percent get an average tax break of over $16,000, while a middle-class family gets only $220 on average. But if interest rates went up because of the congressional majority's plan by even one-third of 1 percent, then mortgage payments for a family with a $100,000 mortgage would go up by $270, leaving them worse off than if they had no tax cut at all.

We should have tax cuts this year, but they should be the right ones, targeted to working families to help our economy grow — not tax breaks that will help only a few while putting our prosperity at risk. I have proposed a program of targeted tax cuts that will give a middle-class American family substantially more benefits than the Republican plan at less than half the cost. Including our carefully targeted marriage penalty relief, two-thirds of the relief will go to the middle 60 percent of American families. Our tax cuts will also help to send our children to college, with a tax deduction or 28 percent tax credit for up to $10,000 in college tuition a year; help to care for family members who need long-term care, through a $3,000 long-term care tax credit; help to pay for child care and to ease the burden on working families with three or more children; and help to fund desperately needed school construction.

And because our plan will cost substantially less than the tax cuts passed by the Congress, we'll still have the resources we need to provide a Medicare prescription drug benefit, to extend the life of Social Security and Medicare, and to pay off the debt by 2012 — so that we can keep interest rates low, keep our economy growing, and provide lower home mortgage, car, and college loan payments for the American people.

This surplus comes from the hard work and ingenuity of the American people. We owe it to them to make the best use of it — for all of them, and for our children's future.

Since the adjournment of the Congress has prevented my return of HR 4810 within the meaning of Article I, section 7, clause 2 of the Constitution, my withholding of approval from the bill precludes its becoming law. *The Pocket Veto Case, 279 U.S. 655 (1929).*

In addition to withholding my signature and thereby invoking my constitutional power to "pocket veto" bills during an adjournment of the Congress, to avoid litigation, I am also sending HR 4810 to the House of Representatives with my objections, to leave no possible doubt that I have vetoed the measure.

WILLIAM J. CLINTON
THE WHITE HOUSE
August 5, 2000

Cheney's Congressional Votes From 1979 to 1989 Reveal Staunch Conservatism

AUGUST 12 — *What follows are votes cast on major issues of the day by former Wyoming Rep. Dick Cheney (1979-89), who is the Republican nominee for vice president. These are his votes, by House vote number, on issues selected by CQ Weekly editors.*

1988

Cheney voted YES

201: To remove a spending bill provision barring discrimination in housing because a family has young children. (June 23)

264: To apologize and authorize $1.25 billion in reparations to surviving Japanese-Americans interned during World War II. (Aug. 4)

231: To strike language seeking a seven-day waiting period for handgun purchases. (Sept. 15)

Cheney voted NO

41: To require institutions to comply with four federal anti-discrimination laws to receive federal funds. (March 22)

79: To ban nuclear tests with an explosive power greater than one kiloton and tests conducted outside designated areas, as long as the Soviet Union observed the same ban. (April 28)

159: To revise procedures to crack down on unfair foreign trade practices and limit import damage to U.S. industries. (May 24)

164: To cap the amounts for which Medicare beneficiaries would be financially liable for Medicare-covered services. (June 2)

196: To shift $400 million in NASA research funding to programs for the homeless and housing-related programs. (June 22)

1987

Cheney voted YES

35: To allow states to raise the speed limit to 65 mph on interstate highways outside urban areas. (March 18)

63: To reduce discretionary spending by an across-the-board cut of 21 percent. (April 23)

83: To increase the borrowing authority of the Federal Savings and Loan Insurance Corporation (FSLIC) from $5 billion to $15 billion over five years. (May 5)

279: To expand the Medicare program to protect beneficiaries from catastrophic medical expenses. (July 22)

371: To reauthorize the independent-counsel law through 1988. (Oct. 21)

454: To postpone economic sanctions against areas that fail to meet pollution standards of the 1970 Clean Air Act (PL 91-604). (Dec. 3)

Cheney voted NO

14: To reauthorize the 1972 clean water act (PL 92-500). (Feb. 3)

482: To convert Aid to Families with Dependent Children into a national education and retraining program for welfare recipients. (Dec. 15)

1986

Cheney voted YES

69: To allow interstate sale of rifles and shotguns and interstate transportation of all firearms. (April 10)

134: To emphasize repair of existing low-income public housing units rather than new construction. (June 5)

178: To provide $100 million in aid to Nicaraguan contras and $300 million in economic aid to Costa Rica. (June 25)

356: To remove restrictions on covert military aid to UNITA rebels in Angola. (Sept. 17)

421: To overhaul immigration laws to penalize employers who hire illegal aliens and to provide legal status to illegal aliens already in the United States. (Oct. 9)

Cheney voted NO

265: To place import restrictions on textile and apparel goods. (Aug. 6)

285: To reduce the fiscal 1987 national defense budget. (Aug. 8)

300: To cut research funds for the Strategic Defense Initiative ("star wars"). (Aug. 12)

311: To prohibit the production of binary chemical weapons (artillery shells and bombs that dispense nerve gas). (Aug. 13)

332: To raise the ceiling on the federal debt. (Aug. 16)

379: To reduce individual and corporate income tax rates. (Sept. 25)

390: To impose economic sanctions against South Africa. (Sept. 29)

1985

Cheney voted YES

156: To produce binary chemical weapons under certain conditions. (June 19)

334: To cut fiscal 1986 spending and new programs. (Oct. 24)

Cheney voted NO

320: To impose new quota restrictions on textile imports. (Oct. 10)

350: To increase the limit on public debt with declining annual limits. (Nov. 1)

381: To require employers to give workers 90 days' notice of any plant shutdown or significant layoff. (Nov. 21)

406: To provide $10 billion over five years for superfund hazardous waste cleanup. (Dec. 10)

425: To reduce individual and corporate income tax rates. (Dec. 17)

1984

Cheney voted YES

74: To impose a one-year physician fee freeze for Medicare services. (April 12)

125: To allow military aid for El Salvador under certain conditions. (May 10)

129: To allow student religious groups to meet in public high schools during non-class hours. (May 15)

226: To impose sanctions on employers who knowingly hire illegal aliens. (June 20)

292: To cut federal funds to high schools that refuse to allow student religious groups to meet on school premises. (July 26)

324: To remove language giving citizens the right to sue in federal court for damages caused by hazardous waste dumping. (Aug. 9)

Cheney voted NO

65: To approve the fiscal 1985 budget resolution, which set fiscal targets but did not reduce deficits. (April 5)

152: To deny funds to test the anti-satellite missile in space unless the Soviet Union conducted a similar test. (May 23)

406: To ban commercial bank loans to the government of South Africa. (Oct. 11)

1983

Cheney voted YES

22: To gradually raise the normal Social Security retirement age from 65 to 67 after 2000. (March 9)

304: To increase funding for the International Monetary Fund. (Aug. 3)

342: To continue U.S. participation in the multinational peacekeeping force in Lebanon. (Sept. 28)

441: To reduce federal dairy price supports to reduce production. (Nov. 9)

453: To phase in an access charge on residential and small business telephone users for the right to long-distance service. (Nov. 10)

Cheney voted NO

42: To approve the fiscal 1984 budget resolution, which called for tax and spending increases. (March 23)

83: To call for a freeze and reduction in nuclear weapons. (May 4)

98: To help unemployed homeowners make their mortgage payments. (May 11)

409: To remove $2.1 billion for the purchase of 21 MX missiles. (Nov. 1)

469: To propose the Equal Rights Amendment. (Nov. 15)

471: To oppose $124.4 million for production facilities for and procurement of chemical munitions. (Nov. 15)

490: To raise $8 billion in revenues in 1984-86 through changes in tax law. (Nov. 17)

1982

Cheney voted YES

134: To approve the fiscal 1983 budget resolution, which set the deficit at $99 billion and called for increases in defense spending. (June 10)

239: To call for a nuclear weapons freeze by the United States and Soviet Union at equal and substantially reduced levels. (Aug. 5)

363: To propose a constitutional amendment requiring Congress to adopt a balanced federal budget every year unless a three-fifths majority agreed to deficit spending. (Oct. 1)

421: To retain the cap on congressional salaries. (Dec. 14)

425: To delete jobs program funding and add $44 million for Radio Liberty. (Dec. 14)

Cheney voted NO

68: To provide $1 billion for mortgage interest subsidy payments to home buyers below a certain family income limit. (May 12)

110: To increase budget authority and outlays to accommodate Medicare funding and to decrease defense programs. (May 27)

299: To add $14.6 billion in new budget authority for federal military and civilian pay raises. (Sept. 9)

396: To increase gasoline and other highway taxes. (Dec. 6)

422: To bar use of funds for research and development, design or construction of the Clinch River breeder reactor. (Dec. 14)

435: To require automakers to use set percentages of U.S. labor and parts in automobiles sold in the United States. (Dec. 15)

444: To cite Environmental Protection Agency Administrator Anne M. Gorsuch for contempt of Congress for withholding documents. (Dec. 16)

1981

Cheney voted YES

7: To increase the public debt limit to $985 billion. (Feb. 5)

30: To decrease budget authority, outlays and revenues for fiscal 1982, resulting in a $31 billion deficit. (May 7)

167: To reduce individual income tax rates by 25 percent across the board over three years. (July 29)

176: To restore minimum Social Security benefits that President Ronald Reagan had proposed to cut for three million recipients. (July 31)

267: To increase the limit on House members' outside earned income from 15 percent to 40 percent of their official salary. (Oct. 28)

351: To reauthorize price support and other farm programs for four years and food stamps for one year. (Dec. 16)

Cheney voted NO

83: To reauthorize the Legal Services Corporation for fiscal 1982-83. (June 18)

147: To delete $189 million in funding for the Tennessee-Tombigbee Waterway. (July 23)

243: To disapprove the sale to Saudi Arabia of Airborne Warning and Control System radar planes and other equipment. (Oct. 14)

299: To delete $1.8 billion intended for procurement of the B-1 bomber. (Nov. 18)

1980

Cheney voted YES

166: To cut U.S. contributions in 1979-82 to several international development banks by $1.5 billion. (April 17)

170: To transfer funds to the Selective Service System to start draft registration of 19- and 20-year-old males in 1980. (April 22)

204: To require families that had annual incomes over 175 percent of the poverty level to repay some or all food stamp benefits received during the year. (May 8)

492: To disapprove the shipment to India by the United States of enriched nuclear fuel. (Sept. 18)

550: To expel Rep. Michael J. (Ozzie) Myers, D-Pa., from the House for his involvement in the FBI's Abscam corruption investigation. (Oct. 2)

Cheney voted NO

124: To raise the percentage of revenue from the crude oil windfall profits tax allocated for energy conservation from 15 percent to 50 percent. (March 12)

186: To increase fiscal 1981 budget authority, outlays and revenues. (April 30)

215: To delete $500 million for continued development of the MX missile. (May 15)

282: To give the Justice Department authority to appoint administrative law judges to handle housing bias cases. (June 11)

586: To permit states to veto federally selected nuclear waste sites within their borders unless both chambers override the veto. (Dec. 3)

1979

Cheney voted YES

25: To conduct relations with Taiwan through a government "liaison office" rather than through the unofficial American Institute in Taiwan. (March 8)

341: To propose a constitutional amendment to prohibit students from being compelled to attend a school other than the one nearest their home to achieve racial desegregation. (July 24)

593: To establish a National Study Commission on Hospital Costs. (Nov. 15)

Cheney voted NO

139: To designate 125.4 million acres in Alaska as national parks, wildlife refuges or forests. (May 15)

289: To establish a separate Department of Education. (July 11)

495: To prohibit agencies from lifting price controls on certain types of domestic crude oil. (Oct. 11)

567: To establish a national minimum welfare benefit and require states to cover unemployed two-parent families with children. (Nov. 7)

615: To impose a moratorium on Nuclear Regulatory Commission issuance of new nuclear plant construction permits through April 1, 1980. (Nov. 29)

661: To authorize $1.5 billion in federal loan guarantees for the Chrysler Corp. (Dec. 18) ◆

Democrats Adopt 'A People's Platform For the People's Party'

What follows is the text of the 2000 platform for the Democratic Party. It was adopted on Aug. 15 by delegates to the Democratic convention in Los Angeles.

Introduction

Today, America finds itself in the midst of prosperity, progress, and peace. We have arrived at this moment because of the hard work of the American people. This election will be about the big choices we have to make to secure prosperity that is broadly shared and progress that reaches all families in this new American century. In the year 2000, the Democratic Party stands ready to meet that challenge and to build on our achievements.

When Thomas Jefferson was elected as our party's first president in 1800, America was a young country trying to find its place in the world. Two hundred years later, Democrats gather at a moment of vast possibility to nominate Al Gore as America's next president. A new economy founded on the force of new technologies and traditional values of work is giving rise to new industries and transforming old ones. Biological breakthroughs give us the chance to unlock the mysteries of humanity's deadliest plagues. While the globe is still beset with tragedies and difficulties, more people live under governments of freedom, liberty, and democracy than ever before in history. America enjoys unparalleled affluence at home and influence abroad.

Yet this moment is clearly one of possibility, not absolute guarantees. We must remember that our achievements were accomplished only with creativity, courage, and conscience; with a willingness to innovate and imagine; and with a recommitment to our basic American values of hard work, community, embracing diversity, faith, family, and personal responsibility. And all of it can be imperiled again.

Let us not forget that America's future did not always seem so bright. Under the Bush-Quayle administration, America was suffering through economic stagnation. Businesses were failing.

Jobs were disappearing. The welfare rolls swelled. Crime exploded in the streets. Hope and optimism were scarce. Most Americans felt that the American Dream was endangered — if not extinct.

But in 1992, Americans elected Bill Clinton and Al Gore with a mandate to turn America around. And that's just what they did. They took on the old thinking that had come to dominate politics and offered new ideas — new ideas that met the challenges of the day, new ideas that kept faith with America's oldest values, new ideas that worked.

Eight years later the record is clear: the longest economic expansion in American history. The most jobs ever created under a single administration. The first real wage growth in 20 years. The highest home ownership rate ever. The lowest African-American and Hispanic-American unemployment rates in American history. The lowest crime rate in 25 years. The lowest number of people on welfare since the 1960's. The largest drop in poverty in nearly 30 years. The lowest level of child poverty in 20 years. And after 15 painful years when the rich were getting richer and the poor were getting poorer, America is finally growing together instead of growing apart.

These are accomplishments, not accidents. They came about because Democrats — from the White House, to the Congress, to State Houses all across America — brought new thinking and new action to our most pressing challenges. We used government as a catalyst to engage the best ideas and energies of the American people. We asked citizens to get involved and they did. They tutored in their children's schools, patrolled on neighborhood crime watches, volunteered in local hospitals, and voiced their opinion on every issue. They shaped effective solutions to real problems. It will take more of this brand of new thinking if we are to build on this record of achievement.

During our nation's darkest hours, Americans have strived mightily and succeeded in meeting the challenges of their times. The question before us is whether we will do the same during this bright moment; whether we will seize this moment to bring more prosperity and progress to more Americans than ever before; whether, having finally conquered our financial deficits, we will have the courage to conquer the other deficits — in health care, in education, in the environment — that challenge us today.

In this platform, today's Democratic Party lays out its plans to do just that. This platform was not written in a dark backroom, but in the light of day; in an open, democratic process that was interactive and inclusive. It was developed both with the guidance of the brightest Democratic leaders and with the voices of thousands of ordinary Americans around the country who contributed their thoughts, ideas, beliefs, and dreams to this platform in person, on paper, and over the Internet. This is a 21st century platform for the 21st century's party. A people's platform for the people's party.

If one theme runs through this 2000 Democratic platform, it is this: If America is to secure prosperity, progress, peace and security for all, we cannot afford to go back. We must move forward together and we must not leave anyone behind. Eight years ago, America was facing a big challenge. Under the Bush-Quayle administration, the American economy was floundering. Slow growth had turned into no growth and into a jobless recovery. Americans in all walks of life were facing a future of less prosperity and more resignation. In 1992, Bill Clinton and Al Gore were elected to turn the American economy around and point upward toward the future.

They took office with a new set of ideas about how to get the economy moving again. They knew that the private sector is the engine of economic growth, but they also knew that, in Franklin Roosevelt's phrase, "the national community" — acting through government — can make a big difference.

Today, the success of these new ideas is clear. After a generation of stagnation for many and decline for some, real wages for all working families have started to rise again. America has the lowest unemployment and fastest economic growth in more than 30 years. The American people have created 22 million new jobs. We have the lowest inflation rate in decades. More Americans own their home than ever before. Looking back on 1992, this much is clear: Americans are better off than we were eight years ago.

But ours is a record to build on, not to rest on. That's because eight years later, we face a new challenge: how to keep prosperity alive — and how to deepen it — in a fast-moving, fast-changing economy. We can never take our economic prosperity for granted nor can we afford to go back to either tax-and-spend or cut-and-run — the failed policies of the past. It took innovative, new Democratic policies to create the environment where prosperity could bloom. It will take more such policies to allow prosperity to blossom — to forge a prosperity that does not leave anyone out and does not leave anyone behind.

During the past decade, the birth of the global, information-based new economy has changed most every aspect of Americans' lives. As we move inexorably from the Industrial Age to the Information Age, the transition will be difficult for some. In the decade to come, Democrats must lead the way in equipping all Americans with new tools for economic success and security.

This is the only sure means of ensuring that America's prosperity is one that is broadly shared.

Time after time, Republicans opposed the ideas that brought prosperity to America. Time after time, they have been proven wrong. But their sorry record does not give them pause, it does not even slow them down. Despite a Democratic record of success, the Republicans now propose to rewind to the policies that brought America the days of deficits, doubt, debt, and decline; a retreat to the thinking of the era of recessions, repossessions, and retrenchment.

Democrats believe that to further our prosperity and make sure all Americans are ready to reap the rewards of the new economy we need thinking as innovative as the moment in which we live. First, we must continue the fiscal discipline that has been the hallmark of the past eight years — that means paying down the debt and offering the right kind of tax cuts. Second, we must use our unprecedented prosperity to secure Social Security and Medicare for future generations.

Third, we must invest in the most precious resource we have — the American people and their skills and ability to innovate. Fourth, we must continue to reinvent government so that it works better and costs less and is in line with the online world. Fifth, we must open new markets to American products at home and around the world. Finally, we must reinforce the basic American bargain of requiring and rewarding hard work and we must provide Americans with the opportunity to participate in key decisions at work and in their communities.

Fiscal Discipline

For the 12 years before Bill Clinton and Al Gore took office, Republicans talked about fiscal discipline while they quadrupled the national debt. They ran up monstrous yearly deficits and nearly ran the American economy into the ground. In 1992, Democrats promised to cut the deficit in half in four years. They did — and went even further. It took Al Gore's tie-breaking vote in the Senate [in 1993] to overcome unanimous Republican opposition to deficit reduction. Today, America has gone from the biggest deficits in history to the biggest surpluses in history. Fiscal discipline keeps interest rates low and investment rates high — and it has helped fuel America's remarkable prosperity.

We must not go back. That's why Democrats now vow to balance the budget every year, barring a national emergency. But even this is not enough. In the 160 years since the very first Democratic platform, America has always struggled under a national debt. Today's Democrats believe we should pay down the debt every year until we can give our children the independence, self-sufficiency, and prosperity that will come from an America that is debt-free.

In 12 years of rule, Republicans quadrupled the national debt. In the next 12 years, Democrats vow to wipe out the publicly-held national debt.

Today, because of the success of the Clinton-Gore Administration, a debt-free America is within reach. This would free businesses to invest and innovate, it would provide an ever more sturdy foundation for future economic growth, and it would create good jobs. That's why Al Gore is determined to completely eliminate the publicly held national debt by the year 2012.

The Right Kind of Tax Cuts. The road to long term prosperity starts with embracing fiscal discipline. Unfortunately, the Republicans eschew fiscal discipline and offer up nothing less than fiscal disaster. They would squander the surplus on a more than trillion-dollar federal government tax giveaway for the well-off and well-connected, while failing to eliminate the national debt, neglecting to shore up Social Security and Medicare, and shirking the need to invest in the education of America's children and the skills of her workers.

For the past eight years, Democrats have been working to offer tax relief to the Americans who need it the most where they need it the most. We cut taxes for working parents who were struggling to make ends meet. We cut taxes for parents who were working hard and trying to raise good kids. We cut taxes for Americans who had studied hard and made it to college. We cut taxes for Americans who were continuing their educations and gaining new skills to stay on the cutting-edge of the economy. We cut taxes for companies that were helping Americans make the transition from welfare to work. We cut taxes for more than 90 percent of America's dynamic small businesses. Today, for most families, the federal tax burden is the lowest it has been in twenty years.

The Bush tax slash takes a different course. It is bigger than any cut Newt Gingrich ever dreamed of. It would let the richest one percent of Americans afford a new sports car and middle class Americans afford a warm soda. It is so out-of-step with reality that the Republican Congress refused to enact it. It would undermine the American economy and undercut our prosperity. Under the leadership of Al Gore, Democrats want to give middle class families tax cuts they can use — tax cuts that will put their own values into action and that will not injure the economic vitality they rely on. Democrats seek the right kind of tax relief — tax cuts that are specifically targeted to help those who need them the most. These tax cuts would let families live their values by helping them save for college, invest in their job skills and lifelong learning, pay for health insurance, afford child care, eliminate the marriage penalty for working families, care for elderly or disabled loved ones, invest in clean cars and clean homes, and build additional security for their retirement.

Retirement Security

Americans' golden years should be times of calm and security, not concern and stress. Few achievements testify more to the ability of government to do good than Social Security. It has lifted millions of elderly Americans out of poverty and helped them make ends meet. Social Security is more than a government program. It is a solemn compact between the generations. It is our nation's most important family protection. The choice for Americans on this vital part of our national heritage has never been more clear: Democrats believe in using our prosperity to save Social Security; the Republicans' tax cut would prevent America from ensuring our senior citizens have a secure retirement. We owe it to America's children and their children to make the strength and solvency of Social Security a major national priority.

That's why Al Gore is committed to making Social Security safe and secure for more than half a century by using the savings from our current unprecedented prosperity to strengthen the Social Security Trust Fund in preparation for the retirement of the Baby Boom generation. We now have an extraordinary opportunity to maintain Social Security. In addition, we can reform it — not the wrong way, with proposals such as raising the retirement age, but the right way — with fiscal discipline and by making it fairer for widows, widowers, and mothers.

Retirement security comes on many fronts. Democrats have successfully passed reforms to simplify the pension process for small businesses, expand pension portability, and protect employee pension funds. Democrats believe that workers' pensions should be protected and more portable. We also believe that changes in every American's pension rights should be fully disclosed. This is becoming increasingly important today, as pensions are progressively being shifted from a workers' benefit plan to a workers' contribution plan. We believe these changes need to be carefully examined by independent agencies to make sure they abide by current federal law. Democrats support President Clinton's veto of the Republican tax scheme that would have diminished anti-discrimination protections for middle-class and lower-income workers.

To build on the success of Social Security, Al Gore has proposed the creation of Retirement Savings Plus — voluntary, tax-free, personally-controlled, privately-managed savings accounts with a government match that would help couples build a nest egg of up to $400,000. Separate from Social Security, Retirement Savings Plus accounts would let Americans save and invest on top of the foundation of Social Security's guaranteed benefit. Under this plan, the federal government would match individual contributions with tax credits, with the hardest-pressed working families getting the most assistance.

The Republicans have a far different idea — a scheme that would come not in addition to Social Security but at the expense of it. Their Social Security privatization plot would siphon $1 trillion in payroll taxes away from the Social Security trust fund, take 14 years off the life of Social Security, eliminate the fundamental guarantee of retirement security, and raise the specter of massive government bailouts. And, according to independent analyses, the Republicans' privatization plan would cut the guaranteed benefits for young workers by as much as 54 percent. It would take the "security" out of Social Security.

Retirement Savings Plus does not threaten Social Security's guaranteed benefit. Social Security may be 65 years old — but it is not ready to be retired. Taken together, George W. Bush's $2 trillion tax cut, his campaign-season spending proposals, his support for an unspecified but unprecedented missile defense system, and his support for privatizing Social Security add up to an assault on the surplus — causing Americans to have to choose between drastic cuts in education and health care or a return to the days of deficit spending. This is not a choice Americans should have to make. With fiscal discipline and a commitment to honoring our values, we can both save Social Security and give Americans the ability to create a nest egg without turning back the clock on our prosperity.

Investing in Americans

Democrats know that today, more than ever before, we need the right kinds of investments — in education, lifelong learning, skill development, and research and development — to take advantage of the vast opportunities of the Information Age. We need to make sure Americans have the skills and tools they need to compete and win in the new knowledge-based, global economy.

A Revolution in Education

Democrats understand that ensuring every child the highest quality education is essential if America is to remain strong and competitive in today's economy. That's why Al Gore's very first campaign speech was about education and that's why Al Gore will make education his top domestic priority. Nine out of every ten children in this country attend a public school. Public education already allows the United States to have one of the highest standards of living in the world, providing equality of opportunity for all regardless of socio-economic status.

The success stories coming from public schools are greater than at any time in their history: higher graduation rates, increasing test scores, and higher student achievement — with especially substantial gains among our neediest students. We must continue to build on this record of success that Democrats have compiled in the last eight years. We have helped states and communities set high academic standards for students and called for an end to social promotion.

We have started hiring 100,000 qualified teachers. We have increased accountability. We have opened the gates of college to millions of Americans.

Now we must do more. Democrats understand that America will not long remain first in the world economically unless we become first in the world educationally. We cannot continue to generate a fifth of the world's economic output if a third of our students do not meet basic reading standards. We cannot stay number one in high technology jobs if we remain last in the percentage of degrees awarded in science. In today's knowledge-based economy, it's just that simple. Education leads to the future success and security of our country and citizenry.

Americans have been told they must choose between investing in education and demanding accountability. This is the type of false choice that drives our government into stalemate and drives Americans up the wall. Americans believe that we need to invest more in our children's educations — and they're right. Americans also believe that we should not be pouring more money into a system that is producing bad results — and they're right about that too. We should do more of what we're doing right and less of what we're doing wrong.

Al Gore and the Democratic Party know that investments without accountability are a waste of money and that accountability without investments are a waste of time. George W. Bush and the Republican Party offer neither real accountability nor reasonable investment. What they do offer are soothing sound-bites and bite-sized solutions. They refuse to invest in America's crumbling schools and crowded classrooms — spending 100 times more on tax cuts than on education. They don't help pay teachers like professionals nor do they insist on higher standards for teachers. They propose blank check block grants without accountability. Their version of accountability relies on private school vouchers that would offer too few dollars to too few children to escape their failing schools. These vouchers would pass the buck on accountability while pulling bucks out of the schools that need them most. When it comes to education, Democrats want to invest more and aim higher, the Republicans invest too little and aim too low.

We cannot afford — materially or morally — to let another generation of American children pass through inadequate schools before we make needed changes that will save them from a lifetime of frustration and limited horizons. The time for action is now.

By the end of the next presidential term, we should have a fully qualified, well trained teacher in every classroom in every school in every part of this country — and every teacher should pass a rigorous test to get there. By the end of the next presidential term, every failing school in America should be turned around — or shut down and reopened under new public leadership.

By the end of the next presidential term, we should ensure that no high school student graduates unless they have mastered the basics of reading and math — so that the diploma they receive really means something.

By the end of the next presidential term, parents across the nation ought to be able to choose the best public school for their children.

By the end of the next presidential term, every eighth grader in America should be computer literate.

By the end of the next presidential term, high-quality, affordable preschool should be fully available to every family, for every child, in every community in America.

By the end of the next presidential term, every child should learn in a safe, modern classroom with the most up-to-date technology.

By the end of the next presidential term, the achievement gap between students of color and the rest of America's students should be eliminated.

All this we pledge — and more. The time for tinkering around the edges has long passed. We need revolutionary improvements in our public schools. This requires a major national investment; a demand of accountability from all; a genuine expansion of public school choice; and a renewed focus on discipline, character, and safety in our schools.

Discipline, Character, and Safety

Education is not just about test scores, but about passing on our values to the next generation of American citizens. Our children and teachers deserve schools of safety and classrooms free of fear. We should have a zero-tolerance policy towards guns in schools. Each school should institute strict, firm, and fair discipline policies that are agreed upon on the first day of the school year at a meeting of teachers, parents, and students.

We should expand the Family Leave Law to make sure parents can attend these meetings and all parent-teacher conferences without being scared they will lose their jobs.

We must do all we can to encourage active parental involvement in our schools — after all, parents are a child's first and best teachers. A parent's job does not end when they drop their child off at the schools front door. They have a responsibility to actively participate in their children's education, to read to their children, and to help their children with their homework.

Schools need to do their part by welcoming parents into the education process and giving them a voice in the education of their children.

Democrats believe in "second-chance schools" where kids expelled from school and those headed for trouble can get the concentrated help, services, and guidance they need to get back on the path to success. If we are serious about fighting school violence, we need a dramatic increase in after-school care for America's children. The average two-parent family works 500 more hours a year than they did a generation ago. Children often come home from school to empty houses. We know that the most dangerous hours for children are those between the end of the school day and the end of the work day. It is in these afternoon hours that children are most likely to get into trouble and fall under bad influences. Democrats have increased after-school assistance 500 times over in the last four years. Al Gore believes in expanding after-school programs and providing Americans with an after-school tax credit so that children have a safe, supervised after-school environment where they can continue to learn and learn right from wrong.

Too often, our culture offers our children a virtual crash course in violence and degradation. It is sometimes a culture of too much meanness and not enough meaning. That's why character education is so important in our schools. Education should not be a morals-free zone. Schools can teach our kids about honesty, hard work, openness to new information, strong discipline, willingness to reason, personal responsibility, and tolerance for different points of view.

Teachers can help children develop the values and the character — as well as the intellectual tools — it takes to succeed and contribute to their communities. The traditional three R's are not enough. Schools need to make sure they teach kids respect, reliability, and responsibility as well.

We must also remember that our schools are not just training the next generation of workers, they are also educating the next generation of citizens. That's why Democrats support democracy education, civic education, and service requirements in our schools.

Strict Accountability for Results, Strong Incentives for Success. Democrats believe that everyone involved in the education system should be held accountable. Accountability means we will no longer tolerate mediocrity and no longer allow failure. Accountability applies to states, school districts, schools, teachers, students, and parents. Everyone must do their part. Nobody can shirk their responsibility.

Consistently bad schools should be shut down. No excuses. No exceptions. Every state and school district should identify failing schools and turn them around with all necessary measures and all necessary resources. Students in those schools should get first priority in transferring to a better-performing public school in the district and getting intensive after-school academic help to make sure they are not left behind while their school is being turned around. Failing schools that do not improve should be quickly shut down and reopened with a new principal and new teachers.

States should be held accountable for reducing drop-out rates, increasing graduation rates, and raising student achievement. Working together with teachers, school principals should be able to hire on the basis of qualifications and fit, not just on the basis of seniority.

Teachers should be answerable for what goes on in their classroom. New teachers who answer the call to join this honorable profession should get the mentors and professional support they need to make the transition into teaching — and then should have to pass a rigorous and fair test before they step foot into a classroom. Teaching is no easy job and we should not expect that everyone is able to make it in the classroom. New teachers should receive ongoing support and mentoring from their more experienced colleagues. Current teachers should receive continuing quality professional development to ensure that their skills and knowledge reflect the most up-to-date information and research.

Those teachers who do not meet the highest quality standards should not be allowed to sully the reputation of the teaching profession. That's why teachers who are not teaching well should receive help in getting up to standards. At its best, teaching is the job of a lifetime. But teaching contracts and licenses should not be an automatic lifetime job guarantee. That's why we need regular evaluations to determine whether a teacher's license should be renewed. Democrats urge faster but fair ways, with due process, to identify, help — and when necessary — speedily remove low performing teachers.

Every student must be given the opportunity to learn. But students have to take responsibility and be accountable for their own educations, as well. We need measurements to make sure students are getting the preparation they require — including voluntary national tests in 4th grade reading and 8th grade math. Democrats insist that no student should graduate with a diploma they cannot read.

The federal government needs to be held accountable, too. In states that do not make progress in improving student performance, the federal government should redirect money from state bureaucrats and transfer it directly to schools that need it. States that do succeed in raising student success should receive bonuses — and schools that are making a positive difference should receive bonuses, as well. In addition, teachers who earn a National Board Certification should be especially rewarded.

Investing in Our Schools. We cannot expect our children to learn all that they need to know in classrooms that are overcrowded, with teachers that are overburdened, and with textbooks and technology that are out-of-date. We need to invest in our schools and our children's' futures.

High-quality pre-school should no longer be a luxury. Research — and the experience of path-breaking states such as North Carolina and Georgia — shows that giving kids a smart start can lead to higher reading and achievement levels, higher graduation rates, and greater success in the workplace.

We need an aggressive national campaign to put one million new well-trained teachers in our classrooms. We must start reducing class size by finishing the job of hiring 100,000 new qualified teachers. In addition, Al Gore has proposed the creation of a new 21st Century Teacher Corps — open to talented people around the country who agree to teach in a school that needs their help. In return, they would get help paying their college tuition, assistance in paying off their student loans, or a hiring bonus for those willing to switch careers. And we need alternative certification so that those who choose to switch into teaching don't have to start their education all over again. Far too many teachers are overstressed and overworked, underpaid and underappreciated. We need to treat teachers like professionals — pay them like professionals and hold them to professional standards. All qualified teachers should get a raise and master teachers should get the biggest raise. We need to provide professional development, training, and support so that all teachers can succeed.

We should rebuild and modernize our school buildings to assure students can attend schools that are modern, safe, and well-equipped for learning. And we need to construct more new schools to meet the needs of the largest generation of students in American history. We cannot convince our children to value education when they are packed into crammed classrooms like sardines in a can and when their facilities are falling down. Al Gore and the Democrats believe we need smaller classes, smaller schools, and "schools within schools" so that impressionable children do not get lost in the shuffle.

We must ensure that children with disabilities are not blocked from having access to free, appropriate education and that the doors to our public schools are not closed to children with special needs. We must, finally, live up to the Federal government's promise to communities to help them defray the expenses of educating children with special needs.

We must assure that schools have the resources to meet the challenges of an increasingly diverse student population with programs for English language learners, including bilingual education, to close the achievement gap. We oppose language-based discrimination in all its forms, including in the provision of education services, and encourage so-called English-plus initiatives because multilingualism is increasingly valuable in the global economy.

We should create new Opportunity Academies around the nation between high school and college where disadvantaged students can get the intensive academic preparation in math, reading, writing, and study skills that will improve their likelihood for success in college and beyond.

Supporting Schools of Innovation. In order to create a world-class educational system for all our students, we must allow experimentation in our public schools to find out what works. The Democratic Party supports expansion of charter schools, magnet schools, site-based schools, year-round schools, and other nontraditional public school options.

Charter schools and other nontraditional public school options can free school leaders, teachers, parents, and community leaders to use their creativity and innovation to help all students meet the highest academic standards. The Democratic Party will triple the number of charter schools in the nation. And, we will ensure that these charter schools are fully accountable — financially and academically — to students and the communities they serve, and that they are indeed making progress in maximizing student achievement. All public schools should have the freedom to design their curriculum within high standards and all public schools should compete for students — and we should start by bringing universal public school choice and competition to our lowest-performing public schools. Let there be no mistake: what America needs are public schools that compete with one another and are held accountable for results, not private school vouchers that drain resources from public schools and hand over the public's hard-earned tax dollars to private schools with no accountability.

Closing the Opportunity Gap

Forty years ago, the Democratic platform discussed a Missile Gap as a measurement of America's competitiveness around the world and our security here at home. Today, too many Americans face an Opportunity Gap — a lack of the skills they need to be competitive in the global economy and have career security in the workplace. The Opportunity Gap is also a chasm created by income disparity, discrimination by race and gender, and the abandonment of our inner cities.

Many of today's workers will need retraining over the next decade. Nearly ninety percent of companies say they already face a shortage of skilled workers. The Opportunity Gap is costing American workers good jobs at good wages — and it must be closed. Al Gore has proposed a broad set of initiatives to provide college education, lifelong learning, and ongoing skill development for all Americans.

College Education and Lifelong Learning for All. With Democratic leadership over the past eight years, the percentage of young people who are entering college has gone up by nearly 20 percent. In the Information Age, it is clear that a college education is more important than ever.

The HOPE Scholarship and Lifetime Learning Tax Credit have opened the gates of college wider than ever before. Pell grants are at their highest level ever.

Now we need to do more. We should make a college education as universal as high school is today. Al Gore has proposed a new National Tuition Savings program to tie together state tuition savings programs in more than 30 states so that parents can save for college tax-free and inflation-free. We propose a tax cut for tuition and fees for post-high school education and training that allows families to choose either a $10,000 a year tax deduction or a $2,800 tax credit.

In today's economy, education should not be a time in a person's life but a way of life. To keep up with the fast-moving, fast-changing economy, workers must have the ability to continue learning and upgrading their skills for a lifetime. The next great frontier in American education is dramatically expanding opportunities for lifelong learning, skill development, and training.

Democrats believe that every hard-working American should have the chance to use their best talents. That is why we support a major new commitment to expanding worker training and skill development, including the creation of national skills standards. Al Gore has called on companies and workers to build more partnerships for skill development. He has proposed incentives for states and employers to expand worker training. We should fund partnerships of employers, colleges, unions, and others that will connect workers to the training they need. We should create a new tax credit for employers who train their workers in the skills needed in the New Economy. We must also give new training allowances that will extend unemployment insurance for those who need time to finish their training courses. Al Gore has called for new 401(j) accounts — like the 401(k)'s which so many Americans use — that would let employers help their employees save tax-free and use those savings for the lifelong learning for the employee or their spouse, or their children's college education. Al Gore has also called for a permanent tax exemption to encourage employers to provide tuition assistance benefits to their workers, and for expanding this exemption so that entire families can benefit from these tuition benefits as well.

Bridging the Digital Divide. Democrats believe that every American — regardless of income, geography, race, or disability — should be able to reach across a computer keyboard, and reach the vast new worlds of knowledge, commerce, and communication that are available at the touch of a fingertip.

That is why Democrats fought for the e-rate to wire every classroom and library to the Internet. In the next four years, we must finish connecting the job and then go further.

We must launch a new crusade — calling on the resources of government, employers, the high-tech industry, community organizations, and unions — to move toward full Internet access in every home, for every family, all across the United States. We must make sure that no family or community is left out. We must not rest until Internet access is universal.

We must also launch a new national effort to provide basic skills in the newest technology. Al Gore has proposed a major initiative to set and achieve a national goal of computer literacy for every child by the time they finish the eighth grade. He has also called for expanded technology training for workers, and supports incentives for employers to provide home computers and Internet access to their workers. And we must do more than merely teaching technology in the classroom and the workplace. We must dramatically expand teacher training in how to use the power of the Internet. We should also use our AmeriCorps national service corps members to teach and promote the Internet in the schools, libraries, and technology centers that need them the most. America was the pioneer of universal education; now America must become the pioneer of universal computer literacy.

Investing in Innovation

Technology is no longer just wondrous gadgets, it is an ever more integral part of our economy — and an enormous part of what has been driving economic growth. We need to harness technology's power and make sure America stays on the cutting-edge.

That means continuing to invest in experimentation, exploration, and innovation. Democrats recognize that a sustained public investment in long term basic research has been the foundation for America's scientific and technological leadership. That's why both public and private investment in research and development is crucial to sustaining our prosperity. On the public side, Democrats believe in doubling the current levels of investment in information technology research and biomedical research and supporting the continued development of the Next Generation Internet — moving 1,000 times faster than today's Internet.

We believe in helping universities and federal laboratories become centers of innovation that support and catalyze private sector growth. We also believe in the use of creative public-private partnerships that will, when appropriate, help bring new products to market faster. We continue to support technology transfer — forming partnerships between industry and government that can help ensure that American companies and workers develop the technological tools needed to compete in tomorrow's global markets.

In the private sector, Democrats believe in supporting the startups, the small businesses, and the entrepreneurs that are making the New Economy go. This means making permanent the Research and Experimentation tax credit and expanding it to make it partially refundable so that small businesses can use it more easily. It also means keeping cyberspace a duty-free zone so that American companies can sell goods around the world and insist that other countries refrain from actions that impede commerce. To expand technology's worldwide potential as a force for good, Al Gore has advanced a bold vision for a new Global Information Infrastructure — a network of networks that sends messages and images at the speed of light, across every continent — to expand access to phone service and communications, further improve the delivery of education and health care, and create new jobs and industries.

Strengthening small business is a vital component of economic innovation, job creation, and supporting entrepreneurship. Small businesses have accounted for more than 90 percent of the 22 million new jobs created with Democratic leadership. The Democratic Party is committed to sustaining and adding to that level of growth of small businesses, including home based businesses. Democrats believe that strengthening small businesses is a vital component of strategies to create opportunity and community economic development. We will build on the tremendous progress of the Clinton-Gore Administration in modernizing the Small Business Administration and improving access to the Federal marketplace. We will fight to reform and strengthen programs to combat discrimination against women and minority entrepreneurs, including federal procurement, because the playing field is still not level.

Americans generate more new technologies, new inventions, and more creative works of software and entertainment than the citizens of any other country in the world. American creativity contributes greatly to improving the quality of daily life, helps us work more efficiently, and enriches our national culture. America's laws and policies must be tailored and equipped to nurture and advance this unique aspect of our national character. This means we must ensure that sound patent and copyright laws motivate our inventors and creators to pursue their vision. Internationally, we must work to build support for strong intellectual property laws among the community of nations, including in trade agreements. We must take all steps necessary to secure effective enforcement of those laws — at home and abroad — to ensure that others do not steal intellectual property through piracy and other forms of theft.

Democrats know that technological innovation is critical to maintaining a strong manufacturing sector as we enter the Information Age. Manufacturing is a principal engine of productivity growth, a provider of jobs that pay family-supportive wages, and a significant source of exports for paying our way in the world economy. Al Gore and the Democratic Party will fight to keep America's basic industries the most competitive in the world.

Protecting American Consumers

As our science and technology advance we must work hard to protect our oldest and most cherished values. That's why Al Gore, while supporting the completion of the Human Genome Project, has championed legislation to ban genetic discrimination. While fighting to expand Internet access, he has led the Administration's efforts to give parents, schools, and communities effective tools to protect children from inappropriate content online. In particular, Al Gore has focused on the challenge of protecting Americans' personal privacy on-line as well as the medical and financial information that can all too easily be intercepted and abused by others.

Al Gore has called for an Electronic Bill of Rights for this electronic age — including the right to choose whether personal information is disclosed; the right to know how, when, and how much of that information is being used; the right to see it yourself; and the right to know if is accurate.

We must protect not only our privacy, but the food we eat, the air we breathe, and the water we drink. That's why Democrats believe we ought to have a modern, science-based food safety system, including meaningful food labeling that also discloses where our food comes from, and that communities should have the right to know about toxins that are released into the air and water.

Investing in Communities

Democrats believe that in building upon the record-breaking prosperity and growth achieved in the past eight years, we must not leave any community behind. Under the leadership of Al Gore, the Empowerment Zones and Enterprise Communities programs have brought new hope to cities and rural areas all across America. Now we need a new round of Empowerment Zones to spread prosperity even further. The Clinton-Gore New Markets Initiative is shining a spotlight on the untapped potential for commerce, tourism, and investment in many communities, and Al Gore will extend these efforts to see that the prosperity of the mainstream economy flows to the Main Streets everywhere. The Clinton-Gore Administration fought to strengthen the Community Reinvestment Act and to create a network of Community Development Banks, and Al Gore will continue that fight. Democrats are committed to building an America in which no neighborhood or town see joblessness and shuttered businesses commonplace or inevitable, and where no families or young adults surrender their God-given right to work hard and live the American dream.

Part of that dream is home ownership. Under Democratic leadership, we have achieved an all-time high in home ownership, including among groups that have historically been left out. We are committed to continuing this progress, because home ownership is a foundation for building wealth and economic security for families, and it provides a vital anchor enabling neighborhoods to thrive. In too many communities, however, owning or renting an affordable home seems an impossible dream. Al Gore and Democrats have long defended the mortgage interest deduction and the Low Income Housing Tax Credit, and believe we must reinvigorate our communities and support our families through partnerships and targeted investments and eliminating community redlining by lenders that will better harness the power of markets to create the housing we need.

We must pay down the debt to keep interest rates low. We need to create a continuum of care for homeless people so that they get help in getting themselves off the streets and back on their feet.

We must ensure that housing costs in thriving communities do not outpace the income of middle class families. We must expand the supply of life cycle housing. We must encourage the renovation and construction of affordable housing closer to places of work and to mass transit so workers can get to their jobs without being tied up in traffic for hours.

In rural America, we have the opportunity to create a rural renewal on our nation's farms with improved transportation and infrastructure, better access to capital and technology, reduced concentration in agribusiness, and an expansion of new markets for our crops, and strengthening our ability to compete in world markets. The Internet can break down barriers of geography and isolation and bring the rural economy into the new economy. Farmers should receive incentives to conserve soil and improving farming and forestry techniques. The Republican Freedom to Farm Act has resulted in years of low prices and necessitated billion dollar bailouts. It is misguided and must be changed. Family farmers who work hard and smart should be able not only to survive but to thrive. Democrats will strengthen, not shred, the safety net for family farmers; we will open markets abroad for them. And we will not turn our backs on rural communities; we will work to ensure that they share in the new prosperity we are building for all of America.

Livable Communities. Across America a new movement is emerging as citizens work together to build more livable communities. These are communities where the streets are safe and schools are good, where high wage jobs are not hours away from home, where people can get to work and run their errands without spending hours stuck in traffic, where they can breathe clean air and drink clean water, where the spirit of community reigns.

Democrats believe communities know best and that they should have the resources and tools they need to act on their decisions, to have the ability to create communities of which families can be proud. We want to transform out-of-control sprawl to well-planned smart growth.

That is why we support the "Better America Bonds" — tax credits for state and local bonds to build more livable communities. We must help communities reconnect to the land around them, preserve open spaces, build parks, improve water quality, and redevelop rusty old brownfields.

We need to help save farms from being turned into strip malls and parks from being paved over.

We should acquire new lands for urban and suburban forests and recreation sites and set aside wetlands, coastal and wildlife preserves. And it is time we enhanced our quality of life by unclogging our nation's roads and airports.

Al Gore and the Democratic Party support the building of high-speed rail systems in major transportation corridors across the nation. High-speed rail reduces highway and airport congestion, improves air quality, stimulates the economy, and broadens the scope of personal choice for traveling between our communities. We support new grants to Amtrak and the states for improving existing and for expanding and completing passenger rail routes and corridors.

Opening Markets Around the World

Exports sustain about 1 in 5 American factory jobs — jobs that pay more than jobs not tied to the global economy. Open markets spur innovation, speed the growth of new industries, and make our businesses more competitive. We must work to knock down barriers to fair trade so other nation's markets are as open as our own.

Trade has been an important part of our economic expansion — about a third of our economic growth in recent years has come from selling American goods and services overseas. There is no doubt that with trade — and with investments in giving American workers the skills they need — we can out-compete workers anywhere in the world.

It's clear we live in a globalized world — and that there is no turning back. But globalization is neither good nor evil. It is a fact — and we have to deal with it. Democrats believe we must be leaders in the new global economy, not followers. We believe that globalization will work for all Americans only if there are rules of the road, as in the domestic economy, that promote both a strong economy and our basic American values.

We need to make the global economy work for all. That means making sure that all trade agreements contain provisions that will protect the environment and labor standards, as well as open markets in other countries. Al Gore will insist on and use the authority to enforce worker rights, human rights, and environmental protections in those agreements. We should use trade to lift up standards around the world not drag down standards here at home.

True open trade is not just about profits, but about people; not a race to the bottom, but a dash to the top; about a rising tide lifting the boats of workers here and abroad; about reinforcing the values of freedom and liberty and the rule of law in the hearts and minds of people everywhere.

The test of open trade in the years ahead is whether it empowers the many and not just the few, whether its blessings are widely shared, whether it helps to lift the poor out of poverty; and whether it works for working people.

Democrats know that to build a new consensus for more open trade, we must give workers the tools they need to compete in the global economy and support rules that will protect workers' rights, human rights, and environmental protections. That's why our lifelong learning and skill development proposals are so important. American workers need access to ongoing skills development so that they have the tools they need to succeed in the New Economy. In addition, our trade adjustment assistance programs should be improved so that all affected workers receive timely and adequate assistance, including measures to address health care coverage and pension protections. With the leadership of Al Gore, Democrats helped America's steel industry weather the effects of the Asian financial crisis. As President, Al Gore will move aggressively to reduce our overall trade deficit and stop the erosion of good paying manufacturing jobs. This includes negotiating tough agreements to reduce our persistent automotive trade imbalances with our major trading partners. We must continue to monitor imports and, consistent with the World Trade Organization, ensure that the United States utilizes all of its trade laws and other mechanisms, including product specific safeguards, to stop quickly and effectively any import surges when they threaten our workers and communities.

The President should be able to negotiate trade agreements with the nations of the world and should include worker rights, human rights, and environmental protections in those agreements, as well as market opening initiatives. At the same time, Al Gore will challenge American companies to ensure labor protections and worker safety at their overseas operations. And U.S. representatives at the International Monetary Fund and the World Bank should also seek to advance fair treatment for workers internationally. We should create an environment in which electronic commerce can flourish globally as it has here in America. We are committed to supporting the rights of workers around the world. And we should vigorously monitor trade agreements to make sure other nations are not shirking their responsibilities.

Democrats are committed to addressing the problem of manipulative corporate tax shelters, including in the international context, that undermine the public's faith in the fairness of our voluntary tax system. At the same time, we must ensure no tax provision has the effect of encouraging corporations to locate in other countries at the expense of American workers.

21st Century Government

Since he took office, Al Gore has led the way in reinventing government — making government more effective in its mission of service to the public. Under his leadership the federal workforce has been cut by 377,000, making it the smallest government since Dwight D. Eisenhower was president. This has been accomplished through cooperation and partnership.

Sixteen thousand pages of regulations were scrapped. From tea testers to mohair subsidies to the Navy's own dairy farm, over 200 outdated and unnecessary government programs have been eliminated. As a percentage of the workforce, the federal government is the smallest it has been since the New Deal.

We have saved over $135 billion — contributing to the surplus and our prosperity. But we have saved something much more precious as well. We have begun to earn back the faith and trust of the American people in their democratic institutions. Trust in government has almost doubled. The first customer survey ever taken of American's satisfaction with the services government delivers found that fully 60 percent felt service had improved in the last two years and rated government services at levels almost as high as services in the private sector.

Today, our government is focused on emphasizing results over red tape, offering Americans quality service, old-fashioned common sense, and working in partnership with the private sector to achieve common goals. Republicans attack public workers and tear down public services. We have empowered government workers and improved public services.

Now we need to go much further. We have ended the era of big government; it's time to end the era of old government. We need to create a government where Americans can easily find the services they need; one that is on-line all the time with no need to wait in line, an open government that's always open. On the Internet, citizens will be able to help cut crime in their neighborhood, notify government of potentially dangerous environmental hazards, or sign up for a clinical trial of the latest advances in medicine. And all of this will be done while protecting everyone's personal privacy and with the highest levels of universal access and security. This new e-government will break down barriers to service, reduce costs, and make government accessible for all.

We must forge partnerships between labor and management that recognize the interests of both sides while uniting both front-line government workers and managers in a common crusade to improve government performance.

We must ensure that government has the tools and expertise necessary to provide high-quality services. Democrats do not believe that privatization is a panacea. Some services are inherently public. Democrats also believe that, to ensure government works better and costs less, public employees must be allowed to compete both for their current work and for new work. When government work is contracted out to private companies, they should adhere to same level of accountability as public agencies and those arrangements must incorporate labor, safety, health, civil rights, and other important safeguards.

We must also continue to decentralize our government, to make it more flexible and responsive towards communities and individuals, and to turn its focus towards empowering Americans to take charge of their own lives.

Faith-based and community-based organizations have always been at the forefront in combating the hardships facing families and communities. Democrats believe it is time that government found ways to harness the power of faith-based organizations in tackling social ills such as drug addiction, juvenile violence, and homelessness. However, in contrast to the Republicans, Democrats believe that partnerships with faith-based organizations should augment — not replace — government programs, should respect First Amendment protections, and should never use taxpayer funds to proselytize or to support discrimination.

Valuing Work

Democrats believe in hard work and we believe that work must pay. It is what has made America great. There is a basic bargain at the heart of the American story — hard work should be both required and rewarded. Democrats also believe that those who do work hard should not be stuck in place — they should get ahead. And those who work hard should have a voice in their workplace.

Supporting Working Families. Democrats know that workers' freedom to choose a voice at work is a fundamental American right that must never be threatened, never be obstructed, never be taken away. From the Industrial Age to the Information Age, unions have given working people the chance to improve their living standards and have a voice on the job. The Clinton-Gore Administration stopped the Team Act, defeated a national right-to-work law, and fought for the resources to enforce worker protections. Al Gore will protect our wage and hour laws, including the forty-hour workweek and overtime requirements, and stand firm in support of the Davis-Bacon act and the Service Contract act. He has also proposed reforming government contracting rules to ensure that taxpayer dollars do not go to companies that break basic labor laws.

Democrats have always believed in making work pay.

We are fighting for a new ergonomic standard and whistle-blower protections. We have stood up for the National Labor Relations Board and fought to protect the right of working families to participate in the political process when it was under attack.

Now we must go further — not just playing defense against misguided Republican attempts to set back the cause of workers' rights, but moving the ball forward. We need a new national law banning permanent striker replacement workers — so that workers' rights to organize into a union and bargain with their employers are never compromised. While we have made the workplace the safest ever, we need to further increase workplace safety. We should stiffen penalties for employer interference with the right to organize and violations of other worker rights. We must also reform labor laws to protect workers' rights to exercise their voices and organize into unions by providing for a more level playing field between management and labor during organizing drives, and facilitating the ability of workers to organize and to bargain collectively.

Rewarding Work for All. Democrats believe in an economy that works for everyone and gives everyone a chance to work. We have made a good start by fighting for the Earned Income Tax Credit which has helped millions of American families work their way out of poverty. We won the battle for increasing the minimum wage.

Now we must do more. We must bring all Americans who are willing to work hard into the circle of prosperity by more fully extend the benefit of the Earned Income Tax Credit to working families, again raising the minimum wage, and giving American workers the skills they need to make it in today's economy. We will vigorously enforce protections against on-the-job discrimination, reassert our belief in an equal day's pay for an equal day's work, seek to prevent the exploitation of workers, and ensure that the nation's worker protection laws are enforced.

Democrats believe that one way we value and reward hard work is to modernize, strengthen, and sustain the nation's unemployment compensation system — a bedrock protection against poverty for millions of workers and their families. Today, the system serves far fewer working families than in the past and many especially vulnerable workers — such as low wage workers, seasonal employees, contingent workers, and women — are especially likely to fall outside the system's protective safety net. Democrats believe we must fight to update and upgrade the nation's unemployment system, to stabilize its funding, extend eligibility to more workers, and improve benefits. We know that even as the economy changes and expands, millions of workers will continue to labor in jobs that pay low wages and may not require significant education or skills. Many of these workers are women, people of color, or recent immigrants. These workers provide invaluable services to American society and their work has great dignity. Democrats are committed to ensuring that these workers — no less than their counterparts in more highly-skilled, better paid positions — are treated with dignity, respect, and fairness on the job. Democrats also believe that workers in temporary, part-time, and contract jobs should be treated fairly and earn the wages and benefits they deserve because of the jobs they do.

Requiring Work from All. With Bill Clinton and Al Gore in the White House, we changed the nation's welfare system — transforming the program into one that encourages and promotes work. Since 1993, the welfare rolls have fallen to their lowest levels in over 30 years. Today, millions of parents now have the dignity of a paycheck, rather than the stigma of a welfare check. The next step is to help these new workers move into the economic mainstream so that they can support their families. It is part of our vision of abolishing poverty. Al Gore is committed to helping new workers and those still on the rolls get help with childcare, transportation and other supports to ensure that anyone who can work, does work. Democrats also believe that we must continue the fight to restore fairness to legal immigrants — these Americans also deserve access to the American dream.

Our fundamental mission is to expand prosperity, not government. But the choices government makes can help or hurt prosperity. For the past eight years, Americans have counted on Democrats to make the right choices. The resulting prosperity is clear. Now, in another moment of big choices, Democrats stand ready to lead again — with a record of results and a vision for the future.

Progress

Eight years ago, many citizens had come to accept the idea that America's best days were behind her: that crime, welfare, teen births, divisiveness and irresponsibility would continue to rise; that our air and water would keep getting dirtier; and that our essential social safety net programs were fated to go broke.

Instead, with the leadership of today's Democratic Party, the past decade has seen not just a rebirth of American prosperity, but a new season of progress in meeting our challenges and living up to our obligations. Crime is down to its lowest levels in a generation — the longest decline on record, teen births are down seven years in a row, adoptions are up by 30 percent, millions of Americans have moved off the welfare rolls and onto the payrolls. America is not just better off, it is better.

But Democrats know that it must be better still. So we want to use this moment to bring even more progress to America. To make America safer, healthier, more secure. To clean up our environment and our politics. To make the job of parents easier and to bring us together as one America.

Fighting Crime

Democrats believe government's most basic duty is to establish law, order, and freedom and keep citizens safe from crime. When crime is rampant, families are forced off the streets and behind closed doors. When children are ducking for cover, they have a hard time reaching for their dreams. When people are afraid to walk in their own neighborhood, communities are robbed of the basic sense of decency and togetherness. When an overburdened justice system lets thugs off easy, good parents have a harder time teaching their children right from wrong.

Bill Clinton and Al Gore took office determined to turn the tide in the battle against crime, drugs, and disorder in our communities. They put in place a tougher more comprehensive strategy than anything tried before, a strategy to fight crime on every single front: more police on the streets to thicken the thin blue line between order and disorder, tougher punishments — including the death penalty — for those that dare to terrorize the innocent, and smarter prevention to stop crime before it even starts.

They stood up to the gun lobby, to pass the Brady Bill and ban deadly assault weapons — and stopped nearly half a million felons, fugitives, and stalkers from buying guns. They fought for and won the biggest anti-drug budgets in history, every single year. They funded new prison cells, and expanded the death penalty for cop killers and terrorists.

Here are the results of that strategy: serious crime is down seven years in a row, to its lowest level in a quarter-century. Violent crime is down by 24 percent. The murder rate is down to levels unseen since the mid-1960's. The number of juveniles committing homicides with guns is down by nearly 60 percent. But we have just begun to fight the forces of lawlessness and violence. We cannot go back to the finger-pointing and failed strategies that led to that steep rise in crime in the Bush-Quayle years. We can't surrender to the right wing Republicans who threatened funding for new police, who tried to gut crime prevention, and who would invite the NRA into the Oval Office. Nor will we go back to the old approach which was tough on the causes of crime, but not tough enough on crime itself.

With Al Gore as President, America won't go back. We will move forward. We will fight to increase the number of community police on our streets. We will fight to give police the high-tech tools and the training they need to keep our streets safe and our families secure. We will toughen the laws against serious and violent crime to restore the sense of order that says to children as well as to criminals: don't even think about committing a crime here. We will reform a justice system that spills half a million prisoners back onto our streets each year — many of them addicted to drugs, unrehabilitated, and just waiting to commit another crime. We will make schools safe havens for students to learn and teachers to teach. We believe that in death penalty cases, DNA testing should be used in all appropriate circumstances, and defendants should have effective assistance of counsel. In all death row cases, we encourage thorough post-conviction reviews. We will put the rights of victims and families first again. And we will push for more crime prevention, to stop the next generation of crime before it's too late.

Victims' Rights. We need a criminal justice system that both upholds our Constitution and reflects our values. Too often, we bend over backward to protect the right of criminals, but pay no attention to those who are hurt the most. Al Gore believes in a Victims' Rights Amendment to the United States Constitution — one that is consistent with fundamental Constitutional protections. Victims must have a voice in trial and other proceedings, their safety must be a factor in the sentencing and release of their attackers, they must be notified when an offender is released back into their community, they must have a right to compensation from their attacker.

Our justice system should place victims and their families in their rightful place.

Ending the Revolving Door. We have to test prisoners for drugs while they are in jail, treat them for addictions, and break up the drug rings inside our prison system. Drug and alcohol abuse are implicated in the crimes of 80 percent of the criminals behind bars. Al Gore believes we should make prisoners a simple deal: get clean to get out, stay clean to stay out. And this deal should be non-negotiable.

We should do even more to make sure that when criminals leave jail, they leave a life of crime behind. We should impose strict supervision of those who have just been released on parole — and insist that they obey the law and stay off drugs. In return, we should help them make it in the workplace. Al Gore believes that ending the revolving door, in combination with more determined efforts at prevention, will both combat crime and ultimately reduce rates of incarceration that are so tragically high in many communities.

Fighting the Scourge of Drugs and Gangs. We should send a strong message to every American child: drugs are wrong, and drugs can kill you. We need to dry up drug demand, hold up drugs at the border, and break up the drug rings that are spreading poison on our streets. We should open more drug courts, to speed justice for drug-related crimes; double the number of drug hotspots where we aggressively target our enforcement efforts; expand drug treatment for at-risk youth; and make sure that all of our school zones are drug-free zones — by stiffening the penalties to those who would use children to peddle drugs, and those who would sell drugs anywhere near our schools. We know that to dry up drug demand, we must provide drug treatment upon demand. To empower communities protect themselves from organized criminal conduct, the Democrats support giving communities relief against gang related crimes. We should be tough on drugs no matter which form they take and should not discriminate in sentencing.

Strong and Sensible Gun Laws. A shocking level of gun violence on our streets and in our schools has shown America the need to keep guns away from those who shouldn't have them — in ways that respect the rights of hunters, sportsmen, and legitimate gun owners. The Columbine tragedy struck America's heart, but in its wake Republicans have done nothing to keep guns away from those who should not have them.

Democrats believe that we should fight gun crime on all fronts — with stronger laws and stronger enforcement. That's why Democrats fought and passed the Brady Law and the Assault Weapons Ban. We increased federal, state, and local gun crime prosecution by 22 percent since 1992. Now gun crime is down by 35 percent.

Now we must do even more. We need mandatory child safety locks, to protect our children.

We should require a photo license I.D., a full background check, and a gun safety test to buy a new handgun in America. We support more federal gun prosecutors, ATF agents and inspectors, and giving states and communities another 10,000 prosecutors to fight gun crime.

Ending Racial Profiling. Good policing demands mutual trust and respect between the community and the police. We shouldn't let the acts of a few rogue officers undermine that trust or the reputation of the outstanding work of the vast majority of our dedicated men and women in blue. That is why we need to end the unjust practice of racial profiling in America — because it's not only unfair, it is inconsistent with America's community policing success, it is a violation of the basic American principle of innocent until proven guilty, it views Americans as members of groups instead of as individuals, and it is just plain shoddy policing. We believe that all law enforcement agencies in America should adopt a zero-tolerance policy toward racial profiling.

Hate Crimes. The very purpose of hate crimes is to dehumanize and stigmatize — not only to wound the victim, but also to distort the American conscience. Every crime is a danger to Americans' lives and liberty. Hate crimes are more than assaults on people, they are assaults on the very idea of America. They should be punished with extra force. Protections should include hate violence based on gender, disability or sexual orientation. And the Republican Congress should stop standing in the way of this pro-civil rights, anti-crime legislation.

Protecting Our Most Vulnerable Citizens. Our most vulnerable deserve special protections. We need tougher penalties against all sex offenders. We should raise the penalties for those who commit crimes against the elderly. We should give federal prosecutors new tools to fight fraud and abuse. We should move aggressively to shut down fraudulent telemarketers who target the elderly. We believe that we must overcome constitutional objections and reenact a strong new law to combat violence against women. And if you commit any violent crime in front of a child, you should pay an even higher price for it: more time in jail.

Ending Domestic Violence. Violence in the home is an often silent terror in the lives of millions.

We have to make sure that all battered women have the legal protection and the support they need to be safe in their own communities, and to keep their attackers away. By stopping domestic violence, we can also break the generational cycle of violence. We know that when children grow up in abusive families, they are more likely to become abusers themselves.

Stopping Crime Before it Starts. Democrats also know that all Americans are better off if we stop crime before it claims new victims, rather than focusing single-mindedly on pursuing perpetrators after the harm is done. That is why we are firmly committed to sound and proven crime-prevention strategies that are good for all Americans. Solid investments in children and youth, in job creation, and in skills development are powerful antidotes to crime.

Judges and the Supreme Court. We will fight to fill the vacancies on the federal bench to make sure we have enough judges to promptly decide all cases and to end Republican delays in the Senate that have kept qualified nominees, especially women and minorities, waiting literally for years for a Senate vote. Democrats oppose efforts to strip the federal courts of jurisdiction to decide critical issues affecting workers, immigrants, veterans and others of access to justice.

And, unlike Republicans, Al Gore will appoint justices to the Supreme Court who have a demonstrated concern for and commitment to the individual rights protected by our Constitution, including the right to privacy.

Valuing our Families

Government does not raise children, families do. But government can help make the hardest job in the world — being a parent — a little easier. Today, families come in all different shapes and sizes, but they all face similar challenges. Government should be on the side of parents — making it easier for them to raise their children and pass down their values. With Democrats in the White House, we have passed the Family and Medical Leave law, which has been used by 20 million Americans to care for a newborn baby or a sick loved one. Al Gore led efforts to create the voluntary TV ratings system, to put the V-chip in all new TV sets sold in America so that parents can stop the assault of graphic images in their children's lives, and to insist on a quick and easy way for all Internet users to be able to make offensive web sites off-limits to their children.

Balancing Work and Family. If we are to value our families, we have to make much more progress. Strengthening America's families means helping parents make time for their children.

We need to find new ways to help parents balance work and family so that they will have time to pass on the right values to their children. Already millions of Americans have benefitted from the Family and Medical Leave law, now we need to expand it so that it covers parent-teacher visits and children's routine medical appointments. And we will extend the law to cover more employers so that more working families enjoy this vital protection during times of family and medical need. We should urge employers to make workplaces more parent-friendly; explore strategies, including voluntary initiatives and policy reforms, that can provide income support for workers during periods of family and medical leave; call on parents to be more involved in their children's learning; and fix the "marriage penalty" so that parents can spend more time at home and less time trying to make ends meet. We should not penalize families by forcing couples to pay more in taxes just because they have made the sacred commitment of marriage to one another. We should also provide grants to community and faith-based organizations to help couples prepare for and strengthen their marriage and relationships, become better parents, and reduce domestic violence.

Child Care and Early Childhood Education. Democrats believe in making child care more affordable through targeted tax cuts and other investments, in improving the safety and quality of child care centers, in requiring accountability so that federal monies and subsidy payments are effectively used to provide quality in child care, in ensuring that children start school ready to read, and in giving a helping hand to parents who decided to stay at home with their children.

We need both higher pay and higher standards for child care workers — and they need to get training so that they can do their jobs well. It is a priority of the Democratic Party to fully fund Head Start.

Eldercare. The Baby Boomers are the first generation with more parents than children. Many families are doing all they can to help for and care for their elderly parents. These families are doing the right thing — and America must be on their side. We must do more to support the families and individuals who are caring for relatives suffering from long-term illnesses at home or at institutions. We should provide Americans with long-term care needs and their caregivers a $3,000 tax credit. We should hold those who care for our nation's elderly to the highest standards and improve these workers' wages, benefits, training, and working conditions. We should make sure that every community in the country has a program to offer caregivers critical information, referrals, and respite from the difficult work of caring for a loved one.

Fatherhood. Promoting responsible fatherhood is the critical next phase of welfare reform and one of the most important things we can do to reduce child poverty. Three times more men acknowledged paternity in 1998 than in 1993. This is a first step toward giving to a child the emotional and financial support a father must give to merit the name.

Democrats believe in cracking down on deadbeats who abandon their children. So we must require all fathers who owe child support to pay or go to work; strengthen child support enforcement, including increasing the amount of child support that gets paid directly to poor families; and make it harder for parents who owe child support to get new credit cards. However, we also recognize that, in addition to dead beat dads there are dead broke dads. Thus Democrats support helping those men who want to reconnect with their families and who want to become a positive force in the lives of their children.

Responsible Entertainment. Parents are struggling to pass on the right values in a culture that sometimes seems to practically scream that chaos and cruelty are cool. Democrats have worked to give parents the tools to have more control over the images their children are exposed to. Parents and the entertainment industry must accept more responsibility. Many parents are not aware of the resources available to them, such as the V-chip technology in television sets and Internet filtering devices, that can help them shield children from violent entertainment. The entertainment industry must accept more responsibility and exercise more self-restraint, by strictly enforcing movie ratings, by taking a close look at violence in its own advertising, and by determining whether the ratings systems are allowing too many children to be exposed to too much violence and cruelty.

Democrats call for the reinstatement of the Fairness Doctrine by the Federal Communications Commission. We believe in public support for the arts, including the National Endowment for the Arts and the National Endowment for the Humanities. Public and private investment in creativity and cultural heritage — the arts and humanities — is an investment in the education of our children, in the well being of our communities, in the strength of our economy, and in spreading the dream of democracy throughout the world.

Accessible, Affordable Quality Health Care

For fifty years, the Democratic Party has been engaged in a battle to provide the kind of health care a great nation owes its people. We reaffirm our commitment to take concrete, specific, realistic steps to move toward the day when every American has affordable health coverage. And we will not rest until the job is done.

During the past eight years, Democrats have helped Americans keep their doctor when they lose or change jobs. We passed the Child Health Insurance Program to help states provide health coverage to millions of uninsured children — the largest single investment in children's health in a 35 years. We kept solvent a Medicare system that was scheduled to go bankrupt this year. We brought immunization rates to an all-time high.

In contrast, the Republican Party has refused to use one penny of the surplus to secure the solvency of Medicare and has supported plans that would increase Medicare premiums, force elderly patients into HMOs and raise the eligibility age for Medicare to 67. They have adamantly opposed the Patients' Bill of Rights and proposed instead a mirage "Patients' Bill of Goods" that would leave out a real guarantee of the right to see a specialist and assurances that you can go to the nearest emergency room — and leave out 135 million Americans in the cold.

Instead of the guaranteed, universal prescription drug benefit that Democrats believe should be added to Medicare, Republicans are proposing to leave to insurance companies the decisions about whether and where a drug benefit might be offered, what it would include, and how much it would cost. Studies suggest that less than half of seniors will be able to use this benefit.

Universal Health Coverage. There is much more left to do. We must redouble our efforts to bring the uninsured into coverage step-by-step and as soon as possible. We should guarantee access to affordable health care for every child in America. We should expand coverage to working families, including more Medicaid assistance to help with the transition from welfare to work. And we should also seek to ensure that dislocated workers are provided affordable health care. We should make health care accessible and affordable for small businesses. In addition, Americans aged 55 to 65 — the fastest growing group of uninsured — should be allowed to buy into the Medicare program to get the coverage they need. By taking these steps, we can move our nation closer to the goal of providing universal health coverage for all Americans.

A Real Patients' Bill of Rights. Medical decisions should be made by patients and their doctors and nurses, not accountants and bureaucrats at the end of a phone line a thousand miles away. It is time we meaningfully addressed concerns about the quality of care and about the decline of patient, access, trust, and satisfaction. People need to get the health care they need, when they need it, without having to leap endless hurdles. Americans need a real, enforceable Patients' Bill of Rights with the right to see a specialist, the right to appeal decisions to an outside board, guaranteed coverage of emergency room care, and the right to sue when they are unfairly denied coverage.

Al Gore will work with a wide range of stakeholders to develop a national strategy to reduce medical errors, including appropriate public reporting, analysis of root causes, and development of error prevention models. Democrats also believe that doctors, nurses, and other health care practitioners must be allowed to advocate freely on behalf of their patients.

Protecting and Strengthening Medicare. It is time we ended the tragedy of elderly Americans being forced to choose between meals and medication. It is time we modernized Medicare with a new prescription drug benefit. This is an essential step in making sure that the best new cures and therapies are available to our seniors and disabled Americans. We cannot afford to permit our seniors to receive only part of the medical care they need.

Democrats believe Medicare is worth fighting for — and worth saving. With the number of Americans on Medicare expected to double in the next 35 years, Al Gore has stepped up and taken responsibility by proposing a Medicare Lock Box that would insure Medicare surpluses are used for Medicare — and not for pork barrel spending or tax giveaways. We should also modernize Medicare by promoting competitive prices and remain vigilant against Medicare fraud.

Fighting Diseases. Our newest medical miracles give us the chance to make significant progress in battling some of the most dreaded diseases. Democrats believe that we must invest in biomedical research and continue to fight and conquer everything from AIDS to Alzheimer's to Diabetes to Parkinson's to spinal cord injuries. We must speed up the development of new drugs and get them to patients sooner while maintaining essential health and safety standards. We should allow stem cell research to make important new discoveries. We should expand prevention and widen access to clinical trials. And we should devote more resources to eliminating disease disparities among racial and ethnic groups.

Our nation must do all it can to focus its efforts on fighting HIV and AIDS. A top priority for Democrats will be the continued investment in research, prevention, care, treatment, and we are deeply committed to the search for a cure. Democrats continue to support important programs such as the Ryan White CARE Act, the Housing Opportunities for People with AIDS program, and incentives to return Americans with HIV/AIDS to work.

For a generation, America has been waging a war on cancer. Al Gore believes it is time we started winning it. Because of astonishing scientific breakthroughs, the day that America is cancer-free is within reach. With the completion of the draft of the human genome, we are on the verge of cracking cancer's secret code. Democrats believe in taking advantage of this progress by doubling federal cancer research.

Fighting Teen Smoking. Al Gore is committed to dramatically reducing teen smoking in America. It is time we treated underage tobacco use like the health crisis it is. That's why we need to give the FDA full authority to keep cigarettes away from children. We must match the power of big tobacco's advertising dollars with a counter-campaign that tells kids the truth about the dangers of smoking and the risks of cancer to themselves and to others through second-hand smoke. And we should double our investment in efforts to prevent teen smoking and break the deadly grip of nicotine addiction.

State attorneys general across America have recovered billions of dollars from the tobacco industry for damages caused by tobaccos' advertising directed at our children and for the death and disease created by cigarettes. Now Republicans are trying to stop the United States Justice Department from pursuing similar litigation to hold the tobacco companies accountable for the damages they have caused to American taxpayers. We believe it is wrong to insulate the tobacco companies from liability for their wrongdoing.

Mental Health. Mental illness has long been concealed behind a shroud of silence and shame.

Mental illness affects nearly one in five Americans each year, but nearly two-thirds of those Americans affected by mental disorders do not receive help. When mental illness goes untreated, undiagnosed, and unmentioned, people are denied the opportunity to live full lives and our nation is denied their full contribution. Democrats believe in supporting families caring for loved ones with mental illness by strengthening our community mental health system, providing access to full mental health coverage for every child in America, giving teachers and schools more mental health resources, and ensuring that mental illness and physical illness are treated equally by our nation's health plans.

Disabilities. Democrats believe that we must fight to ensure that people with disabilities can meet their full potential and participate fully in the American dream. For people with disabilities accessing affordable health insurance is the greatest barrier to returning to work. That is why we fought to assure that people with disabilities do not lose their health care when they return to work. Democrats also support tax credits and grants to pay for rehabilitation and work-related expenses for people with disabilities. And we support all efforts to implement the Supreme Court's Olmstead decision and to make personal assistance services and supports available to people with disabilities in their homes and communities — because no one should be kept in a nursing home or institution if they prefer to live in the community with the necessary supports.

Choice

The Democratic Party stands behind the right of every woman to choose, consistent with Roe v. Wade, and regardless of ability to pay. We believe it is a fundamental constitutional liberty that individual Americans — not government — can best take responsibility for making the most difficult and intensely personal decisions regarding reproduction. This year's Supreme Court rulings show to us all that eliminating a woman's right to choose is only one justice away. That's why the stakes in this election are as high as ever.

Our goal is to make abortion less necessary and more rare, not more difficult and more dangerous. We support contraceptive research, family planning, comprehensive family life education, and policies that support healthy childbearing. The abortion rate is dropping. Now we must continue to support efforts to reduce unintended pregnancies, and we call on all Americans to take personal responsibility to meet this important goal.

The Democratic Party is a party of inclusion. We respect the individual conscience of each American on this difficult issue, and we welcome all our members to participate at every level of our party. This is why we are proud to put into our platform the very words which Republicans refused to let Bob Dole put into their 1996 platform and which they refused to even consider putting in their platform in 2000: "While the party remains steadfast in its commitment to advancing its historic principles and ideals, we also recognize that members of our party have deeply held and sometimes differing views on issues of personal conscience like abortion and capital punishment. We view this diversity of views as a source of strength, not as a sign of weakness, and we welcome into our ranks all Americans who may hold differing positions on these and other issues. Recognizing that tolerance is a virtue, we are committed to resolving our differences in a spirit of civility, hope and mutual respect."

Protecting Our Environment

Democrats know that for all of us there is no more solemn responsibility than that of stewards of God's creation. That is why we have worked for eight years to produce the cleanest environment in decades: with cleaner air, cleaner water, and a safer food supply; a record number of toxic waste dumps cleaned up; new smog and soot standards so that children with asthma and the elderly would be able to live better lives; and a strong international treaty to begin combating global warming — in a way that is market-based and realistic, and does not lead to economic cooling.

From the Redwood forests to the Florida Everglades, from the Grand Canyon to Yellowstone to Yosemite, we have protected millions of acres of our precious natural lands. We stopped development in America's last wild places. Teddy Roosevelt saw our national parks as the playground of the people — there for average families to enjoy with camping and hiking. Today's Republicans see them as the playground of the powerful — there for big businesses to exploit with drilling and mining. The Republicans have tried to sell off national parks; gut air, water, and endangered species protections; let polluters off the hook; and put the special interests ahead of the people's interest. They are wrong. Out natural environment is too precious and too important to waste. Al Gore is committed to restoring the Everglades; protecting the coasts of California and Florida and the Arctic National Wildlife Refuge from oil and gas drilling; and preserving our untouched forests, including the Tongass, from logging and development. With regard to public lands, Democrats believe that communities, environmental interests, and government agencies should work together to protect our public resources, critical habitat areas, and wildlands while ensuring the vitality of local economies. We will work together to find land-based alternatives and decontamination technologies that will permanently end the ocean disposal of contaminated dredge spoils.

Once Americans were led to believe they had to make a choice between the economy and the environment. They now know that this is a false choice. But there is a real choice to make in 2000: whether we will protect our environment in ways that are practical and achievable or go back to the policies that led to generations of environmental devastation and degradation.

We have to do what's right for our Earth because it is the moral thing to do. It involves all of our lives — from the simple security of having clean safe, reliable, affordable electricity for your home; to America's ability to build and sell the best new clean cars, trucks, and technology to the world; to guarding our children from the summer smog that is made worse by global warming, and securing for our grandchildren the expectation of a joyful array of seasons that we took for granted when we grew up ourselves.

Democrats believe we must give Americans incentives to invest in driving more fuel-efficient cars, trucks, and sport utility vehicles; living in more energy-efficient homes, and using more environmentally-sound appliances and equipment. We need to clean up aging power plants. We must invest in rebuilding and improving our transportation infrastructure and ensure that we adequately maintain these systems for the future. Americans need and rely on diverse transportation sources, and our public infrastructure priorities should reflect that diversity.

We should invest in roads, bridges, light rail systems, cleaner buses, the aviation system, our national passenger railroad, Amtrak, and high-speed trains that would give Americans choices — freeing them from traffic, smog-choked cities, and being held hostage to foreign oil. We should ensure that urban communities affected by the presence of airports which create increased levels of noise and pollution be provided mitigation support to address these concerns. We must also ensure that we maintain adequate public funding and public administration of publicly operated and delivered transportation services, without gutting collective bargaining agreements or long-standing worker-protections. In these and other areas, we will encourage project labor agreements, fostering labor-management cooperation, quality development, and efficient use of public monies. Today, technology has advanced to the point that we can drive the kind of cars we like and live in the kind of houses we like — while being kind to the earth. We should use some of our budget surplus to help Americans take advantage of these new opportunities. With the right investments, these new environmentally-friendly technologies can create new jobs for American workers.

America is blessed with abundant low-cost sources of coal, petroleum, and natural gas, but we must use them wisely and ensure that changes in the energy sector promote a workforce whose skills are expanded, utilized, and rewarded. Democrats believe that with the right incentives to encourage the development and deployment of clean energy technologies, we can make all our energy sources cleaner, safer, and healthier for our children. This responsibility includes disposing of nuclear waste in a scientifically-sound manner in accordance with standards designed to protect human health and the environment.

And we must dramatically reduce climate-disrupting and health-threatening pollution in this country, while making sure that all nations of the world participate in this effort. Environmental standards should be raised throughout the world in order to preserve the Earth and to prevent a destructive race to the bottom wherein countries compete for production and jobs based on who can do the least to protect the environment. There will be no new bureaucracies, no new agencies, no new organizations. But there will be action and there will be progress. The Earth truly is in the balance — and we are the guardians of that harmony.

Eight of the ten hottest years ever recorded have occurred during the past ten years. Scientists predict a daunting range of likely effects from global warming. Much of Florida and Louisiana submerged underwater. More record floods, droughts, heat waves, and wildfires. Diseases and pests spreading to new areas. Crop failures and famines. Melting glaciers, stronger storms, and rising seas. These are not Biblical plagues. They are the predicted result of human actions. They can be prevented only with a new set of human actions — big choices and new thinking.

Working with the America's great automakers, Al Gore has led the Partnership for a New Generation of Vehicles which has helped spur the development of high-performing cars that get far better gas mileage while meeting emissions standards. Now we need to give Americans help in being able to afford these new cars — getting them out of the showrooms, onto the streets, and into our driveways. At the same time, we are committed to improving fuel economy in a way that preserves and creates jobs for American workers, and delivers products that consumers want to buy. To further this kind of progress, we now need the oil industry to join us in producing much cleaner fuels that will allow automotive environmental equipment to achieve the maximum possible reductions in emissions.

We have also created a new 21st Century Truck Initiative to build highly-efficient heavy duty pick-up and delivery trucks, even long-haul 18-wheelers. Now we need to work in partnership with industry to create a new generation of mass transit and a new generation of cleaner, more reliable power systems. Al Gore wants to swap every dirty, smoke-belching city bus for a cleaner, less polluting one.

Renewing Our Democracy and Campaign Finance Reform

In the year 2000, along with all the other big choices they have to make, Americans will be making a choice about who's running their country: the people or the special interests, the voters or the lobbyists, the many or the few. We must restore American's faith in their own democracy by providing real and comprehensive campaign finance reform, creating fairer and more open elections, and breaking the link between special interests and political influence. The Republicans will have none of this. Instead of limiting the influence of the powerful on our politics, they want to raise contribution limits so even more special interest money can flow into campaigns. The big-time lobbyists and special interest were so eager to invest in George W. Bush and deliver campaign cash to him hand-over-fist that he became the first major party nominee to pull out of the primary election financing structure and refuse to abide by campaign spending limits.

In this year's presidential primaries it became clear that the Republican establishment is violently opposed to John McCain's call for reforming our democracy. Al Gore supports John McCain's campaign for political reform. In fact, the McCain-Feingold bill is the very first piece of legislation that a President Al Gore will submit to Congress — and he will fight for it until it becomes the law of the land.

Then he will go even further — much further. He will insist on tough new lobbying reform, publicly-guaranteed TV time for debates and advocacy by candidates, and a crackdown on special interest issue ads. Most boldly of all, Al Gore has proposed a public-private, nonpartisan Democracy Endowment which will raise money from Americans and finance Congressional elections — with no other contributions allowed to candidates who accept the funding. This will let our politics be free from the influence of special interests and let Americans believe in their own democracy again.

Just as our country has been the chief apostle of democracy in the world, we must lead by example at home. This begins with our nation's capital. The citizens of the District of Columbia are entitled to autonomy in the conduct of their civic affairs, full political representation as Americans who are fully taxed, and statehood. Puerto Rico has been under U.S. sovereignty for over a century and Puerto Ricans have been U.S. citizens since 1917, but the island's ultimate status still has not been determined and its 3.9 million residents still do not have voting representation in their national government. These disenfranchised citizens — who have contributed greatly to our country in war and peace — are entitled to the permanent and fully democratic status of their choice. Democrats will continue to work in the White House and Congress to clarify the options and enable them to choose and to obtain such a status from among all realistic options. Democrats believe the people of Guam, American Samoa, and the Virgin Islands have a right to be fully self-governing. We are committed to fair treatment in economic and social policies as well as improvement in federal-territorial relations in accordance with the needs of each area. Elected representatives of these areas will be regularly consulted on policies, laws, and treaties that affect the areas and we will ensure fair treatment for our fellow citizens in the territories.

Building One America

Democrats believe that God has given the people of our nation not only a chance, but a mission to prove to men and women throughout this world that people of different racial and ethnic backgrounds, of all faiths and creeds, can not only work and live together, but can enrich and ennoble both themselves and our purpose. America's diversity is expanding, yet amidst important signs of progress, there is widespread evidence of persistent discrimination, growing racial segregation of our schools and neighborhoods, and dream-crushing barriers to opportunity.

We cannot — we dare not — remain a nation divided. Our vision is of an America healed of hatreds and misunderstanding, with equality and opportunity so rich that legacies of discrimination and exclusion will be found only in history books, and not in our communities.

To that end, Democrats support creation of a commission of distinguished scholars and civic leaders to examine the history of slavery, discrimination, and exclusion suffered by all minorities; to report on the continuing effects of those tragic chapters in our history; and to make appropriate recommendations on behalf of the American people.

Welcoming Our Newest Americans. Immigrants enrich the tapestry of American life, making our economy more vibrant, our workplaces more productive, and our nation stronger. We believe that all levels of government, in partnership with the private and voluntary sectors, must devise and pursue a comprehensive immigrant integration agenda that will make the newest Americans full participants in the nation's mainstream. That's why Democrats support reforming the INS to provide better services, and investing the resources needed to reduce the backlog of citizenship applications from nearly two years to three months. Democrats also support increased resources for English language courses, which not only help newcomers learn our common language but also help us promote our common values. And, we believe that family reunification should continue to be the cornerstone of our legal immigration system.

Democrats believe in an effective immigration system that balances a strong enforcement of our laws with fair and evenhanded treatment of immigrants and their families. The Clinton-Gore administration provided long overdue leadership in dramatically improving border management and law enforcement, including a major expansion of the Border Patrol and curbs on abuses of the asylum process. We also recognize that the current system fails to effectively control illegal immigration, has serious adverse impacts on state and local services, and on many communities and workers, and has led to an alarming number of deaths of migrants on the border. Democrats are committed to re-examining and fixing these failed policies.

We must punish employers who engage in a pattern and practice of recruiting undocumented workers in order to intimidate and exploit them, and provide strengthened protections for immigrant workers, including whistleblower protections. Doing so enhances conditions for everyone in the workplace. We believe that any increases in H1-B visas must be temporary, must address only genuine shortages of highly skilled workers, and must include worker protections.

They must also be accompanied by other immigration fairness measures and by increased fees to train American workers for high skill jobs. The Democratic Party is committed to assuring an adequate, predictable supply of agricultural labor while protecting American farm workers who are among the poorest and more vulnerable in our society. We reject calls for guest worker programs that lead to exploitation, and instead call for adjusting the status of immigrants with deep roots in the country. We should have equitable asylum policies that treat people the same whether they have fled violence from the right or left. And we support restoration of basic due process protections and essential benefits for legal immigrants, so that immigrants are no longer subject to deportation for minor offenses, often committed decades ago without opportunity for any judicial review, and are eligible to receive safety net services supported by their tax dollars. Fighting for Civil Rights and Inclusion. Passage of the Civil Rights Act of 1964 was one of the proudest moments of our nation's history and a sterling testament to our aspirations as a people. Yet, despite undeniable progress over the last several decades, inequality and polarization nevertheless persist in far too many American workplaces, schools, and communities. Over the last eight years, we have fought hard to end discrimination. We have increased funding for civil rights enforcement — so that the laws on our books are not just pleasant words, but pledges of justice. Al Gore has strongly opposed efforts to roll back affirmative action programs. He knows that the way to lift this nation up is not by pulling the weakest down, but by continuing to expand opportunities for everyone who wants to achieve.

The Clinton-Gore Administration has appointed the most diverse administration in American history, demonstrating that pursuing excellence means including the all of the best that our nation has to offer.

Al Gore and the Democratic Party know that much remains to be done. We must remember we do not have an American to waste. We continue to lead the fight to end discrimination on the basis of race, gender, religion, age, ethnicity, disability, and sexual orientation. The Democratic Party has always supported the Equal Rights Amendment and will continue to do so, and we are committed to ensuring full equality for women and to vigorously enforcing the Americans with Disabilities Act. We support continuation of the White House initiative on Asian Americans and Pacific Islanders. Because every American counts, we will continue to work toward a census that counts every American. We support continued efforts, like the Employment Non-Discrimination Act, to end workplace discrimination against gay men and lesbians. We support the full inclusion of gay and lesbian families in the life of the nation. This would include an equitable alignment of benefits. We recognize the importance of new battles against forms of discrimination and disadvantage that stand as barriers to communities and families, such as environmental injustices and predatory lending practices. And we will fight for full funding and full staffing of the Equal Employment Opportunity Commission and other civil rights enforcement agencies so they can do their job of ensuring that America lives up to its creed of equal rights and equal opportunity for all.

The Democratic Party proudly upholds its tradition of support for the first Americans. The sovereignty of the American Indians and Native Alaskans and a strong affirmation of the relationship are basic to our approach to the tribal governments. As we move into the 21st century, we have to renew our trust obligations and work to improve the lives of the many Indians who live in terrible poverty. The Democratic Party pledges to continue our work to make a difference in the lives of those who occupied this land before us. We affirm the legal and political relationship between the United States and Native Hawaiians as an important step in the continuing process of reconciliation. We will work to pass legislation establishing a process for Native Hawaiians to reorganize a governing body, freely chosen, expressing their rights to self-determination. The justice we provide the first Americans is a measure of our nation's character, and Democrats believe we should build on the progress of the last eight years.

Forging Common Ground. American citizenship entails both rights and responsibilities and we need to ask every American — from every walk of life — to give something back to their communities and their country. We are committed to expanding AmeriCorps so that more Americans both serve their country and further their educations.

America will become much more diverse in the coming century. But while much is changing, much remains. Our common civic culture — one grounded in the values most Americans share: work, family, personal responsibility, individual liberty, and faith — ties us together. Our common ground — our shared civic institutions — makes us whole. In the years to come, we must celebrate our diversity and focus on strengthening the common values and beliefs that make us one America — one nation, under God, with liberty and justice for all.

Peace

Eight years ago, Americans found themselves between two worlds. After half a century in which we stood up for peace and security all over the globe — taking on the forces of tyranny and terror that imperiled our interests and assaulted our values — the Cold War was over and a new global age was beginning. We needed new ideas and new leadership.

Democrats have provided them. Under the leadership of Bill Clinton and Al Gore, the first light of the 21st Century finds America at peace. More of the world's citizens live in freedom than ever before, and our people and our values are protected by the greatest military force the world has ever known.

Democratic leadership has brought peace and security to Americans and to millions of freedom-loving people around the globe. We achieved victory and ended ethnic cleansing in Kosovo — allowing hundreds of thousands of refugees to return to their homes in safety. We helped achieve historic breakthroughs in the Middle East peace process. We led the efforts that produced the Good Friday Accord in Northern Ireland — offering the best hope yet of ending decades of bloodshed. We are working to build a self-sustaining peace in Bosnia through the implementation of the Dayton Peace accords. We have ended the military dictatorship and given democracy a chance in Haiti. We have made Americans safer by reducing Russian nuclear arsenals. We strengthened and expanded NATO for a new century.

But now is not the time to sound the trumpets of triumph. In the wake of the Cold War, America has entered a new Global Age that is altering our security challenges and creating entirely new issues. Globalization is transforming the international order that defined the 20th century. Today, for both good and ill, our destiny and the destinies of billions of people around the world are increasingly intertwined, and our domestic and international challenges are bound together as never before.

The Democratic Party recognizes that globalization will continue shaping our future. We also believe that the United States has the means and the responsibility to shape globalization so that it reflects the needs and the values of the American people.

Al Gore and the Democratic Party know that we must be able to meet any military challenge from a position of dominance. But Al Gore and the Democratic Party also recognize that there is a new security agenda — threats that affect the entire world and transcend political borders.

During the past century, we have learned that if we wish to avoid war, we must be strong enough to deter aggression, but also farsighted enough to invest in peace. Now it is time to apply this lesson to the new global challenges we face — to shape a new strategy of Forward Engagement to guide our conduct around the world. Forward Engagement means addressing problems early in their development before they become crises, addressing them as close to the source of the problem as possible, and having the forces and resources to deal with these threats as soon after their emergence as possible.

While we must always stand prepared to use our military power when all other options fail, Forward Engagement also means addressing societal and political problems before they evolve into threats to our national security and values — before armed conflict becomes the only way to achieve our goals. And Forward Engagement means drawing on all three main sources of American power — military strength, a vibrant, growing economy, and a free and democratic political system — to advance our objectives around the world.

The Democratic Party believes that America's peace and security depend on our unflagging leadership and engagement in global affairs-and that Forward Engagement is the strategy that must guide us. We must maintain America's economic and military strength. We must also form partnerships to help solve global problems and take advantage of new global opportunities. That means we must deepen our key alliances, develop more constructive relationships with former enemies, and bring together diverse coalitions of nations to deal with new problems. America has a responsibility to lead — and should lead from within the international community.

At a time when new conditions require new thinking, the Republican Party offers little more than outdated positions and a narrow worldview that lets international problems fester.

Some Republicans believe America should turn away from the world. They oppose using our armed forces as part of international solutions, even when regional conflicts threaten our interests and our values.

Other Republicans want America to act unilaterally. They attack the Anti-Ballistic Missile Treaty — even at the risk of precipitating a new nuclear arms race. They voted down the Comprehensive Test Ban Treaty, threatening both our security and our global leadership. They have attempted to sabotage the Clinton-Gore administration's efforts to negotiate with other nations by declaring that any arms control agreement — regardless of content — would be "dead on arrival." Mired in the past, the Republican Party fails to realize that ensuring peace and security for Americans today does not just mean guarding against armies on the march. It means investing in building the global peace. It means addressing the fact that more than 1 billion of the Earth's inhabitants live on less than $1 a day — inviting social dislocation, violence, and war. It means meeting new challenges such as international crime and terrorism, environmental degradation, and pandemic diseases head-on. And it means that Forward Engagement must be the new pole-star of our global strategy.

Neutralizing the Forces That Cause Chaos and Instability

The questions of war and peace among sovereign states are as important to our security as ever. But today America also faces a new set of international issues. Technology's unprecedented power means that lawlessness, diseases, and ecological disruptions — which once were localized — now land on America's doorstep even as they also threaten the stability and security of nations all over the world.

Disruption of the World's Ecological System. The disruption of the world's ecological systems — from the rise of global warming and the consequent damage to our climate balance, to the loss of living species and the depletion of ocean fisheries and forest habitats — continues at a frightening rate. We must act now to protect our Earth while preserving and creating jobs for our people. In 1997, we negotiated the historic Kyoto Protocols, an international treaty that will establish a strong, realistic, and effective framework to reduce greenhouse emissions in an environmentally strong and economically sound way. We are working to develop a broad international effort to take action to meet this threat. Al Gore and the Democratic Party believe we must now ratify those Protocols.

Global Epidemics. Global epidemics constitute another major security threat. Malaria is running out of control in Africa, and antibiotic-resistant strains of tuberculosis are ravaging Russia and other countries.

But the most severe global epidemic is HIV/AIDS. It is more than a health tragedy, it is a threat to global security. AIDS now grips 20 million Africans. Fourteen million have already died, a quarter of them children. Each day, 11,000 more men, women, and children become infected. Diseases like AIDS threaten not just individual citizens, but the very institutions that define and defend the character of society. The Democratic Party believes we can and must do more to prevent transmission, care for those who are ill, and lead in knitting together the scores of AIDS-fighting initiatives into a global campaign to defeat this threat.

Fighting Drugs and Organized Crime. International drug networks and other organized crime syndicates represent a growing threat to the survival of democratic governance. They breed corruption and lawlessness, and they erode the institutions that maintain societal order.

Drug producing nations like Colombia have seen their societies torn apart by the intersection of criminal activity, political discord, and terrorism. And our nation is also afflicted with the violence and hopelessness of drugs. We must continue to combat narco-traffickers, increasing our budget to do so. We must continue to have a strong Drug Czar who can bring together the considerable resources of the U.S. Government in this effort. We must continue to fight those who make the financing of this effort possible such as the money launderers who facilitate the drug trade. We must continue to work with our friends and allies and international organizations to fight the blood money of the drug trade by getting a handle on those nations who turn a blind eye to the financial end of this problem.

We must remember that the drug trade, like other criminal enterprises, fundamentally reflects the economics of hopelessness. Farmers have been drawn to cultivate these crops as a means for economic survival in the absence of other viable alternatives. Al Gore and the Democratic Party understand that no policy of interdiction and prosecution will succeed unless it is combined with robust investment in alternative ways to make a living. We must also build on our efforts to expand the rule of law, fight corruption, and improve democratic governance.

Transforming Our Military

A strong, flexible, and modern military force is the ultimate guarantor of our physical survival and the protection of our interests and values. Today, America's military is the best-trained, best-equipped, most capable, and most ready fighting force in the world. With Bill Clinton and Al Gore in the White House, Democrats reversed a decline in defense spending that began under President Bush, boosted pay and allowances, and provided the funding for a new generation of weapons.

The Democratic Party understands that, good as they are, the armed forces must continue to evolve. They must not only remain prepared for conventional military action, but must sharpen their ability to deal with new missions and new kinds of threats. They must become more agile, more versatile, and must more completely incorporate the revolutionary implications and advantages of American supremacy in information technology.

Recruiting, Training, and Retaining Our Troops. A high-tech fighting force must recruit, train, and retain a professional all-volunteer force of the highest caliber. The Democratic Party understands that in order to do this, military pay must continue to increase. We enacted the largest military pay increase in twenty years — and we must raise pay even more. We need to further reform the military retirement system and improve housing, health care, and childcare benefits to support the general competitiveness of military careers during a period of unprecedented prosperity in the civilian economy. While the number of soldiers and families on food stamps is down by two-thirds over the past decade, it is unacceptable that any member of our armed forces should have to rely on food stamps. Al Gore is committed to equal treatment of all service members and believes all patriotic Americans be allowed to serve their country without discrimination, persecution, and violence.

The Democratic Party honors America's veterans for their selfless willingness to defend the United States and promote our values around the world. We must always remember the debt this nation owes its defenders. Al Gore will expand access to health care for all eligible veterans; pursue the causes of illness suffered by Vietnam and Gulf War veterans; press for more research on diseases caused by exposure to toxic battlefields and treat fairly veterans suffering from those ailments; back research efforts to screen and treat hepatitis C; and expand programs in the areas of mental health, spinal cord injury, and vision impairment. We will streamline the disability claims process to ensure that this nation continues to live up to its sacred commitment to the men and women who served in uniform. We support efforts of the Filipino American Veterans who fought in World War II to obtain equity.

Deploying America's Technological Edge. It is imperative that aging weapons systems — which are now the backbone of our military — be replaced by the oncoming generation of advanced, high-tech weapons which are designed to make sure that our armed forces face any future conflict from a posture of dominance. Al Gore and the Democratic Party will make sure that the military has the most advanced weaponry, sophisticated intelligence, and information systems and, in addition, continues to invest in research and development for future supremacy. By contrast, George W. Bush has talked about "skipping" this generation of weapons — which could mean skipping our responsibility to give our fighting men and women the weapons they need.

We must also ensure that investment in the infrastructure needed to support the military, including our maritime capability, is not ignored. And we must ensure a competitive workforce maintaining high-skilled workers and training programs that will ensure the capability to respond to national security emergencies and defense readiness.

Protecting Our Interests and Securing Our Values. The lessons of the past eight years show that the nation must be prepared to use force when American interests and values are truly at stake.

We cannot be the world's policeman, and we must be discriminating in our approach. But where the stakes are high, when we can assure ourselves that nothing short of military engagement can secure our national interest, when we know that we have the military forces available for the task, when we have made our best efforts to join with allies, and when the cost is proportionate to the objective, we must be ready to act.

Closing the Gates of War

In areas where conflict has raged, comprehensive peace agreements are the foundation for lasting security. Bill Clinton and Al Gore have actively pursued peaceful resolutions to conflicts across the world and have been prepared to go the extra mile on behalf of negotiators seeking peace. Al Gore and the Democratic Party are fundamentally committed to the security of our ally, Israel, and the creation of a comprehensive, just, and lasting peace between Israel and its neighbors. We helped broker the Israel-Jordan Peace Treaty, the Wye River accords, and the Sharm el-Sheik Memorandum, and will continue to work with all parties to make progress towards peace. Our special relationship with Israel is based on the unshakable foundation of shared values and a mutual commitment to democracy, and we will ensure that under all circumstances, Israel retains the qualitative military edge for its national security. Jerusalem is the capital of Israel and should remain an undivided city accessible to people of all faiths. In view of the government of Israel's courageous decision to withdraw from Lebanon, we believe special responsibility now resides with Syria to make a contribution toward peace. The recently-held Camp David summit, while failing to bridge all the gaps between Israel and the Palestinians, demonstrated President Clinton's resolve to do all the United States could do to bring an end to that long conflict. Al Gore, as president, will demonstrate the same resolve. We call on both parties to avoid unilateral actions, such as a unilateral declaration of Palestinian statehood, that will prejudge the outcome of negotiations, and we urge the parties to adhere to their joint pledge to resolve all differences only by good faith negotiations.

In Northern Ireland, we helped facilitate multi-party talks and played an instrumental role in brokering the historic Good Friday Accord, which has greatly enhanced the prospect for peace.

We will continue to work toward implementation of the Accord and provide continued political and economic support for the new institutions involving Northern Ireland, the Republic of Ireland, and Great Britain. Our goal is not merely the laying down of arms, but the joining together of hands in a new political relationship that enables former rivals to govern and thrive together.

We have worked hard and successfully to calm dangerous tensions between our allies Greece and Turkey over issues in the Aegean, and we have never ceased our efforts to facilitate a resolution of tensions between the Greek and Turkish communities on Cyprus. This work must continue.

In the Balkans, the Clinton-Gore Administration ended ethnic cleansing in Bosnia and Kosovo by the resolute use of military power and vigorous diplomacy. The Republican Party, having first opposed the Administration's efforts to restore peace in the region, now tries to impede the Administration's efforts to rebuild these shattered societies. We look forward to the day when Serbia will be free from the grip of Slobodan Milosevic, and we will work to make that happen. America did right in the Balkans, and now we must finish the job.

Remembering the historic suffering of the people of Armenia, and recognizing the need of the modern Armenian state for security and economic growth, Al Gore and the Democratic Party are committed to continuing our efforts to bring a permanent end to tensions between Armenia and Azerbaijan over Nagorno-Karabakh, along with the restoration of diplomatic, commercial, and economic ties between Armenia and her neighbors, including Turkey. Al Gore helped bring about a special task force to intensify economic cooperation between the United States and Armenia.

We have helped close the gates of war in other parts of the world as well, and our work continues. We helped settle the Peru-Ecuador border dispute and end the civil war in Guatemala.

We have worked for peace in the Democratic Republic of Congo, the Central African Republic, Sierra Leone, and on the Ethiopia-Eritrea border. And we helped end the violence and protect democracy in East Timor by leading diplomatic efforts and supporting an international peacekeeping mission.

We helped facilitate the dialogue between North and South Korea, without which the recent summit could not have occurred. We continue to work with China and Taiwan to resolve their differences by peaceful means. And we continue our work with India and Pakistan to dampen down a nuclear arms race on the sub-continent and continue to urge them to deal with their differences over their conflict in Kashmir with peaceful means. President Clinton's historic trip to India and Pakistan has created new possibilities for dialogue with these countries, and under a Gore Administration these will be continued vigorously.

Engaging Former Enemies

Democrats understand that we must engage former enemies. This Administration's efforts to design new relationships with the Russian Federation and China have been continuously subjected to every form of harassment and attack by the Republicans — but they have been in America's national interest and they have been the right thing to do. We recognize that Russia's historic transition to a market democracy is difficult — all the more reason we must continue to engage Russia. We recognize that Russian democracy is challenged by corruption that deeply penetrates her society — all the more reason to engage Russia on behalf of reform. We recognize that Russia has her own self-interest and concerns that can and do run contrary to ours — all the more reason to search for constructive forms of cooperation. We deeply disagree with what Russia is doing in Chechnya and remain concerned about signs of Russian efforts to intimidate the press — all the more reason to step up our discussions with them on those issues. The Democratic Party is prepared to pursue American objectives as needed even at the cost of friction with Russia. But it is also of tremendous potential benefit to us if we can nurture a sense of common purpose and trust. Al Gore and the Democratic Party will continue that effort.

Similarly, we must continue to engage China — a nation with 1.3 billion people, a nuclear arsenal, and a role in the 21st Century that is destined to be one of the basic facts of international life. We must search out ways to cooperate across a broad range of issues, such as the environment and trade, while at the same time, insisting on adherence to international standards on human rights, freedom, the persecution of religions, the suppression of Tibet, and bellicose threats directed at Taiwan. China cannot be ignored, and these issues cannot — and must not — be marginalized. A deterioration of the U.S.-China relationship would harm, not help, American national security interests and the promotion of our values. A Gore Administration will fulfill its responsibilities under the Taiwan Relations Act. A Gore Administration will also remain committed to a "One China" policy. We support a resolution of cross-Straits issues that is both peaceful and consistent with the wishes of the people of Taiwan.

Enhancing Exisiting Alliances

The security and stability of Europe is critical to America's national security interests. We will continue to partner with the European Union to address global issues that could benefit from our combined capabilities. Under a Gore Administration, the U.S. will continue to work with our transatlantic allies to make the North Atlantic Treaty Organization (NATO) even stronger, thereby enhancing stability, promoting prosperity, and fostering democracy throughout Europe.

The Democratic Party strongly supported the accession of Poland, the Czech Republic and Hungary as a milestone in building a stronger NATO and a more democratic and unified Europe.

We look forward to bringing in additional qualified members in the future who share our values and are willing to take on the responsibilities of membership. A Gore Administration will ensure that the issue of NATO's future enlargement is part of the Alliance's agenda at the next summit in 2002 and that no non-NATO member has a veto over NATO decisions in this regard.

We must strengthen our alliances and partnerships in Asia, with Japan and with South Korea.

We must intensify our strategic cooperation with our ally Japan, building on our Joint Security Declaration, while finding more avenues to deal with Japan on a range of issues, from supporting democracy in Asia to promoting fair trade. And we remain committed to the defense of South Korea. The Democratic Party views our warm relationship with Australia as an anchor for our security interests in Southeast Asia, and we commend Australia for its leadership, and we applaud other nations for their participation with us in the peacekeeping operation in East Timor. We also are committed to enhancing our alliance with the countries of Latin America. We must build on the work that we began when we hosted the first Summit of the Americas, and we must accelerate implementation of the Plan of Action that will promote hemispheric cooperation on a full spectrum of political, economic, security and social issues.

Preventing New Physical Threats

Preventing Proliferation. We must strengthen our defense against the proliferation of conventional and unconventional weapons that threaten America. Our first priority must be to continue the work we have begun in cutting stockpiles of weapons of mass destruction, halting testing, and ensuring that weapons and weapons-grade material do not fall into the wrong hands.

Working with the government of the Russian Federation, we have helped safeguard nuclear material against the danger of theft. We have made it possible for thousands of Russia's nuclear scientists and weapons experts to find peaceful pursuits. And we have helped deactivate nearly 5,000 nuclear warheads.

We are also equipping our military and continuously preparing our defenses for an unconventional attack. We have been an active player in international efforts to strengthen compliance with the Biological Weapons Convention. We renewed and made permanent the Non-Proliferation Treaty and ratified the Chemical Weapons Convention, but our effort to ratify the Comprehensive Test Ban Treaty was derailed by Senate Republicans. As President, Al Gore will promptly resubmit this treaty to the Senate with a demand from the American people for its ratification.

Al Gore and the Democratic Party recognize the possibility of change in Iran, but we remain focused on the realities. Even as elements in Iran press for reform, the country still supports international terrorism, strives to acquire weapons of mass destruction, and represses its citizens, as evidenced by the immoral trial of 13 Jews in Shiraz. Ultimately, we must judge Iran by its actions. Al Gore will make an all-out effort to halt Iran's acquisition of weapons of mass destruction and delivery systems.

In Iraq, we are committed to working with our international partners to keep Saddam Hussein boxed in, and we will work to see him out of power. Bill Clinton and Al Gore have stood up to Saddam Hussein time and time again. As President, Al Gore will not hesitate to use America's military might against Iraq when and where it is necessary.

In light of the possibility that U.S. forces or our allies will have to contend with hostile tactical range ballistic missiles, we have been working rapidly to develop anti-tactical ballistic missile systems. We are working successfully with Israel on developing and deploying the Arrow anti-tactical ballistic missile system and the Tactical High Energy Laser.

Our diplomacy has helped to halt North Korea's push for nuclear weapons. We got North Korea to stop testing long-range ballistic missiles and are also engaged in continuing negotiations regarding their testing and export of long-range ballistic missiles. The tight coordination between the United States, South Korea, and Japan is critical to our success, and we will maintain it as the two Koreas continue the dialogue began at the recent summit.

We reject Republican plans to endanger our security with massive unilateral cuts in our arsenal and to construct an unproven, expensive, and ill-conceived missile defense system that would plunge us into a new arms race. Al Gore and the Democratic Party support the development of the technology for a limited national missile defense system that will be able to defend the U.S. against a missile attack from a state that has acquired weapons of mass destruction despite our efforts to block their proliferation. A decision to deploy such a system should be made based on four criteria: the nature of the threat, the feasibility of the technology, the cost, and the overall impact on our national security, including arms control. The Democratic Party places a high value on ensuring that any such system is compatible with the Anti-Ballistic Missile Treaty. We also support continued work in significantly reducing strategic and other nuclear weapons, recognizing that the goal is strategic nuclear stability at progressively lower levels.

Battling Terrorism. Whether terrorism is sponsored by a foreign nation or inspired by a single fanatic individual, such as Osama Bin Laden, Forward Engagement requires trying to disrupt terrorist networks, even before they are ready to attack. We must improve coordination internationally and domestically to share intelligence and develop operational plans. We must continue the comprehensive approach that has resulted in the development of a national counter-terrorism strategy involving all arms and levels of our government. We must continue to target terrorist finances, break up support cells, and disrupt training. And we must close avenues of cyber-attack by improving the security of the Internet and the computers upon which our digital economy exists.

As President, Al Gore will tolerate no attack against American interests at home or abroad: terrorists must know that if they attack America, we will never forget. We will scour the world to hunt them down and bring them to justice.

While fighting terrorism, we will protect the civil liberties of all Americans. Our justice system must guarantee fairness with procedures that protect the rights of the accused, even under the unusual circumstances of the investigation of threats to our national security. We must avoid stereotyping, for it defeats the highest purposes of our country if citizens feel automatically suspect by virtue of their ethnic origin. The purpose of terrorism is not only to intimidate, but also to divide and fracture, and we cannot permit that to happen.

Seizing Opportunities

Forward engagement requires investment. But while international assistance and government aid are important — we should do more. There is no way to donate enough money to the parts of the world that are most deeply affected by war, lawlessness, disease, or disorder. What applies to us, applies to them: The only way for them to make real progress is to encourage investment by promoting growth that is sustainable and broadly shared. Latin America and the Caribbean must continue to be a focal point of our efforts. We believe that increased cooperation and trade with our partners in this hemisphere can reduce poverty and the reliance on the drug trade, and ultimately lead to economic development, stability, and prosperity. We have made great strides by helping avert a financial crisis in Mexico. Mexico's ongoing shift to a mature democracy, as demonstrated by her recent election, makes it increasingly possible for us to visualize even stronger relations and more effective relationships between ourselves, Mexico, and Canada, building on our growing economic ties to address environmental and social issues of common concern. A Gore Administration will build on this possibility in order to assure ourselves and the people of the Americas a future of democracy, prosperity, and security built on mutual trust and respect. At the same time, we should continue to safeguard environmental standards, food safety, and worker protections by refusing to allow cross-border trucking and bus operations until appropriate safety and worker fairness standards have been met.

Prosperity and peace in Asia, the Middle East, and Africa will only be possible when those regions are fully integrated into the global economy. In Asia, we are working to promote fair trade with Japan and China. In the Middle East, we are promoting regional trade, particularly among Israel, Jordan, and Egypt. We must continue our work to reach out to moderate Arab states and we must intensify our effort to foster closer ties to the Islamic World.

With respect to sub-Saharan Africa, the Democratic Party believes in supporting what South African President Thabo Mbeki has called "an African renaissance." Notwithstanding this region's many problems, we see the example of South Africa as a great beacon of hope. We are encouraged by the restoration of democracy in Nigeria, the long-term continuation of a stable democratic system in Botswana, and Mozambique's courageous efforts of recovery after years of civil war. Even in the midst of her continuing problems, we see in Zimbabwe's recent election hope for the survival of the ideal of a multi-ethnic society. We regard the recently enacted African Growth and Opportunity Act as a major contribution toward the future.

We believe that the United Nations can play an integral role in our policy of Forward Engagement. We understand that the institution needs both resources and reform if it is to play that role, and we pledge to take the lead on both fronts.

Prosperity Abroad. Globalization must be a tide that lifts all boats, not a wave that overwhelms the most vulnerable among us. We support increasing our investment in the International Labor Organization and expanding the use of trade preferences that are tied to improvement in core labor standards. We also want to reverse the widening gap between rich and poor and nations, which is why Al Gore and the Democratic Party back debt forgiveness for the world's poorest nations.

We must seek to reform international institutions such as the World Trade Organization, the International Monetary Fund, and the World Bank so that core labor standards, human rights, and protections of the environment are integral to their policies and practices. These institutions must also improve their transparency, accountability, and level of consultation with civil society so that citizens around the world can both understand the basis for their decisions and contribute to them. We should use our influence in multilateral development institutions to not only provide emergency assistance for stabilizing economies and to create social safety nets, including unemployment insurance and health care, but also to give people the skills, education, and training they need to compete in the New Economy.

We must make a special effort to help women and children in societies that are devastated by war, disease and poverty. Women are traditionally the backbone of the family. We must also make a special effort to hear women when they rise up courageously to resist or end war in their communities. They are in a sense the front lines — the first affected — by the horrors of war and the misery of disease and poverty. We demand the United States Congress pass the Convention to Eliminate all forms of Discrimination Against Women which has been consistently blocked by the Republican Senate. And children represent the future. When we lose our children, we lose the promise of a future. Our investment programs must be more targeted toward women. And we must end the scourge of child labor by helping societies create educational opportunities for children and, more importantly, economic alternatives to employing the young.

Promoting Democracy, Human Rights, Rule of Law, and Civil Society. American values and freedoms are a beacon unto nations, and we should use the power of our ideals to foster democracy, human rights, rule of law, and civil society throughout the world. The Democratic Party believes that America must continue to work closely with other nations, as well as non-governmental organizations to promote these goals. We aim to rededicate ourselves to the defense of democracy in the Americas at a moment when it is being brought into question in Peru and absent on the island of Cuba. We will continue to work with Haiti to deepen the roots of democracy that we helped replant. We will continue to press for human rights, the rule of law, and political freedom. We will continue to support the spread of democracy across Africa, Asia, and the Middle East and the development of judiciary, legal systems, media and civil society organizations.

To accomplish this, we need the right tools. Al Gore and the Democratic Party support continued funding for the National Endowment for Democracy, Radio Liberty, Radio Free Europe, Radio Free Asia, Radio Marti, and other efforts to promote democracy and the free flow of ideas. We will build on our successful Reinventing Government program, led by Al Gore, to help other nations make their governments more responsive, more open, and more effective. We strongly support international educational exchanges. The students who come to America to study here — at the best academic institutions in the world — learn about our democratic values and institutions, our entrepreneurial skills, and our culture. They learn that Americans are noble dreamers remaining ever inclusive.

Forty years ago, John F. Kennedy came to Los Angeles to accept the Democratic Party's nomination for president. In doing so, he pointed America towards new frontiers at home and abroad. In the year 2000, Al Gore comes to Los Angeles to accept that same nomination and renew our party's determination to accept big challenges and make bold choices. At the edge of a new century, Democrats stand united in our determination to offer prosperity to all who are willing to work for it, to provide progress to all who are willing to live by the values that have made America great, and to bring peace to all those willing to embrace democracy all over the world.

For eight years, the Democratic Party's new thinking has helped America reach unparalleled heights of prosperity, progress, and peace. Now, we say that this is the time to move forward — not to go back. Now, we say that Democrats have just yet begun to fight for a better America and a brighter future. Now, we say to America, "You ain't seen nothing yet." ◆

Gore Calls 'Working Families' His Priority as He Accepts Democratic Nomination

Following are excerpts of Vice President Al Gore's Aug. 17 speech at the Democratic National Convention in Los Angeles. Transcript provided by the Democratic National Committee:

I speak tonight of gratitude, achievement and high hopes for our country. . . .

I'm honored tonight by the support of a leader of high ideals and fundamental decency, who will be an important part of our country's future — [former] Sen. Bill Bradley [D-N.J.].

There's someone else who will shape that future — a leader of character and courage. A defender of the environment and working families — the next vice president of the United States, [Sen.] Joe Lieberman [D-Conn.]. I picked him for one simple reason: He's the best person for the job.

For almost eight years now, I've been the partner of a leader who moved us out of the valley of recession and into the longest period of prosperity in American history. I say to you tonight: Millions of Americans will live better lives for a long time to come because of the job that's been done by President Bill Clinton.

Instead of the biggest deficits in history, we now have the biggest surpluses. The highest home ownership ever. The lowest inflation in a generation. Instead of losing jobs, we have 22 million new jobs. Above all, our success comes from you, the people who have worked hard for your families. Let's not forget that a few years ago you were also working hard. But your hard work was undone by a government that didn't work, didn't put people first, and wasn't on your side.

Together, we changed things to help unleash your potential, and innovation and investment in the private sector, the engine that drives our economic growth. And our progress on the economy is a good chapter in our history.

But now we turn the page and write a new chapter. . . . This election is not an award for past performance. I'm not asking you to vote for me on the basis of the economy we have. Tonight, I ask for your support on the basis of the better, fairer, more prosperous America we can build together. Together, let's make sure that our prosperity enriches not just the few, but all working families. Let's invest in health care, education, a secure retirement, and middle class tax cuts.

I'm happy that the stock market has boomed and so many businesses and new enterprises have done well. This country is richer and stronger. But my focus is on working families — people trying to make house payments and car payments, working overtime to save for college and do right by their kids. . . .

To all the families in America who have to struggle to afford the right education and the skyrocketing cost of prescription drugs, I want you to know this: I've taken on the powerful forces. And as president, I'll stand up to them, and I'll stand up for you.

To all the families who are struggling with things that money can't measure — like trying to find a little more time to spend with your children, or protecting your children from entertainment that you think glorifies violence and indecency — I want you to know: I believe we must challenge a culture with too much meanness and not enough meaning. And as president, I will stand with you for a goal that we share: to give more power back to the parents, to choose what your own children are exposed to, so you can pass on your family's basic lessons of responsibility and decency. . . .

We could squander this moment, but our country would be the poorer for it. Instead, let's lift our eyes and see how wide the American horizon has become. We're entering a new time, we're electing a new president, and I stand here tonight as my own man, and I want you to know me for who I truly am. I grew up in a wonderful family. I have a lot to be thankful for. And the greatest gift my parents gave me was love. When I was a child, it never once occurred to me that the foundation upon which my security depended would ever shake. And of all the lessons my parents taught me, the most powerful one was unspoken: the way they loved one another. . . . My parents taught me that the real values in life aren't material but spiritual. They include faith and family, duty and honor, and trying to make the world a better place.

I finished college at a time when all that seemed to be in doubt, and our nation's spirit was being depleted. We saw the assassination of our best leaders, appeals to racial backlash and the first warning signs of Watergate. I remember the conversations I had with Tipper back then and the doubts we had about the Vietnam War. But I enlisted in the Army because I knew if I didn't go, someone else in the small town of Carthage, Tenn., would have to go in my place. I was an Army reporter in Vietnam. When I was there, I didn't do the most, or run the gravest danger. But I was proud to wear my country's uniform.

When I came home, running for office was the very last thing I ever thought I would do. I studied religion at Vanderbilt and worked nights as a police reporter at the Nashville Tennesseean. And I saw more of what could go wrong in America — not only on the police beat, but as an investigative reporter covering local government. I also saw so much of what could go right — citizens lifting up local communities, family by family, block by block, neighborhood by neighborhood, in churches and charities, on school boards and city councils.

And then, Tipper and I started our own family. And when our first daughter, Karenna, was born, I began to see the future through a fresh set of eyes. . . . And I decided that I could not turn away from service at home — any more than I could have turned away from service in Vietnam.

That's why I ran for Congress. In my first term, a family in Hardeman County, Tenn., wrote a letter and told how worried they were about toxic waste that had been dumped near their home. I held some of the first hearings on the issue. And ever since, I've been there in the fight against the big polluters. . . . On the issue of the environment, I've never given up, I've never backed down, and I never will. And I say it again tonight: We must reverse the silent, rising tide of global warming.

In the Senate and as vice president, I fought for welfare reform. . . . Others talked about welfare reform. We actually reformed welfare and set time limits. Instead of handouts, we gave people training to go from welfare to work. And we have cut the welfare rolls in half and moved millions into good jobs.

For almost 25 years now, I've been fighting for people. And for all that time, I've been listening to people, holding open meetings in the places where they live and work. And you know what? I've learned a lot. . . . I've learned that the issues before us, the problems and the policies, all have names. And I don't mean the big fancy names that we put on programs and legislation. I'm talking about family names like Nystel, Johnson, Gutierrez, and Malone — people and families I've met in the last year, all across this country. . . . And so here tonight, in the name of all the working families who are the strength and soul of America, I accept your nomination for president of the United States.

I'm here to talk seriously about the issues. I believe people deserve to know specifically what a candidate proposes to do. . . . If you entrust me with the presidency, I will put our democracy back in your hands, and get all the special-interest money — all of it — out of our democracy by enacting campaign finance reform. I feel so strongly about this, I promise you that campaign finance reform will be the very first bill that Joe Lieberman and I send to Congress.

Let others try to restore the old guard. We come to this convention as the change we wish to see in America. And what are those changes?

At a time when most Americans will live to know even their great-grandchildren, we will save and strengthen Social Security and Medicare — not only for this generation, but for generations to come.

At a time of almost unimaginable medical breakthroughs, we will fight for affordable health care for all — so patients and ordinary people are not left powerless and broke. We will move toward universal health coverage, step by step, starting with all children. Let's get all children covered by the year 2004. And let's move to the day when we end the stigma of mental illness and treat it like every other illness, everywhere in this nation. Within the next few years, scientists will identify the genes that cause every type of cancer. We need a national commitment equal to the promise of this unequalled moment. So we will double the federal investment in medical research. We will find new medicines and new cures — not just for cancer, but for everything from diabetes to HIV/AIDS.

At a time when there is more computer power in a Palm Pilot than in the spaceship that took Neil Armstrong to the moon, we will offer all our people lifelong learning and new skills for the higher paying jobs of the future.

At a time when the amount of human knowledge is doubling every five years, we will do bold things to make our schools the best in the world. I will fight for the single greatest commitment to education since the G.I. Bill: for revolutionary improvements in our schools. For higher standards and more accountability. To put a fully qualified teacher in every classroom, test all new teachers, and give teachers the training and professional development they deserve. It's time to treat and reward teachers like the professionals they are.

It's not just about more money. It's about higher standards, accountability, new ideas. But we can't do it without new resources. And that's why I will invest far more in our schools — in the long run, a second-class education always costs more than a first-class education. And I will not go along with any plan that would drain taxpayer money away from our public schools and give it to private schools in the form of vouchers. This nation was a pioneer of universal public education. Now let's set a specific new goal for the first decade of the 21st century: high-quality universal pre-school. . . .

We also have to give middle class families help in paying for college with tax-free college savings, and by making most college tuition tax-deductible. Open the doors of learning to all. And all of this — all of this — is the change we wish to see in America.

Not so long ago, a balanced budget seemed impossible. Now our budget surpluses make it possible to give a full range of targeted tax cuts to working families. Not just to help you save for college, but to pay for health insurance or child care. To reform the estate tax, so people can pass on a small business or a family farm. And to end the marriage penalty — the right way, the fair way — because we shouldn't force couples to pay more in income taxes just because they're married.

But let me say it plainly: I will not go along with a huge tax cut for the wealthy at the expense of everyone else and wreck our good economy in the process. Under the tax plan the other side has proposed, for every 10 dollars that goes to the wealthiest 1 percent, middle-class families would get one dime. And lower-income families would get one penny. In fact, if you add it up, the average family would get about enough money to buy one extra Diet Coke a day, about 62 cents in change. Let me tell you: that's not the kind of change I'm working for. . . .

I'll fight for a new, tax-free way to help you save and build a bigger nest egg for your retirement. I'm talking about something extra that you can save and invest for yourself. Something that will supplement Social Security, not be subtracted from it. . . .

In the next four years, we will pay off all the national debt this nation accumulated in our first 200 years. This will put us on the path to completely eliminating the debt by 2012, keeping America prosperous far into the future.

But there's something at stake in this election that's even more important than economic progress. Simply put, it's our values; it's our responsibility to our loved ones, to our families. . . .

Putting both Social Security and

Medicare in an iron-clad lock box where the politicians can't touch them — to me, that kind of common sense is a family value.

Getting cigarettes out of the hands of kids before they get hooked is a family value. I will crack down on the marketing of tobacco to our children, no matter how hard the tobacco companies lobby, no matter how much they spend.

A new prescription drug benefit under Medicare for all our seniors — that's a family value. And let me tell you: I will fight for it, and the other side will not. . . .

There's one other word we've heard a lot of in this campaign, and that word is honor. To me, honor is not just a word, but an obligation. And you have my word: We will honor hard work by raising the minimum wage so that work always pays more than welfare.

We will honor families by expanding child care and after-school care and family and medical leave so working parents have the help they need to care for their children — because one of the most important jobs of all is raising our children. And we'll support the right of parents to decide that one of them will stay home longer with their babies if that's what they believe is best for their families.

We will honor the ideal of equality by standing up for civil rights and defending affirmative action.

We will honor equal rights and fight for an equal day's pay for an equal day's work.

And let there be no doubt: I will protect and defend a woman's right to choose. The last thing this country needs is a Supreme Court that overturns *Roe v. Wade*.

We will remove all the old barriers so that those who are called disabled can develop all their abilities. And we will also widen the circle of opportunity for all Americans and enforce all our civil rights laws. We will pass the Employment Non-Discrimination Act.

And we will honor the memory of Matthew Shepard, Joseph Ileto and James Byrd, whose families all joined us this week, by passing a law against hate crimes.

We will honor the hard work of raising a family by doing all we can to help parents protect their children. Parents deserve the simple security of knowing that their children are safe whether they're walking down the street, surfing the World Wide Web or sitting behind a desk in school.

To make families safer, we passed the toughest crime bill in history, and we're putting 100,000 new community police on our streets. Crime has fallen in every major category for seven years in a row. But there's still too much danger and there's still too much fear. So tonight I want to set another new, specific goal: to cut the crime rate year after year, every single year throughout this decade. That's why I'll fight to add another 50,000 new community police [officers]. . . .

I will fight for a crime victims' bill of rights, including a constitutional amendment to make sure that victims, and not just criminals, are guaranteed rights in our justice system.

I'll fight to toughen penalties on those who misuse the Internet to prey on our children and violate our privacy. And I'll fight to make every school in this nation drug-free and gun-free. I believe in the right of sportsmen and hunters and law-abiding citizens to own firearms. But I want mandatory background checks to keep guns away from criminals and mandatory child safety locks to protect our children. . . .

I'm excited about America's prospects and full of hope for America's future. Our country has come a long way, and I've come a long way since that long ago time when I went to Vietnam. I've never forgotten what I saw there and the bravery of so many young Americans. The price of freedom is sometimes high, but I never believed that America should turn inward.

As a senator, I broke with many in our party and voted to support the Gulf War when Saddam Hussein invaded Kuwait because I believed America's vital interests were at stake.

Early in my public service, I took up the issue of nuclear arms control and nuclear weapons because nothing is more fundamental than protecting our national security.

Now I want to lead America because I love America. I will keep America's defenses strong. I will make sure our armed forces continue to be the best-equipped, best-trained and best-led in the entire world. . . .We must always have the will to defend our enduring interests — from Europe to the Middle East, to Japan and Korea. We must strengthen our partnerships with Africa, Latin America and the rest of the developing world.

We must welcome and promote truly free trade. But I say to you: It must be fair trade. We must set standards to end child labor, to prevent the exploitation of workers and the poisoning of the environment. Free trade can and must be — and if I'm president, will be — a way to lift everyone up, not bring anyone down to the lowest common denominator.

So those are the issues, and that's where I stand. . . . Sometimes in this campaign, when I visit a school and see a hardworking teacher trying to change the world one child at a time — I see the face of my father. And I know that teaching our children well is not just the teacher's job; it's everyone's job. And it has to be our national mission.

I've shaken hands in diners and coffee shops all across this country. And sometimes when I see a waitress working hard and thanking someone for a tip, I see the face of my mother. And I know for that waitress carrying trays, or a construction worker in the winter cold, I will never agree to raise the retirement age to 70, or threaten the promise of Social Security.

I say to you tonight: We've got to win this election because every hardworking American family deserves to open the door to their dream. In our democracy, the future is not something that just happens to us; it is something we make for ourselves — together.

So to the young people watching tonight, I say: This is your time to make new the life of our world. We need your help to rekindle the spirit of America.

And I ask all of you, my fellow citizens: From this city that marked both the end of America's journey westward and the beginning of the New Frontier, let us set out on a new journey to the best America. A new journey on which we advance not by the turning of wheels, but by the turning of our minds, the reach of our vision, the daring grace of the human spirit.

Yes, we have our problems. But the United States of America is the best country ever created — and still, as ever, the hope of humankind. Yes, we're all imperfect. But as Americans we all share in the privilege and challenge of building a more perfect union.

I know my own imperfections. I know that sometimes people say I'm too serious, that I talk too much substance and policy. Maybe I've done that tonight.

But the presidency is more than a popularity contest. It's a day-by-day fight for people. Sometimes, you have to choose to do what's difficult or unpopular. Sometimes, you have to be willing to spend your popularity in order to pick the hard right over the easy wrong.

There are big choices ahead, and our whole future is at stake. . . . If you entrust me with the presidency, I know I won't always be the most exciting politician. But I pledge to you tonight: I will work for you every day, and I will

Clinton Vetoes Bill To Repeal Estate Tax, Calling it 'Fiscally Irresponsible'

Following is the text of President Clinton's Aug. 31 veto message on HR 8:

TO THE HOUSE OF REPRESENTATIVES:

I am returning herewith without my approval HR 8, legislation to phase out federal estate, gift and generation-skipping transfer taxes over a 10-year period. While I support and would sign targeted and fiscally responsible legislation that provides estate tax relief for small businesses, family farms and principal residences along the lines proposed by House and Senate Democrats, this bill is fiscally irresponsible and provides a very expensive tax break for the best-off Americans while doing nothing for the vast majority of working families. Starting in 2010, HR 8 would drain more than $50 billion annually to benefit only tens of thousands of families, taking resources that could have been used to strengthen Social Security and Medicare for tens of millions of families.

This repeal of the estate tax is the latest part in a tax plan that would cost over $2 trillion, spending projected surpluses that may never materialize and returning America to deficits. This would reverse the fiscal discipline that has helped make the American economy the strongest it has been in generations and would leave no resources to strengthen Social Security or Medicare, provide a voluntary Medicare prescription drug benefit, invest in key priorities like education, or pay off the debt held by the public by 2012. This tax plan would threaten our continued economic expansion by raising interest rates and choking off investment.

We should cut taxes this year, but they should be the right tax cuts, targeted to working families to help our economy grow — not tax breaks that will help only the wealthiest few while putting our prosperity at risk. Our tax cuts will help send our children to college, help families with members who need long-term care, help pay for child care, and help fund desperately needed school construction. Overall, my tax program will provide substantially more benefits to middle-income American families than the tax cuts passed by the congressional tax-writing committees this year, at less than half the cost.

HR 8, in particular, suffers from several problems. The true cost of the bill is masked by the backloading of the tax cut. HR 8 would explode in cost from about $100 billion from 2001-2010 to about $750 billion from 2011-2020, just when the Baby Boom generation begins to retire and Social Security and Medicare come under strain.

Repeal would also be unwise because estate and gift taxes play an important role in the overall fairness and progressivity of our tax system. These taxes ensure that the portion of income that is not taxed during life (such as unrealized capital gains) is taxed at death. Estate tax repeal would benefit only about 2 percent of decedents, providing an average tax cut of $800,000 to only 54,000 families in 2010. More than half of the benefits of repeal would go to one-tenth of 1 percent of families, just 3,000 families annually, with an average tax cut of $7 million. Furthermore, research suggests that repeal of the estate and gift taxes is likely to reduce charitable giving by as much as $6 billion per year.

In 1997, I signed legislation that reduced the estate tax for small businesses and family farms, but I believe that the estate tax is still burdensome to some family farms and small businesses. However, only a tiny fraction of the tax relief provided under HR 8 benefits these important sectors of our economy, and much of that relief would not be realized for a decade. In contrast, House and Senate Democrats have proposed alternatives that would provide significant, immediate tax relief to family-owned businesses and farms in a manner that is much more fiscally responsible than outright repeal. For example, the Senate Democratic alternative would take about two-thirds of families off the estate tax entirely, and could eliminate estate taxes for almost all small businesses and family farms. In contrast to HR 8 — which waits until 2010 to repeal the estate tax — most of the relief in the Democratic alternatives is offered immediately.

By providing more targeted and less costly relief, we preserve the resources necessary to provide a Medicare prescription drug benefit, extend the life of Social Security and Medicare, and pay down the debt by 2012. Maintaining fiscal discipline also would continue to provide the best kind of tax relief to all Americans, not just the wealthiest few, by reducing interest rates on home mortgages, student loans and other essential investments.

This surplus comes from the hard work and ingenuity of the American people. We owe it to them — and to their children — to make the best use of it. This bill, in combination with the tax bills already passed and planned for next year, would squander the surplus — without providing the immediate estate tax relief that family farms, small businesses, and other estates could receive under the fiscally responsible alternatives rejected by the Congress. For that reason, I must veto this bill.

Since the adjournment of the Congress has prevented my return of HR 8 within the meaning of Article I, section 7, clause 2 of the Constitution, my withholding of approval from the bill precludes its becoming law. The Pocket Veto Case, 279 U.S. 655

(1929). In addition to withholding my signature and thereby invoking my constitutional power to "pocket veto" bills during an adjournment of the Congress, to avoid litigation, I am also sending HR 8 to the House of Representatives with my objections, to leave no possible doubt that I have vetoed the measure.

I continue to welcome the opportunity to work with the Congress on a bipartisan basis on tax legislation that is targeted, fiscally responsible and geared towards continuing the economic strength we all have worked so hard to achieve.

WILLIAM J. CLINTON
THE WHITE HOUSE,
August 31, 2000

Hastert Agrees to Remove Estate Tax, Pension Provisions in Quest for Deal On Minimum Wage, Business Tax Cuts

Following is the text of an Aug. 28 letter from House Speaker J. Dennis Hastert, R-Ill., to President Clinton:

The President
The White House
Washington, D.C.

Dear Mr. President:

I have enjoyed working with you on several issues where we have found common ground. We have been quite successful this year in working together on repealing the Social Security Earnings Limit, fighting the war on drugs in Colombia, opening new markets in our poorest communities in America, and opening new markets overseas in China, Africa and the Caribbean.

I would like to propose that we work together over the next month to find common ground on your desire to increase the minimum wage by $1 [per hour] and our desire to help alleviate the burdens on small businesses that would shoulder the costs of such an increase.

It is very clear that a vast majority of Congressional Democrats and Republicans would like to see a balanced approach achieved before we adjourn. While the House and Senate have passed legislation that attempts to strike this balance, a variety of procedural hurdles have prevented us from getting that legislation to your desk for signature.

Our proposal is to increase the minimum wage by $1 in 50-cent increments that begin January 1st of next year and the remaining 50 cents on January 1st of 2002. We are also offering to drop the death tax and pension provisions in the bill that you regrettably find objectionable.

The remaining provisions are designed to assist small business with the costs of this wage increase and have a revenue impact of $24 billion over 5 years and roughly $76 billion over the next 10 years. We find this to be a reasonable and balanced offer that deserves your consideration.

I believe that we can work together to pass this legislation when we return in September with strong bipartisan majorities in the House and Senate. I have spoken with Senate Majority Leader Trent Lott [R-Miss.] and I believe he wants to achieve such a balanced approach as well. We would like your input and your assistance in getting this legislation to your desk before we adjourn this year. We will certainly need your help in removing the procedural roadblocks constructed to block such an effort. I look forward to working with you on this issue over the August recess.

Sincerely,

J. DENNIS HASTERT
Speaker of the House

Clinton, Assessing Fall Agenda, Says GOP's Emphasis on Tax Cut Is Unfair and Irresponsible

What follows are excerpts of President Clinton's Sept. 5 comments about the fall legislative agenda. Transcript provided by The Federal Document Clearing House.

CLINTON: . . . We are committed to breaking the legislative logjam, but we have to move forward with fiscal responsibility, with responsible tax cuts and with public investments that give all our people a chance and fuel our prosperity. For seven-and-a-half years now, we have followed that program, and it's worked very well for America. It has paid enormous dividends.

Unfortunately, the strategy pursued by the Republican leaders in Congress, I believe, would squander that remarkable success. Month by month and bill by bill, they are attempting to spend our projected surplus for years to come, an estimated $2 trillion on massive and reckless tax cuts for the privileged few.

This isn't fiscally responsible. It isn't fair. And it doesn't even take into account the cost that would follow on their plans to partially privatize Social Security or any spending promises they have made to the American people in this election season.

I believe we owe it to our children to stay on course to pay off the national debt over the next 12 years. If we do it, interest rates will stay low, businesses can grow, generations will know that Social Security and Medicare will be there for them. And, I might add, as the Counsel of Economic Advisers reported to me, it amounts to a tax cut, because paying off the debt as opposed to spending it all will keep interest rates, at a minimum, 1 percent lower a year over the next decade, and that is worth $250 billion to the average American families in this country in lower home mortgages, $30 billion in lower car payments and $15 billion in lower college loan payments. So that's a $300 billion tax cut real people get just by doing the right thing. . . .

The American people want us to address the pressing issues that affect their daily lives. Yesterday we celebrated Labor Day. Today, it's time to honor the labor of the American people who sent us here. We should do it by raising the minimum wage by a dollar. Congress should stop holding up the process and make it the first order of business.

We should also have sensible tax cuts in the areas of health care, college tuition, long-term care, the environment and, of course, the New Markets [Initiative] tax cut, which is a tax cut that all of us support for upper-income people to encourage them to invest in lower-income people and lower-income neighborhoods that have been left behind by our prosperity.

Congress should pass a strong patients' bill of rights. . . .

Americans and people with disabilities should not have to wait another year for an affordable voluntary Medicare prescription drug benefit. This is — the money is there, we ought to do this. . . .

Our nation's 44 million uninsured citizens shouldn't have to wait for a significant expansion of health care. We have a proposal on the table that would allow the states to enroll the parents of children who are eligible for our Children's Health Insurance Program. We have a proposal on the table that would allow people between the ages of 55 and 65 to enroll in Medicare if they lose their previous health insurance and to give them a tax credit to make it affordable.

Now, these proposals could take care of 25 percent, and, I might say, the most needy 25 percent of those 44 million Americans without health insurance. We have the money to do it.

We need to keep working to put 50,000 more police on the street. The 100,000 police program has worked very well. We have the lowest violent crime rate in 27 years now, and we need to keep doing what has worked.

We should also pass the commonsense gun safety legislation, and, I hope, the hate crimes bill. I applaud the Senate for passing the hate crimes legislation, including the Republicans who joined our unanimous Democratic caucus in voting for it, virtually unanimous. And I hope that the House will follow suit.

We need to strip out the anti-environmental riders and press for cleaner air and cleaner water. We need to pass the measures that will enable the American people to combat global warming. And we need to approve permanent conservation funding to protect our natural heritage.

We also need to strengthen our laws for providing for equal pay for equal work, pass debt relief for the emerging democracies, normalize trade relations with China.

Most important, we should not forget that the Congress comes back at the beginning of the school year, and there are pressing educational needs for America.

The children of this country need more teachers and smaller classes and modern classrooms. We need to continue to support 100,000 good, new teachers to reduce class sizes, and we need Congress to determine finally we're going to do our part to help the school districts of this country replace broken-down buildings and trailers with modern classrooms.

Again I will say, we believe in sensible tax cuts for middle-class families that make education and long-term care more affordable, not cuts that threaten our prosperity.

Last week, I vetoed the Republican estate tax repeal, not because I don't favor reform of the estate tax laws, but because absolute repeal is not fiscally responsible and it's not fair. . . .

They've got a right to try to override any veto that I make. That's the way the Constitution works. But I wish they'd try just as hard to muster up the two-thirds to raise the minimum wage for people who are working 40 hours a week.

This is a great and good country. We should be fair to everybody. I'm for changes in the estate tax. All of us are. They all voted for it. But the Republicans want an issue. They want it to be an all-or-nothing thing. . . . ◆

Clinton Cites Missouri, California Provisions in His Veto Of Energy-Water Appropriations Bill

What follows is the text of President Clinton's Oct. 7 veto of HR 4733, the energy and water appropriations bill for fiscal 2001.

TO THE HOUSE OF REPRESENTATIVES:

I am returning herewith without my approval, HR 4733, the "Energy and Water Development Appropriations Act, 2001." The bill contains an unacceptable rider regarding the Army Corps of Engineers' master operating manual for the Missouri River. In addition, it fails to provide funding for the California-Bay Delta initiative and includes nearly $700 million for over 300 unrequested projects.

Section 103 would prevent the Army Corps of Engineers from revising the operating manual for the Missouri River that is 40 years old and needs to be updated based on the most recent scientific information. In its current form, the manual simply does not provide an appropriate balance among the competing interests, both commercial and recreational, of the many people who seek to use this great American river. The bill would also undermine implementation of the Endangered Species Act by preventing the Corps of Engineers from funding reasonable and much-needed changes to the operating manual for the Missouri River. The Corps and the U.S. Fish and Wildlife Service are entering a critical phase in their Section 7 consultation on the effects of reservoir project operations. This provision could prevent the Corps from carrying out a necessary element of any reasonable and prudent alternative to avoid jeopardizing the continued existence of the endangered least tern and pallid sturgeon, and the threatened piping plover.

In addition to the objectionable restriction placed upon the Corps of Engineers, the bill fails to provide funding for the California-Bay Delta initiative. This decision could significantly hamper ongoing Federal and State efforts to restore this ecosystem, protect the drinking water of 22 million Californians, and enhance water supply and reliability for over 7 million acres of highly productive farmland and growing urban areas across California. The $60 million budget request, all of which would be used to support activities that can be carried out using existing authorities, is the minimum necessary to ensure adequate Federal participation in these initiatives, which are essential to reducing existing conflicts among water users in California. This funding should be provided without legislative restrictions undermining key environmental statutes or disrupting the balanced approach to meeting the needs of water users and the environment that has been carefully developed through almost six years of work with the State of California and interested stakeholders.

The bill also fails to provide sufficient funding necessary to restore endangered salmon in the Pacific Northwest, which would interfere with the Corps of Engineers' ability to comply with the Endangered Species Act, and provides no funds to start the new construction project requested for the Florida Everglades. The bill also fails to fund the Challenge 21 program for environmentally friendly flood damage reduction projects, the program to modernize Corps recreation facilities, and construction of an emergency outlet at Devil's Lake. In addition, it does not fully support efforts to research and develop non-polluting, domestic sources of energy through solar and renewable technologies that are vital to America's energy security.

Finally, the bill provides nearly $700 million for over 300 unrequested projects, including: nearly 80 unrequested projects totaling more than $330 million for the Department of Energy; nearly 240 unrequested projects totaling over $300 million for the Corps of Engineers, and more than 10 unrequested projects totaling in excess of $10 million for the Bureau of Reclamation. For example, more than 80 unrequested Corps of Engineers construction projects included in the bill would have a long-term cost of nearly $2.7 billion. These unrequested projects and earmarks come at the expense of other initiatives important to taxpaying Americans.

The American people deserve Government spending based upon a balanced approach that maintains fiscal discipline, eliminates the national debt, extends the solvency of Social Security and Medicare, provides for an appropriately sized tax cut, establishes a new voluntary Medicare prescription drug benefit in the context of broader reforms, expands health care coverage to more families, and funds critical investments for our future. I urge the Congress to work expeditiously to develop a bill that addresses the needs of the Nation.

WILLIAM J. CLINTON
THE WHITE HOUSE,
October 7, 2000

President Chides Congress In Veto of Combined Appropriations For Not Making People a Priority

Following is the text of President Clinton's Oct. 30 veto message on HR 4516, which combined fiscal 2001 appropriations bills for the legislative branch and the Treasury Department, Postal Service and independent agencies:

TO THE HOUSE OF REPRESENTATIVES:

I am returning herewith without my approval, HR 4516, the Legislative Branch and the Treasury and General Government Appropriations Act, 2001. This bill provides funds for the legislative branch and the White House at a time when the business of the American people remains unfinished.

The Congress' continued refusal to focus on the priorities of the American people leaves me no alternative but to veto this bill. I cannot in good conscience sign a bill that funds the operations of the Congress and the White House before funding our classrooms, fixing our schools, and protecting our workers.

With the largest student enrollment in history, we need a budget that will allow us to repair and modernize crumbling schools, reduce class size, hire more and better-trained teachers, expand after-school programs, and strengthen accountability to turn around failing schools.

I would sign this legislation in the context of a budget that puts the interests of the American people before self interest or special interests.

I urge the Congress to get its priorities in order and send me, without further delay, balanced legislation I can sign.

WILLIAM J. CLINTON
THE WHITE HOUSE,
October 30, 2000

President Vetoes Intelligence Bill, Citing Fear that 'Overbroad' Language Would Hurt Legitimate Flow of Information

What follows is the text of President Clinton's Nov. 4 veto of HR 4392, the fiscal 2001 intelligence authorization bill.

TO THE HOUSE OF REPRESENTATIVES:

Today, I am disapproving H.R. 4392, the "Intelligence Authorization Act for Fiscal Year 2001," because of one badly flawed provision that would have made a felony of unauthorized disclosures of classified information. Although well intentioned, that provision is overbroad and may unnecessarily chill legitimate activities that are at the heart of a democracy.

I agree that unauthorized disclosures can be extraordinarily harmful to United States national security interests and that far too many such disclosures occur. I have been particularly concerned about their potential effects on the sometimes irreplaceable intelligence sources and methods on which we rely to acquire accurate and timely information I need in order to make the most appropriate decisions on matters of national security. Unauthorized disclosures damage our intelligence relationships abroad, compromise intelligence gathering, jeopardize lives, and increase the threat of terrorism. As Justice Stewart stated in the Pentagon Papers case, "it is elementary that the successful conduct of international diplomacy and the maintenance of an effective national defense require both confidentiality and secrecy. Other nations can hardly deal with this Nation in an atmosphere of mutual trust unless they can be assured that their confidences will be kept . . . and the development of considered and intelligent international policies would be impossible if those charged with their formulation could not communicate with each other freely."

Those who disclose classified information inappropriately thus commit a gross breach of the public trust and may recklessly put our national security at risk. To the extent that existing sanctions have proven insufficient to address and deter unauthorized disclosures, they should be strengthened. What is in dispute is not the gravity of the problem, but the best way to respond to it.

In addressing this issue, we must never forget that the free flow of information is essential to a democratic society. Justice Stewart also wrote in the Pentagon Papers case that "the only effective restraint upon executive policy in the areas of national defense and international affairs may lie in an enlightened citizenry — in an informed and critical public opinion which alone can here protect the values of democratic government."

Justice Brandeis reminded us that "those who won our independence believed . . . that public discussion is a political duty, and that this should be a fundamental principle of the American government." His words caution that we must always tread carefully when considering measures that may limit public discussion — even when those measures are intended to achieve laudable, indeed necessary, goals.

As President, therefore, it is my obligation to protect not only our Government's vital information from improper disclosure, but also to protect the rights of citizens to receive the information necessary for democracy to work. Furthering these two goals requires a careful balancing, which must be assessed in light of our system of classifying information over a range of categories. This legislation does not achieve the proper balance. For example, there is a serious risk that this legislation would tend to have a chilling effect on those who engage in legitimate activities. A desire to avoid the risk that their good-faith choice of words — their exercise of judgment — could become the subject of a criminal referral for prosecution might discourage Government officials from engaging even in appropriate public discussion, press briefings, or other legitimate official activities. Similarly, the legislation may unduly restrain the ability of former Government officials to teach, write, or engage in any activity aimed at building public understanding of complex issues. Incurring such risks is unnecessary and inappropriate in a society built on freedom of expression and the consent of the governed and is particularly inadvisable in a context in which the range of classified materials is so extensive. In such circumstances, this criminal provision would, in my view, create an undue chilling effect.

The problem is compounded because this provision was passed without benefit of public hearings — a particular concern given that it is the public that this law seeks ultimately to protect. The Administration shares the process burden since its deliberations lacked the thoroughness this provision warranted, which in turn led to a failure to apprise the Congress of the concerns I am expressing today.

I deeply appreciate the sincere efforts of Members of Congress to address the problem of unauthorized disclosures and I fully share their commitment. When the Congress returns, I encourage it to send me this bill with this provision deleted, and I encourage the Congress as soon as possible to pursue a more narrowly drawn provision tested in public hearings so that those they represent can also be heard on this important issue.

Since the adjournment of the Congress has prevented my return of H.R.

4392 within the meaning of Article I, section 7, clause 2 of the Constitution, my withholding of approval from the bill precludes its becoming law. The Pocket Veto Case, 279 U.S. 655 (1929). In addition to withholding my signature and thereby invoking my constitutional power to "pocket veto" bills during an adjournment of the Congress, to avoid litigation, I am also sending H.R. 4392 to the House of Representatives with my objections, to leave no possible doubt that I have vetoed the measure.

WILLIAM J. CLINTON
THE WHITE HOUSE,
November 4, 2000.

'We're Looking for a Federal Issue': Supreme Court Hears Florida Recount Case

Following are excerpts from the Dec. 1 oral arguments before the U.S. Supreme Court in the appeal brought by Texas Gov. George W. Bush. He challenged a Florida Supreme Court ruling that had delayed certification of Florida's popular vote, and its crucial 25 electoral votes, while manual recounts were under way in several counties. Transcript provided by Federal Document Clearing House.

Theodore B. Olson, attorney for the Bush campaign: And may it please the court. Two weeks after the Nov. 7 presidential election, the Florida Supreme Court overturned and materially rewrote portions of the carefully formulated set of laws enacted by Florida's legislature to govern the conduct of that election and the determination of controversies with respect to who prevailed on Nov. 7. . . .

The election code that the Florida legislature developed conformed to Title 3, Section 5 of the United States Code. That provision invites states to devise rules in advance of an election to govern the counting of votes and the settling of election controversies.

Justice Sandra Day O'Connor: Well, Mr. Olson, isn't Section 5 sort of a safe harbor provision for states? And do you think that it gives some independent right of a candidate to overturn a Florida decision based on that section?

Olson: We do, Justice O'Connor. It is a safe harbor, but it's more than that. And Section 5 of Title 3 needs to be construed in connection with the history that brought it forth . . . in light of the extreme controversy that was faced by this country as a result of the 1876 election. . . . It led to controversy, contests, discord. Congress was very much concerned about the possibility of that happening again. . . .

Justice Anthony M. Kennedy: Well, but we're looking for a federal issue. And I thought that you might have argued that the secretary of State was instructed by the Supreme Court not to jeopardize the state's chances, and it cited 3 U.S.C. Sections 1 through 10. And so if the state Supreme Court relied on a federal issue or a federal background principle and got it wrong, then you can be here.

Olson: Well, I certainly agree that it mentioned those provisions. I'm simply saying that it blew past the important provisions of Section 5 and the benefits that Section 5 gives to the states, to the voters in that state, and to the people running for office in that state. . . .

Justice Antonin Scalia: Mr. Olson, suppose a less controversial federal benefit scheme. Let's say the scheme that says states can get highway funds if they hold their highway speeds to a certain level, all right? And suppose you have a state Supreme Court that, in your view, unreasonably interprets a state statute as not holding the highway speed to the level required in order to get the benefit of that safe harbor. Would you think that that raises a federal question and that you could appeal a state court decision here, because it deprived the state of the benefit of the highway fund?

Olson: No, I don't think so.

Scalia: Why is this any different?

Olson: This is a great deal different, because this is the — first of all, Article II of the Constitution, which vests authority to establish the rules exclusively in the legislatures of the state, tie in with Section 5. Secondly, as this court has stated. . . .

Scalia: . . . Why is Section 5, in that regard, any different from the highway funding?

Olson: I think it can't be divorced from Article II of the Constitution, because it's a part of a plan for the vesting in the legislatures of a state. And Section 5 implements Article II, in the sense that it provides a benefit, not just to the state, but to the voters of this county.

Kennedy: But just talk about the statutory issue. I assume that if we worked long enough with Justice Scalia's hypothetical, we could find a case where a court adjudicated with reference to the federal principle and got the federal principle wrong. Did *Indiana v.* — that kind of thing. Did that happen here?

Olson: Well, I think that the state did not pay — the state Supreme Court did not pay much attention to the federal statute. It was obviously aware of it. It did get the federal. . . .

Kennedy: Well, then there's no federal constitutional issue here.

Chief Justice William H. Rehnquist: Mr. Olson, do you think that Congress, when it passed 3 U.S.C., intended that there would be any judicial involvement with it? I mean, it seems to me it can just as easily be read as a direction to Congress saying what we're going to do when these electoral votes are presented to us for counting.

Olson: I think that it wasn't directed to Congress, but it seems to me that in the context in which it was adopted and the promise that it afforded, that the conclusive effect would be given to the state's selection of electors, that it is a somewhat empty remedy, and it doesn't accomplish Congress' objectives if it cannot be enforced when an agency of the state government steps in, as the Florida Supreme Court did here, and overturn the plan by which the Florida Legislature carefully set forth a program so that disputes could be resolved, and we wouldn't have the controversy, conflict and chaos that we submit exists today in Florida.

Justice Stephen G. Breyer: All right, so then what you're arguing about is a determination by the state court of Florida as to what the circumstances are under state law, where the action of a state official would or would not be reasonable.

Olson: I think that — yes, but I

think that it has to be looked at in the context in which that was done. When the state Supreme Court so constrained and says in its opinion [the Florida secretary of state will] accept these late returns until 5 p.m. on Nov. 26, and in the context there was no discretion left for the secretary of state at all. . . .

Justice Ruth Bader Ginsburg: Mr. Olson, would you agree that, when we read a state court decision, we should read it in the light most favorable to the integrity of the state supreme court? That if there are two possible readings, one that would impute to that court injudicial behavior, lack of integrity, indeed, dishonesty, and the other that would read the opinion to say we think this court is attempting to construe the state law but it may have been wrong, we might have interpreted it differently, but we are not the arbiters, they are?

Olson: I would like to answer that in two ways. In the first place, I don't mean to suggest, and I hope my words didn't, that there was a lack of integrity or any dishonesty by the Florida Supreme Court. What we're saying, that it was acting far outside the scope of its authority in connection with an exercise of power that is vested by the Constitution of the United States. . . .

Ginsburg: But if it tells us — if it tells us, "We see these two provisions in conflict, they need to be reconciled?"

Olson: But under almost any other circumstances, yes, Justice Ginsburg, but in this context — in this context we're talking about a federal right, a federal constitutional right, and the rights of individual citizens under the Constitution.

Souter: We have to separate your statutory argument from your constitutional argument. To the extent that you're relying just on the Constitution, do you think that Congress could by Section 15 exclude the courts from adjudicating the constitutionality of what the state has done?

Olson: No, I don't think so.

Scalia: But it certainly could express its preference for a scheme whereby the initial litigation, if you will, at this level, would take place in the Congress. To acknowledge that is not to say that the issue is judicial or that this court has somehow been necessarily excluded from the process for all time. It is simply to say that the first line of litigation at the federal level seems, under the statute, to be Congress and not the court. . . .

Laurence Tribe, attorney for Vice President Al Gore's campaign: Mr. Chief Justice, and may it please the court, I think I would want to note at the outset that the alleged due process violation, which keeps popping up and then disappearing, and has, as far as I can tell, not appeared at the state Supreme Court, did make one appearance in the reply brief here, is really not before the court, and for understandable reasons. Because although it is part of the popular culture to talk about how unfair it is to change the rules of the game, I think that misses the point when the game is over, and when it's over in a, kind of, photo finish that leaves people unsure who won.

And then the question is: How do you develop great, sort of, greater certainty? And a rather common technique is a recount, sometimes a manual recount, sometimes taking more time. It'd be rather like looking more closely at the film of the photo finish. It's nothing extraordinary, it's not like suddenly moving Heartbreak Hill or adding a mile or subtracting a mile from . . .

Kennedy: You're saying, no important policy in 3 U.S.C., Section 5?

Tribe: No, no.

Kennedy: In fact, we change the rules after. It's not important in popular culture.

Tribe: Certainly not, Justice Kennedy. But I read U.S.C., Section 5 — that is 3 U.S.C., Section 5 — not as a requirement that, for example, one never add resources to checking how a particular ballot was cast. If you look at the language, I think it's really much too casual to say other, that all of the laws must stay fixed in order to have the safe harbor apply — those as I'll try to argue in a few minutes — that's really not a question for this court, but rather for the Congress.

Rehnquist: Let me ask you just a moment, you say you don't think this statute permits this court to get into the matter at this time. Are you suggesting there could be any judicial review of a decision by the Congress to count one set of electoral votes over . . .

Tribe: No, I don't think so, Mr. Chief Justice. It's just that I don't trust my own imagination to have exhausted all possibilities. For example, in the case in I think it was 1890, in *Fitzgerald v. Green*, when this court held that only states can punish fraudulent voting for presidential electors, it got into the act sort of obliquely and at an angle, and that had a bearing on the question of how the presidential electoral slate might be composed, but it certainly didn't get into this.

Kennedy: You suggest in your reply brief that it is — I think you said it's not self-evident that the Florida legislature at this time has the right to appoint any slate of delegates, because the Congress has set the date and the date is the general election day. If that is so, doesn't this mean that when we think about justiciability, we must be very careful to preserve the role of the court?

You have said that the — or suggested here in your reply brief — that the Florida Legislature now has no role. You are now suggesting that this court has no role. That means the Supreme Court of Florida is it, so far as judicial interpretation of the consequences of 3 U.S.C., Section 5.

Tribe: Justice Kennedy, first of all, I do want to be clear that, in our view, the question of whether and when and how the Florida Legislature can enter the picture is in no way presented here. . . .

Secondly, if it were the case that the Florida Legislature could not simply decide, "Well, we're tired of all this counting; we've moving in," and that this court cannot decide whether the conditions of 3 U.S.C., Section 5 are met, it would then remain only for Congress to make a determination. And adding the Florida Legislature would not, after all, have added an adjudication.

Kennedy: And my point is that puts hydraulic pressure on your nonjusticiability argument and makes it a very, very important argument and a critical argument in this case.

Tribe: Well, perhaps, Justice Kennedy, but I, frankly, can't see how it would affect the decision in this case. That is, after all, you have before you a judgment of the highest court of a state. As Justice Ginsburg and others have suggested, it would ordinarily be the case, surely, that one would not go out of one's way to read the judgment as a breach of faith with the duties of trying to reconcile provisions that are intentioned.

O'Connor: Well, I guess in the area, though, of presidential electors, it could be that that court, as all courts would be, have to be informed, at least, by the provisions of Section 5 in reviewing the laws enacted by the legislature of the state. . . . I mean, it had to register somehow with the Florida courts that that statute was there and that it might be in the state's best interest not to go around changing the law after the election.

Tribe: Well, Justice O'Connor, I certainly agree that if the Florida Supreme Court adverted to 3 U.S.C., Section 5, and, as Justice Kennedy asked earlier, got it wrong, then there would be a federal issue for this court.

O'Connor: Well, is there a federal issue if the court doesn't. . . .

Tribe: No. The answer is no. ◆

Bush Evokes Jefferson, Calls for Tackling Society's Problems 'One Person at a Time'

Following is a transcript of President-elect George W. Bush's Dec. 13 televised speech after the concession of Vice President Al Gore. Bush spoke from the chamber of the state House of Representatives in Austin, Tex. Transcript provided by The Federal Document Clearing House.

Thank you all. Thank you very much. Good evening, my fellow Americans. I appreciate so very much the opportunity to speak with you tonight.

Mr. Speaker, Lieutenant Governor, friends, distinguished guests, our country has been through a long and trying period, with the outcome of the presidential election not finalized for longer than any of us could ever imagine.

Vice President Gore and I put our hearts and hopes into our campaigns. We both gave it our all. We shared similar emotions, so I understand how difficult this moment must be for Vice President Gore and his family.

He has a distinguished record of service to our country as a congressman, a senator and a vice president.

This evening I received a gracious call from the vice president. We agreed to meet early next week in Washington, and we agreed to do our best to heal our country after this hard-fought contest.

Tonight I want to thank all the thousands of volunteers and campaign workers who worked so hard on my behalf.

I also salute the vice president and his supporters for waging a spirited campaign. And I thank him for a call that I know was difficult to make. Laura and I wish the vice president and Sen. [Joseph I.] Lieberman and their families the very best.

I have a lot to be thankful for tonight. I'm thankful for America, and thankful that we were able to resolve our electoral differences in a peaceful way.

I'm thankful to the American people for the great privilege of being able to serve as your next president.

I want to thank my wife and our daughters for their love. Laura's active involvement as first lady has made Texas a better place, and she will be a wonderful first lady of America.

I am proud to have Dick Cheney by my side, and America will be proud to have him as our next vice president.

Tonight I chose to speak from the chamber of the Texas House of Representatives because it has been a home to bipartisan cooperation. Here in a place where Democrats have the majority, Republicans and Democrats have worked together to do what is right for the people we represent.

We've had spirited disagreements. And in the end, we found constructive consensus. It is an experience I will always carry with me, an example I will always follow.

I want to thank my friend, House Speaker Pete Laney, a Democrat, who introduced me today. I want to thank the legislators from both political parties with whom I've worked.

Across the hall in our Texas capitol is the state Senate. And I cannot help but think of our mutual friend, the former Democrat lieutenant governor, Bob Bullock. His love for Texas and his ability to work in a bipartisan way continue to be a model for all of us.

The spirit of cooperation I have seen in this hall is what is needed in Washington, D.C. It is the challenge of our moment. After a difficult election, we must put politics behind us and work together to make the promise of America available for every one of our citizens.

I am optimistic that we can change the tone in Washington, D.C.

I believe things happen for a reason, and I hope the long wait of the last five weeks will heighten a desire to move beyond the bitterness and partisanship of the recent past.

Our nation must rise above a house divided. Americans share hopes and goals and values far more important than any political disagreements.

Republicans want the best for our nation, and so do Democrats. Our votes may differ, but not our hopes.

I know America wants reconciliation and unity. I know Americans want progress. And we must seize this moment and deliver.

Together, guided by a spirit of common sense, common courtesy and common goals, we can unite and inspire the American citizens.

Together, we will work to make all our public schools excellent, teaching every student of every background and every accent, so that no child is left behind.

Together we will save Social Security and renew its promise of a secure retirement for generations to come.

Together we will strengthen Medicare and offer prescription drug coverage to all of our seniors.

Together we will give Americans the broad, fair and fiscally responsible tax relief they deserve.

Together we'll have a bipartisan foreign policy true to our values and true to our friends, and we will have a military equal to every challenge and superior to every adversary.

Together we will address some of society's deepest problems one person at a time, by encouraging and empowering the good hearts and good works of the American people.

This is the essence of compassionate conservatism, and it will be a foundation of my administration.

These priorities are not merely Republican concerns or Democratic concerns; they are American responsibilities.

During the fall campaign, we differed about the details of these proposals, but there was remarkable consensus about the important issues before us: excellent schools, retirement and health security, tax relief, a strong military, a more civil society.

We have discussed our differences. Now it is time to find common ground and build consensus to make America a beacon of opportunity in the 21st century.

I'm optimistic this can happen. Our future demands it, and our history proves it. Two hundred years ago, in the election of 1800, America faced another close presidential election. A tie in the Electoral College put the outcome into the hands of Congress.

After six days of voting and 36 ballots, the House of Representatives elected Thomas Jefferson the third president of the United States. That election brought the first transfer of power from one party to another in our new democracy.

Shortly after the election, Jefferson, in a letter titled "Reconciliation and Reform," wrote this: "The steady character of our countrymen is a rock to which we may safely moor; unequivocal in principle, reasonable in manner. We should be able to hope to do a great deal of good to the cause of freedom and harmony."

Two hundred years have only strengthened the steady character of America. And so as we begin the work of healing our nation, tonight I call upon that character: respect for each other; respect for our differences; generosity of spirit, and a willingness to work hard and work together to solve any problem.

I have something else to ask you, to ask every American. I ask for you to pray for this great nation. I ask for your prayers for leaders from both parties. I thank you for your prayers for me and my family, and I ask you to pray for Vice President Gore and his family.

I have faith that with God's help we as a nation will move forward together as one nation, indivisible. And together we will create an America that is open, so every citizen has access to the American dream; an America that is educated, so every child has the keys to realize that dream; and an America that is united in our diversity and our shared American values that are larger than race or party.

I was not elected to serve one party, but to serve one nation.

The president of the United States is the president of every single American, of every race and every background.

Whether you voted for me or not, I will do my best to serve your interests and I will work to earn your respect.

I will be guided by President Jefferson's sense of purpose, to stand for principle, to be reasonable in manner, and above all, to do great good for the cause of freedom and harmony.

The presidency is more than an honor. It is more than an office. It is a charge to keep, and I will give it my all.

Thank you very much and God bless America. ◆

Gore Concedes Protracted Election To Bush, Pledges to Support President-Elect

Following is a transcript of Vice President Al Gore's Dec. 13 televised address conceding the presidency to Texas Gov. George W. Bush. Gore spoke from the Old Executive Office Building in Washington, D.C. Transcript provided by the White House.

Just moments ago, I spoke with George W. Bush and congratulated him on becoming the 43rd president of the United States. And I promised I wouldn't call him back this time.

I offered to meet with him as soon as possible, so that we can start to heal the divisions of the campaign, and the contest through which we have just passed.

Almost a century and a half ago, Sen. Stephen Douglas told Abraham Lincoln, who had just defeated him for the presidency, "Partisan feeling must yield to patriotism. I am with you, Mr. President, and God bless you."

In that same spirit, I say to President-elect Bush that what remains of partisan rancor must now be put aside. And may God bless his stewardship of this country.

Neither he nor I anticipated this long and difficult road. Certainly, neither of us wanted it to happen. Yet it came. And now it has ended, resolved as it must be resolved — through the honored institutions of our democracy.

Over the library of one of our great law schools is inscribed the motto: "Not under man but under God and law." It is the ruling principle of American freedom, the source of our democratic liberties; I have tried to make it my guide throughout this contest, as it has guided America's deliberations of all the complex issues of the past five weeks.

Now the U.S. Supreme Court has spoken. Let there be no doubt: While I strongly disagree with the court's decision, I accept it. I accept the finality of this outcome, which will be ratified next Monday in the Electoral College. And tonight, for the sake of our unity as a people and the strength of our democracy, I offer my concession.

I also accept my responsibility, which I will discharge unconditionally — to honor the new president-elect, and do everything possible to help him bring Americans together in fulfillment of the great vision that our Declaration of Independence defines, and that our Constitution affirms and defends.

Let me say how grateful I am to all those who supported me — and supported the cause for which we have fought.

Tipper and I feel a deep gratitude to Joe and Hadassah Lieberman, who brought passion and high purpose to our partnership — and opened new doors not just for our campaign, but for our country.

This has been an extraordinary election. But in one of God's unforeseen paths, this belatedly broken impasse can point us all to a new common ground. For its very closeness can serve to remind us that we are one people, with a shared history and a shared destiny.

Indeed, that history gives us many examples of contests as hotly debated, as fiercely fought, with their own challenges to the popular will.

Other disputes have dragged on for weeks before reaching resolution. And each time, both the victor and the vanquished have accepted the result peacefully, and in a spirit of reconciliation.

So let it be with us.

I know that many of my supporters are disappointed. I am, too. But our disappointment must be overcome by our love of country.

And I say to our fellow members of the world community: Let no one see this contest as a sign of American weakness. The strength of American democracy is shown most clearly through the difficulties it can overcome.

Some have expressed concern that the unusual nature of this election might hamper the next president in the conduct of his office. I do not believe it need be so.

President-elect Bush inherits a nation whose citizens will be ready to assist him in the conduct of his large responsibilities. I personally will be at his disposal.

And I call on all Americans — I particularly urge all who stood with us — to unite behind our next president.

This is America. Just as we fight hard when the stakes are high, we close ranks and come together when the contest is done.

And while there will be time enough to debate our continuing differences, now is the time to recognize that that which unites us is greater than that which divides us.

While we yet hold and do not yield our opposing beliefs, there is a higher duty than the one we owe to political party.

This is America, and we put country before party. We will stand together behind our new president.

As for what I'll do next, I don't know the answer to that one yet. Like many of you, I'm looking forward to spending the holidays with family and old friends. I know I'll spend time in Tennessee and mend some fences — literally and figuratively.

Some have asked whether I have any regrets, and I do have one regret: that I didn't get the chance to stay and fight for the American people for the next four years. Especially for those who need burdens lifted and barriers removed. Especially for those who feel their voices have not been heard.

I heard you — and I will not forget.

I've seen America in this campaign. And I like what I see. It's worth fighting for. And that's a fight I'll never stop.

As for the battle that ends tonight, I do believe, as my father once said, that no matter how hard the loss, defeat may serve as well as victory to shake the soul and let the glory out.

So for me, this campaign ends as it began: with the love of Tipper and our family; with faith in God and in the country I have been so proud to serve, from Vietnam to the vice presidency; and with gratitude to our truly tireless campaign staff and volunteers, including all those who worked so hard in Florida for the last 36 days.

Now the political struggle is over. And we turn again to the unending struggle for the common good of all Americans, and for those multitudes around the world who look to us for leadership in the cause of freedom.

In the words of our great hymn, "America, America, let us crown thy good with brotherhood, from sea to shining sea."

And now, my friends, in a phrase I once addressed to others — it is time for me to go.

Thank you, and good night. And God bless America. ◆

Appendix E

PUBLIC LAWS

Public Laws

Public laws 106-1 through 106-170 were enacted in the first session of the 106th Congress. (1999 Almanac, p. E-3)

PL 106-171 (S 1733) Amend the Food Stamp Act of 1977 to provide for a national standard of interoperablity and portability applicable to electronic food stamp benefit transactions. Introduced by FITZGERALD, R-Ill., on Oct. 14, 1999. Senate Agriculture, Nutrition, and Forestry discharged. Senate passed, amended, Nov. 19. House passed, under suspension of the rules, Jan. 31, 2000. President signed Feb. 11, 2000.

PL 106-172 (HR 2130) Amend the Controlled Substances Act to direct the emergency scheduling of gamma hydroxybutyric acid and provide for a national awareness campaign. Introduced by UPTON, R-Mich., on June 10, 1999. House Commerce reported, amended, Sept. 27 (H Rept 106-340, Part 1). House Judiciary discharged. House passed, amended, under suspension of the rules, Oct. 12. Senate passed, with amendments, Nov. 19. House agreed to Senate amendments under suspension of the rules, Jan. 31, 2000. President signed Feb. 18, 2000.

PL 106-173 (HR 1451) Establish the Abraham Lincoln Bicentennial Commission. Introduced by LaHOOD, R- Ill., on April 15, 1999. House passed, amended, under suspension of the rules, Oct. 4. Senate Judiciary discharged. Senate passed, with amendment, Nov. 19. House agreed to Senate amendment, under suspension of the rules, Feb. 8, 2000. President signed Feb. 25, 2000.

PL 106-174 (S 632) Provide assistance for poison prevention and stabilize the funding of regional poison control centers. Introduced by DeWINE, R-Ohio, on March 16, 1999. Senate Health, Education, Labor and Pensions reported, amended, Aug. 4 (no written report). Senate passed, amended, Aug. 5. House passed, under suspension of the rules, Feb. 8, 2000. President signed Feb. 25, 2000.

PL 106-175 (HR 3557) Authorize the president to award a gold medal on behalf of the Congress to Cardinal John O'Connor, archbishop of New York, in recognition of his accomplishments as a priest, a chaplain and a humanitarian. Introduced by FOSSELLA, R-N.Y. , on Jan. 31, 2000. House passed, under suspension of the rules, Feb. 15. Senate Banking, Housing and Urban Affairs discharged. Senate passed March 1. President signed March 5, 2000.

PL 106-176 (HR 149) Make technical corrections to the Omnibus Parks and Public Lands Management Act of 1996. Introduced by HANSEN, R-Utah, on Jan. 6, 1999. House Resources reported, amended, Feb. 12 (H Rept 106-17). House passed, amended, under suspension of the rules, Feb. 23. Senate Energy and Natural Resources reported, with amendments, July 28 (S Rept 106-125). Senate passed, amended, Nov. 19. House agreed to Senate amendments, under suspension of the rules, Feb. 15, 2000. President signed March 10, 2000.

PL 106-177 (HR 764) Reduce the incidence of child abuse and neglect. Introduced by PRYCE, R-Ohio, on Feb. 12, 1999. House Judiciary reported Oct. 1 (H Rept 106-360). House passed, amended, Oct. 5. Senate Judiciary reported, with amendment, Oct. 28 (no written report). Senate passed, with amendment, Nov. 19. House agreed to Senate amendment, under suspension of the rules, Feb. 1, 2000. President signed March 10, 2000.

PL 106-178 (HR 1883) Provide for the application of measures to foreign persons who transfer certain goods, services or technology to Iran, Introduced by GILMAN, R-N.Y., on May 20, 1999. House International Relations reported, amended, Sept. 14 (H Rept 106-315, Part 1). House Science discharged. House passed, amended, under suspension of the rules, Sept. 14. Senate passed, with amendment, Feb. 24, 2000. House agreed to Senate amendments March 1. President signed March 14, 2000.

PL 106-179 (S 613) Encourage Indian economic development and provide for the disclosure of Indian tribal sovereign immunity in contracts involving Indian tribes. Introduced by CAMPBELL, R-Colo., on March 15, 1999. Senate Indian Affairs reported, amended, Sept. 8 (S Rept 106-150). Senate passed, amended, Sept. 15. House Resources reported Feb. 29, 2000 (H Rept 106-501). House passed, under suspension of the rules, Feb. 29. President signed March 14, 2000.

PL 106-180 (S 376) Amend the Communications Satellite Act of 1962 to promote competition and privatization in satellite communications. Introduced by BURNS, R-Mont. on Feb. 4, 1999. Senate Commerce, Science and Transportation reported, amended, June 30 (S Rept 106-100). Senate passed, amended, July 1. House Commerce discharged. House passed, with amendment, Nov. 10. Conference report filed in the House March 2, 2000 (H Rept 106-509). Senate agreed to conference report March 2. House agreed to conference report March 9. President signed March 17, 2000.

PL 106-181 (HR 1000) Amend Title 49, U.S. Code, to reauthorize programs of the Federal Aviation Administration. Introduced by SHUSTER, R-PA., on March 4, 1999. House Transportation and Infrastructure reported, amended, May 28 (H Rept 106-167, Part 1). House Transportation and Infrastructure filed supplemental report June 9 (H Rept 106-167, Part 2). House Budget and Rules discharged. House passed, amended, June 15. Senate Commerce, Science and Transportation discharged. Senate passed, with amendment, Oct. 5. Conference report filed in the House March 8, 2000 (H Rept 106-513). Senate agreed to conference report March 8. House agreed to conference report March 15. President signed April 5, 2000.

PL 106-182 (HR 5) Amend Title II of the Social Security Act to eliminate the earnings test for individuals who have attained retirement age. Introduced by JOHNSON, R-Texas, on March 1, 1999. House Ways and Means reported, amended, March 1, 2000 (H Rept 106-507). House passed, amended, March 1. Senate passed with amendment, March 22. House agreed to Senate amendment March 28. President signed April 7, 2000.

PL 106-183 (HR 1374) Designate the U.S. Post Office building located at 680 U.S. Highway 130 in Hamilton N.J., as the "John K. Rafferty Hamilton Post Office Building." Introduced by SMITH, R-N.J., on April 12, 1999. House passed, amended, under suspension of the rules, Oct. 12. Senate Governmental Affairs reported March 27, 2000 (no written report). Senate passed April 3. President signed April 13, 2000.

PL 106-184 (HR 3189) Designate the U.S. Post Office located at 14071 Peyton Drive in Chino Hills, Calif., as the "Joseph Ileto Post Office." Introduced by MILLER, R-Calif., on Nov. 1, 1999. House passed, under suspension of the rules, Nov. 8. Senate Governmental Affairs reported March 27, 2000 (no written report). Senate passed April 3. President signed April 14, 2000.

PL 106-185 (HR 1658) Provide a more just and uniform procedure for federal civil forfeitures. Introduced by HYDE, R-Ill., on May 4, 1999. House Judiciary reported, amended, June 18 (H Rept 106-192). House passed, amended, June 24. Senate Judiciary reported, with amendment, March 23, 2000 (no written report). Senate passed, with amendment, March 27. House agreed to Senate amendment, under suspension of the rules, April 11. President signed April 25, 2000.

PL 106-186 (S J Res 43) Express the sense of Congress that the president of the United States should encourage free and fair elections and respect for democracy in Peru. Introduced by COVERDELL, R-Ga., on March 28, 2000. Senate passed, amended, April 7. House International Relations discharged. House passed April 11. President signed April 25, 2000.

PL 106-187 (HR 1231) Direct the secretary of Agriculture to convey certain National Forest lands to Elko County, Nev., for continued use as a cemetery. Introduced by GIBBONS, R-Nev., on March 23, 1999. House Resources reported, amended, Sept. 8 (H Rept 106-308). House passed, under suspension of the rules, Sept. 21. Senate Energy and Natural Resources reported March 9 (S Rept 106-238). Senate passed April 13. President signed April 28, 2000.

PL 106-188 (HR 2368) Assist in the resettlement and relocation of the people of Bikini Atoll by amending the terms of the trust fund established during the U.S. administration of the Trust Territory of the Pacific Islands. Introduced by YOUNG, R-Alaska, on June 29, 1999. House Resources reported July 27 (H Rept 106-267). House passed, under suspension of the rules, Sept. 13. Senate Energy and Natural Resources reported March 9, 2000 (S Rept 106-240). Senate passed April 13. President signed April 28, 2000.

PL 106-189 (HR 2862) Direct the secretary of the Interior to release reversionary interests held by the United States in certain parcels of land in Washington County, Utah, to facilitate an anticipated land exchange. Introduced by HANSEN, R-Utah, on Sept. 14, 1999. House passed, under suspension of the rules, Nov. 16. Senate Energy and Natural Resources reported March 9, 2000 (S Rept 106-241). Senate passed April 13. President signed April 28, 2000.

PL 106-190 (HR 2863) Clarify the legal effect on the United States of the acquisition of a parcel of land in the Red Cliffs Desert Reserve in Utah. Introduced by HANSEN, R-Utah, on Sept. 14, 1999. House passed, under suspension of the rules, Nov. 16. Senate Energy and Natural Resources reported March 9, 2000 (S Rept 106-242). Senate passed April 13. President signed April 28, 2000.

PL 106-191 (HR 3063) Amend the Mineral Leasing Act to increase the maximum acreage of federal leases for sodium that may be held by an entity in any one state. Introduced by CUBIN, R-Wyo., on Oct. 13, 1999. House Resources reported Nov. 15 (H Rept 106-469). House passed, under suspension of the rules, Nov. 16. Senate Energy and Natural Resources reported April 12, 2000 (S Rept 106-270). Senate passed April 13. President signed April 28, 2000.

PL 106-192 (HR 1615) Amend the Wild and Scenic Rivers Act to extend the designation of a portion of the Lamprey River in New Hampshire as a recreational river to include an additional river segment. Introduced by SUNUNU, R-N.H., on April 28, 1999. House Resources reported Oct. 7 (H Rept 106-368). House passed, under suspension of the rules, Oct. 12. Senate Energy and Natural Resources reported April 12, 2000 (S Rept 106-269). Senate passed April 13. President signed May 2, 2000.

PL 106-193 (HR 1753) Promote the research, identification, assessment, exploration and development of methane hydrate resources. Introduced by DOYLE, D-Pa., on May 11, 1999. House Science reported, amended, Oct. 13 (H Rept 106-377, Part 1). House Resources reported, amended, Oct. 18 (H Rept 106-377, Part 2). House passed, under suspension of the rules, Oct. 26. Senate passed, with amendment, Nov. 19. House agreed to Senate amendment, with an amendment pursuant to H Res 453, April 3, 2000. Senate agreed to House amendment to Senate amendment April 13. President signed May 2, 2000.

PL 106-194 (HR 3090) Amend the Alaska Native Claims Settlement Act to restore certain lands to the Elim Native Corporation. Introduced by YOUNG, R-Alaska, on Oct. 18, 1999. House Resources reported, amended, Nov. 5 (H Rept 106-452). House passed, under suspension of the rules, Nov. 9. Senate Energy and Natural Resources reported April 10, 2000 (S Rept 106-258). Senate passed April 13. President signed May 2, 2000.

PL 106-195 (H J Res 86) Recognize the 50th anniversary of the Korean War and the service by members of the armed forces during that war. Introduced by EWING, R-Ill., on Feb. 1, 2000. House passed, under suspension of the rules, March 8. Senate Judiciary reported April 12 (no written report). Senate passed April 13. President signed May 2, 2000.

PL 106-196 (S 1567) Designate the U.S. courthouse located at 223 Broad St. in Albany, Ga., as the "C.B. King U.S. Courthouse." Introduced by COVERDELL, R-Ga., on Sept. 8, 1999. Senate Environment and Public Works reported Sept. 29 (no written report). Senate passed Oct. 8. House Transportation and Infrastructure reported, with amendments, March 29, 2000 (H Rept 106-552). House passed, under suspension of the rules, April 3. Senate agreed to House amendments April 13. President signed May 2, 2000.

PL 106-197 (S 1769) Continue reporting requirements of Section 2519 of Title 18, U.S. Code, beyond Dec. 21, 1999. Introduced by LEAHY, D-Vt., on Oct. 22, 1999. Senate Judiciary reported, amended, Oct. 28 (no written report). Senate passed, amended, Nov. 5. House Judiciary discharged. House passed, with amendments, Nov. 18. Senate agreed to House amendments April 13, 2000. President signed May 2, 2000.

PL 106-198 (S J Res 40) Provide for the appointment of Alan G. Spoon as a citizen regent of the Board of Regents of the Smithsonian Institution. Introduced by COCHRAN, R-Miss., on Feb. 29, 2000. Senate Rules and Administration discharged. Senate passed April 12. House passed, under suspension of the rules, May 2. President signed May 5, 2000.

PL 106-199 (S J Res 42) Provide for the reappointment of Manuel L. Ibanez as a citizen regent of the Board of Regents of the Smithsonian Institution. Introduced by COCHRAN, R-Miss., on Feb. 29, 2000. Senate Rules and Administration discharged. Senate passed April 12. House passed, under suspension of the rules, May 2. President signed May 5, 2000.

PL 106-200 (HR 434) Authorize a new trade and investment policy for sub-Saharan Africa. Introduced by CRANE, R-Ill., on Feb. 2, 1999. House International Relations reported, amended, Feb. 16 (H Rept 106-19, Part 1). House Ways and Means reported, amended, June 17 (H Rept 106-19, Part 2). House Banking and Financial Services discharged. House passed, amended, July 16. Senate passed, with amendments, Nov. 3. Conference report filed in the House May 4 (H Rept 106-606). House agreed to conference report May 4. Senate agreed to conference report May 11. President signed May 18, 2000.

PL 106-201 (S 1744) Amend the Endangered Species Act of 1973 to provide that certain species conservation reports shall continue to be submitted. Introduced by JOHN R. CHAFEE, R-R.I., on Oct. 18, 1999. Senate Environment and Public Works reported Oct. 18 (S Rept 106-194). Senate passed March 27, 2000. House passed, under suspension of the rules, May 3. President signed May 18, 2000.

PL 106-202 (S 2323) Amend the Fair Labor Standards Act of 1938 to clarify the treatment of stock options under the act. Introduced by McCONNELL, R-Ky., on March 29, 2000. Senate passed April 12. House passed, under suspension of the rules, May 3. President signed May 18, 2000.

PL 106-203 (HR 2412) Designate the federal building and U.S. courthouse located at 1300 South Harrison St. in Fort Wayne, Ind., as the "E. Ross Adair Federal Building and U.S. Courthouse." Introduced by SOUDER, R-Ind., on June 30, 1999. House Transportation and Infrastructure reported March 23, 2000 (H Rept 106-540). House passed, under suspension of the rules, March 28. Senate Environment and Public Works reported April 13 (no written report). Senate passed May 4. President signed May 22, 2000.

PL 106-204 (S 2370) Designate the federal building located at 500 Pearl St. in New York City as the "Daniel Patrick Moynihan U.S. Courthouse." Introduced by SCHUMER, D-N.Y., on April 6, 2000. Senate Environment and Public Works reported April 13 (no written report). Senate passed May 4. House passed, under suspension of the rules, May 15. President signed May 23, 2000.

PL 106-205 (S J Res 44) Support the Day of Honor 2000 to honor and recognize the service of minority veterans in the U.S. armed forces during World War II. Introduced by KENNEDY, D-Mass., on April 6, 2000. Senate Judiciary discharged. Senate passed May 18. House passed May 23. President signed May 26, 2000.

PL 106-206 (HR 154) Provide for the collection of fees for the making of motion pictures, television productions and sound tracks in National Park System and National Wildlife Refuge System units. Introduced by HEFLEY, R-Colo., on Jan. 6, 1999. House Resources reported, amended, March 23 (H Rept 106-75). House passed, under suspension of the rules, April 12. Senate Energy and Natural Resources reported, with amendments, June 7 (S Rept 106-67). Senate passed, with amendments, Nov. 19. House agreed to Senate amendments, under suspension of the rules, May 22, 2000. President signed May 26, 2000.

PL 106-207 (HR 371) Expedite the naturalization of aliens who served with special guerrilla units in Laos. Introduced by VENTO, D-Minn., on Jan. 19, 1999. House Judiciary reported, amended, April 6 (H Rept 106-563). House passed, under suspension of the rules, May 2, 2000. Senate Judiciary reported, with amendment, May 18 (no written report). Senate passed, with amendment, May 18. House agreed to Senate amendment May 23. President signed May 26, 2000.

PL 106-208 (HR 834) Extend the authorization for the Historic Preservation Fund. Introduced by HEFLEY, R-Colo., on Feb. 24, 1999. House Resources reported, amended, July 20 (H Rept 106-241). House passed, under suspension of the rules, Sept. 21. Senate Energy and Natural Resources reported, with amendments, March 9, 2000 (S Rept 106-237). Senate passed, with amendments, April 13. House agreed to Senate amendments, under suspension of the rules, May 22. President signed May 26, 2000.

PL 106-209 (HR 1377) Designate the facility of the U.S. Postal Service at 9308 S. Chicago Ave. in Chicago, Ill., as the "John J. Buchanan Post Office Building." Introduced by WELLER, R-Ill., on April 13, 1999. House passed, under suspension of the rules, May 24. Senate Governmental Affairs reported, with amendments, Nov. 4 (no written report). Senate passed, with amendments, Nov. 19. House agreed to Senate amendments, under suspension of the rules, May 15, 2000. President signed May 26, 2000.

PL 106-210 (HR 1832) Reform unfair and anti-competitive practices in the professional boxing industry. Introduced by OXLEY, R-Ohio, on May 17, 1999. House Commerce reported, amended, Nov. 4 (H Rept 106-449, Part 1). House Education and the Workforce discharged Nov. 4. House passed, under suspension of the rules, Nov. 8. Senate passed, with amendments, April 7, 2000. House agreed to Senate amendments, under suspension of the rules, May 22. President signed May 26, 2000.

PL 106-211 (HR 3629) Amend the Higher Education Act of 1965 to improve the program for American Indian Tribal Colleges and Universities under part A of Title III. Introduced by GREEN, R-Wis., on Feb. 10, 2000. House passed, under suspension of the rules, May 2. Senate passed May 18. President signed May 26, 2000.

PL 106-212 (HR 3707) Authorize funds for the site selection and construction of a facility in Taipei, Taiwan, suitable for the mission of the American Institute in Taiwan. Introduced by BEREUTER, R-Neb., on Feb. 29, 2000. House passed, under suspension of the rules, March 28. Senate Foreign Relations reported, with amendment, April 20 (no written report). Senate passed, with amendment, May 2. House agreed to Senate amendment May 18. President signed May 26, 2000.

PL 106-213 (S 1836) Extend the deadline for starting construction of a hydroelectric project in Alabama. Introduced by HOLLINGS, D-S.C., on Nov. 1, 1999. Senate Energy and Natural Resources reported April 12, 2000 (S Rept 106-265). Senate passed April 13. House Commerce discharged. House passed May 22. President signed May 26, 2000.

PL 106-214 (HR 3293) Amend the law that authorized the Vietnam Veterans Memorial to authorize the placement within the site of the memorial of a plaque to honor those Vietnam veterans who died after their service in the Vietnam war, but as a direct result of that service. Introduced by GALLEGLY, R-Calif., on Nov. 10, 1999. House Resources reported, amended April 13, 2000 (H Rept 106-585). House passed, amended, under suspension of the rules May 9. Senate Energy and Natural Resources discharged. Senate passed May 25. President signed June 15, 2000.

PL 106-215 (HR 4489) Amend Section 110 of the Illegal Immigration Reform and Immigrant Responsibility Act of 1996. Introduced by SMITH, R-Texas, on May 18, 2000. House passed, under suspension of the rules, May 23. Senate passed May 25. President signed June 15, 2000.

PL 106-216 (HR 1953) Authorize leases for terms not to exceed 99 years on land held in trust for the Torres Martinez Desert Cahuilla Indians and the Guidiville Band of Pomo Indians of the Guidiville Indian Rancheria. Introduced by BONO, R-Calif., on May 26, 1999. House passed, amended, under suspension of the rules, Nov. 17. Senate Indian Affairs reported May 18, 2000 (no written report). Senate passed June 8. President signed June 20, 2000.

PL 106-217 (HR 2484) Provide that land owned by the Lower Sioux Indian Community in the state of Minnesota but not held in trust by the United States for the Community may be leased or transferred by the Community without further approval by the United States. Introduced by MINGE, D-Minn., on July 12, 1999. House Resources reported Feb. 29, 2000 (H Rept 106-502). House passed, under suspension of the rules, Feb. 29. Senate Indian Affairs reported May 18 (no written report). Senate passed June 8. President signed June 20, 2000.

PL 106-218 (HR 3639) Designate the federal building located at 2201 C St., N.W., in the District of Columbia, currently headquarters for the Department of State, as the "Harry S Truman Federal Building." Introduced by SKELTON, D-Mo., on Feb. 10, 2000. House passed, amended, under suspension of the rules, May 23. Senate passed June 8. President signed June 20, 2000.

PL 106-219 (HR 4542) Designate the Washington Opera in Washington, D.C., as the National Opera. Introduced by GOODLING, R-Pa., on May 25, 2000. House passed, under suspension of the rules, June 6. Senate passed June 7. President signed June 20, 2000.

PL 106-220 (S 291) Convey certain real property within the Carlsbad Project in New Mexico to the Carlsbad Irrigation District. Introduced by DOMENICI, R-N.M., on Jan. 21, 1999. Senate Energy and Natural Resources reported March 17, 2000 (S Rept 106-19). Senate passed March 25. House passed, under suspension of the rules, June 7. President signed June 20, 2000.

PL 106-221 (S 356) Authorize the secretary of the Interior to convey certain works, facilities, and titles of the Gila Project, and designated lands within or adjacent to the Gila Project, to the Wellton-Mohawk Irrigation and Drainage District. Introduced by KYL, R-Ariz., on Feb. 3, 1999. Senate Energy and Natural Resources reported March 17 (S Rept 106-21). Senate passed March 25. House passed, under suspension of the rules, June 7, 2000. President signed June 20, 2000.

PL 106-222 (S 777) Require the secretary of Agriculture to establish an electronic filing and retrieval system to enable farmers and other persons to file all required paperwork electronically with selected Agriculture Department agencies and to access public information on programs administered by these agencies. Introduced by FITZGERALD, R-Ill., on April 13, 1999. Senate Agriculture discharged. Senate passed, amended, Nov. 4. House passed, amended, under suspension of the rules, April 10, 2000. Senate agreed to House amendments, with amendments, May 18. House agreed to Senate amendment to House amendments June 6. President signed June 20, 2000.

PL 106-223 (S 2722) Authorize the award of the Medal of Honor to Ed W. Freeman, James K. Okubo, and Andrew J. Smith. Introduced by AKAKA, D-Hawaii, on June 13, 2000. Senate passed June 13. House passed June 16. President signed June 20, 2000.

PL 106-224 (HR 2559) Amend the Federal Crop Insurance Act to strengthen the safety net for agricultural producers by providing greater access to more affordable risk management tools and improved protection from production and income loss. Introduced by COMBEST, R-Texas, on July 20, 1999. House Agriculture reported, amended, Aug. 5 (H Rept 106-300, Part 1). Supplemental report filed Sept. 22 (H Rept 106-300, Part 2). House passed, amended, Sept. 29. Senate passed amended, March 23, 2000. Conference report filed in the House on May 29 (H Rept 106-639). House agreed to conference report May 25. Senate agreed to conference report May 25. President signed June 20, 2000.

PL 106-225 (HR 3642) Authorize the president to award posthumously a gold medal on behalf of the Congress to Charles M. Schulz in recognition of his lasting artistic contributions to the nation and the world. Introduced by THOMPSON, D-Calif., on Feb. 10, 2000. House passed, under suspension of the rules, Feb. 15. Senate Banking, Housing, and Urban Affairs discharged. Senate passed, with amendments, May 2. House agreed to Senate amendments June 6. President signed June 20, 2000.

PL 106-226 (HR 4387) Provide that the School Governance Charter Amendment Act of 2000 take effect on the date it is ratified by the voters of the District of Columbia. Introduced by NORTON, D-D.C., on May 4, 2000. House Government Reform reported June 12 (H Rept 106-664). House passed, under suspension of the rules, June 12. Senate passed June 14. President signed June 27, 2000.

PL 106-227 (H J Res 101) Recognize the 225th birthday of the United States Army. Introduced by SPENCE, R-S.C., on June 8, 2000. House passed, under suspension of the rules, June 13. Senate Judiciary discharged. Senate passed June 15. President signed June 29, 2000.

PL 106-228 (S 1967) Make technical corrections to the status of certain land held in trust for the Mississippi Band of Choctaw Indians, and take certain land into trust for that band. Introduced by COCHRAN, R-Miss., on Nov. 18, 1999. Senate Indian Affairs reported June 13, 2000 (S Rept 106-307). Senate passed June 14. House passed, under suspension of the rules, June 19. President signed June 29, 2000.

PL 106-229 (S 761) Regulate interstate commerce by electronic means (including electronic signatures) and permit and encourage the continued expansion of electronic commerce through the operation of free market forces. Introduced by ABRAHAM, R-Mich., on March 25, 1999. Senate Commerce, Science and Transportation reported, with amendments, July 30 (S Rept 106-131). Senate passed, amended, Nov. 19. House passed, amended, Feb. 16, 2000. Conference report filed in the House on June 8 (H Rept 106-661). House agreed to conference report June 14. Senate agreed to conference report June 16. President signed June 30, 2000.

PL 106-230 (HR 4762) Amend the Internal Revenue Code of 1986 to require "527" organizations to disclose their political activities. Introduced by HOUGHTON, R-N.Y., on June 27, 2000. House passed, under suspension of the rules, June 28. Senate passed June 29. President signed July 1, 2000.

PL 106-231 (HR 642) Redesignate the federal building located at 701 South Santa Fe Ave. in Compton, Calif., known as the Compton Main Post Office, as the "Mervyn Malcolm Dymally Post Office Building." Introduced by MILLENDER-McDONALD, D-Calif., on Feb. 9, 1999. House Government Reform discharged. House passed Nov. 18. Senate Governmental Affairs reported June 21, 2000 (no written report). Senate passed June 23. President signed July 6, 2000.

PL 106-232 (HR 643) Redesignate the federal building located at 10301 South Compton Ave. in Los Angeles, Calif., known as the Watts Finance Office, as the "Augustus F. Hawkins Post Office Building." Introduced by MILLENDER-McDONALD, D-Calif., on Feb. 9, 1999. House passed, under suspension of the rules, Oct. 12. Senate Governmental Affairs reported June 21, 2000 (no written report). Senate passed June 23. President signed July 6, 2000.

PL 106-233 (HR 1666) Designate the facility of the U.S. Postal Service at 200 East Pinckney St. in Madison, Fla., as the "Captain Colin P. Kelly, Jr. Post Office." Introduced by BOYD, D-Fla., on May 4, 1999. House passed, under suspension of the rules, March 21, 2000. Senate Governmental Affairs reported June 21 (no written report). Senate passed June 23. President signed July 6, 2000.

PL 106-234 (HR 2307) Designate the building of the U.S. Postal Service located at 5 Cedar St. in Hopkinton, Mass., as the "Thomas J. Brown Post Office Building." Introduced by McGOVERN, D-Mass., on June 22, 1999. House passed, under suspension of the rules, Nov. 8. Senate Governmental Affairs reported June 21, 2000 (no written report). Senate passed June 23. President signed July 6, 2000.

PL 106-235 (HR 2357) Designate the U.S. Post Office located at 3675 Warrensville Center Road in Shaker Heights, Ohio, as the "Louis Stokes Post Office." Introduced by TRAFICANT, D-Ohio, on June 24, 1999. House passed, under suspension of the rules, Oct. 12. Senate Governmental Affairs reported June 21, 2000 (no written report). Senate passed June 23. President signed July 6, 2000.

PL 106-236 (HR 2460) Designate the U.S. Post Office located at 125 Border Ave. West in Wiggins, Miss., as the "Jay Hanna 'Dizzy' Dean Post Office." Introduced by TAYLOR, D-Miss., on July 1, 1999. House passed, under suspension of the rules, Oct. 12. Senate Governmental Affairs reported June 21, 2000 (no written report). Senate passed June 23. President signed July 6, 2000.

PL 106-237 (HR 2591) Designate the United States Post Office located at 713 Elm St. in Wakefield, Kan., as the "William H. Avery Post Office." Introduced by MORAN, R-Kan., on July 22, 1999. House passed, under suspension of the rules, Oct. 12. Senate Governmental Affairs reported June 21, 2000 (no written report). Senate passed June 23. President signed July 6, 2000.

PL 106-238 (HR 2952) Redesignate the facility of the U.S. Postal Service located at 100 Orchard Park Dr. in Greenville, S.C., as the "Keith D. Oglesby Station." Introduced by DEMINT, R-S.C., on Sept. 27, 1999. House passed, under suspension of the rules, March 8, 2000. Senate Governmental Affairs reported June 21 (no written report). Senate passed June 23. President signed July 6, 2000.

PL 106-239 (HR 3018) Designate the U.S. Post Office located at 557 East Bay St. in Charleston, S.C., as the "Marybelle H. Howe Post Office." Introduced by CLYBURN, D-S.C., on Oct. 5, 1999. House passed, amended, under suspension of the rules, March 8, 2000. Senate Governmental Affairs reported June 21 (no written report). Senate passed June 23. President signed July 6, 2000.

PL 106-240 (HR 3699) Designate the facility of the U.S. Postal Service located at 8409 Lee Highway in Merrifield, Va., as the "Joel T. Broyhill Postal Building." Introduced by WOLF, R-Va., on Feb. 29, 2000. House passed, under suspension of the rules, March 14. Senate Governmental Affairs reported June 21 (no written report). Senate passed June 23. President signed July 6, 2000.

PL 106-241 (HR 3701) Designate the facility of the U.S. Postal Service located at 3118 Washington Blvd. in Arlington, Va., as the "Joseph L. Fisher Post Office Building." Introduced by WOLF, R-Va., on Feb. 29, 2000. House passed, under suspension of the rules, March 14. Senate Governmental Affairs reported June 21 (no written report). Senate passed June 23. President signed July 6, 2000.

PL 106-242 (HR 4241) Designate the facility of the U.S. Postal Service located at 1818 Milton Ave. in Janesville, Wis., as the "Les Aspin Post Office Building." Introduced by RYAN, R-Wis., on April 11, 2000. House passed, under suspension of the rules, June 6. Senate Governmental Affairs reported June 21 (no written report). Senate passed June 23. President signed July 6, 2000.

PL 106-243 (HR 3051) Direct the secretary of the Interior and the Bureau of Reclamation to conduct a feasibility study on the Jicarilla Apache Reservation in the state of New Mexico. Introduced by UDALL, D-N.M., on Oct. 7, 1999. House passed, amended, under suspension of the rules, Nov. 17. Senate Indian Affairs reported June 22, 2000 (no written report). Senate passed June 28. President signed July 10, 2000.

PL 106-244 (S 1309) Amend Title I of the Employee Retirement Income Security Act of 1974 and provide for the preemption of state law in certain cases relating to certain church plans. Introduced by SESSIONS, R-Ala., on June 30, 1999. Senate Health, Education, Labor, and Pensions discharged. Senate passed, amended, Nov. 19. House passed, under suspension of the rules, June 26, 2000. President signed July 10, 2000.

PL 106-245 (S 1515) Amend the Radiation Exposure Compensation Act. Introduced by HATCH, R-Utah, on Aug. 5, 1999. Senate Health, Education, Labor, and Pensions discharged. Senate Judiciary reported, amended, Nov. 2 (no written report). Senate passed Nov. 19. House Judiciary reported, with amendments, June 26, 2000 (H Rept 106-697). House passed, under suspension of the rules, June 27. Senate agreed to House amendment June 28. President signed July 10, 2000.

PL 106-246 (HR 4425) Make appropriations for military construction, family housing, and base realignment and closure for the Department of Defense for the fiscal year ending September 30, 2001. Introduced by HOBSON, R-Ohio, on May 11, 2000. House Appropriations reported May 11 (H Rept 106-614). House passed, amended, May 16. Senate passed, with amendment, May 18. Conference report filed in the House on June 29 (H Rept 106-710). House agreed to conference report June 29. Senate agreed to conference report June 30. President signed July 13, 2000.

PL 106-247 (S 148) Require the Secretary of the Interior to establish a program to provide assistance in the conservation of neotropical migratory birds. Introduced by ABRAHAM, R-Mich., on Jan. 19, 1999. Senate Environment and Public Works reported March 26 (S Rept 106-36). Senate passed April 13. House passed, amended, under suspension of the rules, June 26, 2000. Senate agreed to House amendment June 29. President signed July 20, 2000.

PL 106-248 (S 1892) Authorize the acquisition of the Valles Caldera and provide for an effective land and wildlife management program for this resource within the Department of Agriculture. Introduced by DOMENICI, R-N.M., on Nov. 9, 1999. Senate Energy and Natural Resources reported, amended, April 12, 2000 (S Rept 106-267). Senate passed, amended, April 13. House Resources reported July 11 (H Rept 106-724). House passed, under suspension of the rules, July 12. President signed July 25, 2000.

PL 106-249 (S 986) Direct the secretary of the Interior to convey the Griffith Project to the Southern Nevada Water Authority. Introduced by REID, D-Nev., on May 6, 1999. Senate Energy and Natural Resources reported, amended, Oct. 6 (S Rept 106-173). Senate passed, amended, Nov. 19. House Resources reported July 10, 2000 (H Rept 106-717). House passed, under suspension of the rules, July 10. President signed July 26, 2000.

PL 106-250 (HR 3544) Authorize a gold medal to be awarded on behalf of the Congress to Pope John Paul II in recognition of his many and enduring contributions to peace and religious understanding. Introduced by LEACH, R-Iowa, on Jan. 27, 2000. House passed, amended, under suspension of the rules, May 23. Senate passed July 13. President signed July 27, 2000.

PL 106-251 (HR 3591) Provide for the award of a gold medal on behalf of the Congress to former President Ronald Reagan and his wife Nancy Reagan in recognition of their service to the nation. Introduced by GIBBONS, R-Nev., on Feb. 8, 2000. House passed, under suspension of the rules, April 3. Senate passed July 13. President signed July 27, 2000.

PL 106-252 (HR 4391) Amend Title 4 of the U.S. Code to establish sourcing requirements for state and local taxation of mobile telecommunication services. Introduced by HYDE-R-Ill., on May 4, 2000. House Judiciary reported, amended, July 10 (H Rept 106-719). House passed, amended, under suspension of the rules, July 11. Senate passed July 14. President signed July 28, 2000.

PL 106-253 (HR 4437) Grant to the U.S. Postal Service the authority to issue semipostals. Introduced by McHUGH, R-N.Y., on May 11, 2000. House Government Reform reported, amended, July 17 (H Rept 106-734). House Commerce and House Armed Services discharged. House passed, amended, under suspension of the rules, July 17. Senate passed July 26. President signed July 28, 2000.

PL 106-254 (HR 1791) Amend Title 18, U.S. Code, to provide penalties for harming animals used in federal law enforcement. Introduced by WELLER, R-Ill., on May 13, 1999. House Judiciary reported, amended, Oct. 12 (H Rept 106-372). House passed, amended, under suspension of the rules, Oct. 12. Senate Judiciary discharged. Senate passed July 19, 2000. President signed Aug. 2, 2000.

PL 106-255 (HR 4249) Foster cross-border cooperation and environmental cleanup in Northern Europe. Introduced by GEJDENSON, D-Conn., on April 12, 2000. House passed, amended, under suspension of the rules, May 15. Senate Foreign Relations reported June 28 (no written report). Senate passed July 19. President signed Aug. 2, 2000.

PL 106-256 (S 2327) Establish a Commission on Ocean Policy. Introduced by HOLLINGS, D-S.C., on March 29, 2000. Senate Commerce, Science and Transportation reported May 23 (S Rept 106-301). Senate passed, amended, June 26. House passed, under suspension of the rules, July 25. President signed Aug. 7, 2000.

PL 106-257 (S 1629) Provide for the exchange of certain land in the state of Oregon. Introduced by SMITH, R-Ore., on Sept. 23, 1999. Senate Energy and Natural Resources reported, amended, March 22, 2000 (S Rept 106-248). Senate passed, amended, April 13. House Resources reported July 17 (H Rept 106-747). House passed, under suspension of the rules, July 25. President signed Aug. 8, 2000.

PL 106-258 (S 1910) Amend the act establishing the Women's Rights National Historical Park to permit the secretary of the Interior to acquire title in fee simple to the Hunt House located in Waterloo, N.Y. Introduced by MOYNIHAN, D-N.Y., on Nov. 10, 1999. Senate Energy and Natural Resources reported, amended, April 12, 2000 (S Rept 106-268). Senate passed, amended, April 13. House passed, under suspension of the rules, July 25. President signed Aug. 8, 2000.

PL 106-259 (HR 4576) Make appropriations for the Department of Defense for the fiscal year ending Sept. 30, 2001. Introduced by LEWIS, R-Calif., on June 1, 2000. House Appropriations reported June 1 (H Rept 106-644). House passed June 7. Senate passed, with amendment, June 13. House disagreed to Senate amendment July 12. Conference report filed in the House on July 17 (H Rept 106-754). House agreed to conference report July 19. Senate agreed to conference report July 27. President signed Aug. 9, 2000.

PL 106-260 (HR 1167) Amend the Indian Self-Determination and Education Assistance Act to provide for further self-governance by Indian tribes. Introduced by MILLER, D-Calif., on March 17, 1999. House Resources reported, amended, Nov. 17 (H Rept 106-477). House passed, amended, under suspension of the rules, Nov. 17. Senate passed, with amendment, April 4, 2000. House agreed to Senate amendment with amendments pursuant to H Res 562 on July 24. Senate agreed to House amendments to Senate amendment July 26. President signed Aug. 18, 2000.

PL 106-261 (HR 1749) Designate Wilson Creek in Avery and Caldwell counties, N.C., as a component of the National Wild and Scenic Rivers System. Introduced by BALLENGER, R-N.C., on May 11, 1999. House Resources reported, amended, Feb. 29, 2000 (H Rept 106-500). House passed, amended, under suspension of the rules, Feb. 29. Senate Energy and Natural Resources reported June 27 (S Rept 106-320). Senate passed July 27. President signed Aug. 18, 2000.

PL 106-262 (HR 1982) Name the Department of Veterans Affairs outpatient clinic located at 125 Brookley Dr., Rome, N.Y., as the "Donald J. Mitchell Department of Veterans Affairs Outpatient Clinic." Introduced by BOEHLERT, R-N.Y., on May 27, 1999. House passed, amended, under suspension of the rules, July 25, 2000. Senate Veterans' Affairs discharged. Senate passed July 27. President signed Aug. 18, 2000.

PL 106-263 (HR 3291) Provide for the settlement of the water rights claims of the Shivwits Band of the Paiute Indian Tribe of Utah. Introduced by HANSEN, R-Utah, on Nov. 10, 1999. House Resources reported, amended, July 17, 2000 (H Rept 106-743). House passed, amended, under suspension of the rules, July 25. Senate passed July 27. President signed Aug. 18, 2000.

PL 106-264 (HR 3519) Provide for negotiations for the creation of a trust fund to be administered by the International Bank for Reconstruction and Development or the International Development Association to combat the AIDS epidemic. Introduced by LEACH, R-Iowa, on Jan. 24, 2000. House Banking and Financial Services reported, amended, March 28 (H Rept 106-548). House passed, amended, under suspension of the rules, May 15. Senate Foreign Relations discharged. Senate passed, with amendment, July 26. House agreed to Senate amendment July 27. President signed Aug. 19, 2000.

PL 106-265 (HR 4040) Amend Title 5, U.S. Code, to provide for the establishment of a program under which long-term care insurance is made available to federal employees, members of the uniformed services, and civilian and military retirees, and to correct certain retirement coverage errors. Introduced by SCARBOROUGH, R-Fla., on March 21, 2000. House Government Reform reported, amended, May

8 (H Rept 106-610, Part 1). House Armed Services discharged. House passed, amended, under suspension of the rules, May 9. Senate Governmental Affairs discharged. Senate passed, amended, July 25. House agreed to Senate amendments with amendments July 27. Senate agreed to House amendments July 27. President signed Sept. 19, 2000.

PL 106-266 (HR 1729) Designate the federal facility at 1301 Emmet St. in Charlottesville, Va., as the "Pamela B. Gwin Hall." Introduced by GOODE, I-Va., on May 6, 1999. House Transportation and Infrastructure reported April 13, 2000 (H Rept 106-587). House passed, under suspension of the rules, May 3. Senate Environment and Public Works reported July 26 (no written report). Senate passed Sept. 13. President signed Sept. 22, 2000.

PL 106-267 (HR 1901) Designate the U.S. border station in Pharr, Texas, as the "Kika de la Garza United States Border Station." Introduced by TRAFICANT, D-Ohio, on May 20, 1999. House Transportation and Infrastructure reported April 13, 2000 (H Rept 106-586). House passed, under suspension of the rules, May 3. Senate Environment and Public Works reported July 26 (no written report). Senate passed Sept. 13. President signed Sept. 22, 2000.

PL 106-268 (HR 1959) Designate the federal building at 743 East Durango Blvd. in San Antonio, Texas, as the "Adrian A. Spears Judicial Training Center." Introduced by GONZALEZ, D-Texas, on May 26, 1999. House Transportation and Infrastructure reported, amended, June 22, 2000 (H Rept 106-688). House passed, amended, under suspension of the rules, June 27. Senate Environment and Public Works reported July 26 (no written report). Senate passed Sept. 13. President signed Sept. 22, 2000.

PL 106-269 (HR 4608) Designate the U.S. courthouse at 220 West Depot St. in Greeneville, Tenn., as the "James H. Quillen United States Courthouse." Introduced by JENKINS, R-Tenn., on June 8, 2000. House Transportation and Infrastructure reported June 22 (H Rept 106-689). House passed, under suspension of the rules, June 27. Senate Environment and Public Works reported July 26 (no written report). Senate passed Sept. 13. President signed Sept. 22, 2000.

PL 106-270 (S 1027) Reauthorize the participation of the Bureau of Reclamation in the Deschutes Resources Conservancy. Introduced by SMITH, R-Ore., on May 12, 1999. Senate Energy and Natural Resources reported June 24 (S Rept 106-96). Senate passed July 1. House Resources reported Sept. 6, 2000 (H Rept 106-805). House passed, under suspension of the rules, Sept. 12. President signed Sept. 22, 2000.

PL 106-271 (S 1117) Establish the Corinth Unit of Shiloh National Military Park, in the vicinity of the city of Corinth, Miss., and in the state of Tennessee. Introduced by LOTT, R-Miss., on May 25, 1999. Senate Energy and Natural Resources reported, amended, Oct. 14 (S Rept 106-186). Senate passed, amended, Nov. 19. House passed, under suspension of the rules, Sept. 12, 2000. President signed Sept. 22, 2000.

PL 106-272 (S 1374) Authorize the development and maintenance of a multiagency campus project in the town of Jackson, Wyo. Introduced by THOMAS, R-Wyo., on July 15, 1999. Senate Energy and Natural Resources reported, amended, Nov. 5 (S Rept 106-215). Senate passed, amended, Nov. 19. House Resources reported July 17, 2000 (H Rept 106-748). House passed, under suspension of the rules, Sept. 12. President signed Sept. 22, 2000.

PL 106-273 (S 1937) Amend the Pacific Northwest Electric Power Planning and Conservation Act to provide for electricity sales by the Bonneville Power Administration to joint operating entities. Introduced by CRAIG, R-Idaho, on Nov. 17, 1999. Senate Energy and Natural Resources discharged. Senate passed Nov. 19. House Resources reported Sept. 6, 2000 (H Rept 106-820, Part 1). House Commerce discharged. House passed, under suspension of the rules, Sept. 12. President signed Sept. 22, 2000.

PL 106-274 (S 2869) Protect religious liberty. Introduced by HATCH, R-Utah, on July 13, 2000. Senate passed July 27. House passed July 27. President signed Sept. 22, 2000.

PL 106-275 (H J Res 109) Make continuing appropriations for fiscal 2001. Introduced by YOUNG, R-Fla., on Sept. 25, 2000. House passed Sept. 26. Senate passed Sept. 28. President signed Sept. 29, 2000.

PL 106-276 (S 1638) Amend the Omnibus Crime Control and Safe Streets Act of 1968 to extend the retroactive eligibility dates for financial assistance for higher education for spouses and dependent children of federal, state, and local law enforcement officers who are killed in the line of duty. Introduced by ASHCROFT, R-Mo., on Sept. 24, 1999. Senate Judiciary reported Feb. 10, 2000 (no written report). Senate passed, amended, May 15. House passed, under suspension of the rules, Sept. 19. President signed Oct. 2, 2000.

PL 106-277 (S 2460) Authorize the payment of rewards to individuals furnishing information relating to persons subject to indictment for serious violations of international humanitarian law in Rwanda. Introduced by FEINGOLD, D-Wis., on April 25, 2000. Senate Foreign Relations reported

June 12 (no written report). Senate passed June 23. House passed, under suspension of the rules, Sept. 19. President signed Oct. 2, 2000.

PL 106-278 (HR 940) Designate the Lackawanna Valley and Schuylkill River National Heritage Area. Introduced by SHERWOOD, R-Pa., on March 2, 1999. House Resources reported, amended, Aug. 3, 1999 (H Rept 106-285). House passed, amended, under suspension of the rules, Sept. 13. Senate Energy and Natural Resources reported, amended, July 12, 2000 (S Rept 106-342). Senate passed, with amendments, July 27. Proceedings vacated July 27. Senate passed, with amendments, Sept. 18. House agreed to Senate amendments Sept. 21. President signed Oct. 6, 2000.

PL 106-279 (HR 2909) Provide for implementation by the United States of the Hague Convention on Protection of Children and Cooperation in Respect of Intercountry Adoption. Introduced by GILMAN, R-N.Y., on Sept. 22, 1999. House International Relations reported, amended, June 22, 2000 (H Rept 106-691, Part 1). House Judiciary discharged. House Education and the Workforce discharged. House Ways and Means discharged. House passed, amended, under suspension of the rules, July 18. Senate passed, with amendment, July 27. House agreed to Senate amendment, with amendment, Sept.18. Senate agreed to House amendment Sept. 20. President signed Oct. 6, 2000.

PL 106-280 (HR 4919) Amend the Foreign Assistance Act of 1961 and the Arms Export Control Act to make improvements to defense and security assistance provisions under those Acts and authorize the transfer of naval vessels to certain foreign countries. Introduced by GILMAN, R-N.Y., on July 24, 2000. House passed, under suspension of the rules, July 24. Senate Foreign Relations discharged. Senate passed, with amendment, Sept. 7. Conference report filed in the House Sept. 19 (H Rept 106-868). House agreed to conference report Sept. 21. Senate agreed to conference report Sept. 22. President signed Oct. 6, 2000.

PL 106-281 (HR 5193) Amend the National Housing Act to temporarily extend the applicability of the down payment simplification provisions for the FHA single family housing mortgage insurance program. Introduced by LAZIO, R-N.Y., on Sept. 18, 2000. House passed, amended, under suspension of the rules Sept. 19. Senate Banking, Housing and Urban Affairs discharged. Senate passed Sept. 28. President signed Oct. 6, 2000.

PL 106-282 (H J Res 110) Make further continuing appropriations for fiscal 2001. Introduced by YOUNG, R-Fla., on Oct. 2, 2000. House passed Oct. 3. Senate passed Oct. 5. President signed Oct. 6, 2000.

PL 106-283 (S 430) Amend the Alaska Native Claims Settlement Act and provide for a land exchange between the secretary of Agriculture and the Kake Tribal Corporation. Introduced by MURKOWSKI, R-Alaska, on Feb. 22, 1999. Senate Energy and Natural Resources reported, amended, March 22 (S Rept 106-31). Senate passed, amended, April 19. House Resources reported, with amendment, Jan. 27, 2000 (H Rept 106-489). House passed, with amendment, under suspension of the rules, May 22. Senate agreed to House amendment Sept. 22. President signed Oct. 6, 2000.

PL 106-284 (HR 999) Amend the federal Water Pollution Control Act to improve the quality of coastal recreation waters. Introduced by BILBRAY, R-Calif., on March 4, 1999. House Transportation and Infrastructure reported, amended, April 19, 1999 (H Rept 106-98). House passed, amended, April 22. Senate Environment and Public Works reported Aug. 25, 2000 (no written report). Senate passed, with amendment, Sept. 21. House agreed to Senate amendment, under suspension of the rules, Sept. 26. President signed Oct. 10, 2000.

PL 106-285 (HR 2647) Amend the act entitled "An Act relating to the water rights of the Ak-Chin Indian Community" to clarify certain provisions concerning the leasing of such water rights. Introduced by SHADEGG, R-Ariz., on July 29, 1999. House Resources reported May 2, 2000 (H Rept 106-598). House passed May 9, under suspension of the rules. Senate Indian Affairs reported Sept. 19 (S Rept 106-415). Senate passed Sept. 27. President signed Oct. 10, 2000.

PL 106-286 (HR 4444) Authorize extension of nondiscriminatory treatment (normal trade relations treatment) to the People's Republic of China. Introduced by ARCHER, R-Texas, May 15, 2000. House Ways and Means reported, amended, May 22 (H Rept 106-632). House passed, amended, May 24. Senate passed Sept. 19. President signed Oct. 10, 2000.

PL 106-287 (HR 4700) Grant the consent of the Congress to the Kansas and Missouri Metropolitan Culture District Compact. Introduced by McCARTHY, D-Mo., June 20, 2000. House Judiciary reported July 20 (H Rept 106-769). House passed, under suspension of the rules, July 24. Senate passed Sept. 26. President signed Oct. 10, 2000.

PL 106-288 (H J Res 72) Grant the consent of the Congress to the Red River Boundary Compact. Introduced by THORNBERRY, R-Texas, on Oct. 19, 1999. House Judiciary reported, amended, July 20, 2000 (H Rept 106-770). House passed, amended, under suspension of the rules, July 24. Senate passed Sept. 26. President signed Oct. 10, 2000.

PL 106-289 (S 1295) Designate the U.S. Post Office at 3813 Main St. in East Chicago, Indiana, as the "Lance Corporal Harold Gomez Post Office." Introduced by LUGAR, R-Ind., on June 28, 1999. Senate Governmental Affairs reported Nov. 4 (no written report). Senate passed Nov. 19. House passed, under suspension of the rules, Sept. 27, 2000. President signed Oct. 10, 2000.

PL 106-290 (S 1324) Expand the boundaries of the Gettysburg National Military Park to include Wills House. Introduced by SANTORUM, R-Pa., on July 1, 1999. Senate Energy and Natural Resources reported Oct. 14 (S Rept 106-187). Senate passed Nov. 19. House passed, under suspension of the rules, Sept. 26, 2000. President signed Oct. 10, 2000.

PL 106-291 (HR 4578) Make appropriations for the Department of the Interior and related agencies for the fiscal year ending Sept. 30, 2001. Introduced by REGULA, R-Ohio, on June 1, 2000. House Appropriations reported June 1 (H Rept 106-646). House passed, amended, June 16. Senate Appropriations reported, amended, June 19 (S Rept 106-312). Senate passed, amended, July 18. Conference report filed in the House Sept. 29 (H Rept 106-914). House agreed to conference report Oct. 3. Senate agreed to conference report Oct. 5. President signed Oct. 11, 2000.

PL 106-292 (HR 4115) Authorize appropriations for the U.S. Holocaust Memorial Museum. Introduced by CANNON, R-Utah, on March 29, 2000. House Resources reported, amended, July 17 (H Rept 106-751). House passed, amended, Sept. 7. Senate Energy and Natural Resources reported Sept. 28 (S Rept 106-436). Senate passed Sept. 28. President signed Oct. 12, 2000.

PL 106-293 (HR 4931) Provide for the training or orientation of individuals, during a presidential transition, who the president intends to appoint to certain key positions and provide for a study and report on improving the financial disclosure process for certain presidential nominees. Introduced by HORN, R-Calif., on July 24, 2000. House Government Reform discharged. House passed Sept. 13. Senate passed Sept. 28. President signed Oct. 12, 2000.

PL 106-294 (S 704) Amend Title 18, U.S. Code, to combat the overutilization of prison health care services and control rising prisoner health care costs. Introduced by KYL, R-Ariz., on March 24, 1999. Senate Judiciary reported, amended, April 29 (no written report). Senate passed, amended, May 27. House Judiciary discharged. House passed, with amendment, Sept. 19, 2000. Senate agreed to House amendment Sept. 28. President signed Oct. 12, 2000.

PL 106-295 (HR 1162) Designate the bridge on U.S. Route 231 that crosses the Ohio River between Maceo, Ky., and Rockport, Ind., as the "William H. Natcher Bridge." Introduced by LEWIS, R-Ky., on March 17, 1999. House Transportation and Infrastructure reported April 27 (H Rept 106-112). House passed, under suspension of the rules, May 4. Senate Environment and Public Works reported Sept. 28, 2000 (no written report). Senate passed Oct. 4. President signed Oct. 13, 2000.

PL 106-296 (HR 1605) Designate the U.S. courthouse building at 402 N. Walnut St. and Prospect Ave. in Harrison, Ark., as the "J. Smith Henley Federal Building." Introduced by HUTCHINSON, R-Ark., April 28, 1999. House Transportation and Infrastructure reported, amended, March 23, 2000 (H Rept 106-536). House passed, amended, under suspension of the rules, April 3. Senate Environment and Public Works reported Sept. 28 (no written report). Senate passed Oct. 4. President signed Oct. 13, 2000.

PL 106-297 (HR 1800) Amend the Violent Crime Control and Law Enforcement Act of 1994 to ensure that certain information regarding prisoners is reported to the attorney general. Introduced by HUTCHINSON, R-Ark., on May 13, 1999. House passed, amended, under suspension of the rules, July 24, 2000. Senate Judiciary discharged. Senate passed Oct. 3. President signed Oct. 13, 2000.

PL 106-298 (HR 2752) Give Lincoln County, Nev., the right to purchase at fair market value certain public land within that county. Introduced by GIBBONS, R-Nev., on Aug. 5, 1999. House Resources reported, amended, Sept. 14, 2000 (H Rept 106-847). House passed, amended, under suspension of the rules, Sept. 26. Senate passed Oct. 3. President signed Oct. 13, 2000.

PL 106-299 (HR 2773) Amend the Wild and Scenic Rivers Act to designate the Wekiva River and its tributaries of Rock Springs Run and Black Water Creek in the state of Florida as components of the national wild and scenic rivers system. Introduced by McCOLLUM, R-Fla., on Aug. 5, 1999. House Resources reported, amended, July 17, 2000 (H Rept 106-739). House passed, amended, under suspension of the rules, July 24. Senate passed Oct. 3. President signed Oct. 13, 2000.

PL 106-300 (HR 4318) Establish the Red River National Wildlife Refuge. Introduced by McCRERY, R-La., on April 13, 2000. House Resources reported, amended, Sept. 6 (H Rept 106-809). House passed, amended, under suspension of the rules, Sept. 12. Senate Environment and Public Works reported Oct. 2 (S Rept 106-462). Senate passed Oct. 4. President signed Oct. 13, 2000.

PL 106-301 (HR 4579) Provide for the exchange of certain lands within the state of Utah. Introduced by HANSEN, R-Utah, on June 6, 2000. House passed, amended, under suspension of the rules, July 11. Senate Energy and Natural Resources reported Oct. 2 (S Rept 106-463). Senate passed Oct. 3. President signed Oct. 13, 2000.

PL 106-302 (HR 4583) Extend the authorization for the Air Force Memorial Foundation to establish a memorial in the District of Columbia or its environs. Introduced by HANSEN, R-Utah, on June 6, 2000. House Resources reported Sept. 6 (H Rept 106-817). House passed, under suspension of the rules, Sept. 12. Senate Energy and Natural Resources discharged. Senate passed Oct. 3. President signed Oct. 13, 2000.

PL 106-303 (HR 4642) Make certain personnel flexibilities available with respect to the General Accounting Office. Introduced by BURTON, R-Ind., on June 13, 2000. House passed, amended, under suspension of the rules, Sept. 19. Senate Governmental Affairs discharged. Senate passed Oct. 4. President signed Oct. 13, 2000.

PL 106-304 (HR 4806) Designate the federal building at 1710 Alabama Ave. in Jasper, Ala., as the "Carl Elliott Federal Building." Introduced by ADERHOLT, R-Ala., on June 29, 2000. House passed, under suspension of the rules, July 25. Senate Environment and Public Works reported Sept. 28 (no written report). Senate passed Oct. 4. President signed Oct. 13, 2000.

PL 106-305 (HR 5284) Designate the U.S. customhouse at 101 East Main St. in Norfolk, Va., as the "Owen B. Pickett United States Customhouse." Introduced by SCOTT, D-Va., on Sept. 25, 2000. House Transportation and Infrastructure reported Oct. 2 (H Rept 106-922). House passed, under suspension of the rules, Oct. 2. Senate passed Oct. 4. President signed Oct. 13, 2000.

PL 106-306 (H J Res 111) Make further continuing appropriations for fiscal 2001. Introduced by YOUNG, R-Fla., on Oct. 11, 2000. House passed Oct. 12. Senate passed Oct. 12. President signed Oct. 13, 2000.

PL 106-307 (S 366) Amend the National Trails System Act to designate El Camino Real de Tierra Adentro as a National Historic Trail. Introduced by BINGAMAN, D-N.M., on Feb. 4, 1999. Senate Energy and Natural Resources reported, amended, March 17 (S Rept 106-22) Senate passed, amended, Nov. 19. House passed, under suspension of the rules, Oct. 3, 2000. President signed Oct. 13, 2000.

PL 106-308 (S 1794) Designate the federal courthouse at 145 East Simpson Ave. in Jackson, Wyo., as the "Clifford P. Hansen Federal Courthouse." Introduced by THOMAS, R-Wyo., on Oct. 26, 1999. Senate Environment and Public Works reported Feb. 9, 2000 (no written report). Senate passed March 2. House Transportation and Infrastructure reported Sept. 7 (H Rept 106-828). House passed, under suspension of the rules, Oct. 2. President signed Oct. 13, 2000.

PL 106-309 (HR 1143) Establish a program to provide assistance for programs of credit and other financial services for microenterprises in developing countries. Introduced by GILMAN, R-N.Y., on March 17, 1999. House International Relations reported April 12 (H Rept 106-82). House passed, amended, April 13. Senate Foreign Relations discharged. Senate passed, amended, Oct. 3, 2000. House agreed to Senate amendment Oct. 5. President signed Oct. 17, 2000.

PL 106-310 (HR 4365) Amend the Public Health Service Act with respect to children's health. Introduced by BILIRAKIS, R-Fla., on May 3, 2000. House passed, amended, under suspension of the rules, May 9. Senate Health, Education, Labor, and Pensions discharged. Senate passed, with amendment, Sept. 22. House agreed to Senate amendment Sept. 27. President signed Oct. 17, 2000.

PL 106-311 (HR 5362) Increase the fees charged to employers who are petitioners for the employment of H-1B non-immigrant workers. Introduced by DREIER, R-Calif., on Oct. 3, 2000. House Judiciary discharged. House passed Oct. 6. Senate passed Oct. 10. President signed Oct. 17, 2000.

PL 106-312 (S 1198) Establish a three-year pilot project for the General Accounting Office to report to Congress on economically significant agency regulatory actions. Introduced by SHELBY, R-Ala., on June 9, 1999. Senate Governmental Affairs reported, amended, Dec. 7 (S Rept 106-225). Senate passed, amended, May 9, 2000. House passed, under suspension of the rules, Oct. 3. President signed Oct. 17, 2000.

PL 106-313 (S 2045) Amend the Immigration and Nationality Act with respect to H-1B non-immigrant aliens. Introduced by HATCH, R-Utah, on Feb. 9, 2000. Senate Judiciary reported, amended, April 11 (S Rept 106-260). Senate passed, amended, Oct. 3. House passed, under suspension of the rules, Oct. 3. President signed Oct. 17, 2000.

PL 106-314 (S 2272) Improve the administrative efficiency and effectiveness of the nation's abuse and neglect courts. Introduced by DeWINE, R-Ohio, on March 22, 2000. Senate Judiciary reported July 27 (no written report). Senate passed, amended, Sept. 26. House passed, under the suspension of the rules, Oct. 3. President signed Oct. 17, 2000.

PL 106-315 (HR 2302) Designate the building of the U.S. Postal Service at 307 Main St. in Johnson City, N.Y., as the "James W. McCabe Sr. Post Office Building." Introduced by HINCHEY, D-N.Y., on June 22, 1999. House passed, under suspension of the rules, Sept. 6, 2000. Senate Governmental Affairs reported Sept. 29 (no written report). Senate passed Oct. 6. President signed Oct. 19, 2000.

PL 106-316 (HR 2496) Reauthorize the Junior Duck Stamp Conservation and Design Program Act of 1994. Introduced by ORTIZ, D-Texas, on July 13, 1999. House Resources reported, amended, Oct. 18 (H Rept 106-390). House passed, amended, under suspension of the rules, Oct. 26. Senate Environment and Public Works reported Oct. 2, 2000 (S Rept 106-457). Senate passed Oct. 5. President signed Oct. 19, 2000.

PL 106-317 (HR 2641) Make technical corrections to Title X of the Energy Policy Act of 1992. Introduced by CUBIN, R-Wyo., on July 29, 1999. House Commerce reported, amended, Sept. 25, 2000 (H Rept 106-886). House passed, amended, under suspension of the rules, Sept. 27. Senate passed Oct. 5. President signed Oct. 19, 2000.

PL 106-318 (HR 2778) Amend the Wild and Scenic Rivers Act to designate segments of the Taunton River in the Commonwealth of Massachusetts for study for potential addition to the National Wild and Scenic Rivers System. Introduced by MOAKLEY, D-Mass., on Aug. 5, 1999. House Resources reported, amended, June 19, 2000 (H Rept 106-678). House passed, amended, under suspension of the rules, June 19. Senate Energy and Natural Resources discharged. Senate passed Oct. 5. President signed Oct. 19, 2000.

PL 106-319 (HR 2833) Establish the Yuma Crossing National Heritage Area. Introduced by PASTOR, D-Ariz., on Sept. 9, 1999. House Resources reported, amended, July 17, 2000 (H Rept 106-740). House passed, amended, under suspension of the rules, July 25. Senate passed Oct. 5, 2000. President signed Oct. 19, 2000.

PL 106-320 (HR 2938) Designate the facility of the U.S. Postal Service at 424 S. Michigan St. in South Bend, Ind., as the "John Brademas Post Office." Introduced by ROEMER, D-Ind., on Sept., 23 1999. House passed, under suspension of the rules, June 20, 2000. Senate Governmental Affairs discharged. Senate passed Oct. 6. President signed Oct. 19, 2000.

PL 106-321 (HR 3030) Designate the facility of the U.S. Postal Service at 757 Warren Road in Ithaca, N.Y., as the "Matthew F. McHugh Post Office." Introduced by HINCHEY, D-N.Y., on Oct. 6, 1999. House passed, under suspension of the rules, June 6, 2000. Senate Governmental Affairs reported Sept. 29 (no written report). Senate passed Oct. 6. President signed Oct. 19, 2000.

PL 106-322 (HR 3454) Designate the U.S. post office at 451 College St. in Macon, Ga., as the "Henry McNeal Turner Post Office." Introduced by CHAMBLISS, R-Ga., on Nov. 18, 1999. House passed, under suspension of the rules, Sept. 6, 2000. Senate Governmental Affairs reported Sept. 29 (no written report). Senate passed Oct. 6. President signed Oct. 19, 2000.

PL 106-323 (HR 3745) Authorize the addition of certain parcels to the Effigy Mounds National Monument in Iowa. Introduced by NUSSLE, R-Iowa, on Feb. 29, 2000. House Resources reported, amended, Sept. 7 (H Rept 106-826). House passed, amended, under suspension of the rules, Sept. 26. Senate passed Oct. 5. President signed Oct. 19, 2000.

PL 106-324 (HR 3817) Redesignate the Big South Trail in the Comanche Peak Wilderness Area of Roosevelt National Forest in Colorado as the "Jaryd Atadero Legacy Trail." Introduced by TANCREDO, R-Colo., on March 1, 2000. House Resources reported, amended, July 17 (H Rept 106-738). House passed, amended, under suspension of the rules, July 25. Senate Energy and Natural Resources discharged. Senate passed Oct. 5. President signed Oct. 19, 2000.

PL 106-325 (HR 3909) Designate the facility of the U.S. Postal Service at 4601 S. Cottage Grove Ave. in Chicago, Ill., as the "Henry W. McGee Post Office Building." Introduced by RUSH, D-Ill., on March 14, 2000. House passed, under suspension of the rules, July 11. Senate Governmental Affairs reported Sept. 29 (no written report). Senate passed Oct. 6. President signed Oct. 19, 2000.

PL 106-326 (HR 3985) Designate the facility of the U.S. Postal Service located at 14900 S.W. 30th St. in Miramar City, Fla., as the "Vicki Coceano Post Office Building." Introduced by HASTINGS, D-Fla., on March 15, 2000. House passed, amended, under suspension of the rules, July 17. Senate Governmental Affairs reported Sept. 29 (no written report). Senate passed Oct. 6. President signed Oct. 19, 2000.

PL 106-327 (HR 4157) Designate the facility of the U.S. Postal Service located at 600 Lincoln Ave. in Pasadena, Calif., as the "Matthew 'Mack' Robinson Post Office Building." Introduced by ROGAN, R-Calif., on April 3, 2000. House passed, under suspension of the rules, July 18. Senate Governmental Affairs reported Sept. 29 (no written report). Senate passed Oct. 6. President signed Oct. 19, 2000.

PL 106-328 (HR 4169) Designate the facility of the U.S. Postal Service located at 2000 Vassar St. in Reno, Nev., as the "Barbara F. Vucanovich Post Office Building." Introduced by GIBBONS, R-Nev., on April 4, 2000. House passed, under suspension of the rules, July 12. Senate Governmental Affairs reported Sept. 29 (no written report). Senate passed Oct. 6. President signed Oct. 19, 2000.

PL 106-329 (HR 4226) Authorize the secretary of Agriculture to sell or exchange all or part of certain administrative sites and other land in the Black Hills National Forest, and use funds derived from the sale or exchange to acquire replacement sites and to acquire or construct administrative improvements in connection with the Black Hills National Forest. Introduced by THUNE, R-S.D., on April 10, 2000. House Resources reported, amended, Sept. 6 (H Rept 106-816). House passed, amended, under suspension of the rules, Sept. 18. Senate passed Oct. 5. President signed Oct. 19, 2000.

PL 106-330 (HR 4285) Authorize the secretary of Agriculture to convey certain administrative sites for National Forest System lands in Texas and to convey certain National Forest System land to the New Waverly Gulf Coast Trades Center. Introduced by TURNER, D-Texas, on April 13, 2000. House Agriculture discharged. House passed July 27. Senate Energy and Natural Resources reported Sept. 29 (S Rept 106-447). Senate passed Oct. 5. President signed Oct. 19, 2000.

PL 106-331 (HR 4286) Provide for the establishment of the Cahaba River National Wildlife Refuge in Bibb County, Ala. Introduced by BACHUS, R-Ala., on April 13, 2000. House Resources reported, amended, July 10 (H Rept 106-713). House passed, amended, under suspension of the rules, July 10. Senate Environment and Public Works reported Oct. 2 (S Rept 106-461). Senate passed Oct. 5. President signed Oct. 19, 2000.

PL 106-332 (HR 4435) Clarify certain boundaries on the map relating to Unit NC01 of the Coastal Barrier Resources System. Introduced by JONES, R-N.C., on May 11, 2000. House Resources reported June 6 (H Rept 106-648). House passed, amended, under suspension of the rules, June 7. Senate Environment and Public Works reported Oct. 3 (S Rept 106-473). Senate passed Oct. 5. President signed Oct. 19, 2000.

PL 106-333 (HR 4447) Designate the facility of the U.S. Postal Service located at 919 W. 34th St. in Baltimore, Md., as the "Samuel H. Lacy Sr. Post Office Building." Introduced by CUMMINGS, D-Md., on May 15, 2000. House passed, under suspension of the rules, July 12. Senate Governmental Affairs reported Sept. 29 (no written report). Senate passed Oct. 6. President signed Oct. 19, 2000.

PL 106-334 (HR 4448) Designate the facility of the U.S. Postal Service located at 3500 Dolfield Ave. in Baltimore, Md., as the "Judge Robert Bernard Watts Sr. Post Office Building." Introduced by CUMMINGS, D-Md., on May 15, 2000. House passed, under suspension of the rules, Sept. 6. Senate Governmental Affairs reported Sept. 29 (no written report). Senate passed Oct. 6. President signed Oct. 19, 2000.

PL 106-335 (HR 4449) Designate the facility of the U.S. Postal Service located at 1908 N. Ellamont St. in Baltimore, Md., as the "Dr. Flossie McClain Dedmond Post Office Building." Introduced by CUMMINGS, D-Md., on May 15, 2000. House passed, under suspension of the rules, Sept. 6. Senate Governmental Affairs reported Sept. 29 (no written report). Senate passed Oct. 6. President signed Oct. 19, 2000.

PL 106-336 (HR 4484) Designate the facility of the U.S. Postal Service located at 500 N. Washington St. in Rockville, Md., as the "Everett Alvarez Jr. Post Office Building." Introduced by MORELLA, R-Md., on May 17, 2000. House passed, under suspension of the rules, Sept. 6. Senate Governmental Affairs reported Sept. 29 (no written report). Senate passed Oct. 6. President signed Oct. 19, 2000.

PL 106-337 (HR 4517) Designate the facility of the U.S. Postal Service located at 24 Tsienneto Road in Derry, N.H., as the "Alan B. Shepard Jr. Post Office Building." Introduced by SUNUNU, R-N.H., on May 23, 2000. House passed, under suspension of the rules, July 18. Senate Governmental Affairs reported Sept. 29 (no written report). Senate passed Oct. 6. President signed Oct. 19, 2000.

PL 106-338 (HR 4534) Designate the facility of the U.S. Postal Service located at 114 Ridge St. in Lenoir, N.C., as the "James T. Broyhill Post Office Building." Introduced by BURR, R-N.C., on May 24, 2000. House passed, amended, under suspension of the rules, Sept. 6. Senate Governmental Affairs reported Sept. 29 (no written report). Senate passed Oct. 6. President signed Oct. 19, 2000.

PL 106-339 (HR 4554) Redesignate the facility of the U.S. Postal Service located at 1602 Frankford Ave. in Philadelphia, Pa., as the "Joseph F. Smith Post Office Building." Introduced by BORSKI, D-Pa., on May 25, 2000. House passed, under suspension of the rules, July 18. Senate Governmental Affairs reported Sept. 29 (no written report). Senate passed Oct. 6. President signed Oct. 19, 2000.

PL 106-340 (HR 4615) Redesignate the facility of the U.S. Postal Service located at 3030 Meredith Ave. in Omaha, Neb., as the "Reverend J.C. Wade Post Office." Introduced by TERRY, R-Neb., on June 8, 2000. House passed, under suspension of the rules,

Sept. 6. Senate Governmental Affairs reported Sept. 29 (no written report). Senate passed Oct. 6. President signed Oct. 19, 2000.

PL 106-341 (HR 4658) Designate the facility of the U.S. Postal Service located at 301 Green St. in Fayetteville, N.C., as the "J.L. Dawkins Post Office Building." Introduced by HAYES, R-N.C., on June 14, 2000. House passed, under suspension of the rules, July 11. Senate Governmental Affairs reported Sept. 29 (no written report). Senate passed Oct. 6. President signed Oct. 19, 2000.

PL 106-342 (HR 4884) Redesignate the facility of the U.S. Postal Service located at 200 W. 2nd St. in Royal Oak, Mich., as the "William S. Broomfield Post Office Building." Introduced by KNOLLENBERG, R-Mich., on July 19, 2000. House passed, under suspension of the rules, Sept. 6. Senate Governmental Affairs reported Sept. 29 (no written report). Senate passed Oct. 6. President signed Oct. 19, 2000.

PL 106-343 (S 1236) Extend the deadline under the Federal Power Act for commencement of the construction of the Arrowrock Dam Hydroelectric Project in Idaho. Introduced by CRAIG, R-Idaho, on June 17, 1999. Senate Energy and Natural Resources reported Oct. 4 (S Rept 106-170). Senate passed Nov. 19. House Commerce reported, with amendment, May 19, 2000 (H Rept 106-630). House passed, with amendment, under suspension of the rules, May 22. Senate agreed to House amendment Oct. 5. President signed Oct. 19, 2000.

PL 106-344 (H J Res 114) Make further continuing appropriations for fiscal 2001. Introduced by YOUNG, R-Fla., on Oct. 18, 2000. House passed Oct. 19. Senate passed Oct. 19. President signed Oct. 20, 2000.

PL106-345 (S 2311) Revise and extend the Ryan White CARE Act programs under Title XXVI of the Public Health Service Act, to improve access to health care and the quality of health care under such programs and to provide for the development of increased capacity to provide health care and related support services to individuals and families with HIV disease. Introduced by JEFFORDS, R-Vt., on March 29, 2000. Senate Health, Education, Labor, and Pensions reported May 15 (S Rept 106-294). Senate passed, amended, June 6. House passed, with amendments, Oct. 5. Senate agreed to House amendments Oct. 5. President signed Oct. 20, 2000.

PL 106-346 (HR 4475) Make appropriations for the Department of Transportation and related agencies for fiscal 2001. Introduced by WOLF, R-Va., on May 17, 2000. House Appropriations reported May 17 (H Rept 106-622). House passed, amended, May 19. Senate Appropriations discharged. Senate passed, with amendment, June 15. Conference report filed in the House Oct. 5 (H Rept 106-940). House agreed to conference report Oct. 6. Senate agreed to conference report Oct. 6. President signed Oct. 23, 2000.

PL 106-347 (HR 4975) Designate the post office and courthouse located at 2 Federal Square, Newark, N.J., as the "Frank R. Lautenberg Post Office and Courthouse." Introduced by LOBIONDO, R-N.J., on July 26, 2000. House passed, under suspension of the rules, Sept. 19. Senate passed Oct. 6. President signed Oct. 23, 2000.

PL 106-348 (HR 1509) Authorize the Disabled Veterans' LIFE Memorial Foundation to establish a memorial in the District of Columbia or its environs to honor veterans who became disabled while serving in the Armed Forces of the United States. Introduced by JOHNSON, R-Texas, on April 21, 1999. House Resources reported April 13, 2000 (H Rept 106-583). House passed, under suspension of the rules, May 3. Senate Energy and Natural Resources discharged. Senate passed Oct. 5. President signed Oct. 24, 2000.

PL 106-349 (HR 3201) Authorize the secretary of the Interior to study the suitability and feasibility of designating the Carter G. Woodson Home in the District of Columbia as a National Historic Site. Introduced by NORTON, D-D.C., on Nov. 2, 1999. House passed, under suspension of the rules, Feb. 15, 2000. Senate Energy and Natural Resources reported June 27 (S Rept 106-322). Senate passed Oct. 5. President signed Oct. 24, 2000.

PL 106-350 (HR 3632) Revise the boundaries of the Golden Gate National Recreation Area. Introduced by LANTOS, D-Calif., on Feb. 10, 2000. House Resources reported, amended, Sept. 7 (H Rept 106-825). House passed, amended, under suspension of the rules, Sept. 12. Senate passed Oct. 5. President signed Oct. 24, 2000.

PL 106-351 (HR 3676) Establish the Santa Rosa and San Jacinto Mountains National Monument in California. Introduced by BONO, R-Calif., on Feb. 16, 2000. House Resources reported, amended, July 17 (H Rept 106-750). House passed, amended, under suspension of the rules, July 25. Senate Energy and Natural Resources discharged. Senate passed Oct. 5. President signed Oct. 24, 2000.

PL 106-352 (HR 4063) Establish the Rosie the Riveter — World War II Home Front National Historical Park in the State of California. Introduced by MILLER, D-Calif., on March 22, 2000. House Resources reported, amended, July 11 (H Rept 106-723). House passed, amended, under suspension of the rules, July 11. Senate Energy and Natural Resources reported, with amendments, Sept. 29 (S Rept 106-446). Senate passed Oct. 5. President signed Oct. 24, 2000.

PL 106-353 (HR 4275) Establish the Colorado Canyons National Conservation Area and the Black Ridge Canyons Wilderness. Introduced by McINNIS, R-Colo., on April 13, 2000. House passed, amended, under suspension of the rules, July 25. Senate Energy and Natural Resources reported Oct. 2 (S Rept 106-460). Senate passed Oct. 5. President signed Oct. 24, 2000.

PL 106-354 (HR 4386) Amend Title XIX of the Social Security Act to provide medical assistance for certain women screened and found to have breast or cervical cancer under a federally funded screening program and amend the Public Health Service Act and the Federal Food, Drug, and Cosmetic Act with respect to surveillance and information concerning the relationship between cervical cancer and the human papillomavirus (HPV). Introduced by MYRICK, R-N.C., on May 4, 2000. House passed, amended, under suspension of the rules, May 9. Senate passed, with amendment, Oct. 4. House agreed to Senate amendment Oct. 12. President signed Oct. 24, 2000.

PL 106-355 (HR 4613) Amend the National Historic Preservation Act to establish a national historic lighthouse preservation program. Introduced by SOUDER, R-Ind., on June 8, 2000. House Resources reported, amended, Sept. 26 (H Rept 106-890). House passed, amended, under suspension of the rules, Sept. 26. Senate passed Oct. 5. President signed Oct. 24, 2000.

PL 106-356 (HR 5036) Amend the Dayton Aviation Heritage Preservation Act of 1992 to clarify the areas included in the Dayton Aviation Heritage National Historical Park and authorize appropriations for that park. Introduced by HALL, D-Ohio, on July 27, 2000. House Resources reported Sept. 26 (H Rept 106-896). House passed, amended, under suspension of the rules, Sept. 26. Senate passed Oct. 5. President signed Oct. 24, 2000.

PL 106-357 (S 1849) Designate segments and tributaries of White Clay Creek, Del. and Pa., as a component of the National Wild and Scenic Rivers System. Introduced by BIDEN, D-Del., on Nov. 3, 1999. Senate Energy and Natural Resources reported, amended, April 12, 2000 (S Rept 106-266). Senate passed, amended, April 13. House passed, with amendment, under suspension of the rules, Sept. 18. Senate agreed to House amendment Oct. 5. President signed Oct. 24, 2000.

PL 106-358 (H J Res 115) Make further continuing appropriations for fiscal 2001. Introduced by YOUNG, R-Fla., on Oct. 24, 2000. House passed Oct. 25. Senate passed Oct. 25. President signed Oct. 26, 2000.

PL 106-359 (H J Res 116) Make further continuing appropriations for fiscal 2001. Introduced by YOUNG, R-Fla., on Oct. 24, 2000. House passed Oct. 26. Senate passed Oct. 26. President signed Oct. 26, 2000.

PL 106-360 (HR 34) Direct the secretary of the Interior to make technical corrections to a map relating to the Coastal Barrier Resources System. Introduced by GOSS, R-Fla., on Jan. 6, 1999. House Resources discharged. House passed Nov. 18. Senate Environment and Public Works reported, with amendments, Oct. 3, 2000 (S Rept 106-471). Senate passed, with amendments, Oct. 5. House agreed to Senate amendments, under suspension of the rules, Oct. 12. President signed Oct. 27, 2000.

PL 106-361 (HR 208) Amend Title 5, U.S. Code, to allow for the contribution of certain rollover distributions to accounts in the Thrift Savings Plan and eliminate certain waiting-period requirements for participating in the plan. Introduced by MORELLA, R-Md., on Jan. 6, 1999. House Government Reform reported, amended, April 13 (H Rept 106-87). House passed, amended, under suspension of the rules, April 20. Senate Governmental Affairs reported, with amendments, July 13, 2000 (S Rept 106-343). Senate passed, with amendments, July 21. House agreed to Senate amendments, under suspension of the rules, Oct. 10. President signed Oct. 27, 2000.

PL 106-362 (HR 1695) Provide for the conveyance of certain federal public lands in the Ivanpah Valley, Nev., to Clark County, Nev., for the development of an airport facility. Introduced by GIBBONS, R-Nev., on May 5, 1999. House Resources reported, amended, Nov. 16 (H Rept 106-471). House passed, amended, March 9, 2000. Senate Energy and Natural Resources reported, with amendments, Aug. 25 (S Rept 106-394). Senate passed, with amendments, Oct. 5. House agreed to Senate amendments, under suspension of the rules, Oct. 17. President signed Oct. 27, 2000.

PL 106-363 (HR 1715) Extend the expiration date of the Defense Production Act of 1950. Introduced by BACHUS, R-Ala., on May 6, 1999. House passed, amended, under suspension of the rules, Sept. 18, 2000. Senate passed Oct. 12. President signed Oct. 27, 2000.

PL 106-364 (HR 2296) Amend the Revised Organic Act of the Virgin Islands to provide that the number of members on the legislature of the Virgin Islands and the number of such members constituting a quorum shall be determined by the laws of the

Virgin Islands. Introduced by CHRISTENSEN, D-Virgin Is., on June 22, 1999. House Resources reported Sept. 6 (H Rept 106-807). House passed, under suspension of the rules, Sept. 12, 2000. Senate Energy and Natural Resources discharged. Senate passed Oct. 17. President signed Oct. 27, 2000.

PL 106-365 (HR 2879) Provide for the placement at the Lincoln Memorial of a plaque commemorating the speech of the Rev. Dr. Martin Luther King Jr., known as the "I Have A Dream" speech. Introduced by NORTHUP, R-Ky., on Sept. 15, 1999. House Resources reported Nov. 4 (H Rept 106-448). House passed, under suspension of the rules, Nov. 9. Senate Energy and Natural Resources reported, with amendment, July 10, 2000 (S Rept 106-334). Senate passed, with amendment, Oct. 5. House agreed to Senate amendment, under suspension of the rules, Oct. 10. President signed Oct. 27, 2000.

PL 106-366 (HR 2984) Direct the secretary of the Interior, through the Bureau of Reclamation, to convey the assets of the Middle Loup Division of the Missouri River Basin Project in Nebraska to the Loup Basin Reclamation District, the Sargent River Irrigation District and the Farwell Irrigation District, all in Nebraska. Introduced by BARRETT, R-Neb., on Sept. 30, 1999. House Resources reported, amended, Sept. 7, 2000 (H Rept 106-829). House passed, amended, under suspension of the rules, Sept. 18. Senate Energy and Natural Resources discharged. Senate passed Oct. 13. President signed Oct. 27, 2000.

PL 106-367 (HR 3235) Improve academic and social outcomes for youth and reduce both juvenile crime and the risk that youth will become victims of crime by providing productive activities conducted by law enforcement personnel during non-school hours. Introduced by BARRETT, D-Wis., on Nov, 5, 1999. House Judiciary reported, amended, Sept. 18, 2000 (H Rept 106-859). House passed, amended, under suspension of the rules, on Oct. 2. Senate passed Oct. 13. President signed Oct. 27, 2000.

PL 106-368 (HR 3236) Authorize the secretary of the Interior to enter into contracts with the Weber Basin Water Conservancy District, Utah, to use Weber Basin Project facilities for the impounding, storage and carriage of non-project water for domestic, municipal, industrial and other purposes. Introduced by CANNON, R-Utah, on Nov. 5, 1999. House Resources reported, amended, July 17, 2000 (H Rept 106-742). House passed, amended, under suspension of the rules, July 25. Senate Energy and Natural Resources reported Sept. 28 (S Rept 106-434). Senate passed Oct. 13. President signed Oct. 27, 2000.

PL 106-369 (HR 3292) Provide for the establishment of the Cat Island National Wildlife Refuge in West Feliciana Parish, La. Introduced by BAKER, R-La., on Nov. 10, 1999. House Resources reported, amended, June 8, 2000 (H Rept 106-659). House passed, amended, under suspension of the rules, June 19. Senate Environment and Public Works reported, with amendments, Oct. 2 (S Rept 106-459). Senate passed, with amendments, Oct. 5. House agreed to Senate amendments, under suspension of the rules, Oct. 12. President signed Oct. 27, 2000.

PL 106-370 (HR 3468) Direct the secretary of the Interior to convey certain water rights to Duchesne City, Utah. Introduced by CANNON, R-Utah, on Nov. 18, 1999. House Resources reported July 17, 2000 (H Rept 106-737). House passed, amended, under suspension of the rules, July 25. Senate passed Oct. 13. President signed Oct. 27, 2000.

PL 106-371 (HR 3577) Increase the amount authorized to be appropriated for the north side pumping division of the Minidoka reclamation project, Idaho. Introduced by SIMPSON, R-Idaho, on Feb. 3, 2000. House Resources reported May 2 (H Rept 106-599). House passed, under suspension of the rules, May 8. Senate Energy and Natural Resources reported Sept. 28 (S Rept 106-435). Senate passed Oct. 13. President signed Oct. 27, 2000.

PL 106-372 (HR 3986) Provide for a study of the engineering feasibility of a water exchange in lieu of electrification of the Chandler Pumping Plant at Prosser Diversion Dam, Wash. Introduced by HASTINGS, R-Wash., on March 15, 2000. House Resources reported, amended, Sept. 19 (H Rept 106-864). Failed passage under suspension of the rules (two-thirds required) Sept. 19. House passed, amended, Sept. 20. Senate Energy and Natural Resources discharged. Senate passed Oct. 13. President signed Oct. 27, 2000.

PL 106-373 (HR 4002) Amend the Foreign Assistance Act of 1961 to revise and improve provisions relating to famine prevention and freedom from hunger. Introduced by BRADY, R-Texas, on March 16, 2000. House passed, amended, under suspension of the rules, July 24. Senate Foreign Relations reported, amended, Oct. 2 (no written report). Senate passed, amended, Oct. 4. House agreed to Senate amendment Oct. 12. President signed Oct. 27, 2000.

PL 106-374 (HR 4132) Reauthorize grants for water resources research and technology institutes established under the Water Resources Research Act of 1984. Introduced by DOOLITTLE, R-Calif., on March 30, 2000. House Resources reported July 10 (H Rept 106-714). House passed, under suspension of the rules, July 10. Senate Environment and Public Works discharged. Senate passed Oct. 18. President signed Oct. 27, 2000.

PL 106-375 (HR 4259) Require the secretary of the Treasury to mint coins in commemoration of the National Museum of the American Indian of the Smithsonian Institution. Introduced by LUCAS, R-Okla., on April 12, 2000. House passed, under suspension of the rules, Sept. 26. Senate passed Oct. 11. President signed Oct. 27, 2000.

PL 106-376 (HR 4389) Direct the secretary of the Interior to convey certain water distribution facilities to the Northern Colorado Water Conservancy District. Introduced by SCHAFFER, R-Colo., on May 4, 2000. House Resources reported, amended, Sept. 6 (H Rept 106-812). House passed, amended, under suspension of the rules, Oct. 3. Senate passed Oct. 13. President signed Oct. 27, 2000.

PL 106-377 (HR 4635) Make appropriations for the departments of Veterans Affairs and Housing and Urban Development, and for sundry independent agencies, boards, commissions, corporations and offices for fiscal 2001. Introduced by WALSH, R-N.Y., on June 12, 2000. House Appropriations reported June 12 (H Rept 106-674). House passed, amended, June 21. Senate Appropriations reported, with amendment, Sept. 13 (S Rept 106-410). Senate passed, with amendment, Oct. 12. Conference report filed in the House Oct. 18 (H Rept 106-988). House agreed to conference report Oct. 19. Senate agreed to conference report Oct. 19. President signed Oct. 27, 2000.

PL 106-378 (HR 4681) Provide for the adjustment of status of certain Syrian nationals. Introduced by LAZIO, R-N.Y., on June 15, 2000. House passed, amended, under suspension of the rules, July 11. Senate passed Oct. 13. President signed Oct. 27, 2000.

PL 106-379 (HR 5107) Make certain corrections in copyright law. Introduced by COBLE, R-N.C., on Sept. 6, 2000. House Judiciary reported Sept. 18 (H Rept 106-861). House passed, amended, under suspension of the rules, Sept. 19. Senate passed Oct. 12. President signed Oct. 27, 2000.

PL 106-380 (HR 5212) Direct the American Folklife Center at the Library of Congress to establish a program to collect video and audio recordings of personal histories and testimonials of American war veterans. Introduced by KIND, D-Wis., on Sept. 19, 2000. House passed, amended, under suspension of the rules, Oct. 4. Senate passed Oct. 17. President signed Oct. 27, 2000.

PL 106-381 (H J Res 117) Make further continuing appropriations for fiscal 2001. Introduced by YOUNG, R-Fla., on Oct. 24, 2000. House passed Oct. 27. Senate passed Oct. 27. President signed Oct. 27, 2000.

PL 106-382 (S 624) Authorize construction of the Fort Peck Reservation Rural Water System in Montana. Introduced by BURNS, R-Mont., on March 16, 1999. Senate Energy and Natural Resources reported, amended, Oct. 20 (S Rept 106-198). Senate passed, amended, Nov. 19. House Resources reported, with amendment, Sept. 7, 2000 (H Rept 106-823) House passed, with amendment, under suspension of the rules, Sept. 12. Senate agreed to House amendment Oct. 13. President signed Oct. 27, 2000.

PL 106-383 (S 2498) Authorize the Smithsonian Institution to plan, design, construct and equip laboratory, administrative, and support space to house base operations for the Smithsonian Astrophysical Observatory Submillimeter Array on Mauna Kea at Hilo, Hawaii. Introduced by MOYNIHAN, D-N.Y., on May 2, 2000. Senate Rules and Administration discharged. Senate passed June 14. House passed, under suspension of the rules, Oct. 17. President signed Oct. 27, 2000.

PL 106-384 (S 2686) Amend chapter 36 of Title 39, U.S. Code, to modify rates relating to reduced rate mail matter. Introduced by COCHRAN, R-Miss., on June 7, 2000. Senate Governmental Affairs reported Oct. 3 (S Rept 106-468). Senate passed Oct. 6. House Government Reform discharged. House passed Oct. 11. President signed Oct. 27, 2000.

PL 106-385 (S 3201) Rename the National Museum of American Art the Smithsonian American Art Museum. Introduced by FRIST, R-Tenn., on Oct. 12, 2000. Senate passed Oct. 12. House passed, under suspension of the rules, Oct. 17. President signed Oct. 27, 2000.

PL 106-386 (HR 3244) Combat trafficking of persons, especially into the sex trade, slavery and slavery-like conditions in the United States and countries around the world through prevention, through prosecution and enforcement against traffickers and through protection and assistance to victims of trafficking. Introduced by SMITH, R-N.J., on Nov. 8, 1999. House International Relations reported, amended, Nov. 22 (H Rept 106-487, Part 1). House Judiciary reported, amended, April 13, 2000 (H Rept 106-487, Part 2). House Banking and Financial Services discharged. House passed, amended, under suspension of the rules, May 9. Senate passed, with amendment, July 27. Conference report filed in the House Oct. 5 (H Rept 106-939). House agreed to conference report Oct. 6. Senate agreed to conference report Oct. 11. President signed Oct. 28, 2000.

PL 106-387 (HR 4461) Make appropriations for Agriculture, Rural Development, Food and Drug Administration and related agencies programs for fiscal 2001. Introduced by SKEEN, R-N.M., on May

16, 2000. House Appropriations reported May 16 (H Rept 106-619). House passed, amended, July 11. Senate passed, with amendment, July 20. Conference report filed in the House Oct. 6 (H Rept 106-948). House agreed to conference report Oct. 11. Senate agreed to conference report Oct. 18. President signed Oct. 28, 2000.

PL 106-388 (H J Res 118) Make further continuing appropriations for fiscal 2001. Introduced by YOUNG, R-Fla., on Oct. 24, 2000. House passed Oct. 28. Senate passed Oct. 28. President signed Oct. 28, 2000.

PL 106-389 (H J Res 119) Make further continuing appropriations for fiscal 2001. Introduced by YOUNG, R-Fla., on Oct. 24, 2000. House passed Oct. 29. Senate passed Oct. 29. President signed Oct. 29, 2000.

PL 106-390 (HR 707) Amend the Robert T. Stafford Disaster Relief and Emergency Assistance Act to authorize a program for predisaster mitigation, to streamline the administration of disaster relief and to control the federal costs of disaster assistance. Introduced by FOWLER, R-Fla., on Feb. 11, 1999. House Transportation and Infrastructure reported, amended, March 3 (H Rept 106-40) House passed, amended, March 4. Senate Environment and Public Works reported May 16 (no written report). Senate passed, with amendment, July 19, 2000. House agreed to Senate amendment, with amendment, Oct. 3. Senate agreed to House amendment, with amendment, Oct. 5. House agreed to Senate amendment, under suspension of the rules, Oct. 10. President signed Oct. 30, 2000.

PL 106-391 (HR 1654) Authorize appropriations for the National Aeronautics and Space Administration for fiscal years 2000, 2001 and 2002. Introduced by ROHRABACHER, R-Calif., on May 3, 1999. House Science reported, amended, May 18 (H Rept 106-145). House passed, amended, May 19. Senate passed, with amendment, Nov. 5. Conference report filed in the House Sept. 12, 2000 (H Rept 106-843). House agreed to conference report Sept. 14. Senate agreed to conference report Oct. 13. President signed Oct. 30, 2000.

PL 106-392 (HR 2348) Authorize the Bureau of Reclamation to provide cost sharing for the endangered fish recovery implementation programs for the Upper Colorado and San Juan River Basins. Introduced by HANSEN, R-Utah, on June 24, 1999. House Resources reported, amended, July 25, 2000 (H Rept 106-791). House passed, amended, under suspension of the rules, July 25. Senate passed Oct. 13. President signed Oct. 30, 2000.

PL 106-393 (HR 2389) Restore stability and predictability to the annual payments made to states and counties containing National Forest System lands and public domain lands managed by the Bureau of Land Management for use by the counties for the benefit of public schools and roads. Introduced by DEAL, R-Ga., on June 30, 1999. House Agriculture reported, amended, Oct. 18. (H Rept 106-392, Part 1). House Resources discharged. House passed, amended, Nov. 3. Senate Energy and Natural Resources discharged. Senate passed, with amendment, Oct. 6, 2000. House agreed to Senate amendment, under suspension of the rules, Oct. 10. President signed Oct. 30, 2000.

PL 106-394 (HR 2842) Amend Chapter 89 of Title 5, U.S. Code, concerning the Federal Employees Health Benefits Program, to enable the federal government to enroll an employee and his or her family in the program, when a state court orders the employee to provide health insurance coverage for a child of the employee but the employee fails to provide the coverage. Introduced by CUMMINGS, D-Md., on Sept. 13, 1999. House Government Reform reported, amended, July 24, 2000 (H Rept 106-779). House passed, amended, under suspension of the rules, Sept. 19. Senate Governmental Affairs discharged Sept. 20. Senate passed Oct. 13. President signed Oct. 30, 2000.

PL 106-395 (HR 2883) Amend the Immigration and Nationality Act to confer U.S. citizenship automatically and retroactively on certain foreign-born children adopted by citizens of the United States. Introduced by SMITH, R-Texas, on Sept. 21, 1999. House Judiciary reported, amended, Sept. 14, 2000 (H Rept 106-852). House passed, amended, under suspension of the rules, Sept. 19. Senate passed Oct. 12. President signed Oct. 30, 2000.

PL 106-396 (HR 3767) Amend the Immigration and Nationality Act to make improvements to, and permanently authorize, the visa waiver pilot program under section 217. Introduced by SMITH, R-Texas on March 1, 2000. House Judiciary reported, amended, April 6 (H Rept 106-564). House passed, amended, under the suspension of the rules, April 11. Senate passed, with amendments, Oct. 3. House agreed to Senate amendments, under suspension of the rules, Oct. 10. President signed Oct. 30, 2000.

PL 106-397 (HR 3995) Establish procedures governing the responsibilities of court-appointed receivers who administer departments, offices and agencies of the District of Columbia government. Introduced by NORTON, D-D.C., on March 15, 2000. House Government Reform reported, amended, June 12 (H Rept 106-663). House passed, amended, under suspension of the rules, June 12. Senate Governmental Affairs reported Oct. 6 (S Rept 106-493). Senate passed Oct. 12. President signed Oct. 30, 2000.

PL 106-398 (HR 4205) Authorize appropriations for fiscal 2001 for military activities of the Department of Defense, for military construction and for defense activities of the Department of Energy and prescribe military personnel strengths for fiscal 2001. Introduced by SPENCE, R-S.C., on April 6, 2000. House Armed Services reported, amended, May 12 (H Rept 106-616). House passed, amended, May 18. Senate passed, with amendment, July 13. Conference report filed in the House Oct. 6 (H Rept 106-945). House agreed to conference report Oct. 11. Senate agreed to conference report Oct. 12. President signed Oct. 30, 2000.

PL 106-399 (HR 4828) Designate wilderness areas and a cooperative management and protection area in the vicinity of Steens Mountain in Harney County, Ore. Introduced by WALDEN, R-Ore., on July 12, 2000. House Resources reported, amended, Oct. 3 (H Rept 106-929, Part 1). House Agriculture discharged. House passed, amended, Oct. 4. Senate passed Oct. 12. President signed Oct. 30, 2000.

PL 106-400 (HR 5417) Rename the Stewart B. McKinney Homeless Assistance Act as the "McKinney-Vento Homeless Assistance Act." Introduced by LaFALCE, D-N.Y., on Oct. 6, 2000. House Banking and Financial Services discharged. House passed Oct. 11. Senate passed Oct. 13. President signed Oct. 30, 2000.

PL 106-401 (H J Res 120) Make further continuing appropriations for fiscal 2001. Introduced by YOUNG, R-Fla., on Oct. 24, 2000. House passed Oct. 30. Senate passed Oct. 30. President signed Oct. 30, 2000.

PL 106-402 (S 1809) Improve service systems for individuals with developmental disabilities. Introduced by JEFFORDS, R-Vt., on Oct. 27, 1999. Senate Health, Education, Labor, and Pensions reported, amended, Nov. 4 (no written report). Senate passed, amended, Nov. 8. House Education and the Workforce, House Commerce discharged. House passed Oct. 11, 2000. President signed Oct. 30, 2000.

PL 106-403 (H J Res 121) Make further continuing appropriations for fiscal 2001. Introduced by YOUNG, R-Fla., on Oct. 29, 1999. Senate passed Oct. 31, 3000. House passed Oct. 31. President signed Nov. 1, 2000.

PL 106-404 (HR 209) Improve the ability of federal agencies to license federally owned inventions. Introduced by MORELLA, R-Md., on Jan. 6, 1999. House Science reported, amended, May 6 (H Rept 106-129, Part 1). House Judiciary discharged. House passed, amended, under suspension of the rules, May 11. Senate Commerce, Science and Transportation discharged. Senate passed, with amendment, Oct. 5, 2000. House agreed to Senate amendment, under suspension of the rules, Oct. 17. President signed Nov. 1, 2000.

PL 106-405 (HR 2607) Promote the development of the commercial space transportation industry, and authorize appropriations for the Office of the Associate Administrator for Commercial Space Transportation and for the Office of Space Commercialization. Introduced by ROHRABACHER, R-Calif., on July 26, 1999. House passed, amended, under suspension of the rules, Oct. 4. Senate Commerce, Science and Transportation discharged. Senate passed, with amendment, Oct. 13, 2000. House agreed to Senate amendment, under suspension of the rules, Oct. 17. President signed Nov. 1, 2000.

PL 106-406 (HR 2961) Amend the Immigration and Nationality Act to authorize a three-year pilot program under which the attorney general may extend the period during which certain non-immigrant aliens who require medical treatment in the United States and were admitted under the Visa Waiver Pilot Program may remain in the United States. Introduced by BENTSEN, D-Texas, on Sept. 28, 1999. House Judiciary reported July 11, 2000 (H Rept 106-721). House passed, amended, under suspension of the rules, July 18. Senate Judiciary discharged. Senate passed Oct. 19. President signed Nov. 1, 2000.

PL 106-407 (HR 3069) Authorize the administrator of General Services to provide for redevelopment of the Southeast Federal Center in the District of Columbia. Introduced by FRANKS, R-N.J., on Oct. 13, 1999. House Transportation and Infrastructure reported, amended, April 13, 2000 (H Rept 106-591). House passed, amended, under suspension of the rules, May 8. Senate Governmental Affairs reported, with amendments, Oct. 2 (S Rept 106-458). Senate passed, with amendments, Oct. 11. House agreed to Senate amendments, under suspension of the rules, Oct. 17. President signed Nov. 1, 2000.

PL 106-408 (HR 3671) Amend the Pittman-Robertson Wildlife Restoration Act and the Dingell-Johnson Sport Fish Restoration Act to enhance the funds available for grants to states for fish and wildlife conservation projects, to reauthorize and amend the National Fish and Wildlife Foundation Establishment Act, and to commemorate the centennial of the establishment of the first national wildlife refuge in the United States on March 14, 1903. Introduced by YOUNG, R-Alaska, on Feb. 16, 2000. House Resources reported, amended, March 30 (H Rept 106-554). House passed, amended, April 5. Senate Environment and Public Works reported, with amendment, Oct. 10 (S Rept 106-495). Senate passed, with amendments, Oct. 12.

House agreed to Senate amendments, under suspension of the rules, Oct. 18. President signed Nov. 1, 2000.

PL 106-409 (HR 4068) Amend the Immigration and Nationality Act to extend for an additional three years the special immigrant religious worker program. Introduced by PEASE, R-Ind., on March 23, 2000. House passed, under suspension of the rules, Sept. 19. Senate passed Oct. 19. President signed Nov. 1, 2000.

PL 106-410 (HR 4110) Amend Title 44, U.S. Code, to authorize appropriations for the National Historical Publications and Records Commission for fiscal years 2002 through 2005. Introduced by HORN, R-Calif., on March 29, 2000. House Government Reform reported July 20 (H Rept 106-768). House passed, amended, under suspension of the rules, July 24. Senate Governmental Affairs reported Oct. 3 (S Rept 106-466). Senate passed Oct. 19. President signed Nov. 1, 2000.

PL 106-411 (HR 4320) Assist in the conservation of great apes by supporting and providing financial resources for the conservation programs of countries within the range of great apes and projects of persons with demonstrated expertise in the conservation of great apes. Introduced by MILLER, D-Calif., on April 13, 2000. House Resources reported, amended, July 25 (H Rept 106-792). House passed, amended, under suspension of the rules, July 25. Senate Environment and Public Works reported Oct. 3 (S Rept 106-472). Senate passed Oct. 19. President signed Nov. 1, 2000.

PL 106-412 (HR 4835) Authorize the exchange of land between the secretary of the Interior and the director of Central Intelligence at the George Washington Memorial Parkway in McLean, Va. Introduced by MORAN, D-Va., on July 12, 2000. House Resources reported Sept. 26 (H Rept 106-895, Part 1). House passed, under suspension of the rules, Sept. 26. Senate Energy and Natural Resources discharged. Senate passed Oct. 19. President signed Nov. 1, 2000.

PL 106-413 (HR 4850) Increase, effective Dec. 1, 2000, the rates of compensation for veterans with service-connected disabilities and the rates of dependency and indemnity compensation for the survivors of certain disabled veterans. Introduced by STUMP, R-Ariz., on July 13, 2000. House Veterans' Affairs reported July 24 (H Rept 106-783). House passed, under suspension of the rules, July 25. Senate Veterans' Affairs discharged. Senate passed, with amendments, Oct. 12. House agreed to Senate amendments, under suspension of the rules, Oct. 17. President signed Nov. 1, 2000.

PL 106-414 (HR 5164) Amend Title 49, U.S. Code, to require reports concerning defects in motor vehicles, tires or other motor vehicle equipment in foreign countries. Introduced by UPTON, R-Mich., on Sept. 13, 2000. House Commerce reported, amended, Oct. 10 (H Rept 106-954). House passed, amended, under suspension of the rules, Oct. 11. Senate passed Oct. 11. President signed Nov. 1, 2000.

PL 106-415 (HR 5234) Amend the Hmong Veterans' Naturalization Act of 2000 to extend the applicability of that Act to certain former spouses of deceased Hmong veterans. Introduced by RADANOVICH, R-Calif., on Sept. 20, 2000. House passed, under suspension of the rules, Sept. 25. Senate passed Oct. 19. President signed Nov. 1, 2000.

PL 106-416 (H J Res 122) Make further continuing appropriations for fiscal 2001. Introduced by YOUNG, R-Fla, on Oct. 29, 2000. House passed Nov. 1. Senate passed Nov. 1. President signed Nov. 1, 2000.

PL 106-417 (S 406) Amend the Indian Health Care Improvement Act to make permanent the demonstration program that allows for direct billing of Medicare, Medicaid and other third party payers, and to expand the eligibility under such program to other tribes and tribal organizations. Introduced by MURKOWSKI, R-Alaska, on Feb. 10, 1999. Senate Indian Affairs reported, amended, Sept. 8 (S Rept 106-152). Senate passed, amended, Sept. 15. House Resources reported Sept. 6, 2000 (S Rept 106-818 Part 1). House Ways and Means, House Commerce discharged. House passed, under suspension of the rules, Oct. 17. President signed Nov. 1, 2000.

PL 106-418 (S 1296) Designate portions of the lower Delaware River and associated tributaries as a component of the National Wild and Scenic Rivers System. Introduced by LAUTENBERG, D-N.J., on June 28, 1999. Senate Energy and Natural Resources reported, amended, Nov. 2 (S Rept 106-207). Senate passed, amended, Nov. 19. House passed, under suspension of the rules, Oct. 17, 2000. President signed Nov. 1, 2000.

PL 106-419 (S 1402) Amend Title 38, U.S. Code, to increase amounts of education assistance for veterans under the Montgomery GI Bill and to enhance programs providing education benefits for veterans. Introduced by SPECTER, R-Pa., on July 20, 1999. Senate Veterans' Affairs reported July 20 (S Rept 106-114). Senate passed July 26. House passed, amended, under suspension of the rules, May 23, 2000. Senate agreed to House amendments with amendments Oct. 12. House agreed to Senate amendments, under suspension of the rules, Oct. 17. President signed Nov. 1, 2000.

PL 106-420 (S 1455) Enhance protections against fraud in the offering of financial assistance for college education. Introduced by ABRAHAM, R-Mich., on July 28, 1999. Senate Judiciary reported, amended, Oct. 29 (no written report). Senate passed, amended, Nov. 4. House passed, under suspension of the rules, Sept. 25, 2000. President signed Nov. 1, 2000.

PL 106-421 (S 1705) Direct the secretary of the Interior to enter into land exchanges to acquire from the private owner and to convey to the state of Idaho approximately 1,240 acres of land near the City of Rocks National Reserve, Idaho. Introduced by CRAIG, R-Idaho, on Oct. 7, 1999. Senate Energy and Natural Resources reported April 12, 2000 (S Rept 106-262). Senate passed April 13. House Resources reported July 17 (H Rept 106-749). House passed, under suspension of the rules, Oct. 17. President signed Nov. 1, 2000.

PL 106-422 (S 1707) Amend the Inspector General Act of 1978 (5 U.S.C. App.) to provide that certain designated federal entities shall be establishments under the act. Introduced by THOMPSON, R-Tenn., on Oct. 7, 1999. Senate Governmental Affairs reported, amended, Nov. 8 (S Rept 106-218). Senate passed, amended, Nov. 19. House passed, under suspension of the rules, Oct. 17, 2000. President signed Nov. 1, 2000.

PL 106-423 (S 2102) Provide to the Timbisha Shoshone Tribe a permanent land base within its aboriginal homeland. Introduced by INOUYE, D-Hawaii, on Feb. 24, 2000. Senate Indian Affairs reported, amended, June 30 (S Rept 106-327). Senate passed, amended, July 19. House passed, under suspension of the rules, Oct. 17. President signed Nov. 1, 2000.

PL 106-424 (S 2412) Amend Title 49, U.S. Code, to authorize appropriations for the National Transportation Safety Board for fiscal years 2000, 2001, 2002 and 2003. Introduced by McCAIN, R-Ariz., on April 12, 2000. Senate Commerce, Science and Transportation reported Aug. 25 (S Rept 106-386). Senate passed, amended, Oct. 3. House passed, under suspension of the rules, Oct. 17. President signed Nov. 1, 2000.

PL 106-425 (S 2917) Settle the land claims of the Pueblo of Santo Domingo. Introduced by DOMENICI, R-N.M., on July 25, 2000. Senate Indian Affairs discharged. Senate passed Oct. 11. House passed, under suspension of the rules, Oct. 17. Senate Indian Affairs reported Oct. 18 (S Rept 106-506). President signed Nov. 1, 2000.

PL 106-426 (H J Res 123) Make further continuing appropriations for fiscal 2001. Introduced by YOUNG, R-Fla., on Oct. 29, 2000. House passed, amended, Nov. 2. Senate passed Nov. 2. President signed Nov. 3, 2000.

PL 106-427 (H J Res 124) Make further continuing appropriations for fiscal 2001. Introduced by YOUNG, R-Fla., on Oct. 29, 2000. House passed Nov. 3. Senate passed Nov. 3. President signed Nov. 4, 2000.

PL 106-428 (H J Res 84) Make further continuing appropriations for fiscal 2001. Introduced by YOUNG, R-Fla., on Nov. 18, 1999. House passed Nov. 18. Senate passed, with amendments, Nov. 1, 2000. House agreed to Senate amendments Nov. 3. President signed Nov. 4, 2000.

PL 106-429 (HR 4811) Make appropriations for foreign operations, export financing and related programs for fiscal 2001. Introduced by CALLAHAN, R-Ala., on July 10, 2000. House Appropriations reported July 10 (H Rept 106-720). House passed, amended, July 13. Senate passed, with amendment, July 18. Conference report filed in the House Oct. 24 (H Rept 106-997). House agreed to conference report Oct. 25. Senate agreed to conference report Oct. 25. President signed Nov. 6, 2000.

PL 106-430 (HR 5178) Require changes in the bloodborne pathogens standard in effect under the Occupational Safety and Health Act of 1970. Introduced by BALLENGER, R-N.C., on Sept. 14, 2000. House passed, amended, under suspension of the rules, Oct. 3. Senate passed Oct. 26. President signed Nov. 6, 2000.

PL 106-431 (HR 468) Establish the Saint Helena Island National Scenic Area. Introduced by KILDEE, D-Mich., on Feb. 2, 1999. House Resources reported, amended, July 26 (H Rept 106-255). House passed, amended, under suspension of the rules, Sept. 21. Senate Energy and Natural Resources reported, amended, Aug. 25, 2000 (S Rept 106-392). Senate passed, amended, Oct. 5. House failed to agree to Senate amendment, under suspension of the rules, Oct. 12. House agreed to Senate amendment Oct. 24. President signed Nov. 6, 2000.

PL 106-432 (HR 1725) Provide for the conveyance by the Bureau of Land Management to Douglas County, Ore., of a county park and certain adjacent land. Introduced by DeFAZIO, D-Ore., on May 6, 1999. House Resources reported Nov. 4 (H Rept 106-446). House passed, under suspension of the rules, March 21, 2000. Senate passed, amended, Oct. 5. House agreed to Senate amendments, under suspension of the rules, Oct. 23. President signed Nov. 6, 2000.

PL 106-433 (HR 3218) Amend Title 31, U.S. Code, to prohibit the appearance of Social Security account numbers on or through unopened mailings of checks or other drafts issued on public money in the Treasury. Introduced by CALVERT, R-Calif., on Nov. 4, 1999. House passed, under suspension of the rules, Oct. 18, 2000. Senate passed Oct. 25. President signed Nov. 6, 2000.

PL 106-434 (HR 3657) Provide for the conveyance of a small parcel of public domain land in the San Bernardino National Forest in California. Introduced by BONO, R-Calif., on Feb. 15, 2000. House Resources reported, amended, July 17 (H Rept 106-744). House passed, amended, under suspension of the rules, Sept. 12. Senate Energy and Natural Resources discharged. Senate passed, amended, Oct. 19. House agreed to Senate amendment, under suspension of the rules, Oct. 23. President signed Nov. 6, 2000.

PL 106-435 (HR 3679) Provide for the minting of commemorative coins to support the 2002 Salt Lake Olympic Winter Games and the programs of the United States Olympic Committee. Introduced by COOK, R-Utah, on Feb. 16, 2000. House passed, amended, under suspension of the rules, Sept. 19. Senate passed Oct. 23. President signed Nov. 6, 2000.

PL 106-436 (HR 4315) Designate the facility of the U.S. Postal Service at 3695 Green Rd. in Beachwood, Ohio, as the "Larry Small Post Office Building." Introduced by LaTOURETTE, R-Ohio, on April 13, 2000. House passed, under suspension of the rules, Oct. 2. Senate passed Oct. 24. President signed Nov. 6, 2000.

PL 106-437 (HR 4404) Permit the payment of medical expenses incurred by the U.S. Park Police in the performance of duty to be made directly by the National Park Service and allow for waiver and indemnification in mutual law enforcement agreements between the National Park Service and a state or political subdivision when required by state law. Introduced by HANSEN, R-Utah, on May 9, 2000. House Resources reported, amended, Sept. 14 (H Rept 106-854, Part 1). House Government Reform discharged. House passed, amended, under suspension of the rules, Oct. 17. Senate passed Oct. 26. President signed Nov. 6, 2000.

PL 106-438 (HR 4450) Designate the facility of the U.S. Postal Service at 900 E. Fayette St. in Baltimore, Md., as the "Judge Harry Augustus Cole Post Office Building." Introduced by CUMMINGS, D-Md., on May 15, 2000. House passed, under suspension of the rules, Sept. 19. Senate Governmental Affairs discharged. Senate passed Oct. 24. President signed Nov. 6, 2000.

PL 106-439 (HR 4451) Designate the facility of the U.S. Postal Service at 1001 Frederick Rd. in Baltimore, Md., as the "Frederick L. Dewberry Jr. Post Office Building." Introduced by CUMMINGS, D-Md., on May 15, 2000. House passed, under suspension of the rules, on Sept. 25. Senate Governmental Affairs discharged. Senate passed Oct. 24. President signed Nov. 6, 2000.

PL 106-440 (HR 4625) Designate the facility of the U.S. Postal Service at 2108 E. 38th St. in Erie, Pa., as the "Gertrude A. Barber Post Office Building." Introduced by ENGLISH, R-Pa., on June 9, 2000. House passed, under suspension of the rules, Sept. 19. Senate Governmental Affairs discharged. Senate passed Oct. 24. President signed Nov. 6, 2000.

PL 106-441 (HR 4786) Designate the facility of the U.S. Postal Service at 110 Postal Way in Carrollton, Ga., as the "Samuel P. Roberts Post Office Building." Introduced by BARR, R-Ga., on June 29, 2000. House passed, under suspension of the rules, Sept. 19. Senate Governmental Affairs discharged. Senate passed Oct. 24. President signed Nov. 6, 2000.

PL 106-442 (HR 4957) Amend the Omnibus Parks and Public Lands Management Act of 1996 to extend the legislative authority for the Black Patriots Foundation to establish a commemorative work. Introduced by RANGEL, D-N.Y., on July 25, 2000. House passed, under suspension of the rules, Sept. 12. Senate passed Oct. 26. President signed Nov. 6, 2000.

PL 106-443 (HR 5083) Extend the authority of the Los Angeles Unified School District to use certain park lands in the city of South Gate, Calif., which were acquired with amounts provided from the land and water conservation fund, for elementary school purposes. Introduced by ROYBAL-ALLARD, D-Calif., on July 27, 2000. House passed, under suspension of the rules, Oct. 12. Senate passed Oct. 26. President signed Nov. 6, 2000.

PL 106-444 (HR 5157) Amend Title 44, U.S. Code, to ensure preservation of the records of the Freedmen's Bureau. Introduced by MILLENDER-MCDONALD, D-Calif., on Sept. 12, 2000. House Government Reform discharged. House passed, amended, Oct. 19. Senate passed Oct. 26. President signed Nov. 6, 2000.

PL 106-445 (HR 5273) Clarify the intention of the Congress with regard to the authority of the U.S. Mint to produce numismatic coins. Introduced by BACHUS, R-Ala., on Sept. 25, 2000. House passed, under suspension of the rules, Sept. 26. Senate Banking, Housing, and Urban Affairs discharged. Senate passed Oct. 24. President signed Nov. 6, 2000.

PL 106-446 (HR 5314) Require the immediate termination of the Department of Defense practice of euthanizing military working dogs at the end of their useful working life, and facilitate the adoption of retired military working dogs by law enforcement agencies, former handlers of these dogs and other persons capable of caring for them. Introduced by BARTLETT, R-Md., on Sept. 27, 2000. House passed, amended, under suspension of the rules, Oct. 10. Senate passed, with amendment, Oct. 24. House agreed to Senate amendment, under suspension of the rules, Oct. 26. President signed Nov. 6, 2000.

PL 106-447 (S 614) Provide for regulatory reform in order to encourage investment, business, and economic development with respect to activities conducted on Indian lands. Introduced by CAMPBELL, R-Colo., on March 15, 1999. Senate Indian Affairs reported, amended, Sept. 8 (S Rept 106-151). Senate passed, amended, Sept. 15. House passed, under suspension of the rules, Oct. 23, 2000. President signed Nov. 6, 2000.

PL 106-448 (S 2812) Amend the Immigration and Nationality Act to provide a waiver of the oath of renunciation and allegiance for naturalization of aliens having certain disabilities. Introduced by HATCH, R-Utah, on June 29, 2000. Senate Judiciary reported July 20 (no written report). Senate passed July 21. House Judiciary discharged. House passed, with amendment, Oct. 10. Senate agreed to House amendment Oct. 19. President signed Nov. 6, 2000.

PL 106-449 (S 3062) Modify the date on which the mayor of the District of Columbia submits a performance accountability plan to Congress. Introduced by VOINOVICH, R-Ohio, on Sept. 18, 2000. Senate Governmental Affairs reported Oct. 3 (S Rept 106-469). Senate passed Oct. 6. House Government Reform discharged. House passed Oct. 19. President signed Nov. 6, 2000.

PL 106-450 (HR 1651) Amend the Fishermen's Protective Act of 1967 to extend the period during which reimbursement may be provided to owners of U.S. fishing vessels for costs incurred when the vessel is seized and detained by a foreign country. Introduced by YOUNG, R-Alaska, on April 29, 1999. House Resources reported June 23 (H Rept 106-197). House passed, amended, under suspension of the rules, Sept. 13. Senate Commerce, Science and Transportation reported, with amendment, May 23, 2000 (S Rept 106-302). Senate passed, with amendment, June 26. House failed to agree to Senate amendment, under suspension of the rules, July 25. House agreed to Senate amendment, with an amendment, Sept. 18. Senate agreed to House amendment Oct. 25. President signed Nov. 7, 2000.

PL 106-451 (HR 2442) Provide for the preparation of a government report detailing injustices suffered by Italian Americans during World War II and a formal acknowledgment of such injustices by the president. Introduced by LAZIO, R-N.Y., on July 1, 1999. House passed, under suspension of the rules, Nov. 10. Senate Judiciary reported, amended, Sept. 28, 2000 (no written report). Senate passed, with amendments, Oct. 19. House agreed to Senate amendments, under suspension of the rules, Oct. 24. President signed Nov. 7, 2000.

PL 106-452 (HR 4831) Redesignate the facility of the U.S. Postal Service at 2339 N. California St. in Chicago, Ill., as the "Roberto Clemente Post Office." Introduced by GUTIERREZ, D-Ill., on July 12, 2000. House passed, amended, under suspension of the rules, Oct. 10. Senate passed Oct. 24. President signed Nov. 7, 2000.

PL 106-453 (HR 4853) Redesignate the facility of the U.S. Postal Service at 1568 S. Glen Rd. in South Euclid, Ohio, as the "Arnold C. D'Amico Station." Introduced by JONES, D-Ohio, on July 13, 2000. House Government Reform discharged. House passed, amended, Oct. 12. Senate passed Oct. 24. President signed Nov. 7, 2000.

PL 106-454 (HR 5229) Designate the facility of the U.S. Postal Service at 219 S. Church St. in Odum, Ga., as the "Ruth Harris Coleman Post Office." Introduced by KINGSTON, R-Ga., on Sept. 20, 2000. House passed, under suspension of the rules, Oct. 10. Senate passed Oct. 24. President signed Nov. 7, 2000.

PL 106-455 (S 501) Address resource management issues in Glacier Bay National Park, Alaska. Introduced by MURKOWSKI, R-Alaska, on March 2, 1999. Senate Energy and Natural Resources reported, amended, July 29 (S Rept 106-128). Senate passed, amended, Nov. 19. House passed, under suspension of the rules, Oct. 23, 2000. President signed Nov. 7, 2000.

PL 106-456 (S 503) Designate certain land in the San Isabel National Forest in Colorado as the "Spanish Peaks Wilderness." Introduced by ALLARD, R-Colo., on March 2, 1999. Senate Energy and Natural Resources reported, amended, March 9, 2000 (S Rept 106-233). Senate passed, amended, April 13. House passed, under the suspension of the rules, Oct. 23. President signed Nov. 7, 2000.

PL 106-457 (S 835) Encourage the restoration of estuary habitat through more efficient project financing and enhanced coordination of federal and non-federal restoration programs. Introduced by CHAFEE, JOHN H., R-R.I., on April 20, 1999. Senate Environment and Public Works reported, amended, Oct. 14 (S Rept 106-189). Senate passed, amended, March 30, 2000. House passed, with amendment, under suspension of the rules, Sept. 12. Senate agreed to conference report Oct. 23. Conference report filed in the House on Oct. 24 (H

Rept 106-995). House agreed to conference report Oct. 25. President signed Nov. 7, 2000.

PL 106-458 (S 1088) Authorize the secretary of Agriculture to convey certain administrative sites in national forests in Arizona and to convey certain land to the City of Sedona, Ariz., for a wastewater treatment facility. Introduced by KYL, R-Ariz., on May 20, 1999. Senate Energy and Natural Resources reported July 21 (S Rept 106-115). Senate passed, amended, Nov. 19. House passed, under suspension of the rules, Oct. 23, 2000. President signed Nov. 7, 2000.

PL 106-459 (S 1211) Amend the Colorado River Basin Salinity Control Act to authorize additional measures to carry out the control of salinity upstream of Imperial Dam in a cost-effective manner. Introduced by BENNETT, R-Utah, on June 10, 1999. Senate Energy and Natural Resources reported, amended, Oct. 6 (S Rept 106-175). Senate passed, amended, Nov. 19. House Resources reported Sept. 6, 2000 (H Rept 106-814). House passed, under suspension of the rules, Oct. 23. President signed Nov. 7, 2000.

PL 106-460 (S 1218) Direct the secretary of the Interior to issue to the Landusky School District, without consideration, a patent for the surface and mineral estates of certain lots. Introduced by BURNS, R-Mont., on June 14, 1999. Senate Energy and Natural Resources reported, amended, March 20, 2000 (S Rept 106-245). Senate passed, amended, April 13. House passed, under suspension of the rules, Oct. 23. President signed Nov. 7, 2000.

PL 106-461 (S 1275) Authorize the secretary of the Interior to produce and sell products and to sell publications relating to the Hoover Dam and to deposit revenues generated from the sales into the Colorado River Dam fund. Introduced by KYL, R-Ariz., on June 24, 1999. Senate Energy and Natural Resources reported Oct. 18 (S Rept 106-195). Senate passed Nov. 19. House Resources reported Sept. 6, 2000 (H Rept 106-808). House passed, under suspension of the rules, Oct. 23. President signed Nov. 7, 2000.

PL 106-462 (S 1586) Reduce the fractionated ownership of Indian lands. Introduced by CAMPBELL, R-Colo., on Sept. 15, 1999. Senate Indian Affairs reported, amended, July 26, 2000 (S Rept 106-361). Senate passed, amended, July 26. House passed, under suspension of the rules, Oct. 23. President signed Nov. 7, 2000.

PL 106-463 (S 2300) Amend the Mineral Leasing Act to increase the maximum acreage of federal leases for coal that may be held by an entity in any one state. Introduced by THOMAS, R-Wyo., on March 28, 2000. Senate Energy and Natural Resources reported Aug. 25 (S Rept 106-378). Senate passed Oct. 5. House passed, under suspension of the rules, Oct. 23. President signed Nov. 7, 2000.

PL 106-464 (S 2719) Provide for business development and trade promotion for American Indians. Introduced by CAMPBELL, R-Colo., on June 13, 2000. Senate Indian Affairs reported June 26 (no written report). Senate passed June 28. House passed, under suspension of the rules, Oct. 23. President signed Nov. 7, 2000.

PL 106-465 (S 2950) Authorize the secretary of the Interior to establish the Sand Creek Massacre Historic Site in Colorado. Introduced by CAMPBELL, R-Colo., on July 27, 2000. Senate Energy and Natural Resources reported, amended, Sept. 25 (S Rept 106-418). Senate passed, amended, Oct. 5. House passed, under suspension of the rules, Oct. 23. President signed Nov. 7, 2000.

PL 106-466 (S 3022) Direct the secretary of the Interior to convey certain irrigation facilities to the Nampa and Meridian Irrigation District. Introduced by CRAIG, R-Idaho, on Sept. 8, 2000. Senate Energy and Natural Resources reported, amended, Oct. 3 (S Rept 106-480). Senate passed, amended, Oct. 13. House passed, under suspension of the rules, Oct. 23. President signed Nov. 7, 2000.

PL 106-467 (HR 1235) Authorize the secretary of the Interior to enter into contracts with the Solano County Water Agency, Calif., to use Solano Project facilities for impounding, storage and carriage of non-project water for domestic, municipal and industrial purposes. Introduced by MILLER, D-Calif., on March 23, 1999. House Resources reported Nov. 1 (H Rept 106-426). House passed, under suspension of the rules, Nov. 1. Senate Energy and Natural Resources reported Sept. 28, 2000 (S Rept 106-433). Senate passed Oct. 27. President signed Nov. 9, 2000.

PL 106-468 (HR 2780) Authorize the attorney general to provide grants for organizations to find missing adults. Introduced by MYRICK, R-N.C., on Aug. 5, 1999. House passed, under suspension of the rules, Oct. 19, 2000. Senate passed Oct. 26. President signed Nov. 9, 2000.

PL 106-469 (HR 2884) Extend energy conservation programs under the Energy Policy and Conservation Act through fiscal 2003. Introduced by BLILEY, R-Va., on Sept. 21, 1999. House Commerce reported, amended, Oct. 1 (H Rept 106-359). House passed, amended, under suspension of the rules, April 12, 2000. Senate passed, with amendment, Oct. 19. House agreed to Senate amendment, under suspension of the rules, Oct. 24. President signed Nov. 9, 2000.

PL 106-470 (HR 4312) Direct the secretary of the Interior to conduct a study of the suitability and feasibility of establishing an Upper Housatonic Valley National Heritage Area in Connecticut and Massachusetts. Introduced by JOHNSON, R-Conn., on April 13, 2000. House passed, under suspension of the rules, Oct. 17. Senate passed Oct. 27. President signed Nov. 9, 2000.

PL 106-471 (HR 4646) Designate certain National Forest System lands within the boundaries of Virginia as wilderness areas. Introduced by GOODE, I-Va., on June 13, 2000. House passed, amended, under suspension of the rules, Oct. 17. Senate passed Oct. 27. President signed Nov. 9, 2000.

PL 106-472 (HR 4788) Amend the United States Grain Standards Act to extend the authority of the secretary of Agriculture to collect fees to cover the cost of services performed under the act, to extend the authorization of appropriations for the act and to improve the administration of the act. Introduced by BARRETT, R-Neb., on June 29, 2000. House passed, amended, under suspension of the rules, Oct. 10. Senate passed, with amendment, Oct. 12. House agreed to Senate amendment, with an amendment, Oct. 17. Senate agreed to House amendment Oct. 24. President signed Nov. 9, 2000.

PL 106-473 (HR 4794) Require the secretary of the Interior to complete a resource study of the 600 mile route through Connecticut, Delaware, Maryland, Massachusetts, New Jersey, New York, Pennsylvania, Rhode Island and Virginia used by George Washington and Gen. Rochambeau during the American Revolutionary War. Introduced by LARSON, D-Conn., on June 29, 2000. House passed, under suspension of the rules, Oct. 23. Senate passed Oct. 27. President signed Nov. 9, 2000.

PL 106-474 (HR 4846) Establish the National Recording Registry in the Library of Congress to maintain and preserve sound recordings and recording collections that are culturally, historically or aesthetically significant. Introduced by THOMAS, R-Calif., on July 13, 2000. House passed, amended, under suspension of the rules, July 25. Senate passed, with amendments, Oct. 25. House disagreed to Senate amendments Nov. 1. Senate receded from its amendments Nov. 1. President signed Nov. 9, 2000.

PL 106-475 (HR 4864) Amend Title 38, U.S. Code, to reaffirm and clarify the duty of the secretary of Veterans Affairs to assist claimants for benefits under laws administered by the secretary. Introduced by STUMP, R-Ariz., on July 17, 2000. House Veterans' Affairs reported, amended, July 24 (H Rept 106-781). House passed, amended, under suspension of the rules, July 25. Senate Veterans' Affairs discharged. Senate passed, with amendment, Sept. 25. House agreed to Senate amendment, under suspension of the rules, Oct. 17. President signed Nov. 9, 2000.

PL 106-476 (HR 4868) Amend the Harmonized Tariff Schedule of the United States to modify temporarily certain rates of duty and make other technical amendments to the trade laws. Introduced by CRANE, R-Ill., on July 18, 2000. House Ways and Means reported, amended, July 25 (H Rept 106-789). House passed, amended, under suspension of the rules, July 25. Senate Finance reported, with amendment, Oct. 12 (S Rept 106-503). Senate passed, with amendment, Oct. 13. House agreed to Senate amendment, with amendment, Oct. 24. Senate agreed to House amendment Oct. 26. President signed Nov. 9, 2000.

PL 106-477 (HR 5110) Designate the U.S. courthouse at 3470 12th St. in Riverside, Calif., as the "George E. Brown Jr. United States Courthouse." Introduced by CALVERT, R-Calif., on Sept. 6, 2000. House passed, under suspension of the rules, Oct. 17. Senate passed Nov. 1. President signed Nov. 9, 2000.

PL 106-478 (HR 5302) Designate the U.S. courthouse at 1010 Fifth Ave. in Seattle, Wash., as the "William Kenzo Nakamura United States Courthouse." Introduced by McDERMOTT, D-Wash., on Sept. 26, 2000. House passed, under suspension of the rules, Oct. 17. Senate passed Nov. 1. President signed Nov. 9, 2000.

PL 106-479 (HR 5331) Authorize the Frederick Douglass Gardens, Inc., to establish a memorial and gardens on Department of the Interior lands in the District of Columbia or its environs in honor and commemoration of Frederick Douglass. Introduced by DAVIS, D-Ill., on Sept. 28, 2000. House passed, under suspension of the rules, Oct. 3. Senate passed Oct. 26. President signed Nov. 9, 2000.

PL 106-480 (HR 5388) Designate a building proposed to be located within the boundaries of the Chincoteague National Wildlife Refuge in Virginia, as the "Herbert H. Bateman Educational and Administrative Center." Introduced by YOUNG, R-Alaska, on Oct. 4, 2000. House Resources discharged. House passed Oct. 24. Senate passed Nov. 1. President signed Nov. 9, 2000.

PL 106-481 (HR 5410) Establish revolving funds for the operation of certain programs and activities of the Library of Congress. Introduced by THOMAS, R-Calif., on Oct. 6, 2000. House passed, amended, under suspension of the rules, Oct. 17. Senate passed Oct. 31. President signed Nov. 9, 2000.

PL 106-482 (HR 5478) Authorize the secretary of the Interior to acquire by donation suitable land to serve as the new location for the home of Alexander Hamilton, commonly known as the Hamilton Grange, and to authorize the relocation of the Hamilton Grange to the acquired land. Introduced by RANGEL, D-N.Y., on Oct. 17, 2000. House passed, under suspension of the rules, Oct. 24. Senate passed Oct. 27. President signed Nov. 9, 2000.

PL 106-483 (H J Res 102) Recognize that the Birmingham Pledge has made a significant contribution in fostering racial harmony and reconciliation in the United States and around the world. Introduced by BACHUS, R-Ala., on June 14, 2000. House passed, under suspension of the rules, Sept. 12. Senate Judiciary discharged. Senate passed, with amendments, Oct. 26. House agreed to Senate amendments, under suspension of the rules, Oct. 30. President signed Nov. 9, 2000.

PL 106-484 (S 484) Provide for the granting of refugee status in the United States to nationals of certain foreign countries in which American Vietnam War POW/MIAs or American Korean War POW/MIAs may be present, if those nationals assist in the return to the United States of those POW/MIAs alive. Introduced by CAMPBELL, R-Colo., on Feb. 25, 1999. Senate Judiciary reported May 18, 2000 (no written report). Senate passed, amended, May 24. House International Relations, House Judiciary discharged. House passed Oct. 24. President signed Nov. 9, 2000.

PL 106-485 (S 610) Direct the secretary of the Interior to convey certain land under the jurisdiction of the Bureau of Land Management in Washakie County and Big Horn County, Wyo., to the Westside Irrigation District, Wyo. Introduced by ENZI, R-Wyo., on March 15, 1999. Senate Energy and Natural Resources reported, amended, June 27, 2000 (S Rept 106-313). Senate passed, amended, July 27. House passed, under suspension of the rules, Oct. 23. President signed Nov. 9, 2000.

PL 106-486 (S 698) Review the suitability and feasibility of recovering costs of high altitude rescues at Denali National Park and Preserve in Alaska. Introduced by MURKOWSKI, R-Alaska, on March 24, 1999. Senate Energy and Natural Resources reported June 9 (S Rept 106-71). Senate passed Nov. 19. House passed, under suspension of the rules, Oct. 24, 2000. President signed Nov. 9, 2000.

PL 106-487 (S 710) Authorize a feasibility study on the preservation of certain Civil War battlefields along the Vicksburg Campaign Trail. Introduced by LOTT, R-Miss., on March 24, 1999. Senate Energy and Natural Resources reported, amended, Oct. 14 (S Rept 106-184). Senate passed, amended, Nov. 19. House passed, under suspension of the rules, Oct. 23, 2000. President signed Nov. 9, 2000.

PL 106-488 (S 748) Improve American Indian hiring and contracting by the federal government in Alaska. Introduced by MURKOWSKI, R-Alaska, on March 25, 1999. Senate Energy and Natural Resources reported, amended, June 9, 1999 (S Rept 106-72). Senate passed, amended, Nov. 19. House passed, under suspension of the rules, Oct. 23, 2000. President signed Nov. 9, 2000.

PL 106-489 (S 893) Amend Title 46, U.S. Code, to provide equitable treatment with respect to state and local income taxes for certain individuals who perform duties on vessels. Introduced by GORTON, R-Wash., on April 27, 1999. Senate Commerce, Science and Transportation reported Sept. 26, 2000 (S Rept 106-421). Senate passed Sept. 28. House passed, under suspension of the rules, Oct. 24. President signed Nov. 9, 2000.

PL 106-490 (S 1030) Provide that the conveyance by the Bureau of Land Management of the surface estate to certain land in Wyoming in exchange for certain private land will not result in the removal of the land from operation of the mining laws. Introduced by ENZI, R-Wyo., on May 13, 1999. Senate Energy and Natural Resources reported, amended, Oct. 6 (S Rept 106-174). Senate passed, amended, Nov. 19. House Resources reported Sept. 26, 2000 (H Rept 106-898). House passed, under suspension of the rules, Oct. 23. President signed Nov. 9, 2000.

PL 106-491 (S 1367) Amend the act that established the Saint-Gaudens Historic Site in New Hampshire, by modifying the boundary. Introduced by MURKOWSKI, R-Alaska, on July 14, 1999. Senate Energy and Natural Resources reported, amended, June 27, 2000 (S Rept 106-314). Senate passed, amended, Oct. 5. House passed, under suspension of the rules, Oct. 23. President signed Nov. 9, 2000.

PL 106-492 (S 1438) Establish the National Law Enforcement Museum on federal land in the District of Columbia. Introduced by CAMPBELL, R-Colo., on July 27, 1999. Senate Energy and Natural Resources reported, amended, July 10, 2000 (S Rept 106-330). Senate passed, amended, Sept. 28. House passed, under suspension of the rules, Oct. 24. President signed Nov. 9, 2000.

PL 106-493 (S 1778) Provide for equal exchanges of land around the Cascade Reservoir. Introduced by CRAIG, R-Idaho, on Oct. 25, 1999. Senate Energy and Natural Resources reported, amended, April 13, 2000 (S Rept 106-271). Senate passed, amended, April 13. House Resources reported Sept. 20 (H Rept 106-871). House passed, under suspension of the rules, Oct. 23. President signed Nov. 9, 2000.

PL 106-494 (S 1894) Provide for the conveyance of certain land to Park County, Wyo. Introduced by

THOMAS, R-Wyo., on Nov. 9, 1999. Senate Energy and Natural Resources reported, amended, June 27, 2000 (S Rept 106-315). Senate passed, amended, July 27. House passed, under suspension of the rules, Oct. 23. President signed Nov. 9, 2000.

PL 106-495 (S 2069) Permit the conveyance of certain land in Powell, Wyo. Introduced by ENZI, R-Wyo., on Feb. 10, 2000. Senate Energy and Natural Resources reported Sept. 7 (S Rept 106-402). Senate passed Oct. 5. House passed, under suspension of the rules, Oct. 23. President signed Nov. 9, 2000.

PL 106-496 (S 2425) Authorize the Bureau of Reclamation to participate in the planning, design, and construction of the Bend Feed Canal Pipeline Project in Oregon. Introduced by SMITH, R-Ore., on April 13, 2000. Senate Energy and Natural Resources reported, amended, July 24 (S Rept 106-359). Senate passed, amended, Oct. 13. House passed, under suspension of the rules, Oct. 23. President signed Nov. 9, 2000.

PL 106-497 (S 2872) Improve the cause of action for misrepresentation of Indian arts and crafts. Introduced by CAMPBELL, R-Colo., on July 14, 2000. Senate Indian Affairs reported Oct. 2 (S Rept 106-452). Senate passed Oct. 5. House passed, under suspension of the rules, Oct. 23. President signed Nov. 9, 2000.

PL 106-498 (S 2882) Authorize the Bureau of Reclamation to conduct certain feasibility studies to augment water supplies for the Klamath Project in Oregon and California. Introduced by SMITH, R-Ore., on July 17, 2000. Senate Energy and Natural Resources reported, amended, Oct. 4 (S Rept 106-489). Senate passed, amended, Oct. 13. House passed, under suspension of the rules, Oct. 23. President signed Nov. 9, 2000.

PL 106-499 (S 2951) Authorize the secretary of the Interior to conduct a study to investigate opportunities to better manage the water resources in the Salmon Creek watershed of the upper Columbia River. Introduced by GORTON, R-Wash., on July 27, 2000. Senate Energy and Natural Resources reported, amended, Sept. 28 (S Rept 106-431). Senate passed, amended, Oct. 13. House passed, under suspension of the rules, Oct. 23. President signed Nov. 9, 2000.

PL 106-500 (S 2977) Assist in the establishment of an interpretive center and museum in the vicinity of the Diamond Valley Lake in southern California to ensure the protection and interpretation of the paleontology discoveries made at the lake and develop a trail system for the lake for use by pedestrians and non-motorized vehicles. Introduced by FEINSTEIN, D-Calif., on July 27, 2000. Senate Energy and Natural Resources reported Oct. 2 (S Rept 106-455). Senate passed Oct. 5. House passed, under suspension of the rules, Oct. 23. President signed Nov. 9, 2000.

PL 106-501 (HR 782) Amend the Older Americans Act of 1965 to authorize appropriations for fiscal years 2000 through 2003. Introduced by BARRETT, R-Neb., on Feb. 23, 1999. House Education and the Workforce reported, amended, Sept. 28 (H Rept 106-343). House passed, amended, under suspension of the rules, Oct. 25, 2000. Senate passed Oct. 26. President signed Nov. 13, 2000.

PL 106-502 (HR 1444) Authorize the secretary of the Interior to establish a program to plan, design and construct facilities to mitigate adverse impacts associated with irrigation system water diversions by local governmental entities in Oregon, Washington, Montana and Idaho. Introduced by DeFAZIO, D-Ore., on April 15, 1999. House Resources reported, amended, Nov. 5 (H Rept 106-454, Part 1). House passed, amended, under suspension of the rules, Nov. 9. Senate Energy and Natural Resources reported, with amendments, March 9, 2000 (S Rept 106-239). Senate passed, with amendments, April 13. House agreed to Senate amendments with amendments Oct. 17. Senate agreed to House amendments Oct. 27. President signed Nov. 13, 2000.

PL 106-503 (HR 1550) Authorize appropriations for the United States Fire Administration for fiscal years 2000 and 2001. Introduced by SMITH, R-Mich., on April 26, 1999. House Science reported, amended, May 10 (H Rept 106-133). House passed, amended, under suspension of the rules, May 11. Senate Commerce, Science and Transportation discharged. Senate passed, with amendment, Oct. 18, 2000. House agreed to Senate amendment with amendments Oct. 27. Senate agreed to House amendments Oct. 31. President signed Nov. 13, 2000.

PL 106-504 (HR 2462) Amend the Organic Act of Guam. Introduced by UNDERWOOD, D-Guam, on July 1, 1999. House Resources reported, amended, July 25, 2000 (H Rept 106-787). House passed, amended, under suspension of the rules, July 25. Senate Energy and Natural Resources discharged. Senate passed, with amendment, Oct. 24. House agreed to Senate amendment, under suspension of the rules, Oct. 31. President signed Nov. 13, 2000.

PL 106-505 (HR 2498) Amend the Public Health Service Act to provide for recommendations of the secretary of Health and Human Services regarding the placement of automatic external defibrillators in federal buildings to improve survival rates of individuals who experience cardiac arrest, and to establish protections from civil liability arising from the emergency use of the devices. Introduced by STEARNS, R-Fla., on July 13, 1999. House Commerce reported, amended, May 23, 2000 (H Rept

106-634). House passed, amended, under suspension of the rules, May 23. Senate passed, with amendment, Oct. 26. House agreed to Senate amendment, under suspension of the rules, Oct. 27. President signed Nov. 13, 2000.

PL 106-506 (HR 3388) Promote environmental restoration around the Lake Tahoe basin. Introduced by DOOLITTLE, R-Calif., on Nov. 16, 1999. House Resources reported, amended, Sept. 7, 2000 (H Rept 106-833, Part 1). House Agriculture, House Transportation and Infrastructure discharged. House passed, amended, under suspension of the rules, Oct. 23. Senate passed Oct. 27. President signed Nov. 13, 2000.

PL 106-507 (HR 3621) Provide for the posthumous promotion of William Clark of the Commonwealth of Virginia and the Commonwealth of Kentucky, co-leader of the Lewis and Clark Expedition, to the grade of captain in the Regular Army. Introduced by BEREUTER, R-Neb., on Feb. 10, 2000. House passed, under suspension of the rules, Oct. 10. Senate passed Oct. 27. President signed Nov. 13, 2000.

PL 106-508 (HR 5239) Provide for increased penalties for violations of the Export Administration Act of 1979. Introduced by GILMAN, R-N.Y., on Sept. 21, 2000. House passed, amended, under suspension of the rules, Sept. 25. Senate Banking, Housing, and Urban Affairs discharged. Senate passed, with amendment, Oct. 11. House agreed to Senate amendment, under suspension of the rules, Oct. 30. President signed Nov. 13, 2000.

PL 106-509 (S 700) Amend the National Trails System Act to designate the Ala Kahakai Trail as a National Historic Trail. Introduced by AKAKA, D-Hawaii, on March 24, 1999. Senate Energy and Natural Resources reported, amended, June 7 (S Rept 106-65). Senate passed, amended, July 1. House passed, under suspension of the rules, Oct. 24, 2000. President signed Nov. 13, 2000.

PL 106-510 (S 938) Eliminate restrictions on the acquisition of certain land contiguous to Hawaii Volcanoes National Park. Introduced by AKAKA, D-Hawaii, on May 3, 1999. Senate Energy and Natural Resources reported June 24 (S Rept 106-92). Senate passed, amended, Oct. 14. House passed, under suspension of the rules, Oct. 24, 2000. President signed Nov. 13, 2000.

PL 106-511 (S 964) Provide for equitable compensation for the Cheyenne River Sioux Tribe. Introduced by DASCHLE, D-S.D., on May 5, 1999. Senate Indian Affairs reported, amended, Nov. 8 (S Rept 106- 217). Senate passed, amended, Nov. 19. House Resources reported Oct. 6, 2000 (H Rept 106-944). House passed, with amendment, under suspension of the rules, Oct. 18. Senate agreed to House amendment Oct. 24. President signed Nov. 13, 2000.

PL 106-512 (S 1474) Provide conveyance of the Palmetto Bend project to the state of Texas. Introduced by HUTCHISON, R-Texas, on Aug. 2, 1999. Senate Energy and Natural Resources reported, amended, July 24, 2000 (S Rept 106-358). Senate passed, amended, Oct. 13. House passed, under suspension of the rules, Oct. 24. President signed Nov. 13, 2000.

PL 106-513 (S 1482) Amend the National Marine Sanctuaries Act. Introduced by SNOWE, R-Maine, on Aug. 4, 1999. Senate Commerce, Science and Transportation reported, amended, July 21, 2000 (S Rept 106-353). Senate passed, amended, Oct. 17. House passed, under suspension of the rules, Oct. 24. President signed Nov. 13, 2000.

PL 106-514 (S 1752) Reauthorize and amend the Coastal Barrier Resources Act. Introduced by CHAFEE, JOHN H., R-R.I., on Oct. 20, 1999. Senate Environment and Public Works reported, amended, April 4, 2000 (S Rept 106-252). Senate passed, amended, Sept. 27. House passed, under suspension of the rules, Oct. 24. President signed Nov. 13, 2000.

PL 106-515 (S 1865) Provide grants to establish demonstration mental health courts. Introduced by DeWINE, R-Ohio, on Nov. 4, 1999. Senate Judiciary reported, amended, July 27, 2000 (no written report). Senate passed, amended, Sept. 26. House passed, under suspension of the rules, Oct. 24. President signed Nov. 13, 2000.

PL 106-516 (S 2345) Direct the secretary of the Interior to conduct a special resource study concerning the preservation and public use of sites associated with Harriet Tubman in Auburn, N.Y. Introduced by SCHUMER, D-N.Y., on April 4, 2000. Senate Energy and Natural Resources reported, amended, Sept. 29 (S Rept 106-440). Senate passed, amended, Oct. 5. House passed, under suspension of the rules, Oct. 24. President signed Nov. 13, 2000.

PL 106-517 (S 2413) Amend the Omnibus Crime Control and Safe Streets Act of 1968 to clarify the procedures and conditions for the award of matching grants for the purchase of armor vests. Introduced by CAMPBELL, R-Colo., on April 12, 2000. Senate Judiciary reported June 29 (no written report). Senate passed, amended, Oct. 10. House passed Oct. 25. President signed Nov. 13, 2000.

PL 106-518 (S 2915) Make improvements in the operation and administration of the federal courts. Introduced by GRASSLEY, R-Iowa, on July 25, 2000. Senate Judiciary reported, amended, Sept. 28 (no written report). Senate passed, amended, Oct. 19.

House passed, with amendments, Oct. 25. Senate agreed to House amendments Oct. 27. President signed Nov. 13, 2000.

PL 106-519 (HR 4986) Amend the Internal Revenue Code of 1986 to repeal the provisions relating to foreign sales corporations (FSCs) and to exclude extraterritorial income from gross income. Introduced by ARCHER, R-Texas, on July 27, 2000. House Ways and Means reported, amended, Sept. 13 (H Rept 106-845). House passed, amended, under suspension of the rules, Sept. 13. Senate Finance reported, with amendments, Sept. 20 (S Rept 106-416). Senate passed, with amendment, Nov. 1. House agreed to Senate amendment, under suspension of the rules, Nov. 14. President signed Nov. 15, 2000.

PL 106-520 (H J Res 125) Make further continuing appropriations for fiscal 2001. Introduced by YOUNG, R-Fla., on Nov. 13, 2000. House Appropriations discharged. House passed Nov. 13. Senate passed Nov. 14. President signed Nov. 15, 2000.

PL 106-521 (HR 2346) Authorize the enforcement by state and local governments of certain Federal Communications Commission regulations regarding use of citizens band radio equipment. Introduced by EHLERS, R-Mich., on June 24, 1999. House Commerce reported Sept. 22, 2000 (H Rept 106-883). House passed, under suspension of the rules, Sept. 27. Senate passed, with amendment, Oct. 31. House agreed to Senate amendment, under suspension of the rules, Nov. 13. President signed Nov. 22, 2000.

PL 106-522 (HR 5633) Make appropriations for the government of the District of Columbia and other activities chargeable in whole or in part against the revenues of the District for the fiscal year ending September 30, 2001. Introduced by ISTOOK, R-Okla., on Nov. 14, 2000. House Appropriations discharged. House passed Nov. 14. Senate passed Nov. 14. President signed Nov. 22, 2000.

PL 106-523 (S 768) Establish court-martial jurisdiction over civilians serving with the armed forces during contingency operations, and establish federal jurisdiction over crimes committed outside the United States by former members of the armed forces and civilians accompanying them. Introduced by SESSIONS, R-Ala., on April 13, 1999. Senate Judiciary reported, amended, June 24 (no written report). Senate passed, with amendments, July 1. House Armed Services and House Judiciary discharged. House passed, with amendments, July 25, 2000. Senate agreed to House amendments Oct. 26. President signed Nov. 22, 2000.

PL 106-524 (S 1670) Revise the boundary of Fort Matanzas National Monument. Introduced by GRAHAM, D-Fla., on Sept. 30, 1999. Senate Energy and Natural Resources reported July 10, 2000 (S Rept 106-331). Senate passed Oct. 5. House passed, under suspension of the rules, Oct. 31. President signed Nov. 22, 2000.

PL 106-525 (S 1880) Amend the Public Health Service Act to improve the health of minority individuals. Introduced by KENNEDY, D-Mass., on Nov. 8, 1999. Senate Health, Education, Labor, and Pensions discharged. Senate passed Oct. 26, 2000. House passed, under suspension of the rules, Oct. 31. President signed Nov. 22, 2000.

PL 106-526 (S 1936) Authorize the secretary of Agriculture to sell or exchange all or part of certain administrative sites and other National Forest System land in Oregon and use the resulting proceeds for National Forest System purposes. Introduced by WYDEN, D-Ore., on Nov. 16, 1999. Senate Energy and Natural Resources reported, amended, April 6, 2000 (S Rept 106-256). Senate passed July 27. House Resources reported, with amendment, Oct. 5 (H Rept 106-938). House passed, amended, under suspension of the rules, Oct. 17. Senate agreed to House amendment Oct. 27. President signed Nov. 22, 2000.

PL 106-527 (S 2020) Adjust the boundary of the Natchez Trace Parkway in Mississippi. Introduced by COCHRAN, R-Miss., on Feb. 1, 2000. Senate Energy and Natural Resources reported July 10 (S Rept 106-332). Senate passed July 27. House passed, under suspension of the rules, Oct. 31. President signed Nov. 22, 2000.

PL 106-528 (S 2440) Amend Title 49, U.S. Code, to improve airport security. Introduced by HUTCHISON, R-Texas, on April 13, 2000. Senate Commerce, Science and Transportation reported, amended, Aug. 25 (S Rept 106-388). Senate passed, amended, Oct. 3. House passed, with amendment, under suspension of the rules, Oct. 23. Senate agreed to House amendment Oct. 25. President signed Nov. 22, 2000.

PL 106-529 (S 2485) Direct the secretary of the Interior to provide assistance in planning and constructing a regional heritage center in Calais, Maine. Introduced by COLLINS, R-Maine, on April 27, 2000. Senate Energy and Natural Resources reported, amended, June 27 (S Rept 106-319). Senate passed, amended, Oct. 5. House passed Oct. 30. President signed Nov. 22, 2000.

PL 106-530 (S 2547) Provide for the establishment of the Great Sand Dunes National Park and Preserve and the Baca National Wildlife Refuge in Colorado. Introduced by ALLARD, R-Colo., on May 11, 2000. Senate Energy and Natural Resources reported, amended, Oct. 3 (S Rept 106-479). Senate passed, amended, Oct. 5. House passed, under suspension of the rules, Oct. 25. President signed Nov. 22, 2000.

PL 106-531 (S 2712) Amend chapter 35 of Title 31, U.S. Code, to authorize the consolidation of certain financial and performance management reports required of federal agencies. Introduced by THOMPSON, R-Tenn., on June 12, 2000. Senate Governmental Affairs reported July 11 (S Rept 106-337). Senate passed July 19. House passed, under suspension of the rules, Oct. 27. President signed Nov. 22, 2000.

PL 106-532 (S 2773) Amend the Agricultural Marketing Act of 1946 to enhance dairy markets through dairy product mandatory reporting. Introduced by FEINGOLD, D-Wis., on June 22, 2000. Senate Agriculture, Nutrition and Forestry discharged. Senate passed, amended, Oct. 25. House passed Oct. 25. President signed Nov. 22, 2000.

PL 106-533 (S 2789) Amend the Congressional Award Act to establish a Congressional Recognition for Excellence in Arts Education Board. Introduced by COCHRAN, R-Miss., on June 26, 2000. Senate Governmental Affairs discharged. Senate passed, amended, Oct. 27. House passed, under suspension of the rules, Oct. 31. President signed Nov. 22, 2000.

PL 106-534 (S 3164) Protect seniors from fraud. Introduced by BAYH, D-Ind., on Oct. 5, 2000. Senate Judiciary discharged. Senate passed Oct. 24. House passed, under suspension of the rules, Oct. 30. President signed Nov. 22, 2000.

PL 106-535 (S 3194) Designate the facility of the U.S. Postal Service at 431 George St. in Millersville, Pa., as the "Robert S. Walker Post Office." Introduced by SANTORUM, R-Pa., on Oct. 12, 2000. Senate Governmental Affairs discharged. Senate passed Oct. 24. House passed, under suspension of the rules, Oct. 27. President signed Nov. 22, 2000.

PL 106-536 (S 3239) Amend the Immigration and Nationality Act to provide special immigrant status for certain U.S. international broadcasting employees. Introduced by HELMS, R-N.C., on Oct. 25, 2000. Senate passed Oct. 25. House passed, under suspension of the rules, Oct. 31. President signed Nov. 22, 2000.

PL 106-537 (H J Res 126) Make further continuing appropriations for fiscal 2001. Introduced by YOUNG, R-Fla., on Dec. 4, 2000. House passed Dec. 5. Senate passed Dec. 5. President signed Dec. 5, 2000.

PL 106-538 (HR 2941) Establish the Las Cienegas National Conservation Area in Arizona. Introduced by KOLBE, R-Ariz., on Sept. 24, 1999. House Resources reported, amended, Oct. 4, 2000 (H Rept 106-934). House passed, amended, Oct. 5. Senate passed Oct. 27. President signed Dec. 6, 2000.

PL 106-539 (H J Res 127) Make further continuing appropriations for fiscal 2001. Introduced by YOUNG-R-Fla., on Dec. 6, 2000. House passed Dec. 7. Senate passed Dec. 7. President signed Dec. 7, 2000.

PL 106-540 (H J Res 128) Make further continuing appropriations for fiscal 2001. Introduced by YOUNG, R-Fla., on Dec. 7, 2000. House passed Dec. 8. Senate passed Dec. 8. President signed Dec. 8, 2000.

PL 106-541 (S 2796) Provide for the conservation and development of water and related resources and authorize the secretary of the Army to construct various projects for improvements to U.S. rivers and harbors. Introduced by VOINOVICH, R-Ohio, on June 27, 2000. Senate Environment and Public Works reported, amended, July 27 (S Rept 106-362). Senate passed, with amendments, Sept. 25. House passed, with amendments, Oct. 19. Conference report filed in the House on Oct. 31 (H Rept 106-1020). Senate agreed to conference report Oct. 31. House agreed to conference report Nov. 3. President signed Dec. 11, 2000.

PL 106-542 (H J Res 129) Make further continuing appropriations for fiscal 2001. Introduced by YOUNG, R-Fla., on Dec. 7, 2000. House passed Dec. 11. Senate passed Dec. 11. President signed Dec. 11, 2000.

PL 106-543 (H J Res 133) Make further continuing appropriations for fiscal 2001. Introduced by YOUNG, R-Fla., on Dec. 14, 2000. House Appropriations discharged. House passed Dec. 15. Senate passed Dec. 15. President signed Dec. 15, 2000.

PL 106-544 (HR 3048) Amend section 879 of Title 18, U.S. Code, to clarify the authority of the Secret Service regarding threats against former presidents and members of their families. Introduced by McCOLLUM, R-Fla., on Oct. 7, 1999. House Judiciary reported, amended, June 12, 2000 (H Rept 106-669). House passed, amended, under suspension of the rules, June 26. Senate passed, with amendments, Oct. 13. House disagreed to some Senate amendments and added an amendment, Oct. 25. Senate receded and agreed to the House amendment Dec. 6. President signed Dec. 19, 2000.

PL 106-545 (HR 4281) Establish, where feasible, guidelines, recommendations and regulations that promote the regulatory acceptance of new and revised toxicological tests that protect human and animal health and the environment while reducing, refining or replacing animal tests and ensuring human safety and product effectiveness. Introduced by CALVERT, R-Calif., on April 13, 2000. House Commerce reported, amended, Oct. 16 (H Rept 106-980). House passed, amended, under suspension of the rules, Oct. 17. Senate passed Dec. 6. President signed Dec. 19, 2000.

PL 106-546 (HR 4640) Authorize grants to states for carrying out DNA analyses for use in the FBI's Combined DNA Index System, and provide for the collection and analysis of DNA samples from certain violent and sexual offenders for use in such system. Introduced by McCOLLUM, R-Fla., on June 12, 2000. House Judiciary reported, amended, Sept. 26 (H Rept 106-900, Part 1). House Armed Services discharged. House passed, amended, under suspension of the rules, Oct. 2. Senate passed, with amendment, Dec. 6. House agreed to Senate amendment Dec. 7. President signed Dec. 19, 2000.

PL 106-547 (HR 4827) Amend Title 18, U.S. Code, to prevent entry by false pretenses to any U.S. property, vessel or aircraft or to secure area of any airport, and to prevent the misuse of genuine and counterfeit police badges by those seeking to commit a crime. Introduced by HORN, R-Calif., on July 12, 2000. House Judiciary reported, amended, Sept. 28 (H Rept 106-913). House passed, amended, under suspension of the rules, Oct. 2. Senate passed Dec. 6. President signed Dec. 19, 2000.

PL 106-548 (S 1972) Direct the secretary of Agriculture to convey to the town of Dolores, Colo., the current site of the Joe Rowell Park. Introduced by ALLARD, R-Colo., on Nov. 19, 1999. Senate Energy and Natural Resources reported, amended, Aug. 25, 2000 (S Rept 106-375). Senate passed, amended, Oct. 5. House failed to pass, under suspension of the rules, Nov. 13. House Resources discharged. House passed Dec. 4. President signed Dec. 19, 2000.

PL 106-549 (S 2594) Authorize the secretary of the Interior to contract with the Mancos Water Conservancy District to use the Mancos Project facilities for impounding, storing, diverting and carrying non-project water for irrigation, domestic, municipal, industrial, and any other beneficial purposes. Introduced by ALLARD, R-Colo., on May 18, 2000. Senate Energy and Natural Resources reported, amended, Sept. 28 (S Rept 106-427). Senate passed, amended, Oct. 13. House Resources discharged. House passed Dec. 4. President signed Dec. 19, 2000.

PL 106-550 (S 3137) Establish a commission to commemorate the 250th anniversary of the birth of James Madison. Introduced by SESSIONS, R-Ala., on Sept. 28, 2000. Senate passed Oct. 25. House passed, under suspension of the rules, Dec. 4. President signed Dec. 19, 2000.

PL 106-551 (HR 3514) Amend the Public Health Service Act to provide for a system of sanctuaries for chimpanzees that have been designated as no longer needed in research conducted or supported by the Public Health Service. Introduced by GREENWOOD, R-Pa., on Nov. 22, 1999. House passed, amended, under suspension of the rules, Oct. 24, 2000. Senate passed Dec. 6. President signed Dec. 20, 2000.

PL 106-552 (HR 5016) Redesignate the facility of the U.S. Postal Service located at 514 Express Center Dr. in Chicago, Ill., as the "J.T. Weeker Service Center." Introduced by BLAGOJEVICH, D-Ill., on July 27, 2000. House passed, amended, under suspension of the rules, Oct. 17. Senate passed Dec. 14. President signed Dec. 20, 2000.

PL 106-553 (HR 4942) Make appropriations for the government of the District of Columbia and other activities chargeable in whole or in part against the revenues of the District for fiscal 2001. Introduced by ISTOOK, R-Okla., on July 25, 2000. House Appropriations reported July 25 (H Rept 106-786). House passed, amended, Sept. 14. Senate passed, with amendment, Sept. 27. Conference report filed in the House Oct. 26 (H Rept 106-1005). House agreed to conference report Oct. 26. Senate agreed to conference report Oct. 27. President signed Dec. 21, 2000.

PL 106-554 (HR 4577) Make appropriations for the departments of Labor, Health and Human Services, and Education and related agencies for fiscal 2001. Introduced by PORTER, R-Ill., on June 1, 2000. House Appropriations reported June 1 (H Rept 106-645). House passed, amended, June 14. Senate passed, with amendment, June 30. Conference report filed in the House Dec. 15 (H Rept 106-1033). House agreed to conference report Dec. 15. Senate agreed to conference report Dec. 15. President signed Dec. 21, 2000.

PL 106-555 (HR 2903) Reauthorize the Striped Bass Conservation Act. Introduced by SAXTON, R-N.J., on Sept. 21, 1999. House passed, amended, under suspension of the rules, Oct. 31, 2000. Senate passed Dec. 8. President signed Dec. 21, 2000.

PL 106-556 (HR 5210) Designate the facility of the U.S. Postal Service at 200 S. George St. in York, Pa., as the "George Atlee Goodling Post Office Building." Introduced by GOODLING, R-Pa., on Sept. 19, 2000. House passed, under suspension of the rules, Oct. 17. Senate passed Dec. 14. President signed Dec. 21, 2000.

PL 106-557 (HR 5461) Amend the Magnuson-Stevens Fishery Conservation and Management Act to eliminate the wasteful and unsportsmanlike practice of shark finning. Introduced by CUNNINGHAM, R-Calif., on Oct. 12, 2000. House passed, under suspension of the rules, Oct. 30. Senate passed Dec. 7. President signed Dec. 21, 2000.

PL 106-558 (S 439) Amend the National Forest and Public Lands of Nevada Enhancement Act of 1988 to adjust the boundary of the Toiyabe National Forest, Nev., and amend Chapter 55 of Title 5, U.S. Code, to authorize equal overtime pay provisions for all federal employees engaged in wildland fire suppression operations. Introduced by BRYAN, D-Nev., on Feb. 22, 1999. Senate Energy and Natural Resources reported Nov. 2 (S Rept 106-205). Senate passed Nov. 19. House Resources reported July 17, 2000 (H Rept 106-746). House passed, as amended, under suspension of the rules, Oct. 23. Senate agreed to House amendments Dec. 7. President signed Dec. 21, 2000.

PL 106-559 (S 1508) Provide technical and legal assistance for tribal justice systems and members of Indian tribes. Introduced by CAMPBELL, R-Colo., on Aug. 5, 1999. Senate Indian Affairs reported, amended, Nov. 8 (S Rept 106-219). Senate passed, amended, Nov. 19. House Resources reported Sept. 6, 2000 (H Rept 106-819, Part 1). House Judiciary discharged. House passed, with amendment, under suspension of the rules, Oct. 23. Senate agreed to House amendment Dec. 11. President signed Dec. 21, 2000.

PL 106-560 (S 1898) Provide protection against the risks to the public inherent in the interstate transportation of violent prisoners. Introduced by DORGAN, D-N.D., on Nov. 9, 1999. Senate Judiciary reported, amended, Sept. 28, 2000 (no written report). Senate passed, amended, Oct. 25. House Judiciary discharged. House passed Dec. 7. President signed Dec. 21, 2000.

PL 106-561 (S 3045) Improve the quality, timeliness and credibility of forensic science services for criminal justice purposes. Introduced by SESSIONS, R-Ala., on Sept. 14, 2000. Senate Judiciary discharged. Senate passed, amended, Oct. 26. House Judiciary discharged. House passed Dec. 7. President signed Dec. 21, 2000.

PL 106-562 (HR 1653) Approve a governing international fishery agreement between the United States and the Russian Federation. Introduced by YOUNG, R-Alaska, on April 29, 1999. House Resources reported June 22 (H Rept 106-195). House passed, amended, under suspension of the rules, Oct. 31, 2000. Senate passed Dec. 14. President signed Dec. 23, 2000.

PL 106-563 (HR 2570) Require the secretary of the Interior to undertake a study of ways to commemorate the national significance of the U.S. roadways that comprise the Lincoln Highway. Introduced by REGULA, R-Ohio, on July 20, 1999. House Resources reported Sept. 28, 2000 (H Rept 106-912). House passed, under suspension of the rules, Oct. 17. Senate passed Dec. 15. President signed Dec. 23, 2000. ◆

CQ

Appendix H

HOUSE ROLL CALL VOTES

House Roll Call Votes By Bill Number

House Bills

Senate Bills

House Votes 2, 3, 4, 5, 6, 7 *

1. Quorum Call.* A quorum was present with 313 members responding (121 members did not respond). Jan. 27, 2000.

2. H Con Res 244. Use of Rotunda for Holocaust Memorial/Adoption. Boehner, R-Ohio, motion to suspend the rules and adopt the concurrent resolution to permit the use of the rotunda of the Capitol on May 4 for a ceremony commemorating victims of the Holocaust. Motion agreed to 339-0: R 167-0; D 171-0 (ND 126-0, SD 45-0); I 1-0. A two-thirds majority of those present and voting (226 in this case) is required for adoption under suspension of the rules. Jan. 31, 2000.

3. HR 2130. Date-Rape Drugs/Passage. Upton, R-Mich., motion to suspend the rules and pass the bill to stiffen criminal penalties for possession of drugs associated with date rape. The measure would allow law enforcement to track the drugs more closely, and would classify gamma hydroxybutyric acid (GHB) as a Schedule I drug under the Controlled Substance Act, thereby increasing criminal penalties for illicit manufacture, possession or distribution of GHB. Motion agreed to 339-2: R 164-2; D 173-0 (ND 128-0, SD 45-0); I 2-0. A two-thirds majority of those present and voting (228 in this case) is required for passage under suspension of the rules. Jan. 31, 2000.

4. HR 764. Child Abuse Prevention/Passage. Jenkins, R-Tenn., motion to suspend the rules and adopt the Senate amendments to the bill to increase resources for child abuse victims and abuse prevention programs. The bill would increase to $20 million the amount to be earmarked from the Crime Victims' Fund for grants to programs that assist abuse victims in any year in which deposits to the fund exceed fiscal 1998 levels. It would also authorize $2 million per year for fiscal 2000 through 2002 for state grants to improve information-sharing on unidentified deceased persons. Motion agreed to 410-2: R 208-2; D 200-0 (ND 150-0, SD 50-0); I 2-0. A two-thirds majority of those present and voting (275 in this case) is required for passage under suspension of the rules. Feb. 1, 2000.

5. HR 1838. U.S.-Taiwan Military Ties/Passage. Passage of the bill to increase U.S.-Taiwan military relations. The measure would require the secretary of Defense to establish direct military communication with forces in Taiwan, increase the number of Taiwanese military officials trained at U.S. military academies and require the Pentagon to issue annual reports detailing threats to Taiwan's security. Passed 341-70: R 200-10; D 140-59 (ND 99-50, SD 41-9); I 1-1. Feb. 1, 2000. A "nay" was a vote in support of the president's position.

6. HR 2990. Access to Care for the Uninsured/Motion to Instruct. Berry, D-Ark., motion to instruct House conferees to "take all necessary steps" to begin meetings of the conference, to insist upon the provisions of HR 2990 as passed by the House, and to insist that the provisions be paid for. Motion agreed to 207-175: R 6-173; D 200-1 (ND 150-1, SD 50-0); I 1-1. Feb. 1, 2000.

7. HR 2005. Liability Limits for Durable Goods Makers/Passage. Passage of the bill to impose an 18-year limit on lawsuits against manufacturers of durable goods, such as machine tools, for injuries caused by their products. The time limit would begin when the product first enters the stream of commerce and would apply only to employees eligible for workers' compensation. Passed 222-194: R 198-17; D 23-176 (ND 10-138, SD 13-38); I 1-1. Feb. 2, 2000. A "nay" was a vote in favor of the president's position.

** CQ does not include quorum calls in its vote charts.*

Key

Y	Voted for (yea).
#	Paired for.
+	Announced for.
N	Voted against (nay).
X	Paired against.
–	Announced against.
P	Voted "present."
C	Voted "present" to avoid possible conflict of interest.
?	Did not vote or otherwise make a position known.

•

Democrats ***Republicans***
Independents

	2	3	4	5	6	7
ALABAMA						
1 ***Callahan***	Y	Y	Y	Y	N	Y
2 ***Everett***	+	+	Y	Y	N	Y
3 ***Riley***	Y	Y	Y	Y	N	Y
4 ***Aderholt***	Y	Y	Y	Y	N	Y
5 Cramer	Y	Y	Y	Y	Y	Y
6 ***Bachus***	Y	Y	Y	Y	P	Y
7 Hilliard	Y	Y	Y	Y	Y	N
ALASKA						
AL ***Young***	?	?	Y	Y	N	Y
ARIZONA						
1 ***Salmon***	Y	Y	Y	N	N	Y
2 Pastor	Y	Y	Y	Y	Y	N
3 ***Stump***	Y	Y	Y	Y	N	Y
4 ***Shadegg***	?	?	Y	Y	N	Y
5 ***Kolbe***	Y	Y	Y	N	N	Y
6 ***Hayworth***	Y	Y	Y	Y	N	Y
ARKANSAS						
1 Berry	Y	Y	Y	Y	Y	N
2 Snyder	Y	Y	Y	N	Y	N
3 ***Hutchinson***	Y	Y	Y	Y	N	Y
4 ***Dickey***	Y	Y	Y	Y	N	Y
CALIFORNIA						
1 Thompson	Y	Y	Y	N	Y	N
2 ***Herger***	Y	Y	Y	Y	N	Y
3 ***Ose***	Y	Y	Y	Y	N	Y
4 ***Doolittle***	Y	Y	Y	Y	N	Y
5 Matsui	?	?	Y	N	Y	N
6 Woolsey	Y	Y	Y	Y	Y	N
7 Miller, George	?	?	Y	Y	Y	N
8 Pelosi	Y	Y	Y	Y	Y	N
9 Lee	Y	Y	Y	N	Y	N
10 Tauscher	Y	Y	Y	Y	Y	Y
11 ***Pombo***	?	?	Y	Y	N	Y
12 Lantos	Y	Y	Y	N	Y	N
13 Stark	Y	Y	Y	N	Y	N
14 Eshoo	Y	Y	Y	Y	Y	N
15 ***Campbell***	?	?	?	?	?	?
16 Lofgren	Y	Y	Y	N	Y	N
17 Farr	Y	Y	Y	Y	Y	N
18 Condit	Y	Y	Y	N	Y	Y
19 ***Radanovich***	Y	Y	Y	Y	N	Y
20 Dooley	Y	Y	Y	N	Y	Y
21 ***Thomas***	Y	Y	Y	Y	N	Y
22 Capps	Y	Y	Y	Y	Y	N
23 ***Gallegly***	Y	Y	Y	Y	N	Y
24 Sherman	Y	Y	Y	Y	Y	N
25 ***McKeon***	Y	Y	Y	Y	N	Y
26 Berman	?	?	Y	Y	Y	N
27 ***Rogan***	Y	Y	Y	Y	N	Y
28 ***Dreier***	Y	Y	Y	Y	N	Y
29 Waxman	Y	Y	Y	Y	Y	N
30 Becerra	+	+	Y	Y	Y	N
31 Martinez	Y	Y	Y	Y	Y	N
32 Dixon	Y	Y	Y	Y	Y	N
33 Roybal-Allard	Y	Y	Y	Y	Y	N
34 Napolitano	Y	Y	Y	Y	Y	N
35 Waters	Y	Y	Y	N	?	N
36 ***Kuykendall***	Y	Y	Y	Y	N	Y
37 Millender-McD.	Y	Y	Y	Y	Y	N
38 ***Horn***	Y	Y	Y	Y	Y	N
39 ***Royce***	Y	Y	Y	Y	N	Y
40 ***Lewis***	?	?	Y	N	N	Y
41 ***Miller, Gary***	Y	Y	Y	Y	N	Y
42 Baca	Y	Y	Y	N	Y	N
43 ***Calvert***	Y	Y	Y	Y	N	Y
44 ***Bono***	Y	Y	Y	Y	P	Y
45 ***Rohrabacher***	Y	Y	Y	Y	N	Y
46 Sanchez	+	+	+	+	+	–
47 ***Cox***	?	?	Y	Y	N	Y
48 ***Packard***	Y	Y	Y	Y	N	Y
49 ***Bilbray***	Y	Y	Y	Y	Y	Y
50 Filner	Y	Y	Y	N	Y	N
51 ***Cunningham***	Y	Y	Y	Y	N	Y
52 ***Hunter***	?	?	Y	Y	P	Y
COLORADO						
1 DeGette	?	?	Y	Y	Y	N
2 Udall	Y	Y	Y	Y	Y	N
3 ***McInnis***	Y	Y	Y	Y	N	Y
4 ***Schaffer***	?	?	Y	Y	N	Y
5 ***Hefley***	?	?	Y	Y	N	Y
6 ***Tancredo***	Y	Y	Y	Y	N	Y
CONNECTICUT						
1 Larson	?	?	Y	Y	Y	N
2 Gejdenson	?	?	Y	Y	Y	N
3 DeLauro	Y	Y	Y	Y	Y	N
4 ***Shays***	Y	Y	Y	Y	N	Y
5 Maloney	Y	Y	Y	Y	Y	N
6 ***Johnson***	?	?	Y	Y	N	Y
DELAWARE						
AL ***Castle***	Y	Y	Y	Y	N	Y
FLORIDA						
1 ***Scarborough***	+	+	Y	Y	N	Y
2 Boyd	Y	Y	Y	Y	Y	N
3 Brown	?	?	?	?	Y	N
4 ***Fowler***	+	+	Y	Y	N	Y
5 Thurman	Y	Y	Y	Y	Y	N
6 ***Stearns***	Y	Y	Y	Y	N	Y
7 ***Mica***	Y	Y	Y	Y	N	Y
8 ***McCollum***	?	?	Y	Y	P	Y
9 ***Bilirakis***	Y	Y	Y	Y	N	Y
10 ***Young***	?	?	?	?	?	Y
11 Davis	Y	Y	Y	Y	Y	?
12 ***Canady***	Y	Y	Y	Y	N	Y
13 ***Miller***	?	?	Y	Y	N	Y
14 ***Goss***	Y	Y	Y	Y	N	Y
15 ***Weldon***	?	?	Y	Y	P	Y
16 ***Foley***	Y	Y	Y	Y	P	Y
17 Meek	Y	Y	Y	N	Y	N
18 ***Ros-Lehtinen***	Y	Y	Y	Y	N	Y
19 Wexler	?	?	Y	Y	Y	N
20 Deutsch	Y	Y	Y	Y	Y	N
21 ***Diaz-Balart***	?	?	Y	Y	N	N
22 ***Shaw***	Y	Y	Y	Y	N	Y
23 Hastings	Y	Y	Y	N	Y	N
GEORGIA						
1 ***Kingston***	?	?	Y	Y	N	Y
2 Bishop	Y	Y	Y	Y	Y	N
3 ***Collins***	Y	Y	Y	Y	N	Y
4 McKinney	Y	Y	Y	N	Y	N
5 Lewis	Y	Y	Y	Y	Y	N
6 ***Isakson***	+	+	Y	Y	N	Y
7 ***Barr***	Y	Y	Y	Y	P	Y
8 ***Chambliss***	?	?	?	?	N	Y
9 ***Deal***	?	?	Y	Y	N	Y
10 ***Norwood***	Y	Y	Y	Y	P	Y
11 ***Linder***	Y	Y	Y	Y	N	Y
HAWAII						
1 Abercrombie	?	?	Y	N	Y	N
2 Mink	?	?	Y	N	Y	N
IDAHO						
1 ***Chenoweth-Hage***	Y	N	N	Y	N	Y
2 ***Simpson***	Y	Y	Y	Y	N	Y
ILLINOIS						
1 Rush	Y	Y	Y	N	Y	N
2 Jackson	Y	Y	Y	N	Y	N
3 Lipinski	Y	Y	Y	Y	Y	N
4 Gutierrez	Y	Y	Y	?	Y	N
5 Blagojevich	Y	Y	Y	Y	Y	N
6 ***Hyde***	Y	Y	Y	Y	N	Y
7 Davis	?	?	Y	N	Y	N
8 ***Crane***	Y	Y	Y	Y	N	Y
9 Schakowsky	Y	Y	Y	N	Y	N
10 ***Porter***	Y	Y	Y	Y	–	Y
11 ***Weller***	Y	+	Y	Y	N	Y
12 Costello	Y	Y	Y	Y	Y	N
13 ***Biggert***	Y	Y	Y	Y	N	Y

ND Northern Democrats SD Southern Democrats

	2	3	4	5	6	7
14 ***Hastert***			Y			
15 ***Ewing***	Y	Y	Y	Y	N	N
16 ***Manzullo***	Y	Y	Y	Y	N	Y
17 Evans	Y	Y	Y	N	Y	N
18 ***LaHood***	Y	Y	Y	Y	N	N
19 Phelps	Y	Y	Y	Y	Y	N
20 ***Shimkus***	Y	Y	Y	Y	N	Y
INDIANA						
1 Visclosky	Y	Y	Y	Y	Y	N
2 ***McIntosh***	?	?	Y	Y	N	Y
3 Roemer	Y	Y	Y	N	Y	N
4 ***Souder***	Y	Y	Y	Y	N	Y
5 ***Buyer***	Y	Y	Y	Y	N	Y
6 ***Burton***	+	?	Y	Y	N	Y
7 ***Pease***	Y	Y	Y	Y	N	Y
8 ***Hostettler***	Y	Y	Y	Y	N	Y
9 Hill	Y	Y	Y	N	Y	N
10 Carson	?	?	?	?	?	?
IOWA						
1 ***Leach***	Y	Y	Y	Y	Y	?
2 ***Nussle***	Y	Y	Y	N	N	Y
3 Boswell	Y	Y	Y	Y	Y	N
4 ***Ganske***	Y	Y	Y	Y	P	Y
5 ***Latham***	Y	Y	Y	Y	N	Y
KANSAS						
1 ***Moran***	Y	Y	Y	Y	N	Y
2 ***Ryun***	Y	Y	Y	Y	N	Y
3 Moore	Y	Y	Y	Y	Y	N
4 ***Tiahrt***	+	+	+	+	–	Y
KENTUCKY						
1 ***Whitfield***	Y	Y	Y	Y	N	Y
2 ***Lewis***	Y	Y	Y	Y	N	Y
3 ***Northup***	Y	Y	Y	Y	N	Y
4 Lucas	Y	Y	Y	Y	Y	Y
5 ***Rogers***	Y	Y	Y	Y	N	Y
6 ***Fletcher***	Y	Y	Y	Y	N	Y
LOUISIANA						
1 ***Vitter***	Y	Y	Y	Y	N	Y
2 Jefferson	?	?	Y	Y	Y	N
3 ***Tauzin***	Y	Y	Y	Y	N	?
4 ***McCrery***	?	Y	Y	Y	N	Y
5 ***Cooksey***	?	?	Y	Y	P	Y
6 ***Baker***	Y	Y	Y	Y	N	Y
7 John	Y	Y	Y	Y	Y	Y
MAINE						
1 Allen	Y	Y	Y	Y	Y	N
2 Baldacci	Y	Y	Y	Y	Y	N
MARYLAND						
1 ***Gilchrest***	Y	Y	Y	Y	N	Y
2 ***Ehrlich***	?	?	Y	Y	N	N
3 Cardin	Y	Y	Y	Y	Y	N
4 Wynn	Y	Y	Y	Y	Y	N
5 Hoyer	Y	Y	Y	Y	Y	N
6 ***Bartlett***	Y	Y	Y	Y	N	Y
7 Cummings	Y	Y	Y	Y	Y	N
8 ***Morella***	Y	Y	Y	Y	Y	Y
MASSACHUSETTS						
1 Olver	Y	Y	Y	N	Y	N
2 Neal	?	?	Y	N	Y	N
3 McGovern	Y	Y	Y	N	Y	N
4 Frank	Y	Y	Y	Y	Y	Y
5 Meehan	?	?	Y	Y	Y	?
6 Tierney	Y	Y	Y	N	Y	N
7 Markey	?	?	Y	Y	Y	N
8 Capuano	Y	Y	Y	N	Y	N
9 Moakley	Y	Y	Y	Y	Y	N
10 Delahunt	?	Y	Y	N	Y	N
MICHIGAN						
1 Stupak	Y	Y	Y	Y	Y	N
2 ***Hoekstra***	Y	Y	Y	Y	N	Y
3 ***Ehlers***	Y	Y	Y	N	N	Y
4 ***Camp***	Y	Y	Y	Y	N	Y
5 Barcia	?	?	Y	Y	Y	Y
6 ***Upton***	Y	Y	Y	Y	N	Y
7 ***Smith***	Y	Y	Y	Y	N	Y
8 Stabenow	Y	Y	Y	Y	Y	N
9 Kildee	Y	Y	Y	Y	Y	N
10 Bonior	Y	Y	Y	Y	Y	N
11 ***Knollenberg***	Y	Y	Y	Y	N	Y
12 Levin	Y	Y	Y	Y	Y	N
13 Rivers	?	?	?	?	?	?
14 Conyers	Y	Y	Y	N	Y	N
15 Kilpatrick	+	+	Y	Y	Y	N
16 Dingell	?	?	Y	Y	Y	Y

	2	3	4	5	6	7
MINNESOTA						
1 ***Gutknecht***	Y	Y	Y	Y	–	Y
2 Minge	Y	Y	Y	N	Y	N
3 ***Ramstad***	Y	Y	Y	Y	N	Y
4 Vento	?	?	?	?	?	?
5 Sabo	Y	Y	Y	N	Y	N
6 Luther	Y	Y	Y	Y	Y	N
7 Peterson	Y	Y	Y	N	N	Y
8 Oberstar	Y	Y	Y	N	Y	N
MISSISSIPPI						
1 ***Wicker***	Y	Y	Y	Y	N	Y
2 Thompson	Y	Y	Y	Y	Y	N
3 ***Pickering***	Y	Y	Y	Y	N	Y
4 Shows	Y	Y	Y	Y	Y	N
5 Taylor	Y	Y	Y	Y	Y	Y
MISSOURI						
1 Clay	Y	Y	Y	Y	Y	N
2 ***Talent***	Y	Y	Y	Y	N	Y
3 Gephardt	?	?	Y	Y	Y	N
4 Skelton	Y	Y	Y	N	Y	N
5 McCarthy	Y	Y	Y	Y	Y	N
6 Danner	Y	Y	Y	Y	Y	N
7 ***Blunt***	Y	Y	Y	Y	N	Y
8 ***Emerson***	Y	Y	Y	Y	N	Y
9 ***Hulshof***	?	?	Y	Y	N	Y
MONTANA						
AL ***Hill***	Y	Y	Y	Y	N	N
NEBRASKA						
1 ***Bereuter***	Y	Y	Y	Y	N	Y
2 ***Terry***	Y	Y	Y	Y	N	N
3 ***Barrett***	?	?	?	?	?	Y
NEVADA						
1 Berkley	Y	Y	Y	Y	Y	N
2 ***Gibbons***	Y	Y	Y	Y	Y	N
NEW HAMPSHIRE						
1 ***Sununu***	Y	Y	Y	Y	N	Y
2 ***Bass***	+	+	?	?	?	Y
NEW JERSEY						
1 Andrews	+	Y	Y	Y	Y	N
2 ***LoBiondo***	Y	Y	Y	Y	P	N
3 ***Saxton***	Y	Y	Y	Y	P	?
4 ***Smith***	Y	Y	Y	Y	P	N
5 ***Roukema***	?	?	Y	Y	P	Y
6 Pallone	Y	Y	Y	Y	Y	N
7 ***Franks***	?	?	Y	Y	P	Y
8 Pascrell	Y	Y	Y	Y	Y	N
9 Rothman	Y	Y	Y	Y	Y	N
10 Payne	?	?	Y	N	Y	N
11 ***Frelinghuysen***	Y	Y	Y	Y	P	Y
12 Holt	Y	Y	Y	Y	Y	N
13 Menendez	Y	Y	Y	Y	Y	N
NEW MEXICO						
1 ***Wilson***	?	?	Y	Y	N	Y
2 ***Skeen***	Y	Y	Y	Y	N	Y
3 Udall	Y	Y	Y	Y	Y	N
NEW YORK						
1 Forbes	Y	Y	Y	Y	Y	N
2 ***Lazio***	Y	Y	Y	Y	N	N
3 ***King***	Y	Y	Y	Y	P	N
4 McCarthy	Y	Y	Y	Y	Y	N
5 Ackerman	Y	Y	Y	Y	Y	N
6 Meeks	Y	Y	Y	Y	Y	N
7 Crowley	Y	Y	Y	Y	Y	N
8 Nadler	Y	Y	Y	N	Y	N
9 Weiner	Y	Y	Y	Y	Y	N
10 Towns	Y	Y	Y	Y	Y	?
11 Owens	+	+	Y	N	Y	N
12 Velázquez	Y	Y	Y	Y	Y	N
13 ***Fossella***	Y	Y	Y	Y	N	Y
14 Maloney	Y	Y	Y	Y	Y	N
15 Rangel	Y	Y	Y	Y	Y	N
16 Serrano	Y	Y	Y	N	Y	N
17 Engel	Y	Y	Y	Y	Y	N
18 Lowey	?	?	Y	Y	Y	N
19 ***Kelly***	Y	Y	Y	Y	P	Y
20 ***Gilman***	Y	Y	Y	Y	P	N
21 McNulty	Y	Y	Y	Y	Y	N
22 ***Sweeney***	?	?	Y	Y	N	Y
23 ***Boehlert***	Y	Y	Y	Y	P	Y
24 ***McHugh***	Y	Y	Y	Y	P	Y
25 ***Walsh***	Y	Y	Y	Y	N	Y
26 Hinchey	Y	Y	Y	N	Y	N
27 ***Reynolds***	Y	Y	Y	Y	N	Y
28 Slaughter	+	+	Y	Y	Y	Y
29 LaFalce	Y	Y	Y	N	Y	N

	2	3	4	5	6	7
30 ***Quinn***	Y	Y	Y	Y	?	N
31 ***Houghton***	Y	Y	Y	N	N	Y
NORTH CAROLINA						
1 Clayton	Y	Y	Y	Y	Y	N
2 Etheridge	Y	Y	Y	Y	Y	N
3 ***Jones***	Y	Y	Y	Y	P	Y
4 Price	?	?	Y	Y	Y	N
5 ***Burr***	Y	Y	Y	Y	N	Y
6 ***Coble***	Y	Y	Y	Y	N	N
7 McIntyre	Y	Y	Y	Y	Y	N
8 ***Hayes***	Y	Y	Y	Y	N	Y
9 ***Myrick***	?	?	?	?	?	?
10 ***Ballenger***	Y	Y	Y	Y	N	Y
11 ***Taylor***	?	?	Y	Y	N	Y
12 Watt	Y	Y	Y	Y	Y	N
NORTH DAKOTA						
AL Pomeroy	Y	Y	Y	N	Y	N
OHIO						
1 ***Chabot***	Y	Y	Y	Y	N	Y
2 ***Portman***	Y	Y	Y	Y	N	Y
3 Hall	Y	Y	Y	Y	Y	?
4 ***Oxley***	Y	Y	Y	N	N	Y
5 ***Gillmor***	Y	Y	Y	Y	N	Y
6 Strickland	Y	Y	Y	N	Y	N
7 ***Hobson***	Y	Y	Y	Y	N	Y
8 ***Boehner***	Y	Y	Y	N	N	Y
9 Kaptur	?	?	?	?	Y	Y
10 Kucinich	Y	Y	Y	N	Y	N
11 Jones	Y	Y	Y	N	Y	N
12 ***Kasich***	Y	Y	Y	Y	N	Y
13 Brown	?	?	?	?	?	?
14 Sawyer	Y	Y	Y	Y	Y	N
15 ***Pryce***	Y	Y	Y	Y	N	Y
16 ***Regula***	Y	Y	Y	Y	N	Y
17 Traficant	Y	Y	Y	Y	Y	N
18 ***Ney***	Y	Y	Y	Y	N	Y
19 ***LaTourette***	Y	Y	Y	Y	P	Y
OKLAHOMA						
1 ***Largent***	?	?	Y	Y	N	Y
2 ***Coburn***	?	?	Y	Y	N	Y
3 ***Watkins***	?	?	Y	Y	N	Y
4 ***Watts***	?	?	Y	Y	N	Y
5 ***Istook***	?	?	Y	Y	?	Y
6 ***Lucas***	?	?	Y	Y	N	Y
OREGON						
1 Wu	Y	Y	Y	Y	Y	Y
2 ***Walden***	Y	Y	Y	Y	N	Y
3 Blumenauer	Y	Y	Y	N	Y	N
4 DeFazio	Y	Y	Y	N	Y	N
5 Hooley	Y	Y	Y	N	Y	N
PENNSYLVANIA						
1 Brady	Y	Y	Y	Y	Y	N
2 Fattah	?	?	?	?	?	N
3 Borski	Y	Y	Y	N	Y	N
4 Klink	Y	Y	Y	Y	Y	N
5 ***Peterson***	?	?	Y	Y	N	Y
6 Holden	Y	Y	Y	Y	Y	N
7 ***Weldon***	Y	Y	Y	Y	N	Y
8 ***Greenwood***	Y	Y	Y	Y	N	Y
9 ***Shuster***	?	?	Y	Y	N	Y
10 ***Sherwood***	Y	Y	Y	Y	N	Y
11 Kanjorski	Y	Y	Y	N	Y	N
12 Murtha	Y	Y	Y	Y	Y	N
13 Hoeffel	Y	Y	Y	Y	Y	N
14 Coyne	Y	Y	Y	Y	Y	N
15 ***Toomey***	Y	Y	Y	Y	N	Y
16 ***Pitts***	Y	Y	Y	Y	N	Y
17 ***Gekas***	Y	Y	Y	Y	N	Y
18 Doyle	Y	Y	Y	Y	Y	?
19 ***Goodling***	?	?	Y	Y	N	Y
20 Mascara	Y	Y	Y	Y	Y	N
21 ***English***	Y	Y	Y	Y	N	Y
RHODE ISLAND						
1 Kennedy	+	+	Y	Y	Y	N
2 Weygand	Y	Y	Y	Y	Y	N
SOUTH CAROLINA						
1 ***Sanford***	?	?	?	?	?	Y
2 ***Spence***	?	?	Y	Y	N	Y
3 ***Graham***	?	?	?	?	?	Y
4 ***DeMint***	+	+	+	+	–	Y
5 Spratt	Y	Y	Y	Y	Y	Y
6 Clyburn	Y	Y	Y	Y	Y	N
SOUTH DAKOTA						
AL ***Thune***	Y	Y	Y	Y	N	Y

	2	3	4	5	6	7
TENNESSEE						
1 ***Jenkins***	Y	Y	Y	Y	P	Y
2 ***Duncan***	Y	Y	Y	Y	Y	Y
3 ***Wamp***	Y	Y	Y	Y	N	?
4 ***Hilleary***	Y	Y	Y	Y	N	Y
5 Clement	Y	Y	Y	Y	Y	Y
6 Gordon	Y	Y	Y	Y	Y	Y
7 ***Bryant***	?	?	?	?	?	Y
8 Tanner	Y	Y	Y	Y	Y	Y
9 Ford	Y	Y	Y	Y	Y	N
TEXAS						
1 Sandlin	Y	Y	Y	Y	Y	N
2 Turner	?	?	?	?	?	?
3 ***Johnson, Sam***	Y	Y	Y	Y	N	Y
4 Hall	Y	Y	Y	Y	Y	Y
5 ***Sessions***	Y	Y	Y	Y	N	Y
6 ***Barton***	Y	Y	?	Y	N	Y
7 ***Archer***	Y	Y	Y	N	N	Y
8 ***Brady***	Y	Y	Y	Y	P	Y
9 Lampson	Y	Y	Y	Y	Y	N
10 Doggett	Y	Y	Y	N	Y	N
11 Edwards	Y	Y	Y	Y	Y	N
12 ***Granger***	Y	Y	Y	Y	N	Y
13 ***Thornberry***	Y	Y	Y	Y	N	Y
14 ***Paul***	Y	N	N	N	N	N
15 Hinojosa	?	?	?	?	?	?
16 Reyes	Y	Y	Y	Y	Y	N
17 Stenholm	Y	Y	Y	Y	Y	Y
18 Jackson-Lee	Y	Y	?	?	?	N
19 ***Combest***	Y	Y	Y	Y	N	Y
20 Gonzalez	Y	Y	Y	Y	Y	N
21 ***Smith***	Y	Y	Y	Y	N	Y
22 ***DeLay***	Y	Y	Y	Y	N	Y
23 ***Bonilla***	Y	Y	Y	Y	N	Y
24 Frost	Y	Y	Y	Y	Y	N
25 Bentsen	Y	Y	Y	Y	Y	N
26 ***Armey***	Y	Y	Y	Y	N	Y
27 Ortiz	Y	Y	Y	Y	Y	N
28 Rodriguez	?	?	Y	Y	Y	N
29 Green	Y	Y	Y	Y	Y	N
30 Johnson, E.B.	Y	Y	Y	Y	Y	N
UTAH						
1 ***Hansen***	?	?	Y	Y	N	Y
2 ***Cook***	Y	Y	Y	Y	P	Y
3 ***Cannon***	Y	?	Y	Y	N	Y
VERMONT						
AL *Sanders*	?	Y	Y	N	Y	N
VIRGINIA						
1 ***Bateman***	+	+	Y	Y	N	Y
2 Pickett	Y	Y	Y	N	Y	Y
3 Scott	?	?	Y	N	Y	N
4 Sisisky	Y	Y	Y	Y	Y	Y
5 *Goode*	Y	Y	Y	Y	N	Y
6 ***Goodlatte***	Y	Y	Y	Y	N	Y
7 ***Bliley***	Y	Y	Y	Y	N	Y
8 Moran	Y	Y	Y	N	Y	Y
9 Boucher	?	?	Y	Y	Y	N
10 ***Wolf***	Y	Y	Y	Y	P	Y
11 ***Davis***	Y	Y	Y	Y	N	Y
WASHINGTON						
1 Inslee	Y	Y	Y	Y	Y	N
2 ***Metcalf***	Y	Y	Y	Y	P	N
3 Baird	Y	Y	Y	Y	Y	N
4 ***Hastings***	Y	Y	Y	Y	N	Y
5 ***Nethercutt***	?	?	Y	Y	N	Y
6 Dicks	Y	Y	Y	Y	Y	N
7 McDermott	Y	Y	Y	N	Y	N
8 ***Dunn***	Y	Y	Y	Y	N	Y
9 Smith	Y	Y	Y	Y	Y	N
WEST VIRGINIA						
1 Mollohan	Y	Y	Y	Y	Y	N
2 Wise	Y	Y	Y	Y	Y	N
3 Rahall	Y	Y	Y	Y	Y	N
WISCONSIN						
1 ***Ryan***	Y	Y	Y	Y	N	Y
2 Baldwin	Y	Y	Y	N	Y	N
3 Kind	Y	Y	Y	Y	Y	N
4 Kleczka	Y	Y	Y	Y	Y	N
5 Barrett	Y	Y	Y	N	Y	N
6 ***Petri***	Y	Y	Y	Y	N	Y
7 Obey	Y	Y	Y	N	Y	N
8 ***Green***	Y	Y	Y	Y	N	Y
9 ***Sensenbrenner***	Y	Y	Y	Y	N	Y
WYOMING						
AL ***Cubin***	Y	Y	Y	Y	N	Y

Southern states - Ala., Ark., Fla., Ga., Ky., La., Miss., N.C., Okla., S.C., Tenn., Texas, Va.

8. HR 1451. Abraham Lincoln Bicentennial Commission/Passage. Biggert, R-Ill., motion to suspend the rules and agree to the Senate amendments to the bill to create a commission to study the best way to honor the 200th anniversary of the birth of Abraham Lincoln. Motion agreed (thus clearing the bill for the president) to 385-9: R 194-9; D 189-0 (ND 139-0, SD 50-0); I 2-0 A two-thirds majority of those present and voting (263 in this case) is required for passage under suspension of the rules. Feb. 8, 2000.

9. S 632. Poison Control Center Enhancement/Passage. Upton, R-Mich., motion to suspend the rules and pass the bill to authorize $25 million a year in fiscal 2000-04 to provide grants to regional poison control centers, develop education programs and expand physician and toxicologist supervision of poison control centers. Motion agreed to 378-16: R 187-16; D 189-0 (ND 139-0, SD 50-0); I 2-0. A two-thirds majority of those present and voting (263 in this case) is required for passage under suspension of the rules. Feb. 8, 2000.

10. H Res 418. Honoring Former Speaker Carl Albert/Adoption. Adoption of the resolution to express the condolences of the House on the death of former Rep. Carl Albert, D-Okla. (1947-1977), who served as Speaker from 1971-77. Adopted 390-0: R 202-0; D 186-0 (ND 138-0, SD 48-0); I 2-0. Feb. 8, 2000.

11. Procedural Motion/Journal. Approval of the House Journal of Wednesday, Feb. 9, 2000. Approved 362-37: R 188-14; D 172-23 (ND 125-19, SD 47-4); I 2-0. Feb. 10, 2000.

12. HR 6. Alleviate "Marriage Penalty" Tax/Rule. Adoption of the rule (H Res 419) to provide for House floor consideration of the bill to alleviate the tax code's so-called marriage penalty. Adopted 255-165: R 216-0; D 38-164 (ND 29-122, SD 9-42); I 1-1. Feb. 10, 2000.

13. HR 6. Alleviate "Marriage Penalty" Tax/Rangel Substitute. Rangel, D-N.Y., substitute amendment to reduce taxes for married couples by approximately $95 billion over 10 years. The amendment would increase the standard deduction for married couples to twice that for singles, and would increase the eligibility limit for couples for the earned income tax credit by $2,000 in 2001 and by $2,500 in 2002. The measure would not make any changes to the lowest income tax bracket. Rejected 192-233: R 0-219; D 191-13 (ND 143-9, SD 48-4); I 1-1. Feb. 10, 2000.

14. HR 6. Alleviate "Marriage Penalty" Tax/Recommit. Hill, D-Ind., motion to recommit the measure to the Ways and Means Committee with instructions to repay the national debt before reducing tax rates. Motion rejected 196-230: R 0-219; D 195-10 (ND 143-9, SD 52-1); I 1-1. Feb. 10, 2000.

15. HR 6. Alleviate "Marriage Penalty" Tax/Passage. Passage of the bill to reduce taxes for married couples by approximately $182 billion over 10 years. The measure would increase the standard deduction claimed by married couples to twice the amount claimed by single taxpayers. The upper boundary of the 15 percent tax bracket would gradually increase from 2003 to 2008 to twice the limit for singles. The measure also would allow couples to earn an additional $2,000 before being disqualified from receiving the earned income tax credit. Passed 268-158: R 219-0; D 48-157 (ND 31-121, SD 17-36); I 1-1. Feb. 10, 2000. A "nay" was a vote in support of the president's position.

Key

Y	Voted for (yea).
#	Paired for.
+	Announced for.
N	Voted against (nay).
X	Paired against.
–	Announced against.
P	Voted "present."
C	Voted "present" to avoid possible conflict of interest.
?	Did not vote or otherwise make a position known.

•

Democrats ***Republicans***
Independents

	8	9	10	11	12	13	14	15
ALABAMA								
1 ***Callahan***	Y	Y	Y	Y	Y	N	N	Y
2 ***Everett***	Y	Y	Y	?	?	?	?	?
3 ***Riley***	Y	Y	Y	Y	Y	N	N	Y
4 ***Aderholt***	Y	Y	Y	N	Y	N	N	Y
5 Cramer	Y	Y	Y	Y	N	Y	Y	Y
6 ***Bachus***	Y	Y	Y	Y	Y	N	N	Y
7 Hilliard	Y	Y	Y	N	N	Y	Y	N
ALASKA								
AL ***Young***	?	?	?	Y	Y	N	N	Y
ARIZONA								
1 ***Salmon***	?	?	?	Y	Y	N	N	Y
2 Pastor	Y	Y	Y	Y	N	Y	Y	N
3 ***Stump***	Y	Y	Y	Y	Y	N	N	Y
4 ***Shadegg***	Y	Y	Y	Y	Y	N	N	Y
5 ***Kolbe***	Y	Y	Y	Y	Y	N	N	Y
6 ***Hayworth***	Y	Y	Y	Y	Y	N	N	Y
ARKANSAS								
1 Berry	Y	Y	Y	+	+	N	Y	N
2 Snyder	Y	Y	Y	Y	N	N	Y	N
3 ***Hutchinson***	Y	N	Y	Y	Y	N	N	Y
4 ***Dickey***	Y	Y	Y	Y	Y	N	N	Y
CALIFORNIA								
1 Thompson	Y	Y	Y	N	N	Y	Y	N
2 ***Herger***	Y	N	Y	Y	Y	N	N	Y
3 ***Ose***	Y	Y	Y	Y	Y	N	N	Y
4 ***Doolittle***	Y	N	Y	Y	Y	N	N	Y
5 Matsui	Y	Y	Y	Y	N	Y	Y	N
6 Woolsey	Y	Y	Y	Y	N	Y	Y	N
7 Miller, George	Y	Y	Y	?	N	Y	Y	N
8 Pelosi	Y	Y	Y	Y	Y	Y	Y	N
9 Lee	Y	Y	Y	Y	N	Y	Y	N
10 Tauscher	?	?	?	Y	N	Y	Y	N
11 ***Pombo***	Y	Y	Y	Y	Y	N	N	Y
12 Lantos	Y	Y	Y	Y	N	Y	Y	N
13 Stark	Y	Y	Y	Y	N	Y	Y	N
14 Eshoo	Y	Y	Y	Y	Y	Y	Y	N
15 ***Campbell***	Y	Y	Y	Y	Y	N	N	Y
16 Lofgren	Y	Y	Y	?	?	?	?	?
17 Farr	Y	Y	Y	Y	?	Y	Y	N
18 Condit	Y	Y	Y	Y	N	Y	Y	Y
19 ***Radanovich***	Y	Y	Y	?	Y	N	N	Y
20 Dooley	?	?	?	Y	N	Y	Y	N
21 ***Thomas***	Y	N	Y	Y	Y	N	N	Y
22 Capps	?	?	?	?	?	?	?	?
23 ***Gallegly***	Y	Y	Y	Y	Y	N	N	Y
24 Sherman	Y	Y	Y	Y	N	Y	Y	N
25 ***McKeon***	Y	Y	Y	Y	Y	N	N	Y
26 Berman	Y	Y	Y	Y	N	Y	Y	N
27 ***Rogan***	Y	Y	Y	N	Y	N	N	Y
28 ***Dreier***	Y	Y	Y	Y	Y	N	N	Y
29 Waxman	Y	Y	Y	Y	N	Y	Y	N
30 Becerra	Y	Y	Y	Y	N	Y	Y	N
31 Martinez	Y	Y	Y	Y	N	Y	Y	Y
32 Dixon	Y	Y	Y	Y	N	Y	Y	N
33 Roybal-Allard	Y	Y	Y	Y	N	Y	Y	N
34 Napolitano	Y	Y	Y	Y	N	Y	Y	N
35 Waters	Y	Y	Y	Y	N	Y	Y	N
36 ***Kuykendall***	Y	Y	Y	Y	Y	N	N	Y
37 Millender-McD.	+	+	?	Y	N	Y	Y	N
38 ***Horn***	Y	Y	Y	Y	Y	N	N	Y
39 ***Royce***	N	Y	Y	Y	Y	N	N	Y
40 ***Lewis***	Y	Y	Y	Y	Y	N	N	Y
41 ***Miller, Gary***	Y	Y	Y	Y	Y	N	N	Y
42 Baca	Y	Y	Y	Y	Y	Y	Y	N
43 ***Calvert***	Y	Y	Y	Y	Y	N	N	Y
44 ***Bono***	Y	Y	Y	Y	Y	N	N	Y
45 ***Rohrabacher***	Y	Y	Y	Y	Y	N	N	Y
46 Sanchez	Y	Y	Y	Y	N	Y	Y	N
47 ***Cox***	Y	Y	Y	Y	Y	N	N	Y
48 ***Packard***	Y	Y	Y	Y	Y	N	N	Y
49 ***Bilbray***	Y	Y	Y	Y	Y	N	N	Y
50 Filner	Y	Y	Y	N	N	Y	Y	N
51 ***Cunningham***	Y	Y	Y	Y	Y	N	N	Y
52 ***Hunter***	Y	Y	Y	Y	Y	N	N	Y
COLORADO								
1 DeGette	Y	Y	Y	Y	N	Y	Y	N
2 Udall	Y	Y	Y	Y	N	Y	Y	Y
3 ***McInnis***	Y	Y	Y	Y	Y	N	N	Y
4 ***Schaffer***	N	N	Y	N	Y	N	N	Y
5 ***Hefley***	Y	Y	Y	N	Y	N	N	Y
6 ***Tancredo***	N	Y	Y	P	Y	N	N	Y
CONNECTICUT								
1 Larson	Y	Y	Y	Y	N	Y	Y	N
2 Gejdenson	Y	Y	Y	Y	N	Y	Y	N
3 DeLauro	Y	Y	Y	Y	N	Y	Y	N
4 ***Shays***	Y	Y	Y	Y	Y	N	N	Y
5 Maloney	Y	Y	Y	Y	Y	Y	N	Y
6 ***Johnson***	Y	Y	Y	Y	Y	N	N	Y
DELAWARE								
AL ***Castle***	Y	Y	Y	Y	Y	N	N	Y
FLORIDA								
1 ***Scarborough***	?	?	?	Y	Y	N	N	Y
2 Boyd	Y	Y	Y	Y	N	Y	Y	N
3 Brown	Y	Y	Y	Y	N	Y	Y	N
4 ***Fowler***	Y	Y	Y	Y	Y	N	N	Y
5 Thurman	Y	Y	Y	Y	N	Y	Y	N
6 ***Stearns***	Y	Y	Y	Y	Y	N	N	Y
7 ***Mica***	Y	Y	Y	Y	Y	N	N	Y
8 ***McCollum***	Y	Y	Y	+	+	?	–	+
9 ***Bilirakis***	Y	Y	Y	Y	Y	N	N	Y
10 ***Young***	Y	Y	Y	Y	Y	N	N	Y
11 Davis	Y	Y	Y	Y	N	Y	Y	N
12 ***Canady***	Y	Y	Y	Y	Y	N	N	Y
13 ***Miller***	Y	Y	Y	Y	Y	N	N	Y
14 ***Goss***	Y	Y	Y	Y	Y	N	N	Y
15 ***Weldon***	Y	Y	Y	Y	Y	N	N	Y
16 ***Foley***	Y	Y	Y	?	Y	N	N	Y
17 Meek	Y	Y	Y	Y	N	Y	Y	N
18 ***Ros-Lehtinen***	?	?	?	Y	Y	N	N	Y
19 Wexler	Y	Y	Y	Y	N	Y	Y	N
20 Deutsch	Y	Y	Y	Y	N	Y	Y	N
21 ***Diaz-Balart***	Y	Y	Y	Y	Y	N	N	Y
22 ***Shaw***	Y	Y	Y	Y	Y	N	N	Y
23 Hastings	Y	Y	Y	Y	N	Y	Y	N
GEORGIA								
1 ***Kingston***	Y	Y	Y	Y	Y	N	N	Y
2 Bishop	Y	Y	Y	Y	Y	Y	Y	Y
3 ***Collins***	Y	Y	Y	Y	Y	N	N	Y
4 McKinney	Y	Y	Y	Y	Y	Y	Y	Y
5 Lewis	Y	Y	Y	Y	N	Y	Y	N
6 ***Isakson***	Y	Y	Y	Y	Y	N	N	Y
7 ***Barr***	?	?	?	Y	Y	N	N	Y
8 ***Chambliss***	Y	Y	Y	Y	Y	N	N	Y
9 ***Deal***	?	?	?	Y	Y	N	N	Y
10 ***Norwood***	Y	Y	Y	Y	Y	N	N	Y
11 ***Linder***	Y	Y	Y	Y	Y	N	N	Y
HAWAII								
1 Abercrombie	Y	Y	Y	Y	N	Y	Y	N
2 Mink	Y	Y	Y	Y	N	Y	Y	N
IDAHO								
1 ***Chenoweth-Hage***	N	N	Y	?	Y	N	N	Y
2 ***Simpson***	Y	Y	Y	Y	Y	N	N	Y
ILLINOIS								
1 Rush	?	?	?	Y	N	Y	Y	N
2 Jackson	Y	Y	Y	Y	Y	Y	Y	N
3 Lipinski	?	?	?	?	Y	Y	Y	Y
4 Gutierrez	Y	Y	Y	Y	N	Y	Y	N
5 Blagojevich	Y	Y	Y	Y	N	Y	Y	Y
6 ***Hyde***	Y	Y	Y	Y	Y	N	N	Y
7 Davis	Y	Y	Y	Y	N	Y	Y	N
8 ***Crane***	Y	Y	Y	N	Y	N	N	Y
9 Schakowsky	Y	Y	Y	Y	N	Y	Y	N
10 ***Porter***	Y	Y	Y	Y	Y	N	N	Y
11 ***Weller***	Y	Y	Y	N	Y	N	N	Y
12 Costello	Y	Y	Y	N	N	Y	Y	Y
13 ***Biggert***	Y	Y	Y	Y	Y	N	N	Y

ND Northern Democrats SD Southern Democrats

	8	9	10	11	12	13	14	15
14 **Hastert**				Y				Y
15 **Ewing**	Y	Y	Y	Y	Y	N	N	Y
16 **Manzullo**	Y	Y	Y	Y	Y	N	N	Y
17 Evans	Y	Y	Y	Y	N	Y	Y	N
18 **LaHood**	Y	Y	Y	Y	Y	N	N	Y
19 Phelps	Y	Y	Y	Y	Y	Y	Y	Y
20 **Shimkus**	Y	Y	Y	Y	Y	N	N	Y
INDIANA								
1 Visclosky	Y	Y	Y	N	N	N	Y	N
2 **McIntosh**	?	?	?	Y	Y	N	N	Y
3 Roemer	Y	Y	Y	Y	Y	Y	Y	Y
4 **Souder**	Y	Y	Y	Y	Y	N	N	Y
5 **Buyer**	Y	Y	Y	Y	Y	N	N	Y
6 **Burton**	Y	Y	Y	?	Y	N	N	Y
7 **Pease**	Y	Y	Y	Y	Y	N	N	Y
8 **Hostettler**	Y	Y	Y	Y	Y	N	N	Y
9 Hill	Y	Y	Y	Y	Y	Y	Y	N
10 Carson	Y	Y	Y	Y	Y	Y	Y	Y
IOWA								
1 **Leach**	Y	Y	Y	Y	Y	N	N	Y
2 **Nussle**	Y	Y	Y	Y	Y	N	N	Y
3 Boswell	Y	Y	Y	Y	N	Y	Y	Y
4 **Ganske**	Y	Y	Y	Y	Y	N	N	Y
5 **Latham**	Y	Y	Y	Y	Y	N	N	Y
KANSAS								
1 **Moran**	Y	Y	Y	Y	Y	N	N	Y
2 **Ryun**	Y	Y	Y	Y	Y	N	N	Y
3 Moore	Y	Y	Y	N	Y	Y	Y	Y
4 **Tiahrt**	Y	Y	Y	Y	Y	N	N	Y
KENTUCKY								
1 **Whitfield**	Y	Y	Y	Y	Y	N	N	Y
2 **Lewis**	Y	Y	Y	Y	Y	N	N	Y
3 **Northup**	Y	Y	Y	Y	Y	N	N	Y
4 Lucas	Y	Y	Y	Y	Y	N	Y	Y
5 **Rogers**	?	?	?	Y	Y	N	N	Y
6 **Fletcher**	Y	Y	Y	Y	Y	N	N	Y
LOUISIANA								
1 **Vitter**	Y	Y	Y	?	Y	N	N	Y
2 Jefferson	?	?	?	?	?	?	Y	N
3 **Tauzin**	Y	Y	Y	Y	Y	N	N	Y
4 **McCrery**	?	?	?	?	Y	N	N	Y
5 **Cooksey**	Y	Y	Y	?	Y	N	N	Y
6 **Baker**	Y	Y	Y	Y	Y	N	N	Y
7 John	Y	Y	Y	Y	N	Y	Y	Y
MAINE								
1 Allen	Y	Y	Y	Y	N	Y	Y	N
2 Baldacci	Y	Y	Y	Y	N	Y	Y	N
MARYLAND								
1 **Gilchrest**	Y	Y	Y	Y	Y	N	N	Y
2 **Ehrlich**	Y	Y	Y	Y	Y	N	N	Y
3 Cardin	Y	Y	Y	Y	N	Y	Y	N
4 Wynn	Y	Y	Y	Y	N	Y	Y	N
5 Hoyer	Y	Y	Y	Y	N	Y	Y	N
6 **Bartlett**	Y	Y	Y	Y	Y	N	N	Y
7 Cummings	Y	Y	Y	Y	N	Y	Y	N
8 **Morella**	Y	Y	Y	Y	Y	N	N	Y
MASSACHUSETTS								
1 Olver	Y	Y	Y	Y	N	Y	Y	N
2 Neal	Y	Y	Y	Y	N	Y	Y	N
3 McGovern	Y	Y	Y	Y	N	Y	Y	N
4 Frank	Y	Y	Y	Y	N	Y	Y	N
5 Meehan	Y	Y	Y	Y	N	Y	Y	N
6 Tierney	Y	Y	Y	Y	N	Y	Y	N
7 Markey	Y	Y	Y	Y	N	Y	Y	N
8 Capuano	Y	Y	Y	Y	N	Y	Y	N
9 Moakley	?	?	?	Y	Y	Y	Y	N
10 Delahunt	Y	Y	Y	Y	N	Y	Y	N
MICHIGAN								
1 Stupak	?	?	?	N	Y	Y	Y	Y
2 **Hoekstra**	N	Y	Y	Y	Y	N	N	Y
3 **Ehlers**	Y	Y	Y	Y	Y	N	N	Y
4 **Camp**	Y	Y	Y	Y	Y	N	N	Y
5 Barcia	Y	Y	Y	Y	Y	N	N	Y
6 **Upton**	Y	Y	Y	Y	Y	N	N	Y
7 **Smith**	Y	Y	Y	Y	Y	N	N	Y
8 Stabenow	Y	Y	Y	Y	N	Y	Y	Y
9 Kildee	Y	Y	Y	Y	Y	Y	Y	N
10 Bonior	Y	Y	Y	Y	Y	Y	Y	N
11 **Knollenberg**	Y	Y	Y	Y	Y	N	N	Y
12 Levin	Y	Y	Y	Y	N	Y	Y	N
13 Rivers	Y	Y	Y	Y	N	Y	Y	N
14 Conyers	?	Y	?	?	N	Y	Y	N
15 Kilpatrick	Y	Y	Y	Y	Y	Y	Y	N
16 Dingell	Y	Y	Y	?	N	Y	Y	N
MINNESOTA								
1 **Gutknecht**	Y	Y	Y	N	Y	N	N	Y
2 Minge	Y	Y	Y	Y	N	Y	Y	N
3 **Ramstad**	Y	Y	Y	N	Y	N	N	Y
4 Vento	?	?	?	?	?	?	?	?
5 Sabo	Y	Y	Y	N	N	Y	N	N
6 Luther	Y	Y	Y	Y	N	Y	Y	N
7 Peterson	Y	Y	Y	N	N	Y	Y	N
8 Oberstar	Y	Y	Y	N	N	Y	Y	N
MISSISSIPPI								
1 **Wicker**	Y	Y	?	Y	Y	N	N	Y
2 Thompson	Y	Y	Y	N	N	Y	Y	Y
3 **Pickering**	Y	Y	Y	Y	Y	N	N	Y
4 Shows	Y	Y	Y	Y	Y	Y	Y	Y
5 Taylor	Y	Y	Y	Y	N	Y	Y	N
MISSOURI								
1 Clay	Y	Y	Y	?	N	Y	Y	N
2 **Talent**	Y	Y	Y	?	Y	N	N	Y
3 Gephardt	Y	Y	Y	Y	N	Y	Y	N
4 Skelton	Y	Y	Y	Y	N	Y	Y	Y
5 McCarthy	Y	Y	Y	Y	N	Y	Y	N
6 Danner	?	?	?	?	Y	N	N	Y
7 **Blunt**	Y	Y	Y	?	Y	N	N	Y
8 **Emerson**	Y	Y	Y	Y	Y	N	N	Y
9 **Hulshof**	Y	Y	Y	Y	Y	N	N	Y
MONTANA								
AL **Hill**	Y	Y	Y	N	Y	N	N	Y
NEBRASKA								
1 **Bereuter**	Y	Y	Y	Y	Y	N	N	Y
2 **Terry**	Y	Y	Y	Y	Y	N	N	Y
3 **Barrett**	Y	Y	Y	Y	Y	N	N	Y
NEVADA								
1 Berkley	Y	Y	Y	Y	N	Y	N	Y
2 **Gibbons**	Y	Y	Y	N	Y	N	N	Y
NEW HAMPSHIRE								
1 **Sununu**	Y	N	Y	Y	Y	N	N	Y
2 **Bass**	Y	Y	Y	Y	Y	N	N	Y
NEW JERSEY								
1 Andrews	Y	Y	Y	Y	N	N	Y	N
2 **LoBiondo**	Y	Y	Y	N	Y	N	N	Y
3 **Saxton**	Y	Y	Y	Y	Y	N	N	Y
4 **Smith**	Y	Y	Y	Y	?	N	N	Y
5 **Roukema**	Y	Y	Y	Y	Y	N	N	Y
6 Pallone	Y	Y	Y	Y	N	Y	Y	N
7 **Franks**	Y	Y	Y	Y	Y	N	N	Y
8 Pascrell	Y	Y	Y	Y	N	Y	Y	Y
9 Rothman	Y	Y	Y	N	N	Y	Y	N
10 Payne	Y	Y	Y	Y	N	Y	Y	N
11 **Frelinghuysen**	Y	Y	Y	Y	Y	N	N	Y
12 Holt	Y	Y	Y	Y	N	Y	Y	N
13 Menendez	Y	Y	Y	Y	N	Y	Y	N
NEW MEXICO								
1 **Wilson**	Y	Y	Y	Y	Y	N	N	Y
2 **Skeen**	Y	Y	Y	Y	Y	N	N	Y
3 Udall	Y	Y	Y	N	Y	Y	Y	N
NEW YORK								
1 Forbes	Y	Y	Y	Y	N	Y	N	Y
2 **Lazio**	Y	Y	Y	Y	Y	N	N	Y
3 **King**	Y	Y	Y	Y	Y	N	N	Y
4 McCarthy	Y	Y	Y	Y	N	N	Y	N
5 Ackerman	?	?	?	Y	N	Y	Y	N
6 Meeks	Y	Y	Y	Y	N	Y	Y	N
7 Crowley	Y	Y	Y	N	Y	Y	Y	N
8 Nadler	?	?	?	Y	N	Y	Y	N
9 Weiner	Y	Y	Y	Y	N	Y	Y	N
10 Towns	Y	Y	Y	Y	N	Y	Y	N
11 Owens	Y	Y	Y	Y	N	Y	Y	N
12 Velázquez	Y	Y	Y	Y	N	Y	Y	N
13 **Fossella**	Y	Y	Y	?	?	N	N	Y
14 Maloney	Y	Y	Y	Y	N	Y	Y	N
15 Rangel	Y	Y	Y	Y	N	Y	Y	N
16 Serrano	?	?	?	Y	N	Y	Y	N
17 Engel	Y	Y	Y	Y	Y	Y	Y	N
18 Lowey	Y	Y	Y	Y	N	Y	Y	N
19 **Kelly**	Y	Y	Y	Y	Y	N	N	Y
20 **Gilman**	Y	Y	Y	Y	Y	N	N	Y
21 McNulty	?	?	?	Y	Y	Y	Y	N
22 **Sweeney**	Y	Y	Y	?	Y	N	N	Y
23 **Boehlert**	Y	Y	Y	Y	Y	N	N	Y
24 **McHugh**	Y	Y	Y	Y	Y	N	N	Y
25 **Walsh**	Y	Y	Y	Y	Y	N	N	Y
26 Hinchey	Y	Y	Y	Y	N	Y	Y	N
27 **Reynolds**	Y	Y	Y	Y	Y	N	N	Y
28 Slaughter	Y	Y	Y	Y	N	Y	Y	N
29 LaFalce	Y	Y	Y	Y	N	Y	Y	N
30 **Quinn**	Y	Y	Y	Y	Y	N	N	Y
31 **Houghton**	Y	Y	Y	Y	Y	N	N	Y
NORTH CAROLINA								
1 Clayton	+	+	+	Y	N	Y	Y	N
2 Etheridge	Y	Y	Y	Y	N	Y	Y	Y
3 **Jones**	Y	Y	Y	Y	Y	N	N	Y
4 Price	Y	Y	Y	Y	N	Y	Y	N
5 **Burr**	Y	Y	Y	Y	Y	N	N	Y
6 **Coble**	N	N	Y	Y	Y	N	N	Y
7 McIntyre	Y	Y	Y	Y	Y	Y	Y	Y
8 **Hayes**	Y	Y	Y	Y	Y	N	N	Y
9 **Myrick**	?	?	?	?	Y	N	N	Y
10 **Ballenger**	Y	Y	Y	Y	Y	N	N	Y
11 **Taylor**	?	?	?	?	Y	N	N	Y
12 Watt	Y	Y	Y	Y	N	Y	Y	N
NORTH DAKOTA								
AL Pomeroy	Y	Y	Y	Y	N	Y	Y	N
OHIO								
1 **Chabot**	Y	Y	Y	Y	Y	N	N	Y
2 **Portman**	Y	Y	Y	Y	Y	N	N	Y
3 Hall	Y	Y	Y	?	N	Y	Y	N
4 **Oxley**	Y	Y	Y	Y	Y	N	N	Y
5 **Gillmor**	Y	Y	Y	Y	Y	N	N	?
6 Strickland	Y	Y	Y	N	N	Y	Y	N
7 **Hobson**	Y	Y	Y	Y	Y	N	N	Y
8 **Boehner**	Y	Y	Y	Y	Y	N	N	Y
9 Kaptur	Y	Y	Y	Y	N	N	Y	N
10 Kucinich	Y	Y	Y	N	N	Y	Y	N
11 Jones	Y	Y	Y	Y	N	Y	Y	N
12 **Kasich**	Y	Y	Y	Y	?	N	N	Y
13 Brown	?	?	?	?	?	?	?	?
14 Sawyer	Y	Y	Y	Y	N	Y	Y	N
15 **Pryce**	Y	Y	Y	Y	Y	N	N	Y
16 **Regula**	Y	Y	Y	Y	Y	N	N	Y
17 Traficant	Y	Y	Y	Y	Y	Y	Y	Y
18 **Ney**	Y	Y	Y	Y	Y	N	N	Y
19 **LaTourette**	Y	Y	Y	Y	Y	N	N	Y
OKLAHOMA								
1 **Largent**	?	?	?	Y	Y	N	N	Y
2 **Coburn**	?	?	?	N	Y	N	N	Y
3 **Watkins**	Y	Y	Y	Y	Y	N	N	Y
4 **Watts**	Y	Y	Y	Y	Y	N	N	Y
5 **Istook**	Y	Y	Y	Y	Y	N	N	Y
6 **Lucas**	Y	Y	Y	Y	Y	N	N	Y
OREGON								
1 Wu	Y	Y	Y	N	N	Y	Y	Y
2 **Walden**	Y	Y	Y	Y	Y	N	N	Y
3 Blumenauer	Y	Y	Y	Y	N	Y	Y	N
4 DeFazio	?	?	?	?	?	?	?	?
5 Hooley	Y	Y	Y	Y	N	Y	Y	Y
PENNSYLVANIA								
1 Brady	Y	Y	Y	N	N	Y	Y	N
2 Fattah	Y	?	?	Y	N	Y	Y	N
3 Borski	Y	Y	Y	N	N	Y	Y	N
4 Klink	Y	Y	Y	?	N	Y	Y	N
5 **Peterson**	Y	Y	Y	Y	Y	N	N	Y
6 Holden	Y	Y	Y	Y	N	Y	Y	N
7 **Weldon**	Y	Y	Y	Y	Y	N	N	Y
8 **Greenwood**	Y	Y	Y	Y	Y	N	N	Y
9 **Shuster**	Y	Y	Y	Y	Y	N	N	Y
10 **Sherwood**	Y	Y	Y	Y	Y	N	N	Y
11 Kanjorski	Y	Y	Y	Y	N	N	Y	N
12 Murtha	Y	Y	Y	Y	N	N	Y	N
13 Hoeffel	Y	Y	Y	Y	N	Y	Y	N
14 Coyne	Y	Y	Y	Y	N	Y	Y	N
15 **Toomey**	Y	N	Y	Y	Y	N	N	Y
16 **Pitts**	Y	Y	Y	Y	Y	N	N	Y
17 **Gekas**	?	?	?	Y	?	N	N	Y
18 Doyle	Y	Y	Y	Y	N	Y	Y	Y
19 **Goodling**	?	?	?	Y	Y	N	N	Y
20 Mascara	Y	Y	Y	Y	N	Y	Y	Y
21 **English**	Y	Y	Y	N	Y	N	N	Y
RHODE ISLAND								
1 Kennedy	Y	Y	Y	Y	N	Y	Y	N
2 Weygand	Y	Y	Y	Y	N	Y	Y	N
SOUTH CAROLINA								
1 **Sanford**	N	N	Y	?	Y	N	N	Y
2 **Spence**	Y	Y	?	Y	Y	N	N	Y
3 **Graham**	Y	Y	Y	?	Y	N	N	Y
4 **DeMint**	+	+	+	Y	Y	N	N	Y
5 Spratt	Y	Y	Y	Y	N	Y	Y	N
6 Clyburn	Y	Y	Y	N	N	Y	Y	Y
SOUTH DAKOTA								
AL **Thune**	Y	Y	Y	Y	Y	N	N	Y
TENNESSEE								
1 **Jenkins**	Y	Y	Y	Y	Y	N	N	Y
2 **Duncan**	Y	N	Y	Y	Y	N	N	Y
3 **Wamp**	Y	Y	Y	Y	Y	N	N	Y
4 **Hilleary**	Y	Y	Y	Y	Y	N	N	Y
5 Clement	Y	Y	Y	Y	N	Y	Y	Y
6 Gordon	Y	Y	Y	Y	N	Y	Y	Y
7 **Bryant**	Y	Y	Y	Y	Y	N	N	Y
8 Tanner	Y	Y	Y	Y	N	N	Y	N
9 Ford	Y	Y	Y	Y	N	Y	Y	N
TEXAS								
1 Sandlin	Y	Y	Y	Y	Y	Y	Y	Y
2 Turner	Y	Y	Y	Y	N	Y	Y	N
3 **Johnson, Sam**	Y	N	Y	Y	Y	N	N	Y
4 Hall	Y	Y	Y	Y	N	Y	N	Y
5 **Sessions**	Y	Y	Y	Y	Y	N	N	Y
6 **Barton**	Y	Y	Y	?	Y	N	N	Y
7 **Archer**	Y	N	Y	Y	Y	N	N	Y
8 **Brady**	Y	Y	Y	Y	Y	N	N	Y
9 Lampson	Y	Y	Y	Y	N	Y	Y	N
10 Doggett	Y	Y	?	Y	N	Y	Y	N
11 Edwards	Y	Y	Y	Y	N	Y	Y	N
12 **Granger**	Y	Y	Y	Y	Y	N	N	Y
13 **Thornberry**	Y	Y	Y	Y	Y	N	N	Y
14 **Paul**	N	N	Y	Y	Y	N	N	Y
15 Hinojosa	?	?	?	?	?	?	?	?
16 Reyes	Y	Y	Y	Y	N	Y	Y	N
17 Stenholm	Y	Y	Y	Y	N	Y	Y	N
18 Jackson-Lee	Y	Y	Y	Y	N	Y	Y	N
19 **Combest**	Y	Y	Y	Y	Y	N	N	Y
20 Gonzalez	?	?	?	Y	N	Y	Y	N
21 **Smith**	Y	Y	Y	Y	Y	N	N	Y
22 **DeLay**	Y	Y	Y	Y	Y	N	N	Y
23 **Bonilla**	Y	Y	Y	Y	Y	N	N	Y
24 Frost	Y	Y	Y	Y	Y	Y	Y	N
25 Bentsen	Y	Y	Y	Y	N	Y	Y	N
26 **Armey**	Y	Y	Y	Y	Y	N	N	Y
27 Ortiz	Y	Y	Y	Y	N	Y	Y	N
28 Rodriguez	Y	Y	Y	Y	N	Y	Y	N
29 Green	Y	Y	Y	Y	N	Y	Y	N
30 Johnson, E.B.	Y	Y	Y	Y	N	Y	Y	N
UTAH								
1 **Hansen**	Y	Y	Y	Y	Y	N	N	Y
2 **Cook**	Y	Y	Y	Y	Y	N	N	Y
3 **Cannon**	Y	Y	Y	Y	Y	N	N	Y
VERMONT								
AL *Sanders*	Y	Y	Y	Y	N	Y	Y	N
VIRGINIA								
1 **Bateman**	Y	Y	Y	Y	Y	N	N	Y
2 Pickett	Y	Y	Y	N	N	Y	Y	Y
3 Scott	Y	Y	?	Y	N	Y	Y	N
4 Sisisky	Y	Y	Y	Y	Y	Y	Y	Y
5 *Goode*	Y	Y	Y	Y	Y	N	N	Y
6 **Goodlatte**	Y	Y	Y	Y	Y	N	N	Y
7 **Bliley**	Y	Y	Y	N	Y	N	N	Y
8 Moran	Y	Y	Y	Y	N	Y	Y	N
9 Boucher	Y	Y	Y	Y	N	Y	Y	N
10 **Wolf**	Y	Y	Y	Y	Y	N	N	Y
11 **Davis**	Y	Y	Y	Y	Y	N	N	Y
WASHINGTON								
1 Inslee	Y	Y	Y	Y	Y	Y	Y	Y
2 **Metcalf**	?	Y	Y	Y	Y	N	N	Y
3 Baird	Y	Y	Y	N	Y	Y	Y	Y
4 **Hastings**	Y	Y	Y	Y	Y	N	N	Y
5 **Nethercutt**	Y	Y	Y	Y	Y	N	N	Y
6 Dicks	Y	Y	Y	Y	Y	Y	Y	N
7 McDermott	Y	Y	Y	N	N	Y	Y	N
8 **Dunn**	Y	Y	Y	Y	Y	N	N	Y
9 Smith	Y	Y	Y	Y	Y	Y	Y	Y
WEST VIRGINIA								
1 Mollohan	?	?	?	Y	N	N	N	N
2 Wise	Y	Y	Y	?	N	Y	Y	Y
3 Rahall	Y	Y	Y	Y	N	N	Y	N
WISCONSIN								
1 **Ryan**	Y	N	Y	Y	Y	N	N	Y
2 Baldwin	Y	Y	Y	Y	N	Y	Y	N
3 Kind	Y	Y	Y	Y	N	Y	Y	N
4 Kleczka	Y	Y	Y	Y	N	Y	Y	N
5 Barrett	Y	Y	Y	Y	N	Y	Y	N
6 **Petri**	Y	?	Y	Y	Y	N	N	Y
7 Obey	Y	Y	Y	Y	N	Y	N	N
8 **Green**	Y	Y	Y	Y	Y	N	N	Y
9 **Sensenbrenner**	N	N	Y	Y	Y	N	N	Y
WYOMING								
AL **Cubin**	+	+	+	Y	Y	N	N	Y

Southern states - Ala., Ark., Fla., Ga., Ky., La., Miss., N.C., Okla., S.C., Tenn., Texas, Va.

16. H Con Res 247. Organ Donors/Adoption. Upton, R-Mich., motion to suspend the rules and adopt the concurrent resolution to express the sense of Congress regarding the importance of organ, tissue, bone marrow and blood donation. Motion agreed to 379-0: R 197-0; D 180-0 (ND 132-0, SD 48-0); I 2-0. A two-thirds majority of those present and voting (253 in this case) is required for adoption under suspension of the rules. Feb. 14, 2000.

17. H Con Res 76. Child Abuse/Adoption. Salmon, R-Ariz., motion to suspend the rules and adopt the concurrent resolution to recognize the social impact of child abuse and neglect, urge Americans to work to end child abuse, and recognize the nonprofit organization Childhelp USA for its efforts on behalf of abused and neglected children. Motion agreed to 378-0: R 196-0; D 180-0 (ND 132-0, SD 48-0); I 2-0. A two-thirds majority of those present and voting (252 in this case) is required for adoption under suspension of the rules. Feb. 14, 2000.

18. HR 3557. John Cardinal O'Connor Gold Medal/Passage. Bachus, R-Ala., motion to suspend the rules and pass the bill to authorize the president to award a gold medal honoring John Cardinal O'Connor, Archbishop of New York, in recognition of his accomplishments as a priest, chaplain and humanitarian. Motion agreed to 413-1: R 215-1; D 196-0 (ND 143-0, SD 53-0); I 2-0. A two-thirds majority of those present and voting (276 in this case) is required for passage under suspension of the rules. Feb. 15, 2000.

19. HR 3642. Charles M. Schulz Medal/Passage. Lucas, R-Okla., motion to suspend the rules and pass the bill to authorize the president to award a gold medal honoring Charles M. Schulz in recognition of his artistic contributions. Motion agreed to 410-1: R 213-1; D 195-0 (ND 143-0, SD 52-0); I 2-0. A two-thirds majority of those present and voting (274 in this case) is required for passage under suspension of the rules. Feb. 15, 2000.

20. HR 3201. Historic Site Study/Passage. Hansen, R-Utah, motion to suspend the rules and pass the bill to authorize the Interior Department to study the feasibility of designating the home of Dr. Carter G. Woodson as a national historic landmark. Motion agreed to 413-1: R 211-1; D 200-0 (ND 147-0, SD 53-0); I 2-0. A two-thirds majority of those present and voting (276 in this case) is required for passage under suspension of the rules. Feb. 15, 2000.

Key

- Y Voted for (yea).
- # Paired for.
- \+ Announced for.
- N Voted against (nay).
- X Paired against.
- – Announced against.
- P Voted "present."
- C Voted "present" to avoid possible conflict of interest.
- ? Did not vote or otherwise make a position known.

•

Democrats ***Republicans***
Independents

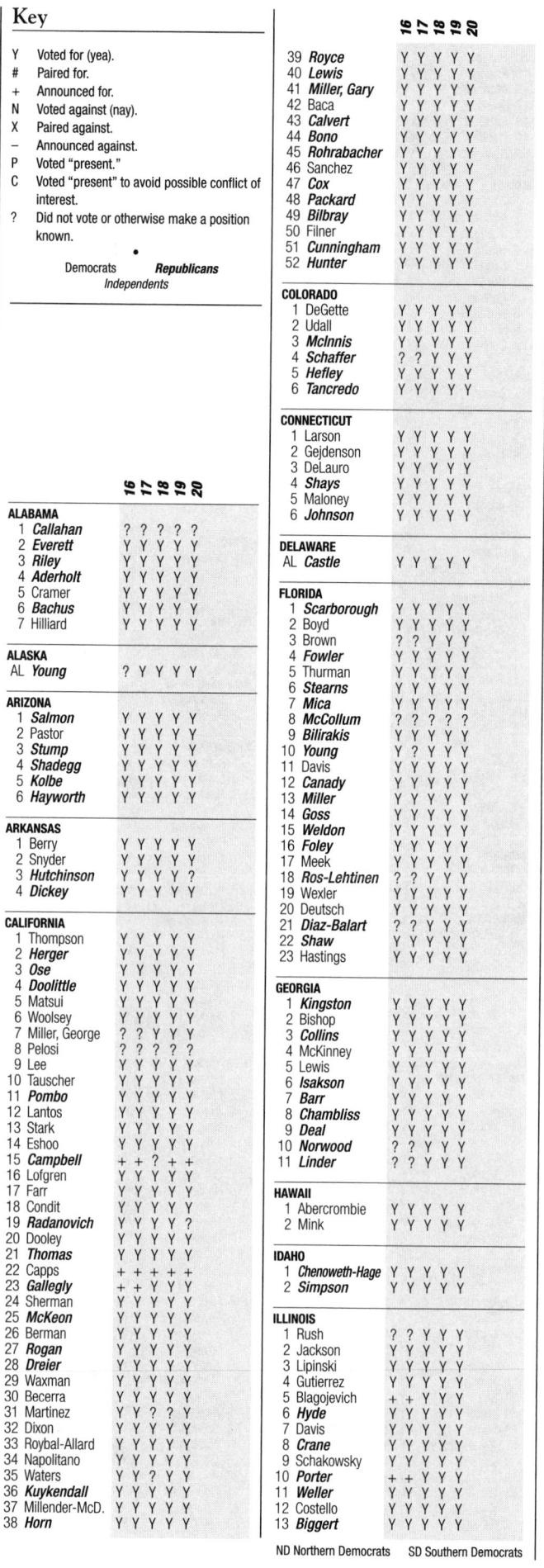

	16	17	18	19	20
ALABAMA					
1 ***Callahan***	?	?	?	?	?
2 ***Everett***	Y	Y	Y	Y	Y
3 ***Riley***	Y	Y	Y	Y	Y
4 ***Aderholt***	Y	Y	Y	Y	Y
5 Cramer	Y	Y	Y	Y	Y
6 ***Bachus***	Y	Y	Y	Y	Y
7 Hilliard	Y	Y	Y	Y	Y
ALASKA					
AL ***Young***	?	Y	Y	Y	Y
ARIZONA					
1 ***Salmon***	Y	Y	Y	Y	Y
2 Pastor	Y	Y	Y	Y	Y
3 ***Stump***	Y	Y	Y	Y	Y
4 ***Shadegg***	Y	Y	Y	Y	Y
5 ***Kolbe***	Y	Y	Y	Y	Y
6 ***Hayworth***	Y	Y	Y	Y	Y
ARKANSAS					
1 Berry	Y	Y	Y	Y	Y
2 Snyder	Y	Y	Y	Y	Y
3 ***Hutchinson***	Y	Y	Y	Y	?
4 ***Dickey***	Y	Y	Y	Y	Y
CALIFORNIA					
1 Thompson	Y	Y	Y	Y	Y
2 ***Herger***	Y	Y	Y	Y	Y
3 ***Ose***	Y	Y	Y	Y	Y
4 ***Doolittle***	Y	Y	Y	Y	Y
5 Matsui	Y	Y	Y	Y	Y
6 Woolsey	Y	Y	Y	Y	Y
7 Miller, George	?	?	Y	Y	Y
8 Pelosi	?	?	?	?	?
9 Lee	Y	Y	Y	Y	Y
10 Tauscher	Y	Y	Y	Y	Y
11 ***Pombo***	Y	Y	Y	Y	Y
12 Lantos	Y	Y	Y	Y	Y
13 Stark	Y	Y	Y	Y	Y
14 Eshoo	Y	Y	Y	Y	Y
15 ***Campbell***	+	+	?	+	+
16 Lofgren	Y	Y	Y	Y	Y
17 Farr	Y	Y	Y	Y	Y
18 Condit	Y	Y	Y	Y	Y
19 ***Radanovich***	Y	Y	Y	Y	?
20 Dooley	Y	Y	Y	Y	Y
21 ***Thomas***	Y	Y	Y	Y	Y
22 Capps	+	+	+	+	+
23 ***Gallegly***	+	+	Y	Y	Y
24 Sherman	Y	Y	Y	Y	Y
25 ***McKeon***	Y	Y	Y	Y	Y
26 Berman	Y	Y	Y	Y	Y
27 ***Rogan***	Y	Y	Y	Y	Y
28 ***Dreier***	Y	Y	Y	Y	Y
29 Waxman	Y	Y	Y	Y	Y
30 Becerra	Y	Y	Y	Y	Y
31 Martinez	Y	Y	?	?	Y
32 Dixon	Y	Y	Y	Y	Y
33 Roybal-Allard	Y	Y	Y	Y	Y
34 Napolitano	Y	Y	Y	Y	Y
35 Waters	Y	Y	?	Y	Y
36 ***Kuykendall***	Y	Y	Y	Y	Y
37 Millender-McD.	Y	Y	Y	Y	Y
38 ***Horn***	Y	Y	Y	Y	Y
39 ***Royce***	Y	Y	Y	Y	Y
40 ***Lewis***	Y	Y	Y	Y	Y
41 ***Miller, Gary***	Y	Y	Y	Y	Y
42 Baca	Y	Y	Y	Y	Y
43 ***Calvert***	Y	Y	Y	Y	Y
44 ***Bono***	Y	Y	Y	Y	Y
45 ***Rohrabacher***	Y	Y	Y	Y	Y
46 Sanchez	Y	Y	Y	Y	Y
47 ***Cox***	Y	Y	Y	Y	Y
48 ***Packard***	Y	Y	Y	Y	Y
49 ***Bilbray***	Y	Y	Y	Y	Y
50 Filner	Y	Y	Y	Y	Y
51 ***Cunningham***	Y	Y	Y	Y	Y
52 ***Hunter***	Y	Y	Y	Y	Y
COLORADO					
1 DeGette	Y	Y	Y	Y	Y
2 Udall	Y	Y	Y	Y	Y
3 ***McInnis***	Y	Y	Y	Y	Y
4 ***Schaffer***	?	?	Y	Y	Y
5 ***Hefley***	Y	Y	Y	Y	Y
6 ***Tancredo***	Y	Y	Y	Y	Y
CONNECTICUT					
1 Larson	Y	Y	Y	Y	Y
2 Gejdenson	Y	Y	Y	Y	Y
3 DeLauro	Y	Y	Y	Y	Y
4 ***Shays***	Y	Y	Y	Y	Y
5 Maloney	Y	Y	Y	Y	Y
6 ***Johnson***	Y	Y	Y	Y	Y
DELAWARE					
AL ***Castle***	Y	Y	Y	Y	Y
FLORIDA					
1 ***Scarborough***	Y	Y	Y	Y	Y
2 Boyd	Y	Y	Y	Y	Y
3 Brown	?	?	Y	Y	Y
4 ***Fowler***	Y	Y	Y	Y	Y
5 Thurman	Y	Y	Y	Y	Y
6 ***Stearns***	Y	Y	Y	Y	Y
7 ***Mica***	Y	Y	Y	Y	Y
8 ***McCollum***	?	?	?	?	?
9 ***Bilirakis***	Y	Y	Y	Y	Y
10 ***Young***	Y	?	Y	Y	Y
11 Davis	Y	Y	Y	Y	Y
12 ***Canady***	Y	Y	Y	Y	Y
13 ***Miller***	Y	Y	Y	Y	Y
14 ***Goss***	Y	Y	Y	Y	Y
15 ***Weldon***	Y	Y	Y	Y	Y
16 ***Foley***	Y	Y	Y	Y	Y
17 Meek	Y	Y	Y	Y	Y
18 ***Ros-Lehtinen***	?	?	Y	Y	Y
19 Wexler	Y	Y	Y	Y	Y
20 Deutsch	Y	Y	Y	Y	Y
21 ***Diaz-Balart***	?	?	Y	Y	Y
22 ***Shaw***	Y	Y	Y	Y	Y
23 Hastings	Y	Y	Y	Y	Y
GEORGIA					
1 ***Kingston***	Y	Y	Y	Y	Y
2 Bishop	Y	Y	Y	Y	Y
3 ***Collins***	Y	Y	Y	Y	Y
4 McKinney	Y	Y	Y	Y	Y
5 Lewis	Y	Y	Y	Y	Y
6 ***Isakson***	Y	Y	Y	Y	Y
7 ***Barr***	Y	Y	Y	Y	Y
8 ***Chambliss***	Y	Y	Y	Y	Y
9 ***Deal***	Y	Y	Y	Y	Y
10 ***Norwood***	?	?	Y	Y	Y
11 ***Linder***	?	?	Y	Y	Y
HAWAII					
1 Abercrombie	Y	Y	Y	Y	Y
2 Mink	Y	Y	Y	Y	Y
IDAHO					
1 ***Chenoweth-Hage***	Y	Y	Y	Y	Y
2 ***Simpson***	Y	Y	Y	Y	Y
ILLINOIS					
1 Rush	?	?	Y	Y	Y
2 Jackson	Y	Y	Y	Y	Y
3 Lipinski	Y	Y	Y	Y	Y
4 Gutierrez	Y	Y	Y	Y	Y
5 Blagojevich	+	+	Y	Y	Y
6 ***Hyde***	Y	Y	Y	Y	Y
7 Davis	Y	Y	Y	Y	Y
8 ***Crane***	Y	Y	Y	Y	Y
9 Schakowsky	Y	Y	Y	Y	Y
10 ***Porter***	+	+	Y	Y	Y
11 ***Weller***	Y	Y	Y	Y	Y
12 Costello	Y	Y	Y	Y	Y
13 ***Biggert***	Y	Y	Y	Y	Y

ND Northern Democrats SD Southern Democrats

	16	17	18	19	20
14 ***Hastert***			Y	Y	
15 ***Ewing***	Y	Y	Y	Y	Y
16 ***Manzullo***	?	?	Y	Y	Y
17 Evans	?	?	Y	Y	Y
18 ***LaHood***	Y	Y	Y	Y	Y
19 Phelps	Y	Y	Y	Y	Y
20 ***Shimkus***	Y	Y	Y	Y	Y
INDIANA					
1 Visclosky	Y	Y	Y	Y	Y
2 ***McIntosh***	Y	Y	Y	Y	Y
3 Roemer	Y	Y	Y	Y	Y
4 ***Souder***	Y	Y	Y	Y	Y
5 ***Buyer***	Y	Y	Y	Y	Y
6 ***Burton***	Y	Y	Y	Y	Y
7 ***Pease***	Y	Y	Y	Y	Y
8 ***Hostettler***	Y	Y	Y	Y	Y
9 Hill	Y	Y	Y	Y	Y
10 Carson	+	+	Y	Y	Y
IOWA					
1 ***Leach***	Y	Y	Y	Y	Y
2 ***Nussle***	Y	Y	Y	Y	Y
3 Boswell	Y	Y	Y	Y	Y
4 ***Ganske***	Y	Y	Y	Y	Y
5 ***Latham***	Y	Y	Y	Y	Y
KANSAS					
1 ***Moran***	Y	Y	Y	Y	Y
2 ***Ryun***	Y	Y	Y	Y	Y
3 Moore	Y	Y	Y	Y	Y
4 ***Tiahrt***	Y	Y	Y	Y	Y
KENTUCKY					
1 ***Whitfield***	Y	Y	Y	Y	Y
2 ***Lewis***	Y	Y	Y	Y	Y
3 ***Northup***	Y	Y	Y	Y	Y
4 Lucas	Y	Y	Y	Y	Y
5 ***Rogers***	Y	Y	Y	Y	Y
6 ***Fletcher***	Y	Y	Y	Y	Y
LOUISIANA					
1 ***Vitter***	Y	Y	Y	Y	Y
2 Jefferson	?	?	Y	Y	Y
3 ***Tauzin***	Y	+	Y	Y	Y
4 ***McCrery***	Y	Y	Y	Y	Y
5 ***Cooksey***	Y	Y	Y	Y	Y
6 ***Baker***	Y	Y	Y	Y	Y
7 John	Y	Y	Y	Y	Y
MAINE					
1 Allen	Y	Y	Y	Y	Y
2 Baldacci	Y	Y	Y	Y	Y
MARYLAND					
1 ***Gilchrest***	Y	Y	Y	Y	Y
2 ***Ehrlich***	?	?	Y	Y	Y
3 Cardin	Y	Y	Y	Y	Y
4 Wynn	Y	Y	Y	Y	Y
5 Hoyer	Y	Y	Y	Y	Y
6 ***Bartlett***	Y	Y	Y	Y	Y
7 Cummings	Y	Y	?	?	Y
8 ***Morella***	Y	Y	Y	Y	Y
MASSACHUSETTS					
1 Olver	Y	Y	Y	Y	Y
2 Neal	?	?	Y	Y	Y
3 McGovern	Y	Y	Y	Y	Y
4 Frank	Y	Y	Y	Y	Y
5 Meehan	Y	Y	Y	Y	Y
6 Tierney	Y	Y	Y	Y	Y
7 Markey	Y	Y	Y	Y	Y
8 Capuano	Y	Y	Y	Y	Y
9 Moakley	?	?	?	?	Y
10 Delahunt	Y	Y	Y	Y	Y
MICHIGAN					
1 Stupak	?	?	Y	Y	Y
2 ***Hoekstra***	Y	Y	Y	Y	Y
3 ***Ehlers***	Y	Y	Y	Y	Y
4 ***Camp***	Y	Y	Y	Y	Y
5 Barcia	Y	Y	Y	Y	Y
6 ***Upton***	Y	Y	Y	Y	Y
7 ***Smith***	Y	Y	Y	Y	Y
8 Stabenow	Y	Y	Y	Y	Y
9 Kildee	Y	Y	Y	Y	Y
10 Bonior	?	?	?	?	?
11 ***Knollenberg***	Y	Y	Y	Y	Y
12 Levin	Y	Y	Y	Y	Y
13 Rivers	Y	Y	Y	Y	Y
14 Conyers	Y	Y	Y	Y	Y
15 Kilpatrick	+	+	Y	Y	Y
16 Dingell	Y	Y	Y	Y	Y
MINNESOTA					
1 ***Gutknecht***	Y	Y	Y	Y	Y
2 Minge	Y	Y	Y	Y	Y
3 ***Ramstad***	Y	Y	Y	Y	Y
4 Vento	?	?	?	?	?
5 Sabo	Y	Y	Y	Y	Y
6 Luther	Y	Y	Y	Y	Y
7 Peterson	Y	Y	Y	Y	Y
8 Oberstar	Y	Y	Y	Y	Y
MISSISSIPPI					
1 ***Wicker***	Y	Y	Y	Y	Y
2 Thompson	Y	Y	Y	Y	Y
3 ***Pickering***	Y	Y	Y	Y	Y
4 Shows	Y	Y	Y	Y	Y
5 Taylor	Y	Y	Y	?	Y
MISSOURI					
1 Clay	?	?	?	?	?
2 ***Talent***	Y	Y	Y	Y	Y
3 Gephardt	Y	Y	Y	Y	?
4 Skelton	Y	Y	Y	Y	Y
5 McCarthy	Y	Y	Y	Y	Y
6 Danner	Y	Y	Y	Y	Y
7 ***Blunt***	Y	Y	Y	Y	Y
8 ***Emerson***	?	?	Y	Y	Y
9 ***Hulshof***	Y	Y	Y	Y	Y
MONTANA					
AL ***Hill***	Y	Y	Y	Y	Y
NEBRASKA					
1 ***Bereuter***	Y	Y	Y	Y	Y
2 ***Terry***	Y	Y	Y	Y	Y
3 ***Barrett***	Y	Y	Y	Y	Y
NEVADA					
1 Berkley	Y	Y	Y	Y	Y
2 ***Gibbons***	?	?	Y	Y	Y
NEW HAMPSHIRE					
1 ***Sununu***	?	?	Y	Y	Y
2 ***Bass***	Y	Y	Y	Y	Y
NEW JERSEY					
1 Andrews	Y	Y	Y	Y	Y
2 ***LoBiondo***	Y	Y	Y	Y	Y
3 ***Saxton***	?	?	Y	Y	Y
4 ***Smith***	Y	Y	Y	Y	Y
5 ***Roukema***	Y	Y	Y	Y	Y
6 Pallone	Y	Y	Y	Y	Y
7 ***Franks***	Y	Y	Y	Y	Y
8 Pascrell	Y	Y	Y	Y	Y
9 Rothman	Y	Y	Y	Y	Y
10 Payne	?	?	Y	Y	Y
11 ***Frelinghuysen***	Y	Y	Y	Y	Y
12 Holt	Y	Y	Y	Y	Y
13 Menendez	Y	Y	Y	Y	Y
NEW MEXICO					
1 ***Wilson***	Y	Y	Y	Y	Y
2 ***Skeen***	Y	Y	Y	Y	Y
3 Udall	Y	Y	Y	Y	Y
NEW YORK					
1 Forbes	Y	Y	Y	Y	Y
2 ***Lazio***	Y	Y	Y	Y	Y
3 ***King***	Y	Y	Y	Y	Y
4 McCarthy	Y	Y	Y	Y	Y
5 Ackerman	Y	Y	Y	Y	Y
6 Meeks	Y	Y	Y	Y	Y
7 Crowley	Y	Y	Y	Y	Y
8 Nadler	Y	Y	Y	Y	Y
9 Weiner	Y	Y	Y	Y	Y
10 Towns	Y	Y	Y	Y	Y
11 Owens	+	+	Y	Y	Y
12 Velázquez	Y	Y	Y	Y	Y
13 ***Fossella***	Y	Y	Y	Y	Y
14 Maloney	Y	Y	Y	Y	Y
15 Rangel	Y	Y	Y	Y	Y
16 Serrano	Y	Y	Y	Y	Y
17 Engel	Y	Y	Y	Y	Y
18 Lowey	?	?	?	?	?
19 ***Kelly***	Y	Y	Y	Y	Y
20 ***Gilman***	Y	Y	Y	Y	Y
21 McNulty	Y	Y	Y	Y	Y
22 ***Sweeney***	Y	Y	Y	Y	Y
23 ***Boehlert***	Y	Y	Y	Y	Y
24 ***McHugh***	Y	Y	Y	Y	Y
25 ***Walsh***	Y	Y	Y	Y	Y
26 Hinchey	Y	Y	Y	?	Y
27 ***Reynolds***	Y	Y	Y	Y	Y
28 Slaughter	Y	Y	Y	Y	Y
29 LaFalce	Y	Y	Y	Y	Y
30 ***Quinn***	Y	Y	Y	Y	Y
31 ***Houghton***	Y	Y	Y	Y	Y
NORTH CAROLINA					
1 Clayton	Y	Y	Y	Y	Y
2 Etheridge	Y	Y	Y	Y	Y
3 ***Jones***	Y	Y	Y	Y	Y
4 Price	Y	Y	Y	Y	Y
5 ***Burr***	Y	Y	Y	Y	Y
6 ***Coble***	Y	Y	Y	Y	Y
7 McIntyre	Y	Y	Y	Y	Y
8 ***Hayes***	Y	Y	Y	Y	Y
9 ***Myrick***	Y	Y	Y	Y	Y
10 ***Ballenger***	Y	Y	Y	Y	Y
11 ***Taylor***	Y	Y	Y	Y	Y
12 Watt	Y	Y	Y	Y	Y
NORTH DAKOTA					
AL Pomeroy	Y	Y	Y	Y	Y
OHIO					
1 ***Chabot***	Y	Y	Y	Y	Y
2 ***Portman***	Y	Y	Y	Y	Y
3 Hall	Y	Y	Y	Y	Y
4 ***Oxley***	?	?	Y	Y	Y
5 ***Gillmor***	Y	Y	Y	Y	Y
6 Strickland	Y	Y	Y	Y	Y
7 ***Hobson***	Y	Y	Y	Y	Y
8 ***Boehner***	Y	Y	Y	Y	Y
9 Kaptur	Y	Y	Y	Y	Y
10 Kucinich	Y	Y	Y	Y	Y
11 Jones	?	?	Y	Y	Y
12 ***Kasich***	?	?	?	?	?
13 Brown	?	?	?	?	?
14 Sawyer	Y	Y	Y	Y	Y
15 ***Pryce***	?	?	Y	Y	Y
16 ***Regula***	Y	Y	Y	Y	Y
17 Traficant	Y	Y	Y	Y	Y
18 ***Ney***	Y	Y	Y	?	Y
19 ***LaTourette***	Y	Y	?	Y	Y
OKLAHOMA					
1 ***Largent***	Y	Y	Y	Y	Y
2 ***Coburn***	?	?	Y	Y	Y
3 ***Watkins***	Y	Y	Y	Y	Y
4 ***Watts***	Y	Y	Y	Y	Y
5 ***Istook***	Y	Y	Y	Y	Y
6 ***Lucas***	Y	Y	Y	Y	Y
OREGON					
1 Wu	Y	Y	Y	Y	Y
2 ***Walden***	Y	Y	Y	Y	Y
3 Blumenauer	Y	Y	Y	Y	Y
4 DeFazio	?	?	?	?	?
5 Hooley	Y	Y	Y	Y	Y
PENNSYLVANIA					
1 Brady	?	?	Y	Y	Y
2 Fattah	Y	Y	Y	Y	Y
3 Borski	Y	Y	Y	Y	Y
4 Klink	?	?	Y	Y	Y
5 ***Peterson***	Y	Y	Y	Y	Y
6 Holden	Y	Y	Y	Y	Y
7 ***Weldon***	Y	Y	Y	Y	Y
8 ***Greenwood***	Y	Y	Y	Y	Y
9 ***Shuster***	Y	Y	Y	Y	Y
10 ***Sherwood***	Y	Y	Y	Y	Y
11 Kanjorski	Y	Y	Y	Y	Y
12 Murtha	Y	Y	Y	Y	Y
13 Hoeffel	Y	Y	Y	Y	Y
14 Coyne	Y	Y	Y	Y	Y
15 ***Toomey***	Y	Y	Y	Y	Y
16 ***Pitts***	Y	Y	Y	Y	Y
17 ***Gekas***	Y	Y	Y	Y	Y
18 Doyle	Y	Y	Y	Y	Y
19 ***Goodling***	Y	Y	Y	Y	Y
20 Mascara	Y	Y	Y	Y	Y
21 ***English***	Y	Y	Y	Y	Y
RHODE ISLAND					
1 Kennedy	+	+	Y	Y	Y
2 Weygand	Y	Y	Y	Y	Y
SOUTH CAROLINA					
1 ***Sanford***	Y	Y	Y	Y	?
2 ***Spence***	Y	Y	Y	Y	Y
3 ***Graham***	?	?	?	?	?
4 ***DeMint***	Y	Y	Y	Y	Y
5 Spratt	Y	Y	Y	Y	Y
6 Clyburn	Y	Y	Y	Y	Y
SOUTH DAKOTA					
AL ***Thune***	Y	Y	Y	Y	Y
TENNESSEE					
1 ***Jenkins***	Y	Y	Y	Y	Y
2 ***Duncan***	Y	Y	Y	Y	Y
3 ***Wamp***	Y	Y	Y	Y	Y
4 ***Hilleary***	Y	Y	Y	Y	Y
5 Clement	Y	Y	Y	Y	Y
6 Gordon	Y	Y	Y	Y	Y
7 ***Bryant***	Y	Y	Y	Y	Y
8 Tanner	Y	Y	Y	Y	Y
9 Ford	Y	Y	Y	Y	Y
TEXAS					
1 Sandlin	Y	Y	Y	Y	Y
2 Turner	Y	Y	Y	Y	Y
3 ***Johnson, Sam***	Y	Y	Y	Y	Y
4 Hall	Y	Y	Y	Y	Y
5 ***Sessions***	Y	Y	Y	Y	Y
6 ***Barton***	Y	Y	Y	Y	Y
7 ***Archer***	Y	Y	Y	?	Y
8 ***Brady***	Y	Y	Y	Y	Y
9 Lampson	?	?	Y	Y	Y
10 Doggett	Y	Y	Y	Y	Y
11 Edwards	?	?	Y	Y	Y
12 ***Granger***	?	?	Y	Y	Y
13 ***Thornberry***	Y	Y	Y	Y	Y
14 ***Paul***	Y	Y	N	N	N
15 Hinojosa	+	+	+	+	+
16 Reyes	Y	Y	Y	Y	Y
17 Stenholm	Y	Y	Y	Y	Y
18 Jackson-Lee	Y	Y	Y	Y	Y
19 ***Combest***	Y	Y	Y	Y	Y
20 Gonzalez	Y	Y	Y	Y	Y
21 ***Smith***	Y	Y	Y	Y	Y
22 ***DeLay***	Y	Y	Y	Y	Y
23 ***Bonilla***	?	?	Y	Y	Y
24 Frost	?	?	Y	Y	Y
25 Bentsen	Y	Y	Y	Y	Y
26 ***Armey***	Y	Y	Y	Y	Y
27 Ortiz	Y	Y	Y	Y	Y
28 Rodriguez	Y	Y	Y	Y	Y
29 Green	Y	Y	Y	Y	Y
30 Johnson, E.B.	Y	Y	Y	Y	Y
UTAH					
1 ***Hansen***	Y	Y	Y	Y	Y
2 ***Cook***	Y	Y	Y	Y	Y
3 ***Cannon***	Y	Y	Y	Y	Y
VERMONT					
AL *Sanders*	Y	Y	Y	Y	Y
VIRGINIA					
1 ***Bateman***	Y	Y	Y	Y	Y
2 Pickett	Y	Y	Y	Y	Y
3 Scott	Y	Y	Y	Y	Y
4 Sisisky	Y	Y	Y	Y	Y
5 *Goode*	Y	Y	Y	Y	Y
6 ***Goodlatte***	Y	Y	Y	Y	Y
7 ***Bliley***	Y	Y	Y	Y	Y
8 Moran	Y	Y	Y	Y	Y
9 Boucher	Y	Y	Y	Y	Y
10 ***Wolf***	Y	Y	Y	Y	Y
11 ***Davis***	Y	Y	Y	Y	Y
WASHINGTON					
1 Inslee	Y	Y	Y	Y	Y
2 ***Metcalf***	Y	Y	Y	?	Y
3 Baird	?	?	?	?	?
4 ***Hastings***	Y	Y	Y	Y	Y
5 ***Nethercutt***	Y	Y	Y	Y	Y
6 Dicks	Y	Y	Y	Y	Y
7 McDermott	Y	Y	Y	Y	Y
8 ***Dunn***	Y	Y	Y	Y	Y
9 Smith	Y	Y	Y	Y	Y
WEST VIRGINIA					
1 Mollohan	Y	Y	?	?	Y
2 Wise	?	?	Y	Y	Y
3 Rahall	Y	Y	Y	Y	Y
WISCONSIN					
1 ***Ryan***	Y	Y	Y	Y	Y
2 Baldwin	Y	Y	Y	Y	Y
3 Kind	Y	Y	Y	Y	Y
4 Kleczka	Y	Y	Y	Y	Y
5 Barrett	Y	Y	Y	Y	Y
6 ***Petri***	Y	Y	Y	Y	Y
7 Obey	Y	Y	Y	Y	Y
8 ***Green***	Y	Y	Y	Y	+
9 ***Sensenbrenner***	Y	Y	Y	Y	Y
WYOMING					
AL ***Cubin***	Y	Y	Y	Y	Y

Southern states - Ala., Ark., Fla., Ga., Ky., La., Miss., N.C., Okla., S.C., Tenn., Texas, Va.

21. Procedural Motion/Journal. Approval of the House Journal of Feb. 14, 2000. Approved 375-33: R 194-16; D 179-17 (ND 133-12, SD 46-5); I 2-0. Feb. 15, 2000.

22. Procedural Motion/Journal. Approval of the House Journal of Feb. 15, 2000. Approved 354-46: R 191-15; D 161-31 (ND 117-23, SD 44-8); I 2-0. Feb. 16, 2000.

23. HR 2366. Product Liability/Rule. Adoption of the rule (H Res 423) to provide for House floor consideration of the bill to place new limits on punitive damages against small businesses and curb product liability claims against retailers. Adopted 223-187: R 211-1; D 11-185 (ND 4-142, SD 7-43); I 1-1. Feb. 16, 2000.

24. HR 2366. Product Liability/Small Business. Conyers, D-Mich., amendment to change the bill's definition of "small business" to businesses that have fewer than 25 full-time employees and that had revenues of $5 million or less in each of the previous two years. It also would restrict the bill's provisions to product liability cases. Rejected 178-237: R 4-209; D 173-27 (ND 137-11, SD 36-16); I 1-1. Feb. 16, 2000.

25. HR 2366. Product Liability/Passage. Passage of the bill to cap punitive damages against small businesses, defined as those with fewer than 25 full-time employees, at $250,000 or three times the economic and non-economic award (such as pain and suffering), whichever is less. The bill, as amended, would allow the cap to be broken if a court ruled that a business intentionally acted to cause harm. The bill would also curb product liability claims against retailers. Passed 221-193: R 197-17; D 23-175 (ND 10-136, SD 13-39); I 1-1. Feb. 16, 2000. A "nay" was a vote in support of the president's position.

Key

- Y Voted for (yea).
- # Paired for.
- + Announced for.
- N Voted against (nay).
- X Paired against.
- – Announced against.
- P Voted "present."
- C Voted "present" to avoid possible conflict of interest.
- ? Did not vote or otherwise make a position known.

•

Democrats ***Republicans***
Independents

	21	22	23	24	25
ALABAMA					
1 ***Callahan***	?	?	?	?	?
2 ***Everett***	Y	Y	Y	?	?
3 ***Riley***	Y	Y	Y	N	Y
4 ***Aderholt***	Y	N	Y	N	Y
5 Cramer	Y	Y	Y	N	Y
6 ***Bachus***	Y	Y	Y	N	Y
7 Hilliard	N	N	N	Y	N
ALASKA					
AL ***Young***	Y	?	Y	N	Y
ARIZONA					
1 ***Salmon***	Y	Y	Y	N	Y
2 Pastor	Y	Y	N	Y	N
3 ***Stump***	Y	Y	Y	N	Y
4 ***Shadegg***	Y	Y	Y	N	N
5 ***Kolbe***	Y	Y	Y	N	Y
6 ***Hayworth***	Y	Y	Y	N	Y
ARKANSAS					
1 Berry	Y	Y	N	N	N
2 Snyder	Y	?	?	?	?
3 ***Hutchinson***	Y	?	Y	N	Y
4 ***Dickey***	N	Y	Y	N	Y
CALIFORNIA					
1 Thompson	N	N	N	Y	N
2 ***Herger***	Y	Y	Y	N	Y
3 ***Ose***	Y	Y	Y	N	Y
4 ***Doolittle***	Y	Y	Y	N	N
5 Matsui	Y	Y	N	Y	N
6 Woolsey	Y	Y	N	Y	N
7 Miller, George	Y	Y	N	Y	N
8 Pelosi	?	Y	N	Y	N
9 Lee	Y	Y	N	Y	N
10 Tauscher	Y	Y	N	Y	N
11 ***Pombo***	Y	Y	Y	N	Y
12 Lantos	Y	Y	N	Y	N
13 Stark	Y	Y	N	Y	N
14 Eshoo	Y	Y	N	Y	N
15 ***Campbell***	+	?	?	?	?
16 Lofgren	Y	Y	N	Y	N
17 Farr	Y	Y	N	Y	N
18 Condit	Y	Y	Y	N	Y
19 ***Radanovich***	?	Y	Y	N	Y
20 Dooley	Y	Y	N	N	Y
21 ***Thomas***	Y	Y	Y	N	Y
22 Capps	+	+	–	+	–
23 ***Gallegly***	Y	Y	Y	N	Y
24 Sherman	Y	Y	N	Y	N
25 ***McKeon***	Y	Y	Y	N	Y
26 Berman	Y	Y	N	Y	N
27 ***Rogan***	N	N	Y	N	Y
28 ***Dreier***	Y	Y	Y	N	Y
29 Waxman	Y	Y	N	Y	N
30 Becerra	Y	Y	N	Y	N
31 Martinez	Y	?	?	?	?
32 Dixon	Y	Y	N	Y	N
33 Roybal-Allard	Y	Y	N	Y	N
34 Napolitano	Y	Y	N	Y	N
35 Waters	N	N	N	Y	N
36 ***Kuykendall***	Y	Y	Y	N	Y
37 Millender-McD.	Y	Y	N	Y	N
38 ***Horn***	Y	Y	Y	N	Y
39 ***Royce***	Y	?	Y	N	Y
40 ***Lewis***	Y	Y	Y	N	Y
41 ***Miller, Gary***	Y	Y	Y	N	Y
42 Baca	Y	Y	N	N	N
43 ***Calvert***	Y	Y	Y	N	Y
44 ***Bono***	Y	Y	Y	N	Y
45 ***Rohrabacher***	Y	Y	Y	N	Y
46 Sanchez	Y	Y	N	Y	N
47 ***Cox***	Y	Y	Y	N	Y
48 ***Packard***	Y	Y	Y	N	Y
49 ***Bilbray***	N	N	Y	N	Y
50 Filner	N	N	N	Y	N
51 ***Cunningham***	Y	Y	Y	N	Y
52 ***Hunter***	Y	Y	Y	N	N
COLORADO					
1 DeGette	Y	Y	N	Y	N
2 Udall	Y	N	N	Y	N
3 ***McInnis***	Y	Y	Y	N	Y
4 ***Schaffer***	N	N	Y	N	Y
5 ***Hefley***	N	N	Y	N	Y
6 ***Tancredo***	P	Y	Y	N	Y
CONNECTICUT					
1 Larson	Y	Y	N	Y	N
2 Gejdenson	Y	?	N	Y	N
3 DeLauro	Y	Y	N	Y	N
4 ***Shays***	Y	Y	Y	N	Y
5 Maloney	Y	Y	N	Y	N
6 ***Johnson***	Y	Y	Y	N	Y
DELAWARE					
AL ***Castle***	Y	Y	Y	N	Y
FLORIDA					
1 ***Scarborough***	Y	Y	Y	N	Y
2 Boyd	Y	Y	Y	N	Y
3 Brown	Y	Y	N	Y	N
4 ***Fowler***	Y	Y	Y	N	Y
5 Thurman	Y	Y	N	Y	N
6 ***Stearns***	Y	Y	Y	N	Y
7 ***Mica***	Y	Y	Y	N	Y
8 ***McCollum***	?	?	?	?	?
9 ***Bilirakis***	Y	Y	Y	N	Y
10 ***Young***	Y	Y	Y	N	Y
11 Davis	Y	Y	N	Y	N
12 ***Canady***	Y	Y	Y	N	Y
13 ***Miller***	Y	Y	Y	N	Y
14 ***Goss***	Y	Y	Y	N	Y
15 ***Weldon***	Y	Y	Y	N	Y
16 ***Foley***	Y	Y	Y	N	Y
17 Meek	Y	Y	N	Y	N
18 ***Ros-Lehtinen***	Y	Y	Y	N	Y
19 Wexler	Y	Y	N	Y	N
20 Deutsch	Y	Y	N	Y	N
21 ***Diaz-Balart***	Y	Y	Y	N	N
22 ***Shaw***	Y	Y	Y	N	Y
23 Hastings	N	Y	N	Y	N
GEORGIA					
1 ***Kingston***	Y	Y	Y	N	Y
2 Bishop	Y	?	?	?	?
3 ***Collins***	Y	Y	Y	N	Y
4 McKinney	?	Y	N	Y	N
5 Lewis	Y	Y	N	Y	N
6 ***Isakson***	Y	Y	Y	N	Y
7 ***Barr***	Y	Y	Y	N	Y
8 ***Chambliss***	Y	Y	Y	N	Y
9 ***Deal***	Y	Y	Y	N	Y
10 ***Norwood***	Y	Y	Y	N	Y
11 ***Linder***	Y	Y	Y	N	Y
HAWAII					
1 Abercrombie	Y	Y	N	Y	N
2 Mink	Y	Y	N	Y	N
IDAHO					
1 ***Chenoweth-Hage***	Y	?	Y	N	Y
2 ***Simpson***	Y	Y	Y	N	Y
ILLINOIS					
1 Rush	Y	Y	N	Y	N
2 Jackson	Y	Y	N	Y	N
3 Lipinski	Y	Y	N	Y	N
4 Gutierrez	Y	N	?	Y	?
5 Blagojevich	Y	Y	N	Y	N
6 ***Hyde***	Y	Y	Y	N	Y
7 Davis	Y	Y	N	Y	N
8 ***Crane***	Y	N	Y	N	Y
9 Schakowsky	Y	Y	N	Y	N
10 ***Porter***	Y	Y	Y	N	Y
11 ***Weller***	N	N	Y	N	Y
12 Costello	N	N	N	Y	N
13 ***Biggert***	Y	Y	Y	N	Y

ND Northern Democrats SD Southern Democrats

	21	22	23	24	25
14 ***Hastert***					
15 ***Ewing***	Y	Y	Y	N	Y
16 ***Manzullo***	Y	Y	Y	N	Y
17 Evans	Y	Y	N	Y	N
18 ***LaHood***	Y	Y	Y	N	Y
19 Phelps	Y	Y	N	Y	N
20 ***Shimkus***	Y	Y	Y	N	Y
INDIANA					
1 Visclosky	N	N	N	Y	N
2 ***McIntosh***	Y	Y	Y	N	Y
3 Roemer	Y	Y	Y	N	Y
4 ***Souder***	Y	Y	Y	N	Y
5 ***Buyer***	Y	Y	Y	N	Y
6 ***Burton***	Y	Y	Y	N	Y
7 ***Pease***	Y	Y	Y	N	Y
8 ***Hostettler***	Y	Y	Y	N	Y
9 Hill	Y	Y	N	Y	N
10 Carson	P	Y	N	Y	N
IOWA					
1 ***Leach***	Y	Y	Y	N	Y
2 ***Nussle***	Y	Y	Y	N	Y
3 Boswell	Y	Y	N	Y	N
4 ***Ganske***	Y	Y	Y	N	Y
5 ***Latham***	Y	Y	Y	N	Y
KANSAS					
1 ***Moran***	Y	Y	Y	N	Y
2 ***Ryun***	Y	Y	Y	N	Y
3 Moore	Y	N	N	Y	N
4 ***Tiahrt***	Y	+	+	N	Y
KENTUCKY					
1 ***Whitfield***	Y	Y	Y	N	Y
2 ***Lewis***	Y	Y	Y	N	Y
3 ***Northup***	Y	Y	Y	N	Y
4 Lucas	Y	Y	Y	N	Y
5 ***Rogers***	Y	Y	Y	N	Y
6 ***Fletcher***	Y	Y	Y	N	Y
LOUISIANA					
1 ***Vitter***	Y	Y	Y	N	Y
2 Jefferson	Y	Y	N	Y	N
3 ***Tauzin***	Y	Y	Y	N	Y
4 ***McCrery***	Y	Y	Y	N	Y
5 ***Cooksey***	Y	?	?	?	?
6 ***Baker***	Y	Y	Y	N	Y
7 John	Y	Y	N	N	Y
MAINE					
1 Allen	Y	Y	N	Y	N
2 Baldacci	Y	?	?	?	?
MARYLAND					
1 ***Gilchrest***	Y	Y	Y	N	Y
2 ***Ehrlich***	Y	Y	Y	N	N
3 Cardin	Y	Y	N	Y	N
4 Wynn	Y	Y	N	Y	N
5 Hoyer	Y	Y	N	Y	N
6 ***Bartlett***	Y	Y	Y	N	Y
7 Cummings	Y	Y	N	Y	N
8 ***Morella***	Y	Y	N	Y	N
MASSACHUSETTS					
1 Olver	Y	Y	N	Y	N
2 Neal	Y	Y	N	Y	N
3 McGovern	Y	Y	N	Y	N
4 Frank	Y	Y	N	Y	Y
5 Meehan	Y	Y	N	Y	N
6 Tierney	Y	?	N	Y	N
7 Markey	Y	Y	N	Y	N
8 Capuano	Y	Y	N	Y	N
9 Moakley	Y	Y	N	Y	N
10 Delahunt	Y	Y	N	Y	N
MICHIGAN					
1 Stupak	Y	Y	N	Y	N
2 ***Hoekstra***	Y	Y	Y	N	Y
3 ***Ehlers***	Y	Y	Y	N	Y
4 ***Camp***	Y	Y	Y	N	Y
5 Barcia	Y	Y	N	N	Y
6 ***Upton***	Y	Y	Y	N	Y
7 ***Smith***	Y	Y	Y	N	Y
8 Stabenow	Y	Y	N	Y	N
9 Kildee	Y	Y	N	Y	N
10 Bonior	?	Y	N	Y	N
11 ***Knollenberg***	Y	Y	Y	N	Y
12 Levin	Y	Y	N	Y	N
13 Rivers	Y	Y	N	Y	N
14 Conyers	Y	Y	N	Y	N
15 Kilpatrick	Y	Y	N	Y	N
16 Dingell	Y	Y	N	Y	N

	21	22	23	24	25
MINNESOTA					
1 ***Gutknecht***	N	N	Y	N	Y
2 Minge	Y	Y	N	Y	N
3 ***Ramstad***	N	N	Y	N	Y
4 Vento	?	?	?	?	?
5 Sabo	N	N	N	Y	N
6 Luther	Y	Y	N	Y	N
7 Peterson	N	N	Y	N	Y
8 Oberstar	Y	N	N	Y	?
MISSISSIPPI					
1 ***Wicker***	N	Y	Y	N	Y
2 Thompson	N	N	N	Y	N
3 ***Pickering***	Y	Y	Y	N	Y
4 Shows	Y	Y	N	N	N
5 Taylor	Y	N	Y	N	Y
MISSOURI					
1 Clay	?	?	?	?	?
2 ***Talent***	Y	Y	Y	N	Y
3 Gephardt	?	?	N	Y	N
4 Skelton	Y	Y	N	N	N
5 McCarthy	Y	Y	N	Y	N
6 Danner	Y	?	N	N	Y
7 ***Blunt***	?	Y	Y	N	Y
8 ***Emerson***	Y	Y	Y	N	Y
9 ***Hulshof***	Y	N	Y	N	Y
MONTANA					
AL ***Hill***	Y	N	Y	N	Y
NEBRASKA					
1 ***Bereuter***	Y	Y	Y	N	Y
2 ***Terry***	Y	Y	Y	N	N
3 ***Barrett***	Y	Y	Y	N	Y
NEVADA					
1 Berkley	Y	Y	N	Y	N
2 ***Gibbons***	N	N	Y	N	Y
NEW HAMPSHIRE					
1 ***Sununu***	Y	Y	Y	N	N
2 ***Bass***	Y	Y	Y	N	Y
NEW JERSEY					
1 Andrews	Y	Y	N	Y	N
2 ***LoBiondo***	N	N	Y	N	Y
3 ***Saxton***	Y	Y	Y	N	Y
4 ***Smith***	Y	Y	?	N	Y
5 ***Roukema***	Y	Y	Y	N	Y
6 Pallone	Y	Y	N	Y	N
7 ***Franks***	Y	Y	Y	N	Y
8 Pascrell	?	Y	N	Y	N
9 Rothman	Y	Y	N	Y	N
10 Payne	Y	Y	N	Y	N
11 ***Frelinghuysen***	Y	Y	Y	N	Y
12 Holt	Y	Y	N	Y	N
13 Menendez	Y	Y	N	Y	N
NEW MEXICO					
1 ***Wilson***	Y	Y	Y	N	Y
2 ***Skeen***	Y	Y	Y	N	Y
3 Udall	N	N	N	Y	N
NEW YORK					
1 Forbes	Y	Y	N	N	N
2 ***Lazio***	Y	Y	Y	Y	Y
3 ***King***	Y	Y	Y	N	N
4 McCarthy	Y	Y	N	Y	N
5 Ackerman	Y	Y	N	Y	N
6 Meeks	Y	N	N	Y	N
7 Crowley	Y	Y	N	Y	N
8 Nadler	Y	Y	N	Y	N
9 Weiner	Y	Y	N	Y	N
10 Towns	Y	Y	N	Y	N
11 Owens	Y	?	N	Y	N
12 Velázquez	Y	Y	N	Y	N
13 ***Fossella***	Y	?	Y	N	Y
14 Maloney	Y	Y	N	Y	N
15 Rangel	Y	Y	N	Y	N
16 Serrano	Y	Y	N	Y	N
17 Engel	Y	Y	N	Y	N
18 Lowey	?	?	?	?	?
19 ***Kelly***	Y	Y	Y	N	Y
20 ***Gilman***	Y	Y	Y	Y	N
21 McNulty	Y	N	N	N	Y
22 ***Sweeney***	N	Y	Y	N	Y
23 ***Boehlert***	Y	Y	Y	N	Y
24 ***McHugh***	Y	Y	Y	N	Y
25 ***Walsh***	Y	Y	Y	N	Y
26 Hinchey	Y	Y	N	Y	N
27 ***Reynolds***	Y	Y	Y	N	Y
28 Slaughter	Y	N	N	Y	N
29 LaFalce	Y	N	N	Y	N

	21	22	23	24	25
30 ***Quinn***	Y	Y	Y	N	Y
31 ***Houghton***	Y	Y	Y	N	Y
NORTH CAROLINA					
1 Clayton	Y	Y	N	Y	N
2 Etheridge	Y	N	N	N	N
3 ***Jones***	Y	Y	Y	N	Y
4 Price	Y	Y	N	Y	N
5 ***Burr***	Y	Y	Y	N	Y
6 ***Coble***	Y	Y	Y	N	N
7 McIntyre	Y	Y	?	Y	N
8 ***Hayes***	Y	Y	Y	N	Y
9 ***Myrick***	Y	?	?	N	Y
10 ***Ballenger***	Y	Y	Y	N	Y
11 ***Taylor***	N	Y	Y	N	Y
12 Watt	Y	Y	N	Y	N
NORTH DAKOTA					
AL Pomeroy	Y	Y	N	Y	N
OHIO					
1 ***Chabot***	Y	Y	Y	N	Y
2 ***Portman***	Y	Y	Y	N	Y
3 Hall	Y	Y	N	Y	Y
4 ***Oxley***	?	Y	Y	N	Y
5 ***Gillmor***	Y	N	Y	N	Y
6 Strickland	N	N	N	Y	N
7 ***Hobson***	Y	Y	Y	N	Y
8 ***Boehner***	Y	?	Y	N	Y
9 Kaptur	Y	Y	N	Y	N
10 Kucinich	Y	N	N	Y	N
11 Jones	Y	?	N	Y	N
12 ***Kasich***	?	Y	Y	N	Y
13 Brown	?	?	?	?	?
14 Sawyer	Y	Y	N	Y	N
15 ***Pryce***	Y	Y	Y	N	Y
16 ***Regula***	Y	Y	Y	N	Y
17 Traficant	Y	Y	Y	Y	N
18 ***Ney***	Y	Y	Y	N	Y
19 ***LaTourette***	Y	Y	Y	N	Y
OKLAHOMA					
1 ***Largent***	Y	Y	Y	N	Y
2 ***Coburn***	N	Y	Y	N	N
3 ***Watkins***	Y	Y	Y	N	Y
4 ***Watts***	Y	Y	Y	?	Y
5 ***Istook***	Y	Y	Y	N	N
6 ***Lucas***	Y	Y	Y	N	Y
OREGON					
1 Wu	Y	N	N	Y	N
2 ***Walden***	Y	Y	Y	N	Y
3 Blumenauer	Y	Y	N	Y	N
4 DeFazio	?	?	?	?	?
5 Hooley	Y	Y	N	Y	N
PENNSYLVANIA					
1 Brady	N	N	N	Y	N
2 Fattah	Y	Y	N	Y	N
3 Borski	N	N	N	Y	N
4 Klink	Y	N	N	Y	N
5 ***Peterson***	Y	Y	Y	N	Y
6 Holden	Y	Y	N	N	Y
7 ***Weldon***	Y	Y	Y	N	Y
8 ***Greenwood***	Y	Y	Y	N	Y
9 ***Shuster***	Y	Y	Y	N	Y
10 ***Sherwood***	Y	Y	Y	N	Y
11 Kanjorski	Y	Y	N	Y	N
12 Murtha	Y	Y	N	Y	N
13 Hoeffel	Y	Y	N	Y	N
14 Coyne	Y	Y	N	Y	N
15 ***Toomey***	Y	Y	Y	N	N
16 ***Pitts***	Y	Y	Y	N	Y
17 ***Gekas***	Y	Y	Y	N	Y
18 Doyle	Y	?	N	Y	N
19 ***Goodling***	Y	Y	Y	N	Y
20 Mascara	Y	Y	N	Y	N
21 ***English***	N	N	Y	Y	N
RHODE ISLAND					
1 Kennedy	Y	Y	N	Y	N
2 Weygand	Y	?	?	Y	N
SOUTH CAROLINA					
1 ***Sanford***	?	?	?	?	?
2 ***Spence***	Y	Y	Y	N	Y
3 ***Graham***	?	?	?	?	?
4 ***DeMint***	Y	Y	Y	N	Y
5 Spratt	Y	Y	N	Y	N
6 Clyburn	Y	N	N	Y	N
SOUTH DAKOTA					
AL ***Thune***	Y	Y	Y	N	Y

	21	22	23	24	25
TENNESSEE					
1 ***Jenkins***	Y	Y	Y	N	Y
2 ***Duncan***	Y	Y	Y	Y	Y
3 ***Wamp***	Y	Y	Y	N	Y
4 ***Hilleary***	N	Y	Y	N	Y
5 Clement	Y	Y	N	N	Y
6 Gordon	Y	Y	N	N	Y
7 ***Bryant***	Y	Y	Y	N	Y
8 Tanner	Y	Y	N	N	Y
9 Ford	N	N	N	Y	Y
TEXAS					
1 Sandlin	Y	Y	N	Y	N
2 Turner	Y	Y	N	Y	N
3 ***Johnson, Sam***	Y	Y	Y	N	Y
4 Hall	?	Y	N	N	Y
5 ***Sessions***	Y	Y	Y	N	Y
6 ***Barton***	Y	?	Y	N	Y
7 ***Archer***	Y	Y	Y	N	Y
8 ***Brady***	Y	Y	Y	N	Y
9 Lampson	Y	Y	N	Y	N
10 Doggett	Y	Y	N	Y	N
11 Edwards	Y	Y	N	Y	N
12 ***Granger***	Y	Y	Y	N	Y
13 ***Thornberry***	Y	Y	Y	N	Y
14 ***Paul***	Y	Y	Y	N	N
15 Hinojosa	+	Y	N	Y	N
16 Reyes	Y	Y	N	Y	N
17 Stenholm	Y	N	Y	N	Y
18 Jackson-Lee	Y	Y	N	Y	N
19 ***Combest***	Y	Y	Y	N	Y
20 Gonzalez	Y	Y	N	Y	N
21 ***Smith***	Y	Y	Y	N	Y
22 ***DeLay***	Y	Y	Y	N	Y
23 ***Bonilla***	Y	Y	Y	N	Y
24 Frost	Y	Y	?	Y	N
25 Bentsen	Y	Y	N	Y	N
26 ***Armey***	Y	Y	Y	N	Y
27 Ortiz	Y	Y	N	Y	N
28 Rodriguez	Y	Y	N	Y	N
29 Green	Y	Y	N	Y	N
30 Johnson, E.B.	Y	Y	N	Y	N
UTAH					
1 ***Hansen***	Y	Y	Y	N	Y
2 ***Cook***	Y	Y	Y	N	Y
3 ***Cannon***	Y	Y	Y	N	Y
VERMONT					
AL *Sanders*	Y	Y	N	Y	N
VIRGINIA					
1 ***Bateman***	Y	Y	Y	N	Y
2 Pickett	N	N	N	N	N
3 Scott	Y	Y	N	Y	N
4 Sisisky	Y	Y	Y	N	Y
5 *Goode*	Y	Y	Y	N	Y
6 ***Goodlatte***	Y	Y	Y	N	Y
7 ***Bliley***	Y	Y	Y	N	Y
8 Moran	Y	Y	Y	N	Y
9 Boucher	Y	Y	N	Y	N
10 ***Wolf***	Y	Y	Y	N	Y
11 ***Davis***	Y	Y	Y	N	Y
WASHINGTON					
1 Inslee	Y	Y	N	Y	N
2 ***Metcalf***	Y	Y	Y	N	Y
3 Baird	?	?	?	?	?
4 ***Hastings***	Y	Y	Y	N	Y
5 ***Nethercutt***	Y	Y	Y	N	N
6 Dicks	Y	Y	N	Y	N
7 McDermott	N	N	N	Y	N
8 ***Dunn***	Y	Y	Y	N	Y
9 Smith	Y	Y	N	Y	N
WEST VIRGINIA					
1 Mollohan	Y	Y	N	Y	N
2 Wise	Y	Y	N	Y	N
3 Rahall	Y	Y	N	Y	N
WISCONSIN					
1 ***Ryan***	Y	Y	Y	N	Y
2 Baldwin	Y	Y	N	Y	N
3 Kind	Y	Y	N	Y	N
4 Kleczka	Y	Y	N	Y	N
5 Barrett	Y	Y	N	Y	N
6 ***Petri***	Y	Y	Y	N	Y
7 Obey	Y	Y	N	Y	N
8 ***Green***	+	Y	Y	N	Y
9 ***Sensenbrenner***	Y	Y	Y	N	Y
WYOMING					
AL ***Cubin***	Y	Y	Y	N	Y

Southern states - Ala., Ark., Fla., Ga., Ky., La., Miss., N.C., Okla., S.C., Tenn., Texas, Va.

26. S 613. Indian Tribe Land Development Contracts/Passage. Sherwood, R-Pa., motion to suspend the rules and pass the bill to amend current law requiring Indian tribes to seek federal approval before entering into certain land development contracts. Under the legislation, federal approval would be necessary for contracts lasting seven years or longer. The bill also would eliminate any requirement for federal review of contracts between Indian tribes and attorneys. Motion agreed to 406-2: R 209-1; D 195-1 (ND 144-1, SD 51-0); I 2-0. A two-thirds majority of those present and voting (272 in this case) is required for passage under suspension of the rules. Feb. 29, 2000.

27. HR 5. Eliminate Social Security Earnings Test/Passage. Passage of the bill that would allow senior citizens ages 65 through 69 to earn money without having their Social Security benefits reduced. Under current law, retirees ages 65 through 69 lose $1 in Social Security benefits for every $3 they earn each year above a certain level (currently $17,000). Passed 422-0: R 215-0; D 205-0 (ND 152-0, SD 53-0); I 2-0. March 1, 2000. A "yea" was a vote in support of the president's position.

28. HR 1883. Russia/Iran Sanctions/Senate Amendments. Gilman, R-N.Y., motion to agree to the Senate amendments to the bill that would authorize the president to impose sanctions against entities found responsible for the transfer of missiles or missile technology to Iran. The bill also would allow the president to withhold "extraordinary" payments to Russia for the International Space Station if Russia spreads missile or nuclear weapons technology to Iran. Motion agreed to 420-0: R 216-0; D 202-0 (ND 149-0, SD 53-0); I 2-0. March 1, 2000.

Key

- Y Voted for (yea).
- # Paired for.
- + Announced for.
- N Voted against (nay).
- X Paired against.
- – Announced against.
- P Voted "present."
- C Voted "present" to avoid possible conflict of interest.
- ? Did not vote or otherwise make a position known.

•

Democrats ***Republicans***
Independents

	26	27	28
ALABAMA			
1 ***Callahan***	Y	Y	Y
2 ***Everett***	Y	Y	Y
3 ***Riley***	Y	Y	Y
4 ***Aderholt***	Y	Y	Y
5 Cramer	Y	Y	Y
6 ***Bachus***	Y	Y	Y
7 Hilliard	Y	Y	Y
ALASKA			
AL ***Young***	Y	Y	Y
ARIZONA			
1 ***Salmon***	Y	Y	Y
2 Pastor	Y	Y	Y
3 ***Stump***	Y	Y	Y
4 ***Shadegg***	Y	Y	Y
5 ***Kolbe***	Y	Y	Y
6 ***Hayworth***	Y	Y	Y
ARKANSAS			
1 Berry	Y	Y	Y
2 Snyder	Y	Y	Y
3 ***Hutchinson***	Y	Y	Y
4 ***Dickey***	Y	Y	Y
CALIFORNIA			
1 Thompson	Y	Y	Y
2 ***Herger***	Y	Y	Y
3 ***Ose***	Y	Y	Y
4 ***Doolittle***	Y	Y	Y
5 Matsui	Y	Y	Y
6 Woolsey	Y	Y	Y
7 Miller, George	Y	Y	Y
8 Pelosi	Y	Y	Y
9 Lee	Y	Y	Y
10 Tauscher	Y	Y	Y
11 ***Pombo***	Y	Y	Y
12 Lantos	Y	Y	Y
13 Stark	Y	Y	Y
14 Eshoo	Y	Y	Y
15 ***Campbell***	+	+	+
16 Lofgren	?	Y	Y
17 Farr	Y	Y	Y
18 Condit	Y	Y	Y
19 ***Radanovich***	Y	Y	Y
20 Dooley	Y	Y	Y
21 ***Thomas***	Y	Y	Y
22 Capps	?	Y	Y
23 ***Gallegly***	Y	Y	Y
24 Sherman	Y	Y	Y
25 ***McKeon***	Y	Y	Y
26 Berman	Y	Y	Y
27 ***Rogan***	Y	Y	Y
28 ***Dreier***	Y	Y	Y
29 Waxman	Y	Y	Y
30 Becerra	Y	Y	Y
31 Martinez	Y	Y	Y
32 Dixon	Y	Y	Y
33 Roybal-Allard	+	Y	Y
34 Napolitano	Y	Y	Y
35 Waters	?	?	?
36 ***Kuykendall***	Y	Y	Y
37 Millender-McD.	?	?	?
38 ***Horn***	Y	+	Y
39 ***Royce***	Y	Y	Y
40 ***Lewis***	Y	Y	Y
41 ***Miller, Gary***	+	Y	Y
42 Baca	Y	Y	Y
43 ***Calvert***	Y	Y	Y
44 ***Bono***	Y	Y	Y
45 ***Rohrabacher***	Y	Y	Y
46 Sanchez	Y	Y	Y
47 ***Cox***	Y	Y	Y
48 ***Packard***	Y	Y	Y
49 ***Bilbray***	Y	Y	Y
50 Filner	Y	Y	Y
51 ***Cunningham***	Y	Y	Y
52 ***Hunter***	Y	Y	Y
COLORADO			
1 DeGette	Y	Y	Y
2 Udall	Y	Y	Y
3 ***McInnis***	Y	Y	Y
4 ***Schaffer***	Y	Y	Y
5 ***Hefley***	Y	Y	Y
6 ***Tancredo***	Y	Y	Y
CONNECTICUT			
1 Larson	Y	Y	?
2 Gejdenson	Y	Y	Y
3 DeLauro	Y	Y	Y
4 ***Shays***	Y	Y	Y
5 Maloney	Y	Y	Y
6 ***Johnson***	Y	Y	Y
DELAWARE			
AL ***Castle***	Y	Y	Y
FLORIDA			
1 ***Scarborough***	Y	Y	Y
2 Boyd	Y	Y	Y
3 Brown	Y	Y	Y
4 ***Fowler***	Y	Y	?
5 Thurman	Y	Y	Y
6 ***Stearns***	Y	Y	Y
7 ***Mica***	Y	+	Y
8 ***McCollum***	Y	Y	Y
9 ***Bilirakis***	Y	Y	Y
10 ***Young***	Y	Y	Y
11 Davis	Y	Y	Y
12 ***Canady***	Y	Y	Y
13 ***Miller***	Y	Y	Y
14 ***Goss***	Y	Y	Y
15 ***Weldon***	Y	Y	Y
16 ***Foley***	Y	Y	Y
17 Meek	Y	Y	Y
18 ***Ros-Lehtinen***	Y	Y	Y
19 Wexler	?	Y	Y
20 Deutsch	+	Y	Y
21 ***Diaz-Balart***	Y	Y	Y
22 ***Shaw***	Y	Y	Y
23 Hastings	Y	Y	Y
GEORGIA			
1 ***Kingston***	Y	Y	Y
2 Bishop	Y	Y	Y
3 ***Collins***	Y	Y	Y
4 McKinney	Y	Y	Y
5 Lewis	Y	Y	Y
6 ***Isakson***	Y	Y	Y
7 ***Barr***	Y	Y	Y
8 ***Chambliss***	Y	Y	Y
9 ***Deal***	Y	Y	Y
10 ***Norwood***	Y	+	+
11 ***Linder***	Y	Y	Y
HAWAII			
1 Abercrombie	Y	Y	Y
2 Mink	Y	Y	Y
IDAHO			
1 ***Chenoweth-Hage***	N	Y	Y
2 ***Simpson***	Y	Y	Y
ILLINOIS			
1 Rush	?	Y	Y
2 Jackson	Y	Y	Y
3 Lipinski	Y	Y	Y
4 Gutierrez	Y	Y	Y
5 Blagojevich	Y	Y	Y
6 ***Hyde***	Y	Y	Y
7 Davis	Y	Y	Y
8 ***Crane***	Y	Y	Y
9 Schakowsky	Y	Y	Y
10 ***Porter***	Y	Y	Y
11 ***Weller***	Y	Y	Y
12 Costello	Y	Y	Y
13 ***Biggert***	Y	Y	Y

ND Northern Democrats SD Southern Democrats

	26	27	28
14 ***Hastert***		Y	
15 ***Ewing***	Y	Y	Y
16 ***Manzullo***	Y	Y	Y
17 Evans	Y	Y	Y
18 ***LaHood***	Y	Y	Y
19 Phelps	Y	Y	Y
20 ***Shimkus***	?	Y	Y
INDIANA			
1 Visclosky	Y	Y	Y
2 ***McIntosh***	Y	Y	Y
3 Roemer	Y	Y	Y
4 ***Souder***	Y	Y	Y
5 ***Buyer***	Y	Y	Y
6 ***Burton***	Y	Y	Y
7 ***Pease***	Y	Y	Y
8 ***Hostettler***	Y	Y	Y
9 Hill	Y	Y	Y
10 Carson	Y	Y	Y
IOWA			
1 ***Leach***	Y	Y	Y
2 ***Nussle***	Y	Y	Y
3 Boswell	Y	Y	Y
4 ***Ganske***	Y	Y	Y
5 ***Latham***	Y	Y	Y
KANSAS			
1 ***Moran***	Y	Y	Y
2 ***Ryun***	Y	Y	Y
3 Moore	Y	Y	Y
4 ***Tiahrt***	Y	Y	Y
KENTUCKY			
1 ***Whitfield***	Y	Y	Y
2 ***Lewis***	Y	Y	Y
3 ***Northup***	Y	Y	Y
4 Lucas	Y	Y	Y
5 ***Rogers***	Y	Y	Y
6 ***Fletcher***	Y	Y	Y
LOUISIANA			
1 ***Vitter***	Y	Y	Y
2 Jefferson	Y	Y	Y
3 ***Tauzin***	Y	Y	Y
4 ***McCrery***	Y	Y	Y
5 ***Cooksey***	Y	Y	Y
6 ***Baker***	Y	Y	Y
7 John	Y	Y	Y
MAINE			
1 Allen	Y	Y	Y
2 Baldacci	Y	Y	Y
MARYLAND			
1 ***Gilchrest***	Y	Y	Y
2 ***Ehrlich***	?	Y	Y
3 Cardin	Y	Y	Y
4 Wynn	Y	Y	Y
5 Hoyer	Y	Y	Y
6 ***Bartlett***	Y	Y	Y
7 Cummings	Y	Y	Y
8 ***Morella***	Y	Y	Y
MASSACHUSETTS			
1 Olver	Y	Y	Y
2 Neal	Y	Y	Y
3 McGovern	Y	Y	Y
4 Frank	Y	Y	Y
5 Meehan	Y	Y	Y
6 Tierney	Y	Y	Y
7 Markey	Y	Y	Y
8 Capuano	Y	Y	Y
9 Moakley	Y	Y	Y
10 Delahunt	Y	Y	Y
MICHIGAN			
1 Stupak	Y	Y	Y
2 ***Hoekstra***	Y	Y	Y
3 ***Ehlers***	Y	Y	Y
4 ***Camp***	Y	Y	Y
5 Barcia	Y	Y	Y
6 ***Upton***	Y	Y	Y
7 ***Smith***	Y	Y	Y
8 Stabenow	Y	Y	Y
9 Kildee	Y	Y	Y
10 Bonior	Y	Y	Y
11 ***Knollenberg***	Y	Y	Y
12 Levin	Y	Y	Y
13 Rivers	Y	Y	Y
14 Conyers	Y	Y	Y
15 Kilpatrick	+	+	+
16 Dingell	Y	Y	?

	26	27	28
MINNESOTA			
1 ***Gutknecht***	Y	Y	Y
2 Minge	Y	Y	Y
3 ***Ramstad***	Y	Y	Y
4 Vento	?	?	?
5 Sabo	Y	Y	Y
6 Luther	Y	Y	Y
7 Peterson	Y	Y	Y
8 Oberstar	Y	Y	Y
MISSISSIPPI			
1 ***Wicker***	Y	Y	Y
2 Thompson	Y	Y	Y
3 ***Pickering***	Y	Y	Y
4 Shows	+	Y	Y
5 Taylor	Y	Y	Y
MISSOURI			
1 Clay	Y	Y	Y
2 ***Talent***	Y	Y	Y
3 Gephardt	Y	Y	Y
4 Skelton	Y	Y	Y
5 McCarthy	Y	Y	Y
6 Danner	Y	Y	Y
7 ***Blunt***	Y	Y	Y
8 ***Emerson***	Y	Y	Y
9 ***Hulshof***	?	Y	Y
MONTANA			
AL ***Hill***	Y	Y	Y
NEBRASKA			
1 ***Bereuter***	Y	Y	Y
2 ***Terry***	Y	Y	Y
3 ***Barrett***	Y	Y	Y
NEVADA			
1 Berkley	Y	Y	Y
2 ***Gibbons***	?	Y	Y
NEW HAMPSHIRE			
1 ***Sununu***	Y	Y	Y
2 ***Bass***	Y	Y	Y
NEW JERSEY			
1 Andrews	Y	Y	Y
2 ***LoBiondo***	Y	Y	Y
3 ***Saxton***	Y	Y	Y
4 ***Smith***	Y	Y	Y
5 ***Roukema***	Y	Y	Y
6 Pallone	Y	Y	Y
7 ***Franks***	Y	Y	Y
8 Pascrell	Y	Y	Y
9 Rothman	Y	Y	Y
10 Payne	Y	Y	Y
11 ***Frelinghuysen***	Y	Y	Y
12 Holt	Y	Y	Y
13 Menendez	Y	Y	Y
NEW MEXICO			
1 ***Wilson***	Y	Y	Y
2 ***Skeen***	Y	Y	Y
3 Udall	Y	Y	Y
NEW YORK			
1 Forbes	Y	Y	Y
2 ***Lazio***	Y	Y	Y
3 ***King***	Y	Y	Y
4 McCarthy	Y	Y	Y
5 Ackerman	Y	Y	Y
6 Meeks	Y	Y	Y
7 Crowley	Y	Y	Y
8 Nadler	Y	Y	Y
9 Weiner	Y	Y	Y
10 Towns	Y	Y	Y
11 Owens	?	Y	Y
12 Velázquez	Y	Y	Y
13 ***Fossella***	Y	Y	Y
14 Maloney	Y	Y	Y
15 Rangel	Y	Y	Y
16 Serrano	Y	Y	Y
17 Engel	Y	Y	Y
18 Lowey	Y	Y	Y
19 ***Kelly***	Y	Y	Y
20 ***Gilman***	Y	Y	Y
21 McNulty	Y	Y	Y
22 ***Sweeney***	Y	Y	Y
23 ***Boehlert***	Y	Y	Y
24 ***McHugh***	Y	Y	Y
25 ***Walsh***	Y	Y	Y
26 Hinchey	Y	Y	Y
27 ***Reynolds***	Y	Y	Y
28 Slaughter	Y	Y	Y
29 LaFalce	Y	Y	Y

	26	27	28
30 ***Quinn***	Y	Y	Y
31 ***Houghton***	Y	Y	Y
NORTH CAROLINA			
1 Clayton	Y	Y	Y
2 Etheridge	Y	Y	Y
3 ***Jones***	Y	Y	Y
4 Price	Y	Y	Y
5 ***Burr***	Y	Y	Y
6 ***Coble***	Y	Y	Y
7 McIntyre	Y	Y	Y
8 ***Hayes***	Y	Y	Y
9 ***Myrick***	Y	Y	Y
10 ***Ballenger***	Y	Y	Y
11 ***Taylor***	Y	Y	Y
12 Watt	Y	Y	Y
NORTH DAKOTA			
AL Pomeroy	Y	Y	Y
OHIO			
1 ***Chabot***	Y	Y	Y
2 ***Portman***	+	Y	Y
3 Hall	Y	Y	Y
4 ***Oxley***	?	Y	Y
5 ***Gillmor***	Y	Y	Y
6 Strickland	N	Y	Y
7 ***Hobson***	Y	Y	Y
8 ***Boehner***	Y	Y	Y
9 Kaptur	?	Y	Y
10 Kucinich	Y	Y	Y
11 Jones	Y	Y	Y
12 ***Kasich***	Y	Y	Y
13 Brown	?	?	?
14 Sawyer	Y	Y	Y
15 ***Pryce***	Y	Y	Y
16 ***Regula***	Y	Y	Y
17 Traficant	Y	Y	Y
18 ***Ney***	Y	Y	Y
19 ***LaTourette***	Y	Y	Y
OKLAHOMA			
1 ***Largent***	Y	Y	Y
2 ***Coburn***	Y	Y	Y
3 ***Watkins***	Y	Y	Y
4 ***Watts***	Y	Y	Y
5 ***Istook***	Y	Y	Y
6 ***Lucas***	Y	Y	Y
OREGON			
1 Wu	Y	Y	Y
2 ***Walden***	Y	Y	Y
3 Blumenauer	Y	Y	Y
4 DeFazio	Y	Y	Y
5 Hooley	Y	Y	Y
PENNSYLVANIA			
1 Brady	Y	Y	Y
2 Fattah	Y	Y	Y
3 Borski	Y	Y	Y
4 Klink	Y	Y	Y
5 ***Peterson***	Y	Y	Y
6 Holden	Y	Y	Y
7 ***Weldon***	Y	Y	Y
8 ***Greenwood***	Y	Y	Y
9 ***Shuster***	Y	Y	Y
10 ***Sherwood***	Y	Y	Y
11 Kanjorski	Y	Y	Y
12 Murtha	?	Y	Y
13 Hoeffel	Y	Y	Y
14 Coyne	Y	Y	Y
15 ***Toomey***	Y	Y	Y
16 ***Pitts***	Y	Y	Y
17 ***Gekas***	Y	Y	Y
18 Doyle	Y	Y	Y
19 ***Goodling***	Y	Y	Y
20 Mascara	Y	Y	Y
21 ***English***	Y	Y	Y
RHODE ISLAND			
1 Kennedy	Y	Y	Y
2 Weygand	Y	Y	Y
SOUTH CAROLINA			
1 ***Sanford***	Y	Y	Y
2 ***Spence***	Y	Y	Y
3 ***Graham***	Y	Y	Y
4 ***DeMint***	Y	Y	Y
5 Spratt	Y	+	Y
6 Clyburn	Y	Y	Y
SOUTH DAKOTA			
AL ***Thune***	Y	Y	Y

	26	27	28
TENNESSEE			
1 ***Jenkins***	Y	Y	Y
2 ***Duncan***	Y	Y	Y
3 ***Wamp***	Y	Y	Y
4 ***Hilleary***	Y	Y	Y
5 Clement	Y	Y	Y
6 Gordon	Y	Y	Y
7 ***Bryant***	Y	Y	Y
8 Tanner	Y	Y	Y
9 Ford	Y	Y	Y
TEXAS			
1 Sandlin	Y	Y	Y
2 Turner	Y	Y	Y
3 ***Johnson, Sam***	Y	Y	Y
4 Hall	Y	Y	?
5 ***Sessions***	Y	Y	Y
6 ***Barton***	?	Y	Y
7 ***Archer***	Y	Y	Y
8 ***Brady***	Y	+	Y
9 Lampson	Y	Y	Y
10 Doggett	Y	Y	Y
11 Edwards	Y	Y	Y
12 ***Granger***	Y	Y	Y
13 ***Thornberry***	Y	Y	Y
14 ***Paul***	?	Y	?
15 Hinojosa	Y	Y	Y
16 Reyes	Y	Y	Y
17 Stenholm	Y	Y	Y
18 Jackson-Lee	Y	Y	Y
19 ***Combest***	Y	Y	Y
20 Gonzalez	Y	Y	Y
21 ***Smith***	Y	Y	Y
22 ***DeLay***	Y	Y	Y
23 ***Bonilla***	Y	Y	Y
24 Frost	Y	Y	Y
25 Bentsen	Y	Y	Y
26 ***Armey***	Y	Y	Y
27 Ortiz	Y	Y	Y
28 Rodriguez	Y	Y	Y
29 Green	Y	Y	Y
30 Johnson, E.B.	Y	Y	Y
UTAH			
1 ***Hansen***	Y	Y	Y
2 ***Cook***	?	?	?
3 ***Cannon***	Y	Y	Y
VERMONT			
AL *Sanders*	Y	Y	Y
VIRGINIA			
1 ***Bateman***	Y	Y	Y
2 Pickett	Y	Y	Y
3 Scott	Y	Y	Y
4 Sisisky	Y	Y	Y
5 *Goode*	Y	Y	Y
6 ***Goodlatte***	Y	Y	Y
7 ***Bliley***	Y	+	Y
8 Moran	Y	Y	Y
9 Boucher	Y	Y	Y
10 ***Wolf***	Y	Y	Y
11 ***Davis***	Y	Y	Y
WASHINGTON			
1 Inslee	Y	Y	Y
2 ***Metcalf***	Y	Y	Y
3 Baird	Y	Y	Y
4 ***Hastings***	Y	Y	Y
5 ***Nethercutt***	Y	Y	Y
6 Dicks	Y	Y	Y
7 McDermott	Y	Y	Y
8 ***Dunn***	Y	Y	Y
9 Smith	Y	Y	Y
WEST VIRGINIA			
1 Mollohan	Y	Y	Y
2 Wise	Y	Y	Y
3 Rahall	Y	Y	Y
WISCONSIN			
1 ***Ryan***	Y	Y	Y
2 Baldwin	Y	Y	Y
3 Kind	Y	Y	Y
4 Kleczka	Y	Y	?
5 Barrett	Y	Y	Y
6 ***Petri***	Y	Y	Y
7 Obey	Y	Y	Y
8 ***Green***	Y	Y	Y
9 ***Sensenbrenner***	Y	Y	Y
WYOMING			
AL ***Cubin***	Y	Y	Y

Southern states - Ala., Ark., Fla., Ga., Ky., La., Miss., N.C., Okla., S.C., Tenn., Texas, Va.

29. HR 1827. Recovery Auditing/Passage. Passage of the bill that would require federal agencies to audit accounts that purchase at least $500 million of goods and services annually from the private sector for government use. The audits could be done in-house or contracted out to private firms. Passed 375-0: R 192-0; D 181-0 (ND 131-0, SD 50-0); I 2-0. March 8, 2000.

30. HR 2952. Keith D. Oglesby Post Office/Passage. Terry, R-Neb., motion to suspend the rules and pass the bill to designate a post office in Greenville, S.C., as the Keith D. Oglesby Station. Motion agreed to 377-0: R 195-0; D 180-0 (ND 130-0, SD 50-0); I 2-0. A two-thirds majority of those present and voting (252 in this case) is required for passage under suspension of the rules. March 8, 2000.

31. HR 3018. Marybelle H. Howe Post Office/Passage. Terry, R-Neb., motion to suspend the rules and pass the bill to designate a post office in Charleston, S.C., as the Marybelle H. Howe Post Office. The bill also would designate post offices in Columbia, S.C., as the Mamie G. Floyd Post Office, in Eastover, S.C., as the Layford R. Johnson Post Office and in Charleston, S.C., as the Richard E. Fields Post Office. Motion agreed to 375-0: R 195-0; D 178-0 (ND 129-0, SD 49-0); I 2-0. A two-thirds majority of those present and voting (250 in this case) is required for passage under suspension of the rules. March 8, 2000.

32. S Con Res 91. Lithuanian Independence Anniversary/Adoption. Gilman, R-N.Y., motion to suspend the rules and agree to the concurrent resolution to congratulate Lithuania on the 10th anniversary of the re-establishment of its independence and on its leading role in the disintegration of the Soviet Union. The resolution also commends Lithuania for its success in implementing political and economic reforms. Motion agreed to 384-0: R 199-0; D 184-0 (ND 132-0, SD 52-0); I 1-0. A two-thirds majority of those present and voting (256 in this case) is required for passage under suspension of the rules. March 8, 2000.

33. H J Res 86. Korean War 50th Anniversary/Passage. Buyer, R-Ind., motion to suspend the rules and pass the joint resolution to recognize the historic significance of the 50th anniversary of the Korean War. Motion agreed to 383-0: R 198-0; D 183-0 (ND 133-0, SD 50-0); I 2-0. A two-thirds majority of those present and voting (256 in this case) is required for passage under suspension of the rules. March 8, 2000.

34. H Res 433. Ivanpah Valley Airport/Rule. Adoption of the rule (H Res 433) to provide for House floor consideration of the bill to direct the Interior Department to convey to Clark County, Nev., about 6,400 acres of public land to develop an airport. Adopted 406-0: R 207-0; D 197-0 (ND 147-0, SD 50-0); I 2-0. March 9, 2000.

Key

- Y Voted for (yea).
- # Paired for.
- + Announced for.
- N Voted against (nay).
- X Paired against.
- – Announced against.
- P Voted "present."
- C Voted "present" to avoid possible conflict of interest.
- ? Did not vote or otherwise make a position known.

•

Democrats ***Republicans***
Independents

	29	30	31	32	33	34
ALABAMA						
1 ***Callahan***	Y	Y	Y	Y	Y	Y
2 ***Everett***	Y	Y	Y	Y	Y	Y
3 ***Riley***	Y	Y	Y	Y	Y	Y
4 ***Aderholt***	Y	Y	Y	Y	Y	Y
5 Cramer	Y	Y	Y	Y	Y	Y
6 ***Bachus***	Y	Y	Y	Y	Y	Y
7 Hilliard	Y	Y	Y	Y	Y	Y
ALASKA						
AL ***Young***	Y	Y	Y	Y	Y	?
ARIZONA						
1 ***Salmon***	Y	Y	Y	Y	Y	?
2 Pastor	Y	Y	Y	Y	Y	Y
3 ***Stump***	Y	Y	Y	Y	Y	Y
4 ***Shadegg***	Y	Y	Y	Y	Y	Y
5 ***Kolbe***	Y	Y	Y	Y	Y	Y
6 ***Hayworth***	Y	Y	Y	Y	Y	Y
ARKANSAS						
1 Berry	Y	Y	Y	Y	Y	Y
2 Snyder	Y	Y	Y	Y	Y	Y
3 ***Hutchinson***	Y	Y	Y	Y	Y	Y
4 ***Dickey***	Y	Y	Y	Y	Y	Y
CALIFORNIA						
1 Thompson	Y	Y	Y	Y	Y	Y
2 ***Herger***	?	Y	Y	Y	Y	?
3 ***Ose***	Y	Y	Y	Y	Y	Y
4 ***Doolittle***	?	Y	Y	Y	Y	Y
5 Matsui	Y	Y	?	Y	Y	Y
6 Woolsey	+	+	+	+	+	Y
7 Miller, George	?	?	?	?	?	Y
8 Pelosi	Y	Y	Y	Y	Y	Y
9 Lee	Y	?	Y	Y	Y	Y
10 Tauscher	Y	Y	Y	Y	Y	Y
11 ***Pombo***	Y	Y	Y	Y	Y	Y
12 Lantos	?	?	?	?	?	Y
13 Stark	Y	Y	Y	Y	Y	Y
14 Eshoo	?	?	?	?	?	Y
15 ***Campbell***	?	?	?	?	?	Y
16 Lofgren	Y	Y	Y	Y	Y	Y
17 Farr	Y	Y	Y	Y	Y	Y
18 Condit	Y	Y	Y	Y	Y	Y
19 ***Radanovich***	?	?	?	?	?	Y
20 Dooley	?	?	?	?	?	Y
21 ***Thomas***	Y	Y	Y	Y	Y	Y
22 Capps	?	?	?	?	?	Y
23 ***Gallegly***	?	?	?	Y	Y	Y
24 Sherman	Y	Y	Y	Y	Y	Y
25 ***McKeon***	?	?	?	?	?	Y
26 Berman	?	?	?	Y	Y	Y
27 ***Rogan***	?	?	?	?	?	Y
28 ***Dreier***	Y	Y	Y	Y	Y	Y
29 Waxman	Y	Y	Y	Y	Y	Y
30 Becerra	Y	Y	Y	Y	Y	Y
31 Martinez	?	?	?	?	?	Y
32 Dixon	Y	Y	Y	Y	Y	?
33 Roybal-Allard	+	+	+	+	+	Y
34 Napolitano	+	+	+	+	+	Y
35 Waters	?	?	?	?	?	Y
36 ***Kuykendall***	+	+	+	+	+	Y
37 Millender-McD.	+	+	+	+	+	Y
38 ***Horn***	Y	Y	Y	Y	Y	Y
39 ***Royce***	+	?	?	Y	Y	Y
40 ***Lewis***	Y	Y	Y	Y	Y	Y
41 ***Miller, Gary***	+	+	+	Y	Y	Y
42 Baca	Y	Y	Y	Y	Y	Y
43 ***Calvert***	?	?	?	?	?	Y
44 ***Bono***	?	?	?	?	?	Y
45 ***Rohrabacher***	?	?	?	?	?	Y
46 Sanchez	Y	Y	Y	Y	Y	+
47 ***Cox***	?	?	?	?	?	Y
48 ***Packard***	?	Y	Y	Y	Y	Y
49 ***Bilbray***	?	?	?	?	Y	Y
50 Filner	?	?	?	?	?	Y
51 ***Cunningham***	?	?	?	+	+	Y
52 ***Hunter***	?	Y	Y	Y	Y	Y
COLORADO						
1 DeGette	Y	Y	Y	Y	Y	Y
2 Udall	Y	Y	Y	Y	Y	Y
3 ***McInnis***	Y	Y	Y	Y	Y	Y
4 ***Schaffer***	?	?	?	?	?	?
5 ***Hefley***	Y	Y	Y	Y	Y	Y
6 ***Tancredo***	Y	Y	Y	Y	Y	Y
CONNECTICUT						
1 Larson	Y	Y	Y	?	?	?
2 Gejdenson	Y	Y	Y	Y	Y	Y
3 DeLauro	Y	Y	Y	Y	Y	Y
4 ***Shays***	Y	Y	Y	Y	Y	Y
5 Maloney	Y	Y	Y	Y	Y	Y
6 ***Johnson***	Y	Y	Y	Y	Y	Y
DELAWARE						
AL ***Castle***	Y	Y	Y	Y	Y	Y
FLORIDA						
1 ***Scarborough***	?	?	?	?	?	?
2 Boyd	Y	Y	Y	Y	Y	Y
3 Brown	Y	Y	?	Y	Y	Y
4 ***Fowler***	Y	Y	Y	Y	Y	Y
5 Thurman	Y	Y	Y	Y	Y	Y
6 ***Stearns***	Y	Y	Y	Y	Y	Y
7 ***Mica***	Y	Y	Y	Y	Y	Y
8 ***McCollum***	Y	Y	Y	Y	Y	?
9 ***Bilirakis***	Y	Y	Y	Y	Y	Y
10 ***Young***	Y	Y	Y	Y	Y	Y
11 Davis	Y	Y	Y	Y	Y	Y
12 ***Canady***	Y	Y	Y	Y	Y	Y
13 ***Miller***	Y	Y	Y	Y	Y	Y
14 ***Goss***	Y	Y	Y	Y	Y	Y
15 ***Weldon***	Y	Y	?	Y	Y	Y
16 ***Foley***	Y	Y	Y	Y	Y	Y
17 Meek	Y	Y	Y	Y	Y	Y
18 ***Ros-Lehtinen***	Y	Y	Y	Y	Y	Y
19 Wexler	Y	Y	Y	Y	Y	Y
20 Deutsch	Y	Y	Y	Y	Y	Y
21 ***Diaz-Balart***	Y	Y	Y	Y	Y	Y
22 ***Shaw***	Y	Y	Y	Y	Y	Y
23 Hastings	Y	Y	Y	Y	Y	Y
GEORGIA						
1 ***Kingston***	Y	Y	Y	Y	Y	Y
2 Bishop	Y	Y	Y	Y	Y	Y
3 ***Collins***	Y	Y	Y	Y	Y	Y
4 McKinney	?	?	Y	Y	Y	Y
5 Lewis	Y	Y	Y	Y	Y	Y
6 ***Isakson***	Y	Y	Y	Y	Y	Y
7 ***Barr***	Y	Y	Y	Y	Y	?
8 ***Chambliss***	Y	Y	Y	Y	Y	Y
9 ***Deal***	?	Y	Y	Y	Y	Y
10 ***Norwood***	?	?	?	?	?	Y
11 ***Linder***	Y	Y	Y	Y	Y	Y
HAWAII						
1 Abercrombie	Y	Y	Y	Y	Y	Y
2 Mink	Y	Y	Y	Y	Y	Y
IDAHO						
1 ***Chenoweth-Hage***	Y	Y	Y	Y	Y	Y
2 ***Simpson***	Y	Y	Y	Y	Y	Y
ILLINOIS						
1 Rush	?	?	?	?	?	Y
2 Jackson	Y	Y	Y	Y	Y	Y
3 Lipinski	Y	Y	Y	Y	Y	Y
4 Gutierrez	Y	Y	Y	Y	Y	Y
5 Blagojevich	Y	Y	Y	Y	Y	Y
6 ***Hyde***	Y	Y	Y	Y	Y	Y
7 Davis	?	?	?	?	Y	Y
8 ***Crane***	Y	Y	Y	Y	Y	Y
9 Schakowsky	Y	Y	Y	Y	Y	Y
10 ***Porter***	Y	Y	Y	Y	Y	Y
11 ***Weller***	Y	Y	Y	Y	Y	Y
12 Costello	Y	Y	Y	Y	Y	Y
13 ***Biggert***	Y	Y	Y	Y	Y	Y

ND Northern Democrats SD Southern Democrats

	29	30	31	32	33	34
14 ***Hastert***						
15 ***Ewing***	Y	Y	Y	Y	Y	Y
16 ***Manzullo***	Y	Y	Y	Y	Y	Y
17 Evans	Y	Y	Y	Y	Y	Y
18 ***LaHood***	Y	Y	Y	Y	Y	Y
19 Phelps	Y	Y	Y	Y	Y	Y
20 ***Shimkus***	Y	Y	Y	Y	Y	Y
INDIANA						
1 Visclosky	Y	Y	Y	Y	Y	Y
2 ***McIntosh***	Y	Y	Y	Y	Y	?
3 Roemer	Y	Y	Y	Y	Y	Y
4 ***Souder***	?	?	?	?	?	Y
5 ***Buyer***	Y	Y	?	Y	Y	Y
6 ***Burton***	Y	Y	Y	Y	Y	Y
7 ***Pease***	Y	Y	Y	Y	Y	Y
8 ***Hostettler***	Y	Y	Y	Y	Y	Y
9 Hill	Y	Y	Y	Y	Y	Y
10 Carson	Y	Y	Y	Y	Y	Y
IOWA						
1 ***Leach***	Y	Y	Y	Y	Y	Y
2 ***Nussle***	Y	Y	Y	Y	Y	Y
3 Boswell	Y	Y	Y	Y	Y	?
4 ***Ganske***	Y	Y	Y	Y	Y	Y
5 ***Latham***	Y	Y	Y	Y	Y	Y
KANSAS						
1 ***Moran***	Y	Y	Y	Y	Y	Y
2 ***Ryun***	Y	Y	Y	Y	Y	Y
3 Moore	Y	Y	Y	Y	Y	Y
4 ***Tiahrt***	Y	Y	Y	Y	Y	Y
KENTUCKY						
1 ***Whitfield***	Y	Y	Y	Y	Y	Y
2 ***Lewis***	Y	Y	Y	Y	Y	Y
3 ***Northup***	Y	Y	Y	Y	Y	Y
4 Lucas	Y	Y	Y	Y	Y	Y
5 ***Rogers***	Y	Y	Y	Y	Y	Y
6 ***Fletcher***	Y	Y	Y	Y	?	Y
LOUISIANA						
1 ***Vitter***	Y	Y	Y	Y	Y	Y
2 Jefferson	Y	Y	Y	Y	Y	Y
3 ***Tauzin***	Y	Y	Y	Y	Y	Y
4 ***McCrery***	Y	Y	Y	Y	Y	Y
5 ***Cooksey***	Y	Y	Y	?	?	?
6 ***Baker***	Y	Y	Y	Y	Y	Y
7 John	Y	Y	Y	Y	Y	Y
MAINE						
1 Allen	Y	Y	Y	Y	Y	Y
2 Baldacci	Y	Y	?	Y	Y	Y
MARYLAND						
1 ***Gilchrest***	Y	Y	Y	Y	Y	Y
2 ***Ehrlich***	?	Y	Y	Y	Y	Y
3 Cardin	Y	Y	Y	Y	Y	Y
4 Wynn	Y	Y	Y	Y	Y	Y
5 Hoyer	Y	Y	Y	Y	Y	Y
6 ***Bartlett***	Y	Y	Y	Y	Y	Y
7 Cummings	Y	Y	Y	Y	Y	Y
8 ***Morella***	Y	Y	Y	Y	Y	Y
MASSACHUSETTS						
1 Olver	Y	Y	Y	Y	Y	Y
2 Neal	Y	Y	Y	Y	Y	Y
3 McGovern	Y	Y	Y	Y	Y	Y
4 Frank	Y	Y	Y	Y	Y	Y
5 Meehan	Y	Y	Y	Y	Y	Y
6 Tierney	Y	Y	Y	Y	Y	Y
7 Markey	Y	Y	Y	Y	Y	Y
8 Capuano	Y	Y	Y	Y	Y	Y
9 Moakley	Y	Y	Y	Y	Y	Y
10 Delahunt	Y	Y	Y	Y	Y	Y
MICHIGAN						
1 Stupak	Y	Y	Y	Y	Y	+
2 ***Hoekstra***	Y	Y	Y	Y	Y	Y
3 ***Ehlers***	Y	Y	Y	Y	Y	Y
4 ***Camp***	Y	Y	Y	Y	Y	Y
5 Barcia	Y	Y	Y	Y	Y	Y
6 ***Upton***	Y	Y	Y	Y	Y	Y
7 ***Smith***	Y	Y	Y	Y	Y	Y
8 Stabenow	Y	Y	Y	Y	Y	Y
9 Kildee	Y	Y	Y	Y	Y	Y
10 Bonior	Y	Y	Y	Y	Y	Y
11 ***Knollenberg***	Y	Y	Y	Y	Y	Y
12 Levin	Y	Y	Y	Y	Y	Y
13 Rivers	Y	Y	Y	Y	Y	Y
14 Conyers	Y	Y	Y	Y	Y	Y
15 Kilpatrick	Y	Y	Y	Y	Y	Y
16 Dingell	Y	Y	Y	Y	Y	Y
MINNESOTA						
1 ***Gutknecht***	Y	Y	Y	Y	Y	Y
2 Minge	Y	Y	Y	Y	Y	Y
3 ***Ramstad***	Y	Y	Y	Y	Y	Y
4 Vento	?	?	?	?	?	?
5 Sabo	Y	Y	Y	Y	Y	Y
6 Luther	Y	Y	Y	Y	Y	Y
7 Peterson	Y	Y	Y	Y	Y	Y
8 Oberstar	Y	Y	Y	Y	Y	Y
MISSISSIPPI						
1 ***Wicker***	Y	Y	Y	Y	Y	Y
2 Thompson	Y	Y	Y	Y	Y	Y
3 ***Pickering***	Y	Y	Y	Y	Y	?
4 Shows	Y	Y	Y	Y	Y	Y
5 Taylor	Y	Y	Y	Y	Y	Y
MISSOURI						
1 Clay	Y	Y	Y	Y	Y	Y
2 ***Talent***	Y	Y	Y	Y	Y	Y
3 Gephardt	Y	Y	Y	Y	Y	Y
4 Skelton	Y	Y	Y	Y	Y	Y
5 McCarthy	Y	Y	Y	Y	Y	Y
6 Danner	?	?	?	Y	Y	Y
7 ***Blunt***	Y	Y	Y	Y	Y	Y
8 ***Emerson***	Y	Y	Y	Y	Y	Y
9 ***Hulshof***	Y	Y	Y	Y	Y	Y
MONTANA						
AL ***Hill***	Y	Y	Y	Y	Y	Y
NEBRASKA						
1 ***Bereuter***	Y	Y	Y	Y	Y	Y
2 ***Terry***	Y	Y	Y	Y	Y	Y
3 ***Barrett***	Y	Y	Y	Y	Y	Y
NEVADA						
1 Berkley	Y	Y	Y	Y	Y	Y
2 ***Gibbons***	Y	Y	Y	Y	Y	Y
NEW HAMPSHIRE						
1 ***Sununu***	Y	Y	Y	Y	Y	Y
2 ***Bass***	Y	Y	Y	Y	Y	Y
NEW JERSEY						
1 Andrews	Y	Y	Y	Y	Y	Y
2 ***LoBiondo***	Y	Y	Y	Y	Y	Y
3 ***Saxton***	Y	Y	Y	?	?	Y
4 ***Smith***	Y	?	Y	Y	Y	Y
5 ***Roukema***	Y	Y	Y	Y	Y	Y
6 Pallone	Y	Y	Y	Y	Y	Y
7 ***Franks***	Y	Y	Y	Y	Y	Y
8 Pascrell	+	+	+	+	+	Y
9 Rothman	Y	Y	Y	Y	Y	Y
10 Payne	?	?	?	?	?	?
11 ***Frelinghuysen***	Y	Y	Y	Y	Y	Y
12 Holt	Y	Y	Y	Y	Y	Y
13 Menendez	Y	Y	Y	Y	Y	Y
NEW MEXICO						
1 ***Wilson***	Y	Y	Y	Y	Y	Y
2 ***Skeen***	Y	Y	Y	Y	Y	Y
3 Udall	Y	Y	Y	Y	Y	Y
NEW YORK						
1 Forbes	Y	Y	Y	Y	Y	Y
2 ***Lazio***	Y	Y	Y	Y	Y	Y
3 ***King***	Y	Y	Y	Y	Y	Y
4 McCarthy	Y	Y	Y	Y	Y	Y
5 Ackerman	Y	Y	Y	Y	Y	Y
6 Meeks	Y	Y	Y	Y	Y	Y
7 Crowley	Y	Y	Y	Y	Y	Y
8 Nadler	Y	Y	Y	Y	Y	Y
9 Weiner	Y	Y	Y	Y	Y	Y
10 Towns	Y	Y	Y	Y	Y	Y
11 Owens	+	+	+	Y	Y	Y
12 Velázquez	Y	Y	Y	+	+	Y
13 ***Fossella***	Y	Y	Y	Y	Y	Y
14 Maloney	Y	Y	Y	Y	Y	Y
15 Rangel	Y	Y	Y	?	?	Y
16 Serrano	Y	Y	Y	Y	Y	Y
17 Engel	Y	Y	Y	Y	Y	Y
18 Lowey	Y	Y	Y	Y	Y	Y
19 ***Kelly***	Y	Y	Y	Y	Y	Y
20 ***Gilman***	Y	Y	Y	Y	Y	Y
21 McNulty	Y	Y	Y	Y	Y	Y
22 ***Sweeney***	Y	Y	Y	Y	Y	Y
23 ***Boehlert***	Y	Y	Y	Y	Y	Y
24 ***McHugh***	Y	Y	Y	Y	Y	Y
25 ***Walsh***	Y	Y	Y	Y	Y	Y
26 Hinchey	Y	Y	Y	Y	Y	Y
27 ***Reynolds***	Y	Y	?	Y	Y	Y
28 Slaughter	Y	Y	Y	Y	Y	Y
29 LaFalce	Y	Y	Y	Y	Y	Y
30 ***Quinn***	Y	Y	Y	Y	Y	Y
31 ***Houghton***	Y	Y	Y	Y	Y	Y
NORTH CAROLINA						
1 Clayton	Y	Y	Y	Y	Y	Y
2 Etheridge	Y	Y	Y	Y	Y	Y
3 ***Jones***	Y	Y	Y	Y	Y	Y
4 Price	Y	Y	Y	Y	Y	Y
5 ***Burr***	Y	Y	Y	Y	Y	Y
6 ***Coble***	Y	Y	Y	Y	Y	Y
7 McIntyre	Y	Y	?	Y	Y	Y
8 ***Hayes***	Y	Y	Y	Y	Y	Y
9 ***Myrick***	Y	Y	Y	Y	Y	Y
10 ***Ballenger***	Y	Y	Y	Y	Y	Y
11 ***Taylor***	Y	Y	Y	Y	Y	Y
12 Watt	Y	Y	Y	Y	Y	Y
NORTH DAKOTA						
AL Pomeroy	Y	Y	Y	Y	Y	Y
OHIO						
1 ***Chabot***	Y	Y	Y	Y	Y	Y
2 ***Portman***	Y	Y	Y	Y	Y	Y
3 Hall	Y	Y	Y	Y	Y	Y
4 ***Oxley***	Y	Y	Y	Y	Y	Y
5 ***Gillmor***	?	?	Y	Y	Y	Y
6 Strickland	Y	Y	Y	Y	Y	Y
7 ***Hobson***	Y	Y	Y	Y	Y	Y
8 ***Boehner***	Y	Y	Y	Y	Y	Y
9 Kaptur	Y	Y	Y	Y	Y	Y
10 Kucinich	+	+	+	+	+	Y
11 Jones	?	?	?	?	?	Y
12 ***Kasich***	?	?	?	Y	Y	Y
13 Brown	?	?	?	?	?	?
14 Sawyer	Y	Y	Y	Y	Y	Y
15 ***Pryce***	Y	Y	Y	Y	Y	Y
16 ***Regula***	Y	Y	Y	Y	Y	Y
17 Traficant	Y	Y	Y	Y	Y	Y
18 ***Ney***	Y	Y	Y	Y	Y	Y
19 ***LaTourette***	?	?	?	?	?	?
OKLAHOMA						
1 ***Largent***	Y	Y	Y	Y	Y	Y
2 ***Coburn***	Y	Y	Y	Y	Y	Y
3 ***Watkins***	Y	Y	Y	Y	Y	Y
4 ***Watts***	Y	Y	Y	Y	?	Y
5 ***Istook***	Y	Y	Y	Y	Y	Y
6 ***Lucas***	Y	Y	Y	Y	Y	Y
OREGON						
1 Wu	Y	Y	Y	Y	Y	Y
2 ***Walden***	Y	Y	Y	Y	Y	Y
3 Blumenauer	Y	Y	Y	Y	Y	Y
4 DeFazio	?	?	?	?	?	Y
5 Hooley	Y	Y	Y	Y	Y	Y
PENNSYLVANIA						
1 Brady	Y	Y	Y	Y	Y	Y
2 Fattah	Y	Y	Y	Y	Y	Y
3 Borski	Y	Y	Y	Y	Y	Y
4 Klink	?	?	?	?	?	Y
5 ***Peterson***	Y	Y	Y	Y	Y	Y
6 Holden	Y	Y	Y	Y	Y	Y
7 ***Weldon***	Y	Y	Y	Y	Y	Y
8 ***Greenwood***	Y	Y	Y	Y	Y	Y
9 ***Shuster***	Y	Y	Y	Y	Y	Y
10 ***Sherwood***	Y	Y	Y	?	Y	Y
11 Kanjorski	Y	Y	Y	Y	Y	Y
12 Murtha	Y	Y	Y	Y	Y	Y
13 Hoeffel	Y	Y	Y	Y	Y	Y
14 Coyne	Y	Y	Y	Y	Y	Y
15 ***Toomey***	Y	Y	Y	Y	Y	Y
16 ***Pitts***	Y	Y	Y	Y	Y	Y
17 ***Gekas***	Y	Y	Y	Y	Y	Y
18 Doyle	Y	Y	Y	Y	Y	?
19 ***Goodling***	Y	Y	Y	Y	Y	Y
20 Mascara	Y	Y	Y	Y	Y	Y
21 ***English***	Y	Y	Y	Y	Y	Y
RHODE ISLAND						
1 Kennedy	Y	Y	Y	Y	Y	Y
2 Weygand	Y	Y	Y	Y	Y	Y
SOUTH CAROLINA						
1 ***Sanford***	Y	Y	Y	Y	Y	Y
2 ***Spence***	?	?	?	?	?	?
3 ***Graham***	Y	Y	Y	Y	Y	Y
4 ***DeMint***	Y	Y	Y	Y	Y	Y
5 Spratt	Y	Y	Y	Y	?	Y
6 Clyburn	Y	Y	Y	Y	Y	Y
SOUTH DAKOTA						
AL ***Thune***	Y	Y	Y	Y	Y	Y
TENNESSEE						
1 ***Jenkins***	Y	Y	Y	Y	Y	Y
2 ***Duncan***	Y	Y	Y	Y	Y	Y
3 ***Wamp***	Y	Y	Y	Y	Y	Y
4 ***Hilleary***	Y	Y	Y	Y	Y	Y
5 Clement	Y	Y	Y	Y	Y	?
6 Gordon	Y	Y	Y	Y	Y	Y
7 ***Bryant***	Y	Y	Y	Y	Y	Y
8 Tanner	?	?	?	?	Y	Y
9 Ford	?	?	?	?	?	Y
TEXAS						
1 Sandlin	Y	Y	Y	Y	Y	Y
2 Turner	Y	Y	Y	Y	Y	Y
3 ***Johnson, Sam***	Y	Y	Y	Y	Y	Y
4 Hall	Y	Y	Y	Y	Y	Y
5 ***Sessions***	Y	Y	Y	Y	Y	Y
6 ***Barton***	Y	Y	Y	Y	Y	Y
7 ***Archer***	Y	Y	Y	Y	Y	Y
8 ***Brady***	Y	?	Y	Y	Y	Y
9 Lampson	Y	Y	Y	Y	Y	Y
10 Doggett	Y	Y	Y	Y	Y	Y
11 Edwards	Y	Y	Y	Y	Y	Y
12 ***Granger***	Y	Y	Y	?	?	?
13 ***Thornberry***	Y	Y	Y	Y	Y	Y
14 ***Paul***	Y	Y	Y	Y	Y	Y
15 Hinojosa	+	+	+	+	+	Y
16 Reyes	Y	Y	Y	Y	+	Y
17 Stenholm	Y	Y	Y	Y	Y	Y
18 Jackson-Lee	Y	Y	Y	Y	Y	Y
19 ***Combest***	Y	Y	Y	Y	Y	Y
20 Gonzalez	Y	Y	Y	Y	Y	Y
21 ***Smith***	Y	Y	Y	Y	Y	Y
22 ***DeLay***	Y	Y	Y	Y	Y	Y
23 ***Bonilla***	Y	Y	Y	Y	Y	Y
24 Frost	Y	Y	Y	Y	Y	?
25 Bentsen	Y	Y	Y	Y	Y	Y
26 ***Armey***	Y	?	?	Y	Y	Y
27 Ortiz	Y	Y	Y	Y	Y	Y
28 Rodriguez	Y	Y	Y	Y	Y	Y
29 Green	Y	Y	Y	Y	Y	Y
30 Johnson, E.B.	Y	Y	Y	Y	Y	Y
UTAH						
1 ***Hansen***	Y	Y	Y	Y	Y	Y
2 ***Cook***	Y	Y	Y	Y	Y	Y
3 ***Cannon***	Y	Y	Y	Y	Y	Y
VERMONT						
AL *Sanders*	Y	Y	Y	?	Y	Y
VIRGINIA						
1 ***Bateman***	Y	Y	Y	Y	Y	Y
2 Pickett	Y	Y	Y	Y	Y	Y
3 Scott	Y	Y	Y	Y	Y	?
4 Sisisky	Y	Y	Y	Y	Y	Y
5 *Goode*	Y	Y	Y	Y	Y	Y
6 ***Goodlatte***	Y	Y	Y	Y	Y	Y
7 ***Bliley***	Y	Y	Y	Y	?	Y
8 Moran	Y	Y	Y	Y	Y	?
9 Boucher	Y	Y	Y	Y	Y	Y
10 ***Wolf***	Y	Y	Y	Y	Y	Y
11 ***Davis***	Y	Y	Y	Y	Y	Y
WASHINGTON						
1 Inslee	Y	Y	Y	Y	Y	Y
2 ***Metcalf***	Y	Y	Y	Y	Y	Y
3 Baird	Y	Y	Y	Y	Y	Y
4 ***Hastings***	Y	Y	Y	Y	Y	Y
5 ***Nethercutt***	Y	Y	Y	Y	Y	Y
6 Dicks	Y	Y	Y	Y	Y	Y
7 McDermott	Y	Y	Y	Y	Y	Y
8 ***Dunn***	?	?	?	?	?	?
9 Smith	Y	Y	Y	Y	Y	Y
WEST VIRGINIA						
1 Mollohan	Y	Y	Y	Y	Y	Y
2 Wise	Y	Y	Y	Y	Y	Y
3 Rahall	Y	Y	Y	Y	Y	Y
WISCONSIN						
1 ***Ryan***	Y	Y	Y	Y	Y	Y
2 Baldwin	Y	Y	Y	Y	Y	Y
3 Kind	?	?	?	Y	Y	Y
4 Kleczka	Y	Y	Y	Y	Y	?
5 Barrett	Y	Y	Y	Y	Y	Y
6 ***Petri***	Y	Y	Y	Y	Y	Y
7 Obey	Y	Y	Y	Y	Y	Y
8 ***Green***	Y	Y	Y	Y	Y	Y
9 ***Sensenbrenner***	Y	Y	Y	Y	Y	Y
WYOMING						
AL ***Cubin***	Y	Y	Y	Y	Y	Y

Southern states - Ala., Ark., Fla., Ga., Ky., La., Miss., N.C., Okla., S.C., Tenn., Texas, Va.

35. Procedural Motion/Journal. Approval of the House Journal of March 8, 2000. Approved 369-45: R 195-15; D 172-30 (ND 129-23, SD 43-7); I 2-0. March 9, 2000.

36. HR 1695. Ivanpah Valley Airport/En bloc amendments. Hansen, R-Utah, amendment that would ease the transference of land back to the federal government if Clark County, Nev., decided not to use the property; permit a study to be performed after the land is conveyed to Clark County and make the Department of Interior a study leader; and allow the county to regain its money, less interest, from the federal government if the land transfer did not occur. Adopted 417-3: R 208-3; D 207-0 (ND 153-0, SD 54-0); I 2-0. March 9, 2000.

37. HR 1695. Ivanpah Valley Airport/Passage. Passage of the bill that would direct the Interior Department to convey to Clark County, Nev., about 6,400 acres of public land to develop an airport. Passed 420-1: R 210-1; D 208-0 (ND 154-0, SD 54-0); I 2-0. March 9, 2000.

38. HR 3081. Mininum Wage/Tax Revisions/Previous Question. Sessions, R-Texas, motion to order the previous question (thus ending debate and possibility of amendment) on adoption of the rule (H Res 434) to provide for House floor consideration of two bills. One would increase the federal hourly minimum wage by $1 over three years. The other would provide nearly $122.7 billion over 10 years in tax cuts, including reductions of estate and gift taxes totaling $78.7 billion. Motion agreed to 216-208: R 213-1; D 2-206 (ND 2-153, SD 0-53); I 1-1. March 9, 2000.

39. HR 3081. Minimum Wage/Tax Revisions/Rule. Adoption of the rule (H Res 434) to provide for the House floor consideration of two bills. One would increase the federal hourly minimum wage by $1 over three years. The other bill would provide nearly $122.7 billion over 10 years in tax cuts, including reductions of estate and gift taxes totaling $78.7 billion. The rule also struck a provision of the minimum wage measure that would have allowed states to opt out of the bill's wage increase under certain conditions. Adopted 214-211: R 211-3; D 2-207 (ND 2-153, SD 0-54); I 1-1. March 9, 2000.

40. HR 3081. Tax Revisions/Recommit. Rangel, D-N.Y., motion to recommit the bill to the House Ways and Means Committee with instructions to add an amendment that would strike the text of the bill and insert language that would permanently extend the work opportunities tax credit and the welfare-to-work credit. The amendment would also allow self-employed individuals to deduct their entire health insurance costs. Motion rejected 207-218: R 1-213; D 205-4 (ND 152-4, SD 53-0); I 1-1. March 9, 2000.

Key

Y Voted for (yea).
\# Paired for.
\+ Announced for.
N Voted against (nay).
X Paired against.
– Announced against.
P Voted "present."
C Voted "present" to avoid possible conflict of interest.
? Did not vote or otherwise make a position known.

•

Democrats ***Republicans***
Independents

	35	36	37	38	39	40
ALABAMA						
1 ***Callahan***	Y	Y	Y	Y	Y	N
2 ***Everett***	Y	Y	Y	Y	Y	N
3 ***Riley***	Y	Y	Y	Y	Y	N
4 ***Aderholt***	N	Y	Y	Y	Y	N
5 Cramer	Y	Y	Y	N	N	Y
6 ***Bachus***	Y	Y	Y	Y	Y	N
7 Hilliard	N	Y	Y	N	N	Y
ALASKA						
AL ***Young***	Y	Y	Y	Y	Y	N
ARIZONA						
1 ***Salmon***	Y	Y	Y	Y	Y	N
2 Pastor	Y	Y	Y	N	N	Y
3 ***Stump***	Y	Y	Y	Y	Y	N
4 ***Shadegg***	Y	Y	Y	Y	Y	N
5 ***Kolbe***	Y	Y	Y	Y	Y	N
6 ***Hayworth***	Y	Y	Y	Y	Y	N
ARKANSAS						
1 Berry	Y	Y	Y	N	N	Y
2 Snyder	Y	Y	Y	N	N	Y
3 ***Hutchinson***	Y	Y	Y	Y	Y	N
4 ***Dickey***	N	Y	Y	Y	Y	N
CALIFORNIA						
1 Thompson	N	Y	Y	N	N	Y
2 ***Herger***	Y	Y	Y	Y	Y	N
3 ***Ose***	Y	Y	Y	Y	Y	N
4 ***Doolittle***	Y	Y	Y	Y	Y	N
5 Matsui	Y	Y	Y	N	N	Y
6 Woolsey	Y	Y	Y	N	N	Y
7 Miller, George	N	Y	Y	N	N	Y
8 Pelosi	Y	Y	Y	N	N	Y
9 Lee	Y	Y	Y	N	N	Y
10 Tauscher	Y	Y	Y	N	N	Y
11 ***Pombo***	Y	Y	Y	Y	Y	N
12 Lantos	Y	Y	Y	N	N	Y
13 Stark	Y	Y	Y	N	N	Y
14 Eshoo	Y	Y	Y	N	N	Y
15 ***Campbell***	Y	Y	Y	Y	Y	N
16 Lofgren	Y	Y	Y	N	N	Y
17 Farr	Y	Y	Y	N	N	Y
18 Condit	Y	Y	Y	N	N	Y
19 ***Radanovich***	Y	Y	Y	Y	Y	N
20 Dooley	Y	Y	Y	N	N	Y
21 ***Thomas***	Y	Y	Y	Y	Y	N
22 Capps	Y	Y	Y	N	N	Y
23 ***Gallegly***	Y	Y	Y	Y	Y	N
24 Sherman	Y	Y	Y	N	N	Y
25 ***McKeon***	Y	Y	Y	Y	Y	N
26 Berman	Y	Y	Y	N	N	Y
27 ***Rogan***	Y	Y	Y	Y	Y	N
28 ***Dreier***	Y	Y	Y	Y	Y	N
29 Waxman	Y	Y	Y	N	N	Y
30 Becerra	Y	Y	Y	N	N	Y
31 Martinez	Y	Y	Y	Y	Y	N
32 Dixon	Y	Y	Y	N	N	Y
33 Roybal-Allard	Y	Y	Y	N	N	Y
34 Napolitano	Y	Y	Y	N	N	Y
35 Waters	N	Y	?	N	N	Y
36 ***Kuykendall***	Y	Y	Y	Y	Y	N
37 Millender-McD.	Y	Y	Y	N	N	Y
38 ***Horn***	Y	?	Y	Y	Y	N
39 ***Royce***	Y	Y	Y	Y	Y	N
40 ***Lewis***	Y	Y	Y	Y	Y	N
41 ***Miller, Gary***	Y	Y	Y	Y	Y	N
42 Baca	Y	Y	Y	N	N	Y
43 ***Calvert***	Y	Y	Y	Y	Y	N
44 ***Bono***	?	Y	Y	Y	Y	N
45 ***Rohrabacher***	Y	Y	Y	Y	Y	N
46 Sanchez	Y	Y	Y	N	N	Y
47 ***Cox***	Y	Y	Y	Y	Y	N
48 ***Packard***	Y	Y	Y	Y	Y	N
49 ***Bilbray***	N	Y	Y	Y	Y	N
50 Filner	N	Y	Y	N	N	Y
51 ***Cunningham***	Y	Y	Y	Y	Y	N
52 ***Hunter***	Y	?	Y	Y	Y	N
COLORADO						
1 DeGette	Y	Y	Y	N	N	Y
2 Udall	Y	Y	Y	N	N	Y
3 ***McInnis***	Y	Y	Y	Y	Y	N
4 ***Schaffer***	?	?	?	?	?	?
5 ***Hefley***	N	Y	Y	Y	N	N
6 ***Tancredo***	P	Y	Y	Y	Y	N
CONNECTICUT						
1 Larson	Y	Y	Y	N	N	Y
2 Gejdenson	Y	Y	Y	N	N	Y
3 DeLauro	Y	Y	Y	N	N	Y
4 ***Shays***	Y	Y	Y	Y	Y	N
5 Maloney	Y	Y	Y	N	N	Y
6 ***Johnson***	Y	Y	Y	Y	Y	N
DELAWARE						
AL ***Castle***	Y	Y	Y	Y	Y	N
FLORIDA						
1 ***Scarborough***	?	?	?	?	?	?
2 Boyd	Y	Y	Y	N	N	Y
3 Brown	Y	Y	Y	N	N	Y
4 ***Fowler***	Y	Y	Y	Y	Y	N
5 Thurman	Y	Y	Y	N	N	Y
6 ***Stearns***	Y	Y	Y	Y	Y	N
7 ***Mica***	Y	Y	Y	Y	Y	N
8 ***McCollum***	?	?	?	?	?	?
9 ***Bilirakis***	Y	Y	Y	Y	Y	N
10 ***Young***	Y	Y	Y	Y	Y	N
11 Davis	Y	Y	Y	N	N	Y
12 ***Canady***	Y	Y	Y	Y	Y	N
13 ***Miller***	Y	Y	Y	Y	Y	N
14 ***Goss***	Y	Y	Y	Y	Y	N
15 ***Weldon***	Y	Y	Y	Y	Y	N
16 ***Foley***	Y	Y	Y	Y	Y	N
17 Meek	Y	Y	Y	?	N	Y
18 ***Ros-Lehtinen***	Y	Y	Y	Y	Y	N
19 Wexler	Y	Y	Y	N	N	Y
20 Deutsch	Y	Y	Y	N	N	Y
21 ***Diaz-Balart***	Y	Y	Y	Y	Y	N
22 ***Shaw***	Y	Y	Y	Y	Y	N
23 Hastings	N	Y	Y	N	N	Y
GEORGIA						
1 ***Kingston***	Y	Y	Y	Y	Y	N
2 Bishop	Y	Y	Y	N	N	Y
3 ***Collins***	Y	Y	Y	Y	Y	N
4 McKinney	Y	Y	Y	N	N	Y
5 Lewis	N	Y	Y	N	N	Y
6 ***Isakson***	Y	Y	Y	Y	Y	N
7 ***Barr***	Y	Y	Y	Y	Y	N
8 ***Chambliss***	Y	Y	Y	Y	Y	N
9 ***Deal***	Y	Y	Y	Y	Y	N
10 ***Norwood***	Y	Y	Y	Y	Y	N
11 ***Linder***	Y	Y	Y	Y	Y	N
HAWAII						
1 Abercrombie	Y	Y	Y	N	N	Y
2 Mink	Y	Y	Y	N	N	Y
IDAHO						
1 ***Chenoweth-Hage***	N	N	Y	Y	Y	N
2 ***Simpson***	Y	Y	Y	Y	Y	N
ILLINOIS						
1 Rush	Y	Y	Y	N	N	Y
2 Jackson	Y	Y	Y	N	N	Y
3 Lipinski	Y	Y	Y	N	N	N
4 Gutierrez	N	Y	Y	N	N	Y
5 Blagojevich	Y	Y	Y	N	N	Y
6 ***Hyde***	Y	Y	Y	Y	Y	N
7 Davis	Y	Y	Y	N	N	Y
8 ***Crane***	N	Y	Y	Y	Y	N
9 Schakowsky	Y	Y	Y	N	N	Y
10 ***Porter***	Y	Y	Y	Y	Y	N
11 ***Weller***	N	Y	Y	Y	Y	N
12 Costello	N	Y	Y	N	N	Y
13 ***Biggert***	Y	Y	Y	Y	Y	N

ND Northern Democrats SD Southern Democrats

	35	36	37	38	39	40
14 ***Hastert***					Y	
15 ***Ewing***	Y	Y	Y	Y	Y	N
16 ***Manzullo***	Y	Y	Y	Y	Y	N
17 Evans	Y	Y	Y	N	N	Y
18 ***LaHood***	Y	Y	Y	Y	Y	N
19 Phelps	Y	Y	Y	N	N	Y
20 ***Shimkus***	Y	Y	Y	Y	Y	N
INDIANA						
1 Visclosky	N	Y	Y	N	N	Y
2 ***McIntosh***	?	Y	Y	Y	Y	N
3 Roemer	Y	Y	Y	N	N	Y
4 ***Souder***	Y	Y	Y	Y	Y	N
5 ***Buyer***	Y	Y	Y	Y	Y	N
6 ***Burton***	Y	Y	Y	Y	Y	N
7 ***Pease***	Y	Y	Y	Y	Y	N
8 ***Hostettler***	Y	Y	Y	Y	Y	N
9 Hill	Y	Y	Y	N	N	Y
10 Carson	Y	Y	Y	N	N	Y
IOWA						
1 ***Leach***	Y	Y	Y	Y	Y	N
2 ***Nussle***	Y	Y	Y	Y	Y	N
3 Boswell	Y	Y	Y	N	N	Y
4 ***Ganske***	Y	Y	Y	Y	Y	?
5 ***Latham***	Y	Y	Y	Y	Y	N
KANSAS						
1 ***Moran***	Y	Y	Y	Y	Y	N
2 ***Ryun***	Y	Y	Y	Y	Y	N
3 Moore	N	Y	Y	N	N	Y
4 ***Tiahrt***	Y	Y	?	Y	Y	N
KENTUCKY						
1 ***Whitfield***	Y	Y	Y	Y	Y	N
2 ***Lewis***	Y	Y	Y	Y	Y	N
3 ***Northup***	Y	Y	Y	Y	Y	N
4 Lucas	Y	Y	Y	N	N	Y
5 ***Rogers***	Y	Y	Y	Y	Y	N
6 ***Fletcher***	Y	Y	Y	Y	Y	N
LOUISIANA						
1 ***Vitter***	Y	Y	Y	Y	Y	N
2 Jefferson	Y	Y	Y	N	N	Y
3 ***Tauzin***	Y	Y	Y	Y	Y	N
4 ***McCrery***	Y	Y	Y	Y	Y	N
5 ***Cooksey***	?	?	?	?	?	?
6 ***Baker***	Y	Y	Y	Y	Y	N
7 John	Y	Y	Y	N	N	Y
MAINE						
1 Allen	Y	Y	Y	N	N	Y
2 Baldacci	Y	Y	Y	N	N	Y
MARYLAND						
1 ***Gilchrest***	Y	Y	Y	Y	Y	N
2 ***Ehrlich***	Y	Y	Y	Y	Y	N
3 Cardin	Y	Y	Y	N	N	Y
4 Wynn	Y	Y	Y	N	N	Y
5 Hoyer	Y	Y	Y	N	N	Y
6 ***Bartlett***	Y	Y	Y	Y	Y	N
7 Cummings	Y	Y	Y	N	N	Y
8 ***Morella***	Y	Y	Y	Y	Y	Y
MASSACHUSETTS						
1 Olver	Y	Y	Y	N	N	Y
2 Neal	Y	Y	Y	N	N	Y
3 McGovern	Y	Y	Y	N	N	Y
4 Frank	?	Y	Y	N	N	Y
5 Meehan	Y	Y	Y	N	N	Y
6 Tierney	Y	Y	Y	N	N	Y
7 Markey	Y	Y	Y	N	N	Y
8 Capuano	?	Y	Y	N	N	Y
9 Moakley	Y	Y	Y	N	N	Y
10 Delahunt	Y	Y	Y	N	N	Y
MICHIGAN						
1 Stupak	N	Y	Y	N	N	Y
2 ***Hoekstra***	Y	Y	Y	Y	Y	N
3 ***Ehlers***	Y	Y	Y	Y	Y	N
4 ***Camp***	Y	Y	Y	Y	Y	N
5 Barcia	Y	Y	Y	N	N	N
6 ***Upton***	Y	Y	Y	Y	Y	N
7 ***Smith***	Y	Y	Y	Y	Y	N
8 Stabenow	Y	Y	Y	N	N	Y
9 Kildee	Y	Y	Y	N	N	Y
10 Bonior	Y	Y	Y	N	N	Y
11 ***Knollenberg***	Y	Y	Y	Y	Y	N
12 Levin	Y	Y	Y	N	N	Y
13 Rivers	Y	Y	Y	N	N	Y
14 Conyers	Y	Y	Y	N	N	Y
15 Kilpatrick	Y	Y	Y	N	N	Y
16 Dingell	Y	Y	Y	N	N	Y
MINNESOTA						
1 ***Gutknecht***	Y	Y	Y	N	N	N
2 Minge	Y	Y	Y	N	N	Y
3 ***Ramstad***	N	Y	Y	Y	Y	N
4 Vento	?	?	?	?	?	?
5 Sabo	N	Y	Y	N	N	Y
6 Luther	Y	Y	Y	N	N	Y
7 Peterson	N	Y	Y	N	N	Y
8 Oberstar	N	Y	Y	N	N	Y
MISSISSIPPI						
1 ***Wicker***	Y	Y	Y	Y	Y	N
2 Thompson	N	Y	Y	N	N	Y
3 ***Pickering***	Y	Y	Y	Y	Y	N
4 Shows	Y	Y	Y	N	N	Y
5 Taylor	N	Y	Y	N	N	Y
MISSOURI						
1 Clay	N	Y	Y	N	N	Y
2 ***Talent***	Y	Y	Y	Y	Y	N
3 Gephardt	Y	Y	Y	N	N	Y
4 Skelton	Y	Y	Y	N	N	Y
5 McCarthy	Y	Y	Y	N	N	Y
6 Danner	Y	Y	Y	N	N	Y
7 ***Blunt***	Y	Y	Y	Y	Y	N
8 ***Emerson***	Y	Y	Y	Y	Y	N
9 ***Hulshof***	Y	Y	Y	Y	Y	N
MONTANA						
AL ***Hill***	N	Y	Y	Y	Y	N
NEBRASKA						
1 ***Bereuter***	Y	Y	Y	Y	Y	N
2 ***Terry***	Y	Y	Y	Y	+	N
3 ***Barrett***	Y	Y	Y	Y	Y	N
NEVADA						
1 Berkley	Y	Y	Y	N	N	Y
2 ***Gibbons***	N	Y	Y	Y	Y	N
NEW HAMPSHIRE						
1 ***Sununu***	Y	Y	Y	Y	Y	N
2 ***Bass***	Y	Y	Y	Y	Y	N
NEW JERSEY						
1 Andrews	Y	Y	Y	N	N	Y
2 ***LoBiondo***	N	Y	Y	Y	Y	N
3 ***Saxton***	Y	Y	?	Y	Y	N
4 ***Smith***	Y	Y	Y	Y	Y	N
5 ***Roukema***	Y	Y	Y	Y	Y	N
6 Pallone	Y	Y	Y	N	N	Y
7 ***Franks***	Y	Y	Y	Y	Y	N
8 Pascrell	N	Y	Y	N	N	Y
9 Rothman	Y	Y	Y	N	N	Y
10 Payne	?	Y	Y	N	N	Y
11 ***Frelinghuysen***	Y	Y	Y	Y	Y	N
12 Holt	Y	Y	Y	N	N	Y
13 Menendez	Y	Y	Y	N	N	Y
NEW MEXICO						
1 ***Wilson***	Y	Y	Y	Y	Y	N
2 ***Skeen***	Y	Y	Y	Y	Y	N
3 Udall	N	Y	Y	N	N	Y
NEW YORK						
1 Forbes	Y	Y	Y	N	N	Y
2 ***Lazio***	Y	Y	Y	Y	Y	N
3 ***King***	Y	Y	Y	Y	Y	N
4 McCarthy	Y	Y	Y	N	N	Y
5 Ackerman	Y	Y	Y	N	N	Y
6 Meeks	Y	Y	Y	N	N	Y
7 Crowley	Y	Y	Y	N	N	Y
8 Nadler	Y	Y	Y	N	N	Y
9 Weiner	Y	Y	Y	N	N	Y
10 Towns	Y	Y	Y	N	N	Y
11 Owens	Y	Y	Y	N	N	Y
12 Velazquez	Y	Y	Y	N	N	Y
13 ***Fossella***	Y	Y	Y	Y	Y	N
14 Maloney	Y	Y	Y	N	N	Y
15 Rangel	Y	Y	Y	N	N	Y
16 Serrano	Y	Y	Y	N	N	Y
17 Engel	Y	Y	Y	N	N	Y
18 Lowey	Y	Y	Y	N	N	Y
19 ***Kelly***	Y	Y	Y	Y	Y	N
20 ***Gilman***	Y	Y	Y	Y	Y	N
21 McNulty	Y	Y	Y	N	N	Y
22 ***Sweeney***	N	Y	Y	Y	Y	N
23 ***Boehlert***	Y	Y	Y	Y	Y	N
24 ***McHugh***	Y	Y	Y	Y	Y	N
25 ***Walsh***	Y	Y	Y	Y	Y	N
26 Hinchey	N	Y	Y	N	N	Y
27 ***Reynolds***	Y	Y	Y	Y	Y	N
28 Slaughter	Y	Y	Y	N	N	Y
29 LaFalce	Y	Y	Y	N	N	Y
30 ***Quinn***	Y	Y	Y	Y	Y	N
31 ***Houghton***	Y	Y	Y	Y	Y	N
NORTH CAROLINA						
1 Clayton	Y	Y	Y	N	N	Y
2 Etheridge	Y	Y	Y	N	N	Y
3 ***Jones***	Y	Y	Y	Y	Y	N
4 Price	Y	Y	Y	N	N	Y
5 ***Burr***	Y	Y	Y	Y	Y	N
6 ***Coble***	Y	Y	N	Y	Y	N
7 McIntyre	Y	Y	Y	N	N	Y
8 ***Hayes***	Y	Y	Y	Y	Y	N
9 ***Myrick***	Y	Y	Y	?	?	N
10 ***Ballenger***	Y	Y	Y	Y	Y	N
11 ***Taylor***	Y	Y	Y	Y	Y	N
12 Watt	Y	Y	Y	N	N	Y
NORTH DAKOTA						
AL Pomeroy	Y	Y	Y	N	N	Y
OHIO						
1 ***Chabot***	Y	Y	Y	Y	Y	N
2 ***Portman***	Y	Y	Y	Y	Y	N
3 Hall	Y	Y	Y	N	N	Y
4 ***Oxley***	Y	Y	Y	Y	Y	N
5 ***Gillmor***	Y	Y	Y	Y	Y	N
6 Strickland	N	Y	Y	N	N	Y
7 ***Hobson***	Y	Y	Y	Y	Y	N
8 ***Boehner***	Y	Y	Y	Y	Y	N
9 Kaptur	Y	Y	Y	N	N	Y
10 Kucinich	N	Y	Y	N	N	Y
11 Jones	Y	Y	Y	N	N	Y
12 ***Kasich***	?	Y	Y	Y	Y	N
13 Brown	?	?	?	?	?	Y
14 Sawyer	Y	Y	Y	N	N	Y
15 ***Pryce***	Y	Y	Y	Y	Y	N
16 ***Regula***	Y	Y	Y	Y	Y	N
17 Traficant	Y	Y	Y	Y	Y	N
18 ***Ney***	Y	Y	Y	Y	Y	N
19 ***LaTourette***	?	?	?	Y	Y	N
OKLAHOMA						
1 ***Largent***	Y	Y	Y	Y	Y	N
2 ***Coburn***	N	N	Y	Y	Y	N
3 ***Watkins***	Y	Y	Y	Y	Y	N
4 ***Watts***	Y	Y	Y	Y	Y	N
5 ***Istook***	Y	Y	Y	Y	N	N
6 ***Lucas***	Y	Y	Y	Y	Y	N
OREGON						
1 Wu	N	Y	Y	N	N	Y
2 ***Walden***	Y	Y	Y	Y	Y	N
3 Blumenauer	Y	Y	Y	N	N	Y
4 DeFazio	Y	Y	Y	N	N	Y
5 Hooley	Y	Y	Y	N	N	Y
PENNSYLVANIA						
1 Brady	N	Y	Y	N	N	Y
2 Fattah	Y	Y	Y	N	N	Y
3 Borski	N	Y	Y	N	N	Y
4 Klink	Y	Y	Y	N	N	Y
5 ***Peterson***	Y	Y	Y	Y	Y	N
6 Holden	Y	Y	Y	N	N	Y
7 ***Weldon***	Y	Y	Y	Y	Y	N
8 ***Greenwood***	Y	Y	Y	Y	Y	N
9 ***Shuster***	Y	Y	Y	Y	Y	N
10 ***Sherwood***	Y	Y	Y	Y	Y	N
11 Kanjorski	Y	Y	Y	N	N	Y
12 Murtha	Y	?	Y	N	N	Y
13 Hoeffel	Y	Y	Y	N	N	Y
14 Coyne	Y	Y	Y	N	N	Y
15 ***Toomey***	Y	Y	Y	Y	Y	N
16 ***Pitts***	Y	Y	Y	Y	Y	N
17 ***Gekas***	Y	Y	Y	Y	Y	N
18 Doyle	Y	Y	Y	N	N	Y
19 ***Goodling***	Y	Y	Y	Y	Y	N
20 Mascara	Y	Y	Y	N	N	Y
21 ***English***	N	Y	Y	Y	Y	N
RHODE ISLAND						
1 Kennedy	Y	Y	Y	N	N	Y
2 Weygand	Y	Y	Y	N	N	Y
SOUTH CAROLINA						
1 ***Sanford***	Y	Y	Y	Y	Y	N
2 ***Spence***	?	?	?	?	?	?
3 ***Graham***	Y	Y	Y	Y	Y	N
4 ***DeMint***	Y	Y	Y	Y	Y	N
5 Spratt	Y	Y	Y	N	N	Y
6 Clyburn	N	Y	Y	N	N	Y
SOUTH DAKOTA						
AL ***Thune***	Y	Y	Y	Y	Y	N
TENNESSEE						
1 ***Jenkins***	Y	Y	Y	Y	Y	N
2 ***Duncan***	Y	Y	Y	Y	Y	N
3 ***Wamp***	Y	Y	Y	Y	Y	N
4 ***Hilleary***	N	Y	Y	Y	Y	N
5 Clement	?	Y	Y	N	N	Y
6 Gordon	Y	Y	Y	N	N	Y
7 ***Bryant***	Y	Y	Y	Y	Y	N
8 Tanner	Y	Y	Y	N	N	Y
9 Ford	Y	Y	Y	N	N	Y
TEXAS						
1 Sandlin	Y	Y	Y	N	N	Y
2 Turner	Y	Y	Y	N	N	Y
3 ***Johnson, Sam***	Y	?	?	?	Y	N
4 Hall	Y	Y	Y	N	N	Y
5 ***Sessions***	Y	Y	Y	Y	Y	N
6 ***Barton***	Y	Y	Y	Y	Y	N
7 ***Archer***	Y	Y	Y	Y	Y	N
8 ***Brady***	Y	Y	Y	Y	Y	N
9 Lampson	Y	Y	Y	N	N	Y
10 Doggett	Y	Y	Y	N	N	Y
11 Edwards	Y	Y	Y	N	N	Y
12 ***Granger***	?	?	?	?	?	?
13 ***Thornberry***	Y	Y	Y	Y	Y	N
14 ***Paul***	Y	N	Y	Y	Y	N
15 Hinojosa	Y	Y	Y	N	N	Y
16 Reyes	Y	Y	Y	N	N	Y
17 Stenholm	Y	Y	Y	N	N	Y
18 Jackson-Lee	Y	Y	Y	N	N	Y
19 ***Combest***	Y	Y	Y	Y	Y	N
20 Gonzalez	Y	Y	Y	N	N	Y
21 ***Smith***	Y	Y	Y	Y	Y	N
22 ***DeLay***	Y	Y	Y	Y	Y	N
23 ***Bonilla***	Y	Y	Y	Y	Y	N
24 Frost	?	Y	Y	N	N	Y
25 Bentsen	Y	Y	Y	N	N	Y
26 ***Armey***	Y	Y	Y	Y	Y	N
27 Ortiz	Y	Y	Y	N	N	Y
28 Rodriguez	Y	Y	Y	N	N	Y
29 Green	Y	Y	Y	N	N	Y
30 Johnson, E.B.	Y	Y	Y	N	N	?
UTAH						
1 ***Hansen***	Y	Y	Y	Y	Y	N
2 ***Cook***	Y	Y	Y	Y	Y	N
3 ***Cannon***	Y	Y	Y	Y	Y	N
VERMONT						
AL *Sanders*	Y	Y	Y	N	N	Y
VIRGINIA						
1 ***Bateman***	Y	Y	Y	Y	Y	N
2 Pickett	N	Y	Y	N	N	Y
3 Scott	?	Y	Y	N	N	Y
4 Sisisky	Y	Y	Y	N	N	Y
5 *Goode*	Y	Y	Y	Y	Y	N
6 ***Goodlatte***	Y	Y	Y	Y	Y	N
7 ***Bliley***	Y	Y	Y	Y	Y	N
8 Moran	?	Y	Y	N	N	Y
9 Boucher	Y	Y	Y	N	N	Y
10 ***Wolf***	Y	Y	Y	Y	Y	N
11 ***Davis***	Y	Y	Y	Y	Y	N
WASHINGTON						
1 Inslee	Y	Y	Y	N	N	Y
2 ***Metcalf***	Y	Y	Y	Y	Y	N
3 Baird	N	Y	Y	N	N	Y
4 ***Hastings***	Y	Y	Y	Y	Y	N
5 ***Nethercutt***	Y	Y	Y	Y	Y	N
6 Dicks	Y	Y	Y	N	N	Y
7 McDermott	N	Y	Y	N	N	Y
8 ***Dunn***	Y	Y	Y	Y	Y	N
9 Smith	Y	Y	Y	N	N	Y
WEST VIRGINIA						
1 Mollohan	Y	Y	Y	N	N	Y
2 Wise	Y	?	Y	N	N	Y
3 Rahall	Y	Y	Y	N	N	Y
WISCONSIN						
1 ***Ryan***	Y	Y	Y	Y	Y	N
2 Baldwin	Y	Y	Y	N	N	Y
3 Kind	Y	Y	Y	N	N	Y
4 Kleczka	Y	Y	Y	N	N	Y
5 Barrett	Y	Y	Y	N	N	Y
6 ***Petri***	Y	Y	Y	Y	Y	N
7 Obey	Y	Y	Y	N	N	Y
8 ***Green***	Y	Y	Y	Y	Y	N
9 ***Sensenbrenner***	Y	Y	Y	Y	Y	N
WYOMING						
AL ***Cubin***	Y	Y	Y	Y	Y	N

Southern states - Ala., Ark., Fla., Ga., Ky., La., Miss., N.C., Okla., S.C., Tenn., Texas, Va.

41. HR 3081. Tax Revisions/Passage. Passage of the bill that would provide about $122.7 billion over 10 years in tax cuts, including reductions of estate and gift taxes totaling $78.7 billion. The bill would also increase the deduction for health insurance for self-employed individuals to 100 percent beginning in 2001, authorize the Housing and Urban Development secretary to designate 15 renewal communities in both urban and rural areas, and increase the deductible percentage of business meal expenses to 60 percent in 2002. (The business meal deduction would be increased to 55 percent in 2001). Passed 257-169: R 215-1; D 41-167 (ND 26-129, SD 15-38); I 1-1. March 9, 2000. A "nay" was a vote in support of the president's position.

42. HR 3846. Minimum Wage/Question of Continued Consideration. Judgment of the House to continue consideration of the bill, despite a point of order raised by Largent, R-Okla., that the bill constituted an unfunded mandate. Continued consideration agreed to 274-141: R 72-137; D 201-3 (ND 152-0, SD 49-3); I 1-1. March 9, 2000.

43. HR 3846. Minimum Wage/Two-Year Increase. Traficant, D-Ohio, amendment that would increase the minimum wage by $1 over two years. Adopted 246-179: R 42-173; D 203-5 (ND 155-0, SD 48-5); I 1-1. March 9, 2000. A "yea" was a vote in support of the president's position.

44. HR 3846. Minimum Wage/Recommit. Clay, D-Mo., motion to recommit the bill to the Committee on Education and the Workforce with instructions to report the bill back to the House with an amendment that would strike the exemption from minimum wage guidelines for computer professionals, funeral directors and certain sales employees and gradually phase in the minimum wage in the Commonwealth of the Northern Mariana Islands. Motion rejected 181-243: R 0-214; D 180-28 (ND 141-14, SD 39-14); I 1-1. March 9, 2000.

45. HR 3846. Minimum Wage/Passage. Passage of the bill, as amended, that would increase the federal hourly minimum wage by $1 over two years. It would also exempt computer professionals, funeral directors and certain sales employees from minimum wage guidelines. Passed 282-143: R 78-137; D 203-5 (ND 155-0, SD 48-5); I 1-1. March 9, 2000.

Key

- Y Voted for (yea).
- # Paired for.
- + Announced for.
- N Voted against (nay).
- X Paired against.
- – Announced against.
- P Voted "present."
- C Voted "present" to avoid possible conflict of interest.
- ? Did not vote or otherwise make a position known.

Democrats ***Republicans*** *Independents*

	41	42	43	44	45
ALABAMA					
1 ***Callahan***	Y	Y	N	N	N
2 ***Everett***	Y	N	N	N	Y
3 ***Riley***	Y	N	N	N	Y
4 ***Aderholt***	Y	Y	Y	N	Y
5 Cramer	Y	Y	Y	N	Y
6 ***Bachus***	Y	N	N	N	N
7 Hilliard	N	Y	Y	Y	Y
ALASKA					
AL ***Young***	Y	Y	Y	N	Y
ARIZONA					
1 ***Salmon***	Y	N	N	N	N
2 Pastor	N	Y	Y	Y	Y
3 ***Stump***	Y	N	N	N	N
4 ***Shadegg***	Y	N	N	N	N
5 ***Kolbe***	Y	N	N	N	N
6 ***Hayworth***	Y	N	N	N	N
ARKANSAS					
1 Berry	N	Y	Y	N	Y
2 Snyder	N	Y	Y	Y	Y
3 ***Hutchinson***	Y	Y	N	N	N
4 ***Dickey***	Y	N	N	N	N
CALIFORNIA					
1 Thompson	Y	Y	Y	Y	Y
2 ***Herger***	Y	N	N	N	N
3 ***Ose***	Y	Y	N	N	N
4 ***Doolittle***	Y	N	N	N	N
5 Matsui	N	Y	Y	Y	Y
6 Woolsey	N	Y	Y	Y	Y
7 Miller, George	N	Y	Y	Y	Y
8 Pelosi	N	Y	Y	Y	Y
9 Lee	N	Y	Y	Y	Y
10 Tauscher	Y	?	Y	N	Y
11 ***Pombo***	Y	N	N	N	N
12 Lantos	N	Y	Y	Y	Y
13 Stark	N	Y	Y	Y	Y
14 Eshoo	N	Y	Y	N	Y
15 ***Campbell***	Y	N	N	N	N
16 Lofgren	N	Y	Y	N	Y
17 Farr	N	Y	Y	N	Y
18 Condit	Y	Y	Y	N	Y
19 ***Radanovich***	Y	N	N	N	N
20 Dooley	Y	?	Y	Y	Y
21 ***Thomas***	Y	Y	N	N	N
22 Capps	Y	Y	Y	Y	Y
23 ***Gallegly***	Y	Y	N	N	Y
24 Sherman	N	Y	Y	Y	Y
25 ***McKeon***	Y	N	N	N	N
26 Berman	N	Y	Y	Y	Y
27 ***Rogan***	Y	N	N	N	N
28 ***Dreier***	Y	N	N	N	N
29 Waxman	N	Y	Y	Y	Y
30 Becerra	N	Y	Y	Y	Y
31 Martinez	Y	Y	Y	N	Y
32 Dixon	N	Y	Y	Y	Y
33 Roybal-Allard	N	Y	Y	Y	Y
34 Napolitano	N	Y	Y	Y	Y
35 Waters	N	Y	Y	Y	Y
36 ***Kuykendall***	Y	Y	N	N	N
37 Millender-McD.	N	Y	Y	Y	Y
38 ***Horn***	Y	Y	Y	N	Y
39 ***Royce***	Y	N	N	N	N
40 ***Lewis***	Y	Y	N	N	Y
41 ***Miller, Gary***	Y	N	N	N	N
42 Baca	N	Y	Y	Y	Y
43 ***Calvert***	Y	N	N	N	N
44 ***Bono***	Y	Y	N	N	Y
45 ***Rohrabacher***	Y	N	N	N	N
46 Sanchez	Y	Y	Y	Y	Y
47 ***Cox***	Y	N	N	N	N
48 ***Packard***	Y	N	N	N	N
49 ***Bilbray***	Y	Y	Y	N	Y
50 Filner	N	Y	Y	Y	Y
51 ***Cunningham***	Y	N	N	N	N
52 ***Hunter***	Y	Y	N	N	Y
COLORADO					
1 DeGette	N	Y	Y	Y	Y
2 Udall	N	Y	Y	Y	Y
3 ***McInnis***	Y	N	N	N	N
4 ***Schaffer***	?	?	?	?	?
5 ***Hefley***	Y	N	N	N	N
6 ***Tancredo***	Y	N	N	N	N
CONNECTICUT					
1 Larson	N	Y	Y	Y	Y
2 Gejdenson	N	Y	Y	Y	Y
3 DeLauro	N	Y	Y	Y	Y
4 ***Shays***	Y	Y	Y	N	Y
5 Maloney	Y	Y	Y	Y	Y
6 ***Johnson***	Y	Y	Y	N	Y
DELAWARE					
AL ***Castle***	Y	Y	Y	N	Y
FLORIDA					
1 ***Scarborough***	?	?	?	?	?
2 Boyd	N	Y	N	N	N
3 Brown	N	Y	Y	Y	Y
4 ***Fowler***	Y	N	N	N	N
5 Thurman	N	?	Y	Y	Y
6 ***Stearns***	Y	N	N	N	N
7 ***Mica***	Y	N	N	N	N
8 ***McCollum***	?	?	?	?	?
9 ***Bilirakis***	Y	Y	N	N	Y
10 ***Young***	Y	Y	Y	N	Y
11 Davis	N	Y	Y	N	Y
12 ***Canady***	Y	Y	N	N	Y
13 ***Miller***	Y	N	N	N	N
14 ***Goss***	Y	N	N	N	N
15 ***Weldon***	Y	N	N	N	N
16 ***Foley***	Y	Y	N	N	Y
17 Meek	N	Y	Y	Y	Y
18 ***Ros-Lehtinen***	Y	Y	Y	N	Y
19 Wexler	N	Y	Y	Y	Y
20 Deutsch	N	Y	Y	Y	Y
21 ***Diaz-Balart***	Y	Y	Y	N	Y
22 ***Shaw***	Y	Y	N	N	Y
23 Hastings	N	Y	Y	Y	Y
GEORGIA					
1 ***Kingston***	Y	N	N	N	N
2 Bishop	Y	Y	Y	N	Y
3 ***Collins***	Y	N	N	N	N
4 McKinney	N	Y	Y	Y	Y
5 Lewis	N	Y	Y	Y	Y
6 ***Isakson***	Y	N	N	N	N
7 ***Barr***	Y	N	N	N	N
8 ***Chambliss***	Y	N	N	N	N
9 ***Deal***	Y	N	N	N	N
10 ***Norwood***	Y	N	N	N	N
11 ***Linder***	Y	?	N	N	N
HAWAII					
1 Abercrombie	N	Y	Y	Y	Y
2 Mink	N	Y	Y	Y	Y
IDAHO					
1 ***Chenoweth-Hage***	Y	N	N	N	N
2 ***Simpson***	Y	N	N	N	N
ILLINOIS					
1 Rush	N	Y	Y	Y	Y
2 Jackson	N	Y	Y	Y	Y
3 Lipinski	N	Y	Y	Y	Y
4 Gutierrez	N	Y	Y	Y	Y
5 Blagojevich	N	Y	Y	Y	Y
6 ***Hyde***	Y	Y	Y	N	Y
7 Davis	N	Y	Y	Y	Y
8 ***Crane***	Y	N	N	N	N
9 Schakowsky	N	Y	Y	Y	Y
10 ***Porter***	Y	Y	N	N	N
11 ***Weller***	Y	Y	Y	N	Y
12 Costello	N	Y	Y	Y	Y
13 ***Biggert***	Y	N	N	N	N

ND Northern Democrats SD Southern Democrats

	41	42	43	44	45
14 ***Hastert***	Y				
15 ***Ewing***	Y	N	N	N	N
16 ***Manzullo***	Y	N	N	N	N
17 Evans	N	Y	Y	Y	Y
18 ***LaHood***	Y	Y	Y	N	Y
19 Phelps	N	Y	Y	Y	Y
20 ***Shimkus***	Y	Y	Y	N	Y
INDIANA					
1 Visclosky	N	Y	Y	Y	Y
2 ***McIntosh***	Y	N	N	N	N
3 Roemer	Y	Y	Y	N	Y
4 ***Souder***	Y	N	N	N	N
5 ***Buyer***	Y	Y	N	N	Y
6 ***Burton***	Y	N	N	?	N
7 ***Pease***	Y	N	N	N	Y
8 ***Hostettler***	Y	N	N	N	N
9 Hill	N	Y	Y	N	Y
10 Carson	N	Y	Y	Y	Y
IOWA					
1 ***Leach***	Y	Y	Y	N	Y
2 ***Nussle***	Y	N	N	N	Y
3 Boswell	Y	Y	Y	Y	Y
4 ***Ganske***	Y	Y	Y	N	Y
5 ***Latham***	Y	N	N	N	N
KANSAS					
1 ***Moran***	Y	N	N	N	N
2 ***Ryun***	Y	N	N	N	N
3 Moore	Y	Y	Y	N	Y
4 ***Tiahrt***	Y	N	N	N	N
KENTUCKY					
1 ***Whitfield***	Y	Y	N	N	N
2 ***Lewis***	Y	N	N	N	N
3 ***Northup***	Y	Y	N	N	N
4 Lucas	Y	Y	N	N	N
5 ***Rogers***	Y	Y	N	N	Y
6 ***Fletcher***	Y	Y	N	N	Y
LOUISIANA					
1 ***Vitter***	Y	N	N	N	N
2 Jefferson	Y	Y	Y	Y	Y
3 ***Tauzin***	Y	Y	N	N	N
4 ***McCrery***	Y	N	N	N	N
5 ***Cooksey***	?	?	?	?	?
6 ***Baker***	Y	Y	N	N	N
7 John	Y	Y	Y	N	Y
MAINE					
1 Allen	N	Y	Y	Y	Y
2 Baldacci	N	Y	Y	Y	Y
MARYLAND					
1 ***Gilchrest***	Y	Y	Y	N	Y
2 ***Ehrlich***	Y	N	N	N	N
3 Cardin	N	Y	Y	Y	Y
4 Wynn	N	Y	Y	Y	Y
5 Hoyer	N	Y	Y	Y	Y
6 ***Bartlett***	Y	N	N	N	N
7 Cummings	N	Y	Y	Y	Y
8 ***Morella***	Y	Y	Y	N	Y
MASSACHUSETTS					
1 Olver	N	Y	Y	Y	Y
2 Neal	N	Y	Y	Y	Y
3 McGovern	N	Y	Y	Y	Y
4 Frank	N	Y	Y	Y	Y
5 Meehan	N	Y	Y	Y	Y
6 Tierney	N	Y	Y	Y	Y
7 Markey	N	Y	Y	Y	Y
8 Capuano	N	Y	Y	Y	Y
9 Moakley	N	Y	Y	Y	Y
10 Delahunt	N	Y	Y	Y	Y
MICHIGAN					
1 Stupak	N	Y	Y	Y	Y
2 ***Hoekstra***	Y	N	N	N	N
3 ***Ehlers***	Y	N	Y	N	Y
4 ***Camp***	Y	N	N	N	Y
5 Barcia	Y	Y	Y	Y	Y
6 ***Upton***	Y	Y	Y	N	Y
7 ***Smith***	Y	N	N	N	N
8 Stabenow	N	Y	Y	Y	Y
9 Kildee	N	Y	Y	Y	Y
10 Bonior	N	Y	Y	Y	Y
11 ***Knollenberg***	Y	N	N	N	N
12 Levin	N	Y	Y	Y	Y
13 Rivers	Y	Y	Y	Y	Y
14 Conyers	N	Y	Y	Y	Y
15 Kilpatrick	N	Y	Y	Y	Y
16 Dingell	N	Y	Y	Y	Y
MINNESOTA					
1 ***Gutknecht***	N	N	N	N	N
2 Minge	N	Y	Y	N	Y
3 ***Ramstad***	Y	N	N	N	N
4 Vento	?	?	?	?	?
5 Sabo	N	Y	Y	Y	Y
6 Luther	N	Y	Y	Y	Y
7 Peterson	Y	Y	Y	N	Y
8 Oberstar	N	Y	Y	Y	Y
MISSISSIPPI					
1 ***Wicker***	Y	N	N	N	Y
2 Thompson	N	Y	Y	Y	Y
3 ***Pickering***	Y	N	N	N	N
4 Shows	Y	Y	Y	N	Y
5 Taylor	N	Y	Y	N	Y
MISSOURI					
1 Clay	N	Y	Y	Y	Y
2 ***Talent***	Y	N	N	N	N
3 Gephardt	N	?	Y	Y	Y
4 Skelton	N	Y	Y	Y	Y
5 McCarthy	N	Y	Y	Y	Y
6 Danner	Y	Y	Y	Y	Y
7 ***Blunt***	Y	N	N	N	N
8 ***Emerson***	Y	N	N	N	Y
9 ***Hulshof***	Y	N	N	N	N
MONTANA					
AL ***Hill***	Y	N	N	N	N
NEBRASKA					
1 ***Bereuter***	Y	Y	N	N	Y
2 ***Terry***	Y	N	N	N	N
3 ***Barrett***	Y	Y	N	N	N
NEVADA					
1 Berkley	Y	Y	Y	Y	Y
2 ***Gibbons***	Y	N	Y	N	Y
NEW HAMPSHIRE					
1 ***Sununu***	Y	N	N	N	N
2 ***Bass***	Y	N	N	N	N
NEW JERSEY					
1 Andrews	N	Y	Y	Y	Y
2 ***LoBiondo***	Y	Y	Y	N	Y
3 ***Saxton***	Y	Y	Y	N	Y
4 ***Smith***	Y	Y	Y	N	Y
5 ***Roukema***	Y	Y	N	N	Y
6 Pallone	N	Y	Y	Y	Y
7 ***Franks***	Y	Y	Y	N	Y
8 Pascrell	N	Y	Y	Y	Y
9 Rothman	N	Y	Y	Y	Y
10 Payne	N	Y	Y	Y	Y
11 ***Frelinghuysen***	Y	Y	Y	N	Y
12 Holt	Y	Y	Y	Y	Y
13 Menendez	N	Y	Y	Y	Y
NEW MEXICO					
1 ***Wilson***	Y	Y	Y	N	Y
2 ***Skeen***	Y	N	N	N	N
3 Udall	N	Y	Y	N	Y
NEW YORK					
1 Forbes	Y	Y	Y	Y	Y
2 ***Lazio***	Y	Y	Y	N	Y
3 ***King***	Y	Y	Y	N	Y
4 McCarthy	Y	Y	Y	Y	Y
5 Ackerman	N	Y	Y	Y	Y
6 Meeks	N	Y	Y	Y	Y
7 Crowley	N	Y	Y	Y	Y
8 Nadler	N	Y	Y	Y	Y
9 Weiner	N	Y	Y	Y	Y
10 Towns	N	Y	Y	Y	Y
11 Owens	N	Y	Y	Y	Y
12 Velázquez	N	Y	Y	Y	Y
13 ***Fossella***	Y	Y	N	N	N
14 Maloney	N	Y	Y	Y	Y
15 Rangel	N	Y	Y	Y	Y
16 Serrano	N	Y	Y	Y	Y
17 Engel	N	Y	Y	Y	Y
18 Lowey	N	Y	Y	Y	Y
19 ***Kelly***	Y	Y	N	N	Y
20 ***Gilman***	Y	Y	Y	N	Y
21 McNulty	N	Y	Y	Y	Y
22 ***Sweeney***	Y	Y	N	N	N
23 ***Boehlert***	Y	Y	Y	N	Y
24 ***McHugh***	Y	Y	Y	N	Y
25 ***Walsh***	Y	Y	Y	N	Y
26 Hinchey	N	Y	Y	Y	Y
27 ***Reynolds***	Y	N	N	N	N
28 Slaughter	N	Y	Y	Y	Y
29 LaFalce	N	Y	Y	Y	Y
30 ***Quinn***	Y	Y	Y	N	Y
31 ***Houghton***	Y	Y	Y	N	Y
NORTH CAROLINA					
1 Clayton	N	Y	Y	Y	Y
2 Etheridge	Y	Y	Y	Y	Y
3 ***Jones***	Y	N	N	N	N
4 Price	Y	Y	Y	Y	Y
5 ***Burr***	Y	N	N	N	N
6 ***Coble***	Y	N	N	N	N
7 McIntyre	Y	Y	Y	Y	Y
8 ***Hayes***	Y	N	N	N	Y
9 ***Myrick***	Y	N	N	N	Y
10 ***Ballenger***	Y	N	N	N	N
11 ***Taylor***	Y	N	N	N	N
12 Watt	N	Y	Y	Y	Y
NORTH DAKOTA					
AL Pomeroy	N	Y	Y	Y	Y
OHIO					
1 ***Chabot***	Y	N	N	N	N
2 ***Portman***	Y	N	N	N	N
3 Hall	Y	Y	Y	Y	Y
4 ***Oxley***	Y	?	N	N	N
5 ***Gillmor***	Y	N	N	N	Y
6 Strickland	?	Y	Y	Y	Y
7 ***Hobson***	Y	Y	N	N	Y
8 ***Boehner***	Y	N	N	N	N
9 Kaptur	N	Y	Y	Y	Y
10 Kucinich	N	Y	Y	Y	Y
11 Jones	N	Y	Y	Y	Y
12 ***Kasich***	Y	N	N	N	N
13 Brown	N	Y	Y	Y	Y
14 Sawyer	N	Y	Y	Y	Y
15 ***Pryce***	Y	N	N	N	N
16 ***Regula***	Y	Y	N	N	Y
17 Traficant	Y	Y	Y	N	Y
18 ***Ney***	Y	Y	Y	N	Y
19 ***LaTourette***	Y	Y	N	N	Y
OKLAHOMA					
1 ***Largent***	Y	N	N	N	N
2 ***Coburn***	Y	N	N	N	N
3 ***Watkins***	Y	N	N	N	N
4 ***Watts***	Y	N	N	N	N
5 ***Istook***	Y	?	N	N	N
6 ***Lucas***	Y	N	N	N	N
OREGON					
1 Wu	Y	Y	Y	Y	Y
2 ***Walden***	Y	N	N	N	N
3 Blumenauer	N	Y	Y	Y	Y
4 DeFazio	N	Y	Y	Y	Y
5 Hooley	Y	Y	Y	Y	Y
PENNSYLVANIA					
1 Brady	N	Y	Y	Y	Y
2 Fattah	N	Y	Y	Y	Y
3 Borski	N	Y	Y	Y	Y
4 Klink	N	Y	Y	Y	Y
5 ***Peterson***	Y	N	N	N	N
6 Holden	N	Y	Y	Y	Y
7 ***Weldon***	Y	Y	Y	N	Y
8 ***Greenwood***	Y	Y	Y	N	Y
9 ***Shuster***	Y	?	N	N	Y
10 ***Sherwood***	Y	Y	Y	N	Y
11 Kanjorski	N	Y	Y	Y	Y
12 Murtha	N	Y	Y	Y	Y
13 Hoeffel	N	Y	Y	Y	Y
14 Coyne	N	Y	Y	Y	Y
15 ***Toomey***	Y	N	N	N	N
16 ***Pitts***	Y	N	N	N	N
17 ***Gekas***	Y	N	N	N	Y
18 Doyle	N	Y	Y	Y	Y
19 ***Goodling***	Y	N	N	N	Y
20 Mascara	N	Y	Y	Y	Y
21 ***English***	Y	Y	Y	N	Y
RHODE ISLAND					
1 Kennedy	N	Y	Y	Y	Y
2 Weygand	N	Y	Y	Y	Y
SOUTH CAROLINA					
1 ***Sanford***	Y	N	N	N	N
2 ***Spence***	?	?	?	?	?
3 ***Graham***	Y	N	N	N	N
4 ***DeMint***	Y	N	N	N	N
5 Spratt	N	Y	Y	Y	Y
6 Clyburn	N	Y	Y	Y	Y
SOUTH DAKOTA					
AL ***Thune***	Y	Y	Y	N	Y
TENNESSEE					
1 ***Jenkins***	Y	N	N	N	N
2 ***Duncan***	Y	Y	N	N	Y
3 ***Wamp***	Y	N	N	N	N
4 ***Hilleary***	Y	N	N	N	Y
5 Clement	N	N	Y	Y	Y
6 Gordon	Y	Y	Y	Y	Y
7 ***Bryant***	Y	N	N	N	N
8 Tanner	N	Y	Y	Y	Y
9 Ford	N	Y	Y	Y	Y
TEXAS					
1 Sandlin	Y	Y	Y	Y	Y
2 Turner	N	Y	Y	Y	Y
3 ***Johnson, Sam***	Y	N	N	N	N
4 Hall	Y	N	N	N	N
5 ***Sessions***	Y	N	N	N	N
6 ***Barton***	Y	N	N	N	N
7 ***Archer***	Y	N	N	N	N
8 ***Brady***	Y	N	N	N	N
9 Lampson	N	Y	Y	Y	Y
10 Doggett	N	Y	Y	N	Y
11 Edwards	N	Y	Y	Y	Y
12 ***Granger***	?	?	?	?	?
13 ***Thornberry***	Y	N	N	N	N
14 ***Paul***	Y	N	N	N	N
15 Hinojosa	N	Y	Y	Y	Y
16 Reyes	N	Y	Y	Y	Y
17 Stenholm	N	N	N	N	N
18 Jackson-Lee	N	Y	Y	Y	Y
19 ***Combest***	Y	N	N	N	N
20 Gonzalez	N	Y	Y	Y	Y
21 ***Smith***	Y	N	N	N	N
22 ***DeLay***	Y	N	N	N	N
23 ***Bonilla***	Y	N	N	N	N
24 Frost	N	Y	Y	Y	Y
25 Bentsen	N	Y	Y	Y	Y
26 ***Armey***	Y	N	N	N	N
27 Ortiz	N	Y	Y	Y	Y
28 Rodriguez	N	Y	Y	Y	Y
29 Green	N	Y	Y	Y	Y
30 Johnson, E.B.	?	?	?	?	?
UTAH					
1 ***Hansen***	Y	N	N	N	N
2 ***Cook***	Y	N	N	N	N
3 ***Cannon***	Y	N	N	N	N
VERMONT					
AL *Sanders*	N	Y	Y	Y	Y
VIRGINIA					
1 ***Bateman***	Y	N	N	N	N
2 Pickett	Y	Y	Y	N	Y
3 Scott	N	Y	Y	Y	Y
4 Sisisky	Y	Y	Y	N	Y
5 *Goode*	Y	N	N	N	N
6 ***Goodlatte***	Y	N	N	N	N
7 ***Bliley***	Y	Y	N	N	N
8 Moran	N	Y	Y	N	Y
9 Boucher	Y	Y	Y	Y	Y
10 ***Wolf***	Y	Y	N	N	Y
11 ***Davis***	Y	?	N	N	N
WASHINGTON					
1 Inslee	Y	Y	Y	Y	Y
2 ***Metcalf***	Y	?	Y	N	Y
3 Baird	Y	Y	Y	Y	Y
4 ***Hastings***	Y	N	N	N	N
5 ***Nethercutt***	Y	N	N	N	N
6 Dicks	N	Y	Y	Y	Y
7 McDermott	N	Y	Y	Y	Y
8 ***Dunn***	Y	N	N	N	N
9 Smith	Y	?	?	?	?
WEST VIRGINIA					
1 Mollohan	N	Y	Y	Y	Y
2 Wise	N	Y	Y	Y	Y
3 Rahall	N	Y	Y	Y	Y
WISCONSIN					
1 ***Ryan***	Y	N	N	N	Y
2 Baldwin	N	Y	Y	Y	Y
3 Kind	N	Y	Y	N	Y
4 Kleczka	N	Y	Y	Y	Y
5 Barrett	N	Y	Y	Y	Y
6 ***Petri***	Y	N	N	N	Y
7 Obey	N	Y	Y	Y	Y
8 ***Green***	Y	N	N	N	Y
9 ***Sensenbrenner***	Y	N	N	N	N
WYOMING					
AL ***Cubin***	Y	N	N	N	N

Southern states - Ala., Ark., Fla., Ga., Ky., La., Miss., N.C., Okla., S.C., Tenn., Texas, Va.

46. HR 3699. Joel T. Broyhill Post Office/Passage. McHugh, R-N.Y., motion to suspend the rules and pass the bill to designate a post office in Merrifield, Va., as the Joel T. Broyhill Postal Building. Motion agreed to 405-0: R 210-0; D 193-0 (ND 148-0, SD 45-0); I 2-0. A two-thirds majority of those present and voting (270 in this case) is required for passage under suspension of the rules. March 14, 2000.

47. HR 3701. Joseph L. Fisher Post Office/Passage. McHugh, R-N.Y., motion to suspend the rules and pass the bill to designate a post office in Arlington, Va., as the Joseph L. Fisher Post Office Building. Motion agreed to 400-0: R 207-0; D 191-0 (ND 146-0, SD 45-0); I 2-0. A two-thirds majority of those present and voting (267 in this case) is required for passage under suspension of the rules. March 14, 2000.

48. HR 1000. Federal Aviation Administration Reauthorization/Conference Report. Adoption of the conference report on the bill that would authorize about $40 billion for aviation programs for fiscal years 2001 through 2003. The agreement would provide $3.2 billion in fiscal 2001, $3.3 billion in fiscal 2002 and $3.4 billion in fiscal 2003 for airport construction grants. Airports would be allowed to increase the local fee on an airline ticket from $3 to $4.50 per segment. The bill would also allow additional flights into Chicago O'Hare International, John F. Kennedy International, LaGuardia and Ronald Reagan Washington National airports. Adopted (thus cleared for the president) 319-101: R 149-68; D 169-32 (ND 127-27, SD 42-5); I 1-1. March 15, 2000.

49. HR 3843. Small Business Programs Reauthorization/Passage. Passage of a bill that would reauthorize programs operated by the Small Business Administration through fiscal 2003. The measure would authorize $14.5 billion for the 7(a) loan program in fiscal 2001, with funding levels increasing to $15 billion in fiscal 2002, and $16 billion in fiscal 2003. It would authorize $4 billion for the 504 loan program in fiscal 2001, with $4.5 billion and $5 billion authorized in subsequent years. The bill also would authorize $60 million for direct loans in 2001, $80 million the next year and $100 million the following year. Passed 410-11: R 205-11; D 203-0 (ND 155-0, SD 48-0); I 2-0. March 15, 2000.

50. HR 1501. Juvenile Justice/Motion to Instruct. Lofgren, D-Calif., motion to instruct House conferees to insist that the conference committee have its first substantive meeting on amendments and motions within two weeks. Motion agreed to 218-205: R 46-172; D 171-32 (ND 138-15, SD 33-17); I 1-1. March 15, 2000.

Key

Y Voted for (yea).
\# Paired for.
\+ Announced for.
N Voted against (nay).
X Paired against.
– Announced against.
P Voted "present."
C Voted "present" to avoid possible conflict of interest.
? Did not vote or otherwise make a position known.

•

Democrats ***Republicans***
Independents

	46	47	48	49	50
ALABAMA					
1 ***Callahan***	Y	Y	Y	Y	N
2 ***Everett***	Y	Y	Y	Y	N
3 ***Riley***	Y	Y	N	Y	N
4 ***Aderholt***	Y	Y	N	Y	N
5 Cramer	Y	Y	Y	Y	N
6 ***Bachus***	Y	Y	Y	Y	N
7 Hilliard	Y	Y	Y	Y	Y
ALASKA					
AL ***Young***	Y	Y	Y	Y	N
ARIZONA					
1 ***Salmon***	Y	Y	N	Y	N
2 Pastor	Y	Y	N	Y	Y
3 ***Stump***	Y	Y	N	Y	N
4 ***Shadegg***	Y	Y	N	N	N
5 ***Kolbe***	Y	Y	N	Y	N
6 ***Hayworth***	Y	Y	N	Y	N
ARKANSAS					
1 Berry	Y	Y	Y	Y	Y
2 Snyder	?	Y	Y	Y	Y
3 ***Hutchinson***	Y	Y	Y	Y	N
4 ***Dickey***	Y	Y	Y	Y	N
CALIFORNIA					
1 Thompson	Y	Y	Y	Y	Y
2 ***Herger***	Y	Y	N	Y	N
3 ***Ose***	Y	Y	Y	Y	Y
4 ***Doolittle***	Y	Y	Y	N	N
5 Matsui	Y	Y	Y	Y	Y
6 Woolsey	Y	Y	Y	Y	Y
7 Miller, George	Y	Y	Y	Y	Y
8 Pelosi	Y	Y	N	Y	Y
9 Lee	Y	Y	Y	Y	Y
10 Tauscher	Y	Y	Y	Y	Y
11 ***Pombo***	Y	Y	Y	Y	N
12 Lantos	Y	Y	Y	Y	Y
13 Stark	?	?	N	Y	?
14 Eshoo	Y	Y	N	Y	Y
15 ***Campbell***	Y	Y	Y	Y	Y
16 Lofgren	Y	Y	N	Y	Y
17 Farr	Y	Y	N	Y	Y
18 Condit	Y	Y	Y	Y	Y
19 ***Radanovich***	Y	Y	Y	Y	N
20 Dooley	Y	Y	Y	Y	Y
21 ***Thomas***	Y	?	Y	Y	N
22 Capps	Y	Y	Y	Y	Y
23 ***Gallegly***	Y	Y	Y	Y	Y
24 Sherman	Y	Y	Y	Y	Y
25 ***McKeon***	Y	Y	Y	Y	N
26 Berman	Y	Y	Y	Y	Y
27 ***Rogan***	Y	Y	Y	Y	Y
28 ***Dreier***	Y	Y	Y	Y	N
29 Waxman	?	?	Y	Y	Y
30 Becerra	Y	?	Y	Y	Y
31 Martinez	Y	Y	Y	Y	N
32 Dixon	Y	Y	N	Y	Y
33 Roybal-Allard	Y	Y	N	Y	Y
34 Napolitano	Y	Y	Y	Y	Y
35 Waters	Y	Y	N	Y	Y
36 ***Kuykendall***	Y	Y	Y	Y	Y
37 Millender-McD.	Y	Y	Y	Y	Y
38 ***Horn***	Y	Y	Y	Y	Y
39 ***Royce***	Y	?	N	N	N
40 ***Lewis***	Y	Y	N	Y	N
41 ***Miller, Gary***	Y	Y	Y	Y	N
42 Baca	Y	Y	Y	Y	N
43 ***Calvert***	Y	Y	Y	Y	N
44 ***Bono***	Y	Y	Y	Y	N
45 ***Rohrabacher***	Y	Y	N	N	N
46 Sanchez	Y	Y	Y	Y	Y
47 ***Cox***	?	?	N	Y	N
48 ***Packard***	?	Y	N	Y	N
49 ***Bilbray***	Y	Y	Y	Y	Y
50 Filner	Y	Y	Y	Y	Y
51 ***Cunningham***	Y	Y	Y	Y	N
52 ***Hunter***	Y	Y	Y	Y	N
COLORADO					
1 DeGette	Y	Y	Y	Y	Y
2 Udall	Y	Y	Y	Y	Y
3 ***McInnis***	Y	Y	N	Y	N
4 ***Schaffer***	Y	Y	Y	Y	N
5 ***Hefley***	Y	Y	Y	Y	N
6 ***Tancredo***	Y	Y	N	Y	Y
CONNECTICUT					
1 Larson	Y	Y	Y	Y	Y
2 Gejdenson	Y	Y	Y	Y	Y
3 DeLauro	Y	Y	Y	Y	Y
4 ***Shays***	Y	Y	N	Y	Y
5 Maloney	?	Y	Y	Y	Y
6 ***Johnson***	Y	Y	Y	Y	Y
DELAWARE					
AL ***Castle***	Y	Y	N	Y	N
FLORIDA					
1 ***Scarborough***	Y	Y	N	Y	N
2 Boyd	Y	Y	N	+	–
3 Brown	Y	Y	Y	?	Y
4 ***Fowler***	Y	Y	Y	Y	N
5 Thurman	Y	Y	Y	Y	Y
6 ***Stearns***	Y	Y	Y	Y	N
7 ***Mica***	Y	Y	Y	Y	N
8 ***McCollum***	?	?	?	Y	N
9 ***Bilirakis***	Y	Y	Y	Y	N
10 ***Young***	Y	Y	N	Y	N
11 Davis	Y	Y	Y	Y	Y
12 ***Canady***	Y	Y	Y	N	N
13 ***Miller***	Y	Y	N	Y	N
14 ***Goss***	Y	Y	N	Y	N
15 ***Weldon***	Y	Y	Y	Y	N
16 ***Foley***	Y	Y	N	Y	Y
17 Meek	Y	Y	Y	Y	Y
18 ***Ros-Lehtinen***	+	+	Y	Y	Y
19 Wexler	Y	Y	Y	Y	Y
20 Deutsch	+	+	Y	Y	Y
21 ***Diaz-Balart***	Y	Y	Y	Y	Y
22 ***Shaw***	Y	Y	Y	Y	Y
23 Hastings	Y	Y	Y	Y	Y
GEORGIA					
1 ***Kingston***	Y	Y	N	Y	Y
2 Bishop	Y	Y	Y	Y	N
3 ***Collins***	Y	Y	N	?	N
4 McKinney	Y	Y	Y	Y	Y
5 Lewis	Y	Y	Y	Y	Y
6 ***Isakson***	Y	Y	Y	Y	N
7 ***Barr***	Y	Y	Y	N	N
8 ***Chambliss***	Y	Y	Y	Y	N
9 ***Deal***	Y	Y	Y	Y	N
10 ***Norwood***	Y	Y	Y	Y	N
11 ***Linder***	Y	Y	Y	Y	N
HAWAII					
1 Abercrombie	Y	Y	Y	Y	Y
2 Mink	Y	Y	Y	Y	Y
IDAHO					
1 ***Chenoweth-Hage***	Y	Y	N	N	N
2 ***Simpson***	Y	Y	Y	Y	N
ILLINOIS					
1 Rush	?	?	?	?	?
2 Jackson	Y	Y	N	Y	Y
3 Lipinski	Y	Y	Y	Y	Y
4 Gutierrez	Y	Y	?	Y	Y
5 Blagojevich	Y	Y	Y	Y	Y
6 ***Hyde***	Y	Y	N	Y	N
7 Davis	Y	Y	N	Y	Y
8 ***Crane***	Y	Y	N	Y	N
9 Schakowsky	Y	Y	Y	Y	Y
10 ***Porter***	Y	Y	N	Y	Y
11 ***Weller***	Y	Y	N	Y	Y
12 Costello	Y	Y	Y	Y	N
13 ***Biggert***	Y	Y	Y	Y	N

ND Northern Democrats SD Southern Democrats

	46	47	48	49	50
14 ***Hastert***					
15 ***Ewing***	Y	Y	Y	Y	N
16 ***Manzullo***	Y	Y	Y	Y	N
17 Evans	Y	Y	Y	Y	Y
18 ***LaHood***	Y	Y	Y	Y	N
19 Phelps	Y	Y	Y	Y	N
20 ***Shimkus***	Y	Y	Y	Y	N
INDIANA					
1 Visclosky	Y	Y	N	Y	Y
2 ***McIntosh***	?	Y	N	Y	N
3 Roemer	Y	Y	N	Y	Y
4 ***Souder***	Y	Y	Y	Y	N
5 ***Buyer***	Y	Y	Y	Y	N
6 ***Burton***	Y	Y	Y	Y	N
7 ***Pease***	Y	Y	Y	Y	N
8 ***Hostettler***	Y	Y	Y	N	N
9 Hill	Y	Y	Y	Y	N
10 Carson	Y	Y	Y	Y	Y
IOWA					
1 ***Leach***	Y	Y	Y	Y	Y
2 ***Nussle***	Y	Y	Y	Y	Y
3 Boswell	?	?	Y	Y	N
4 ***Ganske***	Y	Y	Y	Y	Y
5 ***Latham***	Y	Y	N	Y	N
KANSAS					
1 ***Moran***	Y	Y	Y	Y	N
2 ***Ryun***	Y	Y	Y	Y	N
3 Moore	Y	Y	Y	Y	Y
4 ***Tiahrt***	Y	Y	N	Y	N
KENTUCKY					
1 ***Whitfield***	Y	Y	Y	Y	N
2 ***Lewis***	Y	Y	Y	Y	N
3 ***Northup***	Y	Y	Y	Y	Y
4 Lucas	Y	Y	Y	Y	N
5 ***Rogers***	Y	Y	N	Y	N
6 ***Fletcher***	Y	Y	Y	Y	N
LOUISIANA					
1 ***Vitter***	Y	Y	Y	Y	N
2 Jefferson	Y	Y	Y	Y	Y
3 ***Tauzin***	Y	Y	Y	Y	N
4 ***McCrery***	Y	Y	Y	Y	N
5 ***Cooksey***	Y	Y	Y	Y	N
6 ***Baker***	Y	Y	Y	Y	N
7 John	Y	Y	Y	?	?
MAINE					
1 Allen	Y	Y	Y	Y	Y
2 Baldacci	Y	Y	Y	Y	Y
MARYLAND					
1 ***Gilchrest***	Y	Y	Y	Y	Y
2 ***Ehrlich***	Y	Y	Y	Y	Y
3 Cardin	Y	Y	N	Y	Y
4 Wynn	Y	Y	Y	Y	Y
5 Hoyer	Y	Y	N	Y	Y
6 ***Bartlett***	Y	Y	Y	Y	N
7 Cummings	Y	Y	Y	Y	Y
8 ***Morella***	Y	Y	N	Y	Y
MASSACHUSETTS					
1 Olver	Y	Y	Y	Y	Y
2 Neal	Y	Y	Y	Y	Y
3 McGovern	Y	Y	Y	Y	Y
4 Frank	Y	Y	Y	Y	Y
5 Meehan	Y	Y	Y	Y	Y
6 Tierney	Y	Y	N	Y	Y
7 Markey	Y	Y	Y	Y	Y
8 Capuano	Y	Y	Y	Y	Y
9 Moakley	Y	Y	Y	Y	Y
10 Delahunt	Y	Y	Y	Y	Y
MICHIGAN					
1 Stupak	Y	Y	Y	Y	Y
2 ***Hoekstra***	Y	Y	Y	Y	N
3 ***Ehlers***	Y	Y	Y	Y	Y
4 ***Camp***	Y	Y	Y	Y	Y
5 Barcia	Y	Y	Y	Y	N
6 ***Upton***	Y	Y	Y	Y	Y
7 ***Smith***	Y	Y	Y	Y	N
8 Stabenow	Y	Y	Y	Y	Y
9 Kildee	Y	Y	Y	Y	Y
10 Bonior	Y	Y	Y	Y	Y
11 ***Knollenberg***	Y	Y	Y	Y	N
12 Levin	Y	Y	Y	Y	Y
13 Rivers	Y	Y	Y	Y	Y
14 Conyers	Y	Y	Y	Y	Y
15 Kilpatrick	Y	Y	N	Y	Y
16 Dingell	Y	Y	Y	Y	Y

	46	47	48	49	50
MINNESOTA					
1 ***Gutknecht***	Y	Y	Y	Y	N
2 Minge	Y	Y	Y	Y	Y
3 ***Ramstad***	Y	Y	N	Y	Y
4 Vento	Y	Y	Y	Y	Y
5 Sabo	Y	Y	N	Y	Y
6 Luther	Y	Y	Y	Y	Y
7 Peterson	Y	Y	Y	Y	N
8 Oberstar	Y	Y	Y	Y	Y
MISSISSIPPI					
1 ***Wicker***	?	?	N	Y	N
2 Thompson	Y	Y	Y	Y	Y
3 ***Pickering***	Y	Y	Y	Y	N
4 Shows	Y	Y	Y	Y	N
5 Taylor	Y	Y	Y	Y	N
MISSOURI					
1 Clay	Y	Y	Y	Y	Y
2 ***Talent***	Y	Y	Y	Y	N
3 Gephardt	Y	Y	Y	Y	Y
4 Skelton	Y	Y	Y	Y	N
5 McCarthy	Y	Y	Y	Y	Y
6 Danner	Y	Y	Y	Y	N
7 ***Blunt***	Y	Y	Y	Y	N
8 ***Emerson***	Y	Y	N	Y	N
9 ***Hulshof***	Y	Y	Y	Y	N
MONTANA					
AL ***Hill***	Y	Y	Y	Y	N
NEBRASKA					
1 ***Bereuter***	Y	Y	Y	Y	Y
2 ***Terry***	Y	Y	Y	Y	N
3 ***Barrett***	Y	Y	N	Y	N
NEVADA					
1 Berkley	Y	Y	Y	Y	Y
2 ***Gibbons***	Y	Y	Y	Y	N
NEW HAMPSHIRE					
1 ***Sununu***	Y	Y	N	Y	N
2 ***Bass***	Y	Y	Y	Y	N
NEW JERSEY					
1 Andrews	Y	Y	Y	Y	Y
2 ***LoBiondo***	Y	Y	Y	Y	N
3 ***Saxton***	Y	Y	Y	Y	Y
4 ***Smith***	Y	Y	Y	Y	Y
5 ***Roukema***	Y	?	N	Y	Y
6 Pallone	Y	Y	Y	Y	Y
7 ***Franks***	?	?	Y	Y	Y
8 Pascrell	Y	Y	Y	Y	Y
9 Rothman	Y	Y	Y	Y	Y
10 Payne	Y	Y	Y	Y	Y
11 ***Frelinghuysen***	Y	Y	N	Y	Y
12 Holt	Y	Y	Y	Y	Y
13 Menendez	Y	Y	Y	Y	Y
NEW MEXICO					
1 ***Wilson***	Y	Y	Y	Y	Y
2 ***Skeen***	Y	Y	N	Y	N
3 Udall	Y	Y	Y	Y	Y
NEW YORK					
1 Forbes	Y	Y	Y	Y	Y
2 ***Lazio***	Y	Y	Y	Y	N
3 ***King***	Y	Y	Y	Y	N
4 McCarthy	Y	Y	Y	Y	Y
5 Ackerman	Y	Y	Y	Y	Y
6 Meeks	?	?	Y	Y	Y
7 Crowley	Y	Y	Y	Y	Y
8 Nadler	Y	Y	Y	Y	Y
9 Weiner	Y	Y	Y	Y	Y
10 Towns	Y	Y	Y	Y	Y
11 Owens	Y	Y	Y	Y	Y
12 Velázquez	Y	Y	Y	Y	Y
13 ***Fossella***	Y	Y	Y	Y	N
14 Maloney	Y	Y	Y	Y	Y
15 Rangel	Y	Y	Y	Y	Y
16 Serrano	Y	Y	Y	Y	Y
17 Engel	Y	Y	Y	Y	Y
18 Lowey	Y	Y	N	Y	Y
19 ***Kelly***	Y	Y	Y	Y	Y
20 ***Gilman***	Y	Y	Y	Y	Y
21 McNulty	Y	Y	Y	Y	Y
22 ***Sweeney***	Y	Y	Y	Y	N
23 ***Boehlert***	Y	Y	Y	Y	Y
24 ***McHugh***	Y	Y	Y	Y	Y
25 ***Walsh***	Y	Y	N	Y	N
26 Hinchey	Y	Y	N	Y	Y
27 ***Reynolds***	Y	Y	Y	Y	N
28 Slaughter	Y	Y	Y	Y	Y
29 LaFalce	Y	Y	Y	Y	Y

	46	47	48	49	50
30 ***Quinn***	Y	Y	Y	Y	Y
31 ***Houghton***	Y	Y	Y	Y	N
NORTH CAROLINA					
1 Clayton	Y	Y	Y	Y	Y
2 Etheridge	Y	Y	Y	Y	Y
3 ***Jones***	Y	Y	N	Y	N
4 Price	Y	Y	Y	Y	Y
5 ***Burr***	Y	Y	Y	Y	N
6 ***Coble***	Y	Y	Y	Y	N
7 McIntyre	Y	Y	Y	Y	N
8 ***Hayes***	Y	Y	Y	Y	N
9 ***Myrick***	?	?	?	?	?
10 ***Ballenger***	Y	Y	Y	Y	N
11 ***Taylor***	?	?	N	Y	N
12 Watt	Y	Y	Y	Y	Y
NORTH DAKOTA					
AL Pomeroy	Y	Y	Y	Y	Y
OHIO					
1 ***Chabot***	Y	Y	N	Y	N
2 ***Portman***	Y	Y	N	Y	N
3 Hall	Y	Y	Y	Y	Y
4 ***Oxley***	Y	Y	Y	Y	N
5 ***Gillmor***	Y	Y	Y	Y	N
6 Strickland	Y	Y	Y	Y	N
7 ***Hobson***	Y	Y	N	Y	N
8 ***Boehner***	Y	Y	N	Y	N
9 Kaptur	Y	Y	N	Y	Y
10 Kucinich	Y	Y	Y	Y	Y
11 Jones	Y	Y	Y	Y	Y
12 ***Kasich***	Y	?	Y	Y	N
13 Brown	Y	Y	Y	Y	Y
14 Sawyer	Y	Y	Y	Y	Y
15 ***Pryce***	Y	Y	Y	Y	N
16 ***Regula***	Y	Y	N	Y	N
17 Traficant	Y	Y	Y	Y	N
18 ***Ney***	Y	Y	Y	Y	N
19 ***LaTourette***	Y	Y	Y	Y	N
OKLAHOMA					
1 ***Largent***	Y	Y	N	Y	N
2 ***Coburn***	Y	Y	N	N	N
3 ***Watkins***	Y	Y	Y	Y	N
4 ***Watts***	Y	Y	Y	Y	Y
5 ***Istook***	Y	Y	Y	Y	N
6 ***Lucas***	Y	Y	Y	Y	N
OREGON					
1 Wu	Y	Y	Y	Y	Y
2 ***Walden***	Y	Y	?	?	?
3 Blumenauer	Y	?	Y	Y	Y
4 DeFazio	Y	Y	Y	Y	Y
5 Hooley	Y	Y	Y	Y	Y
PENNSYLVANIA					
1 Brady	Y	Y	Y	Y	Y
2 Fattah	Y	Y	Y	Y	Y
3 Borski	Y	Y	Y	Y	Y
4 Klink	?	?	?	?	?
5 ***Peterson***	Y	Y	Y	Y	N
6 Holden	Y	Y	Y	Y	Y
7 ***Weldon***	Y	Y	Y	Y	N
8 ***Greenwood***	Y	Y	Y	Y	Y
9 ***Shuster***	Y	Y	Y	Y	N
10 ***Sherwood***	Y	Y	Y	Y	N
11 Kanjorski	Y	Y	Y	Y	Y
12 Murtha	Y	Y	Y	Y	Y
13 Hoeffel	Y	Y	Y	Y	Y
14 Coyne	Y	Y	Y	Y	Y
15 ***Toomey***	Y	Y	N	Y	N
16 ***Pitts***	Y	Y	N	Y	N
17 ***Gekas***	Y	Y	Y	Y	N
18 Doyle	Y	Y	Y	Y	Y
19 ***Goodling***	Y	Y	Y	Y	N
20 Mascara	Y	Y	Y	Y	?
21 ***English***	Y	Y	Y	Y	N
RHODE ISLAND					
1 Kennedy	Y	Y	N	Y	Y
2 Weygand	?	?	Y	Y	Y
SOUTH CAROLINA					
1 ***Sanford***	Y	Y	N	N	N
2 ***Spence***	Y	Y	Y	Y	N
3 ***Graham***	Y	Y	N	Y	N
4 ***DeMint***	Y	Y	Y	Y	N
5 Spratt	Y	Y	Y	Y	Y
6 Clyburn	Y	Y	Y	Y	Y
SOUTH DAKOTA					
AL ***Thune***	Y	Y	Y	Y	N

	46	47	48	49	50
TENNESSEE					
1 ***Jenkins***	Y	Y	Y	Y	N
2 ***Duncan***	Y	?	Y	Y	N
3 ***Wamp***	Y	Y	N	Y	N
4 ***Hilleary***	Y	Y	Y	Y	N
5 Clement	Y	Y	Y	Y	Y
6 Gordon	Y	Y	Y	Y	N
7 ***Bryant***	Y	Y	Y	Y	N
8 Tanner	Y	Y	?	?	?
9 Ford	Y	Y	Y	Y	Y
TEXAS					
1 Sandlin	Y	Y	Y	Y	N
2 Turner	Y	Y	Y	Y	N
3 ***Johnson, Sam***	+	+	N	Y	N
4 Hall	Y	Y	N	Y	N
5 ***Sessions***	Y	Y	N	Y	N
6 ***Barton***	Y	Y	Y	Y	N
7 ***Archer***	Y	Y	N	Y	N
8 ***Brady***	Y	Y	N	Y	N
9 Lampson	Y	Y	Y	Y	N
10 Doggett	Y	Y	N	Y	Y
11 Edwards	Y	Y	Y	Y	Y
12 ***Granger***	Y	Y	Y	Y	N
13 ***Thornberry***	Y	Y	N	Y	N
14 ***Paul***	Y	Y	N	N	N
15 Hinojosa	?	?	?	?	?
16 Reyes	?	?	?	?	Y
17 Stenholm	Y	Y	N	Y	N
18 Jackson-Lee	+	+	Y	Y	Y
19 ***Combest***	Y	Y	Y	Y	N
20 Gonzalez	+	+	+	Y	Y
21 ***Smith***	Y	Y	Y	Y	N
22 ***DeLay***	Y	Y	N	Y	N
23 ***Bonilla***	Y	Y	N	Y	N
24 Frost	Y	Y	Y	Y	Y
25 Bentsen	Y	Y	Y	Y	Y
26 ***Armey***	Y	Y	Y	Y	N
27 Ortiz	?	+	+	Y	N
28 Rodriguez	?	?	+	Y	Y
29 Green	Y	Y	Y	Y	N
30 Johnson, E.B.	Y	Y	Y	Y	Y
UTAH					
1 ***Hansen***	?	?	Y	Y	N
2 ***Cook***	?	?	?	?	?
3 ***Cannon***	Y	Y	Y	Y	N
VERMONT					
AL *Sanders*	Y	Y	Y	Y	Y
VIRGINIA					
1 ***Bateman***	Y	Y	Y	Y	Y
2 Pickett	Y	?	Y	Y	N
3 Scott	Y	Y	Y	Y	Y
4 Sisisky	Y	Y	Y	Y	N
5 *Goode*	Y	Y	N	Y	N
6 ***Goodlatte***	Y	Y	Y	Y	N
7 ***Bliley***	Y	Y	Y	Y	N
8 Moran	Y	Y	N	Y	Y
9 Boucher	Y	Y	?	Y	N
10 ***Wolf***	Y	Y	N	Y	Y
11 ***Davis***	Y	Y	Y	Y	Y
WASHINGTON					
1 Inslee	Y	Y	N	Y	Y
2 ***Metcalf***	Y	Y	Y	Y	N
3 Baird	Y	Y	Y	Y	Y
4 ***Hastings***	Y	Y	Y	Y	N
5 ***Nethercutt***	Y	Y	N	?	N
6 Dicks	Y	Y	N	Y	Y
7 McDermott	Y	Y	N	Y	Y
8 ***Dunn***	Y	Y	Y	Y	Y
9 Smith	Y	?	Y	Y	Y
WEST VIRGINIA					
1 Mollohan	?	?	Y	Y	N
2 Wise	Y	Y	Y	Y	N
3 Rahall	Y	Y	Y	Y	N
WISCONSIN					
1 ***Ryan***	Y	Y	Y	Y	N
2 Baldwin	Y	Y	N	Y	Y
3 Kind	Y	Y	Y	Y	Y
4 Kleczka	Y	Y	Y	Y	Y
5 Barrett	Y	Y	Y	Y	Y
6 ***Petri***	Y	Y	Y	Y	N
7 Obey	Y	Y	N	Y	Y
8 ***Green***	Y	Y	Y	Y	N
9 ***Sensenbrenner***	Y	Y	N	Y	N
WYOMING					
AL ***Cubin***	Y	Y	Y	Y	N

Southern states - Ala., Ark., Fla., Ga., Ky., La., Miss., N.C., Okla., S.C., Tenn., Texas, Va.

51. HR 2372. Property Rights/Rule. Adoption of the rule (H Res 441) to provide for House floor consideration of the bill to expedite the process that landowners must use to bring local land use cases involving the "takings" clause of the Fifth Amendment to federal courts. Adopted 276-145: R 214-1; D 61-143 (ND 31-120, SD 30-23); I 1-1. March 16, 2000.

52. HR 2372. Property Rights/Individual Rights. Watt, D-N.C., amendment that would strike references to the word "property" so that anyone with a civil rights claim would have the same access to federal courts. Rejected 170-251: R 0-213; D 169-37 (ND 131-23, SD 38-14); I 1-1. March 16, 2000.

53. HR 2372. Property Rights/Boehlert Substitute. Boehlert, R-N.Y., substitute amendment to strike language in the bill that would expedite the process under which landowners can appeal local land use decisions in federal court. The amendment would maintain bill language establishing an expedited process for filing suit in federal court over land disputes in which the federal government is a defendant, or cases under the jurisdiction of the Court of Federal Claims. Rejected 179-234: R 36-173; D 142-60 (ND 122-29, SD 20-31); I 1-1. March 16, 2000.

54. HR 2372. Property Rights/Recommit. Conyers, D-Mich., motion to recommit the bill to the Committee on the Judiciary with instructions to report the bill back to the House with an amendment specifying that the bill would not apply to claims against local governments arising from an action to protect the public from prostitution or illegal drugs, control adult book stores and the distribution of pornography, or protect against environmental degradation such as illegal ground water contamination. It also would limit the bill's application if the action is a voter initiative or referendum to control development that threatens to "overburden" community resources. Motion rejected 155-254: R 0-209; D 154-44 (ND 128-20, SD 26-24); I 1-1. March 16, 2000.

55. HR 2372. Property Rights/Passage. Passage of the bill that would expedite the process that landowners must use to bring local land use cases involving the "takings" clause of the Fifth Amendment to federal courts. Property owners would be able to take their claim to federal court if the local government had denied the initial application to develop property, an appeal and a request for a waiver. The bill, as amended, would also require federal agencies to notify affected property owners of their rights and procedures for obtaining any compensation due to them within 30 days of an agency decision. Passed 226-182: R 173-33; D 52-148 (ND 22-127, SD 30-21); I 1-1. March 16, 2000. A "nay" was a vote in support of the president's position.

Key

Y Voted for (yea).
\# Paired for.
\+ Announced for.
N Voted against (nay).
X Paired against.
– Announced against.
P Voted "present."
C Voted "present" to avoid possible conflict of interest.
? Did not vote or otherwise make a position known.

•

Democrats ***Republicans***
Independents

	51	52	53	54	55
ALABAMA					
1 ***Callahan***	Y	N	N	N	Y
2 ***Everett***	Y	N	N	N	Y
3 ***Riley***	Y	N	N	N	Y
4 ***Aderholt***	Y	N	N	N	Y
5 Cramer	Y	N	N	N	Y
6 ***Bachus***	Y	N	N	N	N
7 Hilliard	Y	Y	N	Y	Y
ALASKA					
AL ***Young***	Y	N	N	N	Y
ARIZONA					
1 ***Salmon***	Y	N	N	N	Y
2 Pastor	N	Y	Y	Y	N
3 ***Stump***	Y	N	N	N	Y
4 ***Shadegg***	Y	N	N	N	Y
5 ***Kolbe***	Y	N	N	N	Y
6 ***Hayworth***	Y	N	N	N	Y
ARKANSAS					
1 Berry	Y	N	N	N	Y
2 Snyder	N	Y	Y	N	N
3 ***Hutchinson***	Y	N	N	N	Y
4 ***Dickey***	Y	N	N	N	Y
CALIFORNIA					
1 Thompson	Y	N	N	Y	N
2 ***Herger***	Y	N	N	N	Y
3 ***Ose***	Y	N	N	N	Y
4 ***Doolittle***	Y	N	N	N	Y
5 Matsui	N	Y	Y	Y	N
6 Woolsey	N	Y	Y	Y	N
7 Miller, George	N	Y	Y	Y	N
8 Pelosi	N	Y	Y	Y	N
9 Lee	N	Y	Y	Y	N
10 Tauscher	N	Y	N	Y	N
11 ***Pombo***	Y	N	N	N	Y
12 Lantos	N	Y	Y	Y	N
13 Stark	?	?	?	?	?
14 Eshoo	N	Y	Y	Y	N
15 ***Campbell***	Y	N	N	N	Y
16 Lofgren	N	Y	Y	Y	N
17 Farr	N	Y	Y	Y	N
18 Condit	Y	N	N	N	Y
19 ***Radanovich***	Y	N	N	N	Y
20 Dooley	Y	Y	N	N	Y
21 ***Thomas***	Y	N	N	N	Y
22 Capps	N	Y	Y	Y	N
23 ***Gallegly***	Y	N	N	N	Y
24 Sherman	N	Y	Y	Y	N
25 ***McKeon***	Y	N	N	N	Y
26 Berman	N	Y	+	+	–
27 ***Rogan***	Y	N	N	N	Y
28 ***Dreier***	Y	N	N	N	Y
29 Waxman	?	Y	Y	Y	N
30 Becerra	N	Y	N	Y	N
31 Martinez	Y	N	N	N	Y
32 Dixon	N	Y	Y	Y	N
33 Roybal-Allard	N	Y	Y	Y	N
34 Napolitano	Y	Y	Y	Y	N
35 Waters	N	Y	Y	Y	N
36 ***Kuykendall***	Y	N	N	N	Y
37 Millender-McD.	N	Y	Y	Y	N
38 ***Horn***	Y	N	Y	N	N
39 ***Royce***	Y	N	N	N	Y
40 ***Lewis***	Y	N	N	N	Y
41 ***Miller, Gary***	Y	N	?	?	?
42 Baca	Y	N	N	N	Y
43 ***Calvert***	Y	N	N	N	Y
44 ***Bono***	Y	N	N	N	Y
45 ***Rohrabacher***	Y	N	N	N	Y
46 Sanchez	N	Y	N	N	N
47 ***Cox***	Y	N	N	N	+
48 ***Packard***	Y	N	N	N	Y
49 ***Bilbray***	Y	N	Y	N	N
50 Filner	N	Y	Y	Y	N
51 ***Cunningham***	Y	N	N	N	Y
52 ***Hunter***	Y	N	N	N	Y
COLORADO					
1 DeGette	N	Y	Y	Y	N
2 Udall	N	Y	Y	Y	N
3 ***McInnis***	Y	N	N	N	Y
4 ***Schaffer***	Y	N	N	N	Y
5 ***Hefley***	Y	N	N	N	Y
6 ***Tancredo***	Y	N	N	N	Y
CONNECTICUT					
1 Larson	N	Y	Y	Y	N
2 Gejdenson	N	N	Y	Y	N
3 DeLauro	N	Y	Y	Y	N
4 ***Shays***	Y	N	Y	N	N
5 Maloney	N	Y	Y	Y	N
6 ***Johnson***	Y	N	Y	N	N
DELAWARE					
AL ***Castle***	N	N	Y	N	N
FLORIDA					
1 ***Scarborough***	Y	N	N	N	Y
2 Boyd	Y	N	N	N	Y
3 Brown	Y	Y	Y	Y	N
4 ***Fowler***	Y	N	N	N	Y
5 Thurman	Y	Y	Y	Y	N
6 ***Stearns***	Y	N	N	N	Y
7 ***Mica***	Y	N	N	N	Y
8 ***McCollum***	Y	?	?	?	?
9 ***Bilirakis***	Y	N	N	N	Y
10 ***Young***	Y	N	Y	N	Y
11 Davis	Y	N	Y	N	N
12 ***Canady***	Y	N	N	N	Y
13 ***Miller***	Y	N	Y	N	Y
14 ***Goss***	Y	N	Y	N	N
15 ***Weldon***	Y	N	N	N	Y
16 ***Foley***	Y	N	N	N	Y
17 Meek	N	Y	Y	Y	N
18 ***Ros-Lehtinen***	Y	N	N	N	Y
19 Wexler	N	Y	Y	Y	N
20 Deutsch	N	Y	Y	Y	N
21 ***Diaz-Balart***	Y	N	N	N	Y
22 ***Shaw***	Y	N	Y	N	Y
23 Hastings	N	Y	?	?	?
GEORGIA					
1 ***Kingston***	Y	N	N	N	Y
2 Bishop	Y	Y	N	N	Y
3 ***Collins***	Y	N	N	N	Y
4 McKinney	N	?	Y	Y	N
5 Lewis	N	Y	?	?	?
6 ***Isakson***	Y	N	N	N	Y
7 ***Barr***	Y	N	N	N	Y
8 ***Chambliss***	Y	N	N	N	Y
9 ***Deal***	Y	N	N	N	Y
10 ***Norwood***	Y	N	N	N	Y
11 ***Linder***	Y	N	N	N	Y
HAWAII					
1 Abercrombie	N	Y	Y	Y	N
2 Mink	N	Y	Y	Y	N
IDAHO					
1 ***Chenoweth-Hage***	Y	N	?	?	?
2 ***Simpson***	Y	N	N	N	Y
ILLINOIS					
1 Rush	?	?	?	?	?
2 Jackson	N	Y	Y	Y	N
3 Lipinski	Y	N	Y	Y	?
4 Gutierrez	N	Y	Y	Y	N
5 Blagojevich	N	Y	Y	Y	N
6 ***Hyde***	Y	?	?	?	+
7 Davis	N	Y	Y	Y	N
8 ***Crane***	?	?	?	?	?
9 Schakowsky	N	Y	Y	Y	N
10 ***Porter***	Y	N	Y	N	N
11 ***Weller***	Y	N	N	N	Y
12 Costello	Y	Y	Y	Y	N
13 ***Biggert***	Y	?	?	?	?

ND Northern Democrats SD Southern Democrats

	51	52	53	54	55
14 Hastert					
15 Ewing	Y	N	N	N	Y
16 Manzullo	Y	N	N	N	Y
17 Evans	N	Y	Y	Y	N
18 LaHood	Y	N	N	N	Y
19 Phelps	Y	N	N	Y	Y
20 Shimkus	Y	N	N	N	Y
INDIANA					
1 Visclosky	N	Y	Y	Y	N
2 McIntosh	Y	N	N	N	Y
3 Roemer	Y	Y	Y	N	Y
4 Souder	Y	N	N	N	Y
5 Buyer	Y	N	N	N	Y
6 Burton	Y	N	N	N	Y
7 Pease	Y	N	N	N	Y
8 Hostettler	Y	N	N	N	Y
9 Hill	Y	Y	N	Y	Y
10 Carson	N	Y	Y	Y	N
IOWA					
1 Leach	Y	N	Y	N	N
2 Nussle	Y	N	N	N	Y
3 Boswell	Y	N	N	N	Y
4 Ganske	Y	N	Y	N	N
5 Latham	Y	N	N	N	Y
KANSAS					
1 Moran	Y	N	N	N	Y
2 Ryun	Y	N	N	N	Y
3 Moore	N	Y	Y	Y	N
4 Tiahrt	Y	N	N	N	Y
KENTUCKY					
1 Whitfield	?	?	?	?	?
2 Lewis	Y	N	N	N	Y
3 Northup	Y	N	N	N	Y
4 Lucas	Y	N	N	N	Y
5 Rogers	Y	N	N	N	Y
6 Fletcher	Y	N	N	N	Y
LOUISIANA					
1 Vitter	Y	N	N	N	Y
2 Jefferson	N	Y	N	Y	Y
3 Tauzin	Y	N	N	N	Y
4 McCrery	Y	N	N	N	Y
5 Cooksey	Y	N	Y	N	N
6 Baker	Y	N	N	N	Y
7 John	Y	N	N	N	Y
MAINE					
1 Allen	N	Y	Y	Y	N
2 Baldacci	Y	Y	Y	Y	Y
MARYLAND					
1 Gilchrest	Y	N	Y	N	N
2 Ehrlich	Y	N	N	N	Y
3 Cardin	N	N	Y	Y	N
4 Wynn	N	Y	Y	?	N
5 Hoyer	N	N	N	N	Y
6 Bartlett	Y	N	N	N	Y
7 Cummings	N	Y	Y	Y	N
8 Morella	Y	N	Y	N	N
MASSACHUSETTS					
1 Olver	N	Y	Y	Y	N
2 Neal	N	Y	Y	Y	N
3 McGovern	N	Y	Y	Y	N
4 Frank	N	Y	Y	N	N
5 Meehan	N	Y	Y	Y	N
6 Tierney	N	Y	Y	Y	N
7 Markey	N	Y	Y	Y	N
8 Capuano	N	Y	Y	Y	N
9 Moakley	N	Y	Y	Y	N
10 Delahunt	N	Y	Y	Y	N
MICHIGAN					
1 Stupak	Y	Y	Y	Y	N
2 Hoekstra	Y	N	N	N	Y
3 Ehlers	Y	N	Y	N	N
4 Camp	Y	N	N	N	Y
5 Barcia	Y	Y	N	Y	N
6 Upton	Y	N	Y	N	Y
7 Smith	Y	N	N	N	Y
8 Stabenow	N	Y	Y	Y	N
9 Kildee	N	Y	Y	Y	N
10 Bonior	N	Y	Y	Y	N
11 Knollenberg	Y	N	N	N	Y
12 Levin	N	N	Y	Y	N
13 Rivers	N	Y	Y	Y	N
14 Conyers	N	Y	Y	Y	N
15 Kilpatrick	N	Y	Y	Y	N
16 Dingell	N	Y	Y	Y	N

	51	52	53	54	55
MINNESOTA					
1 Gutknecht	Y	N	N	N	Y
2 Minge	Y	N	Y	Y	N
3 Ramstad	Y	N	Y	N	N
4 Vento	N	Y	?	?	?
5 Sabo	N	Y	Y	Y	N
6 Luther	N	Y	Y	Y	N
7 Peterson	N	N	N	Y	N
8 Oberstar	N	Y	Y	Y	N
MISSISSIPPI					
1 Wicker	Y	N	N	N	Y
2 Thompson	N	Y	N	Y	Y
3 Pickering	Y	N	N	N	Y
4 Shows	Y	Y	N	N	Y
5 Taylor	Y	N	N	N	Y
MISSOURI					
1 Clay	N	Y	Y	Y	N
2 Talent	Y	N	N	N	Y
3 Gephardt	N	Y	Y	Y	N
4 Skelton	Y	N	?	?	?
5 McCarthy	N	Y	Y	Y	N
6 Danner	Y	N	N	N	Y
7 Blunt	Y	?	N	N	Y
8 Emerson	Y	N	N	N	Y
9 Hulshof	Y	N	N	N	Y
MONTANA					
AL Hill	Y	N	N	N	Y
NEBRASKA					
1 Bereuter	Y	N	Y	N	N
2 Terry	Y	N	N	N	Y
3 Barrett	Y	N	N	N	Y
NEVADA					
1 Berkley	Y	Y	N	N	Y
2 Gibbons	Y	N	N	N	Y
NEW HAMPSHIRE					
1 Sununu	Y	N	N	N	Y
2 Bass	Y	N	Y	N	N
NEW JERSEY					
1 Andrews	N	Y	Y	Y	N
2 LoBiondo	Y	N	N	N	Y
3 Saxton	Y	N	Y	N	N
4 Smith	Y	N	Y	N	N
5 Roukema	Y	N	Y	N	N
6 Pallone	N	Y	Y	Y	N
7 Franks	Y	N	N	N	Y
8 Pascrell	Y	N	N	Y	N
9 Rothman	Y	Y	N	N	Y
10 Payne	N	Y	Y	?	?
11 Frelinghuysen	Y	N	Y	N	N
12 Holt	N	Y	Y	Y	N
13 Menendez	N	Y	Y	Y	N
NEW MEXICO					
1 Wilson	Y	N	N	N	Y
2 Skeen	Y	N	N	N	Y
3 Udall	N	Y	Y	Y	N
NEW YORK					
1 Forbes	N	Y	Y	Y	N
2 Lazio	Y	N	Y	N	N
3 King	Y	N	N	N	Y
4 McCarthy	N	Y	N	Y	N
5 Ackerman	N	Y	Y	Y	N
6 Meeks	N	Y	Y	Y	Y
7 Crowley	N	Y	N	Y	N
8 Nadler	N	Y	Y	Y	N
9 Weiner	N	Y	Y	Y	N
10 Towns	N	Y	Y	Y	N
11 Owens	?	Y	Y	Y	N
12 Velázquez	N	Y	Y	Y	N
13 Fossella	Y	N	N	N	Y
14 Maloney	Y	Y	Y	Y	Y
15 Rangel	?	Y	Y	Y	N
16 Serrano	N	Y	Y	Y	N
17 Engel	N	Y	Y	Y	N
18 Lowey	N	Y	Y	Y	N
19 Kelly	Y	N	Y	N	N
20 Gilman	Y	N	Y	N	N
21 McNulty	N	Y	Y	Y	N
22 Sweeney	Y	N	N	N	Y
23 Boehlert	Y	N	Y	N	N
24 McHugh	Y	N	N	N	Y
25 Walsh	Y	N	Y	N	N
26 Hinchey	Y	Y	Y	Y	N
27 Reynolds	Y	N	N	N	Y
28 Slaughter	N	Y	Y	Y	N
29 LaFalce	N	Y	Y	?	N

	51	52	53	54	55
30 Quinn	Y	N	N	N	N
31 Houghton	Y	N	N	N	Y
NORTH CAROLINA					
1 Clayton	N	Y	Y	Y	N
2 Etheridge	Y	Y	N	Y	Y
3 Jones	?	N	N	N	Y
4 Price	N	Y	Y	Y	N
5 Burr	Y	N	N	N	Y
6 Coble	Y	N	N	N	Y
7 McIntyre	Y	Y	N	N	Y
8 Hayes	Y	N	N	N	Y
9 Myrick	?	?	?	?	?
10 Ballenger	Y	N	N	N	Y
11 Taylor	Y	N	N	N	Y
12 Watt	N	Y	Y	Y	N
NORTH DAKOTA					
AL Pomeroy	Y	Y	Y	Y	N
OHIO					
1 Chabot	Y	N	N	N	Y
2 Portman	Y	N	Y	N	N
3 Hall	N	N	Y	N	Y
4 Oxley	Y	N	N	N	Y
5 Gillmor	Y	N	N	N	Y
6 Strickland	N	N	Y	Y	N
7 Hobson	Y	N	N	N	Y
8 Boehner	Y	N	N	N	Y
9 Kaptur	N	Y	Y	Y	N
10 Kucinich	N	Y	Y	Y	N
11 Jones	N	Y	Y	Y	N
12 Kasich	Y	N	?	?	?
13 Brown	N	Y	Y	Y	N
14 Sawyer	N	Y	Y	Y	N
15 Pryce	Y	N	N	N	Y
16 Regula	Y	N	Y	N	N
17 Traficant	Y	Y	N	N	Y
18 Ney	Y	N	N	N	Y
19 LaTourette	Y	N	N	N	Y
OKLAHOMA					
1 Largent	Y	N	N	N	Y
2 Coburn	Y	N	N	N	Y
3 Watkins	Y	N	N	N	Y
4 Watts	Y	N	N	N	Y
5 Istook	Y	N	N	N	?
6 Lucas	Y	N	N	N	Y
OREGON					
1 Wu	N	N	N	N	N
2 Walden	Y	N	N	N	Y
3 Blumenauer	N	Y	Y	Y	N
4 DeFazio	N	Y	Y	Y	N
5 Hooley	N	Y	N	Y	N
PENNSYLVANIA					
1 Brady	N	Y	Y	Y	N
2 Fattah	N	Y	Y	Y	N
3 Borski	N	Y	Y	Y	N
4 Klink	?	?	?	?	?
5 Peterson	Y	N	N	N	Y
6 Holden	Y	Y	N	N	Y
7 Weldon	Y	N	Y	N	N
8 Greenwood	Y	N	Y	?	?
9 Shuster	Y	N	N	N	Y
10 Sherwood	Y	N	N	N	Y
11 Kanjorski	N	Y	Y	Y	N
12 Murtha	Y	N	N	N	Y
13 Hoeffel	N	Y	Y	Y	N
14 Coyne	N	Y	Y	Y	N
15 Toomey	Y	N	N	N	Y
16 Pitts	Y	N	N	N	N
17 Gekas	Y	N	N	N	Y
18 Doyle	Y	N	N	N	Y
19 Goodling	Y	N	N	N	Y
20 Mascara	Y	N	N	N	Y
21 English	Y	N	N	N	Y
RHODE ISLAND					
1 Kennedy	N	Y	Y	Y	N
2 Weygand	Y	Y	Y	N	Y
SOUTH CAROLINA					
1 Sanford	Y	N	N	N	Y
2 Spence	Y	N	N	N	Y
3 Graham	Y	N	N	N	Y
4 DeMint	Y	N	N	N	Y
5 Spratt	N	Y	N	Y	N
6 Clyburn	N	Y	Y	Y	N
SOUTH DAKOTA					
AL Thune	Y	N	N	N	Y

	51	52	53	54	55
TENNESSEE					
1 Jenkins	Y	N	N	N	Y
2 Duncan	Y	N	N	N	Y
3 Wamp	Y	N	N	N	Y
4 Hilleary	Y	N	N	N	Y
5 Clement	Y	Y	N	N	Y
6 Gordon	Y	N	N	N	Y
7 Bryant	Y	N	N	N	Y
8 Tanner	Y	N	N	N	Y
9 Ford	Y	Y	Y	Y	Y
TEXAS					
1 Sandlin	Y	Y	N	N	Y
2 Turner	Y	N	N	N	Y
3 Johnson, Sam	Y	N	N	N	Y
4 Hall	N	N	N	N	Y
5 Sessions	Y	N	N	N	Y
6 Barton	Y	N	N	N	Y
7 Archer	Y	N	?	?	?
8 Brady	Y	N	N	N	Y
9 Lampson	Y	Y	N	N	Y
10 Doggett	N	Y	Y	Y	N
11 Edwards	Y	Y	N	Y	Y
12 Granger	Y	N	N	N	Y
13 Thornberry	Y	N	N	N	Y
14 Paul	Y	N	N	N	?
15 Hinojosa	?	?	?	?	?
16 Reyes	Y	Y	Y	Y	N
17 Stenholm	Y	N	N	N	Y
18 Jackson-Lee	N	Y	Y	Y	N
19 Combest	Y	N	N	N	Y
20 Gonzalez	N	Y	N	Y	N
21 Smith	Y	N	N	N	Y
22 DeLay	?	N	N	N	Y
23 Bonilla	Y	N	N	N	Y
24 Frost	Y	Y	N	N	Y
25 Bentsen	N	N	N	Y	N
26 Armey	Y	N	?	N	Y
27 Ortiz	Y	Y	N	N	Y
28 Rodriguez	Y	Y	Y	Y	N
29 Green	N	Y	N	N	Y
30 Johnson, E.B.	N	Y	Y	Y	Y
UTAH					
1 Hansen	Y	N	N	N	Y
2 Cook	?	?	?	?	?
3 Cannon	Y	N	N	N	Y
VERMONT					
AL Sanders	N	Y	Y	Y	N
VIRGINIA					
1 Bateman	Y	N	Y	N	Y
2 Pickett	Y	N	N	N	Y
3 Scott	N	Y	N	Y	Y
4 Sisisky	Y	Y	N	N	Y
5 Goode	Y	N	N	N	Y
6 Goodlatte	Y	N	N	N	Y
7 Bliley	Y	N	N	N	Y
8 Moran	Y	Y	Y	?	N
9 Boucher	N	Y	Y	Y	N
10 Wolf	Y	N	Y	N	N
11 Davis	Y	N	N	N	Y
WASHINGTON					
1 Inslee	N	Y	Y	Y	N
2 Metcalf	Y	N	Y	N	N
3 Baird	N	Y	Y	Y	N
4 Hastings	Y	N	N	N	Y
5 Nethercutt	Y	N	N	N	Y
6 Dicks	N	Y	Y	Y	N
7 McDermott	N	Y	Y	Y	N
8 Dunn	Y	N	N	N	Y
9 Smith	N	Y	Y	Y	N
WEST VIRGINIA					
1 Mollohan	N	N	Y	Y	N
2 Wise	N	Y	Y	Y	N
3 Rahall	N	Y	N	Y	N
WISCONSIN					
1 Ryan	Y	N	N	N	Y
2 Baldwin	N	Y	Y	Y	N
3 Kind	N	Y	N	Y	N
4 Kleczka	N	Y	Y	Y	N
5 Barrett	N	Y	Y	Y	N
6 Petri	Y	N	N	N	Y
7 Obey	Y	Y	Y	Y	N
8 Green	Y	N	N	N	Y
9 Sensenbrenner	Y	N	N	N	Y
WYOMING					
AL Cubin	Y	N	N	N	Y

Southern states - Ala., Ark., Fla., Ga., Ky., La., Miss., N.C., Okla., S.C., Tenn., Texas, Va.

56. H Con Res 288. National Family Day/Adoption. Goodling, R-Pa., motion to suspend the rules and adopt the concurrent resolution providing for an annual National Family Day on a Sunday in March. Motion agreed to 392-0: R 206-0; D 184-0 (ND 134-0, SD 50-0); I 2-0. A two-thirds majority of those present and voting (262 in this case) is required for adoption under suspension of the rules. March 21, 2000.

57. H Res 182. National Park Service/Adoption. Hansen, R-Utah, motion to suspend the rules and adopt the resolution urging the National Park Service to utilize, per current law, the Defense Department's resources to help the park service address its approximate $6 billion maintenance backlog. Motion agreed to 392-2: R 206-2; D 184-0 (ND 133-0, SD 51-0); I 2-0. A two-thirds majority of those present and voting (263 in this case) is required for adoption under suspension of the rules. March 21, 2000.

58. Procedural Motion/Journal. Approval of the House Journal for March 21, 2000. Approved 352-49: R 190-14; D 160-35 (ND 115-28, SD 45-7); I 2-0. March 22, 2000.

59. S 1287. Nuclear Waste Storage/Previous Question. Hastings, R-Wash., motion to order the previous question (thus ending debate and possibility of amendment) on adoption of the rule (H Res 444) to provide for House floor consideration of the bill that would provide for the completion of siting and licensing activities for a permanent nuclear waste repository at Yucca Mountain, Nev. Motion agreed to 219-195: R 213-0; D 5-194 (ND 2-145, SD 3-49); I 1-1. March 22, 2000.

60. S 1287. Nuclear Waste Storage/Rule. Adoption of the rule (H Res 444) to provide for House floor consideration of the bill to provide for the completion of siting and licensing activities for a permanent nuclear waste repository at Yucca Mountain, Nev. Adopted 220-191: R 211-1; D 8-189 (ND 2-143, SD 6-46); I 1-1. March 22, 2000.

61. S 1287. Nuclear Waste Storage/Question of Consideration. Judgment of the House to consider the bill despite a point of order raised by Gibbons, R-Nev., that the bill constitutes an unfunded mandate. Consideration agreed to 206-205: R 197-15; D 8-189 (ND 3-144, SD 5-45); I 1-1. March 22, 2000.

62. S 1287. Nuclear Waste Storage/Commit. Berkley, D-Nev., motion to commit the bill to the House Commerce Committee for the purpose of holding hearings. Motion rejected 188-233: R 4-215; D 183-17 (ND 142-7, SD 41-10); I 1-1. March 22, 2000.

Key

- Y Voted for (yea).
- # Paired for.
- \+ Announced for.
- N Voted against (nay).
- X Paired against.
- – Announced against.
- P Voted "present."
- C Voted "present" to avoid possible conflict of interest.
- ? Did not vote or otherwise make a position known.

•

Democrats ***Republicans***
Independents

	56	57	58	59	60	61	62
ALABAMA							
1 ***Callahan***	Y	Y	Y	Y	Y	Y	N
2 ***Everett***	Y	Y	Y	Y	Y	Y	N
3 ***Riley***	Y	Y	Y	Y	Y	Y	N
4 ***Aderholt***	Y	Y	N	Y	Y	Y	N
5 Cramer	Y	Y	Y	N	N	N	N
6 ***Bachus***	?	?	Y	Y	Y	Y	N
7 Hilliard	Y	Y	N	Y	Y	N	N
ALASKA							
AL ***Young***	Y	Y	?	Y	Y	N	N
ARIZONA							
1 ***Salmon***	Y	Y	Y	Y	?	Y	N
2 Pastor	Y	Y	Y	Y	Y	N	N
3 ***Stump***	Y	Y	Y	Y	Y	Y	N
4 ***Shadegg***	Y	Y	Y	Y	Y	Y	N
5 ***Kolbe***	Y	Y	Y	Y	Y	Y	N
6 ***Hayworth***	Y	Y	Y	Y	Y	Y	N
ARKANSAS							
1 Berry	Y	Y	Y	N	N	?	Y
2 Snyder	Y	Y	Y	N	N	N	Y
3 ***Hutchinson***	Y	Y	?	Y	Y	Y	N
4 ***Dickey***	Y	Y	Y	Y	Y	Y	N
CALIFORNIA							
1 Thompson	Y	Y	N	N	N	N	Y
2 ***Herger***	Y	Y	Y	Y	Y	Y	N
3 ***Ose***	Y	Y	Y	Y	Y	?	N
4 ***Doolittle***	?	?	Y	Y	Y	Y	N
5 Matsui	?	?	Y	N	N	N	Y
6 Woolsey	Y	Y	Y	N	N	N	Y
7 Miller, George	Y	Y	N	N	N	N	Y
8 Pelosi	Y	Y	Y	N	N	N	Y
9 Lee	Y	Y	Y	N	N	N	Y
10 Tauscher	Y	Y	Y	N	N	N	Y
11 ***Pombo***	Y	Y	Y	?	?	Y	N
12 Lantos	Y	Y	Y	N	N	N	Y
13 Stark	Y	Y	N	N	N	N	Y
14 Eshoo	+	+	Y	N	N	N	Y
15 ***Campbell***	Y	Y	Y	Y	Y	N	N
16 Lofgren	Y	Y	Y	N	N	N	Y
17 Farr	Y	Y	Y	N	N	N	Y
18 Condit	Y	Y	Y	N	N	N	Y
19 ***Radanovich***	Y	Y	Y	Y	Y	N	N
20 Dooley	Y	Y	Y	N	N	N	Y
21 ***Thomas***	Y	Y	Y	Y	Y	Y	N
22 Capps	Y	Y	Y	N	N	N	Y
23 ***Gallegly***	Y	Y	Y	Y	Y	Y	N
24 Sherman	Y	Y	Y	N	N	N	Y
25 ***McKeon***	Y	Y	Y	Y	?	Y	N
26 Berman	?	?	Y	N	N	N	Y
27 ***Rogan***	Y	Y	N	Y	Y	Y	N
28 ***Dreier***	Y	Y	Y	Y	Y	Y	N
29 Waxman	Y	Y	Y	N	N	N	Y
30 Becerra	+	+	Y	N	?	N	Y
31 Martinez	?	?	?	Y	Y	Y	N
32 Dixon	Y	Y	Y	N	N	N	Y
33 Roybal-Allard	Y	Y	Y	N	N	N	Y
34 Napolitano	Y	Y	Y	N	N	N	Y
35 Waters	Y	Y	N	N	N	N	Y
36 ***Kuykendall***	Y	Y	Y	Y	Y	N	N
37 Millender-McD.	Y	Y	Y	N	N	N	Y
38 ***Horn***	Y	Y	Y	Y	Y	Y	N
39 ***Royce***	?	?	?	?	?	?	?
40 ***Lewis***	Y	Y	Y	Y	Y	N	N
41 ***Miller, Gary***	Y	Y	Y	Y	Y	Y	N
42 Baca	Y	Y	Y	N	N	N	Y
43 ***Calvert***	Y	Y	Y	Y	Y	Y	N
44 ***Bono***	Y	Y	Y	Y	Y	Y	N
45 ***Rohrabacher***	Y	Y	Y	Y	Y	Y	N
46 Sanchez	Y	Y	Y	N	N	N	Y
47 ***Cox***	Y	Y	Y	Y	Y	Y	N
48 ***Packard***	Y	Y	Y	Y	Y	Y	N
49 ***Bilbray***	Y	Y	N	Y	Y	Y	N
50 Filner	Y	Y	N	N	N	N	Y
51 ***Cunningham***	Y	Y	Y	Y	Y	Y	N
52 ***Hunter***	Y	Y	Y	Y	Y	Y	N
COLORADO							
1 DeGette	Y	Y	Y	N	N	N	Y
2 Udall	Y	Y	N	N	N	N	Y
3 ***McInnis***	Y	Y	Y	Y	Y	Y	Y
4 ***Schaffer***	Y	Y	N	Y	Y	Y	N
5 ***Hefley***	Y	Y	N	Y	Y	N	N
6 ***Tancredo***	Y	Y	P	Y	Y	Y	N
CONNECTICUT							
1 Larson	Y	Y	Y	N	N	N	Y
2 Gejdenson	Y	Y	Y	N	N	Y	N
3 DeLauro	Y	Y	Y	N	N	N	Y
4 ***Shays***	Y	Y	Y	Y	Y	Y	N
5 Maloney	Y	Y	Y	N	N	N	Y
6 ***Johnson***	Y	Y	Y	Y	Y	Y	N
DELAWARE							
AL ***Castle***	Y	Y	Y	Y	Y	Y	N
FLORIDA							
1 ***Scarborough***	Y	Y	?	Y	Y	Y	N
2 Boyd	Y	Y	?	?	?	?	?
3 Brown	Y	Y	Y	N	Y	N	Y
4 ***Fowler***	Y	Y	Y	Y	Y	Y	N
5 Thurman	Y	Y	Y	N	N	N	Y
6 ***Stearns***	Y	Y	Y	Y	Y	Y	N
7 ***Mica***	Y	Y	Y	Y	Y	Y	N
8 ***McCollum***	?	?	?	?	?	?	N
9 ***Bilirakis***	Y	Y	Y	Y	Y	Y	N
10 ***Young***	?	?	Y	Y	Y	Y	N
11 Davis	Y	Y	Y	N	N	N	Y
12 ***Canady***	Y	Y	Y	Y	Y	Y	N
13 ***Miller***	Y	Y	Y	Y	Y	Y	N
14 ***Goss***	Y	Y	Y	Y	Y	Y	N
15 ***Weldon***	Y	Y	Y	Y	Y	Y	N
16 ***Foley***	Y	Y	Y	Y	Y	Y	N
17 Meek	Y	Y	Y	N	Y	N	?
18 ***Ros-Lehtinen***	Y	Y	Y	Y	Y	Y	N
19 Wexler	Y	Y	Y	N	N	N	Y
20 Deutsch	Y	Y	Y	N	N	N	Y
21 ***Diaz-Balart***	Y	Y	Y	Y	Y	Y	N
22 ***Shaw***	Y	Y	Y	Y	Y	Y	N
23 Hastings	Y	Y	N	N	Y	N	Y
GEORGIA							
1 ***Kingston***	Y	Y	Y	Y	Y	?	N
2 Bishop	Y	Y	Y	Y	Y	Y	N
3 ***Collins***	Y	Y	Y	Y	Y	N	N
4 McKinney	Y	Y	Y	N	N	N	Y
5 Lewis	Y	Y	N	N	N	N	Y
6 ***Isakson***	Y	Y	Y	Y	Y	Y	N
7 ***Barr***	Y	Y	Y	Y	Y	Y	N
8 ***Chambliss***	Y	Y	Y	Y	Y	Y	N
9 ***Deal***	Y	Y	Y	Y	Y	Y	N
10 ***Norwood***	Y	Y	Y	Y	Y	Y	N
11 ***Linder***	Y	Y	Y	Y	Y	Y	N
HAWAII							
1 Abercrombie	Y	Y	Y	N	N	N	Y
2 Mink	Y	Y	Y	N	N	N	Y
IDAHO							
1 ***Chenoweth-Hage***	Y	N	N	Y	Y	N	N
2 ***Simpson***	Y	Y	Y	Y	Y	Y	N
ILLINOIS							
1 Rush	?	?	?	?	?	?	?
2 Jackson	Y	Y	Y	N	N	N	Y
3 Lipinski	?	?	Y	N	N	N	Y
4 Gutierrez	?	?	?	N	N	?	Y
5 Blagojevich	?	?	Y	N	N	N	Y
6 ***Hyde***	Y	Y	Y	Y	Y	Y	N
7 Davis	?	?	?	?	?	N	Y
8 ***Crane***	?	?	?	?	?	?	?
9 Schakowsky	?	?	?	?	?	?	?
10 ***Porter***	?	?	?	?	?	Y	N
11 ***Weller***	Y	Y	N	Y	Y	Y	N
12 Costello	Y	Y	N	N	N	N	Y
13 ***Biggert***	Y	Y	Y	Y	Y	Y	N

ND Northern Democrats SD Southern Democrats

	56	57	58	59	60	61	62
14 ***Hastert***						Y	N
15 ***Ewing***	?	?	?	?	?	?	N
16 ***Manzullo***	Y	Y	Y	Y	Y	Y	N
17 Evans	Y	Y	Y	N	N	N	Y
18 ***LaHood***	Y	Y	?	Y	Y	Y	N
19 Phelps	Y	Y	Y	N	N	N	Y
20 ***Shimkus***	Y	Y	Y	Y	Y	Y	N
INDIANA							
1 Visclosky	Y	Y	N	N	N	N	Y
2 ***McIntosh***	Y	Y	Y	Y	Y	N	Y
3 Roemer	Y	Y	Y	N	N	N	Y
4 ***Souder***	Y	Y	Y	Y	Y	Y	N
5 ***Buyer***	Y	Y	Y	Y	Y	Y	N
6 ***Burton***	Y	Y	?	Y	Y	Y	N
7 ***Pease***	Y	Y	Y	Y	Y	Y	N
8 ***Hostettler***	Y	Y	Y	Y	Y	N	N
9 Hill	Y	Y	Y	N	?	?	?
10 Carson	Y	Y	Y	N	N	N	Y
IOWA							
1 ***Leach***	Y	Y	Y	Y	Y	Y	N
2 ***Nussle***	Y	Y	Y	Y	Y	Y	N
3 Boswell	Y	Y	Y	N	N	N	Y
4 ***Ganske***	Y	Y	Y	Y	Y	Y	N
5 ***Latham***	Y	Y	Y	Y	Y	Y	N
KANSAS							
1 ***Moran***	Y	Y	Y	Y	Y	Y	N
2 ***Ryun***	Y	Y	Y	Y	Y	Y	N
3 Moore	Y	Y	N	N	N	N	Y
4 ***Tiahrt***	Y	Y	Y	Y	Y	Y	N
KENTUCKY							
1 ***Whitfield***	Y	Y	Y	Y	Y	Y	N
2 ***Lewis***	Y	Y	Y	Y	Y	Y	N
3 ***Northup***	Y	Y	Y	Y	Y	Y	N
4 Lucas	Y	Y	Y	N	N	N	Y
5 ***Rogers***	Y	Y	Y	Y	Y	Y	N
6 ***Fletcher***	Y	Y	Y	Y	Y	Y	N
LOUISIANA							
1 ***Vitter***	Y	Y	Y	Y	Y	Y	N
2 Jefferson	Y	Y	Y	N	N	N	Y
3 ***Tauzin***	Y	Y	Y	Y	Y	Y	N
4 ***McCrery***	Y	Y	Y	Y	Y	Y	N
5 ***Cooksey***	Y	Y	Y	Y	Y	Y	N
6 ***Baker***	Y	Y	Y	Y	Y	Y	N
7 John	Y	Y	Y	N	N	N	Y
MAINE							
1 Allen	Y	Y	Y	N	N	N	Y
2 Baldacci	Y	Y	Y	N	N	N	Y
MARYLAND							
1 ***Gilchrest***	Y	Y	Y	Y	Y	Y	N
2 ***Ehrlich***	Y	Y	Y	Y	Y	Y	N
3 Cardin	Y	Y	Y	N	N	N	Y
4 Wynn	Y	Y	Y	N	N	N	Y
5 Hoyer	Y	Y	Y	N	N	N	Y
6 ***Bartlett***	Y	Y	Y	Y	Y	Y	N
7 Cummings	Y	Y	Y	N	N	N	Y
8 ***Morella***	Y	Y	Y	Y	Y	Y	N
MASSACHUSETTS							
1 Olver	Y	Y	Y	N	N	N	Y
2 Neal	Y	Y	Y	N	N	N	Y
3 McGovern	Y	Y	N	N	N	N	Y
4 Frank	Y	Y	?	N	N	N	Y
5 Meehan	Y	?	Y	N	N	N	Y
6 Tierney	Y	Y	?	?	N	N	Y
7 Markey	Y	Y	Y	N	N	N	Y
8 Capuano	Y	Y	Y	N	N	N	Y
9 Moakley	Y	Y	Y	N	N	N	Y
10 Delahunt	?	?	Y	N	N	N	Y
MICHIGAN							
1 Stupak	Y	Y	N	N	N	N	Y
2 ***Hoekstra***	Y	Y	Y	Y	Y	Y	N
3 ***Ehlers***	Y	Y	Y	Y	Y	Y	N
4 ***Camp***	Y	Y	Y	Y	Y	Y	N
5 Barcia	Y	Y	Y	N	N	N	Y
6 ***Upton***	Y	Y	Y	Y	Y	Y	N
7 ***Smith***	Y	Y	Y	Y	Y	Y	N
8 Stabenow	Y	Y	Y	N	N	N	Y
9 Kildee	Y	Y	Y	N	N	N	Y
10 Bonior	Y	Y	N	N	N	N	Y
11 ***Knollenberg***	Y	Y	Y	Y	Y	Y	N
12 Levin	Y	Y	Y	N	N	N	Y
13 Rivers	Y	Y	Y	N	N	N	Y
14 Conyers	Y	Y	Y	N	N	N	Y
15 Kilpatrick	Y	Y	Y	N	N	N	Y
16 Dingell	Y	Y	Y	N	N	N	Y

	56	57	58	59	60	61	62
MINNESOTA							
1 ***Gutknecht***	Y	Y	N	Y	Y	Y	N
2 Minge	Y	Y	Y	N	N	N	Y
3 ***Ramstad***	Y	Y	N	Y	Y	Y	N
4 Vento	Y	Y	Y	N	N	N	Y
5 Sabo	Y	Y	N	N	N	N	Y
6 Luther	Y	Y	Y	N	N	N	Y
7 Peterson	Y	Y	N	N	N	N	N
8 Oberstar	Y	Y	N	N	N	N	Y
MISSISSIPPI							
1 ***Wicker***	Y	Y	Y	Y	Y	Y	N
2 Thompson	Y	Y	N	N	N	N	Y
3 ***Pickering***	Y	Y	Y	Y	Y	Y	N
4 Shows	Y	Y	Y	N	N	Y	N
5 Taylor	?	Y	N	N	N	Y	N
MISSOURI							
1 Clay	Y	Y	N	N	N	N	Y
2 ***Talent***	Y	Y	Y	Y	Y	N	N
3 Gephardt	Y	Y	Y	N	N	N	Y
4 Skelton	Y	Y	Y	N	N	N	Y
5 McCarthy	Y	Y	Y	N	N	N	Y
6 Danner	Y	Y	Y	N	N	N	Y
7 ***Blunt***	Y	?	Y	Y	Y	Y	N
8 ***Emerson***	Y	Y	Y	Y	Y	Y	N
9 ***Hulshof***	Y	Y	N	Y	Y	Y	N
MONTANA							
AL ***Hill***	Y	Y	N	Y	Y	Y	N
NEBRASKA							
1 ***Bereuter***	Y	Y	Y	Y	Y	Y	N
2 ***Terry***	Y	Y	Y	Y	Y	Y	N
3 ***Barrett***	Y	Y	Y	Y	Y	Y	N
NEVADA							
1 Berkley	Y	Y	Y	N	N	N	Y
2 ***Gibbons***	Y	Y	N	Y	N	N	Y
NEW HAMPSHIRE							
1 ***Sununu***	Y	Y	Y	Y	Y	Y	N
2 ***Bass***	Y	Y	Y	Y	Y	Y	N
NEW JERSEY							
1 Andrews	Y	Y	Y	N	N	N	Y
2 ***LoBiondo***	Y	Y	N	Y	Y	Y	N
3 ***Saxton***	Y	Y	Y	Y	Y	Y	N
4 ***Smith***	Y	Y	Y	Y	Y	Y	Y
5 ***Roukema***	Y	Y	Y	Y	Y	Y	N
6 Pallone	?	?	?	?	?	?	?
7 ***Franks***	Y	Y	Y	Y	Y	?	N
8 Pascrell	Y	Y	Y	N	N	N	Y
9 Rothman	?	?	Y	N	N	N	Y
10 Payne	?	?	Y	N	N	N	Y
11 ***Frelinghuysen***	Y	Y	Y	Y	Y	Y	N
12 Holt	Y	Y	Y	N	N	N	Y
13 Menendez	Y	Y	Y	N	N	N	Y
NEW MEXICO							
1 ***Wilson***	Y	Y	Y	Y	Y	Y	N
2 ***Skeen***	Y	Y	Y	Y	Y	Y	N
3 Udall	Y	Y	N	N	N	N	Y
NEW YORK							
1 Forbes	Y	Y	Y	N	N	N	Y
2 ***Lazio***	Y	Y	Y	Y	Y	Y	N
3 ***King***	Y	Y	Y	Y	Y	Y	N
4 McCarthy	Y	Y	Y	N	N	N	Y
5 Ackerman	?	?	?	?	?	?	?
6 Meeks	Y	Y	Y	N	N	N	Y
7 Crowley	Y	Y	N	–	N	N	Y
8 Nadler	Y	Y	Y	N	N	N	Y
9 Weiner	?	?	Y	N	N	N	Y
10 Towns	Y	Y	Y	N	N	N	Y
11 Owens	Y	Y	Y	N	?	N	Y
12 Velázquez	Y	Y	N	N	N	N	Y
13 ***Fossella***	+	Y	?	Y	Y	Y	N
14 Maloney	Y	Y	Y	N	N	N	Y
15 Rangel	Y	Y	Y	N	N	N	Y
16 Serrano	Y	Y	Y	N	N	N	Y
17 Engel	?	?	Y	N	N	?	Y
18 Lowey	?	?	?	?	?	?	?
19 ***Kelly***	Y	Y	Y	Y	Y	Y	N
20 ***Gilman***	Y	Y	Y	Y	Y	Y	N
21 McNulty	?	?	Y	N	N	N	Y
22 ***Sweeney***	Y	Y	N	Y	Y	Y	N
23 ***Boehlert***	Y	Y	Y	Y	Y	Y	N
24 ***McHugh***	Y	Y	Y	Y	Y	Y	N
25 ***Walsh***	Y	Y	Y	Y	Y	Y	N
26 Hinchey	Y	Y	N	N	N	N	Y
27 ***Reynolds***	Y	Y	Y	Y	Y	Y	N
28 Slaughter	Y	Y	?	N	N	N	Y
29 LaFalce	Y	Y	Y	N	N	N	Y

	56	57	58	59	60	61	62
30 ***Quinn***	Y	Y	Y	Y	Y	Y	N
31 ***Houghton***	?	?	Y	Y	Y	Y	N
NORTH CAROLINA							
1 Clayton	Y	Y	Y	N	N	N	Y
2 Etheridge	Y	Y	Y	N	N	N	Y
3 ***Jones***	Y	Y	Y	Y	Y	Y	N
4 Price	Y	Y	Y	N	N	N	Y
5 ***Burr***	Y	Y	Y	Y	Y	Y	N
6 ***Coble***	Y	Y	Y	Y	Y	Y	N
7 McIntyre	Y	Y	Y	N	N	N	Y
8 ***Hayes***	Y	Y	Y	Y	Y	Y	N
9 ***Myrick***	Y	Y	Y	Y	Y	Y	N
10 ***Ballenger***	Y	Y	Y	Y	Y	Y	N
11 ***Taylor***	Y	Y	Y	Y	Y	Y	N
12 Watt	Y	Y	Y	N	N	N	Y
NORTH DAKOTA							
AL Pomeroy	Y	Y	Y	N	N	N	?
OHIO							
1 ***Chabot***	Y	Y	Y	Y	Y	Y	N
2 ***Portman***	Y	Y	Y	Y	Y	N	N
3 Hall	Y	Y	Y	N	N	N	Y
4 ***Oxley***	Y	Y	Y	Y	Y	Y	N
5 ***Gillmor***	Y	Y	Y	Y	Y	Y	N
6 Strickland	Y	Y	N	N	N	N	Y
7 ***Hobson***	Y	Y	Y	Y	Y	Y	N
8 ***Boehner***	Y	Y	Y	Y	Y	Y	N
9 Kaptur	Y	Y	Y	N	N	N	Y
10 Kucinich	Y	Y	Y	N	N	N	Y
11 Jones	?	?	?	N	N	N	Y
12 ***Kasich***	Y	Y	Y	Y	Y	Y	N
13 Brown	Y	Y	N	N	N	N	Y
14 Sawyer	Y	Y	Y	N	N	N	Y
15 ***Pryce***	Y	Y	Y	Y	Y	Y	N
16 ***Regula***	Y	Y	Y	Y	Y	Y	N
17 Traficant	Y	Y	Y	N	N	N	Y
18 ***Ney***	Y	Y	Y	Y	Y	Y	N
19 ***LaTourette***	Y	Y	Y	Y	Y	Y	N
OKLAHOMA							
1 ***Largent***	Y	Y	?	Y	Y	Y	N
2 ***Coburn***	Y	Y	Y	Y	Y	Y	N
3 ***Watkins***	Y	Y	Y	Y	Y	Y	N
4 ***Watts***	Y	Y	Y	Y	Y	Y	N
5 ***Istook***	Y	Y	Y	Y	Y	Y	N
6 ***Lucas***	Y	Y	?	Y	Y	Y	N
OREGON							
1 Wu	Y	Y	N	N	N	N	Y
2 ***Walden***	Y	Y	Y	Y	Y	Y	N
3 Blumenauer	Y	Y	Y	N	N	N	Y
4 DeFazio	Y	Y	N	N	N	N	Y
5 Hooley	Y	Y	Y	N	N	N	Y
PENNSYLVANIA							
1 Brady	Y	Y	N	N	N	N	Y
2 Fattah	Y	Y	Y	N	N	N	Y
3 Borski	Y	Y	N	N	N	N	Y
4 Klink	?	?	?	?	?	?	Y
5 ***Peterson***	Y	Y	Y	Y	Y	Y	N
6 Holden	Y	Y	Y	N	N	N	Y
7 ***Weldon***	Y	Y	Y	Y	Y	Y	N
8 ***Greenwood***	?	?	?	?	?	?	?
9 ***Shuster***	Y	Y	Y	Y	Y	Y	N
10 ***Sherwood***	Y	Y	Y	Y	Y	Y	N
11 Kanjorski	Y	Y	Y	N	N	Y	N
12 Murtha	Y	Y	Y	N	N	N	N
13 Hoeffel	Y	Y	Y	N	N	N	Y
14 Coyne	Y	Y	N	N	N	N	Y
15 ***Toomey***	Y	Y	Y	Y	Y	Y	N
16 ***Pitts***	Y	Y	Y	Y	Y	Y	N
17 ***Gekas***	Y	Y	Y	Y	Y	Y	N
18 Doyle	Y	Y	Y	N	N	N	Y
19 ***Goodling***	Y	Y	?	Y	Y	Y	N
20 Mascara	Y	Y	Y	N	N	N	Y
21 ***English***	Y	Y	Y	Y	Y	Y	N
RHODE ISLAND							
1 Kennedy	Y	Y	Y	N	N	N	Y
2 Weygand	Y	Y	Y	N	N	N	Y
SOUTH CAROLINA							
1 ***Sanford***	Y	Y	Y	Y	Y	Y	N
2 ***Spence***	Y	Y	Y	Y	Y	Y	N
3 ***Graham***	Y	Y	Y	Y	Y	Y	N
4 ***DeMint***	Y	Y	Y	Y	Y	Y	N
5 Spratt	Y	Y	Y	N	N	N	N
6 Clyburn	Y	Y	N	N	N	N	N
SOUTH DAKOTA							
AL ***Thune***	Y	Y	Y	Y	Y	Y	N

	56	57	58	59	60	61	62
TENNESSEE							
1 ***Jenkins***	Y	Y	Y	Y	Y	Y	N
2 ***Duncan***	Y	Y	Y	Y	Y	Y	N
3 ***Wamp***	Y	Y	Y	Y	Y	Y	N
4 ***Hilleary***	Y	Y	Y	Y	Y	Y	N
5 Clement	Y	Y	Y	N	N	N	Y
6 Gordon	?	?	Y	N	N	N	Y
7 ***Bryant***	Y	Y	Y	Y	Y	Y	N
8 Tanner	Y	Y	Y	N	N	N	Y
9 Ford	Y	Y	Y	N	N	N	Y
TEXAS							
1 Sandlin	Y	Y	Y	N	N	N	Y
2 Turner	Y	Y	Y	N	N	N	Y
3 ***Johnson, Sam***	?	Y	Y	Y	Y	N	N
4 Hall	Y	Y	Y	N	N	Y	N
5 ***Sessions***	Y	Y	Y	Y	Y	Y	N
6 ***Barton***	Y	Y	Y	Y	Y	?	N
7 ***Archer***	Y	Y	Y	Y	Y	Y	N
8 ***Brady***	Y	Y	Y	Y	Y	Y	N
9 Lampson	Y	Y	Y	N	N	N	Y
10 Doggett	Y	Y	Y	N	N	N	Y
11 Edwards	Y	Y	Y	N	N	N	Y
12 ***Granger***	?	Y	Y	Y	Y	Y	N
13 ***Thornberry***	Y	Y	Y	Y	Y	Y	N
14 ***Paul***	Y	N	Y	Y	Y	Y	N
15 Hinojosa	Y	Y	Y	N	N	N	Y
16 Reyes	Y	Y	Y	N	N	N	Y
17 Stenholm	Y	Y	Y	N	N	N	N
18 Jackson-Lee	?	?	?	?	?	?	?
19 ***Combest***	Y	Y	Y	Y	Y	Y	N
20 Gonzalez	Y	Y	Y	N	N	N	Y
21 ***Smith***	?	?	Y	Y	Y	Y	N
22 ***DeLay***	Y	Y	Y	Y	Y	Y	N
23 ***Bonilla***	Y	Y	Y	Y	Y	Y	N
24 Frost	Y	Y	Y	N	N	N	Y
25 Bentsen	Y	Y	Y	N	N	N	Y
26 ***Armey***	Y	Y	Y	Y	Y	Y	N
27 Ortiz	Y	Y	Y	N	N	N	Y
28 Rodriguez	Y	Y	Y	N	N	N	Y
29 Green	Y	Y	Y	N	N	N	Y
30 Johnson, E.B.	?	?	Y	N	N	N	Y
UTAH							
1 ***Hansen***	Y	Y	Y	Y	Y	Y	N
2 ***Cook***	Y	Y	Y	Y	Y	Y	N
3 ***Cannon***	Y	Y	Y	Y	Y	Y	N
VERMONT							
AL *Sanders*	Y	Y	Y	N	N	N	Y
VIRGINIA							
1 ***Bateman***	+	+	Y	?	Y	Y	N
2 Pickett	Y	Y	N	Y	Y	Y	N
3 Scott	Y	Y	Y	N	N	N	Y
4 Sisisky	Y	Y	Y	N	N	N	Y
5 *Goode*	Y	Y	Y	Y	Y	Y	N
6 ***Goodlatte***	Y	Y	Y	Y	Y	Y	N
7 ***Bliley***	Y	Y	Y	Y	Y	Y	N
8 Moran	Y	Y	Y	N	N	?	Y
9 Boucher	Y	Y	Y	N	N	N	Y
10 ***Wolf***	Y	Y	Y	Y	Y	Y	N
11 ***Davis***	Y	Y	Y	Y	Y	Y	N
WASHINGTON							
1 Inslee	Y	Y	Y	N	N	N	Y
2 ***Metcalf***	Y	Y	Y	Y	Y	Y	N
3 Baird	Y	Y	N	N	–	N	Y
4 ***Hastings***	Y	Y	Y	Y	Y	Y	N
5 ***Nethercutt***	Y	Y	Y	Y	Y	Y	N
6 Dicks	Y	Y	Y	N	N	N	Y
7 McDermott	?	?	?	?	?	?	?
8 ***Dunn***	Y	Y	Y	Y	Y	?	N
9 Smith	Y	Y	Y	N	N	N	Y
WEST VIRGINIA							
1 Mollohan	Y	Y	Y	N	N	N	Y
2 Wise	Y	Y	Y	N	N	N	Y
3 Rahall	Y	Y	Y	N	N	N	Y
WISCONSIN							
1 ***Ryan***	Y	Y	Y	Y	Y	Y	N
2 Baldwin	Y	Y	Y	N	N	N	Y
3 Kind	Y	Y	Y	N	N	N	N
4 Kleczka	Y	Y	Y	N	N	N	Y
5 Barrett	Y	Y	Y	N	N	N	Y
6 ***Petri***	Y	Y	Y	Y	Y	Y	N
7 Obey	Y	Y	Y	N	N	N	Y
8 ***Green***	Y	Y	?	Y	Y	Y	N
9 ***Sensenbrenner***	Y	Y	Y	Y	Y	Y	N
WYOMING							
AL ***Cubin***	Y	Y	Y	Y	Y	N	N

Southern states - Ala., Ark., Fla., Ga., Ky., La., Miss., N.C., Okla., S.C., Tenn., Texas, Va.

63. S 1287. Nuclear Waste Storage/Passage. Passage of the bill that would provide for the completion of siting and licensing activities for a permanent nuclear waste repository at Yucca Mountain, Nev., and establish a timetable for the development of the proposed site. Passed (thus cleared for the president) 253-167: R 199-18; D 53-148 (ND 19-130, SD 34-18); I 1-1. March 22, 2000. A "nay" was a vote in support of the president's position.

64. HR 3822. Oil Price Fixing/Previous Question. Diaz-Balart, R-Fla., motion to order the previous question (thus ending debate and possibility of amendment) on adoption of the rule (H Res 445) to provide for House floor consideration of the bill to require the president to report to Congress on price-fixing by oil exporters and to undertake a diplomatic campaign with U.S. allies to combat rising oil and gasoline prices. Motion agreed to 222-200: R 217-0; D 4-199 (ND 1-149, SD 3-50); I 1-1. (Subsequently, the rule was adopted by voice vote.) March 22, 2000.

65. HR 3822. Oil Price Fixing/Passage. Passage of the bill that would require the president to report to Congress on price-fixing by oil exporters and to undertake a diplomatic campaign with U.S. allies to combat rising oil and gasoline prices. Passed 382-38: R 193-23; D 187-15 (ND 138-11, SD 49-4); I 2-0. A "nay" was a vote in support of the president's position. March 22, 2000.

66. Procedural Motion/Journal. Approval of the House Journal of March 22, 2000. Approved 345-58: R 189-17; D 154-41 (ND 112-31, SD 42-10); I 2-0. March 23, 2000.

67. H Con Res 290. Fiscal 2001 Budget Resolution/Previous Question. Goss, R-Fla., motion to order the previous question (thus ending debate and the possibility of amendment) on adoption of the rule (H Res 446) to provide for House floor consideration of the resolution to set spending and revenue targets for fiscal year 2001. Motion agreed to 220-203: R 217-0; D 2-202 (ND 2-149, SD 0-53); I 1-1. March 23, 2000.

68. H Con Res 290. Fiscal 2001 Budget Resolution/Rule. Adoption of the rule (H Res 446) to provide for House floor consideration, as amended, of the resolution to set spending and revenue targets for fiscal year 2001. Adopted 228-194: R 209-8; D 18-185 (ND 4-146, SD 14-39); I 1-1. March 23, 2000.

69. H Con Res 290. Fiscal 2001 Budget Resolution/Motion to Rise. Saxton, R-N.J., motion to rise from the Committee of the Whole. Motion agreed to 245-165: R 212-0; D 32-164 (ND 29-115, SD 3-49); I 1-1. March 23, 2000.

Key

- Y Voted for (yea).
- # Paired for.
- \+ Announced for.
- N Voted against (nay).
- X Paired against.
- – Announced against.
- P Voted "present."
- C Voted "present" to avoid possible conflict of interest.
- ? Did not vote or otherwise make a position known.

•

Democrats ***Republicans***
Independents

	63	64	65	66	67	68	69
ALABAMA							
1 ***Callahan***	Y	Y	Y	Y	Y	Y	Y
2 ***Everett***	Y	Y	Y	Y	Y	Y	Y
3 ***Riley***	Y	Y	Y	Y	Y	Y	Y
4 ***Aderholt***	Y	Y	Y	N	Y	Y	Y
5 Cramer	Y	N	Y	Y	N	N	N
6 ***Bachus***	Y	Y	Y	Y	Y	Y	Y
7 Hilliard	Y	N	Y	N	N	N	N
ALASKA							
AL ***Young***	Y	Y	Y	?	Y	Y	Y
ARIZONA							
1 ***Salmon***	Y	Y	Y	Y	Y	Y	Y
2 Pastor	Y	N	Y	Y	N	N	N
3 ***Stump***	Y	Y	Y	Y	Y	Y	Y
4 ***Shadegg***	Y	Y	Y	Y	Y	N	Y
5 ***Kolbe***	Y	Y	N	Y	Y	Y	Y
6 ***Hayworth***	Y	Y	Y	Y	Y	Y	Y
ARKANSAS							
1 Berry	Y	N	Y	Y	N	Y	N
2 Snyder	Y	N	Y	N	N	N	N
3 ***Hutchinson***	Y	Y	Y	Y	Y	Y	Y
4 ***Dickey***	Y	Y	Y	Y	Y	Y	Y
CALIFORNIA							
1 Thompson	N	N	Y	N	N	N	N
2 ***Herger***	?	Y	Y	?	Y	Y	Y
3 ***Ose***	Y	Y	Y	Y	Y	Y	Y
4 ***Doolittle***	Y	Y	Y	Y	Y	Y	Y
5 Matsui	N	N	Y	Y	N	N	N
6 Woolsey	N	N	Y	Y	N	N	N
7 Miller, George	N	N	N	N	N	N	N
8 Pelosi	N	N	Y	Y	N	N	N
9 Lee	N	N	Y	Y	N	N	N
10 Tauscher	N	N	Y	Y	N	N	N
11 ***Pombo***	Y	Y	Y	Y	Y	Y	Y
12 Lantos	N	N	Y	Y	N	N	N
13 Stark	N	N	Y	Y	N	N	N
14 Eshoo	N	N	Y	Y	N	N	Y
15 ***Campbell***	Y	Y	Y	Y	Y	Y	Y
16 Lofgren	N	N	Y	Y	N	N	N
17 Farr	N	N	Y	Y	N	N	Y
18 Condit	N	N	N	N	N	N	N
19 ***Radanovich***	N	Y	Y	Y	Y	Y	Y
20 Dooley	N	N	Y	?	N	N	?
21 ***Thomas***	Y	Y	Y	Y	Y	Y	?
22 Capps	N	N	Y	Y	N	N	Y
23 ***Gallegly***	Y	Y	Y	Y	Y	Y	Y
24 Sherman	N	N	Y	Y	N	N	N
25 ***McKeon***	N	Y	Y	Y	Y	Y	Y
26 Berman	N	N	Y	Y	N	N	N
27 ***Rogan***	Y	Y	Y	N	Y	Y	Y
28 ***Dreier***	Y	Y	Y	Y	Y	Y	Y
29 Waxman	N	N	Y	Y	N	N	N
30 Becerra	N	N	Y	Y	N	N	Y
31 Martinez	Y	Y	Y	?	Y	Y	?
32 Dixon	N	N	Y	?	?	?	?
33 Roybal-Allard	N	N	Y	Y	N	N	N
34 Napolitano	N	N	Y	Y	N	N	N
35 Waters	?	N	Y	N	N	N	N
36 ***Kuykendall***	N	Y	Y	?	Y	Y	Y
37 Millender-McD.	N	N	Y	Y	N	N	N
38 ***Horn***	Y	Y	Y	Y	Y	Y	Y
39 ***Royce***	?	?	?	?	?	?	?
40 ***Lewis***	Y	Y	Y	Y	Y	Y	Y
41 ***Miller, Gary***	Y	Y	Y	Y	Y	Y	Y
42 Baca	N	N	Y	Y	N	N	Y
43 ***Calvert***	Y	Y	Y	Y	Y	Y	Y
44 ***Bono***	Y	Y	Y	?	Y	Y	Y
45 ***Rohrabacher***	Y	Y	Y	Y	Y	Y	Y
46 Sanchez	N	N	Y	Y	N	N	N
47 ***Cox***	Y	Y	Y	Y	Y	Y	Y
48 ***Packard***	Y	Y	Y	Y	Y	Y	Y
49 ***Bilbray***	Y	Y	Y	N	Y	Y	Y
50 Filner	N	N	Y	N	N	N	N
51 ***Cunningham***	Y	Y	Y	Y	Y	Y	Y
52 ***Hunter***	Y	Y	Y	Y	Y	Y	Y
COLORADO							
1 DeGette	N	N	Y	Y	N	N	N
2 Udall	N	N	Y	Y	N	N	N
3 ***McInnis***	N	Y	Y	Y	Y	Y	Y
4 ***Schaffer***	Y	Y	Y	N	Y	Y	Y
5 ***Hefley***	Y	Y	N	N	Y	Y	Y
6 ***Tancredo***	Y	Y	Y	Y	Y	Y	Y
CONNECTICUT							
1 Larson	N	N	Y	N	N	N	N
2 Gejdenson	Y	N	Y	Y	N	N	N
3 DeLauro	N	N	Y	Y	N	N	N
4 ***Shays***	N	Y	Y	Y	Y	Y	Y
5 Maloney	Y	N	Y	Y	N	N	N
6 ***Johnson***	Y	Y	Y	Y	Y	Y	Y
DELAWARE							
AL ***Castle***	Y	Y	Y	Y	Y	Y	Y
FLORIDA							
1 ***Scarborough***	Y	Y	Y	Y	Y	Y	Y
2 Boyd	?	N	Y	Y	N	Y	N
3 Brown	Y	N	Y	Y	N	N	N
4 ***Fowler***	Y	Y	Y	Y	Y	Y	Y
5 Thurman	Y	N	Y	Y	N	N	Y
6 ***Stearns***	Y	Y	Y	Y	Y	Y	Y
7 ***Mica***	Y	Y	Y	Y	Y	Y	Y
8 ***McCollum***	Y	Y	Y	?	?	?	?
9 ***Bilirakis***	Y	Y	Y	Y	Y	Y	Y
10 ***Young***	Y	Y	Y	Y	Y	Y	Y
11 Davis	Y	N	Y	Y	N	N	N
12 ***Canady***	Y	Y	Y	Y	Y	Y	Y
13 ***Miller***	Y	Y	Y	Y	Y	Y	Y
14 ***Goss***	Y	Y	Y	Y	Y	Y	Y
15 ***Weldon***	Y	Y	Y	Y	Y	Y	Y
16 ***Foley***	Y	Y	Y	Y	Y	Y	Y
17 Meek	Y	N	Y	Y	N	N	N
18 ***Ros-Lehtinen***	Y	Y	Y	Y	Y	Y	Y
19 Wexler	Y	N	Y	Y	N	N	N
20 Deutsch	Y	N	Y	Y	N	N	N
21 ***Diaz-Balart***	Y	Y	Y	Y	Y	Y	Y
22 ***Shaw***	+	Y	Y	Y	Y	Y	Y
23 Hastings	Y	N	N	Y	N	N	?
GEORGIA							
1 ***Kingston***	Y	Y	Y	Y	Y	Y	Y
2 Bishop	Y	N	Y	Y	N	Y	Y
3 ***Collins***	Y	Y	Y	Y	Y	Y	Y
4 McKinney	N	N	N	N	N	N	N
5 Lewis	N	N	Y	N	N	N	N
6 ***Isakson***	Y	Y	Y	Y	Y	Y	Y
7 ***Barr***	Y	Y	Y	Y	Y	Y	Y
8 ***Chambliss***	Y	Y	Y	Y	Y	Y	Y
9 ***Deal***	Y	Y	Y	Y	Y	Y	Y
10 ***Norwood***	Y	Y	Y	Y	Y	Y	Y
11 ***Linder***	Y	Y	Y	?	Y	Y	Y
HAWAII							
1 Abercrombie	N	N	Y	Y	N	N	Y
2 Mink	N	N	Y	Y	N	N	Y
IDAHO							
1 ***Chenoweth-Hage***	Y	Y	Y	Y	Y	N	Y
2 ***Simpson***	Y	Y	Y	Y	Y	Y	Y
ILLINOIS							
1 Rush	?	?	?	Y	N	N	N
2 Jackson	N	N	Y	Y	N	N	N
3 Lipinski	Y	N	Y	Y	N	N	Y
4 Gutierrez	N	N	Y	Y	N	N	N
5 Blagojevich	N	N	Y	Y	N	N	Y
6 ***Hyde***	Y	Y	Y	Y	Y	Y	Y
7 Davis	N	N	Y	Y	N	N	N
8 ***Crane***	?	?	?	?	?	?	?
9 Schakowsky	?	?	?	?	?	?	?
10 ***Porter***	Y	Y	Y	Y	Y	Y	Y
11 ***Weller***	Y	Y	Y	N	Y	Y	Y
12 Costello	Y	N	Y	N	N	N	Y
13 ***Biggert***	Y	Y	Y	Y	Y	Y	Y

ND Northern Democrats SD Southern Democrats

	63	64	65	66	67	68	69
14 ***Hastert***	Y						
15 ***Ewing***	Y	Y	Y	Y	Y	Y	Y
16 ***Manzullo***	Y	Y	Y	Y	Y	Y	Y
17 Evans	N	N	Y	Y	N	N	N
18 ***LaHood***	Y	Y	Y	Y	Y	Y	Y
19 Phelps	Y	N	Y	Y	N	N	Y
20 ***Shimkus***	Y	Y	Y	Y	Y	Y	Y
INDIANA							
1 Visclosky	N	N	Y	N	N	N	N
2 ***McIntosh***	N	Y	Y	Y	Y	N	Y
3 Roemer	N	N	Y	Y	N	N	N
4 ***Souder***	N	Y	Y	Y	Y	Y	Y
5 ***Buyer***	Y	Y	Y	Y	Y	Y	Y
6 ***Burton***	Y	Y	Y	Y	Y	Y	Y
7 ***Pease***	N	Y	Y	Y	Y	Y	Y
8 ***Hostettler***	Y	Y	Y	Y	Y	N	Y
9 Hill	?	?	?	?	N	N	N
10 Carson	N	N	Y	Y	N	N	N
IOWA							
1 ***Leach***	Y	Y	Y	Y	Y	Y	Y
2 ***Nussle***	Y	Y	Y	Y	Y	Y	Y
3 Boswell	N	N	Y	Y	N	N	N
4 ***Ganske***	Y	Y	Y	Y	Y	Y	Y
5 ***Latham***	Y	Y	Y	N	Y	Y	Y
KANSAS							
1 ***Moran***	Y	Y	N	Y	Y	Y	Y
2 ***Ryun***	Y	Y	Y	Y	Y	Y	Y
3 Moore	N	N	Y	N	N	N	Y
4 ***Tiahrt***	Y	Y	Y	?	Y	Y	Y
KENTUCKY							
1 ***Whitfield***	Y	Y	Y	Y	Y	Y	Y
2 ***Lewis***	Y	Y	Y	Y	Y	Y	Y
3 ***Northup***	Y	Y	Y	Y	Y	Y	Y
4 Lucas	Y	N	Y	Y	N	Y	N
5 ***Rogers***	Y	Y	Y	Y	Y	Y	Y
6 ***Fletcher***	Y	Y	Y	Y	Y	Y	Y
LOUISIANA							
1 ***Vitter***	Y	Y	Y	Y	Y	Y	Y
2 Jefferson	Y	N	Y	?	N	N	N
3 ***Tauzin***	Y	Y	N	Y	Y	Y	Y
4 ***McCrery***	Y	Y	N	Y	Y	Y	Y
5 ***Cooksey***	Y	Y	N	Y	Y	Y	Y
6 ***Baker***	Y	Y	N	Y	Y	Y	Y
7 John	Y	N	Y	Y	N	Y	N
MAINE							
1 Allen	N	N	Y	Y	N	N	N
2 Baldacci	N	N	Y	Y	N	N	Y
MARYLAND							
1 ***Gilchrest***	Y	Y	Y	Y	Y	Y	Y
2 ***Ehrlich***	Y	Y	Y	Y	Y	Y	Y
3 Cardin	N	N	Y	Y	N	N	N
4 Wynn	Y	N	Y	Y	N	N	N
5 Hoyer	N	N	Y	Y	N	N	N
6 ***Bartlett***	Y	Y	Y	Y	Y	N	Y
7 Cummings	N	N	Y	Y	N	N	N
8 ***Morella***	Y	Y	Y	Y	Y	Y	Y
MASSACHUSETTS							
1 Olver	Y	N	Y	Y	N	N	N
2 Neal	Y	N	Y	Y	N	N	Y
3 McGovern	N	N	Y	N	N	N	N
4 Frank	N	N	P	Y	N	N	Y
5 Meehan	N	N	Y	Y	N	N	Y
6 Tierney	N	N	Y	Y	N	N	N
7 Markey	N	N	Y	Y	N	N	N
8 Capuano	N	N	Y	Y	N	N	Y
9 Moakley	N	N	Y	Y	N	N	Y
10 Delahunt	N	N	Y	Y	N	N	N
MICHIGAN							
1 Stupak	N	N	Y	N	N	N	N
2 ***Hoekstra***	Y	Y	Y	Y	Y	Y	Y
3 ***Ehlers***	Y	Y	Y	Y	Y	Y	Y
4 ***Camp***	Y	Y	Y	Y	Y	Y	Y
5 Barcia	N	N	Y	Y	N	N	Y
6 ***Upton***	Y	Y	Y	Y	Y	Y	Y
7 ***Smith***	Y	Y	Y	Y	Y	Y	Y
8 Stabenow	N	N	Y	Y	N	N	N
9 Kildee	N	N	Y	Y	N	N	Y
10 Bonior	N	N	Y	N	N	N	?
11 ***Knollenberg***	Y	Y	Y	Y	Y	Y	Y
12 Levin	N	N	Y	Y	N	N	N
13 Rivers	N	N	Y	Y	N	N	N
14 Conyers	N	N	N	Y	N	N	N
15 Kilpatrick	N	N	Y	Y	N	N	N
16 Dingell	N	N	N	?	N	N	Y

	63	64	65	66	67	68	69
MINNESOTA							
1 ***Gutknecht***	Y	Y	Y	N	Y	Y	Y
2 Minge	N	N	Y	Y	N	N	N
3 ***Ramstad***	Y	Y	Y	N	Y	Y	Y
4 Vento	N	N	Y	Y	N	N	?
5 Sabo	N	N	N	N	N	N	N
6 Luther	N	N	Y	Y	N	N	N
7 Peterson	N	N	N	N	N	Y	N
8 Oberstar	N	N	N	N	N	N	N
MISSISSIPPI							
1 ***Wicker***	Y	Y	Y	N	Y	Y	Y
2 Thompson	Y	N	Y	N	N	Y	N
3 ***Pickering***	Y	Y	N	Y	Y	Y	Y
4 Shows	Y	Y	Y	Y	N	Y	N
5 Taylor	Y	Y	Y	N	N	Y	N
MISSOURI							
1 Clay	N	N	Y	N	N	N	N
2 ***Talent***	N	Y	Y	Y	Y	Y	Y
3 Gephardt	N	N	Y	Y	N	N	Y
4 Skelton	N	N	Y	Y	N	N	Y
5 McCarthy	N	N	Y	Y	N	N	N
6 Danner	N	N	Y	Y	N	N	N
7 ***Blunt***	Y	Y	Y	Y	Y	Y	Y
8 ***Emerson***	Y	Y	Y	Y	Y	Y	Y
9 ***Hulshof***	Y	Y	Y	N	Y	Y	Y
MONTANA							
AL ***Hill***	Y	Y	Y	N	Y	Y	Y
NEBRASKA							
1 ***Bereuter***	Y	Y	?	Y	Y	Y	Y
2 ***Terry***	Y	Y	Y	Y	Y	Y	Y
3 ***Barrett***	Y	Y	Y	Y	Y	Y	Y
NEVADA							
1 Berkley	N	N	Y	Y	N	N	N
2 ***Gibbons***	N	Y	Y	Y	Y	Y	Y
NEW HAMPSHIRE							
1 ***Sununu***	Y	Y	N	Y	Y	Y	Y
2 ***Bass***	Y	Y	Y	Y	Y	Y	Y
NEW JERSEY							
1 Andrews	N	N	Y	Y	N	N	N
2 ***LoBiondo***	Y	Y	Y	N	Y	Y	Y
3 ***Saxton***	Y	Y	Y	Y	Y	Y	Y
4 ***Smith***	N	Y	Y	Y	Y	Y	Y
5 ***Roukema***	Y	Y	Y	Y	Y	Y	Y
6 Pallone	?	?	?	?	?	?	?
7 ***Franks***	Y	?	?	Y	Y	Y	Y
8 Pascrell	N	N	Y	Y	N	N	N
9 Rothman	N	N	Y	Y	N	N	N
10 Payne	N	N	Y	Y	N	N	N
11 ***Frelinghuysen***	Y	Y	Y	Y	Y	Y	Y
12 Holt	N	N	Y	Y	N	N	N
13 Menendez	N	N	Y	Y	N	N	N
NEW MEXICO							
1 ***Wilson***	Y	Y	Y	Y	Y	Y	Y
2 ***Skeen***	Y	Y	Y	Y	Y	Y	Y
3 Udall	N	N	Y	N	N	N	N
NEW YORK							
1 Forbes	N	N	Y	Y	N	N	?
2 ***Lazio***	Y	Y	Y	Y	Y	Y	Y
3 ***King***	Y	Y	Y	Y	Y	Y	Y
4 McCarthy	Y	N	Y	Y	N	N	N
5 Ackerman	?	?	?	?	?	?	?
6 Meeks	N	N	Y	Y	N	N	N
7 Crowley	N	N	Y	N	N	N	N
8 Nadler	N	N	Y	Y	N	N	N
9 Weiner	N	N	Y	Y	N	N	N
10 Towns	N	N	Y	N	N	N	N
11 Owens	N	N	Y	Y	N	N	N
12 Velázquez	N	N	Y	N	N	N	N
13 ***Fossella***	Y	Y	Y	Y	Y	Y	Y
14 Maloney	N	N	Y	Y	N	N	N
15 Rangel	N	N	Y	Y	N	?	N
16 Serrano	N	N	Y	Y	N	N	N
17 Engel	N	N	Y	?	N	N	N
18 Lowey	?	?	?	?	?	?	?
19 ***Kelly***	N	Y	Y	Y	Y	Y	Y
20 ***Gilman***	Y	Y	Y	Y	Y	Y	Y
21 McNulty	N	N	Y	N	N	N	N
22 ***Sweeney***	Y	Y	Y	N	Y	Y	Y
23 ***Boehlert***	Y	Y	Y	Y	Y	Y	Y
24 ***McHugh***	Y	Y	Y	Y	Y	Y	?
25 ***Walsh***	Y	Y	Y	Y	Y	Y	Y
26 Hinchey	N	N	N	Y	N	N	N
27 ***Reynolds***	Y	Y	Y	Y	Y	Y	Y
28 Slaughter	N	N	Y	N	N	N	N
29 LaFalce	N	N	Y	N	N	N	N

	63	64	65	66	67	68	69
30 ***Quinn***	Y	Y	Y	Y	Y	Y	?
31 ***Houghton***	Y	Y	N	Y	Y	Y	Y
NORTH CAROLINA							
1 Clayton	Y	N	Y	Y	N	N	N
2 Etheridge	Y	N	Y	Y	N	N	N
3 ***Jones***	Y	Y	Y	Y	Y	N	Y
4 Price	Y	N	Y	Y	N	N	N
5 ***Burr***	Y	Y	Y	Y	Y	Y	Y
6 ***Coble***	Y	Y	Y	Y	Y	Y	Y
7 McIntyre	Y	N	Y	Y	N	N	N
8 ***Hayes***	Y	Y	Y	Y	Y	Y	Y
9 ***Myrick***	Y	Y	Y	Y	Y	Y	Y
10 ***Ballenger***	Y	Y	Y	Y	Y	Y	Y
11 ***Taylor***	Y	Y	Y	Y	Y	Y	Y
12 Watt	Y	N	Y	Y	N	N	N
NORTH DAKOTA							
AL Pomeroy	N	N	Y	?	N	N	N
OHIO							
1 ***Chabot***	Y	Y	Y	Y	Y	Y	Y
2 ***Portman***	Y	Y	Y	Y	Y	Y	Y
3 Hall	N	N	Y	Y	N	N	N
4 ***Oxley***	Y	Y	Y	Y	Y	Y	Y
5 ***Gillmor***	Y	Y	Y	N	Y	Y	Y
6 Strickland	N	N	Y	N	N	N	N
7 ***Hobson***	Y	Y	Y	Y	Y	Y	Y
8 ***Boehner***	Y	Y	Y	Y	Y	Y	Y
9 Kaptur	N	N	Y	Y	N	N	N
10 Kucinich	N	N	Y	N	N	N	N
11 Jones	N	N	Y	Y	N	N	N
12 ***Kasich***	N	Y	Y	Y	Y	Y	Y
13 Brown	N	N	Y	N	N	N	N
14 Sawyer	N	N	Y	Y	N	N	N
15 ***Pryce***	Y	Y	Y	Y	Y	Y	Y
16 ***Regula***	Y	Y	Y	Y	Y	Y	Y
17 Traficant	N	N	Y	Y	Y	Y	Y
18 ***Ney***	N	Y	Y	Y	Y	Y	Y
19 ***LaTourette***	N	Y	Y	Y	Y	Y	Y
OKLAHOMA							
1 ***Largent***	Y	Y	N	Y	Y	N	Y
2 ***Coburn***	Y	Y	N	Y	Y	N	Y
3 ***Watkins***	Y	Y	N	Y	Y	Y	Y
4 ***Watts***	Y	Y	Y	Y	Y	Y	Y
5 ***Istook***	Y	Y	Y	Y	Y	Y	Y
6 ***Lucas***	Y	Y	Y	Y	Y	Y	Y
OREGON							
1 Wu	N	N	Y	Y	N	N	N
2 ***Walden***	Y	Y	Y	Y	Y	Y	Y
3 Blumenauer	N	N	N	Y	N	N	N
4 DeFazio	N	N	Y	N	N	Y	N
5 Hooley	N	N	Y	N	N	N	N
PENNSYLVANIA							
1 Brady	Y	N	Y	N	N	N	N
2 Fattah	N	N	Y	Y	N	N	N
3 Borski	N	N	Y	Y	N	N	N
4 Klink	Y	N	Y	?	N	N	N
5 ***Peterson***	Y	Y	Y	Y	Y	Y	Y
6 Holden	Y	N	Y	Y	N	N	N
7 ***Weldon***	Y	Y	Y	Y	Y	Y	Y
8 ***Greenwood***	?	?	?	?	?	?	?
9 ***Shuster***	Y	Y	Y	Y	Y	Y	Y
10 ***Sherwood***	Y	Y	Y	Y	Y	Y	Y
11 Kanjorski	Y	N	Y	Y	N	N	N
12 Murtha	Y	N	N	Y	N	N	?
13 Hoeffel	N	N	Y	Y	N	N	N
14 Coyne	N	N	Y	Y	N	N	N
15 ***Toomey***	Y	Y	Y	?	Y	Y	Y
16 ***Pitts***	Y	Y	Y	Y	Y	Y	Y
17 ***Gekas***	Y	Y	Y	Y	Y	Y	Y
18 Doyle	Y	N	Y	Y	N	N	?
19 ***Goodling***	Y	Y	Y	Y	Y	Y	Y
20 Mascara	Y	N	Y	Y	N	N	N
21 ***English***	Y	Y	Y	N	Y	Y	Y
RHODE ISLAND							
1 Kennedy	N	N	Y	Y	N	N	N
2 Weygand	N	N	Y	Y	N	N	N
SOUTH CAROLINA							
1 ***Sanford***	Y	Y	N	Y	Y	Y	Y
2 ***Spence***	Y	Y	Y	Y	Y	Y	Y
3 ***Graham***	Y	Y	Y	Y	Y	Y	Y
4 ***DeMint***	Y	Y	Y	Y	Y	Y	?
5 Spratt	Y	N	Y	Y	N	N	N
6 Clyburn	Y	N	Y	N	N	Y	N
SOUTH DAKOTA							
AL ***Thune***	Y	Y	Y	Y	Y	Y	Y

	63	64	65	66	67	68	69
TENNESSEE							
1 ***Jenkins***	Y	Y	Y	Y	Y	Y	Y
2 ***Duncan***	Y	Y	Y	Y	Y	Y	Y
3 ***Wamp***	Y	Y	Y	Y	Y	Y	Y
4 ***Hilleary***	Y	Y	Y	Y	Y	Y	Y
5 Clement	Y	N	Y	Y	N	N	N
6 Gordon	Y	N	Y	Y	N	N	N
7 ***Bryant***	Y	Y	Y	Y	Y	Y	Y
8 Tanner	Y	N	Y	Y	N	Y	N
9 Ford	N	N	Y	Y	N	Y	N
TEXAS							
1 Sandlin	Y	N	Y	Y	N	N	N
2 Turner	N	N	Y	Y	N	Y	N
3 ***Johnson, Sam***	Y	Y	Y	Y	Y	Y	Y
4 Hall	Y	Y	Y	Y	N	N	N
5 ***Sessions***	Y	Y	N	?	Y	Y	Y
6 ***Barton***	N	Y	N	?	Y	Y	Y
7 ***Archer***	N	Y	N	Y	Y	Y	?
8 ***Brady***	Y	Y	N	Y	Y	Y	Y
9 Lampson	N	N	Y	Y	N	N	N
10 Doggett	N	N	Y	Y	N	N	N
11 Edwards	N	N	Y	Y	N	N	N
12 ***Granger***	Y	Y	Y	Y	Y	Y	Y
13 ***Thornberry***	Y	Y	N	Y	Y	Y	Y
14 ***Paul***	N	Y	Y	Y	Y	Y	Y
15 Hinojosa	N	N	Y	Y	N	N	N
16 Reyes	N	N	Y	Y	N	N	N
17 Stenholm	Y	N	N	N	N	Y	N
18 Jackson-Lee	?	?	?	?	?	?	?
19 ***Combest***	Y	Y	N	Y	Y	Y	Y
20 Gonzalez	N	N	Y	Y	N	N	N
21 ***Smith***	Y	Y	N	Y	Y	Y	Y
22 ***DeLay***	Y	Y	Y	Y	Y	Y	Y
23 ***Bonilla***	Y	Y	N	Y	Y	Y	Y
24 Frost	N	N	Y	Y	N	N	N
25 Bentsen	N	N	N	Y	N	N	N
26 ***Armey***	Y	Y	Y	?	Y	Y	Y
27 Ortiz	N	N	Y	Y	N	N	N
28 Rodriguez	N	N	Y	Y	N	N	N
29 Green	N	N	Y	Y	N	N	N
30 Johnson, E.B.	N	N	Y	Y	N	N	N
UTAH							
1 ***Hansen***	Y	Y	Y	Y	Y	Y	Y
2 ***Cook***	Y	Y	Y	Y	Y	Y	Y
3 ***Cannon***	Y	Y	N	Y	Y	Y	Y
VERMONT							
AL *Sanders*	N	N	Y	Y	N	N	N
VIRGINIA							
1 ***Bateman***	Y	Y	Y	Y	Y	Y	Y
2 Pickett	Y	N	Y	N	N	N	N
3 Scott	N	N	Y	N	N	N	N
4 Sisisky	Y	N	Y	Y	N	Y	Y
5 *Goode*	Y	Y	Y	Y	Y	Y	Y
6 ***Goodlatte***	Y	Y	Y	Y	Y	Y	Y
7 ***Bliley***	Y	Y	Y	?	Y	Y	Y
8 Moran	Y	N	Y	Y	N	N	N
9 Boucher	N	N	Y	Y	N	N	N
10 ***Wolf***	Y	Y	Y	Y	Y	Y	Y
11 ***Davis***	Y	Y	Y	Y	Y	Y	Y
WASHINGTON							
1 Inslee	N	N	Y	Y	N	N	N
2 ***Metcalf***	Y	Y	Y	N	Y	Y	Y
3 Baird	N	N	Y	N	N	N	N
4 ***Hastings***	Y	Y	Y	Y	Y	Y	Y
5 ***Nethercutt***	Y	Y	Y	Y	Y	Y	Y
6 Dicks	N	N	Y	Y	N	N	N
7 McDermott	?	?	?	?	?	?	?
8 ***Dunn***	Y	Y	Y	Y	Y	Y	Y
9 Smith	N	N	Y	Y	N	N	N
WEST VIRGINIA							
1 Mollohan	N	N	Y	Y	N	N	N
2 Wise	N	N	Y	?	N	N	Y
3 Rahall	N	N	N	Y	N	N	N
WISCONSIN							
1 ***Ryan***	Y	Y	Y	Y	Y	Y	Y
2 Baldwin	N	N	Y	Y	N	N	N
3 Kind	Y	N	Y	Y	N	N	Y
4 Kleczka	N	N	Y	Y	N	N	Y
5 Barrett	N	N	Y	Y	N	N	Y
6 ***Petri***	Y	Y	Y	Y	Y	Y	Y
7 Obey	N	N	Y	Y	N	N	Y
8 ***Green***	Y	Y	Y	Y	Y	Y	Y
9 ***Sensenbrenner***	Y	Y	Y	Y	Y	Y	Y
WYOMING							
AL ***Cubin***	Y	Y	Y	Y	Y	Y	Y

Southern states - Ala., Ark., Fla., Ga., Ky., La., Miss., N.C., Okla., S.C., Tenn., Texas, Va.

70. H Con Res 290. Fiscal 2001 Budget Resolution/Owens Substitute. Owens, D-N.Y., substitute amendment on behalf of the Congressional Black Caucus that calls for cuts in defense spending, compared to the resolution, while increasing domestic spending on education, housing and economic development. Rejected 70-348: R 0-212; D 69-135 (ND 54-97, SD 15-38); I 1-1. March 23, 2000.

71. H Con Res 290. Fiscal 2001 Budget Resolution/DeFazio Substitute. DeFazio, D-Ore., substitute amendment on behalf of the Congressional Progressive Caucus that calls for cuts in defense spending, compared to the resolution, while increasing funding for education, health care and veterans. Rejected 61-351: R 0-211; D 60-139 (ND 48-100, SD 12-39); I 1-1. March 23, 2000.

72. H Con Res 290. Fiscal 2001 Budget Resolution/Stenholm Substitute. Stenholm, D-Texas, substitute amendment on behalf of The Coalition, also known as the Blue Dogs, that commits 50 percent of the surplus to pay down the national debt, 25 percent for Social Security and Medicare, and 25 percent for tax cuts. Rejected 171-243: R 33-178; D 138-63 (ND 96-53, SD 42-10); I 0-2. March 23, 2000.

73. H Con Res 290. Fiscal 2001 Budget Resolution/Sununu Substitute. Sununu, R-N.H., substitute amendment on behalf of the Conservative Action Team (CAT) that freezes non-defense discretionary spending while increasing defense spending and tax cuts over those levels provided in the resolution. Rejected 78-339: R 77-135; D 0-203 (ND 0-150, SD 0-53); I 1-1. March 23, 2000.

74. H Con Res 290. Fiscal 2001 Budget Resolution/Democratic Substitute. Spratt, D-S.C., substitute amendment that calls for extending the solvency of the Social Security and Medicare programs, repaying the public debt and providing targeted tax cuts. The plan calls for $306.3 billion overall in defense discretionary spending. The plan would allow $2.6 billion in net tax cuts next year. Rejected 184-233: R 0-212; D 184-19 (ND 137-13, SD 47-6); I 0-2. March 23, 2000.

75. H Con Res 290. Fiscal 2001 Budget Resolution/Adoption. Adoption of the resolution to set broad spending and revenue targets for the next five years. The resolution calls for cutting taxes by $150 billion over five years, and creating a "reserve fund" of $50 billion that could also be used for tax cuts. It would create a $40 billion reserve fund for unspecified changes in Medicare, possibly including the addition of prescription drug coverage. The resolution would create a "lockbox" aimed at ensuring that Social Security surpluses are not spent on other programs. It calls for $596.5 billion in discretionary spending, a 2 percent increase over the current level, and would allow $307.3 billion in defense spending, a 6 percent increase over current levels. Adopted 211-207: R 208-5; D 2-201 (ND 1-149, SD 1-52); I 1-1. March 24, 2000 (after midnight on the day that began March 23).

Key

- Y Voted for (yea).
- \# Paired for.
- \+ Announced for.
- N Voted against (nay).
- X Paired against.
- – Announced against.
- P Voted "present."
- C Voted "present" to avoid possible conflict of interest.
- ? Did not vote or otherwise make a position known.

•

Democrats ***Republicans***
Independents

	70	71	72	73	74	75
ALABAMA						
1 ***Callahan***	N	N	N	N	N	N
2 ***Everett***	N	N	N	N	N	Y
3 ***Riley***	N	N	N	Y	N	Y
4 ***Aderholt***	N	N	Y	Y	N	Y
5 Cramer	N	N	Y	N	N	N
6 ***Bachus***	N	N	N	N	N	Y
7 Hilliard	Y	Y	N	N	Y	N
ALASKA						
AL ***Young***	N	N	N	Y	N	Y
ARIZONA						
1 ***Salmon***	N	N	N	Y	N	Y
2 Pastor	Y	N	Y	N	Y	N
3 ***Stump***	N	N	N	Y	N	Y
4 ***Shadegg***	N	N	N	Y	N	Y
5 ***Kolbe***	N	N	N	N	N	Y
6 ***Hayworth***	N	N	N	Y	N	Y
ARKANSAS						
1 Berry	N	N	Y	N	Y	N
2 Snyder	N	N	Y	N	Y	N
3 ***Hutchinson***	N	N	N	N	N	Y
4 ***Dickey***	N	N	N	Y	N	Y
CALIFORNIA						
1 Thompson	N	N	Y	N	Y	N
2 ***Herger***	N	N	N	Y	N	Y
3 ***Ose***	N	N	N	N	N	Y
4 ***Doolittle***	N	N	N	N	N	Y
5 Matsui	N	N	Y	N	Y	N
6 Woolsey	Y	Y	N	N	Y	N
7 Miller, George	N	Y	Y	N	Y	N
8 Pelosi	Y	Y	Y	N	Y	N
9 Lee	Y	Y	N	N	N	N
10 Tauscher	N	N	Y	N	Y	N
11 ***Pombo***	N	N	N	Y	N	Y
12 Lantos	N	N	Y	N	Y	N
13 Stark	Y	Y	Y	N	N	N
14 Eshoo	N	N	Y	N	Y	N
15 ***Campbell***	N	N	N	N	N	Y
16 Lofgren	Y	N	Y	N	Y	N
17 Farr	Y	Y	Y	N	Y	N
18 Condit	N	N	Y	N	Y	Y
19 ***Radanovich***	N	N	N	Y	N	Y
20 Dooley	N	N	Y	N	Y	N
21 ***Thomas***	N	N	N	N	N	Y
22 Capps	N	N	Y	N	Y	N
23 ***Gallegly***	N	N	N	N	N	Y
24 Sherman	N	N	Y	N	Y	N
25 ***McKeon***	N	N	N	Y	N	Y
26 Berman	Y	N	Y	N	Y	N
27 ***Rogan***	N	N	N	N	N	Y
28 ***Dreier***	N	N	N	Y	N	Y
29 Waxman	Y	N	Y	N	Y	N
30 Becerra	Y	Y	Y	N	Y	N
31 Martinez	Y	?	?	?	?	?
32 Dixon	?	?	?	?	?	?
33 Roybal-Allard	Y	Y	Y	N	Y	N
34 Napolitano	Y	N	Y	N	Y	N
35 Waters	Y	Y	N	N	Y	N
36 ***Kuykendall***	N	N	N	N	N	Y
37 Millender-McD.	Y	Y	Y	N	Y	N
38 ***Horn***	N	N	N	N	N	Y
39 ***Royce***	?	?	?	?	?	?
40 ***Lewis***	N	N	N	N	N	Y
41 ***Miller, Gary***	N	N	N	Y	N	Y
42 Baca	N	N	Y	N	Y	N
43 ***Calvert***	N	N	N	N	N	Y
44 ***Bono***	N	N	N	N	N	Y
45 ***Rohrabacher***	N	N	N	Y	N	Y
46 Sanchez	N	N	Y	N	Y	N
47 ***Cox***	N	N	N	Y	N	Y
48 ***Packard***	N	N	N	N	N	Y
49 ***Bilbray***	N	N	Y	N	N	Y
50 Filner	Y	Y	Y	N	Y	N
51 ***Cunningham***	N	N	N	Y	N	Y
52 ***Hunter***	N	N	Y	Y	N	Y
COLORADO						
1 DeGette	N	N	N	N	Y	N
2 Udall	N	N	N	N	Y	N
3 ***McInnis***	N	N	N	Y	N	Y
4 ***Schaffer***	N	N	N	Y	N	Y
5 ***Hefley***	N	N	N	Y	N	Y
6 ***Tancredo***	N	N	N	Y	N	Y
CONNECTICUT						
1 Larson	Y	N	Y	N	Y	N
2 Gejdenson	N	N	N	N	Y	N
3 DeLauro	N	N	Y	N	Y	N
4 ***Shays***	N	N	N	N	N	Y
5 Maloney	N	N	N	N	Y	N
6 ***Johnson***	N	N	N	N	N	Y
DELAWARE						
AL ***Castle***	N	N	Y	N	N	Y
FLORIDA						
1 ***Scarborough***	N	N	Y	Y	N	Y
2 Boyd	N	N	Y	N	N	N
3 Brown	Y	Y	Y	N	Y	N
4 ***Fowler***	N	N	N	N	N	Y
5 Thurman	N	N	Y	N	Y	N
6 ***Stearns***	N	N	N	Y	N	Y
7 ***Mica***	N	N	N	N	N	Y
8 ***McCollum***	?	?	?	?	?	?
9 ***Bilirakis***	N	N	Y	N	N	Y
10 ***Young***	N	N	Y	N	N	Y
11 Davis	N	N	Y	N	Y	N
12 ***Canady***	N	N	N	N	N	Y
13 ***Miller***	N	N	N	N	N	Y
14 ***Goss***	N	N	N	Y	N	Y
15 ***Weldon***	N	N	N	N	N	Y
16 ***Foley***	N	N	Y	N	N	Y
17 Meek	Y	Y	Y	N	Y	N
18 ***Ros-Lehtinen***	N	N	N	N	N	Y
19 Wexler	N	N	N	N	Y	N
20 Deutsch	N	N	N	N	Y	N
21 ***Diaz-Balart***	N	N	N	N	N	Y
22 ***Shaw***	N	N	N	N	N	Y
23 Hastings	Y	Y	Y	N	Y	N
GEORGIA						
1 ***Kingston***	N	N	N	Y	N	Y
2 Bishop	Y	N	Y	N	Y	N
3 ***Collins***	N	N	N	Y	N	Y
4 McKinney	Y	Y	N	N	Y	N
5 Lewis	Y	Y	N	N	Y	N
6 ***Isakson***	N	N	N	N	N	Y
7 ***Barr***	N	N	N	Y	N	Y
8 ***Chambliss***	N	N	N	N	N	Y
9 ***Deal***	N	N	N	Y	N	Y
10 ***Norwood***	N	N	Y	Y	N	Y
11 ***Linder***	N	N	N	N	N	Y
HAWAII						
1 Abercrombie	N	N	Y	N	Y	N
2 Mink	Y	Y	Y	N	Y	N
IDAHO						
1 ***Chenoweth-Hage***	N	N	N	Y	N	Y
2 ***Simpson***	N	N	N	N	N	Y
ILLINOIS						
1 Rush	Y	Y	N	N	Y	N
2 Jackson	Y	Y	N	N	Y	N
3 Lipinski	N	N	N	N	N	N
4 Gutierrez	Y	Y	N	N	Y	N
5 Blagojevich	N	N	N	N	Y	N
6 ***Hyde***	N	N	N	N	N	Y
7 Davis	Y	Y	N	N	Y	N
8 ***Crane***	?	?	?	?	?	?
9 Schakowsky	?	?	?	?	?	?
10 ***Porter***	N	N	?	?	?	?
11 ***Weller***	N	N	N	N	N	Y
12 Costello	N	N	N	N	N	N
13 ***Biggert***	N	N	N	N	N	Y

ND Northern Democrats SD Southern Democrats

	70	71	72	73	74	75
14 ***Hastert***						Y
15 ***Ewing***	N	N	N	Y	N	Y
16 ***Manzullo***	N	N	N	Y	N	Y
17 Evans	N	N	Y	N	Y	N
18 ***LaHood***	N	N	Y	N	N	Y
19 Phelps	N	N	Y	N	N	N
20 ***Shimkus***	N	N	Y	N	N	Y
INDIANA						
1 Visclosky	N	N	Y	N	N	N
2 ***McIntosh***	N	N	N	Y	N	Y
3 Roemer	N	N	Y	N	Y	N
4 ***Souder***	N	N	N	Y	N	Y
5 ***Buyer***	N	N	N	N	N	Y
6 ***Burton***	N	N	N	Y	N	Y
7 ***Pease***	N	N	N	N	N	Y
8 ***Hostettler***	N	N	N	N	N	N
9 Hill	N	N	Y	N	Y	N
10 Carson	Y	Y	Y	N	Y	N
IOWA						
1 ***Leach***	N	N	N	N	N	Y
2 ***Nussle***	N	N	N	Y	N	Y
3 Boswell	N	N	Y	N	Y	N
4 ***Ganske***	N	N	N	N	N	Y
5 ***Latham***	N	N	N	Y	N	Y
KANSAS						
1 ***Moran***	N	N	Y	N	N	Y
2 ***Ryun***	N	N	N	Y	N	Y
3 Moore	N	N	Y	N	N	N
4 ***Tiahrt***	N	N	Y	Y	N	Y
KENTUCKY						
1 ***Whitfield***	N	N	N	Y	N	Y
2 ***Lewis***	N	N	N	Y	N	Y
3 ***Northup***	N	N	N	N	N	Y
4 Lucas	N	N	Y	N	N	N
5 ***Rogers***	N	N	N	N	N	Y
6 ***Fletcher***	N	N	N	N	N	Y
LOUISIANA						
1 ***Vitter***	N	N	N	Y	N	Y
2 Jefferson	Y	Y	Y	N	Y	N
3 ***Tauzin***	N	N	N	Y	N	Y
4 ***McCrery***	N	N	N	N	N	Y
5 ***Cooksey***	N	N	N	N	N	Y
6 ***Baker***	N	N	N	N	N	Y
7 John	N	N	Y	N	N	N
MAINE						
1 Allen	N	N	N	N	Y	N
2 Baldacci	N	N	Y	N	Y	N
MARYLAND						
1 ***Gilchrest***	N	N	N	N	N	Y
2 ***Ehrlich***	N	N	N	N	N	Y
3 Cardin	N	N	Y	N	Y	N
4 Wynn	Y	Y	Y	N	Y	N
5 Hoyer	N	N	Y	N	Y	N
6 ***Bartlett***	N	N	N	Y	N	Y
7 Cummings	Y	Y	N	N	Y	N
8 ***Morella***	N	N	Y	N	N	N
MASSACHUSETTS						
1 Olver	Y	Y	Y	N	Y	N
2 Neal	N	N	Y	N	Y	N
3 McGovern	Y	Y	N	N	Y	N
4 Frank	Y	Y	N	N	Y	N
5 Meehan	N	N	Y	N	Y	N
6 Tierney	N	N	N	N	N	N
7 Markey	Y	Y	Y	N	Y	N
8 Capuano	Y	Y	Y	N	Y	N
9 Moakley	N	N	Y	N	Y	N
10 Delahunt	N	?	Y	N	Y	N
MICHIGAN						
1 Stupak	N	N	Y	N	Y	N
2 ***Hoekstra***	N	N	N	N	N	Y
3 ***Ehlers***	N	N	N	N	N	Y
4 ***Camp***	N	N	N	N	N	Y
5 Barcia	N	N	Y	N	Y	N
6 ***Upton***	N	N	Y	N	N	Y
7 ***Smith***	N	N	N	N	N	Y
8 Stabenow	N	N	Y	N	Y	N
9 Kildee	N	N	N	N	Y	N
10 Bonior	Y	Y	Y	N	Y	N
11 ***Knollenberg***	N	N	N	N	N	Y
12 Levin	N	N	Y	N	Y	N
13 Rivers	N	N	Y	N	Y	N
14 Conyers	Y	Y	N	N	Y	N
15 Kilpatrick	Y	Y	N	N	Y	N
16 Dingell	N	N	Y	N	Y	N

	70	71	72	73	74	75
MINNESOTA						
1 ***Gutknecht***	N	N	N	N	N	Y
2 Minge	N	Y	Y	N	Y	N
3 ***Ramstad***	N	N	N	N	N	Y
4 Vento	?	?	?	?	?	?
5 Sabo	Y	Y	Y	N	Y	N
6 Luther	N	N	Y	N	Y	N
7 Peterson	N	N	Y	N	Y	N
8 Oberstar	N	Y	Y	N	Y	N
MISSISSIPPI						
1 ***Wicker***	N	N	N	N	N	Y
2 Thompson	Y	Y	N	N	Y	N
3 ***Pickering***	N	N	Y	Y	N	Y
4 Shows	N	N	Y	N	Y	N
5 Taylor	N	N	Y	N	Y	N
MISSOURI						
1 Clay	Y	N	N	N	N	N
2 ***Talent***	N	N	Y	N	N	Y
3 Gephardt	N	N	N	N	Y	N
4 Skelton	N	N	Y	N	Y	N
5 McCarthy	N	N	Y	N	Y	N
6 Danner	N	N	Y	N	N	N
7 ***Blunt***	N	N	N	N	N	Y
8 ***Emerson***	N	N	Y	N	N	Y
9 ***Hulshof***	N	N	N	N	N	Y
MONTANA						
AL ***Hill***	N	N	N	N	N	Y
NEBRASKA						
1 ***Bereuter***	N	N	Y	N	N	Y
2 ***Terry***	N	N	N	Y	N	Y
3 ***Barrett***	N	N	Y	Y	N	Y
NEVADA						
1 Berkley	N	N	Y	N	Y	N
2 ***Gibbons***	N	N	N	Y	N	Y
NEW HAMPSHIRE						
1 ***Sununu***	N	N	N	Y	N	Y
2 ***Bass***	N	N	N	N	N	Y
NEW JERSEY						
1 Andrews	N	N	Y	N	Y	N
2 ***LoBiondo***	N	N	N	N	N	Y
3 ***Saxton***	N	N	N	N	N	Y
4 ***Smith***	N	N	N	N	N	Y
5 ***Roukema***	N	N	N	N	N	Y
6 Pallone	N	N	Y	N	Y	N
7 ***Franks***	N	N	N	N	N	Y
8 Pascrell	N	N	Y	N	Y	N
9 Rothman	N	N	N	N	Y	N
10 Payne	Y	Y	N	N	Y	N
11 ***Frelinghuysen***	N	N	N	N	N	Y
12 Holt	N	N	Y	N	Y	N
13 Menendez	N	N	Y	N	Y	N
NEW MEXICO						
1 ***Wilson***	N	N	N	N	N	Y
2 ***Skeen***	N	N	N	N	N	Y
3 Udall	N	N	N	N	Y	N
NEW YORK						
1 Forbes	N	N	Y	N	Y	N
2 ***Lazio***	N	N	N	N	N	Y
3 ***King***	N	N	N	N	N	Y
4 McCarthy	N	N	Y	N	Y	N
5 Ackerman	?	?	?	?	?	?
6 Meeks	Y	Y	N	N	Y	N
7 Crowley	N	N	Y	N	Y	N
8 Nadler	Y	N	N	N	Y	N
9 Weiner	N	Y	N	N	Y	N
10 Towns	Y	Y	N	N	Y	N
11 Owens	Y	Y	N	N	Y	N
12 Velázquez	Y	Y	N	N	Y	N
13 ***Fossella***	N	N	N	N	N	Y
14 Maloney	N	N	N	N	Y	N
15 Rangel	Y	Y	?	N	Y	N
16 Serrano	Y	Y	Y	N	Y	N
17 Engel	Y	Y	Y	N	Y	N
18 Lowey	?	?	?	?	?	?
19 ***Kelly***	N	N	Y	N	N	Y
20 ***Gilman***	N	N	Y	N	N	Y
21 McNulty	N	N	N	N	Y	N
22 ***Sweeney***	N	N	N	N	N	Y
23 ***Boehlert***	N	N	N	N	N	Y
24 ***McHugh***	?	?	?	?	?	?
25 ***Walsh***	N	N	N	N	N	Y
26 Hinchey	Y	?	Y	N	Y	N
27 ***Reynolds***	N	N	N	N	N	Y
28 Slaughter	N	Y	Y	N	Y	N
29 LaFalce	N	N	Y	N	Y	N

	70	71	72	73	74	75
30 ***Quinn***	?	?	?	?	?	?
31 ***Houghton***	N	N	Y	N	N	Y
NORTH CAROLINA						
1 Clayton	Y	Y	Y	N	Y	N
2 Etheridge	N	N	Y	N	Y	N
3 ***Jones***	N	N	N	Y	N	Y
4 Price	N	N	Y	N	Y	N
5 ***Burr***	N	N	N	Y	N	Y
6 ***Coble***	N	N	N	N	N	Y
7 McIntyre	N	N	Y	N	Y	N
8 ***Hayes***	N	N	Y	N	N	Y
9 ***Myrick***	N	N	N	Y	N	Y
10 ***Ballenger***	N	N	N	Y	N	Y
11 ***Taylor***	N	?	N	Y	N	Y
12 Watt	Y	Y	Y	N	Y	N
NORTH DAKOTA						
AL Pomeroy	N	N	Y	N	Y	N
OHIO						
1 ***Chabot***	N	N	N	Y	N	Y
2 ***Portman***	N	N	N	N	N	Y
3 Hall	N	N	Y	N	Y	N
4 ***Oxley***	N	N	N	N	N	Y
5 ***Gillmor***	N	N	N	N	N	Y
6 Strickland	N	N	N	N	Y	N
7 ***Hobson***	N	N	N	N	N	Y
8 ***Boehner***	N	N	N	Y	N	Y
9 Kaptur	N	N	Y	N	Y	N
10 Kucinich	Y	N	N	N	Y	N
11 Jones	Y	Y	N	N	Y	N
12 ***Kasich***	N	N	N	N	N	Y
13 Brown	N	N	N	N	Y	N
14 Sawyer	N	N	Y	N	Y	N
15 ***Pryce***	N	N	N	N	N	Y
16 ***Regula***	N	N	N	N	N	Y
17 Traficant	N	N	N	N	Y	N
18 ***Ney***	N	N	N	N	N	Y
19 ***LaTourette***	N	N	N	N	N	Y
OKLAHOMA						
1 ***Largent***	?	N	N	Y	N	Y
2 ***Coburn***	N	N	Y	Y	N	Y
3 ***Watkins***	N	N	Y	N	N	Y
4 ***Watts***	N	N	N	N	N	Y
5 ***Istook***	N	N	N	Y	N	Y
6 ***Lucas***	N	N	N	N	N	Y
OREGON						
1 Wu	N	N	Y	N	Y	N
2 ***Walden***	N	N	N	N	N	Y
3 Blumenauer	Y	Y	Y	N	Y	N
4 DeFazio	Y	Y	N	N	N	N
5 Hooley	N	N	N	N	Y	N
PENNSYLVANIA						
1 Brady	Y	Y	Y	N	Y	N
2 Fattah	Y	Y	Y	N	Y	N
3 Borski	N	N	N	N	Y	N
4 Klink	N	N	Y	N	Y	N
5 ***Peterson***	N	N	N	N	N	Y
6 Holden	N	N	Y	N	N	N
7 ***Weldon***	N	N	Y	N	N	Y
8 ***Greenwood***	?	?	?	?	?	?
9 ***Shuster***	N	N	N	N	N	Y
10 ***Sherwood***	N	N	N	N	N	Y
11 Kanjorski	N	N	Y	N	Y	N
12 Murtha	N	N	Y	N	Y	N
13 Hoeffel	N	N	N	N	Y	N
14 Coyne	Y	Y	N	N	Y	N
15 ***Toomey***	N	N	N	Y	N	Y
16 ***Pitts***	N	N	N	Y	N	Y
17 ***Gekas***	N	N	N	Y	N	Y
18 Doyle	N	N	Y	N	Y	N
19 ***Goodling***	N	N	N	N	N	Y
20 Mascara	N	N	Y	N	Y	N
21 ***English***	N	N	N	N	N	Y
RHODE ISLAND						
1 Kennedy	N	N	N	N	Y	N
2 Weygand	N	N	N	N	Y	N
SOUTH CAROLINA						
1 ***Sanford***	N	N	N	N	N	N
2 ***Spence***	N	N	Y	N	N	Y
3 ***Graham***	N	N	N	Y	N	Y
4 ***DeMint***	N	N	N	Y	N	Y
5 Spratt	N	N	Y	N	Y	N
6 Clyburn	Y	Y	N	N	Y	N
SOUTH DAKOTA						
AL ***Thune***	N	N	Y	N	N	Y

	70	71	72	73	74	75
TENNESSEE						
1 ***Jenkins***	N	N	N	N	N	Y
2 ***Duncan***	N	N	N	N	N	Y
3 ***Wamp***	N	N	Y	N	N	Y
4 ***Hilleary***	N	N	N	Y	N	Y
5 Clement	N	N	Y	N	Y	N
6 Gordon	N	N	?	N	Y	N
7 ***Bryant***	N	N	Y	Y	N	Y
8 Tanner	N	N	Y	N	N	N
9 Ford	Y	Y	Y	N	Y	N
TEXAS						
1 Sandlin	N	N	Y	N	Y	N
2 Turner	N	N	Y	N	Y	N
3 ***Johnson, Sam***	N	N	N	Y	N	Y
4 Hall	N	N	Y	N	Y	Y
5 ***Sessions***	N	N	N	Y	N	Y
6 ***Barton***	N	N	Y	Y	N	Y
7 ***Archer***	?	?	?	?	?	?
8 ***Brady***	N	N	N	Y	N	Y
9 Lampson	N	N	Y	N	Y	N
10 Doggett	N	N	Y	N	Y	N
11 Edwards	N	N	Y	N	Y	N
12 ***Granger***	N	N	Y	N	N	Y
13 ***Thornberry***	N	N	N	N	N	Y
14 ***Paul***	N	N	N	Y	N	N
15 Hinojosa	N	N	Y	N	Y	N
16 Reyes	N	N	Y	N	Y	N
17 Stenholm	N	N	Y	N	Y	N
18 Jackson-Lee	?	?	?	?	?	?
19 ***Combest***	N	N	N	N	N	Y
20 Gonzalez	N	N	Y	N	Y	N
21 ***Smith***	N	N	N	Y	N	Y
22 ***DeLay***	N	N	N	N	N	Y
23 ***Bonilla***	?	?	?	?	?	?
24 Frost	N	N	Y	N	Y	N
25 Bentsen	N	N	Y	N	Y	N
26 ***Armey***	N	N	N	N	N	Y
27 Ortiz	N	N	Y	N	Y	N
28 Rodriguez	N	N	Y	N	Y	N
29 Green	N	N	Y	N	Y	N
30 Johnson, E.B.	Y	N	N	N	Y	N
UTAH						
1 ***Hansen***	N	N	N	Y	N	Y
2 ***Cook***	N	N	N	N	N	Y
3 ***Cannon***	N	N	N	Y	N	Y
VERMONT						
AL *Sanders*	Y	Y	N	N	N	N
VIRGINIA						
1 ***Bateman***	N	N	P	N	N	Y
2 Pickett	N	N	N	N	N	N
3 Scott	Y	N	Y	N	Y	N
4 Sisisky	N	N	Y	N	Y	N
5 *Goode*	N	N	N	Y	N	Y
6 ***Goodlatte***	N	N	N	Y	N	Y
7 ***Bliley***	N	N	N	N	N	Y
8 Moran	N	?	Y	N	Y	N
9 Boucher	N	?	N	N	Y	N
10 ***Wolf***	N	N	N	N	N	Y
11 ***Davis***	N	?	N	N	N	Y
WASHINGTON						
1 Inslee	N	N	Y	N	Y	N
2 ***Metcalf***	N	N	N	N	N	Y
3 Baird	N	N	Y	N	Y	N
4 ***Hastings***	N	N	N	N	N	Y
5 ***Nethercutt***	N	N	N	N	N	Y
6 Dicks	N	N	Y	N	Y	N
7 McDermott	?	?	?	?	?	?
8 ***Dunn***	N	N	N	N	N	Y
9 Smith	N	N	Y	N	Y	N
WEST VIRGINIA						
1 Mollohan	N	N	N	N	N	N
2 Wise	N	N	N	N	Y	N
3 Rahall	Y	Y	N	N	Y	N
WISCONSIN						
1 ***Ryan***	N	N	N	N	N	Y
2 Baldwin	N	Y	N	N	Y	N
3 Kind	N	N	Y	N	Y	N
4 Kleczka	N	N	Y	N	Y	N
5 Barrett	Y	N	N	N	Y	N
6 ***Petri***	N	N	N	N	N	Y
7 Obey	N	N	N	N	Y	N
8 ***Green***	N	N	N	N	N	Y
9 ***Sensenbrenner***	N	N	N	N	N	Y
WYOMING						
AL ***Cubin***	N	N	N	Y	N	Y

Southern states - Ala., Ark., Fla., Ga., Ky., La., Miss., N.C., Okla., S.C., Tenn., Texas, Va.

76. HR 2412. E. Ross Adair Federal Building/Passage. LaTourette, R-Ohio, motion to suspend the rules and pass the bill designating the federal building and courthouse in Fort Wayne, Ind., the "E. Ross Adair Federal Building and United States Courthouse." Motion agreed to 417-0: R 209-0; D 206-0 (ND 152-0, SD 54-0); I 2-0. A two-thirds majority of those present and voting (278 in this case) is required for passage under suspension of the rules. March 28, 2000.

77. H Con Res 292. Taiwanese Presidential Election/Adoption. Gilman, R-N.Y., motion to suspend the rules and adopt the concurrent resolution congratulating Taiwan on its March 18 presidential elections and expressing the sense of Congress that the People's Republic of China should refrain from making provocative threats against Taiwan, renounce the use of force against Taiwan and protect human and religious rights in China. Motion agreed to 418-1: R 210-1; D 206-0 (ND 153-0, SD 53-0); I 2-0. A two-thirds majority of those present and voting (280 in this case) is required for adoption under suspension of the rules. March 28, 2000.

78. H Con Res 269. Library of Congress Commendation/Adoption. Ehlers, R-Mich., motion to suspend the rules and adopt the concurrent resolution commending the Library of Congress for its service to Congress and the nation in its bicentennial year. Motion agreed to 416-0: R 207-0; D 207-0 (ND 153-0, SD 54-0); I 2-0. A two-thirds majority of those present and voting (278 in this case) is required for adoption under suspension of the rules. March 28, 2000.

79. HR 5. Eliminate Social Security Earnings Test/Senate Amendment. Shaw, R-Fla., motion to agree to the Senate amendment to the bill that would allow senior citizens ages 65 through 69 to earn money without having their Social Security benefits reduced. The Senate amendment would lift the earnings limit at the beginning of the year in which a senior reaches retirement age. Motion agreed to 419-0: R 210-0; D 207-0 (ND 153-0, SD 54-0); I 2-0. March 28, 2000.

80. Procedural/Journal. Approval of the House Journal of March 28, 2000. Approved 356-47: R 183-18; D 172-29 (ND 127-23, SD 45-6); I 1-0. March 29, 2000.

81. HR 3908. Fiscal 2000 Supplemental Appropriations/Rule. Adoption of the rule (H Res 450) to provide for House floor consideration of the bill to provide emergency supplemental funding for fiscal 2000. Adopted 241-182: R 214-0; D 26-181 (ND 17-137, SD 9-44); I 1-1. March 29, 2000.

82. HR 3908. Fiscal 2000 Supplemental Appropriations/Spending Caps. Sanford, R-S.C., amendment that would cut $1.6 billion from the bill. The amendment would strike all references in HR 3908 to emergency designation, thereby making all funds subject to the spending caps. Rejected 108-315: R 86-128; D 21-186 (ND 11-142, SD 10-44); I 1-1. March 29, 2000. A "nay" was a vote in support of the president's position.

Key

Y	Voted for (yea).
#	Paired for.
+	Announced for.
N	Voted against (nay).
X	Paired against.
–	Announced against.
P	Voted "present."
C	Voted "present" to avoid possible conflict of interest.
?	Did not vote or otherwise make a position known.

•

Democrats ***Republicans***
Independents

	76	77	78	79	80	81	82
ALABAMA							
1 ***Callahan***	Y	Y	Y	Y	Y	Y	N
2 ***Everett***	Y	Y	Y	Y	?	?	?
3 ***Riley***	Y	Y	Y	Y	N	Y	N
4 ***Aderholt***	Y	Y	Y	Y	N	Y	N
5 Cramer	Y	Y	Y	Y	Y	N	N
6 ***Bachus***	Y	Y	Y	Y	Y	Y	N
7 Hilliard	Y	Y	Y	Y	N	N	N
ALASKA							
AL ***Young***	Y	Y	Y	Y	?	Y	N
ARIZONA							
1 ***Salmon***	+	+	+	+	+	+	+
2 Pastor	Y	Y	Y	Y	Y	N	N
3 ***Stump***	Y	Y	Y	Y	Y	Y	N
4 ***Shadegg***	Y	Y	Y	Y	Y	Y	Y
5 ***Kolbe***	Y	Y	Y	Y	Y	Y	N
6 ***Hayworth***	Y	Y	Y	Y	Y	Y	Y
ARKANSAS							
1 Berry	Y	Y	Y	Y	Y	N	Y
2 Snyder	Y	Y	Y	Y	Y	N	N
3 ***Hutchinson***	Y	Y	Y	Y	Y	Y	N
4 ***Dickey***	Y	Y	Y	Y	Y	Y	N
CALIFORNIA							
1 Thompson	Y	Y	Y	Y	N	N	N
2 ***Herger***	Y	Y	?	Y	Y	Y	Y
3 ***Ose***	Y	Y	Y	Y	Y	Y	N
4 ***Doolittle***	Y	Y	Y	Y	Y	Y	N
5 Matsui	Y	Y	Y	Y	Y	N	N
6 Woolsey	Y	Y	Y	Y	Y	N	N
7 Miller, George	?	?	?	?	Y	N	Y
8 Pelosi	Y	Y	Y	Y	Y	N	N
9 Lee	Y	Y	Y	Y	Y	N	N
10 Tauscher	Y	Y	Y	Y	Y	Y	N
11 ***Pombo***	Y	Y	Y	Y	Y	Y	Y
12 Lantos	Y	Y	Y	Y	Y	N	N
13 Stark	Y	Y	Y	Y	N	N	N
14 Eshoo	Y	Y	Y	Y	Y	N	N
15 ***Campbell***	Y	Y	Y	Y	Y	Y	Y
16 Lofgren	Y	Y	Y	Y	Y	N	N
17 Farr	Y	Y	Y	Y	Y	Y	N
18 Condit	Y	Y	Y	Y	Y	N	N
19 ***Radanovich***	Y	Y	Y	Y	Y	Y	Y
20 Dooley	Y	Y	Y	Y	Y	N	N
21 ***Thomas***	Y	Y	Y	Y	Y	Y	N
22 Capps	Y	Y	Y	Y	Y	N	N
23 ***Gallegly***	Y	Y	Y	Y	Y	Y	N
24 Sherman	Y	Y	Y	Y	Y	N	Y
25 ***McKeon***	Y	Y	Y	Y	Y	Y	N
26 Berman	Y	Y	Y	Y	Y	N	N
27 ***Rogan***	Y	Y	Y	Y	N	Y	N
28 ***Dreier***	Y	Y	Y	Y	Y	Y	N
29 Waxman	Y	Y	Y	Y	Y	N	N
30 Becerra	Y	Y	Y	Y	Y	N	N
31 Martinez	Y	Y	Y	Y	Y	Y	N
32 Dixon	Y	Y	Y	Y	Y	N	N
33 Roybal-Allard	Y	Y	Y	Y	Y	N	N
34 Napolitano	Y	Y	Y	Y	Y	N	N
35 Waters	Y	Y	Y	Y	N	N	N
36 ***Kuykendall***	Y	Y	Y	Y	Y	Y	N
37 Millender-McD.	Y	Y	Y	Y	Y	N	N
38 ***Horn***	Y	Y	Y	Y	Y	Y	Y
39 ***Royce***	Y	Y	Y	Y	Y	Y	Y
40 ***Lewis***	Y	Y	Y	Y	Y	Y	N
41 ***Miller, Gary***	Y	Y	Y	Y	Y	Y	Y
42 Baca	Y	Y	Y	Y	Y	N	N
43 ***Calvert***	Y	Y	Y	Y	Y	Y	N
44 ***Bono***	Y	Y	Y	Y	Y	Y	N
45 ***Rohrabacher***	Y	Y	Y	Y	Y	Y	Y
46 Sanchez	Y	Y	Y	Y	Y	N	N
47 ***Cox***	Y	Y	Y	Y	Y	Y	Y
48 ***Packard***	Y	Y	Y	Y	Y	Y	N
49 ***Bilbray***	Y	Y	Y	Y	N	Y	Y
50 Filner	Y	Y	Y	Y	N	N	N
51 ***Cunningham***	Y	Y	Y	Y	Y	Y	N
52 ***Hunter***	Y	Y	Y	Y	Y	Y	N
COLORADO							
1 DeGette	Y	Y	Y	Y	Y	N	N
2 Udall	Y	Y	Y	Y	Y	N	N
3 ***McInnis***	Y	Y	Y	Y	Y	Y	Y
4 ***Schaffer***	Y	Y	Y	Y	N	Y	Y
5 ***Hefley***	Y	Y	Y	Y	N	Y	Y
6 ***Tancredo***	Y	Y	Y	Y	P	Y	Y
CONNECTICUT							
1 Larson	Y	Y	Y	Y	Y	Y	?
2 Gejdenson	Y	Y	Y	Y	Y	N	N
3 DeLauro	Y	Y	Y	Y	Y	Y	N
4 ***Shays***	Y	Y	Y	Y	Y	Y	Y
5 Maloney	Y	Y	Y	Y	Y	Y	N
6 ***Johnson***	Y	Y	+	Y	Y	Y	N
DELAWARE							
AL ***Castle***	Y	Y	Y	Y	Y	Y	Y
FLORIDA							
1 ***Scarborough***	Y	Y	Y	Y	Y	Y	Y
2 Boyd	Y	Y	Y	Y	Y	Y	N
3 Brown	Y	Y	Y	Y	?	N	N
4 ***Fowler***	?	?	?	Y	Y	Y	N
5 Thurman	Y	Y	Y	Y	Y	N	Y
6 ***Stearns***	Y	Y	Y	Y	Y	Y	Y
7 ***Mica***	Y	Y	Y	Y	Y	Y	N
8 ***McCollum***	Y	Y	Y	Y	Y	Y	N
9 ***Bilirakis***	Y	Y	Y	Y	Y	Y	N
10 ***Young***	Y	Y	Y	Y	Y	Y	N
11 Davis	Y	Y	Y	Y	Y	N	N
12 ***Canady***	Y	Y	Y	?	Y	Y	N
13 ***Miller***	Y	Y	Y	Y	Y	Y	N
14 ***Goss***	Y	Y	Y	Y	Y	Y	N
15 ***Weldon***	Y	Y	Y	Y	Y	Y	N
16 ***Foley***	Y	Y	Y	Y	Y	Y	N
17 Meek	Y	Y	Y	Y	Y	N	N
18 ***Ros-Lehtinen***	Y	Y	Y	Y	Y	Y	N
19 Wexler	Y	Y	Y	Y	Y	N	N
20 Deutsch	Y	Y	Y	Y	Y	N	Y
21 ***Diaz-Balart***	Y	Y	Y	Y	Y	Y	N
22 ***Shaw***	Y	Y	Y	Y	Y	Y	N
23 Hastings	Y	Y	Y	Y	Y	N	N
GEORGIA							
1 ***Kingston***	Y	Y	Y	Y	N	Y	Y
2 Bishop	Y	Y	Y	Y	Y	Y	N
3 ***Collins***	Y	Y	Y	Y	Y	Y	Y
4 McKinney	Y	Y	Y	Y	Y	N	Y
5 Lewis	Y	Y	Y	Y	N	N	N
6 ***Isakson***	Y	Y	Y	Y	Y	Y	N
7 ***Barr***	Y	Y	Y	Y	Y	Y	Y
8 ***Chambliss***	Y	Y	Y	Y	Y	Y	Y
9 ***Deal***	?	?	?	?	Y	Y	Y
10 ***Norwood***	Y	Y	Y	Y	?	Y	Y
11 ***Linder***	Y	Y	Y	?	Y	Y	N
HAWAII							
1 Abercrombie	Y	Y	Y	Y	Y	N	N
2 Mink	Y	Y	Y	Y	Y	N	N
IDAHO							
1 ***Chenoweth-Hage***	Y	Y	Y	Y	N	Y	Y
2 ***Simpson***	Y	Y	Y	Y	Y	Y	N
ILLINOIS							
1 Rush	Y	Y	Y	Y	Y	N	N
2 Jackson	Y	Y	Y	Y	Y	N	N
3 Lipinski	Y	Y	Y	Y	Y	N	N
4 Gutierrez	Y	Y	Y	Y	N	N	N
5 Blagojevich	Y	Y	Y	Y	Y	N	N
6 ***Hyde***	Y	Y	Y	Y	?	Y	N
7 Davis	Y	Y	Y	Y	Y	N	N
8 ***Crane***	?	?	?	?	?	?	?
9 Schakowsky	Y	Y	Y	Y	Y	N	N
10 ***Porter***	Y	Y	Y	Y	Y	Y	N
11 ***Weller***	Y	Y	Y	Y	N	Y	N
12 Costello	Y	Y	Y	Y	N	N	N
13 ***Biggert***	Y	Y	Y	Y	Y	Y	N

ND Northern Democrats SD Southern Democrats

	76	77	78	79	80	81	82
14 ***Hastert***				Y		Y	
15 ***Ewing***	Y	Y	Y	Y	Y	Y	Y
16 ***Manzullo***	Y	Y	Y	Y	Y	Y	Y
17 Evans	Y	Y	Y	Y	Y	N	N
18 ***LaHood***	Y	Y	Y	Y	Y	Y	Y
19 Phelps	Y	Y	Y	Y	Y	N	N
20 ***Shimkus***	Y	Y	Y	Y	Y	Y	Y
INDIANA							
1 Visclosky	Y	Y	Y	Y	N	N	N
2 ***McIntosh***	?	?	?	?	Y	?	Y
3 Roemer	Y	Y	Y	Y	Y	N	Y
4 ***Souder***	Y	Y	Y	Y	Y	Y	N
5 ***Buyer***	Y	Y	Y	Y	Y	Y	N
6 ***Burton***	Y	Y	Y	Y	Y	Y	N
7 ***Pease***	Y	Y	Y	Y	Y	Y	Y
8 ***Hostettler***	Y	Y	Y	Y	Y	Y	Y
9 Hill	Y	Y	Y	Y	Y	N	Y
10 Carson	Y	Y	Y	Y	Y	N	N
IOWA							
1 ***Leach***	Y	Y	Y	Y	Y	Y	N
2 ***Nussle***	Y	Y	Y	Y	Y	Y	Y
3 Boswell	Y	Y	Y	Y	Y	N	N
4 ***Ganske***	Y	Y	Y	Y	Y	Y	Y
5 ***Latham***	Y	Y	Y	Y	Y	Y	N
KANSAS							
1 ***Moran***	Y	Y	Y	Y	N	Y	Y
2 ***Ryun***	Y	Y	Y	Y	Y	Y	Y
3 Moore	Y	Y	Y	Y	Y	N	N
4 ***Tiahrt***	Y	Y	Y	Y	Y	Y	N
KENTUCKY							
1 ***Whitfield***	Y	Y	Y	Y	Y	Y	N
2 ***Lewis***	Y	Y	Y	Y	Y	Y	N
3 ***Northup***	Y	Y	Y	Y	Y	Y	N
4 Lucas	Y	Y	Y	Y	Y	N	N
5 ***Rogers***	Y	Y	Y	Y	Y	Y	N
6 ***Fletcher***	Y	Y	Y	Y	Y	Y	N
LOUISIANA							
1 ***Vitter***	Y	Y	Y	Y	?	Y	N
2 Jefferson	Y	Y	Y	Y	?	N	N
3 ***Tauzin***	Y	Y	Y	Y	Y	Y	N
4 ***McCrery***	Y	Y	Y	Y	?	Y	N
5 ***Cooksey***	Y	Y	Y	Y	Y	Y	N
6 ***Baker***	Y	Y	Y	Y	Y	Y	N
7 John	Y	Y	Y	Y	Y	N	N
MAINE							
1 Allen	Y	Y	Y	Y	Y	N	N
2 Baldacci	Y	Y	Y	Y	Y	Y	N
MARYLAND							
1 ***Gilchrest***	Y	Y	Y	Y	Y	Y	N
2 ***Ehrlich***	Y	Y	Y	Y	Y	Y	Y
3 Cardin	Y	Y	Y	Y	Y	N	N
4 Wynn	Y	Y	Y	Y	Y	N	N
5 Hoyer	Y	Y	Y	Y	Y	N	N
6 ***Bartlett***	Y	Y	Y	Y	Y	Y	Y
7 Cummings	Y	Y	Y	Y	Y	N	N
8 ***Morella***	Y	Y	Y	Y	Y	Y	N
MASSACHUSETTS							
1 Olver	Y	Y	Y	Y	Y	N	N
2 Neal	Y	Y	Y	Y	Y	N	N
3 McGovern	Y	Y	Y	Y	Y	N	N
4 Frank	Y	Y	Y	Y	Y	N	N
5 Meehan	Y	Y	Y	Y	Y	N	Y
6 Tierney	Y	Y	Y	Y	Y	N	N
7 Markey	Y	Y	Y	Y	N	N	N
8 Capuano	Y	Y	Y	Y	Y	N	N
9 Moakley	Y	Y	Y	Y	Y	N	N
10 Delahunt	Y	Y	Y	Y	Y	Y	N
MICHIGAN							
1 Stupak	Y	Y	Y	Y	N	N	N
2 ***Hoekstra***	Y	Y	Y	Y	Y	Y	Y
3 ***Ehlers***	Y	Y	Y	Y	Y	Y	N
4 ***Camp***	Y	Y	Y	Y	Y	Y	N
5 Barcia	Y	Y	Y	Y	Y	N	N
6 ***Upton***	Y	Y	Y	Y	Y	Y	Y
7 ***Smith***	Y	Y	Y	Y	Y	Y	Y
8 Stabenow	Y	Y	Y	Y	Y	N	N
9 Kildee	Y	Y	Y	Y	Y	N	N
10 Bonior	Y	Y	Y	Y	N	N	N
11 ***Knollenberg***	Y	Y	Y	Y	Y	Y	N
12 Levin	Y	Y	Y	Y	Y	N	N
13 Rivers	Y	Y	Y	Y	Y	N	Y
14 Conyers	Y	Y	Y	Y	Y	?	N
15 Kilpatrick	Y	Y	Y	Y	Y	N	N
16 Dingell	Y	Y	Y	Y	Y	N	N

	76	77	78	79	80	81	82
MINNESOTA							
1 ***Gutknecht***	Y	Y	Y	Y	N	Y	Y
2 Minge	Y	Y	Y	Y	Y	N	Y
3 ***Ramstad***	Y	Y	Y	Y	N	Y	Y
4 Vento	Y	Y	Y	Y	Y	N	N
5 Sabo	Y	Y	Y	Y	N	N	N
6 Luther	Y	Y	Y	Y	Y	N	Y
7 Peterson	Y	Y	Y	Y	N	N	Y
8 Oberstar	Y	Y	Y	Y	N	N	N
MISSISSIPPI							
1 ***Wicker***	Y	Y	Y	Y	Y	Y	N
2 Thompson	Y	Y	Y	Y	N	N	N
3 ***Pickering***	Y	Y	Y	Y	Y	Y	Y
4 Shows	Y	Y	Y	Y	Y	N	Y
5 Taylor	Y	Y	Y	Y	N	N	Y
MISSOURI							
1 Clay	Y	Y	Y	Y	?	N	N
2 ***Talent***	Y	Y	Y	Y	Y	Y	N
3 Gephardt	Y	Y	Y	Y	Y	N	N
4 Skelton	Y	Y	Y	Y	Y	Y	N
5 McCarthy	Y	Y	Y	Y	Y	N	N
6 Danner	Y	Y	Y	Y	Y	N	N
7 ***Blunt***	Y	Y	Y	Y	Y	Y	Y
8 ***Emerson***	Y	Y	Y	Y	Y	Y	N
9 ***Hulshof***	Y	Y	Y	Y	?	Y	Y
MONTANA							
AL ***Hill***	Y	Y	Y	Y	N	Y	Y
NEBRASKA							
1 ***Bereuter***	Y	Y	Y	Y	Y	Y	Y
2 ***Terry***	Y	Y	Y	Y	Y	Y	Y
3 ***Barrett***	Y	Y	Y	Y	?	Y	N
NEVADA							
1 Berkley	Y	Y	Y	Y	Y	N	N
2 ***Gibbons***	Y	Y	Y	Y	N	Y	Y
NEW HAMPSHIRE							
1 ***Sununu***	Y	Y	Y	Y	Y	Y	Y
2 ***Bass***	Y	Y	Y	Y	Y	Y	N
NEW JERSEY							
1 Andrews	Y	Y	Y	Y	Y	Y	N
2 ***LoBiondo***	Y	Y	Y	Y	N	Y	Y
3 ***Saxton***	Y	Y	Y	Y	Y	Y	N
4 ***Smith***	Y	Y	Y	Y	Y	Y	N
5 ***Roukema***	Y	Y	Y	Y	Y	Y	Y
6 Pallone	Y	Y	Y	Y	N	N	N
7 ***Franks***	?	?	?	?	?	?	?
8 Pascrell	Y	Y	Y	Y	Y	N	N
9 Rothman	Y	Y	Y	Y	Y	N	N
10 Payne	Y	Y	Y	Y	Y	N	N
11 ***Frelinghuysen***	Y	Y	Y	Y	Y	Y	N
12 Holt	Y	Y	Y	Y	Y	N	N
13 Menendez	Y	Y	Y	Y	Y	N	N
NEW MEXICO							
1 ***Wilson***	Y	Y	Y	Y	Y	Y	N
2 ***Skeen***	Y	Y	Y	Y	Y	Y	N
3 Udall	Y	Y	Y	Y	N	N	N
NEW YORK							
1 Forbes	Y	Y	Y	Y	Y	N	Y
2 ***Lazio***	Y	Y	Y	Y	Y	Y	Y
3 ***King***	Y	Y	Y	Y	Y	Y	N
4 McCarthy	Y	Y	Y	Y	Y	N	N
5 Ackerman	Y	Y	Y	Y	Y	N	N
6 Meeks	?	?	?	?	Y	N	N
7 Crowley	Y	Y	Y	Y	N	N	N
8 Nadler	Y	Y	Y	Y	Y	N	N
9 Weiner	Y	Y	Y	Y	Y	N	N
10 Towns	Y	Y	Y	Y	Y	N	N
11 Owens	Y	Y	Y	Y	Y	N	N
12 Velázquez	Y	Y	Y	Y	Y	N	N
13 ***Fossella***	Y	Y	Y	Y	Y	Y	Y
14 Maloney	Y	Y	Y	Y	Y	N	N
15 Rangel	Y	Y	Y	Y	?	N	N
16 Serrano	Y	Y	Y	Y	Y	N	N
17 Engel	Y	Y	Y	Y	Y	N	N
18 Lowey	Y	Y	Y	Y	Y	N	N
19 ***Kelly***	Y	Y	Y	Y	Y	Y	N
20 ***Gilman***	Y	Y	Y	Y	Y	Y	N
21 McNulty	Y	Y	Y	Y	Y	N	N
22 ***Sweeney***	Y	Y	Y	Y	N	Y	N
23 ***Boehlert***	Y	Y	Y	Y	Y	Y	N
24 ***McHugh***	Y	Y	Y	Y	Y	Y	N
25 ***Walsh***	Y	Y	Y	Y	Y	Y	N
26 Hinchey	Y	Y	Y	Y	Y	N	N
27 ***Reynolds***	Y	Y	Y	Y	Y	Y	N
28 Slaughter	Y	Y	Y	Y	?	N	N
29 LaFalce	Y	Y	Y	Y	Y	N	N

	76	77	78	79	80	81	82
30 ***Quinn***	?	?	?	?	?	?	?
31 ***Houghton***	Y	Y	Y	Y	Y	Y	N
NORTH CAROLINA							
1 Clayton	Y	Y	Y	Y	Y	N	N
2 Etheridge	Y	Y	Y	Y	Y	N	N
3 ***Jones***	?	Y	Y	Y	Y	Y	N
4 Price	Y	Y	Y	Y	Y	N	N
5 ***Burr***	Y	Y	?	Y	Y	Y	N
6 ***Coble***	Y	Y	Y	Y	Y	Y	N
7 McIntyre	Y	Y	Y	Y	Y	Y	N
8 ***Hayes***	Y	Y	Y	Y	Y	Y	N
9 ***Myrick***	Y	Y	Y	Y	Y	Y	Y
10 ***Ballenger***	Y	Y	Y	Y	Y	Y	N
11 ***Taylor***	+	+	+	+	Y	Y	N
12 Watt	Y	Y	Y	Y	Y	N	N
NORTH DAKOTA							
AL Pomeroy	Y	Y	Y	Y	Y	N	N
OHIO							
1 ***Chabot***	Y	Y	Y	Y	Y	Y	Y
2 ***Portman***	Y	Y	Y	Y	Y	Y	Y
3 Hall	Y	Y	Y	Y	Y	N	N
4 ***Oxley***	Y	Y	Y	Y	Y	Y	N
5 ***Gillmor***	?	?	?	?	Y	Y	N
6 Strickland	Y	Y	Y	Y	N	N	N
7 ***Hobson***	Y	Y	Y	Y	Y	Y	N
8 ***Boehner***	Y	Y	Y	Y	Y	Y	N
9 Kaptur	Y	Y	Y	Y	Y	N	N
10 Kucinich	Y	Y	Y	Y	+	–	–
11 Jones	Y	Y	Y	Y	Y	N	?
12 ***Kasich***	Y	Y	Y	Y	?	Y	N
13 Brown	Y	Y	Y	Y	N	N	N
14 Sawyer	Y	Y	Y	Y	Y	N	N
15 ***Pryce***	Y	Y	Y	Y	Y	Y	Y
16 ***Regula***	Y	Y	Y	Y	Y	Y	N
17 Traficant	Y	Y	Y	Y	Y	Y	N
18 ***Ney***	Y	Y	Y	Y	Y	Y	N
19 ***LaTourette***	Y	Y	Y	Y	?	Y	N
OKLAHOMA							
1 ***Largent***	Y	Y	Y	Y	Y	Y	Y
2 ***Coburn***	Y	Y	Y	Y	?	Y	Y
3 ***Watkins***	Y	Y	Y	Y	Y	Y	N
4 ***Watts***	Y	Y	Y	Y	Y	Y	N
5 ***Istook***	Y	Y	Y	Y	Y	Y	N
6 ***Lucas***	Y	Y	Y	Y	Y	Y	N
OREGON							
1 Wu	Y	Y	Y	Y	N	N	N
2 ***Walden***	Y	Y	Y	Y	Y	Y	N
3 Blumenauer	Y	Y	Y	Y	Y	N	N
4 DeFazio	Y	Y	Y	Y	N	N	N
5 Hooley	Y	Y	Y	Y	Y	N	N
PENNSYLVANIA							
1 Brady	Y	Y	Y	Y	N	Y	N
2 Fattah	Y	Y	Y	Y	Y	N	N
3 Borski	Y	Y	Y	Y	N	N	N
4 Klink	?	?	?	?	?	?	?
5 ***Peterson***	Y	Y	Y	Y	Y	Y	Y
6 Holden	Y	Y	Y	Y	Y	N	N
7 ***Weldon***	Y	Y	Y	?	Y	Y	N
8 ***Greenwood***	Y	Y	Y	Y	Y	Y	N
9 ***Shuster***	Y	Y	Y	Y	Y	Y	N
10 ***Sherwood***	Y	Y	Y	Y	Y	Y	N
11 Kanjorski	Y	Y	Y	Y	Y	Y	N
12 Murtha	Y	Y	Y	Y	Y	Y	N
13 Hoeffel	Y	Y	Y	Y	Y	Y	N
14 Coyne	Y	Y	Y	Y	Y	N	N
15 ***Toomey***	Y	Y	Y	Y	Y	Y	Y
16 ***Pitts***	Y	Y	Y	Y	Y	Y	Y
17 ***Gekas***	Y	Y	Y	Y	?	Y	N
18 Doyle	Y	Y	Y	Y	Y	N	N
19 ***Goodling***	Y	Y	Y	Y	Y	Y	N
20 Mascara	Y	Y	Y	Y	Y	N	N
21 ***English***	Y	Y	Y	Y	N	Y	N
RHODE ISLAND							
1 Kennedy	Y	Y	Y	Y	Y	N	N
2 Weygand	Y	Y	Y	Y	Y	N	N
SOUTH CAROLINA							
1 ***Sanford***	Y	Y	Y	Y	Y	Y	Y
2 ***Spence***	Y	Y	Y	Y	?	Y	N
3 ***Graham***	Y	Y	Y	Y	Y	Y	Y
4 ***DeMint***	Y	Y	Y	Y	Y	Y	Y
5 Spratt	Y	Y	Y	Y	Y	N	N
6 Clyburn	Y	Y	Y	Y	Y	N	N
SOUTH DAKOTA							
AL ***Thune***	Y	Y	Y	Y	Y	Y	N

	76	77	78	79	80	81	82
TENNESSEE							
1 ***Jenkins***	Y	Y	Y	Y	Y	Y	N
2 ***Duncan***	Y	Y	Y	Y	Y	Y	Y
3 ***Wamp***	Y	Y	Y	Y	Y	Y	N
4 ***Hilleary***	Y	Y	Y	Y	N	Y	N
5 Clement	Y	Y	Y	Y	Y	N	N
6 Gordon	Y	Y	Y	Y	Y	N	N
7 ***Bryant***	Y	Y	Y	Y	Y	Y	N
8 Tanner	Y	Y	Y	Y	Y	N	Y
9 Ford	Y	Y	Y	Y	Y	N	N
TEXAS							
1 Sandlin	Y	Y	Y	Y	N	N	N
2 Turner	Y	Y	Y	Y	Y	N	N
3 ***Johnson, Sam***	Y	Y	Y	Y	Y	Y	Y
4 Hall	Y	Y	Y	Y	Y	Y	Y
5 ***Sessions***	Y	Y	Y	Y	Y	Y	Y
6 ***Barton***	Y	Y	Y	Y	Y	?	?
7 ***Archer***	Y	Y	Y	Y	Y	Y	Y
8 ***Brady***	Y	Y	Y	Y	Y	Y	Y
9 Lampson	Y	Y	Y	Y	Y	N	N
10 Doggett	Y	Y	Y	Y	Y	N	Y
11 Edwards	Y	Y	Y	Y	Y	N	N
12 ***Granger***	Y	Y	Y	Y	?	?	?
13 ***Thornberry***	Y	Y	Y	Y	Y	Y	N
14 ***Paul***	Y	N	Y	Y	Y	Y	Y
15 Hinojosa	Y	Y	Y	Y	Y	N	N
16 Reyes	Y	Y	Y	Y	Y	Y	N
17 Stenholm	Y	Y	Y	Y	Y	N	Y
18 Jackson-Lee	Y	Y	Y	Y	Y	N	N
19 ***Combest***	?	Y	Y	Y	Y	Y	N
20 Gonzalez	Y	Y	Y	Y	Y	N	N
21 ***Smith***	Y	Y	Y	Y	Y	Y	N
22 ***DeLay***	Y	Y	Y	Y	Y	Y	N
23 ***Bonilla***	Y	Y	Y	Y	Y	Y	N
24 Frost	Y	Y	Y	Y	Y	N	N
25 Bentsen	Y	Y	Y	Y	Y	N	N
26 ***Armey***	Y	Y	Y	Y	Y	Y	N
27 Ortiz	Y	Y	Y	Y	Y	Y	N
28 Rodriguez	Y	Y	Y	Y	Y	N	N
29 Green	Y	Y	Y	Y	Y	N	N
30 Johnson, E.B.	Y	Y	Y	Y	Y	N	N
UTAH							
1 ***Hansen***	Y	Y	Y	Y	Y	Y	N
2 ***Cook***	Y	Y	Y	Y	Y	Y	Y
3 ***Cannon***	Y	Y	Y	Y	Y	Y	Y
VERMONT							
AL *Sanders*	Y	Y	Y	Y	?	N	N
VIRGINIA							
1 ***Bateman***	Y	Y	Y	Y	?	Y	N
2 Pickett	Y	?	?	Y	N	Y	N
3 Scott	Y	Y	Y	Y	?	N	N
4 Sisisky	Y	Y	Y	Y	Y	Y	N
5 *Goode*	Y	Y	Y	Y	Y	Y	Y
6 ***Goodlatte***	Y	Y	Y	Y	Y	Y	Y
7 ***Bliley***	Y	Y	Y	Y	Y	Y	N
8 Moran	Y	Y	Y	Y	Y	Y	N
9 Boucher	Y	Y	Y	Y	Y	?	N
10 ***Wolf***	Y	Y	Y	Y	Y	Y	N
11 ***Davis***	Y	Y	Y	Y	Y	Y	N
WASHINGTON							
1 Inslee	Y	Y	Y	Y	Y	N	Y
2 ***Metcalf***	+	+	+	+	Y	Y	Y
3 Baird	Y	Y	Y	Y	N	N	N
4 ***Hastings***	Y	Y	?	Y	Y	Y	N
5 ***Nethercutt***	Y	Y	Y	Y	Y	Y	Y
6 Dicks	Y	Y	Y	Y	Y	Y	N
7 McDermott	Y	Y	Y	Y	?	N	N
8 ***Dunn***	Y	Y	Y	Y	Y	Y	N
9 Smith	Y	Y	Y	Y	Y	N	N
WEST VIRGINIA							
1 Mollohan	?	?	?	?	Y	Y	N
2 Wise	Y	Y	Y	Y	?	N	N
3 Rahall	Y	Y	Y	Y	Y	N	N
WISCONSIN							
1 ***Ryan***	Y	Y	Y	Y	Y	Y	Y
2 Baldwin	Y	Y	Y	Y	Y	N	N
3 Kind	Y	Y	Y	Y	Y	N	N
4 Kleczka	Y	Y	Y	Y	Y	N	N
5 Barrett	Y	Y	Y	Y	Y	N	N
6 ***Petri***	Y	Y	Y	Y	Y	Y	Y
7 Obey	?	Y	Y	Y	Y	N	N
8 ***Green***	Y	Y	Y	Y	Y	Y	Y
9 ***Sensenbrenner***	Y	Y	Y	Y	Y	Y	Y
WYOMING							
AL ***Cubin***	Y	Y	Y	Y	Y	Y	Y

Southern states - Ala., Ark., Fla., Ga., Ky., La., Miss., N.C., Okla., S.C., Tenn., Texas, Va.

83. HR 3908. Fiscal 2000 Supplemental Appropriations/Debt Reduction. Toomey, R-Pa., amendment that would dedicate $4 billion in fiscal 2000 funds to reducing the national debt. Adopted 420-0: R 214-0; D 204-0 (ND 151-0, SD 53-0); I 2-0. March 29, 2000.

84. HR 3908. Fiscal 2000 Supplemental Appropriations/Colombian Drug-Fighting Cut. Obey, D-Wis., amendment that would reduce the bill's Colombian anti-drug allotment by $552 million. Rejected 186-239: R 58-157; D 127-81 (ND 103-52, SD 24-29); I 1-1. March 29, 2000. A "nay" was a vote in support of the president's position.

85. HR 3908. Fiscal 2000 Supplemental Appropriations/Defense Spending. Lewis, R-Calif., amendment that would increase defense spending by $4 billion, including $1.2 billion for military equipment maintenance, $1.2 billion for military deployment support, $750 million for military health care and $231 million for military "quality of life" programs. Adopted 289-130: R 180-34; D 108-95 (ND 66-84, SD 42-11); I 1-1. March 29, 2000.

86. HR 3908. Fiscal 2000 Supplemental Appropriations/Colombian Anti-Drug Aid Elimination. Ramstad, R-Minn., amendment that would strike the bill's $1.7 billion for Colombian anti-drug efforts. Rejected 158-262: R 68-145; D 89-116 (ND 76-76, SD 13-40); I 1-1. March 29, 2000. A "nay" was a vote in support of the president's position.

87. HR 3908. Fiscal 2000 Supplemental Appropriations/Military Assistance to Colombia. Gilman, R-N.Y., amendment that would make delivery of military assistance to Colombia contingent upon implementation by the Colombian government of a strategy to eliminate illicit drug cultivation by 2005. The amendment would also require specific actions to crack down on human rights violations by the Colombian Armed Forces. Adopted 380-39: R 207-5; D 171-34 (ND 123-29, SD 48-5); I 2-0. March 29, 2000.

88. HR 3908. Fiscal 2000 Supplemental Appropriations/Vieques. Fowler, R-Fla., amendment that would strike the provision permitting the use of $40 million for a public referendum on the Puerto Rican island of Vieques on the question of whether to allow continued use of the island by the U.S. Navy. Rejected 183-232: R 173-39; D 9-192 (ND 1-147, SD 8-45); I 1-1. March 29, 2000.

89. HR 3908. Fiscal 2000 Supplemental Appropriations/European Kosovo Aid. Kasich, R-Ohio, amendment that would withhold up to half of the $2.1 billion provided in the bill for Kosovo operations until the president certified that European nations were fulfilling their commitments toward this effort. Rejected 200-219: R 152-59; D 46-160 (ND 36-116, SD 10-44); I 2-0. March 30, 2000. A "nay" was a vote in support of the president's position.

Key

- Y Voted for (yea).
- # Paired for.
- \+ Announced for.
- N Voted against (nay).
- X Paired against.
- – Announced against.
- P Voted "present."
- C Voted "present" to avoid possible conflict of interest.
- ? Did not vote or otherwise make a position known.

•

Democrats ***Republicans***
Independents

	83	84	85	86	87	88	89
ALABAMA							
1 ***Callahan***	Y	N	Y	N	Y	Y	N
2 ***Everett***	?	?	?	?	?	?	?
3 ***Riley***	Y	N	Y	N	Y	Y	Y
4 ***Aderholt***	Y	N	Y	N	Y	Y	N
5 Cramer	Y	N	Y	N	Y	N	N
6 ***Bachus***	Y	Y	Y	N	Y	Y	Y
7 Hilliard	Y	Y	N	N	Y	N	N
ALASKA							
AL ***Young***	Y	N	Y	N	Y	N	?
ARIZONA							
1 ***Salmon***	+	+	Y	Y	Y	Y	Y
2 Pastor	Y	Y	Y	N	Y	N	N
3 ***Stump***	Y	N	Y	N	Y	Y	Y
4 ***Shadegg***	Y	Y	Y	N	Y	Y	Y
5 ***Kolbe***	Y	N	Y	N	Y	Y	N
6 ***Hayworth***	Y	N	Y	N	Y	Y	Y
ARKANSAS							
1 Berry	Y	Y	N	Y	Y	N	Y
2 Snyder	Y	N	Y	N	N	N	N
3 ***Hutchinson***	Y	N	Y	N	Y	Y	Y
4 ***Dickey***	Y	Y	Y	Y	Y	Y	N
CALIFORNIA							
1 Thompson	Y	Y	Y	Y	Y	N	N
2 ***Herger***	Y	N	Y	N	Y	?	Y
3 ***Ose***	Y	N	Y	N	Y	Y	N
4 ***Doolittle***	Y	N	Y	N	Y	Y	Y
5 Matsui	Y	Y	Y	Y	Y	N	N
6 Woolsey	Y	Y	N	Y	N	N	Y
7 Miller, George	Y	Y	N	Y	N	N	Y
8 Pelosi	Y	Y	N	Y	N	N	Y
9 Lee	Y	Y	N	Y	N	N	Y
10 Tauscher	Y	N	Y	N	Y	N	N
11 ***Pombo***	Y	N	Y	N	Y	Y	Y
12 Lantos	Y	N	Y	N	Y	N	N
13 Stark	Y	Y	N	Y	N	N	Y
14 Eshoo	Y	Y	N	Y	N	N	Y
15 ***Campbell***	Y	Y	Y	Y	Y	N	Y
16 Lofgren	Y	Y	N	Y	Y	N	Y
17 Farr	Y	Y	N	N	Y	N	N
18 Condit	Y	N	Y	Y	Y	N	Y
19 ***Radanovich***	Y	N	Y	N	Y	Y	Y
20 Dooley	Y	N	Y	N	Y	N	N
21 ***Thomas***	Y	N	Y	N	Y	Y	Y
22 Capps	Y	Y	Y	N	Y	N	N
23 ***Gallegly***	Y	N	Y	N	Y	N	Y
24 Sherman	Y	Y	N	N	Y	N	Y
25 ***McKeon***	Y	N	Y	N	Y	Y	N
26 Berman	Y	N	N	N	Y	N	N
27 ***Rogan***	Y	N	Y	N	Y	Y	Y
28 ***Dreier***	Y	N	Y	N	Y	Y	N
29 Waxman	Y	Y	N	Y	Y	?	N
30 Becerra	Y	Y	N	N	Y	N	?
31 Martinez	?	N	?	?	?	?	N
32 Dixon	Y	Y	N	N	Y	N	N
33 Roybal-Allard	Y	Y	N	N	Y	N	N
34 Napolitano	Y	N	N	N	Y	N	N
35 Waters	Y	N	N	Y	N	N	N
36 ***Kuykendall***	Y	N	Y	N	Y	Y	N
37 Millender-McD.	Y	Y	N	N	Y	N	N
38 ***Horn***	Y	Y	Y	Y	Y	N	N
39 ***Royce***	Y	Y	Y	Y	Y	Y	Y
40 ***Lewis***	Y	N	Y	N	Y	N	N
41 ***Miller, Gary***	Y	N	Y	N	Y	Y	N
42 Baca	Y	N	Y	N	Y	N	N
43 ***Calvert***	Y	N	Y	N	Y	N	N
44 ***Bono***	?	N	Y	N	Y	Y	N
45 ***Rohrabacher***	Y	Y	Y	Y	Y	Y	Y
46 Sanchez	Y	Y	Y	Y	Y	N	N
47 ***Cox***	Y	Y	Y	Y	N	Y	Y
48 ***Packard***	Y	N	Y	N	Y	N	N
49 ***Bilbray***	Y	N	Y	N	Y	Y	Y
50 Filner	Y	Y	N	Y	Y	N	N
51 ***Cunningham***	Y	N	Y	N	Y	Y	N
52 ***Hunter***	Y	N	Y	?	Y	Y	N
COLORADO							
1 DeGette	Y	Y	N	N	N	N	N
2 Udall	Y	Y	N	Y	Y	N	N
3 ***McInnis***	Y	Y	Y	Y	Y	Y	Y
4 ***Schaffer***	Y	Y	Y	Y	Y	Y	Y
5 ***Hefley***	Y	Y	Y	Y	Y	Y	Y
6 ***Tancredo***	Y	Y	Y	Y	Y	Y	Y
CONNECTICUT							
1 Larson	Y	N	Y	N	Y	N	N
2 Gejdenson	Y	N	Y	N	Y	N	N
3 DeLauro	Y	N	Y	N	Y	N	N
4 ***Shays***	Y	N	N	N	Y	Y	Y
5 Maloney	Y	N	Y	N	Y	N	N
6 ***Johnson***	Y	N	Y	N	Y	Y	N
DELAWARE							
AL ***Castle***	Y	Y	N	Y	Y	Y	Y
FLORIDA							
1 ***Scarborough***	Y	N	Y	Y	Y	Y	Y
2 Boyd	Y	Y	Y	N	Y	N	Y
3 Brown	Y	N	Y	Y	Y	N	N
4 ***Fowler***	Y	N	Y	N	Y	Y	Y
5 Thurman	Y	N	Y	N	Y	N	Y
6 ***Stearns***	Y	Y	Y	Y	Y	Y	Y
7 ***Mica***	Y	N	Y	N	Y	Y	Y
8 ***McCollum***	Y	N	Y	N	Y	N	Y
9 ***Bilirakis***	Y	N	Y	N	Y	Y	N
10 ***Young***	Y	N	Y	N	Y	N	N
11 Davis	Y	N	N	N	N	N	N
12 ***Canady***	Y	N	Y	N	Y	Y	Y
13 ***Miller***	Y	N	Y	N	Y	Y	Y
14 ***Goss***	Y	N	Y	N	Y	Y	Y
15 ***Weldon***	Y	N	Y	N	Y	Y	Y
16 ***Foley***	Y	N	Y	Y	Y	Y	Y
17 Meek	Y	Y	Y	Y	Y	N	N
18 ***Ros-Lehtinen***	Y	N	Y	N	Y	N	Y
19 Wexler	Y	Y	N	N	N	N	N
20 Deutsch	Y	Y	N	N	Y	N	Y
21 ***Diaz-Balart***	Y	N	Y	N	Y	N	N
22 ***Shaw***	Y	N	Y	N	Y	Y	N
23 Hastings	Y	Y	Y	Y	Y	N	N
GEORGIA							
1 ***Kingston***	Y	Y	N	N	Y	Y	Y
2 Bishop	Y	N	Y	N	Y	N	N
3 ***Collins***	Y	Y	N	Y	Y	Y	Y
4 McKinney	Y	Y	N	Y	N	N	Y
5 Lewis	Y	Y	N	Y	Y	N	Y
6 ***Isakson***	Y	N	Y	N	Y	Y	Y
7 ***Barr***	Y	N	Y	N	Y	Y	Y
8 ***Chambliss***	Y	N	Y	N	Y	Y	Y
9 ***Deal***	Y	Y	N	Y	Y	Y	Y
10 ***Norwood***	Y	N	Y	Y	Y	Y	?
11 ***Linder***	Y	N	Y	Y	Y	Y	Y
HAWAII							
1 Abercrombie	Y	Y	Y	Y	Y	N	N
2 Mink	Y	Y	Y	Y	Y	?	Y
IDAHO							
1 ***Chenoweth-Hage***	Y	N	Y	N	Y	Y	?
2 ***Simpson***	Y	N	Y	Y	Y	Y	N
ILLINOIS							
1 Rush	Y	Y	?	?	?	?	?
2 Jackson	Y	Y	N	Y	N	N	Y
3 Lipinski	Y	Y	Y	Y	Y	N	N
4 Gutierrez	Y	Y	N	Y	Y	N	N
5 Blagojevich	Y	Y	N	N	N	N	N
6 ***Hyde***	Y	N	Y	N	Y	Y	N
7 Davis	Y	Y	N	Y	Y	N	N
8 ***Crane***	?	?	?	?	?	?	?
9 Schakowsky	P	Y	N	Y	N	N	N
10 ***Porter***	Y	Y	N	Y	Y	N	N
11 ***Weller***	Y	N	Y	N	Y	Y	N
12 Costello	Y	Y	Y	Y	Y	N	N
13 ***Biggert***	Y	N	N	N	Y	Y	Y

ND Northern Democrats SD Southern Democrats

	83	84	85	86	87	88	89
14 ***Hastert***	Y	N					
15 ***Ewing***	Y	N	N	N	Y	Y	Y
16 ***Manzullo***	Y	Y	Y	Y	Y	Y	Y
17 Evans	Y	Y	Y	Y	Y	N	Y
18 ***LaHood***	Y	N	Y	N	Y	N	Y
19 Phelps	Y	Y	Y	Y	Y	N	N
20 ***Shimkus***	Y	N	Y	N	Y	Y	Y
INDIANA							
1 Visclosky	Y	Y	Y	Y	Y	N	N
2 ***McIntosh***	Y	N	Y	N	Y	N	Y
3 Roemer	Y	Y	Y	Y	Y	N	Y
4 ***Souder***	Y	N	Y	N	Y	Y	Y
5 ***Buyer***	Y	N	Y	N	Y	Y	N
6 ***Burton***	Y	N	Y	N	Y	N	Y
7 ***Pease***	Y	N	Y	N	Y	Y	Y
8 ***Hostettler***	Y	N	Y	N	Y	Y	Y
9 Hill	Y	N	N	N	N	N	N
10 Carson	Y	Y	Y	Y	Y	N	N
IOWA							
1 ***Leach***	Y	Y	N	Y	Y	Y	Y
2 ***Nussle***	Y	N	N	Y	Y	Y	Y
3 Boswell	Y	N	N	N	Y	Y	Y
4 ***Ganske***	Y	Y	N	Y	Y	Y	Y
5 ***Latham***	Y	N	Y	N	Y	Y	Y
KANSAS							
1 ***Moran***	Y	Y	Y	Y	Y	Y	Y
2 ***Ryun***	Y	N	Y	N	Y	Y	Y
3 Moore	Y	N	Y	N	Y	N	Y
4 ***Tiahrt***	Y	Y	Y	Y	Y	Y	N
KENTUCKY							
1 ***Whitfield***	Y	N	Y	N	Y	Y	N
2 ***Lewis***	Y	N	N	Y	N	Y	Y
3 ***Northup***	Y	N	Y	N	Y	N	N
4 Lucas	Y	N	Y	N	Y	Y	N
5 ***Rogers***	Y	N	Y	N	Y	Y	Y
6 ***Fletcher***	Y	N	Y	N	Y	Y	Y
LOUISIANA							
1 ***Vitter***	Y	N	Y	N	Y	Y	Y
2 Jefferson	Y	N	Y	N	Y	N	N
3 ***Tauzin***	Y	N	Y	N	Y	Y	Y
4 ***McCrery***	Y	N	Y	N	Y	Y	Y
5 ***Cooksey***	Y	N	Y	N	Y	Y	Y
6 ***Baker***	Y	N	Y	N	Y	Y	Y
7 John	Y	N	Y	N	Y	N	N
MAINE							
1 Allen	Y	Y	Y	N	Y	N	N
2 Baldacci	Y	Y	Y	N	Y	N	N
MARYLAND							
1 ***Gilchrest***	Y	N	Y	N	Y	N	N
2 ***Ehrlich***	Y	N	Y	N	Y	Y	Y
3 Cardin	Y	N	N	N	Y	N	N
4 Wynn	Y	Y	Y	N	Y	N	N
5 Hoyer	Y	Y	Y	N	Y	N	N
6 ***Bartlett***	Y	N	Y	N	Y	Y	Y
7 Cummings	Y	N	N	N	Y	N	N
8 ***Morella***	Y	Y	N	Y	Y	N	N
MASSACHUSETTS							
1 Olver	Y	Y	N	Y	N	N	N
2 Neal	Y	Y	N	Y	Y	N	Y
3 McGovern	Y	Y	N	Y	N	N	N
4 Frank	P	N	N	N	Y	N	Y
5 Meehan	Y	Y	N	Y	Y	N	Y
6 Tierney	Y	Y	N	Y	N	N	Y
7 Markey	Y	Y	N	Y	N	N	Y
8 Capuano	Y	Y	N	Y	N	N	N
9 Moakley	Y	Y	N	Y	N	N	N
10 Delahunt	Y	Y	N	N	Y	N	Y
MICHIGAN							
1 Stupak	Y	Y	Y	Y	Y	N	N
2 ***Hoekstra***	Y	Y	N	Y	Y	Y	Y
3 ***Ehlers***	Y	Y	N	Y	Y	Y	Y
4 ***Camp***	Y	Y	N	Y	Y	Y	Y
5 Barcia	Y	N	Y	Y	Y	N	Y
6 ***Upton***	Y	Y	N	Y	Y	Y	Y
7 ***Smith***	Y	Y	N	Y	Y	Y	Y
8 Stabenow	Y	N	Y	N	Y	N	N
9 Kildee	Y	Y	Y	N	Y	N	N
10 Bonior	Y	Y	Y	Y	Y	N	N
11 ***Knollenberg***	Y	N	Y	N	N	Y	N
12 Levin	Y	Y	N	N	Y	N	N
13 Rivers	Y	Y	N	N	Y	N	Y
14 Conyers	Y	Y	?	Y	Y	N	Y
15 Kilpatrick	Y	Y	N	Y	Y	N	N
16 Dingell	Y	Y	N	N	Y	N	N

	83	84	85	86	87	88	89
MINNESOTA							
1 ***Gutknecht***	Y	Y	N	Y	Y	N	Y
2 Minge	Y	Y	N	Y	Y	N	Y
3 ***Ramstad***	Y	Y	N	Y	Y	Y	Y
4 Vento	Y	Y	?	?	?	?	?
5 Sabo	Y	Y	N	Y	Y	N	N
6 Luther	Y	Y	N	Y	Y	N	Y
7 Peterson	Y	N	N	Y	Y	N	Y
8 Oberstar	Y	Y	N	Y	N	N	N
MISSISSIPPI							
1 ***Wicker***	Y	Y	Y	Y	Y	N	Y
2 Thompson	Y	N	Y	N	Y	N	N
3 ***Pickering***	Y	N	Y	N	Y	Y	Y
4 Shows	Y	N	Y	N	Y	Y	N
5 Taylor	Y	Y	Y	N	Y	Y	N
MISSOURI							
1 Clay	Y	N	N	Y	Y	?	N
2 ***Talent***	Y	N	Y	N	Y	Y	Y
3 Gephardt	Y	Y	Y	N	Y	N	N
4 Skelton	Y	Y	Y	N	Y	N	N
5 McCarthy	Y	Y	N	Y	Y	N	N
6 Danner	Y	N	Y	Y	Y	N	Y
7 ***Blunt***	Y	N	Y	N	Y	Y	Y
8 ***Emerson***	Y	N	Y	N	Y	N	Y
9 ***Hulshof***	Y	Y	Y	Y	Y	Y	Y
MONTANA							
AL ***Hill***	Y	Y	N	Y	Y	Y	Y
NEBRASKA							
1 ***Bereuter***	Y	Y	Y	Y	Y	Y	N
2 ***Terry***	Y	N	Y	Y	Y	Y	Y
3 ***Barrett***	Y	N	Y	N	Y	Y	Y
NEVADA							
1 Berkley	Y	N	Y	N	Y	N	N
2 ***Gibbons***	Y	N	Y	N	Y	Y	Y
NEW HAMPSHIRE							
1 ***Sununu***	Y	N	Y	Y	Y	Y	Y
2 ***Bass***	Y	N	Y	N	Y	Y	Y
NEW JERSEY							
1 Andrews	Y	Y	Y	N	Y	N	N
2 ***LoBiondo***	Y	N	Y	N	Y	N	N
3 ***Saxton***	Y	N	Y	N	Y	N	Y
4 ***Smith***	Y	N	Y	N	Y	N	N
5 ***Roukema***	Y	N	N	N	Y	Y	Y
6 Pallone	Y	N	Y	N	Y	N	N
7 ***Franks***	?	?	?	?	?	?	?
8 Pascrell	Y	N	Y	N	Y	N	N
9 Rothman	Y	N	?	?	?	?	N
10 Payne	Y	N	Y	N	Y	N	N
11 ***Frelinghuysen***	Y	N	Y	N	Y	N	N
12 Holt	Y	Y	N	N	Y	N	N
13 Menendez	Y	N	Y	N	Y	N	N
NEW MEXICO							
1 ***Wilson***	Y	N	Y	N	Y	N	N
2 ***Skeen***	Y	N	Y	N	Y	Y	N
3 Udall	Y	Y	N	Y	Y	N	Y
NEW YORK							
1 Forbes	Y	N	Y	N	Y	N	N
2 ***Lazio***	Y	N	N	N	Y	N	N
3 ***King***	Y	N	Y	N	Y	N	N
4 McCarthy	Y	N	Y	N	Y	N	N
5 Ackerman	Y	Y	N	N	Y	N	N
6 Meeks	Y	N	N	N	Y	N	N
7 Crowley	Y	Y	N	N	Y	N	N
8 Nadler	Y	Y	N	Y	N	N	N
9 Weiner	Y	Y	N	N	Y	N	N
10 Towns	Y	Y	N	N	Y	N	N
11 Owens	Y	Y	N	Y	Y	N	Y
12 Velázquez	Y	Y	N	N	Y	N	N
13 ***Fossella***	Y	Y	Y	Y	Y	N	Y
14 Maloney	Y	N	N	Y	Y	N	N
15 Rangel	Y	N	N	N	Y	N	N
16 Serrano	Y	Y	N	Y	Y	N	N
17 Engel	Y	Y	N	N	Y	N	N
18 Lowey	Y	Y	N	N	Y	N	N
19 ***Kelly***	Y	N	Y	Y	Y	N	N
20 ***Gilman***	Y	N	?	N	Y	Y	N
21 McNulty	Y	Y	N	Y	Y	N	Y
22 ***Sweeney***	Y	N	Y	N	Y	N	Y
23 ***Boehlert***	Y	N	Y	N	Y	Y	N
24 ***McHugh***	Y	N	Y	N	Y	Y	N
25 ***Walsh***	Y	N	Y	N	Y	N	N
26 Hinchey	Y	Y	N	Y	Y	N	N
27 ***Reynolds***	Y	N	Y	N	Y	N	Y
28 Slaughter	Y	Y	Y	N	Y	N	N
29 LaFalce	Y	Y	Y	N	Y	N	N

	83	84	85	86	87	88	89
30 ***Quinn***	?	?	?	?	?	?	?
31 ***Houghton***	Y	N	Y	N	Y	Y	N
NORTH CAROLINA							
1 Clayton	Y	Y	Y	Y	Y	N	N
2 Etheridge	Y	N	Y	N	Y	N	N
3 ***Jones***	Y	N	Y	N	Y	Y	Y
4 Price	Y	Y	Y	N	Y	N	N
5 ***Burr***	Y	N	Y	N	?	Y	?
6 ***Coble***	Y	N	Y	N	Y	Y	Y
7 McIntyre	Y	N	Y	N	Y	Y	N
8 ***Hayes***	Y	N	Y	N	Y	Y	Y
9 ***Myrick***	Y	N	Y	N	Y	Y	Y
10 ***Ballenger***	Y	N	Y	N	Y	Y	Y
11 ***Taylor***	Y	N	Y	N	Y	Y	N
12 Watt	Y	Y	N	Y	Y	N	N
NORTH DAKOTA							
AL Pomeroy	Y	N	Y	N	Y	N	N
OHIO							
1 ***Chabot***	Y	Y	N	Y	Y	Y	Y
2 ***Portman***	Y	N	N	N	Y	N	Y
3 Hall	Y	Y	Y	Y	Y	?	N
4 ***Oxley***	Y	N	Y	N	Y	Y	N
5 ***Gillmor***	Y	N	Y	N	Y	Y	N
6 Strickland	Y	N	Y	N	Y	N	N
7 ***Hobson***	Y	N	Y	N	Y	Y	N
8 ***Boehner***	Y	N	Y	N	Y	?	N
9 Kaptur	Y	Y	N	Y	N	N	N
10 Kucinich	+	+	−	Y	Y	N	Y
11 Jones	Y	Y	N	Y	Y	N	N
12 ***Kasich***	Y	N	N	N	Y	Y	Y
13 Brown	Y	Y	N	Y	N	N	N
14 Sawyer	Y	N	N	N	Y	N	N
15 ***Pryce***	Y	N	Y	N	?	Y	Y
16 ***Regula***	Y	N	N	N	Y	Y	N
17 Traficant	Y	N	Y	N	Y	N	N
18 ***Ney***	Y	N	Y	N	Y	Y	Y
19 ***LaTourette***	Y	N	N	Y	Y	Y	Y
OKLAHOMA							
1 ***Largent***	Y	Y	N	Y	Y	Y	Y
2 ***Coburn***	Y	Y	Y	Y	Y	Y	Y
3 ***Watkins***	Y	N	Y	N	Y	Y	Y
4 ***Watts***	Y	N	Y	N	Y	Y	Y
5 ***Istook***	Y	Y	Y	Y	Y	Y	Y
6 ***Lucas***	Y	N	Y	N	Y	Y	Y
OREGON							
1 Wu	Y	Y	N	Y	N	N	N
2 ***Walden***	Y	N	Y	Y	Y	Y	Y
3 Blumenauer	Y	Y	N	Y	Y	N	N
4 DeFazio	Y	Y	N	Y	N	N	Y
5 Hooley	Y	Y	N	N	Y	N	Y
PENNSYLVANIA							
1 Brady	Y	N	Y	N	Y	N	N
2 Fattah	Y	N	N	Y	Y	N	N
3 Borski	Y	N	Y	N	Y	N	N
4 Klink	?	?	?	?	?	?	?
5 ***Peterson***	Y	N	Y	N	Y	Y	N
6 Holden	Y	N	Y	N	Y	N	N
7 ***Weldon***	Y	Y	Y	N	Y	Y	Y
8 ***Greenwood***	Y	N	Y	N	Y	Y	Y
9 ***Shuster***	Y	N	Y	N	Y	?	Y
10 ***Sherwood***	Y	N	Y	N	Y	Y	N
11 Kanjorski	Y	N	Y	N	Y	N	N
12 Murtha	Y	N	Y	N	Y	N	N
13 Hoeffel	Y	N	Y	N	Y	N	N
14 Coyne	Y	Y	N	Y	Y	N	N
15 ***Toomey***	Y	Y	Y	Y	Y	Y	Y
16 ***Pitts***	Y	Y	Y	Y	Y	Y	Y
17 ***Gekas***	Y	N	Y	Y	Y	Y	Y
18 Doyle	Y	N	Y	N	Y	N	N
19 ***Goodling***	Y	N	Y	Y	Y	Y	Y
20 Mascara	Y	N	Y	N	Y	N	N
21 ***English***	Y	N	Y	N	Y	N	Y
RHODE ISLAND							
1 Kennedy	Y	Y	Y	Y	Y	N	N
2 Weygand	Y	N	Y	N	Y	N	?
SOUTH CAROLINA							
1 ***Sanford***	Y	Y	N	Y	Y	Y	Y
2 ***Spence***	Y	N	Y	?	?	?	?
3 ***Graham***	Y	N	Y	Y	Y	Y	Y
4 ***DeMint***	Y	N	Y	Y	Y	Y	Y
5 Spratt	Y	Y	Y	Y	Y	N	N
6 Clyburn	?	?	?	?	?	?	N
SOUTH DAKOTA							
AL ***Thune***	Y	N	Y	N	Y	Y	Y

	83	84	85	86	87	88	89
TENNESSEE							
1 ***Jenkins***	Y	Y	Y	N	Y	Y	Y
2 ***Duncan***	Y	Y	N	Y	Y	Y	Y
3 ***Wamp***	Y	N	Y	N	Y	Y	Y
4 ***Hilleary***	Y	Y	Y	Y	Y	Y	Y
5 Clement	Y	N	Y	N	Y	N	N
6 Gordon	Y	N	Y	N	Y	N	Y
7 ***Bryant***	Y	N	Y	N	Y	Y	Y
8 Tanner	Y	N	Y	N	Y	N	N
9 Ford	Y	N	N	Y	Y	N	N
TEXAS							
1 Sandlin	Y	N	Y	N	Y	N	N
2 Turner	Y	N	Y	N	Y	N	N
3 ***Johnson, Sam***	Y	N	Y	N	Y	Y	Y
4 Hall	Y	Y	Y	N	Y	Y	Y
5 ***Sessions***	Y	N	Y	N	Y	Y	Y
6 ***Barton***	?	?	?	?	?	Y	Y
7 ***Archer***	Y	Y	Y	Y	Y	Y	Y
8 ***Brady***	Y	Y	Y	N	Y	Y	Y
9 Lampson	Y	N	Y	N	Y	N	N
10 Doggett	Y	Y	N	Y	N	N	Y
11 Edwards	Y	N	Y	N	Y	N	N
12 ***Granger***	?	?	?	?	?	?	?
13 ***Thornberry***	Y	Y	Y	N	Y	Y	Y
14 ***Paul***	Y	Y	N	Y	N	Y	Y
15 Hinojosa	Y	N	N	N	Y	N	N
16 Reyes	Y	N	Y	N	Y	N	N
17 Stenholm	Y	Y	Y	N	Y	Y	N
18 Jackson-Lee	Y	Y	Y	N	Y	N	N
19 ***Combest***	Y	Y	Y	Y	Y	Y	Y
20 Gonzalez	Y	N	Y	N	Y	N	N
21 ***Smith***	Y	N	Y	N	Y	Y	Y
22 ***DeLay***	Y	N	Y	N	N	Y	Y
23 ***Bonilla***	Y	N	Y	N	Y	N	N
24 Frost	Y	Y	Y	N	Y	N	N
25 Bentsen	Y	Y	Y	N	Y	N	N
26 ***Armey***	Y	N	Y	N	Y	Y	Y
27 Ortiz	Y	N	Y	N	Y	N	N
28 Rodriguez	Y	Y	Y	N	Y	N	N
29 Green	Y	N	Y	N	Y	N	Y
30 Johnson, E.B.	Y	Y	Y	Y	Y	N	N
UTAH							
1 ***Hansen***	Y	N	Y	N	Y	Y	Y
2 ***Cook***	Y	Y	N	Y	Y	Y	Y
3 ***Cannon***	Y	N	Y	N	Y	Y	Y
VERMONT							
AL *Sanders*	Y	Y	N	Y	Y	N	Y
VIRGINIA							
1 ***Bateman***	Y	N	Y	N	Y	Y	N
2 Pickett	Y	N	Y	N	Y	Y	N
3 Scott	Y	Y	Y	Y	Y	N	N
4 Sisisky	Y	N	Y	N	Y	Y	N
5 *Goode*	Y	N	Y	N	Y	Y	Y
6 ***Goodlatte***	Y	N	Y	N	Y	Y	Y
7 ***Bliley***	Y	N	Y	N	N	Y	N
8 Moran	Y	N	Y	N	Y	N	N
9 Boucher	Y	Y	Y	Y	Y	N	N
10 ***Wolf***	Y	N	Y	N	Y	Y	N
11 ***Davis***	Y	N	Y	N	Y	N	N
WASHINGTON							
1 Inslee	Y	Y	Y	Y	Y	N	Y
2 ***Metcalf***	Y	Y	Y	Y	Y	Y	Y
3 Baird	Y	Y	N	Y	N	N	N
4 ***Hastings***	Y	N	Y	N	Y	Y	Y
5 ***Nethercutt***	Y	Y	Y	N	Y	Y	N
6 Dicks	Y	Y	Y	Y	Y	N	N
7 McDermott	Y	Y	N	Y	N	N	N
8 ***Dunn***	Y	N	Y	N	Y	Y	Y
9 Smith	Y	N	Y	N	Y	N	N
WEST VIRGINIA							
1 Mollohan	Y	N	Y	N	Y	N	N
2 Wise	Y	N	Y	N	Y	N	N
3 Rahall	Y	N	Y	N	Y	N	N
WISCONSIN							
1 ***Ryan***	Y	Y	Y	Y	Y	Y	Y
2 Baldwin	Y	Y	N	Y	N	N	Y
3 Kind	Y	Y	N	Y	Y	N	N
4 Kleczka	Y	Y	N	Y	Y	N	N
5 Barrett	Y	Y	N	Y	N	N	N
6 ***Petri***	Y	Y	N	Y	Y	Y	Y
7 Obey	P	Y	N	Y	N	N	N
8 ***Green***	Y	N	Y	Y	Y	Y	Y
9 ***Sensenbrenner***	Y	Y	N	Y	Y	N	Y
WYOMING							
AL ***Cubin***	Y	N	Y	N	Y	Y	Y

Southern states - Ala., Ark., Fla., Ga., Ky., La., Miss., N.C., Okla., S.C., Tenn., Texas, Va.

90. HR 3908. Fiscal 2000 Supplemental Appropriations/Firefighter Aid. Weldon, R-Pa., amendment that would provide $100 million for fire departments, firefighting programs and burn victims. The amendment, as modified, would not allow fire departments to tap Community Development Block Grants to fund the programs. Adopted 386-28: R 180-28; D 204-0 (ND 151-0, SD 53-0); I 2-0. March 30, 2000.

91. HR 3908. Fiscal 2000 Supplemental Appropriations/Reduction. Stearns, R-Fla., amendment that would cut all appropriations by 10 percent except for emergency and Defense Department spending. Rejected 126-291: R 100-110; D 25-180 (ND 17-135, SD 8-45); I 1-1. March 30, 2000.

92. HR 3908. Fiscal 2000 Supplemental Appropriations/DEA Funding Cuts. Paul, R-Texas, amendment that would cut Drug Enforcement Administration funding by $293 million, Defense Department drug-fighting by $186 million and economic aid to Colombia by $1.1 billion. The amendment also would prohibit funding for military construction outside of the United States, as well as funding for Kosovo and East Timor operations unless the purpose was to bring U.S. troops stationed there home. Rejected 45-367: R 41-168; D 4-197 (ND 4-144, SD 0-53); I 0-2. March 30, 2000.

93. HR 3908. Fiscal 2000 Supplemental Appropriations/Los Angeles FDA Building. Tancredo, R-Colo., amendment that would strike $20 million in the bill designated for replacing the Food and Drug Administration building in Los Angeles. Rejected 146-267: R 127-81; D 18-185 (ND 12-138, SD 6-47); I 1-1. March 30, 2000.

94. HR 3908. Fiscal 2000 Supplemental Appropriations/Motion to Recommit. Obey, D-Wis., motion to recommit the bill to the House Appropriations Committee with instructions to report the bill back to the House with provisions that appropriate $262 million for the Office of National Drug Control Policy for grants to recognized national, state or local prevention and treatment organizations. Motion rejected 194-220: R 6-204; D 187-15 (ND 142-7, SD 45-8); I 1-1. March 30, 2000.

95. HR 3908. Fiscal 2000 Supplemental Appropriations/Passage. Passage of the bill to provide $13.2 billion principally for operations in Kosovo, anti-drug assistance to Colombia and natural disaster relief. Specifically, the bill would appropriate $5 billion for operations in Kosovo and East Timor; $1.7 billion for anti-drug measures in Colombia. The bill as amended also would provide an additional $4 billion for the Defense Department. Passed 263-146: R 143-61; D 119-84 (ND 74-77, SD 45-7); I 1-1. March 30, 2000.

Key

- Y Voted for (yea).
- # Paired for.
- \+ Announced for.
- N Voted against (nay).
- X Paired against.
- – Announced against.
- P Voted "present."
- C Voted "present" to avoid possible conflict of interest.
- ? Did not vote or otherwise make a position known.

•

Democrats ***Republicans***
Independents

	90	91	92	93	94	95
ALABAMA						
1 ***Callahan***	Y	N	N	N	N	Y
2 ***Everett***	?	?	?	?	?	?
3 ***Riley***	Y	Y	N	Y	N	Y
4 ***Aderholt***	Y	N	N	Y	Y	Y
5 Cramer	Y	N	N	N	N	Y
6 ***Bachus***	Y	Y	N	N	N	Y
7 Hilliard	Y	N	N	N	Y	Y
ALASKA						
AL ***Young***	?	N	N	Y	N	Y
ARIZONA						
1 ***Salmon***	N	Y	Y	Y	N	N
2 Pastor	Y	N	N	N	Y	Y
3 ***Stump***	Y	N	N	Y	N	Y
4 ***Shadegg***	N	Y	Y	Y	N	N
5 ***Kolbe***	Y	N	N	N	N	Y
6 ***Hayworth***	Y	Y	N	Y	N	Y
ARKANSAS						
1 Berry	Y	N	N	N	Y	N
2 Snyder	Y	N	N	N	Y	Y
3 ***Hutchinson***	Y	N	N	Y	N	Y
4 ***Dickey***	Y	N	Y	Y	N	Y
CALIFORNIA						
1 Thompson	Y	N	N	N	Y	Y
2 ***Herger***	N	Y	N	N	N	Y
3 ***Ose***	Y	N	N	N	N	Y
4 ***Doolittle***	Y	Y	N	Y	N	N
5 Matsui	Y	N	N	N	Y	Y
6 Woolsey	Y	N	N	N	Y	N
7 Miller, George	Y	N	N	N	Y	N
8 Pelosi	Y	N	N	N	Y	N
9 Lee	Y	N	N	N	Y	N
10 Tauscher	Y	N	N	N	Y	Y
11 ***Pombo***	Y	Y	N	N	N	Y
12 Lantos	Y	N	N	N	Y	Y
13 Stark	Y	N	Y	N	Y	N
14 Eshoo	Y	N	N	N	Y	N
15 ***Campbell***	Y	Y	Y	N	N	N
16 Lofgren	Y	N	N	N	Y	N
17 Farr	Y	N	N	N	Y	Y
18 Condit	Y	Y	N	N	Y	Y
19 ***Radanovich***	Y	Y	N	N	N	Y
20 Dooley	Y	Y	N	N	Y	Y
21 ***Thomas***	Y	N	N	N	N	Y
22 Capps	Y	N	N	N	Y	Y
23 ***Gallegly***	Y	N	N	N	N	Y
24 Sherman	Y	N	N	N	Y	Y
25 ***McKeon***	Y	N	N	N	N	Y
26 Berman	Y	N	N	N	Y	Y
27 ***Rogan***	Y	?	?	?	?	+
28 ***Dreier***	Y	N	N	N	N	Y
29 Waxman	Y	N	?	N	Y	N
30 Becerra	?	?	?	?	?	?
31 Martinez	Y	N	N	?	N	Y
32 Dixon	Y	N	N	N	Y	Y
33 Roybal-Allard	Y	N	N	N	Y	Y
34 Napolitano	Y	N	N	N	Y	Y
35 Waters	Y	N	N	N	Y	N
36 ***Kuykendall***	Y	N	N	N	N	Y
37 Millender-McD.	Y	N	N	N	Y	Y
38 ***Horn***	Y	N	N	N	N	Y
39 ***Royce***	N	Y	Y	Y	N	N
40 ***Lewis***	Y	N	N	N	N	Y
41 ***Miller, Gary***	N	Y	N	N	N	Y
42 Baca	Y	N	N	N	Y	Y
43 ***Calvert***	Y	N	N	N	N	Y
44 ***Bono***	Y	N	N	N	N	Y
45 ***Rohrabacher***	N	Y	Y	N	N	N
46 Sanchez	Y	Y	N	N	Y	Y
47 ***Cox***	N	Y	N	N	N	N
48 ***Packard***	Y	N	N	N	N	Y
49 ***Bilbray***	Y	N	N	N	N	+
50 Filner	Y	N	N	N	Y	N
51 ***Cunningham***	Y	Y	N	N	N	Y
52 ***Hunter***	Y	Y	N	N	N	Y
COLORADO						
1 DeGette	Y	N	N	N	Y	N
2 Udall	Y	N	N	Y	Y	N
3 ***McInnis***	Y	Y	N	Y	N	N
4 ***Schaffer***	N	Y	N	Y	N	N
5 ***Hefley***	N	Y	N	Y	N	N
6 ***Tancredo***	–	Y	Y	Y	N	N
CONNECTICUT						
1 Larson	Y	N	N	N	Y	Y
2 Gejdenson	Y	N	N	N	Y	Y
3 DeLauro	Y	N	N	N	Y	Y
4 ***Shays***	Y	Y	N	Y	N	N
5 Maloney	Y	Y	N	N	Y	Y
6 ***Johnson***	Y	N	N	N	N	Y
DELAWARE						
AL ***Castle***	Y	Y	N	N	N	N
FLORIDA						
1 ***Scarborough***	N	Y	Y	Y	Y	Y
2 Boyd	Y	N	N	N	N	Y
3 Brown	Y	N	N	N	Y	?
4 ***Fowler***	Y	N	N	Y	N	Y
5 Thurman	Y	N	N	N	Y	N
6 ***Stearns***	Y	Y	N	Y	N	N
7 ***Mica***	Y	N	N	Y	N	Y
8 ***McCollum***	Y	N	N	N	N	Y
9 ***Bilirakis***	Y	N	N	N	N	Y
10 ***Young***	Y	N	N	N	N	Y
11 Davis	Y	N	N	N	N	N
12 ***Canady***	Y	N	N	N	N	Y
13 ***Miller***	–	Y	N	Y	N	Y
14 ***Goss***	Y	Y	N	N	N	Y
15 ***Weldon***	Y	Y	N	Y	N	Y
16 ***Foley***	Y	Y	N	Y	N	Y
17 Meek	Y	N	N	N	Y	Y
18 ***Ros-Lehtinen***	Y	–	–	–	+	+
19 Wexler	Y	N	N	Y	Y	Y
20 Deutsch	Y	Y	N	Y	Y	Y
21 ***Diaz-Balart***	Y	N	N	N	N	+
22 ***Shaw***	Y	N	N	N	N	Y
23 Hastings	Y	N	N	N	Y	N
GEORGIA						
1 ***Kingston***	Y	Y	N	N	N	Y
2 Bishop	Y	N	N	N	N	Y
3 ***Collins***	N	Y	Y	Y	N	N
4 McKinney	Y	Y	N	N	Y	N
5 Lewis	Y	Y	N	N	Y	N
6 ***Isakson***	Y	N	N	Y	N	Y
7 ***Barr***	Y	Y	N	Y	N	N
8 ***Chambliss***	Y	N	N	Y	N	+
9 ***Deal***	Y	Y	Y	Y	N	N
10 ***Norwood***	?	Y	N	Y	N	Y
11 ***Linder***	N	Y	Y	Y	N	Y
HAWAII						
1 Abercrombie	Y	N	N	N	Y	Y
2 Mink	Y	N	N	N	Y	N
IDAHO						
1 ***Chenoweth-Hage***	?	?	?	?	?	?
2 ***Simpson***	Y	N	Y	Y	N	N
ILLINOIS						
1 Rush	?	?	?	?	?	?
2 Jackson	Y	N	N	N	Y	N
3 Lipinski	Y	N	N	N	Y	N
4 Gutierrez	Y	N	N	N	Y	N
5 Blagojevich	Y	N	N	N	Y	N
6 ***Hyde***	Y	N	N	N	N	Y
7 Davis	Y	N	N	N	Y	N
8 ***Crane***	?	?	?	?	?	?
9 Schakowsky	Y	N	N	N	Y	N
10 ***Porter***	Y	N	N	N	Y	N
11 ***Weller***	Y	N	N	Y	N	Y
12 Costello	Y	Y	N	N	Y	N
13 ***Biggert***	Y	N	N	Y	N	Y

ND Northern Democrats SD Southern Democrats

	90	91	92	93	94	95
14 ***Hastert***					N	Y
15 ***Ewing***	Y	Y	Y	N	N	?
16 ***Manzullo***	Y	Y	Y	Y	N	N
17 Evans	Y	N	N	N	Y	Y
18 ***LaHood***	Y	Y	N	Y	N	N
19 Phelps	Y	N	N	N	Y	N
20 ***Shimkus***	Y	Y	N	Y	N	Y
INDIANA						
1 Visclosky	Y	N	N	N	Y	N
2 ***McIntosh***	Y	?	?	?	?	?
3 Roemer	Y	Y	N	Y	Y	N
4 ***Souder***	Y	N	N	Y	N	Y
5 ***Buyer***	Y	N	N	N	N	Y
6 ***Burton***	Y	Y	N	Y	N	Y
7 ***Pease***	Y	Y	N	N	N	Y
8 ***Hostettler***	N	Y	N	Y	N	Y
9 Hill	Y	N	N	N	N	N
10 Carson	Y	N	N	N	Y	Y
IOWA						
1 ***Leach***	Y	N	N	N	N	N
2 ***Nussle***	Y	Y	N	Y	N	N
3 Boswell	Y	N	N	N	Y	N
4 ***Ganske***	Y	Y	N	Y	Y	N
5 ***Latham***	Y	N	N	N	N	Y
KANSAS						
1 ***Moran***	Y	Y	Y	Y	N	N
2 ***Ryun***	Y	Y	N	Y	N	Y
3 Moore	Y	Y	N	N	Y	N
4 ***Tiahrt***	Y	Y	N	Y	N	Y
KENTUCKY						
1 ***Whitfield***	Y	N	N	N	N	Y
2 ***Lewis***	Y	N	N	Y	N	Y
3 ***Northup***	Y	N	N	N	N	Y
4 Lucas	Y	N	N	N	N	Y
5 ***Rogers***	Y	N	N	Y	N	Y
6 ***Fletcher***	Y	N	N	Y	N	Y
LOUISIANA						
1 ***Vitter***	Y	Y	N	Y	N	Y
2 Jefferson	Y	N	N	N	Y	Y
3 ***Tauzin***	Y	N	N	Y	N	Y
4 ***McCrery***	Y	N	N	N	N	Y
5 ***Cooksey***	Y	N	N	N	N	Y
6 ***Baker***	Y	N	N	Y	N	Y
7 John	Y	N	N	N	Y	Y
MAINE						
1 Allen	Y	N	N	N	Y	Y
2 Baldacci	Y	N	N	N	Y	Y
MARYLAND						
1 ***Gilchrest***	Y	N	N	N	N	Y
2 ***Ehrlich***	Y	Y	N	Y	N	Y
3 Cardin	Y	N	N	N	Y	Y
4 Wynn	Y	N	N	N	Y	Y
5 Hoyer	Y	N	?	N	Y	Y
6 ***Bartlett***	Y	Y	N	Y	N	Y
7 Cummings	?	N	N	N	Y	Y
8 ***Morella***	Y	N	N	N	Y	Y
MASSACHUSETTS						
1 Olver	Y	N	N	N	Y	N
2 Neal	Y	N	N	N	Y	Y
3 McGovern	Y	N	N	N	Y	Y
4 Frank	Y	N	N	N	Y	N
5 Meehan	Y	Y	N	N	Y	N
6 Tierney	Y	N	N	N	Y	N
7 Markey	Y	N	N	N	Y	N
8 Capuano	Y	N	N	N	Y	N
9 Moakley	Y	N	N	N	Y	Y
10 Delahunt	Y	N	N	N	Y	N
MICHIGAN						
1 Stupak	Y	N	N	Y	Y	N
2 ***Hoekstra***	Y	Y	Y	Y	N	Y
3 ***Ehlers***	Y	N	N	–	N	N
4 ***Camp***	Y	Y	N	Y	N	Y
5 Barcia	Y	Y	N	N	Y	Y
6 ***Upton***	Y	Y	N	Y	N	N
7 ***Smith***	Y	Y	N	Y	N	Y
8 Stabenow	Y	N	N	N	Y	Y
9 Kildee	Y	N	N	N	Y	Y
10 Bonior	Y	N	N	N	Y	Y
11 ***Knollenberg***	Y	N	N	N	N	Y
12 Levin	Y	N	N	N	Y	Y
13 Rivers	Y	N	N	Y	Y	N
14 Conyers	Y	N	N	N	Y	N
15 Kilpatrick	Y	N	N	N	Y	N
16 Dingell	Y	N	N	N	Y	Y
MINNESOTA						
1 ***Gutknecht***	Y	Y	Y	Y	N	N
2 Minge	Y	Y	N	Y	N	N
3 ***Ramstad***	Y	Y	Y	Y	Y	N
4 Vento	?	?	?	?	?	?
5 Sabo	Y	N	N	N	Y	N
6 Luther	Y	Y	N	Y	Y	N
7 Peterson	Y	Y	Y	N	Y	N
8 Oberstar	Y	N	N	N	Y	N
MISSISSIPPI						
1 ***Wicker***	Y	N	N	Y	N	Y
2 Thompson	Y	?	?	?	?	?
3 ***Pickering***	Y	Y	N	Y	N	Y
4 Shows	Y	N	N	Y	Y	Y
5 Taylor	Y	N	N	N	N	Y
MISSOURI						
1 Clay	Y	N	N	N	Y	N
2 ***Talent***	Y	N	N	Y	N	Y
3 Gephardt	Y	N	N	N	Y	Y
4 Skelton	Y	N	N	N	Y	Y
5 McCarthy	Y	N	N	N	Y	Y
6 Danner	Y	N	Y	N	Y	N
7 ***Blunt***	Y	N	N	Y	N	Y
8 ***Emerson***	Y	N	N	N	N	Y
9 ***Hulshof***	Y	Y	Y	Y	N	N
MONTANA						
AL ***Hill***	Y	N	Y	Y	N	N
NEBRASKA						
1 ***Bereuter***	Y	Y	N	N	N	N
2 ***Terry***	Y	Y	Y	Y	N	N
3 ***Barrett***	Y	Y	N	N	N	Y
NEVADA						
1 Berkley	Y	N	N	N	Y	Y
2 ***Gibbons***	Y	Y	N	Y	N	Y
NEW HAMPSHIRE						
1 ***Sununu***	N	Y	N	Y	N	N
2 ***Bass***	Y	Y	N	Y	N	Y
NEW JERSEY						
1 Andrews	Y	N	N	N	Y	Y
2 ***LoBiondo***	Y	N	N	Y	N	Y
3 ***Saxton***	Y	N	N	N	N	Y
4 ***Smith***	Y	N	N	N	N	Y
5 ***Roukema***	Y	N	N	Y	N	Y
6 Pallone	Y	N	N	N	Y	Y
7 ***Franks***	?	?	?	?	?	?
8 Pascrell	Y	N	N	N	Y	Y
9 Rothman	Y	N	N	N	Y	Y
10 Payne	Y	N	N	N	Y	N
11 ***Frelinghuysen***	Y	N	N	N	N	Y
12 Holt	Y	N	N	N	Y	N
13 Menendez	Y	N	N	N	Y	Y
NEW MEXICO						
1 ***Wilson***	Y	N	N	Y	N	Y
2 ***Skeen***	Y	N	N	N	N	Y
3 Udall	Y	N	N	Y	Y	N
NEW YORK						
1 Forbes	Y	N	N	N	Y	Y
2 ***Lazio***	Y	Y	N	Y	N	N
3 ***King***	Y	N	N	N	N	Y
4 McCarthy	Y	N	N	N	Y	Y
5 Ackerman	Y	N	N	N	Y	Y
6 Meeks	Y	N	N	N	Y	Y
7 Crowley	Y	N	N	N	Y	N
8 Nadler	Y	N	N	N	Y	N
9 Weiner	Y	?	?	?	?	?
10 Towns	Y	N	N	N	Y	N
11 Owens	Y	N	N	N	Y	N
12 Velázquez	Y	N	N	P	Y	N
13 ***Fossella***	Y	Y	N	Y	N	N
14 Maloney	Y	N	N	N	Y	N
15 Rangel	Y	N	N	N	?	Y
16 Serrano	Y	N	N	N	Y	N
17 Engel	Y	N	N	N	Y	Y
18 Lowey	Y	N	N	N	Y	Y
19 ***Kelly***	Y	N	N	Y	N	Y
20 ***Gilman***	Y	N	N	N	N	Y
21 McNulty	Y	N	N	N	?	?
22 ***Sweeney***	Y	N	N	Y	N	Y
23 ***Boehlert***	Y	N	N	N	N	Y
24 ***McHugh***	Y	N	N	N	N	Y
25 ***Walsh***	Y	N	N	N	N	?
26 Hinchey	Y	N	?	N	Y	N
27 ***Reynolds***	Y	N	N	Y	N	Y
28 Slaughter	Y	N	N	N	Y	N
29 LaFalce	Y	N	N	N	Y	Y
30 ***Quinn***	?	?	?	?	?	?
31 ***Houghton***	Y	Y	N	N	N	Y
NORTH CAROLINA						
1 Clayton	Y	N	N	N	Y	Y
2 Etheridge	Y	N	N	N	Y	Y
3 ***Jones***	Y	N	Y	Y	N	Y
4 Price	Y	N	N	N	Y	Y
5 ***Burr***	?	?	?	?	?	–
6 ***Coble***	Y	Y	N	Y	N	Y
7 McIntyre	Y	N	N	N	Y	Y
8 ***Hayes***	Y	N	N	Y	N	Y
9 ***Myrick***	N	Y	N	Y	N	Y
10 ***Ballenger***	Y	N	N	Y	N	Y
11 ***Taylor***	Y	N	N	N	N	Y
12 Watt	Y	N	N	N	Y	Y
NORTH DAKOTA						
AL Pomeroy	Y	N	N	N	Y	Y
OHIO						
1 ***Chabot***	N	Y	Y	Y	N	N
2 ***Portman***	Y	Y	N	Y	N	Y
3 Hall	Y	N	N	N	Y	N
4 ***Oxley***	Y	N	N	Y	N	Y
5 ***Gillmor***	Y	N	N	Y	N	Y
6 Strickland	Y	N	N	N	N	Y
7 ***Hobson***	Y	N	N	N	N	Y
8 ***Boehner***	Y	N	N	N	N	Y
9 Kaptur	Y	N	?	N	Y	N
10 Kucinich	Y	N	N	N	Y	N
11 Jones	Y	N	N	N	Y	N
12 ***Kasich***	N	Y	N	Y	N	Y
13 Brown	Y	N	N	N	Y	N
14 Sawyer	Y	N	N	N	Y	Y
15 ***Pryce***	Y	Y	N	N	N	Y
16 ***Regula***	Y	N	N	N	N	Y
17 Traficant	Y	N	N	N	N	Y
18 ***Ney***	Y	N	N	Y	N	Y
19 ***LaTourette***	Y	N	N	N	N	N
OKLAHOMA						
1 ***Largent***	Y	Y	Y	Y	N	?
2 ***Coburn***	N	Y	Y	Y	N	N
3 ***Watkins***	Y	N	N	Y	N	Y
4 ***Watts***	Y	N	N	Y	N	Y
5 ***Istook***	Y	N	?	Y	N	Y
6 ***Lucas***	Y	N	N	N	N	Y
OREGON						
1 Wu	Y	Y	N	N	Y	N
2 ***Walden***	Y	N	N	Y	N	Y
3 Blumenauer	Y	N	N	N	Y	N
4 DeFazio	Y	N	N	N	Y	N
5 Hooley	Y	N	N	N	Y	N
PENNSYLVANIA						
1 Brady	Y	N	N	N	Y	N
2 Fattah	Y	N	N	N	Y	N
3 Borski	Y	N	N	N	Y	Y
4 Klink	?	?	?	?	?	?
5 ***Peterson***	Y	N	N	N	N	Y
6 Holden	Y	N	N	N	Y	N
7 ***Weldon***	Y	N	N	Y	N	Y
8 ***Greenwood***	Y	Y	N	Y	N	Y
9 ***Shuster***	Y	N	N	N	N	Y
10 ***Sherwood***	Y	N	N	Y	N	Y
11 Kanjorski	Y	N	N	N	N	Y
12 Murtha	Y	N	N	N	N	Y
13 Hoeffel	Y	N	N	N	Y	Y
14 Coyne	Y	N	N	N	Y	N
15 ***Toomey***	Y	Y	Y	Y	N	Y
16 ***Pitts***	Y	Y	Y	Y	N	N
17 ***Gekas***	Y	Y	Y	N	N	N
18 Doyle	Y	N	N	N	Y	Y
19 ***Goodling***	Y	N	N	N	N	Y
20 Mascara	Y	N	N	N	Y	Y
21 ***English***	Y	Y	N	Y	N	Y
RHODE ISLAND						
1 Kennedy	Y	N	N	N	Y	Y
2 Weygand	?	N	N	N	Y	Y
SOUTH CAROLINA						
1 ***Sanford***	N	Y	Y	Y	N	N
2 ***Spence***	?	?	?	?	?	?
3 ***Graham***	N	Y	Y	Y	N	N
4 ***DeMint***	N	Y	Y	Y	N	N
5 Spratt	?	N	N	N	Y	Y
6 Clyburn	Y	N	N	N	Y	Y
SOUTH DAKOTA						
AL ***Thune***	Y	N	N	Y	N	Y
TENNESSEE						
1 ***Jenkins***	Y	N	N	N	N	Y
2 ***Duncan***	Y	Y	Y	Y	N	N
3 ***Wamp***	Y	N	N	N	N	Y
4 ***Hilleary***	Y	Y	Y	Y	N	Y
5 Clement	Y	N	N	N	Y	Y
6 Gordon	Y	N	N	N	Y	Y
7 ***Bryant***	Y	N	N	Y	N	Y
8 Tanner	Y	Y	N	N	Y	Y
9 Ford	Y	N	N	N	Y	Y
TEXAS						
1 Sandlin	Y	N	N	N	Y	Y
2 Turner	Y	Y	N	N	Y	Y
3 ***Johnson, Sam***	N	Y	N	Y	N	N
4 Hall	Y	Y	N	Y	Y	Y
5 ***Sessions***	Y	Y	N	Y	N	N
6 ***Barton***	N	Y	N	N	N	–
7 ***Archer***	N	Y	Y	Y	?	N
8 ***Brady***	Y	Y	N	Y	N	N
9 Lampson	Y	N	N	N	Y	Y
10 Doggett	Y	Y	N	Y	Y	N
11 Edwards	Y	N	N	N	Y	Y
12 ***Granger***	?	?	?	?	?	?
13 ***Thornberry***	Y	N	N	N	N	Y
14 ***Paul***	N	Y	Y	Y	N	N
15 Hinojosa	Y	N	N	N	Y	Y
16 Reyes	Y	N	N	N	Y	Y
17 Stenholm	Y	Y	N	N	Y	Y
18 Jackson-Lee	Y	N	N	N	Y	Y
19 ***Combest***	Y	N	Y	Y	N	N
20 Gonzalez	Y	N	N	N	Y	Y
21 ***Smith***	Y	N	N	Y	N	Y
22 ***DeLay***	N	N	N	Y	N	Y
23 ***Bonilla***	N	N	N	N	N	Y
24 Frost	Y	N	N	N	Y	Y
25 Bentsen	Y	N	N	Y	Y	Y
26 ***Armey***	Y	N	N	Y	N	Y
27 Ortiz	Y	N	N	N	Y	Y
28 Rodriguez	Y	N	N	N	Y	Y
29 Green	Y	N	N	N	Y	Y
30 Johnson, E.B.	Y	N	N	N	Y	Y
UTAH						
1 ***Hansen***	Y	N	N	Y	N	N
2 ***Cook***	Y	Y	Y	Y	N	N
3 ***Cannon***	N	N	Y	Y	N	N
VERMONT						
AL *Sanders*	Y	N	N	N	Y	N
VIRGINIA						
1 ***Bateman***	?	N	N	?	N	Y
2 Pickett	Y	N	N	N	N	Y
3 Scott	Y	N	N	N	Y	Y
4 Sisisky	Y	N	N	N	N	Y
5 *Goode*	Y	Y	N	Y	N	Y
6 ***Goodlatte***	Y	N	N	Y	N	N
7 ***Bliley***	Y	N	N	N	N	Y
8 Moran	Y	N	N	N	Y	Y
9 Boucher	Y	N	N	N	Y	Y
10 ***Wolf***	Y	N	N	N	N	Y
11 ***Davis***	Y	N	N	Y	N	Y
WASHINGTON						
1 Inslee	Y	Y	N	Y	Y	N
2 ***Metcalf***	Y	Y	Y	Y	N	Y
3 Baird	Y	N	N	N	Y	N
4 ***Hastings***	Y	Y	N	Y	N	Y
5 ***Nethercutt***	Y	N	N	N	N	Y
6 Dicks	Y	N	N	N	Y	Y
7 McDermott	Y	N	N	N	+	N
8 ***Dunn***	Y	N	N	N	N	N
9 Smith	Y	Y	N	Y	Y	Y
WEST VIRGINIA						
1 Mollohan	Y	N	N	N	Y	Y
2 Wise	Y	N	N	N	Y	Y
3 Rahall	Y	N	N	N	Y	Y
WISCONSIN						
1 ***Ryan***	Y	Y	N	Y	N	N
2 Baldwin	Y	N	N	N	Y	N
3 Kind	Y	Y	N	Y	Y	N
4 Kleczka	Y	Y	N	Y	Y	N
5 Barrett	Y	N	N	Y	Y	N
6 ***Petri***	Y	Y	Y	Y	N	N
7 Obey	Y	N	N	N	Y	N
8 ***Green***	Y	Y	N	Y	N	Y
9 ***Sensenbrenner***	Y	Y	Y	Y	N	N
WYOMING						
AL ***Cubin***	Y	Y	N	Y	N	N

Southern states - Ala., Ark., Fla., Ga., Ky., La., Miss., N.C., Okla., S.C., Tenn., Texas, Va.

96. HR 1089. Mutual Fund Reporting/Passage. Gillmor, R-Ohio, motion to suspend the rules and pass the bill to direct the Securities and Exchange Commission, within 18 months, to require mutual fund companies to disclose after-tax returns to investors in their annual reports. Motion agreed to 358-2: R 184-2; D 172-0 (ND 128-0, SD 44-0); I 2-0. A two-thirds majority of those present and voting (240 in this case) is required for passage under suspension of the rules. April 3, 2000.

97. HR 3591. Reagan Gold Medal/Passage. Bachus, R-Ala., motion to suspend the rules and pass the bill awarding gold medals, on behalf of Congress, to former President Ronald Reagan and former first lady Nancy Reagan. Motion agreed to 350-8: R 184-1; D 164-7 (ND 121-6, SD 43-1); I 2-0. A two-thirds majority of those present and voting (239 in this case) is required for passage under suspension of the rules. April 3, 2000.

98. HR 2418. Organ Procurement/HHS Review. LaHood, R-Ill., amendment that would specify that the rules and policies of the Organ Procurement and Transplantation Network are subject to Department of Health and Human Services review and approval. Rejected 160-260: R 32-180; D 127-79 (ND 116-36, SD 11-43); I 1-1. April 4, 2000. A "yea" was a vote in support of the president's position.

99. HR 2418. Organ Procurement/Children's Needs. DeGette, D-Colo., amendment that would ensure the organ transplantation system recognizes the unique health care needs of child transplant recipients. Adopted 420-0: R 212-0; D 206-0 (ND 152-0, SD 54-0); I 2-0. April 4, 2000.

100. HR 2418. Organ Procurement/State Pre-emption. Luther, D-Minn., amendment that would prohibit state or local law from pre-empting Organ Procurement and Transplantation Network policies. It would pre-empt state laws that give priority to state residents over out-of-state residents. Rejected 137-284: R 22-190; D 114-93 (ND 108-45, SD 6-48); I 1-1. April 4, 2000.

101. HR 2418. Organ Procurement/Passage. Passage of the bill that would authorize the Organ Procurement and Transplantation Network to make decisions about organ distribution to patients. The bill, as amended, would nullify the Department of Health and Human Services' rule giving that department final authority over organ allocation policies. It also would create new incentives for people to become organ donors. Passed 275-147: R 187-26; D 87-120 (ND 43-110, SD 44-10); I 1-1. April 4, 2000. A "nay" was a vote in support of the president's position.

102. HR 3660. Abortion Procedure Ban/Rule. Adoption of the rule (H Res 457) to provide for House floor consideration of the bill that would ban a certain medical procedure used in some late-term abortions. Adopted 244-179: R 202-14; D 41-164 (ND 30-122, SD 11-42); I 1-1. April 5, 2000.

103. HR 3660. Abortion Procedure Ban/Recommit. Frank, D-Mass., motion to recommit the bill to the House Judiciary Committee with instructions to have the committee report the bill back to the House with language providing for an exception to the ban when necessary to avoid serious, long-term health consequences to the woman. Motion rejected 140-289: R 17-200; D 123-87 (ND 95-61, SD 28-26); I 0-2. April 5, 2000.

Key

Y Voted for (yea).
\# Paired for.
\+ Announced for.
N Voted against (nay).
X Paired against.
– Announced against.
P Voted "present."
C Voted "present" to avoid possible conflict of interest.
? Did not vote or otherwise make a position known.

•

Democrats ***Republicans***
Independents

	96	97	98	99	100	101	102	103
ALABAMA								
1 ***Callahan***	?	?	N	Y	N	Y	Y	N
2 ***Everett***	Y	Y	N	Y	N	Y	Y	N
3 ***Riley***	Y	Y	N	Y	N	Y	Y	N
4 ***Aderholt***	Y	Y	N	Y	N	Y	Y	N
5 Cramer	Y	Y	N	Y	N	Y	N	N
6 ***Bachus***	Y	Y	N	Y	N	Y	Y	N
7 Hilliard	?	?	N	Y	N	Y	N	Y
ALASKA								
AL ***Young***	Y	Y	N	Y	N	Y	Y	N
ARIZONA								
1 ***Salmon***	Y	Y	N	Y	N	Y	Y	N
2 Pastor	Y	Y	N	Y	N	Y	N	Y
3 ***Stump***	Y	Y	N	Y	N	Y	Y	N
4 ***Shadegg***	Y	Y	N	Y	N	Y	Y	N
5 ***Kolbe***	Y	Y	N	Y	N	Y	N	Y
6 ***Hayworth***	Y	Y	N	Y	N	Y	Y	N
ARKANSAS								
1 Berry	Y	Y	N	Y	N	Y	Y	N
2 Snyder	Y	Y	N	Y	Y	Y	N	Y
3 ***Hutchinson***	Y	Y	N	Y	N	Y	Y	N
4 ***Dickey***	Y	Y	N	Y	N	Y	Y	N
CALIFORNIA								
1 Thompson	Y	Y	Y	Y	Y	N	N	N
2 ***Herger***	Y	Y	N	Y	N	Y	Y	N
3 ***Ose***	Y	Y	N	Y	N	Y	N	Y
4 ***Doolittle***	?	?	N	Y	N	Y	Y	N
5 Matsui	Y	Y	Y	Y	Y	Y	N	Y
6 Woolsey	Y	Y	Y	Y	Y	N	N	Y
7 Miller, George	?	?	Y	Y	Y	N	N	Y
8 Pelosi	?	?	Y	?	Y	N	N	Y
9 Lee	Y	N	Y	Y	Y	N	N	N
10 Tauscher	Y	Y	Y	Y	N	N	N	Y
11 ***Pombo***	Y	Y	N	Y	N	Y	Y	N
12 Lantos	Y	Y	Y	Y	Y	N	N	Y
13 Stark	Y	N	Y	Y	Y	N	N	N
14 Eshoo	?	?	Y	Y	Y	N	N	Y
15 ***Campbell***	?	?	?	?	?	?	?	?
16 Lofgren	?	?	Y	Y	Y	N	N	N
17 Farr	Y	Y	Y	Y	Y	N	N	Y
18 Condit	Y	Y	Y	Y	N	N	N	N
19 ***Radanovich***	Y	Y	Y	Y	N	Y	Y	N
20 Dooley	?	?	Y	Y	Y	N	N	Y
21 ***Thomas***	Y	+	N	Y	N	Y	Y	N
22 Capps	Y	Y	Y	Y	Y	N	N	Y
23 ***Gallegly***	Y	Y	N	Y	N	Y	Y	N
24 Sherman	Y	Y	Y	Y	Y	N	N	Y
25 ***McKeon***	Y	Y	N	Y	N	Y	Y	N
26 Berman	?	?	Y	Y	Y	N	N	Y
27 ***Rogan***	Y	Y	N	Y	N	Y	Y	N
28 ***Dreier***	Y	Y	Y	Y	Y	Y	Y	N
29 Waxman	?	?	Y	Y	Y	N	N	Y
30 Becerra	Y	Y	Y	Y	Y	N	N	Y
31 Martinez	?	?	?	?	?	?	?	N
32 Dixon	Y	Y	Y	Y	Y	N	N	Y
33 Roybal-Allard	?	?	Y	Y	Y	N	N	Y
34 Napolitano	Y	Y	Y	Y	Y	N	N	Y
35 Waters	Y	N	Y	Y	Y	N	N	Y
36 ***Kuykendall***	Y	Y	N	Y	N	Y	N	N
37 Millender-McD.	Y	Y	Y	Y	Y	N	N	Y
38 ***Horn***	Y	Y	Y	Y	N	Y	N	Y
39 ***Royce***	Y	Y	N	Y	N	Y	Y	N
40 ***Lewis***	Y	Y	N	Y	N	Y	Y	N
41 ***Miller, Gary***	Y	Y	N	Y	N	Y	Y	N
42 Baca	Y	Y	Y	Y	N	N	N	Y
43 ***Calvert***	Y	Y	N	Y	N	Y	Y	N
44 ***Bono***	Y	Y	Y	Y	N	Y	Y	N
45 ***Rohrabacher***	Y	Y	N	Y	N	Y	Y	N
46 Sanchez	Y	Y	Y	Y	Y	N	N	N
47 ***Cox***	Y	Y	N	Y	N	Y	Y	?
48 ***Packard***	Y	Y	N	Y	N	Y	Y	N
49 ***Bilbray***	Y	Y	N	Y	N	Y	N	Y
50 Filner	Y	Y	Y	Y	Y	N	N	Y
51 ***Cunningham***	Y	Y	N	Y	N	Y	Y	N
52 ***Hunter***	?	?	Y	Y	N	Y	Y	N
COLORADO								
1 DeGette	Y	Y	Y	Y	Y	Y	N	N
2 Udall	Y	Y	Y	Y	Y	N	N	N
3 ***McInnis***	Y	Y	N	Y	N	Y	Y	N
4 ***Schaffer***	Y	Y	N	Y	N	Y	Y	N
5 ***Hefley***	Y	Y	N	Y	N	Y	Y	N
6 ***Tancredo***	Y	Y	N	Y	N	Y	Y	N
CONNECTICUT								
1 Larson	Y	Y	Y	Y	Y	N	N	Y
2 Gejdenson	Y	Y	Y	Y	Y	N	N	Y
3 DeLauro	Y	Y	Y	Y	Y	N	N	Y
4 ***Shays***	Y	Y	N	Y	Y	Y	Y	Y
5 Maloney	Y	Y	Y	Y	Y	N	N	Y
6 ***Johnson***	Y	Y	N	Y	Y	Y	N	Y
DELAWARE								
AL ***Castle***	Y	Y	Y	Y	Y	N	N	Y
FLORIDA								
1 ***Scarborough***	?	?	N	Y	N	Y	Y	N
2 Boyd	Y	Y	N	Y	N	Y	N	Y
3 Brown	Y	Y	N	Y	N	N	N	N
4 ***Fowler***	?	?	N	Y	N	Y	Y	N
5 Thurman	?	?	N	Y	N	Y	N	Y
6 ***Stearns***	Y	Y	N	Y	N	Y	Y	N
7 ***Mica***	Y	Y	N	Y	N	Y	Y	N
8 ***McCollum***	?	?	N	Y	N	Y	Y	N
9 ***Bilirakis***	Y	Y	N	Y	N	Y	Y	N
10 ***Young***	?	?	N	Y	N	Y	Y	N
11 Davis	?	?	N	Y	N	Y	N	Y
12 ***Canady***	Y	Y	N	Y	N	Y	Y	N
13 ***Miller***	Y	Y	N	Y	N	Y	Y	N
14 ***Goss***	Y	Y	N	Y	N	Y	Y	N
15 ***Weldon***	Y	Y	N	Y	N	Y	Y	N
16 ***Foley***	Y	Y	N	Y	N	Y	Y	N
17 Meek	Y	Y	N	Y	N	Y	?	N
18 ***Ros-Lehtinen***	Y	Y	N	Y	N	Y	Y	N
19 Wexler	Y	Y	N	Y	N	Y	N	Y
20 Deutsch	Y	Y	N	Y	N	Y	N	N
21 ***Diaz-Balart***	?	?	?	?	?	?	Y	N
22 ***Shaw***	Y	Y	N	Y	N	Y	Y	N
23 Hastings	Y	N	N	Y	N	N	N	N
GEORGIA								
1 ***Kingston***	Y	Y	N	Y	N	Y	Y	N
2 Bishop	Y	Y	N	Y	N	Y	Y	N
3 ***Collins***	Y	Y	N	Y	N	Y	Y	N
4 McKinney	Y	Y	N	Y	N	Y	N	Y
5 Lewis	Y	Y	N	Y	N	Y	N	Y
6 ***Isakson***	Y	Y	N	Y	N	Y	Y	N
7 ***Barr***	Y	Y	N	Y	N	Y	Y	N
8 ***Chambliss***	Y	Y	N	Y	N	Y	Y	N
9 ***Deal***	Y	Y	N	Y	N	Y	Y	N
10 ***Norwood***	Y	Y	N	Y	N	Y	Y	N
11 ***Linder***	Y	Y	N	Y	N	Y	Y	N
HAWAII								
1 Abercrombie	Y	Y	N	Y	N	Y	N	Y
2 Mink	Y	Y	N	Y	N	Y	N	Y
IDAHO								
1 ***Chenoweth-Hage***	Y	Y	N	Y	N	Y	Y	N
2 ***Simpson***	Y	Y	N	Y	N	Y	Y	N
ILLINOIS								
1 Rush	Y	Y	Y	Y	Y	N	N	Y
2 Jackson	Y	Y	Y	Y	Y	N	N	Y
3 Lipinski	Y	Y	Y	Y	Y	N	Y	N
4 Gutierrez	Y	P	Y	Y	Y	N	N	Y
5 Blagojevich	Y	Y	Y	Y	Y	N	N	Y
6 ***Hyde***	Y	Y	Y	Y	N	N	Y	N
7 Davis	Y	Y	Y	Y	Y	N	N	Y
8 ***Crane***	?	?	?	?	?	?	?	?
9 Schakowsky	Y	Y	Y	Y	Y	N	N	N
10 ***Porter***	Y	Y	Y	Y	Y	N	N	Y
11 ***Weller***	Y	Y	Y	Y	N	N	Y	N
12 Costello	Y	Y	Y	Y	Y	N	Y	N
13 ***Biggert***	Y	Y	Y	Y	Y	N	Y	N

ND Northern Democrats SD Southern Democrats

	96	97	98	99	100	101	102	103
14 ***Hastert***								
15 ***Ewing***	Y	Y	Y	Y	N	Y	Y	N
16 ***Manzullo***	?	?	N	Y	N	Y	Y	N
17 Evans	Y	Y	Y	Y	Y	N	N	Y
18 ***LaHood***	Y	Y	Y	Y	Y	N	Y	N
19 Phelps	Y	Y	Y	Y	Y	N	Y	N
20 ***Shimkus***	Y	Y	Y	Y	N	N	Y	N
INDIANA								
1 Visclosky	Y	Y	Y	Y	Y	N	N	N
2 ***McIntosh***	?	?	N	Y	N	Y	Y	N
3 Roemer	Y	Y	N	Y	N	N	Y	N
4 ***Souder***	?	?	N	Y	N	Y	Y	N
5 ***Buyer***	Y	Y	N	Y	N	Y	N	N
6 ***Burton***	Y	Y	N	Y	N	Y	Y	N
7 ***Pease***	Y	Y	N	Y	N	Y	Y	N
8 ***Hostettler***	Y	Y	N	Y	N	Y	Y	N
9 Hill	Y	Y	N	Y	N	Y	N	Y
10 Carson	?	?	Y	Y	Y	N	N	Y
IOWA								
1 ***Leach***	Y	Y	N	Y	N	Y	Y	N
2 ***Nussle***	Y	Y	N	Y	?	Y	Y	N
3 Boswell	Y	Y	N	Y	N	Y	Y	N
4 ***Ganske***	Y	Y	N	Y	N	Y	Y	N
5 ***Latham***	Y	Y	N	Y	N	Y	Y	N
KANSAS								
1 ***Moran***	Y	Y	N	Y	N	Y	Y	N
2 ***Ryun***	Y	Y	N	Y	N	Y	Y	N
3 Moore	Y	Y	N	Y	N	Y	N	N
4 ***Tiahrt***	Y	Y	N	Y	N	Y	Y	N
KENTUCKY								
1 ***Whitfield***	Y	Y	N	Y	N	Y	Y	N
2 ***Lewis***	Y	Y	N	Y	N	Y	Y	N
3 ***Northup***	?	?	–	+	–	Y	Y	N
4 Lucas	Y	Y	N	Y	N	Y	Y	N
5 ***Rogers***	Y	Y	N	Y	N	Y	Y	N
6 ***Fletcher***	Y	Y	N	Y	N	Y	Y	N
LOUISIANA								
1 ***Vitter***	Y	Y	N	Y	N	Y	Y	N
2 Jefferson	Y	Y	N	Y	N	Y	N	N
3 ***Tauzin***	Y	Y	N	Y	N	Y	Y	N
4 ***McCrery***	Y	Y	N	Y	N	Y	Y	N
5 ***Cooksey***	?	?	N	Y	N	Y	Y	N
6 ***Baker***	Y	Y	N	Y	N	Y	Y	N
7 John	Y	Y	N	Y	N	Y	Y	N
MAINE								
1 Allen	Y	Y	N	Y	Y	Y	N	N
2 Baldacci	Y	Y	N	Y	Y	Y	N	Y
MARYLAND								
1 ***Gilchrest***	Y	Y	Y	Y	Y	N	Y	N
2 ***Ehrlich***	Y	Y	Y	Y	N	N	Y	N
3 Cardin	Y	Y	Y	Y	Y	N	N	Y
4 Wynn	Y	Y	Y	Y	Y	N	N	Y
5 Hoyer	Y	Y	Y	Y	Y	N	N	Y
6 ***Bartlett***	Y	Y	Y	Y	N	N	Y	N
7 Cummings	Y	Y	Y	Y	Y	N	N	Y
8 ***Morella***	Y	Y	Y	Y	Y	N	?	Y
MASSACHUSETTS								
1 Olver	Y	Y	Y	Y	Y	N	N	Y
2 Neal	?	?	Y	Y	Y	N	N	N
3 McGovern	Y	Y	Y	Y	N	Y	N	Y
4 Frank	Y	Y	Y	Y	Y	N	N	Y
5 Meehan	Y	Y	Y	Y	Y	N	N	Y
6 Tierney	Y	Y	Y	Y	Y	N	N	Y
7 Markey	Y	Y	Y	Y	Y	N	?	Y
8 Capuano	Y	Y	Y	Y	Y	N	N	Y
9 Moakley	Y	Y	Y	Y	Y	N	N	N
10 Delahunt	Y	Y	Y	Y	Y	N	N	Y
MICHIGAN								
1 Stupak	?	?	Y	Y	Y	N	Y	N
2 ***Hoekstra***	Y	Y	N	Y	N	Y	Y	N
3 ***Ehlers***	Y	Y	N	Y	N	Y	Y	N
4 ***Camp***	Y	Y	N	Y	N	Y	Y	N
5 Barcia	Y	Y	N	Y	N	Y	Y	N
6 ***Upton***	Y	Y	N	Y	N	Y	Y	N
7 ***Smith***	Y	Y	N	Y	N	Y	Y	N
8 Stabenow	Y	Y	Y	Y	Y	N	N	Y
9 Kildee	Y	Y	Y	Y	Y	N	N	Y
10 Bonior	Y	Y	Y	Y	Y	N	N	Y
11 ***Knollenberg***	Y	Y	N	Y	N	Y	Y	N
12 Levin	Y	Y	Y	Y	Y	N	N	Y
13 Rivers	Y	Y	N	Y	N	N	N	Y
14 Conyers	?	?	Y	Y	N	N	N	Y
15 Kilpatrick	+	+	N	Y	N	Y	N	N
16 Dingell	Y	Y	Y	Y	Y	N	Y	N

	96	97	98	99	100	101	102	103
MINNESOTA								
1 ***Gutknecht***	Y	Y	N	Y	N	Y	Y	N
2 Minge	Y	Y	N	Y	Y	N	Y	N
3 ***Ramstad***	Y	Y	N	Y	N	Y	Y	N
4 Vento	?	?	?	?	?	?	?	?
5 Sabo	Y	Y	Y	Y	Y	N	N	Y
6 Luther	Y	Y	Y	Y	Y	N	N	Y
7 Peterson	Y	Y	N	Y	N	N	Y	N
8 Oberstar	Y	Y	Y	Y	Y	N	?	N
MISSISSIPPI								
1 ***Wicker***	Y	Y	N	Y	N	Y	Y	N
2 Thompson	Y	Y	Y	Y	Y	N	N	Y
3 ***Pickering***	?	?	N	Y	N	Y	Y	N
4 Shows	?	?	N	Y	N	Y	Y	N
5 Taylor	Y	Y	N	Y	N	Y	Y	N
MISSOURI								
1 Clay	Y	N	Y	Y	Y	N	N	Y
2 ***Talent***	Y	Y	N	Y	N	Y	Y	N
3 Gephardt	Y	Y	Y	Y	Y	Y	N	Y
4 Skelton	Y	Y	N	Y	N	Y	Y	N
5 McCarthy	Y	Y	Y	Y	Y	N	N	Y
6 Danner	Y	Y	N	Y	N	Y	Y	N
7 ***Blunt***	Y	Y	N	Y	N	Y	Y	N
8 ***Emerson***	Y	Y	N	Y	N	Y	Y	N
9 ***Hulshof***	Y	Y	N	Y	N	Y	Y	N
MONTANA								
AL ***Hill***	Y	Y	N	Y	N	Y	Y	N
NEBRASKA								
1 ***Bereuter***	Y	Y	Y	Y	Y	N	Y	N
2 ***Terry***	Y	Y	N	Y	Y	N	Y	N
3 ***Barrett***	Y	Y	Y	Y	Y	N	Y	N
NEVADA								
1 Berkley	Y	Y	N	Y	N	Y	N	Y
2 ***Gibbons***	Y	Y	N	Y	N	Y	Y	N
NEW HAMPSHIRE								
1 ***Sununu***	Y	Y	N	Y	N	Y	Y	N
2 ***Bass***	Y	Y	N	Y	N	Y	Y	Y
NEW JERSEY								
1 Andrews	Y	Y	N	Y	N	Y	N	Y
2 ***LoBiondo***	Y	Y	N	Y	N	Y	Y	N
3 ***Saxton***	Y	Y	N	Y	N	Y	Y	N
4 ***Smith***	Y	Y	N	Y	N	Y	Y	N
5 ***Roukema***	?	?	?	Y	N	Y	Y	N
6 Pallone	Y	Y	N	Y	N	Y	N	Y
7 ***Franks***	?	?	N	Y	N	Y	Y	N
8 Pascrell	Y	Y	N	Y	N	Y	N	N
9 Rothman	Y	Y	N	Y	N	Y	N	Y
10 Payne	?	?	Y	Y	Y	N	N	Y
11 ***Frelinghuysen***	Y	Y	N	Y	N	Y	Y	N
12 Holt	Y	Y	N	Y	N	Y	N	Y
13 Menendez	Y	Y	N	Y	N	Y	N	Y
NEW MEXICO								
1 ***Wilson***	Y	Y	N	Y	N	Y	Y	N
2 ***Skeen***	Y	Y	N	Y	N	Y	Y	N
3 Udall	Y	Y	Y	Y	Y	N	N	N
NEW YORK								
1 Forbes	Y	Y	Y	Y	Y	N	Y	N
2 ***Lazio***	Y	Y	N	Y	N	Y	Y	N
3 ***King***	Y	Y	Y	Y	N	N	Y	N
4 McCarthy	Y	Y	Y	Y	N	N	N	Y
5 Ackerman	Y	Y	Y	Y	Y	N	N	Y
6 Meeks	Y	N	Y	Y	Y	N	N	Y
7 Crowley	Y	Y	Y	Y	Y	N	N	Y
8 Nadler	Y	N	Y	Y	Y	N	N	N
9 Weiner	Y	Y	Y	Y	Y	N	N	Y
10 Towns	Y	Y	Y	Y	Y	N	N	Y
11 Owens	?	?	Y	Y	Y	N	N	Y
12 Velázquez	Y	Y	Y	Y	N	N	N	N
13 ***Fossella***	Y	Y	N	Y	N	Y	Y	N
14 Maloney	Y	Y	Y	Y	N	N	N	Y
15 Rangel	?	?	Y	Y	Y	N	N	Y
16 Serrano	Y	Y	Y	Y	Y	N	N	Y
17 Engel	Y	Y	Y	Y	Y	N	N	Y
18 Lowey	Y	Y	Y	Y	Y	N	N	N
19 ***Kelly***	Y	Y	N	Y	N	Y	N	Y
20 ***Gilman***	Y	Y	N	Y	N	Y	N	Y
21 McNulty	Y	Y	Y	Y	Y	Y	Y	N
22 ***Sweeney***	?	?	N	Y	N	Y	Y	N
23 ***Boehlert***	Y	Y	Y	Y	Y	N	N	Y
24 ***McHugh***	Y	Y	N	Y	N	Y	Y	N
25 ***Walsh***	Y	Y	N	Y	N	Y	Y	N
26 Hinchey	Y	Y	Y	Y	Y	N	N	N
27 ***Reynolds***	Y	Y	N	Y	N	Y	Y	N
28 Slaughter	Y	Y	Y	Y	Y	N	N	N
29 LaFalce	Y	Y	Y	Y	N	Y	Y	N

	96	97	98	99	100	101	102	103
30 ***Quinn***	Y	Y	Y	Y	Y	?	Y	N
31 ***Houghton***	Y	Y	Y	Y	N	Y	Y	N
NORTH CAROLINA								
1 Clayton	Y	Y	Y	Y	Y	N	N	N
2 Etheridge	Y	Y	Y	Y	Y	N	N	Y
3 ***Jones***	Y	Y	N	Y	N	Y	Y	N
4 Price	?	?	Y	Y	Y	N	N	Y
5 ***Burr***	Y	Y	N	Y	N	Y	Y	N
6 ***Coble***	Y	Y	N	Y	N	Y	Y	N
7 McIntyre	Y	Y	Y	Y	Y	N	Y	N
8 ***Hayes***	Y	Y	N	Y	N	Y	Y	N
9 ***Myrick***	?	?	?	?	?	?	?	N
10 ***Ballenger***	Y	Y	N	Y	N	Y	Y	N
11 ***Taylor***	+	+	N	Y	N	Y	Y	N
12 Watt	Y	Y	Y	Y	N	N	N	Y
NORTH DAKOTA								
AL Pomeroy	Y	Y	Y	Y	Y	N	N	N
OHIO								
1 ***Chabot***	Y	Y	N	Y	N	Y	Y	N
2 ***Portman***	Y	Y	N	Y	N	Y	Y	N
3 Hall	Y	Y	Y	Y	N	N	Y	N
4 ***Oxley***	Y	Y	N	Y	N	Y	Y	N
5 ***Gillmor***	Y	Y	N	Y	N	Y	Y	N
6 Strickland	Y	Y	Y	Y	Y	N	N	N
7 ***Hobson***	?	?	N	Y	N	Y	Y	N
8 ***Boehner***	Y	Y	N	Y	N	Y	Y	N
9 Kaptur	Y	Y	P	Y	N	Y	N	N
10 Kucinich	Y	Y	Y	Y	N	N	Y	N
11 Jones	Y	Y	Y	Y	Y	N	N	Y
12 ***Kasich***	Y	Y	N	Y	N	Y	Y	N
13 Brown	?	?	Y	Y	Y	N	N	Y
14 Sawyer	Y	Y	Y	Y	Y	N	N	Y
15 ***Pryce***	?	?	N	Y	N	Y	Y	Y
16 ***Regula***	Y	Y	Y	Y	N	Y	Y	N
17 Traficant	Y	Y	N	Y	N	Y	Y	N
18 ***Ney***	Y	Y	N	Y	N	Y	Y	N
19 ***LaTourette***	Y	Y	N	Y	N	Y	Y	N
OKLAHOMA								
1 ***Largent***	Y	Y	N	Y	N	Y	Y	N
2 ***Coburn***	?	?	N	Y	N	Y	Y	Y
3 ***Watkins***	Y	Y	N	Y	N	Y	Y	N
4 ***Watts***	?	?	N	Y	N	Y	Y	N
5 ***Istook***	Y	Y	N	Y	N	Y	Y	N
6 ***Lucas***	Y	Y	N	Y	N	Y	Y	N
OREGON								
1 Wu	Y	Y	N	Y	N	Y	N	Y
2 ***Walden***	Y	Y	N	Y	Y	Y	Y	N
3 Blumenauer	Y	Y	N	Y	Y	Y	N	Y
4 DeFazio	Y	Y	N	Y	N	Y	N	N
5 Hooley	Y	Y	N	Y	N	Y	N	Y
PENNSYLVANIA								
1 Brady	?	?	?	?	?	?	N	Y
2 Fattah	?	?	?	?	?	?	N	Y
3 Borski	?	?	Y	Y	Y	N	Y	N
4 Klink	?	?	Y	Y	Y	N	?	N
5 ***Peterson***	Y	Y	Y	Y	Y	N	Y	N
6 Holden	Y	Y	Y	Y	Y	N	Y	N
7 ***Weldon***	?	?	Y	Y	N	N	Y	N
8 ***Greenwood***	?	?	?	?	?	?	N	Y
9 ***Shuster***	?	?	?	?	?	?	Y	N
10 ***Sherwood***	Y	Y	Y	Y	Y	N	Y	N
11 Kanjorski	Y	Y	Y	Y	Y	N	Y	N
12 Murtha	?	?	Y	Y	Y	N	Y	N
13 Hoeffel	Y	Y	Y	Y	Y	N	N	Y
14 Coyne	?	?	Y	Y	Y	N	N	Y
15 ***Toomey***	Y	Y	Y	Y	Y	N	Y	N
16 ***Pitts***	Y	Y	N	Y	N	Y	Y	N
17 ***Gekas***	Y	Y	Y	Y	Y	N	Y	N
18 Doyle	?	?	Y	Y	Y	N	Y	N
19 ***Goodling***	?	?	Y	Y	Y	N	Y	N
20 Mascara	Y	Y	Y	Y	Y	N	Y	N
21 ***English***	Y	Y	Y	Y	Y	N	Y	N
RHODE ISLAND								
1 Kennedy	Y	Y	Y	Y	Y	N	N	Y
2 Weygand	?	?	Y	Y	Y	N	Y	N
SOUTH CAROLINA								
1 ***Sanford***	N	Y	N	Y	N	Y	Y	N
2 ***Spence***	Y	Y	N	Y	N	Y	Y	N
3 ***Graham***	?	?	N	Y	N	Y	Y	N
4 ***DeMint***	Y	Y	N	Y	N	Y	Y	N
5 Spratt	Y	Y	N	Y	N	Y	N	Y
6 Clyburn	Y	Y	N	Y	N	Y	N	Y
SOUTH DAKOTA								
AL ***Thune***	Y	Y	N	Y	N	Y	Y	N

	96	97	98	99	100	101	102	103
TENNESSEE								
1 ***Jenkins***	Y	Y	N	Y	N	Y	Y	N
2 ***Duncan***	Y	Y	N	Y	N	Y	Y	N
3 ***Wamp***	Y	Y	N	Y	N	Y	Y	N
4 ***Hilleary***	?	?	N	Y	N	Y	Y	N
5 Clement	Y	Y	N	Y	N	Y	Y	N
6 Gordon	Y	Y	N	Y	N	Y	N	Y
7 ***Bryant***	Y	Y	N	Y	N	Y	Y	N
8 Tanner	Y	Y	N	Y	N	Y	N	N
9 Ford	Y	Y	N	Y	N	Y	N	N
TEXAS								
1 Sandlin	Y	Y	N	Y	N	Y	N	Y
2 Turner	Y	Y	N	Y	N	Y	N	N
3 ***Johnson, Sam***	Y	Y	N	Y	N	Y	Y	N
4 Hall	Y	Y	N	Y	N	Y	Y	N
5 ***Sessions***	Y	Y	Y	Y	Y	N	Y	N
6 ***Barton***	?	?	N	Y	N	Y	Y	N
7 ***Archer***	Y	Y	N	Y	N	Y	Y	N
8 ***Brady***	Y	Y	N	Y	N	Y	Y	N
9 Lampson	?	?	N	Y	N	Y	N	N
10 Doggett	Y	Y	Y	Y	N	N	N	N
11 Edwards	Y	Y	N	Y	N	Y	N	Y
12 ***Granger***	Y	Y	N	Y	N	Y	Y	N
13 ***Thornberry***	Y	Y	N	Y	N	Y	Y	N
14 ***Paul***	N	N	N	Y	N	N	Y	N
15 Hinojosa	Y	Y	N	Y	N	Y	N	Y
16 Reyes	Y	Y	N	Y	N	Y	N	Y
17 Stenholm	Y	Y	Y	Y	N	N	Y	N
18 Jackson-Lee	Y	Y	N	Y	N	Y	N	Y
19 ***Combest***	Y	Y	N	Y	N	Y	Y	N
20 Gonzalez	?	?	N	Y	N	Y	N	Y
21 ***Smith***	Y	Y	N	Y	N	Y	Y	N
22 ***DeLay***	Y	Y	N	Y	N	Y	Y	N
23 ***Bonilla***	Y	Y	N	Y	N	Y	Y	N
24 Frost	?	?	Y	Y	N	Y	N	Y
25 Bentsen	Y	Y	N	Y	N	Y	N	Y
26 ***Armey***	Y	Y	N	Y	N	Y	Y	N
27 Ortiz	?	?	N	Y	N	Y	N	N
28 Rodriguez	Y	Y	Y	Y	N	Y	N	Y
29 Green	Y	Y	N	Y	N	Y	N	Y
30 Johnson, E.B.	Y	Y	Y	Y	Y	Y	N	N
UTAH								
1 ***Hansen***	?	?	N	Y	N	N	Y	N
2 ***Cook***	?	?	?	?	?	?	?	?
3 ***Cannon***	?	?	N	Y	N	Y	Y	N
VERMONT								
AL *Sanders*	Y	Y	Y	Y	Y	N	N	N
VIRGINIA								
1 ***Bateman***	Y	Y	N	Y	N	Y	Y	N
2 Pickett	Y	Y	N	Y	N	Y	N	N
3 Scott	Y	Y	N	Y	N	Y	N	Y
4 Sisisky	Y	Y	N	Y	N	Y	Y	N
5 *Goode*	Y	Y	N	Y	N	Y	Y	N
6 ***Goodlatte***	Y	Y	N	Y	N	Y	Y	N
7 ***Bliley***	Y	Y	N	+	N	Y	Y	N
8 Moran	?	?	N	Y	N	Y	N	Y
9 Boucher	Y	Y	N	Y	N	N	N	Y
10 ***Wolf***	Y	Y	N	Y	N	Y	Y	N
11 ***Davis***	Y	Y	N	Y	N	Y	Y	N
WASHINGTON								
1 Inslee	Y	Y	N	Y	Y	Y	N	Y
2 ***Metcalf***	Y	Y	N	Y	N	Y	Y	N
3 Baird	Y	Y	N	Y	N	Y	N	Y
4 ***Hastings***	Y	Y	N	Y	N	Y	Y	N
5 ***Nethercutt***	Y	Y	N	Y	N	Y	Y	N
6 Dicks	Y	Y	Y	Y	Y	Y	N	Y
7 McDermott	Y	Y	Y	Y	N	Y	N	Y
8 ***Dunn***	Y	Y	N	Y	N	Y	Y	N
9 Smith	Y	Y	Y	Y	N	Y	N	Y
WEST VIRGINIA								
1 Mollohan	Y	Y	Y	Y	Y	N	Y	N
2 Wise	?	?	N	Y	Y	N	N	Y
3 Rahall	?	?	Y	Y	Y	N	Y	N
WISCONSIN								
1 ***Ryan***	Y	Y	N	Y	N	Y	Y	N
2 Baldwin	Y	Y	N	Y	N	Y	N	N
3 Kind	Y	Y	Y	Y	N	Y	N	Y
4 Kleczka	Y	Y	N	Y	N	Y	Y	N
5 Barrett	Y	Y	N	Y	N	Y	N	Y
6 ***Petri***	Y	Y	N	Y	N	Y	Y	N
7 Obey	Y	Y	Y	Y	N	Y	N	Y
8 ***Green***	Y	Y	N	Y	N	Y	Y	N
9 ***Sensenbrenner***	Y	Y	N	Y	N	Y	Y	N
WYOMING								
AL ***Cubin***	Y	Y	N	Y	N	Y	Y	N

Southern states - Ala., Ark., Fla., Ga., Ky., La., Miss., N.C., Okla., S.C., Tenn., Texas, Va.

104. HR 3660. Abortion Procedure Ban/Passage. Passage of the bill that would ban a certain late-term abortion procedure, in which the physician partially delivers the fetus before completing the abortion. A physician convicted of performing such an abortion would be subject to a fine and up to two years in prison. The bill would allow the father, if he is married to the woman, or the woman's parents if the woman is under age 18, to file a civil lawsuit against the doctor for monetary damages. The penalties would not apply if the abortion were necessary to save the woman's life. Passed 287-141: R 209-8; D 77-132 (ND 50-105, SD 27-27); I 1-1. April 5, 2000. A "nay" was a vote in support of the president's position.

105. HR 3671. Fish and Wildlife Grants/Passage. Passage of the bill that would set a ceiling on administrative spending for two Fish and Wildlife Service programs. The programs generally provide grants to states in their efforts to conserve and manage fish and wildlife resources. The measure also would restrict how those funds may be spent. Passed 423-2: R 216-0; D 205-2 (ND 152-2, SD 53-0); I 2-0. April 5, 2000.

106. HR 1776. Home Ownership Expansion/Eligibility. Coburn, R-Okla., amendment that would expand the definition of who is eligible for special assistance under the bill to include federal employees, unionized employees, small-business owners and others. Rejected 72-355: R 69-147; D 2-207 (ND 1-155, SD 1-52); I 1-1. April 6, 2000.

107. HR 1776. Home Ownership Expansion/CDBG Requirements. Waters, D-Calif., amendment that would hold teachers and uniformed municipal employees to existing Community Development Block Grant standards for home ownership assistance (80 percent of the national median income) instead of raising it to 115 percent of area median income as proposed by HR 1776. Rejected 60-367: R 15-202; D 44-164 (ND 29-126, SD 15-38); I 1-1. April 6, 2000.

108. HR 1776. Home Ownership Expansion/Community Center. Traficant, D-Ohio, amendment that would authorize an additional $35 million in Community Development Block Grant funds for the construction of a community center in Youngstown, Ohio. Adopted 225-201: R 129-87; D 96-112 (ND 73-82, SD 23-30); I 0-2. April 6, 2000.

109. HR 1776. Home Ownership Expansion/Religious Organizations. Souder, R-Ind., amendment that would enable religious organizations to compete for federal housing program grants. Adopted 299-124: R 209-5; D 89-118 (ND 60-94, SD 29-24); I 1-1. April 6, 2000.

110. HR 1776. Home Ownership Expansion/Passage. Passage of the bill that would expand home ownership opportunities for low- and moderate-income families by authorizing $1.65 billion for the Department of Housing and Urban Development's HOME program and $4.9 billion for its Community Development Block Grant program. The bill would make special provisions for teachers, police officers and firefighters as well as other municipal employees. It would also allow public housing authorities to provide single grants instead of monthly checks to Section 8 recipients for use as a down payment to buy a home. Passed 417-8: R 207-8; D 208-0 (ND 155-0, SD 53-0); I 2-0. April 6, 2000.

Key

Y Voted for (yea).
\# Paired for.
\+ Announced for.
N Voted against (nay).
X Paired against.
– Announced against.
P Voted "present."
C Voted "present" to avoid possible conflict of interest.
? Did not vote or otherwise make a position known.

•

Democrats ***Republicans***
Independents

	104	105	106	107	108	109	110
ALABAMA							
1 ***Callahan***	Y	Y	Y	N	Y	?	?
2 ***Everett***	Y	Y	N	N	Y	Y	Y
3 ***Riley***	Y	Y	Y	N	Y	Y	Y
4 ***Aderholt***	Y	Y	Y	N	Y	Y	Y
5 Cramer	Y	Y	N	N	Y	Y	Y
6 ***Bachus***	Y	Y	N	N	N	Y	Y
7 Hilliard	N	Y	N	N	N	N	Y
ALASKA							
AL ***Young***	Y	Y	N	N	Y	Y	Y
ARIZONA							
1 ***Salmon***	Y	Y	N	N	N	Y	Y
2 Pastor	N	Y	N	N	Y	N	Y
3 ***Stump***	Y	Y	Y	N	Y	Y	Y
4 ***Shadegg***	Y	Y	Y	Y	N	Y	N
5 ***Kolbe***	N	Y	N	N	N	Y	Y
6 ***Hayworth***	Y	Y	Y	N	N	Y	Y
ARKANSAS							
1 Berry	Y	Y	N	N	N	Y	Y
2 Snyder	N	Y	N	N	N	N	Y
3 ***Hutchinson***	Y	Y	N	N	N	Y	Y
4 ***Dickey***	Y	Y	N	N	Y	Y	Y
CALIFORNIA							
1 Thompson	N	Y	N	N	N	Y	Y
2 ***Herger***	Y	Y	N	N	N	Y	Y
3 ***Ose***	Y	Y	N	N	Y	Y	Y
4 ***Doolittle***	Y	Y	Y	N	Y	Y	Y
5 Matsui	N	Y	N	N	N	N	Y
6 Woolsey	N	Y	N	N	N	N	Y
7 Miller, George	N	Y	N	N	N	N	Y
8 Pelosi	N	Y	N	N	N	N	Y
9 Lee	N	Y	N	Y	Y	N	Y
10 Tauscher	N	Y	N	N	N	Y	Y
11 ***Pombo***	Y	Y	Y	N	?	Y	Y
12 Lantos	N	Y	N	N	N	Y	Y
13 Stark	N	Y	N	Y	N	N	Y
14 Eshoo	N	Y	N	N	N	Y	Y
15 ***Campbell***	?	?	?	?	?	?	?
16 Lofgren	N	Y	N	N	Y	N	Y
17 Farr	N	Y	N	N	N	N	Y
18 Condit	Y	Y	N	N	N	Y	Y
19 ***Radanovich***	Y	Y	Y	N	Y	Y	Y
20 Dooley	N	Y	N	N	N	Y	Y
21 ***Thomas***	Y	Y	Y	N	Y	?	Y
22 Capps	N	Y	N	N	N	Y	Y
23 ***Gallegly***	Y	Y	N	N	Y	Y	Y
24 Sherman	N	Y	N	N	Y	N	Y
25 ***McKeon***	Y	Y	N	N	Y	Y	Y
26 Berman	N	Y	N	N	N	Y	Y
27 ***Rogan***	Y	Y	Y	N	Y	Y	Y
28 ***Dreier***	Y	Y	Y	N	Y	Y	Y
29 Waxman	N	Y	N	N	N	N	Y
30 Becerra	N	Y	N	N	N	N	Y
31 Martinez	Y	Y	N	N	Y	Y	Y
32 Dixon	N	Y	N	Y	N	N	Y
33 Roybal-Allard	N	Y	N	N	N	N	Y
34 Napolitano	N	Y	N	N	Y	Y	Y
35 Waters	N	N	N	Y	Y	N	Y
36 ***Kuykendall***	N	Y	N	N	Y	Y	Y
37 Millender-McD.	N	Y	N	N	Y	N	Y
38 ***Horn***	N	Y	N	N	Y	Y	Y
39 ***Royce***	Y	Y	N	N	N	Y	Y
40 ***Lewis***	Y	Y	N	N	Y	Y	Y
41 ***Miller, Gary***	Y	Y	N	N	Y	Y	Y
42 Baca	Y	Y	N	N	Y	Y	Y
43 ***Calvert***	Y	Y	N	N	Y	Y	Y
44 ***Bono***	Y	Y	N	N	N	Y	Y
45 ***Rohrabacher***	Y	Y	Y	N	Y	Y	Y
46 Sanchez	N	Y	N	N	N	N	Y
47 ***Cox***	Y	Y	N	Y	N	Y	Y
48 ***Packard***	Y	Y	N	N	Y	Y	Y
49 ***Bilbray***	Y	Y	N	N	Y	Y	Y
50 Filner	N	Y	N	Y	N	N	Y
51 ***Cunningham***	Y	Y	Y	N	Y	Y	Y
52 ***Hunter***	Y	Y	Y	N	Y	Y	Y
COLORADO							
1 DeGette	N	Y	N	Y	N	N	Y
2 Udall	N	Y	N	N	N	N	Y
3 ***McInnis***	Y	Y	N	N	N	Y	Y
4 ***Schaffer***	Y	Y	Y	N	N	Y	Y
5 ***Hefley***	Y	Y	N	N	N	Y	N
6 ***Tancredo***	Y	Y	Y	N	N	Y	Y
CONNECTICUT							
1 Larson	N	Y	N	N	N	N	Y
2 Gejdenson	N	Y	N	N	N	N	Y
3 DeLauro	N	Y	N	N	N	N	Y
4 ***Shays***	Y	Y	N	N	N	Y	Y
5 Maloney	Y	Y	N	N	Y	Y	Y
6 ***Johnson***	N	Y	N	N	N	Y	Y
DELAWARE							
AL ***Castle***	Y	Y	N	N	N	Y	Y
FLORIDA							
1 ***Scarborough***	Y	Y	Y	Y	Y	Y	Y
2 Boyd	Y	Y	N	N	N	Y	Y
3 Brown	N	Y	N	Y	Y	N	Y
4 ***Fowler***	Y	Y	N	N	Y	Y	Y
5 Thurman	N	Y	N	Y	Y	N	Y
6 ***Stearns***	Y	Y	N	N	N	Y	Y
7 ***Mica***	Y	Y	N	N	Y	Y	Y
8 ***McCollum***	Y	Y	N	N	Y	Y	Y
9 ***Bilirakis***	Y	Y	N	N	Y	Y	Y
10 ***Young***	Y	?	N	N	Y	Y	Y
11 Davis	Y	Y	N	N	N	N	Y
12 ***Canady***	Y	Y	N	N	Y	Y	Y
13 ***Miller***	Y	Y	Y	N	N	Y	Y
14 ***Goss***	Y	Y	Y	N	N	Y	Y
15 ***Weldon***	Y	Y	?	?	?	?	?
16 ***Foley***	Y	Y	N	N	Y	Y	Y
17 Meek	N	Y	N	Y	N	N	Y
18 ***Ros-Lehtinen***	Y	Y	N	N	Y	Y	Y
19 Wexler	N	Y	N	N	Y	N	Y
20 Deutsch	N	Y	N	N	Y	N	Y
21 ***Diaz-Balart***	Y	Y	N	N	Y	Y	Y
22 ***Shaw***	Y	Y	N	N	Y	Y	Y
23 Hastings	N	Y	N	Y	N	N	Y
GEORGIA							
1 ***Kingston***	Y	Y	Y	N	Y	Y	Y
2 Bishop	Y	Y	N	Y	Y	Y	Y
3 ***Collins***	Y	Y	Y	N	Y	Y	Y
4 McKinney	N	Y	N	Y	Y	N	Y
5 Lewis	N	Y	N	Y	N	N	Y
6 ***Isakson***	Y	Y	N	N	N	Y	Y
7 ***Barr***	Y	Y	N	N	N	Y	Y
8 ***Chambliss***	Y	Y	N	N	N	Y	Y
9 ***Deal***	Y	Y	N	N	Y	Y	Y
10 ***Norwood***	Y	Y	N	N	Y	Y	Y
11 ***Linder***	Y	Y	Y	N	N	Y	Y
HAWAII							
1 Abercrombie	N	Y	N	Y	N	N	Y
2 Mink	N	Y	N	N	Y	N	Y
IDAHO							
1 ***Chenoweth-Hage***	Y	Y	Y	Y	Y	N	Y
2 ***Simpson***	Y	Y	N	N	N	Y	Y
ILLINOIS							
1 Rush	N	Y	N	Y	N	Y	Y
2 Jackson	N	N	N	Y	N	N	Y
3 Lipinski	Y	Y	N	N	Y	Y	Y
4 Gutierrez	N	Y	N	N	N	N	Y
5 Blagojevich	N	Y	N	N	N	N	Y
6 ***Hyde***	Y	Y	N	N	Y	Y	Y
7 Davis	N	Y	N	Y	N	N	Y
8 ***Crane***	?	?	?	?	?	?	?
9 Schakowsky	N	Y	N	N	Y	N	Y
10 ***Porter***	Y	Y	N	N	N	Y	Y
11 ***Weller***	Y	Y	N	N	Y	Y	Y
12 Costello	Y	Y	N	N	Y	Y	Y
13 ***Biggert***	Y	Y	N	N	Y	Y	Y

ND Northern Democrats SD Southern Democrats

	104	105	106	107	108	109	110
14 ***Hastert***	Y						
15 ***Ewing***	Y	Y	N	N	Y	Y	Y
16 ***Manzullo***	Y	Y	Y	N	Y	Y	Y
17 Evans	N	Y	N	N	Y	Y	Y
18 ***LaHood***	Y	Y	N	N	N	Y	Y
19 Phelps	Y	Y	N	N	N	Y	Y
20 ***Shimkus***	Y	Y	N	N	Y	Y	Y
INDIANA							
1 Visclosky	Y	Y	N	N	Y	Y	Y
2 ***McIntosh***	Y	Y	Y	Y	Y	Y	Y
3 Roemer	Y	Y	N	N	N	Y	Y
4 ***Souder***	Y	Y	N	N	Y	Y	Y
5 ***Buyer***	Y	Y	Y	N	Y	Y	Y
6 ***Burton***	Y	Y	N	N	Y	Y	Y
7 ***Pease***	Y	Y	Y	Y	Y	Y	Y
8 ***Hostettler***	Y	Y	Y	N	N	Y	N
9 Hill	Y	Y	N	N	N	Y	Y
10 Carson	N	Y	N	Y	N	N	Y
IOWA							
1 ***Leach***	Y	Y	N	N	N	Y	Y
2 ***Nussle***	Y	Y	Y	N	Y	Y	Y
3 Boswell	Y	Y	N	N	N	N	Y
4 ***Ganske***	Y	Y	N	N	N	Y	Y
5 ***Latham***	Y	Y	Y	N	Y	Y	Y
KANSAS							
1 ***Moran***	Y	Y	Y	N	N	Y	Y
2 ***Ryun***	Y	Y	Y	N	Y	Y	Y
3 Moore	N	Y	N	N	N	Y	Y
4 ***Tiahrt***	Y	Y	Y	N	N	Y	Y
KENTUCKY							
1 ***Whitfield***	Y	Y	N	N	N	Y	Y
2 ***Lewis***	Y	Y	Y	N	Y	Y	Y
3 ***Northup***	Y	Y	N	N	N	Y	Y
4 Lucas	Y	Y	N	N	N	Y	Y
5 ***Rogers***	Y	Y	N	N	N	Y	Y
6 ***Fletcher***	Y	Y	N	N	Y	Y	Y
LOUISIANA							
1 ***Vitter***	Y	Y	N	N	N	Y	Y
2 Jefferson	Y	Y	N	Y	N	Y	Y
3 ***Tauzin***	Y	Y	N	N	Y	Y	Y
4 ***McCrery***	Y	Y	N	N	N	Y	Y
5 ***Cooksey***	Y	Y	Y	N	Y	Y	Y
6 ***Baker***	Y	Y	N	N	N	Y	Y
7 John	Y	Y	N	N	N	Y	Y
MAINE							
1 Allen	N	Y	N	N	N	N	Y
2 Baldacci	N	Y	N	N	N	N	Y
MARYLAND							
1 ***Gilchrest***	Y	Y	N	N	Y	Y	Y
2 ***Ehrlich***	Y	Y	N	N	Y	Y	Y
3 Cardin	N	Y	N	N	Y	N	Y
4 Wynn	N	?	N	N	Y	N	Y
5 Hoyer	N	Y	N	N	Y	N	Y
6 ***Bartlett***	Y	Y	N	N	Y	Y	Y
7 Cummings	N	Y	N	Y	N	N	Y
8 ***Morella***	N	Y	N	N	N	N	Y
MASSACHUSETTS							
1 Olver	N	Y	N	N	N	N	Y
2 Neal	Y	Y	N	N	Y	Y	Y
3 McGovern	N	Y	N	N	Y	N	Y
4 Frank	N	Y	N	N	N	N	Y
5 Meehan	N	Y	N	N	N	Y	Y
6 Tierney	N	Y	N	N	N	N	Y
7 Markey	N	Y	N	N	Y	Y	Y
8 Capuano	N	Y	N	N	N	N	Y
9 Moakley	Y	Y	N	N	Y	Y	Y
10 Delahunt	N	Y	N	N	Y	Y	Y
MICHIGAN							
1 Stupak	Y	Y	N	N	N	N	Y
2 ***Hoekstra***	Y	Y	Y	N	N	Y	Y
3 ***Ehlers***	Y	Y	N	N	N	Y	Y
4 ***Camp***	Y	Y	N	N	Y	Y	Y
5 Barcia	Y	Y	N	N	Y	Y	Y
6 ***Upton***	Y	Y	N	N	N	Y	Y
7 ***Smith***	Y	Y	Y	N	N	Y	Y
8 Stabenow	N	Y	N	N	Y	N	Y
9 Kildee	Y	Y	N	N	Y	Y	Y
10 Bonior	Y	Y	N	N	Y	N	Y
11 ***Knollenberg***	Y	Y	N	N	Y	Y	Y
12 Levin	N	Y	N	N	Y	N	Y
13 Rivers	N	Y	N	N	N	N	Y
14 Conyers	N	Y	N	Y	N	N	Y
15 Kilpatrick	N	Y	N	Y	N	N	Y
16 Dingell	Y	Y	N	N	N	N	Y

	104	105	106	107	108	109	110
MINNESOTA							
1 ***Gutknecht***	Y	Y	Y	Y	Y	Y	Y
2 Minge	Y	Y	N	N	N	N	Y
3 ***Ramstad***	Y	Y	N	N	N	Y	Y
4 Vento	?	?	?	?	?	?	?
5 Sabo	N	Y	N	N	N	N	Y
6 Luther	N	Y	N	N	N	N	Y
7 Peterson	Y	Y	N	N	N	Y	Y
8 Oberstar	Y	Y	N	N	Y	N	Y
MISSISSIPPI							
1 ***Wicker***	Y	Y	N	N	Y	Y	Y
2 Thompson	N	Y	N	Y	N	N	Y
3 ***Pickering***	Y	Y	N	N	Y	Y	Y
4 Shows	Y	Y	N	N	N	Y	Y
5 Taylor	Y	Y	N	N	Y	Y	Y
MISSOURI							
1 Clay	N	Y	N	Y	N	N	Y
2 ***Talent***	Y	Y	N	N	N	Y	Y
3 Gephardt	Y	Y	N	Y	Y	N	Y
4 Skelton	Y	Y	N	N	Y	Y	Y
5 McCarthy	N	Y	N	Y	N	Y	Y
6 Danner	Y	Y	N	?	?	?	?
7 ***Blunt***	Y	Y	Y	N	Y	Y	Y
8 ***Emerson***	Y	Y	N	N	Y	Y	Y
9 ***Hulshof***	Y	Y	N	N	N	Y	Y
MONTANA							
AL ***Hill***	Y	Y	Y	N	N	Y	Y
NEBRASKA							
1 ***Bereuter***	Y	Y	N	N	N	Y	Y
2 ***Terry***	Y	Y	N	N	N	Y	Y
3 ***Barrett***	Y	Y	N	N	N	Y	Y
NEVADA							
1 Berkley	N	Y	N	N	N	Y	Y
2 ***Gibbons***	Y	Y	N	N	Y	Y	Y
NEW HAMPSHIRE							
1 ***Sununu***	Y	Y	Y	Y	N	Y	Y
2 ***Bass***	Y	Y	N	N	Y	Y	Y
NEW JERSEY							
1 Andrews	N	Y	N	N	Y	N	Y
2 ***LoBiondo***	Y	Y	N	N	N	Y	Y
3 ***Saxton***	Y	Y	N	N	N	Y	Y
4 ***Smith***	Y	Y	N	N	Y	Y	Y
5 ***Roukema***	Y	Y	N	N	N	Y	Y
6 Pallone	N	Y	N	N	Y	N	Y
7 ***Franks***	Y	Y	N	N	N	Y	Y
8 Pascrell	Y	Y	N	N	Y	Y	Y
9 Rothman	N	Y	N	N	Y	N	Y
10 Payne	N	Y	N	Y	Y	N	Y
11 ***Frelinghuysen***	Y	Y	N	N	N	Y	Y
12 Holt	N	Y	N	N	N	N	Y
13 Menendez	N	Y	N	N	Y	N	Y
NEW MEXICO							
1 ***Wilson***	Y	Y	N	N	Y	Y	Y
2 ***Skeen***	Y	Y	N	N	Y	Y	Y
3 Udall	N	Y	N	N	N	N	Y
NEW YORK							
1 Forbes	Y	Y	N	N	Y	Y	Y
2 ***Lazio***	Y	Y	N	N	Y	Y	Y
3 ***King***	Y	Y	N	N	Y	Y	Y
4 McCarthy	N	Y	N	N	Y	Y	Y
5 Ackerman	N	Y	N	N	Y	N	Y
6 Meeks	N	Y	N	N	N	Y	Y
7 Crowley	Y	Y	N	N	Y	Y	Y
8 Nadler	N	Y	N	N	Y	N	Y
9 Weiner	N	Y	N	N	Y	Y	Y
10 Towns	N	Y	N	Y	Y	N	Y
11 Owens	N	Y	N	Y	Y	N	Y
12 Velázquez	?	Y	N	N	N	N	Y
13 ***Fossella***	Y	Y	N	N	Y	Y	Y
14 Maloney	N	Y	N	N	Y	Y	Y
15 Rangel	N	?	N	Y	Y	?	Y
16 Serrano	N	Y	N	N	Y	N	Y
17 Engel	N	Y	N	Y	Y	N	Y
18 Lowey	N	Y	N	N	Y	N	Y
19 ***Kelly***	Y	Y	N	N	Y	Y	Y
20 ***Gilman***	N	Y	N	N	Y	Y	?
21 McNulty	Y	Y	N	Y	Y	Y	Y
22 ***Sweeney***	Y	Y	N	N	Y	Y	Y
23 ***Boehlert***	N	Y	N	N	N	Y	Y
24 ***McHugh***	Y	Y	N	N	Y	Y	Y
25 ***Walsh***	Y	Y	N	N	Y	Y	Y
26 Hinchey	N	Y	N	N	N	N	Y
27 ***Reynolds***	Y	Y	N	N	Y	Y	Y
28 Slaughter	N	Y	N	Y	N	N	Y
29 LaFalce	Y	Y	N	Y	Y	Y	Y

	104	105	106	107	108	109	110
30 ***Quinn***	Y	Y	N	N	Y	Y	Y
31 ***Houghton***	Y	Y	N	N	Y	Y	Y
NORTH CAROLINA							
1 Clayton	N	Y	N	Y	N	N	Y
2 Etheridge	Y	Y	N	N	N	N	Y
3 ***Jones***	Y	Y	Y	N	N	Y	Y
4 Price	N	Y	N	N	N	Y	Y
5 ***Burr***	Y	Y	N	N	Y	Y	Y
6 ***Coble***	Y	Y	N	N	N	Y	Y
7 McIntyre	Y	Y	N	N	N	Y	Y
8 ***Hayes***	Y	Y	Y	N	N	Y	Y
9 ***Myrick***	Y	Y	N	N	N	Y	Y
10 ***Ballenger***	Y	Y	N	N	Y	Y	Y
11 ***Taylor***	Y	Y	N	N	N	Y	Y
12 Watt	N	Y	N	Y	N	N	Y
NORTH DAKOTA							
AL Pomeroy	Y	Y	N	N	N	N	Y
OHIO							
1 ***Chabot***	Y	Y	Y	N	N	Y	Y
2 ***Portman***	?	Y	Y	N	Y	Y	Y
3 Hall	Y	Y	N	N	Y	Y	Y
4 ***Oxley***	Y	Y	N	N	N	Y	Y
5 ***Gillmor***	Y	Y	N	N	Y	Y	Y
6 Strickland	Y	Y	N	N	Y	N	Y
7 ***Hobson***	Y	Y	N	N	Y	?	Y
8 ***Boehner***	Y	Y	Y	N	Y	Y	Y
9 Kaptur	Y	Y	N	N	Y	N	Y
10 Kucinich	Y	Y	N	N	Y	Y	Y
11 Jones	N	Y	N	Y	Y	N	Y
12 ***Kasich***	Y	Y	Y	Y	Y	Y	Y
13 Brown	N	Y	N	N	Y	N	Y
14 Sawyer	N	Y	N	N	Y	N	Y
15 ***Pryce***	Y	Y	N	N	Y	Y	Y
16 ***Regula***	Y	Y	N	N	Y	Y	Y
17 Traficant	Y	Y	N	N	Y	Y	Y
18 ***Ney***	Y	Y	N	N	Y	Y	Y
19 ***LaTourette***	Y	Y	N	N	Y	Y	Y
OKLAHOMA							
1 ***Largent***	Y	Y	Y	N	N	Y	Y
2 ***Coburn***	Y	Y	Y	Y	Y	Y	N
3 ***Watkins***	Y	Y	N	N	Y	Y	Y
4 ***Watts***	Y	Y	Y	N	Y	Y	Y
5 ***Istook***	Y	Y	N	N	Y	Y	N
6 ***Lucas***	Y	Y	N	N	Y	Y	Y
OREGON							
1 Wu	N	Y	N	N	N	N	Y
2 ***Walden***	Y	Y	N	N	N	Y	Y
3 Blumenauer	N	Y	N	N	N	N	Y
4 DeFazio	N	Y	N	N	N	Y	Y
5 Hooley	N	Y	N	N	N	N	Y
PENNSYLVANIA							
1 Brady	N	Y	N	Y	Y	Y	Y
2 Fattah	N	Y	N	Y	Y	Y	Y
3 Borski	Y	Y	N	N	Y	Y	Y
4 Klink	Y	Y	N	N	Y	Y	Y
5 ***Peterson***	Y	Y	Y	N	Y	Y	Y
6 Holden	Y	Y	N	N	N	Y	Y
7 ***Weldon***	Y	Y	N	N	Y	Y	Y
8 ***Greenwood***	N	Y	N	N	N	Y	Y
9 ***Shuster***	Y	Y	?	N	Y	Y	Y
10 ***Sherwood***	Y	Y	N	N	Y	Y	Y
11 Kanjorski	Y	Y	N	N	Y	Y	Y
12 Murtha	Y	Y	N	N	Y	Y	Y
13 Hoeffel	N	Y	N	N	N	N	Y
14 Coyne	N	Y	N	N	N	N	Y
15 ***Toomey***	Y	Y	Y	Y	N	Y	Y
16 ***Pitts***	Y	Y	Y	N	N	Y	Y
17 ***Gekas***	Y	Y	N	N	N	Y	Y
18 Doyle	Y	Y	N	N	Y	Y	Y
19 ***Goodling***	Y	Y	N	N	Y	Y	Y
20 Mascara	Y	Y	N	N	Y	Y	Y
21 ***English***	Y	Y	N	N	Y	Y	Y
RHODE ISLAND							
1 Kennedy	Y	Y	N	N	Y	N	Y
2 Weygand	Y	Y	N	N	N	Y	Y
SOUTH CAROLINA							
1 ***Sanford***	Y	Y	Y	Y	N	Y	N
2 ***Spence***	Y	Y	N	N	Y	Y	Y
3 ***Graham***	Y	Y	Y	N	N	Y	Y
4 ***DeMint***	Y	Y	Y	N	N	Y	Y
5 Spratt	Y	Y	N	N	N	Y	Y
6 Clyburn	N	Y	N	Y	Y	N	Y
SOUTH DAKOTA							
AL ***Thune***	Y	Y	N	N	Y	Y	Y

	104	105	106	107	108	109	110
TENNESSEE							
1 ***Jenkins***	Y	Y	N	N	Y	Y	Y
2 ***Duncan***	Y	Y	Y	N	Y	Y	Y
3 ***Wamp***	Y	Y	N	N	Y	Y	Y
4 ***Hilleary***	Y	Y	N	N	N	Y	Y
5 Clement	Y	?	N	N	Y	Y	Y
6 Gordon	Y	Y	Y	N	Y	Y	Y
7 ***Bryant***	Y	Y	Y	N	Y	Y	Y
8 Tanner	Y	Y	N	N	N	Y	Y
9 Ford	Y	Y	N	N	Y	N	Y
TEXAS							
1 Sandlin	Y	Y	N	N	N	Y	Y
2 Turner	Y	Y	N	N	N	Y	Y
3 ***Johnson, Sam***	Y	Y	N	Y	N	Y	Y
4 Hall	Y	Y	N	Y	Y	Y	Y
5 ***Sessions***	Y	Y	N	N	Y	Y	Y
6 ***Barton***	Y	Y	Y	N	N	Y	Y
7 ***Archer***	Y	?	Y	N	Y	Y	Y
8 ***Brady***	Y	Y	Y	N	N	Y	Y
9 Lampson	Y	Y	N	N	Y	Y	Y
10 Doggett	N	Y	N	N	N	N	Y
11 Edwards	N	Y	N	N	Y	N	Y
12 ***Granger***	?	Y	N	N	Y	Y	Y
13 ***Thornberry***	Y	Y	N	N	N	Y	Y
14 ***Paul***	Y	Y	N	Y	N	N	N
15 Hinojosa	Y	Y	N	N	Y	Y	Y
16 Reyes	Y	Y	N	N	Y	Y	Y
17 Stenholm	Y	Y	N	N	N	Y	Y
18 Jackson-Lee	N	Y	N	Y	Y	Y	Y
19 ***Combest***	Y	Y	N	N	N	Y	Y
20 Gonzalez	N	Y	N	N	N	N	Y
21 ***Smith***	Y	Y	N	N	Y	Y	Y
22 ***DeLay***	Y	Y	Y	N	Y	Y	Y
23 ***Bonilla***	Y	Y	N	N	Y	Y	Y
24 Frost	N	Y	N	N	Y	N	Y
25 Bentsen	N	Y	N	N	N	Y	Y
26 ***Armey***	Y	Y	Y	N	Y	Y	Y
27 Ortiz	Y	Y	N	N	Y	Y	Y
28 Rodriguez	N	Y	?	?	?	?	?
29 Green	N	Y	N	N	Y	Y	Y
30 Johnson, E.B.	N	Y	N	Y	Y	N	Y
UTAH							
1 ***Hansen***	Y	Y	N	N	N	N	Y
2 ***Cook***	?	?	?	?	?	?	?
3 ***Cannon***	Y	Y	Y	N	Y	Y	Y
VERMONT							
AL *Sanders*	N	Y	N	Y	N	N	Y
VIRGINIA							
1 ***Bateman***	Y	Y	N	N	N	N	Y
2 Pickett	N	Y	N	N	N	N	Y
3 Scott	N	Y	N	N	N	N	Y
4 Sisisky	Y	Y	N	N	Y	Y	Y
5 *Goode*	Y	Y	Y	N	N	Y	Y
6 ***Goodlatte***	Y	Y	Y	N	N	Y	Y
7 ***Bliley***	Y	Y	Y	N	Y	Y	Y
8 Moran	Y	Y	N	N	N	Y	Y
9 Boucher	N	Y	N	N	N	N	Y
10 ***Wolf***	Y	Y	Y	N	Y	Y	Y
11 ***Davis***	Y	Y	N	N	Y	Y	Y
WASHINGTON							
1 Inslee	N	Y	N	N	N	N	Y
2 ***Metcalf***	Y	Y	N	N	Y	Y	Y
3 Baird	N	Y	N	N	N	N	Y
4 ***Hastings***	Y	Y	Y	Y	N	Y	Y
5 ***Nethercutt***	Y	Y	N	N	Y	Y	Y
6 Dicks	N	Y	N	N	N	Y	Y
7 McDermott	N	Y	N	Y	N	N	Y
8 ***Dunn***	Y	Y	N	N	N	Y	Y
9 Smith	N	Y	N	N	N	Y	Y
WEST VIRGINIA							
1 Mollohan	Y	Y	N	N	Y	Y	Y
2 Wise	N	Y	N	N	N	N	Y
3 Rahall	Y	Y	N	N	Y	Y	Y
WISCONSIN							
1 ***Ryan***	Y	Y	N	N	Y	Y	Y
2 Baldwin	N	Y	N	N	N	N	Y
3 Kind	Y	Y	N	N	N	N	Y
4 Kleczka	Y	Y	N	N	N	N	Y
5 Barrett	Y	Y	N	N	N	N	Y
6 ***Petri***	Y	Y	N	N	N	Y	Y
7 Obey	Y	Y	N	N	N	N	Y
8 ***Green***	Y	Y	N	N	N	Y	Y
9 ***Sensenbrenner***	Y	Y	N	N	N	Y	N
WYOMING							
AL ***Cubin***	Y	Y	N	N	Y	Y	Y

Southern states - Ala., Ark., Fla., Ga., Ky., La., Miss., N.C., Okla., S.C., Tenn., Texas, Va.

111. H Con Res 282. Person of the Century/Adoption. Hayes, R-N.C., motion to suspend the rules and adopt the concurrent resolution declaring the American GI — collectively referring to all members of the U.S. armed services — as the "person of the century" for their service in world wars and conflicts during the 20th century. Motion agreed to 397-0: R 202-0; D 193-0 (ND 144-0, SD 49-0); I 2-0. A two-thirds majority of those present and voting (265 in this case) is required for adoption under suspension of the rules. April 10, 2000.

112. H Con Res 228. Vietnam Era Honorees/Adoption. Kuykendall, R-Calif., motion to suspend the rules and adopt the concurrent resolution recognizing members of the armed forces and federal civilian employees who served the United States during the Vietnam era. Motion agreed to 399-0: R 204-0; D 193-0 (ND 145-0, SD 48-0); I 2-0. A two-thirds majority of those present and voting (266 in this case) is required for adoption under suspension of the rules. April 10, 2000.

113. S 777. USDA Electronic Filing/Passage. Goodlatte, R-Va., motion to suspend the rules and pass the bill requiring the Department of Agriculture to establish an electronic filing and retrieval system allowing farmers to complete required paperwork via computer. The bill would apply to the USDA's Farm Service Agency, Natural Resource Conservation Service, Risk Management Agency and rural development field offices. The bill would allocate $5 million for the project and require its completion within two years. Motion agreed to 397-1: R 203-1; D 192-0 (ND 144-0, SD 48-0); I 2-0. A two-thirds majority of those present and voting (266 in this case) is required for passage under suspension of the rules. April 10, 2000.

114. H Con Res 290. Fiscal 2001 Budget Resolution/Motion to Instruct. Spratt, D-S.C., motion to instruct conferees to insist that the House Ways and Means Committee not report its tax cuts before Sept. 22, allowing Congress enough time to enact legislation to establish a Medicare prescription drug program. The motion also calls upon the conferees to use the Senate's tax-cut figure, which does not include the House-passed $50 billion "reserve" fund that could be put toward tax cuts. Motion rejected 198-201: R 5-200; D 192-0 (ND 144-0, SD 48-0); I 1-1. April 10, 2000.

115. HR 4051. Project Exile/Passage. McCollum, R-Fla., motion to suspend the rules and pass the bill that would authorize $100 million over five years in block grants to states that meet requirements regarding five-year mandatory minimum prison sentences for the use or possession of firearms in commission of a crime. Motion agreed to 358-60: R 208-3; D 149-56 (ND 110-43, SD 39-13); I 1-1. A two-thirds majority of those present and voting (279 in this case) is required for passage under suspension of the rules. April 11, 2000.

116. HR 4163. Tax Code Changes/Passage. Archer, R-Texas, motion to suspend the rules and pass the bill that would increase privacy protection for taxpayers and strengthen rules regarding disclosure of information by the IRS. The measure also would reduce the penalties and interest payments individuals must pay. Motion agreed to 424-0: R 216-0; D 206-0 (ND 154-0, SD 52-0); I 2-0. A two-thirds majority of those present and voting (283 in this case) is required for passage under suspension of the rules. April 11, 2000.

117. H Res 467. President's Tax Proposal/Adoption. McInnis, R-Colo., motion to suspend the rules and adopt the resolution expressing the sense of the House that the tax and user-fee increases proposed by the president in the fiscal year 2001 budget should be adopted. Motion rejected 1-420: R 0-216; D 1-202 (ND 1-151, SD 0-51); I 0-2. A two-thirds majority of those present and voting (281 in this case) is necessary for adoption under suspension of the rules. April 11, 2000.

Key

- Y Voted for (yea).
- # Paired for.
- + Announced for.
- N Voted against (nay).
- X Paired against.
- – Announced against.
- P Voted "present."
- C Voted "present" to avoid possible conflict of interest.
- ? Did not vote or otherwise make a position known.

•

Democrats ***Republicans***
Independents

	111	112	113	114	115	116	117
ALABAMA							
1 ***Callahan***	Y	Y	Y	N	Y	Y	N
2 ***Everett***	Y	Y	Y	N	Y	Y	N
3 ***Riley***	Y	Y	Y	N	Y	Y	N
4 ***Aderholt***	Y	Y	Y	Y	Y	Y	N
5 Cramer	Y	Y	Y	Y	Y	Y	N
6 ***Bachus***	Y	Y	Y	Y	Y	Y	N
7 Hilliard	Y	Y	Y	Y	Y	Y	N
ALASKA							
AL ***Young***	Y	Y	Y	N	Y	?	?
ARIZONA							
1 ***Salmon***	Y	Y	Y	N	Y	Y	N
2 Pastor	Y	Y	Y	Y	Y	Y	N
3 ***Stump***	Y	Y	Y	N	Y	Y	N
4 ***Shadegg***	Y	Y	Y	N	Y	Y	N
5 ***Kolbe***	Y	Y	Y	N	Y	Y	N
6 ***Hayworth***	Y	Y	Y	N	Y	Y	N
ARKANSAS							
1 Berry	Y	Y	Y	Y	Y	Y	N
2 Snyder	Y	Y	Y	Y	N	Y	N
3 ***Hutchinson***	Y	Y	Y	N	Y	Y	N
4 ***Dickey***	Y	Y	Y	N	Y	Y	N
CALIFORNIA							
1 Thompson	Y	Y	Y	Y	Y	Y	N
2 ***Herger***	Y	Y	?	N	Y	Y	N
3 ***Ose***	Y	Y	Y	N	Y	Y	N
4 ***Doolittle***	Y	Y	Y	N	Y	Y	N
5 Matsui	Y	Y	Y	Y	Y	Y	Y
6 Woolsey	Y	Y	Y	Y	N	Y	N
7 Miller, George	Y	Y	Y	Y	Y	?	?
8 Pelosi	Y	Y	Y	Y	N	Y	N
9 Lee	Y	Y	Y	+	N	Y	N
10 Tauscher	Y	Y	Y	Y	Y	Y	N
11 ***Pombo***	Y	Y	Y	N	Y	Y	N
12 Lantos	Y	Y	Y	Y	Y	Y	N
13 Stark	?	Y	Y	Y	N	Y	N
14 Eshoo	Y	Y	Y	Y	Y	Y	N
15 ***Campbell***	?	?	?	?	N	Y	N
16 Lofgren	Y	Y	Y	Y	N	Y	N
17 Farr	Y	Y	Y	Y	Y	Y	N
18 Condit	Y	Y	Y	Y	Y	Y	N
19 ***Radanovich***	Y	Y	Y	N	Y	Y	N
20 Dooley	Y	Y	Y	Y	Y	Y	N
21 ***Thomas***	Y	Y	Y	N	Y	Y	N
22 Capps	Y	Y	Y	Y	Y	Y	N
23 ***Gallegly***	Y	Y	Y	N	Y	Y	N
24 Sherman	Y	Y	Y	Y	Y	Y	N
25 ***McKeon***	Y	Y	Y	N	Y	Y	N
26 Berman	Y	Y	Y	Y	N	Y	N
27 ***Rogan***	Y	Y	Y	N	Y	Y	N
28 ***Dreier***	Y	Y	Y	N	Y	Y	N
29 Waxman	Y	Y	Y	Y	Y	Y	N
30 Becerra	Y	Y	Y	Y	Y	Y	N
31 Martinez	?	?	?	?	?	Y	N
32 Dixon	Y	Y	Y	Y	Y	Y	N
33 Roybal-Allard	Y	Y	Y	Y	Y	Y	N
34 Napolitano	Y	Y	Y	Y	Y	Y	N
35 Waters	Y	Y	Y	Y	N	Y	N
36 ***Kuykendall***	Y	Y	Y	N	Y	Y	N
37 Millender-McD.	Y	Y	Y	Y	N	Y	N
38 ***Horn***	Y	Y	Y	N	Y	Y	N
39 ***Royce***	Y	Y	Y	N	Y	Y	N
40 ***Lewis***	Y	Y	Y	N	Y	Y	N
41 ***Miller, Gary***	Y	Y	Y	N	Y	Y	N
42 Baca	Y	Y	Y	Y	Y	Y	N
43 ***Calvert***	Y	Y	Y	N	Y	+	N
44 ***Bono***	Y	Y	Y	N	Y	Y	N
45 ***Rohrabacher***	Y	Y	Y	N	Y	Y	N
46 Sanchez	Y	Y	Y	Y	Y	Y	N
47 ***Cox***	?	?	?	?	Y	Y	N
48 ***Packard***	Y	Y	Y	N	Y	Y	N
49 ***Bilbray***	+	+	Y	N	Y	Y	N
50 Filner	Y	Y	Y	Y	N	Y	N
51 ***Cunningham***	Y	Y	Y	N	Y	Y	N
52 ***Hunter***	Y	Y	Y	N	Y	Y	N
COLORADO							
1 DeGette	?	?	?	?	?	?	?
2 Udall	Y	Y	Y	Y	Y	Y	N
3 ***McInnis***	Y	Y	Y	N	Y	Y	N
4 ***Schaffer***	?	?	?	?	Y	Y	N
5 ***Hefley***	Y	Y	Y	N	?	Y	N
6 ***Tancredo***	Y	Y	Y	N	Y	Y	N
CONNECTICUT							
1 Larson	Y	Y	Y	Y	Y	Y	P
2 Gejdenson	Y	Y	Y	Y	Y	Y	N
3 DeLauro	Y	Y	Y	Y	Y	Y	N
4 ***Shays***	Y	Y	Y	N	Y	Y	N
5 Maloney	Y	Y	Y	Y	Y	Y	N
6 ***Johnson***	Y	Y	Y	N	Y	Y	N
DELAWARE							
AL ***Castle***	Y	Y	Y	N	Y	Y	N
FLORIDA							
1 ***Scarborough***	Y	Y	Y	N	Y	Y	N
2 Boyd	Y	Y	Y	Y	Y	Y	N
3 Brown	Y	Y	Y	Y	Y	Y	N
4 ***Fowler***	Y	Y	Y	N	Y	Y	N
5 Thurman	Y	Y	Y	Y	Y	Y	N
6 ***Stearns***	Y	Y	Y	N	Y	Y	N
7 ***Mica***	Y	Y	Y	N	Y	Y	N
8 ***McCollum***	?	?	?	?	Y	Y	N
9 ***Bilirakis***	Y	Y	Y	N	Y	Y	N
10 ***Young***	Y	Y	Y	N	Y	Y	N
11 Davis	Y	Y	Y	Y	Y	Y	N
12 ***Canady***	?	?	?	?	Y	Y	N
13 ***Miller***	Y	Y	Y	N	Y	Y	N
14 ***Goss***	Y	Y	Y	N	Y	Y	N
15 ***Weldon***	Y	Y	Y	N	Y	Y	N
16 ***Foley***	Y	Y	Y	N	Y	Y	N
17 Meek	Y	Y	Y	Y	N	Y	N
18 ***Ros-Lehtinen***	Y	Y	Y	N	Y	Y	N
19 Wexler	Y	Y	Y	Y	Y	Y	N
20 Deutsch	Y	Y	Y	Y	Y	Y	N
21 ***Diaz-Balart***	Y	Y	Y	N	Y	Y	N
22 ***Shaw***	Y	Y	Y	N	Y	Y	N
23 Hastings	Y	Y	Y	Y	N	Y	N
GEORGIA							
1 ***Kingston***	Y	Y	Y	N	Y	Y	N
2 Bishop	Y	Y	Y	Y	Y	Y	N
3 ***Collins***	Y	Y	Y	N	Y	Y	N
4 McKinney	Y	Y	Y	Y	N	Y	N
5 Lewis	Y	Y	Y	Y	N	Y	N
6 ***Isakson***	Y	Y	Y	N	Y	Y	N
7 ***Barr***	Y	Y	Y	N	Y	Y	N
8 ***Chambliss***	Y	Y	Y	N	Y	Y	N
9 ***Deal***	Y	Y	Y	N	Y	Y	N
10 ***Norwood***	Y	Y	Y	N	Y	Y	N
11 ***Linder***	Y	Y	Y	N	Y	Y	N
HAWAII							
1 Abercrombie	Y	Y	Y	Y	Y	Y	N
2 Mink	?	?	?	?	Y	Y	N
IDAHO							
1 ***Chenoweth-Hage***	Y	Y	Y	N	Y	Y	N
2 ***Simpson***	Y	Y	Y	N	Y	Y	N
ILLINOIS							
1 Rush	Y	Y	Y	Y	N	Y	N
2 Jackson	Y	Y	Y	Y	N	Y	N
3 Lipinski	Y	Y	Y	Y	Y	Y	N
4 Gutierrez	?	?	?	?	Y	Y	N
5 Blagojevich	Y	Y	Y	Y	Y	Y	N
6 ***Hyde***	Y	Y	Y	N	Y	Y	N
7 Davis	Y	Y	Y	Y	N	Y	N
8 ***Crane***	Y	Y	Y	N	Y	Y	N
9 Schakowsky	Y	Y	Y	Y	N	Y	N
10 ***Porter***	Y	Y	Y	Y	Y	Y	N
11 ***Weller***	Y	Y	Y	N	Y	Y	N
12 Costello	Y	Y	Y	Y	Y	Y	N
13 ***Biggert***	Y	Y	Y	N	Y	Y	N

ND Northern Democrats SD Southern Democrats

	111	112	113	114	115	116	117
14 ***Hastert***							
15 ***Ewing***	Y	Y	Y	N	+	Y	N
16 ***Manzullo***	Y	Y	Y	N	Y	Y	N
17 Evans	Y	Y	Y	Y	Y	Y	N
18 ***LaHood***	Y	Y	Y	N	Y	Y	N
19 Phelps	Y	Y	Y	Y	Y	Y	N
20 ***Shimkus***	Y	Y	Y	N	Y	Y	N
INDIANA							
1 Visclosky	Y	Y	Y	Y	Y	Y	N
2 ***McIntosh***	?	?	?	?	?	?	?
3 Roemer	Y	Y	Y	Y	Y	Y	N
4 ***Souder***	Y	Y	Y	N	Y	Y	N
5 ***Buyer***	?	?	?	?	Y	Y	N
6 ***Burton***	Y	Y	Y	N	Y	Y	N
7 ***Pease***	Y	Y	Y	N	Y	Y	N
8 ***Hostettler***	Y	Y	Y	N	Y	Y	N
9 Hill	Y	Y	Y	Y	Y	Y	N
10 Carson	Y	Y	Y	Y	N	Y	N
IOWA							
1 ***Leach***	Y	Y	Y	N	Y	Y	N
2 ***Nussle***	Y	Y	Y	N	Y	Y	N
3 Boswell	Y	Y	Y	Y	Y	Y	N
4 ***Ganske***	Y	Y	Y	Y	Y	Y	N
5 ***Latham***	Y	Y	Y	N	Y	Y	N
KANSAS							
1 ***Moran***	Y	Y	Y	N	Y	Y	N
2 ***Ryun***	+	+	+	–	Y	Y	N
3 Moore	Y	Y	Y	Y	Y	Y	N
4 ***Tiahrt***	Y	Y	Y	N	Y	Y	N
KENTUCKY							
1 ***Whitfield***	Y	Y	Y	N	Y	Y	N
2 ***Lewis***	Y	Y	Y	N	Y	Y	N
3 ***Northup***	Y	Y	Y	N	Y	Y	N
4 Lucas	Y	Y	Y	Y	Y	Y	N
5 ***Rogers***	Y	Y	Y	N	Y	Y	?
6 ***Fletcher***	Y	Y	Y	N	Y	Y	N
LOUISIANA							
1 ***Vitter***	Y	Y	Y	N	Y	Y	N
2 Jefferson	Y	Y	Y	Y	Y	Y	N
3 ***Tauzin***	Y	Y	Y	N	Y	Y	N
4 ***McCrery***	Y	Y	Y	N	Y	Y	N
5 ***Cooksey***	?	?	?	?	Y	Y	N
6 ***Baker***	Y	Y	Y	N	Y	Y	N
7 John	Y	Y	Y	Y	Y	+	–
MAINE							
1 Allen	Y	Y	Y	Y	N	Y	N
2 Baldacci	Y	Y	Y	Y	Y	Y	N
MARYLAND							
1 ***Gilchrest***	Y	Y	Y	N	Y	Y	N
2 ***Ehrlich***	Y	Y	Y	N	Y	Y	N
3 Cardin	Y	Y	Y	Y	N	Y	N
4 Wynn	Y	Y	Y	Y	?	Y	N
5 Hoyer	Y	Y	Y	Y	Y	Y	N
6 ***Bartlett***	Y	Y	Y	N	Y	Y	N
7 Cummings	Y	Y	Y	Y	N	Y	N
8 ***Morella***	Y	Y	Y	Y	?	Y	N
MASSACHUSETTS							
1 Olver	Y	Y	Y	Y	N	Y	N
2 Neal	?	?	?	?	Y	Y	N
3 McGovern	Y	Y	Y	Y	N	Y	N
4 Frank	Y	Y	Y	Y	N	Y	N
5 Meehan	Y	Y	Y	Y	Y	Y	N
6 Tierney	Y	Y	?	Y	N	Y	N
7 Markey	Y	Y	Y	Y	N	Y	N
8 Capuano	Y	Y	Y	Y	N	Y	N
9 Moakley	?	?	?	?	Y	Y	N
10 Delahunt	Y	Y	Y	Y	N	Y	N
MICHIGAN							
1 Stupak	Y	Y	Y	Y	Y	Y	N
2 ***Hoekstra***	Y	Y	Y	N	Y	Y	N
3 ***Ehlers***	Y	Y	Y	N	Y	Y	N
4 ***Camp***	Y	Y	Y	N	Y	Y	N
5 Barcia	Y	Y	Y	Y	Y	Y	N
6 ***Upton***	Y	Y	Y	N	Y	Y	N
7 ***Smith***	Y	Y	Y	N	Y	Y	N
8 Stabenow	Y	Y	Y	Y	Y	Y	N
9 Kildee	Y	Y	Y	Y	Y	Y	N
10 Bonior	Y	Y	Y	Y	Y	Y	N
11 ***Knollenberg***	Y	Y	Y	N	Y	Y	N
12 Levin	Y	Y	Y	Y	Y	Y	N
13 Rivers	Y	Y	Y	Y	Y	Y	N
14 Conyers	Y	Y	Y	Y	N	Y	N
15 Kilpatrick	Y	Y	Y	Y	N	Y	N
16 Dingell	Y	Y	Y	Y	Y	?	?

	111	112	113	114	115	116	117
MINNESOTA							
1 ***Gutknecht***	Y	Y	Y	N	Y	Y	N
2 Minge	Y	Y	Y	Y	Y	Y	N
3 ***Ramstad***	Y	Y	Y	N	Y	Y	N
4 Vento	Y	Y	Y	Y	Y	Y	N
5 Sabo	Y	Y	Y	Y	N	Y	N
6 Luther	Y	Y	Y	Y	Y	Y	N
7 Peterson	Y	Y	Y	Y	Y	Y	N
8 Oberstar	Y	Y	Y	Y	Y	Y	N
MISSISSIPPI							
1 ***Wicker***	Y	Y	Y	N	Y	Y	N
2 Thompson	Y	Y	Y	Y	N	Y	N
3 ***Pickering***	Y	Y	Y	N	Y	Y	N
4 Shows	Y	Y	Y	Y	Y	Y	N
5 Taylor	Y	Y	Y	Y	Y	Y	N
MISSOURI							
1 Clay	Y	Y	Y	Y	N	Y	N
2 ***Talent***	Y	Y	Y	N	Y	Y	N
3 Gephardt	Y	Y	Y	Y	Y	Y	N
4 Skelton	Y	Y	Y	Y	Y	Y	N
5 McCarthy	Y	Y	Y	Y	N	Y	N
6 Danner	Y	Y	Y	Y	Y	Y	N
7 ***Blunt***	?	?	?	?	Y	Y	N
8 ***Emerson***	Y	Y	Y	N	Y	Y	N
9 ***Hulshof***	Y	Y	Y	N	Y	Y	N
MONTANA							
AL ***Hill***	Y	Y	Y	N	Y	Y	N
NEBRASKA							
1 ***Bereuter***	Y	Y	Y	N	Y	Y	N
2 ***Terry***	Y	Y	Y	N	Y	Y	N
3 ***Barrett***	Y	Y	Y	N	Y	Y	N
NEVADA							
1 Berkley	Y	Y	Y	Y	Y	Y	N
2 ***Gibbons***	Y	Y	Y	N	Y	Y	N
NEW HAMPSHIRE							
1 ***Sununu***	Y	Y	Y	N	Y	Y	N
2 ***Bass***	Y	Y	Y	N	Y	Y	N
NEW JERSEY							
1 Andrews	Y	Y	Y	Y	Y	Y	N
2 ***LoBiondo***	Y	Y	Y	N	Y	Y	N
3 ***Saxton***	Y	Y	Y	N	Y	Y	N
4 ***Smith***	Y	Y	Y	N	Y	Y	N
5 ***Roukema***	Y	Y	Y	N	Y	Y	N
6 Pallone	Y	Y	Y	Y	Y	Y	N
7 ***Franks***	Y	Y	Y	N	Y	Y	N
8 Pascrell	Y	Y	Y	Y	Y	Y	N
9 Rothman	Y	Y	Y	Y	Y	Y	N
10 Payne	Y	Y	Y	Y	N	Y	N
11 ***Frelinghuysen***	Y	Y	Y	N	Y	Y	N
12 Holt	Y	Y	Y	Y	Y	Y	N
13 Menendez	Y	Y	Y	Y	Y	Y	N
NEW MEXICO							
1 ***Wilson***	Y	Y	Y	N	Y	Y	N
2 ***Skeen***	Y	Y	Y	N	Y	Y	N
3 Udall	Y	Y	Y	Y	Y	Y	N
NEW YORK							
1 Forbes	Y	Y	Y	Y	Y	Y	N
2 ***Lazio***	Y	Y	Y	N	Y	Y	N
3 ***King***	Y	Y	Y	N	Y	Y	N
4 McCarthy	Y	Y	Y	Y	Y	Y	N
5 Ackerman	?	?	Y	Y	Y	Y	N
6 Meeks	Y	Y	Y	Y	N	Y	N
7 Crowley	Y	Y	Y	Y	Y	Y	N
8 Nadler	?	?	?	?	Y	Y	N
9 Weiner	Y	Y	Y	Y	Y	Y	N
10 Towns	Y	Y	Y	Y	N	Y	N
11 Owens	?	?	?	?	N	Y	N
12 Velázquez	Y	Y	Y	Y	N	Y	N
13 ***Fossella***	Y	Y	Y	N	Y	Y	N
14 Maloney	Y	Y	?	Y	Y	Y	N
15 Rangel	Y	Y	Y	Y	N	Y	N
16 Serrano	Y	Y	Y	Y	N	Y	N
17 Engel	Y	Y	Y	Y	Y	Y	N
18 Lowey	Y	Y	Y	Y	Y	Y	N
19 ***Kelly***	Y	Y	Y	N	Y	Y	N
20 ***Gilman***	Y	Y	Y	N	+	Y	N
21 McNulty	Y	Y	Y	Y	Y	Y	N
22 ***Sweeney***	Y	Y	Y	N	Y	Y	N
23 ***Boehlert***	Y	Y	Y	N	Y	Y	N
24 ***McHugh***	Y	Y	Y	N	Y	Y	N
25 ***Walsh***	Y	Y	Y	N	Y	Y	N
26 Hinchey	Y	Y	Y	Y	N	Y	N
27 ***Reynolds***	Y	Y	Y	N	Y	Y	N
28 Slaughter	Y	Y	Y	Y	Y	Y	N
29 LaFalce	Y	Y	Y	Y	N	Y	N

	111	112	113	114	115	116	117
30 ***Quinn***	Y	Y	Y	N	Y	Y	N
31 ***Houghton***	Y	Y	Y	N	Y	Y	N
NORTH CAROLINA							
1 Clayton	Y	Y	Y	Y	N	Y	N
2 Etheridge	Y	Y	Y	Y	Y	Y	N
3 ***Jones***	Y	Y	Y	N	Y	Y	N
4 Price	Y	Y	Y	Y	Y	Y	N
5 ***Burr***	Y	Y	Y	N	Y	Y	N
6 ***Coble***	Y	Y	Y	N	Y	Y	N
7 McIntyre	Y	Y	Y	Y	Y	Y	N
8 ***Hayes***	Y	Y	Y	N	Y	Y	N
9 ***Myrick***	Y	Y	Y	N	Y	+	–
10 ***Ballenger***	Y	Y	Y	N	Y	Y	N
11 ***Taylor***	Y	Y	Y	N	Y	Y	N
12 Watt	Y	Y	Y	Y	N	Y	N
NORTH DAKOTA							
AL Pomeroy	Y	Y	Y	Y	Y	Y	N
OHIO							
1 ***Chabot***	Y	Y	Y	N	Y	Y	N
2 ***Portman***	Y	Y	Y	N	Y	Y	N
3 Hall	Y	Y	Y	Y	Y	Y	N
4 ***Oxley***	+	+	+	?	Y	Y	N
5 ***Gillmor***	Y	Y	Y	N	Y	Y	N
6 Strickland	Y	Y	Y	Y	Y	Y	N
7 ***Hobson***	Y	Y	Y	N	Y	Y	N
8 ***Boehner***	Y	Y	Y	N	Y	Y	N
9 Kaptur	Y	Y	Y	Y	Y	Y	N
10 Kucinich	Y	Y	Y	Y	Y	Y	N
11 Jones	?	?	?	?	N	Y	N
12 ***Kasich***	Y	Y	Y	N	Y	Y	N
13 Brown	Y	Y	Y	Y	Y	Y	N
14 Sawyer	Y	Y	Y	Y	Y	Y	N
15 ***Pryce***	?	?	?	?	Y	Y	N
16 ***Regula***	Y	Y	Y	N	Y	Y	N
17 Traficant	Y	Y	Y	Y	Y	Y	N
18 ***Ney***	Y	Y	Y	N	Y	Y	N
19 ***LaTourette***	Y	Y	Y	N	Y	Y	N
OKLAHOMA							
1 ***Largent***	Y	Y	Y	N	Y	Y	N
2 ***Coburn***	?	?	?	?	Y	Y	N
3 ***Watkins***	Y	Y	Y	N	Y	Y	N
4 ***Watts***	Y	Y	Y	N	Y	Y	N
5 ***Istook***	Y	Y	Y	N	Y	Y	N
6 ***Lucas***	Y	Y	Y	N	Y	Y	N
OREGON							
1 Wu	Y	Y	Y	Y	Y	Y	N
2 ***Walden***	Y	Y	Y	N	?	Y	N
3 Blumenauer	Y	Y	Y	Y	Y	Y	P
4 DeFazio	Y	Y	Y	Y	Y	Y	N
5 Hooley	Y	Y	Y	Y	Y	Y	N
PENNSYLVANIA							
1 Brady	Y	Y	Y	Y	N	Y	N
2 Fattah	Y	Y	Y	Y	N	Y	N
3 Borski	?	?	?	?	Y	Y	N
4 Klink	Y	Y	Y	Y	Y	Y	N
5 ***Peterson***	Y	Y	Y	N	Y	Y	N
6 Holden	Y	Y	Y	Y	Y	Y	N
7 ***Weldon***	?	Y	Y	N	Y	Y	N
8 ***Greenwood***	Y	Y	Y	N	Y	Y	N
9 ***Shuster***	Y	Y	Y	N	Y	Y	N
10 ***Sherwood***	Y	Y	Y	N	Y	Y	N
11 Kanjorski	Y	Y	Y	Y	Y	Y	N
12 Murtha	Y	Y	Y	Y	Y	Y	N
13 Hoeffel	Y	Y	Y	Y	Y	Y	N
14 Coyne	Y	Y	Y	Y	Y	Y	N
15 ***Toomey***	Y	Y	Y	N	Y	Y	N
16 ***Pitts***	Y	Y	Y	N	Y	Y	N
17 ***Gekas***	Y	Y	Y	N	Y	Y	N
18 Doyle	Y	Y	Y	Y	Y	Y	N
19 ***Goodling***	Y	Y	Y	N	?	Y	N
20 Mascara	Y	Y	Y	Y	Y	Y	N
21 ***English***	Y	Y	Y	N	Y	Y	N
RHODE ISLAND							
1 Kennedy	Y	Y	Y	Y	N	Y	N
2 Weygand	Y	Y	Y	Y	Y	Y	N
SOUTH CAROLINA							
1 ***Sanford***	Y	Y	N	N	N	Y	N
2 ***Spence***	Y	Y	Y	N	Y	Y	N
3 ***Graham***	Y	Y	Y	N	Y	Y	N
4 ***DeMint***	Y	Y	Y	N	Y	Y	N
5 Spratt	Y	Y	Y	Y	Y	Y	N
6 Clyburn	Y	Y	Y	Y	N	Y	N
SOUTH DAKOTA							
AL ***Thune***	Y	Y	Y	N	Y	Y	N

	111	112	113	114	115	116	117
TENNESSEE							
1 ***Jenkins***	+	+	+	–	Y	Y	N
2 ***Duncan***	Y	Y	Y	N	Y	Y	N
3 ***Wamp***	Y	Y	Y	N	Y	Y	N
4 ***Hilleary***	Y	Y	Y	N	Y	Y	N
5 Clement	?	?	?	?	Y	Y	N
6 Gordon	Y	Y	Y	Y	Y	Y	N
7 ***Bryant***	Y	Y	Y	N	Y	Y	N
8 Tanner	?	?	?	?	Y	Y	N
9 Ford	Y	Y	Y	Y	N	Y	?
TEXAS							
1 Sandlin	Y	Y	Y	Y	Y	Y	N
2 Turner	Y	Y	Y	Y	Y	Y	N
3 ***Johnson, Sam***	Y	Y	Y	N	?	Y	N
4 Hall	Y	Y	Y	Y	Y	Y	N
5 ***Sessions***	Y	Y	Y	N	Y	Y	N
6 ***Barton***	Y	Y	Y	N	Y	Y	N
7 ***Archer***	Y	Y	Y	N	Y	Y	N
8 ***Brady***	Y	Y	Y	N	Y	Y	N
9 Lampson	Y	Y	Y	Y	Y	Y	N
10 Doggett	Y	Y	Y	Y	Y	Y	N
11 Edwards	Y	Y	Y	Y	Y	Y	N
12 ***Granger***	Y	Y	Y	N	Y	Y	N
13 ***Thornberry***	P	Y	Y	N	Y	Y	N
14 ***Paul***	Y	Y	Y	N	N	Y	N
15 Hinojosa	Y	Y	Y	Y	Y	Y	N
16 Reyes	?	?	?	?	?	Y	N
17 Stenholm	Y	Y	Y	Y	Y	Y	N
18 Jackson-Lee	Y	Y	Y	Y	N	Y	N
19 ***Combest***	Y	Y	Y	N	Y	Y	N
20 Gonzalez	Y	Y	Y	Y	Y	Y	N
21 ***Smith***	Y	Y	Y	N	Y	Y	N
22 ***DeLay***	Y	Y	Y	N	Y	Y	N
23 ***Bonilla***	Y	Y	Y	N	Y	Y	N
24 Frost	?	?	?	?	Y	Y	N
25 Bentsen	Y	Y	Y	Y	Y	Y	N
26 ***Armey***	Y	Y	Y	N	Y	Y	N
27 Ortiz	Y	Y	Y	Y	Y	Y	N
28 Rodriguez	?	?	?	?	?	?	?
29 Green	Y	Y	Y	Y	Y	Y	N
30 Johnson, E.B.	Y	Y	Y	Y	N	Y	N
UTAH							
1 ***Hansen***	Y	Y	Y	N	Y	Y	N
2 ***Cook***	?	?	?	?	?	?	?
3 ***Cannon***	?	?	?	?	Y	Y	N
VERMONT							
AL *Sanders*	Y	Y	Y	Y	N	Y	N
VIRGINIA							
1 ***Bateman***	Y	Y	Y	N	Y	Y	N
2 Pickett	Y	Y	Y	Y	Y	Y	N
3 Scott	Y	Y	Y	Y	N	Y	N
4 Sisisky	Y	?	?	?	Y	Y	N
5 *Goode*	Y	Y	Y	N	Y	Y	N
6 ***Goodlatte***	Y	Y	Y	N	Y	Y	N
7 ***Bliley***	Y	Y	Y	N	Y	Y	N
8 Moran	Y	Y	Y	Y	Y	Y	N
9 Boucher	Y	Y	Y	Y	Y	Y	N
10 ***Wolf***	Y	Y	Y	N	Y	Y	N
11 ***Davis***	Y	Y	Y	N	Y	Y	N
WASHINGTON							
1 Inslee	Y	Y	Y	Y	Y	Y	N
2 ***Metcalf***	Y	Y	Y	N	Y	Y	N
3 Baird	Y	Y	Y	Y	Y	Y	N
4 ***Hastings***	Y	Y	Y	N	Y	Y	N
5 ***Nethercutt***	Y	Y	Y	N	Y	Y	N
6 Dicks	Y	Y	Y	Y	Y	Y	N
7 McDermott	Y	Y	Y	Y	N	Y	N
8 ***Dunn***	Y	Y	Y	N	Y	Y	N
9 Smith	Y	Y	Y	Y	Y	Y	N
WEST VIRGINIA							
1 Mollohan	Y	Y	Y	?	Y	Y	N
2 Wise	?	?	?	?	Y	Y	N
3 Rahall	Y	Y	Y	Y	Y	Y	N
WISCONSIN							
1 ***Ryan***	Y	Y	Y	N	Y	Y	N
2 Baldwin	Y	Y	Y	Y	Y	Y	N
3 Kind	Y	Y	Y	Y	Y	Y	N
4 Kleczka	Y	Y	Y	Y	?	Y	N
5 Barrett	Y	Y	Y	Y	Y	Y	N
6 ***Petri***	Y	Y	Y	N	Y	Y	N
7 Obey	Y	Y	Y	Y	Y	Y	N
8 ***Green***	Y	Y	Y	N	Y	Y	N
9 ***Sensenbrenner***	Y	Y	Y	N	Y	Y	N
WYOMING							
AL ***Cubin***	Y	Y	Y	N	?	Y	N

Southern states - Ala., Ark., Fla., Ga., Ky., La., Miss., N.C., Okla., S.C., Tenn., Texas, Va.

118. HR 1501. Juvenile Justice/Motion to Instruct. Conyers, D-Mich., motion to instruct conferees to insist that the conference report include measures that would aid in effective gun safety law enforcement as well as gun safety provisions that would prevent felons, fugitives and stalkers from obtaining guns and children from getting access to guns. Motion agreed to 406-22: R 199-18; D 206-3 (ND 153-3, SD 53-0); I 1-1. April 11, 2000.

119. H J Res 94. Tax Limitation Constitutional Amendment/Passage. Passage of the joint resolution to propose a constitutional amendment to require a two-thirds majority vote of those present and voting in the House and Senate to pass any legislation that increases federal revenues by more than a "de minimis" amount, except in times of war or military conflict threatening national security. Rejected 234-192: R 204-14; D 29-177 (ND 16-136, SD 13-41); I 1-1. A two-thirds majority vote of those present and voting (284 in this case) is required to pass a joint resolution proposing an amendment to the Constitution. April 12, 2000. A "nay" was a vote in support of the president's position.

120. HR 2328. Clean Lakes/Passage. Passage of the bill that would reauthorize the Clean Lakes Program for five years, appropriating $50 million a year through fiscal year 2005 with a one-time expenditure of $25 million for grants to states to help mitigate the effects of acid rain and mine drainage on lakes. Passed 420-5: R 213-5; D 205-0 (ND 151-0, SD 54-0); I 2-0. April 12, 2000.

121. HR 3039. Chesapeake Bay/Passage. Passage of the bill that would reauthorize federal participation in the Chesapeake Bay program — an effort to restore and protect the estuary — allowing $30 million a year for six years for Environmental Protection Agency activities under the program. Passed 418-7: R 210-7; D 206-0 (ND 152-0, SD 54-0); I 2-0. April 12, 2000.

122. HR 2884. Energy Policy and Conservation Act Reauthorization/Passage. Barton, R-Texas, motion to suspend the rules and pass the bill that would reauthorize the Energy Policy and Conservation Act through 2003. The measure also would renew presidential authority to operate the Strategic Petroleum Reserve. Finally, the bill would authorize the secretary of Energy to purchase oil from marginal wells at $15 per barrel whenever the price of oil drops below that amount. Motion agreed to 416-8: R 209-8; D 205-0 (ND 151-0, SD 54-0); I 2-0. A two-thirds majority of those present and voting (283 in this case) is required for passage under suspension of the rules. April 12, 2000.

123. Procedural Motion/Journal. Approval of the House Journal of April 12, 2000. Approved 365-49: R 196-15; D 167-34 (ND 123-24, SD 44-10); I 2-0. April 13, 2000.

124. H Con Res 290. Fiscal 2001 Budget Resolution/Rule. Adoption of the rule (H Res 474) to provide for House floor consideration of the conference report on the fiscal 2001 concurrent resolution on the budget. Adopted 221-205: R 216-0; D 4-204 (ND 2-152, SD 2-52); I 1-1. April 13, 2000.

Key

Y	Voted for (yea).
#	Paired for.
+	Announced for.
N	Voted against (nay).
X	Paired against.
–	Announced against.
P	Voted "present."
C	Voted "present" to avoid possible conflict of interest.
?	Did not vote or otherwise make a position known.

•

Democrats ***Republicans***
Independents

	118	119	120	121	122	123	124
ALABAMA							
1 ***Callahan***	Y	Y	Y	Y	Y	Y	Y
2 ***Everett***	Y	Y	Y	Y	Y	Y	Y
3 ***Riley***	N	Y	Y	Y	Y	N	Y
4 ***Aderholt***	Y	Y	Y	Y	Y	N	Y
5 Cramer	Y	Y	Y	Y	Y	Y	N
6 ***Bachus***	Y	Y	Y	Y	Y	Y	Y
7 Hilliard	Y	N	Y	Y	Y	N	N
ALASKA							
AL ***Young***	N	Y	Y	Y	Y	?	Y
ARIZONA							
1 ***Salmon***	Y	Y	Y	Y	Y	Y	Y
2 Pastor	Y	N	Y	Y	Y	Y	N
3 ***Stump***	N	Y	Y	Y	Y	Y	Y
4 ***Shadegg***	Y	Y	Y	Y	Y	Y	Y
5 ***Kolbe***	Y	Y	Y	Y	Y	Y	Y
6 ***Hayworth***	N	Y	Y	Y	Y	Y	Y
ARKANSAS							
1 Berry	Y	Y	Y	Y	Y	Y	N
2 Snyder	Y	N	Y	Y	Y	Y	N
3 ***Hutchinson***	Y	Y	Y	Y	Y	Y	Y
4 ***Dickey***	Y	Y	Y	Y	Y	N	Y
CALIFORNIA							
1 Thompson	Y	N	Y	Y	Y	N	N
2 ***Herger***	Y	Y	Y	Y	Y	?	Y
3 ***Ose***	Y	Y	Y	Y	Y	Y	Y
4 ***Doolittle***	Y	Y	Y	Y	Y	Y	Y
5 Matsui	Y	N	Y	Y	Y	Y	N
6 Woolsey	Y	N	Y	Y	Y	Y	N
7 Miller, George	Y	N	Y	Y	Y	Y	N
8 Pelosi	Y	N	Y	Y	Y	Y	N
9 Lee	Y	N	Y	Y	Y	Y	N
10 Tauscher	Y	N	Y	Y	Y	Y	N
11 ***Pombo***	N	Y	Y	Y	Y	Y	Y
12 Lantos	Y	N	Y	Y	Y	Y	N
13 Stark	Y	N	Y	Y	Y	?	?
14 Eshoo	Y	N	Y	Y	Y	Y	N
15 ***Campbell***	Y	N	Y	Y	Y	Y	Y
16 Lofgren	Y	N	Y	Y	Y	Y	N
17 Farr	Y	N	Y	Y	Y	Y	N
18 Condit	Y	Y	Y	Y	Y	Y	N
19 ***Radanovich***	Y	Y	Y	Y	Y	Y	Y
20 Dooley	Y	N	Y	Y	Y	Y	N
21 ***Thomas***	Y	Y	Y	Y	Y	Y	Y
22 Capps	Y	N	Y	Y	Y	Y	N
23 ***Gallegly***	Y	Y	Y	Y	Y	Y	Y
24 Sherman	Y	Y	Y	Y	Y	Y	N
25 ***McKeon***	Y	Y	Y	Y	Y	Y	Y
26 Berman	Y	N	Y	Y	Y	Y	N
27 ***Rogan***	Y	Y	Y	Y	Y	N	Y
28 ***Dreier***	Y	N	Y	Y	Y	Y	Y
29 Waxman	Y	N	Y	Y	Y	Y	N
30 Becerra	Y	N	Y	Y	Y	Y	N
31 Martinez	Y	Y	Y	Y	Y	?	Y
32 Dixon	Y	?	Y	Y	Y	Y	N
33 Roybal-Allard	Y	N	Y	Y	Y	Y	N
34 Napolitano	Y	N	Y	Y	Y	Y	N
35 Waters	Y	N	Y	Y	Y	N	N
36 ***Kuykendall***	Y	Y	Y	Y	Y	Y	Y
37 Millender-McD.	Y	N	Y	Y	Y	Y	N
38 ***Horn***	Y	Y	Y	Y	Y	Y	Y
39 ***Royce***	Y	Y	N	Y	N	Y	Y
40 ***Lewis***	Y	Y	Y	Y	Y	Y	Y
41 ***Miller, Gary***	Y	Y	Y	Y	Y	Y	Y
42 Baca	Y	N	Y	Y	Y	Y	N
43 ***Calvert***	Y	Y	Y	Y	Y	Y	Y
44 ***Bono***	Y	Y	Y	Y	Y	Y	Y
45 ***Rohrabacher***	Y	Y	Y	Y	Y	Y	Y
46 Sanchez	Y	Y	Y	Y	Y	?	N
47 ***Cox***	Y	Y	Y	Y	Y	Y	Y
48 ***Packard***	Y	Y	Y	Y	Y	Y	Y
49 ***Bilbray***	Y	Y	Y	Y	Y	N	Y
50 Filner	Y	N	Y	Y	Y	N	N
51 ***Cunningham***	Y	Y	Y	Y	Y	Y	Y
52 ***Hunter***	Y	Y	Y	Y	Y	Y	Y
COLORADO							
1 DeGette	?	?	?	?	?	Y	N
2 Udall	Y	N	Y	Y	Y	Y	N
3 ***McInnis***	Y	Y	Y	Y	Y	Y	Y
4 ***Schaffer***	Y	Y	Y	N	Y	N	Y
5 ***Hefley***	Y	Y	Y	Y	Y	N	Y
6 ***Tancredo***	Y	Y	Y	Y	Y	P	Y
CONNECTICUT							
1 Larson	Y	N	Y	Y	Y	+	N
2 Gejdenson	Y	N	Y	Y	Y	Y	N
3 DeLauro	Y	N	Y	Y	Y	Y	N
4 ***Shays***	Y	Y	Y	Y	Y	Y	Y
5 Maloney	Y	Y	Y	Y	Y	Y	N
6 ***Johnson***	Y	N	Y	Y	Y	Y	Y
DELAWARE							
AL ***Castle***	Y	Y	Y	Y	Y	Y	Y
FLORIDA							
1 ***Scarborough***	Y	Y	Y	Y	Y	Y	Y
2 Boyd	Y	N	Y	Y	Y	Y	N
3 Brown	Y	N	Y	Y	Y	Y	N
4 ***Fowler***	Y	Y	Y	Y	Y	Y	Y
5 Thurman	Y	N	Y	Y	Y	Y	N
6 ***Stearns***	Y	Y	Y	Y	Y	?	Y
7 ***Mica***	Y	Y	Y	Y	Y	Y	Y
8 ***McCollum***	Y	Y	Y	Y	Y	Y	Y
9 ***Bilirakis***	Y	Y	Y	Y	Y	Y	Y
10 ***Young***	Y	Y	Y	Y	Y	Y	Y
11 Davis	Y	N	Y	Y	Y	Y	N
12 ***Canady***	Y	Y	Y	Y	Y	Y	Y
13 ***Miller***	Y	Y	Y	Y	Y	Y	Y
14 ***Goss***	Y	Y	Y	Y	Y	Y	Y
15 ***Weldon***	Y	Y	Y	Y	Y	Y	Y
16 ***Foley***	Y	Y	Y	Y	Y	Y	Y
17 Meek	Y	N	Y	Y	Y	Y	N
18 ***Ros-Lehtinen***	Y	Y	Y	Y	Y	Y	Y
19 Wexler	Y	N	Y	Y	Y	Y	N
20 Deutsch	Y	N	Y	Y	Y	Y	N
21 ***Diaz-Balart***	Y	Y	Y	Y	Y	Y	Y
22 ***Shaw***	Y	N	Y	Y	Y	Y	Y
23 Hastings	Y	N	Y	Y	Y	N	N
GEORGIA							
1 ***Kingston***	Y	Y	Y	Y	Y	Y	Y
2 Bishop	Y	Y	Y	Y	Y	Y	N
3 ***Collins***	Y	Y	Y	Y	Y	Y	Y
4 McKinney	Y	N	Y	Y	Y	Y	N
5 Lewis	Y	N	Y	Y	Y	N	N
6 ***Isakson***	Y	Y	Y	Y	Y	Y	Y
7 ***Barr***	N	Y	Y	Y	Y	Y	Y
8 ***Chambliss***	Y	Y	Y	Y	Y	Y	Y
9 ***Deal***	Y	Y	Y	Y	Y	Y	Y
10 ***Norwood***	Y	Y	Y	Y	Y	Y	Y
11 ***Linder***	Y	Y	Y	Y	Y	Y	Y
HAWAII							
1 Abercrombie	Y	N	+	+	+	Y	N
2 Mink	Y	N	Y	Y	Y	Y	N
IDAHO							
1 ***Chenoweth-Hage***	N	Y	Y	N	Y	Y	Y
2 ***Simpson***	Y	Y	Y	Y	Y	Y	Y
ILLINOIS							
1 Rush	Y	N	Y	Y	Y	Y	N
2 Jackson	Y	N	Y	Y	Y	Y	N
3 Lipinski	Y	N	Y	Y	Y	Y	N
4 Gutierrez	Y	N	Y	Y	Y	N	N
5 Blagojevich	Y	N	Y	Y	Y	Y	N
6 ***Hyde***	Y	N	Y	Y	?	Y	Y
7 Davis	Y	N	Y	Y	Y	Y	N
8 ***Crane***	Y	Y	Y	Y	Y	N	Y
9 Schakowsky	Y	N	Y	Y	Y	Y	N
10 ***Porter***	Y	N	Y	Y	Y	Y	Y
11 ***Weller***	Y	Y	Y	Y	Y	?	Y
12 Costello	Y	N	Y	Y	Y	N	N
13 ***Biggert***	Y	Y	Y	Y	Y	Y	Y

ND Northern Democrats SD Southern Democrats

	118	119	120	121	122	123	124
14 ***Hastert***							
15 ***Ewing***	Y	Y	Y	Y	Y	Y	Y
16 ***Manzullo***	Y	Y	Y	Y	Y	Y	Y
17 Evans	Y	N	Y	Y	Y	Y	N
18 ***LaHood***	Y	Y	Y	Y	Y	Y	Y
19 Phelps	Y	N	Y	Y	Y	N	N
20 ***Shimkus***	Y	Y	Y	Y	Y	Y	Y
INDIANA							
1 Visclosky	Y	N	Y	Y	Y	N	N
2 ***McIntosh***	?	Y	?	?	?	Y	Y
3 Roemer	Y	Y	Y	Y	Y	Y	N
4 ***Souder***	N	Y	Y	Y	Y	Y	Y
5 ***Buyer***	Y	Y	Y	Y	Y	Y	Y
6 ***Burton***	Y	Y	Y	Y	Y	Y	Y
7 ***Pease***	Y	Y	Y	Y	Y	Y	Y
8 ***Hostettler***	N	N	N	N	N	Y	Y
9 Hill	Y	N	Y	Y	Y	Y	N
10 Carson	Y	N	Y	Y	Y	Y	N
IOWA							
1 ***Leach***	Y	Y	Y	Y	Y	Y	Y
2 ***Nussle***	Y	Y	Y	Y	Y	Y	Y
3 Boswell	Y	Y	Y	Y	Y	Y	N
4 ***Ganske***	Y	Y	Y	Y	Y	Y	Y
5 ***Latham***	Y	Y	Y	Y	Y	Y	Y
KANSAS							
1 ***Moran***	Y	Y	Y	Y	Y	Y	Y
2 ***Ryun***	Y	Y	Y	Y	Y	Y	Y
3 Moore	Y	N	Y	Y	Y	N	N
4 ***Tiahrt***	Y	Y	Y	Y	Y	Y	Y
KENTUCKY							
1 ***Whitfield***	Y	Y	Y	Y	Y	Y	Y
2 ***Lewis***	Y	Y	Y	Y	Y	Y	Y
3 ***Northup***	Y	Y	Y	Y	Y	Y	?
4 Lucas	Y	Y	Y	Y	Y	Y	N
5 ***Rogers***	Y	Y	Y	Y	Y	Y	Y
6 ***Fletcher***	Y	Y	Y	Y	Y	Y	Y
LOUISIANA							
1 ***Vitter***	Y	Y	Y	Y	Y	Y	Y
2 Jefferson	Y	N	Y	Y	Y	Y	N
3 ***Tauzin***	Y	Y	Y	Y	Y	Y	Y
4 ***McCrery***	Y	Y	Y	Y	Y	Y	Y
5 ***Cooksey***	Y	Y	Y	Y	Y	Y	Y
6 ***Baker***	Y	Y	Y	Y	Y	Y	Y
7 John	Y	Y	Y	Y	Y	Y	N
MAINE							
1 Allen	Y	N	Y	Y	Y	Y	N
2 Baldacci	Y	N	Y	Y	Y	Y	N
MARYLAND							
1 ***Gilchrest***	Y	Y	Y	Y	Y	Y	Y
2 ***Ehrlich***	Y	Y	Y	Y	Y	Y	Y
3 Cardin	Y	N	Y	Y	Y	Y	N
4 Wynn	Y	N	Y	Y	Y	?	?
5 Hoyer	Y	N	Y	Y	Y	Y	N
6 ***Bartlett***	Y	Y	Y	Y	Y	Y	Y
7 Cummings	Y	?	?	?	?	Y	N
8 ***Morella***	Y	N	Y	Y	Y	Y	Y
MASSACHUSETTS							
1 Olver	Y	N	Y	Y	Y	Y	N
2 Neal	Y	N	Y	Y	Y	Y	N
3 McGovern	Y	N	Y	Y	Y	Y	N
4 Frank	Y	N	Y	Y	Y	Y	N
5 Meehan	Y	N	Y	Y	Y	Y	N
6 Tierney	Y	N	Y	Y	Y	Y	N
7 Markey	Y	N	Y	Y	Y	Y	N
8 Capuano	Y	N	Y	Y	Y	Y	N
9 Moakley	Y	N	Y	Y	?	Y	N
10 Delahunt	Y	N	Y	Y	Y	Y	N
MICHIGAN							
1 Stupak	Y	N	Y	Y	Y	N	N
2 ***Hoekstra***	Y	Y	Y	Y	Y	Y	Y
3 ***Ehlers***	Y	Y	Y	Y	Y	Y	Y
4 ***Camp***	Y	Y	Y	Y	Y	Y	Y
5 Barcia	Y	Y	Y	Y	Y	Y	N
6 ***Upton***	Y	Y	Y	Y	Y	Y	Y
7 ***Smith***	Y	Y	Y	?	Y	Y	Y
8 Stabenow	Y	N	Y	Y	Y	Y	N
9 Kildee	Y	N	Y	Y	Y	Y	N
10 Bonior	Y	N	Y	Y	Y	N	N
11 ***Knollenberg***	Y	Y	Y	Y	Y	Y	Y
12 Levin	Y	N	Y	Y	Y	Y	N
13 Rivers	Y	N	Y	Y	Y	Y	N
14 Conyers	Y	N	Y	Y	Y	Y	N
15 Kilpatrick	Y	N	Y	Y	Y	Y	N
16 Dingell	Y	N	Y	Y	Y	Y	N

	118	119	120	121	122	123	124
MINNESOTA							
1 ***Gutknecht***	Y	Y	Y	Y	Y	N	Y
2 Minge	Y	N	Y	Y	Y	Y	N
3 ***Ramstad***	Y	Y	Y	Y	Y	N	Y
4 Vento	Y	N	Y	Y	Y	Y	N
5 Sabo	Y	N	Y	Y	Y	N	N
6 Luther	Y	N	Y	Y	Y	Y	N
7 Peterson	N	N	Y	Y	Y	N	N
8 Oberstar	Y	N	Y	Y	Y	N	N
MISSISSIPPI							
1 ***Wicker***	Y	Y	Y	Y	Y	N	Y
2 Thompson	Y	N	Y	Y	Y	N	N
3 ***Pickering***	Y	Y	Y	Y	Y	Y	Y
4 Shows	Y	Y	Y	Y	Y	Y	N
5 Taylor	Y	Y	Y	Y	Y	N	N
MISSOURI							
1 Clay	Y	N	Y	Y	Y	?	N
2 ***Talent***	Y	Y	Y	Y	Y	Y	Y
3 Gephardt	Y	?	?	?	?	Y	N
4 Skelton	Y	Y	Y	Y	Y	Y	N
5 McCarthy	Y	N	Y	Y	Y	Y	N
6 Danner	Y	Y	Y	Y	Y	Y	N
7 ***Blunt***	Y	Y	Y	Y	Y	Y	Y
8 ***Emerson***	Y	Y	Y	Y	Y	Y	Y
9 ***Hulshof***	Y	Y	Y	Y	Y	N	Y
MONTANA							
AL ***Hill***	N	N	Y	Y	Y	N	Y
NEBRASKA							
1 ***Bereuter***	Y	N	Y	Y	Y	Y	Y
2 ***Terry***	Y	Y	Y	Y	Y	Y	Y
3 ***Barrett***	Y	Y	Y	Y	Y	Y	Y
NEVADA							
1 Berkley	Y	Y	Y	Y	Y	Y	N
2 ***Gibbons***	Y	Y	Y	Y	Y	Y	Y
NEW HAMPSHIRE							
1 ***Sununu***	Y	Y	Y	Y	Y	Y	Y
2 ***Bass***	Y	Y	Y	Y	Y	Y	Y
NEW JERSEY							
1 Andrews	Y	Y	Y	Y	Y	Y	N
2 ***LoBiondo***	Y	Y	Y	Y	Y	N	Y
3 ***Saxton***	Y	Y	Y	Y	Y	Y	Y
4 ***Smith***	Y	Y	Y	Y	Y	Y	Y
5 ***Roukema***	Y	Y	Y	Y	Y	Y	Y
6 Pallone	Y	Y	Y	Y	Y	N	N
7 ***Franks***	Y	Y	Y	Y	Y	Y	Y
8 Pascrell	Y	N	Y	Y	Y	Y	N
9 Rothman	Y	N	Y	Y	Y	Y	N
10 Payne	Y	N	Y	Y	Y	Y	N
11 ***Frelinghuysen***	Y	Y	Y	Y	Y	Y	Y
12 Holt	Y	N	Y	Y	Y	Y	N
13 Menendez	Y	N	Y	Y	Y	Y	N
NEW MEXICO							
1 ***Wilson***	Y	Y	Y	Y	Y	Y	Y
2 ***Skeen***	Y	Y	Y	Y	Y	Y	Y
3 Udall	Y	N	Y	Y	Y	N	N
NEW YORK							
1 Forbes	Y	Y	Y	Y	Y	?	N
2 ***Lazio***	Y	Y	Y	Y	Y	Y	Y
3 ***King***	Y	Y	Y	Y	Y	Y	Y
4 McCarthy	Y	Y	Y	Y	Y	Y	N
5 Ackerman	Y	N	Y	Y	Y	Y	N
6 Meeks	Y	N	Y	Y	Y	Y	N
7 Crowley	Y	N	Y	Y	Y	Y	N
8 Nadler	Y	N	Y	Y	Y	Y	N
9 Weiner	Y	N	Y	Y	Y	Y	N
10 Towns	Y	N	Y	Y	Y	Y	N
11 Owens	Y	N	Y	Y	Y	Y	N
12 Velázquez	Y	N	Y	Y	Y	Y	N
13 ***Fossella***	Y	Y	Y	Y	Y	Y	Y
14 Maloney	Y	N	Y	Y	Y	Y	N
15 Rangel	Y	N	Y	Y	Y	Y	N
16 Serrano	Y	N	Y	Y	Y	Y	N
17 Engel	Y	N	Y	Y	Y	Y	N
18 Lowey	Y	N	Y	Y	Y	Y	N
19 ***Kelly***	Y	Y	Y	Y	Y	Y	Y
20 ***Gilman***	Y	Y	Y	Y	Y	Y	Y
21 McNulty	Y	N	Y	Y	Y	N	N
22 ***Sweeney***	Y	Y	Y	Y	Y	Y	Y
23 ***Boehlert***	Y	N	Y	Y	Y	Y	Y
24 ***McHugh***	Y	Y	Y	Y	Y	Y	Y
25 ***Walsh***	Y	N	Y	Y	Y	Y	Y
26 Hinchey	Y	N	Y	Y	Y	Y	N
27 ***Reynolds***	Y	Y	Y	Y	Y	Y	Y
28 Slaughter	Y	N	Y	Y	Y	Y	N
29 LaFalce	Y	N	Y	Y	Y	Y	N

	118	119	120	121	122	123	124
30 ***Quinn***	Y	Y	Y	Y	Y	Y	Y
31 ***Houghton***	Y	?	?	?	?	?	?
NORTH CAROLINA							
1 Clayton	Y	N	Y	Y	Y	Y	N
2 Etheridge	Y	Y	Y	Y	Y	N	N
3 ***Jones***	N	Y	Y	Y	Y	Y	Y
4 Price	Y	N	Y	Y	Y	Y	N
5 ***Burr***	Y	Y	Y	Y	Y	Y	Y
6 ***Coble***	Y	Y	Y	Y	Y	Y	Y
7 McIntyre	Y	Y	Y	Y	Y	Y	N
8 ***Hayes***	Y	Y	Y	Y	Y	Y	Y
9 ***Myrick***	+	Y	Y	Y	Y	?	?
10 ***Ballenger***	Y	Y	Y	Y	Y	Y	Y
11 ***Taylor***	Y	Y	Y	Y	Y	Y	Y
12 Watt	Y	N	Y	Y	Y	Y	N
NORTH DAKOTA							
AL Pomeroy	Y	N	Y	Y	Y	Y	N
OHIO							
1 ***Chabot***	Y	Y	Y	Y	Y	Y	Y
2 ***Portman***	Y	Y	Y	Y	Y	Y	Y
3 Hall	Y	N	Y	Y	Y	?	N
4 ***Oxley***	Y	Y	Y	Y	Y	?	Y
5 ***Gillmor***	Y	N	Y	Y	Y	Y	Y
6 Strickland	Y	N	Y	Y	Y	N	N
7 ***Hobson***	Y	Y	Y	Y	Y	Y	Y
8 ***Boehner***	Y	Y	Y	Y	Y	Y	Y
9 Kaptur	Y	?	Y	Y	Y	Y	N
10 Kucinich	Y	N	Y	Y	Y	Y	N
11 Jones	Y	N	Y	Y	Y	Y	N
12 ***Kasich***	Y	Y	Y	Y	Y	Y	Y
13 Brown	Y	N	Y	Y	Y	N	N
14 Sawyer	Y	N	Y	Y	Y	Y	N
15 ***Pryce***	Y	Y	Y	Y	Y	Y	Y
16 ***Regula***	Y	Y	Y	Y	Y	Y	Y
17 Traficant	Y	Y	Y	Y	Y	Y	Y
18 ***Ney***	Y	Y	Y	Y	Y	Y	Y
19 ***LaTourette***	Y	Y	Y	Y	Y	Y	Y
OKLAHOMA							
1 ***Largent***	Y	Y	Y	Y	Y	Y	Y
2 ***Coburn***	N	Y	Y	Y	Y	Y	Y
3 ***Watkins***	Y	+	Y	Y	Y	Y	Y
4 ***Watts***	Y	Y	Y	Y	Y	Y	Y
5 ***Istook***	Y	Y	Y	Y	Y	Y	Y
6 ***Lucas***	Y	Y	Y	Y	Y	Y	Y
OREGON							
1 Wu	Y	N	Y	Y	Y	N	N
2 ***Walden***	Y	Y	Y	Y	Y	Y	Y
3 Blumenauer	Y	N	Y	Y	Y	Y	N
4 DeFazio	Y	N	Y	Y	Y	N	N
5 Hooley	Y	N	Y	Y	Y	N	N
PENNSYLVANIA							
1 Brady	Y	N	Y	Y	Y	N	N
2 Fattah	Y	N	Y	Y	Y	?	N
3 Borski	Y	N	Y	Y	Y	?	?
4 Klink	Y	N	Y	Y	Y	Y	N
5 ***Peterson***	Y	Y	Y	Y	Y	Y	Y
6 Holden	Y	N	Y	Y	Y	Y	N
7 ***Weldon***	Y	Y	Y	Y	Y	Y	Y
8 ***Greenwood***	Y	Y	Y	Y	Y	Y	Y
9 ***Shuster***	Y	Y	Y	Y	Y	Y	Y
10 ***Sherwood***	Y	Y	Y	Y	Y	Y	Y
11 Kanjorski	Y	N	Y	Y	Y	Y	N
12 Murtha	Y	N	Y	Y	Y	Y	N
13 Hoeffel	Y	N	Y	Y	Y	Y	N
14 Coyne	Y	N	Y	Y	Y	Y	N
15 ***Toomey***	Y	Y	Y	Y	N	Y	Y
16 ***Pitts***	Y	Y	Y	Y	N	Y	Y
17 ***Gekas***	Y	Y	Y	Y	Y	Y	Y
18 Doyle	Y	N	Y	Y	Y	Y	N
19 ***Goodling***	Y	Y	Y	Y	Y	Y	Y
20 Mascara	Y	N	Y	Y	Y	Y	N
21 ***English***	Y	Y	Y	Y	Y	N	Y
RHODE ISLAND							
1 Kennedy	Y	N	Y	Y	Y	Y	N
2 Weygand	Y	N	Y	Y	Y	Y	N
SOUTH CAROLINA							
1 ***Sanford***	N	Y	N	N	N	Y	Y
2 ***Spence***	Y	Y	Y	Y	Y	Y	Y
3 ***Graham***	Y	Y	Y	Y	Y	Y	Y
4 ***DeMint***	N	Y	Y	Y	Y	Y	Y
5 Spratt	Y	N	Y	Y	Y	Y	N
6 Clyburn	Y	N	Y	Y	Y	N	N
SOUTH DAKOTA							
AL ***Thune***	Y	Y	Y	Y	Y	Y	Y

	118	119	120	121	122	123	124
TENNESSEE							
1 ***Jenkins***	N	Y	Y	Y	Y	Y	Y
2 ***Duncan***	Y	Y	Y	N	N	Y	Y
3 ***Wamp***	N	Y	Y	Y	Y	Y	Y
4 ***Hilleary***	Y	Y	Y	Y	Y	Y	Y
5 Clement	Y	N	Y	Y	Y	Y	N
6 Gordon	Y	Y	Y	Y	Y	Y	N
7 ***Bryant***	Y	Y	Y	Y	Y	Y	Y
8 Tanner	Y	N	Y	Y	Y	Y	N
9 Ford	Y	N	Y	Y	Y	Y	N
TEXAS							
1 Sandlin	Y	Y	Y	Y	Y	Y	N
2 Turner	Y	N	Y	Y	Y	Y	N
3 ***Johnson, Sam***	Y	Y	Y	Y	Y	Y	Y
4 Hall	Y	Y	Y	Y	Y	Y	N
5 ***Sessions***	Y	Y	Y	Y	Y	Y	Y
6 ***Barton***	Y	Y	Y	Y	Y	Y	Y
7 ***Archer***	Y	Y	Y	Y	Y	Y	Y
8 ***Brady***	Y	Y	Y	Y	Y	Y	Y
9 Lampson	Y	N	Y	Y	Y	Y	N
10 Doggett	Y	N	Y	Y	Y	Y	N
11 Edwards	Y	N	Y	Y	Y	Y	N
12 ***Granger***	Y	Y	Y	Y	Y	Y	Y
13 ***Thornberry***	Y	Y	Y	Y	Y	Y	Y
14 ***Paul***	N	Y	N	N	N	Y	Y
15 Hinojosa	Y	N	Y	Y	Y	Y	N
16 Reyes	Y	N	Y	Y	Y	Y	N
17 Stenholm	Y	N	Y	Y	Y	N	N
18 Jackson-Lee	Y	N	Y	Y	Y	Y	N
19 ***Combest***	Y	Y	Y	Y	Y	?	?
20 Gonzalez	Y	N	Y	Y	Y	Y	N
21 ***Smith***	Y	Y	Y	Y	Y	Y	Y
22 ***DeLay***	Y	Y	Y	Y	Y	Y	Y
23 ***Bonilla***	Y	Y	Y	Y	Y	Y	Y
24 Frost	Y	N	Y	Y	Y	Y	N
25 Bentsen	Y	N	Y	Y	Y	Y	N
26 ***Armey***	Y	Y	Y	Y	Y	Y	Y
27 Ortiz	Y	N	Y	Y	Y	Y	N
28 Rodriguez	?	N	Y	Y	Y	Y	N
29 Green	Y	Y	Y	Y	Y	Y	N
30 Johnson, E.B.	Y	N	Y	Y	Y	N	N
UTAH							
1 ***Hansen***	Y	Y	Y	Y	Y	Y	Y
2 ***Cook***	?	?	?	?	?	?	?
3 ***Cannon***	Y	Y	Y	Y	Y	Y	Y
VERMONT							
AL *Sanders*	Y	N	Y	Y	Y	Y	N
VIRGINIA							
1 ***Bateman***	Y	N	Y	Y	Y	Y	Y
2 Pickett	Y	N	Y	Y	Y	N	Y
3 Scott	Y	N	Y	Y	Y	Y	N
4 Sisisky	Y	N	Y	Y	Y	Y	Y
5 *Goode*	N	Y	Y	Y	Y	Y	Y
6 ***Goodlatte***	Y	Y	Y	Y	Y	Y	Y
7 ***Bliley***	?	Y	Y	Y	Y	Y	Y
8 Moran	Y	N	Y	Y	Y	Y	N
9 Boucher	Y	N	Y	Y	Y	Y	N
10 ***Wolf***	Y	Y	Y	Y	Y	Y	Y
11 ***Davis***	Y	Y	Y	Y	Y	Y	Y
WASHINGTON							
1 Inslee	Y	N	Y	Y	Y	Y	N
2 ***Metcalf***	N	Y	Y	Y	Y	Y	Y
3 Baird	Y	N	Y	Y	Y	N	N
4 ***Hastings***	Y	Y	Y	Y	Y	Y	Y
5 ***Nethercutt***	Y	Y	Y	Y	Y	Y	Y
6 Dicks	Y	N	Y	Y	Y	Y	N
7 McDermott	Y	N	Y	Y	Y	N	N
8 ***Dunn***	Y	Y	Y	Y	Y	Y	Y
9 Smith	Y	N	Y	Y	Y	Y	N
WEST VIRGINIA							
1 Mollohan	N	N	?	?	?	Y	N
2 Wise	Y	N	Y	Y	Y	Y	N
3 Rahall	N	N	Y	Y	Y	Y	N
WISCONSIN							
1 ***Ryan***	Y	Y	Y	Y	Y	Y	Y
2 Baldwin	Y	N	Y	Y	Y	Y	N
3 Kind	Y	N	Y	Y	Y	Y	N
4 Kleczka	Y	N	Y	Y	Y	Y	N
5 Barrett	Y	N	Y	Y	Y	Y	N
6 ***Petri***	Y	Y	Y	Y	Y	Y	Y
7 Obey	Y	N	?	Y	Y	Y	N
8 ***Green***	Y	Y	Y	Y	Y	Y	Y
9 ***Sensenbrenner***	Y	Y	N	N	N	Y	Y
WYOMING							
AL ***Cubin***	Y	Y	Y	Y	Y	Y	Y

Southern states - Ala., Ark., Fla., Ga., Ky., La., Miss., N.C., Okla., S.C., Tenn., Texas, Va.

125. H Con Res 290. Fiscal 2001 Budget Resolution/Conference Report. Adoption of the conference report on the fiscal 2001 concurrent resolution on the budget. The resolution calls for cutting taxes by $150 billion over five years and creates a 'reserve fund' of $25 billion that could also be used for tax cuts. It also would establish a $40 billion reserve fund for Medicare overhaul and to provide prescription drug coverage for seniors. The plan calls for $600.3 billion in discretionary spending and allows for $310.8 billion in defense appropriations. It sets non-defense discretionary spending at $289.5 billion. Adopted (thus sent to the Senate) 220-208: R 213-5; D 6-202 (ND 3-152, SD 3-50); I 1-1. April 13, 2000.

126. HR 4199. Tax Code Termination/Recommit. Rangel, D-N.Y., motion to recommit the bill to the House Ways and Means Committee with instructions to ensure that reform of the tax system is fiscally responsible, that it not endanger a balanced budget nor use funds devoted to Social Security, and that it be fair to all income classes and simplify the tax code. Motion rejected 191-228: R 0-214; D 190-13 (ND 142-9, SD 48-4); I 1-1. April 13, 2000.

127. HR 4199. Tax Code Termination/Passage. Passage of the bill to abolish the tax code, except for the provisions that fund Social Security and Medicare, by Dec. 31, 2004. The bill would recommend that Congress enact a new tax code by July 4, 2004. Passed 229-187: R 211-2; D 17-184 (ND 10-141, SD 7-43); I 1-1. April 13, 2000.

128. HR 3615. Rural Television/Passage. Passage of the bill that would amend the Rural Electrification Act of 1936 to authorize the Agriculture Department to issue up to $1.25 billion in loan guarantees to providers of local television who would provide broadcasting to rural and underserved areas. The measure also establishes a three-member board to review and approve loan applications. Passed 375-37: R 174-32; D 199-5 (ND 146-5, SD 53-0); I 2-0. April 13, 2000.

129. HR 3439. Low-Power FM Radio/Signal Interference Testing. Barrett, D-Wis., amendment that would restore Federal Communications Commission authority to modify low-power FM signal interference standards, once signal interference field tests are completed and Congress has had six months to act. Rejected 142-245: R 3-187; D 138-57 (ND 112-31, SD 26-26); I 1-1. April 13, 2000.

130. HR 3439. Low-Power FM Radio/Passage. Passage of the bill that would modify the Federal Communications Commission (FCC) rules authorizing low-power FM radio stations. The bill would require congressional authority for the FCC to eliminate or reduce any interference standards on the radio dial. Additionally, the bill calls for a pilot program to study the effects of the introduction of low-power stations on already established stations. Passed 274-110: R 188-3; D 85-106 (ND 57-82, SD 28-24); I 1-1. April 13, 2000. A "nay" was a vote in support of the president's position.

Key

Y	Voted for (yea).
#	Paired for.
+	Announced for.
N	Voted against (nay).
X	Paired against.
–	Announced against.
P	Voted "present."
C	Voted "present" to avoid possible conflict of interest.
?	Did not vote or otherwise make a position known.

•

Democrats ***Republicans***
Independents

	125	126	127	128	129	130
ALABAMA						
1 ***Callahan***	Y	?	?	?	?	?
2 ***Everett***	Y	N	Y	Y	N	Y
3 ***Riley***	Y	N	Y	Y	N	Y
4 ***Aderholt***	Y	N	Y	Y	N	Y
5 Cramer	N	Y	Y	Y	N	Y
6 ***Bachus***	Y	N	Y	Y	N	Y
7 Hilliard	N	?	?	Y	Y	N
ALASKA						
AL ***Young***	Y	N	Y	Y	N	Y
ARIZONA						
1 ***Salmon***	Y	N	Y	N	N	Y
2 Pastor	N	Y	N	Y	Y	N
3 ***Stump***	Y	N	Y	Y	N	Y
4 ***Shadegg***	Y	N	Y	N	N	Y
5 ***Kolbe***	Y	N	Y	Y	?	?
6 ***Hayworth***	Y	N	Y	Y	N	Y
ARKANSAS						
1 Berry	N	Y	N	Y	N	Y
2 Snyder	N	Y	N	Y	Y	N
3 ***Hutchinson***	Y	N	Y	Y	N	Y
4 ***Dickey***	Y	N	Y	Y	N	Y
CALIFORNIA						
1 Thompson	N	Y	N	Y	Y	Y
2 ***Herger***	Y	N	Y	Y	?	Y
3 ***Ose***	Y	N	Y	Y	N	Y
4 ***Doolittle***	Y	N	Y	N	N	Y
5 Matsui	N	Y	N	Y	Y	N
6 Woolsey	N	Y	N	Y	Y	N
7 Miller, George	N	?	?	?	?	?
8 Pelosi	N	Y	N	Y	Y	N
9 Lee	N	Y	N	Y	Y	N
10 Tauscher	N	Y	N	Y	Y	N
11 ***Pombo***	Y	N	Y	Y	N	Y
12 Lantos	N	Y	N	Y	Y	N
13 Stark	?	?	?	?	?	?
14 Eshoo	N	Y	N	Y	Y	N
15 ***Campbell***	?	N	Y	Y	N	Y
16 Lofgren	N	Y	N	Y	?	?
17 Farr	N	Y	N	Y	Y	N
18 Condit	Y	N	Y	Y	N	Y
19 ***Radanovich***	Y	N	Y	Y	N	Y
20 Dooley	N	Y	N	Y	Y	N
21 ***Thomas***	Y	N	Y	Y	N	Y
22 Capps	N	Y	N	Y	Y	Y
23 ***Gallegly***	Y	N	Y	?	?	?
24 Sherman	N	Y	N	Y	Y	Y
25 ***McKeon***	Y	N	Y	Y	N	Y
26 Berman	N	Y	N	Y	Y	N
27 ***Rogan***	Y	N	Y	Y	?	?
28 ***Dreier***	Y	N	Y	Y	N	Y
29 Waxman	N	Y	N	Y	Y	N
30 Becerra	N	Y	N	Y	Y	N
31 Martinez	Y	N	Y	Y	?	?
32 Dixon	N	Y	N	Y	Y	N
33 Roybal-Allard	N	Y	N	Y	Y	N
34 Napolitano	N	Y	N	Y	Y	N
35 Waters	N	Y	N	Y	Y	N
36 ***Kuykendall***	Y	N	Y	Y	N	Y
37 Millender-McD.	N	Y	N	Y	Y	N
38 ***Horn***	Y	N	Y	Y	N	Y
39 ***Royce***	Y	N	Y	N	N	N
40 ***Lewis***	Y	N	Y	Y	N	Y
41 ***Miller, Gary***	Y	N	Y	N	?	?
42 Baca	N	Y	N	Y	Y	Y
43 ***Calvert***	Y	N	Y	Y	N	Y
44 ***Bono***	Y	N	Y	Y	N	Y
45 ***Rohrabacher***	Y	N	Y	N	N	Y
46 Sanchez	N	Y	N	Y	+	–
47 ***Cox***	Y	N	Y	N	N	Y
48 ***Packard***	Y	N	Y	Y	N	Y
49 ***Bilbray***	Y	N	Y	Y	N	Y
50 Filner	N	Y	N	Y	Y	N
51 ***Cunningham***	Y	N	Y	Y	N	Y
52 ***Hunter***	Y	N	Y	Y	N	Y
COLORADO						
1 DeGette	N	Y	N	Y	Y	N
2 Udall	N	Y	N	Y	Y	N
3 ***McInnis***	Y	N	Y	?	?	?
4 ***Schaffer***	Y	N	Y	Y	N	Y
5 ***Hefley***	Y	N	Y	Y	N	Y
6 ***Tancredo***	Y	N	Y	Y	N	Y
CONNECTICUT						
1 Larson	N	Y	N	Y	Y	N
2 Gejdenson	N	Y	N	Y	Y	Y
3 DeLauro	N	Y	N	Y	Y	N
4 ***Shays***	Y	N	Y	N	N	Y
5 Maloney	N	Y	Y	Y	Y	Y
6 ***Johnson***	N	N	Y	Y	N	Y
DELAWARE						
AL ***Castle***	Y	N	Y	Y	N	Y
FLORIDA						
1 ***Scarborough***	Y	N	Y	Y	N	Y
2 Boyd	N	Y	N	Y	N	Y
3 Brown	N	Y	N	Y	Y	N
4 ***Fowler***	Y	N	Y	Y	?	?
5 Thurman	N	Y	N	Y	Y	Y
6 ***Stearns***	Y	N	Y	N	N	Y
7 ***Mica***	Y	N	Y	Y	N	Y
8 ***McCollum***	Y	N	Y	Y	?	?
9 ***Bilirakis***	Y	N	Y	Y	?	?
10 ***Young***	Y	?	?	?	?	?
11 Davis	N	Y	N	Y	Y	N
12 ***Canady***	Y	N	Y	Y	?	?
13 ***Miller***	Y	N	Y	N	N	Y
14 ***Goss***	Y	N	Y	Y	N	Y
15 ***Weldon***	Y	N	Y	Y	?	?
16 ***Foley***	Y	N	Y	Y	N	Y
17 Meek	N	Y	N	Y	Y	N
18 ***Ros-Lehtinen***	Y	N	Y	?	?	?
19 Wexler	?	?	?	?	?	?
20 Deutsch	N	Y	N	Y	N	Y
21 ***Diaz-Balart***	Y	N	Y	Y	N	Y
22 ***Shaw***	Y	N	Y	Y	N	Y
23 Hastings	N	Y	N	Y	Y	N
GEORGIA						
1 ***Kingston***	Y	N	Y	Y	N	Y
2 Bishop	N	Y	+	Y	Y	N
3 ***Collins***	Y	N	Y	N	N	Y
4 McKinney	N	Y	N	Y	Y	N
5 Lewis	N	Y	N	Y	Y	N
6 ***Isakson***	Y	N	Y	Y	N	Y
7 ***Barr***	Y	N	Y	Y	N	Y
8 ***Chambliss***	Y	N	Y	Y	N	Y
9 ***Deal***	Y	N	Y	Y	N	Y
10 ***Norwood***	Y	N	Y	Y	N	Y
11 ***Linder***	Y	N	Y	N	N	Y
HAWAII						
1 Abercrombie	N	Y	N	Y	Y	Y
2 Mink	N	Y	N	Y	N	Y
IDAHO						
1 ***Chenoweth-Hage***	Y	N	Y	N	N	Y
2 ***Simpson***	Y	N	Y	Y	N	Y
ILLINOIS						
1 Rush	N	Y	N	Y	Y	N
2 Jackson	N	Y	N	Y	Y	N
3 Lipinski	N	Y	N	Y	N	?
4 Gutierrez	N	Y	N	Y	Y	?
5 Blagojevich	N	Y	N	Y	N	Y
6 ***Hyde***	Y	N	Y	Y	N	Y
7 Davis	N	Y	N	Y	Y	N
8 ***Crane***	Y	N	Y	Y	?	Y
9 Schakowsky	N	Y	N	Y	Y	N
10 ***Porter***	N	N	Y	Y	N	Y
11 ***Weller***	Y	N	Y	Y	N	Y
12 Costello	N	Y	N	Y	?	?
13 ***Biggert***	Y	N	Y	Y	N	Y

ND Northern Democrats SD Southern Democrats

	125	126	127	128	129	130
14 ***Hastert***	Y					
15 ***Ewing***	Y	N	Y	Y	N	Y
16 ***Manzullo***	Y	N	Y	N	N	Y
17 Evans	N	+	–	Y	Y	N
18 ***LaHood***	Y	N	Y	Y	N	Y
19 Phelps	N	Y	N	Y	N	Y
20 ***Shimkus***	Y	N	Y	Y	N	Y
INDIANA						
1 Visclosky	N	Y	N	Y	N	Y
2 ***McIntosh***	Y	N	Y	?	?	?
3 Roemer	N	Y	N	Y	N	Y
4 ***Souder***	Y	N	Y	Y	N	Y
5 ***Buyer***	Y	N	Y	Y	N	Y
6 ***Burton***	Y	N	Y	Y	N	Y
7 ***Pease***	Y	N	Y	Y	N	Y
8 ***Hostettler***	Y	N	Y	Y	N	Y
9 Hill	N	Y	N	Y	N	Y
10 Carson	N	Y	N	Y	Y	N
IOWA						
1 ***Leach***	Y	N	Y	Y	?	?
2 ***Nussle***	Y	N	Y	Y	N	Y
3 Boswell	N	Y	N	Y	N	Y
4 ***Ganske***	Y	N	Y	?	?	?
5 ***Latham***	Y	N	Y	Y	N	Y
KANSAS						
1 ***Moran***	Y	N	Y	Y	N	Y
2 ***Ryun***	Y	N	Y	Y	N	Y
3 Moore	N	Y	N	Y	Y	Y
4 ***Tiahrt***	Y	N	Y	Y	N	Y
KENTUCKY						
1 ***Whitfield***	Y	N	Y	Y	N	Y
2 ***Lewis***	Y	N	Y	Y	N	Y
3 ***Northup***	Y	N	Y	Y	N	Y
4 Lucas	N	Y	Y	Y	N	Y
5 ***Rogers***	Y	N	Y	Y	N	Y
6 ***Fletcher***	Y	N	Y	Y	N	Y
LOUISIANA						
1 ***Vitter***	Y	N	Y	Y	N	Y
2 Jefferson	N	Y	N	Y	Y	Y
3 ***Tauzin***	Y	N	Y	Y	N	Y
4 ***McCrery***	Y	N	Y	Y	N	Y
5 ***Cooksey***	Y	N	Y	+	–	+
6 ***Baker***	Y	N	Y	?	?	?
7 John	N	Y	N	Y	N	Y
MAINE						
1 Allen	N	Y	N	Y	N	Y
2 Baldacci	N	Y	N	Y	N	Y
MARYLAND						
1 ***Gilchrest***	Y	N	Y	Y	N	Y
2 ***Ehrlich***	Y	N	Y	Y	N	Y
3 Cardin	N	Y	N	Y	Y	N
4 Wynn	N	Y	N	Y	Y	N
5 Hoyer	N	Y	N	Y	Y	N
6 ***Bartlett***	Y	N	Y	Y	N	Y
7 Cummings	N	Y	N	Y	Y	N
8 ***Morella***	N	N	N	Y	N	Y
MASSACHUSETTS						
1 Olver	N	Y	N	Y	Y	Y
2 Neal	N	Y	N	Y	Y	Y
3 McGovern	N	Y	N	Y	Y	N
4 Frank	N	Y	N	N	Y	N
5 Meehan	N	Y	N	Y	Y	Y
6 Tierney	N	Y	N	Y	Y	N
7 Markey	N	Y	N	Y	Y	N
8 Capuano	N	Y	N	N	Y	N
9 Moakley	N	Y	N	Y	Y	N
10 Delahunt	N	Y	N	Y	Y	N
MICHIGAN						
1 Stupak	N	Y	N	Y	N	Y
2 ***Hoekstra***	Y	N	Y	Y	N	Y
3 ***Ehlers***	Y	N	Y	N	Y	Y
4 ***Camp***	Y	N	Y	Y	N	Y
5 Barcia	N	N	Y	Y	N	Y
6 ***Upton***	Y	N	Y	Y	N	Y
7 ***Smith***	Y	N	Y	Y	N	Y
8 Stabenow	N	Y	N	Y	Y	Y
9 Kildee	N	Y	N	Y	Y	N
10 Bonior	N	Y	N	Y	Y	N
11 ***Knollenberg***	Y	N	Y	Y	N	Y
12 Levin	N	Y	N	Y	Y	N
13 Rivers	N	Y	N	Y	Y	N
14 Conyers	N	Y	N	Y	Y	N
15 Kilpatrick	N	Y	N	Y	Y	N
16 Dingell	N	Y	N	Y	N	Y

	125	126	127	128	129	130
MINNESOTA						
1 ***Gutknecht***	Y	N	Y	Y	N	Y
2 Minge	N	Y	Y	Y	Y	Y
3 ***Ramstad***	Y	N	Y	Y	N	Y
4 Vento	N	Y	N	?	?	?
5 Sabo	N	Y	N	Y	Y	N
6 Luther	N	Y	N	Y	Y	Y
7 Peterson	N	N	Y	Y	N	Y
8 Oberstar	N	Y	N	Y	N	Y
MISSISSIPPI						
1 ***Wicker***	Y	N	Y	Y	N	Y
2 Thompson	N	Y	N	Y	Y	N
3 ***Pickering***	Y	N	Y	Y	N	Y
4 Shows	N	N	Y	Y	N	Y
5 Taylor	N	Y	Y	Y	N	Y
MISSOURI						
1 Clay	N	?	?	?	?	?
2 ***Talent***	Y	N	Y	Y	N	Y
3 Gephardt	N	Y	N	Y	Y	N
4 Skelton	N	Y	N	Y	N	Y
5 McCarthy	N	Y	N	Y	+	–
6 Danner	N	Y	Y	Y	N	Y
7 ***Blunt***	Y	N	Y	Y	N	Y
8 ***Emerson***	Y	N	Y	Y	N	Y
9 ***Hulshof***	Y	N	Y	Y	N	Y
MONTANA						
AL ***Hill***	Y	N	Y	Y	N	Y
NEBRASKA						
1 ***Bereuter***	Y	N	Y	Y	N	Y
2 ***Terry***	Y	N	Y	Y	N	Y
3 ***Barrett***	Y	N	Y	Y	N	Y
NEVADA						
1 Berkley	N	Y	N	Y	N	Y
2 ***Gibbons***	Y	N	Y	Y	N	Y
NEW HAMPSHIRE						
1 ***Sununu***	Y	N	Y	N	N	Y
2 ***Bass***	Y	N	Y	Y	N	Y
NEW JERSEY						
1 Andrews	N	Y	N	Y	Y	Y
2 ***LoBiondo***	Y	N	Y	Y	N	Y
3 ***Saxton***	Y	N	Y	Y	N	Y
4 ***Smith***	Y	N	Y	Y	N	Y
5 ***Roukema***	Y	N	Y	Y	N	Y
6 Pallone	N	Y	N	Y	N	Y
7 ***Franks***	Y	N	Y	Y	N	Y
8 Pascrell	N	Y	N	Y	Y	N
9 Rothman	N	Y	N	Y	Y	Y
10 Payne	N	Y	N	Y	Y	N
11 ***Frelinghuysen***	Y	N	Y	N	N	Y
12 Holt	N	Y	N	Y	Y	N
13 Menendez	N	Y	N	Y	Y	N
NEW MEXICO						
1 ***Wilson***	Y	N	Y	Y	N	Y
2 ***Skeen***	Y	N	Y	Y	N	Y
3 Udall	N	Y	N	Y	Y	Y
NEW YORK						
1 Forbes	N	N	Y	Y	N	Y
2 ***Lazio***	Y	N	?	Y	N	Y
3 ***King***	Y	N	Y	Y	N	Y
4 McCarthy	N	Y	N	Y	Y	N
5 Ackerman	N	Y	N	Y	Y	N
6 Meeks	N	Y	N	Y	Y	N
7 Crowley	N	Y	N	Y	Y	N
8 Nadler	N	Y	N	Y	Y	N
9 Weiner	N	Y	N	Y	Y	N
10 Towns	N	Y	N	Y	Y	N
11 Owens	N	Y	–	Y	Y	N
12 Velázquez	N	Y	N	Y	Y	N
13 ***Fossella***	Y	N	Y	N	N	Y
14 Maloney	N	Y	N	Y	Y	Y
15 Rangel	N	Y	N	Y	?	?
16 Serrano	N	?	N	Y	Y	N
17 Engel	N	Y	N	Y	Y	Y
18 Lowey	N	Y	N	Y	N	Y
19 ***Kelly***	Y	N	Y	Y	N	Y
20 ***Gilman***	Y	N	Y	Y	N	Y
21 McNulty	N	Y	N	Y	Y	Y
22 ***Sweeney***	Y	N	Y	Y	N	Y
23 ***Boehlert***	Y	N	N	Y	N	Y
24 ***McHugh***	Y	N	Y	Y	N	Y
25 ***Walsh***	Y	N	Y	Y	N	Y
26 Hinchey	N	Y	N	Y	Y	N
27 ***Reynolds***	Y	N	Y	Y	N	Y
28 Slaughter	N	Y	N	Y	Y	N
29 LaFalce	N	Y	N	N	Y	N

	125	126	127	128	129	130
30 ***Quinn***	Y	?	?	?	?	?
31 ***Houghton***	?	?	?	?	?	?
NORTH CAROLINA						
1 Clayton	N	Y	N	Y	Y	N
2 Etheridge	N	Y	N	Y	N	Y
3 ***Jones***	Y	N	Y	Y	N	Y
4 Price	N	Y	N	Y	N	Y
5 ***Burr***	Y	N	Y	Y	N	Y
6 ***Coble***	Y	N	Y	Y	N	Y
7 McIntyre	N	N	Y	Y	N	Y
8 ***Hayes***	Y	N	Y	Y	N	Y
9 ***Myrick***	?	?	?	?	?	?
10 ***Ballenger***	Y	N	Y	Y	N	Y
11 ***Taylor***	Y	N	Y	Y	N	Y
12 Watt	N	Y	N	Y	Y	N
NORTH DAKOTA						
AL Pomeroy	N	Y	N	Y	Y	Y
OHIO						
1 ***Chabot***	Y	N	Y	N	N	Y
2 ***Portman***	Y	N	Y	Y	N	Y
3 Hall	N	Y	N	Y	?	?
4 ***Oxley***	Y	N	Y	Y	N	Y
5 ***Gillmor***	Y	N	Y	Y	N	Y
6 Strickland	N	N	Y	Y	N	Y
7 ***Hobson***	Y	N	Y	Y	N	Y
8 ***Boehner***	Y	N	Y	Y	N	Y
9 Kaptur	N	Y	N	Y	Y	N
10 Kucinich	N	Y	N	Y	Y	N
11 Jones	N	Y	N	Y	Y	N
12 ***Kasich***	Y	N	Y	N	N	Y
13 Brown	N	Y	N	Y	Y	N
14 Sawyer	N	Y	N	Y	Y	Y
15 ***Pryce***	Y	N	Y	Y	N	Y
16 ***Regula***	Y	N	Y	Y	N	Y
17 Traficant	Y	N	Y	Y	N	Y
18 ***Ney***	Y	N	Y	Y	N	Y
19 ***LaTourette***	Y	N	Y	?	?	?
OKLAHOMA						
1 ***Largent***	Y	N	Y	N	N	Y
2 ***Coburn***	Y	N	Y	N	?	?
3 ***Watkins***	Y	N	Y	Y	N	Y
4 ***Watts***	Y	N	Y	Y	N	Y
5 ***Istook***	Y	N	Y	Y	N	Y
6 ***Lucas***	Y	N	Y	Y	?	?
OREGON						
1 Wu	N	Y	N	N	Y	Y
2 ***Walden***	Y	N	Y	Y	N	Y
3 Blumenauer	N	Y	N	Y	Y	N
4 DeFazio	N	Y	N	Y	Y	N
5 Hooley	N	Y	N	Y	Y	Y
PENNSYLVANIA						
1 Brady	N	Y	N	Y	Y	N
2 Fattah	N	Y	N	Y	?	?
3 Borski	?	?	?	?	?	?
4 Klink	N	Y	N	Y	Y	Y
5 ***Peterson***	Y	N	Y	Y	N	Y
6 Holden	N	Y	N	Y	N	N
7 ***Weldon***	Y	N	Y	Y	N	Y
8 ***Greenwood***	Y	N	Y	Y	?	?
9 ***Shuster***	Y	N	Y	Y	?	?
10 ***Sherwood***	Y	N	Y	Y	N	?
11 Kanjorski	N	Y	N	Y	N	Y
12 Murtha	N	N	N	Y	N	Y
13 Hoeffel	N	Y	N	Y	Y	Y
14 Coyne	N	Y	N	Y	Y	N
15 ***Toomey***	Y	N	Y	N	N	Y
16 ***Pitts***	Y	N	Y	Y	N	Y
17 ***Gekas***	Y	N	Y	Y	N	Y
18 Doyle	N	Y	N	?	Y	N
19 ***Goodling***	Y	N	Y	Y	?	?
20 Mascara	N	Y	N	Y	Y	N
21 ***English***	Y	N	Y	Y	N	Y
RHODE ISLAND						
1 Kennedy	N	Y	N	Y	Y	N
2 Weygand	N	Y	N	Y	Y	Y
SOUTH CAROLINA						
1 ***Sanford***	N	N	Y	N	N	Y
2 ***Spence***	Y	N	Y	Y	N	Y
3 ***Graham***	Y	N	Y	Y	N	Y
4 ***DeMint***	Y	N	Y	N	N	Y
5 Spratt	N	Y	N	Y	N	Y
6 Clyburn	N	Y	N	Y	Y	N
SOUTH DAKOTA						
AL ***Thune***	Y	N	Y	Y	N	Y

	125	126	127	128	129	130
TENNESSEE						
1 ***Jenkins***	Y	N	Y	Y	N	Y
2 ***Duncan***	Y	N	Y	N	N	Y
3 ***Wamp***	Y	N	Y	Y	N	Y
4 ***Hilleary***	Y	N	Y	Y	N	Y
5 Clement	N	Y	N	Y	?	?
6 Gordon	N	Y	N	Y	N	Y
7 ***Bryant***	Y	N	Y	Y	N	Y
8 Tanner	N	Y	N	Y	N	Y
9 Ford	N	Y	N	Y	N	Y
TEXAS						
1 Sandlin	N	Y	+	Y	N	Y
2 Turner	N	N	Y	Y	N	Y
3 ***Johnson, Sam***	Y	N	Y	N	N	Y
4 Hall	Y	Y	Y	Y	N	Y
5 ***Sessions***	Y	N	Y	Y	N	Y
6 ***Barton***	Y	N	Y	Y	N	Y
7 ***Archer***	Y	N	Y	N	N	Y
8 ***Brady***	Y	N	Y	Y	N	Y
9 Lampson	N	Y	N	Y	N	Y
10 Doggett	N	Y	N	Y	Y	N
11 Edwards	N	Y	N	Y	N	Y
12 ***Granger***	Y	N	Y	Y	N	Y
13 ***Thornberry***	Y	N	Y	Y	N	Y
14 ***Paul***	N	N	Y	N	N	N
15 Hinojosa	N	Y	N	Y	Y	N
16 Reyes	N	Y	N	Y	Y	N
17 Stenholm	N	Y	N	Y	N	Y
18 Jackson-Lee	N	Y	N	Y	Y	N
19 ***Combest***	Y	N	Y	Y	N	Y
20 Gonzalez	N	Y	N	Y	Y	N
21 ***Smith***	Y	N	Y	Y	N	Y
22 ***DeLay***	Y	N	Y	N	N	Y
23 ***Bonilla***	Y	N	Y	Y	N	Y
24 Frost	N	Y	N	Y	N	Y
25 Bentsen	N	Y	N	Y	Y	N
26 ***Armey***	Y	N	Y	N	N	Y
27 Ortiz	N	Y	N	Y	Y	N
28 Rodriguez	N	Y	N	Y	Y	N
29 Green	N	Y	N	Y	N	Y
30 Johnson, E.B.	N	Y	N	Y	Y	N
UTAH						
1 ***Hansen***	Y	N	Y	Y	N	Y
2 ***Cook***	?	?	?	?	?	?
3 ***Cannon***	Y	N	Y	Y	N	Y
VERMONT						
AL *Sanders*	N	Y	N	Y	Y	N
VIRGINIA						
1 ***Bateman***	Y	N	Y	Y	N	Y
2 Pickett	Y	N	N	Y	N	Y
3 Scott	N	Y	N	Y	Y	N
4 Sisisky	Y	Y	N	Y	N	Y
5 *Goode*	Y	N	Y	Y	N	Y
6 ***Goodlatte***	Y	N	Y	Y	N	Y
7 ***Bliley***	Y	?	?	?	?	?
8 Moran	N	Y	N	Y	Y	N
9 Boucher	N	Y	N	Y	N	Y
10 ***Wolf***	Y	N	Y	Y	N	Y
11 ***Davis***	Y	N	Y	Y	N	Y
WASHINGTON						
1 Inslee	N	Y	N	Y	Y	N
2 ***Metcalf***	Y	N	Y	Y	Y	N
3 Baird	N	Y	N	Y	N	Y
4 ***Hastings***	Y	N	Y	Y	N	Y
5 ***Nethercutt***	Y	N	Y	Y	N	Y
6 Dicks	N	Y	N	Y	Y	?
7 McDermott	N	Y	N	Y	Y	N
8 ***Dunn***	Y	N	Y	Y	N	Y
9 Smith	N	Y	N	Y	Y	?
WEST VIRGINIA						
1 Mollohan	N	N	N	Y	?	?
2 Wise	N	Y	N	Y	N	Y
3 Rahall	N	Y	N	Y	N	Y
WISCONSIN						
1 ***Ryan***	Y	N	Y	Y	N	Y
2 Baldwin	N	Y	N	Y	Y	N
3 Kind	N	Y	N	Y	N	Y
4 Kleczka	N	Y	N	N	Y	Y
5 Barrett	N	Y	N	Y	Y	N
6 ***Petri***	Y	N	Y	Y	Y	Y
7 Obey	N	Y	N	Y	Y	N
8 ***Green***	Y	N	Y	Y	N	Y
9 ***Sensenbrenner***	Y	N	Y	N	N	Y
WYOMING						
AL ***Cubin***	Y	N	Y	Y	N	Y

Southern states - Ala., Ark., Fla., Ga., Ky., La., Miss., N.C., Okla., S.C., Tenn., Texas, Va.

131. H Con Res 300. Y2K Commendation/Adoption. Horn, R-Calif., motion to suspend the rules and adopt the concurrent resolution recognizing and commending the federal work force for its efforts in addressing the Y2K computer problem. Motion agreed to 409-0: R 204-0; D 203-0 (ND 152-0, SD 51-0); I 2-0. A two-thirds majority of those present and voting (273 in this case) is required for adoption under suspension of the rules. May 2, 2000.

132. HR 2932. Golden Spike/Passage. Hansen, R-Utah, motion to suspend the rules and pass the bill that would establish the Crossroads of the West Historic District in Ogden, Utah, to preserve and interpret historic features related to the convergence of the Union Pacific and Central Pacific railroads, and to study the possibility of establishing a Golden Spike/Crossroads of the West National Heritage Area. Motion agreed to 400-9: R 197-9; D 201-0 (ND 150-0, SD 51-0); I 2-0. A two-thirds majority of those present and voting (273 in this case) is required for passage under suspension of the rules. May 2, 2000.

133. H Con Res 295. South Vietnam Resolution/Adoption. Gilman, R-N.Y., motion to suspend the rules and adopt the concurrent resolution that would request the president to remind Vietnam leaders of the American people's commitment to political, religious and economic freedom for the Vietnamese people and to ask the government to release all political prisoners. Motion agreed to 415-3: R 210-3; D 204-0 (ND 150-0, SD 54-0); I 1-0. A two-thirds majority of those present and voting (279 in this case) is required for adoption under suspension of the rules. May 3, 2000.

134. H Con Res 304. Belarus Condemnation/Adoption. Gilman, R-N.Y., motion to suspend the rules and adopt the concurrent resolution that would condemn human rights violations by the government of Belarus and urge it to hold free elections. Motion agreed to 409-2: R 204-2; D 204-0 (ND 150-0, SD 54-0); I 1-0. A two-thirds majority of those present and voting (274 in this case) is required for adoption under suspension of the rules. May 3, 2000.

135. S 1744. Endangered Species Act Reporting/Passage. Hansen, R-Utah, motion to suspend the rules and pass the bill that would require the Interior Department to continue filing an annual report enumerating how much federal money was spent on efforts to conserve endangered and threatened species. The measure would be retroactive to Dec. 19, 1999. Motion agreed to 420-0: R 213-0; D 205-0 (ND 152-0, SD 53-0); I 2-0. A two-thirds majority of those present and voting (280 in this case) is required for passage under suspension of the rules. May 3, 2000.

136. HR 1509. Disabled Veterans' Memorial/Passage. Hansen, R-Utah, motion to suspend the rules and pass the bill that would authorize the Disabled Veterans' LIFE Memorial Foundation to establish a memorial in the District of Columbia or its environs to honor veterans who became disabled while serving in the U.S. armed forces. No federal funds could be used. Motion agreed to 421-0: R 212-0; D 207-0 (ND 153-0, SD 54-0); I 2-0. A two-thirds majority of those present and voting (281 in this case) is required for passage under suspension of the rules. May 3, 2000.

137. H Con Res 310. National Charter Schools Week/Adoption. Petri, R-Wis., motion to suspend the rules and adopt the resolution that would commend the charter school movement and express the sense of Congress that a National Charter Schools Week should be established. Motion agreed to 397-20: R 210-0; D 185-20 (ND 133-18, SD 52-2); I 2-0. A two-thirds majority of those present and voting (278 in this case) is necessary for adoption under suspension of the rules. May 3, 2000.

Key

Y	Voted for (yea).
#	Paired for.
+	Announced for.
N	Voted against (nay).
X	Paired against.
–	Announced against.
P	Voted "present."
C	Voted "present" to avoid possible conflict of interest.
?	Did not vote or otherwise make a position known.

•

Democrats ***Republicans***
Independents

	131	132	133	134	135	136	137
ALABAMA							
1 ***Callahan***	Y	Y	Y	Y	Y	Y	Y
2 ***Everett***	Y	Y	Y	Y	Y	Y	Y
3 ***Riley***	Y	Y	Y	Y	Y	Y	Y
4 ***Aderholt***	Y	Y	Y	Y	Y	Y	Y
5 Cramer	Y	Y	Y	Y	Y	Y	Y
6 ***Bachus***	Y	Y	Y	Y	Y	Y	Y
7 Hilliard	Y	Y	Y	Y	?	Y	N
ALASKA							
AL ***Young***	?	?	?	?	?	?	?
ARIZONA							
1 ***Salmon***	Y	Y	Y	Y	Y	Y	Y
2 Pastor	Y	Y	Y	Y	Y	Y	Y
3 ***Stump***	Y	Y	Y	Y	Y	Y	Y
4 ***Shadegg***	Y	Y	Y	Y	Y	Y	Y
5 ***Kolbe***	Y	Y	Y	Y	Y	Y	Y
6 ***Hayworth***	Y	Y	Y	Y	Y	Y	Y
ARKANSAS							
1 Berry	Y	Y	Y	Y	Y	Y	Y
2 Snyder	Y	Y	Y	Y	Y	Y	Y
3 ***Hutchinson***	Y	Y	Y	?	?	Y	Y
4 ***Dickey***	Y	Y	Y	Y	Y	Y	Y
CALIFORNIA							
1 Thompson	Y	Y	Y	Y	Y	Y	Y
2 ***Herger***	Y	Y	Y	Y	Y	Y	Y
3 ***Ose***	Y	Y	Y	Y	Y	Y	Y
4 ***Doolittle***	Y	Y	Y	Y	Y	Y	?
5 Matsui	Y	Y	Y	Y	Y	Y	Y
6 Woolsey	Y	Y	?	?	Y	Y	Y
7 Miller, George	Y	Y	Y	Y	Y	Y	Y
8 Pelosi	Y	Y	Y	Y	Y	Y	Y
9 Lee	Y	Y	Y	Y	Y	Y	N
10 Tauscher	Y	Y	Y	Y	Y	Y	Y
11 ***Pombo***	Y	Y	Y	Y	Y	Y	Y
12 Lantos	Y	Y	Y	Y	Y	Y	Y
13 Stark	Y	Y	Y	Y	Y	Y	Y
14 Eshoo	Y	Y	Y	Y	Y	Y	Y
15 ***Campbell***	Y	N	Y	Y	Y	Y	Y
16 Lofgren	Y	Y	Y	Y	Y	Y	Y
17 Farr	Y	Y	Y	Y	Y	Y	Y
18 Condit	Y	Y	Y	Y	Y	Y	Y
19 ***Radanovich***	Y	Y	Y	Y	Y	Y	Y
20 Dooley	Y	Y	Y	Y	Y	Y	Y
21 ***Thomas***	Y	Y	Y	Y	Y	Y	Y
22 Capps	Y	Y	Y	Y	Y	Y	Y
23 ***Gallegly***	Y	Y	Y	Y	Y	Y	Y
24 Sherman	Y	Y	Y	Y	Y	Y	Y
25 ***McKeon***	Y	Y	Y	Y	Y	Y	Y
26 Berman	Y	Y	Y	Y	Y	Y	Y
27 ***Rogan***	Y	Y	Y	Y	Y	Y	Y
28 ***Dreier***	Y	Y	Y	Y	Y	Y	Y
29 Waxman	Y	Y	Y	Y	Y	Y	Y
30 Becerra	Y	Y	Y	Y	Y	Y	Y
31 Martinez	Y	Y	Y	Y	Y	Y	Y
32 Dixon	Y	Y	Y	Y	Y	Y	Y
33 Roybal-Allard	Y	Y	Y	Y	Y	Y	Y
34 Napolitano	Y	Y	Y	+	Y	Y	Y
35 Waters	Y	Y	Y	Y	Y	Y	Y
36 ***Kuykendall***	Y	Y	Y	Y	Y	Y	Y
37 Millender-McD.	Y	Y	Y	Y	Y	Y	Y
38 ***Horn***	Y	Y	Y	Y	Y	Y	Y
39 ***Royce***	Y	N	Y	Y	Y	Y	Y
40 ***Lewis***	Y	Y	Y	Y	Y	Y	Y
41 ***Miller, Gary***	Y	N	Y	Y	Y	Y	Y
42 Baca	Y	Y	Y	Y	Y	Y	Y
43 ***Calvert***	Y	Y	Y	Y	Y	Y	Y
44 ***Bono***	Y	Y	Y	Y	Y	Y	Y
45 ***Rohrabacher***	Y	Y	Y	Y	Y	Y	Y
46 Sanchez	Y	Y	Y	Y	Y	Y	Y
47 ***Cox***	Y	Y	Y	Y	Y	?	Y
48 ***Packard***	Y	Y	Y	Y	Y	Y	Y
49 ***Bilbray***	Y	Y	Y	Y	Y	Y	Y
50 Filner	Y	Y	Y	Y	Y	Y	?
51 ***Cunningham***	Y	Y	Y	Y	Y	Y	Y
52 ***Hunter***	Y	Y	Y	Y	Y	Y	Y
COLORADO							
1 DeGette	Y	Y	Y	Y	Y	Y	Y
2 Udall	Y	Y	Y	Y	Y	Y	Y
3 ***McInnis***	Y	Y	Y	Y	Y	Y	Y
4 ***Schaffer***	Y	N	Y	Y	Y	Y	Y
5 ***Hefley***	Y	Y	Y	Y	Y	Y	Y
6 ***Tancredo***	Y	Y	Y	Y	Y	Y	Y
CONNECTICUT							
1 Larson	Y	Y	Y	Y	Y	Y	Y
2 Gejdenson	Y	Y	Y	Y	Y	Y	Y
3 DeLauro	Y	Y	Y	Y	Y	Y	Y
4 ***Shays***	Y	Y	Y	Y	Y	Y	Y
5 Maloney	Y	Y	Y	Y	Y	Y	Y
6 ***Johnson***	Y	Y	Y	Y	Y	Y	Y
DELAWARE							
AL ***Castle***	Y	Y	Y	Y	Y	Y	Y
FLORIDA							
1 ***Scarborough***	Y	Y	Y	Y	Y	Y	Y
2 Boyd	Y	Y	Y	Y	Y	Y	Y
3 Brown	Y	Y	Y	Y	Y	Y	Y
4 ***Fowler***	Y	Y	Y	Y	Y	Y	Y
5 Thurman	Y	Y	Y	Y	Y	Y	Y
6 ***Stearns***	Y	Y	Y	Y	Y	Y	Y
7 ***Mica***	Y	Y	Y	Y	Y	Y	Y
8 ***McCollum***	?	?	Y	Y	Y	Y	Y
9 ***Bilirakis***	Y	Y	Y	Y	Y	Y	Y
10 ***Young***	Y	Y	Y	Y	Y	Y	Y
11 Davis	Y	Y	Y	Y	Y	Y	Y
12 ***Canady***	Y	Y	Y	Y	Y	Y	Y
13 ***Miller***	Y	Y	Y	Y	Y	Y	Y
14 ***Goss***	Y	Y	Y	Y	Y	Y	Y
15 ***Weldon***	?	?	Y	Y	Y	Y	Y
16 ***Foley***	Y	Y	Y	Y	Y	Y	Y
17 Meek	Y	Y	Y	Y	Y	Y	Y
18 ***Ros-Lehtinen***	Y	Y	Y	Y	Y	Y	Y
19 Wexler	Y	Y	Y	Y	Y	Y	Y
20 Deutsch	Y	Y	Y	Y	Y	Y	Y
21 ***Diaz-Balart***	Y	Y	Y	Y	Y	Y	Y
22 ***Shaw***	Y	Y	Y	Y	Y	Y	Y
23 Hastings	Y	Y	Y	Y	Y	Y	Y
GEORGIA							
1 ***Kingston***	Y	Y	Y	Y	Y	Y	Y
2 Bishop	Y	Y	Y	Y	Y	Y	Y
3 ***Collins***	Y	Y	Y	?	Y	Y	Y
4 McKinney	Y	Y	Y	Y	Y	Y	Y
5 Lewis	Y	Y	Y	Y	Y	Y	Y
6 ***Isakson***	Y	Y	Y	Y	Y	Y	Y
7 ***Barr***	Y	Y	Y	P	Y	Y	Y
8 ***Chambliss***	Y	Y	Y	Y	Y	Y	Y
9 ***Deal***	Y	Y	Y	Y	Y	Y	Y
10 ***Norwood***	Y	Y	Y	Y	Y	Y	Y
11 ***Linder***	Y	Y	Y	Y	Y	Y	Y
HAWAII							
1 Abercrombie	Y	Y	Y	Y	Y	Y	Y
2 Mink	Y	Y	Y	Y	Y	Y	N
IDAHO							
1 ***Chenoweth-Hage***	Y	N	N	N	Y	Y	Y
2 ***Simpson***	Y	Y	Y	Y	Y	Y	Y
ILLINOIS							
1 Rush	Y	Y	Y	Y	Y	Y	Y
2 Jackson	Y	Y	Y	Y	Y	Y	Y
3 Lipinski	Y	Y	Y	Y	Y	Y	Y
4 Gutierrez	?	?	?	?	?	?	?
5 Blagojevich	Y	Y	Y	Y	Y	Y	Y
6 ***Hyde***	Y	Y	Y	Y	Y	Y	Y
7 Davis	Y	Y	Y	Y	Y	Y	Y
8 ***Crane***	Y	Y	Y	Y	Y	Y	Y
9 Schakowsky	Y	Y	Y	Y	Y	Y	Y
10 ***Porter***	Y	Y	Y	Y	Y	Y	Y
11 ***Weller***	Y	Y	Y	Y	Y	Y	Y
12 Costello	Y	Y	Y	Y	Y	Y	Y
13 ***Biggert***	Y	Y	Y	Y	Y	Y	Y

ND Northern Democrats SD Southern Democrats

	131	132	133	134	135	136	137
14 ***Hastert***							
15 ***Ewing***	Y	Y	Y	Y	Y	Y	Y
16 ***Manzullo***	?	?	Y	Y	Y	Y	Y
17 Evans	Y	Y	Y	Y	Y	Y	?
18 ***LaHood***	Y	Y	Y	Y	Y	Y	Y
19 Phelps	Y	Y	Y	Y	Y	Y	Y
20 ***Shimkus***	Y	Y	Y	Y	Y	Y	Y
INDIANA							
1 Visclosky	+	?	Y	Y	Y	Y	N
2 ***McIntosh***	?	?	?	?	?	?	?
3 Roemer	Y	Y	Y	Y	Y	Y	Y
4 ***Souder***	?	?	?	?	?	?	?
5 ***Buyer***	Y	Y	Y	Y	Y	Y	Y
6 ***Burton***	Y	Y	Y	Y	Y	Y	Y
7 ***Pease***	Y	Y	Y	Y	Y	Y	Y
8 ***Hostettler***	Y	Y	Y	Y	Y	Y	Y
9 Hill	Y	Y	?	Y	Y	Y	Y
10 Carson	+	+	Y	Y	Y	Y	N
IOWA							
1 ***Leach***	Y	Y	Y	Y	Y	Y	Y
2 ***Nussle***	Y	Y	Y	Y	Y	Y	Y
3 Boswell	Y	Y	Y	Y	Y	Y	Y
4 ***Ganske***	Y	Y	Y	Y	Y	Y	Y
5 ***Latham***	Y	Y	Y	Y	Y	Y	Y
KANSAS							
1 ***Moran***	Y	Y	Y	Y	Y	Y	Y
2 ***Ryun***	Y	Y	Y	Y	Y	Y	Y
3 Moore	Y	Y	+	+	+	Y	Y
4 ***Tiahrt***	Y	Y	Y	Y	Y	Y	Y
KENTUCKY							
1 ***Whitfield***	Y	Y	Y	Y	Y	Y	Y
2 ***Lewis***	Y	Y	Y	Y	Y	Y	Y
3 ***Northup***	Y	Y	Y	Y	Y	Y	Y
4 Lucas	Y	Y	Y	Y	Y	Y	Y
5 ***Rogers***	Y	Y	Y	Y	Y	Y	Y
6 ***Fletcher***	Y	Y	Y	Y	Y	Y	Y
LOUISIANA							
1 ***Vitter***	Y	Y	Y	Y	Y	Y	Y
2 Jefferson	Y	Y	Y	Y	Y	Y	Y
3 ***Tauzin***	?	?	Y	Y	Y	Y	Y
4 ***McCrery***	Y	Y	Y	Y	Y	Y	Y
5 ***Cooksey***	Y	Y	Y	?	Y	?	Y
6 ***Baker***	Y	Y	Y	Y	Y	Y	Y
7 John	Y	Y	Y	Y	Y	Y	Y
MAINE							
1 Allen	Y	Y	Y	Y	Y	Y	Y
2 Baldacci	Y	Y	Y	Y	Y	Y	Y
MARYLAND							
1 ***Gilchrest***	Y	Y	Y	Y	Y	Y	Y
2 ***Ehrlich***	Y	Y	Y	Y	Y	Y	Y
3 Cardin	Y	Y	Y	Y	Y	Y	Y
4 Wynn	Y	Y	Y	Y	Y	Y	Y
5 Hoyer	Y	Y	Y	Y	Y	Y	Y
6 ***Bartlett***	Y	Y	Y	Y	Y	Y	Y
7 Cummings	Y	Y	Y	Y	Y	Y	?
8 ***Morella***	Y	Y	Y	Y	Y	Y	Y
MASSACHUSETTS							
1 Olver	Y	Y	Y	Y	Y	Y	N
2 Neal	Y	Y	Y	Y	Y	Y	Y
3 McGovern	Y	Y	Y	Y	Y	Y	Y
4 Frank	Y	Y	Y	Y	Y	Y	Y
5 Meehan	Y	Y	Y	Y	Y	Y	Y
6 Tierney	Y	Y	Y	Y	Y	Y	N
7 Markey	Y	Y	Y	Y	Y	Y	Y
8 Capuano	Y	Y	Y	Y	Y	Y	N
9 Moakley	Y	Y	Y	Y	Y	Y	Y
10 Delahunt	Y	Y	Y	Y	Y	Y	Y
MICHIGAN							
1 Stupak	Y	Y	Y	Y	Y	Y	Y
2 ***Hoekstra***	Y	Y	Y	Y	Y	Y	Y
3 ***Ehlers***	Y	Y	Y	Y	Y	Y	Y
4 ***Camp***	Y	Y	Y	Y	Y	Y	Y
5 Barcia	Y	Y	Y	Y	Y	Y	Y
6 ***Upton***	Y	Y	Y	Y	Y	Y	Y
7 ***Smith***	Y	Y	Y	Y	Y	Y	Y
8 Stabenow	Y	Y	Y	Y	Y	Y	Y
9 Kildee	Y	Y	Y	Y	Y	Y	Y
10 Bonior	Y	Y	Y	Y	Y	Y	N
11 ***Knollenberg***	Y	Y	Y	Y	Y	Y	Y
12 Levin	Y	Y	Y	Y	Y	Y	Y
13 Rivers	Y	Y	Y	Y	Y	Y	N
14 Conyers	Y	Y	Y	Y	Y	Y	N
15 Kilpatrick	Y	?	Y	Y	Y	Y	Y
16 Dingell	Y	Y	Y	Y	Y	Y	Y
MINNESOTA							
1 ***Gutknecht***	Y	Y	Y	Y	Y	Y	Y
2 Minge	Y	Y	Y	Y	Y	Y	Y
3 ***Ramstad***	Y	Y	Y	Y	Y	Y	Y
4 Vento	Y	Y	Y	Y	Y	Y	Y
5 Sabo	Y	Y	Y	Y	Y	Y	Y
6 Luther	Y	Y	Y	Y	Y	Y	Y
7 Peterson	Y	Y	Y	Y	Y	Y	Y
8 Oberstar	Y	Y	Y	Y	Y	Y	Y
MISSISSIPPI							
1 ***Wicker***	Y	Y	Y	P	Y	Y	Y
2 Thompson	Y	Y	Y	Y	Y	Y	Y
3 ***Pickering***	Y	Y	Y	Y	Y	Y	Y
4 Shows	Y	Y	Y	Y	Y	Y	Y
5 Taylor	Y	Y	Y	Y	Y	Y	Y
MISSOURI							
1 Clay	Y	Y	Y	Y	Y	Y	N
2 ***Talent***	Y	Y	Y	Y	Y	Y	Y
3 Gephardt	Y	Y	Y	Y	Y	Y	Y
4 Skelton	Y	Y	Y	Y	Y	Y	Y
5 McCarthy	Y	Y	Y	Y	Y	Y	Y
6 Danner	Y	Y	Y	Y	Y	Y	Y
7 ***Blunt***	Y	Y	Y	Y	Y	Y	Y
8 ***Emerson***	Y	Y	Y	Y	Y	Y	Y
9 ***Hulshof***	Y	Y	Y	Y	Y	Y	Y
MONTANA							
AL ***Hill***	Y	Y	Y	Y	Y	Y	Y
NEBRASKA							
1 ***Bereuter***	Y	Y	Y	Y	Y	Y	Y
2 ***Terry***	Y	Y	Y	Y	Y	Y	Y
3 ***Barrett***	Y	Y	Y	Y	Y	Y	Y
NEVADA							
1 Berkley	Y	Y	Y	Y	Y	Y	Y
2 ***Gibbons***	Y	Y	Y	Y	Y	Y	Y
NEW HAMPSHIRE							
1 ***Sununu***	Y	Y	Y	Y	Y	Y	Y
2 ***Bass***	Y	Y	Y	Y	Y	Y	Y
NEW JERSEY							
1 Andrews	Y	Y	Y	Y	Y	Y	Y
2 ***LoBiondo***	Y	Y	Y	Y	Y	Y	Y
3 ***Saxton***	?	Y	Y	Y	Y	Y	Y
4 ***Smith***	Y	Y	Y	Y	Y	Y	Y
5 ***Roukema***	Y	Y	Y	Y	Y	Y	Y
6 Pallone	Y	Y	Y	Y	Y	Y	Y
7 ***Franks***	Y	Y	Y	Y	Y	Y	Y
8 Pascrell	Y	Y	Y	Y	Y	Y	Y
9 Rothman	Y	Y	Y	Y	Y	Y	Y
10 Payne	Y	Y	Y	Y	Y	Y	N
11 ***Frelinghuysen***	Y	Y	Y	?	Y	Y	Y
12 Holt	Y	Y	Y	Y	Y	Y	Y
13 Menendez	Y	Y	Y	Y	Y	Y	Y
NEW MEXICO							
1 ***Wilson***	Y	Y	Y	Y	Y	Y	Y
2 ***Skeen***	Y	Y	Y	Y	Y	Y	Y
3 Udall	Y	Y	Y	Y	Y	Y	Y
NEW YORK							
1 Forbes	Y	Y	Y	Y	Y	Y	Y
2 ***Lazio***	Y	Y	Y	Y	Y	Y	Y
3 ***King***	Y	Y	Y	Y	Y	Y	Y
4 McCarthy	Y	Y	Y	Y	Y	Y	Y
5 Ackerman	Y	Y	Y	Y	Y	Y	Y
6 Meeks	Y	Y	Y	Y	Y	Y	Y
7 Crowley	Y	Y	Y	Y	Y	Y	Y
8 Nadler	Y	Y	Y	Y	Y	Y	Y
9 Weiner	Y	Y	Y	Y	Y	Y	Y
10 Towns	Y	Y	Y	Y	Y	Y	N
11 Owens	Y	Y	Y	Y	Y	Y	Y
12 Velázquez	+	+	+	+	+	+	+
13 ***Fossella***	Y	Y	Y	Y	Y	Y	Y
14 Maloney	Y	Y	Y	Y	Y	Y	Y
15 Rangel	Y	?	Y	Y	Y	Y	Y
16 Serrano	Y	Y	Y	Y	Y	Y	N
17 Engel	Y	Y	Y	Y	Y	Y	Y
18 Lowey	Y	Y	Y	Y	Y	Y	Y
19 ***Kelly***	Y	Y	Y	Y	Y	Y	Y
20 ***Gilman***	Y	Y	Y	Y	Y	Y	Y
21 McNulty	Y	Y	Y	Y	Y	Y	Y
22 ***Sweeney***	?	?	Y	Y	Y	Y	Y
23 ***Boehlert***	Y	Y	Y	Y	Y	Y	Y
24 ***McHugh***	Y	Y	Y	Y	Y	Y	Y
25 ***Walsh***	Y	Y	Y	Y	Y	Y	Y
26 Hinchey	Y	Y	Y	Y	Y	Y	N
27 ***Reynolds***	Y	Y	Y	Y	Y	Y	Y
28 Slaughter	Y	Y	Y	Y	Y	Y	N
29 LaFalce	Y	Y	Y	Y	Y	Y	Y
30 ***Quinn***	Y	Y	Y	Y	Y	Y	Y
31 ***Houghton***	Y	Y	Y	Y	Y	Y	Y
NORTH CAROLINA							
1 Clayton	Y	Y	Y	Y	Y	Y	Y
2 Etheridge	Y	Y	Y	Y	Y	Y	Y
3 ***Jones***	Y	Y	Y	Y	Y	Y	Y
4 Price	Y	Y	Y	Y	Y	Y	Y
5 ***Burr***	Y	Y	Y	?	Y	Y	Y
6 ***Coble***	Y	N	Y	Y	Y	Y	Y
7 McIntyre	+	+	Y	Y	Y	Y	Y
8 ***Hayes***	Y	Y	Y	Y	Y	Y	Y
9 ***Myrick***	+	+	+	+	+	+	+
10 ***Ballenger***	Y	Y	Y	Y	Y	Y	Y
11 ***Taylor***	Y	Y	Y	Y	Y	Y	Y
12 Watt	Y	Y	Y	Y	Y	Y	Y
NORTH DAKOTA							
AL Pomeroy	Y	Y	Y	Y	Y	Y	Y
OHIO							
1 ***Chabot***	Y	Y	Y	Y	Y	Y	Y
2 ***Portman***	Y	Y	Y	Y	Y	Y	Y
3 Hall	Y	Y	Y	Y	Y	Y	Y
4 ***Oxley***	?	?	?	Y	Y	Y	Y
5 ***Gillmor***	Y	Y	N	Y	Y	Y	Y
6 Strickland	Y	Y	Y	Y	Y	Y	Y
7 ***Hobson***	Y	Y	Y	Y	Y	Y	Y
8 ***Boehner***	Y	Y	Y	Y	Y	Y	Y
9 Kaptur	Y	Y	Y	Y	Y	Y	Y
10 Kucinich	Y	Y	Y	Y	Y	Y	N
11 Jones	Y	Y	Y	Y	Y	Y	Y
12 ***Kasich***	Y	Y	Y	Y	Y	Y	?
13 Brown	Y	Y	Y	Y	Y	Y	Y
14 Sawyer	Y	Y	Y	Y	Y	Y	Y
15 ***Pryce***	Y	Y	Y	Y	Y	Y	Y
16 ***Regula***	Y	Y	Y	Y	Y	Y	Y
17 Traficant	Y	Y	Y	Y	Y	Y	Y
18 ***Ney***	Y	Y	Y	Y	Y	Y	Y
19 ***LaTourette***	Y	Y	Y	Y	Y	Y	Y
OKLAHOMA							
1 ***Largent***	Y	N	Y	Y	Y	Y	?
2 ***Coburn***	?	?	?	?	?	?	?
3 ***Watkins***	Y	Y	Y	Y	Y	Y	Y
4 ***Watts***	Y	Y	Y	Y	Y	Y	Y
5 ***Istook***	?	?	Y	Y	Y	Y	Y
6 ***Lucas***	?	?	?	?	?	?	?
OREGON							
1 Wu	Y	Y	Y	Y	Y	Y	Y
2 ***Walden***	Y	Y	Y	Y	Y	Y	Y
3 Blumenauer	Y	Y	Y	Y	Y	Y	Y
4 DeFazio	Y	Y	Y	Y	Y	Y	Y
5 Hooley	Y	Y	Y	Y	Y	Y	Y
PENNSYLVANIA							
1 Brady	Y	Y	Y	Y	Y	Y	Y
2 Fattah	Y	Y	Y	Y	Y	Y	Y
3 Borski	Y	Y	Y	Y	Y	Y	Y
4 Klink	Y	Y	Y	Y	Y	Y	Y
5 ***Peterson***	Y	Y	Y	Y	Y	Y	Y
6 Holden	Y	Y	Y	Y	Y	Y	Y
7 ***Weldon***	Y	Y	Y	Y	Y	Y	Y
8 ***Greenwood***	Y	Y	Y	Y	Y	Y	Y
9 ***Shuster***	Y	Y	Y	Y	Y	Y	Y
10 ***Sherwood***	Y	Y	Y	Y	Y	Y	Y
11 Kanjorski	Y	Y	Y	Y	Y	Y	Y
12 Murtha	Y	Y	Y	Y	Y	Y	Y
13 Hoeffel	Y	Y	Y	Y	Y	Y	Y
14 Coyne	Y	Y	Y	Y	Y	Y	Y
15 ***Toomey***	Y	Y	Y	Y	Y	Y	Y
16 ***Pitts***	Y	Y	Y	Y	Y	Y	Y
17 ***Gekas***	Y	Y	Y	Y	Y	Y	Y
18 Doyle	Y	Y	Y	Y	Y	Y	Y
19 ***Goodling***	Y	Y	Y	Y	Y	Y	Y
20 Mascara	Y	Y	Y	Y	Y	Y	Y
21 ***English***	Y	Y	Y	Y	Y	Y	Y
RHODE ISLAND							
1 Kennedy	Y	Y	+	+	+	+	Y
2 Weygand	Y	Y	Y	Y	Y	Y	Y
SOUTH CAROLINA							
1 ***Sanford***	Y	N	Y	Y	Y	Y	Y
2 ***Spence***	Y	Y	Y	?	Y	Y	Y
3 ***Graham***	Y	Y	Y	Y	Y	Y	Y
4 ***DeMint***	Y	Y	Y	Y	Y	Y	Y
5 Spratt	Y	Y	Y	Y	Y	Y	Y
6 Clyburn	Y	Y	Y	Y	Y	Y	Y
SOUTH DAKOTA							
AL ***Thune***	Y	Y	Y	Y	Y	Y	Y
TENNESSEE							
1 ***Jenkins***	Y	Y	Y	Y	Y	Y	Y
2 ***Duncan***	Y	Y	Y	Y	Y	Y	Y
3 ***Wamp***	Y	Y	Y	Y	Y	Y	Y
4 ***Hilleary***	Y	Y	Y	Y	Y	Y	Y
5 Clement	Y	Y	Y	Y	Y	Y	Y
6 Gordon	Y	Y	Y	Y	Y	Y	Y
7 ***Bryant***	Y	Y	Y	Y	Y	Y	Y
8 Tanner	Y	Y	Y	Y	Y	Y	Y
9 Ford	?	?	Y	Y	Y	Y	Y
TEXAS							
1 Sandlin	Y	Y	Y	Y	Y	Y	Y
2 Turner	Y	Y	Y	Y	Y	Y	Y
3 ***Johnson, Sam***	Y	Y	Y	Y	Y	Y	Y
4 Hall	Y	Y	Y	Y	Y	Y	Y
5 ***Sessions***	?	?	Y	Y	Y	Y	Y
6 ***Barton***	Y	Y	Y	Y	Y	Y	Y
7 ***Archer***	Y	Y	Y	Y	Y	Y	Y
8 ***Brady***	?	Y	Y	Y	Y	Y	Y
9 Lampson	Y	Y	Y	Y	Y	Y	Y
10 Doggett	Y	Y	Y	Y	Y	Y	Y
11 Edwards	Y	Y	Y	Y	Y	Y	Y
12 ***Granger***	Y	Y	Y	Y	Y	Y	Y
13 ***Thornberry***	Y	Y	Y	Y	Y	Y	Y
14 ***Paul***	Y	N	N	N	Y	Y	Y
15 Hinojosa	Y	Y	Y	Y	Y	Y	Y
16 Reyes	Y	Y	Y	Y	Y	Y	Y
17 Stenholm	Y	Y	Y	Y	Y	Y	Y
18 Jackson-Lee	Y	Y	Y	Y	Y	Y	Y
19 ***Combest***	Y	Y	Y	Y	Y	Y	Y
20 Gonzalez	Y	Y	Y	Y	Y	Y	Y
21 ***Smith***	Y	Y	Y	Y	Y	Y	Y
22 ***DeLay***	Y	Y	Y	Y	Y	Y	?
23 ***Bonilla***	Y	Y	Y	Y	Y	Y	Y
24 Frost	Y	Y	Y	Y	Y	Y	Y
25 Bentsen	Y	Y	Y	Y	Y	Y	Y
26 ***Armey***	Y	Y	Y	Y	Y	Y	Y
27 Ortiz	+	+	Y	Y	Y	Y	Y
28 Rodriguez	Y	Y	Y	Y	Y	Y	Y
29 Green	Y	Y	Y	Y	Y	Y	Y
30 Johnson, E.B.	Y	Y	Y	Y	Y	Y	Y
UTAH							
1 ***Hansen***	Y	Y	Y	Y	Y	Y	Y
2 ***Cook***	?	?	?	?	?	?	?
3 ***Cannon***	Y	Y	Y	Y	Y	Y	Y
VERMONT							
AL *Sanders*	Y	Y	?	?	Y	Y	Y
VIRGINIA							
1 ***Bateman***	Y	Y	Y	Y	Y	Y	Y
2 Pickett	Y	Y	Y	Y	Y	Y	Y
3 Scott	Y	Y	Y	Y	Y	Y	N
4 Sisisky	Y	Y	Y	Y	Y	Y	Y
5 *Goode*	Y	Y	Y	Y	Y	Y	Y
6 ***Goodlatte***	Y	Y	Y	Y	Y	Y	Y
7 ***Bliley***	Y	Y	Y	Y	Y	Y	Y
8 Moran	Y	Y	Y	Y	Y	Y	Y
9 Boucher	Y	Y	Y	Y	Y	Y	Y
10 ***Wolf***	Y	Y	Y	Y	Y	Y	Y
11 ***Davis***	Y	Y	Y	Y	Y	Y	Y
WASHINGTON							
1 Inslee	Y	Y	Y	Y	Y	Y	Y
2 ***Metcalf***	Y	Y	Y	Y	Y	Y	Y
3 Baird	Y	Y	Y	Y	Y	Y	Y
4 ***Hastings***	Y	Y	Y	Y	Y	Y	Y
5 ***Nethercutt***	Y	Y	Y	Y	Y	Y	Y
6 Dicks	Y	Y	Y	Y	Y	Y	Y
7 McDermott	Y	Y	Y	Y	Y	Y	N
8 ***Dunn***	Y	Y	Y	Y	Y	Y	Y
9 Smith	Y	Y	Y	Y	Y	Y	Y
WEST VIRGINIA							
1 Mollohan	Y	Y	Y	Y	Y	Y	Y
2 Wise	?	?	?	?	?	?	?
3 Rahall	Y	Y	Y	Y	Y	Y	Y
WISCONSIN							
1 ***Ryan***	Y	Y	Y	Y	Y	Y	Y
2 Baldwin	Y	Y	Y	Y	Y	Y	Y
3 Kind	Y	Y	Y	Y	Y	Y	Y
4 Kleczka	Y	Y	Y	Y	Y	Y	Y
5 Barrett	Y	Y	Y	Y	Y	Y	Y
6 ***Petri***	Y	Y	Y	Y	Y	Y	Y
7 Obey	Y	Y	Y	Y	Y	Y	Y
8 ***Green***	Y	Y	Y	Y	Y	Y	Y
9 ***Sensenbrenner***	Y	Y	Y	Y	Y	Y	Y
WYOMING							
AL ***Cubin***	Y	Y	Y	Y	Y	Y	Y

Southern states - Ala., Ark., Fla., Ga., Ky., La., Miss., N.C., Okla., S.C., Tenn., Texas, Va.

138. HR 2957. Lake Pontchartrain Basin/Passage. Passage of the bill that would establish the Lake Pontchartrain Basin as an estuary of national importance under the Environmental Protection Agency's National Estuary Program. The bill would authorize $5 million a year through fiscal year 2005 for restoration activities and $100 million for a project to reduce the amount of sewage entering Lake Pontchartrain from New Orleans. Passed 418-6: R 209-6; D 207-0 (ND 154-0, SD 53-0); I 2-0. May 3, 2000.

139. S 2323. Stock Options/Passage. Goodling, R-Pa., motion to suspend the rules and pass the bill that would amend the Fair Labor Standards Act to exclude income derived from an employee's stock option, stock appreciation or stock purchase plan from the employee's regular rate of pay, which is used to calculate overtime pay. Motion agreed to 421-0: R 212-0; D 207-0 (ND 154-0, SD 53-0); I 2-0. A two-thirds majority of those present and voting (281 in this case) is required for passage under suspension of the rules. May 3, 2000.

140. HR 4055. IDEA Funding/Passage. Goodling, R-Pa., motion to suspend the rules and pass the bill that would fund 40 percent of the cost of educating children with disabilities under the Individuals with Disabilities Education Act. The bill would authorize an additional $2 billion a year for 10 years. Motion agreed to 421-3: R 211-3; D 208-0 (ND 154-0, SD 54-0); I 2-0. A two-thirds majority of those present and voting (283 in this case) is required for passage under suspension of the rules. May 3, 2000.

141. HR 1901. Border Station Naming/Passage. LaTourette, R-Ohio, motion to suspend the rules and pass the bill that would designate the border station in Pharr, Texas, the "Kika de la Garza United States Border Station" after the former Texas congressman (1965-97). Motion agreed to 417-1: R 208-1; D 207-0 (ND 153-0, SD 54-0); I 2-0. A two-thirds majority of those present and voting (279 in this case) is required for passage under suspension of the rules. May 3, 2000.

142. HR 1106. Alternative Water Sources/Passage. Passage of the bill that would authorize $375 million over five years to establish a program that would provide federal matching funds for the design and construction of water reclamation, reuse and conservation projects. The funds would be available to state and local governments as well as private utilities and nonprofit entities for alternative water source projects. Passed 416-5: R 209-5; D 205-0 (ND 151-0, SD 54-0); I 2-0. May 4, 2000.

143. HR 673. Florida Keys/Passage. Passage of the bill that would authorize $213 million over five years for grants by the Environmental Protection Agency to replace or improve wastewater treatment and stormwater management systems in the Florida Keys, in order to improve water quality in the Florida Keys National Marine Sanctuary. Passed 411-7: R 207-7; D 202-0 (ND 148-0, SD 54-0); I 2-0. May 4, 2000.

144. HR 434. Africa, Caribbean Trade/Rule. Adoption of the rule (H Res 488) to provide for House floor consideration of the conference report on the bill that would extend certain tariff benefits to the nations of the Caribbean, Central America and sub-Saharan Africa. Adopted 301-114: R 207-4; D 94-108 (ND 67-81, SD 27-27); I 0-2. May 4, 2000.

145. HR 434. Africa, Caribbean Trade/Conference Report. Adoption of the conference report on the bill that would extend certain tariff benefits to the nations of the Caribbean, Central America and sub-Saharan Africa. Adopted 309-110: R 183-30; D 126-78 (ND 82-69, SD 44-9); I 0-2. May 4, 2000. A "yea" was a vote in support of the president's position.

Key

- Y Voted for (yea).
- # Paired for.
- \+ Announced for.
- N Voted against (nay).
- X Paired against.
- – Announced against.
- P Voted "present."
- C Voted "present" to avoid possible conflict of interest.
- ? Did not vote or otherwise make a position known.

•

Democrats ***Republicans***
Independents

	138	139	140	141	142	143	144	145
ALABAMA								
1 ***Callahan***	Y	Y	Y	Y	Y	Y	Y	Y
2 ***Everett***	Y	Y	Y	Y	Y	Y	Y	?
3 ***Riley***	Y	Y	Y	Y	Y	Y	Y	Y
4 ***Aderholt***	Y	Y	Y	Y	Y	Y	Y	Y
5 Cramer	Y	Y	Y	Y	Y	Y	N	Y
6 ***Bachus***	Y	Y	Y	Y	Y	Y	Y	Y
7 Hilliard	Y	Y	Y	Y	Y	Y	Y	Y
ALASKA								
AL ***Young***	?	?	?	?	?	?	?	?
ARIZONA								
1 ***Salmon***	Y	Y	Y	Y	Y	Y	Y	Y
2 Pastor	Y	Y	Y	Y	Y	Y	Y	Y
3 ***Stump***	Y	Y	Y	Y	Y	Y	Y	Y
4 ***Shadegg***	Y	Y	Y	Y	Y	Y	Y	Y
5 ***Kolbe***	Y	Y	Y	Y	Y	Y	Y	Y
6 ***Hayworth***	Y	Y	Y	Y	Y	Y	Y	Y
ARKANSAS								
1 Berry	Y	Y	Y	Y	Y	Y	Y	Y
2 Snyder	Y	Y	Y	Y	Y	Y	Y	Y
3 ***Hutchinson***	Y	Y	Y	Y	Y	Y	Y	Y
4 ***Dickey***	Y	Y	Y	Y	Y	Y	Y	Y
CALIFORNIA								
1 Thompson	Y	Y	Y	Y	Y	Y	N	Y
2 ***Herger***	Y	Y	Y	Y	Y	Y	Y	Y
3 ***Ose***	Y	Y	Y	Y	Y	Y	Y	Y
4 ***Doolittle***	Y	Y	Y	Y	Y	Y	Y	Y
5 Matsui	Y	Y	Y	Y	Y	Y	Y	Y
6 Woolsey	Y	Y	Y	Y	Y	Y	N	N
7 Miller, George	Y	Y	Y	Y	Y	Y	N	N
8 Pelosi	Y	Y	Y	Y	Y	Y	N	Y
9 Lee	Y	Y	Y	Y	Y	Y	N	N
10 Tauscher	Y	Y	Y	Y	Y	Y	Y	Y
11 ***Pombo***	Y	Y	Y	Y	Y	Y	Y	Y
12 Lantos	Y	Y	Y	Y	Y	Y	N	N
13 Stark	Y	Y	Y	Y	Y	Y	N	N
14 Eshoo	Y	Y	Y	Y	Y	Y	N	Y
15 ***Campbell***	Y	Y	Y	Y	Y	Y	Y	Y
16 Lofgren	Y	Y	Y	Y	Y	Y	Y	Y
17 Farr	Y	Y	Y	Y	Y	Y	Y	Y
18 Condit	Y	Y	Y	Y	Y	Y	N	N
19 ***Radanovich***	Y	?	Y	Y	Y	Y	Y	Y
20 Dooley	Y	Y	Y	Y	Y	Y	Y	Y
21 ***Thomas***	Y	Y	Y	Y	Y	Y	?	Y
22 Capps	Y	Y	Y	Y	Y	Y	Y	Y
23 ***Gallegly***	Y	Y	Y	Y	Y	Y	Y	Y
24 Sherman	Y	Y	Y	Y	Y	Y	Y	N
25 ***McKeon***	Y	Y	Y	Y	Y	Y	Y	Y
26 Berman	Y	Y	Y	Y	Y	Y	Y	Y
27 ***Rogan***	Y	Y	Y	Y	Y	Y	Y	Y
28 ***Dreier***	Y	Y	Y	Y	Y	Y	Y	Y
29 Waxman	Y	Y	Y	Y	Y	Y	N	Y
30 Becerra	Y	Y	Y	Y	Y	Y	Y	Y
31 Martinez	Y	Y	Y	Y	Y	Y	Y	Y
32 Dixon	Y	Y	Y	Y	Y	Y	Y	Y
33 Roybal-Allard	Y	Y	Y	Y	Y	Y	N	N
34 Napolitano	Y	Y	Y	Y	Y	Y	N	Y
35 Waters	Y	Y	Y	Y	Y	Y	N	Y
36 ***Kuykendall***	Y	Y	Y	Y	Y	Y	Y	Y
37 Millender-McD.	Y	Y	Y	Y	Y	Y	?	Y
38 ***Horn***	Y	Y	Y	Y	Y	Y	Y	Y
39 ***Royce***	N	Y	Y	Y	N	N	Y	Y
40 ***Lewis***	Y	Y	Y	Y	Y	Y	Y	Y
41 ***Miller, Gary***	Y	Y	Y	Y	Y	Y	Y	Y
42 Baca	Y	Y	Y	Y	Y	Y	–	N
43 ***Calvert***	Y	Y	Y	Y	Y	Y	Y	Y
44 ***Bono***	Y	Y	Y	Y	Y	Y	Y	Y
45 ***Rohrabacher***	Y	Y	Y	Y	Y	Y	Y	N
46 Sanchez	Y	Y	Y	Y	Y	Y	N	Y
47 ***Cox***	Y	Y	Y	?	Y	Y	Y	Y
48 ***Packard***	Y	Y	Y	Y	Y	Y	Y	Y
49 ***Bilbray***	Y	Y	Y	Y	Y	Y	Y	Y
50 Filner	Y	Y	Y	Y	Y	Y	N	N
51 ***Cunningham***	Y	Y	Y	Y	Y	Y	Y	Y
52 ***Hunter***	Y	Y	Y	Y	Y	Y	N	N
COLORADO								
1 DeGette	Y	Y	Y	Y	Y	Y	Y	Y
2 Udall	Y	Y	Y	Y	Y	Y	N	N
3 ***McInnis***	Y	Y	Y	Y	Y	Y	Y	Y
4 ***Schaffer***	N	Y	Y	Y	Y	N	Y	Y
5 ***Hefley***	Y	Y	Y	Y	Y	Y	Y	Y
6 ***Tancredo***	Y	Y	Y	Y	Y	Y	Y	Y
CONNECTICUT								
1 Larson	Y	Y	Y	Y	Y	Y	Y	Y
2 Gejdenson	Y	Y	Y	Y	Y	Y	N	Y
3 DeLauro	Y	Y	Y	Y	Y	Y	N	N
4 ***Shays***	Y	Y	Y	Y	Y	Y	Y	Y
5 Maloney	Y	Y	Y	Y	Y	Y	Y	N
6 ***Johnson***	Y	Y	Y	Y	Y	Y	Y	Y
DELAWARE								
AL ***Castle***	Y	Y	Y	Y	Y	Y	Y	Y
FLORIDA								
1 ***Scarborough***	Y	Y	Y	Y	Y	Y	Y	Y
2 Boyd	Y	Y	Y	Y	Y	Y	N	Y
3 Brown	Y	Y	Y	Y	Y	Y	Y	Y
4 ***Fowler***	Y	Y	Y	Y	Y	Y	Y	Y
5 Thurman	Y	Y	Y	Y	Y	Y	Y	Y
6 ***Stearns***	Y	Y	Y	Y	Y	Y	Y	Y
7 ***Mica***	Y	Y	Y	Y	Y	Y	Y	Y
8 ***McCollum***	Y	Y	Y	Y	Y	Y	Y	Y
9 ***Bilirakis***	Y	Y	Y	Y	Y	Y	Y	N
10 ***Young***	?	?	?	?	Y	Y	Y	Y
11 Davis	Y	Y	Y	Y	Y	Y	Y	Y
12 ***Canady***	Y	Y	Y	Y	Y	Y	Y	Y
13 ***Miller***	Y	Y	Y	Y	Y	Y	Y	Y
14 ***Goss***	Y	Y	Y	Y	Y	Y	Y	Y
15 ***Weldon***	Y	Y	Y	Y	Y	Y	Y	Y
16 ***Foley***	Y	Y	Y	Y	Y	Y	Y	Y
17 Meek	Y	Y	Y	Y	Y	Y	Y	Y
18 ***Ros-Lehtinen***	Y	Y	Y	Y	Y	Y	Y	Y
19 Wexler	Y	Y	Y	Y	Y	Y	Y	Y
20 Deutsch	Y	Y	Y	Y	Y	Y	N	Y
21 ***Diaz-Balart***	Y	Y	Y	Y	Y	Y	Y	Y
22 ***Shaw***	Y	Y	Y	Y	Y	Y	Y	Y
23 Hastings	Y	Y	Y	Y	Y	Y	N	?
GEORGIA								
1 ***Kingston***	Y	Y	Y	Y	Y	Y	Y	N
2 Bishop	Y	Y	Y	Y	Y	Y	Y	Y
3 ***Collins***	Y	Y	Y	Y	Y	Y	Y	Y
4 McKinney	Y	Y	Y	Y	Y	Y	N	N
5 Lewis	Y	Y	Y	Y	Y	Y	N	Y
6 ***Isakson***	Y	Y	Y	Y	Y	Y	Y	Y
7 ***Barr***	Y	Y	Y	Y	Y	Y	Y	N
8 ***Chambliss***	Y	Y	Y	Y	Y	Y	Y	Y
9 ***Deal***	Y	Y	Y	Y	Y	Y	Y	N
10 ***Norwood***	Y	Y	Y	Y	Y	Y	N	N
11 ***Linder***	Y	Y	Y	Y	Y	Y	Y	Y
HAWAII								
1 Abercrombie	Y	Y	Y	Y	Y	Y	Y	N
2 Mink	Y	Y	Y	Y	Y	Y	N	N
IDAHO								
1 ***Chenoweth-Hage***	N	Y	Y	Y	?	N	Y	N
2 ***Simpson***	Y	Y	Y	Y	Y	Y	Y	Y
ILLINOIS								
1 Rush	Y	Y	Y	Y	Y	Y	N	Y
2 Jackson	Y	Y	Y	Y	Y	Y	N	N
3 Lipinski	Y	Y	Y	Y	Y	Y	Y	N
4 Gutierrez	?	?	?	?	?	?	?	?
5 Blagojevich	Y	Y	Y	Y	Y	Y	Y	Y
6 ***Hyde***	Y	Y	Y	Y	Y	Y	Y	Y
7 Davis	Y	Y	Y	Y	Y	Y	Y	Y
8 ***Crane***	Y	Y	Y	Y	Y	Y	Y	Y
9 Schakowsky	Y	Y	Y	Y	Y	Y	N	N
10 ***Porter***	Y	Y	Y	Y	Y	Y	Y	Y
11 ***Weller***	Y	Y	Y	Y	Y	Y	Y	Y
12 Costello	Y	Y	Y	Y	Y	Y	N	N
13 ***Biggert***	Y	Y	Y	Y	Y	Y	Y	Y

ND Northern Democrats SD Southern Democrats

	138	139	140	141	142	143	144	145
14 ***Hastert***	Y							Y
15 ***Ewing***	Y	Y	Y	Y	Y	Y	Y	Y
16 ***Manzullo***	Y	Y	Y	Y	Y	Y	Y	Y
17 Evans	Y	Y	Y	Y	Y	Y	N	N
18 ***LaHood***	Y	Y	Y	Y	Y	Y	Y	Y
19 Phelps	Y	Y	Y	Y	Y	Y	N	N
20 ***Shimkus***	Y	Y	Y	Y	Y	Y	Y	Y
INDIANA								
1 Visclosky	Y	Y	Y	Y	Y	Y	N	N
2 ***McIntosh***	Y	Y	Y	Y	Y	Y	Y	Y
3 Roemer	Y	Y	Y	Y	Y	Y	Y	Y
4 ***Souder***	Y	Y	Y	?	Y	Y	Y	N
5 ***Buyer***	Y	Y	Y	Y	Y	Y	Y	N
6 ***Burton***	Y	Y	Y	Y	Y	Y	Y	Y
7 ***Pease***	Y	Y	Y	Y	Y	Y	Y	Y
8 ***Hostettler***	N	Y	Y	Y	N	N	Y	N
9 Hill	Y	Y	Y	Y	Y	Y	N	Y
10 Carson	Y	Y	Y	Y	Y	Y	Y	Y
IOWA								
1 ***Leach***	Y	Y	Y	Y	Y	Y	Y	Y
2 ***Nussle***	Y	Y	Y	Y	Y	Y	Y	Y
3 Boswell	Y	Y	Y	Y	Y	Y	N	Y
4 ***Ganske***	Y	Y	Y	Y	Y	Y	Y	Y
5 ***Latham***	Y	Y	Y	Y	Y	Y	Y	Y
KANSAS								
1 ***Moran***	Y	Y	Y	Y	Y	Y	Y	Y
2 ***Ryun***	Y	Y	Y	Y	Y	Y	Y	Y
3 Moore	Y	Y	Y	Y	Y	Y	Y	Y
4 ***Tiahrt***	Y	Y	Y	Y	Y	Y	Y	Y
KENTUCKY								
1 ***Whitfield***	Y	Y	Y	Y	Y	Y	Y	Y
2 ***Lewis***	Y	Y	Y	Y	Y	Y	Y	Y
3 ***Northup***	Y	Y	Y	Y	Y	Y	Y	Y
4 Lucas	Y	Y	Y	Y	Y	Y	N	Y
5 ***Rogers***	Y	Y	Y	Y	Y	Y	Y	N
6 ***Fletcher***	Y	Y	Y	+	Y	Y	Y	N
LOUISIANA								
1 ***Vitter***	Y	Y	Y	Y	Y	Y	Y	Y
2 Jefferson	Y	Y	Y	Y	Y	Y	Y	Y
3 ***Tauzin***	Y	?	Y	Y	Y	Y	Y	Y
4 ***McCrery***	Y	Y	Y	Y	Y	Y	Y	Y
5 ***Cooksey***	Y	?	Y	Y	Y	Y	Y	Y
6 ***Baker***	Y	Y	Y	Y	Y	Y	Y	Y
7 John	Y	Y	Y	Y	Y	Y	N	Y
MAINE								
1 Allen	Y	Y	Y	Y	Y	Y	N	Y
2 Baldacci	Y	Y	Y	Y	Y	Y	N	N
MARYLAND								
1 ***Gilchrest***	Y	Y	Y	Y	Y	Y	Y	Y
2 ***Ehrlich***	Y	Y	Y	Y	Y	Y	Y	Y
3 Cardin	Y	Y	Y	Y	Y	Y	Y	Y
4 Wynn	Y	Y	Y	Y	Y	Y	N	Y
5 Hoyer	Y	Y	Y	Y	Y	Y	Y	Y
6 ***Bartlett***	Y	Y	Y	Y	Y	Y	Y	N
7 Cummings	Y	Y	Y	Y	Y	Y	Y	Y
8 ***Morella***	Y	Y	Y	Y	Y	Y	Y	Y
MASSACHUSETTS								
1 Olver	Y	Y	Y	Y	Y	Y	N	Y
2 Neal	Y	Y	Y	Y	Y	Y	N	N
3 McGovern	Y	Y	Y	Y	Y	Y	N	N
4 Frank	Y	Y	Y	Y	Y	Y	N	N
5 Meehan	Y	Y	Y	Y	Y	Y	Y	Y
6 Tierney	Y	Y	Y	Y	Y	Y	N	N
7 Markey	Y	Y	Y	Y	Y	Y	N	N
8 Capuano	Y	Y	Y	Y	Y	Y	N	N
9 Moakley	Y	Y	Y	Y	Y	Y	N	N
10 Delahunt	Y	Y	Y	Y	Y	Y	N	N
MICHIGAN								
1 Stupak	Y	Y	Y	Y	Y	Y	N	N
2 ***Hoekstra***	Y	Y	Y	Y	Y	Y	Y	Y
3 ***Ehlers***	Y	Y	Y	Y	Y	Y	Y	Y
4 ***Camp***	Y	Y	Y	Y	Y	Y	Y	Y
5 Barcia	Y	Y	Y	Y	Y	Y	N	N
6 ***Upton***	Y	Y	Y	Y	Y	Y	Y	Y
7 ***Smith***	Y	Y	Y	Y	Y	Y	?	Y
8 Stabenow	Y	Y	Y	Y	Y	Y	Y	Y
9 Kildee	Y	Y	Y	Y	Y	Y	N	N
10 Bonior	Y	Y	Y	Y	Y	Y	N	N
11 ***Knollenberg***	Y	Y	Y	Y	Y	Y	Y	Y
12 Levin	Y	Y	Y	Y	Y	Y	Y	Y
13 Rivers	Y	Y	Y	Y	Y	Y	Y	Y
14 Conyers	Y	Y	Y	Y	Y	Y	N	N
15 Kilpatrick	Y	Y	Y	Y	Y	Y	Y	Y
16 Dingell	Y	Y	Y	Y	Y	Y	N	N
MINNESOTA								
1 ***Gutknecht***	Y	Y	Y	Y	Y	Y	?	?
2 Minge	Y	Y	Y	Y	Y	Y	Y	Y
3 ***Ramstad***	Y	Y	Y	Y	Y	Y	Y	Y
4 Vento	Y	Y	Y	Y	?	?	?	?
5 Sabo	Y	Y	Y	Y	Y	Y	N	Y
6 Luther	Y	Y	Y	Y	Y	Y	Y	Y
7 Peterson	Y	Y	Y	Y	Y	Y	N	N
8 Oberstar	Y	Y	Y	Y	Y	Y	N	N
MISSISSIPPI								
1 ***Wicker***	?	Y	Y	Y	Y	Y	Y	Y
2 Thompson	Y	Y	Y	Y	Y	Y	Y	?
3 ***Pickering***	Y	Y	Y	Y	Y	Y	Y	Y
4 Shows	Y	Y	Y	Y	Y	Y	N	N
5 Taylor	Y	Y	Y	Y	Y	Y	N	N
MISSOURI								
1 Clay	Y	Y	Y	Y	Y	?	?	Y
2 ***Talent***	Y	Y	Y	Y	Y	Y	Y	Y
3 Gephardt	Y	Y	Y	Y	Y	Y	N	N
4 Skelton	Y	Y	Y	Y	Y	Y	N	Y
5 McCarthy	Y	Y	Y	Y	Y	Y	Y	Y
6 Danner	Y	Y	Y	Y	Y	Y	N	Y
7 ***Blunt***	Y	Y	Y	Y	Y	Y	Y	Y
8 ***Emerson***	Y	Y	Y	Y	Y	Y	Y	Y
9 ***Hulshof***	Y	Y	Y	Y	Y	Y	Y	Y
MONTANA								
AL ***Hill***	Y	Y	Y	Y	Y	Y	Y	Y
NEBRASKA								
1 ***Bereuter***	Y	Y	Y	Y	Y	Y	Y	Y
2 ***Terry***	Y	Y	Y	Y	Y	Y	Y	Y
3 ***Barrett***	Y	Y	Y	Y	Y	Y	Y	Y
NEVADA								
1 Berkley	Y	Y	Y	Y	Y	Y	Y	Y
2 ***Gibbons***	Y	Y	Y	Y	Y	Y	Y	Y
NEW HAMPSHIRE								
1 ***Sununu***	Y	Y	Y	Y	Y	Y	Y	Y
2 ***Bass***	Y	Y	Y	Y	Y	Y	Y	Y
NEW JERSEY								
1 Andrews	Y	Y	Y	Y	Y	?	N	N
2 ***LoBiondo***	Y	Y	Y	Y	Y	Y	Y	N
3 ***Saxton***	Y	Y	Y	Y	Y	Y	Y	N
4 ***Smith***	Y	Y	Y	Y	Y	Y	Y	N
5 ***Roukema***	Y	Y	Y	Y	Y	Y	Y	Y
6 Pallone	Y	Y	Y	Y	Y	Y	N	N
7 ***Franks***	Y	Y	Y	Y	Y	Y	Y	?
8 Pascrell	Y	Y	Y	Y	Y	Y	Y	N
9 Rothman	Y	Y	Y	Y	Y	Y	Y	Y
10 Payne	Y	Y	Y	Y	Y	Y	Y	Y
11 ***Frelinghuysen***	Y	Y	Y	Y	Y	Y	Y	Y
12 Holt	Y	Y	Y	Y	Y	Y	Y	N
13 Menendez	Y	Y	Y	Y	Y	Y	Y	Y
NEW MEXICO								
1 ***Wilson***	Y	Y	Y	Y	Y	Y	Y	Y
2 ***Skeen***	Y	Y	Y	Y	Y	Y	Y	Y
3 Udall	Y	Y	Y	Y	Y	Y	N	N
NEW YORK								
1 Forbes	Y	Y	Y	Y	Y	Y	N	N
2 ***Lazio***	Y	Y	Y	Y	Y	Y	Y	Y
3 ***King***	Y	Y	Y	Y	Y	Y	Y	Y
4 McCarthy	Y	Y	Y	Y	Y	Y	Y	Y
5 Ackerman	Y	Y	Y	Y	Y	Y	Y	Y
6 Meeks	Y	Y	Y	Y	Y	Y	Y	Y
7 Crowley	Y	Y	Y	Y	Y	Y	Y	N
8 Nadler	Y	Y	Y	Y	Y	Y	N	N
9 Weiner	Y	Y	Y	Y	Y	Y	Y	Y
10 Towns	Y	Y	Y	Y	Y	Y	N	Y
11 Owens	Y	Y	Y	Y	Y	Y	Y	Y
12 Velázquez	+	+	+	+	+	+	+	−
13 ***Fossella***	Y	Y	Y	Y	+	+	Y	Y
14 Maloney	Y	Y	Y	Y	Y	Y	N	Y
15 Rangel	Y	Y	Y	Y	Y	Y	Y	Y
16 Serrano	Y	Y	Y	Y	?	?	?	?
17 Engel	Y	Y	Y	Y	?	?	?	Y
18 Lowey	Y	Y	Y	Y	Y	Y	Y	Y
19 ***Kelly***	Y	Y	Y	?	Y	Y	Y	Y
20 ***Gilman***	Y	Y	Y	Y	Y	Y	Y	Y
21 McNulty	Y	Y	Y	Y	Y	Y	Y	Y
22 ***Sweeney***	Y	Y	Y	Y	Y	Y	Y	Y
23 ***Boehlert***	Y	Y	Y	Y	Y	Y	Y	Y
24 ***McHugh***	Y	Y	Y	Y	Y	Y	Y	?
25 ***Walsh***	Y	Y	Y	?	Y	Y	Y	Y
26 Hinchey	Y	Y	Y	Y	Y	Y	N	Y
27 ***Reynolds***	Y	Y	Y	Y	Y	Y	Y	Y
28 Slaughter	Y	Y	Y	Y	Y	Y	Y	Y
29 LaFalce	Y	Y	Y	Y	Y	Y	Y	Y
30 ***Quinn***	Y	Y	Y	Y	Y	Y	Y	Y
31 ***Houghton***	Y	Y	Y	Y	Y	Y	Y	Y
NORTH CAROLINA								
1 Clayton	Y	Y	Y	Y	Y	Y	Y	Y
2 Etheridge	Y	Y	Y	Y	Y	Y	N	N
3 ***Jones***	Y	Y	Y	Y	Y	Y	Y	N
4 Price	Y	Y	Y	Y	Y	Y	N	Y
5 ***Burr***	Y	Y	Y	Y	Y	Y	Y	N
6 ***Coble***	Y	Y	Y	Y	Y	Y	Y	N
7 McIntyre	Y	Y	Y	Y	Y	Y	N	N
8 ***Hayes***	Y	Y	Y	Y	Y	Y	N	N
9 ***Myrick***	+	+	+	+	Y	Y	Y	Y
10 ***Ballenger***	Y	Y	Y	Y	Y	Y	Y	Y
11 ***Taylor***	Y	Y	Y	Y	Y	Y	Y	N
12 Watt	Y	Y	Y	Y	Y	Y	N	N
NORTH DAKOTA								
AL Pomeroy	Y	Y	Y	Y	Y	Y	Y	Y
OHIO								
1 ***Chabot***	Y	Y	Y	Y	Y	Y	Y	Y
2 ***Portman***	Y	Y	Y	Y	Y	Y	Y	Y
3 Hall	Y	Y	Y	Y	Y	?	N	Y
4 ***Oxley***	Y	Y	Y	Y	Y	Y	Y	Y
5 ***Gillmor***	Y	Y	Y	Y	Y	Y	Y	Y
6 Strickland	Y	Y	Y	Y	Y	Y	N	N
7 ***Hobson***	Y	Y	Y	Y	Y	Y	Y	Y
8 ***Boehner***	Y	Y	Y	Y	Y	Y	Y	Y
9 Kaptur	Y	Y	Y	Y	Y	Y	N	N
10 Kucinich	Y	Y	Y	Y	Y	Y	N	N
11 Jones	Y	Y	Y	Y	Y	Y	Y	Y
12 ***Kasich***	Y	Y	Y	Y	Y	Y	Y	Y
13 Brown	Y	Y	Y	Y	Y	Y	Y	N
14 Sawyer	Y	Y	Y	Y	Y	Y	Y	Y
15 ***Pryce***	Y	Y	Y	Y	Y	Y	Y	Y
16 ***Regula***	Y	Y	Y	Y	Y	Y	Y	Y
17 Traficant	Y	Y	Y	Y	Y	Y	Y	N
18 ***Ney***	Y	Y	Y	Y	Y	Y	Y	N
19 ***LaTourette***	Y	Y	Y	Y	?	?	Y	Y
OKLAHOMA								
1 ***Largent***	Y	Y	Y	Y	Y	Y	Y	Y
2 ***Coburn***	?	?	?	?	?	?	?	?
3 ***Watkins***	Y	Y	Y	Y	Y	Y	Y	Y
4 ***Watts***	Y	Y	Y	Y	Y	Y	Y	Y
5 ***Istook***	Y	Y	Y	Y	Y	Y	Y	Y
6 ***Lucas***	?	?	?	?	?	?	?	?
OREGON								
1 Wu	Y	Y	Y	Y	Y	Y	Y	Y
2 ***Walden***	Y	Y	Y	Y	Y	Y	Y	Y
3 Blumenauer	Y	Y	Y	Y	Y	Y	N	Y
4 DeFazio	Y	Y	Y	Y	Y	Y	N	N
5 Hooley	Y	Y	Y	Y	Y	Y	N	Y
PENNSYLVANIA								
1 Brady	Y	Y	Y	Y	Y	Y	Y	N
2 Fattah	Y	Y	Y	Y	Y	Y	Y	Y
3 Borski	Y	Y	Y	Y	Y	Y	Y	Y
4 Klink	Y	Y	Y	Y	Y	Y	N	N
5 ***Peterson***	Y	Y	Y	Y	Y	Y	Y	Y
6 Holden	Y	Y	Y	Y	Y	Y	N	N
7 ***Weldon***	Y	Y	Y	Y	Y	Y	Y	Y
8 ***Greenwood***	Y	Y	Y	Y	Y	Y	Y	Y
9 ***Shuster***	Y	Y	Y	Y	Y	Y	Y	Y
10 ***Sherwood***	Y	Y	Y	Y	Y	Y	Y	Y
11 Kanjorski	Y	Y	Y	Y	Y	Y	N	N
12 Murtha	Y	Y	Y	Y	Y	Y	Y	N
13 Hoeffel	Y	Y	Y	Y	Y	Y	Y	Y
14 Coyne	Y	Y	Y	Y	Y	Y	N	N
15 ***Toomey***	Y	Y	Y	Y	Y	Y	Y	Y
16 ***Pitts***	Y	Y	Y	Y	Y	Y	Y	Y
17 ***Gekas***	Y	Y	Y	Y	Y	Y	Y	Y
18 Doyle	Y	Y	Y	?	Y	Y	N	N
19 ***Goodling***	Y	Y	Y	Y	Y	Y	?	Y
20 Mascara	Y	Y	Y	Y	Y	Y	N	N
21 ***English***	Y	Y	Y	Y	Y	Y	Y	Y
RHODE ISLAND								
1 Kennedy	Y	Y	Y	Y	Y	Y	N	N
2 Weygand	Y	Y	Y	Y	Y	Y	N	N
SOUTH CAROLINA								
1 ***Sanford***	N	Y	N	N	N	N	Y	N
2 ***Spence***	Y	Y	Y	Y	Y	Y	?	?
3 ***Graham***	Y	Y	Y	Y	Y	Y	Y	Y
4 ***DeMint***	Y	Y	Y	Y	Y	Y	Y	Y
5 Spratt	Y	Y	Y	Y	Y	Y	N	N
6 Clyburn	Y	Y	Y	Y	Y	Y	N	Y
SOUTH DAKOTA								
AL ***Thune***	Y	Y	Y	Y	Y	Y	Y	Y
TENNESSEE								
1 ***Jenkins***	Y	Y	Y	Y	Y	Y	Y	N
2 ***Duncan***	Y	Y	Y	N	Y	Y	Y	N
3 ***Wamp***	Y	Y	Y	Y	Y	Y	N	N
4 ***Hilleary***	Y	Y	Y	Y	Y	Y	Y	N
5 Clement	Y	Y	Y	Y	Y	Y	Y	Y
6 Gordon	Y	Y	Y	Y	Y	Y	N	Y
7 ***Bryant***	Y	Y	Y	Y	Y	Y	Y	Y
8 Tanner	Y	Y	Y	Y	Y	Y	Y	Y
9 Ford	Y	Y	Y	Y	Y	Y	Y	Y
TEXAS								
1 Sandlin	Y	Y	Y	Y	Y	Y	N	Y
2 Turner	Y	Y	Y	Y	Y	Y	Y	Y
3 ***Johnson, Sam***	Y	Y	Y	Y	Y	Y	Y	Y
4 Hall	Y	Y	Y	Y	Y	Y	Y	Y
5 ***Sessions***	Y	Y	Y	Y	Y	Y	Y	Y
6 ***Barton***	Y	Y	Y	Y	Y	Y	Y	Y
7 ***Archer***	Y	Y	Y	Y	Y	Y	Y	Y
8 ***Brady***	Y	Y	Y	Y	Y	Y	Y	Y
9 Lampson	Y	Y	Y	Y	Y	Y	Y	Y
10 Doggett	Y	Y	Y	Y	Y	Y	N	Y
11 Edwards	Y	Y	Y	Y	Y	Y	N	Y
12 ***Granger***	Y	Y	Y	Y	Y	Y	Y	Y
13 ***Thornberry***	Y	Y	Y	Y	Y	Y	Y	Y
14 ***Paul***	N	Y	N	Y	N	N	Y	N
15 Hinojosa	Y	Y	Y	Y	Y	Y	Y	Y
16 Reyes	Y	Y	Y	Y	Y	Y	N	Y
17 Stenholm	Y	Y	Y	Y	Y	Y	Y	Y
18 Jackson-Lee	Y	Y	Y	Y	Y	Y	Y	Y
19 ***Combest***	Y	Y	Y	Y	Y	Y	Y	Y
20 Gonzalez	Y	Y	Y	Y	Y	Y	N	Y
21 ***Smith***	Y	Y	Y	Y	Y	Y	Y	Y
22 ***DeLay***	Y	Y	Y	Y	Y	Y	?	Y
23 ***Bonilla***	Y	Y	Y	Y	Y	Y	Y	Y
24 Frost	?	?	Y	Y	Y	Y	N	Y
25 Bentsen	Y	Y	Y	Y	Y	Y	Y	Y
26 ***Armey***	Y	Y	Y	Y	Y	Y	Y	Y
27 Ortiz	Y	Y	Y	Y	Y	Y	Y	Y
28 Rodriguez	Y	Y	Y	Y	Y	Y	N	Y
29 Green	Y	Y	Y	Y	Y	Y	N	N
30 Johnson, E.B.	Y	Y	Y	Y	Y	Y	Y	Y
UTAH								
1 ***Hansen***	Y	Y	Y	Y	Y	Y	Y	Y
2 ***Cook***	?	?	?	?	?	?	?	?
3 ***Cannon***	Y	Y	Y	Y	Y	Y	Y	Y
VERMONT								
AL *Sanders*	Y	Y	Y	Y	Y	Y	N	N
VIRGINIA								
1 ***Bateman***	Y	Y	?	?	Y	Y	Y	Y
2 Pickett	Y	Y	Y	Y	Y	Y	N	Y
3 Scott	Y	Y	Y	Y	Y	Y	Y	Y
4 Sisisky	Y	Y	Y	Y	Y	Y	Y	Y
5 *Goode*	Y	Y	Y	Y	Y	Y	N	N
6 ***Goodlatte***	Y	Y	Y	Y	Y	Y	Y	Y
7 ***Bliley***	Y	Y	Y	Y	Y	Y	Y	Y
8 Moran	Y	Y	Y	Y	Y	Y	Y	Y
9 Boucher	Y	Y	Y	Y	Y	Y	N	N
10 ***Wolf***	Y	Y	Y	Y	Y	Y	Y	Y
11 ***Davis***	Y	Y	Y	Y	Y	Y	Y	Y
WASHINGTON								
1 Inslee	Y	Y	Y	Y	Y	Y	Y	Y
2 ***Metcalf***	Y	Y	Y	Y	Y	?	Y	N
3 Baird	Y	Y	Y	Y	Y	Y	Y	Y
4 ***Hastings***	Y	Y	Y	Y	Y	Y	Y	Y
5 ***Nethercutt***	Y	Y	Y	Y	Y	Y	Y	Y
6 Dicks	Y	Y	Y	Y	Y	Y	Y	Y
7 McDermott	Y	Y	Y	Y	Y	Y	N	Y
8 ***Dunn***	Y	Y	Y	Y	Y	Y	Y	Y
9 Smith	Y	Y	Y	Y	Y	Y	Y	Y
WEST VIRGINIA								
1 Mollohan	Y	Y	Y	Y	Y	Y	Y	N
2 Wise	?	?	?	?	?	?	?	?
3 Rahall	Y	Y	Y	Y	Y	Y	N	N
WISCONSIN								
1 ***Ryan***	Y	Y	Y	Y	Y	Y	Y	Y
2 Baldwin	Y	Y	Y	Y	Y	Y	N	N
3 Kind	Y	Y	Y	Y	Y	Y	Y	Y
4 Kleczka	Y	Y	Y	Y	Y	Y	N	N
5 Barrett	Y	Y	Y	Y	Y	Y	N	N
6 ***Petri***	Y	Y	Y	Y	Y	Y	Y	Y
7 Obey	Y	Y	Y	Y	Y	Y	N	?
8 ***Green***	Y	Y	Y	Y	Y	Y	Y	Y
9 ***Sensenbrenner***	Y	Y	N	Y	Y	N	Y	Y
WYOMING								
AL ***Cubin***	Y	Y	Y	Y	Y	Y	Y	Y

Southern states - Ala., Ark., Fla., Ga., Ky., La., Miss., N.C., Okla., S.C., Tenn., Texas, Va.

House Votes 146, 147, 148, 149, 150, 151, 152

146. H Con Res 296. USDA Discrimination/Adoption. Simpson, R-Idaho, motion to suspend the rules and adopt the concurrent resolution expressing the sense of Congress that the settlement process and claims of African-American farmers against the Department of Agriculture should be resolved expeditiously. Motion rejected 216-180: R 197-0; D 18-179 (ND 12-133, SD 6-46); I 1-1. A two-thirds majority of those present and voting (264 in this case) is required for adoption under suspension of the rules. May 8, 2000.

147. HR 3577. Minidoka Reclamation Project/Passage. Simpson, R-Idaho, motion to suspend the rules and pass the bill that would increase the authorization for the Minidoka water reclamation project in Idaho from $11.4 million to $14.2 million. Motion agreed to 385-6: R 190-6; D 193-0 (ND 142-0, SD 51-0); I 2-0. A two-thirds majority of those present and voting (261 in this case) is required for passage under suspension of the rules. May 8, 2000.

148. H Con Res 89. German Heritage/Adoption. Simpson, R-Idaho, motion to suspend the rules and adopt the concurrent resolution recognizing the Hermann Monument and Hermann Heights Park in New Ulm, Minn., as a national symbol of the contributions of Americans of German heritage. Motion agreed to 389-0: R 194-0; D 193-0 (ND 143-0, SD 50-0); I 2-0. A two-thirds majority of those present and voting (260 in this case) is required for adoption under suspension of the rules. May 8, 2000.

149. H Res 492. Teacher Appreciation/Adoption. McKeon, R-Calif., motion to suspend the rules and adopt the resolution that would honor and recognize the unique and important achievement of teachers and urge Americans to pay tribute to the nation's teachers. Motion agreed to 422-0: R 213-0; D 207-0 (ND 153-0, SD 54-0); I 2-0. A two-thirds majority of those present and voting (282 in this case) is required for adoption under suspension of the rules. May 9, 2000.

150. HR 3293. Vietnam Memorial Plaque/Passage. Gallegly, R-Calif., motion to suspend the rules and pass the bill that would authorize a plaque commemorating Vietnam veterans who died after the conflict ended but as a direct result of their service at the Vietnam Veterans Memorial. No federal funds could be used for the design, procurement or installation of the plaque. Motion agreed to 421-0: R 212-0; D 207-0 (ND 153-0, SD 54-0); I 2-0. A two-thirds majority of those present and voting (281 in this case) is required for passage under suspension of the rules. May 9, 2000.

151. HR 4386. Breast and Cervical Cancer Treatment/Passage. Lazio, R-N.Y., motion to suspend the rules and pass the bill that would allow states to provide Medicaid coverage for treatment to women who have been screened under the Centers for Disease Control and Prevention's national breast and cervical cancer early detection program for low-income women and found to have cancer. It would require the federal government to pay states 75 percent of the cost of Medicaid coverage. Motion agreed to 421-1: R 212-1; D 207-0 (ND 153-0, SD 54-0); I 2-0. A two-thirds majority of those present and voting (282 in this case) is required for passage under suspension of the rules. May 9, 2000.

152. HR 4365. Children's Health Care/Passage. Bilirakis, R-Fla., motion to suspend the rules and pass the bill that would require the National Institutes of Health to establish a Pediatric Research Initiative to provide funding for increased pediatric biomedical research into such areas as autism, juvenile diabetes, asthma, epilepsy and birth defects. It also would increase adoption information and referral training for workers in adoption organizations, health centers and family planning clinics. Motion agreed to 419-2: R 210-2; D 207-0 (ND 153-0, SD 54-0); I 2-0. A two-thirds majority of those present and voting (281 in this case) is required for passage under suspension of the rules. May 9, 2000.

Key

Y Voted for (yea).
Paired for.
\+ Announced for.
N Voted against (nay).
X Paired against.
– Announced against.
P Voted "present."
C Voted "present" to avoid possible conflict of interest.
? Did not vote or otherwise make a position known.

•

Democrats ***Republicans***
Independents

	146	147	148	149	150	151	152
ALABAMA							
1 ***Callahan***	Y	Y	Y	Y	Y	Y	Y
2 ***Everett***	?	?	?	Y	Y	Y	Y
3 ***Riley***	Y	Y	Y	Y	Y	Y	Y
4 ***Aderholt***	Y	Y	Y	Y	Y	Y	Y
5 Cramer	N	Y	Y	Y	Y	Y	Y
6 ***Bachus***	Y	Y	Y	Y	Y	Y	Y
7 Hilliard	N	Y	Y	Y	Y	Y	Y
ALASKA							
AL ***Young***	Y	Y	Y	Y	Y	Y	Y
ARIZONA							
1 ***Salmon***	Y	Y	Y	Y	Y	Y	Y
2 Pastor	N	Y	Y	Y	Y	Y	Y
3 ***Stump***	Y	Y	Y	Y	Y	Y	Y
4 ***Shadegg***	Y	Y	Y	Y	Y	Y	Y
5 ***Kolbe***	Y	Y	Y	Y	Y	Y	Y
6 ***Hayworth***	Y	Y	Y	Y	Y	Y	Y
ARKANSAS							
1 Berry	N	Y	Y	Y	Y	Y	Y
2 Snyder	N	Y	Y	Y	Y	Y	Y
3 ***Hutchinson***	Y	Y	Y	Y	Y	Y	Y
4 ***Dickey***	Y	Y	Y	Y	Y	Y	Y
CALIFORNIA							
1 Thompson	N	Y	Y	Y	Y	Y	Y
2 ***Herger***	?	?	?	Y	Y	Y	Y
3 ***Ose***	Y	Y	Y	Y	Y	Y	Y
4 ***Doolittle***	?	?	?	Y	Y	Y	Y
5 Matsui	N	Y	Y	Y	Y	Y	Y
6 Woolsey	N	Y	Y	Y	Y	Y	Y
7 Miller, George	N	Y	Y	Y	Y	Y	Y
8 Pelosi	N	Y	Y	Y	Y	Y	Y
9 Lee	N	Y	Y	Y	Y	Y	Y
10 Tauscher	N	Y	Y	Y	Y	Y	Y
11 ***Pombo***	Y	Y	Y	Y	Y	Y	Y
12 Lantos	N	Y	Y	Y	Y	Y	Y
13 Stark	?	?	?	Y	Y	Y	Y
14 Eshoo	N	Y	Y	Y	Y	Y	Y
15 ***Campbell***	?	?	?	?	?	?	?
16 Lofgren	N	Y	Y	Y	Y	Y	Y
17 Farr	N	Y	Y	Y	Y	Y	Y
18 Condit	N	Y	Y	Y	Y	Y	Y
19 ***Radanovich***	Y	Y	Y	Y	Y	Y	Y
20 Dooley	?	?	?	Y	Y	Y	Y
21 ***Thomas***	Y	Y	Y	Y	Y	Y	Y
22 Capps	N	Y	Y	Y	Y	Y	Y
23 ***Gallegly***	Y	Y	Y	Y	Y	Y	Y
24 Sherman	N	Y	Y	Y	Y	Y	Y
25 ***McKeon***	Y	Y	Y	Y	Y	Y	Y
26 Berman	N	Y	Y	Y	Y	Y	Y
27 ***Rogan***	Y	Y	Y	Y	Y	Y	Y
28 ***Dreier***	Y	Y	Y	Y	Y	Y	Y
29 Waxman	N	Y	Y	Y	Y	Y	Y
30 Becerra	N	Y	Y	Y	Y	Y	Y
31 Martinez	?	?	?	Y	Y	Y	Y
32 Dixon	N	Y	Y	Y	Y	Y	Y
33 Roybal-Allard	N	Y	Y	Y	Y	Y	Y
34 Napolitano	N	Y	Y	Y	Y	Y	Y
35 Waters	N	Y	Y	Y	Y	Y	Y
36 ***Kuykendall***	+	+	+	+	+	+	+
37 Millender-McD.	N	Y	Y	Y	Y	Y	Y
38 ***Horn***	Y	Y	?	Y	Y	Y	Y
39 ***Royce***	Y	N	Y	Y	Y	Y	Y
40 ***Lewis***	Y	Y	Y	Y	Y	Y	Y
41 ***Miller, Gary***	Y	Y	Y	Y	Y	Y	Y
42 Baca	N	Y	Y	Y	Y	Y	Y
43 ***Calvert***	Y	Y	Y	Y	Y	Y	Y
44 ***Bono***	Y	Y	Y	Y	Y	Y	Y
45 ***Rohrabacher***	Y	Y	Y	Y	Y	Y	Y
46 Sanchez	N	Y	Y	Y	Y	Y	Y
47 ***Cox***	Y	Y	Y	Y	Y	Y	Y
48 ***Packard***	Y	Y	Y	Y	Y	Y	Y
49 ***Bilbray***	Y	Y	Y	Y	Y	Y	Y
50 Filner	N	Y	Y	Y	Y	Y	Y
51 ***Cunningham***	Y	Y	Y	Y	Y	Y	Y
52 ***Hunter***	Y	Y	Y	Y	Y	Y	Y
COLORADO							
1 DeGette	?	?	?	Y	Y	Y	Y
2 Udall	N	Y	Y	Y	Y	Y	Y
3 ***McInnis***	Y	Y	Y	Y	Y	Y	Y
4 ***Schaffer***	?	?	?	Y	Y	Y	Y
5 ***Hefley***	Y	Y	Y	Y	Y	Y	Y
6 ***Tancredo***	Y	Y	Y	Y	Y	Y	Y
CONNECTICUT							
1 Larson	N	Y	Y	Y	Y	Y	Y
2 Gejdenson	N	Y	Y	Y	Y	Y	Y
3 DeLauro	N	Y	Y	Y	Y	Y	Y
4 ***Shays***	Y	Y	Y	Y	Y	Y	Y
5 Maloney	N	Y	Y	Y	Y	Y	Y
6 ***Johnson***	Y	Y	Y	Y	Y	Y	Y
DELAWARE							
AL ***Castle***	Y	Y	Y	Y	Y	Y	Y
FLORIDA							
1 ***Scarborough***	Y	Y	Y	Y	Y	Y	Y
2 Boyd	N	Y	Y	Y	Y	Y	Y
3 Brown	N	Y	Y	Y	Y	Y	Y
4 ***Fowler***	Y	Y	Y	Y	Y	Y	Y
5 Thurman	N	Y	Y	Y	Y	Y	Y
6 ***Stearns***	Y	Y	Y	Y	Y	Y	Y
7 ***Mica***	Y	Y	Y	Y	Y	Y	Y
8 ***McCollum***	?	?	?	?	?	?	?
9 ***Bilirakis***	Y	Y	Y	Y	Y	Y	Y
10 ***Young***	Y	Y	Y	?	?	?	?
11 Davis	N	Y	Y	Y	Y	Y	Y
12 ***Canady***	Y	Y	Y	Y	Y	Y	Y
13 ***Miller***	Y	Y	Y	Y	Y	Y	Y
14 ***Goss***	Y	Y	Y	Y	Y	Y	Y
15 ***Weldon***	Y	Y	Y	Y	Y	Y	Y
16 ***Foley***	Y	Y	Y	Y	Y	Y	Y
17 Meek	N	Y	Y	Y	Y	Y	Y
18 ***Ros-Lehtinen***	Y	Y	Y	Y	Y	Y	Y
19 Wexler	N	?	?	Y	Y	Y	Y
20 Deutsch	N	Y	Y	Y	Y	Y	Y
21 ***Diaz-Balart***	Y	Y	Y	Y	Y	Y	Y
22 ***Shaw***	Y	Y	Y	Y	Y	Y	Y
23 Hastings	N	Y	Y	Y	Y	Y	Y
GEORGIA							
1 ***Kingston***	Y	Y	Y	Y	Y	Y	Y
2 Bishop	N	Y	Y	Y	Y	Y	Y
3 ***Collins***	Y	Y	Y	Y	Y	Y	Y
4 McKinney	N	Y	Y	Y	Y	Y	Y
5 Lewis	N	Y	Y	Y	Y	Y	Y
6 ***Isakson***	Y	Y	Y	Y	Y	Y	Y
7 ***Barr***	Y	Y	Y	Y	Y	Y	Y
8 ***Chambliss***	?	?	?	Y	Y	Y	Y
9 ***Deal***	Y	Y	Y	Y	Y	Y	Y
10 ***Norwood***	Y	Y	Y	Y	Y	Y	Y
11 ***Linder***	Y	Y	Y	Y	Y	Y	Y
HAWAII							
1 Abercrombie	N	Y	Y	Y	Y	Y	Y
2 Mink	N	Y	Y	Y	Y	Y	Y
IDAHO							
1 ***Chenoweth-Hage***	Y	Y	Y	Y	Y	Y	Y
2 ***Simpson***	Y	Y	Y	Y	Y	Y	Y
ILLINOIS							
1 Rush	N	Y	Y	Y	Y	Y	Y
2 Jackson	N	Y	Y	Y	Y	Y	Y
3 Lipinski	?	?	?	Y	Y	Y	Y
4 Gutierrez	N	Y	Y	Y	Y	Y	Y
5 Blagojevich	N	Y	Y	Y	Y	Y	Y
6 ***Hyde***	Y	Y	Y	Y	Y	Y	Y
7 Davis	N	Y	Y	Y	Y	Y	Y
8 ***Crane***	Y	Y	Y	Y	Y	Y	Y
9 Schakowsky	N	Y	Y	Y	Y	Y	Y
10 ***Porter***	Y	Y	Y	Y	Y	Y	Y
11 ***Weller***	Y	Y	Y	Y	Y	Y	Y
12 Costello	N	Y	Y	Y	Y	Y	Y
13 ***Biggert***	Y	Y	Y	Y	Y	Y	Y

ND Northern Democrats SD Southern Democrats

	146	147	148	149	150	151	152
14 ***Hastert***							
15 ***Ewing***	Y	Y	Y	Y	Y	Y	Y
16 ***Manzullo***	Y	Y	Y	Y	Y	Y	Y
17 Evans	N	Y	Y	Y	Y	Y	Y
18 ***LaHood***	Y	Y	Y	Y	Y	Y	Y
19 Phelps	N	Y	Y	Y	Y	Y	Y
20 ***Shimkus***	Y	Y	Y	Y	Y	Y	Y
INDIANA							
1 Visclosky	N	Y	Y	Y	Y	Y	Y
2 ***McIntosh***	?	?	?	?	?	?	?
3 Roemer	N	Y	Y	Y	Y	Y	Y
4 ***Souder***	?	?	?	Y	Y	Y	Y
5 ***Buyer***	?	?	?	?	?	?	?
6 ***Burton***	Y	Y	Y	Y	Y	Y	+
7 ***Pease***	Y	Y	Y	Y	Y	Y	Y
8 ***Hostettler***	Y	Y	Y	Y	Y	Y	Y
9 Hill	N	?	?	Y	Y	Y	Y
10 Carson	N	Y	Y	Y	Y	Y	Y
IOWA							
1 ***Leach***	Y	Y	Y	Y	Y	Y	Y
2 ***Nussle***	Y	Y	Y	Y	Y	Y	Y
3 Boswell	N	Y	Y	Y	Y	Y	Y
4 ***Ganske***	Y	Y	Y	Y	Y	Y	Y
5 ***Latham***	Y	Y	Y	Y	Y	Y	Y
KANSAS							
1 ***Moran***	Y	Y	Y	Y	Y	Y	Y
2 ***Ryun***	Y	Y	Y	Y	Y	Y	Y
3 Moore	N	Y	Y	Y	Y	Y	Y
4 ***Tiahrt***	Y	Y	Y	Y	Y	Y	Y
KENTUCKY							
1 ***Whitfield***	Y	Y	Y	Y	Y	Y	Y
2 ***Lewis***	Y	Y	Y	Y	Y	Y	Y
3 ***Northup***	Y	Y	Y	Y	Y	Y	Y
4 Lucas	Y	Y	Y	Y	Y	Y	Y
5 ***Rogers***	Y	Y	Y	Y	Y	Y	Y
6 ***Fletcher***	Y	Y	Y	Y	Y	Y	Y
LOUISIANA							
1 ***Vitter***	Y	Y	Y	Y	Y	Y	Y
2 Jefferson	N	Y	Y	Y	Y	Y	Y
3 ***Tauzin***	Y	Y	Y	Y	Y	Y	Y
4 ***McCrery***	Y	Y	Y	Y	Y	Y	Y
5 ***Cooksey***	?	?	?	Y	?	Y	Y
6 ***Baker***	Y	Y	Y	Y	Y	Y	Y
7 John	N	Y	Y	Y	Y	Y	Y
MAINE							
1 Allen	N	Y	Y	Y	Y	Y	Y
2 Baldacci	Y	Y	Y	Y	Y	Y	Y
MARYLAND							
1 ***Gilchrest***	Y	Y	Y	Y	Y	Y	Y
2 ***Ehrlich***	?	?	?	Y	Y	Y	Y
3 Cardin	N	Y	Y	Y	Y	Y	Y
4 Wynn	N	Y	Y	Y	Y	Y	Y
5 Hoyer	N	Y	Y	Y	Y	Y	Y
6 ***Bartlett***	Y	Y	Y	Y	Y	Y	Y
7 Cummings	N	Y	Y	Y	Y	Y	Y
8 ***Morella***	?	?	?	Y	Y	Y	Y
MASSACHUSETTS							
1 Olver	N	Y	Y	Y	Y	Y	Y
2 Neal	N	Y	Y	Y	Y	Y	Y
3 McGovern	N	Y	Y	Y	Y	Y	Y
4 Frank	N	Y	Y	Y	Y	Y	Y
5 Meehan	N	Y	Y	Y	Y	Y	Y
6 Tierney	N	Y	Y	Y	Y	Y	Y
7 Markey	N	Y	Y	Y	Y	Y	Y
8 Capuano	N	Y	Y	Y	Y	Y	Y
9 Moakley	?	?	?	?	?	?	?
10 Delahunt	N	Y	Y	Y	Y	Y	Y
MICHIGAN							
1 Stupak	N	Y	Y	Y	Y	Y	Y
2 ***Hoekstra***	Y	Y	Y	Y	Y	Y	Y
3 ***Ehlers***	Y	Y	Y	Y	Y	Y	Y
4 ***Camp***	Y	Y	Y	Y	Y	Y	Y
5 Barcia	N	Y	Y	Y	Y	Y	Y
6 ***Upton***	Y	Y	Y	Y	Y	Y	Y
7 ***Smith***	Y	N	Y	Y	Y	Y	Y
8 Stabenow	Y	Y	Y	Y	Y	Y	Y
9 Kildee	N	Y	Y	Y	Y	Y	Y
10 Bonior	N	Y	Y	Y	Y	Y	Y
11 ***Knollenberg***	Y	Y	Y	Y	Y	Y	Y
12 Levin	N	Y	Y	Y	Y	Y	Y
13 Rivers	Y	Y	Y	Y	Y	Y	Y
14 Conyers	N	Y	Y	Y	Y	Y	Y
15 Kilpatrick	N	Y	Y	Y	Y	Y	Y
16 Dingell	Y	Y	Y	Y	Y	Y	Y
MINNESOTA							
1 ***Gutknecht***	Y	Y	Y	Y	Y	Y	Y
2 Minge	N	Y	Y	Y	Y	Y	Y
3 ***Ramstad***	Y	Y	Y	Y	Y	Y	Y
4 Vento	N	Y	Y	Y	Y	Y	Y
5 Sabo	N	Y	Y	Y	Y	Y	Y
6 Luther	Y	Y	Y	Y	Y	Y	Y
7 Peterson	N	Y	Y	Y	Y	Y	Y
8 Oberstar	N	Y	Y	Y	Y	Y	Y
MISSISSIPPI							
1 ***Wicker***	Y	Y	Y	Y	Y	Y	Y
2 Thompson	N	Y	Y	Y	Y	Y	Y
3 ***Pickering***	Y	Y	?	Y	Y	Y	Y
4 Shows	N	Y	Y	Y	Y	Y	Y
5 Taylor	Y	Y	Y	Y	Y	Y	Y
MISSOURI							
1 Clay	?	?	?	Y	Y	Y	Y
2 ***Talent***	Y	Y	Y	Y	Y	Y	Y
3 Gephardt	N	Y	Y	?	?	?	?
4 Skelton	N	Y	Y	Y	Y	Y	Y
5 McCarthy	N	Y	Y	Y	Y	Y	Y
6 Danner	N	Y	Y	Y	Y	Y	Y
7 ***Blunt***	Y	Y	Y	Y	Y	Y	Y
8 ***Emerson***	Y	Y	Y	Y	Y	Y	Y
9 ***Hulshof***	Y	Y	Y	Y	Y	Y	Y
MONTANA							
AL ***Hill***	Y	Y	Y	Y	Y	Y	Y
NEBRASKA							
1 ***Bereuter***	Y	Y	Y	Y	Y	Y	Y
2 ***Terry***	Y	Y	Y	Y	Y	Y	Y
3 ***Barrett***	Y	Y	Y	Y	Y	Y	Y
NEVADA							
1 Berkley	N	Y	Y	Y	Y	Y	Y
2 ***Gibbons***	Y	Y	Y	Y	Y	Y	Y
NEW HAMPSHIRE							
1 ***Sununu***	Y	Y	Y	Y	Y	Y	Y
2 ***Bass***	Y	Y	Y	Y	Y	Y	Y
NEW JERSEY							
1 Andrews	?	?	?	Y	Y	Y	Y
2 ***LoBiondo***	Y	Y	Y	Y	Y	Y	Y
3 ***Saxton***	Y	Y	Y	Y	Y	Y	Y
4 ***Smith***	Y	Y	Y	Y	Y	Y	Y
5 ***Roukema***	Y	Y	Y	Y	Y	Y	Y
6 Pallone	N	Y	Y	Y	Y	Y	Y
7 ***Franks***	?	?	?	Y	Y	Y	Y
8 Pascrell	N	Y	Y	Y	Y	Y	Y
9 Rothman	N	Y	Y	Y	Y	Y	Y
10 Payne	N	?	?	?	?	?	?
11 ***Frelinghuysen***	Y	Y	Y	Y	Y	Y	Y
12 Holt	N	Y	Y	Y	Y	Y	Y
13 Menendez	N	Y	Y	Y	Y	Y	Y
NEW MEXICO							
1 ***Wilson***	?	?	?	Y	Y	Y	Y
2 ***Skeen***	Y	Y	Y	Y	Y	Y	Y
3 Udall	N	?	Y	Y	Y	Y	Y
NEW YORK							
1 Forbes	N	Y	Y	Y	Y	Y	Y
2 ***Lazio***	Y	Y	Y	Y	Y	Y	Y
3 ***King***	Y	Y	Y	Y	Y	Y	Y
4 McCarthy	N	Y	Y	Y	Y	Y	Y
5 Ackerman	N	Y	Y	Y	Y	Y	Y
6 Meeks	N	Y	Y	Y	Y	Y	Y
7 Crowley	N	Y	Y	Y	Y	Y	Y
8 Nadler	N	Y	Y	Y	Y	Y	Y
9 Weiner	N	Y	Y	Y	Y	Y	Y
10 Towns	N	Y	Y	Y	Y	Y	Y
11 Owens	+	+	–	Y	Y	Y	Y
12 Velázquez	N	Y	Y	Y	Y	Y	Y
13 ***Fossella***	Y	Y	Y	Y	Y	Y	Y
14 Maloney	N	Y	Y	Y	Y	Y	Y
15 Rangel	N	Y	Y	Y	Y	Y	Y
16 Serrano	?	?	?	Y	Y	Y	Y
17 Engel	Y	Y	Y	Y	Y	Y	Y
18 Lowey	N	Y	Y	Y	Y	Y	Y
19 ***Kelly***	Y	Y	Y	Y	Y	Y	Y
20 ***Gilman***	Y	Y	Y	Y	Y	Y	Y
21 McNulty	N	Y	Y	Y	Y	Y	Y
22 ***Sweeney***	?	?	?	Y	Y	Y	Y
23 ***Boehlert***	Y	Y	Y	Y	Y	Y	Y
24 ***McHugh***	Y	Y	Y	Y	Y	Y	Y
25 ***Walsh***	Y	Y	Y	Y	Y	Y	Y
26 Hinchey	N	Y	Y	Y	Y	Y	Y
27 ***Reynolds***	Y	Y	Y	Y	Y	Y	Y
28 Slaughter	N	Y	Y	Y	Y	Y	Y
29 LaFalce	N	Y	Y	Y	Y	Y	Y
30 ***Quinn***	Y	Y	Y	Y	Y	Y	Y
31 ***Houghton***	Y	Y	Y	Y	Y	Y	Y
NORTH CAROLINA							
1 Clayton	N	Y	Y	Y	Y	Y	Y
2 Etheridge	N	Y	Y	Y	Y	Y	Y
3 ***Jones***	Y	Y	Y	Y	Y	Y	Y
4 Price	N	Y	Y	Y	Y	Y	Y
5 ***Burr***	Y	Y	Y	Y	Y	Y	Y
6 ***Coble***	Y	N	Y	Y	Y	Y	Y
7 McIntyre	N	Y	Y	Y	Y	Y	Y
8 ***Hayes***	Y	Y	Y	Y	Y	Y	Y
9 ***Myrick***	+	+	+	Y	Y	Y	Y
10 ***Ballenger***	Y	Y	Y	Y	Y	Y	Y
11 ***Taylor***	Y	Y	Y	Y	Y	Y	Y
12 Watt	N	Y	Y	Y	Y	Y	Y
NORTH DAKOTA							
AL Pomeroy	N	Y	Y	Y	Y	Y	Y
OHIO							
1 ***Chabot***	Y	Y	Y	Y	Y	Y	Y
2 ***Portman***	Y	Y	Y	Y	Y	Y	Y
3 Hall	N	Y	Y	Y	Y	Y	Y
4 ***Oxley***	Y	Y	Y	Y	Y	Y	Y
5 ***Gillmor***	Y	Y	Y	Y	Y	Y	Y
6 Strickland	N	Y	Y	Y	Y	Y	Y
7 ***Hobson***	Y	Y	Y	Y	Y	Y	Y
8 ***Boehner***	Y	Y	Y	Y	Y	Y	Y
9 Kaptur	N	Y	Y	Y	Y	Y	Y
10 Kucinich	N	Y	Y	Y	Y	Y	Y
11 Jones	N	Y	Y	Y	Y	Y	Y
12 ***Kasich***	?	?	?	Y	Y	Y	Y
13 Brown	N	Y	Y	Y	Y	Y	Y
14 Sawyer	N	Y	Y	Y	Y	Y	Y
15 ***Pryce***	?	?	?	Y	Y	Y	Y
16 ***Regula***	Y	Y	Y	Y	Y	Y	Y
17 Traficant	Y	Y	Y	Y	Y	Y	Y
18 ***Ney***	Y	Y	Y	Y	Y	Y	Y
19 ***LaTourette***	Y	Y	Y	Y	Y	Y	Y
OKLAHOMA							
1 ***Largent***	Y	Y	Y	Y	Y	Y	Y
2 ***Coburn***	?	?	?	Y	Y	Y	Y
3 ***Watkins***	Y	Y	Y	Y	Y	Y	Y
4 ***Watts***	Y	Y	Y	Y	Y	Y	Y
5 ***Istook***	Y	Y	Y	Y	Y	Y	Y
6 ***Lucas***	?	?	?	?	?	?	?
OREGON							
1 Wu	N	Y	Y	Y	Y	Y	Y
2 ***Walden***	Y	Y	Y	Y	Y	Y	Y
3 Blumenauer	N	Y	Y	Y	Y	Y	Y
4 DeFazio	N	Y	Y	Y	Y	Y	Y
5 Hooley	N	Y	Y	Y	Y	Y	Y
PENNSYLVANIA							
1 Brady	N	Y	Y	Y	Y	Y	Y
2 Fattah	N	Y	Y	Y	Y	Y	Y
3 Borski	N	Y	Y	Y	Y	Y	Y
4 Klink	N	Y	Y	Y	Y	Y	Y
5 ***Peterson***	Y	Y	Y	Y	Y	Y	Y
6 Holden	N	Y	Y	Y	Y	Y	Y
7 ***Weldon***	Y	Y	Y	Y	Y	Y	Y
8 ***Greenwood***	Y	Y	Y	Y	Y	Y	Y
9 ***Shuster***	Y	Y	Y	Y	Y	Y	Y
10 ***Sherwood***	Y	Y	Y	Y	Y	Y	Y
11 Kanjorski	Y	Y	Y	Y	Y	Y	Y
12 Murtha	Y	Y	Y	Y	Y	Y	Y
13 Hoeffel	N	Y	Y	Y	Y	Y	Y
14 Coyne	N	Y	Y	Y	Y	Y	Y
15 ***Toomey***	Y	Y	Y	Y	Y	Y	Y
16 ***Pitts***	Y	Y	Y	Y	Y	Y	Y
17 ***Gekas***	Y	Y	Y	Y	Y	Y	Y
18 Doyle	N	Y	Y	Y	Y	Y	Y
19 ***Goodling***	Y	Y	Y	Y	Y	Y	Y
20 Mascara	N	Y	Y	Y	Y	Y	Y
21 ***English***	Y	Y	Y	Y	Y	Y	Y
RHODE ISLAND							
1 Kennedy	N	Y	Y	Y	Y	Y	Y
2 Weygand	N	Y	Y	Y	Y	Y	Y
SOUTH CAROLINA							
1 ***Sanford***	Y	N	Y	Y	Y	N	N
2 ***Spence***	Y	Y	Y	Y	Y	Y	Y
3 ***Graham***	Y	Y	Y	Y	Y	Y	Y
4 ***DeMint***	Y	Y	Y	Y	Y	Y	Y
5 Spratt	N	Y	Y	Y	Y	Y	Y
6 Clyburn	N	Y	Y	Y	Y	Y	Y
SOUTH DAKOTA							
AL ***Thune***	Y	Y	Y	Y	Y	Y	Y
TENNESSEE							
1 ***Jenkins***	Y	Y	Y	Y	Y	Y	Y
2 ***Duncan***	Y	Y	Y	Y	Y	Y	Y
3 ***Wamp***	Y	Y	Y	Y	Y	Y	Y
4 ***Hilleary***	Y	Y	Y	Y	Y	Y	Y
5 Clement	?	?	?	Y	Y	Y	Y
6 Gordon	N	Y	Y	Y	Y	Y	Y
7 ***Bryant***	Y	Y	Y	Y	Y	Y	Y
8 Tanner	N	Y	Y	Y	Y	Y	Y
9 Ford	N	Y	Y	Y	Y	Y	Y
TEXAS							
1 Sandlin	Y	Y	Y	Y	Y	Y	Y
2 Turner	Y	Y	Y	Y	Y	Y	Y
3 ***Johnson, Sam***	Y	Y	Y	Y	Y	Y	Y
4 Hall	Y	Y	Y	Y	Y	Y	Y
5 ***Sessions***	Y	Y	Y	Y	Y	Y	Y
6 ***Barton***	Y	Y	Y	Y	Y	Y	Y
7 ***Archer***	Y	Y	Y	Y	Y	Y	Y
8 ***Brady***	Y	Y	Y	Y	Y	Y	Y
9 Lampson	N	Y	Y	Y	Y	Y	Y
10 Doggett	N	Y	Y	Y	Y	Y	Y
11 Edwards	N	Y	Y	Y	Y	Y	Y
12 ***Granger***	Y	Y	Y	Y	Y	Y	Y
13 ***Thornberry***	Y	Y	Y	Y	Y	Y	Y
14 ***Paul***	Y	N	Y	Y	Y	Y	N
15 Hinojosa	N	Y	Y	Y	Y	Y	Y
16 Reyes	N	Y	Y	Y	Y	Y	Y
17 Stenholm	N	Y	Y	Y	Y	Y	Y
18 Jackson-Lee	N	Y	Y	Y	Y	Y	Y
19 ***Combest***	Y	Y	Y	Y	Y	Y	Y
20 Gonzalez	N	Y	Y	Y	Y	Y	Y
21 ***Smith***	Y	Y	Y	Y	Y	Y	Y
22 ***DeLay***	Y	Y	Y	Y	Y	Y	Y
23 ***Bonilla***	Y	Y	Y	Y	Y	Y	Y
24 Frost	N	Y	Y	Y	Y	Y	Y
25 Bentsen	N	Y	Y	Y	Y	Y	Y
26 ***Armey***	Y	Y	Y	Y	Y	Y	Y
27 Ortiz	N	Y	Y	Y	Y	Y	Y
28 Rodriguez	N	Y	Y	Y	Y	Y	Y
29 Green	N	Y	Y	Y	Y	Y	Y
30 Johnson, E.B.	N	Y	Y	Y	Y	Y	Y
UTAH							
1 ***Hansen***	?	?	?	Y	Y	Y	Y
2 ***Cook***	Y	Y	Y	Y	Y	Y	Y
3 ***Cannon***	Y	Y	Y	Y	Y	Y	Y
VERMONT							
AL *Sanders*	N	Y	Y	Y	Y	Y	Y
VIRGINIA							
1 ***Bateman***	Y	Y	Y	Y	Y	Y	Y
2 Pickett	Y	Y	Y	Y	Y	Y	Y
3 Scott	N	Y	Y	Y	Y	Y	Y
4 Sisisky	?	?	?	Y	Y	Y	Y
5 *Goode*	Y	Y	Y	Y	Y	Y	Y
6 ***Goodlatte***	Y	Y	Y	Y	Y	Y	Y
7 ***Bliley***	Y	Y	Y	Y	Y	Y	Y
8 Moran	N	Y	Y	Y	Y	Y	Y
9 Boucher	N	Y	?	Y	Y	Y	Y
10 ***Wolf***	Y	Y	Y	Y	Y	Y	Y
11 ***Davis***	Y	?	?	Y	Y	Y	Y
WASHINGTON							
1 Inslee	N	Y	Y	Y	Y	Y	Y
2 ***Metcalf***	Y	Y	Y	Y	Y	Y	Y
3 Baird	N	Y	Y	Y	Y	Y	Y
4 ***Hastings***	Y	Y	Y	Y	Y	Y	Y
5 ***Nethercutt***	Y	Y	Y	Y	Y	Y	Y
6 Dicks	N	Y	Y	Y	Y	Y	Y
7 McDermott	N	Y	Y	Y	Y	Y	Y
8 ***Dunn***	Y	Y	Y	Y	Y	Y	Y
9 Smith	N	Y	Y	Y	Y	Y	Y
WEST VIRGINIA							
1 Mollohan	?	?	?	Y	Y	Y	Y
2 Wise	?	?	?	?	?	?	?
3 Rahall	Y	Y	Y	Y	Y	Y	Y
WISCONSIN							
1 ***Ryan***	Y	Y	Y	Y	Y	Y	Y
2 Baldwin	N	Y	Y	Y	Y	Y	Y
3 Kind	Y	Y	Y	Y	Y	Y	Y
4 Kleczka	Y	Y	Y	Y	Y	Y	Y
5 Barrett	N	Y	Y	Y	Y	Y	Y
6 ***Petri***	Y	Y	Y	Y	Y	Y	Y
7 Obey	N	Y	Y	Y	Y	Y	Y
8 ***Green***	Y	Y	Y	Y	Y	Y	Y
9 ***Sensenbrenner***	Y	N	Y	Y	Y	Y	Y
WYOMING							
AL ***Cubin***	?	?	?	?	?	?	?

Southern states - Ala., Ark., Fla., Ga., Ky., La., Miss., N.C., Okla., S.C., Tenn., Texas, Va.

153. HR 3313. Long Island Sound/Passage. Shuster, R-Pa., motion to suspend the rules and pass the bill that would reauthorize the Environmental Protection Agency's Long Island Sound program office between 2000 and 2003 and increase to $80 million per year the amount authorized for grants to create a conservation and management plan for Long Island Sound under the National Estuary program. Motion agreed to 391-29: R 182-29; D 207-0 (ND 153-0, SD 54-0); I 2-0. A two-thirds majority of those present and voting (280 in this case) is required for passage under suspension of the rules. May 9, 2000.

154. HR 3709. Internet Tax Moratorium/Question of Consideration. Judgment of the House to consider the bill that would impose a five-year moratorium on state and local taxes on Internet access, despite a point of order raised by Conyers, D-Mich., that the bill would impose an unfunded mandate. Consideration agreed to 271-129: R 211-3; D 59-125 (ND 40-96, SD 19-29); I 1-1. May 10, 2000.

155. HR 3709. Internet Tax Moratorium/Long-Term Extension. Chabot, R-Ohio, amendment to the Delahunt, D-Mass., amendment to provide for a 99-year extension of the moratorium on state and local taxes on the Internet. The Delahunt amendment would extend the moratorium for two years. Rejected 90-336: R 85-134; D 4-201 (ND 3-151, SD 1-50); I 1-1. May 10, 2000.

156. HR 3709. Internet Tax Moratorium/Two-Year Extension. Delahunt, D-Mass., amendment that would extend the current moratorium on new state and local Internet taxes until Oct. 21, 2003. Rejected 208-219: R 36-182; D 171-36 (ND 127-28, SD 44-8); I 1-1. May 10, 2000. A "yea" was a vote in support of the president's position.

157. HR 3709. Internet Tax Moratorium/State Taxes. Istook, R-Okla., amendment expressing the sense of Congress that states should develop a tax system for electronic commerce that includes a centralized, multistate registration for sellers, with uniform definitions, procedures and rules. Adopted 289-138: R 93-126; D 195-11 (ND 144-10, SD 51-1); I 1-1. May 10, 2000.

158. HR 3709. Internet Tax Moratorium/Recommit. Conyers, D-Mich., motion to recommit the bill to the House Committee on the Judiciary with instructions to report it back with an amendment that extends the moratorium on state and local taxes on the Internet for two years instead of five years. Motion rejected 177-250: R 5-213; D 171-36 (ND 131-24, SD 40-12); I 1-1. May 10, 2000.

159. HR 3709. Internet Tax Moratorium/Passage. Passage of the bill that would impose a five-year moratorium on state and local taxes on Internet access, ending Oct. 21, 2006. It would also eliminate the grandfather clause that currently allows certain states to collect taxes on Internet access. Passed 352-75: R 209-9; D 142-65 (ND 104-51, SD 38-14); I 1-1. May 10, 2000.

Key

- Y Voted for (yea).
- # Paired for.
- \+ Announced for.
- N Voted against (nay).
- X Paired against.
- – Announced against.
- P Voted "present."
- C Voted "present" to avoid possible conflict of interest.
- ? Did not vote or otherwise make a position known.

•

Democrats ***Republicans***
Independents

	153	154	155	156	157	158	159
ALABAMA							
1 ***Callahan***	Y	Y	N	N	N	N	Y
2 ***Everett***	N	Y	N	N	N	N	Y
3 ***Riley***	Y	Y	N	N	Y	N	Y
4 ***Aderholt***	Y	Y	Y	N	Y	N	Y
5 Cramer	Y	N	N	Y	Y	N	Y
6 ***Bachus***	Y	Y	N	?	Y	N	Y
7 Hilliard	Y	N	N	N	Y	Y	N
ALASKA							
AL ***Young***	Y	Y	N	N	Y	N	Y
ARIZONA							
1 ***Salmon***	N	Y	Y	N	N	N	Y
2 Pastor	Y	N	N	Y	Y	Y	Y
3 ***Stump***	N	Y	N	N	N	N	Y
4 ***Shadegg***	N	Y	Y	N	N	N	Y
5 ***Kolbe***	Y	Y	N	N	N	N	Y
6 ***Hayworth***	?	Y	Y	N	N	N	Y
ARKANSAS							
1 Berry	Y	N	N	Y	Y	Y	Y
2 Snyder	Y	Y	N	Y	Y	Y	N
3 ***Hutchinson***	Y	Y	N	N	Y	N	Y
4 ***Dickey***	Y	Y	Y	Y	N	N	Y
CALIFORNIA							
1 Thompson	Y	N	N	Y	Y	Y	Y
2 ***Herger***	N	Y	Y	N	N	N	Y
3 ***Ose***	Y	Y	N	N	Y	N	Y
4 ***Doolittle***	N	Y	Y	N	N	N	Y
5 Matsui	Y	N	N	Y	Y	Y	N
6 Woolsey	Y	?	N	Y	Y	Y	Y
7 Miller, George	Y	N	N	Y	Y	Y	N
8 Pelosi	Y	Y	N	N	Y	N	Y
9 Lee	Y	N	N	Y	Y	Y	N
10 Tauscher	Y	Y	N	Y	Y	N	Y
11 ***Pombo***	Y	Y	Y	N	N	N	Y
12 Lantos	Y	N	N	Y	Y	Y	Y
13 Stark	Y	N	N	Y	?	Y	N
14 Eshoo	Y	Y	N	N	Y	N	Y
15 ***Campbell***	?	?	?	?	?	?	?
16 Lofgren	Y	Y	N	N	N	N	Y
17 Farr	Y	N	N	Y	Y	Y	Y
18 Condit	Y	N	N	Y	Y	Y	N
19 ***Radanovich***	Y	Y	Y	N	N	N	Y
20 Dooley	Y	N	N	Y	Y	Y	Y
21 ***Thomas***	Y	Y	N	N	Y	N	Y
22 Capps	Y	+	N	Y	Y	Y	Y
23 ***Gallegly***	Y	Y	N	N	Y	N	Y
24 Sherman	Y	Y	N	Y	Y	Y	Y
25 ***McKeon***	Y	Y	N	N	N	N	Y
26 Berman	Y	Y	N	Y	Y	Y	Y
27 ***Rogan***	Y	Y	Y	N	N	N	Y
28 ***Dreier***	Y	Y	N	N	N	N	Y
29 Waxman	Y	?	N	Y	Y	Y	Y
30 Becerra	Y	Y	N	Y	Y	Y	Y
31 Martinez	Y	Y	Y	N	Y	N	Y
32 Dixon	Y	Y	N	Y	Y	Y	Y
33 Roybal-Allard	Y	N	N	Y	Y	Y	N
34 Napolitano	Y	N	N	Y	Y	Y	Y
35 Waters	Y	N	N	Y	Y	Y	Y
36 ***Kuykendall***	+	Y	Y	N	N	N	Y
37 Millender-McD.	Y	N	N	Y	Y	Y	Y
38 ***Horn***	Y	Y	Y	N	N	N	Y
39 ***Royce***	N	Y	Y	N	N	N	Y
40 ***Lewis***	Y	Y	N	N	Y	N	Y
41 ***Miller, Gary***	Y	Y	Y	N	N	N	Y
42 Baca	Y	–	N	Y	Y	Y	Y
43 ***Calvert***	Y	Y	N	N	N	N	Y
44 ***Bono***	Y	Y	Y	N	N	N	Y
45 ***Rohrabacher***	Y	Y	Y	N	N	N	Y
46 Sanchez	Y	N	N	Y	Y	Y	Y
47 ***Cox***	Y	Y	Y	N	N	N	Y
48 ***Packard***	Y	Y	Y	N	N	N	Y
49 ***Bilbray***	Y	Y	Y	N	N	N	Y
50 Filner	Y	N	N	Y	Y	Y	Y
51 ***Cunningham***	Y	Y	Y	N	N	N	Y
52 ***Hunter***	Y	Y	N	N	N	N	Y
COLORADO							
1 DeGette	Y	Y	N	Y	Y	Y	Y
2 Udall	Y	Y	N	Y	Y	Y	Y
3 ***McInnis***	Y	Y	Y	N	N	N	Y
4 ***Schaffer***	N	Y	Y	N	N	N	Y
5 ***Hefley***	Y	Y	Y	N	N	N	Y
6 ***Tancredo***	Y	Y	Y	N	N	N	Y
CONNECTICUT							
1 Larson	Y	N	N	Y	Y	Y	Y
2 Gejdenson	Y	Y	N	N	Y	N	Y
3 DeLauro	Y	N	N	Y	Y	Y	Y
4 ***Shays***	Y	Y	Y	N	N	N	Y
5 Maloney	Y	N	N	Y	Y	Y	Y
6 ***Johnson***	Y	Y	N	N	Y	N	Y
DELAWARE							
AL ***Castle***	Y	Y	N	Y	Y	N	Y
FLORIDA							
1 ***Scarborough***	Y	Y	Y	N	N	N	Y
2 Boyd	Y	N	N	Y	Y	Y	N
3 Brown	Y	N	N	Y	Y	Y	Y
4 ***Fowler***	Y	Y	N	Y	Y	N	Y
5 Thurman	Y	N	N	Y	Y	Y	Y
6 ***Stearns***	N	Y	Y	N	N	N	Y
7 ***Mica***	Y	Y	Y	N	N	N	Y
8 ***McCollum***	?	Y	Y	N	N	N	Y
9 ***Bilirakis***	Y	Y	N	N	Y	N	Y
10 ***Young***	?	Y	N	N	Y	N	Y
11 Davis	Y	N	N	Y	Y	Y	Y
12 ***Canady***	Y	Y	N	N	N	N	Y
13 ***Miller***	Y	Y	Y	N	N	N	Y
14 ***Goss***	Y	Y	N	N	N	N	Y
15 ***Weldon***	Y	Y	Y	N	N	N	Y
16 ***Foley***	Y	Y	N	Y	Y	N	Y
17 Meek	Y	?	?	?	?	?	?
18 ***Ros-Lehtinen***	Y	Y	Y	N	Y	N	Y
19 Wexler	Y	N	N	Y	Y	N	Y
20 Deutsch	Y	?	N	N	Y	N	Y
21 ***Diaz-Balart***	Y	Y	Y	N	Y	N	Y
22 ***Shaw***	Y	Y	N	N	Y	N	Y
23 Hastings	Y	N	N	Y	Y	Y	N
GEORGIA							
1 ***Kingston***	Y	Y	Y	N	N	N	Y
2 Bishop	Y	Y	N	Y	Y	Y	Y
3 ***Collins***	N	?	Y	N	N	N	Y
4 McKinney	Y	Y	Y	Y	Y	Y	Y
5 Lewis	Y	?	?	Y	Y	Y	Y
6 ***Isakson***	Y	Y	N	N	Y	N	Y
7 ***Barr***	Y	Y	Y	N	N	N	Y
8 ***Chambliss***	Y	Y	Y	N	Y	N	Y
9 ***Deal***	Y	Y	N	N	N	N	Y
10 ***Norwood***	Y	Y	N	N	Y	N	Y
11 ***Linder***	Y	Y	Y	N	N	?	Y
HAWAII							
1 Abercrombie	Y	N	N	Y	N	Y	N
2 Mink	Y	Y	N	Y	Y	Y	Y
IDAHO							
1 ***Chenoweth-Hage***	N	Y	Y	N	Y	N	Y
2 ***Simpson***	Y	Y	Y	N	N	N	Y
ILLINOIS							
1 Rush	Y	?	N	Y	Y	Y	N
2 Jackson	Y	N	N	Y	Y	Y	N
3 Lipinski	Y	N	N	N	N	N	N
4 Gutierrez	Y	N	N	Y	N	Y	Y
5 Blagojevich	Y	Y	N	Y	Y	Y	N
6 ***Hyde***	Y	Y	N	N	Y	N	Y
7 Davis	Y	N	N	Y	Y	Y	N
8 ***Crane***	N	Y	Y	N	N	N	Y
9 Schakowsky	Y	N	N	Y	Y	Y	N
10 ***Porter***	Y	Y	N	Y	Y	N	N
11 ***Weller***	Y	Y	Y	N	N	N	Y
12 Costello	Y	N	N	N	Y	Y	Y
13 ***Biggert***	Y	Y	N	N	N	N	Y

ND Northern Democrats SD Southern Democrats

	153	154	155	156	157	158	159
14 ***Hastert***				N			
15 ***Ewing***	Y	Y	N	N	Y	N	Y
16 ***Manzullo***	Y	Y	N	N	N	N	Y
17 Evans	Y	N	N	Y	Y	Y	Y
18 ***LaHood***	Y	Y	N	N	Y	N	N
19 Phelps	Y	N	N	N	Y	N	Y
20 ***Shimkus***	Y	Y	N	N	Y	N	Y
INDIANA							
1 Visclosky	Y	N	N	Y	Y	Y	Y
2 ***McIntosh***	?	Y	N	N	N	N	Y
3 Roemer	Y	Y	N	Y	Y	Y	Y
4 ***Souder***	Y	Y	Y	N	Y	N	Y
5 ***Buyer***	?	Y	N	N	Y	N	Y
6 ***Burton***	+	Y	Y	N	Y	N	Y
7 ***Pease***	Y	Y	Y	N	N	N	Y
8 ***Hostettler***	N	Y	N	N	Y	N	Y
9 Hill	Y	N	N	Y	Y	Y	Y
10 Carson	Y	N	N	Y	Y	Y	Y
IOWA							
1 ***Leach***	Y	Y	N	Y	Y	N	Y
2 ***Nussle***	Y	Y	N	Y	Y	N	Y
3 Boswell	Y	N	N	Y	Y	N	Y
4 ***Ganske***	Y	Y	N	Y	Y	Y	N
5 ***Latham***	Y	Y	N	Y	Y	N	Y
KANSAS							
1 ***Moran***	Y	N	N	Y	Y	N	N
2 ***Ryun***	Y	Y	N	N	N	N	Y
3 Moore	Y	N	N	Y	Y	Y	N
4 ***Tiahrt***	N	Y	N	N	N	N	Y
KENTUCKY							
1 ***Whitfield***	Y	Y	N	Y	N	N	Y
2 ***Lewis***	Y	Y	N	Y	Y	N	Y
3 ***Northup***	Y	Y	N	N	N	N	Y
4 Lucas	Y	Y	N	N	Y	N	Y
5 ***Rogers***	Y	Y	N	Y	Y	N	Y
6 ***Fletcher***	Y	Y	Y	N	N	N	Y
LOUISIANA							
1 ***Vitter***	Y	Y	N	N	Y	N	Y
2 Jefferson	Y	Y	N	N	Y	N	Y
3 ***Tauzin***	Y	Y	Y	N	N	N	Y
4 ***McCrery***	Y	Y	N	N	Y	N	Y
5 ***Cooksey***	Y	Y	N	N	N	N	Y
6 ***Baker***	Y	Y	N	Y	Y	N	Y
7 John	Y	Y	N	Y	Y	N	Y
MAINE							
1 Allen	Y	?	N	Y	Y	Y	N
2 Baldacci	Y	?	N	Y	Y	Y	Y
MARYLAND							
1 ***Gilchrest***	Y	Y	N	N	Y	N	Y
2 ***Ehrlich***	Y	Y	N	N	N	N	Y
3 Cardin	Y	N	N	Y	Y	Y	Y
4 Wynn	Y	?	N	Y	Y	Y	Y
5 Hoyer	Y	Y	N	Y	Y	Y	Y
6 ***Bartlett***	Y	Y	Y	N	N	N	Y
7 Cummings	Y	N	N	Y	Y	Y	Y
8 ***Morella***	Y	Y	N	N	Y	N	Y
MASSACHUSETTS							
1 Olver	Y	N	N	Y	Y	Y	N
2 Neal	Y	N	N	Y	Y	Y	N
3 McGovern	Y	N	N	Y	Y	Y	Y
4 Frank	Y	N	N	Y	Y	Y	N
5 Meehan	Y	N	N	Y	N	Y	N
6 Tierney	Y	N	N	Y	Y	Y	N
7 Markey	Y	N	N	Y	Y	Y	N
8 Capuano	Y	N	N	Y	N	Y	N
9 Moakley	?	?	N	Y	Y	Y	Y
10 Delahunt	Y	N	N	Y	Y	Y	N
MICHIGAN							
1 Stupak	Y	N	N	Y	Y	Y	Y
2 ***Hoekstra***	Y	Y	N	N	Y	N	Y
3 ***Ehlers***	Y	Y	N	N	Y	N	Y
4 ***Camp***	Y	Y	N	N	N	N	Y
5 Barcia	Y	?	N	N	Y	N	Y
6 ***Upton***	Y	Y	Y	N	N	N	Y
7 ***Smith***	N	Y	Y	N	Y	N	Y
8 Stabenow	Y	Y	N	Y	Y	N	Y
9 Kildee	Y	Y	N	Y	Y	Y	Y
10 Bonior	Y	N	N	Y	Y	Y	N
11 ***Knollenberg***	Y	Y	N	N	N	N	Y
12 Levin	Y	N	N	Y	N	Y	N
13 Rivers	Y	Y	N	N	Y	N	Y
14 Conyers	Y	N	N	Y	Y	Y	N
15 Kilpatrick	Y	–	N	Y	Y	Y	N
16 Dingell	Y	?	N	N	Y	Y	Y

	153	154	155	156	157	158	159
MINNESOTA							
1 ***Gutknecht***	Y	Y	N	N	N	N	Y
2 Minge	Y	N	N	Y	Y	Y	N
3 ***Ramstad***	Y	Y	N	N	Y	N	Y
4 Vento	Y	N	N	Y	Y	Y	N
5 Sabo	Y	N	N	Y	Y	Y	N
6 Luther	Y	N	N	Y	Y	Y	Y
7 Peterson	Y	N	N	Y	Y	Y	N
8 Oberstar	Y	?	N	Y	Y	Y	N
MISSISSIPPI							
1 ***Wicker***	Y	Y	N	N	Y	N	Y
2 Thompson	Y	N	N	Y	Y	Y	Y
3 ***Pickering***	Y	Y	N	N	N	N	Y
4 Shows	Y	Y	N	Y	Y	N	Y
5 Taylor	Y	Y	N	N	Y	N	Y
MISSOURI							
1 Clay	Y	N	N	Y	Y	Y	N
2 ***Talent***	Y	Y	N	N	Y	N	Y
3 Gephardt	?	?	N	Y	Y	Y	Y
4 Skelton	Y	Y	N	Y	Y	Y	Y
5 McCarthy	Y	N	N	Y	Y	Y	N
6 Danner	Y	N	N	Y	Y	Y	N
7 ***Blunt***	Y	Y	N	N	N	N	Y
8 ***Emerson***	Y	Y	N	Y	Y	N	Y
9 ***Hulshof***	Y	Y	N	N	Y	N	Y
MONTANA							
AL ***Hill***	Y	Y	Y	N	N	N	Y
NEBRASKA							
1 ***Bereuter***	Y	Y	N	N	Y	N	Y
2 ***Terry***	Y	Y	Y	N	N	N	Y
3 ***Barrett***	Y	Y	Y	N	Y	N	Y
NEVADA							
1 Berkley	Y	N	N	Y	Y	Y	Y
2 ***Gibbons***	Y	Y	N	N	N	N	Y
NEW HAMPSHIRE							
1 ***Sununu***	Y	Y	Y	N	N	N	Y
2 ***Bass***	Y	Y	N	N	N	N	Y
NEW JERSEY							
1 Andrews	Y	N	N	Y	Y	N	Y
2 ***LoBiondo***	Y	Y	N	N	N	N	Y
3 ***Saxton***	Y	Y	N	N	N	N	Y
4 ***Smith***	Y	Y	Y	N	N	N	Y
5 ***Roukema***	Y	Y	N	N	N	N	Y
6 Pallone	Y	+	N	Y	Y	Y	Y
7 ***Franks***	Y	Y	Y	N	N	N	Y
8 Pascrell	Y	N	N	Y	Y	Y	Y
9 Rothman	Y	N	N	Y	Y	Y	N
10 Payne	?	N	N	Y	Y	Y	N
11 ***Frelinghuysen***	Y	Y	N	N	N	N	Y
12 Holt	Y	Y	N	Y	Y	Y	Y
13 Menendez	Y	Y	N	N	Y	N	Y
NEW MEXICO							
1 ***Wilson***	Y	Y	N	Y	Y	N	Y
2 ***Skeen***	Y	Y	Y	N	N	N	Y
3 Udall	Y	N	N	Y	Y	N	Y
NEW YORK							
1 Forbes	Y	Y	Y	N	N	N	Y
2 ***Lazio***	Y	Y	N	N	N	N	Y
3 ***King***	Y	Y	N	N	N	N	Y
4 McCarthy	Y	Y	N	N	Y	N	Y
5 Ackerman	Y	N	N	Y	Y	Y	Y
6 Meeks	Y	N	N	N	Y	Y	Y
7 Crowley	Y	N	N	Y	Y	Y	Y
8 Nadler	Y	Y	N	Y	Y	Y	Y
9 Weiner	Y	Y	N	Y	Y	Y	Y
10 Towns	Y	N	N	N	Y	Y	Y
11 Owens	Y	N	N	Y	Y	Y	Y
12 Velázquez	Y	N	N	Y	Y	Y	Y
13 ***Fossella***	Y	+	Y	N	N	N	Y
14 Maloney	Y	N	N	Y	Y	Y	Y
15 Rangel	Y	N	N	Y	Y	Y	Y
16 Serrano	Y	N	N	Y	Y	Y	Y
17 Engel	Y	?	N	Y	Y	Y	Y
18 Lowey	Y	N	N	Y	Y	Y	Y
19 ***Kelly***	Y	Y	N	N	N	N	Y
20 ***Gilman***	Y	Y	N	N	N	N	Y
21 McNulty	Y	N	N	Y	Y	Y	Y
22 ***Sweeney***	Y	Y	N	N	Y	N	Y
23 ***Boehlert***	Y	Y	N	N	Y	N	Y
24 ***McHugh***	Y	Y	N	N	N	N	Y
25 ***Walsh***	Y	Y	N	N	Y	N	Y
26 Hinchey	Y	?	N	Y	Y	Y	N
27 ***Reynolds***	Y	Y	N	N	N	N	Y
28 Slaughter	Y	N	N	Y	Y	Y	N
29 LaFalce	Y	N	N	Y	Y	Y	N

	153	154	155	156	157	158	159
30 ***Quinn***	Y	Y	N	N	N	N	Y
31 ***Houghton***	Y	?	N	N	N	N	Y
NORTH CAROLINA							
1 Clayton	Y	N	N	Y	Y	Y	N
2 Etheridge	Y	Y	N	Y	Y	Y	Y
3 ***Jones***	N	Y	N	Y	Y	N	Y
4 Price	Y	Y	N	Y	Y	Y	Y
5 ***Burr***	Y	Y	N	Y	N	N	Y
6 ***Coble***	N	Y	N	Y	N	N	Y
7 McIntyre	Y	Y	N	N	Y	Y	Y
8 ***Hayes***	Y	Y	N	N	N	N	Y
9 ***Myrick***	Y	?	N	Y	Y	N	Y
10 ***Ballenger***	N	Y	N	Y	N	N	Y
11 ***Taylor***	N	Y	Y	N	Y	N	Y
12 Watt	Y	N	N	Y	Y	Y	N
NORTH DAKOTA							
AL Pomeroy	Y	N	N	N	Y	Y	Y
OHIO							
1 ***Chabot***	N	Y	Y	N	N	N	Y
2 ***Portman***	Y	Y	N	N	N	N	Y
3 Hall	Y	N	N	Y	Y	Y	Y
4 ***Oxley***	Y	Y	N	N	N	N	Y
5 ***Gillmor***	Y	Y	N	Y	Y	N	Y
6 Strickland	Y	Y	N	N	N	N	Y
7 ***Hobson***	Y	Y	N	N	N	N	Y
8 ***Boehner***	Y	Y	Y	N	N	N	Y
9 Kaptur	Y	Y	N	Y	N	Y	Y
10 Kucinich	Y	N	N	Y	Y	Y	N
11 Jones	Y	N	N	Y	Y	Y	N
12 ***Kasich***	Y	Y	Y	N	N	N	Y
13 Brown	Y	N	N	Y	Y	Y	N
14 Sawyer	Y	N	N	Y	Y	Y	Y
15 ***Pryce***	Y	Y	N	Y	Y	N	Y
16 ***Regula***	Y	Y	N	Y	Y	N	Y
17 Traficant	Y	Y	N	N	Y	N	Y
18 ***Ney***	Y	Y	N	Y	Y	N	N
19 ***LaTourette***	Y	Y	N	N	Y	Y	Y
OKLAHOMA							
1 ***Largent***	N	Y	N	N	Y	N	Y
2 ***Coburn***	N	Y	Y	N	Y	N	Y
3 ***Watkins***	Y	Y	N	Y	Y	Y	Y
4 ***Watts***	Y	Y	N	N	Y	N	Y
5 ***Istook***	Y	N	N	Y	Y	Y	Y
6 ***Lucas***	?	?	?	?	?	?	?
OREGON							
1 Wu	Y	Y	N	N	Y	Y	Y
2 ***Walden***	Y	Y	Y	N	N	N	Y
3 Blumenauer	Y	N	N	Y	Y	Y	Y
4 DeFazio	Y	Y	N	N	Y	N	Y
5 Hooley	Y	Y	N	N	Y	N	Y
PENNSYLVANIA							
1 Brady	Y	N	N	Y	Y	Y	N
2 Fattah	Y	?	?	?	?	?	?
3 Borski	Y	N	N	Y	Y	Y	N
4 Klink	Y	N	N	Y	Y	Y	Y
5 ***Peterson***	Y	Y	Y	N	N	N	Y
6 Holden	Y	N	N	Y	Y	Y	Y
7 ***Weldon***	Y	Y	N	N	Y	N	Y
8 ***Greenwood***	Y	Y	N	Y	Y	N	Y
9 ***Shuster***	Y	Y	N	Y	Y	Y	N
10 ***Sherwood***	Y	Y	Y	N	N	N	Y
11 Kanjorski	Y	?	N	Y	Y	Y	N
12 Murtha	Y	N	N	N	Y	Y	Y
13 Hoeffel	Y	Y	N	Y	Y	Y	Y
14 Coyne	Y	N	N	Y	Y	Y	N
15 ***Toomey***	Y	Y	Y	N	N	N	Y
16 ***Pitts***	Y	Y	Y	N	N	N	Y
17 ***Gekas***	Y	Y	N	?	N	N	Y
18 Doyle	Y	Y	N	Y	Y	Y	Y
19 ***Goodling***	Y	Y	Y	N	N	N	Y
20 Mascara	Y	?	N	Y	Y	Y	Y
21 ***English***	Y	Y	N	N	N	N	Y
RHODE ISLAND							
1 Kennedy	Y	N	?	Y	Y	Y	N
2 Weygand	Y	N	N	Y	Y	Y	Y
SOUTH CAROLINA							
1 ***Sanford***	N	Y	N	Y	N	N	N
2 ***Spence***	Y	Y	N	N	Y	N	Y
3 ***Graham***	Y	Y	Y	N	N	N	Y
4 ***DeMint***	Y	Y	Y	N	N	N	Y
5 Spratt	Y	Y	N	Y	Y	Y	N
6 Clyburn	Y	N	N	Y	Y	Y	N
SOUTH DAKOTA							
AL ***Thune***	Y	N	N	Y	Y	Y	N

	153	154	155	156	157	158	159
TENNESSEE							
1 ***Jenkins***	Y	Y	N	Y	Y	N	Y
2 ***Duncan***	N	Y	N	Y	Y	N	Y
3 ***Wamp***	Y	Y	N	Y	N	N	Y
4 ***Hilleary***	Y	Y	Y	N	Y	N	Y
5 Clement	Y	N	N	Y	Y	N	Y
6 Gordon	Y	N	N	Y	Y	Y	N
7 ***Bryant***	Y	Y	N	N	Y	N	Y
8 Tanner	Y	Y	N	Y	Y	Y	Y
9 Ford	Y	N	N	Y	Y	Y	Y
TEXAS							
1 Sandlin	Y	Y	N	Y	Y	Y	Y
2 Turner	Y	?	N	Y	Y	Y	Y
3 ***Johnson, Sam***	N	Y	N	N	N	N	Y
4 Hall	Y	Y	N	Y	Y	Y	N
5 ***Sessions***	Y	Y	N	N	N	N	Y
6 ***Barton***	Y	Y	N	N	Y	N	Y
7 ***Archer***	Y	Y	N	N	N	N	Y
8 ***Brady***	N	Y	N	Y	Y	N	Y
9 Lampson	Y	N	N	Y	Y	Y	Y
10 Doggett	Y	N	N	Y	N	Y	Y
11 Edwards	Y	Y	N	Y	Y	Y	Y
12 ***Granger***	Y	Y	N	N	N	N	Y
13 ***Thornberry***	Y	Y	N	N	N	N	Y
14 ***Paul***	N	Y	N	Y	Y	N	N
15 Hinojosa	Y	Y	N	Y	Y	Y	Y
16 Reyes	Y	N	N	Y	Y	Y	Y
17 Stenholm	Y	N	N	Y	Y	Y	N
18 Jackson-Lee	Y	N	N	Y	Y	N	N
19 ***Combest***	Y	Y	Y	N	N	N	N
20 Gonzalez	Y	N	N	Y	Y	Y	Y
21 ***Smith***	Y	Y	Y	N	N	N	Y
22 ***DeLay***	Y	Y	Y	N	N	N	Y
23 ***Bonilla***	Y	Y	N	N	N	N	Y
24 Frost	Y	N	N	Y	Y	Y	Y
25 Bentsen	Y	N	N	Y	Y	Y	N
26 ***Armey***	Y	Y	N	N	N	N	Y
27 Ortiz	Y	N	N	Y	Y	Y	Y
28 Rodriguez	Y	N	N	Y	Y	Y	Y
29 Green	Y	?	N	Y	Y	Y	Y
30 Johnson, E.B.	Y	N	N	Y	Y	Y	Y
UTAH							
1 ***Hansen***	Y	Y	N	N	N	N	Y
2 ***Cook***	Y	Y	Y	N	N	N	Y
3 ***Cannon***	Y	Y	Y	N	N	N	Y
VERMONT							
AL *Sanders*	Y	N	N	Y	Y	Y	N
VIRGINIA							
1 ***Bateman***	Y	Y	N	N	Y	N	Y
2 Pickett	Y	Y	N	Y	Y	N	Y
3 Scott	Y	N	N	Y	Y	Y	N
4 Sisisky	Y	Y	N	N	Y	N	Y
5 *Goode*	Y	Y	Y	N	N	N	Y
6 ***Goodlatte***	Y	Y	Y	N	N	N	Y
7 ***Bliley***	Y	Y	N	N	N	N	Y
8 Moran	Y	?	?	?	?	?	?
9 Boucher	Y	N	N	N	Y	N	Y
10 ***Wolf***	Y	Y	N	N	N	N	Y
11 ***Davis***	N	Y	Y	N	N	N	Y
WASHINGTON							
1 Inslee	Y	Y	N	N	N	N	Y
2 ***Metcalf***	Y	Y	Y	N	Y	N	Y
3 Baird	Y	N	N	Y	Y	Y	N
4 ***Hastings***	Y	Y	Y	N	Y	N	Y
5 ***Nethercutt***	Y	Y	Y	N	Y	N	?
6 Dicks	Y	N	N	Y	Y	Y	Y
7 McDermott	Y	N	N	Y	Y	Y	N
8 ***Dunn***	Y	Y	N	N	Y	N	Y
9 Smith	Y	Y	N	N	Y	N	Y
WEST VIRGINIA							
1 Mollohan	Y	Y	N	N	Y	N	Y
2 Wise	?	?	?	?	?	?	?
3 Rahall	Y	N	N	Y	Y	Y	Y
WISCONSIN							
1 ***Ryan***	Y	Y	Y	N	Y	N	Y
2 Baldwin	Y	N	N	Y	Y	Y	N
3 Kind	Y	Y	N	Y	Y	Y	Y
4 Kleczka	Y	N	N	Y	Y	Y	Y
5 Barrett	Y	Y	N	Y	Y	Y	Y
6 ***Petri***	Y	Y	N	N	Y	N	Y
7 Obey	Y	N	N	Y	Y	Y	N
8 ***Green***	Y	Y	N	N	N	N	Y
9 ***Sensenbrenner***	N	Y	Y	N	N	N	Y
WYOMING							
AL ***Cubin***	?	?	N	N	Y	N	Y

Southern states - Ala., Ark., Fla., Ga., Ky., La., Miss., N.C., Okla., S.C., Tenn., Texas, Va.

160. HR 701. Land Conservation/Coastal States. Regula, R-Ohio, amendment allowing states that currently permit offshore drilling to receive the majority of their funding under the impact assistance and coastal conservation section of the bill. Rejected 109-317: R 99-117; D 10-198 (ND 5-149, SD 5-49); I 0-2. May 10, 2000.

161. HR 701. Land Conservation/Local Payments. Radanovich, R-Calif., amendment that would require full funding of the payments in lieu of taxes and refuge revenue sharing programs before other projects are provided with assistance from the Conservation and Reinvestment Act fund. Rejected 153-273: R 144-72; D 8-200 (ND 5-149, SD 3-51); I 1-1. May 10, 2000.

162. HR 701. Land Conservation/CARA Fund Reduction. Tancredo, R-Colo., amendment that would redirect the $450 million allocated for land acquisition to boost funding for urban parks and recreation programs, farmland protection programs, and threatened and endangered species recovery projects. Rejected 109-315: R 107-107; D 2-206 (ND 0-154, SD 2-52); I 0-2. May 10, 2000.

163. HR 701. Land Conservation/Debt Reduction. Shadegg, R-Ariz., amendment that would prohibit the Treasury Department from transferring offshore drilling royalties to the Conservation and Reinvestment Act fund unless the Congressional Budget Office certifies that Congress is on track to eliminate the publicly held debt by 2013 and that there is no on-budget deficit, and that neither Social Security nor Medicare is scheduled to run a deficit within the next five years. Adopted 216-208: R 177-38; D 38-169 (ND 20-134, SD 18-35); I 1-1. May 10, 2000.

164. HR 701. Land Conservation/Antiquities Act. Chenoweth-Hage, R-Idaho, amendment that would prohibit the use of funds in the bill to establish or manage any national monument designated after 1995 under the Antiquities Act. Rejected 160-265: R 154-61; D 5-203 (ND 1-153, SD 4-50); I 1-1. May 10, 2000.

165. HR 701. Land Conservation/Property Rights. Pombo, R-Calif., amendment stating that the property rights of landowners shall not be diminished because their property borders lands that are subsequently acquired by the federal government as a result of the bill. Rejected 171-253: R 154-61; D 16-191 (ND 6-147, SD 10-44); I 1-1. May 10, 2000.

166. HR 701. Land Conservation/Private Land Acquisition. Peterson, R-Pa., amendment that would prohibit using the funds in the bill for the purpose of acquiring non-federal land, unless the land already lies within federally held park, wilderness or recreation areas. Rejected 108-310: R 104-108; D 3-201 (ND 0-152, SD 3-49); I 1-1. May 11, 2000.

Key

Y	Voted for (yea).
#	Paired for.
+	Announced for.
N	Voted against (nay).
X	Paired against.
–	Announced against.
P	Voted "present."
C	Voted "present" to avoid possible conflict of interest.
?	Did not vote or otherwise make a position known.

•

Democrats ***Republicans***
Independents

	160	161	162	163	164	165	166
ALABAMA							
1 ***Callahan***	N	N	N	N	N	N	N
2 ***Everett***	N	Y	Y	Y	Y	Y	Y
3 ***Riley***	N	N	N	Y	Y	Y	Y
4 ***Aderholt***	N	Y	Y	Y	Y	Y	Y
5 Cramer	N	N	N	N	N	N	N
6 ***Bachus***	N	N	N	N	N	N	N
7 Hilliard	N	N	N	N	N	N	N
ALASKA							
AL ***Young***	N	N	N	N	N	N	N
ARIZONA							
1 ***Salmon***	Y	Y	Y	Y	Y	Y	Y
2 Pastor	N	Y	N	N	N	N	N
3 ***Stump***	Y	Y	Y	Y	Y	Y	Y
4 ***Shadegg***	Y	Y	Y	Y	Y	Y	Y
5 ***Kolbe***	Y	Y	N	Y	Y	Y	N
6 ***Hayworth***	Y	Y	Y	Y	Y	Y	Y
ARKANSAS							
1 Berry	N	Y	Y	Y	Y	Y	Y
2 Snyder	N	N	N	N	N	N	N
3 ***Hutchinson***	Y	Y	N	Y	Y	Y	Y
4 ***Dickey***	Y	Y	Y	Y	Y	Y	Y
CALIFORNIA							
1 Thompson	N	N	N	N	N	N	N
2 ***Herger***	Y	Y	Y	Y	Y	Y	Y
3 ***Ose***	N	Y	Y	Y	Y	Y	Y
4 ***Doolittle***	Y	Y	Y	Y	Y	Y	Y
5 Matsui	N	N	N	N	N	N	N
6 Woolsey	N	N	N	N	N	N	N
7 Miller, George	N	N	N	N	N	N	N
8 Pelosi	N	N	N	N	N	N	N
9 Lee	N	N	N	N	N	N	N
10 Tauscher	N	N	N	N	N	N	N
11 ***Pombo***	Y	Y	Y	Y	Y	Y	Y
12 Lantos	N	N	N	N	N	N	N
13 Stark	N	N	N	N	N	N	N
14 Eshoo	N	N	N	N	N	N	N
15 ***Campbell***	?	?	?	?	?	?	?
16 Lofgren	N	N	N	N	N	N	?
17 Farr	N	N	N	N	N	N	N
18 Condit	N	Y	N	Y	N	N	N
19 ***Radanovich***	Y	Y	Y	Y	Y	Y	Y
20 Dooley	N	N	N	N	N	N	N
21 ***Thomas***	N	Y	Y	Y	Y	Y	Y
22 Capps	N	N	N	N	N	N	N
23 ***Gallegly***	N	Y	N	Y	Y	Y	N
24 Sherman	N	N	N	N	N	N	N
25 ***McKeon***	N	Y	Y	Y	Y	Y	Y
26 Berman	?	?	?	?	?	?	N
27 ***Rogan***	N	N	Y	Y	Y	Y	N
28 ***Dreier***	N	Y	N	Y	Y	Y	N
29 Waxman	N	N	N	N	N	N	N
30 Becerra	N	N	N	N	N	N	N
31 Martinez	?	?	?	?	?	?	N
32 Dixon	N	N	N	N	N	N	N
33 Roybal-Allard	N	N	N	N	N	N	N
34 Napolitano	N	N	N	N	N	N	N
35 Waters	N	N	N	N	N	N	N
36 ***Kuykendall***	N	N	N	Y	N	N	N
37 Millender-McD.	N	N	N	N	N	N	N
38 ***Horn***	N	Y	N	N	N	N	N

	160	161	162	163	164	165	166
39 ***Royce***	N	Y	Y	Y	Y	Y	Y
40 ***Lewis***	N	Y	Y	Y	Y	Y	Y
41 ***Miller, Gary***	Y	Y	Y	Y	Y	Y	Y
42 Baca	N	N	N	N	N	Y	N
43 ***Calvert***	N	Y	Y	Y	Y	Y	N
44 ***Bono***	N	N	N	N	N	N	N
45 ***Rohrabacher***	N	Y	Y	Y	Y	Y	Y
46 Sanchez	N	N	N	N	N	N	N
47 ***Cox***	N	N	N	Y	Y	Y	N
48 ***Packard***	N	Y	N	Y	Y	Y	N
49 ***Bilbray***	N	N	N	N	N	N	N
50 Filner	N	N	N	N	N	N	N
51 ***Cunningham***	N	Y	Y	Y	Y	Y	N
52 ***Hunter***	N	Y	Y	Y	Y	Y	?
COLORADO							
1 DeGette	N	N	N	N	N	N	?
2 Udall	N	N	N	N	N	N	N
3 ***McInnis***	Y	Y	N	N	Y	Y	N
4 ***Schaffer***	Y	Y	Y	Y	Y	Y	Y
5 ***Hefley***	Y	Y	Y	Y	Y	Y	N
6 ***Tancredo***	Y	Y	Y	Y	Y	Y	N
CONNECTICUT							
1 Larson	N	N	N	N	N	N	N
2 Gejdenson	N	N	N	N	N	N	N
3 DeLauro	N	N	N	N	N	N	N
4 ***Shays***	N	N	N	N	N	N	N
5 Maloney	N	N	N	N	N	N	N
6 ***Johnson***	N	Y	N	N	Y	N	N
DELAWARE							
AL ***Castle***	N	N	N	N	N	N	N
FLORIDA							
1 ***Scarborough***	N	N	N	Y	N	N	N
2 Boyd	N	N	N	Y	N	N	N
3 Brown	N	N	N	N	N	N	N
4 ***Fowler***	N	Y	N	Y	Y	Y	N
5 Thurman	N	N	N	Y	N	N	N
6 ***Stearns***	N	Y	Y	Y	Y	Y	Y
7 ***Mica***	N	Y	N	Y	Y	Y	N
8 ***McCollum***	N	Y	N	Y	Y	Y	N
9 ***Bilirakis***	N	N	N	Y	N	Y	N
10 ***Young***	N	Y	N	Y	Y	Y	Y
11 Davis	N	N	N	N	N	N	N
12 ***Canady***	N	Y	N	Y	Y	Y	N
13 ***Miller***	N	N	N	Y	Y	Y	N
14 ***Goss***	N	Y	N	Y	Y	Y	N
15 ***Weldon***	N	Y	Y	Y	Y	Y	Y
16 ***Foley***	N	N	N	N	N	N	N
17 Meek	N	N	N	N	N	N	N
18 ***Ros-Lehtinen***	N	N	N	N	N	N	N
19 Wexler	N	N	N	N	N	N	N
20 Deutsch	N	N	N	N	N	N	N
21 ***Diaz-Balart***	N	N	N	N	N	N	N
22 ***Shaw***	N	N	N	Y	N	N	N
23 Hastings	N	N	N	N	N	N	N
GEORGIA							
1 ***Kingston***	N	Y	Y	Y	Y	Y	Y
2 Bishop	N	N	N	Y	N	N	N
3 ***Collins***	N	Y	Y	Y	Y	Y	Y
4 McKinney	N	N	N	N	N	N	N
5 Lewis	N	N	N	N	N	N	N
6 ***Isakson***	N	N	N	Y	N	N	N
7 ***Barr***	Y	Y	Y	Y	Y	Y	Y
8 ***Chambliss***	N	Y	N	Y	N	Y	N
9 ***Deal***	N	Y	N	Y	Y	N	N
10 ***Norwood***	N	Y	Y	Y	Y	Y	Y
11 ***Linder***	Y	Y	Y	Y	Y	Y	Y
HAWAII							
1 Abercrombie	N	N	N	N	N	N	N
2 Mink	N	N	N	N	N	N	N
IDAHO							
1 ***Chenoweth-Hage***	Y	Y	Y	Y	Y	Y	Y
2 ***Simpson***	Y	Y	Y	Y	Y	Y	Y
ILLINOIS							
1 Rush	N	N	N	N	N	N	N
2 Jackson	N	N	N	N	N	N	N
3 Lipinski	N	N	N	N	N	N	N
4 Gutierrez	N	N	N	N	N	N	N
5 Blagojevich	N	N	N	N	N	N	N
6 ***Hyde***	N	Y	N	N	Y	Y	N
7 Davis	N	N	N	N	N	N	N
8 ***Crane***	N	N	N	Y	Y	Y	N
9 Schakowsky	N	N	N	N	N	N	N
10 ***Porter***	N	N	N	N	N	N	N
11 ***Weller***	N	N	N	N	N	N	N
12 Costello	N	N	N	Y	N	N	N
13 ***Biggert***	N	N	N	N	N	N	N

ND Northern Democrats SD Southern Democrats

	160	161	162	163	164	165	166
14 ***Hastert***							
15 ***Ewing***	Y	N	N	Y	N	Y	N
16 ***Manzullo***	Y	Y	Y	Y	Y	Y	Y
17 Evans	N	N	N	Y	N	N	N
18 ***LaHood***	N	N	N	Y	N	N	Y
19 Phelps	N	N	N	Y	N	N	N
20 ***Shimkus***	N	Y	Y	Y	Y	Y	Y
INDIANA							
1 Visclosky	Y	N	N	N	N	N	N
2 ***McIntosh***	N	Y	N	Y	N	N	N
3 Roemer	N	N	N	Y	N	N	N
4 ***Souder***	N	N	N	Y	Y	N	N
5 ***Buyer***	Y	Y	Y	Y	Y	Y	Y
6 ***Burton***	Y	Y	Y	Y	Y	Y	+
7 ***Pease***	Y	Y	N	Y	N	N	N
8 ***Hostettler***	Y	Y	Y	Y	Y	Y	Y
9 Hill	N	N	N	Y	N	N	N
10 Carson	N	N	N	N	N	N	N
IOWA							
1 ***Leach***	Y	N	N	N	N	N	N
2 ***Nussle***	Y	Y	N	Y	Y	Y	Y
3 Boswell	N	N	N	Y	N	N	N
4 ***Ganske***	Y	N	N	Y	Y	Y	N
5 ***Latham***	Y	Y	Y	Y	Y	Y	Y
KANSAS							
1 ***Moran***	N	N	Y	Y	Y	Y	N
2 ***Ryun***	Y	Y	Y	Y	Y	Y	Y
3 Moore	N	N	N	N	N	N	N
4 ***Tiahrt***	Y	Y	Y	Y	Y	Y	Y
KENTUCKY							
1 ***Whitfield***	Y	Y	N	Y	N	N	N
2 ***Lewis***	Y	Y	Y	Y	Y	Y	N
3 ***Northup***	N	N	Y	Y	Y	Y	N
4 Lucas	N	N	N	Y	N	Y	N
5 ***Rogers***	N	Y	N	Y	Y	Y	N
6 ***Fletcher***	Y	Y	Y	Y	Y	Y	N
LOUISIANA							
1 ***Vitter***	N	N	N	Y	N	N	N
2 Jefferson	N	N	N	?	N	N	?
3 ***Tauzin***	N	N	N	N	N	N	N
4 ***McCrery***	N	N	N	N	N	N	N
5 ***Cooksey***	N	N	N	Y	N	N	N
6 ***Baker***	N	N	N	N	N	N	N
7 John	N	N	N	N	N	N	N
MAINE							
1 Allen	N	N	N	N	N	N	N
2 Baldacci	N	N	N	N	N	Y	N
MARYLAND							
1 ***Gilchrest***	N	N	N	N	N	N	N
2 ***Ehrlich***	N	Y	N	Y	Y	N	N
3 Cardin	N	N	N	N	N	N	N
4 Wynn	N	N	N	N	N	N	N
5 Hoyer	N	N	N	N	N	N	N
6 ***Bartlett***	Y	Y	Y	Y	Y	Y	Y
7 Cummings	N	N	N	N	N	N	?
8 ***Morella***	N	N	N	N	N	N	N
MASSACHUSETTS							
1 Olver	N	N	N	N	N	N	N
2 Neal	N	N	N	N	N	N	N
3 McGovern	N	N	N	N	N	N	N
4 Frank	N	N	N	N	N	N	N
5 Meehan	N	N	N	N	N	N	N
6 Tierney	N	N	N	N	N	N	N
7 Markey	N	N	N	N	N	N	N
8 Capuano	N	N	N	N	N	N	N
9 Moakley	N	N	N	N	N	N	N
10 Delahunt	N	N	N	N	N	N	N
MICHIGAN							
1 Stupak	N	Y	N	Y	N	N	N
2 ***Hoekstra***	Y	Y	Y	Y	Y	Y	N
3 ***Ehlers***	Y	N	N	N	N	N	N
4 ***Camp***	N	Y	?	Y	Y	Y	N
5 Barcia	N	N	N	Y	N	N	N
6 ***Upton***	N	N	N	Y	N	N	N
7 ***Smith***	Y	Y	Y	Y	Y	Y	N
8 Stabenow	N	N	N	N	N	N	N
9 Kildee	N	N	N	N	N	N	N
10 Bonior	N	N	N	N	N	N	N
11 ***Knollenberg***	Y	Y	Y	Y	Y	Y	Y
12 Levin	N	N	N	N	N	N	N
13 Rivers	N	N	N	N	N	N	N
14 Conyers	N	N	N	N	N	N	N
15 Kilpatrick	N	N	N	N	N	N	N
16 Dingell	N	N	N	N	N	N	N

	160	161	162	163	164	165	166
MINNESOTA							
1 ***Gutknecht***	Y	Y	Y	Y	Y	Y	N
2 Minge	N	N	N	Y	N	N	N
3 ***Ramstad***	N	N	N	Y	N	N	N
4 Vento	N	N	N	N	N	N	N
5 Sabo	N	N	N	Y	N	N	N
6 Luther	N	N	N	Y	N	N	N
7 Peterson	N	N	N	Y	N	N	N
8 Oberstar	N	N	N	N	N	N	N
MISSISSIPPI							
1 ***Wicker***	Y	Y	Y	Y	Y	Y	Y
2 Thompson	N	N	N	N	N	N	?
3 ***Pickering***	Y	N	N	Y	Y	Y	N
4 Shows	N	N	N	Y	Y	Y	N
5 Taylor	N	N	N	Y	N	Y	N
MISSOURI							
1 Clay	N	N	N	N	N	N	N
2 ***Talent***	Y	Y	N	Y	Y	Y	N
3 Gephardt	N	N	N	N	N	N	N
4 Skelton	N	N	N	Y	N	N	?
5 McCarthy	N	N	N	N	N	N	N
6 Danner	N	N	N	Y	N	Y	N
7 ***Blunt***	Y	Y	Y	Y	Y	Y	Y
8 ***Emerson***	Y	Y	Y	Y	Y	Y	Y
9 ***Hulshof***	Y	Y	Y	Y	Y	Y	Y
MONTANA							
AL ***Hill***	Y	Y	Y	Y	Y	Y	Y
NEBRASKA							
1 ***Bereuter***	Y	N	N	Y	N	N	N
2 ***Terry***	Y	Y	Y	Y	Y	Y	Y
3 ***Barrett***	Y	N	Y	Y	Y	Y	Y
NEVADA							
1 Berkley	N	N	N	N	N	N	N
2 ***Gibbons***	Y	Y	Y	Y	Y	Y	Y
NEW HAMPSHIRE							
1 ***Sununu***	Y	Y	N	Y	Y	Y	Y
2 ***Bass***	N	N	N	N	N	N	N
NEW JERSEY							
1 Andrews	N	N	N	N	N	N	N
2 ***LoBiondo***	N	N	N	Y	N	N	N
3 ***Saxton***	N	N	N	Y	N	N	N
4 ***Smith***	N	N	N	Y	N	N	N
5 ***Roukema***	N	N	N	Y	N	N	N
6 Pallone	N	N	N	N	N	N	N
7 ***Franks***	?	?	?	?	?	?	N
8 Pascrell	N	N	N	N	N	N	N
9 Rothman	N	N	N	N	N	N	N
10 Payne	N	N	N	N	N	N	N
11 ***Frelinghuysen***	N	N	N	N	N	N	N
12 Holt	N	N	N	N	N	N	N
13 Menendez	N	N	N	N	N	N	N
NEW MEXICO							
1 ***Wilson***	N	Y	N	Y	Y	Y	N
2 ***Skeen***	Y	Y	N	Y	Y	Y	N
3 Udall	N	N	N	N	N	N	N
NEW YORK							
1 Forbes	N	N	N	N	N	N	N
2 ***Lazio***	N	N	N	N	N	N	N
3 ***King***	N	N	N	Y	N	Y	Y
4 McCarthy	N	N	N	N	N	N	N
5 Ackerman	N	N	N	N	N	N	N
6 Meeks	N	N	N	N	N	N	N
7 Crowley	N	N	N	N	N	N	N
8 Nadler	N	N	N	N	N	N	N
9 Weiner	N	N	N	N	N	N	N
10 Towns	N	N	N	N	N	N	N
11 Owens	N	N	N	N	N	N	N
12 Velázquez	N	N	N	N	N	N	N
13 ***Fossella***	N	Y	Y	Y	Y	Y	Y
14 Maloney	N	N	N	N	N	N	N
15 Rangel	N	N	N	N	N	N	N
16 Serrano	N	N	N	N	N	N	N
17 Engel	N	N	N	N	N	N	N
18 Lowey	N	N	N	N	N	N	N
19 ***Kelly***	N	N	N	N	N	N	N
20 ***Gilman***	N	N	N	N	N	N	N
21 McNulty	N	N	N	N	N	N	N
22 ***Sweeney***	N	Y	Y	Y	Y	Y	Y
23 ***Boehlert***	N	N	N	N	N	N	N
24 ***McHugh***	N	Y	Y	Y	Y	Y	N
25 ***Walsh***	N	N	N	N	N	N	N
26 Hinchey	N	N	N	N	N	N	N
27 ***Reynolds***	N	N	Y	Y	Y	Y	Y
28 Slaughter	N	N	N	N	N	N	N
29 LaFalce	N	N	N	N	N	N	N

	160	161	162	163	164	165	166
30 ***Quinn***	N	N	N	N	N	N	N
31 ***Houghton***	N	N	N	N	N	N	N
NORTH CAROLINA							
1 Clayton	N	N	N	N	N	N	N
2 Etheridge	N	N	N	N	N	N	N
3 ***Jones***	N	N	N	Y	Y	Y	N
4 Price	N	N	N	N	N	N	N
5 ***Burr***	N	N	N	Y	N	N	N
6 ***Coble***	?	?	?	?	?	?	?
7 McIntyre	N	N	N	Y	N	N	N
8 ***Hayes***	N	N	N	Y	N	Y	N
9 ***Myrick***	N	Y	N	Y	Y	Y	Y
10 ***Ballenger***	N	Y	N	Y	Y	Y	Y
11 ***Taylor***	Y	Y	Y	Y	Y	Y	N
12 Watt	N	N	N	N	N	N	N
NORTH DAKOTA							
AL Pomeroy	N	Y	N	Y	N	Y	N
OHIO							
1 ***Chabot***	Y	Y	Y	Y	Y	Y	Y
2 ***Portman***	Y	N	N	Y	Y	N	N
3 Hall	N	N	N	N	N	?	N
4 ***Oxley***	Y	Y	Y	Y	Y	Y	Y
5 ***Gillmor***	Y	N	N	Y	N	Y	N
6 Strickland	N	N	N	N	N	N	N
7 ***Hobson***	Y	Y	Y	Y	Y	Y	Y
8 ***Boehner***	Y	Y	Y	Y	Y	Y	Y
9 Kaptur	N	N	N	N	N	N	N
10 Kucinich	N	N	N	N	N	N	N
11 Jones	N	N	N	N	N	N	N
12 ***Kasich***	Y	Y	N	Y	N	Y	?
13 Brown	N	N	N	N	N	N	N
14 Sawyer	N	N	N	N	N	N	N
15 ***Pryce***	Y	N	Y	Y	Y	Y	Y
16 ***Regula***	Y	Y	Y	Y	Y	Y	Y
17 Traficant	N	N	N	Y	Y	N	N
18 ***Ney***	Y	Y	Y	Y	Y	Y	Y
19 ***LaTourette***	Y	N	N	Y	N	N	N
OKLAHOMA							
1 ***Largent***	Y	Y	Y	Y	Y	Y	Y
2 ***Coburn***	Y	Y	Y	Y	Y	Y	Y
3 ***Watkins***	Y	Y	Y	Y	Y	Y	Y
4 ***Watts***	N	Y	Y	Y	Y	Y	Y
5 ***Istook***	Y	Y	?	?	?	?	Y
6 ***Lucas***	?	?	?	?	?	?	?
OREGON							
1 Wu	N	N	N	N	N	N	N
2 ***Walden***	N	Y	Y	Y	Y	Y	Y
3 Blumenauer	N	N	N	N	N	N	N
4 DeFazio	N	N	N	N	N	N	N
5 Hooley	N	N	N	N	N	N	N
PENNSYLVANIA							
1 Brady	N	N	N	N	N	N	N
2 Fattah	N	N	N	N	N	N	N
3 Borski	N	N	N	N	N	N	N
4 Klink	N	N	N	Y	N	N	N
5 ***Peterson***	Y	Y	N	Y	Y	Y	Y
6 Holden	N	N	N	Y	N	Y	N
7 ***Weldon***	N	N	N	Y	N	N	?
8 ***Greenwood***	N	N	N	N	N	N	N
9 ***Shuster***	N	N	N	N	N	N	Y
10 ***Sherwood***	Y	N	Y	Y	Y	Y	?
11 Kanjorski	N	N	N	N	N	N	N
12 Murtha	Y	N	N	N	N	Y	N
13 Hoeffel	N	N	N	N	N	N	N
14 Coyne	N	N	N	N	N	N	N
15 ***Toomey***	Y	Y	Y	Y	Y	Y	Y
16 ***Pitts***	Y	Y	Y	Y	Y	Y	Y
17 ***Gekas***	Y	Y	N	Y	N	Y	Y
18 Doyle	Y	N	N	N	N	N	N
19 ***Goodling***	N	Y	Y	Y	Y	Y	Y
20 Mascara	N	N	N	N	N	N	N
21 ***English***	N	N	N	N	N	N	N
RHODE ISLAND							
1 Kennedy	N	N	N	N	N	N	N
2 Weygand	N	N	N	N	N	N	N
SOUTH CAROLINA							
1 ***Sanford***	N	N	N	Y	Y	Y	Y
2 ***Spence***	N	Y	Y	Y	Y	Y	?
3 ***Graham***	N	Y	Y	Y	Y	Y	Y
4 ***DeMint***	Y	Y	Y	Y	Y	Y	Y
5 Spratt	N	N	N	Y	N	N	N
6 Clyburn	N	N	N	N	N	N	N
SOUTH DAKOTA							
AL ***Thune***	N	Y	Y	Y	Y	Y	N

	160	161	162	163	164	165	166
TENNESSEE							
1 ***Jenkins***	Y	Y	N	Y	Y	Y	N
2 ***Duncan***	Y	Y	N	Y	Y	Y	Y
3 ***Wamp***	Y	Y	Y	Y	Y	Y	N
4 ***Hilleary***	Y	Y	Y	Y	Y	Y	Y
5 Clement	N	N	N	N	N	N	N
6 Gordon	N	N	N	Y	N	N	Y
7 ***Bryant***	Y	Y	N	Y	Y	Y	N
8 Tanner	N	N	N	Y	N	N	N
9 Ford	N	N	N	N	N	N	N
TEXAS							
1 Sandlin	N	N	N	Y	N	Y	N
2 Turner	N	N	N	N	N	N	N
3 ***Johnson, Sam***	Y	Y	Y	Y	Y	Y	Y
4 Hall	Y	Y	N	Y	Y	Y	N
5 ***Sessions***	Y	Y	Y	Y	Y	Y	Y
6 ***Barton***	Y	Y	Y	Y	Y	Y	Y
7 ***Archer***	Y	Y	Y	Y	Y	Y	Y
8 ***Brady***	Y	Y	Y	Y	Y	Y	Y
9 Lampson	N	N	N	N	N	N	N
10 Doggett	N	N	N	Y	N	N	N
11 Edwards	N	N	N	Y	N	Y	N
12 ***Granger***	Y	Y	Y	Y	Y	Y	Y
13 ***Thornberry***	Y	Y	Y	Y	Y	Y	Y
14 ***Paul***	Y	Y	Y	Y	Y	Y	Y
15 Hinojosa	Y	N	N	N	N	N	N
16 Reyes	N	N	N	N	N	N	N
17 Stenholm	Y	Y	Y	Y	Y	Y	Y
18 Jackson-Lee	N	N	N	N	N	N	N
19 ***Combest***	Y	Y	Y	Y	Y	Y	Y
20 Gonzalez	N	N	N	N	N	N	N
21 ***Smith***	Y	Y	Y	Y	Y	Y	Y
22 ***DeLay***	Y	Y	Y	Y	Y	Y	Y
23 ***Bonilla***	Y	Y	Y	Y	Y	Y	Y
24 Frost	N	N	N	N	N	N	N
25 Bentsen	N	N	N	N	N	N	N
26 ***Armey***	Y	Y	Y	Y	Y	Y	Y
27 Ortiz	Y	N	N	N	N	N	N
28 Rodriguez	N	N	N	N	N	N	N
29 Green	Y	N	N	Y	N	Y	N
30 Johnson, E.B.	N	N	N	N	N	N	N
UTAH							
1 ***Hansen***	N	Y	N	N	Y	Y	N
2 ***Cook***	Y	Y	Y	Y	Y	Y	Y
3 ***Cannon***	N	Y	Y	Y	Y	Y	Y
VERMONT							
AL *Sanders*	N	N	N	N	N	N	N
VIRGINIA							
1 ***Bateman***	?	?	?	?	?	?	N
2 Pickett	N	N	N	N	N	N	N
3 Scott	N	N	N	N	N	N	N
4 Sisisky	N	N	N	Y	N	Y	N
5 *Goode*	N	Y	N	Y	Y	Y	Y
6 ***Goodlatte***	Y	Y	Y	Y	Y	Y	Y
7 ***Bliley***	N	Y	Y	Y	Y	Y	Y
8 Moran	N	N	N	N	N	N	N
9 Boucher	N	N	N	N	N	N	N
10 ***Wolf***	N	N	N	Y	Y	N	N
11 ***Davis***	N	N	N	Y	N	N	N
WASHINGTON							
1 Inslee	N	N	N	N	N	N	N
2 ***Metcalf***	N	Y	Y	Y	Y	Y	N
3 Baird	N	N	N	N	N	N	N
4 ***Hastings***	Y	Y	Y	Y	Y	Y	Y
5 ***Nethercutt***	N	Y	Y	Y	Y	Y	Y
6 Dicks	N	N	N	N	N	N	N
7 McDermott	N	N	N	N	N	N	N
8 ***Dunn***	N	Y	N	Y	Y	Y	N
9 Smith	N	N	N	N	N	N	N
WEST VIRGINIA							
1 Mollohan	Y	N	N	N	N	N	N
2 Wise	?	?	?	?	?	?	?
3 Rahall	N	N	N	N	N	N	N
WISCONSIN							
1 ***Ryan***	Y	Y	N	Y	Y	Y	Y
2 Baldwin	N	N	N	N	N	N	N
3 Kind	N	N	N	N	N	N	N
4 Kleczka	N	N	N	N	N	N	N
5 Barrett	N	N	N	N	N	N	N
6 ***Petri***	N	Y	Y	Y	Y	Y	Y
7 Obey	Y	Y	N	Y	N	N	N
8 ***Green***	N	Y	N	Y	Y	Y	N
9 ***Sensenbrenner***	N	Y	Y	Y	Y	Y	Y
WYOMING							
AL ***Cubin***	Y	Y	Y	Y	Y	Y	Y

Southern states - Ala., Ark., Fla., Ga., Ky., La., Miss., N.C., Okla., S.C., Tenn., Texas, Va.

167. HR 701. Land Conservation/Annual Appropriations. Chambliss, R-Ga., amendment that would make the bill's funding subject to annual appropriations until 2006. Afterward, the funds would be available without appropriations. Rejected 142-281: R 124-91; D 17-189 (ND 11-142, SD 6-47); I 1-1. May 11, 2000.

168. HR 701. Land Conservation/Contra Costa County. Chenoweth-Hage, R-Idaho, amendment that would prevent Contra Costa County in California from receiving coastal impact assistance because it does not lie within 200 miles of a leased oil drilling tract. Rejected 166-259: R 162-54; D 3-204 (ND 1-153, SD 2-51); I 1-1. May 11, 2000.

169. HR 701. Land Conservation/Parks Maintenance. Hastings, R-Wash., amendment that would dedicate at least half of the Land and Water Conservation Fund to maintain and manage lands already under federal ownership. Rejected 169-256: R 159-56; D 9-199 (ND 4-150, SD 5-49); I 1-1. May 11, 2000.

170. HR 701. Land Conservation/Local Control. Sweeney, R-N.Y., amendment that would allow local governments to veto proposed land acquisition projects under the Land and Water Conservation Fund within 90 days of notification. Rejected 187-238: R 171-45; D 15-192 (ND 10-143, SD 5-49); I 1-1. May 11, 2000.

171. HR 701. Land Conservation/Federal Ownership Limitations. Simpson, R-Idaho, amendment that would prohibit the use of funds in the bill to acquire more federal land in a state where 50 percent or more of the land is already owned by the federal government. Rejected 157-266: R 148-69; D 8-196 (ND 4-147, SD 4-49); I 1-1. May 11, 2000.

172. HR 701. Land Conservation/Property Condemnation. Calvert, R-Calif., amendment that would prohibit any level of government from using the bill's coastal impact assistance or conservation funds to condemn property. Rejected 158-261: R 144-68; D 13-192 (ND 7-144, SD 6-48); I 1-1. May 11, 2000.

173. HR 701. Land Conservation/Outreach Organizations. Chenoweth-Hage, R-Idaho, amendment that would prohibit "Pittman-Robertston" wildlife program funds from being given to organizations that engage in public outreach, species re-introduction or other activities not currently covered by the law. Rejected 107-317: R 102-113; D 4-203 (ND 3-150, SD 1-53); I 1-1. May 11, 2000.

Key

Y Voted for (yea).
\# Paired for.
\+ Announced for.
N Voted against (nay).
X Paired against.
– Announced against.
P Voted "present."
C Voted "present" to avoid possible conflict of interest.
? Did not vote or otherwise make a position known.

•

Democrats ***Republicans***
Independents

	167	168	169	170	171	172	173
ALABAMA							
1 ***Callahan***	N	N	N	Y	Y	N	N
2 ***Everett***	N	Y	Y	Y	Y	Y	Y
3 ***Riley***	N	Y	N	Y	Y	Y	Y
4 ***Aderholt***	N	Y	Y	Y	Y	Y	Y
5 Cramer	N	N	N	N	N	N	N
6 ***Bachus***	N	N	N	Y	N	N	N
7 Hilliard	N	N	N	N	N	N	N
ALASKA							
AL ***Young***	N	N	N	N	N	N	N
ARIZONA							
1 ***Salmon***	Y	Y	Y	Y	Y	Y	Y
2 Pastor	N	N	N	N	N	N	N
3 ***Stump***	Y	Y	Y	Y	Y	Y	Y
4 ***Shadegg***	Y	Y	Y	Y	Y	Y	Y
5 ***Kolbe***	Y	Y	Y	Y	N	Y	Y
6 ***Hayworth***	Y	Y	Y	Y	Y	Y	Y
ARKANSAS							
1 Berry	Y	N	Y	Y	Y	Y	N
2 Snyder	N	N	N	N	N	N	N
3 ***Hutchinson***	Y	Y	Y	Y	Y	N	N
4 ***Dickey***	Y	Y	?	Y	Y	Y	N
CALIFORNIA							
1 Thompson	N	N	N	N	N	N	N
2 ***Herger***	Y	Y	Y	Y	Y	Y	Y
3 ***Ose***	Y	Y	Y	Y	Y	Y	N
4 ***Doolittle***	Y	Y	Y	Y	Y	Y	Y
5 Matsui	N	N	N	N	N	N	N
6 Woolsey	N	N	N	N	N	N	N
7 Miller, George	N	N	N	N	N	N	N
8 Pelosi	N	N	N	N	N	N	N
9 Lee	N	N	N	N	N	N	N
10 Tauscher	N	N	N	N	N	N	N
11 ***Pombo***	Y	Y	Y	Y	Y	Y	Y
12 Lantos	N	N	N	N	N	N	N
13 Stark	N	N	N	N	N	N	N
14 Eshoo	N	N	N	N	N	N	N
15 ***Campbell***	?	?	?	?	?	?	?
16 Lofgren	?	?	?	?	?	?	?
17 Farr	N	N	N	N	N	N	N
18 Condit	N	N	N	N	N	Y	N
19 ***Radanovich***	Y	Y	Y	Y	Y	Y	Y
20 Dooley	N	N	N	N	N	N	N
21 ***Thomas***	N	Y	Y	Y	Y	Y	Y
22 Capps	N	N	N	N	N	N	N
23 ***Gallegly***	N	N	N	Y	Y	Y	N
24 Sherman	N	N	N	N	N	N	N
25 ***McKeon***	Y	Y	Y	Y	Y	Y	Y
26 Berman	N	N	N	N	N	N	N
27 ***Rogan***	N	N	N	Y	Y	N	N
28 ***Dreier***	N	Y	Y	Y	Y	Y	N
29 Waxman	N	N	N	N	N	N	N
30 Becerra	N	N	N	N	N	N	N
31 Martinez	N	N	N	Y	Y	Y	N
32 Dixon	Y	N	N	N	N	N	N
33 Roybal-Allard	Y	N	N	N	N	N	N
34 Napolitano	N	N	N	N	N	N	N
35 Waters	N	N	N	N	N	N	N
36 ***Kuykendall***	N	N	N	N	N	N	N
37 Millender-McD.	N	N	N	N	?	N	N
38 ***Horn***	N	N	N	N	N	Y	N
39 ***Royce***	Y	Y	Y	Y	Y	Y	Y
40 ***Lewis***	Y	Y	Y	Y	Y	Y	Y
41 ***Miller, Gary***	Y	Y	Y	Y	Y	Y	Y
42 Baca	N	N	N	Y	N	Y	N
43 ***Calvert***	Y	Y	Y	Y	Y	Y	Y
44 ***Bono***	N	N	N	N	N	Y	Y
45 ***Rohrabacher***	Y	Y	Y	Y	Y	Y	Y
46 Sanchez	N	N	N	N	N	N	N
47 ***Cox***	Y	Y	Y	Y	Y	Y	N
48 ***Packard***	Y	Y	Y	Y	Y	Y	N
49 ***Bilbray***	N	N	N	N	N	N	N
50 Filner	N	N	N	N	N	N	N
51 ***Cunningham***	Y	Y	Y	Y	Y	Y	N
52 ***Hunter***	?	Y	Y	Y	Y	Y	Y
COLORADO							
1 DeGette	?	?	?	?	?	?	?
2 Udall	N	N	N	N	N	N	N
3 ***McInnis***	N	Y	Y	Y	N	Y	N
4 ***Schaffer***	Y	Y	Y	Y	Y	Y	Y
5 ***Hefley***	Y	Y	Y	Y	Y	Y	N
6 ***Tancredo***	Y	Y	Y	Y	N	Y	N
CONNECTICUT							
1 Larson	N	N	N	N	N	N	N
2 Gejdenson	N	N	N	N	N	N	N
3 DeLauro	N	N	N	N	N	N	N
4 ***Shays***	N	N	N	N	N	N	N
5 Maloney	N	N	N	N	N	N	N
6 ***Johnson***	N	Y	N	N	N	N	N
DELAWARE							
AL ***Castle***	N	N	N	N	N	N	N
FLORIDA							
1 ***Scarborough***	Y	Y	Y	Y	Y	N	N
2 Boyd	N	N	N	N	N	N	N
3 Brown	N	N	N	N	N	N	N
4 ***Fowler***	N	Y	Y	Y	N	N	Y
5 Thurman	N	N	N	N	N	N	N
6 ***Stearns***	Y	Y	Y	Y	Y	Y	Y
7 ***Mica***	N	N	Y	Y	N	Y	N
8 ***McCollum***	N	Y	Y	Y	N	N	N
9 ***Bilirakis***	N	Y	Y	Y	N	N	N
10 ***Young***	Y	Y	Y	Y	Y	Y	Y
11 Davis	N	N	N	N	N	N	N
12 ***Canady***	N	Y	N	Y	Y	N	N
13 ***Miller***	Y	Y	Y	Y	Y	N	N
14 ***Goss***	Y	Y	Y	Y	N	N	N
15 ***Weldon***	Y	Y	Y	Y	Y	Y	Y
16 ***Foley***	N	N	Y	Y	N	N	N
17 Meek	N	N	N	N	N	N	N
18 ***Ros-Lehtinen***	N	N	N	N	N	Y	N
19 Wexler	N	N	N	N	N	N	N
20 Deutsch	N	N	N	N	N	N	N
21 ***Diaz-Balart***	N	Y	Y	N	N	Y	N
22 ***Shaw***	N	N	Y	Y	N	N	N
23 Hastings	N	N	N	N	N	N	N
GEORGIA							
1 ***Kingston***	Y	Y	Y	Y	Y	Y	Y
2 Bishop	N	N	N	N	N	N	N
3 ***Collins***	Y	Y	Y	Y	Y	Y	N
4 McKinney	N	N	N	N	N	N	N
5 Lewis	N	N	N	N	N	N	N
6 ***Isakson***	Y	Y	N	N	N	N	N
7 ***Barr***	Y	Y	Y	Y	Y	Y	Y
8 ***Chambliss***	Y	Y	Y	Y	N	Y	N
9 ***Deal***	Y	Y	Y	Y	Y	N	N
10 ***Norwood***	Y	Y	Y	Y	Y	Y	Y
11 ***Linder***	Y	Y	Y	Y	Y	Y	N
HAWAII							
1 Abercrombie	N	N	N	N	N	N	N
2 Mink	N	N	N	N	N	N	N
IDAHO							
1 ***Chenoweth-Hage***	Y	Y	Y	Y	Y	Y	+
2 ***Simpson***	Y	Y	Y	Y	Y	Y	Y
ILLINOIS							
1 Rush	N	N	N	N	N	N	N
2 Jackson	Y	N	N	N	N	N	N
3 Lipinski	N	N	N	N	N	N	N
4 Gutierrez	N	N	N	N	N	N	N
5 Blagojevich	N	N	N	N	N	N	N
6 ***Hyde***	N	Y	N	Y	Y	N	Y
7 Davis	N	N	N	N	N	N	N
8 ***Crane***	N	N	Y	Y	Y	N	N
9 Schakowsky	N	N	N	N	N	N	N
10 ***Porter***	N	N	N	N	N	N	N
11 ***Weller***	N	Y	?	N	N	?	N
12 Costello	N	N	N	N	N	N	N
13 ***Biggert***	N	N	N	N	N	N	N

ND Northern Democrats SD Southern Democrats

	167	168	169	170	171	172	173
14 ***Hastert***							
15 ***Ewing***	Y	Y	Y	Y	Y	Y	N
16 ***Manzullo***	Y	Y	Y	Y	Y	Y	Y
17 Evans	N	N	N	N	N	?	N
18 ***LaHood***	Y	Y	Y	Y	Y	Y	N
19 Phelps	N	N	N	N	N	N	N
20 ***Shimkus***	N	N	Y	Y	Y	Y	Y
INDIANA							
1 Visclosky	N	N	N	N	N	N	N
2 ***McIntosh***	N	Y	N	Y	N	?	?
3 Roemer	N	N	N	N	N	N	N
4 ***Souder***	N	N	N	N	N	N	N
5 ***Buyer***	?	Y	Y	Y	Y	Y	Y
6 ***Burton***	Y	Y	Y	Y	Y	Y	Y
7 ***Pease***	N	Y	N	N	N	N	N
8 ***Hostettler***	Y	Y	Y	Y	Y	Y	Y
9 Hill	N	N	N	N	N	N	N
10 Carson	N	N	N	N	N	N	N
IOWA							
1 ***Leach***	N	N	N	N	N	N	N
2 ***Nussle***	Y	Y	Y	Y	Y	Y	Y
3 Boswell	N	N	N	Y	N	N	N
4 ***Ganske***	N	Y	Y	Y	Y	N	N
5 ***Latham***	Y	Y	Y	Y	Y	Y	Y
KANSAS							
1 ***Moran***	Y	Y	Y	Y	Y	Y	N
2 ***Ryun***	Y	Y	Y	Y	Y	Y	Y
3 Moore	N	N	N	N	N	N	N
4 ***Tiahrt***	Y	Y	Y	Y	Y	Y	Y
KENTUCKY							
1 ***Whitfield***	N	Y	Y	Y	Y	N	N
2 ***Lewis***	N	Y	Y	Y	Y	Y	N
3 ***Northup***	Y	Y	Y	Y	Y	N	N
4 Lucas	N	N	N	N	N	N	N
5 ***Rogers***	Y	Y	Y	Y	Y	Y	N
6 ***Fletcher***	N	Y	Y	Y	Y	N	N
LOUISIANA							
1 ***Vitter***	N	N	N	N	N	N	N
2 Jefferson	?	?	Y	N	N	N	N
3 ***Tauzin***	N	N	N	N	N	N	N
4 ***McCrery***	N	N	N	N	N	N	N
5 ***Cooksey***	N	Y	N	N	N	N	N
6 ***Baker***	N	N	N	N	Y	N	Y
7 John	N	N	N	N	N	N	N
MAINE							
1 Allen	N	N	N	N	N	N	N
2 Baldacci	N	N	N	N	N	N	N
MARYLAND							
1 ***Gilchrest***	N	N	N	N	N	N	N
2 ***Ehrlich***	N	N	Y	Y	N	Y	N
3 Cardin	N	N	N	N	N	N	N
4 Wynn	N	N	N	N	N	N	N
5 Hoyer	Y	N	N	N	N	N	N
6 ***Bartlett***	Y	Y	Y	Y	Y	Y	Y
7 Cummings	?	N	N	N	N	N	N
8 ***Morella***	N	N	N	N	N	N	N
MASSACHUSETTS							
1 Olver	N	N	N	N	N	N	N
2 Neal	N	N	N	N	N	N	N
3 McGovern	N	N	N	N	N	N	N
4 Frank	N	N	N	N	?	N	N
5 Meehan	N	N	N	N	N	N	N
6 Tierney	N	N	N	N	N	N	N
7 Markey	N	N	N	N	N	N	N
8 Capuano	N	N	N	N	N	N	N
9 Moakley	N	N	N	N	N	N	N
10 Delahunt	N	N	N	N	N	N	N
MICHIGAN							
1 Stupak	N	N	Y	Y	Y	N	N
2 ***Hoekstra***	Y	Y	Y	Y	Y	Y	Y
3 ***Ehlers***	N	N	N	N	N	N	N
4 ***Camp***	N	Y	Y	Y	Y	Y	N
5 Barcia	N	N	Y	Y	N	Y	N
6 ***Upton***	N	N	N	N	N	N	N
7 ***Smith***	Y	Y	Y	Y	Y	Y	Y
8 Stabenow	N	N	N	N	N	N	N
9 Kildee	N	N	N	N	N	N	N
10 Bonior	N	N	N	N	N	N	N
11 ***Knollenberg***	Y	Y	Y	Y	Y	Y	Y
12 Levin	N	N	N	N	N	N	N
13 Rivers	N	N	N	N	N	N	N
14 Conyers	N	N	N	N	N	N	N
15 Kilpatrick	N	N	N	N	N	N	N
16 Dingell	N	N	N	N	N	N	N

	167	168	169	170	171	172	173
MINNESOTA							
1 ***Gutknecht***	N	Y	N	Y	Y	Y	Y
2 Minge	Y	N	N	N	N	N	N
3 ***Ramstad***	N	Y	N	N	N	N	N
4 Vento	N	N	N	N	N	N	N
5 Sabo	Y	N	N	N	N	N	N
6 Luther	Y	N	N	N	N	N	N
7 Peterson	N	N	N	N	N	Y	N
8 Oberstar	N	N	N	N	N	N	N
MISSISSIPPI							
1 ***Wicker***	Y	Y	Y	Y	Y	?	Y
2 Thompson	N	N	N	N	N	N	N
3 ***Pickering***	Y	Y	Y	Y	Y	Y	Y
4 Shows	Y	N	Y	Y	Y	Y	N
5 Taylor	N	N	N	N	N	N	N
MISSOURI							
1 Clay	N	N	N	N	N	N	N
2 ***Talent***	Y	Y	Y	Y	Y	Y	Y
3 Gephardt	N	N	N	N	N	N	N
4 Skelton	N	N	Y	N	N	N	Y
5 McCarthy	N	N	N	N	N	–	–
6 Danner	N	N	Y	Y	Y	Y	Y
7 ***Blunt***	Y	Y	Y	Y	Y	Y	Y
8 ***Emerson***	Y	Y	Y	Y	Y	Y	Y
9 ***Hulshof***	Y	Y	Y	Y	Y	Y	Y
MONTANA							
AL ***Hill***	Y	N	Y	Y	Y	Y	Y
NEBRASKA							
1 ***Bereuter***	N	Y	Y	N	N	N	N
2 ***Terry***	N	Y	Y	Y	Y	Y	Y
3 ***Barrett***	Y	Y	Y	Y	Y	Y	Y
NEVADA							
1 Berkley	N	N	N	N	N	N	N
2 ***Gibbons***	Y	Y	Y	Y	Y	Y	Y
NEW HAMPSHIRE							
1 ***Sununu***	Y	Y	Y	Y	Y	Y	Y
2 ***Bass***	N	N	N	N	N	N	N
NEW JERSEY							
1 Andrews	N	N	N	N	N	N	N
2 ***LoBiondo***	N	N	N	N	N	N	N
3 ***Saxton***	N	N	N	N	N	N	N
4 ***Smith***	N	N	N	N	N	N	N
5 ***Roukema***	N	N	Y	N	N	Y	N
6 Pallone	N	N	N	N	N	N	N
7 ***Franks***	N	N	N	N	N	N	N
8 Pascrell	N	N	N	N	N	N	N
9 Rothman	N	N	N	N	N	N	N
10 Payne	N	N	N	N	N	N	N
11 ***Frelinghuysen***	N	N	N	N	N	N	N
12 Holt	N	N	N	N	N	N	N
13 Menendez	N	N	N	N	N	N	N
NEW MEXICO							
1 ***Wilson***	N	Y	N	Y	Y	Y	N
2 ***Skeen***	Y	Y	Y	Y	Y	Y	Y
3 Udall	N	N	N	N	N	N	N
NEW YORK							
1 Forbes	N	N	N	N	N	N	N
2 ***Lazio***	N	N	N	N	N	N	N
3 ***King***	N	N	N	Y	N	N	N
4 McCarthy	N	N	N	N	N	N	N
5 Ackerman	N	N	N	N	N	N	N
6 Meeks	N	N	N	Y	N	N	N
7 Crowley	N	N	N	N	N	Y	N
8 Nadler	N	N	N	N	N	N	N
9 Weiner	N	N	N	N	N	N	N
10 Towns	N	N	N	N	N	N	N
11 Owens	N	N	N	N	N	N	N
12 Velázquez	N	N	N	N	N	N	N
13 ***Fossella***	N	Y	Y	Y	N	Y	N
14 Maloney	N	N	N	N	N	N	N
15 Rangel	N	N	N	?	N	N	N
16 Serrano	N	N	N	N	N	N	N
17 Engel	N	N	N	Y	N	N	N
18 Lowey	N	N	N	N	N	N	N
19 ***Kelly***	N	N	Y	N	N	N	N
20 ***Gilman***	N	N	N	N	N	N	N
21 McNulty	N	N	N	N	N	N	N
22 ***Sweeney***	N	Y	Y	Y	Y	Y	Y
23 ***Boehlert***	N	N	N	N	N	N	N
24 ***McHugh***	N	Y	Y	Y	Y	Y	Y
25 ***Walsh***	N	N	N	N	N	N	N
26 Hinchey	N	N	N	N	?	N	N
27 ***Reynolds***	N	Y	Y	Y	Y	Y	Y
28 Slaughter	N	N	N	N	N	N	N
29 LaFalce	N	N	N	N	N	N	N

	167	168	169	170	171	172	173
30 ***Quinn***	N	N	N	Y	N	N	N
31 ***Houghton***	N	N	N	Y	N	N	N
NORTH CAROLINA							
1 Clayton	N	N	N	N	N	N	N
2 Etheridge	N	N	N	N	N	N	N
3 ***Jones***	Y	Y	Y	Y	Y	Y	N
4 Price	N	N	N	N	N	N	N
5 ***Burr***	N	N	N	Y	Y	N	N
6 ***Coble***	?	?	?	?	?	?	?
7 McIntyre	N	N	N	N	N	N	N
8 ***Hayes***	N	N	N	N	N	N	N
9 ***Myrick***	Y	Y	Y	Y	Y	Y	N
10 ***Ballenger***	Y	Y	Y	Y	Y	Y	Y
11 ***Taylor***	Y	Y	Y	Y	Y	Y	Y
12 Watt	N	N	N	N	N	N	N
NORTH DAKOTA							
AL Pomeroy	N	N	N	Y	N	N	N
OHIO							
1 ***Chabot***	Y	Y	Y	Y	Y	Y	Y
2 ***Portman***	Y	Y	N	Y	N	N	N
3 Hall	N	N	N	N	N	N	N
4 ***Oxley***	Y	Y	Y	Y	Y	Y	N
5 ***Gillmor***	N	Y	N	Y	N	Y	N
6 Strickland	N	N	N	N	N	N	N
7 ***Hobson***	Y	Y	Y	Y	Y	Y	N
8 ***Boehner***	Y	Y	Y	Y	Y	Y	Y
9 Kaptur	N	N	N	N	N	N	N
10 Kucinich	N	N	N	N	N	N	N
11 Jones	N	N	N	N	N	N	N
12 ***Kasich***	Y	Y	Y	Y	Y	Y	N
13 Brown	N	N	N	N	N	N	N
14 Sawyer	N	N	N	N	N	N	N
15 ***Pryce***	Y	Y	Y	Y	Y	Y	N
16 ***Regula***	Y	Y	Y	Y	Y	Y	N
17 Traficant	N	N	N	Y	Y	N	Y
18 ***Ney***	Y	Y	Y	Y	Y	Y	N
19 ***LaTourette***	Y	N	Y	Y	N	N	N
OKLAHOMA							
1 ***Largent***	Y	Y	Y	Y	Y	Y	Y
2 ***Coburn***	Y	Y	Y	Y	Y	Y	Y
3 ***Watkins***	Y	Y	Y	Y	Y	Y	Y
4 ***Watts***	Y	Y	Y	Y	Y	+	Y
5 ***Istook***	Y	Y	Y	Y	Y	Y	Y
6 ***Lucas***	?	?	?	?	?	?	?
OREGON							
1 Wu	N	N	N	N	N	N	N
2 ***Walden***	Y	Y	Y	Y	Y	Y	Y
3 Blumenauer	N	N	N	N	N	N	N
4 DeFazio	N	N	N	N	N	N	N
5 Hooley	N	N	N	N	N	N	N
PENNSYLVANIA							
1 Brady	N	N	N	N	N	N	N
2 Fattah	N	N	N	N	N	N	N
3 Borski	N	N	N	N	N	N	N
4 Klink	N	N	N	N	N	N	N
5 ***Peterson***	Y	Y	Y	Y	Y	Y	Y
6 Holden	N	N	N	N	N	N	N
7 ***Weldon***	N	N	N	Y	N	N	N
8 ***Greenwood***	N	?	N	N	N	N	N
9 ***Shuster***	Y	Y	Y	Y	Y	Y	N
10 ***Sherwood***	?	?	?	?	?	?	?
11 Kanjorski	N	N	N	N	N	N	N
12 Murtha	Y	N	N	N	N	N	N
13 Hoeffel	N	N	N	N	N	N	N
14 Coyne	N	N	N	N	N	N	N
15 ***Toomey***	Y	Y	Y	Y	Y	Y	Y
16 ***Pitts***	Y	Y	Y	Y	Y	Y	N
17 ***Gekas***	Y	Y	N	?	Y	Y	N
18 Doyle	N	N	N	N	N	?	N
19 ***Goodling***	Y	Y	Y	Y	Y	Y	Y
20 Mascara	N	N	N	N	N	N	N
21 ***English***	N	Y	N	N	N	N	N
RHODE ISLAND							
1 Kennedy	N	N	N	N	N	N	N
2 Weygand	N	N	N	N	N	N	N
SOUTH CAROLINA							
1 ***Sanford***	Y	Y	Y	N	Y	Y	Y
2 ***Spence***	Y	Y	Y	Y	Y	Y	Y
3 ***Graham***	Y	Y	Y	Y	Y	Y	Y
4 ***DeMint***	Y	Y	Y	Y	Y	Y	Y
5 Spratt	N	N	N	N	N	N	N
6 Clyburn	N	N	N	N	N	N	N
SOUTH DAKOTA							
AL ***Thune***	N	N	Y	Y	N	N	N

	167	168	169	170	171	172	173
TENNESSEE							
1 ***Jenkins***	N	Y	Y	Y	Y	Y	N
2 ***Duncan***	Y	Y	Y	Y	Y	Y	Y
3 ***Wamp***	Y	Y	Y	Y	Y	Y	N
4 ***Hilleary***	Y	Y	Y	Y	Y	Y	Y
5 Clement	N	N	N	N	N	N	N
6 Gordon	N	N	N	N	N	N	N
7 ***Bryant***	N	Y	Y	Y	Y	Y	N
8 Tanner	N	N	N	N	N	Y	N
9 Ford	N	N	N	N	?	N	N
TEXAS							
1 Sandlin	N	N	N	Y	N	Y	N
2 Turner	N	N	N	N	N	N	N
3 ***Johnson, Sam***	Y	Y	Y	Y	Y	Y	Y
4 Hall	Y	Y	Y	Y	Y	Y	Y
5 ***Sessions***	Y	Y	Y	Y	Y	Y	Y
6 ***Barton***	Y	Y	Y	Y	Y	Y	Y
7 ***Archer***	Y	Y	Y	Y	Y	Y	Y
8 ***Brady***	Y	Y	Y	Y	Y	Y	Y
9 Lampson	N	N	N	N	N	N	N
10 Doggett	Y	N	N	N	N	N	N
11 Edwards	N	N	N	N	N	N	N
12 ***Granger***	Y	Y	Y	Y	Y	Y	Y
13 ***Thornberry***	Y	Y	Y	Y	Y	Y	Y
14 ***Paul***	Y	Y	Y	Y	Y	Y	Y
15 Hinojosa	N	N	N	N	N	N	N
16 Reyes	N	N	N	N	N	N	N
17 Stenholm	Y	N	Y	Y	Y	Y	N
18 Jackson-Lee	N	N	N	N	N	N	N
19 ***Combest***	Y	Y	Y	Y	Y	?	Y
20 Gonzalez	N	N	N	N	N	N	N
21 ***Smith***	Y	Y	Y	Y	Y	Y	Y
22 ***DeLay***	Y	Y	Y	Y	Y	Y	Y
23 ***Bonilla***	Y	Y	Y	Y	Y	Y	Y
24 Frost	N	N	N	N	N	N	N
25 Bentsen	N	N	N	N	N	N	N
26 ***Armey***	Y	Y	Y	Y	Y	Y	N
27 Ortiz	N	N	N	N	N	N	N
28 Rodriguez	N	N	N	N	N	N	N
29 Green	N	N	N	N	N	N	N
30 Johnson, E.B.	N	N	N	N	N	N	N
UTAH							
1 ***Hansen***	Y	Y	Y	Y	Y	Y	N
2 ***Cook***	Y	Y	Y	Y	Y	Y	Y
3 ***Cannon***	Y	Y	Y	Y	Y	Y	Y
VERMONT							
AL *Sanders*	N	N	N	N	N	N	N
VIRGINIA							
1 ***Bateman***	N	N	Y	N	N	N	N
2 Pickett	N	Y	N	N	N	N	N
3 Scott	N	N	N	N	N	N	N
4 Sisisky	N	N	N	N	N	N	N
5 *Goode*	Y	Y	Y	Y	Y	Y	Y
6 ***Goodlatte***	Y	Y	Y	Y	Y	Y	Y
7 ***Bliley***	Y	Y	Y	Y	Y	Y	Y
8 Moran	Y	N	N	N	N	N	N
9 Boucher	N	N	N	N	N	N	N
10 ***Wolf***	Y	N	Y	Y	Y	N	N
11 ***Davis***	N	N	Y	Y	Y	N	N
WASHINGTON							
1 Inslee	N	N	N	N	N	N	N
2 ***Metcalf***	N	Y	Y	Y	Y	Y	Y
3 Baird	N	N	N	N	N	N	N
4 ***Hastings***	Y	Y	Y	Y	Y	Y	Y
5 ***Nethercutt***	Y	Y	Y	Y	Y	Y	Y
6 Dicks	Y	N	N	N	N	N	N
7 McDermott	N	N	N	N	N	N	N
8 ***Dunn***	N	Y	Y	Y	Y	Y	N
9 Smith	N	N	N	N	N	N	N
WEST VIRGINIA							
1 Mollohan	Y	N	N	N	N	N	N
2 Wise	?	?	?	?	?	?	?
3 Rahall	N	N	N	N	N	N	N
WISCONSIN							
1 ***Ryan***	Y	Y	Y	Y	Y	Y	Y
2 Baldwin	N	N	N	N	N	N	N
3 Kind	N	N	N	N	N	N	N
4 Kleczka	N	N	N	N	N	N	N
5 Barrett	N	N	N	N	N	N	N
6 ***Petri***	Y	Y	Y	Y	Y	Y	N
7 Obey	Y	Y	N	N	N	N	N
8 ***Green***	N	Y	Y	Y	Y	Y	N
9 ***Sensenbrenner***	Y	Y	Y	Y	Y	Y	Y
WYOMING							
AL ***Cubin***	Y	Y	Y	Y	Y	Y	Y

Southern states - Ala., Ark., Fla., Ga., Ky., La., Miss., N.C., Okla., S.C., Tenn., Texas, Va.

174. HR 701. Land Conservation/Urban Parks. Udall, D-Colo., amendment that would add the Forest Service's urban and community forestry assistance program to the list of those eligible to receive funds under the bill's farmland protection and forest legacy program. Adopted 306-116: R 103-111; D 202-4 (ND 150-2, SD 52-2); I 1-1. May 11, 2000.

175. HR 701. Land Conservation/Land Auctions. Gibbons, R-Nev., amendment that would allow the Bureau of Land Management to auction off federally held lands. The property would first be offered to state and local governments for recreational purposes. Profits from the sale of lands to private owners would be shared among federal, state and local governments. Rejected 170-250: R 161-54; D 8-195 (ND 4-146, SD 4-49); I 1-1. May 11, 2000.

176. HR 701. Land Conservation/Population Requirements. Ose, R-Calif., amendment that would make funds available only to areas with a population of 100,000 or more. It also would prohibit expenditures until certain criteria are met, such as alleviating maintenance backlogs in national parks, monuments and forests. Rejected 56-365: R 55-158; D 1-205 (ND 1-152, SD 0-53); I 0-2. May 11, 2000.

177. HR 701. Land Conservation/Maintenance Backlog. Thornberry, R-Texas, substitute amendment that would require funding to be subject to annual appropriations until 2006, would establish a dedicated annual fund to address the maintenance backlog on federal properties, and would require that backlog be reduced by 5 percent a year. Additionally, it would make the payment in lieu of taxes program mandatory and provide more private property rights. Rejected 126-291: R 119-92; D 6-198 (ND 1-149, SD 5-49); I 1-1. May 11, 2000.

178. HR 701. Land Conservation/Recommit. DeFazio, D-Ore., motion to recommit to the House Resources Committee with instructions to report the bill back to the House with an amendment that prohibits the expenditure of funds if such expenditures diminish the benefit obligations of Social Security and Medicare. Motion agreed to 413-3: R 208-3; D 203-0 (ND 151-0, SD 52-0); I 2-0. (Subsequently, Young, R-Alaska, reported back with an amendment that would prohibit the expenditure of funds if such expenditures diminish the benefit obligations of Social Security and Medicare.) May 11, 2000.

179. HR 701. Land Conservation/Passage. Passage of the bill that would set aside about $2.8 billion a year in royalties, gained from oil and gas drilling on federal lands, for the purchase of environmentally sensitive land and other conservation programs. Passed 315-102: R 118-93; D 196-8 (ND 147-5, SD 49-3); I 1-1. May 11, 2000.

Key

- Y Voted for (yea).
- # Paired for.
- \+ Announced for.
- N Voted against (nay).
- X Paired against.
- – Announced against.
- P Voted "present."
- C Voted "present" to avoid possible conflict of interest.
- ? Did not vote or otherwise make a position known.

•

Democrats ***Republicans***
Independents

	174	175	176	177	178	179
ALABAMA						
1 ***Callahan***	Y	N	N	N	Y	Y
2 ***Everett***	N	Y	N	Y	Y	N
3 ***Riley***	N	Y	N	N	Y	Y
4 ***Aderholt***	N	Y	N	Y	Y	N
5 Cramer	Y	N	?	N	Y	Y
6 ***Bachus***	N	N	N	N	Y	Y
7 Hilliard	Y	N	N	N	Y	Y
ALASKA						
AL ***Young***	Y	N	N	N	Y	Y
ARIZONA						
1 ***Salmon***	N	Y	Y	Y	Y	N
2 Pastor	Y	N	N	N	Y	Y
3 ***Stump***	N	Y	Y	Y	Y	N
4 ***Shadegg***	N	Y	Y	Y	Y	N
5 ***Kolbe***	Y	Y	N	Y	Y	N
6 ***Hayworth***	N	Y	Y	Y	Y	N
ARKANSAS						
1 Berry	N	Y	N	Y	Y	N
2 Snyder	Y	N	N	N	Y	Y
3 ***Hutchinson***	Y	Y	N	Y	Y	N
4 ***Dickey***	Y	Y	Y	Y	Y	N
CALIFORNIA						
1 Thompson	Y	N	N	N	Y	Y
2 ***Herger***	N	Y	Y	Y	Y	N
3 ***Ose***	Y	Y	Y	Y	Y	N
4 ***Doolittle***	N	Y	Y	Y	Y	N
5 Matsui	Y	?	N	N	Y	Y
6 Woolsey	Y	N	N	N	Y	Y
7 Miller, George	Y	N	N	N	Y	Y
8 Pelosi	Y	N	N	N	Y	Y
9 Lee	N	N	N	N	Y	Y
10 Tauscher	Y	N	N	N	Y	Y
11 ***Pombo***	N	Y	Y	Y	Y	N
12 Lantos	Y	N	N	N	Y	Y
13 Stark	Y	N	N	N	Y	Y
14 Eshoo	Y	N	N	N	Y	Y
15 ***Campbell***	?	?	?	?	?	?
16 Lofgren	?	?	?	?	?	?
17 Farr	Y	N	N	N	Y	Y
18 Condit	Y	N	N	N	Y	Y
19 ***Radanovich***	N	Y	Y	Y	Y	N
20 Dooley	Y	N	N	N	Y	Y
21 ***Thomas***	N	Y	Y	?	Y	N
22 Capps	Y	N	N	N	Y	Y
23 ***Gallegly***	Y	Y	N	N	Y	Y
24 Sherman	Y	N	N	N	Y	Y
25 ***McKeon***	N	Y	Y	Y	Y	N
26 Berman	?	N	N	N	Y	Y
27 ***Rogan***	N	Y	N	N	Y	Y
28 ***Dreier***	N	Y	Y	N	Y	Y
29 Waxman	Y	N	N	N	Y	Y
30 Becerra	Y	N	N	N	Y	Y
31 Martinez	Y	Y	N	Y	Y	Y
32 Dixon	Y	N	N	N	Y	Y
33 Roybal-Allard	Y	N	N	N	Y	Y
34 Napolitano	Y	N	N	N	Y	Y
35 Waters	Y	N	N	N	Y	Y
36 ***Kuykendall***	Y	N	N	N	Y	Y
37 Millender-McD.	Y	N	N	N	Y	Y
38 ***Horn***	Y	N	N	N	Y	Y
39 ***Royce***	N	Y	Y	Y	Y	N
40 ***Lewis***	Y	Y	Y	Y	Y	N
41 ***Miller, Gary***	N	Y	N	N	Y	N
42 Baca	Y	N	N	N	Y	Y
43 ***Calvert***	N	Y	Y	Y	Y	N
44 ***Bono***	Y	N	N	N	Y	Y
45 ***Rohrabacher***	N	Y	Y	Y	Y	N
46 Sanchez	Y	?	N	N	Y	Y
47 ***Cox***	Y	Y	N	Y	Y	N
48 ***Packard***	N	N	N	Y	Y	N
49 ***Bilbray***	N	N	N	N	Y	Y
50 Filner	Y	N	N	N	Y	Y
51 ***Cunningham***	N	Y	N	N	Y	Y
52 ***Hunter***	N	Y	Y	Y	Y	N
COLORADO						
1 DeGette	?	?	?	?	?	?
2 Udall	Y	N	N	N	Y	Y
3 ***McInnis***	Y	Y	N	?	?	?
4 ***Schaffer***	N	Y	N	Y	Y	N
5 ***Hefley***	Y	Y	N	Y	Y	Y
6 ***Tancredo***	Y	Y	N	Y	Y	Y
CONNECTICUT						
1 Larson	Y	N	N	N	Y	Y
2 Gejdenson	Y	N	N	N	Y	Y
3 DeLauro	Y	N	N	N	Y	Y
4 ***Shays***	Y	N	N	N	Y	Y
5 Maloney	Y	N	N	N	Y	Y
6 ***Johnson***	Y	N	N	N	Y	Y
DELAWARE						
AL ***Castle***	N	N	N	N	Y	Y
FLORIDA						
1 ***Scarborough***	Y	N	N	N	Y	Y
2 Boyd	Y	N	N	N	Y	Y
3 Brown	Y	N	N	N	Y	Y
4 ***Fowler***	N	N	N	Y	Y	Y
5 Thurman	Y	N	N	N	Y	Y
6 ***Stearns***	Y	Y	N	Y	Y	N
7 ***Mica***	Y	Y	N	Y	Y	Y
8 ***McCollum***	Y	Y	N	N	Y	Y
9 ***Bilirakis***	Y	Y	N	N	Y	Y
10 ***Young***	Y	Y	N	Y	Y	N
11 Davis	N	N	N	N	Y	Y
12 ***Canady***	N	Y	N	N	Y	Y
13 ***Miller***	Y	Y	N	Y	Y	Y
14 ***Goss***	Y	Y	N	N	Y	Y
15 ***Weldon***	Y	Y	Y	Y	Y	N
16 ***Foley***	+	N	N	N	Y	Y
17 Meek	Y	N	N	N	?	?
18 ***Ros-Lehtinen***	Y	N	N	N	Y	Y
19 Wexler	Y	N	N	N	Y	Y
20 Deutsch	Y	N	N	N	Y	Y
21 ***Diaz-Balart***	Y	Y	N	N	Y	Y
22 ***Shaw***	Y	Y	N	N	Y	Y
23 Hastings	Y	N	N	N	Y	Y
GEORGIA						
1 ***Kingston***	N	Y	N	Y	Y	N
2 Bishop	Y	N	N	N	Y	Y
3 ***Collins***	Y	Y	N	Y	Y	Y
4 McKinney	Y	N	N	N	Y	Y
5 Lewis	Y	N	N	N	?	Y
6 ***Isakson***	Y	N	N	N	Y	Y
7 ***Barr***	Y	Y	N	Y	Y	Y
8 ***Chambliss***	N	Y	N	N	Y	Y
9 ***Deal***	N	Y	N	N	Y	Y
10 ***Norwood***	N	Y	Y	Y	Y	Y
11 ***Linder***	Y	Y	Y	Y	Y	N
HAWAII						
1 Abercrombie	Y	N	N	N	Y	Y
2 Mink	Y	N	N	N	Y	Y
IDAHO						
1 ***Chenoweth-Hage***	N	Y	Y	Y	Y	N
2 ***Simpson***	N	Y	Y	Y	Y	N
ILLINOIS						
1 Rush	Y	N	N	N	Y	Y
2 Jackson	Y	N	N	N	Y	Y
3 Lipinski	Y	N	N	N	Y	Y
4 Gutierrez	Y	N	N	N	Y	Y
5 Blagojevich	Y	N	N	N	Y	Y
6 ***Hyde***	Y	Y	N	N	Y	Y
7 Davis	Y	N	N	N	Y	Y
8 ***Crane***	Y	Y	N	N	Y	Y
9 Schakowsky	Y	N	N	N	Y	Y
10 ***Porter***	Y	N	N	N	Y	Y
11 ***Weller***	Y	N	N	N	Y	Y
12 Costello	Y	N	N	N	Y	Y
13 ***Biggert***	Y	N	N	N	Y	Y

ND Northern Democrats SD Southern Democrats

	174	175	176	177	178	179
14 *Hastert*						
15 *Ewing*	N	N	N	N	Y	N
16 *Manzullo*	N	Y	Y	Y	Y	N
17 Evans	Y	N	N	N	Y	Y
18 *LaHood*	Y	Y	N	N	Y	Y
19 Phelps	Y	N	N	N	Y	Y
20 *Shimkus*	N	Y	Y	Y	Y	Y
INDIANA						
1 Visclosky	Y	N	N	N	Y	N
2 *McIntosh*	?	?	?	?	?	?
3 Roemer	N	N	N	N	Y	Y
4 *Souder*	N	N	N	N	Y	Y
5 *Buyer*	N	Y	Y	Y	Y	N
6 *Burton*	N	Y	Y	Y	Y	N
7 *Pease*	Y	N	N	N	Y	Y
8 *Hostettler*	N	Y	Y	Y	Y	N
9 Hill	Y	N	N	N	Y	Y
10 Carson	Y	N	N	N	Y	Y
IOWA						
1 *Leach*	Y	N	N	N	Y	Y
2 *Nussle*	N	Y	N	Y	Y	Y
3 Boswell	Y	N	N	N	Y	Y
4 *Ganske*	Y	Y	N	N	Y	Y
5 *Latham*	N	Y	N	Y	Y	N
KANSAS						
1 *Moran*	Y	Y	N	Y	Y	N
2 *Ryun*	N	Y	Y	Y	Y	N
3 Moore	Y	N	N	N	Y	Y
4 *Tiahrt*	N	Y	Y	Y	Y	N
KENTUCKY						
1 *Whitfield*	Y	Y	N	N	Y	Y
2 *Lewis*	Y	Y	N	N	Y	Y
3 *Northup*	N	Y	N	Y	Y	Y
4 Lucas	Y	N	N	N	Y	Y
5 *Rogers*	Y	Y	N	N	Y	Y
6 *Fletcher*	Y	Y	N	N	Y	Y
LOUISIANA						
1 *Vitter*	Y	N	N	N	Y	Y
2 Jefferson	Y	N	N	N	Y	Y
3 *Tauzin*	Y	N	N	N	Y	Y
4 *McCrery*	Y	N	N	N	Y	Y
5 *Cooksey*	Y	Y	N	N	Y	Y
6 *Baker*	Y	Y	N	N	Y	Y
7 John	Y	N	N	N	Y	Y
MAINE						
1 Allen	Y	N	N	N	Y	Y
2 Baldacci	Y	N	N	N	Y	Y
MARYLAND						
1 *Gilchrest*	N	N	N	N	Y	Y
2 *Ehrlich*	Y	Y	N	N	Y	Y
3 Cardin	Y	N	N	N	Y	Y
4 Wynn	Y	N	N	N	Y	Y
5 Hoyer	Y	N	N	N	Y	N
6 *Bartlett*	Y	Y	N	Y	Y	N
7 Cummings	Y	N	N	N	Y	Y
8 *Morella*	Y	N	N	N	Y	Y
MASSACHUSETTS						
1 Olver	Y	N	N	N	Y	Y
2 Neal	Y	N	N	N	Y	Y
3 McGovern	Y	N	N	N	Y	Y
4 Frank	Y	N	N	N	Y	Y
5 Meehan	Y	N	N	N	Y	Y
6 Tierney	Y	N	N	N	Y	Y
7 Markey	Y	N	N	N	Y	Y
8 Capuano	Y	N	N	N	Y	Y
9 Moakley	Y	N	N	N	Y	Y
10 Delahunt	Y	N	N	N	Y	Y
MICHIGAN						
1 Stupak	Y	N	N	N	Y	Y
2 *Hoekstra*	N	Y	Y	Y	Y	N
3 *Ehlers*	Y	N	N	N	Y	Y
4 *Camp*	Y	N	N	N	Y	Y
5 Barcia	Y	N	N	N	Y	Y
6 *Upton*	Y	N	N	N	Y	Y
7 *Smith*	Y	Y	Y	N	Y	N
8 Stabenow	Y	N	N	N	Y	Y
9 Kildee	Y	N	N	N	Y	Y
10 Bonior	Y	N	N	N	Y	Y
11 *Knollenberg*	N	Y	N	Y	Y	N
12 Levin	Y	N	N	N	Y	Y
13 Rivers	Y	N	N	N	Y	Y
14 Conyers	Y	N	N	N	Y	Y
15 Kilpatrick	Y	N	N	N	Y	Y
16 Dingell	Y	N	N	?	Y	Y
MINNESOTA						
1 *Gutknecht*	Y	Y	N	N	Y	Y
2 Minge	Y	N	N	N	Y	Y
3 *Ramstad*	Y	N	N	N	Y	Y
4 Vento	Y	N	N	?	?	?
5 Sabo	Y	N	N	N	Y	N
6 Luther	Y	N	N	N	Y	Y
7 Peterson	Y	N	N	N	Y	Y
8 Oberstar	Y	N	N	N	Y	Y
MISSISSIPPI						
1 *Wicker*	N	Y	N	Y	Y	N
2 Thompson	Y	N	N	N	Y	Y
3 *Pickering*	N	Y	N	Y	Y	Y
4 Shows	Y	Y	N	Y	Y	Y
5 Taylor	Y	N	N	N	Y	Y
MISSOURI						
1 Clay	Y	N	N	N	Y	Y
2 *Talent*	N	Y	N	Y	Y	N
3 Gephardt	Y	N	N	N	Y	Y
4 Skelton	Y	N	N	N	Y	Y
5 McCarthy	+	−	−	−	+	+
6 Danner	Y	N	N	N	Y	Y
7 *Blunt*	N	Y	N	Y	Y	N
8 *Emerson*	N	Y	N	Y	Y	N
9 *Hulshof*	Y	Y	N	Y	Y	N
MONTANA						
AL *Hill*	N	Y	N	Y	Y	Y
NEBRASKA						
1 *Bereuter*	N	N	N	N	Y	Y
2 *Terry*	N	Y	N	Y	Y	Y
3 *Barrett*	N	Y	N	Y	Y	N
NEVADA						
1 Berkley	Y	Y	N	N	Y	Y
2 *Gibbons*	N	Y	Y	Y	Y	N
NEW HAMPSHIRE						
1 *Sununu*	N	Y	N	Y	Y	N
2 *Bass*	Y	N	N	N	Y	Y
NEW JERSEY						
1 Andrews	Y	N	N	?	Y	Y
2 *LoBiondo*	Y	N	N	N	Y	Y
3 *Saxton*	Y	N	?	N	Y	Y
4 *Smith*	Y	N	N	N	Y	Y
5 *Roukema*	N	N	N	N	Y	Y
6 Pallone	Y	N	N	N	Y	Y
7 *Franks*	N	N	N	N	Y	Y
8 Pascrell	Y	N	N	N	Y	Y
9 Rothman	Y	N	N	N	Y	Y
10 Payne	Y	N	N	N	Y	Y
11 *Frelinghuysen*	Y	N	N	N	Y	Y
12 Holt	Y	N	N	N	Y	Y
13 Menendez	Y	N	N	N	Y	Y
NEW MEXICO						
1 *Wilson*	Y	Y	Y	N	Y	Y
2 *Skeen*	Y	Y	Y	Y	Y	Y
3 Udall	Y	N	N	N	Y	Y
NEW YORK						
1 Forbes	Y	N	N	N	Y	Y
2 *Lazio*	Y	Y	N	N	Y	Y
3 *King*	N	N	N	N	Y	Y
4 McCarthy	Y	N	N	N	Y	Y
5 Ackerman	Y	N	N	N	Y	Y
6 Meeks	Y	N	N	N	Y	Y
7 Crowley	Y	N	N	N	Y	Y
8 Nadler	Y	N	N	N	Y	Y
9 Weiner	Y	N	N	N	Y	Y
10 Towns	Y	N	N	N	Y	Y
11 Owens	Y	N	N	N	Y	Y
12 Velázquez	Y	N	N	N	Y	Y
13 *Fossella*	Y	Y	N	N	Y	Y
14 Maloney	Y	N	N	N	Y	Y
15 Rangel	Y	N	N	N	Y	Y
16 Serrano	Y	N	N	N	Y	Y
17 Engel	Y	N	N	N	Y	Y
18 Lowey	Y	N	N	N	Y	Y
19 *Kelly*	Y	N	N	N	Y	Y
20 *Gilman*	N	N	N	Y	Y	Y
21 McNulty	Y	N	N	N	Y	Y
22 *Sweeney*	N	Y	N	N	Y	Y
23 *Boehlert*	Y	N	N	N	Y	Y
24 *McHugh*	N	Y	N	N	Y	Y
25 *Walsh*	Y	N	N	?	?	?
26 Hinchey	Y	?	N	N	Y	Y
27 *Reynolds*	Y	Y	N	N	Y	Y
28 Slaughter	Y	N	N	N	Y	Y
29 LaFalce	Y	N	N	N	Y	Y
30 *Quinn*	N	N	N	N	Y	Y
31 *Houghton*	N	N	N	N	Y	Y
NORTH CAROLINA						
1 Clayton	Y	N	N	N	Y	Y
2 Etheridge	Y	N	N	N	Y	Y
3 *Jones*	Y	Y	N	Y	Y	Y
4 Price	Y	N	N	N	Y	Y
5 *Burr*	N	Y	N	N	Y	Y
6 *Coble*	?	?	?	?	?	?
7 McIntyre	Y	N	N	N	Y	Y
8 *Hayes*	Y	N	N	N	Y	Y
9 *Myrick*	Y	Y	N	Y	Y	Y
10 *Ballenger*	N	Y	N	Y	Y	Y
11 *Taylor*	N	Y	N	Y	Y	N
12 Watt	Y	N	N	N	Y	Y
NORTH DAKOTA						
AL Pomeroy	Y	N	N	N	Y	Y
OHIO						
1 *Chabot*	N	Y	N	Y	Y	N
2 *Portman*	Y	Y	N	N	Y	Y
3 Hall	Y	N	N	N	Y	Y
4 *Oxley*	Y	Y	N	Y	Y	N
5 *Gillmor*	N	Y	N	N	Y	Y
6 Strickland	Y	N	N	N	Y	Y
7 *Hobson*	?	Y	Y	Y	Y	N
8 *Boehner*	N	Y	Y	?	Y	N
9 Kaptur	Y	N	N	N	?	Y
10 Kucinich	Y	N	N	N	Y	Y
11 Jones	Y	N	N	N	Y	Y
12 *Kasich*	Y	N	N	Y	Y	N
13 Brown	Y	N	N	N	Y	Y
14 Sawyer	Y	N	N	N	Y	Y
15 *Pryce*	Y	Y	Y	Y	Y	Y
16 *Regula*	Y	Y	Y	Y	Y	N
17 Traficant	Y	Y	Y	N	Y	Y
18 *Ney*	Y	Y	N	Y	Y	Y
19 *LaTourette*	Y	N	?	N	Y	Y
OKLAHOMA						
1 *Largent*	N	Y	Y	Y	Y	N
2 *Coburn*	N	Y	N	Y	Y	N
3 *Watkins*	N	Y	N	Y	Y	N
4 *Watts*	N	Y	N	Y	Y	N
5 *Istook*	N	Y	N	Y	Y	N
6 *Lucas*	?	?	?	?	?	?
OREGON						
1 Wu	Y	N	N	N	Y	Y
2 *Walden*	N	Y	N	Y	Y	N
3 Blumenauer	Y	N	N	N	Y	Y
4 DeFazio	Y	N	N	N	Y	Y
5 Hooley	Y	N	N	N	Y	Y
PENNSYLVANIA						
1 Brady	Y	N	N	N	Y	Y
2 Fattah	Y	N	N	N	Y	Y
3 Borski	Y	N	N	N	Y	Y
4 Klink	Y	N	N	N	Y	Y
5 *Peterson*	N	Y	N	Y	Y	N
6 Holden	Y	N	N	N	Y	Y
7 *Weldon*	Y	N	N	N	Y	Y
8 *Greenwood*	Y	N	N	N	Y	Y
9 *Shuster*	N	Y	N	Y	Y	Y
10 *Sherwood*	?	?	?	?	?	?
11 Kanjorski	Y	N	N	N	Y	Y
12 Murtha	Y	N	N	N	Y	N
13 Hoeffel	Y	N	N	N	Y	Y
14 Coyne	Y	N	N	N	Y	Y
15 *Toomey*	N	Y	N	Y	Y	N
16 *Pitts*	N	Y	N	Y	Y	Y
17 *Gekas*	Y	Y	N	N	Y	Y
18 Doyle	Y	N	N	N	Y	Y
19 *Goodling*	N	?	Y	Y	N	N
20 Mascara	Y	N	N	N	Y	Y
21 *English*	Y	N	N	N	Y	Y
RHODE ISLAND						
1 Kennedy	Y	N	N	N	Y	Y
2 Weygand	Y	N	N	N	Y	Y
SOUTH CAROLINA						
1 *Sanford*	N	Y	N	Y	Y	N
2 *Spence*	N	Y	N	Y	Y	N
3 *Graham*	N	Y	N	Y	Y	?
4 *DeMint*	N	Y	N	Y	+	−
5 Spratt	Y	N	N	N	Y	Y
6 Clyburn	Y	N	N	N	Y	Y
SOUTH DAKOTA						
AL *Thune*	Y	Y	N	N	Y	Y
TENNESSEE						
1 *Jenkins*	N	Y	N	N	Y	Y
2 *Duncan*	Y	Y	N	Y	Y	N
3 *Wamp*	Y	Y	N	Y	Y	N
4 *Hilleary*	Y	Y	Y	Y	Y	N
5 Clement	Y	N	N	N	Y	Y
6 Gordon	Y	N	N	N	Y	Y
7 *Bryant*	Y	Y	N	Y	Y	N
8 Tanner	Y	N	N	N	Y	Y
9 Ford	Y	N	N	N	Y	?
TEXAS						
1 Sandlin	Y	N	N	Y	Y	Y
2 Turner	Y	N	N	N	Y	Y
3 *Johnson, Sam*	N	Y	Y	Y	Y	N
4 Hall	Y	Y	N	Y	Y	N
5 *Sessions*	N	Y	Y	Y	Y	Y
6 *Barton*	Y	Y	Y	Y	?	?
7 *Archer*	N	Y	?	Y	Y	N
8 *Brady*	N	Y	N	Y	Y	Y
9 Lampson	Y	N	N	N	Y	Y
10 Doggett	Y	N	N	N	Y	Y
11 Edwards	Y	N	N	N	Y	Y
12 *Granger*	N	Y	Y	Y	Y	N
13 *Thornberry*	N	Y	Y	Y	Y	N
14 *Paul*	N	Y	N	Y	Y	N
15 Hinojosa	Y	N	N	N	Y	Y
16 Reyes	Y	N	N	N	Y	Y
17 Stenholm	Y	Y	N	Y	Y	N
18 Jackson-Lee	Y	N	N	N	Y	Y
19 *Combest*	N	Y	N	Y	?	Y
20 Gonzalez	Y	N	N	N	Y	Y
21 *Smith*	N	Y	Y	Y	Y	N
22 *DeLay*	N	Y	Y	Y	Y	N
23 *Bonilla*	N	Y	N	Y	Y	N
24 Frost	Y	N	N	N	Y	Y
25 Bentsen	Y	N	N	N	Y	Y
26 *Armey*	N	Y	Y	Y	Y	N
27 Ortiz	Y	N	N	N	Y	Y
28 Rodriguez	Y	N	N	N	Y	Y
29 Green	Y	N	N	N	Y	Y
30 Johnson, E.B.	Y	N	N	N	Y	Y
UTAH						
1 *Hansen*	N	Y	N	N	Y	Y
2 *Cook*	Y	Y	Y	Y	Y	N
3 *Cannon*	Y	Y	Y	Y	Y	N
VERMONT						
AL Sanders	Y	N	N	N	Y	Y
VIRGINIA						
1 *Bateman*	Y	Y	N	N	Y	Y
2 Pickett	Y	N	N	N	Y	Y
3 Scott	Y	N	N	N	Y	Y
4 Sisisky	Y	N	N	N	Y	Y
5 Goode	N	Y	N	Y	Y	N
6 *Goodlatte*	N	Y	N	Y	Y	N
7 *Bliley*	Y	Y	N	?	Y	N
8 Moran	Y	N	N	N	Y	Y
9 Boucher	Y	?	N	N	Y	Y
10 *Wolf*	Y	N	N	Y	Y	N
11 *Davis*	Y	Y	N	N	Y	Y
WASHINGTON						
1 Inslee	Y	N	N	N	Y	Y
2 *Metcalf*	Y	Y	N	Y	N	Y
3 Baird	Y	N	N	N	Y	Y
4 *Hastings*	N	Y	Y	Y	Y	N
5 *Nethercutt*	N	Y	Y	Y	Y	N
6 Dicks	Y	N	N	N	Y	Y
7 McDermott	Y	N	N	N	Y	Y
8 *Dunn*	N	Y	N	N	Y	Y
9 Smith	Y	N	N	N	Y	Y
WEST VIRGINIA						
1 Mollohan	Y	N	N	N	Y	Y
2 Wise	?	?	?	?	?	?
3 Rahall	Y	N	N	N	Y	Y
WISCONSIN						
1 *Ryan*	N	Y	N	Y	Y	Y
2 Baldwin	Y	N	N	N	Y	Y
3 Kind	Y	N	N	N	Y	Y
4 Kleczka	Y	N	N	N	Y	Y
5 Barrett	Y	N	N	N	Y	Y
6 *Petri*	N	Y	N	Y	Y	Y
7 Obey	Y	N	N	N	Y	N
8 *Green*	N	Y	N	N	Y	Y
9 *Sensenbrenner*	Y	Y	Y	Y	Y	N
WYOMING						
AL *Cubin*	N	Y	Y	Y	Y	N

Southern states - Ala., Ark., Fla., Ga., Ky., La., Miss., N.C., Okla., S.C., Tenn., Texas, Va.

House Votes 180, 181, 182, 183, 184, 185, 186

180. H Res 491. G.V. "Sonny" Montgomery Room/Adoption. Shuster, R-Pa., motion to suspend the rules and adopt the resolution naming Room H-130 in the Capitol building the G.V. "Sonny" Montgomery room in honor of the former congressman (1967-97) who has facilitated a prayer breakfast in that room since 1967. Although he has retired, he continues the tradition. Motion agreed to 380-0: R 196-0; D 182-0 (ND 131-0, SD 51-0); I 2-0. A two-thirds majority of those present and voting (254 in this case) is required for adoption under suspension of the rules. May 15, 2000.

181. HR 4251. North Korean Nuclear Transfers/Passage. Gilman, R-N.Y., motion to suspend the rules and pass the bill that would require Congress to concur before a nuclear cooperation agreement with North Korea can take effect. The bill would provide expedited procedures for consideration of a joint resolution concurring in the president's certification. Motion agreed to 374-6: R 196-0; D 176-6 (ND 126-5, SD 50-1); I 2-0. A two-thirds majority of those present and voting (254 in this case) is required for passage under suspension of the rules. May 15, 2000.

182. H Con Res 309. Children's Safety/Adoption. Castle, R-Del., motion to suspend the rules and adopt the concurrent resolution expressing the sense of Congress that states should encourage their primary and secondary schools to implement quality personal safety education programs. Motion agreed to 383-0: R 198-0; D 183-0 (ND 132-0, SD 51-0); I 2-0. A two-thirds majority of those present and voting (256 in this case) is required for adoption under suspension of the rules. May 15, 2000.

183. H Con Res 326. New Mexico Fires/Adoption. Chenoweth-Hage, R-Idaho, motion to suspend the rules and adopt the concurrent resolution expressing the sense of Congress that the federal government should take full responsibility for the fires near Los Alamos, N.M., that were intentionally set by the Park Service and grew out of control. Motion agreed to 404-0: R 207-0; D 195-0 (ND 143-0, SD 52-0); I 2-0. A two-thirds majority of those present and voting (270 in this case) is required for passage under suspension of the rules. May 16, 2000.

184. HR 4425. Fiscal 2001 Military Construction Appropriations/Passage. Passage of the bill to provide $8.6 billion for military construction programs in fiscal 2001, including $3.7 billion for general construction, $3.6 billion for family housing and $1.2 billion for activities associated with the most recent round of base closure and realignment. The bill would also fund the first construction stage of a new ballistic missile defense system. Passed 386-22: R 207-4; D 177-18 (ND 125-17, SD 52-1); I 2-0. May 16, 2000.

185. HR 853. Budget Process Changes/Previous Question. Goss, R-Fla., motion to order the previous question (thus ending debate and possibility of amendment) on adoption of the rule (H Res 499) to provide for House floor consideration of the bill to amend the Congressional Budget Act of 1974 to provide for joint resolutions on the budget, instead of non-binding concurrent resolutions. Motion agreed to 221-200: R 215-0; D 5-199 (ND 5-145, SD 0-54); I 1-1. (Subsequently, the rule was adopted by voice vote.) May 16, 2000.

186. HR 853. Budget Process Changes/Biennial System. Dreier, R-Calif., amendment that would replace the annual budgeting and appropriations system with a biennial one. Rejected 201-217: R 176-42; D 24-174 (ND 17-128, SD 7-46); I 1-1. May 16, 2000.

Key

- Y Voted for (yea).
- # Paired for.
- + Announced for.
- N Voted against (nay).
- X Paired against.
- – Announced against.
- P Voted "present."
- C Voted "present" to avoid possible conflict of interest.
- ? Did not vote or otherwise make a position known.

•

Democrats ***Republicans***
Independents

	180	181	182	183	184	185	186
ALABAMA							
1 ***Callahan***	?	?	?	?	Y	Y	Y
2 ***Everett***	Y	Y	Y	Y	Y	Y	N
3 ***Riley***	Y	Y	Y	Y	Y	Y	Y
4 ***Aderholt***	Y	Y	Y	Y	Y	Y	N
5 Cramer	Y	Y	Y	Y	Y	N	N
6 ***Bachus***	Y	Y	Y	Y	Y	Y	Y
7 Hilliard	Y	Y	Y	Y	Y	N	N
ALASKA							
AL ***Young***	Y	Y	Y	Y	Y	Y	Y
ARIZONA							
1 ***Salmon***	Y	Y	Y	Y	+	Y	Y
2 Pastor	Y	Y	Y	Y	Y	N	N
3 ***Stump***	Y	Y	Y	Y	Y	Y	Y
4 ***Shadegg***	Y	Y	Y	Y	Y	Y	Y
5 ***Kolbe***	Y	Y	Y	Y	Y	Y	Y
6 ***Hayworth***	Y	Y	Y	Y	Y	Y	Y
ARKANSAS							
1 Berry	Y	Y	Y	Y	Y	N	N
2 Snyder	Y	Y	Y	Y	Y	N	N
3 ***Hutchinson***	Y	Y	Y	P	Y	Y	Y
4 ***Dickey***	Y	Y	Y	Y	Y	Y	N
CALIFORNIA							
1 Thompson	Y	Y	Y	Y	Y	N	Y
2 ***Herger***	Y	Y	Y	Y	Y	Y	Y
3 ***Ose***	Y	Y	Y	Y	Y	Y	Y
4 ***Doolittle***	Y	Y	Y	Y	Y	Y	N
5 Matsui	Y	Y	Y	Y	Y	N	N
6 Woolsey	Y	Y	Y	Y	Y	N	N
7 Miller, George	Y	Y	Y	Y	Y	N	N
8 Pelosi	Y	Y	Y	Y	Y	N	N
9 Lee	Y	Y	Y	Y	N	N	N
10 Tauscher	Y	Y	Y	Y	Y	N	Y
11 ***Pombo***	Y	Y	Y	Y	Y	Y	N
12 Lantos	Y	Y	Y	Y	Y	N	N
13 Stark	Y	Y	Y	Y	N	N	N
14 Eshoo	Y	Y	Y	Y	Y	N	N
15 ***Campbell***	?	?	?	?	?	?	?
16 Lofgren	Y	Y	Y	Y	N	N	N
17 Farr	?	?	?	Y	Y	N	N
18 Condit	Y	Y	Y	Y	Y	N	Y
19 ***Radanovich***	Y	Y	Y	Y	Y	Y	Y
20 Dooley	Y	Y	Y	?	?	N	N
21 ***Thomas***	?	?	?	Y	Y	Y	Y
22 Capps	Y	Y	Y	Y	Y	N	N
23 ***Gallegly***	Y	Y	Y	Y	Y	Y	Y
24 Sherman	Y	Y	Y	Y	Y	N	N
25 ***McKeon***	Y	Y	Y	Y	Y	Y	Y
26 Berman	Y	Y	Y	Y	Y	N	N
27 ***Rogan***	Y	Y	Y	Y	Y	Y	Y
28 ***Dreier***	Y	Y	Y	Y	Y	Y	Y
29 Waxman	?	?	?	Y	Y	N	N
30 Becerra	+	+	+	Y	Y	N	N
31 Martinez	Y	Y	Y	?	Y	Y	Y
32 Dixon	Y	Y	Y	Y	Y	N	N
33 Roybal-Allard	Y	Y	Y	Y	Y	N	N
34 Napolitano	Y	Y	Y	Y	Y	N	Y
35 Waters	Y	Y	Y	Y	Y	N	N
36 ***Kuykendall***	Y	Y	Y	Y	Y	Y	Y
37 Millender-McD.	Y	Y	Y	Y	Y	–	N
38 ***Horn***	Y	Y	Y	Y	Y	Y	Y
39 ***Royce***	Y	Y	Y	Y	N	Y	Y
40 ***Lewis***	Y	Y	Y	Y	Y	Y	N
41 ***Miller, Gary***	Y	Y	Y	Y	Y	Y	Y
42 Baca	Y	Y	Y	Y	Y	N	N
43 ***Calvert***	Y	Y	Y	Y	Y	Y	Y
44 ***Bono***	Y	Y	Y	Y	Y	Y	Y
45 ***Rohrabacher***	Y	Y	Y	Y	Y	Y	Y
46 Sanchez	Y	Y	Y	Y	Y	N	N
47 ***Cox***	Y	Y	Y	Y	Y	Y	N
48 ***Packard***	Y	Y	Y	Y	Y	Y	N
49 ***Bilbray***	Y	Y	Y	Y	Y	Y	Y
50 Filner	Y	Y	Y	Y	Y	N	N
51 ***Cunningham***	Y	Y	Y	Y	Y	Y	N
52 ***Hunter***	Y	Y	Y	Y	Y	Y	N
COLORADO							
1 DeGette	Y	Y	Y	Y	Y	N	N
2 Udall	Y	Y	Y	Y	Y	N	N
3 ***McInnis***	Y	Y	Y	Y	Y	Y	Y
4 ***Schaffer***	?	?	?	Y	Y	Y	Y
5 ***Hefley***	?	?	?	Y	Y	Y	Y
6 ***Tancredo***	Y	Y	Y	Y	Y	Y	Y
CONNECTICUT							
1 Larson	Y	Y	Y	Y	Y	N	N
2 Gejdenson	Y	Y	Y	Y	Y	N	N
3 DeLauro	Y	Y	Y	Y	Y	N	N
4 ***Shays***	Y	Y	Y	Y	Y	Y	Y
5 Maloney	Y	Y	Y	Y	?	N	N
6 ***Johnson***	Y	Y	Y	Y	Y	Y	Y
DELAWARE							
AL ***Castle***	Y	Y	Y	Y	Y	Y	Y
FLORIDA							
1 ***Scarborough***	Y	Y	Y	Y	Y	Y	Y
2 Boyd	Y	Y	Y	Y	Y	N	N
3 Brown	?	?	?	?	Y	N	N
4 ***Fowler***	Y	Y	Y	Y	Y	Y	Y
5 Thurman	Y	Y	Y	Y	Y	N	?
6 ***Stearns***	Y	Y	Y	Y	Y	Y	Y
7 ***Mica***	Y	Y	Y	Y	Y	Y	Y
8 ***McCollum***	?	?	?	?	?	?	?
9 ***Bilirakis***	Y	Y	Y	Y	Y	Y	Y
10 ***Young***	Y	Y	Y	Y	Y	Y	Y
11 Davis	Y	Y	Y	Y	Y	N	N
12 ***Canady***	Y	Y	Y	Y	Y	Y	Y
13 ***Miller***	Y	Y	Y	Y	Y	Y	Y
14 ***Goss***	Y	Y	Y	Y	Y	Y	Y
15 ***Weldon***	Y	Y	Y	Y	Y	Y	Y
16 ***Foley***	Y	Y	Y	Y	Y	Y	Y
17 Meek	Y	Y	Y	Y	Y	N	N
18 ***Ros-Lehtinen***	Y	Y	Y	Y	Y	Y	Y
19 Wexler	?	?	?	Y	Y	N	N
20 Deutsch	Y	Y	Y	Y	Y	N	N
21 ***Diaz-Balart***	Y	Y	Y	Y	Y	Y	Y
22 ***Shaw***	Y	Y	Y	Y	Y	Y	Y
23 Hastings	Y	Y	Y	Y	Y	N	N
GEORGIA							
1 ***Kingston***	?	?	?	Y	Y	Y	N
2 Bishop	Y	Y	Y	Y	Y	N	N
3 ***Collins***	Y	Y	Y	Y	Y	Y	N
4 McKinney	Y	Y	Y	Y	N	N	N
5 Lewis	Y	Y	Y	Y	Y	N	N
6 ***Isakson***	Y	Y	Y	Y	Y	Y	Y
7 ***Barr***	Y	Y	Y	Y	Y	Y	Y
8 ***Chambliss***	Y	Y	Y	Y	Y	Y	Y
9 ***Deal***	Y	Y	Y	Y	Y	Y	Y
10 ***Norwood***	Y	Y	Y	?	Y	Y	Y
11 ***Linder***	Y	Y	Y	Y	Y	Y	Y
HAWAII							
1 Abercrombie	+	+	+	+	+	N	N
2 Mink	Y	Y	Y	Y	Y	N	N
IDAHO							
1 ***Chenoweth-Hage***	?	?	?	Y	Y	Y	N
2 ***Simpson***	Y	Y	Y	Y	Y	Y	Y
ILLINOIS							
1 Rush	?	?	?	Y	Y	N	N
2 Jackson	Y	Y	Y	Y	Y	N	N
3 Lipinski	Y	Y	Y	Y	Y	N	N
4 Gutierrez	?	?	?	Y	Y	N	N
5 Blagojevich	?	?	?	Y	Y	N	N
6 ***Hyde***	Y	Y	Y	Y	Y	Y	Y
7 Davis	Y	Y	Y	Y	Y	N	N
8 ***Crane***	Y	Y	Y	Y	Y	Y	Y
9 Schakowsky	Y	Y	Y	Y	Y	N	N
10 ***Porter***	Y	Y	Y	Y	Y	Y	Y
11 ***Weller***	Y	Y	Y	Y	Y	Y	Y
12 Costello	Y	Y	Y	Y	Y	N	N
13 ***Biggert***	Y	Y	Y	Y	Y	Y	Y

ND Northern Democrats SD Southern Democrats

	180	181	182	183	184	185	186
14 ***Hastert***							Y
15 ***Ewing***	Y	Y	Y	Y	Y	Y	Y
16 ***Manzullo***	Y	Y	Y	Y	Y	Y	N
17 Evans	Y	Y	Y	Y	Y	N	N
18 ***LaHood***	Y	Y	Y	Y	Y	Y	Y
19 Phelps	Y	Y	Y	Y	Y	N	N
20 ***Shimkus***	Y	Y	Y	Y	Y	Y	Y
INDIANA							
1 Visclosky	Y	Y	Y	Y	Y	N	N
2 ***McIntosh***	?	?	?	?	?	?	?
3 Roemer	Y	Y	Y	Y	Y	N	Y
4 ***Souder***	Y	Y	Y	Y	Y	Y	Y
5 ***Buyer***	?	?	?	Y	Y	Y	Y
6 ***Burton***	Y	Y	Y	Y	Y	Y	Y
7 ***Pease***	Y	Y	Y	Y	Y	Y	Y
8 ***Hostettler***	Y	Y	Y	Y	Y	Y	Y
9 Hill	Y	Y	Y	Y	Y	N	N
10 Carson	Y	Y	Y	Y	Y	N	N
IOWA							
1 ***Leach***	Y	Y	Y	Y	Y	Y	Y
2 ***Nussle***	Y	Y	Y	?	Y	Y	N
3 Boswell	Y	Y	Y	Y	Y	N	N
4 ***Ganske***	?	Y	Y	Y	Y	Y	Y
5 ***Latham***	Y	Y	Y	Y	Y	Y	Y
KANSAS							
1 ***Moran***	Y	Y	Y	Y	Y	Y	Y
2 ***Ryun***	?	?	?	Y	Y	Y	Y
3 Moore	Y	Y	Y	Y	Y	Y	N
4 ***Tiahrt***	Y	+	Y	Y	Y	Y	Y
KENTUCKY							
1 ***Whitfield***	Y	Y	Y	Y	Y	Y	Y
2 ***Lewis***	Y	Y	Y	Y	Y	Y	N
3 ***Northup***	Y	Y	Y	Y	Y	Y	Y
4 Lucas	Y	Y	Y	Y	Y	N	N
5 ***Rogers***	Y	Y	Y	Y	Y	Y	N
6 ***Fletcher***	Y	Y	Y	Y	Y	Y	N
LOUISIANA							
1 ***Vitter***	Y	Y	Y	Y	Y	Y	Y
2 Jefferson	Y	Y	Y	Y	Y	N	N
3 ***Tauzin***	Y	Y	Y	Y	Y	Y	Y
4 ***McCrery***	Y	Y	Y	Y	Y	Y	Y
5 ***Cooksey***	?	?	?	Y	Y	Y	Y
6 ***Baker***	Y	Y	Y	Y	Y	Y	Y
7 John	Y	Y	Y	Y	Y	N	N
MAINE							
1 Allen	Y	Y	Y	Y	Y	N	N
2 Baldacci	Y	Y	Y	Y	Y	N	N
MARYLAND							
1 ***Gilchrest***	Y	Y	Y	Y	Y	Y	Y
2 ***Ehrlich***	Y	Y	Y	Y	Y	Y	Y
3 Cardin	Y	Y	Y	Y	Y	Y	N
4 Wynn	Y	Y	Y	Y	Y	N	N
5 Hoyer	Y	Y	Y	Y	Y	N	N
6 ***Bartlett***	Y	Y	Y	Y	Y	Y	Y
7 Cummings	Y	Y	Y	Y	Y	N	N
8 ***Morella***	Y	Y	Y	Y	Y	Y	Y
MASSACHUSETTS							
1 Olver	Y	Y	Y	Y	Y	N	N
2 Neal	Y	Y	Y	Y	?	N	N
3 McGovern	Y	Y	Y	Y	Y	N	N
4 Frank	Y	N	Y	Y	N	N	N
5 Meehan	Y	Y	Y	Y	Y	N	Y
6 Tierney	Y	Y	Y	Y	N	N	N
7 Markey	Y	Y	Y	Y	N	N	N
8 Capuano	+	–	+	Y	N	N	N
9 Moakley	?	?	?	Y	Y	N	N
10 Delahunt	Y	Y	Y	Y	Y	N	N
MICHIGAN							
1 Stupak	?	?	?	?	?	?	?
2 ***Hoekstra***	?	?	?	Y	Y	Y	Y
3 ***Ehlers***	Y	Y	Y	Y	Y	Y	Y
4 ***Camp***	Y	Y	Y	Y	Y	Y	Y
5 Barcia	Y	Y	Y	Y	Y	N	N
6 ***Upton***	Y	Y	Y	Y	Y	Y	Y
7 ***Smith***	?	?	?	Y	Y	Y	N
8 Stabenow	Y	Y	Y	Y	Y	N	N
9 Kildee	Y	Y	Y	Y	Y	N	N
10 Bonior	Y	Y	Y	Y	Y	N	N
11 ***Knollenberg***	Y	Y	Y	Y	Y	Y	N
12 Levin	Y	Y	Y	Y	Y	N	N
13 Rivers	Y	Y	Y	Y	N	N	N
14 Conyers	Y	Y	Y	Y	N	N	N
15 Kilpatrick	+	+	+	Y	Y	N	N
16 Dingell	Y	Y	Y	Y	Y	N	N
MINNESOTA							
1 ***Gutknecht***	Y	Y	Y	Y	+	Y	Y
2 Minge	Y	Y	Y	Y	Y	N	Y
3 ***Ramstad***	Y	Y	Y	Y	Y	Y	Y
4 Vento	?	?	?	?	?	N	Y
5 Sabo	Y	Y	Y	Y	Y	N	N
6 Luther	Y	Y	Y	Y	Y	N	Y
7 Peterson	Y	Y	Y	Y	Y	N	N
8 Oberstar	Y	Y	Y	Y	Y	N	N
MISSISSIPPI							
1 ***Wicker***	Y	Y	Y	Y	Y	Y	N
2 Thompson	Y	Y	Y	Y	Y	N	N
3 ***Pickering***	Y	Y	Y	Y	Y	Y	Y
4 Shows	Y	Y	Y	Y	+	N	N
5 Taylor	Y	Y	Y	Y	Y	N	N
MISSOURI							
1 Clay	Y	Y	Y	?	?	N	N
2 ***Talent***	Y	Y	Y	Y	Y	Y	Y
3 Gephardt	Y	Y	Y	Y	Y	N	N
4 Skelton	Y	Y	Y	Y	?	N	N
5 McCarthy	Y	Y	Y	Y	Y	N	Y
6 Danner	?	?	?	?	?	?	N
7 ***Blunt***	Y	Y	Y	Y	Y	Y	Y
8 ***Emerson***	Y	Y	Y	Y	Y	Y	N
9 ***Hulshof***	Y	Y	Y	Y	Y	Y	Y
MONTANA							
AL ***Hill***	Y	Y	Y	Y	Y	Y	N
NEBRASKA							
1 ***Bereuter***	Y	Y	Y	Y	Y	Y	Y
2 ***Terry***	Y	Y	Y	Y	Y	Y	Y
3 ***Barrett***	Y	Y	Y	Y	Y	Y	Y
NEVADA							
1 Berkley	?	?	?	Y	Y	N	N
2 ***Gibbons***	Y	Y	Y	Y	Y	Y	Y
NEW HAMPSHIRE							
1 ***Sununu***	Y	Y	Y	Y	Y	Y	Y
2 ***Bass***	Y	Y	Y	Y	Y	Y	Y
NEW JERSEY							
1 Andrews	Y	Y	Y	Y	Y	N	N
2 ***LoBiondo***	Y	Y	Y	+	+	+	Y
3 ***Saxton***	Y	Y	Y	Y	Y	Y	N
4 ***Smith***	Y	Y	Y	Y	Y	Y	Y
5 ***Roukema***	Y	Y	Y	Y	Y	Y	Y
6 Pallone	Y	Y	Y	Y	Y	N	N
7 ***Franks***	?	?	?	?	?	?	Y
8 Pascrell	Y	Y	Y	Y	Y	N	N
9 Rothman	?	?	?	Y	Y	N	N
10 Payne	?	?	?	Y	N	N	N
11 ***Frelinghuysen***	Y	Y	Y	Y	Y	Y	N
12 Holt	Y	Y	Y	Y	Y	N	N
13 Menendez	Y	Y	Y	Y	Y	N	N
NEW MEXICO							
1 ***Wilson***	?	?	?	Y	Y	Y	Y
2 ***Skeen***	Y	Y	Y	Y	Y	Y	N
3 Udall	?	?	?	?	?	?	?
NEW YORK							
1 Forbes	?	?	?	Y	Y	N	N
2 ***Lazio***	Y	Y	Y	Y	Y	Y	Y
3 ***King***	Y	Y	Y	Y	Y	Y	Y
4 McCarthy	Y	Y	Y	+	Y	N	N
5 Ackerman	?	?	?	?	?	?	?
6 Meeks	Y	Y	Y	Y	Y	N	?
7 Crowley	Y	Y	Y	Y	Y	N	N
8 Nadler	Y	N	Y	Y	N	?	?
9 Weiner	Y	Y	Y	Y	Y	N	N
10 Towns	Y	Y	Y	Y	Y	N	N
11 Owens	+	–	+	Y	N	N	?
12 Velázquez	Y	Y	Y	Y	Y	N	N
13 ***Fossella***	Y	Y	Y	Y	Y	Y	Y
14 Maloney	Y	Y	Y	Y	Y	N	?
15 Rangel	Y	Y	Y	Y	Y	N	?
16 Serrano	Y	Y	Y	Y	?	N	?
17 Engel	?	?	?	Y	Y	N	?
18 Lowey	?	?	?	P	Y	N	?
19 ***Kelly***	Y	Y	Y	P	Y	Y	N
20 ***Gilman***	Y	Y	Y	Y	Y	Y	Y
21 McNulty	?	?	?	?	?	?	?
22 ***Sweeney***	Y	Y	Y	Y	Y	Y	Y
23 ***Boehlert***	Y	Y	Y	Y	Y	Y	Y
24 ***McHugh***	Y	Y	Y	Y	Y	Y	Y
25 ***Walsh***	Y	Y	Y	Y	Y	Y	N
26 Hinchey	Y	Y	Y	Y	?	N	N
27 ***Reynolds***	?	?	?	Y	Y	Y	Y
28 Slaughter	Y	Y	Y	+	Y	N	N
29 LaFalce	Y	N	Y	Y	?	N	N
30 ***Quinn***	Y	Y	Y	Y	Y	Y	Y
31 ***Houghton***	Y	Y	Y	Y	?	Y	Y
NORTH CAROLINA							
1 Clayton	Y	Y	Y	Y	Y	N	N
2 Etheridge	Y	Y	Y	Y	Y	N	N
3 ***Jones***	Y	Y	Y	Y	Y	Y	Y
4 Price	Y	Y	Y	Y	Y	N	N
5 ***Burr***	Y	Y	Y	Y	Y	Y	Y
6 ***Coble***	Y	Y	Y	Y	Y	Y	Y
7 McIntyre	Y	Y	Y	Y	Y	N	N
8 ***Hayes***	Y	Y	Y	Y	Y	Y	N
9 ***Myrick***	Y	Y	Y	Y	Y	Y	Y
10 ***Ballenger***	Y	Y	Y	Y	Y	Y	Y
11 ***Taylor***	Y	Y	Y	Y	Y	Y	N
12 Watt	Y	Y	Y	Y	Y	N	N
NORTH DAKOTA							
AL Pomeroy	Y	Y	Y	Y	Y	N	N
OHIO							
1 ***Chabot***	Y	Y	Y	Y	Y	Y	Y
2 ***Portman***	Y	Y	Y	Y	Y	Y	Y
3 Hall	Y	N	Y	Y	Y	Y	Y
4 ***Oxley***	Y	Y	Y	Y	Y	Y	Y
5 ***Gillmor***	Y	Y	Y	Y	Y	Y	Y
6 Strickland	Y	Y	Y	Y	Y	N	N
7 ***Hobson***	Y	Y	Y	Y	Y	Y	N
8 ***Boehner***	Y	Y	Y	Y	Y	Y	Y
9 Kaptur	?	?	Y	Y	Y	N	N
10 Kucinich	Y	Y	Y	Y	N	N	N
11 Jones	Y	Y	Y	Y	Y	N	N
12 ***Kasich***	Y	Y	Y	Y	Y	Y	N
13 Brown	Y	Y	Y	Y	Y	N	N
14 Sawyer	Y	Y	Y	Y	Y	N	N
15 ***Pryce***	Y	Y	Y	Y	Y	Y	Y
16 ***Regula***	Y	Y	Y	Y	Y	Y	Y
17 Traficant	Y	Y	Y	Y	Y	Y	N
18 ***Ney***	Y	Y	Y	Y	Y	Y	Y
19 ***LaTourette***	Y	Y	Y	Y	Y	Y	Y
OKLAHOMA							
1 ***Largent***	Y	Y	Y	?	?	?	?
2 ***Coburn***	Y	Y	Y	Y	Y	Y	Y
3 ***Watkins***	Y	Y	Y	Y	Y	Y	N
4 ***Watts***	Y	Y	Y	Y	Y	Y	Y
5 ***Istook***	Y	Y	Y	Y	Y	Y	N
6 ***Lucas***	?	?	?	Y	Y	Y	Y
OREGON							
1 Wu	Y	Y	Y	Y	N	N	N
2 ***Walden***	Y	Y	Y	Y	Y	Y	Y
3 Blumenauer	Y	Y	Y	Y	Y	N	N
4 DeFazio	Y	Y	Y	Y	Y	N	Y
5 Hooley	Y	Y	Y	Y	Y	N	N
PENNSYLVANIA							
1 Brady	Y	Y	Y	Y	Y	N	N
2 Fattah	Y	Y	Y	Y	Y	N	N
3 Borski	Y	Y	Y	Y	Y	N	N
4 Klink	Y	Y	Y	Y	N	N	N
5 ***Peterson***	?	?	?	Y	Y	Y	Y
6 Holden	Y	Y	Y	Y	Y	N	N
7 ***Weldon***	Y	Y	Y	Y	?	Y	Y
8 ***Greenwood***	Y	Y	Y	Y	Y	Y	Y
9 ***Shuster***	Y	Y	Y	Y	Y	Y	N
10 ***Sherwood***	Y	Y	Y	Y	Y	Y	N
11 Kanjorski	Y	Y	Y	Y	Y	N	N
12 Murtha	Y	Y	Y	Y	Y	N	N
13 Hoeffel	Y	Y	Y	Y	Y	N	N
14 Coyne	Y	Y	Y	Y	Y	N	N
15 ***Toomey***	Y	Y	Y	Y	Y	Y	Y
16 ***Pitts***	Y	Y	Y	Y	Y	Y	Y
17 ***Gekas***	Y	Y	Y	Y	Y	Y	Y
18 Doyle	Y	Y	Y	Y	Y	N	N
19 ***Goodling***	Y	Y	Y	Y	Y	Y	Y
20 Mascara	Y	Y	Y	Y	Y	N	N
21 ***English***	?	?	Y	Y	Y	Y	Y
RHODE ISLAND							
1 Kennedy	Y	Y	Y	Y	Y	N	N
2 Weygand	Y	Y	Y	Y	Y	N	N
SOUTH CAROLINA							
1 ***Sanford***	Y	Y	Y	P	Y	Y	Y
2 ***Spence***	Y	Y	Y	Y	Y	Y	N
3 ***Graham***	Y	Y	Y	Y	Y	Y	Y
4 ***DeMint***	Y	Y	Y	Y	Y	Y	Y
5 Spratt	Y	Y	Y	Y	Y	N	N
6 Clyburn	Y	Y	Y	Y	Y	N	N
SOUTH DAKOTA							
AL ***Thune***	Y	Y	Y	Y	Y	Y	Y
TENNESSEE							
1 ***Jenkins***	Y	Y	Y	Y	Y	Y	Y
2 ***Duncan***	Y	Y	Y	Y	N	Y	N
3 ***Wamp***	Y	Y	Y	Y	Y	Y	Y
4 ***Hilleary***	Y	Y	Y	Y	Y	Y	Y
5 Clement	Y	Y	Y	Y	Y	N	Y
6 Gordon	Y	Y	Y	Y	Y	N	N
7 ***Bryant***	Y	Y	Y	Y	Y	Y	Y
8 Tanner	Y	Y	Y	Y	Y	N	Y
9 Ford	Y	Y	Y	Y	Y	N	N
TEXAS							
1 Sandlin	Y	Y	Y	Y	Y	N	Y
2 Turner	Y	Y	Y	Y	Y	N	N
3 ***Johnson, Sam***	Y	Y	Y	Y	Y	Y	Y
4 Hall	Y	Y	Y	Y	Y	N	Y
5 ***Sessions***	Y	Y	Y	Y	Y	Y	Y
6 ***Barton***	Y	Y	Y	Y	Y	Y	Y
7 ***Archer***	Y	Y	Y	Y	Y	Y	Y
8 ***Brady***	Y	Y	Y	Y	Y	Y	Y
9 Lampson	Y	Y	Y	Y	Y	N	N
10 Doggett	Y	Y	Y	Y	Y	N	Y
11 Edwards	Y	Y	Y	Y	Y	N	N
12 ***Granger***	Y	Y	Y	Y	Y	Y	Y
13 ***Thornberry***	Y	Y	Y	Y	Y	Y	Y
14 ***Paul***	Y	Y	Y	Y	N	Y	N
15 Hinojosa	Y	Y	Y	Y	Y	N	N
16 Reyes	Y	Y	Y	Y	Y	N	N
17 Stenholm	Y	Y	Y	Y	Y	N	N
18 Jackson-Lee	Y	Y	Y	Y	Y	N	N
19 ***Combest***	Y	Y	Y	Y	Y	Y	Y
20 Gonzalez	Y	Y	Y	Y	Y	N	N
21 ***Smith***	Y	Y	Y	Y	Y	Y	Y
22 ***DeLay***	?	?	?	?	Y	Y	Y
23 ***Bonilla***	Y	Y	Y	Y	Y	Y	N
24 Frost	Y	Y	Y	Y	Y	N	N
25 Bentsen	Y	Y	Y	Y	Y	N	N
26 ***Armey***	Y	Y	Y	Y	Y	Y	Y
27 Ortiz	Y	Y	Y	Y	Y	N	N
28 Rodriguez	Y	Y	Y	Y	Y	N	N
29 Green	Y	Y	Y	Y	Y	N	N
30 Johnson, E.B.	Y	N	Y	Y	Y	N	N
UTAH							
1 ***Hansen***	?	?	?	Y	Y	Y	Y
2 ***Cook***	?	?	?	Y	Y	Y	Y
3 ***Cannon***	Y	Y	Y	Y	Y	Y	Y
VERMONT							
AL *Sanders*	Y	Y	Y	Y	Y	N	N
VIRGINIA							
1 ***Bateman***	?	?	?	P	Y	Y	Y
2 Pickett	Y	Y	Y	Y	Y	N	N
3 Scott	Y	Y	Y	Y	Y	N	N
4 Sisisky	Y	Y	Y	Y	Y	N	Y
5 *Goode*	Y	Y	Y	Y	Y	Y	Y
6 ***Goodlatte***	Y	Y	Y	Y	Y	Y	Y
7 ***Bliley***	Y	Y	Y	Y	Y	Y	Y
8 Moran	Y	Y	Y	Y	Y	N	N
9 Boucher	?	?	?	?	Y	N	Y
10 ***Wolf***	Y	Y	Y	Y	Y	Y	N
11 ***Davis***	Y	Y	Y	Y	Y	Y	Y
WASHINGTON							
1 Inslee	Y	Y	Y	Y	Y	N	Y
2 ***Metcalf***	Y	Y	Y	Y	Y	Y	Y
3 Baird	Y	Y	Y	Y	Y	N	N
4 ***Hastings***	Y	Y	Y	Y	Y	Y	Y
5 ***Nethercutt***	Y	Y	Y	Y	Y	Y	Y
6 Dicks	Y	Y	Y	Y	Y	N	N
7 McDermott	Y	Y	Y	Y	N	N	N
8 ***Dunn***	Y	Y	Y	Y	Y	Y	Y
9 Smith	Y	Y	Y	Y	Y	N	Y
WEST VIRGINIA							
1 Mollohan	Y	Y	Y	P	Y	N	N
2 Wise	Y	Y	Y	Y	Y	N	N
3 Rahall	?	?	?	Y	Y	N	N
WISCONSIN							
1 ***Ryan***	Y	Y	Y	Y	Y	Y	Y
2 Baldwin	Y	Y	Y	Y	Y	N	N
3 Kind	Y	Y	Y	Y	Y	N	Y
4 Kleczka	Y	Y	Y	Y	Y	N	Y
5 Barrett	?	?	?	Y	N	N	N
6 ***Petri***	Y	Y	Y	Y	Y	Y	N
7 Obey	Y	N	Y	Y	Y	N	N
8 ***Green***	Y	Y	Y	Y	Y	Y	Y
9 ***Sensenbrenner***	Y	Y	Y	Y	N	Y	Y
WYOMING							
AL ***Cubin***	Y	Y	Y	Y	Y	Y	Y

Southern states - Ala., Ark., Fla., Ga., Ky., La., Miss., N.C., Okla., S.C., Tenn., Texas, Va.

Key

Y Voted for (yea).
\# Paired for.
\+ Announced for.
N Voted against (nay).
X Paired against.
– Announced against.
P Voted "present."
C Voted "present" to avoid possible conflict of interest.
? Did not vote or otherwise make a position known.

•

Democrats ***Republicans***
Independents

187. HR 853. Budget Process Changes/Government Shutdowns. Gekas, R-Pa., amendment that would automatically enact continuing resolutions to fund programs at the previous year's level when appropriations bills are not enacted by the start of the fiscal year. Rejected 173-236: R 164-48; D 8-187 (ND 5-136, SD 3-51); I 1-1. May 16, 2000. A "nay" was a vote in support of the president's position.

188. HR 853. Budget Process Changes/Budget Functions. Jackson-Lee, D-Texas, amendment that would eliminate a provision in the bill that would move the analysis of budget functions from the budget resolution to the committee report. Rejected 188-225: R 7-207; D 180-17 (ND 130-13, SD 50-4); I 1-1. May 16, 2000.

189. HR 853. Budget Process Changes/Passage. Passage of the bill that would change the budget resolution from a non-binding concurrent resolution to a joint resolution requiring presidential signature and having the force of law. The bill would create an emergency reserve fund at least equal to the average amount spent on emergencies over the past five years. The bill also would limit reauthorization on all programs to 10 years. Rejected 166-250: R 153-63; D 12-186 (ND 8-136, SD 4-50); I 1-1. May 16, 2000.

190. HR 4205. Fiscal 2001 Defense Authorization/Rule. Adoption of the rule (H Res 503) to provide for House floor consideration of the bill to authorize $309.9 billion for defense programs. Adopted 220-201: R 215-0; D 4-200 (ND 4-146, SD 0-54); I 1-1. May 17, 2000.

191. HR 4205. Fiscal 2001 Defense Authorization/Motion to Rise. Taylor, D-Miss., motion to rise from the Committee of the Whole. Motion rejected 204-216: R 0-214; D 203-1 (ND 149-1, SD 54-0); I 1-1. May 17, 2000.

192. HR 4205. Fiscal 2001 Defense Authorization/Motion to Rise. Taylor, D-Miss., motion to rise from the Committee of the Whole. Motion rejected 200-215: R 0-212; D 199-2 (ND 146-2, SD 53-0); I 1-1. May 17, 2000.

193. HR 4205. Fiscal 2001 Defense Authorization/Kosovo Operations. Kasich, R-Ohio, amendment that would withhold the bill's funding authorization for Kosovo operations, unless extenuating circumstances arise, until the president certifies that European nations are meeting specific burden-sharing targets by April 1, 2001. Kosovo funds could be used only for withdrawing U.S. ground forces from Kosovo if the president failed to provide such certification. Adopted 264-153: R 195-18; D 67-135 (ND 49-100, SD 18-35); I 2-0. May 17, 2000. A "nay" was a vote in support of the president's position.

	187	188	189	190	191	192	193
ALABAMA							
1 ***Callahan***	N	N	N	Y	N	N	N
2 ***Everett***	Y	N	N	Y	N	N	Y
3 ***Riley***	Y	?	N	Y	N	N	Y
4 ***Aderholt***	Y	N	Y	Y	N	N	Y
5 Cramer	N	Y	N	N	Y	Y	N
6 ***Bachus***	Y	N	N	Y	N	N	Y
7 Hilliard	N	Y	N	N	Y	Y	N
ALASKA							
AL ***Young***	Y	N	N	Y	N	N	Y
ARIZONA							
1 ***Salmon***	Y	N	Y	Y	N	N	Y
2 Pastor	N	Y	N	N	Y	Y	N
3 ***Stump***	Y	N	N	Y	N	N	N
4 ***Shadegg***	Y	N	Y	Y	N	N	Y
5 ***Kolbe***	N	N	N	Y	N	N	N
6 ***Hayworth***	Y	N	Y	Y	N	N	Y
ARKANSAS							
1 Berry	N	Y	N	N	Y	Y	Y
2 Snyder	N	Y	N	N	Y	Y	N
3 ***Hutchinson***	Y	N	Y	Y	N	N	Y
4 ***Dickey***	N	N	N	Y	N	N	Y
CALIFORNIA							
1 Thompson	N	Y	N	N	Y	Y	Y
2 ***Herger***	Y	N	Y	Y	N	N	?
3 ***Ose***	N	N	N	Y	N	N	Y
4 ***Doolittle***	Y	N	N	Y	N	N	Y
5 Matsui	N	Y	N	N	Y	Y	N
6 Woolsey	N	Y	N	N	Y	Y	Y
7 Miller, George	N	Y	N	N	Y	Y	Y
8 Pelosi	N	Y	N	N	Y	Y	Y
9 Lee	N	Y	N	N	Y	Y	Y
10 Tauscher	N	Y	N	N	Y	Y	N
11 ***Pombo***	Y	N	Y	Y	N	N	Y
12 Lantos	N	Y	N	N	Y	Y	N
13 Stark	N	Y	N	N	Y	Y	Y
14 Eshoo	N	Y	N	N	Y	Y	Y
15 ***Campbell***	?	?	?	?	?	?	?
16 Lofgren	N	Y	N	N	Y	Y	Y
17 Farr	N	Y	N	N	Y	Y	Y
18 Condit	N	N	Y	N	Y	Y	Y
19 ***Radanovich***	Y	N	Y	Y	?	N	Y
20 Dooley	N	Y	N	N	Y	Y	N
21 ***Thomas***	Y	N	Y	Y	N	N	Y
22 Capps	N	Y	N	N	Y	Y	N
23 ***Gallegly***	Y	N	Y	Y	N	N	Y
24 Sherman	N	Y	N	N	Y	Y	Y
25 ***McKeon***	Y	N	Y	Y	N	N	Y
26 Berman	N	Y	N	N	Y	Y	N
27 ***Rogan***	Y	N	Y	Y	N	N	Y
28 ***Dreier***	Y	N	Y	Y	N	N	Y
29 Waxman	N	Y	N	N	Y	Y	N
30 Becerra	N	Y	N	N	Y	Y	Y
31 Martinez	?	?	?	Y	N	N	Y
32 Dixon	N	Y	N	N	Y	Y	N
33 Roybal-Allard	N	Y	N	N	Y	Y	N
34 Napolitano	N	Y	N	N	Y	Y	N
35 Waters	N	Y	N	N	Y	Y	N
36 ***Kuykendall***	N	N	N	Y	N	N	Y
37 Millender-McD.	N	Y	N	N	Y	Y	N
38 ***Horn***	Y	N	Y	Y	N	N	Y
39 ***Royce***	Y	N	Y	Y	N	N	Y
40 ***Lewis***	N	N	N	Y	N	N	N
41 ***Miller, Gary***	Y	N	Y	Y	N	N	Y
42 Baca	N	Y	N	N	Y	Y	N
43 ***Calvert***	N	N	N	Y	N	N	Y
44 ***Bono***	Y	N	Y	Y	N	N	Y
45 ***Rohrabacher***	Y	N	Y	Y	N	N	Y
46 Sanchez	N	Y	N	N	Y	Y	N
47 ***Cox***	Y	N	Y	Y	N	N	Y
48 ***Packard***	N	N	N	Y	N	N	Y
49 ***Bilbray***	Y	Y	Y	Y	N	N	Y
50 Filner	N	Y	N	N	Y	Y	N
51 ***Cunningham***	Y	N	N	Y	N	N	Y
52 ***Hunter***	N	N	N	Y	N	N	N
COLORADO							
1 DeGette	N	Y	N	N	Y	Y	N
2 Udall	N	Y	N	Y	Y	Y	Y
3 ***McInnis***	Y	N	Y	Y	N	N	Y
4 ***Schaffer***	Y	N	Y	Y	N	N	Y
5 ***Hefley***	Y	N	Y	Y	N	N	Y
6 ***Tancredo***	Y	N	Y	Y	N	N	Y
CONNECTICUT							
1 Larson	N	Y	N	N	Y	Y	N
2 Gejdenson	N	Y	N	N	Y	Y	N
3 DeLauro	N	Y	N	N	Y	Y	N
4 ***Shays***	Y	N	Y	Y	N	N	Y
5 Maloney	N	Y	N	N	Y	Y	N
6 ***Johnson***	Y	Y	Y	Y	N	N	Y
DELAWARE							
AL ***Castle***	Y	N	Y	Y	N	N	Y
FLORIDA							
1 ***Scarborough***	Y	N	Y	Y	N	?	Y
2 Boyd	N	Y	N	N	Y	Y	Y
3 Brown	N	Y	N	N	Y	Y	Y
4 ***Fowler***	Y	N	N	Y	N	N	Y
5 Thurman	N	Y	N	N	Y	Y	Y
6 ***Stearns***	Y	N	Y	Y	N	N	Y
7 ***Mica***	Y	N	Y	Y	N	N	Y
8 ***McCollum***	?	?	?	Y	N	N	Y
9 ***Bilirakis***	Y	N	N	Y	?	N	Y
10 ***Young***	N	N	N	Y	N	N	Y
11 Davis	N	Y	N	N	Y	Y	N
12 ***Canady***	Y	N	Y	Y	N	N	Y
13 ***Miller***	Y	N	N	Y	N	N	Y
14 ***Goss***	Y	N	Y	Y	N	N	Y
15 ***Weldon***	Y	N	Y	Y	N	N	Y
16 ***Foley***	Y	N	Y	Y	N	N	Y
17 Meek	N	Y	N	N	Y	Y	Y
18 ***Ros-Lehtinen***	Y	N	Y	Y	N	N	Y
19 Wexler	N	Y	N	N	Y	Y	N
20 Deutsch	N	Y	N	N	Y	Y	Y
21 ***Diaz-Balart***	Y	N	Y	Y	N	N	N
22 ***Shaw***	Y	N	Y	Y	N	N	Y
23 Hastings	N	Y	N	N	Y	Y	N
GEORGIA							
1 ***Kingston***	Y	N	Y	Y	N	N	Y
2 Bishop	N	Y	N	N	Y	Y	Y
3 ***Collins***	N	N	Y	?	N	N	Y
4 McKinney	N	Y	N	N	Y	Y	?
5 Lewis	N	Y	N	N	Y	Y	N
6 ***Isakson***	Y	N	Y	Y	N	N	Y
7 ***Barr***	Y	N	Y	Y	N	N	Y
8 ***Chambliss***	Y	N	Y	Y	N	N	Y
9 ***Deal***	Y	N	Y	Y	N	N	Y
10 ***Norwood***	Y	N	Y	Y	N	N	Y
11 ***Linder***	Y	Y	Y	Y	N	N	Y
HAWAII							
1 Abercrombie	N	Y	N	N	Y	Y	N
2 Mink	N	Y	N	N	Y	Y	Y
IDAHO							
1 ***Chenoweth-Hage***	N	N	N	Y	N	N	Y
2 ***Simpson***	Y	Y	Y	Y	N	N	Y
ILLINOIS							
1 Rush	N	Y	N	N	Y	Y	N
2 Jackson	N	Y	N	N	Y	Y	Y
3 Lipinski	N	Y	N	?	Y	Y	Y
4 Gutierrez	N	Y	N	N	Y	Y	Y
5 Blagojevich	N	Y	N	N	Y	Y	Y
6 ***Hyde***	Y	N	N	Y	N	N	Y
7 Davis	N	Y	N	N	Y	Y	Y
8 ***Crane***	Y	N	Y	Y	N	N	Y
9 Schakowsky	N	Y	N	N	Y	Y	N
10 ***Porter***	Y	N	N	Y	N	N	N
11 ***Weller***	Y	N	Y	Y	N	N	Y
12 Costello	N	Y	N	N	Y	Y	Y
13 ***Biggert***	N	N	N	Y	N	N	Y

ND Northern Democrats SD Southern Democrats

	187	188	189	190	191	192	193
14 ***Hastert***				Y			
15 ***Ewing***	Y	N	Y	Y	N	N	Y
16 ***Manzullo***	N	N	Y	Y	N	N	Y
17 Evans	N	Y	N	N	Y	Y	Y
18 ***LaHood***	Y	N	Y	Y	N	N	Y
19 Phelps	N	Y	N	N	Y	Y	Y
20 ***Shimkus***	Y	N	Y	Y	N	N	Y
INDIANA							
1 Visclosky	N	N	N	N	Y	Y	N
2 ***McIntosh***	?	?	?	?	?	?	?
3 Roemer	N	Y	N	N	Y	Y	Y
4 ***Souder***	Y	N	Y	Y	N	N	Y
5 ***Buyer***	Y	N	Y	Y	N	N	Y
6 ***Burton***	Y	N	Y	Y	N	N	Y
7 ***Pease***	Y	N	Y	Y	N	N	Y
8 ***Hostettler***	Y	N	Y	Y	N	N	Y
9 Hill	N	Y	N	N	Y	Y	N
10 Carson	N	Y	N	N	Y	Y	Y
IOWA							
1 ***Leach***	Y	N	Y	Y	N	N	Y
2 ***Nussle***	Y	N	Y	Y	N	N	Y
3 Boswell	N	Y	N	N	Y	Y	Y
4 ***Ganske***	?	?	Y	Y	N	N	Y
5 ***Latham***	N	N	Y	Y	N	N	Y
KANSAS							
1 ***Moran***	Y	N	Y	Y	N	N	Y
2 ***Ryun***	Y	N	Y	Y	N	N	Y
3 Moore	N	Y	N	N	Y	Y	Y
4 ***Tiahrt***	N	N	N	Y	N	N	Y
KENTUCKY							
1 ***Whitfield***	Y	N	Y	Y	N	N	Y
2 ***Lewis***	Y	N	N	Y	N	N	Y
3 ***Northup***	N	N	N	Y	N	N	Y
4 Lucas	N	Y	Y	N	Y	Y	N
5 ***Rogers***	N	N	N	Y	N	N	Y
6 ***Fletcher***	Y	N	Y	Y	N	N	Y
LOUISIANA							
1 ***Vitter***	Y	N	Y	Y	N	N	Y
2 Jefferson	N	Y	N	N	Y	Y	N
3 ***Tauzin***	Y	N	Y	Y	N	N	Y
4 ***McCrery***	?	N	Y	Y	N	N	Y
5 ***Cooksey***	N	N	Y	Y	N	N	Y
6 ***Baker***	?	N	Y	Y	N	N	Y
7 John	N	Y	N	N	Y	Y	N
MAINE							
1 Allen	N	Y	N	N	Y	Y	N
2 Baldacci	N	Y	N	–	+	+	–
MARYLAND							
1 ***Gilchrest***	N	N	Y	Y	N	N	Y
2 ***Ehrlich***	Y	N	Y	Y	N	N	Y
3 Cardin	N	N	Y	N	Y	Y	N
4 Wynn	Y	Y	N	N	Y	Y	N
5 Hoyer	N	Y	N	N	Y	Y	N
6 ***Bartlett***	Y	N	Y	Y	N	N	Y
7 Cummings	N	Y	N	N	Y	Y	N
8 ***Morella***	Y	N	N	Y	N	N	Y
MASSACHUSETTS							
1 Olver	N	Y	N	N	Y	Y	N
2 Neal	N	Y	N	N	Y	Y	Y
3 McGovern	N	Y	N	N	Y	Y	N
4 Frank	N	Y	N	N	Y	Y	N
5 Meehan	N	Y	Y	N	Y	Y	Y
6 Tierney	N	Y	N	N	Y	Y	Y
7 Markey	N	Y	N	N	Y	?	N
8 Capuano	N	Y	N	N	Y	Y	N
9 Moakley	N	Y	N	N	Y	Y	Y
10 Delahunt	?	Y	N	?	Y	Y	Y
MICHIGAN							
1 Stupak	?	?	?	?	?	?	?
2 ***Hoekstra***	Y	N	Y	Y	N	N	Y
3 ***Ehlers***	Y	Y	N	Y	N	N	Y
4 ***Camp***	Y	N	Y	Y	N	N	Y
5 Barcia	N	Y	N	N	Y	Y	Y
6 ***Upton***	N	N	Y	Y	N	N	Y
7 ***Smith***	Y	N	Y	Y	N	N	Y
8 Stabenow	N	Y	N	N	Y	Y	N
9 Kildee	N	Y	N	N	Y	Y	N
10 Bonior	N	Y	N	N	Y	Y	N
11 ***Knollenberg***	N	N	N	Y	N	N	N
12 Levin	N	Y	N	N	Y	Y	N
13 Rivers	N	N	N	N	Y	Y	Y
14 Conyers	N	Y	N	N	Y	Y	N
15 Kilpatrick	N	Y	N	N	Y	Y	N
16 Dingell	N	Y	N	N	Y	Y	N

	187	188	189	190	191	192	193
MINNESOTA							
1 ***Gutknecht***	Y	N	Y	Y	N	N	Y
2 Minge	Y	N	Y	N	Y	Y	Y
3 ***Ramstad***	Y	N	Y	Y	N	N	Y
4 Vento	N	Y	N	N	Y	Y	N
5 Sabo	N	Y	N	N	Y	Y	N
6 Luther	N	N	Y	N	Y	Y	Y
7 Peterson	N	N	N	N	Y	Y	Y
8 Oberstar	N	N	N	N	Y	Y	N
MISSISSIPPI							
1 ***Wicker***	Y	N	N	Y	N	N	Y
2 Thompson	N	Y	N	N	Y	Y	N
3 ***Pickering***	Y	N	Y	Y	N	N	Y
4 Shows	Y	N	N	N	Y	Y	Y
5 Taylor	Y	N	N	N	Y	Y	N
MISSOURI							
1 Clay	N	Y	N	N	Y	?	N
2 ***Talent***	Y	N	Y	Y	N	N	Y
3 Gephardt	N	Y	N	N	Y	Y	N
4 Skelton	N	Y	N	N	Y	Y	N
5 McCarthy	N	Y	N	N	Y	Y	N
6 Danner	N	N	N	N	Y	Y	Y
7 ***Blunt***	Y	N	Y	Y	N	N	Y
8 ***Emerson***	N	N	N	Y	N	N	Y
9 ***Hulshof***	Y	N	Y	Y	N	N	Y
MONTANA							
AL ***Hill***	Y	N	Y	Y	N	N	Y
NEBRASKA							
1 ***Bereuter***	Y	N	N	Y	N	N	Y
2 ***Terry***	Y	N	Y	Y	N	N	Y
3 ***Barrett***	N	Y	N	Y	N	N	Y
NEVADA							
1 Berkley	N	Y	N	N	Y	Y	N
2 ***Gibbons***	N	N	Y	Y	N	N	Y
NEW HAMPSHIRE							
1 ***Sununu***	Y	N	Y	Y	N	N	Y
2 ***Bass***	Y	N	Y	Y	N	N	Y
NEW JERSEY							
1 Andrews	N	Y	N	N	Y	Y	N
2 ***LoBiondo***	Y	N	Y	Y	N	N	Y
3 ***Saxton***	N	N	Y	Y	N	N	Y
4 ***Smith***	Y	N	Y	Y	N	N	Y
5 ***Roukema***	Y	N	Y	Y	N	N	Y
6 Pallone	N	Y	N	N	Y	Y	N
7 ***Franks***	Y	N	Y	Y	N	N	Y
8 Pascrell	N	Y	N	N	Y	Y	N
9 Rothman	N	Y	N	N	?	Y	N
10 Payne	N	Y	N	N	Y	Y	N
11 ***Frelinghuysen***	N	N	Y	Y	N	N	Y
12 Holt	N	Y	N	N	Y	Y	N
13 Menendez	N	Y	N	N	Y	Y	N
NEW MEXICO							
1 ***Wilson***	Y	N	Y	Y	N	N	Y
2 ***Skeen***	N	N	N	Y	N	N	Y
3 Udall	?	?	?	?	?	?	?
NEW YORK							
1 Forbes	Y	Y	N	N	Y	Y	N
2 ***Lazio***	Y	N	Y	Y	N	N	Y
3 ***King***	Y	N	N	Y	N	N	N
4 McCarthy	N	Y	N	N	Y	Y	N
5 Ackerman	?	?	?	N	Y	Y	N
6 Meeks	?	?	?	N	Y	Y	N
7 Crowley	N	Y	N	–	+	+	–
8 Nadler	?	?	?	N	Y	Y	N
9 Weiner	N	Y	N	N	Y	Y	N
10 Towns	N	Y	N	N	Y	Y	N
11 Owens	?	?	?	N	Y	Y	N
12 Velázquez	N	Y	N	N	Y	Y	N
13 ***Fossella***	Y	N	Y	Y	N	N	N
14 Maloney	?	?	?	N	Y	Y	N
15 Rangel	?	?	?	N	Y	Y	N
16 Serrano	?	?	?	N	Y	Y	N
17 Engel	?	?	?	N	Y	Y	N
18 Lowey	?	?	?	N	Y	Y	N
19 ***Kelly***	Y	N	N	Y	N	N	N
20 ***Gilman***	N	N	N	Y	N	N	N
21 McNulty	?	?	?	N	Y	Y	N
22 ***Sweeney***	Y	N	Y	Y	N	N	Y
23 ***Boehlert***	Y	N	N	Y	N	N	N
24 ***McHugh***	Y	N	Y	Y	N	N	Y
25 ***Walsh***	N	N	N	Y	N	N	Y
26 Hinchey	N	Y	N	N	Y	Y	N
27 ***Reynolds***	Y	N	Y	Y	N	N	Y
28 Slaughter	–	Y	N	N	Y	+	N
29 LaFalce	N	Y	N	N	Y	Y	?

	187	188	189	190	191	192	193
30 ***Quinn***	Y	N	N	Y	N	N	Y
31 ***Houghton***	Y	N	Y	Y	N	N	N
NORTH CAROLINA							
1 Clayton	N	Y	N	N	Y	Y	Y
2 Etheridge	N	Y	N	N	Y	Y	N
3 ***Jones***	Y	N	Y	Y	N	N	Y
4 Price	N	Y	N	N	Y	Y	N
5 ***Burr***	Y	N	Y	Y	N	N	Y
6 ***Coble***	Y	N	Y	Y	N	N	Y
7 McIntyre	N	Y	N	N	Y	Y	N
8 ***Hayes***	N	N	Y	Y	N	N	Y
9 ***Myrick***	Y	N	Y	Y	N	N	Y
10 ***Ballenger***	Y	N	Y	Y	N	?	?
11 ***Taylor***	N	N	N	Y	N	N	Y
12 Watt	N	Y	N	N	Y	Y	Y
NORTH DAKOTA							
AL Pomeroy	N	Y	N	N	Y	?	N
OHIO							
1 ***Chabot***	Y	N	Y	Y	N	N	Y
2 ***Portman***	N	N	Y	Y	N	N	Y
3 Hall	Y	Y	N	N	Y	Y	?
4 ***Oxley***	?	N	Y	Y	N	N	Y
5 ***Gillmor***	Y	N	N	Y	N	N	Y
6 Strickland	N	Y	N	N	Y	Y	N
7 ***Hobson***	N	N	N	Y	N	N	N
8 ***Boehner***	N	N	N	Y	N	N	Y
9 Kaptur	N	?	N	N	Y	Y	N
10 Kucinich	N	Y	N	N	Y	Y	Y
11 Jones	N	Y	N	N	Y	Y	N
12 ***Kasich***	Y	N	Y	Y	N	N	Y
13 Brown	N	Y	N	N	Y	Y	Y
14 Sawyer	N	Y	N	N	Y	Y	N
15 ***Pryce***	N	N	Y	Y	N	N	Y
16 ***Regula***	N	N	N	Y	N	N	Y
17 Traficant	N	N	N	Y	Y	N	Y
18 ***Ney***	Y	N	N	Y	N	?	Y
19 ***LaTourette***	Y	N	N	Y	N	N	Y
OKLAHOMA							
1 ***Largent***	?	?	?	?	?	?	?
2 ***Coburn***	Y	N	Y	?	?	?	?
3 ***Watkins***	N	N	N	Y	N	N	Y
4 ***Watts***	N	N	Y	Y	N	N	Y
5 ***Istook***	Y	N	N	Y	N	N	Y
6 ***Lucas***	Y	N	Y	Y	N	N	Y
OREGON							
1 Wu	N	Y	N	N	Y	Y	Y
2 ***Walden***	Y	N	Y	Y	N	N	Y
3 Blumenauer	N	Y	N	N	Y	Y	N
4 DeFazio	N	Y	Y	N	Y	Y	Y
5 Hooley	N	Y	N	N	Y	Y	Y
PENNSYLVANIA							
1 Brady	N	Y	N	N	Y	Y	N
2 Fattah	N	Y	N	N	Y	Y	N
3 Borski	N	Y	N	N	Y	Y	N
4 Klink	N	Y	N	N	Y	Y	N
5 ***Peterson***	Y	N	Y	Y	N	N	Y
6 Holden	N	Y	N	N	Y	Y	N
7 ***Weldon***	Y	N	N	Y	N	N	Y
8 ***Greenwood***	Y	N	Y	Y	N	N	Y
9 ***Shuster***	Y	N	N	Y	N	N	Y
10 ***Sherwood***	N	N	N	Y	N	N	Y
11 Kanjorski	N	N	N	N	Y	Y	N
12 Murtha	N	N	N	N	Y	Y	N
13 Hoeffel	N	Y	N	N	Y	Y	N
14 Coyne	N	Y	N	N	Y	Y	N
15 ***Toomey***	Y	N	Y	Y	N	N	Y
16 ***Pitts***	Y	N	Y	Y	N	N	Y
17 ***Gekas***	Y	N	Y	Y	N	N	Y
18 Doyle	N	Y	N	?	?	?	?
19 ***Goodling***	Y	N	Y	Y	N	N	Y
20 Mascara	N	Y	N	N	Y	Y	N
21 ***English***	Y	N	Y	Y	N	N	Y
RHODE ISLAND							
1 Kennedy	N	Y	N	N	Y	Y	N
2 Weygand	N	Y	N	N	Y	Y	N
SOUTH CAROLINA							
1 ***Sanford***	Y	N	Y	Y	N	?	?
2 ***Spence***	N	N	N	Y	N	N	Y
3 ***Graham***	Y	N	Y	Y	N	N	Y
4 ***DeMint***	Y	N	Y	Y	N	N	Y
5 Spratt	N	Y	N	N	Y	Y	N
6 Clyburn	N	Y	N	N	Y	Y	N
SOUTH DAKOTA							
AL ***Thune***	Y	N	Y	Y	N	N	Y

	187	188	189	190	191	192	193
TENNESSEE							
1 ***Jenkins***	Y	N	Y	Y	N	N	Y
2 ***Duncan***	Y	N	N	Y	N	N	Y
3 ***Wamp***	N	N	Y	?	?	?	?
4 ***Hilleary***	Y	N	Y	Y	N	N	Y
5 Clement	N	Y	N	N	Y	Y	N
6 Gordon	N	Y	N	N	Y	Y	Y
7 ***Bryant***	Y	N	Y	Y	N	N	Y
8 Tanner	N	Y	Y	N	Y	Y	Y
9 Ford	N	Y	N	N	Y	Y	Y
TEXAS							
1 Sandlin	N	Y	N	N	Y	Y	N
2 Turner	N	Y	N	N	Y	Y	N
3 ***Johnson, Sam***	Y	N	Y	Y	N	N	Y
4 Hall	N	Y	N	N	Y	Y	Y
5 ***Sessions***	Y	N	Y	Y	N	N	Y
6 ***Barton***	Y	N	Y	Y	N	N	Y
7 ***Archer***	Y	N	Y	Y	N	N	Y
8 ***Brady***	Y	N	Y	Y	N	N	Y
9 Lampson	N	Y	N	N	Y	Y	N
10 Doggett	Y	Y	Y	N	Y	Y	Y
11 Edwards	N	Y	N	N	Y	Y	N
12 ***Granger***	N	N	N	Y	N	N	Y
13 ***Thornberry***	N	N	Y	Y	N	N	Y
14 ***Paul***	N	Y	N	Y	N	N	Y
15 Hinojosa	N	Y	N	N	Y	Y	N
16 Reyes	N	Y	N	N	Y	Y	N
17 Stenholm	N	N	Y	N	Y	Y	N
18 Jackson-Lee	N	Y	N	N	Y	Y	N
19 ***Combest***	Y	N	Y	Y	N	N	Y
20 Gonzalez	N	Y	N	N	Y	Y	N
21 ***Smith***	Y	N	Y	Y	N	N	Y
22 ***DeLay***	N	N	Y	Y	N	N	Y
23 ***Bonilla***	N	N	N	Y	N	N	N
24 Frost	N	Y	N	N	Y	?	N
25 Bentsen	N	Y	N	N	Y	Y	N
26 ***Armey***	Y	N	Y	Y	N	N	Y
27 Ortiz	N	Y	N	N	Y	Y	N
28 Rodriguez	N	Y	N	N	Y	Y	Y
29 Green	N	Y	N	N	Y	Y	Y
30 Johnson, E.B.	N	Y	N	N	Y	Y	N
UTAH							
1 ***Hansen***	Y	N	Y	Y	N	N	Y
2 ***Cook***	Y	N	N	Y	N	N	Y
3 ***Cannon***	Y	N	Y	Y	N	N	Y
VERMONT							
AL *Sanders*	N	Y	N	N	Y	Y	Y
VIRGINIA							
1 ***Bateman***	Y	N	N	Y	N	N	Y
2 Pickett	N	N	N	N	Y	Y	N
3 Scott	N	Y	N	N	Y	Y	N
4 Sisisky	N	Y	N	N	Y	Y	N
5 *Goode*	Y	N	Y	Y	N	N	Y
6 ***Goodlatte***	Y	N	Y	Y	N	N	Y
7 ***Bliley***	?	?	?	Y	N	N	N
8 Moran	N	Y	N	N	Y	Y	N
9 Boucher	N	Y	N	N	Y	Y	Y
10 ***Wolf***	N	N	N	Y	N	N	N
11 ***Davis***	Y	N	Y	?	N	N	Y
WASHINGTON							
1 Inslee	N	Y	Y	N	Y	Y	Y
2 ***Metcalf***	Y	N	Y	Y	N	N	Y
3 Baird	N	Y	N	Y	Y	Y	N
4 ***Hastings***	Y	N	Y	Y	N	N	Y
5 ***Nethercutt***	Y	N	Y	Y	N	N	Y
6 Dicks	N	Y	N	N	Y	Y	N
7 McDermott	N	Y	N	N	Y	Y	N
8 ***Dunn***	Y	N	Y	Y	N	N	Y
9 Smith	N	Y	Y	N	Y	Y	N
WEST VIRGINIA							
1 Mollohan	N	N	N	N	Y	Y	N
2 Wise	N	Y	N	N	?	Y	?
3 Rahall	N	Y	N	N	Y	Y	N
WISCONSIN							
1 ***Ryan***	Y	N	Y	Y	N	N	Y
2 Baldwin	N	Y	N	N	Y	Y	Y
3 Kind	N	Y	N	N	Y	Y	N
4 Kleczka	Y	Y	N	N	Y	Y	Y
5 Barrett	?	Y	N	N	Y	Y	Y
6 ***Petri***	Y	N	Y	Y	N	N	Y
7 Obey	N	Y	N	N	Y	Y	N
8 ***Green***	Y	N	Y	Y	N	N	Y
9 ***Sensenbrenner***	Y	N	Y	Y	N	N	Y
WYOMING							
AL ***Cubin***	Y	N	N	Y	N	N	Y

Southern states - Ala., Ark., Fla., Ga., Ky., La., Miss., N.C., Okla., S.C., Tenn., Texas, Va.

194. HR 4205. Fiscal 2001 Defense Authorization/One-Percent Reduction. Frank, D-Mass., amendment that would reduce the bill's total authorization by 1 percent. No cuts could be made in the operations and maintenance accounts or from personnel accounts. Rejected 88-331: R 14-201; D 73-129 (ND 67-82, SD 6-47); I 1-1. May 18, 2000.

195. HR 4205. Fiscal 2001 Defense Authorization/Congressional Waiting Period. Dreier, R-Calif., amendment that would shorten the waiting period from 180 days to 60 days for Congress to review a proposed adjustment in the performance level that defines high-speed computers and would exclude any days in which the House or Senate is in sine die adjournment. Adopted 415-8: R 211-5; D 202-3 (ND 150-2, SD 52-1); I 2-0. May 18, 2000.

196. HR 4205. Fiscal 2001 Defense Authorization/Missile Production. Luther, D-Minn., amendment that would end Trident II (D-5) submarine-launched ballistic missile production and terminate the program after fiscal year 2002. Rejected 112-313: R 16-199; D 95-113 (ND 87-67, SD 8-46); I 1-1. May 18, 2000.

197. HR 4205. Fiscal 2001 Defense Authorization/Military Border Patrols. Traficant, D-Ohio, amendment that would allow the Defense Department to assign military patrols to the Immigration and Naturalization Service and Customs Service for the purpose of monitoring U.S. borders. The attorney general could request the assistance to prevent terrorists and drug traffickers from entering the United States. The Treasury Department could request assistance for inspecting cargo, vehicles and aircraft. Adopted 243-183: R 184-31; D 58-151 (ND 39-116, SD 19-35); I 1-1. May 18, 2000.

198. HR 4205. Fiscal 2001 Defense Authorization/Health Coverage. Stearns, R-Fla., amendment that would require the Defense Department to conduct a study comparing its health care program's physical, speech and occupational therapy coverage and reimbursement with that available in the plan for federal civilian employees. Adopted 426-0: R 218-0; D 206-0 (ND 153-0, SD 53-0); I 2-0. May 18, 2000.

199. HR 4205. Fiscal 2001 Defense Authorization/Military Property. Sanford, R-S.C., amendment that would prohibit the Defense Department from offering military property to local governments at prices below fair market price. Rejected 56-368: R 45-171; D 11-195 (ND 11-141, SD 0-54); I 0-2. May 18, 2000.

200. HR 4205. Fiscal 2001 Defense Authorization/Previous Question. Sessions, R-Texas, motion to order the previous question (thus ending debate and possibility of amendment) on adoption of the rule (H Res 504) to provide for House floor consideration of the bill that would authorize $309.9 billion for defense programs. Motion agreed to 226-200: R 219-0; D 6-199 (ND 3-148, SD 3-51); I 1-1. May 18, 2000.

Key

- Y Voted for (yea).
- # Paired for.
- \+ Announced for.
- N Voted against (nay).
- X Paired against.
- – Announced against.
- P Voted "present."
- C Voted "present" to avoid possible conflict of interest.
- ? Did not vote or otherwise make a position known.

•

Democrats ***Republicans***
Independents

	194	195	196	197	198	199	200
ALABAMA							
1 ***Callahan***	N	Y	N	Y	Y	N	Y
2 ***Everett***	N	Y	N	Y	Y	N	Y
3 ***Riley***	N	Y	N	Y	Y	N	Y
4 ***Aderholt***	N	Y	N	Y	Y	N	Y
5 Cramer	N	Y	N	Y	Y	N	N
6 ***Bachus***	N	Y	N	Y	Y	N	Y
7 Hilliard	N	Y	N	Y	Y	N	N
ALASKA							
AL ***Young***	?	?	?	Y	Y	N	Y
ARIZONA							
1 ***Salmon***	?	?	?	?	?	?	?
2 Pastor	N	Y	N	N	Y	N	N
3 ***Stump***	N	Y	N	N	Y	N	Y
4 ***Shadegg***	N	Y	N	Y	Y	Y	Y
5 ***Kolbe***	N	Y	N	N	Y	N	Y
6 ***Hayworth***	N	N	N	N	Y	N	Y
ARKANSAS							
1 Berry	N	Y	N	N	Y	N	N
2 Snyder	N	Y	N	N	Y	N	N
3 ***Hutchinson***	N	Y	?	Y	Y	N	Y
4 ***Dickey***	N	Y	N	Y	Y	N	Y
CALIFORNIA							
1 Thompson	N	Y	Y	N	Y	N	N
2 ***Herger***	N	Y	N	Y	Y	N	Y
3 ***Ose***	N	Y	N	N	Y	N	Y
4 ***Doolittle***	N	Y	N	?	Y	N	Y
5 Matsui	N	Y	N	N	Y	N	N
6 Woolsey	Y	Y	Y	N	Y	N	N
7 Miller, George	Y	Y	Y	N	Y	N	N
8 Pelosi	Y	Y	Y	N	Y	N	N
9 Lee	Y	Y	Y	N	Y	N	N
10 Tauscher	N	Y	N	Y	Y	N	N
11 ***Pombo***	N	Y	N	Y	Y	N	Y
12 Lantos	N	Y	N	N	Y	N	N
13 Stark	Y	Y	Y	N	Y	Y	N
14 Eshoo	Y	Y	Y	N	Y	N	N
15 ***Campbell***	?	?	?	?	?	?	?
16 Lofgren	Y	Y	Y	N	Y	N	N
17 Farr	N	Y	Y	N	Y	N	N
18 Condit	N	Y	N	N	Y	N	N
19 ***Radanovich***	N	Y	N	Y	Y	N	Y
20 Dooley	N	Y	N	N	Y	N	N
21 ***Thomas***	N	Y	N	Y	Y	N	Y
22 Capps	N	Y	Y	N	Y	N	N
23 ***Gallegly***	N	Y	N	Y	Y	N	Y
24 Sherman	N	Y	Y	N	Y	Y	N
25 ***McKeon***	N	Y	N	Y	Y	N	Y
26 Berman	Y	Y	Y	N	Y	N	N
27 ***Rogan***	N	Y	N	Y	Y	Y	Y
28 ***Dreier***	N	Y	N	N	Y	N	Y
29 Waxman	Y	Y	Y	N	Y	N	N
30 Becerra	Y	Y	Y	N	Y	N	N
31 Martinez	N	Y	N	Y	Y	N	Y
32 Dixon	N	Y	N	N	Y	N	?
33 Roybal-Allard	Y	Y	N	N	Y	N	N
34 Napolitano	N	Y	Y	N	Y	N	N
35 Waters	Y	Y	?	N	Y	N	N
36 ***Kuykendall***	N	Y	N	Y	Y	N	Y
37 Millender-McD.	Y	Y	N	N	Y	N	N
38 ***Horn***	N	Y	N	Y	Y	Y	Y
39 ***Royce***	Y	Y	N	Y	Y	Y	Y
40 ***Lewis***	N	Y	N	Y	Y	N	Y
41 ***Miller, Gary***	N	Y	N	Y	Y	N	Y
42 Baca	N	Y	N	N	Y	N	N
43 ***Calvert***	N	Y	N	Y	Y	N	Y
44 ***Bono***	N	Y	N	Y	Y	N	Y
45 ***Rohrabacher***	N	Y	Y	Y	Y	Y	Y
46 Sanchez	Y	Y	N	N	Y	N	N
47 ***Cox***	N	Y	N	N	Y	Y	Y
48 ***Packard***	N	Y	N	Y	Y	Y	Y
49 ***Bilbray***	N	Y	N	Y	Y	N	Y
50 Filner	Y	Y	Y	N	Y	N	N
51 ***Cunningham***	N	Y	Y	Y	Y	N	Y
52 ***Hunter***	N	N	N	Y	Y	Y	Y
COLORADO							
1 DeGette	Y	Y	Y	N	Y	N	N
2 Udall	Y	Y	Y	N	Y	N	N
3 ***McInnis***	N	Y	N	Y	Y	N	Y
4 ***Schaffer***	N	Y	N	Y	Y	Y	Y
5 ***Hefley***	N	Y	N	Y	Y	N	Y
6 ***Tancredo***	N	Y	N	Y	Y	Y	Y
CONNECTICUT							
1 Larson	N	Y	N	N	Y	N	N
2 Gejdenson	N	Y	N	N	Y	N	N
3 DeLauro	N	Y	N	N	Y	N	N
4 ***Shays***	Y	Y	Y	Y	Y	N	Y
5 Maloney	N	Y	N	Y	Y	N	N
6 ***Johnson***	N	Y	N	Y	Y	N	Y
DELAWARE							
AL ***Castle***	N	Y	N	Y	Y	N	Y
FLORIDA							
1 ***Scarborough***	N	Y	N	Y	Y	N	Y
2 Boyd	N	Y	N	Y	Y	N	Y
3 Brown	N	Y	N	N	Y	N	N
4 ***Fowler***	N	Y	N	Y	Y	N	Y
5 Thurman	N	Y	N	Y	Y	N	N
6 ***Stearns***	N	Y	N	Y	Y	Y	Y
7 ***Mica***	N	Y	N	Y	Y	N	Y
8 ***McCollum***	N	Y	N	Y	Y	N	Y
9 ***Bilirakis***	N	Y	N	Y	Y	N	Y
10 ***Young***	N	Y	N	Y	Y	N	Y
11 Davis	N	Y	N	N	Y	N	N
12 ***Canady***	N	Y	N	Y	Y	N	Y
13 ***Miller***	N	Y	N	Y	Y	Y	Y
14 ***Goss***	N	Y	N	Y	Y	N	Y
15 ***Weldon***	N	Y	N	Y	Y	N	Y
16 ***Foley***	N	Y	N	Y	Y	Y	Y
17 Meek	?	?	N	N	Y	N	N
18 ***Ros-Lehtinen***	N	Y	N	Y	Y	N	Y
19 Wexler	N	Y	N	Y	Y	N	N
20 Deutsch	N	Y	N	Y	Y	N	N
21 ***Diaz-Balart***	N	Y	N	Y	Y	N	Y
22 ***Shaw***	N	Y	N	Y	Y	N	Y
23 Hastings	N	Y	N	N	Y	N	N
GEORGIA							
1 ***Kingston***	N	Y	N	Y	Y	Y	Y
2 Bishop	N	Y	N	Y	Y	N	Y
3 ***Collins***	N	Y	N	Y	Y	N	Y
4 McKinney	Y	Y	Y	N	Y	N	N
5 Lewis	Y	Y	Y	N	Y	N	N
6 ***Isakson***	N	Y	N	Y	Y	N	Y
7 ***Barr***	N	Y	N	Y	Y	N	Y
8 ***Chambliss***	N	Y	N	Y	Y	N	Y
9 ***Deal***	N	Y	N	Y	Y	N	Y
10 ***Norwood***	N	Y	N	Y	Y	N	Y
11 ***Linder***	N	Y	N	N	Y	Y	Y
HAWAII							
1 Abercrombie	N	Y	N	N	Y	N	N
2 Mink	N	Y	Y	N	Y	N	N
IDAHO							
1 ***Chenoweth-Hage***	N	Y	N	N	Y	Y	Y
2 ***Simpson***	N	Y	N	Y	Y	N	Y
ILLINOIS							
1 Rush	Y	Y	Y	N	Y	N	N
2 Jackson	Y	Y	Y	N	Y	N	N
3 Lipinski	N	Y	N	Y	Y	N	N
4 Gutierrez	Y	Y	Y	N	Y	N	N
5 Blagojevich	N	Y	N	N	Y	N	N
6 ***Hyde***	N	Y	N	Y	Y	N	Y
7 Davis	Y	Y	Y	N	Y	N	N
8 ***Crane***	N	Y	N	Y	Y	Y	Y
9 Schakowsky	Y	Y	Y	N	Y	N	N
10 ***Porter***	N	Y	Y	Y	Y	N	Y
11 ***Weller***	N	Y	N	Y	Y	?	Y
12 Costello	N	Y	N	Y	Y	N	N
13 ***Biggert***	N	Y	N	Y	Y	N	Y

ND Northern Democrats SD Southern Democrats

	194	195	196	197	198	199	200
14 ***Hastert***							
15 ***Ewing***	N	Y	N	N	Y	N	Y
16 ***Manzullo***	N	Y	N	Y	Y	N	Y
17 Evans	N	Y	Y	N	Y	N	N
18 ***LaHood***	N	Y	N	Y	Y	N	Y
19 Phelps	N	Y	N	Y	Y	N	N
20 ***Shimkus***	N	Y	N	Y	Y	N	Y
INDIANA							
1 Visclosky	N	Y	N	N	Y	N	N
2 ***McIntosh***	N	Y	N	Y	Y	N	Y
3 Roemer	N	Y	Y	Y	Y	N	N
4 ***Souder***	N	Y	N	Y	Y	N	Y
5 ***Buyer***	N	Y	N	?	Y	N	Y
6 ***Burton***	N	Y	N	Y	Y	N	Y
7 ***Pease***	N	Y	N	Y	Y	N	Y
8 ***Hostettler***	N	N	N	Y	Y	Y	Y
9 Hill	N	Y	N	N	Y	N	N
10 Carson	N	Y	Y	N	Y	N	N
IOWA							
1 ***Leach***	?	?	?	?	?	?	Y
2 ***Nussle***	N	Y	Y	Y	Y	N	Y
3 Boswell	N	Y	N	Y	Y	N	N
4 ***Ganske***	Y	N	N	N	Y	Y	Y
5 ***Latham***	N	Y	N	Y	Y	N	Y
KANSAS							
1 ***Moran***	N	Y	N	Y	Y	N	Y
2 ***Ryun***	N	Y	N	Y	Y	N	Y
3 Moore	N	Y	N	N	Y	N	N
4 ***Tiahrt***	N	Y	N	Y	Y	Y	Y
KENTUCKY							
1 ***Whitfield***	N	Y	N	N	Y	N	Y
2 ***Lewis***	N	Y	N	Y	Y	N	Y
3 ***Northup***	N	Y	N	Y	Y	Y	Y
4 Lucas	N	Y	N	Y	Y	N	N
5 ***Rogers***	N	Y	N	Y	Y	N	Y
6 ***Fletcher***	N	Y	N	Y	Y	N	Y
LOUISIANA							
1 ***Vitter***	N	Y	N	N	Y	Y	Y
2 Jefferson	N	Y	N	N	Y	N	N
3 ***Tauzin***	N	Y	N	Y	Y	N	Y
4 ***McCrery***	N	Y	N	Y	Y	N	Y
5 ***Cooksey***	N	Y	N	Y	Y	N	Y
6 ***Baker***	N	Y	N	Y	Y	N	Y
7 John	N	Y	N	N	Y	N	N
MAINE							
1 Allen	N	Y	Y	N	Y	N	N
2 Baldacci	N	Y	N	N	Y	N	N
MARYLAND							
1 ***Gilchrest***	N	Y	N	Y	Y	N	Y
2 ***Ehrlich***	N	Y	N	N	Y	N	Y
3 Cardin	N	Y	Y	N	Y	N	N
4 Wynn	N	Y	N	N	Y	N	N
5 Hoyer	–	+	N	N	Y	N	N
6 ***Bartlett***	N	Y	N	Y	Y	N	Y
7 Cummings	N	Y	Y	N	Y	N	N
8 ***Morella***	Y	Y	Y	N	Y	N	Y
MASSACHUSETTS							
1 Olver	Y	Y	N	N	Y	N	N
2 Neal	Y	Y	Y	N	Y	N	N
3 McGovern	Y	Y	Y	N	Y	Y	N
4 Frank	Y	Y	Y	N	Y	N	N
5 Meehan	Y	Y	Y	N	Y	N	N
6 Tierney	Y	Y	Y	N	Y	N	N
7 Markey	?	Y	Y	N	Y	N	N
8 Capuano	Y	Y	Y	N	Y	Y	N
9 Moakley	N	Y	N	Y	Y	N	N
10 Delahunt	Y	Y	Y	N	?	?	N
MICHIGAN							
1 Stupak	?	?	?	?	?	?	?
2 ***Hoekstra***	Y	Y	Y	N	Y	Y	Y
3 ***Ehlers***	Y	Y	Y	N	Y	Y	Y
4 ***Camp***	N	Y	N	Y	Y	N	Y
5 Barcia	N	Y	N	Y	Y	N	Y
6 ***Upton***	Y	Y	Y	Y	Y	Y	Y
7 ***Smith***	Y	Y	N	N	Y	Y	Y
8 Stabenow	N	Y	Y	Y	Y	N	N
9 Kildee	N	Y	N	Y	Y	N	N
10 Bonior	Y	Y	Y	N	Y	N	N
11 ***Knollenberg***	N	Y	N	Y	Y	N	Y
12 Levin	N	Y	Y	Y	Y	N	N
13 Rivers	Y	Y	Y	Y	Y	N	N
14 Conyers	Y	Y	Y	N	Y	Y	N
15 Kilpatrick	Y	Y	N	Y	Y	N	N
16 Dingell	Y	Y	N	N	Y	N	N
MINNESOTA							
1 ***Gutknecht***	N	Y	N	Y	Y	N	Y
2 Minge	Y	Y	Y	N	Y	Y	N
3 ***Ramstad***	Y	Y	Y	Y	Y	Y	Y
4 Vento	Y	Y	Y	N	Y	Y	N
5 Sabo	N	Y	Y	N	Y	N	N
6 Luther	Y	Y	Y	Y	Y	N	N
7 Peterson	N	Y	Y	Y	Y	?	N
8 Oberstar	Y	Y	Y	N	Y	N	?
MISSISSIPPI							
1 ***Wicker***	N	Y	N	Y	Y	N	Y
2 Thompson	N	Y	N	N	Y	N	N
3 ***Pickering***	N	Y	N	Y	Y	N	Y
4 Shows	N	Y	N	Y	Y	N	N
5 Taylor	N	N	N	N	Y	N	Y
MISSOURI							
1 Clay	Y	Y	Y	N	Y	N	N
2 ***Talent***	N	Y	N	Y	Y	N	Y
3 Gephardt	Y	Y	Y	Y	Y	N	N
4 Skelton	N	Y	N	N	Y	N	N
5 McCarthy	N	Y	Y	N	Y	N	N
6 Danner	N	Y	N	N	Y	N	N
7 ***Blunt***	N	Y	N	Y	Y	N	Y
8 ***Emerson***	N	Y	N	Y	Y	N	Y
9 ***Hulshof***	N	Y	N	Y	Y	N	Y
MONTANA							
AL ***Hill***	N	Y	N	Y	Y	N	Y
NEBRASKA							
1 ***Bereuter***	N	Y	N	N	Y	N	Y
2 ***Terry***	N	Y	N	N	Y	N	Y
3 ***Barrett***	N	Y	N	Y	Y	N	Y
NEVADA							
1 Berkley	N	Y	N	N	Y	N	N
2 ***Gibbons***	N	Y	N	Y	Y	N	Y
NEW HAMPSHIRE							
1 ***Sununu***	N	Y	N	Y	Y	Y	Y
2 ***Bass***	N	Y	N	Y	Y	N	Y
NEW JERSEY							
1 Andrews	N	Y	N	N	Y	N	N
2 ***LoBiondo***	N	Y	N	Y	Y	N	Y
3 ***Saxton***	N	Y	N	Y	Y	N	Y
4 ***Smith***	N	Y	N	Y	Y	N	Y
5 ***Roukema***	N	Y	N	Y	Y	N	Y
6 Pallone	N	Y	Y	Y	Y	N	N
7 ***Franks***	N	Y	N	Y	Y	N	Y
8 Pascrell	N	Y	N	Y	Y	N	N
9 Rothman	N	N	N	N	Y	N	N
10 Payne	Y	N	Y	N	Y	N	N
11 ***Frelinghuysen***	N	Y	N	Y	Y	N	Y
12 Holt	Y	Y	Y	N	Y	N	N
13 Menendez	N	Y	Y	N	Y	N	N
NEW MEXICO							
1 ***Wilson***	N	Y	N	Y	Y	N	Y
2 ***Skeen***	N	Y	N	Y	Y	N	Y
3 Udall	?	?	?	?	?	?	?
NEW YORK							
1 Forbes	N	Y	N	Y	Y	N	N
2 ***Lazio***	N	Y	N	Y	Y	N	Y
3 ***King***	N	Y	N	Y	Y	N	Y
4 McCarthy	N	Y	N	Y	Y	N	N
5 Ackerman	N	Y	N	N	Y	N	N
6 Meeks	N	Y	Y	N	Y	N	N
7 Crowley	Y	Y	N	N	Y	N	N
8 Nadler	Y	Y	Y	N	Y	N	N
9 Weiner	Y	Y	Y	N	Y	N	N
10 Towns	Y	Y	Y	N	Y	N	N
11 Owens	Y	Y	Y	N	Y	N	?
12 Velázquez	Y	Y	Y	N	Y	N	N
13 ***Fossella***	?	Y	N	Y	Y	N	Y
14 Maloney	N	Y	Y	N	Y	?	N
15 Rangel	Y	Y	Y	N	Y	N	N
16 Serrano	N	Y	Y	N	Y	N	N
17 Engel	Y	Y	N	Y	Y	N	N
18 Lowey	Y	Y	Y	Y	Y	N	N
19 ***Kelly***	N	Y	N	Y	Y	N	Y
20 ***Gilman***	N	Y	N	Y	Y	N	Y
21 McNulty	N	Y	N	Y	Y	N	N
22 ***Sweeney***	N	Y	N	Y	Y	N	Y
23 ***Boehlert***	N	Y	N	Y	Y	N	Y
24 ***McHugh***	N	Y	N	Y	Y	N	Y
25 ***Walsh***	N	Y	N	Y	Y	N	Y
26 Hinchey	Y	Y	Y	N	Y	N	N
27 ***Reynolds***	N	Y	N	Y	Y	N	Y
28 Slaughter	?	Y	Y	N	?	N	N
29 LaFalce	N	Y	N	Y	Y	N	N
30 ***Quinn***	N	Y	N	Y	Y	N	Y
31 ***Houghton***	N	Y	N	N	Y	N	Y
NORTH CAROLINA							
1 Clayton	N	Y	N	N	Y	N	N
2 Etheridge	N	Y	N	Y	Y	N	N
3 ***Jones***	N	Y	N	Y	Y	N	Y
4 Price	N	Y	Y	Y	Y	N	N
5 ***Burr***	N	Y	N	N	Y	N	Y
6 ***Coble***	N	Y	N	Y	Y	N	Y
7 McIntyre	N	Y	N	Y	Y	N	N
8 ***Hayes***	N	Y	N	N	Y	N	Y
9 ***Myrick***	N	Y	N	Y	Y	N	Y
10 ***Ballenger***	N	Y	N	Y	Y	N	Y
11 ***Taylor***	N	Y	N	Y	Y	N	Y
12 Watt	Y	Y	Y	N	Y	N	N
NORTH DAKOTA							
AL Pomeroy	N	Y	Y	N	Y	N	?
OHIO							
1 ***Chabot***	N	Y	N	Y	Y	Y	Y
2 ***Portman***	N	Y	N	Y	Y	N	Y
3 Hall	N	Y	Y	Y	Y	N	N
4 ***Oxley***	N	Y	N	Y	Y	N	Y
5 ***Gillmor***	N	Y	N	Y	Y	N	Y
6 Strickland	N	Y	Y	Y	Y	N	N
7 ***Hobson***	N	Y	N	Y	Y	N	Y
8 ***Boehner***	N	Y	N	N	Y	N	Y
9 Kaptur	?	?	N	Y	Y	N	N
10 Kucinich	Y	Y	Y	Y	Y	N	N
11 Jones	Y	Y	Y	N	Y	N	N
12 ***Kasich***	N	Y	N	Y	Y	Y	Y
13 Brown	Y	Y	Y	N	Y	N	N
14 Sawyer	N	Y	Y	N	Y	N	N
15 ***Pryce***	N	Y	N	Y	Y	N	Y
16 ***Regula***	N	Y	N	Y	Y	N	Y
17 Traficant	N	Y	N	Y	Y	N	Y
18 ***Ney***	N	Y	N	Y	Y	N	Y
19 ***LaTourette***	N	Y	N	Y	Y	N	Y
OKLAHOMA							
1 ***Largent***	N	Y	N	Y	Y	N	Y
2 ***Coburn***	N	Y	N	Y	Y	Y	Y
3 ***Watkins***	N	Y	N	Y	Y	N	Y
4 ***Watts***	N	Y	N	Y	Y	N	Y
5 ***Istook***	N	Y	N	Y	Y	N	Y
6 ***Lucas***	N	Y	N	Y	Y	N	Y
OREGON							
1 Wu	Y	Y	Y	N	Y	Y	N
2 ***Walden***	N	Y	N	Y	Y	N	Y
3 Blumenauer	Y	Y	Y	N	Y	N	N
4 DeFazio	Y	Y	Y	Y	Y	N	N
5 Hooley	Y	Y	Y	N	Y	N	N
PENNSYLVANIA							
1 Brady	N	Y	N	N	Y	N	N
2 Fattah	?	Y	Y	N	Y	N	N
3 Borski	N	Y	N	N	Y	N	N
4 Klink	N	Y	Y	Y	Y	N	N
5 ***Peterson***	N	Y	N	Y	Y	N	Y
6 Holden	N	Y	N	Y	Y	N	N
7 ***Weldon***	N	Y	N	Y	Y	N	Y
8 ***Greenwood***	N	Y	N	Y	Y	Y	Y
9 ***Shuster***	N	Y	N	Y	Y	N	Y
10 ***Sherwood***	N	Y	N	Y	Y	N	Y
11 Kanjorski	N	Y	N	N	Y	N	N
12 Murtha	N	Y	N	N	Y	N	N
13 Hoeffel	N	Y	N	N	Y	N	N
14 Coyne	Y	Y	N	N	Y	N	N
15 ***Toomey***	N	Y	N	N	Y	Y	Y
16 ***Pitts***	N	Y	N	Y	Y	N	Y
17 ***Gekas***	N	Y	N	Y	Y	N	Y
18 Doyle	N	Y	N	Y	Y	N	N
19 ***Goodling***	N	Y	N	Y	Y	N	Y
20 Mascara	N	Y	N	Y	Y	N	N
21 ***English***	N	Y	N	Y	Y	N	Y
RHODE ISLAND							
1 Kennedy	N	Y	N	N	Y	N	N
2 Weygand	N	Y	N	N	Y	N	N
SOUTH CAROLINA							
1 ***Sanford***	Y	Y	Y	N	Y	Y	Y
2 ***Spence***	N	Y	N	Y	Y	N	Y
3 ***Graham***	N	Y	N	Y	Y	N	Y
4 ***DeMint***	N	Y	N	Y	Y	Y	Y
5 Spratt	N	Y	N	N	Y	N	N
6 Clyburn	N	Y	N	N	Y	N	N
SOUTH DAKOTA							
AL ***Thune***	N	Y	N	Y	Y	N	Y
TENNESSEE							
1 ***Jenkins***	N	Y	N	N	Y	N	Y
2 ***Duncan***	Y	Y	Y	Y	Y	N	Y
3 ***Wamp***	N	Y	N	Y	Y	N	Y
4 ***Hilleary***	N	Y	N	Y	Y	N	Y
5 Clement	N	Y	N	N	Y	N	N
6 Gordon	N	Y	N	Y	Y	N	N
7 ***Bryant***	N	Y	N	Y	Y	N	Y
8 Tanner	N	Y	N	Y	Y	N	N
9 Ford	N	Y	N	Y	Y	N	N
TEXAS							
1 Sandlin	N	Y	Y	N	Y	N	N
2 Turner	N	Y	N	N	Y	N	N
3 ***Johnson, Sam***	N	Y	N	Y	Y	Y	Y
4 Hall	N	Y	N	Y	Y	N	N
5 ***Sessions***	N	Y	N	Y	Y	Y	Y
6 ***Barton***	–	+	–	+	Y	N	Y
7 ***Archer***	N	Y	N	Y	Y	Y	Y
8 ***Brady***	N	Y	N	Y	Y	N	Y
9 Lampson	N	Y	N	N	Y	N	N
10 Doggett	Y	Y	Y	N	Y	N	N
11 Edwards	N	Y	N	N	Y	N	N
12 ***Granger***	N	Y	N	Y	Y	N	Y
13 ***Thornberry***	N	Y	N	N	Y	N	Y
14 ***Paul***	Y	Y	Y	N	Y	Y	Y
15 Hinojosa	N	Y	N	N	Y	N	N
16 Reyes	N	Y	N	N	Y	N	N
17 Stenholm	N	Y	N	N	Y	N	N
18 Jackson-Lee	Y	Y	N	N	Y	N	N
19 ***Combest***	N	Y	N	Y	Y	N	Y
20 Gonzalez	N	Y	N	N	Y	N	N
21 ***Smith***	N	Y	N	Y	Y	N	Y
22 ***DeLay***	N	Y	N	Y	Y	Y	Y
23 ***Bonilla***	N	Y	N	N	Y	N	Y
24 Frost	N	Y	N	N	Y	N	N
25 Bentsen	N	Y	Y	N	Y	N	N
26 ***Armey***	N	Y	N	Y	Y	Y	Y
27 Ortiz	N	Y	N	N	Y	N	N
28 Rodriguez	N	Y	N	N	Y	N	N
29 Green	Y	Y	Y	N	Y	N	N
30 Johnson, E.B.	N	Y	N	N	Y	N	N
UTAH							
1 ***Hansen***	N	Y	N	Y	Y	N	Y
2 ***Cook***	N	Y	N	Y	Y	N	Y
3 ***Cannon***	N	Y	N	Y	Y	Y	Y
VERMONT							
AL *Sanders*	Y	Y	Y	N	Y	N	N
VIRGINIA							
1 ***Bateman***	N	Y	N	N	Y	N	Y
2 Pickett	N	Y	N	N	?	N	N
3 Scott	N	Y	N	N	Y	N	N
4 Sisisky	N	Y	N	Y	Y	N	N
5 *Goode*	N	Y	N	Y	Y	N	Y
6 ***Goodlatte***	N	Y	N	Y	Y	Y	Y
7 ***Bliley***	N	Y	N	Y	Y	N	Y
8 Moran	N	Y	N	Y	Y	N	N
9 Boucher	N	Y	N	Y	Y	N	N
10 ***Wolf***	N	Y	N	Y	Y	N	Y
11 ***Davis***	N	Y	N	Y	Y	N	Y
WASHINGTON							
1 Inslee	N	Y	N	N	Y	N	N
2 ***Metcalf***	N	Y	N	Y	Y	?	Y
3 Baird	N	Y	Y	N	Y	N	N
4 ***Hastings***	N	Y	N	Y	Y	N	Y
5 ***Nethercutt***	N	Y	N	Y	Y	N	Y
6 Dicks	N	Y	N	N	Y	N	N
7 McDermott	Y	Y	Y	N	Y	N	N
8 ***Dunn***	N	Y	N	Y	Y	N	Y
9 Smith	N	Y	N	Y	Y	N	N
WEST VIRGINIA							
1 Mollohan	?	?	N	N	Y	N	N
2 Wise	N	Y	N	N	Y	N	N
3 Rahall	N	Y	N	Y	Y	N	N
WISCONSIN							
1 ***Ryan***	N	Y	N	Y	Y	Y	Y
2 Baldwin	Y	Y	Y	N	Y	N	N
3 Kind	Y	Y	Y	Y	Y	Y	N
4 Kleczka	Y	Y	N	N	Y	N	N
5 Barrett	Y	Y	Y	N	Y	Y	N
6 ***Petri***	Y	Y	Y	Y	Y	N	Y
7 Obey	Y	Y	Y	N	Y	Y	N
8 ***Green***	N	N	Y	Y	Y	N	Y
9 ***Sensenbrenner***	Y	Y	Y	Y	Y	Y	Y
WYOMING							
AL ***Cubin***	N	Y	N	N	Y	N	Y

Southern states - Ala., Ark., Fla., Ga., Ky., La., Miss., N.C., Okla., S.C., Tenn., Texas, Va.

201. HR 4205. Fiscal 2001 Defense Authorization/Rule. Adoption of the rule (H Res 504) to provide for further House floor consideration of the bill to authorize $309.9 billion for defense programs. Adopted 254-169: R 217-0; D 36-168 (ND 18-133, SD 18-35); I 1-1. May 18, 2000.

202. HR 4205. Fiscal 2001 Defense Authorization/Vieques Island. Skelton, D-Mo., amendment that would allow the Navy to transfer land on the western end of the Puerto Rican island of Vieques in accordance with the president's agreement negotiated with the government of Puerto Rico. Adopted 218-201: R 23-193; D 194-7 (ND 149-2, SD 45-5); I 1-1. May 18, 2000. A "yea" was a vote in support of the president's position.

203. HR 4205. Fiscal 2001 Defense Authorization/Military Base Abortions. Sanchez, D-Calif., amendment that would allow service members and their dependents to have abortions in overseas Defense Department medical facilities, provided the service members or their dependents pay for the procedure. Rejected 195-221: R 31-184; D 163-36 (ND 123-27, SD 40-9); I 1-1. May 18, 2000.

204. HR 4205. Fiscal 2001 Defense Authorization/School of the Americas. Moakley, D-Mass., amendment that would close the Army's School of the Americas in Georgia and prohibit the establishment of a successor school for at least 10 months. A congressional task force would be charged with assessing the training of Latin American soldiers by the United States government and reporting to Congress within six months. Rejected 204-214: R 48-167; D 154-47 (ND 133-17, SD 21-30); I 2-0. May 18, 2000.

205. HR 4205. Fiscal 2001 Defense Authorization/Nuclear Reactors. Cox, R-Calif., amendment that would prohibit the government from providing guarantees or insurance for potential liability claims if nuclear reactors provided to North Korea are involved in accidents. Adopted 334-85: R 213-1; D 119-84 (ND 82-69, SD 37-15); I 2-0. May 18, 2000.

206. HR 4205. Fiscal 2001 Defense Authorization/Retiree Health Care. Buyer, R-Ind., substitute to the Taylor, D-Miss., amendment that would expand the Defense Department's Medicare subvention demonstration program to seven additional sites comprising up to 24 military treatment facilities. Rejected 95-323: R 93-123; D 2-198 (ND 2-146, SD 0-52); I 0-2. May 18, 2000.

207. HR 4205. Fiscal 2001 Defense Authorization/Retiree Health Care. Taylor, D-Miss., amendment that would expand the Defense Department Medicare subvention demonstration program and make it permanent. The program would be available to all Medicare-eligible military retirees and their dependents by Jan. 1, 2006. Adopted 406-10: R 207-9; D 197-1 (ND 145-1, SD 52-0); I 2-0. May 18, 2000.

208. HR 4205. Fiscal 2001 Defense Authorization/Passage. Passage of the bill that would authorize $309.9 billion for defense programs, 7 percent more than the fiscal 2000 authorization. It would provide $62.3 billion for weapons procurement, $39.3 billion for research and development, $109.4 billion for operations and maintenance, $8.4 billion for military construction and family housing, and $12.8 billion for the Energy Department. Passed 353-63: R 208-6; D 144-56 (ND 95-53, SD 49-3); I 1-1. May 18, 2000.

Key

- Y Voted for (yea).
- # Paired for.
- \+ Announced for.
- N Voted against (nay).
- X Paired against.
- – Announced against.
- P Voted "present."
- C Voted "present" to avoid possible conflict of interest.
- ? Did not vote or otherwise make a position known.

•

Democrats ***Republicans***
Independents

	201	202	203	204	205	206	207	208
ALABAMA								
1 ***Callahan***	Y	N	N	N	Y	N	Y	Y
2 ***Everett***	Y	N	N	N	Y	Y	Y	Y
3 ***Riley***	Y	N	N	N	Y	N	Y	Y
4 ***Aderholt***	Y	N	N	N	Y	N	Y	Y
5 Cramer	N	Y	Y	N	Y	N	Y	Y
6 ***Bachus***	Y	N	N	N	Y	N	Y	Y
7 Hilliard	N	Y	Y	Y	Y	N	Y	Y
ALASKA								
AL ***Young***	Y	Y	N	N	Y	N	Y	Y
ARIZONA								
1 ***Salmon***	?	?	?	?	?	?	?	?
2 Pastor	Y	Y	Y	Y	N	N	Y	Y
3 ***Stump***	Y	N	N	N	Y	Y	N	Y
4 ***Shadegg***	Y	?	?	?	?	?	?	?
5 ***Kolbe***	Y	N	Y	N	Y	N	Y	Y
6 ***Hayworth***	Y	N	N	N	Y	N	Y	Y
ARKANSAS								
1 Berry	N	Y	N	N	N	N	Y	Y
2 Snyder	N	Y	Y	N	N	N	Y	Y
3 ***Hutchinson***	Y	N	N	N	Y	Y	Y	Y
4 ***Dickey***	Y	N	N	N	Y	N	Y	Y
CALIFORNIA								
1 Thompson	N	Y	Y	Y	Y	N	Y	Y
2 ***Herger***	Y	N	N	N	Y	Y	Y	Y
3 ***Ose***	Y	N	Y	N	Y	Y	Y	Y
4 ***Doolittle***	Y	N	N	N	Y	Y	Y	Y
5 Matsui	N	Y	Y	Y	N	N	Y	Y
6 Woolsey	N	Y	Y	Y	Y	N	?	?
7 Miller, George	N	Y	Y	Y	N	N	Y	N
8 Pelosi	N	Y	Y	Y	N	N	Y	N
9 Lee	N	Y	Y	Y	Y	N	Y	N
10 Tauscher	N	Y	Y	Y	N	N	Y	Y
11 ***Pombo***	Y	N	N	N	Y	N	Y	Y
12 Lantos	N	Y	Y	Y	N	N	Y	Y
13 Stark	N	Y	Y	Y	Y	Y	N	N
14 Eshoo	N	Y	Y	Y	N	N	Y	N
15 ***Campbell***	?	?	?	?	?	?	?	?
16 Lofgren	N	Y	Y	Y	N	N	Y	N
17 Farr	N	Y	Y	Y	N	N	Y	Y
18 Condit	N	Y	Y	N	Y	N	Y	Y
19 ***Radanovich***	Y	N	N	N	Y	Y	Y	Y
20 Dooley	N	Y	Y	Y	N	N	Y	Y
21 ***Thomas***	Y	N	Y	N	Y	Y	N	Y
22 Capps	N	Y	Y	Y	Y	N	Y	Y
23 ***Gallegly***	Y	Y	N	N	Y	N	Y	Y
24 Sherman	N	Y	Y	Y	Y	N	Y	Y
25 ***McKeon***	Y	N	N	N	Y	Y	Y	Y
26 Berman	N	Y	Y	Y	N	N	Y	Y
27 ***Rogan***	Y	N	N	N	Y	N	Y	Y
28 ***Dreier***	Y	N	N	N	Y	Y	Y	Y
29 Waxman	N	Y	Y	Y	N	N	Y	N
30 Becerra	N	Y	Y	Y	N	N	Y	Y
31 Martinez	Y	Y	N	N	Y	Y	Y	Y
32 Dixon	?	Y	Y	N	N	N	Y	Y
33 Roybal-Allard	N	Y	Y	N	Y	N	Y	Y
34 Napolitano	N	Y	Y	N	Y	N	Y	Y
35 Waters	N	Y	Y	Y	Y	N	?	N
36 ***Kuykendall***	Y	N	Y	N	Y	N	Y	Y
37 Millender-McD.	N	Y	Y	N	N	N	Y	Y
38 ***Horn***	Y	N	Y	N	Y	N	Y	Y
39 ***Royce***	Y	N	N	N	Y	N	Y	Y
40 ***Lewis***	Y	N	N	N	Y	Y	Y	Y
41 ***Miller, Gary***	Y	N	N	N	Y	Y	Y	Y
42 Baca	Y	Y	Y	N	Y	N	Y	Y
43 ***Calvert***	Y	N	N	N	Y	N	Y	Y
44 ***Bono***	Y	N	Y	N	Y	N	Y	Y
45 ***Rohrabacher***	Y	N	N	N	Y	N	Y	Y
46 Sanchez	N	Y	Y	Y	Y	N	Y	Y
47 ***Cox***	Y	N	N	N	Y	Y	Y	Y
48 ***Packard***	Y	N	N	N	Y	Y	N	Y
49 ***Bilbray***	Y	N	N	N	Y	N	Y	Y
50 Filner	N	Y	Y	Y	N	N	Y	N
51 ***Cunningham***	Y	N	N	N	Y	Y	Y	Y
52 ***Hunter***	Y	N	N	N	Y	Y	Y	Y
COLORADO								
1 DeGette	N	Y	Y	Y	Y	N	Y	N
2 Udall	N	Y	Y	Y	Y	N	Y	Y
3 ***McInnis***	Y	N	N	Y	Y	N	Y	Y
4 ***Schaffer***	Y	N	N	Y	Y	N	Y	Y
5 ***Hefley***	Y	N	N	Y	Y	N	Y	Y
6 ***Tancredo***	Y	N	N	N	Y	N	Y	Y
CONNECTICUT								
1 Larson	Y	Y	Y	Y	N	N	Y	Y
2 Gejdenson	N	Y	Y	Y	N	N	Y	Y
3 DeLauro	N	Y	Y	Y	N	N	Y	Y
4 ***Shays***	Y	N	Y	Y	Y	Y	N	N
5 Maloney	Y	Y	Y	Y	N	N	Y	Y
6 ***Johnson***	Y	N	Y	Y	Y	Y	Y	Y
DELAWARE								
AL ***Castle***	Y	N	Y	N	Y	Y	Y	Y
FLORIDA								
1 ***Scarborough***	Y	N	N	Y	Y	N	Y	Y
2 Boyd	Y	Y	Y	N	Y	N	Y	Y
3 Brown	Y	Y	Y	N	Y	N	Y	Y
4 ***Fowler***	Y	N	Y	N	Y	Y	Y	Y
5 Thurman	N	Y	Y	Y	N	N	Y	Y
6 ***Stearns***	Y	N	N	N	Y	Y	Y	Y
7 ***Mica***	Y	N	N	N	Y	Y	Y	Y
8 ***McCollum***	Y	Y	N	N	Y	Y	Y	Y
9 ***Bilirakis***	Y	N	N	N	Y	N	Y	Y
10 ***Young***	Y	N	N	N	Y	N	Y	Y
11 Davis	N	Y	Y	N	Y	N	Y	Y
12 ***Canady***	Y	N	N	N	Y	N	Y	Y
13 ***Miller***	Y	N	Y	Y	Y	N	Y	Y
14 ***Goss***	Y	N	N	N	Y	Y	Y	Y
15 ***Weldon***	Y	N	N	N	Y	N	Y	Y
16 ***Foley***	Y	N	Y	Y	Y	N	Y	Y
17 Meek	N	Y	Y	N	Y	N	Y	Y
18 ***Ros-Lehtinen***	Y	Y	N	N	Y	N	Y	Y
19 Wexler	N	Y	Y	Y	N	N	Y	Y
20 Deutsch	N	Y	Y	N	N	N	Y	Y
21 ***Diaz-Balart***	Y	Y	N	N	Y	N	Y	Y
22 ***Shaw***	Y	N	Y	N	Y	N	Y	Y
23 Hastings	N	+	+	–	N	N	Y	Y
GEORGIA								
1 ***Kingston***	Y	N	N	N	Y	Y	Y	Y
2 Bishop	Y	Y	Y	N	Y	N	Y	Y
3 ***Collins***	Y	N	N	N	Y	N	Y	Y
4 McKinney	N	Y	Y	Y	Y	N	Y	N
5 Lewis	N	?	?	?	?	?	?	?
6 ***Isakson***	Y	N	Y	N	Y	N	Y	Y
7 ***Barr***	Y	N	N	N	Y	N	Y	Y
8 ***Chambliss***	Y	N	N	N	Y	N	Y	Y
9 ***Deal***	Y	N	N	N	Y	N	Y	Y
10 ***Norwood***	Y	N	N	N	Y	N	Y	Y
11 ***Linder***	Y	N	N	N	Y	N	Y	Y
HAWAII								
1 Abercrombie	N	Y	Y	Y	Y	N	Y	Y
2 Mink	Y	Y	Y	Y	Y	N	Y	Y
IDAHO								
1 ***Chenoweth-Hage***	Y	N	N	N	Y	Y	Y	Y
2 ***Simpson***	Y	N	N	N	Y	Y	Y	Y
ILLINOIS								
1 Rush	N	Y	Y	Y	N	N	Y	N
2 Jackson	N	Y	Y	Y	N	N	Y	N
3 Lipinski	Y	?	?	?	?	?	?	?
4 Gutierrez	N	Y	Y	?	Y	N	Y	Y
5 Blagojevich	N	Y	Y	Y	Y	N	Y	Y
6 ***Hyde***	Y	N	N	N	Y	N	Y	Y
7 Davis	N	Y	Y	Y	N	N	Y	N
8 ***Crane***	Y	N	N	N	Y	Y	Y	Y
9 Schakowsky	N	Y	Y	Y	N	N	Y	N
10 ***Porter***	Y	Y	Y	Y	Y	N	Y	Y
11 ***Weller***	?	N	N	Y	Y	N	Y	Y
12 Costello	Y	Y	N	Y	Y	N	Y	Y
13 ***Biggert***	Y	N	Y	Y	Y	N	Y	Y

ND Northern Democrats SD Southern Democrats

	201	202	203	204	205	206	207	208
14 ***Hastert***								Y
15 ***Ewing***	Y	N	N	N	Y	Y	Y	Y
16 ***Manzullo***	Y	N	N	Y	Y	N	Y	Y
17 Evans	N	Y	Y	Y	Y	N	Y	Y
18 ***LaHood***	Y	N	N	Y	Y	N	Y	Y
19 Phelps	Y	Y	N	Y	Y	N	Y	Y
20 ***Shimkus***	Y	N	N	N	Y	N	Y	Y
INDIANA								
1 Visclosky	N	Y	Y	Y	N	N	Y	Y
2 ***McIntosh***	Y	N	N	N	Y	N	Y	Y
3 Roemer	N	Y	N	Y	Y	N	Y	Y
4 ***Souder***	Y	N	N	N	Y	Y	Y	Y
5 ***Buyer***	Y	N	N	N	Y	Y	N	Y
6 ***Burton***	Y	Y	N	N	Y	Y	Y	Y
7 ***Pease***	Y	N	N	N	Y	Y	Y	Y
8 ***Hostettler***	Y	N	N	N	Y	Y	Y	Y
9 Hill	N	Y	Y	Y	N	N	Y	Y
10 Carson	N	Y	Y	Y	Y	N	Y	N
IOWA								
1 ***Leach***	Y	N	Y	Y	Y	N	Y	Y
2 ***Nussle***	Y	N	N	Y	Y	N	Y	Y
3 Boswell	N	N	Y	N	Y	N	Y	Y
4 ***Ganske***	Y	N	N	N	Y	N	Y	Y
5 ***Latham***	Y	N	N	N	Y	N	Y	Y
KANSAS								
1 ***Moran***	Y	N	N	N	Y	N	Y	Y
2 ***Ryun***	Y	N	N	N	Y	Y	Y	Y
3 Moore	Y	Y	Y	Y	Y	N	Y	Y
4 ***Tiahrt***	Y	N	N	N	Y	Y	Y	Y
KENTUCKY								
1 ***Whitfield***	Y	N	N	N	Y	N	Y	Y
2 ***Lewis***	Y	N	N	N	Y	N	Y	Y
3 ***Northup***	Y	N	N	N	Y	N	Y	Y
4 Lucas	N	Y	N	Y	Y	N	Y	Y
5 ***Rogers***	Y	N	N	N	Y	N	Y	Y
6 ***Fletcher***	Y	N	N	Y	Y	N	Y	Y
LOUISIANA								
1 ***Vitter***	Y	N	N	N	Y	Y	Y	Y
2 Jefferson	?	Y	?	Y	Y	N	Y	Y
3 ***Tauzin***	Y	N	N	N	Y	Y	Y	Y
4 ***McCrery***	Y	N	N	N	Y	N	Y	Y
5 ***Cooksey***	Y	N	N	N	Y	N	Y	Y
6 ***Baker***	Y	N	N	N	Y	N	Y	Y
7 John	N	Y	N	N	Y	N	Y	Y
MAINE								
1 Allen	N	Y	Y	Y	N	N	Y	Y
2 Baldacci	N	Y	Y	Y	Y	N	Y	Y
MARYLAND								
1 ***Gilchrest***	Y	N	Y	N	Y	Y	Y	Y
2 ***Ehrlich***	Y	Y	Y	N	Y	Y	Y	Y
3 Cardin	N	Y	Y	Y	Y	N	Y	Y
4 Wynn	?	Y	Y	Y	Y	N	Y	Y
5 Hoyer	N	Y	Y	N	Y	N	Y	Y
6 ***Bartlett***	Y	N	N	N	Y	N	Y	Y
7 Cummings	N	Y	Y	Y	Y	N	Y	Y
8 ***Morella***	Y	Y	Y	Y	?	N	Y	Y
MASSACHUSETTS								
1 Olver	N	Y	Y	Y	N	N	Y	N
2 Neal	N	Y	Y	Y	Y	N	Y	N
3 McGovern	N	Y	Y	Y	N	N	Y	N
4 Frank	N	Y	Y	Y	N	N	Y	N
5 Meehan	N	Y	Y	Y	N	?	?	Y
6 Tierney	N	Y	Y	Y	Y	N	Y	N
7 Markey	N	Y	Y	Y	Y	N	Y	N
8 Capuano	N	Y	Y	Y	Y	N	Y	N
9 Moakley	N	Y	N	Y	Y	N	Y	N
10 Delahunt	N	Y	Y	Y	N	N	Y	N
MICHIGAN								
1 Stupak	?	?	?	?	?	?	?	?
2 ***Hoekstra***	Y	N	N	N	Y	Y	Y	Y
3 ***Ehlers***	Y	N	N	Y	Y	Y	Y	N
4 ***Camp***	Y	N	N	Y	Y	N	Y	Y
5 Barcia	Y	Y	N	Y	Y	N	Y	Y
6 ***Upton***	Y	N	N	Y	Y	N	Y	Y
7 ***Smith***	Y	N	N	Y	Y	N	Y	Y
8 Stabenow	N	Y	Y	Y	Y	N	Y	Y
9 Kildee	N	Y	N	Y	Y	N	Y	Y
10 Bonior	N	Y	Y	Y	Y	N	Y	Y
11 ***Knollenberg***	Y	Y	N	N	Y	Y	Y	?
12 Levin	N	Y	Y	Y	Y	N	Y	Y
13 Rivers	N	Y	Y	Y	Y	N	Y	N
14 Conyers	N	Y	Y	Y	N	N	Y	N
15 Kilpatrick	N	Y	Y	Y	N	N	Y	Y
16 Dingell	N	Y	Y	N	Y	N	Y	Y
MINNESOTA								
1 ***Gutknecht***	Y	N	N	Y	Y	N	Y	Y
2 Minge	N	Y	Y	Y	N	N	Y	N
3 ***Ramstad***	Y	N	Y	Y	Y	N	Y	Y
4 Vento	N	?	?	?	?	?	?	?
5 Sabo	N	Y	Y	Y	N	N	Y	N
6 Luther	N	Y	Y	Y	Y	N	Y	N
7 Peterson	N	Y	N	Y	Y	N	Y	Y
8 Oberstar	?	Y	Y	Y	N	N	Y	N
MISSISSIPPI								
1 ***Wicker***	Y	Y	N	N	Y	N	Y	Y
2 Thompson	N	Y	Y	Y	Y	N	Y	Y
3 ***Pickering***	Y	N	N	N	Y	N	Y	Y
4 Shows	N	N	N	N	Y	N	Y	Y
5 Taylor	Y	N	N	N	Y	N	Y	Y
MISSOURI								
1 Clay	N	Y	Y	Y	N	N	Y	Y
2 ***Talent***	Y	N	N	Y	Y	N	Y	Y
3 Gephardt	N	Y	Y	Y	N	N	Y	Y
4 Skelton	N	Y	N	N	Y	N	Y	Y
5 McCarthy	N	Y	Y	Y	Y	N	Y	Y
6 Danner	N	Y	N	Y	Y	N	Y	Y
7 ***Blunt***	Y	N	N	N	Y	Y	Y	Y
8 ***Emerson***	Y	N	N	N	Y	N	Y	Y
9 ***Hulshof***	Y	N	N	Y	Y	N	Y	Y
MONTANA								
AL ***Hill***	Y	N	N	N	Y	N	Y	Y
NEBRASKA								
1 ***Bereuter***	Y	N	N	N	Y	N	Y	Y
2 ***Terry***	Y	N	N	N	Y	N	Y	Y
3 ***Barrett***	Y	N	N	N	Y	Y	Y	Y
NEVADA								
1 Berkley	N	Y	Y	Y	Y	N	Y	Y
2 ***Gibbons***	Y	N	N	N	Y	N	Y	N
NEW HAMPSHIRE								
1 ***Sununu***	Y	N	N	N	Y	Y	Y	Y
2 ***Bass***	Y	N	Y	N	Y	N	Y	Y
NEW JERSEY								
1 Andrews	N	Y	Y	Y	Y	N	Y	Y
2 ***LoBiondo***	Y	N	N	Y	Y	N	Y	Y
3 ***Saxton***	Y	N	N	N	Y	N	Y	Y
4 ***Smith***	Y	N	N	Y	Y	N	Y	Y
5 ***Roukema***	Y	N	Y	N	Y	N	Y	Y
6 Pallone	N	Y	Y	Y	Y	N	Y	Y
7 ***Franks***	?	?	?	?	?	?	?	?
8 Pascrell	Y	Y	Y	Y	Y	N	Y	Y
9 Rothman	N	Y	Y	Y	Y	N	Y	Y
10 Payne	N	Y	Y	Y	N	N	Y	N
11 ***Frelinghuysen***	Y	N	Y	N	Y	N	Y	Y
12 Holt	N	Y	Y	Y	N	N	Y	N
13 Menendez	N	Y	Y	Y	Y	N	Y	Y
NEW MEXICO								
1 ***Wilson***	Y	N	N	?	?	N	Y	Y
2 ***Skeen***	Y	N	N	N	Y	N	Y	Y
3 Udall	?	?	?	?	?	?	?	?
NEW YORK								
1 Forbes	N	Y	N	Y	Y	N	Y	Y
2 ***Lazio***	Y	Y	N	Y	Y	N	Y	Y
3 ***King***	Y	Y	N	N	Y	N	Y	Y
4 McCarthy	N	Y	Y	Y	Y	N	Y	Y
5 Ackerman	N	Y	Y	Y	N	?	?	?
6 Meeks	N	Y	Y	Y	N	N	Y	N
7 Crowley	N	Y	N	Y	N	N	Y	Y
8 Nadler	N	Y	Y	Y	N	N	Y	N
9 Weiner	N	Y	Y	Y	N	N	Y	N
10 Towns	N	?	?	?	?	?	?	?
11 Owens	?	Y	Y	Y	N	N	Y	N
12 Velázquez	N	Y	Y	Y	Y	N	Y	N
13 ***Fossella***	Y	N	N	N	Y	N	Y	Y
14 Maloney	N	Y	Y	Y	Y	N	Y	Y
15 Rangel	N	?	?	?	?	?	?	?
16 Serrano	N	Y	Y	Y	N	N	Y	Y
17 Engel	N	Y	Y	Y	N	N	Y	N
18 Lowey	N	Y	Y	Y	N	N	Y	N
19 ***Kelly***	Y	N	Y	Y	Y	Y	Y	Y
20 ***Gilman***	Y	Y	Y	N	Y	N	Y	Y
21 McNulty	N	Y	N	Y	Y	N	Y	Y
22 ***Sweeney***	Y	N	N	N	Y	N	Y	Y
23 ***Boehlert***	Y	Y	Y	Y	Y	N	Y	Y
24 ***McHugh***	Y	N	N	N	Y	N	Y	Y
25 ***Walsh***	Y	Y	N	Y	Y	N	Y	Y
26 Hinchey	N	Y	Y	Y	Y	N	Y	Y
27 ***Reynolds***	Y	N	N	N	Y	Y	Y	Y
28 Slaughter	N	Y	Y	Y	Y	N	Y	N
29 LaFalce	N	Y	N	N	N	N	Y	Y
30 ***Quinn***	Y	?	?	?	?	?	?	?
31 ***Houghton***	Y	N	N	N	Y	Y	N	Y
NORTH CAROLINA								
1 Clayton	Y	Y	Y	N	Y	N	Y	Y
2 Etheridge	N	Y	Y	Y	N	N	Y	Y
3 ***Jones***	Y	N	N	N	Y	N	Y	Y
4 Price	N	Y	Y	Y	N	N	Y	Y
5 ***Burr***	Y	N	N	N	Y	N	Y	Y
6 ***Coble***	Y	N	N	Y	Y	N	Y	Y
7 McIntyre	N	N	N	N	Y	N	Y	Y
8 ***Hayes***	Y	N	N	N	Y	N	Y	Y
9 ***Myrick***	Y	N	N	N	Y	N	Y	Y
10 ***Ballenger***	Y	N	N	N	Y	Y	Y	Y
11 ***Taylor***	Y	N	N	N	Y	Y	Y	Y
12 Watt	N	Y	Y	Y	N	N	Y	N
NORTH DAKOTA								
AL Pomeroy	N	Y	Y	Y	N	N	Y	Y
OHIO								
1 ***Chabot***	Y	N	N	Y	Y	Y	Y	Y
2 ***Portman***	Y	N	N	N	Y	Y	Y	Y
3 Hall	N	Y	N	Y	N	N	Y	Y
4 ***Oxley***	Y	N	N	N	Y	Y	Y	Y
5 ***Gillmor***	Y	N	N	N	Y	Y	Y	Y
6 Strickland	Y	Y	Y	Y	Y	N	Y	Y
7 ***Hobson***	Y	N	N	N	Y	Y	Y	Y
8 ***Boehner***	Y	N	N	Y	Y	Y	Y	Y
9 Kaptur	N	Y	?	N	Y	N	Y	Y
10 Kucinich	N	Y	N	Y	Y	N	Y	N
11 Jones	N	Y	Y	Y	N	N	Y	Y
12 ***Kasich***	Y	N	N	N	Y	Y	Y	?
13 Brown	N	Y	Y	Y	N	N	Y	N
14 Sawyer	N	Y	Y	Y	N	N	Y	Y
15 ***Pryce***	Y	N	Y	Y	Y	Y	Y	Y
16 ***Regula***	Y	N	N	Y	Y	Y	Y	Y
17 Traficant	Y	N	N	Y	Y	N	Y	Y
18 ***Ney***	Y	N	?	Y	Y	N	Y	Y
19 ***LaTourette***	Y	N	N	Y	Y	Y	Y	Y
OKLAHOMA								
1 ***Largent***	Y	N	N	N	Y	Y	Y	Y
2 ***Coburn***	Y	N	N	N	Y	N	Y	Y
3 ***Watkins***	Y	N	N	N	Y	N	Y	Y
4 ***Watts***	Y	N	N	N	Y	N	Y	Y
5 ***Istook***	Y	N	N	N	Y	Y	Y	Y
6 ***Lucas***	Y	N	N	N	Y	N	Y	Y
OREGON								
1 Wu	N	Y	Y	Y	Y	N	Y	N
2 ***Walden***	Y	N	Y	N	Y	Y	Y	Y
3 Blumenauer	N	Y	Y	Y	N	N	Y	N
4 DeFazio	N	Y	Y	Y	Y	N	Y	N
5 Hooley	N	Y	Y	Y	Y	N	Y	N
PENNSYLVANIA								
1 Brady	N	Y	Y	Y	N	N	Y	Y
2 Fattah	N	Y	Y	Y	Y	N	Y	N
3 Borski	N	Y	N	Y	N	N	Y	Y
4 Klink	N	Y	N	Y	Y	N	Y	Y
5 ***Peterson***	Y	N	N	N	Y	N	Y	Y
6 Holden	Y	Y	N	Y	Y	N	Y	Y
7 ***Weldon***	Y	N	N	N	Y	Y	Y	Y
8 ***Greenwood***	Y	N	Y	N	Y	Y	Y	Y
9 ***Shuster***	Y	Y	N	N	Y	Y	Y	Y
10 ***Sherwood***	Y	N	N	Y	Y	Y	Y	Y
11 Kanjorski	Y	Y	N	N	Y	N	Y	Y
12 Murtha	Y	Y	N	N	N	?	?	?
13 Hoeffel	N	Y	Y	Y	Y	N	Y	Y
14 Coyne	N	Y	Y	Y	N	N	Y	N
15 ***Toomey***	Y	N	N	N	Y	Y	Y	Y
16 ***Pitts***	Y	N	N	N	Y	Y	Y	Y
17 ***Gekas***	Y	N	N	N	Y	Y	Y	Y
18 Doyle	N	Y	N	Y	Y	N	Y	Y
19 ***Goodling***	Y	N	N	N	Y	Y	Y	Y
20 Mascara	Y	Y	N	Y	Y	N	Y	Y
21 ***English***	Y	N	N	Y	Y	N	Y	Y
RHODE ISLAND								
1 Kennedy	N	Y	Y	Y	Y	N	Y	Y
2 Weygand	N	Y	N	Y	Y	N	Y	Y
SOUTH CAROLINA								
1 ***Sanford***	Y	N	N	Y	Y	Y	N	N
2 ***Spence***	Y	N	N	N	Y	Y	Y	Y
3 ***Graham***	Y	N	N	N	Y	Y	Y	Y
4 ***DeMint***	Y	N	N	N	Y	Y	Y	Y
5 Spratt	Y	Y	Y	N	Y	N	Y	Y
6 Clyburn	Y	Y	Y	N	Y	N	Y	Y
SOUTH DAKOTA								
AL ***Thune***	Y	N	N	N	Y	N	Y	Y
TENNESSEE								
1 ***Jenkins***	Y	N	N	N	Y	N	Y	Y
2 ***Duncan***	Y	N	N	Y	Y	N	Y	Y
3 ***Wamp***	Y	N	N	Y	Y	N	Y	Y
4 ***Hilleary***	Y	N	N	N	Y	N	Y	Y
5 Clement	Y	Y	Y	Y	Y	N	Y	Y
6 Gordon	Y	Y	Y	Y	Y	N	Y	Y
7 ***Bryant***	Y	N	N	N	Y	Y	Y	Y
8 Tanner	N	Y	Y	N	Y	N	Y	Y
9 Ford	N	?	?	?	?	?	?	?
TEXAS								
1 Sandlin	Y	Y	Y	N	Y	N	Y	Y
2 Turner	Y	Y	?	N	Y	N	Y	Y
3 ***Johnson, Sam***	Y	N	N	N	Y	Y	Y	Y
4 Hall	N	N	N	N	Y	N	Y	Y
5 ***Sessions***	Y	N	N	N	Y	N	Y	Y
6 ***Barton***	Y	N	N	N	Y	N	Y	Y
7 ***Archer***	Y	N	N	N	Y	Y	N	Y
8 ***Brady***	Y	N	N	N	Y	Y	Y	Y
9 Lampson	Y	Y	Y	Y	N	N	Y	Y
10 Doggett	N	Y	Y	Y	Y	N	Y	N
11 Edwards	N	Y	Y	N	N	N	Y	Y
12 ***Granger***	Y	N	N	N	Y	Y	Y	Y
13 ***Thornberry***	Y	N	N	N	Y	Y	Y	Y
14 ***Paul***	Y	Y	N	Y	Y	N	Y	N
15 Hinojosa	N	Y	Y	Y	Y	N	Y	Y
16 Reyes	Y	Y	Y	N	Y	N	Y	Y
17 Stenholm	N	N	N	N	Y	N	Y	Y
18 Jackson-Lee	N	Y	Y	Y	N	N	Y	Y
19 ***Combest***	Y	N	N	N	Y	Y	Y	Y
20 Gonzalez	N	Y	Y	N	N	N	Y	Y
21 ***Smith***	Y	N	N	N	Y	N	Y	Y
22 ***DeLay***	Y	N	N	N	Y	Y	Y	Y
23 ***Bonilla***	Y	N	N	N	Y	Y	Y	Y
24 Frost	Y	Y	Y	N	Y	N	Y	Y
25 Bentsen	N	Y	Y	Y	Y	N	Y	Y
26 ***Armey***	Y	N	N	N	Y	Y	Y	Y
27 Ortiz	N	Y	N	N	Y	N	Y	Y
28 Rodriguez	N	Y	Y	N	Y	N	Y	Y
29 Green	Y	Y	Y	Y	Y	N	Y	Y
30 Johnson, E.B.	N	Y	Y	N	N	N	Y	Y
UTAH								
1 ***Hansen***	Y	N	N	N	Y	Y	Y	Y
2 ***Cook***	Y	N	N	N	Y	Y	Y	Y
3 ***Cannon***	Y	N	N	N	Y	Y	Y	?
VERMONT								
AL *Sanders*	N	Y	Y	Y	Y	N	Y	N
VIRGINIA								
1 ***Bateman***	Y	N	N	N	N	Y	Y	Y
2 Pickett	Y	?	Y	N	Y	N	Y	Y
3 Scott	N	Y	Y	Y	Y	N	Y	Y
4 Sisisky	Y	Y	Y	N	Y	N	Y	Y
5 *Goode*	Y	N	N	Y	Y	N	Y	Y
6 ***Goodlatte***	Y	N	N	N	Y	N	Y	Y
7 ***Bliley***	Y	N	N	N	Y	N	Y	Y
8 Moran	Y	Y	Y	Y	N	N	Y	Y
9 Boucher	N	Y	Y	Y	Y	N	Y	Y
10 ***Wolf***	Y	N	N	N	Y	N	Y	Y
11 ***Davis***	Y	Y	N	N	Y	N	Y	Y
WASHINGTON								
1 Inslee	N	Y	Y	Y	N	N	Y	Y
2 ***Metcalf***	Y	N	N	Y	Y	Y	Y	Y
3 Baird	N	Y	Y	Y	Y	N	Y	Y
4 ***Hastings***	Y	N	N	N	Y	N	Y	Y
5 ***Nethercutt***	Y	N	N	N	Y	N	Y	Y
6 Dicks	N	Y	Y	Y	N	N	Y	Y
7 McDermott	N	Y	Y	Y	N	N	Y	N
8 ***Dunn***	Y	N	Y	N	Y	Y	Y	Y
9 Smith	N	Y	Y	Y	N	N	Y	Y
WEST VIRGINIA								
1 Mollohan	N	Y	N	N	N	N	Y	Y
2 Wise	N	Y	Y	N	Y	N	Y	Y
3 Rahall	N	Y	N	Y	Y	N	Y	Y
WISCONSIN								
1 ***Ryan***	Y	Y	N	Y	Y	N	Y	Y
2 Baldwin	N	Y	Y	Y	N	N	Y	N
3 Kind	N	Y	Y	Y	Y	N	Y	N
4 Kleczka	N	Y	Y	Y	N	N	Y	Y
5 Barrett	N	Y	Y	Y	Y	N	Y	N
6 ***Petri***	Y	Y	N	Y	Y	N	Y	Y
7 Obey	N	Y	Y	Y	N	N	Y	N
8 ***Green***	Y	Y	N	N	Y	N	Y	Y
9 ***Sensenbrenner***	Y	Y	N	Y	Y	Y	N	N
WYOMING								
AL ***Cubin***	Y	N	N	N	Y	N	Y	Y

Southern states - Ala., Ark., Fla., Ga., Ky., La., Miss., N.C., Okla., S.C., Tenn., Texas, Va.

Key

Y Voted for (yea).
\# Paired for.
\+ Announced for.
N Voted against (nay).
X Paired against.
– Announced against.
P Voted "present."
C Voted "present" to avoid possible conflict of interest.
? Did not vote or otherwise make a position known.

•

Democrats ***Republicans***
Independents

209. HR 4475. Fiscal 2001 Transportation Appropriations/New Orleans Airport. Vitter, R-La., amendment that would prohibit using Department of Transportation funds for engineering work related to an additional runway at New Orleans International Airport. Adopted 218-187: R 211-0; D 6-186 (ND 3-135, SD 3-51); I 1-1. May 19, 2000.

210. HR 4475. Fiscal 2001 Transportation Appropriations/Passage. Passage of the bill that would appropriate $55.2 billion for transportation programs for fiscal 2001, including $30.7 billion for highway programs, $12.6 billion for the Federal Aviation Administration, $4.6 billion for the Coast Guard and $521 million for Amtrak. Passed 395-13: R 206-7; D 187-6 (ND 137-2, SD 50-4); I 2-0. May 19, 2000.

211. HR 3852. Alabama Hydroelectric Project/Passage. Oxley, R-Ohio, motion to suspend the rules and pass the bill that would require the Federal Energy Regulatory Commission to push back the start date for construction of a hydroelectric project in Alabama. Motion agreed to 354-0: R 180-0; D 173-0 (ND 128-0, SD 45-0); I 1-0. A two-thirds majority of those present and voting (236 in this case) is required for passage under suspension of the rules. May 22, 2000.

212. S 1236. Idaho Hydroelectric Project/Passage. Oxley, R-Ohio, motion to suspend the rules and pass the bill that would require the Federal Energy Regulatory Commission to push back the start date for construction of the Arrowrock Dam hydroelectric project in Idaho. Motion agreed to 356-0: R 180-0; D 175-0 (ND 130-0, SD 45-0); I 1-0. A two-thirds majority of those present and voting (238 in this case) is required for passage under suspension of the rules. May 22, 2000.

213. H Con Res 302. Memorial Day/Adoption. Biggert, R-Ill., motion to suspend the rules and adopt the concurrent resolution calling for a national moment of remembrance, for those who died in the pursuit of freedom and peace, at 3 p.m. local time on each Memorial Day. Motion agreed to 362-0: R 185-0; D 176-0 (ND 131-0, SD 45-0); I 1-0. A two-thirds majority of those present and voting (242 in this case) is required for adoption under suspension of the rules. May 22, 2000.

214. HR 4392. Fiscal 2001 Intelligence Authorization/Disclosure. Roemer, D-Ind., amendment that would require the director of Central Intelligence to submit a report to Congress by Feb. 1 each year containing an unclassified statement of the aggregate appropriations for U.S. intelligence activities the previous fiscal year. Rejected 175-225: R 17-187; D 156-38 (ND 123-18, SD 33-20); I 2-0. May 23, 2000.

215. HR 4392. Fiscal 2001 Intelligence Authorization/Espionage. Traficant, D-Ohio, amendment that would require the director of Central Intelligence to report to Congress on the effects of foreign espionage on U.S. trade secrets, patents and technology development. Adopted 407-1: R 208-1; D 197-0 (ND 144-0, SD 53-0); I 2-0. May 23, 2000.

	209	210	211	212	213	214	215
ALABAMA							
1 ***Callahan***	Y	Y	?	?	?	N	Y
2 ***Everett***	Y	Y	Y	Y	Y	N	Y
3 ***Riley***	Y	Y	+	+	+	N	Y
4 ***Aderholt***	Y	Y	Y	Y	Y	N	Y
5 Cramer	N	Y	Y	Y	Y	N	Y
6 ***Bachus***	Y	Y	Y	Y	Y	N	?
7 Hilliard	N	Y	Y	Y	Y	Y	Y
ALASKA							
AL ***Young***	Y	Y	Y	Y	Y	?	?
ARIZONA							
1 ***Salmon***	?	?	Y	Y	Y	N	Y
2 Pastor	N	Y	Y	Y	Y	Y	Y
3 ***Stump***	Y	Y	Y	Y	Y	N	Y
4 ***Shadegg***	+	+	+	+	+	N	Y
5 ***Kolbe***	Y	Y	Y	Y	Y	N	Y
6 ***Hayworth***	Y	Y	Y	Y	Y	N	Y
ARKANSAS							
1 Berry	N	Y	Y	Y	Y	Y	Y
2 Snyder	N	Y	Y	Y	Y	Y	Y
3 ***Hutchinson***	Y	Y	Y	Y	Y	N	Y
4 ***Dickey***	Y	Y	Y	Y	Y	?	Y
CALIFORNIA							
1 Thompson	N	Y	Y	Y	Y	N	Y
2 ***Herger***	Y	Y	Y	Y	Y	N	Y
3 ***Ose***	Y	Y	Y	Y	Y	N	Y
4 ***Doolittle***	Y	Y	Y	Y	Y	N	Y
5 Matsui	N	Y	Y	Y	Y	Y	Y
6 Woolsey	–	+	Y	Y	Y	Y	Y
7 Miller, George	?	?	Y	Y	Y	Y	Y
8 Pelosi	N	Y	Y	Y	Y	Y	Y
9 Lee	N	Y	Y	Y	Y	Y	Y
10 Tauscher	N	Y	Y	Y	Y	Y	Y
11 ***Pombo***	Y	Y	Y	Y	Y	?	Y
12 Lantos	N	Y	Y	Y	Y	Y	Y
13 Stark	N	N	Y	Y	Y	Y	Y
14 Eshoo	N	Y	Y	Y	Y	Y	Y
15 ***Campbell***	?	?	Y	Y	Y	Y	Y
16 Lofgren	?	+	Y	Y	Y	Y	Y
17 Farr	N	Y	Y	Y	Y	Y	Y
18 Condit	N	Y	Y	Y	Y	Y	Y
19 ***Radanovich***	Y	Y	Y	?	Y	N	Y
20 Dooley	N	Y	Y	Y	Y	Y	Y
21 ***Thomas***	Y	Y	Y	Y	Y	N	Y
22 Capps	–	+	Y	Y	Y	Y	Y
23 ***Gallegly***	Y	Y	Y	Y	Y	N	Y
24 Sherman	N	Y	Y	Y	Y	Y	Y
25 ***McKeon***	Y	Y	Y	Y	Y	N	Y
26 Berman	N	Y	Y	Y	Y	Y	Y
27 ***Rogan***	?	?	Y	Y	Y	N	Y
28 ***Dreier***	Y	Y	Y	Y	Y	N	Y
29 Waxman	N	Y	Y	Y	Y	?	?
30 Becerra	N	Y	Y	Y	Y	Y	Y
31 Martinez	N	Y	?	?	?	?	?
32 Dixon	N	Y	Y	Y	Y	Y	Y
33 Roybal-Allard	N	Y	Y	Y	Y	Y	Y
34 Napolitano	N	Y	Y	Y	Y	Y	Y
35 Waters	N	Y	Y	Y	Y	Y	Y
36 ***Kuykendall***	Y	Y	Y	Y	Y	N	Y
37 Millender-McD.	N	Y	Y	Y	Y	Y	Y
38 ***Horn***	Y	Y	Y	Y	Y	N	Y
39 ***Royce***	Y	N	Y	Y	Y	N	Y
40 ***Lewis***	Y	Y	Y	Y	Y	N	Y
41 ***Miller, Gary***	Y	Y	Y	Y	Y	N	Y
42 Baca	N	Y	Y	Y	Y	N	Y
43 ***Calvert***	Y	Y	Y	Y	Y	N	Y
44 ***Bono***	Y	Y	Y	Y	Y	N	Y
45 ***Rohrabacher***	Y	Y	Y	Y	Y	Y	Y
46 Sanchez	N	Y	Y	Y	Y	Y	Y
47 ***Cox***	Y	Y	Y	Y	Y	N	Y
48 ***Packard***	Y	Y	Y	Y	Y	N	Y
49 ***Bilbray***	Y	Y	Y	Y	Y	N	Y
50 Filner	N	Y	Y	Y	Y	Y	Y
51 ***Cunningham***	Y	Y	Y	Y	Y	N	Y
52 ***Hunter***	Y	Y	Y	Y	Y	N	Y
COLORADO							
1 DeGette	N	Y	?	Y	Y	Y	Y
2 Udall	N	Y	Y	Y	Y	Y	Y
3 ***McInnis***	Y	Y	Y	Y	Y	N	Y
4 ***Schaffer***	Y	Y	Y	Y	Y	Y	Y
5 ***Hefley***	Y	Y	Y	Y	Y	N	Y
6 ***Tancredo***	Y	Y	Y	Y	Y	N	Y
CONNECTICUT							
1 Larson	N	Y	Y	Y	Y	?	?
2 Gejdenson	N	Y	Y	Y	Y	N	Y
3 DeLauro	N	Y	Y	Y	Y	Y	Y
4 ***Shays***	Y	Y	+	+	+	N	Y
5 Maloney	N	Y	Y	Y	Y	Y	Y
6 ***Johnson***	Y	Y	Y	Y	Y	N	Y
DELAWARE							
AL ***Castle***	Y	Y	Y	Y	Y	N	Y
FLORIDA							
1 ***Scarborough***	Y	N	?	?	?	?	?
2 Boyd	N	Y	Y	Y	Y	Y	Y
3 Brown	N	Y	?	?	?	Y	Y
4 ***Fowler***	Y	Y	Y	Y	Y	N	Y
5 Thurman	N	Y	Y	Y	Y	Y	Y
6 ***Stearns***	Y	N	Y	Y	Y	N	Y
7 ***Mica***	Y	Y	Y	Y	Y	N	Y
8 ***McCollum***	Y	Y	Y	Y	Y	N	Y
9 ***Bilirakis***	Y	Y	+	+	+	N	Y
10 ***Young***	Y	Y	Y	Y	Y	?	Y
11 Davis	N	Y	Y	Y	Y	Y	Y
12 ***Canady***	Y	Y	Y	Y	Y	N	Y
13 ***Miller***	Y	Y	Y	Y	Y	N	Y
14 ***Goss***	Y	Y	Y	Y	Y	N	Y
15 ***Weldon***	Y	Y	Y	Y	Y	N	Y
16 ***Foley***	Y	Y	Y	Y	Y	N	Y
17 Meek	N	Y	Y	Y	Y	Y	Y
18 ***Ros-Lehtinen***	Y	Y	Y	Y	Y	N	Y
19 Wexler	N	Y	Y	Y	Y	Y	Y
20 Deutsch	N	Y	Y	Y	Y	Y	Y
21 ***Diaz-Balart***	Y	Y	Y	Y	Y	N	Y
22 ***Shaw***	Y	Y	Y	Y	Y	N	Y
23 Hastings	N	Y	Y	Y	Y	Y	Y
GEORGIA							
1 ***Kingston***	Y	Y	?	?	?	N	Y
2 Bishop	N	Y	Y	Y	Y	N	Y
3 ***Collins***	Y	Y	?	?	?	N	Y
4 McKinney	N	Y	?	?	?	Y	Y
5 Lewis	N	Y	Y	Y	Y	Y	Y
6 ***Isakson***	Y	Y	Y	Y	Y	N	Y
7 ***Barr***	Y	Y	Y	Y	Y	N	Y
8 ***Chambliss***	Y	Y	Y	Y	Y	N	Y
9 ***Deal***	Y	Y	?	?	Y	N	Y
10 ***Norwood***	?	?	Y	Y	Y	N	Y
11 ***Linder***	Y	Y	Y	Y	Y	N	Y
HAWAII							
1 Abercrombie	N	Y	Y	Y	Y	Y	Y
2 Mink	N	Y	Y	Y	Y	Y	Y
IDAHO							
1 ***Chenoweth-Hage***	Y	N	?	?	?	?	Y
2 ***Simpson***	Y	Y	Y	Y	Y	N	Y
ILLINOIS							
1 Rush	N	Y	?	?	?	Y	Y
2 Jackson	N	Y	Y	Y	Y	Y	Y
3 Lipinski	?	?	Y	Y	Y	Y	Y
4 Gutierrez	N	Y	+	+	+	Y	Y
5 Blagojevich	N	Y	Y	Y	Y	Y	Y
6 ***Hyde***	Y	Y	Y	Y	Y	N	Y
7 Davis	N	Y	Y	Y	Y	Y	Y
8 ***Crane***	Y	Y	Y	Y	Y	N	Y
9 Schakowsky	N	Y	?	?	?	Y	Y
10 ***Porter***	Y	Y	Y	Y	Y	Y	Y
11 ***Weller***	Y	Y	Y	Y	Y	N	Y
12 Costello	N	Y	Y	Y	Y	Y	Y
13 ***Biggert***	Y	Y	Y	Y	Y	N	Y

ND Northern Democrats SD Southern Democrats

	209	210	211	212	213	214	215
14 ***Hastert***		Y					
15 ***Ewing***	Y	Y	Y	Y	Y	N	Y
16 ***Manzullo***	Y	Y	Y	Y	Y	Y	Y
17 Evans	N	Y	Y	Y	Y	Y	Y
18 ***LaHood***	Y	Y	Y	Y	Y	N	Y
19 Phelps	N	Y	Y	Y	Y	Y	Y
20 ***Shimkus***	Y	Y	Y	Y	Y	N	Y
INDIANA							
1 Visclosky	N	Y	Y	Y	Y	Y	Y
2 ***McIntosh***	?	?	?	?	?	?	?
3 Roemer	N	Y	Y	Y	Y	Y	Y
4 ***Souder***	Y	Y	?	?	?	N	Y
5 ***Buyer***	Y	Y	Y	Y	Y	N	Y
6 ***Burton***	Y	Y	Y	Y	Y	N	Y
7 ***Pease***	Y	Y	Y	Y	Y	N	Y
8 ***Hostettler***	Y	Y	Y	Y	Y	N	Y
9 Hill	N	Y	Y	Y	Y	Y	Y
10 Carson	N	Y	Y	Y	Y	Y	Y
IOWA							
1 ***Leach***	Y	Y	Y	Y	Y	Y	Y
2 ***Nussle***	Y	Y	Y	Y	Y	N	Y
3 Boswell	N	Y	Y	Y	Y	N	Y
4 ***Ganske***	Y	Y	Y	Y	Y	Y	Y
5 ***Latham***	Y	Y	Y	Y	Y	N	Y
KANSAS							
1 ***Moran***	Y	Y	Y	Y	Y	N	Y
2 ***Ryun***	Y	Y	+	+	+	N	Y
3 Moore	N	Y	Y	Y	Y	Y	Y
4 ***Tiahrt***	Y	Y	Y	Y	Y	–	+
KENTUCKY							
1 ***Whitfield***	Y	Y	Y	Y	Y	N	Y
2 ***Lewis***	Y	Y	Y	Y	Y	N	Y
3 ***Northup***	Y	Y	Y	Y	Y	N	Y
4 Lucas	N	Y	Y	Y	Y	N	Y
5 ***Rogers***	Y	Y	?	?	?	N	Y
6 ***Fletcher***	Y	Y	Y	Y	Y	N	Y
LOUISIANA							
1 ***Vitter***	Y	Y	Y	Y	Y	N	Y
2 Jefferson	N	N	Y	Y	Y	Y	Y
3 ***Tauzin***	Y	Y	Y	Y	Y	N	Y
4 ***McCrery***	Y	Y	Y	Y	Y	N	Y
5 ***Cooksey***	Y	Y	?	?	?	?	?
6 ***Baker***	Y	Y	?	?	?	N	Y
7 John	N	Y	Y	Y	Y	N	Y
MAINE							
1 Allen	N	Y	Y	Y	Y	Y	Y
2 Baldacci	N	Y	Y	Y	Y	Y	Y
MARYLAND							
1 ***Gilchrest***	Y	Y	Y	Y	Y	N	Y
2 ***Ehrlich***	Y	Y	Y	Y	Y	N	Y
3 Cardin	N	Y	Y	Y	Y	N	Y
4 Wynn	N	Y	Y	Y	Y	Y	Y
5 Hoyer	N	Y	Y	Y	Y	N	Y
6 ***Bartlett***	Y	Y	Y	Y	Y	N	Y
7 Cummings	N	Y	Y	Y	Y	Y	Y
8 ***Morella***	Y	Y	Y	Y	Y	Y	Y
MASSACHUSETTS							
1 Olver	N	Y	Y	Y	Y	Y	Y
2 Neal	N	Y	Y	Y	Y	Y	Y
3 McGovern	N	Y	Y	Y	Y	Y	Y
4 Frank	N	Y	?	?	?	Y	Y
5 Meehan	N	Y	?	?	?	?	Y
6 Tierney	N	Y	?	?	?	Y	Y
7 Markey	N	Y	?	?	?	Y	Y
8 Capuano	N	Y	+	+	+	?	?
9 Moakley	N	Y	?	?	?	?	Y
10 Delahunt	N	Y	Y	Y	Y	Y	Y
MICHIGAN							
1 Stupak	?	?	?	?	?	?	?
2 ***Hoekstra***	Y	Y	Y	Y	Y	N	Y
3 ***Ehlers***	Y	Y	Y	Y	Y	N	Y
4 ***Camp***	Y	Y	Y	Y	Y	N	Y
5 Barcia	N	Y	Y	Y	Y	Y	Y
6 ***Upton***	Y	Y	Y	Y	Y	Y	Y
7 ***Smith***	Y	Y	Y	Y	Y	N	Y
8 Stabenow	N	Y	Y	Y	Y	Y	Y
9 Kildee	N	Y	Y	Y	Y	Y	Y
10 Bonior	N	Y	Y	Y	Y	Y	Y
11 ***Knollenberg***	Y	Y	Y	Y	Y	N	Y
12 Levin	N	Y	Y	Y	Y	Y	Y
13 Rivers	N	Y	Y	Y	Y	Y	Y
14 Conyers	N	Y	Y	Y	Y	Y	Y
15 Kilpatrick	N	Y	Y	Y	Y	Y	Y
16 Dingell	N	Y	Y	Y	Y	Y	Y
MINNESOTA							
1 ***Gutknecht***	Y	Y	?	?	?	N	Y
2 Minge	N	Y	+	+	+	?	?
3 ***Ramstad***	Y	Y	+	+	+	N	Y
4 Vento	?	?	Y	Y	Y	Y	Y
5 Sabo	N	Y	Y	Y	Y	Y	Y
6 Luther	N	Y	Y	Y	Y	Y	Y
7 Peterson	Y	Y	Y	Y	Y	Y	Y
8 Oberstar	N	Y	Y	Y	Y	+	+
MISSISSIPPI							
1 ***Wicker***	Y	Y	?	?	?	N	Y
2 Thompson	N	Y	?	?	?	Y	Y
3 ***Pickering***	Y	Y	Y	Y	Y	N	Y
4 Shows	Y	Y	?	?	?	N	Y
5 Taylor	N	Y	?	?	?	N	Y
MISSOURI							
1 Clay	N	Y	Y	Y	Y	Y	Y
2 ***Talent***	Y	Y	Y	Y	Y	N	Y
3 Gephardt	?	Y	Y	Y	Y	Y	Y
4 Skelton	N	Y	Y	Y	Y	N	Y
5 McCarthy	N	Y	Y	Y	Y	Y	Y
6 Danner	N	Y	Y	Y	Y	Y	Y
7 ***Blunt***	Y	Y	Y	Y	Y	?	?
8 ***Emerson***	Y	Y	Y	Y	Y	N	Y
9 ***Hulshof***	Y	Y	Y	Y	Y	N	Y
MONTANA							
AL ***Hill***	Y	Y	Y	Y	Y	N	Y
NEBRASKA							
1 ***Bereuter***	Y	Y	Y	Y	Y	N	Y
2 ***Terry***	Y	Y	Y	Y	Y	N	Y
3 ***Barrett***	Y	Y	Y	Y	Y	N	Y
NEVADA							
1 Berkley	N	Y	Y	Y	Y	Y	Y
2 ***Gibbons***	Y	Y	Y	Y	Y	N	Y
NEW HAMPSHIRE							
1 ***Sununu***	Y	Y	Y	Y	Y	N	Y
2 ***Bass***	Y	Y	Y	Y	Y	N	Y
NEW JERSEY							
1 Andrews	N	Y	Y	Y	Y	N	Y
2 ***LoBiondo***	Y	Y	Y	Y	Y	N	Y
3 ***Saxton***	Y	Y	Y	Y	Y	N	Y
4 ***Smith***	Y	Y	Y	Y	Y	N	Y
5 ***Roukema***	Y	Y	Y	Y	Y	N	Y
6 Pallone	N	Y	Y	Y	Y	Y	Y
7 ***Franks***	Y	Y	?	?	?	N	Y
8 Pascrell	N	Y	Y	Y	Y	Y	Y
9 Rothman	N	Y	Y	Y	Y	Y	Y
10 Payne	N	Y	Y	Y	Y	Y	Y
11 ***Frelinghuysen***	Y	Y	Y	Y	Y	N	Y
12 Holt	N	Y	Y	Y	Y	Y	Y
13 Menendez	N	Y	Y	Y	Y	Y	Y
NEW MEXICO							
1 ***Wilson***	Y	Y	Y	Y	Y	N	Y
2 ***Skeen***	Y	Y	Y	Y	Y	N	Y
3 Udall	?	?	Y	Y	Y	Y	Y
NEW YORK							
1 Forbes	N	Y	?	?	?	?	?
2 ***Lazio***	Y	Y	?	?	?	?	?
3 ***King***	Y	Y	Y	Y	Y	N	Y
4 McCarthy	N	Y	?	?	?	?	?
5 Ackerman	?	?	?	?	?	?	?
6 Meeks	N	Y	Y	Y	Y	Y	Y
7 Crowley	N	Y	Y	Y	Y	Y	Y
8 Nadler	N	Y	Y	Y	Y	Y	Y
9 Weiner	N	Y	?	?	?	?	?
10 Towns	?	?	?	?	Y	Y	Y
11 Owens	–	+	Y	Y	Y	Y	Y
12 Velázquez	N	Y	Y	Y	Y	Y	Y
13 ***Fossella***	Y	Y	Y	Y	Y	–	Y
14 Maloney	N	N	Y	Y	Y	Y	Y
15 Rangel	N	Y	?	?	?	Y	Y
16 Serrano	N	Y	Y	Y	Y	Y	Y
17 Engel	N	Y	Y	Y	Y	Y	Y
18 Lowey	N	Y	Y	Y	Y	Y	Y
19 ***Kelly***	Y	Y	Y	Y	Y	N	Y
20 ***Gilman***	Y	Y	Y	Y	Y	N	Y
21 McNulty	N	Y	?	?	?	N	Y
22 ***Sweeney***	Y	Y	?	Y	Y	N	Y
23 ***Boehlert***	Y	Y	Y	Y	Y	N	Y
24 ***McHugh***	Y	Y	Y	Y	Y	N	Y
25 ***Walsh***	Y	Y	Y	Y	Y	N	Y
26 Hinchey	N	Y	Y	Y	Y	Y	Y
27 ***Reynolds***	Y	Y	?	?	?	N	Y
28 Slaughter	N	Y	Y	Y	Y	Y	Y
29 LaFalce	N	Y	Y	Y	Y	Y	Y
30 ***Quinn***	?	?	Y	Y	Y	N	Y
31 ***Houghton***	Y	Y	?	?	?	N	Y
NORTH CAROLINA							
1 Clayton	N	Y	Y	Y	Y	Y	Y
2 Etheridge	N	Y	Y	Y	Y	Y	Y
3 ***Jones***	Y	Y	Y	Y	Y	N	Y
4 Price	N	Y	Y	Y	Y	Y	Y
5 ***Burr***	Y	Y	Y	Y	Y	N	Y
6 ***Coble***	Y	Y	Y	Y	Y	N	Y
7 McIntyre	N	Y	Y	Y	Y	N	Y
8 ***Hayes***	Y	Y	Y	Y	Y	N	Y
9 ***Myrick***	Y	Y	Y	Y	Y	Y	Y
10 ***Ballenger***	Y	Y	+	+	Y	N	Y
11 ***Taylor***	Y	Y	Y	Y	Y	N	Y
12 Watt	N	Y	Y	Y	Y	Y	Y
NORTH DAKOTA							
AL Pomeroy	N	Y	?	?	?	Y	Y
OHIO							
1 ***Chabot***	Y	Y	Y	Y	Y	Y	Y
2 ***Portman***	Y	Y	Y	Y	Y	N	Y
3 Hall	N	Y	Y	Y	Y	N	Y
4 ***Oxley***	Y	Y	Y	Y	Y	N	Y
5 ***Gillmor***	Y	Y	?	?	?	N	Y
6 Strickland	N	Y	Y	Y	Y	Y	Y
7 ***Hobson***	Y	Y	?	?	?	N	Y
8 ***Boehner***	Y	Y	Y	Y	Y	N	Y
9 Kaptur	N	Y	?	?	?	Y	Y
10 Kucinich	N	Y	Y	Y	Y	Y	Y
11 Jones	?	?	?	?	?	?	Y
12 ***Kasich***	Y	Y	Y	Y	Y	N	Y
13 Brown	N	Y	?	?	?	?	?
14 Sawyer	N	Y	Y	Y	Y	Y	Y
15 ***Pryce***	Y	Y	?	?	?	N	Y
16 ***Regula***	Y	Y	Y	Y	Y	?	Y
17 Traficant	Y	Y	Y	Y	Y	N	Y
18 ***Ney***	Y	Y	Y	Y	Y	N	Y
19 ***LaTourette***	Y	Y	Y	Y	Y	N	Y
OKLAHOMA							
1 ***Largent***	Y	Y	Y	Y	Y	N	Y
2 ***Coburn***	Y	Y	?	?	?	N	Y
3 ***Watkins***	Y	Y	?	?	?	N	Y
4 ***Watts***	Y	Y	Y	Y	Y	N	Y
5 ***Istook***	Y	Y	Y	Y	Y	Y	Y
6 ***Lucas***	Y	Y	?	?	Y	N	Y
OREGON							
1 Wu	N	Y	Y	Y	Y	N	Y
2 ***Walden***	Y	Y	+	Y	Y	N	Y
3 Blumenauer	N	Y	Y	Y	Y	Y	Y
4 DeFazio	N	Y	Y	Y	Y	Y	Y
5 Hooley	N	Y	?	?	Y	Y	Y
PENNSYLVANIA							
1 Brady	?	?	Y	Y	Y	Y	Y
2 Fattah	?	?	Y	Y	Y	Y	Y
3 Borski	?	?	Y	Y	Y	Y	Y
4 Klink	?	?	?	?	?	N	Y
5 ***Peterson***	Y	Y	?	?	?	N	Y
6 Holden	?	Y	Y	Y	Y	Y	Y
7 ***Weldon***	?	Y	Y	Y	Y	N	Y
8 ***Greenwood***	Y	Y	Y	Y	Y	N	Y
9 ***Shuster***	Y	Y	Y	Y	Y	N	N
10 ***Sherwood***	Y	Y	Y	?	Y	N	Y
11 Kanjorski	N	Y	Y	Y	Y	Y	Y
12 Murtha	?	?	Y	Y	Y	N	Y
13 Hoeffel	N	Y	Y	Y	Y	Y	Y
14 Coyne	N	Y	?	?	?	Y	Y
15 ***Toomey***	Y	Y	?	?	?	N	Y
16 ***Pitts***	Y	Y	Y	Y	Y	N	Y
17 ***Gekas***	Y	Y	Y	Y	Y	N	Y
18 Doyle	N	Y	Y	Y	Y	N	Y
19 ***Goodling***	Y	Y	?	?	?	N	Y
20 Mascara	N	Y	Y	Y	Y	Y	Y
21 ***English***	Y	Y	Y	Y	Y	N	Y
RHODE ISLAND							
1 Kennedy	N	Y	Y	Y	Y	Y	Y
2 Weygand	N	Y	Y	Y	Y	Y	Y
SOUTH CAROLINA							
1 ***Sanford***	Y	N	Y	Y	Y	N	Y
2 ***Spence***	Y	Y	Y	Y	Y	N	Y
3 ***Graham***	Y	Y	Y	Y	Y	N	Y
4 ***DeMint***	Y	Y	Y	Y	Y	N	Y
5 Spratt	N	Y	Y	Y	Y	Y	Y
6 Clyburn	N	Y	Y	Y	Y	Y	Y
SOUTH DAKOTA							
AL ***Thune***	Y	Y	Y	Y	Y	N	Y
TENNESSEE							
1 ***Jenkins***	Y	Y	Y	Y	Y	N	Y
2 ***Duncan***	Y	Y	Y	Y	Y	Y	Y
3 ***Wamp***	Y	Y	Y	Y	Y	N	Y
4 ***Hilleary***	Y	Y	?	?	?	N	Y
5 Clement	N	Y	Y	Y	Y	N	Y
6 Gordon	N	Y	Y	Y	Y	N	Y
7 ***Bryant***	Y	Y	?	?	?	?	?
8 Tanner	N	Y	Y	Y	Y	Y	Y
9 Ford	N	Y	?	?	?	Y	Y
TEXAS							
1 Sandlin	N	Y	Y	Y	Y	Y	Y
2 Turner	N	Y	?	?	?	N	Y
3 ***Johnson, Sam***	Y	Y	Y	Y	Y	N	Y
4 Hall	Y	Y	Y	Y	Y	N	Y
5 ***Sessions***	Y	Y	Y	Y	Y	N	Y
6 ***Barton***	Y	?	?	?	?	?	?
7 ***Archer***	Y	Y	Y	Y	Y	N	Y
8 ***Brady***	Y	Y	Y	Y	Y	N	Y
9 Lampson	N	Y	?	?	?	Y	Y
10 Doggett	N	N	Y	Y	Y	Y	Y
11 Edwards	N	Y	Y	Y	Y	N	Y
12 ***Granger***	Y	Y	Y	Y	Y	N	Y
13 ***Thornberry***	Y	Y	Y	Y	Y	N	Y
14 ***Paul***	Y	N	?	?	?	Y	Y
15 Hinojosa	N	Y	Y	Y	Y	N	Y
16 Reyes	N	Y	Y	Y	Y	N	Y
17 Stenholm	N	Y	Y	Y	Y	N	Y
18 Jackson-Lee	N	N	Y	Y	Y	Y	Y
19 ***Combest***	Y	Y	Y	Y	Y	N	Y
20 Gonzalez	N	Y	Y	Y	Y	Y	Y
21 ***Smith***	Y	Y	Y	Y	Y	N	Y
22 ***DeLay***	Y	Y	?	?	?	?	?
23 ***Bonilla***	Y	Y	Y	Y	Y	N	Y
24 Frost	N	Y	Y	Y	Y	Y	Y
25 Bentsen	N	N	Y	Y	Y	N	Y
26 ***Armey***	Y	Y	Y	Y	Y	?	?
27 Ortiz	N	Y	Y	Y	Y	N	Y
28 Rodriguez	N	Y	?	?	?	?	?
29 Green	N	Y	Y	Y	Y	Y	Y
30 Johnson, E.B.	N	Y	Y	Y	Y	Y	Y
UTAH							
1 ***Hansen***	Y	Y	?	?	?	N	Y
2 ***Cook***	Y	Y	Y	Y	Y	N	Y
3 ***Cannon***	?	Y	Y	Y	Y	N	Y
VERMONT							
AL *Sanders*	N	Y	?	?	?	Y	Y
VIRGINIA							
1 ***Bateman***	Y	Y	Y	Y	Y	N	Y
2 Pickett	N	Y	Y	Y	Y	N	Y
3 Scott	N	Y	Y	Y	Y	N	Y
4 Sisisky	N	Y	Y	Y	Y	N	Y
5 *Goode*	Y	Y	Y	Y	Y	Y	Y
6 ***Goodlatte***	Y	Y	Y	Y	Y	N	Y
7 ***Bliley***	Y	Y	Y	Y	Y	N	Y
8 Moran	N	Y	Y	Y	Y	Y	Y
9 Boucher	Y	Y	Y	Y	Y	Y	Y
10 ***Wolf***	Y	Y	Y	Y	Y	N	Y
11 ***Davis***	Y	Y	Y	Y	Y	N	Y
WASHINGTON							
1 Inslee	N	Y	Y	Y	Y	Y	Y
2 ***Metcalf***	Y	Y	Y	Y	Y	Y	Y
3 Baird	N	Y	Y	Y	Y	Y	Y
4 ***Hastings***	Y	Y	Y	Y	Y	N	Y
5 ***Nethercutt***	+	+	Y	Y	Y	N	Y
6 Dicks	Y	?	Y	Y	Y	Y	Y
7 McDermott	N	Y	Y	Y	Y	Y	Y
8 ***Dunn***	Y	Y	Y	Y	Y	N	Y
9 Smith	N	Y	Y	Y	Y	Y	Y
WEST VIRGINIA							
1 Mollohan	N	Y	Y	Y	Y	N	Y
2 Wise	N	Y	?	?	?	?	?
3 Rahall	N	Y	Y	Y	Y	N	Y
WISCONSIN							
1 ***Ryan***	Y	Y	Y	Y	Y	N	Y
2 Baldwin	N	Y	Y	Y	Y	Y	Y
3 Kind	N	Y	+	Y	Y	Y	Y
4 Kleczka	N	Y	Y	Y	Y	N	Y
5 Barrett	N	Y	Y	Y	Y	Y	Y
6 ***Petri***	Y	Y	Y	Y	Y	Y	Y
7 Obey	N	Y	Y	Y	?	Y	Y
8 ***Green***	Y	Y	Y	Y	Y	N	Y
9 ***Sensenbrenner***	Y	N	Y	Y	Y	N	Y
WYOMING							
AL ***Cubin***	Y	Y	Y	Y	Y	N	Y

Southern states - Ala., Ark., Fla., Ga., Ky., La., Miss., N.C., Okla., S.C., Tenn., Texas, Va.

House Votes 216, 217, 218, 219, 220, 221

216. HR 4392. Fiscal 2001 Intelligence Authorization/China. Traficant, D-Ohio, amendment that would require the director of Central Intelligence to report to Congress within 60 days of enactment whether or not China's goals and policies constitute a threat to U.S. national security. Adopted 404-8: R 208-5; D 194-3 (ND 142-2, SD 52-1); I 2-0. (Subsequently, the bill that would authorize classified amounts in fiscal 2001 for 11 intelligence agencies including the CIA and National Security Agency, was passed by voice vote.) May 23, 2000.

217. HR 297. Rural Water System/Passage. Doolittle, R-Calif., motion to suspend the rules and pass the bill that would authorize $214 million to construct the Lewis and Clark Rural Water System, which would provide drinking water to rural communities in southeastern South Dakota, northwestern Iowa and southwestern Minnesota. Motion agreed to 400-13: R 200-12; D 198-1 (ND 145-1, SD 53-0); I 2-0. A two-thirds majority of those present and voting (276 in this case) is required for passage under suspension of the rules. May 23, 2000.

218. H Res 443. American Samoa/Adoption. Doolittle, R-Calif., motion to suspend the rules and adopt the resolution recognizing the historical significance of the centennial of the U.S. flag flying over American Samoa. Motion agreed to 417-0: R 216-0; D 199-0 (ND 147-0, SD 52-0); I 2-0. A two-thirds majority of those present and voting (278 in this case) is required for adoption under suspension of the rules. May 23, 2000.

219. HR 3544. Pope John Paul II Gold Medal/Passage. Leach, R-Iowa, motion to suspend the rules and pass the bill that would award a gold medal, on behalf of Congress, to Pope John Paul II. Motion agreed to 416-1: R 215-1; D 199-0 (ND 147-0, SD 52-0); I 2-0. A two-thirds majority of those present and voting (278 in this case) is required for passage under suspension of the rules. May 23, 2000.

220. S 1402. GI Bill/Passage. Stump, R-Ariz., motion to suspend the rules and pass the bill that would increase the amount of educational reimbursement that veterans receive under the Montgomery GI Bill. Motion agreed to 417-0: R 216-0; D 199-0 (ND 147-0, SD 52-0); I 2-0. A two-thirds majority of those present and voting (278 in this case) is required for passage under suspension of the rules. May 23, 2000.

221. H Con Res 293. Child Abduction/Adoption. Gilman, R-N.Y., motion to suspend the rules and adopt the concurrent resolution that would urge all parties of the Hague Convention to comply with its provision to return abducted children and to ensure parental access rights. The resolution would single out Austria, Germany and Sweden as countries that routinely ignore the convention. Motion agreed to 416-0: R 216-0; D 198-0 (ND 147-0, SD 51-0); I 2-0. A two-thirds majority of those present and voting (278 in this case) is required for adoption under suspension of the rules. May 23, 2000.

Key

- Y Voted for (yea).
- # Paired for.
- \+ Announced for.
- N Voted against (nay).
- X Paired against.
- – Announced against.
- P Voted "present."
- C Voted "present" to avoid possible conflict of interest.
- ? Did not vote or otherwise make a position known.

Democrats • ***Republicans***
Independents

	216	217	218	219	220	221
ALABAMA						
1 ***Callahan***	Y	Y	Y	Y	Y	Y
2 ***Everett***	Y	Y	Y	Y	Y	Y
3 ***Riley***	Y	Y	Y	Y	Y	Y
4 ***Aderholt***	Y	Y	Y	Y	Y	Y
5 Cramer	Y	Y	Y	Y	Y	Y
6 ***Bachus***	Y	Y	Y	Y	?	Y
7 Hilliard	Y	Y	Y	Y	Y	?
ALASKA						
AL ***Young***	?	Y	Y	Y	Y	Y
ARIZONA						
1 ***Salmon***	Y	N	Y	Y	Y	Y
2 Pastor	Y	Y	Y	Y	Y	Y
3 ***Stump***	Y	Y	Y	Y	Y	Y
4 ***Shadegg***	Y	N	Y	Y	Y	Y
5 ***Kolbe***	N	Y	Y	Y	Y	Y
6 ***Hayworth***	Y	Y	Y	Y	Y	Y
ARKANSAS						
1 Berry	Y	Y	Y	Y	Y	Y
2 Snyder	Y	Y	Y	Y	Y	Y
3 ***Hutchinson***	Y	Y	Y	Y	Y	Y
4 ***Dickey***	Y	Y	Y	Y	Y	Y
CALIFORNIA						
1 Thompson	Y	Y	Y	Y	Y	Y
2 ***Herger***	Y	Y	Y	Y	Y	Y
3 ***Ose***	Y	Y	Y	Y	Y	Y
4 ***Doolittle***	Y	Y	Y	Y	Y	Y
5 Matsui	Y	Y	Y	Y	Y	Y
6 Woolsey	Y	Y	Y	Y	Y	Y
7 Miller, George	Y	Y	Y	Y	Y	Y
8 Pelosi	Y	Y	Y	Y	Y	Y
9 Lee	Y	Y	Y	Y	Y	Y
10 Tauscher	Y	Y	Y	Y	Y	Y
11 ***Pombo***	Y	Y	Y	Y	Y	Y
12 Lantos	Y	Y	Y	Y	Y	Y
13 Stark	Y	Y	Y	Y	Y	Y
14 Eshoo	Y	Y	Y	Y	Y	Y
15 ***Campbell***	Y	N	Y	Y	Y	Y
16 Lofgren	Y	Y	Y	Y	Y	Y
17 Farr	Y	Y	Y	Y	Y	Y
18 Condit	Y	Y	Y	Y	Y	Y
19 ***Radanovich***	Y	Y	Y	Y	Y	Y
20 Dooley	Y	Y	Y	Y	Y	Y
21 ***Thomas***	Y	Y	Y	Y	Y	Y
22 Capps	Y	Y	Y	Y	Y	Y
23 ***Gallegly***	Y	Y	Y	Y	Y	Y
24 Sherman	Y	Y	Y	Y	Y	Y
25 ***McKeon***	Y	Y	Y	Y	Y	Y
26 Berman	Y	Y	Y	Y	Y	Y
27 ***Rogan***	Y	Y	Y	Y	Y	Y
28 ***Dreier***	Y	Y	Y	Y	Y	Y
29 Waxman	?	?	?	?	?	?
30 Becerra	Y	Y	Y	Y	Y	Y
31 Martinez	?	?	?	?	?	?
32 Dixon	Y	Y	Y	Y	Y	Y
33 Roybal-Allard	Y	Y	Y	Y	Y	Y
34 Napolitano	Y	+	Y	Y	Y	Y
35 Waters	Y	Y	Y	Y	Y	Y
36 ***Kuykendall***	Y	Y	Y	Y	Y	Y
37 Millender-McD.	Y	Y	Y	Y	Y	Y
38 ***Horn***	Y	Y	Y	Y	Y	Y
39 ***Royce***	Y	N	Y	Y	Y	Y
40 ***Lewis***	Y	Y	Y	Y	Y	Y
41 ***Miller, Gary***	Y	Y	Y	Y	Y	Y
42 Baca	Y	Y	Y	Y	Y	Y
43 ***Calvert***	Y	Y	Y	Y	Y	Y
44 ***Bono***	Y	Y	Y	Y	Y	Y
45 ***Rohrabacher***	Y	Y	Y	Y	Y	Y
46 Sanchez	Y	Y	Y	Y	Y	Y
47 ***Cox***	Y	?	Y	Y	Y	Y
48 ***Packard***	Y	Y	Y	Y	Y	Y
49 ***Bilbray***	Y	Y	Y	Y	Y	Y
50 Filner	Y	Y	Y	Y	Y	Y
51 ***Cunningham***	Y	Y	Y	Y	Y	Y
52 ***Hunter***	Y	Y	Y	Y	Y	Y
COLORADO						
1 DeGette	Y	Y	Y	Y	Y	Y
2 Udall	Y	Y	Y	Y	Y	Y
3 ***McInnis***	Y	Y	Y	Y	Y	Y
4 ***Schaffer***	Y	Y	Y	Y	Y	Y
5 ***Hefley***	Y	Y	Y	Y	Y	Y
6 ***Tancredo***	Y	Y	Y	Y	Y	Y
CONNECTICUT						
1 Larson	?	?	?	?	?	?
2 Gejdenson	Y	Y	Y	Y	Y	Y
3 DeLauro	Y	Y	Y	Y	Y	Y
4 ***Shays***	Y	N	Y	Y	Y	Y
5 Maloney	Y	Y	Y	Y	Y	Y
6 ***Johnson***	N	Y	Y	Y	Y	Y
DELAWARE						
AL ***Castle***	Y	Y	Y	Y	Y	Y
FLORIDA						
1 ***Scarborough***	?	Y	Y	Y	Y	Y
2 Boyd	Y	Y	Y	Y	Y	Y
3 Brown	Y	Y	Y	Y	Y	Y
4 ***Fowler***	Y	Y	Y	Y	Y	Y
5 Thurman	Y	Y	Y	Y	Y	Y
6 ***Stearns***	Y	Y	Y	Y	Y	Y
7 ***Mica***	Y	Y	Y	Y	Y	Y
8 ***McCollum***	Y	?	?	?	?	?
9 ***Bilirakis***	Y	Y	Y	Y	Y	Y
10 ***Young***	Y	Y	Y	Y	Y	Y
11 Davis	Y	Y	Y	Y	Y	Y
12 ***Canady***	Y	Y	Y	Y	Y	Y
13 ***Miller***	Y	Y	Y	Y	Y	Y
14 ***Goss***	Y	Y	Y	Y	Y	Y
15 ***Weldon***	Y	Y	Y	Y	Y	Y
16 ***Foley***	Y	Y	Y	Y	Y	Y
17 Meek	Y	Y	Y	Y	Y	Y
18 ***Ros-Lehtinen***	Y	Y	Y	Y	Y	Y
19 Wexler	Y	Y	Y	Y	Y	Y
20 Deutsch	Y	Y	Y	Y	Y	Y
21 ***Diaz-Balart***	Y	Y	Y	Y	Y	Y
22 ***Shaw***	Y	Y	Y	Y	Y	Y
23 Hastings	Y	Y	Y	Y	Y	Y
GEORGIA						
1 ***Kingston***	Y	Y	Y	Y	Y	Y
2 Bishop	Y	Y	Y	Y	Y	Y
3 ***Collins***	Y	Y	Y	Y	Y	Y
4 McKinney	Y	Y	Y	Y	Y	Y
5 Lewis	Y	Y	Y	Y	Y	Y
6 ***Isakson***	Y	Y	Y	Y	Y	Y
7 ***Barr***	Y	Y	Y	Y	Y	Y
8 ***Chambliss***	Y	Y	Y	Y	Y	Y
9 ***Deal***	Y	Y	Y	Y	Y	Y
10 ***Norwood***	Y	Y	Y	Y	Y	Y
11 ***Linder***	Y	Y	Y	Y	Y	Y
HAWAII						
1 Abercrombie	Y	Y	Y	Y	Y	Y
2 Mink	Y	Y	Y	Y	Y	Y
IDAHO						
1 ***Chenoweth-Hage***	Y	N	Y	Y	Y	Y
2 ***Simpson***	Y	Y	Y	Y	Y	Y
ILLINOIS						
1 Rush	Y	Y	Y	Y	Y	Y
2 Jackson	Y	Y	Y	Y	Y	Y
3 Lipinski	Y	Y	Y	Y	Y	Y
4 Gutierrez	Y	Y	Y	Y	Y	Y
5 Blagojevich	Y	Y	Y	Y	Y	Y
6 ***Hyde***	Y	Y	Y	Y	Y	Y
7 Davis	Y	Y	Y	Y	Y	Y
8 ***Crane***	Y	Y	Y	Y	Y	Y
9 Schakowsky	Y	Y	Y	Y	Y	Y
10 ***Porter***	Y	Y	Y	Y	Y	Y
11 ***Weller***	Y	?	Y	Y	Y	Y
12 Costello	Y	Y	Y	Y	Y	Y
13 ***Biggert***	Y	Y	Y	Y	Y	Y

ND Northern Democrats SD Southern Democrats

	216	217	218	219	220	221
14 ***Hastert***						
15 ***Ewing***	Y	Y	Y	Y	Y	Y
16 ***Manzullo***	Y	Y	Y	Y	Y	Y
17 Evans	Y	Y	Y	Y	Y	Y
18 ***LaHood***	Y	Y	Y	Y	Y	Y
19 Phelps	Y	Y	Y	Y	Y	Y
20 ***Shimkus***	Y	Y	Y	Y	Y	Y
INDIANA						
1 Visclosky	Y	Y	Y	Y	Y	Y
2 ***McIntosh***	?	?	?	?	?	?
3 Roemer	Y	Y	Y	Y	Y	Y
4 ***Souder***	Y	Y	Y	Y	Y	Y
5 ***Buyer***	Y	Y	Y	Y	Y	Y
6 ***Burton***	Y	Y	Y	Y	Y	Y
7 ***Pease***	Y	?	?	?	?	?
8 ***Hostettler***	Y	N	Y	Y	Y	Y
9 Hill	Y	Y	Y	Y	Y	Y
10 Carson	Y	Y	Y	Y	Y	Y
IOWA						
1 ***Leach***	Y	Y	Y	Y	Y	Y
2 ***Nussle***	Y	Y	Y	Y	Y	Y
3 Boswell	Y	Y	Y	Y	Y	Y
4 ***Ganske***	Y	Y	Y	Y	Y	Y
5 ***Latham***	Y	Y	Y	Y	Y	Y
KANSAS						
1 ***Moran***	Y	Y	Y	Y	Y	Y
2 ***Ryun***	Y	Y	Y	Y	Y	Y
3 Moore	Y	Y	Y	Y	Y	Y
4 ***Tiahrt***	+	Y	Y	Y	Y	Y
KENTUCKY						
1 ***Whitfield***	Y	Y	Y	Y	Y	Y
2 ***Lewis***	Y	Y	Y	Y	Y	Y
3 ***Northup***	Y	Y	Y	Y	Y	Y
4 Lucas	Y	Y	Y	Y	Y	Y
5 ***Rogers***	Y	Y	Y	Y	Y	Y
6 ***Fletcher***	Y	Y	Y	Y	Y	Y
LOUISIANA						
1 ***Vitter***	Y	Y	Y	Y	Y	Y
2 Jefferson	Y	Y	Y	Y	Y	Y
3 ***Tauzin***	Y	Y	Y	Y	Y	Y
4 ***McCrery***	Y	Y	Y	Y	Y	Y
5 ***Cooksey***	?	Y	Y	Y	Y	Y
6 ***Baker***	Y	Y	Y	Y	Y	Y
7 John	Y	Y	Y	Y	Y	Y
MAINE						
1 Allen	Y	Y	Y	Y	Y	Y
2 Baldacci	Y	Y	Y	Y	Y	Y
MARYLAND						
1 ***Gilchrest***	Y	Y	Y	Y	Y	Y
2 ***Ehrlich***	Y	Y	Y	Y	Y	Y
3 Cardin	Y	Y	Y	Y	Y	Y
4 Wynn	Y	Y	Y	Y	Y	Y
5 Hoyer	Y	Y	Y	Y	Y	Y
6 ***Bartlett***	Y	Y	Y	Y	Y	Y
7 Cummings	Y	Y	Y	Y	Y	Y
8 ***Morella***	Y	Y	Y	Y	Y	Y
MASSACHUSETTS						
1 Olver	Y	Y	Y	Y	Y	Y
2 Neal	Y	Y	Y	Y	Y	Y
3 McGovern	Y	Y	Y	Y	Y	Y
4 Frank	N	Y	Y	Y	Y	Y
5 Meehan	Y	Y	Y	Y	Y	Y
6 Tierney	Y	Y	Y	Y	Y	Y
7 Markey	Y	Y	Y	Y	Y	Y
8 Capuano	+	+	+	+	+	+
9 Moakley	Y	Y	Y	Y	Y	Y
10 Delahunt	Y	Y	Y	Y	Y	Y
MICHIGAN						
1 Stupak	?	?	?	?	?	?
2 ***Hoekstra***	Y	Y	Y	Y	Y	Y
3 ***Ehlers***	Y	Y	Y	Y	Y	Y
4 ***Camp***	Y	Y	Y	Y	Y	Y
5 Barcia	Y	Y	Y	Y	Y	Y
6 ***Upton***	Y	Y	Y	Y	Y	Y
7 ***Smith***	Y	Y	Y	Y	Y	Y
8 Stabenow	Y	Y	Y	Y	Y	Y
9 Kildee	Y	Y	Y	Y	Y	Y
10 Bonior	Y	Y	Y	Y	Y	Y
11 ***Knollenberg***	Y	Y	Y	Y	Y	Y
12 Levin	Y	Y	Y	Y	Y	Y
13 Rivers	Y	Y	Y	Y	Y	Y
14 Conyers	Y	Y	Y	Y	Y	Y
15 Kilpatrick	Y	Y	Y	Y	Y	Y
16 Dingell	Y	Y	Y	Y	Y	Y
MINNESOTA						
1 ***Gutknecht***	Y	N	Y	Y	Y	Y
2 Minge	?	Y	Y	Y	Y	Y
3 ***Ramstad***	Y	Y	Y	Y	Y	Y
4 Vento	Y	Y	Y	Y	Y	Y
5 Sabo	Y	Y	Y	Y	Y	Y
6 Luther	Y	Y	Y	Y	Y	Y
7 Peterson	Y	N	Y	Y	Y	Y
8 Oberstar	+	Y	Y	Y	Y	Y
MISSISSIPPI						
1 ***Wicker***	Y	Y	Y	Y	Y	Y
2 Thompson	Y	Y	Y	Y	Y	Y
3 ***Pickering***	Y	Y	Y	Y	Y	Y
4 Shows	Y	Y	Y	Y	Y	Y
5 Taylor	Y	Y	Y	Y	Y	Y
MISSOURI						
1 Clay	Y	Y	Y	Y	Y	Y
2 ***Talent***	Y	Y	Y	Y	Y	Y
3 Gephardt	Y	Y	Y	Y	Y	Y
4 Skelton	Y	Y	Y	Y	Y	Y
5 McCarthy	Y	Y	Y	Y	Y	Y
6 Danner	Y	Y	Y	Y	Y	Y
7 ***Blunt***	Y	Y	Y	Y	Y	Y
8 ***Emerson***	Y	Y	Y	Y	Y	Y
9 ***Hulshof***	Y	Y	Y	Y	Y	Y
MONTANA						
AL ***Hill***	Y	Y	Y	Y	Y	Y
NEBRASKA						
1 ***Bereuter***	N	Y	Y	Y	Y	Y
2 ***Terry***	Y	Y	Y	Y	Y	Y
3 ***Barrett***	Y	Y	Y	Y	Y	Y
NEVADA						
1 Berkley	Y	Y	Y	Y	Y	Y
2 ***Gibbons***	Y	Y	Y	Y	Y	Y
NEW HAMPSHIRE						
1 ***Sununu***	Y	Y	Y	Y	Y	Y
2 ***Bass***	Y	Y	Y	Y	Y	Y
NEW JERSEY						
1 Andrews	Y	Y	Y	Y	Y	Y
2 ***LoBiondo***	Y	Y	Y	Y	Y	Y
3 ***Saxton***	Y	Y	Y	Y	Y	Y
4 ***Smith***	Y	Y	Y	Y	Y	Y
5 ***Roukema***	Y	Y	Y	Y	Y	Y
6 Pallone	Y	Y	Y	Y	Y	Y
7 ***Franks***	Y	Y	Y	Y	Y	Y
8 Pascrell	Y	Y	Y	Y	Y	Y
9 Rothman	Y	Y	Y	Y	Y	Y
10 Payne	Y	Y	Y	Y	Y	Y
11 ***Frelinghuysen***	Y	Y	Y	Y	Y	Y
12 Holt	Y	Y	Y	Y	Y	Y
13 Menendez	Y	Y	Y	Y	Y	Y
NEW MEXICO						
1 ***Wilson***	Y	Y	Y	Y	Y	Y
2 ***Skeen***	Y	Y	Y	Y	Y	Y
3 Udall	Y	Y	Y	Y	Y	Y
NEW YORK						
1 Forbes	?	?	?	?	?	?
2 ***Lazio***	?	Y	Y	Y	Y	Y
3 ***King***	Y	Y	Y	Y	Y	Y
4 McCarthy	?	?	?	?	?	?
5 Ackerman	?	?	?	?	?	?
6 Meeks	Y	Y	Y	Y	Y	Y
7 Crowley	Y	Y	Y	Y	Y	Y
8 Nadler	Y	Y	Y	Y	Y	Y
9 Weiner	?	?	?	?	?	?
10 Towns	Y	Y	Y	Y	Y	Y
11 Owens	Y	Y	Y	Y	Y	Y
12 Velázquez	Y	Y	Y	Y	Y	Y
13 ***Fossella***	Y	Y	Y	Y	Y	Y
14 Maloney	Y	Y	Y	Y	Y	Y
15 Rangel	Y	Y	Y	Y	Y	Y
16 Serrano	Y	Y	Y	Y	Y	Y
17 Engel	Y	Y	Y	Y	Y	Y
18 Lowey	Y	Y	Y	Y	Y	Y
19 ***Kelly***	Y	Y	Y	Y	Y	Y
20 ***Gilman***	Y	Y	Y	Y	Y	Y
21 McNulty	Y	Y	Y	Y	Y	Y
22 ***Sweeney***	Y	Y	Y	Y	Y	Y
23 ***Boehlert***	Y	Y	Y	Y	Y	Y
24 ***McHugh***	Y	Y	Y	Y	Y	+
25 ***Walsh***	Y	Y	Y	Y	Y	Y
26 Hinchey	Y	Y	Y	Y	Y	Y
27 ***Reynolds***	Y	Y	Y	Y	Y	Y
28 Slaughter	Y	Y	Y	Y	Y	Y
29 LaFalce	Y	Y	Y	Y	Y	Y
30 ***Quinn***	Y	Y	Y	Y	Y	Y
31 ***Houghton***	N	Y	Y	Y	Y	Y
NORTH CAROLINA						
1 Clayton	Y	Y	Y	Y	Y	Y
2 Etheridge	Y	Y	Y	Y	Y	Y
3 ***Jones***	Y	Y	Y	Y	Y	Y
4 Price	Y	Y	Y	Y	Y	Y
5 ***Burr***	Y	Y	Y	Y	Y	Y
6 ***Coble***	Y	N	Y	Y	Y	Y
7 McIntyre	Y	Y	Y	Y	Y	Y
8 ***Hayes***	Y	Y	Y	Y	Y	Y
9 ***Myrick***	Y	Y	Y	Y	Y	Y
10 ***Ballenger***	Y	Y	Y	Y	Y	Y
11 ***Taylor***	Y	Y	Y	Y	Y	Y
12 Watt	N	Y	Y	Y	Y	Y
NORTH DAKOTA						
AL Pomeroy	Y	Y	Y	Y	Y	Y
OHIO						
1 ***Chabot***	Y	Y	Y	Y	Y	Y
2 ***Portman***	Y	Y	Y	Y	Y	Y
3 Hall	Y	Y	Y	Y	Y	Y
4 ***Oxley***	Y	Y	Y	Y	Y	Y
5 ***Gillmor***	Y	Y	Y	Y	Y	Y
6 Strickland	Y	Y	Y	Y	Y	Y
7 ***Hobson***	Y	Y	Y	Y	Y	Y
8 ***Boehner***	Y	Y	Y	Y	Y	Y
9 Kaptur	Y	Y	Y	Y	Y	Y
10 Kucinich	Y	Y	Y	Y	Y	Y
11 Jones	Y	Y	Y	Y	Y	Y
12 ***Kasich***	Y	Y	Y	Y	Y	Y
13 Brown	?	?	?	?	?	?
14 Sawyer	Y	Y	Y	Y	Y	Y
15 ***Pryce***	Y	Y	Y	?	Y	Y
16 ***Regula***	Y	Y	Y	Y	Y	Y
17 Traficant	Y	Y	Y	Y	Y	Y
18 ***Ney***	Y	Y	Y	Y	Y	Y
19 ***LaTourette***	Y	Y	Y	Y	Y	Y
OKLAHOMA						
1 ***Largent***	Y	Y	Y	Y	Y	Y
2 ***Coburn***	Y	Y	Y	Y	Y	Y
3 ***Watkins***	Y	Y	Y	Y	Y	Y
4 ***Watts***	Y	Y	Y	Y	Y	Y
5 ***Istook***	Y	Y	Y	Y	Y	Y
6 ***Lucas***	Y	Y	Y	Y	Y	Y
OREGON						
1 Wu	Y	Y	Y	Y	Y	Y
2 ***Walden***	Y	Y	Y	Y	Y	Y
3 Blumenauer	Y	Y	Y	Y	Y	Y
4 DeFazio	Y	Y	Y	Y	Y	Y
5 Hooley	Y	Y	Y	Y	Y	Y
PENNSYLVANIA						
1 Brady	Y	Y	Y	Y	Y	Y
2 Fattah	Y	Y	Y	Y	Y	Y
3 Borski	Y	Y	Y	Y	Y	Y
4 Klink	Y	Y	Y	Y	Y	Y
5 ***Peterson***	Y	Y	Y	Y	Y	Y
6 Holden	Y	Y	Y	Y	Y	Y
7 ***Weldon***	Y	Y	Y	Y	Y	Y
8 ***Greenwood***	Y	Y	Y	Y	Y	Y
9 ***Shuster***	N	Y	Y	Y	Y	Y
10 ***Sherwood***	Y	Y	Y	Y	Y	Y
11 Kanjorski	Y	Y	Y	Y	Y	Y
12 Murtha	Y	Y	Y	Y	Y	Y
13 Hoeffel	Y	Y	Y	Y	Y	Y
14 Coyne	N	Y	Y	Y	Y	Y
15 ***Toomey***	Y	Y	Y	Y	Y	Y
16 ***Pitts***	Y	Y	Y	Y	Y	Y
17 ***Gekas***	Y	Y	Y	Y	Y	Y
18 Doyle	Y	Y	Y	Y	Y	Y
19 ***Goodling***	Y	Y	Y	Y	Y	Y
20 Mascara	Y	Y	Y	Y	Y	Y
21 ***English***	Y	Y	Y	Y	Y	Y
RHODE ISLAND						
1 Kennedy	Y	Y	Y	Y	Y	Y
2 Weygand	Y	Y	Y	Y	Y	Y
SOUTH CAROLINA						
1 ***Sanford***	Y	N	Y	Y	Y	Y
2 ***Spence***	Y	Y	Y	Y	Y	Y
3 ***Graham***	Y	Y	Y	Y	Y	Y
4 ***DeMint***	Y	Y	Y	Y	Y	Y
5 Spratt	Y	Y	Y	Y	Y	Y
6 Clyburn	Y	Y	Y	Y	Y	Y
SOUTH DAKOTA						
AL ***Thune***	Y	Y	Y	Y	Y	Y
TENNESSEE						
1 ***Jenkins***	Y	Y	Y	Y	Y	Y
2 ***Duncan***	Y	Y	Y	Y	Y	Y
3 ***Wamp***	Y	Y	Y	Y	Y	Y
4 ***Hilleary***	Y	Y	Y	Y	Y	Y
5 Clement	Y	Y	Y	Y	Y	Y
6 Gordon	Y	Y	Y	Y	Y	Y
7 ***Bryant***	?	Y	Y	Y	Y	Y
8 Tanner	Y	Y	Y	Y	Y	Y
9 Ford	Y	Y	Y	Y	Y	Y
TEXAS						
1 Sandlin	Y	Y	Y	Y	Y	Y
2 Turner	Y	Y	Y	Y	Y	Y
3 ***Johnson, Sam***	Y	Y	Y	Y	Y	Y
4 Hall	Y	Y	Y	Y	Y	Y
5 ***Sessions***	Y	Y	Y	Y	Y	Y
6 ***Barton***	?	Y	Y	Y	Y	Y
7 ***Archer***	Y	?	Y	Y	Y	Y
8 ***Brady***	Y	?	Y	Y	Y	Y
9 Lampson	Y	Y	Y	Y	Y	Y
10 Doggett	Y	Y	Y	Y	Y	Y
11 Edwards	Y	Y	Y	Y	Y	Y
12 ***Granger***	Y	Y	Y	Y	Y	Y
13 ***Thornberry***	Y	Y	Y	Y	Y	Y
14 ***Paul***	Y	N	Y	N	Y	Y
15 Hinojosa	Y	Y	Y	Y	Y	Y
16 Reyes	Y	Y	Y	Y	Y	Y
17 Stenholm	Y	Y	Y	Y	Y	Y
18 Jackson-Lee	Y	Y	Y	Y	Y	Y
19 ***Combest***	Y	Y	Y	Y	Y	Y
20 Gonzalez	Y	Y	Y	Y	Y	Y
21 ***Smith***	Y	Y	Y	Y	Y	Y
22 ***DeLay***	Y	Y	Y	Y	Y	Y
23 ***Bonilla***	Y	Y	Y	Y	Y	Y
24 Frost	Y	Y	Y	Y	Y	Y
25 Bentsen	Y	Y	Y	Y	Y	Y
26 ***Armey***	Y	Y	Y	Y	Y	Y
27 Ortiz	Y	Y	Y	Y	Y	Y
28 Rodriguez	?	?	?	?	?	?
29 Green	Y	Y	Y	?	Y	Y
30 Johnson, E.B.	Y	Y	Y	Y	Y	Y
UTAH						
1 ***Hansen***	Y	Y	Y	Y	Y	Y
2 ***Cook***	Y	Y	Y	Y	Y	Y
3 ***Cannon***	Y	Y	Y	Y	Y	Y
VERMONT						
AL *Sanders*	Y	Y	Y	Y	Y	Y
VIRGINIA						
1 ***Bateman***	Y	Y	Y	Y	Y	Y
2 Pickett	Y	Y	?	Y	?	?
3 Scott	Y	Y	Y	Y	Y	Y
4 Sisisky	Y	Y	Y	Y	Y	Y
5 *Goode*	Y	Y	Y	Y	Y	Y
6 ***Goodlatte***	Y	Y	Y	Y	Y	Y
7 ***Bliley***	Y	Y	Y	Y	Y	Y
8 Moran	Y	Y	Y	Y	Y	Y
9 Boucher	Y	Y	Y	Y	Y	Y
10 ***Wolf***	Y	Y	Y	Y	Y	Y
11 ***Davis***	Y	Y	Y	Y	Y	Y
WASHINGTON						
1 Inslee	Y	Y	Y	Y	Y	Y
2 ***Metcalf***	Y	Y	Y	Y	Y	Y
3 Baird	Y	Y	Y	Y	Y	Y
4 ***Hastings***	Y	Y	Y	Y	Y	Y
5 ***Nethercutt***	Y	?	?	Y	Y	Y
6 Dicks	Y	Y	Y	Y	Y	Y
7 McDermott	Y	Y	Y	Y	Y	Y
8 ***Dunn***	Y	Y	Y	Y	Y	Y
9 Smith	Y	Y	Y	Y	Y	Y
WEST VIRGINIA						
1 Mollohan	Y	Y	Y	Y	Y	Y
2 Wise	?	Y	Y	Y	Y	Y
3 Rahall	Y	Y	Y	Y	Y	Y
WISCONSIN						
1 ***Ryan***	Y	Y	Y	Y	Y	Y
2 Baldwin	Y	Y	Y	Y	Y	Y
3 Kind	Y	Y	Y	Y	Y	Y
4 Kleczka	Y	Y	Y	Y	Y	Y
5 Barrett	Y	Y	Y	Y	Y	Y
6 ***Petri***	Y	Y	Y	Y	Y	Y
7 Obey	Y	Y	Y	Y	Y	Y
8 ***Green***	Y	Y	Y	Y	Y	Y
9 ***Sensenbrenner***	Y	N	Y	Y	Y	Y
WYOMING						
AL ***Cubin***	Y	?	?	?	?	?

Southern states - Ala., Ark., Fla., Ga., Ky., La., Miss., N.C., Okla., S.C., Tenn., Texas, Va.

House Votes **222, 223, 224, 225, 227 ***

222. HR 2498. Heart Attack Victims/Passage. Stearns, R-Fla., motion to suspend the rules and pass the bill that would place automatic external defibrillators in federal buildings to assist heart-attack victims, and provide limited immunity from civil liability for anyone who uses the devices in an emergency. Motion agreed to 415-2: R 214-2; D 199-0 (ND 147-0, SD 52-0); I 2-0. A two-thirds majority of those present and voting (278 in this case) is required for passage under suspension of the rules. May 23, 2000.

223. HR 3639. Harry S Truman Building/Passage. Shuster, R-Pa., motion to suspend the rules and pass the bill that would designate the federal building that currently houses the State Department the "Harry S Truman Federal Building." Motion agreed to 413-0: R 215-0; D 196-0 (ND 146-0, SD 50-0); I 2-0. A two-thirds majority of those present and voting (276 in this case) is required for passage under suspension of the rules. May 23, 2000.

224. Procedural Motion/Journal. Approval of the House Journal of May 23, 2000. Approved 345-54: R 188-15; D 155-39 (ND 111-31, SD 44-8); I 2-0. May 24, 2000.

225. HR 4444. China Trade/Rule. Adoption of the rule (H Res 510) to provide for House floor consideration of the bill that would grant permanent normal trade relations to the People's Republic of China. Adopted 294-136: R 217-2; D 77-132 (ND 44-111, SD 33-21); I 0-2. May 24, 2000.

226. Procedural Motion/Quorum Call. * A quorum was present with 419 members (15 did not respond). May 24, 2000.

227. HR 4444. China Trade/Motion to Recommit. Bonior, D-Mich., motion to recommit the bill to the House Ways and Means and International Relations committees with instructions to add language revoking China's permanent normal trade relations status if China invades, blockades or attacks Taiwan. Motion rejected 176-258: R 44-177; D 130-81 (ND 108-49, SD 22-32); I 2-0. May 24, 2000.

* *CQ does not include quorum calls in its vote charts.*

Key

- Y Voted for (yea).
- # Paired for.
- \+ Announced for.
- N Voted against (nay).
- X Paired against.
- – Announced against.
- P Voted "present."
- C Voted "present" to avoid possible conflict of interest.
- ? Did not vote or otherwise make a position known.

Democrats • ***Republicans*** *Independents*

	222	223	224	225	227
ALABAMA					
1 ***Callahan***	Y	Y	Y	Y	N
2 ***Everett***	Y	Y	Y	Y	N
3 ***Riley***	Y	Y	Y	Y	Y
4 ***Aderholt***	Y	Y	N	Y	Y
5 Cramer	Y	Y	Y	Y	N
6 ***Bachus***	Y	Y	Y	Y	N
7 Hilliard	?	?	N	N	Y
ALASKA					
AL ***Young***	Y	Y	?	Y	N
ARIZONA					
1 ***Salmon***	Y	Y	Y	Y	N
2 Pastor	Y	Y	Y	Y	N
3 ***Stump***	Y	Y	Y	Y	N
4 ***Shadegg***	Y	Y	Y	Y	Y
5 ***Kolbe***	Y	Y	Y	Y	N
6 ***Hayworth***	Y	Y	Y	Y	N
ARKANSAS					
1 Berry	Y	Y	Y	Y	N
2 Snyder	Y	Y	Y	Y	N
3 ***Hutchinson***	Y	?	Y	Y	N
4 ***Dickey***	Y	Y	N	Y	N
CALIFORNIA					
1 Thompson	Y	Y	N	Y	N
2 ***Herger***	Y	Y	Y	Y	N
3 ***Ose***	Y	Y	Y	Y	N
4 ***Doolittle***	Y	Y	Y	Y	N
5 Matsui	Y	Y	Y	Y	N
6 Woolsey	Y	Y	Y	N	Y
7 Miller, George	Y	Y	N	N	Y
8 Pelosi	Y	Y	Y	N	Y
9 Lee	Y	Y	Y	N	Y
10 Tauscher	Y	Y	Y	Y	N
11 ***Pombo***	Y	Y	Y	Y	Y
12 Lantos	Y	Y	Y	N	Y
13 Stark	Y	Y	N	N	Y
14 Eshoo	Y	Y	Y	Y	N
15 ***Campbell***	Y	Y	Y	Y	N
16 Lofgren	Y	Y	Y	Y	N
17 Farr	Y	Y	Y	N	Y
18 Condit	Y	Y	Y	N	Y
19 ***Radanovich***	Y	Y	Y	Y	N
20 Dooley	Y	Y	Y	Y	N
21 ***Thomas***	Y	Y	Y	Y	N
22 Capps	Y	Y	Y	Y	N
23 ***Gallegly***	Y	Y	Y	Y	N
24 Sherman	Y	Y	Y	N	Y
25 ***McKeon***	Y	Y	Y	Y	N
26 Berman	Y	Y	Y	N	Y
27 ***Rogan***	Y	Y	N	Y	Y
28 ***Dreier***	Y	Y	Y	Y	N
29 Waxman	?	?	Y	N	Y
30 Becerra	Y	Y	Y	Y	N
31 Martinez	?	?	?	Y	N
32 Dixon	Y	Y	Y	Y	N
33 Roybal-Allard	Y	Y	Y	N	Y
34 Napolitano	Y	Y	Y	Y	N
35 Waters	Y	Y	N	N	Y
36 ***Kuykendall***	Y	Y	Y	Y	N
37 Millender-McD.	Y	Y	Y	N	Y
38 ***Horn***	Y	Y	Y	Y	Y
39 ***Royce***	?	Y	Y	Y	N
40 ***Lewis***	Y	Y	Y	Y	N
41 ***Miller, Gary***	Y	Y	Y	Y	N
42 Baca	Y	Y	Y	N	Y
43 ***Calvert***	Y	Y	Y	Y	N
44 ***Bono***	Y	Y	Y	Y	N
45 ***Rohrabacher***	Y	Y	Y	Y	Y
46 Sanchez	Y	Y	Y	N	Y
47 ***Cox***	Y	Y	Y	Y	N
48 ***Packard***	Y	Y	Y	Y	N
49 ***Bilbray***	Y	Y	N	Y	N
50 Filner	Y	Y	N	N	N
51 ***Cunningham***	Y	Y	Y	Y	N
52 ***Hunter***	Y	Y	Y	Y	Y
COLORADO					
1 DeGette	Y	Y	Y	Y	N
2 Udall	Y	Y	?	Y	Y
3 ***McInnis***	Y	Y	Y	Y	N
4 ***Schaffer***	Y	Y	N	Y	Y
5 ***Hefley***	Y	Y	N	Y	Y
6 ***Tancredo***	Y	Y	P	Y	Y
CONNECTICUT					
1 Larson	?	?	?	N	N
2 Gejdenson	Y	Y	Y	N	Y
3 DeLauro	Y	Y	Y	N	Y
4 ***Shays***	Y	Y	Y	Y	N
5 Maloney	Y	Y	Y	Y	N
6 ***Johnson***	Y	Y	Y	Y	N
DELAWARE					
AL ***Castle***	Y	Y	Y	Y	N
FLORIDA					
1 ***Scarborough***	Y	Y	?	?	?
2 Boyd	Y	Y	Y	Y	N
3 Brown	Y	Y	Y	N	Y
4 ***Fowler***	Y	Y	Y	Y	N
5 Thurman	Y	Y	Y	Y	Y
6 ***Stearns***	Y	Y	Y	Y	Y
7 ***Mica***	Y	Y	Y	Y	N
8 ***McCollum***	?	?	Y	Y	N
9 ***Bilirakis***	Y	Y	Y	Y	N
10 ***Young***	Y	Y	Y	Y	N
11 Davis	Y	?	Y	Y	N
12 ***Canady***	Y	Y	Y	Y	N
13 ***Miller***	Y	Y	Y	Y	N
14 ***Goss***	Y	Y	Y	Y	N
15 ***Weldon***	Y	Y	Y	Y	Y
16 ***Foley***	Y	Y	Y	Y	N
17 Meek	Y	Y	Y	N	N
18 ***Ros-Lehtinen***	Y	Y	Y	Y	N
19 Wexler	Y	Y	Y	N	Y
20 Deutsch	Y	Y	Y	N	Y
21 ***Diaz-Balart***	Y	Y	Y	Y	N
22 ***Shaw***	Y	Y	Y	Y	N
23 Hastings	Y	Y	N	N	N
GEORGIA					
1 ***Kingston***	Y	Y	Y	Y	Y
2 Bishop	Y	Y	Y	Y	N
3 ***Collins***	Y	Y	Y	Y	N
4 McKinney	Y	Y	?	N	Y
5 Lewis	Y	Y	N	N	Y
6 ***Isakson***	Y	Y	Y	Y	N
7 ***Barr***	Y	Y	Y	Y	Y
8 ***Chambliss***	Y	Y	Y	Y	N
9 ***Deal***	Y	Y	Y	Y	N
10 ***Norwood***	Y	Y	Y	Y	Y
11 ***Linder***	Y	Y	Y	Y	N
HAWAII					
1 Abercrombie	Y	Y	Y	N	Y
2 Mink	Y	Y	Y	N	Y
IDAHO					
1 ***Chenoweth-Hage***	Y	?	?	Y	Y
2 ***Simpson***	Y	Y	Y	Y	N
ILLINOIS					
1 Rush	Y	Y	?	N	Y
2 Jackson	Y	Y	Y	N	Y
3 Lipinski	Y	Y	N	N	Y
4 Gutierrez	Y	Y	N	N	Y
5 Blagojevich	Y	Y	Y	N	Y
6 ***Hyde***	Y	Y	Y	Y	N
7 Davis	Y	Y	Y	N	Y
8 ***Crane***	Y	Y	N	Y	N
9 Schakowsky	Y	Y	Y	N	Y
10 ***Porter***	Y	Y	Y	Y	N
11 ***Weller***	Y	Y	N	Y	N
12 Costello	Y	Y	N	N	Y
13 ***Biggert***	Y	Y	Y	Y	N

ND Northern Democrats SD Southern Democrats

	222	223	224	225	227
14 ***Hastert***				Y	N
15 ***Ewing***	Y	Y	Y	Y	N
16 ***Manzullo***	Y	Y	Y	Y	N
17 Evans	Y	Y	Y	N	Y
18 ***LaHood***	Y	Y	Y	Y	N
19 Phelps	Y	Y	N	N	Y
20 ***Shimkus***	Y	Y	Y	Y	N
INDIANA					
1 Visclosky	Y	Y	N	N	Y
2 ***McIntosh***	?	?	Y	Y	N
3 Roemer	Y	Y	Y	Y	N
4 ***Souder***	Y	Y	Y	Y	Y
5 ***Buyer***	Y	Y	Y	Y	Y
6 ***Burton***	Y	Y	?	Y	Y
7 ***Pease***	?	?	?	?	N
8 ***Hostettler***	Y	Y	Y	Y	Y
9 Hill	Y	Y	Y	Y	N
10 Carson	Y	Y	Y	Y	N
IOWA					
1 ***Leach***	Y	Y	Y	Y	N
2 ***Nussle***	Y	Y	Y	Y	N
3 Boswell	Y	Y	Y	Y	N
4 ***Ganske***	Y	Y	?	Y	N
5 ***Latham***	Y	Y	Y	Y	N
KANSAS					
1 ***Moran***	Y	Y	Y	Y	N
2 ***Ryun***	Y	Y	Y	Y	N
3 Moore	Y	Y	N	Y	N
4 ***Tiahrt***	Y	Y	Y	Y	N
KENTUCKY					
1 ***Whitfield***	Y	Y	Y	Y	N
2 ***Lewis***	Y	Y	Y	Y	N
3 ***Northup***	Y	Y	Y	Y	N
4 Lucas	Y	Y	Y	Y	N
5 ***Rogers***	Y	Y	Y	Y	Y
6 ***Fletcher***	Y	Y	Y	Y	N
LOUISIANA					
1 ***Vitter***	Y	Y	Y	Y	N
2 Jefferson	Y	Y	Y	Y	N
3 ***Tauzin***	Y	Y	?	Y	N
4 ***McCrery***	Y	Y	Y	Y	N
5 ***Cooksey***	Y	Y	Y	Y	N
6 ***Baker***	Y	Y	Y	Y	N
7 John	Y	Y	Y	Y	N
MAINE					
1 Allen	Y	Y	Y	Y	N
2 Baldacci	Y	Y	Y	N	Y
MARYLAND					
1 ***Gilchrest***	Y	Y	?	Y	N
2 ***Ehrlich***	Y	Y	?	Y	N
3 Cardin	Y	Y	Y	N	N
4 Wynn	Y	Y	Y	N	Y
5 Hoyer	Y	Y	Y	Y	N
6 ***Bartlett***	Y	Y	Y	Y	Y
7 Cummings	Y	Y	?	N	Y
8 ***Morella***	Y	Y	?	Y	N
MASSACHUSETTS					
1 Olver	Y	Y	N	N	Y
2 Neal	Y	Y	Y	Y	N
3 McGovern	Y	Y	Y	N	Y
4 Frank	Y	Y	Y	N	Y
5 Meehan	Y	Y	Y	Y	N
6 Tierney	Y	Y	Y	N	Y
7 Markey	Y	Y	Y	N	Y
8 Capuano	?	?	Y	N	Y
9 Moakley	Y	Y	Y	N	Y
10 Delahunt	Y	Y	?	N	Y
MICHIGAN					
1 Stupak	?	?	?	?	Y
2 ***Hoekstra***	Y	Y	Y	Y	Y
3 ***Ehlers***	Y	Y	Y	Y	N
4 ***Camp***	Y	Y	Y	Y	N
5 Barcia	Y	Y	Y	N	Y
6 ***Upton***	Y	Y	Y	Y	N
7 ***Smith***	Y	Y	Y	Y	Y
8 Stabenow	Y	Y	Y	N	Y
9 Kildee	Y	Y	Y	N	Y
10 Bonior	Y	Y	N	N	Y
11 ***Knollenberg***	Y	Y	Y	Y	N
12 Levin	Y	Y	Y	Y	N
13 Rivers	Y	Y	Y	N	Y
14 Conyers	Y	Y	Y	N	Y
15 Kilpatrick	Y	Y	Y	N	Y
16 Dingell	Y	Y	Y	N	Y

	222	223	224	225	227
MINNESOTA					
1 ***Gutknecht***	Y	Y	N	Y	N
2 Minge	Y	Y	?	Y	N
3 ***Ramstad***	Y	Y	N	Y	N
4 Vento	Y	Y	Y	N	Y
5 Sabo	Y	Y	N	N	Y
6 Luther	Y	Y	Y	N	Y
7 Peterson	Y	Y	N	N	Y
8 Oberstar	Y	Y	N	N	Y
MISSISSIPPI					
1 ***Wicker***	Y	Y	Y	Y	N
2 Thompson	Y	Y	N	N	Y
3 ***Pickering***	Y	Y	Y	Y	N
4 Shows	Y	Y	Y	N	Y
5 Taylor	Y	Y	N	N	Y
MISSOURI					
1 Clay	Y	Y	N	N	Y
2 ***Talent***	Y	Y	Y	Y	N
3 Gephardt	Y	Y	Y	N	Y
4 Skelton	Y	Y	Y	Y	N
5 McCarthy	Y	Y	Y	N	N
6 Danner	Y	Y	Y	N	Y
7 ***Blunt***	Y	Y	?	Y	N
8 ***Emerson***	Y	Y	Y	Y	N
9 ***Hulshof***	Y	Y	?	Y	N
MONTANA					
AL ***Hill***	Y	Y	N	Y	N
NEBRASKA					
1 ***Bereuter***	Y	Y	Y	Y	N
2 ***Terry***	Y	Y	Y	Y	N
3 ***Barrett***	Y	Y	Y	Y	N
NEVADA					
1 Berkley	Y	Y	Y	N	Y
2 ***Gibbons***	Y	Y	?	Y	Y
NEW HAMPSHIRE					
1 ***Sununu***	Y	Y	Y	Y	N
2 ***Bass***	Y	Y	Y	Y	N
NEW JERSEY					
1 Andrews	Y	Y	Y	N	Y
2 ***LoBiondo***	Y	Y	N	Y	Y
3 ***Saxton***	Y	Y	Y	Y	Y
4 ***Smith***	Y	Y	Y	N	Y
5 ***Roukema***	Y	Y	Y	Y	N
6 Pallone	Y	Y	Y	N	Y
7 ***Franks***	Y	Y	Y	Y	N
8 Pascrell	Y	Y	?	N	Y
9 Rothman	Y	Y	Y	N	Y
10 Payne	Y	Y	Y	N	Y
11 ***Frelinghuysen***	Y	Y	Y	Y	N
12 Holt	Y	Y	Y	N	Y
13 Menendez	Y	Y	Y	N	Y
NEW MEXICO					
1 ***Wilson***	Y	Y	Y	Y	N
2 ***Skeen***	Y	Y	Y	Y	N
3 Udall	Y	Y	N	N	Y
NEW YORK					
1 Forbes	?	?	Y	N	Y
2 ***Lazio***	Y	Y	?	?	N
3 ***King***	Y	Y	Y	Y	N
4 McCarthy	?	?	Y	N	Y
5 Ackerman	?	?	Y	Y	N
6 Meeks	Y	Y	Y	Y	N
7 Crowley	Y	Y	Y	N	Y
8 Nadler	Y	Y	?	N	Y
9 Weiner	?	?	?	?	N
10 Towns	Y	Y	Y	N	Y
11 Owens	Y	Y	Y	N	Y
12 Velázquez	Y	Y	Y	N	Y
13 ***Fossella***	Y	Y	?	Y	N
14 Maloney	Y	Y	?	Y	N
15 Rangel	Y	Y	Y	Y	N
16 Serrano	Y	Y	Y	Y	N
17 Engel	Y	Y	?	N	Y
18 Lowey	Y	Y	Y	Y	N
19 ***Kelly***	Y	Y	Y	Y	N
20 ***Gilman***	Y	Y	Y	Y	Y
21 McNulty	Y	Y	Y	N	Y
22 ***Sweeney***	Y	Y	N	Y	N
23 ***Boehlert***	Y	Y	Y	Y	N
24 ***McHugh***	Y	Y	Y	Y	N
25 ***Walsh***	Y	Y	Y	Y	N
26 Hinchey	Y	Y	Y	N	Y
27 ***Reynolds***	Y	Y	Y	Y	N
28 Slaughter	Y	Y	N	N	Y
29 LaFalce	Y	Y	Y	Y	N

	222	223	224	225	227
30 ***Quinn***	Y	Y	Y	Y	N
31 ***Houghton***	Y	Y	Y	Y	N
NORTH CAROLINA					
1 Clayton	Y	Y	Y	Y	N
2 Etheridge	Y	Y	Y	Y	N
3 ***Jones***	Y	Y	?	N	Y
4 Price	Y	Y	Y	Y	N
5 ***Burr***	Y	Y	Y	Y	N
6 ***Coble***	Y	Y	Y	Y	N
7 McIntyre	Y	Y	Y	N	Y
8 ***Hayes***	Y	Y	Y	Y	N
9 ***Myrick***	Y	Y	Y	Y	N
10 ***Ballenger***	Y	Y	Y	Y	N
11 ***Taylor***	Y	Y	Y	Y	Y
12 Watt	Y	Y	Y	N	N
NORTH DAKOTA					
AL Pomeroy	Y	Y	N	Y	N
OHIO					
1 ***Chabot***	Y	Y	Y	Y	Y
2 ***Portman***	Y	Y	Y	Y	N
3 Hall	Y	Y	Y	N	Y
4 ***Oxley***	Y	Y	Y	Y	N
5 ***Gillmor***	Y	Y	Y	Y	N
6 Strickland	Y	Y	N	N	Y
7 ***Hobson***	Y	Y	Y	Y	N
8 ***Boehner***	Y	Y	Y	Y	N
9 Kaptur	Y	Y	Y	N	Y
10 Kucinich	Y	Y	N	N	Y
11 Jones	Y	?	N	N	Y
12 ***Kasich***	Y	Y	?	Y	Y
13 Brown	?	?	Y	N	Y
14 Sawyer	Y	Y	Y	N	Y
15 ***Pryce***	Y	Y	Y	Y	N
16 ***Regula***	Y	Y	Y	Y	N
17 Traficant	Y	Y	Y	N	Y
18 ***Ney***	Y	Y	Y	Y	Y
19 ***LaTourette***	Y	Y	Y	Y	N
OKLAHOMA					
1 ***Largent***	Y	Y	Y	Y	N
2 ***Coburn***	Y	Y	Y	Y	Y
3 ***Watkins***	Y	Y	Y	Y	N
4 ***Watts***	Y	Y	Y	Y	N
5 ***Istook***	Y	Y	Y	Y	N
6 ***Lucas***	Y	Y	Y	Y	N
OREGON					
1 Wu	Y	Y	N	N	Y
2 ***Walden***	Y	Y	Y	Y	N
3 Blumenauer	Y	Y	Y	Y	N
4 DeFazio	Y	Y	N	N	Y
5 Hooley	Y	Y	Y	Y	N
PENNSYLVANIA					
1 Brady	Y	Y	N	N	Y
2 Fattah	Y	Y	?	N	N
3 Borski	Y	Y	N	N	Y
4 Klink	Y	Y	N	N	Y
5 ***Peterson***	Y	Y	Y	Y	N
6 Holden	Y	Y	N	N	Y
7 ***Weldon***	Y	Y	Y	Y	N
8 ***Greenwood***	Y	Y	Y	Y	N
9 ***Shuster***	Y	Y	Y	Y	N
10 ***Sherwood***	Y	Y	Y	Y	N
11 Kanjorski	Y	Y	Y	N	Y
12 Murtha	Y	Y	Y	N	Y
13 Hoeffel	Y	Y	Y	N	Y
14 Coyne	Y	Y	Y	N	Y
15 ***Toomey***	Y	Y	Y	Y	N
16 ***Pitts***	Y	Y	Y	Y	N
17 ***Gekas***	Y	Y	Y	Y	N
18 Doyle	Y	Y	Y	N	Y
19 ***Goodling***	Y	Y	Y	Y	N
20 Mascara	Y	Y	Y	N	Y
21 ***English***	Y	Y	N	Y	N
RHODE ISLAND					
1 Kennedy	Y	Y	Y	N	Y
2 Weygand	Y	Y	Y	N	Y
SOUTH CAROLINA					
1 ***Sanford***	N	Y	Y	Y	N
2 ***Spence***	Y	Y	Y	Y	Y
3 ***Graham***	Y	Y	Y	Y	Y
4 ***DeMint***	Y	Y	Y	Y	N
5 Spratt	Y	?	?	N	Y
6 Clyburn	Y	Y	N	N	Y
SOUTH DAKOTA					
AL ***Thune***	Y	Y	Y	Y	N

	222	223	224	225	227
TENNESSEE					
1 ***Jenkins***	Y	Y	Y	Y	N
2 ***Duncan***	Y	Y	Y	Y	Y
3 ***Wamp***	Y	Y	Y	Y	Y
4 ***Hilleary***	Y	Y	N	Y	N
5 Clement	Y	Y	Y	Y	Y
6 Gordon	Y	Y	Y	Y	Y
7 ***Bryant***	Y	Y	Y	Y	N
8 Tanner	Y	Y	Y	Y	N
9 Ford	Y	Y	N	Y	N
TEXAS					
1 Sandlin	Y	Y	Y	Y	Y
2 Turner	Y	Y	Y	Y	N
3 ***Johnson, Sam***	Y	Y	Y	Y	N
4 Hall	Y	Y	Y	Y	N
5 ***Sessions***	Y	Y	Y	Y	N
6 ***Barton***	Y	Y	Y	Y	Y
7 ***Archer***	Y	Y	Y	Y	N
8 ***Brady***	Y	Y	Y	Y	N
9 Lampson	Y	Y	Y	N	Y
10 Doggett	Y	Y	Y	Y	N
11 Edwards	Y	Y	Y	Y	N
12 ***Granger***	Y	Y	Y	Y	N
13 ***Thornberry***	Y	Y	Y	Y	N
14 ***Paul***	N	Y	Y	Y	N
15 Hinojosa	Y	Y	Y	Y	N
16 Reyes	Y	Y	Y	Y	N
17 Stenholm	Y	Y	Y	Y	N
18 Jackson-Lee	Y	Y	Y	N	Y
19 ***Combest***	Y	Y	Y	Y	N
20 Gonzalez	Y	Y	Y	Y	N
21 ***Smith***	Y	Y	Y	Y	N
22 ***DeLay***	Y	Y	Y	Y	N
23 ***Bonilla***	Y	Y	Y	Y	N
24 Frost	Y	Y	Y	Y	N
25 Bentsen	Y	Y	Y	Y	N
26 ***Armey***	Y	Y	Y	Y	N
27 Ortiz	Y	Y	Y	Y	N
28 Rodriguez	?	?	?	N	Y
29 Green	Y	Y	Y	N	Y
30 Johnson, E.B.	Y	Y	Y	Y	N
UTAH					
1 ***Hansen***	Y	Y	Y	Y	N
2 ***Cook***	Y	Y	Y	Y	Y
3 ***Cannon***	Y	Y	Y	Y	N
VERMONT					
AL *Sanders*	Y	Y	Y	N	Y
VIRGINIA					
1 ***Bateman***	Y	Y	Y	Y	N
2 Pickett	Y	Y	N	Y	N
3 Scott	Y	Y	Y	Y	N
4 Sisisky	Y	Y	Y	N	Y
5 *Goode*	Y	Y	Y	N	Y
6 ***Goodlatte***	Y	Y	Y	Y	N
7 ***Bliley***	Y	Y	Y	Y	N
8 Moran	Y	Y	Y	Y	N
9 Boucher	Y	Y	Y	N	Y
10 ***Wolf***	Y	Y	Y	Y	Y
11 ***Davis***	Y	Y	Y	Y	N
WASHINGTON					
1 Inslee	Y	Y	Y	Y	N
2 ***Metcalf***	Y	Y	Y	Y	N
3 Baird	Y	Y	N	Y	N
4 ***Hastings***	Y	Y	Y	Y	N
5 ***Nethercutt***	Y	Y	Y	Y	N
6 Dicks	Y	Y	Y	Y	N
7 McDermott	Y	Y	N	Y	N
8 ***Dunn***	Y	Y	Y	Y	N
9 Smith	Y	Y	Y	Y	N
WEST VIRGINIA					
1 Mollohan	Y	Y	?	N	Y
2 Wise	Y	Y	Y	N	Y
3 Rahall	Y	Y	Y	N	Y
WISCONSIN					
1 ***Ryan***	Y	Y	Y	Y	N
2 Baldwin	Y	Y	Y	N	Y
3 Kind	Y	Y	Y	Y	N
4 Kleczka	Y	Y	Y	N	Y
5 Barrett	Y	Y	Y	N	Y
6 ***Petri***	Y	Y	Y	Y	N
7 Obey	Y	Y	Y	N	Y
8 ***Green***	Y	Y	Y	Y	N
9 ***Sensenbrenner***	Y	Y	Y	Y	Y
WYOMING					
AL ***Cubin***	?	?	Y	Y	N

Southern states - Ala., Ark., Fla., Ga., Ky., La., Miss., N.C., Okla., S.C., Tenn., Texas, Va.

228. HR 4444. China Trade/Passage. Passage of the bill that would make normal trade relations with the People's Republic of China permanent. The bill includes provisions to protect U.S. businesses and workers from import surges; establish a commission to monitor human rights, labor standards and religious freedom in China; require the administration to report annually on China's compliance with trade agreements; and express the sense of Congress that Taiwan should be admitted to the World Trade Organization. The measure would also authorize $99 million for Radio Free Asia and the Voice of America to expand broadcasts to China and neighboring countries. Passed 237-197: R 164-57; D 73-138 (ND 43-114, SD 30-24); I 0-2. May 24, 2000. A "yea" was a vote in support of the president's position.

229. HR 3916. Telephone Tax/Previous Question. Linder, R-Ga., motion to order the previous question (thus ending debate and possibility of amendment) on adoption of the rule (H Res 511) for House floor consideration of the bill that would repeal the telephone tax. Motion agreed to 221-201: R 215-0; D 5-200 (ND 4-149, SD 1-51); I 1-1. May 25, 2000.

230. HR 3916. Telephone Tax/Rule. Adoption of the rule (H Res 511) to provide for House floor consideration of the bill that would repeal the telephone tax. Adopted 404-15: R 214-0; D 188-15 (ND 140-12, SD 48-3); I 2-0. May 25, 2000.

231. H Con Res 331. Israeli Pullout/Adoption. Adoption of the resolution commending Israel for its withdrawal of military forces from southern Lebanon. It also calls on the United Nations to establish an interim force to help restore Lebanese sovereignty. Adopted 403-3: R 203-3; D 198-0 (ND 147-0, SD 51-0); I 2-0. May 25, 2000.

232. HR 3916. Telephone Tax/Recommit. Doggett, D-Texas, motion to recommit the bill to the House Ways and Means Committee with instructions to include a provision barring organizations that exist under the Internal Revenue Code's section 527 from benefiting from the bill unless such organizations disclose donors and affiliation. Motion rejected 208-214: R 6-210; D 201-3 (ND 150-2, SD 51-1); I 1-1. May 25, 2000.

233. HR 3916. Telephone Tax/Passage. Passage of the bill that would eliminate the 3 percent excise tax on telecommunications services. Under the bill, the tax would be phased out by 1 percent each year. Passed 420-2: R 216-0; D 202-2 (ND 150-2, SD 52-0); I 2-0. May 25, 2000.

Key

- Y Voted for (yea).
- \# Paired for.
- \+ Announced for.
- N Voted against (nay).
- X Paired against.
- – Announced against.
- P Voted "present."
- C Voted "present" to avoid possible conflict of interest.
- ? Did not vote or otherwise make a position known.

Democrats • ***Republicans***
Independents

	228	229	230	231	232	233
ALABAMA						
1 ***Callahan***	Y	Y	Y	Y	N	Y
2 ***Everett***	Y	Y	Y	Y	N	Y
3 ***Riley***	N	Y	Y	Y	N	Y
4 ***Aderholt***	N	Y	Y	Y	N	Y
5 Cramer	Y	N	Y	Y	Y	Y
6 ***Bachus***	Y	Y	Y	Y	N	Y
7 Hilliard	N	?	?	?	Y	Y
ALASKA						
AL ***Young***	N	Y	Y	Y	N	Y
ARIZONA						
1 ***Salmon***	Y	Y	Y	Y	N	Y
2 Pastor	N	N	Y	Y	Y	Y
3 ***Stump***	Y	Y	Y	Y	N	Y
4 ***Shadegg***	Y	Y	Y	Y	N	Y
5 ***Kolbe***	Y	Y	Y	Y	N	Y
6 ***Hayworth***	N	Y	Y	Y	N	Y
ARKANSAS						
1 Berry	Y	N	N	Y	Y	Y
2 Snyder	Y	N	Y	Y	Y	Y
3 ***Hutchinson***	Y	Y	Y	Y	N	Y
4 ***Dickey***	Y	Y	Y	Y	N	Y
CALIFORNIA						
1 Thompson	Y	N	Y	Y	Y	Y
2 ***Herger***	Y	Y	Y	Y	N	Y
3 ***Ose***	Y	Y	Y	Y	N	Y
4 ***Doolittle***	Y	Y	Y	Y	N	Y
5 Matsui	Y	N	Y	Y	Y	Y
6 Woolsey	N	N	Y	Y	Y	Y
7 Miller, George	N	N	Y	Y	Y	Y
8 Pelosi	N	N	Y	Y	Y	Y
9 Lee	N	N	Y	Y	Y	Y
10 Tauscher	Y	N	Y	Y	Y	Y
11 ***Pombo***	N	Y	Y	Y	N	Y
12 Lantos	N	N	Y	Y	Y	Y
13 Stark	N	N	Y	Y	Y	N
14 Eshoo	Y	Y	Y	Y	Y	Y
15 ***Campbell***	Y	Y	Y	Y	N	Y
16 Lofgren	Y	N	Y	Y	Y	Y
17 Farr	N	N	Y	Y	Y	Y
18 Condit	N	N	Y	Y	Y	Y
19 ***Radanovich***	Y	Y	Y	Y	N	Y
20 Dooley	Y	N	Y	Y	Y	Y
21 ***Thomas***	Y	Y	Y	Y	N	Y
22 Capps	Y	N	Y	+	Y	Y
23 ***Gallegly***	Y	Y	Y	Y	N	Y
24 Sherman	N	N	Y	Y	Y	Y
25 ***McKeon***	Y	Y	Y	Y	N	Y
26 Berman	N	N	Y	?	Y	Y
27 ***Rogan***	Y	Y	Y	Y	N	Y
28 ***Dreier***	Y	Y	Y	Y	N	Y
29 Waxman	Y	N	Y	Y	Y	Y
30 Becerra	Y	–	+	+	Y	Y
31 Martinez	Y	Y	Y	Y	N	Y
32 Dixon	Y	N	Y	Y	Y	Y
33 Roybal-Allard	N	N	Y	Y	Y	Y
34 Napolitano	N	N	Y	Y	Y	Y
35 Waters	N	N	N	Y	Y	Y
36 ***Kuykendall***	Y	Y	Y	Y	N	Y
37 Millender-McD.	N	N	Y	Y	Y	Y
38 ***Horn***	N	Y	Y	Y	Y	Y
39 ***Royce***	Y	Y	Y	Y	N	Y
40 ***Lewis***	Y	Y	Y	Y	N	Y
41 ***Miller, Gary***	Y	Y	Y	Y	N	Y
42 Baca	N	N	Y	Y	Y	Y
43 ***Calvert***	Y	Y	Y	Y	N	Y
44 ***Bono***	Y	Y	Y	Y	N	Y
45 ***Rohrabacher***	N	Y	Y	Y	N	Y
46 Sanchez	N	N	Y	Y	Y	Y
47 ***Cox***	Y	Y	Y	Y	N	Y
48 ***Packard***	Y	Y	Y	Y	N	Y
49 ***Bilbray***	Y	Y	Y	Y	Y	Y
50 Filner	N	N	Y	Y	Y	Y
51 ***Cunningham***	Y	Y	Y	Y	N	Y
52 ***Hunter***	N	Y	Y	Y	N	Y
COLORADO						
1 DeGette	Y	N	Y	Y	Y	Y
2 Udall	N	N	Y	Y	Y	Y
3 ***McInnis***	Y	?	?	?	?	?
4 ***Schaffer***	Y	Y	Y	Y	N	Y
5 ***Hefley***	N	Y	Y	Y	N	Y
6 ***Tancredo***	N	Y	Y	Y	N	Y
CONNECTICUT						
1 Larson	N	N	Y	Y	Y	Y
2 Gejdenson	N	N	Y	Y	Y	Y
3 DeLauro	N	N	Y	Y	Y	Y
4 ***Shays***	Y	Y	Y	Y	N	Y
5 Maloney	N	N	Y	Y	Y	Y
6 ***Johnson***	Y	Y	Y	Y	N	Y
DELAWARE						
AL ***Castle***	Y	Y	Y	Y	N	Y
FLORIDA						
1 ***Scarborough***	?	?	?	?	?	?
2 Boyd	Y	N	Y	Y	Y	Y
3 Brown	N	N	Y	Y	Y	Y
4 ***Fowler***	Y	Y	Y	Y	N	Y
5 Thurman	Y	N	Y	Y	Y	Y
6 ***Stearns***	N	Y	Y	Y	N	Y
7 ***Mica***	N	Y	Y	Y	N	Y
8 ***McCollum***	Y	Y	Y	Y	N	Y
9 ***Bilirakis***	N	Y	Y	Y	N	Y
10 ***Young***	Y	Y	Y	Y	N	Y
11 Davis	Y	N	Y	Y	?	Y
12 ***Canady***	Y	Y	Y	Y	N	Y
13 ***Miller***	Y	Y	Y	Y	N	Y
14 ***Goss***	Y	Y	Y	Y	N	Y
15 ***Weldon***	N	Y	Y	Y	N	Y
16 ***Foley***	Y	Y	Y	Y	N	Y
17 Meek	N	N	?	Y	?	?
18 ***Ros-Lehtinen***	N	Y	Y	Y	?	?
19 Wexler	N	N	Y	?	Y	Y
20 Deutsch	N	N	Y	Y	Y	Y
21 ***Diaz-Balart***	N	Y	Y	Y	N	Y
22 ***Shaw***	Y	Y	Y	Y	N	Y
23 Hastings	N	N	Y	Y	Y	Y
GEORGIA						
1 ***Kingston***	N	Y	Y	Y	N	Y
2 Bishop	Y	N	Y	Y	Y	Y
3 ***Collins***	N	Y	Y	Y	N	Y
4 McKinney	N	N	Y	Y	Y	Y
5 Lewis	N	N	Y	Y	Y	Y
6 ***Isakson***	Y	Y	Y	Y	N	Y
7 ***Barr***	N	Y	Y	P	N	Y
8 ***Chambliss***	Y	Y	Y	Y	N	Y
9 ***Deal***	N	Y	Y	Y	N	Y
10 ***Norwood***	N	Y	Y	Y	N	Y
11 ***Linder***	Y	Y	Y	Y	N	Y
HAWAII						
1 Abercrombie	N	N	Y	Y	Y	Y
2 Mink	N	N	Y	?	Y	Y
IDAHO						
1 ***Chenoweth-Hage***	N	Y	Y	Y	N	Y
2 ***Simpson***	Y	Y	Y	Y	N	Y
ILLINOIS						
1 Rush	N	N	Y	Y	Y	Y
2 Jackson	N	N	Y	Y	Y	Y
3 Lipinski	N	N	Y	Y	Y	Y
4 Gutierrez	N	N	Y	Y	Y	Y
5 Blagojevich	N	N	Y	Y	Y	Y
6 ***Hyde***	Y	Y	Y	Y	N	Y
7 Davis	N	N	Y	Y	Y	Y
8 ***Crane***	Y	Y	Y	Y	N	Y
9 Schakowsky	N	N	?	Y	Y	Y
10 ***Porter***	Y	Y	Y	Y	N	Y
11 ***Weller***	Y	Y	Y	Y	N	Y
12 Costello	N	N	Y	Y	Y	Y
13 ***Biggert***	Y	Y	Y	Y	N	Y

ND Northern Democrats SD Southern Democrats

	228	229	230	231	232	233
14 ***Hastert***	Y				N	Y
15 ***Ewing***	Y	Y	Y	Y	N	Y
16 ***Manzullo***	Y	Y	Y	Y	N	Y
17 Evans	N	N	Y	Y	Y	Y
18 ***LaHood***	Y	Y	Y	Y	N	Y
19 Phelps	N	N	Y	Y	Y	Y
20 ***Shimkus***	Y	Y	Y	Y	N	Y
INDIANA						
1 Visclosky	N	N	Y	Y	Y	Y
2 ***McIntosh***	Y	Y	Y	Y	N	Y
3 Roemer	Y	N	Y	Y	Y	Y
4 ***Souder***	N	Y	Y	Y	N	Y
5 ***Buyer***	N	Y	Y	Y	N	Y
6 ***Burton***	N	Y	Y	Y	N	Y
7 ***Pease***	Y	Y	Y	Y	N	Y
8 ***Hostettler***	N	Y	Y	Y	N	Y
9 Hill	Y	N	Y	Y	Y	Y
10 Carson	Y	N	Y	Y	Y	Y
IOWA						
1 ***Leach***	Y	Y	Y	Y	Y	Y
2 ***Nussle***	Y	Y	Y	Y	N	Y
3 Boswell	Y	Y	Y	Y	Y	Y
4 ***Ganske***	Y	Y	Y	Y	Y	Y
5 ***Latham***	Y	Y	Y	Y	N	Y
KANSAS						
1 ***Moran***	Y	Y	Y	Y	N	Y
2 ***Ryun***	Y	Y	Y	Y	N	Y
3 Moore	Y	N	Y	Y	Y	Y
4 ***Tiahrt***	Y	Y	Y	Y	N	Y
KENTUCKY						
1 ***Whitfield***	Y	Y	Y	Y	N	Y
2 ***Lewis***	Y	Y	Y	Y	N	Y
3 ***Northup***	Y	Y	Y	Y	N	Y
4 Lucas	Y	N	Y	Y	Y	Y
5 ***Rogers***	N	Y	Y	Y	N	Y
6 ***Fletcher***	Y	Y	Y	Y	N	Y
LOUISIANA						
1 ***Vitter***	Y	Y	Y	Y	N	Y
2 Jefferson	Y	N	Y	Y	Y	Y
3 ***Tauzin***	Y	Y	Y	Y	N	Y
4 ***McCrery***	Y	Y	Y	Y	N	Y
5 ***Cooksey***	Y	Y	Y	?	N	Y
6 ***Baker***	Y	Y	Y	Y	N	Y
7 John	Y	N	Y	Y	Y	Y
MAINE						
1 Allen	Y	N	Y	Y	Y	Y
2 Baldacci	N	N	Y	Y	Y	Y
MARYLAND						
1 ***Gilchrest***	Y	Y	Y	Y	N	Y
2 ***Ehrlich***	N	Y	Y	Y	N	Y
3 Cardin	Y	N	Y	Y	Y	Y
4 Wynn	N	N	N	Y	Y	Y
5 Hoyer	Y	N	Y	Y	Y	Y
6 ***Bartlett***	N	Y	Y	Y	N	Y
7 Cummings	N	N	Y	Y	Y	Y
8 ***Morella***	Y	Y	Y	Y	Y	Y
MASSACHUSETTS						
1 Olver	N	N	Y	Y	Y	Y
2 Neal	Y	N	Y	Y	Y	Y
3 McGovern	N	N	Y	Y	Y	Y
4 Frank	N	N	Y	Y	Y	Y
5 Meehan	Y	N	Y	Y	Y	Y
6 Tierney	N	N	N	Y	Y	Y
7 Markey	N	N	N	Y	Y	Y
8 Capuano	N	N	Y	Y	Y	Y
9 Moakley	N	N	Y	Y	Y	Y
10 Delahunt	N	N	Y	Y	Y	Y
MICHIGAN						
1 Stupak	N	N	Y	Y	Y	Y
2 ***Hoekstra***	N	Y	Y	Y	N	Y
3 ***Ehlers***	Y	Y	Y	Y	N	Y
4 ***Camp***	Y	Y	Y	Y	N	Y
5 Barcia	N	N	Y	Y	Y	Y
6 ***Upton***	Y	Y	Y	Y	N	Y
7 ***Smith***	Y	Y	Y	Y	N	Y
8 Stabenow	N	N	Y	Y	Y	Y
9 Kildee	N	N	Y	Y	Y	Y
10 Bonior	N	N	Y	Y	Y	Y
11 ***Knollenberg***	Y	Y	Y	Y	N	Y
12 Levin	Y	N	Y	Y	Y	Y
13 Rivers	N	N	Y	Y	Y	Y
14 Conyers	N	N	Y	Y	Y	Y
15 Kilpatrick	N	N	Y	Y	Y	Y
16 Dingell	N	N	N	Y	Y	Y
MINNESOTA						
1 ***Gutknecht***	Y	Y	Y	Y	N	Y
2 Minge	Y	–	+	+	+	+
3 ***Ramstad***	Y	Y	Y	Y	N	Y
4 Vento	N	N	Y	Y	Y	?
5 Sabo	N	N	Y	Y	Y	Y
6 Luther	N	N	Y	Y	Y	Y
7 Peterson	N	N	Y	Y	Y	Y
8 Oberstar	N	N	Y	Y	Y	Y
MISSISSIPPI						
1 ***Wicker***	Y	Y	Y	P	N	Y
2 Thompson	N	N	Y	Y	Y	Y
3 ***Pickering***	Y	Y	Y	Y	N	Y
4 Shows	N	N	Y	Y	Y	Y
5 Taylor	N	N	N	Y	Y	Y
MISSOURI						
1 Clay	N	N	Y	?	?	?
2 ***Talent***	Y	Y	Y	?	N	Y
3 Gephardt	N	N	Y	Y	Y	Y
4 Skelton	Y	N	Y	Y	Y	Y
5 McCarthy	N	N	Y	Y	Y	Y
6 Danner	N	N	Y	Y	Y	Y
7 ***Blunt***	Y	Y	Y	Y	N	Y
8 ***Emerson***	Y	Y	Y	Y	N	Y
9 ***Hulshof***	Y	Y	Y	Y	N	Y
MONTANA						
AL ***Hill***	Y	Y	Y	Y	N	Y
NEBRASKA						
1 ***Bereuter***	Y	Y	Y	+	N	Y
2 ***Terry***	Y	Y	Y	Y	N	Y
3 ***Barrett***	Y	Y	Y	Y	N	Y
NEVADA						
1 Berkley	N	N	Y	Y	Y	Y
2 ***Gibbons***	N	Y	Y	Y	N	Y
NEW HAMPSHIRE						
1 ***Sununu***	Y	Y	Y	Y	N	Y
2 ***Bass***	Y	Y	Y	Y	N	Y
NEW JERSEY						
1 Andrews	N	N	Y	Y	Y	Y
2 ***LoBiondo***	N	Y	Y	Y	N	Y
3 ***Saxton***	N	Y	Y	Y	N	Y
4 ***Smith***	N	Y	Y	Y	N	Y
5 ***Roukema***	Y	Y	Y	Y	N	Y
6 Pallone	N	N	Y	Y	Y	Y
7 ***Franks***	Y	Y	Y	Y	N	Y
8 Pascrell	N	N	Y	Y	Y	Y
9 Rothman	N	N	Y	Y	Y	Y
10 Payne	N	N	Y	Y	Y	Y
11 ***Frelinghuysen***	Y	Y	Y	Y	N	Y
12 Holt	N	N	Y	Y	Y	Y
13 Menendez	N	N	Y	Y	Y	Y
NEW MEXICO						
1 ***Wilson***	Y	Y	Y	Y	N	Y
2 ***Skeen***	Y	Y	Y	Y	N	Y
3 Udall	N	N	Y	Y	Y	Y
NEW YORK						
1 Forbes	N	N	Y	Y	Y	Y
2 ***Lazio***	Y	Y	Y	Y	N	Y
3 ***King***	N	Y	Y	Y	N	Y
4 McCarthy	N	N	Y	Y	Y	Y
5 Ackerman	Y	N	Y	Y	Y	Y
6 Meeks	Y	N	N	Y	Y	Y
7 Crowley	N	N	Y	Y	Y	Y
8 Nadler	N	N	Y	Y	Y	Y
9 Weiner	Y	?	?	?	?	?
10 Towns	N	N	N	Y	Y	Y
11 Owens	N	N	N	?	Y	Y
12 Velázquez	N	N	Y	Y	Y	Y
13 ***Fossella***	Y	Y	Y	Y	N	Y
14 Maloney	Y	N	Y	Y	Y	Y
15 Rangel	Y	N	Y	Y	Y	Y
16 Serrano	Y	N	Y	Y	Y	Y
17 Engel	N	N	N	Y	Y	Y
18 Lowey	Y	N	Y	Y	Y	Y
19 ***Kelly***	Y	Y	Y	Y	N	Y
20 ***Gilman***	N	Y	Y	Y	N	Y
21 McNulty	N	N	Y	Y	Y	Y
22 ***Sweeney***	Y	Y	Y	Y	N	Y
23 ***Boehlert***	Y	Y	Y	Y	N	Y
24 ***McHugh***	Y	Y	Y	Y	N	Y
25 ***Walsh***	Y	Y	Y	Y	N	Y
26 Hinchey	N	N	N	Y	Y	Y
27 ***Reynolds***	Y	Y	Y	Y	N	Y
28 Slaughter	N	N	Y	Y	Y	Y
29 LaFalce	Y	N	Y	?	Y	Y
30 ***Quinn***	N	Y	Y	Y	N	Y
31 ***Houghton***	Y	Y	Y	?	N	Y
NORTH CAROLINA						
1 Clayton	N	N	Y	Y	Y	Y
2 Etheridge	Y	N	Y	Y	Y	Y
3 ***Jones***	N	Y	Y	Y	N	Y
4 Price	Y	N	Y	Y	Y	Y
5 ***Burr***	N	Y	Y	Y	N	Y
6 ***Coble***	N	Y	Y	?	N	Y
7 McIntyre	N	N	Y	Y	Y	Y
8 ***Hayes***	N	Y	Y	Y	N	Y
9 ***Myrick***	Y	Y	Y	Y	N	Y
10 ***Ballenger***	Y	Y	Y	Y	N	Y
11 ***Taylor***	N	Y	?	Y	N	Y
12 Watt	N	N	Y	Y	Y	Y
NORTH DAKOTA						
AL Pomeroy	Y	N	Y	Y	Y	Y
OHIO						
1 ***Chabot***	Y	Y	Y	Y	N	Y
2 ***Portman***	Y	Y	Y	Y	N	Y
3 Hall	N	N	Y	Y	Y	Y
4 ***Oxley***	Y	Y	Y	Y	N	Y
5 ***Gillmor***	Y	Y	Y	Y	N	Y
6 Strickland	N	N	Y	Y	Y	Y
7 ***Hobson***	Y	Y	Y	Y	N	Y
8 ***Boehner***	Y	Y	Y	Y	N	Y
9 Kaptur	N	N	Y	Y	Y	Y
10 Kucinich	N	N	Y	Y	Y	Y
11 Jones	N	N	Y	Y	Y	Y
12 ***Kasich***	Y	Y	Y	Y	N	Y
13 Brown	N	N	Y	Y	Y	Y
14 Sawyer	Y	N	Y	Y	Y	Y
15 ***Pryce***	Y	Y	Y	Y	N	Y
16 ***Regula***	Y	Y	Y	Y	N	Y
17 Traficant	N	Y	Y	Y	N	Y
18 ***Ney***	N	Y	Y	Y	N	Y
19 ***LaTourette***	N	Y	Y	Y	N	Y
OKLAHOMA						
1 ***Largent***	Y	Y	Y	Y	N	Y
2 ***Coburn***	N	?	?	?	?	?
3 ***Watkins***	Y	Y	Y	Y	N	Y
4 ***Watts***	Y	Y	Y	Y	N	Y
5 ***Istook***	Y	Y	Y	Y	N	Y
6 ***Lucas***	Y	Y	Y	Y	N	Y
OREGON						
1 Wu	N	N	Y	Y	Y	Y
2 ***Walden***	Y	Y	Y	Y	N	Y
3 Blumenauer	Y	N	Y	Y	Y	Y
4 DeFazio	N	N	Y	Y	Y	Y
5 Hooley	Y	N	Y	Y	Y	Y
PENNSYLVANIA						
1 Brady	N	N	Y	Y	Y	Y
2 Fattah	N	N	Y	Y	Y	Y
3 Borski	N	N	Y	Y	Y	Y
4 Klink	N	N	N	Y	Y	Y
5 ***Peterson***	Y	Y	Y	Y	N	Y
6 Holden	N	N	Y	Y	Y	Y
7 ***Weldon***	Y	Y	Y	Y	N	Y
8 ***Greenwood***	Y	Y	Y	Y	N	Y
9 ***Shuster***	Y	Y	Y	Y	N	Y
10 ***Sherwood***	Y	Y	Y	Y	N	Y
11 Kanjorski	N	N	Y	Y	Y	Y
12 Murtha	N	N	Y	Y	Y	N
13 Hoeffel	N	N	Y	Y	Y	Y
14 Coyne	N	N	Y	Y	Y	Y
15 ***Toomey***	Y	Y	Y	Y	N	Y
16 ***Pitts***	Y	Y	Y	?	N	Y
17 ***Gekas***	Y	Y	Y	Y	N	Y
18 Doyle	N	N	Y	Y	Y	Y
19 ***Goodling***	N	Y	Y	N	N	Y
20 Mascara	N	N	Y	Y	Y	Y
21 ***English***	Y	Y	Y	Y	N	Y
RHODE ISLAND						
1 Kennedy	N	–	+	+	+	+
2 Weygand	N	N	Y	Y	Y	Y
SOUTH CAROLINA						
1 ***Sanford***	N	Y	Y	Y	N	Y
2 ***Spence***	N	?	?	?	?	?
3 ***Graham***	N	Y	Y	Y	N	Y
4 ***DeMint***	Y	Y	Y	Y	N	Y
5 Spratt	N	N	Y	Y	Y	Y
6 Clyburn	N	?	?	?	Y	Y
SOUTH DAKOTA						
AL ***Thune***	Y	Y	Y	Y	N	Y
TENNESSEE						
1 ***Jenkins***	Y	Y	Y	Y	N	Y
2 ***Duncan***	N	Y	Y	Y	N	Y
3 ***Wamp***	N	Y	Y	Y	N	Y
4 ***Hilleary***	Y	Y	Y	Y	N	Y
5 Clement	N	N	Y	Y	Y	Y
6 Gordon	N	N	Y	Y	Y	Y
7 ***Bryant***	Y	Y	Y	Y	N	Y
8 Tanner	Y	N	Y	Y	Y	Y
9 Ford	Y	N	Y	Y	Y	Y
TEXAS						
1 Sandlin	Y	N	Y	Y	Y	Y
2 Turner	Y	N	Y	Y	Y	Y
3 ***Johnson, Sam***	Y	?	?	?	N	Y
4 Hall	Y	Y	Y	Y	N	Y
5 ***Sessions***	Y	Y	Y	Y	N	Y
6 ***Barton***	N	Y	Y	Y	N	Y
7 ***Archer***	Y	Y	Y	Y	N	Y
8 ***Brady***	Y	Y	Y	?	N	Y
9 Lampson	N	N	Y	Y	Y	Y
10 Doggett	Y	N	Y	Y	Y	Y
11 Edwards	Y	N	Y	Y	Y	Y
12 ***Granger***	Y	Y	Y	Y	N	Y
13 ***Thornberry***	Y	Y	Y	Y	N	Y
14 ***Paul***	N	Y	Y	N	N	Y
15 Hinojosa	Y	N	Y	Y	Y	Y
16 Reyes	Y	N	Y	Y	Y	Y
17 Stenholm	Y	N	N	Y	Y	Y
18 Jackson-Lee	Y	N	Y	Y	Y	Y
19 ***Combest***	Y	Y	Y	Y	N	Y
20 Gonzalez	Y	N	Y	Y	Y	Y
21 ***Smith***	Y	Y	Y	Y	N	Y
22 ***DeLay***	Y	Y	Y	N	N	Y
23 ***Bonilla***	Y	Y	Y	Y	N	Y
24 Frost	Y	N	Y	Y	Y	Y
25 Bentsen	Y	N	Y	Y	Y	Y
26 ***Armey***	Y	Y	Y	Y	N	Y
27 Ortiz	Y	N	Y	Y	Y	?
28 Rodriguez	N	N	Y	Y	Y	Y
29 Green	N	N	Y	Y	Y	Y
30 Johnson, E.B.	Y	N	Y	Y	Y	Y
UTAH						
1 ***Hansen***	Y	Y	Y	Y	N	Y
2 ***Cook***	N	Y	Y	Y	N	Y
3 ***Cannon***	Y	Y	Y	Y	N	Y
VERMONT						
AL *Sanders*	N	N	Y	Y	Y	Y
VIRGINIA						
1 ***Bateman***	Y	?	?	?	?	?
2 Pickett	Y	N	Y	Y	Y	Y
3 Scott	N	N	Y	Y	Y	Y
4 Sisisky	N	N	Y	Y	Y	Y
5 *Goode*	N	Y	Y	Y	N	Y
6 ***Goodlatte***	Y	Y	Y	Y	N	Y
7 ***Bliley***	Y	Y	Y	Y	N	Y
8 Moran	Y	N	Y	Y	Y	Y
9 Boucher	N	N	Y	Y	Y	Y
10 ***Wolf***	N	Y	Y	Y	N	Y
11 ***Davis***	Y	Y	Y	Y	N	Y
WASHINGTON						
1 Inslee	Y	N	Y	Y	Y	Y
2 ***Metcalf***	N	Y	Y	Y	N	Y
3 Baird	Y	N	Y	Y	Y	Y
4 ***Hastings***	Y	Y	Y	Y	N	Y
5 ***Nethercutt***	Y	Y	Y	Y	Y	Y
6 Dicks	Y	N	Y	Y	Y	Y
7 McDermott	Y	N	Y	Y	Y	Y
8 ***Dunn***	Y	Y	Y	Y	N	Y
9 Smith	Y	N	Y	Y	Y	Y
WEST VIRGINIA						
1 Mollohan	N	N	Y	Y	?	Y
2 Wise	N	N	Y	Y	Y	Y
3 Rahall	N	N	Y	Y	Y	Y
WISCONSIN						
1 ***Ryan***	Y	Y	Y	Y	N	Y
2 Baldwin	N	N	Y	Y	Y	Y
3 Kind	Y	N	Y	Y	Y	Y
4 Kleczka	N	N	Y	Y	Y	Y
5 Barrett	N	N	Y	Y	Y	Y
6 ***Petri***	Y	Y	Y	Y	N	Y
7 Obey	N	N	N	Y	Y	Y
8 ***Green***	Y	Y	Y	Y	N	Y
9 ***Sensenbrenner***	N	Y	Y	Y	N	Y
WYOMING						
AL ***Cubin***	Y	Y	Y	Y	N	Y

Southern states - Ala., Ark., Fla., Ga., Ky., La., Miss., N.C., Okla., S.C., Tenn., Texas, Va.

234. H Res 509. African-American Music/Adoption. Goodling, R-Pa., motion to suspend the rules and adopt the resolution recognizing the contributions of African-American music to global culture and commerce. Motion agreed to 382-0: R 194-0; D 186-0 (ND 138-0, SD 48-0); I 2-0. A two-thirds majority of those present and voting (255 in this case) is required for adoption under suspension of the rules. June 6, 2000.

235. HR 4241. Les Aspin Post Office/Passage. Ryan, R-Wis., motion to suspend the rules and pass the bill designating the U.S. Post Office in Janesville, Wis., the "Les Aspin Post Office." Motion agreed to 378-6: R 187-6; D 189-0 (ND 141-0, SD 48-0); I 2-0. A two-thirds majority of those present and voting (256 in this case) is required for passage under suspension of the rules. June 6, 2000.

236. HR 3030. Matthew F. McHugh Post Office/Passage. Morella, R-Md., motion to suspend the rules and pass the bill designating the U.S. Post Office in Ithaca, N.Y., the "Matthew F. McHugh Post Office." Motion agreed to 385-2: R 194-2; D 189-0 (ND 140-0, SD 49-0); I 2-0 . A two-thirds majority of those present and voting (258 in this case) is required for passage under suspension of the rules. June 6, 2000.

237. HR 3535. Shark Finning/Passage. Sherwood, R-Pa., motion to suspend the rules and pass the bill that would ban the practice of cutting off a shark's fin and discarding the carcass into the sea in federal waters of the Pacific Ocean. Motion agreed to 390-1: R 198-1; D 190-0 (ND 141-0, SD 49-0); I 2-0. A two-thirds majority of those present and voting (261 in this case) is required for passage under suspension of the rules. June 6, 2000.

238. HR 3605. San Rafael Legacy District/Protective Status. Boehlert, R-N.Y., substitute amendment to the Udall, D-Colo., amendment. The Boehlert amendment would instruct the Interior secretary to maintain at least the existing level of protection in each section of the conservation area, pending completion of a management plan. The Udall amendment would designate more than 1 million acres in Utah for protection as wilderness study areas. Adopted 212-211: R 208-5; D 3-205 (ND 3-151, SD 0-54); I 1-1. (The Udall amendment, as amended by Boehlert, was subsequently adopted by voice vote.) June 7, 2000.

239. HR 3605. San Rafael Legacy District/Conservation Area Boundaries. Inslee, D-Wash., amendment that would define the conservation area as the 1,288,570 acres of land depicted in the Bureau of Land Management map titled "San Rafael Western Legacy District and National Conservation Area" dated March 28, 2000. Adopted 228-194: R 23-189; D 204-4 (ND 151-3, SD 53-1); I 1-1. June 7, 2000.

Key

Y Voted for (yea).
\# Paired for.
\+ Announced for.
N Voted against (nay).
X Paired against.
– Announced against.
P Voted "present."
C Voted "present" to avoid possible conflict of interest.
? Did not vote or otherwise make a position known.

Democrats • ***Republicans***
Independents

	234	235	236	237	238	239
ALABAMA						
1 ***Callahan***	Y	Y	Y	Y	Y	N
2 ***Everett***	Y	Y	Y	Y	Y	N
3 ***Riley***	Y	Y	Y	Y	Y	N
4 ***Aderholt***	Y	Y	Y	Y	Y	N
5 Cramer	Y	Y	Y	Y	N	Y
6 ***Bachus***	Y	Y	Y	Y	Y	N
7 Hilliard	?	?	?	?	N	Y
ALASKA						
AL ***Young***	Y	Y	Y	Y	Y	N
ARIZONA						
1 ***Salmon***	?	?	?	?	?	?
2 Pastor	?	?	?	?	N	Y
3 ***Stump***	Y	Y	Y	Y	Y	N
4 ***Shadegg***	Y	Y	Y	Y	Y	N
5 ***Kolbe***	Y	Y	Y	Y	Y	N
6 ***Hayworth***	Y	Y	Y	Y	Y	N
ARKANSAS						
1 Berry	Y	Y	Y	Y	N	Y
2 Snyder	Y	Y	Y	Y	N	Y
3 ***Hutchinson***	Y	Y	Y	Y	Y	N
4 ***Dickey***	Y	Y	Y	Y	Y	N
CALIFORNIA						
1 Thompson	Y	Y	Y	Y	N	Y
2 ***Herger***	Y	Y	Y	Y	Y	N
3 ***Ose***	Y	Y	Y	Y	Y	N
4 ***Doolittle***	Y	Y	Y	Y	Y	N
5 Matsui	Y	Y	Y	Y	N	Y
6 Woolsey	Y	Y	Y	Y	N	Y
7 Miller, George	Y	Y	Y	Y	N	Y
8 Pelosi	Y	Y	Y	Y	N	Y
9 Lee	Y	Y	Y	Y	N	Y
10 Tauscher	Y	Y	Y	Y	N	Y
11 ***Pombo***	Y	Y	Y	Y	Y	N
12 Lantos	Y	Y	Y	Y	N	Y
13 Stark	Y	Y	Y	Y	N	Y
14 Eshoo	Y	Y	Y	Y	N	Y
15 ***Campbell***	?	Y	Y	Y	N	Y
16 Lofgren	?	Y	Y	Y	N	Y
17 Farr	Y	Y	Y	Y	N	Y
18 Condit	?	?	?	?	N	Y
19 ***Radanovich***	Y	Y	Y	Y	Y	N
20 Dooley	Y	Y	Y	Y	N	Y
21 ***Thomas***	Y	Y	Y	Y	Y	N
22 Capps	Y	Y	Y	Y	N	Y
23 ***Gallegly***	Y	Y	Y	Y	Y	N
24 Sherman	Y	Y	Y	Y	N	Y
25 ***McKeon***	Y	Y	Y	Y	Y	N
26 Berman	Y	Y	Y	Y	N	Y
27 ***Rogan***	Y	Y	Y	Y	Y	N
28 ***Dreier***	Y	Y	Y	Y	Y	N
29 Waxman	?	?	?	?	N	Y
30 Becerra	Y	Y	Y	Y	N	Y
31 Martinez	Y	Y	Y	Y	Y	N
32 Dixon	Y	Y	Y	Y	N	Y
33 Roybal-Allard	Y	Y	Y	?	N	Y
34 Napolitano	Y	Y	Y	Y	N	Y
35 Waters	Y	Y	Y	Y	N	Y
36 ***Kuykendall***	Y	Y	Y	Y	Y	N
37 Millender-McD.	Y	Y	Y	Y	N	Y
38 ***Horn***	Y	Y	Y	Y	Y	Y
39 ***Royce***	?	?	?	?	Y	N
40 ***Lewis***	Y	Y	Y	Y	Y	N
41 ***Miller, Gary***	Y	Y	Y	Y	Y	N
42 Baca	Y	Y	Y	Y	N	Y
43 ***Calvert***	Y	Y	Y	Y	Y	N
44 ***Bono***	Y	Y	Y	Y	Y	N
45 ***Rohrabacher***	Y	Y	Y	Y	Y	N
46 Sanchez	+	+	+	+	N	Y
47 ***Cox***	Y	Y	Y	Y	Y	N
48 ***Packard***	Y	Y	Y	Y	Y	N
49 ***Bilbray***	Y	Y	Y	Y	Y	Y
50 Filner	Y	Y	Y	Y	N	Y
51 ***Cunningham***	Y	N	Y	Y	Y	N
52 ***Hunter***	Y	Y	Y	Y	Y	N
COLORADO						
1 DeGette	Y	Y	Y	Y	N	Y
2 Udall	Y	Y	Y	Y	N	Y
3 ***McInnis***	Y	Y	Y	Y	Y	N
4 ***Schaffer***	Y	Y	Y	Y	Y	N
5 ***Hefley***	Y	Y	Y	Y	Y	N
6 ***Tancredo***	Y	Y	Y	Y	Y	N
CONNECTICUT						
1 Larson	Y	Y	Y	Y	N	Y
2 Gejdenson	Y	Y	Y	Y	N	Y
3 DeLauro	Y	Y	Y	Y	N	Y
4 ***Shays***	Y	Y	Y	Y	Y	Y
5 Maloney	Y	Y	Y	Y	N	Y
6 ***Johnson***	?	?	?	Y	Y	Y
DELAWARE						
AL ***Castle***	Y	Y	Y	Y	Y	Y
FLORIDA						
1 ***Scarborough***	Y	N	Y	Y	Y	N
2 Boyd	Y	Y	Y	Y	N	Y
3 Brown	Y	Y	Y	Y	N	Y
4 ***Fowler***	Y	Y	Y	Y	Y	N
5 Thurman	Y	Y	Y	Y	N	Y
6 ***Stearns***	Y	Y	Y	Y	Y	N
7 ***Mica***	Y	Y	Y	Y	Y	N
8 ***McCollum***	?	?	?	?	Y	N
9 ***Bilirakis***	Y	Y	Y	Y	Y	N
10 ***Young***	Y	Y	Y	Y	Y	N
11 Davis	Y	Y	Y	Y	N	Y
12 ***Canady***	Y	Y	Y	Y	Y	N
13 ***Miller***	Y	Y	Y	Y	Y	N
14 ***Goss***	Y	Y	Y	Y	Y	N
15 ***Weldon***	Y	Y	Y	Y	Y	N
16 ***Foley***	Y	+	Y	Y	Y	N
17 Meek	?	?	?	?	N	Y
18 ***Ros-Lehtinen***	?	?	Y	Y	Y	N
19 Wexler	Y	Y	Y	Y	N	Y
20 Deutsch	Y	Y	Y	Y	N	Y
21 ***Diaz-Balart***	Y	Y	Y	Y	Y	N
22 ***Shaw***	Y	Y	Y	Y	Y	N
23 Hastings	Y	Y	Y	Y	N	Y
GEORGIA						
1 ***Kingston***	Y	Y	Y	Y	Y	N
2 Bishop	Y	Y	Y	Y	N	Y
3 ***Collins***	Y	N	Y	Y	Y	N
4 McKinney	Y	Y	Y	Y	N	Y
5 Lewis	Y	Y	Y	Y	N	Y
6 ***Isakson***	Y	Y	Y	Y	Y	N
7 ***Barr***	Y	Y	Y	Y	Y	N
8 ***Chambliss***	?	?	?	?	Y	N
9 ***Deal***	Y	Y	Y	Y	Y	N
10 ***Norwood***	?	?	?	?	Y	N
11 ***Linder***	Y	Y	Y	Y	Y	N
HAWAII						
1 Abercrombie	Y	Y	Y	Y	N	Y
2 Mink	Y	Y	Y	Y	N	Y
IDAHO						
1 ***Chenoweth-Hage***	Y	N	N	Y	Y	N
2 ***Simpson***	Y	Y	Y	Y	Y	N
ILLINOIS						
1 Rush	Y	Y	Y	Y	N	Y
2 Jackson	Y	Y	Y	Y	N	Y
3 Lipinski	Y	Y	Y	Y	N	Y
4 Gutierrez	Y	Y	Y	Y	N	Y
5 Blagojevich	Y	Y	Y	Y	N	Y
6 ***Hyde***	Y	Y	Y	Y	Y	N
7 Davis	Y	Y	Y	Y	N	Y
8 ***Crane***	Y	Y	Y	Y	Y	N
9 Schakowsky	Y	Y	Y	Y	N	Y
10 ***Porter***	Y	Y	Y	Y	N	Y
11 ***Weller***	Y	Y	Y	Y	Y	N
12 Costello	?	?	?	?	N	Y
13 ***Biggert***	Y	Y	Y	Y	Y	N

ND Northern Democrats SD Southern Democrats

	234	235	236	237	238	239
14 ***Hastert***					Y	
15 ***Ewing***	Y	Y	Y	Y	Y	N
16 ***Manzullo***	Y	Y	Y	Y	Y	N
17 Evans	Y	Y	Y	Y	N	Y
18 ***LaHood***	Y	Y	Y	Y	Y	N
19 Phelps	Y	Y	Y	Y	N	Y
20 ***Shimkus***	Y	Y	Y	Y	Y	N
INDIANA						
1 Visclosky	Y	Y	Y	Y	N	Y
2 ***McIntosh***	?	?	?	?	Y	N
3 Roemer	Y	Y	Y	Y	N	Y
4 ***Souder***	Y	Y	Y	Y	Y	N
5 ***Buyer***	Y	Y	Y	Y	Y	N
6 ***Burton***	Y	?	Y	Y	Y	N
7 ***Pease***	Y	Y	Y	Y	Y	Y
8 ***Hostettler***	Y	Y	Y	Y	Y	N
9 Hill	Y	Y	Y	Y	N	Y
10 Carson	Y	Y	Y	Y	N	Y
IOWA						
1 ***Leach***	Y	Y	Y	?	Y	Y
2 ***Nussle***	Y	Y	?	Y	Y	N
3 Boswell	Y	Y	Y	Y	N	Y
4 ***Ganske***	Y	Y	Y	Y	Y	Y
5 ***Latham***	Y	Y	Y	Y	Y	N
KANSAS						
1 ***Moran***	Y	Y	Y	Y	Y	N
2 ***Ryun***	Y	Y	Y	Y	Y	N
3 Moore	Y	Y	Y	Y	N	Y
4 ***Tiahrt***	Y	Y	Y	Y	Y	N
KENTUCKY						
1 ***Whitfield***	Y	Y	Y	Y	Y	N
2 ***Lewis***	Y	Y	Y	Y	Y	N
3 ***Northup***	Y	Y	Y	Y	Y	N
4 Lucas	Y	Y	Y	Y	N	Y
5 ***Rogers***	Y	Y	Y	Y	Y	N
6 ***Fletcher***	Y	Y	Y	Y	Y	N
LOUISIANA						
1 ***Vitter***	?	?	?	?	Y	N
2 Jefferson	?	?	?	?	N	Y
3 ***Tauzin***	?	?	?	?	Y	N
4 ***McCrery***	Y	Y	Y	Y	Y	N
5 ***Cooksey***	?	?	?	?	Y	N
6 ***Baker***	Y	Y	Y	Y	Y	N
7 John	Y	Y	Y	Y	N	Y
MAINE						
1 Allen	Y	Y	Y	Y	N	Y
2 Baldacci	Y	Y	Y	Y	N	Y
MARYLAND						
1 ***Gilchrest***	Y	Y	Y	Y	Y	N
2 ***Ehrlich***	Y	Y	Y	Y	Y	N
3 Cardin	Y	Y	Y	Y	N	Y
4 Wynn	Y	Y	Y	Y	N	Y
5 Hoyer	Y	Y	Y	Y	N	Y
6 ***Bartlett***	Y	Y	Y	Y	Y	N
7 Cummings	Y	Y	Y	Y	N	Y
8 ***Morella***	Y	?	?	Y	N	Y
MASSACHUSETTS						
1 Olver	Y	Y	Y	Y	N	Y
2 Neal	?	?	?	Y	N	Y
3 McGovern	Y	Y	Y	Y	N	Y
4 Frank	Y	Y	Y	Y	N	Y
5 Meehan	Y	Y	Y	Y	N	Y
6 Tierney	Y	Y	Y	Y	N	Y
7 Markey	?	?	?	?	?	?
8 Capuano	Y	Y	Y	Y	N	Y
9 Moakley	Y	Y	Y	Y	N	Y
10 Delahunt	Y	Y	Y	Y	N	Y
MICHIGAN						
1 Stupak	Y	Y	Y	Y	N	Y
2 ***Hoekstra***	Y	Y	Y	Y	Y	N
3 ***Ehlers***	Y	Y	Y	Y	Y	Y
4 ***Camp***	Y	Y	Y	Y	Y	N
5 Barcia	Y	Y	Y	Y	N	N
6 ***Upton***	Y	Y	Y	Y	Y	Y
7 ***Smith***	?	?	?	?	?	?
8 Stabenow	Y	Y	Y	Y	N	Y
9 Kildee	Y	Y	Y	Y	N	Y
10 Bonior	Y	Y	Y	Y	N	Y
11 ***Knollenberg***	Y	Y	Y	Y	Y	N
12 Levin	Y	Y	Y	Y	N	Y
13 Rivers	Y	Y	Y	Y	N	Y
14 Conyers	?	Y	Y	Y	N	Y
15 Kilpatrick	Y	Y	Y	Y	N	Y
16 Dingell	Y	Y	Y	Y	N	Y
MINNESOTA						
1 ***Gutknecht***	Y	Y	Y	Y	Y	N
2 Minge	Y	Y	Y	Y	N	Y
3 ***Ramstad***	Y	Y	Y	Y	N	Y
4 Vento	?	?	?	?	?	?
5 Sabo	Y	Y	Y	Y	N	Y
6 Luther	Y	Y	Y	Y	N	Y
7 Peterson	Y	Y	Y	Y	N	Y
8 Oberstar	Y	Y	Y	Y	N	Y
MISSISSIPPI						
1 ***Wicker***	Y	Y	Y	Y	Y	N
2 Thompson	Y	Y	Y	Y	N	Y
3 ***Pickering***	Y	Y	Y	Y	Y	N
4 Shows	Y	Y	Y	Y	N	Y
5 Taylor	?	?	?	?	N	Y
MISSOURI						
1 Clay	Y	Y	Y	Y	N	Y
2 ***Talent***	Y	Y	Y	Y	Y	N
3 Gephardt	Y	Y	Y	Y	N	Y
4 Skelton	?	?	?	?	?	?
5 McCarthy	Y	Y	Y	Y	N	Y
6 Danner	Y	Y	Y	Y	N	Y
7 ***Blunt***	Y	Y	Y	Y	Y	N
8 ***Emerson***	Y	Y	Y	Y	Y	N
9 ***Hulshof***	Y	Y	Y	Y	Y	N
MONTANA						
AL ***Hill***	Y	Y	Y	Y	Y	N
NEBRASKA						
1 ***Bereuter***	Y	Y	Y	Y	Y	N
2 ***Terry***	+	Y	Y	Y	Y	N
3 ***Barrett***	Y	Y	Y	Y	Y	N
NEVADA						
1 Berkley	Y	Y	Y	Y	N	Y
2 ***Gibbons***	Y	Y	Y	Y	Y	N
NEW HAMPSHIRE						
1 ***Sununu***	Y	Y	Y	Y	Y	N
2 ***Bass***	Y	Y	Y	Y	Y	Y
NEW JERSEY						
1 Andrews	Y	Y	Y	Y	N	Y
2 ***LoBiondo***	Y	Y	Y	Y	Y	Y
3 ***Saxton***	Y	Y	Y	Y	N	Y
4 ***Smith***	Y	Y	Y	Y	Y	Y
5 ***Roukema***	?	?	?	?	?	?
6 Pallone	Y	Y	Y	Y	N	Y
7 ***Franks***	?	?	?	?	?	?
8 Pascrell	?	?	?	?	N	Y
9 Rothman	Y	Y	Y	Y	N	Y
10 Payne	?	?	?	?	N	Y
11 ***Frelinghuysen***	Y	Y	Y	Y	Y	Y
12 Holt	Y	Y	Y	Y	N	Y
13 Menendez	?	?	?	?	N	Y
NEW MEXICO						
1 ***Wilson***	Y	Y	Y	Y	Y	N
2 ***Skeen***	Y	Y	Y	Y	Y	N
3 Udall	?	?	?	?	N	Y
NEW YORK						
1 Forbes	Y	Y	Y	Y	N	Y
2 ***Lazio***	Y	Y	Y	Y	Y	Y
3 ***King***	Y	Y	Y	Y	Y	N
4 McCarthy	Y	Y	Y	Y	N	Y
5 Ackerman	Y	Y	Y	Y	N	Y
6 Meeks	Y	Y	Y	Y	N	Y
7 Crowley	Y	Y	Y	Y	N	Y
8 Nadler	Y	Y	Y	Y	N	Y
9 Weiner	Y	Y	Y	Y	N	Y
10 Towns	Y	Y	Y	Y	N	Y
11 Owens	Y	Y	Y	Y	N	Y
12 Velázquez	Y	Y	Y	Y	N	Y
13 ***Fossella***	Y	Y	Y	Y	Y	N
14 Maloney	Y	Y	Y	Y	N	Y
15 Rangel	Y	Y	Y	Y	N	Y
16 Serrano	Y	Y	Y	Y	N	Y
17 Engel	Y	Y	Y	Y	N	Y
18 Lowey	Y	Y	Y	Y	N	Y
19 ***Kelly***	Y	Y	Y	Y	Y	N
20 ***Gilman***	Y	Y	Y	Y	Y	Y
21 McNulty	?	?	?	?	N	Y
22 ***Sweeney***	?	?	?	?	?	?
23 ***Boehlert***	Y	Y	Y	Y	Y	N
24 ***McHugh***	Y	Y	Y	Y	Y	N
25 ***Walsh***	Y	N	Y	Y	Y	N
26 Hinchey	Y	Y	Y	Y	N	Y
27 ***Reynolds***	Y	Y	Y	Y	Y	N
28 Slaughter	Y	Y	Y	Y	N	Y
29 LaFalce	Y	Y	Y	Y	N	Y
30 ***Quinn***	Y	Y	Y	Y	Y	N
31 ***Houghton***	?	?	?	?	?	?
NORTH CAROLINA						
1 Clayton	Y	Y	Y	Y	N	Y
2 Etheridge	Y	Y	Y	Y	N	Y
3 ***Jones***	Y	Y	Y	Y	Y	N
4 Price	?	?	Y	Y	N	Y
5 ***Burr***	Y	Y	Y	Y	Y	N
6 ***Coble***	Y	Y	Y	Y	Y	N
7 McIntyre	Y	Y	Y	Y	N	Y
8 ***Hayes***	Y	Y	Y	Y	Y	N
9 ***Myrick***	Y	Y	Y	Y	Y	N
10 ***Ballenger***	Y	Y	Y	Y	Y	N
11 ***Taylor***	Y	Y	Y	Y	Y	N
12 Watt	Y	Y	Y	Y	N	Y
NORTH DAKOTA						
AL Pomeroy	Y	Y	Y	Y	N	Y
OHIO						
1 ***Chabot***	Y	Y	Y	Y	Y	N
2 ***Portman***	Y	Y	Y	Y	Y	N
3 Hall	Y	Y	Y	Y	N	Y
4 ***Oxley***	Y	Y	Y	Y	Y	N
5 ***Gillmor***	Y	Y	Y	Y	Y	N
6 Strickland	Y	Y	Y	Y	N	Y
7 ***Hobson***	Y	Y	Y	Y	Y	N
8 ***Boehner***	Y	Y	Y	Y	Y	N
9 Kaptur	Y	Y	Y	Y	N	Y
10 Kucinich	Y	Y	Y	Y	N	Y
11 Jones	?	?	?	?	N	Y
12 ***Kasich***	Y	Y	Y	Y	Y	N
13 Brown	Y	Y	Y	Y	N	Y
14 Sawyer	Y	Y	Y	Y	N	Y
15 ***Pryce***	Y	Y	Y	Y	Y	N
16 ***Regula***	Y	Y	Y	Y	Y	N
17 Traficant	Y	Y	Y	Y	Y	N
18 ***Ney***	Y	Y	Y	Y	Y	N
19 ***LaTourette***	Y	Y	Y	Y	Y	N
OKLAHOMA						
1 ***Largent***	Y	Y	Y	Y	Y	N
2 ***Coburn***	?	?	?	?	Y	N
3 ***Watkins***	Y	Y	Y	Y	Y	N
4 ***Watts***	Y	Y	Y	Y	Y	N
5 ***Istook***	Y	Y	Y	Y	Y	N
6 ***Lucas***	Y	Y	Y	Y	Y	N
OREGON						
1 Wu	Y	Y	Y	Y	N	Y
2 ***Walden***	Y	Y	Y	Y	Y	N
3 Blumenauer	Y	Y	Y	Y	N	Y
4 DeFazio	Y	Y	Y	Y	N	Y
5 Hooley	Y	Y	Y	Y	N	Y
PENNSYLVANIA						
1 Brady	Y	Y	Y	Y	N	Y
2 Fattah	Y	Y	Y	Y	N	Y
3 Borski	Y	Y	Y	Y	N	Y
4 Klink	Y	Y	Y	Y	N	Y
5 ***Peterson***	Y	Y	Y	Y	Y	N
6 Holden	Y	Y	Y	Y	N	Y
7 ***Weldon***	Y	Y	Y	Y	Y	N
8 ***Greenwood***	?	?	?	?	?	?
9 ***Shuster***	Y	Y	Y	Y	Y	N
10 ***Sherwood***	Y	?	Y	Y	Y	N
11 Kanjorski	Y	Y	Y	Y	N	Y
12 Murtha	Y	Y	?	Y	Y	Y
13 Hoeffel	Y	Y	Y	Y	N	Y
14 Coyne	Y	Y	Y	Y	N	Y
15 ***Toomey***	Y	Y	Y	Y	Y	N
16 ***Pitts***	?	?	?	?	Y	N
17 ***Gekas***	Y	Y	Y	Y	Y	N
18 Doyle	?	?	?	?	N	Y
19 ***Goodling***	Y	Y	Y	Y	Y	N
20 Mascara	Y	Y	Y	Y	N	Y
21 ***English***	?	?	?	?	?	?
RHODE ISLAND						
1 Kennedy	Y	Y	Y	Y	N	Y
2 Weygand	Y	Y	Y	Y	N	Y
SOUTH CAROLINA						
1 ***Sanford***	Y	N	N	Y	Y	N
2 ***Spence***	Y	Y	Y	Y	Y	N
3 ***Graham***	Y	Y	Y	Y	Y	N
4 ***DeMint***	Y	Y	Y	Y	Y	N
5 Spratt	Y	Y	Y	Y	N	Y
6 Clyburn	Y	Y	Y	Y	N	Y
SOUTH DAKOTA						
AL ***Thune***	Y	Y	Y	Y	Y	N
TENNESSEE						
1 ***Jenkins***	Y	Y	Y	Y	Y	N
2 ***Duncan***	Y	Y	Y	Y	Y	N
3 ***Wamp***	Y	Y	Y	Y	Y	N
4 ***Hilleary***	?	?	?	?	Y	N
5 Clement	Y	Y	Y	Y	N	Y
6 Gordon	Y	Y	Y	Y	N	Y
7 ***Bryant***	Y	Y	Y	Y	Y	N
8 Tanner	Y	Y	Y	Y	N	Y
9 Ford	?	?	?	?	N	Y
TEXAS						
1 Sandlin	Y	Y	Y	Y	N	Y
2 Turner	Y	Y	Y	Y	N	Y
3 ***Johnson, Sam***	Y	Y	Y	Y	Y	N
4 Hall	Y	Y	Y	Y	N	N
5 ***Sessions***	Y	Y	Y	Y	Y	N
6 ***Barton***	Y	Y	Y	Y	Y	N
7 ***Archer***	Y	Y	Y	Y	Y	N
8 ***Brady***	?	Y	Y	Y	Y	N
9 Lampson	Y	Y	Y	Y	N	Y
10 Doggett	Y	Y	Y	Y	N	Y
11 Edwards	Y	Y	Y	Y	N	Y
12 ***Granger***	Y	Y	Y	Y	Y	N
13 ***Thornberry***	Y	Y	Y	Y	Y	N
14 ***Paul***	Y	Y	Y	N	Y	N
15 Hinojosa	Y	Y	Y	Y	N	Y
16 Reyes	Y	Y	Y	Y	N	Y
17 Stenholm	Y	Y	Y	Y	N	Y
18 Jackson-Lee	Y	Y	Y	Y	N	Y
19 ***Combest***	Y	Y	Y	Y	Y	N
20 Gonzalez	Y	Y	Y	Y	N	Y
21 ***Smith***	Y	Y	Y	Y	Y	N
22 ***DeLay***	Y	Y	Y	Y	Y	N
23 ***Bonilla***	Y	Y	Y	Y	Y	N
24 Frost	Y	Y	Y	Y	N	Y
25 Bentsen	Y	Y	Y	Y	N	Y
26 ***Armey***	Y	Y	Y	Y	Y	N
27 Ortiz	Y	Y	Y	Y	N	Y
28 Rodriguez	Y	Y	Y	Y	N	Y
29 Green	Y	Y	Y	Y	N	Y
30 Johnson, E.B.	Y	Y	Y	Y	N	Y
UTAH						
1 ***Hansen***	Y	Y	Y	Y	Y	N
2 ***Cook***	?	?	?	?	Y	N
3 ***Cannon***	Y	Y	Y	Y	Y	N
VERMONT						
AL *Sanders*	Y	Y	Y	Y	N	Y
VIRGINIA						
1 ***Bateman***	Y	Y	?	Y	Y	N
2 Pickett	Y	Y	Y	Y	N	Y
3 Scott	Y	Y	Y	Y	N	Y
4 Sisisky	Y	Y	Y	Y	N	Y
5 *Goode*	Y	Y	Y	Y	Y	N
6 ***Goodlatte***	Y	Y	Y	Y	Y	N
7 ***Bliley***	?	?	?	?	Y	N
8 Moran	Y	Y	Y	Y	N	Y
9 Boucher	Y	Y	Y	Y	N	Y
10 ***Wolf***	Y	Y	Y	Y	Y	Y
11 ***Davis***	Y	Y	Y	Y	Y	Y
WASHINGTON						
1 Inslee	Y	Y	Y	Y	N	Y
2 ***Metcalf***	?	?	Y	Y	Y	N
3 Baird	Y	Y	Y	Y	N	Y
4 ***Hastings***	Y	Y	Y	Y	Y	N
5 ***Nethercutt***	Y	Y	Y	Y	?	?
6 Dicks	Y	Y	Y	Y	N	Y
7 McDermott	Y	Y	Y	Y	N	Y
8 ***Dunn***	Y	Y	Y	Y	Y	N
9 Smith	Y	Y	Y	Y	N	Y
WEST VIRGINIA						
1 Mollohan	Y	Y	Y	Y	N	Y
2 Wise	?	Y	Y	Y	N	Y
3 Rahall	Y	Y	Y	Y	N	Y
WISCONSIN						
1 ***Ryan***	Y	Y	Y	Y	Y	N
2 Baldwin	Y	Y	Y	Y	N	Y
3 Kind	Y	Y	Y	Y	N	Y
4 Kleczka	Y	Y	Y	Y	N	Y
5 Barrett	Y	Y	Y	Y	N	Y
6 ***Petri***	Y	Y	Y	Y	Y	N
7 Obey	Y	Y	Y	Y	N	Y
8 ***Green***	Y	Y	Y	Y	Y	N
9 ***Sensenbrenner***	Y	Y	Y	Y	Y	N
WYOMING						
AL ***Cubin***	Y	Y	Y	Y	Y	N

Southern states - Ala., Ark., Fla., Ga., Ky., La., Miss., N.C., Okla., S.C., Tenn., Texas, Va.

240. HR 3605. San Rafael Legacy District/Cars. Boehlert, R-N.Y., substitute amendment to the Holt, D-N.J., amendment. The Boehlert amendment would permit the use of motorized vehicles where authorized by the Bureau of Land Management. The Holt amendment would limit motorized vehicles within a conservation area to those used for administrative purposes or emergencies. Rejected 210-214: R 204-9; D 5-204 (ND 3-152, SD 2-52); I 1-1. June 7, 2000.

241. HR 4576. Fiscal 2001 Defense Appropriations/Passage. Passage of the bill to appropriate $288.5 billion in defense spending for fiscal 2001, which is $4 billion more than the president's request and represents an 8 percent increase over fiscal 2000 spending. The bill would provide $4.6 billion for missile defense and $2.1 billion for 10 F-22 Raptor tactical aircraft. The measure would fund a 3.7 percent pay increase for military personnel and provide $97.5 billion for operations and maintenance. Passed 367-58: R 208-8; D 158-49 (ND 107-46, SD 51-3); I 1-1. June 7, 2000.

242. S 291. Carlsbad Irrigation/Passage. Sherwood, R-Pa., motion to suspend the rules and pass the bill that would authorize the Interior secretary to convey the irrigation and drainage system of the Carlsbad Project and related land in Eddy County, N.M., to the Carlsbad Irrigation District, a quasi-municipal corporation. Motion agreed to 422-0: R 215-0; D 205-0 (ND 151-0, SD 54-0); I 2-0. A two-thirds majority of those present and voting (282 in this case) is necessary for passage under suspension of the rules. June 7, 2000.

243. S 356. Wellton-Mohawk Land Transfer/Passage. Sherwood, R-Pa., motion to suspend the rules and pass the bill that would authorize the Interior secretary to transfer certain works, facilities and titles of the Gila Project, including certain federally owned lands within or adjacent to the project, to the Wellton-Mohawk Irrigation and Drainage District of Yuma County, Ariz. Motion agreed to 423-0: R 215-0; D 206-0 (ND 152-0, SD 54-0); I 2-0. A two-thirds majority of those present and voting (282 in this case) is required for passage under suspension of the rules. June 7, 2000.

244. HR 4435. North Carolina Coastal Barrier/Passage. Sherwood, R-Pa., motion to suspend the rules and pass the bill that would clarify the boundary of the Coastal Barrier Resources System in Dare and Currituck counties in North Carolina to remove publicly and privately developed areas and add adjacent aquatic habitats. Motion agreed to 421-1: R 216-0; D 203-1 (ND 150-1, SD 53-0); I 2-0. A two-thirds majority of those present and voting (282 in this case) is required for passage under suspension of the rules. June 7, 2000.

245. HR 3176. Kealia Pond Refuge/Passage. Sherwood, R-Pa., motion to suspend the rules and pass the bill that would direct the Fish and Wildlife Service to study how to return conditions in the Kealia Pond National Wildlife Refuge to its natural wetland state and authorize $250,000 for that study. Motion agreed to 406-14: R 201-14; D 203-0 (ND 151-0, SD 52-0); I 2-0. A two-thirds majority of those present and voting (280 in this case) is required for passage under suspension of the rules. June 7, 2000.

Key

- Y Voted for (yea).
- # Paired for.
- + Announced for.
- N Voted against (nay).
- X Paired against.
- – Announced against.
- P Voted "present."
- C Voted "present" to avoid possible conflict of interest.
- ? Did not vote or otherwise make a position known.

•

Democrats ***Republicans***
Independents

	240	241	242	243	244	245
ALABAMA						
1 ***Callahan***	Y	Y	Y	Y	Y	Y
2 ***Everett***	Y	Y	Y	Y	Y	Y
3 ***Riley***	Y	Y	Y	Y	Y	Y
4 ***Aderholt***	Y	Y	Y	Y	Y	Y
5 Cramer	N	Y	Y	Y	Y	Y
6 ***Bachus***	Y	Y	Y	Y	Y	Y
7 Hilliard	N	Y	Y	Y	Y	Y
ALASKA						
AL ***Young***	Y	Y	Y	Y	Y	Y
ARIZONA						
1 ***Salmon***	?	Y	Y	Y	Y	Y
2 Pastor	N	Y	Y	Y	Y	Y
3 ***Stump***	Y	Y	Y	Y	Y	Y
4 ***Shadegg***	Y	Y	Y	Y	Y	Y
5 ***Kolbe***	Y	Y	Y	Y	Y	Y
6 ***Hayworth***	Y	Y	Y	Y	Y	Y
ARKANSAS						
1 Berry	N	Y	Y	Y	Y	Y
2 Snyder	N	Y	Y	Y	Y	Y
3 ***Hutchinson***	Y	Y	Y	Y	Y	Y
4 ***Dickey***	Y	Y	Y	Y	Y	Y
CALIFORNIA						
1 Thompson	N	Y	Y	Y	Y	Y
2 ***Herger***	Y	Y	Y	Y	Y	Y
3 ***Ose***	Y	Y	Y	Y	Y	Y
4 ***Doolittle***	Y	Y	Y	Y	Y	Y
5 Matsui	N	Y	Y	Y	Y	Y
6 Woolsey	N	Y	Y	Y	Y	Y
7 Miller, George	N	N	Y	Y	Y	Y
8 Pelosi	N	Y	Y	Y	Y	Y
9 Lee	N	N	Y	Y	Y	Y
10 Tauscher	N	Y	Y	Y	Y	Y
11 ***Pombo***	Y	Y	Y	Y	Y	N
12 Lantos	N	Y	Y	Y	Y	Y
13 Stark	N	N	Y	Y	Y	Y
14 Eshoo	N	N	Y	Y	Y	Y
15 ***Campbell***	N	N	Y	Y	Y	Y
16 Lofgren	N	N	Y	Y	Y	Y
17 Farr	N	Y	Y	Y	Y	Y
18 Condit	N	Y	Y	Y	Y	Y
19 ***Radanovich***	Y	Y	Y	Y	Y	Y
20 Dooley	N	Y	Y	Y	Y	Y
21 ***Thomas***	Y	Y	Y	Y	Y	Y
22 Capps	N	Y	Y	Y	Y	Y
23 ***Gallegly***	Y	Y	Y	Y	Y	Y
24 Sherman	N	Y	Y	Y	Y	Y
25 ***McKeon***	Y	Y	Y	Y	Y	Y
26 Berman	N	Y	Y	Y	Y	Y
27 ***Rogan***	Y	Y	Y	Y	Y	Y
28 ***Dreier***	Y	Y	Y	Y	Y	Y
29 Waxman	N	N	Y	Y	Y	Y
30 Becerra	N	Y	Y	Y	Y	Y
31 Martinez	Y	Y	Y	Y	Y	Y
32 Dixon	N	Y	Y	Y	Y	Y
33 Roybal-Allard	N	Y	Y	Y	Y	Y
34 Napolitano	N	Y	Y	Y	Y	Y
35 Waters	N	Y	Y	Y	Y	Y
36 ***Kuykendall***	Y	Y	Y	Y	Y	Y
37 Millender-McD.	N	Y	Y	Y	Y	Y
38 ***Horn***	Y	Y	Y	Y	Y	Y
39 ***Royce***	Y	Y	Y	Y	Y	N
40 ***Lewis***	Y	Y	Y	Y	Y	Y
41 ***Miller, Gary***	Y	Y	Y	Y	Y	Y
42 Baca	N	Y	Y	Y	Y	Y
43 ***Calvert***	Y	Y	Y	Y	Y	Y
44 ***Bono***	Y	Y	Y	Y	Y	Y
45 ***Rohrabacher***	Y	Y	Y	Y	Y	Y
46 Sanchez	N	Y	Y	Y	Y	Y
47 ***Cox***	Y	Y	Y	Y	Y	Y
48 ***Packard***	Y	Y	Y	Y	Y	Y
49 ***Bilbray***	Y	Y	Y	Y	Y	Y
50 Filner	N	N	Y	Y	Y	Y
51 ***Cunningham***	Y	Y	?	Y	Y	Y
52 ***Hunter***	Y	Y	Y	Y	Y	Y
COLORADO						
1 DeGette	N	N	Y	Y	Y	Y
2 Udall	N	N	Y	Y	Y	Y
3 ***McInnis***	Y	?	Y	Y	Y	Y
4 ***Schaffer***	Y	Y	Y	Y	Y	N
5 ***Hefley***	Y	Y	Y	Y	Y	Y
6 ***Tancredo***	Y	Y	Y	Y	Y	Y
CONNECTICUT						
1 Larson	N	Y	Y	Y	Y	Y
2 Gejdenson	N	Y	Y	Y	Y	Y
3 DeLauro	N	Y	Y	Y	Y	Y
4 ***Shays***	Y	N	Y	Y	Y	Y
5 Maloney	N	Y	Y	Y	Y	Y
6 ***Johnson***	Y	Y	Y	Y	Y	Y
DELAWARE						
AL ***Castle***	Y	Y	Y	Y	Y	Y
FLORIDA						
1 ***Scarborough***	Y	Y	Y	Y	Y	Y
2 Boyd	Y	Y	Y	Y	Y	Y
3 Brown	N	Y	Y	Y	Y	Y
4 ***Fowler***	Y	Y	Y	Y	Y	Y
5 Thurman	N	Y	Y	Y	Y	Y
6 ***Stearns***	Y	Y	Y	Y	Y	N
7 ***Mica***	Y	Y	Y	Y	Y	Y
8 ***McCollum***	Y	Y	Y	Y	Y	Y
9 ***Bilirakis***	Y	Y	Y	Y	Y	Y
10 ***Young***	Y	Y	Y	Y	Y	Y
11 Davis	N	Y	Y	Y	Y	Y
12 ***Canady***	Y	Y	Y	Y	Y	Y
13 ***Miller***	Y	Y	Y	Y	Y	Y
14 ***Goss***	Y	Y	Y	Y	Y	Y
15 ***Weldon***	Y	Y	Y	Y	Y	Y
16 ***Foley***	Y	Y	Y	Y	Y	Y
17 Meek	N	Y	Y	Y	Y	Y
18 ***Ros-Lehtinen***	Y	Y	Y	Y	Y	Y
19 Wexler	N	Y	Y	Y	Y	Y
20 Deutsch	N	Y	Y	Y	Y	Y
21 ***Diaz-Balart***	Y	Y	Y	Y	Y	Y
22 ***Shaw***	Y	Y	Y	Y	Y	Y
23 Hastings	N	Y	Y	Y	Y	Y
GEORGIA						
1 ***Kingston***	Y	Y	Y	Y	Y	Y
2 Bishop	N	Y	Y	Y	Y	Y
3 ***Collins***	Y	Y	Y	Y	Y	Y
4 McKinney	N	N	Y	Y	Y	Y
5 Lewis	N	Y	Y	Y	Y	Y
6 ***Isakson***	Y	Y	Y	Y	Y	Y
7 ***Barr***	Y	Y	Y	Y	Y	Y
8 ***Chambliss***	Y	Y	Y	Y	Y	Y
9 ***Deal***	Y	Y	Y	Y	Y	Y
10 ***Norwood***	Y	Y	Y	Y	Y	Y
11 ***Linder***	Y	Y	Y	Y	Y	Y
HAWAII						
1 Abercrombie	N	Y	Y	Y	Y	Y
2 Mink	N	Y	Y	Y	Y	Y
IDAHO						
1 ***Chenoweth-Hage***	Y	Y	Y	Y	Y	N
2 ***Simpson***	Y	Y	Y	Y	Y	Y
ILLINOIS						
1 Rush	N	Y	Y	Y	Y	Y
2 Jackson	N	N	Y	Y	Y	Y
3 Lipinski	N	Y	Y	Y	Y	Y
4 Gutierrez	N	N	Y	Y	Y	Y
5 Blagojevich	N	Y	Y	Y	Y	Y
6 ***Hyde***	Y	Y	Y	Y	Y	Y
7 Davis	N	N	Y	Y	Y	Y
8 ***Crane***	Y	Y	Y	Y	Y	Y
9 Schakowsky	N	N	Y	Y	Y	Y
10 ***Porter***	N	Y	Y	Y	Y	Y
11 ***Weller***	Y	Y	Y	Y	Y	Y
12 Costello	N	Y	Y	Y	Y	Y
13 ***Biggert***	Y	Y	Y	Y	Y	Y

ND Northern Democrats SD Southern Democrats

	240	241	242	243	244	245
14 ***Hastert***	Y					
15 ***Ewing***	Y	Y	Y	Y	Y	Y
16 ***Manzullo***	Y	Y	Y	Y	Y	Y
17 Evans	N	Y	Y	Y	Y	Y
18 ***LaHood***	Y	Y	Y	Y	Y	Y
19 Phelps	N	Y	Y	Y	Y	Y
20 ***Shimkus***	Y	Y	Y	Y	Y	Y
INDIANA						
1 Visclosky	N	Y	Y	Y	Y	Y
2 ***McIntosh***	Y	Y	Y	Y	Y	Y
3 Roemer	N	Y	Y	Y	Y	Y
4 ***Souder***	Y	Y	Y	Y	Y	Y
5 ***Buyer***	Y	Y	Y	Y	Y	Y
6 ***Burton***	Y	Y	Y	Y	Y	Y
7 ***Pease***	Y	Y	Y	Y	Y	Y
8 ***Hostettler***	Y	Y	Y	Y	Y	Y
9 Hill	N	Y	Y	Y	Y	Y
10 Carson	N	Y	Y	Y	Y	Y
IOWA						
1 ***Leach***	N	Y	Y	Y	Y	Y
2 ***Nussle***	Y	Y	Y	Y	Y	Y
3 Boswell	N	Y	Y	Y	Y	Y
4 ***Ganske***	Y	N	Y	Y	Y	Y
5 ***Latham***	Y	Y	Y	Y	Y	Y
KANSAS						
1 ***Moran***	Y	Y	Y	Y	Y	Y
2 ***Ryun***	Y	Y	Y	Y	Y	Y
3 Moore	N	Y	Y	Y	Y	Y
4 ***Tiahrt***	Y	Y	Y	Y	Y	N
KENTUCKY						
1 ***Whitfield***	Y	Y	Y	Y	Y	Y
2 ***Lewis***	Y	Y	Y	?	Y	Y
3 ***Northup***	Y	Y	Y	Y	Y	Y
4 Lucas	N	Y	Y	Y	Y	Y
5 ***Rogers***	Y	Y	Y	Y	Y	Y
6 ***Fletcher***	Y	Y	Y	Y	Y	Y
LOUISIANA						
1 ***Vitter***	Y	Y	Y	Y	Y	Y
2 Jefferson	N	Y	Y	Y	Y	?
3 ***Tauzin***	Y	Y	Y	Y	Y	Y
4 ***McCrery***	Y	Y	Y	Y	Y	Y
5 ***Cooksey***	Y	Y	Y	Y	Y	Y
6 ***Baker***	Y	Y	Y	Y	Y	Y
7 John	N	Y	Y	Y	Y	Y
MAINE						
1 Allen	N	Y	Y	Y	Y	Y
2 Baldacci	N	Y	Y	Y	Y	Y
MARYLAND						
1 ***Gilchrest***	Y	Y	?	Y	Y	Y
2 ***Ehrlich***	Y	Y	Y	Y	Y	?
3 Cardin	N	Y	Y	Y	Y	Y
4 Wynn	N	Y	Y	Y	Y	Y
5 Hoyer	N	Y	Y	Y	Y	Y
6 ***Bartlett***	Y	Y	Y	Y	Y	Y
7 Cummings	N	Y	Y	Y	Y	Y
8 ***Morella***	N	Y	Y	Y	Y	Y
MASSACHUSETTS						
1 Olver	N	Y	Y	Y	Y	Y
2 Neal	N	Y	Y	Y	Y	Y
3 McGovern	N	N	?	Y	Y	Y
4 Frank	N	N	Y	Y	Y	Y
5 Meehan	N	Y	Y	Y	Y	Y
6 Tierney	N	N	Y	Y	Y	Y
7 Markey	?	?	?	?	?	?
8 Capuano	N	N	Y	Y	Y	Y
9 Moakley	N	Y	Y	Y	Y	Y
10 Delahunt	N	N	Y	Y	Y	Y
MICHIGAN						
1 Stupak	N	Y	Y	Y	Y	Y
2 ***Hoekstra***	Y	Y	Y	Y	Y	Y
3 ***Ehlers***	N	N	Y	Y	Y	Y
4 ***Camp***	Y	Y	Y	Y	Y	Y
5 Barcia	Y	Y	Y	Y	Y	Y
6 ***Upton***	Y	Y	Y	Y	Y	Y
7 ***Smith***	?	?	?	?	?	?
8 Stabenow	N	Y	Y	Y	Y	Y
9 Kildee	N	Y	Y	Y	Y	Y
10 Bonior	N	Y	Y	Y	Y	Y
11 ***Knollenberg***	Y	Y	Y	Y	Y	Y
12 Levin	N	Y	Y	Y	Y	Y
13 Rivers	N	N	Y	Y	Y	Y
14 Conyers	N	N	Y	Y	Y	Y
15 Kilpatrick	N	Y	Y	Y	Y	Y
16 Dingell	N	Y	Y	Y	Y	Y

Southern states - Ala., Ark., Fla., Ga., Ky., La., Miss., N.C., Okla., S.C., Tenn., Texas, Va.

	240	241	242	243	244	245
MINNESOTA						
1 ***Gutknecht***	Y	Y	Y	Y	Y	Y
2 Minge	N	N	Y	Y	Y	Y
3 ***Ramstad***	N	N	Y	Y	Y	Y
4 Vento	?	?	?	?	?	?
5 Sabo	N	Y	Y	Y	Y	Y
6 Luther	N	N	Y	Y	Y	Y
7 Peterson	N	N	Y	Y	Y	Y
8 Oberstar	N	N	Y	Y	Y	Y
MISSISSIPPI						
1 ***Wicker***	Y	Y	Y	Y	Y	Y
2 Thompson	N	Y	Y	Y	Y	Y
3 ***Pickering***	Y	Y	Y	Y	Y	Y
4 Shows	N	Y	Y	Y	Y	Y
5 Taylor	N	Y	Y	Y	Y	Y
MISSOURI						
1 Clay	N	Y	Y	Y	?	?
2 ***Talent***	Y	Y	Y	Y	Y	Y
3 Gephardt	N	Y	?	?	?	?
4 Skelton	N	Y	Y	Y	Y	Y
5 McCarthy	N	Y	Y	Y	Y	Y
6 Danner	N	?	?	?	?	?
7 ***Blunt***	Y	Y	Y	Y	Y	Y
8 ***Emerson***	Y	Y	Y	Y	Y	N
9 ***Hulshof***	Y	Y	Y	Y	Y	Y
MONTANA						
AL ***Hill***	Y	Y	Y	Y	Y	Y
NEBRASKA						
1 ***Bereuter***	Y	Y	Y	Y	Y	Y
2 ***Terry***	Y	Y	Y	Y	Y	Y
3 ***Barrett***	Y	Y	Y	Y	Y	Y
NEVADA						
1 Berkley	N	Y	Y	Y	Y	Y
2 ***Gibbons***	Y	Y	Y	Y	Y	Y
NEW HAMPSHIRE						
1 ***Sununu***	Y	Y	Y	Y	Y	Y
2 ***Bass***	Y	Y	Y	Y	Y	Y
NEW JERSEY						
1 Andrews	N	Y	Y	Y	Y	Y
2 ***LoBiondo***	N	Y	Y	Y	Y	Y
3 ***Saxton***	Y	Y	Y	Y	Y	Y
4 ***Smith***	N	Y	Y	Y	Y	Y
5 ***Roukema***	?	Y	Y	Y	Y	Y
6 Pallone	N	Y	Y	Y	Y	Y
7 ***Franks***	?	Y	Y	Y	Y	Y
8 Pascrell	N	Y	Y	Y	Y	Y
9 Rothman	N	Y	Y	Y	Y	Y
10 Payne	N	N	Y	Y	Y	Y
11 ***Frelinghuysen***	N	Y	Y	Y	Y	Y
12 Holt	N	Y	Y	Y	Y	Y
13 Menendez	N	Y	Y	Y	Y	Y
NEW MEXICO						
1 ***Wilson***	Y	Y	Y	Y	Y	Y
2 ***Skeen***	Y	Y	Y	Y	Y	Y
3 Udall	N	Y	Y	Y	Y	Y
NEW YORK						
1 Forbes	N	Y	Y	Y	Y	Y
2 ***Lazio***	Y	Y	Y	Y	Y	Y
3 ***King***	Y	Y	Y	Y	Y	Y
4 McCarthy	N	Y	Y	Y	Y	Y
5 Ackerman	N	Y	Y	Y	Y	Y
6 Meeks	N	N	Y	Y	Y	Y
7 Crowley	N	Y	Y	Y	Y	Y
8 Nadler	N	N	Y	Y	Y	Y
9 Weiner	N	N	Y	Y	Y	Y
10 Towns	N	N	Y	Y	Y	Y
11 Owens	N	N	Y	Y	Y	Y
12 Velázquez	N	N	Y	Y	Y	Y
13 ***Fossella***	Y	Y	Y	Y	Y	Y
14 Maloney	N	Y	Y	Y	Y	Y
15 Rangel	N	N	Y	Y	Y	Y
16 Serrano	N	N	Y	Y	Y	Y
17 Engel	N	Y	Y	Y	Y	Y
18 Lowey	N	Y	Y	Y	Y	Y
19 ***Kelly***	Y	Y	Y	Y	Y	Y
20 ***Gilman***	Y	Y	Y	Y	Y	Y
21 McNulty	N	Y	Y	Y	Y	Y
22 ***Sweeney***	?	Y	Y	Y	Y	Y
23 ***Boehlert***	Y	Y	Y	Y	Y	Y
24 ***McHugh***	Y	Y	Y	Y	Y	Y
25 ***Walsh***	Y	Y	Y	Y	Y	Y
26 Hinchey	N	N	Y	Y	Y	Y
27 ***Reynolds***	Y	Y	Y	Y	Y	Y
28 Slaughter	N	Y	Y	Y	Y	Y
29 LaFalce	N	Y	Y	Y	Y	Y

	240	241	242	243	244	245
30 ***Quinn***	Y	Y	Y	Y	Y	Y
31 ***Houghton***	?	?	?	?	?	?
NORTH CAROLINA						
1 Clayton	N	Y	Y	Y	Y	Y
2 Etheridge	N	Y	Y	Y	Y	Y
3 ***Jones***	Y	Y	Y	Y	Y	Y
4 Price	N	Y	Y	Y	Y	Y
5 ***Burr***	Y	Y	Y	Y	Y	Y
6 ***Coble***	Y	Y	Y	Y	Y	Y
7 McIntyre	N	Y	Y	Y	Y	Y
8 ***Hayes***	Y	Y	Y	Y	Y	Y
9 ***Myrick***	Y	Y	Y	Y	Y	Y
10 ***Ballenger***	Y	Y	Y	Y	Y	Y
11 ***Taylor***	Y	Y	Y	Y	Y	Y
12 Watt	N	N	Y	Y	Y	Y
NORTH DAKOTA						
AL Pomeroy	N	Y	Y	Y	Y	Y
OHIO						
1 ***Chabot***	Y	Y	Y	Y	Y	Y
2 ***Portman***	Y	Y	Y	Y	Y	Y
3 Hall	N	Y	Y	Y	Y	Y
4 ***Oxley***	Y	Y	Y	Y	Y	Y
5 ***Gillmor***	Y	Y	Y	Y	Y	Y
6 Strickland	N	Y	Y	Y	Y	Y
7 ***Hobson***	Y	Y	Y	Y	Y	Y
8 ***Boehner***	Y	Y	Y	Y	Y	Y
9 Kaptur	N	Y	Y	Y	Y	Y
10 Kucinich	N	N	Y	Y	Y	Y
11 Jones	N	Y	Y	Y	Y	Y
12 ***Kasich***	Y	Y	Y	Y	Y	Y
13 Brown	N	N	Y	Y	Y	Y
14 Sawyer	N	Y	Y	Y	Y	Y
15 ***Pryce***	Y	Y	Y	Y	Y	Y
16 ***Regula***	Y	Y	Y	Y	Y	Y
17 Traficant	Y	Y	Y	Y	Y	Y
18 ***Ney***	Y	Y	Y	Y	Y	Y
19 ***LaTourette***	Y	Y	Y	Y	Y	Y
OKLAHOMA						
1 ***Largent***	Y	Y	Y	Y	Y	Y
2 ***Coburn***	Y	Y	Y	Y	Y	Y
3 ***Watkins***	Y	Y	Y	Y	Y	Y
4 ***Watts***	Y	Y	Y	Y	Y	Y
5 ***Istook***	Y	+	?	?	?	?
6 ***Lucas***	Y	Y	Y	Y	Y	Y
OREGON						
1 Wu	N	Y	Y	Y	Y	Y
2 ***Walden***	Y	Y	Y	Y	Y	Y
3 Blumenauer	N	N	Y	Y	N	Y
4 DeFazio	N	N	Y	Y	Y	Y
5 Hooley	N	N	Y	Y	Y	Y
PENNSYLVANIA						
1 Brady	N	Y	Y	Y	Y	Y
2 Fattah	N	N	Y	Y	Y	Y
3 Borski	N	Y	Y	Y	Y	Y
4 Klink	N	Y	Y	Y	Y	Y
5 ***Peterson***	Y	Y	Y	Y	Y	Y
6 Holden	N	Y	Y	Y	Y	Y
7 ***Weldon***	Y	Y	Y	Y	Y	Y
8 ***Greenwood***	?	?	?	?	?	?
9 ***Shuster***	Y	Y	Y	Y	Y	Y
10 ***Sherwood***	Y	Y	Y	Y	Y	Y
11 Kanjorski	N	Y	Y	Y	Y	Y
12 Murtha	N	Y	Y	Y	Y	Y
13 Hoeffel	N	Y	Y	Y	Y	Y
14 Coyne	N	N	Y	Y	Y	Y
15 ***Toomey***	Y	Y	Y	Y	Y	Y
16 ***Pitts***	Y	Y	Y	Y	Y	Y
17 ***Gekas***	Y	Y	Y	Y	Y	Y
18 Doyle	N	Y	Y	Y	Y	Y
19 ***Goodling***	Y	Y	Y	Y	Y	Y
20 Mascara	N	Y	Y	Y	Y	Y
21 ***English***	?	Y	Y	Y	Y	Y
RHODE ISLAND						
1 Kennedy	N	Y	Y	Y	Y	Y
2 Weygand	N	Y	Y	Y	Y	Y
SOUTH CAROLINA						
1 ***Sanford***	Y	N	Y	Y	Y	N
2 ***Spence***	Y	Y	Y	Y	Y	Y
3 ***Graham***	Y	Y	Y	Y	Y	Y
4 ***DeMint***	Y	Y	Y	Y	Y	Y
5 Spratt	N	Y	Y	Y	Y	Y
6 Clyburn	N	Y	Y	Y	Y	Y
SOUTH DAKOTA						
AL ***Thune***	Y	Y	Y	Y	Y	Y

	240	241	242	243	244	245
TENNESSEE						
1 ***Jenkins***	Y	Y	Y	Y	Y	Y
2 ***Duncan***	Y	Y	Y	Y	Y	Y
3 ***Wamp***	Y	Y	Y	Y	Y	Y
4 ***Hilleary***	Y	Y	Y	Y	Y	Y
5 Clement	N	Y	Y	Y	Y	Y
6 Gordon	N	Y	Y	Y	Y	Y
7 ***Bryant***	Y	Y	Y	Y	Y	Y
8 Tanner	N	Y	Y	Y	Y	Y
9 Ford	N	Y	Y	Y	Y	Y
TEXAS						
1 Sandlin	N	Y	Y	Y	Y	Y
2 Turner	N	Y	Y	Y	Y	Y
3 ***Johnson, Sam***	Y	Y	Y	Y	Y	N
4 Hall	N	Y	Y	Y	Y	Y
5 ***Sessions***	Y	Y	Y	Y	Y	Y
6 ***Barton***	Y	Y	Y	Y	Y	Y
7 ***Archer***	Y	Y	Y	?	?	?
8 ***Brady***	Y	Y	Y	Y	Y	Y
9 Lampson	N	Y	Y	Y	Y	Y
10 Doggett	N	N	Y	Y	Y	Y
11 Edwards	N	Y	Y	Y	Y	Y
12 ***Granger***	Y	Y	Y	Y	Y	Y
13 ***Thornberry***	Y	Y	Y	Y	Y	Y
14 ***Paul***	Y	N	Y	Y	Y	N
15 Hinojosa	N	Y	Y	Y	Y	Y
16 Reyes	N	Y	Y	Y	Y	Y
17 Stenholm	N	Y	Y	Y	Y	Y
18 Jackson-Lee	N	Y	Y	Y	Y	Y
19 ***Combest***	Y	Y	Y	Y	Y	Y
20 Gonzalez	N	Y	Y	Y	Y	Y
21 ***Smith***	Y	Y	Y	Y	Y	Y
22 ***DeLay***	Y	Y	Y	Y	Y	N
23 ***Bonilla***	Y	Y	Y	Y	Y	Y
24 Frost	N	Y	Y	Y	Y	Y
25 Bentsen	N	Y	Y	Y	Y	Y
26 ***Armey***	Y	Y	Y	Y	Y	N
27 Ortiz	N	Y	Y	Y	Y	Y
28 Rodriguez	N	Y	Y	Y	Y	Y
29 Green	N	Y	Y	Y	Y	Y
30 Johnson, E.B.	N	Y	Y	Y	Y	Y
UTAH						
1 ***Hansen***	Y	Y	Y	Y	Y	Y
2 ***Cook***	Y	Y	Y	Y	Y	Y
3 ***Cannon***	Y	Y	Y	Y	Y	Y
VERMONT						
AL *Sanders*	N	N	Y	Y	Y	Y
VIRGINIA						
1 ***Bateman***	Y	Y	Y	Y	Y	Y
2 Pickett	Y	Y	Y	Y	Y	Y
3 Scott	N	Y	Y	Y	Y	Y
4 Sisisky	N	Y	Y	Y	?	?
5 *Goode*	Y	Y	Y	Y	Y	Y
6 ***Goodlatte***	Y	Y	Y	Y	Y	Y
7 ***Bliley***	Y	Y	Y	Y	Y	Y
8 Moran	N	Y	Y	Y	Y	Y
9 Boucher	N	Y	Y	Y	Y	Y
10 ***Wolf***	Y	Y	Y	Y	Y	Y
11 ***Davis***	Y	Y	Y	Y	Y	Y
WASHINGTON						
1 Inslee	N	Y	Y	Y	Y	Y
2 ***Metcalf***	Y	Y	Y	Y	Y	Y
3 Baird	N	Y	Y	Y	Y	Y
4 ***Hastings***	Y	Y	Y	Y	Y	Y
5 ***Nethercutt***	?	Y	Y	Y	Y	Y
6 Dicks	N	Y	Y	Y	Y	Y
7 McDermott	N	N	Y	Y	Y	Y
8 ***Dunn***	Y	Y	Y	Y	Y	Y
9 Smith	N	Y	Y	Y	Y	Y
WEST VIRGINIA						
1 Mollohan	N	Y	Y	Y	Y	Y
2 Wise	N	?	?	?	?	?
3 Rahall	N	Y	Y	Y	Y	Y
WISCONSIN						
1 ***Ryan***	Y	Y	Y	Y	Y	Y
2 Baldwin	N	N	Y	Y	Y	Y
3 Kind	N	N	Y	Y	Y	Y
4 Kleczka	N	Y	Y	Y	Y	Y
5 Barrett	N	N	Y	Y	Y	Y
6 ***Petri***	Y	Y	Y	Y	Y	Y
7 Obey	N	N	Y	Y	Y	Y
8 ***Green***	Y	Y	Y	Y	Y	Y
9 ***Sensenbrenner***	Y	N	Y	Y	Y	N
WYOMING						
AL ***Cubin***	Y	Y	Y	Y	Y	N

House Votes **246, 247, 248, 249, 250**

246. Procedural Motion/Journal. Approval of the House Journal of Wednesday, June 7, 2000. Approved 363-45: R 198-12; D 163-33 (ND 119-25, SD 44-8); I 2-0. June 8, 2000.

247. HR 4577. Fiscal 2001 Labor-HHS-Education Appropriations/Rule. Adoption of the rule (H Res 518) to provide for House floor consideration of the bill to appropriate $351.8 billion for the departments of Labor, Health and Human Services, Education and related agencies. Adopted 218-204: R 215-1; D 2-202 (ND 2-148, SD 0-54); I 1-1. June 8, 2000.

248. HR 8. Estate Tax Repeal/Previous Question. Reynolds, R-Ky., motion to order the previous question (thus ending debate and possibility of amendment) on adoption of the rule (H Res 519) to provide for House floor consideration of the bill that would amend the Internal Revenue Code of 1986 to phase out estate and gift taxes over a 10-year period. Motion agreed to 225-199: R 216-0; D 8-198 (ND 5-147, SD 3-51); I 1-1. June 8, 2000.

249. HR 8. Estate Tax Repeal/Rule. Adoption of the rule (H Res 519) to provide for House floor consideration of the bill that would amend the Internal Revenue Code of 1986 to phase out estate and gift taxes over a 10-year period. Adopted 242-180: R 215-0; D 26-179 (ND 16-135, SD 10-44); I 1-1. June 8, 2000.

250. HR 4577. Fiscal 2001 Labor-HHS-Education Appropriations/Ergonomic Standards. Traficant, R-Ohio, amendment to strike a provision that would prohibit the Occupational Safety and Health Administration from using funds to establish a standard on ergonomic protection. Rejected 203-220: R 14-203; D 188-16 (ND 147-3, SD 41-13); I 1-1. June 8, 2000. A "yea" was a vote in support of the president's position.

Key

Y	Voted for (yea).
#	Paired for.
+	Announced for.
N	Voted against (nay).
X	Paired against.
–	Announced against.
P	Voted "present."
C	Voted "present" to avoid possible conflict of interest.
?	Did not vote or otherwise make a position known.

•

Democrats ***Republicans***
Independents

	246	247	248	249	250
ALABAMA					
1 ***Callahan***	Y	Y	Y	Y	N
2 ***Everett***	Y	Y	Y	Y	N
3 ***Riley***	Y	Y	Y	Y	N
4 ***Aderholt***	N	Y	Y	Y	N
5 Cramer	Y	N	N	Y	Y
6 ***Bachus***	Y	Y	Y	Y	N
7 Hilliard	N	N	N	N	Y
ALASKA					
AL ***Young***	Y	Y	Y	Y	N
ARIZONA					
1 ***Salmon***	Y	Y	Y	Y	N
2 Pastor	Y	N	N	N	Y
3 ***Stump***	Y	Y	Y	Y	N
4 ***Shadegg***	Y	Y	Y	Y	N
5 ***Kolbe***	Y	Y	Y	Y	N
6 ***Hayworth***	Y	Y	Y	Y	N
ARKANSAS					
1 Berry	Y	N	N	N	N
2 Snyder	Y	N	N	N	Y
3 ***Hutchinson***	Y	Y	Y	Y	N
4 ***Dickey***	N	Y	Y	Y	N
CALIFORNIA					
1 Thompson	N	N	N	N	Y
2 ***Herger***	Y	Y	Y	Y	N
3 ***Ose***	Y	Y	Y	Y	N
4 ***Doolittle***	Y	Y	Y	Y	N
5 Matsui	Y	N	N	N	Y
6 Woolsey	Y	N	N	N	Y
7 Miller, George	Y	N	N	N	Y
8 Pelosi	Y	N	N	N	Y
9 Lee	Y	N	N	N	Y
10 Tauscher	Y	N	N	Y	Y
11 ***Pombo***	Y	Y	Y	Y	N
12 Lantos	Y	N	N	N	Y
13 Stark	N	N	N	?	Y
14 Eshoo	Y	N	Y	Y	Y
15 ***Campbell***	Y	Y	Y	Y	Y
16 Lofgren	Y	N	N	Y	Y
17 Farr	Y	N	N	N	Y
18 Condit	Y	N	N	N	Y
19 ***Radanovich***	?	Y	Y	Y	N
20 Dooley	Y	N	N	Y	N
21 ***Thomas***	Y	Y	Y	Y	N
22 Capps	Y	N	N	N	Y
23 ***Gallegly***	Y	Y	Y	Y	N
24 Sherman	Y	N	N	N	Y
25 ***McKeon***	Y	Y	Y	Y	N
26 Berman	Y	N	N	N	Y
27 ***Rogan***	Y	Y	Y	Y	N
28 ***Dreier***	Y	Y	Y	Y	N
29 Waxman	Y	N	N	N	Y
30 Becerra	Y	N	N	N	Y
31 Martinez	Y	Y	Y	Y	?
32 Dixon	Y	N	N	N	Y
33 Roybal-Allard	Y	N	N	N	Y
34 Napolitano	Y	N	N	N	Y
35 Waters	N	N	N	N	Y
36 ***Kuykendall***	Y	Y	Y	Y	N
37 Millender-McD.	Y	N	N	N	Y
38 ***Horn***	Y	Y	Y	Y	Y
39 ***Royce***	Y	Y	Y	Y	N
40 ***Lewis***	Y	Y	Y	Y	N
41 ***Miller, Gary***	Y	Y	Y	Y	N
42 Baca	Y	N	N	N	Y
43 ***Calvert***	Y	Y	Y	Y	N
44 ***Bono***	Y	Y	Y	Y	N
45 ***Rohrabacher***	?	Y	Y	Y	N
46 Sanchez	Y	N	N	N	Y
47 ***Cox***	Y	Y	Y	Y	N
48 ***Packard***	Y	Y	Y	Y	N
49 ***Bilbray***	N	Y	Y	Y	N
50 Filner	N	N	N	N	Y
51 ***Cunningham***	Y	Y	Y	Y	N
52 ***Hunter***	Y	Y	Y	Y	N
COLORADO					
1 DeGette	Y	N	N	N	Y
2 Udall	Y	N	N	N	Y
3 ***McInnis***	Y	Y	Y	Y	N
4 ***Schaffer***	Y	Y	Y	Y	N
5 ***Hefley***	N	Y	Y	Y	N
6 ***Tancredo***	P	Y	Y	Y	N
CONNECTICUT					
1 Larson	Y	N	N	N	Y
2 Gejdenson	?	?	N	N	Y
3 DeLauro	Y	N	N	N	Y
4 ***Shays***	Y	Y	Y	Y	N
5 Maloney	Y	N	N	N	Y
6 ***Johnson***	Y	Y	Y	Y	N
DELAWARE					
AL ***Castle***	Y	Y	Y	Y	N
FLORIDA					
1 ***Scarborough***	Y	Y	Y	Y	N
2 Boyd	Y	N	N	N	N
3 Brown	Y	N	N	N	Y
4 ***Fowler***	Y	Y	Y	Y	N
5 Thurman	N	N	N	N	Y
6 ***Stearns***	Y	Y	Y	Y	N
7 ***Mica***	Y	Y	Y	Y	N
8 ***McCollum***	Y	Y	Y	Y	N
9 ***Bilirakis***	Y	Y	Y	Y	N
10 ***Young***	Y	Y	Y	Y	N
11 Davis	Y	N	N	Y	Y
12 ***Canady***	Y	Y	Y	Y	N
13 ***Miller***	Y	Y	Y	Y	N
14 ***Goss***	Y	Y	Y	Y	N
15 ***Weldon***	Y	Y	Y	Y	N
16 ***Foley***	Y	Y	Y	Y	N
17 Meek	Y	N	N	N	Y
18 ***Ros-Lehtinen***	Y	Y	Y	Y	N
19 Wexler	Y	N	N	N	Y
20 Deutsch	Y	N	N	N	Y
21 ***Diaz-Balart***	Y	Y	Y	Y	N
22 ***Shaw***	Y	Y	Y	Y	N
23 Hastings	N	N	N	N	Y
GEORGIA					
1 ***Kingston***	Y	Y	Y	Y	N
2 Bishop	Y	N	N	Y	Y
3 ***Collins***	Y	Y	Y	Y	N
4 McKinney	Y	N	N	N	Y
5 Lewis	N	N	N	N	Y
6 ***Isakson***	Y	Y	Y	Y	N
7 ***Barr***	Y	Y	Y	Y	N
8 ***Chambliss***	Y	Y	Y	Y	N
9 ***Deal***	Y	Y	Y	Y	N
10 ***Norwood***	Y	Y	Y	Y	N
11 ***Linder***	Y	Y	Y	Y	N
HAWAII					
1 Abercrombie	Y	N	N	N	Y
2 Mink	Y	N	N	N	Y
IDAHO					
1 ***Chenoweth-Hage***	Y	Y	Y	Y	N
2 ***Simpson***	Y	Y	Y	Y	N
ILLINOIS					
1 Rush	Y	N	N	N	Y
2 Jackson	Y	N	N	N	Y
3 Lipinski	Y	N	N	N	Y
4 Gutierrez	N	N	N	N	Y
5 Blagojevich	Y	N	N	Y	Y
6 ***Hyde***	Y	Y	Y	Y	N
7 Davis	Y	N	N	N	Y
8 ***Crane***	N	Y	Y	Y	N
9 Schakowsky	Y	N	N	N	Y
10 ***Porter***	Y	Y	Y	Y	N
11 ***Weller***	N	Y	Y	Y	Y
12 Costello	N	N	N	N	Y
13 ***Biggert***	Y	Y	Y	Y	N

ND Northern Democrats SD Southern Democrats

	246	247	248	249	250
14 ***Hastert***		Y			N
15 ***Ewing***	Y	Y	Y	Y	N
16 ***Manzullo***	?	Y	Y	Y	N
17 Evans	Y	N	N	N	Y
18 ***LaHood***	Y	Y	Y	Y	N
19 Phelps	Y	N	N	N	Y
20 ***Shimkus***	Y	Y	Y	Y	N
INDIANA					
1 Visclosky	N	N	N	N	Y
2 ***McIntosh***	?	Y	Y	Y	N
3 Roemer	Y	N	N	N	Y
4 ***Souder***	Y	Y	Y	Y	N
5 ***Buyer***	Y	Y	Y	Y	N
6 ***Burton***	Y	Y	Y	Y	N
7 ***Pease***	Y	Y	Y	Y	N
8 ***Hostettler***	Y	Y	Y	Y	N
9 Hill	Y	N	N	N	Y
10 Carson	P	N	N	N	Y
IOWA					
1 ***Leach***	Y	Y	Y	Y	N
2 ***Nussle***	Y	Y	Y	Y	N
3 Boswell	Y	N	N	N	Y
4 ***Ganske***	Y	Y	Y	Y	N
5 ***Latham***	Y	Y	Y	Y	N
KANSAS					
1 ***Moran***	Y	Y	Y	Y	N
2 ***Ryun***	Y	Y	Y	Y	N
3 Moore	Y	N	N	N	Y
4 ***Tiahrt***	Y	Y	Y	Y	N
KENTUCKY					
1 ***Whitfield***	Y	Y	Y	Y	N
2 ***Lewis***	Y	Y	Y	Y	N
3 ***Northup***	Y	Y	Y	Y	N
4 Lucas	Y	N	N	Y	Y
5 ***Rogers***	Y	Y	Y	Y	N
6 ***Fletcher***	Y	Y	Y	Y	N
LOUISIANA					
1 ***Vitter***	Y	Y	Y	Y	N
2 Jefferson	?	N	N	N	Y
3 ***Tauzin***	Y	Y	Y	Y	N
4 ***McCrery***	Y	Y	Y	Y	N
5 ***Cooksey***	Y	Y	Y	Y	N
6 ***Baker***	Y	Y	Y	Y	N
7 John	Y	N	N	N	N
MAINE					
1 Allen	Y	N	N	N	Y
2 Baldacci	Y	N	N	N	Y
MARYLAND					
1 ***Gilchrest***	Y	Y	Y	Y	N
2 ***Ehrlich***	Y	Y	Y	Y	N
3 Cardin	Y	N	N	N	Y
4 Wynn	Y	N	N	N	Y
5 Hoyer	Y	N	N	N	Y
6 ***Bartlett***	Y	Y	Y	Y	N
7 Cummings	?	N	N	N	Y
8 ***Morella***	Y	N	Y	Y	N
MASSACHUSETTS					
1 Olver	Y	N	N	N	Y
2 Neal	Y	N	N	N	Y
3 McGovern	Y	N	N	N	Y
4 Frank	Y	N	N	N	Y
5 Meehan	Y	N	N	N	Y
6 Tierney	?	N	N	N	Y
7 Markey	?	?	?	?	?
8 Capuano	Y	N	N	N	Y
9 Moakley	Y	N	N	N	Y
10 Delahunt	Y	N	N	N	Y
MICHIGAN					
1 Stupak	N	N	N	N	Y
2 ***Hoekstra***	Y	Y	Y	Y	N
3 ***Ehlers***	Y	Y	Y	Y	N
4 ***Camp***	Y	Y	Y	Y	N
5 Barcia	Y	N	N	Y	N
6 ***Upton***	Y	Y	Y	Y	N
7 ***Smith***	?	?	?	?	?
8 Stabenow	Y	N	N	N	Y
9 Kildee	Y	N	N	N	Y
10 Bonior	Y	N	N	N	Y
11 ***Knollenberg***	Y	Y	Y	Y	N
12 Levin	P	N	N	N	Y
13 Rivers	Y	N	N	N	Y
14 Conyers	P	N	N	N	Y
15 Kilpatrick	Y	N	N	N	Y
16 Dingell	Y	N	N	N	Y
MINNESOTA					
1 ***Gutknecht***	Y	Y	Y	Y	N
2 Minge	Y	N	N	N	Y
3 ***Ramstad***	N	Y	Y	Y	N
4 Vento	?	?	?	?	?
5 Sabo	N	N	N	N	Y
6 Luther	Y	N	N	N	Y
7 Peterson	N	N	N	N	Y
8 Oberstar	N	N	N	N	Y
MISSISSIPPI					
1 ***Wicker***	N	Y	Y	Y	N
2 Thompson	N	N	N	N	Y
3 ***Pickering***	Y	Y	Y	Y	N
4 Shows	Y	N	N	N	N
5 Taylor	N	N	N	N	N
MISSOURI					
1 Clay	?	?	?	?	?
2 ***Talent***	Y	Y	Y	Y	N
3 Gephardt	Y	N	N	N	Y
4 Skelton	Y	N	N	Y	N
5 McCarthy	Y	N	N	N	Y
6 Danner	?	?	?	?	?
7 ***Blunt***	Y	Y	Y	Y	N
8 ***Emerson***	Y	Y	Y	Y	N
9 ***Hulshof***	Y	Y	Y	Y	N
MONTANA					
AL ***Hill***	N	Y	Y	Y	N
NEBRASKA					
1 ***Bereuter***	Y	Y	Y	Y	N
2 ***Terry***	Y	Y	Y	Y	N
3 ***Barrett***	P	Y	Y	Y	N
NEVADA					
1 Berkley	Y	N	N	Y	Y
2 ***Gibbons***	Y	Y	Y	Y	N
NEW HAMPSHIRE					
1 ***Sununu***	Y	Y	Y	Y	N
2 ***Bass***	Y	Y	Y	Y	N
NEW JERSEY					
1 Andrews	Y	N	N	N	Y
2 ***LoBiondo***	N	Y	Y	Y	Y
3 ***Saxton***	Y	Y	Y	Y	Y
4 ***Smith***	Y	Y	Y	Y	Y
5 ***Roukema***	Y	Y	Y	Y	N
6 Pallone	Y	N	N	N	Y
7 ***Franks***	Y	?	Y	Y	N
8 Pascrell	Y	N	N	N	Y
9 Rothman	Y	N	N	N	Y
10 Payne	Y	N	N	N	Y
11 ***Frelinghuysen***	Y	Y	Y	Y	N
12 Holt	Y	N	N	N	Y
13 Menendez	Y	N	N	N	Y
NEW MEXICO					
1 ***Wilson***	Y	Y	Y	Y	N
2 ***Skeen***	Y	Y	Y	Y	N
3 Udall	N	N	N	N	Y
NEW YORK					
1 Forbes	Y	N	Y	Y	Y
2 ***Lazio***	Y	Y	Y	Y	?
3 ***King***	Y	Y	Y	Y	Y
4 McCarthy	Y	N	N	N	Y
5 Ackerman	Y	N	N	N	Y
6 Meeks	Y	?	N	N	Y
7 Crowley	Y	N	N	N	Y
8 Nadler	Y	N	N	N	Y
9 Weiner	Y	N	N	N	Y
10 Towns	Y	N	N	N	Y
11 Owens	Y	N	N	N	Y
12 Velázquez	Y	N	N	N	Y
13 ***Fossella***	?	?	Y	Y	N
14 Maloney	Y	N	N	N	Y
15 Rangel	?	N	N	Y	Y
16 Serrano	Y	N	N	N	Y
17 Engel	Y	N	N	N	Y
18 Lowey	Y	N	N	N	Y
19 ***Kelly***	Y	Y	Y	Y	N
20 ***Gilman***	Y	Y	Y	Y	?
21 McNulty	Y	N	N	N	Y
22 ***Sweeney***	Y	Y	Y	Y	N
23 ***Boehlert***	Y	Y	Y	Y	Y
24 ***McHugh***	Y	Y	Y	Y	Y
25 ***Walsh***	Y	Y	Y	Y	N
26 Hinchey	Y	N	N	N	Y
27 ***Reynolds***	Y	Y	Y	Y	N
28 Slaughter	N	N	N	N	Y
29 LaFalce	Y	N	N	N	Y
30 ***Quinn***	Y	Y	Y	Y	Y
31 ***Houghton***	?	?	?	?	N
NORTH CAROLINA					
1 Clayton	Y	N	N	N	Y
2 Etheridge	Y	N	N	N	Y
3 ***Jones***	Y	Y	Y	Y	N
4 Price	Y	N	N	N	Y
5 ***Burr***	Y	Y	Y	Y	N
6 ***Coble***	Y	Y	Y	Y	N
7 McIntyre	Y	N	Y	Y	N
8 ***Hayes***	Y	Y	Y	Y	N
9 ***Myrick***	Y	?	Y	Y	N
10 ***Ballenger***	Y	Y	Y	Y	N
11 ***Taylor***	Y	Y	Y	Y	N
12 Watt	Y	N	N	N	Y
NORTH DAKOTA					
AL Pomeroy	N	N	N	N	Y
OHIO					
1 ***Chabot***	Y	Y	Y	Y	N
2 ***Portman***	Y	Y	Y	Y	N
3 Hall	N	N	N	N	Y
4 ***Oxley***	Y	Y	Y	Y	N
5 ***Gillmor***	Y	Y	Y	Y	N
6 Strickland	N	N	N	N	Y
7 ***Hobson***	Y	Y	Y	Y	N
8 ***Boehner***	Y	Y	Y	Y	N
9 Kaptur	Y	N	N	N	Y
10 Kucinich	N	N	N	N	Y
11 Jones	Y	N	N	N	Y
12 ***Kasich***	Y	Y	Y	Y	N
13 Brown	Y	N	N	N	Y
14 Sawyer	Y	N	N	N	Y
15 ***Pryce***	Y	Y	Y	Y	N
16 ***Regula***	Y	Y	Y	Y	N
17 Traficant	Y	Y	Y	Y	Y
18 ***Ney***	Y	Y	Y	Y	N
19 ***LaTourette***	Y	Y	Y	Y	N
OKLAHOMA					
1 ***Largent***	Y	Y	Y	Y	N
2 ***Coburn***	Y	Y	Y	Y	N
3 ***Watkins***	Y	Y	?	?	N
4 ***Watts***	Y	Y	Y	Y	N
5 ***Istook***	Y	Y	?	?	?
6 ***Lucas***	Y	Y	Y	Y	N
OREGON					
1 Wu	N	N	N	N	Y
2 ***Walden***	Y	Y	Y	Y	N
3 Blumenauer	Y	N	N	N	Y
4 DeFazio	N	N	N	N	Y
5 Hooley	Y	N	N	N	Y
PENNSYLVANIA					
1 Brady	N	N	N	N	Y
2 Fattah	N	N	N	N	Y
3 Borski	N	N	N	N	Y
4 Klink	?	?	?	?	?
5 ***Peterson***	?	Y	Y	Y	N
6 Holden	Y	N	N	N	Y
7 ***Weldon***	Y	Y	Y	Y	Y
8 ***Greenwood***	?	?	?	?	?
9 ***Shuster***	Y	Y	Y	Y	N
10 ***Sherwood***	Y	Y	Y	Y	N
11 Kanjorski	Y	N	N	N	Y
12 Murtha	Y	N	N	N	Y
13 Hoeffel	Y	N	N	N	Y
14 Coyne	Y	N	N	N	Y
15 ***Toomey***	Y	Y	Y	Y	N
16 ***Pitts***	Y	Y	Y	Y	N
17 ***Gekas***	Y	Y	Y	Y	N
18 Doyle	Y	N	N	N	Y
19 ***Goodling***	Y	Y	Y	Y	N
20 Mascara	Y	N	N	N	Y
21 ***English***	N	Y	Y	Y	Y
RHODE ISLAND					
1 Kennedy	Y	N	N	N	Y
2 Weygand	Y	N	N	N	Y
SOUTH CAROLINA					
1 ***Sanford***	Y	Y	Y	Y	N
2 ***Spence***	Y	Y	Y	Y	N
3 ***Graham***	Y	Y	Y	Y	N
4 ***DeMint***	Y	Y	Y	Y	N
5 Spratt	Y	N	N	N	Y
6 Clyburn	Y	N	N	N	Y
SOUTH DAKOTA					
AL ***Thune***	Y	Y	Y	Y	N
TENNESSEE					
1 ***Jenkins***	Y	Y	Y	Y	N
2 ***Duncan***	Y	Y	Y	Y	N
3 ***Wamp***	Y	Y	Y	Y	N
4 ***Hilleary***	N	Y	Y	Y	N
5 Clement	Y	N	N	Y	N
6 Gordon	Y	N	Y	Y	Y
7 ***Bryant***	Y	Y	Y	Y	N
8 Tanner	Y	N	Y	Y	N
9 Ford	Y	N	N	N	Y
TEXAS					
1 Sandlin	Y	N	N	Y	Y
2 Turner	Y	N	N	N	N
3 ***Johnson, Sam***	Y	Y	Y	Y	N
4 Hall	Y	N	N	N	N
5 ***Sessions***	Y	Y	Y	Y	N
6 ***Barton***	Y	Y	Y	Y	N
7 ***Archer***	Y	Y	Y	Y	N
8 ***Brady***	Y	Y	Y	Y	N
9 Lampson	Y	N	N	N	Y
10 Doggett	Y	N	N	N	Y
11 Edwards	Y	N	N	N	Y
12 ***Granger***	Y	Y	Y	Y	N
13 ***Thornberry***	Y	Y	Y	Y	N
14 ***Paul***	Y	Y	Y	Y	N
15 Hinojosa	?	N	N	N	Y
16 Reyes	Y	N	N	N	Y
17 Stenholm	Y	N	N	N	N
18 Jackson-Lee	Y	N	N	N	Y
19 ***Combest***	Y	Y	Y	Y	N
20 Gonzalez	Y	N	N	N	Y
21 ***Smith***	Y	Y	Y	Y	N
22 ***DeLay***	Y	Y	Y	Y	N
23 ***Bonilla***	Y	Y	Y	Y	N
24 Frost	Y	N	N	N	Y
25 Bentsen	Y	N	N	N	Y
26 ***Armey***	Y	Y	Y	Y	N
27 Ortiz	Y	N	N	N	Y
28 Rodriguez	Y	N	N	N	Y
29 Green	N	N	N	N	Y
30 Johnson, E.B.	Y	N	N	N	Y
UTAH					
1 ***Hansen***	Y	Y	Y	Y	N
2 ***Cook***	Y	Y	Y	Y	N
3 ***Cannon***	Y	Y	Y	Y	N
VERMONT					
AL *Sanders*	Y	N	N	N	Y
VIRGINIA					
1 ***Bateman***	Y	Y	Y	Y	N
2 Pickett	N	N	N	N	N
3 Scott	Y	N	N	N	Y
4 Sisisky	Y	N	N	N	N
5 *Goode*	Y	Y	Y	Y	N
6 ***Goodlatte***	Y	Y	Y	Y	N
7 ***Bliley***	Y	Y	Y	Y	N
8 Moran	Y	N	N	N	Y
9 Boucher	Y	N	N	Y	Y
10 ***Wolf***	Y	Y	Y	Y	N
11 ***Davis***	Y	Y	Y	Y	N
WASHINGTON					
1 Inslee	Y	N	N	N	Y
2 ***Metcalf***	Y	Y	Y	Y	Y
3 Baird	N	N	N	N	Y
4 ***Hastings***	Y	Y	Y	Y	N
5 ***Nethercutt***	Y	Y	Y	Y	N
6 Dicks	Y	N	N	Y	Y
7 McDermott	N	N	N	N	Y
8 ***Dunn***	Y	Y	Y	Y	N
9 Smith	Y	N	Y	Y	?
WEST VIRGINIA					
1 Mollohan	Y	N	N	N	Y
2 Wise	Y	N	N	Y	Y
3 Rahall	Y	N	N	Y	Y
WISCONSIN					
1 ***Ryan***	Y	Y	Y	Y	N
2 Baldwin	N	N	N	N	Y
3 Kind	Y	N	N	N	Y
4 Kleczka	Y	N	N	N	Y
5 Barrett	Y	N	N	N	Y
6 ***Petri***	Y	Y	Y	Y	Y
7 Obey	?	N	N	N	Y
8 ***Green***	Y	Y	Y	+	N
9 ***Sensenbrenner***	Y	Y	Y	Y	N
WYOMING					
AL ***Cubin***	Y	Y	Y	Y	N

Southern states - Ala., Ark., Fla., Ga., Ky., La., Miss., N.C., Okla., S.C., Tenn., Texas, Va.

251. Procedural Motion/Journal. Approval of the House Journal of Thursday, June 8, 2000. Approved 330-51: R 176-13; D 152-38 (ND 110-28, SD 42-10); I 2-0. June 9, 2000.

252. HR 8. Estate Tax Repeal/Democratic Substitute. Rangel, D-N.Y., amendment that would reduce all estate tax rates by 20 percent and raise the estate and gift-tax exemption to $4 million for family farmers and small-business owners as well as immediately increase the exemption for everyone from $675,000 to $1.1 million. Rejected 196-222: R 3-213; D 192-8 (ND 142-5, SD 50-3); I 1-1. June 9, 2000.

253. HR 8. Estate Tax Repeal/Recommit. Doggett, D-Texas, motion to recommit the bill to the House Ways and Means Committee with instructions to deny the gift-tax exclusion to organizations that exist under Section 527 of the Internal Revenue Code unless such organizations disclose their donors. Motion rejected 202-216: R 6-210; D 195-5 (ND 144-3, SD 51-2); I 1-1. June 9, 2000.

254. HR 8. Estate Tax Repeal/Passage. Passage of the bill that would amend the Internal Revenue Code of 1986 to phase out the estate and gift taxes, repealing them entirely by 2010. Passed 279-136: R 213-0; D 65-135 (ND 43-104, SD 22-31); I 1-1. June 9, 2000. A "nay" was a vote in support of the president's position.

255. HR 4577. Fiscal 2001 Labor-HHS-Education Appropriations/Motion to Rise. Obey, D-Wis., motion to rise from the Committee of the Whole, thus prohibiting the possibility of further amendments being offered for the day. Motion rejected 187-202: R 0-195; D 186-6 (ND 135-5, SD 51-1); I 1-1. June 12, 2000.

256. HR 4577. Fiscal 2001 Labor-HHS-Education Appropriations/Motion to Rise. Obey, D-Wis, motion to rise from the Committee of the Whole, thus prohibiting the possibility of further amendments being offered for the day. Motion rejected 182-196: R 0-189; D 181-6 (ND 131-4, SD 50-2); I 1-1. June 12, 2000.

257. Procedural Motion/Journal. Approval of the House Journal of Tuesday, June 12, 2000. Approved 329-66: R 182-20; D 146-46 (ND 110-34, SD 36-12); I 1-0. June 13, 2000.

258. HR 4079. Education Department Audit/Passage. Hoekstra, R-Mich., motion to suspend the rules and pass the bill that would require the Comptroller General to conduct a comprehensive fraud audit of the Education Department and report on the results within six months of enactment. Motion agreed to 380-19: R 205-0; D 174-19 (ND 131-12, SD 43-7); I 1-0. A two-thirds majority of those present and voting (266 in this case) is required for passage under suspension of the rules. June 13, 2000.

Key

Y Voted for (yea).
\# Paired for.
\+ Announced for.
N Voted against (nay).
X Paired against.
– Announced against.
P Voted "present."
C Voted "present" to avoid possible conflict of interest.
? Did not vote or otherwise make a position known.

Democrats • ***Republicans***
Independents

	251	252	253	254	255	256	257	258
ALABAMA								
1 ***Callahan***	Y	N	N	Y	N	N	Y	Y
2 ***Everett***	Y	N	N	Y	N	N	Y	Y
3 ***Riley***	Y	N	N	Y	N	N	N	Y
4 ***Aderholt***	N	N	N	Y	N	N	N	Y
5 Cramer	Y	Y	Y	Y	Y	Y	?	Y
6 ***Bachus***	Y	N	N	Y	N	N	Y	Y
7 Hilliard	N	Y	Y	N	Y	Y	N	N
ALASKA								
AL ***Young***	?	N	N	Y	N	N	?	?
ARIZONA								
1 ***Salmon***	Y	N	N	Y	N	N	Y	Y
2 Pastor	Y	Y	Y	N	Y	Y	Y	Y
3 ***Stump***	Y	N	N	Y	N	N	Y	Y
4 ***Shadegg***	Y	N	N	Y	N	N	Y	Y
5 ***Kolbe***	Y	N	N	Y	N	N	Y	Y
6 ***Hayworth***	Y	N	N	Y	N	N	Y	Y
ARKANSAS								
1 Berry	Y	Y	Y	Y	Y	Y	Y	Y
2 Snyder	Y	Y	Y	N	Y	Y	Y	Y
3 ***Hutchinson***	Y	N	N	Y	N	N	Y	Y
4 ***Dickey***	N	N	N	Y	N	N	N	Y
CALIFORNIA								
1 Thompson	N	Y	Y	Y	Y	Y	N	Y
2 ***Herger***	Y	N	N	Y	N	N	Y	Y
3 ***Ose***	Y	N	N	Y	N	N	Y	Y
4 ***Doolittle***	Y	N	N	Y	N	N	Y	Y
5 Matsui	?	Y	Y	N	Y	Y	Y	Y
6 Woolsey	Y	Y	Y	N	Y	Y	Y	Y
7 Miller, George	N	Y	Y	N	Y	Y	N	Y
8 Pelosi	?	Y	Y	N	Y	?	Y	Y
9 Lee	Y	Y	Y	N	Y	Y	Y	N
10 Tauscher	Y	Y	Y	Y	Y	Y	N	Y
11 ***Pombo***	Y	N	N	Y	N	N	Y	Y
12 Lantos	Y	Y	Y	Y	Y	Y	Y	Y
13 Stark	N	Y	Y	N	?	?	N	Y
14 Eshoo	Y	Y	Y	Y	Y	Y	Y	Y
15 ***Campbell***	Y	N	Y	Y	?	?	?	?
16 Lofgren	Y	Y	Y	Y	Y	Y	Y	N
17 Farr	Y	Y	Y	Y	Y	Y	Y	Y
18 Condit	Y	Y	Y	Y	N	N	N	Y
19 ***Radanovich***	?	N	N	Y	N	N	Y	Y
20 Dooley	?	Y	Y	Y	?	?	Y	Y
21 ***Thomas***	Y	N	N	Y	N	N	Y	Y
22 Capps	Y	Y	Y	Y	Y	Y	Y	Y
23 ***Gallegly***	Y	N	N	Y	N	N	Y	Y
24 Sherman	Y	Y	Y	N	Y	Y	Y	Y
25 ***McKeon***	Y	N	N	Y	N	N	Y	Y
26 Berman	Y	Y	Y	N	Y	Y	Y	Y
27 ***Rogan***	?	N	N	Y	N	N	N	Y
28 ***Dreier***	Y	N	N	Y	N	N	Y	Y
29 Waxman	?	Y	Y	N	?	?	Y	Y
30 Becerra	Y	Y	Y	N	Y	Y	Y	Y
31 Martinez	Y	Y	N	Y	?	?	Y	Y
32 Dixon	?	Y	Y	N	Y	Y	Y	Y
33 Roybal-Allard	Y	Y	Y	N	Y	Y	Y	Y
34 Napolitano	Y	Y	Y	N	Y	Y	Y	Y
35 Waters	N	Y	Y	N	Y	Y	?	?
36 ***Kuykendall***	Y	N	N	Y	N	N	Y	Y
37 Millender-McD.	Y	Y	Y	N	Y	Y	Y	Y
38 ***Horn***	Y	N	N	Y	N	N	Y	Y
39 ***Royce***	Y	N	N	Y	N	N	Y	Y
40 ***Lewis***	Y	N	N	Y	N	N	Y	Y
41 ***Miller, Gary***	Y	N	N	Y	N	N	Y	Y
42 Baca	Y	Y	Y	Y	Y	Y	Y	Y
43 ***Calvert***	Y	N	N	Y	N	N	Y	Y
44 ***Bono***	Y	N	N	Y	N	N	?	Y
45 ***Rohrabacher***	Y	N	N	Y	N	N	Y	Y
46 Sanchez	Y	Y	Y	Y	Y	N	N	Y
47 ***Cox***	Y	N	N	Y	?	?	?	?
48 ***Packard***	Y	N	N	?	N	N	Y	Y
49 ***Bilbray***	N	N	N	Y	N	N	N	Y
50 Filner	N	Y	Y	N	Y	Y	N	N
51 ***Cunningham***	?	?	?	?	N	N	Y	Y
52 ***Hunter***	Y	N	N	Y	N	N	Y	Y
COLORADO								
1 DeGette	Y	Y	Y	N	Y	Y	Y	Y
2 Udall	N	Y	Y	Y	Y	Y	N	Y
3 ***McInnis***	Y	N	N	Y	N	N	Y	Y
4 ***Schaffer***	N	N	N	Y	N	N	N	Y
5 ***Hefley***	N	N	N	Y	N	?	N	Y
6 ***Tancredo***	P	N	N	Y	N	N	P	Y
CONNECTICUT								
1 Larson	Y	Y	Y	N	Y	Y	Y	Y
2 Gejdenson	Y	Y	Y	N	Y	Y	Y	Y
3 DeLauro	Y	Y	Y	N	?	?	Y	Y
4 ***Shays***	Y	N	Y	Y	N	N	Y	Y
5 Maloney	Y	Y	Y	Y	Y	Y	Y	Y
6 ***Johnson***	Y	N	N	Y	N	N	Y	Y
DELAWARE								
AL ***Castle***	Y	N	N	Y	N	N	Y	Y
FLORIDA								
1 ***Scarborough***	Y	N	N	Y	N	N	Y	Y
2 Boyd	Y	Y	Y	Y	Y	Y	Y	Y
3 Brown	Y	Y	Y	N	Y	Y	Y	Y
4 ***Fowler***	Y	N	N	Y	N	N	Y	Y
5 Thurman	N	Y	Y	N	Y	Y	N	Y
6 ***Stearns***	?	N	N	Y	N	?	?	Y
7 ***Mica***	Y	N	N	Y	N	N	Y	Y
8 ***McCollum***	?	N	N	Y	?	?	?	?
9 ***Bilirakis***	Y	N	N	Y	N	N	Y	Y
10 ***Young***	Y	N	N	Y	N	N	Y	Y
11 Davis	Y	Y	Y	N	Y	Y	Y	Y
12 ***Canady***	Y	N	N	Y	N	N	Y	Y
13 ***Miller***	Y	N	N	Y	N	N	Y	Y
14 ***Goss***	?	N	N	Y	N	N	Y	Y
15 ***Weldon***	Y	N	N	Y	N	N	Y	Y
16 ***Foley***	Y	N	N	Y	N	N	Y	Y
17 Meek	Y	Y	Y	N	Y	Y	Y	Y
18 ***Ros-Lehtinen***	Y	N	N	Y	N	N	Y	Y
19 Wexler	Y	Y	Y	N	Y	Y	Y	Y
20 Deutsch	Y	N	Y	Y	Y	Y	+	+
21 ***Diaz-Balart***	Y	N	N	Y	N	N	Y	Y
22 ***Shaw***	Y	N	N	Y	N	N	Y	Y
23 Hastings	N	Y	Y	N	Y	Y	N	N
GEORGIA								
1 ***Kingston***	Y	N	N	Y	N	N	Y	Y
2 Bishop	Y	Y	Y	Y	Y	Y	?	?
3 ***Collins***	Y	N	N	Y	N	N	Y	Y
4 McKinney	Y	Y	Y	N	Y	Y	Y	Y
5 Lewis	N	Y	Y	N	Y	Y	N	Y
6 ***Isakson***	Y	N	N	Y	N	N	Y	Y
7 ***Barr***	Y	N	N	Y	N	N	Y	Y
8 ***Chambliss***	Y	N	N	Y	N	N	Y	Y
9 ***Deal***	Y	N	N	Y	N	N	Y	Y
10 ***Norwood***	?	N	N	Y	N	N	Y	Y
11 ***Linder***	Y	N	N	Y	?	?	Y	Y
HAWAII								
1 Abercrombie	Y	N	N	Y	Y	Y	Y	Y
2 Mink	Y	Y	Y	Y	Y	Y	Y	Y
IDAHO								
1 ***Chenoweth-Hage***	?	N	N	Y	?	N	?	?
2 ***Simpson***	Y	N	N	Y	N	N	Y	Y
ILLINOIS								
1 Rush	Y	Y	Y	N	Y	Y	Y	Y
2 Jackson	Y	Y	Y	N	Y	Y	Y	Y
3 Lipinski	Y	Y	Y	Y	Y	Y	Y	Y
4 Gutierrez	N	Y	Y	N	N	?	Y	Y
5 Blagojevich	Y	Y	Y	Y	Y	Y	Y	Y
6 ***Hyde***	Y	N	N	Y	N	N	Y	Y
7 Davis	Y	Y	Y	N	Y	Y	Y	Y
8 ***Crane***	?	N	N	Y	N	N	N	Y
9 Schakowsky	Y	Y	Y	N	Y	Y	Y	Y
10 ***Porter***	?	N	N	Y	N	N	Y	Y
11 ***Weller***	N	N	N	Y	N	N	N	Y
12 Costello	N	Y	Y	Y	Y	Y	N	Y
13 ***Biggert***	Y	N	N	Y	N	N	Y	Y

ND Northern Democrats SD Southern Democrats

	251	252	253	254	255	256	257	258
14 ***Hastert***		N	N	Y				
15 ***Ewing***	Y	N	N	Y	?	N	Y	Y
16 ***Manzullo***	Y	N	N	Y	N	N	?	+
17 Evans	Y	Y	Y	N	Y	Y	Y	Y
18 ***LaHood***	Y	N	N	Y	N	N	Y	Y
19 Phelps	Y	Y	Y	Y	Y	Y	N	Y
20 ***Shimkus***	Y	N	N	Y	N	N	Y	Y
INDIANA								
1 Visclosky	N	Y	Y	N	Y	Y	N	Y
2 ***McIntosh***	Y	N	N	Y	?	?	Y	Y
3 Roemer	Y	Y	Y	Y	N	N	Y	Y
4 ***Souder***	Y	N	N	Y	N	N	Y	Y
5 ***Buyer***	Y	N	N	Y	N	N	Y	Y
6 ***Burton***	Y	N	N	Y	N	N	Y	Y
7 ***Pease***	Y	N	N	Y	N	N	Y	Y
8 ***Hostettler***	Y	N	N	Y	N	N	Y	Y
9 Hill	Y	Y	Y	N	Y	Y	Y	Y
10 Carson	Y	Y	Y	N	Y	Y	Y	Y
IOWA								
1 ***Leach***	Y	Y	N	Y	N	N	Y	Y
2 ***Nussle***	Y	N	N	Y	N	N	Y	Y
3 Boswell	Y	Y	Y	Y	N	Y	Y	Y
4 ***Ganske***	Y	N	Y	Y	N	?	Y	Y
5 ***Latham***	N	N	N	Y	N	N	Y	Y
KANSAS								
1 ***Moran***	Y	N	N	Y	N	N	N	Y
2 ***Ryun***	Y	N	N	Y	N	N	Y	Y
3 Moore	Y	Y	Y	Y	Y	Y	Y	Y
4 ***Tiahrt***	Y	N	N	Y	N	N	Y	Y
KENTUCKY								
1 ***Whitfield***	Y	N	N	+	N	N	Y	Y
2 ***Lewis***	Y	N	N	Y	N	N	Y	Y
3 ***Northup***	Y	N	N	Y	N	N	Y	Y
4 Lucas	Y	Y	Y	Y	Y	Y	Y	Y
5 ***Rogers***	Y	N	N	Y	N	N	Y	Y
6 ***Fletcher***	Y	N	N	Y	N	N	Y	Y
LOUISIANA								
1 ***Vitter***	Y	N	N	Y	N	N	Y	Y
2 Jefferson	?	Y	Y	Y	Y	Y	N	Y
3 ***Tauzin***	Y	N	N	Y	N	N	Y	Y
4 ***McCrery***	Y	N	N	Y	N	N	Y	Y
5 ***Cooksey***	Y	N	N	Y	N	N	Y	Y
6 ***Baker***	Y	N	N	Y	?	?	Y	Y
7 John	Y	Y	Y	Y	Y	Y	?	Y
MAINE								
1 Allen	Y	Y	Y	N	Y	Y	Y	Y
2 Baldacci	Y	Y	Y	N	Y	Y	+	+
MARYLAND								
1 ***Gilchrest***	Y	N	N	Y	N	N	Y	Y
2 ***Ehrlich***	?	N	N	Y	N	N	Y	Y
3 Cardin	Y	Y	Y	N	Y	Y	Y	Y
4 Wynn	Y	Y	Y	Y	Y	Y	Y	N
5 Hoyer	Y	Y	Y	N	Y	Y	Y	N
6 ***Bartlett***	Y	N	N	Y	N	N	Y	Y
7 Cummings	?	Y	Y	N	Y	Y	Y	Y
8 ***Morella***	Y	N	Y	Y	N	N	Y	Y
MASSACHUSETTS								
1 Olver	N	Y	Y	N	Y	Y	N	Y
2 Neal	Y	Y	Y	N	Y	Y	Y	Y
3 McGovern	Y	Y	Y	N	Y	Y	Y	Y
4 Frank	Y	Y	Y	N	Y	Y	Y	P
5 Meehan	Y	Y	Y	N	Y	Y	Y	Y
6 Tierney	Y	Y	Y	N	Y	Y	Y	Y
7 Markey	?	?	?	?	Y	Y	?	?
8 Capuano	N	Y	Y	N	Y	Y	N	N
9 Moakley	Y	Y	Y	N	Y	Y	Y	Y
10 Delahunt	?	Y	Y	Y	Y	Y	Y	Y
MICHIGAN								
1 Stupak	N	Y	Y	N	Y	Y	N	Y
2 ***Hoekstra***	?	N	N	Y	N	N	Y	Y
3 ***Ehlers***	Y	N	N	Y	N	N	Y	Y
4 ***Camp***	Y	N	N	Y	N	N	Y	Y
5 Barcia	Y	Y	Y	Y	Y	Y	Y	Y
6 ***Upton***	Y	N	N	Y	N	N	Y	Y
7 ***Smith***	?	?	?	?	N	N	Y	Y
8 Stabenow	Y	Y	Y	N	Y	Y	Y	Y
9 Kildee	Y	Y	Y	N	Y	Y	Y	Y
10 Bonior	Y	Y	Y	N	Y	Y	Y	Y
11 ***Knollenberg***	Y	N	N	Y	N	N	Y	Y
12 Levin	Y	Y	Y	N	Y	Y	Y	Y
13 Rivers	Y	Y	Y	N	Y	Y	Y	Y
14 Conyers	+	+	+	−	Y	Y	Y	N
15 Kilpatrick	Y	Y	Y	N	Y	Y	Y	Y
16 Dingell	Y	Y	Y	N	Y	?	Y	Y
MINNESOTA								
1 ***Gutknecht***	N	Y	N	Y	N	N	N	Y
2 Minge	Y	Y	Y	N	Y	Y	Y	Y
3 ***Ramstad***	N	N	N	Y	N	N	N	Y
4 Vento	?	?	?	?	?	?	?	?
5 Sabo	N	Y	Y	N	?	?	N	Y
6 Luther	Y	Y	Y	N	Y	Y	Y	Y
7 Peterson	?	Y	Y	Y	Y	Y	N	Y
8 Oberstar	N	Y	Y	N	Y	Y	N	Y
MISSISSIPPI								
1 ***Wicker***	N	N	N	Y	N	N	Y	Y
2 Thompson	N	Y	Y	N	Y	Y	N	Y
3 ***Pickering***	Y	N	N	Y	N	N	Y	Y
4 Shows	Y	Y	Y	Y	Y	N	Y	Y
5 Taylor	N	Y	Y	N	Y	Y	N	Y
MISSOURI								
1 Clay	?	?	?	?	Y	Y	N	N
2 ***Talent***	Y	N	N	Y	N	N	?	?
3 Gephardt	Y	Y	Y	N	?	?	?	?
4 Skelton	Y	Y	Y	Y	Y	Y	Y	Y
5 McCarthy	Y	Y	Y	N	Y	+	Y	Y
6 Danner	?	?	?	?	?	?	?	?
7 ***Blunt***	Y	N	N	Y	N	N	Y	Y
8 ***Emerson***	Y	N	N	Y	N	?	Y	Y
9 ***Hulshof***	Y	N	N	Y	N	N	N	Y
MONTANA								
AL ***Hill***	N	N	N	Y	N	N	N	Y
NEBRASKA								
1 ***Bereuter***	Y	N	N	Y	N	N	Y	Y
2 ***Terry***	Y	N	N	Y	N	N	Y	Y
3 ***Barrett***	Y	N	N	Y	N	N	Y	Y
NEVADA								
1 Berkley	Y	N	Y	Y	Y	Y	Y	Y
2 ***Gibbons***	Y	N	N	Y	N	N	N	Y
NEW HAMPSHIRE								
1 ***Sununu***	Y	N	N	Y	N	N	Y	Y
2 ***Bass***	Y	N	N	Y	N	N	Y	Y
NEW JERSEY								
1 Andrews	Y	Y	Y	Y	?	?	Y	Y
2 ***LoBiondo***	N	N	N	Y	N	N	N	Y
3 ***Saxton***	Y	N	N	Y	N	N	Y	Y
4 ***Smith***	Y	N	N	Y	N	N	Y	Y
5 ***Roukema***	Y	N	N	Y	N	?	Y	Y
6 Pallone	N	Y	Y	N	Y	Y	N	Y
7 ***Franks***	?	N	Y	Y	N	N	Y	Y
8 Pascrell	N	Y	Y	Y	Y	Y	Y	Y
9 Rothman	Y	Y	Y	N	Y	Y	N	Y
10 Payne	Y	Y	Y	N	?	?	Y	N
11 ***Frelinghuysen***	Y	N	N	Y	N	N	Y	Y
12 Holt	N	Y	Y	Y	Y	Y	Y	Y
13 Menendez	Y	Y	Y	N	Y	Y	Y	Y
NEW MEXICO								
1 ***Wilson***	Y	N	N	Y	N	N	Y	Y
2 ***Skeen***	Y	N	N	Y	N	N	Y	Y
3 Udall	N	Y	Y	N	Y	Y	N	Y
NEW YORK								
1 Forbes	Y	N	Y	Y	Y	Y	Y	Y
2 ***Lazio***	?	?	?	?	?	N	Y	Y
3 ***King***	Y	N	Y	Y	N	N	Y	Y
4 McCarthy	Y	Y	Y	N	Y	Y	Y	Y
5 Ackerman	Y	Y	Y	N	Y	Y	Y	Y
6 Meeks	Y	Y	Y	N	Y	Y	Y	Y
7 Crowley	Y	Y	Y	N	Y	Y	Y	Y
8 Nadler	Y	Y	Y	N	Y	Y	Y	N
9 Weiner	Y	Y	Y	N	Y	Y	Y	Y
10 Towns	?	Y	Y	N	?	?	Y	N
11 Owens	Y	Y	Y	N	?	?	+	+
12 Velázquez	Y	Y	Y	Y	Y	Y	N	Y
13 ***Fossella***	Y	N	N	Y	N	N	Y	Y
14 Maloney	Y	Y	Y	N	?	?	Y	Y
15 Rangel	Y	Y	Y	N	Y	Y	Y	Y
16 Serrano	Y	Y	Y	N	Y	Y	Y	Y
17 Engel	Y	Y	Y	N	Y	Y	?	?
18 Lowey	Y	Y	Y	N	Y	Y	Y	Y
19 ***Kelly***	Y	N	N	Y	N	N	Y	Y
20 ***Gilman***	?	?	?	?	N	N	Y	Y
21 McNulty	N	Y	Y	Y	Y	Y	N	Y
22 ***Sweeney***	N	N	N	Y	N	N	N	Y
23 ***Boehlert***	Y	N	N	Y	N	N	Y	Y
24 ***McHugh***	Y	N	N	Y	N	N	Y	Y
25 ***Walsh***	Y	N	N	Y	N	N	Y	Y
26 Hinchey	Y	Y	Y	N	Y	Y	?	Y
27 ***Reynolds***	Y	N	N	Y	N	N	Y	Y
28 Slaughter	Y	Y	Y	N	Y	Y	N	Y
29 LaFalce	Y	Y	Y	N	Y	Y	Y	Y
30 ***Quinn***	Y	N	N	Y	N	N	Y	Y
31 ***Houghton***	Y	N	N	Y	N	N	Y	Y
NORTH CAROLINA								
1 Clayton	Y	Y	Y	Y	Y	Y	Y	N
2 Etheridge	Y	Y	Y	Y	Y	Y	N	Y
3 ***Jones***	Y	N	N	Y	N	N	Y	Y
4 Price	Y	Y	Y	N	Y	Y	N	Y
5 ***Burr***	Y	N	N	Y	N	N	Y	Y
6 ***Coble***	Y	N	N	Y	N	N	Y	Y
7 McIntyre	Y	Y	Y	Y	Y	Y	Y	Y
8 ***Hayes***	Y	N	N	Y	N	N	Y	Y
9 ***Myrick***	Y	N	N	Y	?	?	Y	Y
10 ***Ballenger***	?	N	N	Y	N	N	Y	Y
11 ***Taylor***	Y	N	N	Y	N	N	Y	Y
12 Watt	Y	?	?	?	Y	Y	Y	Y
NORTH DAKOTA								
AL Pomeroy	N	Y	Y	N	Y	Y	N	Y
OHIO								
1 ***Chabot***	Y	N	N	Y	N	N	Y	Y
2 ***Portman***	Y	N	N	Y	N	N	Y	Y
3 Hall	Y	Y	Y	N	Y	?	Y	Y
4 ***Oxley***	Y	N	N	Y	N	?	Y	Y
5 ***Gillmor***	?	?	?	?	?	?	?	?
6 Strickland	N	Y	Y	N	Y	Y	?	?
7 ***Hobson***	Y	N	N	Y	N	N	Y	Y
8 ***Boehner***	Y	N	N	?	N	?	?	?
9 Kaptur	?	Y	Y	N	Y	Y	Y	Y
10 Kucinich	N	Y	Y	N	Y	Y	N	Y
11 Jones	Y	Y	Y	N	Y	Y	?	?
12 ***Kasich***	?	N	N	Y	?	?	Y	Y
13 Brown	Y	Y	Y	N	Y	Y	Y	Y
14 Sawyer	Y	Y	Y	N	Y	Y	Y	Y
15 ***Pryce***	Y	N	N	Y	N	N	Y	Y
16 ***Regula***	Y	N	N	Y	N	N	Y	Y
17 Traficant	Y	N	N	Y	N	N	Y	Y
18 ***Ney***	Y	N	N	Y	−	−	Y	Y
19 ***LaTourette***	Y	N	N	Y	N	N	?	?
OKLAHOMA								
1 ***Largent***	Y	N	N	Y	?	N	Y	Y
2 ***Coburn***	Y	N	N	Y	?	?	N	Y
3 ***Watkins***	Y	N	N	Y	N	N	Y	Y
4 ***Watts***	?	N	N	Y	?	?	?	+
5 ***Istook***	?	?	?	+	N	N	Y	Y
6 ***Lucas***	Y	N	N	Y	N	N	Y	Y
OREGON								
1 Wu	Y	Y	Y	N	Y	Y	N	Y
2 ***Walden***	Y	N	N	Y	N	N	Y	Y
3 Blumenauer	?	?	?	?	Y	Y	Y	Y
4 DeFazio	N	Y	Y	N	Y	Y	N	Y
5 Hooley	N	Y	Y	Y	Y	Y	N	Y
PENNSYLVANIA								
1 Brady	N	Y	Y	N	Y	Y	N	Y
2 Fattah	N	Y	Y	N	?	?	?	?
3 Borski	N	Y	Y	N	Y	Y	N	Y
4 Klink	?	?	?	?	Y	Y	N	Y
5 ***Peterson***	Y	N	N	Y	N	?	Y	Y
6 Holden	Y	Y	Y	N	Y	Y	Y	Y
7 ***Weldon***	?	N	N	Y	?	?	?	?
8 ***Greenwood***	Y	N	N	Y	N	N	Y	Y
9 ***Shuster***	?	N	N	Y	?	?	Y	Y
10 ***Sherwood***	Y	Y	N	Y	N	N	Y	Y
11 Kanjorski	Y	Y	Y	N	Y	Y	Y	Y
12 Murtha	Y	N	Y	N	Y	Y	Y	Y
13 Hoeffel	Y	Y	Y	N	+	+	Y	Y
14 Coyne	Y	Y	Y	N	Y	Y	Y	Y
15 ***Toomey***	Y	N	N	Y	?	?	?	?
16 ***Pitts***	Y	N	N	Y	N	?	Y	Y
17 ***Gekas***	?	N	N	Y	N	?	Y	Y
18 Doyle	Y	Y	Y	N	Y	Y	?	?
19 ***Goodling***	Y	N	N	Y	N	N	Y	Y
20 Mascara	Y	Y	Y	N	Y	Y	Y	Y
21 ***English***	?	N	N	Y	N	N	N	Y
RHODE ISLAND								
1 Kennedy	Y	Y	Y	N	Y	Y	Y	Y
2 Weygand	Y	Y	Y	N	Y	Y	Y	Y
SOUTH CAROLINA								
1 ***Sanford***	Y	N	N	Y	N	N	N	Y
2 ***Spence***	Y	N	N	Y	N	N	Y	Y
3 ***Graham***	Y	N	N	Y	N	N	Y	Y
4 ***DeMint***	Y	N	N	Y	?	?	?	?
5 Spratt	Y	Y	Y	N	Y	Y	Y	Y
6 Clyburn	Y	Y	Y	N	Y	Y	Y	N
SOUTH DAKOTA								
AL ***Thune***	Y	N	N	Y	N	N	Y	Y
TENNESSEE								
1 ***Jenkins***	Y	N	N	Y	N	N	Y	Y
2 ***Duncan***	Y	N	N	Y	N	N	Y	Y
3 ***Wamp***	Y	N	N	Y	?	N	Y	Y
4 ***Hilleary***	?	N	N	Y	N	N	Y	Y
5 Clement	?	Y	Y	Y	Y	Y	Y	Y
6 Gordon	Y	Y	Y	Y	?	?	?	?
7 ***Bryant***	Y	N	N	Y	N	N	Y	Y
8 Tanner	Y	N	N	Y	Y	Y	Y	Y
9 Ford	Y	Y	Y	Y	Y	Y	Y	Y
TEXAS								
1 Sandlin	Y	Y	Y	Y	Y	Y	Y	Y
2 Turner	Y	Y	Y	N	Y	Y	?	?
3 ***Johnson, Sam***	?	N	N	Y	N	N	Y	Y
4 Hall	Y	Y	N	Y	N	N	Y	Y
5 ***Sessions***	Y	N	N	Y	N	N	Y	Y
6 ***Barton***	Y	N	N	Y	N	N	Y	Y
7 ***Archer***	Y	N	N	Y	N	?	Y	Y
8 ***Brady***	?	N	N	Y	N	N	Y	Y
9 Lampson	Y	Y	Y	Y	Y	Y	Y	Y
10 Doggett	Y	Y	Y	N	Y	Y	Y	Y
11 Edwards	Y	Y	Y	N	Y	Y	Y	Y
12 ***Granger***	Y	N	N	Y	N	N	Y	Y
13 ***Thornberry***	Y	N	N	Y	N	N	Y	Y
14 ***Paul***	Y	N	N	Y	N	N	Y	Y
15 Hinojosa	Y	Y	Y	N	Y	Y	Y	Y
16 Reyes	Y	Y	Y	N	Y	Y	Y	Y
17 Stenholm	Y	Y	Y	N	Y	Y	Y	Y
18 Jackson-Lee	N	Y	Y	N	Y	Y	Y	N
19 ***Combest***	Y	N	N	Y	N	N	Y	Y
20 Gonzalez	Y	Y	Y	N	Y	Y	Y	Y
21 ***Smith***	Y	N	N	Y	N	N	Y	Y
22 ***DeLay***	?	N	N	Y	N	N	Y	Y
23 ***Bonilla***	Y	N	N	Y	N	N	Y	Y
24 Frost	Y	Y	Y	N	Y	Y	Y	Y
25 Bentsen	Y	Y	Y	N	Y	Y	Y	Y
26 ***Armey***	Y	N	N	Y	N	N	Y	Y
27 Ortiz	Y	Y	Y	N	Y	Y	Y	Y
28 Rodriguez	Y	Y	Y	N	Y	Y	Y	Y
29 Green	Y	Y	Y	N	Y	Y	N	Y
30 Johnson, E.B.	N	Y	Y	N	Y	Y	N	N
UTAH								
1 ***Hansen***	Y	N	N	Y	?	?	Y	Y
2 ***Cook***	Y	N	N	Y	?	?	?	?
3 ***Cannon***	Y	N	N	Y	N	N	Y	Y
VERMONT								
AL *Sanders*	Y	Y	Y	N	Y	Y	?	?
VIRGINIA								
1 ***Bateman***	Y	N	N	Y	?	?	Y	Y
2 Pickett	N	N	N	Y	N	?	N	Y
3 Scott	Y	Y	Y	N	Y	Y	Y	N
4 Sisisky	Y	Y	Y	Y	Y	Y	Y	Y
5 *Goode*	Y	N	N	Y	N	N	Y	Y
6 ***Goodlatte***	Y	N	N	Y	?	?	?	?
7 ***Bliley***	Y	N	N	Y	N	N	Y	Y
8 Moran	Y	Y	Y	Y	Y	Y	Y	Y
9 Boucher	Y	Y	Y	Y	Y	Y	Y	Y
10 ***Wolf***	Y	N	N	Y	N	N	Y	Y
11 ***Davis***	Y	N	N	Y	N	N	Y	Y
WASHINGTON								
1 Inslee	Y	Y	Y	Y	Y	Y	Y	Y
2 ***Metcalf***	P	N	N	Y	?	?	Y	Y
3 Baird	Y	Y	Y	Y	Y	Y	N	Y
4 ***Hastings***	Y	N	N	Y	N	N	Y	Y
5 ***Nethercutt***	Y	N	N	Y	N	N	Y	Y
6 Dicks	Y	Y	Y	N	Y	Y	Y	Y
7 McDermott	?	+	+	−	Y	Y	N	N
8 ***Dunn***	Y	N	N	Y	N	N	Y	Y
9 Smith	+	+	+	+	Y	Y	Y	Y
WEST VIRGINIA								
1 Mollohan	Y	Y	Y	Y	Y	Y	Y	Y
2 Wise	Y	Y	Y	Y	?	?	Y	Y
3 Rahall	Y	Y	Y	Y	Y	Y	Y	Y
WISCONSIN								
1 ***Ryan***	Y	N	N	Y	N	N	Y	Y
2 Baldwin	Y	Y	Y	N	Y	Y	Y	Y
3 Kind	Y	?	?	?	Y	Y	Y	Y
4 Kleczka	Y	Y	Y	N	Y	Y	Y	Y
5 Barrett	Y	Y	Y	N	Y	Y	Y	Y
6 ***Petri***	Y	N	N	Y	N	N	Y	Y
7 Obey	N	Y	Y	N	Y	Y	Y	?
8 ***Green***	Y	N	N	Y	N	N	Y	Y
9 ***Sensenbrenner***	Y	N	N	Y	N	N	Y	Y
WYOMING								
AL ***Cubin***	Y	N	N	Y	N	N	Y	Y

Southern states - Ala., Ark., Fla., Ga., Ky., La., Miss., N.C., Okla., S.C., Tenn., Texas, Va.

259. **HR 4577. Fiscal 2001 Labor-HHS-Education Appropriations/Special Education Funding.** Bass, R-N.H., amendment that would increase funding for special education by $200 million, offset by an equal reduction in funding for the Gear Up education program. Rejected 98-319: R 93-116; D 4-202 (ND 3-150, SD 1-52); I 1-1. June 13, 2000.

260. **HR 4577. Fiscal 2001 Labor-HHS-Education Appropriations/Special Education Funding.** Ryan, R-Wis., amendment that would cut the bill's funding for 21st Century Community Learning Centers in half to $300 million and increase funding for special education state grants by $300 million. Rejected 124-293: R 119-91; D 4-201 (ND 3-150, SD 1-51); I 1-1. June 13, 2000.

261. **HR 4577. Fiscal 2001 Labor-HHS-Education Appropriations/Special Education Funding.** Miller, R-Calif., amendment that would increase funding for special education state grants by $16 million, offset by an equal reduction in funds for the Ready to Learn television program. Rejected 150-267: R 139-72; D 10-194 (ND 9-142, SD 1-52); I 1-1. June 13, 2000.

262. **HR 4577. Fiscal 2001 Labor-HHS-Education Appropriations/Special Education Funding.** Schaffer, R-Colo., amendment that would increase funding for special education by $10.4 million, offset by an equal reduction in Education Department research funds. Rejected 132-287: R 124-87; D 8-198 (ND 4-149, SD 4-49); I 0-2. June 13, 2000.

263. **HR 4577. Fiscal 2001 Labor-HHS-Education Appropriations/Corporation for Public Broadcasting.** Oxley, R-Ohio, amendment that would reduce the bill's advance appropriation for the Corporation for Public Broadcasting by 1 percent, or $3.65 million. Rejected 110-305: R 108-100; D 2-203 (ND 1-151, SD 1-52); I 0-2. June 13, 2000.

264. **HR 4577. Fiscal 2001 Labor-HHS-Education Appropriations/Special Education Funding.** Schaffer, R-Colo., amendment that would increase funding for special education state grants by $42.2 million, offset by an equal reduction in funding for the Job Corps. Rejected 103-315: R 101-110; D 2-203 (ND 2-151, SD 0-52); I 0-2. June 13, 2000.

265. **HR 4577. Fiscal 2001 Labor-HHS-Education Appropriations/Native Hawaiian Schools.** Boehner, R-Ohio, amendment that would prohibit the use of funds for the Native Hawaiian Education program, which provides funds to the Bishop Estate Trust. Rejected 202-220: R 200-13; D 1-206 (ND 1-152, SD 0-54); I 1-1. June 13, 2000.

Key

Y	Voted for (yea).
#	Paired for.
+	Announced for.
N	Voted against (nay).
X	Paired against.
–	Announced against.
P	Voted "present."
C	Voted "present" to avoid possible conflict of interest.
?	Did not vote or otherwise make a position known.

Democrats • ***Republicans***
Independents

	259	260	261	262	263	264	265
ALABAMA							
1 ***Callahan***	N	N	N	N	N	N	Y
2 ***Everett***	N	Y	Y	N	Y	Y	Y
3 ***Riley***	Y	Y	Y	Y	Y	Y	Y
4 ***Aderholt***	Y	Y	Y	Y	Y	Y	Y
5 Cramer	N	N	N	N	N	N	N
6 ***Bachus***	N	N	N	Y	Y	N	Y
7 Hilliard	N	N	N	N	N	N	N
ALASKA							
AL ***Young***	N	N	N	N	N	N	N
ARIZONA							
1 ***Salmon***	Y	Y	Y	Y	Y	Y	Y
2 Pastor	N	N	Y	N	N	N	N
3 ***Stump***	Y	Y	Y	N	Y	Y	Y
4 ***Shadegg***	Y	Y	Y	Y	Y	Y	Y
5 ***Kolbe***	Y	N	N	N	N	N	Y
6 ***Hayworth***	Y	Y	Y	Y	Y	Y	Y
ARKANSAS							
1 Berry	N	N	N	N	N	N	N
2 Snyder	N	N	N	N	N	N	N
3 ***Hutchinson***	N	N	N	N	N	N	Y
4 ***Dickey***	Y	N	Y	Y	Y	Y	Y
CALIFORNIA							
1 Thompson	N	N	N	N	N	N	N
2 ***Herger***	N	Y	Y	Y	Y	Y	Y
3 ***Ose***	N	N	N	N	N	N	Y
4 ***Doolittle***	Y	Y	Y	Y	Y	Y	N
5 Matsui	N	N	N	N	N	N	N
6 Woolsey	N	N	N	N	N	N	N
7 Miller, George	N	N	N	N	N	N	N
8 Pelosi	N	N	N	N	N	N	N
9 Lee	N	N	N	N	N	N	N
10 Tauscher	N	N	N	N	N	N	N
11 ***Pombo***	Y	N	Y	Y	Y	Y	Y
12 Lantos	N	N	N	N	N	N	N
13 Stark	N	N	N	N	N	N	N
14 Eshoo	N	N	N	N	N	N	N
15 ***Campbell***	?	?	?	?	?	?	?
16 Lofgren	N	N	N	N	N	N	N
17 Farr	N	N	N	N	N	N	N
18 Condit	N	N	N	N	N	N	N
19 ***Radanovich***	N	Y	Y	Y	Y	Y	Y
20 Dooley	N	N	N	N	N	N	N
21 ***Thomas***	N	N	Y	N	N	N	Y
22 Capps	N	N	N	N	N	N	N
23 ***Gallegly***	N	N	N	N	N	N	N
24 Sherman	N	N	N	N	N	N	N
25 ***McKeon***	N	N	N	N	N	N	Y
26 Berman	N	N	N	N	N	N	N
27 ***Rogan***	Y	N	Y	N	Y	N	Y
28 ***Dreier***	Y	Y	Y	Y	Y	Y	Y
29 Waxman	N	N	N	N	N	N	N
30 Becerra	N	N	N	N	N	N	N
31 Martinez	N	N	N	N	N	N	N
32 Dixon	N	N	N	N	N	N	N
33 Roybal-Allard	N	N	N	N	N	N	N
34 Napolitano	N	N	N	N	N	N	N
35 Waters	N	N	N	N	N	N	N
36 ***Kuykendall***	Y	Y	Y	Y	Y	N	Y
37 Millender-McD.	N	N	N	N	N	N	N
38 ***Horn***	N	Y	N	Y	N	N	Y
39 ***Royce***	N	Y	Y	Y	Y	Y	Y
40 ***Lewis***	N	N	N	N	N	N	N
41 ***Miller, Gary***	Y	Y	Y	Y	Y	Y	Y
42 Baca	N	N	N	N	N	N	N
43 ***Calvert***	N	N	Y	N	N	N	Y
44 ***Bono***	N	Y	Y	Y	N	Y	Y
45 ***Rohrabacher***	Y	Y	Y	Y	Y	Y	Y
46 Sanchez	N	N	N	N	N	N	N
47 ***Cox***	?	?	?	?	?	?	Y
48 ***Packard***	N	N	N	N	N	N	Y
49 ***Bilbray***	N	N	N	N	N	N	Y
50 Filner	N	N	N	N	N	N	N
51 ***Cunningham***	N	N	N	Y	Y	Y	Y
52 ***Hunter***	Y	Y	Y	Y	Y	Y	Y
COLORADO							
1 DeGette	N	N	N	N	N	N	N
2 Udall	N	N	N	N	N	N	N
3 ***McInnis***	Y	Y	Y	Y	Y	N	Y
4 ***Schaffer***	Y	Y	Y	Y	Y	Y	Y
5 ***Hefley***	Y	Y	Y	Y	Y	Y	Y
6 ***Tancredo***	Y	Y	Y	Y	Y	Y	Y
CONNECTICUT							
1 Larson	N	N	N	N	N	N	N
2 Gejdenson	N	N	N	N	N	N	N
3 DeLauro	N	N	N	N	N	N	N
4 ***Shays***	N	N	Y	N	N	N	Y
5 Maloney	Y	Y	Y	Y	N	Y	N
6 ***Johnson***	N	N	Y	N	N	N	N
DELAWARE							
AL ***Castle***	N	N	N	N	N	N	Y
FLORIDA							
1 ***Scarborough***	N	Y	Y	Y	Y	Y	Y
2 Boyd	N	N	N	N	N	N	N
3 Brown	N	N	N	N	N	N	N
4 ***Fowler***	Y	N	N	Y	N	N	Y
5 Thurman	N	N	N	N	N	N	N
6 ***Stearns***	N	Y	Y	Y	Y	N	Y
7 ***Mica***	N	Y	Y	Y	Y	Y	Y
8 ***McCollum***	?	?	?	?	?	?	?
9 ***Bilirakis***	N	N	Y	N	Y	N	Y
10 ***Young***	N	N	N	N	N	N	Y
11 Davis	N	N	N	N	N	N	N
12 ***Canady***	N	Y	Y	N	Y	N	Y
13 ***Miller***	Y	Y	Y	Y	Y	Y	Y
14 ***Goss***	N	N	N	Y	Y	Y	Y
15 ***Weldon***	Y	Y	Y	Y	Y	Y	Y
16 ***Foley***	N	N	Y	N	N	Y	Y
17 Meek	N	N	N	N	N	N	N
18 ***Ros-Lehtinen***	N	N	Y	N	N	N	Y
19 Wexler	N	N	N	N	N	N	N
20 Deutsch	N	N	N	N	N	N	N
21 ***Diaz-Balart***	N	N	Y	N	N	N	Y
22 ***Shaw***	N	Y	N	Y	N	N	Y
23 Hastings	N	N	N	N	N	N	N
GEORGIA							
1 ***Kingston***	N	N	Y	Y	Y	N	Y
2 Bishop	N	N	N	N	N	N	N
3 ***Collins***	N	Y	Y	Y	Y	Y	Y
4 McKinney	N	N	N	N	N	N	N
5 Lewis	N	N	N	N	N	N	N
6 ***Isakson***	N	N	N	N	N	N	Y
7 ***Barr***	Y	Y	Y	Y	Y	Y	Y
8 ***Chambliss***	N	Y	Y	N	N	N	Y
9 ***Deal***	N	N	N	N	N	Y	Y
10 ***Norwood***	Y	Y	Y	Y	Y	Y	Y
11 ***Linder***	N	N	Y	N	Y	Y	Y
HAWAII							
1 Abercrombie	N	N	N	N	N	N	N
2 Mink	N	N	N	N	N	N	N
IDAHO							
1 ***Chenoweth-Hage***	Y	Y	Y	Y	Y	Y	Y
2 ***Simpson***	Y	Y	Y	N	N	N	Y
ILLINOIS							
1 Rush	N	N	N	N	N	N	N
2 Jackson	N	N	N	N	N	N	N
3 Lipinski	N	N	N	N	N	N	N
4 Gutierrez	N	N	N	N	N	N	N
5 Blagojevich	N	N	N	N	N	N	N
6 ***Hyde***	N	N	N	N	Y	N	Y
7 Davis	N	N	N	N	N	N	N
8 ***Crane***	Y	Y	Y	Y	Y	Y	Y
9 Schakowsky	N	N	N	N	N	N	N
10 ***Porter***	N	N	N	N	N	N	Y
11 ***Weller***	N	N	N	N	?	Y	Y
12 Costello	N	N	N	N	N	N	N
13 ***Biggert***	N	N	N	N	N	N	Y

ND Northern Democrats SD Southern Democrats

	259	260	261	262	263	264	265
14 ***Hastert***							
15 ***Ewing***	N	Y	N	N	?	Y	Y
16 ***Manzullo***	Y	Y	Y	Y	Y	Y	Y
17 Evans	N	N	N	N	N	N	N
18 ***LaHood***	N	N	N	Y	N	N	Y
19 Phelps	N	N	N	N	N	N	N
20 ***Shimkus***	Y	Y	Y	Y	Y	Y	Y
INDIANA							
1 Visclosky	N	N	N	N	N	N	+
2 ***McIntosh***	Y	Y	Y	Y	Y	N	Y
3 Roemer	N	N	Y	N	N	N	N
4 ***Souder***	N	Y	Y	Y	Y	N	Y
5 ***Buyer***	N	Y	Y	Y	Y	N	Y
6 ***Burton***	Y	Y	Y	Y	Y	Y	Y
7 ***Pease***	N	Y	Y	N	Y	Y	Y
8 ***Hostettler***	Y	Y	Y	Y	Y	Y	Y
9 Hill	N	N	N	N	N	N	N
10 Carson	N	N	N	N	N	N	N
IOWA							
1 ***Leach***	N	Y	Y	Y	N	N	Y
2 ***Nussle***	Y	Y	Y	Y	N	Y	Y
3 Boswell	N	N	N	N	N	N	N
4 ***Ganske***	N	Y	Y	N	N	N	Y
5 ***Latham***	Y	Y	Y	Y	Y	N	Y
KANSAS							
1 ***Moran***	Y	Y	N	Y	N	N	Y
2 ***Ryun***	Y	Y	Y	Y	Y	Y	Y
3 Moore	N	Y	Y	N	N	N	N
4 ***Tiahrt***	Y	Y	Y	Y	N	Y	Y
KENTUCKY							
1 ***Whitfield***	N	N	N	N	N	N	Y
2 ***Lewis***	N	N	Y	Y	N	Y	Y
3 ***Northup***	N	N	N	N	N	N	Y
4 Lucas	N	N	N	N	N	N	N
5 ***Rogers***	N	N	N	N	N	N	Y
6 ***Fletcher***	?	N	N	N	N	N	Y
LOUISIANA							
1 ***Vitter***	Y	Y	Y	Y	N	Y	Y
2 Jefferson	N	N	N	N	N	N	N
3 ***Tauzin***	N	Y	Y	Y	N	N	Y
4 ***McCrery***	N	N	Y	Y	Y	N	Y
5 ***Cooksey***	Y	N	N	N	N	N	Y
6 ***Baker***	N	Y	Y	Y	N	N	Y
7 John	N	?	N	N	N	N	N
MAINE							
1 Allen	N	N	N	N	N	N	N
2 Baldacci	N	N	N	N	N	N	N
MARYLAND							
1 ***Gilchrest***	N	N	N	N	N	N	Y
2 ***Ehrlich***	Y	Y	Y	Y	Y	N	Y
3 Cardin	N	N	N	N	N	N	N
4 Wynn	N	N	N	N	N	N	N
5 Hoyer	N	N	N	N	N	N	N
6 ***Bartlett***	N	Y	Y	Y	Y	Y	Y
7 Cummings	N	N	N	N	N	N	N
8 ***Morella***	N	N	N	N	N	N	N
MASSACHUSETTS							
1 Olver	N	N	N	N	N	N	N
2 Neal	N	N	N	N	N	N	N
3 McGovern	N	N	N	N	N	N	N
4 Frank	N	N	N	N	N	N	N
5 Meehan	N	N	N	N	N	N	N
6 Tierney	N	N	Y	N	N	N	N
7 Markey	?	?	?	?	?	?	N
8 Capuano	N	N	N	N	N	N	N
9 Moakley	N	N	N	N	N	N	N
10 Delahunt	N	N	N	N	N	N	N
MICHIGAN							
1 Stupak	N	N	N	N	N	N	N
2 ***Hoekstra***	Y	Y	Y	Y	Y	Y	Y
3 ***Ehlers***	Y	N	N	N	N	N	Y
4 ***Camp***	N	N	Y	Y	Y	Y	Y
5 Barcia	N	N	Y	N	N	N	N
6 ***Upton***	N	Y	Y	Y	Y	N	Y
7 ***Smith***	Y	Y	Y	N	Y	Y	Y
8 Stabenow	N	N	N	N	N	N	N
9 Kildee	N	N	N	N	N	N	N
10 Bonior	N	N	N	N	N	N	N
11 ***Knollenberg***	N	N	N	N	N	N	Y
12 Levin	N	N	N	N	N	N	N
13 Rivers	Y	Y	Y	N	N	N	N
14 Conyers	N	N	N	N	N	N	N
15 Kilpatrick	N	N	N	N	N	N	N
16 Dingell	N	N	N	N	N	N	N

	259	260	261	262	263	264	265
MINNESOTA							
1 ***Gutknecht***	Y	N	Y	Y	Y	Y	Y
2 Minge	N	N	N	N	N	N	N
3 ***Ramstad***	Y	Y	Y	Y	N	Y	Y
4 Vento	?	?	?	?	?	?	?
5 Sabo	N	N	N	N	N	N	N
6 Luther	N	N	N	Y	N	N	N
7 Peterson	N	N	?	N	N	N	Y
8 Oberstar	N	N	N	N	N	N	N
MISSISSIPPI							
1 ***Wicker***	N	N	N	N	N	N	Y
2 Thompson	N	N	N	N	N	N	N
3 ***Pickering***	N	Y	Y	Y	N	N	Y
4 Shows	N	N	N	N	N	N	N
5 Taylor	Y	Y	N	Y	N	N	N
MISSOURI							
1 Clay	N	N	N	N	N	N	N
2 ***Talent***	Y	Y	Y	Y	Y	N	Y
3 Gephardt	N	N	N	N	N	N	N
4 Skelton	N	N	N	N	N	N	N
5 McCarthy	N	N	N	N	N	N	N
6 Danner	?	?	?	?	?	?	?
7 ***Blunt***	Y	Y	Y	Y	N	Y	Y
8 ***Emerson***	N	N	N	Y	N	N	Y
9 ***Hulshof***	N	Y	Y	Y	Y	N	Y
MONTANA							
AL ***Hill***	N	Y	Y	Y	Y	Y	N
NEBRASKA							
1 ***Bereuter***	Y	Y	N	N	N	Y	Y
2 ***Terry***	Y	Y	Y	Y	Y	N	Y
3 ***Barrett***	N	N	N	N	Y	N	Y
NEVADA							
1 Berkley	N	N	N	N	N	N	N
2 ***Gibbons***	Y	Y	Y	Y	N	N	Y
NEW HAMPSHIRE							
1 ***Sununu***	Y	Y	Y	Y	N	Y	Y
2 ***Bass***	Y	Y	Y	Y	N	Y	Y
NEW JERSEY							
1 Andrews	N	N	N	N	N	N	N
2 ***LoBiondo***	N	N	N	N	Y	N	Y
3 ***Saxton***	N	N	N	N	N	N	Y
4 ***Smith***	N	N	N	N	N	N	N
5 ***Roukema***	Y	N	Y	Y	N	Y	Y
6 Pallone	?	?	?	?	?	?	?
7 ***Franks***	?	?	?	?	?	?	?
8 Pascrell	N	N	N	N	N	N	N
9 Rothman	N	N	N	N	N	N	N
10 Payne	N	N	N	N	N	N	N
11 ***Frelinghuysen***	Y	N	N	N	N	N	N
12 Holt	N	N	N	N	N	N	N
13 Menendez	N	N	N	N	N	N	N
NEW MEXICO							
1 ***Wilson***	N	N	Y	N	N	N	N
2 ***Skeen***	N	N	N	N	N	N	Y
3 Udall	N	N	Y	N	N	N	N
NEW YORK							
1 Forbes	N	N	N	N	N	N	N
2 ***Lazio***	N	N	N	N	N	N	Y
3 ***King***	N	N	N	N	N	N	N
4 McCarthy	N	N	N	N	N	N	N
5 Ackerman	N	N	N	N	N	N	N
6 Meeks	N	N	N	N	N	N	N
7 Crowley	N	N	N	N	N	N	N
8 Nadler	N	N	N	N	N	N	N
9 Weiner	N	N	N	N	N	N	N
10 Towns	N	N	N	N	N	N	N
11 Owens	N	N	N	N	N	N	N
12 Velázquez	N	N	N	N	N	N	N
13 ***Fossella***	N	N	Y	Y	N	N	Y
14 Maloney	N	N	N	N	N	N	N
15 Rangel	N	N	N	N	N	N	N
16 Serrano	N	N	N	N	N	N	N
17 Engel	N	N	N	N	N	N	N
18 Lowey	N	N	N	N	N	N	N
19 ***Kelly***	Y	Y	Y	Y	N	Y	Y
20 ***Gilman***	N	N	N	N	N	N	Y
21 McNulty	N	N	N	N	N	N	N
22 ***Sweeney***	N	Y	Y	Y	N	N	Y
23 ***Boehlert***	N	N	N	N	N	N	N
24 ***McHugh***	N	Y	Y	Y	N	N	Y
25 ***Walsh***	N	N	N	N	N	N	Y
26 Hinchey	N	N	N	N	N	N	N
27 ***Reynolds***	Y	N	Y	Y	N	N	Y
28 Slaughter	N	N	N	N	N	N	N
29 LaFalce	N	N	N	N	N	N	N

	259	260	261	262	263	264	265
30 ***Quinn***	N	N	Y	Y	N	N	Y
31 ***Houghton***	N	N	N	N	N	N	Y
NORTH CAROLINA							
1 Clayton	N	N	N	N	N	N	N
2 Etheridge	N	N	N	N	N	N	N
3 ***Jones***	Y	Y	Y	Y	Y	Y	Y
4 Price	N	N	N	N	N	N	N
5 ***Burr***	N	Y	Y	N	Y	Y	Y
6 ***Coble***	Y	Y	Y	Y	Y	Y	Y
7 McIntyre	N	N	N	N	N	N	N
8 ***Hayes***	Y	N	N	N	Y	N	Y
9 ***Myrick***	Y	Y	Y	Y	Y	Y	Y
10 ***Ballenger***	N	Y	Y	N	Y	N	Y
11 ***Taylor***	N	Y	N	Y	Y	Y	Y
12 Watt	N	N	N	N	N	N	N
NORTH DAKOTA							
AL Pomeroy	N	N	N	N	N	N	N
OHIO							
1 ***Chabot***	Y	Y	Y	Y	Y	Y	Y
2 ***Portman***	N	Y	Y	Y	Y	Y	Y
3 Hall	N	N	N	N	N	N	N
4 ***Oxley***	Y	Y	Y	Y	Y	Y	Y
5 ***Gillmor***	?	?	?	?	?	?	?
6 Strickland	N	N	N	N	N	N	N
7 ***Hobson***	N	N	N	N	N	N	Y
8 ***Boehner***	Y	Y	Y	Y	Y	Y	Y
9 Kaptur	N	N	N	N	N	N	N
10 Kucinich	N	N	N	N	N	N	N
11 Jones	N	N	N	N	N	N	N
12 ***Kasich***	Y	Y	Y	Y	?	Y	Y
13 Brown	N	N	N	N	N	N	N
14 Sawyer	N	N	N	N	N	N	N
15 ***Pryce***	Y	N	N	N	N	N	Y
16 ***Regula***	N	N	N	N	N	N	Y
17 Traficant	N	N	N	N	N	N	N
18 ***Ney***	N	N	N	N	N	N	Y
19 ***LaTourette***	N	N	N	N	N	N	Y
OKLAHOMA							
1 ***Largent***	Y	Y	Y	Y	Y	Y	Y
2 ***Coburn***	Y	Y	Y	Y	Y	Y	Y
3 ***Watkins***	N	Y	Y	N	N	N	Y
4 ***Watts***	–	+	+	+	+	–	+
5 ***Istook***	N	Y	Y	N	Y	Y	Y
6 ***Lucas***	N	N	Y	Y	N	N	Y
OREGON							
1 Wu	N	N	N	N	N	N	N
2 ***Walden***	Y	Y	Y	Y	N	N	Y
3 Blumenauer	N	N	N	N	N	N	N
4 DeFazio	N	N	N	N	N	N	N
5 Hooley	N	N	N	N	N	N	N
PENNSYLVANIA							
1 Brady	N	N	N	N	N	N	N
2 Fattah	N	N	N	N	N	N	N
3 Borski	N	N	N	N	N	N	N
4 Klink	N	N	N	N	N	N	N
5 ***Peterson***	N	N	N	N	N	N	Y
6 Holden	N	N	N	N	N	N	N
7 ***Weldon***	?	?	?	?	?	?	N
8 ***Greenwood***	N	N	N	N	N	N	Y
9 ***Shuster***	N	N	N	N	Y	N	Y
10 ***Sherwood***	N	N	N	N	N	N	Y
11 Kanjorski	N	N	N	N	N	N	N
12 Murtha	N	N	N	N	?	N	N
13 Hoeffel	N	N	N	N	N	N	N
14 Coyne	N	N	N	N	N	N	N
15 ***Toomey***	Y	Y	Y	Y	Y	Y	Y
16 ***Pitts***	Y	Y	Y	Y	Y	Y	Y
17 ***Gekas***	N	?	N	Y	N	N	Y
18 Doyle	N	N	N	N	N	N	N
19 ***Goodling***	N	Y	N	N	N	N	Y
20 Mascara	N	N	N	N	N	N	N
21 ***English***	N	N	N	N	N	N	Y
RHODE ISLAND							
1 Kennedy	N	N	N	N	N	N	N
2 Weygand	N	N	N	N	N	N	N
SOUTH CAROLINA							
1 ***Sanford***	Y	Y	Y	Y	Y	Y	Y
2 ***Spence***	N	N	Y	Y	Y	Y	Y
3 ***Graham***	N	Y	Y	Y	Y	Y	Y
4 ***DeMint***	?	?	?	?	?	?	?
5 Spratt	N	N	N	N	N	N	N
6 Clyburn	N	N	N	N	N	N	N
SOUTH DAKOTA							
AL ***Thune***	?	N	Y	Y	N	N	Y

	259	260	261	262	263	264	265
TENNESSEE							
1 ***Jenkins***	Y	Y	Y	Y	N	N	Y
2 ***Duncan***	Y	Y	Y	Y	Y	Y	Y
3 ***Wamp***	Y	Y	Y	Y	Y	Y	Y
4 ***Hilleary***	Y	Y	Y	Y	Y	Y	Y
5 Clement	N	N	N	N	N	N	N
6 Gordon	?	?	?	?	?	?	N
7 ***Bryant***	Y	N	Y	N	Y	Y	Y
8 Tanner	N	N	N	N	N	N	N
9 Ford	N	N	N	N	N	?	N
TEXAS							
1 Sandlin	N	N	N	N	N	N	N
2 Turner	N	N	N	Y	N	N	N
3 ***Johnson, Sam***	Y	Y	Y	Y	Y	Y	Y
4 Hall	N	N	Y	N	N	N	N
5 ***Sessions***	Y	Y	Y	Y	Y	Y	Y
6 ***Barton***	N	Y	Y	N	Y	Y	Y
7 ***Archer***	N	Y	Y	Y	Y	Y	Y
8 ***Brady***	Y	Y	Y	Y	Y	Y	Y
9 Lampson	N	N	N	N	N	N	N
10 Doggett	N	N	N	N	N	N	N
11 Edwards	N	N	N	Y	N	N	N
12 ***Granger***	N	N	N	N	N	N	Y
13 ***Thornberry***	Y	Y	Y	Y	Y	Y	Y
14 ***Paul***	Y	Y	Y	Y	Y	Y	Y
15 Hinojosa	N	N	N	N	N	N	N
16 Reyes	N	N	N	N	N	N	N
17 Stenholm	N	N	N	N	Y	N	N
18 Jackson-Lee	N	N	N	N	N	N	N
19 ***Combest***	N	Y	Y	Y	Y	Y	Y
20 Gonzalez	N	N	N	N	N	N	N
21 ***Smith***	N	Y	Y	Y	Y	Y	Y
22 ***DeLay***	Y	Y	Y	Y	Y	Y	Y
23 ***Bonilla***	N	N	N	N	N	N	Y
24 Frost	N	N	N	N	N	N	N
25 Bentsen	N	N	N	N	N	N	N
26 ***Armey***	N	Y	Y	Y	Y	Y	Y
27 Ortiz	N	N	N	N	N	N	N
28 Rodriguez	N	N	N	N	N	N	N
29 Green	N	N	N	Y	N	N	N
30 Johnson, E.B.	N	N	N	N	N	N	N
UTAH							
1 ***Hansen***	Y	Y	Y	N	N	N	Y
2 ***Cook***	?	?	?	?	?	?	?
3 ***Cannon***	Y	Y	Y	Y	Y	Y	Y
VERMONT							
AL *Sanders*	N	N	N	N	N	N	N
VIRGINIA							
1 ***Bateman***	N	N	N	N	N	N	Y
2 Pickett	N	N	N	N	N	N	N
3 Scott	N	N	N	N	N	N	N
4 Sisisky	N	N	N	N	N	N	N
5 *Goode*	Y	Y	N	N	N	N	N
6 ***Goodlatte***	?	?	?	?	?	?	?
7 ***Bliley***	N	N	N	N	Y	N	Y
8 Moran	N	N	N	N	N	N	N
9 Boucher	N	N	N	N	N	N	N
10 ***Wolf***	N	N	N	N	N	N	Y
11 ***Davis***	N	N	N	Y	N	N	N
WASHINGTON							
1 Inslee	Y	N	Y	Y	N	N	N
2 ***Metcalf***	Y	Y	Y	Y	N	N	Y
3 Baird	N	N	N	N	N	Y	N
4 ***Hastings***	Y	Y	Y	Y	Y	N	Y
5 ***Nethercutt***	Y	Y	Y	N	Y	N	Y
6 Dicks	N	N	N	N	N	N	N
7 McDermott	N	N	N	N	N	N	N
8 ***Dunn***	Y	N	Y	Y	N	Y	Y
9 Smith	N	N	N	Y	N	N	N
WEST VIRGINIA							
1 Mollohan	N	N	N	N	N	N	N
2 Wise	N	N	N	N	N	N	N
3 Rahall	N	N	N	N	N	N	N
WISCONSIN							
1 ***Ryan***	Y	Y	Y	Y	Y	Y	Y
2 Baldwin	N	N	N	N	N	N	N
3 Kind	N	N	N	N	N	N	N
4 Kleczka	N	N	N	N	N	N	N
5 Barrett	N	N	N	N	N	N	N
6 ***Petri***	N	Y	Y	N	Y	Y	Y
7 Obey	N	N	?	N	N	N	N
8 ***Green***	Y	N	Y	Y	Y	Y	Y
9 ***Sensenbrenner***	Y	Y	Y	Y	Y	Y	Y
WYOMING							
AL ***Cubin***	Y	Y	Y	N	Y	Y	Y

Southern states - Ala., Ark., Fla., Ga., Ky., La., Miss., N.C., Okla., S.C., Tenn., Texas, Va.

Key

Y Voted for (yea).
Paired for.
+ Announced for.
N Voted against (nay).
X Paired against.
– Announced against.
P Voted "present."
C Voted "present" to avoid possible conflict of interest.
? Did not vote or otherwise make a position known.

Democrats ***Republicans***
Independents

266. HR 4577. Fiscal 2001 Labor-HHS-Education Appropriations/Military Recruiting. Stearns, R-Fla., amendment that would prohibit the use of funds to bar military recruiting at secondary schools. Adopted 381-41: R 210-3; D 170-37 (ND 119-34, SD 51-3); I 1-1. June 13, 2000.

267. HR 4577. Fiscal 2001 Labor-HHS-Education Appropriations/21st Century Teachers. Wilson, R-N.M., amendment that would appropriate $25 million for the 21st Century Teacher Scholarship Act, pending authorization of the program, offset by an equal reduction for the Occupational Safety and Health Administration. Rejected 156-267: R 147-66; D 8-200 (ND 3-151, SD 5-49); I 1-1. June 13, 2000. A "nay" was a vote in support of the president's position.

268. HR 4577. Fiscal 2001 Labor-HHS-Education Appropriations/NIH. Sanders, I-Vt., amendment that would prohibit the National Institutes of Health (NIH) from using funds to grant a license on federally owned research or federally owned prescription drugs, except where NIH has determined that the drug will be made available to the public on reasonable terms. Adopted 313-109: R 118-95; D 193-14 (ND 144-10, SD 49-4); I 2-0. June 13, 2000.

269. HR 4577. Fiscal 2001 Labor-HHS-Education Appropriations/Across-the-Board Cut. Young, R-Fla., amendment that would reduce all discretionary account levels by 0.617 percent to keep the bill within its 302(b) allocation. Rejected 186-236: R 182-31; D 3-204 (ND 0-153, SD 3-51); I 1-1. June 13, 2000.

270. Procedural Motion/Journal. Approval of the House Journal of Tuesday, June 13, 2000. Approved 352-59: R 188-19; D 162-40 (ND 116-34, SD 46-6); I 2-0. June 14, 2000.

271. S 761. Electronic Signatures/Conference Report. Adoption of the conference report on the bill to promote electronic commerce and establish a minimum federal standard for the use and recognition of electronic signatures. The bill would ensure that electronic signatures are given the same legal validity and enforceability as written ones. Consumers would have to consent to the use of electronic records and be provided with information on how to access those records. Adopted 426-4: R 216-3; D 208-1 (ND 155-0, SD 53-1); I 2-0. June 14, 2000.

272. HR 4577. Fiscal 2001 Labor-HHS-Education Appropriations/Recommit. Obey, D-Wis., motion to recommit the bill to the House Appropriations Committee with instructions to reinstate fiscal 2002 funds for state block grants for child care that were eliminated under the rule for debate on the bill. Motion rejected 212-219: R 3-217; D 208-1 (ND 154-1, SD 54-0); I 1-1. June 14, 2000.

	266	267	268	269	270	271	272
ALABAMA							
1 ***Callahan***	Y	Y	N	Y	Y	Y	N
2 ***Everett***	Y	Y	Y	Y	Y	Y	N
3 ***Riley***	Y	Y	N	Y	N	Y	N
4 ***Aderholt***	Y	Y	Y	N	N	Y	N
5 Cramer	Y	N	Y	N	Y	Y	Y
6 ***Bachus***	Y	Y	Y	Y	Y	Y	N
7 Hilliard	Y	N	Y	N	N	Y	Y
ALASKA							
AL ***Young***	Y	Y	Y	Y	?	Y	N
ARIZONA							
1 ***Salmon***	Y	Y	N	Y	Y	Y	N
2 Pastor	Y	Y	Y	N	Y	Y	Y
3 ***Stump***	Y	Y	N	Y	Y	N	N
4 ***Shadegg***	Y	N	N	Y	Y	Y	N
5 ***Kolbe***	Y	Y	N	Y	Y	Y	N
6 ***Hayworth***	Y	Y	N	Y	Y	Y	N
ARKANSAS							
1 Berry	Y	N	Y	N	Y	Y	Y
2 Snyder	Y	N	N	N	Y	Y	Y
3 ***Hutchinson***	Y	N	Y	Y	?	Y	N
4 ***Dickey***	Y	Y	Y	Y	N	Y	N
CALIFORNIA							
1 Thompson	Y	N	Y	N	N	Y	Y
2 ***Herger***	Y	Y	Y	Y	Y	Y	N
3 ***Ose***	Y	Y	N	Y	Y	Y	N
4 ***Doolittle***	Y	Y	Y	Y	Y	Y	N
5 Matsui	Y	N	Y	?	Y	Y	Y
6 Woolsey	N	N	Y	N	Y	Y	Y
7 Miller, George	N	N	Y	N	N	Y	Y
8 Pelosi	N	N	Y	N	Y	Y	Y
9 Lee	N	N	Y	N	Y	Y	Y
10 Tauscher	Y	N	Y	N	Y	Y	Y
11 ***Pombo***	Y	Y	N	Y	Y	Y	N
12 Lantos	Y	N	Y	N	Y	Y	Y
13 Stark	N	N	Y	N	N	Y	Y
14 Eshoo	Y	N	N	N	Y	Y	Y
15 ***Campbell***	?	?	?	?	Y	Y	N
16 Lofgren	N	N	N	N	Y	Y	Y
17 Farr	N	N	N	N	Y	Y	Y
18 Condit	Y	N	Y	N	N	Y	Y
19 ***Radanovich***	Y	Y	Y	Y	Y	Y	N
20 Dooley	Y	N	N	N	Y	Y	Y
21 ***Thomas***	Y	Y	N	Y	Y	Y	N
22 Capps	Y	N	Y	N	Y	Y	Y
23 ***Gallegly***	Y	N	Y	N	Y	Y	N
24 Sherman	Y	N	N	N	Y	Y	Y
25 ***McKeon***	Y	N	N	Y	Y	Y	N
26 Berman	Y	N	Y	N	Y	Y	Y
27 ***Rogan***	Y	Y	Y	N	N	Y	N
28 ***Dreier***	Y	Y	N	Y	Y	Y	N
29 Waxman	Y	N	Y	N	Y	Y	Y
30 Becerra	Y	N	Y	N	Y	Y	Y
31 Martinez	Y	Y	Y	N	Y	Y	N
32 Dixon	Y	N	Y	N	Y	Y	Y
33 Roybal-Allard	Y	N	Y	N	Y	Y	Y
34 Napolitano	Y	N	Y	N	Y	Y	Y
35 Waters	N	N	Y	N	N	Y	Y
36 ***Kuykendall***	Y	Y	Y	N	Y	Y	N
37 Millender-McD.	Y	N	Y	N	Y	Y	Y
38 ***Horn***	Y	Y	Y	N	Y	Y	N
39 ***Royce***	Y	Y	Y	Y	Y	Y	N
40 ***Lewis***	Y	N	N	Y	Y	Y	N
41 ***Miller, Gary***	Y	N	N	Y	Y	Y	N
42 Baca	Y	N	Y	N	Y	Y	Y
43 ***Calvert***	Y	N	N	Y	Y	Y	N
44 ***Bono***	Y	Y	Y	Y	Y	Y	N
45 ***Rohrabacher***	Y	N	Y	Y	Y	Y	N
46 Sanchez	N	N	Y	N	Y	Y	Y
47 ***Cox***	Y	Y	N	Y	Y	Y	N
48 ***Packard***	Y	Y	N	Y	Y	Y	N
49 ***Bilbray***	Y	Y	Y	N	N	Y	N
50 Filner	N	N	Y	N	N	Y	Y
51 ***Cunningham***	Y	Y	N	Y	Y	Y	N
52 ***Hunter***	Y	Y	Y	Y	?	Y	N
COLORADO							
1 DeGette	N	N	Y	N	Y	Y	Y
2 Udall	N	N	Y	N	N	Y	Y
3 ***McInnis***	Y	Y	Y	Y	Y	Y	N
4 ***Schaffer***	Y	N	Y	Y	N	Y	N
5 ***Hefley***	Y	Y	Y	Y	N	Y	N
6 ***Tancredo***	Y	Y	Y	Y	P	Y	N
CONNECTICUT							
1 Larson	Y	N	Y	N	Y	Y	Y
2 Gejdenson	Y	N	Y	N	Y	Y	Y
3 DeLauro	Y	N	Y	N	Y	Y	Y
4 ***Shays***	Y	N	Y	Y	Y	Y	N
5 Maloney	Y	N	N	N	Y	Y	Y
6 ***Johnson***	Y	N	N	N	Y	Y	N
DELAWARE							
AL ***Castle***	Y	N	N	Y	Y	Y	N
FLORIDA							
1 ***Scarborough***	Y	Y	N	Y	Y	Y	N
2 Boyd	Y	N	Y	N	Y	Y	Y
3 Brown	Y	N	Y	N	Y	Y	Y
4 ***Fowler***	Y	Y	N	Y	Y	Y	N
5 Thurman	Y	N	Y	N	Y	Y	Y
6 ***Stearns***	Y	Y	N	Y	Y	Y	N
7 ***Mica***	Y	Y	N	Y	Y	Y	N
8 ***McCollum***	?	?	?	?	Y	Y	N
9 ***Bilirakis***	Y	Y	Y	Y	Y	Y	N
10 ***Young***	Y	Y	N	Y	N	Y	N
11 Davis	Y	N	Y	N	Y	Y	Y
12 ***Canady***	Y	Y	Y	Y	Y	Y	N
13 ***Miller***	Y	Y	Y	Y	Y	Y	N
14 ***Goss***	Y	Y	Y	Y	Y	Y	N
15 ***Weldon***	Y	N	N	N	Y	Y	N
16 ***Foley***	Y	Y	Y	Y	Y	Y	N
17 Meek	Y	N	Y	N	Y	Y	Y
18 ***Ros-Lehtinen***	Y	N	Y	Y	Y	Y	N
19 Wexler	Y	N	Y	N	?	Y	Y
20 Deutsch	Y	N	Y	N	Y	Y	Y
21 ***Diaz-Balart***	Y	N	Y	Y	Y	Y	N
22 ***Shaw***	Y	Y	Y	Y	Y	Y	N
23 Hastings	Y	N	Y	N	N	Y	Y
GEORGIA							
1 ***Kingston***	Y	Y	Y	Y	Y	Y	N
2 Bishop	Y	N	Y	N	Y	Y	Y
3 ***Collins***	Y	N	Y	Y	Y	Y	N
4 McKinney	N	N	Y	N	Y	Y	Y
5 Lewis	Y	N	Y	N	Y	Y	Y
6 ***Isakson***	Y	N	Y	Y	Y	Y	N
7 ***Barr***	Y	Y	Y	Y	Y	Y	N
8 ***Chambliss***	Y	Y	Y	Y	Y	Y	N
9 ***Deal***	Y	Y	Y	Y	Y	Y	N
10 ***Norwood***	Y	Y	Y	Y	Y	Y	N
11 ***Linder***	Y	Y	Y	Y	Y	Y	N
HAWAII							
1 Abercrombie	Y	N	Y	N	Y	Y	Y
2 Mink	Y	N	Y	N	Y	Y	Y
IDAHO							
1 ***Chenoweth-Hage***	Y	N	Y	Y	N	N	N
2 ***Simpson***	Y	Y	Y	Y	Y	Y	N
ILLINOIS							
1 Rush	Y	N	Y	N	Y	Y	Y
2 Jackson	N	N	Y	N	Y	Y	Y
3 Lipinski	Y	N	Y	N	Y	Y	Y
4 Gutierrez	Y	N	Y	N	N	Y	Y
5 Blagojevich	Y	N	Y	N	Y	Y	Y
6 ***Hyde***	Y	Y	Y	Y	Y	Y	N
7 Davis	Y	N	Y	N	Y	Y	Y
8 ***Crane***	Y	Y	N	Y	N	Y	N
9 Schakowsky	Y	N	Y	N	Y	Y	Y
10 ***Porter***	Y	N	N	Y	Y	Y	N
11 ***Weller***	Y	N	Y	Y	N	Y	N
12 Costello	Y	N	Y	N	N	Y	Y
13 ***Biggert***	Y	N	N	Y	Y	Y	N

ND Northern Democrats SD Southern Democrats

	266	267	268	269	270	271	272
14 ***Hastert***							N
15 ***Ewing***	Y	N	Y	Y	Y	Y	N
16 ***Manzullo***	Y	Y	Y	Y	Y	Y	N
17 Evans	Y	N	Y	N	N	Y	Y
18 ***LaHood***	Y	Y	Y	N	Y	Y	N
19 Phelps	Y	N	Y	N	Y	Y	Y
20 ***Shimkus***	Y	Y	Y	N	Y	Y	N
INDIANA							
1 Visclosky	Y	N	Y	N	N	Y	Y
2 ***McIntosh***	Y	Y	N	Y	?	Y	Y
3 Roemer	Y	N	Y	N	Y	Y	Y
4 ***Souder***	Y	Y	Y	Y	?	Y	N
5 ***Buyer***	Y	Y	N	Y	Y	Y	N
6 ***Burton***	Y	Y	Y	Y	?	Y	N
7 ***Pease***	Y	Y	N	Y	Y	Y	N
8 ***Hostettler***	Y	Y	N	Y	Y	Y	N
9 Hill	Y	N	Y	N	Y	Y	Y
10 Carson	Y	N	Y	N	Y	Y	Y
IOWA							
1 ***Leach***	Y	N	Y	N	Y	Y	N
2 ***Nussle***	Y	Y	Y	Y	Y	Y	N
3 Boswell	Y	N	Y	N	Y	Y	Y
4 ***Ganske***	Y	N	Y	N	Y	Y	N
5 ***Latham***	Y	Y	Y	Y	Y	Y	N
KANSAS							
1 ***Moran***	Y	Y	Y	Y	Y	Y	N
2 ***Ryun***	Y	N	N	Y	Y	Y	N
3 Moore	Y	N	Y	N	N	Y	Y
4 ***Tiahrt***	Y	Y	N	Y	Y	Y	N
KENTUCKY							
1 ***Whitfield***	Y	N	Y	Y	N	Y	N
2 ***Lewis***	Y	Y	Y	Y	Y	Y	N
3 ***Northup***	Y	N	Y	Y	Y	Y	N
4 Lucas	Y	N	N	N	Y	Y	Y
5 ***Rogers***	Y	Y	N	N	Y	Y	N
6 ***Fletcher***	Y	Y	Y	N	Y	Y	N
LOUISIANA							
1 ***Vitter***	Y	N	N	Y	Y	Y	N
2 Jefferson	Y	N	Y	N	?	Y	Y
3 ***Tauzin***	Y	Y	N	Y	Y	Y	N
4 ***McCrery***	Y	Y	N	Y	Y	Y	N
5 ***Cooksey***	Y	Y	N	Y	Y	Y	N
6 ***Baker***	Y	Y	N	Y	Y	Y	N
7 John	Y	N	Y	N	Y	Y	Y
MAINE							
1 Allen	Y	N	Y	N	Y	Y	Y
2 Baldacci	Y	N	Y	N	Y	Y	Y
MARYLAND							
1 ***Gilchrest***	Y	Y	Y	Y	Y	Y	N
2 ***Ehrlich***	Y	Y	Y	Y	Y	Y	N
3 Cardin	Y	N	Y	N	Y	Y	Y
4 Wynn	Y	N	Y	N	Y	Y	Y
5 Hoyer	Y	N	Y	N	Y	Y	Y
6 ***Bartlett***	Y	Y	Y	Y	Y	Y	N
7 Cummings	Y	N	Y	N	?	Y	Y
8 ***Morella***	N	N	N	N	Y	Y	Y
MASSACHUSETTS							
1 Olver	N	N	Y	N	N	Y	Y
2 Neal	Y	N	Y	N	Y	Y	Y
3 McGovern	N	N	Y	N	Y	Y	Y
4 Frank	N	N	Y	N	Y	Y	Y
5 Meehan	Y	N	Y	N	Y	Y	Y
6 Tierney	Y	N	Y	N	?	Y	Y
7 Markey	Y	N	Y	N	Y	Y	Y
8 Capuano	Y	N	Y	N	N	Y	Y
9 Moakley	Y	N	Y	N	Y	Y	Y
10 Delahunt	N	N	Y	N	?	Y	Y
MICHIGAN							
1 Stupak	Y	N	Y	N	N	Y	Y
2 ***Hoekstra***	Y	N	Y	Y	Y	Y	N
3 ***Ehlers***	Y	Y	Y	Y	Y	Y	N
4 ***Camp***	Y	Y	Y	N	Y	Y	N
5 Barcia	Y	N	Y	N	Y	Y	Y
6 ***Upton***	Y	Y	Y	N	Y	Y	N
7 ***Smith***	Y	N	N	Y	Y	Y	N
8 Stabenow	Y	N	Y	N	Y	Y	Y
9 Kildee	Y	N	Y	N	Y	Y	Y
10 Bonior	Y	N	Y	N	Y	Y	Y
11 ***Knollenberg***	Y	N	N	Y	Y	Y	N
12 Levin	Y	N	Y	N	Y	Y	Y
13 Rivers	N	N	Y	N	Y	Y	Y
14 Conyers	N	N	Y	N	Y	Y	Y
15 Kilpatrick	Y	N	Y	N	Y	Y	Y
16 Dingell	Y	N	Y	N	Y	Y	Y

	266	267	268	269	270	271	272
MINNESOTA							
1 ***Gutknecht***	Y	Y	Y	Y	N	Y	N
2 Minge	Y	N	Y	N	Y	Y	Y
3 ***Ramstad***	Y	Y	Y	N	N	Y	N
4 Vento	?	?	?	?	?	?	?
5 Sabo	Y	N	Y	N	N	Y	Y
6 Luther	Y	N	Y	N	Y	Y	Y
7 Peterson	Y	N	Y	N	N	Y	Y
8 Oberstar	Y	N	Y	N	N	Y	Y
MISSISSIPPI							
1 ***Wicker***	Y	Y	Y	Y	N	Y	N
2 Thompson	Y	N	Y	N	N	Y	Y
3 ***Pickering***	Y	Y	Y	Y	Y	Y	N
4 Shows	Y	N	Y	N	Y	Y	Y
5 Taylor	Y	Y	Y	Y	N	N	Y
MISSOURI							
1 Clay	Y	N	Y	N	N	Y	Y
2 ***Talent***	Y	Y	Y	Y	Y	Y	N
3 Gephardt	Y	N	Y	N	Y	Y	Y
4 Skelton	Y	N	Y	N	Y	Y	Y
5 McCarthy	Y	N	Y	N	Y	Y	Y
6 Danner	?	?	?	?	?	?	?
7 ***Blunt***	Y	Y	N	Y	Y	Y	N
8 ***Emerson***	Y	Y	Y	Y	Y	Y	N
9 ***Hulshof***	Y	Y	N	Y	N	Y	N
MONTANA							
AL ***Hill***	Y	Y	Y	Y	?	Y	N
NEBRASKA							
1 ***Bereuter***	Y	Y	N	Y	Y	Y	N
2 ***Terry***	Y	Y	N	Y	Y	Y	N
3 ***Barrett***	Y	Y	N	Y	Y	Y	N
NEVADA							
1 Berkley	Y	N	Y	N	Y	Y	Y
2 ***Gibbons***	Y	Y	N	Y	Y	Y	N
NEW HAMPSHIRE							
1 ***Sununu***	Y	N	N	Y	Y	Y	N
2 ***Bass***	Y	Y	Y	Y	Y	Y	N
NEW JERSEY							
1 Andrews	Y	N	Y	N	Y	Y	Y
2 ***LoBiondo***	Y	N	Y	N	N	Y	N
3 ***Saxton***	Y	N	Y	Y	Y	Y	N
4 ***Smith***	Y	N	Y	N	Y	Y	N
5 ***Roukema***	Y	N	N	Y	Y	Y	N
6 Pallone	?	?	?	?	Y	Y	Y
7 ***Franks***	?	?	?	?	Y	Y	N
8 Pascrell	Y	N	Y	N	Y	Y	Y
9 Rothman	Y	N	N	N	Y	Y	Y
10 Payne	N	N	Y	N	Y	Y	Y
11 ***Frelinghuysen***	Y	N	N	Y	Y	Y	N
12 Holt	N	N	N	N	Y	Y	Y
13 Menendez	Y	N	Y	N	Y	Y	Y
NEW MEXICO							
1 ***Wilson***	Y	Y	Y	N	Y	Y	N
2 ***Skeen***	Y	Y	N	Y	Y	Y	N
3 Udall	Y	N	Y	N	Y	Y	Y
NEW YORK							
1 Forbes	Y	N	Y	N	Y	Y	Y
2 ***Lazio***	Y	Y	Y	N	Y	Y	Y
3 ***King***	Y	N	Y	N	Y	Y	N
4 McCarthy	Y	N	Y	N	Y	Y	Y
5 Ackerman	Y	N	Y	N	Y	Y	Y
6 Meeks	Y	N	Y	N	Y	Y	Y
7 Crowley	Y	N	Y	N	Y	Y	Y
8 Nadler	N	N	Y	N	Y	Y	Y
9 Weiner	Y	N	Y	N	Y	Y	Y
10 Towns	N	N	Y	N	N	Y	Y
11 Owens	N	N	Y	N	?	Y	Y
12 Velázquez	Y	N	Y	N	N	Y	Y
13 ***Fossella***	Y	N	Y	Y	Y	Y	N
14 Maloney	Y	N	Y	N	Y	Y	Y
15 Rangel	N	N	N	N	Y	Y	Y
16 Serrano	N	N	Y	N	Y	Y	Y
17 Engel	Y	N	Y	N	Y	Y	Y
18 Lowey	Y	N	Y	N	Y	Y	Y
19 ***Kelly***	Y	N	N	N	Y	Y	N
20 ***Gilman***	Y	N	Y	N	Y	Y	N
21 McNulty	Y	N	Y	N	N	Y	Y
22 ***Sweeney***	Y	Y	Y	Y	N	Y	N
23 ***Boehlert***	Y	N	Y	Y	Y	Y	N
24 ***McHugh***	Y	N	Y	N	Y	Y	N
25 ***Walsh***	Y	N	Y	Y	Y	Y	N
26 Hinchey	Y	N	Y	N	N	Y	Y
27 ***Reynolds***	Y	Y	N	Y	Y	Y	N
28 Slaughter	Y	N	Y	N	N	Y	Y
29 LaFalce	Y	N	Y	N	Y	Y	Y

	266	267	268	269	270	271	272
30 ***Quinn***	Y	N	Y	N	Y	Y	N
31 ***Houghton***	Y	N	Y	N	Y	Y	N
NORTH CAROLINA							
1 Clayton	N	N	Y	N	Y	Y	Y
2 Etheridge	Y	N	Y	N	Y	Y	Y
3 ***Jones***	Y	N	Y	Y	Y	Y	N
4 Price	Y	N	Y	N	Y	Y	Y
5 ***Burr***	Y	Y	Y	Y	Y	Y	N
6 ***Coble***	Y	Y	Y	Y	Y	Y	N
7 McIntyre	Y	N	Y	N	Y	Y	Y
8 ***Hayes***	Y	Y	Y	N	Y	Y	N
9 ***Myrick***	Y	Y	N	Y	Y	Y	N
10 ***Ballenger***	Y	Y	N	Y	Y	Y	N
11 ***Taylor***	Y	Y	N	Y	Y	Y	N
12 Watt	N	N	Y	N	Y	Y	Y
NORTH DAKOTA							
AL Pomeroy	Y	N	Y	N	?	Y	Y
OHIO							
1 ***Chabot***	Y	N	Y	Y	Y	Y	N
2 ***Portman***	Y	Y	N	Y	Y	Y	N
3 Hall	Y	N	Y	N	Y	Y	Y
4 ***Oxley***	Y	Y	N	Y	Y	Y	N
5 ***Gillmor***	?	?	?	?	Y	Y	N
6 Strickland	Y	N	Y	N	N	Y	Y
7 ***Hobson***	Y	Y	Y	Y	Y	Y	N
8 ***Boehner***	Y	Y	N	Y	Y	Y	N
9 Kaptur	Y	N	Y	N	Y	Y	Y
10 Kucinich	N	N	Y	N	N	Y	Y
11 Jones	N	N	Y	N	N	Y	Y
12 ***Kasich***	Y	Y	N	Y	?	Y	N
13 Brown	N	N	Y	N	Y	Y	Y
14 Sawyer	Y	N	Y	N	Y	Y	Y
15 ***Pryce***	Y	Y	N	Y	Y	Y	N
16 ***Regula***	Y	Y	N	Y	Y	Y	N
17 Traficant	Y	N	Y	N	Y	Y	Y
18 ***Ney***	Y	N	Y	Y	Y	Y	N
19 ***LaTourette***	Y	N	Y	Y	Y	Y	N
OKLAHOMA							
1 ***Largent***	Y	Y	N	Y	Y	Y	N
2 ***Coburn***	Y	N	Y	Y	?	Y	N
3 ***Watkins***	Y	Y	N	Y	Y	Y	N
4 ***Watts***	+	+	−	+	Y	Y	N
5 ***Istook***	Y	Y	N	Y	Y	Y	N
6 ***Lucas***	Y	Y	N	Y	Y	Y	N
OREGON							
1 Wu	N	N	Y	N	N	Y	Y
2 ***Walden***	Y	Y	Y	Y	Y	Y	N
3 Blumenauer	P	N	Y	N	Y	Y	Y
4 DeFazio	N	Y	Y	N	N	Y	Y
5 Hooley	N	N	Y	N	N	Y	Y
PENNSYLVANIA							
1 Brady	Y	N	Y	N	N	Y	Y
2 Fattah	Y	N	Y	N	Y	Y	Y
3 Borski	Y	N	Y	N	N	Y	Y
4 Klink	Y	N	Y	N	Y	Y	Y
5 ***Peterson***	Y	Y	N	Y	Y	Y	N
6 Holden	Y	N	Y	N	Y	Y	Y
7 ***Weldon***	Y	N	Y	Y	Y	Y	N
8 ***Greenwood***	Y	Y	N	Y	Y	Y	N
9 ***Shuster***	Y	Y	N	Y	Y	Y	N
10 ***Sherwood***	Y	N	Y	Y	Y	Y	N
11 Kanjorski	Y	N	Y	N	Y	Y	Y
12 Murtha	Y	N	Y	N	Y	Y	Y
13 Hoeffel	Y	N	Y	N	Y	Y	Y
14 Coyne	Y	N	Y	N	Y	Y	Y
15 ***Toomey***	Y	N	Y	Y	Y	Y	N
16 ***Pitts***	Y	Y	N	Y	Y	Y	N
17 ***Gekas***	Y	N	Y	Y	Y	Y	N
18 Doyle	Y	N	Y	N	Y	Y	Y
19 ***Goodling***	Y	N	Y	Y	Y	Y	N
20 Mascara	Y	N	Y	N	Y	Y	Y
21 ***English***	Y	N	Y	Y	N	Y	N
RHODE ISLAND							
1 Kennedy	Y	N	Y	N	Y	Y	Y
2 Weygand	Y	N	Y	N	Y	Y	Y
SOUTH CAROLINA							
1 ***Sanford***	Y	N	N	Y	Y	Y	N
2 ***Spence***	Y	Y	Y	N	Y	Y	N
3 ***Graham***	Y	Y	Y	Y	Y	Y	N
4 ***DeMint***	?	?	?	?	Y	Y	N
5 Spratt	Y	N	Y	N	Y	Y	Y
6 Clyburn	Y	N	Y	N	Y	Y	Y
SOUTH DAKOTA							
AL ***Thune***	Y	Y	Y	Y	Y	Y	N

	266	267	268	269	270	271	272
TENNESSEE							
1 ***Jenkins***	Y	Y	Y	Y	Y	Y	N
2 ***Duncan***	Y	Y	Y	Y	Y	Y	N
3 ***Wamp***	Y	Y	Y	Y	Y	Y	N
4 ***Hilleary***	Y	Y	Y	N	Y	Y	N
5 Clement	Y	N	Y	N	Y	Y	Y
6 Gordon	Y	N	Y	N	Y	Y	Y
7 ***Bryant***	Y	Y	Y	Y	Y	Y	N
8 Tanner	Y	N	Y	N	Y	Y	Y
9 Ford	Y	N	Y	N	Y	Y	Y
TEXAS							
1 Sandlin	Y	N	Y	N	Y	Y	Y
2 Turner	Y	N	Y	N	Y	Y	Y
3 ***Johnson, Sam***	Y	N	N	Y	Y	Y	N
4 Hall	Y	Y	Y	Y	Y	Y	Y
5 ***Sessions***	Y	Y	Y	Y	Y	Y	N
6 ***Barton***	Y	Y	N	Y	?	Y	N
7 ***Archer***	Y	Y	N	Y	Y	Y	N
8 ***Brady***	Y	Y	N	Y	Y	Y	N
9 Lampson	Y	N	Y	N	Y	Y	Y
10 Doggett	Y	N	Y	N	Y	Y	Y
11 Edwards	Y	N	+	N	Y	Y	Y
12 ***Granger***	Y	Y	N	Y	Y	Y	N
13 ***Thornberry***	Y	Y	N	Y	Y	Y	N
14 ***Paul***	N	N	Y	Y	Y	N	N
15 Hinojosa	Y	N	Y	N	Y	Y	Y
16 Reyes	Y	N	Y	N	Y	Y	Y
17 Stenholm	Y	Y	Y	Y	N	Y	Y
18 Jackson-Lee	Y	N	Y	N	Y	Y	Y
19 ***Combest***	Y	Y	N	Y	Y	Y	N
20 Gonzalez	Y	N	N	N	Y	Y	Y
21 ***Smith***	Y	Y	N	Y	Y	Y	N
22 ***DeLay***	Y	Y	N	Y	?	Y	N
23 ***Bonilla***	Y	Y	N	Y	Y	Y	N
24 Frost	Y	N	Y	N	Y	Y	Y
25 Bentsen	Y	N	N	N	Y	Y	Y
26 ***Armey***	Y	Y	N	Y	Y	Y	N
27 Ortiz	Y	N	Y	N	Y	Y	Y
28 Rodriguez	Y	N	Y	N	Y	Y	Y
29 Green	Y	N	Y	N	Y	Y	Y
30 Johnson, E.B.	Y	N	Y	N	Y	Y	Y
UTAH							
1 ***Hansen***	Y	Y	N	Y	Y	Y	N
2 ***Cook***	?	?	?	?	?	?	?
3 ***Cannon***	Y	Y	N	Y	Y	Y	N
VERMONT							
AL *Sanders*	N	N	Y	N	Y	Y	Y
VIRGINIA							
1 ***Bateman***	N	N	N	Y	Y	Y	N
2 Pickett	Y	Y	Y	N	N	Y	Y
3 Scott	Y	N	Y	N	Y	Y	Y
4 Sisisky	Y	Y	Y	N	Y	Y	Y
5 *Goode*	Y	Y	Y	Y	Y	Y	N
6 ***Goodlatte***	?	?	?	?	Y	Y	N
7 ***Bliley***	Y	Y	N	Y	Y	Y	N
8 Moran	Y	N	Y	N	Y	Y	Y
9 Boucher	Y	N	Y	N	Y	Y	Y
10 ***Wolf***	Y	Y	Y	Y	Y	Y	N
11 ***Davis***	Y	Y	Y	Y	Y	Y	N
WASHINGTON							
1 Inslee	Y	N	Y	N	Y	Y	Y
2 ***Metcalf***	Y	N	Y	Y	Y	Y	N
3 Baird	Y	N	Y	N	N	Y	Y
4 ***Hastings***	Y	Y	N	Y	Y	Y	N
5 ***Nethercutt***	Y	Y	N	Y	Y	Y	N
6 Dicks	Y	N	Y	N	Y	Y	Y
7 McDermott	N	N	Y	N	N	Y	Y
8 ***Dunn***	Y	Y	N	Y	Y	Y	N
9 Smith	Y	N	N	N	Y	Y	Y
WEST VIRGINIA							
1 Mollohan	Y	N	Y	N	Y	Y	Y
2 Wise	Y	N	Y	N	Y	Y	Y
3 Rahall	Y	N	Y	N	Y	Y	Y
WISCONSIN							
1 ***Ryan***	Y	N	N	Y	Y	Y	N
2 Baldwin	N	N	Y	N	Y	Y	Y
3 Kind	Y	N	Y	N	Y	Y	Y
4 Kleczka	Y	N	Y	N	Y	Y	Y
5 Barrett	Y	N	Y	N	Y	Y	Y
6 ***Petri***	Y	N	Y	Y	Y	Y	N
7 Obey	Y	N	Y	N	Y	Y	Y
8 ***Green***	Y	N	Y	Y	Y	Y	N
9 ***Sensenbrenner***	Y	Y	N	Y	?	?	?
WYOMING							
AL ***Cubin***	Y	Y	N	Y	Y	Y	N

Southern states - Ala., Ark., Fla., Ga., Ky., La., Miss., N.C., Okla., S.C., Tenn., Texas, Va.

273. HR 4577. Fiscal 2001 Labor-HHS-Education Appropriations/Passage. Passage of the bill that would appropriate $351.8 billion for the Labor, Health and Human Services and Education departments and related agencies, which is a $12.3 billion increase in discretionary spending and an $11.5 billion increase in mandatory spending. The bill includes $20.5 billion for the National Institutes of Health, $8.3 billion for Pell grants and $6.6 billion for special education programs. The measure also would prohibit the Occupational Safety and Health Administration from using funds to establish any standards on ergonomic protection. Passed 217-214: R 213-7; D 3-206 (ND 2-153, SD 1-53); I 1-1. June 14, 2000.

274. HR 4578. Fiscal 2001 Interior Appropriations/Gas Efficiency. Sununu, R-N.H., amendment that would eliminate funding for the Energy Department's partnership for a new generation of vehicles program. A portion of the savings would go to the federal Treasury and the remainder would be split among the payment in lieu of taxes program for states and localities and the maintenance accounts of the Forest Service and the National Park Service. Adopted 214-211: R 145-71; D 67-140 (ND 51-102, SD 16-38); I 2-0. June 14, 2000. A "nay" was a vote in support of the president's position.

275. HR 4578. Fiscal 2001 Interior Appropriations/Fire Fighting. Hefley, R-Colo., amendment that would increase the Forest Service's fire-fighting fund by $4 million, offset by an equal reduction in funding for the Bureau of Land Management's wild horse and burro program. Adopted 364-55: R 174-41; D 188-14 (ND 141-9, SD 47-5); I 2-0. June 14, 2000.

276. HR 4578. Fiscal 2001 Interior Appropriations/Forestry. DeFazio, D-Ore., amendment that would increase National Forest System funding by $26 million and reduce funding for fossil energy research and development activities in the Energy Resource, Supply and Efficiency program by $53 million. Rejected 167-254: R 33-181; D 133-72 (ND 115-36, SD 18-36); I 1-1. June 14, 2000.

277. HR 4578. Fiscal 2001 Interior Appropriations/Tree Harvesting. Wu, D-Ore., amendment that would increase funding for the Forest Service's fish and wildlife management program by $15 million, offset by an equal reduction in the Forest Service's forest products account. Rejected 173-249: R 38-179; D 134-69 (ND 116-34, SD 18-35); I 1-1. June 14, 2000.

278. HR 4635. Fiscal 2001 VA-HUD Appropriations/Rule. Adoption of the rule (H Res 525) to provide for House floor consideration of the bill to appropriate $101.3 billion in fiscal 2001 for the departments of Veterans Affairs, Housing and Urban Development and other independent agencies. Adopted 232-182: R 215-0; D 16-181 (ND 10-136, SD 6-45); I 1-1. June 15, 2000.

279. HR 4578. Fiscal 2001 Interior Appropriations/Columbia Basin. Nethercutt, R-Wash., amendment to the Dicks, D-Wash., amendment that would reinstate a provision in the bill that would prevent funds from being used to continue developing a management plan for the Interior Department's Columbia basin ecosystem management project until federal agencies have completed an analysis of the project's impact on affected communities. Rejected 206-221: R 202-16; D 3-204 (ND 2-152, SD 1-52); I 1-1. June 15, 2000. A "nay" was a vote in support of the president's position.

Key

- Y Voted for (yea).
- # Paired for.
- + Announced for.
- N Voted against (nay).
- X Paired against.
- – Announced against.
- P Voted "present."
- C Voted "present" to avoid possible conflict of interest.
- ? Did not vote or otherwise make a position known.

•

Democrats ***Republicans***
Independents

	273	274	275	276	277	278	279
ALABAMA							
1 ***Callahan***	Y	?	?	N	N	Y	Y
2 ***Everett***	Y	Y	N	N	N	Y	Y
3 ***Riley***	Y	Y	Y	N	N	Y	Y
4 ***Aderholt***	Y	Y	Y	N	N	Y	Y
5 Cramer	N	N	Y	N	N	N	N
6 ***Bachus***	Y	N	Y	?	N	Y	Y
7 Hilliard	N	Y	?	Y	N	N	N
ALASKA							
AL ***Young***	Y	N	N	N	N	Y	Y
ARIZONA							
1 ***Salmon***	Y	Y	Y	Y	N	Y	Y
2 Pastor	N	N	N	N	Y	N	N
3 ***Stump***	Y	Y	Y	N	N	Y	Y
4 ***Shadegg***	Y	Y	Y	N	N	Y	Y
5 ***Kolbe***	Y	Y	N	N	N	Y	Y
6 ***Hayworth***	Y	Y	Y	N	N	Y	Y
ARKANSAS							
1 Berry	N	N	N	N	N	N	N
2 Snyder	N	N	Y	N	N	N	N
3 ***Hutchinson***	Y	Y	N	N	N	Y	Y
4 ***Dickey***	Y	Y	Y	N	N	Y	Y
CALIFORNIA							
1 Thompson	N	Y	Y	Y	N	N	N
2 ***Herger***	Y	Y	Y	N	N	Y	Y
3 ***Ose***	Y	N	N	N	N	Y	Y
4 ***Doolittle***	Y	Y	Y	N	N	?	Y
5 Matsui	N	N	Y	Y	Y	N	N
6 Woolsey	N	Y	Y	Y	Y	N	N
7 Miller, George	N	Y	Y	Y	Y	N	N
8 Pelosi	N	Y	Y	Y	Y	N	N
9 Lee	N	Y	Y	Y	Y	N	N
10 Tauscher	N	N	Y	Y	Y	N	N
11 ***Pombo***	Y	Y	Y	N	N	Y	Y
12 Lantos	N	N	Y	Y	Y	N	N
13 Stark	N	N	Y	Y	Y	N	N
14 Eshoo	N	Y	Y	Y	Y	N	N
15 ***Campbell***	Y	?	?	?	?	?	?
16 Lofgren	N	?	?	?	?	?	?
17 Farr	N	Y	N	Y	Y	N	N
18 Condit	N	Y	Y	Y	N	N	N
19 ***Radanovich***	Y	Y	Y	N	N	Y	Y
20 Dooley	N	N	Y	N	N	Y	N
21 ***Thomas***	Y	N	Y	N	N	Y	Y
22 Capps	N	Y	Y	Y	Y	N	N
23 ***Gallegly***	Y	Y	Y	N	N	Y	Y
24 Sherman	N	N	Y	Y	N	N	N
25 ***McKeon***	Y	N	Y	N	N	Y	Y
26 Berman	N	N	Y	Y	N	N	N
27 ***Rogan***	Y	Y	Y	N	N	Y	Y
28 ***Dreier***	Y	N	Y	N	N	Y	Y
29 Waxman	N	N	Y	Y	Y	N	N
30 Becerra	N	Y	Y	Y	Y	N	N
31 Martinez	Y	N	Y	?	?	Y	Y
32 Dixon	N	N	Y	Y	N	N	N
33 Roybal-Allard	N	N	Y	Y	Y	N	N
34 Napolitano	N	N	Y	N	Y	N	N
35 Waters	N	Y	Y	Y	Y	N	N
36 ***Kuykendall***	Y	N	Y	N	N	Y	Y
37 Millender-McD.	N	N	Y	Y	N	N	N
38 ***Horn***	Y	Y	Y	N	Y	Y	Y
39 ***Royce***	Y	Y	Y	Y	N	Y	Y
40 ***Lewis***	Y	N	Y	?	N	Y	Y
41 ***Miller, Gary***	Y	Y	N	N	N	Y	Y
42 Baca	N	N	Y	N	N	N	N
43 ***Calvert***	Y	Y	Y	N	N	Y	Y
44 ***Bono***	Y	Y	Y	N	N	Y	Y
45 ***Rohrabacher***	Y	Y	Y	Y	N	Y	Y
46 Sanchez	N	N	Y	Y	Y	N	N
47 ***Cox***	Y	Y	Y	Y	N	Y	Y
48 ***Packard***	Y	N	N	N	N	Y	Y
49 ***Bilbray***	Y	Y	Y	Y	Y	Y	Y
50 Filner	N	Y	Y	Y	Y	N	N
51 ***Cunningham***	Y	Y	Y	N	N	Y	Y
52 ***Hunter***	Y	Y	Y	N	N	Y	Y
COLORADO							
1 DeGette	N	N	Y	Y	Y	N	N
2 Udall	N	N	Y	Y	Y	N	N
3 ***McInnis***	Y	Y	Y	N	N	Y	Y
4 ***Schaffer***	N	Y	Y	N	N	Y	Y
5 ***Hefley***	Y	Y	Y	N	N	Y	Y
6 ***Tancredo***	Y	Y	Y	N	N	Y	Y
CONNECTICUT							
1 Larson	N	Y	Y	Y	Y	N	N
2 Gejdenson	N	N	Y	Y	Y	N	N
3 DeLauro	N	Y	Y	Y	Y	N	N
4 ***Shays***	Y	Y	Y	Y	Y	Y	N
5 Maloney	N	Y	Y	Y	Y	N	N
6 ***Johnson***	Y	Y	Y	N	Y	Y	N
DELAWARE							
AL ***Castle***	Y	N	N	Y	Y	Y	Y
FLORIDA							
1 ***Scarborough***	Y	Y	Y	Y	Y	Y	Y
2 Boyd	N	Y	?	N	N	N	N
3 Brown	N	N	Y	Y	Y	N	N
4 ***Fowler***	Y	Y	Y	N	N	Y	Y
5 Thurman	N	N	Y	N	N	?	N
6 ***Stearns***	Y	Y	Y	N	N	Y	Y
7 ***Mica***	Y	Y	Y	Y	N	Y	Y
8 ***McCollum***	Y	Y	Y	N	N	Y	Y
9 ***Bilirakis***	Y	N	Y	N	N	Y	Y
10 ***Young***	Y	N	N	N	N	?	?
11 Davis	N	N	Y	Y	Y	N	N
12 ***Canady***	Y	Y	N	N	N	Y	Y
13 ***Miller***	Y	Y	N	N	Y	Y	Y
14 ***Goss***	Y	N	N	N	Y	Y	Y
15 ***Weldon***	Y	Y	Y	N	N	Y	Y
16 ***Foley***	Y	Y	Y	Y	Y	Y	Y
17 Meek	N	N	N	Y	?	N	N
18 ***Ros-Lehtinen***	Y	N	Y	N	N	Y	Y
19 Wexler	N	Y	Y	Y	Y	N	N
20 Deutsch	N	Y	Y	Y	Y	N	N
21 ***Diaz-Balart***	Y	N	Y	N	N	Y	Y
22 ***Shaw***	Y	Y	Y	N	Y	Y	Y
23 Hastings	N	N	Y	Y	Y	N	N
GEORGIA							
1 ***Kingston***	Y	Y	Y	N	N	Y	Y
2 Bishop	N	N	Y	Y	N	N	N
3 ***Collins***	Y	Y	Y	N	N	Y	Y
4 McKinney	N	Y	Y	Y	Y	?	N
5 Lewis	N	Y	Y	Y	Y	N	N
6 ***Isakson***	Y	N	Y	N	N	Y	Y
7 ***Barr***	N	Y	Y	N	N	Y	Y
8 ***Chambliss***	Y	N	Y	N	N	Y	Y
9 ***Deal***	Y	Y	Y	N	N	Y	Y
10 ***Norwood***	Y	Y	Y	N	N	Y	Y
11 ***Linder***	Y	Y	Y	?	?	Y	Y
HAWAII							
1 Abercrombie	N	Y	Y	Y	Y	?	N
2 Mink	N	N	Y	Y	Y	N	N
IDAHO							
1 ***Chenoweth-Hage***	Y	Y	Y	N	N	?	Y
2 ***Simpson***	Y	N	N	N	N	Y	Y
ILLINOIS							
1 Rush	N	N	Y	N	Y	N	N
2 Jackson	N	N	Y	Y	Y	N	N
3 Lipinski	N	N	Y	Y	N	N	N
4 Gutierrez	N	N	Y	Y	Y	N	N
5 Blagojevich	N	Y	Y	Y	Y	N	N
6 ***Hyde***	Y	N	Y	N	N	Y	Y
7 Davis	N	N	Y	N	Y	N	N
8 ***Crane***	Y	Y	Y	N	N	Y	Y
9 Schakowsky	N	N	?	Y	Y	N	N
10 ***Porter***	Y	N	N	N	Y	Y	N
11 ***Weller***	Y	N	Y	N	N	Y	Y
12 Costello	N	Y	Y	Y	N	N	N
13 ***Biggert***	Y	N	N	N	N	Y	Y

ND Northern Democrats SD Southern Democrats

Member	273	274	275	276	277	278	279
14 **Hastert**	Y						
15 **Ewing**	Y	N	Y	N	N	Y	Y
16 **Manzullo**	Y	N	Y	N	N	Y	Y
17 Evans	N	Y	Y	Y	Y	N	N
18 **LaHood**	Y	N	N	N	N	Y	Y
19 Phelps	N	Y	Y	Y	N	N	N
20 **Shimkus**	Y	Y	Y	N	N	Y	Y
INDIANA							
1 Visclosky	N	N	N	N	N	+	N
2 **McIntosh**	Y	Y	Y	N	N	Y	Y
3 Roemer	N	N	Y	N	Y	N	N
4 **Souder**	Y	Y	Y	N	N	Y	Y
5 **Buyer**	Y	N	Y	N	N	Y	Y
6 **Burton**	Y	Y	Y	N	N	Y	Y
7 **Pease**	Y	Y	Y	N	Y	Y	Y
8 **Hostettler**	N	Y	Y	Y	N	Y	Y
9 Hill	N	N	Y	N	Y	N	N
10 Carson	N	N	Y	Y	Y	N	N
IOWA							
1 **Leach**	Y	Y	Y	Y	Y	Y	N
2 **Nussle**	Y	Y	N	N	N	Y	Y
3 Boswell	N	N	Y	Y	N	N	N
4 **Ganske**	Y	Y	Y	N	N	Y	Y
5 **Latham**	Y	Y	Y	N	N	Y	Y
KANSAS							
1 **Moran**	Y	Y	Y	N	Y	Y	Y
2 **Ryun**	Y	Y	Y	N	N	Y	Y
3 Moore	N	Y	Y	N	Y	N	N
4 **Tiahrt**	Y	Y	Y	N	N	Y	Y
KENTUCKY							
1 **Whitfield**	Y	Y	Y	N	N	Y	Y
2 **Lewis**	Y	Y	Y	N	N	Y	Y
3 **Northup**	Y	N	Y	N	N	Y	Y
4 Lucas	N	N	Y	N	N	N	N
5 **Rogers**	Y	N	Y	N	N	Y	Y
6 **Fletcher**	Y	Y	Y	N	N	Y	Y
LOUISIANA							
1 **Vitter**	Y	Y	Y	N	N	Y	Y
2 Jefferson	N	N	Y	N	Y	N	N
3 **Tauzin**	Y	Y	Y	N	N	Y	Y
4 **McCrery**	Y	Y	Y	N	N	Y	Y
5 **Cooksey**	Y	N	N	N	N	Y	Y
6 **Baker**	Y	N	Y	N	N	Y	Y
7 John	N	N	Y	N	N	N	N
MAINE							
1 Allen	N	N	Y	Y	Y	N	N
2 Baldacci	N	N	Y	N	N	N	N
MARYLAND							
1 **Gilchrest**	Y	N	Y	N	N	Y	Y
2 **Ehrlich**	Y	Y	Y	N	N	Y	Y
3 Cardin	N	N	Y	Y	Y	N	N
4 Wynn	N	N	Y	Y	Y	N	N
5 Hoyer	N	N	?	Y	Y	N	N
6 **Bartlett**	Y	Y	Y	N	N	Y	Y
7 Cummings	N	Y	Y	Y	Y	?	N
8 **Morella**	N	N	Y	Y	Y	Y	N
MASSACHUSETTS							
1 Olver	N	Y	Y	Y	Y	N	N
2 Neal	N	Y	Y	Y	Y	N	N
3 McGovern	N	Y	Y	Y	Y	N	N
4 Frank	N	N	Y	Y	Y	N	N
5 Meehan	N	Y	Y	Y	Y	N	N
6 Tierney	N	Y	Y	Y	Y	N	N
7 Markey	N	N	Y	Y	Y	N	N
8 Capuano	N	N	Y	Y	Y	N	N
9 Moakley	N	Y	Y	Y	Y	N	N
10 Delahunt	N	N	Y	Y	Y	N	N
MICHIGAN							
1 Stupak	N	N	Y	N	N	N	N
2 **Hoekstra**	Y	N	N	N	N	Y	Y
3 **Ehlers**	Y	N	Y	Y	Y	Y	Y
4 **Camp**	Y	N	Y	N	N	Y	Y
5 Barcia	N	N	Y	Y	Y	N	N
6 **Upton**	Y	N	Y	N	Y	Y	Y
7 **Smith**	Y	N	Y	N	N	Y	Y
8 Stabenow	N	N	Y	N	Y	N	N
9 Kildee	N	N	Y	Y	Y	N	N
10 Bonior	N	N	Y	Y	Y	N	N
11 **Knollenberg**	Y	N	N	N	N	Y	Y
12 Levin	N	N	Y	Y	Y	N	N
13 Rivers	N	N	N	Y	Y	N	N
14 Conyers	N	N	Y	Y	Y	N	N
15 Kilpatrick	N	N	Y	Y	Y	N	N
16 Dingell	N	N	Y	N	N	N	N
MINNESOTA							
1 **Gutknecht**	Y	Y	Y	N	N	Y	Y
2 Minge	N	Y	Y	Y	N	Y	N
3 **Ramstad**	Y	Y	Y	N	Y	Y	N
4 Vento	?	?	?	?	?	?	?
5 Sabo	N	N	N	Y	Y	N	N
6 Luther	N	Y	Y	Y	Y	N	N
7 Peterson	N	Y	Y	N	N	N	N
8 Oberstar	N	N	Y	Y	N	N	N
MISSISSIPPI							
1 **Wicker**	Y	Y	Y	N	N	Y	Y
2 Thompson	N	N	Y	Y	Y	N	N
3 **Pickering**	Y	Y	Y	N	N	Y	Y
4 Shows	N	Y	Y	N	N	Y	N
5 Taylor	N	Y	Y	Y	N	N	N
MISSOURI							
1 Clay	N	N	Y	?	?	N	N
2 **Talent**	Y	Y	Y	N	N	Y	Y
3 Gephardt	N	N	Y	Y	Y	N	N
4 Skelton	N	N	Y	N	N	N	N
5 McCarthy	N	N	Y	N	Y	N	N
6 Danner	?	?	?	?	?	?	?
7 **Blunt**	Y	N	N	N	N	Y	Y
8 **Emerson**	Y	Y	Y	N	N	Y	Y
9 **Hulshof**	Y	Y	Y	Y	N	Y	Y
MONTANA							
AL **Hill**	Y	Y	Y	N	N	Y	Y
NEBRASKA							
1 **Bereuter**	Y	Y	Y	N	N	Y	Y
2 **Terry**	Y	Y	Y	N	N	Y	Y
3 **Barrett**	Y	N	N	?	N	Y	Y
NEVADA							
1 Berkley	N	Y	N	Y	Y	N	N
2 **Gibbons**	Y	Y	N	N	N	Y	Y
NEW HAMPSHIRE							
1 **Sununu**	Y	Y	Y	Y	N	Y	Y
2 **Bass**	Y	Y	Y	Y	N	Y	Y
NEW JERSEY							
1 Andrews	N	Y	Y	Y	Y	N	N
2 **LoBiondo**	Y	Y	Y	Y	Y	Y	N
3 **Saxton**	Y	Y	Y	Y	Y	Y	N
4 **Smith**	Y	Y	Y	Y	Y	Y	N
5 **Roukema**	Y	Y	Y	N	Y	Y	N
6 Pallone	N	Y	Y	Y	Y	N	N
7 **Franks**	Y	N	Y	N	Y	Y	N
8 Pascrell	N	Y	Y	Y	Y	N	N
9 Rothman	N	Y	Y	Y	Y	N	N
10 Payne	N	Y	Y	Y	Y	N	N
11 **Frelinghuysen**	Y	Y	Y	N	Y	Y	Y
12 Holt	N	Y	Y	Y	Y	N	N
13 Menendez	N	Y	Y	Y	Y	N	N
NEW MEXICO							
1 **Wilson**	Y	N	Y	N	N	Y	Y
2 **Skeen**	Y	N	Y	N	N	Y	Y
3 Udall	N	Y	Y	N	Y	N	N
NEW YORK							
1 Forbes	N	Y	Y	Y	Y	N	N
2 **Lazio**	N	N	Y	Y	Y	Y	N
3 **King**	Y	N	Y	N	N	Y	Y
4 McCarthy	N	N	Y	N	Y	N	N
5 Ackerman	N	?	?	?	?	N	N
6 Meeks	N	N	Y	Y	Y	N	N
7 Crowley	N	N	Y	Y	Y	N	N
8 Nadler	N	N	N	Y	Y	?	N
9 Weiner	N	N	Y	Y	Y	N	N
10 Towns	N	N	Y	N	Y	N	N
11 Owens	N	N	Y	Y	Y	N	N
12 Velázquez	N	N	Y	Y	Y	N	N
13 **Fossella**	Y	Y	Y	N	Y	Y	Y
14 Maloney	N	N	Y	Y	Y	N	N
15 Rangel	N	N	?	N	N	N	N
16 Serrano	N	Y	Y	Y	Y	?	N
17 Engel	N	N	Y	Y	Y	N	N
18 Lowey	N	N	Y	Y	Y	N	N
19 **Kelly**	Y	N	Y	Y	Y	Y	N
20 **Gilman**	Y	N	Y	N	Y	Y	N
21 McNulty	N	N	Y	Y	Y	N	N
22 **Sweeney**	Y	N	Y	N	N	Y	Y
23 **Boehlert**	Y	N	Y	N	Y	Y	Y
24 **McHugh**	Y	N	Y	N	N	Y	Y
25 **Walsh**	Y	Y	Y	N	Y	Y	N
26 Hinchey	N	N	Y	Y	Y	N	N
27 **Reynolds**	Y	N	N	N	N	Y	Y
28 Slaughter	N	Y	Y	Y	Y	N	N
29 LaFalce	N	N	Y	Y	Y	N	N
30 **Quinn**	Y	N	N	N	N	Y	Y
31 **Houghton**	Y	N	Y	N	N	?	Y
NORTH CAROLINA							
1 Clayton	N	Y	Y	Y	N	N	N
2 Etheridge	N	N	Y	Y	Y	N	N
3 **Jones**	Y	Y	Y	Y	N	Y	Y
4 Price	N	Y	Y	Y	Y	N	N
5 **Burr**	Y	Y	Y	N	Y	N	Y
6 **Coble**	Y	Y	Y	N	N	Y	Y
7 McIntyre	N	N	Y	N	N	N	N
8 **Hayes**	Y	Y	Y	N	N	Y	Y
9 **Myrick**	Y	Y	Y	N	N	Y	?
10 **Ballenger**	Y	Y	Y	N	N	Y	Y
11 **Taylor**	Y	N	N	N	N	Y	Y
12 Watt	N	Y	Y	Y	Y	N	N
NORTH DAKOTA							
AL Pomeroy	N	N	Y	N	N	N	N
OHIO							
1 **Chabot**	Y	Y	Y	Y	Y	Y	Y
2 **Portman**	Y	N	Y	N	Y	Y	Y
3 Hall	N	N	Y	N	Y	N	N
4 **Oxley**	Y	N	Y	N	N	Y	Y
5 **Gillmor**	Y	Y	N	N	N	Y	Y
6 Strickland	N	Y	Y	N	N	N	N
7 **Hobson**	Y	N	N	N	N	Y	Y
8 **Boehner**	Y	N	Y	N	N	Y	Y
9 Kaptur	N	N	Y	N	Y	?	N
10 Kucinich	N	N	Y	Y	Y	N	N
11 Jones	N	N	Y	Y	Y	N	N
12 **Kasich**	Y	Y	Y	Y	N	Y	Y
13 Brown	N	Y	Y	Y	Y	N	N
14 Sawyer	N	N	Y	Y	Y	?	N
15 **Pryce**	Y	N	N	N	N	Y	Y
16 **Regula**	Y	N	N	N	N	Y	Y
17 Traficant	Y	N	Y	N	N	Y	Y
18 **Ney**	Y	N	Y	N	N	Y	Y
19 **LaTourette**	Y	N	N	N	N	Y	Y
OKLAHOMA							
1 **Largent**	Y	Y	Y	N	N	Y	Y
2 **Coburn**	Y	Y	Y	N	N	Y	Y
3 **Watkins**	Y	Y	Y	N	N	Y	Y
4 **Watts**	Y	Y	Y	N	N	Y	Y
5 **Istook**	Y	Y	Y	N	N	Y	Y
6 **Lucas**	Y	Y	Y	N	N	Y	Y
OREGON							
1 Wu	N	N	Y	Y	Y	N	N
2 **Walden**	Y	Y	N	Y	N	Y	Y
3 Blumenauer	N	Y	Y	Y	Y	N	N
4 DeFazio	N	N	Y	Y	Y	N	N
5 Hooley	N	N	Y	Y	Y	N	N
PENNSYLVANIA							
1 Brady	N	N	Y	N	N	N	N
2 Fattah	N	N	Y	Y	Y	N	N
3 Borski	N	N	Y	Y	Y	N	N
4 Klink	N	N	Y	N	N	N	N
5 **Peterson**	Y	Y	Y	N	N	Y	Y
6 Holden	N	N	Y	N	N	Y	N
7 **Weldon**	Y	Y	Y	N	Y	Y	Y
8 **Greenwood**	Y	?	?	N	Y	Y	Y
9 **Shuster**	Y	?	?	?	?	Y	Y
10 **Sherwood**	Y	N	Y	N	N	Y	Y
11 Kanjorski	N	N	Y	N	N	Y	N
12 Murtha	N	N	Y	N	?	Y	N
13 Hoeffel	N	Y	Y	Y	Y	N	N
14 Coyne	N	N	Y	Y	Y	N	N
15 **Toomey**	Y	Y	Y	N	N	Y	Y
16 **Pitts**	Y	Y	Y	N	N	Y	Y
17 **Gekas**	Y	Y	Y	N	N	Y	Y
18 Doyle	N	N	Y	N	N	Y	N
19 **Goodling**	Y	Y	N	N	N	Y	Y
20 Mascara	N	N	Y	N	N	N	N
21 **English**	Y	Y	Y	N	N	Y	Y
RHODE ISLAND							
1 Kennedy	N	N	Y	Y	Y	N	N
2 Weygand	N	N	Y	Y	Y	N	N
SOUTH CAROLINA							
1 **Sanford**	N	Y	Y	Y	Y	Y	Y
2 **Spence**	Y	Y	Y	N	N	Y	Y
3 **Graham**	Y	Y	Y	N	N	Y	Y
4 **DeMint**	Y	Y	Y	N	N	Y	Y
5 Spratt	N	N	Y	N	N	N	N
6 Clyburn	N	Y	Y	Y	Y	N	N
SOUTH DAKOTA							
AL **Thune**	Y	Y	Y	N	N	Y	Y
TENNESSEE							
1 **Jenkins**	Y	Y	Y	N	N	Y	Y
2 **Duncan**	Y	Y	Y	N	N	Y	Y
3 **Wamp**	Y	N	Y	N	N	Y	Y
4 **Hilleary**	Y	Y	Y	N	N	Y	Y
5 Clement	N	N	N	N	N	N	N
6 Gordon	N	N	Y	N	N	N	N
7 **Bryant**	Y	Y	Y	N	N	Y	Y
8 Tanner	N	Y	Y	N	N	Y	N
9 Ford	N	N	Y	Y	N	N	N
TEXAS							
1 Sandlin	N	N	Y	N	N	N	N
2 Turner	N	N	Y	N	N	N	N
3 **Johnson, Sam**	Y	Y	Y	N	N	Y	Y
4 Hall	N	Y	Y	N	N	N	N
5 **Sessions**	Y	Y	Y	N	N	Y	Y
6 **Barton**	Y	N	Y	N	N	Y	Y
7 **Archer**	Y	Y	Y	N	N	Y	Y
8 **Brady**	Y	N	Y	N	N	Y	Y
9 Lampson	N	N	Y	N	N	N	N
10 Doggett	N	Y	Y	Y	Y	N	N
11 Edwards	N	N	Y	N	N	N	N
12 **Granger**	Y	N	Y	N	N	Y	Y
13 **Thornberry**	Y	Y	Y	N	N	Y	Y
14 **Paul**	N	Y	Y	Y	Y	Y	Y
15 Hinojosa	N	N	Y	N	N	?	?
16 Reyes	N	N	Y	N	N	N	N
17 Stenholm	N	Y	Y	N	N	Y	Y
18 Jackson-Lee	N	N	Y	N	N	N	N
19 **Combest**	Y	Y	N	N	N	Y	Y
20 Gonzalez	N	N	N	N	Y	N	N
21 **Smith**	Y	Y	Y	N	Y	Y	Y
22 **DeLay**	Y	Y	Y	N	N	Y	Y
23 **Bonilla**	Y	N	N	N	N	Y	Y
24 Frost	N	N	Y	N	N	N	N
25 Bentsen	N	N	Y	N	N	N	N
26 **Armey**	Y	Y	N	N	N	?	Y
27 Ortiz	N	N	Y	N	N	N	N
28 Rodriguez	N	N	Y	N	N	N	N
29 Green	N	N	Y	N	N	N	N
30 Johnson, E.B.	N	N	Y	N	N	N	N
UTAH							
1 **Hansen**	Y	Y	Y	N	N	Y	Y
2 **Cook**	?	?	?	?	?	Y	Y
3 **Cannon**	Y	Y	N	N	N	Y	Y
VERMONT							
AL Sanders	N	Y	Y	Y	Y	N	N
VIRGINIA							
1 **Bateman**	Y	N	N	N	N	Y	Y
2 Pickett	Y	N	Y	N	N	N	N
3 Scott	N	N	Y	N	Y	N	N
4 Sisisky	N	N	Y	N	N	Y	N
5 Goode	Y	Y	Y	N	N	Y	Y
6 **Goodlatte**	Y	Y	Y	N	N	Y	Y
7 **Bliley**	Y	N	Y	N	N	Y	Y
8 Moran	N	N	N	N	Y	N	N
9 Boucher	N	N	Y	N	Y	Y	N
10 **Wolf**	Y	N	N	N	N	Y	Y
11 **Davis**	Y	Y	N	N	N	Y	Y
WASHINGTON							
1 Inslee	N	N	Y	Y	Y	N	N
2 **Metcalf**	Y	Y	Y	Y	N	Y	Y
3 Baird	N	N	Y	Y	N	N	N
4 **Hastings**	Y	Y	Y	N	N	Y	Y
5 **Nethercutt**	Y	Y	Y	N	N	Y	Y
6 Dicks	N	N	N	N	N	N	N
7 McDermott	N	N	Y	Y	Y	N	N
8 **Dunn**	Y	Y	Y	N	N	Y	Y
9 Smith	N	N	Y	Y	Y	N	N
WEST VIRGINIA							
1 Mollohan	N	N	N	N	N	Y	N
2 Wise	N	N	Y	N	N	N	N
3 Rahall	N	Y	Y	Y	Y	N	N
WISCONSIN							
1 **Ryan**	Y	Y	?	Y	N	Y	Y
2 Baldwin	N	Y	Y	Y	Y	N	N
3 Kind	N	Y	Y	Y	Y	N	N
4 Kleczka	N	N	Y	Y	Y	N	N
5 Barrett	N	Y	Y	Y	Y	?	N
6 **Petri**	Y	Y	Y	N	Y	Y	N
7 Obey	N	N	Y	Y	N	N	N
8 **Green**	Y	Y	Y	Y	N	Y	Y
9 **Sensenbrenner**	?	Y	Y	Y	Y	Y	Y
WYOMING							
AL **Cubin**	Y	Y	Y	N	N	Y	Y

Southern states - Ala., Ark., Fla., Ga., Ky., La., Miss., N.C., Okla., S.C., Tenn., Texas, Va.

Key

- Y Voted for (yea).
- \# Paired for.
- \+ Announced for.
- N Voted against (nay).
- X Paired against.
- – Announced against.
- P Voted "present."
- C Voted "present" to avoid possible conflict of interest.
- ? Did not vote or otherwise make a position known.

Democrats ***Republicans*** *Independents*

280. HR 4578. Fiscal 2001 Interior Appropriations/National Monuments. Hansen, R-Utah, amendment to the Dicks, D-Wash., amendment that would reinstate the bill's provision that would prohibit the Interior Department from using funds to design, plan or manage federal lands as national monuments that have been designated since 1999 under the Antiquities Act. Rejected 187-234: R 177-38; D 9-195 (ND 4-148, SD 5-47); I 1-1. June 15, 2000. A "nay" was a vote in support of the president's position.

281. HR 4578. Fiscal 2001 Interior Appropriations/National Monuments and Columbia Basin. Dicks, D-Wash., amendment that would nullify the bill's provision prohibiting the Interior Department from planning or managing national monuments, designating new wildlife refuges or finishing the Columbia basin ecosystem management plan. Adopted 243-177: R 46-169; D 196-7 (ND 149-3, SD 47-4); I 1-1. A "yea" was a vote in support of the president's position. June 15, 2000.

282. HR 4578. Fiscal 2001 Interior Appropriations/NEA. Stearns, R-Fla., amendment that would decrease the bill's appropriation for the National Endowment for the Arts by approximately $1.96 million and increase funds for wildland fire management. Rejected 152-256: R 139-74; D 12-181 (ND 5-140, SD 7-41); I 1-1. June 15, 2000.

283. HR 4578. Fiscal 2001 Interior Appropriations/Clean Coal Deferral. Slaughter, D-N.Y., amendment that would increase the amount of the deferral for clean coal technology program of the Department of Energy by $22 million from $67 million to $89 million. Adopted 207-204: R 25-189; D 181-14 (ND 139-6, SD 42-8); I 1-1. June 15, 2000.

284. HR 4578. Fiscal 2001 Interior Appropriations/Motion to Rise. Obey, D-Wis., motion to rise from the Committee of the Whole. Motion rejected 183-218: R 0-208; D 182-9 (ND 136-6, SD 46-3); I 1-1. June 15, 2000.

285. Quorum Call.* A quorum was present with 362 members (73 did not respond). June 15, 2000.

286. HR 4578. Fiscal 2001 Interior Appropriations/Heating Oil Reserve. Sanders, I-Vt., amendment that would provide $10 million for the creation of a home heating oil reserve in the Northeast. Rejected 193-195: R 23-181; D 169-13 (ND 129-8, SD 40-5); I 1-1. June 15, 2000.

**CQ does not include quorum calls in its vote charts.*

	280	281	282	283	284	286
ALABAMA						
1 ***Callahan***	Y	N	Y	N	N	?
2 ***Everett***	Y	N	Y	N	N	N
3 ***Riley***	Y	N	Y	N	N	N
4 ***Aderholt***	Y	N	Y	N	N	N
5 Cramer	N	Y	N	Y	Y	Y
6 ***Bachus***	Y	N	Y	N	N	N
7 Hilliard	N	Y	N	Y	Y	Y
ALASKA						
AL ***Young***	Y	N	Y	N	N	N
ARIZONA						
1 ***Salmon***	Y	N	Y	N	N	N
2 Pastor	N	Y	N	Y	Y	N
3 ***Stump***	Y	N	Y	N	N	N
4 ***Shadegg***	Y	N	Y	N	N	N
5 ***Kolbe***	Y	N	N	N	N	N
6 ***Hayworth***	Y	N	Y	N	N	N
ARKANSAS						
1 Berry	N	Y	N	Y	Y	N
2 Snyder	N	Y	N	Y	Y	Y
3 ***Hutchinson***	Y	N	N	N	N	N
4 ***Dickey***	Y	N	Y	N	N	N
CALIFORNIA						
1 Thompson	N	Y	N	Y	Y	Y
2 ***Herger***	Y	N	Y	N	N	N
3 ***Ose***	Y	N	N	N	N	N
4 ***Doolittle***	Y	N	Y	N	N	N
5 Matsui	N	Y	N	Y	Y	Y
6 Woolsey	N	Y	N	Y	Y	Y
7 Miller, George	N	Y	N	Y	Y	Y
8 Pelosi	N	Y	N	Y	Y	Y
9 Lee	N	Y	N	Y	Y	Y
10 Tauscher	N	Y	N	Y	Y	Y
11 ***Pombo***	Y	N	Y	N	N	N
12 Lantos	N	Y	N	Y	Y	Y
13 Stark	N	Y	N	Y	Y	?
14 Eshoo	N	Y	N	Y	Y	Y
15 ***Campbell***	?	?	?	?	?	?
16 Lofgren	?	?	?	?	?	?
17 Farr	N	Y	N	Y	Y	Y
18 Condit	N	Y	Y	N	Y	Y
19 ***Radanovich***	Y	N	Y	N	N	N
20 Dooley	Y	N	N	Y	Y	N
21 ***Thomas***	Y	N	N	N	N	N
22 Capps	N	Y	N	Y	Y	Y
23 ***Gallegly***	Y	N	N	N	N	N
24 Sherman	N	Y	N	Y	Y	Y
25 ***McKeon***	Y	N	N	N	N	N
26 Berman	N	Y	N	Y	Y	Y
27 ***Rogan***	Y	N	Y	N	N	N
28 ***Dreier***	Y	N	Y	N	N	N
29 Waxman	N	Y	N	Y	Y	Y
30 Becerra	?	?	?	?	?	?
31 Martinez	Y	N	N	Y	?	?
32 Dixon	N	Y	N	Y	Y	Y
33 Roybal-Allard	N	Y	N	Y	Y	Y
34 Napolitano	N	Y	N	Y	Y	Y
35 Waters	N	Y	N	Y	Y	Y
36 ***Kuykendall***	N	Y	N	Y	N	N
37 Millender-McD.	N	Y	N	Y	Y	Y
38 ***Horn***	N	Y	N	Y	?	N
39 ***Royce***	Y	N	Y	N	N	N
40 ***Lewis***	Y	Y	N	N	N	N
41 ***Miller, Gary***	Y	N	Y	N	N	N
42 Baca	N	Y	N	Y	N	Y
43 ***Calvert***	Y	N	Y	N	N	N
44 ***Bono***	Y	N	N	N	N	N
45 ***Rohrabacher***	Y	N	Y	N	N	N
46 Sanchez	N	Y	N	Y	Y	Y
47 ***Cox***	Y	N	Y	N	N	N
48 ***Packard***	Y	N	Y	N	N	N
49 ***Bilbray***	N	Y	N	Y	N	N
50 Filner	N	Y	N	Y	Y	?
51 ***Cunningham***	Y	N	Y	N	N	N
52 ***Hunter***	Y	N	Y	N	N	N
COLORADO						
1 DeGette	N	Y	Y	Y	Y	Y
2 Udall	N	Y	Y	Y	Y	Y
3 ***McInnis***	N	Y	Y	N	N	N
4 ***Schaffer***	Y	N	Y	N	N	N
5 ***Hefley***	Y	N	Y	N	N	N
6 ***Tancredo***	Y	N	Y	N	N	N
CONNECTICUT						
1 Larson	N	Y	N	Y	Y	Y
2 Gejdenson	N	Y	N	Y	Y	Y
3 DeLauro	N	Y	N	Y	Y	Y
4 ***Shays***	N	Y	N	Y	N	Y
5 Maloney	N	Y	N	Y	Y	Y
6 ***Johnson***	Y	Y	N	Y	N	Y
DELAWARE						
AL ***Castle***	N	Y	N	Y	N	N
FLORIDA						
1 ***Scarborough***	N	Y	Y	N	N	N
2 Boyd	N	Y	Y	Y	Y	Y
3 Brown	N	Y	N	Y	Y	Y
4 ***Fowler***	Y	N	N	N	N	N
5 Thurman	N	Y	Y	Y	Y	Y
6 ***Stearns***	Y	N	Y	N	N	N
7 ***Mica***	Y	N	N	N	N	N
8 ***McCollum***	?	?	?	?	?	?
9 ***Bilirakis***	Y	N	Y	N	N	N
10 ***Young***	?	?	?	?	?	N
11 Davis	N	Y	N	Y	Y	Y
12 ***Canady***	Y	N	Y	N	N	N
13 ***Miller***	Y	N	Y	N	N	N
14 ***Goss***	Y	N	Y	N	N	N
15 ***Weldon***	Y	N	Y	N	N	N
16 ***Foley***	N	Y	N	Y	N	N
17 Meek	N	Y	N	Y	Y	Y
18 ***Ros-Lehtinen***	Y	N	N	N	N	N
19 Wexler	N	Y	?	Y	Y	Y
20 Deutsch	N	Y	N	Y	Y	Y
21 ***Diaz-Balart***	Y	N	N	N	N	N
22 ***Shaw***	Y	N	N	N	N	N
23 Hastings	N	Y	N	Y	Y	Y
GEORGIA						
1 ***Kingston***	Y	N	Y	N	N	N
2 Bishop	N	Y	Y	Y	Y	Y
3 ***Collins***	Y	N	Y	N	N	N
4 McKinney	N	Y	N	Y	Y	Y
5 Lewis	N	Y	?	Y	Y	Y
6 ***Isakson***	Y	N	N	N	N	N
7 ***Barr***	Y	N	Y	N	N	N
8 ***Chambliss***	Y	N	Y	N	N	N
9 ***Deal***	Y	N	N	N	N	N
10 ***Norwood***	?	Y	Y	N	N	N
11 ***Linder***	Y	N	Y	N	N	N
HAWAII						
1 Abercrombie	N	Y	N	Y	Y	Y
2 Mink	N	Y	N	Y	Y	Y
IDAHO						
1 ***Chenoweth-Hage***	Y	N	Y	N	N	N
2 ***Simpson***	Y	Y	Y	N	N	N
ILLINOIS						
1 Rush	N	Y	N	Y	Y	Y
2 Jackson	N	Y	N	Y	Y	Y
3 Lipinski	N	Y	N	N	Y	N
4 Gutierrez	N	Y	N	Y	Y	Y
5 Blagojevich	N	Y	N	Y	Y	Y
6 ***Hyde***	Y	N	Y	N	N	N
7 Davis	N	Y	N	Y	Y	Y
8 ***Crane***	Y	N	Y	N	N	?
9 Schakowsky	N	Y	N	Y	Y	Y
10 ***Porter***	N	Y	N	Y	N	N
11 ***Weller***	Y	Y	Y	N	N	N
12 Costello	N	Y	?	?	?	?
13 ***Biggert***	N	Y	N	N	N	N

ND Northern Democrats SD Southern Democrats

	280	281	282	283	284	286
14 ***Hastert***				N	N	N
15 ***Ewing***	Y	N	N	N	N	N
16 ***Manzullo***	Y	N	Y	N	N	N
17 Evans	N	Y	N	Y	Y	Y
18 ***LaHood***	Y	Y	N	Y	N	N
19 Phelps	N	Y	N	Y	Y	Y
20 ***Shimkus***	Y	N	N	N	N	N
INDIANA						
1 Visclosky	N	Y	N	Y	Y	Y
2 ***McIntosh***	Y	Y	?	?	?	N
3 Roemer	N	Y	N	Y	N	?
4 ***Souder***	Y	N	N	N	N	N
5 ***Buyer***	Y	N	Y	N	N	N
6 ***Burton***	Y	N	Y	N	N	N
7 ***Pease***	Y	Y	Y	N	N	N
8 ***Hostettler***	Y	N	Y	N	N	N
9 Hill	N	Y	N	Y	Y	Y
10 Carson	N	Y	N	Y	Y	Y
IOWA						
1 ***Leach***	N	Y	N	Y	N	?
2 ***Nussle***	Y	?	Y	N	N	N
3 Boswell	N	Y	N	Y	N	Y
4 ***Ganske***	N	Y	N	N	N	N
5 ***Latham***	Y	Y	Y	N	N	N
KANSAS						
1 ***Moran***	Y	N	N	N	N	N
2 ***Ryun***	Y	N	Y	N	N	N
3 Moore	N	Y	N	Y	Y	Y
4 ***Tiahrt***	Y	N	Y	N	N	N
KENTUCKY						
1 ***Whitfield***	Y	N	Y	N	N	N
2 ***Lewis***	Y	N	Y	N	N	N
3 ***Northup***	Y	N	N	N	N	N
4 Lucas	N	Y	N	Y	Y	Y
5 ***Rogers***	Y	N	Y	N	N	N
6 ***Fletcher***	Y	N	Y	N	N	N
LOUISIANA						
1 ***Vitter***	Y	N	Y	N	N	N
2 Jefferson	N	?	?	?	?	?
3 ***Tauzin***	Y	N	Y	N	N	N
4 ***McCrery***	Y	N	Y	N	N	N
5 ***Cooksey***	Y	N	?	?	?	?
6 ***Baker***	Y	N	N	N	N	N
7 John	N	Y	N	Y	Y	N
MAINE						
1 Allen	N	Y	N	Y	Y	Y
2 Baldacci	N	Y	N	Y	Y	Y
MARYLAND						
1 ***Gilchrest***	N	Y	Y	N	N	N
2 ***Ehrlich***	Y	N	Y	N	N	N
3 Cardin	N	Y	N	Y	Y	Y
4 Wynn	N	Y	N	Y	Y	Y
5 Hoyer	N	Y	N	Y	Y	Y
6 ***Bartlett***	Y	N	Y	N	N	N
7 Cummings	N	Y	N	Y	Y	Y
8 ***Morella***	N	Y	N	Y	N	Y
MASSACHUSETTS						
1 Olver	N	Y	N	Y	Y	Y
2 Neal	N	Y	N	Y	Y	Y
3 McGovern	N	Y	N	Y	Y	Y
4 Frank	N	Y	N	Y	Y	Y
5 Meehan	N	Y	N	Y	Y	Y
6 Tierney	N	Y	N	Y	Y	Y
7 Markey	N	Y	N	Y	Y	Y
8 Capuano	N	Y	N	Y	Y	Y
9 Moakley	N	Y	N	Y	Y	Y
10 Delahunt	N	Y	N	Y	Y	Y
MICHIGAN						
1 Stupak	N	Y	N	N	Y	Y
2 ***Hoekstra***	N	Y	N	N	N	?
3 ***Ehlers***	N	Y	N	N	N	N
4 ***Camp***	Y	N	N	N	N	N
5 Barcia	N	Y	N	Y	Y	Y
6 ***Upton***	N	Y	N	N	N	N
7 ***Smith***	Y	N	N	N	?	N
8 Stabenow	N	Y	N	Y	Y	Y
9 Kildee	N	Y	N	Y	Y	Y
10 Bonior	N	Y	N	Y	Y	Y
11 ***Knollenberg***	Y	N	N	N	N	N
12 Levin	N	Y	N	Y	Y	Y
13 Rivers	N	Y	N	Y	Y	Y
14 Conyers	N	Y	N	Y	Y	Y
15 Kilpatrick	N	Y	N	Y	Y	Y
16 Dingell	N	Y	N	Y	Y	Y

	280	281	282	283	284	286
MINNESOTA						
1 ***Gutknecht***	Y	N	Y	N	N	N
2 Minge	N	Y	N	Y	N	Y
3 ***Ramstad***	N	Y	N	Y	N	N
4 Vento	?	?	?	?	?	?
5 Sabo	N	Y	N	Y	Y	Y
6 Luther	N	Y	N	Y	Y	Y
7 Peterson	Y	Y	N	N	Y	Y
8 Oberstar	N	Y	N	Y	Y	Y
MISSISSIPPI						
1 ***Wicker***	Y	N	Y	N	N	?
2 Thompson	N	Y	N	Y	Y	Y
3 ***Pickering***	Y	N	Y	N	N	N
4 Shows	?	?	?	?	?	?
5 Taylor	N	Y	Y	N	Y	Y
MISSOURI						
1 Clay	N	Y	N	Y	Y	Y
2 ***Talent***	Y	N	Y	N	N	Y
3 Gephardt	N	Y	N	Y	Y	Y
4 Skelton	N	Y	Y	N	Y	?
5 McCarthy	N	Y	N	Y	Y	Y
6 Danner	?	?	?	?	?	?
7 ***Blunt***	Y	N	Y	N	N	N
8 ***Emerson***	Y	N	Y	N	N	N
9 ***Hulshof***	Y	N	Y	N	N	N
MONTANA						
AL ***Hill***	Y	N	Y	N	N	N
NEBRASKA						
1 ***Bereuter***	Y	N	N	Y	N	N
2 ***Terry***	Y	N	Y	N	N	N
3 ***Barrett***	Y	N	Y	N	N	N
NEVADA						
1 Berkley	N	Y	N	Y	Y	Y
2 ***Gibbons***	Y	N	Y	N	N	N
NEW HAMPSHIRE						
1 ***Sununu***	Y	N	Y	N	N	N
2 ***Bass***	N	Y	N	N	N	Y
NEW JERSEY						
1 Andrews	N	Y	N	Y	Y	Y
2 ***LoBiondo***	N	Y	N	Y	N	Y
3 ***Saxton***	N	Y	N	N	N	Y
4 ***Smith***	N	Y	Y	N	N	Y
5 ***Roukema***	N	Y	N	Y	N	?
6 Pallone	N	Y	N	Y	Y	Y
7 ***Franks***	?	?	N	Y	N	Y
8 Pascrell	N	Y	N	Y	Y	Y
9 Rothman	N	Y	N	Y	Y	Y
10 Payne	N	Y	N	Y	Y	Y
11 ***Frelinghuysen***	N	Y	N	Y	N	Y
12 Holt	N	Y	N	Y	Y	Y
13 Menendez	N	Y	N	Y	Y	Y
NEW MEXICO						
1 ***Wilson***	Y	N	Y	N	N	N
2 ***Skeen***	Y	N	N	N	N	N
3 Udall	N	Y	Y	Y	Y	Y
NEW YORK						
1 Forbes	N	Y	N	Y	Y	Y
2 ***Lazio***	N	Y	N	Y	N	?
3 ***King***	Y	N	Y	N	N	Y
4 McCarthy	N	Y	N	Y	Y	Y
5 Ackerman	N	Y	N	Y	Y	Y
6 Meeks	N	Y	N	Y	Y	Y
7 Crowley	N	Y	N	Y	Y	Y
8 Nadler	N	Y	N	Y	?	?
9 Weiner	N	Y	N	Y	Y	Y
10 Towns	N	Y	N	Y	Y	Y
11 Owens	N	Y	N	Y	Y	Y
12 Velázquez	N	Y	?	?	?	?
13 ***Fossella***	Y	N	Y	N	N	Y
14 Maloney	N	Y	N	Y	Y	Y
15 Rangel	N	Y	?	?	?	?
16 Serrano	N	Y	?	?	?	?
17 Engel	N	Y	?	?	?	?
18 Lowey	N	Y	N	Y	Y	Y
19 ***Kelly***	N	Y	N	Y	N	Y
20 ***Gilman***	N	Y	N	Y	N	Y
21 McNulty	N	Y	N	Y	Y	Y
22 ***Sweeney***	Y	N	N	N	N	Y
23 ***Boehlert***	N	Y	N	Y	N	Y
24 ***McHugh***	Y	N	N	N	N	Y
25 ***Walsh***	N	Y	N	N	N	Y
26 Hinchey	N	Y	N	Y	Y	Y
27 ***Reynolds***	N	N	N	N	N	Y
28 Slaughter	N	Y	N	Y	Y	Y
29 LaFalce	N	Y	N	Y	Y	Y

	280	281	282	283	284	286
30 ***Quinn***	N	Y	N	N	N	Y
31 ***Houghton***	N	N	N	Y	N	Y
NORTH CAROLINA						
1 Clayton	N	Y	N	Y	Y	Y
2 Etheridge	N	Y	N	Y	Y	Y
3 ***Jones***	Y	N	Y	N	N	N
4 Price	N	Y	N	Y	Y	Y
5 ***Burr***	Y	N	N	N	N	N
6 ***Coble***	Y	N	Y	N	N	N
7 McIntyre	N	Y	N	N	Y	?
8 ***Hayes***	Y	N	Y	N	N	N
9 ***Myrick***	Y	N	Y	N	N	?
10 ***Ballenger***	Y	N	N	Y	N	N
11 ***Taylor***	Y	N	Y	N	N	N
12 Watt	N	Y	N	Y	N	Y
NORTH DAKOTA						
AL Pomeroy	N	Y	N	Y	Y	Y
OHIO						
1 ***Chabot***	Y	N	Y	N	N	N
2 ***Portman***	Y	N	Y	N	N	N
3 Hall	N	Y	N	Y	Y	?
4 ***Oxley***	Y	N	?	?	?	?
5 ***Gillmor***	Y	N	N	N	N	N
6 Strickland	N	Y	N	Y	Y	Y
7 ***Hobson***	N	Y	N	N	N	N
8 ***Boehner***	Y	N	Y	N	N	N
9 Kaptur	N	Y	N	Y	Y	Y
10 Kucinich	N	Y	N	Y	Y	Y
11 Jones	?	Y	N	Y	Y	Y
12 ***Kasich***	N	Y	Y	N	?	?
13 Brown	N	Y	N	Y	Y	Y
14 Sawyer	N	Y	N	Y	Y	N
15 ***Pryce***	Y	N	N	N	N	N
16 ***Regula***	Y	N	N	N	N	N
17 Traficant	Y	N	N	N	N	N
18 ***Ney***	Y	N	Y	N	N	N
19 ***LaTourette***	Y	Y	N	N	N	N
OKLAHOMA						
1 ***Largent***	Y	N	Y	N	N	N
2 ***Coburn***	Y	N	Y	N	N	N
3 ***Watkins***	Y	N	Y	N	N	N
4 ***Watts***	Y	N	Y	N	N	N
5 ***Istook***	Y	N	Y	N	?	N
6 ***Lucas***	Y	N	Y	N	N	N
OREGON						
1 Wu	N	Y	N	Y	Y	N
2 ***Walden***	Y	N	Y	N	N	N
3 Blumenauer	N	Y	?	?	?	?
4 DeFazio	N	Y	N	Y	Y	Y
5 Hooley	N	Y	?	?	?	?
PENNSYLVANIA						
1 Brady	N	Y	N	Y	Y	Y
2 Fattah	N	Y	N	Y	Y	Y
3 Borski	N	Y	N	Y	Y	Y
4 Klink	N	Y	?	?	?	?
5 ***Peterson***	Y	N	Y	N	N	N
6 Holden	N	Y	N	Y	Y	Y
7 ***Weldon***	N	Y	Y	N	N	N
8 ***Greenwood***	?	?	?	?	?	?
9 ***Shuster***	Y	N	Y	N	?	?
10 ***Sherwood***	Y	N	N	N	N	Y
11 Kanjorski	N	Y	N	Y	Y	Y
12 Murtha	N	Y	N	Y	Y	N
13 Hoeffel	N	Y	N	Y	Y	Y
14 Coyne	N	Y	N	Y	Y	Y
15 ***Toomey***	Y	N	?	?	?	?
16 ***Pitts***	Y	N	Y	N	N	N
17 ***Gekas***	Y	N	Y	N	N	N
18 Doyle	N	Y	N	Y	Y	Y
19 ***Goodling***	Y	N	Y	N	N	Y
20 Mascara	N	Y	N	Y	Y	Y
21 ***English***	N	Y	N	N	N	N
RHODE ISLAND						
1 Kennedy	N	Y	N	Y	Y	Y
2 Weygand	N	Y	N	Y	Y	Y
SOUTH CAROLINA						
1 ***Sanford***	Y	N	Y	N	N	N
2 ***Spence***	Y	N	Y	N	N	N
3 ***Graham***	Y	N	Y	N	N	N
4 ***DeMint***	Y	N	Y	N	N	N
5 Spratt	N	Y	N	Y	Y	?
6 Clyburn	N	Y	N	Y	Y	Y
SOUTH DAKOTA						
AL ***Thune***	Y	N	N	N	N	N

	280	281	282	283	284	286
TENNESSEE						
1 ***Jenkins***	Y	N	Y	N	N	N
2 ***Duncan***	Y	N	Y	N	N	N
3 ***Wamp***	Y	N	Y	N	N	N
4 ***Hilleary***	Y	N	Y	N	N	N
5 Clement	N	Y	N	Y	Y	Y
6 Gordon	N	Y	N	Y	Y	Y
7 ***Bryant***	Y	N	Y	N	N	N
8 Tanner	N	Y	N	N	Y	Y
9 Ford	N	Y	N	Y	Y	Y
TEXAS						
1 Sandlin	N	Y	N	Y	Y	N
2 Turner	N	Y	Y	Y	Y	Y
3 ***Johnson, Sam***	Y	N	Y	N	N	N
4 Hall	Y	N	Y	N	N	N
5 ***Sessions***	Y	N	Y	N	N	N
6 ***Barton***	Y	N	Y	N	N	?
7 ***Archer***	Y	N	Y	N	N	N
8 ***Brady***	Y	N	Y	N	N	N
9 Lampson	N	Y	N	Y	Y	Y
10 Doggett	N	Y	N	Y	Y	Y
11 Edwards	N	Y	N	Y	Y	Y
12 ***Granger***	Y	N	N	N	N	N
13 ***Thornberry***	Y	N	Y	N	N	N
14 ***Paul***	Y	N	Y	N	N	N
15 Hinojosa	?	?	?	?	?	?
16 Reyes	N	Y	N	Y	Y	Y
17 Stenholm	Y	N	N	N	Y	Y
18 Jackson-Lee	N	Y	N	Y	N	Y
19 ***Combest***	Y	N	Y	N	N	N
20 Gonzalez	N	Y	N	Y	Y	Y
21 ***Smith***	Y	N	Y	N	N	N
22 ***DeLay***	Y	N	Y	N	N	N
23 ***Bonilla***	Y	N	Y	N	N	N
24 Frost	N	Y	N	Y	Y	Y
25 Bentsen	N	Y	N	Y	Y	Y
26 ***Armey***	Y	N	Y	N	N	N
27 Ortiz	Y	Y	N	Y	Y	Y
28 Rodriguez	N	Y	N	Y	Y	Y
29 Green	N	Y	N	Y	Y	?
30 Johnson, E.B.	N	Y	N	Y	Y	Y
UTAH						
1 ***Hansen***	Y	N	Y	N	N	N
2 ***Cook***	Y	N	N	Y	N	N
3 ***Cannon***	Y	N	Y	N	N	N
VERMONT						
AL *Sanders*	N	Y	N	Y	Y	Y
VIRGINIA						
1 ***Bateman***	Y	N	Y	N	N	N
2 Pickett	Y	N	N	N	Y	N
3 Scott	N	Y	N	Y	?	Y
4 Sisisky	Y	N	N	N	Y	?
5 *Goode*	Y	N	Y	N	N	N
6 ***Goodlatte***	Y	N	Y	N	N	N
7 ***Bliley***	Y	N	Y	N	?	?
8 Moran	N	Y	N	Y	Y	?
9 Boucher	N	Y	?	?	?	?
10 ***Wolf***	Y	N	N	N	N	N
11 ***Davis***	N	Y	N	N	N	N
WASHINGTON						
1 Inslee	N	Y	N	Y	Y	Y
2 ***Metcalf***	Y	N	Y	N	N	N
3 Baird	N	Y	N	Y	Y	Y
4 ***Hastings***	Y	N	Y	N	N	N
5 ***Nethercutt***	Y	N	N	N	N	N
6 Dicks	N	Y	N	Y	Y	Y
7 McDermott	N	Y	N	Y	?	?
8 ***Dunn***	Y	N	Y	N	N	N
9 Smith	N	Y	N	N	Y	N
WEST VIRGINIA						
1 Mollohan	N	?	N	Y	Y	Y
2 Wise	N	Y	N	Y	Y	Y
3 Rahall	N	Y	N	Y	Y	Y
WISCONSIN						
1 ***Ryan***	Y	N	Y	N	N	N
2 Baldwin	N	Y	N	Y	Y	Y
3 Kind	N	Y	N	Y	N	Y
4 Kleczka	N	Y	N	Y	Y	Y
5 Barrett	N	Y	N	Y	Y	Y
6 ***Petri***	N	Y	Y	N	N	N
7 Obey	N	Y	N	Y	Y	Y
8 ***Green***	Y	N	Y	N	N	N
9 ***Sensenbrenner***	Y	N	Y	N	N	N
WYOMING						
AL ***Cubin***	Y	N	Y	N	N	N

Southern states - Ala., Ark., Fla., Ga., Ky., La., Miss., N.C., Okla., S.C., Tenn., Texas, Va.

287. HR 4578. Fiscal 2001 Interior Appropriations/Motion to Rise. Doggett, D-Texas, motion to rise from the Committee of the Whole. Motion rejected 169-214: R 2-201; D 166-12 (ND 125-9, SD 41-3); I 1-1. June 15, 2000.

288. HR 4578. Fiscal 2001 Interior Appropriations/Columbia Basin. Nethercutt, R-Wash., amendment that would prevent funds from being used to continue developing a management plan for the Interior Department's Columbia basin ecosystem management project until federal agencies have completed an analysis of the project's impact on affected communities. Adopted 197-180: R 194-13; D 2-166 (ND 1-129, SD 1-37); I 1-1. June 15, 2000. A "nay" was a vote in support of the president's position.

289. HR 4578. Fiscal 2001 Interior Appropriations/Indian Casinos. Weldon, R-Fla., amendment that would prohibit "casino-style" gambling on Native American lands under Interior Department regulations issued in April 1999 until two federal court cases have been adjudicated. Rejected 167-205: R 148-56; D 18-148 (ND 9-119, SD 9-29); I 1-1. June 16, 2000.

290. HR 4578. Fiscal 2001 Interior Appropriations/Recommit. Dicks, D-Wash., motion to recommit the bill to the House Appropriations Committee with instructions to defer an additional $22 million from the clean coal technology program to increase funding for the National Endowment for the Arts, National Endowment for the Humanities and Institute for Museum and Library Services. Motion rejected 184-188: R 21-182; D 162-5 (ND 127-2, SD 35-3); I 1-1. June 16, 2000.

291. HR 4578. Fiscal 2001 Interior Appropriations/Passage. Passage of the bill that would appropriate $14.6 billion for the Interior Department, related agencies and cultural programs and agencies in fiscal 2001. The funding represents a 2 percent decrease from fiscal 2000 appropriations. Passed 204-172: R 194-13; D 9-158 (ND 8-120, SD 1-38); I 1-1. June 16, 2000.

Key

- Y Voted for (yea).
- # Paired for.
- + Announced for.
- N Voted against (nay).
- X Paired against.
- – Announced against.
- P Voted "present."
- C Voted "present" to avoid possible conflict of interest.
- ? Did not vote or otherwise make a position known.

•

Democrats ***Republicans***
Independents

	287	288	289	290	291
ALABAMA					
1 ***Callahan***	?	Y	N	N	Y
2 ***Everett***	N	Y	Y	N	Y
3 ***Riley***	N	Y	Y	N	Y
4 ***Aderholt***	N	Y	Y	N	Y
5 Cramer	Y	N	Y	Y	N
6 ***Bachus***	N	Y	Y	N	Y
7 Hilliard	Y	?	?	?	?
ALASKA					
AL ***Young***	N	Y	N	N	Y
ARIZONA					
1 ***Salmon***	?	Y	Y	N	Y
2 Pastor	Y	N	N	Y	N
3 ***Stump***	N	Y	Y	N	Y
4 ***Shadegg***	N	Y	Y	N	Y
5 ***Kolbe***	N	Y	N	Y	Y
6 ***Hayworth***	N	Y	N	N	Y
ARKANSAS					
1 Berry	Y	N	N	N	N
2 Snyder	Y	N	N	Y	N
3 ***Hutchinson***	N	Y	Y	N	Y
4 ***Dickey***	N	Y	Y	N	Y
CALIFORNIA					
1 Thompson	Y	N	N	Y	N
2 ***Herger***	N	Y	Y	N	N
3 ***Ose***	N	Y	Y	N	Y
4 ***Doolittle***	N	Y	Y	N	Y
5 Matsui	Y	N	N	Y	N
6 Woolsey	Y	N	N	Y	N
7 Miller, George	Y	N	N	Y	N
8 Pelosi	Y	N	N	Y	N
9 Lee	Y	N	N	Y	N
10 Tauscher	Y	N	N	Y	N
11 ***Pombo***	N	Y	Y	N	Y
12 Lantos	Y	N	N	Y	N
13 Stark	?	?	N	Y	N
14 Eshoo	Y	N	N	Y	N
15 ***Campbell***	?	?	?	?	?
16 Lofgren	?	?	?	?	?
17 Farr	Y	N	N	Y	N
18 Condit	Y	N	N	N	N
19 ***Radanovich***	?	Y	N	N	Y
20 Dooley	Y	N	N	Y	N
21 ***Thomas***	N	Y	Y	N	Y
22 Capps	Y	N	N	Y	N
23 ***Gallegly***	N	Y	N	N	Y
24 Sherman	Y	N	N	Y	N
25 ***McKeon***	N	Y	Y	N	Y
26 Berman	Y	N	N	Y	N
27 ***Rogan***	?	Y	N	N	Y
28 ***Dreier***	N	Y	N	N	Y
29 Waxman	Y	N	N	Y	N
30 Becerra	?	?	?	?	?
31 Martinez	?	?	?	?	?
32 Dixon	Y	N	N	Y	N
33 Roybal-Allard	Y	N	N	Y	N
34 Napolitano	Y	N	N	Y	N
35 Waters	Y	N	N	Y	N
36 ***Kuykendall***	N	Y	N	Y	Y
37 Millender-McD.	Y	?	?	?	?
38 ***Horn***	N	N	N	Y	Y
39 ***Royce***	N	Y	N	N	N
40 ***Lewis***	N	Y	N	N	Y
41 ***Miller, Gary***	N	?	?	?	?
42 Baca	N	N	N	Y	N
43 ***Calvert***	N	Y	N	N	Y
44 ***Bono***	N	Y	N	N	Y
45 ***Rohrabacher***	N	Y	N	N	N
46 Sanchez	Y	N	N	Y	N
47 ***Cox***	N	Y	Y	N	Y
48 ***Packard***	N	Y	Y	N	Y
49 ***Bilbray***	N	Y	N	Y	Y
50 Filner	?	?	?	?	?
51 ***Cunningham***	N	Y	N	N	N
52 ***Hunter***	N	Y	Y	N	Y
COLORADO					
1 DeGette	Y	N	N	Y	N
2 Udall	Y	N	N	Y	N
3 ***McInnis***	N	Y	Y	N	Y
4 ***Schaffer***	N	Y	Y	N	Y
5 ***Hefley***	N	Y	Y	N	N
6 ***Tancredo***	N	Y	Y	N	Y
CONNECTICUT					
1 Larson	Y	N	N	Y	N
2 Gejdenson	Y	N	N	Y	N
3 DeLauro	Y	N	N	Y	N
4 ***Shays***	N	N	Y	Y	Y
5 Maloney	Y	N	N	Y	N
6 ***Johnson***	N	Y	Y	Y	Y
DELAWARE					
AL ***Castle***	N	Y	Y	Y	Y
FLORIDA					
1 ***Scarborough***	Y	Y	Y	N	Y
2 Boyd	Y	N	N	Y	N
3 Brown	Y	N	N	Y	N
4 ***Fowler***	N	Y	Y	N	Y
5 Thurman	Y	N	N	Y	N
6 ***Stearns***	N	Y	Y	N	Y
7 ***Mica***	N	Y	Y	N	Y
8 ***McCollum***	?	?	?	?	?
9 ***Bilirakis***	N	Y	Y	N	Y
10 ***Young***	N	Y	Y	N	Y
11 Davis	Y	N	N	Y	N
12 ***Canady***	N	Y	Y	N	Y
13 ***Miller***	N	Y	Y	N	Y
14 ***Goss***	N	Y	Y	N	Y
15 ***Weldon***	N	Y	Y	N	Y
16 ***Foley***	N	Y	N	N	Y
17 Meek	Y	?	?	?	?
18 ***Ros-Lehtinen***	N	Y	?	N	Y
19 Wexler	Y	N	Y	Y	N
20 Deutsch	Y	N	N	Y	N
21 ***Diaz-Balart***	N	Y	N	N	Y
22 ***Shaw***	N	Y	Y	N	Y
23 Hastings	Y	N	N	Y	N
GEORGIA					
1 ***Kingston***	N	Y	Y	N	Y
2 Bishop	Y	?	?	?	?
3 ***Collins***	N	Y	Y	N	Y
4 McKinney	Y	N	N	?	N
5 Lewis	Y	N	N	Y	N
6 ***Isakson***	N	Y	Y	N	Y
7 ***Barr***	?	Y	Y	N	N
8 ***Chambliss***	N	Y	Y	N	Y
9 ***Deal***	N	?	?	?	?
10 ***Norwood***	?	Y	Y	N	Y
11 ***Linder***	N	?	?	?	?
HAWAII					
1 Abercrombie	Y	N	N	Y	N
2 Mink	Y	N	N	Y	N
IDAHO					
1 ***Chenoweth-Hage***	N	Y	Y	N	N
2 ***Simpson***	N	Y	N	N	Y
ILLINOIS					
1 Rush	Y	N	N	Y	N
2 Jackson	Y	N	N	Y	N
3 Lipinski	Y	N	N	Y	N
4 Gutierrez	N	N	N	Y	?
5 Blagojevich	Y	N	N	Y	N
6 ***Hyde***	N	Y	Y	N	Y
7 Davis	Y	N	N	Y	N
8 ***Crane***	N	Y	Y	N	Y
9 Schakowsky	Y	N	N	Y	N
10 ***Porter***	N	Y	Y	Y	Y
11 ***Weller***	N	Y	N	N	Y
12 Costello	?	?	?	?	?
13 ***Biggert***	N	Y	Y	N	Y

ND Northern Democrats SD Southern Democrats

	287	288	289	290	291
14 ***Hastert***	N	Y		N	Y
15 ***Ewing***	N	Y	?	?	?
16 ***Manzullo***	N	Y	Y	N	Y
17 Evans	Y	N	N	Y	N
18 ***LaHood***	N	Y	Y	?	Y
19 Phelps	Y	N	N	Y	N
20 ***Shimkus***	N	Y	Y	N	Y
INDIANA					
1 Visclosky	Y	N	N	Y	N
2 ***McIntosh***	N	Y	Y	N	Y
3 Roemer	?	N	Y	Y	N
4 ***Souder***	N	Y	Y	N	Y
5 ***Buyer***	N	Y	Y	N	Y
6 ***Burton***	N	Y	Y	N	Y
7 ***Pease***	N	Y	Y	N	Y
8 ***Hostettler***	N	Y	Y	N	N
9 Hill	Y	N	N	Y	N
10 Carson	Y	N	N	Y	N
IOWA					
1 ***Leach***	N	N	N	Y	Y
2 ***Nussle***	N	Y	N	N	Y
3 Boswell	?	N	Y	Y	N
4 ***Ganske***	?	Y	Y	?	Y
5 ***Latham***	N	Y	N	N	Y
KANSAS					
1 ***Moran***	N	Y	Y	N	Y
2 ***Ryun***	N	Y	Y	N	Y
3 Moore	N	N	?	Y	N
4 ***Tiahrt***	N	Y	Y	N	N
KENTUCKY					
1 ***Whitfield***	N	Y	Y	N	Y
2 ***Lewis***	N	Y	Y	N	Y
3 ***Northup***	N	Y	Y	N	Y
4 Lucas	Y	N	Y	N	N
5 ***Rogers***	N	Y	Y	N	Y
6 ***Fletcher***	N	Y	Y	N	Y
LOUISIANA					
1 ***Vitter***	N	Y	Y	N	Y
2 Jefferson	?	?	?	?	?
3 ***Tauzin***	N	Y	N	N	Y
4 ***McCrery***	N	Y	N	N	Y
5 ***Cooksey***	?	?	?	?	?
6 ***Baker***	N	Y	N	N	Y
7 John	Y	N	N	Y	N
MAINE					
1 Allen	Y	N	N	Y	N
2 Baldacci	Y	N	N	Y	N
MARYLAND					
1 ***Gilchrest***	N	Y	Y	N	Y
2 ***Ehrlich***	N	Y	N	N	Y
3 Cardin	Y	N	N	Y	N
4 Wynn	Y	N	N	Y	N
5 Hoyer	Y	N	N	Y	N
6 ***Bartlett***	N	Y	Y	N	Y
7 Cummings	Y	N	N	Y	N
8 ***Morella***	N	N	N	Y	Y
MASSACHUSETTS					
1 Olver	Y	N	N	Y	N
2 Neal	Y	N	?	?	?
3 McGovern	Y	N	N	Y	N
4 Frank	Y	N	N	Y	N
5 Meehan	Y	N	N	Y	N
6 Tierney	Y	N	N	Y	N
7 Markey	Y	N	N	Y	N
8 Capuano	Y	?	?	?	?
9 Moakley	Y	N	N	Y	N
10 Delahunt	Y	N	N	Y	N
MICHIGAN					
1 Stupak	Y	N	N	Y	N
2 ***Hoekstra***	N	Y	Y	N	Y
3 ***Ehlers***	N	Y	Y	Y	Y
4 ***Camp***	N	Y	N	N	Y
5 Barcia	Y	N	N	Y	N
6 ***Upton***	N	Y	Y	Y	Y
7 ***Smith***	?	Y	Y	N	Y
8 Stabenow	Y	N	N	Y	N
9 Kildee	Y	N	N	Y	N
10 Bonior	Y	N	N	Y	N
11 ***Knollenberg***	N	Y	N	N	Y
12 Levin	Y	N	N	Y	N
13 Rivers	Y	N	N	Y	N
14 Conyers	Y	N	N	Y	N
15 Kilpatrick	?	N	N	Y	N
16 Dingell	Y	N	N	Y	N

	287	288	289	290	291
MINNESOTA					
1 ***Gutknecht***	N	Y	Y	N	Y
2 Minge	N	N	N	Y	N
3 ***Ramstad***	N	N	N	Y	Y
4 Vento	?	?	?	?	?
5 Sabo	Y	N	N	Y	N
6 Luther	Y	N	N	Y	N
7 Peterson	Y	N	N	Y	N
8 Oberstar	Y	N	N	Y	Y
MISSISSIPPI					
1 ***Wicker***	?	Y	Y	N	Y
2 Thompson	Y	?	?	?	?
3 ***Pickering***	N	Y	Y	N	Y
4 Shows	?	?	?	?	?
5 Taylor	Y	N	N	N	Y
MISSOURI					
1 Clay	Y	?	?	?	?
2 ***Talent***	N	Y	Y	N	Y
3 Gephardt	Y	N	N	Y	N
4 Skelton	?	?	?	?	?
5 McCarthy	Y	N	N	Y	N
6 Danner	?	?	?	?	?
7 ***Blunt***	N	Y	Y	N	Y
8 ***Emerson***	N	Y	Y	N	Y
9 ***Hulshof***	N	Y	Y	N	Y
MONTANA					
AL ***Hill***	N	Y	Y	N	Y
NEBRASKA					
1 ***Bereuter***	N	Y	Y	N	Y
2 ***Terry***	N	Y	Y	N	Y
3 ***Barrett***	N	Y	N	N	Y
NEVADA					
1 Berkley	Y	N	Y	Y	N
2 ***Gibbons***	N	Y	Y	N	N
NEW HAMPSHIRE					
1 ***Sununu***	N	Y	Y	N	Y
2 ***Bass***	N	Y	Y	Y	Y
NEW JERSEY					
1 Andrews	Y	N	Y	Y	N
2 ***LoBiondo***	N	N	Y	Y	Y
3 ***Saxton***	N	N	N	Y	Y
4 ***Smith***	N	Y	Y	N	Y
5 ***Roukema***	N	Y	Y	Y	Y
6 Pallone	Y	N	N	Y	N
7 ***Franks***	N	N	Y	Y	Y
8 Pascrell	N	N	N	Y	N
9 Rothman	Y	N	Y	Y	N
10 Payne	Y	?	?	?	?
11 ***Frelinghuysen***	N	Y	Y	Y	Y
12 Holt	Y	N	N	Y	N
13 Menendez	N	N	N	Y	N
NEW MEXICO					
1 ***Wilson***	N	Y	N	N	Y
2 ***Skeen***	N	Y	N	N	Y
3 Udall	Y	N	N	Y	N
NEW YORK					
1 Forbes	?	N	N	Y	N
2 ***Lazio***	?	?	?	?	?
3 ***King***	N	Y	N	N	Y
4 McCarthy	Y	N	N	Y	N
5 Ackerman	Y	N	N	Y	N
6 Meeks	Y	?	?	?	?
7 Crowley	?	N	N	Y	N
8 Nadler	?	?	?	?	?
9 Weiner	Y	N	N	Y	N
10 Towns	Y	?	?	?	?
11 Owens	Y	?	?	?	?
12 Velázquez	?	?	?	?	?
13 ***Fossella***	N	Y	Y	N	Y
14 Maloney	Y	N	N	Y	N
15 Rangel	?	?	?	?	?
16 Serrano	?	?	?	?	?
17 Engel	?	?	?	?	?
18 Lowey	Y	N	N	Y	N
19 ***Kelly***	N	N	Y	Y	Y
20 ***Gilman***	N	N	N	Y	Y
21 McNulty	Y	N	N	Y	N
22 ***Sweeney***	N	Y	N	N	Y
23 ***Boehlert***	N	N	Y	Y	Y
24 ***McHugh***	N	Y	Y	N	Y
25 ***Walsh***	N	Y	Y	N	Y
26 Hinchey	Y	N	N	Y	N
27 ***Reynolds***	N	Y	Y	N	Y
28 Slaughter	Y	N	N	Y	N
29 LaFalce	Y	?	?	?	?

	287	288	289	290	291
30 ***Quinn***	N	Y	Y	N	Y
31 ***Houghton***	N	Y	N	N	Y
NORTH CAROLINA					
1 Clayton	Y	?	?	?	?
2 Etheridge	Y	N	?	Y	N
3 ***Jones***	N	Y	Y	N	Y
4 Price	Y	N	Y	Y	N
5 ***Burr***	N	Y	Y	N	Y
6 ***Coble***	N	Y	Y	N	Y
7 McIntyre	?	?	?	?	?
8 ***Hayes***	N	Y	Y	N	Y
9 ***Myrick***	N	Y	Y	N	Y
10 ***Ballenger***	N	Y	Y	?	Y
11 ***Taylor***	N	Y	Y	N	Y
12 Watt	N	?	?	?	?
NORTH DAKOTA					
AL Pomeroy	Y	N	N	Y	N
OHIO					
1 ***Chabot***	N	Y	Y	N	Y
2 ***Portman***	N	Y	Y	N	Y
3 Hall	Y	N	?	?	?
4 ***Oxley***	?	?	?	?	?
5 ***Gillmor***	N	Y	Y	N	Y
6 Strickland	Y	N	N	Y	N
7 ***Hobson***	N	Y	Y	N	Y
8 ***Boehner***	N	Y	N	N	Y
9 Kaptur	Y	N	N	Y	N
10 Kucinich	Y	N	N	Y	N
11 Jones	Y	?	?	?	?
12 ***Kasich***	N	Y	Y	N	Y
13 Brown	Y	N	N	Y	N
14 Sawyer	Y	N	N	Y	N
15 ***Pryce***	N	Y	N	N	Y
16 ***Regula***	N	Y	N	N	Y
17 Traficant	N	Y	Y	N	Y
18 ***Ney***	N	Y	N	N	Y
19 ***LaTourette***	N	Y	N	N	Y
OKLAHOMA					
1 ***Largent***	N	Y	Y	N	Y
2 ***Coburn***	N	Y	?	N	Y
3 ***Watkins***	N	Y	Y	N	Y
4 ***Watts***	N	Y	Y	?	Y
5 ***Istook***	N	?	Y	N	Y
6 ***Lucas***	N	Y	Y	N	Y
OREGON					
1 Wu	Y	N	N	Y	N
2 ***Walden***	N	Y	N	N	Y
3 Blumenauer	?	?	?	?	?
4 DeFazio	Y	N	N	Y	N
5 Hooley	?	?	?	?	?
PENNSYLVANIA					
1 Brady	Y	N	N	Y	N
2 Fattah	Y	N	N	Y	N
3 Borski	Y	N	N	Y	N
4 Klink	?	?	?	?	?
5 ***Peterson***	N	Y	Y	N	Y
6 Holden	Y	N	N	Y	Y
7 ***Weldon***	N	Y	N	N	Y
8 ***Greenwood***	?	?	?	?	?
9 ***Shuster***	?	?	?	?	?
10 ***Sherwood***	N	Y	N	N	Y
11 Kanjorski	Y	N	N	Y	N
12 Murtha	Y	N	N	Y	Y
13 Hoeffel	Y	N	N	Y	N
14 Coyne	Y	N	N	Y	N
15 ***Toomey***	?	?	?	?	?
16 ***Pitts***	N	Y	Y	N	Y
17 ***Gekas***	N	Y	N	N	Y
18 Doyle	Y	N	N	Y	Y
19 ***Goodling***	Y	N	Y	Y	Y
20 Mascara	Y	N	N	Y	Y
21 ***English***	N	Y	N	N	Y
RHODE ISLAND					
1 Kennedy	Y	N	N	Y	N
2 Weygand	Y	N	Y	Y	N
SOUTH CAROLINA					
1 ***Sanford***	N	Y	Y	N	Y
2 ***Spence***	N	Y	Y	N	Y
3 ***Graham***	N	Y	Y	N	Y
4 ***DeMint***	N	Y	Y	N	Y
5 Spratt	?	N	Y	Y	N
6 Clyburn	Y	?	?	?	?
SOUTH DAKOTA					
AL ***Thune***	N	Y	Y	N	Y

	287	288	289	290	291
TENNESSEE					
1 ***Jenkins***	N	Y	Y	N	Y
2 ***Duncan***	N	Y	Y	N	Y
3 ***Wamp***	N	Y	Y	N	Y
4 ***Hilleary***	N	Y	N	N	Y
5 Clement	?	?	N	Y	N
6 Gordon	Y	N	N	Y	N
7 ***Bryant***	N	Y	Y	N	Y
8 Tanner	Y	N	N	Y	N
9 Ford	Y	N	N	Y	N
TEXAS					
1 Sandlin	Y	N	N	Y	N
2 Turner	Y	N	N	Y	N
3 ***Johnson, Sam***	N	Y	Y	N	Y
4 Hall	N	Y	Y	Y	N
5 ***Sessions***	N	Y	Y	N	Y
6 ***Barton***	?	?	?	?	?
7 ***Archer***	N	Y	Y	N	Y
8 ***Brady***	N	Y	Y	N	Y
9 Lampson	Y	N	N	Y	N
10 Doggett	Y	N	N	Y	N
11 Edwards	Y	N	Y	Y	N
12 ***Granger***	N	Y	N	N	Y
13 ***Thornberry***	N	Y	Y	N	Y
14 ***Paul***	N	Y	N	N	N
15 Hinojosa	?	?	?	?	?
16 Reyes	Y	N	N	Y	N
17 Stenholm	Y	N	Y	Y	N
18 Jackson-Lee	Y	?	?	?	?
19 ***Combest***	N	Y	Y	N	Y
20 Gonzalez	Y	N	N	Y	N
21 ***Smith***	N	Y	Y	N	Y
22 ***DeLay***	N	Y	Y	N	Y
23 ***Bonilla***	N	Y	Y	N	Y
24 Frost	Y	N	N	Y	N
25 Bentsen	Y	N	N	Y	N
26 ***Armey***	N	Y	Y	N	Y
27 Ortiz	N	N	N	Y	N
28 Rodriguez	Y	N	N	Y	N
29 Green	?	?	?	?	?
30 Johnson, E.B.	Y	?	?	?	?
UTAH					
1 ***Hansen***	N	Y	Y	N	N
2 ***Cook***	N	?	Y	N	Y
3 ***Cannon***	N	Y	Y	N	Y
VERMONT					
AL *Sanders*	Y	Y	N	Y	N
VIRGINIA					
1 ***Bateman***	N	Y	Y	N	Y
2 Pickett	Y	N	N	Y	N
3 Scott	Y	N	N	Y	N
4 Sisisky	?	N	Y	Y	N
5 *Goode*	N	N	Y	N	Y
6 ***Goodlatte***	N	Y	Y	N	Y
7 ***Bliley***	?	?	?	?	?
8 Moran	?	N	N	Y	N
9 Boucher	?	?	?	?	?
10 ***Wolf***	N	Y	Y	N	Y
11 ***Davis***	N	Y	N	N	Y
WASHINGTON					
1 Inslee	Y	N	N	Y	N
2 ***Metcalf***	N	Y	N	N	Y
3 Baird	Y	N	N	Y	N
4 ***Hastings***	N	Y	Y	N	Y
5 ***Nethercutt***	N	Y	N	N	Y
6 Dicks	Y	N	N	Y	N
7 McDermott	?	?	?	?	?
8 ***Dunn***	N	Y	Y	N	Y
9 Smith	Y	N	N	Y	N
WEST VIRGINIA					
1 Mollohan	Y	N	N	Y	Y
2 Wise	Y	N	N	Y	N
3 Rahall	N	N	Y	Y	Y
WISCONSIN					
1 ***Ryan***	N	Y	Y	N	Y
2 Baldwin	Y	N	N	Y	N
3 Kind	N	N	N	Y	N
4 Kleczka	Y	N	N	Y	N
5 Barrett	Y	N	N	Y	N
6 ***Petri***	N	N	N	Y	Y
7 Obey	Y	N	Y	Y	N
8 ***Green***	N	Y	Y	N	Y
9 ***Sensenbrenner***	N	N	?	?	?
WYOMING					
AL ***Cubin***	N	Y	Y	N	Y

Southern states - Ala., Ark., Fla., Ga., Ky., La., Miss., N.C., Okla., S.C., Tenn., Texas, Va.

292. HR 4635. Fiscal 2001 VA-HUD Appropriations/Motion to Rise. Waxman, D-Calif., motion to rise from the Committee of the Whole. Motion rejected 138-243: R 0-185; D 137-57 (ND 105-36, SD 32-21); I 1-1. June 19, 2000.

293. HR 4635. Fiscal 2001 VA-HUD Appropriations/Tobacco Lawsuit. Waxman, D-Calif., amendment that would strike language in the bill that would prohibit the Veteran's Administration from transferring any medical care funding to the Justice Department for use in government lawsuits against tobacco companies. Rejected 197-207: R 34-173; D 162-33 (ND 133-10, SD 29-23); I 1-1. June 19, 2000. A "yea" was a vote in support of the president's position.

294. HR 4201. Religious Broadcasting/Educational Programming. Markey, D- Mass., amendment that would only allow nonprofit educational organizations to hold non-commercial broadcast licenses. The organizations would be required to broadcast primarily educational, instructional, cultural or educational religious materials. Rejected 174-250: R 7-207; D 166-42 (ND 133-22, SD 33-20); I 1-1. June 20, 2000.

295. HR 4201. Religious Broadcasting/Passage. Passage of the bill that would establish broader eligibility standards for broadcasters seeking non-commercial educational broadcast channels, limit the Federal Communications Commission's authority to regulate the content of those broadcasts and allow religious broadcasters easier access to such channels. Passed 264-159: R 207-6; D 56-152 (ND 30-124, SD 26-28); I 1-1. June 20, 2000.

296. HR 4601. Debt Reduction/Passage. Archer, R-Texas, motion to suspend the rules and pass the bill that would set aside a portion of the fiscal year 2000 non-Social Security surplus to be used only for debt reduction. Motion agreed to 419-5: R 214-0; D 203-5 (ND 150-4, SD 53-1); I 2-0. A two-thirds majority of those present and voting (283 in this case) is required for passage under suspension of the rules. June 20, 2000.

297. HR 3859. Social Security-Medicare "Lockbox"/Passage. Herger, R-Calif., motion to suspend the rules and pass the bill that would permit the Social Security and Medicare hospital insurance trust fund surpluses to be used only to pay down the national debt until legislation to overhaul both programs is enacted. Motion agreed to 420-2: R 213-0; D 205-2 (ND 151-2, SD 54-0); I 2-0. A two-thirds majority of those present and voting (282 in this case) is required for passage under suspension of the rules. June 20, 2000.

Key

- Y Voted for (yea).
- # Paired for.
- + Announced for.
- N Voted against (nay).
- X Paired against.
- – Announced against.
- P Voted "present."
- C Voted "present" to avoid possible conflict of interest.
- ? Did not vote or otherwise make a position known.

•

Democrats ***Republicans***
Independents

	292	293	294	295	296	297
ALABAMA						
1 ***Callahan***	N	N	N	Y	Y	Y
2 ***Everett***	N	N	N	Y	Y	Y
3 ***Riley***	N	N	N	Y	Y	Y
4 ***Aderholt***	N	N	N	Y	Y	Y
5 Cramer	Y	N	N	Y	Y	Y
6 ***Bachus***	?	N	N	Y	Y	Y
7 Hilliard	Y	N	Y	N	Y	Y
ALASKA						
AL ***Young***	N	N	N	Y	Y	Y
ARIZONA						
1 ***Salmon***	N	Y	N	Y	Y	Y
2 Pastor	Y	Y	Y	N	Y	Y
3 ***Stump***	N	N	N	Y	Y	Y
4 ***Shadegg***	N	N	N	Y	Y	Y
5 ***Kolbe***	N	N	N	Y	Y	Y
6 ***Hayworth***	N	N	N	Y	Y	Y
ARKANSAS						
1 Berry	Y	Y	N	Y	Y	Y
2 Snyder	Y	Y	N	N	Y	Y
3 ***Hutchinson***	N	N	N	Y	Y	Y
4 ***Dickey***	N	N	N	Y	Y	Y
CALIFORNIA						
1 Thompson	N	Y	Y	N	Y	Y
2 ***Herger***	N	N	N	?	Y	Y
3 ***Ose***	N	N	N	Y	Y	Y
4 ***Doolittle***	N	N	N	Y	Y	Y
5 Matsui	Y	Y	Y	N	Y	Y
6 Woolsey	Y	Y	Y	N	Y	Y
7 Miller, George	Y	Y	Y	N	Y	?
8 Pelosi	?	?	Y	N	Y	Y
9 Lee	Y	Y	Y	N	Y	Y
10 Tauscher	Y	Y	Y	N	Y	Y
11 ***Pombo***	N	N	N	Y	Y	Y
12 Lantos	Y	Y	Y	N	Y	Y
13 Stark	Y	Y	Y	N	Y	Y
14 Eshoo	Y	Y	Y	N	Y	Y
15 ***Campbell***	?	?	?	?	?	?
16 Lofgren	?	Y	Y	N	Y	Y
17 Farr	Y	Y	Y	N	Y	Y
18 Condit	N	Y	N	Y	Y	Y
19 ***Radanovich***	N	N	N	Y	Y	Y
20 Dooley	Y	Y	Y	N	Y	Y
21 ***Thomas***	N	N	N	Y	Y	Y
22 Capps	Y	Y	Y	N	Y	Y
23 ***Gallegly***	N	Y	N	Y	Y	Y
24 Sherman	Y	Y	Y	N	Y	Y
25 ***McKeon***	N	N	N	Y	Y	Y
26 Berman	Y	Y	Y	N	Y	Y
27 ***Rogan***	?	N	N	Y	Y	Y
28 ***Dreier***	N	N	N	Y	Y	Y
29 Waxman	Y	Y	Y	N	Y	Y
30 Becerra	Y	Y	Y	N	Y	Y
31 Martinez	?	?	N	Y	Y	Y
32 Dixon	Y	Y	Y	N	Y	Y
33 Roybal-Allard	?	?	?	?	?	?
34 Napolitano	Y	Y	Y	Y	Y	Y
35 Waters	Y	Y	Y	Y	Y	Y
36 ***Kuykendall***	N	Y	N	Y	Y	Y
37 Millender-McD.	Y	+	Y	N	Y	Y
38 ***Horn***	N	Y	Y	N	Y	Y
39 ***Royce***	N	N	N	Y	Y	Y
40 ***Lewis***	N	N	N	Y	Y	Y
41 ***Miller, Gary***	N	N	N	Y	Y	Y
42 Baca	Y	N	N	Y	Y	Y
43 ***Calvert***	N	N	N	Y	Y	Y
44 ***Bono***	N	N	N	Y	Y	Y
45 ***Rohrabacher***	N	N	N	Y	Y	Y
46 Sanchez	Y	N	Y	N	Y	Y
47 ***Cox***	N	N	N	Y	Y	Y
48 ***Packard***	N	N	N	Y	Y	Y
49 ***Bilbray***	?	+	N	Y	Y	Y
50 Filner	Y	Y	Y	N	Y	Y
51 ***Cunningham***	N	N	N	?	Y	Y
52 ***Hunter***	?	N	N	Y	Y	Y
COLORADO						
1 DeGette	N	Y	Y	N	Y	Y
2 Udall	Y	Y	Y	N	Y	Y
3 ***McInnis***	N	N	N	Y	Y	Y
4 ***Schaffer***	N	N	N	Y	Y	Y
5 ***Hefley***	N	N	N	Y	Y	Y
6 ***Tancredo***	N	N	N	Y	Y	Y
CONNECTICUT						
1 Larson	Y	Y	Y	N	Y	Y
2 Gejdenson	Y	Y	Y	N	Y	Y
3 DeLauro	Y	Y	Y	N	Y	Y
4 ***Shays***	?	Y	N	Y	Y	Y
5 Maloney	Y	N	Y	N	Y	Y
6 ***Johnson***	N	Y	Y	N	Y	Y
DELAWARE						
AL ***Castle***	N	Y	N	Y	Y	Y
FLORIDA						
1 ***Scarborough***	N	Y	N	Y	Y	Y
2 Boyd	Y	N	N	Y	Y	Y
3 Brown	?	?	Y	N	Y	Y
4 ***Fowler***	?	?	N	Y	Y	Y
5 Thurman	Y	Y	Y	N	N	Y
6 ***Stearns***	N	N	N	Y	Y	Y
7 ***Mica***	N	N	N	Y	Y	Y
8 ***McCollum***	?	?	?	?	?	?
9 ***Bilirakis***	N	N	N	Y	Y	Y
10 ***Young***	N	N	N	Y	Y	Y
11 Davis	Y	Y	Y	Y	Y	Y
12 ***Canady***	N	N	N	Y	Y	Y
13 ***Miller***	N	N	N	Y	Y	Y
14 ***Goss***	N	N	N	Y	Y	Y
15 ***Weldon***	N	N	N	Y	Y	Y
16 ***Foley***	N	Y	N	Y	Y	Y
17 Meek	Y	Y	Y	N	Y	Y
18 ***Ros-Lehtinen***	N	N	N	Y	Y	?
19 Wexler	Y	Y	Y	N	Y	Y
20 Deutsch	Y	Y	Y	N	Y	Y
21 ***Diaz-Balart***	N	N	N	Y	Y	Y
22 ***Shaw***	N	N	N	Y	Y	Y
23 Hastings	Y	Y	Y	N	Y	Y
GEORGIA						
1 ***Kingston***	?	N	N	Y	Y	Y
2 Bishop	N	N	N	Y	Y	Y
3 ***Collins***	N	N	N	Y	Y	Y
4 McKinney	Y	Y	Y	N	Y	Y
5 Lewis	Y	Y	Y	N	Y	Y
6 ***Isakson***	N	N	N	Y	Y	Y
7 ***Barr***	N	N	N	Y	Y	Y
8 ***Chambliss***	N	N	N	Y	Y	Y
9 ***Deal***	N	N	N	Y	Y	Y
10 ***Norwood***	N	N	N	Y	Y	Y
11 ***Linder***	N	N	N	Y	Y	Y
HAWAII						
1 Abercrombie	N	Y	Y	N	Y	Y
2 Mink	N	Y	Y	N	Y	Y
IDAHO						
1 ***Chenoweth-Hage***	N	N	N	Y	Y	Y
2 ***Simpson***	N	N	N	Y	Y	Y
ILLINOIS						
1 Rush	Y	Y	Y	N	Y	Y
2 Jackson	Y	Y	Y	N	Y	Y
3 Lipinski	Y	Y	N	Y	Y	Y
4 Gutierrez	N	Y	Y	N	Y	Y
5 Blagojevich	Y	Y	Y	N	Y	Y
6 ***Hyde***	N	N	N	Y	Y	Y
7 Davis	Y	Y	Y	N	Y	Y
8 ***Crane***	N	N	N	Y	Y	Y
9 Schakowsky	Y	Y	Y	N	Y	Y
10 ***Porter***	N	Y	Y	N	Y	Y
11 ***Weller***	N	N	N	Y	Y	Y
12 Costello	N	Y	N	Y	Y	Y
13 ***Biggert***	N	N	Y	Y	Y	Y

ND Northern Democrats SD Southern Democrats

	292	293	294	295	296	297
14 ***Hastert***						
15 ***Ewing***	?	?	?	?	?	?
16 ***Manzullo***	N	N	N	Y	Y	Y
17 Evans	N	Y	Y	N	Y	Y
18 ***LaHood***	N	N	N	Y	Y	Y
19 Phelps	N	N	N	Y	Y	Y
20 ***Shimkus***	N	N	N	Y	Y	Y
INDIANA						
1 Visclosky	Y	Y	Y	N	Y	Y
2 ***McIntosh***	?	?	?	?	?	?
3 Roemer	N	Y	N	N	Y	Y
4 ***Souder***	N	N	N	Y	Y	Y
5 ***Buyer***	N	N	N	Y	Y	Y
6 ***Burton***	?	N	N	Y	Y	Y
7 ***Pease***	N	N	N	Y	Y	Y
8 ***Hostettler***	N	N	N	Y	Y	Y
9 Hill	N	N	Y	N	Y	Y
10 Carson	Y	Y	Y	N	Y	Y
IOWA						
1 ***Leach***	?	Y	N	Y	Y	Y
2 ***Nussle***	N	N	N	Y	Y	Y
3 Boswell	N	Y	N	Y	Y	Y
4 ***Ganske***	N	Y	N	Y	Y	Y
5 ***Latham***	N	N	N	Y	Y	Y
KANSAS						
1 ***Moran***	N	Y	N	Y	Y	Y
2 ***Ryun***	N	N	N	Y	Y	Y
3 Moore	N	Y	Y	Y	Y	Y
4 ***Tiahrt***	N	N	N	Y	Y	Y
KENTUCKY						
1 ***Whitfield***	N	N	N	Y	Y	Y
2 ***Lewis***	N	N	N	Y	Y	Y
3 ***Northup***	N	N	N	Y	Y	Y
4 Lucas	Y	N	N	Y	Y	Y
5 ***Rogers***	N	N	N	Y	Y	Y
6 ***Fletcher***	?	N	N	Y	Y	Y
LOUISIANA						
1 ***Vitter***	N	N	N	Y	Y	Y
2 Jefferson	Y	Y	Y	N	Y	Y
3 ***Tauzin***	N	N	N	Y	Y	Y
4 ***McCrery***	N	N	N	Y	Y	Y
5 ***Cooksey***	?	N	N	Y	Y	Y
6 ***Baker***	N	N	N	Y	Y	Y
7 John	N	N	N	Y	Y	Y
MAINE						
1 Allen	Y	Y	Y	N	Y	Y
2 Baldacci	Y	Y	Y	Y	Y	Y
MARYLAND						
1 ***Gilchrest***	N	Y	N	Y	Y	Y
2 ***Ehrlich***	?	N	N	Y	Y	Y
3 Cardin	Y	Y	Y	N	N	Y
4 Wynn	Y	Y	Y	N	Y	Y
5 Hoyer	Y	Y	Y	N	Y	Y
6 ***Bartlett***	N	N	N	Y	Y	Y
7 Cummings	Y	Y	Y	N	Y	Y
8 ***Morella***	N	Y	Y	N	Y	Y
MASSACHUSETTS						
1 Olver	Y	Y	Y	N	Y	Y
2 Neal	Y	Y	Y	N	Y	Y
3 McGovern	Y	Y	Y	N	Y	Y
4 Frank	Y	Y	Y	N	Y	Y
5 Meehan	Y	Y	Y	N	Y	Y
6 Tierney	Y	Y	Y	N	Y	Y
7 Markey	Y	Y	Y	N	Y	Y
8 Capuano	Y	Y	Y	N	Y	Y
9 Moakley	Y	Y	Y	N	Y	Y
10 Delahunt	Y	Y	Y	N	Y	Y
MICHIGAN						
1 Stupak	N	Y	Y	Y	Y	Y
2 ***Hoekstra***	N	N	N	Y	Y	Y
3 ***Ehlers***	N	Y	N	Y	Y	Y
4 ***Camp***	N	N	N	Y	Y	Y
5 Barcia	Y	Y	N	Y	Y	Y
6 ***Upton***	N	Y	N	Y	Y	Y
7 ***Smith***	N	N	N	Y	Y	Y
8 Stabenow	Y	Y	Y	N	Y	Y
9 Kildee	Y	Y	N	Y	Y	Y
10 Bonior	Y	Y	Y	N	Y	Y
11 ***Knollenberg***	N	N	N	Y	Y	Y
12 Levin	N	Y	Y	N	Y	Y
13 Rivers	N	Y	Y	N	Y	Y
14 Conyers	Y	Y	Y	?	Y	Y
15 Kilpatrick	Y	Y	Y	N	Y	Y
16 Dingell	N	Y	Y	N	Y	Y

	292	293	294	295	296	297
MINNESOTA						
1 ***Gutknecht***	N	N	N	Y	Y	Y
2 Minge	N	Y	Y	N	Y	Y
3 ***Ramstad***	N	Y	N	Y	Y	Y
4 Vento	?	?	?	?	?	?
5 Sabo	Y	Y	Y	N	N	N
6 Luther	Y	Y	Y	N	Y	Y
7 Peterson	N	Y	N	Y	Y	Y
8 Oberstar	Y	?	Y	N	N	Y
MISSISSIPPI						
1 ***Wicker***	N	N	N	Y	Y	Y
2 Thompson	N	N	Y	N	Y	Y
3 ***Pickering***	N	N	N	Y	Y	Y
4 Shows	N	N	N	Y	Y	Y
5 Taylor	Y	Y	N	Y	Y	Y
MISSOURI						
1 Clay	N	N	Y	N	Y	Y
2 ***Talent***	N	N	N	Y	Y	Y
3 Gephardt	?	?	Y	N	Y	Y
4 Skelton	Y	Y	N	Y	Y	Y
5 McCarthy	Y	Y	Y	N	Y	Y
6 Danner	Y	N	Y	N	Y	Y
7 ***Blunt***	N	N	N	Y	Y	Y
8 ***Emerson***	–	–	–	+	+	+
9 ***Hulshof***	N	N	N	Y	Y	Y
MONTANA						
AL ***Hill***	N	N	N	Y	Y	Y
NEBRASKA						
1 ***Bereuter***	N	N	N	Y	Y	Y
2 ***Terry***	N	N	N	Y	Y	Y
3 ***Barrett***	N	N	N	Y	Y	Y
NEVADA						
1 Berkley	N	N	Y	N	Y	Y
2 ***Gibbons***	N	N	N	Y	Y	Y
NEW HAMPSHIRE						
1 ***Sununu***	N	N	N	Y	Y	Y
2 ***Bass***	N	N	N	Y	Y	Y
NEW JERSEY						
1 Andrews	Y	Y	Y	N	Y	Y
2 ***LoBiondo***	N	Y	N	Y	Y	Y
3 ***Saxton***	N	Y	N	Y	Y	Y
4 ***Smith***	N	Y	N	Y	Y	Y
5 ***Roukema***	N	Y	N	Y	Y	Y
6 Pallone	Y	Y	Y	N	Y	Y
7 ***Franks***	N	Y	N	Y	Y	Y
8 Pascrell	Y	Y	Y	N	Y	Y
9 Rothman	?	?	Y	N	Y	Y
10 Payne	?	?	Y	N	Y	Y
11 ***Frelinghuysen***	N	N	N	Y	Y	Y
12 Holt	Y	Y	Y	N	Y	Y
13 Menendez	N	Y	Y	N	Y	Y
NEW MEXICO						
1 ***Wilson***	N	N	N	Y	Y	Y
2 ***Skeen***	N	N	N	Y	Y	Y
3 Udall	N	Y	Y	N	Y	Y
NEW YORK						
1 Forbes	N	N	N	Y	Y	Y
2 ***Lazio***	?	Y	N	Y	Y	Y
3 ***King***	N	Y	N	Y	Y	Y
4 McCarthy	N	Y	Y	N	Y	Y
5 Ackerman	Y	Y	Y	N	Y	Y
6 Meeks	?	Y	Y	N	Y	Y
7 Crowley	Y	Y	Y	N	Y	Y
8 Nadler	Y	Y	Y	N	N	N
9 Weiner	Y	?	?	N	Y	Y
10 Towns	Y	Y	Y	N	Y	Y
11 Owens	+	+	Y	N	Y	Y
12 Velázquez	Y	Y	Y	N	Y	Y
13 ***Fossella***	?	N	N	Y	Y	Y
14 Maloney	?	Y	Y	N	Y	Y
15 Rangel	Y	Y	Y	N	Y	Y
16 Serrano	N	Y	Y	N	Y	Y
17 Engel	?	?	Y	N	Y	Y
18 Lowey	Y	Y	Y	N	Y	Y
19 ***Kelly***	N	N	N	Y	Y	Y
20 ***Gilman***	?	Y	Y	N	Y	Y
21 McNulty	Y	Y	Y	N	Y	Y
22 ***Sweeney***	N	N	N	Y	Y	Y
23 ***Boehlert***	N	N	Y	N	Y	Y
24 ***McHugh***	N	N	N	Y	Y	Y
25 ***Walsh***	N	N	N	Y	Y	Y
26 Hinchey	Y	Y	Y	N	Y	Y
27 ***Reynolds***	N	N	N	Y	Y	Y
28 Slaughter	Y	Y	Y	N	Y	Y
29 LaFalce	Y	Y	Y	N	Y	Y

	292	293	294	295	296	297
30 ***Quinn***	?	N	N	Y	Y	Y
31 ***Houghton***	N	N	N	Y	Y	Y
NORTH CAROLINA						
1 Clayton	Y	N	Y	N	Y	Y
2 Etheridge	N	N	Y	Y	Y	Y
3 ***Jones***	N	N	N	Y	Y	Y
4 Price	N	N	Y	N	Y	Y
5 ***Burr***	N	N	N	Y	Y	Y
6 ***Coble***	N	N	N	Y	Y	Y
7 McIntyre	Y	N	N	Y	Y	Y
8 ***Hayes***	–	–	N	Y	Y	Y
9 ***Myrick***	?	N	N	Y	Y	Y
10 ***Ballenger***	N	N	N	Y	Y	Y
11 ***Taylor***	N	N	N	Y	Y	Y
12 Watt	Y	Y	Y	N	Y	Y
NORTH DAKOTA						
AL Pomeroy	Y	Y	Y	N	Y	Y
OHIO						
1 ***Chabot***	N	N	N	Y	Y	Y
2 ***Portman***	N	N	N	Y	Y	Y
3 Hall	Y	Y	Y	Y	Y	Y
4 ***Oxley***	?	N	N	Y	Y	Y
5 ***Gillmor***	N	N	N	Y	Y	Y
6 Strickland	Y	Y	N	Y	Y	Y
7 ***Hobson***	N	N	N	Y	Y	Y
8 ***Boehner***	N	N	N	Y	Y	Y
9 Kaptur	Y	Y	Y	N	Y	Y
10 Kucinich	Y	Y	N	Y	Y	Y
11 Jones	Y	Y	Y	Y	Y	Y
12 ***Kasich***	?	N	N	Y	Y	Y
13 Brown	Y	Y	Y	N	Y	Y
14 Sawyer	Y	Y	Y	N	Y	Y
15 ***Pryce***	N	Y	N	Y	Y	Y
16 ***Regula***	N	N	N	Y	Y	Y
17 Traficant	N	Y	N	Y	Y	Y
18 ***Ney***	N	Y	N	Y	Y	Y
19 ***LaTourette***	N	Y	N	Y	Y	Y
OKLAHOMA						
1 ***Largent***	?	?	N	Y	Y	Y
2 ***Coburn***	?	?	N	Y	Y	Y
3 ***Watkins***	N	N	N	Y	Y	Y
4 ***Watts***	N	N	N	Y	Y	Y
5 ***Istook***	N	N	N	Y	Y	Y
6 ***Lucas***	N	N	N	Y	Y	Y
OREGON						
1 Wu	Y	Y	Y	N	Y	Y
2 ***Walden***	N	N	N	Y	Y	Y
3 Blumenauer	Y	Y	Y	N	Y	Y
4 DeFazio	N	Y	Y	N	Y	Y
5 Hooley	–	?	Y	N	Y	Y
PENNSYLVANIA						
1 Brady	Y	Y	Y	N	Y	Y
2 Fattah	?	?	Y	N	Y	Y
3 Borski	Y	Y	Y	N	Y	Y
4 Klink	?	Y	Y	N	?	?
5 ***Peterson***	N	N	N	Y	Y	Y
6 Holden	Y	Y	N	Y	Y	Y
7 ***Weldon***	N	N	?	Y	Y	Y
8 ***Greenwood***	?	Y	N	Y	Y	Y
9 ***Shuster***	?	?	N	Y	Y	Y
10 ***Sherwood***	N	Y	N	Y	Y	Y
11 Kanjorski	Y	Y	Y	N	Y	Y
12 Murtha	?	Y	N	Y	Y	Y
13 Hoeffel	Y	Y	Y	N	Y	Y
14 Coyne	Y	Y	Y	N	Y	Y
15 ***Toomey***	N	N	N	Y	Y	Y
16 ***Pitts***	N	N	N	Y	Y	Y
17 ***Gekas***	N	N	N	Y	Y	Y
18 Doyle	Y	Y	N	Y	Y	Y
19 ***Goodling***	N	N	N	Y	Y	Y
20 Mascara	Y	Y	Y	Y	Y	Y
21 ***English***	N	N	N	Y	Y	Y
RHODE ISLAND						
1 Kennedy	Y	Y	Y	N	Y	Y
2 Weygand	Y	Y	Y	Y	Y	Y
SOUTH CAROLINA						
1 ***Sanford***	N	N	N	Y	Y	Y
2 ***Spence***	N	N	N	Y	Y	Y
3 ***Graham***	N	N	N	Y	Y	Y
4 ***DeMint***	N	N	N	Y	Y	Y
5 Spratt	Y	N	?	Y	Y	Y
6 Clyburn	N	N	Y	N	Y	Y
SOUTH DAKOTA						
AL ***Thune***	N	Y	N	Y	Y	Y

	292	293	294	295	296	297
TENNESSEE						
1 ***Jenkins***	?	N	N	Y	Y	Y
2 ***Duncan***	N	N	N	Y	Y	Y
3 ***Wamp***	N	N	N	Y	Y	Y
4 ***Hilleary***	N	N	N	Y	Y	Y
5 Clement	N	N	N	Y	Y	Y
6 Gordon	N	N	Y	Y	Y	Y
7 ***Bryant***	N	N	N	Y	Y	Y
8 Tanner	N	N	Y	Y	Y	Y
9 Ford	Y	Y	Y	N	Y	Y
TEXAS						
1 Sandlin	Y	Y	N	Y	Y	Y
2 Turner	N	Y	N	Y	Y	Y
3 ***Johnson, Sam***	N	N	N	Y	Y	Y
4 Hall	N	N	N	Y	Y	Y
5 ***Sessions***	N	N	N	Y	Y	Y
6 ***Barton***	N	N	N	Y	Y	Y
7 ***Archer***	N	N	N	Y	Y	Y
8 ***Brady***	N	N	N	Y	Y	Y
9 Lampson	Y	Y	N	Y	Y	Y
10 Doggett	Y	Y	Y	N	Y	Y
11 Edwards	Y	Y	Y	N	Y	Y
12 ***Granger***	?	N	N	Y	Y	Y
13 ***Thornberry***	N	N	N	Y	Y	Y
14 ***Paul***	N	N	N	Y	Y	Y
15 Hinojosa	Y	Y	Y	N	Y	Y
16 Reyes	N	Y	N	Y	Y	Y
17 Stenholm	N	N	N	Y	Y	Y
18 Jackson-Lee	N	Y	Y	Y	Y	Y
19 ***Combest***	N	N	N	Y	Y	Y
20 Gonzalez	Y	Y	Y	N	Y	Y
21 ***Smith***	N	N	N	Y	Y	Y
22 ***DeLay***	?	N	N	Y	Y	Y
23 ***Bonilla***	N	N	N	Y	Y	Y
24 Frost	N	Y	Y	Y	Y	Y
25 Bentsen	N	Y	Y	N	Y	Y
26 ***Armey***	N	N	N	Y	Y	Y
27 Ortiz	N	Y	N	Y	Y	Y
28 Rodriguez	N	Y	Y	N	Y	Y
29 Green	Y	Y	N	Y	Y	Y
30 Johnson, E.B.	Y	Y	Y	N	Y	Y
UTAH						
1 ***Hansen***	N	Y	N	Y	Y	Y
2 ***Cook***	?	?	?	?	?	?
3 ***Cannon***	?	?	N	Y	Y	Y
VERMONT						
AL *Sanders*	Y	Y	Y	N	Y	Y
VIRGINIA						
1 ***Bateman***	N	N	N	Y	Y	Y
2 Pickett	Y	N	Y	N	Y	Y
3 Scott	N	N	Y	N	Y	Y
4 Sisisky	N	N	N	Y	Y	Y
5 *Goode*	N	N	N	Y	Y	Y
6 ***Goodlatte***	N	N	N	Y	Y	Y
7 ***Bliley***	N	N	N	Y	Y	Y
8 Moran	Y	+	Y	N	Y	Y
9 Boucher	Y	N	Y	N	Y	Y
10 ***Wolf***	N	Y	N	Y	Y	Y
11 ***Davis***	N	N	N	Y	+	+
WASHINGTON						
1 Inslee	N	Y	Y	N	Y	Y
2 ***Metcalf***	N	N	N	Y	Y	Y
3 Baird	Y	Y	Y	N	Y	Y
4 ***Hastings***	N	N	N	Y	Y	Y
5 ***Nethercutt***	N	N	N	Y	Y	Y
6 Dicks	Y	Y	Y	N	Y	Y
7 McDermott	Y	Y	Y	N	Y	Y
8 ***Dunn***	–	+	N	Y	Y	Y
9 Smith	N	Y	Y	N	Y	Y
WEST VIRGINIA						
1 Mollohan	N	N	N	Y	Y	Y
2 Wise	N	Y	N	Y	Y	Y
3 Rahall	N	Y	N	Y	Y	Y
WISCONSIN						
1 ***Ryan***	N	N	N	Y	Y	Y
2 Baldwin	Y	Y	Y	N	Y	Y
3 Kind	N	Y	Y	N	Y	Y
4 Kleczka	N	Y	Y	N	Y	Y
5 Barrett	N	Y	Y	N	Y	Y
6 ***Petri***	N	N	N	Y	Y	Y
7 Obey	Y	Y	Y	N	Y	Y
8 ***Green***	?	N	N	Y	Y	Y
9 ***Sensenbrenner***	N	N	N	Y	Y	Y
WYOMING						
AL ***Cubin***	N	N	N	Y	Y	Y

Southern states - Ala., Ark., Fla., Ga., Ky., La., Miss., N.C., Okla., S.C., Tenn., Texas, Va.

298. H J Res 90. World Trade Organization/Rule. Adoption of the rule (H Res 528) to provide for House floor consideration of the joint resolution that would withdraw congressional approval from the agreement establishing the World Trade Organization. Adopted 343-61: R 205-2; D 137-58 (ND 98-48, SD 39-10); I 1-1. June 21, 2000.

299. HR 4635. Fiscal 2001 VA-HUD Appropriations/Public Housing. Kelly, R-N.Y., amendment that would increase the public housing operating fund by $1 million, offset by decreasing the salaries and expenses for management and administration by an equal amount. Adopted 250-170: R 212-2; D 37-167 (ND 28-122, SD 9-45); I 1-1. June 21, 2000.

300. HR 4635. Fiscal 2001 VA-HUD Appropriations/Fannie Mae-Freddie Mac. Hinchey, D-N.Y., amendment that would increase the bill's appropriation for the Office of Federal Housing Enterprise Oversight, which oversees Fannie Mae and Freddie Mac, by $4.8 million. Rejected 207-211: R 16-198; D 190-12 (ND 142-8, SD 48-4); I 1-1. June 21, 2000.

301. HR 4635. Fiscal 2001 VA-HUD Appropriations/Kyoto Protocol. Olver, D-Mass., amendment that would clarify that the bill's restrictions on the EPA related to implementing the Kyoto Protocol do not apply to activities already authorized by law. Adopted 314-108: R 118-97; D 195-10 (ND 148-3, SD 47-7); I 1-1. June 21, 2000.

302. HR 4635. Fiscal 2001 VA-HUD Appropriations/Space Station. Roemer, D-Ind., amendment that would terminate the International Space Station and put the savings from that project into other programs and toward debt reduction. Rejected 98-325: R 46-170; D 50-155 (ND 48-103, SD 2-52); I 2-0. June 21, 2000. A "nay" was a vote in support of the president's position.

303. HR 4635. Fiscal 2001 VA-HUD Appropriations/Veterans' Benefits. Hinchey, D-N.Y., amendment that would prohibit the Veterans Affairs Department from using any funds in the bill to implement or administer its veterans equitable resource allocation system. Rejected 145-277: R 58-157; D 86-119 (ND 86-65, SD 0-54); I 1-1. June 21, 2000.

Key

- Y Voted for (yea).
- \# Paired for.
- \+ Announced for.
- N Voted against (nay).
- X Paired against.
- – Announced against.
- P Voted "present."
- C Voted "present" to avoid possible conflict of interest.
- ? Did not vote or otherwise make a position known.

•

Democrats ***Republicans***
Independents

	298	299	300	301	302	303
ALABAMA						
1 ***Callahan***	Y	Y	N	N	N	N
2 ***Everett***	Y	Y	N	N	N	N
3 ***Riley***	Y	Y	Y	N	N	N
4 ***Aderholt***	Y	Y	N	N	N	N
5 Cramer	Y	N	N	N	N	N
6 ***Bachus***	Y	Y	N	N	N	N
7 Hilliard	N	N	Y	Y	N	N
ALASKA						
AL ***Young***	?	Y	N	N	Y	N
ARIZONA						
1 ***Salmon***	Y	Y	N	N	N	N
2 Pastor	Y	Y	Y	Y	N	N
3 ***Stump***	Y	Y	N	N	N	N
4 ***Shadegg***	Y	Y	N	N	N	N
5 ***Kolbe***	Y	Y	N	Y	Y	N
6 ***Hayworth***	Y	Y	N	N	N	N
ARKANSAS						
1 Berry	Y	Y	Y	N	N	N
2 Snyder	Y	N	Y	Y	N	N
3 ***Hutchinson***	Y	Y	?	N	N	N
4 ***Dickey***	Y	Y	N	Y	N	N
CALIFORNIA						
1 Thompson	Y	N	Y	Y	N	N
2 ***Herger***	Y	Y	N	N	Y	N
3 ***Ose***	Y	Y	N	Y	N	N
4 ***Doolittle***	Y	Y	N	Y	N	N
5 Matsui	Y	?	Y	Y	N	N
6 Woolsey	N	N	Y	Y	Y	N
7 Miller, George	N	N	Y	Y	Y	N
8 Pelosi	Y	N	Y	Y	Y	N
9 Lee	N	N	Y	Y	Y	N
10 Tauscher	Y	N	Y	Y	N	?
11 ***Pombo***	Y	Y	N	N	N	N
12 Lantos	Y	N	Y	Y	N	N
13 Stark	N	N	Y	Y	Y	N
14 Eshoo	Y	Y	Y	Y	N	N
15 ***Campbell***	?	?	?	?	?	?
16 Lofgren	N	N	Y	Y	N	N
17 Farr	Y	N	Y	Y	N	N
18 Condit	Y	N	Y	Y	N	N
19 ***Radanovich***	Y	Y	N	N	N	N
20 Dooley	Y	N	N	Y	N	N
21 ***Thomas***	Y	Y	N	Y	N	N
22 Capps	Y	N	Y	Y	N	N
23 ***Gallegly***	Y	Y	N	Y	N	N
24 Sherman	N	N	Y	Y	N	N
25 ***McKeon***	Y	Y	N	N	N	N
26 Berman	?	N	Y	Y	N	N
27 ***Rogan***	Y	Y	N	N	N	N
28 ***Dreier***	Y	Y	N	Y	N	N
29 Waxman	Y	N	Y	Y	Y	N
30 Becerra	Y	N	Y	Y	N	N
31 Martinez	?	Y	N	N	N	Y
32 Dixon	Y	N	Y	Y	N	N
33 Roybal-Allard	?	?	?	?	?	?
34 Napolitano	N	N	Y	Y	N	N
35 Waters	N	N	Y	Y	N	Y
36 ***Kuykendall***	Y	Y	N	Y	N	–
37 Millender-McD.	Y	N	Y	Y	N	N
38 ***Horn***	Y	Y	Y	Y	N	Y
39 ***Royce***	Y	Y	N	Y	N	N
40 ***Lewis***	Y	Y	N	Y	N	N
41 ***Miller, Gary***	Y	Y	N	N	N	N
42 Baca	Y	N	Y	Y	N	N
43 ***Calvert***	Y	Y	N	Y	N	N
44 ***Bono***	Y	Y	N	N	N	N
45 ***Rohrabacher***	Y	Y	N	N	N	N
46 Sanchez	Y	N	Y	Y	N	N
47 ***Cox***	Y	Y	?	Y	N	N
48 ***Packard***	?	Y	N	Y	N	N
49 ***Bilbray***	Y	Y	N	Y	Y	N
50 Filner	N	N	Y	Y	N	N
51 ***Cunningham***	Y	Y	N	Y	N	N
52 ***Hunter***	Y	Y	N	Y	N	N
COLORADO						
1 DeGette	Y	N	Y	Y	N	N
2 Udall	Y	N	Y	Y	N	N
3 ***McInnis***	Y	Y	N	N	Y	N
4 ***Schaffer***	Y	Y	N	Y	Y	N
5 ***Hefley***	Y	Y	Y	N	Y	N
6 ***Tancredo***	Y	Y	N	Y	Y	N
CONNECTICUT						
1 Larson	Y	N	Y	Y	N	Y
2 Gejdenson	N	N	Y	Y	N	Y
3 DeLauro	N	N	Y	Y	N	Y
4 ***Shays***	Y	Y	N	Y	Y	Y
5 Maloney	N	N	Y	Y	N	Y
6 ***Johnson***	Y	Y	N	Y	N	Y
DELAWARE						
AL ***Castle***	Y	Y	N	Y	N	Y
FLORIDA						
1 ***Scarborough***	Y	Y	N	N	N	N
2 Boyd	Y	N	N	Y	N	N
3 Brown	N	N	Y	Y	N	N
4 ***Fowler***	Y	Y	N	Y	N	N
5 Thurman	Y	N	Y	Y	N	N
6 ***Stearns***	Y	Y	N	N	N	N
7 ***Mica***	+	Y	N	N	N	N
8 ***McCollum***	Y	Y	N	Y	N	?
9 ***Bilirakis***	Y	Y	N	N	N	N
10 ***Young***	Y	Y	N	Y	N	N
11 Davis	Y	N	Y	Y	N	N
12 ***Canady***	Y	Y	N	N	N	N
13 ***Miller***	Y	Y	N	Y	N	N
14 ***Goss***	Y	Y	N	Y	N	N
15 ***Weldon***	Y	Y	N	Y	N	N
16 ***Foley***	Y	Y	N	Y	N	N
17 Meek	N	N	Y	Y	N	N
18 ***Ros-Lehtinen***	Y	Y	N	Y	N	N
19 Wexler	?	N	Y	Y	N	N
20 Deutsch	Y	N	+	Y	N	N
21 ***Diaz-Balart***	Y	Y	N	N	N	N
22 ***Shaw***	Y	Y	N	Y	N	N
23 Hastings	Y	N	Y	Y	N	N
GEORGIA						
1 ***Kingston***	Y	Y	N	N	Y	N
2 Bishop	Y	Y	Y	Y	N	N
3 ***Collins***	Y	Y	N	Y	N	N
4 McKinney	Y	N	Y	Y	N	N
5 Lewis	N	N	Y	Y	N	N
6 ***Isakson***	Y	Y	N	Y	N	N
7 ***Barr***	Y	Y	N	N	N	N
8 ***Chambliss***	Y	Y	N	N	N	N
9 ***Deal***	Y	Y	N	N	N	N
10 ***Norwood***	Y	Y	N	N	N	N
11 ***Linder***	Y	Y	N	N	N	N
HAWAII						
1 Abercrombie	?	N	?	?	?	N
2 Mink	Y	N	Y	Y	Y	Y
IDAHO						
1 ***Chenoweth-Hage***	Y	Y	N	Y	N	N
2 ***Simpson***	Y	Y	N	N	N	N
ILLINOIS						
1 Rush	N	N	Y	Y	N	Y
2 Jackson	N	N	Y	Y	N	Y
3 Lipinski	N	N	Y	Y	N	Y
4 Gutierrez	N	N	Y	Y	Y	Y
5 Blagojevich	?	N	Y	Y	Y	Y
6 ***Hyde***	Y	Y	N	Y	N	Y
7 Davis	N	N	Y	Y	N	Y
8 ***Crane***	Y	Y	N	N	N	Y
9 Schakowsky	N	N	Y	Y	N	Y
10 ***Porter***	?	Y	N	Y	Y	Y
11 ***Weller***	Y	Y	N	Y	N	Y
12 Costello	N	N	Y	Y	N	Y
13 ***Biggert***	Y	Y	N	N	N	Y

ND Northern Democrats SD Southern Democrats

	298	299	300	301	302	303
14 ***Hastert***						
15 ***Ewing***	Y	?	N	Y	N	Y
16 ***Manzullo***	Y	Y	Y	N	Y	Y
17 Evans	Y	N	Y	Y	Y	N
18 ***LaHood***	N	Y	N	Y	N	Y
19 Phelps	Y	N	Y	Y	Y	N
20 ***Shimkus***	Y	Y	N	Y	N	Y
INDIANA						
1 Visclosky	N	N	Y	Y	Y	N
2 ***McIntosh***	?	?	?	?	?	Y
3 Roemer	Y	Y	N	Y	Y	N
4 ***Souder***	Y	Y	N	N	N	N
5 ***Buyer***	Y	Y	N	N	N	N
6 ***Burton***	+	Y	N	N	N	N
7 ***Pease***	Y	Y	N	Y	Y	N
8 ***Hostettler***	Y	Y	N	N	N	N
9 Hill	Y	Y	Y	Y	N	N
10 Carson	?	N	Y	Y	Y	Y
IOWA						
1 ***Leach***	N	Y	Y	Y	Y	Y
2 ***Nussle***	Y	Y	N	Y	Y	N
3 Boswell	Y	Y	Y	Y	N	Y
4 ***Ganske***	Y	Y	Y	Y	Y	Y
5 ***Latham***	Y	Y	N	Y	Y	Y
KANSAS						
1 ***Moran***	Y	Y	N	N	N	N
2 ***Ryun***	Y	Y	N	N	N	N
3 Moore	Y	Y	N	Y	N	Y
4 ***Tiahrt***	Y	Y	N	N	N	N
KENTUCKY						
1 ***Whitfield***	Y	Y	N	N	N	N
2 ***Lewis***	Y	Y	N	N	N	N
3 ***Northup***	Y	Y	N	Y	N	N
4 Lucas	Y	Y	Y	Y	N	N
5 ***Rogers***	Y	Y	N	Y	N	N
6 ***Fletcher***	Y	Y	N	Y	N	N
LOUISIANA						
1 ***Vitter***	Y	Y	Y	N	N	N
2 Jefferson	?	N	Y	Y	N	N
3 ***Tauzin***	Y	Y	N	N	N	N
4 ***McCrery***	Y	Y	N	N	N	N
5 ***Cooksey***	Y	Y	N	Y	N	N
6 ***Baker***	Y	Y	N	Y	N	N
7 John	Y	N	Y	Y	N	N
MAINE						
1 Allen	Y	N	Y	Y	N	Y
2 Baldacci	Y	Y	Y	Y	N	Y
MARYLAND						
1 ***Gilchrest***	Y	Y	N	Y	N	N
2 ***Ehrlich***	Y	Y	N	Y	N	N
3 Cardin	Y	N	Y	Y	N	N
4 Wynn	?	?	?	?	?	?
5 Hoyer	Y	N	Y	Y	N	N
6 ***Bartlett***	Y	Y	N	Y	N	N
7 Cummings	Y	N	Y	Y	N	N
8 ***Morella***	Y	N	Y	Y	N	N
MASSACHUSETTS						
1 Olver	N	N	Y	Y	Y	Y
2 Neal	Y	Y	Y	Y	N	Y
3 McGovern	N	N	Y	Y	N	Y
4 Frank	N	N	N	Y	Y	Y
5 Meehan	Y	Y	Y	Y	Y	Y
6 Tierney	N	N	Y	Y	Y	Y
7 Markey	N	N	Y	Y	N	Y
8 Capuano	N	N	Y	Y	N	Y
9 Moakley	Y	Y	Y	Y	N	Y
10 Delahunt	Y	N	Y	Y	Y	Y
MICHIGAN						
1 Stupak	Y	Y	Y	Y	N	Y
2 ***Hoekstra***	Y	Y	N	Y	Y	Y
3 ***Ehlers***	Y	Y	N	Y	N	Y
4 ***Camp***	Y	Y	N	Y	Y	Y
5 Barcia	Y	N	Y	Y	N	Y
6 ***Upton***	Y	Y	N	Y	Y	Y
7 ***Smith***	Y	Y	N	Y	Y	N
8 Stabenow	Y	Y	Y	Y	N	Y
9 Kildee	Y	N	Y	Y	Y	Y
10 Bonior	N	N	Y	Y	N	Y
11 ***Knollenberg***	Y	Y	N	Y	N	N
12 Levin	Y	N	Y	Y	Y	Y
13 Rivers	Y	N	Y	Y	Y	Y
14 Conyers	Y	N	Y	Y	N	Y
15 Kilpatrick	Y	N	Y	Y	N	Y
16 Dingell	N	N	Y	N	Y	Y

	298	299	300	301	302	303
MINNESOTA						
1 ***Gutknecht***	Y	Y	Y	Y	N	N
2 Minge	Y	N	Y	Y	Y	N
3 ***Ramstad***	Y	Y	N	Y	Y	N
4 Vento	?	?	?	?	?	?
5 Sabo	Y	N	Y	Y	N	N
6 Luther	Y	Y	Y	Y	Y	N
7 Peterson	N	Y	Y	Y	N	N
8 Oberstar	Y	N	Y	Y	Y	N
MISSISSIPPI						
1 ***Wicker***	Y	Y	N	N	N	N
2 Thompson	N	N	Y	Y	N	N
3 ***Pickering***	Y	Y	N	N	N	N
4 Shows	Y	Y	Y	Y	N	N
5 Taylor	Y	Y	Y	Y	N	N
MISSOURI						
1 Clay	N	N	Y	Y	N	Y
2 ***Talent***	Y	Y	N	Y	N	N
3 Gephardt	Y	N	Y	Y	N	N
4 Skelton	N	N	Y	Y	N	N
5 McCarthy	Y	Y	Y	Y	N	N
6 Danner	Y	Y	Y	Y	Y	Y
7 ***Blunt***	Y	Y	N	N	N	N
8 ***Emerson***	Y	Y	N	Y	N	N
9 ***Hulshof***	Y	Y	N	N	N	Y
MONTANA						
AL ***Hill***	Y	Y	N	Y	N	N
NEBRASKA						
1 ***Bereuter***	Y	Y	Y	Y	Y	Y
2 ***Terry***	Y	Y	Y	Y	N	Y
3 ***Barrett***	Y	Y	N	Y	N	Y
NEVADA						
1 Berkley	N	N	Y	Y	N	N
2 ***Gibbons***	Y	Y	N	Y	N	N
NEW HAMPSHIRE						
1 ***Sununu***	Y	Y	N	Y	N	Y
2 ***Bass***	Y	Y	N	Y	Y	Y
NEW JERSEY						
1 Andrews	?	N	Y	Y	N	Y
2 ***LoBiondo***	Y	Y	N	Y	Y	Y
3 ***Saxton***	Y	Y	N	Y	N	Y
4 ***Smith***	?	Y	N	Y	N	Y
5 ***Roukema***	Y	Y	N	Y	Y	Y
6 Pallone	N	N	Y	Y	Y	Y
7 ***Franks***	Y	Y	N	Y	Y	Y
8 Pascrell	Y	Y	Y	Y	Y	Y
9 Rothman	N	Y	Y	Y	N	Y
10 Payne	N	N	Y	Y	N	Y
11 ***Frelinghuysen***	Y	Y	N	Y	N	Y
12 Holt	N	N	Y	Y	Y	Y
13 Menendez	Y	N	Y	Y	N	Y
NEW MEXICO						
1 ***Wilson***	Y	Y	N	Y	N	N
2 ***Skeen***	Y	Y	N	N	N	N
3 Udall	N	N	Y	Y	Y	N
NEW YORK						
1 Forbes	Y	N	Y	Y	N	Y
2 ***Lazio***	Y	Y	N	Y	Y	Y
3 ***King***	Y	Y	N	Y	N	Y
4 McCarthy	Y	N	Y	Y	N	Y
5 Ackerman	Y	N	Y	Y	N	Y
6 Meeks	?	N	Y	Y	N	Y
7 Crowley	Y	N	Y	Y	N	Y
8 Nadler	N	N	Y	Y	Y	Y
9 Weiner	Y	N	Y	Y	N	Y
10 Towns	N	N	Y	Y	N	Y
11 Owens	N	N	Y	Y	N	Y
12 Velázquez	N	N	Y	Y	N	Y
13 ***Fossella***	+	Y	N	Y	N	Y
14 Maloney	Y	N	Y	Y	Y	Y
15 Rangel	Y	?	?	?	?	?
16 Serrano	Y	?	?	?	?	?
17 Engel	?	N	Y	Y	N	Y
18 Lowey	Y	N	Y	Y	Y	Y
19 ***Kelly***	Y	Y	Y	Y	Y	Y
20 ***Gilman***	Y	Y	N	Y	N	Y
21 McNulty	Y	N	Y	Y	N	Y
22 ***Sweeney***	?	Y	N	Y	N	Y
23 ***Boehlert***	Y	Y	N	Y	N	Y
24 ***McHugh***	Y	Y	N	Y	N	Y
25 ***Walsh***	Y	Y	N	Y	N	Y
26 Hinchey	N	N	Y	Y	N	Y
27 ***Reynolds***	Y	?	?	?	?	Y
28 Slaughter	N	?	Y	Y	N	Y
29 LaFalce	Y	N	Y	Y	N	Y

	298	299	300	301	302	303
30 ***Quinn***	Y	Y	N	Y	N	Y
31 ***Houghton***	Y	Y	N	Y	N	Y
NORTH CAROLINA						
1 Clayton	?	N	Y	Y	N	N
2 Etheridge	Y	N	Y	Y	N	N
3 ***Jones***	Y	Y	N	N	N	N
4 Price	Y	N	Y	Y	N	N
5 ***Burr***	Y	Y	N	N	N	N
6 ***Coble***	Y	Y	N	N	Y	N
7 McIntyre	Y	N	Y	N	N	N
8 ***Hayes***	Y	Y	N	N	N	N
9 ***Myrick***	Y	Y	N	N	Y	N
10 ***Ballenger***	Y	Y	N	N	N	N
11 ***Taylor***	Y	Y	N	N	N	N
12 Watt	N	N	Y	Y	N	N
NORTH DAKOTA						
AL Pomeroy	Y	N	Y	Y	Y	N
OHIO						
1 ***Chabot***	Y	Y	N	N	Y	Y
2 ***Portman***	Y	Y	N	Y	Y	N
3 Hall	Y	N	Y	Y	N	N
4 ***Oxley***	Y	Y	N	Y	N	N
5 ***Gillmor***	Y	Y	N	Y	N	N
6 Strickland	N	N	N	Y	Y	N
7 ***Hobson***	Y	Y	N	Y	N	N
8 ***Boehner***	Y	Y	N	Y	N	N
9 Kaptur	Y	N	Y	Y	Y	Y
10 Kucinich	N	N	Y	Y	N	N
11 Jones	Y	N	Y	Y	N	N
12 ***Kasich***	Y	N	Y	Y	N	N
13 Brown	N	N	Y	Y	Y	N
14 Sawyer	Y	N	Y	Y	N	N
15 ***Pryce***	Y	Y	N	Y	N	N
16 ***Regula***	Y	Y	N	Y	N	N
17 Traficant	Y	Y	N	N	N	N
18 ***Ney***	Y	Y	N	N	N	N
19 ***LaTourette***	Y	Y	N	Y	N	N
OKLAHOMA						
1 ***Largent***	?	Y	N	Y	Y	N
2 ***Coburn***	Y	Y	N	N	N	N
3 ***Watkins***	Y	Y	N	N	N	N
4 ***Watts***	Y	Y	N	N	N	N
5 ***Istook***	Y	Y	N	N	N	N
6 ***Lucas***	Y	Y	Y	N	N	N
OREGON						
1 Wu	Y	N	Y	Y	N	N
2 ***Walden***	Y	Y	N	N	N	N
3 Blumenauer	Y	N	Y	Y	Y	N
4 DeFazio	N	N	Y	Y	Y	N
5 Hooley	Y	N	Y	Y	N	N
PENNSYLVANIA						
1 Brady	Y	N	Y	Y	N	Y
2 Fattah	Y	N	Y	Y	N	Y
3 Borski	Y	N	Y	Y	N	Y
4 Klink	Y	Y	Y	Y	N	Y
5 ***Peterson***	Y	Y	N	N	N	N
6 Holden	Y	N	Y	Y	Y	Y
7 ***Weldon***	Y	Y	N	Y	N	Y
8 ***Greenwood***	Y	?	N	Y	N	Y
9 ***Shuster***	Y	Y	N	N	Y	Y
10 ***Sherwood***	Y	Y	N	Y	N	Y
11 Kanjorski	Y	N	Y	Y	Y	Y
12 Murtha	Y	N	Y	Y	N	Y
13 Hoeffel	Y	Y	Y	Y	N	Y
14 Coyne	Y	N	Y	Y	Y	Y
15 ***Toomey***	Y	Y	Y	Y	N	Y
16 ***Pitts***	Y	Y	N	N	N	Y
17 ***Gekas***	Y	Y	N	?	N	N
18 Doyle	Y	Y	Y	Y	N	Y
19 ***Goodling***	Y	Y	N	N	Y	Y
20 Mascara	Y	Y	Y	Y	N	Y
21 ***English***	Y	Y	N	Y	N	Y
RHODE ISLAND						
1 Kennedy	Y	N	?	Y	N	Y
2 Weygand	Y	Y	Y	Y	N	Y
SOUTH CAROLINA						
1 ***Sanford***	Y	Y	N	Y	Y	N
2 ***Spence***	Y	Y	N	Y	N	N
3 ***Graham***	Y	Y	N	N	N	N
4 ***DeMint***	Y	Y	N	N	N	N
5 Spratt	Y	N	Y	Y	Y	N
6 Clyburn	N	N	Y	Y	N	N
SOUTH DAKOTA						
AL ***Thune***	Y	Y	N	Y	N	N

	298	299	300	301	302	303
TENNESSEE						
1 ***Jenkins***	Y	Y	N	N	N	N
2 ***Duncan***	Y	Y	N	N	Y	N
3 ***Wamp***	Y	Y	N	N	N	N
4 ***Hilleary***	Y	Y	N	N	Y	N
5 Clement	Y	Y	Y	Y	N	N
6 Gordon	Y	N	N	Y	N	N
7 ***Bryant***	Y	Y	N	Y	Y	N
8 Tanner	Y	N	Y	Y	N	N
9 Ford	?	N	Y	Y	Y	N
TEXAS						
1 Sandlin	Y	N	Y	N	N	N
2 Turner	Y	N	Y	Y	N	N
3 ***Johnson, Sam***	Y	Y	N	N	N	N
4 Hall	Y	Y	Y	N	N	N
5 ***Sessions***	Y	Y	N	N	N	N
6 ***Barton***	?	Y	N	N	N	N
7 ***Archer***	Y	Y	N	N	N	N
8 ***Brady***	Y	Y	N	N	N	N
9 Lampson	Y	N	Y	Y	N	N
10 Doggett	Y	N	Y	Y	N	N
11 Edwards	Y	N	Y	Y	N	N
12 ***Granger***	Y	Y	N	N	N	N
13 ***Thornberry***	Y	Y	N	N	N	?
14 ***Paul***	Y	Y	N	N	Y	N
15 Hinojosa	Y	N	Y	Y	N	N
16 Reyes	Y	N	Y	Y	N	N
17 Stenholm	Y	Y	Y	N	N	N
18 Jackson-Lee	N	N	Y	Y	N	N
19 ***Combest***	Y	Y	N	N	N	N
20 Gonzalez	Y	N	Y	Y	N	N
21 ***Smith***	Y	Y	N	N	N	N
22 ***DeLay***	Y	?	?	?	?	?
23 ***Bonilla***	Y	Y	N	N	Y	N
24 Frost	N	N	Y	Y	N	N
25 Bentsen	Y	N	Y	Y	N	N
26 ***Armey***	Y	Y	N	N	N	N
27 Ortiz	Y	N	Y	Y	N	N
28 Rodriguez	Y	N	Y	Y	N	N
29 Green	Y	N	Y	Y	N	N
30 Johnson, E.B.	N	N	Y	Y	N	N
UTAH						
1 ***Hansen***	Y	Y	N	Y	N	N
2 ***Cook***	?	?	?	?	?	?
3 ***Cannon***	Y	Y	N	Y	N	N
VERMONT						
AL *Sanders*	N	N	Y	Y	Y	Y
VIRGINIA						
1 ***Bateman***	Y	Y	N	N	N	N
2 Pickett	Y	Y	N	Y	N	N
3 Scott	Y	N	Y	Y	N	N
4 Sisisky	Y	N	Y	Y	N	N
5 *Goode*	Y	Y	N	N	Y	N
6 ***Goodlatte***	Y	Y	N	N	Y	N
7 ***Bliley***	Y	Y	N	N	N	N
8 Moran	?	N	?	Y	N	N
9 Boucher	Y	N	Y	N	N	N
10 ***Wolf***	Y	Y	N	Y	N	N
11 ***Davis***	Y	Y	N	Y	N	N
WASHINGTON						
1 Inslee	Y	Y	Y	Y	N	N
2 ***Metcalf***	Y	Y	N	Y	N	N
3 Baird	Y	N	Y	Y	N	N
4 ***Hastings***	Y	Y	N	N	N	N
5 ***Nethercutt***	Y	Y	N	Y	N	N
6 Dicks	Y	N	Y	Y	N	N
7 McDermott	Y	N	Y	Y	N	N
8 ***Dunn***	Y	Y	N	Y	N	N
9 Smith	Y	Y	Y	Y	N	N
WEST VIRGINIA						
1 Mollohan	Y	N	N	Y	N	Y
2 Wise	Y	Y	Y	Y	N	N
3 Rahall	Y	N	Y	Y	N	N
WISCONSIN						
1 ***Ryan***	Y	Y	N	Y	Y	Y
2 Baldwin	Y	N	Y	Y	N	Y
3 Kind	Y	N	Y	Y	Y	Y
4 Kleczka	Y	N	Y	Y	N	Y
5 Barrett	Y	N	Y	Y	Y	Y
6 ***Petri***	Y	Y	N	Y	Y	Y
7 Obey	N	N	Y	Y	N	Y
8 ***Green***	Y	Y	N	Y	Y	Y
9 ***Sensenbrenner***	Y	Y	N	N	N	Y
WYOMING						
AL ***Cubin***	?	Y	N	N	N	N

Southern states - Ala., Ark., Fla., Ga., Ky., La., Miss., N.C., Okla., S.C., Tenn., Texas, Va.

304. HR 4635. Fiscal 2001 VA-HUD Appropriations/EPA. Hinchey, D-N.Y., amendment that would delete language in the bill that would prevent the EPA from encouraging the use of dredging, enforcing arsenic drinking water standards and issuing radon water standards. Rejected 208-216: R 28-188; D 179-27 (ND 142-10, SD 37-17); I 1-1. A "yea" was a vote in support of the president's position. June 21, 2000.

305. HR 4635. Fiscal 2001 VA-HUD Appropriations/EPA. Collins, R-Ga., amendment that would delay until June 15, 2001, the use of funds by the EPA to designate ozone non-attainment areas under the more strict national ambient air quality standards issued by the EPA in 1997. Adopted 225-199: R 167-49; D 57-149 (ND 30-122, SD 27-27); I 1-1. June 21, 2000. A "nay" was a vote in support of the president's position.

306. HR 4635. Fiscal 2001 VA-HUD Appropriations/Gun Safety. Hostettler, R-Ind., amendment that would prohibit the Department of Housing and Urban Development from using funds to administer its communities for safer guns coalition. Under the program, municipalities would give preference to gun manufacturers, which would agree to abide by a code of conduct when purchasing weapons for municipal police forces. Adopted 218-207: R 173-44; D 44-162 (ND 22-130, SD 22-32); I 1-1. June 21, 2000.

307. HR 4635. Fiscal 2001 VA-HUD Appropriations/Low-Income Housing. Nadler, D-N.Y., amendment that would appropriate an additional $344 million to the Department of Housing and Urban Development to use for Section 8 low-income housing vouchers. The increase would be offset by an equal decrease in funding for the International Space Station. Rejected 138-286: R 31-185; D 106-100 (ND 100-52, SD 6-48); I 1-1. June 21, 2000.

308. HR 4635. Fiscal 2001 VA-HUD Appropriations/Gun Safety. Hostettler, R-Ind., amendment that would prohibit the Department of Housing and Urban Development (HUD) from using funds to enforce, implement or administer the settlement reached in March between HUD and Smith & Wesson. The agreement states HUD would give preference to gun manufacturers that agree to abide by a code of conduct when purchasing weapons for housing authority security forces. Rejected 206-219: R 163-54; D 42-164 (ND 20-132, SD 22-32); I 1-1. June 21, 2000.

Key

- Y Voted for (yea).
- # Paired for.
- + Announced for.
- N Voted against (nay).
- X Paired against.
- – Announced against.
- P Voted "present."
- C Voted "present" to avoid possible conflict of interest.
- ? Did not vote or otherwise make a position known.

Democrats ***Republicans*** *Independents*

	304	305	306	307	308
ALABAMA					
1 ***Callahan***	N	Y	Y	N	Y
2 ***Everett***	N	Y	Y	N	Y
3 ***Riley***	N	Y	Y	N	Y
4 ***Aderholt***	N	Y	Y	N	Y
5 Cramer	N	Y	Y	N	Y
6 ***Bachus***	N	Y	Y	N	Y
7 Hilliard	Y	N	N	Y	N
ALASKA					
AL ***Young***	N	Y	Y	N	Y
ARIZONA					
1 ***Salmon***	N	Y	Y	N	Y
2 Pastor	Y	Y	N	Y	N
3 ***Stump***	N	Y	Y	N	Y
4 ***Shadegg***	N	Y	Y	N	Y
5 ***Kolbe***	N	N	Y	N	Y
6 ***Hayworth***	N	Y	Y	N	Y
ARKANSAS					
1 Berry	N	Y	Y	N	Y
2 Snyder	Y	N	N	N	N
3 ***Hutchinson***	N	Y	Y	N	Y
4 ***Dickey***	N	Y	Y	N	Y
CALIFORNIA					
1 Thompson	Y	N	Y	Y	N
2 ***Herger***	N	Y	Y	N	Y
3 ***Ose***	N	Y	Y	N	Y
4 ***Doolittle***	N	Y	Y	N	Y
5 Matsui	Y	N	N	N	N
6 Woolsey	Y	N	N	Y	N
7 Miller, George	Y	N	N	Y	N
8 Pelosi	Y	N	N	Y	N
9 Lee	Y	N	N	Y	N
10 Tauscher	Y	N	N	N	N
11 ***Pombo***	N	Y	Y	N	Y
12 Lantos	Y	N	N	Y	N
13 Stark	Y	N	N	Y	N
14 Eshoo	Y	N	N	N	N
15 ***Campbell***	?	?	?	?	?
16 Lofgren	Y	N	N	N	N
17 Farr	Y	N	N	Y	N
18 Condit	Y	N	N	N	N
19 ***Radanovich***	N	Y	Y	N	N
20 Dooley	N	Y	N	Y	N
21 ***Thomas***	N	Y	Y	N	Y
22 Capps	Y	N	N	Y	N
23 ***Gallegly***	N	N	Y	N	N
24 Sherman	Y	N	N	N	N
25 ***McKeon***	N	Y	Y	N	Y
26 Berman	Y	N	N	Y	N
27 ***Rogan***	N	Y	N	N	N
28 ***Dreier***	N	Y	Y	N	Y
29 Waxman	Y	N	N	Y	N
30 Becerra	Y	N	N	Y	N
31 Martinez	N	Y	Y	N	Y
32 Dixon	Y	N	N	Y	N
33 Roybal-Allard	?	?	?	?	?
34 Napolitano	Y	N	N	Y	N
35 Waters	Y	N	N	Y	N
36 ***Kuykendall***	–	–	–	–	–
37 Millender-McD.	Y	N	N	Y	N
38 ***Horn***	Y	N	N	?	N
39 ***Royce***	N	Y	Y	N	Y
40 ***Lewis***	Y	N	Y	N	Y
41 ***Miller, Gary***	N	Y	Y	N	Y
42 Baca	Y	Y	Y	N	Y
43 ***Calvert***	N	N	Y	N	Y
44 ***Bono***	N	Y	Y	N	Y
45 ***Rohrabacher***	N	Y	Y	N	Y
46 Sanchez	Y	N	N	Y	N
47 ***Cox***	N	Y	Y	N	Y
48 ***Packard***	N	Y	Y	N	N
49 ***Bilbray***	Y	N	N	Y	N
50 Filner	Y	N	N	Y	N
51 ***Cunningham***	N	Y	Y	N	Y
52 ***Hunter***	N	Y	Y	N	Y
COLORADO					
1 DeGette	Y	N	N	Y	N
2 Udall	Y	N	N	Y	N
3 ***McInnis***	N	N	Y	N	Y
4 ***Schaffer***	N	Y	Y	Y	Y
5 ***Hefley***	N	Y	Y	Y	Y
6 ***Tancredo***	N	Y	Y	Y	N
CONNECTICUT					
1 Larson	Y	N	N	N	N
2 Gejdenson	Y	N	N	N	N
3 DeLauro	Y	N	N	Y	N
4 ***Shays***	Y	N	N	Y	N
5 Maloney	Y	N	N	N	N
6 ***Johnson***	Y	N	N	N	N
DELAWARE					
AL ***Castle***	Y	N	N	N	N
FLORIDA					
1 ***Scarborough***	Y	N	Y	N	Y
2 Boyd	N	Y	Y	N	Y
3 Brown	Y	N	N	N	N
4 ***Fowler***	N	Y	Y	N	Y
5 Thurman	Y	N	N	N	N
6 ***Stearns***	N	Y	Y	N	Y
7 ***Mica***	N	Y	Y	N	Y
8 ***McCollum***	?	Y	Y	N	N
9 ***Bilirakis***	Y	N	Y	N	Y
10 ***Young***	N	Y	Y	N	N
11 Davis	Y	N	N	N	N
12 ***Canady***	N	Y	Y	N	Y
13 ***Miller***	N	N	Y	N	N
14 ***Goss***	N	N	Y	N	Y
15 ***Weldon***	N	Y	Y	N	Y
16 ***Foley***	N	Y	N	N	N
17 Meek	Y	N	N	N	N
18 ***Ros-Lehtinen***	N	Y	Y	N	N
19 Wexler	Y	N	N	N	N
20 Deutsch	Y	N	N	N	N
21 ***Diaz-Balart***	N	Y	Y	N	N
22 ***Shaw***	N	N	N	N	N
23 Hastings	Y	N	N	N	N
GEORGIA					
1 ***Kingston***	N	Y	Y	N	Y
2 Bishop	N	Y	Y	N	Y
3 ***Collins***	N	Y	Y	N	Y
4 McKinney	Y	N	N	Y	N
5 Lewis	Y	N	N	Y	N
6 ***Isakson***	N	Y	Y	N	N
7 ***Barr***	N	Y	Y	N	Y
8 ***Chambliss***	N	Y	Y	N	Y
9 ***Deal***	N	Y	Y	N	Y
10 ***Norwood***	N	Y	Y	N	Y
11 ***Linder***	N	Y	Y	N	Y
HAWAII					
1 Abercrombie	Y	N	N	Y	N
2 Mink	Y	N	N	Y	N
IDAHO					
1 ***Chenoweth-Hage***	N	?	Y	N	Y
2 ***Simpson***	N	Y	Y	N	Y
ILLINOIS					
1 Rush	Y	N	N	Y	N
2 Jackson	Y	N	N	Y	N
3 Lipinski	Y	Y	N	N	N
4 Gutierrez	Y	N	N	Y	N
5 Blagojevich	Y	N	N	Y	N
6 ***Hyde***	N	Y	N	N	N
7 Davis	Y	N	N	Y	N
8 ***Crane***	N	Y	Y	N	Y
9 Schakowsky	Y	N	N	Y	N
10 ***Porter***	N	N	N	Y	N
11 ***Weller***	N	N	N	N	N
12 Costello	N	N	Y	Y	Y
13 ***Biggert***	N	Y	Y	N	Y

ND Northern Democrats SD Southern Democrats

	304	305	306	307	308
14 ***Hastert***					
15 ***Ewing***	N	Y	N	N	N
16 ***Manzullo***	N	Y	Y	N	Y
17 Evans	Y	N	N	Y	N
18 ***LaHood***	N	Y	Y	N	Y
19 Phelps	N	Y	Y	Y	Y
20 ***Shimkus***	N	Y	Y	N	Y
INDIANA					
1 Visclosky	Y	N	N	Y	N
2 ***McIntosh***	N	Y	Y	N	Y
3 Roemer	Y	Y	N	Y	N
4 ***Souder***	N	Y	Y	N	Y
5 ***Buyer***	N	Y	Y	N	Y
6 ***Burton***	N	Y	Y	N	Y
7 ***Pease***	N	Y	Y	N	Y
8 ***Hostettler***	N	Y	Y	N	Y
9 Hill	Y	Y	Y	N	Y
10 Carson	Y	Y	N	Y	N
IOWA					
1 ***Leach***	Y	N	N	Y	N
2 ***Nussle***	N	N	Y	Y	Y
3 Boswell	Y	Y	Y	N	Y
4 ***Ganske***	N	N	Y	Y	N
5 ***Latham***	N	Y	Y	Y	Y
KANSAS					
1 ***Moran***	N	Y	Y	N	Y
2 ***Ryun***	N	Y	Y	N	Y
3 Moore	Y	N	N	Y	N
4 ***Tiahrt***	N	Y	Y	N	Y
KENTUCKY					
1 ***Whitfield***	N	Y	Y	Y	Y
2 ***Lewis***	N	Y	Y	N	Y
3 ***Northup***	N	Y	N	N	N
4 Lucas	N	Y	Y	N	Y
5 ***Rogers***	N	Y	Y	N	Y
6 ***Fletcher***	N	Y	Y	N	Y
LOUISIANA					
1 ***Vitter***	N	Y	Y	N	Y
2 Jefferson	Y	N	N	N	N
3 ***Tauzin***	N	Y	Y	N	Y
4 ***McCrery***	N	Y	Y	N	Y
5 ***Cooksey***	N	Y	Y	N	Y
6 ***Baker***	N	Y	Y	N	Y
7 John	N	Y	Y	N	Y
MAINE					
1 Allen	Y	N	N	N	N
2 Baldacci	Y	N	N	N	N
MARYLAND					
1 ***Gilchrest***	Y	N	N	N	N
2 ***Ehrlich***	N	Y	Y	N	Y
3 Cardin	Y	N	N	N	N
4 Wynn	?	?	?	?	?
5 Hoyer	Y	N	N	N	N
6 ***Bartlett***	N	Y	Y	N	Y
7 Cummings	Y	N	N	N	N
8 ***Morella***	Y	N	N	N	N
MASSACHUSETTS					
1 Olver	Y	N	N	Y	N
2 Neal	Y	N	N	N	N
3 McGovern	Y	N	N	N	N
4 Frank	Y	N	N	N	N
5 Meehan	Y	N	N	Y	N
6 Tierney	Y	N	N	Y	N
7 Markey	Y	N	N	Y	N
8 Capuano	Y	N	N	Y	N
9 Moakley	Y	N	N	N	N
10 Delahunt	Y	N	N	Y	N
MICHIGAN					
1 Stupak	Y	Y	N	Y	N
2 ***Hoekstra***	N	Y	Y	N	Y
3 ***Ehlers***	Y	N	N	N	N
4 ***Camp***	N	Y	Y	Y	Y
5 Barcia	N	Y	Y	N	Y
6 ***Upton***	N	Y	N	Y	N
7 ***Smith***	N	Y	Y	N	Y
8 Stabenow	Y	Y	N	Y	N
9 Kildee	Y	Y	N	Y	N
10 Bonior	Y	N	N	Y	N
11 ***Knollenberg***	N	Y	Y	N	Y
12 Levin	Y	Y	N	Y	N
13 Rivers	Y	N	N	Y	N
14 Conyers	Y	Y	N	Y	N
15 Kilpatrick	Y	Y	N	Y	N
16 Dingell	Y	Y	Y	Y	Y

	304	305	306	307	308
MINNESOTA					
1 ***Gutknecht***	N	N	Y	N	Y
2 Minge	Y	N	N	Y	N
3 ***Ramstad***	Y	N	N	Y	N
4 Vento	?	?	?	?	?
5 Sabo	Y	N	N	Y	N
6 Luther	Y	N	N	Y	N
7 Peterson	N	N	Y	N	Y
8 Oberstar	Y	N	N	Y	N
MISSISSIPPI					
1 ***Wicker***	N	Y	Y	N	Y
2 Thompson	Y	N	N	N	N
3 ***Pickering***	N	Y	Y	N	Y
4 Shows	N	Y	Y	N	Y
5 Taylor	N	N	Y	N	Y
MISSOURI					
1 Clay	Y	N	N	Y	N
2 ***Talent***	N	Y	Y	N	Y
3 Gephardt	Y	N	N	N	N
4 Skelton	Y	Y	Y	N	Y
5 McCarthy	N	N	N	N	N
6 Danner	N	Y	Y	Y	Y
7 ***Blunt***	N	Y	Y	N	Y
8 ***Emerson***	N	Y	Y	N	Y
9 ***Hulshof***	N	Y	Y	N	Y
MONTANA					
AL ***Hill***	N	Y	Y	N	Y
NEBRASKA					
1 ***Bereuter***	N	N	Y	Y	N
2 ***Terry***	N	Y	Y	N	Y
3 ***Barrett***	N	Y	Y	N	Y
NEVADA					
1 Berkley	Y	N	N	Y	N
2 ***Gibbons***	N	Y	Y	N	Y
NEW HAMPSHIRE					
1 ***Sununu***	N	N	Y	N	Y
2 ***Bass***	N	N	Y	Y	Y
NEW JERSEY					
1 Andrews	Y	N	N	N	N
2 ***LoBiondo***	Y	N	N	N	N
3 ***Saxton***	Y	N	N	N	N
4 ***Smith***	Y	N	N	Y	N
5 ***Roukema***	Y	N	N	N	N
6 Pallone	Y	N	N	Y	N
7 ***Franks***	Y	N	N	Y	N
8 Pascrell	Y	N	N	Y	N
9 Rothman	Y	N	N	N	N
10 Payne	Y	N	N	Y	N
11 ***Frelinghuysen***	Y	N	N	N	N
12 Holt	Y	N	N	Y	N
13 Menendez	Y	N	N	Y	N
NEW MEXICO					
1 ***Wilson***	Y	Y	N	Y	Y
2 ***Skeen***	N	Y	Y	N	Y
3 Udall	Y	N	N	Y	N
NEW YORK					
1 Forbes	Y	N	N	N	N
2 ***Lazio***	Y	N	N	Y	N
3 ***King***	N	N	N	N	N
4 McCarthy	Y	N	N	N	N
5 Ackerman	Y	N	N	Y	N
6 Meeks	Y	N	N	Y	N
7 Crowley	Y	N	N	Y	N
8 Nadler	Y	N	N	Y	N
9 Weiner	Y	N	N	Y	N
10 Towns	Y	N	N	Y	N
11 Owens	Y	N	N	Y	N
12 Velázquez	Y	N	N	Y	N
13 ***Fossella***	N	N	N	N	N
14 Maloney	Y	N	N	Y	N
15 Rangel	?	?	?	?	?
16 Serrano	?	?	?	?	?
17 Engel	Y	N	N	Y	N
18 Lowey	Y	N	N	Y	N
19 ***Kelly***	Y	N	Y	N	N
20 ***Gilman***	Y	N	N	N	N
21 McNulty	Y	N	N	Y	N
22 ***Sweeney***	N	N	N	N	Y
23 ***Boehlert***	Y	N	N	N	N
24 ***McHugh***	N	N	N	Y	Y
25 ***Walsh***	N	N	N	N	N
26 Hinchey	Y	N	N	Y	N
27 ***Reynolds***	N	Y	Y	N	Y
28 Slaughter	Y	N	N	Y	N
29 LaFalce	Y	N	N	Y	N

	304	305	306	307	308
30 ***Quinn***	N	N	N	Y	N
31 ***Houghton***	N	N	N	N	N
NORTH CAROLINA					
1 Clayton	Y	N	N	Y	N
2 Etheridge	Y	N	N	N	N
3 ***Jones***	N	Y	Y	N	Y
4 Price	Y	N	N	N	N
5 ***Burr***	N	Y	Y	N	Y
6 ***Coble***	N	Y	Y	N	Y
7 McIntyre	N	Y	Y	N	Y
8 ***Hayes***	N	Y	Y	N	Y
9 ***Myrick***	N	Y	Y	Y	Y
10 ***Ballenger***	N	Y	Y	N	Y
11 ***Taylor***	N	Y	Y	N	Y
12 Watt	Y	N	N	Y	N
NORTH DAKOTA					
AL Pomeroy	N	N	N	Y	N
OHIO					
1 ***Chabot***	N	Y	Y	Y	Y
2 ***Portman***	N	Y	Y	N	Y
3 Hall	Y	N	N	N	N
4 ***Oxley***	N	Y	Y	N	Y
5 ***Gillmor***	N	Y	N	N	N
6 Strickland	Y	Y	Y	Y	Y
7 ***Hobson***	N	Y	N	N	Y
8 ***Boehner***	N	Y	Y	N	Y
9 Kaptur	Y	N	N	Y	N
10 Kucinich	Y	N	N	N	N
11 Jones	Y	N	N	Y	N
12 ***Kasich***	Y	Y	Y	N	Y
13 Brown	Y	N	N	Y	N
14 Sawyer	Y	N	N	N	N
15 ***Pryce***	N	Y	N	N	N
16 ***Regula***	N	Y	N	N	N
17 Traficant	N	Y	Y	N	Y
18 ***Ney***	N	Y	Y	N	Y
19 ***LaTourette***	Y	Y	Y	N	N
OKLAHOMA					
1 ***Largent***	N	Y	Y	N	Y
2 ***Coburn***	N	Y	Y	N	Y
3 ***Watkins***	N	Y	Y	N	Y
4 ***Watts***	N	Y	Y	N	Y
5 ***Istook***	N	Y	Y	N	Y
6 ***Lucas***	N	Y	Y	N	Y
OREGON					
1 Wu	Y	N	N	N	N
2 ***Walden***	N	Y	Y	N	Y
3 Blumenauer	Y	N	N	Y	N
4 DeFazio	Y	N	Y	Y	N
5 Hooley	Y	N	N	N	N
PENNSYLVANIA					
1 Brady	Y	N	N	Y	N
2 Fattah	Y	N	N	Y	N
3 Borski	Y	N	N	N	N
4 Klink	Y	Y	N	N	N
5 ***Peterson***	N	Y	Y	N	Y
6 Holden	Y	Y	Y	N	Y
7 ***Weldon***	N	Y	Y	N	Y
8 ***Greenwood***	Y	N	N	N	N
9 ***Shuster***	N	Y	Y	N	Y
10 ***Sherwood***	Y	N	Y	N	Y
11 Kanjorski	Y	N	Y	N	Y
12 Murtha	Y	Y	Y	N	Y
13 Hoeffel	Y	N	N	Y	N
14 Coyne	Y	N	N	Y	N
15 ***Toomey***	N	Y	Y	N	Y
16 ***Pitts***	N	Y	Y	N	Y
17 ***Gekas***	N	Y	Y	N	Y
18 Doyle	Y	Y	N	N	N
19 ***Goodling***	N	Y	Y	N	Y
20 Mascara	Y	Y	Y	N	Y
21 ***English***	N	Y	Y	Y	Y
RHODE ISLAND					
1 Kennedy	Y	N	N	Y	N
2 Weygand	Y	N	N	Y	N
SOUTH CAROLINA					
1 ***Sanford***	N	Y	Y	N	Y
2 ***Spence***	N	Y	Y	N	Y
3 ***Graham***	N	Y	Y	N	Y
4 ***DeMint***	N	Y	Y	N	Y
5 Spratt	Y	Y	N	N	N
6 Clyburn	Y	Y	N	N	N
SOUTH DAKOTA					
AL ***Thune***	N	Y	Y	N	Y

	304	305	306	307	308
TENNESSEE					
1 ***Jenkins***	N	Y	Y	N	Y
2 ***Duncan***	N	Y	Y	Y	Y
3 ***Wamp***	N	Y	Y	N	Y
4 ***Hilleary***	N	Y	Y	Y	Y
5 Clement	N	Y	Y	N	Y
6 Gordon	Y	Y	Y	N	Y
7 ***Bryant***	N	Y	Y	Y	Y
8 Tanner	N	Y	Y	N	Y
9 Ford	Y	Y	N	Y	N
TEXAS					
1 Sandlin	N	Y	Y	N	Y
2 Turner	N	Y	Y	N	Y
3 ***Johnson, Sam***	N	Y	Y	N	Y
4 Hall	N	Y	Y	N	Y
5 ***Sessions***	N	Y	Y	N	Y
6 ***Barton***	N	Y	Y	N	Y
7 ***Archer***	N	Y	Y	N	Y
8 ***Brady***	N	Y	Y	N	Y
9 Lampson	Y	Y	Y	N	Y
10 Doggett	Y	N	N	N	N
11 Edwards	Y	Y	N	N	N
12 ***Granger***	N	Y	Y	N	Y
13 ***Thornberry***	N	Y	Y	N	Y
14 ***Paul***	N	Y	Y	N	Y
15 Hinojosa	Y	N	N	N	N
16 Reyes	Y	N	N	N	N
17 Stenholm	N	Y	Y	N	Y
18 Jackson-Lee	Y	N	N	N	N
19 ***Combest***	N	Y	Y	N	Y
20 Gonzalez	Y	N	N	N	N
21 ***Smith***	N	Y	Y	N	Y
22 ***DeLay***	?	?	?	?	?
23 ***Bonilla***	N	Y	Y	N	Y
24 Frost	N	Y	N	N	N
25 Bentsen	Y	N	N	N	N
26 ***Armey***	N	Y	Y	N	Y
27 Ortiz	Y	Y	Y	N	Y
28 Rodriguez	Y	Y	N	N	N
29 Green	Y	Y	Y	N	Y
30 Johnson, E.B.	Y	N	N	N	N
UTAH					
1 ***Hansen***	N	Y	Y	N	Y
2 ***Cook***	?	?	?	?	?
3 ***Cannon***	N	Y	Y	N	Y
VERMONT					
AL *Sanders*	Y	N	N	Y	N
VIRGINIA					
1 ***Bateman***	N	Y	Y	N	Y
2 Pickett	Y	Y	Y	N	Y
3 Scott	Y	N	N	N	N
4 Sisisky	N	Y	Y	N	Y
5 *Goode*	N	Y	Y	N	Y
6 ***Goodlatte***	N	Y	Y	N	Y
7 ***Bliley***	N	Y	Y	N	Y
8 Moran	Y	N	N	N	N
9 Boucher	Y	Y	Y	N	Y
10 ***Wolf***	N	N	Y	N	Y
11 ***Davis***	N	N	N	N	N
WASHINGTON					
1 Inslee	Y	N	N	N	N
2 ***Metcalf***	N	Y	Y	N	Y
3 Baird	Y	N	N	N	N
4 ***Hastings***	N	Y	Y	N	Y
5 ***Nethercutt***	N	Y	Y	N	Y
6 Dicks	Y	N	N	N	N
7 McDermott	Y	N	N	N	N
8 ***Dunn***	N	Y	N	N	N
9 Smith	Y	N	N	N	N
WEST VIRGINIA					
1 Mollohan	Y	Y	Y	N	Y
2 Wise	Y	Y	Y	N	Y
3 Rahall	Y	Y	Y	Y	Y
WISCONSIN					
1 ***Ryan***	N	Y	Y	Y	Y
2 Baldwin	Y	N	N	Y	N
3 Kind	Y	N	N	Y	N
4 Kleczka	Y	N	N	N	N
5 Barrett	Y	N	N	Y	N
6 ***Petri***	N	Y	Y	Y	Y
7 Obey	Y	N	N	Y	N
8 ***Green***	N	Y	Y	N	Y
9 ***Sensenbrenner***	N	Y	Y	N	Y
WYOMING					
AL ***Cubin***	N	Y	Y	N	Y

Southern states - Ala., Ark., Fla., Ga., Ky., La., Miss., N.C., Okla., S.C., Tenn., Texas, Va.

309. HR 4635. Fiscal 2001 VA-HUD Appropriations/Passage. Passage of the bill that would appropriate $101.3 billion in fiscal year 2001 for the departments of Veterans Affairs and Housing and Urban Development and other independent agencies, representing a 2 percent increase over fiscal 2000. The total includes $46.8 billion for VA programs and benefits, $30 billion for HUD programs and $7.1 billion for the EPA. Passed 256-169: R 212-5; D 43-163 (ND 26-126, SD 17-37); I 1-1. June 21, 2000.

310. H J Res 90. World Trade Organization/Adoption. Adoption of the joint resolution that would withdraw congressional approval from the agreement establishing the World Trade Organization. Rejected 56-363: R 33-182; D 21-181 (ND 18-131, SD 3-50); I 2-0. June 21, 2000. A "nay" was a vote in support of the president's position.

311. HR 4516. Fiscal 2001 Legislative Branch Appropriations/Rule. Adoption of the rule (H Res 530) to provide for House floor consideration of the bill to appropriate $1.9 billion for the legislative branch (excluding the Senate) for fiscal 2001. Adopted 234-173: R 207-0; D 26-172 (ND 16-128, SD 10-44); I 1-1. June 22, 2000.

312. HR 4516. Fiscal 2001 Legislative Branch Appropriations/Debt Reduction. Ryan, R-Wis., amendment that would put all fiscal 2001 appropriations cuts approved in amendments toward debt reduction unless the amendment specifies that the savings be applied elsewhere. Rejected 184-235: R 150-65; D 33-169 (ND 24-124, SD 9-45); I 1-1. June 22, 2000.

313. HR 4516. Fiscal 2001 Legislative Branch Appropriations/Passage. Passage of the bill that would appropriate $1.9 billion in fiscal year 2001 for legislative branch operations (excluding the Senate). Passed 373-50: R 207-9; D 164-41 (ND 119-32, SD 45-9); I 2-0. June 22, 2000.

Key

- Y Voted for (yea).
- # Paired for.
- + Announced for.
- N Voted against (nay).
- X Paired against.
- – Announced against.
- P Voted "present."
- C Voted "present" to avoid possible conflict of interest.
- ? Did not vote or otherwise make a position known.

•

Democrats ***Republicans***
Independents

	309	310	311	312	313
ALABAMA					
1 ***Callahan***	Y	N	Y	N	Y
2 ***Everett***	Y	Y	Y	Y	Y
3 ***Riley***	Y	N	Y	Y	Y
4 ***Aderholt***	Y	Y	Y	Y	Y
5 Cramer	Y	N	N	N	Y
6 ***Bachus***	Y	N	Y	N	Y
7 Hilliard	N	N	N	N	Y
ALASKA					
AL ***Young***	Y	Y	?	N	Y
ARIZONA					
1 ***Salmon***	Y	N	Y	Y	Y
2 Pastor	N	N	Y	N	Y
3 ***Stump***	Y	N	Y	Y	Y
4 ***Shadegg***	Y	N	Y	Y	Y
5 ***Kolbe***	Y	N	Y	N	Y
6 ***Hayworth***	Y	N	Y	Y	Y
ARKANSAS					
1 Berry	Y	N	N	N	Y
2 Snyder	N	N	N	N	Y
3 ***Hutchinson***	Y	N	Y	N	Y
4 ***Dickey***	Y	N	Y	N	Y
CALIFORNIA					
1 Thompson	N	N	N	N	Y
2 ***Herger***	Y	N	Y	Y	Y
3 ***Ose***	Y	N	Y	N	Y
4 ***Doolittle***	Y	Y	Y	N	Y
5 Matsui	N	N	N	N	Y
6 Woolsey	N	N	N	N	Y
7 Miller, George	N	N	N	N	N
8 Pelosi	N	N	N	N	N
9 Lee	N	N	N	N	N
10 Tauscher	N	N	N	N	Y
11 ***Pombo***	Y	Y	Y	N	Y
12 Lantos	N	N	N	N	Y
13 Stark	N	N	N	N	N
14 Eshoo	N	N	Y	N	Y
15 ***Campbell***	?	?	Y	Y	Y
16 Lofgren	N	N	N	N	N
17 Farr	N	N	N	N	N
18 Condit	N	N	N	Y	Y
19 ***Radanovich***	Y	N	Y	Y	Y
20 Dooley	Y	N	N	N	Y
21 ***Thomas***	Y	N	?	Y	Y
22 Capps	N	N	N	N	Y
23 ***Gallegly***	Y	N	Y	Y	Y
24 Sherman	N	N	N	N	Y
25 ***McKeon***	Y	N	Y	N	Y
26 Berman	N	N	N	N	Y
27 ***Rogan***	Y	N	Y	Y	Y
28 ***Dreier***	Y	N	Y	Y	Y
29 Waxman	N	N	N	N	N
30 Becerra	N	N	N	N	N
31 Martinez	Y	N	Y	N	Y
32 Dixon	N	N	N	N	Y
33 Roybal-Allard	?	?	?	?	?
34 Napolitano	N	N	N	N	Y
35 Waters	N	Y	N	N	N
36 ***Kuykendall***	+	–	+	+	+
37 Millender-McD.	N	N	N	N	Y
38 ***Horn***	Y	N	Y	Y	Y
39 ***Royce***	Y	N	Y	Y	N
40 ***Lewis***	Y	N	Y	N	Y
41 ***Miller, Gary***	Y	N	Y	Y	Y
42 Baca	N	N	N	N	Y
43 ***Calvert***	Y	N	Y	N	Y
44 ***Bono***	Y	N	Y	N	Y
45 ***Rohrabacher***	Y	Y	Y	Y	Y
46 Sanchez	N	N	N	N	Y
47 ***Cox***	Y	N	Y	Y	Y
48 ***Packard***	Y	N	Y	N	Y
49 ***Bilbray***	Y	N	Y	Y	Y
50 Filner	N	N	?	?	?
51 ***Cunningham***	Y	N	Y	Y	Y
52 ***Hunter***	Y	Y	?	Y	Y
COLORADO					
1 DeGette	N	N	N	N	Y
2 Udall	N	N	N	N	Y
3 ***McInnis***	Y	N	Y	Y	Y
4 ***Schaffer***	Y	Y	Y	Y	N
5 ***Hefley***	Y	N	Y	Y	Y
6 ***Tancredo***	Y	Y	Y	Y	Y
CONNECTICUT					
1 Larson	N	N	N	N	Y
2 Gejdenson	N	N	N	N	N
3 DeLauro	N	N	N	N	Y
4 ***Shays***	Y	N	Y	Y	N
5 Maloney	Y	N	Y	Y	Y
6 ***Johnson***	Y	N	Y	N	Y
DELAWARE					
AL ***Castle***	Y	N	Y	Y	Y
FLORIDA					
1 ***Scarborough***	Y	Y	Y	Y	Y
2 Boyd	Y	N	Y	N	Y
3 Brown	N	N	Y	N	Y
4 ***Fowler***	Y	N	Y	N	Y
5 Thurman	Y	N	N	N	Y
6 ***Stearns***	Y	N	Y	Y	Y
7 ***Mica***	Y	N	Y	Y	Y
8 ***McCollum***	Y	N	?	?	?
9 ***Bilirakis***	Y	Y	Y	N	Y
10 ***Young***	Y	N	Y	N	Y
11 Davis	Y	N	N	N	N
12 ***Canady***	Y	N	Y	Y	Y
13 ***Miller***	Y	N	Y	Y	Y
14 ***Goss***	Y	N	Y	Y	Y
15 ***Weldon***	N	Y	Y	Y	Y
16 ***Foley***	Y	N	Y	Y	Y
17 Meek	Y	N	Y	N	Y
18 ***Ros-Lehtinen***	Y	N	Y	Y	Y
19 Wexler	N	N	N	N	Y
20 Deutsch	N	N	N	Y	Y
21 ***Diaz-Balart***	Y	N	Y	N	Y
22 ***Shaw***	Y	N	Y	Y	Y
23 Hastings	Y	N	N	N	Y
GEORGIA					
1 ***Kingston***	Y	N	Y	Y	Y
2 Bishop	N	N	N	N	Y
3 ***Collins***	Y	N	Y	Y	Y
4 McKinney	N	Y	N	N	Y
5 Lewis	N	N	N	N	Y
6 ***Isakson***	Y	N	Y	Y	Y
7 ***Barr***	Y	Y	Y	Y	Y
8 ***Chambliss***	Y	N	Y	Y	Y
9 ***Deal***	Y	Y	Y	Y	Y
10 ***Norwood***	Y	Y	Y	Y	Y
11 ***Linder***	Y	N	Y	Y	Y
HAWAII					
1 Abercrombie	Y	Y	Y	N	Y
2 Mink	Y	Y	N	N	Y
IDAHO					
1 ***Chenoweth-Hage***	Y	Y	Y	Y	N
2 ***Simpson***	Y	N	Y	N	Y
ILLINOIS					
1 Rush	N	N	N	N	Y
2 Jackson	N	Y	N	N	Y
3 Lipinski	Y	Y	N	N	Y
4 Gutierrez	N	N	N	N	Y
5 Blagojevich	N	N	Y	N	Y
6 ***Hyde***	Y	N	Y	?	?
7 Davis	N	N	N	?	Y
8 ***Crane***	Y	N	Y	Y	Y
9 Schakowsky	N	N	N	N	Y
10 ***Porter***	Y	N	?	N	Y
11 ***Weller***	Y	N	Y	Y	Y
12 Costello	N	N	N	N	N
13 ***Biggert***	Y	N	Y	N	Y

ND Northern Democrats SD Southern Democrats

	309	310	311	312	313
14 ***Hastert***					Y
15 ***Ewing***	Y	N	Y	Y	Y
16 ***Manzullo***	Y	N	Y	Y	Y
17 Evans	Y	N	N	N	N
18 ***LaHood***	Y	N	Y	Y	Y
19 Phelps	N	N	N	N	N
20 ***Shimkus***	Y	N	Y	Y	Y
INDIANA					
1 Visclosky	N	N	?	N	Y
2 ***McIntosh***	Y	?	Y	Y	Y
3 Roemer	N	N	N	Y	N
4 ***Souder***	Y	N	Y	Y	Y
5 ***Buyer***	Y	N	Y	N	Y
6 ***Burton***	Y	Y	Y	Y	Y
7 ***Pease***	Y	N	Y	Y	Y
8 ***Hostettler***	Y	Y	Y	Y	Y
9 Hill	Y	N	N	Y	Y
10 Carson	N	P	N	N	Y
IOWA					
1 ***Leach***	Y	N	Y	Y	Y
2 ***Nussle***	Y	N	Y	Y	Y
3 Boswell	Y	N	Y	Y	Y
4 ***Ganske***	Y	N	Y	Y	Y
5 ***Latham***	Y	N	Y	N	Y
KANSAS					
1 ***Moran***	Y	N	Y	Y	N
2 ***Ryun***	Y	N	Y	Y	Y
3 Moore	Y	N	N	Y	Y
4 ***Tiahrt***	Y	N	Y	N	Y
KENTUCKY					
1 ***Whitfield***	Y	N	Y	Y	Y
2 ***Lewis***	Y	N	Y	Y	Y
3 ***Northup***	Y	N	Y	N	Y
4 Lucas	Y	N	N	Y	N
5 ***Rogers***	Y	N	Y	N	Y
6 ***Fletcher***	Y	N	Y	Y	Y
LOUISIANA					
1 ***Vitter***	Y	N	Y	Y	Y
2 Jefferson	N	?	N	N	Y
3 ***Tauzin***	Y	N	?	Y	Y
4 ***McCrery***	Y	N	?	N	Y
5 ***Cooksey***	Y	N	Y	N	Y
6 ***Baker***	Y	N	?	Y	Y
7 John	Y	N	N	N	Y
MAINE					
1 Allen	N	N	N	N	Y
2 Baldacci	N	N	N	N	Y
MARYLAND					
1 ***Gilchrest***	Y	N	Y	N	Y
2 ***Ehrlich***	Y	N	Y	Y	Y
3 Cardin	N	N	Y	N	Y
4 Wynn	?	?	?	?	?
5 Hoyer	N	N	N	N	N
6 ***Bartlett***	Y	Y	Y	Y	Y
7 Cummings	N	N	?	N	Y
8 ***Morella***	N	N	Y	N	Y
MASSACHUSETTS					
1 Olver	N	N	N	N	Y
2 Neal	N	N	N	N	Y
3 McGovern	N	N	N	N	Y
4 Frank	N	N	N	N	Y
5 Meehan	N	N	N	N	Y
6 Tierney	N	N	N	N	Y
7 Markey	N	N	N	N	Y
8 Capuano	N	N	N	N	Y
9 Moakley	N	N	N	N	Y
10 Delahunt	N	N	N	N	N
MICHIGAN					
1 Stupak	N	Y	N	N	Y
2 ***Hoekstra***	Y	N	Y	Y	Y
3 ***Ehlers***	Y	N	Y	N	Y
4 ***Camp***	Y	N	Y	Y	Y
5 Barcia	Y	N	N	N	Y
6 ***Upton***	Y	N	Y	Y	Y
7 ***Smith***	Y	N	Y	Y	Y
8 Stabenow	N	N	N	Y	Y
9 Kildee	N	N	N	N	Y
10 Bonior	N	Y	N	N	Y
11 ***Knollenberg***	Y	N	Y	N	Y
12 Levin	N	N	N	N	Y
13 Rivers	N	P	N	N	Y
14 Conyers	N	N	N	N	N
15 Kilpatrick	N	N	N	N	Y
16 Dingell	N	N	N	N	N

	309	310	311	312	313
MINNESOTA					
1 ***Gutknecht***	Y	N	Y	Y	Y
2 Minge	N	N	N	Y	N
3 ***Ramstad***	Y	N	Y	Y	Y
4 Vento	?	?	?	?	?
5 Sabo	N	N	N	N	Y
6 Luther	N	N	N	Y	N
7 Peterson	N	Y	N	Y	N
8 Oberstar	N	Y	N	N	Y
MISSISSIPPI					
1 ***Wicker***	Y	N	Y	N	Y
2 Thompson	N	N	N	N	Y
3 ***Pickering***	Y	N	Y	Y	Y
4 Shows	Y	N	Y	Y	Y
5 Taylor	Y	Y	N	Y	Y
MISSOURI					
1 Clay	N	N	N	N	Y
2 ***Talent***	Y	N	Y	Y	Y
3 Gephardt	N	N	N	N	N
4 Skelton	Y	N	Y	N	Y
5 McCarthy	N	N	N	N	Y
6 Danner	Y	N	N	Y	Y
7 ***Blunt***	Y	N	Y	Y	Y
8 ***Emerson***	Y	N	Y	N	Y
9 ***Hulshof***	Y	N	Y	Y	N
MONTANA					
AL ***Hill***	Y	N	Y	Y	Y
NEBRASKA					
1 ***Bereuter***	Y	N	Y	Y	Y
2 ***Terry***	Y	N	Y	Y	Y
3 ***Barrett***	Y	N	Y	Y	Y
NEVADA					
1 Berkley	N	N	N	Y	Y
2 ***Gibbons***	Y	Y	Y	Y	Y
NEW HAMPSHIRE					
1 ***Sununu***	Y	N	Y	Y	Y
2 ***Bass***	Y	N	Y	Y	Y
NEW JERSEY					
1 Andrews	N	N	N	Y	N
2 ***LoBiondo***	Y	N	Y	Y	Y
3 ***Saxton***	Y	N	Y	Y	Y
4 ***Smith***	Y	Y	Y	Y	Y
5 ***Roukema***	Y	N	Y	Y	Y
6 Pallone	N	N	N	N	Y
7 ***Franks***	Y	N	Y	Y	Y
8 Pascrell	N	N	Y	N	Y
9 Rothman	N	N	N	N	N
10 Payne	N	N	N	N	N
11 ***Frelinghuysen***	Y	N	Y	N	Y
12 Holt	N	N	N	Y	Y
13 Menendez	N	N	N	N	Y
NEW MEXICO					
1 ***Wilson***	Y	N	Y	N	Y
2 ***Skeen***	Y	N	Y	N	Y
3 Udall	N	N	N	N	Y
NEW YORK					
1 Forbes	Y	N	Y	Y	Y
2 ***Lazio***	N	N	Y	Y	Y
3 ***King***	Y	N	Y	N	Y
4 McCarthy	N	N	N	N	Y
5 Ackerman	N	N	N	N	Y
6 Meeks	N	N	N	N	Y
7 Crowley	N	N	N	N	Y
8 Nadler	N	N	N	N	Y
9 Weiner	N	N	N	N	Y
10 Towns	N	N	?	?	N
11 Owens	N	N	N	N	Y
12 Velázquez	N	N	N	N	Y
13 ***Fossella***	Y	N	?	Y	Y
14 Maloney	N	N	N	N	Y
15 Rangel	?	?	?	?	?
16 Serrano	?	?	N	N	Y
17 Engel	N	N	?	?	?
18 Lowey	N	N	N	N	Y
19 ***Kelly***	Y	N	Y	Y	Y
20 ***Gilman***	Y	N	Y	N	Y
21 McNulty	N	N	Y	N	Y
22 ***Sweeney***	Y	N	Y	N	Y
23 ***Boehlert***	Y	N	Y	N	Y
24 ***McHugh***	Y	N	Y	N	Y
25 ***Walsh***	Y	N	Y	N	Y
26 Hinchey	N	P	N	N	Y
27 ***Reynolds***	Y	N	Y	N	Y
28 Slaughter	N	N	N	N	Y
29 LaFalce	N	N	N	N	Y

	309	310	311	312	313
30 ***Quinn***	Y	N	Y	N	Y
31 ***Houghton***	Y	N	Y	N	Y
NORTH CAROLINA					
1 Clayton	N	N	N	N	Y
2 Etheridge	N	N	N	Y	Y
3 ***Jones***	Y	Y	Y	Y	Y
4 Price	Y	N	N	N	Y
5 ***Burr***	Y	N	Y	Y	Y
6 ***Coble***	Y	N	Y	Y	Y
7 McIntyre	N	N	Y	Y	Y
8 ***Hayes***	Y	N	Y	Y	Y
9 ***Myrick***	Y	N	Y	Y	Y
10 ***Ballenger***	Y	N	Y	Y	Y
11 ***Taylor***	Y	Y	Y	N	Y
12 Watt	N	N	N	N	N
NORTH DAKOTA					
AL Pomeroy	N	N	N	N	Y
OHIO					
1 ***Chabot***	Y	N	Y	Y	Y
2 ***Portman***	Y	N	Y	Y	Y
3 Hall	N	N	N	N	Y
4 ***Oxley***	Y	N	Y	N	Y
5 ***Gillmor***	Y	N	Y	N	Y
6 Strickland	N	Y	N	N	Y
7 ***Hobson***	Y	N	?	?	?
8 ***Boehner***	Y	N	Y	Y	Y
9 Kaptur	Y	Y	N	N	Y
10 Kucinich	N	Y	N	N	Y
11 Jones	N	N	N	N	Y
12 ***Kasich***	Y	N	Y	Y	Y
13 Brown	N	Y	N	N	N
14 Sawyer	N	N	N	N	Y
15 ***Pryce***	Y	N	Y	Y	Y
16 ***Regula***	Y	N	Y	N	Y
17 Traficant	Y	Y	Y	N	Y
18 ***Ney***	Y	Y	Y	Y	Y
19 ***LaTourette***	Y	N	Y	N	Y
OKLAHOMA					
1 ***Largent***	Y	N	Y	Y	Y
2 ***Coburn***	Y	Y	Y	Y	Y
3 ***Watkins***	Y	N	Y	N	Y
4 ***Watts***	Y	N	Y	Y	Y
5 ***Istook***	Y	Y	Y	N	Y
6 ***Lucas***	Y	N	Y	N	Y
OREGON					
1 Wu	N	N	N	N	Y
2 ***Walden***	Y	N	Y	Y	Y
3 Blumenauer	N	N	N	N	Y
4 DeFazio	N	Y	N	Y	Y
5 Hooley	N	N	N	Y	Y
PENNSYLVANIA					
1 Brady	N	N	N	N	Y
2 Fattah	N	N	?	N	N
3 Borski	N	N	N	N	Y
4 Klink	N	N	?	N	Y
5 ***Peterson***	Y	N	Y	N	Y
6 Holden	Y	N	N	N	Y
7 ***Weldon***	Y	N	Y	Y	Y
8 ***Greenwood***	Y	N	Y	N	Y
9 ***Shuster***	Y	?	Y	N	Y
10 ***Sherwood***	Y	N	Y	Y	Y
11 Kanjorski	Y	N	Y	N	Y
12 Murtha	Y	N	Y	N	Y
13 Hoeffel	N	N	Y	N	Y
14 Coyne	N	N	N	N	Y
15 ***Toomey***	Y	N	Y	Y	Y
16 ***Pitts***	Y	N	Y	Y	Y
17 ***Gekas***	Y	N	Y	Y	Y
18 Doyle	Y	N	N	N	Y
19 ***Goodling***	Y	Y	Y	Y	Y
20 Mascara	Y	N	N	N	Y
21 ***English***	Y	N	?	Y	Y
RHODE ISLAND					
1 Kennedy	N	Y	N	N	N
2 Weygand	N	N	N	Y	Y
SOUTH CAROLINA					
1 ***Sanford***	N	N	Y	Y	N
2 ***Spence***	Y	N	Y	N	Y
3 ***Graham***	Y	N	Y	Y	Y
4 ***DeMint***	Y	N	Y	Y	Y
5 Spratt	N	N	N	N	Y
6 Clyburn	N	N	N	N	Y
SOUTH DAKOTA					
AL ***Thune***	Y	N	Y	Y	Y

	309	310	311	312	313
TENNESSEE					
1 ***Jenkins***	Y	N	Y	Y	Y
2 ***Duncan***	Y	Y	Y	Y	Y
3 ***Wamp***	Y	Y	Y	N	Y
4 ***Hilleary***	Y	Y	Y	Y	Y
5 Clement	N	N	N	N	Y
6 Gordon	N	N	N	N	Y
7 ***Bryant***	Y	N	Y	Y	Y
8 Tanner	N	N	N	N	N
9 Ford	N	N	Y	N	N
TEXAS					
1 Sandlin	N	N	N	N	Y
2 Turner	Y	N	N	N	Y
3 ***Johnson, Sam***	Y	N	Y	Y	Y
4 Hall	N	Y	Y	Y	Y
5 ***Sessions***	Y	N	Y	Y	Y
6 ***Barton***	Y	N	Y	Y	Y
7 ***Archer***	Y	N	?	Y	Y
8 ***Brady***	Y	N	Y	Y	Y
9 Lampson	N	N	N	N	Y
10 Doggett	N	N	N	Y	N
11 Edwards	N	N	N	N	Y
12 ***Granger***	Y	N	Y	Y	Y
13 ***Thornberry***	Y	N	Y	Y	Y
14 ***Paul***	N	Y	Y	Y	N
15 Hinojosa	N	N	N	N	Y
16 Reyes	N	N	N	N	Y
17 Stenholm	N	N	N	N	Y
18 Jackson-Lee	N	N	N	N	Y
19 ***Combest***	Y	N	Y	Y	Y
20 Gonzalez	N	N	N	N	Y
21 ***Smith***	Y	N	Y	Y	Y
22 ***DeLay***	?	?	Y	Y	Y
23 ***Bonilla***	Y	N	Y	N	Y
24 Frost	N	N	N	N	N
25 Bentsen	N	N	N	N	Y
26 ***Armey***	Y	N	Y	Y	Y
27 Ortiz	N	N	Y	N	Y
28 Rodriguez	N	N	N	N	Y
29 Green	N	N	N	N	N
30 Johnson, E.B.	N	N	N	N	Y
UTAH					
1 ***Hansen***	Y	N	Y	N	Y
2 ***Cook***	?	?	?	?	?
3 ***Cannon***	Y	N	Y	Y	Y
VERMONT					
AL *Sanders*	N	Y	N	N	Y
VIRGINIA					
1 ***Bateman***	Y	N	Y	N	Y
2 Pickett	Y	N	Y	N	Y
3 Scott	N	N	N	N	Y
4 Sisisky	Y	N	Y	Y	Y
5 *Goode*	Y	Y	Y	Y	Y
6 ***Goodlatte***	Y	N	Y	Y	Y
7 ***Bliley***	Y	N	Y	Y	Y
8 Moran	Y	N	N	N	N
9 Boucher	Y	N	N	N	Y
10 ***Wolf***	Y	N	Y	N	Y
11 ***Davis***	Y	N	Y	Y	Y
WASHINGTON					
1 Inslee	Y	N	N	Y	N
2 ***Metcalf***	Y	Y	Y	Y	Y
3 Baird	N	N	N	N	Y
4 ***Hastings***	Y	N	Y	Y	Y
5 ***Nethercutt***	Y	N	Y	N	Y
6 Dicks	Y	N	N	?	Y
7 McDermott	N	N	N	N	Y
8 ***Dunn***	Y	N	Y	Y	Y
9 Smith	N	N	N	Y	N
WEST VIRGINIA					
1 Mollohan	Y	N	?	N	Y
2 Wise	Y	N	?	N	Y
3 Rahall	Y	N	N	N	Y
WISCONSIN					
1 ***Ryan***	Y	N	Y	Y	Y
2 Baldwin	N	Y	N	N	Y
3 Kind	N	N	N	N	N
4 Kleczka	N	N	N	Y	Y
5 Barrett	N	N	N	Y	Y
6 ***Petri***	Y	N	Y	Y	Y
7 Obey	N	Y	N	N	Y
8 ***Green***	Y	N	Y	Y	Y
9 ***Sensenbrenner***	Y	Y	Y	Y	N
WYOMING					
AL ***Cubin***	Y	N	Y	?	?

Southern states - Ala., Ark., Fla., Ga., Ky., La., Miss., N.C., Okla., S.C., Tenn., Texas, Va.

314. HR 4690. Fiscal 2001 Commerce, Justice, State Appropriations/Rule. Adoption of the rule (H Res 529) to provide for House floor consideration of the bill that would appropriate $37.4 billion for the departments of Commerce, Justice and State, and other agencies. Adopted 225-188: R 213-0; D 11-187 (ND 7-140, SD 4-47); I 1-1. June 22, 2000.

315. HR 4690. Fiscal 2001 Commerce, Justice, State Appropriations/Secret Evidence. Campbell, R-Calif., amendment that would reduce by $173,000 the funding for federal prison system salaries and expenses to protest when the Immigration and Naturalization Service denies bond, asylum or other relief to non-citizens based on evidence kept secret from them. Adopted 239-173: R 74-140; D 164-32 (ND 126-17, SD 38-15); I 1-1. June 22, 2000.

316. HR 4690. Fiscal 2001 Commerce, Justice, State Appropriations/Economic Development. Hinchey, D-N.Y., amendment that would increase the appropriation for the Economic Development Administration by $50 million, offset by an equal reduction in funding for violent offender imprisonment and truth-in-sentencing grants. Rejected 128-284: R 4-210; D 123-73 (ND 99-45, SD 24-28); I 1-1. June 22, 2000.

317. HR 4690. Fiscal 2001 Commerce, Justice, State Appropriations/Prison Fund Reduction. Scott, D-Va., amendment that would increase the appropriation for Boys and Girls Clubs and drug courts by $61 million each, offset by an equal reduction in funding for violent offender imprisonment and truth-in-sentencing grants. Rejected 184-226: R 35-176; D 148-49 (ND 108-36, SD 40-13); I 1-1. June 22, 2000.

318. HR 4690. Fiscal 2001 Commerce, Justice, State Appropriations/Prison Abortions. DeGette, D-Colo., amendment that would strike the provision banning the use of federal funds for abortion services for female federal prisoners. Rejected 156-254: R 15-198; D 140-55 (ND 105-37, SD 35-18); I 1-1. June 22, 2000.

Key

- Y Voted for (yea).
- # Paired for.
- \+ Announced for.
- N Voted against (nay).
- X Paired against.
- – Announced against.
- P Voted "present."
- C Voted "present" to avoid possible conflict of interest.
- ? Did not vote or otherwise make a position known.

Democrats ***Republicans***
Independents

	314	315	316	317	318
ALABAMA					
1 ***Callahan***	Y	N	N	N	N
2 ***Everett***	Y	N	N	N	N
3 ***Riley***	Y	N	N	N	N
4 ***Aderholt***	Y	N	N	N	N
5 Cramer	N	N	N	Y	N
6 ***Bachus***	Y	Y	N	N	N
7 Hilliard	N	Y	Y	Y	Y
ALASKA					
AL ***Young***	Y	N	N	N	N
ARIZONA					
1 ***Salmon***	Y	N	N	N	N
2 Pastor	N	Y	Y	Y	Y
3 ***Stump***	Y	N	N	N	N
4 ***Shadegg***	Y	N	N	N	N
5 ***Kolbe***	Y	N	N	Y	N
6 ***Hayworth***	Y	Y	N	N	N
ARKANSAS					
1 Berry	N	Y	N	N	N
2 Snyder	N	Y	N	Y	N
3 ***Hutchinson***	Y	N	N	Y	N
4 ***Dickey***	Y	N	N	N	N
CALIFORNIA					
1 Thompson	N	Y	N	N	Y
2 ***Herger***	Y	Y	N	N	N
3 ***Ose***	Y	N	N	N	N
4 ***Doolittle***	Y	Y	N	N	N
5 Matsui	N	Y	Y	Y	Y
6 Woolsey	N	Y	Y	Y	Y
7 Miller, George	N	Y	Y	Y	Y
8 Pelosi	N	Y	Y	Y	Y
9 Lee	N	Y	Y	Y	Y
10 Tauscher	N	Y	N	N	Y
11 ***Pombo***	Y	Y	N	N	N
12 Lantos	N	Y	Y	Y	Y
13 Stark	N	Y	Y	Y	Y
14 Eshoo	Y	Y	Y	Y	Y
15 ***Campbell***	Y	Y	Y	Y	Y
16 Lofgren	N	Y	Y	Y	Y
17 Farr	N	Y	Y	Y	Y
18 Condit	Y	Y	N	Y	Y
19 ***Radanovich***	Y	N	N	N	N
20 Dooley	?	Y	N	Y	Y
21 ***Thomas***	Y	Y	N	N	?
22 Capps	N	Y	N	Y	Y
23 ***Gallegly***	Y	N	N	N	N
24 Sherman	N	N	N	N	Y
25 ***McKeon***	Y	N	N	N	N
26 Berman	N	?	?	?	?
27 ***Rogan***	Y	N	N	N	N
28 ***Dreier***	Y	N	N	N	N
29 Waxman	N	N	Y	Y	Y
30 Becerra	N	Y	Y	Y	Y
31 Martinez	Y	?	?	?	?
32 Dixon	N	?	?	?	?
33 Roybal-Allard	?	?	?	?	?
34 Napolitano	N	Y	Y	Y	Y
35 Waters	N	Y	Y	Y	Y
36 ***Kuykendall***	+	+	–	–	+
37 Millender-McD.	N	Y	Y	Y	Y
38 ***Horn***	Y	Y	N	N	Y
39 ***Royce***	Y	N	N	N	N
40 ***Lewis***	Y	N	N	?	N
41 ***Miller, Gary***	Y	N	N	N	N
42 Baca	N	Y	N	Y	Y
43 ***Calvert***	Y	N	N	N	N
44 ***Bono***	Y	Y	N	N	N
45 ***Rohrabacher***	Y	N	N	N	N
46 Sanchez	N	Y	Y	Y	Y
47 ***Cox***	Y	Y	N	N	N
48 ***Packard***	Y	N	N	N	N
49 ***Bilbray***	Y	N	N	Y	N
50 Filner	?	?	?	?	?
51 ***Cunningham***	Y	Y	N	N	N
52 ***Hunter***	Y	N	N	N	N
COLORADO					
1 DeGette	N	Y	Y	Y	Y
2 Udall	N	Y	Y	Y	Y
3 ***McInnis***	Y	N	N	Y	N
4 ***Schaffer***	Y	N	N	N	N
5 ***Hefley***	Y	N	N	N	N
6 ***Tancredo***	Y	N	N	N	N
CONNECTICUT					
1 Larson	N	Y	Y	N	Y
2 Gejdenson	N	Y	Y	N	Y
3 DeLauro	N	Y	Y	N	Y
4 ***Shays***	Y	Y	N	Y	Y
5 Maloney	N	Y	Y	N	Y
6 ***Johnson***	Y	Y	N	N	Y
DELAWARE					
AL ***Castle***	Y	Y	N	Y	N
FLORIDA					
1 ***Scarborough***	Y	Y	N	N	N
2 Boyd	N	Y	Y	Y	N
3 Brown	?	Y	N	Y	Y
4 ***Fowler***	Y	N	N	N	N
5 Thurman	N	N	Y	Y	N
6 ***Stearns***	Y	N	N	N	N
7 ***Mica***	Y	N	N	N	N
8 ***McCollum***	?	?	?	?	?
9 ***Bilirakis***	Y	N	N	N	N
10 ***Young***	Y	N	N	N	N
11 Davis	N	N	N	Y	Y
12 ***Canady***	Y	N	N	N	N
13 ***Miller***	Y	N	N	N	N
14 ***Goss***	Y	N	N	N	N
15 ***Weldon***	Y	N	N	N	N
16 ***Foley***	Y	N	N	Y	N
17 Meek	?	Y	Y	Y	Y
18 ***Ros-Lehtinen***	Y	N	N	N	N
19 Wexler	N	N	N	Y	Y
20 Deutsch	N	N	N	N	Y
21 ***Diaz-Balart***	Y	N	N	?	N
22 ***Shaw***	Y	N	N	N	N
23 Hastings	N	Y	Y	Y	Y
GEORGIA					
1 ***Kingston***	Y	N	N	N	N
2 Bishop	N	Y	Y	Y	Y
3 ***Collins***	Y	N	N	N	N
4 McKinney	N	Y	Y	Y	Y
5 Lewis	N	Y	Y	Y	Y
6 ***Isakson***	Y	N	N	N	N
7 ***Barr***	Y	Y	N	N	N
8 ***Chambliss***	Y	N	N	N	N
9 ***Deal***	Y	N	N	N	N
10 ***Norwood***	Y	N	N	N	N
11 ***Linder***	?	N	N	N	N
HAWAII					
1 Abercrombie	N	Y	Y	Y	Y
2 Mink	N	Y	Y	Y	Y
IDAHO					
1 ***Chenoweth-Hage***	Y	Y	N	N	N
2 ***Simpson***	Y	Y	N	N	N
ILLINOIS					
1 Rush	N	Y	Y	Y	Y
2 Jackson	N	Y	Y	Y	Y
3 Lipinski	N	Y	N	N	N
4 Gutierrez	N	Y	Y	Y	Y
5 Blagojevich	N	Y	N	N	Y
6 ***Hyde***	?	N	N	N	N
7 Davis	N	Y	Y	Y	Y
8 ***Crane***	Y	N	N	N	N
9 Schakowsky	N	Y	Y	Y	Y
10 ***Porter***	Y	Y	N	N	Y
11 ***Weller***	Y	N	N	N	N
12 Costello	N	Y	N	N	N
13 ***Biggert***	Y	N	N	N	Y

ND Northern Democrats SD Southern Democrats

	314	315	316	317	318
14 ***Hastert***					
15 ***Ewing***	Y	N	N	N	N
16 ***Manzullo***	Y	Y	N	N	N
17 Evans	N	Y	Y	Y	Y
18 ***LaHood***	Y	Y	N	Y	N
19 Phelps	N	Y	N	N	N
20 ***Shimkus***	Y	N	Y	N	N
INDIANA					
1 Visclosky	N	Y	Y	Y	N
2 ***McIntosh***	Y	?	?	?	?
3 Roemer	N	Y	N	N	N
4 ***Souder***	Y	N	N	Y	N
5 ***Buyer***	Y	N	N	N	N
6 ***Burton***	Y	N	N	N	N
7 ***Pease***	Y	Y	Y	N	N
8 ***Hostettler***	Y	Y	N	N	N
9 Hill	N	Y	Y	Y	N
10 Carson	N	Y	Y	Y	Y
IOWA					
1 ***Leach***	Y	Y	N	Y	N
2 ***Nussle***	Y	N	N	N	N
3 Boswell	N	N	N	N	Y
4 ***Ganske***	Y	Y	N	N	N
5 ***Latham***	Y	N	N	N	N
KANSAS					
1 ***Moran***	Y	Y	N	N	N
2 ***Ryun***	?	N	N	N	N
3 Moore	Y	Y	N	Y	N
4 ***Tiahrt***	Y	Y	N	N	N
KENTUCKY					
1 ***Whitfield***	Y	Y	N	Y	N
2 ***Lewis***	Y	N	N	N	N
3 ***Northup***	Y	N	N	Y	N
4 Lucas	N	N	N	N	N
5 ***Rogers***	Y	N	N	N	N
6 ***Fletcher***	Y	N	N	N	N
LOUISIANA					
1 ***Vitter***	Y	N	N	N	N
2 Jefferson	N	Y	Y	Y	Y
3 ***Tauzin***	Y	N	N	N	N
4 ***McCrery***	Y	Y	N	N	N
5 ***Cooksey***	Y	Y	N	N	N
6 ***Baker***	Y	N	N	N	N
7 John	N	Y	N	N	N
MAINE					
1 Allen	N	Y	Y	Y	Y
2 Baldacci	N	Y	Y	Y	Y
MARYLAND					
1 ***Gilchrest***	Y	N	N	N	Y
2 ***Ehrlich***	Y	Y	N	N	N
3 Cardin	N	Y	Y	Y	Y
4 Wynn	?	?	?	?	?
5 Hoyer	N	Y	Y	Y	Y
6 ***Bartlett***	Y	Y	N	N	N
7 Cummings	N	Y	Y	Y	Y
8 ***Morella***	Y	N	N	Y	Y
MASSACHUSETTS					
1 Olver	N	Y	Y	Y	Y
2 Neal	N	Y	Y	Y	N
3 McGovern	N	Y	Y	Y	Y
4 Frank	N	Y	Y	Y	Y
5 Meehan	N	Y	Y	Y	Y
6 Tierney	N	Y	Y	Y	Y
7 Markey	N	Y	Y	Y	Y
8 Capuano	N	Y	Y	Y	Y
9 Moakley	N	Y	Y	Y	N
10 Delahunt	N	Y	Y	Y	Y
MICHIGAN					
1 Stupak	N	Y	Y	Y	N
2 ***Hoekstra***	Y	Y	N	Y	N
3 ***Ehlers***	Y	Y	N	Y	N
4 ***Camp***	Y	Y	N	Y	N
5 Barcia	?	Y	N	Y	N
6 ***Upton***	Y	Y	N	Y	N
7 ***Smith***	Y	Y	N	N	N
8 Stabenow	N	Y	N	N	Y
9 Kildee	N	Y	N	Y	N
10 Bonior	N	Y	Y	Y	N
11 ***Knollenberg***	Y	N	N	N	N
12 Levin	N	Y	N	Y	Y
13 Rivers	N	Y	Y	Y	Y
14 Conyers	N	Y	Y	Y	Y
15 Kilpatrick	N	Y	Y	Y	Y
16 Dingell	N	Y	Y	N	N

	314	315	316	317	318
MINNESOTA					
1 ***Gutknecht***	Y	Y	N	N	N
2 Minge	N	Y	Y	Y	Y
3 ***Ramstad***	Y	N	N	N	N
4 Vento	?	?	?	?	?
5 Sabo	N	Y	Y	Y	Y
6 Luther	N	Y	Y	Y	Y
7 Peterson	N	Y	Y	N	N
8 Oberstar	N	Y	Y	Y	N
MISSISSIPPI					
1 ***Wicker***	Y	N	N	Y	N
2 Thompson	N	Y	Y	Y	Y
3 ***Pickering***	Y	N	N	N	N
4 Shows	Y	N	N	N	N
5 Taylor	N	N	N	N	N
MISSOURI					
1 Clay	N	Y	Y	Y	Y
2 ***Talent***	Y	Y	N	N	N
3 Gephardt	N	Y	N	N	Y
4 Skelton	N	Y	N	Y	N
5 McCarthy	N	Y	Y	Y	Y
6 Danner	N	Y	N	N	N
7 ***Blunt***	Y	N	N	N	N
8 ***Emerson***	Y	N	N	N	N
9 ***Hulshof***	Y	N	N	N	N
MONTANA					
AL ***Hill***	Y	N	N	N	N
NEBRASKA					
1 ***Bereuter***	Y	N	N	Y	N
2 ***Terry***	Y	N	N	N	N
3 ***Barrett***	Y	N	N	N	N
NEVADA					
1 Berkley	N	N	N	Y	Y
2 ***Gibbons***	Y	N	N	N	N
NEW HAMPSHIRE					
1 ***Sununu***	Y	Y	N	N	N
2 ***Bass***	Y	N	N	N	Y
NEW JERSEY					
1 Andrews	N	N	N	N	Y
2 ***LoBiondo***	Y	N	N	N	N
3 ***Saxton***	Y	N	N	N	N
4 ***Smith***	Y	N	N	N	N
5 ***Roukema***	Y	N	N	N	N
6 Pallone	N	N	N	N	Y
7 ***Franks***	Y	N	N	N	N
8 Pascrell	N	Y	Y	Y	Y
9 Rothman	N	N	N	N	Y
10 Payne	N	Y	Y	Y	Y
11 ***Frelinghuysen***	Y	Y	N	N	Y
12 Holt	N	Y	N	Y	Y
13 Menendez	N	N	N	N	Y
NEW MEXICO					
1 ***Wilson***	Y	Y	N	Y	N
2 ***Skeen***	Y	N	N	N	N
3 Udall	N	Y	Y	Y	N
NEW YORK					
1 Forbes	N	Y	N	N	N
2 ***Lazio***	Y	N	N	N	N
3 ***King***	Y	Y	N	N	N
4 McCarthy	Y	Y	N	N	Y
5 Ackerman	N	Y	Y	Y	Y
6 Meeks	N	?	?	?	?
7 Crowley	N	N	N	Y	N
8 Nadler	N	Y	Y	Y	Y
9 Weiner	N	N	N	Y	Y
10 Towns	N	Y	Y	Y	Y
11 Owens	N	Y	Y	Y	Y
12 Velázquez	N	Y	N	Y	Y
13 ***Fossella***	Y	N	N	N	N
14 Maloney	N	N	Y	Y	Y
15 Rangel	?	?	?	?	?
16 Serrano	N	Y	Y	Y	?
17 Engel	?	N	Y	Y	Y
18 Lowey	N	N	Y	Y	Y
19 ***Kelly***	Y	N	N	N	Y
20 ***Gilman***	Y	N	N	N	Y
21 McNulty	N	Y	Y	Y	N
22 ***Sweeney***	Y	Y	N	N	N
23 ***Boehlert***	Y	N	N	N	Y
24 ***McHugh***	Y	Y	N	N	N
25 ***Walsh***	Y	N	N	Y	N
26 Hinchey	N	Y	Y	Y	Y
27 ***Reynolds***	Y	N	N	N	N
28 Slaughter	N	?	?	?	?
29 LaFalce	N	Y	Y	Y	N

	314	315	316	317	318
30 ***Quinn***	Y	Y	N	Y	N
31 ***Houghton***	Y	Y	N	Y	Y
NORTH CAROLINA					
1 Clayton	N	Y	Y	Y	Y
2 Etheridge	N	Y	N	N	N
3 ***Jones***	Y	N	N	N	N
4 Price	N	Y	N	Y	Y
5 ***Burr***	Y	Y	N	N	N
6 ***Coble***	Y	Y	N	N	N
7 McIntyre	N	N	N	Y	N
8 ***Hayes***	Y	N	N	N	N
9 ***Myrick***	Y	?	?	?	?
10 ***Ballenger***	Y	Y	N	N	N
11 ***Taylor***	Y	Y	N	N	N
12 Watt	N	Y	Y	Y	Y
NORTH DAKOTA					
AL Pomeroy	N	Y	Y	N	N
OHIO					
1 ***Chabot***	Y	N	N	N	N
2 ***Portman***	Y	N	N	N	N
3 Hall	N	?	?	?	?
4 ***Oxley***	Y	N	N	N	N
5 ***Gillmor***	Y	N	N	N	N
6 Strickland	N	Y	Y	Y	Y
7 ***Hobson***	Y	Y	N	N	N
8 ***Boehner***	Y	N	N	N	N
9 Kaptur	N	Y	Y	Y	N
10 Kucinich	N	Y	Y	Y	N
11 Jones	N	?	?	?	?
12 ***Kasich***	Y	Y	N	N	N
13 Brown	N	Y	Y	Y	Y
14 Sawyer	N	Y	Y	Y	Y
15 ***Pryce***	Y	N	N	N	N
16 ***Regula***	Y	N	N	N	N
17 Traficant	Y	N	N	N	N
18 ***Ney***	Y	Y	N	N	N
19 ***LaTourette***	Y	Y	N	N	N
OKLAHOMA					
1 ***Largent***	Y	N	N	N	N
2 ***Coburn***	Y	?	?	?	?
3 ***Watkins***	Y	N	N	N	N
4 ***Watts***	Y	Y	N	N	N
5 ***Istook***	Y	Y	N	Y	N
6 ***Lucas***	Y	N	N	N	N
OREGON					
1 Wu	N	Y	N	N	Y
2 ***Walden***	Y	N	N	N	N
3 Blumenauer	N	Y	Y	Y	Y
4 DeFazio	N	Y	N	Y	Y
5 Hooley	N	Y	N	Y	Y
PENNSYLVANIA					
1 Brady	N	Y	Y	Y	Y
2 Fattah	N	Y	Y	Y	Y
3 Borski	N	N	N	N	Y
4 Klink	N	?	?	?	?
5 ***Peterson***	Y	Y	N	N	N
6 Holden	N	Y	Y	N	N
7 ***Weldon***	Y	Y	N	Y	N
8 ***Greenwood***	Y	Y	Y	Y	Y
9 ***Shuster***	Y	?	?	?	?
10 ***Sherwood***	Y	Y	N	N	N
11 Kanjorski	N	Y	Y	N	N
12 Murtha	?	Y	N	N	N
13 Hoeffel	N	Y	N	N	Y
14 Coyne	N	Y	Y	Y	Y
15 ***Toomey***	Y	Y	N	N	N
16 ***Pitts***	Y	N	N	N	N
17 ***Gekas***	Y	N	N	N	N
18 Doyle	N	Y	N	N	N
19 ***Goodling***	Y	N	N	N	N
20 Mascara	N	Y	N	Y	N
21 ***English***	Y	Y	N	N	N
RHODE ISLAND					
1 Kennedy	N	Y	Y	Y	Y
2 Weygand	N	Y	Y	Y	N
SOUTH CAROLINA					
1 ***Sanford***	Y	Y	N	Y	N
2 ***Spence***	Y	N	N	N	N
3 ***Graham***	Y	Y	N	N	N
4 ***DeMint***	Y	Y	N	N	N
5 Spratt	N	Y	N	Y	Y
6 Clyburn	N	Y	Y	Y	Y
SOUTH DAKOTA					
AL ***Thune***	Y	N	N	N	N

	314	315	316	317	318
TENNESSEE					
1 ***Jenkins***	Y	N	N	N	N
2 ***Duncan***	Y	N	N	Y	N
3 ***Wamp***	Y	N	N	N	N
4 ***Hilleary***	Y	N	N	N	N
5 Clement	?	Y	N	Y	N
6 Gordon	N	?	?	?	?
7 ***Bryant***	Y	N	N	N	N
8 Tanner	N	Y	N	N	Y
9 Ford	N	Y	Y	Y	Y
TEXAS					
1 Sandlin	N	Y	N	Y	Y
2 Turner	N	Y	N	Y	N
3 ***Johnson, Sam***	Y	N	N	Y	N
4 Hall	Y	Y	N	N	N
5 ***Sessions***	Y	N	N	N	N
6 ***Barton***	Y	N	N	N	N
7 ***Archer***	Y	N	N	N	N
8 ***Brady***	Y	N	N	N	N
9 Lampson	N	Y	Y	Y	N
10 Doggett	N	Y	N	Y	Y
11 Edwards	N	Y	N	Y	N
12 ***Granger***	Y	N	N	Y	N
13 ***Thornberry***	Y	N	N	N	N
14 ***Paul***	Y	Y	N	Y	N
15 Hinojosa	N	Y	Y	Y	Y
16 Reyes	N	N	Y	N	Y
17 Stenholm	Y	Y	N	N	N
18 Jackson-Lee	N	Y	Y	Y	Y
19 ***Combest***	Y	N	N	N	N
20 Gonzalez	N	Y	N	N	Y
21 ***Smith***	Y	N	N	N	N
22 ***DeLay***	Y	N	N	N	N
23 ***Bonilla***	Y	N	N	N	N
24 Frost	N	N	N	Y	Y
25 Bentsen	N	Y	N	Y	Y
26 ***Armey***	Y	N	N	N	N
27 Ortiz	N	N	Y	Y	N
28 Rodriguez	N	Y	Y	Y	Y
29 Green	N	N	Y	Y	Y
30 Johnson, E.B.	N	Y	Y	Y	Y
UTAH					
1 ***Hansen***	Y	N	N	N	N
2 ***Cook***	?	?	?	?	?
3 ***Cannon***	?	N	N	?	N
VERMONT					
AL *Sanders*	N	Y	Y	Y	Y
VIRGINIA					
1 ***Bateman***	Y	N	N	N	N
2 Pickett	N	N	N	Y	Y
3 Scott	N	Y	Y	Y	Y
4 Sisisky	Y	N	N	Y	Y
5 *Goode*	Y	N	N	N	N
6 ***Goodlatte***	Y	N	N	N	N
7 ***Bliley***	Y	N	N	N	N
8 Moran	N	Y	Y	Y	Y
9 Boucher	N	Y	?	N	Y
10 ***Wolf***	Y	Y	N	Y	N
11 ***Davis***	Y	Y	N	N	N
WASHINGTON					
1 Inslee	N	N	N	Y	Y
2 ***Metcalf***	Y	N	N	N	N
3 Baird	N	Y	Y	N	Y
4 ***Hastings***	Y	N	N	N	N
5 ***Nethercutt***	Y	Y	N	Y	N
6 Dicks	N	Y	Y	Y	Y
7 McDermott	N	Y	Y	Y	Y
8 ***Dunn***	Y	N	N	Y	N
9 Smith	N	Y	N	N	Y
WEST VIRGINIA					
1 Mollohan	Y	N	N	N	N
2 Wise	N	?	N	N	Y
3 Rahall	N	Y	Y	Y	N
WISCONSIN					
1 ***Ryan***	Y	Y	N	N	N
2 Baldwin	N	Y	Y	Y	Y
3 Kind	N	Y	Y	Y	Y
4 Kleczka	?	Y	Y	Y	N
5 Barrett	N	Y	Y	Y	Y
6 ***Petri***	Y	Y	N	N	N
7 Obey	N	Y	Y	Y	?
8 ***Green***	Y	Y	N	N	N
9 ***Sensenbrenner***	Y	Y	N	N	N
WYOMING					
AL ***Cubin***	?	N	N	N	N

Southern states - Ala., Ark., Fla., Ga., Ky., La., Miss., N.C., Okla., S.C., Tenn., Texas, Va.

319. HR 4690. Fiscal 2001 Commerce, Justice, State Appropriations/Tobacco Lawsuit. Waxman, D-Calif., amendment that would exempt a pending federal suit against tobacco companies from a provision that would prohibit the Justice Department from taking funds from other departments to support high-cost federal lawsuits. Adopted 215-183: R 55-147; D 159-35 (ND 133-10, SD 26-25); I 1-1. June 23, 2000. A "yea" was a vote in support of the president's position.

320. HR 4690. Fiscal 2001 Commerce, Justice, State Appropriations/Attorney Overtime Pay. Davis, R-Va., amendment that would strike a provision prohibiting the Justice Department from using funds to pay its attorneys overtime for any work performed in fiscal 2001. Rejected 103-288: R 33-162; D 69-125 (ND 55-87, SD 14-38); I 1-1. June 23, 2000.

321. HR 4690. Fiscal 2001 Commerce, Justice, State Appropriations/Patent Office. Coble, R-N.C., amendment that would increase the Patent and Trademark Office appropriation by $134 million and reduce the Commerce Department's economic and statistical analysis programs by $10 million, census statistic funds by $40 million and the State Department's educational and cultural exchange program by $99 million. Rejected 145-223: R 106-76; D 38-146 (ND 32-103, SD 6-43); I 1-1. June 23 2000.

322. HR 4690. Fiscal 2001 Commerce, Justice, State Appropriations/Asia Foundation. Sanford, R-S.C., amendment that would eliminate funding for the Asia Foundation. Rejected 86-312: R 74-135; D 11-176 (ND 9-126, SD 2-50); I 1-1. June 26, 2000.

323. HR 4690. Fiscal 2001 Commerce, Justice, State Appropriations/Kyoto Protocol. Olver, D-Mass., amendment that would clarify that the bill's restrictions on implementing the Kyoto climate change treaty would not apply to activities that are otherwise authorized by law. Adopted 217-181: R 44-164; D 172-16 (ND 131-5, SD 41-11); I 1-1. June 26, 2000.

324. HR 4690. Fiscal 2001 Commerce, Justice, State Appropriations/Gun Safety. Hostettler, R-Ind., amendment that would prohibit the Justice Department from using funds to implement or administer the settlement reached between the federal government and gun manufacturer Smith & Wesson. Rejected 196-201: R 156-50; D 39-150 (ND 17-120, SD 22-30); I 1-1. June 26, 2000. A "nay" was a vote in support of the president's position.

325. HR 4690. Fiscal 2001 Commerce, Justice, State Appropriations/Xinhua News Agency. Vitter, R-La., amendment that would prohibit the State Department from using funds to approve the purchase by the Chinese government's Xinhua News Agency of property in Arlington, Va., overlooking the Pentagon. Adopted 367-34: R 210-0; D 155-34 (ND 111-26, SD 44-8); I 2-0. June 26, 2000.

326. HR 4690. Fiscal 2001 Commerce, Justice, State Appropriations/Passage. Passage of the bill that would appropriate $37.4 billion for the departments of Commerce, Justice and State and the federal judiciary and related agencies in fiscal 2001, 5.5 percent less than in fiscal year 2000. Passed 214-195: R 188-22; D 26-171 (ND 14-130, SD 12-41); I 0-2. June 26, 2000.

Key

Y	Voted for (yea).
#	Paired for.
+	Announced for.
N	Voted against (nay).
X	Paired against.
–	Announced against.
P	Voted "present."
C	Voted "present" to avoid possible conflict of interest.
?	Did not vote or otherwise make a position known.

•

Democrats ***Republicans***
Independents

	319	320	321	322	323	324	325	326
ALABAMA								
1 ***Callahan***	N	N	?	N	N	Y	Y	Y
2 ***Everett***	N	N	?	Y	N	Y	Y	Y
3 ***Riley***	N	N	N	Y	N	?	Y	Y
4 ***Aderholt***	N	N	N	Y	N	Y	Y	Y
5 Cramer	N	N	N	N	N	Y	Y	Y
6 ***Bachus***	?	?	?	Y	N	Y	Y	Y
7 Hilliard	N	N	N	N	N	Y	N	N
ALASKA								
AL ***Young***	?	Y	Y	N	N	Y	Y	Y
ARIZONA								
1 ***Salmon***	?	N	N	N	N	Y	Y	Y
2 Pastor	Y	N	N	Y	Y	N	Y	Y
3 ***Stump***	N	N	Y	N	N	Y	Y	Y
4 ***Shadegg***	N	N	Y	Y	N	Y	Y	N
5 ***Kolbe***	N	N	N	N	Y	Y	Y	Y
6 ***Hayworth***	N	N	Y	Y	N	Y	Y	Y
ARKANSAS								
1 Berry	Y	N	N	N	N	Y	Y	Y
2 Snyder	Y	N	N	N	Y	N	Y	N
3 ***Hutchinson***	N	?	?	N	N	Y	Y	Y
4 ***Dickey***	N	N	Y	N	Y	Y	Y	Y
CALIFORNIA								
1 Thompson	Y	Y	Y	N	Y	N	Y	N
2 ***Herger***	N	?	?	Y	N	Y	Y	P
3 ***Ose***	Y	N	Y	N	N	Y	Y	Y
4 ***Doolittle***	N	N	Y	Y	N	Y	Y	Y
5 Matsui	Y	N	N	N	Y	N	Y	N
6 Woolsey	Y	N	N	N	Y	N	N	N
7 Miller, George	Y	Y	N	N	Y	N	Y	N
8 Pelosi	Y	Y	Y	N	Y	N	Y	N
9 Lee	Y	Y	N	N	Y	N	N	N
10 Tauscher	Y	Y	N	N	Y	N	Y	N
11 ***Pombo***	N	N	Y	Y	N	Y	Y	Y
12 Lantos	Y	N	N	N	Y	N	P	N
13 Stark	Y	N	N	N	Y	N	N	N
14 Eshoo	Y	Y	Y	N	Y	N	Y	N
15 ***Campbell***	Y	?	?	?	?	?	?	?
16 Lofgren	Y	N	Y	N	Y	N	Y	N
17 Farr	Y	Y	Y	N	Y	N	N	N
18 Condit	N	N	Y	N	N	N	Y	N
19 ***Radanovich***	?	N	Y	Y	N	Y	Y	Y
20 Dooley	Y	Y	Y	N	Y	N	Y	N
21 ***Thomas***	N	N	N	N	N	Y	Y	Y
22 Capps	Y	N	N	N	Y	N	Y	N
23 ***Gallegly***	Y	?	?	N	Y	N	Y	Y
24 Sherman	Y	N	Y	N	Y	N	Y	N
25 ***McKeon***	Y	N	Y	N	N	Y	Y	Y
26 Berman	?	?	?	N	Y	N	N	N
27 ***Rogan***	N	Y	?	N	N	N	Y	Y
28 ***Dreier***	N	N	Y	N	N	Y	Y	Y
29 Waxman	Y	N	N	?	?	?	?	?
30 Becerra	Y	N	N	N	Y	N	Y	Y
31 Martinez	N	Y	Y	?	?	?	?	?
32 Dixon	?	?	?	N	Y	N	P	N
33 Roybal-Allard	+	+	–	N	Y	N	Y	N
34 Napolitano	Y	N	Y	N	Y	N	Y	N
35 Waters	Y	Y	?	N	Y	N	N	N
36 ***Kuykendall***	+	–	+	N	Y	N	Y	Y
37 Millender-McD.	Y	N	N	N	Y	N	Y	N
38 ***Horn***	Y	Y	Y	N	Y	N	Y	Y
39 ***Royce***	Y	N	Y	N	N	Y	Y	N
40 ***Lewis***	N	N	N	N	N	Y	Y	Y
41 ***Miller, Gary***	N	N	Y	N	N	Y	Y	Y
42 Baca	N	N	N	N	Y	Y	Y	N
43 ***Calvert***	Y	N	Y	N	N	Y	Y	Y
44 ***Bono***	Y	N	Y	N	N	Y	Y	Y
45 ***Rohrabacher***	N	N	Y	Y	N	Y	Y	Y
46 Sanchez	Y	Y	N	N	Y	N	Y	N
47 ***Cox***	?	N	Y	N	N	Y	Y	Y
48 ***Packard***	N	N	N	N	N	Y	Y	Y
49 ***Bilbray***	Y	Y	Y	N	Y	N	Y	Y
50 Filner	?	?	?	N	Y	N	Y	N
51 ***Cunningham***	Y	N	Y	N	N	Y	Y	Y
52 ***Hunter***	N	Y	Y	Y	N	Y	Y	Y
COLORADO								
1 DeGette	Y	N	Y	N	Y	N	Y	N
2 Udall	Y	Y	N	N	Y	N	Y	N
3 ***McInnis***	N	N	Y	N	N	N	Y	N
4 ***Schaffer***	Y	N	Y	Y	N	Y	Y	N
5 ***Hefley***	N	N	Y	Y	N	Y	Y	N
6 ***Tancredo***	N	N	Y	Y	N	N	Y	N
CONNECTICUT								
1 Larson	Y	N	Y	N	Y	N	P	N
2 Gejdenson	Y	Y	N	N	Y	N	Y	N
3 DeLauro	Y	Y	N	N	Y	N	Y	N
4 ***Shays***	Y	N	Y	Y	Y	N	Y	Y
5 Maloney	Y	Y	N	N	Y	N	N	N
6 ***Johnson***	Y	N	Y	N	?	N	Y	Y
DELAWARE								
AL ***Castle***	Y	Y	Y	N	Y	N	Y	Y
FLORIDA								
1 ***Scarborough***	Y	Y	?	Y	N	Y	Y	Y
2 Boyd	N	N	N	Y	Y	Y	Y	Y
3 Brown	Y	N	N	?	?	?	Y	N
4 ***Fowler***	N	N	?	N	N	Y	Y	Y
5 Thurman	Y	N	Y	N	Y	N	Y	N
6 ***Stearns***	N	N	Y	Y	N	Y	Y	Y
7 ***Mica***	N	N	Y	Y	N	Y	Y	Y
8 ***McCollum***	?	?	?	?	?	?	?	?
9 ***Bilirakis***	Y	N	N	N	N	Y	Y	Y
10 ***Young***	Y	?	?	N	N	Y	Y	Y
11 Davis	Y	Y	N	N	Y	N	Y	N
12 ***Canady***	?	?	?	N	N	Y	Y	Y
13 ***Miller***	N	N	N	Y	N	N	Y	Y
14 ***Goss***	N	?	?	N	Y	Y	Y	Y
15 ***Weldon***	N	N	Y	Y	Y	Y	Y	Y
16 ***Foley***	Y	N	N	Y	Y	N	Y	Y
17 Meek	Y	N	N	N	Y	N	N	Y
18 ***Ros-Lehtinen***	N	N	?	N	Y	N	Y	Y
19 Wexler	Y	N	Y	N	Y	N	Y	N
20 Deutsch	Y	Y	N	N	Y	N	Y	N
21 ***Diaz-Balart***	N	N	N	N	N	N	Y	Y
22 ***Shaw***	N	N	N	N	N	N	Y	Y
23 Hastings	Y	?	?	N	Y	N	N	Y
GEORGIA								
1 ***Kingston***	N	N	Y	Y	N	Y	Y	Y
2 Bishop	N	N	?	N	N	Y	Y	N
3 ***Collins***	N	N	N	Y	N	Y	Y	Y
4 McKinney	Y	Y	N	N	Y	N	Y	N
5 Lewis	Y	N	N	N	Y	N	Y	N
6 ***Isakson***	N	Y	Y	N	N	N	Y	Y
7 ***Barr***	N	Y	Y	Y	N	Y	Y	N
8 ***Chambliss***	N	N	N	N	N	Y	Y	N
9 ***Deal***	N	N	?	N	N	Y	Y	Y
10 ***Norwood***	N	N	Y	N	N	Y	Y	N
11 ***Linder***	N	N	N	N	N	Y	Y	Y
HAWAII								
1 Abercrombie	Y	Y	N	N	Y	N	Y	Y
2 Mink	Y	N	N	N	Y	N	N	Y
IDAHO								
1 ***Chenoweth-Hage***	N	?	?	Y	N	Y	Y	N
2 ***Simpson***	N	N	Y	N	N	N	Y	Y
ILLINOIS								
1 Rush	Y	N	N	?	?	?	?	N
2 Jackson	Y	Y	N	N	Y	N	Y	N
3 Lipinski	Y	N	N	?	?	?	?	?
4 Gutierrez	Y	N	N	?	?	?	?	?
5 Blagojevich	Y	N	N	?	?	?	?	?
6 ***Hyde***	N	Y	Y	N	N	N	Y	Y
7 Davis	Y	N	N	?	?	?	N	N
8 ***Crane***	N	N	Y	Y	N	Y	Y	N
9 Schakowsky	Y	Y	N	?	?	?	?	N
10 ***Porter***	Y	Y	N	N	Y	N	Y	Y
11 ***Weller***	N	N	Y	N	Y	N	Y	Y
12 Costello	Y	N	N	N	Y	Y	Y	N
13 ***Biggert***	N	N	N	N	N	Y	Y	Y

ND Northern Democrats SD Southern Democrats

	319	320	321	322	323	324	325	326
14 ***Hastert***								Y
15 ***Ewing***	N	?	?	N	N	Y	Y	Y
16 ***Manzullo***	Y	N	Y	?	?	?	?	?
17 Evans	Y	N	N	N	Y	N	Y	N
18 ***LaHood***	Y	?	?	N	Y	Y	Y	Y
19 Phelps	N	N	N	N	Y	Y	Y	N
20 ***Shimkus***	N	N	N	N	N	Y	Y	Y
INDIANA								
1 Visclosky	Y	N	N	N	Y	N	Y	Y
2 ***McIntosh***	?	?	?	?	?	?	?	?
3 Roemer	Y	N	N	N	Y	N	Y	N
4 ***Souder***	N	N	N	N	N	Y	Y	Y
5 ***Buyer***	N	N	Y	Y	N	Y	Y	Y
6 ***Burton***	N	Y	Y	Y	N	Y	Y	Y
7 ***Pease***	N	N	Y	Y	N	Y	Y	Y
8 ***Hostettler***	N	N	Y	Y	N	Y	Y	Y
9 Hill	N	N	N	N	Y	Y	Y	N
10 Carson	Y	N	N	–	+	N	N	N
IOWA								
1 ***Leach***	?	Y	N	N	N	N	Y	Y
2 ***Nussle***	N	N	N	N	N	Y	Y	Y
3 Boswell	Y	Y	N	–	+	+	Y	N
4 ***Ganske***	Y	N	N	N	Y	N	Y	Y
5 ***Latham***	N	N	N	N	N	Y	Y	Y
KANSAS								
1 ***Moran***	N	N	Y	Y	N	Y	Y	Y
2 ***Ryun***	N	N	Y	+	–	+	+	+
3 Moore	Y	N	N	Y	Y	N	Y	N
4 ***Tiahrt***	N	N	N	N	N	Y	Y	Y
KENTUCKY								
1 ***Whitfield***	N	N	N	?	?	?	Y	Y
2 ***Lewis***	N	N	Y	N	N	Y	Y	Y
3 ***Northup***	N	N	N	N	N	N	Y	Y
4 Lucas	N	N	N	N	Y	Y	Y	Y
5 ***Rogers***	N	N	N	N	N	Y	Y	Y
6 ***Fletcher***	N	N	Y	N	N	Y	Y	Y
LOUISIANA								
1 ***Vitter***	N	N	Y	N	N	Y	Y	Y
2 Jefferson	Y	N	N	N	Y	N	Y	N
3 ***Tauzin***	?	?	?	N	N	Y	Y	Y
4 ***McCrery***	?	N	N	N	N	Y	Y	Y
5 ***Cooksey***	N	N	N	N	N	Y	Y	Y
6 ***Baker***	N	?	?	N	N	Y	Y	Y
7 John	N	N	N	N	N	Y	Y	Y
MAINE								
1 Allen	Y	Y	N	N	Y	N	Y	N
2 Baldacci	Y	Y	N	N	Y	N	Y	N
MARYLAND								
1 ***Gilchrest***	Y	Y	N	N	Y	N	Y	Y
2 ***Ehrlich***	N	Y	Y	Y	Y	Y	Y	Y
3 Cardin	Y	N	N	N	Y	N	Y	N
4 Wynn	+	+	–	N	Y	N	Y	N
5 Hoyer	Y	Y	N	N	Y	N	Y	N
6 ***Bartlett***	N	N	Y	Y	N	Y	Y	Y
7 Cummings	Y	Y	N	N	Y	N	Y	N
8 ***Morella***	Y	Y	N	–	+	–	Y	N
MASSACHUSETTS								
1 Olver	Y	N	N	N	Y	N	N	N
2 Neal	Y	N	N	N	Y	N	Y	N
3 McGovern	Y	Y	N	N	Y	N	Y	N
4 Frank	Y	Y	Y	N	Y	N	P	N
5 Meehan	Y	Y	?	N	Y	N	P	N
6 Tierney	?	Y	N	N	Y	N	Y	N
7 Markey	Y	N	?	?	?	?	?	?
8 Capuano	Y	Y	N	N	Y	N	N	N
9 Moakley	Y	N	?	N	Y	N	Y	N
10 Delahunt	Y	Y	Y	N	Y	N	Y	N
MICHIGAN								
1 Stupak	Y	N	?	N	Y	N	Y	N
2 ***Hoekstra***	N	N	N	Y	N	Y	Y	Y
3 ***Ehlers***	Y	N	Y	N	Y	N	Y	Y
4 ***Camp***	N	N	Y	N	N	Y	Y	Y
5 Barcia	Y	N	Y	N	N	Y	Y	Y
6 ***Upton***	Y	N	N	N	N	N	Y	Y
7 ***Smith***	N	Y	N	Y	N	Y	Y	Y
8 Stabenow	Y	N	?	N	Y	N	Y	Y
9 Kildee	Y	N	N	N	Y	N	Y	N
10 Bonior	Y	N	N	N	Y	N	Y	N
11 ***Knollenberg***	N	N	N	N	N	N	Y	Y
12 Levin	Y	N	N	N	Y	N	Y	N
13 Rivers	Y	Y	N	N	Y	N	Y	N
14 Conyers	Y	Y	Y	N	Y	N	N	N
15 Kilpatrick	Y	N	?	–	+	–	+	–
16 Dingell	Y	Y	N	?	?	?	N	N
MINNESOTA								
1 ***Gutknecht***	N	N	N	Y	Y	Y	Y	Y
2 Minge	Y	N	Y	N	Y	N	Y	N
3 ***Ramstad***	Y	N	Y	Y	Y	N	Y	Y
4 Vento	?	?	?	?	?	?	?	?
5 Sabo	Y	N	N	N	Y	N	Y	N
6 Luther	Y	N	Y	Y	Y	N	Y	N
7 Peterson	N	N	Y	N	N	Y	Y	N
8 Oberstar	Y	N	N	N	Y	N	N	N
MISSISSIPPI								
1 ***Wicker***	N	N	N	N	N	Y	Y	Y
2 Thompson	N	N	?	N	Y	N	N	N
3 ***Pickering***	N	?	?	N	N	Y	Y	Y
4 Shows	N	N	N	?	?	?	?	?
5 Taylor	Y	N	N	Y	N	Y	Y	Y
MISSOURI								
1 Clay	Y	?	N	N	Y	N	N	N
2 ***Talent***	N	N	N	?	?	?	?	?
3 Gephardt	Y	N	N	N	Y	N	Y	N
4 Skelton	Y	N	N	N	Y	Y	Y	N
5 McCarthy	Y	Y	Y	N	Y	N	Y	Y
6 Danner	N	Y	N	N	N	Y	Y	N
7 ***Blunt***	N	N	N	N	N	Y	Y	Y
8 ***Emerson***	N	N	N	N	N	Y	Y	Y
9 ***Hulshof***	N	N	N	Y	N	Y	Y	Y
MONTANA								
AL ***Hill***	N	N	Y	N	N	Y	Y	Y
NEBRASKA								
1 ***Bereuter***	Y	N	N	N	Y	N	Y	Y
2 ***Terry***	N	N	N	N	N	Y	Y	Y
3 ***Barrett***	N	N	N	N	N	Y	Y	Y
NEVADA								
1 Berkley	Y	Y	N	N	Y	N	Y	N
2 ***Gibbons***	N	N	?	Y	N	Y	Y	Y
NEW HAMPSHIRE								
1 ***Sununu***	N	N	?	Y	N	Y	Y	Y
2 ***Bass***	N	N	Y	N	Y	Y	Y	Y
NEW JERSEY								
1 Andrews	Y	N	N	Y	Y	N	Y	N
2 ***LoBiondo***	Y	N	N	Y	Y	N	Y	Y
3 ***Saxton***	Y	N	Y	N	Y	N	Y	Y
4 ***Smith***	Y	N	N	N	Y	N	Y	Y
5 ***Roukema***	Y	N	Y	N	Y	N	Y	Y
6 Pallone	Y	N	N	N	Y	N	Y	N
7 ***Franks***	Y	Y	?	N	Y	N	Y	Y
8 Pascrell	Y	N	?	N	Y	N	Y	N
9 Rothman	?	?	?	N	Y	N	Y	N
10 Payne	Y	N	N	N	Y	N	N	N
11 ***Frelinghuysen***	Y	Y	N	N	Y	N	Y	Y
12 Holt	Y	N	N	N	Y	N	Y	N
13 Menendez	Y	N	N	N	Y	N	Y	N
NEW MEXICO								
1 ***Wilson***	Y	N	Y	N	Y	Y	Y	Y
2 ***Skeen***	N	N	N	N	N	Y	Y	Y
3 Udall	Y	N	N	N	Y	N	Y	N
NEW YORK								
1 Forbes	N	N	Y	Y	Y	N	Y	Y
2 ***Lazio***	?	?	?	?	?	?	?	?
3 ***King***	Y	N	Y	N	Y	N	Y	Y
4 McCarthy	Y	N	Y	N	Y	N	Y	N
5 Ackerman	Y	N	N	N	Y	N	N	N
6 Meeks	Y	N	N	N	Y	N	Y	N
7 Crowley	Y	Y	N	N	Y	N	Y	N
8 Nadler	Y	Y	Y	N	Y	N	Y	N
9 Weiner	Y	Y	Y	N	Y	N	Y	N
10 Towns	?	N	N	?	?	?	N	N
11 Owens	Y	N	N	N	Y	N	Y	N
12 Velázquez	Y	N	N	N	Y	N	N	N
13 ***Fossella***	N	N	Y	N	N	N	Y	Y
14 Maloney	Y	N	N	N	Y	N	Y	N
15 Rangel	?	?	?	?	?	?	?	?
16 Serrano	Y	N	N	N	Y	N	Y	N
17 Engel	Y	N	N	N	Y	N	Y	N
18 Lowey	Y	Y	N	N	Y	N	Y	N
19 ***Kelly***	Y	Y	Y	Y	Y	N	Y	Y
20 ***Gilman***	Y	Y	N	N	N	N	Y	Y
21 McNulty	Y	Y	N	N	Y	N	Y	N
22 ***Sweeney***	N	Y	N	N	N	N	Y	Y
23 ***Boehlert***	Y	N	Y	N	Y	N	Y	Y
24 ***McHugh***	Y	Y	N	N	N	N	Y	Y
25 ***Walsh***	Y	N	N	N	N	N	Y	Y
26 Hinchey	Y	Y	N	?	?	?	?	?
27 ***Reynolds***	N	N	N	N	Y	Y	Y	Y
28 Slaughter	Y	Y	Y	N	Y	N	Y	N
29 LaFalce	Y	Y	N	N	Y	N	Y	N
30 ***Quinn***	Y	N	N	N	Y	N	Y	Y
31 ***Houghton***	N	N	Y	N	Y	N	Y	Y
NORTH CAROLINA								
1 Clayton	?	Y	Y	N	Y	N	N	N
2 Etheridge	N	Y	?	N	Y	N	Y	N
3 ***Jones***	N	?	?	Y	N	Y	Y	N
4 Price	N	Y	N	N	Y	N	Y	N
5 ***Burr***	N	N	Y	N	N	Y	Y	N
6 ***Coble***	N	N	Y	Y	N	Y	Y	N
7 McIntyre	N	N	N	N	N	Y	Y	N
8 ***Hayes***	N	N	Y	N	N	Y	Y	Y
9 ***Myrick***	?	?	?	N	N	Y	Y	Y
10 ***Ballenger***	N	N	Y	N	N	Y	Y	Y
11 ***Taylor***	N	N	?	N	N	Y	Y	Y
12 Watt	N	Y	N	N	Y	N	P	N
NORTH DAKOTA								
AL Pomeroy	?	?	?	?	?	?	?	?
OHIO								
1 ***Chabot***	N	N	Y	Y	N	Y	Y	Y
2 ***Portman***	Y	N	Y	N	Y	Y	Y	Y
3 Hall	Y	N	N	N	Y	N	Y	N
4 ***Oxley***	N	Y	Y	N	N	N	Y	Y
5 ***Gillmor***	N	N	N	N	N	Y	Y	Y
6 Strickland	Y	N	N	N	Y	Y	Y	N
7 ***Hobson***	Y	N	N	N	Y	Y	Y	Y
8 ***Boehner***	N	?	?	N	N	Y	Y	Y
9 Kaptur	Y	N	N	?	?	?	Y	N
10 Kucinich	Y	N	N	N	Y	N	N	N
11 Jones	?	?	?	?	?	?	N	N
12 ***Kasich***	?	N	Y	Y	N	Y	Y	Y
13 Brown	Y	N	N	N	Y	N	Y	N
14 Sawyer	Y	N	N	N	Y	N	Y	N
15 ***Pryce***	Y	N	Y	N	N	N	Y	Y
16 ***Regula***	Y	N	N	N	Y	Y	Y	Y
17 Traficant	Y	Y	Y	N	N	Y	Y	Y
18 ***Ney***	N	N	Y	Y	N	?	Y	Y
19 ***LaTourette***	N	?	?	N	N	N	Y	Y
OKLAHOMA								
1 ***Largent***	N	N	Y	Y	N	Y	Y	Y
2 ***Coburn***	?	?	?	Y	N	Y	Y	N
3 ***Watkins***	N	N	?	N	N	Y	Y	Y
4 ***Watts***	N	N	N	N	N	Y	Y	Y
5 ***Istook***	?	?	?	N	N	Y	Y	Y
6 ***Lucas***	N	N	Y	N	N	Y	Y	Y
OREGON								
1 Wu	Y	Y	Y	N	Y	N	Y	N
2 ***Walden***	N	N	Y	N	N	Y	Y	Y
3 Blumenauer	Y	N	Y	N	Y	N	P	N
4 DeFazio	Y	Y	Y	Y	Y	N	Y	N
5 Hooley	Y	N	N	N	Y	N	Y	N
PENNSYLVANIA								
1 Brady	Y	Y	N	N	Y	N	Y	N
2 Fattah	Y	Y	N	N	Y	N	Y	N
3 Borski	Y	N	N	N	Y	N	Y	N
4 Klink	?	?	?	?	?	?	?	?
5 ***Peterson***	Y	N	N	Y	N	Y	?	Y
6 Holden	Y	N	N	N	Y	Y	Y	N
7 ***Weldon***	N	N	N	Y	Y	Y	Y	Y
8 ***Greenwood***	Y	N	N	N	Y	N	Y	Y
9 ***Shuster***	N	N	Y	N	Y	Y	?	?
10 ***Sherwood***	Y	N	N	N	N	Y	Y	Y
11 Kanjorski	Y	N	N	Y	Y	Y	Y	N
12 Murtha	N	?	?	N	N	Y	N	Y
13 Hoeffel	Y	N	N	N	Y	N	Y	N
14 Coyne	Y	Y	N	N	Y	N	N	N
15 ***Toomey***	N	N	Y	Y	N	Y	Y	N
16 ***Pitts***	N	N	Y	?	?	?	Y	Y
17 ***Gekas***	?	Y	N	N	N	Y	Y	Y
18 Doyle	Y	N	N	Y	Y	N	Y	N
19 ***Goodling***	N	N	Y	N	N	Y	Y	Y
20 Mascara	Y	N	N	N	Y	Y	Y	N
21 ***English***	N	N	N	N	N	Y	Y	Y
RHODE ISLAND								
1 Kennedy	Y	Y	N	?	Y	N	Y	–
2 Weygand	Y	N	N	N	Y	N	Y	N
SOUTH CAROLINA								
1 ***Sanford***	N	N	Y	Y	N	Y	Y	N
2 ***Spence***	N	N	Y	N	N	Y	Y	Y
3 ***Graham***	N	N	N	N	N	Y	Y	N
4 ***DeMint***	N	N	Y	Y	N	Y	Y	Y
5 Spratt	N	N	N	N	Y	N	Y	N
6 Clyburn	N	N	N	N	Y	N	N	N
SOUTH DAKOTA								
AL ***Thune***	Y	N	Y	N	N	Y	Y	Y
TENNESSEE								
1 ***Jenkins***	N	N	N	Y	N	Y	Y	?
2 ***Duncan***	N	N	N	Y	N	Y	Y	N
3 ***Wamp***	N	Y	N	N	N	Y	Y	Y
4 ***Hilleary***	N	N	Y	Y	N	Y	Y	Y
5 Clement	N	N	N	N	Y	Y	Y	N
6 Gordon	N	N	N	N	Y	Y	Y	N
7 ***Bryant***	N	Y	Y	Y	N	Y	Y	Y
8 Tanner	N	N	N	N	Y	Y	Y	N
9 Ford	Y	Y	N	N	Y	N	Y	N
TEXAS								
1 Sandlin	N	N	N	N	N	Y	Y	N
2 Turner	Y	N	N	N	Y	Y	Y	N
3 ***Johnson, Sam***	N	Y	Y	Y	N	Y	Y	Y
4 Hall	N	Y	Y	N	N	Y	Y	Y
5 ***Sessions***	N	N	Y	Y	N	Y	Y	Y
6 ***Barton***	N	N	Y	Y	N	Y	Y	Y
7 ***Archer***	N	N	Y	N	N	?	Y	Y
8 ***Brady***	N	N	N	N	N	Y	Y	Y
9 Lampson	Y	N	N	N	Y	Y	Y	N
10 Doggett	Y	Y	N	N	Y	N	Y	N
11 Edwards	Y	N	N	N	Y	N	Y	N
12 ***Granger***	N	N	?	N	N	Y	Y	Y
13 ***Thornberry***	N	N	Y	N	N	Y	Y	Y
14 ***Paul***	N	N	Y	Y	N	Y	Y	N
15 Hinojosa	Y	N	N	N	Y	N	Y	N
16 Reyes	?	?	?	N	Y	N	Y	Y
17 Stenholm	N	N	N	N	N	Y	Y	N
18 Jackson-Lee	Y	Y	N	N	Y	N	Y	N
19 ***Combest***	N	N	Y	Y	N	Y	Y	Y
20 Gonzalez	Y	N	N	N	Y	N	Y	N
21 ***Smith***	N	N	Y	N	N	Y	Y	Y
22 ***DeLay***	N	N	N	N	N	Y	Y	Y
23 ***Bonilla***	N	N	N	N	N	Y	Y	Y
24 Frost	Y	N	N	N	Y	N	Y	N
25 Bentsen	Y	N	N	N	Y	N	Y	N
26 ***Armey***	N	N	Y	Y	N	Y	Y	Y
27 Ortiz	N	N	N	N	Y	Y	Y	N
28 Rodriguez	Y	N	N	N	Y	N	Y	N
29 Green	Y	N	N	N	Y	Y	Y	N
30 Johnson, E.B.	?	N	N	N	Y	N	N	N
UTAH								
1 ***Hansen***	Y	N	Y	?	?	?	?	?
2 ***Cook***	?	?	?	?	?	?	?	?
3 ***Cannon***	N	N	Y	N	N	Y	Y	Y
VERMONT								
AL *Sanders*	Y	Y	N	N	Y	N	Y	N
VIRGINIA								
1 ***Bateman***	N	Y	N	N	N	Y	Y	Y
2 Pickett	N	N	N	N	Y	Y	Y	N
3 Scott	N	Y	N	N	Y	N	Y	N
4 Sisisky	N	Y	N	N	Y	Y	Y	N
5 *Goode*	N	N	Y	Y	N	Y	Y	N
6 ***Goodlatte***	N	N	Y	Y	N	Y	Y	Y
7 ***Bliley***	N	Y	N	N	N	Y	Y	Y
8 Moran	Y	Y	Y	N	Y	N	N	N
9 Boucher	N	N	Y	N	N	Y	Y	Y
10 ***Wolf***	Y	Y	Y	N	N	Y	Y	Y
11 ***Davis***	N	Y	Y	N	Y	N	Y	Y
WASHINGTON								
1 Inslee	Y	N	Y	N	Y	N	Y	N
2 ***Metcalf***	Y	N	Y	Y	N	Y	Y	Y
3 Baird	Y	N	N	N	Y	N	Y	N
4 ***Hastings***	N	N	N	Y	N	Y	Y	Y
5 ***Nethercutt***	Y	?	?	Y	N	Y	Y	Y
6 Dicks	Y	?	?	N	Y	N	Y	Y
7 McDermott	Y	Y	N	N	Y	N	N	N
8 ***Dunn***	Y	Y	N	N	N	N	Y	Y
9 Smith	?	?	?	Y	Y	N	Y	N
WEST VIRGINIA								
1 Mollohan	N	N	N	N	Y	Y	Y	Y
2 Wise	Y	N	Y	N	Y	Y	Y	N
3 Rahall	Y	Y	N	N	Y	Y	Y	N
WISCONSIN								
1 ***Ryan***	N	N	N	Y	N	Y	Y	Y
2 Baldwin	Y	Y	Y	N	Y	N	Y	N
3 Kind	Y	N	N	N	Y	N	Y	N
4 Kleczka	Y	N	N	N	Y	N	Y	N
5 Barrett	Y	N	N	N	Y	N	Y	N
6 ***Petri***	N	N	N	N	N	Y	Y	Y
7 Obey	Y	N	N	N	Y	N	Y	N
8 ***Green***	N	N	N	N	N	Y	Y	Y
9 ***Sensenbrenner***	N	N	Y	Y	N	Y	Y	N
WYOMING								
AL ***Cubin***	N	N	Y	Y	N	Y	Y	Y

Southern states - Ala., Ark., Fla., Ga., Ky., La., Miss., N.C., Okla., S.C., Tenn., Texas, Va.

327. HR 3417. Pribilof Islands/Passage. Sherwood, R-Pa., motion to suspend the rules and pass the bill that would end federal involvement in the civil administration of Alaska's Pribilof Islands and provide federal payments associated with the land transfer from federal to local control. Motion agreed to 400-3: R 202-3; D 196-0 (ND 143-0, SD 53-0); I 2-0. A two-thirds majority of those present and voting (269 in this case) is required for passage under suspension of the rules. June 26, 2000.

328. S 148. Bird Conservation/Passage. Sherwood, R-Pa., motion to suspend the rules and pass the bill that would establish a grant program for the conservation of neotropical migratory birds. Private and public organizations as well as domestic and international governments would be eligible to apply for grants, although the federal government's share would not exceed 25 percent of the total cost. Motion agreed to 384-22: R 185-22; D 197-0 (ND 144-0, SD 53-0); I 2-0. A two-thirds majority of those present and voting (271 in this case) is required for passage under suspension of the rules. June 26, 2000.

329. HR 4408. Bass Conservation/Passage. Sherwood, R-Pa., motion to suspend the rules and pass the bill that would reauthorize the Atlantic Striped Bass Conservation Act through fiscal 2003, authorizing $1 million a year for the Commerce Department and $250,000 a year for the Interior Department to conduct studies on the bass population. Motion agreed to 393-12: R 195-12; D 196-0 (ND 143-0, SD 53-0); I 2-0. A two-thirds majority of those present and voting (270 in this case) is required for passage under suspension of the rules. June 26, 2000.

330. HR 3023. Yuma Port Authority/Passage. Sherwood, R-Pa., motion to suspend the rules and pass the bill that would authorize the secretary of the Interior to convey property to the Greater Yuma Port Authority of Yuma County, Ariz., for use as an international port of entry. Motion agreed to 404-1: R 206-0; D 196-1 (ND 145-0, SD 51-1); I 2-0. A two-thirds majority of those present and voting (270 in this case) is required for passage under suspension of the rules. June 26, 2000.

331. H Con Res 312. Title Loans/Adoption. Roukema, R-N.J., motion to suspend the rules and adopt the concurrent resolution expressing the sense of Congress that states and the federal government should oversee title loan and title pawn transactions more closely. Motion agreed to 420-6: R 209-6; D 209-0 (ND 155-0, SD 54-0); I 2-0. A two-thirds majority of those present and voting (284 in this case) is required for adoption under suspension of the rules. June 27, 2000.

332. H Res 494. Ohio State Motto/Adoption. Chabot, R-Ohio, motion to suspend the rules and adopt the resolution expressing the sense of the House that the Ohio state motto is constitutional and urges the courts to uphold its constitutionality. Motion agreed to 333-27: R 213-2; D 119-25 (ND 83-17, SD 36-8); I 1-0. A two-thirds majority of those present and voting (240 in this case) is required for adoption under suspension of the rules. June 27, 2000.

333. HR 4608. James H. Quillen Courthouse/Passage. LaTourette, R-Ohio, motion to suspend the rules and pass the bill that would designate the federal courthouse located at 220 W. Depot St., Greenville, Tenn., as the "James H. Quillen U.S. Courthouse." Motion agreed to 421-2: R 212-2; D 207-0 (ND 153-0, SD 54-0); I 2-0. A two-thirds majority of those present and voting (282 in this case) is required for passage under suspension of the rules. June 27, 2000.

334. HR 4733. Fiscal 2001 Energy, Water Appropriations/Mississippi River. Hulshof, R-Mo., amendment that would designate $2 million in Army Corps of Engineers funding for the upper Mississippi River comprehensive plan. Rejected 165-262: R 96-121; D 68-140 (ND 50-105, SD 18-35); I 1-1. June 27, 2000.

Key

- Y Voted for (yea).
- # Paired for.
- + Announced for.
- N Voted against (nay).
- X Paired against.
- – Announced against.
- P Voted "present."
- C Voted "present" to avoid possible conflict of interest.
- ? Did not vote or otherwise make a position known.

•

Democrats ***Republicans***
Independents

	327	328	329	330	331	332	333	334
ALABAMA								
1 ***Callahan***	Y	Y	Y	Y	Y	Y	Y	N
2 ***Everett***	Y	Y	Y	Y	Y	Y	Y	N
3 ***Riley***	Y	Y	Y	Y	Y	Y	Y	Y
4 ***Aderholt***	Y	Y	Y	Y	Y	Y	Y	Y
5 Cramer	Y	Y	Y	Y	Y	Y	Y	N
6 ***Bachus***	Y	Y	Y	Y	Y	Y	Y	N
7 Hilliard	Y	Y	Y	Y	Y	P	Y	Y
ALASKA								
AL ***Young***	?	?	?	?	?	?	?	N
ARIZONA								
1 ***Salmon***	Y	N	N	Y	Y	Y	Y	Y
2 Pastor	Y	Y	Y	Y	Y	Y	Y	N
3 ***Stump***	Y	Y	Y	Y	Y	Y	Y	N
4 ***Shadegg***	Y	Y	Y	Y	Y	Y	Y	Y
5 ***Kolbe***	Y	Y	Y	Y	Y	Y	Y	N
6 ***Hayworth***	Y	Y	Y	Y	Y	Y	Y	N
ARKANSAS								
1 Berry	Y	Y	Y	Y	Y	Y	Y	Y
2 Snyder	Y	Y	Y	Y	Y	Y	Y	N
3 ***Hutchinson***	Y	Y	Y	Y	Y	Y	Y	Y
4 ***Dickey***	Y	?	Y	Y	Y	Y	Y	N
CALIFORNIA								
1 Thompson	Y	Y	Y	Y	Y	N	Y	Y
2 ***Herger***	Y	N	Y	Y	Y	Y	Y	N
3 ***Ose***	Y	Y	Y	Y	Y	Y	Y	N
4 ***Doolittle***	Y	N	Y	Y	N	Y	Y	N
5 Matsui	Y	Y	Y	Y	Y	Y	Y	N
6 Woolsey	Y	Y	Y	Y	Y	P	Y	N
7 Miller, George	Y	Y	Y	Y	Y	P	Y	Y
8 Pelosi	Y	Y	?	Y	Y	P	Y	Y
9 Lee	Y	Y	Y	Y	Y	N	Y	Y
10 Tauscher	Y	Y	Y	Y	Y	P	Y	N
11 ***Pombo***	Y	N	Y	Y	N	Y	Y	N
12 Lantos	Y	Y	Y	Y	Y	P	Y	Y
13 Stark	Y	Y	Y	Y	Y	N	Y	Y
14 Eshoo	Y	Y	Y	Y	Y	Y	Y	Y
15 ***Campbell***	?	?	?	?	Y	N	Y	N
16 Lofgren	Y	Y	Y	Y	Y	P	Y	N
17 Farr	Y	Y	Y	Y	Y	Y	Y	Y
18 Condit	Y	Y	Y	Y	Y	Y	Y	N
19 ***Radanovich***	Y	Y	Y	Y	Y	Y	Y	N
20 Dooley	Y	Y	Y	Y	Y	Y	Y	Y
21 ***Thomas***	Y	Y	Y	Y	Y	Y	Y	?
22 Capps	Y	Y	Y	Y	Y	Y	Y	Y
23 ***Gallegly***	Y	Y	Y	Y	Y	Y	Y	N
24 Sherman	Y	Y	Y	Y	Y	Y	Y	Y
25 ***McKeon***	Y	Y	Y	Y	Y	Y	Y	N
26 Berman	Y	Y	Y	Y	Y	P	Y	Y
27 ***Rogan***	Y	Y	Y	Y	Y	Y	Y	Y
28 ***Dreier***	Y	Y	Y	Y	Y	Y	Y	N
29 Waxman	?	?	?	?	Y	P	Y	N
30 Becerra	Y	Y	Y	Y	Y	P	Y	Y
31 Martinez	?	?	?	?	Y	Y	Y	N
32 Dixon	Y	Y	Y	Y	Y	Y	Y	N
33 Roybal-Allard	Y	Y	Y	Y	Y	Y	Y	N
34 Napolitano	Y	Y	Y	Y	Y	Y	Y	N
35 Waters	Y	Y	Y	Y	Y	N	Y	N
36 ***Kuykendall***	Y	Y	Y	Y	Y	Y	Y	N
37 Millender-McD.	Y	Y	Y	Y	Y	P	Y	N
38 ***Horn***	Y	Y	?	Y	Y	Y	Y	N
39 ***Royce***	N	N	N	Y	Y	Y	Y	N
40 ***Lewis***	Y	Y	Y	Y	Y	Y	Y	N
41 ***Miller, Gary***	Y	N	N	Y	Y	Y	Y	N
42 Baca	Y	Y	Y	Y	Y	Y	Y	Y
43 ***Calvert***	Y	Y	Y	Y	Y	Y	Y	N
44 ***Bono***	Y	Y	Y	Y	Y	Y	Y	N
45 ***Rohrabacher***	Y	N	N	Y	N	Y	Y	N
46 Sanchez	Y	Y	Y	Y	Y	P	?	N
47 ***Cox***	Y	Y	Y	Y	Y	Y	Y	N
48 ***Packard***	Y	Y	Y	Y	Y	Y	Y	N
49 ***Bilbray***	Y	Y	Y	Y	Y	Y	Y	N
50 Filner	Y	Y	Y	Y	Y	Y	Y	N
51 ***Cunningham***	Y	Y	Y	Y	Y	Y	Y	N
52 ***Hunter***	Y	Y	Y	Y	Y	Y	Y	N
COLORADO								
1 DeGette	Y	Y	Y	Y	Y	P	Y	N
2 Udall	Y	Y	Y	Y	Y	P	Y	Y
3 ***McInnis***	Y	Y	Y	Y	Y	Y	Y	Y
4 ***Schaffer***	Y	N	N	Y	Y	Y	Y	N
5 ***Hefley***	P	Y	Y	P	Y	Y	N	N
6 ***Tancredo***	Y	N	Y	Y	Y	Y	Y	Y
CONNECTICUT								
1 Larson	Y	Y	Y	Y	Y	P	Y	N
2 Gejdenson	Y	Y	Y	Y	Y	N	Y	Y
3 DeLauro	Y	Y	Y	Y	Y	Y	Y	N
4 ***Shays***	Y	Y	Y	Y	Y	Y	Y	Y
5 Maloney	Y	Y	Y	Y	Y	Y	Y	N
6 ***Johnson***	Y	Y	Y	Y	Y	Y	Y	N
DELAWARE								
AL ***Castle***	Y	Y	Y	Y	Y	Y	Y	N
FLORIDA								
1 ***Scarborough***	Y	Y	Y	Y	Y	Y	Y	Y
2 Boyd	Y	Y	Y	Y	Y	P	Y	N
3 Brown	Y	Y	Y	Y	Y	Y	Y	Y
4 ***Fowler***	Y	Y	Y	Y	Y	Y	Y	N
5 Thurman	Y	Y	Y	Y	Y	P	Y	Y
6 ***Stearns***	Y	N	N	Y	Y	Y	Y	N
7 ***Mica***	Y	Y	Y	Y	Y	Y	Y	N
8 ***McCollum***	?	?	?	?	Y	Y	Y	N
9 ***Bilirakis***	Y	Y	Y	Y	Y	Y	Y	N
10 ***Young***	Y	Y	Y	Y	Y	Y	Y	N
11 Davis	Y	Y	Y	Y	Y	Y	Y	Y
12 ***Canady***	Y	Y	Y	Y	Y	Y	Y	Y
13 ***Miller***	Y	Y	Y	Y	Y	Y	Y	N
14 ***Goss***	Y	Y	Y	Y	Y	Y	Y	N
15 ***Weldon***	Y	Y	Y	Y	Y	Y	Y	N
16 ***Foley***	Y	Y	Y	Y	Y	Y	Y	Y
17 Meek	Y	Y	Y	Y	Y	Y	Y	Y
18 ***Ros-Lehtinen***	Y	Y	Y	Y	Y	Y	Y	Y
19 Wexler	Y	Y	Y	Y	Y	Y	Y	Y
20 Deutsch	Y	Y	Y	Y	Y	Y	Y	Y
21 ***Diaz-Balart***	Y	Y	Y	Y	Y	Y	Y	Y
22 ***Shaw***	Y	Y	Y	Y	Y	Y	Y	N
23 Hastings	Y	Y	Y	Y	Y	N	Y	Y
GEORGIA								
1 ***Kingston***	Y	Y	Y	Y	Y	Y	Y	N
2 Bishop	Y	Y	Y	Y	Y	Y	Y	N
3 ***Collins***	Y	Y	Y	Y	Y	Y	Y	N
4 McKinney	Y	Y	Y	Y	Y	N	Y	Y
5 Lewis	Y	Y	Y	Y	Y	P	Y	Y
6 ***Isakson***	Y	Y	Y	Y	Y	Y	Y	Y
7 ***Barr***	Y	Y	Y	Y	Y	Y	Y	Y
8 ***Chambliss***	Y	Y	Y	Y	Y	Y	Y	Y
9 ***Deal***	Y	Y	Y	Y	Y	Y	Y	Y
10 ***Norwood***	Y	Y	Y	Y	Y	Y	Y	Y
11 ***Linder***	Y	Y	Y	Y	?	?	Y	Y
HAWAII								
1 Abercrombie	Y	Y	Y	Y	Y	P	Y	N
2 Mink	Y	Y	Y	Y	Y	P	Y	N
IDAHO								
1 ***Chenoweth-Hage***	Y	N	N	Y	Y	N	Y	N
2 ***Simpson***	Y	Y	Y	Y	Y	Y	Y	N
ILLINOIS								
1 Rush	Y	Y	Y	Y	Y	Y	Y	N
2 Jackson	Y	Y	Y	Y	Y	N	Y	N
3 Lipinski	?	?	?	?	Y	Y	Y	N
4 Gutierrez	?	?	?	?	Y	Y	Y	N
5 Blagojevich	?	?	?	?	Y	Y	Y	Y
6 ***Hyde***	Y	Y	Y	Y	Y	Y	Y	Y
7 Davis	Y	Y	Y	Y	Y	N	Y	Y
8 ***Crane***	Y	Y	Y	Y	Y	Y	Y	Y
9 Schakowsky	Y	Y	Y	Y	Y	P	Y	Y
10 ***Porter***	Y	Y	Y	Y	Y	Y	Y	Y
11 ***Weller***	Y	Y	Y	Y	Y	Y	Y	Y
12 Costello	Y	Y	Y	Y	Y	Y	Y	Y
13 ***Biggert***	Y	Y	Y	Y	Y	Y	Y	Y

ND Northern Democrats SD Southern Democrats

	327	328	329	330	331	332	333	334
14 Hastert								
15 Ewing	Y	Y	Y	Y	Y	Y	Y	Y
16 Manzullo	Y	Y	Y	?	Y	Y	Y	Y
17 Evans	Y	Y	Y	Y	Y	Y	Y	Y
18 LaHood	Y	Y	Y	Y	Y	Y	Y	Y
19 Phelps	Y	Y	Y	Y	Y	Y	Y	Y
20 Shimkus	Y	Y	Y	Y	Y	Y	Y	Y
INDIANA								
1 Visclosky	Y	Y	Y	Y	Y	Y	Y	N
2 McIntosh	?	?	?	?	?	?	?	?
3 Roemer	Y	Y	Y	Y	Y	Y	Y	N
4 Souder	Y	Y	Y	Y	Y	Y	Y	Y
5 Buyer	Y	Y	Y	Y	Y	Y	Y	Y
6 Burton	Y	Y	Y	Y	Y	Y	Y	Y
7 Pease	Y	Y	Y	Y	Y	Y	Y	N
8 Hostettler	Y	N	N	Y	Y	Y	Y	Y
9 Hill	P	Y	Y	Y	Y	Y	Y	N
10 Carson	Y	Y	Y	Y	Y	P	Y	Y
IOWA								
1 Leach	Y	Y	Y	Y	Y	Y	Y	Y
2 Nussle	Y	Y	Y	Y	Y	Y	Y	Y
3 Boswell	Y	Y	Y	Y	Y	Y	Y	Y
4 Ganske	Y	Y	Y	Y	Y	Y	Y	Y
5 Latham	Y	Y	Y	Y	Y	Y	Y	Y
KANSAS								
1 Moran	Y	Y	Y	Y	Y	Y	Y	Y
2 Ryun	+	Y	Y	Y	Y	Y	Y	N
3 Moore	Y	Y	Y	Y	Y	Y	Y	N
4 Tiahrt	Y	Y	Y	Y	+	+	+	Y
KENTUCKY								
1 Whitfield	Y	Y	Y	Y	Y	Y	Y	Y
2 Lewis	Y	Y	Y	Y	Y	Y	Y	N
3 Northup	Y	Y	Y	Y	Y	Y	Y	Y
4 Lucas	Y	Y	Y	Y	Y	Y	Y	N
5 Rogers	Y	Y	Y	Y	Y	Y	Y	N
6 Fletcher	Y	Y	Y	Y	Y	Y	Y	N
LOUISIANA								
1 Vitter	Y	Y	Y	Y	Y	Y	Y	Y
2 Jefferson	Y	Y	Y	?	Y	Y	Y	N
3 Tauzin	Y	Y	Y	Y	Y	Y	Y	Y
4 McCrery	Y	Y	Y	Y	Y	Y	Y	Y
5 Cooksey	Y	Y	Y	Y	Y	Y	Y	Y
6 Baker	Y	Y	Y	Y	Y	Y	Y	N
7 John	Y	Y	Y	Y	Y	Y	Y	N
MAINE								
1 Allen	Y	Y	Y	Y	Y	Y	Y	N
2 Baldacci	Y	Y	Y	Y	Y	Y	Y	N
MARYLAND								
1 Gilchrest	Y	Y	Y	Y	Y	Y	Y	Y
2 Ehrlich	Y	Y	Y	Y	Y	Y	Y	Y
3 Cardin	Y	Y	Y	Y	Y	Y	Y	N
4 Wynn	Y	Y	Y	Y	Y	Y	Y	Y
5 Hoyer	Y	Y	Y	Y	Y	P	Y	Y
6 Bartlett	Y	Y	Y	Y	Y	Y	Y	Y
7 Cummings	Y	Y	Y	Y	Y	Y	Y	N
8 Morella	Y	Y	Y	Y	Y	Y	Y	N
MASSACHUSETTS								
1 Olver	Y	Y	Y	Y	Y	P	Y	N
2 Neal	Y	Y	Y	Y	Y	P	Y	N
3 McGovern	Y	Y	Y	Y	Y	P	Y	N
4 Frank	Y	Y	Y	Y	Y	P	Y	N
5 Meehan	Y	Y	Y	Y	Y	P	Y	N
6 Tierney	Y	Y	Y	Y	Y	P	Y	N
7 Markey	?	?	?	?	?	?	?	?
8 Capuano	Y	Y	Y	Y	Y	P	Y	N
9 Moakley	Y	Y	Y	Y	Y	Y	Y	N
10 Delahunt	Y	Y	Y	Y	Y	P	Y	N
MICHIGAN								
1 Stupak	Y	Y	Y	Y	Y	P	Y	N
2 Hoekstra	Y	Y	Y	Y	Y	Y	Y	Y
3 Ehlers	Y	Y	Y	Y	Y	Y	Y	Y
4 Camp	Y	Y	Y	Y	Y	Y	?	Y
5 Barcia	Y	Y	Y	Y	Y	Y	Y	N
6 Upton	Y	Y	Y	Y	Y	Y	Y	N
7 Smith	Y	Y	Y	Y	N	Y	Y	Y
8 Stabenow	Y	Y	Y	Y	Y	Y	Y	N
9 Kildee	Y	Y	Y	Y	Y	Y	Y	Y
10 Bonior	Y	Y	Y	Y	Y	Y	Y	N
11 Knollenberg	Y	Y	Y	Y	Y	Y	Y	N
12 Levin	Y	Y	Y	Y	Y	P	Y	N
13 Rivers	Y	Y	Y	Y	Y	P	Y	N
14 Conyers	Y	Y	?	Y	Y	N	Y	N
15 Kilpatrick	?	?	Y	Y	Y	Y	?	N
16 Dingell	Y	Y	Y	Y	Y	P	Y	N

	327	328	329	330	331	332	333	334
MINNESOTA								
1 Gutknecht	Y	Y	Y	Y	Y	Y	Y	Y
2 Minge	Y	Y	Y	Y	Y	P	Y	Y
3 Ramstad	Y	Y	Y	Y	Y	Y	Y	Y
4 Vento	?	?	?	?	?	?	?	?
5 Sabo	?	?	?	?	Y	P	Y	Y
6 Luther	Y	Y	Y	Y	Y	Y	Y	Y
7 Peterson	Y	Y	Y	Y	Y	Y	Y	N
8 Oberstar	Y	Y	Y	Y	Y	N	Y	N
MISSISSIPPI								
1 Wicker	Y	Y	Y	Y	Y	Y	Y	N
2 Thompson	Y	Y	Y	Y	Y	Y	Y	Y
3 Pickering	Y	Y	Y	Y	Y	Y	Y	Y
4 Shows	?	?	?	?	Y	Y	Y	Y
5 Taylor	Y	Y	Y	N	Y	Y	Y	N
MISSOURI								
1 Clay	Y	Y	Y	Y	Y	N	Y	Y
2 Talent	?	?	?	?	Y	Y	Y	Y
3 Gephardt	Y	Y	Y	Y	Y	Y	Y	Y
4 Skelton	Y	Y	Y	Y	Y	Y	Y	Y
5 McCarthy	Y	Y	Y	Y	Y	P	Y	Y
6 Danner	Y	Y	Y	Y	Y	Y	Y	Y
7 Blunt	Y	Y	Y	Y	Y	Y	Y	N
8 Emerson	Y	Y	Y	Y	Y	Y	Y	Y
9 Hulshof	Y	Y	Y	Y	Y	Y	Y	Y
MONTANA								
AL Hill	Y	Y	Y	Y	Y	Y	Y	Y
NEBRASKA								
1 Bereuter	Y	Y	Y	Y	Y	Y	Y	N
2 Terry	Y	Y	Y	Y	Y	Y	Y	N
3 Barrett	Y	Y	Y	Y	Y	Y	Y	N
NEVADA								
1 Berkley	Y	Y	Y	Y	Y	Y	Y	N
2 Gibbons	Y	Y	Y	Y	Y	Y	Y	Y
NEW HAMPSHIRE								
1 Sununu	Y	Y	Y	Y	Y	Y	Y	Y
2 Bass	Y	Y	Y	Y	Y	Y	Y	N
NEW JERSEY								
1 Andrews	Y	Y	Y	Y	Y	Y	Y	Y
2 LoBiondo	Y	Y	Y	Y	Y	Y	Y	N
3 Saxton	Y	Y	Y	Y	Y	Y	Y	N
4 Smith	Y	Y	Y	Y	Y	Y	Y	N
5 Roukema	?	?	?	?	Y	Y	Y	N
6 Pallone	Y	Y	Y	Y	Y	Y	Y	N
7 Franks	Y	Y	Y	Y	Y	Y	Y	N
8 Pascrell	Y	Y	Y	Y	Y	Y	Y	N
9 Rothman	Y	Y	Y	Y	Y	Y	Y	N
10 Payne	Y	Y	Y	Y	Y	N	Y	N
11 Frelinghuysen	Y	Y	Y	Y	Y	Y	Y	N
12 Holt	Y	Y	Y	Y	Y	Y	Y	Y
13 Menendez	Y	Y	Y	Y	Y	Y	Y	N
NEW MEXICO								
1 Wilson	Y	Y	Y	Y	Y	Y	Y	N
2 Skeen	Y	Y	Y	Y	Y	Y	Y	N
3 Udall	Y	Y	Y	Y	Y	Y	Y	N
NEW YORK								
1 Forbes	Y	Y	Y	Y	Y	Y	Y	N
2 Lazio	?	?	?	?	?	?	?	?
3 King	Y	Y	Y	Y	Y	Y	Y	N
4 McCarthy	Y	Y	Y	Y	Y	Y	Y	N
5 Ackerman	Y	Y	Y	Y	Y	N	N	N
6 Meeks	Y	Y	Y	Y	Y	P	Y	N
7 Crowley	Y	Y	Y	Y	Y	Y	Y	N
8 Nadler	Y	Y	Y	Y	Y	N	Y	Y
9 Weiner	Y	Y	Y	Y	Y	Y	Y	N
10 Towns	Y	Y	Y	Y	Y	Y	Y	N
11 Owens	Y	Y	Y	Y	Y	P	Y	N
12 Velázquez	Y	Y	Y	Y	Y	N	Y	N
13 Fossella	Y	Y	Y	Y	Y	Y	Y	N
14 Maloney	Y	Y	Y	Y	Y	Y	Y	N
15 Rangel	?	?	?	?	Y	P	Y	Y
16 Serrano	Y	Y	Y	Y	Y	Y	Y	Y
17 Engel	Y	Y	Y	Y	Y	P	Y	N
18 Lowey	Y	Y	Y	Y	Y	P	Y	N
19 Kelly	Y	Y	Y	Y	Y	Y	Y	N
20 Gilman	Y	Y	Y	Y	Y	Y	Y	N
21 McNulty	Y	Y	Y	Y	Y	Y	Y	Y
22 Sweeney	Y	Y	Y	Y	Y	Y	Y	Y
23 Boehlert	Y	Y	Y	Y	Y	Y	Y	N
24 McHugh	Y	Y	Y	Y	Y	Y	Y	Y
25 Walsh	Y	Y	Y	Y	Y	Y	Y	N
26 Hinchey	?	?	?	?	Y	P	Y	Y
27 Reynolds	Y	Y	Y	Y	Y	Y	Y	N
28 Slaughter	Y	Y	Y	Y	Y	P	Y	N
29 LaFalce	Y	Y	Y	Y	Y	Y	Y	N

	327	328	329	330	331	332	333	334
30 Quinn	Y	Y	Y	Y	Y	Y	Y	N
31 Houghton	Y	Y	Y	Y	Y	Y	Y	N
NORTH CAROLINA								
1 Clayton	Y	Y	Y	Y	Y	P	Y	N
2 Etheridge	Y	Y	Y	Y	Y	Y	Y	Y
3 Jones	Y	Y	Y	Y	Y	Y	Y	Y
4 Price	Y	Y	Y	Y	Y	Y	Y	Y
5 Burr	Y	Y	Y	Y	Y	Y	Y	Y
6 Coble	Y	N	Y	Y	Y	Y	Y	N
7 McIntyre	Y	Y	Y	Y	Y	Y	Y	N
8 Hayes	Y	Y	Y	Y	Y	Y	Y	N
9 Myrick	Y	Y	Y	Y	Y	Y	Y	Y
10 Ballenger	Y	Y	Y	Y	Y	Y	Y	N
11 Taylor	?	Y	Y	Y	Y	Y	Y	N
12 Watt	Y	Y	Y	Y	Y	P	Y	N
NORTH DAKOTA								
AL Pomeroy	?	?	?	?	Y	Y	Y	N
OHIO								
1 Chabot	Y	Y	Y	Y	Y	Y	Y	N
2 Portman	Y	Y	Y	Y	Y	Y	Y	Y
3 Hall	Y	Y	Y	Y	Y	Y	Y	Y
4 Oxley	Y	Y	Y	Y	Y	Y	Y	Y
5 Gillmor	Y	Y	Y	Y	Y	Y	Y	N
6 Strickland	Y	Y	Y	Y	Y	Y	Y	N
7 Hobson	Y	Y	Y	Y	Y	Y	Y	N
8 Boehner	Y	Y	Y	Y	Y	Y	Y	Y
9 Kaptur	Y	Y	Y	Y	Y	Y	Y	N
10 Kucinich	Y	Y	Y	Y	Y	Y	Y	N
11 Jones	Y	Y	Y	Y	Y	N	Y	N
12 Kasich	Y	Y	Y	Y	Y	Y	Y	N
13 Brown	Y	Y	Y	Y	Y	Y	Y	N
14 Sawyer	Y	Y	Y	Y	Y	Y	Y	N
15 Pryce	Y	Y	Y	Y	Y	Y	Y	N
16 Regula	Y	Y	Y	Y	Y	Y	Y	N
17 Traficant	Y	Y	Y	Y	Y	Y	Y	N
18 Ney	Y	Y	Y	Y	Y	Y	Y	Y
19 LaTourette	Y	Y	Y	Y	Y	Y	Y	N
OKLAHOMA								
1 Largent	Y	Y	Y	Y	Y	Y	Y	Y
2 Coburn	Y	N	Y	Y	Y	Y	Y	Y
3 Watkins	Y	Y	Y	Y	Y	Y	Y	N
4 Watts	Y	N	Y	Y	Y	Y	Y	N
5 Istook	Y	Y	Y	Y	Y	Y	Y	N
6 Lucas	Y	Y	Y	Y	Y	Y	Y	N
OREGON								
1 Wu	Y	Y	Y	Y	Y	Y	Y	N
2 Walden	Y	Y	Y	Y	Y	Y	Y	N
3 Blumenauer	Y	Y	Y	Y	Y	P	Y	N
4 DeFazio	Y	Y	Y	Y	Y	P	Y	Y
5 Hooley	Y	Y	Y	Y	Y	P	Y	N
PENNSYLVANIA								
1 Brady	Y	Y	Y	Y	Y	Y	Y	N
2 Fattah	Y	Y	Y	Y	Y	Y	Y	N
3 Borski	Y	Y	Y	Y	Y	Y	Y	N
4 Klink	?	?	?	?	Y	Y	Y	N
5 Peterson	Y	Y	Y	Y	Y	Y	Y	Y
6 Holden	Y	Y	Y	Y	Y	Y	Y	N
7 Weldon	Y	Y	Y	Y	Y	Y	Y	N
8 Greenwood	Y	Y	Y	Y	Y	Y	Y	N
9 Shuster	?	?	?	?	Y	Y	Y	Y
10 Sherwood	Y	Y	Y	Y	Y	Y	Y	N
11 Kanjorski	Y	Y	Y	Y	Y	N	Y	N
12 Murtha	Y	Y	Y	Y	Y	Y	Y	N
13 Hoeffel	Y	Y	Y	Y	Y	Y	Y	N
14 Coyne	Y	Y	Y	Y	Y	P	Y	N
15 Toomey	Y	N	Y	Y	Y	Y	Y	N
16 Pitts	Y	Y	Y	Y	Y	Y	Y	Y
17 Gekas	Y	Y	Y	Y	Y	Y	Y	N
18 Doyle	Y	Y	Y	Y	Y	Y	Y	N
19 Goodling	Y	Y	Y	Y	Y	Y	Y	N
20 Mascara	Y	Y	Y	Y	Y	Y	Y	N
21 English	Y	Y	Y	Y	Y	Y	Y	Y
RHODE ISLAND								
1 Kennedy	Y	Y	Y	Y	Y	P	Y	Y
2 Weygand	Y	Y	Y	Y	Y	Y	Y	N
SOUTH CAROLINA								
1 Sanford	N	N	N	Y	N	Y	N	Y
2 Spence	Y	Y	Y	Y	Y	Y	Y	Y
3 Graham	Y	Y	Y	Y	Y	Y	Y	Y
4 DeMint	Y	N	Y	Y	Y	Y	Y	N
5 Spratt	Y	Y	Y	Y	Y	Y	Y	N
6 Clyburn	Y	Y	Y	Y	Y	Y	Y	Y
SOUTH DAKOTA								
AL Thune	Y	Y	Y	Y	Y	Y	Y	Y

	327	328	329	330	331	332	333	334
TENNESSEE								
1 Jenkins	Y	Y	Y	Y	Y	Y	Y	Y
2 Duncan	Y	Y	Y	Y	Y	Y	Y	N
3 Wamp	Y	Y	Y	Y	Y	Y	Y	N
4 Hilleary	Y	Y	Y	Y	Y	Y	Y	N
5 Clement	Y	Y	Y	Y	Y	Y	Y	N
6 Gordon	Y	Y	Y	Y	Y	Y	Y	N
7 Bryant	Y	Y	Y	Y	Y	Y	Y	Y
8 Tanner	Y	Y	Y	Y	Y	Y	Y	N
9 Ford	Y	Y	Y	Y	Y	Y	Y	N
TEXAS								
1 Sandlin	Y	Y	Y	Y	Y	Y	Y	Y
2 Turner	Y	Y	Y	Y	Y	Y	Y	N
3 Johnson, Sam	Y	Y	Y	Y	Y	Y	Y	Y
4 Hall	Y	Y	Y	Y	Y	Y	Y	N
5 Sessions	Y	Y	Y	Y	Y	Y	Y	N
6 Barton	?	?	?	?	Y	Y	Y	Y
7 Archer	Y	Y	Y	Y	Y	Y	Y	Y
8 Brady	Y	Y	Y	Y	Y	Y	Y	Y
9 Lampson	Y	Y	Y	Y	Y	Y	Y	N
10 Doggett	Y	Y	Y	Y	Y	P	Y	Y
11 Edwards	Y	Y	Y	Y	Y	N	Y	N
12 Granger	Y	Y	Y	Y	Y	Y	Y	N
13 Thornberry	Y	Y	Y	Y	Y	Y	Y	N
14 Paul	Y	N	N	Y	N	Y	Y	Y
15 Hinojosa	Y	Y	Y	Y	Y	Y	Y	?
16 Reyes	Y	Y	Y	Y	Y	Y	Y	N
17 Stenholm	Y	Y	Y	Y	Y	Y	Y	N
18 Jackson-Lee	Y	Y	Y	Y	Y	N	Y	N
19 Combest	?	?	?	?	Y	Y	Y	N
20 Gonzalez	Y	Y	Y	Y	Y	N	Y	N
21 Smith	Y	Y	Y	Y	Y	Y	Y	Y
22 DeLay	Y	Y	Y	Y	Y	Y	Y	N
23 Bonilla	Y	Y	Y	Y	Y	Y	Y	N
24 Frost	Y	Y	Y	Y	Y	Y	Y	N
25 Bentsen	Y	Y	Y	Y	Y	Y	Y	N
26 Armey	Y	Y	Y	Y	Y	Y	Y	N
27 Ortiz	Y	Y	Y	Y	Y	Y	Y	N
28 Rodriguez	Y	Y	Y	Y	Y	Y	Y	N
29 Green	Y	Y	Y	Y	Y	Y	Y	N
30 Johnson, E.B.	Y	Y	Y	Y	Y	N	Y	N
UTAH								
1 Hansen	?	?	?	?	Y	Y	Y	Y
2 Cook	?	?	?	?	?	?	?	?
3 Cannon	Y	N	N	Y	Y	Y	Y	Y
VERMONT								
AL Sanders	Y	Y	Y	Y	Y	P	Y	Y
VIRGINIA								
1 Bateman	?	?	?	?	Y	Y	Y	N
2 Pickett	Y	Y	Y	Y	Y	N	Y	N
3 Scott	Y	Y	Y	Y	Y	N	Y	N
4 Sisisky	Y	Y	Y	Y	Y	P	Y	N
5 Goode	Y	Y	Y	Y	Y	Y	Y	N
6 Goodlatte	Y	Y	Y	Y	Y	Y	Y	N
7 Bliley	Y	Y	Y	Y	Y	Y	Y	Y
8 Moran	Y	Y	Y	Y	Y	P	Y	N
9 Boucher	Y	Y	Y	Y	Y	P	Y	N
10 Wolf	Y	Y	Y	Y	Y	Y	Y	N
11 Davis	Y	Y	Y	Y	Y	Y	Y	N
WASHINGTON								
1 Inslee	Y	Y	Y	Y	Y	P	Y	N
2 Metcalf	Y	Y	Y	Y	Y	Y	P	N
3 Baird	Y	Y	Y	Y	Y	P	Y	N
4 Hastings	Y	Y	Y	Y	Y	Y	Y	N
5 Nethercutt	Y	Y	Y	Y	Y	Y	Y	N
6 Dicks	Y	Y	Y	Y	Y	P	Y	N
7 McDermott	Y	Y	Y	Y	Y	N	Y	Y
8 Dunn	Y	Y	Y	Y	Y	Y	Y	N
9 Smith	Y	Y	Y	Y	Y	P	Y	N
WEST VIRGINIA								
1 Mollohan	Y	Y	Y	Y	Y	Y	Y	N
2 Wise	Y	Y	Y	Y	Y	Y	Y	N
3 Rahall	Y	Y	Y	Y	Y	Y	Y	N
WISCONSIN								
1 Ryan	Y	Y	Y	Y	Y	Y	Y	Y
2 Baldwin	Y	Y	Y	Y	Y	P	Y	Y
3 Kind	Y	Y	Y	Y	Y	P	Y	Y
4 Kleczka	Y	Y	Y	Y	Y	P	Y	Y
5 Barrett	Y	Y	Y	Y	Y	P	Y	Y
6 Petri	Y	Y	Y	Y	Y	Y	Y	Y
7 Obey	Y	Y	Y	Y	Y	P	Y	N
8 Green	Y	Y	Y	Y	Y	Y	Y	Y
9 Sensenbrenner	N	N	N	Y	Y	Y	Y	Y
WYOMING								
AL Cubin	Y	N	Y	Y	Y	Y	Y	Y

Southern states - Ala., Ark., Fla., Ga., Ky., La., Miss., N.C., Okla., S.C., Tenn., Texas, Va.

335. HR 4733. Fiscal 2001 Energy, Water Appropriations/Chesapeake and Delaware Canal. Gilchrest, R-Md., amendment that would reduce by $100,000 the Army Corps of Engineers funding for a project to deepen the Chesapeake and Delaware canal. Rejected 153-273: R 134-82; D 18-190 (ND 16-139, SD 2-51); I 1-1. June 27, 2000.

336. HR 4733. Fiscal 2001 Energy, Water Appropriations/Chesapeake Bay. Gilchrest, R-Md., amendment that would reduce by $6.8 million the Army Corps of Engineers funding for a project to straighten a channel in the upper Chesapeake Bay. Rejected 145-281: R 126-91; D 18-189 (ND 16-138, SD 2-51); I 1-1. June 27, 2000.

337. HR 4733. Fiscal 2001 Energy, Water Appropriations/Nuclear Energy Research. Foley, R-Fla., amendment that would eliminate funding for the Energy Department's nuclear energy research initiative. Rejected 71-356: R 29-190; D 41-165 (ND 35-117, SD 6-48); I 1-1. June 27, 2000.

338. HR 4733. Fiscal 2001 Energy, Water Appropriations/Delaware River Channel. Andrews, D-N.J., amendment that would prohibit using funds to dredge the Delaware River main channel before June 1, 2001. Rejected 176-249: R 97-121; D 77-128 (ND 63-89, SD 14-39); I 2-0. June 27, 2000.

339. HR 4733. Fiscal 2001 Energy, Water Appropriations/Strategic Petroleum Reserve. Sherwood, R-Pa., amendment that would reauthorize the Strategic Petroleum Reserve for three years and authorize the Energy Department to buy oil from small or marginal wells when oil prices fall below $15 a barrel. It would also establish a regional home heating oil reserve in the Northeast. Adopted 393-33: R 186-32; D 205-1 (ND 151-1, SD 54-0); I 2-0. June 27, 2000.

340. HR 4733. Fiscal 2001 Energy, Water Appropriations/Dual-Hatting. Ryun, R-Kan., amendment that would withhold pay from any employee who simultaneously holds or carries out the responsibilities of a position within the National Nuclear Security Administration and a position within the Department of Energy. Adopted 239-187: R 203-15; D 35-171 (ND 22-130, SD 13-41); I 1-1. June 27, 2000.

341. HR 4762. Campaign Finance Disclosure/Passage. Passage of the bill that would require groups organized under section 527 of the tax code to disclose contribution and expenditure information to the Treasury Department. Passed 385-39: R 178-39; D 205-0 (ND 151-0, SD 54-0); I 2-0. A two-thirds majority of those present and voting (283 in this case) is required for passage under suspension of the rules. June 28, 2000 (after midnight on the day that began June 27).

342. HR 4733. Fiscal 2001 Energy, Water Appropriations/Passage. Passage of the bill that would appropriate $21.7 billion for the Energy Department, the Army Corps of Engineers, water projects and other independent agencies in fiscal 2001, $546 million more than in fiscal year 2000. Passed 407-19: R 206-12; D 199-7 (ND 147-5, SD 52-2); I 2-0. June 28, 2000 (after midnight on the day that began June 27).

Key

Y Voted for (yea).
\# Paired for.
\+ Announced for.
N Voted against (nay).
X Paired against.
– Announced against.
P Voted "present."
C Voted "present" to avoid possible conflict of interest.
? Did not vote or otherwise make a position known.

•

Democrats ***Republicans***
Independents

	335	336	337	338	339	340	341	342
ALABAMA								
1 ***Callahan***	N	N	N	N	Y	Y	Y	Y
2 ***Everett***	N	N	N	Y	Y	Y	Y	Y
3 ***Riley***	Y	N	N	N	Y	Y	Y	Y
4 ***Aderholt***	N	N	N	Y	Y	Y	Y	Y
5 Cramer	N	N	N	N	Y	N	Y	Y
6 ***Bachus***	N	N	N	N	Y	Y	Y	Y
7 Hilliard	N	N	N	N	Y	N	Y	Y
ALASKA								
AL ***Young***	N	N	N	N	Y	Y	?	?
ARIZONA								
1 ***Salmon***	Y	Y	N	Y	N	Y	Y	Y
2 Pastor	N	N	N	N	Y	N	Y	Y
3 ***Stump***	Y	N	N	N	Y	Y	N	Y
4 ***Shadegg***	Y	Y	N	Y	Y	Y	Y	Y
5 ***Kolbe***	Y	Y	N	Y	Y	N	Y	Y
6 ***Hayworth***	N	N	N	N	Y	Y	N	Y
ARKANSAS								
1 Berry	N	N	N	N	Y	Y	Y	Y
2 Snyder	N	N	N	N	Y	N	Y	Y
3 ***Hutchinson***	N	N	N	N	Y	Y	Y	Y
4 ***Dickey***	N	N	N	N	Y	Y	N	Y
CALIFORNIA								
1 Thompson	N	N	Y	Y	Y	N	Y	Y
2 ***Herger***	N	N	N	N	Y	Y	N	Y
3 ***Ose***	N	Y	N	N	Y	N	Y	Y
4 ***Doolittle***	N	N	N	N	N	Y	N	Y
5 Matsui	N	N	N	N	Y	N	Y	Y
6 Woolsey	N	N	Y	Y	Y	N	Y	Y
7 Miller, George	N	N	Y	N	Y	N	Y	Y
8 Pelosi	N	N	Y	N	Y	N	Y	Y
9 Lee	N	N	Y	Y	Y	N	Y	Y
10 Tauscher	N	N	N	Y	Y	Y	Y	Y
11 ***Pombo***	Y	N	Y	N	N	Y	N	Y
12 Lantos	N	N	?	N	Y	?	Y	Y
13 Stark	N	N	?	?	?	?	Y	Y
14 Eshoo	N	N	Y	Y	Y	N	Y	Y
15 ***Campbell***	Y	Y	N	N	Y	Y	Y	Y
16 Lofgren	N	N	N	Y	Y	Y	Y	Y
17 Farr	Y	Y	N	N	Y	N	Y	Y
18 Condit	N	N	N	Y	Y	N	Y	Y
19 ***Radanovich***	N	N	N	Y	Y	Y	N	Y
20 Dooley	N	N	N	Y	Y	N	Y	Y
21 ***Thomas***	?	N	N	N	Y	Y	N	Y
22 Capps	N	N	Y	Y	Y	N	Y	Y
23 ***Gallegly***	N	N	N	Y	Y	Y	Y	Y
24 Sherman	N	N	N	Y	Y	N	Y	Y
25 ***McKeon***	Y	Y	N	N	Y	Y	Y	Y
26 Berman	N	N	N	Y	Y	N	Y	Y
27 ***Rogan***	N	N	N	N	Y	Y	Y	Y
28 ***Dreier***	N	N	N	N	Y	Y	Y	Y
29 Waxman	N	N	N	Y	Y	N	Y	Y
30 Becerra	N	N	N	Y	Y	N	Y	Y
31 Martinez	Y	Y	?	?	?	?	?	?
32 Dixon	N	N	N	N	Y	N	Y	Y
33 Roybal-Allard	N	N	N	N	Y	N	Y	Y
34 Napolitano	N	N	N	Y	Y	N	Y	Y
35 Waters	N	N	Y	N	Y	N	+	Y
36 ***Kuykendall***	Y	Y	N	N	Y	Y	Y	Y
37 Millender-McD.	N	N	N	N	Y	N	Y	Y
38 ***Horn***	Y	Y	Y	Y	Y	Y	Y	Y
39 ***Royce***	Y	Y	Y	Y	N	Y	Y	N
40 ***Lewis***	Y	N	N	N	Y	Y	N	Y
41 ***Miller, Gary***	Y	Y	N	N	N	Y	Y	Y
42 Baca	N	N	N	N	Y	Y	Y	Y
43 ***Calvert***	Y	N	N	N	Y	Y	Y	Y
44 ***Bono***	Y	N	N	Y	Y	Y	Y	Y
45 ***Rohrabacher***	Y	Y	Y	N	N	Y	Y	Y
46 Sanchez	N	N	Y	Y	Y	N	Y	Y
47 ***Cox***	Y	Y	Y	Y	N	Y	Y	Y
48 ***Packard***	N	N	N	N	Y	N	Y	Y
49 ***Bilbray***	Y	Y	N	Y	Y	Y	Y	Y
50 Filner	N	N	N	N	Y	N	Y	Y
51 ***Cunningham***	Y	Y	N	Y	N	Y	Y	Y
52 ***Hunter***	Y	Y	N	N	Y	Y	Y	Y
COLORADO								
1 DeGette	N	Y	N	Y	Y	N	Y	Y
2 Udall	Y	Y	Y	Y	Y	N	Y	Y
3 ***McInnis***	Y	Y	N	Y	Y	Y	Y	Y
4 ***Schaffer***	N	N	Y	Y	N	Y	?	N
5 ***Hefley***	Y	Y	N	Y	N	Y	N	Y
6 ***Tancredo***	Y	Y	Y	Y	N	Y	N	N
CONNECTICUT								
1 Larson	N	N	N	N	Y	N	Y	Y
2 Gejdenson	N	N	N	N	Y	N	Y	Y
3 DeLauro	N	N	N	N	Y	N	Y	Y
4 ***Shays***	Y	Y	Y	Y	Y	Y	Y	N
5 Maloney	N	N	N	Y	Y	Y	Y	Y
6 ***Johnson***	Y	Y	N	Y	Y	Y	Y	Y
DELAWARE								
AL ***Castle***	Y	Y	N	Y	Y	Y	Y	N
FLORIDA								
1 ***Scarborough***	Y	Y	Y	Y	Y	Y	Y	Y
2 Boyd	N	N	N	N	Y	N	Y	Y
3 Brown	N	N	N	N	Y	N	Y	Y
4 ***Fowler***	N	N	N	N	Y	Y	Y	Y
5 Thurman	N	N	N	N	Y	N	Y	Y
6 ***Stearns***	N	N	N	Y	Y	Y	Y	N
7 ***Mica***	Y	Y	N	N	Y	Y	N	Y
8 ***McCollum***	Y	Y	N	N	Y	Y	Y	Y
9 ***Bilirakis***	Y	Y	N	Y	Y	Y	Y	Y
10 ***Young***	N	Y	N	N	Y	N	Y	Y
11 Davis	N	N	N	Y	Y	N	Y	Y
12 ***Canady***	Y	Y	N	N	Y	Y	N	Y
13 ***Miller***	Y	Y	N	Y	Y	Y	Y	Y
14 ***Goss***	Y	Y	Y	Y	N	Y	Y	Y
15 ***Weldon***	Y	N	N	N	Y	N	Y	Y
16 ***Foley***	Y	Y	Y	Y	Y	Y	Y	Y
17 Meek	N	N	N	N	Y	N	Y	Y
18 ***Ros-Lehtinen***	Y	Y	Y	Y	Y	Y	Y	Y
19 Wexler	N	N	Y	Y	Y	N	Y	Y
20 Deutsch	N	N	Y	Y	Y	N	Y	Y
21 ***Diaz-Balart***	Y	Y	N	Y	Y	Y	Y	Y
22 ***Shaw***	Y	Y	N	N	Y	Y	Y	Y
23 Hastings	N	N	N	Y	Y	N	Y	Y
GEORGIA								
1 ***Kingston***	N	Y	Y	Y	Y	Y	N	Y
2 Bishop	N	N	N	N	Y	N	Y	Y
3 ***Collins***	Y	Y	N	Y	Y	Y	Y	Y
4 McKinney	N	N	Y	Y	Y	Y	Y	Y
5 Lewis	Y	Y	Y	Y	Y	N	Y	Y
6 ***Isakson***	Y	Y	N	N	Y	Y	Y	Y
7 ***Barr***	Y	N	N	Y	Y	Y	N	Y
8 ***Chambliss***	Y	Y	N	Y	Y	Y	Y	Y
9 ***Deal***	Y	Y	N	Y	Y	Y	Y	Y
10 ***Norwood***	Y	Y	N	Y	Y	Y	Y	Y
11 ***Linder***	Y	Y	N	Y	Y	Y	N	Y
HAWAII								
1 Abercrombie	Y	Y	Y	N	Y	Y	Y	Y
2 Mink	N	N	N	Y	Y	N	Y	Y
IDAHO								
1 ***Chenoweth-Hage***	N	N	N	N	Y	Y	N	Y
2 ***Simpson***	N	N	N	N	Y	Y	Y	Y
ILLINOIS								
1 Rush	N	N	N	Y	Y	N	Y	Y
2 Jackson	N	N	Y	Y	Y	N	Y	Y
3 Lipinski	N	N	N	N	Y	N	Y	Y
4 Gutierrez	N	N	N	Y	Y	N	Y	Y
5 Blagojevich	N	N	N	Y	Y	Y	Y	Y
6 ***Hyde***	Y	Y	N	N	Y	Y	Y	Y
7 Davis	N	N	N	Y	Y	N	Y	Y
8 ***Crane***	N	N	N	N	Y	N	N	Y
9 Schakowsky	N	N	N	Y	Y	N	Y	Y
10 ***Porter***	Y	Y	N	Y	Y	Y	Y	Y
11 ***Weller***	Y	Y	N	N	Y	Y	Y	Y
12 Costello	N	N	N	N	Y	N	Y	Y
13 ***Biggert***	Y	Y	N	Y	Y	Y	Y	Y

ND Northern Democrats SD Southern Democrats

	335	336	337	338	339	340	341	342
14 ***Hastert***							Y	
15 ***Ewing***	Y	Y	N	N	Y	Y	Y	Y
16 ***Manzullo***	Y	Y	N	Y	Y	Y	N	Y
17 Evans	N	N	N	N	Y	N	Y	Y
18 ***LaHood***	Y	Y	N	Y	Y	Y	Y	Y
19 Phelps	N	N	N	N	Y	N	Y	Y
20 ***Shimkus***	Y	N	N	Y	N	Y	Y	Y
INDIANA								
1 Visclosky	N	N	N	N	Y	N	Y	Y
2 ***McIntosh***	?	?	?	?	?	?	?	?
3 Roemer	N	N	N	Y	Y	N	Y	Y
4 ***Souder***	N	N	N	N	N	Y	N	Y
5 ***Buyer***	N	N	N	N	Y	Y	Y	Y
6 ***Burton***	Y	Y	N	N	N	Y	N	Y
7 ***Pease***	Y	Y	N	Y	N	Y	Y	Y
8 ***Hostettler***	N	N	N	N	N	Y	N	Y
9 Hill	Y	N	N	Y	Y	N	Y	Y
10 Carson	N	N	N	Y	Y	N	Y	Y
IOWA								
1 ***Leach***	Y	Y	N	Y	Y	Y	Y	Y
2 ***Nussle***	Y	Y	N	N	Y	Y	Y	Y
3 Boswell	N	N	N	N	Y	Y	Y	Y
4 ***Ganske***	Y	Y	N	?	?	?	Y	Y
5 ***Latham***	N	N	N	N	Y	Y	Y	Y
KANSAS								
1 ***Moran***	Y	Y	Y	Y	Y	Y	Y	Y
2 ***Ryun***	N	N	N	N	Y	Y	N	Y
3 Moore	N	N	N	Y	Y	N	Y	Y
4 ***Tiahrt***	N	N	N	Y	Y	Y	N	Y
KENTUCKY								
1 ***Whitfield***	Y	Y	N	N	Y	Y	Y	Y
2 ***Lewis***	N	N	N	Y	Y	Y	Y	Y
3 ***Northup***	N	N	N	N	Y	Y	+	Y
4 Lucas	N	N	N	Y	Y	Y	Y	Y
5 ***Rogers***	N	N	N	N	Y	Y	Y	Y
6 ***Fletcher***	N	N	N	Y	Y	Y	Y	Y
LOUISIANA								
1 ***Vitter***	N	N	N	N	Y	Y	Y	Y
2 Jefferson	N	N	N	N	Y	N	Y	Y
3 ***Tauzin***	Y	N	N	N	Y	Y	Y	Y
4 ***McCrery***	Y	N	N	N	Y	Y	Y	Y
5 ***Cooksey***	Y	Y	N	N	Y	Y	N	Y
6 ***Baker***	N	N	N	N	Y	Y	Y	Y
7 John	N	N	N	N	Y	Y	Y	Y
MAINE								
1 Allen	N	N	N	N	Y	N	Y	Y
2 Baldacci	N	N	N	N	Y	N	Y	Y
MARYLAND								
1 ***Gilchrest***	Y	Y	N	Y	Y	Y	Y	Y
2 ***Ehrlich***	N	N	N	N	Y	Y	Y	Y
3 Cardin	N	N	N	N	Y	N	Y	Y
4 Wynn	N	N	N	N	Y	N	Y	Y
5 Hoyer	N	N	N	N	Y	N	Y	Y
6 ***Bartlett***	Y	Y	N	Y	Y	Y	Y	Y
7 Cummings	N	N	N	N	Y	N	Y	Y
8 ***Morella***	Y	Y	N	Y	Y	N	Y	Y
MASSACHUSETTS								
1 Olver	Y	Y	Y	Y	Y	N	Y	Y
2 Neal	N	N	N	N	Y	N	Y	Y
3 McGovern	N	N	Y	Y	Y	N	Y	Y
4 Frank	N	N	Y	N	Y	N	Y	Y
5 Meehan	N	N	Y	Y	Y	N	Y	Y
6 Tierney	N	N	Y	N	Y	N	Y	Y
7 Markey	?	?	?	?	?	?	?	?
8 Capuano	N	N	Y	N	Y	N	Y	Y
9 Moakley	N	?	N	N	Y	N	Y	Y
10 Delahunt	Y	Y	Y	N	Y	N	Y	?
MICHIGAN								
1 Stupak	N	N	N	N	Y	N	Y	Y
2 ***Hoekstra***	Y	Y	N	Y	Y	Y	Y	Y
3 ***Ehlers***	Y	Y	N	Y	Y	N	Y	Y
4 ***Camp***	N	N	N	N	Y	Y	Y	Y
5 Barcia	N	N	N	N	?	Y	Y	Y
6 ***Upton***	Y	Y	N	Y	Y	Y	Y	Y
7 ***Smith***	Y	Y	N	Y	Y	Y	Y	Y
8 Stabenow	N	N	N	N	Y	N	Y	Y
9 Kildee	N	N	N	N	Y	Y	Y	Y
10 Bonior	N	N	N	?	Y	N	Y	Y
11 ***Knollenberg***	?	N	N	N	Y	N	Y	Y
12 Levin	N	N	N	N	Y	N	Y	Y
13 Rivers	Y	N	N	Y	Y	N	Y	Y
14 Conyers	N	N	Y	Y	Y	N	Y	Y
15 Kilpatrick	N	N	N	N	Y	N	Y	Y
16 Dingell	N	N	N	N	Y	N	Y	Y

	335	336	337	338	339	340	341	342
MINNESOTA								
1 ***Gutknecht***	Y	Y	N	Y	N	Y	Y	Y
2 Minge	N	Y	Y	Y	Y	Y	Y	Y
3 ***Ramstad***	Y	Y	N	Y	Y	Y	Y	N
4 Vento	?	?	?	?	?	?	?	?
5 Sabo	N	N	N	N	Y	N	Y	Y
6 Luther	Y	Y	Y	Y	Y	Y	Y	N
7 Peterson	N	N	N	N	Y	Y	Y	N
8 Oberstar	N	N	N	N	Y	N	?	Y
MISSISSIPPI								
1 ***Wicker***	N	N	N	N	Y	Y	Y	Y
2 Thompson	N	N	N	N	Y	N	Y	Y
3 ***Pickering***	Y	N	N	N	Y	Y	Y	Y
4 Shows	N	N	N	N	Y	Y	Y	Y
5 Taylor	Y	Y	Y	?	Y	Y	Y	Y
MISSOURI								
1 Clay	N	N	N	Y	Y	N	Y	?
2 ***Talent***	N	N	N	N	Y	Y	Y	Y
3 Gephardt	N	N	N	N	Y	N	Y	Y
4 Skelton	N	N	N	Y	Y	Y	Y	Y
5 McCarthy	Y	Y	N	Y	Y	N	+	Y
6 Danner	N	N	N	N	Y	Y	Y	Y
7 ***Blunt***	N	N	N	N	Y	Y	Y	Y
8 ***Emerson***	N	N	N	N	Y	N	Y	Y
9 ***Hulshof***	N	N	N	N	Y	Y	Y	Y
MONTANA								
AL ***Hill***	Y	Y	N	Y	N	Y	Y	Y
NEBRASKA								
1 ***Bereuter***	Y	Y	N	Y	Y	Y	Y	Y
2 ***Terry***	Y	Y	N	Y	Y	Y	Y	Y
3 ***Barrett***	Y	Y	N	Y	Y	N	Y	Y
NEVADA								
1 Berkley	N	N	N	N	Y	N	Y	Y
2 ***Gibbons***	N	N	N	N	Y	Y	Y	N
NEW HAMPSHIRE								
1 ***Sununu***	Y	Y	Y	Y	N	Y	Y	Y
2 ***Bass***	Y	Y	N	Y	Y	Y	Y	Y
NEW JERSEY								
1 Andrews	Y	Y	N	Y	Y	Y	Y	N
2 ***LoBiondo***	Y	Y	N	Y	Y	Y	Y	Y
3 ***Saxton***	Y	Y	N	Y	Y	Y	Y	Y
4 ***Smith***	Y	Y	N	Y	Y	Y	Y	Y
5 ***Roukema***	Y	Y	N	N	Y	Y	Y	Y
6 Pallone	N	N	Y	Y	Y	Y	Y	Y
7 ***Franks***	N	N	N	N	Y	Y	Y	Y
8 Pascrell	N	N	N	Y	Y	N	Y	Y
9 Rothman	N	N	N	N	Y	N	Y	Y
10 Payne	N	N	Y	N	Y	N	Y	Y
11 ***Frelinghuysen***	N	N	N	N	Y	N	Y	Y
12 Holt	N	N	N	Y	Y	N	Y	Y
13 Menendez	N	N	N	N	Y	N	Y	Y
NEW MEXICO								
1 ***Wilson***	Y	N	N	Y	Y	Y	Y	Y
2 ***Skeen***	N	Y	N	N	Y	Y	Y	Y
3 Udall	N	N	N	Y	Y	N	Y	Y
NEW YORK								
1 Forbes	N	N	N	N	Y	N	Y	Y
2 ***Lazio***	?	?	Y	Y	Y	Y	Y	Y
3 ***King***	N	N	N	N	Y	Y	Y	Y
4 McCarthy	N	N	N	N	Y	N	Y	Y
5 Ackerman	N	N	N	N	Y	N	Y	Y
6 Meeks	N	N	N	Y	Y	N	Y	Y
7 Crowley	N	N	N	N	Y	Y	Y	Y
8 Nadler	N	N	Y	N	Y	N	Y	Y
9 Weiner	N	N	N	N	Y	N	Y	Y
10 Towns	N	N	N	Y	Y	N	Y	Y
11 Owens	N	N	Y	Y	Y	N	Y	Y
12 Velázquez	N	N	Y	Y	Y	N	Y	Y
13 ***Fossella***	N	Y	N	N	Y	Y	Y	Y
14 Maloney	N	N	Y	Y	Y	N	Y	Y
15 Rangel	N	N	Y	N	Y	N	Y	Y
16 Serrano	N	N	N	Y	Y	N	Y	Y
17 Engel	N	N	N	N	Y	N	Y	Y
18 Lowey	N	N	N	N	Y	N	Y	Y
19 ***Kelly***	Y	Y	Y	Y	Y	Y	Y	Y
20 ***Gilman***	Y	Y	Y	Y	Y	Y	Y	Y
21 McNulty	N	N	N	Y	Y	N	Y	Y
22 ***Sweeney***	N	N	N	Y	Y	Y	Y	Y
23 ***Boehlert***	Y	Y	N	N	Y	Y	Y	Y
24 ***McHugh***	N	N	N	N	Y	Y	Y	Y
25 ***Walsh***	N	N	N	Y	Y	Y	Y	Y
26 Hinchey	N	N	N	Y	Y	N	Y	Y
27 ***Reynolds***	N	N	N	N	Y	Y	Y	Y
28 Slaughter	N	N	N	Y	Y	N	Y	Y
29 LaFalce	N	N	N	N	Y	N	Y	Y

	335	336	337	338	339	340	341	342
30 ***Quinn***	N	N	N	N	Y	N	Y	Y
31 ***Houghton***	Y	Y	N	N	Y	Y	Y	Y
NORTH CAROLINA								
1 Clayton	N	N	N	N	Y	N	Y	Y
2 Etheridge	N	N	N	N	Y	N	Y	Y
3 ***Jones***	Y	Y	N	N	N	Y	Y	Y
4 Price	N	N	N	N	Y	N	Y	Y
5 ***Burr***	N	N	N	Y	Y	Y	Y	Y
6 ***Coble***	Y	Y	N	Y	N	Y	Y	Y
7 McIntyre	N	N	N	N	Y	N	Y	Y
8 ***Hayes***	N	Y	N	Y	Y	Y	Y	Y
9 ***Myrick***	Y	Y	N	Y	Y	Y	N	Y
10 ***Ballenger***	N	N	N	Y	N	Y	Y	Y
11 ***Taylor***	N	N	N	N	Y	Y	Y	Y
12 Watt	N	N	N	Y	Y	N	Y	Y
NORTH DAKOTA								
AL Pomeroy	N	N	N	N	Y	N	Y	Y
OHIO								
1 ***Chabot***	Y	Y	N	Y	Y	Y	Y	Y
2 ***Portman***	N	N	N	Y	Y	Y	Y	Y
3 Hall	N	N	N	Y	Y	N	Y	Y
4 ***Oxley***	Y	Y	N	N	Y	Y	N	Y
5 ***Gillmor***	Y	Y	N	Y	Y	Y	Y	Y
6 Strickland	N	N	N	N	Y	N	Y	Y
7 ***Hobson***	Y	Y	N	N	Y	Y	Y	Y
8 ***Boehner***	N	N	N	Y	Y	Y	Y	Y
9 Kaptur	N	N	N	N	Y	N	Y	Y
10 Kucinich	N	N	Y	Y	Y	N	Y	Y
11 Jones	N	N	N	N	Y	N	Y	Y
12 ***Kasich***	N	N	N	N	Y	Y	Y	Y
13 Brown	N	N	N	Y	Y	N	Y	Y
14 Sawyer	N	N	N	N	Y	N	Y	Y
15 ***Pryce***	Y	Y	N	N	Y	Y	Y	Y
16 ***Regula***	N	N	N	N	Y	Y	Y	Y
17 Traficant	Y	Y	N	N	Y	Y	Y	Y
18 ***Ney***	N	Y	N	N	Y	Y	Y	Y
19 ***LaTourette***	Y	Y	N	N	Y	Y	Y	Y
OKLAHOMA								
1 ***Largent***	N	N	N	N	Y	Y	Y	Y
2 ***Coburn***	Y	Y	N	N	N	Y	N	Y
3 ***Watkins***	N	N	N	N	Y	Y	Y	Y
4 ***Watts***	Y	Y	N	N	Y	Y	Y	Y
5 ***Istook***	N	N	N	Y	Y	Y	Y	Y
6 ***Lucas***	Y	Y	N	Y	Y	Y	Y	Y
OREGON								
1 Wu	N	N	N	N	N	N	Y	Y
2 ***Walden***	Y	Y	N	N	N	Y	Y	Y
3 Blumenauer	Y	Y	Y	N	Y	N	Y	Y
4 DeFazio	Y	Y	Y	N	Y	Y	Y	Y
5 Hooley	N	N	N	N	Y	N	Y	Y
PENNSYLVANIA								
1 Brady	N	N	N	N	Y	N	Y	Y
2 Fattah	N	N	N	N	Y	N	Y	Y
3 Borski	N	N	N	N	Y	N	Y	Y
4 Klink	N	N	N	N	Y	N	Y	Y
5 ***Peterson***	Y	?	N	N	Y	Y	N	Y
6 Holden	N	N	N	N	Y	N	Y	Y
7 ***Weldon***	Y	N	N	N	Y	Y	Y	Y
8 ***Greenwood***	Y	Y	N	N	Y	Y	Y	Y
9 ***Shuster***	N	N	N	N	Y	Y	Y	Y
10 ***Sherwood***	Y	Y	N	N	Y	Y	Y	Y
11 Kanjorski	N	N	N	N	Y	N	Y	Y
12 Murtha	N	N	N	N	Y	N	Y	Y
13 Hoeffel	N	N	Y	N	Y	N	Y	Y
14 Coyne	N	N	N	N	Y	N	Y	Y
15 ***Toomey***	Y	N	Y	N	N	Y	N	Y
16 ***Pitts***	N	N	N	N	N	Y	N	Y
17 ***Gekas***	N	N	N	N	Y	Y	Y	Y
18 Doyle	N	N	N	N	Y	N	Y	Y
19 ***Goodling***	N	Y	Y	N	Y	Y	Y	Y
20 Mascara	N	N	N	N	Y	N	Y	Y
21 ***English***	N	N	N	N	Y	Y	Y	Y
RHODE ISLAND								
1 Kennedy	N	N	N	N	Y	N	Y	Y
2 Weygand	N	N	N	Y	Y	N	Y	Y
SOUTH CAROLINA								
1 ***Sanford***	Y	Y	Y	Y	N	Y	Y	N
2 ***Spence***	Y	N	N	N	Y	Y	Y	Y
3 ***Graham***	Y	Y	N	Y	Y	Y	Y	Y
4 ***DeMint***	N	N	N	Y	Y	Y	Y	Y
5 Spratt	N	N	N	N	Y	N	Y	Y
6 Clyburn	N	N	N	Y	Y	N	Y	Y
SOUTH DAKOTA								
AL ***Thune***	N	Y	Y	Y	Y	Y	Y	Y

	335	336	337	338	339	340	341	342
TENNESSEE								
1 ***Jenkins***	Y	N	N	N	Y	Y	N	Y
2 ***Duncan***	Y	Y	N	Y	N	Y	Y	Y
3 ***Wamp***	Y	Y	N	Y	Y	Y	Y	Y
4 ***Hilleary***	Y	Y	N	N	Y	Y	Y	Y
5 Clement	N	N	N	N	Y	N	Y	Y
6 Gordon	N	N	N	N	Y	Y	Y	Y
7 ***Bryant***	Y	Y	N	N	Y	Y	Y	Y
8 Tanner	N	N	N	N	Y	Y	Y	Y
9 Ford	N	N	N	Y	Y	N	Y	Y
TEXAS								
1 Sandlin	N	N	N	N	Y	Y	Y	Y
2 Turner	N	N	N	N	Y	Y	Y	Y
3 ***Johnson, Sam***	Y	Y	N	N	N	Y	N	Y
4 Hall	N	N	N	Y	Y	Y	Y	Y
5 ***Sessions***	Y	Y	Y	Y	Y	Y	Y	Y
6 ***Barton***	Y	N	N	N	Y	Y	N	Y
7 ***Archer***	Y	Y	N	N	Y	Y	Y	Y
8 ***Brady***	Y	Y	N	N	Y	Y	Y	Y
9 Lampson	N	N	N	N	Y	N	Y	Y
10 Doggett	N	N	Y	Y	Y	N	Y	N
11 Edwards	N	N	N	N	Y	N	Y	Y
12 ***Granger***	N	N	N	N	Y	Y	Y	Y
13 ***Thornberry***	N	Y	N	N	Y	Y	N	Y
14 ***Paul***	Y	Y	Y	Y	N	Y	N	N
15 Hinojosa	?	?	N	N	Y	N	Y	Y
16 Reyes	N	N	N	N	Y	N	Y	Y
17 Stenholm	N	N	N	Y	Y	Y	Y	Y
18 Jackson-Lee	N	N	N	N	Y	N	Y	Y
19 ***Combest***	Y	Y	N	Y	Y	Y	N	Y
20 Gonzalez	N	N	N	N	Y	N	Y	Y
21 ***Smith***	N	Y	N	N	Y	Y	Y	Y
22 ***DeLay***	Y	Y	N	N	Y	Y	N	Y
23 ***Bonilla***	Y	Y	N	N	Y	Y	N	Y
24 Frost	N	N	N	N	Y	N	Y	Y
25 Bentsen	N	N	N	N	Y	N	Y	Y
26 ***Armey***	N	Y	N	N	Y	Y	Y	Y
27 Ortiz	N	N	N	N	Y	N	Y	Y
28 Rodriguez	N	N	N	N	Y	N	Y	Y
29 Green	N	N	N	N	Y	N	Y	Y
30 Johnson, E.B.	N	N	N	N	Y	N	Y	N
UTAH								
1 ***Hansen***	Y	Y	N	N	Y	Y	Y	Y
2 ***Cook***	?	?	?	?	?	?	?	?
3 ***Cannon***	Y	Y	N	N	Y	Y	Y	Y
VERMONT								
AL *Sanders*	N	N	Y	Y	Y	N	Y	Y
VIRGINIA								
1 ***Bateman***	N	N	N	N	Y	N	Y	Y
2 Pickett	N	N	N	N	Y	N	Y	Y
3 Scott	N	N	N	N	Y	N	Y	Y
4 Sisisky	N	N	N	N	Y	Y	Y	Y
5 *Goode*	Y	Y	N	Y	Y	Y	Y	Y
6 ***Goodlatte***	Y	Y	N	Y	Y	Y	Y	N
7 ***Bliley***	Y	N	N	Y	Y	Y	Y	Y
8 Moran	N	N	N	Y	Y	N	Y	Y
9 Boucher	N	N	N	N	Y	N	Y	Y
10 ***Wolf***	Y	Y	N	N	Y	N	Y	Y
11 ***Davis***	Y	Y	N	Y	Y	Y	Y	Y
WASHINGTON								
1 Inslee	Y	Y	Y	Y	Y	Y	Y	N
2 ***Metcalf***	N	Y	Y	Y	Y	Y	Y	Y
3 Baird	N	N	N	N	Y	N	Y	Y
4 ***Hastings***	N	N	N	N	Y	Y	Y	Y
5 ***Nethercutt***	Y	Y	N	N	Y	Y	Y	Y
6 Dicks	N	N	N	N	Y	N	Y	Y
7 McDermott	N	N	Y	Y	Y	N	Y	Y
8 ***Dunn***	N	N	N	N	Y	Y	Y	Y
9 Smith	Y	Y	N	Y	Y	Y	Y	N
WEST VIRGINIA								
1 Mollohan	N	N	N	N	Y	N	Y	Y
2 Wise	N	N	N	N	Y	N	Y	Y
3 Rahall	N	N	Y	N	Y	N	Y	Y
WISCONSIN								
1 ***Ryan***	Y	Y	Y	Y	Y	Y	Y	Y
2 Baldwin	N	N	N	Y	Y	N	Y	Y
3 Kind	N	N	N	N	Y	N	Y	Y
4 Kleczka	N	N	N	N	Y	N	Y	Y
5 Barrett	N	N	N	N	Y	N	Y	Y
6 ***Petri***	Y	Y	Y	Y	Y	Y	Y	Y
7 Obey	N	N	N	N	Y	N	Y	Y
8 ***Green***	N	N	Y	N	Y	Y	Y	Y
9 ***Sensenbrenner***	Y	Y	Y	Y	N	Y	Y	N
WYOMING								
AL ***Cubin***	Y	N	N	N	Y	Y	Y	Y

Southern states - Ala., Ark., Fla., Ga., Ky., La., Miss., N.C., Okla., S.C., Tenn., Texas, Va.

343. Procedural Motion/Adjourn. Bonior, D-Mich., motion to adjourn. Motion rejected 166-237: R 0-207; D 165-29 (ND 122-21, SD 43-8); I 1-1. June 28, 2000.

344. HR 4680. Prescription Drugs/Consideration of Rule. Judgment of the House on proceeding to the consideration of the rule (H Res 539) to provide for House floor consideration of the bill to provide prescription drug coverage for Medicare beneficiaries, despite the Stenholm, D-Texas, point of order regarding unfunded mandates. Agreed to consider the rule 224-200: R 215-1; D 8-198 (ND 7-147, SD 1-51); I 1-1. June 28, 2000.

345. HR 4680. Prescription Drugs/Motion to Reconsider. Goss, R-Fla., motion to table the Frank, D-Mass., motion to reconsider the vote on the motion to consider the resolution (H Res 539) to provide for House floor consideration of the bill to provide prescription drug coverage for Medicare beneficiaries. Motion agreed to 219-200: R 211-1; D 7-198 (ND 6-147, SD 1-51); I 1-1. June 28, 2000.

346. Procedural Motion/Adjourn. Frank, D-Mass., motion to adjourn. Motion rejected 174-242: R 0-211; D 173-30 (ND 127-24, SD 46-6); I 1-1. June 28, 2000.

347. HR 4680. Prescription Drugs/Previous Question. Goss, R-Fla., motion to order the previous question (thus ending debate and possibility of amendment) on adoption of the rule (H Res 539) to provide for House floor consideration of the bill that would provide prescription drug coverage to Medicare beneficiaries. Motion agreed to 227-204: R 221-0; D 5-203 (ND 4-150, SD 1-53); I 1-1. June 28, 2000.

348. HR 4680. Prescription Drugs/Motion to Reconsider. Dreier, R-Calif., motion to table the Moakley, D-Mass., motion to reconsider the vote on ordering the previous question (thus ending debate and possibility of amendment) on adoption of the rule (H Res 539) to provide for House floor consideration of the bill to provide prescription drug coverage for Medicare beneficiaries. Motion agreed to 220-205: R 214-2; D 5-202 (ND 4-149, SD 1-53); I 1-1. June 28, 2000.

349. HR 4680. Prescription Drugs/Rule. Adoption of the rule (H Res 539) to provide for House floor consideration of the bill to provide prescription drug coverage for Medicare beneficiaries. Adopted 216-213: R 212-7; D 3-205 (ND 3-151, SD 0-54); I 1-1. June 28, 2000.

350. HR 4680. Prescription Drugs/Motion to Reconsider. Dreier, R-Calif., motion to table the Goss, R-Fla., motion to reconsider the vote on adoption of the rule (H Res 539) to provide for House floor consideration of the bill to provide prescription drug coverage for Medicare beneficiaries. Motion agreed to 222-204: R 218-0; D 3-203 (ND 3-150, SD 0-53); I 1-1. June 28, 2000.

Key

- Y Voted for (yea).
- # Paired for.
- + Announced for.
- N Voted against (nay).
- X Paired against.
- – Announced against.
- P Voted "present."
- C Voted "present" to avoid possible conflict of interest.
- ? Did not vote or otherwise make a position known.

•

Democrats ***Republicans***
Independents

	343	344	345	346	347	348	349	350
ALABAMA								
1 ***Callahan***	N	Y	Y	N	Y	Y	Y	Y
2 ***Everett***	N	Y	Y	N	Y	Y	Y	Y
3 ***Riley***	N	Y	Y	N	Y	Y	Y	Y
4 ***Aderholt***	N	Y	Y	N	Y	Y	Y	Y
5 Cramer	Y	N	N	Y	N	N	N	N
6 ***Bachus***	N	Y	Y	N	Y	Y	Y	Y
7 Hilliard	Y	N	N	Y	N	N	N	N
ALASKA								
AL ***Young***	?	Y	Y	N	Y	Y	Y	Y
ARIZONA								
1 ***Salmon***	N	Y	Y	N	Y	Y	Y	Y
2 Pastor	Y	N	N	Y	N	N	N	N
3 ***Stump***	N	Y	Y	N	Y	Y	Y	Y
4 ***Shadegg***	N	Y	Y	N	Y	Y	N	Y
5 ***Kolbe***	N	Y	Y	N	Y	Y	Y	Y
6 ***Hayworth***	N	Y	Y	N	Y	Y	Y	Y
ARKANSAS								
1 Berry	Y	N	N	Y	N	N	N	N
2 Snyder	Y	N	N	N	N	N	N	N
3 ***Hutchinson***	N	Y	Y	?	Y	Y	Y	Y
4 ***Dickey***	N	Y	Y	N	Y	Y	Y	Y
CALIFORNIA								
1 Thompson	Y	N	N	Y	N	N	N	N
2 ***Herger***	N	Y	Y	N	Y	Y	Y	Y
3 ***Ose***	N	Y	Y	N	Y	Y	Y	Y
4 ***Doolittle***	N	Y	Y	N	Y	Y	Y	Y
5 Matsui	Y	Y	N	Y	N	N	N	N
6 Woolsey	Y	N	N	Y	N	N	N	N
7 Miller, George	Y	N	N	Y	N	N	N	N
8 Pelosi	Y	N	N	Y	N	N	N	N
9 Lee	Y	N	N	Y	N	N	N	N
10 Tauscher	Y	N	N	Y	N	N	N	N
11 ***Pombo***	N	Y	Y	N	Y	Y	Y	Y
12 Lantos	Y	N	Y	Y	N	N	N	N
13 Stark	Y	N	N	Y	N	N	N	N
14 Eshoo	Y	N	N	Y	N	N	N	N
15 ***Campbell***	N	Y	Y	N	Y	Y	Y	Y
16 Lofgren	Y	N	N	Y	N	N	N	N
17 Farr	N	N	N	Y	N	N	N	N
18 Condit	Y	N	N	Y	N	N	N	N
19 ***Radanovich***	N	Y	?	N	Y	Y	Y	Y
20 Dooley	Y	N	N	Y	N	N	N	N
21 ***Thomas***	N	Y	Y	N	Y	Y	Y	Y
22 Capps	Y	N	N	Y	N	N	N	N
23 ***Gallegly***	N	Y	Y	N	Y	Y	Y	Y
24 Sherman	Y	N	N	Y	N	N	N	N
25 ***McKeon***	N	Y	Y	N	Y	Y	Y	Y
26 Berman	Y	N	N	Y	N	N	N	N
27 ***Rogan***	N	Y	Y	N	Y	Y	Y	Y
28 ***Dreier***	N	Y	Y	N	Y	Y	Y	Y
29 Waxman	?	N	N	Y	N	N	N	N
30 Becerra	Y	N	N	Y	N	N	N	N
31 Martinez	?	Y	Y	N	Y	Y	Y	Y
32 Dixon	?	N	N	Y	N	N	N	N
33 Roybal-Allard	Y	N	N	Y	N	N	N	N
34 Napolitano	Y	N	N	Y	N	N	N	N
35 Waters	Y	N	N	Y	N	N	N	N
36 ***Kuykendall***	N	Y	Y	N	Y	Y	Y	Y
37 Millender-McD.	Y	N	N	Y	N	N	N	N
38 ***Horn***	N	Y	Y	N	Y	Y	Y	Y
39 ***Royce***	N	Y	Y	N	Y	Y	Y	Y
40 ***Lewis***	N	Y	Y	N	Y	Y	Y	Y
41 ***Miller, Gary***	N	Y	Y	N	Y	Y	Y	Y
42 Baca	Y	N	N	Y	N	N	N	N
43 ***Calvert***	N	Y	Y	N	Y	Y	Y	Y
44 ***Bono***	N	Y	Y	N	Y	Y	Y	Y
45 ***Rohrabacher***	N	Y	Y	N	Y	Y	Y	Y
46 Sanchez	Y	N	N	Y	N	N	N	N
47 ***Cox***	N	Y	Y	N	Y	Y	Y	Y
48 ***Packard***	N	Y	Y	N	Y	Y	Y	Y
49 ***Bilbray***	N	Y	Y	N	Y	Y	Y	Y
50 Filner	Y	N	N	Y	N	N	N	N
51 ***Cunningham***	N	Y	Y	N	Y	Y	Y	Y
52 ***Hunter***	N	Y	Y	N	Y	?	Y	Y
COLORADO								
1 DeGette	N	N	N	Y	N	N	N	N
2 Udall	Y	N	N	Y	N	N	N	N
3 ***McInnis***	N	Y	Y	N	Y	Y	Y	Y
4 ***Schaffer***	N	Y	Y	?	Y	Y	Y	Y
5 ***Hefley***	N	Y	Y	N	Y	Y	Y	Y
6 ***Tancredo***	N	Y	Y	N	Y	Y	Y	Y
CONNECTICUT								
1 Larson	Y	N	N	Y	N	N	N	N
2 Gejdenson	Y	N	N	Y	N	N	N	N
3 DeLauro	Y	N	N	Y	N	N	N	N
4 ***Shays***	N	Y	Y	N	Y	Y	Y	Y
5 Maloney	Y	N	N	N	N	N	N	N
6 ***Johnson***	N	Y	Y	N	Y	Y	Y	Y
DELAWARE								
AL ***Castle***	N	Y	Y	N	Y	Y	Y	Y
FLORIDA								
1 ***Scarborough***	N	Y	Y	N	Y	Y	Y	Y
2 Boyd	Y	N	N	Y	N	N	N	N
3 Brown	Y	N	N	Y	N	N	N	N
4 ***Fowler***	N	Y	Y	N	Y	Y	Y	Y
5 Thurman	Y	N	N	Y	N	N	N	N
6 ***Stearns***	N	Y	Y	N	Y	?	Y	Y
7 ***Mica***	N	Y	Y	N	Y	Y	Y	Y
8 ***McCollum***	N	Y	Y	N	Y	Y	Y	Y
9 ***Bilirakis***	N	Y	Y	N	Y	Y	Y	Y
10 ***Young***	?	Y	Y	N	Y	Y	Y	Y
11 Davis	Y	N	N	Y	N	N	N	N
12 ***Canady***	?	Y	Y	N	Y	Y	Y	Y
13 ***Miller***	N	Y	Y	N	Y	Y	Y	Y
14 ***Goss***	N	Y	Y	N	Y	Y	Y	Y
15 ***Weldon***	N	Y	Y	N	Y	Y	Y	Y
16 ***Foley***	N	Y	Y	N	Y	Y	Y	Y
17 Meek	?	N	N	Y	N	N	N	N
18 ***Ros-Lehtinen***	N	Y	Y	N	Y	Y	Y	Y
19 Wexler	Y	N	N	Y	N	N	N	N
20 Deutsch	Y	N	N	Y	N	N	N	N
21 ***Diaz-Balart***	N	Y	Y	N	Y	Y	Y	Y
22 ***Shaw***	N	Y	Y	N	Y	Y	Y	Y
23 Hastings	Y	N	N	Y	N	N	N	N
GEORGIA								
1 ***Kingston***	N	Y	Y	N	Y	Y	Y	Y
2 Bishop	Y	N	N	Y	N	N	N	N
3 ***Collins***	N	Y	Y	N	Y	Y	Y	Y
4 McKinney	Y	N	N	Y	N	N	N	N
5 Lewis	Y	N	N	Y	N	N	N	N
6 ***Isakson***	N	Y	Y	N	Y	Y	Y	Y
7 ***Barr***	N	Y	Y	N	Y	Y	Y	Y
8 ***Chambliss***	N	Y	Y	N	Y	Y	Y	Y
9 ***Deal***	N	Y	Y	N	Y	Y	Y	Y
10 ***Norwood***	?	Y	Y	N	Y	Y	Y	Y
11 ***Linder***	?	Y	Y	N	Y	Y	Y	Y
HAWAII								
1 Abercrombie	N	N	N	N	N	N	N	N
2 Mink	Y	N	N	Y	N	N	N	N
IDAHO								
1 ***Chenoweth-Hage***	N	Y	Y	N	Y	Y	N	Y
2 ***Simpson***	N	Y	Y	N	Y	Y	Y	Y
ILLINOIS								
1 Rush	Y	N	N	Y	N	N	N	N
2 Jackson	Y	N	N	N	N	N	N	Y
3 Lipinski	Y	N	N	Y	N	N	N	N
4 Gutierrez	Y	N	N	Y	N	N	N	N
5 Blagojevich	N	N	N	Y	N	Y	N	N
6 ***Hyde***	N	?	?	?	Y	Y	Y	Y
7 Davis	N	N	N	Y	N	N	N	N
8 ***Crane***	N	Y	Y	N	Y	Y	Y	Y
9 Schakowsky	Y	N	N	Y	N	N	N	N
10 ***Porter***	?	?	?	?	Y	Y	Y	Y
11 ***Weller***	N	Y	Y	N	Y	Y	Y	Y
12 Costello	N	N	N	N	N	N	N	N
13 ***Biggert***	N	Y	Y	N	Y	Y	Y	Y

ND Northern Democrats SD Southern Democrats

	343	344	345	346	347	348	349	350
14 ***Hastert***	N				Y	Y	Y	Y
15 ***Ewing***	N	Y	Y	N	Y	Y	Y	Y
16 ***Manzullo***	N	Y	Y	N	Y	Y	Y	Y
17 Evans	Y	N	N	N	N	N	N	N
18 ***LaHood***	N	Y	Y	N	Y	Y	Y	Y
19 Phelps	Y	N	N	Y	N	N	N	N
20 ***Shimkus***	N	Y	Y	N	Y	Y	Y	Y
INDIANA								
1 Visclosky	Y	N	N	Y	N	N	N	N
2 ***McIntosh***	?	?	?	?	Y	Y	Y	Y
3 Roemer	N	N	N	N	N	N	N	N
4 ***Souder***	N	Y	Y	N	Y	Y	?	Y
5 ***Buyer***	N	Y	Y	N	Y	?	Y	Y
6 ***Burton***	–	+	Y	N	Y	Y	Y	Y
7 ***Pease***	N	Y	Y	N	Y	Y	Y	Y
8 ***Hostettler***	N	Y	Y	N	Y	Y	N	Y
9 Hill	Y	N	N	Y	N	N	N	N
10 Carson	Y	N	N	Y	N	N	N	N
IOWA								
1 ***Leach***	N	Y	Y	N	Y	Y	Y	Y
2 ***Nussle***	N	Y	Y	N	Y	Y	Y	Y
3 Boswell	Y	N	N	N	N	N	N	N
4 ***Ganske***	N	Y	Y	N	Y	Y	N	Y
5 ***Latham***	N	Y	Y	N	Y	Y	Y	Y
KANSAS								
1 ***Moran***	N	Y	Y	N	Y	N	Y	Y
2 ***Ryun***	N	Y	Y	N	Y	Y	Y	Y
3 Moore	N	N	N	Y	N	N	N	N
4 ***Tiahrt***	N	Y	Y	N	Y	Y	Y	Y
KENTUCKY								
1 ***Whitfield***	N	Y	Y	N	Y	Y	Y	Y
2 ***Lewis***	N	Y	Y	N	Y	Y	Y	Y
3 ***Northup***	N	Y	Y	N	Y	Y	Y	Y
4 Lucas	Y	N	N	Y	N	N	N	N
5 ***Rogers***	N	Y	Y	N	Y	Y	Y	Y
6 ***Fletcher***	N	Y	Y	N	Y	Y	Y	Y
LOUISIANA								
1 ***Vitter***	?	Y	Y	N	Y	Y	Y	Y
2 Jefferson	Y	N	N	Y	N	N	N	N
3 ***Tauzin***	N	Y	?	N	Y	Y	Y	Y
4 ***McCrery***	N	Y	Y	N	Y	Y	Y	Y
5 ***Cooksey***	N	Y	Y	N	Y	Y	Y	Y
6 ***Baker***	N	Y	Y	N	Y	Y	Y	Y
7 John	N	N	N	N	N	N	N	N
MAINE								
1 Allen	Y	N	N	Y	N	N	N	N
2 Baldacci	Y	N	N	Y	N	N	N	N
MARYLAND								
1 ***Gilchrest***	N	Y	Y	N	Y	Y	Y	Y
2 ***Ehrlich***	N	Y	Y	N	Y	Y	Y	Y
3 Cardin	Y	Y	N	Y	N	N	N	N
4 Wynn	Y	N	N	Y	N	N	N	N
5 Hoyer	Y	N	N	Y	N	N	N	N
6 ***Bartlett***	N	Y	Y	N	Y	Y	Y	Y
7 Cummings	?	N	N	Y	N	N	N	N
8 ***Morella***	N	Y	Y	N	Y	Y	N	Y
MASSACHUSETTS								
1 Olver	Y	N	?	Y	N	N	N	N
2 Neal	Y	N	N	Y	N	N	N	N
3 McGovern	Y	N	N	Y	N	N	N	N
4 Frank	Y	Y	N	Y	N	N	N	N
5 Meehan	Y	N	N	Y	N	N	N	N
6 Tierney	Y	N	N	Y	N	N	N	N
7 Markey	?	?	?	?	?	?	?	?
8 Capuano	Y	N	N	Y	N	N	N	N
9 Moakley	Y	N	N	Y	N	N	N	N
10 Delahunt	?	N	N	?	N	N	N	N
MICHIGAN								
1 Stupak	Y	N	N	Y	N	N	N	N
2 ***Hoekstra***	N	Y	Y	N	Y	Y	Y	Y
3 ***Ehlers***	N	Y	Y	N	Y	Y	Y	Y
4 ***Camp***	N	Y	Y	N	Y	Y	Y	Y
5 Barcia	N	N	N	N	N	N	N	N
6 ***Upton***	N	Y	Y	N	Y	Y	Y	Y
7 ***Smith***	N	Y	Y	N	Y	Y	Y	Y
8 Stabenow	N	N	N	Y	N	N	N	N
9 Kildee	Y	N	N	Y	N	N	N	N
10 Bonior	Y	N	N	Y	N	N	N	N
11 ***Knollenberg***	N	Y	Y	N	Y	Y	Y	Y
12 Levin	Y	N	N	Y	N	N	N	N
13 Rivers	Y	N	N	Y	N	N	N	N
14 Conyers	Y	N	N	?	N	N	N	N
15 Kilpatrick	N	N	N	Y	N	N	N	N
16 Dingell	Y	N	N	?	N	N	N	N

	343	344	345	346	347	348	349	350
MINNESOTA								
1 ***Gutknecht***	N	Y	Y	N	Y	N	Y	Y
2 Minge	N	N	N	Y	N	N	N	N
3 ***Ramstad***	N	Y	Y	N	Y	Y	Y	Y
4 Vento	?	?	?	?	?	?	?	?
5 Sabo	Y	N	N	Y	N	N	N	N
6 Luther	Y	N	N	Y	N	N	N	N
7 Peterson	N	Y	Y	N	Y	Y	Y	?
8 Oberstar	Y	N	N	Y	N	N	N	N
MISSISSIPPI								
1 ***Wicker***	N	Y	Y	?	Y	Y	Y	Y
2 Thompson	Y	N	N	Y	N	N	N	N
3 ***Pickering***	N	Y	Y	N	Y	Y	Y	Y
4 Shows	N	N	N	Y	N	N	N	N
5 Taylor	Y	N	N	Y	N	N	N	N
MISSOURI								
1 Clay	?	N	N	Y	N	N	N	N
2 ***Talent***	N	Y	Y	N	Y	Y	Y	Y
3 Gephardt	Y	N	N	Y	N	N	N	N
4 Skelton	Y	N	N	Y	N	N	N	N
5 McCarthy	Y	N	N	Y	N	N	N	N
6 Danner	Y	N	N	Y	N	N	N	N
7 ***Blunt***	N	Y	Y	N	Y	Y	Y	Y
8 ***Emerson***	?	Y	Y	?	Y	Y	N	Y
9 ***Hulshof***	N	Y	Y	N	Y	Y	Y	Y
MONTANA								
AL ***Hill***	N	Y	Y	N	Y	Y	Y	Y
NEBRASKA								
1 ***Bereuter***	N	Y	Y	N	Y	Y	Y	Y
2 ***Terry***	N	Y	Y	N	Y	Y	Y	Y
3 ***Barrett***	N	Y	Y	N	Y	Y	Y	Y
NEVADA								
1 Berkley	Y	N	N	Y	N	N	N	N
2 ***Gibbons***	N	Y	Y	N	Y	Y	Y	Y
NEW HAMPSHIRE								
1 ***Sununu***	N	Y	Y	N	Y	Y	Y	Y
2 ***Bass***	N	Y	Y	N	Y	Y	Y	Y
NEW JERSEY								
1 Andrews	Y	N	N	Y	N	N	N	N
2 ***LoBiondo***	N	Y	Y	N	Y	Y	Y	Y
3 ***Saxton***	N	Y	Y	N	Y	Y	Y	Y
4 ***Smith***	N	Y	Y	N	Y	Y	Y	Y
5 ***Roukema***	N	Y	Y	N	Y	Y	Y	Y
6 Pallone	Y	N	N	Y	N	N	N	N
7 ***Franks***	N	Y	Y	N	Y	Y	Y	?
8 Pascrell	Y	N	N	Y	N	N	N	N
9 Rothman	Y	N	N	Y	N	N	N	N
10 Payne	Y	N	N	Y	N	N	N	N
11 ***Frelinghuysen***	N	Y	Y	N	Y	Y	Y	Y
12 Holt	Y	N	N	Y	N	N	N	N
13 Menendez	Y	N	N	Y	N	N	N	N
NEW MEXICO								
1 ***Wilson***	N	Y	Y	N	Y	Y	Y	Y
2 ***Skeen***	N	Y	Y	N	Y	Y	Y	Y
3 Udall	N	N	N	N	N	N	N	N
NEW YORK								
1 Forbes	Y	N	N	Y	N	N	N	N
2 ***Lazio***	N	Y	Y	?	Y	Y	Y	Y
3 ***King***	N	Y	Y	N	Y	Y	Y	Y
4 McCarthy	Y	N	N	Y	N	N	N	N
5 Ackerman	Y	N	N	Y	N	N	N	N
6 Meeks	Y	N	N	Y	N	?	N	N
7 Crowley	Y	N	N	Y	N	N	N	N
8 Nadler	Y	N	N	Y	N	N	N	N
9 Weiner	Y	N	N	Y	N	N	N	N
10 Towns	Y	N	N	N	N	N	N	N
11 Owens	Y	N	N	Y	N	N	N	N
12 Velázquez	Y	N	N	Y	N	N	N	N
13 ***Fossella***	N	Y	Y	N	Y	Y	Y	Y
14 Maloney	Y	N	N	Y	N	N	N	N
15 Rangel	Y	N	N	Y	N	N	N	N
16 Serrano	?	N	N	N	N	N	N	N
17 Engel	Y	N	N	Y	N	N	N	N
18 Lowey	Y	N	Y	Y	N	N	N	N
19 ***Kelly***	N	Y	Y	N	Y	Y	Y	Y
20 ***Gilman***	N	Y	N	Y	Y	Y	Y	Y
21 McNulty	Y	N	N	Y	N	N	N	N
22 ***Sweeney***	N	Y	Y	N	Y	Y	Y	Y
23 ***Boehlert***	N	Y	Y	N	Y	Y	Y	Y
24 ***McHugh***	N	Y	Y	N	Y	Y	Y	Y
25 ***Walsh***	N	Y	Y	N	Y	Y	Y	Y
26 Hinchey	?	N	N	Y	N	N	N	N
27 ***Reynolds***	?	Y	Y	N	Y	Y	Y	Y
28 Slaughter	Y	N	N	Y	N	N	N	N
29 LaFalce	Y	N	N	Y	N	N	N	N

	343	344	345	346	347	348	349	350
30 ***Quinn***	N	Y	Y	N	Y	Y	Y	Y
31 ***Houghton***	N	Y	Y	N	Y	Y	Y	Y
NORTH CAROLINA								
1 Clayton	Y	N	N	Y	N	N	N	N
2 Etheridge	Y	N	N	Y	N	N	N	N
3 ***Jones***	N	Y	Y	?	Y	N	?	Y
4 Price	Y	N	N	Y	N	N	N	N
5 ***Burr***	N	Y	Y	N	Y	Y	Y	Y
6 ***Coble***	N	Y	Y	N	Y	Y	Y	Y
7 McIntyre	Y	N	N	Y	N	N	N	N
8 ***Hayes***	N	Y	Y	N	Y	Y	Y	Y
9 ***Myrick***	?	Y	Y	N	Y	Y	Y	Y
10 ***Ballenger***	N	Y	Y	N	Y	Y	Y	Y
11 ***Taylor***	N	Y	Y	N	Y	Y	Y	Y
12 Watt	N	N	N	N	N	N	N	N
NORTH DAKOTA								
AL Pomeroy	Y	N	N	Y	N	N	N	N
OHIO								
1 ***Chabot***	N	Y	Y	N	Y	Y	Y	Y
2 ***Portman***	N	Y	Y	N	Y	Y	Y	Y
3 Hall	Y	N	N	Y	N	N	N	N
4 ***Oxley***	N	Y	Y	N	Y	Y	Y	Y
5 ***Gillmor***	N	Y	Y	N	Y	Y	Y	Y
6 Strickland	?	?	?	?	?	?	?	?
7 ***Hobson***	N	Y	Y	N	Y	Y	Y	Y
8 ***Boehner***	?	Y	Y	N	Y	Y	Y	Y
9 Kaptur	?	N	N	Y	N	N	N	N
10 Kucinich	N	N	N	N	N	N	N	N
11 Jones	Y	N	N	Y	N	N	N	N
12 ***Kasich***	N	Y	Y	N	Y	Y	Y	Y
13 Brown	Y	N	N	N	N	N	N	N
14 Sawyer	Y	N	N	Y	N	N	N	N
15 ***Pryce***	N	Y	Y	N	Y	Y	Y	Y
16 ***Regula***	N	Y	Y	N	Y	Y	Y	Y
17 Traficant	N	Y	Y	N	Y	Y	Y	Y
18 ***Ney***	N	Y	Y	N	Y	Y	Y	Y
19 ***LaTourette***	N	Y	Y	N	Y	Y	Y	Y
OKLAHOMA								
1 ***Largent***	N	Y	Y	N	Y	Y	Y	Y
2 ***Coburn***	N	Y	Y	N	Y	Y	N	Y
3 ***Watkins***	N	Y	Y	N	Y	Y	Y	Y
4 ***Watts***	N	Y	Y	N	Y	Y	Y	Y
5 ***Istook***	N	Y	Y	N	Y	Y	Y	Y
6 ***Lucas***	N	Y	Y	N	Y	Y	Y	Y
OREGON								
1 Wu	N	N	N	N	N	N	N	N
2 ***Walden***	N	Y	Y	N	Y	Y	Y	Y
3 Blumenauer	Y	N	N	N	N	N	N	N
4 DeFazio	Y	N	N	Y	N	N	N	N
5 Hooley	N	N	N	Y	N	N	N	N
PENNSYLVANIA								
1 Brady	Y	N	N	Y	N	N	N	N
2 Fattah	Y	N	N	Y	N	N	N	N
3 Borski	Y	N	N	Y	N	N	N	N
4 Klink	N	N	N	N	N	N	N	N
5 ***Peterson***	N	Y	Y	N	Y	Y	Y	Y
6 Holden	Y	N	N	Y	N	N	N	N
7 ***Weldon***	N	Y	Y	N	Y	Y	Y	Y
8 ***Greenwood***	N	Y	Y	N	Y	Y	Y	Y
9 ***Shuster***	N	Y	Y	N	Y	Y	Y	Y
10 ***Sherwood***	N	Y	Y	N	Y	Y	Y	Y
11 Kanjorski	Y	N	N	Y	N	N	N	N
12 Murtha	?	N	N	Y	N	N	N	N
13 Hoeffel	Y	N	N	Y	N	N	N	N
14 Coyne	Y	N	N	Y	N	N	N	N
15 ***Toomey***	N	Y	Y	N	Y	Y	Y	Y
16 ***Pitts***	N	Y	Y	N	Y	Y	Y	Y
17 ***Gekas***	N	Y	Y	N	Y	?	Y	?
18 Doyle	Y	N	N	Y	N	N	N	N
19 ***Goodling***	N	Y	Y	N	Y	Y	Y	?
20 Mascara	Y	N	N	Y	N	N	N	N
21 ***English***	N	Y	Y	N	Y	Y	Y	Y
RHODE ISLAND								
1 Kennedy	Y	N	N	Y	N	N	N	N
2 Weygand	Y	N	N	Y	N	N	N	N
SOUTH CAROLINA								
1 ***Sanford***	N	Y	Y	N	Y	Y	Y	Y
2 ***Spence***	N	Y	Y	N	Y	Y	Y	Y
3 ***Graham***	N	Y	Y	N	Y	Y	Y	Y
4 ***DeMint***	N	Y	Y	N	Y	Y	Y	Y
5 Spratt	Y	N	N	Y	N	N	N	N
6 Clyburn	Y	N	N	Y	N	N	N	N
SOUTH DAKOTA								
AL ***Thune***	N	Y	Y	N	Y	Y	Y	Y

	343	344	345	346	347	348	349	350
TENNESSEE								
1 ***Jenkins***	N	Y	Y	N	Y	Y	Y	Y
2 ***Duncan***	N	N	Y	N	Y	Y	Y	Y
3 ***Wamp***	N	Y	Y	N	Y	Y	Y	Y
4 ***Hilleary***	N	Y	Y	N	Y	Y	Y	Y
5 Clement	?	N	N	Y	N	N	N	N
6 Gordon	N	N	N	Y	N	N	N	N
7 ***Bryant***	N	Y	Y	N	Y	Y	Y	Y
8 Tanner	Y	N	N	Y	N	N	N	N
9 Ford	Y	N	N	Y	N	N	N	N
TEXAS								
1 Sandlin	Y	N	N	Y	N	N	N	N
2 Turner	Y	N	N	Y	N	N	N	N
3 ***Johnson, Sam***	N	Y	Y	N	Y	Y	Y	Y
4 Hall	N	N	Y	N	Y	Y	N	N
5 ***Sessions***	N	Y	Y	N	Y	Y	Y	Y
6 ***Barton***	N	Y	Y	N	Y	Y	Y	Y
7 ***Archer***	N	Y	Y	N	Y	Y	Y	Y
8 ***Brady***	N	Y	Y	N	Y	Y	Y	Y
9 Lampson	Y	N	N	Y	N	N	N	N
10 Doggett	Y	N	N	Y	N	N	N	N
11 Edwards	Y	N	N	Y	N	N	N	?
12 ***Granger***	N	Y	Y	N	Y	Y	Y	Y
13 ***Thornberry***	N	Y	Y	N	Y	Y	Y	Y
14 ***Paul***	N	Y	Y	N	Y	Y	Y	Y
15 Hinojosa	Y	?	?	?	N	N	N	N
16 Reyes	N	N	N	Y	N	N	N	N
17 Stenholm	Y	N	N	Y	N	N	N	N
18 Jackson-Lee	Y	N	N	Y	N	N	N	N
19 ***Combest***	N	Y	Y	N	Y	Y	Y	Y
20 Gonzalez	Y	N	N	Y	N	N	N	N
21 ***Smith***	?	Y	Y	N	Y	Y	Y	Y
22 ***DeLay***	N	Y	?	N	Y	Y	Y	Y
23 ***Bonilla***	N	Y	Y	N	Y	Y	Y	Y
24 Frost	Y	N	N	Y	N	N	N	N
25 Bentsen	Y	N	N	Y	N	N	N	N
26 ***Armey***	N	Y	Y	N	Y	Y	Y	Y
27 Ortiz	N	N	N	Y	N	N	N	N
28 Rodriguez	N	N	N	Y	N	N	N	N
29 Green	Y	N	N	N	N	N	N	N
30 Johnson, E.B.	Y	N	N	Y	N	N	N	N
UTAH								
1 ***Hansen***	N	Y	?	N	Y	Y	Y	Y
2 ***Cook***	?	?	?	?	?	?	?	?
3 ***Cannon***	N	Y	?	N	Y	Y	Y	Y
VERMONT								
AL *Sanders*	Y	N	N	Y	N	N	N	N
VIRGINIA								
1 ***Bateman***	N	Y	Y	N	Y	Y	Y	Y
2 Pickett	Y	N	N	Y	N	N	N	N
3 Scott	Y	?	?	?	N	N	N	N
4 Sisisky	Y	Y	N	N	N	N	N	N
5 *Goode*	N	Y	Y	N	Y	Y	Y	Y
6 ***Goodlatte***	N	Y	Y	N	Y	?	Y	Y
7 ***Bliley***	N	Y	Y	N	Y	Y	Y	Y
8 Moran	?	N	N	Y	N	N	N	N
9 Boucher	Y	N	N	Y	N	N	N	N
10 ***Wolf***	N	Y	Y	N	Y	Y	Y	Y
11 ***Davis***	N	Y	Y	N	Y	Y	Y	Y
WASHINGTON								
1 Inslee	Y	N	N	Y	N	N	N	N
2 ***Metcalf***	N	Y	Y	N	Y	Y	Y	Y
3 Baird	Y	N	N	Y	N	N	N	N
4 ***Hastings***	N	Y	Y	N	Y	Y	Y	Y
5 ***Nethercutt***	N	Y	Y	N	Y	Y	Y	Y
6 Dicks	Y	N	Y	Y	N	N	N	N
7 McDermott	Y	N	N	Y	N	N	N	N
8 ***Dunn***	N	Y	Y	N	Y	Y	Y	Y
9 Smith	Y	N	N	Y	N	N	N	N
WEST VIRGINIA								
1 Mollohan	Y	Y	N	N	N	N	N	N
2 Wise	?	N	N	N	N	N	N	N
3 Rahall	N	N	N	N	N	N	N	N
WISCONSIN								
1 ***Ryan***	N	Y	Y	N	Y	Y	Y	Y
2 Baldwin	Y	N	N	Y	N	N	N	N
3 Kind	N	N	N	N	N	N	N	N
4 Kleczka	Y	N	N	N	N	N	N	N
5 Barrett	Y	N	N	Y	N	N	N	N
6 ***Petri***	N	Y	Y	N	Y	Y	Y	Y
7 Obey	Y	N	N	Y	N	N	N	N
8 ***Green***	N	Y	Y	N	Y	Y	Y	Y
9 ***Sensenbrenner***	N	Y	Y	N	Y	Y	Y	Y
WYOMING								
AL ***Cubin***	N	Y	Y	N	Y	Y	Y	Y

Southern states - Ala., Ark., Fla., Ga., Ky., La., Miss., N.C., Okla., S.C., Tenn., Texas, Va.

351. Procedural Motion/Adjourn. Moakley, D-Mass., motion to adjourn. Motion rejected 178-244: R 0-215; D 177-28 (ND 129-22, SD 48-6); I 1-1. June 28, 2000.

352. HR 4680. Procedural Motion/Use of Exhibits. Judgment of the House as to whether Menendez, D-N.J., shall be permitted to use an exhibit on the House floor during debate on the bill to provide prescription drug coverage for Medicare beneficiaries. Agreed to use of the exhibit 371-48: R 196-18; D 173-30 (ND 129-22, SD 44-8); I 2-0. June 28, 2000.

353. HR 4680. Procedural Motion/Use of Exhibits. Judgment of the House as to whether Olver, D-Mass., shall be permitted to use an exhibit on the House floor during debate on the bill to provide prescription drug coverage for Medicare beneficiaries. Agreed to use of the exhibit 326-92: R 132-80; D 192-12 (ND 141-10, SD 51-2); I 2-0. June 28, 2000.

354. HR 4680. Procedural Motion/Use of Exhibits. Judgment of the House as to whether Hooley, D-Ore., shall be permitted to use an exhibit on the House floor during debate on the bill to provide prescription drug coverage for Medicare beneficiaries. Agreed to use of the exhibit 224-191: R 36-177; D 187-13 (ND 139-9, SD 48-4); I 1-1. June 28, 2000.

355. HR 4680. Prescription Drugs/Appeal Ruling of the Chair. Thomas, R-Calif., motion to table (kill) the Weygand, D-R.I., appeal of the ruling of the chair sustaining the Thomas point of order that the Stark, D-Calif., motion to recommit with instructions violates the Budget Act and the Ways and Means Committee's allocation of new budget authority. Motion agreed to 224-202: R 219-0; D 4-201 (ND 4-149, SD 0-52); I 1-1. June 28, 2000.

356. HR 4680. Prescription Drugs/Recommit. Stark, D-Calif., motion to recommit the bill to the House Ways and Means Committee with instructions to report it back with a Medicare prescription plan made available to all Medicare beneficiaries. Motion rejected 204-222: R 0-219; D 203-2 (ND 149-2, SD 54-0); I 1-1. June 28, 2000.

357. HR 4680. Prescription Drugs/Passage. Passage of the bill that would provide prescription drug coverage for Medicare beneficiaries and establish the Medicare Benefits Administration within the Department of Health and Human Services to administer the program. The benefit would be provided by private insurers with a choice between at least two plans. Passed 217-214: R 211-10; D 5-203 (ND 4-150, SD 1-53); I 1-1. June 28, 2000. A "nay" was a vote in support of the president's position.

358. HR 4461. Fiscal 2001 Agriculture Appropriations/Rule. Adoption of the rule (H Res 538) to provide for House floor consideration of the bill to appropriate funds for the Agriculture Department in fiscal year 2001. Adopted 232-179: R 216-0; D 15-178 (ND 11-132, SD 4-46); I 1-1. June 28, 2000.

Key

Y Voted for (yea).
\# Paired for.
\+ Announced for.
N Voted against (nay).
X Paired against.
– Announced against.
P Voted "present."
C Voted "present" to avoid possible conflict of interest.
? Did not vote or otherwise make a position known.

•

Democrats ***Republicans***
Independents

	351	352	353	354	355	356	357	358
ALABAMA								
1 ***Callahan***	N	Y	Y	P	Y	N	Y	Y
2 ***Everett***	N	Y	N	N	Y	N	Y	Y
3 ***Riley***	N	Y	Y	N	Y	N	Y	Y
4 ***Aderholt***	N	Y	Y	Y	Y	N	Y	Y
5 Cramer	Y	Y	Y	Y	N	Y	N	N
6 ***Bachus***	N	Y	Y	N	Y	N	Y	Y
7 Hilliard	Y	Y	Y	Y	N	Y	N	N
ALASKA								
AL ***Young***	N	Y	?	N	Y	N	Y	Y
ARIZONA								
1 ***Salmon***	N	Y	Y	Y	Y	N	Y	Y
2 Pastor	Y	Y	Y	Y	N	Y	N	N
3 ***Stump***	N	Y	Y	N	Y	N	Y	Y
4 ***Shadegg***	N	Y	N	N	Y	N	Y	Y
5 ***Kolbe***	N	Y	Y	N	Y	N	Y	Y
6 ***Hayworth***	N	Y	N	N	Y	N	Y	Y
ARKANSAS								
1 Berry	Y	Y	Y	Y	N	Y	N	N
2 Snyder	Y	Y	Y	Y	N	Y	N	N
3 ***Hutchinson***	N	N	Y	N	Y	N	Y	Y
4 ***Dickey***	N	Y	Y	N	Y	N	Y	Y
CALIFORNIA								
1 Thompson	Y	Y	Y	Y	N	Y	N	N
2 ***Herger***	?	Y	Y	N	Y	N	Y	Y
3 ***Ose***	N	Y	Y	N	Y	N	Y	Y
4 ***Doolittle***	N	Y	Y	N	Y	N	Y	Y
5 Matsui	Y	N	Y	Y	N	Y	N	?
6 Woolsey	Y	Y	Y	Y	N	Y	N	N
7 Miller, George	Y	Y	Y	Y	N	Y	N	?
8 Pelosi	Y	?	Y	Y	N	Y	N	?
9 Lee	Y	Y	Y	Y	N	Y	N	N
10 Tauscher	Y	Y	Y	Y	N	Y	N	N
11 ***Pombo***	?	Y	N	N	Y	N	Y	Y
12 Lantos	Y	Y	Y	Y	N	Y	N	N
13 Stark	Y	Y	N	Y	N	Y	N	?
14 Eshoo	Y	Y	Y	Y	N	Y	N	N
15 ***Campbell***	N	Y	Y	N	Y	N	Y	Y
16 Lofgren	N	Y	Y	Y	N	Y	N	N
17 Farr	Y	Y	Y	Y	N	Y	N	N
18 Condit	Y	Y	Y	Y	N	Y	N	N
19 ***Radanovich***	?	N	N	N	Y	N	Y	Y
20 Dooley	Y	Y	?	?	N	Y	N	N
21 ***Thomas***	N	N	N	N	Y	N	Y	Y
22 Capps	Y	Y	Y	Y	N	Y	N	N
23 ***Gallegly***	N	Y	Y	Y	Y	N	Y	Y
24 Sherman	Y	Y	Y	Y	N	Y	N	N
25 ***McKeon***	N	Y	Y	N	Y	N	Y	Y
26 Berman	Y	Y	Y	Y	N	Y	N	N
27 ***Rogan***	N	Y	N	N	Y	N	Y	Y
28 ***Dreier***	N	Y	Y	N	Y	N	Y	Y
29 Waxman	Y	?	Y	Y	N	Y	N	?
30 Becerra	Y	Y	Y	Y	N	Y	N	N
31 Martinez	N	Y	Y	?	Y	N	Y	?
32 Dixon	Y	Y	Y	Y	N	Y	N	N
33 Roybal-Allard	Y	Y	Y	Y	N	Y	N	N
34 Napolitano	Y	Y	Y	Y	N	Y	N	N
35 Waters	Y	Y	Y	Y	N	Y	N	N
36 ***Kuykendall***	N	Y	Y	N	Y	N	Y	Y
37 Millender-McD.	Y	Y	Y	Y	N	Y	N	N
38 ***Horn***	N	Y	Y	Y	Y	N	Y	Y
39 ***Royce***	N	Y	Y	N	Y	N	Y	Y
40 ***Lewis***	N	Y	Y	N	Y	N	Y	Y
41 ***Miller, Gary***	N	N	Y	N	Y	N	Y	Y
42 Baca	Y	Y	Y	Y	N	Y	N	N
43 ***Calvert***	N	Y	Y	N	Y	N	Y	Y
44 ***Bono***	N	Y	Y	N	Y	N	Y	Y
45 ***Rohrabacher***	N	Y	N	N	Y	N	Y	Y
46 Sanchez	Y	Y	Y	Y	N	Y	N	N
47 ***Cox***	N	N	N	Y	Y	N	Y	Y
48 ***Packard***	N	Y	N	N	Y	N	Y	Y
49 ***Bilbray***	N	Y	N	N	Y	N	Y	Y
50 Filner	Y	?	?	?	?	?	?	N
51 ***Cunningham***	N	Y	Y	N	Y	N	Y	Y
52 ***Hunter***	N	Y	Y	N	Y	N	Y	Y
COLORADO								
1 DeGette	Y	Y	Y	Y	N	?	N	N
2 Udall	Y	Y	Y	Y	N	Y	N	N
3 ***McInnis***	N	Y	Y	N	Y	N	Y	Y
4 ***Schaffer***	N	Y	N	N	Y	N	N	Y
5 ***Hefley***	N	N	N	N	Y	N	Y	?
6 ***Tancredo***	N	N	N	N	Y	N	Y	Y
CONNECTICUT								
1 Larson	N	Y	Y	Y	N	Y	N	N
2 Gejdenson	Y	Y	Y	Y	N	Y	N	N
3 DeLauro	Y	Y	Y	Y	N	Y	N	N
4 ***Shays***	N	Y	Y	Y	Y	N	Y	Y
5 Maloney	?	?	?	?	N	Y	Y	N
6 ***Johnson***	N	Y	Y	Y	Y	N	Y	Y
DELAWARE								
AL ***Castle***	N	Y	N	N	Y	N	Y	Y
FLORIDA								
1 ***Scarborough***	N	Y	Y	Y	Y	N	Y	Y
2 Boyd	Y	Y	Y	Y	N	Y	N	N
3 Brown	Y	Y	Y	Y	N	Y	N	N
4 ***Fowler***	N	Y	N	N	?	N	Y	Y
5 Thurman	N	Y	Y	Y	N	Y	N	N
6 ***Stearns***	N	?	Y	N	Y	N	Y	?
7 ***Mica***	N	N	N	N	Y	N	Y	Y
8 ***McCollum***	N	Y	Y	N	Y	N	Y	Y
9 ***Bilirakis***	N	Y	N	N	Y	N	Y	Y
10 ***Young***	N	Y	Y	N	Y	N	Y	Y
11 Davis	Y	Y	Y	?	N	Y	N	N
12 ***Canady***	N	Y	N	N	Y	N	Y	Y
13 ***Miller***	N	Y	Y	N	Y	N	Y	Y
14 ***Goss***	N	Y	N	N	Y	N	Y	Y
15 ***Weldon***	N	Y	N	?	Y	N	Y	Y
16 ***Foley***	N	Y	Y	Y	Y	N	Y	Y
17 Meek	Y	N	Y	Y	N	Y	N	N
18 ***Ros-Lehtinen***	N	Y	N	N	Y	N	Y	Y
19 Wexler	Y	Y	Y	Y	N	Y	N	Y
20 Deutsch	Y	N	Y	Y	N	Y	N	Y
21 ***Diaz-Balart***	N	Y	N	N	Y	N	Y	Y
22 ***Shaw***	N	Y	N	N	Y	N	Y	Y
23 Hastings	Y	Y	Y	Y	N	Y	N	N
GEORGIA								
1 ***Kingston***	N	Y	Y	Y	Y	N	Y	Y
2 Bishop	Y	Y	Y	Y	N	Y	N	N
3 ***Collins***	N	Y	N	N	Y	N	Y	Y
4 McKinney	Y	Y	Y	Y	N	Y	N	N
5 Lewis	Y	Y	Y	Y	N	Y	N	N
6 ***Isakson***	N	Y	N	N	Y	N	Y	Y
7 ***Barr***	N	N	N	N	Y	N	Y	Y
8 ***Chambliss***	N	Y	Y	Y	Y	N	Y	Y
9 ***Deal***	N	Y	N	N	Y	N	Y	Y
10 ***Norwood***	N	Y	Y	N	Y	N	Y	Y
11 ***Linder***	N	Y	Y	N	Y	N	Y	Y
HAWAII								
1 Abercrombie	Y	Y	Y	?	N	Y	N	N
2 Mink	Y	N	N	N	N	Y	N	N
IDAHO								
1 ***Chenoweth-Hage***	N	Y	N	N	Y	N	N	Y
2 ***Simpson***	N	Y	N	N	Y	N	Y	Y
ILLINOIS								
1 Rush	Y	Y	Y	Y	N	Y	N	N
2 Jackson	Y	Y	Y	Y	N	Y	N	N
3 Lipinski	N	Y	Y	Y	N	Y	N	N
4 Gutierrez	Y	Y	Y	?	N	Y	N	Y
5 Blagojevich	Y	Y	Y	Y	N	Y	N	N
6 ***Hyde***	N	Y	N	N	Y	N	Y	Y
7 Davis	Y	N	Y	Y	N	Y	N	N
8 ***Crane***	N	?	?	N	Y	N	Y	Y
9 Schakowsky	Y	Y	Y	Y	N	Y	N	N
10 ***Porter***	N	Y	N	N	Y	N	Y	Y
11 ***Weller***	N	Y	Y	N	Y	N	Y	Y
12 Costello	N	Y	Y	Y	N	Y	N	N
13 ***Biggert***	N	Y	N	N	Y	N	Y	Y

ND Northern Democrats SD Southern Democrats

	351	352	353	354	355	356	357	358
14 ***Hastert***	N					N	Y	Y
15 ***Ewing***	N	N	?	?	Y	N	Y	Y
16 ***Manzullo***	N	Y	Y	N	Y	N	Y	Y
17 Evans	N	N	Y	Y	N	Y	N	N
18 ***LaHood***	N	Y	Y	Y	Y	N	Y	Y
19 Phelps	N	Y	Y	Y	N	Y	N	N
20 ***Shimkus***	N	Y	N	N	Y	N	Y	Y
INDIANA								
1 Visclosky	Y	Y	Y	Y	N	Y	N	N
2 ***McIntosh***	N	?	?	N	Y	N	Y	Y
3 Roemer	N	Y	Y	Y	N	Y	N	N
4 ***Souder***	N	Y	N	?	Y	N	Y	Y
5 ***Buyer***	N	Y	Y	N	Y	N	Y	Y
6 ***Burton***	N	Y	Y	N	Y	N	Y	Y
7 ***Pease***	N	Y	N	N	Y	N	Y	Y
8 ***Hostettler***	N	Y	Y	N	Y	N	N	Y
9 Hill	Y	Y	Y	Y	N	Y	N	N
10 Carson	Y	Y	Y	Y	N	Y	N	N
IOWA								
1 ***Leach***	N	Y	Y	Y	Y	N	Y	Y
2 ***Nussle***	N	Y	Y	Y	Y	N	Y	Y
3 Boswell	Y	Y	Y	Y	N	Y	N	N
4 ***Ganske***	N	Y	Y	Y	Y	N	N	Y
5 ***Latham***	N	Y	Y	N	Y	N	Y	Y
KANSAS								
1 ***Moran***	N	Y	N	N	Y	N	Y	Y
2 ***Ryun***	N	Y	N	N	Y	N	Y	Y
3 Moore	Y	Y	Y	Y	N	Y	N	N
4 ***Tiahrt***	N	Y	N	N	Y	N	Y	Y
KENTUCKY								
1 ***Whitfield***	N	Y	N	N	Y	N	Y	Y
2 ***Lewis***	N	Y	N	N	Y	N	Y	Y
3 ***Northup***	N	Y	Y	N	Y	N	Y	Y
4 Lucas	Y	Y	Y	Y	N	Y	N	N
5 ***Rogers***	N	Y	N	N	Y	N	Y	Y
6 ***Fletcher***	N	Y	Y	N	Y	N	Y	Y
LOUISIANA								
1 ***Vitter***	N	Y	Y	N	Y	N	Y	Y
2 Jefferson	Y	Y	Y	Y	?	Y	N	N
3 ***Tauzin***	N	Y	Y	N	Y	N	Y	Y
4 ***McCrery***	N	Y	Y	Y	Y	N	Y	Y
5 ***Cooksey***	N	Y	N	N	Y	N	Y	Y
6 ***Baker***	N	Y	N	N	Y	N	Y	Y
7 John	Y	Y	Y	Y	N	Y	N	N
MAINE								
1 Allen	Y	N	Y	Y	N	Y	N	N
2 Baldacci	Y	N	Y	Y	N	Y	N	N
MARYLAND								
1 ***Gilchrest***	N	Y	Y	N	Y	N	Y	Y
2 ***Ehrlich***	N	Y	Y	N	Y	N	Y	Y
3 Cardin	Y	Y	Y	Y	N	Y	N	N
4 Wynn	Y	Y	Y	Y	N	Y	N	N
5 Hoyer	Y	Y	Y	Y	N	Y	N	N
6 ***Bartlett***	N	Y	Y	N	Y	N	Y	Y
7 Cummings	Y	Y	Y	Y	N	Y	N	N
8 ***Morella***	N	Y	Y	Y	Y	N	N	Y
MASSACHUSETTS								
1 Olver	?	Y	N	N	N	Y	N	N
2 Neal	Y	N	Y	Y	N	Y	N	N
3 McGovern	Y	Y	Y	Y	N	Y	N	N
4 Frank	Y	Y	Y	Y	N	Y	N	N
5 Meehan	Y	Y	Y	Y	N	Y	N	N
6 Tierney	Y	N	N	Y	N	Y	N	N
7 Markey	?	?	?	?	?	?	?	?
8 Capuano	Y	N	N	N	N	Y	N	N
9 Moakley	Y	Y	Y	Y	N	Y	N	N
10 Delahunt	Y	Y	Y	Y	N	Y	N	N
MICHIGAN								
1 Stupak	Y	Y	Y	Y	N	Y	N	N
2 ***Hoekstra***	N	Y	Y	N	Y	N	Y	Y
3 ***Ehlers***	N	Y	Y	N	Y	N	Y	Y
4 ***Camp***	N	Y	Y	Y	Y	N	Y	Y
5 Barcia	N	Y	Y	Y	Y	N	N	N
6 ***Upton***	N	Y	Y	N	Y	N	Y	Y
7 ***Smith***	N	Y	Y	Y	Y	N	N	Y
8 Stabenow	Y	Y	Y	Y	N	Y	N	N
9 Kildee	Y	Y	Y	Y	N	Y	N	N
10 Bonior	Y	N	Y	Y	N	Y	N	N
11 ***Knollenberg***	N	Y	Y	N	Y	?	Y	Y
12 Levin	Y	Y	Y	Y	N	Y	N	N
13 Rivers	Y	Y	Y	Y	N	Y	N	N
14 Conyers	Y	Y	Y	Y	N	Y	N	N
15 Kilpatrick	Y	Y	Y	Y	N	Y	N	N
16 Dingell	Y	N	Y	Y	N	Y	N	N

	351	352	353	354	355	356	357	358
MINNESOTA								
1 ***Gutknecht***	N	Y	N	N	Y	N	Y	Y
2 Minge	Y	Y	Y	Y	N	Y	N	N
3 ***Ramstad***	N	Y	Y	N	Y	N	Y	Y
4 Vento	?	?	?	?	?	?	?	?
5 Sabo	Y	Y	Y	Y	N	Y	N	N
6 Luther	Y	Y	Y	Y	N	Y	N	N
7 Peterson	N	Y	Y	N	Y	Y	Y	N
8 Oberstar	Y	Y	Y	Y	N	Y	N	N
MISSISSIPPI								
1 ***Wicker***	N	Y	N	N	Y	N	Y	Y
2 Thompson	Y	Y	Y	Y	N	Y	N	N
3 ***Pickering***	N	Y	N	N	Y	N	Y	Y
4 Shows	Y	Y	Y	Y	N	Y	N	N
5 Taylor	Y	N	Y	N	N	Y	N	N
MISSOURI								
1 Clay	Y	Y	Y	Y	N	Y	N	?
2 ***Talent***	N	Y	Y	Y	Y	N	Y	Y
3 Gephardt	Y	Y	Y	Y	N	Y	N	N
4 Skelton	Y	Y	Y	Y	N	Y	N	N
5 McCarthy	Y	Y	Y	Y	N	Y	N	N
6 Danner	Y	N	Y	Y	N	Y	N	?
7 ***Blunt***	N	Y	Y	N	Y	N	Y	Y
8 ***Emerson***	N	N	Y	N	Y	N	Y	Y
9 ***Hulshof***	N	Y	N	N	Y	N	Y	Y
MONTANA								
AL ***Hill***	N	Y	Y	N	Y	N	Y	Y
NEBRASKA								
1 ***Bereuter***	N	Y	Y	N	Y	N	Y	Y
2 ***Terry***	N	N	N	N	Y	N	Y	Y
3 ***Barrett***	N	Y	Y	N	Y	N	Y	Y
NEVADA								
1 Berkley	Y	Y	Y	Y	N	Y	N	N
2 ***Gibbons***	N	Y	Y	N	Y	N	Y	Y
NEW HAMPSHIRE								
1 ***Sununu***	N	Y	N	N	Y	N	Y	Y
2 ***Bass***	N	Y	N	N	Y	?	Y	Y
NEW JERSEY								
1 Andrews	Y	Y	Y	Y	N	Y	N	Y
2 ***LoBiondo***	N	Y	Y	N	Y	N	Y	Y
3 ***Saxton***	N	Y	Y	N	Y	N	Y	Y
4 ***Smith***	N	Y	Y	Y	Y	N	Y	Y
5 ***Roukema***	N	Y	N	N	Y	N	Y	Y
6 Pallone	Y	Y	Y	Y	N	Y	N	Y
7 ***Franks***	N	Y	Y	N	Y	N	Y	Y
8 Pascrell	Y	Y	Y	Y	N	Y	N	Y
9 Rothman	Y	Y	Y	Y	N	Y	N	Y
10 Payne	Y	Y	Y	Y	N	Y	N	N
11 ***Frelinghuysen***	N	Y	Y	N	Y	N	Y	Y
12 Holt	N	Y	Y	Y	N	Y	N	Y
13 Menendez	Y	Y	Y	Y	N	Y	N	Y
NEW MEXICO								
1 ***Wilson***	N	Y	Y	P	Y	N	Y	Y
2 ***Skeen***	N	Y	Y	N	Y	N	Y	Y
3 Udall	N	Y	Y	Y	N	Y	N	N
NEW YORK								
1 Forbes	Y	Y	Y	?	N	Y	N	Y
2 ***Lazio***	N	Y	Y	Y	Y	N	Y	Y
3 ***King***	N	Y	Y	N	Y	N	Y	Y
4 McCarthy	Y	N	N	N	N	Y	N	N
5 Ackerman	Y	Y	Y	Y	N	Y	N	N
6 Meeks	Y	Y	Y	Y	N	Y	N	N
7 Crowley	Y	Y	Y	Y	N	Y	N	N
8 Nadler	Y	Y	Y	Y	N	Y	N	N
9 Weiner	Y	Y	Y	Y	N	Y	N	N
10 Towns	N	N	Y	Y	N	Y	N	N
11 Owens	N	Y	Y	Y	N	Y	N	N
12 Velázquez	Y	Y	Y	Y	N	Y	N	N
13 ***Fossella***	N	Y	Y	N	Y	N	Y	Y
14 Maloney	?	Y	Y	Y	N	Y	N	N
15 Rangel	Y	Y	Y	Y	N	Y	N	N
16 Serrano	Y	Y	Y	Y	?	+	N	N
17 Engel	Y	Y	Y	Y	N	Y	N	N
18 Lowey	Y	Y	Y	Y	N	Y	N	N
19 ***Kelly***	N	N	N	N	Y	N	Y	Y
20 ***Gilman***	?	Y	Y	Y	Y	N	Y	Y
21 McNulty	Y	Y	Y	Y	N	Y	N	N
22 ***Sweeney***	N	N	Y	N	Y	N	Y	Y
23 ***Boehlert***	N	Y	Y	Y	Y	N	Y	Y
24 ***McHugh***	N	Y	Y	N	Y	N	Y	Y
25 ***Walsh***	N	Y	Y	N	Y	N	Y	Y
26 Hinchey	Y	Y	Y	Y	N	Y	N	N
27 ***Reynolds***	N	Y	Y	N	Y	N	Y	Y
28 Slaughter	Y	N	Y	Y	N	Y	N	N
29 LaFalce	Y	Y	Y	Y	N	Y	N	N

	351	352	353	354	355	356	357	358
30 ***Quinn***	N	Y	Y	N	Y	N	Y	Y
31 ***Houghton***	N	Y	Y	N	Y	N	Y	Y
NORTH CAROLINA								
1 Clayton	Y	N	Y	Y	N	Y	N	N
2 Etheridge	N	Y	Y	Y	N	Y	N	N
3 ***Jones***	N	Y	Y	N	Y	N	Y	Y
4 Price	Y	Y	Y	Y	N	Y	N	N
5 ***Burr***	N	Y	N	N	Y	N	Y	Y
6 ***Coble***	N	Y	Y	N	Y	N	Y	Y
7 McIntyre	Y	Y	Y	Y	N	Y	N	Y
8 ***Hayes***	N	Y	Y	N	Y	N	Y	Y
9 ***Myrick***	?	Y	N	N	Y	N	Y	Y
10 ***Ballenger***	N	Y	N	N	Y	N	Y	Y
11 ***Taylor***	N	Y	N	N	Y	N	Y	Y
12 Watt	N	Y	Y	Y	N	Y	N	N
NORTH DAKOTA								
AL Pomeroy	Y	Y	Y	Y	N	Y	N	N
OHIO								
1 ***Chabot***	N	Y	Y	Y	Y	N	Y	Y
2 ***Portman***	N	Y	Y	Y	Y	N	Y	Y
3 Hall	Y	Y	Y	Y	N	Y	N	?
4 ***Oxley***	N	Y	Y	N	Y	N	Y	?
5 ***Gillmor***	N	Y	Y	N	Y	N	Y	Y
6 Strickland	?	Y	Y	Y	N	Y	N	N
7 ***Hobson***	N	Y	Y	Y	Y	N	Y	Y
8 ***Boehner***	N	Y	Y	N	Y	N	Y	Y
9 Kaptur	Y	Y	Y	Y	N	Y	N	N
10 Kucinich	N	Y	Y	Y	N	Y	N	N
11 Jones	Y	Y	Y	Y	N	Y	N	N
12 ***Kasich***	N	?	Y	N	Y	N	Y	Y
13 Brown	Y	N	Y	Y	N	Y	N	N
14 Sawyer	Y	Y	Y	Y	N	Y	N	N
15 ***Pryce***	N	Y	Y	N	Y	N	Y	Y
16 ***Regula***	N	Y	N	N	Y	N	Y	Y
17 Traficant	N	Y	Y	Y	Y	N	Y	Y
18 ***Ney***	N	Y	N	Y	Y	N	Y	Y
19 ***LaTourette***	N	Y	Y	N	Y	N	Y	Y
OKLAHOMA								
1 ***Largent***	N	Y	N	N	Y	N	Y	Y
2 ***Coburn***	N	N	Y	?	Y	N	N	Y
3 ***Watkins***	N	Y	N	N	Y	N	Y	Y
4 ***Watts***	N	Y	N	N	Y	N	Y	Y
5 ***Istook***	N	Y	Y	N	Y	N	N	Y
6 ***Lucas***	N	Y	N	N	Y	N	Y	Y
OREGON								
1 Wu	Y	N	N	N	Y	Y	N	Y
2 ***Walden***	N	Y	Y	Y	Y	N	Y	Y
3 Blumenauer	Y	Y	Y	Y	N	Y	N	N
4 DeFazio	Y	Y	Y	Y	N	Y	N	N
5 Hooley	N	N	Y	Y	N	?	N	N
PENNSYLVANIA								
1 Brady	Y	Y	Y	Y	N	Y	N	N
2 Fattah	Y	Y	Y	Y	N	Y	N	?
3 Borski	Y	Y	Y	Y	N	Y	N	N
4 Klink	N	Y	Y	Y	N	Y	N	N
5 ***Peterson***	N	Y	N	N	Y	N	Y	Y
6 Holden	Y	Y	Y	Y	N	Y	N	N
7 ***Weldon***	N	N	N	N	Y	N	Y	Y
8 ***Greenwood***	N	Y	N	N	Y	N	Y	Y
9 ***Shuster***	N	Y	Y	N	Y	N	Y	?
10 ***Sherwood***	N	N	N	N	Y	N	Y	Y
11 Kanjorski	Y	N	N	Y	N	Y	N	N
12 Murtha	Y	N	N	N	N	Y	N	?
13 Hoeffel	Y	Y	Y	Y	N	Y	N	N
14 Coyne	Y	Y	Y	Y	N	Y	N	N
15 ***Toomey***	N	Y	N	N	Y	N	Y	Y
16 ***Pitts***	N	Y	N	N	Y	N	Y	Y
17 ***Gekas***	N	Y	?	N	Y	N	Y	Y
18 Doyle	Y	Y	Y	Y	N	Y	N	N
19 ***Goodling***	?	?	?	N	Y	N	Y	?
20 Mascara	Y	Y	Y	Y	N	Y	N	N
21 ***English***	N	N	Y	N	Y	N	Y	Y
RHODE ISLAND								
1 Kennedy	Y	Y	?	Y	N	Y	N	N
2 Weygand	Y	N	N	N	N	Y	N	N
SOUTH CAROLINA								
1 ***Sanford***	N	Y	Y	N	Y	N	N	Y
2 ***Spence***	N	Y	N	N	Y	N	Y	Y
3 ***Graham***	N	Y	Y	N	Y	N	Y	Y
4 ***DeMint***	N	Y	N	N	Y	N	Y	Y
5 Spratt	Y	Y	Y	Y	N	Y	N	N
6 Clyburn	Y	Y	Y	Y	N	Y	N	N
SOUTH DAKOTA								
AL ***Thune***	N	Y	Y	N	Y	N	Y	Y

	351	352	353	354	355	356	357	358
TENNESSEE								
1 ***Jenkins***	N	Y	Y	N	Y	N	Y	Y
2 ***Duncan***	N	Y	Y	N	Y	N	Y	Y
3 ***Wamp***	N	Y	Y	N	Y	N	Y	Y
4 ***Hilleary***	N	Y	N	N	Y	N	Y	Y
5 Clement	Y	Y	Y	Y	N	Y	N	?
6 Gordon	N	Y	Y	Y	N	Y	N	?
7 ***Bryant***	N	Y	Y	N	Y	N	Y	Y
8 Tanner	Y	N	N	Y	N	Y	N	N
9 Ford	Y	Y	Y	Y	N	Y	N	N
TEXAS								
1 Sandlin	Y	Y	Y	Y	N	Y	N	N
2 Turner	Y	Y	Y	Y	N	Y	N	N
3 ***Johnson, Sam***	N	Y	Y	N	Y	N	Y	Y
4 Hall	N	Y	Y	Y	N	Y	Y	Y
5 ***Sessions***	N	Y	N	N	Y	N	Y	Y
6 ***Barton***	N	Y	Y	Y	Y	N	Y	Y
7 ***Archer***	N	?	?	N	Y	N	Y	Y
8 ***Brady***	N	Y	N	?	Y	N	Y	Y
9 Lampson	Y	Y	Y	N	N	Y	N	N
10 Doggett	Y	Y	Y	Y	N	Y	N	N
11 Edwards	Y	?	Y	Y	N	Y	N	N
12 ***Granger***	N	Y	N	N	Y	N	Y	Y
13 ***Thornberry***	N	Y	N	N	Y	N	Y	Y
14 ***Paul***	N	Y	N	Y	Y	N	N	Y
15 Hinojosa	Y	Y	Y	Y	?	Y	N	N
16 Reyes	Y	Y	Y	Y	N	Y	N	N
17 Stenholm	Y	Y	Y	Y	N	Y	N	N
18 Jackson-Lee	Y	N	Y	Y	N	Y	N	N
19 ***Combest***	N	Y	Y	N	Y	N	Y	Y
20 Gonzalez	Y	Y	Y	Y	N	Y	N	N
21 ***Smith***	N	Y	Y	N	Y	N	Y	Y
22 ***DeLay***	N	Y	N	N	Y	N	Y	Y
23 ***Bonilla***	N	Y	Y	N	Y	N	Y	Y
24 Frost	Y	Y	Y	Y	N	Y	N	N
25 Bentsen	Y	N	N	N	N	Y	N	N
26 ***Armey***	N	Y	N	N	Y	N	Y	Y
27 Ortiz	Y	Y	Y	N	N	Y	N	N
28 Rodriguez	Y	Y	Y	Y	N	Y	N	N
29 Green	N	N	Y	Y	N	Y	N	N
30 Johnson, E.B.	Y	Y	Y	Y	N	Y	N	N
UTAH								
1 ***Hansen***	N	Y	Y	N	Y	N	Y	Y
2 ***Cook***	?	?	?	?	?	?	?	?
3 ***Cannon***	N	Y	Y	N	Y	N	Y	Y
VERMONT								
AL *Sanders*	Y	Y	Y	Y	N	Y	N	N
VIRGINIA								
1 ***Bateman***	N	Y	?	N	Y	N	Y	Y
2 Pickett	Y	Y	Y	Y	N	Y	N	?
3 Scott	Y	Y	Y	Y	N	Y	N	N
4 Sisisky	Y	Y	Y	Y	N	Y	N	N
5 *Goode*	N	Y	Y	N	Y	N	Y	Y
6 ***Goodlatte***	N	Y	Y	Y	Y	N	Y	Y
7 ***Bliley***	N	Y	Y	N	Y	N	Y	Y
8 Moran	Y	?	?	?	N	Y	N	N
9 Boucher	Y	Y	Y	Y	N	Y	N	?
10 ***Wolf***	N	Y	Y	Y	Y	N	Y	Y
11 ***Davis***	N	Y	Y	Y	Y	N	Y	Y
WASHINGTON								
1 Inslee	Y	Y	Y	Y	N	Y	N	N
2 ***Metcalf***	N	Y	Y	Y	Y	N	Y	Y
3 Baird	Y	Y	Y	Y	N	Y	N	N
4 ***Hastings***	N	Y	Y	N	Y	N	Y	Y
5 ***Nethercutt***	N	Y	Y	N	Y	N	Y	Y
6 Dicks	Y	Y	Y	Y	N	Y	N	?
7 McDermott	Y	N	Y	Y	N	Y	N	N
8 ***Dunn***	N	Y	Y	Y	Y	N	Y	Y
9 Smith	Y	Y	Y	Y	N	Y	N	N
WEST VIRGINIA								
1 Mollohan	N	Y	Y	Y	N	Y	N	Y
2 Wise	N	Y	Y	Y	N	Y	N	N
3 Rahall	N	Y	Y	Y	N	Y	N	N
WISCONSIN								
1 ***Ryan***	N	Y	Y	N	Y	N	Y	Y
2 Baldwin	Y	Y	Y	Y	N	Y	N	N
3 Kind	N	Y	Y	Y	N	Y	N	N
4 Kleczka	N	Y	Y	Y	N	Y	N	N
5 Barrett	Y	Y	Y	Y	N	Y	N	N
6 ***Petri***	N	Y	Y	Y	Y	N	Y	Y
7 Obey	Y	Y	Y	Y	N	Y	N	N
8 ***Green***	N	Y	Y	N	Y	N	Y	Y
9 ***Sensenbrenner***	N	Y	N	N	Y	N	Y	Y
WYOMING								
AL ***Cubin***	N	Y	Y	N	Y	N	Y	Y

Southern states - Ala., Ark., Fla., Ga., Ky., La., Miss., N.C., Okla., S.C., Tenn., Texas, Va.

359. HR 4461. Fiscal 2001 Agriculture Appropriations/Appalachian Watershed Station. Ney, R-Ohio, amendment that would increase the North Appalachian Experimental Watershed Research Station appropriation by $100,000 offset by reducing funding for the Agriculture Department's Inspector General and Communications offices. Rejected 94-326: R 81-135; D 13-189 (ND 11-138, SD 2-51); I 0-2. June 29, 2000.

360. HR 4461. Fiscal 2001 Agriculture Appropriations/Asparagus Research. Hefley, R-Colo., amendment that would reduce the Agriculture Department's appropriation for special research and grant programs by $200,000 to try to eliminate a grant for "international asparagus competitiveness." Rejected 132-287: R 107-108; D 24-178 (ND 18-131, SD 6-47); I 1-1. June 29, 2000.

361. HR 4461. Fiscal 2001 Agriculture Appropriations/Agri-tourism. Hefley, R-Colo., amendment that would eliminate the Agriculture Department's agri-tourism program by reducing the entire $2 million appropriation. Rejected 94-319: R 83-130; D 11-187 (ND 9-136, SD 2-51); I 0-2. June 29, 2000.

362. HR 4425. Military Construction/Supplemental Appropriations/Conference Report. Adoption of the conference report on the bill that would appropriate $11.2 billion in emergency spending for fiscal 2000 and $8.83 billion for military construction for fiscal year 2001. Adopted (thus sent to the Senate) 306-110: R 171-44; D 135-64 (ND 92-54, SD 43-10); I 0-2. June 29, 2000.

363. H Res 535. Medicare Supplemental Funding/Adoption. Thomas, R-Calif., motion to suspend the rules and adopt the resolution expressing the sense of the House that upon receiving the Congressional Budget Office's mid-year re-estimates, the House shall promptly assess the figures and provide appropriate adjustments to the Medicare program during the second session of the 106th Congress. Adopted 404-8: R 210-4; D 192-4 (ND 141-4, SD 51-0); I 2-0. A two-thirds majority of those present and voting (275 in this case) is required for adoption under suspension of the rules. June 29, 2000.

364. HR 1304. Physician Collective Bargaining/Previous Question. Motion to order the previous question (thus ending debate and possibility of amendment) on adoption of the rule (H Res 542) to provide for House floor consideration of the bill to allow doctors to bargain collectively with insurance plans. Motion agreed to 241-174: R 210-1; D 30-172 (ND 22-127, SD 8-45); I 1-1. June 29, 2000.

365. HR 1304. Physician Collective Bargaining/Rule. Adoption of the rule (H Res 542) to provide for House floor consideration of the bill to allow doctors to bargain collectively with insurance plans. Adopted 225-197: R 143-73; D 81-123 (ND 58-93, SD 23-30); I 1-1. June 29, 2000.

Key

- Y Voted for (yea).
- # Paired for.
- \+ Announced for.
- N Voted against (nay).
- X Paired against.
- – Announced against.
- P Voted "present."
- C Voted "present" to avoid possible conflict of interest.
- ? Did not vote or otherwise make a position known.

•

Democrats ***Republicans***
Independents

	359	360	361	362	363	364	365
ALABAMA							
1 ***Callahan***	N	Y	N	Y	Y	Y	Y
2 ***Everett***	N	N	N	Y	Y	Y	Y
3 ***Riley***	Y	N	N	Y	Y	Y	Y
4 ***Aderholt***	Y	N	N	Y	Y	Y	Y
5 Cramer	N	N	N	Y	Y	N	Y
6 ***Bachus***	Y	Y	N	Y	Y	Y	Y
7 Hilliard	N	N	N	N	Y	N	N
ALASKA							
AL ***Young***	?	?	?	Y	Y	Y	N
ARIZONA							
1 ***Salmon***	N	Y	Y	Y	Y	Y	Y
2 Pastor	N	N	N	Y	Y	N	N
3 ***Stump***	N	Y	Y	Y	Y	Y	Y
4 ***Shadegg***	N	Y	Y	N	Y	Y	N
5 ***Kolbe***	N	N	N	Y	Y	Y	N
6 ***Hayworth***	Y	Y	Y	Y	Y	Y	N
ARKANSAS							
1 Berry	N	N	N	Y	Y	Y	Y
2 Snyder	N	N	N	Y	Y	N	Y
3 ***Hutchinson***	N	Y	N	Y	Y	Y	Y
4 ***Dickey***	N	Y	Y	Y	Y	Y	Y
CALIFORNIA							
1 Thompson	N	N	N	Y	Y	N	N
2 ***Herger***	N	N	N	Y	Y	Y	Y
3 ***Ose***	N	N	N	Y	Y	Y	Y
4 ***Doolittle***	N	N	N	N	Y	Y	Y
5 Matsui	N	N	?	Y	Y	N	N
6 Woolsey	N	N	N	N	Y	N	N
7 Miller, George	N	N	N	N	Y	N	N
8 Pelosi	N	N	N	N	Y	N	N
9 Lee	N	N	N	N	Y	N	N
10 Tauscher	N	N	N	Y	Y	N	N
11 ***Pombo***	N	N	N	N	Y	Y	Y
12 Lantos	N	N	N	Y	Y	N	N
13 Stark	N	N	N	N	N	Y	N
14 Eshoo	N	N	N	N	Y	N	N
15 ***Campbell***	Y	Y	Y	N	Y	N	Y
16 Lofgren	?	?	?	N	Y	N	N
17 Farr	N	N	N	Y	Y	N	N
18 Condit	N	N	N	Y	Y	N	N
19 ***Radanovich***	N	N	N	Y	Y	Y	Y
20 Dooley	N	N	N	Y	Y	N	N
21 ***Thomas***	Y	N	N	Y	Y	?	Y
22 Capps	N	N	N	Y	Y	N	N
23 ***Gallegly***	Y	N	N	Y	Y	Y	Y
24 Sherman	N	N	N	Y	Y	N	N
25 ***McKeon***	Y	N	N	Y	Y	Y	Y
26 Berman	N	N	N	Y	Y	N	N
27 ***Rogan***	N	Y	N	Y	Y	Y	Y
28 ***Dreier***	N	Y	Y	Y	Y	Y	Y
29 Waxman	N	N	N	Y	Y	N	N
30 Becerra	N	N	N	Y	Y	N	N
31 Martinez	Y	Y	N	?	?	Y	N
32 Dixon	N	N	N	Y	Y	N	N
33 Roybal-Allard	N	N	N	Y	Y	N	N
34 Napolitano	N	N	N	Y	Y	N	N
35 Waters	N	N	N	Y	Y	N	Y
36 ***Kuykendall***	Y	N	N	Y	Y	Y	Y
37 Millender-McD.	N	N	N	Y	Y	N	N
38 ***Horn***	Y	Y	Y	Y	Y	Y	Y
39 ***Royce***	N	Y	Y	N	Y	Y	N
40 ***Lewis***	N	N	N	Y	Y	?	N
41 ***Miller, Gary***	N	Y	Y	Y	Y	Y	N
42 Baca	N	N	N	Y	Y	N	Y
43 ***Calvert***	N	N	N	Y	Y	Y	Y
44 ***Bono***	N	N	N	Y	Y	Y	N
45 ***Rohrabacher***	N	N	Y	N	Y	Y	Y
46 Sanchez	N	N	N	Y	Y	N	Y
47 ***Cox***	N	Y	Y	N	Y	Y	Y
48 ***Packard***	N	N	N	Y	Y	Y	N
49 ***Bilbray***	Y	N	Y	Y	Y	Y	Y
50 Filner	?	?	?	?	?	?	?
51 ***Cunningham***	N	N	N	Y	Y	Y	N
52 ***Hunter***	Y	N	N	Y	Y	Y	N
COLORADO							
1 DeGette	N	Y	N	N	Y	N	N
2 Udall	N	Y	N	N	Y	N	N
3 ***McInnis***	Y	Y	Y	Y	Y	Y	N
4 ***Schaffer***	N	Y	Y	Y	Y	Y	N
5 ***Hefley***	N	Y	Y	Y	Y	Y	N
6 ***Tancredo***	N	Y	N	Y	Y	Y	Y
CONNECTICUT							
1 Larson	N	N	N	Y	Y	N	N
2 Gejdenson	N	Y	N	Y	Y	N	N
3 DeLauro	N	N	N	Y	Y	N	N
4 ***Shays***	N	Y	Y	Y	Y	Y	N
5 Maloney	N	N	N	Y	Y	N	Y
6 ***Johnson***	Y	Y	N	Y	Y	Y	N
DELAWARE							
AL ***Castle***	N	N	N	Y	Y	Y	Y
FLORIDA							
1 ***Scarborough***	Y	Y	Y	Y	Y	Y	Y
2 Boyd	N	N	N	N	Y	N	N
3 Brown	N	N	N	Y	Y	N	N
4 ***Fowler***	Y	N	Y	Y	Y	Y	Y
5 Thurman	N	N	N	N	Y	N	N
6 ***Stearns***	Y	Y	Y	Y	Y	Y	Y
7 ***Mica***	N	Y	Y	Y	Y	Y	Y
8 ***McCollum***	N	Y	N	Y	Y	Y	Y
9 ***Bilirakis***	Y	Y	N	Y	Y	Y	Y
10 ***Young***	N	N	N	Y	Y	?	?
11 Davis	N	N	N	N	Y	N	N
12 ***Canady***	N	N	N	?	Y	Y	Y
13 ***Miller***	Y	Y	Y	Y	Y	Y	Y
14 ***Goss***	N	Y	Y	Y	Y	Y	Y
15 ***Weldon***	N	N	N	Y	Y	Y	Y
16 ***Foley***	Y	N	N	Y	Y	Y	Y
17 Meek	N	N	N	Y	?	N	N
18 ***Ros-Lehtinen***	Y	Y	Y	Y	Y	Y	Y
19 Wexler	N	N	N	N	Y	N	N
20 Deutsch	N	N	N	N	Y	N	N
21 ***Diaz-Balart***	N	Y	Y	Y	Y	Y	Y
22 ***Shaw***	Y	Y	Y	Y	Y	Y	Y
23 Hastings	N	N	N	N	Y	N	N
GEORGIA							
1 ***Kingston***	Y	Y	Y	N	Y	Y	N
2 Bishop	?	?	?	?	?	?	?
3 ***Collins***	Y	N	N	Y	Y	Y	Y
4 McKinney	N	N	N	N	Y	N	Y
5 Lewis	N	N	N	N	Y	N	N
6 ***Isakson***	Y	N	N	Y	Y	Y	Y
7 ***Barr***	Y	Y	Y	Y	Y	Y	Y
8 ***Chambliss***	N	N	N	Y	Y	Y	N
9 ***Deal***	N	N	N	Y	Y	Y	Y
10 ***Norwood***	N	N	N	Y	Y	Y	Y
11 ***Linder***	N	Y	Y	Y	Y	Y	Y
HAWAII							
1 Abercrombie	N	N	N	N	Y	Y	Y
2 Mink	N	N	N	Y	Y	N	N
IDAHO							
1 ***Chenoweth-Hage***	N	N	N	N	Y	Y	Y
2 ***Simpson***	N	N	N	Y	Y	Y	Y
ILLINOIS							
1 Rush	N	N	N	N	Y	N	N
2 Jackson	Y	N	N	N	Y	N	N
3 Lipinski	N	N	?	Y	Y	N	Y
4 Gutierrez	N	N	N	N	Y	N	N
5 Blagojevich	N	N	N	Y	Y	N	N
6 ***Hyde***	N	N	N	Y	Y	Y	Y
7 Davis	N	N	N	N	Y	N	N
8 ***Crane***	Y	Y	Y	Y	Y	Y	Y
9 Schakowsky	N	N	N	N	Y	N	N
10 ***Porter***	N	Y	N	N	Y	Y	Y
11 ***Weller***	Y	Y	N	Y	Y	Y	Y
12 Costello	N	Y	N	N	Y	N	Y
13 ***Biggert***	Y	N	N	Y	Y	Y	N

ND Northern Democrats SD Southern Democrats

	359	360	361	362	363	364	365
14 ***Hastert***				Y		Y	Y
15 ***Ewing***	N	Y	Y	?	Y	Y	N
16 ***Manzullo***	Y	Y	?	N	Y	Y	Y
17 Evans	N	N	N	Y	Y	N	N
18 ***LaHood***	N	N	N	Y	Y	Y	N
19 Phelps	N	N	N	N	Y	N	Y
20 ***Shimkus***	Y	N	N	Y	Y	Y	Y
INDIANA							
1 Visclosky	N	N	N	N	Y	N	N
2 ***McIntosh***	?	?	?	?	?	?	?
3 Roemer	N	N	N	N	Y	N	Y
4 ***Souder***	N	N	Y	Y	Y	Y	Y
5 ***Buyer***	Y	N	N	Y	Y	Y	N
6 ***Burton***	N	N	N	Y	Y	Y	N
7 ***Pease***	N	N	N	Y	Y	Y	N
8 ***Hostettler***	Y	Y	N	Y	Y	Y	N
9 Hill	N	N	N	N	Y	N	N
10 Carson	N	N	N	Y	Y	N	N
IOWA							
1 ***Leach***	N	Y	Y	Y	Y	Y	Y
2 ***Nussle***	N	N	N	N	Y	Y	N
3 Boswell	N	N	N	N	Y	N	Y
4 ***Ganske***	N	Y	Y	N	Y	P	Y
5 ***Latham***	N	N	N	Y	Y	Y	N
KANSAS							
1 ***Moran***	N	N	Y	N	Y	Y	Y
2 ***Ryun***	N	Y	N	N	Y	Y	N
3 Moore	N	Y	N	Y	Y	N	N
4 ***Tiahrt***	N	Y	N	Y	Y	Y	N
KENTUCKY							
1 ***Whitfield***	Y	N	N	Y	Y	Y	Y
2 ***Lewis***	N	N	N	Y	Y	Y	N
3 ***Northup***	N	N	N	Y	Y	Y	N
4 Lucas	N	N	N	Y	Y	Y	Y
5 ***Rogers***	N	N	N	Y	Y	Y	Y
6 ***Fletcher***	N	N	N	Y	Y	Y	Y
LOUISIANA							
1 ***Vitter***	Y	Y	Y	Y	Y	Y	Y
2 Jefferson	N	N	N	Y	Y	N	N
3 ***Tauzin***	Y	N	N	Y	Y	Y	Y
4 ***McCrery***	Y	N	N	Y	Y	Y	N
5 ***Cooksey***	N	N	N	Y	Y	Y	Y
6 ***Baker***	N	Y	Y	Y	Y	Y	Y
7 John	N	N	N	Y	Y	N	N
MAINE							
1 Allen	N	N	N	Y	Y	N	N
2 Baldacci	N	N	N	Y	Y	N	N
MARYLAND							
1 ***Gilchrest***	Y	Y	N	Y	Y	Y	Y
2 ***Ehrlich***	Y	Y	Y	Y	Y	Y	N
3 Cardin	N	N	N	Y	Y	N	Y
4 Wynn	?	N	?	?	?	N	N
5 Hoyer	N	N	N	Y	Y	N	N
6 ***Bartlett***	Y	Y	N	Y	Y	Y	Y
7 Cummings	N	N	N	Y	Y	N	N
8 ***Morella***	N	Y	N	Y	Y	Y	Y
MASSACHUSETTS							
1 Olver	N	N	N	Y	Y	N	N
2 Neal	N	N	N	Y	Y	N	Y
3 McGovern	N	N	N	Y	Y	N	N
4 Frank	N	Y	Y	N	N	N	Y
5 Meehan	N	Y	Y	N	Y	N	Y
6 Tierney	N	N	Y	N	Y	N	N
7 Markey	?	?	?	?	?	?	?
8 Capuano	N	N	N	N	Y	N	N
9 Moakley	N	N	N	Y	Y	Y	Y
10 Delahunt	N	N	N	Y	Y	N	N
MICHIGAN							
1 Stupak	N	N	N	Y	Y	Y	Y
2 ***Hoekstra***	Y	N	Y	N	Y	Y	N
3 ***Ehlers***	Y	N	Y	N	N	Y	Y
4 ***Camp***	N	N	N	Y	Y	Y	N
5 Barcia	N	N	N	Y	Y	?	Y
6 ***Upton***	Y	N	N	N	Y	Y	Y
7 ***Smith***	N	N	N	N	Y	Y	Y
8 Stabenow	N	N	N	Y	Y	N	N
9 Kildee	N	N	N	Y	Y	Y	Y
10 Bonior	N	N	N	Y	Y	N	Y
11 ***Knollenberg***	N	N	N	Y	Y	Y	Y
12 Levin	N	N	N	Y	Y	N	Y
13 Rivers	N	N	N	N	Y	N	N
14 Conyers	N	N	N	N	?	N	Y
15 Kilpatrick	N	N	N	Y	Y	N	Y
16 Dingell	N	N	N	Y	Y	Y	Y

	359	360	361	362	363	364	365
MINNESOTA							
1 ***Gutknecht***	N	N	N	Y	Y	Y	N
2 Minge	N	Y	N	N	Y	N	N
3 ***Ramstad***	N	Y	Y	N	Y	Y	N
4 Vento	?	?	?	?	?	?	?
5 Sabo	N	N	N	N	Y	N	N
6 Luther	N	Y	N	N	Y	N	N
7 Peterson	N	N	N	N	Y	Y	N
8 Oberstar	N	N	N	Y	Y	Y	Y
MISSISSIPPI							
1 ***Wicker***	N	N	N	N	Y	Y	N
2 Thompson	N	N	N	Y	Y	N	N
3 ***Pickering***	N	Y	Y	Y	Y	Y	Y
4 Shows	N	Y	Y	Y	Y	Y	Y
5 Taylor	Y	Y	Y	Y	Y	N	Y
MISSOURI							
1 Clay	?	?	?	?	?	?	?
2 ***Talent***	N	N	N	Y	Y	Y	Y
3 Gephardt	N	N	N	Y	Y	N	Y
4 Skelton	N	N	N	Y	Y	N	N
5 McCarthy	N	N	N	Y	Y	N	N
6 Danner	N	N	N	N	Y	N	N
7 ***Blunt***	Y	Y	N	Y	Y	Y	Y
8 ***Emerson***	N	N	N	Y	Y	Y	Y
9 ***Hulshof***	N	N	N	N	Y	Y	Y
MONTANA							
AL ***Hill***	N	N	N	N	Y	Y	Y
NEBRASKA							
1 ***Bereuter***	N	Y	N	Y	Y	Y	N
2 ***Terry***	N	Y	Y	N	Y	Y	N
3 ***Barrett***	N	Y	N	Y	Y	Y	N
NEVADA							
1 Berkley	N	Y	Y	Y	Y	N	Y
2 ***Gibbons***	N	N	Y	Y	Y	Y	Y
NEW HAMPSHIRE							
1 ***Sununu***	Y	Y	Y	Y	Y	Y	N
2 ***Bass***	N	Y	N	Y	Y	Y	Y
NEW JERSEY							
1 Andrews	N	N	N	Y	Y	N	Y
2 ***LoBiondo***	N	Y	Y	Y	Y	Y	Y
3 ***Saxton***	N	N	N	Y	Y	Y	Y
4 ***Smith***	N	Y	N	Y	Y	Y	Y
5 ***Roukema***	N	Y	Y	Y	Y	Y	Y
6 Pallone	N	N	N	Y	Y	N	Y
7 ***Franks***	Y	Y	Y	Y	Y	Y	Y
8 Pascrell	N	Y	N	Y	Y	N	Y
9 Rothman	N	N	N	Y	Y	N	N
10 Payne	N	N	N	N	Y	N	Y
11 ***Frelinghuysen***	N	Y	Y	Y	Y	Y	Y
12 Holt	N	N	N	Y	Y	N	Y
13 Menendez	N	N	Y	Y	Y	N	N
NEW MEXICO							
1 ***Wilson***	N	Y	N	Y	Y	Y	Y
2 ***Skeen***	N	N	N	Y	Y	Y	N
3 Udall	N	Y	Y	Y	Y	N	N
NEW YORK							
1 Forbes	N	Y	N	Y	Y	Y	Y
2 ***Lazio***	?	?	?	?	?	Y	Y
3 ***King***	Y	N	N	Y	Y	Y	Y
4 McCarthy	N	Y	N	Y	Y	N	Y
5 Ackerman	N	N	N	N	Y	N	N
6 Meeks	N	N	N	Y	Y	N	N
7 Crowley	N	N	N	N	Y	N	N
8 Nadler	N	N	N	N	Y	N	Y
9 Weiner	N	N	N	Y	Y	N	Y
10 Towns	N	N	N	N	N	N	N
11 Owens	N	N	N	N	Y	N	N
12 Velázquez	N	N	N	N	Y	N	N
13 ***Fossella***	Y	Y	Y	Y	Y	Y	Y
14 Maloney	N	N	N	Y	Y	N	Y
15 Rangel	N	N	N	N	N	N	Y
16 Serrano	N	N	N	Y	Y	N	N
17 Engel	N	N	N	Y	Y	N	N
18 Lowey	N	N	N	Y	Y	N	N
19 ***Kelly***	Y	Y	Y	Y	Y	Y	Y
20 ***Gilman***	N	N	N	Y	Y	Y	Y
21 McNulty	?	?	?	?	?	?	?
22 ***Sweeney***	Y	Y	N	Y	Y	Y	Y
23 ***Boehlert***	N	N	N	Y	Y	Y	N
24 ***McHugh***	Y	N	N	Y	Y	Y	N
25 ***Walsh***	N	N	N	Y	Y	Y	N
26 Hinchey	N	N	N	Y	Y	N	Y
27 ***Reynolds***	N	N	N	Y	Y	Y	Y
28 Slaughter	N	N	N	N	Y	N	N
29 LaFalce	N	N	N	Y	Y	Y	Y

	359	360	361	362	363	364	365
30 ***Quinn***	Y	N	N	Y	Y	Y	N
31 ***Houghton***	Y	N	N	Y	Y	Y	N
NORTH CAROLINA							
1 Clayton	N	N	N	Y	Y	N	N
2 Etheridge	N	N	N	Y	Y	N	N
3 ***Jones***	N	Y	Y	Y	Y	Y	Y
4 Price	N	N	N	Y	Y	N	N
5 ***Burr***	Y	Y	Y	Y	Y	Y	N
6 ***Coble***	N	Y	N	Y	Y	Y	Y
7 McIntyre	N	N	N	Y	Y	Y	Y
8 ***Hayes***	N	N	N	Y	Y	Y	Y
9 ***Myrick***	N	Y	Y	Y	Y	Y	Y
10 ***Ballenger***	Y	Y	Y	Y	Y	Y	N
11 ***Taylor***	N	Y	Y	Y	?	?	?
12 Watt	N	N	N	Y	?	N	N
NORTH DAKOTA							
AL Pomeroy	N	N	N	Y	Y	N	N
OHIO							
1 ***Chabot***	Y	Y	Y	N	Y	Y	Y
2 ***Portman***	Y	Y	Y	Y	Y	Y	Y
3 Hall	Y	N	N	Y	Y	Y	Y
4 ***Oxley***	Y	Y	N	Y	Y	Y	N
5 ***Gillmor***	Y	N	N	Y	Y	Y	Y
6 Strickland	Y	N	N	?	?	N	Y
7 ***Hobson***	Y	Y	Y	Y	Y	Y	N
8 ***Boehner***	Y	N	N	Y	Y	Y	N
9 Kaptur	N	N	N	N	Y	N	N
10 Kucinich	Y	N	N	N	Y	P	N
11 Jones	N	N	N	?	?	N	N
12 ***Kasich***	Y	Y	Y	N	Y	Y	Y
13 Brown	N	N	N	N	Y	N	N
14 Sawyer	Y	N	N	Y	Y	N	Y
15 ***Pryce***	Y	N	N	Y	Y	Y	Y
16 ***Regula***	Y	N	N	Y	Y	Y	Y
17 Traficant	Y	N	Y	Y	Y	Y	Y
18 ***Ney***	Y	N	N	Y	Y	Y	Y
19 ***LaTourette***	Y	N	N	Y	Y	Y	Y
OKLAHOMA							
1 ***Largent***	N	Y	Y	N	Y	Y	N
2 ***Coburn***	N	Y	Y	N	Y	Y	Y
3 ***Watkins***	N	N	N	Y	Y	Y	N
4 ***Watts***	N	N	N	Y	Y	Y	N
5 ***Istook***	N	N	N	Y	Y	Y	Y
6 ***Lucas***	N	N	N	Y	Y	Y	Y
OREGON							
1 Wu	N	N	N	N	Y	N	N
2 ***Walden***	N	N	N	Y	Y	Y	Y
3 Blumenauer	N	N	N	N	Y	N	Y
4 DeFazio	N	N	N	N	Y	N	Y
5 Hooley	N	N	N	Y	Y	N	N
PENNSYLVANIA							
1 Brady	N	N	N	Y	Y	N	N
2 Fattah	Y	N	N	Y	Y	N	N
3 Borski	N	N	N	Y	Y	Y	N
4 Klink	?	?	?	?	?	?	?
5 ***Peterson***	Y	N	N	Y	Y	Y	Y
6 Holden	Y	N	N	Y	Y	Y	Y
7 ***Weldon***	N	Y	N	Y	Y	?	Y
8 ***Greenwood***	N	Y	N	Y	Y	P	Y
9 ***Shuster***	Y	N	N	?	?	?	?
10 ***Sherwood***	N	N	N	Y	Y	Y	Y
11 Kanjorski	N	N	N	Y	Y	N	Y
12 Murtha	N	N	N	Y	Y	Y	N
13 Hoeffel	N	N	N	Y	Y	N	Y
14 Coyne	N	N	?	N	Y	N	Y
15 ***Toomey***	N	Y	Y	Y	Y	Y	Y
16 ***Pitts***	N	N	N	N	Y	Y	N
17 ***Gekas***	N	N	N	N	Y	Y	N
18 Doyle	N	N	N	Y	Y	Y	Y
19 ***Goodling***	?	?	?	Y	?	Y	N
20 Mascara	N	N	N	Y	Y	Y	Y
21 ***English***	Y	Y	N	Y	Y	Y	Y
RHODE ISLAND							
1 Kennedy	N	N	N	Y	Y	N	Y
2 Weygand	N	N	?	Y	Y	Y	Y
SOUTH CAROLINA							
1 ***Sanford***	N	Y	Y	N	N	Y	Y
2 ***Spence***	N	Y	N	Y	Y	Y	N
3 ***Graham***	N	Y	N	Y	Y	Y	Y
4 ***DeMint***	Y	Y	Y	N	Y	Y	N
5 Spratt	N	N	N	Y	Y	N	Y
6 Clyburn	N	N	N	Y	Y	N	N
SOUTH DAKOTA							
AL ***Thune***	N	N	N	Y	Y	Y	Y

	359	360	361	362	363	364	365
TENNESSEE							
1 ***Jenkins***	N	N	N	Y	Y	Y	Y
2 ***Duncan***	Y	Y	Y	N	Y	Y	Y
3 ***Wamp***	Y	Y	Y	Y	Y	Y	Y
4 ***Hilleary***	Y	Y	Y	Y	Y	Y	Y
5 Clement	N	N	N	Y	Y	N	N
6 Gordon	N	N	N	Y	Y	N	Y
7 ***Bryant***	Y	Y	Y	Y	Y	Y	Y
8 Tanner	N	N	N	Y	Y	N	N
9 Ford	Y	N	N	Y	Y	N	N
TEXAS							
1 Sandlin	N	N	N	Y	Y	N	Y
2 Turner	N	N	N	Y	Y	Y	Y
3 ***Johnson, Sam***	N	Y	Y	Y	Y	Y	N
4 Hall	N	Y	N	Y	Y	Y	Y
5 ***Sessions***	N	Y	Y	Y	Y	Y	Y
6 ***Barton***	N	Y	Y	N	Y	Y	N
7 ***Archer***	N	Y	Y	Y	Y	Y	N
8 ***Brady***	N	Y	Y	N	Y	Y	Y
9 Lampson	N	N	N	Y	Y	N	Y
10 Doggett	N	Y	N	N	Y	N	Y
11 Edwards	N	Y	N	Y	Y	N	Y
12 ***Granger***	N	N	N	Y	Y	Y	Y
13 ***Thornberry***	N	N	N	Y	Y	Y	Y
14 ***Paul***	N	Y	Y	N	N	Y	Y
15 Hinojosa	N	N	N	Y	Y	N	N
16 Reyes	N	N	N	Y	Y	N	N
17 Stenholm	N	N	N	Y	Y	Y	Y
18 Jackson-Lee	N	N	N	Y	Y	N	Y
19 ***Combest***	N	N	N	N	Y	Y	N
20 Gonzalez	N	N	N	Y	Y	N	N
21 ***Smith***	N	N	N	Y	Y	Y	Y
22 ***DeLay***	Y	N	Y	Y	Y	Y	Y
23 ***Bonilla***	N	N	?	Y	Y	Y	N
24 Frost	N	N	N	Y	Y	N	Y
25 Bentsen	N	N	N	Y	Y	N	N
26 ***Armey***	Y	Y	Y	Y	Y	Y	Y
27 Ortiz	N	N	N	Y	Y	N	Y
28 Rodriguez	N	N	N	Y	Y	N	N
29 Green	N	N	N	Y	Y	N	Y
30 Johnson, E.B.	N	N	N	Y	Y	N	N
UTAH							
1 ***Hansen***	N	N	Y	Y	Y	Y	Y
2 ***Cook***	?	?	?	?	?	?	?
3 ***Cannon***	N	Y	Y	Y	N	Y	N
VERMONT							
AL *Sanders*	N	N	N	N	Y	N	N
VIRGINIA							
1 ***Bateman***	N	Y	N	Y	Y	Y	N
2 Pickett	N	N	N	Y	Y	Y	N
3 Scott	N	N	N	Y	Y	N	Y
4 Sisisky	N	Y	N	Y	Y	N	N
5 *Goode*	N	Y	N	N	Y	Y	Y
6 ***Goodlatte***	N	Y	N	N	Y	Y	Y
7 ***Bliley***	Y	Y	N	Y	Y	Y	N
8 Moran	N	N	N	Y	Y	N	N
9 Boucher	N	N	N	Y	Y	Y	Y
10 ***Wolf***	N	N	N	Y	Y	Y	Y
11 ***Davis***	N	Y	Y	Y	Y	Y	Y
WASHINGTON							
1 Inslee	N	Y	Y	Y	Y	N	N
2 ***Metcalf***	Y	N	N	Y	Y	Y	Y
3 Baird	N	N	N	N	Y	N	N
4 ***Hastings***	Y	N	?	?	?	?	?
5 ***Nethercutt***	Y	N	N	Y	Y	Y	Y
6 Dicks	N	N	N	Y	Y	N	N
7 McDermott	N	N	N	N	Y	N	N
8 ***Dunn***	N	N	N	N	Y	Y	N
9 Smith	N	N	Y	Y	Y	N	N
WEST VIRGINIA							
1 Mollohan	Y	N	N	?	Y	Y	Y
2 Wise	Y	?	N	Y	Y	N	Y
3 Rahall	Y	N	N	Y	Y	Y	Y
WISCONSIN							
1 ***Ryan***	N	Y	N	N	Y	Y	N
2 Baldwin	N	N	N	N	Y	N	N
3 Kind	N	Y	N	N	Y	N	N
4 Kleczka	N	N	N	N	?	N	Y
5 Barrett	N	Y	N	N	Y	N	N
6 ***Petri***	N	N	Y	N	Y	Y	Y
7 Obey	N	N	N	Y	Y	N	Y
8 ***Green***	N	Y	N	N	Y	Y	N
9 ***Sensenbrenner***	Y	Y	Y	N	Y	Y	N
WYOMING							
AL ***Cubin***	N	?	N	Y	Y	Y	Y

Southern states - Ala., Ark., Fla., Ga., Ky., La., Miss., N.C., Okla., S.C., Tenn., Texas, Va.

366. **Procedural Motion/Adjourn.** LaHood, R-Ill., motion to adjourn. Motion rejected 135-279: R 41-171; D 93-107 (ND 67-79, SD 26-28); I 1-1. June 29, 2000.

367. **HR 1304. Physician Collective Bargaining/Boycotts.** Ballenger, R-N.C., amendment to provide that the bill's antitrust exemptions would not apply to certain negotiations concerning pay or to health care professionals who have not submitted certain plans, disclosed certain information or engaged in boycotts of health plans. Rejected 71-345: R 69-144; D 2-199 (ND 1-147, SD 1-52); I 0-2. June 30, 2000 (after midnight on the day that began June 29).

368. **HR 1304. Physician Collective Bargaining/Antitrust Laws.** Stearns, R-Fla., amendment that would exempt groups of health care professionals engaged in negotiations with health plans from federal antitrust laws under certain conditions. Rejected 94-320: R 87-124; D 7-194 (ND 6-142, SD 1-52); I 0-2. June 30, 2000 (after midnight on the day that began June 29).

369. **HR 1304. Physician Collective Bargaining/Unions.** Cox, R-Calif., amendment that would clarify that a health care plan may not force a physician to join a union as a condition of employment. Rejected 201-214: R 185-27; D 15-186 (ND 1-147, SD 14-39); I 1-1. June 30, 2000 (after midnight on the day that began June 29).

370. **HR 1304. Physician Collective Bargaining/Fees.** Terry, R-Neb., amendment that would not apply the bill to negotiations between health care professionals and health insurance companies regarding fees. Rejected 78-338: R 76-136; D 2-200 (ND 2-147, SD 0-53); I 0-2 June 30, 2000 (after midnight on the day that began June 29).

371. **HR 1304. Physician Collective Bargaining/Abortions.** Coburn, R-Okla., amendment to exempt discussions regarding abortion coverage from collective bargaining. Adopted 213-202: R 177-34; D 35-167 (ND 26-123, SD 9-44); I 1-1. June 30, 2000 (after midnight on the day that began June 29).

372. **HR 1304. Physician Collective Bargaining/Passage.** Passage of the bill that would allow doctors to bargain collectively with insurance plans. They would be given the same treatment under antitrust laws that are given to labor organizations under the National Labor Relations Act although it would not amend that act in any way. Passed 276-136: R 123-87; D 151-49 (ND 105-42, SD 46-7); I 2-0. June 30, 2000 (after midnight on the day that began June 29).

Key

- Y Voted for (yea).
- # Paired for.
- + Announced for.
- N Voted against (nay).
- X Paired against.
- – Announced against.
- P Voted "present."
- C Voted "present" to avoid possible conflict of interest.
- ? Did not vote or otherwise make a position known.

•

Democrats *Republicans*
Independents

	366	367	368	369	370	371	372
ALABAMA							
1 *Callahan*	?	N	N	Y	N	Y	Y
2 *Everett*	N	N	N	Y	N	Y	Y
3 *Riley*	N	N	N	Y	N	Y	Y
4 *Aderholt*	N	N	N	Y	N	Y	Y
5 Cramer	N	N	N	N	N	N	Y
6 *Bachus*	N	N	N	Y	N	Y	Y
7 Hilliard	N	N	N	N	N	N	Y
ALASKA							
AL *Young*	Y	N	Y	Y	N	Y	N
ARIZONA							
1 *Salmon*	N	N	Y	Y	N	Y	Y
2 Pastor	N	N	N	N	N	N	Y
3 *Stump*	N	Y	Y	Y	Y	Y	N
4 *Shadegg*	Y	Y	Y	Y	Y	Y	N
5 *Kolbe*	N	Y	Y	Y	Y	N	Y
6 *Hayworth*	N	Y	Y	Y	Y	Y	N
ARKANSAS							
1 Berry	N	N	N	N	N	Y	Y
2 Snyder	Y	N	N	N	N	N	Y
3 *Hutchinson*	N	N	Y	Y	N	Y	Y
4 *Dickey*	N	N	N	Y	N	Y	Y
CALIFORNIA							
1 Thompson	Y	N	N	N	N	N	Y
2 *Herger*	N	N	Y	Y	N	Y	N
3 *Ose*	N	N	N	Y	N	N	Y
4 *Doolittle*	N	N	N	Y	N	Y	Y
5 Matsui	Y	N	N	N	N	N	Y
6 Woolsey	?	N	N	N	N	N	N
7 Miller, George	N	N	N	N	N	N	N
8 Pelosi	Y	N	N	N	N	N	N
9 Lee	N	N	?	N	N	N	N
10 Tauscher	Y	N	N	N	N	N	Y
11 *Pombo*	N	N	Y	Y	N	Y	Y
12 Lantos	Y	N	N	N	N	N	Y
13 Stark	Y	?	?	?	?	?	?
14 Eshoo	Y	N	N	N	N	N	N
15 *Campbell*	N	N	N	Y	N	N	Y
16 Lofgren	N	N	N	N	N	N	N
17 Farr	Y	N	N	N	N	N	Y
18 Condit	Y	N	N	N	N	N	Y
19 *Radanovich*	Y	Y	Y	Y	Y	Y	N
20 Dooley	Y	N	Y	N	N	N	N
21 *Thomas*	N	Y	Y	Y	Y	Y	N
22 Capps	N	N	N	N	N	N	N
23 *Gallegly*	N	N	N	Y	N	Y	Y
24 Sherman	N	N	N	N	N	N	N
25 *McKeon*	Y	Y	Y	Y	Y	Y	N
26 Berman	?	N	N	N	N	N	N
27 *Rogan*	N	N	N	Y	N	Y	Y
28 *Dreier*	N	Y	Y	Y	Y	Y	N
29 Waxman	Y	N	N	N	N	N	N
30 Becerra	N	N	N	N	N	N	P
31 Martinez	?	?	?	?	?	?	?
32 Dixon	N	N	N	N	N	N	N
33 Roybal-Allard	N	N	N	N	N	N	N
34 Napolitano	Y	N	N	N	N	N	Y
35 Waters	?	N	N	N	N	N	N
36 *Kuykendall*	N	N	N	Y	N	N	Y
37 Millender-McD.	N	N	N	N	N	N	N
38 *Horn*	N	N	N	N	N	N	Y
39 *Royce*	N	N	N	Y	N	Y	Y
40 *Lewis*	N	N	N	Y	N	Y	Y
41 *Miller, Gary*	Y	Y	Y	Y	Y	Y	N
42 Baca	N	N	N	N	N	N	Y
43 *Calvert*	N	N	N	Y	N	Y	Y
44 *Bono*	Y	Y	Y	Y	Y	N	N
45 *Rohrabacher*	N	N	N	Y	N	Y	Y
46 Sanchez	N	N	N	N	N	N	N
47 *Cox*	N	N	N	Y	Y	Y	N
48 *Packard*	N	Y	Y	Y	Y	Y	N
49 *Bilbray*	N	N	N	Y	N	N	Y
50 Filner	?	?	?	?	?	?	?
51 *Cunningham*	N	Y	Y	Y	N	Y	N
52 *Hunter*	N	N	N	Y	N	Y	Y
COLORADO							
1 DeGette	N	N	N	N	N	N	N
2 Udall	Y	N	N	N	N	N	Y
3 *McInnis*	N	N	Y	Y	N	Y	N
4 *Schaffer*	N	Y	N	Y	Y	Y	N
5 *Hefley*	Y	N	Y	Y	N	Y	Y
6 *Tancredo*	N	N	N	Y	Y	Y	Y
CONNECTICUT							
1 Larson	Y	N	Y	N	N	N	N
2 Gejdenson	N	N	N	N	N	N	Y
3 DeLauro	N	N	N	N	N	N	Y
4 *Shays*	N	N	Y	N	N	N	N
5 Maloney	N	N	N	N	N	N	Y
6 *Johnson*	Y	Y	Y	Y	Y	N	N
DELAWARE							
AL *Castle*	N	Y	Y	Y	Y	N	N
FLORIDA							
1 *Scarborough*	N	N	?	Y	N	Y	Y
2 Boyd	Y	N	N	Y	N	N	Y
3 Brown	Y	N	N	N	N	N	Y
4 *Fowler*	N	?	?	?	?	?	?
5 Thurman	Y	N	N	N	N	N	N
6 *Stearns*	N	N	Y	Y	N	Y	N
7 *Mica*	N	N	Y	Y	N	Y	Y
8 *McCollum*	N	N	N	Y	N	Y	Y
9 *Bilirakis*	N	N	Y	Y	Y	Y	N
10 *Young*	?	?	?	?	?	?	?
11 Davis	Y	N	Y	N	N	N	Y
12 *Canady*	N	N	N	Y	N	Y	Y
13 *Miller*	N	N	N	Y	N	N	Y
14 *Goss*	N	Y	Y	Y	Y	Y	N
15 *Weldon*	N	N	N	Y	N	Y	Y
16 *Foley*	N	N	N	Y	N	N	Y
17 Meek	Y	?	?	?	?	?	?
18 *Ros-Lehtinen*	N	N	N	Y	N	Y	Y
19 Wexler	N	N	N	N	N	N	N
20 Deutsch	N	N	N	N	N	N	N
21 *Diaz-Balart*	N	N	N	N	N	Y	Y
22 *Shaw*	N	N	N	Y	N	N	Y
23 Hastings	Y	N	N	N	N	N	N
GEORGIA							
1 *Kingston*	Y	Y	Y	Y	Y	Y	N
2 Bishop	N	N	N	N	N	N	Y
3 *Collins*	N	N	N	Y	N	Y	Y
4 McKinney	N	N	N	N	N	N	Y
5 Lewis	N	N	N	N	N	N	N
6 *Isakson*	N	N	N	Y	N	Y	Y
7 *Barr*	N	N	N	Y	N	Y	Y
8 *Chambliss*	Y	N	N	Y	N	Y	Y
9 *Deal*	N	N	N	Y	N	Y	Y
10 *Norwood*	N	N	N	Y	N	Y	Y
11 *Linder*	N	Y	N	?	?	Y	Y
HAWAII							
1 Abercrombie	Y	N	N	N	N	N	Y
2 Mink	Y	N	Y	N	N	N	N
IDAHO							
1 *Chenoweth-Hage*	N	N	N	Y	N	Y	Y
2 *Simpson*	N	N	N	Y	N	Y	Y
ILLINOIS							
1 Rush	N	N	N	?	N	N	Y
2 Jackson	Y	N	N	N	N	N	N
3 Lipinski	Y	N	N	N	N	Y	Y
4 Gutierrez	N	N	N	N	N	N	N
5 Blagojevich	Y	N	N	N	N	N	Y
6 *Hyde*	N	N	N	Y	N	Y	Y
7 Davis	N	N	N	N	N	N	Y
8 *Crane*	N	N	Y	Y	Y	Y	N
9 Schakowsky	Y	N	N	N	N	N	N
10 *Porter*	Y	N	N	Y	N	N	Y
11 *Weller*	N	N	N	N	N	Y	Y
12 Costello	N	N	N	N	N	Y	Y
13 *Biggert*	N	Y	Y	Y	Y	N	N

ND Northern Democrats SD Southern Democrats

	366	367	368	369	370	371	372
14 ***Hastert***	N	Y	Y	Y	Y	Y	
15 ***Ewing***	N	Y	N	Y	Y	Y	N
16 ***Manzullo***	N	N	N	Y	N	Y	Y
17 Evans	Y	N	N	N	N	N	Y
18 ***LaHood***	Y	Y	N	Y	N	Y	N
19 Phelps	N	N	N	N	N	Y	Y
20 ***Shimkus***	N	N	N	Y	N	Y	Y
INDIANA							
1 Visclosky	Y	N	N	N	N	N	N
2 ***McIntosh***	?	?	?	?	?	?	?
3 Roemer	N	N	N	N	N	Y	Y
4 ***Souder***	N	N	Y	Y	Y	Y	Y
5 ***Buyer***	Y	Y	Y	Y	Y	Y	N
6 ***Burton***	Y	Y	Y	Y	Y	Y	N
7 ***Pease***	N	Y	Y	Y	Y	Y	N
8 ***Hostettler***	Y	Y	Y	Y	Y	Y	N
9 Hill	Y	N	Y	N	N	N	Y
10 Carson	Y	N	N	N	N	N	Y
IOWA							
1 ***Leach***	N	N	N	Y	N	Y	Y
2 ***Nussle***	N	Y	Y	Y	Y	Y	N
3 Boswell	N	N	N	N	N	N	Y
4 ***Ganske***	N	N	N	Y	N	?	Y
5 ***Latham***	N	N	Y	Y	Y	Y	N
KANSAS							
1 ***Moran***	N	N	Y	Y	N	Y	Y
2 ***Ryun***	N	Y	Y	Y	Y	Y	N
3 Moore	Y	N	N	Y	N	N	Y
4 ***Tiahrt***	N	Y	Y	Y	Y	Y	N
KENTUCKY							
1 ***Whitfield***	N	N	N	Y	N	Y	Y
2 ***Lewis***	Y	Y	Y	Y	Y	Y	Y
3 ***Northup***	Y	N	Y	Y	N	Y	N
4 Lucas	N	N	N	N	N	Y	Y
5 ***Rogers***	N	Y	N	Y	Y	Y	N
6 ***Fletcher***	N	N	N	Y	N	Y	Y
LOUISIANA							
1 ***Vitter***	N	N	N	Y	N	Y	Y
2 Jefferson	Y	N	N	N	N	N	Y
3 ***Tauzin***	N	N	N	Y	N	Y	Y
4 ***McCrery***	N	Y	Y	Y	Y	Y	N
5 ***Cooksey***	N	N	N	Y	N	N	Y
6 ***Baker***	Y	N	N	Y	N	Y	Y
7 John	Y	N	N	Y	N	Y	Y
MAINE							
1 Allen	Y	N	N	N	N	N	Y
2 Baldacci	N	N	N	N	N	N	Y
MARYLAND							
1 ***Gilchrest***	N	N	N	Y	N	N	Y
2 ***Ehrlich***	N	N	Y	Y	N	Y	Y
3 Cardin	N	N	N	N	N	N	Y
4 Wynn	N	N	N	N	N	N	Y
5 Hoyer	Y	N	N	N	N	N	Y
6 ***Bartlett***	N	Y	N	Y	Y	Y	Y
7 Cummings	N	N	N	N	N	N	Y
8 ***Morella***	N	N	N	N	N	N	Y
MASSACHUSETTS							
1 Olver	Y	N	N	N	N	N	Y
2 Neal	Y	N	N	N	N	N	Y
3 McGovern	N	N	N	N	N	N	Y
4 Frank	Y	N	N	N	N	N	Y
5 Meehan	Y	N	N	N	N	N	Y
6 Tierney	N	N	N	N	N	N	Y
7 Markey	?	?	?	?	?	?	?
8 Capuano	N	N	N	N	N	N	Y
9 Moakley	N	N	N	N	N	Y	Y
10 Delahunt	Y	N	N	N	N	N	Y
MICHIGAN							
1 Stupak	N	N	N	N	N	Y	Y
2 ***Hoekstra***	Y	Y	Y	Y	Y	Y	N
3 ***Ehlers***	N	N	Y	Y	N	Y	N
4 ***Camp***	Y	N	N	Y	N	Y	Y
5 Barcia	N	N	N	N	N	Y	Y
6 ***Upton***	N	N	N	Y	N	Y	Y
7 ***Smith***	N	N	N	Y	N	Y	Y
8 Stabenow	Y	N	N	N	N	N	Y
9 Kildee	N	N	N	N	N	Y	Y
10 Bonior	N	N	N	N	N	N	Y
11 ***Knollenberg***	N	Y	Y	Y	Y	Y	N
12 Levin	N	N	N	N	N	N	Y
13 Rivers	Y	N	N	N	N	N	Y
14 Conyers	Y	N	N	N	N	N	Y
15 Kilpatrick	Y	N	N	N	N	N	N
16 Dingell	N	N	N	N	N	N	Y
MINNESOTA							
1 ***Gutknecht***	Y	Y	N	Y	N	Y	N
2 Minge	Y	N	N	N	N	N	N
3 ***Ramstad***	N	Y	Y	Y	Y	N	N
4 Vento	?	?	?	?	?	?	?
5 Sabo	Y	N	N	N	N	N	N
6 Luther	N	N	Y	N	N	N	N
7 Peterson	Y	N	N	N	N	Y	Y
8 Oberstar	N	N	N	N	N	Y	Y
MISSISSIPPI							
1 ***Wicker***	N	N	Y	Y	N	Y	Y
2 Thompson	N	N	N	N	N	N	Y
3 ***Pickering***	N	N	N	Y	N	Y	Y
4 Shows	Y	N	N	N	N	Y	Y
5 Taylor	Y	N	N	Y	N	Y	Y
MISSOURI							
1 Clay	?	?	?	?	?	?	?
2 ***Talent***	N	N	N	Y	N	Y	Y
3 Gephardt	Y	N	N	N	N	N	Y
4 Skelton	Y	N	N	N	N	Y	Y
5 McCarthy	Y	N	N	N	N	N	N
6 Danner	Y	N	N	N	N	Y	Y
7 ***Blunt***	N	Y	Y	Y	Y	Y	N
8 ***Emerson***	N	N	N	N	N	Y	Y
9 ***Hulshof***	N	Y	Y	Y	Y	Y	Y
MONTANA							
AL ***Hill***	N	N	N	Y	N	Y	Y
NEBRASKA							
1 ***Bereuter***	Y	Y	Y	Y	Y	Y	N
2 ***Terry***	N	Y	Y	Y	Y	Y	N
3 ***Barrett***	Y	N	N	Y	Y	Y	N
NEVADA							
1 Berkley	Y	N	N	N	N	N	N
2 ***Gibbons***	N	N	N	Y	N	N	Y
NEW HAMPSHIRE							
1 ***Sununu***	N	Y	Y	Y	Y	Y	N
2 ***Bass***	N	Y	Y	Y	Y	N	N
NEW JERSEY							
1 Andrews	N	N	N	N	N	N	Y
2 ***LoBiondo***	N	N	N	N	N	Y	Y
3 ***Saxton***	N	N	N	N	N	Y	Y
4 ***Smith***	N	N	N	N	N	Y	Y
5 ***Roukema***	N	N	N	Y	N	N	Y
6 Pallone	N	N	N	N	N	N	Y
7 ***Franks***	N	N	N	N	N	N	Y
8 Pascrell	N	N	N	N	N	N	Y
9 Rothman	N	N	N	N	N	N	Y
10 Payne	Y	N	N	N	N	N	Y
11 ***Frelinghuysen***	N	N	N	Y	N	N	Y
12 Holt	N	N	N	N	N	N	N
13 Menendez	N	N	N	N	N	N	Y
NEW MEXICO							
1 ***Wilson***	N	N	N	Y	N	Y	Y
2 ***Skeen***	N	N	N	Y	Y	Y	N
3 Udall	N	N	N	N	N	N	Y
NEW YORK							
1 Forbes	Y	N	N	N	N	Y	Y
2 ***Lazio***	N	N	N	Y	N	N	Y
3 ***King***	N	N	N	N	N	Y	Y
4 McCarthy	N	N	N	N	N	N	Y
5 Ackerman	N	N	N	N	N	N	Y
6 Meeks	N	?	N	N	N	N	N
7 Crowley	N	N	N	N	N	N	Y
8 Nadler	Y	N	N	N	N	N	Y
9 Weiner	Y	N	N	N	N	N	Y
10 Towns	Y	N	N	N	N	N	N
11 Owens	N	N	N	N	N	N	P
12 Velázquez	N	N	N	N	N	N	N
13 ***Fossella***	Y	N	N	Y	N	Y	Y
14 Maloney	Y	N	N	N	N	N	Y
15 Rangel	N	N	N	N	N	N	N
16 Serrano	Y	N	N	N	N	N	Y
17 Engel	Y	N	N	N	N	N	Y
18 Lowey	Y	N	N	N	N	N	N
19 ***Kelly***	N	N	N	N	N	N	Y
20 ***Gilman***	N	N	N	N	N	N	Y
21 McNulty	?	?	?	?	?	?	?
22 ***Sweeney***	N	N	N	N	N	N	Y
23 ***Boehlert***	N	N	N	N	N	N	Y
24 ***McHugh***	Y	N	N	N	N	Y	N
25 ***Walsh***	N	N	N	Y	N	Y	N
26 Hinchey	Y	N	N	N	N	N	Y
27 ***Reynolds***	N	N	N	Y	N	Y	Y
28 Slaughter	Y	N	N	N	N	N	Y
29 LaFalce	Y	N	N	N	N	Y	Y
30 ***Quinn***	Y	N	N	N	N	Y	N
31 ***Houghton***	Y	Y	?	N	N	N	N
NORTH CAROLINA							
1 Clayton	N	N	N	N	N	N	Y
2 Etheridge	N	N	N	Y	N	N	Y
3 ***Jones***	N	N	N	Y	N	Y	Y
4 Price	N	N	N	Y	N	N	Y
5 ***Burr***	N	N	N	Y	N	Y	Y
6 ***Coble***	N	Y	Y	Y	Y	Y	N
7 McIntyre	Y	N	N	N	N	Y	Y
8 ***Hayes***	N	N	N	Y	N	Y	Y
9 ***Myrick***	N	Y	Y	Y	Y	Y	N
10 ***Ballenger***	Y	Y	Y	Y	Y	Y	N
11 ***Taylor***	?	?	?	?	?	?	?
12 Watt	Y	Y	N	N	N	N	N
NORTH DAKOTA							
AL Pomeroy	Y	Y	Y	N	Y	N	N
OHIO							
1 ***Chabot***	Y	Y	Y	Y	Y	Y	N
2 ***Portman***	N	N	Y	Y	N	Y	N
3 Hall	Y	N	N	N	N	Y	Y
4 ***Oxley***	Y	N	Y	Y	Y	Y	N
5 ***Gillmor***	N	N	N	Y	N	Y	Y
6 Strickland	N	N	N	N	N	N	Y
7 ***Hobson***	Y	N	N	Y	N	Y	N
8 ***Boehner***	Y	Y	Y	Y	Y	Y	N
9 Kaptur	Y	N	N	N	N	N	Y
10 Kucinich	N	N	N	N	N	Y	Y
11 Jones	N	N	N	N	N	N	N
12 ***Kasich***	N	N	N	Y	N	Y	Y
13 Brown	N	N	N	N	N	N	Y
14 Sawyer	Y	N	N	N	N	N	Y
15 ***Pryce***	N	Y	Y	Y	Y	N	N
16 ***Regula***	N	N	N	N	N	Y	Y
17 Traficant	N	N	N	N	N	Y	Y
18 ***Ney***	N	N	N	N	N	Y	Y
19 ***LaTourette***	N	N	N	N	N	Y	Y
OKLAHOMA							
1 ***Largent***	N	Y	Y	Y	Y	Y	N
2 ***Coburn***	Y	Y	Y	Y	Y	Y	N
3 ***Watkins***	N	Y	Y	Y	Y	Y	N
4 ***Watts***	N	N	N	Y	N	Y	N
5 ***Istook***	N	N	N	Y	N	Y	Y
6 ***Lucas***	N	N	Y	Y	N	Y	Y
OREGON							
1 Wu	N	N	N	N	N	N	Y
2 ***Walden***	N	N	N	N	Y	N	N
3 Blumenauer	N	N	N	N	N	N	Y
4 DeFazio	N	N	N	N	N	N	Y
5 Hooley	N	N	N	N	N	N	Y
PENNSYLVANIA							
1 Brady	Y	N	N	N	N	N	Y
2 Fattah	Y	N	N	N	N	N	Y
3 Borski	Y	N	N	N	N	Y	Y
4 Klink	?	?	?	?	?	?	?
5 ***Peterson***	N	N	N	Y	N	Y	Y
6 Holden	?	N	N	N	N	Y	Y
7 ***Weldon***	?	N	N	N	N	Y	N
8 ***Greenwood***	N	N	N	Y	N	N	Y
9 ***Shuster***	?	?	?	?	?	?	?
10 ***Sherwood***	N	N	N	N	N	Y	N
11 Kanjorski	N	N	N	N	N	Y	Y
12 Murtha	Y	N	N	N	N	Y	Y
13 Hoeffel	N	N	N	N	N	N	Y
14 Coyne	N	N	N	N	N	N	Y
15 ***Toomey***	N	N	Y	Y	Y	Y	N
16 ***Pitts***	Y	Y	Y	Y	Y	Y	N
17 ***Gekas***	N	Y	Y	Y	Y	Y	N
18 Doyle	N	N	N	N	N	Y	Y
19 ***Goodling***	?	Y	Y	Y	Y	Y	N
20 Mascara	N	N	N	N	N	Y	Y
21 ***English***	N	N	N	N	N	Y	Y
RHODE ISLAND							
1 Kennedy	Y	N	N	N	N	N	Y
2 Weygand	N	N	N	N	N	Y	Y
SOUTH CAROLINA							
1 ***Sanford***	N	Y	Y	Y	Y	Y	N
2 ***Spence***	N	N	Y	Y	N	Y	?
3 ***Graham***	N	N	N	Y	N	Y	Y
4 ***DeMint***	Y	Y	Y	Y	Y	Y	N
5 Spratt	Y	N	N	Y	N	N	Y
6 Clyburn	Y	N	N	N	N	N	Y
SOUTH DAKOTA							
AL ***Thune***	N	N	N	Y	N	Y	Y
TENNESSEE							
1 ***Jenkins***	?	N	N	Y	N	Y	Y
2 ***Duncan***	N	N	N	Y	N	Y	Y
3 ***Wamp***	N	N	N	Y	N	Y	Y
4 ***Hilleary***	N	N	N	Y	N	Y	Y
5 Clement	N	N	N	Y	N	N	Y
6 Gordon	N	N	N	N	N	N	Y
7 ***Bryant***	N	N	N	Y	N	Y	Y
8 Tanner	Y	N	N	Y	N	N	Y
9 Ford	Y	N	N	N	N	N	Y
TEXAS							
1 Sandlin	Y	N	N	N	N	N	Y
2 Turner	N	N	N	N	N	N	Y
3 ***Johnson, Sam***	Y	?	?	?	?	?	?
4 Hall	N	N	N	Y	N	Y	Y
5 ***Sessions***	N	N	N	Y	N	Y	Y
6 ***Barton***	Y	Y	Y	Y	Y	Y	N
7 ***Archer***	Y	?	?	?	?	?	?
8 ***Brady***	N	N	Y	Y	N	Y	N
9 Lampson	Y	N	N	N	N	N	Y
10 Doggett	N	N	N	N	N	N	N
11 Edwards	Y	N	N	Y	N	N	Y
12 ***Granger***	N	N	N	Y	N	N	Y
13 ***Thornberry***	N	N	N	Y	N	Y	Y
14 ***Paul***	N	N	N	N	N	P	Y
15 Hinojosa	N	N	N	N	N	N	Y
16 Reyes	N	N	N	N	N	N	Y
17 Stenholm	N	N	N	Y	N	Y	Y
18 Jackson-Lee	N	N	N	N	N	N	Y
19 ***Combest***	N	Y	Y	Y	Y	Y	N
20 Gonzalez	Y	N	N	N	N	N	Y
21 ***Smith***	N	N	N	Y	N	Y	Y
22 ***DeLay***	N	Y	Y	Y	Y	Y	N
23 ***Bonilla***	N	Y	Y	Y	Y	Y	N
24 Frost	N	N	N	N	N	N	Y
25 Bentsen	Y	N	N	N	N	N	Y
26 ***Armey***	N	Y	Y	Y	Y	Y	N
27 Ortiz	N	N	N	N	N	Y	Y
28 Rodriguez	Y	N	N	N	N	N	Y
29 Green	N	N	N	N	N	N	Y
30 Johnson, E.B.	N	N	N	N	N	N	Y
UTAH							
1 ***Hansen***	N	N	Y	Y	N	Y	Y
2 ***Cook***	?	?	?	?	?	?	?
3 ***Cannon***	N	Y	Y	Y	Y	Y	N
VERMONT							
AL *Sanders*	Y	N	N	N	N	N	Y
VIRGINIA							
1 ***Bateman***	N	Y	N	Y	N	Y	N
2 Pickett	Y	N	N	Y	N	N	Y
3 Scott	N	N	N	N	N	N	Y
4 Sisisky	Y	N	N	Y	N	N	Y
5 *Goode*	N	N	N	Y	N	Y	Y
6 ***Goodlatte***	N	N	Y	Y	Y	Y	Y
7 ***Bliley***	N	Y	Y	Y	Y	Y	N
8 Moran	Y	N	N	Y	N	N	Y
9 Boucher	N	N	N	N	N	N	Y
10 ***Wolf***	N	N	N	Y	N	Y	Y
11 ***Davis***	N	N	N	Y	N	Y	Y
WASHINGTON							
1 Inslee	N	N	N	N	N	N	N
2 ***Metcalf***	N	N	N	Y	N	Y	?
3 Baird	N	N	N	N	N	N	N
4 ***Hastings***	?	?	?	?	?	?	?
5 ***Nethercutt***	N	N	N	Y	N	Y	Y
6 Dicks	Y	N	N	N	N	N	Y
7 McDermott	Y	N	N	N	N	N	Y
8 ***Dunn***	N	Y	N	Y	Y	Y	N
9 Smith	N	N	N	N	N	N	N
WEST VIRGINIA							
1 Mollohan	N	N	N	N	N	Y	Y
2 Wise	N	N	N	N	N	N	Y
3 Rahall	N	N	N	N	N	Y	Y
WISCONSIN							
1 ***Ryan***	Y	Y	Y	Y	Y	Y	Y
2 Baldwin	N	N	N	N	N	N	N
3 Kind	N	N	N	N	N	N	Y
4 Kleczka	N	N	N	N	N	N	Y
5 Barrett	N	N	N	N	Y	N	N
6 ***Petri***	N	N	N	Y	N	Y	Y
7 Obey	N	N	N	N	N	N	Y
8 ***Green***	Y	N	Y	N	Y	Y	Y
9 ***Sensenbrenner***	Y	Y	Y	Y	Y	Y	N
WYOMING							
AL ***Cubin***	N	N	N	Y	N	Y	Y

Southern states - Ala., Ark., Fla., Ga., Ky., La., Miss., N.C., Okla., S.C., Tenn., Texas, Va.

373. HR 4461. Fiscal 2001 Agriculture Appropriations/Abortion Pill. Coburn, R-Okla., amendment that would prohibit the Food and Drug Administration from using funds to test, develop or approve any drug for the chemical inducement of abortion. Rejected 182-187: R 149-34; D 32-152 (ND 25-112, SD 7-40); I 1-1. A "nay" was a vote in support of the president's position. July 10, 2000.

374. HR 4461. Fiscal 2001 Agriculture Appropriations/Across-the-Board Cut. Royce, R-Calif., amendment that would enact a 1 percent across-the-board cut in fiscal 2001 Agriculture Department appropriations. Rejected 53-316: R 52-131; D 0-184 (ND 0-136, SD 0-48); I 1-1. July 10, 2000.

375. HR 4461. Fiscal 2001 Agriculture Appropriations/Imported Prescription Drugs. Crowley, D-N.Y., amendment that would overturn the current Food and Drug Administration prohibition on U.S. citizens traveling to other countries to purchase prescription drugs for individual use. Adopted 363-12: R 178-9; D 183-3 (ND 134-3, SD 49-0); I 2-0. July 10, 2000.

376. HR 4461. Fiscal 2001 Agriculture Appropriations/Market Access Program. Royce, R-Calif., amendment that would prohibit using funds for the Market Access Program, which gives grants to businesses and trade associations to promote agricultural exports. Rejected 77-301: R 53-136; D 24-163 (ND 21-116, SD 3-47); I 0-2. July 10, 2000.

377. HR 4461. Fiscal 2001 Agriculture Appropriations/Imported Prescriptions Drugs. Coburn, R-Okla., amendment that would prohibit the Food and Drug Administration from using funds to interfere with the importation of drugs that have been approved for use in the United States, Mexico or Canada. Adopted 370-12: R 184-6; D 184-6 (ND 133-6, SD 51-0); I 2-0. July 10, 2000.

378. HR 4461. Fiscal 2001 Agriculture Appropriations/School Breakfast Study. Sanford, R-S.C., amendment that would prohibit the Agriculture Department from conducting a child nutrition pilot program to study the effects of providing free breakfasts to students without regard to family income. Rejected 59-323: R 57-133; D 1-189 (ND 1-138, SD 0-51); I 1-1. July 10, 2000.

379. H Con Res 253. Vatican U.N. Seat/Adoption. Smith, R-N.J., motion to suspend the rules and adopt the concurrent resolution expressing the sense of Congress strongly objecting to any effort to expel the Holy See from the United Nations by removing its status as a permanent observer. Motion agreed to 416-1: R 215-0; D 199-1 (ND 148-1, SD 51-0); I 2-0. A two-thirds majority of those present and voting (278 in this case) is required for adoption under suspension of the rules. July 11, 2000.

Key

- Y Voted for (yea).
- # Paired for.
- + Announced for.
- N Voted against (nay).
- X Paired against.
- – Announced against.
- P Voted "present."
- C Voted "present" to avoid possible conflict of interest.
- ? Did not vote or otherwise make a position known.

•

Democrats ***Republicans***
Independents

	373	374	375	376	377	378	379
ALABAMA							
1 ***Callahan***	Y	N	Y	N	Y	Y	Y
2 ***Everett***	Y	N	Y	N	Y	N	Y
3 ***Riley***	Y	N	Y	N	Y	N	Y
4 ***Aderholt***	Y	N	Y	N	Y	N	Y
5 Cramer	N	N	Y	N	Y	N	Y
6 ***Bachus***	Y	N	Y	N	Y	N	Y
7 Hilliard	N	N	Y	N	Y	N	Y
ALASKA							
AL ***Young***	?	?	?	?	?	?	?
ARIZONA							
1 ***Salmon***	Y	Y	Y	Y	Y	Y	Y
2 Pastor	N	N	Y	N	Y	N	Y
3 ***Stump***	Y	N	Y	N	Y	Y	Y
4 ***Shadegg***	Y	Y	Y	Y	Y	Y	Y
5 ***Kolbe***	N	N	Y	N	Y	N	Y
6 ***Hayworth***	Y	Y	Y	Y	Y	Y	Y
ARKANSAS							
1 Berry	Y	N	Y	N	Y	N	Y
2 Snyder	N	N	Y	N	Y	N	Y
3 ***Hutchinson***	Y	N	Y	?	Y	N	Y
4 ***Dickey***	Y	N	Y	N	Y	N	Y
CALIFORNIA							
1 Thompson	N	N	Y	N	Y	N	Y
2 ***Herger***	Y	Y	Y	N	Y	Y	Y
3 ***Ose***	N	N	Y	N	Y	N	Y
4 ***Doolittle***	Y	N	Y	N	Y	Y	Y
5 Matsui	N	N	Y	N	Y	N	Y
6 Woolsey	N	N	Y	N	Y	N	Y
7 Miller, George	N	N	Y	N	Y	N	Y
8 Pelosi	N	N	Y	?	Y	N	Y
9 Lee	–	–	+	–	+	–	Y
10 Tauscher	N	N	Y	N	Y	N	Y
11 ***Pombo***	Y	N	Y	N	Y	N	Y
12 Lantos	N	N	Y	N	Y	N	Y
13 Stark	N	N	Y	Y	Y	N	N
14 Eshoo	N	N	Y	N	Y	N	Y
15 ***Campbell***	?	?	?	?	?	?	?
16 Lofgren	N	N	Y	N	Y	N	Y
17 Farr	N	N	Y	N	Y	N	Y
18 Condit	N	N	Y	N	Y	N	Y
19 ***Radanovich***	Y	Y	Y	?	Y	N	Y
20 Dooley	N	N	N	N	N	N	Y
21 ***Thomas***	N	N	N	N	N	N	Y
22 Capps	N	N	Y	N	Y	N	Y
23 ***Gallegly***	Y	N	Y	N	Y	N	Y
24 Sherman	N	N	Y	N	Y	N	Y
25 ***McKeon***	Y	N	Y	N	Y	N	Y
26 Berman	N	N	Y	N	Y	N	Y
27 ***Rogan***	Y	N	Y	N	Y	N	Y
28 ***Dreier***	Y	N	N	N	Y	N	Y
29 Waxman	?	?	?	?	?	?	Y
30 Becerra	–	–	+	–	+	–	+
31 Martinez	Y	N	Y	N	Y	N	Y
32 Dixon	N	N	Y	N	Y	N	Y
33 Roybal-Allard	N	N	Y	N	Y	N	Y
34 Napolitano	N	N	Y	N	Y	N	Y
35 Waters	N	?	Y	N	N	N	Y
36 ***Kuykendall***	N	N	Y	N	Y	N	Y
37 Millender-McD.	N	N	Y	N	Y	N	Y
38 ***Horn***	N	N	Y	N	Y	N	Y
39 ***Royce***	Y	Y	Y	Y	Y	Y	Y
40 ***Lewis***	?	?	?	?	?	?	Y
41 ***Miller, Gary***	Y	Y	Y	Y	Y	Y	Y
42 Baca	N	N	Y	N	Y	N	Y
43 ***Calvert***	Y	N	Y	N	Y	N	Y
44 ***Bono***	Y	N	Y	N	Y	N	Y
45 ***Rohrabacher***	Y	Y	Y	Y	Y	Y	Y
46 Sanchez	–	–	–	–	–	–	Y
47 ***Cox***	Y	Y	Y	Y	Y	Y	Y
48 ***Packard***	Y	N	Y	N	Y	N	Y
49 ***Bilbray***	N	Y	Y	N	Y	N	Y
50 Filner	N	N	Y	N	Y	N	Y
51 ***Cunningham***	Y	N	Y	Y	Y	N	Y
52 ***Hunter***	Y	Y	Y	N	Y	Y	Y
COLORADO							
1 DeGette	N	N	Y	N	Y	N	Y
2 Udall	N	N	Y	Y	Y	N	Y
3 ***McInnis***	Y	N	Y	Y	Y	N	Y
4 ***Schaffer***	Y	Y	Y	N	Y	Y	Y
5 ***Hefley***	Y	Y	Y	Y	Y	Y	Y
6 ***Tancredo***	Y	Y	Y	Y	Y	N	Y
CONNECTICUT							
1 Larson	N	N	Y	N	Y	N	Y
2 Gejdenson	N	N	Y	N	Y	N	Y
3 DeLauro	N	N	Y	N	Y	N	Y
4 ***Shays***	–	–	+	–	+	–	Y
5 Maloney	–	–	+	–	+	–	Y
6 ***Johnson***	N	N	Y	N	Y	Y	?
DELAWARE							
AL ***Castle***	N	N	Y	N	Y	N	Y
FLORIDA							
1 ***Scarborough***	?	?	?	Y	Y	N	Y
2 Boyd	N	N	Y	N	Y	N	Y
3 Brown	N	N	Y	N	Y	N	Y
4 ***Fowler***	?	?	?	?	Y	N	Y
5 Thurman	N	N	Y	N	Y	N	Y
6 ***Stearns***	Y	Y	Y	Y	Y	Y	Y
7 ***Mica***	Y	Y	Y	N	Y	Y	Y
8 ***McCollum***	?	?	?	?	?	?	?
9 ***Bilirakis***	Y	N	Y	N	Y	N	Y
10 ***Young***	Y	N	Y	N	Y	N	Y
11 Davis	N	N	Y	N	Y	N	Y
12 ***Canady***	Y	N	Y	N	Y	N	Y
13 ***Miller***	N	Y	Y	Y	Y	N	Y
14 ***Goss***	Y	N	Y	N	Y	N	Y
15 ***Weldon***	Y	N	Y	N	Y	N	Y
16 ***Foley***	N	N	Y	N	Y	N	Y
17 Meek	N	N	Y	N	Y	N	Y
18 ***Ros-Lehtinen***	Y	N	Y	N	Y	N	Y
19 Wexler	N	N	Y	N	Y	N	Y
20 Deutsch	N	N	Y	N	Y	N	Y
21 ***Diaz-Balart***	Y	N	Y	N	Y	N	Y
22 ***Shaw***	Y	N	Y	Y	Y	N	Y
23 Hastings	N	N	Y	N	Y	N	Y
GEORGIA							
1 ***Kingston***	Y	N	Y	N	Y	Y	Y
2 Bishop	N	N	Y	N	Y	N	Y
3 ***Collins***	?	?	?	?	?	?	Y
4 McKinney	N	N	Y	Y	Y	N	?
5 Lewis	N	N	Y	N	Y	N	Y
6 ***Isakson***	–	–	+	–	+	–	Y
7 ***Barr***	?	?	Y	Y	Y	Y	Y
8 ***Chambliss***	+	–	+	–	+	–	Y
9 ***Deal***	?	?	Y	N	Y	N	Y
10 ***Norwood***	?	?	?	?	?	?	Y
11 ***Linder***	Y	Y	Y	Y	Y	?	Y
HAWAII							
1 Abercrombie	N	N	Y	N	Y	N	Y
2 Mink	N	N	Y	N	Y	N	Y
IDAHO							
1 ***Chenoweth-Hage***	?	?	?	?	?	?	?
2 ***Simpson***	Y	N	Y	N	Y	N	Y
ILLINOIS							
1 Rush	?	?	?	?	?	?	Y
2 Jackson	N	N	Y	N	N	N	Y
3 Lipinski	?	?	?	?	?	?	Y
4 Gutierrez	N	N	Y	N	Y	N	Y
5 Blagojevich	N	N	Y	N	Y	N	Y
6 ***Hyde***	Y	N	Y	Y	Y	N	Y
7 Davis	N	N	Y	N	Y	N	Y
8 ***Crane***	Y	Y	Y	Y	N	Y	Y
9 Schakowsky	N	N	Y	N	Y	N	Y
10 ***Porter***	N	N	Y	N	N	N	Y
11 ***Weller***	Y	N	Y	N	?	N	Y
12 Costello	Y	N	Y	N	Y	N	Y
13 ***Biggert***	N	Y	Y	N	Y	N	Y

ND Northern Democrats SD Southern Democrats

	373	374	375	376	377	378	379
14 ***Hastert***							
15 ***Ewing***	Y	N	Y	N	Y	?	Y
16 ***Manzullo***	Y	Y	Y	N	Y	Y	Y
17 Evans	N	N	Y	N	Y	N	Y
18 ***LaHood***	Y	N	Y	N	Y	N	Y
19 Phelps	Y	N	Y	N	Y	N	Y
20 ***Shimkus***	Y	N	Y	N	Y	N	Y
INDIANA							
1 Visclosky	Y	N	Y	Y	Y	N	Y
2 ***McIntosh***	?	?	?	?	?	?	?
3 Roemer	Y	N	Y	N	Y	N	Y
4 ***Souder***	Y	N	Y	N	Y	N	Y
5 ***Buyer***	Y	N	Y	N	Y	Y	Y
6 ***Burton***	Y	Y	Y	N	Y	Y	Y
7 ***Pease***	Y	Y	N	N	Y	Y	Y
8 ***Hostettler***	Y	Y	Y	Y	Y	Y	Y
9 Hill	?	?	?	?	Y	Y	Y
10 Carson	N	N	Y	N	Y	N	Y
IOWA							
1 ***Leach***	N	N	Y	N	Y	N	Y
2 ***Nussle***	Y	N	Y	N	Y	N	Y
3 Boswell	N	N	Y	N	Y	N	Y
4 ***Ganske***	N	N	Y	N	Y	N	Y
5 ***Latham***	Y	N	Y	N	Y	N	Y
KANSAS							
1 ***Moran***	Y	N	Y	N	Y	N	Y
2 ***Ryun***	Y	Y	Y	Y	Y	N	Y
3 Moore	N	N	Y	N	Y	N	Y
4 ***Tiahrt***	Y	N	Y	N	Y	N	Y
KENTUCKY							
1 ***Whitfield***	Y	N	Y	N	Y	N	Y
2 ***Lewis***	Y	N	Y	N	Y	N	Y
3 ***Northup***	Y	N	Y	N	Y	N	Y
4 Lucas	+	–	Y	N	Y	N	Y
5 ***Rogers***	Y	N	Y	N	Y	N	Y
6 ***Fletcher***	Y	N	Y	N	Y	N	Y
LOUISIANA							
1 ***Vitter***	Y	Y	Y	N	Y	N	Y
2 Jefferson	N	N	Y	N	Y	N	?
3 ***Tauzin***	Y	N	Y	N	Y	N	Y
4 ***McCrery***	Y	N	N	N	N	N	Y
5 ***Cooksey***	Y	N	Y	N	?	N	Y
6 ***Baker***	Y	N	Y	N	Y	Y	Y
7 John	Y	N	Y	N	Y	N	Y
MAINE							
1 Allen	N	N	Y	N	Y	N	Y
2 Baldacci	N	N	Y	N	Y	N	Y
MARYLAND							
1 ***Gilchrest***	?	?	?	?	?	?	Y
2 ***Ehrlich***	N	Y	Y	Y	Y	N	Y
3 Cardin	N	N	Y	N	Y	N	Y
4 Wynn	N	N	Y	N	Y	N	Y
5 Hoyer	N	N	Y	N	Y	N	+
6 ***Bartlett***	Y	N	Y	N	Y	Y	Y
7 Cummings	N	N	Y	N	Y	N	Y
8 ***Morella***	N	N	Y	Y	Y	N	Y
MASSACHUSETTS							
1 Olver	N	N	Y	N	Y	N	Y
2 Neal	N	N	Y	N	Y	N	Y
3 McGovern	N	N	Y	N	Y	N	Y
4 Frank	N	N	Y	N	Y	N	Y
5 Meehan	N	N	Y	Y	Y	N	Y
6 Tierney	N	N	Y	Y	Y	N	Y
7 Markey	N	N	Y	N	Y	N	Y
8 Capuano	N	N	Y	N	Y	N	Y
9 Moakley	?	?	?	?	?	?	Y
10 Delahunt	N	N	Y	N	Y	N	Y
MICHIGAN							
1 Stupak	Y	N	Y	N	Y	N	Y
2 ***Hoekstra***	Y	Y	Y	Y	Y	Y	Y
3 ***Ehlers***	Y	N	Y	Y	Y	Y	Y
4 ***Camp***	?	?	?	?	?	?	Y
5 Barcia	Y	N	Y	N	Y	N	Y
6 ***Upton***	N	N	Y	N	Y	N	Y
7 ***Smith***	N	N	Y	N	Y	N	Y
8 Stabenow	N	N	Y	N	Y	N	Y
9 Kildee	Y	N	Y	N	Y	N	Y
10 Bonior	N	N	Y	N	Y	N	Y
11 ***Knollenberg***	Y	N	N	N	N	N	Y
12 Levin	N	N	Y	N	Y	N	Y
13 Rivers	N	N	Y	Y	Y	N	Y
14 Conyers	N	N	Y	N	N	N	Y
15 Kilpatrick	–	+	–	–	+	–	Y
16 Dingell	N	N	N	N	N	N	Y

	373	374	375	376	377	378	379
MINNESOTA							
1 ***Gutknecht***	Y	Y	Y	N	Y	N	Y
2 Minge	N	N	Y	N	Y	N	Y
3 ***Ramstad***	N	Y	Y	Y	Y	N	Y
4 Vento	?	?	?	?	?	?	?
5 Sabo	N	N	Y	N	Y	N	Y
6 Luther	N	N	Y	Y	Y	N	Y
7 Peterson	Y	N	Y	N	Y	N	Y
8 Oberstar	Y	N	Y	N	Y	N	Y
MISSISSIPPI							
1 ***Wicker***	Y	N	Y	N	Y	N	Y
2 Thompson	N	N	Y	N	Y	N	Y
3 ***Pickering***	Y	N	Y	N	Y	N	Y
4 Shows	Y	N	Y	N	Y	N	Y
5 Taylor	+	+	+	+	+	–	Y
MISSOURI							
1 Clay	N	N	Y	N	Y	N	Y
2 ***Talent***	?	?	?	?	?	?	Y
3 Gephardt	N	N	Y	N	Y	N	Y
4 Skelton	Y	N	Y	N	Y	N	Y
5 McCarthy	N	N	Y	N	Y	N	Y
6 Danner	Y	N	Y	N	Y	N	Y
7 ***Blunt***	Y	N	Y	N	Y	N	Y
8 ***Emerson***	Y	N	Y	N	Y	N	Y
9 ***Hulshof***	?	?	?	?	?	?	Y
MONTANA							
AL ***Hill***	Y	N	Y	N	Y	N	Y
NEBRASKA							
1 ***Bereuter***	Y	N	Y	N	Y	N	Y
2 ***Terry***	Y	N	Y	N	Y	N	Y
3 ***Barrett***	Y	N	Y	N	Y	N	Y
NEVADA							
1 Berkley	–	–	+	Y	Y	N	Y
2 ***Gibbons***	N	N	Y	N	Y	N	Y
NEW HAMPSHIRE							
1 ***Sununu***	Y	Y	Y	Y	Y	N	Y
2 ***Bass***	N	N	Y	Y	Y	N	Y
NEW JERSEY							
1 Andrews	N	N	Y	Y	Y	N	Y
2 ***LoBiondo***	Y	N	Y	Y	Y	N	Y
3 ***Saxton***	Y	N	Y	Y	Y	N	Y
4 ***Smith***	Y	N	Y	N	Y	N	Y
5 ***Roukema***	N	N	N	Y	Y	N	Y
6 Pallone	N	N	Y	Y	Y	N	Y
7 ***Franks***	N	Y	N	Y	Y	Y	Y
8 Pascrell	N	N	Y	Y	Y	N	Y
9 Rothman	N	N	Y	Y	Y	N	Y
10 Payne	?	?	?	?	?	?	?
11 ***Frelinghuysen***	N	N	N	Y	Y	N	Y
12 Holt	N	N	N	Y	Y	N	Y
13 Menendez	N	N	Y	N	Y	N	Y
NEW MEXICO							
1 ***Wilson***	N	N	Y	N	Y	N	Y
2 ***Skeen***	Y	N	Y	N	Y	N	Y
3 Udall	N	N	Y	N	Y	N	Y
NEW YORK							
1 Forbes	?	?	?	?	?	?	?
2 ***Lazio***	?	?	?	?	?	?	Y
3 ***King***	Y	N	Y	N	Y	N	Y
4 McCarthy	N	N	Y	N	Y	N	Y
5 Ackerman	N	N	Y	N	Y	N	Y
6 Meeks	N	N	Y	N	Y	N	Y
7 Crowley	N	N	Y	N	Y	N	Y
8 Nadler	N	N	Y	Y	Y	N	Y
9 Weiner	N	N	Y	Y	Y	N	Y
10 Towns	N	N	Y	N	Y	N	Y
11 Owens	–	–	+	–	+	–	+
12 Velázquez	N	N	Y	N	Y	N	Y
13 ***Fossella***	+	?	+	–	+	–	Y
14 Maloney	N	N	Y	N	Y	N	Y
15 Rangel	N	N	Y	N	Y	N	Y
16 Serrano	N	N	Y	N	Y	N	Y
17 Engel	N	N	Y	N	Y	N	Y
18 Lowey	N	N	Y	Y	N	N	Y
19 ***Kelly***	N	N	Y	Y	Y	N	Y
20 ***Gilman***	N	N	Y	N	Y	N	Y
21 McNulty	?	?	?	?	?	?	?
22 ***Sweeney***	N	N	Y	N	Y	N	Y
23 ***Boehlert***	N	N	Y	N	Y	N	Y
24 ***McHugh***	Y	N	Y	N	Y	N	Y
25 ***Walsh***	Y	N	Y	N	Y	N	Y
26 Hinchey	N	N	Y	N	Y	N	Y
27 ***Reynolds***	Y	N	Y	N	Y	N	Y
28 Slaughter	N	N	Y	N	Y	N	Y
29 LaFalce	Y	N	Y	N	Y	N	Y

	373	374	375	376	377	378	379
30 ***Quinn***	Y	N	Y	N	Y	N	Y
31 ***Houghton***	N	N	Y	N	?	?	Y
NORTH CAROLINA							
1 Clayton	N	N	Y	N	Y	N	Y
2 Etheridge	N	N	Y	N	Y	N	Y
3 ***Jones***	Y	N	Y	N	Y	N	Y
4 Price	N	N	Y	N	Y	N	Y
5 ***Burr***	+	?	?	?	?	?	Y
6 ***Coble***	Y	Y	Y	Y	Y	Y	Y
7 McIntyre	Y	N	Y	N	Y	N	Y
8 ***Hayes***	Y	N	Y	N	Y	N	Y
9 ***Myrick***	+	+	+	+	+	+	Y
10 ***Ballenger***	?	?	?	?	Y	N	Y
11 ***Taylor***	+	+	+	–	+	–	Y
12 Watt	?	?	?	N	Y	N	Y
NORTH DAKOTA							
AL Pomeroy	N	N	Y	N	Y	N	Y
OHIO							
1 ***Chabot***	?	?	?	Y	Y	Y	Y
2 ***Portman***	Y	N	Y	Y	Y	N	Y
3 Hall	Y	N	Y	N	Y	N	Y
4 ***Oxley***	Y	N	Y	N	Y	N	Y
5 ***Gillmor***	Y	N	Y	N	Y	N	Y
6 Strickland	N	N	Y	N	Y	N	Y
7 ***Hobson***	Y	N	Y	N	Y	Y	Y
8 ***Boehner***	?	?	Y	N	Y	N	Y
9 Kaptur	N	N	Y	N	Y	N	Y
10 Kucinich	Y	N	Y	N	Y	N	Y
11 Jones	N	N	Y	N	Y	N	Y
12 ***Kasich***	Y	Y	Y	N	Y	Y	Y
13 Brown	N	N	Y	Y	Y	N	Y
14 Sawyer	N	N	Y	N	Y	N	Y
15 ***Pryce***	?	?	?	?	?	?	Y
16 ***Regula***	Y	N	Y	N	Y	N	Y
17 Traficant	Y	N	Y	N	Y	N	Y
18 ***Ney***	Y	N	Y	N	Y	N	Y
19 ***LaTourette***	?	?	?	?	?	?	Y
OKLAHOMA							
1 ***Largent***	Y	N	Y	Y	Y	Y	Y
2 ***Coburn***	Y	Y	Y	Y	Y	N	Y
3 ***Watkins***	+	–	Y	N	Y	N	Y
4 ***Watts***	Y	N	Y	N	Y	Y	Y
5 ***Istook***	Y	Y	Y	Y	Y	N	Y
6 ***Lucas***	Y	N	Y	N	Y	N	Y
OREGON							
1 Wu	N	N	Y	Y	Y	N	Y
2 ***Walden***	Y	N	Y	N	Y	N	Y
3 Blumenauer	N	N	Y	N	Y	N	Y
4 DeFazio	N	N	Y	N	Y	N	Y
5 Hooley	N	N	Y	N	Y	N	Y
PENNSYLVANIA							
1 Brady	N	N	Y	N	Y	N	Y
2 Fattah	?	?	?	?	?	?	Y
3 Borski	Y	N	Y	N	Y	N	Y
4 Klink	?	?	?	?	?	?	Y
5 ***Peterson***	Y	N	Y	N	Y	N	Y
6 Holden	Y	N	Y	N	Y	N	Y
7 ***Weldon***	Y	N	Y	N	Y	N	Y
8 ***Greenwood***	N	N	Y	N	Y	N	Y
9 ***Shuster***	Y	N	Y	N	Y	N	Y
10 ***Sherwood***	Y	N	Y	N	Y	N	Y
11 Kanjorski	Y	N	Y	N	Y	N	Y
12 Murtha	Y	N	Y	N	Y	N	Y
13 Hoeffel	N	N	Y	N	Y	N	Y
14 Coyne	?	?	?	?	?	?	Y
15 ***Toomey***	N	Y	Y	Y	Y	Y	Y
16 ***Pitts***	Y	Y	Y	N	Y	Y	Y
17 ***Gekas***	Y	N	Y	N	Y	N	Y
18 Doyle	Y	N	Y	N	Y	N	Y
19 ***Goodling***	Y	N	Y	N	Y	Y	Y
20 Mascara	Y	N	Y	N	Y	N	Y
21 ***English***	Y	N	Y	Y	Y	N	Y
RHODE ISLAND							
1 Kennedy	N	N	Y	N	Y	N	Y
2 Weygand	Y	N	Y	N	Y	N	Y
SOUTH CAROLINA							
1 ***Sanford***	Y	Y	Y	Y	Y	Y	Y
2 ***Spence***	Y	N	Y	N	Y	N	Y
3 ***Graham***	?	?	?	?	?	?	Y
4 ***DeMint***	+	+	+	+	+	+	Y
5 Spratt	?	?	?	N	Y	N	Y
6 Clyburn	N	N	Y	N	Y	N	Y
SOUTH DAKOTA							
AL ***Thune***	Y	N	Y	N	Y	Y	Y

	373	374	375	376	377	378	379
TENNESSEE							
1 ***Jenkins***	+	–	+	N	Y	N	Y
2 ***Duncan***	?	?	Y	Y	Y	Y	Y
3 ***Wamp***	Y	N	Y	Y	Y	N	Y
4 ***Hilleary***	?	?	?	?	?	?	Y
5 Clement	N	N	Y	N	Y	N	Y
6 Gordon	N	N	Y	N	Y	N	Y
7 ***Bryant***	Y	N	Y	N	Y	N	Y
8 Tanner	–	–	+	–	+	–	Y
9 Ford	?	N	Y	N	Y	N	Y
TEXAS							
1 Sandlin	N	N	Y	?	Y	N	Y
2 Turner	N	N	Y	N	Y	N	Y
3 ***Johnson, Sam***	Y	Y	Y	N	Y	Y	Y
4 Hall	Y	N	Y	N	Y	N	Y
5 ***Sessions***	Y	Y	Y	N	Y	N	Y
6 ***Barton***	Y	Y	Y	N	Y	N	Y
7 ***Archer***	Y	Y	N	Y	N	N	Y
8 ***Brady***	Y	Y	Y	N	Y	Y	Y
9 Lampson	N	N	Y	N	Y	N	Y
10 Doggett	N	N	Y	Y	Y	N	Y
11 Edwards	N	N	Y	N	Y	N	Y
12 ***Granger***	N	N	Y	N	Y	Y	Y
13 ***Thornberry***	Y	N	Y	N	Y	N	Y
14 ***Paul***	Y	Y	Y	Y	Y	Y	Y
15 Hinojosa	–	–	+	–	+	–	+
16 Reyes	N	N	Y	N	Y	N	Y
17 Stenholm	Y	N	Y	N	Y	N	Y
18 Jackson-Lee	N	N	Y	N	Y	N	Y
19 ***Combest***	Y	N	Y	N	Y	Y	Y
20 Gonzalez	N	N	Y	N	Y	N	Y
21 ***Smith***	N	N	Y	N	Y	N	Y
22 ***DeLay***	Y	Y	Y	Y	Y	Y	Y
23 ***Bonilla***	Y	N	Y	N	Y	Y	Y
24 Frost	N	N	Y	N	Y	N	Y
25 Bentsen	N	N	Y	N	Y	N	Y
26 ***Armey***	Y	Y	Y	Y	Y	Y	Y
27 Ortiz	Y	N	Y	N	Y	N	Y
28 Rodriguez	N	N	Y	N	Y	N	Y
29 Green	N	N	Y	Y	Y	N	Y
30 Johnson, E.B.	N	N	Y	N	Y	N	Y
UTAH							
1 ***Hansen***	?	?	?	?	?	?	Y
2 ***Cook***	?	?	?	?	?	?	Y
3 ***Cannon***	Y	Y	Y	Y	Y	Y	Y
VERMONT							
AL *Sanders*	N	N	Y	N	Y	N	Y
VIRGINIA							
1 ***Bateman***	Y	N	+	N	Y	N	Y
2 Pickett	N	N	Y	N	Y	N	Y
3 Scott	N	N	Y	N	Y	N	Y
4 Sisisky	N	N	Y	N	Y	N	Y
5 *Goode*	Y	Y	Y	N	Y	Y	Y
6 ***Goodlatte***	Y	N	Y	N	Y	Y	Y
7 ***Bliley***	Y	N	Y	N	Y	N	Y
8 Moran	N	N	Y	N	Y	N	Y
9 Boucher	N	N	Y	N	Y	N	Y
10 ***Wolf***	Y	N	Y	N	Y	N	Y
11 ***Davis***	?	?	?	?	?	?	Y
WASHINGTON							
1 Inslee	N	N	Y	N	Y	N	Y
2 ***Metcalf***	Y	Y	Y	N	Y	N	Y
3 Baird	N	N	Y	N	Y	N	Y
4 ***Hastings***	Y	N	Y	N	Y	Y	Y
5 ***Nethercutt***	Y	N	Y	N	Y	N	Y
6 Dicks	N	N	Y	N	Y	N	Y
7 McDermott	N	N	Y	N	Y	N	Y
8 ***Dunn***	Y	N	Y	N	Y	Y	Y
9 Smith	?	?	?	?	?	?	?
WEST VIRGINIA							
1 Mollohan	Y	N	Y	N	Y	N	Y
2 Wise	N	N	Y	N	Y	N	Y
3 Rahall	Y	N	Y	N	Y	N	Y
WISCONSIN							
1 ***Ryan***	Y	Y	Y	N	Y	Y	Y
2 Baldwin	N	N	Y	N	Y	N	Y
3 Kind	N	N	Y	Y	Y	N	Y
4 Kleczka	N	N	Y	Y	Y	N	Y
5 Barrett	N	N	Y	Y	Y	N	Y
6 ***Petri***	Y	Y	Y	Y	Y	N	Y
7 Obey	N	N	Y	N	Y	N	Y
8 ***Green***	Y	N	Y	N	Y	N	Y
9 ***Sensenbrenner***	Y	Y	Y	Y	Y	Y	Y
WYOMING							
AL ***Cubin***	Y	N	Y	N	Y	Y	Y

Southern states - Ala., Ark., Fla., Ga., Ky., La., Miss., N.C., Okla., S.C., Tenn., Texas, Va.

380. HR 4442. Wildlife Refuge System Centennial/Passage. Walden, R-Ore., motion to suspend the rules and pass the bill that would establish a National Wildlife Refuge System Centennial Commission to promote public awareness of the system in preparation of its 100th anniversary in 2003. It would also require the U.S. Fish and Wildlife Service to develop a long-term plan to address the system's construction and maintenance needs. Motion agreed to 403-15: R 200-15; D 201-0 (ND 149-0, SD 52-0); I 2-0. A two-thirds majority of those present and voting (279 in this case) is required for passage under suspension of the rules. July 11, 2000.

381. H Res 415. National Ocean Day/Adoption. Walden, R-Ore., motion to suspend the rules and adopt the resolution expressing the sense of the House that a National Ocean Day should be created in order to recognize the significance of the ocean. Motion agreed to 387-28: R 186-28; D 199-0 (ND 146-0, SD 53-0); I 2-0. A two-thirds majority of those present and voting (277 in this case) is required for adoption under suspension of the rules. July 11, 2000.

382. HR 4461. Fiscal 2001 Agriculture Appropriations/Wild Animals. DeFazio, D-Ore., amendment that would reduce funding for the Agriculture Department's Wildlife Services program by $7 million and specify that none of the program's funds could be used to conduct campaigns for the destruction of wild predatory animals, such as mountain lions and bobcats, for the purpose of protecting livestock. Rejected 190-228: R 56-159; D 133-68 (ND 112-36, SD 21-32); I 1-1. July 11, 2000.

383. HR 4461. Fiscal 2001 Agriculture Appropriations/Mohair Subsidies. Sanford, R-S.C., amendment that would prevent the Agriculture Department from making payments to producers of wool and mohair. Rejected 166-255: R 106-110; D 60-143 (ND 49-100, SD 11-43); I 0-2. July 11, 2000.

384. HR 4461. Fiscal 2001 Agriculture Appropriations/Conflict of Interest. Burton, R-Ind., amendment that would prohibit members of a federal advisory committee on vaccines from being granted a waiver from conflict-of-interest rules. Rejected 168-253: R 146-69; D 21-183 (ND 18-132, SD 3-51); I 1-1. July 11, 2000.

385. HR 4461. Fiscal 2001 Agriculture Appropriations/Passage. Passage of the bill that would appropriate $75.4 billion in fiscal 2001, including $35 billion for domestic food programs, $21.2 billion for the food stamp program, $1.2 billion for the Food and Drug Administration and $812 million for conservation programs, as well as $890 million for the Agriculture Research Service and $1.4 billion for the Rural Housing Service. Passed 339-82: R 200-16; D 137-66 (ND 88-61, SD 49-5); I 2-0. July 11, 2000.

386. Procedural Motion/Journal. Approval of the House Journal of Tuesday, July 11, 2000. Approved 354-50: R 191-14; D 161-36 (ND 117-28, SD 44-8); I 2-0. July 12, 2000.

Key

- Y Voted for (yea).
- # Paired for.
- + Announced for.
- N Voted against (nay).
- X Paired against.
- – Announced against.
- P Voted "present."
- C Voted "present" to avoid possible conflict of interest.
- ? Did not vote or otherwise make a position known.

•

Democrats ***Republicans***
Independents

	380	381	382	383	384	385	386
ALABAMA							
1 ***Callahan***	Y	Y	?	N	Y	Y	Y
2 ***Everett***	Y	Y	N	N	Y	Y	Y
3 ***Riley***	Y	Y	N	N	Y	Y	Y
4 ***Aderholt***	Y	Y	N	N	Y	Y	N
5 Cramer	Y	Y	N	N	N	Y	Y
6 ***Bachus***	Y	Y	N	N	Y	Y	Y
7 Hilliard	Y	Y	N	N	N	Y	N
ALASKA							
AL ***Young***	?	?	N	N	Y	Y	?
ARIZONA							
1 ***Salmon***	Y	Y	N	Y	Y	N	Y
2 Pastor	Y	Y	N	N	N	Y	Y
3 ***Stump***	N	N	N	N	Y	Y	Y
4 ***Shadegg***	Y	Y	N	Y	Y	Y	Y
5 ***Kolbe***	Y	Y	N	Y	N	Y	Y
6 ***Hayworth***	Y	Y	N	Y	Y	Y	Y
ARKANSAS							
1 Berry	Y	Y	N	N	N	Y	Y
2 Snyder	Y	Y	Y	N	N	Y	Y
3 ***Hutchinson***	?	?	N	Y	Y	Y	Y
4 ***Dickey***	Y	Y	N	N	Y	Y	Y
CALIFORNIA							
1 Thompson	Y	Y	N	N	N	Y	N
2 ***Herger***	N	N	N	Y	?	Y	Y
3 ***Ose***	Y	Y	N	N	Y	Y	Y
4 ***Doolittle***	Y	Y	N	N	Y	Y	Y
5 Matsui	Y	Y	Y	N	N	Y	Y
6 Woolsey	Y	Y	Y	N	N	Y	Y
7 Miller, George	Y	Y	Y	Y	Y	N	Y
8 Pelosi	Y	Y	Y	N	N	N	Y
9 Lee	Y	Y	Y	N	N	N	Y
10 Tauscher	Y	Y	Y	N	N	N	Y
11 ***Pombo***	N	N	N	N	Y	Y	N
12 Lantos	Y	Y	Y	N	N	N	Y
13 Stark	Y	Y	Y	Y	N	N	N
14 Eshoo	Y	Y	Y	Y	N	N	Y
15 ***Campbell***	?	?	?	?	?	?	?
16 Lofgren	Y	Y	Y	Y	N	N	Y
17 Farr	Y	Y	Y	N	N	Y	Y
18 Condit	Y	Y	N	N	N	Y	Y
19 ***Radanovich***	Y	N	N	N	Y	Y	Y
20 Dooley	Y	Y	N	N	N	Y	Y
21 ***Thomas***	Y	N	N	N	N	Y	Y
22 Capps	Y	Y	N	Y	N	Y	Y
23 ***Gallegly***	Y	Y	Y	N	N	Y	Y
24 Sherman	Y	Y	Y	N	N	Y	Y
25 ***McKeon***	Y	Y	N	N	N	Y	Y
26 Berman	Y	Y	Y	N	N	N	Y
27 ***Rogan***	Y	Y	N	Y	Y	Y	N
28 ***Dreier***	Y	Y	N	N	N	Y	Y
29 Waxman	Y	Y	Y	N	N	N	Y
30 Becerra	+	+	+	–	–	+	Y
31 Martinez	Y	Y	N	N	N	Y	Y
32 Dixon	Y	Y	Y	N	N	Y	Y
33 Roybal-Allard	Y	Y	Y	N	N	Y	Y
34 Napolitano	Y	Y	Y	N	N	Y	Y
35 Waters	Y	Y	Y	N	Y	N	N
36 ***Kuykendall***	Y	Y	Y	N	Y	Y	Y
37 Millender-McD.	Y	Y	Y	N	N	Y	Y
38 ***Horn***	Y	Y	Y	N	Y	Y	Y
39 ***Royce***	N	Y	Y	Y	Y	N	Y
40 ***Lewis***	Y	Y	N	N	N	Y	Y
41 ***Miller, Gary***	Y	Y	N	Y	Y	Y	Y
42 Baca	Y	Y	N	N	N	Y	Y
43 ***Calvert***	Y	Y	N	N	N	Y	Y
44 ***Bono***	Y	Y	N	Y	N	Y	Y
45 ***Rohrabacher***	N	Y	Y	Y	Y	N	Y
46 Sanchez	Y	Y	N	N	N	Y	Y
47 ***Cox***	Y	Y	Y	Y	Y	Y	Y
48 ***Packard***	Y	Y	N	N	N	Y	Y
49 ***Bilbray***	Y	Y	Y	Y	Y	Y	N
50 Filner	Y	Y	Y	N	Y	N	N
51 ***Cunningham***	Y	Y	N	Y	N	Y	Y
52 ***Hunter***	Y	Y	N	N	Y	Y	Y
COLORADO							
1 DeGette	Y	Y	Y	Y	N	N	Y
2 Udall	Y	Y	Y	N	N	N	Y
3 ***McInnis***	Y	Y	N	N	Y	N	Y
4 ***Schaffer***	Y	Y	N	Y	Y	Y	N
5 ***Hefley***	Y	Y	Y	Y	Y	N	N
6 ***Tancredo***	Y	Y	Y	Y	Y	N	P
CONNECTICUT							
1 Larson	Y	Y	Y	N	N	Y	Y
2 Gejdenson	Y	Y	Y	Y	N	Y	Y
3 DeLauro	Y	Y	Y	N	N	Y	Y
4 ***Shays***	Y	Y	Y	Y	Y	N	Y
5 Maloney	Y	Y	Y	Y	N	N	Y
6 ***Johnson***	Y	Y	Y	Y	Y	Y	Y
DELAWARE							
AL ***Castle***	Y	Y	Y	Y	N	Y	Y
FLORIDA							
1 ***Scarborough***	Y	Y	?	?	?	Y	Y
2 Boyd	Y	Y	N	N	N	Y	Y
3 Brown	Y	Y	N	N	N	Y	Y
4 ***Fowler***	Y	Y	N	Y	Y	Y	Y
5 Thurman	Y	Y	N	N	N	Y	Y
6 ***Stearns***	Y	Y	N	Y	Y	Y	Y
7 ***Mica***	Y	Y	Y	Y	Y	N	Y
8 ***McCollum***	?	?	?	?	?	?	Y
9 ***Bilirakis***	Y	Y	N	N	N	Y	Y
10 ***Young***	Y	Y	N	N	Y	Y	Y
11 Davis	Y	Y	?	Y	N	Y	Y
12 ***Canady***	Y	Y	N	N	N	Y	Y
13 ***Miller***	Y	Y	N	Y	Y	Y	Y
14 ***Goss***	Y	Y	N	Y	Y	Y	Y
15 ***Weldon***	Y	Y	N	Y	Y	Y	Y
16 ***Foley***	Y	Y	N	N	Y	Y	Y
17 Meek	Y	Y	N	N	N	Y	Y
18 ***Ros-Lehtinen***	Y	Y	N	N	Y	Y	Y
19 Wexler	Y	Y	Y	Y	N	Y	N
20 Deutsch	Y	Y	Y	Y	N	N	N
21 ***Diaz-Balart***	Y	Y	N	N	Y	Y	Y
22 ***Shaw***	Y	Y	N	Y	Y	Y	Y
23 Hastings	Y	Y	Y	Y	N	Y	N
GEORGIA							
1 ***Kingston***	Y	N	N	N	N	Y	Y
2 Bishop	Y	Y	N	N	N	Y	Y
3 ***Collins***	Y	N	N	Y	Y	Y	Y
4 McKinney	?	?	Y	Y	Y	N	Y
5 Lewis	Y	Y	Y	Y	N	N	Y
6 ***Isakson***	Y	Y	N	N	Y	Y	Y
7 ***Barr***	N	N	N	Y	Y	Y	Y
8 ***Chambliss***	Y	Y	N	N	N	Y	Y
9 ***Deal***	Y	N	N	Y	Y	Y	Y
10 ***Norwood***	Y	N	N	N	Y	?	Y
11 ***Linder***	Y	Y	N	Y	Y	Y	Y
HAWAII							
1 Abercrombie	Y	Y	N	N	N	Y	Y
2 Mink	Y	Y	N	N	Y	Y	Y
IDAHO							
1 ***Chenoweth-Hage***	?	?	?	?	?	?	?
2 ***Simpson***	Y	Y	N	N	Y	Y	Y
ILLINOIS							
1 Rush	Y	Y	Y	N	N	N	Y
2 Jackson	Y	Y	Y	N	N	N	Y
3 Lipinski	Y	Y	Y	Y	Y	Y	Y
4 Gutierrez	Y	Y	Y	N	N	N	N
5 Blagojevich	Y	Y	Y	N	N	Y	Y
6 ***Hyde***	Y	Y	Y	N	Y	Y	Y
7 Davis	Y	Y	Y	N	N	N	Y
8 ***Crane***	Y	Y	Y	Y	Y	N	N
9 Schakowsky	Y	Y	Y	Y	N	N	N
10 ***Porter***	Y	Y	Y	Y	N	Y	Y
11 ***Weller***	Y	Y	Y	N	N	Y	N
12 Costello	Y	Y	Y	N	Y	Y	?
13 ***Biggert***	Y	Y	Y	Y	Y	Y	Y

ND Northern Democrats SD Southern Democrats

	380	381	382	383	384	385	386
14 *Hastert*							
15 *Ewing*	Y	Y	N	N	N	Y	Y
16 *Manzullo*	Y	Y	N	Y	Y	Y	Y
17 Evans	Y	Y	Y	N	Y	Y	Y
18 *LaHood*	N	N	N	N	Y	Y	Y
19 Phelps	Y	Y	Y	N	Y	Y	Y
20 *Shimkus*	Y	Y	N	N	Y	Y	Y
INDIANA							
1 Visclosky	Y	Y	N	N	N	Y	N
2 *McIntosh*	?	?	?	?	?	?	Y
3 Roemer	Y	Y	Y	Y	N	Y	Y
4 *Souder*	Y	Y	N	Y	N	Y	?
5 *Buyer*	Y	Y	N	N	N	Y	Y
6 *Burton*	Y	Y	N	N	Y	Y	Y
7 *Pease*	Y	N	Y	Y	Y	Y	Y
8 *Hostettler*	Y	Y	N	Y	Y	Y	Y
9 Hill	Y	Y	Y	N	N	Y	Y
10 Carson	Y	Y	Y	N	N	N	?
IOWA							
1 *Leach*	Y	Y	Y	N	Y	Y	?
2 *Nussle*	Y	Y	N	N	Y	Y	Y
3 Boswell	Y	Y	N	N	N	Y	Y
4 *Ganske*	Y	Y	N	Y	Y	Y	Y
5 *Latham*	Y	Y	N	N	N	Y	Y
KANSAS							
1 *Moran*	Y	N	N	N	Y	Y	Y
2 *Ryun*	Y	Y	N	N	Y	Y	Y
3 Moore	Y	Y	Y	N	N	Y	N
4 *Tiahrt*	Y	Y	N	N	Y	Y	Y
KENTUCKY							
1 *Whitfield*	Y	Y	Y	N	N	Y	?
2 *Lewis*	Y	Y	N	N	N	Y	Y
3 *Northup*	Y	Y	Y	Y	Y	Y	Y
4 Lucas	Y	Y	N	N	N	Y	Y
5 *Rogers*	Y	Y	N	N	N	Y	Y
6 *Fletcher*	Y	Y	N	N	N	Y	Y
LOUISIANA							
1 *Vitter*	Y	Y	N	N	Y	Y	Y
2 Jefferson	Y	Y	Y	N	N	Y	Y
3 *Tauzin*	Y	?	Y	N	Y	Y	Y
4 *McCrery*	Y	Y	N	Y	N	Y	Y
5 *Cooksey*	Y	Y	N	N	N	Y	Y
6 *Baker*	Y	Y	N	Y	Y	Y	?
7 John	Y	Y	N	N	N	Y	Y
MAINE							
1 Allen	Y	Y	Y	N	N	Y	Y
2 Baldacci	Y	Y	N	N	Y	Y	Y
MARYLAND							
1 *Gilchrest*	Y	Y	N	N	N	Y	Y
2 *Ehrlich*	Y	Y	N	Y	N	Y	Y
3 Cardin	Y	Y	Y	N	N	Y	Y
4 Wynn	Y	Y	Y	N	N	Y	?
5 Hoyer	+	+	Y	N	N	Y	Y
6 *Bartlett*	Y	Y	N	Y	Y	Y	Y
7 Cummings	Y	Y	Y	N	N	N	Y
8 *Morella*	Y	Y	Y	Y	N	Y	Y
MASSACHUSETTS							
1 Olver	Y	Y	Y	Y	N	Y	Y
2 Neal	Y	Y	Y	Y	N	N	Y
3 McGovern	Y	Y	Y	Y	N	N	Y
4 Frank	Y	P	Y	Y	N	N	Y
5 Meehan	Y	Y	Y	Y	N	N	Y
6 Tierney	Y	Y	Y	Y	N	N	Y
7 Markey	Y	Y	Y	Y	N	N	Y
8 Capuano	Y	Y	Y	Y	N	N	N
9 Moakley	Y	Y	Y	Y	N	Y	Y
10 Delahunt	Y	Y	Y	Y	N	N	Y
MICHIGAN							
1 Stupak	Y	Y	N	N	N	Y	N
2 *Hoekstra*	Y	Y	N	Y	Y	Y	Y
3 *Ehlers*	Y	Y	N	Y	Y	Y	Y
4 *Camp*	Y	Y	N	Y	Y	Y	Y
5 Barcia	Y	Y	Y	Y	N	Y	Y
6 *Upton*	Y	Y	N	Y	N	Y	Y
7 *Smith*	Y	N	N	N	Y	Y	Y
8 Stabenow	Y	Y	N	Y	N	Y	Y
9 Kildee	Y	Y	Y	Y	N	Y	Y
10 Bonior	Y	Y	Y	N	N	Y	N
11 *Knollenberg*	Y	N	N	Y	N	Y	?
12 Levin	Y	Y	Y	N	N	Y	Y
13 Rivers	Y	Y	Y	Y	N	N	Y
14 Conyers	Y	?	Y	Y	N	N	Y
15 Kilpatrick	Y	Y	Y	N	N	Y	Y
16 Dingell	Y	Y	N	N	N	Y	Y

	380	381	382	383	384	385	386
MINNESOTA							
1 *Gutknecht*	Y	Y	N	Y	Y	Y	Y
2 Minge	Y	Y	N	N	N	N	Y
3 *Ramstad*	Y	Y	Y	Y	Y	Y	N
4 Vento	?	?	?	?	?	?	?
5 Sabo	Y	Y	Y	N	Y	N	N
6 Luther	Y	Y	Y	Y	N	N	Y
7 Peterson	Y	Y	N	N	Y	N	N
8 Oberstar	Y	Y	N	N	N	N	N
MISSISSIPPI							
1 *Wicker*	Y	Y	N	N	Y	Y	Y
2 Thompson	Y	Y	N	N	N	Y	N
3 *Pickering*	Y	Y	N	N	Y	Y	Y
4 Shows	Y	Y	N	N	N	Y	Y
5 Taylor	Y	Y	Y	Y	Y	Y	N
MISSOURI							
1 Clay	Y	Y	Y	N	N	N	N
2 *Talent*	Y	Y	N	N	N	Y	Y
3 Gephardt	Y	Y	Y	N	N	N	Y
4 Skelton	Y	Y	N	N	N	Y	Y
5 McCarthy	Y	Y	Y	N	N	Y	Y
6 Danner	Y	Y	N	N	N	Y	Y
7 *Blunt*	Y	N	N	N	Y	Y	Y
8 *Emerson*	Y	Y	N	N	Y	Y	Y
9 *Hulshof*	Y	Y	Y	Y	Y	Y	N
MONTANA							
AL *Hill*	Y	Y	N	N	Y	Y	N
NEBRASKA							
1 *Bereuter*	Y	Y	N	Y	N	Y	Y
2 *Terry*	Y	Y	N	Y	Y	Y	Y
3 *Barrett*	Y	Y	N	Y	Y	Y	Y
NEVADA							
1 Berkley	Y	Y	Y	Y	N	N	Y
2 *Gibbons*	Y	Y	N	N	Y	Y	Y
NEW HAMPSHIRE							
1 *Sununu*	Y	Y	Y	Y	Y	N	Y
2 *Bass*	Y	Y	Y	Y	N	Y	Y
NEW JERSEY							
1 Andrews	Y	Y	Y	Y	N	N	Y
2 *LoBiondo*	Y	Y	Y	Y	Y	Y	N
3 *Saxton*	Y	Y	N	Y	Y	Y	Y
4 *Smith*	Y	Y	Y	Y	Y	Y	Y
5 *Roukema*	Y	Y	Y	Y	N	Y	Y
6 Pallone	Y	Y	Y	N	N	Y	Y
7 *Franks*	Y	Y	Y	Y	N	Y	Y
8 Pascrell	Y	Y	Y	N	N	Y	Y
9 Rothman	Y	Y	Y	N	N	Y	Y
10 Payne	?	?	?	?	N	N	Y
11 *Frelinghuysen*	Y	Y	Y	Y	N	Y	Y
12 Holt	Y	Y	Y	Y	N	Y	N
13 Menendez	Y	Y	Y	Y	N	Y	Y
NEW MEXICO							
1 *Wilson*	Y	Y	N	N	Y	Y	Y
2 *Skeen*	Y	Y	N	N	Y	Y	Y
3 Udall	Y	Y	N	N	N	Y	Y
NEW YORK							
1 Forbes	?	?	?	?	?	?	?
2 *Lazio*	Y	Y	Y	N	Y	Y	Y
3 *King*	Y	Y	Y	Y	N	Y	Y
4 McCarthy	Y	Y	Y	N	N	Y	Y
5 Ackerman	Y	P	Y	Y	N	Y	?
6 Meeks	Y	Y	Y	N	N	Y	Y
7 Crowley	Y	Y	Y	Y	N	Y	Y
8 Nadler	Y	Y	Y	Y	N	Y	Y
9 Weiner	Y	Y	Y	Y	N	Y	Y
10 Towns	Y	Y	N	N	N	N	Y
11 Owens	+	+	+	−	−	?	+
12 Velázquez	Y	Y	Y	Y	N	N	N
13 *Fossella*	Y	Y	Y	Y	N	Y	Y
14 Maloney	Y	Y	Y	N	N	N	Y
15 Rangel	Y	Y	Y	N	N	Y	Y
16 Serrano	Y	Y	Y	N	N	Y	Y
17 Engel	Y	Y	Y	N	N	Y	Y
18 Lowey	Y	Y	N	Y	N	Y	Y
19 *Kelly*	Y	Y	Y	Y	Y	Y	Y
20 *Gilman*	Y	Y	Y	Y	N	Y	Y
21 McNulty	?	?	?	?	?	?	?
22 *Sweeney*	Y	Y	N	N	N	Y	Y
23 *Boehlert*	Y	Y	Y	N	N	Y	Y
24 *McHugh*	Y	Y	N	N	Y	Y	Y
25 *Walsh*	Y	Y	N	N	N	Y	Y
26 Hinchey	Y	Y	Y	N	N	Y	Y
27 *Reynolds*	Y	Y	N	N	Y	Y	Y
28 Slaughter	Y	Y	+	+	−	+	?
29 LaFalce	Y	Y	Y	Y	N	Y	Y

	380	381	382	383	384	385	386
30 *Quinn*	Y	Y	N	N	Y	Y	Y
31 *Houghton*	Y	Y	Y	Y	N	Y	Y
NORTH CAROLINA							
1 Clayton	Y	Y	N	N	N	Y	Y
2 Etheridge	Y	Y	Y	N	N	Y	Y
3 *Jones*	Y	Y	Y	Y	Y	Y	Y
4 Price	Y	Y	Y	N	N	Y	Y
5 *Burr*	Y	Y	N	N	Y	Y	Y
6 *Coble*	N	Y	N	Y	N	Y	Y
7 McIntyre	Y	Y	N	N	N	Y	Y
8 *Hayes*	Y	Y	N	N	Y	Y	Y
9 *Myrick*	Y	Y	N	Y	Y	Y	Y
10 *Ballenger*	Y	Y	N	N	Y	Y	Y
11 *Taylor*	Y	Y	N	N	N	Y	Y
12 Watt	Y	Y	N	N	N	Y	Y
NORTH DAKOTA							
AL Pomeroy	Y	Y	N	N	N	Y	N
OHIO							
1 *Chabot*	Y	N	Y	Y	Y	Y	Y
2 *Portman*	Y	Y	N	Y	N	Y	Y
3 Hall	Y	Y	Y	N	N	Y	N
4 *Oxley*	Y	Y	N	Y	Y	Y	?
5 *Gillmor*	Y	Y	N	N	N	Y	Y
6 Strickland	Y	Y	N	Y	Y	Y	N
7 *Hobson*	Y	Y	N	N	N	Y	Y
8 *Boehner*	Y	Y	N	Y	N	Y	Y
9 Kaptur	Y	Y	N	N	N	Y	Y
10 Kucinich	Y	Y	Y	N	Y	N	N
11 Jones	Y	Y	Y	N	N	Y	Y
12 *Kasich*	Y	Y	N	Y	Y	Y	Y
13 Brown	Y	Y	Y	Y	N	N	Y
14 Sawyer	Y	Y	Y	N	N	Y	Y
15 *Pryce*	Y	Y	N	Y	Y	Y	Y
16 *Regula*	Y	Y	N	N	N	Y	Y
17 Traficant	Y	Y	N	N	Y	Y	Y
18 *Ney*	Y	Y	N	N	N	Y	Y
19 *LaTourette*	Y	Y	N	Y	N	Y	Y
OKLAHOMA							
1 *Largent*	Y	Y	N	N	Y	Y	Y
2 *Coburn*	N	N	N	Y	Y	N	Y
3 *Watkins*	Y	Y	N	N	N	Y	Y
4 *Watts*	Y	Y	N	N	Y	Y	Y
5 *Istook*	Y	Y	N	Y	Y	Y	Y
6 *Lucas*	Y	Y	N	N	N	Y	Y
OREGON							
1 Wu	Y	Y	Y	Y	N	N	N
2 *Walden*	Y	Y	N	N	Y	Y	Y
3 Blumenauer	Y	Y	Y	Y	N	N	Y
4 DeFazio	Y	Y	Y	Y	Y	Y	N
5 Hooley	Y	Y	Y	N	N	Y	Y
PENNSYLVANIA							
1 Brady	Y	Y	Y	N	N	N	N
2 Fattah	Y	Y	Y	N	N	N	N
3 Borski	Y	Y	Y	N	N	Y	N
4 Klink	Y	Y	N	N	N	Y	Y
5 *Peterson*	Y	Y	N	N	N	Y	Y
6 Holden	Y	Y	N	N	N	Y	Y
7 *Weldon*	Y	Y	Y	N	Y	Y	Y
8 *Greenwood*	Y	Y	Y	Y	N	Y	Y
9 *Shuster*	Y	Y	N	Y	Y	Y	Y
10 *Sherwood*	Y	Y	N	N	Y	Y	Y
11 Kanjorski	Y	Y	N	N	N	Y	Y
12 Murtha	Y	Y	N	N	N	Y	Y
13 Hoeffel	Y	Y	Y	Y	N	Y	Y
14 Coyne	Y	Y	Y	N	N	N	Y
15 *Toomey*	Y	Y	Y	Y	Y	Y	Y
16 *Pitts*	Y	Y	N	Y	Y	Y	Y
17 *Gekas*	Y	Y	N	N	Y	Y	Y
18 Doyle	Y	Y	Y	N	N	Y	Y
19 *Goodling*	Y	Y	N	Y	Y	Y	Y
20 Mascara	Y	Y	N	N	N	Y	Y
21 *English*	Y	Y	Y	Y	Y	Y	N
RHODE ISLAND							
1 Kennedy	Y	Y	Y	N	N	N	Y
2 Weygand	Y	Y	Y	N	N	N	Y
SOUTH CAROLINA							
1 *Sanford*	Y	N	Y	Y	Y	N	Y
2 *Spence*	Y	Y	N	Y	N	Y	Y
3 *Graham*	Y	Y	N	Y	Y	Y	Y
4 *DeMint*	Y	Y	N	Y	Y	Y	Y
5 Spratt	Y	Y	Y	N	Y	Y	Y
6 Clyburn	Y	Y	Y	Y	N	Y	Y
SOUTH DAKOTA							
AL *Thune*	Y	Y	N	N	Y	Y	Y

	380	381	382	383	384	385	386
TENNESSEE							
1 *Jenkins*	Y	Y	N	N	Y	Y	Y
2 *Duncan*	N	Y	Y	Y	Y	Y	Y
3 *Wamp*	Y	Y	Y	Y	Y	Y	Y
4 *Hilleary*	Y	N	N	Y	Y	Y	N
5 Clement	Y	Y	Y	N	N	Y	Y
6 Gordon	Y	Y	N	N	N	Y	Y
7 *Bryant*	Y	Y	N	Y	Y	Y	Y
8 Tanner	Y	Y	N	N	N	Y	Y
9 Ford	Y	Y	Y	N	N	Y	N
TEXAS							
1 Sandlin	Y	Y	N	N	N	Y	Y
2 Turner	Y	Y	N	N	N	Y	Y
3 *Johnson, Sam*	N	N	N	N	Y	Y	?
4 Hall	Y	Y	N	N	Y	Y	Y
5 *Sessions*	Y	Y	N	N	Y	Y	?
6 *Barton*	Y	N	N	N	Y	N	?
7 *Archer*	Y	N	N	Y	Y	Y	?
8 *Brady*	Y	Y	N	N	N	Y	Y
9 Lampson	Y	Y	N	N	N	Y	Y
10 Doggett	Y	Y	Y	Y	N	N	Y
11 Edwards	Y	Y	N	N	N	Y	Y
12 *Granger*	Y	Y	N	N	N	Y	Y
13 *Thornberry*	N	N	N	N	N	Y	Y
14 *Paul*	N	N	Y	Y	Y	N	?
15 Hinojosa	+	Y	N	N	N	Y	Y
16 Reyes	Y	Y	N	N	N	Y	Y
17 Stenholm	Y	Y	N	N	N	Y	Y
18 Jackson-Lee	Y	Y	Y	N	N	Y	Y
19 *Combest*	Y	Y	N	N	N	Y	Y
20 Gonzalez	Y	Y	Y	N	N	Y	Y
21 *Smith*	Y	Y	N	N	Y	Y	Y
22 *DeLay*	N	N	N	Y	Y	Y	Y
23 *Bonilla*	N	Y	N	N	N	Y	Y
24 Frost	Y	Y	N	N	N	Y	?
25 Bentsen	Y	Y	N	N	N	Y	Y
26 *Armey*	Y	N	N	N	Y	Y	Y
27 Ortiz	Y	Y	N	N	N	Y	Y
28 Rodriguez	Y	Y	N	N	N	Y	Y
29 Green	Y	Y	Y	N	N	Y	Y
30 Johnson, E.B.	Y	Y	Y	N	N	Y	Y
UTAH							
1 *Hansen*	Y	Y	N	N	Y	Y	Y
2 *Cook*	Y	Y	N	N	Y	Y	Y
3 *Cannon*	Y	N	N	N	Y	Y	Y
VERMONT							
AL *Sanders*	Y	Y	Y	N	N	Y	Y
VIRGINIA							
1 *Bateman*	Y	Y	N	N	Y	Y	?
2 Pickett	Y	Y	N	N	N	Y	N
3 Scott	Y	Y	Y	N	N	Y	Y
4 Sisisky	Y	Y	N	N	N	Y	?
5 *Goode*	Y	Y	N	N	Y	Y	Y
6 *Goodlatte*	Y	Y	N	N	Y	Y	Y
7 *Bliley*	Y	Y	N	Y	N	Y	Y
8 Moran	Y	Y	Y	Y	N	N	Y
9 Boucher	Y	Y	N	N	N	Y	Y
10 *Wolf*	Y	Y	N	Y	Y	Y	Y
11 *Davis*	Y	Y	Y	Y	Y	Y	Y
WASHINGTON							
1 Inslee	Y	Y	Y	Y	Y	N	Y
2 *Metcalf*	Y	Y	Y	Y	Y	Y	Y
3 Baird	Y	Y	Y	N	N	Y	N
4 *Hastings*	Y	Y	N	N	Y	Y	Y
5 *Nethercutt*	Y	Y	N	N	N	Y	Y
6 Dicks	Y	Y	N	N	N	Y	Y
7 McDermott	Y	Y	Y	Y	N	N	N
8 *Dunn*	Y	Y	N	Y	Y	Y	Y
9 Smith	?	?	?	?	?	?	?
WEST VIRGINIA							
1 Mollohan	Y	Y	?	N	N	Y	Y
2 Wise	Y	Y	N	N	N	Y	?
3 Rahall	Y	Y	N	N	N	?	Y
WISCONSIN							
1 *Ryan*	Y	Y	Y	Y	Y	Y	Y
2 Baldwin	Y	Y	Y	Y	N	N	Y
3 Kind	Y	Y	Y	Y	N	N	Y
4 Kleczka	Y	Y	Y	Y	N	Y	Y
5 Barrett	Y	Y	Y	Y	N	N	Y
6 *Petri*	Y	Y	Y	Y	N	N	Y
7 Obey	Y	Y	Y	N	N	N	?
8 *Green*	Y	Y	Y	Y	Y	Y	Y
9 *Sensenbrenner*	Y	Y	Y	Y	Y	N	Y
WYOMING							
AL *Cubin*	Y	Y	N	N	Y	Y	Y

Southern states - Ala., Ark., Fla., Ga., Ky., La., Miss., N.C., Okla., S.C., Tenn., Texas, Va.

387. HR 4810. 'Marriage Penalty' Tax Relief/Rule. Adoption of the rule (H Res 545) to provide for House floor consideration of the bill that would modify the tax code in order to reduce the so-called marriage penalty. Adopted 407-16: R 219-0; D 186-16 (ND 134-14, SD 52-2); I 2-0. July 12, 2000.

388. S 1892. Valles Caldera National Preserve/Passage. Hansen, R-Utah, motion to suspend the rules and pass the bill that would authorize the Agriculture Department to buy the 95,000-acre Baca Ranch in New Mexico for the purpose of creating the Valles Caldera National Preserve. Motion agreed to (thus cleared for the president) 377-45: R 174-44; D 202-0 (ND 148-0, SD 54-0); I 1-1. A two-thirds majority of those present and voting (282 in this case) is required for passage under suspension of the rules. July 12, 2000.

389. HR 4169. Barbara F. Vucanovich Post Office/Passage. McHugh, R-N.Y., motion to suspend the rules and pass the bill that would designate a post office in Reno, Nev., as the "Barbara F. Vucanovich Post Office Building." Motion agreed to 418-1: R 216-1; D 200-0 (ND 146-0, SD 54-0); I 2-0. A two-thirds majority of those present and voting (280 in this case) is required for passage under suspension of the rules. July 12, 2000.

390. HR 4810. 'Marriage Penalty' Tax Relief/Democratic Substitute. Rangel, D-N.Y., substitute amendment to reduce taxes for married couples by $95 billion over 10 years. The amendment would increase the standard deduction for married couples to twice that for singles, and would increase the eligibility limit for couples for the earned income tax credit by $2,000 in 2001 and by $2,500 in 2002. The measure would not make any changes to the lowest income tax bracket. Rejected 198-228: R 0-219; D 197-8 (ND 145-6, SD 52-2); I 1-1. July 12, 2000.

391. HR 4810. 'Marriage Penalty' Tax Relief/Motion to Recommit. Rangel, D-N.Y., motion to recommit the bill to the House Ways and Means Committee with instructions to add language that would not put the tax reduction into effect until a Medicare prescription drug benefit meeting certain criteria was enacted. Motion rejected 197-230: R 0-219; D 196-10 (ND 144-8, SD 52-2); I 1-1. July 12, 2000.

392. HR 4810. 'Marriage Penalty' Tax Relief/Passage. Passage of the bill to reduce taxes for married couples by approximately $182.3 billion over 10 years. The measure would increase the standard deduction claimed by married couples to twice the amount claimed by single taxpayers. The upper boundary of the 15 percent tax bracket would gradually increase from 2003 to 2008 to twice the limit for singles. The measure also would allow couples to earn an additional $2,000 before being disqualified from receiving the earned income tax credit. Passed 269-159: R 220-0; D 48-158 (ND 31-121, SD 17-37); I 1-1. July 12, 2000. A "nay" was a vote in support of the president's position.

393. HR 4447. Samuel H. Lacy Sr. Post Office/Passage. McHugh, R-N.Y., motion to suspend the rules and pass the bill designating a post office in Baltimore, Md., as the "Samuel H. Lacy Sr. Post Office Building." Motion agreed to 412-0: R 208-0; D 202-0 (ND 148-0, SD 54-0); I 2-0. A two-thirds majority of those present and voting (275 in this case) is required for passage under suspension of the rules. July 12, 2000.

Key

Y	Voted for (yea).
#	Paired for.
+	Announced for.
N	Voted against (nay).
X	Paired against.
–	Announced against.
P	Voted "present."
C	Voted "present" to avoid possible conflict of interest.
?	Did not vote or otherwise make a position known.

•

Democrats ***Republicans***
Independents

	387	388	389	390	391	392	393
ALABAMA							
1 ***Callahan***	Y	Y	Y	N	N	Y	?
2 ***Everett***	Y	N	Y	N	N	Y	Y
3 ***Riley***	Y	Y	Y	N	N	Y	Y
4 ***Aderholt***	Y	Y	Y	N	N	Y	Y
5 Cramer	Y	Y	Y	Y	Y	Y	Y
6 ***Bachus***	Y	Y	?	N	N	Y	Y
7 Hilliard	N	Y	Y	Y	Y	N	Y
ALASKA							
AL ***Young***	Y	Y	Y	N	N	Y	Y
ARIZONA							
1 ***Salmon***	Y	N	Y	N	N	Y	Y
2 Pastor	Y	Y	Y	Y	Y	N	Y
3 ***Stump***	Y	Y	Y	N	N	Y	Y
4 ***Shadegg***	Y	N	Y	N	N	Y	Y
5 ***Kolbe***	Y	Y	Y	N	N	Y	Y
6 ***Hayworth***	Y	Y	Y	N	N	Y	Y
ARKANSAS							
1 Berry	Y	Y	Y	N	Y	N	Y
2 Snyder	Y	Y	Y	Y	Y	N	Y
3 ***Hutchinson***	Y	Y	Y	N	N	Y	Y
4 ***Dickey***	Y	Y	Y	N	N	Y	Y
CALIFORNIA							
1 Thompson	Y	Y	Y	Y	Y	N	Y
2 ***Herger***	Y	N	Y	N	N	Y	Y
3 ***Ose***	Y	Y	Y	N	N	Y	Y
4 ***Doolittle***	Y	N	Y	N	N	Y	Y
5 Matsui	Y	Y	Y	Y	Y	N	Y
6 Woolsey	N	Y	Y	Y	Y	N	Y
7 Miller, George	N	Y	Y	Y	Y	N	Y
8 Pelosi	Y	Y	Y	Y	Y	N	Y
9 Lee	Y	Y	Y	Y	Y	N	Y
10 Tauscher	Y	Y	Y	Y	Y	Y	Y
11 ***Pombo***	Y	N	Y	N	N	Y	Y
12 Lantos	Y	Y	Y	Y	Y	N	Y
13 Stark	Y	Y	Y	Y	Y	N	Y
14 Eshoo	Y	Y	Y	Y	Y	N	Y
15 ***Campbell***	?	?	?	?	?	?	?
16 Lofgren	Y	Y	Y	Y	Y	N	Y
17 Farr	Y	Y	Y	Y	Y	N	Y
18 Condit	Y	Y	Y	Y	Y	Y	Y
19 ***Radanovich***	Y	Y	Y	N	N	Y	Y
20 Dooley	Y	Y	Y	Y	Y	N	?
21 ***Thomas***	Y	Y	Y	N	N	Y	Y
22 Capps	Y	Y	Y	Y	Y	Y	Y
23 ***Gallegly***	Y	Y	Y	N	N	Y	Y
24 Sherman	Y	Y	Y	Y	Y	N	Y
25 ***McKeon***	Y	Y	Y	N	N	Y	Y
26 Berman	Y	Y	Y	Y	Y	N	Y
27 ***Rogan***	Y	Y	Y	N	N	Y	Y
28 ***Dreier***	Y	N	Y	N	N	Y	Y
29 Waxman	Y	Y	Y	Y	Y	N	Y
30 Becerra	Y	Y	Y	Y	Y	N	Y
31 Martinez	Y	Y	Y	N	N	Y	Y
32 Dixon	Y	Y	Y	Y	Y	N	Y
33 Roybal-Allard	Y	Y	Y	Y	Y	N	Y
34 Napolitano	Y	Y	Y	Y	Y	N	Y
35 Waters	Y	Y	Y	?	Y	N	Y
36 ***Kuykendall***	Y	Y	Y	N	N	Y	Y
37 Millender-McD.	Y	Y	Y	Y	Y	N	Y
38 ***Horn***	Y	Y	Y	N	N	Y	+
39 ***Royce***	Y	N	Y	N	N	Y	Y
40 ***Lewis***	Y	Y	Y	N	N	Y	?
41 ***Miller, Gary***	Y	Y	Y	N	N	Y	Y
42 Baca	Y	Y	Y	Y	Y	N	Y
43 ***Calvert***	Y	Y	Y	N	N	Y	Y
44 ***Bono***	Y	Y	Y	N	N	Y	Y
45 ***Rohrabacher***	Y	Y	Y	N	N	Y	Y
46 Sanchez	Y	Y	Y	Y	Y	N	Y
47 ***Cox***	Y	Y	Y	N	N	Y	Y
48 ***Packard***	Y	Y	Y	N	N	Y	Y
49 ***Bilbray***	Y	Y	Y	N	N	Y	Y
50 Filner	N	Y	Y	Y	Y	N	Y
51 ***Cunningham***	Y	Y	Y	N	N	Y	Y
52 ***Hunter***	Y	N	Y	N	N	Y	Y
COLORADO							
1 DeGette	Y	Y	Y	Y	Y	N	Y
2 Udall	N	Y	Y	Y	Y	Y	Y
3 ***McInnis***	Y	Y	Y	N	N	Y	Y
4 ***Schaffer***	Y	N	Y	N	N	Y	Y
5 ***Hefley***	Y	Y	Y	N	N	Y	Y
6 ***Tancredo***	Y	Y	Y	N	N	Y	Y
CONNECTICUT							
1 Larson	Y	Y	Y	Y	Y	N	Y
2 Gejdenson	Y	Y	Y	Y	Y	N	Y
3 DeLauro	Y	Y	Y	Y	Y	N	Y
4 ***Shays***	Y	Y	Y	N	N	Y	Y
5 Maloney	Y	Y	Y	Y	Y	Y	Y
6 ***Johnson***	Y	Y	Y	N	N	Y	Y
DELAWARE							
AL ***Castle***	Y	Y	Y	N	N	Y	Y
FLORIDA							
1 ***Scarborough***	Y	Y	Y	N	N	Y	Y
2 Boyd	Y	Y	Y	Y	Y	N	Y
3 Brown	Y	Y	Y	Y	Y	N	Y
4 ***Fowler***	Y	Y	Y	N	N	Y	Y
5 Thurman	Y	Y	Y	Y	Y	N	Y
6 ***Stearns***	Y	Y	Y	N	N	Y	Y
7 ***Mica***	Y	Y	Y	N	N	Y	Y
8 ***McCollum***	Y	Y	Y	N	N	Y	Y
9 ***Bilirakis***	Y	Y	Y	N	N	Y	Y
10 ***Young***	Y	Y	Y	N	N	Y	Y
11 Davis	Y	Y	Y	Y	Y	N	Y
12 ***Canady***	Y	Y	Y	N	N	Y	Y
13 ***Miller***	Y	Y	Y	N	N	Y	Y
14 ***Goss***	Y	Y	Y	N	N	Y	Y
15 ***Weldon***	Y	Y	Y	N	N	Y	Y
16 ***Foley***	Y	Y	Y	N	N	Y	Y
17 Meek	Y	Y	Y	Y	Y	N	Y
18 ***Ros-Lehtinen***	Y	Y	Y	N	N	Y	Y
19 Wexler	Y	Y	Y	Y	Y	N	Y
20 Deutsch	Y	Y	Y	Y	Y	N	Y
21 ***Diaz-Balart***	Y	Y	Y	N	N	Y	Y
22 ***Shaw***	Y	Y	Y	N	N	Y	Y
23 Hastings	Y	Y	Y	Y	Y	N	Y
GEORGIA							
1 ***Kingston***	Y	N	Y	N	N	Y	Y
2 Bishop	Y	Y	Y	Y	Y	Y	Y
3 ***Collins***	Y	Y	Y	N	N	Y	Y
4 McKinney	Y	Y	Y	Y	Y	Y	Y
5 Lewis	Y	Y	Y	Y	Y	N	Y
6 ***Isakson***	Y	Y	Y	N	N	Y	Y
7 ***Barr***	Y	Y	Y	N	N	Y	Y
8 ***Chambliss***	Y	Y	Y	N	N	Y	Y
9 ***Deal***	Y	Y	Y	N	N	Y	Y
10 ***Norwood***	Y	Y	Y	N	N	Y	Y
11 ***Linder***	Y	Y	Y	N	N	Y	Y
HAWAII							
1 Abercrombie	Y	Y	Y	Y	Y	N	Y
2 Mink	Y	Y	Y	Y	Y	Y	Y
IDAHO							
1 ***Chenoweth-Hage***	?	?	?	?	?	?	?
2 ***Simpson***	Y	Y	Y	N	N	Y	Y
ILLINOIS							
1 Rush	Y	Y	Y	Y	Y	N	Y
2 Jackson	N	Y	Y	Y	Y	N	Y
3 Lipinski	Y	Y	Y	Y	Y	Y	Y
4 Gutierrez	N	Y	Y	Y	Y	N	Y
5 Blagojevich	Y	Y	Y	Y	Y	Y	Y
6 ***Hyde***	Y	Y	Y	N	N	Y	Y
7 Davis	Y	Y	Y	Y	Y	N	Y
8 ***Crane***	Y	Y	Y	N	N	Y	Y
9 Schakowsky	Y	Y	Y	Y	Y	N	Y
10 ***Porter***	Y	Y	Y	N	N	Y	Y
11 ***Weller***	Y	Y	Y	N	N	Y	Y
12 Costello	Y	Y	Y	Y	Y	Y	Y
13 ***Biggert***	Y	Y	Y	N	N	Y	Y

ND Northern Democrats SD Southern Democrats

	387	388	389	390	391	392	393
14 ***Hastert***						Y	
15 ***Ewing***	Y	Y	Y	N	N	Y	?
16 ***Manzullo***	Y	N	Y	N	N	Y	Y
17 Evans	Y	Y	?	Y	Y	N	Y
18 ***LaHood***	Y	Y	Y	N	N	Y	Y
19 Phelps	Y	Y	Y	Y	Y	Y	Y
20 ***Shimkus***	Y	Y	Y	N	N	Y	Y
INDIANA							
1 Visclosky	Y	Y	Y	N	Y	N	Y
2 ***McIntosh***	Y	Y	Y	N	N	Y	Y
3 Roemer	Y	Y	Y	Y	Y	Y	Y
4 ***Souder***	Y	Y	Y	N	N	Y	Y
5 ***Buyer***	Y	Y	Y	N	N	Y	Y
6 ***Burton***	Y	Y	Y	N	N	Y	Y
7 ***Pease***	Y	Y	Y	N	N	Y	Y
8 ***Hostettler***	Y	N	Y	N	N	Y	Y
9 Hill	Y	Y	Y	Y	N	N	Y
10 Carson	?	?	?	?	?	?	?
IOWA							
1 ***Leach***	Y	Y	Y	N	N	Y	Y
2 ***Nussle***	Y	Y	Y	N	N	Y	Y
3 Boswell	Y	Y	Y	Y	Y	Y	Y
4 ***Ganske***	Y	N	Y	N	N	Y	Y
5 ***Latham***	Y	Y	Y	N	N	Y	Y
KANSAS							
1 ***Moran***	Y	Y	Y	N	N	Y	Y
2 ***Ryun***	Y	N	Y	N	N	Y	Y
3 Moore	Y	Y	Y	Y	Y	Y	Y
4 ***Tiahrt***	Y	Y	Y	N	N	Y	Y
KENTUCKY							
1 ***Whitfield***	Y	N	Y	N	N	Y	Y
2 ***Lewis***	Y	N	Y	N	N	Y	Y
3 ***Northup***	Y	Y	Y	N	N	Y	Y
4 Lucas	Y	Y	Y	N	Y	Y	Y
5 ***Rogers***	Y	Y	Y	N	N	Y	Y
6 ***Fletcher***	Y	Y	Y	N	N	Y	Y
LOUISIANA							
1 ***Vitter***	Y	N	Y	N	N	Y	Y
2 Jefferson	Y	Y	Y	Y	Y	N	Y
3 ***Tauzin***	Y	Y	Y	N	N	Y	Y
4 ***McCrery***	Y	Y	Y	N	N	Y	Y
5 ***Cooksey***	Y	Y	Y	N	N	Y	Y
6 ***Baker***	Y	Y	Y	N	N	Y	Y
7 John	Y	Y	Y	Y	Y	Y	Y
MAINE							
1 Allen	Y	Y	Y	Y	Y	N	Y
2 Baldacci	Y	Y	Y	Y	Y	N	Y
MARYLAND							
1 ***Gilchrest***	Y	Y	Y	N	N	Y	Y
2 ***Ehrlich***	Y	Y	Y	N	N	Y	Y
3 Cardin	Y	Y	Y	Y	Y	N	Y
4 Wynn	?	?	?	Y	Y	N	Y
5 Hoyer	Y	Y	Y	Y	Y	N	Y
6 ***Bartlett***	Y	N	Y	N	N	Y	Y
7 Cummings	Y	Y	Y	Y	Y	N	Y
8 ***Morella***	Y	Y	Y	N	N	Y	Y
MASSACHUSETTS							
1 Olver	Y	Y	Y	Y	Y	N	Y
2 Neal	Y	Y	Y	Y	Y	N	Y
3 McGovern	Y	Y	Y	Y	Y	N	Y
4 Frank	N	Y	Y	Y	Y	N	Y
5 Meehan	Y	Y	Y	Y	Y	N	Y
6 Tierney	Y	Y	Y	Y	Y	N	Y
7 Markey	Y	Y	Y	Y	Y	N	Y
8 Capuano	Y	Y	Y	Y	Y	N	Y
9 Moakley	Y	Y	Y	Y	Y	N	Y
10 Delahunt	Y	Y	Y	Y	Y	N	Y
MICHIGAN							
1 Stupak	Y	Y	Y	Y	Y	Y	Y
2 ***Hoekstra***	Y	Y	Y	N	N	Y	Y
3 ***Ehlers***	Y	Y	Y	N	N	Y	Y
4 ***Camp***	Y	Y	Y	N	N	Y	Y
5 Barcia	Y	Y	Y	N	N	Y	Y
6 ***Upton***	Y	Y	Y	N	N	Y	Y
7 ***Smith***	Y	Y	Y	N	N	Y	Y
8 Stabenow	Y	Y	Y	Y	Y	Y	Y
9 Kildee	Y	Y	Y	Y	Y	N	Y
10 Bonior	Y	Y	Y	Y	Y	N	Y
11 ***Knollenberg***	Y	Y	Y	N	N	Y	Y
12 Levin	Y	Y	Y	Y	Y	N	Y
13 Rivers	Y	Y	Y	Y	Y	N	Y
14 Conyers	N	Y	Y	Y	Y	N	Y
15 Kilpatrick	Y	Y	Y	Y	Y	N	Y
16 Dingell	Y	Y	Y	Y	Y	N	Y
MINNESOTA							
1 ***Gutknecht***	Y	Y	Y	N	N	Y	Y
2 Minge	Y	Y	Y	Y	Y	N	Y
3 ***Ramstad***	Y	Y	Y	N	N	Y	Y
4 Vento	?	?	?	?	?	?	?
5 Sabo	N	Y	Y	Y	Y	N	Y
6 Luther	Y	Y	Y	Y	Y	N	Y
7 Peterson	Y	Y	Y	Y	N	N	Y
8 Oberstar	N	Y	Y	Y	Y	N	Y
MISSISSIPPI							
1 ***Wicker***	Y	Y	Y	N	N	Y	Y
2 Thompson	Y	Y	Y	Y	Y	Y	Y
3 ***Pickering***	Y	Y	Y	N	N	Y	Y
4 Shows	Y	Y	Y	Y	Y	Y	Y
5 Taylor	Y	Y	Y	Y	N	N	Y
MISSOURI							
1 Clay	Y	Y	Y	Y	Y	N	?
2 ***Talent***	Y	Y	Y	N	N	Y	Y
3 Gephardt	Y	Y	Y	Y	Y	N	Y
4 Skelton	Y	Y	Y	Y	Y	Y	Y
5 McCarthy	Y	Y	Y	Y	Y	N	Y
6 Danner	Y	Y	Y	N	Y	Y	Y
7 ***Blunt***	Y	Y	Y	N	N	Y	Y
8 ***Emerson***	Y	Y	Y	N	N	Y	Y
9 ***Hulshof***	Y	Y	Y	N	N	Y	Y
MONTANA							
AL ***Hill***	Y	Y	Y	N	N	Y	Y
NEBRASKA							
1 ***Bereuter***	Y	Y	Y	N	N	Y	Y
2 ***Terry***	Y	N	Y	N	N	Y	?
3 ***Barrett***	Y	Y	Y	N	N	Y	Y
NEVADA							
1 Berkley	Y	Y	Y	Y	Y	Y	Y
2 ***Gibbons***	Y	N	Y	N	N	Y	Y
NEW HAMPSHIRE							
1 ***Sununu***	Y	Y	Y	N	N	Y	Y
2 ***Bass***	Y	Y	Y	N	N	Y	Y
NEW JERSEY							
1 Andrews	Y	Y	Y	Y	Y	N	Y
2 ***LoBiondo***	Y	Y	Y	N	N	Y	Y
3 ***Saxton***	Y	Y	Y	N	N	Y	Y
4 ***Smith***	Y	Y	Y	N	N	Y	Y
5 ***Roukema***	Y	Y	Y	N	N	Y	Y
6 Pallone	N	Y	Y	Y	Y	N	Y
7 ***Franks***	Y	Y	Y	N	N	Y	Y
8 Pascrell	Y	Y	Y	Y	Y	Y	Y
9 Rothman	Y	Y	Y	Y	Y	N	Y
10 Payne	Y	Y	Y	Y	Y	N	Y
11 ***Frelinghuysen***	Y	Y	Y	N	N	Y	Y
12 Holt	Y	Y	Y	Y	Y	Y	Y
13 Menendez	Y	Y	Y	Y	Y	N	Y
NEW MEXICO							
1 ***Wilson***	Y	Y	Y	N	N	Y	Y
2 ***Skeen***	Y	Y	Y	N	N	Y	Y
3 Udall	Y	Y	Y	Y	Y	N	Y
NEW YORK							
1 Forbes	?	?	?	?	?	?	?
2 ***Lazio***	Y	Y	Y	N	N	Y	Y
3 ***King***	Y	Y	Y	N	N	Y	Y
4 McCarthy	Y	Y	Y	Y	Y	Y	Y
5 Ackerman	?	?	?	Y	Y	N	Y
6 Meeks	Y	Y	Y	Y	Y	N	Y
7 Crowley	Y	Y	Y	Y	Y	N	?
8 Nadler	Y	Y	Y	Y	Y	N	Y
9 Weiner	Y	Y	Y	Y	Y	N	Y
10 Towns	Y	Y	Y	Y	Y	N	Y
11 Owens	+	+	+	Y	Y	N	Y
12 Velázquez	Y	Y	Y	Y	Y	N	Y
13 ***Fossella***	Y	Y	Y	N	N	Y	Y
14 Maloney	Y	Y	Y	Y	Y	N	Y
15 Rangel	Y	Y	Y	Y	Y	N	?
16 Serrano	Y	Y	Y	Y	Y	N	Y
17 Engel	Y	Y	Y	Y	Y	N	Y
18 Lowey	Y	Y	Y	Y	Y	N	Y
19 ***Kelly***	Y	Y	Y	N	N	Y	Y
20 ***Gilman***	Y	Y	Y	N	N	Y	Y
21 McNulty	?	?	?	?	?	?	?
22 ***Sweeney***	Y	Y	Y	N	N	Y	Y
23 ***Boehlert***	Y	Y	Y	N	N	Y	Y
24 ***McHugh***	Y	Y	Y	N	N	Y	Y
25 ***Walsh***	Y	Y	Y	N	N	Y	Y
26 Hinchey	N	Y	Y	Y	Y	N	Y
27 ***Reynolds***	Y	Y	Y	N	N	Y	Y
28 Slaughter	+	+	+	Y	Y	N	Y
29 LaFalce	Y	Y	Y	Y	Y	N	Y
30 ***Quinn***	Y	Y	Y	N	N	Y	Y
31 ***Houghton***	Y	?	Y	N	N	Y	Y
NORTH CAROLINA							
1 Clayton	Y	Y	Y	Y	Y	N	Y
2 Etheridge	Y	Y	Y	Y	Y	Y	Y
3 ***Jones***	Y	N	Y	N	N	Y	Y
4 Price	Y	Y	Y	Y	Y	N	Y
5 ***Burr***	Y	Y	Y	N	N	Y	Y
6 ***Coble***	Y	N	Y	N	N	Y	Y
7 McIntyre	Y	Y	Y	Y	Y	Y	Y
8 ***Hayes***	Y	N	Y	N	N	Y	Y
9 ***Myrick***	Y	Y	Y	N	N	Y	Y
10 ***Ballenger***	Y	Y	Y	N	N	Y	Y
11 ***Taylor***	Y	Y	Y	N	N	Y	Y
12 Watt	Y	Y	Y	Y	Y	N	Y
NORTH DAKOTA							
AL Pomeroy	Y	Y	Y	Y	Y	N	Y
OHIO							
1 ***Chabot***	Y	N	Y	N	N	Y	Y
2 ***Portman***	Y	Y	Y	N	N	Y	Y
3 Hall	Y	Y	Y	Y	Y	N	Y
4 ***Oxley***	Y	Y	Y	N	N	Y	?
5 ***Gillmor***	Y	Y	Y	N	N	Y	Y
6 Strickland	Y	Y	Y	Y	Y	N	Y
7 ***Hobson***	Y	Y	Y	N	N	Y	Y
8 ***Boehner***	Y	Y	Y	N	N	Y	Y
9 Kaptur	Y	Y	Y	Y	Y	N	Y
10 Kucinich	N	Y	Y	Y	Y	N	Y
11 Jones	Y	Y	Y	Y	Y	N	Y
12 ***Kasich***	Y	N	Y	N	N	Y	Y
13 Brown	Y	Y	Y	Y	Y	N	Y
14 Sawyer	Y	Y	Y	Y	Y	N	Y
15 ***Pryce***	Y	Y	Y	N	N	Y	Y
16 ***Regula***	Y	Y	Y	N	N	Y	Y
17 Traficant	Y	Y	Y	N	N	Y	Y
18 ***Ney***	Y	Y	Y	N	N	Y	Y
19 ***LaTourette***	Y	Y	Y	N	N	Y	Y
OKLAHOMA							
1 ***Largent***	Y	N	Y	N	N	Y	Y
2 ***Coburn***	Y	N	Y	N	N	Y	Y
3 ***Watkins***	Y	Y	Y	N	N	Y	Y
4 ***Watts***	Y	Y	Y	N	N	Y	Y
5 ***Istook***	Y	Y	Y	N	N	Y	Y
6 ***Lucas***	Y	Y	Y	N	N	Y	Y
OREGON							
1 Wu	Y	Y	Y	Y	Y	Y	Y
2 ***Walden***	Y	Y	Y	N	N	Y	Y
3 Blumenauer	Y	Y	Y	Y	Y	N	Y
4 DeFazio	Y	Y	Y	Y	Y	N	Y
5 Hooley	Y	Y	Y	Y	Y	Y	Y
PENNSYLVANIA							
1 Brady	Y	Y	Y	Y	Y	N	Y
2 Fattah	Y	Y	Y	Y	Y	N	Y
3 Borski	Y	Y	Y	Y	Y	N	Y
4 Klink	Y	Y	Y	Y	Y	N	Y
5 ***Peterson***	Y	Y	Y	N	N	Y	Y
6 Holden	Y	Y	Y	Y	Y	N	Y
7 ***Weldon***	Y	Y	Y	N	N	Y	Y
8 ***Greenwood***	Y	Y	Y	N	N	Y	Y
9 ***Shuster***	Y	Y	Y	N	N	Y	Y
10 ***Sherwood***	Y	Y	Y	N	N	Y	Y
11 Kanjorski	Y	Y	Y	Y	Y	N	Y
12 Murtha	Y	Y	Y	N	N	N	Y
13 Hoeffel	Y	Y	Y	Y	Y	N	Y
14 Coyne	Y	Y	Y	Y	Y	N	Y
15 ***Toomey***	Y	N	Y	N	N	Y	Y
16 ***Pitts***	Y	Y	Y	N	N	Y	Y
17 ***Gekas***	Y	Y	Y	N	N	Y	Y
18 Doyle	Y	Y	?	Y	Y	Y	Y
19 ***Goodling***	Y	Y	Y	N	N	Y	Y
20 Mascara	Y	Y	Y	Y	Y	Y	Y
21 ***English***	Y	Y	Y	N	N	Y	Y
RHODE ISLAND							
1 Kennedy	Y	Y	Y	Y	Y	N	Y
2 Weygand	Y	Y	Y	Y	Y	N	Y
SOUTH CAROLINA							
1 ***Sanford***	Y	N	N	N	N	Y	Y
2 ***Spence***	Y	Y	Y	N	N	Y	Y
3 ***Graham***	Y	N	Y	N	N	Y	Y
4 ***DeMint***	Y	N	Y	N	N	Y	Y
5 Spratt	Y	Y	Y	Y	Y	Y	Y
6 Clyburn	Y	Y	Y	Y	Y	Y	Y
SOUTH DAKOTA							
AL ***Thune***	Y	Y	Y	N	N	Y	Y
TENNESSEE							
1 ***Jenkins***	Y	N	Y	N	N	Y	Y
2 ***Duncan***	Y	N	Y	N	N	Y	?
3 ***Wamp***	Y	N	Y	N	N	Y	Y
4 ***Hilleary***	Y	Y	Y	N	N	Y	Y
5 Clement	Y	Y	Y	Y	Y	Y	Y
6 Gordon	Y	Y	Y	Y	Y	Y	Y
7 ***Bryant***	Y	Y	Y	N	N	Y	Y
8 Tanner	Y	Y	Y	Y	Y	N	Y
9 Ford	Y	Y	Y	Y	Y	N	Y
TEXAS							
1 Sandlin	Y	Y	Y	Y	Y	Y	Y
2 Turner	Y	Y	Y	Y	Y	N	Y
3 ***Johnson, Sam***	Y	N	Y	N	N	Y	Y
4 Hall	Y	Y	Y	Y	Y	Y	Y
5 ***Sessions***	Y	Y	Y	N	N	Y	Y
6 ***Barton***	Y	Y	Y	N	N	Y	Y
7 ***Archer***	Y	N	Y	N	N	Y	Y
8 ***Brady***	Y	N	Y	N	N	Y	Y
9 Lampson	Y	Y	Y	Y	Y	N	Y
10 Doggett	N	Y	Y	Y	Y	N	Y
11 Edwards	Y	Y	Y	Y	Y	N	Y
12 ***Granger***	Y	Y	Y	N	N	Y	Y
13 ***Thornberry***	Y	N	Y	N	N	Y	Y
14 ***Paul***	Y	N	Y	N	N	Y	Y
15 Hinojosa	Y	Y	Y	Y	Y	N	Y
16 Reyes	Y	Y	Y	Y	Y	N	Y
17 Stenholm	Y	Y	Y	Y	N	N	Y
18 Jackson-Lee	Y	Y	Y	Y	Y	N	Y
19 ***Combest***	Y	Y	Y	N	N	Y	Y
20 Gonzalez	Y	Y	Y	Y	Y	N	Y
21 ***Smith***	Y	Y	Y	N	N	Y	Y
22 ***DeLay***	Y	Y	Y	N	N	Y	Y
23 ***Bonilla***	Y	Y	Y	N	N	Y	Y
24 Frost	Y	Y	Y	Y	Y	N	Y
25 Bentsen	Y	Y	Y	Y	Y	N	Y
26 ***Armey***	Y	Y	Y	N	N	Y	?
27 Ortiz	Y	Y	Y	Y	Y	N	Y
28 Rodriguez	Y	Y	Y	Y	Y	N	Y
29 Green	Y	Y	Y	Y	Y	N	Y
30 Johnson, E.B.	Y	Y	Y	Y	Y	N	Y
UTAH							
1 ***Hansen***	Y	Y	Y	N	N	Y	?
2 ***Cook***	Y	N	Y	N	N	Y	?
3 ***Cannon***	Y	Y	Y	N	N	Y	Y
VERMONT							
AL *Sanders*	Y	Y	Y	Y	Y	N	Y
VIRGINIA							
1 ***Bateman***	Y	Y	Y	N	N	Y	Y
2 Pickett	Y	Y	Y	Y	Y	Y	Y
3 Scott	Y	Y	Y	Y	Y	N	Y
4 Sisisky	Y	Y	Y	Y	Y	Y	Y
5 *Goode*	Y	N	Y	N	N	Y	Y
6 ***Goodlatte***	Y	N	Y	N	N	Y	Y
7 ***Bliley***	Y	Y	Y	N	N	Y	Y
8 Moran	Y	Y	Y	Y	Y	N	Y
9 Boucher	Y	Y	Y	Y	Y	N	Y
10 ***Wolf***	Y	Y	Y	N	N	Y	Y
11 ***Davis***	Y	Y	Y	N	N	Y	Y
WASHINGTON							
1 Inslee	Y	Y	Y	Y	N	Y	Y
2 ***Metcalf***	Y	Y	?	N	N	Y	Y
3 Baird	Y	Y	Y	Y	Y	Y	Y
4 ***Hastings***	Y	N	Y	N	N	Y	Y
5 ***Nethercutt***	Y	Y	Y	N	N	Y	Y
6 Dicks	Y	Y	Y	Y	Y	N	Y
7 McDermott	Y	Y	Y	Y	Y	N	Y
8 ***Dunn***	Y	Y	Y	N	N	Y	Y
9 Smith	?	?	?	?	?	?	?
WEST VIRGINIA							
1 Mollohan	Y	Y	Y	Y	Y	N	Y
2 Wise	Y	Y	Y	Y	Y	Y	Y
3 Rahall	Y	Y	Y	Y	Y	N	Y
WISCONSIN							
1 ***Ryan***	Y	Y	Y	N	N	Y	Y
2 Baldwin	Y	Y	Y	Y	Y	N	Y
3 Kind	Y	Y	Y	Y	Y	N	Y
4 Kleczka	Y	Y	Y	Y	Y	N	Y
5 Barrett	Y	Y	Y	Y	Y	N	Y
6 ***Petri***	Y	Y	Y	N	N	Y	Y
7 Obey	N	Y	Y	Y	Y	N	Y
8 ***Green***	Y	Y	Y	N	N	Y	?
9 ***Sensenbrenner***	Y	N	Y	N	N	Y	Y
WYOMING							
AL ***Cubin***	Y	Y	Y	N	N	Y	Y

Southern states - Ala., Ark., Fla., Ga., Ky., La., Miss., N.C., Okla., S.C., Tenn., Texas, Va.

394. HR 4811. Fiscal 2001 Foreign Operations Appropriations/Rule. Adoption of the rule (H Res 546) to provide for House floor consideration of the bill that would appropriate $13.3 billion in fiscal year 2001 for foreign operations. Adopted 225-199: R 218-0; D 6-198 (ND 5-145, SD 1-53); I 1-1. July 12, 2000.

395. HR 4576. Fiscal 2001 Defense Appropriations/Closed Conference. Young, R-Fla., motion to close portions of the conference to the public during consideration of national security issues. Motion agreed to 407-7: R 211-0; D 194-7 (ND 142-5, SD 52-2); I 2-0. July 12, 2000.

396. HR 4811. Fiscal 2001 Foreign Operations Appropriations/Overseas Abortions. Greenwood, R-Pa., amendment that would strike the bill's "Mexico City" restrictions on international family planning, which restricts U.S. funding to any private, non-governmental or multilateral organization that uses its own funds to directly or indirectly perform abortions in a foreign country. Rejected 206-221: R 35-185; D 170-35 (ND 125-26, SD 45-9); I 1-1. July 13, 2000. A "yea" was a vote in support of the president's position.

397. HR 4811. Fiscal 2001 Foreign Operations Appropriations/Debt Relief. Waters, D-Calif., amendment that would increase funding for the Heavily Indebted Poor Countries Trust Fund by $156 million and offset it with cuts to various other programs. The fund was created to help debtor countries write off most of the money owed to multilateral agencies. Adopted 216-211: R26-194; D 189-16 (ND 142-9, SD 47-7); I 1-1. July 13, 2000.

398. HR 4811. Fiscal 2001 Foreign Operations Appropriations/AIDS Marshall Plan. Lee, D-Calif., amendment that would provide an additional $42 million to the World Bank's AIDS Marshall Plan Trust Fund. The increase would be offset by cuts to foreign military financing. Adopted 267-156: R 72-146; D 194-9 (ND 144-5, SD 50-4); I 1-1. July 13, 2000.

399. HR 4811. Fiscal 2001 Foreign Operations Appropriations/Nuclear Accident Liability. Bereuter, R-Neb., amendment that would prohibit the government from providing guarantees or insurance for whatever liability claims might be made if nuclear reactors provided to North Korea are involved in a catastrophic nuclear accident. Adopted 298-125: R 214-5; D 82-120 (ND 56-93, SD 26-27); I 2-0. July 13, 2000.

400. HR 4811. Fiscal 2001 Foreign Operations Appropriations/Passage. Passage of the bill that would appropriate $13.3 billion for foreign aid and export assistance, $451 million less than the current level. Passed 239-185: R 191-29; D 48-154 (ND 31-118, SD 17-36); I 0-2. July 13, 2000.

Key

- Y Voted for (yea).
- # Paired for.
- + Announced for.
- N Voted against (nay).
- X Paired against.
- – Announced against.
- P Voted "present."
- C Voted "present" to avoid possible conflict of interest.
- ? Did not vote or otherwise make a position known.

•

Democrats ***Republicans***
Independents

	394	395	396	397	398	399	400
ALABAMA							
1 ***Callahan***	Y	Y	N	N	N	N	Y
2 ***Everett***	Y	Y	N	N	N	Y	Y
3 ***Riley***	Y	Y	N	N	N	Y	Y
4 ***Aderholt***	Y	Y	N	Y	N	Y	Y
5 Cramer	N	Y	Y	N	Y	N	Y
6 ***Bachus***	Y	Y	N	Y	Y	Y	Y
7 Hilliard	N	Y	Y	Y	Y	N	N
ALASKA							
AL ***Young***	Y	Y	N	N	N	Y	Y
ARIZONA							
1 ***Salmon***	Y	Y	N	N	N	Y	Y
2 Pastor	N	Y	Y	Y	Y	N	N
3 ***Stump***	Y	Y	N	N	N	Y	N
4 ***Shadegg***	Y	Y	N	N	N	Y	Y
5 ***Kolbe***	Y	Y	Y	N	Y	Y	Y
6 ***Hayworth***	Y	Y	N	N	N	Y	Y
ARKANSAS							
1 Berry	N	Y	N	Y	Y	Y	N
2 Snyder	N	Y	Y	Y	Y	N	N
3 ***Hutchinson***	Y	Y	N	N	N	Y	Y
4 ***Dickey***	Y	Y	N	N	N	Y	Y
CALIFORNIA							
1 Thompson	N	Y	Y	Y	Y	Y	N
2 ***Herger***	Y	Y	N	N	N	Y	N
3 ***Ose***	Y	Y	Y	N	N	Y	Y
4 ***Doolittle***	Y	Y	N	N	N	Y	N
5 Matsui	?	?	Y	Y	Y	N	N
6 Woolsey	N	Y	Y	Y	Y	Y	N
7 Miller, George	N	Y	Y	Y	Y	N	N
8 Pelosi	N	Y	Y	Y	Y	N	N
9 Lee	N	Y	Y	Y	Y	N	N
10 Tauscher	N	Y	Y	Y	Y	N	N
11 ***Pombo***	Y	Y	N	N	N	Y	N
12 Lantos	N	Y	Y	Y	Y	N	N
13 Stark	N	N	Y	Y	Y	Y	N
14 Eshoo	N	Y	Y	Y	Y	N	N
15 ***Campbell***	?	?	Y	Y	Y	Y	N
16 Lofgren	N	Y	Y	Y	Y	N	N
17 Farr	N	Y	Y	Y	Y	N	N
18 Condit	N	Y	Y	N	Y	N	N
19 ***Radanovich***	Y	Y	N	N	N	Y	Y
20 Dooley	N	Y	Y	Y	Y	N	N
21 ***Thomas***	Y	Y	Y	N	N	Y	Y
22 Capps	N	Y	Y	Y	Y	Y	N
23 ***Gallegly***	Y	Y	N	N	Y	Y	Y
24 Sherman	N	Y	Y	Y	Y	Y	Y
25 ***McKeon***	Y	Y	N	N	N	Y	Y
26 Berman	N	Y	Y	Y	Y	N	Y
27 ***Rogan***	Y	Y	N	N	N	Y	Y
28 ***Dreier***	Y	Y	N	N	Y	Y	Y
29 Waxman	N	Y	Y	Y	Y	N	N
30 Becerra	N	Y	Y	Y	Y	N	N
31 Martinez	Y	Y	N	N	N	Y	Y
32 Dixon	N	Y	Y	Y	Y	N	N
33 Roybal-Allard	N	Y	Y	Y	Y	N	N
34 Napolitano	N	Y	Y	Y	Y	N	N
35 Waters	N	N	Y	Y	Y	N	N
36 ***Kuykendall***	Y	Y	Y	N	Y	Y	Y
37 Millender-McD.	N	Y	Y	Y	Y	N	N
38 ***Horn***	Y	Y	Y	Y	Y	Y	Y
39 ***Royce***	Y	Y	N	N	Y	Y	N
40 ***Lewis***	Y	Y	N	N	N	N	Y
41 ***Miller, Gary***	Y	Y	N	N	N	Y	Y
42 Baca	N	?	Y	Y	Y	N	N
43 ***Calvert***	Y	Y	N	N	N	Y	Y
44 ***Bono***	Y	Y	N	N	Y	Y	Y
45 ***Rohrabacher***	Y	Y	N	N	Y	Y	N
46 Sanchez	N	Y	Y	Y	Y	N	N
47 ***Cox***	Y	Y	N	N	N	Y	Y
48 ***Packard***	Y	Y	N	N	N	Y	Y
49 ***Bilbray***	Y	Y	Y	N	Y	Y	Y
50 Filner	N	Y	Y	Y	Y	N	N
51 ***Cunningham***	Y	Y	N	N	N	Y	N
52 ***Hunter***	Y	?	N	N	N	Y	Y
COLORADO							
1 DeGette	N	Y	Y	Y	Y	N	N
2 Udall	N	Y	Y	Y	Y	N	N
3 ***McInnis***	Y	Y	N	N	N	Y	N
4 ***Schaffer***	Y	Y	N	Y	Y	Y	N
5 ***Hefley***	Y	Y	N	N	N	Y	N
6 ***Tancredo***	Y	Y	N	N	N	Y	Y
CONNECTICUT							
1 Larson	N	Y	Y	Y	Y	N	N
2 Gejdenson	N	Y	Y	Y	Y	N	N
3 DeLauro	N	Y	Y	Y	Y	N	N
4 ***Shays***	Y	Y	Y	Y	Y	Y	Y
5 Maloney	N	Y	Y	N	Y	N	Y
6 ***Johnson***	Y	Y	Y	N	Y	Y	Y
DELAWARE							
AL ***Castle***	Y	Y	Y	Y	Y	Y	Y
FLORIDA							
1 ***Scarborough***	Y	Y	N	N	N	Y	Y
2 Boyd	N	Y	Y	N	N	Y	Y
3 Brown	N	Y	Y	Y	Y	N	N
4 ***Fowler***	Y	Y	Y	N	N	Y	Y
5 Thurman	N	Y	Y	Y	Y	N	N
6 ***Stearns***	Y	Y	N	N	N	Y	N
7 ***Mica***	Y	Y	N	N	Y	Y	Y
8 ***McCollum***	Y	Y	N	N	N	Y	Y
9 ***Bilirakis***	Y	Y	N	N	N	Y	Y
10 ***Young***	Y	Y	N	N	N	N	Y
11 Davis	N	Y	Y	Y	Y	Y	Y
12 ***Canady***	Y	Y	N	N	Y	Y	Y
13 ***Miller***	Y	Y	N	N	N	Y	Y
14 ***Goss***	Y	Y	N	N	N	Y	Y
15 ***Weldon***	Y	Y	N	N	N	Y	Y
16 ***Foley***	Y	Y	Y	N	Y	Y	Y
17 Meek	N	Y	Y	Y	Y	N	N
18 ***Ros-Lehtinen***	Y	Y	N	N	Y	Y	Y
19 Wexler	N	Y	Y	Y	Y	N	Y
20 Deutsch	N	Y	Y	Y	Y	N	Y
21 ***Diaz-Balart***	Y	?	N	N	N	Y	Y
22 ***Shaw***	Y	Y	N	N	N	Y	Y
23 Hastings	N	Y	Y	Y	Y	N	N
GEORGIA							
1 ***Kingston***	Y	Y	N	N	Y	Y	Y
2 Bishop	N	Y	Y	Y	Y	Y	N
3 ***Collins***	Y	Y	N	N	N	Y	Y
4 McKinney	N	Y	Y	Y	Y	Y	N
5 Lewis	N	Y	Y	Y	Y	N	N
6 ***Isakson***	Y	Y	Y	N	N	Y	Y
7 ***Barr***	Y	Y	N	N	N	Y	N
8 ***Chambliss***	Y	Y	N	N	?	Y	Y
9 ***Deal***	Y	Y	N	N	N	Y	Y
10 ***Norwood***	Y	Y	N	N	N	Y	Y
11 ***Linder***	Y	Y	N	N	N	Y	Y
HAWAII							
1 Abercrombie	N	Y	Y	Y	Y	Y	N
2 Mink	N	Y	Y	Y	Y	N	N
IDAHO							
1 ***Chenoweth-Hage***	?	?	–	–	–	+	–
2 ***Simpson***	Y	?	N	N	N	Y	Y
ILLINOIS							
1 Rush	N	Y	Y	Y	Y	N	N
2 Jackson	N	Y	Y	Y	Y	N	N
3 Lipinski	N	Y	N	Y	N	Y	N
4 Gutierrez	N	Y	Y	Y	Y	N	N
5 Blagojevich	N	Y	Y	Y	Y	Y	Y
6 ***Hyde***	Y	Y	N	N	Y	Y	Y
7 Davis	N	Y	Y	Y	Y	N	N
8 ***Crane***	Y	Y	N	N	N	Y	Y
9 Schakowsky	N	Y	Y	Y	Y	Y	Y
10 ***Porter***	Y	Y	Y	Y	Y	Y	Y
11 ***Weller***	Y	Y	N	N	N	Y	Y
12 Costello	N	Y	N	Y	Y	Y	N
13 ***Biggert***	Y	Y	Y	N	N	Y	Y

ND Northern Democrats SD Southern Democrats

	394	395	396	397	398	399	400
14 ***Hastert***			N	N			Y
15 ***Ewing***	Y	Y	N	N	N	Y	Y
16 ***Manzullo***	Y	Y	N	N	N	Y	Y
17 Evans	N	Y	Y	Y	Y	Y	N
18 ***LaHood***	Y	Y	N	N	N	Y	Y
19 Phelps	N	Y	N	Y	Y	Y	N
20 ***Shimkus***	Y	Y	N	N	N	Y	Y
INDIANA							
1 Visclosky	N	Y	Y	Y	Y	N	N
2 ***McIntosh***	Y	Y	?	?	?	?	?
3 Roemer	N	Y	N	N	Y	N	N
4 ***Souder***	Y	Y	N	N	N	Y	Y
5 ***Buyer***	Y	Y	N	N	N	Y	Y
6 ***Burton***	Y	Y	N	N	N	Y	Y
7 ***Pease***	Y	Y	N	N	Y	Y	Y
8 ***Hostettler***	Y	Y	N	N	N	Y	Y
9 Hill	N	Y	Y	N	N	N	N
10 Carson	?	?	Y	Y	Y	N	N
IOWA							
1 ***Leach***	Y	Y	Y	Y	Y	Y	Y
2 ***Nussle***	Y	?	N	Y	Y	Y	Y
3 Boswell	N	Y	Y	Y	N	Y	N
4 ***Ganske***	Y	Y	N	Y	Y	Y	Y
5 ***Latham***	Y	Y	N	Y	N	Y	Y
KANSAS							
1 ***Moran***	Y	Y	N	N	Y	Y	Y
2 ***Ryun***	Y	Y	N	N	N	Y	Y
3 Moore	Y	Y	Y	Y	Y	Y	N
4 ***Tiahrt***	Y	Y	N	N	N	Y	Y
KENTUCKY							
1 ***Whitfield***	Y	Y	N	N	Y	Y	Y
2 ***Lewis***	Y	Y	N	N	N	Y	N
3 ***Northup***	Y	Y	N	N	N	Y	Y
4 Lucas	N	Y	N	Y	N	Y	Y
5 ***Rogers***	Y	Y	N	N	N	Y	Y
6 ***Fletcher***	Y	Y	N	N	Y	Y	Y
LOUISIANA							
1 ***Vitter***	Y	Y	N	N	N	Y	Y
2 Jefferson	N	Y	Y	Y	Y	N	N
3 ***Tauzin***	Y	Y	N	N	N	Y	Y
4 ***McCrery***	Y	Y	N	N	N	Y	Y
5 ***Cooksey***	?	Y	N	N	N	Y	Y
6 ***Baker***	Y	Y	N	N	N	N	Y
7 John	N	Y	N	Y	Y	Y	Y
MAINE							
1 Allen	N	Y	Y	Y	Y	N	N
2 Baldacci	N	Y	Y	Y	Y	N	N
MARYLAND							
1 ***Gilchrest***	Y	Y	Y	Y	Y	Y	Y
2 ***Ehrlich***	Y	Y	Y	N	Y	Y	Y
3 Cardin	N	Y	Y	Y	Y	N	N
4 Wynn	N	Y	Y	Y	Y	Y	N
5 Hoyer	N	Y	Y	Y	Y	N	N
6 ***Bartlett***	Y	Y	N	N	N	Y	Y
7 Cummings	N	Y	+	+	+	N	N
8 ***Morella***	Y	Y	Y	Y	Y	N	Y
MASSACHUSETTS							
1 Olver	N	Y	Y	Y	Y	N	N
2 Neal	N	Y	Y	Y	Y	N	N
3 McGovern	N	Y	Y	Y	Y	N	N
4 Frank	N	Y	Y	Y	Y	N	N
5 Meehan	N	Y	Y	Y	Y	Y	N
6 Tierney	N	Y	Y	Y	Y	Y	N
7 Markey	N	Y	Y	Y	Y	?	?
8 Capuano	N	Y	Y	Y	Y	N	N
9 Moakley	N	Y	Y	Y	Y	N	N
10 Delahunt	N	Y	Y	Y	Y	N	N
MICHIGAN							
1 Stupak	N	Y	N	Y	Y	Y	Y
2 ***Hoekstra***	Y	Y	N	N	Y	Y	Y
3 ***Ehlers***	Y	Y	N	Y	Y	Y	Y
4 ***Camp***	Y	Y	N	N	Y	Y	Y
5 Barcia	N	Y	N	Y	Y	Y	Y
6 ***Upton***	Y	Y	N	N	Y	Y	Y
7 ***Smith***	Y	Y	N	N	N	Y	Y
8 Stabenow	N	Y	Y	Y	Y	Y	Y
9 Kildee	N	Y	N	Y	Y	N	N
10 Bonior	N	Y	Y	Y	Y	N	N
11 ***Knollenberg***	Y	Y	N	N	N	Y	Y
12 Levin	N	Y	Y	Y	Y	Y	N
13 Rivers	N	Y	Y	Y	Y	Y	N
14 Conyers	N	Y	Y	Y	Y	N	N
15 Kilpatrick	N	Y	Y	Y	Y	N	N
16 Dingell	N	Y	Y	Y	Y	N	N
MINNESOTA							
1 ***Gutknecht***	Y	Y	N	N	Y	Y	Y
2 Minge	N	Y	Y	Y	Y	Y	N
3 ***Ramstad***	Y	Y	Y	Y	Y	Y	Y
4 Vento	?	?	?	?	?	?	?
5 Sabo	N	Y	Y	Y	Y	N	N
6 Luther	N	Y	Y	Y	Y	Y	N
7 Peterson	Y	Y	N	Y	Y	N	N
8 Oberstar	N	Y	N	Y	Y	N	N
MISSISSIPPI							
1 ***Wicker***	Y	Y	N	N	N	Y	Y
2 Thompson	N	Y	Y	Y	Y	N	N
3 ***Pickering***	Y	Y	N	N	Y	Y	Y
4 Shows	N	Y	N	N	Y	Y	Y
5 Taylor	N	Y	N	N	Y	Y	N
MISSOURI							
1 Clay	?	?	?	?	?	?	?
2 ***Talent***	Y	Y	N	N	N	Y	Y
3 Gephardt	N	Y	Y	Y	Y	N	N
4 Skelton	N	Y	N	Y	Y	Y	N
5 McCarthy	N	Y	Y	Y	Y	Y	N
6 Danner	N	Y	N	N	N	Y	N
7 ***Blunt***	Y	Y	N	N	N	Y	Y
8 ***Emerson***	Y	Y	N	N	Y	Y	Y
9 ***Hulshof***	Y	Y	N	N	Y	Y	Y
MONTANA							
AL ***Hill***	Y	Y	N	N	N	Y	Y
NEBRASKA							
1 ***Bereuter***	Y	Y	N	N	N	Y	Y
2 ***Terry***	Y	Y	N	N	N	Y	Y
3 ***Barrett***	Y	Y	N	N	N	Y	Y
NEVADA							
1 Berkley	N	Y	Y	Y	Y	Y	Y
2 ***Gibbons***	Y	Y	Y	N	N	Y	Y
NEW HAMPSHIRE							
1 ***Sununu***	Y	Y	N	Y	Y	Y	Y
2 ***Bass***	Y	Y	Y	N	N	Y	Y
NEW JERSEY							
1 Andrews	N	Y	Y	Y	Y	Y	N
2 ***LoBiondo***	Y	Y	N	N	N	Y	Y
3 ***Saxton***	Y	Y	N	N	N	Y	Y
4 ***Smith***	Y	Y	N	Y	Y	Y	Y
5 ***Roukema***	Y	Y	Y	N	N	Y	Y
6 Pallone	N	Y	Y	Y	Y	N	N
7 ***Franks***	Y	Y	Y	N	N	Y	Y
8 Pascrell	N	Y	Y	Y	Y	Y	Y
9 Rothman	N	Y	Y	Y	Y	Y	N
10 Payne	N	Y	Y	Y	Y	N	N
11 ***Frelinghuysen***	Y	Y	Y	N	N	Y	Y
12 Holt	N	Y	Y	Y	Y	Y	Y
13 Menendez	N	Y	Y	Y	Y	Y	N
NEW MEXICO							
1 ***Wilson***	Y	Y	N	N	N	Y	Y
2 ***Skeen***	Y	Y	N	N	N	Y	Y
3 Udall	N	Y	Y	Y	Y	Y	N
NEW YORK							
1 Forbes	?	?	?	?	?	?	?
2 ***Lazio***	Y	Y	Y	N	N	Y	Y
3 ***King***	Y	Y	N	N	N	Y	Y
4 McCarthy	N	Y	Y	Y	Y	N	Y
5 Ackerman	N	Y	Y	Y	Y	N	N
6 Meeks	N	Y	Y	Y	Y	N	N
7 Crowley	N	Y	Y	Y	Y	N	Y
8 Nadler	N	Y	Y	Y	Y	Y	Y
9 Weiner	N	Y	Y	Y	Y	N	Y
10 Towns	N	Y	Y	Y	Y	N	Y
11 Owens	N	Y	Y	Y	Y	N	Y
12 Velázquez	N	Y	Y	Y	?	Y	N
13 ***Fossella***	Y	Y	N	N	Y	Y	Y
14 Maloney	N	Y	Y	Y	Y	N	Y
15 Rangel	N	Y	Y	Y	Y	N	N
16 Serrano	N	Y	Y	Y	?	Y	N
17 Engel	N	Y	Y	Y	Y	N	Y
18 Lowey	N	Y	Y	Y	Y	N	Y
19 ***Kelly***	Y	Y	Y	Y	Y	Y	Y
20 ***Gilman***	Y	Y	Y	N	N	Y	Y
21 McNulty	?	?	?	?	?	?	?
22 ***Sweeney***	Y	Y	Y	N	N	Y	Y
23 ***Boehlert***	Y	Y	Y	Y	Y	Y	Y
24 ***McHugh***	Y	Y	N	N	Y	Y	Y
25 ***Walsh***	Y	Y	N	N	N	Y	Y
26 Hinchey	N	Y	Y	Y	Y	Y	N
27 ***Reynolds***	Y	Y	N	N	N	Y	Y
28 Slaughter	N	Y	Y	Y	Y	Y	N
29 LaFalce	N	Y	N	Y	Y	N	Y
30 ***Quinn***	Y	Y	N	N	N	Y	Y
31 ***Houghton***	Y	Y	Y	N	Y	Y	Y
NORTH CAROLINA							
1 Clayton	N	Y	Y	Y	Y	N	N
2 Etheridge	N	Y	Y	Y	Y	N	N
3 ***Jones***	Y	Y	N	N	N	Y	N
4 Price	N	Y	Y	Y	Y	N	N
5 ***Burr***	Y	Y	N	N	N	Y	Y
6 ***Coble***	Y	Y	N	N	N	Y	Y
7 McIntyre	Y	Y	N	N	N	Y	Y
8 ***Hayes***	Y	Y	N	N	Y	Y	N
9 ***Myrick***	Y	Y	N	N	Y	Y	Y
10 ***Ballenger***	Y	Y	N	N	N	Y	Y
11 ***Taylor***	Y	Y	N	N	N	Y	Y
12 Watt	N	N	Y	Y	Y	N	N
NORTH DAKOTA							
AL Pomeroy	N	Y	Y	Y	Y	N	N
OHIO							
1 ***Chabot***	Y	Y	N	N	Y	Y	Y
2 ***Portman***	Y	Y	N	N	Y	Y	Y
3 Hall	N	Y	N	Y	Y	N	N
4 ***Oxley***	Y	Y	N	N	N	Y	Y
5 ***Gillmor***	Y	Y	N	N	N	Y	Y
6 Strickland	N	Y	Y	Y	Y	Y	N
7 ***Hobson***	Y	Y	N	N	Y	Y	Y
8 ***Boehner***	Y	Y	N	N	N	Y	Y
9 Kaptur	N	Y	Y	Y	Y	N	Y
10 Kucinich	N	N	N	N	Y	Y	N
11 Jones	N	?	Y	Y	Y	N	N
12 ***Kasich***	Y	?	N	Y	Y	Y	Y
13 Brown	N	Y	Y	Y	Y	N	N
14 Sawyer	N	Y	Y	Y	Y	N	N
15 ***Pryce***	Y	Y	Y	N	Y	Y	Y
16 ***Regula***	Y	Y	N	N	N	Y	Y
17 Traficant	Y	Y	N	Y	Y	Y	Y
18 ***Ney***	Y	?	N	N	N	Y	Y
19 ***LaTourette***	Y	Y	N	Y	N	Y	Y
OKLAHOMA							
1 ***Largent***	Y	Y	N	N	Y	Y	Y
2 ***Coburn***	Y	Y	N	N	Y	Y	N
3 ***Watkins***	Y	Y	N	N	N	Y	N
4 ***Watts***	Y	Y	N	N	N	Y	Y
5 ***Istook***	Y	Y	N	N	N	Y	Y
6 ***Lucas***	Y	Y	N	N	N	Y	N
OREGON							
1 Wu	N	Y	Y	Y	Y	Y	Y
2 ***Walden***	Y	Y	Y	N	N	Y	Y
3 Blumenauer	N	N	Y	Y	Y	N	N
4 DeFazio	N	N	Y	Y	Y	Y	N
5 Hooley	N	Y	Y	Y	Y	Y	Y
PENNSYLVANIA							
1 Brady	N	Y	Y	Y	Y	N	N
2 Fattah	N	Y	Y	Y	Y	N	N
3 Borski	N	?	N	Y	Y	N	N
4 Klink	N	Y	N	Y	Y	Y	Y
5 ***Peterson***	Y	Y	N	N	N	Y	Y
6 Holden	N	Y	N	N	Y	Y	Y
7 ***Weldon***	Y	Y	N	N	N	Y	Y
8 ***Greenwood***	Y	Y	Y	N	Y	Y	Y
9 ***Shuster***	Y	Y	N	N	N	Y	Y
10 ***Sherwood***	Y	Y	N	N	Y	Y	Y
11 Kanjorski	N	Y	N	Y	Y	N	N
12 Murtha	N	Y	N	Y	Y	N	N
13 Hoeffel	Y	Y	Y	Y	Y	Y	N
14 Coyne	N	Y	Y	Y	Y	N	N
15 ***Toomey***	Y	Y	N	N	N	Y	Y
16 ***Pitts***	Y	Y	N	N	N	Y	Y
17 ***Gekas***	Y	?	N	N	N	Y	Y
18 Doyle	N	Y	N	Y	Y	Y	Y
19 ***Goodling***	Y	Y	N	N	Y	Y	Y
20 Mascara	N	Y	N	Y	Y	Y	Y
21 ***English***	Y	Y	N	Y	N	Y	Y
RHODE ISLAND							
1 Kennedy	N	Y	Y	Y	Y	N	N
2 Weygand	N	Y	N	Y	Y	Y	Y
SOUTH CAROLINA							
1 ***Sanford***	Y	Y	N	N	N	Y	N
2 ***Spence***	Y	Y	N	N	N	Y	Y
3 ***Graham***	Y	Y	N	N	N	Y	Y
4 ***DeMint***	Y	Y	N	N	N	Y	Y
5 Spratt	N	Y	Y	Y	Y	Y	N
6 Clyburn	N	Y	Y	Y	Y	N	N
SOUTH DAKOTA							
AL ***Thune***	Y	Y	N	N	Y	Y	Y
TENNESSEE							
1 ***Jenkins***	Y	Y	N	N	Y	Y	N
2 ***Duncan***	Y	Y	N	N	Y	Y	N
3 ***Wamp***	Y	Y	N	N	Y	Y	Y
4 ***Hilleary***	Y	Y	N	N	Y	Y	Y
5 Clement	N	Y	Y	Y	Y	Y	N
6 Gordon	N	Y	Y	Y	Y	Y	Y
7 ***Bryant***	Y	Y	N	N	Y	Y	Y
8 Tanner	N	Y	Y	Y	Y	Y	N
9 Ford	N	Y	Y	Y	Y	N	N
TEXAS							
1 Sandlin	N	Y	Y	Y	Y	N	N
2 Turner	N	Y	Y	Y	Y	Y	Y
3 ***Johnson, Sam***	Y	Y	N	N	N	Y	Y
4 Hall	N	Y	N	N	Y	Y	N
5 ***Sessions***	Y	Y	N	N	N	Y	Y
6 ***Barton***	Y	Y	N	N	N	Y	Y
7 ***Archer***	Y	?	N	N	N	Y	Y
8 ***Brady***	Y	Y	N	N	N	Y	Y
9 Lampson	N	Y	Y	Y	Y	Y	Y
10 Doggett	N	Y	Y	Y	Y	Y	N
11 Edwards	N	Y	Y	Y	Y	N	N
12 ***Granger***	Y	Y	N	N	N	Y	Y
13 ***Thornberry***	Y	Y	N	N	N	Y	Y
14 ***Paul***	Y	Y	N	N	Y	Y	N
15 Hinojosa	N	Y	Y	Y	Y	N	N
16 Reyes	N	Y	Y	Y	Y	Y	N
17 Stenholm	N	Y	N	Y	Y	Y	N
18 Jackson-Lee	N	N	Y	Y	Y	N	N
19 ***Combest***	Y	Y	N	N	N	Y	N
20 Gonzalez	N	Y	Y	Y	Y	N	N
21 ***Smith***	Y	Y	N	N	N	Y	Y
22 ***DeLay***	Y	Y	N	N	N	Y	Y
23 ***Bonilla***	Y	Y	N	N	N	Y	Y
24 Frost	N	Y	Y	Y	Y	N	Y
25 Bentsen	N	Y	Y	Y	Y	Y	Y
26 ***Armey***	Y	Y	N	N	N	Y	Y
27 Ortiz	N	Y	N	Y	Y	Y	N
28 Rodriguez	N	Y	Y	Y	Y	N	N
29 Green	N	Y	Y	Y	Y	Y	Y
30 Johnson, E.B.	N	Y	Y	Y	Y	N	N
UTAH							
1 ***Hansen***	Y	Y	N	N	N	Y	N
2 ***Cook***	Y	Y	N	N	N	Y	N
3 ***Cannon***	Y	Y	N	N	N	Y	Y
VERMONT							
AL *Sanders*	N	Y	Y	Y	Y	Y	N
VIRGINIA							
1 ***Bateman***	Y	Y	N	N	N	Y	Y
2 Pickett	N	Y	Y	N	N	Y	Y
3 Scott	N	Y	Y	Y	Y	Y	N
4 Sisisky	N	Y	Y	Y	Y	Y	Y
5 *Goode*	Y	Y	N	N	N	Y	N
6 ***Goodlatte***	Y	Y	N	N	N	Y	N
7 ***Bliley***	Y	Y	N	N	N	Y	Y
8 Moran	N	Y	Y	Y	Y	N	N
9 Boucher	N	Y	Y	Y	Y	?	?
10 ***Wolf***	Y	Y	N	Y	N	Y	Y
11 ***Davis***	Y	Y	Y	N	Y	Y	Y
WASHINGTON							
1 Inslee	N	Y	Y	Y	Y	N	N
2 ***Metcalf***	Y	Y	N	N	N	Y	Y
3 Baird	N	Y	Y	Y	Y	Y	N
4 ***Hastings***	Y	Y	N	N	N	Y	Y
5 ***Nethercutt***	Y	Y	N	N	Y	Y	Y
6 Dicks	N	Y	Y	N	Y	N	N
7 McDermott	N	Y	Y	Y	Y	N	N
8 ***Dunn***	Y	Y	N	N	Y	Y	Y
9 Smith	?	?	?	?	?	?	?
WEST VIRGINIA							
1 Mollohan	N	Y	N	Y	Y	?	?
2 Wise	N	Y	Y	Y	Y	?	?
3 Rahall	N	Y	N	Y	Y	N	N
WISCONSIN							
1 ***Ryan***	Y	Y	N	N	N	Y	Y
2 Baldwin	N	Y	Y	Y	Y	N	N
3 Kind	N	Y	Y	Y	Y	Y	N
4 Kleczka	N	Y	Y	Y	Y	Y	N
5 Barrett	N	Y	Y	Y	Y	Y	N
6 ***Petri***	Y	Y	N	N	Y	Y	Y
7 Obey	N	Y	Y	Y	Y	N	N
8 ***Green***	Y	Y	N	N	N	Y	N
9 ***Sensenbrenner***	Y	Y	N	Y	Y	Y	N
WYOMING							
AL ***Cubin***	Y	Y	N	Y	N	Y	Y

Southern states - Ala., Ark., Fla., Ga., Ky., La., Miss., N.C., Okla., S.C., Tenn., Texas, Va.

401. H Res 534. Nuclear Security Lapses/Adoption. Spence, R-S.C., motion to suspend the rules and adopt the resolution expressing the sense of the House that security failures at Los Alamos National Laboratory show that the National Nuclear Security Administration's policies and procedures remain inadequate. The resolution also states that the individuals responsible must be held accountable and immediate action must be taken to correct security deficiencies. Motion agreed to 391-5: R 206-0; D 183-5 (ND 133-5, SD 50-0); I 2-0. A two-thirds majority of those present and voting (264 in this case) is required for adoption under suspension of the rules. July 17, 2000.

402. H Con Res 319. Latvian Independence/Adoption. Bereuter, R-Neb., motion to suspend the rules and adopt the concurrent resolution congratulating Latvia on the 10th anniversary of the reestablishment of its independence, on its role in the disintegration of the former Soviet Union and on its success in implementing political and economic reforms. Motion agreed to 398-0: R 205-0; D 191-0 (ND 139-0, SD 52-0); I 2-0. A two-thirds majority of those present and voting (266 in this case) is required for adoption under suspension of the rules. July 17, 2000.

403. H Res 531. Buenos Aires Bombing/Adoption. Ros-Lehtinen, R-Fla., motion to suspend the rules and adopt the resolution condemning the July 1994 attack on the AMIA Jewish Community Center in Buenos Aires, Argentina, and urging the offer of aid by U.S. law enforcement agencies in resolving it. Motion agreed to 402-1: R 208-1; D 192-0 (ND 140-0, SD 52-0); I 2-0. A two-thirds majority of those present and voting (269 in this case) is required for adoption under suspension of the rules. July 17, 2000.

404. HR 3125. Internet Gambling/Passage. Goodlatte, R-Va., motion to suspend the rules and pass the bill that would prohibit people engaged in a gambling business from using the Internet or any other interactive computer service to place, receive or otherwise make a bet or wager, or to assist in the placing of a bet or wager. The measure would provide penalties for violators. Motion rejected 245-159: R 165-44; D 79-114 (ND 45-95, SD 34-19); I 1-1. A two-thirds majority of those present and voting (270 in this case) is required for passage under suspension of the rules. July 17, 2000. A "nay" was a vote in support of the president's position.

405. H J Res 103. China NTR Disapproval/Passage. Passage of the joint resolution to disapprove of the president's decision to provide normal trade relations (formerly known as most-favored-nation status) for items produced in China for the period July 2000 through July 2001. Rejected 147-281: R 54-164; D 91-117 (ND 78-76, SD 13-41); I 2-0. July 18, 2000. A "nay" was a vote in support of the president's position.

406. HR 3113. Unsolicited E-mail/Passage. Wilson, R-N.M., motion to suspend the rules and pass the bill that would prohibit any person from sending unsolicited commercial e-mail (or spam) unless the messages included a a return e-mail address providing a way for consumers to opt out of future solicitations. Motion agreed to 427-1: R 217-1; D 208-0 (ND 154-0, SD 54-0); I 2-0. A two-thirds majority of those present and voting (286 in this case) is required for passage under suspension of the rules. July 18, 2000.

407. HR 4517. Alan B. Shepard Jr. Post Office/Passage. McHugh, R-N.Y., motion to suspend the rules and pass the bill designating a post office in Derry, N.H., the "Alan B. Shepard Jr. Post Office Building." Motion agreed to 423-0: R 214-0; D 208-0 (ND 154-0, SD 54-0); I 1-0. July 18, 2000.

408. HR 4810. Alleviate 'Marriage Penalty' Tax/Motion to Instruct. Cardin, D-Md., motion to instruct conferees to maximize the amount of relief provided to middle- and low-income taxpayers, minimize the additional marriage bonuses provided to taxpayers already receiving marriage bonuses, and settle differences over effective dates and phase-in amounts in a fiscally responsible manner. Motion rejected 203-222: R 1-215; D 201-6 (ND 147-6, SD 54-0); I 1-1. July 18, 2000.

Key

- Y Voted for (yea).
- # Paired for.
- + Announced for.
- N Voted against (nay).
- X Paired against.
- – Announced against.
- P Voted "present."
- C Voted "present" to avoid possible conflict of interest.
- ? Did not vote or otherwise make a position known.

•

Democrats ***Republicans***
Independents

	401	402	403	404	405	406	407	408
ALABAMA								
1 ***Callahan***	Y	Y	Y	Y	N	Y	Y	N
2 ***Everett***	Y	Y	Y	Y	N	Y	Y	N
3 ***Riley***	Y	Y	Y	Y	Y	Y	Y	N
4 ***Aderholt***	Y	Y	Y	Y	Y	Y	Y	N
5 Cramer	Y	Y	Y	Y	N	Y	Y	Y
6 ***Bachus***	Y	Y	Y	Y	N	Y	Y	N
7 Hilliard	Y	Y	Y	N	Y	Y	Y	Y
ALASKA								
AL ***Young***	Y	Y	Y	Y	Y	Y	Y	N
ARIZONA								
1 ***Salmon***	Y	Y	Y	Y	N	Y	Y	N
2 Pastor	Y	Y	Y	N	N	Y	Y	Y
3 ***Stump***	Y	Y	Y	Y	N	Y	Y	N
4 ***Shadegg***	Y	Y	Y	Y	N	Y	Y	N
5 ***Kolbe***	Y	Y	Y	N	N	Y	Y	N
6 ***Hayworth***	Y	Y	Y	N	Y	Y	Y	N
ARKANSAS								
1 Berry	Y	Y	Y	Y	N	Y	Y	Y
2 Snyder	Y	Y	Y	N	N	Y	Y	Y
3 ***Hutchinson***	?	?	?	?	N	Y	Y	N
4 ***Dickey***	?	Y	Y	Y	N	Y	Y	N
CALIFORNIA								
1 Thompson	Y	Y	Y	N	N	Y	Y	Y
2 ***Herger***	Y	Y	Y	Y	N	Y	Y	N
3 ***Ose***	Y	Y	Y	Y	N	Y	Y	N
4 ***Doolittle***	Y	Y	Y	N	N	Y	Y	N
5 Matsui	Y	Y	Y	N	N	Y	Y	Y
6 Woolsey	Y	Y	Y	N	Y	Y	Y	Y
7 Miller, George	Y	Y	Y	Y	Y	Y	Y	Y
8 Pelosi	Y	Y	Y	N	Y	Y	Y	Y
9 Lee	Y	Y	Y	N	Y	Y	Y	Y
10 Tauscher	Y	Y	Y	N	N	Y	Y	Y
11 ***Pombo***	Y	Y	Y	N	Y	Y	Y	N
12 Lantos	Y	Y	Y	N	Y	Y	Y	Y
13 Stark	N	Y	Y	N	Y	Y	Y	Y
14 Eshoo	Y	Y	Y	N	N	Y	Y	Y
15 ***Campbell***	?	?	?	?	?	?	?	?
16 Lofgren	Y	Y	Y	N	N	Y	Y	Y
17 Farr	Y	Y	Y	Y	N	Y	Y	Y
18 Condit	Y	Y	Y	Y	Y	Y	Y	Y
19 ***Radanovich***	Y	Y	Y	Y	N	Y	Y	N
20 Dooley	Y	Y	Y	Y	N	Y	Y	Y
21 ***Thomas***	Y	Y	Y	Y	N	Y	Y	N
22 Capps	Y	Y	Y	N	N	Y	Y	Y
23 ***Gallegly***	Y	Y	Y	Y	N	Y	Y	N
24 Sherman	Y	Y	Y	N	N	Y	Y	Y
25 ***McKeon***	Y	Y	Y	Y	N	Y	Y	N
26 Berman	Y	Y	Y	N	N	Y	Y	Y
27 ***Rogan***	Y	Y	Y	Y	N	Y	Y	N
28 ***Dreier***	Y	Y	Y	N	N	Y	Y	N
29 Waxman	?	?	?	?	N	Y	Y	Y
30 Becerra	Y	Y	Y	N	N	Y	Y	Y
31 Martinez	?	?	?	?	N	Y	Y	N
32 Dixon	P	Y	Y	Y	N	Y	Y	Y
33 Roybal-Allard	Y	Y	Y	N	N	Y	Y	Y
34 Napolitano	Y	Y	Y	N	N	Y	Y	Y
35 Waters	Y	Y	Y	Y	Y	Y	Y	Y
36 ***Kuykendall***	Y	Y	Y	N	N	Y	?	N
37 Millender-McD.	Y	Y	Y	N	N	Y	Y	Y
38 ***Horn***	Y	Y	Y	Y	Y	Y	Y	?
39 ***Royce***	Y	Y	Y	N	N	Y	Y	N
40 ***Lewis***	Y	Y	Y	Y	N	Y	Y	N
41 ***Miller, Gary***	Y	Y	Y	Y	N	Y	Y	N
42 Baca	Y	Y	Y	N	Y	Y	Y	Y
43 ***Calvert***	?	?	?	?	N	Y	Y	N
44 ***Bono***	Y	Y	Y	N	N	Y	Y	N
45 ***Rohrabacher***	Y	Y	Y	N	Y	Y	Y	N
46 Sanchez	Y	Y	Y	N	Y	Y	Y	Y
47 ***Cox***	Y	Y	Y	N	Y	Y	Y	N
48 ***Packard***	Y	Y	Y	Y	N	Y	Y	N
49 ***Bilbray***	Y	Y	Y	N	N	Y	Y	N
50 Filner	Y	Y	Y	N	N	Y	Y	Y
51 ***Cunningham***	Y	Y	Y	Y	N	Y	Y	N
52 ***Hunter***	Y	Y	Y	Y	Y	Y	Y	N
COLORADO								
1 DeGette	Y	Y	Y	N	N	Y	Y	Y
2 Udall	Y	Y	Y	N	Y	Y	Y	Y
3 ***McInnis***	Y	Y	Y	Y	N	Y	Y	N
4 ***Schaffer***	Y	Y	Y	N	Y	Y	Y	N
5 ***Hefley***	Y	Y	Y	Y	Y	Y	Y	N
6 ***Tancredo***	Y	Y	Y	Y	Y	Y	Y	N
CONNECTICUT								
1 Larson	Y	Y	Y	N	N	Y	Y	Y
2 Gejdenson	Y	Y	Y	N	Y	Y	Y	Y
3 DeLauro	Y	Y	Y	Y	Y	Y	Y	Y
4 ***Shays***	Y	Y	Y	Y	N	Y	Y	N
5 Maloney	Y	Y	Y	Y	N	Y	Y	Y
6 ***Johnson***	Y	Y	Y	Y	N	Y	Y	N
DELAWARE								
AL ***Castle***	Y	Y	Y	Y	N	Y	Y	N
FLORIDA								
1 ***Scarborough***	Y	Y	Y	N	Y	Y	Y	N
2 Boyd	Y	Y	Y	N	N	Y	Y	Y
3 Brown	Y	Y	Y	Y	Y	Y	Y	Y
4 ***Fowler***	Y	Y	Y	Y	N	Y	Y	N
5 Thurman	Y	Y	Y	Y	N	Y	Y	Y
6 ***Stearns***	Y	Y	Y	Y	Y	Y	Y	N
7 ***Mica***	Y	Y	Y	Y	N	Y	Y	N
8 ***McCollum***	?	?	?	?	?	?	?	?
9 ***Bilirakis***	Y	Y	Y	Y	N	Y	Y	N
10 ***Young***	?	?	?	?	N	Y	Y	N
11 Davis	Y	Y	Y	Y	N	Y	Y	Y
12 ***Canady***	Y	Y	Y	Y	N	Y	Y	N
13 ***Miller***	Y	Y	Y	Y	N	Y	Y	N
14 ***Goss***	Y	Y	Y	Y	N	Y	Y	N
15 ***Weldon***	Y	Y	Y	Y	Y	Y	Y	N
16 ***Foley***	Y	Y	Y	Y	N	Y	Y	N
17 Meek	Y	Y	Y	Y	Y	Y	Y	Y
18 ***Ros-Lehtinen***	Y	Y	Y	Y	Y	Y	Y	N
19 Wexler	Y	Y	Y	Y	Y	Y	Y	Y
20 Deutsch	Y	Y	Y	Y	N	Y	Y	Y
21 ***Diaz-Balart***	Y	Y	Y	Y	Y	Y	Y	N
22 ***Shaw***	Y	Y	Y	Y	N	Y	Y	N
23 Hastings	Y	Y	Y	Y	Y	Y	Y	Y
GEORGIA								
1 ***Kingston***	Y	Y	Y	N	Y	Y	Y	N
2 Bishop	Y	Y	Y	Y	N	Y	Y	Y
3 ***Collins***	Y	Y	Y	Y	Y	Y	Y	N
4 McKinney	Y	Y	Y	N	Y	Y	Y	Y
5 Lewis	Y	Y	Y	N	Y	Y	Y	Y
6 ***Isakson***	Y	Y	Y	Y	N	Y	Y	N
7 ***Barr***	Y	Y	Y	N	Y	Y	Y	N
8 ***Chambliss***	Y	Y	Y	Y	N	Y	Y	N
9 ***Deal***	Y	Y	Y	Y	Y	Y	Y	N
10 ***Norwood***	Y	Y	Y	Y	Y	Y	Y	N
11 ***Linder***	Y	Y	Y	Y	N	Y	Y	N
HAWAII								
1 Abercrombie	+	+	+	–	Y	Y	Y	Y
2 Mink	Y	Y	Y	N	Y	Y	Y	Y
IDAHO								
1 ***Chenoweth-Hage***	Y	Y	Y	N	N	Y	Y	N
2 ***Simpson***	Y	Y	Y	N	N	Y	Y	N
ILLINOIS								
1 Rush	?	?	?	?	Y	Y	Y	Y
2 Jackson	Y	Y	Y	N	Y	Y	Y	Y
3 Lipinski	Y	Y	Y	Y	Y	Y	Y	Y
4 Gutierrez	?	?	?	?	Y	Y	Y	Y
5 Blagojevich	?	?	?	?	N	Y	Y	Y
6 ***Hyde***	Y	Y	Y	Y	N	Y	Y	N
7 Davis	Y	Y	Y	N	Y	Y	Y	Y
8 ***Crane***	Y	Y	Y	N	N	Y	Y	N
9 Schakowsky	Y	Y	Y	N	Y	Y	Y	Y
10 ***Porter***	Y	+	Y	Y	N	Y	Y	?
11 ***Weller***	Y	Y	Y	Y	N	Y	?	N
12 Costello	Y	Y	Y	Y	Y	Y	Y	Y
13 ***Biggert***	Y	Y	Y	N	N	Y	Y	N

ND Northern Democrats SD Southern Democrats

	401	402	403	404	405	406	407	408
14 ***Hastert***								
15 ***Ewing***	Y	Y	Y	Y	N	Y	Y	N
16 ***Manzullo***	Y	Y	Y	Y	N	Y	Y	N
17 Evans	Y	Y	Y	N	Y	Y	Y	Y
18 ***LaHood***	Y	Y	Y	Y	N	Y	Y	N
19 Phelps	Y	Y	Y	Y	Y	Y	Y	Y
20 ***Shimkus***	Y	Y	Y	Y	N	Y	Y	N
INDIANA								
1 Visclosky	N	Y	Y	Y	Y	Y	Y	Y
2 ***McIntosh***	?	?	?	?	?	?	?	?
3 Roemer	Y	Y	Y	Y	N	Y	Y	Y
4 ***Souder***	Y	Y	Y	Y	Y	Y	Y	N
5 ***Buyer***	Y	Y	Y	Y	N	Y	Y	N
6 ***Burton***	Y	Y	Y	Y	Y	Y	Y	N
7 ***Pease***	Y	Y	Y	Y	N	Y	Y	N
8 ***Hostettler***	Y	Y	Y	Y	Y	Y	Y	N
9 Hill	Y	Y	Y	Y	N	Y	Y	Y
10 Carson	+	+	+	−	N	Y	Y	Y
IOWA								
1 ***Leach***	Y	Y	Y	Y	N	Y	Y	N
2 ***Nussle***	Y	Y	Y	Y	N	Y	Y	N
3 Boswell	Y	Y	Y	Y	−	+	+	+
4 ***Ganske***	Y	Y	Y	Y	N	Y	Y	N
5 ***Latham***	Y	Y	Y	Y	N	Y	Y	N
KANSAS								
1 ***Moran***	Y	Y	Y	Y	N	Y	Y	N
2 ***Ryun***	Y	Y	Y	Y	N	Y	Y	N
3 Moore	Y	Y	Y	N	N	Y	Y	Y
4 ***Tiahrt***	Y	Y	Y	Y	N	Y	Y	N
KENTUCKY								
1 ***Whitfield***	Y	Y	Y	Y	N	Y	Y	N
2 ***Lewis***	Y	Y	Y	Y	N	Y	Y	N
3 ***Northup***	Y	Y	Y	Y	N	Y	Y	N
4 Lucas	Y	Y	Y	Y	N	Y	Y	Y
5 ***Rogers***	Y	Y	Y	Y	N	Y	Y	N
6 ***Fletcher***	Y	Y	Y	Y	N	Y	Y	N
LOUISIANA								
1 ***Vitter***	Y	Y	Y	Y	N	Y	Y	N
2 Jefferson	Y	Y	Y	N	N	Y	Y	Y
3 ***Tauzin***	Y	Y	Y	Y	N	Y	Y	N
4 ***McCrery***	Y	Y	Y	Y	N	Y	Y	N
5 ***Cooksey***	Y	Y	Y	Y	N	Y	Y	N
6 ***Baker***	Y	Y	Y	Y	N	Y	Y	N
7 John	Y	Y	Y	Y	N	Y	Y	Y
MAINE								
1 Allen	Y	Y	Y	Y	N	Y	Y	Y
2 Baldacci	Y	Y	Y	Y	Y	Y	Y	Y
MARYLAND								
1 ***Gilchrest***	Y	Y	Y	Y	N	Y	Y	N
2 ***Ehrlich***	?	?	?	?	Y	Y	Y	N
3 Cardin	Y	Y	Y	N	N	Y	Y	Y
4 Wynn	Y	Y	Y	N	Y	Y	Y	Y
5 Hoyer	Y	Y	Y	N	N	Y	Y	Y
6 ***Bartlett***	Y	Y	Y	Y	Y	Y	Y	N
7 Cummings	Y	Y	Y	N	Y	Y	Y	Y
8 ***Morella***	Y	Y	Y	Y	N	Y	Y	N
MASSACHUSETTS								
1 Olver	Y	Y	Y	N	Y	Y	Y	Y
2 Neal	Y	Y	Y	N	N	Y	Y	Y
3 McGovern	Y	Y	Y	N	N	Y	Y	Y
4 Frank	N	Y	Y	N	Y	Y	Y	Y
5 Meehan	Y	Y	Y	N	N	Y	Y	Y
6 Tierney	Y	Y	Y	N	Y	Y	Y	Y
7 Markey	?	?	?	?	N	Y	Y	Y
8 Capuano	Y	Y	Y	N	Y	Y	Y	Y
9 Moakley	Y	Y	Y	N	N	Y	Y	Y
10 Delahunt	Y	Y	Y	N	Y	Y	Y	Y
MICHIGAN								
1 Stupak	Y	Y	Y	N	Y	Y	Y	Y
2 ***Hoekstra***	Y	Y	Y	Y	N	Y	Y	N
3 ***Ehlers***	Y	+	Y	Y	N	Y	Y	N
4 ***Camp***	Y	Y	Y	Y	N	Y	Y	N
5 Barcia	Y	Y	Y	Y	Y	Y	Y	N
6 ***Upton***	Y	Y	Y	N	N	Y	Y	N
7 ***Smith***	Y	Y	Y	N	N	Y	Y	N
8 Stabenow	Y	Y	Y	N	Y	Y	Y	Y
9 Kildee	Y	Y	Y	N	Y	Y	Y	Y
10 Bonior	Y	Y	Y	N	Y	Y	Y	Y
11 ***Knollenberg***	Y	Y	Y	N	N	Y	Y	N
12 Levin	Y	Y	Y	N	N	Y	Y	Y
13 Rivers	Y	Y	Y	N	Y	Y	Y	Y
14 Conyers	Y	Y	Y	N	Y	Y	Y	Y
15 Kilpatrick	+	+	+	−	Y	Y	Y	Y
16 Dingell	Y	Y	Y	N	N	Y	Y	Y

	401	402	403	404	405	406	407	408
MINNESOTA								
1 ***Gutknecht***	Y	Y	Y	Y	N	Y	Y	N
2 Minge	Y	Y	Y	Y	N	Y	Y	Y
3 ***Ramstad***	Y	Y	Y	Y	N	Y	Y	N
4 Vento	?	?	?	?	?	?	?	?
5 Sabo	Y	Y	Y	Y	Y	Y	Y	Y
6 Luther	Y	Y	Y	Y	N	Y	Y	Y
7 Peterson	Y	Y	Y	Y	N	Y	Y	Y
8 Oberstar	Y	Y	Y	N	N	Y	Y	Y
MISSISSIPPI								
1 ***Wicker***	Y	Y	Y	Y	N	Y	Y	N
2 Thompson	?	Y	Y	N	Y	Y	Y	Y
3 ***Pickering***	Y	Y	Y	Y	N	Y	Y	N
4 Shows	Y	Y	Y	Y	N	Y	Y	Y
5 Taylor	Y	Y	Y	Y	Y	Y	Y	Y
MISSOURI								
1 Clay	Y	Y	Y	N	Y	Y	Y	Y
2 ***Talent***	Y	Y	Y	Y	N	Y	Y	N
3 Gephardt	Y	Y	Y	N	Y	Y	Y	Y
4 Skelton	Y	Y	Y	Y	N	Y	Y	Y
5 McCarthy	Y	Y	Y	Y	N	Y	Y	Y
6 Danner	?	?	Y	Y	Y	Y	Y	N
7 ***Blunt***	Y	Y	Y	N	N	Y	Y	N
8 ***Emerson***	Y	Y	Y	Y	N	Y	Y	N
9 ***Hulshof***	Y	Y	Y	Y	N	Y	Y	N
MONTANA								
AL ***Hill***	Y	Y	Y	Y	N	Y	Y	N
NEBRASKA								
1 ***Bereuter***	Y	Y	Y	Y	N	Y	Y	N
2 ***Terry***	Y	Y	Y	Y	N	Y	Y	N
3 ***Barrett***	Y	Y	Y	Y	N	Y	Y	N
NEVADA								
1 Berkley	Y	Y	Y	Y	N	Y	Y	Y
2 ***Gibbons***	Y	Y	Y	Y	Y	Y	Y	N
NEW HAMPSHIRE								
1 ***Sununu***	Y	Y	Y	Y	N	Y	Y	N
2 ***Bass***	Y	Y	Y	Y	N	Y	Y	N
NEW JERSEY								
1 Andrews	Y	Y	Y	N	N	Y	Y	Y
2 ***LoBiondo***	Y	Y	Y	Y	Y	Y	Y	N
3 ***Saxton***	Y	Y	Y	Y	Y	Y	?	N
4 ***Smith***	Y	Y	Y	Y	Y	Y	Y	N
5 ***Roukema***	Y	Y	Y	Y	N	Y	Y	N
6 Pallone	Y	Y	Y	Y	Y	Y	Y	Y
7 ***Franks***	Y	Y	Y	Y	N	Y	Y	N
8 Pascrell	Y	Y	Y	Y	Y	Y	Y	Y
9 Rothman	Y	Y	Y	Y	Y	Y	Y	Y
10 Payne	Y	Y	Y	N	Y	Y	Y	Y
11 ***Frelinghuysen***	Y	Y	Y	Y	N	Y	Y	N
12 Holt	Y	Y	Y	Y	N	Y	Y	Y
13 Menendez	Y	Y	Y	Y	Y	Y	Y	Y
NEW MEXICO								
1 ***Wilson***	P	Y	Y	Y	N	Y	Y	Y
2 ***Skeen***	Y	Y	Y	N	N	Y	Y	N
3 Udall	Y	Y	Y	N	Y	Y	Y	Y
NEW YORK								
1 Forbes	Y	Y	Y	Y	Y	Y	Y	N
2 ***Lazio***	Y	Y	Y	Y	Y	Y	Y	N
3 ***King***	Y	Y	Y	Y	Y	Y	Y	N
4 McCarthy	Y	Y	Y	Y	N	Y	Y	Y
5 Ackerman	?	?	?	?	N	Y	Y	Y
6 Meeks	Y	Y	Y	N	N	Y	Y	Y
7 Crowley	Y	Y	Y	N	N	Y	Y	Y
8 Nadler	Y	Y	Y	N	Y	Y	Y	Y
9 Weiner	Y	Y	Y	N	N	Y	Y	Y
10 Towns	Y	Y	Y	N	N	Y	Y	Y
11 Owens	Y	Y	Y	N	Y	Y	Y	Y
12 Velázquez	Y	Y	Y	N	Y	Y	Y	Y
13 ***Fossella***	Y	Y	Y	N	N	Y	Y	N
14 Maloney	Y	Y	Y	N	Y	Y	Y	Y
15 Rangel	Y	Y	Y	N	N	Y	Y	Y
16 Serrano	?	?	?	?	N	Y	Y	Y
17 Engel	Y	Y	Y	N	Y	Y	Y	Y
18 Lowey	Y	Y	Y	N	N	Y	Y	Y
19 ***Kelly***	Y	Y	Y	Y	N	Y	Y	N
20 ***Gilman***	Y	Y	Y	Y	Y	Y	Y	N
21 McNulty	?	?	?	?	N	Y	Y	Y
22 ***Sweeney***	Y	Y	Y	Y	N	Y	Y	N
23 ***Boehlert***	Y	Y	Y	Y	N	Y	Y	N
24 ***McHugh***	Y	Y	Y	Y	N	Y	Y	N
25 ***Walsh***	Y	Y	Y	Y	N	Y	Y	N
26 Hinchey	Y	Y	Y	N	N	Y	Y	Y
27 ***Reynolds***	Y	Y	Y	Y	N	Y	Y	N
28 Slaughter	Y	Y	Y	N	N	Y	Y	Y
29 LaFalce	Y	Y	Y	Y	N	Y	Y	Y

	401	402	403	404	405	406	407	408
30 ***Quinn***	Y	Y	Y	Y	Y	Y	Y	N
31 ***Houghton***	Y	Y	Y	N	N	Y	Y	N
NORTH CAROLINA								
1 Clayton	?	Y	Y	N	N	Y	Y	Y
2 Etheridge	Y	Y	Y	Y	N	Y	Y	Y
3 ***Jones***	Y	Y	Y	Y	Y	Y	Y	N
4 Price	Y	Y	Y	Y	N	Y	Y	Y
5 ***Burr***	Y	Y	Y	Y	Y	Y	Y	N
6 ***Coble***	Y	Y	Y	Y	Y	Y	Y	N
7 McIntyre	Y	Y	Y	Y	Y	Y	Y	Y
8 ***Hayes***	Y	Y	Y	Y	Y	Y	Y	N
9 ***Myrick***	Y	Y	Y	Y	N	Y	Y	N
10 ***Ballenger***	Y	Y	Y	Y	N	Y	Y	N
11 ***Taylor***	Y	Y	Y	Y	Y	Y	Y	N
12 Watt	Y	Y	Y	N	N	Y	Y	Y
NORTH DAKOTA								
AL Pomeroy	Y	Y	Y	Y	N	Y	Y	Y
OHIO								
1 ***Chabot***	Y	Y	Y	N	N	Y	Y	N
2 ***Portman***	Y	Y	Y	N	N	Y	Y	N
3 Hall	Y	Y	Y	Y	Y	Y	Y	Y
4 ***Oxley***	Y	Y	Y	Y	N	Y	Y	N
5 ***Gillmor***	?	?	Y	Y	N	Y	Y	N
6 Strickland	Y	Y	Y	Y	Y	Y	Y	Y
7 ***Hobson***	Y	Y	Y	Y	N	Y	Y	N
8 ***Boehner***	Y	Y	Y	Y	N	Y	Y	N
9 Kaptur	Y	Y	Y	N	Y	Y	Y	Y
10 Kucinich	Y	Y	Y	N	Y	Y	Y	Y
11 Jones	Y	Y	Y	N	Y	Y	Y	Y
12 ***Kasich***	Y	Y	Y	N	N	Y	Y	N
13 Brown	Y	Y	Y	N	Y	Y	Y	?
14 Sawyer	Y	Y	Y	N	N	Y	Y	Y
15 ***Pryce***	Y	Y	Y	Y	N	Y	Y	N
16 ***Regula***	Y	Y	Y	Y	N	Y	Y	N
17 Traficant	Y	Y	Y	Y	Y	Y	Y	N
18 ***Ney***	Y	Y	Y	N	Y	Y	Y	N
19 ***LaTourette***	Y	Y	Y	Y	N	Y	Y	N
OKLAHOMA								
1 ***Largent***	Y	Y	Y	Y	N	Y	Y	N
2 ***Coburn***	?	?	?	?	Y	Y	Y	N
3 ***Watkins***	Y	Y	Y	Y	N	Y	Y	N
4 ***Watts***	Y	Y	Y	Y	N	Y	Y	N
5 ***Istook***	Y	Y	Y	Y	N	Y	Y	N
6 ***Lucas***	Y	Y	Y	Y	N	Y	Y	N
OREGON								
1 Wu	Y	Y	Y	N	Y	Y	Y	Y
2 ***Walden***	Y	Y	Y	Y	N	Y	Y	N
3 Blumenauer	Y	Y	Y	N	N	Y	Y	Y
4 DeFazio	Y	Y	Y	Y	Y	Y	Y	Y
5 Hooley	Y	Y	Y	Y	N	Y	Y	Y
PENNSYLVANIA								
1 Brady	Y	Y	Y	N	Y	Y	Y	Y
2 Fattah	Y	Y	Y	N	N	Y	Y	Y
3 Borski	Y	Y	Y	N	Y	Y	Y	Y
4 Klink	?	?	?	?	Y	Y	Y	Y
5 ***Peterson***	Y	Y	Y	Y	N	Y	Y	N
6 Holden	Y	Y	Y	N	N	Y	Y	Y
7 ***Weldon***	Y	Y	Y	N	N	Y	Y	N
8 ***Greenwood***	Y	Y	Y	N	N	Y	Y	N
9 ***Shuster***	Y	Y	Y	Y	N	Y	Y	N
10 ***Sherwood***	Y	Y	Y	Y	N	Y	Y	N
11 Kanjorski	Y	Y	Y	N	N	Y	Y	Y
12 Murtha	N	Y	Y	N	N	Y	Y	Y
13 Hoeffel	Y	Y	Y	N	N	Y	Y	Y
14 Coyne	Y	Y	Y	N	Y	Y	Y	Y
15 ***Toomey***	Y	Y	Y	Y	N	Y	Y	N
16 ***Pitts***	Y	Y	Y	Y	N	Y	Y	N
17 ***Gekas***	Y	Y	Y	Y	N	Y	Y	N
18 Doyle	Y	Y	Y	N	Y	Y	Y	Y
19 ***Goodling***	Y	?	Y	Y	Y	Y	Y	N
20 Mascara	Y	Y	Y	N	Y	Y	Y	Y
21 ***English***	Y	Y	Y	N	N	Y	Y	N
RHODE ISLAND								
1 Kennedy	Y	Y	Y	N	Y	Y	Y	Y
2 Weygand	Y	Y	Y	N	Y	Y	Y	Y
SOUTH CAROLINA								
1 ***Sanford***	Y	Y	Y	N	Y	Y	Y	N
2 ***Spence***	Y	Y	Y	Y	Y	Y	Y	N
3 ***Graham***	Y	Y	Y	Y	Y	Y	Y	N
4 ***DeMint***	Y	Y	Y	Y	N	Y	Y	N
5 Spratt	?	?	?	Y	Y	Y	Y	Y
6 Clyburn	Y	Y	Y	N	Y	Y	Y	Y
SOUTH DAKOTA								
AL ***Thune***	Y	Y	Y	Y	N	Y	Y	N

	401	402	403	404	405	406	407	408
TENNESSEE								
1 ***Jenkins***	Y	Y	Y	N	N	Y	Y	N
2 ***Duncan***	Y	Y	Y	Y	Y	Y	Y	N
3 ***Wamp***	Y	Y	Y	Y	Y	Y	Y	N
4 ***Hilleary***	Y	Y	Y	Y	Y	Y	Y	N
5 Clement	Y	Y	Y	N	N	Y	Y	Y
6 Gordon	Y	Y	Y	Y	N	Y	Y	Y
7 ***Bryant***	Y	Y	Y	Y	N	Y	Y	N
8 Tanner	Y	Y	Y	Y	N	Y	Y	Y
9 Ford	?	?	?	?	N	Y	Y	Y
TEXAS								
1 Sandlin	Y	Y	Y	Y	N	Y	Y	Y
2 Turner	Y	Y	Y	Y	N	Y	Y	Y
3 ***Johnson, Sam***	Y	Y	Y	N	N	Y	Y	N
4 Hall	Y	Y	Y	Y	N	Y	Y	Y
5 ***Sessions***	?	?	?	?	N	Y	Y	N
6 ***Barton***	?	?	?	?	Y	Y	Y	N
7 ***Archer***	Y	Y	Y	N	N	Y	Y	N
8 ***Brady***	Y	Y	Y	Y	N	Y	Y	N
9 Lampson	Y	Y	Y	Y	N	Y	Y	Y
10 Doggett	Y	Y	Y	N	N	Y	Y	Y
11 Edwards	Y	Y	Y	Y	N	Y	Y	Y
12 ***Granger***	+	+	+	+	N	Y	Y	N
13 ***Thornberry***	Y	Y	Y	Y	N	Y	Y	N
14 ***Paul***	Y	Y	N	N	N	N	Y	N
15 Hinojosa	Y	Y	Y	Y	N	Y	Y	Y
16 Reyes	Y	Y	Y	N	N	Y	Y	Y
17 Stenholm	Y	Y	Y	Y	N	Y	Y	Y
18 Jackson-Lee	Y	Y	Y	Y	N	Y	Y	Y
19 ***Combest***	Y	Y	Y	Y	N	Y	Y	N
20 Gonzalez	Y	Y	Y	N	N	Y	Y	Y
21 ***Smith***	Y	Y	Y	Y	N	Y	Y	N
22 ***DeLay***	Y	Y	Y	N	N	Y	Y	N
23 ***Bonilla***	Y	Y	Y	Y	N	Y	Y	N
24 Frost	Y	Y	Y	Y	N	Y	Y	Y
25 Bentsen	Y	Y	Y	N	N	Y	Y	Y
26 ***Armey***	Y	Y	Y	Y	N	Y	Y	N
27 Ortiz	Y	Y	Y	Y	N	Y	Y	Y
28 Rodriguez	Y	Y	Y	N	N	Y	Y	Y
29 Green	Y	Y	Y	N	N	Y	Y	Y
30 Johnson, E.B.	Y	Y	Y	N	N	Y	Y	Y
UTAH								
1 ***Hansen***	Y	Y	Y	Y	N	Y	Y	N
2 ***Cook***	?	?	?	?	Y	Y	Y	N
3 ***Cannon***	Y	Y	Y	N	N	Y	Y	N
VERMONT								
AL *Sanders*	Y	Y	Y	N	Y	Y	?	Y
VIRGINIA								
1 ***Bateman***	Y	Y	Y	Y	N	Y	Y	N
2 Pickett	Y	Y	Y	Y	N	Y	Y	Y
3 Scott	Y	Y	Y	N	N	Y	Y	Y
4 Sisisky	Y	Y	Y	Y	Y	Y	Y	Y
5 *Goode*	Y	Y	Y	Y	Y	Y	Y	N
6 ***Goodlatte***	Y	Y	Y	Y	N	Y	Y	N
7 ***Bliley***	Y	Y	Y	Y	N	Y	?	N
8 Moran	Y	Y	Y	Y	N	Y	Y	Y
9 Boucher	Y	Y	Y	Y	N	Y	Y	Y
10 ***Wolf***	Y	Y	Y	Y	Y	Y	Y	N
11 ***Davis***	Y	Y	Y	N	N	Y	Y	N
WASHINGTON								
1 Inslee	Y	Y	Y	N	N	Y	Y	N
2 ***Metcalf***	Y	Y	Y	Y	Y	Y	Y	N
3 Baird	Y	Y	Y	N	N	Y	Y	Y
4 ***Hastings***	Y	Y	Y	Y	N	Y	Y	N
5 ***Nethercutt***	Y	Y	Y	Y	N	Y	Y	N
6 Dicks	?	?	?	?	N	Y	Y	Y
7 McDermott	N	Y	Y	N	N	Y	Y	Y
8 ***Dunn***	Y	Y	Y	Y	N	Y	Y	N
9 Smith	?	?	?	?	?	?	?	?
WEST VIRGINIA								
1 Mollohan	Y	Y	Y	Y	Y	Y	Y	Y
2 Wise	?	?	?	?	Y	Y	Y	Y
3 Rahall	Y	Y	Y	Y	Y	Y	Y	Y
WISCONSIN								
1 ***Ryan***	Y	Y	Y	Y	N	Y	Y	N
2 Baldwin	Y	Y	Y	N	Y	Y	Y	Y
3 Kind	Y	Y	Y	N	N	Y	Y	Y
4 Kleczka	Y	Y	Y	N	N	Y	Y	Y
5 Barrett	Y	Y	Y	N	N	Y	Y	Y
6 ***Petri***	Y	Y	Y	N	N	Y	Y	N
7 Obey	Y	Y	Y	N	Y	Y	Y	Y
8 ***Green***	Y	Y	Y	Y	N	Y	Y	N
9 ***Sensenbrenner***	Y	Y	Y	Y	Y	Y	Y	N
WYOMING								
AL ***Cubin***	Y	Y	Y	Y	N	Y	Y	N

Southern states - Ala., Ark., Fla., Ga., Ky., La., Miss., N.C., Okla., S.C., Tenn., Texas, Va.

409. HR 4866. Debt Reduction/Passage. Nussle, R-Iowa, motion to suspend the rules and pass the bill that would establish a Treasury Department account in fiscal 2001 into which $25 billion from the non-Social Security surplus would be deposited, and which could be used only to reduce the national debt. Motion agreed to 422-1: R 217-0; D 203-1 (ND 150-1, SD 53-0); I 2-0. A two-thirds majority of those present and voting (282 in this case) is required for passage under suspension of the rules. July 18, 2000.

410. HR 1102. Pension and Retirement Enhancement/Democratic Substitute. Neal, D-Mass., amendment that would add provisions to provide a refundable credit for low- and middle-income workers, and tax relief for small employers with pension plans. Rejected 200-221: R 0-216; D 200-3 (ND 147-2, SD 53-1); I 0-2. July 19, 2000.

411. HR 1102. Pension and Retirement Enhancement/Recommit. Neal, D-Mass., motion to recommit the bill to the House Ways and Means Committee with instructions to add language specifying that the bill could take effect only if there was no on-budget deficit and if a Medicare prescription drug benefit was in place. Motion rejected 185-239: R 0-218; D 184-20 (ND 137-13, SD 47-7); I 1-1. July 19, 2000.

412. HR 1102. Pension and Retirement Enhancement/Passage. Passage of the bill that would increase, at a cost of $52.2 billion over 10 years, the amount individuals could contribute to traditional and Roth Individual Retirement Accounts and to 401(k) plans and would make it easier for workers to take pension plans with them when they leave their jobs. The bill would increase from $2,000 to $5,000 the limit on annual contributions by 2003. Those age 50 and older could immediately contribute up to $5,000 more annually. After 2003, contribution limits would increase with inflation in $500 increments. Passed 401-25: R 218-1; D 182-23 (ND 128-23, SD 54-0); I 1-1. July 19, 2000. A "nay" was a vote in support of the president's position.

413. HR 4576. Fiscal 2001 Defense Appropriations/Conference Report. Adoption of the conference report on the bill to appropriate $287.8 billion in defense spending for fiscal 2001. The measure would provide $3.3 billion more than President Clinton's request and $21.7 billion more than appropriated in fiscal 2000. The measure includes $3.9 billion for production of the F-22 fighter jet and $689 million for the development of a joint strike fighter jet for the Air Force, Navy and Marine Corps. Adopted (thus sent to the Senate) 367-58: R 207-10; D 159-47 (ND 108-44, SD 51-3); I 1-1. July 19, 2000.

414. HR 4118. Russian Debt Forgiveness/Passage. Passage of the bill that would prohibit the president from rescheduling or forgiving any bilateral debts of Russia until he certifies that Russia has closed its intelligence facility at Lourdes, Cuba. It would allow the president to waive the prohibition under certain conditions. Passed 275-146: R 213-2; D 61-143 (ND 39-112, SD 22-31); I 1-1. July 19, 2000. A "nay" was a vote in support of the president's position.

415. HR 4577. Fiscal 2001 Labor-HHS Appropriations/Motion to Instruct. Obey, D-Wis., motion to instruct conferees to insist that the conference report include certain minimum funding levels for certain Education Department programs, such as Head Start and Pell Grants, and for the National Institutes of Health, as well as other provisions. Motion rejected 207-212: R 4-208; D 202-3 (ND 149-2, SD 53-1); I 1-1. July 19, 2000.

416. HR 2634. Drug Treatment Waiver/Passage. Bliley, R-Va., motion to suspend the rules and pass the bill that would allow doctors to treat heroin addicts with controlled substances that help in their detoxification treatment without first registering with the Drug Enforcement Agency. They would have to apply for a waiver and agree to limit the number of patients they treat at the risk of losing their ability to dispense such drugs. Motion agreed to 412-1: R 210-1; D 200-0 (ND 147-0, SD 53-0); I 2-0. A two-thirds majority of those present and voting (276 in this case) is required for passage under suspension of the rules. July 19, 2000.

Key

- Y Voted for (yea).
- # Paired for.
- + Announced for.
- N Voted against (nay).
- X Paired against.
- – Announced against.
- P Voted "present."
- C Voted "present" to avoid possible conflict of interest.
- ? Did not vote or otherwise make a position known.

•

Democrats ***Republicans***
Independents

	409	410	411	412	413	414	415	416
ALABAMA								
1 ***Callahan***	Y	N	N	Y	Y	Y	N	Y
2 ***Everett***	Y	N	N	Y	Y	Y	N	Y
3 ***Riley***	Y	N	N	Y	Y	Y	N	Y
4 ***Aderholt***	Y	N	N	Y	Y	Y	N	Y
5 Cramer	Y	Y	Y	Y	Y	N	Y	Y
6 ***Bachus***	Y	N	N	Y	Y	Y	N	Y
7 Hilliard	Y	Y	Y	Y	Y	N	Y	Y
ALASKA								
AL ***Young***	Y	N	N	Y	Y	Y	N	Y
ARIZONA								
1 ***Salmon***	Y	N	N	Y	Y	Y	N	?
2 Pastor	Y	Y	Y	Y	Y	N	Y	Y
3 ***Stump***	Y	N	N	Y	Y	Y	N	Y
4 ***Shadegg***	Y	N	N	Y	Y	Y	N	Y
5 ***Kolbe***	Y	N	N	Y	Y	Y	N	?
6 ***Hayworth***	Y	N	N	Y	Y	Y	N	Y
ARKANSAS								
1 Berry	Y	Y	Y	Y	Y	N	Y	Y
2 Snyder	Y	Y	Y	Y	Y	N	Y	Y
3 ***Hutchinson***	Y	N	N	Y	Y	Y	N	Y
4 ***Dickey***	Y	N	N	Y	Y	Y	N	Y
CALIFORNIA								
1 Thompson	Y	Y	Y	Y	Y	N	Y	Y
2 ***Herger***	Y	N	N	Y	Y	Y	N	Y
3 ***Ose***	Y	N	N	Y	Y	Y	N	Y
4 ***Doolittle***	Y	N	N	Y	Y	Y	N	Y
5 Matsui	Y	Y	Y	N	Y	N	Y	Y
6 Woolsey	Y	Y	Y	Y	Y	N	Y	Y
7 Miller, George	Y	Y	Y	Y	N	N	Y	Y
8 Pelosi	Y	Y	Y	Y	Y	N	Y	?
9 Lee	Y	Y	Y	N	N	N	Y	Y
10 Tauscher	Y	Y	N	Y	Y	N	Y	Y
11 ***Pombo***	Y	N	N	Y	Y	Y	N	Y
12 Lantos	Y	Y	Y	Y	Y	N	Y	Y
13 Stark	Y	Y	Y	N	N	N	Y	Y
14 Eshoo	Y	Y	Y	Y	N	N	Y	Y
15 ***Campbell***	?	?	?	?	?	?	?	?
16 Lofgren	Y	Y	Y	Y	N	N	Y	Y
17 Farr	Y	Y	Y	Y	Y	N	Y	Y
18 Condit	Y	Y	Y	Y	Y	Y	Y	Y
19 ***Radanovich***	Y	N	N	Y	Y	Y	N	Y
20 Dooley	Y	Y	Y	Y	Y	N	Y	Y
21 ***Thomas***	Y	N	N	Y	Y	Y	N	Y
22 Capps	Y	Y	Y	Y	Y	Y	Y	Y
23 ***Gallegly***	Y	N	N	Y	Y	Y	N	Y
24 Sherman	Y	Y	Y	Y	Y	N	Y	Y
25 ***McKeon***	Y	N	N	Y	Y	Y	N	Y
26 Berman	Y	Y	Y	Y	Y	N	Y	Y
27 ***Rogan***	Y	N	N	Y	Y	Y	N	Y
28 ***Dreier***	Y	N	N	Y	Y	Y	N	Y
29 Waxman	Y	Y	Y	Y	N	N	Y	Y
30 Becerra	Y	Y	Y	N	Y	N	Y	Y
31 Martinez	Y	?	?	?	Y	Y	N	Y
32 Dixon	Y	Y	Y	Y	Y	N	Y	Y
33 Roybal-Allard	Y	Y	Y	N	Y	N	Y	Y
34 Napolitano	Y	Y	Y	Y	Y	?	Y	Y
35 Waters	Y	Y	Y	Y	N	N	Y	?
36 ***Kuykendall***	Y	N	N	Y	Y	Y	N	Y
37 Millender-McD.	Y	Y	Y	Y	Y	N	Y	Y
38 ***Horn***	?	N	N	Y	Y	Y	N	Y
39 ***Royce***	Y	N	N	Y	Y	Y	N	Y
40 ***Lewis***	Y	N	N	Y	Y	Y	N	Y
41 ***Miller, Gary***	Y	N	N	Y	Y	Y	N	Y
42 Baca	Y	?	?	?	?	?	?	?
43 ***Calvert***	Y	N	N	Y	Y	Y	N	Y
44 ***Bono***	Y	N	N	Y	Y	Y	N	Y
45 ***Rohrabacher***	Y	N	N	Y	Y	Y	N	Y
46 Sanchez	Y	Y	Y	Y	Y	N	Y	Y
47 ***Cox***	Y	N	N	Y	Y	Y	N	Y
48 ***Packard***	Y	N	N	Y	Y	Y	N	Y
49 ***Bilbray***	Y	N	N	Y	Y	Y	Y	Y
50 Filner	Y	Y	Y	N	N	N	Y	Y
51 ***Cunningham***	Y	N	N	Y	Y	Y	N	Y
52 ***Hunter***	Y	N	N	Y	Y	Y	N	Y
COLORADO								
1 DeGette	Y	Y	Y	Y	N	N	Y	Y
2 Udall	Y	Y	Y	Y	N	N	Y	Y
3 ***McInnis***	Y	N	N	Y	Y	Y	N	Y
4 ***Schaffer***	Y	N	N	Y	Y	Y	N	Y
5 ***Hefley***	Y	N	N	Y	Y	Y	N	Y
6 ***Tancredo***	Y	N	N	Y	Y	Y	N	Y
CONNECTICUT								
1 Larson	Y	Y	Y	Y	Y	N	Y	Y
2 Gejdenson	Y	Y	Y	Y	Y	N	Y	Y
3 DeLauro	Y	Y	Y	Y	Y	N	Y	Y
4 ***Shays***	Y	N	N	Y	N	Y	N	Y
5 Maloney	Y	Y	Y	Y	Y	N	Y	Y
6 ***Johnson***	Y	N	N	Y	Y	N	?	Y
DELAWARE								
AL ***Castle***	Y	N	N	Y	Y	Y	N	Y
FLORIDA								
1 ***Scarborough***	Y	N	N	Y	Y	Y	N	Y
2 Boyd	Y	N	Y	Y	Y	Y	Y	Y
3 Brown	Y	Y	Y	Y	Y	N	Y	Y
4 ***Fowler***	Y	N	N	Y	Y	Y	N	Y
5 Thurman	Y	Y	Y	Y	Y	Y	Y	Y
6 ***Stearns***	Y	N	N	Y	Y	Y	N	Y
7 ***Mica***	Y	N	N	Y	Y	Y	N	Y
8 ***McCollum***	?	N	N	Y	Y	Y	N	Y
9 ***Bilirakis***	Y	N	N	Y	Y	Y	N	Y
10 ***Young***	Y	N	N	Y	Y	Y	N	Y
11 Davis	Y	Y	Y	Y	Y	Y	Y	Y
12 ***Canady***	Y	N	N	Y	Y	Y	N	Y
13 ***Miller***	Y	N	N	Y	Y	Y	N	Y
14 ***Goss***	Y	N	N	Y	Y	Y	N	Y
15 ***Weldon***	Y	N	N	Y	Y	Y	N	Y
16 ***Foley***	Y	N	N	Y	Y	Y	N	Y
17 Meek	Y	Y	Y	Y	Y	N	Y	Y
18 ***Ros-Lehtinen***	Y	N	N	Y	Y	Y	N	Y
19 Wexler	Y	Y	Y	Y	Y	Y	Y	Y
20 Deutsch	Y	Y	Y	Y	Y	Y	Y	Y
21 ***Diaz-Balart***	Y	N	N	Y	Y	Y	N	Y
22 ***Shaw***	Y	N	N	Y	Y	Y	N	Y
23 Hastings	Y	Y	Y	Y	Y	N	Y	Y
GEORGIA								
1 ***Kingston***	Y	N	N	Y	Y	Y	N	Y
2 Bishop	Y	Y	Y	Y	Y	Y	Y	Y
3 ***Collins***	Y	N	N	Y	Y	Y	N	Y
4 McKinney	Y	Y	Y	Y	N	N	Y	Y
5 Lewis	Y	Y	Y	Y	Y	N	Y	Y
6 ***Isakson***	Y	N	N	Y	Y	Y	N	Y
7 ***Barr***	Y	N	N	Y	Y	Y	N	Y
8 ***Chambliss***	Y	N	N	Y	Y	Y	N	Y
9 ***Deal***	Y	N	N	Y	Y	Y	N	Y
10 ***Norwood***	Y	N	N	Y	Y	Y	N	Y
11 ***Linder***	Y	N	N	Y	Y	Y	N	Y
HAWAII								
1 Abercrombie	Y	Y	Y	Y	Y	N	Y	Y
2 Mink	Y	Y	Y	Y	Y	N	Y	Y
IDAHO								
1 ***Chenoweth-Hage***	Y	N	N	Y	Y	Y	N	Y
2 ***Simpson***	Y	N	N	Y	Y	Y	N	Y
ILLINOIS								
1 Rush	Y	Y	Y	Y	N	N	Y	?
2 Jackson	Y	Y	Y	N	N	N	Y	Y
3 Lipinski	Y	Y	Y	Y	Y	Y	Y	Y
4 Gutierrez	Y	Y	Y	Y	N	N	Y	Y
5 Blagojevich	Y	Y	Y	Y	Y	N	Y	Y
6 ***Hyde***	Y	N	N	Y	Y	Y	N	Y
7 Davis	Y	Y	Y	Y	N	N	Y	Y
8 ***Crane***	Y	N	N	Y	Y	Y	N	Y
9 Schakowsky	Y	Y	Y	Y	N	N	Y	Y
10 ***Porter***	Y	N	N	Y	Y	Y	N	Y
11 ***Weller***	Y	N	N	Y	Y	Y	N	Y
12 Costello	Y	Y	Y	Y	Y	Y	Y	Y
13 ***Biggert***	Y	N	N	Y	Y	Y	N	Y

ND Northern Democrats SD Southern Democrats

	409	410	411	412	413	414	415	416
14 ***Hastert***				Y				
15 ***Ewing***	Y	N	N	Y	Y	Y	N	Y
16 ***Manzullo***	Y	N	N	Y	Y	Y	N	Y
17 Evans	Y	Y	Y	Y	Y	N	Y	Y
18 ***LaHood***	Y	N	N	Y	Y	Y	N	Y
19 Phelps	Y	Y	Y	Y	Y	Y	Y	Y
20 ***Shimkus***	Y	N	N	Y	Y	Y	N	Y
INDIANA								
1 Visclosky	Y	Y	Y	N	Y	N	Y	Y
2 ***McIntosh***	?	?	?	?	?	?	?	?
3 Roemer	Y	Y	N	Y	Y	N	Y	?
4 ***Souder***	Y	N	N	Y	?	Y	N	Y
5 ***Buyer***	Y	N	N	Y	Y	Y	N	Y
6 ***Burton***	Y	N	N	Y	Y	Y	N	Y
7 ***Pease***	Y	N	N	Y	Y	Y	N	Y
8 ***Hostettler***	Y	N	N	Y	Y	Y	N	Y
9 Hill	Y	Y	N	Y	Y	N	Y	Y
10 Carson	Y	Y	Y	Y	Y	N	Y	Y
IOWA								
1 ***Leach***	Y	N	N	Y	Y	Y	N	Y
2 ***Nussle***	Y	N	N	Y	Y	Y	N	Y
3 Boswell	+	?	?	?	?	?	?	?
4 ***Ganske***	Y	N	N	Y	N	Y	N	Y
5 ***Latham***	Y	N	N	Y	Y	Y	N	Y
KANSAS								
1 ***Moran***	Y	N	N	Y	Y	Y	N	Y
2 ***Ryun***	Y	N	N	Y	Y	Y	N	Y
3 Moore	Y	Y	N	Y	Y	Y	Y	Y
4 ***Tiahrt***	Y	N	N	Y	Y	Y	N	Y
KENTUCKY								
1 ***Whitfield***	Y	N	N	Y	Y	Y	N	Y
2 ***Lewis***	Y	N	N	Y	Y	Y	N	Y
3 ***Northup***	Y	N	N	Y	Y	Y	N	Y
4 Lucas	Y	Y	Y	Y	Y	Y	Y	Y
5 ***Rogers***	Y	N	N	Y	Y	Y	N	Y
6 ***Fletcher***	Y	N	N	Y	Y	Y	Y	Y
LOUISIANA								
1 ***Vitter***	Y	N	N	Y	Y	Y	N	Y
2 Jefferson	Y	Y	Y	Y	Y	N	Y	Y
3 ***Tauzin***	Y	N	N	Y	Y	Y	N	Y
4 ***McCrery***	Y	N	N	Y	Y	Y	N	Y
5 ***Cooksey***	Y	N	N	Y	Y	Y	N	Y
6 ***Baker***	Y	N	N	Y	Y	Y	N	Y
7 John	Y	Y	Y	Y	Y	N	Y	Y
MAINE								
1 Allen	Y	Y	Y	Y	Y	N	Y	Y
2 Baldacci	Y	Y	Y	Y	Y	N	Y	Y
MARYLAND								
1 ***Gilchrest***	Y	N	N	Y	Y	Y	N	Y
2 ***Ehrlich***	Y	N	N	Y	Y	Y	N	Y
3 Cardin	Y	Y	N	Y	Y	N	Y	Y
4 Wynn	Y	Y	Y	Y	Y	N	Y	Y
5 Hoyer	Y	Y	Y	Y	Y	N	Y	Y
6 ***Bartlett***	Y	N	N	Y	Y	Y	N	Y
7 Cummings	Y	Y	Y	Y	Y	N	Y	Y
8 ***Morella***	Y	N	N	Y	Y	Y	Y	Y
MASSACHUSETTS								
1 Olver	Y	Y	Y	N	Y	N	Y	Y
2 Neal	Y	Y	Y	N	Y	N	Y	Y
3 McGovern	Y	Y	Y	Y	N	N	Y	Y
4 Frank	Y	Y	Y	N	N	N	Y	Y
5 Meehan	Y	Y	Y	Y	Y	N	Y	Y
6 Tierney	Y	Y	Y	Y	N	N	Y	Y
7 Markey	Y	Y	Y	N	N	N	Y	Y
8 Capuano	Y	Y	Y	Y	N	N	Y	Y
9 Moakley	Y	Y	Y	Y	Y	N	Y	Y
10 Delahunt	Y	Y	Y	Y	N	N	Y	Y
MICHIGAN								
1 Stupak	Y	Y	Y	Y	Y	Y	Y	Y
2 ***Hoekstra***	Y	N	N	Y	Y	Y	N	Y
3 ***Ehlers***	Y	N	N	Y	N	Y	N	Y
4 ***Camp***	Y	N	N	Y	Y	Y	N	Y
5 Barcia	Y	Y	N	Y	Y	Y	Y	Y
6 ***Upton***	Y	N	N	Y	N	Y	N	Y
7 ***Smith***	Y	N	N	Y	Y	Y	–	Y
8 Stabenow	Y	Y	Y	Y	Y	Y	Y	Y
9 Kildee	Y	Y	Y	Y	Y	Y	Y	Y
10 Bonior	Y	Y	Y	N	Y	N	Y	Y
11 ***Knollenberg***	Y	N	N	Y	Y	Y	N	Y
12 Levin	Y	Y	Y	Y	Y	N	Y	Y
13 Rivers	Y	Y	Y	Y	N	N	Y	Y
14 Conyers	Y	Y	Y	N	N	N	Y	Y
15 Kilpatrick	Y	Y	Y	Y	Y	N	Y	Y
16 Dingell	Y	Y	Y	Y	Y	N	Y	Y
MINNESOTA								
1 ***Gutknecht***	Y	N	N	N	Y	Y	N	Y
2 Minge	Y	Y	N	Y	N	N	Y	Y
3 ***Ramstad***	Y	N	N	Y	N	Y	N	Y
4 Vento	?	?	?	?	?	?	?	?
5 Sabo	Y	Y	Y	N	Y	N	Y	Y
6 Luther	Y	Y	N	Y	N	N	Y	Y
7 Peterson	Y	N	N	Y	N	Y	Y	Y
8 Oberstar	Y	Y	Y	Y	N	N	Y	Y
MISSISSIPPI								
1 ***Wicker***	Y	N	N	Y	Y	Y	N	?
2 Thompson	Y	Y	Y	Y	Y	N	Y	Y
3 ***Pickering***	Y	N	N	Y	Y	Y	N	Y
4 Shows	Y	Y	Y	Y	Y	Y	Y	Y
5 Taylor	Y	Y	N	Y	Y	Y	Y	Y
MISSOURI								
1 Clay	Y	Y	Y	N	Y	N	?	?
2 ***Talent***	Y	N	N	Y	Y	Y	N	Y
3 Gephardt	Y	Y	Y	N	Y	Y	Y	Y
4 Skelton	Y	Y	Y	Y	Y	Y	Y	Y
5 McCarthy	Y	Y	Y	Y	Y	N	Y	Y
6 Danner	Y	Y	Y	Y	Y	Y	Y	Y
7 ***Blunt***	Y	N	N	Y	Y	Y	N	Y
8 ***Emerson***	Y	N	N	Y	Y	Y	N	Y
9 ***Hulshof***	Y	N	N	Y	Y	Y	N	Y
MONTANA								
AL ***Hill***	Y	N	N	Y	Y	Y	N	Y
NEBRASKA								
1 ***Bereuter***	Y	N	N	Y	Y	Y	N	Y
2 ***Terry***	Y	N	N	Y	Y	Y	N	Y
3 ***Barrett***	Y	N	N	Y	Y	Y	N	Y
NEVADA								
1 Berkley	Y	Y	Y	Y	Y	Y	Y	Y
2 ***Gibbons***	Y	N	N	Y	Y	Y	N	Y
NEW HAMPSHIRE								
1 ***Sununu***	Y	N	N	Y	Y	Y	N	Y
2 ***Bass***	Y	N	N	Y	Y	Y	N	Y
NEW JERSEY								
1 Andrews	Y	Y	Y	Y	Y	Y	Y	Y
2 ***LoBiondo***	Y	N	N	Y	Y	Y	N	Y
3 ***Saxton***	Y	N	N	Y	Y	Y	N	Y
4 ***Smith***	Y	N	N	Y	Y	Y	N	Y
5 ***Roukema***	Y	N	N	Y	Y	Y	N	Y
6 Pallone	Y	Y	Y	Y	Y	Y	Y	Y
7 ***Franks***	Y	N	N	Y	Y	Y	N	Y
8 Pascrell	Y	Y	Y	Y	Y	Y	Y	Y
9 Rothman	Y	Y	Y	Y	Y	Y	Y	Y
10 Payne	Y	Y	Y	Y	N	N	Y	Y
11 ***Frelinghuysen***	Y	N	N	Y	Y	Y	N	Y
12 Holt	Y	Y	Y	Y	Y	Y	Y	Y
13 Menendez	Y	Y	Y	Y	Y	Y	Y	Y
NEW MEXICO								
1 ***Wilson***	Y	N	N	Y	Y	Y	N	Y
2 ***Skeen***	Y	N	N	Y	Y	Y	N	Y
3 Udall	Y	Y	Y	Y	Y	N	Y	Y
NEW YORK								
1 Forbes	Y	Y	N	Y	Y	Y	Y	Y
2 ***Lazio***	Y	N	N	Y	Y	?	?	?
3 ***King***	Y	N	N	Y	Y	Y	N	Y
4 McCarthy	Y	Y	Y	Y	Y	Y	Y	Y
5 Ackerman	Y	Y	Y	Y	Y	N	Y	Y
6 Meeks	Y	Y	Y	Y	N	N	Y	Y
7 Crowley	Y	Y	Y	Y	Y	Y	Y	Y
8 Nadler	N	Y	Y	Y	N	N	Y	Y
9 Weiner	Y	Y	Y	Y	N	N	Y	Y
10 Towns	Y	Y	Y	Y	Y	N	Y	Y
11 Owens	Y	Y	Y	Y	N	N	Y	Y
12 Velázquez	Y	Y	Y	Y	N	N	Y	Y
13 ***Fossella***	Y	N	N	Y	Y	Y	N	Y
14 Maloney	Y	Y	Y	Y	Y	N	Y	Y
15 Rangel	Y	Y	Y	N	N	N	Y	Y
16 Serrano	Y	Y	Y	N	Y	N	Y	Y
17 Engel	Y	Y	Y	Y	Y	N	Y	Y
18 Lowey	Y	Y	Y	Y	Y	N	Y	Y
19 ***Kelly***	Y	N	N	Y	Y	Y	N	Y
20 ***Gilman***	Y	N	N	Y	Y	Y	N	Y
21 McNulty	Y	Y	Y	Y	Y	N	Y	Y
22 ***Sweeney***	Y	N	N	Y	Y	Y	N	?
23 ***Boehlert***	Y	N	N	Y	Y	Y	N	Y
24 ***McHugh***	Y	N	N	Y	Y	Y	N	Y
25 ***Walsh***	Y	N	N	Y	Y	Y	N	Y
26 Hinchey	Y	Y	Y	N	Y	N	Y	Y
27 ***Reynolds***	Y	N	N	Y	Y	Y	N	Y
28 Slaughter	Y	Y	Y	Y	Y	N	Y	Y
29 LaFalce	Y	Y	Y	Y	Y	N	Y	Y
30 ***Quinn***	Y	N	N	Y	Y	Y	Y	Y
31 ***Houghton***	Y	N	N	Y	Y	N	N	Y
NORTH CAROLINA								
1 Clayton	Y	Y	Y	Y	Y	N	Y	Y
2 Etheridge	Y	Y	Y	Y	Y	Y	Y	Y
3 ***Jones***	Y	N	N	Y	Y	Y	N	Y
4 Price	Y	Y	Y	Y	Y	N	Y	Y
5 ***Burr***	Y	N	N	Y	Y	Y	N	Y
6 ***Coble***	Y	N	N	Y	Y	Y	N	Y
7 McIntyre	Y	Y	N	Y	Y	Y	Y	Y
8 ***Hayes***	Y	N	N	Y	Y	Y	N	Y
9 ***Myrick***	Y	N	N	Y	Y	Y	N	Y
10 ***Ballenger***	Y	N	N	Y	Y	Y	N	Y
11 ***Taylor***	Y	N	N	Y	Y	Y	N	Y
12 Watt	Y	Y	Y	Y	N	N	Y	Y
NORTH DAKOTA								
AL Pomeroy	Y	Y	N	Y	Y	N	Y	Y
OHIO								
1 ***Chabot***	Y	N	N	Y	Y	Y	N	Y
2 ***Portman***	Y	N	N	Y	Y	Y	N	Y
3 Hall	Y	Y	Y	Y	Y	Y	Y	Y
4 ***Oxley***	Y	N	N	Y	Y	Y	N	Y
5 ***Gillmor***	Y	N	N	Y	Y	Y	N	Y
6 Strickland	Y	Y	Y	Y	Y	Y	Y	Y
7 ***Hobson***	Y	N	N	Y	Y	Y	N	Y
8 ***Boehner***	Y	N	N	Y	Y	Y	N	Y
9 Kaptur	Y	Y	Y	Y	Y	N	Y	Y
10 Kucinich	Y	Y	Y	Y	N	N	Y	Y
11 Jones	Y	Y	Y	Y	Y	N	Y	Y
12 ***Kasich***	Y	N	N	Y	Y	Y	N	Y
13 Brown	?	Y	Y	N	N	N	Y	Y
14 Sawyer	Y	Y	Y	Y	Y	N	Y	Y
15 ***Pryce***	Y	N	N	Y	Y	Y	?	Y
16 ***Regula***	Y	N	N	Y	Y	Y	N	Y
17 Traficant	Y	N	N	Y	Y	Y	N	Y
18 ***Ney***	Y	N	N	Y	Y	Y	N	Y
19 ***LaTourette***	Y	N	N	Y	Y	Y	N	Y
OKLAHOMA								
1 ***Largent***	Y	N	N	Y	Y	Y	N	Y
2 ***Coburn***	Y	N	N	Y	Y	Y	N	Y
3 ***Watkins***	Y	N	N	Y	Y	Y	N	Y
4 ***Watts***	Y	N	N	Y	Y	Y	N	Y
5 ***Istook***	Y	N	N	Y	Y	Y	N	Y
6 ***Lucas***	Y	N	N	Y	Y	Y	N	Y
OREGON								
1 Wu	Y	Y	Y	Y	Y	Y	Y	Y
2 ***Walden***	Y	N	N	Y	Y	Y	N	Y
3 Blumenauer	Y	Y	Y	Y	N	N	Y	Y
4 DeFazio	Y	Y	Y	Y	N	Y	Y	Y
5 Hooley	Y	Y	Y	Y	N	Y	Y	Y
PENNSYLVANIA								
1 Brady	Y	Y	Y	Y	Y	N	Y	Y
2 Fattah	Y	Y	Y	Y	Y	N	Y	Y
3 Borski	Y	Y	Y	Y	Y	Y	Y	Y
4 Klink	Y	?	?	?	?	N	Y	Y
5 ***Peterson***	Y	N	N	Y	Y	Y	N	Y
6 Holden	Y	Y	Y	Y	Y	Y	Y	Y
7 ***Weldon***	Y	?	N	Y	Y	Y	?	Y
8 ***Greenwood***	Y	N	N	Y	Y	Y	?	?
9 ***Shuster***	Y	N	N	Y	Y	Y	N	Y
10 ***Sherwood***	Y	N	N	Y	Y	Y	N	Y
11 Kanjorski	Y	Y	Y	Y	Y	N	Y	Y
12 Murtha	?	Y	Y	Y	Y	?	?	?
13 Hoeffel	Y	Y	Y	Y	Y	Y	Y	Y
14 Coyne	Y	Y	Y	Y	N	N	Y	Y
15 ***Toomey***	Y	N	N	Y	Y	Y	N	Y
16 ***Pitts***	Y	N	N	Y	Y	Y	N	Y
17 ***Gekas***	Y	N	N	Y	Y	Y	N	Y
18 Doyle	Y	Y	Y	Y	Y	Y	Y	Y
19 ***Goodling***	Y	N	N	Y	Y	Y	N	Y
20 Mascara	Y	Y	Y	Y	Y	Y	Y	Y
21 ***English***	Y	N	N	Y	Y	Y	N	Y
RHODE ISLAND								
1 Kennedy	Y	+	Y	N	Y	Y	Y	Y
2 Weygand	Y	?	?	Y	Y	Y	Y	Y
SOUTH CAROLINA								
1 ***Sanford***	Y	N	N	Y	N	Y	N	N
2 ***Spence***	Y	N	N	Y	Y	Y	N	Y
3 ***Graham***	Y	N	N	Y	Y	Y	N	Y
4 ***DeMint***	Y	N	N	Y	Y	Y	N	Y
5 Spratt	Y	Y	Y	Y	Y	?	Y	Y
6 Clyburn	Y	Y	Y	Y	Y	N	Y	Y
SOUTH DAKOTA								
AL ***Thune***	Y	N	N	Y	Y	Y	N	Y
TENNESSEE								
1 ***Jenkins***	Y	N	N	Y	Y	Y	N	Y
2 ***Duncan***	Y	N	N	Y	N	Y	N	Y
3 ***Wamp***	Y	N	N	Y	Y	Y	N	Y
4 ***Hilleary***	Y	N	N	Y	Y	?	N	Y
5 Clement	Y	Y	Y	Y	Y	N	Y	Y
6 Gordon	?	Y	Y	Y	Y	Y	Y	Y
7 ***Bryant***	Y	N	N	Y	Y	Y	N	Y
8 Tanner	Y	Y	Y	Y	Y	N	Y	Y
9 Ford	Y	Y	Y	Y	Y	N	Y	Y
TEXAS								
1 Sandlin	Y	Y	N	Y	Y	Y	Y	Y
2 Turner	Y	Y	Y	Y	Y	Y	Y	Y
3 ***Johnson, Sam***	Y	N	N	Y	Y	Y	N	Y
4 Hall	Y	Y	N	Y	Y	Y	N	Y
5 ***Sessions***	Y	N	N	Y	Y	Y	N	Y
6 ***Barton***	Y	?	?	?	?	?	?	?
7 ***Archer***	Y	N	N	Y	Y	Y	N	Y
8 ***Brady***	Y	N	N	Y	Y	+	N	Y
9 Lampson	Y	Y	Y	Y	Y	Y	Y	Y
10 Doggett	Y	Y	Y	Y	N	N	Y	Y
11 Edwards	Y	Y	N	Y	Y	N	Y	Y
12 ***Granger***	Y	N	N	Y	Y	Y	N	Y
13 ***Thornberry***	Y	N	N	Y	Y	Y	N	Y
14 ***Paul***	Y	N	N	Y	N	Y	N	Y
15 Hinojosa	Y	Y	Y	Y	Y	N	Y	Y
16 Reyes	Y	Y	Y	Y	Y	N	Y	Y
17 Stenholm	Y	Y	N	Y	Y	Y	Y	Y
18 Jackson-Lee	Y	Y	Y	Y	Y	N	Y	Y
19 ***Combest***	Y	N	N	Y	Y	Y	N	Y
20 Gonzalez	Y	Y	Y	Y	Y	N	Y	Y
21 ***Smith***	Y	N	N	Y	Y	Y	N	Y
22 ***DeLay***	Y	N	N	Y	Y	Y	N	Y
23 ***Bonilla***	Y	N	N	Y	Y	Y	N	Y
24 Frost	Y	Y	Y	Y	Y	N	Y	Y
25 Bentsen	Y	Y	N	Y	Y	Y	Y	Y
26 ***Armey***	Y	N	N	Y	Y	Y	N	Y
27 Ortiz	Y	Y	Y	Y	Y	Y	Y	Y
28 Rodriguez	Y	Y	Y	Y	Y	N	Y	Y
29 Green	Y	Y	Y	Y	Y	Y	Y	Y
30 Johnson, E.B.	Y	Y	Y	Y	Y	N	Y	Y
UTAH								
1 ***Hansen***	Y	N	N	Y	Y	Y	N	Y
2 ***Cook***	Y	N	N	Y	Y	Y	N	Y
3 ***Cannon***	Y	N	N	Y	Y	Y	N	?
VERMONT								
AL *Sanders*	Y	N	Y	N	N	N	Y	Y
VIRGINIA								
1 ***Bateman***	Y	?	N	Y	Y	Y	N	Y
2 Pickett	Y	Y	Y	Y	Y	N	Y	Y
3 Scott	Y	Y	Y	Y	Y	N	Y	Y
4 Sisisky	Y	Y	Y	Y	Y	Y	Y	?
5 *Goode*	Y	N	N	Y	Y	Y	N	Y
6 ***Goodlatte***	Y	N	N	Y	Y	Y	N	Y
7 ***Bliley***	Y	N	N	Y	Y	Y	N	Y
8 Moran	Y	Y	Y	Y	Y	Y	Y	Y
9 Boucher	Y	Y	Y	Y	Y	N	Y	Y
10 ***Wolf***	Y	N	N	Y	Y	Y	N	Y
11 ***Davis***	Y	N	N	Y	Y	Y	N	Y
WASHINGTON								
1 Inslee	Y	Y	Y	Y	Y	N	Y	Y
2 ***Metcalf***	Y	N	N	Y	N	Y	N	Y
3 Baird	Y	Y	N	Y	Y	N	Y	Y
4 ***Hastings***	Y	N	N	Y	Y	Y	N	Y
5 ***Nethercutt***	Y	N	N	Y	Y	Y	N	Y
6 Dicks	Y	Y	Y	Y	Y	N	Y	Y
7 McDermott	+	Y	Y	N	N	N	Y	Y
8 ***Dunn***	Y	N	N	Y	Y	Y	N	Y
9 Smith	?	?	?	?	?	?	?	?
WEST VIRGINIA								
1 Mollohan	Y	Y	Y	Y	Y	N	Y	Y
2 Wise	Y	Y	Y	Y	Y	Y	Y	Y
3 Rahall	Y	Y	Y	Y	Y	N	Y	Y
WISCONSIN								
1 ***Ryan***	Y	N	N	Y	Y	Y	N	Y
2 Baldwin	Y	Y	Y	Y	N	N	Y	Y
3 Kind	Y	Y	Y	Y	Y	N	Y	Y
4 Kleczka	Y	Y	Y	Y	Y	N	Y	Y
5 Barrett	Y	Y	Y	Y	N	N	Y	Y
6 ***Petri***	Y	N	N	Y	Y	Y	N	Y
7 Obey	Y	Y	Y	Y	N	N	Y	Y
8 ***Green***	Y	N	N	Y	Y	Y	N	Y
9 ***Sensenbrenner***	Y	N	N	Y	N	Y	N	Y
WYOMING								
AL ***Cubin***	Y	N	N	Y	Y	Y	N	Y

Southern states - Ala., Ark., Fla., Ga., Ky., La., Miss., N.C., Okla., S.C., Tenn., Texas, Va.

417. HR 4810. Alleviate 'Marriage Penalty' Tax/Rule. Adoption of the rule (H Res 559) to provide for House floor consideration of the conference report that would reduce taxes for married couples by approximately $89.8 billion over five years. Adopted 279-140: R 215-0; D 63-139 (ND 40-108, SD 23-31); I 1-1. July 20, 2000.

418. HR 4810. Alleviate 'Marriage Penalty' Tax/Conference Report. Adoption of the conference report of the bill that would reduce taxes for married couples by approximately $89.8 billion over five years. The measure would increase the standard deduction for married couples to twice the amount claimed by single taxpayers. The upper boundary of the 15 percent tax bracket would gradually increase from 2000 to Dec. 31, 2004, to twice the limit for singles. The measure also would allow couples to earn an additional $2,000 before being disqualified from receiving the earned income tax credit. The bill would also allow couples to use family tax credits without paying the alternative minimum tax even if they fell under the alternative minimum tax. Adopted (thus sent to the Senate) 271-156: R 219-0; D 51-155 (ND 33-119, SD 18-36); I 1-1. July 20, 2000. A "nay" was a vote in support of the president's position.

419. HR 4871. Fiscal 2001 Treasury Appropriations/Previous Question. Linder, R-Ga., motion to order the previous question (thus ending debate and possibility of amendment) on adoption of the rule (H Res 560) to provide for House floor consideration of the bill to appropriate $29.1 billion in fiscal 2001 for the Treasury Department, U.S. Postal Service and related agencies. Motion agreed to 250-173: R 124-94; D 126-77 (ND 94-56, SD 32-21); I 0-2. July 20, 2000.

420. HR 4871. Fiscal 2001 Treasury Appropriations/Rule. Adoption of the rule (H Res 560) to provide for House floor consideration of the bill to appropriate $29.1 billion in fiscal 2001 for the Treasury Department, U.S. Postal Service and related agencies. Adopted 282-141: R 160-57; D 122-82 (ND 89-61, SD 33-21); I 0-2. July 20, 2000.

421. HR 4871. Fiscal 2001 Treasury Appropriations/Anti-Drug Funding. Vitter, R-La., amendment that would provide $25 million for High Intensity Drug Trafficking Areas (HIDTA) and offsets the cost with an equal reduction in the Internal Revenue Service's funding. Adopted 284-134: R 175-38; D 108-95 (ND 69-80, SD 39-15); I 1-1. July 20, 2000.

422. HR 4871. Fiscal 2001 Treasury Appropriations/Abortion Funding. DeLauro, D-Conn., amendment that would strike the bill's provision banning funds for an abortion, or the administrative expenses in connection with any health plan under the federal employees health benefit program that provides any benefits or coverage for abortions. Rejected 184-230: R 28-185; D 155-44 (ND 112-33, SD 43-11); I 1-1. July 20, 2000. A "yea" was a vote in support of the president's position.

Key

- Y Voted for (yea).
- # Paired for.
- + Announced for.
- N Voted against (nay).
- X Paired against.
- – Announced against.
- P Voted "present."
- C Voted "present" to avoid possible conflict of interest.
- ? Did not vote or otherwise make a position known.

•

Democrats ***Republicans***
Independents

	417	418	419	420	421	422
ALABAMA						
1 ***Callahan***	Y	Y	Y	Y	Y	N
2 ***Everett***	Y	Y	Y	N	Y	N
3 ***Riley***	Y	Y	N	N	Y	N
4 ***Aderholt***	Y	Y	N	N	Y	N
5 Cramer	Y	Y	N	N	Y	Y
6 ***Bachus***	Y	Y	Y	Y	Y	N
7 Hilliard	N	N	Y	N	N	Y
ALASKA						
AL ***Young***	Y	Y	Y	Y	Y	N
ARIZONA						
1 ***Salmon***	Y	Y	Y	Y	Y	N
2 Pastor	N	N	Y	N	Y	Y
3 ***Stump***	Y	Y	N	Y	Y	N
4 ***Shadegg***	Y	Y	Y	N	Y	N
5 ***Kolbe***	Y	Y	Y	Y	N	N
6 ***Hayworth***	Y	Y	N	N	?	?
ARKANSAS						
1 Berry	N	N	N	N	Y	N
2 Snyder	N	N	N	N	Y	Y
3 ***Hutchinson***	Y	Y	N	Y	Y	N
4 ***Dickey***	Y	Y	Y	Y	Y	N
CALIFORNIA						
1 Thompson	N	N	Y	Y	N	Y
2 ***Herger***	Y	Y	N	N	Y	N
3 ***Ose***	Y	Y	N	Y	Y	Y
4 ***Doolittle***	Y	Y	Y	Y	Y	N
5 Matsui	?	N	Y	Y	N	?
6 Woolsey	N	N	Y	?	N	Y
7 Miller, George	N	N	Y	Y	N	Y
8 Pelosi	N	N	Y	Y	Y	Y
9 Lee	N	N	Y	Y	N	Y
10 Tauscher	Y	Y	Y	Y	Y	Y
11 ***Pombo***	Y	Y	Y	Y	Y	N
12 Lantos	N	N	Y	Y	Y	Y
13 Stark	N	N	Y	Y	N	Y
14 Eshoo	Y	N	Y	Y	Y	Y
15 ***Campbell***	?	?	?	?	?	?
16 Lofgren	N	N	N	Y	Y	Y
17 Farr	N	N	Y	Y	Y	Y
18 Condit	Y	Y	Y	Y	Y	Y
19 ***Radanovich***	?	Y	N	Y	Y	N
20 Dooley	N	N	Y	Y	Y	Y
21 ***Thomas***	Y	Y	Y	Y	Y	Y
22 Capps	Y	Y	N	N	Y	Y
23 ***Gallegly***	Y	Y	N	Y	Y	N
24 Sherman	N	N	N	Y	N	Y
25 ***McKeon***	Y	Y	Y	Y	Y	N
26 Berman	Y	N	Y	Y	?	?
27 ***Rogan***	Y	Y	N	N	Y	N
28 ***Dreier***	Y	Y	Y	Y	Y	N
29 Waxman	N	N	Y	Y	N	Y
30 Becerra	N	N	N	N	N	Y
31 Martinez	Y	Y	Y	Y	Y	N
32 Dixon	N	N	Y	Y	Y	Y
33 Roybal-Allard	N	N	Y	Y	N	Y
34 Napolitano	N	N	N	N	Y	Y
35 Waters	N	N	N	Y	Y	Y
36 ***Kuykendall***	Y	Y	Y	Y	Y	Y
37 Millender-McD.	N	N	Y	Y	Y	Y
38 ***Horn***	Y	Y	N	Y	N	Y
39 ***Royce***	Y	Y	N	N	Y	N
40 ***Lewis***	Y	Y	Y	Y	Y	N
41 ***Miller, Gary***	Y	Y	Y	Y	Y	N
42 Baca	?	?	?	?	?	?
43 ***Calvert***	Y	Y	Y	Y	Y	N
44 ***Bono***	Y	Y	Y	N	Y	N
45 ***Rohrabacher***	Y	Y	Y	Y	Y	N
46 Sanchez	N	N	N	Y	?	?
47 ***Cox***	Y	Y	Y	Y	Y	N
48 ***Packard***	Y	Y	Y	Y	N	N
49 ***Bilbray***	Y	Y	Y	Y	Y	N
50 Filner	N	N	N	N	Y	Y
51 ***Cunningham***	Y	Y	Y	Y	Y	N
52 ***Hunter***	Y	Y	Y	Y	Y	N
COLORADO						
1 DeGette	?	N	Y	N	Y	Y
2 Udall	N	N	N	N	Y	Y
3 ***McInnis***	Y	Y	Y	Y	?	?
4 ***Schaffer***	Y	Y	N	N	Y	N
5 ***Hefley***	Y	Y	Y	Y	Y	N
6 ***Tancredo***	Y	Y	Y	N	Y	N
CONNECTICUT						
1 Larson	N	N	Y	Y	N	Y
2 Gejdenson	N	N	N	N	Y	Y
3 DeLauro	N	N	Y	Y	N	Y
4 ***Shays***	Y	Y	Y	Y	Y	Y
5 Maloney	Y	Y	N	N	Y	Y
6 ***Johnson***	Y	Y	N	Y	N	Y
DELAWARE						
AL ***Castle***	Y	Y	N	Y	N	Y
FLORIDA						
1 ***Scarborough***	Y	Y	N	N	Y	N
2 Boyd	N	N	Y	Y	N	Y
3 Brown	Y	N	Y	Y	Y	Y
4 ***Fowler***	Y	Y	Y	Y	Y	N
5 Thurman	N	N	N	N	Y	Y
6 ***Stearns***	Y	Y	N	N	Y	N
7 ***Mica***	Y	Y	N	Y	Y	N
8 ***McCollum***	Y	Y	Y	Y	Y	N
9 ***Bilirakis***	Y	Y	Y	Y	N	N
10 ***Young***	Y	Y	Y	Y	N	N
11 Davis	N	N	Y	Y	Y	Y
12 ***Canady***	Y	Y	Y	Y	Y	N
13 ***Miller***	Y	Y	Y	Y	N	N
14 ***Goss***	Y	Y	Y	Y	Y	N
15 ***Weldon***	Y	Y	Y	Y	N	N
16 ***Foley***	Y	Y	Y	Y	Y	Y
17 Meek	N	N	Y	Y	N	Y
18 ***Ros-Lehtinen***	Y	Y	Y	Y	Y	N
19 Wexler	N	N	Y	Y	N	Y
20 Deutsch	N	N	N	N	N	Y
21 ***Diaz-Balart***	Y	Y	Y	Y	Y	N
22 ***Shaw***	Y	Y	Y	Y	Y	N
23 Hastings	N	N	Y	Y	N	Y
GEORGIA						
1 ***Kingston***	Y	Y	N	N	Y	N
2 Bishop	Y	Y	N	Y	Y	Y
3 ***Collins***	Y	Y	N	N	Y	N
4 McKinney	Y	Y	N	N	Y	Y
5 Lewis	N	N	Y	Y	N	Y
6 ***Isakson***	Y	Y	Y	Y	Y	N
7 ***Barr***	Y	Y	Y	Y	Y	N
8 ***Chambliss***	Y	Y	N	N	Y	N
9 ***Deal***	Y	Y	N	N	Y	N
10 ***Norwood***	Y	Y	Y	Y	Y	N
11 ***Linder***	Y	Y	Y	Y	Y	N
HAWAII						
1 Abercrombie	Y	Y	Y	Y	Y	Y
2 Mink	Y	Y	Y	Y	Y	Y
IDAHO						
1 ***Chenoweth-Hage***	Y	Y	N	Y	N	N
2 ***Simpson***	Y	Y	Y	Y	N	N
ILLINOIS						
1 Rush	N	N	Y	N	N	?
2 Jackson	N	N	Y	N	N	Y
3 Lipinski	N	Y	Y	Y	N	N
4 Gutierrez	N	N	Y	Y	N	Y
5 Blagojevich	Y	Y	Y	Y	Y	Y
6 ***Hyde***	Y	Y	Y	Y	N	N
7 Davis	?	N	Y	N	N	Y
8 ***Crane***	Y	Y	Y	Y	Y	N
9 Schakowsky	N	N	Y	Y	N	Y
10 ***Porter***	Y	Y	Y	Y	N	Y
11 ***Weller***	Y	Y	N	Y	?	?
12 Costello	Y	Y	N	N	Y	N
13 ***Biggert***	Y	Y	Y	Y	Y	Y

ND Northern Democrats SD Southern Democrats

	417	418	419	420	421	422
14 ***Hastert***		Y	Y			
15 ***Ewing***	Y	Y	Y	Y	Y	N
16 ***Manzullo***	Y	Y	N	Y	N	N
17 Evans	N	N	N	N	Y	Y
18 ***LaHood***	Y	Y	N	Y	Y	N
19 Phelps	Y	Y	N	N	N	N
20 ***Shimkus***	Y	Y	N	N	Y	N
INDIANA						
1 Visclosky	N	N	N	N	N	Y
2 ***McIntosh***	Y	Y	N	N	?	?
3 Roemer	?	?	?	?	?	?
4 ***Souder***	Y	Y	Y	Y	Y	N
5 ***Buyer***	Y	Y	N	Y	Y	N
6 ***Burton***	?	Y	Y	Y	?	?
7 ***Pease***	Y	Y	Y	Y	Y	N
8 ***Hostettler***	Y	Y	N	N	Y	N
9 Hill	N	N	N	N	Y	Y
10 Carson	Y	N	N	N	N	Y
IOWA						
1 ***Leach***	Y	Y	Y	Y	Y	N
2 ***Nussle***	Y	Y	Y	Y	N	N
3 Boswell	Y	Y	N	N	Y	Y
4 ***Ganske***	Y	Y	Y	Y	Y	N
5 ***Latham***	Y	Y	Y	Y	Y	N
KANSAS						
1 ***Moran***	Y	Y	N	N	Y	N
2 ***Ryun***	Y	Y	N	Y	Y	N
3 Moore	Y	Y	N	N	Y	Y
4 ***Tiahrt***	Y	Y	N	N	Y	N
KENTUCKY						
1 ***Whitfield***	Y	Y	N	N	Y	N
2 ***Lewis***	Y	Y	N	N	Y	N
3 ***Northup***	Y	Y	N	Y	Y	N
4 Lucas	Y	Y	N	N	Y	N
5 ***Rogers***	Y	Y	Y	Y	Y	N
6 ***Fletcher***	Y	Y	N	N	Y	N
LOUISIANA						
1 ***Vitter***	Y	Y	N	Y	Y	N
2 Jefferson	N	N	Y	Y	Y	Y
3 ***Tauzin***	Y	Y	Y	Y	Y	N
4 ***McCrery***	Y	Y	Y	Y	Y	N
5 ***Cooksey***	?	?	?	?	?	?
6 ***Baker***	Y	Y	N	N	Y	N
7 John	Y	Y	Y	Y	Y	N
MAINE						
1 Allen	N	N	N	Y	N	Y
2 Baldacci	N	N	N	Y	N	Y
MARYLAND						
1 ***Gilchrest***	Y	Y	Y	Y	Y	Y
2 ***Ehrlich***	Y	Y	?	?	Y	Y
3 Cardin	N	N	Y	Y	N	Y
4 Wynn	N	N	Y	Y	N	Y
5 Hoyer	N	N	Y	Y	N	Y
6 ***Bartlett***	Y	Y	N	Y	Y	N
7 Cummings	Y	N	Y	Y	Y	Y
8 ***Morella***	Y	Y	Y	Y	N	Y
MASSACHUSETTS						
1 Olver	N	N	Y	Y	N	Y
2 Neal	N	N	Y	Y	N	N
3 McGovern	N	N	Y	N	N	Y
4 Frank	N	N	Y	Y	N	Y
5 Meehan	N	N	Y	N	Y	Y
6 Tierney	N	N	N	N	N	Y
7 Markey	N	N	Y	Y	N	Y
8 Capuano	N	N	Y	Y	N	Y
9 Moakley	N	N	Y	Y	N	N
10 Delahunt	N	N	Y	Y	?	?
MICHIGAN						
1 Stupak	Y	Y	Y	N	N	N
2 ***Hoekstra***	Y	Y	Y	Y	Y	N
3 ***Ehlers***	Y	Y	Y	Y	N	N
4 ***Camp***	Y	Y	Y	Y	Y	N
5 Barcia	Y	Y	Y	N	N	N
6 ***Upton***	Y	Y	Y	Y	Y	N
7 ***Smith***	Y	Y	Y	Y	Y	N
8 Stabenow	Y	Y	N	N	Y	Y
9 Kildee	Y	Y	N	N	N	N
10 Bonior	N	N	Y	Y	N	N
11 ***Knollenberg***	Y	Y	Y	Y	N	N
12 Levin	Y	N	Y	N	Y	Y
13 Rivers	N	N	N	N	N	Y
14 Conyers	N	N	Y	Y	N	Y
15 Kilpatrick	?	?	?	?	N	Y
16 Dingell	N	N	Y	Y	N	N

	417	418	419	420	421	422
MINNESOTA						
1 ***Gutknecht***	Y	Y	Y	Y	Y	N
2 Minge	N	N	N	N	N	Y
3 ***Ramstad***	Y	Y	N	N	Y	Y
4 Vento	?	?	?	?	?	?
5 Sabo	N	N	Y	Y	N	Y
6 Luther	N	N	N	N	Y	Y
7 Peterson	N	N	N	Y	N	N
8 Oberstar	N	N	Y	N	N	N
MISSISSIPPI						
1 ***Wicker***	Y	Y	Y	Y	Y	N
2 Thompson	N	Y	Y	N	N	Y
3 ***Pickering***	Y	Y	N	Y	Y	N
4 Shows	Y	Y	N	N	Y	N
5 Taylor	N	N	N	N	Y	N
MISSOURI						
1 Clay	N	N	?	?	?	?
2 ***Talent***	Y	Y	N	Y	Y	N
3 Gephardt	N	N	Y	Y	Y	Y
4 Skelton	Y	Y	Y	Y	Y	N
5 McCarthy	N	N	Y	Y	N	Y
6 Danner	Y	Y	N	N	Y	N
7 ***Blunt***	Y	Y	Y	Y	N	N
8 ***Emerson***	Y	Y	N	Y	Y	N
9 ***Hulshof***	Y	Y	N	N	Y	N
MONTANA						
AL ***Hill***	Y	Y	N	N	Y	N
NEBRASKA						
1 ***Bereuter***	Y	Y	Y	Y	Y	N
2 ***Terry***	Y	Y	N	Y	Y	N
3 ***Barrett***	Y	Y	Y	Y	Y	N
NEVADA						
1 Berkley	Y	Y	N	N	Y	Y
2 ***Gibbons***	Y	Y	N	N	Y	N
NEW HAMPSHIRE						
1 ***Sununu***	Y	Y	Y	Y	Y	N
2 ***Bass***	Y	Y	Y	Y	Y	Y
NEW JERSEY						
1 Andrews	N	N	Y	Y	N	Y
2 ***LoBiondo***	Y	Y	N	N	Y	N
3 ***Saxton***	Y	Y	N	Y	Y	N
4 ***Smith***	Y	Y	Y	Y	Y	N
5 ***Roukema***	Y	Y	N	N	Y	Y
6 Pallone	N	N	Y	Y	Y	Y
7 ***Franks***	Y	Y	N	Y	Y	Y
8 Pascrell	Y	Y	N	N	N	Y
9 Rothman	N	N	Y	N	Y	Y
10 Payne	N	N	Y	N	Y	Y
11 ***Frelinghuysen***	Y	Y	N	Y	N	Y
12 Holt	Y	Y	N	N	Y	Y
13 Menendez	N	N	Y	Y	Y	Y
NEW MEXICO						
1 ***Wilson***	Y	Y	N	N	Y	N
2 ***Skeen***	Y	Y	Y	Y	N	N
3 Udall	N	N	N	N	Y	Y
NEW YORK						
1 Forbes	Y	Y	N	N	Y	N
2 ***Lazio***	Y	Y	N	Y	Y	Y
3 ***King***	Y	Y	Y	Y	Y	Y
4 McCarthy	Y	Y	N	Y	Y	Y
5 Ackerman	N	N	Y	Y	Y	Y
6 Meeks	N	N	Y	Y	Y	Y
7 Crowley	N	N	N	N	Y	N
8 Nadler	N	N	Y	Y	N	Y
9 Weiner	N	N	Y	Y	Y	Y
10 Towns	N	N	Y	Y	N	Y
11 Owens	N	N	Y	N	N	Y
12 Velázquez	N	N	N	N	Y	Y
13 ***Fossella***	Y	Y	N	N	Y	N
14 Maloney	N	N	N	Y	Y	Y
15 Rangel	N	N	Y	Y	N	Y
16 Serrano	N	N	Y	Y	Y	Y
17 Engel	Y	N	Y	Y	Y	Y
18 Lowey	N	N	Y	N	Y	Y
19 ***Kelly***	Y	Y	N	Y	Y	Y
20 ***Gilman***	Y	Y	Y	Y	N	Y
21 McNulty	N	N	Y	Y	Y	N
22 ***Sweeney***	Y	Y	Y	Y	Y	Y
23 ***Boehlert***	Y	Y	Y	Y	Y	Y
24 ***McHugh***	Y	Y	Y	Y	Y	N
25 ***Walsh***	Y	Y	Y	Y	Y	N
26 Hinchey	N	N	Y	N	Y	Y
27 ***Reynolds***	Y	Y	N	Y	Y	N
28 Slaughter	N	N	Y	N	N	Y
29 LaFalce	N	N	Y	N	N	N

	417	418	419	420	421	422
30 ***Quinn***	Y	Y	Y	Y	Y	N
31 ***Houghton***	Y	Y	Y	Y	N	Y
NORTH CAROLINA						
1 Clayton	Y	N	Y	Y	Y	Y
2 Etheridge	N	Y	N	Y	Y	Y
3 ***Jones***	Y	Y	N	N	Y	N
4 Price	N	N	N	Y	Y	Y
5 ***Burr***	Y	Y	Y	Y	Y	N
6 ***Coble***	Y	Y	N	N	Y	N
7 McIntyre	Y	Y	N	N	Y	N
8 ***Hayes***	Y	Y	N	Y	Y	N
9 ***Myrick***	Y	Y	Y	Y	N	N
10 ***Ballenger***	Y	Y	Y	Y	Y	N
11 ***Taylor***	Y	Y	Y	Y	N	N
12 Watt	N	N	Y	Y	Y	Y
NORTH DAKOTA						
AL Pomeroy	N	N	N	N	Y	Y
OHIO						
1 ***Chabot***	Y	Y	N	N	Y	N
2 ***Portman***	Y	Y	N	Y	N	N
3 Hall	N	N	Y	Y	Y	N
4 ***Oxley***	Y	Y	Y	Y	Y	N
5 ***Gillmor***	Y	Y	Y	Y	Y	N
6 Strickland	N	N	N	N	N	Y
7 ***Hobson***	Y	Y	Y	Y	N	N
8 ***Boehner***	Y	Y	Y	Y	Y	N
9 Kaptur	N	Y	N	N	N	?
10 Kucinich	N	N	N	N	N	N
11 Jones	N	N	Y	N	N	Y
12 ***Kasich***	Y	Y	N	N	Y	N
13 Brown	N	N	Y	N	N	?
14 Sawyer	Y	N	Y	Y	N	Y
15 ***Pryce***	Y	Y	Y	Y	Y	Y
16 ***Regula***	Y	Y	Y	Y	Y	N
17 Traficant	Y	Y	Y	Y	Y	N
18 ***Ney***	Y	Y	Y	Y	Y	N
19 ***LaTourette***	Y	Y	Y	Y	Y	N
OKLAHOMA						
1 ***Largent***	Y	Y	N	N	Y	N
2 ***Coburn***	Y	Y	N	N	Y	N
3 ***Watkins***	Y	Y	Y	Y	Y	N
4 ***Watts***	Y	Y	N	Y	Y	N
5 ***Istook***	Y	Y	Y	Y	Y	N
6 ***Lucas***	Y	Y	N	Y	Y	N
OREGON						
1 Wu	N	Y	N	N	Y	Y
2 ***Walden***	Y	Y	N	Y	Y	N
3 Blumenauer	N	N	Y	Y	N	Y
4 DeFazio	N	N	N	N	N	Y
5 Hooley	Y	Y	N	N	Y	Y
PENNSYLVANIA						
1 Brady	N	N	Y	Y	N	Y
2 Fattah	N	N	Y	Y	N	Y
3 Borski	N	N	Y	Y	N	N
4 Klink	N	N	Y	Y	N	N
5 ***Peterson***	Y	Y	N	Y	Y	N
6 Holden	Y	Y	Y	Y	Y	N
7 ***Weldon***	?	Y	Y	Y	Y	N
8 ***Greenwood***	Y	Y	Y	Y	Y	Y
9 ***Shuster***	Y	Y	Y	Y	Y	N
10 ***Sherwood***	Y	Y	N	N	Y	N
11 Kanjorski	N	N	Y	Y	N	N
12 Murtha	Y	N	Y	Y	N	N
13 Hoeffel	N	N	N	N	N	Y
14 Coyne	?	N	Y	Y	N	Y
15 ***Toomey***	Y	Y	N	N	Y	N
16 ***Pitts***	Y	Y	N	Y	Y	N
17 ***Gekas***	Y	Y	N	N	Y	N
18 Doyle	Y	Y	Y	Y	Y	N
19 ***Goodling***	Y	Y	Y	Y	Y	N
20 Mascara	Y	Y	N	Y	Y	N
21 ***English***	Y	Y	N	N	N	N
RHODE ISLAND						
1 Kennedy	N	N	Y	Y	N	Y
2 Weygand	N	N	N	N	Y	N
SOUTH CAROLINA						
1 ***Sanford***	Y	Y	N	N	N	N
2 ***Spence***	Y	Y	Y	Y	Y	N
3 ***Graham***	Y	Y	Y	Y	Y	N
4 ***DeMint***	Y	Y	N	Y	Y	N
5 Spratt	Y	Y	N	Y	Y	Y
6 Clyburn	Y	Y	?	Y	N	Y
SOUTH DAKOTA						
AL ***Thune***	Y	Y	N	N	Y	N

	417	418	419	420	421	422
TENNESSEE						
1 ***Jenkins***	Y	Y	N	N	Y	N
2 ***Duncan***	Y	Y	N	N	Y	N
3 ***Wamp***	Y	Y	N	N	Y	N
4 ***Hilleary***	Y	Y	N	N	Y	N
5 Clement	Y	Y	Y	Y	N	Y
6 Gordon	Y	Y	N	N	Y	Y
7 ***Bryant***	Y	Y	N	N	Y	N
8 Tanner	N	N	N	N	Y	Y
9 Ford	N	N	N	N	Y	Y
TEXAS						
1 Sandlin	Y	Y	N	N	Y	Y
2 Turner	Y	N	Y	Y	Y	Y
3 ***Johnson, Sam***	Y	Y	Y	Y	Y	N
4 Hall	Y	Y	N	N	Y	N
5 ***Sessions***	Y	Y	N	Y	Y	N
6 ***Barton***	?	?	?	?	?	?
7 ***Archer***	Y	Y	Y	Y	N	N
8 ***Brady***	Y	Y	N	Y	N	N
9 Lampson	N	N	Y	Y	Y	N
10 Doggett	N	N	Y	Y	Y	Y
11 Edwards	N	N	N	N	Y	N
12 ***Granger***	Y	Y	Y	Y	Y	N
13 ***Thornberry***	Y	Y	Y	N	Y	N
14 ***Paul***	Y	Y	N	N	N	N
15 Hinojosa	N	N	Y	Y	Y	Y
16 Reyes	N	N	N	N	Y	Y
17 Stenholm	Y	Y	N	Y	Y	N
18 Jackson-Lee	Y	N	Y	Y	Y	Y
19 ***Combest***	Y	Y	N	Y	Y	N
20 Gonzalez	Y	N	Y	N	Y	Y
21 ***Smith***	Y	Y	Y	Y	Y	N
22 ***DeLay***	Y	Y	Y	Y	Y	N
23 ***Bonilla***	Y	Y	Y	Y	N	Y
24 Frost	N	N	Y	Y	Y	Y
25 Bentsen	N	N	Y	Y	Y	Y
26 ***Armey***	Y	Y	Y	Y	Y	N
27 Ortiz	Y	N	Y	Y	Y	N
28 Rodriguez	Y	N	Y	Y	Y	Y
29 Green	N	N	Y	N	Y	Y
30 Johnson, E.B.	N	N	Y	Y	N	Y
UTAH						
1 ***Hansen***	Y	Y	Y	Y	Y	N
2 ***Cook***	Y	Y	N	N	Y	N
3 ***Cannon***	Y	Y	Y	Y	Y	N
VERMONT						
AL *Sanders*	N	N	N	N	N	Y
VIRGINIA						
1 ***Bateman***	Y	Y	Y	Y	N	N
2 Pickett	Y	Y	Y	Y	N	Y
3 Scott	N	N	Y	Y	Y	Y
4 Sisisky	Y	Y	Y	Y	N	Y
5 *Goode*	Y	Y	N	N	Y	N
6 ***Goodlatte***	Y	Y	Y	Y	Y	N
7 ***Bliley***	Y	Y	Y	Y	Y	N
8 Moran	N	N	Y	Y	N	Y
9 Boucher	Y	Y	Y	Y	N	Y
10 ***Wolf***	Y	Y	Y	Y	N	N
11 ***Davis***	Y	Y	Y	Y	N	Y
WASHINGTON						
1 Inslee	Y	Y	N	N	Y	Y
2 ***Metcalf***	Y	Y	N	N	Y	N
3 Baird	N	Y	N	N	Y	Y
4 ***Hastings***	Y	Y	Y	Y	Y	N
5 ***Nethercutt***	Y	Y	N	Y	Y	N
6 Dicks	N	N	Y	Y	Y	Y
7 McDermott	N	N	Y	Y	Y	Y
8 ***Dunn***	Y	Y	Y	Y	Y	N
9 Smith	?	?	?	?	?	?
WEST VIRGINIA						
1 Mollohan	Y	N	?	Y	N	N
2 Wise	Y	Y	N	N	Y	Y
3 Rahall	N	N	Y	Y	Y	N
WISCONSIN						
1 ***Ryan***	Y	Y	N	Y	Y	N
2 Baldwin	N	N	N	N	N	Y
3 Kind	N	N	N	N	N	Y
4 Kleczka	Y	N	N	N	Y	N
5 Barrett	N	N	N	N	Y	Y
6 ***Petri***	Y	Y	N	N	Y	N
7 Obey	N	N	Y	N	N	Y
8 ***Green***	Y	Y	N	Y	Y	N
9 ***Sensenbrenner***	Y	Y	N	N	Y	N
WYOMING						
AL ***Cubin***	Y	Y	Y	Y	Y	N

Southern states - Ala., Ark., Fla., Ga., Ky., La., Miss., N.C., Okla., S.C., Tenn., Texas, Va.

423. HR 4871. Fiscal 2001 Treasury Appropriations/Contractor Regulations. Davis, R-Va., amendment that would block implementation of stricter regulations governing who is eligible for federal contracts until the GAO completes an audit documenting whether there is a problem requiring the proposed rule. Adopted 228-190: R 203-10; D 24-179 (ND 10-139, SD 14-40); I 1-1. July 20, 2000. A "nay" was a vote in support of the president's position.

424. HR 4871. Fiscal 2001 Treasury Appropriations/Cuban Economic Embargo. Rangel, D-N.Y., amendment that would block funding to implement, administer, or enforce the economic embargo of Cuba. Rejected 174-241: R 24-188; D 149-52 (ND 113-36, SD 36-16); I 1-1. July 20, 2000.

425. HR 4871. Fiscal 2001 Treasury Appropriations/Cuban Travel Embargo. Sanford, R-S.C., amendment that would block funding for enforcing restrictions on travel to Cuba. Adopted 232-186: R 60-153; D 171-32 (ND 126-23, SD 45-9); I 1-1. July 20, 2000.

426. HR 4871. Fiscal 2001 Treasury Appropriations/Cuban Sanctions. Moran, R-Kan., amendment that would block funding to implement sanctions on the sales of agricultural commodities, medicine or medicinal supplies to Cuba. Adopted 301-116: R 119-93; D 180-23 (ND 132-17, SD 48-6); I 2-0. July 20, 2000.

427. HR 4871. Fiscal 2001 Treasury Appropriations/Gun Manufacturer Agreement. Hostettler, R-Ind., amendment that would block funding to enforce, implement, or administer provisions of a settlement between Smith & Wesson and the Justice Department. Rejected 204-214: R 163-50; D 40-163 (ND 18-131, SD 22-32); I 1-1. July 20, 2000. A "nay" was a vote in support of the president's position.

428. HR 4871. Fiscal 2001 Treasury Appropriations/Passage. Passage of the bill that would appropriate $29.1 billion in fiscal 2001 for the Treasury Department, U.S. Postal Service, various offices of the Executive Office of the President and certain independent agencies, an $824.5 million increase over fiscal 2000 spending. The total includes $731 million for the Bureau of Alcohol, Tobacco and Firearms and $8.5 billion for the Internal Revenue Service. The bill would also require federal employee health plans that provide prescription drug coverage to include contraceptives. Passed 216-202: R 175-39; D 41-161 (ND 27-121, SD 14-40); I 0-2. July 20, 2000.

Key

- Y Voted for (yea).
- # Paired for.
- + Announced for.
- N Voted against (nay).
- X Paired against.
- – Announced against.
- P Voted "present."
- C Voted "present" to avoid possible conflict of interest.
- ? Did not vote or otherwise make a position known.

•

Democrats ***Republicans***
Independents

	423	424	425	426	427	428
ALABAMA						
1 ***Callahan***	Y	N	N	Y	Y	Y
2 ***Everett***	Y	N	N	Y	Y	Y
3 ***Riley***	Y	N	N	N	Y	Y
4 ***Aderholt***	Y	N	Y	Y	Y	N
5 Cramer	Y	Y	Y	Y	Y	N
6 ***Bachus***	Y	N	N	N	Y	Y
7 Hilliard	N	Y	Y	Y	N	N
ALASKA						
AL ***Young***	Y	N	N	N	Y	Y
ARIZONA						
1 ***Salmon***	Y	Y	Y	Y	Y	Y
2 Pastor	N	Y	Y	Y	N	N
3 ***Stump***	Y	N	N	Y	Y	Y
4 ***Shadegg***	Y	N	N	N	Y	N
5 ***Kolbe***	Y	N	N	N	Y	Y
6 ***Hayworth***	?	?	?	?	?	?
ARKANSAS						
1 Berry	Y	Y	Y	Y	Y	Y
2 Snyder	N	Y	Y	Y	N	N
3 ***Hutchinson***	Y	N	N	Y	Y	Y
4 ***Dickey***	Y	N	N	Y	Y	Y
CALIFORNIA						
1 Thompson	N	Y	Y	Y	N	N
2 ***Herger***	Y	Y	Y	Y	Y	N
3 ***Ose***	Y	N	N	Y	Y	Y
4 ***Doolittle***	Y	N	N	N	Y	Y
5 Matsui	N	Y	Y	Y	N	N
6 Woolsey	N	Y	Y	Y	N	N
7 Miller, George	N	Y	Y	Y	N	N
8 Pelosi	N	Y	Y	Y	N	N
9 Lee	N	Y	Y	Y	N	N
10 Tauscher	Y	Y	Y	Y	N	Y
11 ***Pombo***	Y	N	N	N	Y	Y
12 Lantos	N	Y	Y	Y	N	N
13 Stark	N	Y	Y	Y	N	N
14 Eshoo	Y	Y	Y	Y	N	N
15 ***Campbell***	?	?	?	?	?	?
16 Lofgren	N	Y	Y	Y	N	N
17 Farr	N	Y	Y	Y	N	N
18 Condit	N	Y	Y	Y	N	N
19 ***Radanovich***	Y	N	Y	N	Y	Y
20 Dooley	Y	Y	Y	Y	N	Y
21 ***Thomas***	Y	N	N	Y	Y	Y
22 Capps	N	Y	Y	Y	N	N
23 ***Gallegly***	Y	N	Y	Y	N	Y
24 Sherman	N	N	Y	Y	N	N
25 ***McKeon***	Y	N	N	N	Y	Y
26 Berman	?	?	?	?	?	?
27 ***Rogan***	Y	N	N	N	N	Y
28 ***Dreier***	Y	N	N	N	Y	Y
29 Waxman	N	Y	Y	Y	N	N
30 Becerra	N	Y	Y	Y	N	N
31 Martinez	Y	N	N	N	Y	Y
32 Dixon	N	Y	Y	Y	N	Y
33 Roybal-Allard	N	Y	Y	Y	N	N
34 Napolitano	N	Y	Y	Y	N	N
35 Waters	N	Y	Y	Y	N	?
36 ***Kuykendall***	Y	N	N	Y	N	Y
37 Millender-McD.	N	Y	Y	Y	N	N
38 ***Horn***	Y	N	N	Y	N	Y
39 ***Royce***	Y	N	N	N	Y	Y
40 ***Lewis***	Y	N	N	N	Y	Y
41 ***Miller, Gary***	Y	N	N	N	Y	Y
42 Baca	?	?	?	?	?	?
43 ***Calvert***	Y	N	N	Y	Y	Y
44 ***Bono***	Y	Y	Y	Y	Y	Y
45 ***Rohrabacher***	Y	N	N	N	Y	Y
46 Sanchez	?	?	?	?	?	?
47 ***Cox***	Y	N	N	N	Y	Y
48 ***Packard***	Y	N	N	N	Y	Y
49 ***Bilbray***	Y	N	Y	Y	N	Y
50 Filner	N	Y	Y	Y	N	N
51 ***Cunningham***	Y	N	N	N	Y	Y
52 ***Hunter***	Y	N	N	N	Y	Y
COLORADO						
1 DeGette	N	Y	Y	Y	N	N
2 Udall	Y	Y	Y	Y	N	N
3 ***McInnis***	?	?	?	?	?	?
4 ***Schaffer***	Y	N	N	N	Y	N
5 ***Hefley***	Y	N	N	Y	Y	N
6 ***Tancredo***	Y	N	N	N	N	N
CONNECTICUT						
1 Larson	Y	Y	Y	Y	N	Y
2 Gejdenson	N	Y	Y	Y	N	N
3 DeLauro	N	Y	Y	Y	N	N
4 ***Shays***	Y	Y	Y	Y	N	Y
5 Maloney	N	N	Y	Y	N	N
6 ***Johnson***	Y	Y	Y	Y	Y	Y
DELAWARE						
AL ***Castle***	Y	N	Y	Y	N	Y
FLORIDA						
1 ***Scarborough***	Y	N	N	N	Y	N
2 Boyd	Y	N	Y	Y	Y	Y
3 Brown	N	?	Y	Y	N	Y
4 ***Fowler***	Y	N	N	N	Y	Y
5 Thurman	N	Y	Y	Y	N	N
6 ***Stearns***	Y	N	N	N	Y	N
7 ***Mica***	Y	N	N	Y	Y	Y
8 ***McCollum***	Y	N	N	N	N	N
9 ***Bilirakis***	Y	N	N	N	Y	Y
10 ***Young***	Y	N	N	N	N	Y
11 Davis	Y	N	N	Y	N	N
12 ***Canady***	Y	N	N	N	Y	Y
13 ***Miller***	Y	N	N	N	N	Y
14 ***Goss***	Y	N	N	N	Y	Y
15 ***Weldon***	Y	N	N	N	Y	N
16 ***Foley***	Y	N	N	N	N	N
17 Meek	N	Y	Y	Y	N	Y
18 ***Ros-Lehtinen***	N	N	N	N	N	N
19 Wexler	N	N	N	N	N	N
20 Deutsch	N	N	N	N	N	N
21 ***Diaz-Balart***	N	N	N	N	N	N
22 ***Shaw***	Y	N	N	N	N	Y
23 Hastings	N	Y	Y	Y	N	Y
GEORGIA						
1 ***Kingston***	Y	N	N	N	Y	Y
2 Bishop	N	Y	Y	Y	Y	Y
3 ***Collins***	Y	N	N	Y	Y	Y
4 McKinney	N	Y	Y	Y	N	N
5 Lewis	N	Y	Y	Y	N	N
6 ***Isakson***	Y	N	N	Y	N	Y
7 ***Barr***	Y	N	N	N	Y	N
8 ***Chambliss***	Y	N	N	Y	Y	Y
9 ***Deal***	Y	N	N	Y	Y	Y
10 ***Norwood***	Y	N	N	Y	Y	Y
11 ***Linder***	Y	Y	Y	Y	Y	Y
HAWAII						
1 Abercrombie	N	Y	Y	Y	N	Y
2 Mink	N	Y	Y	Y	N	Y
IDAHO						
1 ***Chenoweth-Hage***	Y	N	N	N	Y	N
2 ***Simpson***	Y	N	Y	Y	Y	Y
ILLINOIS						
1 Rush	N	Y	Y	Y	N	N
2 Jackson	N	Y	Y	Y	N	N
3 Lipinski	N	N	N	N	N	Y
4 Gutierrez	N	N	N	N	N	N
5 Blagojevich	N	N	N	Y	N	N
6 ***Hyde***	N	N	N	N	N	Y
7 Davis	N	Y	Y	Y	N	N
8 ***Crane***	Y	N	N	Y	Y	N
9 Schakowsky	N	Y	Y	Y	N	N
10 ***Porter***	Y	N	Y	Y	N	Y
11 ***Weller***	?	?	?	?	?	?
12 Costello	N	Y	Y	Y	Y	N
13 ***Biggert***	Y	Y	Y	Y	Y	Y

ND Northern Democrats SD Southern Democrats

	423	424	425	426	427	428
14 ***Hastert***			N	N		Y
15 ***Ewing***	Y	N	Y	Y	Y	Y
16 ***Manzullo***	Y	N	Y	Y	Y	Y
17 Evans	N	Y	Y	Y	N	N
18 ***LaHood***	Y	Y	Y	Y	Y	Y
19 Phelps	N	Y	Y	Y	Y	N
20 ***Shimkus***	N	Y	Y	Y	Y	Y
INDIANA						
1 Visclosky	N	Y	Y	Y	N	Y
2 ***McIntosh***	?	?	?	?	?	?
3 Roemer	?	?	?	?	?	?
4 ***Souder***	Y	N	N	N	Y	N
5 ***Buyer***	Y	N	N	Y	Y	Y
6 ***Burton***	?	?	?	?	?	?
7 ***Pease***	Y	N	N	Y	Y	Y
8 ***Hostettler***	Y	N	Y	Y	Y	N
9 Hill	N	Y	Y	Y	Y	N
10 Carson	N	Y	Y	Y	N	N
IOWA						
1 ***Leach***	Y	Y	Y	Y	N	Y
2 ***Nussle***	Y	Y	Y	Y	Y	Y
3 Boswell	N	Y	Y	Y	Y	N
4 ***Ganske***	Y	Y	Y	Y	N	Y
5 ***Latham***	Y	Y	Y	Y	Y	Y
KANSAS						
1 ***Moran***	Y	N	Y	Y	Y	Y
2 ***Ryun***	Y	N	N	Y	Y	N
3 Moore	N	Y	Y	Y	N	N
4 ***Tiahrt***	Y	N	Y	Y	Y	Y
KENTUCKY						
1 ***Whitfield***	Y	N	Y	Y	Y	Y
2 ***Lewis***	Y	N	N	Y	Y	N
3 ***Northup***	Y	N	N	N	N	Y
4 Lucas	Y	N	N	N	Y	N
5 ***Rogers***	Y	N	N	N	Y	Y
6 ***Fletcher***	Y	N	N	Y	Y	Y
LOUISIANA						
1 ***Vitter***	Y	N	N	N	Y	Y
2 Jefferson	N	Y	Y	Y	N	N
3 ***Tauzin***	Y	N	N	N	Y	Y
4 ***McCrery***	Y	N	N	Y	Y	Y
5 ***Cooksey***	?	?	?	?	?	?
6 ***Baker***	Y	N	N	N	Y	N
7 John	Y	+	Y	Y	Y	Y
MAINE						
1 Allen	N	Y	Y	Y	N	N
2 Baldacci	N	Y	Y	Y	N	Y
MARYLAND						
1 ***Gilchrest***	Y	N	Y	Y	N	Y
2 ***Ehrlich***	Y	N	Y	Y	Y	Y
3 Cardin	N	N	Y	Y	N	N
4 Wynn	N	N	Y	Y	N	Y
5 Hoyer	N	N	Y	Y	N	N
6 ***Bartlett***	Y	N	N	N	Y	N
7 Cummings	N	Y	Y	Y	N	N
8 ***Morella***	Y	N	Y	Y	N	Y
MASSACHUSETTS						
1 Olver	N	Y	Y	Y	N	N
2 Neal	N	Y	Y	Y	N	N
3 McGovern	N	Y	Y	Y	N	N
4 Frank	N	Y	Y	Y	N	N
5 Meehan	N	Y	Y	Y	N	N
6 Tierney	N	Y	Y	Y	N	N
7 Markey	N	Y	Y	Y	N	N
8 Capuano	N	Y	Y	Y	N	N
9 Moakley	N	Y	Y	Y	N	N
10 Delahunt	?	?	?	?	?	?
MICHIGAN						
1 Stupak	N	Y	Y	Y	N	N
2 ***Hoekstra***	Y	N	Y	Y	Y	Y
3 ***Ehlers***	Y	N	Y	Y	Y	Y
4 ***Camp***	Y	N	N	Y	Y	Y
5 Barcia	N	Y	N	Y	N	N
6 ***Upton***	Y	Y	Y	Y	N	Y
7 ***Smith***	Y	N	N	Y	Y	Y
8 Stabenow	N	N	N	Y	N	N
9 Kildee	N	N	Y	Y	N	N
10 Bonior	N	Y	Y	Y	N	N
11 ***Knollenberg***	Y	N	N	N	Y	Y
12 Levin	N	N	Y	Y	N	N
13 Rivers	N	Y	Y	Y	N	N
14 Conyers	N	Y	Y	Y	N	N
15 Kilpatrick	N	Y	Y	Y	N	N
16 Dingell	N	N	N	Y	Y	N

	423	424	425	426	427	428
MINNESOTA						
1 ***Gutknecht***	Y	N	Y	Y	Y	Y
2 Minge	N	Y	Y	Y	N	N
3 ***Ramstad***	Y	Y	Y	Y	N	N
4 Vento	?	?	?	?	?	?
5 Sabo	N	Y	Y	Y	N	N
6 Luther	N	Y	Y	Y	N	N
7 Peterson	N	Y	Y	Y	Y	N
8 Oberstar	N	Y	Y	Y	N	N
MISSISSIPPI						
1 ***Wicker***	Y	N	N	N	Y	Y
2 Thompson	N	Y	Y	Y	N	N
3 ***Pickering***	Y	N	Y	Y	Y	Y
4 Shows	N	Y	Y	Y	Y	N
5 Taylor	Y	Y	Y	Y	Y	N
MISSOURI						
1 Clay	?	?	?	?	?	?
2 ***Talent***	Y	N	N	Y	Y	Y
3 Gephardt	N	N	N	N	N	N
4 Skelton	N	N	N	Y	Y	N
5 McCarthy	N	Y	Y	Y	N	N
6 Danner	N	Y	Y	Y	Y	N
7 ***Blunt***	Y	N	N	N	Y	Y
8 ***Emerson***	Y	N	N	P	Y	Y
9 ***Hulshof***	Y	N	N	Y	Y	Y
MONTANA						
AL ***Hill***	Y	N	N	Y	Y	Y
NEBRASKA						
1 ***Bereuter***	Y	N	Y	Y	N	Y
2 ***Terry***	Y	N	Y	Y	Y	Y
3 ***Barrett***	Y	N	Y	Y	Y	Y
NEVADA						
1 Berkley	N	N	N	N	N	N
2 ***Gibbons***	Y	N	N	Y	Y	Y
NEW HAMPSHIRE						
1 ***Sununu***	Y	N	Y	Y	Y	Y
2 ***Bass***	Y	N	Y	Y	Y	Y
NEW JERSEY						
1 Andrews	N	N	N	N	N	N
2 ***LoBiondo***	Y	N	N	Y	N	Y
3 ***Saxton***	Y	N	Y	Y	N	Y
4 ***Smith***	N	N	N	N	N	N
5 ***Roukema***	Y	N	N	Y	N	Y
6 Pallone	N	N	N	N	N	N
7 ***Franks***	Y	N	N	N	N	N
8 Pascrell	N	N	N	N	N	Y
9 Rothman	N	N	N	N	N	N
10 Payne	N	Y	Y	Y	N	Y
11 ***Frelinghuysen***	Y	N	N	N	N	Y
12 Holt	N	Y	Y	Y	N	N
13 Menendez	N	N	N	N	N	N
NEW MEXICO						
1 ***Wilson***	Y	N	N	Y	Y	Y
2 ***Skeen***	Y	N	N	N	Y	Y
3 Udall	N	Y	Y	Y	N	N
NEW YORK						
1 Forbes	N	N	N	N	N	Y
2 ***Lazio***	Y	N	N	N	N	Y
3 ***King***	N	N	N	N	N	Y
4 McCarthy	Y	Y	Y	Y	N	Y
5 Ackerman	N	N	N	N	N	N
6 Meeks	N	Y	Y	Y	N	N
7 Crowley	N	N	N	N	N	N
8 Nadler	N	Y	Y	Y	N	N
9 Weiner	N	Y	Y	Y	N	N
10 Towns	N	Y	Y	Y	N	N
11 Owens	N	Y	Y	Y	N	N
12 Velázquez	N	Y	Y	Y	N	N
13 ***Fossella***	Y	N	N	N	N	Y
14 Maloney	N	N	Y	Y	N	N
15 Rangel	N	Y	Y	Y	N	N
16 Serrano	N	Y	Y	Y	N	Y
17 Engel	N	N	N	N	N	N
18 Lowey	N	Y	Y	Y	N	N
19 ***Kelly***	Y	N	N	N	N	Y
20 ***Gilman***	N	N	N	N	N	Y
21 McNulty	N	Y	Y	Y	N	N
22 ***Sweeney***	N	N	N	Y	Y	Y
23 ***Boehlert***	Y	Y	Y	Y	N	Y
24 ***McHugh***	Y	N	N	Y	Y	Y
25 ***Walsh***	Y	N	Y	Y	N	Y
26 Hinchey	N	Y	Y	Y	N	N
27 ***Reynolds***	Y	N	N	N	Y	Y
28 Slaughter	N	Y	Y	Y	N	N
29 LaFalce	N	Y	Y	Y	N	N

	423	424	425	426	427	428
30 ***Quinn***	N	N	N	Y	N	Y
31 ***Houghton***	Y	N	N	Y	N	Y
NORTH CAROLINA						
1 Clayton	N	Y	Y	Y	N	Y
2 Etheridge	N	N	Y	Y	N	N
3 ***Jones***	Y	N	N	N	Y	N
4 Price	N	Y	Y	Y	N	Y
5 ***Burr***	Y	N	N	N	Y	Y
6 ***Coble***	Y	N	N	Y	Y	Y
7 McIntyre	Y	N	N	Y	Y	N
8 ***Hayes***	Y	N	N	N	Y	Y
9 ***Myrick***	Y	N	N	Y	Y	Y
10 ***Ballenger***	Y	N	N	N	Y	Y
11 ***Taylor***	Y	N	N	N	Y	Y
12 Watt	N	Y	Y	Y	N	Y
NORTH DAKOTA						
AL Pomeroy	N	Y	Y	Y	N	N
OHIO						
1 ***Chabot***	Y	N	N	N	Y	N
2 ***Portman***	Y	N	N	N	Y	Y
3 Hall	N	Y	Y	Y	N	N
4 ***Oxley***	Y	N	Y	Y	N	Y
5 ***Gillmor***	Y	N	N	Y	Y	Y
6 Strickland	N	Y	Y	Y	Y	N
7 ***Hobson***	Y	N	N	N	Y	Y
8 ***Boehner***	Y	N	N	P	Y	Y
9 Kaptur	N	N	Y	Y	N	Y
10 Kucinich	N	Y	Y	Y	N	N
11 Jones	N	Y	Y	Y	N	N
12 ***Kasich***	Y	N	N	N	Y	Y
13 Brown	N	Y	Y	Y	N	N
14 Sawyer	N	Y	Y	Y	N	N
15 ***Pryce***	Y	N	N	N	N	Y
16 ***Regula***	Y	N	N	N	Y	Y
17 Traficant	Y	N	N	N	Y	Y
18 ***Ney***	N	N	Y	Y	Y	Y
19 ***LaTourette***	Y	Y	Y	Y	N	Y
OKLAHOMA						
1 ***Largent***	Y	Y	Y	Y	Y	Y
2 ***Coburn***	Y	N	N	Y	Y	N
3 ***Watkins***	Y	N	N	Y	Y	Y
4 ***Watts***	Y	N	N	N	Y	Y
5 ***Istook***	Y	N	N	Y	Y	Y
6 ***Lucas***	Y	N	N	Y	Y	Y
OREGON						
1 Wu	Y	N	Y	N	N	N
2 ***Walden***	Y	N	N	Y	Y	Y
3 Blumenauer	N	Y	Y	Y	N	N
4 DeFazio	N	Y	Y	Y	N	N
5 Hooley	N	Y	Y	Y	N	N
PENNSYLVANIA						
1 Brady	N	N	Y	Y	N	N
2 Fattah	N	Y	Y	Y	N	N
3 Borski	N	N	Y	Y	N	N
4 Klink	N	Y	Y	Y	N	Y
5 ***Peterson***	Y	N	Y	Y	Y	Y
6 Holden	N	N	Y	Y	Y	Y
7 ***Weldon***	Y	N	N	N	Y	Y
8 ***Greenwood***	Y	N	Y	Y	N	Y
9 ***Shuster***	Y	N	N	N	Y	Y
10 ***Sherwood***	Y	N	Y	Y	Y	Y
11 Kanjorski	N	Y	Y	Y	N	Y
12 Murtha	N	N	N	Y	Y	Y
13 Hoeffel	N	Y	Y	Y	N	N
14 Coyne	N	Y	Y	Y	N	N
15 ***Toomey***	Y	N	Y	Y	Y	N
16 ***Pitts***	Y	N	N	N	Y	Y
17 ***Gekas***	Y	N	N	N	N	N
18 Doyle	N	Y	Y	Y	N	Y
19 ***Goodling***	Y	N	N	N	Y	Y
20 Mascara	N	N	Y	Y	Y	Y
21 ***English***	Y	Y	Y	Y	Y	Y
RHODE ISLAND						
1 Kennedy	N	N	N	N	N	N
2 Weygand	N	Y	Y	Y	N	N
SOUTH CAROLINA						
1 ***Sanford***	Y	N	Y	Y	Y	N
2 ***Spence***	Y	N	?	N	Y	Y
3 ***Graham***	Y	N	N	N	Y	Y
4 ***DeMint***	Y	N	N	Y	Y	Y
5 Spratt	Y	N	Y	Y	N	N
6 Clyburn	N	Y	Y	Y	N	Y
SOUTH DAKOTA						
AL ***Thune***	Y	Y	Y	Y	Y	Y

	423	424	425	426	427	428
TENNESSEE						
1 ***Jenkins***	Y	N	N	N	Y	Y
2 ***Duncan***	Y	N	N	Y	Y	N
3 ***Wamp***	Y	N	Y	Y	Y	Y
4 ***Hilleary***	Y	N	Y	Y	Y	N
5 Clement	N	Y	Y	Y	Y	N
6 Gordon	N	N	Y	Y	Y	N
7 ***Bryant***	Y	N	N	N	Y	Y
8 Tanner	Y	Y	Y	Y	Y	N
9 Ford	N	Y	Y	Y	N	N
TEXAS						
1 Sandlin	N	Y	Y	Y	Y	N
2 Turner	Y	Y	Y	Y	Y	N
3 ***Johnson, Sam***	Y	N	N	N	Y	Y
4 Hall	Y	N	Y	Y	Y	N
5 ***Sessions***	Y	Y	N	Y	Y	Y
6 ***Barton***	?	?	?	?	?	?
7 ***Archer***	Y	N	N	N	N	Y
8 ***Brady***	Y	N	N	N	Y	Y
9 Lampson	N	Y	Y	Y	Y	N
10 Doggett	N	Y	Y	Y	N	Y
11 Edwards	N	Y	Y	Y	N	N
12 ***Granger***	Y	N	N	N	Y	Y
13 ***Thornberry***	Y	N	N	Y	Y	Y
14 ***Paul***	Y	Y	Y	Y	Y	N
15 Hinojosa	N	Y	Y	Y	N	N
16 Reyes	N	N	N	N	N	N
17 Stenholm	Y	Y	Y	Y	Y	Y
18 Jackson-Lee	N	Y	Y	Y	N	N
19 ***Combest***	Y	Y	Y	Y	Y	Y
20 Gonzalez	N	Y	Y	Y	N	N
21 ***Smith***	Y	N	N	Y	Y	Y
22 ***DeLay***	Y	N	N	N	Y	Y
23 ***Bonilla***	Y	N	N	N	Y	Y
24 Frost	N	N	N	Y	N	N
25 Bentsen	N	N	Y	Y	Y	N
26 ***Armey***	Y	N	N	N	Y	Y
27 Ortiz	N	N	N	N	Y	N
28 Rodriguez	N	Y	Y	Y	N	N
29 Green	N	N	N	N	Y	N
30 Johnson, E.B.	N	Y	Y	Y	N	N
UTAH						
1 ***Hansen***	Y	N	N	Y	Y	Y
2 ***Cook***	Y	N	N	N	Y	N
3 ***Cannon***	Y	?	N	N	Y	Y
VERMONT						
AL *Sanders*	N	Y	Y	Y	N	N
VIRGINIA						
1 ***Bateman***	Y	N	N	Y	Y	Y
2 Pickett	N	Y	Y	Y	Y	N
3 Scott	N	Y	Y	Y	N	N
4 Sisisky	N	N	Y	Y	Y	N
5 *Goode*	Y	N	N	Y	Y	N
6 ***Goodlatte***	Y	N	N	Y	Y	N
7 ***Bliley***	Y	N	Y	Y	Y	Y
8 Moran	Y	Y	Y	Y	N	Y
9 Boucher	N	Y	Y	Y	Y	N
10 ***Wolf***	Y	N	N	N	Y	Y
11 ***Davis***	Y	N	N	N	N	Y
WASHINGTON						
1 Inslee	Y	Y	Y	Y	N	N
2 ***Metcalf***	Y	N	N	N	Y	N
3 Baird	N	Y	Y	Y	N	Y
4 ***Hastings***	Y	N	N	N	Y	Y
5 ***Nethercutt***	Y	N	N	N	Y	Y
6 Dicks	N	Y	Y	Y	N	Y
7 McDermott	N	Y	Y	Y	N	N
8 ***Dunn***	Y	N	N	Y	N	Y
9 Smith	?	?	?	?	?	?
WEST VIRGINIA						
1 Mollohan	N	N	Y	Y	Y	Y
2 Wise	N	Y	Y	Y	Y	N
3 Rahall	N	N	N	Y	Y	N
WISCONSIN						
1 ***Ryan***	Y	Y	Y	Y	Y	Y
2 Baldwin	N	Y	Y	Y	N	N
3 Kind	N	Y	Y	Y	N	N
4 Kleczka	N	Y	Y	Y	N	N
5 Barrett	N	Y	Y	Y	N	N
6 ***Petri***	Y	N	N	Y	Y	N
7 Obey	N	Y	Y	Y	N	N
8 ***Green***	Y	N	N	Y	Y	Y
9 ***Sensenbrenner***	Y	N	N	Y	Y	N
WYOMING						
AL ***Cubin***	Y	N	N	Y	Y	Y

Southern states - Ala., Ark., Fla., Ga., Ky., La., Miss., N.C., Okla., S.C., Tenn., Texas, Va.

429. **HR 4700. Kansas City Compact/Passage.** Hutchinson, R-Ark., motion to suspend the rules and pass the bill granting consent to the Kansas and Missouri Metropolitan Culture District Compact, which is a special taxing district created to facilitate cultural development, including sporting activities and facilities, in the greater Kansas City area. Motion agreed to 376-1: R 186-1; D 188-0 (ND 136-0, SD 52-0); I 2-0 . A two-thirds majority of those present and voting (252 in this case) is required for passage under suspension of the rules. July 24, 2000.

430. **HR 4923. Community Renewal Program/Passage.** English, R-Pa., motion to suspend the rules and pass the bill that would provide tax credits and economic incentives to encourage investment and job creation in economically depressed urban and rural communities. Motion agreed to 394-27: R 214-1; D 179-25 (ND 130-23, SD 49-2); I 1-1. A two-thirds majority of those present and voting (281 in this case) is required for passage under suspension of the rules. July 25, 2000. A "yea" was a vote in support of the president's position.

431. **HR 4888. Pregnant Death Row Inmates/Passage.** Hutchinson, R-Ark., motion to suspend the rules and pass the bill that would prohibit state, federal and territorial authorities from carrying out a death sentence on a pregnant woman. Motion agreed to 417-0: R 212-0; D 203-0 (ND 152-0, SD 51-0); I 2-0. A two-thirds majority of those present and voting (278 in this case) is required for passage under suspension of the rules. July 25, 2000.

432. **HR 4864. Expedited Veterans Claims/Passage.** Stump, R-Ariz., motion to suspend the rules and pass the bill that would authorize the Veterans Affairs Department (VA) to assist claimants in obtaining evidence to establish entitlement to a benefit and requires the VA to make reasonable efforts to obtain relevant records that claimants identify and authorize the VA to obtain. Motion agreed to 414-0: R 210-0; D 202-0 (ND 151-0, SD 51-0); I 2-0. A two-thirds majority of those present and voting (276 in this case) is required for passage under suspension of the rules. July 25, 2000.

433. **HR 1651. Fishermen's Reimbursements/Passage.** Saxton, R-N.J., motion to suspend the rules and pass the bill, as amended by the Senate, that would reauthorize through fiscal 2003 the Fishermen's Protective Act, which reimburses owners of U.S. fishing vessels that are illegally seized or detained by other nations. Motion rejected 265-154: R 192-18; D 73-134 (ND 55-99, SD 18-35); I 0-2. A two-thirds majority of those present and voting (280 in this case) is required for passage under suspension of the rules. July 25, 2000.

434. **HR 2919. Underground Railroad Museum/Passage.** Hansen, R-Utah, motion to suspend the rules and pass the bill that would authorize $16 million for the construction and program development for the National Underground Railroad Freedom Center in Cincinnati, Ohio. Motion agreed to 404-11: R 197-11; D 205-0 (ND 152-0, SD 53-0); I 2-0. A two-thirds majority of those present and voting (277 in this case) is required for passage under suspension of the rules. July 25, 2000.

435. **S 1910. Suffrage Historical Home/Passage.** Hansen, R-Utah, motion to suspend the rules and pass the bill that would remove a restriction against the Interior Department acquiring the title to the Hunt House in Waterloo, N.Y., and would allow it to be included in the Women's Rights National Historical Park. Motion agreed to 404-9: R 195-9; D 207-0 (ND 154-0, SD 53-0); I 2-0. A two-thirds majority of those present and voting (276 in this case) is required for passage under suspension of the rules. July 25, 2000.

Key

- Y Voted for (yea).
- # Paired for.
- + Announced for.
- N Voted against (nay).
- X Paired against.
- – Announced against.
- P Voted "present."
- C Voted "present" to avoid possible conflict of interest.
- ? Did not vote or otherwise make a position known.

•

Democrats ***Republicans***
Independents

	429	430	431	432	433	434	435
ALABAMA							
1 ***Callahan***	Y	Y	Y	Y	Y	Y	Y
2 ***Everett***	Y	Y	Y	Y	Y	Y	Y
3 ***Riley***	Y	Y	Y	Y	Y	Y	Y
4 ***Aderholt***	Y	Y	Y	Y	Y	Y	Y
5 Cramer	?	Y	Y	Y	Y	Y	Y
6 ***Bachus***	Y	Y	Y	Y	Y	Y	?
7 Hilliard	Y	Y	Y	Y	N	Y	Y
ALASKA							
AL ***Young***	Y	Y	Y	Y	Y	Y	Y
ARIZONA							
1 ***Salmon***	?	Y	Y	Y	Y	Y	Y
2 Pastor	Y	Y	Y	Y	N	Y	Y
3 ***Stump***	Y	Y	Y	Y	Y	N	Y
4 ***Shadegg***	Y	Y	Y	Y	Y	Y	Y
5 ***Kolbe***	Y	Y	Y	Y	Y	Y	Y
6 ***Hayworth***	Y	Y	Y	Y	Y	Y	Y
ARKANSAS							
1 Berry	Y	Y	Y	Y	Y	Y	Y
2 Snyder	Y	Y	Y	Y	Y	Y	Y
3 ***Hutchinson***	Y	Y	Y	Y	Y	?	Y
4 ***Dickey***	Y	Y	Y	Y	Y	Y	?
CALIFORNIA							
1 Thompson	Y	Y	Y	Y	Y	Y	Y
2 ***Herger***	Y	Y	Y	Y	Y	Y	Y
3 ***Ose***	+	Y	Y	Y	Y	Y	Y
4 ***Doolittle***	?	Y	Y	Y	Y	Y	Y
5 Matsui	Y	Y	Y	Y	N	Y	Y
6 Woolsey	Y	Y	Y	Y	Y	Y	Y
7 Miller, George	Y	N	Y	Y	Y	Y	Y
8 Pelosi	Y	N	Y	Y	Y	Y	Y
9 Lee	Y	Y	Y	Y	N	Y	Y
10 Tauscher	Y	Y	Y	Y	Y	Y	Y
11 ***Pombo***	?	Y	Y	Y	Y	Y	Y
12 Lantos	Y	Y	Y	Y	N	Y	Y
13 Stark	?	N	Y	Y	Y	Y	Y
14 Eshoo	Y	Y	Y	Y	Y	Y	Y
15 ***Campbell***	Y	Y	Y	Y	Y	Y	Y
16 Lofgren	Y	N	Y	Y	Y	Y	Y
17 Farr	Y	N	Y	Y	Y	Y	Y
18 Condit	Y	Y	Y	Y	N	Y	Y
19 ***Radanovich***	Y	Y	Y	Y	Y	Y	Y
20 Dooley	Y	Y	Y	Y	Y	Y	Y
21 ***Thomas***	Y	Y	Y	Y	?	Y	Y
22 Capps	Y	Y	Y	Y	Y	Y	Y
23 ***Gallegly***	Y	Y	Y	Y	Y	Y	Y
24 Sherman	Y	N	Y	Y	Y	Y	Y
25 ***McKeon***	Y	Y	Y	Y	Y	Y	Y
26 Berman	Y	Y	Y	Y	Y	?	Y
27 ***Rogan***	+	Y	Y	Y	Y	Y	Y
28 ***Dreier***	Y	Y	Y	Y	Y	Y	Y
29 Waxman	Y	N	Y	Y	Y	Y	Y
30 Becerra	Y	Y	Y	Y	N	Y	Y
31 Martinez	Y	Y	Y	Y	Y	?	Y
32 Dixon	Y	Y	Y	Y	N	Y	Y
33 Roybal-Allard	Y	Y	Y	Y	Y	Y	Y
34 Napolitano	Y	Y	Y	Y	N	Y	Y
35 Waters	?	N	Y	Y	N	Y	Y
36 ***Kuykendall***	Y	Y	Y	Y	Y	Y	Y
37 Millender-McD.	Y	Y	Y	Y	N	Y	Y
38 ***Horn***	Y	Y	Y	Y	Y	Y	Y
39 ***Royce***	Y	Y	Y	Y	N	Y	Y
40 ***Lewis***	Y	Y	Y	Y	Y	Y	Y
41 ***Miller, Gary***	?	Y	Y	Y	N	Y	Y
42 Baca	?	Y	Y	Y	N	Y	Y
43 ***Calvert***	Y	Y	Y	Y	Y	Y	Y
44 ***Bono***	Y	Y	Y	Y	Y	Y	Y
45 ***Rohrabacher***	Y	Y	Y	Y	N	Y	Y
46 Sanchez	Y	Y	Y	Y	Y	Y	Y
47 ***Cox***	Y	Y	Y	Y	Y	Y	Y
48 ***Packard***	Y	Y	Y	Y	Y	Y	Y
49 ***Bilbray***	Y	Y	Y	?	Y	Y	Y
50 Filner	Y	N	Y	Y	N	Y	Y
51 ***Cunningham***	Y	Y	Y	Y	Y	Y	Y
52 ***Hunter***	Y	Y	Y	Y	Y	Y	Y
COLORADO							
1 DeGette	Y	Y	Y	Y	N	Y	Y
2 Udall	Y	Y	Y	Y	Y	Y	Y
3 ***McInnis***	Y	Y	Y	Y	Y	Y	Y
4 ***Schaffer***	Y	Y	Y	Y	N	N	N
5 ***Hefley***	?	Y	Y	Y	Y	Y	Y
6 ***Tancredo***	Y	Y	Y	Y	Y	Y	Y
CONNECTICUT							
1 Larson	Y	Y	Y	Y	Y	Y	Y
2 Gejdenson	Y	N	Y	Y	Y	Y	Y
3 DeLauro	Y	Y	Y	Y	Y	Y	Y
4 ***Shays***	Y	Y	Y	Y	Y	Y	Y
5 Maloney	Y	Y	Y	Y	N	Y	Y
6 ***Johnson***	Y	Y	P	Y	Y	Y	Y
DELAWARE							
AL ***Castle***	Y	Y	Y	Y	Y	Y	Y
FLORIDA							
1 ***Scarborough***	Y	Y	Y	Y	Y	Y	Y
2 Boyd	Y	Y	Y	Y	Y	Y	Y
3 Brown	Y	Y	Y	Y	N	Y	Y
4 ***Fowler***	?	Y	Y	Y	Y	Y	Y
5 Thurman	Y	Y	Y	Y	N	Y	Y
6 ***Stearns***	?	Y	Y	Y	N	Y	Y
7 ***Mica***	Y	Y	Y	Y	Y	Y	Y
8 ***McCollum***	?	?	?	?	?	?	?
9 ***Bilirakis***	Y	Y	Y	Y	Y	Y	Y
10 ***Young***	?	Y	Y	Y	Y	Y	Y
11 Davis	Y	Y	Y	Y	N	Y	Y
12 ***Canady***	Y	Y	Y	Y	Y	Y	Y
13 ***Miller***	Y	Y	Y	Y	Y	Y	Y
14 ***Goss***	Y	Y	Y	Y	Y	Y	Y
15 ***Weldon***	Y	Y	Y	Y	Y	Y	Y
16 ***Foley***	Y	Y	Y	Y	Y	Y	Y
17 Meek	Y	Y	Y	Y	N	Y	Y
18 ***Ros-Lehtinen***	Y	+	+	+	+	+	+
19 Wexler	Y	Y	Y	Y	N	Y	Y
20 Deutsch	Y	Y	Y	Y	N	Y	Y
21 ***Diaz-Balart***	Y	Y	Y	Y	Y	Y	Y
22 ***Shaw***	Y	Y	Y	Y	Y	Y	Y
23 Hastings	Y	N	Y	Y	N	Y	Y
GEORGIA							
1 ***Kingston***	Y	Y	Y	Y	Y	Y	Y
2 Bishop	Y	Y	Y	Y	Y	Y	Y
3 ***Collins***	Y	Y	Y	Y	Y	Y	Y
4 McKinney	Y	Y	Y	Y	Y	Y	Y
5 Lewis	Y	Y	Y	Y	Y	Y	Y
6 ***Isakson***	Y	Y	Y	Y	Y	Y	Y
7 ***Barr***	Y	Y	Y	Y	Y	Y	Y
8 ***Chambliss***	Y	Y	Y	Y	Y	Y	Y
9 ***Deal***	Y	Y	Y	Y	Y	Y	Y
10 ***Norwood***	?	Y	Y	Y	Y	N	N
11 ***Linder***	Y	Y	Y	Y	Y	Y	Y
HAWAII							
1 Abercrombie	Y	Y	Y	Y	N	Y	Y
2 Mink	Y	Y	Y	Y	Y	Y	Y
IDAHO							
1 ***Chenoweth-Hage***	N	Y	Y	Y	Y	N	N
2 ***Simpson***	Y	Y	Y	Y	Y	Y	Y
ILLINOIS							
1 Rush	Y	Y	Y	Y	N	Y	Y
2 Jackson	Y	N	Y	Y	Y	Y	Y
3 Lipinski	Y	Y	Y	Y	N	Y	Y
4 Gutierrez	Y	N	Y	Y	N	Y	Y
5 Blagojevich	Y	Y	Y	Y	N	Y	Y
6 ***Hyde***	Y	Y	Y	Y	Y	Y	Y
7 Davis	Y	Y	Y	Y	N	Y	Y
8 ***Crane***	Y	Y	Y	Y	Y	Y	Y
9 Schakowsky	Y	N	Y	Y	Y	Y	Y
10 ***Porter***	+	Y	Y	Y	Y	Y	Y
11 ***Weller***	Y	Y	Y	Y	Y	Y	Y
12 Costello	Y	Y	Y	Y	N	Y	Y
13 ***Biggert***	Y	Y	Y	Y	Y	Y	Y

ND Northern Democrats SD Southern Democrats

	429	430	431	432	433	434	435
14 ***Hastert***		Y					
15 ***Ewing***	?	?	?	?	?	?	?
16 ***Manzullo***	Y	Y	Y	Y	Y	Y	Y
17 Evans	Y	Y	Y	Y	N	Y	Y
18 ***LaHood***	Y	Y	Y	Y	Y	Y	Y
19 Phelps	Y	Y	Y	Y	N	Y	Y
20 ***Shimkus***	Y	Y	Y	Y	Y	Y	Y
INDIANA							
1 Visclosky	Y	N	Y	Y	N	Y	Y
2 ***McIntosh***	?	?	?	?	?	?	?
3 Roemer	Y	Y	Y	Y	N	Y	Y
4 ***Souder***	Y	Y	Y	Y	Y	Y	Y
5 ***Buyer***	Y	Y	Y	Y	Y	Y	Y
6 ***Burton***	?	Y	Y	Y	Y	Y	+
7 ***Pease***	Y	Y	Y	Y	Y	Y	Y
8 ***Hostettler***	Y	Y	Y	Y	Y	Y	Y
9 Hill	Y	Y	Y	Y	Y	Y	Y
10 Carson	Y	Y	Y	Y	N	Y	Y
IOWA							
1 ***Leach***	Y	Y	Y	Y	Y	Y	Y
2 ***Nussle***	Y	Y	Y	Y	Y	Y	Y
3 Boswell	Y	Y	Y	Y	N	Y	Y
4 ***Ganske***	Y	Y	?	Y	Y	Y	Y
5 ***Latham***	Y	Y	Y	Y	Y	Y	Y
KANSAS							
1 ***Moran***	Y	Y	Y	Y	Y	Y	Y
2 ***Ryun***	Y	Y	Y	Y	Y	Y	Y
3 Moore	Y	Y	Y	Y	Y	Y	Y
4 ***Tiahrt***	Y	Y	Y	Y	Y	Y	Y
KENTUCKY							
1 ***Whitfield***	Y	Y	Y	Y	Y	Y	Y
2 ***Lewis***	Y	Y	Y	Y	Y	Y	Y
3 ***Northup***	Y	Y	Y	Y	Y	Y	Y
4 Lucas	Y	Y	Y	Y	Y	Y	Y
5 ***Rogers***	Y	Y	Y	Y	Y	Y	Y
6 ***Fletcher***	Y	Y	Y	Y	Y	Y	Y
LOUISIANA							
1 ***Vitter***	Y	Y	Y	Y	Y	Y	Y
2 Jefferson	Y	Y	Y	Y	N	Y	Y
3 ***Tauzin***	Y	Y	Y	Y	Y	Y	Y
4 ***McCrery***	Y	Y	Y	Y	Y	Y	Y
5 ***Cooksey***	Y	Y	Y	Y	Y	Y	Y
6 ***Baker***	Y	Y	Y	Y	Y	Y	Y
7 John	Y	Y	Y	Y	N	Y	Y
MAINE							
1 Allen	Y	Y	Y	Y	Y	Y	Y
2 Baldacci	Y	Y	Y	Y	Y	Y	Y
MARYLAND							
1 ***Gilchrest***	Y	Y	Y	Y	Y	Y	Y
2 ***Ehrlich***	Y	Y	Y	Y	Y	Y	Y
3 Cardin	Y	Y	Y	Y	Y	Y	Y
4 Wynn	Y	Y	Y	Y	N	Y	Y
5 Hoyer	Y	Y	Y	Y	Y	Y	Y
6 ***Bartlett***	Y	Y	Y	Y	Y	Y	Y
7 Cummings	Y	Y	Y	Y	N	Y	Y
8 ***Morella***	?	Y	Y	Y	Y	Y	Y
MASSACHUSETTS							
1 Olver	Y	N	Y	Y	N	Y	Y
2 Neal	Y	Y	Y	Y	N	Y	Y
3 McGovern	Y	Y	Y	Y	N	Y	Y
4 Frank	Y	N	Y	Y	N	Y	Y
5 Meehan	Y	Y	Y	Y	Y	Y	Y
6 Tierney	?	Y	Y	Y	Y	Y	Y
7 Markey	Y	Y	Y	Y	Y	Y	Y
8 Capuano	Y	Y	Y	Y	N	Y	Y
9 Moakley	Y	Y	Y	?	N	Y	Y
10 Delahunt	Y	Y	Y	Y	Y	Y	Y
MICHIGAN							
1 Stupak	Y	Y	Y	Y	N	Y	Y
2 ***Hoekstra***	Y	Y	Y	Y	Y	Y	Y
3 ***Ehlers***	Y	Y	Y	Y	Y	Y	Y
4 ***Camp***	Y	Y	Y	Y	Y	Y	Y
5 Barcia	Y	Y	Y	Y	N	Y	Y
6 ***Upton***	Y	Y	Y	Y	Y	Y	Y
7 ***Smith***	Y	Y	Y	Y	Y	Y	Y
8 Stabenow	Y	Y	Y	Y	N	Y	Y
9 Kildee	Y	Y	Y	Y	N	Y	Y
10 Bonior	Y	Y	Y	Y	N	Y	Y
11 ***Knollenberg***	Y	Y	Y	Y	Y	Y	Y
12 Levin	Y	Y	Y	Y	N	Y	Y
13 Rivers	Y	Y	Y	Y	N	Y	Y
14 Conyers	Y	N	Y	Y	N	Y	Y
15 Kilpatrick	Y	Y	Y	Y	N	Y	Y
16 Dingell	Y	Y	Y	Y	N	Y	Y

	429	430	431	432	433	434	435
MINNESOTA							
1 ***Gutknecht***	Y	Y	Y	Y	Y	Y	Y
2 Minge	Y	Y	Y	Y	Y	Y	Y
3 ***Ramstad***	Y	Y	Y	Y	Y	Y	Y
4 Vento	?	?	?	?	?	?	?
5 Sabo	Y	N	Y	Y	N	Y	Y
6 Luther	Y	Y	Y	Y	Y	Y	Y
7 Peterson	Y	Y	Y	Y	N	Y	Y
8 Oberstar	Y	Y	Y	Y	N	Y	Y
MISSISSIPPI							
1 ***Wicker***	Y	Y	Y	Y	Y	Y	Y
2 Thompson	Y	Y	Y	Y	N	Y	Y
3 ***Pickering***	Y	Y	Y	Y	Y	Y	Y
4 Shows	Y	Y	Y	Y	N	Y	Y
5 Taylor	Y	Y	Y	Y	Y	Y	Y
MISSOURI							
1 Clay	?	Y	Y	Y	N	Y	Y
2 ***Talent***	Y	Y	Y	Y	Y	Y	Y
3 Gephardt	Y	Y	Y	Y	N	Y	Y
4 Skelton	Y	Y	Y	Y	N	Y	Y
5 McCarthy	Y	Y	Y	Y	N	Y	Y
6 Danner	?	?	?	?	N	Y	Y
7 ***Blunt***	Y	Y	Y	Y	Y	Y	Y
8 ***Emerson***	Y	Y	Y	Y	Y	Y	Y
9 ***Hulshof***	Y	Y	Y	Y	Y	Y	Y
MONTANA							
AL ***Hill***	Y	Y	Y	Y	Y	Y	Y
NEBRASKA							
1 ***Bereuter***	Y	Y	Y	Y	Y	Y	Y
2 ***Terry***	Y	Y	Y	Y	Y	Y	Y
3 ***Barrett***	Y	Y	Y	Y	Y	Y	?
NEVADA							
1 Berkley	Y	Y	Y	Y	N	Y	Y
2 ***Gibbons***	Y	Y	Y	Y	Y	Y	Y
NEW HAMPSHIRE							
1 ***Sununu***	Y	Y	Y	Y	Y	Y	Y
2 ***Bass***	Y	Y	Y	Y	Y	Y	Y
NEW JERSEY							
1 Andrews	Y	Y	Y	Y	Y	Y	Y
2 ***LoBiondo***	Y	Y	Y	Y	Y	Y	Y
3 ***Saxton***	Y	Y	Y	Y	Y	Y	Y
4 ***Smith***	Y	Y	Y	Y	Y	Y	Y
5 ***Roukema***	Y	Y	Y	Y	Y	Y	Y
6 Pallone	Y	Y	Y	Y	Y	Y	Y
7 ***Franks***	?	Y	Y	Y	?	?	?
8 Pascrell	Y	Y	Y	Y	N	Y	Y
9 Rothman	Y	Y	Y	Y	Y	Y	Y
10 Payne	?	N	Y	Y	N	Y	Y
11 ***Frelinghuysen***	Y	Y	Y	Y	Y	Y	Y
12 Holt	Y	Y	Y	Y	Y	Y	Y
13 Menendez	?	?	?	?	?	?	?
NEW MEXICO							
1 ***Wilson***	Y	Y	Y	Y	Y	Y	Y
2 ***Skeen***	Y	Y	Y	Y	Y	Y	Y
3 Udall	Y	Y	Y	Y	N	Y	Y
NEW YORK							
1 Forbes	Y	Y	Y	Y	N	Y	Y
2 ***Lazio***	?	Y	Y	Y	?	?	?
3 ***King***	Y	Y	Y	Y	N	Y	Y
4 McCarthy	Y	Y	Y	Y	N	Y	Y
5 Ackerman	Y	N	Y	Y	N	Y	Y
6 Meeks	?	Y	Y	Y	N	Y	Y
7 Crowley	Y	Y	Y	Y	N	Y	Y
8 Nadler	Y	Y	Y	Y	N	Y	Y
9 Weiner	Y	Y	Y	Y	N	Y	Y
10 Towns	Y	Y	Y	Y	N	Y	Y
11 Owens	?	Y	Y	Y	N	Y	Y
12 Velázquez	Y	Y	Y	Y	N	Y	Y
13 ***Fossella***	Y	Y	Y	Y	Y	Y	Y
14 Maloney	?	Y	Y	Y	N	Y	Y
15 Rangel	Y	Y	Y	Y	N	Y	Y
16 Serrano	Y	Y	Y	?	Y	Y	Y
17 Engel	?	Y	Y	Y	N	Y	Y
18 Lowey	Y	Y	Y	Y	Y	Y	Y
19 ***Kelly***	Y	Y	Y	Y	Y	Y	Y
20 ***Gilman***	?	?	?	?	?	?	?
21 McNulty	Y	Y	Y	Y	Y	Y	Y
22 ***Sweeney***	?	Y	Y	Y	Y	Y	Y
23 ***Boehlert***	Y	Y	Y	Y	Y	Y	Y
24 ***McHugh***	Y	Y	Y	Y	Y	Y	Y
25 ***Walsh***	Y	Y	Y	Y	Y	Y	Y
26 Hinchey	Y	Y	Y	Y	Y	Y	Y
27 ***Reynolds***	Y	Y	Y	Y	Y	Y	Y
28 Slaughter	+	Y	Y	Y	N	Y	Y
29 LaFalce	Y	Y	P	Y	N	Y	Y

	429	430	431	432	433	434	435
30 ***Quinn***	Y	Y	Y	Y	Y	Y	Y
31 ***Houghton***	Y	Y	Y	Y	Y	Y	Y
NORTH CAROLINA							
1 Clayton	Y	Y	Y	Y	Y	Y	Y
2 Etheridge	Y	Y	Y	Y	N	Y	Y
3 ***Jones***	Y	Y	Y	Y	N	N	N
4 Price	Y	Y	Y	Y	N	Y	Y
5 ***Burr***	Y	Y	Y	Y	Y	Y	Y
6 ***Coble***	Y	Y	Y	Y	Y	N	Y
7 McIntyre	Y	Y	Y	Y	N	Y	Y
8 ***Hayes***	Y	Y	Y	Y	Y	Y	Y
9 ***Myrick***	Y	Y	Y	Y	Y	Y	Y
10 ***Ballenger***	Y	Y	Y	Y	Y	Y	Y
11 ***Taylor***	?	Y	Y	Y	Y	Y	Y
12 Watt	Y	Y	Y	Y	N	Y	Y
NORTH DAKOTA							
AL Pomeroy	Y	Y	Y	Y	N	Y	Y
OHIO							
1 ***Chabot***	Y	Y	Y	Y	Y	Y	Y
2 ***Portman***	Y	Y	Y	Y	Y	Y	Y
3 Hall	Y	Y	Y	Y	N	Y	Y
4 ***Oxley***	Y	Y	Y	Y	Y	Y	Y
5 ***Gillmor***	Y	Y	Y	Y	Y	Y	Y
6 Strickland	Y	Y	Y	Y	N	Y	Y
7 ***Hobson***	Y	Y	Y	Y	Y	Y	Y
8 ***Boehner***	Y	Y	Y	Y	Y	Y	Y
9 Kaptur	Y	Y	Y	Y	N	Y	Y
10 Kucinich	Y	Y	Y	Y	N	Y	Y
11 Jones	Y	Y	Y	Y	N	Y	Y
12 ***Kasich***	Y	Y	Y	?	N	Y	Y
13 Brown	Y	Y	Y	Y	N	Y	Y
14 Sawyer	Y	Y	Y	Y	N	Y	Y
15 ***Pryce***	Y	Y	Y	Y	Y	Y	?
16 ***Regula***	Y	Y	Y	Y	Y	Y	Y
17 Traficant	Y	Y	Y	Y	Y	Y	Y
18 ***Ney***	Y	Y	Y	Y	Y	Y	Y
19 ***LaTourette***	Y	Y	Y	Y	Y	Y	Y
OKLAHOMA							
1 ***Largent***	Y	Y	Y	Y	N	N	N
2 ***Coburn***	?	Y	Y	?	Y	N	N
3 ***Watkins***	?	Y	Y	?	Y	Y	Y
4 ***Watts***	Y	Y	Y	Y	Y	Y	Y
5 ***Istook***	Y	Y	Y	Y	Y	Y	Y
6 ***Lucas***	Y	Y	Y	Y	Y	Y	Y
OREGON							
1 Wu	Y	Y	Y	Y	Y	Y	Y
2 ***Walden***	Y	Y	Y	Y	Y	Y	Y
3 Blumenauer	Y	Y	Y	Y	Y	Y	Y
4 DeFazio	Y	N	Y	Y	Y	Y	Y
5 Hooley	Y	Y	Y	Y	Y	Y	Y
PENNSYLVANIA							
1 Brady	Y	Y	Y	Y	N	Y	Y
2 Fattah	?	Y	Y	Y	N	Y	Y
3 Borski	Y	Y	Y	Y	N	Y	Y
4 Klink	Y	Y	Y	Y	N	Y	Y
5 ***Peterson***	Y	Y	Y	Y	Y	Y	Y
6 Holden	Y	Y	Y	Y	N	Y	Y
7 ***Weldon***	Y	Y	Y	Y	Y	Y	Y
8 ***Greenwood***	Y	Y	Y	Y	Y	Y	Y
9 ***Shuster***	Y	Y	Y	Y	Y	Y	Y
10 ***Sherwood***	Y	Y	Y	Y	Y	Y	Y
11 Kanjorski	Y	Y	Y	Y	N	Y	Y
12 Murtha	?	Y	Y	Y	N	Y	Y
13 Hoeffel	Y	Y	Y	Y	N	Y	Y
14 Coyne	Y	Y	Y	Y	N	Y	Y
15 ***Toomey***	Y	Y	Y	Y	Y	Y	Y
16 ***Pitts***	Y	Y	Y	Y	Y	Y	Y
17 ***Gekas***	Y	Y	Y	Y	Y	Y	Y
18 Doyle	Y	Y	Y	Y	N	Y	Y
19 ***Goodling***	Y	Y	Y	Y	Y	Y	Y
20 Mascara	Y	Y	Y	Y	N	Y	Y
21 ***English***	Y	Y	Y	Y	Y	Y	Y
RHODE ISLAND							
1 Kennedy	?	Y	Y	Y	N	Y	Y
2 Weygand	Y	Y	Y	Y	N	Y	Y
SOUTH CAROLINA							
1 ***Sanford***	Y	Y	Y	Y	N	N	N
2 ***Spence***	?	Y	Y	Y	Y	P	Y
3 ***Graham***	Y	Y	Y	Y	Y	Y	Y
4 ***DeMint***	Y	Y	Y	Y	Y	Y	Y
5 Spratt	Y	Y	Y	Y	N	Y	Y
6 Clyburn	Y	Y	Y	Y	N	Y	Y
SOUTH DAKOTA							
AL ***Thune***	Y	Y	Y	Y	Y	Y	Y

	429	430	431	432	433	434	435
TENNESSEE							
1 ***Jenkins***	+	+	+	+	−	+	+
2 ***Duncan***	Y	Y	Y	Y	N	Y	Y
3 ***Wamp***	Y	Y	Y	Y	N	Y	Y
4 ***Hilleary***	+	Y	Y	Y	Y	Y	Y
5 Clement	Y	Y	Y	Y	N	Y	Y
6 Gordon	Y	?	?	?	Y	Y	Y
7 ***Bryant***	Y	Y	Y	Y	Y	Y	Y
8 Tanner	Y	Y	Y	Y	Y	Y	Y
9 Ford	Y	Y	Y	Y	Y	Y	Y
TEXAS							
1 Sandlin	Y	Y	Y	Y	N	Y	Y
2 Turner	Y	Y	Y	Y	N	Y	Y
3 ***Johnson, Sam***	Y	Y	Y	Y	Y	Y	Y
4 Hall	Y	Y	Y	Y	Y	Y	Y
5 ***Sessions***	?	Y	Y	Y	Y	Y	Y
6 ***Barton***	?	?	?	?	?	?	?
7 ***Archer***	Y	Y	Y	Y	Y	Y	Y
8 ***Brady***	Y	Y	Y	Y	Y	Y	Y
9 Lampson	?	?	?	?	N	Y	Y
10 Doggett	Y	Y	Y	Y	Y	Y	Y
11 Edwards	Y	?	?	?	?	?	?
12 ***Granger***	?	Y	Y	Y	Y	Y	Y
13 ***Thornberry***	Y	Y	Y	Y	Y	Y	Y
14 ***Paul***	Y	N	Y	Y	N	N	N
15 Hinojosa	Y	Y	Y	Y	N	Y	Y
16 Reyes	Y	Y	Y	Y	N	Y	Y
17 Stenholm	Y	Y	Y	Y	Y	Y	Y
18 Jackson-Lee	Y	Y	Y	Y	N	Y	Y
19 ***Combest***	Y	Y	Y	Y	Y	Y	Y
20 Gonzalez	Y	Y	Y	Y	N	Y	Y
21 ***Smith***	?	Y	Y	Y	Y	Y	Y
22 ***DeLay***	Y	Y	Y	Y	Y	Y	Y
23 ***Bonilla***	Y	Y	Y	Y	Y	Y	Y
24 Frost	Y	Y	Y	Y	N	Y	Y
25 Bentsen	Y	Y	Y	Y	N	Y	Y
26 ***Armey***	?	Y	Y	Y	Y	Y	Y
27 Ortiz	Y	Y	Y	Y	Y	Y	Y
28 Rodriguez	Y	Y	Y	Y	N	Y	Y
29 Green	Y	Y	Y	Y	N	Y	Y
30 Johnson, E.B.	Y	Y	Y	Y	N	Y	Y
UTAH							
1 ***Hansen***	Y	Y	Y	Y	Y	Y	Y
2 ***Cook***	?	Y	Y	Y	N	Y	Y
3 ***Cannon***	Y	Y	Y	Y	Y	Y	?
VERMONT							
AL *Sanders*	Y	N	Y	Y	N	Y	Y
VIRGINIA							
1 ***Bateman***	?	Y	Y	Y	N	P	P
2 Pickett	Y	Y	Y	Y	N	Y	Y
3 Scott	Y	N	Y	Y	N	Y	Y
4 Sisisky	Y	Y	Y	Y	N	Y	Y
5 *Goode*	Y	Y	Y	Y	N	Y	Y
6 ***Goodlatte***	Y	Y	Y	Y	N	Y	Y
7 ***Bliley***	Y	Y	Y	Y	Y	Y	Y
8 Moran	Y	Y	Y	Y	Y	Y	Y
9 Boucher	Y	Y	Y	Y	N	Y	Y
10 ***Wolf***	Y	Y	Y	Y	Y	Y	Y
11 ***Davis***	Y	Y	Y	Y	Y	Y	Y
WASHINGTON							
1 Inslee	Y	Y	Y	Y	N	Y	Y
2 ***Metcalf***	Y	Y	Y	Y	Y	Y	Y
3 Baird	Y	Y	Y	Y	N	Y	Y
4 ***Hastings***	Y	Y	Y	Y	Y	Y	Y
5 ***Nethercutt***	Y	Y	Y	Y	Y	Y	Y
6 Dicks	Y	Y	Y	Y	Y	Y	Y
7 McDermott	Y	N	Y	Y	Y	Y	Y
8 ***Dunn***	Y	Y	Y	Y	Y	Y	Y
9 Smith	?	?	?	?	?	?	?
WEST VIRGINIA							
1 Mollohan	?	Y	Y	Y	N	Y	Y
2 Wise	?	Y	Y	Y	N	Y	Y
3 Rahall	?	Y	Y	Y	N	Y	Y
WISCONSIN							
1 ***Ryan***	Y	Y	Y	Y	Y	Y	Y
2 Baldwin	Y	N	Y	Y	Y	Y	Y
3 Kind	Y	Y	Y	Y	Y	Y	Y
4 Kleczka	Y	Y	Y	Y	N	Y	Y
5 Barrett	Y	Y	Y	Y	Y	Y	Y
6 ***Petri***	Y	Y	Y	Y	N	Y	Y
7 Obey	Y	Y	Y	Y	N	Y	Y
8 ***Green***	Y	Y	Y	Y	Y	Y	Y
9 ***Sensenbrenner***	Y	Y	Y	Y	N	N	N
WYOMING							
AL ***Cubin***	Y	Y	Y	Y	?	?	?

Southern states - Ala., Ark., Fla., Ga., Ky., La., Miss., N.C., Okla., S.C., Tenn., Texas, Va.

436. HR 4806. Carl Elliot Federal Building/Passage. LaTourette, R-Ohio, motion to suspend the rules and pass the bill that would designate a federal building in Jasper, Ala., the "Carl Elliot Federal Building." Motion agreed to 411-0: R 207-0; D 202-0 (ND 150-0, SD 52-0); I 2-0. A two-thirds majority of those present and voting (274 in this case) is required for passage under suspension of the rules. July 25, 2000.

437. H Con Res 372. Coast Guard Commendation/Adoption. Gilchrest, R-Md., motion to suspend the rules and adopt the concurrent resolution recognizing the 210th anniversary of the Coast Guard and commending the people who have served in it. Motion agreed to 409-0: R 205-0; D 202-0 (ND 151-0, SD 51-0); I 2-0. A two-thirds majority of those present and voting (273 in this case) is required for adoption under suspension of the rules. July 25, 2000.

438. HR 4868. Trade and Tariff Changes/Passage. Crane, R-Ill., motion to suspend the rules and pass the bill that would streamline customs laws, make technical corrections to trade laws and temporarily suspend or reduce duties for certain imported products, the majority of them chemicals. Motion agreed to 411-0: R 207-0; D 202-0 (ND 151-0, SD 51-0); I 2-0. A two-thirds majority of those present and voting (274 in this case) is required for passage under suspension of the rules. July 25, 2000.

439. HR 4033. Bulletproof Vests/Passage. Chabot, R-Ohio, motion to suspend the rules and pass the bill that would reauthorize the bulletproof vest matching grant program for fiscal years 2002 through 2004 and double the annual authorization to $50 million a year. Motion agreed to 413-3: R 209-3; D 202-0 (ND 149-0, SD 53-0); I 2-0. A two-thirds majority of those present and voting (278 in this case) is required for passage under suspension of the rules. July 26, 2000.

440. HR 4710. Pornography Prosecution/Passage. Chabot, R-Ohio, motion to suspend the rules and pass the bill that would authorize an additional $5 million in fiscal 2001 for the Justice Department's criminal division child exploitation and obscenity section to hire and train staff for the prosecution of obscenity and child pornography cases. Motion agreed to 412-4: R 211-1; D 199-3 (ND 148-1, SD 51-2); I 2-0. A two-thirds majority of those present and voting (278 in this case) is required for passage under suspension of the rules. July 26, 2000.

441. H J Res 99. Vietnam NTR Disapproval/Adoption. Adoption of the joint resolution disapproving of the annual extension of trade status to Vietnam through July 2, 2001. Rejected 91-332: R 66-148; D 23-184 (ND 16-137, SD 7-47); I 2-0. July 26, 2000. A "nay" was a vote in support of the president's position.

442. HR 4942. Fiscal 2001 DC Appropriations/Rule. Adoption of the rule (H Res 563) to provide for House floor consideration of the bill (HR 4942) that would appropriate $414 million for the District of Columbia in fiscal year 2001. Adopted 217-203: R 213-1; D 3-201 (ND 1-149, SD 2-52); I 1-1. July 26, 2000.

[1] *Rep. Matthew G. Martinez of California switched parties from Democrat to Republican on July 26, 2000. The first vote he cast as a Republican was vote 439.*

Key

- Y Voted for (yea).
- # Paired for.
- \+ Announced for.
- N Voted against (nay).
- X Paired against.
- – Announced against.
- P Voted "present."
- C Voted "present" to avoid possible conflict of interest.
- ? Did not vote or otherwise make a position known.

•

Democrats **_Republicans_**
Independents

	436	437	438	439	440	441	442
ALABAMA							
1 ***Callahan***	Y	Y	Y	Y	Y	N	Y
2 ***Everett***	Y	Y	Y	Y	Y	Y	Y
3 ***Riley***	Y	Y	Y	Y	Y	Y	Y
4 ***Aderholt***	Y	Y	Y	Y	Y	Y	Y
5 Cramer	Y	Y	Y	Y	Y	N	N
6 ***Bachus***	Y	Y	Y	Y	Y	Y	Y
7 Hilliard	Y	Y	Y	Y	Y	N	N
ALASKA							
AL ***Young***	Y	Y	Y	?	?	N	Y
ARIZONA							
1 ***Salmon***	Y	Y	Y	Y	Y	N	Y
2 Pastor	Y	Y	Y	Y	Y	N	N
3 ***Stump***	Y	Y	Y	Y	Y	Y	Y
4 ***Shadegg***	Y	Y	Y	Y	Y	Y	Y
5 ***Kolbe***	Y	Y	Y	Y	Y	N	Y
6 ***Hayworth***	Y	Y	Y	Y	Y	Y	Y
ARKANSAS							
1 Berry	Y	Y	Y	Y	Y	N	N
2 Snyder	Y	Y	Y	Y	Y	N	N
3 ***Hutchinson***	Y	Y	Y	Y	Y	N	Y
4 ***Dickey***	Y	Y	Y	Y	Y	N	Y
CALIFORNIA							
1 Thompson	Y	Y	Y	Y	Y	N	N
2 ***Herger***	Y	Y	Y	Y	Y	N	Y
3 ***Ose***	Y	Y	Y	Y	Y	N	Y
4 ***Doolittle***	Y	Y	Y	Y	Y	Y	Y
5 Matsui	Y	Y	Y	Y	Y	N	N
6 Woolsey	Y	Y	Y	Y	Y	N	N
7 Miller, George	?	?	?	Y	Y	N	N
8 Pelosi	Y	Y	Y	Y	Y	N	N
9 Lee	Y	Y	Y	Y	Y	N	N
10 Tauscher	Y	Y	Y	Y	Y	N	N
11 ***Pombo***	Y	Y	Y	Y	Y	Y	Y
12 Lantos	Y	Y	Y	Y	Y	N	N
13 Stark	Y	Y	Y	?	?	N	N
14 Eshoo	Y	Y	Y	Y	Y	N	N
15 ***Campbell***	Y	Y	Y	Y	Y	N	Y
16 Lofgren	Y	Y	Y	Y	Y	Y	N
17 Farr	Y	Y	Y	Y	Y	N	N
18 Condit	Y	Y	Y	Y	Y	N	N
19 ***Radanovich***	Y	Y	Y	Y	Y	?	Y
20 Dooley	Y	Y	Y	Y	Y	N	N
21 ***Thomas***	Y	Y	Y	Y	Y	N	Y
22 Capps	Y	Y	Y	Y	Y	N	N
23 ***Gallegly***	Y	Y	Y	Y	Y	N	Y
24 Sherman	Y	Y	Y	Y	Y	N	N
25 ***McKeon***	Y	Y	Y	Y	Y	N	Y
26 Berman	Y	Y	Y	Y	Y	N	N
27 ***Rogan***	Y	Y	Y	Y	Y	Y	Y
28 ***Dreier***	Y	Y	Y	Y	Y	N	Y
29 Waxman	Y	Y	Y	Y	Y	N	N
30 Becerra	Y	Y	Y	Y	Y	N	N
31 Martinez [1]	Y	Y	Y	Y	Y	N	Y
32 Dixon	Y	Y	Y	Y	Y	N	N
33 Roybal-Allard	Y	Y	Y	Y	Y	N	N
34 Napolitano	Y	Y	Y	Y	Y	N	N
35 Waters	Y	Y	Y	?	?	N	N
36 ***Kuykendall***	Y	Y	Y	Y	Y	N	Y
37 Millender-McD.	Y	Y	Y	Y	Y	N	N
38 ***Horn***	Y	Y	?	Y	Y	N	Y
39 ***Royce***	?	Y	Y	Y	Y	Y	Y
40 ***Lewis***	Y	Y	Y	Y	Y	N	?
41 ***Miller, Gary***	Y	Y	Y	Y	Y	N	Y
42 Baca	Y	Y	Y	Y	Y	Y	N
43 ***Calvert***	Y	Y	Y	Y	Y	N	Y
44 ***Bono***	Y	Y	Y	Y	Y	N	Y
45 ***Rohrabacher***	Y	Y	Y	Y	Y	Y	Y
46 Sanchez	Y	Y	Y	Y	Y	Y	N
47 ***Cox***	Y	?	Y	Y	Y	Y	Y
48 ***Packard***	Y	Y	Y	Y	Y	N	Y
49 ***Bilbray***	Y	Y	Y	Y	Y	N	Y
50 Filner	Y	Y	Y	Y	Y	N	N
51 ***Cunningham***	Y	Y	Y	Y	Y	N	Y
52 ***Hunter***	Y	Y	Y	Y	Y	Y	Y
COLORADO							
1 DeGette	Y	Y	Y	Y	Y	N	N
2 Udall	Y	Y	Y	Y	Y	N	N
3 ***McInnis***	Y	Y	Y	Y	Y	N	Y
4 ***Schaffer***	Y	Y	Y	Y	Y	Y	Y
5 ***Hefley***	Y	Y	Y	Y	Y	Y	Y
6 ***Tancredo***	Y	Y	Y	Y	Y	N	Y
CONNECTICUT							
1 Larson	Y	Y	Y	Y	Y	N	N
2 Gejdenson	Y	Y	Y	Y	Y	N	N
3 DeLauro	Y	Y	Y	Y	Y	N	N
4 ***Shays***	Y	Y	Y	Y	Y	N	Y
5 Maloney	Y	Y	Y	Y	Y	N	N
6 ***Johnson***	Y	Y	Y	Y	Y	N	Y
DELAWARE							
AL ***Castle***	Y	Y	Y	Y	Y	N	Y
FLORIDA							
1 ***Scarborough***	Y	Y	Y	Y	Y	Y	Y
2 Boyd	Y	Y	Y	Y	Y	N	N
3 Brown	Y	Y	Y	Y	Y	N	N
4 ***Fowler***	Y	Y	Y	Y	Y	N	Y
5 Thurman	Y	Y	Y	Y	Y	N	N
6 ***Stearns***	Y	Y	Y	Y	Y	N	Y
7 ***Mica***	Y	Y	Y	Y	Y	N	Y
8 ***McCollum***	?	?	?	Y	Y	N	Y
9 ***Bilirakis***	Y	Y	Y	Y	Y	N	Y
10 ***Young***	Y	Y	Y	?	?	Y	Y
11 Davis	Y	Y	Y	Y	Y	N	N
12 ***Canady***	Y	Y	Y	Y	Y	Y	Y
13 ***Miller***	Y	Y	Y	Y	Y	N	Y
14 ***Goss***	Y	Y	Y	Y	Y	N	Y
15 ***Weldon***	Y	Y	Y	Y	Y	Y	Y
16 ***Foley***	Y	Y	Y	Y	Y	N	Y
17 Meek	Y	Y	Y	?	+	N	N
18 ***Ros-Lehtinen***	+	+	+	Y	Y	Y	Y
19 Wexler	Y	Y	Y	Y	Y	N	N
20 Deutsch	Y	Y	Y	Y	Y	N	N
21 ***Diaz-Balart***	Y	Y	Y	Y	Y	Y	Y
22 ***Shaw***	Y	Y	Y	Y	Y	N	Y
23 Hastings	Y	Y	Y	Y	Y	N	N
GEORGIA							
1 ***Kingston***	Y	Y	Y	Y	Y	N	Y
2 Bishop	Y	Y	Y	Y	Y	N	N
3 ***Collins***	Y	Y	Y	Y	Y	Y	Y
4 McKinney	Y	?	?	Y	Y	Y	N
5 Lewis	Y	Y	Y	Y	Y	Y	N
6 ***Isakson***	Y	Y	Y	Y	Y	N	Y
7 ***Barr***	Y	Y	Y	Y	Y	Y	Y
8 ***Chambliss***	Y	Y	Y	Y	Y	N	Y
9 ***Deal***	Y	Y	Y	Y	Y	Y	Y
10 ***Norwood***	Y	Y	Y	Y	Y	N	Y
11 ***Linder***	Y	Y	Y	Y	Y	N	Y
HAWAII							
1 Abercrombie	Y	Y	Y	?	Y	N	N
2 Mink	Y	Y	Y	Y	Y	N	N
IDAHO							
1 ***Chenoweth-Hage***	Y	Y	Y	Y	Y	Y	Y
2 ***Simpson***	Y	Y	Y	Y	Y	N	Y
ILLINOIS							
1 Rush	Y	Y	?	Y	Y	N	N
2 Jackson	Y	Y	Y	Y	Y	N	N
3 Lipinski	Y	Y	Y	Y	Y	N	N
4 Gutierrez	Y	Y	Y	Y	Y	N	N
5 Blagojevich	Y	Y	Y	Y	Y	N	N
6 ***Hyde***	Y	Y	Y	Y	Y	Y	Y
7 Davis	Y	Y	Y	Y	Y	N	N
8 ***Crane***	Y	Y	Y	Y	Y	N	Y
9 Schakowsky	Y	Y	Y	Y	Y	N	N
10 ***Porter***	Y	Y	Y	Y	Y	N	Y
11 ***Weller***	Y	Y	Y	Y	Y	N	Y
12 Costello	Y	Y	Y	Y	Y	N	N
13 ***Biggert***	Y	Y	Y	Y	Y	N	Y

ND Northern Democrats SD Southern Democrats

	436	437	438	439	440	441	442
14 ***Hastert***							
15 ***Ewing***	?	?	?	?	?	?	?
16 ***Manzullo***	Y	Y	Y	Y	Y	N	Y
17 Evans	Y	Y	Y	Y	Y	N	N
18 ***LaHood***	Y	Y	Y	Y	Y	Y	Y
19 Phelps	Y	Y	Y	Y	Y	N	N
20 ***Shimkus***	Y	Y	Y	Y	Y	N	Y
INDIANA							
1 Visclosky	Y	Y	Y	Y	Y	N	N
2 ***McIntosh***	?	?	?	?	?	?	?
3 Roemer	Y	Y	Y	Y	Y	N	?
4 ***Souder***	Y	Y	Y	Y	Y	Y	Y
5 ***Buyer***	Y	Y	Y	Y	Y	Y	Y
6 ***Burton***	Y	Y	Y	Y	Y	Y	Y
7 ***Pease***	Y	Y	Y	Y	Y	N	Y
8 ***Hostettler***	Y	Y	Y	Y	Y	N	Y
9 Hill	Y	Y	Y	Y	Y	N	N
10 Carson	Y	Y	Y	Y	Y	N	N
IOWA							
1 ***Leach***	Y	Y	Y	Y	Y	N	Y
2 ***Nussle***	Y	Y	Y	Y	Y	N	Y
3 Boswell	Y	Y	Y	Y	Y	N	N
4 ***Ganske***	Y	Y	Y	Y	Y	N	Y
5 ***Latham***	Y	Y	Y	Y	Y	N	Y
KANSAS							
1 ***Moran***	Y	Y	Y	Y	Y	N	Y
2 ***Ryun***	Y	Y	Y	Y	Y	N	Y
3 Moore	Y	Y	Y	Y	Y	N	N
4 ***Tiahrt***	Y	Y	Y	Y	Y	N	Y
KENTUCKY							
1 ***Whitfield***	Y	Y	Y	Y	Y	N	Y
2 ***Lewis***	Y	Y	Y	Y	Y	N	Y
3 ***Northup***	Y	Y	Y	Y	Y	N	Y
4 Lucas	Y	Y	Y	Y	Y	N	N
5 ***Rogers***	Y	Y	Y	Y	Y	N	Y
6 ***Fletcher***	Y	Y	Y	Y	Y	N	Y
LOUISIANA							
1 ***Vitter***	Y	Y	Y	Y	Y	N	Y
2 Jefferson	Y	Y	Y	Y	Y	N	N
3 ***Tauzin***	Y	Y	Y	Y	Y	N	Y
4 ***McCrery***	Y	Y	Y	Y	Y	N	Y
5 ***Cooksey***	Y	Y	Y	Y	Y	N	Y
6 ***Baker***	Y	Y	Y	?	Y	N	Y
7 John	Y	Y	Y	Y	Y	N	N
MAINE							
1 Allen	Y	Y	Y	Y	Y	N	N
2 Baldacci	Y	Y	Y	Y	Y	N	N
MARYLAND							
1 ***Gilchrest***	Y	Y	Y	Y	Y	N	Y
2 ***Ehrlich***	Y	Y	Y	Y	Y	Y	Y
3 Cardin	Y	Y	Y	Y	Y	N	N
4 Wynn	Y	Y	Y	Y	?	N	N
5 Hoyer	Y	Y	Y	Y	Y	N	N
6 ***Bartlett***	Y	Y	Y	Y	Y	Y	Y
7 Cummings	Y	Y	Y	Y	Y	N	N
8 ***Morella***	Y	Y	Y	Y	Y	N	N
MASSACHUSETTS							
1 Olver	Y	Y	Y	Y	Y	N	N
2 Neal	Y	Y	Y	Y	?	N	N
3 McGovern	Y	Y	Y	Y	Y	N	N
4 Frank	Y	Y	Y	Y	Y	N	N
5 Meehan	Y	Y	Y	Y	Y	N	N
6 Tierney	Y	Y	Y	?	?	N	N
7 Markey	Y	Y	Y	Y	Y	N	N
8 Capuano	Y	Y	Y	Y	Y	N	N
9 Moakley	Y	Y	Y	Y	Y	N	N
10 Delahunt	Y	Y	Y	Y	Y	N	N
MICHIGAN							
1 Stupak	Y	Y	Y	Y	Y	N	N
2 ***Hoekstra***	Y	Y	Y	Y	Y	N	Y
3 ***Ehlers***	Y	Y	Y	Y	Y	N	Y
4 ***Camp***	Y	Y	Y	Y	Y	N	Y
5 Barcia	Y	Y	Y	Y	Y	N	N
6 ***Upton***	Y	Y	Y	Y	Y	N	Y
7 ***Smith***	Y	Y	Y	Y	Y	N	Y
8 Stabenow	Y	Y	Y	Y	Y	N	N
9 Kildee	Y	Y	Y	Y	Y	Y	N
10 Bonior	Y	Y	Y	Y	Y	Y	N
11 ***Knollenberg***	Y	Y	Y	Y	Y	N	Y
12 Levin	Y	Y	Y	Y	Y	N	N
13 Rivers	Y	Y	Y	Y	Y	Y	N
14 Conyers	Y	Y	Y	Y	Y	N	N
15 Kilpatrick	Y	Y	Y	Y	Y	N	N
16 Dingell	Y	Y	Y	Y	Y	N	N
MINNESOTA							
1 ***Gutknecht***	Y	Y	Y	Y	Y	Y	Y
2 Minge	Y	Y	Y	Y	Y	N	N
3 ***Ramstad***	Y	Y	Y	Y	Y	N	Y
4 Vento	?	?	?	?	?	?	?
5 Sabo	Y	Y	Y	Y	Y	N	N
6 Luther	Y	Y	Y	Y	Y	N	N
7 Peterson	Y	Y	Y	Y	Y	N	N
8 Oberstar	Y	Y	Y	Y	Y	N	N
MISSISSIPPI							
1 ***Wicker***	Y	Y	Y	Y	Y	N	Y
2 Thompson	Y	Y	?	Y	Y	N	N
3 ***Pickering***	Y	Y	Y	Y	Y	N	Y
4 Shows	Y	Y	Y	Y	Y	N	Y
5 Taylor	Y	Y	Y	Y	Y	Y	N
MISSOURI							
1 Clay	?	?	Y	Y	Y	?	N
2 ***Talent***	Y	Y	Y	Y	Y	N	Y
3 Gephardt	Y	Y	Y	Y	Y	N	N
4 Skelton	Y	Y	Y	Y	Y	N	N
5 McCarthy	Y	Y	Y	Y	Y	N	N
6 Danner	Y	Y	Y	Y	Y	N	N
7 ***Blunt***	Y	Y	Y	N	Y	N	Y
8 ***Emerson***	Y	Y	Y	Y	Y	N	Y
9 ***Hulshof***	Y	Y	Y	Y	Y	N	Y
MONTANA							
AL ***Hill***	Y	Y	Y	Y	Y	Y	Y
NEBRASKA							
1 ***Bereuter***	Y	Y	Y	Y	Y	N	Y
2 ***Terry***	Y	Y	Y	Y	Y	N	Y
3 ***Barrett***	Y	Y	Y	Y	Y	N	Y
NEVADA							
1 Berkley	Y	Y	Y	Y	Y	N	N
2 ***Gibbons***	Y	Y	Y	Y	Y	N	Y
NEW HAMPSHIRE							
1 ***Sununu***	Y	Y	Y	Y	Y	N	Y
2 ***Bass***	?	?	?	Y	Y	N	Y
NEW JERSEY							
1 Andrews	Y	Y	Y	Y	Y	Y	N
2 ***LoBiondo***	Y	Y	Y	Y	Y	Y	Y
3 ***Saxton***	Y	Y	Y	Y	Y	Y	Y
4 ***Smith***	Y	Y	Y	Y	Y	Y	Y
5 ***Roukema***	Y	Y	Y	Y	Y	N	Y
6 Pallone	Y	Y	Y	Y	Y	N	N
7 ***Franks***	?	?	?	Y	Y	N	Y
8 Pascrell	Y	Y	Y	Y	Y	N	N
9 Rothman	Y	Y	Y	Y	Y	N	N
10 Payne	Y	Y	Y	Y	Y	N	N
11 ***Frelinghuysen***	Y	Y	Y	Y	Y	N	Y
12 Holt	Y	Y	Y	Y	Y	N	N
13 Menendez	?	?	?	Y	Y	Y	N
NEW MEXICO							
1 ***Wilson***	Y	Y	Y	Y	Y	N	Y
2 ***Skeen***	Y	Y	Y	Y	Y	N	Y
3 Udall	Y	Y	Y	Y	Y	N	N
NEW YORK							
1 Forbes	Y	Y	Y	Y	Y	Y	N
2 ***Lazio***	?	?	?	Y	Y	Y	Y
3 ***King***	Y	Y	Y	Y	Y	Y	Y
4 McCarthy	Y	Y	Y	Y	Y	N	N
5 Ackerman	Y	Y	Y	Y	Y	N	N
6 Meeks	Y	Y	Y	Y	Y	N	N
7 Crowley	Y	Y	Y	Y	Y	N	N
8 Nadler	Y	Y	Y	Y	N	N	N
9 Weiner	?	?	?	Y	Y	N	N
10 Towns	Y	Y	Y	Y	Y	N	N
11 Owens	Y	Y	Y	Y	Y	N	N
12 Velázquez	Y	Y	Y	Y	Y	N	N
13 ***Fossella***	Y	+	Y	Y	Y	Y	Y
14 Maloney	Y	Y	Y	Y	Y	N	N
15 Rangel	Y	Y	Y	Y	Y	N	N
16 Serrano	Y	Y	Y	Y	Y	N	N
17 Engel	Y	Y	Y	?	Y	N	N
18 Lowey	Y	Y	Y	Y	Y	N	N
19 ***Kelly***	Y	Y	Y	Y	Y	Y	Y
20 ***Gilman***	?	?	?	?	?	?	?
21 McNulty	Y	Y	Y	Y	Y	Y	N
22 ***Sweeney***	Y	Y	Y	Y	Y	N	Y
23 ***Boehlert***	Y	Y	Y	Y	Y	N	Y
24 ***McHugh***	Y	Y	Y	Y	Y	N	Y
25 ***Walsh***	Y	Y	Y	Y	Y	Y	Y
26 Hinchey	Y	Y	Y	Y	Y	N	N
27 ***Reynolds***	Y	Y	Y	Y	Y	N	Y
28 Slaughter	Y	Y	Y	Y	Y	N	N
29 LaFalce	Y	Y	Y	Y	Y	N	N
30 ***Quinn***	Y	Y	Y	Y	Y	N	Y
31 ***Houghton***	Y	?	Y	Y	Y	N	Y
NORTH CAROLINA							
1 Clayton	Y	Y	Y	Y	Y	N	N
2 Etheridge	Y	Y	Y	Y	Y	N	N
3 ***Jones***	Y	Y	Y	Y	Y	Y	Y
4 Price	Y	Y	Y	Y	Y	N	N
5 ***Burr***	Y	Y	Y	Y	Y	N	Y
6 ***Coble***	Y	Y	Y	Y	Y	Y	Y
7 McIntyre	Y	Y	Y	Y	Y	Y	N
8 ***Hayes***	Y	Y	Y	Y	Y	Y	Y
9 ***Myrick***	Y	Y	Y	Y	Y	N	Y
10 ***Ballenger***	Y	Y	Y	Y	Y	N	Y
11 ***Taylor***	Y	Y	Y	Y	Y	Y	Y
12 Watt	Y	Y	Y	Y	Y	N	N
NORTH DAKOTA							
AL Pomeroy	Y	Y	Y	Y	Y	N	N
OHIO							
1 ***Chabot***	Y	Y	Y	Y	Y	Y	Y
2 ***Portman***	Y	Y	Y	Y	Y	N	Y
3 Hall	Y	Y	Y	Y	Y	N	N
4 ***Oxley***	Y	Y	Y	Y	Y	N	Y
5 ***Gillmor***	Y	Y	Y	Y	Y	N	Y
6 Strickland	Y	Y	Y	Y	Y	Y	N
7 ***Hobson***	Y	Y	Y	Y	Y	N	Y
8 ***Boehner***	Y	Y	Y	Y	Y	N	Y
9 Kaptur	Y	Y	Y	Y	Y	Y	N
10 Kucinich	Y	Y	Y	Y	Y	Y	N
11 Jones	Y	Y	Y	Y	Y	N	?
12 ***Kasich***	Y	Y	Y	Y	Y	Y	Y
13 Brown	Y	Y	Y	Y	Y	Y	N
14 Sawyer	Y	Y	Y	Y	Y	N	N
15 ***Pryce***	Y	Y	Y	Y	Y	N	Y
16 ***Regula***	Y	Y	Y	Y	Y	N	Y
17 Traficant	Y	Y	Y	Y	Y	N	Y
18 ***Ney***	Y	Y	Y	Y	?	N	Y
19 ***LaTourette***	Y	Y	Y	Y	Y	N	Y
OKLAHOMA							
1 ***Largent***	Y	Y	Y	Y	Y	N	Y
2 ***Coburn***	Y	Y	Y	Y	Y	N	Y
3 ***Watkins***	Y	Y	Y	Y	Y	N	Y
4 ***Watts***	Y	Y	Y	Y	Y	N	Y
5 ***Istook***	Y	Y	Y	Y	Y	N	Y
6 ***Lucas***	Y	Y	Y	Y	Y	N	Y
OREGON							
1 Wu	?	Y	Y	Y	Y	N	N
2 ***Walden***	Y	Y	Y	Y	Y	N	Y
3 Blumenauer	Y	Y	Y	Y	Y	N	N
4 DeFazio	Y	Y	Y	Y	Y	N	N
5 Hooley	Y	Y	Y	Y	Y	N	N
PENNSYLVANIA							
1 Brady	Y	Y	Y	Y	Y	N	N
2 Fattah	Y	Y	Y	Y	Y	N	N
3 Borski	Y	Y	Y	Y	Y	N	N
4 Klink	Y	Y	Y	Y	Y	N	?
5 ***Peterson***	Y	Y	Y	Y	Y	N	Y
6 Holden	Y	Y	Y	Y	Y	Y	N
7 ***Weldon***	Y	Y	Y	Y	Y	Y	Y
8 ***Greenwood***	Y	Y	Y	Y	Y	N	Y
9 ***Shuster***	Y	Y	Y	Y	Y	N	Y
10 ***Sherwood***	Y	Y	Y	Y	Y	Y	Y
11 Kanjorski	Y	Y	Y	Y	Y	N	N
12 Murtha	Y	Y	Y	Y	Y	N	N
13 Hoeffel	Y	Y	Y	Y	Y	N	N
14 Coyne	Y	Y	Y	Y	Y	N	N
15 ***Toomey***	Y	Y	Y	Y	Y	N	Y
16 ***Pitts***	Y	Y	Y	Y	Y	Y	Y
17 ***Gekas***	Y	Y	Y	Y	Y	N	Y
18 Doyle	Y	Y	Y	Y	Y	N	N
19 ***Goodling***	Y	Y	Y	Y	Y	Y	Y
20 Mascara	Y	Y	Y	Y	Y	N	N
21 ***English***	Y	Y	Y	Y	Y	N	Y
RHODE ISLAND							
1 Kennedy	Y	Y	Y	Y	Y	Y	N
2 Weygand	Y	Y	Y	Y	Y	N	N
SOUTH CAROLINA							
1 ***Sanford***	Y	Y	Y	N	Y	N	Y
2 ***Spence***	Y	Y	Y	Y	Y	N	Y
3 ***Graham***	Y	Y	Y	Y	Y	Y	Y
4 ***DeMint***	Y	Y	Y	Y	Y	N	Y
5 Spratt	Y	Y	Y	Y	Y	N	N
6 Clyburn	Y	Y	Y	Y	Y	N	N
SOUTH DAKOTA							
AL ***Thune***	Y	Y	Y	Y	Y	N	Y
TENNESSEE							
1 ***Jenkins***	+	+	+	?	?	?	?
2 ***Duncan***	Y	Y	Y	Y	Y	Y	Y
3 ***Wamp***	Y	Y	Y	Y	Y	Y	Y
4 ***Hilleary***	Y	Y	Y	Y	Y	Y	Y
5 Clement	Y	Y	Y	Y	Y	N	N
6 Gordon	Y	Y	Y	Y	Y	N	N
7 ***Bryant***	Y	Y	Y	Y	Y	N	Y
8 Tanner	Y	Y	Y	Y	Y	N	N
9 Ford	Y	Y	Y	Y	Y	N	N
TEXAS							
1 Sandlin	Y	Y	Y	Y	Y	N	N
2 Turner	Y	Y	Y	Y	Y	N	N
3 ***Johnson, Sam***	Y	Y	Y	Y	Y	Y	Y
4 Hall	Y	Y	Y	Y	Y	Y	Y
5 ***Sessions***	Y	Y	Y	Y	Y	N	Y
6 ***Barton***	?	?	?	?	?	?	?
7 ***Archer***	Y	Y	Y	Y	Y	N	Y
8 ***Brady***	Y	Y	Y	Y	Y	N	Y
9 Lampson	Y	Y	Y	Y	Y	N	N
10 Doggett	Y	Y	Y	Y	Y	N	N
11 Edwards	?	?	?	Y	Y	N	N
12 ***Granger***	?	?	?	+	+	–	+
13 ***Thornberry***	Y	Y	Y	Y	Y	N	Y
14 ***Paul***	Y	Y	Y	N	N	Y	Y
15 Hinojosa	Y	Y	Y	Y	Y	N	N
16 Reyes	Y	Y	Y	Y	Y	N	N
17 Stenholm	Y	Y	Y	Y	Y	N	N
18 Jackson-Lee	Y	Y	Y	Y	Y	Y	N
19 ***Combest***	Y	Y	Y	Y	Y	N	Y
20 Gonzalez	Y	Y	Y	Y	Y	N	N
21 ***Smith***	Y	Y	Y	Y	Y	N	Y
22 ***DeLay***	Y	Y	Y	Y	Y	N	Y
23 ***Bonilla***	Y	Y	Y	Y	Y	Y	Y
24 Frost	Y	Y	Y	Y	Y	N	N
25 Bentsen	Y	Y	Y	Y	Y	N	N
26 ***Armey***	Y	Y	Y	Y	Y	N	Y
27 Ortiz	Y	Y	Y	Y	Y	N	N
28 Rodriguez	Y	Y	Y	Y	Y	N	N
29 Green	Y	Y	Y	Y	Y	Y	N
30 Johnson, E.B.	Y	Y	Y	Y	Y	N	N
UTAH							
1 ***Hansen***	Y	Y	Y	Y	Y	N	Y
2 ***Cook***	Y	Y	Y	Y	Y	Y	Y
3 ***Cannon***	Y	Y	Y	Y	Y	N	Y
VERMONT							
AL *Sanders*	Y	Y	Y	Y	Y	Y	N
VIRGINIA							
1 ***Bateman***	?	?	?	Y	Y	N	Y
2 Pickett	?	?	Y	Y	Y	N	N
3 Scott	Y	Y	Y	Y	N	N	N
4 Sisisky	Y	Y	Y	Y	Y	N	N
5 *Goode*	Y	Y	Y	Y	Y	Y	Y
6 ***Goodlatte***	Y	Y	Y	Y	Y	N	Y
7 ***Bliley***	Y	Y	Y	Y	Y	N	Y
8 Moran	Y	Y	Y	Y	N	N	N
9 Boucher	Y	Y	Y	Y	Y	N	N
10 ***Wolf***	Y	Y	Y	Y	Y	Y	Y
11 ***Davis***	Y	Y	Y	Y	Y	Y	Y
WASHINGTON							
1 Inslee	Y	Y	Y	Y	Y	N	N
2 ***Metcalf***	Y	Y	Y	Y	Y	Y	Y
3 Baird	Y	Y	Y	Y	Y	N	N
4 ***Hastings***	Y	Y	Y	Y	Y	N	Y
5 ***Nethercutt***	Y	Y	Y	Y	Y	N	Y
6 Dicks	Y	Y	Y	Y	Y	N	N
7 McDermott	Y	Y	Y	Y	Y	N	–
8 ***Dunn***	Y	Y	Y	Y	Y	N	Y
9 Smith	?	?	?	?	?	?	?
WEST VIRGINIA							
1 Mollohan	Y	Y	Y	Y	Y	N	N
2 Wise	Y	Y	Y	Y	Y	N	N
3 Rahall	Y	Y	Y	Y	Y	N	N
WISCONSIN							
1 ***Ryan***	Y	Y	Y	Y	Y	N	Y
2 Baldwin	Y	Y	Y	Y	Y	N	N
3 Kind	Y	Y	Y	Y	Y	N	N
4 Kleczka	Y	Y	Y	Y	Y	N	N
5 Barrett	Y	Y	Y	Y	Y	N	N
6 ***Petri***	Y	Y	Y	Y	Y	N	Y
7 Obey	Y	Y	Y	Y	Y	N	N
8 ***Green***	Y	Y	Y	Y	Y	Y	Y
9 ***Sensenbrenner***	Y	Y	Y	Y	Y	N	Y
WYOMING							
AL ***Cubin***	?	?	?	?	?	?	?

Southern states - Ala., Ark., Fla., Ga., Ky., La., Miss., N.C., Okla., S.C., Tenn., Texas, Va.

443. Procedural Motion/Journal. Approval of the House Journal of Wednesday, July 26, 2000. Approved 344-55: R 179-18; D 163-37 (ND 118-28, SD 45-9); I 2-0. July 27, 2000.

444. HR 4205. Fiscal 2001 Defense Authorization/Motion to Instruct. Taylor, D-Miss., motion to instruct conferees to insist upon the provisions contained in Section 725 of the House bill, relating to the Medicare subvention project for military retirees and dependents. Motion agreed to 416-2: R 208-2; D 206-0 (ND 152-0, SD 54-0); I 2-0. July 27, 2000.

445. HR 4205. Fiscal 2001 Defense Authorization/Closed Conference. Spence, R-S.C., motion to close portions of the conference to the public during consideration of national security issues. Motion agreed to 411-9: R 212-0; D 197-9 (ND 145-7, SD 52-2); I 2-0. July 27, 2000.

446. HR 4516. Fiscal 2001 Legislative Branch Appropriations /Conference Report. Goss, R-Fla., motion to table (kill) the Archer, R-Texas, resolution (H Res 568) that states the conference report to the fiscal 2001 legislative branch appropriations contains a tax provision that contravenes the constitutional requirement that such measures originate in the House. Motion agreed to 213-212: R 211-5; D 1-206 (ND 1-152, SD 0-54); I 1-1. July 27, 2000.

447. HR 4865. Social Security Tax Repeal/Rule. Adoption of the rule (H Res 564) to provide for House floor consideration of the bill that would repeal the provision in the 1993 law that increased the portion of Social Security benefits subject to taxation from 50 percent to 85 percent for certain income levels. Adopted 232-194: R 217-0; D 14-194 (ND 10-144, SD 4-50); I 1-0. July 27, 2000.

448. HR 4516. Fiscal 2001 Legislative Branch Appropriations/Rule. Adoption of the rule (H Res 565) to provide for House floor consideration of the conference report that would make fiscal 2001 appropriations for the legislative branch. Adopted 214-210: R 212-4; D 1-205 (ND 1-152, SD 0-53); I 1-1. July 27, 2000.

449. HR 4865. Social Security Tax Repeal/Democratic Substitute. Pomeroy, D-N.D., amendment that would strike the bill's language and replace it with a provision that would increase the income thresholds at which 85 percent of Social Security benefits are subject to taxation from $34,000 to $80,000 for single taxpayers, and from $44,000 to $100,000 for married taxpayers filing jointly. The Medicare trust fund would not be affected. Rejected 169-256: R 1-215; D 167-40 (ND 126-28, SD 41-12); I 1-1. July 27, 2000.

450. HR 4865. Social Security Tax Repeal/Passage. Passage of the bill that would repeal the provision in the 1993 law that increased the portion of Social Security benefits subject to taxation from 50 percent to 85 percent for single taxpayers with incomes over $34,000 and married taxpayers filing jointly with incomes over $44,000, effective after Dec. 31, 2000. An amount equal to the revenues that would have been collected had the tax not been repealed would be transferred to the Medicare trust fund from the general fund. Passed 265-159: R 212-3; D 52-155 (ND 37-117, SD 15-38); I 1-1. A "nay" was a vote in support of the president's position. July 27, 2000.

Key

- Y Voted for (yea).
- \# Paired for.
- \+ Announced for.
- N Voted against (nay).
- X Paired against.
- – Announced against.
- P Voted "present."
- C Voted "present" to avoid possible conflict of interest.
- ? Did not vote or otherwise make a position known.

Democrats ***Republicans***
Independents

	443	444	445	446	447	448	449	450
ALABAMA								
1 ***Callahan***	Y	Y	Y	Y	Y	Y	N	Y
2 ***Everett***	N	Y	Y	Y	Y	Y	N	Y
3 ***Riley***	Y	Y	Y	Y	Y	Y	N	Y
4 ***Aderholt***	N	Y	Y	Y	Y	Y	N	Y
5 Cramer	Y	Y	Y	N	N	N	Y	Y
6 ***Bachus***	Y	Y	Y	Y	Y	Y	N	Y
7 Hilliard	N	Y	Y	N	N	N	Y	N
ALASKA								
AL ***Young***	?	?	?	Y	Y	Y	N	Y
ARIZONA								
1 ***Salmon***	Y	Y	Y	Y	Y	Y	N	Y
2 Pastor	Y	Y	Y	N	N	N	Y	N
3 ***Stump***	Y	Y	Y	Y	Y	Y	N	Y
4 ***Shadegg***	Y	Y	Y	Y	Y	Y	N	Y
5 ***Kolbe***	Y	Y	Y	Y	Y	Y	N	Y
6 ***Hayworth***	Y	Y	Y	Y	Y	Y	N	Y
ARKANSAS								
1 Berry	Y	Y	Y	N	N	N	N	N
2 Snyder	Y	Y	Y	N	N	N	N	N
3 ***Hutchinson***	Y	Y	Y	Y	Y	Y	N	Y
4 ***Dickey***	N	Y	Y	Y	Y	Y	N	Y
CALIFORNIA								
1 Thompson	N	Y	Y	N	N	N	Y	N
2 ***Herger***	?	Y	Y	Y	Y	Y	N	Y
3 ***Ose***	Y	Y	Y	Y	Y	Y	N	Y
4 ***Doolittle***	Y	Y	Y	Y	Y	Y	N	Y
5 Matsui	Y	Y	Y	N	N	N	Y	N
6 Woolsey	Y	Y	Y	N	N	N	Y	N
7 Miller, George	Y	Y	N	N	N	N	N	N
8 Pelosi	Y	Y	Y	N	N	N	Y	N
9 Lee	Y	Y	N	N	N	N	Y	N
10 Tauscher	Y	Y	Y	N	N	N	Y	Y
11 ***Pombo***	Y	Y	Y	Y	Y	Y	N	Y
12 Lantos	Y	Y	Y	N	N	N	Y	N
13 Stark	?	Y	N	N	N	N	Y	N
14 Eshoo	Y	Y	Y	N	N	N	Y	N
15 ***Campbell***	Y	Y	Y	N	Y	Y	N	Y
16 Lofgren	Y	Y	Y	N	N	N	Y	N
17 Farr	Y	Y	Y	N	N	N	Y	N
18 Condit	N	Y	Y	N	N	N	Y	Y
19 ***Radanovich***	Y	Y	Y	Y	Y	Y	N	Y
20 Dooley	Y	Y	Y	N	N	N	Y	Y
21 ***Thomas***	?	N	Y	Y	Y	Y	N	Y
22 Capps	Y	Y	Y	N	N	N	Y	Y
23 ***Gallegly***	Y	Y	Y	Y	Y	Y	N	Y
24 Sherman	Y	Y	Y	N	N	N	Y	N
25 ***McKeon***	Y	Y	Y	Y	Y	Y	N	Y
26 Berman	Y	Y	Y	N	N	N	Y	N
27 ***Rogan***	N	Y	Y	Y	Y	Y	N	Y
28 ***Dreier***	Y	Y	Y	Y	Y	Y	N	Y
29 Waxman	Y	Y	Y	N	N	?	Y	N
30 Becerra	Y	Y	Y	N	N	N	Y	N
31 ***Martinez***	Y	Y	Y	Y	Y	Y	N	Y
32 Dixon	Y	Y	Y	N	N	N	Y	N
33 Roybal-Allard	Y	Y	Y	N	N	N	Y	N
34 Napolitano	Y	Y	Y	N	N	N	Y	N
35 Waters	N	Y	Y	N	N	N	N	N
36 ***Kuykendall***	Y	Y	Y	Y	Y	Y	N	Y
37 Millender-McD.	Y	Y	Y	N	N	N	Y	N
38 ***Horn***	Y	Y	Y	Y	Y	Y	N	Y
39 ***Royce***	Y	Y	Y	Y	Y	Y	N	Y
40 ***Lewis***	Y	Y	Y	Y	Y	Y	N	Y
41 ***Miller, Gary***	Y	Y	Y	Y	Y	Y	N	Y
42 Baca	Y	Y	Y	N	N	N	Y	N
43 ***Calvert***	Y	Y	Y	Y	Y	Y	N	Y
44 ***Bono***	Y	Y	Y	Y	?	Y	N	Y
45 ***Rohrabacher***	Y	Y	Y	Y	Y	Y	N	Y
46 Sanchez	Y	Y	Y	N	N	N	Y	Y
47 ***Cox***	Y	Y	Y	Y	Y	?	N	Y
48 ***Packard***	Y	Y	Y	Y	Y	Y	N	Y
49 ***Bilbray***	N	Y	Y	Y	Y	Y	N	Y
50 Filner	N	Y	Y	N	N	N	Y	N
51 ***Cunningham***	Y	Y	Y	Y	Y	Y	N	Y
52 ***Hunter***	?	?	Y	Y	Y	Y	N	Y
COLORADO								
1 DeGette	Y	Y	Y	N	N	N	Y	N
2 Udall	Y	Y	Y	N	N	N	Y	N
3 ***McInnis***	Y	Y	Y	Y	Y	Y	N	Y
4 ***Schaffer***	N	Y	Y	Y	Y	Y	N	Y
5 ***Hefley***	N	Y	Y	Y	Y	Y	N	Y
6 ***Tancredo***	N	Y	Y	Y	Y	Y	N	Y
CONNECTICUT								
1 Larson	Y	Y	Y	N	N	N	Y	Y
2 Gejdenson	Y	Y	Y	N	N	N	Y	Y
3 DeLauro	Y	Y	Y	N	N	N	Y	N
4 ***Shays***	Y	Y	Y	Y	Y	Y	N	Y
5 Maloney	Y	Y	Y	N	Y	N	Y	Y
6 ***Johnson***	?	Y	Y	Y	Y	Y	N	Y
DELAWARE								
AL ***Castle***	Y	Y	Y	Y	Y	Y	N	Y
FLORIDA								
1 ***Scarborough***	Y	Y	Y	Y	Y	Y	N	Y
2 Boyd	Y	Y	Y	N	N	N	N	N
3 Brown	Y	Y	Y	N	N	N	Y	N
4 ***Fowler***	Y	Y	Y	Y	Y	Y	N	Y
5 Thurman	Y	Y	Y	N	N	N	N	N
6 ***Stearns***	Y	Y	Y	Y	Y	Y	N	Y
7 ***Mica***	Y	Y	Y	Y	Y	Y	N	Y
8 ***McCollum***	Y	Y	Y	Y	Y	Y	N	Y
9 ***Bilirakis***	Y	Y	Y	Y	Y	Y	N	Y
10 ***Young***	Y	Y	Y	Y	Y	Y	N	Y
11 Davis	Y	Y	Y	N	N	N	Y	N
12 ***Canady***	Y	Y	Y	Y	Y	Y	N	Y
13 ***Miller***	Y	Y	Y	Y	Y	Y	N	Y
14 ***Goss***	Y	Y	Y	Y	Y	Y	N	Y
15 ***Weldon***	?	Y	Y	Y	Y	Y	N	Y
16 ***Foley***	Y	Y	Y	Y	Y	Y	N	Y
17 Meek	Y	Y	Y	N	N	N	Y	N
18 ***Ros-Lehtinen***	Y	Y	Y	Y	Y	Y	N	Y
19 Wexler	Y	Y	Y	N	N	N	Y	Y
20 Deutsch	Y	Y	Y	N	N	N	Y	Y
21 ***Diaz-Balart***	Y	Y	Y	Y	Y	Y	N	Y
22 ***Shaw***	?	Y	Y	Y	Y	Y	N	Y
23 Hastings	N	Y	Y	N	N	N	N	N
GEORGIA								
1 ***Kingston***	Y	Y	Y	Y	Y	Y	N	Y
2 Bishop	Y	Y	Y	N	Y	N	Y	Y
3 ***Collins***	?	Y	Y	Y	Y	Y	N	Y
4 McKinney	Y	Y	N	N	N	N	Y	Y
5 Lewis	Y	Y	Y	N	N	N	N	N
6 ***Isakson***	Y	Y	Y	Y	Y	Y	N	Y
7 ***Barr***	Y	Y	Y	Y	Y	Y	N	Y
8 ***Chambliss***	Y	Y	Y	Y	Y	Y	N	Y
9 ***Deal***	Y	Y	Y	Y	Y	Y	N	Y
10 ***Norwood***	Y	Y	Y	Y	Y	Y	N	Y
11 ***Linder***	Y	Y	Y	Y	Y	Y	N	Y
HAWAII								
1 Abercrombie	Y	Y	Y	N	N	N	Y	Y
2 Mink	Y	Y	Y	N	N	N	Y	Y
IDAHO								
1 ***Chenoweth-Hage***	N	Y	Y	Y	Y	Y	N	Y
2 ***Simpson***	Y	Y	Y	Y	Y	Y	N	Y
ILLINOIS								
1 Rush	Y	Y	Y	N	N	N	Y	N
2 Jackson	Y	Y	N	N	N	N	Y	N
3 Lipinski	Y	Y	Y	N	N	N	N	N
4 Gutierrez	N	Y	Y	N	N	N	Y	N
5 Blagojevich	Y	Y	Y	N	N	N	Y	Y
6 ***Hyde***	Y	Y	Y	Y	Y	Y	N	Y
7 Davis	Y	Y	Y	N	N	N	Y	N
8 ***Crane***	?	Y	Y	Y	Y	Y	N	Y
9 Schakowsky	Y	Y	Y	N	N	N	Y	Y
10 ***Porter***	?	Y	Y	Y	Y	Y	N	Y
11 ***Weller***	N	Y	Y	Y	Y	Y	N	Y
12 Costello	N	Y	Y	N	N	N	N	N
13 ***Biggert***	Y	Y	Y	Y	Y	Y	N	Y

ND Northern Democrats SD Southern Democrats

	443	444	445	446	447	448	449	450
14 ***Hastert***				Y	Y	Y	N	Y
15 ***Ewing***	?	?	?	?	?	?	?	?
16 ***Manzullo***	Y	Y	Y	Y	Y	P	N	Y
17 Evans	Y	Y	Y	N	N	N	Y	Y
18 ***LaHood***	Y	Y	Y	Y	Y	Y	N	Y
19 Phelps	Y	Y	Y	N	N	N	N	N
20 ***Shimkus***	Y	Y	Y	Y	Y	Y	N	Y
INDIANA								
1 Visclosky	Y	Y	Y	N	N	N	Y	N
2 ***McIntosh***	?	?	?	?	?	?	?	?
3 Roemer	Y	Y	Y	N	N	N	Y	Y
4 ***Souder***	Y	Y	Y	Y	Y	Y	N	Y
5 ***Buyer***	Y	P	?	Y	Y	Y	N	Y
6 ***Burton***	Y	Y	?	Y	Y	Y	N	Y
7 ***Pease***	Y	Y	Y	Y	Y	Y	N	Y
8 ***Hostettler***	Y	Y	Y	Y	Y	Y	N	Y
9 Hill	Y	Y	Y	N	N	N	Y	N
10 Carson	Y	Y	Y	N	N	N	Y	N
IOWA								
1 ***Leach***	Y	Y	Y	Y	Y	Y	N	Y
2 ***Nussle***	?	Y	Y	N	Y	Y	N	Y
3 Boswell	Y	Y	Y	N	Y	N	Y	Y
4 ***Ganske***	Y	Y	Y	Y	Y	N	N	Y
5 ***Latham***	Y	Y	Y	Y	Y	Y	N	Y
KANSAS								
1 ***Moran***	N	Y	Y	Y	Y	Y	N	Y
2 ***Ryun***	Y	Y	Y	Y	Y	Y	N	Y
3 Moore	Y	Y	Y	N	Y	N	Y	Y
4 ***Tiahrt***	Y	Y	Y	Y	Y	Y	N	Y
KENTUCKY								
1 ***Whitfield***	Y	Y	Y	Y	Y	Y	N	Y
2 ***Lewis***	Y	Y	Y	Y	Y	Y	N	Y
3 ***Northup***	Y	Y	Y	Y	Y	Y	N	Y
4 Lucas	Y	Y	Y	N	Y	N	Y	Y
5 ***Rogers***	Y	Y	Y	Y	Y	Y	N	Y
6 ***Fletcher***	Y	Y	Y	Y	Y	Y	N	Y
LOUISIANA								
1 ***Vitter***	Y	Y	Y	Y	Y	Y	N	Y
2 Jefferson	Y	Y	Y	N	N	N	Y	N
3 ***Tauzin***	Y	Y	Y	Y	Y	Y	N	Y
4 ***McCrery***	?	Y	Y	Y	Y	Y	N	Y
5 ***Cooksey***	Y	Y	Y	Y	Y	Y	N	Y
6 ***Baker***	Y	Y	Y	Y	Y	Y	N	Y
7 John	Y	Y	Y	N	N	N	Y	N
MAINE								
1 Allen	Y	Y	Y	N	N	N	N	N
2 Baldacci	Y	Y	Y	N	N	N	Y	N
MARYLAND								
1 ***Gilchrest***	Y	Y	Y	Y	Y	Y	N	Y
2 ***Ehrlich***	Y	Y	Y	Y	Y	Y	N	Y
3 Cardin	Y	Y	Y	N	N	N	N	N
4 Wynn	Y	Y	Y	N	N	N	Y	N
5 Hoyer	Y	Y	Y	N	N	N	N	N
6 ***Bartlett***	Y	Y	Y	Y	Y	Y	N	Y
7 Cummings	Y	Y	Y	N	N	N	Y	N
8 ***Morella***	Y	Y	Y	Y	Y	Y	N	N
MASSACHUSETTS								
1 Olver	N	Y	Y	N	N	N	Y	N
2 Neal	Y	Y	Y	N	N	N	Y	N
3 McGovern	N	Y	Y	N	N	N	Y	N
4 Frank	Y	Y	Y	N	N	N	N	N
5 Meehan	Y	Y	Y	N	N	N	Y	N
6 Tierney	N	Y	Y	N	N	N	Y	N
7 Markey	Y	Y	Y	N	N	N	Y	N
8 Capuano	N	Y	Y	N	N	N	Y	N
9 Moakley	Y	Y	Y	N	N	N	Y	N
10 Delahunt	Y	Y	Y	N	N	N	Y	N
MICHIGAN								
1 Stupak	N	Y	Y	N	N	N	Y	N
2 ***Hoekstra***	Y	Y	Y	Y	Y	Y	N	Y
3 ***Ehlers***	Y	Y	Y	Y	Y	Y	N	Y
4 ***Camp***	Y	Y	Y	Y	Y	Y	N	Y
5 Barcia	Y	Y	Y	N	N	N	Y	Y
6 ***Upton***	Y	Y	Y	Y	Y	Y	N	Y
7 ***Smith***	Y	+	Y	Y	Y	Y	N	Y
8 Stabenow	Y	Y	Y	N	Y	N	Y	Y
9 Kildee	Y	Y	Y	N	N	N	Y	N
10 Bonior	Y	Y	Y	N	N	N	Y	N
11 ***Knollenberg***	Y	Y	Y	Y	Y	Y	N	Y
12 Levin	Y	Y	Y	N	N	N	Y	N
13 Rivers	Y	Y	Y	N	N	N	Y	N
14 Conyers	?	Y	?	N	N	N	Y	N
15 Kilpatrick	Y	Y	Y	N	N	N	Y	N
16 Dingell	Y	Y	Y	N	N	N	Y	N
MINNESOTA								
1 ***Gutknecht***	N	Y	Y	N	Y	Y	N	Y
2 Minge	Y	Y	Y	N	N	N	N	N
3 ***Ramstad***	N	Y	Y	N	Y	Y	N	Y
4 Vento	?	?	?	?	?	?	?	?
5 Sabo	N	Y	Y	N	N	N	N	N
6 Luther	Y	Y	Y	N	N	N	Y	Y
7 Peterson	N	Y	Y	N	N	N	N	N
8 Oberstar	N	Y	Y	N	N	N	Y	N
MISSISSIPPI								
1 ***Wicker***	N	Y	Y	Y	Y	Y	N	Y
2 Thompson	N	Y	Y	N	N	N	Y	N
3 ***Pickering***	Y	Y	Y	Y	Y	Y	N	Y
4 Shows	Y	Y	Y	N	Y	N	Y	Y
5 Taylor	N	Y	Y	N	N	N	N	N
MISSOURI								
1 Clay	N	Y	Y	N	N	N	Y	N
2 ***Talent***	Y	Y	Y	Y	Y	Y	N	Y
3 Gephardt	N	Y	Y	N	N	N	Y	N
4 Skelton	Y	Y	Y	N	N	N	Y	N
5 McCarthy	Y	Y	Y	N	N	N	Y	N
6 Danner	Y	Y	Y	N	N	N	N	Y
7 ***Blunt***	Y	Y	Y	Y	Y	Y	N	Y
8 ***Emerson***	Y	Y	Y	Y	Y	N	N	Y
9 ***Hulshof***	Y	Y	Y	Y	Y	Y	N	Y
MONTANA								
AL ***Hill***	N	Y	Y	Y	Y	Y	N	Y
NEBRASKA								
1 ***Bereuter***	Y	Y	Y	Y	Y	Y	N	Y
2 ***Terry***	Y	Y	Y	Y	Y	Y	N	Y
3 ***Barrett***	Y	Y	Y	Y	Y	Y	N	Y
NEVADA								
1 Berkley	Y	Y	Y	N	Y	N	Y	Y
2 ***Gibbons***	Y	Y	Y	Y	Y	Y	N	Y
NEW HAMPSHIRE								
1 ***Sununu***	Y	+	Y	Y	Y	Y	N	Y
2 ***Bass***	Y	Y	Y	Y	Y	Y	N	Y
NEW JERSEY								
1 Andrews	Y	Y	Y	N	N	N	Y	N
2 ***LoBiondo***	N	Y	Y	Y	Y	Y	N	Y
3 ***Saxton***	Y	Y	Y	Y	Y	Y	N	Y
4 ***Smith***	Y	Y	Y	Y	Y	Y	N	Y
5 ***Roukema***	Y	Y	Y	Y	Y	Y	N	Y
6 Pallone	Y	Y	Y	N	N	N	Y	N
7 ***Franks***	Y	Y	?	Y	Y	Y	N	Y
8 Pascrell	Y	Y	Y	N	N	N	Y	N
9 Rothman	Y	Y	Y	N	N	N	Y	N
10 Payne	Y	Y	Y	N	N	N	Y	N
11 ***Frelinghuysen***	Y	Y	Y	Y	Y	Y	N	Y
12 Holt	Y	Y	Y	N	N	N	Y	Y
13 Menendez	Y	Y	Y	N	N	N	Y	N
NEW MEXICO								
1 ***Wilson***	Y	Y	Y	Y	Y	Y	Y	Y
2 ***Skeen***	Y	Y	Y	Y	Y	Y	N	Y
3 Udall	N	Y	Y	N	N	N	Y	N
NEW YORK								
1 Forbes	Y	Y	Y	N	Y	N	N	Y
2 ***Lazio***	Y	Y	Y	Y	Y	Y	N	Y
3 ***King***	Y	Y	Y	Y	Y	Y	N	Y
4 McCarthy	Y	Y	Y	N	Y	N	Y	Y
5 Ackerman	Y	Y	Y	N	N	N	Y	N
6 Meeks	Y	Y	Y	N	N	N	N	N
7 Crowley	Y	Y	Y	N	N	N	Y	Y
8 Nadler	Y	Y	Y	N	N	N	Y	N
9 Weiner	Y	Y	Y	N	N	N	Y	Y
10 Towns	Y	Y	Y	N	N	N	Y	N
11 Owens	Y	Y	Y	N	N	N	Y	N
12 Velázquez	Y	Y	Y	N	N	N	Y	N
13 ***Fossella***	Y	Y	Y	Y	Y	Y	N	Y
14 Maloney	Y	Y	Y	N	N	N	Y	Y
15 Rangel	?	Y	Y	N	N	N	N	N
16 Serrano	Y	Y	Y	N	N	N	Y	N
17 Engel	?	Y	Y	N	N	N	Y	Y
18 Lowey	Y	Y	Y	N	N	N	Y	Y
19 ***Kelly***	Y	Y	Y	Y	Y	Y	N	Y
20 ***Gilman***	?	?	?	?	?	?	?	?
21 McNulty	N	Y	Y	N	N	N	Y	N
22 ***Sweeney***	Y	Y	Y	Y	Y	Y	N	Y
23 ***Boehlert***	Y	Y	Y	Y	Y	Y	N	Y
24 ***McHugh***	Y	Y	Y	Y	Y	Y	N	Y
25 ***Walsh***	Y	Y	Y	Y	Y	Y	N	Y
26 Hinchey	N	Y	Y	N	N	N	Y	N
27 ***Reynolds***	Y	Y	Y	Y	Y	Y	N	Y
28 Slaughter	N	Y	Y	N	N	N	Y	N
29 LaFalce	Y	Y	Y	N	N	N	Y	N
30 ***Quinn***	Y	Y	Y	Y	Y	Y	N	Y
31 ***Houghton***	?	Y	Y	Y	Y	Y	N	N
NORTH CAROLINA								
1 Clayton	Y	Y	Y	N	N	N	Y	N
2 Etheridge	Y	Y	Y	N	N	N	Y	N
3 ***Jones***	Y	Y	Y	Y	Y	Y	N	Y
4 Price	Y	Y	Y	N	N	N	Y	N
5 ***Burr***	Y	Y	Y	Y	Y	Y	N	Y
6 ***Coble***	Y	Y	Y	Y	Y	Y	N	Y
7 McIntyre	Y	Y	Y	N	N	N	Y	N
8 ***Hayes***	Y	Y	Y	Y	Y	Y	N	Y
9 ***Myrick***	Y	Y	Y	Y	Y	Y	?	?
10 ***Ballenger***	Y	Y	Y	Y	Y	Y	N	Y
11 ***Taylor***	Y	Y	Y	Y	Y	Y	N	Y
12 Watt	Y	Y	N	N	N	N	Y	N
NORTH DAKOTA								
AL Pomeroy	Y	Y	Y	N	Y	N	Y	N
OHIO								
1 ***Chabot***	Y	Y	Y	Y	Y	Y	N	Y
2 ***Portman***	Y	Y	Y	Y	Y	Y	N	Y
3 Hall	Y	Y	?	?	N	N	Y	N
4 ***Oxley***	Y	Y	Y	Y	Y	Y	N	Y
5 ***Gillmor***	N	Y	Y	Y	Y	Y	N	Y
6 Strickland	N	Y	Y	N	N	N	Y	N
7 ***Hobson***	Y	Y	Y	Y	Y	Y	N	Y
8 ***Boehner***	Y	Y	Y	Y	Y	Y	N	Y
9 Kaptur	Y	Y	Y	N	N	N	Y	Y
10 Kucinich	N	Y	N	N	N	N	Y	Y
11 Jones	?	?	Y	N	N	N	Y	N
12 ***Kasich***	Y	?	Y	Y	Y	Y	N	Y
13 Brown	Y	Y	Y	N	N	N	Y	N
14 Sawyer	Y	Y	Y	N	N	N	Y	N
15 ***Pryce***	Y	Y	Y	Y	Y	Y	N	Y
16 ***Regula***	Y	Y	Y	Y	Y	Y	N	Y
17 Traficant	Y	Y	Y	Y	Y	Y	N	Y
18 ***Ney***	Y	Y	Y	Y	Y	Y	N	Y
19 ***LaTourette***	Y	Y	Y	Y	Y	Y	N	Y
OKLAHOMA								
1 ***Largent***	Y	Y	Y	Y	Y	Y	?	?
2 ***Coburn***	Y	Y	Y	Y	Y	Y	N	Y
3 ***Watkins***	?	Y	Y	Y	Y	Y	N	Y
4 ***Watts***	Y	Y	Y	Y	Y	Y	N	Y
5 ***Istook***	Y	Y	Y	Y	Y	Y	N	Y
6 ***Lucas***	Y	Y	Y	Y	Y	Y	N	Y
OREGON								
1 Wu	Y	Y	Y	N	N	N	Y	Y
2 ***Walden***	Y	Y	Y	Y	Y	Y	N	Y
3 Blumenauer	Y	Y	N	N	N	N	N	N
4 DeFazio	N	Y	N	N	N	N	Y	Y
5 Hooley	N	Y	Y	N	N	N	Y	Y
PENNSYLVANIA								
1 Brady	N	Y	Y	N	N	N	N	N
2 Fattah	N	Y	Y	N	N	N	N	N
3 Borski	N	Y	Y	N	N	N	N	N
4 Klink	Y	Y	Y	N	N	N	Y	N
5 ***Peterson***	Y	Y	Y	Y	Y	Y	N	Y
6 Holden	Y	Y	Y	N	N	N	N	N
7 ***Weldon***	Y	Y	Y	Y	Y	Y	N	Y
8 ***Greenwood***	Y	Y	Y	Y	Y	Y	N	Y
9 ***Shuster***	Y	Y	Y	Y	Y	Y	N	Y
10 ***Sherwood***	Y	Y	Y	Y	Y	Y	N	Y
11 Kanjorski	Y	Y	Y	N	N	N	N	N
12 Murtha	Y	Y	Y	N	N	N	N	N
13 Hoeffel	Y	Y	Y	N	N	N	N	N
14 Coyne	Y	Y	Y	N	N	N	N	N
15 ***Toomey***	Y	Y	Y	Y	Y	Y	N	Y
16 ***Pitts***	?	Y	Y	Y	Y	Y	N	Y
17 ***Gekas***	Y	Y	Y	Y	Y	Y	N	Y
18 Doyle	?	Y	Y	N	N	N	Y	N
19 ***Goodling***	?	Y	Y	Y	Y	Y	N	Y
20 Mascara	Y	Y	Y	N	N	N	Y	N
21 ***English***	?	Y	Y	Y	Y	Y	N	Y
RHODE ISLAND								
1 Kennedy	Y	Y	Y	N	N	N	Y	N
2 Weygand	Y	Y	Y	N	N	N	Y	N
SOUTH CAROLINA								
1 ***Sanford***	Y	N	Y	Y	Y	N	N	N
2 ***Spence***	Y	Y	Y	Y	Y	Y	N	Y
3 ***Graham***	Y	Y	Y	Y	Y	Y	N	Y
4 ***DeMint***	Y	Y	Y	Y	Y	Y	N	Y
5 Spratt	Y	Y	Y	N	N	N	?	?
6 Clyburn	N	Y	Y	N	N	N	Y	N
SOUTH DAKOTA								
AL ***Thune***	Y	Y	Y	Y	Y	Y	N	Y
TENNESSEE								
1 ***Jenkins***	?	?	?	?	?	?	?	?
2 ***Duncan***	Y	Y	Y	Y	Y	Y	N	Y
3 ***Wamp***	Y	Y	Y	Y	Y	Y	N	Y
4 ***Hilleary***	N	Y	Y	Y	Y	Y	N	Y
5 Clement	Y	Y	Y	N	N	N	Y	Y
6 Gordon	Y	Y	Y	N	N	N	Y	Y
7 ***Bryant***	Y	Y	Y	Y	Y	Y	N	Y
8 Tanner	Y	Y	Y	N	N	N	N	N
9 Ford	Y	Y	Y	N	N	N	N	N
TEXAS								
1 Sandlin	Y	Y	Y	N	N	N	Y	Y
2 Turner	Y	Y	Y	N	N	N	Y	Y
3 ***Johnson, Sam***	?	Y	Y	Y	Y	Y	N	Y
4 Hall	Y	Y	Y	N	N	N	Y	Y
5 ***Sessions***	Y	Y	Y	Y	Y	Y	N	Y
6 ***Barton***	?	?	Y	?	?	?	?	?
7 ***Archer***	?	Y	Y	N	Y	Y	N	Y
8 ***Brady***	Y	Y	Y	Y	Y	Y	N	Y
9 Lampson	Y	Y	Y	N	N	N	Y	Y
10 Doggett	Y	Y	Y	N	N	N	N	N
11 Edwards	Y	Y	Y	N	N	N	N	N
12 ***Granger***	Y	Y	Y	Y	Y	Y	N	Y
13 ***Thornberry***	Y	Y	Y	Y	Y	Y	N	Y
14 ***Paul***	Y	Y	Y	Y	Y	Y	N	Y
15 Hinojosa	Y	Y	Y	N	N	N	Y	N
16 Reyes	Y	Y	Y	N	N	N	Y	N
17 Stenholm	Y	Y	Y	N	N	N	N	N
18 Jackson-Lee	N	Y	Y	N	N	N	N	N
19 ***Combest***	Y	Y	Y	Y	Y	Y	N	Y
20 Gonzalez	N	Y	Y	N	N	N	Y	N
21 ***Smith***	Y	Y	Y	Y	Y	Y	N	Y
22 ***DeLay***	Y	Y	Y	Y	Y	Y	N	Y
23 ***Bonilla***	Y	Y	Y	Y	Y	Y	N	Y
24 Frost	Y	Y	Y	N	N	N	Y	N
25 Bentsen	Y	Y	Y	N	N	N	Y	N
26 ***Armey***	Y	Y	Y	Y	Y	Y	N	Y
27 Ortiz	N	Y	Y	N	N	N	Y	N
28 Rodriguez	Y	Y	Y	N	N	N	Y	N
29 Green	Y	Y	Y	N	Y	N	Y	N
30 Johnson, E.B.	Y	Y	Y	N	N	N	Y	N
UTAH								
1 ***Hansen***	Y	Y	Y	Y	Y	Y	N	Y
2 ***Cook***	Y	Y	Y	Y	Y	Y	N	Y
3 ***Cannon***	Y	Y	Y	Y	Y	Y	N	Y
VERMONT								
AL *Sanders*	Y	Y	Y	N	?	N	Y	N
VIRGINIA								
1 ***Bateman***	Y	Y	Y	Y	Y	Y	N	Y
2 Pickett	N	Y	Y	N	N	N	Y	N
3 Scott	Y	Y	Y	N	N	N	Y	N
4 Sisisky	Y	Y	Y	N	N	?	Y	Y
5 *Goode*	Y	Y	Y	Y	Y	Y	N	Y
6 ***Goodlatte***	Y	Y	Y	Y	Y	Y	N	Y
7 ***Bliley***	Y	Y	Y	Y	Y	Y	N	Y
8 Moran	Y	Y	Y	N	N	N	Y	N
9 Boucher	Y	Y	Y	N	N	N	Y	Y
10 ***Wolf***	?	?	?	?	Y	Y	N	Y
11 ***Davis***	Y	Y	?	?	Y	Y	N	Y
WASHINGTON								
1 Inslee	Y	Y	Y	N	Y	N	N	Y
2 ***Metcalf***	Y	Y	Y	Y	Y	Y	N	?
3 Baird	?	?	Y	N	N	N	Y	N
4 ***Hastings***	Y	Y	Y	Y	Y	Y	N	Y
5 ***Nethercutt***	Y	Y	Y	Y	Y	Y	N	Y
6 Dicks	Y	Y	Y	N	N	N	Y	N
7 McDermott	N	Y	Y	N	N	N	N	N
8 ***Dunn***	Y	Y	Y	Y	Y	Y	N	Y
9 Smith	?	?	?	?	?	?	?	?
WEST VIRGINIA								
1 Mollohan	Y	Y	Y	N	N	N	N	N
2 Wise	?	Y	Y	N	N	N	Y	Y
3 Rahall	Y	Y	Y	N	N	N	Y	N
WISCONSIN								
1 ***Ryan***	Y	Y	Y	Y	Y	Y	N	Y
2 Baldwin	Y	Y	Y	N	N	N	Y	N
3 Kind	Y	Y	Y	N	N	N	Y	N
4 Kleczka	Y	Y	Y	N	N	N	Y	N
5 Barrett	Y	Y	Y	N	N	N	Y	N
6 ***Petri***	Y	Y	Y	Y	Y	Y	N	Y
7 Obey	Y	Y	Y	N	N	N	Y	N
8 ***Green***	Y	Y	Y	Y	Y	Y	N	Y
9 ***Sensenbrenner***	Y	Y	Y	Y	Y	Y	N	Y
WYOMING								
AL ***Cubin***	Y	Y	Y	Y	Y	Y	N	Y

Southern states - Ala., Ark., Fla., Ga., Ky., La., Miss., N.C., Okla., S.C., Tenn., Texas, Va.

451. HR 4884. William S. Broomfield Post Office/Passage. Morella, R-Md., motion to suspend the rules and pass the bill designating a post office in Royal Oak, Mich., the "William S. Broomfield Post Office Building." Motion agreed to 404-0: R 210-0; D 192-0 (ND 142-0, SD 50-0); I 2-0. Sept. 6, 2000.

452. HR 4484. Everett Alvarez Jr. Post Office/Passage. Morella, R-Md., motion to suspend the rules and pass the bill designating a post office in Rockville, Md., the "Everett Alvarez Jr. Post Office Building." Motion agreed to 403-0: R 207-0; D 194-0 (ND 143-0, SD 51-0); I 2-0. Sept. 6, 2000.

453. HR 4448. Judge Robert Watts Post Office/Passage. Morella, R-Md., motion to suspend the rules and pass the bill designating a post office in Baltimore the "Judge Robert Bernard Watts Sr. Post Office Building." Motion agreed to 404-0: R 206-0; D 196-0 (ND 145-0, SD 51-0); I 2-0. Sept. 6, 2000.

454. HR 4115. Holocaust Memorial/Passage. Passage of the bill that would permanently authorize funding for the United States Holocaust Memorial museum and designate it an independent entity of the federal government. Passed 415-1: R 213-1; D 200-0 (ND 147-0, SD 53-0); I 2-0. Sept. 7, 2000.

455. HR 4678. Welfare Child Support/Religious Organizations. Scott, D-Va., amendment that would prohibit any organization that receives a fatherhood grant from subjecting participants to sectarian worship or instruction during the grant program. If a grant recipient discriminated against a beneficiary, the Justice Department would be allowed to enforce anti-discrimination laws. Rejected 163-257: R 2-214; D 160-42 (ND 126-24, SD 34-18); I 1-1. Sept. 7, 2000.

Key

- Y Voted for (yea).
- # Paired for.
- + Announced for.
- N Voted against (nay).
- X Paired against.
- – Announced against.
- P Voted "present."
- C Voted "present" to avoid possible conflict of interest.
- ? Did not vote or otherwise make a position known.

•

Democrats ***Republicans***
Independents

	451	452	453	454	455
ALABAMA					
1 ***Callahan***	Y	Y	Y	Y	N
2 ***Everett***	Y	Y	Y	?	?
3 ***Riley***	Y	Y	Y	Y	?
4 ***Aderholt***	Y	Y	Y	Y	N
5 Cramer	Y	Y	Y	Y	N
6 ***Bachus***	Y	Y	Y	Y	N
7 Hilliard	Y	Y	Y	Y	Y
ALASKA					
AL ***Young***	?	?	?	?	?
ARIZONA					
1 ***Salmon***	Y	Y	Y	Y	N
2 Pastor	Y	Y	Y	Y	Y
3 ***Stump***	Y	Y	Y	Y	N
4 ***Shadegg***	?	?	?	Y	N
5 ***Kolbe***	Y	Y	Y	Y	N
6 ***Hayworth***	Y	Y	Y	Y	N
ARKANSAS					
1 Berry	Y	Y	Y	Y	N
2 Snyder	Y	Y	Y	Y	N
3 ***Hutchinson***	Y	Y	Y	Y	N
4 ***Dickey***	Y	Y	Y	Y	N
CALIFORNIA					
1 Thompson	Y	Y	Y	Y	Y
2 ***Herger***	Y	Y	Y	?	N
3 ***Ose***	Y	Y	Y	Y	N
4 ***Doolittle***	Y	Y	Y	Y	N
5 Matsui	Y	Y	Y	Y	Y
6 Woolsey	Y	Y	Y	Y	Y
7 Miller, George	Y	Y	Y	Y	Y
8 Pelosi	Y	Y	Y	Y	Y
9 Lee	Y	Y	Y	Y	Y
10 Tauscher	Y	Y	Y	Y	Y
11 ***Pombo***	Y	Y	Y	Y	N
12 Lantos	Y	Y	Y	Y	Y
13 Stark	Y	Y	Y	Y	Y
14 Eshoo	Y	Y	Y	Y	Y
15 ***Campbell***	Y	Y	Y	Y	Y
16 Lofgren	Y	Y	Y	Y	Y
17 Farr	Y	?	Y	Y	Y
18 Condit	Y	Y	Y	Y	N
19 ***Radanovich***	Y	Y	Y	Y	N
20 Dooley	Y	Y	Y	Y	Y
21 ***Thomas***	Y	Y	Y	Y	N
22 Capps	Y	Y	Y	Y	N
23 ***Gallegly***	Y	Y	Y	Y	N
24 Sherman	Y	Y	Y	Y	Y
25 ***McKeon***	Y	Y	Y	Y	N
26 Berman	Y	Y	Y	Y	Y
27 ***Rogan***	Y	Y	Y	Y	N
28 ***Dreier***	Y	Y	Y	Y	N
29 Waxman	Y	Y	Y	Y	Y
30 Becerra	Y	Y	Y	Y	Y
31 ***Martinez***	Y	Y	Y	Y	N
32 Dixon	Y	Y	Y	Y	Y
33 Roybal-Allard	Y	Y	Y	Y	Y
34 Napolitano	Y	Y	Y	Y	Y
35 Waters	Y	Y	Y	Y	Y
36 ***Kuykendall***	Y	Y	Y	Y	N
37 Millender-McD.	Y	Y	Y	Y	Y
38 ***Horn***	Y	Y	Y	Y	Y
39 ***Royce***	Y	Y	Y	Y	N
40 ***Lewis***	Y	Y	Y	Y	N
41 ***Miller, Gary***	Y	Y	Y	Y	N
42 Baca	Y	Y	Y	Y	Y
43 ***Calvert***	Y	Y	Y	Y	N
44 ***Bono***	Y	Y	Y	Y	N
45 ***Rohrabacher***	Y	Y	Y	Y	N
46 Sanchez	Y	Y	Y	Y	Y
47 ***Cox***	Y	Y	Y	Y	N
48 ***Packard***	Y	Y	Y	Y	N
49 ***Bilbray***	Y	Y	Y	Y	N
50 Filner	Y	Y	Y	Y	Y
51 ***Cunningham***	Y	Y	Y	Y	N
52 ***Hunter***	Y	Y	Y	Y	N
COLORADO					
1 DeGette	Y	Y	Y	Y	Y
2 Udall	Y	Y	Y	Y	Y
3 ***McInnis***	Y	Y	Y	Y	N
4 ***Schaffer***	Y	Y	Y	Y	N
5 ***Hefley***	Y	Y	Y	Y	N
6 ***Tancredo***	Y	Y	Y	Y	N
CONNECTICUT					
1 Larson	Y	Y	Y	Y	Y
2 Gejdenson	Y	Y	Y	Y	Y
3 DeLauro	Y	Y	Y	Y	Y
4 ***Shays***	Y	Y	Y	Y	N
5 Maloney	Y	Y	Y	Y	Y
6 ***Johnson***	Y	+	Y	Y	N
DELAWARE					
AL ***Castle***	Y	Y	?	Y	N
FLORIDA					
1 ***Scarborough***	Y	Y	Y	Y	N
2 Boyd	Y	Y	Y	Y	N
3 Brown	Y	Y	Y	Y	Y
4 ***Fowler***	Y	Y	Y	Y	N
5 Thurman	Y	Y	Y	Y	Y
6 ***Stearns***	Y	Y	Y	Y	N
7 ***Mica***	Y	Y	Y	Y	N
8 ***McCollum***	?	?	?	?	?
9 ***Bilirakis***	Y	Y	Y	Y	N
10 ***Young***	Y	Y	Y	Y	N
11 Davis	Y	Y	Y	Y	N
12 ***Canady***	Y	Y	Y	Y	N
13 ***Miller***	Y	Y	Y	Y	N
14 ***Goss***	Y	Y	Y	Y	N
15 ***Weldon***	Y	Y	Y	Y	N
16 ***Foley***	Y	Y	Y	Y	N
17 Meek	Y	Y	Y	Y	Y
18 ***Ros-Lehtinen***	Y	Y	Y	Y	N
19 Wexler	Y	Y	Y	Y	Y
20 Deutsch	Y	Y	Y	Y	Y
21 ***Diaz-Balart***	Y	Y	Y	Y	N
22 ***Shaw***	Y	Y	Y	Y	N
23 Hastings	Y	Y	Y	Y	Y
GEORGIA					
1 ***Kingston***	Y	Y	Y	Y	N
2 Bishop	?	?	?	Y	Y
3 ***Collins***	Y	Y	Y	Y	N
4 McKinney	Y	Y	Y	Y	Y
5 Lewis	Y	Y	Y	Y	Y
6 ***Isakson***	Y	Y	Y	Y	N
7 ***Barr***	Y	Y	Y	Y	N
8 ***Chambliss***	Y	Y	Y	Y	N
9 ***Deal***	Y	Y	Y	Y	N
10 ***Norwood***	Y	Y	Y	Y	N
11 ***Linder***	Y	Y	Y	Y	N
HAWAII					
1 Abercrombie	Y	Y	Y	Y	Y
2 Mink	Y	Y	Y	Y	Y
IDAHO					
1 ***Chenoweth-Hage***	Y	Y	Y	Y	N
2 ***Simpson***	Y	Y	Y	Y	N
ILLINOIS					
1 Rush	Y	Y	Y	Y	Y
2 Jackson	Y	Y	Y	Y	Y
3 Lipinski	Y	Y	Y	Y	N
4 Gutierrez	Y	Y	Y	Y	Y
5 Blagojevich	Y	Y	Y	Y	Y
6 ***Hyde***	Y	Y	Y	Y	N
7 Davis	Y	Y	Y	Y	Y
8 ***Crane***	Y	Y	Y	Y	N
9 Schakowsky	Y	?	Y	Y	Y
10 ***Porter***	Y	Y	Y	Y	N
11 ***Weller***	Y	Y	Y	Y	N
12 Costello	Y	Y	Y	Y	Y
13 ***Biggert***	Y	Y	Y	Y	N

ND Northern Democrats SD Southern Democrats

	451	452	453	454	455
14 ***Hastert***					
15 ***Ewing***	Y	Y	Y	Y	N
16 ***Manzullo***	Y	Y	Y	Y	N
17 Evans	Y	Y	Y	Y	Y
18 ***LaHood***	Y	Y	Y	Y	N
19 Phelps	Y	Y	Y	Y	N
20 ***Shimkus***	Y	Y	Y	Y	N
INDIANA					
1 Visclosky	Y	Y	Y	Y	Y
2 ***McIntosh***	?	?	?	?	?
3 Roemer	Y	Y	Y	Y	N
4 ***Souder***	?	?	?	Y	N
5 ***Buyer***	Y	Y	Y	Y	N
6 ***Burton***	Y	Y	Y	Y	N
7 ***Pease***	Y	Y	Y	Y	N
8 ***Hostettler***	Y	Y	Y	Y	N
9 Hill	Y	Y	Y	Y	N
10 Carson	Y	Y	Y	Y	Y
IOWA					
1 ***Leach***	Y	Y	Y	Y	N
2 ***Nussle***	Y	?	Y	Y	N
3 Boswell	Y	Y	Y	Y	Y
4 ***Ganske***	Y	Y	?	Y	N
5 ***Latham***	Y	Y	Y	Y	N
KANSAS					
1 ***Moran***	Y	Y	Y	Y	N
2 ***Ryun***	Y	Y	Y	Y	N
3 Moore	Y	Y	Y	Y	Y
4 ***Tiahrt***	Y	Y	Y	Y	N
KENTUCKY					
1 ***Whitfield***	Y	Y	Y	Y	N
2 ***Lewis***	Y	Y	Y	Y	N
3 ***Northup***	Y	Y	Y	Y	N
4 Lucas	Y	Y	Y	Y	N
5 ***Rogers***	Y	Y	Y	Y	N
6 ***Fletcher***	Y	Y	Y	Y	N
LOUISIANA					
1 ***Vitter***	Y	Y	Y	Y	N
2 Jefferson	?	Y	Y	?	?
3 ***Tauzin***	Y	Y	Y	Y	N
4 ***McCrery***	Y	Y	Y	Y	N
5 ***Cooksey***	Y	Y	Y	Y	N
6 ***Baker***	Y	Y	Y	Y	N
7 John	Y	Y	Y	Y	N
MAINE					
1 Allen	Y	Y	Y	Y	Y
2 Baldacci	Y	Y	Y	Y	Y
MARYLAND					
1 ***Gilchrest***	Y	Y	Y	Y	N
2 ***Ehrlich***	?	?	?	Y	N
3 Cardin	Y	Y	Y	Y	Y
4 Wynn	Y	Y	Y	Y	Y
5 Hoyer	Y	Y	Y	Y	Y
6 ***Bartlett***	Y	Y	Y	Y	N
7 Cummings	Y	Y	Y	Y	Y
8 ***Morella***	Y	Y	Y	Y	N
MASSACHUSETTS					
1 Olver	Y	Y	Y	Y	Y
2 Neal	Y	Y	Y	Y	Y
3 McGovern	Y	Y	Y	Y	Y
4 Frank	Y	Y	Y	Y	Y
5 Meehan	Y	Y	Y	Y	Y
6 Tierney	Y	Y	Y	Y	Y
7 Markey	Y	Y	Y	Y	Y
8 Capuano	Y	Y	Y	Y	Y
9 Moakley	Y	Y	Y	Y	Y
10 Delahunt	Y	Y	Y	Y	Y
MICHIGAN					
1 Stupak	Y	Y	Y	Y	N
2 ***Hoekstra***	Y	Y	Y	Y	N
3 ***Ehlers***	Y	Y	Y	Y	N
4 ***Camp***	Y	Y	Y	Y	N
5 Barcia	Y	Y	Y	Y	N
6 ***Upton***	Y	Y	Y	Y	N
7 ***Smith***	Y	Y	Y	Y	N
8 Stabenow	Y	Y	Y	Y	Y
9 Kildee	Y	Y	Y	Y	Y
10 Bonior	Y	Y	Y	Y	Y
11 ***Knollenberg***	Y	Y	Y	Y	N
12 Levin	Y	Y	Y	Y	Y
13 Rivers	Y	Y	Y	Y	Y
14 Conyers	Y	Y	Y	Y	Y
15 Kilpatrick	Y	Y	Y	Y	Y
16 Dingell	Y	Y	Y	Y	N

	451	452	453	454	455
MINNESOTA					
1 ***Gutknecht***	Y	Y	Y	Y	N
2 Minge	Y	Y	Y	Y	Y
3 ***Ramstad***	Y	Y	Y	Y	N
4 Vento	?	?	?	?	?
5 Sabo	Y	Y	Y	Y	Y
6 Luther	Y	Y	Y	Y	Y
7 Peterson	Y	Y	Y	Y	N
8 Oberstar	Y	Y	Y	Y	Y
MISSISSIPPI					
1 ***Wicker***	Y	Y	Y	Y	N
2 Thompson	Y	Y	Y	Y	Y
3 ***Pickering***	Y	Y	Y	Y	N
4 Shows	Y	Y	Y	Y	N
5 Taylor	Y	Y	Y	Y	N
MISSOURI					
1 Clay	Y	Y	Y	Y	Y
2 ***Talent***	Y	Y	Y	Y	N
3 Gephardt	Y	Y	Y	Y	Y
4 Skelton	Y	Y	Y	Y	N
5 McCarthy	Y	Y	Y	Y	Y
6 Danner	?	?	?	Y	N
7 ***Blunt***	Y	Y	Y	Y	N
8 ***Emerson***	?	?	?	Y	N
9 ***Hulshof***	Y	Y	Y	Y	N
MONTANA					
AL ***Hill***	Y	Y	Y	Y	N
NEBRASKA					
1 ***Bereuter***	Y	Y	Y	Y	N
2 ***Terry***	Y	Y	Y	Y	N
3 ***Barrett***	Y	Y	Y	Y	N
NEVADA					
1 Berkley	Y	Y	Y	Y	Y
2 ***Gibbons***	Y	Y	Y	Y	N
NEW HAMPSHIRE					
1 ***Sununu***	Y	Y	Y	Y	N
2 ***Bass***	Y	Y	Y	Y	N
NEW JERSEY					
1 Andrews	?	?	?	?	N
2 ***LoBiondo***	Y	Y	Y	Y	N
3 ***Saxton***	Y	Y	Y	Y	N
4 ***Smith***	Y	Y	Y	Y	N
5 ***Roukema***	Y	Y	Y	Y	N
6 Pallone	Y	Y	Y	Y	Y
7 ***Franks***	?	?	?	Y	N
8 Pascrell	Y	Y	Y	Y	Y
9 Rothman	Y	Y	Y	Y	Y
10 Payne	Y	Y	Y	Y	Y
11 ***Frelinghuysen***	Y	Y	Y	Y	N
12 Holt	Y	Y	Y	Y	Y
13 Menendez	Y	Y	Y	Y	Y
NEW MEXICO					
1 ***Wilson***	Y	?	?	Y	N
2 ***Skeen***	Y	Y	Y	Y	N
3 Udall	Y	Y	Y	Y	Y
NEW YORK					
1 Forbes	Y	Y	Y	Y	N
2 ***Lazio***	?	?	?	?	?
3 ***King***	Y	Y	Y	Y	N
4 McCarthy	Y	Y	Y	Y	Y
5 Ackerman	?	?	?	Y	Y
6 Meeks	?	Y	Y	Y	Y
7 Crowley	Y	Y	Y	Y	Y
8 Nadler	Y	Y	Y	Y	Y
9 Weiner	?	?	?	Y	Y
10 Towns	Y	Y	Y	?	?
11 Owens	?	?	?	+	+
12 Velázquez	Y	Y	Y	Y	Y
13 ***Fossella***	Y	Y	Y	Y	N
14 Maloney	Y	Y	Y	Y	Y
15 Rangel	Y	Y	Y	?	Y
16 Serrano	Y	Y	Y	Y	Y
17 Engel	?	?	?	?	?
18 Lowey	?	Y	Y	Y	Y
19 ***Kelly***	Y	Y	Y	Y	N
20 ***Gilman***	Y	Y	Y	Y	N
21 McNulty	Y	Y	Y	Y	Y
22 ***Sweeney***	Y	Y	Y	Y	N
23 ***Boehlert***	Y	Y	Y	Y	N
24 ***McHugh***	Y	Y	Y	Y	N
25 ***Walsh***	Y	Y	Y	Y	N
26 Hinchey	Y	Y	Y	Y	Y
27 ***Reynolds***	Y	Y	Y	Y	N
28 Slaughter	Y	Y	Y	Y	Y
29 LaFalce	Y	Y	Y	Y	Y

	451	452	453	454	455
30 ***Quinn***	Y	Y	Y	Y	N
31 ***Houghton***	Y	Y	Y	Y	N
NORTH CAROLINA					
1 Clayton	Y	Y	Y	Y	Y
2 Etheridge	Y	Y	Y	Y	Y
3 ***Jones***	Y	Y	Y	Y	N
4 Price	Y	Y	Y	Y	Y
5 ***Burr***	Y	Y	Y	Y	N
6 ***Coble***	Y	Y	Y	Y	N
7 McIntyre	Y	Y	Y	Y	N
8 ***Hayes***	Y	Y	Y	Y	N
9 ***Myrick***	Y	Y	Y	Y	N
10 ***Ballenger***	Y	Y	Y	Y	N
11 ***Taylor***	Y	Y	Y	Y	N
12 Watt	Y	Y	Y	Y	Y
NORTH DAKOTA					
AL Pomeroy	Y	Y	Y	Y	Y
OHIO					
1 ***Chabot***	Y	Y	Y	Y	N
2 ***Portman***	Y	Y	Y	Y	N
3 Hall	Y	Y	Y	Y	N
4 ***Oxley***	Y	Y	Y	Y	N
5 ***Gillmor***	Y	Y	Y	Y	N
6 Strickland	?	Y	Y	Y	Y
7 ***Hobson***	Y	Y	Y	Y	N
8 ***Boehner***	Y	Y	Y	Y	N
9 Kaptur	Y	Y	Y	?	P
10 Kucinich	Y	Y	Y	Y	Y
11 Jones	?	?	?	?	?
12 ***Kasich***	Y	Y	Y	Y	N
13 Brown	Y	Y	Y	Y	Y
14 Sawyer	Y	Y	Y	Y	Y
15 ***Pryce***	Y	Y	Y	Y	N
16 ***Regula***	Y	Y	Y	Y	N
17 Traficant	Y	Y	Y	Y	N
18 ***Ney***	Y	Y	Y	Y	N
19 ***LaTourette***	?	?	?	Y	N
OKLAHOMA					
1 ***Largent***	Y	Y	Y	Y	N
2 ***Coburn***	Y	Y	Y	Y	N
3 ***Watkins***	Y	Y	Y	Y	N
4 ***Watts***	Y	Y	Y	Y	N
5 ***Istook***	Y	Y	Y	Y	N
6 ***Lucas***	Y	Y	Y	Y	N
OREGON					
1 Wu	Y	Y	Y	Y	Y
2 ***Walden***	+	+	+	Y	N
3 Blumenauer	Y	Y	Y	Y	Y
4 DeFazio	Y	Y	Y	Y	Y
5 Hooley	Y	Y	Y	Y	Y
PENNSYLVANIA					
1 Brady	Y	Y	Y	Y	Y
2 Fattah	Y	Y	Y	Y	Y
3 Borski	Y	Y	Y	Y	N
4 Klink	?	?	?	?	Y
5 ***Peterson***	Y	Y	Y	Y	N
6 Holden	Y	Y	Y	Y	N
7 ***Weldon***	Y	Y	Y	Y	N
8 ***Greenwood***	Y	Y	Y	Y	N
9 ***Shuster***	Y	Y	Y	Y	N
10 ***Sherwood***	Y	Y	Y	Y	N
11 Kanjorski	Y	Y	Y	Y	Y
12 Murtha	Y	Y	Y	Y	N
13 Hoeffel	Y	Y	Y	Y	Y
14 Coyne	Y	Y	Y	Y	Y
15 ***Toomey***	Y	Y	Y	Y	N
16 ***Pitts***	Y	Y	Y	Y	N
17 ***Gekas***	Y	Y	Y	Y	N
18 Doyle	Y	Y	Y	Y	N
19 ***Goodling***	Y	Y	Y	Y	N
20 Mascara	Y	Y	Y	Y	N
21 ***English***	Y	Y	Y	Y	N
RHODE ISLAND					
1 Kennedy	Y	Y	Y	Y	Y
2 Weygand	Y	Y	Y	Y	Y
SOUTH CAROLINA					
1 ***Sanford***	Y	Y	Y	Y	N
2 ***Spence***	Y	Y	Y	Y	N
3 ***Graham***	Y	Y	Y	Y	N
4 ***DeMint***	Y	Y	Y	Y	N
5 Spratt	Y	Y	Y	Y	N
6 Clyburn	Y	Y	Y	Y	Y
SOUTH DAKOTA					
AL ***Thune***	Y	Y	Y	Y	N

	451	452	453	454	455
TENNESSEE					
1 ***Jenkins***	Y	Y	Y	Y	N
2 ***Duncan***	Y	Y	Y	Y	N
3 ***Wamp***	Y	Y	Y	Y	N
4 ***Hilleary***	Y	Y	Y	Y	N
5 Clement	Y	Y	Y	Y	N
6 Gordon	Y	Y	Y	Y	N
7 ***Bryant***	Y	Y	Y	Y	N
8 Tanner	Y	Y	Y	Y	?
9 Ford	Y	Y	Y	Y	N
TEXAS					
1 Sandlin	Y	Y	Y	Y	Y
2 Turner	Y	Y	Y	Y	Y
3 ***Johnson, Sam***	Y	Y	Y	Y	N
4 Hall	Y	Y	Y	Y	N
5 ***Sessions***	Y	Y	Y	Y	N
6 ***Barton***	Y	Y	Y	?	N
7 ***Archer***	Y	Y	Y	Y	N
8 ***Brady***	Y	Y	Y	Y	N
9 Lampson	?	?	?	?	Y
10 Doggett	Y	Y	Y	Y	Y
11 Edwards	Y	Y	Y	Y	Y
12 ***Granger***	Y	Y	Y	Y	N
13 ***Thornberry***	Y	Y	Y	Y	N
14 ***Paul***	Y	Y	Y	N	N
15 Hinojosa	Y	Y	Y	Y	Y
16 Reyes	?	?	?	Y	Y
17 Stenholm	Y	Y	Y	Y	N
18 Jackson-Lee	Y	Y	Y	Y	Y
19 ***Combest***	Y	Y	Y	Y	N
20 Gonzalez	Y	Y	Y	Y	Y
21 ***Smith***	Y	Y	Y	Y	N
22 ***DeLay***	Y	Y	Y	Y	N
23 ***Bonilla***	Y	Y	Y	Y	N
24 Frost	Y	Y	Y	Y	Y
25 Bentsen	Y	Y	Y	Y	Y
26 ***Armey***	Y	Y	Y	Y	N
27 Ortiz	Y	Y	Y	Y	N
28 Rodriguez	Y	Y	Y	Y	Y
29 Green	Y	Y	Y	Y	Y
30 Johnson, E.B.	Y	Y	Y	Y	Y
UTAH					
1 ***Hansen***	Y	Y	Y	Y	N
2 ***Cook***	?	?	?	Y	N
3 ***Cannon***	Y	Y	Y	Y	N
VERMONT					
AL *Sanders*	Y	Y	Y	Y	Y
VIRGINIA					
1 ***Bateman***	Y	Y	Y	Y	N
2 Pickett	Y	Y	Y	Y	Y
3 Scott	Y	Y	Y	Y	Y
4 Sisisky	Y	Y	Y	Y	Y
5 *Goode*	Y	Y	Y	Y	N
6 ***Goodlatte***	Y	Y	Y	Y	N
7 ***Bliley***	Y	Y	?	Y	N
8 Moran	Y	Y	Y	Y	Y
9 Boucher	Y	Y	Y	Y	N
10 ***Wolf***	Y	Y	Y	Y	N
11 ***Davis***	Y	Y	Y	Y	N
WASHINGTON					
1 Inslee	Y	Y	Y	Y	Y
2 ***Metcalf***	Y	Y	Y	Y	N
3 Baird	Y	Y	Y	Y	Y
4 ***Hastings***	Y	Y	Y	Y	N
5 ***Nethercutt***	Y	Y	Y	Y	N
6 Dicks	Y	Y	Y	Y	Y
7 McDermott	Y	Y	Y	Y	Y
8 ***Dunn***	Y	Y	Y	Y	N
9 Smith	Y	Y	Y	Y	N
WEST VIRGINIA					
1 Mollohan	?	?	?	Y	N
2 Wise	?	?	?	Y	N
3 Rahall	Y	Y	Y	Y	Y
WISCONSIN					
1 ***Ryan***	Y	Y	Y	Y	N
2 Baldwin	Y	Y	Y	Y	Y
3 Kind	Y	Y	Y	Y	Y
4 Kleczka	Y	Y	Y	Y	Y
5 Barrett	Y	Y	Y	Y	Y
6 ***Petri***	Y	Y	Y	Y	N
7 Obey	Y	Y	Y	Y	Y
8 ***Green***	Y	Y	Y	Y	N
9 ***Sensenbrenner***	Y	Y	Y	Y	N
WYOMING					
AL ***Cubin***	Y	Y	Y	?	N

Southern states - Ala., Ark., Fla., Ga., Ky., La., Miss., N.C., Okla., S.C., Tenn., Texas, Va.

House Votes **456, 457, 458, 459**

456. **HR 4678. Welfare Child Support/Recommit.** Scott, D-Va., motion to recommit the bill to the House Ways and Means Committee with instructions to provide that funds in the bill could not be used in the fatherhood programs to discriminate in employment. Motion rejected 175-249: R 0-218; D 174-30 (ND 134-17, SD 40-13); I 1-1. Sept. 7, 2000.

457. **HR 4678. Welfare Child Support/Passage.** Passage of the bill that would give ex-welfare families all overdue child support payments owed them before or after they received welfare. States could also pass on all the child support collected to families still on welfare. The bill would also authorize grants for parenting classes and job training. Passed 405-18: R 206-11; D 197-7 (ND 145-6, SD 52-1); I 2-0. Sept. 7, 2000.

458. **HR 8. Estate Tax Repeal/Veto Override.** Passage, over President Clinton's Aug. 31, 2000, veto, of the bill that would amend the Internal Revenue Code of 1986 to reduce and ultimately repeal the estate and gift tax by 2010. Rejected 274-157: R 220-1; D 53-155 (ND 35-120, SD 18-35); I 1-1. Sept. 7, 2000. A two-thirds majority of those present and voting (288 in this case) of both houses is required to override a veto. A "nay" was a vote in support of the president's position.

459. **HR 4844. Railroad Retirement/Passage.** Shuster, R-Pa., motion to suspend the rules and pass the bill that would allow railroad retirement assets to be invested in private securities, reduce the payroll tax on railroad workers and make other changes in the railroad retirement system. Motion agreed to 391-25: R 191-23; D 198-2 (ND 148-0, SD 50-2); I 2-0. Sept. 7, 2000.

Key

Y	Voted for (yea).
#	Paired for.
+	Announced for.
N	Voted against (nay).
X	Paired against.
–	Announced against.
P	Voted "present."
C	Voted "present" to avoid possible conflict of interest.
?	Did not vote or otherwise make a position known.

•

Democrats ***Republicans***
Independents

	456	457	458	459
ALABAMA				
1 ***Callahan***	N	Y	Y	?
2 ***Everett***	?	?	Y	Y
3 ***Riley***	N	Y	Y	Y
4 ***Aderholt***	N	Y	Y	Y
5 Cramer	N	Y	Y	Y
6 ***Bachus***	N	Y	Y	Y
7 Hilliard	Y	Y	N	Y
ALASKA				
AL ***Young***	?	?	?	?
ARIZONA				
1 ***Salmon***	N	Y	Y	Y
2 Pastor	Y	Y	N	Y
3 ***Stump***	N	Y	Y	Y
4 ***Shadegg***	N	N	Y	Y
5 ***Kolbe***	N	Y	Y	Y
6 ***Hayworth***	N	Y	Y	Y
ARKANSAS				
1 Berry	Y	Y	Y	Y
2 Snyder	Y	Y	N	Y
3 ***Hutchinson***	N	Y	Y	Y
4 ***Dickey***	N	Y	Y	Y
CALIFORNIA				
1 Thompson	Y	Y	Y	Y
2 ***Herger***	N	Y	Y	Y
3 ***Ose***	N	Y	Y	Y
4 ***Doolittle***	N	Y	Y	Y
5 Matsui	Y	Y	N	Y
6 Woolsey	Y	Y	N	Y
7 Miller, George	Y	Y	N	Y
8 Pelosi	Y	Y	N	Y
9 Lee	Y	Y	N	Y
10 Tauscher	Y	Y	Y	Y
11 ***Pombo***	N	Y	Y	Y
12 Lantos	Y	Y	N	Y
13 Stark	Y	Y	N	Y
14 Eshoo	Y	Y	N	Y
15 ***Campbell***	N	Y	Y	?
16 Lofgren	Y	Y	N	Y
17 Farr	Y	Y	N	Y
18 Condit	N	Y	Y	Y
19 ***Radanovich***	N	Y	Y	Y
20 Dooley	Y	Y	Y	Y
21 ***Thomas***	N	Y	Y	Y
22 Capps	Y	Y	Y	Y
23 ***Gallegly***	N	Y	Y	Y
24 Sherman	Y	Y	N	Y
25 ***McKeon***	N	Y	Y	Y
26 Berman	Y	Y	N	Y
27 ***Rogan***	N	Y	Y	Y
28 ***Dreier***	N	Y	Y	Y
29 Waxman	Y	Y	N	Y
30 Becerra	Y	Y	N	Y
31 ***Martinez***	N	Y	Y	Y
32 Dixon	Y	Y	N	Y
33 Roybal-Allard	Y	Y	N	Y
34 Napolitano	Y	Y	N	Y
35 Waters	Y	N	N	Y
36 ***Kuykendall***	N	Y	Y	Y
37 Millender-McD.	Y	Y	N	Y
38 ***Horn***	N	Y	Y	Y
39 ***Royce***	N	Y	Y	N
40 ***Lewis***	N	Y	Y	Y
41 ***Miller, Gary***	N	Y	Y	Y
42 Baca	Y	Y	N	Y
43 ***Calvert***	N	Y	Y	Y
44 ***Bono***	N	Y	Y	Y
45 ***Rohrabacher***	N	Y	Y	N
46 Sanchez	Y	Y	Y	Y
47 ***Cox***	N	Y	Y	N
48 ***Packard***	N	Y	Y	Y
49 ***Bilbray***	N	Y	Y	Y
50 Filner	Y	Y	N	Y
51 ***Cunningham***	N	Y	Y	Y
52 ***Hunter***	N	Y	Y	N
COLORADO				
1 DeGette	Y	Y	N	Y
2 Udall	Y	Y	N	Y
3 ***McInnis***	N	Y	Y	Y
4 ***Schaffer***	N	Y	Y	N
5 ***Hefley***	N	Y	Y	N
6 ***Tancredo***	N	Y	Y	Y
CONNECTICUT				
1 Larson	Y	Y	N	Y
2 Gejdenson	Y	N	N	Y
3 DeLauro	Y	Y	N	Y
4 ***Shays***	N	Y	Y	N
5 Maloney	Y	Y	Y	Y
6 ***Johnson***	N	Y	Y	Y
DELAWARE				
AL ***Castle***	N	Y	Y	Y
FLORIDA				
1 ***Scarborough***	N	Y	Y	Y
2 Boyd	N	Y	N	Y
3 Brown	Y	Y	N	Y
4 ***Fowler***	N	Y	Y	Y
5 Thurman	Y	Y	N	Y
6 ***Stearns***	N	Y	Y	Y
7 ***Mica***	N	Y	Y	Y
8 ***McCollum***	?	?	Y	?
9 ***Bilirakis***	N	Y	Y	Y
10 ***Young***	N	Y	Y	Y
11 Davis	Y	Y	N	?
12 ***Canady***	N	Y	Y	Y
13 ***Miller***	N	Y	Y	N
14 ***Goss***	N	Y	Y	Y
15 ***Weldon***	N	Y	Y	Y
16 ***Foley***	N	Y	Y	Y
17 Meek	Y	Y	N	Y
18 ***Ros-Lehtinen***	N	Y	Y	Y
19 Wexler	Y	Y	N	Y
20 Deutsch	Y	Y	N	Y
21 ***Diaz-Balart***	N	Y	Y	Y
22 ***Shaw***	N	Y	Y	Y
23 Hastings	Y	Y	N	Y
GEORGIA				
1 ***Kingston***	N	Y	Y	Y
2 Bishop	Y	Y	Y	Y
3 ***Collins***	N	Y	Y	Y
4 McKinney	Y	Y	N	Y
5 Lewis	Y	Y	N	Y
6 ***Isakson***	N	Y	Y	Y
7 ***Barr***	N	Y	Y	Y
8 ***Chambliss***	N	Y	Y	Y
9 ***Deal***	N	Y	Y	Y
10 ***Norwood***	N	Y	Y	Y
11 ***Linder***	N	Y	Y	Y
HAWAII				
1 Abercrombie	Y	Y	Y	Y
2 Mink	Y	Y	Y	Y
IDAHO				
1 ***Chenoweth-Hage***	N	N	Y	Y
2 ***Simpson***	N	Y	Y	Y
ILLINOIS				
1 Rush	Y	Y	N	Y
2 Jackson	Y	N	N	Y
3 Lipinski	N	Y	Y	Y
4 Gutierrez	Y	Y	N	Y
5 Blagojevich	Y	Y	Y	Y
6 ***Hyde***	N	Y	Y	Y
7 Davis	Y	Y	N	Y
8 ***Crane***	N	Y	Y	N
9 Schakowsky	Y	Y	N	Y
10 ***Porter***	N	Y	Y	Y
11 ***Weller***	N	Y	Y	Y
12 Costello	Y	Y	Y	Y
13 ***Biggert***	N	Y	Y	Y

ND Northern Democrats SD Southern Democrats

	456	457	458	459
14 ***Hastert***			Y	
15 ***Ewing***	N	?	Y	Y
16 ***Manzullo***	N	N	Y	Y
17 Evans	Y	Y	N	Y
18 ***LaHood***	N	Y	Y	Y
19 Phelps	N	Y	Y	Y
20 ***Shimkus***	N	Y	Y	Y
INDIANA				
1 Visclosky	Y	Y	N	Y
2 ***McIntosh***	?	?	Y	?
3 Roemer	N	Y	Y	Y
4 ***Souder***	N	Y	Y	Y
5 ***Buyer***	N	Y	Y	Y
6 ***Burton***	N	Y	Y	Y
7 ***Pease***	N	Y	Y	Y
8 ***Hostettler***	N	N	Y	N
9 Hill	Y	Y	N	Y
10 Carson	Y	Y	N	Y
IOWA				
1 ***Leach***	N	Y	Y	Y
2 ***Nussle***	N	Y	Y	Y
3 Boswell	Y	Y	Y	Y
4 ***Ganske***	N	Y	Y	Y
5 ***Latham***	N	Y	Y	Y
KANSAS				
1 ***Moran***	N	Y	Y	Y
2 ***Ryun***	N	Y	Y	Y
3 Moore	Y	Y	Y	Y
4 ***Tiahrt***	N	Y	Y	Y
KENTUCKY				
1 ***Whitfield***	N	Y	Y	Y
2 ***Lewis***	N	Y	Y	Y
3 ***Northup***	N	Y	Y	Y
4 Lucas	N	Y	Y	Y
5 ***Rogers***	N	Y	Y	Y
6 ***Fletcher***	N	Y	Y	Y
LOUISIANA				
1 ***Vitter***	N	Y	Y	?
2 Jefferson	?	?	?	?
3 ***Tauzin***	N	Y	Y	Y
4 ***McCrery***	N	Y	Y	Y
5 ***Cooksey***	N	Y	Y	Y
6 ***Baker***	N	Y	Y	Y
7 John	N	Y	Y	Y
MAINE				
1 Allen	Y	Y	N	Y
2 Baldacci	Y	Y	N	Y
MARYLAND				
1 ***Gilchrest***	N	Y	Y	Y
2 ***Ehrlich***	N	Y	Y	Y
3 Cardin	Y	Y	N	Y
4 Wynn	Y	Y	N	Y
5 Hoyer	Y	Y	N	Y
6 ***Bartlett***	N	Y	Y	Y
7 Cummings	Y	Y	N	Y
8 ***Morella***	N	Y	Y	Y
MASSACHUSETTS				
1 Olver	Y	Y	N	Y
2 Neal	Y	Y	N	Y
3 McGovern	Y	Y	N	Y
4 Frank	Y	N	N	Y
5 Meehan	Y	Y	N	Y
6 Tierney	Y	Y	N	Y
7 Markey	Y	Y	N	Y
8 Capuano	Y	Y	N	Y
9 Moakley	Y	Y	N	Y
10 Delahunt	Y	Y	Y	?
MICHIGAN				
1 Stupak	Y	Y	N	Y
2 ***Hoekstra***	N	Y	Y	Y
3 ***Ehlers***	N	Y	Y	Y
4 ***Camp***	N	Y	Y	Y
5 Barcia	N	Y	Y	Y
6 ***Upton***	N	Y	Y	Y
7 ***Smith***	N	Y	Y	N
8 Stabenow	Y	Y	N	Y
9 Kildee	N	Y	N	Y
10 Bonior	Y	Y	N	Y
11 ***Knollenberg***	N	Y	Y	Y
12 Levin	Y	Y	N	Y
13 Rivers	Y	Y	N	Y
14 Conyers	Y	Y	N	Y
15 Kilpatrick	Y	Y	N	Y
16 Dingell	Y	Y	N	Y

	456	457	458	459
MINNESOTA				
1 ***Gutknecht***	N	Y	Y	Y
2 Minge	Y	Y	N	Y
3 ***Ramstad***	N	Y	Y	Y
4 Vento	?	?	?	?
5 Sabo	Y	Y	N	Y
6 Luther	Y	Y	N	Y
7 Peterson	N	Y	Y	Y
8 Oberstar	Y	Y	N	Y
MISSISSIPPI				
1 ***Wicker***	N	Y	Y	Y
2 Thompson	Y	Y	N	Y
3 ***Pickering***	N	Y	Y	Y
4 Shows	N	Y	Y	Y
5 Taylor	N	Y	N	N
MISSOURI				
1 Clay	Y	Y	N	Y
2 ***Talent***	N	Y	Y	Y
3 Gephardt	Y	Y	N	Y
4 Skelton	N	Y	Y	Y
5 McCarthy	Y	Y	N	Y
6 Danner	Y	Y	Y	Y
7 ***Blunt***	N	Y	Y	Y
8 ***Emerson***	N	Y	Y	Y
9 ***Hulshof***	N	Y	Y	Y
MONTANA				
AL ***Hill***	N	Y	Y	Y
NEBRASKA				
1 ***Bereuter***	N	Y	N	Y
2 ***Terry***	N	Y	Y	Y
3 ***Barrett***	N	Y	Y	Y
NEVADA				
1 Berkley	Y	Y	Y	Y
2 ***Gibbons***	N	Y	Y	Y
NEW HAMPSHIRE				
1 ***Sununu***	N	Y	Y	N
2 ***Bass***	N	Y	Y	Y
NEW JERSEY				
1 Andrews	Y	Y	Y	Y
2 ***LoBiondo***	N	Y	Y	Y
3 ***Saxton***	N	Y	Y	Y
4 ***Smith***	N	Y	Y	Y
5 ***Roukema***	N	Y	Y	?
6 Pallone	Y	Y	N	Y
7 ***Franks***	N	Y	Y	Y
8 Pascrell	Y	Y	N	Y
9 Rothman	Y	Y	N	Y
10 Payne	Y	N	N	Y
11 ***Frelinghuysen***	N	Y	Y	Y
12 Holt	Y	Y	Y	Y
13 Menendez	Y	Y	N	Y
NEW MEXICO				
1 ***Wilson***	N	Y	Y	Y
2 ***Skeen***	N	Y	Y	Y
3 Udall	Y	Y	N	Y
NEW YORK				
1 Forbes	N	Y	Y	Y
2 ***Lazio***	N	Y	Y	?
3 ***King***	N	Y	Y	Y
4 McCarthy	Y	Y	Y	Y
5 Ackerman	Y	N	N	?
6 Meeks	Y	Y	N	?
7 Crowley	Y	Y	N	Y
8 Nadler	Y	Y	N	Y
9 Weiner	Y	Y	N	Y
10 Towns	?	?	N	Y
11 Owens	+	+	N	?
12 Velázquez	Y	Y	N	Y
13 ***Fossella***	N	Y	Y	Y
14 Maloney	Y	Y	N	Y
15 Rangel	Y	Y	N	Y
16 Serrano	Y	Y	N	Y
17 Engel	?	?	N	Y
18 Lowey	Y	Y	N	Y
19 ***Kelly***	N	Y	Y	Y
20 ***Gilman***	N	Y	Y	Y
21 McNulty	Y	Y	N	Y
22 ***Sweeney***	N	Y	Y	Y
23 ***Boehlert***	N	Y	Y	Y
24 ***McHugh***	N	Y	Y	Y
25 ***Walsh***	N	Y	Y	Y
26 Hinchey	Y	Y	N	Y
27 ***Reynolds***	N	Y	Y	Y
28 Slaughter	Y	Y	N	Y
29 LaFalce	Y	Y	N	Y

	456	457	458	459
30 ***Quinn***	N	Y	Y	Y
31 ***Houghton***	N	Y	Y	Y
NORTH CAROLINA				
1 Clayton	Y	Y	Y	Y
2 Etheridge	Y	Y	Y	Y
3 ***Jones***	N	N	Y	Y
4 Price	Y	Y	N	Y
5 ***Burr***	N	Y	Y	Y
6 ***Coble***	N	Y	Y	Y
7 McIntyre	N	Y	Y	Y
8 ***Hayes***	N	Y	Y	Y
9 ***Myrick***	N	Y	Y	Y
10 ***Ballenger***	N	Y	Y	Y
11 ***Taylor***	N	Y	Y	Y
12 Watt	Y	Y	N	Y
NORTH DAKOTA				
AL Pomeroy	Y	Y	N	Y
OHIO				
1 ***Chabot***	N	Y	Y	N
2 ***Portman***	N	Y	Y	Y
3 Hall	N	Y	N	Y
4 ***Oxley***	N	Y	Y	Y
5 ***Gillmor***	N	Y	Y	Y
6 Strickland	Y	Y	N	Y
7 ***Hobson***	N	Y	Y	Y
8 ***Boehner***	N	Y	Y	Y
9 Kaptur	N	Y	N	Y
10 Kucinich	Y	Y	N	Y
11 Jones	?	?	N	Y
12 ***Kasich***	N	Y	Y	N
13 Brown	Y	Y	N	Y
14 Sawyer	Y	Y	N	Y
15 ***Pryce***	N	Y	Y	Y
16 ***Regula***	N	Y	Y	Y
17 Traficant	N	Y	Y	Y
18 ***Ney***	N	Y	Y	Y
19 ***LaTourette***	N	Y	Y	Y
OKLAHOMA				
1 ***Largent***	N	Y	Y	N
2 ***Coburn***	N	N	Y	N
3 ***Watkins***	N	Y	Y	Y
4 ***Watts***	N	Y	Y	Y
5 ***Istook***	N	Y	Y	Y
6 ***Lucas***	N	Y	Y	Y
OREGON				
1 Wu	Y	Y	N	Y
2 ***Walden***	N	Y	Y	Y
3 Blumenauer	Y	Y	N	Y
4 DeFazio	Y	Y	N	Y
5 Hooley	Y	Y	Y	Y
PENNSYLVANIA				
1 Brady	Y	Y	N	Y
2 Fattah	Y	Y	N	Y
3 Borski	N	Y	N	Y
4 Klink	Y	Y	Y	?
5 ***Peterson***	N	Y	Y	Y
6 Holden	N	Y	N	?
7 ***Weldon***	N	Y	Y	Y
8 ***Greenwood***	N	Y	?	Y
9 ***Shuster***	N	Y	Y	Y
10 ***Sherwood***	N	Y	Y	Y
11 Kanjorski	Y	Y	N	Y
12 Murtha	Y	Y	N	Y
13 Hoeffel	Y	Y	N	Y
14 Coyne	Y	Y	N	Y
15 ***Toomey***	N	Y	Y	Y
16 ***Pitts***	N	Y	Y	Y
17 ***Gekas***	N	Y	Y	Y
18 Doyle	Y	Y	N	Y
19 ***Goodling***	N	Y	Y	Y
20 Mascara	Y	Y	N	Y
21 ***English***	N	Y	Y	Y
RHODE ISLAND				
1 Kennedy	Y	Y	N	Y
2 Weygand	Y	Y	N	Y
SOUTH CAROLINA				
1 ***Sanford***	N	N	Y	N
2 ***Spence***	N	Y	Y	Y
3 ***Graham***	N	N	Y	Y
4 ***DeMint***	N	Y	Y	Y
5 Spratt	N	Y	N	Y
6 Clyburn	Y	Y	N	Y
SOUTH DAKOTA				
AL ***Thune***	N	Y	Y	Y

	456	457	458	459
TENNESSEE				
1 ***Jenkins***	N	Y	Y	Y
2 ***Duncan***	N	Y	Y	Y
3 ***Wamp***	N	Y	Y	Y
4 ***Hilleary***	N	Y	Y	Y
5 Clement	Y	Y	Y	Y
6 Gordon	N	Y	Y	Y
7 ***Bryant***	N	Y	Y	Y
8 Tanner	N	Y	Y	Y
9 Ford	Y	Y	Y	Y
TEXAS				
1 Sandlin	Y	Y	Y	Y
2 Turner	Y	Y	N	Y
3 ***Johnson, Sam***	N	Y	Y	N
4 Hall	N	Y	Y	Y
5 ***Sessions***	N	Y	Y	Y
6 ***Barton***	N	Y	Y	Y
7 ***Archer***	N	Y	Y	N
8 ***Brady***	N	Y	Y	Y
9 Lampson	Y	Y	Y	Y
10 Doggett	Y	Y	N	Y
11 Edwards	Y	Y	N	Y
12 ***Granger***	N	Y	Y	Y
13 ***Thornberry***	N	Y	Y	Y
14 ***Paul***	N	N	Y	N
15 Hinojosa	Y	Y	N	Y
16 Reyes	Y	Y	N	Y
17 Stenholm	Y	Y	N	N
18 Jackson-Lee	Y	Y	N	Y
19 ***Combest***	N	Y	Y	Y
20 Gonzalez	Y	Y	N	Y
21 ***Smith***	N	Y	Y	Y
22 ***DeLay***	N	Y	Y	N
23 ***Bonilla***	N	Y	Y	Y
24 Frost	Y	Y	N	Y
25 Bentsen	Y	Y	N	Y
26 ***Armey***	N	Y	Y	Y
27 Ortiz	Y	Y	N	Y
28 Rodriguez	Y	Y	N	Y
29 Green	Y	Y	N	Y
30 Johnson, E.B.	Y	Y	N	Y
UTAH				
1 ***Hansen***	N	Y	Y	Y
2 ***Cook***	N	Y	Y	Y
3 ***Cannon***	N	N	Y	N
VERMONT				
AL *Sanders*	Y	Y	N	Y
VIRGINIA				
1 ***Bateman***	N	N	Y	Y
2 Pickett	Y	Y	N	Y
3 Scott	Y	N	N	Y
4 Sisisky	Y	Y	Y	Y
5 *Goode*	N	Y	Y	Y
6 ***Goodlatte***	N	Y	Y	Y
7 ***Bliley***	N	Y	Y	Y
8 Moran	N	Y	N	Y
9 Boucher	Y	Y	Y	Y
10 ***Wolf***	N	Y	Y	Y
11 ***Davis***	N	Y	Y	Y
WASHINGTON				
1 Inslee	Y	Y	Y	Y
2 ***Metcalf***	N	Y	Y	Y
3 Baird	Y	Y	Y	Y
4 ***Hastings***	N	Y	Y	Y
5 ***Nethercutt***	N	Y	Y	Y
6 Dicks	Y	Y	N	Y
7 McDermott	Y	Y	N	+
8 ***Dunn***	N	Y	Y	Y
9 Smith	Y	Y	Y	Y
WEST VIRGINIA				
1 Mollohan	N	Y	Y	Y
2 Wise	N	Y	Y	Y
3 Rahall	N	Y	Y	Y
WISCONSIN				
1 ***Ryan***	N	Y	Y	Y
2 Baldwin	Y	Y	N	Y
3 Kind	Y	Y	N	Y
4 Kleczka	Y	Y	N	Y
5 Barrett	Y	Y	N	Y
6 ***Petri***	N	Y	Y	Y
7 Obey	Y	Y	N	Y
8 ***Green***	N	Y	Y	Y
9 ***Sensenbrenner***	N	Y	Y	N
WYOMING				
AL ***Cubin***	N	Y	Y	Y

Southern states - Ala., Ark., Fla., Ga., Ky., La., Miss., N.C., Okla., S.C., Tenn., Texas, Va.

460. HR 2090. International Ocean Exploration/Passage. Saxton, R-N.J., motion to suspend the rules and pass the bill that would require the Commerce Department to contract with the National Academy of Sciences to establish an advisory panel to study the feasibility and social value of a coordinated international oceanographic exploration and study program. It would authorize $1.5 million for the study. Motion agreed to 390-8: R 201-8; D 187-0 (ND 134-0, SD 53-0); I 2-0. A two-thirds majority of those present and voting (266 in this case) is required for passage under suspension of the rules. Sept. 12, 2000.

461. HR 4957. Black Revolutionary War Memorial/Passage. Hansen, R-Utah, motion to suspend the rules and pass the bill that would extend until 2005 the authority of the Black Revolutionary War Patriots Foundation to complete a memorial to the blacks who fought in that war. Motion agreed to 398-0: R 208-0; D 188-0 (ND 135-0, SD 53-0); I 2-0. A two-thirds majority of those present and voting (266 in this case) is required for passage under suspension of the rules. Sept. 12, 2000.

462. HR 3632. Golden Gate Park Expansion/Passage. Hansen, R-Utah, motion to suspend the rules and pass the bill that would expand the Golden Gate National Recreation Area by approximately 1,200 acres. Motion agreed to 333-68: R 142-67; D 190-0 (ND 137-0, SD 53-0); I 1-1. A two-thirds majority of those present and voting (268 in this case) is required for passage under suspension of the rules. Sept. 12, 2000.

463. HR 4583. Air Force Memorial/Passage. Hansen, R-Utah, motion to suspend the rules and pass the bill that would extend until Dec. 2, 2005, authorization for the Air Force Memorial Foundation to establish a memorial in the District of Columbia. Motion agreed to 398-0: R 206-0; D 190-0 (ND 137-0, SD 53-0); I 2-0. A two-thirds majority of those present and voting (266 in this case) is required for passage under suspension of the rules. Sept. 12, 2000.

464. S 1374. Wyoming Park Facility/Passage. Walden, R-Ore., motion to suspend the rules and pass the bill that would authorize the Interior Department to swap land in the Bridger-Teton National Forest in Wyoming for land and the construction of a multi-agency administrative facility by the town of Jackson, Wyo., and the Wyoming Game and Fish Commission. Motion agreed to 400-0: R 207-0; D 191-0 (ND 138-0, SD 53-0); I 2-0. A two-thirds majority of those present and voting (267 in this case) is required for passage under suspension of the rules. Sept. 12, 2000.

465. Procedural Motion/Journal. Approval of the House Journal of Sept. 12, 2000. Approved 337-51: R 184-13; D 152-38 (ND 108-30, SD 44-8); I 1-0. Sept. 13, 2000.

[1] *Rep. Herbert H. Bateman, R-Va., died on Sept. 11, 2000. The last vote for which he was eligible was 459.*

Key

- Y Voted for (yea).
- # Paired for.
- + Announced for.
- N Voted against (nay).
- X Paired against.
- – Announced against.
- P Voted "present."
- C Voted "present" to avoid possible conflict of interest.
- ? Did not vote or otherwise make a position known.

Democrats **_Republicans_** *Independents*

	460	461	462	463	464	465
ALABAMA						
1 ***Callahan***	Y	Y	Y	Y	Y	Y
2 ***Everett***	Y	Y	Y	Y	Y	Y
3 ***Riley***	Y	Y	Y	Y	Y	Y
4 ***Aderholt***	Y	Y	Y	Y	Y	N
5 Cramer	Y	Y	Y	Y	Y	Y
6 ***Bachus***	Y	Y	Y	Y	Y	Y
7 Hilliard	Y	Y	Y	Y	Y	N
ALASKA						
AL ***Young***	Y	Y	Y	Y	Y	?
ARIZONA						
1 ***Salmon***	Y	Y	Y	Y	Y	Y
2 Pastor	Y	Y	Y	Y	Y	Y
3 ***Stump***	Y	Y	N	Y	Y	Y
4 ***Shadegg***	Y	Y	N	Y	Y	Y
5 ***Kolbe***	Y	Y	Y	Y	Y	Y
6 ***Hayworth***	Y	Y	Y	Y	Y	Y
ARKANSAS						
1 Berry	Y	Y	Y	Y	Y	Y
2 Snyder	Y	Y	Y	Y	Y	Y
3 ***Hutchinson***	Y	Y	Y	Y	Y	Y
4 ***Dickey***	Y	Y	Y	Y	Y	?
CALIFORNIA						
1 Thompson	Y	Y	Y	Y	Y	N
2 ***Herger***	Y	Y	N	Y	Y	Y
3 ***Ose***	Y	Y	N	Y	Y	Y
4 ***Doolittle***	Y	Y	N	Y	Y	?
5 Matsui	Y	Y	Y	Y	Y	Y
6 Woolsey	Y	Y	Y	Y	Y	Y
7 Miller, George	Y	Y	Y	Y	Y	?
8 Pelosi	Y	Y	Y	Y	Y	Y
9 Lee	Y	Y	Y	Y	Y	Y
10 Tauscher	Y	Y	Y	Y	Y	Y
11 ***Pombo***	Y	Y	N	Y	Y	Y
12 Lantos	Y	Y	Y	Y	Y	Y
13 Stark	Y	Y	Y	Y	Y	Y
14 Eshoo	?	?	?	?	?	?
15 ***Campbell***	?	?	?	?	?	Y
16 Lofgren	+	+	+	+	+	Y
17 Farr	Y	Y	Y	Y	Y	Y
18 Condit	Y	Y	Y	Y	Y	Y
19 ***Radanovich***	Y	Y	Y	Y	Y	Y
20 Dooley	Y	Y	Y	Y	Y	Y
21 ***Thomas***	Y	Y	Y	Y	Y	Y
22 Capps	Y	Y	Y	Y	Y	Y
23 ***Gallegly***	Y	Y	Y	Y	Y	Y
24 Sherman	Y	Y	Y	Y	Y	Y
25 ***McKeon***	Y	Y	Y	Y	Y	Y
26 Berman	Y	Y	Y	Y	Y	Y
27 ***Rogan***	Y	Y	Y	Y	Y	Y
28 ***Dreier***	Y	Y	Y	Y	Y	Y
29 Waxman	Y	Y	Y	Y	Y	Y
30 Becerra	+	+	+	+	+	Y
31 ***Martinez***	Y	Y	Y	Y	Y	?
32 Dixon	Y	Y	Y	Y	Y	Y
33 Roybal-Allard	Y	Y	Y	Y	Y	Y
34 Napolitano	Y	Y	Y	Y	Y	Y
35 Waters	Y	Y	Y	Y	Y	N
36 ***Kuykendall***	Y	Y	Y	Y	Y	Y
37 Millender-McD.	Y	Y	Y	Y	Y	Y
38 ***Horn***	Y	Y	Y	Y	Y	Y
39 ***Royce***	N	Y	N	Y	Y	Y
40 ***Lewis***	Y	Y	Y	Y	Y	Y
41 ***Miller, Gary***	Y	Y	N	Y	Y	Y
42 Baca	Y	Y	Y	Y	Y	Y
43 ***Calvert***	Y	Y	Y	Y	Y	Y
44 ***Bono***	Y	Y	Y	Y	Y	Y
45 ***Rohrabacher***	Y	Y	N	Y	Y	Y
46 Sanchez	Y	Y	Y	Y	Y	Y
47 ***Cox***	Y	Y	Y	Y	Y	Y
48 ***Packard***	Y	Y	Y	Y	Y	Y
49 ***Bilbray***	Y	Y	Y	Y	Y	N
50 Filner	+	+	+	+	+	N
51 ***Cunningham***	Y	Y	Y	Y	Y	Y
52 ***Hunter***	Y	Y	Y	Y	Y	Y
COLORADO						
1 DeGette	Y	Y	Y	Y	Y	Y
2 Udall	?	?	?	Y	Y	Y
3 ***McInnis***	Y	Y	Y	Y	Y	Y
4 ***Schaffer***	?	?	?	Y	Y	?
5 ***Hefley***	Y	Y	Y	Y	Y	N
6 ***Tancredo***	Y	Y	N	Y	Y	P
CONNECTICUT						
1 Larson	Y	Y	Y	Y	Y	Y
2 Gejdenson	Y	Y	Y	Y	Y	Y
3 DeLauro	Y	Y	Y	Y	Y	Y
4 ***Shays***	Y	Y	Y	Y	Y	Y
5 Maloney	+	+	+	Y	Y	Y
6 ***Johnson***	Y	Y	Y	Y	Y	Y
DELAWARE						
AL ***Castle***	Y	Y	Y	Y	Y	Y
FLORIDA						
1 ***Scarborough***	Y	Y	Y	Y	Y	Y
2 Boyd	Y	Y	Y	Y	Y	Y
3 Brown	Y	Y	Y	Y	Y	Y
4 ***Fowler***	Y	Y	N	Y	Y	Y
5 Thurman	Y	Y	Y	Y	Y	Y
6 ***Stearns***	Y	Y	N	Y	Y	Y
7 ***Mica***	Y	Y	Y	Y	Y	Y
8 ***McCollum***	?	?	?	?	?	?
9 ***Bilirakis***	Y	Y	Y	Y	Y	Y
10 ***Young***	Y	Y	Y	Y	Y	Y
11 Davis	Y	Y	Y	Y	Y	Y
12 ***Canady***	Y	Y	Y	Y	Y	Y
13 ***Miller***	Y	Y	Y	Y	Y	Y
14 ***Goss***	Y	Y	Y	Y	Y	Y
15 ***Weldon***	Y	Y	Y	Y	?	Y
16 ***Foley***	Y	Y	Y	Y	Y	Y
17 Meek	Y	Y	Y	Y	Y	Y
18 ***Ros-Lehtinen***	Y	Y	Y	Y	Y	Y
19 Wexler	Y	Y	Y	Y	Y	Y
20 Deutsch	Y	Y	Y	Y	Y	Y
21 ***Diaz-Balart***	Y	Y	Y	Y	Y	Y
22 ***Shaw***	Y	Y	Y	Y	Y	Y
23 Hastings	Y	Y	Y	Y	Y	N
GEORGIA						
1 ***Kingston***	Y	Y	N	Y	Y	Y
2 Bishop	Y	Y	Y	Y	Y	Y
3 ***Collins***	Y	Y	Y	Y	Y	Y
4 McKinney	Y	Y	Y	Y	Y	Y
5 Lewis	Y	Y	Y	Y	Y	Y
6 ***Isakson***	Y	Y	Y	Y	Y	Y
7 ***Barr***	N	Y	N	Y	Y	Y
8 ***Chambliss***	Y	Y	Y	Y	?	?
9 ***Deal***	Y	Y	Y	Y	Y	Y
10 ***Norwood***	Y	Y	N	Y	Y	Y
11 ***Linder***	Y	Y	N	Y	Y	Y
HAWAII						
1 Abercrombie	Y	Y	Y	Y	Y	Y
2 Mink	Y	Y	Y	Y	Y	Y
IDAHO						
1 ***Chenoweth-Hage***	N	?	N	Y	Y	Y
2 ***Simpson***	Y	Y	N	Y	Y	Y
ILLINOIS						
1 Rush	Y	Y	Y	?	Y	Y
2 Jackson	Y	Y	Y	Y	Y	Y
3 Lipinski	Y	Y	Y	Y	Y	Y
4 Gutierrez	Y	Y	Y	Y	?	N
5 Blagojevich	Y	Y	Y	Y	Y	Y
6 ***Hyde***	Y	Y	Y	Y	Y	Y
7 Davis	Y	Y	Y	Y	Y	Y
8 ***Crane***	Y	Y	N	Y	Y	?
9 Schakowsky	Y	Y	Y	Y	Y	Y
10 ***Porter***	Y	Y	Y	Y	Y	Y
11 ***Weller***	Y	Y	Y	Y	Y	N
12 Costello	Y	Y	Y	Y	Y	N
13 ***Biggert***	Y	Y	Y	Y	Y	Y

ND Northern Democrats SD Southern Democrats

	460	461	462	463	464	465
14 ***Hastert***						
15 ***Ewing***	Y	Y	N	?	Y	Y
16 ***Manzullo***	Y	Y	N	Y	Y	Y
17 Evans	Y	Y	Y	Y	Y	Y
18 ***LaHood***	Y	Y	Y	Y	Y	Y
19 Phelps	Y	Y	Y	Y	Y	N
20 ***Shimkus***	Y	Y	Y	Y	Y	Y
INDIANA						
1 Visclosky	Y	Y	Y	Y	Y	N
2 ***McIntosh***	?	?	?	?	?	?
3 Roemer	Y	Y	Y	Y	Y	Y
4 ***Souder***	?	?	?	?	?	Y
5 ***Buyer***	Y	Y	Y	Y	Y	Y
6 ***Burton***	Y	Y	Y	Y	Y	Y
7 ***Pease***	Y	Y	N	Y	Y	Y
8 ***Hostettler***	N	Y	N	Y	Y	Y
9 Hill	Y	Y	Y	Y	Y	Y
10 Carson	Y	Y	Y	Y	Y	P
IOWA						
1 ***Leach***	Y	Y	Y	Y	Y	Y
2 ***Nussle***	Y	Y	N	Y	Y	Y
3 Boswell	Y	Y	Y	Y	Y	Y
4 ***Ganske***	Y	Y	Y	Y	Y	Y
5 ***Latham***	Y	Y	N	Y	Y	Y
KANSAS						
1 ***Moran***	Y	Y	N	Y	Y	N
2 ***Ryun***	Y	Y	N	Y	Y	?
3 Moore	Y	Y	Y	Y	Y	Y
4 ***Tiahrt***	Y	Y	N	Y	Y	Y
KENTUCKY						
1 ***Whitfield***	Y	Y	Y	Y	Y	Y
2 ***Lewis***	Y	Y	Y	Y	Y	Y
3 ***Northup***	Y	Y	Y	Y	Y	Y
4 Lucas	Y	Y	Y	Y	Y	Y
5 ***Rogers***	Y	Y	Y	Y	Y	Y
6 ***Fletcher***	Y	Y	Y	Y	Y	Y
LOUISIANA						
1 ***Vitter***	Y	Y	Y	Y	Y	Y
2 Jefferson	Y	Y	Y	Y	Y	Y
3 ***Tauzin***	Y	Y	Y	Y	Y	Y
4 ***McCrery***	Y	Y	Y	Y	Y	Y
5 ***Cooksey***	Y	Y	Y	Y	Y	Y
6 ***Baker***	Y	Y	Y	Y	Y	Y
7 John	Y	Y	Y	Y	Y	Y
MAINE						
1 Allen	Y	Y	Y	Y	Y	Y
2 Baldacci	Y	Y	Y	Y	Y	N
MARYLAND						
1 ***Gilchrest***	Y	Y	Y	Y	Y	?
2 ***Ehrlich***	Y	Y	N	Y	Y	Y
3 Cardin	Y	Y	Y	Y	Y	Y
4 Wynn	Y	Y	Y	?	Y	Y
5 Hoyer	Y	Y	Y	Y	Y	Y
6 ***Bartlett***	Y	Y	N	Y	Y	Y
7 Cummings	Y	Y	Y	Y	Y	N
8 ***Morella***	Y	Y	Y	Y	Y	Y
MASSACHUSETTS						
1 Olver	Y	Y	Y	Y	Y	Y
2 Neal	Y	Y	Y	Y	Y	Y
3 McGovern	Y	Y	Y	Y	Y	N
4 Frank	Y	Y	Y	Y	Y	Y
5 Meehan	Y	Y	Y	Y	Y	Y
6 Tierney	Y	Y	Y	Y	Y	N
7 Markey	Y	Y	Y	Y	Y	N
8 Capuano	Y	Y	Y	Y	Y	N
9 Moakley	Y	Y	Y	Y	Y	Y
10 Delahunt	Y	Y	Y	Y	Y	Y
MICHIGAN						
1 Stupak	Y	Y	Y	Y	Y	N
2 ***Hoekstra***	Y	Y	Y	Y	Y	Y
3 ***Ehlers***	Y	Y	Y	+	Y	Y
4 ***Camp***	Y	Y	N	Y	Y	Y
5 Barcia	Y	Y	Y	Y	Y	Y
6 ***Upton***	Y	Y	Y	Y	Y	Y
7 ***Smith***	Y	Y	N	Y	Y	Y
8 Stabenow	Y	Y	Y	Y	Y	Y
9 Kildee	Y	Y	Y	Y	Y	Y
10 Bonior	Y	Y	Y	Y	Y	Y
11 ***Knollenberg***	Y	Y	Y	Y	Y	Y
12 Levin	Y	Y	Y	Y	Y	Y
13 Rivers	Y	Y	Y	Y	Y	Y
14 Conyers	?	?	Y	Y	Y	?
15 Kilpatrick	Y	Y	Y	Y	Y	Y
16 Dingell	Y	Y	Y	Y	Y	Y

	460	461	462	463	464	465
MINNESOTA						
1 ***Gutknecht***	Y	Y	N	Y	Y	N
2 Minge	Y	Y	Y	Y	Y	Y
3 ***Ramstad***	Y	Y	Y	Y	Y	N
4 Vento	?	?	?	?	?	?
5 Sabo	Y	Y	Y	Y	Y	N
6 Luther	Y	Y	Y	Y	Y	Y
7 Peterson	Y	Y	Y	Y	Y	N
8 Oberstar	Y	Y	Y	Y	Y	N
MISSISSIPPI						
1 ***Wicker***	Y	Y	N	Y	Y	Y
2 Thompson	Y	Y	Y	Y	Y	N
3 ***Pickering***	Y	Y	Y	Y	Y	Y
4 Shows	Y	Y	Y	Y	Y	Y
5 Taylor	Y	Y	Y	Y	Y	N
MISSOURI						
1 Clay	?	?	?	?	?	N
2 ***Talent***	Y	Y	Y	Y	Y	Y
3 Gephardt	Y	Y	Y	Y	Y	Y
4 Skelton	Y	Y	Y	Y	Y	Y
5 McCarthy	Y	Y	Y	Y	Y	Y
6 Danner	Y	Y	Y	Y	Y	Y
7 ***Blunt***	Y	Y	N	Y	Y	Y
8 ***Emerson***	Y	Y	N	Y	Y	Y
9 ***Hulshof***	Y	Y	Y	Y	Y	N
MONTANA						
AL ***Hill***	Y	Y	Y	Y	Y	N
NEBRASKA						
1 ***Bereuter***	Y	Y	Y	?	Y	Y
2 ***Terry***	Y	Y	Y	Y	Y	Y
3 ***Barrett***	Y	Y	Y	Y	Y	Y
NEVADA						
1 Berkley	Y	Y	Y	Y	Y	Y
2 ***Gibbons***	Y	Y	Y	Y	Y	Y
NEW HAMPSHIRE						
1 ***Sununu***	Y	Y	N	Y	Y	?
2 ***Bass***	Y	Y	Y	Y	Y	Y
NEW JERSEY						
1 Andrews	Y	Y	Y	Y	Y	Y
2 ***LoBiondo***	Y	Y	Y	Y	Y	N
3 ***Saxton***	Y	Y	Y	Y	Y	Y
4 ***Smith***	Y	Y	Y	Y	Y	Y
5 ***Roukema***	Y	Y	Y	?	?	Y
6 Pallone	Y	Y	Y	Y	Y	N
7 ***Franks***	?	?	?	?	?	?
8 Pascrell	Y	Y	Y	Y	Y	N
9 Rothman	?	Y	Y	Y	Y	N
10 Payne	Y	Y	Y	Y	Y	Y
11 ***Frelinghuysen***	Y	Y	Y	Y	Y	Y
12 Holt	Y	Y	Y	Y	Y	Y
13 Menendez	Y	Y	Y	Y	Y	Y
NEW MEXICO						
1 ***Wilson***	Y	Y	Y	Y	Y	Y
2 ***Skeen***	Y	Y	Y	Y	Y	Y
3 Udall	Y	Y	Y	Y	Y	N
NEW YORK						
1 Forbes	Y	Y	Y	Y	Y	Y
2 ***Lazio***	?	?	?	?	?	?
3 ***King***	Y	Y	Y	Y	Y	Y
4 McCarthy	Y	Y	Y	Y	Y	Y
5 Ackerman	?	?	?	?	?	Y
6 Meeks	?	?	?	?	?	?
7 Crowley	?	?	Y	Y	Y	N
8 Nadler	Y	Y	Y	Y	Y	Y
9 Weiner	?	?	?	?	?	?
10 Towns	?	?	?	?	?	?
11 Owens	+	+	+	+	+	+
12 Velázquez	?	?	?	?	?	Y
13 ***Fossella***	Y	Y	Y	Y	Y	Y
14 Maloney	Y	Y	Y	Y	Y	Y
15 Rangel	Y	Y	Y	Y	Y	Y
16 Serrano	?	?	?	?	?	?
17 Engel	?	?	?	?	?	?
18 Lowey	Y	Y	Y	Y	Y	Y
19 ***Kelly***	Y	Y	Y	Y	Y	Y
20 ***Gilman***	Y	Y	Y	Y	Y	Y
21 McNulty	Y	Y	Y	Y	Y	N
22 ***Sweeney***	?	?	?	?	?	?
23 ***Boehlert***	?	?	?	?	?	Y
24 ***McHugh***	Y	Y	Y	Y	Y	Y
25 ***Walsh***	Y	Y	Y	Y	Y	Y
26 Hinchey	Y	Y	Y	Y	Y	?
27 ***Reynolds***	Y	Y	Y	Y	Y	Y
28 Slaughter	Y	Y	Y	Y	Y	N
29 LaFalce	Y	Y	Y	Y	Y	N

	460	461	462	463	464	465
30 ***Quinn***	Y	Y	Y	Y	Y	Y
31 ***Houghton***	Y	Y	Y	Y	Y	Y
NORTH CAROLINA						
1 Clayton	Y	Y	Y	Y	Y	Y
2 Etheridge	Y	Y	Y	Y	Y	Y
3 ***Jones***	Y	Y	Y	Y	Y	Y
4 Price	Y	Y	Y	Y	Y	?
5 ***Burr***	Y	Y	Y	Y	Y	Y
6 ***Coble***	Y	Y	N	Y	Y	Y
7 McIntyre	Y	Y	Y	Y	Y	Y
8 ***Hayes***	Y	Y	N	Y	Y	?
9 ***Myrick***	Y	Y	Y	Y	Y	Y
10 ***Ballenger***	Y	Y	Y	Y	Y	Y
11 ***Taylor***	Y	Y	N	Y	Y	Y
12 Watt	Y	Y	Y	Y	Y	Y
NORTH DAKOTA						
AL Pomeroy	Y	Y	Y	Y	Y	Y
OHIO						
1 ***Chabot***	N	Y	N	Y	Y	Y
2 ***Portman***	Y	Y	Y	Y	Y	Y
3 Hall	Y	Y	Y	Y	Y	Y
4 ***Oxley***	Y	Y	Y	Y	Y	Y
5 ***Gillmor***	Y	Y	Y	Y	Y	Y
6 Strickland	Y	Y	Y	Y	Y	Y
7 ***Hobson***	Y	Y	Y	Y	Y	Y
8 ***Boehner***	Y	Y	N	Y	Y	Y
9 Kaptur	Y	Y	Y	Y	Y	Y
10 Kucinich	Y	Y	Y	Y	Y	N
11 Jones	Y	Y	Y	Y	Y	Y
12 ***Kasich***	Y	Y	Y	Y	Y	?
13 Brown	Y	Y	Y	Y	Y	Y
14 Sawyer	Y	Y	Y	Y	Y	Y
15 ***Pryce***	Y	Y	Y	Y	Y	Y
16 ***Regula***	Y	Y	Y	Y	Y	Y
17 Traficant	Y	Y	Y	Y	Y	Y
18 ***Ney***	Y	Y	Y	Y	Y	Y
19 ***LaTourette***	Y	Y	Y	Y	Y	Y
OKLAHOMA						
1 ***Largent***	Y	Y	N	Y	Y	Y
2 ***Coburn***	Y	Y	N	Y	Y	N
3 ***Watkins***	?	?	?	?	?	Y
4 ***Watts***	Y	Y	N	Y	Y	?
5 ***Istook***	Y	Y	Y	Y	Y	Y
6 ***Lucas***	Y	Y	Y	Y	Y	Y
OREGON						
1 Wu	Y	Y	Y	Y	Y	Y
2 ***Walden***	Y	Y	Y	Y	Y	?
3 Blumenauer	Y	Y	Y	Y	Y	Y
4 DeFazio	Y	Y	Y	Y	Y	?
5 Hooley	Y	Y	Y	Y	Y	Y
PENNSYLVANIA						
1 Brady	Y	Y	Y	Y	Y	N
2 Fattah	Y	Y	Y	Y	Y	?
3 Borski	?	?	?	?	?	N
4 Klink	?	?	?	?	?	?
5 ***Peterson***	Y	Y	Y	Y	Y	Y
6 Holden	Y	Y	Y	Y	Y	Y
7 ***Weldon***	Y	Y	Y	Y	Y	Y
8 ***Greenwood***	Y	Y	Y	Y	Y	Y
9 ***Shuster***	Y	Y	Y	Y	Y	Y
10 ***Sherwood***	Y	Y	Y	Y	Y	?
11 Kanjorski	Y	Y	Y	Y	Y	Y
12 Murtha	Y	Y	Y	Y	Y	?
13 Hoeffel	Y	Y	Y	Y	Y	Y
14 Coyne	Y	Y	Y	Y	Y	Y
15 ***Toomey***	Y	Y	N	Y	Y	Y
16 ***Pitts***	Y	Y	Y	Y	Y	Y
17 ***Gekas***	Y	Y	Y	Y	Y	Y
18 Doyle	Y	Y	Y	Y	Y	?
19 ***Goodling***	Y	Y	Y	Y	Y	Y
20 Mascara	Y	Y	Y	Y	Y	Y
21 ***English***	Y	Y	Y	Y	Y	N
RHODE ISLAND						
1 Kennedy	Y	Y	Y	Y	Y	Y
2 Weygand	?	?	?	?	?	?
SOUTH CAROLINA						
1 ***Sanford***	N	Y	N	Y	Y	Y
2 ***Spence***	Y	Y	Y	Y	Y	Y
3 ***Graham***	Y	Y	N	Y	Y	Y
4 ***DeMint***	Y	Y	N	Y	Y	Y
5 Spratt	Y	Y	Y	Y	Y	Y
6 Clyburn	Y	Y	Y	Y	Y	Y
SOUTH DAKOTA						
AL ***Thune***	Y	Y	Y	Y	Y	Y

	460	461	462	463	464	465
TENNESSEE						
1 ***Jenkins***	Y	Y	N	Y	Y	Y
2 ***Duncan***	Y	Y	N	Y	Y	Y
3 ***Wamp***	Y	Y	N	Y	Y	Y
4 ***Hilleary***	Y	Y	N	Y	Y	N
5 Clement	Y	Y	Y	Y	Y	Y
6 Gordon	Y	Y	Y	Y	Y	Y
7 ***Bryant***	Y	Y	N	Y	Y	Y
8 Tanner	Y	Y	Y	Y	Y	Y
9 Ford	Y	Y	Y	Y	Y	N
TEXAS						
1 Sandlin	Y	Y	Y	Y	Y	Y
2 Turner	Y	Y	Y	Y	Y	Y
3 ***Johnson, Sam***	Y	Y	Y	Y	Y	Y
4 Hall	Y	Y	Y	Y	Y	Y
5 ***Sessions***	Y	Y	N	Y	Y	Y
6 ***Barton***	Y	Y	Y	Y	Y	Y
7 ***Archer***	Y	Y	Y	Y	Y	Y
8 ***Brady***	Y	Y	Y	Y	Y	Y
9 Lampson	Y	Y	Y	Y	Y	Y
10 Doggett	Y	Y	Y	Y	Y	Y
11 Edwards	Y	Y	Y	Y	Y	Y
12 ***Granger***	Y	Y	Y	Y	Y	Y
13 ***Thornberry***	Y	Y	N	Y	Y	Y
14 ***Paul***	N	Y	N	Y	Y	Y
15 Hinojosa	Y	Y	Y	Y	Y	Y
16 Reyes	Y	Y	Y	Y	Y	Y
17 Stenholm	Y	Y	Y	Y	Y	Y
18 Jackson-Lee	Y	Y	Y	Y	Y	N
19 ***Combest***	Y	Y	N	Y	Y	Y
20 Gonzalez	Y	Y	Y	Y	Y	Y
21 ***Smith***	Y	Y	Y	Y	Y	Y
22 ***DeLay***	Y	Y	N	Y	Y	?
23 ***Bonilla***	?	?	?	?	?	Y
24 Frost	Y	Y	Y	Y	Y	Y
25 Bentsen	Y	Y	Y	Y	Y	Y
26 ***Armey***	Y	Y	N	Y	Y	Y
27 Ortiz	Y	Y	Y	Y	Y	Y
28 Rodriguez	Y	Y	Y	Y	Y	Y
29 Green	Y	Y	Y	Y	Y	N
30 Johnson, E.B.	?	?	?	?	?	Y
UTAH						
1 ***Hansen***	Y	Y	Y	Y	Y	Y
2 ***Cook***	Y	Y	Y	Y	Y	Y
3 ***Cannon***	Y	Y	Y	Y	Y	Y
VERMONT						
AL *Sanders*	Y	Y	Y	Y	Y	?
VIRGINIA						
1 Vacant[1]						
2 Pickett	Y	Y	Y	Y	Y	N
3 Scott	Y	Y	Y	Y	Y	Y
4 Sisisky	Y	Y	Y	Y	Y	Y
5 *Goode*	Y	Y	N	Y	Y	Y
6 ***Goodlatte***	Y	Y	N	Y	Y	?
7 ***Bliley***	Y	Y	Y	Y	Y	?
8 Moran	Y	Y	Y	Y	Y	Y
9 Boucher	Y	Y	Y	Y	Y	?
10 ***Wolf***	Y	Y	Y	Y	Y	Y
11 ***Davis***	Y	Y	Y	Y	Y	Y
WASHINGTON						
1 Inslee	Y	Y	Y	Y	Y	Y
2 ***Metcalf***	Y	Y	N	Y	Y	Y
3 Baird	Y	Y	Y	Y	Y	Y
4 ***Hastings***	Y	Y	Y	Y	Y	Y
5 ***Nethercutt***	Y	Y	N	Y	Y	Y
6 Dicks	Y	Y	Y	Y	Y	Y
7 McDermott	Y	Y	Y	Y	Y	N
8 ***Dunn***	Y	Y	N	Y	Y	Y
9 Smith	Y	Y	Y	Y	Y	Y
WEST VIRGINIA						
1 Mollohan	Y	Y	Y	Y	Y	Y
2 Wise	?	?	?	?	?	Y
3 Rahall	Y	Y	Y	Y	Y	Y
WISCONSIN						
1 ***Ryan***	Y	Y	Y	Y	Y	Y
2 Baldwin	Y	Y	Y	Y	Y	Y
3 Kind	Y	Y	Y	Y	Y	Y
4 Kleczka	Y	Y	Y	Y	Y	Y
5 Barrett	Y	Y	Y	Y	Y	Y
6 ***Petri***	Y	Y	N	Y	Y	Y
7 Obey	Y	Y	Y	Y	Y	Y
8 ***Green***	Y	Y	Y	Y	Y	Y
9 ***Sensenbrenner***	N	Y	N	Y	Y	Y
WYOMING						
AL ***Cubin***	Y	Y	N	Y	Y	Y

Southern states - Ala., Ark., Fla., Ga., Ky., La., Miss., N.C., Okla., S.C., Tenn., Texas, Va.

466. HR 4810. Alleviate "Marriage Penalty" Tax/Veto Override. Passage, over President Clinton's Aug. 5, 2000, veto of the bill that would reduce taxes for married couples by approximately $89.8 billion over five years. Rejected 270-158: R 220-0; D 49-157 (ND 32-120, SD 17-37); I 1-1. Sept. 13, 2000. A two-thirds majority of those present and voting in each chamber (286 House members in this case) is required to override a veto. A "nay" was a vote in support of the president's position.

467. HR 4986. Foreign Sales Corporations/Passage. Archer, R-Texas, motion to suspend the rules and pass the bill that would repeal portions of the 1984 law (PL 98-369) that created foreign sales corporations (FSCs). The bill would exempt most income earned abroad from federal taxation if a majority of the value of the product or service was derived from U.S. components or labor. Motion agreed to 315-109: R 200-17; D 114-91 (ND 77-74, SD 37-17); I 1-1. A two-thirds majority of those present and voting (283 in this case) is required for passage under suspension of the rules. Sept. 13, 2000. A "yea" was a vote in support of the president's position.

468. HR 4892. Boy Scouts Charter/Passage. Hutchinson, R-Ark., motion to suspend the rules and pass the bill that would repeal the Boy Scouts of America federal charter. Motion rejected 12-362: R 1-216; D 11-144 (ND 7-98, SD 4-46); I 0-2. A two-thirds majority of those present and voting (250 in this case) is required for passage under suspension of the rules. Sept. 13, 2000.

469. H Con Res 327. Merchant Marine/Adoption. Kuykendall, R-Calif., motion to suspend the rules and adopt the concurrent resolution honoring the U.S. merchant marine for its contributions and sacrifices during times of war. Motion agreed to 418-0: R 213-0; D 203-0 (ND 149-0, SD 54-0); I 2-0. A two-thirds majority of those present and voting (279 in this case) is required for adoption under suspension of the rules. Sept. 13, 2000.

470. HR 4205. Fiscal 2001 Defense Authorization/Motion to Instruct. Graham, R-S.C., motion to instruct conferees to not agree to provisions which: fail to recognize that the 14th amendment to the Constitution guarantees all persons equal protection under the law; deny equal protection under the law by conditioning prosecution of certain offenses on the race, color, religion, national origin, gender, sexual orientation, or disability of the victim; and preclude a person convicted of murder from being sentenced to death. Motion rejected 196-227: R 176-39; D 19-187 (ND 8-144, SD 11-43); I 1-1. Sept. 13, 2000.

471. HR 4205. Fiscal 2001 Defense Authorization/Motion to Instruct. Conyers, D-Mich., motion to instruct conferees to agree to the provisions contained in title XV of the Senate amendment which deals with federal hate crime law. Motion agreed to 232-192: R 41-174; D 190-17 (ND 147-6, SD 43-11); I 1-1. Sept. 13, 2000. A "yea" was a vote in support of the president's position.

Key

- Y Voted for (yea).
- # Paired for.
- \+ Announced for.
- N Voted against (nay).
- X Paired against.
- – Announced against.
- P Voted "present."
- C Voted "present" to avoid possible conflict of interest.
- ? Did not vote or otherwise make a position known.

Democrats • ***Republicans***
Independents

	466	467	468	469	470	471
ALABAMA						
1 ***Callahan***	Y	Y	N	Y	Y	N
2 ***Everett***	Y	Y	N	Y	Y	N
3 ***Riley***	Y	Y	N	Y	Y	N
4 ***Aderholt***	Y	Y	N	Y	Y	N
5 Cramer	Y	Y	N	Y	Y	N
6 ***Bachus***	Y	Y	N	Y	Y	N
7 Hilliard	N	Y	P	Y	N	Y
ALASKA						
AL ***Young***	Y	Y	N	Y	Y	N
ARIZONA						
1 ***Salmon***	Y	Y	N	Y	Y	N
2 Pastor	N	Y	P	Y	N	Y
3 ***Stump***	Y	Y	N	Y	Y	N
4 ***Shadegg***	Y	Y	N	Y	Y	N
5 ***Kolbe***	Y	Y	N	Y	N	Y
6 ***Hayworth***	Y	Y	N	Y	Y	N
ARKANSAS						
1 Berry	N	N	N	Y	Y	N
2 Snyder	N	Y	N	Y	N	Y
3 ***Hutchinson***	Y	Y	N	?	Y	N
4 ***Dickey***	Y	Y	N	Y	Y	N
CALIFORNIA						
1 Thompson	N	Y	P	Y	N	Y
2 ***Herger***	Y	Y	N	Y	Y	N
3 ***Ose***	Y	Y	N	Y	Y	N
4 ***Doolittle***	Y	Y	N	?	Y	N
5 Matsui	N	Y	P	Y	N	Y
6 Woolsey	N	N	Y	Y	N	Y
7 Miller, George	N	N	P	Y	N	Y
8 Pelosi	N	Y	P	Y	N	Y
9 Lee	N	N	Y	Y	N	Y
10 Tauscher	Y	Y	N	Y	N	Y
11 ***Pombo***	Y	Y	N	Y	Y	N
12 Lantos	N	N	P	Y	N	Y
13 Stark	N	N	Y	Y	N	Y
14 Eshoo	?	?	?	?	?	?
15 ***Campbell***	Y	Y	N	Y	Y	–
16 Lofgren	N	Y	P	Y	N	Y
17 Farr	N	N	P	Y	N	Y
18 Condit	Y	Y	N	Y	N	Y
19 ***Radanovich***	Y	Y	N	Y	Y	N
20 Dooley	N	Y	N	Y	N	Y
21 ***Thomas***	Y	Y	N	Y	Y	N
22 Capps	Y	Y	N	Y	N	Y
23 ***Gallegly***	Y	Y	N	Y	N	Y
24 Sherman	N	Y	P	Y	N	Y
25 ***McKeon***	Y	Y	N	Y	Y	N
26 Berman	N	Y	N	Y	N	Y
27 ***Rogan***	Y	Y	N	Y	Y	N
28 ***Dreier***	Y	Y	N	Y	Y	N
29 Waxman	N	N	P	Y	N	Y
30 Becerra	N	Y	P	Y	N	Y
31 ***Martinez***	Y	Y	N	Y	Y	N
32 Dixon	N	Y	P	Y	N	Y
33 Roybal-Allard	N	N	Y	Y	N	Y
34 Napolitano	N	Y	N	Y	N	Y
35 Waters	N	N	P	?	N	Y
36 ***Kuykendall***	Y	Y	N	Y	N	Y
37 Millender-McD.	N	Y	N	Y	N	Y
38 ***Horn***	Y	Y	N	Y	Y	Y
39 ***Royce***	Y	Y	N	Y	Y	N
40 ***Lewis***	Y	Y	N	Y	Y	N
41 ***Miller, Gary***	Y	Y	N	Y	Y	N
42 Baca	N	Y	N	Y	N	Y
43 ***Calvert***	Y	Y	N	Y	Y	N
44 ***Bono***	Y	Y	N	Y	N	Y
45 ***Rohrabacher***	Y	Y	N	Y	Y	N
46 Sanchez	N	Y	P	Y	N	Y
47 ***Cox***	Y	Y	N	Y	Y	N
48 ***Packard***	Y	Y	N	Y	Y	N
49 ***Bilbray***	Y	N	N	?	N	Y
50 Filner	N	N	N	Y	N	Y
51 ***Cunningham***	Y	Y	N	Y	Y	N
52 ***Hunter***	Y	N	N	Y	Y	N
COLORADO						
1 DeGette	N	N	P	Y	N	Y
2 Udall	N	N	N	Y	N	Y
3 ***McInnis***	Y	Y	N	Y	Y	N
4 ***Schaffer***	Y	Y	N	Y	Y	N
5 ***Hefley***	Y	Y	N	Y	Y	N
6 ***Tancredo***	Y	Y	N	Y	Y	N
CONNECTICUT						
1 Larson	N	Y	N	Y	N	Y
2 Gejdenson	N	Y	N	Y	N	Y
3 DeLauro	N	Y	N	Y	N	Y
4 ***Shays***	Y	Y	N	Y	N	Y
5 Maloney	Y	N	N	Y	N	Y
6 ***Johnson***	Y	Y	N	Y	N	Y
DELAWARE						
AL ***Castle***	Y	N	N	Y	N	Y
FLORIDA						
1 ***Scarborough***	Y	Y	N	Y	Y	N
2 Boyd	N	Y	N	Y	Y	N
3 Brown	N	N	N	Y	N	Y
4 ***Fowler***	Y	Y	N	Y	Y	N
5 Thurman	N	N	N	Y	N	Y
6 ***Stearns***	Y	Y	N	Y	Y	N
7 ***Mica***	Y	Y	N	Y	Y	N
8 ***McCollum***	Y	Y	N	Y	N	Y
9 ***Bilirakis***	Y	Y	N	Y	Y	N
10 ***Young***	Y	Y	N	Y	Y	N
11 Davis	N	Y	N	Y	N	Y
12 ***Canady***	Y	Y	N	Y	Y	N
13 ***Miller***	Y	Y	N	Y	Y	N
14 ***Goss***	Y	Y	N	Y	Y	N
15 ***Weldon***	Y	Y	N	Y	Y	N
16 ***Foley***	Y	Y	N	Y	N	Y
17 Meek	N	N	N	Y	N	Y
18 ***Ros-Lehtinen***	Y	Y	N	Y	N	Y
19 Wexler	N	N	Y	Y	N	Y
20 Deutsch	Y	N	Y	Y	N	Y
21 ***Diaz-Balart***	Y	Y	N	Y	N	Y
22 ***Shaw***	Y	Y	N	Y	N	Y
23 Hastings	N	N	Y	Y	N	Y
GEORGIA						
1 ***Kingston***	Y	Y	N	Y	Y	N
2 Bishop	Y	Y	N	Y	N	Y
3 ***Collins***	Y	Y	N	Y	Y	N
4 McKinney	Y	N	Y	Y	N	Y
5 Lewis	N	N	N	Y	N	Y
6 ***Isakson***	Y	Y	N	Y	Y	N
7 ***Barr***	Y	Y	N	Y	Y	N
8 ***Chambliss***	Y	Y	N	Y	Y	N
9 ***Deal***	Y	Y	N	Y	Y	N
10 ***Norwood***	Y	Y	N	Y	Y	N
11 ***Linder***	Y	Y	N	Y	Y	N
HAWAII						
1 Abercrombie	N	N	N	Y	N	Y
2 Mink	Y	N	N	Y	N	Y
IDAHO						
1 ***Chenoweth-Hage***	Y	N	N	Y	Y	N
2 ***Simpson***	Y	Y	N	Y	Y	N
ILLINOIS						
1 Rush	N	N	P	?	N	Y
2 Jackson	N	N	P	Y	N	Y
3 Lipinski	Y	N	N	Y	Y	N
4 Gutierrez	N	N	P	Y	N	Y
5 Blagojevich	N	N	N	Y	N	Y
6 ***Hyde***	Y	Y	N	Y	Y	N
7 Davis	N	N	Y	Y	N	Y
8 ***Crane***	Y	Y	N	Y	Y	N
9 Schakowsky	N	N	P	Y	N	Y
10 ***Porter***	Y	Y	N	Y	N	Y
11 ***Weller***	Y	Y	N	Y	Y	Y
12 Costello	Y	N	N	Y	Y	Y
13 ***Biggert***	Y	Y	N	Y	N	Y

ND Northern Democrats SD Southern Democrats

	466	467	468	469	470	471
14 ***Hastert***	Y					
15 ***Ewing***	Y	Y	N	Y	Y	N
16 ***Manzullo***	Y	Y	N	Y	Y	N
17 Evans	N	N	N	Y	N	Y
18 ***LaHood***	Y	Y	N	Y	Y	Y
19 Phelps	Y	N	N	Y	Y	N
20 ***Shimkus***	Y	Y	N	Y	Y	Y
INDIANA						
1 Visclosky	N	N	N	Y	N	Y
2 ***McIntosh***	Y	Y	N	Y	?	N
3 Roemer	Y	N	N	Y	N	Y
4 ***Souder***	Y	Y	N	Y	Y	N
5 ***Buyer***	Y	Y	N	Y	Y	N
6 ***Burton***	Y	N	N	Y	Y	N
7 ***Pease***	Y	Y	N	Y	Y	N
8 ***Hostettler***	Y	N	N	Y	Y	N
9 Hill	N	Y	N	Y	N	Y
10 Carson	N	Y	P	Y	N	Y
IOWA						
1 ***Leach***	Y	Y	N	Y	N	Y
2 ***Nussle***	Y	Y	N	Y	Y	N
3 Boswell	Y	Y	N	Y	N	Y
4 ***Ganske***	Y	N	N	Y	Y	N
5 ***Latham***	Y	Y	N	Y	Y	N
KANSAS						
1 ***Moran***	Y	Y	N	Y	Y	N
2 ***Ryun***	Y	Y	N	Y	Y	N
3 Moore	Y	Y	N	Y	N	Y
4 ***Tiahrt***	Y	Y	N	Y	Y	N
KENTUCKY						
1 ***Whitfield***	Y	Y	N	Y	Y	N
2 ***Lewis***	Y	Y	N	Y	Y	N
3 ***Northup***	Y	Y	N	Y	Y	N
4 Lucas	Y	Y	N	Y	Y	N
5 ***Rogers***	Y	Y	N	Y	Y	N
6 ***Fletcher***	Y	Y	N	Y	Y	N
LOUISIANA						
1 ***Vitter***	Y	Y	N	Y	Y	N
2 Jefferson	N	Y	N	Y	N	Y
3 ***Tauzin***	Y	Y	N	Y	Y	N
4 ***McCrery***	Y	Y	N	Y	Y	Y
5 ***Cooksey***	Y	Y	N	Y	Y	N
6 ***Baker***	Y	Y	N	Y	Y	N
7 John	Y	Y	N	Y	Y	N
MAINE						
1 Allen	N	N	N	Y	N	Y
2 Baldacci	N	N	N	Y	N	Y
MARYLAND						
1 ***Gilchrest***	?	?	?	?	?	?
2 ***Ehrlich***	Y	Y	N	Y	Y	N
3 Cardin	N	Y	N	Y	N	Y
4 Wynn	N	Y	N	Y	N	Y
5 Hoyer	N	Y	N	Y	N	Y
6 ***Bartlett***	Y	Y	N	Y	N	N
7 Cummings	N	N	N	Y	N	Y
8 ***Morella***	Y	Y	P	Y	N	Y
MASSACHUSETTS						
1 Olver	N	N	P	Y	N	Y
2 Neal	N	Y	P	?	N	Y
3 McGovern	N	N	P	Y	N	Y
4 Frank	N	N	P	Y	N	Y
5 Meehan	N	N	P	Y	N	Y
6 Tierney	N	N	P	Y	N	Y
7 Markey	N	N	P	Y	N	Y
8 Capuano	N	N	P	Y	N	Y
9 Moakley	N	N	P	Y	N	Y
10 Delahunt	N	N	P	Y	N	Y
MICHIGAN						
1 Stupak	Y	Y	N	Y	N	Y
2 ***Hoekstra***	Y	Y	N	Y	Y	N
3 ***Ehlers***	Y	N	N	Y	N	N
4 ***Camp***	Y	Y	N	Y	Y	N
5 Barcia	Y	N	N	Y	Y	N
6 ***Upton***	Y	Y	N	Y	N	Y
7 ***Smith***	Y	Y	N	?	Y	N
8 Stabenow	Y	Y	N	Y	N	Y
9 Kildee	N	N	N	Y	N	Y
10 Bonior	N	N	N	Y	N	Y
11 ***Knollenberg***	Y	Y	N	Y	Y	N
12 Levin	N	Y	N	Y	N	Y
13 Rivers	N	N	P	Y	N	Y
14 Conyers	N	N	P	Y	N	Y
15 Kilpatrick	N	Y	N	Y	N	Y
16 Dingell	N	Y	N	Y	N	Y
MINNESOTA						
1 ***Gutknecht***	Y	Y	N	Y	Y	N
2 Minge	N	Y	N	Y	N	Y
3 ***Ramstad***	Y	Y	N	Y	Y	N
4 Vento	?	?	?	?	?	?
5 Sabo	N	Y	P	Y	N	Y
6 Luther	N	N	N	Y	N	Y
7 Peterson	N	N	N	Y	Y	N
8 Oberstar	N	N	N	Y	N	Y
MISSISSIPPI						
1 ***Wicker***	Y	Y	N	Y	Y	N
2 Thompson	N	Y	N	Y	N	Y
3 ***Pickering***	Y	Y	N	Y	Y	N
4 Shows	Y	N	N	Y	Y	N
5 Taylor	N	N	N	Y	Y	N
MISSOURI						
1 Clay	N	Y	P	Y	N	Y
2 ***Talent***	Y	Y	N	Y	Y	N
3 Gephardt	N	Y	N	Y	N	Y
4 Skelton	Y	Y	N	Y	Y	Y
5 McCarthy	N	N	N	Y	N	Y
6 Danner	Y	Y	N	Y	N	Y
7 ***Blunt***	Y	Y	N	Y	Y	N
8 ***Emerson***	Y	N	N	Y	Y	N
9 ***Hulshof***	Y	Y	N	Y	Y	N
MONTANA						
AL ***Hill***	Y	Y	N	Y	Y	N
NEBRASKA						
1 ***Bereuter***	Y	Y	N	Y	Y	N
2 ***Terry***	Y	Y	N	Y	Y	N
3 ***Barrett***	Y	Y	N	Y	Y	N
NEVADA						
1 Berkley	Y	Y	N	Y	N	Y
2 ***Gibbons***	Y	Y	N	Y	Y	Y
NEW HAMPSHIRE						
1 ***Sununu***	Y	Y	N	Y	Y	N
2 ***Bass***	Y	Y	N	Y	N	Y
NEW JERSEY						
1 Andrews	N	N	N	Y	N	Y
2 ***LoBiondo***	Y	N	N	Y	N	Y
3 ***Saxton***	Y	N	N	Y	N	Y
4 ***Smith***	Y	Y	N	Y	N	Y
5 ***Roukema***	Y	Y	N	Y	Y	Y
6 Pallone	N	N	N	Y	N	Y
7 ***Franks***	Y	Y	N	Y	N	?
8 Pascrell	Y	N	N	Y	N	Y
9 Rothman	N	N	N	Y	N	Y
10 Payne	N	N	N	Y	N	Y
11 ***Frelinghuysen***	Y	Y	N	Y	N	Y
12 Holt	Y	N	N	Y	N	Y
13 Menendez	N	N	N	Y	N	Y
NEW MEXICO						
1 ***Wilson***	Y	Y	N	Y	Y	N
2 ***Skeen***	Y	Y	N	Y	Y	N
3 Udall	N	N	N	Y	N	Y
NEW YORK						
1 Forbes	Y	Y	N	Y	N	Y
2 ***Lazio***	Y	?	?	?	?	?
3 ***King***	Y	Y	N	Y	Y	N
4 McCarthy	Y	Y	N	Y	N	Y
5 Ackerman	N	Y	Y	Y	N	Y
6 Meeks	N	Y	P	Y	N	Y
7 Crowley	N	Y	N	Y	N	Y
8 Nadler	N	N	P	Y	N	Y
9 Weiner	N	Y	P	Y	N	Y
10 Towns	N	Y	N	Y	N	Y
11 Owens	–	–	?	+	–	Y
12 Velázquez	N	N	P	Y	N	Y
13 ***Fossella***	Y	Y	N	Y	Y	N
14 Maloney	N	N	P	Y	N	Y
15 Rangel	N	Y	P	Y	N	Y
16 Serrano	N	N	P	Y	N	Y
17 Engel	?	?	?	?	?	?
18 Lowey	N	Y	P	Y	N	Y
19 ***Kelly***	Y	Y	N	Y	N	Y
20 ***Gilman***	Y	N	N	Y	N	Y
21 McNulty	N	Y	N	Y	N	Y
22 ***Sweeney***	Y	Y	N	Y	Y	N
23 ***Boehlert***	Y	Y	N	Y	N	Y
24 ***McHugh***	Y	Y	N	Y	Y	N
25 ***Walsh***	Y	Y	N	Y	N	Y
26 Hinchey	N	N	N	Y	N	Y
27 ***Reynolds***	Y	Y	N	Y	?	?
28 Slaughter	N	N	N	Y	N	Y
29 LaFalce	N	Y	N	Y	N	Y
30 ***Quinn***	Y	Y	N	Y	N	Y
31 ***Houghton***	Y	Y	N	Y	N	Y
NORTH CAROLINA						
1 Clayton	N	Y	N	Y	N	Y
2 Etheridge	Y	Y	N	Y	N	Y
3 ***Jones***	Y	Y	N	Y	Y	N
4 Price	N	Y	N	Y	N	Y
5 ***Burr***	Y	Y	N	Y	Y	N
6 ***Coble***	Y	Y	N	Y	Y	N
7 McIntyre	Y	Y	N	Y	Y	N
8 ***Hayes***	Y	Y	N	Y	Y	N
9 ***Myrick***	Y	Y	N	Y	Y	N
10 ***Ballenger***	Y	Y	N	Y	Y	N
11 ***Taylor***	Y	Y	N	Y	Y	N
12 Watt	N	N	N	Y	N	Y
NORTH DAKOTA						
AL Pomeroy	N	Y	N	Y	N	Y
OHIO						
1 ***Chabot***	Y	N	N	Y	Y	N
2 ***Portman***	Y	Y	N	Y	Y	N
3 Hall	N	Y	?	Y	N	Y
4 ***Oxley***	Y	Y	N	Y	Y	N
5 ***Gillmor***	Y	Y	N	Y	Y	Y
6 Strickland	N	N	N	Y	N	Y
7 ***Hobson***	Y	Y	N	Y	N	N
8 ***Boehner***	Y	Y	N	Y	Y	N
9 Kaptur	N	N	N	Y	N	Y
10 Kucinich	N	N	N	Y	N	Y
11 Jones	N	Y	N	Y	N	Y
12 ***Kasich***	Y	Y	N	Y	Y	N
13 Brown	N	N	N	Y	N	Y
14 Sawyer	N	Y	N	Y	N	Y
15 ***Pryce***	Y	Y	N	Y	N	N
16 ***Regula***	Y	Y	N	Y	N	Y
17 Traficant	Y	N	N	Y	Y	N
18 ***Ney***	Y	Y	N	Y	Y	N
19 ***LaTourette***	Y	Y	N	Y	N	Y
OKLAHOMA						
1 ***Largent***	Y	Y	N	Y	Y	N
2 ***Coburn***	Y	Y	N	?	Y	N
3 ***Watkins***	Y	Y	N	Y	Y	N
4 ***Watts***	Y	Y	N	Y	Y	N
5 ***Istook***	Y	Y	N	Y	Y	N
6 ***Lucas***	Y	Y	N	Y	Y	N
OREGON						
1 Wu	Y	Y	P	Y	N	Y
2 ***Walden***	Y	Y	N	Y	Y	N
3 Blumenauer	N	Y	N	Y	N	Y
4 DeFazio	N	N	N	Y	N	Y
5 Hooley	Y	N	N	Y	N	Y
PENNSYLVANIA						
1 Brady	N	Y	N	Y	N	Y
2 Fattah	N	Y	N	Y	N	Y
3 Borski	N	Y	N	Y	N	Y
4 Klink	N	N	N	Y	N	?
5 ***Peterson***	Y	Y	N	Y	Y	N
6 Holden	Y	Y	N	Y	N	Y
7 ***Weldon***	Y	Y	N	Y	N	N
8 ***Greenwood***	Y	Y	Y	Y	N	Y
9 ***Shuster***	Y	Y	N	Y	Y	N
10 ***Sherwood***	Y	Y	N	Y	N	N
11 Kanjorski	N	Y	N	Y	N	Y
12 Murtha	N	Y	N	Y	N	Y
13 Hoeffel	N	Y	N	Y	N	Y
14 Coyne	N	Y	N	Y	N	Y
15 ***Toomey***	Y	Y	N	Y	Y	N
16 ***Pitts***	Y	Y	N	Y	Y	N
17 ***Gekas***	Y	Y	N	Y	Y	N
18 Doyle	Y	Y	N	Y	N	Y
19 ***Goodling***	Y	Y	N	Y	Y	N
20 Mascara	Y	Y	N	Y	N	Y
21 ***English***	Y	Y	N	Y	Y	Y
RHODE ISLAND						
1 Kennedy	N	Y	Y	Y	N	Y
2 Weygand	?	?	?	?	?	Y
SOUTH CAROLINA						
1 ***Sanford***	Y	Y	N	Y	Y	N
2 ***Spence***	Y	Y	N	Y	Y	N
3 ***Graham***	Y	Y	N	Y	Y	N
4 ***DeMint***	Y	Y	N	Y	Y	N
5 Spratt	Y	Y	N	Y	N	Y
6 Clyburn	N	Y	N	Y	N	Y
SOUTH DAKOTA						
AL ***Thune***	Y	Y	N	Y	Y	N
TENNESSEE						
1 ***Jenkins***	Y	Y	N	Y	Y	N
2 ***Duncan***	Y	N	N	Y	Y	N
3 ***Wamp***	Y	Y	N	Y	Y	N
4 ***Hilleary***	Y	Y	N	Y	Y	N
5 Clement	Y	Y	N	Y	N	Y
6 Gordon	Y	Y	N	Y	N	Y
7 ***Bryant***	Y	Y	N	Y	Y	N
8 Tanner	N	Y	N	Y	Y	N
9 Ford	N	N	N	Y	N	Y
TEXAS						
1 Sandlin	Y	Y	N	Y	N	Y
2 Turner	N	Y	N	Y	N	Y
3 ***Johnson, Sam***	Y	Y	N	Y	?	N
4 Hall	Y	Y	N	Y	Y	N
5 ***Sessions***	Y	Y	N	Y	Y	N
6 ***Barton***	Y	Y	N	Y	Y	N
7 ***Archer***	Y	Y	N	Y	Y	N
8 ***Brady***	Y	Y	N	Y	Y	N
9 Lampson	N	Y	N	Y	N	Y
10 Doggett	N	N	N	Y	N	Y
11 Edwards	N	N	N	Y	N	Y
12 ***Granger***	Y	Y	N	Y	Y	N
13 ***Thornberry***	Y	Y	N	Y	Y	N
14 ***Paul***	Y	P	N	Y	Y	N
15 Hinojosa	N	Y	N	Y	N	Y
16 Reyes	N	Y	N	Y	N	Y
17 Stenholm	N	Y	N	Y	Y	N
18 Jackson-Lee	N	N	P	Y	N	Y
19 ***Combest***	Y	Y	N	Y	Y	N
20 Gonzalez	N	Y	N	Y	N	Y
21 ***Smith***	Y	Y	N	Y	Y	N
22 ***DeLay***	Y	Y	N	Y	Y	N
23 ***Bonilla***	Y	Y	N	Y	Y	N
24 Frost	N	Y	N	Y	N	Y
25 Bentsen	N	Y	N	Y	N	Y
26 ***Armey***	Y	Y	N	Y	Y	N
27 Ortiz	N	Y	N	Y	N	Y
28 Rodriguez	N	Y	N	Y	N	Y
29 Green	N	N	N	Y	N	Y
30 Johnson, E.B.	N	Y	P	Y	N	Y
UTAH						
1 ***Hansen***	Y	N	N	Y	Y	N
2 ***Cook***	Y	N	N	Y	Y	N
3 ***Cannon***	Y	N	N	Y	Y	N
VERMONT						
AL *Sanders*	N	N	N	Y	N	Y
VIRGINIA						
1 Vacant						
2 Pickett	Y	Y	N	Y	N	Y
3 Scott	N	Y	N	Y	N	Y
4 Sisisky	Y	Y	N	Y	N	Y
5 *Goode*	Y	Y	N	Y	Y	N
6 ***Goodlatte***	Y	Y	N	Y	Y	N
7 ***Bliley***	Y	Y	N	Y	Y	N
8 Moran	N	Y	P	Y	N	Y
9 Boucher	Y	Y	N	Y	N	Y
10 ***Wolf***	Y	Y	N	Y	Y	N
11 ***Davis***	Y	Y	N	Y	Y	N
WASHINGTON						
1 Inslee	Y	Y	N	Y	N	Y
2 ***Metcalf***	Y	Y	N	Y	Y	N
3 Baird	Y	Y	N	Y	N	Y
4 ***Hastings***	Y	Y	N	Y	Y	N
5 ***Nethercutt***	Y	Y	N	Y	Y	N
6 Dicks	N	Y	N	Y	N	Y
7 McDermott	N	Y	P	Y	N	Y
8 ***Dunn***	Y	Y	N	Y	Y	N
9 Smith	Y	Y	N	Y	N	Y
WEST VIRGINIA						
1 Mollohan	N	Y	N	Y	N	Y
2 Wise	Y	?	N	Y	N	Y
3 Rahall	N	N	N	Y	N	Y
WISCONSIN						
1 ***Ryan***	Y	Y	N	Y	Y	N
2 Baldwin	N	N	P	Y	N	Y
3 Kind	N	Y	N	Y	N	Y
4 Kleczka	N	Y	N	Y	N	Y
5 Barrett	N	N	P	Y	N	Y
6 ***Petri***	Y	Y	N	Y	Y	N
7 Obey	N	N	N	Y	N	Y
8 ***Green***	Y	Y	N	Y	Y	N
9 ***Sensenbrenner***	Y	Y	N	Y	Y	N
WYOMING						
AL ***Cubin***	Y	Y	N	Y	Y	N

Southern states - Ala., Ark., Fla., Ga., Ky., La., Miss., N.C., Okla., S.C., Tenn., Texas, Va.

472. HR 4942. Fiscal 2001 District of Columbia Appropriations/Tobacco Ban. Bilbray, R-Calif., amendment that would prohibit minors in the District of Columbia from possessing tobacco products unless delivery of such products is part of their job. Adopted 265-155: R 204-13; D 60-141 (ND 37-111, SD 23-30); I 1-1. Sept. 14, 2000.

473. HR 4942. Fiscal 2001 District of Columbia Appropriations/Needle Exchange. Souder, R-Ind., amendment that would expand the bill's restriction on funding needle exchange programs to apply to both federal and local funds. Adopted 239-181: R 196-20; D 42-160 (ND 25-123, SD 17-37); I 1-1. Sept. 14, 2000. A "nay" was a vote in support of the president's position.

474. HR 4942. Fiscal 2001 District of Columbia Appropriations/Passage. Passage of the bill that would appropriate $414 million for the District of Columbia in fiscal 2001. Passed 217-207: R 213-5; D 3-201 (ND 1-149, SD 2-52); I 1-1. Sept. 14, 2000.

475. HR 1654. Fiscal 2001 NASA Authorization/Conference Report. Adoption of the conference report that would authorize $14.2 billion for fiscal 2001 and $14.6 billion for 2002 for the National Aeronautics and Space Administration. The measure would cap spending for the international space station at $25 billion and shuttle missions for space station assembly at $17.7 billion. Adopted (thus sent to the Senate) 399-17: R 205-8; D 193-8 (ND 140-8, SD 53-0); I 1-1. Sept. 14, 2000.

476. HR 4516. Fiscal 2001 Legislative Branch/Treasury, Postal Service Appropriations/Conference Report. Adoption of the conference report to appropriate $2.5 billion in fiscal 2001 for the legislative branch; appropriate $30.4 billion in fiscal 2001 for the Treasury Department, Postal Service, executive office of the president and certain independent agencies; and repeal the 3 percent federal excise tax on telecommunications services by the end of 2002. Adopted (thus sent to the Senate) 212-209: R 197-20; D 15-187 (ND 14-134, SD 1-53); I 0-2. Sept. 14, 2000.

Key

- Y Voted for (yea).
- # Paired for.
- \+ Announced for.
- N Voted against (nay).
- X Paired against.
- – Announced against.
- P Voted "present."
- C Voted "present" to avoid possible conflict of interest.
- ? Did not vote or otherwise make a position known.

•

Democrats ***Republicans***
Independents

	472	473	474	475	476
ALABAMA					
1 ***Callahan***	Y	Y	Y	Y	Y
2 ***Everett***	Y	Y	Y	Y	Y
3 ***Riley***	Y	Y	Y	Y	Y
4 ***Aderholt***	Y	Y	Y	Y	N
5 Cramer	Y	Y	N	Y	N
6 ***Bachus***	Y	Y	Y	Y	Y
7 Hilliard	N	N	N	Y	N
ALASKA					
AL ***Young***	N	Y	Y	Y	Y
ARIZONA					
1 ***Salmon***	Y	Y	Y	Y	Y
2 Pastor	Y	N	N	Y	N
3 ***Stump***	Y	Y	Y	Y	Y
4 ***Shadegg***	Y	Y	Y	Y	Y
5 ***Kolbe***	Y	N	Y	Y	Y
6 ***Hayworth***	Y	Y	Y	Y	Y
ARKANSAS					
1 Berry	N	N	N	Y	N
2 Snyder	N	N	N	Y	N
3 ***Hutchinson***	N	Y	Y	Y	Y
4 ***Dickey***	Y	Y	Y	Y	Y
CALIFORNIA					
1 Thompson	N	N	N	Y	N
2 ***Herger***	Y	Y	Y	Y	Y
3 ***Ose***	Y	Y	Y	Y	Y
4 ***Doolittle***	Y	Y	Y	Y	Y
5 Matsui	N	N	N	Y	N
6 Woolsey	N	N	N	Y	N
7 Miller, George	N	N	N	N	N
8 Pelosi	N	N	N	Y	N
9 Lee	N	N	N	N	N
10 Tauscher	N	N	N	Y	N
11 ***Pombo***	Y	Y	Y	Y	Y
12 Lantos	N	N	N	Y	N
13 Stark	N	N	N	N	N
14 Eshoo	?	?	?	?	?
15 ***Campbell***	?	?	?	?	?
16 Lofgren	Y	N	N	Y	N
17 Farr	N	N	N	Y	N
18 Condit	N	N	N	Y	N
19 ***Radanovich***	Y	Y	Y	Y	Y
20 Dooley	N	N	N	Y	N
21 ***Thomas***	Y	N	Y	Y	Y
22 Capps	Y	N	N	Y	N
23 ***Gallegly***	Y	Y	Y	Y	Y
24 Sherman	N	N	N	Y	N
25 ***McKeon***	Y	Y	Y	Y	Y
26 Berman	N	N	N	Y	N
27 ***Rogan***	Y	Y	Y	Y	N
28 ***Dreier***	Y	Y	Y	Y	Y
29 Waxman	N	N	N	Y	N
30 Becerra	?	?	?	?	?
31 ***Martinez***	Y	Y	Y	?	Y
32 Dixon	N	N	N	Y	N
33 Roybal-Allard	N	N	N	Y	N
34 Napolitano	N	N	N	Y	N
35 Waters	?	?	N	Y	N
36 ***Kuykendall***	Y	Y	Y	Y	Y
37 Millender-McD.	N	N	N	Y	N
38 ***Horn***	Y	N	Y	Y	Y
39 ***Royce***	Y	Y	Y	Y	Y
40 ***Lewis***	Y	Y	Y	Y	Y
41 ***Miller, Gary***	Y	Y	Y	Y	Y
42 Baca	Y	Y	N	Y	N
43 ***Calvert***	Y	Y	Y	Y	Y
44 ***Bono***	Y	Y	Y	Y	Y
45 ***Rohrabacher***	N	Y	Y	Y	Y
46 Sanchez	N	N	N	Y	N
47 ***Cox***	Y	Y	Y	Y	Y
48 ***Packard***	Y	Y	Y	Y	Y
49 ***Bilbray***	Y	Y	Y	Y	Y
50 Filner	N	N	N	Y	N
51 ***Cunningham***	Y	Y	Y	Y	Y
52 ***Hunter***	Y	Y	Y	Y	Y
COLORADO					
1 DeGette	Y	N	N	Y	N
2 Udall	Y	N	N	Y	N
3 ***McInnis***	Y	Y	Y	N	Y
4 ***Schaffer***	Y	Y	Y	N	N
5 ***Hefley***	Y	Y	Y	Y	Y
6 ***Tancredo***	Y	Y	Y	N	Y
CONNECTICUT					
1 Larson	N	N	N	Y	Y
2 Gejdenson	N	N	N	Y	N
3 DeLauro	N	N	N	Y	N
4 ***Shays***	Y	N	Y	Y	Y
5 Maloney	N	N	N	Y	N
6 ***Johnson***	Y	N	Y	Y	Y
DELAWARE					
AL ***Castle***	Y	N	Y	Y	Y
FLORIDA					
1 ***Scarborough***	Y	Y	Y	Y	Y
2 Boyd	N	N	N	Y	N
3 Brown	N	N	N	Y	N
4 ***Fowler***	Y	Y	Y	Y	Y
5 Thurman	N	N	N	Y	N
6 ***Stearns***	Y	Y	Y	Y	Y
7 ***Mica***	Y	Y	Y	Y	Y
8 ***McCollum***	?	?	?	?	?
9 ***Bilirakis***	Y	Y	Y	Y	Y
10 ***Young***	Y	Y	Y	Y	Y
11 Davis	N	N	N	Y	N
12 ***Canady***	Y	Y	Y	Y	Y
13 ***Miller***	Y	N	Y	Y	Y
14 ***Goss***	Y	Y	Y	Y	Y
15 ***Weldon***	Y	Y	Y	Y	Y
16 ***Foley***	Y	N	Y	Y	Y
17 Meek	N	N	N	Y	N
18 ***Ros-Lehtinen***	Y	Y	Y	Y	Y
19 Wexler	N	N	N	Y	N
20 Deutsch	Y	N	N	Y	N
21 ***Diaz-Balart***	Y	Y	Y	Y	Y
22 ***Shaw***	Y	Y	Y	Y	Y
23 Hastings	N	N	N	Y	N
GEORGIA					
1 ***Kingston***	Y	Y	Y	Y	Y
2 Bishop	Y	N	N	Y	N
3 ***Collins***	Y	Y	Y	Y	Y
4 McKinney	Y	N	N	Y	N
5 Lewis	N	N	N	Y	N
6 ***Isakson***	Y	Y	Y	Y	Y
7 ***Barr***	Y	Y	N	Y	N
8 ***Chambliss***	Y	Y	Y	Y	Y
9 ***Deal***	Y	Y	Y	Y	Y
10 ***Norwood***	Y	Y	Y	Y	Y
11 ***Linder***	Y	Y	Y	?	Y
HAWAII					
1 Abercrombie	N	N	N	Y	N
2 Mink	N	N	N	Y	N
IDAHO					
1 ***Chenoweth-Hage***	Y	?	Y	N	N
2 ***Simpson***	Y	Y	Y	Y	Y
ILLINOIS					
1 Rush	N	N	N	Y	N
2 Jackson	N	N	N	Y	N
3 Lipinski	Y	Y	N	Y	N
4 Gutierrez	?	?	?	?	?
5 Blagojevich	N	Y	N	Y	N
6 ***Hyde***	Y	Y	Y	Y	Y
7 Davis	N	N	N	Y	N
8 ***Crane***	Y	Y	Y	Y	Y
9 Schakowsky	N	N	N	Y	N
10 ***Porter***	Y	N	Y	Y	Y
11 ***Weller***	Y	Y	Y	Y	Y
12 Costello	Y	Y	N	Y	N
13 ***Biggert***	Y	Y	Y	Y	Y

ND Northern Democrats SD Southern Democrats

	472	473	474	475	476
14 ***Hastert***		Y	Y		Y
15 ***Ewing***	Y	Y	Y	Y	Y
16 ***Manzullo***	Y	Y	Y	Y	N
17 Evans	N	Y	N	Y	N
18 ***LaHood***	Y	Y	Y	Y	Y
19 Phelps	Y	Y	N	Y	N
20 ***Shimkus***	Y	Y	Y	Y	Y
INDIANA					
1 Visclosky	Y	Y	N	Y	N
2 ***McIntosh***	?	?	?	?	?
3 Roemer	Y	Y	N	N	N
4 ***Souder***	Y	Y	Y	Y	Y
5 ***Buyer***	Y	Y	Y	Y	Y
6 ***Burton***	Y	Y	Y	Y	Y
7 ***Pease***	Y	Y	Y	Y	Y
8 ***Hostettler***	Y	Y	Y	Y	Y
9 Hill	N	Y	N	Y	N
10 Carson	N	N	N	Y	N
IOWA					
1 ***Leach***	Y	Y	Y	Y	Y
2 ***Nussle***	Y	Y	Y	Y	Y
3 Boswell	Y	Y	N	Y	N
4 ***Ganske***	Y	N	Y	Y	N
5 ***Latham***	Y	Y	Y	Y	Y
KANSAS					
1 ***Moran***	Y	Y	Y	Y	Y
2 ***Ryun***	Y	Y	Y	Y	Y
3 Moore	Y	N	N	Y	N
4 ***Tiahrt***	Y	Y	Y	Y	Y
KENTUCKY					
1 ***Whitfield***	Y	Y	Y	Y	Y
2 ***Lewis***	Y	Y	Y	Y	Y
3 ***Northup***	Y	Y	Y	Y	N
4 Lucas	Y	Y	Y	Y	N
5 ***Rogers***	Y	Y	Y	Y	Y
6 ***Fletcher***	Y	Y	Y	Y	N
LOUISIANA					
1 ***Vitter***	Y	Y	Y	Y	Y
2 Jefferson	N	N	N	Y	N
3 ***Tauzin***	Y	Y	Y	Y	Y
4 ***McCrery***	Y	Y	Y	Y	Y
5 ***Cooksey***	N	N	Y	Y	Y
6 ***Baker***	Y	Y	Y	Y	Y
7 John	Y	Y	N	Y	N
MAINE					
1 Allen	N	N	N	Y	N
2 Baldacci	Y	N	N	Y	Y
MARYLAND					
1 ***Gilchrest***	Y	Y	Y	Y	Y
2 ***Ehrlich***	Y	Y	Y	Y	Y
3 Cardin	N	N	N	Y	N
4 Wynn	N	N	N	Y	N
5 Hoyer	N	N	N	Y	N
6 ***Bartlett***	Y	Y	Y	Y	Y
7 Cummings	N	N	N	Y	N
8 ***Morella***	N	N	N	Y	Y
MASSACHUSETTS					
1 Olver	N	N	N	Y	N
2 Neal	?	?	N	Y	N
3 McGovern	N	N	N	Y	N
4 Frank	N	N	N	N	N
5 Meehan	N	N	N	Y	N
6 Tierney	N	N	N	Y	N
7 Markey	N	N	N	Y	N
8 Capuano	N	N	N	Y	N
9 Moakley	N	N	N	Y	N
10 Delahunt	N	N	N	Y	N
MICHIGAN					
1 Stupak	N	N	N	Y	N
2 ***Hoekstra***	Y	Y	Y	Y	Y
3 ***Ehlers***	Y	N	Y	Y	Y
4 ***Camp***	Y	Y	Y	Y	Y
5 Barcia	Y	Y	N	Y	N
6 ***Upton***	Y	N	Y	Y	Y
7 ***Smith***	Y	Y	Y	Y	Y
8 Stabenow	Y	N	N	Y	N
9 Kildee	N	N	N	Y	N
10 Bonior	N	N	N	Y	N
11 ***Knollenberg***	Y	Y	Y	Y	Y
12 Levin	N	N	N	Y	N
13 Rivers	N	N	N	Y	N
14 Conyers	N	N	N	N	N
15 Kilpatrick	N	N	N	Y	N
16 Dingell	N	N	N	Y	N

	472	473	474	475	476
MINNESOTA					
1 ***Gutknecht***	Y	Y	Y	Y	Y
2 Minge	N	N	N	Y	N
3 ***Ramstad***	Y	Y	Y	N	Y
4 Vento	?	?	?	?	?
5 Sabo	N	N	N	Y	N
6 Luther	Y	Y	N	Y	N
7 Peterson	Y	Y	N	Y	Y
8 Oberstar	N	N	N	Y	N
MISSISSIPPI					
1 ***Wicker***	Y	Y	Y	Y	Y
2 Thompson	N	N	N	Y	N
3 ***Pickering***	Y	Y	Y	Y	Y
4 Shows	N	Y	N	Y	N
5 Taylor	Y	Y	N	Y	N
MISSOURI					
1 Clay	Y	N	N	?	?
2 ***Talent***	Y	Y	Y	Y	Y
3 Gephardt	Y	N	N	Y	N
4 Skelton	Y	Y	N	Y	N
5 McCarthy	N	N	N	Y	N
6 Danner	Y	Y	N	Y	N
7 ***Blunt***	Y	Y	Y	Y	Y
8 ***Emerson***	Y	Y	Y	Y	Y
9 ***Hulshof***	Y	Y	Y	Y	Y
MONTANA					
AL ***Hill***	Y	Y	Y	Y	Y
NEBRASKA					
1 ***Bereuter***	Y	Y	Y	Y	Y
2 ***Terry***	Y	Y	Y	Y	Y
3 ***Barrett***	Y	Y	Y	Y	Y
NEVADA					
1 Berkley	N	N	N	Y	N
2 ***Gibbons***	Y	Y	Y	Y	Y
NEW HAMPSHIRE					
1 ***Sununu***	Y	Y	Y	Y	Y
2 ***Bass***	Y	Y	Y	Y	Y
NEW JERSEY					
1 Andrews	N	N	N	Y	N
2 ***LoBiondo***	Y	Y	Y	Y	Y
3 ***Saxton***	Y	Y	Y	Y	Y
4 ***Smith***	Y	Y	Y	Y	Y
5 ***Roukema***	Y	Y	Y	Y	Y
6 Pallone	Y	N	N	Y	N
7 ***Franks***	Y	Y	Y	Y	Y
8 Pascrell	N	Y	N	Y	Y
9 Rothman	Y	N	N	Y	N
10 Payne	Y	N	N	Y	N
11 ***Frelinghuysen***	Y	N	Y	Y	Y
12 Holt	Y	N	N	Y	N
13 Menendez	Y	N	N	Y	N
NEW MEXICO					
1 ***Wilson***	Y	Y	Y	Y	Y
2 ***Skeen***	Y	Y	Y	Y	Y
3 Udall	Y	N	N	Y	N
NEW YORK					
1 Forbes	Y	Y	N	Y	?
2 ***Lazio***	?	?	?	?	?
3 ***King***	Y	Y	Y	Y	Y
4 McCarthy	N	N	N	Y	Y
5 Ackerman	N	N	N	?	N
6 Meeks	N	N	N	Y	N
7 Crowley	N	N	N	Y	N
8 Nadler	N	N	N	Y	N
9 Weiner	N	N	N	Y	N
10 Towns	N	N	N	Y	N
11 Owens	N	N	N	Y	N
12 Velázquez	N	Y	N	Y	N
13 ***Fossella***	Y	Y	Y	Y	Y
14 Maloney	N	N	N	Y	N
15 Rangel	N	N	N	Y	N
16 Serrano	N	N	N	Y	N
17 Engel	N	N	N	Y	N
18 Lowey	N	N	N	Y	N
19 ***Kelly***	Y	Y	Y	Y	Y
20 ***Gilman***	Y	Y	Y	Y	Y
21 McNulty	Y	Y	N	Y	N
22 ***Sweeney***	Y	Y	Y	Y	Y
23 ***Boehlert***	Y	N	Y	Y	Y
24 ***McHugh***	Y	Y	Y	Y	Y
25 ***Walsh***	Y	Y	Y	Y	Y
26 Hinchey	N	N	N	Y	N
27 ***Reynolds***	Y	Y	Y	Y	Y
28 Slaughter	N	N	N	Y	N
29 LaFalce	N	N	N	Y	N

	472	473	474	475	476
30 ***Quinn***	Y	Y	Y	Y	Y
31 ***Houghton***	Y	N	Y	Y	Y
NORTH CAROLINA					
1 Clayton	?	N	N	Y	N
2 Etheridge	Y	Y	N	Y	N
3 ***Jones***	Y	Y	Y	Y	N
4 Price	Y	N	N	Y	N
5 ***Burr***	Y	Y	Y	Y	Y
6 ***Coble***	Y	Y	Y	N	Y
7 McIntyre	Y	Y	Y	Y	N
8 ***Hayes***	Y	Y	Y	Y	N
9 ***Myrick***	Y	Y	Y	Y	Y
10 ***Ballenger***	N	Y	Y	Y	Y
11 ***Taylor***	Y	?	Y	Y	Y
12 Watt	N	N	N	Y	N
NORTH DAKOTA					
AL Pomeroy	N	Y	N	Y	N
OHIO					
1 ***Chabot***	Y	Y	Y	Y	N
2 ***Portman***	Y	Y	Y	Y	Y
3 Hall	N	Y	N	Y	N
4 ***Oxley***	Y	Y	Y	Y	Y
5 ***Gillmor***	Y	N	Y	Y	Y
6 Strickland	N	Y	N	Y	N
7 ***Hobson***	Y	Y	Y	Y	Y
8 ***Boehner***	N	Y	Y	Y	Y
9 Kaptur	N	N	N	Y	N
10 Kucinich	N	N	N	Y	N
11 Jones	N	N	N	Y	N
12 ***Kasich***	Y	Y	Y	Y	Y
13 Brown	N	N	N	Y	N
14 Sawyer	N	N	N	Y	N
15 ***Pryce***	Y	Y	Y	Y	Y
16 ***Regula***	Y	Y	Y	Y	Y
17 Traficant	Y	Y	Y	Y	Y
18 ***Ney***	Y	Y	Y	Y	Y
19 ***LaTourette***	Y	Y	Y	Y	Y
OKLAHOMA					
1 ***Largent***	Y	Y	Y	Y	N
2 ***Coburn***	Y	Y	Y	Y	N
3 ***Watkins***	Y	Y	Y	Y	Y
4 ***Watts***	Y	Y	Y	Y	Y
5 ***Istook***	Y	Y	Y	Y	Y
6 ***Lucas***	Y	Y	Y	Y	Y
OREGON					
1 Wu	Y	N	N	Y	N
2 ***Walden***	Y	Y	Y	Y	Y
3 Blumenauer	N	N	N	Y	N
4 DeFazio	N	N	N	N	N
5 Hooley	Y	N	N	Y	N
PENNSYLVANIA					
1 Brady	N	N	N	Y	Y
2 Fattah	N	N	N	Y	N
3 Borski	N	N	N	Y	N
4 Klink	?	?	?	?	?
5 ***Peterson***	Y	Y	Y	Y	Y
6 Holden	Y	Y	N	Y	Y
7 ***Weldon***	Y	Y	Y	Y	?
8 ***Greenwood***	Y	N	Y	?	Y
9 ***Shuster***	Y	Y	Y	Y	Y
10 ***Sherwood***	Y	Y	Y	Y	Y
11 Kanjorski	N	N	N	Y	N
12 Murtha	N	N	N	Y	Y
13 Hoeffel	N	N	N	Y	N
14 Coyne	N	N	N	Y	N
15 ***Toomey***	Y	Y	Y	Y	N
16 ***Pitts***	Y	Y	Y	Y	Y
17 ***Gekas***	Y	Y	Y	Y	Y
18 Doyle	N	N	N	Y	Y
19 ***Goodling***	Y	Y	Y	Y	Y
20 Mascara	Y	Y	N	Y	Y
21 ***English***	Y	Y	Y	Y	Y
RHODE ISLAND					
1 Kennedy	N	N	N	Y	N
2 Weygand	N	N	N	Y	N
SOUTH CAROLINA					
1 ***Sanford***	N	Y	Y	N	N
2 ***Spence***	Y	Y	Y	Y	Y
3 ***Graham***	Y	Y	Y	Y	Y
4 ***DeMint***	Y	Y	Y	Y	Y
5 Spratt	Y	Y	N	Y	N
6 Clyburn	N	N	N	Y	N
SOUTH DAKOTA					
AL ***Thune***	Y	Y	Y	Y	Y

	472	473	474	475	476
TENNESSEE					
1 ***Jenkins***	N	Y	Y	Y	Y
2 ***Duncan***	N	Y	N	Y	N
3 ***Wamp***	N	Y	Y	Y	Y
4 ***Hilleary***	Y	Y	Y	Y	Y
5 Clement	Y	Y	N	Y	N
6 Gordon	Y	N	N	Y	N
7 ***Bryant***	Y	Y	Y	Y	Y
8 Tanner	N	Y	N	Y	N
9 Ford	N	N	N	?	N
TEXAS					
1 Sandlin	N	Y	N	Y	N
2 Turner	Y	Y	N	Y	N
3 ***Johnson, Sam***	Y	Y	Y	Y	Y
4 Hall	Y	Y	N	Y	N
5 ***Sessions***	Y	Y	Y	Y	Y
6 ***Barton***	Y	Y	Y	Y	Y
7 ***Archer***	Y	Y	Y	Y	Y
8 ***Brady***	Y	Y	Y	Y	Y
9 Lampson	N	N	N	Y	N
10 Doggett	N	N	N	Y	N
11 Edwards	Y	N	N	Y	N
12 ***Granger***	Y	Y	Y	Y	Y
13 ***Thornberry***	Y	Y	Y	Y	Y
14 ***Paul***	N	Y	N	N	N
15 Hinojosa	N	N	N	Y	N
16 Reyes	Y	N	N	Y	N
17 Stenholm	Y	Y	N	Y	N
18 Jackson-Lee	Y	N	N	Y	N
19 ***Combest***	Y	Y	Y	Y	Y
20 Gonzalez	N	N	N	Y	N
21 ***Smith***	Y	Y	Y	Y	Y
22 ***DeLay***	Y	Y	Y	Y	Y
23 ***Bonilla***	N	N	Y	Y	Y
24 Frost	N	N	N	Y	N
25 Bentsen	Y	N	N	Y	N
26 ***Armey***	Y	Y	Y	?	Y
27 Ortiz	Y	Y	N	Y	N
28 Rodriguez	Y	Y	N	Y	N
29 Green	Y	Y	N	Y	N
30 Johnson, E.B.	N	N	N	Y	N
UTAH					
1 ***Hansen***	Y	Y	Y	Y	Y
2 ***Cook***	Y	Y	Y	Y	N
3 ***Cannon***	Y	Y	Y	Y	Y
VERMONT					
AL *Sanders*	N	N	N	N	N
VIRGINIA					
1 Vacant					
2 Pickett	N	N	N	Y	N
3 Scott	N	N	N	Y	N
4 Sisisky	N	N	N	Y	N
5 *Goode*	Y	Y	Y	Y	N
6 ***Goodlatte***	Y	Y	Y	Y	Y
7 ***Bliley***	Y	Y	Y	Y	Y
8 Moran	N	N	N	Y	Y
9 Boucher	N	N	N	Y	N
10 ***Wolf***	Y	Y	Y	Y	Y
11 ***Davis***	Y	Y	Y	Y	Y
WASHINGTON					
1 Inslee	Y	N	N	Y	N
2 ***Metcalf***	Y	Y	Y	Y	Y
3 Baird	N	N	N	Y	N
4 ***Hastings***	Y	Y	Y	Y	Y
5 ***Nethercutt***	Y	Y	Y	Y	Y
6 Dicks	N	N	N	Y	Y
7 McDermott	N	N	N	Y	N
8 ***Dunn***	Y	Y	Y	Y	Y
9 Smith	N	N	N	Y	N
WEST VIRGINIA					
1 Mollohan	N	N	N	Y	Y
2 Wise	?	?	?	?	?
3 Rahall	N	N	N	Y	Y
WISCONSIN					
1 ***Ryan***	Y	Y	Y	Y	Y
2 Baldwin	N	N	N	Y	N
3 Kind	N	N	N	Y	N
4 Kleczka	Y	N	N	Y	N
5 Barrett	N	N	N	N	N
6 ***Petri***	Y	Y	Y	Y	Y
7 Obey	N	N	N	Y	N
8 ***Green***	Y	Y	Y	Y	Y
9 ***Sensenbrenner***	Y	Y	N	Y	N
WYOMING					
AL ***Cubin***	Y	Y	Y	Y	Y

Southern states - Ala., Ark., Fla., Ga., Ky., La., Miss., N.C., Okla., S.C., Tenn., Texas, Va.

477. HR 5173. Debt Reduction/Passage. Herger, R-Calif., motion to suspend the rules and pass the bill that would require all Social Security and Medicare surpluses to be used for debt reduction, pending enactment of legislation to overhaul those programs. In fiscal 2001, $42 billion of the non-Social Security and non-Medicare surplus would have to be used for debt reduction. Motion agreed to 381-3: R 191-0; D 188-3 (ND 139-3, SD 49-0); I 2-0. A two-thirds majority of those present and voting (256 in this case) is required for passage under suspension of the rules. Sept. 18, 2000.

478. HR 5010. Commemorative Quarters/Passage. Bachus, R-Ala., motion to suspend the rules and pass the bill that would create a commemorative quarters program to honor the District of Columbia, Puerto Rico, Guam, American Samoa, the U.S. Virgin Islands and the Northern Mariana Islands, beginning in 2009. Motion agreed to 377-6: R 183-6; D 192-0 (ND 143-0, SD 49-0); I 2-0. A two-thirds majority of those present and voting (256 in this case) is required for passage under suspension of the rules. Sept. 18, 2000.

479. HR 5203. Debt Reduction, Pensions/Passage. Shaw, R-Fla., motion to suspend the rules and pass the bill that would require all Social Security and Medicare surpluses to be used for debt reduction, pending enactment of legislation to overhaul those programs. In fiscal 2001, $42 billion of the non-Social Security and non-Medicare surplus would have to be used for debt reduction. The bill also would increase the amount individuals may contribute to pensions, 401(k)s and Individual Retirement Accounts. Motion agreed to 401-20: R 214-0; D 186-19 (ND 132-19, SD 54-0); I 1-1. A two-thirds majority of those present and voting (281 in this case) is required for passage under suspension of the rules. Sept. 19, 2000.

480. HR 3986. Prosser Dam/Passage. Simpson, R-Idaho, motion to suspend the rules and pass the bill that would authorize the Interior Department to study the feasibility of exchanging water from the Columbia River for water historically diverted from the Yakima River for use by two irrigation districts. Motion rejected 218-201: R 210-3; D 7-197 (ND 7-143, SD 0-54); I 1-1. A two-thirds majority of those present and voting (280 in this case) is required for passage under suspension of the rules. Sept. 19, 2000.

481. HR 4577. Labor-HHS-Education Appropriations/Motion to Instruct. Coburn, R-Okla., motion to instruct conferees to accept language in the Senate version of the fiscal 2001 Labor-HHS-Education appropriations bill that would prohibit use of elementary and secondary school funds in the bill to distribute the so-called morning after pill to minors. Motion agreed to 250-170: R 191-24; D 58-145 (ND 34-115, SD 24-30); I 1-1. Sept. 19, 2000.

Key

- Y Voted for (yea).
- # Paired for.
- \+ Announced for.
- N Voted against (nay).
- X Paired against.
- – Announced against.
- P Voted "present."
- C Voted "present" to avoid possible conflict of interest.
- ? Did not vote or otherwise make a position known.

•

Democrats ***Republicans***
Independents

	477	478	479	480	481
ALABAMA					
1 ***Callahan***	Y	Y	Y	Y	Y
2 ***Everett***	Y	Y	Y	Y	Y
3 ***Riley***	Y	Y	Y	Y	Y
4 ***Aderholt***	Y	Y	Y	Y	Y
5 Cramer	Y	Y	Y	N	Y
6 ***Bachus***	Y	Y	Y	Y	Y
7 Hilliard	Y	Y	Y	N	N
ALASKA					
AL ***Young***	Y	Y	Y	Y	Y
ARIZONA					
1 ***Salmon***	Y	Y	Y	Y	Y
2 Pastor	Y	Y	Y	N	N
3 ***Stump***	Y	Y	Y	Y	Y
4 ***Shadegg***	Y	Y	Y	Y	Y
5 ***Kolbe***	Y	Y	Y	Y	N
6 ***Hayworth***	Y	Y	Y	Y	Y
ARKANSAS					
1 Berry	Y	Y	Y	N	Y
2 Snyder	Y	Y	Y	N	N
3 ***Hutchinson***	Y	Y	Y	Y	Y
4 ***Dickey***	Y	Y	Y	Y	Y
CALIFORNIA					
1 Thompson	Y	Y	Y	Y	N
2 ***Herger***	Y	Y	Y	Y	Y
3 ***Ose***	Y	Y	Y	Y	N
4 ***Doolittle***	Y	Y	Y	Y	Y
5 Matsui	Y	Y	N	N	N
6 Woolsey	Y	Y	Y	N	N
7 Miller, George	Y	Y	Y	N	N
8 Pelosi	?	?	Y	N	N
9 Lee	Y	Y	N	N	N
10 Tauscher	Y	Y	Y	N	N
11 ***Pombo***	Y	Y	Y	Y	Y
12 Lantos	Y	Y	Y	N	N
13 Stark	?	?	N	N	N
14 Eshoo	Y	Y	Y	N	N
15 ***Campbell***	?	?	?	?	?
16 Lofgren	Y	Y	Y	N	N
17 Farr	Y	Y	Y	N	N
18 Condit	Y	Y	Y	N	N
19 ***Radanovich***	Y	Y	Y	Y	Y
20 Dooley	?	?	?	?	?
21 ***Thomas***	Y	Y	Y	Y	Y
22 Capps	Y	Y	Y	N	N
23 ***Gallegly***	Y	Y	Y	Y	Y
24 Sherman	Y	Y	Y	N	N
25 ***McKeon***	Y	Y	Y	Y	Y
26 Berman	Y	Y	Y	N	N
27 ***Rogan***	?	?	Y	Y	Y
28 ***Dreier***	Y	Y	Y	Y	Y
29 Waxman	?	?	Y	N	N
30 Becerra	Y	Y	Y	N	N
31 ***Martinez***	Y	Y	Y	Y	Y
32 Dixon	Y	Y	Y	N	N
33 Roybal-Allard	Y	Y	N	N	N
34 Napolitano	Y	Y	Y	N	N
35 Waters	Y	Y	Y	N	N
36 ***Kuykendall***	Y	Y	Y	Y	N
37 Millender-McD.	Y	Y	Y	N	N
38 ***Horn***	Y	Y	Y	Y	N
39 ***Royce***	Y	N	Y	Y	Y
40 ***Lewis***	?	?	Y	Y	N
41 ***Miller, Gary***	Y	N	Y	Y	Y
42 Baca	Y	Y	Y	N	N
43 ***Calvert***	Y	Y	Y	Y	Y
44 ***Bono***	Y	Y	Y	Y	Y
45 ***Rohrabacher***	Y	Y	Y	Y	Y
46 Sanchez	Y	Y	Y	N	N
47 ***Cox***	Y	Y	Y	Y	Y
48 ***Packard***	Y	Y	Y	Y	Y
49 ***Bilbray***	Y	Y	Y	Y	N
50 Filner	Y	Y	N	N	N
51 ***Cunningham***	Y	Y	Y	Y	Y
52 ***Hunter***	Y	Y	Y	Y	Y
COLORADO					
1 DeGette	Y	Y	Y	N	N
2 Udall	Y	Y	Y	N	N
3 ***McInnis***	Y	Y	Y	Y	Y
4 ***Schaffer***	Y	N	Y	Y	Y
5 ***Hefley***	Y	Y	Y	Y	Y
6 ***Tancredo***	Y	Y	Y	Y	Y
CONNECTICUT					
1 Larson	Y	Y	Y	N	N
2 Gejdenson	Y	Y	Y	N	N
3 DeLauro	Y	Y	Y	N	N
4 ***Shays***	Y	Y	Y	Y	N
5 Maloney	Y	Y	Y	N	Y
6 ***Johnson***	Y	Y	+	Y	N
DELAWARE					
AL ***Castle***	Y	Y	Y	Y	Y
FLORIDA					
1 ***Scarborough***	Y	Y	Y	Y	Y
2 Boyd	Y	Y	Y	N	Y
3 Brown	Y	Y	Y	N	N
4 ***Fowler***	Y	Y	Y	Y	Y
5 Thurman	?	?	Y	N	N
6 ***Stearns***	Y	Y	Y	Y	Y
7 ***Mica***	Y	Y	Y	Y	Y
8 ***McCollum***	?	?	?	?	?
9 ***Bilirakis***	Y	Y	Y	Y	Y
10 ***Young***	Y	Y	Y	Y	Y
11 Davis	Y	Y	Y	N	Y
12 ***Canady***	Y	Y	Y	Y	Y
13 ***Miller***	Y	Y	Y	Y	Y
14 ***Goss***	Y	N	Y	Y	Y
15 ***Weldon***	Y	Y	Y	Y	Y
16 ***Foley***	Y	Y	Y	Y	Y
17 Meek	Y	Y	Y	N	N
18 ***Ros-Lehtinen***	Y	Y	Y	Y	Y
19 Wexler	Y	Y	Y	N	N
20 Deutsch	Y	Y	Y	N	N
21 ***Diaz-Balart***	Y	Y	Y	Y	Y
22 ***Shaw***	Y	Y	Y	Y	Y
23 Hastings	Y	Y	Y	N	N
GEORGIA					
1 ***Kingston***	?	?	Y	Y	Y
2 Bishop	Y	Y	Y	N	Y
3 ***Collins***	Y	Y	Y	Y	Y
4 McKinney	Y	Y	Y	N	N
5 Lewis	?	?	Y	N	N
6 ***Isakson***	Y	Y	Y	Y	Y
7 ***Barr***	Y	Y	Y	Y	Y
8 ***Chambliss***	Y	Y	Y	Y	Y
9 ***Deal***	Y	Y	Y	Y	Y
10 ***Norwood***	?	?	Y	Y	Y
11 ***Linder***	Y	Y	Y	Y	Y
HAWAII					
1 Abercrombie	Y	Y	Y	?	N
2 Mink	Y	Y	Y	N	N
IDAHO					
1 ***Chenoweth-Hage***	+	+	Y	Y	Y
2 ***Simpson***	Y	Y	Y	Y	Y
ILLINOIS					
1 Rush	Y	Y	Y	N	N
2 Jackson	Y	Y	N	N	N
3 Lipinski	Y	Y	Y	N	Y
4 Gutierrez	Y	Y	Y	N	N
5 Blagojevich	Y	Y	Y	N	N
6 ***Hyde***	Y	Y	Y	Y	Y
7 Davis	Y	Y	N	N	N
8 ***Crane***	?	?	Y	Y	Y
9 Schakowsky	Y	Y	Y	N	N
10 ***Porter***	Y	Y	Y	Y	N
11 ***Weller***	Y	Y	Y	Y	Y
12 Costello	Y	Y	Y	N	Y
13 ***Biggert***	Y	Y	Y	Y	N

ND Northern Democrats SD Southern Democrats

	477	478	479	480	481
14 ***Hastert***	Y		Y		
15 ***Ewing***	Y	Y	Y	Y	Y
16 ***Manzullo***	Y	Y	Y	Y	Y
17 Evans	Y	Y	Y	N	N
18 ***LaHood***	Y	Y	Y	Y	Y
19 Phelps	Y	Y	Y	N	Y
20 ***Shimkus***	Y	Y	Y	Y	Y
INDIANA					
1 Visclosky	Y	Y	Y	N	N
2 ***McIntosh***	?	?	?	?	?
3 Roemer	Y	Y	Y	N	Y
4 ***Souder***	Y	Y	Y	Y	Y
5 ***Buyer***	Y	Y	Y	?	Y
6 ***Burton***	Y	Y	Y	Y	Y
7 ***Pease***	Y	Y	Y	Y	Y
8 ***Hostettler***	Y	Y	Y	Y	Y
9 Hill	Y	Y	Y	N	Y
10 Carson	Y	Y	Y	N	N
IOWA					
1 ***Leach***	Y	Y	Y	Y	N
2 ***Nussle***	Y	Y	Y	Y	Y
3 Boswell	Y	Y	Y	Y	N
4 ***Ganske***	Y	Y	Y	Y	N
5 ***Latham***	Y	Y	Y	Y	Y
KANSAS					
1 ***Moran***	Y	Y	Y	Y	Y
2 ***Ryun***	Y	Y	Y	Y	Y
3 Moore	Y	Y	Y	N	N
4 ***Tiahrt***	Y	Y	Y	Y	Y
KENTUCKY					
1 ***Whitfield***	Y	Y	Y	Y	Y
2 ***Lewis***	Y	Y	Y	Y	Y
3 ***Northup***	Y	Y	Y	Y	Y
4 Lucas	Y	Y	Y	N	Y
5 ***Rogers***	Y	Y	Y	Y	Y
6 ***Fletcher***	Y	?	Y	Y	Y
LOUISIANA					
1 ***Vitter***	Y	Y	Y	Y	Y
2 Jefferson	Y	Y	Y	N	N
3 ***Tauzin***	Y	Y	Y	Y	Y
4 ***McCrery***	Y	Y	Y	Y	Y
5 ***Cooksey***	Y	Y	Y	Y	Y
6 ***Baker***	Y	Y	Y	Y	Y
7 John	Y	Y	Y	N	Y
MAINE					
1 Allen	Y	Y	Y	N	N
2 Baldacci	Y	Y	Y	N	N
MARYLAND					
1 ***Gilchrest***	Y	Y	Y	Y	Y
2 ***Ehrlich***	?	?	Y	Y	Y
3 Cardin	Y	Y	Y	N	N
4 Wynn	Y	Y	Y	N	N
5 Hoyer	Y	Y	Y	N	N
6 ***Bartlett***	Y	Y	Y	Y	Y
7 Cummings	Y	Y	Y	N	N
8 ***Morella***	Y	Y	Y	Y	N
MASSACHUSETTS					
1 Olver	Y	Y	N	N	N
2 Neal	?	?	Y	N	Y
3 McGovern	Y	Y	Y	N	N
4 Frank	Y	Y	N	N	N
5 Meehan	Y	Y	Y	N	N
6 Tierney	Y	Y	Y	N	N
7 Markey	Y	Y	Y	N	N
8 Capuano	Y	Y	Y	N	N
9 Moakley	?	?	Y	N	Y
10 Delahunt	Y	Y	Y	N	N
MICHIGAN					
1 Stupak	Y	Y	Y	N	Y
2 ***Hoekstra***	Y	Y	Y	Y	Y
3 ***Ehlers***	Y	Y	Y	Y	Y
4 ***Camp***	Y	Y	Y	Y	Y
5 Barcia	Y	Y	Y	N	Y
6 ***Upton***	Y	Y	Y	Y	N
7 ***Smith***	Y	Y	Y	Y	Y
8 Stabenow	Y	Y	Y	N	N
9 Kildee	Y	Y	Y	N	Y
10 Bonior	Y	Y	Y	N	Y
11 ***Knollenberg***	Y	Y	Y	Y	Y
12 Levin	Y	Y	Y	N	N
13 Rivers	Y	Y	Y	N	N
14 Conyers	Y	Y	N	N	N
15 Kilpatrick	Y	Y	Y	N	N
16 Dingell	Y	Y	Y	N	N
MINNESOTA					
1 ***Gutknecht***	Y	Y	Y	Y	Y
2 Minge	Y	Y	Y	N	N
3 ***Ramstad***	Y	Y	Y	Y	N
4 Vento	?	?	?	?	?
5 Sabo	N	Y	Y	N	N
6 Luther	Y	Y	Y	N	N
7 Peterson	Y	Y	Y	N	Y
8 Oberstar	+	+	Y	N	Y
MISSISSIPPI					
1 ***Wicker***	Y	Y	Y	Y	Y
2 Thompson	Y	Y	Y	N	N
3 ***Pickering***	Y	Y	Y	Y	Y
4 Shows	Y	Y	Y	N	Y
5 Taylor	Y	Y	Y	N	Y
MISSOURI					
1 Clay	Y	Y	N	N	N
2 ***Talent***	?	?	Y	Y	Y
3 Gephardt	Y	Y	Y	N	Y
4 Skelton	Y	Y	Y	N	Y
5 McCarthy	Y	Y	Y	N	N
6 Danner	Y	Y	Y	N	Y
7 ***Blunt***	?	?	Y	Y	Y
8 ***Emerson***	+	+	Y	Y	Y
9 ***Hulshof***	Y	Y	Y	Y	Y
MONTANA					
AL ***Hill***	Y	Y	Y	Y	Y
NEBRASKA					
1 ***Bereuter***	Y	Y	Y	Y	Y
2 ***Terry***	Y	Y	Y	Y	Y
3 ***Barrett***	Y	Y	Y	Y	Y
NEVADA					
1 Berkley	Y	Y	Y	N	N
2 ***Gibbons***	Y	Y	Y	Y	N
NEW HAMPSHIRE					
1 ***Sununu***	Y	Y	Y	Y	Y
2 ***Bass***	Y	Y	Y	Y	N
NEW JERSEY					
1 Andrews	Y	Y	Y	N	N
2 ***LoBiondo***	Y	Y	Y	Y	Y
3 ***Saxton***	?	?	Y	Y	Y
4 ***Smith***	Y	Y	Y	Y	Y
5 ***Roukema***	Y	Y	Y	Y	N
6 Pallone	Y	Y	Y	N	N
7 ***Franks***	?	?	?	?	?
8 Pascrell	?	?	Y	N	N
9 Rothman	Y	Y	Y	N	N
10 Payne	Y	Y	N	N	N
11 ***Frelinghuysen***	Y	Y	Y	Y	N
12 Holt	Y	Y	Y	N	N
13 Menendez	Y	Y	Y	N	N
NEW MEXICO					
1 ***Wilson***	Y	Y	Y	Y	Y
2 ***Skeen***	Y	Y	Y	Y	Y
3 Udall	Y	Y	Y	N	N
NEW YORK					
1 Forbes	Y	Y	Y	N	Y
2 ***Lazio***	?	?	?	?	?
3 ***King***	Y	Y	Y	Y	Y
4 McCarthy	Y	Y	Y	N	N
5 Ackerman	Y	Y	Y	N	N
6 Meeks	Y	Y	Y	N	N
7 Crowley	Y	Y	Y	N	N
8 Nadler	N	Y	N	N	N
9 Weiner	Y	Y	Y	N	N
10 Towns	Y	Y	Y	N	N
11 Owens	?	?	Y	N	N
12 Velázquez	Y	Y	Y	N	N
13 ***Fossella***	Y	Y	Y	Y	Y
14 Maloney	Y	Y	Y	N	N
15 Rangel	Y	Y	N	N	N
16 Serrano	Y	Y	Y	N	N
17 Engel	Y	Y	Y	N	N
18 Lowey	Y	Y	Y	N	N
19 ***Kelly***	Y	Y	Y	Y	N
20 ***Gilman***	Y	Y	Y	Y	N
21 McNulty	Y	Y	?	?	?
22 ***Sweeney***	?	?	Y	Y	Y
23 ***Boehlert***	Y	Y	Y	Y	N
24 ***McHugh***	Y	Y	Y	Y	Y
25 ***Walsh***	?	?	Y	Y	Y
26 Hinchey	?	?	Y	N	N
27 ***Reynolds***	Y	Y	Y	Y	Y
28 Slaughter	Y	Y	Y	N	N
29 LaFalce	Y	Y	N	N	Y
30 ***Quinn***	Y	Y	Y	Y	Y
31 ***Houghton***	Y	Y	Y	?	N
NORTH CAROLINA					
1 Clayton	Y	Y	Y	N	N
2 Etheridge	Y	Y	Y	N	N
3 ***Jones***	+	+	Y	Y	Y
4 Price	Y	Y	Y	N	N
5 ***Burr***	Y	Y	Y	Y	Y
6 ***Coble***	Y	Y	Y	N	Y
7 McIntyre	Y	Y	Y	N	Y
8 ***Hayes***	Y	Y	Y	Y	Y
9 ***Myrick***	Y	Y	Y	Y	Y
10 ***Ballenger***	Y	Y	Y	Y	Y
11 ***Taylor***	+	+	Y	Y	Y
12 Watt	Y	Y	Y	N	N
NORTH DAKOTA					
AL Pomeroy	Y	Y	Y	N	Y
OHIO					
1 ***Chabot***	Y	Y	Y	Y	Y
2 ***Portman***	Y	Y	Y	Y	Y
3 Hall	Y	Y	Y	Y	Y
4 ***Oxley***	?	?	Y	Y	Y
5 ***Gillmor***	Y	Y	Y	Y	Y
6 Strickland	Y	Y	Y	N	Y
7 ***Hobson***	Y	Y	Y	Y	Y
8 ***Boehner***	Y	N	Y	Y	Y
9 Kaptur	Y	Y	Y	N	Y
10 Kucinich	Y	Y	Y	N	Y
11 Jones	Y	Y	Y	N	N
12 ***Kasich***	?	?	Y	Y	Y
13 Brown	Y	Y	Y	N	N
14 Sawyer	Y	Y	Y	N	N
15 ***Pryce***	?	?	Y	Y	Y
16 ***Regula***	Y	Y	Y	Y	Y
17 Traficant	Y	Y	Y	Y	Y
18 ***Ney***	Y	Y	Y	Y	Y
19 ***LaTourette***	Y	Y	Y	Y	Y
OKLAHOMA					
1 ***Largent***	Y	Y	Y	Y	Y
2 ***Coburn***	Y	Y	Y	Y	Y
3 ***Watkins***	Y	Y	?	Y	Y
4 ***Watts***	Y	Y	Y	Y	Y
5 ***Istook***	Y	Y	Y	Y	Y
6 ***Lucas***	Y	Y	Y	Y	Y
OREGON					
1 Wu	Y	Y	Y	N	N
2 ***Walden***	Y	Y	Y	Y	Y
3 Blumenauer	Y	Y	Y	N	N
4 DeFazio	Y	Y	Y	N	N
5 Hooley	Y	Y	Y	N	N
PENNSYLVANIA					
1 Brady	Y	Y	Y	N	N
2 Fattah	?	?	Y	N	N
3 Borski	Y	Y	Y	N	Y
4 Klink	?	?	?	?	?
5 ***Peterson***	Y	Y	Y	Y	Y
6 Holden	Y	Y	Y	N	Y
7 ***Weldon***	Y	Y	Y	Y	Y
8 ***Greenwood***	Y	Y	Y	Y	N
9 ***Shuster***	Y	Y	Y	Y	Y
10 ***Sherwood***	Y	Y	Y	Y	Y
11 Kanjorski	Y	Y	Y	N	Y
12 Murtha	Y	Y	Y	N	?
13 Hoeffel	Y	Y	Y	N	N
14 Coyne	Y	Y	Y	N	N
15 ***Toomey***	Y	Y	Y	Y	Y
16 ***Pitts***	Y	Y	Y	Y	Y
17 ***Gekas***	Y	Y	Y	N	Y
18 Doyle	Y	Y	Y	N	Y
19 ***Goodling***	Y	Y	Y	Y	Y
20 Mascara	Y	Y	Y	N	Y
21 ***English***	Y	Y	Y	Y	Y
RHODE ISLAND					
1 Kennedy	Y	Y	N	N	N
2 Weygand	Y	Y	Y	N	Y
SOUTH CAROLINA					
1 ***Sanford***	Y	Y	Y	Y	Y
2 ***Spence***	Y	Y	Y	Y	Y
3 ***Graham***	Y	Y	Y	Y	Y
4 ***DeMint***	Y	Y	Y	Y	Y
5 Spratt	Y	Y	Y	N	Y
6 Clyburn	Y	Y	Y	N	N
SOUTH DAKOTA					
AL ***Thune***	Y	Y	Y	Y	Y
TENNESSEE					
1 ***Jenkins***	Y	Y	Y	Y	Y
2 ***Duncan***	Y	Y	Y	Y	Y
3 ***Wamp***	?	?	Y	Y	Y
4 ***Hilleary***	+	+	Y	Y	Y
5 Clement	Y	Y	Y	N	Y
6 Gordon	?	?	Y	N	Y
7 ***Bryant***	Y	Y	Y	Y	Y
8 Tanner	Y	Y	Y	N	Y
9 Ford	Y	Y	Y	N	N
TEXAS					
1 Sandlin	Y	Y	Y	N	Y
2 Turner	Y	Y	Y	N	Y
3 ***Johnson, Sam***	?	?	Y	Y	Y
4 Hall	Y	Y	Y	N	Y
5 ***Sessions***	Y	Y	Y	Y	Y
6 ***Barton***	Y	Y	Y	Y	Y
7 ***Archer***	Y	Y	Y	Y	Y
8 ***Brady***	Y	Y	Y	Y	Y
9 Lampson	Y	Y	Y	N	Y
10 Doggett	Y	Y	Y	N	N
11 Edwards	Y	Y	Y	N	Y
12 ***Granger***	Y	Y	Y	Y	Y
13 ***Thornberry***	Y	Y	Y	Y	Y
14 ***Paul***	Y	N	Y	N	Y
15 Hinojosa	Y	Y	Y	N	N
16 Reyes	Y	Y	Y	N	N
17 Stenholm	Y	Y	Y	N	Y
18 Jackson-Lee	Y	Y	Y	N	N
19 ***Combest***	Y	Y	Y	Y	Y
20 Gonzalez	Y	Y	Y	N	N
21 ***Smith***	Y	Y	Y	Y	Y
22 ***DeLay***	Y	Y	Y	Y	Y
23 ***Bonilla***	Y	Y	Y	Y	Y
24 Frost	?	?	Y	N	N
25 Bentsen	Y	Y	Y	N	N
26 ***Armey***	Y	Y	Y	Y	Y
27 Ortiz	Y	Y	Y	N	Y
28 Rodriguez	Y	Y	Y	N	N
29 Green	Y	Y	Y	N	Y
30 Johnson, E.B.	Y	Y	Y	N	N
UTAH					
1 ***Hansen***	Y	Y	Y	Y	Y
2 ***Cook***	?	?	Y	Y	Y
3 ***Cannon***	Y	Y	Y	Y	Y
VERMONT					
AL *Sanders*	Y	Y	N	N	N
VIRGINIA					
1 Vacant					
2 Pickett	Y	Y	Y	N	Y
3 Scott	Y	Y	Y	N	N
4 Sisisky	Y	Y	Y	N	Y
5 *Goode*	Y	Y	Y	Y	Y
6 ***Goodlatte***	Y	Y	Y	Y	Y
7 ***Bliley***	Y	Y	Y	Y	Y
8 Moran	Y	Y	Y	N	N
9 Boucher	?	?	Y	N	N
10 ***Wolf***	Y	Y	Y	Y	Y
11 ***Davis***	Y	Y	Y	Y	Y
WASHINGTON					
1 Inslee	Y	Y	Y	Y	N
2 ***Metcalf***	Y	Y	Y	Y	Y
3 Baird	Y	Y	Y	Y	N
4 ***Hastings***	?	?	Y	Y	Y
5 ***Nethercutt***	?	?	?	?	?
6 Dicks	Y	Y	Y	Y	N
7 McDermott	Y	Y	N	N	N
8 ***Dunn***	?	?	Y	Y	Y
9 Smith	Y	Y	Y	N	N
WEST VIRGINIA					
1 Mollohan	N	Y	N	N	Y
2 Wise	?	?	?	?	?
3 Rahall	Y	Y	Y	N	Y
WISCONSIN					
1 ***Ryan***	Y	Y	Y	Y	Y
2 Baldwin	Y	Y	Y	N	N
3 Kind	Y	Y	Y	N	N
4 Kleczka	Y	Y	Y	N	Y
5 Barrett	Y	Y	Y	N	N
6 ***Petri***	Y	Y	Y	Y	Y
7 Obey	Y	Y	Y	N	P
8 ***Green***	Y	Y	Y	Y	Y
9 ***Sensenbrenner***	Y	Y	Y	Y	Y
WYOMING					
AL ***Cubin***	?	?	Y	Y	Y

Southern states - Ala., Ark., Fla., Ga., Ky., La., Miss., N.C., Okla., S.C., Tenn., Texas, Va.

482. HR 4945. Contract Bundling/Passage. Passage of the bill that would require the Small Business Administration (SBA) to collect and analyze data on federal contracts to determine the number of small businesses that have been displaced as primary contractors by bundling. It would also require the SBA to report to Congress on how much has been saved through bundling. Passed 422-0: R 214-0; D 206-0 (ND 153-0, SD 53-0); I 2-0. Sept. 20, 2000.

483. HR 3986. Prosser Dam/Passage. Passage of the bill that would authorize the Interior Department to study the feasibility of exchanging water from the Columbia River for water historically diverted from the Yakima River for use by two irrigation districts. Passed 418-1: R 212-1; D 204-0 (ND 151-0, SD 53-0); I 2-0. Sept. 20, 2000.

484. HR 4577. Fiscal 2001 Labor-HHS-Education Appropriations/Motion to Instruct. Obey, D-Wis., motion to instruct conferees to insist on disagreeing with provisions in the Senate amendment that would deny the president's request for dedicated resources to reduce class sizes in the early grades and for local school construction and, instead, would broadly expand the Title VI education block grant with limited accountability in the use of funds. Motion agreed to 222-201: R 18-198; D 203-2 (ND 151-1, SD 52-1); I 1-1. Sept. 20, 2000.

485. HR 4919. Defense and Security Assistance/Conference Report. Adoption of the conference report on the bill that would authorize $3.8 billion in fiscal 2001 and $3.9 billion in 2002 for foreign military financing, international military education and training, and anti-terrorism, non-proliferation, and export control assistance. Adopted 396-17: R 201-8; D 194-8 (ND 142-7, SD 52-1); I 1-1. Sept. 21, 2000.

486. HR 5109. Veterans Health Care/Passage. Passage of the bill that would establish a pilot program that would allow veterans who meet certain criteria to receive care at non-Veterans Administration hospitals. It also would guarantee VA nurses the same annual pay raise as other federal workers and prevent the VA from lowering nurses' salaries. Additionally, it would increase pay for dentists who specialize or take on additional responsibilities, and extend their retirement benefits. Passed 411-0: R 210-0; D 199-0 (ND 150-0, SD 49-0); I 2-0. Sept. 21, 2000.

Key

- Y Voted for (yea).
- \# Paired for.
- \+ Announced for.
- N Voted against (nay).
- X Paired against.
- – Announced against.
- P Voted "present."
- C Voted "present" to avoid possible conflict of interest.
- ? Did not vote or otherwise make a position known.

•

Democrats ***Republicans***
Independents

	482	483	484	485	486
ALABAMA					
1 ***Callahan***	Y	Y	N	?	Y
2 ***Everett***	Y	Y	N	Y	Y
3 ***Riley***	Y	Y	N	Y	Y
4 ***Aderholt***	Y	Y	Y	Y	Y
5 Cramer	Y	Y	Y	Y	Y
6 ***Bachus***	Y	Y	N	Y	Y
7 Hilliard	Y	Y	?	Y	Y
ALASKA					
AL ***Young***	Y	Y	N	?	Y
ARIZONA					
1 ***Salmon***	Y	Y	Y	Y	Y
2 Pastor	Y	Y	Y	Y	Y
3 ***Stump***	Y	Y	N	Y	Y
4 ***Shadegg***	Y	Y	N	Y	Y
5 ***Kolbe***	Y	Y	N	Y	Y
6 ***Hayworth***	Y	Y	N	Y	Y
ARKANSAS					
1 Berry	Y	Y	Y	Y	Y
2 Snyder	Y	Y	Y	Y	Y
3 ***Hutchinson***	Y	?	N	Y	?
4 ***Dickey***	Y	Y	N	Y	Y
CALIFORNIA					
1 Thompson	Y	Y	Y	Y	Y
2 ***Herger***	Y	Y	N	Y	Y
3 ***Ose***	Y	Y	N	Y	Y
4 ***Doolittle***	Y	Y	N	Y	Y
5 Matsui	Y	Y	Y	Y	Y
6 Woolsey	Y	Y	Y	Y	Y
7 Miller, George	Y	Y	Y	N	Y
8 Pelosi	Y	Y	Y	Y	Y
9 Lee	Y	Y	Y	Y	Y
10 Tauscher	Y	Y	Y	Y	Y
11 ***Pombo***	Y	Y	N	Y	Y
12 Lantos	Y	Y	Y	Y	Y
13 Stark	Y	Y	Y	N	Y
14 Eshoo	Y	Y	Y	Y	Y
15 ***Campbell***	?	?	?	?	?
16 Lofgren	Y	Y	Y	Y	Y
17 Farr	Y	Y	Y	Y	Y
18 Condit	Y	Y	Y	Y	Y
19 ***Radanovich***	Y	Y	N	Y	Y
20 Dooley	Y	Y	Y	?	?
21 ***Thomas***	Y	Y	N	Y	Y
22 Capps	Y	Y	Y	Y	Y
23 ***Gallegly***	Y	Y	Y	Y	Y
24 Sherman	Y	Y	Y	Y	Y
25 ***McKeon***	Y	Y	N	Y	Y
26 Berman	Y	Y	Y	Y	Y
27 ***Rogan***	Y	Y	N	Y	Y
28 ***Dreier***	Y	Y	N	Y	Y
29 Waxman	Y	Y	Y	?	?
30 Becerra	Y	Y	Y	Y	Y
31 ***Martinez***	Y	Y	N	?	Y
32 Dixon	Y	Y	Y	Y	Y
33 Roybal-Allard	Y	Y	Y	Y	Y
34 Napolitano	Y	Y	Y	+	Y
35 Waters	Y	Y	Y	N	Y
36 ***Kuykendall***	Y	Y	N	Y	Y
37 Millender-McD.	Y	Y	Y	Y	Y
38 ***Horn***	Y	Y	N	Y	Y
39 ***Royce***	Y	Y	N	N	Y
40 ***Lewis***	Y	Y	N	Y	Y
41 ***Miller, Gary***	Y	Y	N	Y	Y
42 Baca	Y	Y	Y	Y	Y
43 ***Calvert***	Y	Y	N	Y	Y
44 ***Bono***	Y	Y	N	Y	Y
45 ***Rohrabacher***	Y	Y	N	Y	Y
46 Sanchez	Y	Y	Y	Y	Y
47 ***Cox***	Y	Y	N	Y	Y
48 ***Packard***	Y	Y	N	Y	Y
49 ***Bilbray***	Y	Y	N	Y	Y
50 Filner	Y	Y	Y	Y	Y
51 ***Cunningham***	Y	Y	N	?	Y
52 ***Hunter***	Y	Y	N	Y	Y
COLORADO					
1 DeGette	Y	Y	Y	Y	Y
2 Udall	Y	Y	Y	Y	Y
3 ***McInnis***	Y	Y	Y	Y	?
4 ***Schaffer***	Y	Y	N	N	Y
5 ***Hefley***	Y	Y	N	Y	Y
6 ***Tancredo***	Y	Y	N	Y	Y
CONNECTICUT					
1 Larson	Y	Y	Y	Y	Y
2 Gejdenson	Y	Y	Y	Y	Y
3 DeLauro	Y	Y	Y	Y	Y
4 ***Shays***	Y	Y	N	Y	Y
5 Maloney	Y	Y	Y	Y	Y
6 ***Johnson***	Y	Y	Y	Y	Y
DELAWARE					
AL ***Castle***	Y	Y	N	Y	Y
FLORIDA					
1 ***Scarborough***	Y	Y	N	Y	Y
2 Boyd	Y	Y	Y	Y	Y
3 Brown	Y	Y	Y	Y	Y
4 ***Fowler***	Y	Y	N	Y	Y
5 Thurman	Y	Y	Y	Y	Y
6 ***Stearns***	Y	Y	N	Y	Y
7 ***Mica***	Y	Y	N	Y	Y
8 ***McCollum***	Y	Y	N	?	?
9 ***Bilirakis***	Y	Y	N	Y	Y
10 ***Young***	Y	Y	N	Y	Y
11 Davis	Y	Y	Y	Y	Y
12 ***Canady***	Y	Y	N	Y	Y
13 ***Miller***	Y	Y	N	Y	Y
14 ***Goss***	Y	Y	N	Y	Y
15 ***Weldon***	Y	Y	N	Y	Y
16 ***Foley***	Y	Y	Y	Y	Y
17 Meek	?	Y	Y	Y	Y
18 ***Ros-Lehtinen***	Y	Y	N	+	+
19 Wexler	Y	Y	Y	Y	?
20 Deutsch	Y	Y	Y	Y	+
21 ***Diaz-Balart***	+	Y	N	Y	+
22 ***Shaw***	Y	Y	Y	Y	Y
23 Hastings	Y	Y	Y	?	?
GEORGIA					
1 ***Kingston***	Y	Y	N	Y	Y
2 Bishop	Y	Y	Y	Y	Y
3 ***Collins***	Y	Y	N	Y	Y
4 McKinney	Y	Y	Y	N	Y
5 Lewis	Y	Y	Y	Y	Y
6 ***Isakson***	Y	Y	N	Y	Y
7 ***Barr***	Y	Y	N	Y	Y
8 ***Chambliss***	Y	Y	N	Y	Y
9 ***Deal***	Y	Y	N	Y	Y
10 ***Norwood***	Y	?	N	Y	Y
11 ***Linder***	Y	Y	N	Y	Y
HAWAII					
1 Abercrombie	Y	Y	Y	Y	Y
2 Mink	Y	Y	Y	Y	Y
IDAHO					
1 ***Chenoweth-Hage***	Y	Y	N	Y	Y
2 ***Simpson***	Y	Y	N	Y	Y
ILLINOIS					
1 Rush	Y	Y	Y	Y	Y
2 Jackson	Y	Y	Y	Y	Y
3 Lipinski	Y	Y	Y	Y	Y
4 Gutierrez	Y	Y	Y	Y	Y
5 Blagojevich	Y	Y	Y	Y	Y
6 ***Hyde***	Y	Y	N	Y	Y
7 Davis	Y	Y	Y	Y	Y
8 ***Crane***	Y	Y	N	Y	Y
9 Schakowsky	Y	Y	Y	Y	Y
10 ***Porter***	Y	Y	N	Y	Y
11 ***Weller***	Y	Y	N	Y	Y
12 Costello	Y	Y	Y	Y	Y
13 ***Biggert***	Y	Y	N	Y	Y

ND Northern Democrats SD Southern Democrats

	482	483	484	485	486
14 ***Hastert***					
15 ***Ewing***	Y	Y	N	Y	Y
16 ***Manzullo***	Y	Y	N	Y	Y
17 Evans	Y	Y	Y	Y	Y
18 ***LaHood***	Y	Y	N	Y	Y
19 Phelps	Y	Y	Y	Y	Y
20 ***Shimkus***	Y	Y	N	Y	Y
INDIANA					
1 Visclosky	Y	Y	Y	Y	Y
2 ***McIntosh***	?	?	?	?	?
3 Roemer	Y	Y	Y	Y	Y
4 ***Souder***	Y	Y	N	Y	Y
5 ***Buyer***	Y	Y	N	Y	Y
6 ***Burton***	Y	Y	?	Y	?
7 ***Pease***	Y	Y	N	Y	Y
8 ***Hostettler***	Y	Y	N	N	Y
9 Hill	Y	Y	Y	Y	Y
10 Carson	Y	Y	Y	Y	Y
IOWA					
1 ***Leach***	Y	Y	N	Y	Y
2 ***Nussle***	Y	Y	N	Y	Y
3 Boswell	Y	Y	Y	Y	Y
4 ***Ganske***	Y	Y	N	Y	Y
5 ***Latham***	Y	Y	N	Y	Y
KANSAS					
1 ***Moran***	Y	Y	N	Y	Y
2 ***Ryun***	Y	Y	N	Y	Y
3 Moore	Y	Y	Y	Y	Y
4 ***Tiahrt***	Y	Y	N	Y	Y
KENTUCKY					
1 ***Whitfield***	Y	Y	N	Y	Y
2 ***Lewis***	Y	Y	N	Y	Y
3 ***Northup***	Y	Y	N	Y	Y
4 Lucas	Y	Y	Y	Y	Y
5 ***Rogers***	Y	Y	N	Y	Y
6 ***Fletcher***	Y	Y	Y	Y	Y
LOUISIANA					
1 ***Vitter***	Y	Y	N	Y	Y
2 Jefferson	Y	Y	Y	Y	Y
3 ***Tauzin***	Y	Y	N	Y	Y
4 ***McCrery***	Y	Y	N	Y	Y
5 ***Cooksey***	Y	Y	N	Y	Y
6 ***Baker***	Y	Y	N	Y	Y
7 John	Y	Y	Y	Y	Y
MAINE					
1 Allen	Y	Y	Y	Y	Y
2 Baldacci	Y	Y	Y	Y	Y
MARYLAND					
1 ***Gilchrest***	Y	Y	N	Y	Y
2 ***Ehrlich***	Y	Y	N	Y	Y
3 Cardin	Y	Y	Y	?	Y
4 Wynn	Y	Y	Y	Y	Y
5 Hoyer	Y	Y	Y	Y	Y
6 ***Bartlett***	Y	Y	N	Y	Y
7 Cummings	Y	Y	Y	Y	Y
8 ***Morella***	Y	Y	Y	Y	Y
MASSACHUSETTS					
1 Olver	Y	Y	Y	Y	Y
2 Neal	Y	Y	Y	Y	Y
3 McGovern	Y	Y	Y	Y	Y
4 Frank	Y	Y	Y	Y	Y
5 Meehan	Y	Y	Y	Y	Y
6 Tierney	Y	Y	Y	Y	Y
7 Markey	Y	Y	Y	Y	Y
8 Capuano	Y	Y	Y	Y	Y
9 Moakley	Y	Y	Y	Y	Y
10 Delahunt	Y	Y	Y	Y	Y
MICHIGAN					
1 Stupak	Y	Y	Y	Y	Y
2 ***Hoekstra***	Y	Y	N	Y	Y
3 ***Ehlers***	Y	Y	N	N	Y
4 ***Camp***	Y	Y	N	Y	Y
5 Barcia	Y	Y	Y	Y	Y
6 ***Upton***	Y	Y	Y	Y	Y
7 ***Smith***	Y	Y	N	Y	Y
8 Stabenow	Y	Y	Y	Y	Y
9 Kildee	Y	Y	Y	Y	Y
10 Bonior	Y	Y	Y	Y	Y
11 ***Knollenberg***	Y	Y	N	Y	Y
12 Levin	Y	Y	Y	Y	Y
13 Rivers	Y	Y	Y	Y	Y
14 Conyers	Y	Y	Y	N	Y
15 Kilpatrick	Y	Y	Y	Y	Y
16 Dingell	Y	Y	Y	Y	Y
MINNESOTA					
1 ***Gutknecht***	Y	Y	N	Y	Y
2 Minge	Y	Y	Y	Y	Y
3 ***Ramstad***	Y	Y	Y	Y	Y
4 Vento	?	?	?	?	?
5 Sabo	Y	Y	?	Y	Y
6 Luther	Y	Y	Y	Y	Y
7 Peterson	Y	Y	Y	Y	Y
8 Oberstar	Y	Y	Y	Y	Y
MISSISSIPPI					
1 ***Wicker***	Y	Y	N	Y	Y
2 Thompson	Y	Y	Y	Y	Y
3 ***Pickering***	Y	Y	N	Y	Y
4 Shows	Y	Y	Y	Y	Y
5 Taylor	Y	Y	Y	Y	Y
MISSOURI					
1 Clay	Y	?	Y	?	?
2 ***Talent***	Y	Y	N	Y	Y
3 Gephardt	Y	?	Y	Y	Y
4 Skelton	Y	Y	Y	Y	Y
5 McCarthy	Y	Y	Y	Y	Y
6 Danner	Y	Y	Y	Y	?
7 ***Blunt***	Y	Y	N	Y	Y
8 ***Emerson***	Y	Y	N	Y	Y
9 ***Hulshof***	Y	Y	N	Y	Y
MONTANA					
AL ***Hill***	Y	Y	N	Y	Y
NEBRASKA					
1 ***Bereuter***	Y	Y	N	Y	Y
2 ***Terry***	Y	Y	N	Y	Y
3 ***Barrett***	Y	Y	N	Y	Y
NEVADA					
1 Berkley	Y	Y	Y	Y	Y
2 ***Gibbons***	Y	Y	N	Y	Y
NEW HAMPSHIRE					
1 ***Sununu***	Y	Y	N	Y	Y
2 ***Bass***	Y	Y	N	Y	Y
NEW JERSEY					
1 Andrews	Y	Y	Y	Y	Y
2 ***LoBiondo***	Y	Y	Y	Y	Y
3 ***Saxton***	Y	Y	N	Y	Y
4 ***Smith***	Y	Y	Y	Y	Y
5 ***Roukema***	Y	Y	N	Y	Y
6 Pallone	Y	Y	Y	Y	Y
7 ***Franks***	Y	Y	N	Y	Y
8 Pascrell	Y	Y	Y	Y	Y
9 Rothman	Y	Y	Y	Y	Y
10 Payne	Y	Y	Y	Y	Y
11 ***Frelinghuysen***	Y	Y	N	Y	Y
12 Holt	Y	Y	Y	Y	Y
13 Menendez	Y	Y	Y	Y	Y
NEW MEXICO					
1 ***Wilson***	Y	?	N	Y	Y
2 ***Skeen***	Y	Y	N	Y	Y
3 Udall	Y	Y	Y	Y	Y
NEW YORK					
1 Forbes	Y	Y	Y	Y	Y
2 ***Lazio***	?	?	?	?	?
3 ***King***	Y	Y	N	Y	Y
4 McCarthy	Y	Y	Y	Y	Y
5 Ackerman	Y	Y	Y	Y	Y
6 Meeks	Y	Y	Y	Y	Y
7 Crowley	Y	Y	Y	Y	Y
8 Nadler	Y	Y	Y	Y	Y
9 Weiner	Y	Y	Y	Y	Y
10 Towns	Y	Y	Y	Y	Y
11 Owens	Y	Y	Y	Y	Y
12 Velázquez	Y	Y	Y	Y	Y
13 ***Fossella***	Y	Y	N	Y	Y
14 Maloney	Y	Y	Y	Y	Y
15 Rangel	Y	Y	Y	Y	Y
16 Serrano	Y	Y	Y	Y	Y
17 Engel	Y	Y	Y	Y	Y
18 Lowey	Y	Y	Y	Y	Y
19 ***Kelly***	Y	Y	Y	Y	Y
20 ***Gilman***	Y	Y	Y	Y	Y
21 McNulty	Y	Y	Y	Y	Y
22 ***Sweeney***	Y	Y	N	Y	Y
23 ***Boehlert***	Y	Y	N	Y	Y
24 ***McHugh***	Y	Y	N	Y	Y
25 ***Walsh***	Y	Y	N	Y	Y
26 Hinchey	Y	Y	Y	Y	Y
27 ***Reynolds***	Y	Y	N	Y	Y
28 Slaughter	Y	Y	Y	Y	Y
29 LaFalce	Y	Y	Y	Y	Y
30 ***Quinn***	Y	Y	Y	Y	Y
31 ***Houghton***	Y	Y	N	Y	Y
NORTH CAROLINA					
1 Clayton	Y	Y	Y	Y	Y
2 Etheridge	Y	Y	Y	Y	Y
3 ***Jones***	Y	Y	N	Y	Y
4 Price	Y	Y	Y	Y	Y
5 ***Burr***	Y	Y	N	Y	Y
6 ***Coble***	Y	Y	N	Y	Y
7 McIntyre	Y	Y	Y	Y	Y
8 ***Hayes***	Y	Y	N	Y	Y
9 ***Myrick***	Y	Y	N	Y	Y
10 ***Ballenger***	Y	Y	N	Y	Y
11 ***Taylor***	Y	Y	N	Y	Y
12 Watt	Y	Y	Y	Y	Y
NORTH DAKOTA					
AL Pomeroy	Y	Y	Y	Y	Y
OHIO					
1 ***Chabot***	Y	Y	N	Y	Y
2 ***Portman***	Y	Y	N	Y	Y
3 Hall	Y	Y	Y	Y	Y
4 ***Oxley***	Y	Y	N	Y	Y
5 ***Gillmor***	Y	Y	N	Y	Y
6 Strickland	Y	Y	Y	Y	Y
7 ***Hobson***	Y	Y	N	Y	Y
8 ***Boehner***	Y	Y	N	Y	Y
9 Kaptur	Y	Y	Y	Y	Y
10 Kucinich	Y	Y	Y	Y	Y
11 Jones	Y	Y	?	Y	Y
12 ***Kasich***	Y	Y	N	?	Y
13 Brown	Y	Y	Y	Y	Y
14 Sawyer	Y	Y	Y	Y	Y
15 ***Pryce***	Y	Y	N	Y	Y
16 ***Regula***	Y	Y	N	Y	Y
17 Traficant	Y	Y	N	Y	Y
18 ***Ney***	Y	Y	Y	Y	Y
19 ***LaTourette***	Y	Y	N	Y	Y
OKLAHOMA					
1 ***Largent***	Y	Y	N	Y	Y
2 ***Coburn***	Y	?	N	Y	Y
3 ***Watkins***	Y	Y	N	Y	Y
4 ***Watts***	Y	Y	N	Y	Y
5 ***Istook***	Y	Y	N	Y	Y
6 ***Lucas***	Y	Y	N	Y	Y
OREGON					
1 Wu	Y	Y	Y	Y	Y
2 ***Walden***	Y	Y	N	Y	Y
3 Blumenauer	Y	Y	Y	Y	Y
4 DeFazio	Y	Y	Y	N	Y
5 Hooley	Y	Y	Y	Y	Y
PENNSYLVANIA					
1 Brady	Y	Y	Y	Y	Y
2 Fattah	Y	Y	Y	Y	Y
3 Borski	Y	Y	Y	Y	Y
4 Klink	?	?	?	?	?
5 ***Peterson***	Y	Y	N	Y	Y
6 Holden	Y	Y	Y	Y	Y
7 ***Weldon***	Y	Y	N	?	Y
8 ***Greenwood***	Y	Y	N	Y	Y
9 ***Shuster***	Y	Y	N	Y	Y
10 ***Sherwood***	Y	Y	Y	Y	Y
11 Kanjorski	Y	Y	Y	Y	Y
12 Murtha	Y	Y	Y	Y	Y
13 Hoeffel	Y	Y	Y	Y	Y
14 Coyne	Y	Y	Y	Y	Y
15 ***Toomey***	Y	Y	N	Y	Y
16 ***Pitts***	Y	Y	N	Y	Y
17 ***Gekas***	Y	Y	N	Y	Y
18 Doyle	Y	Y	Y	Y	Y
19 ***Goodling***	Y	Y	N	Y	Y
20 Mascara	Y	Y	Y	Y	Y
21 ***English***	Y	Y	N	Y	Y
RHODE ISLAND					
1 Kennedy	Y	Y	Y	Y	Y
2 Weygand	Y	Y	Y	Y	Y
SOUTH CAROLINA					
1 ***Sanford***	Y	Y	N	N	Y
2 ***Spence***	Y	Y	N	Y	Y
3 ***Graham***	Y	Y	N	Y	?
4 ***DeMint***	Y	Y	N	Y	Y
5 Spratt	Y	?	Y	Y	Y
6 Clyburn	Y	Y	Y	Y	Y
SOUTH DAKOTA					
AL ***Thune***	Y	Y	N	Y	Y
TENNESSEE					
1 ***Jenkins***	Y	Y	N	Y	Y
2 ***Duncan***	Y	Y	N	N	Y
3 ***Wamp***	Y	Y	N	Y	Y
4 ***Hilleary***	Y	Y	N	Y	Y
5 Clement	Y	Y	Y	Y	Y
6 Gordon	Y	Y	Y	Y	Y
7 ***Bryant***	Y	Y	N	Y	Y
8 Tanner	Y	Y	Y	Y	Y
9 Ford	Y	Y	Y	Y	Y
TEXAS					
1 Sandlin	Y	Y	Y	Y	Y
2 Turner	Y	Y	Y	Y	Y
3 ***Johnson, Sam***	Y	Y	N	Y	Y
4 Hall	Y	Y	N	Y	Y
5 ***Sessions***	Y	Y	N	Y	Y
6 ***Barton***	Y	Y	N	Y	Y
7 ***Archer***	Y	Y	N	Y	Y
8 ***Brady***	?	Y	N	Y	Y
9 Lampson	Y	Y	Y	Y	Y
10 Doggett	Y	Y	Y	Y	Y
11 Edwards	Y	Y	Y	Y	Y
12 ***Granger***	Y	Y	N	Y	Y
13 ***Thornberry***	Y	Y	N	Y	Y
14 ***Paul***	Y	N	N	N	Y
15 Hinojosa	Y	Y	Y	Y	Y
16 Reyes	Y	Y	Y	Y	?
17 Stenholm	Y	Y	Y	Y	Y
18 Jackson-Lee	Y	Y	Y	Y	Y
19 ***Combest***	Y	Y	N	Y	Y
20 Gonzalez	Y	Y	Y	Y	Y
21 ***Smith***	Y	Y	N	Y	Y
22 ***DeLay***	Y	Y	N	Y	Y
23 ***Bonilla***	Y	Y	N	Y	Y
24 Frost	Y	Y	Y	Y	?
25 Bentsen	Y	Y	Y	Y	Y
26 ***Armey***	Y	Y	N	Y	Y
27 Ortiz	Y	Y	Y	Y	Y
28 Rodriguez	Y	Y	Y	Y	Y
29 Green	Y	Y	Y	Y	Y
30 Johnson, E.B.	Y	Y	Y	Y	Y
UTAH					
1 ***Hansen***	Y	Y	N	Y	Y
2 ***Cook***	Y	Y	N	Y	Y
3 ***Cannon***	Y	Y	N	Y	Y
VERMONT					
AL *Sanders*	Y	Y	Y	N	Y
VIRGINIA					
1 Vacant					
2 Pickett	Y	Y	Y	Y	Y
3 Scott	Y	Y	Y	Y	Y
4 Sisisky	Y	Y	Y	Y	Y
5 *Goode*	Y	Y	N	Y	Y
6 ***Goodlatte***	Y	Y	N	Y	Y
7 ***Bliley***	Y	Y	N	Y	Y
8 Moran	Y	Y	Y	Y	Y
9 Boucher	Y	Y	Y	Y	Y
10 ***Wolf***	Y	Y	N	Y	Y
11 ***Davis***	Y	Y	N	Y	Y
WASHINGTON					
1 Inslee	Y	Y	Y	Y	Y
2 ***Metcalf***	Y	Y	N	?	?
3 Baird	Y	Y	Y	Y	Y
4 ***Hastings***	Y	Y	N	Y	Y
5 ***Nethercutt***	?	?	?	Y	Y
6 Dicks	Y	Y	Y	Y	Y
7 McDermott	Y	Y	Y	Y	Y
8 ***Dunn***	Y	Y	N	Y	Y
9 Smith	Y	Y	Y	Y	Y
WEST VIRGINIA					
1 Mollohan	Y	Y	Y	N	Y
2 Wise	?	?	Y	Y	Y
3 Rahall	Y	Y	Y	N	Y
WISCONSIN					
1 ***Ryan***	Y	Y	N	Y	Y
2 Baldwin	Y	Y	Y	Y	Y
3 Kind	Y	Y	Y	Y	Y
4 Kleczka	Y	Y	Y	Y	Y
5 Barrett	Y	Y	Y	Y	Y
6 ***Petri***	Y	Y	N	Y	Y
7 Obey	Y	Y	Y	Y	Y
8 ***Green***	+	Y	N	Y	Y
9 ***Sensenbrenner***	Y	Y	N	N	Y
WYOMING					
AL ***Cubin***	Y	Y	N	Y	Y

Southern states - Ala., Ark., Fla., Ga., Ky., La., Miss., N.C., Okla., S.C., Tenn., Texas, Va.

487. H Con Res 399. IDEA/Adoption. Goodling, R-Pa., motion to suspend the rules and adopt the concurrent resolution recognizing the 25th anniversary of the enactment of the Education for All Handicapped Children Act of 1975 and reaffirming Congress' support for the Individuals with Disabilities Education Act. Motion agreed to 359-2: R 182-2; D 176-0 (ND 127-0, SD 49-0); I 1-0. A two-thirds majority of those present and voting (241 in this case) is required for adoption under suspension of the rules. Sept. 25, 2000.

488. Procedural Motion/Journal. Approval of the House Journal of Monday, Sept. 25, 2000. Approved 332-47: R 177-15; D 154-32 (ND 111-26, SD 43-6); I 1-0. Sept. 26, 2000.

489. HR 5117. Abducted Children Exemption/Passage. Ramstad, R-Minn., motion to suspend the rules and pass the bill that would allow the parents of abducted children to continue claiming the missing child as a dependent for tax purposes. If the child were determined to be dead, or would have turned 18, the provision would cease to apply. Motion agreed to 419-0: R 211-0; D 206-0 (ND 152-0, SD 54-0); I 2-0. A two-thirds majority of those present and voting (280 in this case) is required for passage under suspension of the rules. Sept. 26, 2000.

490. HR 2572. Apollo Award/Passage. Sensenbrenner, R-Wis., motion to suspend the rules and pass the bill that would bestow an Apollo Exploration Award, which would include a lunar rock sample, to the 32 astronauts of the Apollo space program. Motion agreed to 419-0: R 212-0; D 205-0 (ND 152-0, SD 53-0); I 2-0. A two-thirds majority of those present and voting (280 in this case) is required for passage under suspension of the rules. Sept. 26, 2000.

491. HR 1248. Violence Against Women Act/Passage. Hyde, R-Ill., motion to suspend the rules and pass the bill that would reauthorize the Violence Against Women Act and allocate $3.6 billion for programs including shelters, sexual assault prevention and education and training for judges for fiscal years 2001-2005. Motion agreed to 415-3: R 206-3; D 207-0 (ND 153-0, SD 54-0); I 2-0. A two-thirds majority of those present and voting (279 in this case) is required for passage under suspension of the rules. Sept. 26, 2000. A "yea" was a vote in support of the president's position.

492. H J Res 100. Helsinki Act Anniversary/Passage. Gilman, R-N.Y., motion to suspend the rules and pass the joint resolution that calls upon the president to issue a proclamation recognizing the 25th anniversary of the signing of the Final Act of the Conference on Security and Cooperation in Europe and reasserting U.S. commitment to full implementation of the Helsinki Final Act. Motion agreed to 413-0: R 207-0; D 204-0 (ND 151-0, SD 53-0); I 2-0. A two-thirds majority of those present and voting (276 in this case) is required for passage under suspension of the rules. Sept. 26, 2000.

Key

- Y Voted for (yea).
- # Paired for.
- \+ Announced for.
- N Voted against (nay).
- X Paired against.
- – Announced against.
- P Voted "present."
- C Voted "present" to avoid possible conflict of interest.
- ? Did not vote or otherwise make a position known.

•

Democrats ***Republicans***
Independents

	487	488	489	490	491	492
ALABAMA						
1 ***Callahan***	Y	Y	Y	Y	Y	Y
2 ***Everett***	Y	Y	Y	Y	Y	Y
3 ***Riley***	Y	Y	Y	Y	Y	Y
4 ***Aderholt***	Y	Y	Y	Y	Y	Y
5 Cramer	Y	Y	Y	Y	Y	Y
6 ***Bachus***	Y	Y	Y	Y	Y	Y
7 Hilliard	?	N	Y	Y	Y	Y
ALASKA						
AL ***Young***	Y	?	Y	Y	Y	Y
ARIZONA						
1 ***Salmon***	Y	Y	Y	Y	Y	Y
2 Pastor	Y	Y	Y	Y	Y	Y
3 ***Stump***	Y	Y	Y	Y	Y	Y
4 ***Shadegg***	Y	Y	Y	Y	Y	Y
5 ***Kolbe***	Y	Y	Y	Y	Y	Y
6 ***Hayworth***	Y	Y	Y	Y	Y	Y
ARKANSAS						
1 Berry	Y	Y	Y	Y	Y	Y
2 Snyder	Y	Y	Y	Y	Y	Y
3 ***Hutchinson***	Y	Y	Y	Y	Y	Y
4 ***Dickey***	?	N	Y	Y	Y	Y
CALIFORNIA						
1 Thompson	Y	N	Y	Y	Y	Y
2 ***Herger***	Y	Y	Y	Y	Y	Y
3 ***Ose***	Y	Y	Y	Y	Y	Y
4 ***Doolittle***	Y	Y	Y	Y	Y	Y
5 Matsui	?	Y	Y	Y	Y	?
6 Woolsey	+	Y	Y	Y	Y	Y
7 Miller, George	?	Y	Y	Y	Y	Y
8 Pelosi	?	?	Y	Y	Y	Y
9 Lee	+	Y	Y	Y	Y	Y
10 Tauscher	Y	Y	Y	Y	Y	Y
11 ***Pombo***	?	Y	Y	Y	Y	Y
12 Lantos	?	Y	Y	Y	Y	Y
13 Stark	Y	N	Y	Y	Y	Y
14 Eshoo	Y	Y	Y	Y	Y	Y
15 ***Campbell***	?	?	?	?	?	?
16 Lofgren	Y	Y	Y	Y	Y	Y
17 Farr	Y	Y	Y	Y	Y	Y
18 Condit	Y	N	Y	Y	Y	Y
19 ***Radanovich***	Y	Y	Y	Y	?	?
20 Dooley	Y	Y	Y	Y	Y	Y
21 ***Thomas***	Y	Y	Y	Y	Y	Y
22 Capps	+	Y	Y	Y	Y	Y
23 ***Gallegly***	Y	Y	Y	Y	Y	Y
24 Sherman	Y	Y	Y	Y	Y	Y
25 ***McKeon***	Y	Y	Y	Y	Y	Y
26 Berman	Y	Y	Y	Y	Y	Y
27 ***Rogan***	Y	Y	+	+	+	+
28 ***Dreier***	Y	Y	Y	Y	Y	Y
29 Waxman	?	Y	Y	Y	Y	Y
30 Becerra	Y	Y	Y	Y	Y	Y
31 ***Martinez***	Y	Y	Y	Y	Y	Y
32 Dixon	Y	Y	Y	Y	Y	Y
33 Roybal-Allard	Y	Y	Y	Y	Y	Y
34 Napolitano	Y	Y	Y	Y	Y	Y
35 Waters	Y	Y	Y	Y	Y	Y
36 ***Kuykendall***	Y	Y	Y	Y	Y	Y
37 Millender-McD.	Y	?	Y	Y	Y	Y
38 ***Horn***	Y	?	Y	Y	Y	Y
39 ***Royce***	Y	?	Y	Y	Y	Y
40 ***Lewis***	Y	Y	Y	Y	Y	Y
41 ***Miller, Gary***	?	?	?	?	?	?
42 Baca	Y	Y	Y	Y	Y	Y
43 ***Calvert***	Y	Y	Y	Y	Y	Y
44 ***Bono***	Y	Y	Y	Y	Y	Y
45 ***Rohrabacher***	Y	Y	Y	Y	Y	Y
46 Sanchez	Y	Y	Y	Y	Y	Y
47 ***Cox***	Y	Y	Y	Y	Y	Y
48 ***Packard***	Y	Y	Y	Y	Y	Y
49 ***Bilbray***	Y	N	Y	Y	Y	Y
50 Filner	Y	N	Y	Y	Y	Y
51 ***Cunningham***	Y	Y	Y	Y	Y	Y
52 ***Hunter***	Y	Y	Y	Y	Y	Y
COLORADO						
1 DeGette	Y	Y	Y	Y	Y	Y
2 Udall	Y	N	Y	Y	Y	Y
3 ***McInnis***	Y	Y	Y	Y	Y	Y
4 ***Schaffer***	Y	N	Y	Y	Y	Y
5 ***Hefley***	Y	N	Y	Y	Y	Y
6 ***Tancredo***	Y	P	Y	Y	Y	Y
CONNECTICUT						
1 Larson	Y	Y	Y	Y	Y	Y
2 Gejdenson	Y	Y	Y	Y	Y	Y
3 DeLauro	?	Y	Y	Y	Y	Y
4 ***Shays***	Y	Y	Y	Y	Y	Y
5 Maloney	+	Y	Y	Y	Y	Y
6 ***Johnson***	Y	Y	Y	Y	Y	Y
DELAWARE						
AL ***Castle***	Y	Y	Y	Y	Y	Y
FLORIDA						
1 ***Scarborough***	Y	Y	Y	Y	Y	Y
2 Boyd	Y	Y	Y	Y	Y	Y
3 Brown	?	Y	Y	Y	Y	Y
4 ***Fowler***	Y	Y	Y	Y	Y	Y
5 Thurman	Y	Y	Y	Y	Y	Y
6 ***Stearns***	Y	Y	Y	Y	Y	Y
7 ***Mica***	+	Y	Y	Y	Y	Y
8 ***McCollum***	?	?	?	?	?	?
9 ***Bilirakis***	Y	Y	Y	Y	Y	Y
10 ***Young***	Y	Y	Y	Y	Y	Y
11 Davis	Y	Y	Y	Y	Y	Y
12 ***Canady***	Y	Y	Y	Y	Y	Y
13 ***Miller***	Y	Y	Y	Y	Y	Y
14 ***Goss***	Y	Y	Y	Y	Y	Y
15 ***Weldon***	Y	Y	Y	Y	Y	Y
16 ***Foley***	Y	Y	Y	Y	Y	Y
17 Meek	Y	Y	Y	Y	Y	Y
18 ***Ros-Lehtinen***	Y	Y	Y	Y	Y	Y
19 Wexler	Y	?	Y	Y	Y	Y
20 Deutsch	Y	Y	Y	Y	Y	Y
21 ***Diaz-Balart***	Y	Y	Y	Y	Y	?
22 ***Shaw***	Y	Y	Y	Y	Y	Y
23 Hastings	Y	N	Y	Y	Y	Y
GEORGIA						
1 ***Kingston***	Y	Y	Y	Y	Y	Y
2 Bishop	Y	Y	Y	Y	Y	Y
3 ***Collins***	Y	?	Y	Y	Y	Y
4 McKinney	?	Y	Y	?	Y	Y
5 Lewis	Y	Y	Y	Y	Y	Y
6 ***Isakson***	+	Y	Y	Y	Y	Y
7 ***Barr***	?	Y	Y	Y	Y	Y
8 ***Chambliss***	Y	Y	Y	Y	Y	Y
9 ***Deal***	Y	Y	Y	Y	Y	Y
10 ***Norwood***	Y	Y	Y	Y	Y	Y
11 ***Linder***	Y	Y	Y	Y	Y	Y
HAWAII						
1 Abercrombie	Y	Y	Y	Y	Y	Y
2 Mink	?	?	Y	Y	Y	Y
IDAHO						
1 ***Chenoweth-Hage***	Y	?	Y	Y	N	Y
2 ***Simpson***	Y	Y	Y	Y	Y	Y
ILLINOIS						
1 Rush	Y	Y	Y	Y	Y	Y
2 Jackson	Y	Y	Y	Y	Y	Y
3 Lipinski	Y	Y	Y	Y	Y	Y
4 Gutierrez	+	N	Y	Y	Y	Y
5 Blagojevich	Y	Y	Y	Y	Y	Y
6 ***Hyde***	Y	?	Y	Y	Y	Y
7 Davis	Y	Y	Y	Y	Y	Y
8 ***Crane***	Y	N	Y	Y	Y	Y
9 Schakowsky	Y	Y	Y	Y	Y	Y
10 ***Porter***	Y	Y	Y	Y	Y	Y
11 ***Weller***	Y	N	Y	Y	Y	?
12 Costello	Y	?	Y	Y	Y	Y
13 ***Biggert***	Y	Y	Y	Y	Y	Y

ND Northern Democrats SD Southern Democrats

	487	488	489	490	491	492
14 ***Hastert***				Y	Y	
15 ***Ewing***	Y	Y	Y	Y	Y	Y
16 ***Manzullo***	Y	Y	Y	Y	Y	Y
17 Evans	Y	Y	Y	Y	Y	Y
18 ***LaHood***	Y	Y	Y	Y	Y	Y
19 Phelps	Y	Y	Y	Y	Y	Y
20 ***Shimkus***	Y	Y	Y	Y	Y	Y
INDIANA						
1 Visclosky	Y	N	Y	Y	Y	Y
2 ***McIntosh***	?	?	?	?	?	?
3 Roemer	Y	Y	Y	Y	Y	Y
4 ***Souder***	?	Y	Y	Y	Y	Y
5 ***Buyer***	Y	Y	Y	Y	Y	Y
6 ***Burton***	+	+	+	+	+	+
7 ***Pease***	Y	Y	Y	Y	Y	Y
8 ***Hostettler***	Y	Y	Y	Y	N	Y
9 Hill	?	Y	Y	Y	Y	Y
10 Carson	Y	Y	Y	Y	Y	Y
IOWA						
1 ***Leach***	Y	Y	Y	Y	Y	Y
2 ***Nussle***	Y	Y	Y	Y	Y	Y
3 Boswell	Y	Y	Y	Y	Y	Y
4 ***Ganske***	Y	Y	Y	Y	Y	Y
5 ***Latham***	Y	Y	Y	Y	Y	Y
KANSAS						
1 ***Moran***	Y	N	Y	Y	Y	Y
2 ***Ryun***	Y	Y	Y	Y	Y	Y
3 Moore	Y	Y	Y	Y	Y	Y
4 ***Tiahrt***	Y	Y	Y	Y	Y	Y
KENTUCKY						
1 ***Whitfield***	Y	Y	Y	Y	Y	Y
2 ***Lewis***	Y	Y	Y	Y	Y	Y
3 ***Northup***	?	Y	Y	Y	Y	Y
4 Lucas	Y	Y	Y	Y	Y	Y
5 ***Rogers***	Y	Y	Y	Y	Y	Y
6 ***Fletcher***	Y	Y	Y	Y	Y	Y
LOUISIANA						
1 ***Vitter***	?	?	Y	Y	Y	Y
2 Jefferson	Y	?	Y	Y	Y	Y
3 ***Tauzin***	Y	Y	Y	Y	Y	Y
4 ***McCrery***	?	?	Y	Y	Y	Y
5 ***Cooksey***	Y	Y	Y	Y	Y	Y
6 ***Baker***	?	Y	Y	Y	Y	Y
7 John	Y	Y	Y	Y	Y	Y
MAINE						
1 Allen	Y	Y	Y	Y	Y	Y
2 Baldacci	Y	Y	Y	Y	Y	Y
MARYLAND						
1 ***Gilchrest***	Y	Y	Y	Y	Y	Y
2 ***Ehrlich***	Y	Y	Y	Y	Y	Y
3 Cardin	Y	Y	Y	Y	Y	Y
4 Wynn	Y	Y	Y	Y	Y	Y
5 Hoyer	Y	Y	Y	Y	Y	Y
6 ***Bartlett***	Y	Y	Y	Y	Y	Y
7 Cummings	Y	Y	Y	Y	Y	Y
8 ***Morella***	Y	Y	Y	Y	Y	Y
MASSACHUSETTS						
1 Olver	Y	Y	Y	Y	Y	Y
2 Neal	?	Y	Y	Y	Y	Y
3 McGovern	Y	Y	Y	Y	Y	Y
4 Frank	Y	Y	Y	Y	Y	Y
5 Meehan	Y	Y	Y	Y	Y	Y
6 Tierney	?	Y	Y	Y	Y	Y
7 Markey	Y	N	Y	Y	Y	Y
8 Capuano	Y	N	Y	Y	Y	Y
9 Moakley	Y	Y	Y	Y	Y	Y
10 Delahunt	?	Y	Y	Y	Y	Y
MICHIGAN						
1 Stupak	Y	N	Y	Y	Y	?
2 ***Hoekstra***	Y	Y	Y	Y	Y	Y
3 ***Ehlers***	Y	Y	Y	Y	Y	Y
4 ***Camp***	Y	Y	Y	Y	Y	Y
5 Barcia	Y	Y	Y	Y	Y	Y
6 ***Upton***	Y	Y	Y	Y	Y	Y
7 ***Smith***	?	?	?	?	?	?
8 Stabenow	Y	?	Y	Y	Y	Y
9 Kildee	Y	Y	Y	Y	Y	Y
10 Bonior	Y	Y	Y	Y	Y	Y
11 ***Knollenberg***	Y	Y	Y	Y	Y	Y
12 Levin	Y	Y	Y	Y	Y	Y
13 Rivers	Y	Y	Y	Y	Y	Y
14 Conyers	Y	Y	Y	Y	Y	Y
15 Kilpatrick	Y	?	Y	Y	Y	Y
16 Dingell	Y	?	Y	Y	Y	Y
MINNESOTA						
1 ***Gutknecht***	Y	N	Y	Y	Y	Y
2 Minge	Y	Y	Y	Y	Y	Y
3 ***Ramstad***	Y	N	Y	Y	Y	Y
4 Vento	?	?	?	?	?	?
5 Sabo	Y	N	Y	Y	Y	Y
6 Luther	Y	Y	Y	Y	Y	Y
7 Peterson	Y	N	Y	Y	Y	Y
8 Oberstar	Y	N	Y	Y	Y	Y
MISSISSIPPI						
1 ***Wicker***	?	Y	Y	Y	Y	Y
2 Thompson	Y	N	Y	Y	Y	Y
3 ***Pickering***	Y	Y	Y	Y	Y	Y
4 Shows	+	Y	Y	Y	Y	Y
5 Taylor	Y	N	Y	Y	Y	?
MISSOURI						
1 Clay	Y	?	Y	Y	Y	Y
2 ***Talent***	?	?	Y	Y	Y	Y
3 Gephardt	Y	Y	Y	Y	Y	Y
4 Skelton	Y	Y	Y	Y	Y	Y
5 McCarthy	Y	Y	Y	Y	Y	Y
6 Danner	?	?	Y	Y	Y	Y
7 ***Blunt***	?	?	Y	Y	Y	Y
8 ***Emerson***	Y	?	Y	Y	+	Y
9 ***Hulshof***	Y	N	Y	Y	Y	Y
MONTANA						
AL ***Hill***	Y	N	Y	Y	Y	Y
NEBRASKA						
1 ***Bereuter***	Y	Y	Y	Y	Y	Y
2 ***Terry***	Y	Y	Y	Y	Y	Y
3 ***Barrett***	Y	Y	Y	Y	Y	Y
NEVADA						
1 Berkley	Y	Y	Y	Y	Y	Y
2 ***Gibbons***	Y	?	Y	Y	Y	Y
NEW HAMPSHIRE						
1 ***Sununu***	Y	Y	Y	Y	Y	Y
2 ***Bass***	Y	Y	Y	Y	Y	Y
NEW JERSEY						
1 Andrews	Y	Y	Y	Y	Y	Y
2 ***LoBiondo***	Y	N	Y	Y	Y	Y
3 ***Saxton***	Y	Y	Y	Y	Y	Y
4 ***Smith***	Y	Y	Y	Y	Y	Y
5 ***Roukema***	Y	Y	Y	Y	Y	Y
6 Pallone	Y	Y	Y	Y	Y	Y
7 ***Franks***	?	?	Y	Y	Y	?
8 Pascrell	Y	N	Y	Y	Y	Y
9 Rothman	Y	Y	Y	Y	Y	Y
10 Payne	Y	Y	Y	Y	Y	Y
11 ***Frelinghuysen***	Y	Y	Y	Y	Y	Y
12 Holt	Y	N	Y	Y	Y	Y
13 Menendez	Y	Y	Y	Y	Y	Y
NEW MEXICO						
1 ***Wilson***	Y	Y	Y	Y	Y	Y
2 ***Skeen***	Y	Y	Y	Y	Y	Y
3 Udall	?	N	Y	Y	Y	Y
NEW YORK						
1 Forbes	Y	Y	Y	Y	Y	Y
2 ***Lazio***	?	?	?	?	?	?
3 ***King***	Y	Y	Y	Y	Y	Y
4 McCarthy	Y	Y	Y	Y	Y	Y
5 Ackerman	Y	Y	Y	Y	Y	Y
6 Meeks	?	Y	Y	Y	Y	Y
7 Crowley	Y	N	Y	Y	Y	Y
8 Nadler	Y	?	Y	Y	Y	Y
9 Weiner	Y	Y	Y	Y	Y	Y
10 Towns	Y	Y	Y	Y	Y	Y
11 Owens	Y	Y	Y	Y	Y	Y
12 Velázquez	Y	Y	Y	Y	Y	Y
13 ***Fossella***	+	+	Y	Y	Y	Y
14 Maloney	Y	Y	Y	Y	Y	Y
15 Rangel	Y	Y	Y	Y	Y	Y
16 Serrano	?	Y	Y	Y	Y	Y
17 Engel	?	?	Y	Y	Y	Y
18 Lowey	Y	Y	Y	Y	Y	Y
19 ***Kelly***	Y	Y	Y	Y	Y	Y
20 ***Gilman***	Y	Y	Y	Y	?	Y
21 McNulty	?	N	Y	Y	Y	Y
22 ***Sweeney***	?	Y	Y	Y	Y	Y
23 ***Boehlert***	Y	Y	Y	Y	Y	Y
24 ***McHugh***	Y	Y	Y	Y	Y	Y
25 ***Walsh***	Y	Y	Y	Y	Y	Y
26 Hinchey	?	?	Y	Y	Y	Y
27 ***Reynolds***	Y	Y	Y	Y	Y	Y
28 Slaughter	Y	N	Y	Y	Y	Y
29 LaFalce	Y	Y	Y	Y	Y	Y
30 ***Quinn***	?	Y	Y	Y	Y	Y
31 ***Houghton***	Y	Y	Y	Y	Y	Y
NORTH CAROLINA						
1 Clayton	Y	Y	Y	Y	Y	Y
2 Etheridge	Y	Y	Y	Y	Y	Y
3 ***Jones***	Y	Y	Y	Y	Y	Y
4 Price	Y	?	Y	Y	Y	Y
5 ***Burr***	Y	Y	Y	Y	Y	Y
6 ***Coble***	Y	Y	Y	Y	Y	Y
7 McIntyre	Y	Y	Y	Y	Y	Y
8 ***Hayes***	Y	Y	Y	Y	Y	Y
9 ***Myrick***	+	Y	Y	Y	Y	Y
10 ***Ballenger***	?	Y	Y	Y	Y	Y
11 ***Taylor***	+	+	Y	Y	Y	Y
12 Watt	Y	Y	Y	Y	Y	Y
NORTH DAKOTA						
AL Pomeroy	Y	Y	Y	Y	Y	Y
OHIO						
1 ***Chabot***	Y	Y	Y	Y	Y	Y
2 ***Portman***	Y	Y	Y	Y	Y	Y
3 Hall	Y	N	Y	Y	Y	Y
4 ***Oxley***	?	Y	Y	Y	Y	Y
5 ***Gillmor***	?	?	?	?	?	?
6 Strickland	Y	Y	Y	Y	Y	Y
7 ***Hobson***	Y	Y	Y	Y	Y	Y
8 ***Boehner***	Y	Y	Y	Y	Y	Y
9 Kaptur	Y	Y	Y	Y	Y	Y
10 Kucinich	Y	N	Y	Y	Y	Y
11 Jones	?	?	?	?	?	?
12 ***Kasich***	Y	Y	Y	Y	Y	Y
13 Brown	Y	Y	Y	Y	Y	Y
14 Sawyer	Y	Y	Y	Y	Y	Y
15 ***Pryce***	?	?	Y	Y	Y	Y
16 ***Regula***	Y	Y	Y	Y	Y	Y
17 Traficant	Y	Y	Y	Y	Y	Y
18 ***Ney***	Y	Y	Y	Y	Y	Y
19 ***LaTourette***	Y	Y	Y	Y	Y	Y
OKLAHOMA						
1 ***Largent***	Y	Y	Y	Y	Y	Y
2 ***Coburn***	?	?	Y	Y	Y	Y
3 ***Watkins***	Y	Y	Y	Y	Y	Y
4 ***Watts***	Y	Y	Y	Y	Y	Y
5 ***Istook***	Y	Y	Y	Y	Y	Y
6 ***Lucas***	Y	Y	Y	Y	Y	Y
OREGON						
1 Wu	Y	Y	Y	Y	Y	Y
2 ***Walden***	Y	Y	Y	Y	Y	Y
3 Blumenauer	Y	Y	Y	Y	Y	Y
4 DeFazio	?	N	Y	Y	Y	Y
5 Hooley	Y	Y	Y	Y	Y	Y
PENNSYLVANIA						
1 Brady	Y	N	Y	Y	Y	Y
2 Fattah	Y	?	Y	Y	Y	Y
3 Borski	Y	N	Y	Y	Y	Y
4 Klink	?	?	?	?	?	?
5 ***Peterson***	Y	Y	Y	Y	Y	Y
6 Holden	Y	Y	Y	Y	Y	Y
7 ***Weldon***	Y	?	Y	Y	Y	Y
8 ***Greenwood***	Y	Y	Y	Y	Y	Y
9 ***Shuster***	Y	Y	Y	Y	Y	Y
10 ***Sherwood***	Y	Y	Y	Y	Y	Y
11 Kanjorski	Y	Y	Y	Y	Y	Y
12 Murtha	?	Y	Y	Y	Y	Y
13 Hoeffel	Y	Y	Y	Y	Y	Y
14 Coyne	Y	Y	Y	Y	Y	Y
15 ***Toomey***	Y	Y	Y	Y	Y	Y
16 ***Pitts***	Y	Y	Y	Y	Y	Y
17 ***Gekas***	Y	Y	Y	Y	Y	Y
18 Doyle	Y	Y	Y	Y	Y	Y
19 ***Goodling***	Y	Y	Y	Y	Y	Y
20 Mascara	Y	Y	Y	Y	Y	Y
21 ***English***	?	N	Y	Y	Y	Y
RHODE ISLAND						
1 Kennedy	Y	Y	Y	Y	Y	Y
2 Weygand	Y	?	Y	Y	Y	Y
SOUTH CAROLINA						
1 ***Sanford***	N	Y	Y	Y	N	Y
2 ***Spence***	Y	Y	Y	Y	Y	Y
3 ***Graham***	?	Y	Y	Y	Y	Y
4 ***DeMint***	Y	Y	Y	Y	Y	Y
5 Spratt	Y	Y	Y	Y	Y	Y
6 Clyburn	Y	Y	Y	Y	Y	Y
SOUTH DAKOTA						
AL ***Thune***	Y	Y	Y	Y	Y	Y
TENNESSEE						
1 ***Jenkins***	Y	Y	Y	Y	Y	Y
2 ***Duncan***	Y	Y	Y	Y	Y	Y
3 ***Wamp***	Y	N	Y	Y	Y	Y
4 ***Hilleary***	Y	N	Y	Y	Y	Y
5 Clement	+	Y	Y	Y	Y	Y
6 Gordon	Y	Y	Y	Y	Y	Y
7 ***Bryant***	Y	Y	Y	Y	Y	Y
8 Tanner	Y	Y	Y	Y	Y	Y
9 Ford	Y	?	Y	Y	Y	Y
TEXAS						
1 Sandlin	Y	?	Y	Y	Y	Y
2 Turner	Y	Y	Y	Y	Y	Y
3 ***Johnson, Sam***	Y	Y	Y	Y	Y	Y
4 Hall	Y	Y	Y	Y	Y	Y
5 ***Sessions***	Y	Y	Y	Y	Y	Y
6 ***Barton***	Y	Y	Y	Y	Y	Y
7 ***Archer***	Y	?	Y	Y	Y	Y
8 ***Brady***	Y	Y	Y	Y	Y	Y
9 Lampson	Y	Y	Y	Y	Y	Y
10 Doggett	Y	Y	Y	Y	Y	Y
11 Edwards	Y	Y	Y	Y	Y	Y
12 ***Granger***	Y	Y	Y	Y	Y	Y
13 ***Thornberry***	Y	Y	Y	Y	Y	Y
14 ***Paul***	N	?	?	?	?	?
15 Hinojosa	Y	Y	Y	Y	Y	Y
16 Reyes	Y	Y	Y	Y	Y	Y
17 Stenholm	Y	N	Y	Y	Y	Y
18 Jackson-Lee	Y	Y	Y	Y	Y	Y
19 ***Combest***	Y	Y	Y	Y	Y	Y
20 Gonzalez	Y	Y	Y	Y	Y	Y
21 ***Smith***	Y	Y	Y	Y	Y	Y
22 ***DeLay***	Y	Y	Y	Y	Y	Y
23 ***Bonilla***	Y	Y	Y	Y	Y	Y
24 Frost	Y	Y	Y	Y	Y	Y
25 Bentsen	Y	Y	Y	Y	Y	Y
26 ***Armey***	Y	Y	Y	Y	Y	Y
27 Ortiz	Y	Y	Y	Y	Y	Y
28 Rodriguez	Y	Y	Y	Y	Y	Y
29 Green	Y	Y	Y	Y	Y	Y
30 Johnson, E.B.	Y	Y	Y	Y	Y	Y
UTAH						
1 ***Hansen***	Y	Y	Y	Y	Y	Y
2 ***Cook***	?	Y	Y	Y	Y	Y
3 ***Cannon***	Y	Y	Y	Y	Y	Y
VERMONT						
AL *Sanders*	?	?	Y	Y	Y	Y
VIRGINIA						
1 Vacant						
2 Pickett	Y	N	Y	Y	Y	Y
3 Scott	Y	Y	Y	Y	Y	Y
4 Sisisky	Y	Y	Y	Y	Y	Y
5 *Goode*	Y	Y	Y	Y	Y	Y
6 ***Goodlatte***	Y	Y	Y	Y	Y	Y
7 ***Bliley***	?	Y	Y	Y	Y	Y
8 Moran	Y	Y	Y	Y	Y	Y
9 Boucher	Y	Y	Y	Y	Y	Y
10 ***Wolf***	Y	Y	Y	Y	Y	Y
11 ***Davis***	Y	Y	Y	Y	Y	Y
WASHINGTON						
1 Inslee	Y	Y	Y	Y	Y	Y
2 ***Metcalf***	Y	Y	Y	Y	Y	Y
3 Baird	Y	N	Y	Y	Y	Y
4 ***Hastings***	Y	Y	Y	Y	Y	Y
5 ***Nethercutt***	?	Y	Y	Y	Y	Y
6 Dicks	Y	Y	Y	Y	Y	Y
7 McDermott	Y	N	Y	Y	Y	Y
8 ***Dunn***	Y	Y	Y	Y	Y	Y
9 Smith	Y	Y	?	?	Y	Y
WEST VIRGINIA						
1 Mollohan	Y	Y	Y	Y	Y	Y
2 Wise	?	?	Y	Y	Y	Y
3 Rahall	Y	?	Y	Y	Y	Y
WISCONSIN						
1 ***Ryan***	Y	Y	Y	Y	Y	Y
2 Baldwin	Y	Y	Y	Y	Y	Y
3 Kind	Y	Y	Y	Y	Y	Y
4 Kleczka	Y	Y	Y	Y	Y	Y
5 Barrett	Y	Y	Y	Y	Y	Y
6 ***Petri***	Y	Y	Y	Y	Y	Y
7 Obey	Y	Y	Y	Y	Y	Y
8 ***Green***	Y	Y	Y	Y	Y	Y
9 ***Sensenbrenner***	Y	Y	Y	Y	Y	Y
WYOMING						
AL ***Cubin***	?	Y	Y	Y	Y	Y

Southern states - Ala., Ark., Fla., Ga., Ky., La., Miss., N.C., Okla., S.C., Tenn., Texas, Va.

493. H J Res 109. Continuing Resolution/Passage. Passage of the joint resolution that would provide temporary funding authority, at current levels, until Oct. 6, for the departments, agencies and programs for which regular fiscal year 2001 appropriations bills have not been enacted by Oct. 1. Passed 415-2: R 210-0; D 203-2 (ND 149-2, SD 54-0); I 2-0. A two-thirds majority of those present and voting (278 in this case) is required for passage under suspension of the rules. Sept. 26, 2000.

494. HR 5175. Superfund Exemption/Passage. Oxley, R-Ohio, motion to suspend the rules and pass the bill that would exempt small businesses from liability under the superfund hazardous waste cleanup program if the business dumped only a small amount of waste or just ordinary garbage. An expedited settlement procedure would also be established. Motion rejected 253-161: R 206-3; D 46-157 (ND 21-129, SD 25-28); I 1-1. A two-thirds majority of those present and voting (276 in this case) is required for passage under suspension of the rules. Sept. 26, 2000.

495. HR 4292. Live Births/Passage. Canady, R-Fla., motion to suspend the rules and pass the bill that would expand the definition of "person" to include any fetus that has been completely expelled or extracted from the woman and meets other criteria, such as having a beating heart, regardless of whether the birth was a result of an induced abortion. Motion agreed to 380-15: R 200-2; D 178-13 (ND 133-9, SD 45-4); I 2-0. A two-thirds majority of those present and voting (264 in this case) is required for passage under suspension of the rules. Sept. 26, 2000.

496. HR 4365. Children's Health Care/Concur with Senate Amendments. Passage of the bill, as amended by the Senate, that would reauthorize children's research and prevention programs, reauthorize substance abuse and mental health services, and allow some physicians to prescribe certain narcotics in treating narcotics addiction. It also includes provisions to make child care facilities safer and to stiffen penalties for manufacturing methamphetamine and "ecstasy." Passed (thus cleared for the president) 394-25: R 213-1; D 179-24 (ND 135-15, SD 44-9); I 2-0. Sept. 27, 2000.

497. HR 5272. Palestinian Statehood/Passage. Gilman, R-N.Y., motion to suspend the rules and pass the bill that would penalize the Palestinian Authority if it unilaterally declared itself an independent state. It would bar nonhumanitarian assistance to such a government and authorize the president to withhold money from any international organization that recognized it. Motion agreed to 385-27: R 209-2; D 174-25 (ND 129-19, SD 45-6); I 2-0. A two-thirds majority of those present and voting (280 in this case) is required for passage under suspension of the rules. Sept. 27, 2000.

Key

- Y Voted for (yea).
- # Paired for.
- + Announced for.
- N Voted against (nay).
- X Paired against.
- – Announced against.
- P Voted "present."
- C Voted "present" to avoid possible conflict of interest.
- ? Did not vote or otherwise make a position known.

Democrats **_Republicans_** _Independents_

	493	494	495	496	497
ALABAMA					
1 ***Callahan***	Y	Y	Y	Y	Y
2 ***Everett***	Y	Y	Y	Y	Y
3 ***Riley***	Y	Y	Y	Y	Y
4 ***Aderholt***	Y	Y	Y	Y	Y
5 Cramer	Y	Y	Y	Y	Y
6 ***Bachus***	Y	Y	Y	Y	Y
7 Hilliard	Y	N	Y	N	N
ALASKA					
AL ***Young***	Y	Y	Y	Y	Y
ARIZONA					
1 ***Salmon***	Y	Y	Y	Y	Y
2 Pastor	Y	N	Y	Y	Y
3 ***Stump***	Y	Y	Y	Y	Y
4 ***Shadegg***	Y	Y	Y	Y	Y
5 ***Kolbe***	Y	Y	Y	Y	Y
6 ***Hayworth***	Y	Y	Y	Y	Y
ARKANSAS					
1 Berry	Y	Y	Y	Y	Y
2 Snyder	Y	N	Y	Y	Y
3 ***Hutchinson***	Y	Y	Y	Y	Y
4 ***Dickey***	Y	Y	Y	Y	Y
CALIFORNIA					
1 Thompson	Y	N	Y	Y	Y
2 ***Herger***	Y	Y	Y	Y	Y
3 ***Ose***	Y	Y	Y	Y	Y
4 ***Doolittle***	Y	Y	Y	Y	?
5 Matsui	Y	N	Y	Y	Y
6 Woolsey	Y	?	Y	Y	Y
7 Miller, George	Y	N	Y	N	N
8 Pelosi	Y	N	Y	Y	Y
9 Lee	Y	N	N	N	N
10 Tauscher	Y	N	Y	Y	Y
11 ***Pombo***	Y	Y	Y	Y	Y
12 Lantos	Y	N	Y	Y	Y
13 Stark	N	?	?	Y	N
14 Eshoo	Y	N	Y	Y	Y
15 ***Campbell***	?	?	?	?	?
16 Lofgren	Y	N	Y	Y	Y
17 Farr	Y	N	Y	Y	Y
18 Condit	Y	Y	Y	Y	Y
19 ***Radanovich***	Y	Y	Y	Y	Y
20 Dooley	Y	N	Y	Y	Y
21 ***Thomas***	Y	Y	Y	Y	?
22 Capps	Y	N	Y	Y	Y
23 ***Gallegly***	Y	Y	Y	Y	Y
24 Sherman	Y	N	Y	Y	Y
25 ***McKeon***	Y	Y	Y	Y	Y
26 Berman	Y	N	Y	Y	Y
27 ***Rogan***	+	+	+	Y	Y
28 ***Dreier***	Y	Y	Y	Y	Y
29 Waxman	Y	N	Y	Y	Y
30 Becerra	Y	N	Y	Y	Y
31 ***Martinez***	Y	Y	?	Y	Y
32 Dixon	Y	N	Y	Y	Y
33 Roybal-Allard	Y	N	Y	Y	Y
34 Napolitano	Y	Y	Y	Y	Y
35 Waters	Y	N	N	N	N
36 ***Kuykendall***	Y	Y	Y	Y	Y
37 Millender-McD.	Y	N	Y	Y	Y
38 ***Horn***	?	Y	Y	Y	Y
39 ***Royce***	Y	Y	Y	Y	Y
40 ***Lewis***	Y	Y	Y	Y	Y
41 ***Miller, Gary***	Y	Y	Y	Y	Y
42 Baca	Y	Y	Y	Y	Y
43 ***Calvert***	Y	Y	Y	Y	Y
44 ***Bono***	Y	Y	Y	Y	Y
45 ***Rohrabacher***	Y	Y	Y	Y	N
46 Sanchez	Y	N	Y	Y	Y
47 ***Cox***	Y	Y	Y	Y	Y
48 ***Packard***	Y	Y	?	Y	Y
49 ***Bilbray***	Y	Y	Y	Y	Y
50 Filner	Y	N	Y	Y	Y
51 ***Cunningham***	Y	Y	Y	Y	Y
52 ***Hunter***	Y	Y	Y	Y	Y
COLORADO					
1 DeGette	Y	N	Y	Y	Y
2 Udall	Y	N	Y	Y	Y
3 ***McInnis***	Y	Y	Y	Y	Y
4 ***Schaffer***	Y	Y	Y	Y	Y
5 ***Hefley***	Y	Y	Y	Y	Y
6 ***Tancredo***	Y	Y	Y	Y	Y
CONNECTICUT					
1 Larson	Y	N	Y	Y	Y
2 Gejdenson	Y	N	Y	N	Y
3 DeLauro	Y	N	Y	Y	Y
4 ***Shays***	Y	N	Y	Y	Y
5 Maloney	Y	N	Y	Y	Y
6 ***Johnson***	Y	Y	N	Y	Y
DELAWARE					
AL ***Castle***	Y	Y	Y	Y	Y
FLORIDA					
1 ***Scarborough***	Y	Y	Y	Y	Y
2 Boyd	Y	Y	Y	Y	Y
3 Brown	Y	N	Y	Y	Y
4 ***Fowler***	Y	Y	Y	Y	Y
5 Thurman	Y	N	Y	Y	Y
6 ***Stearns***	Y	Y	Y	Y	Y
7 ***Mica***	Y	Y	Y	Y	Y
8 ***McCollum***	?	?	?	?	?
9 ***Bilirakis***	Y	Y	Y	Y	Y
10 ***Young***	Y	Y	Y	Y	Y
11 Davis	Y	N	Y	Y	Y
12 ***Canady***	Y	Y	Y	Y	Y
13 ***Miller***	Y	Y	Y	Y	Y
14 ***Goss***	Y	Y	Y	Y	Y
15 ***Weldon***	Y	Y	Y	Y	Y
16 ***Foley***	Y	Y	Y	Y	Y
17 Meek	Y	N	Y	Y	?
18 ***Ros-Lehtinen***	Y	Y	Y	Y	Y
19 Wexler	Y	N	Y	Y	Y
20 Deutsch	Y	N	Y	Y	Y
21 ***Diaz-Balart***	Y	Y	Y	Y	Y
22 ***Shaw***	Y	Y	Y	Y	Y
23 Hastings	Y	N	N	N	Y
GEORGIA					
1 ***Kingston***	Y	Y	Y	Y	Y
2 Bishop	Y	Y	Y	Y	Y
3 ***Collins***	Y	Y	Y	Y	Y
4 McKinney	Y	N	N	N	N
5 Lewis	Y	N	?	N	Y
6 ***Isakson***	Y	Y	Y	Y	Y
7 ***Barr***	Y	Y	Y	Y	Y
8 ***Chambliss***	Y	Y	Y	Y	Y
9 ***Deal***	Y	Y	Y	Y	Y
10 ***Norwood***	Y	Y	Y	Y	Y
11 ***Linder***	Y	Y	Y	Y	Y
HAWAII					
1 Abercrombie	Y	N	Y	Y	Y
2 Mink	Y	N	Y	Y	Y
IDAHO					
1 ***Chenoweth-Hage***	Y	Y	Y	Y	Y
2 ***Simpson***	Y	Y	Y	Y	Y
ILLINOIS					
1 Rush	Y	N	?	+	Y
2 Jackson	Y	N	N	N	N
3 Lipinski	Y	N	Y	Y	Y
4 Gutierrez	+	N	Y	Y	Y
5 Blagojevich	Y	N	Y	Y	Y
6 ***Hyde***	Y	Y	Y	Y	Y
7 Davis	Y	N	Y	N	Y
8 ***Crane***	Y	Y	Y	Y	Y
9 Schakowsky	Y	N	P	Y	Y
10 ***Porter***	Y	Y	?	Y	Y
11 ***Weller***	Y	Y	Y	Y	Y
12 Costello	Y	N	Y	Y	Y
13 ***Biggert***	Y	Y	Y	Y	Y

ND Northern Democrats SD Southern Democrats

	493	494	495	496	497
14 ***Hastert***					
15 ***Ewing***	Y	+	+	+	+
16 ***Manzullo***	Y	Y	Y	Y	Y
17 Evans	Y	N	Y	Y	Y
18 ***LaHood***	Y	Y	Y	Y	Y
19 Phelps	Y	Y	Y	Y	Y
20 ***Shimkus***	Y	Y	Y	Y	Y
INDIANA					
1 Visclosky	Y	N	Y	Y	Y
2 ***McIntosh***	?	?	?	?	?
3 Roemer	Y	Y	Y	Y	Y
4 ***Souder***	Y	Y	Y	Y	Y
5 ***Buyer***	Y	Y	Y	Y	Y
6 ***Burton***	Y	Y	Y	Y	Y
7 ***Pease***	Y	Y	Y	Y	Y
8 ***Hostettler***	Y	Y	Y	Y	Y
9 Hill	Y	N	Y	Y	Y
10 Carson	Y	N	N	Y	N
IOWA					
1 ***Leach***	Y	Y	Y	Y	Y
2 ***Nussle***	Y	Y	Y	Y	Y
3 Boswell	Y	N	Y	Y	Y
4 ***Ganske***	Y	Y	Y	Y	Y
5 ***Latham***	Y	Y	Y	Y	Y
KANSAS					
1 ***Moran***	Y	Y	Y	Y	Y
2 ***Ryun***	Y	Y	Y	Y	Y
3 Moore	Y	Y	Y	Y	Y
4 ***Tiahrt***	Y	Y	Y	Y	Y
KENTUCKY					
1 ***Whitfield***	Y	Y	Y	Y	Y
2 ***Lewis***	Y	Y	Y	Y	Y
3 ***Northup***	Y	Y	Y	Y	Y
4 Lucas	Y	Y	Y	Y	Y
5 ***Rogers***	Y	Y	Y	Y	Y
6 ***Fletcher***	Y	Y	Y	Y	Y
LOUISIANA					
1 ***Vitter***	Y	Y	Y	Y	Y
2 Jefferson	Y	N	Y	Y	Y
3 ***Tauzin***	Y	Y	Y	Y	Y
4 ***McCrery***	Y	Y	Y	Y	Y
5 ***Cooksey***	Y	Y	Y	Y	Y
6 ***Baker***	Y	?	Y	Y	Y
7 John	Y	Y	Y	Y	Y
MAINE					
1 Allen	Y	N	Y	Y	Y
2 Baldacci	Y	Y	Y	Y	Y
MARYLAND					
1 ***Gilchrest***	Y	Y	Y	Y	Y
2 ***Ehrlich***	Y	Y	Y	Y	Y
3 Cardin	Y	N	Y	Y	Y
4 Wynn	Y	N	Y	?	?
5 Hoyer	Y	N	Y	Y	Y
6 ***Bartlett***	Y	Y	Y	Y	Y
7 Cummings	Y	N	Y	N	Y
8 ***Morella***	Y	N	?	Y	Y
MASSACHUSETTS					
1 Olver	Y	N	Y	Y	Y
2 Neal	Y	N	Y	Y	Y
3 McGovern	Y	N	Y	Y	Y
4 Frank	Y	N	?	Y	Y
5 Meehan	Y	N	Y	Y	Y
6 Tierney	Y	N	Y	Y	Y
7 Markey	Y	N	Y	Y	Y
8 Capuano	Y	N	Y	Y	P
9 Moakley	Y	N	Y	Y	Y
10 Delahunt	Y	N	Y	Y	Y
MICHIGAN					
1 Stupak	Y	N	Y	Y	Y
2 ***Hoekstra***	Y	Y	Y	Y	Y
3 ***Ehlers***	Y	Y	Y	Y	Y
4 ***Camp***	Y	Y	Y	Y	Y
5 Barcia	Y	Y	Y	Y	Y
6 ***Upton***	Y	Y	Y	Y	Y
7 ***Smith***	?	?	?	Y	Y
8 Stabenow	Y	N	Y	Y	Y
9 Kildee	Y	N	Y	Y	Y
10 Bonior	Y	N	Y	Y	N
11 ***Knollenberg***	Y	Y	Y	Y	Y
12 Levin	Y	N	Y	Y	Y
13 Rivers	Y	N	Y	Y	P
14 Conyers	Y	N	Y	N	N
15 Kilpatrick	Y	N	?	N	Y
16 Dingell	Y	N	N	Y	N
MINNESOTA					
1 ***Gutknecht***	Y	Y	Y	Y	Y
2 Minge	Y	Y	Y	Y	Y
3 ***Ramstad***	Y	Y	Y	Y	Y
4 Vento	?	?	?	?	?
5 Sabo	Y	N	Y	Y	N
6 Luther	Y	N	Y	Y	Y
7 Peterson	Y	Y	Y	Y	Y
8 Oberstar	Y	N	Y	Y	Y
MISSISSIPPI					
1 ***Wicker***	Y	Y	Y	Y	Y
2 Thompson	Y	N	Y	Y	Y
3 ***Pickering***	Y	Y	Y	Y	Y
4 Shows	Y	Y	Y	Y	Y
5 Taylor	Y	Y	Y	Y	Y
MISSOURI					
1 Clay	?	?	?	N	N
2 ***Talent***	Y	Y	Y	Y	Y
3 Gephardt	Y	N	Y	Y	Y
4 Skelton	Y	Y	Y	Y	Y
5 McCarthy	Y	N	Y	Y	Y
6 Danner	Y	Y	Y	Y	N
7 ***Blunt***	Y	Y	Y	Y	Y
8 ***Emerson***	Y	Y	Y	Y	Y
9 ***Hulshof***	Y	Y	Y	Y	Y
MONTANA					
AL ***Hill***	Y	Y	Y	Y	Y
NEBRASKA					
1 ***Bereuter***	Y	Y	+	Y	Y
2 ***Terry***	Y	Y	Y	Y	Y
3 ***Barrett***	Y	Y	Y	Y	Y
NEVADA					
1 Berkley	Y	N	Y	Y	Y
2 ***Gibbons***	Y	Y	Y	Y	Y
NEW HAMPSHIRE					
1 ***Sununu***	Y	Y	Y	Y	N
2 ***Bass***	Y	Y	Y	Y	Y
NEW JERSEY					
1 Andrews	Y	N	Y	Y	Y
2 ***LoBiondo***	Y	Y	Y	Y	Y
3 ***Saxton***	Y	?	Y	?	Y
4 ***Smith***	Y	Y	Y	Y	Y
5 ***Roukema***	Y	Y	Y	Y	Y
6 Pallone	Y	N	Y	Y	Y
7 ***Franks***	?	?	?	Y	Y
8 Pascrell	Y	N	Y	Y	Y
9 Rothman	Y	N	Y	Y	Y
10 Payne	Y	N	Y	N	N
11 ***Frelinghuysen***	Y	Y	Y	Y	Y
12 Holt	Y	N	Y	Y	Y
13 Menendez	Y	N	Y	Y	Y
NEW MEXICO					
1 ***Wilson***	Y	Y	Y	Y	Y
2 ***Skeen***	Y	Y	Y	Y	Y
3 Udall	Y	N	Y	Y	Y
NEW YORK					
1 Forbes	Y	N	Y	Y	Y
2 ***Lazio***	?	?	?	?	?
3 ***King***	Y	Y	Y	Y	Y
4 McCarthy	Y	N	Y	Y	Y
5 Ackerman	Y	N	Y	Y	Y
6 Meeks	Y	N	Y	N	Y
7 Crowley	Y	N	Y	Y	Y
8 Nadler	Y	N	Y	Y	Y
9 Weiner	Y	N	Y	Y	Y
10 Towns	Y	N	Y	N	Y
11 Owens	Y	N	Y	Y	Y
12 Velázquez	Y	N	N	Y	Y
13 ***Fossella***	Y	Y	Y	Y	Y
14 Maloney	Y	N	N	Y	Y
15 Rangel	Y	N	Y	Y	Y
16 Serrano	Y	N	Y	Y	N
17 Engel	Y	N	Y	Y	Y
18 Lowey	Y	N	N	Y	Y
19 ***Kelly***	Y	Y	Y	Y	Y
20 ***Gilman***	Y	N	N	Y	Y
21 McNulty	Y	N	Y	Y	Y
22 ***Sweeney***	Y	Y	Y	Y	Y
23 ***Boehlert***	Y	Y	Y	Y	Y
24 ***McHugh***	Y	Y	Y	Y	Y
25 ***Walsh***	Y	Y	Y	Y	Y
26 Hinchey	Y	N	P	Y	Y
27 ***Reynolds***	Y	Y	Y	Y	Y
28 Slaughter	Y	N	P	N	Y
29 LaFalce	Y	N	Y	Y	Y
30 ***Quinn***	Y	Y	?	Y	Y
31 ***Houghton***	Y	Y	?	Y	Y
NORTH CAROLINA					
1 Clayton	Y	N	Y	N	N
2 Etheridge	Y	Y	Y	Y	Y
3 ***Jones***	Y	Y	Y	Y	Y
4 Price	Y	N	Y	Y	Y
5 ***Burr***	Y	Y	Y	Y	Y
6 ***Coble***	Y	Y	Y	Y	Y
7 McIntyre	Y	Y	Y	Y	Y
8 ***Hayes***	Y	Y	Y	Y	Y
9 ***Myrick***	Y	Y	Y	Y	Y
10 ***Ballenger***	Y	Y	Y	Y	Y
11 ***Taylor***	Y	Y	Y	Y	Y
12 Watt	Y	N	N	N	N
NORTH DAKOTA					
AL Pomeroy	Y	Y	Y	Y	Y
OHIO					
1 ***Chabot***	Y	Y	Y	Y	Y
2 ***Portman***	Y	Y	Y	Y	Y
3 Hall	Y	Y	?	Y	Y
4 ***Oxley***	Y	Y	Y	Y	Y
5 ***Gillmor***	?	?	?	Y	Y
6 Strickland	Y	N	Y	Y	Y
7 ***Hobson***	Y	Y	Y	Y	Y
8 ***Boehner***	Y	Y	?	Y	Y
9 Kaptur	Y	N	Y	Y	Y
10 Kucinich	Y	N	Y	Y	P
11 Jones	?	?	?	?	?
12 ***Kasich***	Y	Y	Y	Y	Y
13 Brown	Y	N	?	?	Y
14 Sawyer	Y	N	Y	Y	Y
15 ***Pryce***	Y	Y	Y	Y	Y
16 ***Regula***	Y	Y	Y	Y	Y
17 Traficant	Y	Y	Y	Y	N
18 ***Ney***	Y	Y	Y	Y	Y
19 ***LaTourette***	Y	Y	Y	Y	Y
OKLAHOMA					
1 ***Largent***	Y	Y	Y	Y	Y
2 ***Coburn***	Y	Y	Y	Y	Y
3 ***Watkins***	?	Y	Y	Y	Y
4 ***Watts***	Y	Y	Y	Y	Y
5 ***Istook***	Y	Y	Y	Y	Y
6 ***Lucas***	Y	Y	Y	Y	Y
OREGON					
1 Wu	Y	Y	Y	Y	Y
2 ***Walden***	Y	Y	Y	Y	Y
3 Blumenauer	Y	N	Y	Y	Y
4 DeFazio	N	N	Y	Y	P
5 Hooley	Y	N	Y	Y	Y
PENNSYLVANIA					
1 Brady	Y	N	Y	Y	Y
2 Fattah	Y	N	N	N	Y
3 Borski	Y	N	Y	Y	Y
4 Klink	?	?	?	?	?
5 ***Peterson***	Y	Y	Y	Y	Y
6 Holden	Y	Y	Y	Y	Y
7 ***Weldon***	Y	Y	Y	Y	Y
8 ***Greenwood***	Y	Y	Y	Y	Y
9 ***Shuster***	Y	Y	?	Y	Y
10 ***Sherwood***	Y	Y	Y	Y	Y
11 Kanjorski	Y	N	Y	Y	Y
12 Murtha	Y	Y	?	Y	N
13 Hoeffel	Y	N	Y	Y	Y
14 Coyne	Y	N	Y	Y	Y
15 ***Toomey***	Y	Y	Y	Y	Y
16 ***Pitts***	Y	Y	Y	Y	Y
17 ***Gekas***	Y	Y	Y	Y	Y
18 Doyle	Y	Y	Y	Y	Y
19 ***Goodling***	Y	Y	Y	Y	?
20 Mascara	Y	N	Y	Y	Y
21 ***English***	Y	Y	Y	Y	Y
RHODE ISLAND					
1 Kennedy	Y	N	Y	Y	Y
2 Weygand	Y	N	Y	Y	Y
SOUTH CAROLINA					
1 ***Sanford***	Y	Y	Y	N	Y
2 ***Spence***	Y	Y	Y	Y	Y
3 ***Graham***	Y	Y	Y	Y	Y
4 ***DeMint***	Y	Y	Y	Y	Y
5 Spratt	Y	Y	Y	Y	Y
6 Clyburn	Y	N	Y	N	Y
SOUTH DAKOTA					
AL ***Thune***	Y	Y	Y	Y	Y
TENNESSEE					
1 ***Jenkins***	Y	Y	Y	Y	Y
2 ***Duncan***	Y	Y	Y	Y	Y
3 ***Wamp***	Y	Y	Y	Y	Y
4 ***Hilleary***	Y	Y	Y	Y	?
5 Clement	Y	Y	Y	Y	Y
6 Gordon	Y	Y	Y	Y	Y
7 ***Bryant***	Y	Y	Y	Y	Y
8 Tanner	Y	Y	Y	Y	Y
9 Ford	Y	N	Y	Y	Y
TEXAS					
1 Sandlin	Y	?	?	?	?
2 Turner	Y	Y	Y	Y	Y
3 ***Johnson, Sam***	Y	Y	Y	Y	Y
4 Hall	Y	Y	Y	Y	Y
5 ***Sessions***	Y	Y	Y	Y	Y
6 ***Barton***	Y	Y	Y	Y	Y
7 ***Archer***	Y	Y	Y	Y	Y
8 ***Brady***	Y	Y	Y	Y	Y
9 Lampson	Y	Y	Y	Y	Y
10 Doggett	Y	N	Y	Y	Y
11 Edwards	Y	Y	Y	Y	Y
12 ***Granger***	Y	Y	Y	Y	Y
13 ***Thornberry***	Y	Y	Y	Y	Y
14 ***Paul***	?	?	?	?	?
15 Hinojosa	Y	N	Y	Y	Y
16 Reyes	Y	N	Y	Y	Y
17 Stenholm	Y	Y	Y	Y	Y
18 Jackson-Lee	Y	N	Y	Y	Y
19 ***Combest***	Y	Y	Y	Y	Y
20 Gonzalez	Y	N	N	Y	Y
21 ***Smith***	Y	Y	Y	Y	Y
22 ***DeLay***	Y	Y	Y	Y	Y
23 ***Bonilla***	Y	Y	Y	Y	Y
24 Frost	Y	N	Y	Y	Y
25 Bentsen	Y	Y	Y	Y	Y
26 ***Armey***	Y	Y	Y	Y	Y
27 Ortiz	Y	Y	Y	Y	Y
28 Rodriguez	Y	N	Y	Y	Y
29 Green	Y	Y	Y	Y	Y
30 Johnson, E.B.	Y	N	Y	N	N
UTAH					
1 ***Hansen***	Y	Y	Y	Y	Y
2 ***Cook***	Y	Y	Y	Y	Y
3 ***Cannon***	Y	Y	Y	Y	Y
VERMONT					
AL *Sanders*	Y	N	Y	Y	Y
VIRGINIA					
1 Vacant					
2 Pickett	Y	Y	?	Y	?
3 Scott	Y	N	Y	N	Y
4 Sisisky	Y	Y	?	Y	Y
5 *Goode*	Y	Y	Y	Y	Y
6 ***Goodlatte***	Y	Y	Y	Y	Y
7 ***Bliley***	Y	Y	Y	Y	Y
8 Moran	Y	Y	?	Y	N
9 Boucher	Y	N	Y	Y	Y
10 ***Wolf***	Y	Y	Y	Y	Y
11 ***Davis***	Y	Y	Y	Y	Y
WASHINGTON					
1 Inslee	Y	N	Y	Y	Y
2 ***Metcalf***	Y	Y	Y	Y	Y
3 Baird	Y	N	Y	Y	Y
4 ***Hastings***	Y	Y	Y	Y	Y
5 ***Nethercutt***	Y	Y	Y	Y	Y
6 Dicks	Y	N	Y	Y	Y
7 McDermott	Y	N	Y	Y	N
8 ***Dunn***	Y	Y	Y	Y	Y
9 Smith	Y	N	Y	Y	Y
WEST VIRGINIA					
1 Mollohan	Y	N	Y	Y	Y
2 Wise	Y	Y	Y	Y	Y
3 Rahall	Y	Y	Y	Y	N
WISCONSIN					
1 ***Ryan***	Y	Y	Y	Y	Y
2 Baldwin	Y	N	Y	Y	Y
3 Kind	Y	N	Y	Y	Y
4 Kleczka	Y	N	Y	Y	Y
5 Barrett	Y	N	Y	Y	Y
6 ***Petri***	Y	Y	Y	Y	Y
7 Obey	Y	N	Y	Y	N
8 ***Green***	Y	Y	Y	Y	Y
9 ***Sensenbrenner***	Y	Y	Y	Y	Y
WYOMING					
AL ***Cubin***	Y	Y	Y	Y	Y

Southern states - Ala., Ark., Fla., Ga., Ky., La., Miss., N.C., Okla., S.C., Tenn., Texas, Va.

498. HR 3100. Telephone Solicitations/Passage. Passage of the bill that would make it illegal for telephone solicitors to interfere with or circumvent the transmission of caller identification information. Passed 420-0: R 214-0; D 204-0 (ND 152-0, SD 52-0); I 2-0. A three-fifths majority of those present and voting (280 in this case) is required for passage of a bill called from the Corrections Calendar. Sept. 27, 2000.

499. H Res 576. Children's Cancer Research/Adoption. Burr, R-N.C., motion to suspend the rules and adopt the resolution supporting efforts to increase childhood cancer awareness, treatment and research. Motion agreed to 415-0: R 212-0; D 201-0 (ND 152-0, SD 49-0); I 2-0. A two-thirds majority of those present and voting (277 in this case) is required for adoption under suspension of the rules. Sept. 27, 2000.

500. HR 4733. Fiscal 2001 Energy-Water Appropriations/Rule. Adoption of the rule (H Res 598) to provide for House floor consideration of the conference report of the bill that would appropriate $23.6 billion for the Energy Department, the Army Corps of Engineers and other agencies. Adopted 231-186: R 205-8; D 25-177 (ND 12-136, SD 13-41); I 1-1. Sept. 28, 2000.

501. HR 4733. Fiscal 2001 Energy-Water Appropriations/Conference Report. Adoption of the conference report on the bill that would appropriate $23.6 billion in fiscal 2001 for the Energy Department, the Army Corps of Engineers and other agencies, which is an 11 percent increase over current levels and $890 million more than the president's request. Adopted (thus sent to the Senate) 301-118: R 169-44; D 131-73 (ND 86-64, SD 45-9); I 1-1. Sept. 28, 2000.

502. HR 4461. Fiscal 2001 Agriculture Department Appropriations/Motion to Instruct. Kaptur, D-Ohio, motion to instruct conferees to hold public meetings and fully debate and resolve the differences between the House and Senate versions of the fiscal 2001 Agriculture Department appropriations bills. Motion agreed to 409-0: R 208-0; D 199-0 (ND 147-0, SD 52-0); I 2-0. Sept. 28, 2000.

Key

- Y Voted for (yea).
- # Paired for.
- + Announced for.
- N Voted against (nay).
- X Paired against.
- – Announced against.
- P Voted "present."
- C Voted "present" to avoid possible conflict of interest.
- ? Did not vote or otherwise make a position known.

•

Democrats ***Republicans***
Independents

	498	499	500	501	502
ALABAMA					
1 ***Callahan***	Y	Y	Y	Y	?
2 ***Everett***	Y	Y	Y	Y	?
3 ***Riley***	Y	Y	Y	Y	Y
4 ***Aderholt***	Y	Y	Y	Y	Y
5 Cramer	Y	Y	N	Y	Y
6 ***Bachus***	Y	Y	Y	Y	Y
7 Hilliard	Y	Y	N	Y	Y
ALASKA					
AL ***Young***	Y	Y	Y	?	?
ARIZONA					
1 ***Salmon***	Y	Y	Y	N	Y
2 Pastor	Y	Y	Y	Y	Y
3 ***Stump***	Y	Y	Y	Y	Y
4 ***Shadegg***	Y	Y	Y	N	Y
5 ***Kolbe***	Y	Y	Y	Y	Y
6 ***Hayworth***	Y	Y	Y	Y	Y
ARKANSAS					
1 Berry	Y	Y	N	Y	Y
2 Snyder	Y	Y	N	Y	Y
3 ***Hutchinson***	Y	Y	Y	Y	Y
4 ***Dickey***	Y	Y	Y	Y	Y
CALIFORNIA					
1 Thompson	Y	Y	N	Y	Y
2 ***Herger***	Y	Y	Y	Y	Y
3 ***Ose***	Y	Y	Y	Y	Y
4 ***Doolittle***	Y	Y	Y	Y	Y
5 Matsui	Y	Y	N	Y	Y
6 Woolsey	Y	Y	N	Y	Y
7 Miller, George	Y	Y	N	Y	Y
8 Pelosi	Y	Y	N	Y	Y
9 Lee	Y	Y	N	Y	Y
10 Tauscher	Y	Y	Y	Y	Y
11 ***Pombo***	Y	Y	Y	Y	Y
12 Lantos	Y	Y	N	Y	Y
13 Stark	Y	Y	N	Y	Y
14 Eshoo	Y	Y	?	?	?
15 ***Campbell***	?	?	Y	N	Y
16 Lofgren	Y	Y	N	Y	Y
17 Farr	Y	Y	N	Y	Y
18 Condit	Y	Y	N	Y	Y
19 ***Radanovich***	Y	Y	Y	Y	Y
20 Dooley	Y	Y	Y	Y	Y
21 ***Thomas***	Y	Y	Y	Y	Y
22 Capps	Y	Y	N	Y	Y
23 ***Gallegly***	Y	Y	Y	Y	Y
24 Sherman	Y	Y	N	N	Y
25 ***McKeon***	Y	Y	Y	Y	Y
26 Berman	Y	Y	N	N	Y
27 ***Rogan***	Y	Y	Y	N	Y
28 ***Dreier***	Y	Y	Y	Y	Y
29 Waxman	Y	Y	N	N	Y
30 Becerra	Y	Y	N	Y	Y
31 ***Martinez***	Y	Y	Y	Y	Y
32 Dixon	Y	Y	N	Y	Y
33 Roybal-Allard	Y	Y	N	Y	Y
34 Napolitano	Y	Y	Y	Y	Y
35 Waters	Y	Y	N	N	Y
36 ***Kuykendall***	Y	Y	Y	Y	Y
37 Millender-McD.	Y	Y	N	Y	Y
38 ***Horn***	Y	Y	Y	Y	Y
39 ***Royce***	Y	Y	Y	N	Y
40 ***Lewis***	Y	Y	Y	Y	Y
41 ***Miller, Gary***	Y	Y	Y	Y	Y
42 Baca	Y	Y	N	Y	Y
43 ***Calvert***	Y	Y	Y	Y	Y
44 ***Bono***	Y	Y	Y	Y	Y
45 ***Rohrabacher***	Y	Y	Y	Y	Y
46 Sanchez	Y	Y	N	Y	Y
47 ***Cox***	Y	Y	Y	Y	Y
48 ***Packard***	Y	Y	Y	Y	Y
49 ***Bilbray***	Y	Y	Y	Y	Y
50 Filner	Y	Y	N	Y	Y
51 ***Cunningham***	Y	Y	Y	Y	?
52 ***Hunter***	Y	?	Y	Y	Y
COLORADO					
1 DeGette	Y	Y	N	Y	Y
2 Udall	Y	Y	N	Y	Y
3 ***McInnis***	Y	Y	Y	Y	Y
4 ***Schaffer***	Y	Y	Y	N	Y
5 ***Hefley***	Y	Y	Y	N	Y
6 ***Tancredo***	Y	Y	N	N	Y
CONNECTICUT					
1 Larson	Y	Y	N	N	Y
2 Gejdenson	Y	Y	N	N	Y
3 DeLauro	Y	Y	N	N	Y
4 ***Shays***	Y	Y	Y	N	Y
5 Maloney	Y	Y	N	N	Y
6 ***Johnson***	Y	Y	Y	Y	Y
DELAWARE					
AL ***Castle***	Y	Y	?	N	Y
FLORIDA					
1 ***Scarborough***	Y	Y	Y	Y	?
2 Boyd	Y	Y	N	Y	Y
3 Brown	Y	Y	Y	Y	?
4 ***Fowler***	Y	Y	Y	Y	Y
5 Thurman	Y	Y	N	N	Y
6 ***Stearns***	Y	Y	Y	N	Y
7 ***Mica***	Y	Y	Y	Y	Y
8 ***McCollum***	?	?	?	?	?
9 ***Bilirakis***	Y	Y	Y	Y	Y
10 ***Young***	Y	Y	Y	Y	Y
11 Davis	Y	Y	Y	Y	Y
12 ***Canady***	Y	Y	Y	Y	Y
13 ***Miller***	Y	Y	Y	Y	Y
14 ***Goss***	Y	Y	Y	Y	Y
15 ***Weldon***	Y	Y	Y	Y	Y
16 ***Foley***	Y	Y	Y	Y	Y
17 Meek	Y	Y	Y	Y	Y
18 ***Ros-Lehtinen***	Y	Y	Y	Y	Y
19 Wexler	Y	Y	N	N	Y
20 Deutsch	Y	Y	N	N	Y
21 ***Diaz-Balart***	Y	Y	Y	Y	Y
22 ***Shaw***	Y	Y	Y	Y	Y
23 Hastings	Y	?	N	N	Y
GEORGIA					
1 ***Kingston***	Y	?	Y	Y	Y
2 Bishop	Y	Y	N	Y	Y
3 ***Collins***	Y	Y	Y	Y	Y
4 McKinney	Y	Y	N	N	Y
5 Lewis	Y	Y	N	Y	Y
6 ***Isakson***	Y	Y	Y	Y	Y
7 ***Barr***	Y	Y	Y	Y	Y
8 ***Chambliss***	Y	Y	Y	Y	Y
9 ***Deal***	Y	Y	Y	Y	Y
10 ***Norwood***	Y	Y	?	Y	Y
11 ***Linder***	Y	Y	Y	Y	Y
HAWAII					
1 Abercrombie	Y	Y	N	Y	Y
2 Mink	Y	Y	N	Y	Y
IDAHO					
1 ***Chenoweth-Hage***	Y	Y	Y	N	?
2 ***Simpson***	Y	Y	Y	Y	Y
ILLINOIS					
1 Rush	Y	Y	N	N	Y
2 Jackson	Y	Y	N	Y	Y
3 Lipinski	Y	Y	N	Y	Y
4 Gutierrez	Y	Y	N	N	Y
5 Blagojevich	Y	Y	N	Y	Y
6 ***Hyde***	Y	Y	Y	Y	Y
7 Davis	Y	Y	N	Y	Y
8 ***Crane***	Y	Y	Y	Y	Y
9 Schakowsky	Y	Y	N	Y	Y
10 ***Porter***	Y	Y	Y	Y	Y
11 ***Weller***	Y	Y	Y	Y	Y
12 Costello	Y	Y	N	Y	Y
13 ***Biggert***	Y	Y	Y	Y	Y

ND Northern Democrats SD Southern Democrats

	498	499	500	501	502
14 ***Hastert***					
15 ***Ewing***	+	+	Y	Y	Y
16 ***Manzullo***	Y	Y	Y	Y	Y
17 Evans	Y	Y	N	Y	Y
18 ***LaHood***	Y	Y	Y	Y	Y
19 Phelps	Y	Y	N	Y	Y
20 ***Shimkus***	Y	Y	Y	Y	Y
INDIANA					
1 Visclosky	Y	Y	N	Y	Y
2 ***McIntosh***	?	?	?	?	?
3 Roemer	Y	Y	N	Y	Y
4 ***Souder***	Y	Y	Y	Y	Y
5 ***Buyer***	Y	Y	Y	Y	Y
6 ***Burton***	Y	Y	Y	Y	Y
7 ***Pease***	Y	Y	Y	Y	Y
8 ***Hostettler***	Y	Y	Y	N	Y
9 Hill	Y	Y	N	Y	Y
10 Carson	Y	Y	Y	Y	Y
IOWA					
1 ***Leach***	Y	Y	Y	Y	Y
2 ***Nussle***	Y	Y	Y	Y	Y
3 Boswell	Y	Y	N	N	Y
4 ***Ganske***	Y	?	Y	Y	Y
5 ***Latham***	Y	Y	Y	Y	Y
KANSAS					
1 ***Moran***	Y	Y	Y	N	Y
2 ***Ryun***	Y	Y	Y	N	Y
3 Moore	Y	Y	Y	Y	Y
4 ***Tiahrt***	Y	Y	Y	Y	Y
KENTUCKY					
1 ***Whitfield***	Y	Y	Y	Y	Y
2 ***Lewis***	Y	Y	Y	Y	Y
3 ***Northup***	Y	Y	Y	Y	Y
4 Lucas	Y	Y	N	Y	Y
5 ***Rogers***	Y	Y	Y	Y	Y
6 ***Fletcher***	Y	Y	Y	Y	Y
LOUISIANA					
1 ***Vitter***	Y	Y	Y	Y	Y
2 Jefferson	Y	Y	N	Y	Y
3 ***Tauzin***	Y	Y	Y	Y	Y
4 ***McCrery***	Y	Y	Y	Y	Y
5 ***Cooksey***	Y	Y	Y	Y	Y
6 ***Baker***	Y	Y	Y	Y	Y
7 John	Y	Y	N	Y	Y
MAINE					
1 Allen	Y	Y	N	N	Y
2 Baldacci	Y	Y	N	N	Y
MARYLAND					
1 ***Gilchrest***	Y	Y	Y	?	Y
2 ***Ehrlich***	Y	Y	Y	Y	Y
3 Cardin	Y	Y	N	N	Y
4 Wynn	Y	Y	N	N	Y
5 Hoyer	Y	Y	N	Y	Y
6 ***Bartlett***	Y	Y	Y	Y	Y
7 Cummings	Y	Y	N	Y	Y
8 ***Morella***	Y	Y	Y	?	Y
MASSACHUSETTS					
1 Olver	Y	Y	N	N	Y
2 Neal	Y	Y	N	N	Y
3 McGovern	Y	Y	N	N	Y
4 Frank	Y	Y	N	N	Y
5 Meehan	Y	Y	N	N	Y
6 Tierney	Y	Y	N	N	Y
7 Markey	Y	Y	N	N	Y
8 Capuano	Y	Y	N	N	Y
9 Moakley	Y	Y	N	N	Y
10 Delahunt	Y	Y	N	N	Y
MICHIGAN					
1 Stupak	Y	Y	N	Y	Y
2 ***Hoekstra***	Y	Y	Y	Y	Y
3 ***Ehlers***	Y	Y	Y	Y	Y
4 ***Camp***	Y	Y	Y	Y	Y
5 Barcia	Y	Y	N	Y	Y
6 ***Upton***	Y	Y	Y	N	Y
7 ***Smith***	Y	Y	Y	N	Y
8 Stabenow	Y	Y	?	Y	Y
9 Kildee	Y	Y	N	Y	Y
10 Bonior	Y	Y	N	Y	Y
11 ***Knollenberg***	Y	Y	Y	Y	Y
12 Levin	Y	Y	N	Y	Y
13 Rivers	Y	Y	N	Y	Y
14 Conyers	Y	Y	N	N	Y
15 Kilpatrick	Y	Y	N	Y	Y
16 Dingell	Y	Y	N	?	Y

	498	499	500	501	502
MINNESOTA					
1 ***Gutknecht***	+	Y	Y	Y	Y
2 Minge	Y	Y	N	N	Y
3 ***Ramstad***	Y	Y	Y	N	Y
4 Vento	?	?	?	?	?
5 Sabo	Y	Y	N	N	Y
6 Luther	Y	Y	N	N	Y
7 Peterson	Y	Y	N	Y	Y
8 Oberstar	Y	Y	N	N	Y
MISSISSIPPI					
1 ***Wicker***	Y	Y	Y	Y	Y
2 Thompson	Y	Y	Y	Y	Y
3 ***Pickering***	Y	Y	Y	N	Y
4 Shows	Y	Y	Y	Y	Y
5 Taylor	Y	Y	N	Y	Y
MISSOURI					
1 Clay	Y	Y	?	?	?
2 ***Talent***	Y	Y	?	?	?
3 Gephardt	Y	Y	N	Y	Y
4 Skelton	Y	Y	N	Y	Y
5 McCarthy	Y	Y	N	N	+
6 Danner	Y	Y	N	Y	?
7 ***Blunt***	Y	Y	Y	Y	Y
8 ***Emerson***	Y	Y	Y	Y	Y
9 ***Hulshof***	Y	Y	Y	Y	Y
MONTANA					
AL ***Hill***	Y	Y	Y	Y	Y
NEBRASKA					
1 ***Bereuter***	Y	Y	Y	Y	Y
2 ***Terry***	Y	Y	Y	Y	Y
3 ***Barrett***	Y	Y	Y	Y	Y
NEVADA					
1 Berkley	Y	Y	Y	Y	Y
2 ***Gibbons***	Y	Y	Y	N	Y
NEW HAMPSHIRE					
1 ***Sununu***	Y	Y	Y	N	Y
2 ***Bass***	Y	Y	Y	Y	Y
NEW JERSEY					
1 Andrews	Y	Y	N	N	Y
2 ***LoBiondo***	Y	Y	Y	Y	Y
3 ***Saxton***	Y	Y	Y	Y	Y
4 ***Smith***	Y	Y	Y	Y	Y
5 ***Roukema***	Y	Y	Y	Y	Y
6 Pallone	Y	Y	N	N	Y
7 ***Franks***	Y	Y	Y	Y	?
8 Pascrell	Y	Y	N	N	Y
9 Rothman	Y	Y	N	N	Y
10 Payne	Y	Y	N	N	Y
11 ***Frelinghuysen***	Y	Y	Y	Y	Y
12 Holt	Y	Y	N	N	Y
13 Menendez	Y	Y	N	Y	Y
NEW MEXICO					
1 ***Wilson***	Y	Y	Y	Y	Y
2 ***Skeen***	Y	Y	Y	Y	Y
3 Udall	Y	Y	N	Y	Y
NEW YORK					
1 Forbes	Y	Y	N	Y	?
2 ***Lazio***	?	?	?	?	?
3 ***King***	Y	Y	Y	Y	Y
4 McCarthy	Y	Y	N	Y	Y
5 Ackerman	Y	Y	N	N	Y
6 Meeks	Y	Y	N	N	Y
7 Crowley	Y	Y	N	Y	Y
8 Nadler	Y	Y	N	N	Y
9 Weiner	Y	Y	N	Y	Y
10 Towns	Y	Y	N	N	Y
11 Owens	Y	Y	N	N	Y
12 Velázquez	Y	Y	N	N	Y
13 ***Fossella***	Y	Y	Y	Y	Y
14 Maloney	Y	Y	N	Y	Y
15 Rangel	?	?	N	N	Y
16 Serrano	Y	Y	N	Y	Y
17 Engel	Y	Y	?	N	Y
18 Lowey	Y	Y	N	N	Y
19 ***Kelly***	Y	Y	N	Y	Y
20 ***Gilman***	Y	Y	Y	Y	Y
21 McNulty	Y	Y	N	N	Y
22 ***Sweeney***	Y	Y	N	Y	Y
23 ***Boehlert***	Y	Y	Y	Y	Y
24 ***McHugh***	Y	Y	N	Y	Y
25 ***Walsh***	Y	Y	Y	Y	Y
26 Hinchey	Y	Y	N	N	Y
27 ***Reynolds***	Y	Y	N	Y	Y
28 Slaughter	Y	Y	N	Y	Y
29 LaFalce	Y	Y	?	Y	Y

	498	499	500	501	502
30 ***Quinn***	Y	Y	N	Y	Y
31 ***Houghton***	Y	Y	Y	Y	Y
NORTH CAROLINA					
1 Clayton	Y	Y	N	Y	Y
2 Etheridge	Y	Y	N	Y	Y
3 ***Jones***	Y	Y	Y	Y	Y
4 Price	Y	Y	N	Y	Y
5 ***Burr***	Y	Y	Y	Y	?
6 ***Coble***	Y	Y	Y	Y	Y
7 McIntyre	Y	Y	Y	Y	Y
8 ***Hayes***	Y	Y	Y	Y	Y
9 ***Myrick***	Y	Y	Y	N	Y
10 ***Ballenger***	Y	Y	Y	Y	Y
11 ***Taylor***	Y	Y	Y	Y	Y
12 Watt	Y	Y	N	N	Y
NORTH DAKOTA					
AL Pomeroy	Y	Y	N	Y	Y
OHIO					
1 ***Chabot***	Y	Y	Y	N	Y
2 ***Portman***	Y	Y	Y	N	Y
3 Hall	Y	Y	N	Y	Y
4 ***Oxley***	Y	Y	Y	N	Y
5 ***Gillmor***	Y	Y	Y	Y	Y
6 Strickland	Y	Y	N	Y	Y
7 ***Hobson***	Y	Y	Y	Y	Y
8 ***Boehner***	Y	Y	Y	N	Y
9 Kaptur	Y	Y	N	Y	Y
10 Kucinich	Y	Y	N	N	Y
11 Jones	?	?	?	?	?
12 ***Kasich***	Y	Y	Y	Y	Y
13 Brown	Y	Y	N	N	Y
14 Sawyer	Y	Y	N	Y	Y
15 ***Pryce***	Y	Y	Y	Y	Y
16 ***Regula***	Y	Y	Y	Y	Y
17 Traficant	Y	Y	Y	Y	Y
18 ***Ney***	Y	Y	Y	Y	Y
19 ***LaTourette***	Y	Y	Y	Y	Y
OKLAHOMA					
1 ***Largent***	Y	Y	Y	N	Y
2 ***Coburn***	Y	Y	N	N	Y
3 ***Watkins***	Y	Y	Y	Y	Y
4 ***Watts***	Y	Y	Y	Y	Y
5 ***Istook***	Y	Y	Y	N	Y
6 ***Lucas***	Y	Y	Y	Y	Y
OREGON					
1 Wu	Y	Y	N	Y	Y
2 ***Walden***	Y	Y	Y	Y	Y
3 Blumenauer	Y	Y	N	N	Y
4 DeFazio	Y	Y	N	N	Y
5 Hooley	Y	Y	N	Y	Y
PENNSYLVANIA					
1 Brady	Y	Y	N	Y	Y
2 Fattah	Y	Y	N	Y	Y
3 Borski	Y	Y	N	Y	Y
4 Klink	?	?	?	?	?
5 ***Peterson***	Y	Y	Y	Y	Y
6 Holden	Y	Y	N	N	Y
7 ***Weldon***	Y	Y	Y	Y	Y
8 ***Greenwood***	Y	Y	Y	N	Y
9 ***Shuster***	Y	Y	Y	Y	Y
10 ***Sherwood***	Y	Y	Y	Y	Y
11 Kanjorski	Y	Y	N	N	Y
12 Murtha	Y	Y	N	Y	Y
13 Hoeffel	Y	Y	N	Y	Y
14 Coyne	Y	Y	N	N	Y
15 ***Toomey***	Y	Y	Y	N	Y
16 ***Pitts***	Y	Y	Y	Y	Y
17 ***Gekas***	Y	Y	Y	Y	Y
18 Doyle	Y	Y	N	Y	Y
19 ***Goodling***	Y	Y	Y	N	Y
20 Mascara	Y	Y	N	Y	Y
21 ***English***	Y	Y	Y	Y	Y
RHODE ISLAND					
1 Kennedy	Y	Y	N	N	Y
2 Weygand	Y	Y	N	N	Y
SOUTH CAROLINA					
1 ***Sanford***	Y	Y	Y	N	Y
2 ***Spence***	Y	Y	Y	Y	Y
3 ***Graham***	Y	Y	Y	Y	Y
4 ***DeMint***	Y	Y	Y	N	Y
5 Spratt	Y	Y	N	Y	Y
6 Clyburn	Y	Y	Y	Y	Y
SOUTH DAKOTA					
AL ***Thune***	Y	Y	Y	Y	Y

	498	499	500	501	502
TENNESSEE					
1 ***Jenkins***	Y	Y	Y	Y	Y
2 ***Duncan***	Y	Y	Y	Y	Y
3 ***Wamp***	Y	Y	Y	Y	Y
4 ***Hilleary***	Y	Y	Y	Y	Y
5 Clement	Y	Y	N	Y	Y
6 Gordon	Y	?	N	Y	Y
7 ***Bryant***	Y	Y	Y	Y	Y
8 Tanner	Y	Y	N	Y	Y
9 Ford	Y	Y	N	Y	Y
TEXAS					
1 Sandlin	?	?	Y	Y	Y
2 Turner	Y	Y	N	Y	Y
3 ***Johnson, Sam***	Y	Y	Y	N	Y
4 Hall	Y	Y	Y	Y	Y
5 ***Sessions***	Y	Y	Y	Y	Y
6 ***Barton***	Y	Y	Y	Y	Y
7 ***Archer***	Y	Y	Y	N	Y
8 ***Brady***	Y	Y	Y	N	Y
9 Lampson	Y	Y	Y	Y	Y
10 Doggett	Y	Y	N	N	Y
11 Edwards	Y	Y	N	Y	Y
12 ***Granger***	Y	Y	Y	Y	Y
13 ***Thornberry***	Y	Y	Y	Y	Y
14 ***Paul***	?	?	?	?	?
15 Hinojosa	Y	Y	N	Y	Y
16 Reyes	Y	Y	N	Y	Y
17 Stenholm	Y	Y	N	N	Y
18 Jackson-Lee	?	?	N	Y	Y
19 ***Combest***	Y	Y	Y	Y	Y
20 Gonzalez	Y	Y	N	Y	Y
21 ***Smith***	Y	Y	Y	Y	Y
22 ***DeLay***	Y	Y	Y	Y	Y
23 ***Bonilla***	Y	Y	Y	Y	Y
24 Frost	Y	Y	Y	Y	Y
25 Bentsen	Y	Y	Y	Y	Y
26 ***Armey***	Y	Y	Y	Y	Y
27 Ortiz	Y	Y	N	Y	Y
28 Rodriguez	Y	Y	N	Y	Y
29 Green	Y	Y	Y	Y	Y
30 Johnson, E.B.	Y	Y	N	Y	Y
UTAH					
1 ***Hansen***	Y	Y	Y	Y	Y
2 ***Cook***	Y	Y	Y	N	Y
3 ***Cannon***	Y	Y	Y	Y	Y
VERMONT					
AL *Sanders*	Y	Y	N	N	Y
VIRGINIA					
1 Vacant					
2 Pickett	Y	?	N	Y	?
3 Scott	Y	Y	N	Y	Y
4 Sisisky	Y	Y	N	Y	Y
5 *Goode*	Y	Y	Y	Y	Y
6 ***Goodlatte***	Y	Y	Y	Y	Y
7 ***Bliley***	Y	Y	N	N	Y
8 Moran	Y	Y	N	Y	Y
9 Boucher	Y	Y	N	Y	Y
10 ***Wolf***	Y	Y	Y	Y	Y
11 ***Davis***	Y	Y	Y	Y	Y
WASHINGTON					
1 Inslee	Y	Y	N	N	Y
2 ***Metcalf***	Y	Y	Y	Y	Y
3 Baird	Y	Y	N	Y	Y
4 ***Hastings***	Y	Y	Y	Y	Y
5 ***Nethercutt***	Y	Y	Y	Y	Y
6 Dicks	Y	Y	Y	Y	Y
7 McDermott	Y	Y	N	N	Y
8 ***Dunn***	Y	Y	Y	Y	Y
9 Smith	Y	Y	N	Y	Y
WEST VIRGINIA					
1 Mollohan	Y	Y	Y	Y	Y
2 Wise	Y	Y	Y	Y	?
3 Rahall	Y	Y	Y	Y	Y
WISCONSIN					
1 ***Ryan***	Y	Y	Y	N	Y
2 Baldwin	Y	Y	N	N	Y
3 Kind	Y	Y	N	N	Y
4 Kleczka	Y	Y	N	N	Y
5 Barrett	Y	Y	N	N	Y
6 ***Petri***	Y	Y	Y	N	Y
7 Obey	Y	Y	N	N	Y
8 ***Green***	Y	Y	Y	N	Y
9 ***Sensenbrenner***	Y	Y	Y	N	Y
WYOMING					
AL ***Cubin***	Y	Y	Y	N	Y

Southern states - Ala., Ark., Fla., Ga., Ky., La., Miss., N.C., Okla., S.C., Tenn., Texas, Va.

503. HR 4049. Privacy Commission/Passage. Horn, R-Calif., motion to suspend the rules and pass the bill that would establish a Commission for the Comprehensive Study of Privacy Protection, which would study individual privacy and how to balance the protection of individual privacy with appropriate use of personal information collected by governments and private industry. It would authorize $5 million for the operation of the commission. Motion rejected 250-146: R 182-21; D 67-124 (ND 43-98, SD 24-26); I 1-1. A two-thirds majority of those present and voting (264) is required for passage under suspension of the rules. Oct. 2, 2000. A "nay" was a vote in support of the president's position.

504. HR 4147. Child Pornography/Passage. Canady, R-Fla., motion to suspend the rules and pass the bill that would raise from 16 to 18 the maximum age of minors for whom adults could be penalized for giving obscene materials. Motion agreed to 397-2: R 202-0; D 193-2 (ND 144-0, SD 49-2); I 2-0. A two-thirds majority of those present and voting (266 in this case) is required for passage under suspension of the rules. Oct. 2, 2000.

505. HR 3088. HIV Testing/Passage. Canady, R-Fla., motion to suspend the rules and pass the bill that would allow sexual assault victims to find out the HIV status of their suspected assailant immediately after charges are brought. Motion agreed to 380-19: R 201-1; D 178-17 (ND 131-13, SD 47-4); I 1-1. A two-thirds majority of those present and voting (266 in this case) is required for passage under suspension of the rules. Oct. 2, 2000.

506. HR 4578. Fiscal 2001 Interior Appropriations/Rule. Adoption of the rule (H Res 603) to provide for House floor consideration of the conference report on the bill that would appropriate $18.8 billion for the Interior Department. Adopted 354-65: R 200-13; D 153-51 (ND 112-40, SD 41-11); I 1-1. Oct. 3, 2000.

507. HR 4578. Fiscal 2001 Interior Appropriations/Conference Report. Adoption of the conference report on the bill that would appropriate $18.8 billion for the Interior Department. Adopted (thus sent to the Senate) 348-69: R 148-62; D 199-6 (ND 151-2, SD 48-4); I 1-1. Oct. 3, 2000.

508. H Res 278. Breast Cancer Research/Adoption. Coburn, R-Okla., motion to suspend the rules and adopt the resolution to express the sense of the House regarding the importance of education, early detection and treatment and other efforts in the fight against breast cancer. Motion agreed to 420-0: R 212-0; D 206-0 (ND 154-0, SD 52-0); I 2-0. A two-thirds majority of those present and voting (280 in this case) is required for adoption under suspension of the rules. Oct. 3, 2000.

Key

- Y Voted for (yea).
- # Paired for.
- + Announced for.
- N Voted against (nay).
- X Paired against.
- – Announced against.
- P Voted "present."
- C Voted "present" to avoid possible conflict of interest.
- ? Did not vote or otherwise make a position known.

•

Democrats ***Republicans***
Independents

	503	504	505	506	507	508
ALABAMA						
1 ***Callahan***	Y	Y	Y	N	Y	Y
2 ***Everett***	+	+	+	Y	Y	Y
3 ***Riley***	+	+	+	+	+	+
4 ***Aderholt***	Y	Y	Y	Y	Y	Y
5 Cramer	Y	Y	Y	Y	Y	Y
6 ***Bachus***	Y	Y	Y	Y	Y	Y
7 Hilliard	N	Y	Y	N	Y	Y
ALASKA						
AL ***Young***	Y	Y	Y	N	N	Y
ARIZONA						
1 ***Salmon***	Y	Y	Y	Y	N	Y
2 Pastor	Y	Y	Y	Y	Y	Y
3 ***Stump***	Y	Y	Y	Y	Y	Y
4 ***Shadegg***	Y	Y	Y	Y	N	Y
5 ***Kolbe***	Y	Y	Y	Y	Y	Y
6 ***Hayworth***	Y	Y	Y	Y	N	Y
ARKANSAS						
1 Berry	Y	Y	Y	Y	N	Y
2 Snyder	N	Y	Y	Y	Y	Y
3 ***Hutchinson***	Y	?	Y	Y	N	Y
4 ***Dickey***	Y	Y	Y	Y	Y	Y
CALIFORNIA						
1 Thompson	N	Y	Y	N	Y	Y
2 ***Herger***	Y	Y	Y	Y	Y	Y
3 ***Ose***	Y	Y	Y	Y	Y	Y
4 ***Doolittle***	Y	Y	Y	Y	Y	Y
5 Matsui	N	Y	Y	Y	Y	Y
6 Woolsey	+	+	–	N	Y	Y
7 Miller, George	N	Y	N	N	Y	Y
8 Pelosi	N	Y	N	Y	Y	Y
9 Lee	N	Y	N	N	Y	Y
10 Tauscher	N	Y	Y	N	Y	Y
11 ***Pombo***	N	Y	Y	Y	N	Y
12 Lantos	N	Y	Y	Y	Y	Y
13 Stark	N	Y	N	N	Y	Y
14 Eshoo	?	?	?	?	?	?
15 ***Campbell***	?	?	?	Y	Y	Y
16 Lofgren	N	Y	Y	Y	Y	Y
17 Farr	N	Y	Y	Y	Y	Y
18 Condit	N	Y	Y	Y	Y	Y
19 ***Radanovich***	Y	Y	Y	Y	Y	Y
20 Dooley	Y	Y	Y	Y	Y	Y
21 ***Thomas***	N	Y	Y	Y	Y	Y
22 Capps	Y	Y	Y	Y	Y	Y
23 ***Gallegly***	Y	Y	Y	Y	Y	Y
24 Sherman	N	Y	Y	Y	Y	Y
25 ***McKeon***	Y	Y	Y	Y	Y	Y
26 Berman	N	Y	Y	Y	Y	Y
27 ***Rogan***	Y	Y	Y	Y	Y	Y
28 ***Dreier***	Y	Y	Y	Y	Y	Y
29 Waxman	N	Y	N	N	Y	Y
30 Becerra	N	Y	Y	Y	Y	Y
31 ***Martinez***	?	?	?	Y	?	Y
32 Dixon	N	Y	Y	Y	Y	Y
33 Roybal-Allard	N	Y	N	Y	Y	Y
34 Napolitano	N	Y	Y	+	Y	Y
35 Waters	N	Y	N	Y	Y	Y
36 ***Kuykendall***	Y	Y	Y	Y	Y	Y
37 Millender-McD.	N	Y	Y	Y	Y	Y
38 ***Horn***	Y	Y	Y	Y	Y	Y
39 ***Royce***	N	Y	Y	Y	N	Y
40 ***Lewis***	Y	Y	Y	Y	Y	Y
41 ***Miller, Gary***	Y	Y	Y	Y	N	Y
42 Baca	N	Y	Y	Y	?	Y
43 ***Calvert***	Y	Y	Y	Y	Y	Y
44 ***Bono***	Y	Y	Y	N	Y	Y
45 ***Rohrabacher***	N	Y	Y	Y	N	Y
46 Sanchez	N	Y	Y	N	Y	Y
47 ***Cox***	N	Y	Y	Y	N	Y
48 ***Packard***	Y	Y	Y	Y	Y	Y
49 ***Bilbray***	Y	Y	Y	Y	Y	Y
50 Filner	N	Y	Y	Y	Y	Y
51 ***Cunningham***	Y	Y	Y	Y	Y	Y
52 ***Hunter***	Y	Y	Y	Y	Y	Y
COLORADO						
1 DeGette	Y	Y	Y	N	Y	Y
2 Udall	Y	Y	Y	Y	Y	Y
3 ***McInnis***	Y	Y	Y	Y	Y	Y
4 ***Schaffer***	Y	Y	Y	Y	N	Y
5 ***Hefley***	N	Y	Y	?	?	?
6 ***Tancredo***	Y	Y	Y	Y	N	Y
CONNECTICUT						
1 Larson	Y	Y	Y	Y	Y	Y
2 Gejdenson	N	Y	Y	Y	Y	Y
3 DeLauro	N	Y	Y	Y	Y	Y
4 ***Shays***	Y	Y	Y	Y	Y	Y
5 Maloney	Y	Y	Y	Y	Y	Y
6 ***Johnson***	Y	Y	Y	Y	Y	Y
DELAWARE						
AL ***Castle***	Y	Y	Y	Y	Y	Y
FLORIDA						
1 ***Scarborough***	Y	Y	Y	Y	N	Y
2 Boyd	Y	Y	Y	Y	Y	Y
3 Brown	?	?	?	Y	Y	Y
4 ***Fowler***	Y	Y	Y	Y	Y	Y
5 Thurman	N	Y	Y	Y	Y	Y
6 ***Stearns***	Y	Y	Y	Y	N	Y
7 ***Mica***	Y	Y	Y	Y	Y	Y
8 ***McCollum***	?	?	?	?	?	?
9 ***Bilirakis***	Y	Y	Y	Y	Y	Y
10 ***Young***	Y	Y	Y	Y	Y	Y
11 Davis	Y	Y	Y	Y	Y	Y
12 ***Canady***	Y	Y	Y	Y	Y	Y
13 ***Miller***	Y	Y	Y	Y	Y	Y
14 ***Goss***	Y	Y	Y	Y	Y	Y
15 ***Weldon***	Y	Y	Y	Y	Y	Y
16 ***Foley***	Y	Y	Y	Y	Y	Y
17 Meek	Y	Y	Y	Y	Y	Y
18 ***Ros-Lehtinen***	Y	Y	Y	Y	Y	Y
19 Wexler	N	Y	?	?	?	?
20 Deutsch	N	Y	Y	N	Y	Y
21 ***Diaz-Balart***	Y	Y	Y	Y	Y	Y
22 ***Shaw***	Y	Y	Y	Y	Y	Y
23 Hastings	?	?	?	?	?	?
GEORGIA						
1 ***Kingston***	Y	Y	Y	Y	Y	Y
2 Bishop	Y	Y	Y	Y	Y	Y
3 ***Collins***	Y	Y	Y	Y	Y	Y
4 McKinney	N	Y	Y	N	Y	Y
5 Lewis	N	Y	N	N	Y	Y
6 ***Isakson***	Y	Y	Y	N	Y	Y
7 ***Barr***	N	Y	Y	Y	N	Y
8 ***Chambliss***	Y	Y	Y	N	N	Y
9 ***Deal***	N	Y	Y	Y	Y	Y
10 ***Norwood***	N	Y	Y	N	Y	Y
11 ***Linder***	Y	Y	Y	Y	Y	Y
HAWAII						
1 Abercrombie	N	Y	Y	N	Y	Y
2 Mink	N	Y	Y	N	Y	Y
IDAHO						
1 ***Chenoweth-Hage***	Y	Y	Y	Y	N	Y
2 ***Simpson***	Y	Y	Y	Y	Y	Y
ILLINOIS						
1 Rush	N	Y	Y	Y	Y	Y
2 Jackson	N	Y	N	Y	Y	Y
3 Lipinski	Y	Y	Y	Y	Y	Y
4 Gutierrez	N	Y	Y	Y	Y	Y
5 Blagojevich	?	?	?	N	Y	Y
6 ***Hyde***	Y	Y	Y	Y	Y	Y
7 Davis	N	Y	Y	Y	Y	Y
8 ***Crane***	Y	Y	Y	N	N	Y
9 Schakowsky	N	Y	Y	Y	Y	Y
10 ***Porter***	Y	Y	Y	Y	Y	Y
11 ***Weller***	Y	Y	Y	Y	Y	Y
12 Costello	Y	Y	Y	Y	Y	Y
13 ***Biggert***	Y	Y	Y	Y	Y	Y

ND Northern Democrats SD Southern Democrats

	503	504	505	506	507	508
14 *Hastert*				Y		Y
15 *Ewing*	Y	Y	Y	Y	Y	Y
16 *Manzullo*	Y	Y	Y	Y	Y	Y
17 Evans	N	Y	Y	Y	Y	Y
18 *LaHood*	Y	Y	Y	Y	Y	Y
19 Phelps	Y	Y	Y	N	Y	Y
20 *Shimkus*	Y	Y	Y	Y	Y	Y
INDIANA						
1 Visclosky	N	Y	Y	Y	Y	Y
2 *McIntosh*	?	?	?	?	?	?
3 Roemer	Y	Y	Y	N	Y	Y
4 *Souder*	Y	Y	Y	N	?	Y
5 *Buyer*	Y	Y	Y	Y	Y	Y
6 *Burton*	Y	Y	Y	Y	N	Y
7 *Pease*	Y	Y	Y	Y	Y	Y
8 *Hostettler*	Y	Y	Y	Y	N	Y
9 Hill	Y	Y	Y	N	Y	Y
10 Carson	–	+	+	N	Y	Y
IOWA						
1 *Leach*	Y	Y	Y	Y	Y	Y
2 *Nussle*	Y	Y	Y	Y	Y	Y
3 Boswell	Y	Y	Y	Y	Y	Y
4 *Ganske*	Y	Y	Y	Y	Y	Y
5 *Latham*	Y	Y	Y	Y	Y	Y
KANSAS						
1 *Moran*	Y	Y	Y	Y	Y	Y
2 *Ryun*	Y	Y	Y	Y	N	Y
3 Moore	Y	Y	Y	N	Y	Y
4 *Tiahrt*	Y	Y	Y	Y	N	Y
KENTUCKY						
1 *Whitfield*	Y	Y	Y	Y	Y	Y
2 *Lewis*	Y	Y	Y	Y	Y	Y
3 *Northup*	Y	Y	Y	Y	Y	Y
4 Lucas	Y	Y	Y	Y	Y	Y
5 *Rogers*	Y	Y	Y	Y	Y	Y
6 *Fletcher*	+	+	+	Y	Y	Y
LOUISIANA						
1 *Vitter*	Y	Y	Y	Y	N	Y
2 Jefferson	?	?	Y	N	N	Y
3 *Tauzin*	N	Y	Y	Y	N	Y
4 *McCrery*	Y	Y	Y	Y	Y	Y
5 *Cooksey*	Y	Y	Y	Y	Y	Y
6 *Baker*	Y	Y	Y	Y	Y	Y
7 John	N	Y	Y	N	N	Y
MAINE						
1 Allen	Y	Y	Y	Y	Y	Y
2 Baldacci	?	Y	Y	N	Y	Y
MARYLAND						
1 *Gilchrest*	?	?	?	N	Y	Y
2 *Ehrlich*	N	Y	Y	Y	Y	Y
3 Cardin	N	Y	Y	N	Y	Y
4 Wynn	N	Y	Y	Y	Y	Y
5 Hoyer	N	Y	Y	Y	Y	Y
6 *Bartlett*	Y	Y	Y	Y	Y	Y
7 Cummings	N	Y	Y	Y	Y	Y
8 *Morella*	Y	Y	Y	Y	Y	Y
MASSACHUSETTS						
1 Olver	N	Y	Y	Y	Y	Y
2 Neal	?	?	?	Y	Y	Y
3 McGovern	N	Y	Y	Y	Y	Y
4 Frank	N	?	Y	Y	Y	Y
5 Meehan	N	Y	Y	Y	Y	Y
6 Tierney	N	Y	Y	Y	Y	Y
7 Markey	N	Y	Y	Y	Y	Y
8 Capuano	N	Y	N	Y	Y	Y
9 Moakley	N	Y	Y	Y	Y	Y
10 Delahunt	N	Y	Y	N	Y	Y
MICHIGAN						
1 Stupak	N	Y	Y	N	N	Y
2 *Hoekstra*	Y	Y	Y	Y	N	Y
3 *Ehlers*	Y	Y	Y	Y	Y	Y
4 *Camp*	Y	Y	Y	Y	Y	Y
5 Barcia	Y	Y	Y	N	Y	Y
6 *Upton*	N	Y	Y	Y	Y	Y
7 *Smith*	Y	Y	Y	Y	N	Y
8 Stabenow	Y	Y	Y	Y	Y	Y
9 Kildee	Y	Y	Y	N	Y	Y
10 Bonior	N	Y	Y	Y	Y	Y
11 *Knollenberg*	Y	Y	Y	Y	Y	Y
12 Levin	N	Y	Y	N	Y	Y
13 Rivers	Y	Y	Y	N	Y	Y
14 Conyers	N	Y	?	N	Y	Y
15 Kilpatrick	N	Y	Y	Y	Y	Y
16 Dingell	N	Y	Y	N	Y	Y
MINNESOTA						
1 *Gutknecht*	Y	Y	Y	Y	N	Y
2 Minge	Y	Y	Y	Y	Y	Y
3 *Ramstad*	Y	Y	Y	Y	N	Y
4 Vento	?	?	?	?	?	?
5 Sabo	N	Y	Y	Y	Y	Y
6 Luther	N	Y	Y	N	Y	Y
7 Peterson	Y	Y	Y	N	N	Y
8 Oberstar	N	Y	Y	N	Y	Y
MISSISSIPPI						
1 *Wicker*	Y	Y	Y	Y	Y	Y
2 Thompson	N	Y	Y	Y	Y	Y
3 *Pickering*	N	Y	Y	Y	N	Y
4 Shows	N	Y	Y	Y	Y	Y
5 Taylor	?	Y	Y	Y	Y	Y
MISSOURI						
1 Clay	?	?	?	N	Y	Y
2 *Talent*	Y	Y	Y	Y	N	Y
3 Gephardt	N	Y	Y	Y	Y	Y
4 Skelton	N	Y	Y	Y	Y	Y
5 McCarthy	N	Y	Y	N	Y	Y
6 Danner	N	Y	Y	N	Y	Y
7 *Blunt*	Y	Y	Y	Y	N	Y
8 *Emerson*	Y	Y	Y	Y	N	Y
9 *Hulshof*	Y	Y	Y	Y	N	Y
MONTANA						
AL *Hill*	Y	Y	Y	Y	Y	Y
NEBRASKA						
1 *Bereuter*	Y	Y	Y	Y	Y	Y
2 *Terry*	Y	Y	Y	Y	Y	Y
3 *Barrett*	Y	Y	Y	Y	Y	Y
NEVADA						
1 Berkley	Y	Y	Y	Y	Y	Y
2 *Gibbons*	Y	Y	Y	Y	N	Y
NEW HAMPSHIRE						
1 *Sununu*	Y	Y	Y	Y	Y	Y
2 *Bass*	Y	Y	Y	Y	Y	Y
NEW JERSEY						
1 Andrews	?	Y	Y	N	Y	Y
2 *LoBiondo*	Y	Y	Y	Y	Y	Y
3 *Saxton*	Y	Y	Y	N	Y	Y
4 *Smith*	Y	Y	Y	Y	Y	Y
5 *Roukema*	Y	Y	Y	Y	Y	Y
6 Pallone	N	Y	Y	Y	Y	Y
7 *Franks*	?	?	?	?	?	?
8 Pascrell	Y	Y	Y	Y	Y	Y
9 Rothman	N	Y	Y	Y	Y	Y
10 Payne	N	Y	N	Y	Y	Y
11 *Frelinghuysen*	Y	Y	Y	Y	Y	Y
12 Holt	Y	Y	Y	N	Y	Y
13 Menendez	N	Y	Y	Y	Y	Y
NEW MEXICO						
1 *Wilson*	Y	Y	Y	Y	Y	Y
2 *Skeen*	Y	Y	Y	Y	Y	Y
3 Udall	N	Y	Y	Y	Y	Y
NEW YORK						
1 Forbes	Y	Y	Y	Y	Y	Y
2 *Lazio*	?	?	?	?	?	?
3 *King*	?	?	?	?	?	?
4 McCarthy	Y	Y	Y	Y	Y	Y
5 Ackerman	N	Y	Y	N	Y	Y
6 Meeks	N	Y	Y	N	Y	Y
7 Crowley	Y	Y	Y	Y	Y	Y
8 Nadler	N	Y	N	Y	Y	Y
9 Weiner	Y	Y	Y	Y	Y	Y
10 Towns	?	?	?	Y	Y	Y
11 Owens	–	+	+	Y	Y	Y
12 Velázquez	N	Y	Y	Y	Y	Y
13 *Fossella*	Y	Y	Y	Y	Y	Y
14 Maloney	Y	Y	Y	Y	Y	Y
15 Rangel	N	Y	Y	Y	Y	Y
16 Serrano	?	Y	Y	Y	Y	Y
17 Engel	N	Y	Y	Y	Y	Y
18 Lowey	N	Y	Y	Y	Y	Y
19 *Kelly*	Y	Y	Y	Y	Y	Y
20 *Gilman*	Y	Y	Y	Y	Y	Y
21 McNulty	Y	Y	Y	Y	Y	Y
22 *Sweeney*	Y	Y	Y	Y	Y	Y
23 *Boehlert*	Y	Y	Y	Y	Y	Y
24 *McHugh*	Y	Y	Y	Y	Y	Y
25 *Walsh*	Y	Y	Y	Y	Y	Y
26 Hinchey	N	Y	Y	Y	Y	Y
27 *Reynolds*	Y	Y	Y	Y	Y	Y
28 Slaughter	N	Y	Y	Y	Y	Y
29 LaFalce	N	Y	Y	Y	Y	Y
30 *Quinn*	Y	Y	Y	Y	Y	Y
31 *Houghton*	?	?	?	Y	Y	Y
NORTH CAROLINA						
1 Clayton	N	Y	Y	Y	Y	Y
2 Etheridge	Y	Y	Y	Y	Y	Y
3 *Jones*	Y	Y	Y	N	N	Y
4 Price	Y	Y	Y	Y	Y	Y
5 *Burr*	N	Y	Y	Y	N	Y
6 *Coble*	Y	Y	Y	Y	Y	Y
7 McIntyre	Y	Y	Y	Y	Y	Y
8 *Hayes*	Y	Y	Y	Y	Y	Y
9 *Myrick*	Y	Y	Y	Y	N	Y
10 *Ballenger*	Y	Y	Y	Y	Y	Y
11 *Taylor*	Y	Y	Y	Y	Y	Y
12 Watt	N	N	N	N	Y	Y
NORTH DAKOTA						
AL Pomeroy	N	Y	Y	Y	Y	Y
OHIO						
1 *Chabot*	Y	Y	Y	Y	N	Y
2 *Portman*	–	+	+	Y	Y	Y
3 Hall	N	Y	Y	Y	Y	Y
4 *Oxley*	Y	Y	Y	Y	Y	Y
5 *Gillmor*	N	Y	Y	Y	Y	Y
6 Strickland	N	Y	Y	Y	Y	Y
7 *Hobson*	Y	Y	Y	Y	Y	Y
8 *Boehner*	Y	Y	Y	Y	Y	Y
9 Kaptur	N	Y	Y	Y	Y	Y
10 Kucinich	N	Y	Y	Y	Y	Y
11 Jones	N	Y	N	Y	Y	Y
12 *Kasich*	Y	Y	Y	Y	Y	Y
13 Brown	N	Y	Y	N	Y	Y
14 Sawyer	N	Y	Y	Y	Y	Y
15 *Pryce*	Y	Y	Y	Y	Y	Y
16 *Regula*	Y	Y	Y	Y	Y	Y
17 Traficant	Y	Y	Y	Y	Y	Y
18 *Ney*	Y	Y	Y	Y	Y	Y
19 *LaTourette*	Y	Y	Y	Y	Y	Y
OKLAHOMA						
1 *Largent*	Y	Y	Y	Y	N	Y
2 *Coburn*	N	Y	Y	Y	N	?
3 *Watkins*	Y	Y	Y	Y	Y	Y
4 *Watts*	Y	Y	Y	Y	Y	Y
5 *Istook*	Y	Y	Y	Y	N	Y
6 *Lucas*	Y	Y	Y	Y	Y	Y
OREGON						
1 Wu	Y	Y	Y	Y	Y	Y
2 *Walden*	Y	Y	Y	Y	Y	Y
3 Blumenauer	Y	Y	Y	Y	Y	Y
4 DeFazio	Y	Y	Y	N	Y	Y
5 Hooley	Y	Y	Y	Y	Y	Y
PENNSYLVANIA						
1 Brady	N	Y	Y	Y	Y	Y
2 Fattah	N	Y	Y	Y	Y	Y
3 Borski	N	Y	Y	Y	Y	Y
4 Klink	?	?	?	?	Y	Y
5 *Peterson*	Y	Y	Y	Y	Y	Y
6 Holden	N	Y	Y	Y	Y	Y
7 *Weldon*	Y	Y	Y	Y	Y	Y
8 *Greenwood*	Y	Y	Y	Y	Y	Y
9 *Shuster*	Y	Y	Y	N	Y	Y
10 *Sherwood*	Y	Y	Y	Y	Y	Y
11 Kanjorski	N	Y	Y	Y	Y	Y
12 Murtha	N	Y	Y	Y	Y	Y
13 Hoeffel	–	Y	Y	Y	Y	Y
14 Coyne	N	Y	Y	Y	Y	Y
15 *Toomey*	Y	Y	Y	Y	N	Y
16 *Pitts*	Y	Y	Y	Y	N	Y
17 *Gekas*	Y	Y	Y	Y	Y	Y
18 Doyle	N	Y	Y	Y	Y	Y
19 *Goodling*	?	?	?	Y	Y	Y
20 Mascara	Y	Y	Y	Y	Y	Y
21 *English*	Y	Y	Y	Y	Y	Y
RHODE ISLAND						
1 Kennedy	N	Y	Y	Y	Y	Y
2 Weygand	N	Y	Y	Y	Y	Y
SOUTH CAROLINA						
1 *Sanford*	N	Y	N	Y	N	Y
2 *Spence*	?	?	?	Y	Y	Y
3 *Graham*	Y	Y	Y	Y	N	Y
4 *DeMint*	Y	Y	Y	Y	N	Y
5 Spratt	Y	Y	Y	Y	Y	Y
6 Clyburn	N	Y	Y	Y	Y	Y
SOUTH DAKOTA						
AL *Thune*	Y	Y	Y	Y	Y	Y
TENNESSEE						
1 *Jenkins*	Y	Y	Y	Y	Y	Y
2 *Duncan*	Y	Y	Y	Y	N	Y
3 *Wamp*	Y	Y	Y	Y	Y	Y
4 *Hilleary*	?	?	?	Y	Y	Y
5 Clement	Y	Y	Y	Y	Y	Y
6 Gordon	Y	Y	Y	Y	Y	Y
7 *Bryant*	N	Y	Y	Y	N	Y
8 Tanner	Y	Y	Y	Y	Y	Y
9 Ford	N	Y	Y	Y	Y	Y
TEXAS						
1 Sandlin	Y	Y	Y	N	Y	Y
2 Turner	Y	Y	Y	Y	Y	Y
3 *Johnson, Sam*	Y	Y	Y	Y	N	Y
4 Hall	Y	Y	Y	Y	N	Y
5 *Sessions*	Y	Y	Y	Y	N	Y
6 *Barton*	N	Y	Y	Y	N	Y
7 *Archer*	Y	Y	Y	Y	N	Y
8 *Brady*	Y	Y	Y	Y	N	Y
9 Lampson	Y	Y	Y	Y	Y	Y
10 Doggett	N	Y	Y	Y	Y	Y
11 Edwards	Y	Y	Y	Y	Y	Y
12 *Granger*	Y	Y	Y	Y	Y	Y
13 *Thornberry*	Y	Y	Y	Y	N	Y
14 *Paul*	?	?	?	?	?	?
15 Hinojosa	N	Y	Y	Y	Y	Y
16 Reyes	N	Y	Y	Y	Y	Y
17 Stenholm	N	Y	Y	Y	Y	Y
18 Jackson-Lee	N	Y	N	Y	Y	Y
19 *Combest*	Y	Y	Y	Y	N	Y
20 Gonzalez	Y	Y	Y	N	Y	Y
21 *Smith*	Y	Y	Y	Y	Y	Y
22 *DeLay*	Y	Y	Y	Y	Y	Y
23 *Bonilla*	Y	Y	Y	Y	Y	Y
24 Frost	Y	Y	Y	Y	Y	Y
25 Bentsen	Y	Y	Y	Y	Y	Y
26 *Armey*	Y	Y	Y	Y	Y	Y
27 Ortiz	N	Y	Y	N	Y	Y
28 Rodriguez	N	Y	Y	Y	Y	Y
29 Green	N	Y	Y	Y	Y	Y
30 Johnson, E.B.	N	Y	Y	Y	Y	Y
UTAH						
1 *Hansen*	Y	Y	Y	N	N	Y
2 *Cook*	?	?	?	Y	Y	Y
3 *Cannon*	Y	Y	Y	Y	N	Y
VERMONT						
AL *Sanders*	N	Y	N	N	Y	Y
VIRGINIA						
1 Vacant						
2 Pickett	N	Y	Y	Y	Y	Y
3 Scott	N	N	N	Y	Y	Y
4 Sisisky	Y	Y	Y	Y	Y	Y
5 *Goode*	Y	Y	Y	Y	N	Y
6 *Goodlatte*	N	Y	Y	Y	Y	Y
7 *Bliley*	Y	Y	?	Y	Y	Y
8 Moran	Y	Y	Y	Y	Y	Y
9 Boucher	N	Y	Y	Y	Y	Y
10 *Wolf*	Y	Y	Y	Y	Y	Y
11 *Davis*	Y	Y	Y	Y	Y	Y
WASHINGTON						
1 Inslee	Y	Y	Y	Y	Y	Y
2 *Metcalf*	Y	Y	Y	Y	N	Y
3 Baird	Y	Y	Y	Y	Y	Y
4 *Hastings*	Y	Y	Y	Y	Y	Y
5 *Nethercutt*	Y	Y	Y	Y	Y	Y
6 Dicks	Y	Y	Y	Y	Y	Y
7 McDermott	N	Y	N	N	Y	Y
8 *Dunn*	Y	Y	Y	?	?	?
9 Smith	Y	Y	Y	Y	Y	Y
WEST VIRGINIA						
1 Mollohan	N	Y	Y	Y	Y	Y
2 Wise	?	?	?	Y	Y	Y
3 Rahall	N	Y	Y	Y	Y	Y
WISCONSIN						
1 *Ryan*	Y	Y	Y	Y	N	Y
2 Baldwin	N	Y	Y	Y	Y	Y
3 Kind	Y	Y	Y	N	Y	Y
4 Kleczka	Y	Y	Y	Y	Y	Y
5 Barrett	Y	Y	Y	Y	Y	Y
6 *Petri*	Y	Y	Y	Y	N	Y
7 Obey	N	Y	Y	Y	Y	Y
8 *Green*	Y	Y	Y	Y	N	Y
9 *Sensenbrenner*	Y	Y	Y	Y	N	Y
WYOMING						
AL *Cubin*	N	Y	Y	Y	Y	Y

Southern states - Ala., Ark., Fla., Ga., Ky., La., Miss., N.C., Okla., S.C., Tenn., Texas, Va.

509. H J Res 110. Continuing Resolution/Passage. Passage of the joint resolution that would provide temporary funding authority, at current levels, until Oct. 14 for the departments, agencies and programs for which regular fiscal year 2001 appropriations bills have not been enacted by Oct. 6, 2000. Passed 415-1: R 210-0; D 203-1 (ND 152-1, SD 52-0); I 2-0. Oct. 3, 2000.

510. HR 4942. Fiscal 2001 District of Columbia Appropriations/Motion to Instruct Conferees. Moran, D-Va., motion to instruct conferees to agree with the Senate version of the bill to make fiscal 2001 appropriations for the District of Columbia. Motion rejected 190-219: R 3-205; D 186-13 (ND 140-7, SD 46-6); I 1-1. Oct. 4, 2000.

511. HR 5212. Veterans' Oral History/Passage. Hansen, R-Utah, motion to suspend the rules and pass the bill that would direct the Library of Congress' American Folklife Center to establish a program to collect and catalog video and audio recordings of personal histories and testimonials of American war veterans. The bill would authorize $250,000 for fiscal year 2001 and such sums as may be necessary for each succeeding fiscal year. Motion agreed to 407-0: R 208-0; D 197-0 (ND 146-0, SD 51-0); I 2-0. A two-thirds majority of those present and voting (272 in this case) is required for passage under suspension of the rules. Oct. 4, 2000.

512. S 2311. Ryan White CARE Act/Passage. Passage of the bill that would reauthorize the Ryan White CARE Act programs through fiscal year 2005, distribute funds to states and cities based on the number of both AIDS and HIV cases beginning in 2005, and make other changes. Passed 411-0: R 211-0; D 198-0 (ND 144-0, SD 54-0); I 2-0. Oct. 5, 2000.

513. HR 2941. Las Cienegas Conservation Area/Rule. Adoption of the rule to (H Res 610) to provide for House floor consideration of the bill that would establish 42,000 acres as Las Cienegas National Conservation Area in southern Arizona and 142,800 acres as the Sonoita Valley Acquisition Planning District. Adopted 411-0: R 209-0; D 200-0 (ND 146-0, SD 54-0); I 2-0. (HR 2941 subsequently passed by voice vote.) Oct. 5, 2000.

Key

- Y Voted for (yea).
- # Paired for.
- \+ Announced for.
- N Voted against (nay).
- X Paired against.
- – Announced against.
- P Voted "present."
- C Voted "present" to avoid possible conflict of interest.
- ? Did not vote or otherwise make a position known.

Democrats ***Republicans***
Independents

	509	510	511	512	513
ALABAMA					
1 ***Callahan***	Y	N	Y	Y	Y
2 ***Everett***	Y	N	Y	Y	Y
3 ***Riley***	+	+	+	Y	Y
4 ***Aderholt***	Y	N	Y	Y	Y
5 Cramer	Y	Y	Y	Y	Y
6 ***Bachus***	Y	N	Y	Y	Y
7 Hilliard	Y	Y	Y	Y	Y
ALASKA					
AL ***Young***	Y	N	Y	Y	Y
ARIZONA					
1 ***Salmon***	Y	N	Y	Y	Y
2 Pastor	Y	Y	Y	Y	Y
3 ***Stump***	Y	N	Y	Y	Y
4 ***Shadegg***	Y	N	Y	Y	Y
5 ***Kolbe***	Y	N	Y	Y	Y
6 ***Hayworth***	Y	N	Y	Y	Y
ARKANSAS					
1 Berry	Y	Y	Y	Y	Y
2 Snyder	Y	Y	Y	Y	Y
3 ***Hutchinson***	Y	N	Y	Y	Y
4 ***Dickey***	Y	N	Y	Y	Y
CALIFORNIA					
1 Thompson	Y	Y	Y	Y	Y
2 ***Herger***	Y	N	Y	Y	Y
3 ***Ose***	Y	N	Y	Y	Y
4 ***Doolittle***	Y	N	Y	Y	Y
5 Matsui	Y	Y	Y	Y	Y
6 Woolsey	Y	Y	Y	Y	Y
7 Miller, George	Y	Y	Y	Y	Y
8 Pelosi	Y	Y	Y	Y	Y
9 Lee	Y	Y	Y	Y	Y
10 Tauscher	Y	Y	Y	Y	Y
11 ***Pombo***	Y	N	Y	Y	Y
12 Lantos	Y	Y	Y	Y	Y
13 Stark	Y	Y	Y	Y	Y
14 Eshoo	?	?	?	?	?
15 ***Campbell***	Y	N	Y	Y	Y
16 Lofgren	Y	Y	Y	Y	Y
17 Farr	Y	Y	Y	Y	Y
18 Condit	Y	Y	Y	Y	Y
19 ***Radanovich***	Y	N	Y	Y	Y
20 Dooley	Y	Y	Y	Y	Y
21 ***Thomas***	Y	N	Y	Y	Y
22 Capps	Y	Y	Y	Y	Y
23 ***Gallegly***	Y	N	Y	Y	Y
24 Sherman	Y	Y	Y	Y	Y
25 ***McKeon***	Y	N	Y	Y	Y
26 Berman	Y	Y	Y	Y	Y
27 ***Rogan***	Y	N	Y	Y	Y
28 ***Dreier***	Y	N	Y	Y	Y
29 Waxman	Y	Y	Y	Y	Y
30 Becerra	Y	Y	Y	Y	Y
31 ***Martinez***	Y	N	Y	Y	Y
32 Dixon	Y	Y	Y	Y	Y
33 Roybal-Allard	Y	Y	Y	Y	Y
34 Napolitano	Y	Y	Y	Y	Y
35 Waters	Y	Y	Y	Y	Y
36 ***Kuykendall***	Y	N	Y	Y	Y
37 Millender-McD.	Y	Y	Y	Y	Y
38 ***Horn***	Y	N	Y	Y	Y
39 ***Royce***	Y	N	Y	Y	Y
40 ***Lewis***	Y	N	Y	Y	Y
41 ***Miller, Gary***	Y	N	Y	Y	Y
42 Baca	Y	?	?	Y	Y
43 ***Calvert***	Y	N	Y	Y	Y
44 ***Bono***	Y	N	Y	Y	Y
45 ***Rohrabacher***	Y	N	Y	Y	Y
46 Sanchez	Y	Y	Y	Y	Y
47 ***Cox***	Y	N	Y	Y	Y
48 ***Packard***	Y	N	Y	Y	Y
49 ***Bilbray***	Y	N	Y	Y	Y
50 Filner	Y	Y	Y	Y	Y
51 ***Cunningham***	Y	N	Y	Y	Y
52 ***Hunter***	Y	N	Y	Y	Y
COLORADO					
1 DeGette	Y	Y	Y	Y	Y
2 Udall	Y	Y	Y	Y	Y
3 ***McInnis***	Y	N	Y	Y	Y
4 ***Schaffer***	Y	N	Y	Y	Y
5 ***Hefley***	?	?	?	?	?
6 ***Tancredo***	Y	N	Y	Y	Y
CONNECTICUT					
1 Larson	Y	Y	Y	Y	Y
2 Gejdenson	Y	Y	Y	Y	Y
3 DeLauro	Y	Y	Y	Y	Y
4 ***Shays***	Y	N	Y	Y	Y
5 Maloney	Y	N	Y	+	Y
6 ***Johnson***	Y	N	Y	Y	Y
DELAWARE					
AL ***Castle***	Y	N	Y	Y	Y
FLORIDA					
1 ***Scarborough***	Y	N	Y	Y	Y
2 Boyd	Y	Y	Y	Y	Y
3 Brown	Y	?	?	Y	Y
4 ***Fowler***	Y	N	Y	Y	Y
5 Thurman	Y	Y	Y	Y	Y
6 ***Stearns***	Y	N	Y	Y	Y
7 ***Mica***	Y	N	Y	Y	Y
8 ***McCollum***	?	?	?	?	?
9 ***Bilirakis***	Y	N	Y	Y	Y
10 ***Young***	Y	N	Y	?	Y
11 Davis	Y	Y	Y	Y	Y
12 ***Canady***	Y	N	Y	Y	Y
13 ***Miller***	Y	N	Y	?	?
14 ***Goss***	Y	N	Y	Y	Y
15 ***Weldon***	Y	N	Y	Y	Y
16 ***Foley***	Y	N	Y	Y	Y
17 Meek	Y	Y	Y	Y	Y
18 ***Ros-Lehtinen***	Y	N	Y	Y	Y
19 Wexler	?	Y	Y	Y	Y
20 Deutsch	Y	Y	Y	Y	Y
21 ***Diaz-Balart***	Y	N	Y	Y	Y
22 ***Shaw***	Y	N	Y	Y	Y
23 Hastings	?	?	?	Y	Y
GEORGIA					
1 ***Kingston***	Y	N	Y	Y	Y
2 Bishop	Y	Y	Y	Y	Y
3 ***Collins***	Y	N	Y	Y	Y
4 McKinney	Y	Y	Y	Y	Y
5 Lewis	Y	Y	Y	Y	Y
6 ***Isakson***	Y	N	Y	Y	Y
7 ***Barr***	Y	N	Y	Y	Y
8 ***Chambliss***	Y	N	Y	Y	Y
9 ***Deal***	Y	N	Y	Y	Y
10 ***Norwood***	Y	N	Y	Y	Y
11 ***Linder***	Y	N	Y	Y	Y
HAWAII					
1 Abercrombie	Y	Y	Y	Y	Y
2 Mink	Y	Y	Y	Y	Y
IDAHO					
1 ***Chenoweth-Hage***	Y	N	Y	Y	?
2 ***Simpson***	Y	N	Y	Y	Y
ILLINOIS					
1 Rush	Y	Y	Y	Y	Y
2 Jackson	Y	Y	Y	Y	Y
3 Lipinski	Y	Y	Y	Y	Y
4 Gutierrez	Y	Y	Y	Y	Y
5 Blagojevich	Y	Y	Y	Y	Y
6 ***Hyde***	Y	N	Y	Y	Y
7 Davis	Y	Y	Y	Y	Y
8 ***Crane***	Y	N	Y	Y	Y
9 Schakowsky	Y	Y	Y	Y	Y
10 ***Porter***	Y	Y	Y	Y	Y
11 ***Weller***	Y	N	Y	Y	Y
12 Costello	Y	N	Y	Y	Y
13 ***Biggert***	Y	N	Y	Y	Y

ND Northern Democrats SD Southern Democrats

	509	510	511	512	513
14 ***Hastert***					
15 ***Ewing***	Y	N	Y	Y	Y
16 ***Manzullo***	Y	N	Y	Y	Y
17 Evans	Y	Y	Y	Y	Y
18 ***LaHood***	Y	N	Y	Y	Y
19 Phelps	Y	N	Y	Y	Y
20 ***Shimkus***	Y	N	Y	Y	Y
INDIANA					
1 Visclosky	Y	Y	Y	Y	Y
2 ***McIntosh***	?	?	?	?	?
3 Roemer	Y	N	Y	Y	Y
4 ***Souder***	Y	N	Y	Y	Y
5 ***Buyer***	Y	N	Y	Y	Y
6 ***Burton***	Y	N	Y	Y	Y
7 ***Pease***	Y	N	Y	Y	Y
8 ***Hostettler***	Y	N	Y	Y	Y
9 Hill	Y	Y	Y	Y	Y
10 Carson	Y	Y	Y	Y	Y
IOWA					
1 ***Leach***	Y	N	Y	Y	Y
2 ***Nussle***	Y	N	Y	Y	Y
3 Boswell	Y	Y	Y	Y	Y
4 ***Ganske***	Y	N	Y	Y	Y
5 ***Latham***	Y	N	Y	Y	Y
KANSAS					
1 ***Moran***	Y	N	Y	Y	Y
2 ***Ryun***	Y	N	Y	Y	Y
3 Moore	Y	Y	Y	Y	Y
4 ***Tiahrt***	Y	N	Y	Y	Y
KENTUCKY					
1 ***Whitfield***	Y	N	Y	Y	Y
2 ***Lewis***	Y	N	Y	Y	Y
3 ***Northup***	Y	N	Y	Y	Y
4 Lucas	Y	N	Y	Y	Y
5 ***Rogers***	Y	N	Y	Y	Y
6 ***Fletcher***	Y	N	Y	Y	Y
LOUISIANA					
1 ***Vitter***	Y	N	Y	Y	Y
2 Jefferson	Y	Y	Y	Y	Y
3 ***Tauzin***	Y	N	Y	Y	Y
4 ***McCrery***	Y	N	Y	Y	Y
5 ***Cooksey***	Y	N	Y	Y	Y
6 ***Baker***	Y	N	Y	Y	Y
7 John	Y	Y	Y	Y	Y
MAINE					
1 Allen	Y	Y	Y	Y	Y
2 Baldacci	Y	Y	Y	Y	Y
MARYLAND					
1 ***Gilchrest***	Y	N	Y	Y	Y
2 ***Ehrlich***	Y	N	Y	Y	Y
3 Cardin	Y	Y	Y	Y	Y
4 Wynn	Y	Y	Y	Y	Y
5 Hoyer	Y	?	?	Y	Y
6 ***Bartlett***	Y	N	Y	Y	Y
7 Cummings	Y	Y	Y	Y	Y
8 ***Morella***	Y	Y	Y	Y	Y
MASSACHUSETTS					
1 Olver	Y	Y	Y	Y	Y
2 Neal	Y	Y	Y	Y	Y
3 McGovern	Y	Y	Y	Y	Y
4 Frank	Y	Y	Y	Y	Y
5 Meehan	?	?	?	Y	Y
6 Tierney	Y	Y	Y	Y	Y
7 Markey	Y	Y	Y	Y	Y
8 Capuano	Y	Y	Y	Y	Y
9 Moakley	Y	Y	Y	Y	Y
10 Delahunt	Y	Y	Y	Y	Y
MICHIGAN					
1 Stupak	Y	Y	Y	Y	Y
2 ***Hoekstra***	Y	N	Y	Y	Y
3 ***Ehlers***	Y	N	Y	Y	Y
4 ***Camp***	Y	N	Y	Y	Y
5 Barcia	Y	Y	Y	Y	Y
6 ***Upton***	Y	N	Y	Y	Y
7 ***Smith***	Y	N	Y	Y	Y
8 Stabenow	Y	Y	Y	Y	?
9 Kildee	Y	Y	Y	Y	Y
10 Bonior	Y	Y	Y	?	Y
11 ***Knollenberg***	Y	N	Y	Y	Y
12 Levin	Y	Y	Y	Y	Y
13 Rivers	Y	Y	Y	Y	Y
14 Conyers	Y	Y	Y	Y	Y
15 Kilpatrick	Y	Y	Y	Y	Y
16 Dingell	Y	Y	Y	Y	Y

	509	510	511	512	513
MINNESOTA					
1 ***Gutknecht***	Y	N	Y	Y	Y
2 Minge	Y	Y	Y	Y	Y
3 ***Ramstad***	Y	N	Y	Y	Y
4 Vento	?	?	?	?	?
5 Sabo	Y	Y	Y	Y	Y
6 Luther	Y	Y	Y	Y	Y
7 Peterson	Y	Y	Y	Y	Y
8 Oberstar	Y	Y	Y	Y	Y
MISSISSIPPI					
1 ***Wicker***	Y	N	Y	Y	Y
2 Thompson	Y	Y	Y	Y	Y
3 ***Pickering***	Y	N	Y	Y	Y
4 Shows	Y	N	Y	Y	Y
5 Taylor	Y	N	Y	Y	Y
MISSOURI					
1 Clay	Y	Y	Y	?	?
2 ***Talent***	Y	N	Y	Y	Y
3 Gephardt	Y	?	?	?	Y
4 Skelton	Y	?	?	Y	Y
5 McCarthy	Y	Y	Y	Y	Y
6 Danner	Y	Y	Y	Y	Y
7 ***Blunt***	Y	N	Y	Y	Y
8 ***Emerson***	Y	N	Y	Y	Y
9 ***Hulshof***	Y	N	Y	Y	Y
MONTANA					
AL ***Hill***	Y	N	Y	Y	Y
NEBRASKA					
1 ***Bereuter***	Y	N	Y	Y	Y
2 ***Terry***	Y	N	Y	Y	Y
3 ***Barrett***	Y	N	Y	Y	Y
NEVADA					
1 Berkley	Y	Y	Y	?	Y
2 ***Gibbons***	Y	N	Y	Y	Y
NEW HAMPSHIRE					
1 ***Sununu***	Y	N	Y	Y	Y
2 ***Bass***	Y	N	Y	Y	Y
NEW JERSEY					
1 Andrews	Y	Y	Y	Y	Y
2 ***LoBiondo***	Y	N	Y	Y	Y
3 ***Saxton***	Y	N	Y	Y	Y
4 ***Smith***	Y	N	Y	Y	Y
5 ***Roukema***	Y	N	Y	Y	Y
6 Pallone	Y	Y	Y	Y	Y
7 ***Franks***	?	?	?	?	?
8 Pascrell	Y	Y	Y	Y	Y
9 Rothman	Y	Y	Y	Y	Y
10 Payne	Y	Y	Y	Y	?
11 ***Frelinghuysen***	Y	N	Y	Y	Y
12 Holt	Y	Y	Y	Y	Y
13 Menendez	Y	Y	Y	Y	Y
NEW MEXICO					
1 ***Wilson***	Y	N	Y	Y	Y
2 ***Skeen***	Y	N	Y	Y	Y
3 Udall	Y	Y	Y	Y	Y
NEW YORK					
1 Forbes	Y	N	Y	Y	Y
2 ***Lazio***	?	?	?	?	?
3 ***King***	?	?	?	?	?
4 McCarthy	Y	Y	Y	Y	Y
5 Ackerman	Y	Y	Y	Y	Y
6 Meeks	Y	Y	Y	Y	Y
7 Crowley	Y	Y	Y	Y	Y
8 Nadler	Y	Y	Y	Y	Y
9 Weiner	Y	Y	Y	Y	Y
10 Towns	Y	Y	Y	Y	Y
11 Owens	Y	Y	Y	Y	Y
12 Velázquez	Y	Y	Y	Y	Y
13 ***Fossella***	Y	+	+	Y	Y
14 Maloney	Y	Y	Y	Y	Y
15 Rangel	Y	Y	Y	?	Y
16 Serrano	Y	Y	Y	Y	Y
17 Engel	Y	Y	Y	Y	Y
18 Lowey	Y	Y	Y	Y	Y
19 ***Kelly***	Y	N	Y	Y	Y
20 ***Gilman***	Y	N	Y	Y	Y
21 McNulty	Y	Y	Y	Y	Y
22 ***Sweeney***	Y	?	?	?	?
23 ***Boehlert***	Y	N	Y	Y	Y
24 ***McHugh***	Y	N	Y	Y	Y
25 ***Walsh***	Y	N	Y	Y	Y
26 Hinchey	Y	Y	Y	Y	Y
27 ***Reynolds***	Y	N	Y	Y	Y
28 Slaughter	Y	Y	Y	Y	Y
29 LaFalce	Y	Y	Y	Y	Y

	509	510	511	512	513
30 ***Quinn***	Y	N	Y	Y	Y
31 ***Houghton***	?	?	?	Y	Y
NORTH CAROLINA					
1 Clayton	Y	Y	?	Y	Y
2 Etheridge	Y	Y	Y	Y	Y
3 ***Jones***	Y	N	Y	Y	Y
4 Price	Y	Y	Y	Y	Y
5 ***Burr***	Y	N	Y	Y	Y
6 ***Coble***	Y	N	Y	Y	Y
7 McIntyre	Y	N	Y	Y	Y
8 ***Hayes***	Y	N	Y	Y	Y
9 ***Myrick***	Y	N	Y	Y	Y
10 ***Ballenger***	?	N	Y	Y	Y
11 ***Taylor***	Y	N	Y	Y	Y
12 Watt	Y	Y	Y	Y	Y
NORTH DAKOTA					
AL Pomeroy	Y	Y	Y	Y	Y
OHIO					
1 ***Chabot***	Y	N	Y	Y	Y
2 ***Portman***	Y	N	Y	Y	Y
3 Hall	Y	Y	Y	Y	Y
4 ***Oxley***	Y	N	Y	Y	Y
5 ***Gillmor***	Y	N	Y	Y	Y
6 Strickland	Y	Y	Y	Y	Y
7 ***Hobson***	Y	N	Y	Y	Y
8 ***Boehner***	Y	N	Y	Y	Y
9 Kaptur	Y	Y	Y	Y	Y
10 Kucinich	Y	Y	Y	Y	Y
11 Jones	Y	Y	Y	Y	Y
12 ***Kasich***	Y	N	Y	Y	Y
13 Brown	Y	Y	Y	Y	Y
14 Sawyer	Y	Y	Y	Y	Y
15 ***Pryce***	Y	N	Y	Y	Y
16 ***Regula***	Y	N	Y	Y	Y
17 Traficant	Y	N	Y	Y	Y
18 ***Ney***	Y	N	Y	Y	Y
19 ***LaTourette***	Y	N	Y	Y	Y
OKLAHOMA					
1 ***Largent***	Y	N	Y	Y	Y
2 ***Coburn***	Y	N	Y	Y	Y
3 ***Watkins***	Y	N	Y	Y	Y
4 ***Watts***	Y	N	Y	Y	Y
5 ***Istook***	Y	N	Y	Y	Y
6 ***Lucas***	Y	N	Y	Y	Y
OREGON					
1 Wu	Y	Y	Y	Y	Y
2 ***Walden***	Y	N	Y	Y	Y
3 Blumenauer	Y	Y	Y	Y	Y
4 DeFazio	N	Y	Y	Y	Y
5 Hooley	Y	Y	Y	Y	Y
PENNSYLVANIA					
1 Brady	Y	Y	Y	Y	Y
2 Fattah	Y	Y	Y	Y	Y
3 Borski	Y	Y	Y	Y	Y
4 Klink	Y	?	?	?	?
5 ***Peterson***	Y	N	Y	Y	Y
6 Holden	Y	N	Y	Y	Y
7 ***Weldon***	Y	N	Y	Y	Y
8 ***Greenwood***	Y	Y	Y	Y	Y
9 ***Shuster***	Y	N	Y	Y	Y
10 ***Sherwood***	Y	N	Y	Y	Y
11 Kanjorski	Y	Y	Y	Y	Y
12 Murtha	Y	Y	Y	?	?
13 Hoeffel	Y	Y	Y	Y	Y
14 Coyne	Y	Y	Y	Y	Y
15 ***Toomey***	Y	N	Y	Y	Y
16 ***Pitts***	Y	N	Y	Y	Y
17 ***Gekas***	Y	N	Y	Y	Y
18 Doyle	Y	Y	Y	Y	Y
19 ***Goodling***	Y	N	Y	Y	?
20 Mascara	Y	Y	Y	Y	Y
21 ***English***	Y	?	?	Y	Y
RHODE ISLAND					
1 Kennedy	Y	Y	Y	Y	Y
2 Weygand	Y	Y	Y	Y	Y
SOUTH CAROLINA					
1 ***Sanford***	Y	N	Y	Y	Y
2 ***Spence***	Y	N	Y	Y	Y
3 ***Graham***	Y	N	Y	Y	Y
4 ***DeMint***	Y	N	Y	Y	Y
5 Spratt	Y	Y	Y	Y	Y
6 Clyburn	Y	Y	Y	Y	Y
SOUTH DAKOTA					
AL ***Thune***	Y	N	Y	Y	Y

	509	510	511	512	513
TENNESSEE					
1 ***Jenkins***	Y	N	Y	Y	Y
2 ***Duncan***	Y	N	Y	Y	Y
3 ***Wamp***	Y	N	Y	Y	Y
4 ***Hilleary***	Y	?	?	Y	Y
5 Clement	Y	Y	Y	Y	Y
6 Gordon	Y	Y	Y	Y	Y
7 ***Bryant***	Y	N	Y	Y	Y
8 Tanner	Y	Y	Y	Y	Y
9 Ford	Y	Y	Y	Y	Y
TEXAS					
1 Sandlin	Y	Y	Y	Y	Y
2 Turner	Y	Y	Y	Y	Y
3 ***Johnson, Sam***	Y	N	Y	Y	Y
4 Hall	Y	N	Y	Y	Y
5 ***Sessions***	Y	N	Y	Y	Y
6 ***Barton***	Y	N	Y	Y	Y
7 ***Archer***	Y	N	Y	Y	Y
8 ***Brady***	Y	N	Y	Y	Y
9 Lampson	Y	Y	Y	Y	Y
10 Doggett	Y	Y	Y	Y	Y
11 Edwards	Y	Y	Y	Y	Y
12 ***Granger***	Y	N	Y	Y	?
13 ***Thornberry***	Y	N	Y	Y	Y
14 ***Paul***	?	?	?	?	?
15 Hinojosa	+	Y	Y	Y	Y
16 Reyes	Y	Y	Y	Y	Y
17 Stenholm	Y	Y	Y	Y	Y
18 Jackson-Lee	Y	Y	Y	Y	Y
19 ***Combest***	Y	N	Y	Y	Y
20 Gonzalez	Y	Y	Y	Y	Y
21 ***Smith***	Y	N	Y	Y	Y
22 ***DeLay***	Y	N	Y	Y	Y
23 ***Bonilla***	Y	N	Y	Y	Y
24 Frost	Y	Y	Y	Y	Y
25 Bentsen	Y	Y	Y	Y	Y
26 ***Armey***	Y	N	Y	Y	Y
27 Ortiz	Y	Y	Y	Y	Y
28 Rodriguez	Y	Y	Y	Y	Y
29 Green	Y	Y	Y	Y	Y
30 Johnson, E.B.	Y	Y	Y	Y	Y
UTAH					
1 ***Hansen***	Y	N	Y	Y	Y
2 ***Cook***	Y	N	Y	Y	Y
3 ***Cannon***	Y	N	Y	Y	Y
VERMONT					
AL *Sanders*	Y	Y	Y	Y	Y
VIRGINIA					
1 Vacant					
2 Pickett	Y	N	Y	Y	Y
3 Scott	Y	Y	Y	Y	Y
4 Sisisky	Y	Y	Y	Y	Y
5 *Goode*	Y	N	Y	Y	Y
6 ***Goodlatte***	Y	N	Y	Y	Y
7 ***Bliley***	Y	N	Y	Y	Y
8 Moran	Y	Y	Y	Y	Y
9 Boucher	Y	Y	Y	Y	Y
10 ***Wolf***	Y	N	Y	Y	Y
11 ***Davis***	Y	N	Y	Y	Y
WASHINGTON					
1 Inslee	Y	Y	Y	Y	Y
2 ***Metcalf***	Y	N	Y	Y	Y
3 Baird	Y	Y	Y	Y	?
4 ***Hastings***	Y	N	Y	Y	Y
5 ***Nethercutt***	Y	N	Y	Y	Y
6 Dicks	Y	Y	Y	Y	Y
7 McDermott	Y	Y	Y	Y	Y
8 ***Dunn***	?	N	Y	Y	Y
9 Smith	Y	Y	Y	Y	Y
WEST VIRGINIA					
1 Mollohan	Y	Y	Y	Y	Y
2 Wise	Y	?	?	?	?
3 Rahall	Y	Y	Y	Y	Y
WISCONSIN					
1 ***Ryan***	Y	N	Y	Y	Y
2 Baldwin	Y	Y	Y	Y	Y
3 Kind	Y	Y	Y	Y	Y
4 Kleczka	Y	Y	Y	Y	Y
5 Barrett	Y	Y	?	Y	Y
6 ***Petri***	Y	N	Y	Y	Y
7 Obey	Y	Y	Y	?	?
8 ***Green***	Y	N	Y	Y	Y
9 ***Sensenbrenner***	Y	N	Y	Y	Y
WYOMING					
AL ***Cubin***	Y	N	Y	Y	Y

Southern states - Ala., Ark., Fla., Ga., Ky., La., Miss., N.C., Okla., S.C., Tenn., Texas, Va.

514. Procedural Motion/Journal. Approval of the House Journal of Thursday, Oct. 5, 2000. Approved 267-50: R 141-15; D 125-35 (ND 88-31, SD 37-4); I 1-0. Oct. 6, 2000.

515. HR 4475. Fiscal 2001 Transportation Appropriations/Rule. Adoption of the rule (H Res 612) to provide for House floor consideration of the conference report on the bill that would appropriate $58 billion for the Transportation Department and related agencies in fiscal 2001. Adopted 244-136: R 191-6; D 52-129 (ND 41-93, SD 11-36); I 1-1. Oct. 6, 2000.

516. HR 4475. Fiscal 2001 Transportation Appropriations/Conference Report. Adoption of the conference report on the bill that would provide $58 billion for the Transportation Department and related agencies in fiscal 2001, including $31.4 billion in highway funding. Adopted (thus sent to the Senate) 344-50: R 161-39; D 181-11 (ND 134-7, SD 47-4); I 2-0. Oct. 6, 2000.

517. HR 3244. Human Trafficking/Rule. Adoption of the rule (H Res 613) to provide for House floor consideration of the conference report on the bill to combat human trafficking and establish a new visa for aliens who are victims of human trafficking, as well as several other crime measures. Adopted 356-28: R 187-7; D 168-20 (ND 124-15, SD 44-5); I 1-1. Oct. 6, 2000.

518. HR 3244. Human Trafficking/Conference Report. Adoption of the conference report on the bill to combat human trafficking and establish a new visa for aliens who are victims of human trafficking. The bill also would: reauthorize the Violence Against Women Act and authorize $3.3 billion in fiscal 2001-05 to carry it out; strengthen enforcement of state laws outlawing direct sales of alcohol over the Internet; require states releasing violent sexual offenders who commit similar crimes in another state to reimburse the second state for costs related to the apprehension, prosecution and incarceration of the criminal; and allow terrorism victims to recover judgments from frozen assets of countries listed by the State Department as terrorism sponsors. Adopted (thus sent to the Senate) 371-1: R 187-1; D 182-0 (ND 134-0, SD 48-0); I 2-0. Oct. 6, 2000. A "yea" was a vote in support of the president's position.

519. S 2438. Pipeline Safety/Passage. Shuster, R-Pa., motion to suspend the rules and pass the bill that would reauthorize the Pipeline Safety Act through 2003. Motion rejected 232-158: R 180-20; D 51-137 (ND 24-115, SD 27-22); I 1-1. A two-thirds majority of those present and voting (260 in this case) is required for passage under suspension of the rules. Oct. 10, 2000.

[1] *Bruce F. Vento, D-Minn., died Oct. 10, 2000. The last vote for which he was eligible was 518.*

Key

- Y Voted for (yea).
- # Paired for.
- + Announced for.
- N Voted against (nay).
- X Paired against.
- – Announced against.
- P Voted "present."
- C Voted "present" to avoid possible conflict of interest.
- ? Did not vote or otherwise make a position known.

Democrats ***Republicans***
Independents

	514	515	516	517	518	519
ALABAMA						
1 ***Callahan***	Y	Y	Y	?	?	Y
2 ***Everett***	Y	Y	Y	Y	+	Y
3 ***Riley***	N	Y	Y	Y	Y	+
4 ***Aderholt***	N	Y	Y	Y	Y	Y
5 Cramer	Y	Y	Y	Y	?	Y
6 ***Bachus***	Y	Y	Y	Y	Y	Y
7 Hilliard	N	N	Y	Y	Y	N
ALASKA						
AL ***Young***	?	?	Y	Y	Y	Y
ARIZONA						
1 ***Salmon***	Y	Y	N	Y	Y	Y
2 Pastor	Y	N	Y	Y	Y	N
3 ***Stump***	Y	Y	N	Y	Y	Y
4 ***Shadegg***	Y	?	N	Y	Y	Y
5 ***Kolbe***	Y	Y	Y	+	+	?
6 ***Hayworth***	Y	Y	N	Y	Y	Y
ARKANSAS						
1 Berry	Y	N	Y	Y	Y	N
2 Snyder	Y	N	Y	Y	Y	N
3 ***Hutchinson***	N	Y	?	?	?	Y
4 ***Dickey***	N	Y	Y	Y	Y	Y
CALIFORNIA						
1 Thompson	N	N	Y	N	Y	N
2 ***Herger***	?	Y	N	Y	Y	Y
3 ***Ose***	Y	Y	Y	N	Y	Y
4 ***Doolittle***	?	Y	Y	N	Y	Y
5 Matsui	Y	N	Y	Y	Y	N
6 Woolsey	Y	N	Y	N	Y	N
7 Miller, George	N	N	Y	Y	Y	?
8 Pelosi	Y	N	Y	N	Y	?
9 Lee	Y	N	Y	N	Y	N
10 Tauscher	Y	Y	Y	Y	Y	Y
11 ***Pombo***	?	Y	Y	N	Y	?
12 Lantos	Y	N	Y	Y	Y	N
13 Stark	N	N	Y	?	?	?
14 Eshoo	?	?	?	?	?	?
15 ***Campbell***	Y	Y	?	?	?	?
16 Lofgren	Y	N	Y	N	Y	N
17 Farr	Y	N	Y	Y	?	?
18 Condit	Y	N	Y	Y	Y	Y
19 ***Radanovich***	?	Y	Y	Y	Y	Y
20 Dooley	Y	Y	Y	N	Y	Y
21 ***Thomas***	?	Y	Y	Y	Y	Y
22 Capps	Y	N	Y	Y	Y	N
23 ***Gallegly***	Y	Y	Y	Y	Y	Y
24 Sherman	Y	N	Y	Y	Y	N
25 ***McKeon***	Y	Y	Y	Y	Y	Y
26 Berman	?	?	?	?	?	N
27 ***Rogan***	?	Y	Y	Y	Y	Y
28 ***Dreier***	Y	Y	Y	Y	Y	Y
29 Waxman	?	?	?	?	?	N
30 Becerra	Y	N	Y	Y	Y	N
31 ***Martinez***	?	?	Y	Y	Y	Y
32 Dixon	?	?	Y	Y	Y	N
33 Roybal-Allard	Y	N	Y	Y	Y	N
34 Napolitano	Y	N	Y	Y	Y	Y
35 Waters	?	?	?	?	?	N
36 ***Kuykendall***	Y	Y	Y	Y	Y	Y
37 Millender-McD.	?	N	Y	Y	Y	Y
38 ***Horn***	Y	Y	Y	Y	Y	Y
39 ***Royce***	Y	Y	N	Y	Y	Y
40 ***Lewis***	Y	Y	Y	Y	Y	Y
41 ***Miller, Gary***	Y	Y	Y	Y	Y	Y
42 Baca	Y	N	Y	Y	Y	N
43 ***Calvert***	?	Y	Y	Y	Y	Y
44 ***Bono***	?	Y	Y	Y	Y	?
45 ***Rohrabacher***	Y	Y	N	Y	Y	Y
46 Sanchez	N	N	Y	Y	Y	N
47 ***Cox***	Y	Y	N	Y	Y	Y
48 ***Packard***	Y	Y	Y	Y	Y	Y
49 ***Bilbray***	?	Y	Y	Y	Y	Y
50 Filner	–	N	Y	Y	Y	N
51 ***Cunningham***	Y	Y	Y	Y	Y	Y
52 ***Hunter***	Y	Y	Y	Y	?	Y
COLORADO						
1 DeGette	Y	N	Y	N	Y	N
2 Udall	N	N	Y	Y	Y	N
3 ***McInnis***	Y	Y	Y	Y	Y	Y
4 ***Schaffer***	N	Y	N	Y	Y	Y
5 ***Hefley***	?	?	?	?	?	Y
6 ***Tancredo***	?	Y	Y	Y	Y	Y
CONNECTICUT						
1 Larson	Y	Y	Y	Y	Y	N
2 Gejdenson	Y	N	Y	Y	Y	N
3 DeLauro	Y	N	Y	Y	Y	N
4 ***Shays***	Y	Y	Y	Y	Y	N
5 Maloney	Y	Y	Y	Y	Y	Y
6 ***Johnson***	?	Y	Y	Y	Y	N
DELAWARE						
AL ***Castle***	?	Y	Y	Y	Y	Y
FLORIDA						
1 ***Scarborough***	Y	Y	Y	Y	Y	N
2 Boyd	Y	N	Y	Y	Y	Y
3 Brown	?	N	Y	Y	Y	?
4 ***Fowler***	Y	Y	Y	Y	+	Y
5 Thurman	Y	N	Y	Y	Y	N
6 ***Stearns***	Y	Y	N	Y	Y	Y
7 ***Mica***	Y	Y	Y	Y	+	Y
8 ***McCollum***	?	?	?	?	?	?
9 ***Bilirakis***	?	Y	Y	Y	+	Y
10 ***Young***	Y	Y	Y	Y	Y	Y
11 Davis	?	Y	Y	Y	Y	Y
12 ***Canady***	?	Y	Y	Y	Y	Y
13 ***Miller***	?	?	?	?	?	?
14 ***Goss***	?	?	?	?	?	Y
15 ***Weldon***	?	Y	Y	Y	Y	Y
16 ***Foley***	+	+	Y	Y	Y	Y
17 Meek	?	?	?	?	?	N
18 ***Ros-Lehtinen***	Y	Y	Y	Y	Y	Y
19 Wexler	?	N	Y	Y	Y	N
20 Deutsch	Y	N	Y	Y	Y	N
21 ***Diaz-Balart***	+	+	+	+	+	Y
22 ***Shaw***	Y	Y	Y	Y	Y	Y
23 Hastings	N	N	Y	Y	Y	N
GEORGIA						
1 ***Kingston***	Y	Y	Y	Y	Y	Y
2 Bishop	Y	Y	Y	Y	Y	N
3 ***Collins***	?	Y	Y	Y	Y	Y
4 McKinney	?	?	Y	Y	Y	N
5 Lewis	?	?	?	?	?	N
6 ***Isakson***	Y	Y	Y	?	?	Y
7 ***Barr***	Y	Y	Y	Y	Y	?
8 ***Chambliss***	Y	Y	Y	Y	Y	Y
9 ***Deal***	Y	Y	Y	Y	Y	Y
10 ***Norwood***	?	Y	Y	Y	Y	Y
11 ***Linder***	Y	Y	Y	Y	Y	Y
HAWAII						
1 Abercrombie	Y	Y	Y	Y	Y	N
2 Mink	Y	Y	Y	Y	Y	?
IDAHO						
1 ***Chenoweth-Hage***	?	Y	Y	Y	Y	N
2 ***Simpson***	Y	Y	Y	Y	Y	Y
ILLINOIS						
1 Rush	?	?	Y	Y	Y	N
2 Jackson	Y	N	Y	Y	Y	N
3 Lipinski	N	Y	Y	Y	?	N
4 Gutierrez	N	N	Y	Y	Y	?
5 Blagojevich	Y	Y	Y	Y	Y	?
6 ***Hyde***	Y	Y	Y	Y	Y	Y
7 Davis	Y	Y	Y	Y	Y	N
8 ***Crane***	?	?	Y	Y	Y	?
9 Schakowsky	Y	Y	Y	Y	Y	N
10 ***Porter***	?	?	Y	Y	Y	N
11 ***Weller***	N	Y	Y	Y	Y	Y
12 Costello	N	N	Y	Y	Y	N
13 ***Biggert***	Y	Y	Y	Y	Y	Y

ND Northern Democrats SD Southern Democrats

	514	515	516	517	518	519
14 ***Hastert***	Y				Y	
15 ***Ewing***	Y	Y	Y	Y	Y	Y
16 ***Manzullo***	Y	Y	Y	Y	Y	N
17 Evans	Y	Y	Y	Y	Y	N
18 ***LaHood***	Y	Y	Y	Y	Y	Y
19 Phelps	N	N	Y	Y	Y	N
20 ***Shimkus***	Y	Y	Y	Y	Y	Y
INDIANA						
1 Visclosky	N	N	Y	Y	Y	N
2 ***McIntosh***	?	?	?	?	?	?
3 Roemer	Y	N	Y	Y	Y	Y
4 ***Souder***	?	Y	Y	Y	Y	Y
5 ***Buyer***	Y	Y	Y	Y	Y	Y
6 ***Burton***	?	Y	Y	Y	Y	Y
7 ***Pease***	Y	Y	Y	Y	Y	N
8 ***Hostettler***	Y	Y	N	Y	Y	Y
9 Hill	Y	Y	Y	Y	Y	N
10 Carson	+	−	+	−	+	−
IOWA						
1 ***Leach***	?	Y	Y	Y	Y	Y
2 ***Nussle***	Y	Y	Y	Y	Y	Y
3 Boswell	Y	N	Y	Y	Y	N
4 ***Ganske***	Y	Y	Y	Y	Y	N
5 ***Latham***	Y	Y	Y	Y	Y	Y
KANSAS						
1 ***Moran***	N	Y	Y	Y	Y	Y
2 ***Ryun***	Y	Y	N	Y	Y	Y
3 Moore	Y	Y	Y	Y	Y	N
4 ***Tiahrt***	Y	Y	Y	Y	Y	Y
KENTUCKY						
1 ***Whitfield***	?	Y	Y	Y	Y	Y
2 ***Lewis***	Y	Y	Y	Y	Y	Y
3 ***Northup***	Y	Y	Y	Y	Y	Y
4 Lucas	Y	N	Y	Y	Y	Y
5 ***Rogers***	?	Y	Y	Y	Y	Y
6 ***Fletcher***	Y	Y	Y	Y	Y	Y
LOUISIANA						
1 ***Vitter***	?	Y	Y	Y	Y	Y
2 Jefferson	Y	N	Y	Y	Y	?
3 ***Tauzin***	Y	Y	Y	Y	Y	Y
4 ***McCrery***	Y	Y	Y	Y	Y	Y
5 ***Cooksey***	Y	Y	Y	Y	Y	Y
6 ***Baker***	?	?	?	?	?	Y
7 John	Y	N	Y	Y	Y	Y
MAINE						
1 Allen	Y	N	Y	Y	Y	N
2 Baldacci	N	N	Y	Y	Y	Y
MARYLAND						
1 ***Gilchrest***	?	?	Y	Y	Y	Y
2 ***Ehrlich***	?	Y	Y	Y	Y	Y
3 Cardin	Y	Y	Y	Y	Y	N
4 Wynn	Y	Y	Y	Y	Y	Y
5 Hoyer	?	Y	Y	Y	Y	N
6 ***Bartlett***	Y	Y	Y	Y	Y	Y
7 Cummings	?	?	Y	Y	Y	N
8 ***Morella***	Y	Y	Y	Y	Y	N
MASSACHUSETTS						
1 Olver	Y	Y	Y	Y	Y	N
2 Neal	N	N	Y	Y	Y	Y
3 McGovern	?	N	Y	Y	Y	N
4 Frank	Y	N	Y	Y	Y	N
5 Meehan	?	N	Y	Y	Y	N
6 Tierney	Y	N	Y	Y	Y	N
7 Markey	Y	Y	Y	Y	Y	N
8 Capuano	N	N	Y	Y	Y	Y
9 Moakley	Y	N	Y	Y	Y	Y
10 Delahunt	?	?	Y	Y	Y	Y
MICHIGAN						
1 Stupak	N	N	Y	Y	Y	N
2 ***Hoekstra***	N	N	N	Y	Y	?
3 ***Ehlers***	Y	Y	Y	Y	Y	Y
4 ***Camp***	Y	Y	Y	Y	Y	Y
5 Barcia	Y	N	N	Y	Y	Y
6 ***Upton***	Y	Y	Y	Y	Y	Y
7 ***Smith***	P	Y	Y	Y	Y	Y
8 Stabenow	?	Y	Y	Y	Y	N
9 Kildee	Y	N	Y	Y	Y	N
10 Bonior	?	N	Y	Y	Y	N
11 ***Knollenberg***	Y	Y	Y	Y	?	?
12 Levin	Y	N	Y	Y	Y	N
13 Rivers	Y	N	Y	Y	Y	N
14 Conyers	?	?	Y	N	Y	N
15 Kilpatrick	Y	N	Y	Y	Y	N
16 Dingell	Y	N	Y	Y	Y	N

	514	515	516	517	518	519
MINNESOTA						
1 ***Gutknecht***	N	Y	N	Y	Y	Y
2 Minge	Y	N	Y	N	Y	Y
3 ***Ramstad***	N	Y	Y	Y	Y	Y
4 Vento[1]	?	?	?	?	?	
5 Sabo	N	N	Y	Y	Y	N
6 Luther	Y	N	Y	Y	Y	N
7 Peterson	?	Y	Y	Y	Y	N
8 Oberstar	N	N	Y	N	Y	N
MISSISSIPPI						
1 ***Wicker***	?	Y	Y	Y	Y	Y
2 Thompson	N	N	Y	?	?	N
3 ***Pickering***	Y	Y	Y	Y	Y	Y
4 Shows	Y	+	Y	Y	Y	Y
5 Taylor	N	N	N	Y	Y	Y
MISSOURI						
1 Clay	?	?	?	?	?	N
2 ***Talent***	Y	Y	?	?	?	?
3 Gephardt	?	N	Y	Y	Y	N
4 Skelton	Y	Y	Y	Y	Y	N
5 McCarthy	+	N	Y	Y	Y	N
6 Danner	Y	Y	Y	Y	?	?
7 ***Blunt***	Y	Y	Y	Y	Y	Y
8 ***Emerson***	Y	Y	Y	Y	Y	Y
9 ***Hulshof***	?	Y	Y	N	Y	Y
MONTANA						
AL ***Hill***	N	N	Y	Y	Y	Y
NEBRASKA						
1 ***Bereuter***	Y	Y	Y	Y	Y	N
2 ***Terry***	Y	Y	Y	Y	Y	Y
3 ***Barrett***	Y	Y	Y	Y	Y	Y
NEVADA						
1 Berkley	Y	N	Y	Y	Y	N
2 ***Gibbons***	N	Y	Y	Y	Y	Y
NEW HAMPSHIRE						
1 ***Sununu***	Y	Y	Y	Y	Y	Y
2 ***Bass***	Y	Y	Y	Y	Y	Y
NEW JERSEY						
1 Andrews	Y	N	Y	Y	Y	N
2 ***LoBiondo***	N	Y	Y	Y	Y	N
3 ***Saxton***	Y	Y	Y	Y	Y	N
4 ***Smith***	Y	Y	Y	Y	Y	N
5 ***Roukema***	Y	Y	Y	Y	Y	N
6 Pallone	Y	N	Y	Y	Y	N
7 ***Franks***	?	?	?	?	?	?
8 Pascrell	Y	Y	Y	Y	+	N
9 Rothman	Y	N	Y	Y	Y	N
10 Payne	Y	N	Y	N	Y	N
11 ***Frelinghuysen***	Y	Y	Y	Y	Y	N
12 Holt	N	N	Y	Y	Y	N
13 Menendez	Y	Y	Y	Y	Y	N
NEW MEXICO						
1 ***Wilson***	Y	Y	Y	Y	Y	?
2 ***Skeen***	Y	Y	Y	Y	Y	Y
3 Udall	N	N	Y	Y	Y	N
NEW YORK						
1 Forbes	Y	N	Y	?	?	N
2 ***Lazio***	?	?	?	?	?	?
3 ***King***	?	?	?	?	?	Y
4 McCarthy	Y	N	Y	Y	Y	N
5 Ackerman	?	?	?	?	?	N
6 Meeks	?	?	?	?	?	?
7 Crowley	N	N	Y	Y	Y	N
8 Nadler	Y	N	Y	Y	Y	N
9 Weiner	Y	N	Y	Y	Y	N
10 Towns	Y	N	Y	Y	Y	N
11 Owens	+	N	Y	Y	Y	N
12 Velázquez	Y	N	N	Y	Y	N
13 ***Fossella***	?	Y	Y	Y	Y	Y
14 Maloney	Y	N	Y	N	Y	N
15 Rangel	?	?	?	?	?	N
16 Serrano	Y	Y	Y	Y	Y	N
17 Engel	?	?	Y	Y	Y	N
18 Lowey	?	?	Y	Y	Y	N
19 ***Kelly***	Y	Y	Y	Y	Y	Y
20 ***Gilman***	Y	Y	Y	Y	Y	Y
21 McNulty	N	Y	Y	Y	Y	N
22 ***Sweeney***	N	N	Y	Y	Y	Y
23 ***Boehlert***	?	Y	Y	Y	Y	Y
24 ***McHugh***	Y	Y	Y	Y	Y	Y
25 ***Walsh***	Y	Y	Y	Y	Y	Y
26 Hinchey	?	N	Y	Y	Y	N
27 ***Reynolds***	Y	Y	Y	Y	Y	Y
28 Slaughter	N	N	Y	Y	Y	Y
29 LaFalce	N	Y	Y	Y	Y	N

	514	515	516	517	518	519
30 ***Quinn***	?	Y	Y	Y	Y	Y
31 ***Houghton***	Y	Y	Y	Y	Y	Y
NORTH CAROLINA						
1 Clayton	Y	N	Y	N	Y	N
2 Etheridge	Y	N	Y	Y	Y	?
3 ***Jones***	Y	Y	N	Y	Y	Y
4 Price	Y	N	Y	Y	Y	Y
5 ***Burr***	Y	Y	Y	Y	Y	Y
6 ***Coble***	Y	Y	Y	Y	Y	Y
7 McIntyre	Y	N	Y	Y	Y	Y
8 ***Hayes***	?	Y	Y	Y	Y	Y
9 ***Myrick***	Y	Y	Y	Y	Y	Y
10 ***Ballenger***	Y	Y	+	+	+	Y
11 ***Taylor***	Y	Y	Y	Y	Y	Y
12 Watt	?	N	Y	N	Y	N
NORTH DAKOTA						
AL Pomeroy	Y	Y	Y	Y	Y	Y
OHIO						
1 ***Chabot***	Y	Y	N	Y	Y	Y
2 ***Portman***	Y	Y	Y	Y	Y	Y
3 Hall	Y	Y	Y	Y	Y	N
4 ***Oxley***	Y	Y	N	Y	Y	Y
5 ***Gillmor***	Y	Y	N	Y	Y	Y
6 Strickland	?	?	?	?	?	N
7 ***Hobson***	Y	Y	Y	Y	Y	Y
8 ***Boehner***	Y	Y	N	Y	Y	Y
9 Kaptur	?	Y	Y	Y	Y	N
10 Kucinich	N	N	Y	Y	Y	N
11 Jones	Y	N	Y	N	Y	N
12 ***Kasich***	Y	Y	N	Y	Y	?
13 Brown	Y	N	Y	Y	Y	N
14 Sawyer	N	N	Y	Y	Y	N
15 ***Pryce***	Y	Y	Y	Y	Y	Y
16 ***Regula***	Y	Y	Y	Y	Y	Y
17 Traficant	Y	Y	Y	Y	Y	Y
18 ***Ney***	Y	Y	Y	Y	Y	Y
19 ***LaTourette***	Y	Y	Y	N	?	Y
OKLAHOMA						
1 ***Largent***	?	Y	N	Y	Y	?
2 ***Coburn***	Y	N	N	Y	Y	Y
3 ***Watkins***	Y	Y	Y	Y	Y	Y
4 ***Watts***	Y	Y	Y	Y	Y	Y
5 ***Istook***	Y	Y	Y	Y	Y	Y
6 ***Lucas***	Y	Y	Y	Y	Y	Y
OREGON						
1 Wu	N	N	Y	N	Y	−
2 ***Walden***	Y	Y	Y	Y	Y	Y
3 Blumenauer	?	?	?	?	?	N
4 DeFazio	N	Y	Y	Y	Y	N
5 Hooley	Y	N	Y	Y	Y	Y
PENNSYLVANIA						
1 Brady	N	N	Y	Y	Y	N
2 Fattah	Y	N	Y	Y	Y	?
3 Borski	N	N	Y	Y	Y	N
4 Klink	?	?	?	?	?	?
5 ***Peterson***	Y	Y	Y	?	+	Y
6 Holden	Y	N	Y	Y	Y	N
7 ***Weldon***	Y	Y	?	?	Y	Y
8 ***Greenwood***	Y	Y	Y	Y	Y	Y
9 ***Shuster***	?	?	?	?	?	Y
10 ***Sherwood***	Y	Y	Y	Y	Y	N
11 Kanjorski	Y	Y	Y	Y	Y	Y
12 Murtha	Y	Y	Y	N	Y	Y
13 Hoeffel	Y	Y	Y	Y	Y	N
14 Coyne	Y	Y	Y	Y	Y	N
15 ***Toomey***	Y	Y	N	Y	Y	Y
16 ***Pitts***	Y	Y	N	Y	Y	Y
17 ***Gekas***	Y	Y	Y	Y	Y	Y
18 Doyle	Y	Y	Y	Y	Y	Y
19 ***Goodling***	Y	Y	Y	Y	?	Y
20 Mascara	Y	Y	Y	Y	Y	N
21 ***English***	?	Y	Y	Y	Y	Y
RHODE ISLAND						
1 Kennedy	Y	N	Y	Y	?	N
2 Weygand	Y	Y	Y	Y	Y	?
SOUTH CAROLINA						
1 ***Sanford***	Y	Y	N	N	N	N
2 ***Spence***	?	?	?	?	?	Y
3 ***Graham***	?	Y	N	Y	Y	Y
4 ***DeMint***	Y	Y	N	Y	Y	Y
5 Spratt	Y	Y	Y	Y	Y	Y
6 Clyburn	Y	Y	Y	Y	Y	N
SOUTH DAKOTA						
AL ***Thune***	Y	Y	Y	Y	Y	Y

	514	515	516	517	518	519
TENNESSEE						
1 ***Jenkins***	Y	Y	Y	?	Y	Y
2 ***Duncan***	Y	Y	Y	Y	Y	Y
3 ***Wamp***	Y	Y	Y	Y	Y	N
4 ***Hilleary***	N	Y	Y	Y	Y	Y
5 Clement	Y	Y	Y	Y	Y	Y
6 Gordon	Y	N	Y	N	Y	N
7 ***Bryant***	Y	Y	N	Y	Y	Y
8 Tanner	Y	N	Y	Y	Y	Y
9 Ford	?	N	Y	Y	Y	?
TEXAS						
1 Sandlin	Y	N	Y	Y	Y	Y
2 Turner	Y	N	Y	Y	Y	Y
3 ***Johnson, Sam***	?	Y	N	Y	Y	Y
4 Hall	Y	Y	Y	Y	Y	Y
5 ***Sessions***	Y	Y	N	Y	Y	Y
6 ***Barton***	?	Y	N	?	?	Y
7 ***Archer***	?	Y	N	Y	Y	?
8 ***Brady***	Y	Y	N	Y	Y	Y
9 Lampson	Y	N	Y	Y	Y	Y
10 Doggett	Y	N	N	Y	Y	N
11 Edwards	?	N	Y	Y	Y	Y
12 ***Granger***	Y	Y	Y	Y	Y	Y
13 ***Thornberry***	Y	Y	N	Y	Y	Y
14 ***Paul***	?	?	?	?	?	N
15 Hinojosa	Y	N	Y	Y	Y	N
16 Reyes	?	?	?	?	?	?
17 Stenholm	Y	N	Y	Y	Y	Y
18 Jackson-Lee	Y	N	Y	N	Y	Y
19 ***Combest***	Y	Y	Y	Y	Y	Y
20 Gonzalez	Y	N	Y	Y	Y	Y
21 ***Smith***	?	?	?	?	?	Y
22 ***DeLay***	?	Y	Y	Y	Y	Y
23 ***Bonilla***	Y	Y	Y	Y	Y	Y
24 Frost	Y	N	Y	Y	Y	Y
25 Bentsen	Y	N	N	Y	Y	Y
26 ***Armey***	?	Y	Y	Y	Y	Y
27 Ortiz	Y	Y	Y	Y	Y	Y
28 Rodriguez	?	?	Y	Y	Y	N
29 Green	Y	N	N	Y	Y	Y
30 Johnson, E.B.	Y	N	Y	Y	Y	N
UTAH						
1 ***Hansen***	?	?	?	?	?	Y
2 ***Cook***	Y	Y	Y	Y	Y	?
3 ***Cannon***	?	?	Y	Y	Y	Y
VERMONT						
AL *Sanders*	?	N	Y	N	Y	N
VIRGINIA						
1 Vacant						
2 Pickett	Y	Y	Y	?	?	Y
3 Scott	?	N	Y	N	Y	N
4 Sisisky	Y	Y	Y	Y	Y	Y
5 *Goode*	Y	Y	Y	Y	Y	Y
6 ***Goodlatte***	Y	Y	Y	Y	Y	Y
7 ***Bliley***	Y	Y	Y	Y	?	?
8 Moran	Y	Y	Y	Y	Y	Y
9 Boucher	?	?	Y	Y	Y	N
10 ***Wolf***	Y	Y	Y	Y	Y	Y
11 ***Davis***	?	Y	Y	Y	Y	Y
WASHINGTON						
1 Inslee	Y	Y	Y	Y	Y	N
2 ***Metcalf***	?	?	?	?	?	N
3 Baird	N	N	Y	Y	Y	N
4 ***Hastings***	Y	Y	Y	Y	Y	Y
5 ***Nethercutt***	Y	Y	Y	N	Y	Y
6 Dicks	?	?	?	?	?	Y
7 McDermott	N	N	Y	Y	Y	N
8 ***Dunn***	?	Y	Y	Y	Y	Y
9 Smith	Y	N	Y	Y	Y	N
WEST VIRGINIA						
1 Mollohan	?	N	Y	Y	Y	Y
2 Wise	?	?	?	?	?	?
3 Rahall	Y	Y	Y	Y	Y	N
WISCONSIN						
1 ***Ryan***	Y	Y	N	Y	Y	Y
2 Baldwin	Y	N	N	Y	Y	N
3 Kind	Y	N	N	Y	Y	N
4 Kleczka	?	N	N	Y	Y	N
5 Barrett	Y	N	N	Y	Y	N
6 ***Petri***	Y	N	N	Y	Y	Y
7 Obey	N	N	N	Y	Y	N
8 ***Green***	Y	Y	N	Y	Y	Y
9 ***Sensenbrenner***	Y	N	N	Y	Y	Y
WYOMING						
AL ***Cubin***	?	Y	N	Y	Y	Y

Southern states - Ala., Ark., Fla., Ga., Ky., La., Miss., N.C., Okla., S.C., Tenn., Texas, Va.

520. HR 208. Federal Employee Retirement/Passage. Morella, R-Md., motion to suspend the rules and concur with the Senate amendments to the bill that would allow federal employees to participate in the Thrift Savings Plan (TSP) immediately upon being hired. It also would allow new employees to transfer some "rollover" funds from other tax-deferred savings plans, including 401(k) accounts, into the TSP. Motion agreed to 382-0: R 194-0; D 186-0 (ND 138-0, SD 48-0); I 2-0. A two-thirds majority of those present and voting (255 in this case) is required for passage under suspension of the rules. Oct. 10, 2000.

521. HR 762. Lupus Research/Passage. Bilirakis, R-Fla., motion to suspend the rules and pass the bill that would authorize in fiscal 2001-03 a program to expand and intensify research on lupus at the National Institutes of Health and for a program to help people afflicted with lupus, and their families. Motion agreed to 385-2: R 197-2; D 186-0 (ND 138-0, SD 48-0); I 2-0. A two-thirds majority of those present and voting (258 in this case) is required for passage under suspension of the rules. Oct. 10, 2000.

522. HR 4205. Fiscal 2001 Defense Department Authorization/Conference Report. Adoption of the conference report on the bill that would authorize $309.9 billion for the Defense Department, including $4.8 billion for ballistic missile defense programs. It also would entitle military retirees to lifetime health care benefits and would restore prescription coverage to most Medicare-eligible retirees. Adopted (thus sent to the Senate) 382-31: R 206-4; D 175-26 (ND 123-24, SD 52-2); I 1-1. Oct. 11, 2000.

523. HR 4733. Fiscal 2001 Energy-Water Appropriations/Veto Override. Passage, over President Clinton's Oct. 7, 2000, veto of the conference report on the bill that would appropriate $23.6 billion for the Energy Department, the Army Corps of Engineers and other agencies. Passed 315-98: R 182-28; D 132-69 (ND 90-58, SD 42-11); I 1-1. A two-thirds majority of those present and voting (276 House members in this case) of both houses is required to override a veto. A "nay" was a vote in support of the president's position. Oct. 11, 2000.

524. HR 4461. Fiscal 2001 Agriculture Appropriations/Rule. Diaz-Balart, R-Fla., motion to order the previous question (thus ending debate and the possiblity of amendment) on adoption of the rule (H Res 617) to provide for House floor consideration of the conference report on the bill that would appropriate $78.5 billion for the Agriculture Department and related agencies. Adopted 214-201: R 210-2; D 3-198 (ND 1-147, SD 2-51); I 1-1. Oct. 11, 2000. (Subsequently, the rule was adopted by voice vote.)

525. HR 4461. Fiscal 2001 Agriculture Appropriations/Conference Report. Adoption of the conference report on the bill that would appropriate $78.5 billion for the Agriculture Department and related agencies. The agreement includes $3.6 billion in emergency aid for farmers and a deal that would allow the sale of food and medicine to five nations including Cuba but bar public or private U.S. financing of Cuban purchases. It also would codify the executive order restricting travel to Cuba. U.S. pharmacies and wholesalers would be allowed to re-import U.S.-made prescription drugs that are sold abroad for less than they cost in the United States. Adopted (thus sent to the Senate) 340-75: R 176-36; D 162-39 (ND 113-35, SD 49-4); I 2-0. Oct. 11, 2000.)

Key

- Y Voted for (yea).
- # Paired for.
- \+ Announced for.
- N Voted against (nay).
- X Paired against.
- – Announced against.
- P Voted "present."
- C Voted "present" to avoid possible conflict of interest.
- ? Did not vote or otherwise make a position known.

•

Democrats **Republicans**
Independents

	520	521	522	523	524	525
ALABAMA						
1 ***Callahan***	Y	Y	Y	Y	Y	Y
2 ***Everett***	Y	Y	Y	Y	Y	Y
3 ***Riley***	+	+	Y	Y	Y	Y
4 ***Aderholt***	Y	Y	Y	Y	Y	Y
5 Cramer	Y	Y	Y	Y	N	Y
6 ***Bachus***	Y	Y	Y	Y	Y	Y
7 Hilliard	Y	Y	Y	N	N	Y
ALASKA						
AL ***Young***	Y	Y	Y	Y	Y	Y
ARIZONA						
1 ***Salmon***	?	Y	Y	Y	Y	N
2 Pastor	Y	Y	Y	Y	N	?
3 ***Stump***	Y	Y	Y	Y	Y	Y
4 ***Shadegg***	Y	Y	Y	Y	Y	N
5 ***Kolbe***	?	?	Y	Y	Y	N
6 ***Hayworth***	Y	Y	Y	Y	Y	Y
ARKANSAS						
1 Berry	Y	Y	Y	Y	N	Y
2 Snyder	Y	Y	Y	Y	N	Y
3 ***Hutchinson***	Y	Y	?	Y	Y	Y
4 ***Dickey***	Y	Y	Y	Y	Y	Y
CALIFORNIA						
1 Thompson	Y	Y	Y	Y	N	Y
2 ***Herger***	Y	Y	Y	Y	Y	Y
3 ***Ose***	Y	Y	Y	Y	Y	Y
4 ***Doolittle***	Y	Y	Y	Y	Y	Y
5 Matsui	Y	Y	Y	Y	N	Y
6 Woolsey	Y	Y	N	Y	N	Y
7 Miller, George	?	?	N	Y	N	N
8 Pelosi	?	Y	Y	Y	N	N
9 Lee	Y	Y	N	Y	N	N
10 Tauscher	Y	Y	Y	Y	N	Y
11 ***Pombo***	?	?	Y	Y	Y	Y
12 Lantos	Y	Y	Y	Y	N	N
13 Stark	?	?	N	Y	N	N
14 Eshoo	?	?	?	?	?	?
15 ***Campbell***	?	?	?	?	?	?
16 Lofgren	Y	Y	N	Y	N	N
17 Farr	?	?	Y	Y	N	Y
18 Condit	Y	Y	Y	Y	N	Y
19 ***Radanovich***	Y	Y	Y	Y	Y	Y
20 Dooley	Y	Y	Y	Y	N	Y
21 ***Thomas***	Y	Y	Y	Y	Y	Y
22 Capps	Y	Y	Y	Y	N	Y
23 ***Gallegly***	Y	Y	Y	Y	Y	Y
24 Sherman	Y	Y	Y	N	N	N
25 ***McKeon***	Y	Y	Y	Y	Y	Y
26 Berman	Y	Y	Y	N	N	N
27 ***Rogan***	Y	Y	Y	Y	Y	Y
28 ***Dreier***	Y	Y	Y	Y	Y	Y
29 Waxman	Y	Y	?	?	N	N
30 Becerra	Y	Y	Y	N	N	Y
31 ***Martinez***	Y	Y	Y	Y	Y	Y
32 Dixon	Y	Y	Y	Y	N	Y
33 Roybal-Allard	Y	Y	Y	N	N	Y
34 Napolitano	Y	Y	Y	N	N	N
35 Waters	Y	Y	N	N	N	N
36 ***Kuykendall***	Y	Y	Y	Y	Y	Y
37 Millender-McD.	Y	Y	Y	Y	N	Y
38 ***Horn***	Y	Y	Y	Y	N	Y
39 ***Royce***	Y	Y	Y	N	Y	N
40 ***Lewis***	Y	Y	Y	Y	Y	Y
41 ***Miller, Gary***	Y	Y	Y	Y	Y	Y
42 Baca	Y	Y	Y	Y	N	Y
43 ***Calvert***	Y	Y	Y	Y	Y	Y
44 ***Bono***	?	?	Y	Y	Y	Y
45 ***Rohrabacher***	Y	Y	Y	Y	Y	N
46 Sanchez	Y	Y	Y	Y	N	Y
47 ***Cox***	Y	Y	Y	Y	Y	N
48 ***Packard***	Y	Y	Y	Y	Y	Y
49 ***Bilbray***	Y	Y	Y	Y	Y	Y
50 Filner	Y	Y	Y	N	N	N
51 ***Cunningham***	Y	Y	Y	Y	Y	Y
52 ***Hunter***	Y	Y	Y	Y	Y	?
COLORADO						
1 DeGette	Y	Y	N	Y	N	Y
2 Udall	Y	Y	Y	Y	N	Y
3 ***McInnis***	Y	Y	Y	Y	Y	Y
4 ***Schaffer***	Y	Y	Y	?	Y	N
5 ***Hefley***	Y	Y	Y	Y	Y	N
6 ***Tancredo***	Y	Y	Y	N	Y	N
CONNECTICUT						
1 Larson	Y	Y	Y	Y	N	Y
2 Gejdenson	Y	Y	Y	N	N	N
3 DeLauro	Y	Y	Y	N	N	Y
4 ***Shays***	Y	Y	N	N	Y	N
5 Maloney	Y	Y	Y	N	N	Y
6 ***Johnson***	Y	Y	Y	Y	Y	Y
DELAWARE						
AL ***Castle***	Y	Y	Y	N	Y	Y
FLORIDA						
1 ***Scarborough***	Y	Y	Y	Y	Y	N
2 Boyd	Y	Y	Y	Y	N	Y
3 Brown	?	?	Y	Y	N	Y
4 ***Fowler***	Y	Y	Y	Y	Y	Y
5 Thurman	Y	Y	Y	Y	N	Y
6 ***Stearns***	+	Y	Y	N	Y	Y
7 ***Mica***	Y	Y	Y	Y	Y	Y
8 ***McCollum***	?	?	?	?	?	?
9 ***Bilirakis***	Y	Y	Y	Y	Y	Y
10 ***Young***	Y	Y	Y	Y	Y	Y
11 Davis	?	Y	Y	Y	N	Y
12 ***Canady***	Y	Y	Y	Y	Y	Y
13 ***Miller***	?	?	?	?	?	?
14 ***Goss***	Y	Y	Y	Y	Y	N
15 ***Weldon***	?	Y	Y	Y	Y	N
16 ***Foley***	Y	Y	Y	Y	Y	Y
17 Meek	Y	Y	Y	Y	N	Y
18 ***Ros-Lehtinen***	Y	Y	Y	Y	Y	Y
19 Wexler	Y	Y	Y	N	N	Y
20 Deutsch	Y	Y	Y	N	N	Y
21 ***Diaz-Balart***	Y	Y	Y	Y	Y	Y
22 ***Shaw***	Y	Y	Y	Y	Y	Y
23 Hastings	Y	Y	Y	Y	N	Y
GEORGIA						
1 ***Kingston***	Y	Y	Y	Y	Y	Y
2 Bishop	Y	Y	Y	Y	Y	Y
3 ***Collins***	Y	Y	Y	Y	Y	Y
4 McKinney	Y	Y	N	N	N	N
5 Lewis	Y	Y	N	N	N	Y
6 ***Isakson***	Y	Y	Y	Y	Y	Y
7 ***Barr***	?	?	Y	Y	Y	Y
8 ***Chambliss***	Y	Y	Y	Y	Y	Y
9 ***Deal***	Y	Y	Y	Y	Y	Y
10 ***Norwood***	Y	Y	Y	Y	Y	Y
11 ***Linder***	Y	Y	Y	Y	Y	Y
HAWAII						
1 Abercrombie	Y	Y	Y	Y	N	Y
2 Mink	?	?	Y	Y	N	Y
IDAHO						
1 ***Chenoweth-Hage***	Y	Y	Y	Y	Y	N
2 ***Simpson***	Y	Y	Y	Y	Y	Y
ILLINOIS						
1 Rush	Y	Y	Y	N	N	Y
2 Jackson	Y	Y	N	Y	N	N
3 Lipinski	Y	Y	Y	Y	N	Y
4 Gutierrez	?	?	N	N	N	Y
5 Blagojevich	?	?	Y	N	N	Y
6 ***Hyde***	Y	Y	Y	Y	Y	Y
7 Davis	Y	Y	N	N	N	N
8 ***Crane***	?	?	Y	Y	Y	N
9 Schakowsky	Y	?	N	Y	N	N
10 ***Porter***	Y	Y	Y	Y	Y	Y
11 ***Weller***	Y	Y	Y	Y	Y	Y
12 Costello	Y	Y	Y	Y	N	Y
13 ***Biggert***	Y	Y	Y	Y	Y	Y

ND Northern Democrats SD Southern Democrats

	520	521	522	523	524	525
14 ***Hastert***						Y
15 ***Ewing***	Y	Y	Y	Y	Y	Y
16 ***Manzullo***	?	Y	Y	Y	Y	Y
17 Evans	Y	?	Y	Y	N	Y
18 ***LaHood***	Y	Y	Y	Y	Y	Y
19 Phelps	Y	Y	Y	Y	N	Y
20 ***Shimkus***	Y	Y	Y	Y	Y	Y
INDIANA						
1 Visclosky	Y	Y	Y	Y	N	Y
2 ***McIntosh***	?	?	?	?	?	?
3 Roemer	Y	Y	Y	Y	N	Y
4 ***Souder***	Y	Y	Y	Y	Y	Y
5 ***Buyer***	Y	Y	Y	Y	Y	Y
6 ***Burton***	Y	Y	Y	Y	Y	Y
7 ***Pease***	Y	Y	Y	Y	Y	Y
8 ***Hostettler***	Y	Y	Y	N	Y	N
9 Hill	Y	Y	Y	Y	N	Y
10 Carson	+	+	Y	Y	N	N
IOWA						
1 ***Leach***	Y	Y	Y	Y	Y	Y
2 ***Nussle***	Y	Y	Y	Y	Y	Y
3 Boswell	Y	Y	Y	Y	N	Y
4 ***Ganske***	Y	Y	Y	Y	N	Y
5 ***Latham***	Y	Y	Y	Y	Y	Y
KANSAS						
1 ***Moran***	Y	Y	Y	N	Y	Y
2 ***Ryun***	Y	Y	Y	N	Y	Y
3 Moore	Y	Y	Y	Y	N	Y
4 ***Tiahrt***	Y	Y	Y	Y	Y	Y
KENTUCKY						
1 ***Whitfield***	Y	Y	Y	Y	Y	Y
2 ***Lewis***	Y	Y	Y	Y	Y	Y
3 ***Northup***	Y	Y	Y	Y	Y	Y
4 Lucas	Y	Y	Y	Y	N	Y
5 ***Rogers***	Y	Y	Y	Y	Y	Y
6 ***Fletcher***	Y	Y	Y	Y	Y	Y
LOUISIANA						
1 ***Vitter***	Y	Y	Y	Y	Y	Y
2 Jefferson	?	?	Y	N	N	Y
3 ***Tauzin***	Y	Y	Y	Y	Y	Y
4 ***McCrery***	Y	Y	Y	Y	Y	N
5 ***Cooksey***	Y	Y	Y	Y	Y	Y
6 ***Baker***	Y	Y	Y	Y	Y	Y
7 John	Y	Y	Y	Y	N	Y
MAINE						
1 Allen	Y	Y	Y	N	N	Y
2 Baldacci	Y	Y	Y	N	N	Y
MARYLAND						
1 ***Gilchrest***	Y	Y	Y	Y	Y	Y
2 ***Ehrlich***	Y	Y	Y	Y	Y	Y
3 Cardin	Y	Y	Y	Y	N	Y
4 Wynn	Y	Y	Y	N	N	Y
5 Hoyer	Y	Y	Y	Y	N	Y
6 ***Bartlett***	?	Y	Y	Y	Y	Y
7 Cummings	Y	Y	Y	Y	N	Y
8 ***Morella***	Y	Y	Y	Y	Y	Y
MASSACHUSETTS						
1 Olver	Y	Y	Y	Y	N	N
2 Neal	Y	Y	?	?	?	?
3 McGovern	Y	Y	Y	Y	N	Y
4 Frank	Y	Y	N	N	?	?
5 Meehan	Y	Y	?	?	?	?
6 Tierney	Y	Y	Y	Y	N	N
7 Markey	Y	Y	N	N	N	N
8 Capuano	Y	Y	Y	Y	N	Y
9 Moakley	Y	Y	Y	Y	N	Y
10 Delahunt	Y	Y	Y	Y	N	Y
MICHIGAN						
1 Stupak	Y	Y	Y	Y	N	Y
2 ***Hoekstra***	?	?	Y	Y	Y	N
3 ***Ehlers***	Y	Y	N	Y	Y	Y
4 ***Camp***	Y	Y	Y	Y	Y	Y
5 Barcia	Y	Y	Y	Y	N	Y
6 ***Upton***	Y	Y	Y	Y	Y	N
7 ***Smith***	Y	Y	Y	Y	Y	Y
8 Stabenow	Y	Y	Y	Y	N	Y
9 Kildee	Y	Y	Y	Y	N	Y
10 Bonior	Y	Y	Y	Y	N	Y
11 ***Knollenberg***	?	?	Y	Y	Y	Y
12 Levin	Y	Y	Y	Y	N	Y
13 Rivers	Y	Y	Y	Y	N	Y
14 Conyers	Y	Y	N	N	N	N
15 Kilpatrick	Y	Y	Y	Y	N	Y
16 Dingell	Y	Y	Y	N	N	N

	520	521	522	523	524	525
MINNESOTA						
1 ***Gutknecht***	Y	Y	Y	N	Y	Y
2 Minge	Y	Y	Y	N	N	Y
3 ***Ramstad***	Y	Y	Y	N	Y	Y
4 Vacant						
5 Sabo	Y	Y	Y	N	N	Y
6 Luther	Y	Y	Y	N	N	Y
7 Peterson	Y	Y	Y	Y	N	Y
8 Oberstar	Y	Y	Y	N	N	Y
MISSISSIPPI						
1 ***Wicker***	Y	Y	Y	Y	Y	Y
2 Thompson	Y	Y	Y	Y	N	Y
3 ***Pickering***	Y	Y	Y	Y	Y	Y
4 Shows	Y	Y	Y	Y	N	Y
5 Taylor	Y	Y	Y	Y	N	Y
MISSOURI						
1 Clay	Y	Y	Y	Y	N	Y
2 ***Talent***	?	?	?	Y	Y	Y
3 Gephardt	Y	Y	Y	Y	N	Y
4 Skelton	Y	Y	Y	Y	N	Y
5 McCarthy	Y	Y	Y	N	N	Y
6 Danner	?	?	+	+	+	Y
7 ***Blunt***	Y	Y	Y	Y	Y	Y
8 ***Emerson***	Y	Y	Y	Y	Y	Y
9 ***Hulshof***	Y	Y	Y	Y	Y	Y
MONTANA						
AL ***Hill***	Y	Y	Y	Y	Y	Y
NEBRASKA						
1 ***Bereuter***	Y	Y	Y	Y	Y	Y
2 ***Terry***	Y	Y	Y	Y	Y	Y
3 ***Barrett***	Y	Y	Y	Y	Y	Y
NEVADA						
1 Berkley	Y	Y	Y	Y	N	N
2 ***Gibbons***	Y	Y	Y	N	Y	Y
NEW HAMPSHIRE						
1 ***Sununu***	Y	Y	Y	N	Y	N
2 ***Bass***	Y	Y	Y	Y	Y	Y
NEW JERSEY						
1 Andrews	Y	Y	Y	N	N	N
2 ***LoBiondo***	Y	Y	Y	Y	Y	Y
3 ***Saxton***	Y	Y	Y	Y	Y	Y
4 ***Smith***	Y	Y	Y	Y	Y	Y
5 ***Roukema***	Y	Y	Y	Y	Y	N
6 Pallone	Y	Y	Y	N	N	Y
7 ***Franks***	?	?	?	?	?	?
8 Pascrell	Y	Y	Y	Y	N	Y
9 Rothman	Y	Y	Y	N	N	Y
10 Payne	Y	Y	N	N	N	N
11 ***Frelinghuysen***	Y	Y	Y	Y	Y	N
12 Holt	Y	Y	Y	N	N	Y
13 Menendez	Y	Y	Y	Y	N	Y
NEW MEXICO						
1 ***Wilson***	?	?	Y	Y	Y	Y
2 ***Skeen***	Y	Y	Y	Y	Y	Y
3 Udall	Y	Y	Y	Y	N	Y
NEW YORK						
1 Forbes	Y	Y	Y	N	N	Y
2 ***Lazio***	?	?	?	?	Y	Y
3 ***King***	Y	Y	Y	Y	Y	Y
4 McCarthy	Y	Y	Y	Y	N	Y
5 Ackerman	Y	Y	Y	N	N	N
6 Meeks	?	?	Y	N	N	Y
7 Crowley	Y	Y	Y	Y	N	N
8 Nadler	Y	Y	N	N	N	N
9 Weiner	Y	Y	Y	Y	N	N
10 Towns	Y	Y	Y	N	N	N
11 Owens	Y	Y	N	N	N	N
12 Velázquez	Y	Y	N	N	N	Y
13 ***Fossella***	Y	Y	Y	Y	Y	Y
14 Maloney	Y	Y	Y	Y	N	Y
15 Rangel	?	Y	Y	N	N	N
16 Serrano	Y	Y	Y	Y	N	Y
17 Engel	Y	Y	Y	N	N	Y
18 Lowey	Y	Y	Y	N	N	Y
19 ***Kelly***	Y	Y	Y	Y	Y	Y
20 ***Gilman***	Y	Y	Y	Y	Y	Y
21 McNulty	Y	Y	Y	N	N	Y
22 ***Sweeney***	Y	Y	Y	Y	Y	Y
23 ***Boehlert***	Y	Y	Y	Y	Y	Y
24 ***McHugh***	Y	Y	Y	Y	Y	Y
25 ***Walsh***	Y	Y	Y	Y	Y	Y
26 Hinchey	Y	Y	Y	N	N	Y
27 ***Reynolds***	Y	Y	Y	Y	Y	Y
28 Slaughter	Y	Y	Y	N	N	Y
29 LaFalce	Y	Y	Y	Y	N	Y

	520	521	522	523	524	525
30 ***Quinn***	Y	Y	Y	Y	Y	Y
31 ***Houghton***	Y	Y	Y	Y	Y	Y
NORTH CAROLINA						
1 Clayton	Y	Y	Y	Y	N	Y
2 Etheridge	?	?	Y	Y	N	Y
3 ***Jones***	Y	Y	Y	Y	Y	Y
4 Price	Y	Y	Y	Y	N	Y
5 ***Burr***	Y	Y	Y	Y	?	?
6 ***Coble***	Y	Y	Y	?	?	?
7 McIntyre	Y	Y	Y	Y	N	Y
8 ***Hayes***	Y	Y	Y	Y	Y	Y
9 ***Myrick***	Y	Y	Y	N	?	?
10 ***Ballenger***	Y	Y	Y	Y	Y	Y
11 ***Taylor***	Y	Y	Y	Y	Y	Y
12 Watt	Y	Y	Y	N	N	Y
NORTH DAKOTA						
AL Pomeroy	Y	Y	Y	N	N	Y
OHIO						
1 ***Chabot***	Y	Y	Y	N	Y	N
2 ***Portman***	Y	Y	Y	N	Y	Y
3 Hall	Y	Y	Y	Y	N	Y
4 ***Oxley***	Y	Y	Y	Y	Y	Y
5 ***Gillmor***	?	Y	Y	Y	Y	Y
6 Strickland	Y	Y	Y	Y	N	Y
7 ***Hobson***	Y	Y	Y	Y	Y	Y
8 ***Boehner***	Y	Y	Y	Y	Y	N
9 Kaptur	Y	Y	Y	Y	N	Y
10 Kucinich	Y	Y	N	N	N	Y
11 Jones	Y	Y	Y	Y	N	Y
12 ***Kasich***	?	?	Y	Y	Y	N
13 Brown	Y	Y	Y	N	N	Y
14 Sawyer	Y	Y	Y	Y	N	Y
15 ***Pryce***	Y	Y	Y	Y	Y	Y
16 ***Regula***	Y	Y	Y	Y	Y	Y
17 Traficant	Y	Y	Y	Y	Y	Y
18 ***Ney***	Y	Y	Y	Y	Y	Y
19 ***LaTourette***	Y	Y	Y	Y	Y	Y
OKLAHOMA						
1 ***Largent***	?	?	?	N	Y	N
2 ***Coburn***	Y	?	Y	N	Y	N
3 ***Watkins***	Y	Y	Y	Y	Y	Y
4 ***Watts***	Y	Y	Y	Y	Y	Y
5 ***Istook***	Y	Y	Y	Y	Y	N
6 ***Lucas***	Y	Y	Y	Y	Y	Y
OREGON						
1 Wu	+	+	Y	Y	N	Y
2 ***Walden***	Y	Y	Y	Y	Y	Y
3 Blumenauer	Y	Y	N	N	N	N
4 DeFazio	Y	Y	N	N	N	Y
5 Hooley	Y	Y	Y	Y	N	Y
PENNSYLVANIA						
1 Brady	Y	Y	Y	Y	N	Y
2 Fattah	?	?	Y	N	N	Y
3 Borski	Y	Y	Y	Y	N	Y
4 Klink	?	?	?	?	?	?
5 ***Peterson***	Y	Y	Y	Y	Y	Y
6 Holden	Y	Y	Y	N	N	Y
7 ***Weldon***	Y	Y	Y	Y	Y	Y
8 ***Greenwood***	Y	Y	Y	Y	Y	Y
9 ***Shuster***	Y	Y	?	?	?	Y
10 ***Sherwood***	Y	Y	Y	Y	Y	Y
11 Kanjorski	Y	Y	Y	Y	N	Y
12 Murtha	Y	Y	Y	Y	N	Y
13 Hoeffel	Y	Y	Y	Y	N	Y
14 Coyne	Y	Y	N	Y	N	Y
15 ***Toomey***	Y	Y	Y	N	Y	N
16 ***Pitts***	Y	Y	Y	Y	Y	Y
17 ***Gekas***	Y	Y	Y	Y	Y	Y
18 Doyle	Y	Y	Y	Y	N	Y
19 ***Goodling***	Y	Y	Y	Y	Y	Y
20 Mascara	Y	Y	Y	Y	N	Y
21 ***English***	Y	Y	Y	Y	Y	Y
RHODE ISLAND						
1 Kennedy	Y	Y	Y	Y	N	Y
2 Weygand	?	?	?	N	N	Y
SOUTH CAROLINA						
1 ***Sanford***	Y	N	Y	N	Y	N
2 ***Spence***	Y	Y	Y	Y	Y	Y
3 ***Graham***	Y	Y	Y	Y	Y	Y
4 ***DeMint***	Y	Y	Y	N	Y	N
5 Spratt	Y	?	Y	Y	?	?
6 Clyburn	Y	Y	Y	Y	N	N
SOUTH DAKOTA						
AL ***Thune***	Y	Y	Y	Y	Y	Y

	520	521	522	523	524	525
TENNESSEE						
1 ***Jenkins***	Y	Y	Y	Y	Y	Y
2 ***Duncan***	Y	Y	Y	Y	Y	Y
3 ***Wamp***	Y	Y	Y	Y	Y	Y
4 ***Hilleary***	Y	Y	Y	Y	Y	Y
5 Clement	Y	Y	Y	Y	N	Y
6 Gordon	Y	Y	Y	Y	N	Y
7 ***Bryant***	Y	Y	Y	Y	Y	Y
8 Tanner	Y	Y	Y	Y	N	Y
9 Ford	?	?	Y	Y	N	Y
TEXAS						
1 Sandlin	Y	Y	Y	Y	N	Y
2 Turner	Y	Y	Y	Y	N	Y
3 ***Johnson, Sam***	Y	Y	Y	N	Y	N
4 Hall	Y	Y	Y	Y	Y	Y
5 ***Sessions***	Y	Y	Y	Y	Y	Y
6 ***Barton***	Y	Y	Y	?	Y	Y
7 ***Archer***	?	?	Y	?	Y	?
8 ***Brady***	Y	Y	Y	Y	Y	Y
9 Lampson	Y	Y	Y	Y	N	Y
10 Doggett	Y	Y	Y	N	N	N
11 Edwards	Y	Y	Y	Y	N	Y
12 ***Granger***	Y	Y	Y	Y	Y	Y
13 ***Thornberry***	Y	Y	Y	Y	Y	Y
14 ***Paul***	Y	N	N	N	Y	N
15 Hinojosa	Y	Y	Y	Y	N	Y
16 Reyes	?	?	Y	Y	N	Y
17 Stenholm	Y	Y	Y	N	N	Y
18 Jackson-Lee	Y	Y	Y	N	N	Y
19 ***Combest***	Y	Y	Y	Y	Y	Y
20 Gonzalez	Y	Y	Y	Y	N	Y
21 ***Smith***	Y	Y	Y	Y	Y	Y
22 ***DeLay***	Y	Y	Y	Y	Y	Y
23 ***Bonilla***	Y	Y	Y	Y	Y	Y
24 Frost	Y	Y	Y	Y	N	Y
25 Bentsen	Y	Y	Y	Y	N	Y
26 ***Armey***	Y	Y	Y	Y	Y	Y
27 Ortiz	Y	Y	Y	Y	N	Y
28 Rodriguez	Y	Y	Y	Y	N	Y
29 Green	Y	Y	Y	Y	N	Y
30 Johnson, E.B.	Y	Y	Y	N	N	Y
UTAH						
1 ***Hansen***	Y	Y	Y	Y	Y	Y
2 ***Cook***	?	?	Y	N	Y	Y
3 ***Cannon***	Y	Y	+	Y	Y	Y
VERMONT						
AL *Sanders*	Y	Y	N	N	N	Y
VIRGINIA						
1 Vacant						
2 Pickett	Y	Y	Y	Y	N	Y
3 Scott	Y	Y	Y	Y	N	Y
4 Sisisky	Y	Y	Y	Y	N	Y
5 *Goode*	Y	Y	Y	Y	Y	Y
6 ***Goodlatte***	Y	Y	Y	Y	Y	Y
7 ***Bliley***	?	?	Y	Y	Y	Y
8 Moran	Y	Y	Y	–	N	N
9 Boucher	Y	Y	Y	Y	N	Y
10 ***Wolf***	Y	Y	Y	Y	Y	Y
11 ***Davis***	Y	Y	Y	Y	Y	N
WASHINGTON						
1 Inslee	Y	Y	Y	Y	N	Y
2 ***Metcalf***	Y	Y	Y	Y	Y	N
3 Baird	Y	Y	Y	Y	N	Y
4 ***Hastings***	Y	Y	Y	Y	Y	Y
5 ***Nethercutt***	Y	Y	Y	Y	Y	Y
6 Dicks	Y	Y	Y	Y	N	Y
7 McDermott	Y	Y	N	N	N	N
8 ***Dunn***	Y	Y	Y	Y	Y	Y
9 Smith	Y	Y	Y	Y	N	Y
WEST VIRGINIA						
1 Mollohan	Y	Y	Y	Y	N	Y
2 Wise	?	?	?	?	?	?
3 Rahall	Y	Y	Y	Y	N	Y
WISCONSIN						
1 ***Ryan***	Y	Y	Y	N	Y	Y
2 Baldwin	Y	Y	N	N	N	Y
3 Kind	Y	Y	Y	N	N	Y
4 Kleczka	Y	Y	Y	N	N	N
5 Barrett	Y	Y	Y	N	N	Y
6 ***Petri***	Y	Y	Y	N	Y	Y
7 Obey	Y	Y	Y	N	N	Y
8 ***Green***	Y	Y	Y	N	Y	Y
9 ***Sensenbrenner***	Y	Y	N	N	Y	N
WYOMING						
AL ***Cubin***	Y	Y	Y	N	Y	Y

Southern states - Ala., Ark., Fla., Ga., Ky., La., Miss., N.C., Okla., S.C., Tenn., Texas, Va.

526. HR 2415. State Department Authorization/Motion to Instruct. Nadler, D-N.Y., motion to instruct conferees to insist that all conference meetings be open to the public and media, and that managers provide conferees sufficient time to offer and review proposed amendments. Motion agreed to 398-1: R 207-1; D 189-0 (ND 141-0, SD 48-0); I 2-0. Oct. 11, 2000.

527. H J Res 111. Continuing Resolution/Passage. Passage of the joint resolution that would provide temporary funding authority, at current levels through Oct. 20, for the departments, agencies and programs for which regular fiscal year 2001 appropriations bills will not be enacted by Oct. 14. Passed 407-2: R 210-0; D 195-2 (ND 143-2, SD 52-0); I 2-0. Oct. 12, 2000.

528. HR 5174. Base Polling Sites/Passage. Bartlett, R-Md., motion to suspend the rules and pass the bill that would allow the Defense Department to use buildings at military or reserve facilities as polling places in federal, state and local elections. Once designated as a polling place, the particular site would have to continue to be used as a site. Motion agreed to 297-113: R 209-0; D 86-113 (ND 62-84, SD 24-29); I 2-0. A two-thirds majority of those present and voting (274 in this case) is required for passage under suspension of the rules. Oct. 12, 2000.

529. HR 4656. Lake Tahoe Basin/Passage. Hansen, R-Utah, motion to suspend the rules and pass the bill that would authorize the Forest Service to convey approximately 8.7 acres of land in Nevada to the Washoe County school district for the construction of an elementary school. The Forest Service would have to use the proceeds to buy environmentally sensitive land in the Lake Tahoe basin. Motion rejected 248-160: R 206-1; D 41-158 (ND 29-117, SD 12-41); I 1-1. A two-thirds majority of those present and voting (272 in this case) is required for passage under suspension of the rules. Oct. 12, 2000.

530. HR 34. Floridian Coastal Barrier/Passage. Hansen, R-Utah, motion to suspend the rules and agree to the Senate amendments to the bill that would direct the Interior Department to correct a map portraying the boundaries of an "otherwise protected area" of the coastal barrier resources system on Captiva Island in Lee County, Fla. Motion agreed to 407-1: R 207-0; D 198-1 (ND 145-1, SD 53-0); I 2-0. A two-thirds majority of those present and voting (272 in this case) is required for passage under suspension of the rules. Oct. 12, 2000.

Key

Y Voted for (yea).
Paired for.
+ Announced for.
N Voted against (nay).
X Paired against.
– Announced against.
P Voted "present."
C Voted "present" to avoid possible conflict of interest.
? Did not vote or otherwise make a position known.

•

Democrats ***Republicans***
Independents

	526	527	528	529	530
ALABAMA					
1 ***Callahan***	Y	Y	Y	Y	Y
2 ***Everett***	Y	Y	Y	Y	Y
3 ***Riley***	Y	Y	Y	Y	Y
4 ***Aderholt***	Y	Y	Y	Y	Y
5 Cramer	Y	Y	Y	N	Y
6 ***Bachus***	Y	Y	Y	?	Y
7 Hilliard	Y	Y	N	N	Y
ALASKA					
AL ***Young***	Y	Y	Y	Y	Y
ARIZONA					
1 ***Salmon***	Y	Y	Y	Y	Y
2 Pastor	?	Y	N	N	Y
3 ***Stump***	Y	Y	Y	Y	Y
4 ***Shadegg***	Y	Y	Y	Y	Y
5 ***Kolbe***	Y	Y	Y	Y	Y
6 ***Hayworth***	Y	Y	Y	Y	Y
ARKANSAS					
1 Berry	Y	Y	N	N	Y
2 Snyder	Y	Y	N	Y	Y
3 ***Hutchinson***	Y	Y	Y	Y	Y
4 ***Dickey***	Y	Y	?	?	?
CALIFORNIA					
1 Thompson	Y	Y	N	Y	Y
2 ***Herger***	Y	Y	Y	Y	Y
3 ***Ose***	Y	Y	Y	Y	Y
4 ***Doolittle***	Y	Y	Y	Y	Y
5 Matsui	Y	Y	N	N	Y
6 Woolsey	Y	Y	N	N	Y
7 Miller, George	Y	Y	Y	N	Y
8 Pelosi	Y	Y	N	N	Y
9 Lee	Y	Y	N	N	Y
10 Tauscher	Y	Y	Y	N	Y
11 ***Pombo***	Y	Y	Y	Y	Y
12 Lantos	Y	Y	N	N	Y
13 Stark	?	?	?	?	?
14 Eshoo	?	?	?	?	?
15 ***Campbell***	?	?	?	?	?
16 Lofgren	Y	Y	Y	N	Y
17 Farr	Y	Y	N	N	Y
18 Condit	Y	Y	Y	Y	Y
19 ***Radanovich***	Y	Y	Y	Y	Y
20 Dooley	Y	Y	Y	Y	Y
21 ***Thomas***	Y	Y	Y	Y	Y
22 Capps	Y	Y	Y	N	Y
23 ***Gallegly***	Y	Y	Y	Y	Y
24 Sherman	Y	Y	N	N	Y
25 ***McKeon***	Y	Y	Y	Y	Y
26 Berman	Y	Y	N	N	Y
27 ***Rogan***	Y	Y	Y	Y	Y
28 ***Dreier***	Y	Y	Y	Y	Y
29 Waxman	Y	Y	Y	N	Y
30 Becerra	Y	Y	Y	N	Y
31 ***Martinez***	Y	?	Y	Y	Y
32 Dixon	Y	Y	N	N	Y
33 Roybal-Allard	Y	Y	Y	Y	Y
34 Napolitano	Y	Y	N	N	Y
35 Waters	Y	Y	N	N	Y
36 ***Kuykendall***	Y	Y	Y	Y	Y
37 Millender-McD.	Y	Y	N	N	Y
38 ***Horn***	Y	+	Y	Y	Y
39 ***Royce***	Y	Y	Y	Y	Y
40 ***Lewis***	Y	Y	Y	Y	Y
41 ***Miller, Gary***	Y	Y	Y	Y	Y
42 Baca	Y	?	?	?	?
43 ***Calvert***	Y	Y	Y	Y	Y
44 ***Bono***	Y	Y	Y	Y	Y
45 ***Rohrabacher***	Y	Y	Y	Y	Y
46 Sanchez	Y	Y	Y	N	Y
47 ***Cox***	Y	Y	Y	Y	Y
48 ***Packard***	Y	Y	Y	Y	Y
49 ***Bilbray***	Y	Y	Y	Y	Y
50 Filner	Y	Y	N	N	Y
51 ***Cunningham***	Y	Y	Y	Y	Y
52 ***Hunter***	Y	Y	Y	Y	Y
COLORADO					
1 DeGette	Y	Y	N	N	Y
2 Udall	Y	Y	N	N	Y
3 ***McInnis***	Y	Y	Y	Y	?
4 ***Schaffer***	Y	Y	Y	Y	Y
5 ***Hefley***	Y	Y	Y	Y	Y
6 ***Tancredo***	Y	Y	Y	Y	Y
CONNECTICUT					
1 Larson	Y	Y	N	N	Y
2 Gejdenson	Y	Y	Y	N	Y
3 DeLauro	?	Y	Y	N	Y
4 ***Shays***	Y	Y	Y	Y	Y
5 Maloney	Y	+	Y	Y	Y
6 ***Johnson***	Y	Y	Y	Y	Y
DELAWARE					
AL ***Castle***	Y	Y	Y	Y	Y
FLORIDA					
1 ***Scarborough***	Y	Y	Y	Y	Y
2 Boyd	Y	Y	N	N	Y
3 Brown	Y	Y	N	N	Y
4 ***Fowler***	Y	Y	Y	Y	Y
5 Thurman	Y	Y	Y	N	Y
6 ***Stearns***	Y	Y	Y	Y	Y
7 ***Mica***	Y	+	Y	Y	Y
8 ***McCollum***	?	?	?	?	?
9 ***Bilirakis***	Y	Y	Y	Y	Y
10 ***Young***	?	Y	Y	Y	Y
11 Davis	Y	Y	Y	N	Y
12 ***Canady***	Y	Y	Y	Y	Y
13 ***Miller***	?	Y	Y	Y	Y
14 ***Goss***	Y	Y	Y	Y	Y
15 ***Weldon***	Y	Y	Y	Y	Y
16 ***Foley***	Y	Y	Y	Y	Y
17 Meek	Y	Y	N	N	Y
18 ***Ros-Lehtinen***	Y	Y	Y	Y	Y
19 Wexler	Y	Y	N	N	Y
20 Deutsch	Y	Y	N	N	Y
21 ***Diaz-Balart***	Y	Y	Y	Y	Y
22 ***Shaw***	Y	Y	Y	Y	Y
23 Hastings	Y	Y	N	N	Y
GEORGIA					
1 ***Kingston***	Y	Y	Y	Y	Y
2 Bishop	Y	Y	Y	Y	Y
3 ***Collins***	Y	Y	Y	Y	Y
4 McKinney	Y	Y	N	N	Y
5 Lewis	Y	Y	N	N	Y
6 ***Isakson***	Y	Y	Y	Y	Y
7 ***Barr***	Y	Y	Y	Y	Y
8 ***Chambliss***	Y	Y	Y	Y	Y
9 ***Deal***	Y	Y	Y	Y	Y
10 ***Norwood***	Y	Y	?	?	?
11 ***Linder***	Y	Y	Y	Y	Y
HAWAII					
1 Abercrombie	Y	Y	N	N	Y
2 Mink	Y	Y	N	N	Y
IDAHO					
1 ***Chenoweth-Hage***	Y	Y	Y	Y	Y
2 ***Simpson***	Y	Y	Y	Y	Y
ILLINOIS					
1 Rush	Y	Y	N	N	Y
2 Jackson	Y	Y	N	N	Y
3 Lipinski	Y	Y	Y	N	Y
4 Gutierrez	Y	Y	N	N	Y
5 Blagojevich	Y	Y	Y	N	Y
6 ***Hyde***	Y	Y	Y	Y	Y
7 Davis	Y	Y	N	N	Y
8 ***Crane***	Y	Y	Y	Y	Y
9 Schakowsky	Y	Y	N	N	Y
10 ***Porter***	Y	Y	Y	Y	Y
11 ***Weller***	Y	Y	Y	Y	Y
12 Costello	Y	Y	Y	N	Y
13 ***Biggert***	Y	Y	Y	Y	Y

ND Northern Democrats SD Southern Democrats

	526	527	528	529	530
14 ***Hastert***					
15 ***Ewing***	Y	Y	Y	Y	Y
16 ***Manzullo***	Y	Y	Y	Y	Y
17 Evans	Y	Y	N	N	Y
18 ***LaHood***	Y	Y	Y	Y	Y
19 Phelps	Y	Y	Y	N	Y
20 ***Shimkus***	Y	Y	Y	Y	Y
INDIANA					
1 Visclosky	Y	Y	N	N	Y
2 ***McIntosh***	?	?	?	?	?
3 Roemer	Y	Y	Y	N	Y
4 ***Souder***	N	Y	Y	Y	Y
5 ***Buyer***	Y	Y	Y	Y	Y
6 ***Burton***	Y	Y	Y	Y	Y
7 ***Pease***	Y	Y	Y	Y	Y
8 ***Hostettler***	Y	Y	Y	Y	Y
9 Hill	Y	Y	Y	Y	Y
10 Carson	Y	Y	Y	N	Y
IOWA					
1 ***Leach***	Y	Y	Y	Y	Y
2 ***Nussle***	Y	Y	Y	Y	Y
3 Boswell	Y	Y	Y	Y	Y
4 ***Ganske***	Y	Y	Y	Y	Y
5 ***Latham***	Y	Y	Y	Y	Y
KANSAS					
1 ***Moran***	Y	Y	Y	Y	Y
2 ***Ryun***	Y	Y	Y	Y	Y
3 Moore	Y	Y	Y	Y	Y
4 ***Tiahrt***	Y	Y	Y	Y	Y
KENTUCKY					
1 ***Whitfield***	Y	Y	Y	Y	Y
2 ***Lewis***	Y	Y	Y	Y	Y
3 ***Northup***	Y	Y	Y	Y	Y
4 Lucas	Y	Y	N	Y	Y
5 ***Rogers***	Y	Y	Y	Y	Y
6 ***Fletcher***	Y	Y	Y	Y	Y
LOUISIANA					
1 ***Vitter***	Y	Y	Y	Y	Y
2 Jefferson	Y	Y	N	N	Y
3 ***Tauzin***	Y	Y	Y	Y	Y
4 ***McCrery***	Y	Y	Y	Y	Y
5 ***Cooksey***	Y	Y	Y	Y	Y
6 ***Baker***	Y	Y	Y	Y	Y
7 John	Y	Y	Y	Y	Y
MAINE					
1 Allen	Y	Y	Y	N	Y
2 Baldacci	Y	Y	Y	N	Y
MARYLAND					
1 ***Gilchrest***	Y	Y	Y	Y	Y
2 ***Ehrlich***	Y	Y	Y	Y	Y
3 Cardin	Y	Y	Y	N	Y
4 Wynn	Y	Y	Y	Y	Y
5 Hoyer	Y	Y	Y	N	Y
6 ***Bartlett***	Y	Y	Y	Y	Y
7 Cummings	Y	Y	N	N	Y
8 ***Morella***	Y	Y	Y	Y	Y
MASSACHUSETTS					
1 Olver	Y	Y	N	N	Y
2 Neal	?	Y	N	N	Y
3 McGovern	Y	Y	N	N	Y
4 Frank	?	Y	N	N	Y
5 Meehan	?	?	?	?	?
6 Tierney	Y	Y	N	N	Y
7 Markey	Y	Y	N	N	Y
8 Capuano	Y	Y	N	N	Y
9 Moakley	Y	Y	N	N	Y
10 Delahunt	Y	Y	N	N	Y
MICHIGAN					
1 Stupak	Y	Y	N	N	Y
2 ***Hoekstra***	Y	Y	Y	Y	Y
3 ***Ehlers***	Y	Y	Y	Y	Y
4 ***Camp***	Y	Y	Y	Y	Y
5 Barcia	Y	Y	Y	Y	Y
6 ***Upton***	Y	Y	Y	Y	Y
7 ***Smith***	Y	Y	Y	Y	Y
8 Stabenow	Y	Y	Y	N	Y
9 Kildee	Y	Y	Y	Y	Y
10 Bonior	Y	Y	N	N	Y
11 ***Knollenberg***	Y	Y	Y	Y	Y
12 Levin	Y	Y	N	N	Y
13 Rivers	Y	Y	Y	Y	Y
14 Conyers	Y	Y	N	N	Y
15 Kilpatrick	Y	Y	N	N	Y
16 Dingell	Y	Y	N	N	Y
MINNESOTA					
1 ***Gutknecht***	Y	Y	Y	Y	Y
2 Minge	Y	Y	Y	Y	Y
3 ***Ramstad***	Y	Y	Y	Y	Y
4 Vacant					
5 Sabo	Y	Y	N	N	Y
6 Luther	Y	Y	Y	Y	Y
7 Peterson	Y	Y	Y	Y	Y
8 Oberstar	Y	Y	Y	Y	Y
MISSISSIPPI					
1 ***Wicker***	Y	Y	Y	Y	Y
2 Thompson	Y	Y	N	N	Y
3 ***Pickering***	Y	Y	Y	Y	Y
4 Shows	Y	Y	Y	Y	Y
5 Taylor	Y	Y	Y	N	Y
MISSOURI					
1 Clay	?	Y	N	N	Y
2 ***Talent***	?	?	?	?	?
3 Gephardt	Y	Y	N	N	Y
4 Skelton	Y	Y	N	N	Y
5 McCarthy	Y	Y	N	N	Y
6 Danner	?	Y	?	?	?
7 ***Blunt***	Y	Y	Y	Y	Y
8 ***Emerson***	Y	Y	Y	Y	Y
9 ***Hulshof***	Y	Y	Y	Y	Y
MONTANA					
AL ***Hill***	Y	Y	Y	Y	Y
NEBRASKA					
1 ***Bereuter***	Y	Y	Y	Y	Y
2 ***Terry***	Y	Y	Y	Y	Y
3 ***Barrett***	Y	Y	Y	Y	Y
NEVADA					
1 Berkley	Y	Y	Y	Y	Y
2 ***Gibbons***	Y	Y	Y	Y	Y
NEW HAMPSHIRE					
1 ***Sununu***	Y	Y	Y	Y	Y
2 ***Bass***	Y	Y	Y	Y	Y
NEW JERSEY					
1 Andrews	Y	Y	N	N	Y
2 ***LoBiondo***	Y	Y	Y	Y	Y
3 ***Saxton***	Y	Y	Y	Y	Y
4 ***Smith***	Y	Y	Y	Y	Y
5 ***Roukema***	Y	Y	Y	Y	Y
6 Pallone	Y	Y	N	N	Y
7 ***Franks***	?	?	?	?	?
8 Pascrell	Y	Y	Y	Y	Y
9 Rothman	Y	Y	N	N	Y
10 Payne	Y	Y	N	N	Y
11 ***Frelinghuysen***	Y	Y	Y	Y	Y
12 Holt	?	Y	N	N	Y
13 Menendez	Y	Y	N	N	Y
NEW MEXICO					
1 ***Wilson***	Y	Y	Y	Y	Y
2 ***Skeen***	Y	Y	Y	Y	Y
3 Udall	Y	Y	N	N	Y
NEW YORK					
1 Forbes	Y	?	?	?	?
2 ***Lazio***	Y	?	?	?	?
3 ***King***	Y	Y	Y	Y	Y
4 McCarthy	Y	Y	Y	N	Y
5 Ackerman	Y	Y	N	N	Y
6 Meeks	Y	Y	N	N	Y
7 Crowley	Y	Y	N	N	Y
8 Nadler	Y	?	?	?	?
9 Weiner	Y	Y	N	N	Y
10 Towns	Y	Y	N	N	Y
11 Owens	Y	Y	N	N	Y
12 Velázquez	Y	Y	N	N	Y
13 ***Fossella***	?	Y	+	+	Y
14 Maloney	Y	Y	Y	N	Y
15 Rangel	Y	Y	N	N	Y
16 Serrano	Y	Y	N	N	Y
17 Engel	Y	Y	N	N	Y
18 Lowey	Y	Y	N	N	Y
19 ***Kelly***	Y	Y	Y	Y	Y
20 ***Gilman***	Y	Y	Y	Y	Y
21 McNulty	Y	Y	Y	N	Y
22 ***Sweeney***	Y	Y	Y	Y	Y
23 ***Boehlert***	Y	Y	Y	Y	Y
24 ***McHugh***	Y	Y	Y	Y	Y
25 ***Walsh***	Y	Y	Y	Y	Y
26 Hinchey	Y	Y	N	N	Y
27 ***Reynolds***	Y	?	?	?	?
28 Slaughter	Y	Y	N	N	Y
29 LaFalce	Y	Y	N	N	Y
30 ***Quinn***	Y	Y	Y	Y	Y
31 ***Houghton***	Y	Y	Y	Y	Y
NORTH CAROLINA					
1 Clayton	?	Y	N	N	Y
2 Etheridge	Y	Y	Y	N	Y
3 ***Jones***	Y	Y	Y	Y	Y
4 Price	Y	Y	N	N	Y
5 ***Burr***	?	Y	Y	Y	Y
6 ***Coble***	?	Y	Y	Y	Y
7 McIntyre	?	Y	Y	Y	Y
8 ***Hayes***	?	Y	Y	Y	Y
9 ***Myrick***	?	Y	Y	Y	Y
10 ***Ballenger***	Y	Y	Y	Y	Y
11 ***Taylor***	Y	Y	Y	Y	Y
12 Watt	?	Y	Y	N	Y
NORTH DAKOTA					
AL Pomeroy	Y	Y	Y	Y	Y
OHIO					
1 ***Chabot***	Y	Y	Y	Y	Y
2 ***Portman***	Y	Y	Y	Y	Y
3 Hall	Y	Y	Y	Y	Y
4 ***Oxley***	Y	?	?	?	?
5 ***Gillmor***	Y	Y	Y	Y	Y
6 Strickland	Y	Y	Y	N	Y
7 ***Hobson***	Y	Y	Y	Y	Y
8 ***Boehner***	Y	Y	Y	Y	Y
9 Kaptur	Y	?	N	N	Y
10 Kucinich	Y	Y	Y	N	Y
11 Jones	Y	Y	N	N	Y
12 ***Kasich***	Y	Y	Y	Y	Y
13 Brown	Y	Y	Y	N	Y
14 Sawyer	Y	Y	N	N	Y
15 ***Pryce***	Y	Y	Y	Y	Y
16 ***Regula***	Y	Y	Y	Y	Y
17 Traficant	Y	Y	Y	Y	Y
18 ***Ney***	Y	Y	Y	Y	Y
19 ***LaTourette***	Y	Y	Y	Y	Y
OKLAHOMA					
1 ***Largent***	Y	Y	Y	Y	Y
2 ***Coburn***	Y	Y	Y	Y	Y
3 ***Watkins***	Y	Y	Y	Y	Y
4 ***Watts***	Y	Y	Y	Y	Y
5 ***Istook***	Y	Y	Y	Y	Y
6 ***Lucas***	Y	Y	Y	Y	Y
OREGON					
1 Wu	Y	Y	Y	Y	Y
2 ***Walden***	Y	Y	Y	Y	Y
3 Blumenauer	Y	Y	Y	Y	N
4 DeFazio	Y	N	Y	Y	Y
5 Hooley	?	Y	Y	Y	Y
PENNSYLVANIA					
1 Brady	Y	Y	Y	N	Y
2 Fattah	Y	Y	Y	N	Y
3 Borski	Y	Y	Y	N	Y
4 Klink	?	?	?	?	?
5 ***Peterson***	Y	Y	Y	Y	Y
6 Holden	?	Y	Y	N	Y
7 ***Weldon***	Y	Y	Y	Y	Y
8 ***Greenwood***	Y	Y	Y	Y	Y
9 ***Shuster***	Y	Y	Y	Y	Y
10 ***Sherwood***	Y	Y	Y	Y	Y
11 Kanjorski	Y	Y	N	N	Y
12 Murtha	Y	Y	N	N	Y
13 Hoeffel	Y	Y	Y	N	Y
14 Coyne	Y	Y	N	N	Y
15 ***Toomey***	Y	Y	Y	Y	Y
16 ***Pitts***	Y	Y	Y	Y	Y
17 ***Gekas***	Y	Y	Y	Y	Y
18 Doyle	Y	Y	Y	N	Y
19 ***Goodling***	Y	Y	Y	Y	Y
20 Mascara	Y	Y	Y	N	Y
21 ***English***	Y	Y	Y	Y	Y
RHODE ISLAND					
1 Kennedy	Y	Y	N	N	Y
2 Weygand	Y	Y	N	N	Y
SOUTH CAROLINA					
1 ***Sanford***	Y	Y	Y	N	Y
2 ***Spence***	Y	Y	Y	Y	Y
3 ***Graham***	Y	Y	Y	Y	Y
4 ***DeMint***	Y	Y	Y	Y	Y
5 Spratt	?	Y	Y	N	Y
6 Clyburn	?	Y	N	N	Y
SOUTH DAKOTA					
AL ***Thune***	Y	Y	Y	Y	Y
TENNESSEE					
1 ***Jenkins***	Y	Y	Y	Y	Y
2 ***Duncan***	Y	Y	Y	Y	Y
3 ***Wamp***	Y	Y	Y	Y	Y
4 ***Hilleary***	Y	Y	Y	Y	Y
5 Clement	Y	Y	Y	N	Y
6 Gordon	Y	Y	N	N	Y
7 ***Bryant***	Y	Y	Y	Y	Y
8 Tanner	Y	Y	N	N	Y
9 Ford	?	Y	N	N	Y
TEXAS					
1 Sandlin	Y	Y	N	N	Y
2 Turner	Y	Y	Y	Y	Y
3 ***Johnson, Sam***	Y	Y	Y	Y	Y
4 Hall	Y	Y	Y	Y	Y
5 ***Sessions***	Y	Y	Y	Y	Y
6 ***Barton***	Y	Y	Y	Y	Y
7 ***Archer***	Y	Y	Y	Y	Y
8 ***Brady***	Y	Y	Y	Y	Y
9 Lampson	Y	Y	Y	Y	Y
10 Doggett	Y	Y	Y	N	Y
11 Edwards	Y	Y	Y	N	Y
12 ***Granger***	Y	Y	Y	Y	Y
13 ***Thornberry***	Y	Y	Y	Y	Y
14 ***Paul***	Y	Y	Y	Y	Y
15 Hinojosa	Y	Y	Y	N	Y
16 Reyes	Y	Y	Y	N	Y
17 Stenholm	Y	Y	N	N	Y
18 Jackson-Lee	Y	Y	N	N	Y
19 ***Combest***	Y	Y	Y	Y	Y
20 Gonzalez	Y	Y	Y	N	Y
21 ***Smith***	Y	Y	Y	Y	Y
22 ***DeLay***	Y	Y	Y	Y	Y
23 ***Bonilla***	Y	Y	Y	?	?
24 Frost	Y	Y	Y	N	Y
25 Bentsen	Y	Y	N	N	Y
26 ***Armey***	Y	Y	Y	Y	Y
27 Ortiz	Y	Y	Y	N	Y
28 Rodriguez	Y	Y	Y	N	Y
29 Green	Y	?	?	?	?
30 Johnson, E.B.	Y	Y	N	N	Y
UTAH					
1 ***Hansen***	Y	Y	Y	Y	Y
2 ***Cook***	Y	Y	?	?	?
3 ***Cannon***	Y	Y	Y	Y	Y
VERMONT					
AL *Sanders*	Y	Y	Y	N	Y
VIRGINIA					
1 Vacant					
2 Pickett	Y	Y	N	Y	Y
3 Scott	Y	Y	N	N	Y
4 Sisisky	Y	Y	N	Y	Y
5 *Goode*	Y	Y	Y	Y	Y
6 ***Goodlatte***	?	Y	Y	Y	Y
7 ***Bliley***	Y	Y	Y	Y	Y
8 Moran	Y	Y	Y	N	Y
9 Boucher	Y	?	N	Y	Y
10 ***Wolf***	Y	Y	Y	Y	Y
11 ***Davis***	Y	Y	Y	Y	Y
WASHINGTON					
1 Inslee	Y	Y	Y	N	Y
2 ***Metcalf***	Y	Y	Y	Y	Y
3 Baird	Y	N	Y	N	Y
4 ***Hastings***	Y	Y	Y	Y	Y
5 ***Nethercutt***	Y	Y	Y	Y	Y
6 Dicks	Y	Y	N	N	Y
7 McDermott	Y	Y	N	N	Y
8 ***Dunn***	Y	Y	Y	Y	?
9 Smith	Y	Y	Y	N	Y
WEST VIRGINIA					
1 Mollohan	Y	Y	N	N	Y
2 Wise	?	?	?	?	?
3 Rahall	Y	Y	Y	Y	Y
WISCONSIN					
1 ***Ryan***	Y	Y	Y	Y	Y
2 Baldwin	Y	Y	N	N	Y
3 Kind	Y	Y	Y	Y	Y
4 Kleczka	Y	Y	N	Y	Y
5 Barrett	Y	Y	N	Y	Y
6 ***Petri***	Y	Y	Y	Y	Y
7 Obey	Y	Y	N	N	Y
8 ***Green***	Y	Y	Y	Y	Y
9 ***Sensenbrenner***	Y	Y	Y	Y	Y
WYOMING					
AL ***Cubin***	Y	Y	Y	Y	Y

Southern states - Ala., Ark., Fla., Ga., Ky., La., Miss., N.C., Okla., S.C., Tenn., Texas, Va.

531. H Res 631. Honoring USS *Cole* Victims/Adoption. Adoption of the resolution that honors the crew members of the USS *Cole* who were killed or wounded in the terrorist bombing attack in Aden, Yemen. Adopted 386-0: R 199-0; D 187-0 (ND 137-0, SD 50-0); I 0-0. Oct. 18, 2000.

532. H Con Res 415. Children's Memorial Day/Adoption. Ose, R-Calif., motion to suspend the rules and adopt the concurrent resolution that expresses the sense of Congress that a National Children's Memorial Day should be established and requests the president to issue a proclamation declaring it. Motion agreed to 376-0: R 190-0; D 186-0 (ND 136-0, SD 50-0); I 0-0. A two-thirds majority of those present and voting (251 in this case) is required for adoption under suspension of the rules. Oct. 18, 2000.

533. HR 3218. Identity Protection/Passage. Ose, R-Calif., motion to suspend the rules and pass the bill that would prohibit the Treasury Department from displaying Social Security numbers on or through windows on Social Security check envelopes. Motion agreed to 385-0: R 196-0; D 189-0 (ND 138-0, SD 51-0); I 0-0. A two-thirds majority of those present and voting (257 in this case) is required for passage under suspension of the rules. Oct. 18, 2000.

534. S 2796. Water Resources Development/Passage. Passage of the bill that would authorize Army Corps of Engineers' water projects for flood and beach erosion control, navigation, and environmental restoration. It also would authorize $7.8 billion for the 35-year Everglades restoration project. It would require the corps to: conduct a pilot program for peer reviews of corps project feasibility studies; take inventory of and assess the condition of all Depression-era dams; and move forward on a comprehensive river restoration plan for the Missouri River Basin. Passed 394-14: R 196-11; D 196-3 (ND 146-2, SD 50-1); I 2-0. Oct. 19, 2000.

535. HR 4635. Fiscal 2001 VA-HUD and Energy-Water Appropriations/Rule. Adoption of the rule (H Res 638) for the conference report on the bill that would appropriate $107.3 billion in fiscal year 2001 for the Veterans Affairs and Housing and Urban Development departments as well as $23.6 billion for energy and water programs. Adopted 400-7: R 202-5; D 196-2 (ND 147-2, SD 49-0); I 2-0. Oct. 19, 2000.

Key

Y Voted for (yea).
\# Paired for.
\+ Announced for.
N Voted against (nay).
X Paired against.
– Announced against.
P Voted "present."
C Voted "present" to avoid possible conflict of interest.
? Did not vote or otherwise make a position known.

•

Democrats ***Republicans***
Independents

	531	532	533	534	535
ALABAMA					
1 ***Callahan***	Y	Y	Y	Y	Y
2 ***Everett***	Y	Y	Y	Y	Y
3 ***Riley***	Y	Y	Y	Y	Y
4 ***Aderholt***	Y	Y	Y	Y	Y
5 Cramer	Y	Y	Y	Y	Y
6 ***Bachus***	Y	Y	Y	Y	Y
7 Hilliard	Y	Y	Y	?	?
ALASKA					
AL ***Young***	Y	Y	Y	Y	Y
ARIZONA					
1 ***Salmon***	Y	Y	Y	Y	Y
2 Pastor	Y	Y	Y	Y	Y
3 ***Stump***	Y	Y	Y	Y	Y
4 ***Shadegg***	Y	Y	Y	Y	Y
5 ***Kolbe***	+	+	+	Y	Y
6 ***Hayworth***	Y	Y	Y	Y	Y
ARKANSAS					
1 Berry	Y	Y	Y	Y	Y
2 Snyder	Y	Y	Y	Y	Y
3 ***Hutchinson***	Y	Y	Y	Y	Y
4 ***Dickey***	Y	Y	?	Y	Y
CALIFORNIA					
1 Thompson	Y	Y	Y	Y	Y
2 ***Herger***	Y	?	Y	Y	Y
3 ***Ose***	Y	Y	Y	Y	Y
4 ***Doolittle***	Y	Y	Y	Y	Y
5 Matsui	Y	Y	Y	Y	Y
6 Woolsey	Y	Y	Y	Y	Y
7 Miller, George	Y	Y	Y	Y	Y
8 Pelosi	Y	Y	Y	Y	?
9 Lee	Y	Y	Y	Y	Y
10 Tauscher	Y	Y	Y	Y	Y
11 ***Pombo***	Y	Y	Y	Y	Y
12 Lantos	Y	Y	Y	Y	Y
13 Stark	Y	Y	Y	?	Y
14 Eshoo	Y	Y	Y	Y	Y
15 ***Campbell***	?	?	?	?	?
16 Lofgren	Y	Y	Y	Y	Y
17 Farr	Y	Y	Y	Y	Y
18 Condit	Y	Y	Y	Y	Y
19 ***Radanovich***	Y	?	Y	Y	Y
20 Dooley	?	?	?	Y	Y
21 ***Thomas***	Y	Y	Y	Y	Y
22 Capps	Y	Y	Y	Y	Y
23 ***Gallegly***	Y	Y	Y	Y	Y
24 Sherman	Y	Y	Y	Y	Y
25 ***McKeon***	Y	Y	Y	Y	Y
26 Berman	Y	Y	Y	Y	Y
27 ***Rogan***	Y	Y	Y	Y	Y
28 ***Dreier***	Y	Y	Y	Y	Y
29 Waxman	Y	Y	Y	Y	Y
30 Becerra	+	Y	Y	Y	Y
31 ***Martinez***	Y	Y	Y	Y	Y
32 Dixon	Y	Y	Y	Y	Y
33 Roybal-Allard	Y	Y	Y	Y	Y
34 Napolitano	Y	?	Y	Y	Y
35 Waters	Y	Y	Y	Y	Y
36 ***Kuykendall***	Y	Y	Y	Y	Y
37 Millender-McD.	Y	Y	Y	Y	Y
38 ***Horn***	Y	Y	Y	Y	Y
39 ***Royce***	Y	Y	Y	N	Y
40 ***Lewis***	Y	Y	Y	Y	?
41 ***Miller, Gary***	Y	Y	Y	Y	Y
42 Baca	Y	Y	Y	Y	Y
43 ***Calvert***	Y	Y	Y	Y	Y
44 ***Bono***	Y	Y	Y	Y	Y
45 ***Rohrabacher***	Y	Y	Y	Y	Y
46 Sanchez	Y	Y	Y	Y	Y
47 ***Cox***	Y	Y	Y	Y	Y
48 ***Packard***	Y	?	Y	Y	Y
49 ***Bilbray***	Y	?	Y	Y	Y
50 Filner	Y	Y	Y	Y	Y
51 ***Cunningham***	Y	Y	?	Y	Y
52 ***Hunter***	Y	Y	Y	Y	Y
COLORADO					
1 DeGette	Y	Y	Y	Y	Y
2 Udall	Y	Y	Y	Y	Y
3 ***McInnis***	Y	Y	Y	Y	Y
4 ***Schaffer***	Y	Y	Y	N	Y
5 ***Hefley***	Y	Y	Y	Y	Y
6 ***Tancredo***	Y	Y	Y	N	N
CONNECTICUT					
1 Larson	Y	Y	Y	Y	Y
2 Gejdenson	Y	Y	Y	Y	Y
3 DeLauro	Y	Y	Y	Y	Y
4 ***Shays***	Y	Y	Y	N	?
5 Maloney	Y	Y	Y	Y	Y
6 ***Johnson***	Y	Y	Y	Y	Y
DELAWARE					
AL ***Castle***	Y	Y	Y	Y	Y
FLORIDA					
1 ***Scarborough***	Y	Y	Y	Y	Y
2 Boyd	Y	Y	Y	Y	Y
3 Brown	?	?	?	Y	Y
4 ***Fowler***	Y	Y	Y	Y	Y
5 Thurman	Y	Y	Y	Y	Y
6 ***Stearns***	Y	+	Y	Y	Y
7 ***Mica***	Y	Y	Y	Y	Y
8 ***McCollum***	?	?	?	?	?
9 ***Bilirakis***	Y	Y	Y	Y	Y
10 ***Young***	Y	Y	Y	Y	Y
11 Davis	Y	Y	Y	Y	Y
12 ***Canady***	Y	Y	Y	Y	Y
13 ***Miller***	?	?	?	?	?
14 ***Goss***	Y	Y	Y	Y	Y
15 ***Weldon***	Y	Y	Y	Y	Y
16 ***Foley***	Y	Y	Y	Y	Y
17 Meek	Y	Y	Y	Y	Y
18 ***Ros-Lehtinen***	+	+	+	Y	Y
19 Wexler	Y	Y	Y	Y	Y
20 Deutsch	Y	Y	Y	Y	Y
21 ***Diaz-Balart***	Y	Y	Y	Y	Y
22 ***Shaw***	?	?	?	Y	Y
23 Hastings	Y	Y	Y	Y	Y
GEORGIA					
1 ***Kingston***	Y	Y	Y	Y	Y
2 Bishop	Y	Y	Y	Y	Y
3 ***Collins***	Y	Y	Y	Y	Y
4 McKinney	Y	Y	Y	Y	Y
5 Lewis	Y	Y	Y	Y	Y
6 ***Isakson***	Y	Y	Y	Y	Y
7 ***Barr***	Y	Y	Y	Y	Y
8 ***Chambliss***	Y	Y	Y	Y	Y
9 ***Deal***	Y	Y	Y	Y	Y
10 ***Norwood***	Y	Y	Y	Y	Y
11 ***Linder***	Y	Y	Y	Y	Y
HAWAII					
1 Abercrombie	Y	Y	Y	Y	Y
2 Mink	Y	Y	Y	Y	Y
IDAHO					
1 ***Chenoweth-Hage***	?	?	?	?	?
2 ***Simpson***	Y	Y	Y	?	Y
ILLINOIS					
1 Rush	Y	Y	Y	Y	Y
2 Jackson	Y	Y	Y	Y	Y
3 Lipinski	?	?	?	?	?
4 Gutierrez	?	?	?	Y	Y
5 Blagojevich	Y	Y	Y	Y	Y
6 ***Hyde***	Y	Y	Y	Y	Y
7 Davis	Y	Y	Y	Y	Y
8 ***Crane***	Y	Y	Y	Y	Y
9 Schakowsky	Y	?	Y	Y	Y
10 ***Porter***	Y	Y	Y	Y	Y
11 ***Weller***	Y	Y	Y	Y	Y
12 Costello	Y	Y	Y	Y	Y
13 ***Biggert***	Y	Y	Y	Y	Y

ND Northern Democrats SD Southern Democrats

	531	532	533	534	535
14 ***Hastert***					
15 ***Ewing***	Y	Y	Y	Y	Y
16 ***Manzullo***	Y	Y	Y	Y	Y
17 Evans	Y	Y	Y	Y	Y
18 ***LaHood***	Y	Y	Y	Y	Y
19 Phelps	Y	Y	Y	Y	Y
20 ***Shimkus***	Y	Y	Y	Y	Y
INDIANA					
1 Visclosky	Y	Y	Y	Y	Y
2 ***McIntosh***	?	?	?	?	?
3 Roemer	Y	Y	Y	Y	N
4 ***Souder***	Y	Y	Y	Y	Y
5 ***Buyer***	Y	Y	Y	Y	Y
6 ***Burton***	Y	Y	Y	Y	Y
7 ***Pease***	Y	Y	Y	Y	Y
8 ***Hostettler***	?	?	?	Y	Y
9 Hill	Y	Y	Y	Y	Y
10 Carson	Y	Y	Y	Y	Y
IOWA					
1 ***Leach***	Y	Y	Y	Y	Y
2 ***Nussle***	Y	Y	Y	Y	N
3 Boswell	Y	Y	Y	Y	Y
4 ***Ganske***	Y	Y	Y	Y	Y
5 ***Latham***	Y	Y	Y	Y	N
KANSAS					
1 ***Moran***	Y	Y	Y	Y	Y
2 ***Ryun***	Y	Y	Y	Y	Y
3 Moore	Y	Y	Y	Y	Y
4 ***Tiahrt***	Y	Y	Y	Y	Y
KENTUCKY					
1 ***Whitfield***	Y	Y	Y	Y	Y
2 ***Lewis***	Y	Y	Y	Y	Y
3 ***Northup***	Y	Y	Y	Y	Y
4 Lucas	Y	Y	Y	Y	Y
5 ***Rogers***	Y	Y	Y	Y	Y
6 ***Fletcher***	Y	Y	Y	Y	Y
LOUISIANA					
1 ***Vitter***	Y	Y	Y	Y	Y
2 Jefferson	Y	Y	Y	Y	Y
3 ***Tauzin***	Y	Y	Y	Y	Y
4 ***McCrery***	Y	Y	Y	Y	Y
5 ***Cooksey***	Y	Y	Y	Y	Y
6 ***Baker***	Y	Y	Y	Y	Y
7 John	Y	Y	Y	Y	Y
MAINE					
1 Allen	Y	Y	Y	Y	Y
2 Baldacci	Y	Y	Y	Y	Y
MARYLAND					
1 ***Gilchrest***	Y	Y	Y	Y	Y
2 ***Ehrlich***	Y	Y	Y	Y	Y
3 Cardin	?	?	?	Y	Y
4 Wynn	Y	Y	Y	Y	Y
5 Hoyer	Y	?	Y	Y	Y
6 ***Bartlett***	Y	Y	Y	Y	Y
7 Cummings	Y	Y	Y	Y	Y
8 ***Morella***	Y	Y	Y	+	Y
MASSACHUSETTS					
1 Olver	Y	Y	Y	Y	Y
2 Neal	Y	Y	Y	Y	Y
3 McGovern	Y	Y	Y	Y	Y
4 Frank	Y	Y	Y	Y	Y
5 Meehan	Y	Y	Y	Y	Y
6 Tierney	Y	Y	Y	Y	Y
7 Markey	Y	Y	Y	Y	Y
8 Capuano	Y	Y	Y	Y	Y
9 Moakley	Y	Y	Y	Y	Y
10 Delahunt	?	?	?	Y	Y
MICHIGAN					
1 Stupak	?	?	?	N	Y
2 ***Hoekstra***	Y	Y	Y	Y	Y
3 ***Ehlers***	Y	Y	Y	Y	Y
4 ***Camp***	Y	Y	Y	Y	Y
5 Barcia	Y	Y	Y	Y	Y
6 ***Upton***	Y	Y	Y	Y	Y
7 ***Smith***	Y	Y	Y	Y	Y
8 Stabenow	Y	Y	Y	Y	?
9 Kildee	Y	Y	Y	Y	Y
10 Bonior	Y	Y	Y	Y	Y
11 ***Knollenberg***	Y	Y	Y	Y	Y
12 Levin	Y	Y	Y	Y	Y
13 Rivers	Y	Y	Y	Y	Y
14 Conyers	?	?	?	Y	Y
15 Kilpatrick	Y	Y	Y	Y	Y
16 Dingell	Y	Y	Y	?	Y
MINNESOTA					
1 ***Gutknecht***	Y	Y	Y	Y	Y
2 Minge	Y	Y	Y	Y	Y
3 ***Ramstad***	Y	Y	Y	N	Y
4 Vacant					
5 Sabo	Y	Y	Y	Y	Y
6 Luther	Y	Y	Y	Y	Y
7 Peterson	Y	Y	Y	Y	Y
8 Oberstar	Y	Y	Y	Y	Y
MISSISSIPPI					
1 ***Wicker***	Y	Y	Y	Y	Y
2 Thompson	Y	Y	Y	Y	?
3 ***Pickering***	Y	Y	Y	Y	Y
4 Shows	Y	Y	Y	Y	Y
5 Taylor	Y	Y	Y	Y	Y
MISSOURI					
1 Clay	Y	Y	Y	?	?
2 ***Talent***	?	?	?	?	?
3 Gephardt	?	?	?	?	Y
4 Skelton	Y	Y	Y	Y	Y
5 McCarthy	Y	Y	Y	Y	Y
6 Danner	Y	Y	Y	Y	N
7 ***Blunt***	Y	Y	Y	Y	Y
8 ***Emerson***	Y	Y	Y	Y	Y
9 ***Hulshof***	Y	Y	Y	Y	N
MONTANA					
AL ***Hill***	Y	Y	Y	N	N
NEBRASKA					
1 ***Bereuter***	Y	Y	Y	Y	Y
2 ***Terry***	Y	Y	Y	Y	Y
3 ***Barrett***	Y	Y	Y	Y	Y
NEVADA					
1 Berkley	Y	Y	Y	Y	Y
2 ***Gibbons***	Y	Y	Y	Y	Y
NEW HAMPSHIRE					
1 ***Sununu***	Y	Y	Y	Y	Y
2 ***Bass***	Y	Y	Y	Y	Y
NEW JERSEY					
1 Andrews	Y	Y	Y	N	Y
2 ***LoBiondo***	Y	Y	Y	Y	Y
3 ***Saxton***	Y	Y	Y	Y	Y
4 ***Smith***	Y	Y	Y	Y	Y
5 ***Roukema***	Y	Y	Y	Y	Y
6 Pallone	Y	Y	Y	Y	Y
7 ***Franks***	?	?	?	?	?
8 Pascrell	?	?	?	Y	Y
9 Rothman	Y	Y	Y	Y	Y
10 Payne	Y	Y	Y	Y	Y
11 ***Frelinghuysen***	Y	Y	Y	Y	Y
12 Holt	Y	Y	Y	Y	Y
13 Menendez	Y	Y	Y	Y	Y
NEW MEXICO					
1 ***Wilson***	Y	Y	Y	Y	Y
2 ***Skeen***	Y	Y	Y	Y	Y
3 Udall	Y	Y	Y	Y	Y
NEW YORK					
1 Forbes	?	?	?	Y	Y
2 ***Lazio***	?	?	?	?	?
3 ***King***	Y	Y	Y	Y	Y
4 McCarthy	Y	Y	Y	Y	Y
5 Ackerman	Y	Y	Y	Y	Y
6 Meeks	Y	Y	Y	Y	Y
7 Crowley	Y	Y	Y	Y	Y
8 Nadler	Y	Y	Y	Y	Y
9 Weiner	Y	Y	Y	Y	Y
10 Towns	Y	Y	Y	Y	Y
11 Owens	Y	Y	Y	Y	Y
12 Velázquez	Y	Y	Y	Y	Y
13 ***Fossella***	Y	Y	Y	Y	Y
14 Maloney	Y	Y	Y	Y	Y
15 Rangel	Y	Y	Y	Y	Y
16 Serrano	Y	Y	Y	Y	Y
17 Engel	Y	Y	Y	Y	Y
18 Lowey	Y	Y	Y	Y	Y
19 ***Kelly***	Y	Y	Y	Y	Y
20 ***Gilman***	Y	Y	Y	Y	Y
21 McNulty	Y	Y	Y	Y	Y
22 ***Sweeney***	Y	Y	Y	Y	Y
23 ***Boehlert***	Y	Y	Y	Y	Y
24 ***McHugh***	Y	Y	Y	Y	Y
25 ***Walsh***	?	?	Y	Y	Y
26 Hinchey	Y	Y	Y	Y	Y
27 ***Reynolds***	Y	Y	Y	Y	Y
28 Slaughter	Y	Y	Y	Y	Y
29 LaFalce	Y	Y	Y	Y	Y
30 ***Quinn***	Y	Y	Y	Y	Y
31 ***Houghton***	?	?	?	?	?
NORTH CAROLINA					
1 Clayton	Y	Y	Y	Y	Y
2 Etheridge	Y	Y	Y	Y	Y
3 ***Jones***	Y	Y	?	Y	Y
4 Price	Y	Y	Y	Y	Y
5 ***Burr***	Y	Y	Y	Y	Y
6 ***Coble***	Y	Y	Y	Y	Y
7 McIntyre	Y	Y	Y	Y	Y
8 ***Hayes***	Y	Y	Y	Y	Y
9 ***Myrick***	Y	Y	Y	Y	Y
10 ***Ballenger***	Y	Y	Y	+	Y
11 ***Taylor***	Y	Y	Y	Y	Y
12 Watt	Y	?	Y	Y	Y
NORTH DAKOTA					
AL Pomeroy	Y	Y	Y	Y	Y
OHIO					
1 ***Chabot***	Y	Y	Y	Y	Y
2 ***Portman***	Y	Y	Y	Y	Y
3 Hall	Y	Y	Y	Y	Y
4 ***Oxley***	?	?	?	?	?
5 ***Gillmor***	Y	Y	Y	Y	Y
6 Strickland	Y	Y	Y	Y	Y
7 ***Hobson***	Y	Y	Y	Y	Y
8 ***Boehner***	Y	Y	Y	Y	Y
9 Kaptur	Y	Y	Y	Y	Y
10 Kucinich	Y	Y	Y	Y	Y
11 Jones	?	Y	Y	?	?
12 ***Kasich***	?	?	?	Y	Y
13 Brown	Y	Y	Y	Y	Y
14 Sawyer	Y	Y	Y	Y	Y
15 ***Pryce***	Y	Y	Y	Y	Y
16 ***Regula***	Y	Y	Y	Y	Y
17 Traficant	Y	Y	Y	Y	Y
18 ***Ney***	+	?	+	Y	Y
19 ***LaTourette***	Y	Y	Y	Y	Y
OKLAHOMA					
1 ***Largent***	Y	Y	Y	Y	Y
2 ***Coburn***	Y	Y	Y	N	Y
3 ***Watkins***	Y	Y	Y	Y	Y
4 ***Watts***	Y	Y	Y	Y	Y
5 ***Istook***	Y	Y	Y	Y	Y
6 ***Lucas***	Y	?	Y	Y	Y
OREGON					
1 Wu	Y	Y	Y	Y	Y
2 ***Walden***	Y	Y	Y	Y	Y
3 Blumenauer	Y	Y	Y	Y	Y
4 DeFazio	Y	Y	Y	Y	Y
5 Hooley	Y	Y	Y	Y	Y
PENNSYLVANIA					
1 Brady	Y	Y	Y	Y	Y
2 Fattah	?	?	?	Y	Y
3 Borski	Y	Y	Y	Y	Y
4 Klink	?	?	?	Y	Y
5 ***Peterson***	Y	Y	Y	Y	Y
6 Holden	Y	Y	Y	Y	Y
7 ***Weldon***	Y	Y	Y	Y	Y
8 ***Greenwood***	Y	Y	Y	Y	Y
9 ***Shuster***	Y	Y	Y	Y	Y
10 ***Sherwood***	Y	?	Y	Y	Y
11 Kanjorski	Y	Y	Y	Y	Y
12 Murtha	Y	Y	Y	Y	Y
13 Hoeffel	Y	Y	Y	Y	Y
14 Coyne	Y	Y	Y	Y	Y
15 ***Toomey***	Y	Y	Y	Y	Y
16 ***Pitts***	?	?	?	Y	Y
17 ***Gekas***	Y	Y	Y	Y	Y
18 Doyle	Y	Y	Y	Y	Y
19 ***Goodling***	Y	Y	Y	Y	Y
20 Mascara	Y	Y	Y	Y	Y
21 ***English***	?	?	?	Y	Y
RHODE ISLAND					
1 Kennedy	?	?	?	Y	Y
2 Weygand	?	?	?	Y	Y
SOUTH CAROLINA					
1 ***Sanford***	Y	Y	Y	N	?
2 ***Spence***	Y	Y	Y	Y	Y
3 ***Graham***	?	?	?	Y	Y
4 ***DeMint***	Y	Y	Y	Y	Y
5 Spratt	?	Y	Y	Y	Y
6 Clyburn	Y	Y	Y	Y	Y
SOUTH DAKOTA					
AL ***Thune***	Y	Y	Y	Y	Y
TENNESSEE					
1 ***Jenkins***	Y	Y	Y	Y	Y
2 ***Duncan***	Y	Y	Y	Y	Y
3 ***Wamp***	Y	Y	Y	Y	Y
4 ***Hilleary***	Y	Y	Y	Y	Y
5 Clement	Y	Y	Y	Y	Y
6 Gordon	Y	Y	Y	Y	Y
7 ***Bryant***	Y	Y	Y	Y	Y
8 Tanner	Y	Y	Y	Y	Y
9 Ford	Y	Y	Y	Y	Y
TEXAS					
1 Sandlin	Y	Y	Y	Y	Y
2 Turner	?	?	?	?	?
3 ***Johnson, Sam***	Y	Y	Y	N	Y
4 Hall	Y	Y	Y	Y	Y
5 ***Sessions***	Y	Y	Y	Y	Y
6 ***Barton***	Y	Y	Y	Y	Y
7 ***Archer***	Y	Y	Y	Y	Y
8 ***Brady***	Y	Y	Y	Y	Y
9 Lampson	Y	Y	Y	Y	Y
10 Doggett	Y	Y	Y	N	Y
11 Edwards	Y	Y	Y	Y	Y
12 ***Granger***	Y	Y	Y	Y	Y
13 ***Thornberry***	Y	Y	Y	Y	Y
14 ***Paul***	Y	Y	Y	N	Y
15 Hinojosa	Y	Y	Y	Y	Y
16 Reyes	Y	Y	Y	Y	Y
17 Stenholm	Y	Y	Y	Y	Y
18 Jackson-Lee	Y	Y	Y	Y	Y
19 ***Combest***	Y	Y	Y	Y	Y
20 Gonzalez	Y	Y	Y	Y	Y
21 ***Smith***	Y	Y	Y	Y	Y
22 ***DeLay***	Y	Y	Y	Y	Y
23 ***Bonilla***	Y	?	Y	Y	Y
24 Frost	Y	Y	Y	Y	Y
25 Bentsen	Y	Y	Y	Y	Y
26 ***Armey***	Y	Y	Y	Y	Y
27 Ortiz	Y	Y	Y	Y	Y
28 Rodriguez	?	?	?	?	?
29 Green	Y	Y	Y	Y	Y
30 Johnson, E.B.	Y	Y	Y	Y	Y
UTAH					
1 ***Hansen***	?	?	?	?	?
2 ***Cook***	Y	Y	Y	Y	Y
3 ***Cannon***	Y	Y	Y	Y	Y
VERMONT					
AL *Sanders*	?	?	?	Y	Y
VIRGINIA					
1 Vacant					
2 Pickett	Y	Y	Y	Y	Y
3 Scott	Y	Y	Y	Y	Y
4 Sisisky	Y	Y	Y	Y	Y
5 *Goode*	?	?	?	Y	Y
6 ***Goodlatte***	Y	Y	Y	Y	Y
7 ***Bliley***	Y	Y	Y	Y	Y
8 Moran	Y	Y	Y	Y	?
9 Boucher	Y	Y	Y	Y	Y
10 ***Wolf***	Y	Y	Y	Y	Y
11 ***Davis***	Y	Y	Y	Y	Y
WASHINGTON					
1 Inslee	Y	Y	Y	Y	Y
2 ***Metcalf***	Y	Y	Y	Y	Y
3 Baird	Y	Y	Y	Y	Y
4 ***Hastings***	Y	Y	Y	Y	Y
5 ***Nethercutt***	+	+	?	Y	Y
6 Dicks	Y	Y	Y	Y	Y
7 McDermott	Y	Y	Y	Y	Y
8 ***Dunn***	Y	Y	Y	Y	Y
9 Smith	Y	Y	Y	Y	Y
WEST VIRGINIA					
1 Mollohan	Y	Y	Y	Y	Y
2 Wise	?	?	?	?	?
3 Rahall	Y	Y	Y	Y	Y
WISCONSIN					
1 ***Ryan***	Y	Y	Y	Y	Y
2 Baldwin	Y	Y	Y	Y	Y
3 Kind	Y	Y	Y	Y	Y
4 Kleczka	Y	Y	?	Y	Y
5 Barrett	?	?	+	Y	Y
6 ***Petri***	Y	Y	Y	Y	Y
7 Obey	Y	Y	Y	Y	Y
8 ***Green***	Y	Y	Y	Y	Y
9 ***Sensenbrenner***	Y	Y	Y	N	Y
WYOMING					
AL ***Cubin***	Y	?	?	Y	Y

Southern states - Ala., Ark., Fla., Ga., Ky., La., Miss., N.C., Okla., S.C., Tenn., Texas, Va.

536. HR 4635. Fiscal 2001 VA-HUD and Energy-Water Appropriations/Conference Report. Adoption of the conference report on the bill that would appropriate $107.3 billion in fiscal 2001 for the Veterans Affairs and Housing and Urban Development departments and independent agencies. The bill also includes a slightly revised version of a bill (HR 4733) to appropriate $23.6 billion for the Energy Department and Army Corps of Engineers, and other independent agencies. Adopted (thus sent to the Senate) 386-24: R 185-22; D 199-2 (ND 149-1, SD 50-1); I 2-0. Oct. 19, 2000.

537. H J Res 114. Continuing Resolution/Previous Question. Linder, R-Ga., motion to order the previous question (thus ending debate and possibility of amendment) on adoption of the rule (H Res 637) to provide for House floor consideration of the joint resolution that would make further continuing appropriations for fiscal year 2001. Motion agreed to 212-193: R 208-0; D 3-192 (ND 3-142, SD 0-50); I 1-1. Oct. 19, 2000.

538. H J Res 114. Continuing Resolution/Rule. Adoption of the rule (H Res 637) providing for House floor consideration of the joint resolution that would provide temporary funding authority, at current levels through Oct. 25, for the departments, agencies and programs for which regular fiscal year 2001 appropriations bills will not be enacted by Oct. 20. Adopted 209-187: R 201-0; D 7-186 (ND 7-137, SD 0-49); I 1-1. Oct. 19, 2000.

539. H J Res 114. Continuing Resolution/Passage. Passage of the joint resolution that would provide temporary funding authority, at current levels, through Oct. 25, for the departments, agencies and programs for which regular fiscal year 2001 appropriations bills will not be enacted by Oct. 20. Passed 262-136: R 208-0; D 53-135 (ND 41-97, SD 12-38); I 1-1. Oct. 19, 2000.

540. HR 4541. Commodities Exchanges/Passage. Combest, R-Texas, motion to suspend the rules and pass the bill that would reauthorize activities of the Commodity Futures Trading Commission (CFTC), modify regulation of the futures market, provide "legal certainty" to over-the-counter (OTC) derivatives and authorize the trading of single-stock futures. Motion agreed to 377-4: R 194-2; D 181-2 (ND 136-1, SD 45-1); I 2-0. A two-thirds majority of those present and voting (254 in this case) is required for passage under suspension of the rules. Oct. 19, 2000. A "yea" was a vote in support of the president's position.

Key

- Y Voted for (yea).
- # Paired for.
- + Announced for.
- N Voted against (nay).
- X Paired against.
- – Announced against.
- P Voted "present."
- C Voted "present" to avoid possible conflict of interest.
- ? Did not vote or otherwise make a position known.

•

Democrats ***Republicans***
Independents

	536	537	538	539	540
ALABAMA					
1 ***Callahan***	Y	Y	Y	Y	Y
2 ***Everett***	Y	Y	Y	Y	?
3 ***Riley***	Y	Y	Y	Y	Y
4 ***Aderholt***	Y	Y	Y	Y	Y
5 Cramer	Y	N	N	N	Y
6 ***Bachus***	Y	Y	Y	Y	Y
7 Hilliard	Y	N	N	N	Y
ALASKA					
AL ***Young***	Y	Y	Y	Y	Y
ARIZONA					
1 ***Salmon***	N	Y	Y	Y	Y
2 Pastor	Y	N	N	N	Y
3 ***Stump***	Y	Y	Y	Y	Y
4 ***Shadegg***	N	Y	Y	Y	Y
5 ***Kolbe***	Y	Y	Y	Y	Y
6 ***Hayworth***	Y	Y	Y	Y	Y
ARKANSAS					
1 Berry	Y	N	N	N	Y
2 Snyder	Y	N	N	Y	Y
3 ***Hutchinson***	Y	Y	Y	Y	Y
4 ***Dickey***	Y	Y	Y	Y	Y
CALIFORNIA					
1 Thompson	Y	N	N	N	Y
2 ***Herger***	Y	Y	Y	Y	Y
3 ***Ose***	Y	Y	Y	Y	Y
4 ***Doolittle***	Y	Y	Y	Y	Y
5 Matsui	Y	N	N	N	Y
6 Woolsey	Y	N	N	N	Y
7 Miller, George	Y	N	N	N	Y
8 Pelosi	Y	N	N	N	Y
9 Lee	Y	N	N	N	Y
10 Tauscher	Y	N	N	Y	Y
11 ***Pombo***	Y	Y	Y	Y	Y
12 Lantos	Y	N	N	N	Y
13 Stark	Y	N	N	N	Y
14 Eshoo	Y	N	N	Y	Y
15 ***Campbell***	?	?	?	?	?
16 Lofgren	Y	N	N	N	Y
17 Farr	Y	N	N	Y	Y
18 Condit	Y	N	N	Y	Y
19 ***Radanovich***	Y	Y	?	Y	Y
20 Dooley	Y	N	N	Y	Y
21 ***Thomas***	Y	Y	Y	Y	Y
22 Capps	Y	N	N	Y	Y
23 ***Gallegly***	Y	Y	Y	Y	Y
24 Sherman	Y	N	N	N	Y
25 ***McKeon***	Y	Y	Y	Y	Y
26 Berman	Y	N	N	Y	Y
27 ***Rogan***	Y	Y	Y	Y	?
28 ***Dreier***	Y	Y	Y	Y	Y
29 Waxman	Y	N	N	N	Y
30 Becerra	Y	N	N	N	Y
31 ***Martinez***	Y	Y	Y	Y	Y
32 Dixon	Y	N	N	N	Y
33 Roybal-Allard	Y	N	N	N	Y
34 Napolitano	Y	N	N	N	Y
35 Waters	Y	N	N	N	Y
36 ***Kuykendall***	Y	Y	Y	Y	Y
37 Millender-McD.	Y	N	N	N	Y
38 ***Horn***	Y	Y	Y	Y	Y
39 ***Royce***	Y	Y	Y	Y	Y
40 ***Lewis***	?	?	?	?	?
41 ***Miller, Gary***	Y	Y	Y	Y	Y
42 Baca	Y	N	N	N	Y
43 ***Calvert***	Y	Y	Y	Y	Y
44 ***Bono***	Y	Y	Y	Y	Y
45 ***Rohrabacher***	Y	Y	Y	Y	Y
46 Sanchez	Y	N	N	+	+
47 ***Cox***	N	Y	Y	Y	Y
48 ***Packard***	Y	Y	Y	Y	Y
49 ***Bilbray***	Y	Y	Y	Y	Y
50 Filner	Y	N	N	N	+
51 ***Cunningham***	Y	Y	Y	Y	Y
52 ***Hunter***	Y	Y	Y	Y	Y
COLORADO					
1 DeGette	Y	N	N	N	Y
2 Udall	Y	N	N	N	Y
3 ***McInnis***	Y	Y	Y	Y	?
4 ***Schaffer***	N	Y	Y	Y	Y
5 ***Hefley***	Y	Y	Y	Y	Y
6 ***Tancredo***	N	Y	Y	Y	Y
CONNECTICUT					
1 Larson	Y	N	N	N	Y
2 Gejdenson	Y	N	N	N	Y
3 DeLauro	Y	N	N	N	Y
4 ***Shays***	?	?	?	?	?
5 Maloney	Y	N	N	N	Y
6 ***Johnson***	Y	Y	Y	Y	Y
DELAWARE					
AL ***Castle***	N	Y	Y	Y	Y
FLORIDA					
1 ***Scarborough***	Y	Y	Y	Y	Y
2 Boyd	Y	N	N	N	Y
3 Brown	Y	N	N	N	Y
4 ***Fowler***	Y	Y	Y	Y	Y
5 Thurman	Y	N	N	N	Y
6 ***Stearns***	Y	Y	Y	Y	Y
7 ***Mica***	Y	Y	Y	Y	Y
8 ***McCollum***	?	?	?	?	?
9 ***Bilirakis***	Y	Y	Y	Y	?
10 ***Young***	Y	Y	Y	Y	Y
11 Davis	Y	N	N	N	Y
12 ***Canady***	Y	Y	Y	Y	Y
13 ***Miller***	?	?	?	?	?
14 ***Goss***	Y	Y	Y	Y	Y
15 ***Weldon***	Y	Y	Y	Y	Y
16 ***Foley***	Y	Y	Y	Y	Y
17 Meek	Y	N	N	N	Y
18 ***Ros-Lehtinen***	Y	Y	Y	Y	Y
19 Wexler	Y	N	N	N	Y
20 Deutsch	Y	N	N	N	Y
21 ***Diaz-Balart***	Y	Y	Y	?	+
22 ***Shaw***	Y	Y	Y	Y	?
23 Hastings	Y	N	N	N	Y
GEORGIA					
1 ***Kingston***	Y	Y	Y	Y	Y
2 Bishop	Y	N	N	Y	Y
3 ***Collins***	Y	Y	Y	Y	Y
4 McKinney	Y	N	N	N	Y
5 Lewis	Y	N	N	N	Y
6 ***Isakson***	Y	Y	Y	Y	Y
7 ***Barr***	Y	Y	Y	Y	Y
8 ***Chambliss***	Y	Y	Y	Y	Y
9 ***Deal***	Y	Y	Y	Y	Y
10 ***Norwood***	Y	Y	Y	Y	Y
11 ***Linder***	Y	Y	Y	Y	Y
HAWAII					
1 Abercrombie	Y	N	Y	Y	Y
2 Mink	Y	N	N	N	Y
IDAHO					
1 ***Chenoweth-Hage***	?	?	?	?	?
2 ***Simpson***	Y	Y	Y	Y	Y
ILLINOIS					
1 Rush	Y	?	?	?	?
2 Jackson	Y	N	N	N	Y
3 Lipinski	?	?	?	?	?
4 Gutierrez	Y	N	N	N	Y
5 Blagojevich	Y	N	Y	Y	Y
6 ***Hyde***	Y	Y	Y	Y	Y
7 Davis	Y	N	N	N	?
8 ***Crane***	Y	Y	Y	Y	Y
9 Schakowsky	Y	N	N	N	Y
10 ***Porter***	Y	Y	Y	Y	Y
11 ***Weller***	Y	Y	Y	Y	Y
12 Costello	Y	N	N	N	Y
13 ***Biggert***	Y	Y	Y	Y	Y

ND Northern Democrats SD Southern Democrats

	536	537	538	539	540
14 ***Hastert***					
15 ***Ewing***	Y	Y	Y	Y	Y
16 ***Manzullo***	Y	Y	Y	Y	Y
17 Evans	Y	N	N	N	Y
18 ***LaHood***	Y	Y	Y	Y	Y
19 Phelps	Y	N	N	N	Y
20 ***Shimkus***	Y	Y	Y	Y	Y
INDIANA					
1 Visclosky	Y	N	N	N	Y
2 ***McIntosh***	?	?	?	?	?
3 Roemer	Y	N	Y	Y	Y
4 ***Souder***	Y	Y	Y	Y	Y
5 ***Buyer***	Y	Y	Y	Y	Y
6 ***Burton***	Y	Y	Y	Y	Y
7 ***Pease***	Y	Y	Y	Y	Y
8 ***Hostettler***	N	Y	Y	Y	Y
9 Hill	Y	N	N	Y	Y
10 Carson	Y	N	N	N	Y
IOWA					
1 ***Leach***	Y	Y	Y	Y	Y
2 ***Nussle***	Y	Y	Y	Y	Y
3 Boswell	Y	N	N	Y	Y
4 ***Ganske***	Y	Y	Y	Y	Y
5 ***Latham***	Y	Y	Y	Y	Y
KANSAS					
1 ***Moran***	Y	Y	Y	Y	Y
2 ***Ryun***	N	Y	Y	Y	Y
3 Moore	Y	Y	Y	Y	Y
4 ***Tiahrt***	Y	Y	Y	Y	Y
KENTUCKY					
1 ***Whitfield***	Y	Y	Y	Y	Y
2 ***Lewis***	Y	Y	Y	Y	Y
3 ***Northup***	Y	Y	Y	Y	Y
4 Lucas	Y	N	N	Y	Y
5 ***Rogers***	Y	Y	Y	Y	Y
6 ***Fletcher***	Y	Y	Y	Y	Y
LOUISIANA					
1 ***Vitter***	Y	Y	Y	Y	Y
2 Jefferson	Y	N	N	N	Y
3 ***Tauzin***	Y	Y	?	Y	Y
4 ***McCrery***	Y	Y	Y	Y	Y
5 ***Cooksey***	Y	?	Y	Y	?
6 ***Baker***	Y	Y	Y	Y	?
7 John	Y	N	N	N	Y
MAINE					
1 Allen	Y	N	N	N	Y
2 Baldacci	Y	N	N	Y	Y
MARYLAND					
1 ***Gilchrest***	Y	Y	Y	Y	Y
2 ***Ehrlich***	Y	Y	Y	Y	Y
3 Cardin	Y	N	N	N	Y
4 Wynn	Y	N	N	N	Y
5 Hoyer	Y	N	N	N	Y
6 ***Bartlett***	Y	Y	Y	Y	Y
7 Cummings	Y	N	N	N	Y
8 ***Morella***	Y	Y	Y	Y	Y
MASSACHUSETTS					
1 Olver	Y	N	N	N	Y
2 Neal	Y	N	N	N	Y
3 McGovern	Y	N	N	N	Y
4 Frank	Y	N	N	N	Y
5 Meehan	Y	N	N	N	Y
6 Tierney	Y	N	N	N	Y
7 Markey	Y	N	N	N	Y
8 Capuano	Y	N	N	N	Y
9 Moakley	Y	N	N	N	Y
10 Delahunt	Y	N	N	N	Y
MICHIGAN					
1 Stupak	Y	N	N	N	Y
2 ***Hoekstra***	Y	Y	Y	Y	Y
3 ***Ehlers***	Y	Y	Y	Y	Y
4 ***Camp***	Y	Y	Y	Y	Y
5 Barcia	Y	N	N	?	Y
6 ***Upton***	Y	Y	Y	Y	Y
7 ***Smith***	Y	Y	Y	Y	N
8 Stabenow	Y	N	N	Y	Y
9 Kildee	Y	N	N	N	Y
10 Bonior	Y	N	N	N	Y
11 ***Knollenberg***	Y	Y	Y	Y	Y
12 Levin	Y	N	N	N	Y
13 Rivers	Y	N	N	N	Y
14 Conyers	?	?	?	?	?
15 Kilpatrick	Y	N	N	N	Y
16 Dingell	Y	N	N	?	Y

	536	537	538	539	540
MINNESOTA					
1 ***Gutknecht***	Y	Y	Y	Y	Y
2 Minge	Y	N	N	Y	Y
3 ***Ramstad***	Y	Y	Y	Y	Y
4 Vacant					
5 Sabo	Y	N	N	N	Y
6 Luther	Y	N	N	Y	Y
7 Peterson	Y	N	N	Y	Y
8 Oberstar	Y	?	?	?	?
MISSISSIPPI					
1 ***Wicker***	Y	Y	Y	Y	Y
2 Thompson	?	?	?	?	?
3 ***Pickering***	Y	Y	?	Y	Y
4 Shows	Y	N	N	N	Y
5 Taylor	Y	N	N	Y	N
MISSOURI					
1 Clay	?	?	?	?	?
2 ***Talent***	?	?	?	?	?
3 Gephardt	Y	?	?	?	?
4 Skelton	Y	N	N	N	Y
5 McCarthy	Y	N	N	N	Y
6 Danner	Y	N	N	Y	Y
7 ***Blunt***	Y	Y	Y	Y	Y
8 ***Emerson***	Y	Y	Y	Y	Y
9 ***Hulshof***	Y	Y	Y	Y	Y
MONTANA					
AL ***Hill***	Y	Y	Y	Y	Y
NEBRASKA					
1 ***Bereuter***	Y	Y	Y	Y	Y
2 ***Terry***	Y	Y	Y	Y	Y
3 ***Barrett***	Y	Y	Y	Y	Y
NEVADA					
1 Berkley	Y	N	N	Y	Y
2 ***Gibbons***	N	Y	Y	Y	Y
NEW HAMPSHIRE					
1 ***Sununu***	Y	Y	Y	Y	Y
2 ***Bass***	Y	Y	Y	Y	Y
NEW JERSEY					
1 Andrews	N	N	N	N	Y
2 ***LoBiondo***	Y	Y	Y	Y	Y
3 ***Saxton***	Y	Y	Y	Y	Y
4 ***Smith***	Y	Y	Y	Y	Y
5 ***Roukema***	Y	Y	Y	Y	Y
6 Pallone	Y	N	N	N	Y
7 ***Franks***	?	?	?	?	?
8 Pascrell	Y	N	N	N	?
9 Rothman	Y	N	N	N	Y
10 Payne	Y	N	N	N	Y
11 ***Frelinghuysen***	Y	Y	Y	Y	Y
12 Holt	Y	N	N	N	Y
13 Menendez	Y	N	N	N	Y
NEW MEXICO					
1 ***Wilson***	Y	Y	Y	Y	Y
2 ***Skeen***	Y	Y	Y	Y	Y
3 Udall	Y	N	N	N	Y
NEW YORK					
1 Forbes	Y	N	N	?	?
2 ***Lazio***	?	?	?	?	?
3 ***King***	Y	Y	Y	Y	Y
4 McCarthy	Y	N	N	N	Y
5 Ackerman	Y	N	N	?	?
6 Meeks	Y	N	N	N	Y
7 Crowley	Y	N	N	N	Y
8 Nadler	Y	N	N	N	Y
9 Weiner	Y	N	N	N	Y
10 Towns	Y	N	N	N	Y
11 Owens	Y	N	N	?	?
12 Velázquez	Y	N	N	N	Y
13 ***Fossella***	Y	Y	Y	Y	Y
14 Maloney	Y	N	N	Y	Y
15 Rangel	Y	N	N	N	Y
16 Serrano	Y	N	N	Y	Y
17 Engel	Y	N	N	N	Y
18 Lowey	Y	N	N	N	Y
19 ***Kelly***	Y	Y	Y	Y	Y
20 ***Gilman***	Y	Y	?	Y	Y
21 McNulty	Y	N	N	N	Y
22 ***Sweeney***	Y	Y	Y	Y	Y
23 ***Boehlert***	Y	Y	Y	Y	Y
24 ***McHugh***	Y	Y	Y	Y	Y
25 ***Walsh***	Y	Y	Y	Y	Y
26 Hinchey	Y	N	N	N	Y
27 ***Reynolds***	Y	Y	Y	Y	Y
28 Slaughter	Y	N	N	N	Y
29 LaFalce	Y	N	N	N	Y

	536	537	538	539	540
30 ***Quinn***	Y	Y	Y	Y	Y
31 ***Houghton***	?	Y	Y	Y	Y
NORTH CAROLINA					
1 Clayton	Y	N	N	N	Y
2 Etheridge	Y	N	N	N	Y
3 ***Jones***	Y	Y	Y	Y	Y
4 Price	Y	N	N	N	Y
5 ***Burr***	Y	Y	Y	Y	Y
6 ***Coble***	Y	Y	Y	Y	Y
7 McIntyre	Y	N	N	Y	Y
8 ***Hayes***	Y	Y	Y	Y	Y
9 ***Myrick***	Y	Y	Y	Y	Y
10 ***Ballenger***	Y	Y	Y	Y	Y
11 ***Taylor***	Y	Y	Y	Y	Y
12 Watt	Y	N	N	N	Y
NORTH DAKOTA					
AL Pomeroy	Y	N	N	N	Y
OHIO					
1 ***Chabot***	N	Y	Y	Y	Y
2 ***Portman***	Y	Y	Y	Y	Y
3 Hall	Y	N	N	N	Y
4 ***Oxley***	?	?	?	?	?
5 ***Gillmor***	Y	Y	Y	Y	Y
6 Strickland	Y	N	N	N	Y
7 ***Hobson***	Y	Y	Y	Y	Y
8 ***Boehner***	Y	Y	Y	Y	Y
9 Kaptur	Y	N	N	N	Y
10 Kucinich	Y	N	N	Y	Y
11 Jones	?	?	?	?	?
12 ***Kasich***	N	Y	Y	Y	Y
13 Brown	Y	N	N	N	Y
14 Sawyer	Y	N	N	N	Y
15 ***Pryce***	Y	Y	Y	Y	Y
16 ***Regula***	Y	Y	?	Y	Y
17 Traficant	Y	Y	Y	Y	Y
18 ***Ney***	Y	Y	Y	Y	Y
19 ***LaTourette***	Y	Y	Y	Y	Y
OKLAHOMA					
1 ***Largent***	Y	Y	Y	Y	Y
2 ***Coburn***	N	Y	Y	Y	Y
3 ***Watkins***	Y	Y	Y	Y	Y
4 ***Watts***	Y	Y	Y	Y	Y
5 ***Istook***	Y	Y	Y	Y	Y
6 ***Lucas***	Y	Y	Y	Y	Y
OREGON					
1 Wu	Y	N	N	N	Y
2 ***Walden***	Y	Y	Y	Y	Y
3 Blumenauer	Y	N	N	N	Y
4 DeFazio	Y	N	N	N	N
5 Hooley	Y	N	N	N	Y
PENNSYLVANIA					
1 Brady	Y	N	N	?	?
2 Fattah	Y	N	N	N	Y
3 Borski	Y	N	N	N	Y
4 Klink	Y	?	?	?	?
5 ***Peterson***	Y	Y	Y	Y	Y
6 Holden	Y	N	N	Y	Y
7 ***Weldon***	Y	Y	Y	Y	Y
8 ***Greenwood***	Y	Y	Y	Y	Y
9 ***Shuster***	Y	Y	Y	Y	?
10 ***Sherwood***	Y	Y	Y	Y	Y
11 Kanjorski	Y	N	N	Y	Y
12 Murtha	Y	N	Y	Y	Y
13 Hoeffel	Y	N	N	Y	Y
14 Coyne	Y	N	N	N	Y
15 ***Toomey***	N	Y	Y	Y	Y
16 ***Pitts***	N	Y	Y	Y	Y
17 ***Gekas***	Y	Y	?	Y	Y
18 Doyle	Y	N	N	N	Y
19 ***Goodling***	?	Y	Y	Y	Y
20 Mascara	Y	N	N	N	Y
21 ***English***	Y	Y	Y	Y	Y
RHODE ISLAND					
1 Kennedy	Y	N	N	N	Y
2 Weygand	Y	?	?	?	?
SOUTH CAROLINA					
1 ***Sanford***	N	Y	Y	Y	Y
2 ***Spence***	Y	Y	Y	Y	Y
3 ***Graham***	Y	Y	Y	Y	Y
4 ***DeMint***	N	Y	Y	Y	?
5 Spratt	Y	?	?	?	?
6 Clyburn	Y	N	N	N	Y
SOUTH DAKOTA					
AL ***Thune***	Y	Y	Y	Y	Y

	536	537	538	539	540
TENNESSEE					
1 ***Jenkins***	Y	Y	Y	Y	Y
2 ***Duncan***	Y	Y	Y	Y	Y
3 ***Wamp***	Y	Y	Y	Y	Y
4 ***Hilleary***	Y	Y	Y	Y	Y
5 Clement	Y	N	?	N	Y
6 Gordon	Y	N	N	Y	Y
7 ***Bryant***	Y	Y	Y	Y	Y
8 Tanner	Y	N	N	N	Y
9 Ford	Y	N	N	N	Y
TEXAS					
1 Sandlin	Y	N	N	Y	Y
2 Turner	?	?	?	?	?
3 ***Johnson, Sam***	N	Y	Y	Y	Y
4 Hall	Y	N	N	Y	Y
5 ***Sessions***	Y	Y	Y	Y	Y
6 ***Barton***	N	Y	Y	Y	Y
7 ***Archer***	N	Y	Y	Y	Y
8 ***Brady***	Y	Y	Y	Y	Y
9 Lampson	Y	N	N	N	Y
10 Doggett	Y	N	N	N	Y
11 Edwards	Y	N	N	N	Y
12 ***Granger***	Y	Y	Y	Y	Y
13 ***Thornberry***	Y	Y	Y	Y	Y
14 ***Paul***	N	Y	Y	Y	N
15 Hinojosa	Y	N	N	N	Y
16 Reyes	Y	N	N	N	Y
17 Stenholm	N	N	N	N	Y
18 Jackson-Lee	Y	N	N	N	?
19 ***Combest***	Y	Y	Y	Y	Y
20 Gonzalez	Y	N	N	N	Y
21 ***Smith***	Y	Y	Y	Y	Y
22 ***DeLay***	Y	Y	Y	Y	?
23 ***Bonilla***	Y	Y	Y	Y	Y
24 Frost	Y	N	N	N	Y
25 Bentsen	Y	N	N	Y	Y
26 ***Armey***	Y	Y	Y	Y	Y
27 Ortiz	Y	N	N	N	Y
28 Rodriguez	?	?	?	?	?
29 Green	Y	N	N	N	?
30 Johnson, E.B.	Y	N	N	N	Y
UTAH					
1 ***Hansen***	?	?	?	?	?
2 ***Cook***	Y	Y	Y	Y	Y
3 ***Cannon***	Y	Y	Y	Y	Y
VERMONT					
AL *Sanders*	Y	N	N	N	Y
VIRGINIA					
1 Vacant					
2 Pickett	Y	N	N	Y	Y
3 Scott	Y	N	N	N	Y
4 Sisisky	Y	N	N	Y	?
5 *Goode*	Y	Y	Y	Y	Y
6 ***Goodlatte***	Y	Y	Y	Y	Y
7 ***Bliley***	N	Y	Y	Y	Y
8 Moran	Y	N	N	N	Y
9 Boucher	Y	N	N	Y	?
10 ***Wolf***	Y	Y	Y	Y	Y
11 ***Davis***	Y	Y	?	Y	?
WASHINGTON					
1 Inslee	Y	N	N	Y	Y
2 ***Metcalf***	Y	Y	Y	Y	?
3 Baird	Y	N	N	N	Y
4 ***Hastings***	Y	Y	Y	Y	Y
5 ***Nethercutt***	Y	Y	Y	Y	Y
6 Dicks	Y	N	N	Y	Y
7 McDermott	Y	N	N	N	Y
8 ***Dunn***	Y	Y	?	Y	Y
9 Smith	Y	N	N	Y	Y
WEST VIRGINIA					
1 Mollohan	Y	N	Y	Y	Y
2 Wise	?	?	?	?	?
3 Rahall	Y	N	N	Y	Y
WISCONSIN					
1 ***Ryan***	Y	Y	Y	Y	Y
2 Baldwin	Y	N	N	Y	Y
3 Kind	Y	Y	N	Y	Y
4 Kleczka	Y	N	N	Y	Y
5 Barrett	Y	N	N	Y	Y
6 ***Petri***	Y	Y	Y	Y	Y
7 Obey	Y	N	?	N	Y
8 ***Green***	Y	Y	Y	Y	Y
9 ***Sensenbrenner***	N	Y	Y	Y	Y
WYOMING					
AL ***Cubin***	Y	Y	Y	Y	Y

Southern states - Ala., Ark., Fla., Ga., Ky., La., Miss., N.C., Okla., S.C., Tenn., Texas, Va.

541. HR 4656. Lake Tahoe Basin/Rule. Adoption of the rule (H Res 634) to provide for floor consideration of the bill that would authorize the U.S. Forest Service to transfer land in the Lake Tahoe Basin to the Washoe County School District for an elementary school site. Adopted 196-181: R 189-0; D 7-180 (ND 5-132, SD 2-48); I 0-1. Oct. 24, 2000. (Subsequently, the bill passed by voice vote.)

542. H Con Res 414. Afghan Democracy/Adoption. Gilman, R-N.Y., motion to suspend the rules and adopt the concurrent resolution expressing U.S. support for the right of Afghans to determine their own destiny through a democratic process and free and fair elections. Motion agreed to 381-0: R 191-0; D 189-0 (ND 139-0, SD 50-0); I 1-0. A two-thirds majority of those present and voting (254 in this case) is required for adoption under suspension of the rules. Oct. 24, 2000.

543. HR 4271. Science Education/Passage. Sensenbrenner, R-Wis., motion to suspend the rules and pass the bill that would authorize funding for programs intended to enhance math and science education, particularly in elementary and secondary schools. Motion rejected 215-156: R 171-15; D 44-140 (ND 34-103, SD 10-37); I 0-1. A two-thirds majority of those present and voting (248 in this case) is required for passage under suspension of the rules. Oct. 24, 2000.

544. Procedural Motion/Journal. Approval of the House Journal of Tuesday, Oct. 24, 2000. Approved 332-51: R 177-16; D 154-35 (ND 112-28, SD 42-7); I 1-0. Oct. 25, 2000.

545. HR 4811. Fiscal 2001 Foreign Operations Appropriations/Previous Question. Diaz-Balart, R-Fla., motion to order the previous question (thus ending debate and possibility of amendment) on adoption of the rule (H Res 647) to provide for House floor consideration of the conference report on the bill to appropriate $14.9 billion for foreign aid and export assistance. Motion agreed to 210-197: R 208-0; D 1-196 (ND 1-145, SD 0-51); I 1-1. Oct. 25, 2000.

546. HR 4811. Fiscal 2001 Foreign Operations Appropriations/Conference Report. Adoption of the conference report on the bill that would appropriate $14.9 billion in fiscal year 2001 for foreign operations. It includes $2.9 billion for Israel, almost $2 billion for Egypt, $1.1 billion for international financial institutions and $435 million to restructure and forgive the debt of the world's poorest nations. Adopted (thus sent to the Senate) 307-101: R 133-77; D 173-23 (ND 131-13, SD 42-10); I 1-1. Oct. 25, 2000.

547. HR 782. Older Americans Act/Passage. McKeon, R-Calif., motion to suspend the rules and pass the bill that would reauthorize programs under the Older Americans Act and set aside $125 million for a new family caregiver program. Motion agreed to 405-2: R 208-2; D 195-0 (ND 143-0, SD 52-0); I 2-0. A two-thirds majority of those present and voting (272 in this case) is required for passage under suspension of the rules. Oct. 25, 2000.

548. HR 5375. Erie Canal/Passage. Hansen, R-Utah, motion to suspend the rules and pass the bill that would establish the Erie Canalway National Heritage Corridor in New York. It would establish a commission charged with creating a comprehensive plan for preserving the canal-related history and culture. Motion rejected 223-183: R 198-10; D 24-172 (ND 15-129, SD 9-43); I 1-1. A two-thirds majority of those present and voting (271 in this case) is required for passage under suspension of the rules. Oct. 25, 2000.

Key

Y Voted for (yea).
\# Paired for.
\+ Announced for.
N Voted against (nay).
X Paired against.
– Announced against.
P Voted "present."
C Voted "present" to avoid possible conflict of interest.
? Did not vote or otherwise make a position known.

•

Democrats ***Republicans***
Independents

	541	542	543	544	545	546	547	548
ALABAMA								
1 ***Callahan***	Y	Y	Y	Y	Y	Y	Y	Y
2 ***Everett***	Y	Y	Y	Y	Y	N	Y	Y
3 ***Riley***	Y	Y	Y	N	Y	N	Y	Y
4 ***Aderholt***	Y	Y	Y	N	Y	N	Y	Y
5 Cramer	N	Y	Y	Y	N	Y	Y	Y
6 ***Bachus***	Y	Y	Y	Y	Y	Y	Y	Y
7 Hilliard	N	Y	N	N	N	Y	Y	N
ALASKA								
AL ***Young***	Y	Y	Y	?	Y	Y	Y	Y
ARIZONA								
1 ***Salmon***	Y	Y	Y	Y	Y	N	Y	N
2 Pastor	N	Y	N	Y	N	Y	Y	N
3 ***Stump***	Y	Y	?	Y	Y	N	Y	Y
4 ***Shadegg***	Y	Y	Y	?	?	?	?	?
5 ***Kolbe***	+	+	+	Y	Y	Y	Y	Y
6 ***Hayworth***	Y	Y	Y	Y	Y	N	Y	Y
ARKANSAS								
1 Berry	N	Y	N	Y	N	N	Y	N
2 Snyder	N	Y	Y	Y	N	Y	Y	N
3 ***Hutchinson***	Y	Y	Y	Y	Y	N	Y	Y
4 ***Dickey***	?	?	?	?	?	Y	Y	Y
CALIFORNIA								
1 Thompson	N	Y	N	N	N	Y	Y	N
2 ***Herger***	Y	Y	Y	Y	Y	N	Y	Y
3 ***Ose***	Y	Y	Y	Y	Y	Y	Y	Y
4 ***Doolittle***	Y	Y	Y	Y	Y	N	Y	Y
5 Matsui	N	Y	N	Y	N	Y	Y	N
6 Woolsey	N	Y	N	Y	N	Y	Y	N
7 Miller, George	N	Y	N	N	N	Y	Y	N
8 Pelosi	N	Y	N	Y	N	Y	Y	Y
9 Lee	N	Y	N	Y	N	Y	Y	N
10 Tauscher	N	Y	Y	N	N	Y	Y	N
11 ***Pombo***	Y	Y	Y	Y	Y	N	Y	N
12 Lantos	N	Y	N	Y	N	Y	Y	N
13 Stark	N	Y	N	N	N	N	Y	N
14 Eshoo	N	Y	N	Y	N	Y	Y	N
15 ***Campbell***	?	?	?	?	?	?	?	?
16 Lofgren	N	Y	N	Y	N	Y	Y	N
17 Farr	N	Y	N	Y	N	Y	Y	N
18 Condit	N	Y	N	Y	N	N	Y	N
19 ***Radanovich***	Y	Y	Y	Y	Y	Y	Y	Y
20 Dooley	N	Y	N	Y	N	Y	Y	N
21 ***Thomas***	Y	Y	Y	Y	Y	Y	Y	Y
22 Capps	N	Y	N	Y	N	Y	Y	N
23 ***Gallegly***	Y	Y	Y	Y	Y	Y	Y	Y
24 Sherman	N	Y	N	Y	N	Y	Y	N
25 ***McKeon***	Y	Y	Y	Y	Y	Y	Y	Y
26 Berman	N	Y	N	Y	N	Y	Y	N
27 ***Rogan***	Y	Y	Y	Y	Y	Y	Y	Y
28 ***Dreier***	Y	Y	Y	Y	Y	Y	Y	Y
29 Waxman	N	Y	N	Y	N	Y	?	?
30 Becerra	+	–	+	N	N	Y	Y	N
31 ***Martinez***	Y	Y	Y	Y	Y	Y	Y	Y
32 Dixon	N	Y	N	?	N	Y	Y	N
33 Roybal-Allard	N	Y	N	Y	N	Y	Y	N
34 Napolitano	N	Y	N	Y	N	Y	Y	N
35 Waters	N	Y	N	N	N	Y	Y	N
36 ***Kuykendall***	Y	Y	Y	Y	Y	Y	Y	Y
37 Millender-McD.	N	Y	N	Y	N	Y	Y	N
38 ***Horn***	Y	Y	Y	Y	Y	Y	Y	Y
39 ***Royce***	Y	Y	Y	Y	Y	Y	Y	?
40 ***Lewis***	?	?	?	Y	Y	Y	Y	?
41 ***Miller, Gary***	Y	Y	N	Y	Y	N	Y	Y
42 Baca	N	Y	N	Y	N	Y	Y	N
43 ***Calvert***	Y	Y	Y	Y	Y	Y	Y	Y
44 ***Bono***	Y	Y	Y	Y	Y	Y	Y	Y
45 ***Rohrabacher***	Y	Y	Y	Y	Y	N	Y	Y
46 Sanchez	N	Y	N	N	N	Y	Y	N
47 ***Cox***	Y	Y	Y	Y	Y	N	Y	Y
48 ***Packard***	Y	Y	Y	Y	Y	Y	Y	Y
49 ***Bilbray***	+	+	+	N	Y	Y	Y	Y
50 Filner	N	Y	N	N	N	Y	Y	N
51 ***Cunningham***	Y	Y	Y	Y	Y	N	Y	N
52 ***Hunter***	Y	Y	?	Y	Y	N	Y	Y
COLORADO								
1 DeGette	?	Y	N	Y	N	Y	Y	N
2 Udall	N	Y	Y	Y	N	Y	Y	N
3 ***McInnis***	Y	Y	Y	Y	Y	N	Y	Y
4 ***Schaffer***	Y	Y	N	N	Y	N	Y	N
5 ***Hefley***	Y	Y	N	N	Y	N	Y	Y
6 ***Tancredo***	Y	Y	N	Y	Y	N	Y	Y
CONNECTICUT								
1 Larson	N	Y	P	Y	N	Y	Y	N
2 Gejdenson	N	Y	N	Y	N	Y	Y	N
3 DeLauro	N	Y	N	Y	N	Y	Y	N
4 ***Shays***	?	Y	Y	Y	Y	Y	Y	Y
5 Maloney	N	Y	Y	Y	N	Y	Y	Y
6 ***Johnson***	Y	Y	Y	Y	Y	Y	Y	Y
DELAWARE								
AL ***Castle***	?	?	?	Y	Y	Y	Y	Y
FLORIDA								
1 ***Scarborough***	Y	Y	Y	Y	Y	N	Y	Y
2 Boyd	N	Y	Y	Y	N	N	Y	N
3 Brown	?	?	?	Y	N	Y	Y	N
4 ***Fowler***	?	?	?	Y	Y	Y	Y	Y
5 Thurman	N	Y	N	Y	N	Y	Y	N
6 ***Stearns***	Y	Y	Y	Y	Y	N	Y	Y
7 ***Mica***	+	+	+	+	+	+	+	+
8 ***McCollum***	?	?	?	?	?	?	?	?
9 ***Bilirakis***	+	+	+	Y	Y	Y	Y	Y
10 ***Young***	Y	Y	Y	Y	Y	Y	Y	Y
11 Davis	N	Y	N	Y	N	Y	Y	N
12 ***Canady***	Y	Y	Y	Y	Y	N	Y	Y
13 ***Miller***	Y	Y	Y	Y	Y	N	Y	Y
14 ***Goss***	Y	Y	Y	Y	Y	N	Y	Y
15 ***Weldon***	Y	Y	Y	Y	Y	N	Y	Y
16 ***Foley***	Y	Y	Y	Y	Y	Y	Y	Y
17 Meek	?	?	?	?	N	Y	Y	N
18 ***Ros-Lehtinen***	Y	Y	Y	Y	Y	Y	Y	Y
19 Wexler	N	Y	N	Y	N	Y	Y	N
20 Deutsch	N	Y	N	Y	N	Y	Y	N
21 ***Diaz-Balart***	Y	Y	Y	Y	Y	Y	Y	Y
22 ***Shaw***	?	?	?	?	Y	Y	Y	Y
23 Hastings	?	?	?	?	?	?	?	?
GEORGIA								
1 ***Kingston***	Y	Y	Y	Y	Y	Y	Y	Y
2 Bishop	N	Y	Y	Y	N	Y	Y	N
3 ***Collins***	Y	Y	Y	Y	Y	N	Y	Y
4 McKinney	N	Y	N	Y	N	Y	Y	N
5 Lewis	N	Y	N	N	N	Y	Y	N
6 ***Isakson***	Y	Y	Y	Y	Y	Y	Y	Y
7 ***Barr***	Y	Y	?	Y	Y	N	Y	Y
8 ***Chambliss***	Y	Y	Y	Y	Y	N	Y	Y
9 ***Deal***	?	?	?	Y	Y	N	Y	Y
10 ***Norwood***	Y	Y	Y	Y	Y	N	Y	Y
11 ***Linder***	Y	Y	Y	Y	Y	Y	Y	Y
HAWAII								
1 Abercrombie	N	Y	N	Y	N	Y	Y	N
2 Mink	N	Y	N	Y	N	Y	Y	N
IDAHO								
1 ***Chenoweth-Hage***	?	?	?	?	?	?	?	?
2 ***Simpson***	Y	Y	Y	Y	Y	Y	Y	Y
ILLINOIS								
1 Rush	N	Y	N	Y	N	Y	Y	N
2 Jackson	N	Y	Y	Y	N	Y	Y	N
3 Lipinski	N	Y	Y	Y	N	Y	Y	N
4 Gutierrez	N	Y	?	Y	N	Y	Y	N
5 Blagojevich	N	Y	Y	Y	N	Y	Y	N
6 ***Hyde***	?	?	?	Y	Y	Y	Y	Y
7 Davis	N	Y	N	Y	N	Y	Y	N
8 ***Crane***	Y	Y	N	N	Y	Y	Y	Y
9 Schakowsky	N	Y	N	Y	N	Y	Y	N
10 ***Porter***	Y	Y	Y	?	Y	Y	Y	Y
11 ***Weller***	Y	Y	Y	N	Y	Y	Y	Y
12 Costello	Y	Y	Y	N	N	Y	Y	N
13 ***Biggert***	Y	Y	Y	Y	Y	Y	Y	Y

ND Northern Democrats SD Southern Democrats

	541	542	543	544	545	546	547	548
14 ***Hastert***								
15 ***Ewing***	Y	Y	Y	Y	Y	Y	Y	Y
16 ***Manzullo***	Y	Y	N	Y	Y	N	Y	Y
17 Evans	N	Y	N	Y	N	Y	Y	N
18 ***LaHood***	Y	Y	Y	Y	Y	Y	Y	Y
19 Phelps	N	Y	Y	Y	N	N	Y	N
20 ***Shimkus***	Y	Y	Y	Y	Y	Y	Y	Y
INDIANA								
1 Visclosky	?	?	?	N	N	Y	Y	N
2 ***McIntosh***	?	?	?	?	?	?	?	?
3 Roemer	N	Y	N	Y	N	N	Y	Y
4 ***Souder***	Y	Y	Y	Y	Y	Y	Y	Y
5 ***Buyer***	Y	Y	Y	Y	Y	Y	Y	Y
6 ***Burton***	Y	Y	?	?	Y	Y	Y	Y
7 ***Pease***	Y	Y	Y	Y	Y	Y	Y	Y
8 ***Hostettler***	Y	Y	N	Y	Y	N	Y	Y
9 Hill	N	Y	N	Y	N	Y	Y	N
10 Carson	N	Y	N	Y	N	Y	Y	N
IOWA								
1 ***Leach***	Y	Y	Y	Y	Y	Y	Y	Y
2 ***Nussle***	+	+	+	Y	Y	Y	Y	Y
3 Boswell	N	Y	Y	Y	N	Y	Y	N
4 ***Ganske***	Y	Y	Y	Y	Y	Y	Y	Y
5 ***Latham***	Y	Y	Y	Y	Y	Y	Y	Y
KANSAS								
1 ***Moran***	Y	Y	Y	N	Y	N	Y	Y
2 ***Ryun***	Y	Y	Y	Y	Y	N	Y	Y
3 Moore	N	Y	Y	Y	N	Y	Y	N
4 ***Tiahrt***	Y	Y	N	Y	Y	N	Y	Y
KENTUCKY								
1 ***Whitfield***	Y	Y	Y	Y	Y	N	Y	Y
2 ***Lewis***	Y	Y	Y	Y	Y	N	Y	Y
3 ***Northup***	Y	Y	Y	Y	Y	Y	Y	Y
4 Lucas	N	Y	N	Y	N	Y	Y	N
5 ***Rogers***	Y	Y	Y	Y	Y	Y	Y	Y
6 ***Fletcher***	+	Y	Y	Y	Y	Y	Y	Y
LOUISIANA								
1 ***Vitter***	Y	Y	Y	Y	Y	N	Y	Y
2 Jefferson	N	Y	N	Y	N	N	Y	N
3 ***Tauzin***	Y	Y	Y	Y	Y	Y	Y	Y
4 ***McCrery***	Y	Y	Y	Y	Y	Y	Y	Y
5 ***Cooksey***	Y	Y	Y	Y	Y	Y	Y	Y
6 ***Baker***	Y	Y	Y	Y	Y	Y	Y	Y
7 John	?	?	?	?	?	?	?	?
MAINE								
1 Allen	N	Y	Y	Y	N	Y	Y	N
2 Baldacci	N	Y	N	Y	N	Y	Y	N
MARYLAND								
1 ***Gilchrest***	Y	Y	Y	Y	Y	Y	Y	Y
2 ***Ehrlich***	Y	Y	Y	Y	Y	Y	Y	Y
3 Cardin	N	Y	N	Y	N	Y	Y	N
4 Wynn	N	Y	N	Y	N	Y	Y	N
5 Hoyer	N	Y	N	Y	N	Y	Y	N
6 ***Bartlett***	Y	Y	Y	Y	Y	Y	Y	Y
7 Cummings	N	Y	N	Y	N	Y	Y	N
8 ***Morella***	Y	Y	N	?	Y	Y	Y	Y
MASSACHUSETTS								
1 Olver	N	Y	Y	Y	N	Y	Y	N
2 Neal	N	Y	N	Y	N	Y	Y	N
3 McGovern	N	Y	N	?	?	+	+	?
4 Frank	N	Y	N	Y	N	Y	Y	N
5 Meehan	N	Y	N	Y	N	Y	Y	N
6 Tierney	N	Y	N	Y	N	Y	Y	N
7 Markey	N	Y	N	Y	N	Y	Y	N
8 Capuano	N	Y	N	N	N	Y	Y	N
9 Moakley	N	Y	N	Y	N	Y	Y	N
10 Delahunt	?	?	?	?	?	?	?	?
MICHIGAN								
1 Stupak	?	?	?	?	?	?	?	?
2 ***Hoekstra***	Y	Y	Y	Y	Y	N	Y	Y
3 ***Ehlers***	Y	Y	Y	Y	Y	Y	Y	Y
4 ***Camp***	Y	Y	Y	Y	Y	Y	Y	Y
5 Barcia	N	Y	Y	Y	N	Y	Y	Y
6 ***Upton***	Y	Y	Y	Y	Y	Y	Y	Y
7 ***Smith***	Y	Y	Y	Y	Y	N	Y	Y
8 Stabenow	N	Y	Y	?	N	Y	Y	Y
9 Kildee	Y	Y	N	Y	N	Y	Y	N
10 Bonior	N	Y	N	Y	N	Y	Y	N
11 ***Knollenberg***	Y	Y	Y	Y	Y	Y	Y	Y
12 Levin	N	Y	N	Y	N	Y	Y	N
13 Rivers	N	Y	N	Y	N	N	Y	N
14 Conyers	N	Y	N	Y	N	?	Y	N
15 Kilpatrick	N	Y	N	Y	N	Y	Y	N
16 Dingell	N	Y	Y	Y	N	Y	Y	N

	541	542	543	544	545	546	547	548
MINNESOTA								
1 ***Gutknecht***	Y	Y	Y	N	Y	Y	Y	Y
2 Minge	N	Y	N	Y	N	Y	Y	N
3 ***Ramstad***	Y	Y	Y	N	Y	Y	Y	Y
4 Vacant								
5 Sabo	N	Y	N	N	N	Y	Y	N
6 Luther	N	Y	N	Y	N	N	Y	N
7 Peterson	Y	Y	N	?	N	N	Y	N
8 Oberstar	N	Y	N	N	N	N	Y	N
MISSISSIPPI								
1 ***Wicker***	Y	Y	Y	N	Y	Y	Y	Y
2 Thompson	N	Y	N	N	N	Y	Y	N
3 ***Pickering***	Y	Y	Y	Y	Y	N	Y	Y
4 Shows	N	Y	N	Y	N	N	Y	Y
5 Taylor	N	Y	Y	?	N	N	Y	Y
MISSOURI								
1 Clay	N	Y	N	N	N	Y	Y	N
2 ***Talent***	?	?	?	?	?	?	?	?
3 Gephardt	N	Y	Y	Y	N	?	?	?
4 Skelton	N	Y	N	Y	N	Y	Y	N
5 McCarthy	N	Y	N	Y	N	Y	Y	N
6 Danner	?	?	?	?	?	?	?	?
7 ***Blunt***	Y	Y	Y	Y	Y	N	Y	Y
8 ***Emerson***	Y	Y	Y	Y	Y	N	Y	Y
9 ***Hulshof***	Y	Y	Y	N	Y	Y	Y	Y
MONTANA								
AL ***Hill***	Y	Y	Y	N	Y	Y	Y	Y
NEBRASKA								
1 ***Bereuter***	Y	Y	Y	Y	Y	Y	Y	Y
2 ***Terry***	Y	Y	Y	Y	Y	Y	Y	Y
3 ***Barrett***	Y	Y	Y	Y	Y	N	Y	Y
NEVADA								
1 Berkley	Y	Y	Y	Y	N	Y	Y	N
2 ***Gibbons***	Y	Y	Y	Y	Y	Y	Y	Y
NEW HAMPSHIRE								
1 ***Sununu***	Y	Y	Y	Y	Y	Y	Y	Y
2 ***Bass***	Y	Y	Y	Y	Y	Y	Y	Y
NEW JERSEY								
1 Andrews	N	Y	N	Y	N	Y	Y	N
2 ***LoBiondo***	Y	Y	N	N	Y	Y	Y	Y
3 ***Saxton***	Y	Y	Y	Y	Y	Y	Y	Y
4 ***Smith***	Y	Y	Y	Y	Y	Y	Y	Y
5 ***Roukema***	Y	Y	?	Y	Y	Y	Y	Y
6 Pallone	N	Y	N	N	N	Y	Y	N
7 ***Franks***	?	?	?	?	?	?	?	?
8 Pascrell	N	Y	Y	Y	N	Y	Y	N
9 Rothman	N	Y	N	Y	N	Y	Y	N
10 Payne	N	Y	N	Y	N	Y	Y	N
11 ***Frelinghuysen***	Y	Y	Y	Y	Y	Y	Y	Y
12 Holt	N	Y	Y	Y	N	Y	Y	N
13 Menendez	?	?	?	Y	N	Y	Y	Y
NEW MEXICO								
1 ***Wilson***	Y	Y	Y	Y	Y	Y	Y	Y
2 ***Skeen***	Y	Y	Y	Y	Y	Y	Y	Y
3 Udall	N	Y	N	N	N	Y	Y	N
NEW YORK								
1 Forbes	?	?	?	?	N	Y	Y	N
2 ***Lazio***	?	?	?	?	?	?	?	?
3 ***King***	?	?	?	Y	Y	Y	Y	Y
4 McCarthy	N	Y	N	Y	N	Y	Y	Y
5 Ackerman	N	Y	N	Y	N	Y	Y	N
6 Meeks	N	Y	N	?	?	?	?	?
7 Crowley	?	?	?	?	N	Y	Y	N
8 Nadler	N	Y	N	Y	N	Y	Y	N
9 Weiner	?	?	?	Y	N	Y	Y	N
10 Towns	N	Y	N	Y	N	Y	Y	N
11 Owens	N	Y	N	Y	N	Y	Y	N
12 Velázquez	N	Y	N	N	N	Y	Y	N
13 ***Fossella***	Y	Y	Y	Y	Y	Y	Y	Y
14 Maloney	N	Y	N	Y	N	Y	Y	N
15 Rangel	N	Y	N	Y	N	Y	Y	N
16 Serrano	N	Y	N	Y	N	Y	Y	Y
17 Engel	?	?	?	?	?	?	?	?
18 Lowey	N	Y	N	Y	N	Y	Y	N
19 ***Kelly***	Y	Y	Y	Y	Y	Y	Y	Y
20 ***Gilman***	?	Y	Y	Y	Y	Y	Y	Y
21 McNulty	N	Y	Y	N	N	Y	Y	N
22 ***Sweeney***	Y	Y	Y	N	Y	Y	Y	Y
23 ***Boehlert***	Y	Y	Y	Y	Y	Y	Y	Y
24 ***McHugh***	Y	Y	Y	Y	Y	Y	Y	Y
25 ***Walsh***	Y	Y	Y	Y	Y	Y	Y	Y
26 Hinchey	N	Y	N	Y	N	Y	?	N
27 ***Reynolds***	Y	Y	Y	Y	Y	Y	Y	Y
28 Slaughter	N	Y	N	N	N	Y	Y	Y
29 LaFalce	N	Y	Y	Y	N	Y	Y	Y

	541	542	543	544	545	546	547	548
30 ***Quinn***	Y	Y	Y	Y	Y	Y	Y	Y
31 ***Houghton***	Y	?	Y	Y	Y	Y	Y	Y
NORTH CAROLINA								
1 Clayton	N	Y	N	Y	N	Y	Y	N
2 Etheridge	N	Y	N	N	N	Y	Y	N
3 ***Jones***	Y	Y	Y	Y	Y	N	Y	Y
4 Price	N	Y	N	?	N	Y	Y	N
5 ***Burr***	Y	Y	Y	Y	Y	Y	Y	Y
6 ***Coble***	Y	Y	Y	Y	Y	Y	Y	N
7 McIntyre	N	Y	Y	Y	N	Y	Y	Y
8 ***Hayes***	Y	Y	Y	Y	Y	N	Y	Y
9 ***Myrick***	Y	Y	Y	Y	Y	N	Y	Y
10 ***Ballenger***	Y	Y	Y	Y	Y	Y	Y	Y
11 ***Taylor***	Y	Y	Y	Y	Y	Y	Y	Y
12 Watt	N	Y	N	Y	N	Y	Y	N
NORTH DAKOTA								
AL Pomeroy	N	Y	N	Y	N	Y	Y	N
OHIO								
1 ***Chabot***	Y	Y	Y	Y	Y	N	Y	Y
2 ***Portman***	Y	Y	Y	Y	Y	Y	Y	Y
3 Hall	?	Y	Y	Y	N	Y	Y	Y
4 ***Oxley***	Y	Y	Y	Y	Y	Y	Y	Y
5 ***Gillmor***	Y	Y	Y	Y	Y	Y	Y	Y
6 Strickland	N	Y	N	Y	N	Y	Y	N
7 ***Hobson***	Y	Y	Y	Y	Y	Y	Y	Y
8 ***Boehner***	Y	Y	Y	Y	Y	Y	Y	Y
9 Kaptur	N	Y	N	Y	N	Y	Y	N
10 Kucinich	N	Y	N	N	N	N	Y	N
11 Jones	N	Y	N	Y	N	Y	Y	N
12 ***Kasich***	Y	Y	Y	?	Y	Y	Y	Y
13 Brown	?	?	?	?	?	?	?	?
14 Sawyer	N	Y	N	N	N	Y	Y	N
15 ***Pryce***	Y	Y	Y	Y	Y	Y	Y	Y
16 ***Regula***	Y	Y	Y	Y	Y	Y	Y	Y
17 Traficant	Y	Y	Y	Y	Y	Y	Y	Y
18 ***Ney***	+	+	+	?	Y	Y	Y	Y
19 ***LaTourette***	Y	Y	Y	Y	Y	Y	Y	Y
OKLAHOMA								
1 ***Largent***	Y	Y	Y	?	?	?	?	?
2 ***Coburn***	Y	Y	P	?	Y	N	Y	N
3 ***Watkins***	Y	Y	Y	Y	Y	N	Y	Y
4 ***Watts***	?	?	?	?	?	Y	Y	Y
5 ***Istook***	Y	Y	Y	Y	Y	N	Y	Y
6 ***Lucas***	Y	Y	Y	Y	Y	N	Y	Y
OREGON								
1 Wu	N	Y	N	N	N	Y	Y	N
2 ***Walden***	Y	Y	Y	Y	Y	N	Y	Y
3 Blumenauer	N	Y	N	Y	N	Y	Y	Y
4 DeFazio	N	Y	N	N	N	N	Y	N
5 Hooley	N	Y	N	N	N	Y	Y	N
PENNSYLVANIA								
1 Brady	?	?	?	N	N	Y	Y	N
2 Fattah	?	?	?	N	N	Y	Y	N
3 Borski	N	Y	Y	N	N	Y	Y	N
4 Klink	?	?	?	?	?	?	?	?
5 ***Peterson***	?	?	?	?	?	?	?	?
6 Holden	N	Y	Y	Y	N	Y	Y	N
7 ***Weldon***	Y	Y	Y	Y	Y	Y	Y	Y
8 ***Greenwood***	Y	Y	Y	?	Y	Y	Y	Y
9 ***Shuster***	Y	Y	Y	Y	Y	Y	Y	Y
10 ***Sherwood***	Y	Y	Y	Y	Y	Y	Y	Y
11 Kanjorski	N	Y	Y	Y	N	Y	Y	N
12 Murtha	N	Y	N	?	N	Y	Y	N
13 Hoeffel	N	Y	Y	Y	N	Y	Y	N
14 Coyne	N	Y	N	Y	N	Y	Y	N
15 ***Toomey***	Y	Y	N	Y	Y	N	Y	Y
16 ***Pitts***	Y	Y	Y	Y	Y	N	Y	Y
17 ***Gekas***	Y	Y	Y	Y	Y	Y	Y	Y
18 Doyle	N	Y	Y	Y	N	Y	Y	N
19 ***Goodling***	Y	Y	Y	?	Y	Y	Y	Y
20 Mascara	N	Y	N	Y	N	Y	Y	N
21 ***English***	Y	Y	Y	N	Y	Y	Y	Y
RHODE ISLAND								
1 Kennedy	N	Y	N	Y	N	Y	Y	N
2 Weygand	?	?	?	Y	N	Y	Y	N
SOUTH CAROLINA								
1 ***Sanford***	Y	Y	N	Y	Y	N	N	N
2 ***Spence***	Y	Y	Y	Y	Y	N	Y	Y
3 ***Graham***	Y	Y	Y	Y	Y	N	Y	Y
4 ***DeMint***	Y	Y	N	Y	Y	N	Y	Y
5 Spratt	N	Y	N	Y	N	Y	Y	N
6 Clyburn	N	Y	N	N	N	Y	Y	N
SOUTH DAKOTA								
AL ***Thune***	Y	Y	Y	Y	Y	N	Y	Y

	541	542	543	544	545	546	547	548
TENNESSEE								
1 ***Jenkins***	Y	Y	Y	Y	Y	N	Y	Y
2 ***Duncan***	?	?	?	?	Y	N	Y	Y
3 ***Wamp***	Y	Y	Y	Y	Y	Y	Y	Y
4 ***Hilleary***	?	?	?	?	Y	N	Y	Y
5 Clement	N	Y	N	Y	N	Y	Y	Y
6 Gordon	N	Y	N	Y	N	Y	Y	Y
7 ***Bryant***	Y	Y	Y	Y	Y	Y	Y	Y
8 Tanner	N	Y	Y	Y	N	N	Y	N
9 Ford	N	Y	N	Y	N	Y	Y	N
TEXAS								
1 Sandlin	N	Y	N	Y	N	N	Y	N
2 Turner	N	Y	N	Y	N	Y	Y	N
3 ***Johnson, Sam***	Y	Y	Y	Y	Y	N	Y	N
4 Hall	Y	Y	Y	Y	N	N	Y	N
5 ***Sessions***	Y	Y	Y	Y	Y	Y	Y	Y
6 ***Barton***	Y	Y	Y	Y	Y	N	Y	Y
7 ***Archer***	Y	Y	N	Y	Y	N	Y	Y
8 ***Brady***	Y	Y	Y	Y	Y	N	Y	Y
9 Lampson	N	Y	N	Y	N	Y	Y	N
10 Doggett	N	Y	N	Y	N	Y	Y	N
11 Edwards	N	Y	N	Y	?	N	Y	N
12 ***Granger***	Y	Y	Y	Y	Y	Y	Y	Y
13 ***Thornberry***	Y	Y	Y	Y	Y	N	Y	Y
14 ***Paul***	Y	Y	N	Y	Y	N	N	N
15 Hinojosa	N	Y	N	Y	N	Y	Y	N
16 Reyes	N	Y	N	Y	N	Y	Y	N
17 Stenholm	N	Y	N	Y	N	N	Y	N
18 Jackson-Lee	N	Y	P	Y	N	Y	Y	N
19 ***Combest***	Y	Y	Y	Y	Y	N	Y	Y
20 Gonzalez	N	Y	N	Y	N	Y	Y	N
21 ***Smith***	Y	Y	Y	Y	Y	Y	Y	Y
22 ***DeLay***	?	?	?	?	Y	N	Y	Y
23 ***Bonilla***	Y	Y	Y	Y	Y	Y	Y	Y
24 Frost	N	Y	N	Y	N	Y	Y	N
25 Bentsen	N	Y	N	Y	N	Y	Y	N
26 ***Armey***	Y	Y	Y	Y	Y	Y	Y	Y
27 Ortiz	N	Y	N	Y	N	Y	Y	N
28 Rodriguez	N	Y	N	Y	N	Y	Y	N
29 Green	N	Y	N	N	N	Y	Y	N
30 Johnson, E.B.	N	Y	P	Y	N	Y	Y	N
UTAH								
1 ***Hansen***	Y	Y	Y	Y	Y	N	Y	Y
2 ***Cook***	Y	Y	Y	Y	Y	N	Y	Y
3 ***Cannon***	Y	Y	Y	?	Y	N	Y	Y
VERMONT								
AL ***Sanders***	N	Y	N	Y	N	Y	Y	N
VIRGINIA								
1 Vacant								
2 Pickett	Y	Y	?	N	N	Y	Y	Y
3 Scott	N	Y	N	Y	N	Y	Y	N
4 Sisisky	N	Y	N	Y	N	Y	Y	Y
5 ***Goode***	?	?	?	?	Y	N	Y	Y
6 ***Goodlatte***	Y	Y	Y	Y	Y	N	Y	Y
7 ***Bliley***	Y	Y	Y	Y	Y	Y	Y	Y
8 Moran	N	Y	Y	Y	N	Y	Y	N
9 Boucher	N	Y	Y	Y	N	Y	Y	N
10 ***Wolf***	?	?	?	Y	Y	Y	Y	Y
11 ***Davis***	Y	Y	Y	Y	Y	Y	Y	Y
WASHINGTON								
1 Inslee	N	Y	Y	Y	N	Y	Y	N
2 ***Metcalf***	Y	Y	Y	?	Y	Y	Y	Y
3 Baird	N	Y	N	Y	N	Y	Y	N
4 ***Hastings***	Y	Y	Y	Y	Y	Y	Y	Y
5 ***Nethercutt***	Y	Y	Y	Y	Y	Y	Y	Y
6 Dicks	N	Y	N	Y	N	Y	Y	N
7 McDermott	N	Y	N	N	N	N	Y	N
8 ***Dunn***	Y	Y	Y	Y	Y	Y	Y	Y
9 Smith	N	Y	Y	Y	N	Y	Y	N
WEST VIRGINIA								
1 Mollohan	N	Y	Y	Y	N	Y	Y	Y
2 Wise	?	?	?	?	?	?	?	?
3 Rahall	N	Y	N	Y	N	N	Y	N
WISCONSIN								
1 ***Ryan***	Y	Y	Y	Y	Y	Y	Y	Y
2 Baldwin	N	Y	N	Y	N	Y	Y	N
3 Kind	N	Y	N	Y	N	N	Y	N
4 Kleczka	N	Y	Y	Y	N	Y	Y	N
5 Barrett	N	Y	Y	Y	N	Y	Y	N
6 ***Petri***	Y	Y	Y	Y	Y	Y	Y	Y
7 Obey	N	Y	Y	Y	N	Y	Y	N
8 ***Green***	+	+	+	Y	Y	Y	Y	Y
9 ***Sensenbrenner***	Y	Y	Y	Y	Y	N	Y	N
WYOMING								
AL ***Cubin***	?	?	?	Y	Y	N	Y	Y

Southern states - Ala., Ark., Fla., Ga., Ky., La., Miss., N.C., Okla., S.C., Tenn., Texas, Va.

549. H Con Res 426. Middle East Violence/Adoption. Gilman, R-N.Y., motion to suspend the rules and adopt the concurrent resolution expressing Congress' solidarity with Israel and condemning the Palestinian leadership for encouraging the violence that has erupted in the Middle East. Motion agreed to 365-30: R 198-9; D 166-21 (ND 126-13, SD 40-8); I 1-0. A two-thirds majority of those present and voting (in this case 264) is required for adoption under suspension of the rules. Oct. 25, 2000.

550. S 2547. Great Sand Dunes/Passage. Hansen, R-Utah, motion to suspend the rules and pass the bill that would establish the Great Sand Dunes National Park in Colorado when sufficient lands have been acquired to warrant the designation. Motion agreed to 366-34: R 179-27; D 185-7 (ND 138-4, SD 47-3); I 2-0. A two-thirds majority of those present and voting (in this case 267) is required for passage under suspension of the rules. Oct. 25, 2000.

551. H J Res 115. Continuing Resolution/Rule. Adoption of the rule (H Res 646) to provide for House floor consideration of the joint resolution that would provide temporary funding authority, at current levels, through Oct. 26, for the departments, agencies and programs for which regular fiscal year 2001 appropriations bills have not been enacted by Oct. 25. Adopted 205-191: R 203-0; D 1-190 (ND 1-137, SD 0-53); I 1-1. Oct. 25, 2000.

552. H J Res 115. Continuing Resolution/Passage. Passage of the joint resolution that would provide temporary funding authority, at current levels, through Oct. 26, for the departments, agencies and programs for which regular fiscal year 2001 appropriations bills have not been enacted by Oct. 25. Passed 395-9: R 204-1; D 189-8 (ND 137-7, SD 52-1); I 2-0. Oct. 25, 2000.

553. Procedural Motion/Adjourn. McNulty, D-N.Y., motion to adjourn. Motion rejected 8-349: R 4-181; D 4-167 (ND 3-118, SD 1-49); I 0-1. Oct. 26, 2000.

554. Procedural Motion/Journal. Approval of the House Journal of Wednesday, Oct. 25, 2000. Approved 300-67: R 166-17; D 132-50 (ND 90-40, SD 42-10); I 2-0. Oct. 26, 2000.

555. HR 2614. Tax Cut Package/Previous Question. Motion to order the previous question (thus ending debate and possibility of amendment) on adoption of the rule (H Res 652) to provide for House floor consideration of the conference report on the bill that would increase the minimum wage $1 over two years, increase payments to Medicare-funded health care providers, and provide a total of $240.4 billion in tax cuts over 10 years. It also would expand contribution limits for IRAs and other retirement savings, bring U.S. export tax regulations in line with international trade rules, and ban physician-assisted suicide. Adopted 209-195: R 207-0; D 1-194 (ND 1-142, SD 0-52); I 1-1. Oct. 26, 2000.

Key

- Y Voted for (yea).
- # Paired for.
- + Announced for.
- N Voted against (nay).
- X Paired against.
- – Announced against.
- P Voted "present."
- C Voted "present" to avoid possible conflict of interest.
- ? Did not vote or otherwise make a position known.

•

Democrats ***Republicans***
Independents

	549	550	551	552	553	554	555
ALABAMA							
1 ***Callahan***	Y	Y	Y	Y	N	Y	Y
2 ***Everett***	Y	Y	Y	Y	N	Y	Y
3 ***Riley***	Y	N	Y	Y	N	Y	Y
4 ***Aderholt***	Y	Y	Y	Y	N	N	Y
5 Cramer	Y	Y	N	Y	N	Y	N
6 ***Bachus***	Y	Y	Y	Y	N	Y	Y
7 Hilliard	N	Y	N	Y	N	N	N
ALASKA							
AL ***Young***	Y	Y	Y	Y	N	Y	Y
ARIZONA							
1 ***Salmon***	Y	Y	Y	Y	Y	Y	Y
2 Pastor	Y	Y	N	Y	N	Y	N
3 ***Stump***	Y	Y	Y	Y	N	Y	Y
4 ***Shadegg***	?	?	?	?	?	Y	Y
5 ***Kolbe***	Y	Y	Y	Y	N	Y	Y
6 ***Hayworth***	Y	Y	Y	Y	N	Y	Y
ARKANSAS							
1 Berry	Y	N	N	Y	N	Y	N
2 Snyder	P	Y	N	Y	N	Y	N
3 ***Hutchinson***	Y	Y	Y	Y	N	Y	Y
4 ***Dickey***	Y	Y	Y	Y	N	Y	Y
CALIFORNIA							
1 Thompson	Y	Y	N	Y	N	N	N
2 ***Herger***	Y	N	Y	Y	N	Y	Y
3 ***Ose***	Y	Y	Y	Y	N	Y	Y
4 ***Doolittle***	Y	Y	Y	Y	N	Y	Y
5 Matsui	Y	Y	N	Y	N	Y	N
6 Woolsey	Y	Y	N	Y	N	Y	N
7 Miller, George	Y	Y	N	N	N	N	N
8 Pelosi	Y	Y	N	Y	N	Y	N
9 Lee	N	Y	N	Y	N	N	N
10 Tauscher	Y	Y	N	Y	N	Y	N
11 ***Pombo***	Y	N	Y	Y	N	Y	Y
12 Lantos	Y	Y	N	Y	N	Y	N
13 Stark	N	Y	N	Y	N	N	N
14 Eshoo	Y	Y	N	Y	N	Y	N
15 ***Campbell***	?	?	?	?	?	?	?
16 Lofgren	P	Y	N	Y	N	Y	N
17 Farr	Y	Y	N	Y	Y	Y	N
18 Condit	Y	Y	N	Y	N	Y	N
19 ***Radanovich***	Y	Y	?	Y	N	Y	Y
20 Dooley	Y	Y	N	Y	N	Y	N
21 ***Thomas***	Y	Y	Y	Y	N	Y	Y
22 Capps	Y	Y	N	Y	N	Y	N
23 ***Gallegly***	Y	Y	Y	Y	N	Y	Y
24 Sherman	Y	Y	N	Y	N	Y	N
25 ***McKeon***	Y	Y	Y	Y	N	Y	Y
26 Berman	Y	Y	N	Y	N	Y	N
27 ***Rogan***	Y	Y	Y	Y	N	?	Y
28 ***Dreier***	Y	Y	Y	Y	N	Y	Y
29 Waxman	?	?	?	?	?	?	?
30 Becerra	Y	Y	N	Y	–	N	N
31 ***Martinez***	N	Y	Y	Y	Y	?	Y
32 Dixon	Y	Y	N	Y	?	Y	N
33 Roybal-Allard	Y	Y	N	Y	N	Y	N
34 Napolitano	Y	Y	N	Y	N	Y	N
35 Waters	N	Y	N	Y	N	N	N
36 ***Kuykendall***	Y	Y	Y	Y	N	Y	Y
37 Millender-McD.	Y	?	N	Y	N	Y	N
38 ***Horn***	Y	?	Y	Y	N	Y	Y
39 ***Royce***	?	?	Y	Y	N	Y	Y
40 ***Lewis***	Y	Y	Y	Y	N	Y	Y
41 ***Miller, Gary***	Y	N	Y	Y	N	Y	Y
42 Baca	Y	Y	N	Y	?	?	N
43 ***Calvert***	Y	Y	Y	Y	N	Y	Y
44 ***Bono***	Y	Y	Y	Y	N	Y	Y
45 ***Rohrabacher***	N	N	Y	Y	N	Y	Y
46 Sanchez	Y	Y	N	Y	N	Y	N
47 ***Cox***	Y	Y	Y	Y	N	Y	Y
48 ***Packard***	Y	Y	Y	Y	?	?	?
49 ***Bilbray***	Y	Y	Y	Y	?	N	Y
50 Filner	Y	Y	N	Y	N	N	N
51 ***Cunningham***	Y	Y	Y	Y	N	Y	Y
52 ***Hunter***	Y	Y	Y	Y	N	Y	Y
COLORADO							
1 DeGette	Y	Y	N	Y	N	Y	N
2 Udall	Y	Y	N	Y	?	?	N
3 ***McInnis***	Y	Y	Y	Y	N	Y	Y
4 ***Schaffer***	Y	N	Y	Y	N	N	Y
5 ***Hefley***	Y	N	Y	Y	N	N	Y
6 ***Tancredo***	Y	Y	Y	Y	N	P	Y
CONNECTICUT							
1 Larson	Y	Y	N	Y	N	Y	N
2 Gejdenson	Y	Y	N	Y	N	Y	N
3 DeLauro	Y	Y	N	Y	N	Y	N
4 ***Shays***	Y	Y	Y	Y	?	?	?
5 Maloney	Y	Y	?	?	N	Y	N
6 ***Johnson***	Y	Y	?	Y	N	?	Y
DELAWARE							
AL ***Castle***	Y	Y	Y	Y	N	Y	Y
FLORIDA							
1 ***Scarborough***	Y	Y	Y	Y	N	Y	Y
2 Boyd	Y	N	N	Y	N	Y	N
3 Brown	Y	Y	N	Y	N	Y	N
4 ***Fowler***	Y	Y	Y	Y	?	?	Y
5 Thurman	P	Y	N	Y	N	Y	N
6 ***Stearns***	Y	N	Y	Y	N	Y	Y
7 ***Mica***	+	+	+	+	N	Y	Y
8 ***McCollum***	?	?	?	?	?	?	?
9 ***Bilirakis***	Y	Y	Y	Y	N	Y	Y
10 ***Young***	Y	Y	Y	Y	N	Y	Y
11 Davis	Y	Y	N	Y	N	Y	N
12 ***Canady***	Y	Y	Y	Y	N	Y	Y
13 ***Miller***	Y	Y	Y	Y	N	Y	Y
14 ***Goss***	Y	Y	Y	Y	N	Y	Y
15 ***Weldon***	Y	Y	Y	Y	N	Y	Y
16 ***Foley***	Y	Y	Y	Y	N	?	Y
17 Meek	Y	Y	N	Y	N	Y	N
18 ***Ros-Lehtinen***	Y	Y	Y	Y	N	Y	Y
19 Wexler	Y	Y	N	Y	?	Y	N
20 Deutsch	Y	Y	N	Y	N	Y	N
21 ***Diaz-Balart***	Y	Y	Y	Y	N	Y	Y
22 ***Shaw***	Y	Y	Y	Y	N	Y	Y
23 Hastings	?	?	?	?	N	Y	N
GEORGIA							
1 ***Kingston***	Y	Y	Y	Y	N	N	Y
2 Bishop	Y	Y	N	Y	N	Y	N
3 ***Collins***	Y	?	?	?	?	?	Y
4 McKinney	N	Y	N	Y	N	Y	N
5 Lewis	Y	Y	N	Y	N	N	N
6 ***Isakson***	Y	Y	Y	Y	N	Y	Y
7 ***Barr***	Y	Y	Y	Y	N	Y	Y
8 ***Chambliss***	Y	Y	Y	Y	N	Y	Y
9 ***Deal***	Y	Y	Y	Y	N	Y	Y
10 ***Norwood***	Y	Y	Y	Y	N	Y	Y
11 ***Linder***	Y	Y	Y	Y	N	Y	Y
HAWAII							
1 Abercrombie	Y	N	N	Y	?	Y	N
2 Mink	Y	Y	N	Y	?	Y	N
IDAHO							
1 ***Chenoweth-Hage***	?	?	?	?	?	?	?
2 ***Simpson***	Y	N	Y	Y	N	Y	Y
ILLINOIS							
1 Rush	Y	N	N	Y	N	Y	N
2 Jackson	N	Y	N	Y	N	Y	N
3 Lipinski	Y	Y	N	Y	N	Y	N
4 Gutierrez	Y	Y	?	Y	N	Y	N
5 Blagojevich	Y	Y	N	Y	?	?	?
6 ***Hyde***	Y	Y	Y	Y	N	Y	Y
7 Davis	Y	Y	N	Y	N	Y	N
8 ***Crane***	Y	Y	Y	Y	?	N	Y
9 Schakowsky	Y	Y	N	Y	N	Y	N
10 ***Porter***	Y	Y	Y	Y	?	?	Y
11 ***Weller***	Y	Y	Y	Y	N	N	Y
12 Costello	Y	Y	N	N	N	N	N
13 ***Biggert***	Y	Y	Y	Y	N	Y	Y

ND Northern Democrats SD Southern Democrats

	549	550	551	552	553	554	555
14 ***Hastert***							Y
15 ***Ewing***	Y	Y	Y	Y	N	Y	Y
16 ***Manzullo***	Y	Y	Y	Y	N	?	Y
17 Evans	Y	Y	N	Y	N	Y	N
18 ***LaHood***	P	Y	Y	Y	N	Y	Y
19 Phelps	Y	Y	N	Y	N	Y	N
20 ***Shimkus***	Y	Y	Y	Y	N	Y	Y
INDIANA							
1 Visclosky	Y	Y	N	N	N	N	N
2 ***McIntosh***	?	?	?	?	?	?	?
3 Roemer	Y	Y	N	Y	N	Y	N
4 ***Souder***	Y	Y	Y	Y	N	Y	Y
5 ***Buyer***	Y	?	Y	Y	N	Y	Y
6 ***Burton***	Y	N	Y	Y	–	+	Y
7 ***Pease***	Y	Y	Y	Y	N	Y	Y
8 ***Hostettler***	N	N	Y	Y	N	Y	Y
9 Hill	Y	Y	N	Y	N	N	N
10 Carson	Y	Y	N	Y	N	Y	N
IOWA							
1 ***Leach***	Y	Y	Y	Y	N	Y	Y
2 ***Nussle***	Y	Y	Y	Y	N	Y	Y
3 Boswell	Y	Y	N	Y	N	Y	N
4 ***Ganske***	Y	Y	Y	Y	N	Y	Y
5 ***Latham***	Y	Y	Y	Y	N	N	Y
KANSAS							
1 ***Moran***	Y	N	Y	Y	N	N	Y
2 ***Ryun***	Y	Y	Y	Y	N	?	Y
3 Moore	Y	Y	N	Y	N	Y	N
4 ***Tiahrt***	Y	N	Y	Y	N	Y	Y
KENTUCKY							
1 ***Whitfield***	Y	Y	Y	Y	N	Y	Y
2 ***Lewis***	Y	Y	Y	Y	N	Y	Y
3 ***Northup***	Y	Y	Y	Y	N	Y	Y
4 Lucas	Y	Y	N	Y	N	Y	N
5 ***Rogers***	Y	Y	Y	Y	N	Y	Y
6 ***Fletcher***	Y	Y	Y	Y	N	Y	Y
LOUISIANA							
1 ***Vitter***	Y	Y	Y	Y	N	Y	Y
2 Jefferson	Y	Y	N	Y	?	Y	N
3 ***Tauzin***	Y	Y	Y	Y	N	Y	Y
4 ***McCrery***	Y	Y	Y	Y	N	?	Y
5 ***Cooksey***	Y	Y	Y	Y	N	Y	Y
6 ***Baker***	Y	Y	Y	Y	N	Y	Y
7 John	?	?	N	Y	N	Y	N
MAINE							
1 Allen	Y	Y	N	Y	N	N	N
2 Baldacci	Y	Y	N	Y	?	?	N
MARYLAND							
1 ***Gilchrest***	N	Y	Y	Y	?	Y	Y
2 ***Ehrlich***	Y	Y	?	Y	?	Y	Y
3 Cardin	Y	Y	N	Y	N	Y	N
4 Wynn	Y	Y	N	Y	N	N	N
5 Hoyer	Y	Y	N	Y	N	Y	N
6 ***Bartlett***	Y	Y	Y	Y	N	Y	Y
7 Cummings	Y	Y	N	Y	?	Y	N
8 ***Morella***	Y	Y	Y	Y	?	?	Y
MASSACHUSETTS							
1 Olver	Y	Y	N	Y	N	N	N
2 Neal	Y	Y	N	Y	?	?	?
3 McGovern	?	?	?	Y	N	N	N
4 Frank	Y	Y	N	Y	N	Y	N
5 Meehan	Y	Y	N	Y	?	Y	N
6 Tierney	Y	Y	N	Y	N	Y	N
7 Markey	Y	Y	N	Y	N	Y	N
8 Capuano	Y	Y	N	N	N	N	N
9 Moakley	Y	Y	N	Y	N	Y	N
10 Delahunt	?	?	?	?	?	?	N
MICHIGAN							
1 Stupak	?	?	?	?	?	?	?
2 ***Hoekstra***	Y	Y	Y	Y	?	?	?
3 ***Ehlers***	Y	Y	Y	Y	N	Y	Y
4 ***Camp***	Y	Y	Y	Y	N	Y	Y
5 Barcia	Y	Y	N	Y	N	Y	N
6 ***Upton***	Y	Y	Y	Y	N	Y	Y
7 ***Smith***	Y	Y	Y	Y	N	Y	Y
8 Stabenow	Y	Y	?	Y	?	?	N
9 Kildee	Y	Y	N	Y	N	Y	N
10 Bonior	N	Y	N	Y	N	?	N
11 ***Knollenberg***	Y	Y	Y	Y	N	Y	Y
12 Levin	Y	Y	N	Y	N	N	N
13 Rivers	P	Y	N	Y	N	Y	N
14 Conyers	N	N	N	Y	N	Y	N
15 Kilpatrick	N	Y	N	Y	N	Y	N
16 Dingell	N	Y	N	Y	N	Y	N

	549	550	551	552	553	554	555
MINNESOTA							
1 ***Gutknecht***	Y	Y	Y	Y	N	N	Y
2 Minge	Y	?	N	Y	N	Y	N
3 ***Ramstad***	Y	Y	Y	Y	N	N	Y
4 Vacant							
5 Sabo	Y	N	N	Y	N	N	N
6 Luther	Y	Y	N	Y	N	Y	N
7 Peterson	Y	Y	N	Y	N	N	N
8 Oberstar	Y	Y	N	Y	N	N	N
MISSISSIPPI							
1 ***Wicker***	Y	Y	Y	Y	N	N	Y
2 Thompson	N	?	N	Y	?	?	?
3 ***Pickering***	Y	Y	Y	Y	?	Y	Y
4 Shows	Y	Y	N	Y	N	N	N
5 Taylor	Y	Y	N	Y	N	N	N
MISSOURI							
1 Clay	N	Y	N	Y	?	N	N
2 ***Talent***	?	?	?	?	?	?	?
3 Gephardt	?	?	?	Y	N	Y	N
4 Skelton	Y	Y	N	Y	N	Y	N
5 McCarthy	Y	Y	N	Y	N	Y	N
6 Danner	?	?	?	?	?	?	?
7 ***Blunt***	Y	Y	Y	Y	N	Y	Y
8 ***Emerson***	Y	Y	Y	Y	?	?	Y
9 ***Hulshof***	Y	Y	Y	Y	N	N	Y
MONTANA							
AL ***Hill***	Y	Y	Y	Y	N	Y	Y
NEBRASKA							
1 ***Bereuter***	Y	Y	Y	Y	N	Y	Y
2 ***Terry***	Y	Y	Y	Y	N	Y	Y
3 ***Barrett***	Y	Y	Y	Y	N	Y	Y
NEVADA							
1 Berkley	Y	Y	N	Y	N	Y	N
2 ***Gibbons***	Y	Y	Y	Y	N	Y	Y
NEW HAMPSHIRE							
1 ***Sununu***	P	Y	Y	Y	N	Y	Y
2 ***Bass***	Y	Y	Y	Y	N	Y	Y
NEW JERSEY							
1 Andrews	Y	Y	N	Y	N	N	N
2 ***LoBiondo***	Y	Y	Y	Y	N	N	Y
3 ***Saxton***	Y	Y	Y	Y	N	Y	Y
4 ***Smith***	Y	Y	Y	Y	N	Y	Y
5 ***Roukema***	Y	Y	Y	Y	N	Y	Y
6 Pallone	Y	Y	N	Y	N	N	N
7 ***Franks***	?	?	?	?	?	?	?
8 Pascrell	Y	Y	N	Y	N	N	N
9 Rothman	Y	Y	N	Y	N	Y	N
10 Payne	N	Y	N	Y	N	Y	N
11 ***Frelinghuysen***	Y	Y	Y	Y	N	Y	Y
12 Holt	Y	Y	N	Y	N	N	N
13 Menendez	Y	Y	N	Y	N	Y	N
NEW MEXICO							
1 ***Wilson***	Y	Y	Y	Y	N	Y	Y
2 ***Skeen***	Y	Y	Y	Y	N	Y	Y
3 Udall	Y	Y	N	Y	N	N	N
NEW YORK							
1 Forbes	Y	Y	N	Y	?	?	N
2 ***Lazio***	?	?	?	?	?	?	?
3 ***King***	Y	Y	Y	Y	N	Y	Y
4 McCarthy	Y	Y	N	Y	N	Y	N
5 Ackerman	Y	Y	N	Y	?	?	?
6 Meeks	?	?	?	?	?	Y	N
7 Crowley	Y	Y	N	Y	?	?	?
8 Nadler	Y	Y	N	Y	?	Y	N
9 Weiner	Y	Y	N	Y	?	?	?
10 Towns	Y	Y	N	Y	N	Y	N
11 Owens	Y	Y	N	Y	?	?	?
12 Velázquez	Y	Y	N	Y	Y	N	N
13 ***Fossella***	Y	Y	Y	?	?	?	Y
14 Maloney	Y	Y	N	Y	N	Y	N
15 Rangel	Y	Y	N	Y	N	Y	N
16 Serrano	N	Y	N	Y	N	Y	N
17 Engel	?	?	?	?	?	?	?
18 Lowey	Y	Y	N	Y	N	Y	N
19 ***Kelly***	Y	Y	Y	Y	N	Y	Y
20 ***Gilman***	Y	Y	Y	Y	N	Y	Y
21 McNulty	Y	Y	N	Y	N	N	N
22 ***Sweeney***	Y	Y	Y	Y	N	N	Y
23 ***Boehlert***	Y	Y	Y	Y	N	Y	Y
24 ***McHugh***	Y	Y	Y	Y	N	Y	Y
25 ***Walsh***	Y	Y	Y	Y	N	Y	Y
26 Hinchey	Y	Y	N	Y	N	N	N
27 ***Reynolds***	Y	Y	Y	Y	N	Y	Y
28 Slaughter	Y	Y	–	+	?	?	N
29 LaFalce	Y	Y	N	Y	N	N	N

	549	550	551	552	553	554	555
30 ***Quinn***	Y	Y	Y	Y	N	Y	Y
31 ***Houghton***	Y	Y	Y	Y	N	Y	Y
NORTH CAROLINA							
1 Clayton	N	Y	N	Y	N	Y	N
2 Etheridge	Y	Y	N	Y	N	Y	N
3 ***Jones***	Y	N	Y	Y	N	Y	Y
4 Price	Y	Y	N	Y	N	Y	N
5 ***Burr***	Y	Y	Y	Y	N	Y	Y
6 ***Coble***	Y	N	Y	Y	N	Y	Y
7 McIntyre	Y	Y	N	Y	N	Y	N
8 ***Hayes***	Y	Y	Y	Y	N	Y	Y
9 ***Myrick***	Y	Y	Y	Y	N	Y	Y
10 ***Ballenger***	Y	Y	Y	Y	N	Y	Y
11 ***Taylor***	Y	Y	Y	Y	N	Y	Y
12 Watt	P	Y	N	Y	N	Y	N
NORTH DAKOTA							
AL Pomeroy	Y	Y	N	Y	N	Y	N
OHIO							
1 ***Chabot***	Y	N	Y	Y	N	Y	Y
2 ***Portman***	Y	Y	Y	Y	N	?	Y
3 Hall	Y	Y	N	Y	?	N	N
4 ***Oxley***	Y	Y	Y	Y	N	Y	Y
5 ***Gillmor***	Y	Y	Y	Y	N	Y	Y
6 Strickland	Y	Y	N	Y	N	N	N
7 ***Hobson***	Y	Y	Y	Y	N	Y	Y
8 ***Boehner***	Y	Y	Y	Y	N	Y	Y
9 Kaptur	Y	Y	N	N	N	?	N
10 Kucinich	N	Y	N	Y	N	N	N
11 Jones	P	Y	N	Y	?	N	N
12 ***Kasich***	Y	Y	Y	Y	?	?	Y
13 Brown	?	?	?	Y	N	Y	N
14 Sawyer	P	Y	N	Y	N	Y	N
15 ***Pryce***	Y	Y	Y	Y	N	Y	Y
16 ***Regula***	Y	Y	Y	Y	N	Y	Y
17 Traficant	Y	Y	Y	Y	N	Y	Y
18 ***Ney***	Y	Y	Y	Y	N	Y	?
19 ***LaTourette***	Y	Y	Y	Y	N	Y	?
OKLAHOMA							
1 ***Largent***	?	?	?	?	?	?	Y
2 ***Coburn***	N	N	Y	Y	N	Y	Y
3 ***Watkins***	Y	Y	Y	Y	N	Y	Y
4 ***Watts***	Y	Y	Y	Y	N	?	Y
5 ***Istook***	Y	Y	?	Y	N	Y	Y
6 ***Lucas***	Y	Y	Y	Y	N	Y	Y
OREGON							
1 Wu	Y	Y	N	Y	N	N	N
2 ***Walden***	Y	Y	Y	Y	N	Y	Y
3 Blumenauer	Y	Y	N	Y	N	Y	N
4 DeFazio	P	Y	N	N	N	N	N
5 Hooley	Y	Y	N	Y	N	N	N
PENNSYLVANIA							
1 Brady	Y	Y	N	Y	?	?	?
2 Fattah	Y	Y	N	Y	N	N	N
3 Borski	Y	Y	N	Y	N	N	N
4 Klink	?	?	?	?	?	?	?
5 ***Peterson***	?	?	?	?	?	?	?
6 Holden	Y	Y	N	Y	N	Y	N
7 ***Weldon***	Y	Y	Y	Y	?	?	?
8 ***Greenwood***	Y	Y	?	?	?	?	Y
9 ***Shuster***	Y	Y	Y	Y	Y	Y	Y
10 ***Sherwood***	Y	Y	Y	Y	N	Y	Y
11 Kanjorski	Y	Y	N	Y	N	Y	N
12 Murtha	Y	Y	N	Y	N	Y	N
13 Hoeffel	Y	Y	N	Y	N	Y	N
14 Coyne	Y	Y	N	Y	?	Y	N
15 ***Toomey***	Y	N	Y	Y	?	Y	Y
16 ***Pitts***	Y	Y	Y	Y	N	Y	Y
17 ***Gekas***	Y	Y	Y	Y	N	Y	Y
18 Doyle	Y	Y	N	Y	?	?	N
19 ***Goodling***	N	Y	Y	Y	?	Y	Y
20 Mascara	Y	Y	N	Y	N	Y	N
21 ***English***	Y	Y	Y	Y	N	N	Y
RHODE ISLAND							
1 Kennedy	Y	Y	N	Y	N	Y	N
2 Weygand	Y	Y	N	Y	N	Y	N
SOUTH CAROLINA							
1 ***Sanford***	N	N	Y	Y	?	Y	Y
2 ***Spence***	Y	Y	Y	Y	Y	Y	Y
3 ***Graham***	Y	Y	Y	Y	?	?	Y
4 ***DeMint***	Y	N	Y	Y	N	Y	Y
5 Spratt	Y	Y	N	Y	?	?	?
6 Clyburn	Y	Y	N	Y	N	N	N
SOUTH DAKOTA							
AL ***Thune***	Y	Y	Y	Y	N	Y	Y

	549	550	551	552	553	554	555
TENNESSEE							
1 ***Jenkins***	Y	Y	Y	Y	N	Y	Y
2 ***Duncan***	Y	N	Y	Y	N	Y	Y
3 ***Wamp***	Y	Y	Y	Y	?	?	Y
4 ***Hilleary***	Y	Y	Y	Y	N	N	Y
5 Clement	Y	Y	N	Y	N	Y	N
6 Gordon	Y	Y	N	Y	N	Y	N
7 ***Bryant***	Y	Y	Y	Y	N	Y	Y
8 Tanner	Y	Y	N	Y	N	Y	N
9 Ford	N	Y	N	N	Y	N	N
TEXAS							
1 Sandlin	Y	Y	N	Y	N	Y	N
2 Turner	Y	Y	N	Y	N	Y	N
3 ***Johnson, Sam***	Y	Y	Y	Y	N	Y	Y
4 Hall	Y	Y	N	Y	N	Y	N
5 ***Sessions***	Y	Y	Y	Y	N	Y	Y
6 ***Barton***	Y	Y	Y	N	?	Y	Y
7 ***Archer***	Y	Y	Y	Y	?	?	Y
8 ***Brady***	Y	Y	Y	Y	N	Y	Y
9 Lampson	Y	Y	N	Y	N	Y	N
10 Doggett	Y	Y	N	Y	N	Y	N
11 Edwards	N	Y	N	Y	N	Y	N
12 ***Granger***	Y	Y	Y	Y	N	Y	Y
13 ***Thornberry***	Y	Y	Y	Y	N	Y	Y
14 ***Paul***	N	N	Y	Y	N	Y	Y
15 Hinojosa	Y	Y	N	Y	N	Y	N
16 Reyes	Y	Y	N	Y	N	Y	N
17 Stenholm	Y	N	N	Y	N	N	N
18 Jackson-Lee	Y	Y	N	Y	N	N	N
19 ***Combest***	Y	Y	Y	?	N	Y	Y
20 Gonzalez	Y	Y	N	Y	N	Y	N
21 ***Smith***	Y	Y	Y	Y	N	Y	Y
22 ***DeLay***	Y	Y	Y	Y	N	Y	Y
23 ***Bonilla***	Y	Y	?	?	N	Y	Y
24 Frost	Y	Y	N	Y	N	Y	N
25 Bentsen	Y	Y	N	Y	N	Y	N
26 ***Armey***	Y	Y	Y	Y	N	?	Y
27 Ortiz	Y	Y	N	Y	N	Y	N
28 Rodriguez	Y	Y	N	Y	N	Y	N
29 Green	Y	Y	N	Y	N	N	N
30 Johnson, E.B.	Y	Y	N	Y	N	Y	N
UTAH							
1 ***Hansen***	Y	N	Y	Y	N	Y	Y
2 ***Cook***	Y	N	Y	Y	N	Y	Y
3 ***Cannon***	Y	Y	Y	Y	N	Y	Y
VERMONT							
AL ***Sanders***	P	Y	N	Y	?	Y	N
VIRGINIA							
1 Vacant							
2 Pickett	?	?	N	Y	N	N	N
3 Scott	Y	Y	N	Y	N	Y	N
4 Sisisky	Y	Y	N	Y	N	Y	N
5 ***Goode***	Y	Y	Y	Y	N	Y	Y
6 ***Goodlatte***	Y	Y	Y	Y	N	Y	Y
7 ***Bliley***	Y	Y	Y	Y	N	Y	Y
8 Moran	N	Y	N	Y	N	Y	N
9 Boucher	N	Y	N	Y	N	Y	N
10 ***Wolf***	Y	Y	Y	Y	N	Y	Y
11 ***Davis***	Y	Y	Y	Y	N	?	Y
WASHINGTON							
1 Inslee	Y	Y	N	Y	N	Y	N
2 ***Metcalf***	N	N	Y	Y	?	?	?
3 Baird	Y	Y	N	N	N	Y	N
4 ***Hastings***	Y	Y	Y	Y	N	Y	Y
5 ***Nethercutt***	Y	Y	Y	Y	N	Y	Y
6 Dicks	Y	Y	N	Y	N	Y	N
7 McDermott	Y	Y	+	Y	Y	N	N
8 ***Dunn***	Y	Y	Y	Y	N	Y	Y
9 Smith	Y	Y	N	Y	N	Y	N
WEST VIRGINIA							
1 Mollohan	Y	Y	?	Y	N	Y	N
2 Wise	?	?	?	?	?	?	N
3 Rahall	N	Y	N	Y	N	Y	N
WISCONSIN							
1 ***Ryan***	Y	Y	Y	Y	N	Y	Y
2 Baldwin	Y	Y	N	Y	N	Y	N
3 Kind	Y	Y	N	Y	?	?	N
4 Kleczka	Y	Y	N	Y	N	Y	N
5 Barrett	Y	Y	N	Y	N	Y	N
6 ***Petri***	Y	Y	Y	Y	N	Y	Y
7 Obey	Y	Y	N	Y	N	N	N
8 ***Green***	Y	Y	Y	Y	N	Y	Y
9 ***Sensenbrenner***	Y	N	Y	Y	N	Y	Y
WYOMING							
AL ***Cubin***	Y	N	Y	Y	N	Y	Y

Southern states - Ala., Ark., Fla., Ga., Ky., La., Miss., N.C., Okla., S.C., Tenn., Texas, Va.

House Votes 556, 557, 558, 559, 560, 561, 562

556. HR 2614. Tax Cut Package/Rule. Adoption of the rule (H Res 652) to provide for House floor consideration of the conference report on the bill that would increase the minimum wage $1 over two years, increase payments to Medicare-funded health care providers, and provide a total of $240.4 billion in tax cuts over 10 years. It also would expand contribution limits for IRAs and other retirement savings, bring U.S. export tax regulations in line with international trade rules, and ban physician-assisted suicide. Motion agreed to 207-200: R 204-4; D 2-195 (ND 2-143, SD 0-52); I 1-1. Oct. 26, 2000.

557. HR 4942. Fiscal 2001 Commerce-Justice-State and District of Columbia Appropriations/Previous Question. Motion to order the previous question (thus ending debate and possibility of amendment) on adoption of the rule (H Res 653) to provide for House floor consideration of the conference report on the bill that would appropriate $39.9 billion for the departments of Commerce, Justice, State and other independent agencies, and $445 million for the District of Columbia. Motion agreed to 214-194: R 211-0; D 2-193 (ND 1-143, SD 1-50); I 1-1. Oct. 26, 2000.

558. HR 4942. Fiscal 2001 Commerce-Justice-State and District of Columbia Appropriations/Rule. Adoption of the rule (H Res 653) to provide for House floor consideration of the conference report on the bill that would appropriate would appropriate $39.9 billion for the departments of Commerce, Justice, State and other independent agencies, and $445 million for the District of Columbia. Adopted 212-192: R 208-0; D 3-191 (ND 1-143, SD 2-48); I 1-1. Oct. 26, 2000.

559. Suspensions/Rule. Adoption of the rule (H Res 651) to provide for House floor consideration of motions to suspend the rules and pass legislation. Adopted 221-190: R 212-0; D 8-189 (ND 6-139, SD 2-50); I 1-1. Oct. 26, 2000.

560. HR 2614. Tax Cut Package/Conference Report. Adoption of the conference report on the bill that would increase the minimum wage $1 over two years, increase payments to Medicare-funded health care providers, and provide a total of $240.4 billion in tax cuts over 10 years. It also would expand contribution limits for IRAs and other retirement savings, bring U.S. export tax regulations in line with international trade rules, and ban physician-assisted suicide. Adopted (thus sent to the Senate) 237-174: R 203-6; D 33-167 (ND 21-127, SD 12-40); I 1-1. A "nay" was a vote in support of the president's position. Oct. 26, 2000.

561. H J Res 116. Continuing Resolution/Passage. Passage of the joint resolution that would provide temporary funding authority, at current levels, until Oct. 27, for the departments, agencies and programs for which regular fiscal year 2001 appropriations bills have not been enacted by Oct. 26. Passed 392-10: R 202-1; D 188-9 (ND 136-9, SD 52-0); I 2-0. Oct. 26, 2000.

562. HR 4942. Fiscal 2001 Commerce-Justice-State and District of Columbia Appropriations/Conference Report. Adoption of the conference report on the bill that would appropriate $445 million in federal funds for the District of Columbia and approve the expenditure of $6.7 billion of District funds. It also would appropriate $39.9 billion for the departments of Commerce, Justice, State and other independent agencies. It also would allow certain illegal aliens to seek legal status through the courts and to permit the families of legal resident aliens to remain in the United States while their applications for permanent residency are being processed. Adopted (thus sent to the Senate) 206-198: R 185-19; D 20-178 (ND 12-134, SD 8-44); I 1-1. Oct. 26, 2000. A "nay" was a vote in support of the president's position.

Key

Y	Voted for (yea).
#	Paired for.
+	Announced for.
N	Voted against (nay).
X	Paired against.
–	Announced against.
P	Voted "present."
C	Voted "present" to avoid possible conflict of interest.
?	Did not vote or otherwise make a position known.

•

Democrats ***Republicans***
Independents

	556	557	558	559	560	561	562
ALABAMA							
1 ***Callahan***	Y	Y	Y	Y	Y	Y	Y
2 ***Everett***	Y	Y	Y	Y	Y	Y	Y
3 ***Riley***	Y	Y	Y	Y	Y	Y	N
4 ***Aderholt***	Y	Y	Y	Y	Y	Y	N
5 Cramer	N	N	N	N	Y	Y	Y
6 ***Bachus***	Y	Y	Y	Y	Y	Y	Y
7 Hilliard	N	N	N	N	N	Y	N
ALASKA							
AL ***Young***	Y	Y	Y	Y	Y	Y	Y
ARIZONA							
1 ***Salmon***	Y	Y	Y	Y	N	Y	N
2 Pastor	N	N	N	N	N	Y	N
3 ***Stump***	Y	Y	Y	Y	N	Y	?
4 ***Shadegg***	Y	Y	Y	Y	Y	Y	N
5 ***Kolbe***	Y	Y	Y	Y	Y	Y	Y
6 ***Hayworth***	Y	Y	Y	Y	Y	Y	Y
ARKANSAS							
1 Berry	N	N	N	N	N	Y	Y
2 Snyder	N	N	N	N	N	Y	N
3 ***Hutchinson***	Y	Y	Y	Y	Y	?	Y
4 ***Dickey***	Y	Y	Y	Y	Y	Y	Y
CALIFORNIA							
1 Thompson	N	N	N	N	Y	Y	N
2 ***Herger***	Y	Y	Y	Y	Y	Y	Y
3 ***Ose***	Y	Y	Y	Y	Y	Y	Y
4 ***Doolittle***	Y	Y	Y	Y	Y	Y	Y
5 Matsui	N	N	N	N	N	Y	N
6 Woolsey	N	N	N	N	N	Y	N
7 Miller, George	N	N	N	Y	N	N	N
8 Pelosi	N	N	N	N	N	Y	N
9 Lee	N	N	N	N	N	Y	N
10 Tauscher	N	N	N	N	Y	Y	N
11 ***Pombo***	Y	Y	Y	Y	Y	Y	Y
12 Lantos	N	N	N	N	N	Y	N
13 Stark	N	N	N	N	N	Y	N
14 Eshoo	N	N	N	N	N	Y	N
15 ***Campbell***	?	?	?	?	?	?	?
16 Lofgren	N	N	N	N	N	Y	N
17 Farr	N	N	N	N	N	Y	N
18 Condit	N	N	N	N	Y	Y	N
19 ***Radanovich***	Y	Y	Y	Y	Y	Y	Y
20 Dooley	N	N	N	N	Y	Y	N
21 ***Thomas***	Y	Y	Y	Y	Y	Y	Y
22 Capps	N	N	N	N	Y	Y	N
23 ***Gallegly***	Y	Y	Y	Y	Y	Y	Y
24 Sherman	N	N	N	N	N	Y	N
25 ***McKeon***	Y	Y	Y	Y	Y	Y	Y
26 Berman	N	N	N	N	N	Y	N
27 ***Rogan***	Y	Y	Y	Y	Y	Y	Y
28 ***Dreier***	Y	Y	Y	Y	Y	Y	Y
29 Waxman	?	?	?	?	?	?	?
30 Becerra	N	N	N	N	N	Y	N
31 ***Martinez***	Y	Y	Y	Y	?	?	?
32 Dixon	N	N	N	N	N	Y	Y
33 Roybal-Allard	N	N	N	N	N	Y	N
34 Napolitano	N	N	N	N	N	Y	N
35 Waters	N	N	N	?	N	?	N
36 ***Kuykendall***	Y	Y	Y	Y	Y	Y	Y
37 Millender-McD.	N	N	N	N	N	Y	N
38 ***Horn***	Y	Y	?	Y	Y	Y	Y
39 ***Royce***	Y	Y	Y	Y	Y	Y	N
40 ***Lewis***	?	Y	Y	Y	Y	Y	Y
41 ***Miller, Gary***	Y	Y	Y	Y	Y	Y	Y
42 Baca	N	N	N	N	N	Y	N
43 ***Calvert***	Y	Y	Y	Y	Y	Y	Y
44 ***Bono***	Y	Y	Y	Y	Y	Y	Y
45 ***Rohrabacher***	Y	Y	Y	Y	Y	Y	Y
46 Sanchez	N	N	N	N	N	Y	N
47 ***Cox***	Y	Y	Y	Y	Y	Y	Y
48 ***Packard***	?	?	?	?	?	?	?
49 ***Bilbray***	Y	Y	Y	Y	Y	Y	?
50 Filner	N	N	N	N	N	Y	N
51 ***Cunningham***	Y	Y	Y	Y	Y	Y	Y
52 ***Hunter***	Y	Y	Y	Y	Y	Y	Y
COLORADO							
1 DeGette	N	N	N	N	N	Y	N
2 Udall	N	N	N	N	N	Y	N
3 ***McInnis***	Y	Y	Y	Y	Y	Y	Y
4 ***Schaffer***	Y	Y	Y	Y	Y	?	N
5 ***Hefley***	Y	Y	Y	Y	Y	Y	Y
6 ***Tancredo***	Y	Y	Y	Y	Y	Y	N
CONNECTICUT							
1 Larson	N	N	?	N	N	Y	N
2 Gejdenson	N	N	N	N	N	Y	N
3 DeLauro	N	N	N	N	N	Y	N
4 ***Shays***	Y	Y	Y	Y	Y	Y	Y
5 Maloney	N	N	N	N	Y	Y	N
6 ***Johnson***	Y	Y	Y	Y	Y	Y	Y
DELAWARE							
AL ***Castle***	Y	Y	Y	Y	Y	Y	Y
FLORIDA							
1 ***Scarborough***	Y	Y	Y	Y	Y	Y	Y
2 Boyd	N	N	N	N	Y	Y	N
3 Brown	N	N	N	N	N	Y	N
4 ***Fowler***	Y	Y	Y	Y	Y	?	?
5 Thurman	N	N	N	N	N	Y	N
6 ***Stearns***	Y	Y	Y	Y	Y	Y	Y
7 ***Mica***	Y	Y	Y	Y	Y	Y	Y
8 ***McCollum***	?	?	?	?	?	?	?
9 ***Bilirakis***	Y	Y	Y	Y	Y	Y	Y
10 ***Young***	Y	Y	Y	Y	Y	Y	Y
11 Davis	N	N	N	N	N	Y	N
12 ***Canady***	Y	Y	Y	Y	Y	Y	Y
13 ***Miller***	Y	Y	Y	Y	Y	Y	Y
14 ***Goss***	Y	Y	Y	Y	Y	Y	Y
15 ***Weldon***	Y	Y	Y	Y	Y	Y	N
16 ***Foley***	Y	Y	Y	Y	Y	Y	Y
17 Meek	N	?	?	N	N	Y	N
18 ***Ros-Lehtinen***	Y	Y	Y	Y	Y	Y	Y
19 Wexler	N	N	N	N	N	Y	N
20 Deutsch	N	N	N	N	N	Y	N
21 ***Diaz-Balart***	Y	Y	Y	Y	Y	Y	Y
22 ***Shaw***	Y	Y	Y	Y	Y	Y	Y
23 Hastings	N	N	N	N	N	Y	N
GEORGIA							
1 ***Kingston***	Y	Y	Y	Y	Y	Y	Y
2 Bishop	N	N	?	N	Y	Y	Y
3 ***Collins***	Y	Y	Y	Y	Y	Y	N
4 McKinney	N	N	N	N	N	Y	N
5 Lewis	N	N	N	N	N	Y	N
6 ***Isakson***	Y	Y	Y	Y	Y	Y	Y
7 ***Barr***	Y	Y	Y	Y	Y	Y	N
8 ***Chambliss***	Y	Y	Y	Y	Y	Y	Y
9 ***Deal***	Y	Y	Y	Y	Y	Y	N
10 ***Norwood***	Y	Y	Y	Y	Y	Y	Y
11 ***Linder***	Y	Y	Y	Y	Y	Y	Y
HAWAII							
1 Abercrombie	N	N	N	N	N	Y	Y
2 Mink	N	N	N	N	N	Y	N
IDAHO							
1 ***Chenoweth-Hage***	?	?	?	?	?	?	?
2 ***Simpson***	Y	Y	Y	Y	Y	Y	Y
ILLINOIS							
1 Rush	N	N	N	N	N	Y	Y
2 Jackson	N	N	N	N	N	Y	N
3 Lipinski	N	N	N	N	N	Y	N
4 Gutierrez	N	N	N	N	N	Y	N
5 Blagojevich	?	?	?	?	?	?	?
6 ***Hyde***	Y	Y	Y	Y	Y	Y	Y
7 Davis	N	N	N	N	N	Y	N
8 ***Crane***	Y	Y	Y	Y	Y	Y	Y
9 Schakowsky	N	N	N	N	N	Y	N
10 ***Porter***	Y	Y	Y	Y	Y	Y	Y
11 ***Weller***	Y	Y	Y	Y	Y	Y	Y
12 Costello	N	N	N	N	N	N	N
13 ***Biggert***	Y	Y	Y	Y	Y	Y	Y

ND Northern Democrats SD Southern Democrats

	556	557	558	559	560	561	562
14 ***Hastert***	Y			Y	Y		Y
15 ***Ewing***	Y	Y	Y	Y	Y	Y	Y
16 ***Manzullo***	Y	Y	Y	Y	Y	Y	Y
17 Evans	N	N	?	N	N	Y	N
18 ***LaHood***	Y	Y	Y	Y	Y	Y	Y
19 Phelps	N	N	N	N	N	Y	N
20 ***Shimkus***	Y	Y	Y	Y	Y	Y	Y
INDIANA							
1 Visclosky	N	N	N	N	N	N	N
2 ***McIntosh***	?	?	?	?	?	?	?
3 Roemer	N	N	N	N	Y	Y	N
4 ***Souder***	Y	Y	Y	Y	Y	Y	Y
5 ***Buyer***	Y	Y	Y	Y	Y	Y	Y
6 ***Burton***	Y	Y	Y	Y	Y	Y	Y
7 ***Pease***	Y	Y	Y	Y	Y	Y	Y
8 ***Hostettler***	Y	Y	Y	Y	Y	Y	Y
9 Hill	N	N	N	N	N	Y	N
10 Carson	N	N	N	N	N	Y	N
IOWA							
1 ***Leach***	Y	Y	?	Y	Y	Y	Y
2 ***Nussle***	Y	Y	Y	Y	Y	Y	Y
3 Boswell	N	N	N	N	Y	Y	N
4 ***Ganske***	Y	Y	Y	Y	Y	Y	Y
5 ***Latham***	Y	Y	Y	Y	Y	Y	Y
KANSAS							
1 ***Moran***	Y	Y	Y	Y	Y	Y	Y
2 ***Ryun***	Y	Y	Y	Y	Y	Y	Y
3 Moore	N	N	N	N	Y	Y	N
4 ***Tiahrt***	Y	Y	Y	Y	Y	Y	Y
KENTUCKY							
1 ***Whitfield***	Y	Y	Y	Y	Y	Y	Y
2 ***Lewis***	Y	Y	Y	Y	Y	Y	Y
3 ***Northup***	Y	Y	Y	Y	Y	Y	Y
4 Lucas	N	N	N	N	Y	Y	Y
5 ***Rogers***	Y	Y	Y	Y	Y	Y	Y
6 ***Fletcher***	Y	Y	Y	Y	Y	Y	Y
LOUISIANA							
1 ***Vitter***	Y	Y	Y	Y	Y	Y	Y
2 Jefferson	N	N	N	N	N	Y	N
3 ***Tauzin***	Y	Y	Y	Y	Y	?	?
4 ***McCrery***	Y	Y	Y	Y	Y	Y	Y
5 ***Cooksey***	Y	Y	?	Y	Y	Y	Y
6 ***Baker***	Y	Y	Y	Y	Y	Y	Y
7 John	N	N	N	N	N	Y	N
MAINE							
1 Allen	N	N	N	N	N	Y	N
2 Baldacci	N	N	N	N	N	Y	N
MARYLAND							
1 ***Gilchrest***	Y	Y	Y	Y	Y	Y	Y
2 ***Ehrlich***	Y	Y	Y	Y	Y	Y	Y
3 Cardin	N	N	N	N	N	Y	N
4 Wynn	N	N	N	N	N	Y	N
5 Hoyer	N	N	N	N	N	Y	N
6 ***Bartlett***	Y	Y	Y	Y	Y	Y	Y
7 Cummings	N	N	N	N	N	Y	N
8 ***Morella***	Y	Y	Y	Y	Y	Y	N
MASSACHUSETTS							
1 Olver	N	N	N	N	N	Y	N
2 Neal	?	N	N	N	N	Y	N
3 McGovern	N	N	N	N	N	Y	N
4 Frank	N	N	N	N	N	Y	N
5 Meehan	N	N	N	N	N	Y	N
6 Tierney	N	N	N	N	N	Y	N
7 Markey	N	N	N	N	N	Y	N
8 Capuano	N	N	N	N	N	N	N
9 Moakley	N	N	N	N	N	Y	N
10 Delahunt	N	N	N	N	N	Y	N
MICHIGAN							
1 Stupak	?	?	?	?	N	N	N
2 ***Hoekstra***	?	Y	Y	Y	Y	Y	Y
3 ***Ehlers***	Y	Y	Y	Y	Y	Y	Y
4 ***Camp***	Y	Y	Y	Y	Y	Y	Y
5 Barcia	N	N	N	Y	Y	Y	N
6 ***Upton***	Y	Y	Y	Y	Y	Y	Y
7 ***Smith***	Y	Y	Y	Y	Y	Y	Y
8 Stabenow	N	?	N	?	Y	Y	Y
9 Kildee	N	N	N	N	N	Y	N
10 Bonior	N	N	N	N	N	Y	N
11 ***Knollenberg***	Y	Y	Y	Y	Y	Y	Y
12 Levin	N	N	N	N	N	Y	N
13 Rivers	N	N	N	N	N	Y	N
14 Conyers	N	N	N	N	N	Y	N
15 Kilpatrick	N	N	N	N	N	Y	N
16 Dingell	N	N	N	N	N	N	N

	556	557	558	559	560	561	562
MINNESOTA							
1 ***Gutknecht***	Y	Y	Y	Y	Y	Y	Y
2 Minge	N	N	N	N	Y	Y	N
3 ***Ramstad***	Y	Y	Y	Y	Y	Y	Y
4 Vacant							
5 Sabo	N	N	N	N	Y	Y	N
6 Luther	N	N	N	N	Y	Y	N
7 Peterson	N	N	N	N	Y	Y	Y
8 Oberstar	N	N	N	N	N	Y	N
MISSISSIPPI							
1 ***Wicker***	Y	Y	Y	Y	Y	Y	Y
2 Thompson	?	?	?	?	?	?	?
3 ***Pickering***	Y	Y	Y	Y	Y	Y	Y
4 Shows	N	N	Y	Y	Y	Y	Y
5 Taylor	N	N	N	Y	N	Y	N
MISSOURI							
1 Clay	N	N	N	N	N	Y	N
2 ***Talent***	?	Y	Y	Y	Y	?	?
3 Gephardt	N	N	N	N	N	Y	N
4 Skelton	N	N	N	N	N	Y	N
5 McCarthy	N	N	N	N	N	Y	N
6 Danner	?	?	?	?	?	?	?
7 ***Blunt***	Y	Y	Y	Y	Y	Y	Y
8 ***Emerson***	Y	Y	Y	Y	Y	Y	Y
9 ***Hulshof***	Y	Y	Y	Y	Y	Y	Y
MONTANA							
AL ***Hill***	Y	Y	Y	Y	Y	Y	N
NEBRASKA							
1 ***Bereuter***	Y	Y	Y	Y	Y	Y	Y
2 ***Terry***	Y	Y	Y	Y	Y	Y	Y
3 ***Barrett***	Y	Y	Y	Y	Y	Y	Y
NEVADA							
1 Berkley	N	N	N	N	Y	Y	N
2 ***Gibbons***	Y	Y	Y	Y	Y	Y	Y
NEW HAMPSHIRE							
1 ***Sununu***	Y	Y	Y	Y	Y	Y	Y
2 ***Bass***	Y	Y	Y	Y	Y	Y	Y
NEW JERSEY							
1 Andrews	N	N	N	N	N	Y	N
2 ***LoBiondo***	Y	Y	Y	Y	Y	Y	Y
3 ***Saxton***	Y	Y	Y	Y	Y	Y	Y
4 ***Smith***	N	Y	Y	Y	Y	Y	Y
5 ***Roukema***	Y	Y	Y	Y	Y	Y	Y
6 Pallone	N	?	N	N	N	Y	N
7 ***Franks***	?	?	?	?	?	?	?
8 Pascrell	N	N	N	N	N	Y	N
9 Rothman	N	N	N	N	N	Y	N
10 Payne	N	N	N	N	?	?	?
11 ***Frelinghuysen***	Y	Y	Y	Y	Y	Y	Y
12 Holt	N	N	N	N	N	Y	N
13 Menendez	N	N	N	N	N	Y	N
NEW MEXICO							
1 ***Wilson***	Y	Y	Y	Y	Y	Y	Y
2 ***Skeen***	Y	Y	Y	Y	Y	Y	Y
3 Udall	N	N	N	N	N	Y	N
NEW YORK							
1 Forbes	N	N	N	N	N	Y	N
2 ***Lazio***	?	?	?	?	?	?	?
3 ***King***	N	Y	Y	Y	Y	Y	Y
4 McCarthy	N	N	N	N	N	Y	N
5 Ackerman	N	N	N	N	N	Y	?
6 Meeks	N	N	N	N	N	Y	N
7 Crowley	?	?	?	?	?	?	?
8 Nadler	N	N	N	N	N	Y	N
9 Weiner	N	N	N	N	N	Y	N
10 Towns	N	N	N	N	N	Y	N
11 Owens	?	?	?	?	N	Y	N
12 Velázquez	N	N	N	N	N	Y	N
13 ***Fossella***	Y	Y	Y	Y	Y	Y	Y
14 Maloney	N	N	N	N	N	Y	N
15 Rangel	N	N	N	N	N	Y	N
16 Serrano	N	N	N	N	N	Y	Y
17 Engel	?	N	N	N	N	Y	N
18 Lowey	N	N	N	N	N	Y	N
19 ***Kelly***	Y	Y	Y	Y	Y	Y	Y
20 ***Gilman***	Y	Y	Y	Y	Y	Y	Y
21 McNulty	N	N	N	N	N	Y	N
22 ***Sweeney***	Y	Y	Y	Y	Y	Y	Y
23 ***Boehlert***	N	Y	Y	Y	Y	Y	Y
24 ***McHugh***	N	Y	Y	Y	Y	Y	Y
25 ***Walsh***	Y	Y	Y	Y	Y	Y	Y
26 Hinchey	N	N	N	N	N	Y	N
27 ***Reynolds***	Y	Y	Y	Y	Y	Y	Y
28 Slaughter	N	N	N	N	N	Y	Y
29 LaFalce	N	N	N	N	N	Y	N

	556	557	558	559	560	561	562
30 ***Quinn***	Y	Y	Y	Y	Y	Y	Y
31 ***Houghton***	Y	Y	Y	Y	Y	Y	Y
NORTH CAROLINA							
1 Clayton	N	N	N	N	N	Y	N
2 Etheridge	N	N	N	N	N	Y	N
3 ***Jones***	Y	Y	Y	Y	Y	Y	Y
4 Price	N	N	N	N	N	Y	N
5 ***Burr***	Y	Y	Y	Y	Y	Y	Y
6 ***Coble***	Y	Y	Y	Y	Y	Y	Y
7 McIntyre	N	N	N	N	Y	Y	Y
8 ***Hayes***	Y	Y	Y	Y	Y	Y	Y
9 ***Myrick***	Y	Y	Y	Y	Y	Y	Y
10 ***Ballenger***	Y	Y	Y	Y	Y	Y	Y
11 ***Taylor***	Y	Y	Y	Y	Y	Y	Y
12 Watt	N	N	N	N	N	Y	N
NORTH DAKOTA							
AL Pomeroy	N	N	N	N	N	Y	N
OHIO							
1 ***Chabot***	Y	Y	Y	Y	Y	Y	Y
2 ***Portman***	Y	Y	Y	Y	Y	Y	Y
3 Hall	N	N	N	N	N	?	N
4 ***Oxley***	Y	Y	Y	Y	Y	Y	Y
5 ***Gillmor***	Y	Y	Y	Y	Y	Y	Y
6 Strickland	N	N	N	N	N	Y	N
7 ***Hobson***	Y	Y	Y	Y	Y	Y	Y
8 ***Boehner***	Y	Y	Y	Y	Y	Y	Y
9 Kaptur	N	N	N	N	N	N	N
10 Kucinich	N	N	N	N	N	N	N
11 Jones	N	?	N	N	N	Y	N
12 ***Kasich***	Y	Y	Y	Y	Y	Y	Y
13 Brown	N	N	N	N	N	Y	N
14 Sawyer	N	N	N	N	N	Y	N
15 ***Pryce***	Y	Y	Y	Y	Y	Y	Y
16 ***Regula***	Y	Y	Y	Y	Y	Y	Y
17 Traficant	Y	Y	Y	Y	Y	Y	Y
18 ***Ney***	Y	Y	Y	Y	Y	?	Y
19 ***LaTourette***	?	Y	Y	Y	Y	Y	Y
OKLAHOMA							
1 ***Largent***	Y	Y	Y	Y	Y	Y	Y
2 ***Coburn***	Y	Y	Y	Y	Y	Y	N
3 ***Watkins***	Y	Y	Y	Y	Y	Y	Y
4 ***Watts***	Y	Y	Y	Y	Y	Y	Y
5 ***Istook***	Y	Y	Y	Y	Y	Y	Y
6 ***Lucas***	Y	Y	Y	Y	Y	Y	Y
OREGON							
1 Wu	N	N	N	Y	N	Y	N
2 ***Walden***	Y	Y	Y	Y	N	Y	Y
3 Blumenauer	N	N	N	N	N	Y	N
4 DeFazio	N	N	N	N	N	N	N
5 Hooley	N	N	N	N	N	Y	N
PENNSYLVANIA							
1 Brady	?	?	?	?	?	?	?
2 Fattah	N	N	N	N	N	Y	N
3 Borski	N	N	?	N	N	Y	N
4 Klink	?	?	?	?	?	?	?
5 ***Peterson***	?	?	?	?	?	?	?
6 Holden	N	N	N	N	N	Y	N
7 ***Weldon***	?	?	?	Y	Y	Y	Y
8 ***Greenwood***	Y	Y	Y	Y	Y	Y	Y
9 ***Shuster***	Y	Y	Y	Y	N	Y	?
10 ***Sherwood***	Y	Y	Y	Y	Y	Y	Y
11 Kanjorski	N	N	N	N	N	Y	Y
12 Murtha	N	N	N	N	N	Y	Y
13 Hoeffel	N	N	N	N	N	Y	N
14 Coyne	N	N	N	N	N	Y	N
15 ***Toomey***	Y	Y	Y	Y	Y	Y	N
16 ***Pitts***	Y	Y	Y	Y	Y	Y	Y
17 ***Gekas***	Y	Y	Y	Y	Y	Y	Y
18 Doyle	N	N	N	N	N	Y	N
19 ***Goodling***	Y	Y	Y	Y	Y	Y	Y
20 Mascara	N	N	N	N	N	Y	N
21 ***English***	Y	Y	Y	Y	Y	Y	Y
RHODE ISLAND							
1 Kennedy	N	N	N	N	N	Y	N
2 Weygand	N	N	N	N	Y	Y	N
SOUTH CAROLINA							
1 ***Sanford***	Y	Y	Y	Y	N	Y	N
2 ***Spence***	Y	Y	Y	Y	Y	Y	Y
3 ***Graham***	Y	Y	Y	Y	Y	Y	Y
4 ***DeMint***	Y	Y	Y	Y	Y	Y	Y
5 Spratt	?	?	?	?	?	?	?
6 Clyburn	N	N	N	N	N	Y	N
SOUTH DAKOTA							
AL ***Thune***	Y	Y	Y	Y	Y	Y	Y

	556	557	558	559	560	561	562
TENNESSEE							
1 ***Jenkins***	Y	Y	Y	Y	Y	Y	Y
2 ***Duncan***	Y	Y	Y	Y	Y	Y	Y
3 ***Wamp***	Y	Y	Y	Y	Y	Y	Y
4 ***Hilleary***	Y	Y	Y	Y	Y	Y	Y
5 Clement	N	N	N	N	N	Y	N
6 Gordon	N	N	N	N	Y	Y	N
7 ***Bryant***	Y	Y	Y	Y	Y	Y	Y
8 Tanner	N	N	N	N	N	Y	N
9 Ford	N	N	N	N	N	Y	N
TEXAS							
1 Sandlin	N	N	N	N	N	Y	N
2 Turner	N	N	N	N	N	Y	N
3 ***Johnson, Sam***	Y	Y	Y	Y	?	?	?
4 Hall	N	N	N	N	Y	Y	N
5 ***Sessions***	Y	Y	Y	Y	Y	Y	Y
6 ***Barton***	Y	Y	Y	Y	Y	N	N
7 ***Archer***	Y	Y	Y	Y	N	Y	Y
8 ***Brady***	Y	Y	Y	Y	Y	Y	Y
9 Lampson	N	N	N	N	N	Y	N
10 Doggett	N	N	N	N	N	Y	N
11 Edwards	N	N	N	N	Y	Y	N
12 ***Granger***	Y	Y	Y	Y	Y	Y	Y
13 ***Thornberry***	Y	Y	Y	Y	Y	Y	Y
14 ***Paul***	Y	Y	Y	Y	P	Y	N
15 Hinojosa	N	N	N	N	N	Y	N
16 Reyes	N	N	N	N	N	Y	N
17 Stenholm	N	N	N	N	N	Y	N
18 Jackson-Lee	N	N	N	N	N	Y	N
19 ***Combest***	Y	Y	Y	Y	Y	Y	Y
20 Gonzalez	N	N	N	N	N	Y	N
21 ***Smith***	Y	Y	Y	Y	Y	Y	Y
22 ***DeLay***	Y	Y	Y	Y	Y	Y	Y
23 ***Bonilla***	Y	Y	Y	Y	Y	Y	Y
24 Frost	N	N	N	N	N	Y	N
25 Bentsen	N	N	N	N	Y	Y	N
26 ***Armey***	Y	Y	Y	Y	Y	Y	Y
27 Ortiz	N	N	N	N	N	Y	N
28 Rodriguez	N	N	N	N	N	Y	N
29 Green	N	N	N	N	N	Y	N
30 Johnson, E.B.	N	N	N	N	N	Y	N
UTAH							
1 ***Hansen***	Y	Y	Y	Y	Y	Y	Y
2 ***Cook***	Y	Y	Y	Y	Y	Y	Y
3 ***Cannon***	Y	Y	Y	Y	Y	Y	Y
VERMONT							
AL ***Sanders***	N	N	N	N	N	Y	N
VIRGINIA							
1 Vacant							
2 Pickett	N	N	N	N	N	Y	N
3 Scott	N	N	N	N	N	Y	N
4 Sisisky	N	N	N	N	Y	Y	Y
5 ***Goode***	Y	Y	Y	Y	Y	Y	Y
6 ***Goodlatte***	Y	Y	Y	Y	Y	Y	Y
7 ***Bliley***	Y	Y	Y	?	?	?	?
8 Moran	N	N	N	N	N	Y	N
9 Boucher	N	Y	Y	N	Y	Y	Y
10 ***Wolf***	Y	Y	Y	Y	Y	Y	N
11 ***Davis***	Y	Y	Y	Y	Y	Y	Y
WASHINGTON							
1 Inslee	N	N	N	Y	N	Y	N
2 ***Metcalf***	?	?	?	?	?	?	?
3 Baird	N	N	N	N	N	N	N
4 ***Hastings***	Y	Y	Y	Y	Y	Y	Y
5 ***Nethercutt***	Y	Y	Y	Y	Y	Y	Y
6 Dicks	N	N	N	N	N	Y	Y
7 McDermott	N	N	N	N	N	Y	N
8 ***Dunn***	Y	Y	Y	Y	Y	Y	Y
9 Smith	N	N	N	N	N	Y	N
WEST VIRGINIA							
1 Mollohan	N	N	N	N	N	Y	Y
2 Wise	Y	N	N	N	Y	?	?
3 Rahall	N	N	N	N	N	Y	N
WISCONSIN							
1 ***Ryan***	Y	Y	Y	Y	Y	Y	Y
2 Baldwin	N	N	N	N	N	Y	N
3 Kind	N	N	N	Y	N	Y	N
4 Kleczka	N	N	N	N	N	Y	N
5 Barrett	N	N	N	N	N	Y	N
6 ***Petri***	Y	Y	Y	Y	Y	Y	Y
7 Obey	N	N	N	N	N	Y	N
8 ***Green***	Y	Y	Y	Y	Y	Y	Y
9 ***Sensenbrenner***	Y	Y	Y	Y	Y	Y	Y
WYOMING							
AL ***Cubin***	Y	Y	Y	Y	Y	Y	Y

Southern states - Ala., Ark., Fla., Ga., Ky., La., Miss., N.C., Okla., S.C., Tenn., Texas, Va.

563. H J Res 117. Continuing Resolution/Passage. Passage of the joint resolution that would provide temporary funding authority, at current levels, until Oct. 28, for the departments, agencies and programs for which regular fiscal year 2001 appropriations bills are not enacted by Oct. 27. Passed 366-13: R 188-0; D 177-13 (ND 130-11, SD 47-2); I 1-0. Oct. 27, 2000.

564. S 2943. International Malaria Control/Passage. Gilman, R-N.Y. motion to suspend the rules and pass the bill that would authorize $50 million a year in fiscal 2001 and 2002 for international malaria-prevention programs overseen by the U.S. Agency for International Development (USAID). Motion agreed to 385-2: R 187-2; D 196-0 (ND 145-0, SD 51-0); I 2-0. A two-thirds majority of those present and voting (in this case 258) is required for passage under suspension of the rules. Oct. 27, 2000.

565. HR 2498. Cardiac Arrest Survival/Passage. Bilirakis, R-Fla., motion to suspend the rules and pass the bill that would authorize a variety of public health programs, including boosting research on both clinical lupus and prostate cancer. Other programs would seek to combat biological terrorist attacks, renovate biomedical and behavioral research facilities, authorize grants to increase defibrillator access in rural areas and require the Department of Health and Human Services to revise how it certifies organ procurement groups. Motion agreed to 384-2: R 187-2; D 195-0 (ND 144-0, SD 51-0); I 2-0. A two-thirds majority of those present and voting (in this case 257) is required for passage under suspension of the rules. Oct. 27, 2000.

566. HR 1550. Fire Administration Reauthorization/Adoption. Sensenbrenner, R-Wis., motion to suspend the rules and adopt the resolution (H Res 655) that would concur with the House and Senate amendments to the bill to authorize programs within the U.S. Fire Administration and to authorize funding for the National Earthquake Hazards Reduction Program. Motion agreed to 384-5: R 187-4; D 195-1 (ND 145-0, SD 50-1); I 2-0. A two-thirds majority of those present and voting (260 in this case) is required for adoption under suspension of the rules. Oct. 27, 2000.

567. S 2712. Reports Consolidation Act/Passage. Horn, R-Calif., motion to suspend the rules and pass the bill that would authorize and encourage the consolidation of financial and performance management reports into one annual report. Motion agreed to 385-0: R 188-0; D 195-0 (ND 144-0, SD 51-0); I 2-0. A two-thirds majority of those present and voting (in this case 257) is required for passage under suspension of the rules. Oct. 27, 2000.

568. HR 5309. Ronald Reagan Post Office/Passage. McHugh, R-N.Y., motion to suspend the rules and pass the bill naming a post office in West Melbourne, Fla., the "Ronald W. Reagan Post Office Building." Motion agreed to 376-8: R 190-0; D 184-8 (ND 133-8, SD 51-0); I 2-0. A two-thirds majority of those present and voting (256 in this case) is required for passage under suspension of the rules. Oct. 27, 2000.

569. S 3194. Robert Walker Post Office/Passage. McHugh, R-N.Y., motion to suspend the rules and pass the bill naming a post office in Millersville, Pa., the "Robert S. Walker Post Office." Motion agreed to 379-7: R 188-2; D 189-5 (ND 138-5, SD 51-0); I 2-0. A two-thirds majority of those present and voting (258 in this case) is required for passage under suspension of the rules. Oct. 27, 2000.

570. Procedural Motion/Journal. Approval of the House Journal of Friday, Oct. 27, 2000. Approved 256-60: R 151-12; D 103-48 (ND 72-41, SD 31-7); I 2-0. Oct. 28, 2000.

Key

Y Voted for (yea).
\# Paired for.
\+ Announced for.
N Voted against (nay).
X Paired against.
– Announced against.
P Voted "present."
C Voted "present" to avoid possible conflict of interest.
? Did not vote or otherwise make a position known.

•

Democrats ***Republicans***
Independents

	563	564	565	566	567	568	569	570
ALABAMA								
1 ***Callahan***	Y	Y	Y	Y	Y	Y	Y	Y
2 ***Everett***	Y	Y	Y	Y	Y	Y	Y	Y
3 ***Riley***	Y	Y	Y	Y	Y	Y	Y	Y
4 ***Aderholt***	Y	Y	Y	Y	Y	Y	Y	Y
5 Cramer	?	?	?	?	?	?	?	N
6 ***Bachus***	Y	Y	Y	Y	Y	Y	Y	N
7 Hilliard	N	Y	Y	Y	Y	Y	Y	?
ALASKA								
AL ***Young***	Y	Y	Y	Y	Y	Y	Y	?
ARIZONA								
1 ***Salmon***	Y	Y	Y	Y	Y	Y	Y	Y
2 Pastor	N	Y	Y	Y	Y	Y	Y	N
3 ***Stump***	Y	Y	Y	N	Y	Y	Y	Y
4 ***Shadegg***	Y	Y	Y	N	Y	Y	Y	Y
5 ***Kolbe***	+	+	+	?	?	+	+	+
6 ***Hayworth***	Y	Y	Y	Y	Y	Y	Y	Y
ARKANSAS								
1 Berry	Y	Y	Y	Y	Y	Y	Y	N
2 Snyder	Y	Y	Y	Y	Y	Y	Y	Y
3 ***Hutchinson***	?	Y	Y	Y	Y	Y	Y	Y
4 ***Dickey***	?	?	?	?	?	?	?	?
CALIFORNIA								
1 Thompson	Y	Y	Y	Y	Y	Y	Y	N
2 ***Herger***	Y	Y	Y	Y	Y	Y	Y	?
3 ***Ose***	Y	Y	Y	Y	Y	Y	Y	Y
4 ***Doolittle***	Y	Y	Y	Y	Y	Y	Y	?
5 Matsui	Y	Y	Y	Y	Y	Y	Y	Y
6 Woolsey	Y	Y	Y	Y	Y	Y	Y	Y
7 Miller, George	N	Y	?	Y	Y	Y	Y	Y
8 Pelosi	Y	Y	Y	Y	Y	Y	Y	Y
9 Lee	Y	Y	Y	Y	Y	N	Y	Y
10 Tauscher	Y	Y	Y	Y	Y	Y	Y	Y
11 ***Pombo***	Y	Y	Y	Y	Y	Y	Y	?
12 Lantos	Y	Y	Y	Y	Y	Y	Y	?
13 Stark	?	?	?	?	?	?	?	?
14 Eshoo	Y	Y	Y	Y	Y	Y	Y	Y
15 ***Campbell***	?	?	?	?	?	?	?	?
16 Lofgren	Y	Y	Y	Y	Y	N	N	Y
17 Farr	Y	Y	Y	Y	Y	Y	Y	Y
18 Condit	Y	Y	Y	Y	Y	Y	Y	Y
19 ***Radanovich***	Y	Y	Y	Y	Y	Y	N	?
20 Dooley	Y	Y	Y	Y	Y	Y	Y	Y
21 ***Thomas***	Y	Y	Y	Y	Y	Y	Y	Y
22 Capps	Y	Y	Y	Y	Y	Y	Y	Y
23 ***Gallegly***	Y	Y	Y	Y	Y	Y	Y	Y
24 Sherman	Y	Y	Y	Y	Y	Y	Y	Y
25 ***McKeon***	Y	?	?	?	?	?	?	?
26 Berman	Y	Y	Y	Y	Y	Y	Y	Y
27 ***Rogan***	Y	Y	Y	Y	Y	Y	Y	N
28 ***Dreier***	Y	Y	Y	Y	Y	Y	Y	Y
29 Waxman	?	?	?	?	?	?	?	Y
30 Becerra	Y	Y	Y	Y	Y	Y	Y	+
31 ***Martinez***	?	?	?	?	?	?	?	?
32 Dixon	?	Y	Y	Y	Y	Y	Y	?
33 Roybal-Allard	Y	Y	Y	Y	Y	Y	Y	Y
34 Napolitano	Y	Y	Y	Y	Y	Y	Y	Y
35 Waters	Y	Y	Y	Y	Y	Y	Y	N
36 ***Kuykendall***	Y	Y	Y	Y	Y	Y	Y	Y
37 Millender-McD.	Y	Y	Y	Y	Y	Y	Y	Y
38 ***Horn***	Y	Y	Y	Y	Y	Y	Y	Y
39 ***Royce***	Y	Y	Y	Y	Y	Y	Y	Y
40 ***Lewis***	Y	Y	Y	Y	Y	Y	Y	Y
41 ***Miller, Gary***	Y	Y	Y	Y	Y	Y	Y	Y
42 Baca	Y	Y	Y	Y	Y	Y	Y	?
43 ***Calvert***	Y	Y	Y	Y	Y	Y	Y	Y
44 ***Bono***	Y	Y	Y	Y	Y	Y	Y	Y
45 ***Rohrabacher***	Y	Y	Y	Y	Y	Y	Y	Y
46 Sanchez	Y	Y	Y	Y	Y	Y	Y	N
47 ***Cox***	?	?	?	?	?	?	?	?
48 ***Packard***	Y	?	?	Y	Y	Y	Y	Y
49 ***Bilbray***	?	?	?	?	?	?	?	?
50 Filner	Y	Y	Y	Y	Y	N	Y	N
51 ***Cunningham***	Y	Y	Y	Y	Y	Y	Y	Y
52 ***Hunter***	Y	Y	Y	Y	Y	?	Y	Y
COLORADO								
1 DeGette	Y	Y	Y	Y	Y	Y	Y	Y
2 Udall	Y	Y	Y	Y	Y	Y	Y	N
3 ***McInnis***	?	?	?	?	?	?	?	?
4 ***Schaffer***	Y	Y	Y	Y	Y	Y	Y	N
5 ***Hefley***	?	?	?	?	?	?	?	?
6 ***Tancredo***	Y	Y	Y	Y	Y	Y	Y	P
CONNECTICUT								
1 Larson	Y	Y	Y	Y	Y	Y	Y	Y
2 Gejdenson	Y	Y	Y	Y	Y	Y	Y	N
3 DeLauro	Y	Y	Y	Y	Y	Y	Y	Y
4 ***Shays***	?	?	?	?	?	?	?	?
5 Maloney	Y	Y	Y	Y	Y	Y	Y	Y
6 ***Johnson***	Y	Y	Y	Y	Y	Y	Y	Y
DELAWARE								
AL ***Castle***	Y	Y	Y	Y	Y	Y	Y	Y
FLORIDA								
1 ***Scarborough***	Y	Y	Y	Y	Y	Y	Y	Y
2 Boyd	Y	Y	Y	Y	Y	Y	Y	Y
3 Brown	Y	Y	Y	Y	Y	Y	Y	?
4 ***Fowler***	?	?	?	?	?	?	?	?
5 Thurman	Y	Y	Y	Y	Y	Y	Y	Y
6 ***Stearns***	Y	Y	Y	Y	Y	Y	Y	Y
7 ***Mica***	Y	Y	Y	Y	Y	Y	Y	Y
8 ***McCollum***	?	?	?	?	?	?	?	?
9 ***Bilirakis***	Y	Y	Y	Y	Y	Y	Y	Y
10 ***Young***	Y	Y	Y	Y	Y	Y	Y	Y
11 Davis	Y	Y	Y	Y	Y	Y	Y	Y
12 ***Canady***	Y	Y	Y	Y	Y	Y	Y	Y
13 ***Miller***	Y	Y	Y	Y	Y	Y	Y	Y
14 ***Goss***	Y	Y	Y	Y	Y	Y	Y	Y
15 ***Weldon***	Y	Y	Y	Y	Y	Y	Y	?
16 ***Foley***	Y	Y	Y	Y	Y	Y	Y	Y
17 Meek	Y	Y	Y	Y	Y	Y	Y	?
18 ***Ros-Lehtinen***	Y	Y	Y	Y	Y	Y	Y	?
19 Wexler	Y	Y	Y	Y	Y	Y	Y	Y
20 Deutsch	Y	Y	Y	Y	Y	Y	Y	Y
21 ***Diaz-Balart***	Y	Y	Y	Y	Y	Y	Y	?
22 ***Shaw***	Y	Y	Y	Y	Y	Y	Y	?
23 Hastings	Y	Y	Y	Y	Y	Y	Y	?
GEORGIA								
1 ***Kingston***	?	?	?	?	?	?	?	Y
2 Bishop	Y	Y	Y	Y	Y	Y	Y	?
3 ***Collins***	Y	Y	Y	Y	Y	Y	Y	Y
4 McKinney	Y	Y	Y	Y	Y	Y	Y	Y
5 Lewis	Y	Y	Y	Y	Y	Y	Y	Y
6 ***Isakson***	?	?	?	?	?	?	?	Y
7 ***Barr***	?	?	?	?	?	?	?	?
8 ***Chambliss***	Y	Y	Y	Y	Y	Y	Y	Y
9 ***Deal***	Y	Y	Y	Y	Y	Y	Y	Y
10 ***Norwood***	Y	Y	Y	Y	Y	Y	Y	Y
11 ***Linder***	Y	Y	Y	Y	Y	Y	Y	Y
HAWAII								
1 Abercrombie	Y	+	+	+	+	+	+	Y
2 Mink	Y	Y	Y	Y	Y	Y	Y	?
IDAHO								
1 ***Chenoweth-Hage***	?	?	?	?	?	?	?	Y
2 ***Simpson***	Y	Y	Y	Y	Y	Y	Y	Y
ILLINOIS								
1 Rush	Y	Y	Y	Y	Y	Y	Y	?
2 Jackson	Y	Y	Y	Y	Y	Y	Y	Y
3 Lipinski	Y	Y	Y	Y	Y	Y	Y	?
4 Gutierrez	Y	Y	Y	Y	Y	?	Y	Y
5 Blagojevich	Y	Y	Y	Y	Y	Y	Y	?
6 ***Hyde***	Y	Y	Y	Y	Y	Y	Y	Y
7 Davis	Y	Y	Y	Y	Y	Y	Y	?
8 ***Crane***	Y	Y	Y	Y	Y	Y	Y	?
9 Schakowsky	Y	Y	Y	Y	Y	Y	Y	Y
10 ***Porter***	Y	Y	Y	Y	Y	Y	Y	?
11 ***Weller***	Y	Y	Y	Y	Y	Y	Y	N
12 Costello	N	Y	Y	Y	Y	Y	Y	N
13 ***Biggert***	Y	Y	Y	Y	Y	Y	Y	Y

ND Northern Democrats SD Southern Democrats

	563	564	565	566	567	568	569	570
14 ***Hastert***								
15 ***Ewing***	Y	Y	Y	Y	Y	Y	Y	Y
16 ***Manzullo***	Y	Y	Y	Y	Y	Y	Y	?
17 Evans	Y	Y	Y	Y	Y	Y	Y	Y
18 ***LaHood***	Y	Y	Y	Y	Y	Y	Y	Y
19 Phelps	Y	Y	Y	Y	Y	Y	Y	Y
20 ***Shimkus***	Y	Y	Y	Y	Y	Y	Y	Y
INDIANA								
1 Visclosky	N	Y	Y	Y	Y	Y	Y	?
2 ***McIntosh***	?	?	?	?	?	?	?	?
3 Roemer	Y	Y	Y	Y	Y	Y	Y	Y
4 ***Souder***	Y	Y	Y	Y	Y	Y	Y	Y
5 ***Buyer***	Y	Y	Y	Y	Y	Y	Y	?
6 ***Burton***	Y	Y	Y	Y	Y	Y	Y	?
7 ***Pease***	Y	Y	Y	Y	Y	Y	Y	Y
8 ***Hostettler***	Y	Y	Y	Y	Y	Y	Y	Y
9 Hill	Y	Y	Y	Y	Y	Y	Y	Y
10 Carson	Y	Y	Y	Y	Y	Y	Y	N
IOWA								
1 ***Leach***	Y	Y	Y	Y	Y	Y	Y	Y
2 ***Nussle***	Y	Y	Y	Y	Y	Y	Y	Y
3 Boswell	Y	Y	Y	Y	Y	Y	Y	Y
4 ***Ganske***	?	?	?	?	?	?	?	?
5 ***Latham***	Y	Y	Y	Y	Y	Y	Y	N
KANSAS								
1 ***Moran***	Y	Y	Y	Y	Y	Y	Y	N
2 ***Ryun***	Y	Y	Y	Y	Y	Y	Y	Y
3 Moore	Y	Y	Y	Y	Y	Y	Y	Y
4 ***Tiahrt***	Y	Y	Y	Y	Y	Y	Y	Y
KENTUCKY								
1 ***Whitfield***	Y	Y	Y	Y	Y	Y	Y	Y
2 ***Lewis***	Y	Y	Y	Y	Y	Y	Y	Y
3 ***Northup***	Y	Y	Y	Y	Y	Y	Y	Y
4 Lucas	Y	Y	Y	Y	Y	Y	Y	Y
5 ***Rogers***	Y	Y	Y	Y	Y	Y	Y	?
6 ***Fletcher***	Y	Y	Y	Y	Y	Y	Y	Y
LOUISIANA								
1 ***Vitter***	Y	Y	Y	Y	Y	Y	Y	?
2 Jefferson	?	Y	Y	Y	Y	Y	Y	N
3 ***Tauzin***	+	Y	Y	Y	Y	Y	Y	Y
4 ***McCrery***	?	Y	Y	Y	Y	Y	Y	Y
5 ***Cooksey***	?	Y	Y	Y	Y	Y	Y	Y
6 ***Baker***	Y	Y	Y	Y	Y	Y	Y	Y
7 John	Y	Y	Y	Y	Y	Y	Y	Y
MAINE								
1 Allen	Y	Y	Y	Y	Y	Y	Y	N
2 Baldacci	Y	Y	Y	Y	Y	Y	Y	N
MARYLAND								
1 ***Gilchrest***	?	Y	Y	Y	Y	Y	Y	Y
2 ***Ehrlich***	Y	Y	Y	Y	Y	Y	Y	?
3 Cardin	Y	Y	Y	Y	Y	Y	Y	Y
4 Wynn	Y	Y	Y	Y	Y	Y	Y	?
5 Hoyer	Y	Y	Y	Y	Y	Y	Y	Y
6 ***Bartlett***	Y	Y	Y	Y	Y	Y	Y	Y
7 Cummings	Y	Y	Y	Y	Y	Y	Y	Y
8 ***Morella***	Y	Y	Y	Y	Y	Y	Y	?
MASSACHUSETTS								
1 Olver	?	Y	Y	Y	Y	Y	N	N
2 Neal	Y	Y	Y	Y	Y	Y	Y	?
3 McGovern	Y	Y	Y	Y	Y	Y	Y	N
4 Frank	N	Y	Y	Y	Y	Y	Y	Y
5 Meehan	Y	Y	Y	Y	Y	Y	Y	?
6 Tierney	Y	Y	Y	Y	?	?	?	N
7 Markey	Y	Y	Y	Y	Y	Y	Y	?
8 Capuano	N	Y	Y	Y	Y	Y	Y	N
9 Moakley	Y	Y	Y	Y	Y	Y	Y	N
10 Delahunt	Y	Y	Y	Y	Y	Y	Y	?
MICHIGAN								
1 Stupak	N	Y	Y	Y	Y	Y	Y	N
2 ***Hoekstra***	Y	Y	Y	Y	Y	Y	Y	Y
3 ***Ehlers***	Y	Y	Y	Y	Y	Y	Y	Y
4 ***Camp***	Y	Y	Y	Y	Y	Y	Y	Y
5 Barcia	Y	Y	Y	Y	Y	Y	Y	?
6 ***Upton***	Y	Y	Y	Y	Y	Y	Y	Y
7 ***Smith***	Y	Y	Y	Y	Y	Y	Y	Y
8 Stabenow	Y	Y	Y	Y	Y	Y	Y	?
9 Kildee	Y	Y	Y	Y	Y	Y	Y	?
10 Bonior	Y	Y	Y	Y	Y	Y	?	?
11 ***Knollenberg***	Y	Y	Y	Y	Y	Y	Y	Y
12 Levin	Y	Y	Y	Y	Y	Y	Y	Y
13 Rivers	Y	Y	Y	Y	Y	Y	Y	Y
14 Conyers	Y	?	?	?	?	?	?	Y
15 Kilpatrick	Y	Y	Y	Y	Y	Y	Y	Y
16 Dingell	N	Y	Y	Y	Y	Y	Y	Y

	563	564	565	566	567	568	569	570
MINNESOTA								
1 ***Gutknecht***	Y	Y	Y	Y	Y	Y	Y	N
2 Minge	Y	Y	Y	Y	Y	?	Y	Y
3 ***Ramstad***	Y	Y	Y	Y	Y	Y	Y	N
4 Vacant								
5 Sabo	Y	Y	Y	Y	Y	N	Y	N
6 Luther	Y	Y	Y	Y	Y	Y	Y	Y
7 Peterson	Y	Y	Y	Y	Y	Y	Y	N
8 Oberstar	Y	Y	Y	Y	Y	N	Y	N
MISSISSIPPI								
1 ***Wicker***	Y	Y	Y	Y	Y	Y	Y	N
2 Thompson	?	Y	Y	Y	Y	Y	Y	?
3 ***Pickering***	Y	Y	Y	Y	Y	Y	Y	?
4 Shows	Y	Y	Y	Y	Y	Y	Y	Y
5 Taylor	Y	Y	Y	N	Y	Y	Y	?
MISSOURI								
1 Clay	?	Y	Y	Y	Y	Y	Y	?
2 ***Talent***	?	?	?	?	?	?	?	?
3 Gephardt	Y	Y	Y	Y	Y	Y	Y	Y
4 Skelton	Y	Y	Y	Y	Y	Y	Y	Y
5 McCarthy	Y	Y	Y	Y	Y	Y	Y	+
6 Danner	?	?	?	?	?	?	?	?
7 ***Blunt***	Y	Y	Y	Y	Y	Y	Y	Y
8 ***Emerson***	Y	Y	Y	Y	Y	Y	Y	Y
9 ***Hulshof***	Y	Y	Y	Y	Y	Y	Y	?
MONTANA								
AL ***Hill***	Y	Y	Y	Y	Y	Y	Y	N
NEBRASKA								
1 ***Bereuter***	Y	Y	Y	Y	Y	Y	Y	Y
2 ***Terry***	Y	Y	Y	Y	Y	Y	Y	Y
3 ***Barrett***	Y	Y	Y	Y	Y	Y	Y	Y
NEVADA								
1 Berkley	Y	Y	Y	Y	Y	Y	Y	Y
2 ***Gibbons***	Y	Y	Y	Y	Y	Y	Y	Y
NEW HAMPSHIRE								
1 ***Sununu***	Y	Y	Y	Y	Y	Y	Y	Y
2 ***Bass***	Y	Y	Y	Y	Y	Y	Y	Y
NEW JERSEY								
1 Andrews	Y	Y	Y	Y	Y	Y	Y	?
2 ***LoBiondo***	Y	Y	Y	Y	Y	Y	Y	N
3 ***Saxton***	Y	Y	Y	Y	Y	Y	Y	Y
4 ***Smith***	Y	Y	Y	Y	Y	Y	Y	Y
5 ***Roukema***	Y	Y	Y	Y	+	Y	Y	Y
6 Pallone	Y	Y	Y	Y	Y	Y	Y	N
7 ***Franks***	?	?	?	?	?	?	?	?
8 Pascrell	Y	Y	Y	Y	Y	Y	Y	N
9 Rothman	Y	Y	Y	Y	Y	Y	Y	N
10 Payne	Y	Y	Y	Y	Y	Y	Y	?
11 ***Frelinghuysen***	Y	Y	Y	Y	Y	Y	Y	?
12 Holt	Y	Y	Y	Y	Y	Y	Y	N
13 Menendez	Y	Y	Y	Y	Y	Y	Y	?
NEW MEXICO								
1 ***Wilson***	Y	Y	Y	Y	Y	Y	Y	Y
2 ***Skeen***	Y	Y	Y	Y	Y	Y	Y	Y
3 Udall	Y	Y	Y	Y	Y	Y	Y	N
NEW YORK								
1 Forbes	Y	Y	Y	Y	Y	Y	Y	Y
2 ***Lazio***	?	?	?	?	?	?	?	?
3 ***King***	Y	Y	Y	Y	Y	Y	Y	?
4 McCarthy	Y	Y	Y	Y	Y	Y	Y	Y
5 Ackerman	Y	Y	Y	Y	Y	Y	Y	?
6 Meeks	Y	Y	Y	Y	Y	N	Y	N
7 Crowley	?	Y	Y	Y	Y	Y	Y	Y
8 Nadler	Y	Y	Y	Y	Y	N	Y	Y
9 Weiner	?	Y	Y	Y	Y	Y	Y	Y
10 Towns	Y	Y	Y	Y	Y	Y	Y	Y
11 Owens	Y	Y	Y	Y	Y	Y	Y	?
12 Velázquez	Y	Y	Y	Y	Y	Y	Y	N
13 ***Fossella***	Y	Y	Y	Y	Y	Y	Y	?
14 Maloney	Y	Y	Y	Y	Y	Y	Y	Y
15 Rangel	Y	Y	Y	Y	Y	Y	Y	Y
16 Serrano	?	Y	Y	Y	Y	Y	Y	Y
17 Engel	Y	Y	Y	Y	Y	Y	Y	?
18 Lowey	Y	Y	Y	Y	Y	Y	Y	Y
19 ***Kelly***	Y	Y	Y	Y	Y	Y	Y	Y
20 ***Gilman***	Y	Y	Y	Y	Y	Y	Y	Y
21 McNulty	Y	Y	Y	Y	Y	Y	Y	N
22 ***Sweeney***	Y	Y	Y	Y	Y	Y	Y	Y
23 ***Boehlert***	Y	Y	Y	Y	Y	Y	Y	Y
24 ***McHugh***	Y	Y	Y	Y	Y	Y	Y	Y
25 ***Walsh***	Y	?	?	Y	Y	Y	Y	Y
26 Hinchey	?	Y	Y	Y	Y	Y	Y	?
27 ***Reynolds***	Y	Y	Y	Y	Y	Y	Y	?
28 Slaughter	Y	Y	Y	Y	Y	Y	Y	N
29 LaFalce	Y	Y	Y	Y	Y	Y	Y	?

	563	564	565	566	567	568	569	570
30 ***Quinn***	Y	?	?	?	?	?	?	Y
31 ***Houghton***	Y	Y	Y	Y	Y	Y	Y	Y
NORTH CAROLINA								
1 Clayton	Y	Y	Y	Y	Y	Y	Y	Y
2 Etheridge	Y	Y	Y	Y	Y	Y	Y	N
3 ***Jones***	Y	Y	Y	Y	Y	Y	Y	Y
4 Price	Y	Y	Y	Y	Y	Y	Y	Y
5 ***Burr***	Y	Y	Y	Y	Y	Y	Y	Y
6 ***Coble***	Y	Y	Y	Y	Y	Y	Y	Y
7 McIntyre	?	Y	Y	Y	Y	Y	Y	+
8 ***Hayes***	Y	Y	Y	Y	Y	Y	Y	Y
9 ***Myrick***	Y	Y	Y	Y	Y	Y	Y	Y
10 ***Ballenger***	Y	Y	Y	Y	Y	Y	Y	Y
11 ***Taylor***	Y	Y	Y	Y	Y	Y	Y	?
12 Watt	Y	Y	Y	Y	Y	Y	Y	?
NORTH DAKOTA								
AL Pomeroy	Y	Y	Y	Y	Y	Y	Y	Y
OHIO								
1 ***Chabot***	Y	Y	Y	Y	Y	Y	Y	Y
2 ***Portman***	Y	Y	Y	Y	Y	Y	Y	Y
3 Hall	Y	Y	Y	Y	Y	Y	Y	N
4 ***Oxley***	Y	Y	Y	Y	Y	Y	Y	Y
5 ***Gillmor***	Y	Y	Y	Y	Y	Y	Y	Y
6 Strickland	Y	Y	Y	Y	Y	Y	Y	N
7 ***Hobson***	Y	Y	Y	Y	Y	Y	Y	Y
8 ***Boehner***	Y	Y	Y	Y	Y	Y	Y	Y
9 Kaptur	N	Y	Y	Y	Y	?	Y	?
10 Kucinich	Y	Y	Y	Y	Y	Y	Y	N
11 Jones	Y	Y	Y	Y	Y	Y	Y	N
12 ***Kasich***	?	?	?	?	?	?	?	?
13 Brown	Y	Y	Y	Y	Y	Y	Y	?
14 Sawyer	Y	Y	Y	Y	Y	Y	Y	Y
15 ***Pryce***	Y	Y	Y	Y	Y	Y	Y	?
16 ***Regula***	?	Y	Y	Y	Y	Y	Y	Y
17 Traficant	Y	Y	Y	Y	Y	Y	Y	Y
18 ***Ney***	Y	Y	Y	Y	Y	Y	Y	Y
19 ***LaTourette***	Y	Y	Y	Y	Y	Y	Y	Y
OKLAHOMA								
1 ***Largent***	Y	Y	Y	Y	Y	Y	Y	?
2 ***Coburn***	Y	?	?	?	?	?	?	Y
3 ***Watkins***	?	Y	Y	Y	Y	Y	Y	Y
4 ***Watts***	+	+	+	+	+	+	+	+
5 ***Istook***	Y	Y	Y	Y	Y	Y	Y	Y
6 ***Lucas***	Y	Y	Y	Y	Y	Y	Y	Y
OREGON								
1 Wu	Y	Y	Y	Y	Y	Y	N	N
2 ***Walden***	Y	Y	Y	Y	Y	Y	Y	Y
3 Blumenauer	Y	Y	Y	Y	Y	Y	Y	Y
4 DeFazio	N	Y	Y	Y	Y	Y	N	N
5 Hooley	Y	Y	Y	Y	Y	Y	Y	N
PENNSYLVANIA								
1 Brady	Y	?	?	?	?	?	?	N
2 Fattah	?	Y	Y	Y	Y	Y	Y	?
3 Borski	Y	Y	Y	Y	Y	Y	Y	N
4 Klink	?	?	?	?	?	?	?	?
5 ***Peterson***	?	?	?	?	?	?	?	?
6 Holden	Y	Y	Y	Y	Y	Y	Y	Y
7 ***Weldon***	Y	Y	Y	Y	Y	Y	Y	Y
8 ***Greenwood***	Y	Y	Y	Y	Y	Y	Y	?
9 ***Shuster***	Y	Y	Y	Y	Y	Y	Y	?
10 ***Sherwood***	Y	Y	Y	Y	Y	Y	Y	Y
11 Kanjorski	Y	Y	Y	Y	Y	Y	Y	?
12 Murtha	Y	Y	Y	Y	Y	Y	Y	Y
13 Hoeffel	Y	Y	Y	Y	Y	Y	Y	Y
14 Coyne	Y	?	?	?	?	?	?	Y
15 ***Toomey***	Y	Y	Y	Y	Y	Y	Y	Y
16 ***Pitts***	Y	Y	Y	Y	Y	Y	Y	Y
17 ***Gekas***	Y	Y	Y	Y	Y	Y	Y	Y
18 Doyle	Y	Y	Y	Y	Y	Y	Y	Y
19 ***Goodling***	Y	Y	Y	Y	Y	Y	Y	Y
20 Mascara	Y	Y	Y	Y	Y	Y	Y	Y
21 ***English***	Y	Y	Y	Y	Y	Y	Y	N
RHODE ISLAND								
1 Kennedy	Y	Y	Y	Y	Y	Y	Y	?
2 Weygand	Y	Y	Y	Y	Y	Y	Y	?
SOUTH CAROLINA								
1 ***Sanford***	Y	N	N	Y	Y	Y	N	Y
2 ***Spence***	Y	Y	Y	Y	Y	Y	Y	Y
3 ***Graham***	Y	?	?	?	?	?	?	Y
4 ***DeMint***	Y	Y	Y	Y	Y	Y	Y	Y
5 Spratt	?	?	?	?	?	?	?	?
6 Clyburn	Y	Y	Y	Y	Y	Y	Y	?
SOUTH DAKOTA								
AL ***Thune***	Y	Y	Y	Y	Y	Y	Y	Y

	563	564	565	566	567	568	569	570
TENNESSEE								
1 ***Jenkins***	Y	Y	Y	Y	Y	Y	Y	Y
2 ***Duncan***	Y	Y	Y	Y	Y	Y	Y	?
3 ***Wamp***	Y	Y	Y	Y	Y	Y	Y	Y
4 ***Hilleary***	Y	Y	Y	Y	Y	Y	Y	Y
5 Clement	Y	Y	Y	Y	Y	Y	Y	Y
6 Gordon	Y	Y	Y	Y	Y	Y	Y	Y
7 ***Bryant***	Y	Y	Y	Y	Y	Y	Y	Y
8 Tanner	Y	Y	Y	Y	Y	Y	Y	Y
9 Ford	N	Y	Y	Y	Y	Y	Y	Y
TEXAS								
1 Sandlin	Y	Y	Y	Y	Y	Y	Y	?
2 Turner	Y	Y	Y	Y	Y	Y	Y	Y
3 ***Johnson, Sam***	?	Y	Y	N	Y	Y	Y	Y
4 Hall	Y	Y	Y	Y	Y	Y	Y	Y
5 ***Sessions***	Y	?	?	?	?	?	?	?
6 ***Barton***	?	Y	Y	Y	Y	Y	Y	?
7 ***Archer***	Y	Y	Y	Y	Y	Y	Y	Y
8 ***Brady***	Y	Y	Y	Y	?	Y	Y	Y
9 Lampson	Y	Y	Y	Y	Y	Y	Y	Y
10 Doggett	Y	Y	Y	Y	Y	Y	Y	Y
11 Edwards	Y	Y	Y	Y	Y	Y	Y	?
12 ***Granger***	Y	Y	Y	Y	Y	Y	Y	Y
13 ***Thornberry***	Y	Y	Y	Y	Y	Y	Y	Y
14 ***Paul***	Y	N	N	N	Y	Y	Y	Y
15 Hinojosa	Y	Y	Y	Y	Y	Y	Y	Y
16 Reyes	Y	Y	Y	Y	Y	Y	Y	Y
17 Stenholm	Y	Y	Y	Y	Y	Y	Y	N
18 Jackson-Lee	Y	Y	Y	Y	Y	Y	Y	N
19 ***Combest***	Y	Y	Y	Y	Y	Y	Y	Y
20 Gonzalez	Y	Y	Y	Y	Y	Y	Y	Y
21 ***Smith***	Y	Y	Y	Y	Y	Y	Y	Y
22 ***DeLay***	Y	Y	Y	Y	?	?	Y	Y
23 ***Bonilla***	Y	Y	Y	Y	Y	Y	Y	Y
24 Frost	Y	Y	Y	Y	Y	Y	Y	Y
25 Bentsen	Y	Y	Y	Y	Y	Y	Y	?
26 ***Armey***	Y	Y	Y	Y	Y	Y	Y	Y
27 Ortiz	Y	Y	Y	Y	Y	Y	Y	Y
28 Rodriguez	Y	Y	Y	Y	Y	Y	Y	Y
29 Green	Y	Y	Y	Y	Y	Y	Y	Y
30 Johnson, E.B.	Y	Y	Y	Y	Y	Y	Y	N
UTAH								
1 ***Hansen***	Y	Y	Y	Y	Y	Y	Y	Y
2 ***Cook***	Y	Y	Y	Y	Y	Y	Y	Y
3 ***Cannon***	Y	Y	Y	Y	Y	Y	Y	Y
VERMONT								
AL *Sanders*	?	Y	Y	Y	Y	Y	Y	Y
VIRGINIA								
1 Vacant								
2 Pickett	Y	?	?	?	?	?	?	?
3 Scott	Y	Y	Y	Y	Y	Y	Y	Y
4 Sisisky	Y	Y	Y	Y	Y	Y	Y	Y
5 *Goode*	Y	Y	Y	Y	Y	Y	Y	Y
6 ***Goodlatte***	Y	Y	Y	Y	Y	Y	Y	Y
7 ***Bliley***	Y	Y	Y	Y	Y	Y	Y	Y
8 Moran	Y	Y	Y	Y	Y	Y	Y	Y
9 Boucher	Y	Y	Y	Y	Y	Y	Y	?
10 ***Wolf***	Y	Y	Y	Y	Y	Y	Y	Y
11 ***Davis***	Y	Y	Y	Y	Y	Y	Y	?
WASHINGTON								
1 Inslee	Y	Y	Y	Y	Y	Y	Y	Y
2 ***Metcalf***	?	?	?	?	?	?	?	?
3 Baird	N	Y	Y	Y	Y	Y	Y	N
4 ***Hastings***	Y	Y	Y	Y	Y	Y	Y	Y
5 ***Nethercutt***	Y	Y	Y	Y	Y	Y	Y	?
6 Dicks	Y	Y	Y	Y	Y	Y	Y	Y
7 McDermott	Y	Y	Y	Y	Y	N	N	N
8 ***Dunn***	?	?	?	?	?	?	?	?
9 Smith	Y	Y	Y	Y	Y	Y	Y	Y
WEST VIRGINIA								
1 Mollohan	?	?	?	?	?	?	?	Y
2 Wise	?	?	?	?	?	?	?	?
3 Rahall	Y	Y	Y	Y	Y	Y	Y	Y
WISCONSIN								
1 ***Ryan***	Y	Y	Y	Y	Y	Y	Y	Y
2 Baldwin	Y	Y	Y	Y	Y	Y	Y	N
3 Kind	Y	Y	Y	Y	Y	Y	Y	Y
4 Kleczka	Y	Y	Y	Y	Y	Y	Y	Y
5 Barrett	Y	Y	Y	Y	Y	Y	Y	?
6 ***Petri***	Y	Y	Y	Y	Y	Y	Y	Y
7 Obey	Y	Y	Y	Y	Y	Y	Y	N
8 ***Green***	Y	Y	Y	Y	Y	Y	Y	Y
9 ***Sensenbrenner***	Y	Y	Y	Y	Y	Y	Y	Y
WYOMING								
AL ***Cubin***	Y	Y	Y	Y	Y	Y	Y	Y

Southern states - Ala., Ark., Fla., Ga., Ky., La., Miss., N.C., Okla., S.C., Tenn., Texas, Va.

571. H J Res 118. Continuing Resolution/Passage. Passage of the joint resolution that would provide temporary funding authority, at current levels, until Oct. 29, for the departments and programs for which regular fiscal 2001 appropriations are not enacted by Oct. 28. Passed 339-7: R 179-0; D 158-7 (ND 120-6, SD 38-1); I 2-0. Oct. 28, 2000.

572. HR 4577. Fiscal 2001 Labor-HHS-Education Appropriations/Motion to Instruct. DeLauro, D-Conn., motion to instruct House conferees to insist on the highest funding level possible for the Low-Income Home Energy Assistance Program in fiscal 2001 and 2002. Motion agreed to 305-18: R 148-18; D 155-0 (ND 119-0, SD 36-0); I 2-0. Oct. 28, 2000.

573. HR 4577. Fiscal 2001 Labor-HHS-Education Appropriations/Motion to Instruct. Lowey, D-N.Y., motion to instruct House conferees to insist on disagreeing with provisions in the Senate bill that deny the president's requests for dedicated resources to reduce class size in the early grades and for local school construction. Motion rejected 150-159: R 4-154; D 145-4 (ND 112-3, SD 33-1); I 1-1. Oct. 28, 2000.

574. Procedural Motion/Journal. Approval of the House Journal of Saturday, Oct. 28, 2000. Approved 286-42: R 168-12; D 117-30 (ND 83-26, SD 34-4); I 1-0. Oct. 29, 2000.

575. H J Res 119. Continuing Resolution/Passage. Passage of the joint resolution that would provide temporary funding authority, at current levels, until Oct. 30, for the departments and programs for which regular fiscal 2001 appropriations are not enacted by Oct. 29. Passed 342-7: R 187-1; D 153-6 (ND 115-6, SD 38-0); I 2-0. Oct. 29, 2000.

576. HR 4577. Fiscal 2001 Labor-HHS-Education Appropriations/Motion to Instruct. Pallone, D-N.J., motion to instruct House conferees to require Medicare+Choice organizations to offer plans for a minimum contract period of three years, and to maintain the benefits specified under the contract for three years. Motion rejected 170-183: R 14-176; D 155-6 (ND 115-6, SD 40-0); I 1-1. Oct. 29, 2000.

577. Procedural Motion/Journal. Approval of the House Journal of Sunday, Oct. 29, 2000. Approved 298-47: R 174-11; D 122-36 (ND 85-32, SD 38-3); I 2-0. Oct. 30, 2000.

578. H J Res 120. Continuing Resolution/Passage. Passage of the joint resolution that would provide temporary funding authority, at current levels, until Oct. 31, for the departments and programs for which regular fiscal 2001 appropriations are not enacted by Oct. 30. Passed 339-9: R 185-1; D 152-8 (ND 111-7, SD 41-1); I 2-0. Oct. 30, 2000.

Key

- Y Voted for (yea).
- \# Paired for.
- \+ Announced for.
- N Voted against (nay).
- X Paired against.
- – Announced against.
- P Voted "present."
- C Voted "present" to avoid possible conflict of interest.
- ? Did not vote or otherwise make a position known.

Democrats ***Republicans***
Independents

	571	572	573	574	575	576	577	578
ALABAMA								
1 ***Callahan***	Y	Y	N	Y	Y	N	Y	Y
2 ***Everett***	Y	Y	N	Y	Y	N	+	+
3 ***Riley***	Y	Y	N	+	+	–	+	+
4 ***Aderholt***	Y	Y	N	Y	Y	Y	N	Y
5 Cramer	Y	Y	Y	Y	Y	Y	Y	Y
6 ***Bachus***	Y	Y	N	Y	Y	N	Y	Y
7 Hilliard	?	?	?	?	?	?	?	?
ALASKA								
AL ***Young***	Y	Y	N	Y	Y	N	?	Y
ARIZONA								
1 ***Salmon***	Y	N	N	Y	Y	N	Y	Y
2 Pastor	Y	Y	Y	N	Y	Y	Y	Y
3 ***Stump***	Y	Y	N	Y	Y	N	Y	Y
4 ***Shadegg***	Y	Y	N	Y	Y	N	Y	Y
5 ***Kolbe***	+	–	–	+	+	–	+	+
6 ***Hayworth***	Y	Y	N	Y	Y	N	Y	Y
ARKANSAS								
1 Berry	Y	Y	Y	Y	Y	Y	Y	Y
2 Snyder	Y	Y	Y	?	?	?	?	?
3 ***Hutchinson***	Y	Y	N	Y	Y	N	Y	Y
4 ***Dickey***	?	?	?	?	?	?	?	?
CALIFORNIA								
1 Thompson	Y	Y	Y	N	Y	Y	N	Y
2 ***Herger***	Y	Y	N	Y	Y	N	Y	Y
3 ***Ose***	Y	Y	N	Y	Y	N	Y	Y
4 ***Doolittle***	Y	N	N	Y	Y	N	Y	Y
5 Matsui	Y	Y	Y	Y	Y	Y	Y	Y
6 Woolsey	Y	Y	Y	Y	Y	Y	Y	Y
7 Miller, George	N	Y	Y	N	N	Y	N	N
8 Pelosi	Y	Y	Y	Y	Y	Y	Y	Y
9 Lee	Y	Y	Y	N	Y	Y	Y	Y
10 Tauscher	Y	Y	Y	Y	Y	Y	Y	Y
11 ***Pombo***	Y	Y	N	Y	Y	N	Y	Y
12 Lantos	?	?	?	?	?	?	?	?
13 Stark	?	?	?	?	?	?	?	?
14 Eshoo	Y	Y	Y	Y	Y	Y	Y	Y
15 ***Campbell***	?	?	?	?	?	?	?	?
16 Lofgren	Y	Y	Y	Y	Y	Y	Y	Y
17 Farr	Y	Y	Y	Y	Y	Y	Y	Y
18 Condit	Y	Y	Y	N	Y	Y	N	Y
19 ***Radanovich***	?	?	?	Y	Y	N	Y	Y
20 Dooley	Y	Y	?	?	?	?	Y	Y
21 ***Thomas***	Y	Y	N	Y	Y	N	Y	Y
22 Capps	Y	Y	Y	Y	Y	Y	Y	Y
23 ***Gallegly***	Y	Y	N	Y	Y	N	Y	Y
24 Sherman	Y	Y	Y	Y	Y	Y	Y	Y
25 ***McKeon***	?	?	?	Y	Y	N	Y	Y
26 Berman	Y	Y	Y	Y	Y	Y	Y	?
27 ***Rogan***	Y	Y	N	Y	Y	N	N	Y
28 ***Dreier***	Y	Y	N	Y	Y	N	Y	Y
29 Waxman	Y	Y	Y	Y	Y	Y	Y	?
30 Becerra	+	+	+	+	+	+	+	+
31 ***Martinez***	?	?	?	?	?	?	?	?
32 Dixon	Y	Y	Y	Y	Y	Y	Y	Y
33 Roybal-Allard	Y	Y	Y	Y	Y	Y	Y	?
34 Napolitano	Y	Y	Y	Y	Y	Y	Y	Y
35 Waters	?	Y	Y	Y	Y	Y	?	Y
36 ***Kuykendall***	Y	?	?	Y	Y	N	Y	Y
37 Millender-McD.	Y	Y	Y	?	Y	Y	Y	Y
38 ***Horn***	Y	Y	N	Y	Y	Y	Y	Y
39 ***Royce***	Y	N	N	Y	Y	N	Y	Y
40 ***Lewis***	Y	Y	N	Y	Y	N	Y	Y
41 ***Miller, Gary***	Y	Y	N	Y	Y	N	Y	Y
42 Baca	?	?	?	Y	Y	Y	Y	Y
43 ***Calvert***	?	?	?	Y	Y	N	Y	Y
44 ***Bono***	Y	Y	N	Y	Y	N	Y	Y
45 ***Rohrabacher***	Y	N	N	Y	Y	N	Y	Y
46 Sanchez	Y	Y	Y	+	+	+	N	Y
47 ***Cox***	?	?	?	Y	Y	N	?	Y
48 ***Packard***	Y	Y	N	Y	Y	N	Y	Y
49 ***Bilbray***	?	?	?	N	Y	Y	N	Y
50 Filner	Y	Y	Y	N	Y	Y	N	Y
51 ***Cunningham***	Y	Y	N	Y	Y	N	Y	Y
52 ***Hunter***	Y	Y	N	Y	Y	N	Y	Y
COLORADO								
1 DeGette	Y	Y	Y	Y	Y	Y	Y	Y
2 Udall	Y	Y	Y	Y	Y	Y	N	Y
3 ***McInnis***	?	?	?	?	?	?	?	?
4 ***Schaffer***	Y	Y	N	N	Y	N	N	Y
5 ***Hefley***	?	?	?	?	?	?	?	?
6 ***Tancredo***	Y	?	?	?	?	?	Y	Y
CONNECTICUT								
1 Larson	Y	Y	Y	Y	Y	Y	Y	Y
2 Gejdenson	Y	?	?	N	Y	Y	N	Y
3 DeLauro	Y	Y	Y	Y	Y	Y	Y	Y
4 ***Shays***	?	?	?	?	?	?	?	?
5 Maloney	Y	+	+	+	+	Y	Y	Y
6 ***Johnson***	Y	Y	Y	?	?	N	Y	Y
DELAWARE								
AL ***Castle***	Y	Y	N	Y	Y	N	Y	Y
FLORIDA								
1 ***Scarborough***	Y	Y	N	Y	Y	N	?	Y
2 Boyd	Y	Y	Y	Y	Y	Y	Y	Y
3 Brown	?	?	?	?	?	?	?	?
4 ***Fowler***	?	?	?	?	?	?	?	?
5 Thurman	Y	Y	Y	Y	Y	Y	Y	Y
6 ***Stearns***	Y	Y	N	Y	Y	N	Y	+
7 ***Mica***	Y	Y	N	Y	Y	N	Y	Y
8 ***McCollum***	?	?	?	?	?	?	?	?
9 ***Bilirakis***	Y	Y	N	Y	Y	N	Y	Y
10 ***Young***	Y	Y	N	Y	Y	N	Y	Y
11 Davis	Y	Y	Y	Y	Y	Y	Y	Y
12 ***Canady***	Y	Y	N	Y	Y	N	Y	Y
13 ***Miller***	Y	N	N	Y	Y	N	Y	Y
14 ***Goss***	Y	Y	N	Y	Y	N	Y	Y
15 ***Weldon***	?	?	?	Y	Y	N	Y	Y
16 ***Foley***	Y	Y	N	Y	Y	N	Y	Y
17 Meek	?	?	?	?	?	?	?	?
18 ***Ros-Lehtinen***	?	?	?	Y	Y	N	Y	Y
19 Wexler	Y	Y	?	Y	Y	Y	Y	Y
20 Deutsch	Y	Y	Y	Y	Y	Y	Y	Y
21 ***Diaz-Balart***	?	?	?	Y	Y	N	Y	Y
22 ***Shaw***	?	?	?	?	?	?	?	?
23 Hastings	?	?	?	?	?	?	?	?
GEORGIA								
1 ***Kingston***	Y	Y	?	N	Y	N	Y	Y
2 Bishop	?	?	?	?	?	?	Y	Y
3 ***Collins***	Y	Y	?	Y	Y	N	Y	Y
4 McKinney	Y	Y	Y	Y	Y	Y	Y	?
5 Lewis	Y	Y	Y	?	?	Y	Y	Y
6 ***Isakson***	Y	Y	N	Y	Y	N	Y	Y
7 ***Barr***	?	?	?	?	?	?	?	?
8 ***Chambliss***	Y	Y	N	Y	Y	N	Y	?
9 ***Deal***	Y	N	N	Y	Y	N	Y	Y
10 ***Norwood***	Y	Y	N	Y	Y	N	Y	Y
11 ***Linder***	Y	N	N	Y	Y	N	Y	Y
HAWAII								
1 Abercrombie	Y	Y	Y	+	+	+	+	+
2 Mink	Y	Y	Y	Y	Y	Y	Y	Y
IDAHO								
1 ***Chenoweth-Hage***	Y	Y	N	?	Y	N	Y	Y
2 ***Simpson***	Y	N	N	Y	Y	N	Y	Y
ILLINOIS								
1 Rush	?	?	?	Y	Y	Y	Y	?
2 Jackson	Y	Y	Y	Y	Y	Y	Y	Y
3 Lipinski	?	?	?	?	?	?	?	?
4 Gutierrez	Y	Y	?	?	?	?	?	?
5 Blagojevich	?	?	?	Y	Y	Y	Y	Y
6 ***Hyde***	Y	?	?	?	Y	?	Y	Y
7 Davis	?	?	?	?	?	?	?	?
8 ***Crane***	?	?	?	?	?	?	?	?
9 Schakowsky	Y	Y	Y	N	Y	Y	Y	Y
10 ***Porter***	?	?	?	Y	Y	N	?	?
11 ***Weller***	Y	+	+	N	Y	N	N	Y
12 Costello	Y	Y	Y	N	N	Y	N	N
13 ***Biggert***	Y	Y	N	Y	Y	N	Y	Y

ND Northern Democrats SD Southern Democrats

	571	572	573	574	575	576	577	578
14 ***Hastert***								
15 ***Ewing***	Y	Y	N	Y	Y	N	Y	Y
16 ***Manzullo***	Y	Y	N	Y	Y	N	Y	Y
17 Evans	Y	Y	Y	Y	Y	Y	Y	Y
18 ***LaHood***	Y	Y	?	Y	Y	N	Y	Y
19 Phelps	Y	Y	?	Y	Y	Y	N	N
20 ***Shimkus***	Y	?	?	Y	Y	N	Y	Y
INDIANA								
1 Visclosky	?	?	?	?	?	?	?	?
2 ***McIntosh***	?	?	?	?	?	?	?	?
3 Roemer	Y	Y	Y	Y	Y	Y	Y	Y
4 ***Souder***	Y	Y	N	Y	Y	N	Y	Y
5 ***Buyer***	Y	Y	N	Y	Y	N	Y	Y
6 ***Burton***	Y	Y	N	Y	Y	N	?	?
7 ***Pease***	Y	Y	N	Y	Y	N	Y	Y
8 ***Hostettler***	Y	N	N	Y	Y	N	Y	Y
9 Hill	Y	Y	Y	Y	Y	Y	Y	Y
10 Carson	Y	Y	Y	Y	Y	Y	Y	Y
IOWA								
1 ***Leach***	Y	Y	N	Y	Y	Y	Y	Y
2 ***Nussle***	Y	Y	N	Y	Y	N	Y	Y
3 Boswell	Y	Y	Y	Y	Y	Y	Y	Y
4 ***Ganske***	?	Y	N	Y	Y	Y	Y	Y
5 ***Latham***	Y	Y	N	N	Y	N	N	Y
KANSAS								
1 ***Moran***	Y	Y	N	N	Y	N	N	Y
2 ***Ryun***	Y	Y	N	Y	Y	N	Y	Y
3 Moore	Y	Y	Y	Y	Y	Y	Y	Y
4 ***Tiahrt***	Y	Y	N	Y	Y	N	Y	Y
KENTUCKY								
1 ***Whitfield***	Y	Y	N	Y	Y	N	Y	Y
2 ***Lewis***	Y	Y	N	Y	Y	N	Y	Y
3 ***Northup***	Y	Y	N	Y	Y	N	Y	Y
4 Lucas	Y	Y	Y	Y	Y	Y	Y	Y
5 ***Rogers***	Y	Y	N	Y	Y	N	Y	Y
6 ***Fletcher***	Y	Y	?	Y	Y	N	Y	Y
LOUISIANA								
1 ***Vitter***	Y	Y	N	Y	Y	N	Y	Y
2 Jefferson	Y	Y	Y	Y	Y	Y	?	Y
3 ***Tauzin***	Y	Y	N	Y	Y	N	Y	Y
4 ***McCrery***	Y	Y	N	Y	Y	N	Y	Y
5 ***Cooksey***	Y	Y	N	?	?	?	?	?
6 ***Baker***	Y	Y	N	Y	Y	N	Y	Y
7 John	Y	Y	Y	Y	Y	Y	Y	Y
MAINE								
1 Allen	Y	Y	Y	?	?	?	?	?
2 Baldacci	Y	Y	Y	Y	Y	Y	Y	Y
MARYLAND								
1 ***Gilchrest***	Y	Y	N	Y	Y	N	Y	Y
2 ***Ehrlich***	Y	Y	N	Y	Y	N	Y	Y
3 Cardin	Y	Y	Y	Y	Y	Y	?	?
4 Wynn	?	?	?	?	?	?	Y	Y
5 Hoyer	Y	Y	Y	?	Y	Y	Y	Y
6 ***Bartlett***	Y	Y	N	Y	Y	N	Y	Y
7 Cummings	Y	Y	Y	Y	Y	Y	Y	Y
8 ***Morella***	?	?	?	Y	Y	Y	?	?
MASSACHUSETTS								
1 Olver	Y	Y	Y	N	Y	Y	N	Y
2 Neal	?	?	?	N	Y	Y	?	?
3 McGovern	Y	Y	Y	N	Y	Y	N	Y
4 Frank	?	?	?	?	?	?	?	?
5 Meehan	Y	Y	Y	?	?	?	?	?
6 Tierney	Y	Y	Y	Y	Y	Y	Y	Y
7 Markey	Y	Y	Y	Y	Y	Y	N	Y
8 Capuano	N	Y	Y	N	N	Y	N	Y
9 Moakley	Y	Y	Y	Y	Y	Y	Y	Y
10 Delahunt	?	?	?	?	?	?	?	?
MICHIGAN								
1 Stupak	N	?	?	?	?	?	N	N
2 ***Hoekstra***	Y	Y	N	Y	Y	N	Y	Y
3 ***Ehlers***	Y	+	–	Y	Y	N	Y	Y
4 ***Camp***	Y	Y	N	Y	Y	N	Y	Y
5 Barcia	Y	Y	Y	Y	Y	Y	Y	Y
6 ***Upton***	Y	Y	N	Y	Y	N	Y	Y
7 ***Smith***	Y	N	N	Y	Y	N	Y	Y
8 Stabenow	Y	Y	Y	?	Y	Y	?	Y
9 Kildee	Y	Y	Y	Y	Y	Y	Y	Y
10 Bonior	Y	Y	Y	Y	Y	Y	Y	Y
11 ***Knollenberg***	Y	Y	N	Y	Y	N	Y	Y
12 Levin	Y	Y	Y	Y	Y	Y	Y	Y
13 Rivers	Y	Y	Y	Y	Y	Y	Y	Y
14 Conyers	Y	Y	Y	?	?	?	?	?
15 Kilpatrick	Y	Y	Y	?	?	?	?	?
16 Dingell	N	Y	Y	Y	N	Y	?	N

	571	572	573	574	575	576	577	578
MINNESOTA								
1 ***Gutknecht***	Y	Y	N	N	Y	N	Y	Y
2 Minge	Y	Y	Y	Y	Y	N	Y	Y
3 ***Ramstad***	Y	Y	N	N	Y	N	N	Y
4 Vacant								
5 Sabo	Y	Y	?	N	Y	N	N	Y
6 Luther	Y	Y	Y	Y	Y	Y	Y	Y
7 Peterson	Y	Y	N	N	Y	N	N	Y
8 Oberstar	Y	Y	Y	N	Y	N	N	Y
MISSISSIPPI								
1 ***Wicker***	Y	Y	N	N	Y	N	Y	Y
2 Thompson	?	?	?	?	?	?	?	?
3 ***Pickering***	?	?	?	Y	Y	N	?	?
4 Shows	Y	Y	Y	Y	Y	Y	Y	Y
5 Taylor	?	?	?	N	Y	Y	?	Y
MISSOURI								
1 Clay	?	?	?	?	?	?	?	?
2 ***Talent***	?	?	?	?	?	?	?	?
3 Gephardt	Y	?	?	Y	Y	Y	?	Y
4 Skelton	Y	Y	Y	Y	Y	Y	Y	Y
5 McCarthy	+	+	+	Y	Y	Y	Y	Y
6 Danner	?	?	?	?	?	?	?	?
7 ***Blunt***	Y	Y	N	Y	Y	N	Y	Y
8 ***Emerson***	Y	Y	N	Y	Y	Y	Y	Y
9 ***Hulshof***	?	?	?	?	?	?	?	?
MONTANA								
AL ***Hill***	Y	Y	N	Y	Y	N	Y	Y
NEBRASKA								
1 ***Bereuter***	Y	Y	N	?	?	?	Y	Y
2 ***Terry***	Y	Y	N	Y	Y	N	Y	Y
3 ***Barrett***	Y	Y	N	Y	Y	N	Y	Y
NEVADA								
1 Berkley	Y	Y	Y	Y	Y	Y	Y	Y
2 ***Gibbons***	Y	Y	N	Y	Y	N	Y	Y
NEW HAMPSHIRE								
1 ***Sununu***	Y	Y	N	Y	Y	N	Y	Y
2 ***Bass***	Y	Y	N	Y	Y	N	Y	Y
NEW JERSEY								
1 Andrews	?	?	?	Y	Y	Y	Y	Y
2 ***LoBiondo***	Y	Y	Y	N	Y	Y	N	Y
3 ***Saxton***	Y	Y	N	Y	Y	Y	Y	Y
4 ***Smith***	Y	Y	N	Y	Y	Y	Y	Y
5 ***Roukema***	Y	?	?	Y	Y	Y	Y	Y
6 Pallone	Y	Y	Y	?	Y	Y	N	Y
7 ***Franks***	?	?	?	?	?	?	?	?
8 Pascrell	Y	?	?	Y	Y	?	?	?
9 Rothman	Y	Y	Y	N	Y	Y	N	Y
10 Payne	Y	Y	Y	Y	Y	Y	Y	?
11 ***Frelinghuysen***	Y	Y	N	Y	Y	N	Y	Y
12 Holt	Y	Y	Y	N	Y	Y	N	Y
13 Menendez	Y	Y	Y	?	?	?	?	Y
NEW MEXICO								
1 ***Wilson***	Y	Y	N	Y	Y	Y	Y	Y
2 ***Skeen***	Y	Y	N	Y	Y	N	Y	Y
3 Udall	Y	Y	Y	N	Y	Y	N	Y
NEW YORK								
1 Forbes	Y	Y	Y	?	?	?	?	?
2 ***Lazio***	?	?	?	?	?	?	?	?
3 ***King***	?	?	?	Y	Y	N	?	?
4 McCarthy	Y	Y	Y	Y	Y	Y	Y	Y
5 Ackerman	?	?	?	?	Y	Y	?	?
6 Meeks	Y	Y	Y	Y	Y	Y	Y	Y
7 Crowley	?	?	?	?	?	?	?	?
8 Nadler	Y	Y	Y	Y	Y	Y	Y	Y
9 Weiner	Y	Y	Y	?	?	Y	Y	Y
10 Towns	Y	Y	Y	?	Y	Y	Y	Y
11 Owens	?	?	?	?	?	?	Y	Y
12 Velázquez	Y	Y	Y	?	Y	Y	N	Y
13 ***Fossella***	?	?	?	?	Y	N	Y	Y
14 Maloney	Y	Y	Y	?	Y	Y	+	+
15 Rangel	Y	Y	Y	Y	Y	Y	Y	Y
16 Serrano	Y	Y	Y	Y	Y	Y	Y	Y
17 Engel	Y	Y	Y	?	Y	Y	Y	Y
18 Lowey	Y	Y	Y	?	Y	Y	Y	Y
19 ***Kelly***	Y	Y	N	Y	Y	N	Y	Y
20 ***Gilman***	Y	Y	Y	?	Y	Y	Y	Y
21 McNulty	Y	Y	Y	Y	Y	Y	Y	Y
22 ***Sweeney***	Y	Y	N	?	Y	N	N	Y
23 ***Boehlert***	Y	Y	N	Y	Y	N	Y	Y
24 ***McHugh***	Y	?	?	Y	Y	Y	Y	Y
25 ***Walsh***	Y	Y	N	Y	Y	N	Y	Y
26 Hinchey	Y	Y	Y	+	+	Y	?	Y
27 ***Reynolds***	Y	Y	N	Y	Y	N	Y	Y
28 Slaughter	Y	Y	Y	?	Y	Y	N	Y
29 LaFalce	?	?	?	?	?	?	?	?

	571	572	573	574	575	576	577	578
30 ***Quinn***	Y	Y	Y	?	Y	N	Y	Y
31 ***Houghton***	Y	?	?	Y	?	N	Y	Y
NORTH CAROLINA								
1 Clayton	Y	Y	Y	?	?	?	Y	Y
2 Etheridge	Y	Y	Y	Y	Y	Y	Y	Y
3 ***Jones***	Y	?	?	Y	Y	Y	Y	Y
4 Price	Y	Y	Y	Y	Y	Y	Y	Y
5 ***Burr***	Y	Y	N	Y	Y	N	Y	Y
6 ***Coble***	Y	N	N	Y	Y	N	Y	Y
7 McIntyre	+	+	+	+	+	+	+	+
8 ***Hayes***	Y	Y	N	Y	Y	N	Y	Y
9 ***Myrick***	Y	Y	N	Y	Y	N	Y	Y
10 ***Ballenger***	Y	Y	N	Y	Y	N	Y	Y
11 ***Taylor***	?	?	?	Y	Y	N	Y	Y
12 Watt	?	?	?	Y	Y	Y	Y	Y
NORTH DAKOTA								
AL Pomeroy	Y	Y	Y	Y	Y	Y	Y	Y
OHIO								
1 ***Chabot***	Y	Y	N	Y	Y	N	Y	Y
2 ***Portman***	Y	Y	?	Y	Y	N	Y	Y
3 Hall	Y	Y	Y	Y	Y	Y	Y	Y
4 ***Oxley***	Y	Y	N	?	?	?	?	?
5 ***Gillmor***	?	?	?	?	?	?	Y	Y
6 Strickland	Y	Y	Y	Y	Y	Y	N	Y
7 ***Hobson***	Y	Y	N	Y	Y	N	Y	Y
8 ***Boehner***	Y	Y	N	Y	Y	N	Y	Y
9 Kaptur	?	?	?	?	?	?	?	?
10 Kucinich	Y	Y	Y	N	Y	Y	N	Y
11 Jones	Y	Y	Y	Y	Y	Y	?	?
12 ***Kasich***	?	?	?	?	?	?	?	?
13 Brown	?	?	?	Y	Y	Y	Y	Y
14 Sawyer	Y	?	?	Y	Y	Y	Y	Y
15 ***Pryce***	Y	Y	N	?	Y	N	Y	Y
16 ***Regula***	Y	Y	N	Y	Y	N	Y	Y
17 Traficant	Y	Y	N	Y	Y	N	Y	Y
18 ***Ney***	Y	Y	N	Y	Y	N	Y	Y
19 ***LaTourette***	Y	?	?	?	?	?	Y	Y
OKLAHOMA								
1 ***Largent***	Y	N	N	Y	Y	N	Y	Y
2 ***Coburn***	Y	Y	?	N	Y	N	Y	Y
3 ***Watkins***	Y	?	?	?	?	?	?	?
4 ***Watts***	+	+	–	?	+	–	?	+
5 ***Istook***	Y	Y	N	Y	Y	N	Y	Y
6 ***Lucas***	Y	Y	N	Y	Y	N	Y	Y
OREGON								
1 Wu	Y	Y	Y	N	Y	Y	N	Y
2 ***Walden***	Y	Y	N	Y	Y	N	Y	Y
3 Blumenauer	Y	Y	Y	Y	Y	Y	Y	Y
4 DeFazio	N	Y	Y	N	N	Y	N	N
5 Hooley	Y	Y	Y	Y	Y	Y	N	Y
PENNSYLVANIA								
1 Brady	Y	Y	Y	N	Y	?	?	?
2 Fattah	Y	Y	Y	?	Y	Y	?	?
3 Borski	Y	Y	Y	N	Y	Y	N	Y
4 Klink	?	?	?	?	?	?	?	?
5 ***Peterson***	?	?	?	Y	Y	N	Y	Y
6 Holden	Y	Y	Y	Y	Y	Y	Y	Y
7 ***Weldon***	Y	Y	N	Y	Y	N	Y	Y
8 ***Greenwood***	Y	Y	N	?	?	N	Y	?
9 ***Shuster***	?	?	?	?	?	?	?	?
10 ***Sherwood***	Y	Y	N	Y	Y	N	Y	Y
11 Kanjorski	?	?	?	?	?	?	?	?
12 Murtha	Y	Y	?	Y	Y	?	Y	Y
13 Hoeffel	Y	Y	Y	Y	Y	Y	Y	Y
14 Coyne	Y	Y	Y	Y	Y	Y	Y	Y
15 ***Toomey***	Y	N	N	Y	Y	N	Y	Y
16 ***Pitts***	Y	Y	N	Y	Y	N	Y	Y
17 ***Gekas***	Y	Y	N	Y	Y	N	Y	Y
18 Doyle	Y	Y	Y	Y	Y	Y	Y	Y
19 ***Goodling***	Y	Y	N	?	Y	N	Y	Y
20 Mascara	Y	Y	Y	Y	Y	Y	Y	Y
21 ***English***	Y	Y	N	N	Y	N	N	Y
RHODE ISLAND								
1 Kennedy	?	?	?	?	?	?	Y	Y
2 Weygand	?	?	?	?	?	?	?	?
SOUTH CAROLINA								
1 ***Sanford***	Y	N	N	Y	Y	N	Y	Y
2 ***Spence***	Y	Y	N	Y	Y	N	Y	Y
3 ***Graham***	Y	Y	N	Y	Y	N	Y	Y
4 ***DeMint***	Y	Y	N	Y	Y	N	Y	Y
5 Spratt	?	?	?	?	?	?	?	?
6 Clyburn	?	?	?	N	Y	Y	N	Y
SOUTH DAKOTA								
AL ***Thune***	Y	Y	N	Y	Y	N	Y	Y

	571	572	573	574	575	576	577	578
TENNESSEE								
1 ***Jenkins***	Y	Y	N	Y	Y	N	Y	Y
2 ***Duncan***	?	?	?	Y	Y	N	Y	?
3 ***Wamp***	Y	Y	N	Y	Y	N	Y	Y
4 ***Hilleary***	Y	Y	N	Y	Y	N	Y	Y
5 Clement	Y	Y	Y	Y	Y	Y	Y	Y
6 Gordon	?	?	?	Y	Y	?	Y	Y
7 ***Bryant***	Y	?	?	Y	Y	N	Y	Y
8 Tanner	Y	Y	Y	Y	Y	Y	Y	Y
9 Ford	N	Y	Y	?	?	Y	N	N
TEXAS								
1 Sandlin	Y	Y	Y	Y	Y	Y	Y	Y
2 Turner	Y	Y	Y	Y	Y	Y	Y	Y
3 ***Johnson, Sam***	Y	N	N	Y	Y	N	?	Y
4 Hall	Y	Y	N	Y	Y	Y	Y	Y
5 ***Sessions***	?	?	?	Y	Y	N	Y	Y
6 ***Barton***	?	?	?	Y	N	N	?	N
7 ***Archer***	Y	N	N	?	?	?	Y	Y
8 ***Brady***	Y	Y	N	Y	Y	N	Y	Y
9 Lampson	Y	Y	Y	Y	Y	Y	Y	Y
10 Doggett	Y	Y	Y	Y	Y	Y	Y	Y
11 Edwards	Y	?	?	Y	Y	Y	?	Y
12 ***Granger***	Y	Y	N	Y	Y	N	Y	Y
13 ***Thornberry***	Y	Y	N	Y	Y	N	Y	Y
14 ***Paul***	Y	N	N	Y	Y	N	Y	Y
15 Hinojosa	Y	Y	Y	Y	Y	Y	Y	Y
16 Reyes	Y	Y	Y	Y	Y	Y	Y	Y
17 Stenholm	Y	Y	Y	N	Y	Y	N	Y
18 Jackson-Lee	Y	Y	Y	N	Y	Y	Y	Y
19 ***Combest***	Y	Y	N	Y	Y	N	Y	Y
20 Gonzalez	Y	Y	Y	Y	Y	Y	Y	Y
21 ***Smith***	Y	Y	N	Y	Y	N	Y	Y
22 ***DeLay***	Y	Y	N	Y	Y	N	Y	Y
23 ***Bonilla***	Y	Y	N	Y	Y	N	Y	Y
24 Frost	Y	?	?	Y	Y	Y	Y	Y
25 Bentsen	?	?	?	Y	Y	Y	Y	Y
26 ***Armey***	Y	Y	N	Y	Y	N	Y	Y
27 Ortiz	Y	Y	Y	Y	Y	Y	Y	Y
28 Rodriguez	Y	Y	Y	Y	Y	Y	Y	Y
29 Green	Y	?	?	Y	Y	Y	Y	Y
30 Johnson, E.B.	Y	Y	Y	+	+	Y	?	?
UTAH								
1 ***Hansen***	Y	Y	N	Y	Y	N	Y	Y
2 ***Cook***	Y	Y	N	Y	Y	N	Y	Y
3 ***Cannon***	Y	N	N	Y	Y	N	Y	Y
VERMONT								
AL *Sanders*	Y	Y	Y	Y	Y	Y	Y	Y
VIRGINIA								
1 Vacant								
2 Pickett	?	?	?	?	?	?	?	?
3 Scott	Y	Y	Y	Y	Y	Y	Y	Y
4 Sisisky	Y	Y	?	Y	Y	Y	Y	Y
5 *Goode*	Y	Y	N	?	Y	N	Y	Y
6 ***Goodlatte***	Y	Y	?	?	Y	N	Y	Y
7 ***Bliley***	Y	Y	N	Y	Y	N	Y	Y
8 Moran	Y	Y	Y	?	?	?	Y	Y
9 Boucher	?	?	?	?	?	?	?	?
10 ***Wolf***	Y	Y	N	Y	Y	N	Y	Y
11 ***Davis***	Y	Y	?	Y	Y	N	Y	Y
WASHINGTON								
1 Inslee	Y	Y	Y	Y	Y	Y	Y	Y
2 ***Metcalf***	?	?	?	?	?	?	?	?
3 Baird	N	Y	Y	N	N	Y	N	N
4 ***Hastings***	Y	Y	N	Y	Y	N	Y	Y
5 ***Nethercutt***	Y	Y	N	Y	Y	N	Y	Y
6 Dicks	Y	Y	Y	Y	Y	Y	Y	Y
7 McDermott	Y	Y	Y	N	Y	Y	N	Y
8 ***Dunn***	?	?	?	Y	Y	N	Y	Y
9 Smith	Y	Y	N	Y	Y	N	Y	Y
WEST VIRGINIA								
1 Mollohan	Y	?	Y	Y	Y	Y	Y	Y
2 Wise	?	?	?	?	?	?	?	?
3 Rahall	Y	Y	Y	Y	Y	Y	Y	Y
WISCONSIN								
1 ***Ryan***	Y	Y	N	Y	Y	N	Y	Y
2 Baldwin	Y	Y	Y	Y	Y	Y	Y	Y
3 Kind	Y	?	?	?	Y	Y	Y	Y
4 Kleczka	Y	Y	Y	Y	Y	Y	Y	Y
5 Barrett	Y	Y	Y	Y	Y	Y	Y	Y
6 ***Petri***	Y	Y	N	Y	Y	N	Y	Y
7 Obey	Y	Y	Y	Y	Y	Y	N	Y
8 ***Green***	Y	Y	N	Y	Y	N	Y	Y
9 ***Sensenbrenner***	Y	?	?	Y	Y	N	Y	Y
WYOMING								
AL ***Cubin***	Y	Y	N	Y	Y	N	Y	Y

Southern states - Ala., Ark., Fla., Ga., Ky., La., Miss., N.C., Okla., S.C., Tenn., Texas, Va.

579. Procedural Motion/Hour of Meeting. Linder, R-Ga., motion that when the House adjourns Oct. 30, it reconvene at 6 p.m. on Tuesday, Oct. 31. Motion agreed to 199-159: R 189-1; D 9-157 (ND 8-115, SD 1-42); I 1-1. Oct. 30, 2000.

580. H J Res 121, H J Res 122, H J Res 123, H J Res 142. Continuing Resolutions/Previous Question. Linder, R-Ga., motion to order the previous question (thus ending debate and possibility of amendment) on adoption of the rule (H Res 662) to provide for House floor consideration of the joint resolutions that would make further continuing appropriations for fiscal year 2001. Motion agreed to 286-73: R 190-0; D 94-73 (ND 79-46, SD 15-27); I 2-0. Oct. 30, 2000.

581. H J Res 121, H J Res 122, H J Res 123, H J Res 142. Continuing Resolutions/Rule. Adoption of the rule (H Res 662) to provide for House floor consideration of the joint resolutions that would make further continuing appropriations for fiscal year 2001. Adopted 296-64: R 189-0; D 105-64 (ND 82-45, SD 23-19); I 2-0. Oct. 30, 2000.

582. S 2485. St. Croix Islands Heritage Center/Previous Question. Diaz-Balart, R-Fla., motion to order the previous question (thus ending debate and possibility of amendment) on adoption of the rule (H Res 663) to provide for House floor consideration of the bill that would direct the Interior secretary to provide assistance in planning and constructing a regional heritage center in Calais, Maine, and would also amend HR 2614 to reinstate the minimum wage from June 30 through Dec. 31, 2000. Motion agreed to 189-169: R 184-0; D 4-168 (ND 3-123, SD 1-45); I 1-1. Oct. 30, 2000. (Subsequently, S 2485 passed by voice vote.)

583. S 2485. St. Croix Islands Heritage Center/Rule. Adoption of the rule (H Res 663) to provide for House floor consideration of the bill that would direct the Interior secretary to provide assistance in planning and constructing a regional heritage center in Calais, Maine, and would also amend HR 2614 to reinstate the minimum wage from June 30 through Dec. 31, 2000. Adopted 348-0: R 181-0; D 165-0 (ND 123-0, SD 42-0); I 2-0. Oct. 30, 2000.

584. Procedural Motion/Journal. Approval of the House Journal of Monday, Oct. 30, 2000. Approved 291-70: R 167-16; D 123-54 (ND 87-44, SD 36-10); I 1-0. Oct. 31, 2000.

585. H J Res 121. Continuing Resolution/Passage. Passage of the joint resolution that would provide temporary funding authority, at current levels, until Nov. 1, for the departments and programs for which regular fiscal 2001 appropriations are not enacted by Oct. 31. Passed 361-13: R 187-1; D 172-12 (ND 125-10, SD 47-2); I 2-0. Oct. 31, 2000.

586. Procedural Motion/Journal. Approval of the House Journal of Tuesday, Oct. 31, 2000. Approved 313-58: R 172-14; D 139-44 (ND 99-38, SD 40-6); I 2-0. Nov. 1, 2000.

Key

- Y Voted for (yea).
- # Paired for.
- + Announced for.
- N Voted against (nay).
- X Paired against.
- – Announced against.
- P Voted "present."
- C Voted "present" to avoid possible conflict of interest.
- ? Did not vote or otherwise make a position known.

•

Democrats ***Republicans***
Independents

	579	580	581	582	583	584	585	586
ALABAMA								
1 ***Callahan***	Y	Y	Y	Y	Y	Y	Y	Y
2 ***Everett***	+	+	+	+	+	Y	Y	Y
3 ***Riley***	+	+	+	?	?	Y	Y	Y
4 ***Aderholt***	Y	Y	Y	Y	Y	Y	Y	Y
5 Cramer	N	Y	Y	N	Y	Y	Y	Y
6 ***Bachus***	Y	Y	Y	Y	Y	Y	Y	Y
7 Hilliard	?	?	?	?	?	N	N	N
ALASKA								
AL ***Young***	Y	Y	Y	Y	Y	Y	Y	?
ARIZONA								
1 ***Salmon***	Y	Y	Y	Y	Y	?	?	?
2 Pastor	N	N	N	N	Y	Y	Y	Y
3 ***Stump***	Y	Y	Y	Y	Y	Y	Y	Y
4 ***Shadegg***	Y	Y	Y	Y	Y	Y	Y	Y
5 ***Kolbe***	+	+	+	+	+	Y	Y	Y
6 ***Hayworth***	Y	Y	Y	Y	Y	Y	Y	Y
ARKANSAS								
1 Berry	N	N	N	N	Y	N	Y	Y
2 Snyder	?	?	?	?	?	Y	Y	Y
3 ***Hutchinson***	Y	Y	Y	Y	Y	Y	Y	Y
4 ***Dickey***	?	?	?	?	?	?	?	?
CALIFORNIA								
1 Thompson	N	N	N	N	Y	N	Y	N
2 ***Herger***	Y	Y	Y	Y	Y	Y	Y	Y
3 ***Ose***	Y	Y	Y	?	?	?	?	?
4 ***Doolittle***	Y	Y	Y	Y	Y	Y	Y	Y
5 Matsui	N	Y	Y	N	Y	Y	Y	Y
6 Woolsey	N	N	N	N	Y	Y	Y	Y
7 Miller, George	N	N	N	N	Y	N	N	N
8 Pelosi	N	N	N	N	Y	Y	Y	Y
9 Lee	N	N	N	N	Y	Y	Y	Y
10 Tauscher	N	N	Y	N	Y	Y	Y	Y
11 ***Pombo***	Y	Y	Y	Y	Y	Y	Y	Y
12 Lantos	?	?	?	?	?	?	?	?
13 Stark	?	?	?	?	?	Y	?	N
14 Eshoo	N	Y	Y	N	Y	Y	Y	Y
15 ***Campbell***	?	?	?	?	?	?	?	?
16 Lofgren	N	Y	N	N	Y	Y	Y	Y
17 Farr	N	N	Y	N	Y	Y	Y	Y
18 Condit	N	N	N	N	Y	Y	Y	N
19 ***Radanovich***	Y	?	?	?	?	Y	Y	Y
20 Dooley	N	Y	Y	N	Y	?	?	?
21 ***Thomas***	Y	Y	Y	Y	Y	Y	Y	Y
22 Capps	N	Y	Y	N	Y	Y	Y	Y
23 ***Gallegly***	Y	Y	Y	Y	Y	Y	Y	Y
24 Sherman	N	Y	Y	N	Y	Y	Y	Y
25 ***McKeon***	Y	Y	Y	Y	Y	Y	Y	Y
26 Berman	N	N	Y	N	Y	Y	Y	Y
27 ***Rogan***	Y	Y	Y	Y	Y	Y	Y	Y
28 ***Dreier***	Y	Y	Y	Y	Y	Y	Y	Y
29 Waxman	N	N	Y	N	Y	?	?	?
30 Becerra	N	N	N	N	Y	N	Y	N
31 ***Martinez***	?	?	?	?	?	Y	Y	?
32 Dixon	N	Y	Y	N	Y	Y	Y	Y
33 Roybal-Allard	N	N	Y	N	Y	Y	Y	Y
34 Napolitano	N	Y	Y	N	Y	Y	Y	Y
35 Waters	N	N	N	N	?	?	?	?
36 ***Kuykendall***	Y	Y	Y	Y	Y	Y	Y	Y
37 Millender-McD.	N	Y	Y	N	Y	Y	Y	Y
38 ***Horn***	Y	Y	?	Y	Y	Y	Y	Y
39 ***Royce***	Y	Y	Y	Y	Y	Y	Y	Y
40 ***Lewis***	Y	Y	Y	Y	Y	Y	Y	Y
41 ***Miller, Gary***	Y	Y	Y	Y	Y	Y	Y	Y
42 Baca	N	Y	Y	N	Y	Y	Y	Y
43 ***Calvert***	Y	Y	Y	Y	Y	Y	Y	Y
44 ***Bono***	Y	Y	Y	Y	Y	Y	Y	Y
45 ***Rohrabacher***	Y	Y	Y	Y	Y	Y	Y	Y
46 Sanchez	N	Y	Y	N	Y	N	Y	N
47 ***Cox***	Y	Y	Y	Y	Y	Y	Y	?
48 ***Packard***	Y	Y	Y	Y	Y	Y	Y	Y
49 ***Bilbray***	Y	Y	Y	Y	Y	N	?	?
50 Filner	N	N	N	N	Y	N	Y	N
51 ***Cunningham***	Y	Y	Y	Y	?	Y	Y	Y
52 ***Hunter***	Y	Y	Y	Y	Y	Y	Y	?
COLORADO								
1 DeGette	N	N	N	N	Y	?	?	Y
2 Udall	N	Y	N	N	Y	N	Y	Y
3 ***McInnis***	?	?	?	?	?	Y	Y	Y
4 ***Schaffer***	Y	Y	Y	Y	Y	Y	Y	N
5 ***Hefley***	?	?	?	?	?	N	Y	N
6 ***Tancredo***	Y	Y	Y	Y	Y	P	Y	P
CONNECTICUT								
1 Larson	N	Y	Y	N	Y	Y	Y	Y
2 Gejdenson	N	Y	Y	N	Y	N	Y	N
3 DeLauro	N	Y	N	N	Y	Y	Y	Y
4 ***Shays***	?	?	?	?	?	Y	Y	?
5 Maloney	N	Y	Y	N	Y	Y	Y	Y
6 ***Johnson***	Y	Y	Y	Y	Y	Y	Y	Y
DELAWARE								
AL ***Castle***	Y	Y	Y	Y	Y	Y	Y	Y
FLORIDA								
1 ***Scarborough***	Y	Y	Y	?	?	?	?	?
2 Boyd	N	–	–	N	Y	Y	Y	Y
3 Brown	?	?	?	?	?	?	?	?
4 ***Fowler***	?	?	?	?	?	?	?	?
5 Thurman	N	N	Y	N	Y	Y	Y	Y
6 ***Stearns***	?	+	+	+	+	Y	Y	Y
7 ***Mica***	Y	Y	Y	?	+	?	Y	?
8 ***McCollum***	?	?	?	?	?	?	?	?
9 ***Bilirakis***	Y	Y	Y	Y	Y	Y	Y	Y
10 ***Young***	Y	Y	Y	Y	Y	Y	Y	Y
11 Davis	N	Y	N	N	Y	N	Y	Y
12 ***Canady***	Y	Y	Y	Y	Y	?	?	?
13 ***Miller***	Y	Y	Y	Y	Y	Y	Y	Y
14 ***Goss***	Y	Y	Y	Y	Y	Y	Y	Y
15 ***Weldon***	Y	Y	Y	?	?	?	Y	Y
16 ***Foley***	Y	Y	Y	Y	Y	Y	Y	Y
17 Meek	?	Y	N	N	Y	Y	Y	Y
18 ***Ros-Lehtinen***	Y	Y	Y	Y	Y	?	?	Y
19 Wexler	N	Y	Y	N	Y	Y	Y	?
20 Deutsch	N	Y	Y	N	Y	Y	Y	Y
21 ***Diaz-Balart***	?	Y	Y	Y	Y	Y	Y	Y
22 ***Shaw***	?	?	?	?	?	?	?	?
23 Hastings	?	?	?	?	?	?	?	?
GEORGIA								
1 ***Kingston***	Y	Y	Y	Y	Y	?	?	Y
2 Bishop	N	Y	Y	N	?	Y	Y	Y
3 ***Collins***	Y	Y	Y	Y	Y	?	?	?
4 McKinney	N	N	Y	N	Y	Y	Y	Y
5 Lewis	N	N	N	N	Y	Y	Y	Y
6 ***Isakson***	Y	Y	Y	Y	Y	?	+	Y
7 ***Barr***	?	?	?	?	?	Y	Y	Y
8 ***Chambliss***	Y	Y	Y	Y	Y	Y	Y	Y
9 ***Deal***	Y	Y	Y	Y	Y	Y	Y	Y
10 ***Norwood***	Y	Y	Y	Y	Y	Y	Y	Y
11 ***Linder***	Y	Y	Y	Y	Y	Y	Y	Y
HAWAII								
1 Abercrombie	–	–	+	–	+	Y	Y	Y
2 Mink	N	Y	N	N	Y	Y	Y	Y
IDAHO								
1 ***Chenoweth-Hage***	Y	Y	Y	Y	Y	N	Y	Y
2 ***Simpson***	Y	Y	Y	Y	Y	Y	Y	Y
ILLINOIS								
1 Rush	N	N	Y	N	Y	Y	Y	Y
2 Jackson	N	N	N	N	Y	Y	Y	Y
3 Lipinski	?	?	?	?	?	Y	Y	Y
4 Gutierrez	?	N	Y	N	Y	N	Y	N
5 Blagojevich	N	Y	Y	N	Y	?	?	Y
6 ***Hyde***	Y	Y	Y	Y	Y	Y	Y	Y
7 Davis	?	?	?	?	?	Y	Y	Y
8 ***Crane***	?	?	?	?	?	N	Y	N
9 Schakowsky	N	Y	Y	N	Y	Y	Y	Y
10 ***Porter***	Y	Y	Y	Y	Y	Y	Y	Y
11 ***Weller***	Y	Y	Y	Y	Y	N	Y	N
12 Costello	N	N	N	N	Y	N	N	N
13 ***Biggert***	Y	Y	Y	Y	Y	Y	Y	Y

ND Northern Democrats SD Southern Democrats

	579	580	581	582	583	584	585	586
14 ***Hastert***	Y							
15 ***Ewing***	Y	Y	Y	Y	Y	Y	Y	Y
16 ***Manzullo***	Y	Y	Y	Y	Y	Y	Y	Y
17 Evans	N	Y	Y	N	Y	Y	Y	Y
18 ***LaHood***	Y	Y	Y	Y	Y	Y	Y	Y
19 Phelps	N	N	N	N	Y	Y	N	Y
20 ***Shimkus***	Y	Y	Y	Y	Y	Y	Y	Y
INDIANA								
1 Visclosky	?	?	N	N	Y	N	N	N
2 ***McIntosh***	?	?	?	?	?	?	?	?
3 Roemer	N	Y	Y	N	Y	Y	Y	Y
4 ***Souder***	Y	Y	Y	Y	Y	Y	Y	Y
5 ***Buyer***	Y	Y	Y	Y	Y	Y	Y	Y
6 ***Burton***	?	Y	Y	Y	Y	Y	Y	?
7 ***Pease***	Y	Y	Y	Y	Y	Y	Y	Y
8 ***Hostettler***	Y	Y	Y	Y	Y	?	?	Y
9 Hill	N	Y	Y	N	Y	Y	Y	Y
10 Carson	N	Y	N	N	Y	Y	Y	Y
IOWA								
1 ***Leach***	Y	Y	Y	Y	Y	Y	Y	Y
2 ***Nussle***	Y	Y	Y	Y	Y	Y	Y	Y
3 Boswell	N	N	Y	N	Y	Y	Y	Y
4 ***Ganske***	Y	Y	Y	Y	Y	Y	Y	Y
5 ***Latham***	Y	Y	Y	Y	Y	N	Y	N
KANSAS								
1 ***Moran***	Y	Y	Y	Y	Y	N	Y	N
2 ***Ryun***	Y	Y	Y	Y	Y	Y	Y	Y
3 Moore	N	Y	Y	N	Y	N	Y	Y
4 ***Tiahrt***	Y	Y	Y	Y	Y	?	+	Y
KENTUCKY								
1 ***Whitfield***	Y	Y	Y	?	?	Y	Y	Y
2 ***Lewis***	Y	Y	Y	Y	Y	Y	Y	Y
3 ***Northup***	Y	Y	Y	Y	Y	Y	Y	Y
4 Lucas	N	Y	Y	N	Y	Y	Y	Y
5 ***Rogers***	Y	Y	Y	Y	Y	Y	Y	Y
6 ***Fletcher***	Y	Y	Y	Y	Y	Y	Y	Y
LOUISIANA								
1 ***Vitter***	Y	Y	Y	Y	Y	Y	Y	Y
2 Jefferson	N	Y	Y	N	Y	Y	Y	Y
3 ***Tauzin***	Y	Y	Y	Y	Y	Y	Y	Y
4 ***McCrery***	Y	Y	Y	Y	Y	?	?	?
5 ***Cooksey***	?	?	?	?	?	Y	Y	Y
6 ***Baker***	Y	Y	Y	Y	Y	Y	Y	Y
7 John	N	Y	Y	N	Y	Y	Y	Y
MAINE								
1 Allen	?	?	?	?	?	Y	Y	Y
2 Baldacci	N	Y	Y	Y	Y	Y	Y	Y
MARYLAND								
1 ***Gilchrest***	Y	Y	Y	Y	Y	Y	Y	Y
2 ***Ehrlich***	Y	Y	Y	Y	Y	Y	Y	Y
3 Cardin	?	?	?	N	Y	Y	Y	Y
4 Wynn	N	Y	Y	N	Y	?	?	N
5 Hoyer	N	?	?	N	Y	Y	Y	Y
6 ***Bartlett***	Y	Y	Y	Y	Y	Y	Y	Y
7 Cummings	N	Y	Y	N	Y	?	Y	Y
8 ***Morella***	?	Y	Y	Y	Y	Y	Y	Y
MASSACHUSETTS								
1 Olver	N	N	N	N	Y	N	Y	N
2 Neal	?	?	?	?	?	N	Y	N
3 McGovern	N	Y	Y	N	Y	N	Y	N
4 Frank	?	?	?	?	?	Y	Y	Y
5 Meehan	?	Y	Y	N	Y	Y	Y	Y
6 Tierney	N	Y	N	N	Y	Y	Y	Y
7 Markey	N	Y	N	N	Y	N	Y	Y
8 Capuano	N	Y	N	N	Y	N	N	N
9 Moakley	N	Y	N	N	Y	Y	Y	Y
10 Delahunt	?	?	?	?	?	Y	Y	Y
MICHIGAN								
1 Stupak	N	N	N	N	Y	N	N	N
2 ***Hoekstra***	Y	Y	Y	Y	Y	Y	Y	Y
3 ***Ehlers***	Y	Y	Y	Y	Y	Y	Y	Y
4 ***Camp***	Y	Y	Y	Y	Y	?	?	Y
5 Barcia	N	Y	Y	N	?	Y	Y	?
6 ***Upton***	Y	Y	Y	Y	Y	Y	Y	Y
7 ***Smith***	Y	Y	Y	Y	Y	Y	Y	Y
8 Stabenow	Y	Y	Y	N	Y	?	Y	?
9 Kildee	N	N	N	N	Y	Y	Y	Y
10 Bonior	N	N	N	N	Y	N	Y	Y
11 ***Knollenberg***	Y	Y	Y	Y	Y	Y	Y	Y
12 Levin	N	Y	Y	N	Y	Y	Y	Y
13 Rivers	N	Y	Y	N	Y	Y	Y	Y
14 Conyers	?	?	?	?	?	?	?	?
15 Kilpatrick	?	Y	Y	N	Y	?	Y	Y
16 Dingell	N	N	N	N	Y	Y	N	?

	579	580	581	582	583	584	585	586
MINNESOTA								
1 ***Gutknecht***	Y	Y	Y	Y	Y	N	Y	N
2 Minge	N	Y	Y	N	Y	Y	Y	Y
3 ***Ramstad***	Y	Y	Y	Y	Y	N	Y	N
4 Vacant								
5 Sabo	N	Y	Y	N	Y	N	Y	N
6 Luther	N	Y	Y	N	Y	Y	Y	Y
7 Peterson	N	Y	Y	Y	Y	N	Y	?
8 Oberstar	N	N	N	N	Y	N	Y	N
MISSISSIPPI								
1 ***Wicker***	Y	Y	Y	Y	Y	N	Y	N
2 Thompson	?	?	?	N	Y	N	Y	N
3 ***Pickering***	?	Y	Y	Y	Y	?	?	Y
4 Shows	N	Y	Y	N	Y	Y	Y	Y
5 Taylor	N	N	N	N	Y	N	Y	N
MISSOURI								
1 Clay	?	N	N	N	Y	?	Y	N
2 ***Talent***	?	?	?	?	?	?	?	?
3 Gephardt	N	N	N	N	Y	?	?	Y
4 Skelton	Y	Y	Y	N	Y	Y	Y	Y
5 McCarthy	Y	Y	Y	+	+	Y	Y	Y
6 Danner	?	?	?	?	?	?	?	?
7 ***Blunt***	Y	Y	Y	Y	Y	?	?	Y
8 ***Emerson***	Y	Y	Y	Y	Y	Y	Y	Y
9 ***Hulshof***	?	?	?	?	?	N	Y	N
MONTANA								
AL ***Hill***	Y	Y	Y	Y	Y	?	?	?
NEBRASKA								
1 ***Bereuter***	Y	Y	Y	Y	Y	Y	Y	Y
2 ***Terry***	Y	Y	Y	Y	Y	Y	Y	Y
3 ***Barrett***	Y	Y	Y	Y	Y	Y	Y	Y
NEVADA								
1 Berkley	N	Y	Y	N	Y	Y	Y	Y
2 ***Gibbons***	Y	Y	Y	Y	Y	Y	Y	Y
NEW HAMPSHIRE								
1 ***Sununu***	Y	Y	Y	Y	Y	Y	Y	Y
2 ***Bass***	Y	Y	Y	Y	Y	Y	Y	Y
NEW JERSEY								
1 Andrews	N	N	Y	N	Y	Y	Y	Y
2 ***LoBiondo***	Y	Y	Y	Y	Y	N	Y	N
3 ***Saxton***	Y	Y	Y	Y	Y	Y	Y	Y
4 ***Smith***	Y	Y	Y	Y	Y	Y	Y	?
5 ***Roukema***	Y	Y	Y	Y	Y	Y	Y	Y
6 Pallone	N	Y	N	N	Y	N	Y	N
7 ***Franks***	?	?	?	?	?	?	?	?
8 Pascrell	?	?	?	?	?	Y	Y	Y
9 Rothman	N	Y	Y	N	Y	N	Y	N
10 Payne	N	N	Y	?	?	?	Y	Y
11 ***Frelinghuysen***	Y	Y	Y	Y	Y	Y	Y	Y
12 Holt	N	N	N	N	Y	N	Y	N
13 Menendez	N	N	Y	N	Y	N	Y	N
NEW MEXICO								
1 ***Wilson***	N	Y	Y	Y	Y	Y	Y	Y
2 ***Skeen***	Y	Y	Y	Y	Y	Y	Y	Y
3 Udall	N	Y	Y	N	Y	N	Y	N
NEW YORK								
1 Forbes	?	?	?	?	?	Y	?	Y
2 ***Lazio***	?	?	?	?	?	?	?	?
3 ***King***	?	?	?	?	?	Y	Y	Y
4 McCarthy	N	Y	Y	N	Y	Y	Y	Y
5 Ackerman	?	?	?	?	?	Y	Y	Y
6 Meeks	N	N	Y	N	Y	?	?	Y
7 Crowley	?	?	?	?	?	Y	Y	Y
8 Nadler	N	Y	Y	N	Y	Y	Y	Y
9 Weiner	N	Y	Y	N	Y	Y	Y	Y
10 Towns	N	N	Y	N	Y	?	?	Y
11 Owens	N	N	N	N	Y	Y	Y	Y
12 Velázquez	N	N	N	N	Y	N	Y	Y
13 ***Fossella***	Y	Y	Y	Y	Y	?	Y	Y
14 Maloney	–	–	+	–	+	N	Y	Y
15 Rangel	N	N	N	N	?	N	Y	Y
16 Serrano	N	N	Y	N	Y	N	Y	N
17 Engel	N	Y	Y	N	Y	Y	Y	Y
18 Lowey	N	Y	Y	N	Y	N	Y	Y
19 ***Kelly***	Y	Y	Y	Y	Y	Y	Y	Y
20 ***Gilman***	Y	Y	Y	Y	?	Y	Y	Y
21 McNulty	N	Y	Y	N	Y	N	Y	N
22 ***Sweeney***	Y	Y	Y	Y	Y	N	Y	N
23 ***Boehlert***	Y	Y	Y	Y	Y	Y	Y	Y
24 ***McHugh***	Y	Y	Y	Y	Y	Y	Y	Y
25 ***Walsh***	Y	Y	Y	Y	Y	Y	Y	Y
26 Hinchey	N	Y	Y	N	Y	Y	Y	Y
27 ***Reynolds***	Y	Y	Y	Y	Y	Y	Y	Y
28 Slaughter	?	Y	Y	N	Y	N	Y	N
29 LaFalce	?	?	?	?	?	N	N	N

	579	580	581	582	583	584	585	586
30 ***Quinn***	Y	Y	Y	Y	Y	Y	Y	Y
31 ***Houghton***	Y	Y	Y	Y	Y	Y	Y	Y
NORTH CAROLINA								
1 Clayton	N	N	N	N	Y	Y	Y	Y
2 Etheridge	N	N	Y	N	Y	?	?	Y
3 ***Jones***	Y	Y	Y	Y	Y	Y	Y	Y
4 Price	N	N	Y	N	?	N	Y	Y
5 ***Burr***	Y	Y	Y	Y	Y	Y	Y	Y
6 ***Coble***	Y	Y	Y	Y	Y	Y	Y	Y
7 McIntyre	–	+	+	N	Y	Y	Y	Y
8 ***Hayes***	Y	Y	Y	Y	Y	Y	Y	N
9 ***Myrick***	Y	Y	Y	Y	Y	Y	Y	Y
10 ***Ballenger***	Y	Y	Y	Y	Y	Y	Y	Y
11 ***Taylor***	Y	Y	?	?	?	?	?	Y
12 Watt	N	N	N	N	Y	Y	Y	Y
NORTH DAKOTA								
AL Pomeroy	N	Y	Y	N	Y	Y	Y	?
OHIO								
1 ***Chabot***	Y	Y	Y	Y	Y	Y	Y	Y
2 ***Portman***	Y	Y	Y	Y	Y	+	+	Y
3 Hall	N	Y	Y	N	Y	N	Y	?
4 ***Oxley***	?	?	?	?	?	?	Y	Y
5 ***Gillmor***	Y	Y	Y	Y	Y	Y	Y	Y
6 Strickland	N	N	N	N	Y	N	Y	N
7 ***Hobson***	Y	Y	Y	Y	Y	Y	Y	Y
8 ***Boehner***	Y	Y	Y	Y	Y	Y	Y	Y
9 Kaptur	?	?	?	?	?	N	Y	Y
10 Kucinich	N	Y	N	N	Y	N	Y	N
11 Jones	?	?	?	?	?	Y	Y	Y
12 ***Kasich***	?	?	?	?	?	Y	Y	?
13 Brown	N	Y	Y	?	?	?	?	?
14 Sawyer	N	Y	Y	?	?	?	Y	Y
15 ***Pryce***	Y	Y	Y	Y	Y	Y	Y	Y
16 ***Regula***	Y	Y	Y	Y	Y	Y	Y	Y
17 Traficant	Y	Y	Y	Y	Y	Y	Y	Y
18 ***Ney***	Y	Y	Y	Y	Y	Y	Y	Y
19 ***LaTourette***	Y	Y	Y	Y	Y	Y	Y	Y
OKLAHOMA								
1 ***Largent***	Y	Y	Y	Y	Y	Y	Y	Y
2 ***Coburn***	Y	Y	Y	Y	Y	Y	Y	?
3 ***Watkins***	?	?	?	?	?	N	Y	Y
4 ***Watts***	+	Y	Y	Y	Y	Y	Y	?
5 ***Istook***	Y	Y	Y	Y	Y	Y	Y	Y
6 ***Lucas***	Y	Y	Y	Y	Y	Y	Y	Y
OREGON								
1 Wu	N	Y	N	N	Y	N	Y	N
2 ***Walden***	Y	?	Y	Y	Y	Y	Y	Y
3 Blumenauer	N	?	Y	N	Y	Y	Y	Y
4 DeFazio	N	?	?	N	Y	N	N	N
5 Hooley	N	?	?	N	Y	N	Y	N
PENNSYLVANIA								
1 Brady	?	Y	Y	N	Y	N	Y	N
2 Fattah	?	Y	Y	?	?	?	Y	Y
3 Borski	N	Y	Y	N	Y	?	?	N
4 Klink	?	?	?	?	?	?	?	?
5 ***Peterson***	Y	Y	Y	Y	Y	Y	Y	Y
6 Holden	N	Y	Y	N	Y	Y	Y	Y
7 ***Weldon***	Y	Y	Y	Y	Y	Y	Y	Y
8 ***Greenwood***	Y	Y	Y	Y	Y	?	?	?
9 ***Shuster***	?	?	?	?	?	Y	Y	Y
10 ***Sherwood***	Y	Y	Y	Y	Y	Y	Y	Y
11 Kanjorski	?	?	?	?	?	Y	Y	Y
12 Murtha	Y	Y	Y	N	Y	Y	Y	Y
13 Hoeffel	Y	Y	Y	N	Y	Y	Y	Y
14 Coyne	N	Y	Y	N	Y	Y	Y	Y
15 ***Toomey***	Y	Y	Y	Y	Y	Y	Y	Y
16 ***Pitts***	Y	Y	Y	Y	Y	Y	Y	Y
17 ***Gekas***	Y	Y	Y	Y	Y	Y	Y	Y
18 Doyle	N	Y	Y	N	Y	Y	Y	Y
19 ***Goodling***	Y	Y	Y	Y	Y	Y	Y	Y
20 Mascara	Y	+	+	–	+	Y	Y	Y
21 ***English***	Y	Y	Y	Y	Y	N	Y	N
RHODE ISLAND								
1 Kennedy	N	Y	Y	N	Y	?	?	?
2 Weygand	?	?	?	?	?	Y	Y	Y
SOUTH CAROLINA								
1 ***Sanford***	Y	Y	Y	Y	Y	?	?	Y
2 ***Spence***	Y	Y	Y	Y	Y	Y	Y	Y
3 ***Graham***	Y	Y	Y	Y	Y	Y	Y	Y
4 ***DeMint***	Y	Y	Y	Y	Y	+	+	Y
5 Spratt	?	?	?	?	?	?	?	Y
6 Clyburn	N	N	N	N	Y	N	Y	Y
SOUTH DAKOTA								
AL ***Thune***	Y	Y	Y	Y	Y	Y	Y	Y

	579	580	581	582	583	584	585	586
TENNESSEE								
1 ***Jenkins***	Y	Y	Y	Y	Y	Y	Y	Y
2 ***Duncan***	Y	Y	Y	Y	Y	Y	Y	Y
3 ***Wamp***	Y	Y	Y	Y	Y	Y	Y	Y
4 ***Hilleary***	Y	Y	Y	Y	Y	N	Y	Y
5 Clement	N	Y	Y	N	Y	Y	Y	Y
6 Gordon	N	Y	Y	N	Y	Y	Y	Y
7 ***Bryant***	Y	Y	Y	Y	Y	Y	Y	Y
8 Tanner	N	N	Y	N	Y	Y	Y	Y
9 Ford	N	N	N	N	Y	N	N	Y
TEXAS								
1 Sandlin	N	N	Y	N	Y	Y	Y	Y
2 Turner	N	?	?	N	Y	Y	Y	?
3 ***Johnson, Sam***	Y	Y	Y	Y	Y	Y	Y	Y
4 Hall	N	Y	Y	Y	Y	Y	Y	Y
5 ***Sessions***	Y	Y	Y	Y	Y	Y	Y	Y
6 ***Barton***	Y	Y	Y	Y	?	Y	N	Y
7 ***Archer***	Y	Y	Y	?	?	?	?	?
8 ***Brady***	Y	?	?	?	?	Y	Y	Y
9 Lampson	N	N	N	N	Y	Y	Y	Y
10 Doggett	N	N	N	N	Y	Y	Y	Y
11 Edwards	N	N	Y	N	Y	Y	Y	Y
12 ***Granger***	Y	Y	Y	Y	Y	Y	Y	Y
13 ***Thornberry***	Y	Y	Y	Y	Y	Y	Y	Y
14 ***Paul***	Y	Y	Y	Y	P	Y	Y	Y
15 Hinojosa	N	Y	Y	N	Y	Y	Y	Y
16 Reyes	N	N	Y	N	Y	Y	Y	?
17 Stenholm	N	N	N	N	?	?	Y	N
18 Jackson-Lee	N	N	N	N	Y	Y	Y	+
19 ***Combest***	Y	Y	Y	Y	Y	Y	Y	Y
20 Gonzalez	N	N	N	N	Y	Y	Y	Y
21 ***Smith***	Y	Y	Y	Y	Y	Y	Y	Y
22 ***DeLay***	Y	Y	Y	Y	Y	Y	Y	Y
23 ***Bonilla***	Y	Y	Y	Y	Y	Y	Y	Y
24 Frost	N	N	N	N	Y	Y	Y	Y
25 Bentsen	N	Y	N	N	Y	?	Y	Y
26 ***Armey***	Y	Y	Y	Y	Y	Y	Y	Y
27 Ortiz	N	N	Y	N	Y	Y	Y	Y
28 Rodriguez	N	N	N	N	Y	Y	Y	Y
29 Green	Y	N	N	N	+	Y	Y	N
30 Johnson, E.B.	?	?	?	?	?	N	Y	Y
UTAH								
1 ***Hansen***	Y	Y	Y	Y	Y	Y	Y	?
2 ***Cook***	Y	Y	Y	Y	Y	Y	Y	?
3 ***Cannon***	Y	Y	Y	Y	Y	Y	Y	Y
VERMONT								
AL *Sanders*	N	Y	Y	N	Y	Y	Y	Y
VIRGINIA								
1 Vacant								
2 Pickett	?	?	?	?	?	N	Y	N
3 Scott	N	N	Y	N	Y	Y	Y	?
4 Sisisky	N	N	N	N	Y	Y	Y	Y
5 *Goode*	Y	Y	Y	Y	Y	?	Y	Y
6 ***Goodlatte***	Y	?	?	Y	Y	Y	Y	Y
7 ***Bliley***	Y	Y	Y	Y	Y	Y	Y	Y
8 Moran	N	N	Y	N	Y	?	Y	Y
9 Boucher	?	?	?	?	?	?	?	?
10 ***Wolf***	Y	Y	Y	?	Y	Y	Y	Y
11 ***Davis***	Y	Y	Y	Y	Y	Y	Y	Y
WASHINGTON								
1 Inslee	N	N	N	N	Y	Y	Y	Y
2 ***Metcalf***	?	?	?	?	?	?	?	?
3 Baird	N	N	N	N	Y	N	N	N
4 ***Hastings***	Y	Y	Y	Y	Y	Y	Y	Y
5 ***Nethercutt***	Y	Y	Y	Y	Y	Y	Y	Y
6 Dicks	N	N	N	N	Y	Y	Y	?
7 McDermott	N	N	N	N	Y	N	Y	N
8 ***Dunn***	Y	Y	Y	Y	Y	?	?	?
9 Smith	N	Y	Y	N	Y	Y	Y	Y
WEST VIRGINIA								
1 Mollohan	N	Y	Y	N	Y	?	?	?
2 Wise	?	?	?	?	?	?	?	?
3 Rahall	N	Y	Y	N	Y	Y	Y	Y
WISCONSIN								
1 ***Ryan***	Y	Y	Y	Y	Y	Y	Y	Y
2 Baldwin	N	Y	Y	N	Y	Y	Y	Y
3 Kind	N	Y	Y	N	Y	Y	Y	Y
4 Kleczka	N	Y	Y	N	Y	Y	Y	Y
5 Barrett	Y	Y	Y	N	Y	Y	Y	Y
6 ***Petri***	Y	Y	Y	Y	Y	Y	Y	Y
7 Obey	N	N	N	N	Y	N	Y	N
8 ***Green***	Y	Y	Y	Y	Y	Y	Y	Y
9 ***Sensenbrenner***	Y	Y	Y	Y	Y	?	Y	Y
WYOMING								
AL ***Cubin***	Y	Y	Y	Y	Y	Y	Y	Y

Southern states - Ala., Ark., Fla., Ga., Ky., La., Miss., N.C., Okla., S.C., Tenn., Texas, Va.

587. H J Res 122. Continuing Resolution/Passage. Passage of the joint resolution that would provide temporary funding authority, at current levels, until Nov. 2, for the departments and programs for which regular fiscal 2001 appropriations will not be enacted by Nov. 1. Passed 371-13: R 196-1; D 173-12 (ND 129-9, SD 44-3); I 2-0. Nov. 1, 2000.

588. Procedural Motion/Hour of Meeting. Young, R-Alaska, motion that when the House adjourns Nov. 1, it reconvene at 6 p.m. on Thursday, Nov. 2. Motion agreed to 239-130: R 186-2; D 52-127 (ND 39-96, SD 13-31); I 1-1. Nov. 1, 2000.

589. H Con Res 397. Central Asian Leaders/Adoption. Bereuter, R-Neb., motion to suspend the rules and adopt the concurrent resolution expressing Congress' concern about the tendency of some Central Asian leaders to seek to remain in power indefinitely and their willingness to manipulate constitutions, elections, and legislative and judicial systems. Motion agreed to 362-3: R 182-3; D 178-0 (ND 134-0, SD 44-0); I 2-0. A two-thirds majority of those present and voting (244 in this case) is required for adoption under suspension of the rules. Nov. 1, 2000.

590. HR 4577. Fiscal 2001 Labor-HHS-Education Appropriations/Motion to Instruct. Holt, D-N.J., motion to instruct conferees to disagree with provisions in the Senate bill that would deny the president's request for dedicated resources for local school construction and instead broadly expand the Title VI education block grant, which has limited accountability in the use of funds. Motion rejected 176-183: R 7-176; D 168-6 (ND 131-3, SD 37-3); I 1-1. Nov. 1, 2000.

591. HR 4577. Fiscal 2001 Labor-HHS-Education Appropriations/Motion to Instruct. Wu, D-Ore., motion to instruct conferees to disagree with provisions in the Senate bill that would deny the president's request for dedicated resources to reduce class sizes in the early grades and instead broadly expand the Title VI education block grant, which has limited accountability in the use of funds. Motion rejected 168-170: R 7-165; D 160-4 (ND 122-3, SD 38-1); I 1-1. Nov. 1, 2000.

592. H J Res 123. Continuing Resolution/Passage. Passage of the joint resolution that would provide temporary funding authority, at current levels, until Nov. 3, for the departments and programs for which regular fiscal 2001 appropriations are not enacted by Nov. 2. It would also provide $7 million for expenses related to the presidential transition. Passed 310-7: R 179-0; D 129-7 (ND 95-4, SD 34-3); I 2-0. Nov. 2, 2000.

Key

- Y Voted for (yea).
- # Paired for.
- \+ Announced for.
- N Voted against (nay).
- X Paired against.
- – Announced against.
- P Voted "present."
- C Voted "present" to avoid possible conflict of interest.
- ? Did not vote or otherwise make a position known.

•

Democrats ***Republicans***
Independents

	587	588	589	590	591	592
ALABAMA						
1 ***Callahan***	Y	Y	Y	N	N	Y
2 ***Everett***	Y	Y	Y	N	N	Y
3 ***Riley***	Y	Y	Y	N	N	?
4 ***Aderholt***	Y	Y	Y	N	N	Y
5 Cramer	Y	Y	Y	Y	Y	Y
6 ***Bachus***	Y	Y	Y	N	N	Y
7 Hilliard	N	N	Y	Y	Y	Y
ALASKA						
AL ***Young***	Y	Y	Y	N	N	Y
ARIZONA						
1 ***Salmon***	?	?	?	?	?	?
2 Pastor	Y	N	Y	Y	Y	Y
3 ***Stump***	Y	Y	Y	N	N	Y
4 ***Shadegg***	Y	Y	Y	N	N	Y
5 ***Kolbe***	Y	Y	Y	N	N	Y
6 ***Hayworth***	Y	Y	Y	N	N	Y
ARKANSAS						
1 Berry	Y	N	Y	Y	Y	N
2 Snyder	Y	Y	Y	Y	Y	Y
3 ***Hutchinson***	Y	Y	?	N	N	Y
4 ***Dickey***	?	?	?	?	?	?
CALIFORNIA						
1 Thompson	Y	Y	Y	Y	Y	Y
2 ***Herger***	Y	Y	Y	N	N	Y
3 ***Ose***	?	?	?	?	?	?
4 ***Doolittle***	Y	Y	Y	N	N	Y
5 Matsui	Y	N	Y	Y	Y	Y
6 Woolsey	Y	N	Y	Y	Y	Y
7 Miller, George	N	N	Y	Y	Y	?
8 Pelosi	Y	N	Y	Y	Y	Y
9 Lee	Y	N	Y	Y	Y	Y
10 Tauscher	Y	N	Y	Y	Y	Y
11 ***Pombo***	Y	Y	Y	N	N	Y
12 Lantos	?	?	?	?	?	?
13 Stark	Y	Y	Y	Y	?	?
14 Eshoo	Y	Y	Y	Y	Y	Y
15 ***Campbell***	?	?	?	?	?	?
16 Lofgren	Y	N	Y	Y	Y	Y
17 Farr	Y	N	Y	Y	Y	Y
18 Condit	Y	Y	Y	N	N	Y
19 ***Radanovich***	Y	Y	Y	N	N	Y
20 Dooley	?	?	?	?	?	?
21 ***Thomas***	Y	Y	Y	N	N	Y
22 Capps	Y	Y	Y	Y	Y	+
23 ***Gallegly***	Y	Y	Y	N	N	Y
24 Sherman	Y	N	Y	Y	Y	Y
25 ***McKeon***	Y	?	?	?	?	Y
26 Berman	Y	Y	Y	Y	Y	?
27 ***Rogan***	Y	Y	Y	N	N	Y
28 ***Dreier***	Y	Y	Y	N	N	Y
29 Waxman	?	?	?	?	?	?
30 Becerra	Y	N	Y	Y	Y	?
31 ***Martinez***	Y	Y	Y	N	N	Y
32 Dixon	Y	Y	Y	Y	Y	Y
33 Roybal-Allard	Y	N	Y	Y	Y	Y
34 Napolitano	Y	N	Y	Y	Y	Y
35 Waters	?	?	?	?	?	?
36 ***Kuykendall***	Y	Y	Y	N	N	Y
37 Millender-McD.	Y	N	Y	Y	Y	Y
38 ***Horn***	Y	Y	Y	N	Y	Y
39 ***Royce***	Y	Y	Y	N	N	Y
40 ***Lewis***	Y	Y	Y	N	N	Y
41 ***Miller, Gary***	Y	Y	Y	N	N	Y
42 Baca	Y	N	Y	Y	Y	Y
43 ***Calvert***	Y	Y	Y	N	?	?
44 ***Bono***	Y	Y	Y	N	N	Y
45 ***Rohrabacher***	Y	Y	Y	N	?	Y
46 Sanchez	Y	N	?	Y	Y	Y
47 ***Cox***	Y	?	Y	N	N	Y
48 ***Packard***	Y	Y	Y	N	N	Y
49 ***Bilbray***	?	?	?	?	?	?
50 Filner	Y	N	Y	Y	Y	Y
51 ***Cunningham***	Y	N	?	N	N	Y
52 ***Hunter***	Y	Y	Y	N	N	?
COLORADO						
1 DeGette	Y	N	Y	Y	Y	Y
2 Udall	Y	N	Y	Y	Y	Y
3 ***McInnis***	Y	Y	Y	N	N	Y
4 ***Schaffer***	Y	Y	Y	N	?	?
5 ***Hefley***	Y	Y	Y	N	N	?
6 ***Tancredo***	Y	Y	Y	N	?	?
CONNECTICUT						
1 Larson	Y	N	?	Y	?	Y
2 Gejdenson	Y	N	Y	?	?	?
3 DeLauro	Y	N	Y	Y	Y	Y
4 ***Shays***	?	?	?	?	?	?
5 Maloney	Y	N	Y	Y	Y	Y
6 ***Johnson***	Y	Y	Y	?	N	Y
DELAWARE						
AL ***Castle***	Y	Y	Y	N	N	Y
FLORIDA						
1 ***Scarborough***	?	?	?	?	?	?
2 Boyd	Y	Y	+	+	+	Y
3 Brown	?	?	?	?	?	?
4 ***Fowler***	?	?	?	?	?	?
5 Thurman	Y	N	Y	Y	Y	Y
6 ***Stearns***	Y	Y	Y	N	N	Y
7 ***Mica***	?	?	?	?	N	Y
8 ***McCollum***	?	?	?	?	?	?
9 ***Bilirakis***	Y	Y	Y	N	N	Y
10 ***Young***	Y	Y	Y	N	N	Y
11 Davis	Y	?	Y	?	?	Y
12 ***Canady***	?	?	?	N	N	Y
13 ***Miller***	Y	Y	Y	N	N	Y
14 ***Goss***	Y	Y	Y	N	N	Y
15 ***Weldon***	Y	Y	?	N	?	?
16 ***Foley***	Y	Y	Y	N	N	Y
17 Meek	Y	?	?	Y	Y	?
18 ***Ros-Lehtinen***	Y	Y	Y	N	?	Y
19 Wexler	?	?	?	?	?	?
20 Deutsch	Y	N	Y	Y	Y	Y
21 ***Diaz-Balart***	Y	Y	Y	N	N	?
22 ***Shaw***	?	?	?	?	?	Y
23 Hastings	?	?	?	?	?	?
GEORGIA						
1 ***Kingston***	Y	Y	Y	N	N	Y
2 Bishop	Y	Y	Y	?	?	?
3 ***Collins***	?	?	?	?	?	?
4 McKinney	Y	Y	Y	Y	Y	Y
5 Lewis	Y	N	Y	Y	Y	Y
6 ***Isakson***	Y	Y	Y	N	N	Y
7 ***Barr***	Y	Y	Y	N	?	Y
8 ***Chambliss***	Y	Y	?	?	?	Y
9 ***Deal***	Y	Y	Y	N	?	Y
10 ***Norwood***	Y	Y	Y	N	N	Y
11 ***Linder***	Y	Y	Y	N	N	Y
HAWAII						
1 Abercrombie	Y	Y	Y	Y	Y	Y
2 Mink	Y	N	Y	Y	Y	Y
IDAHO						
1 ***Chenoweth-Hage***	Y	Y	N	N	N	Y
2 ***Simpson***	Y	Y	Y	N	N	Y
ILLINOIS						
1 Rush	Y	Y	Y	Y	Y	?
2 Jackson	Y	Y	Y	Y	Y	Y
3 Lipinski	Y	Y	Y	Y	Y	Y
4 Gutierrez	Y	N	Y	Y	?	Y
5 Blagojevich	Y	Y	Y	Y	Y	Y
6 ***Hyde***	Y	Y	Y	N	?	Y
7 Davis	Y	Y	Y	Y	Y	?
8 ***Crane***	Y	Y	Y	N	N	Y
9 Schakowsky	Y	N	Y	Y	Y	Y
10 ***Porter***	Y	Y	Y	N	N	Y
11 ***Weller***	Y	Y	Y	N	N	Y
12 Costello	N	N	Y	Y	Y	?
13 ***Biggert***	Y	Y	Y	N	N	Y

ND Northern Democrats SD Southern Democrats

	587	588	589	590	591	592
14 **Hastert**	Y					Y
15 **Ewing**	Y	Y	Y	N	?	?
16 **Manzullo**	Y	Y	Y	N	N	Y
17 Evans	?	N	Y	Y	Y	Y
18 **LaHood**	Y	Y	Y	N	N	Y
19 Phelps	N	N	Y	Y	?	N
20 **Shimkus**	Y	Y	Y	N	N	Y
INDIANA						
1 Visclosky	N	N	Y	Y	Y	?
2 **McIntosh**	?	?	?	?	?	?
3 Roemer	Y	Y	Y	Y	Y	Y
4 **Souder**	Y	Y	Y	Y	N	Y
5 **Buyer**	Y	Y	Y	N	N	Y
6 **Burton**	Y	?	Y	N	N	Y
7 **Pease**	Y	Y	Y	N	N	Y
8 **Hostettler**	Y	Y	Y	N	N	Y
9 Hill	Y	N	Y	Y	Y	Y
10 Carson	Y	N	Y	Y	Y	Y
IOWA						
1 **Leach**	Y	Y	Y	N	N	Y
2 **Nussle**	Y	?	?	N	N	Y
3 Boswell	Y	Y	Y	Y	Y	Y
4 **Ganske**	Y	Y	Y	N	N	?
5 **Latham**	Y	Y	Y	N	N	Y
KANSAS						
1 **Moran**	Y	Y	Y	N	N	Y
2 **Ryun**	Y	Y	Y	N	N	Y
3 Moore	?	Y	Y	Y	Y	Y
4 **Tiahrt**	Y	Y	Y	N	N	Y
KENTUCKY						
1 **Whitfield**	Y	Y	Y	N	N	Y
2 **Lewis**	Y	Y	Y	N	N	Y
3 **Northup**	Y	Y	Y	?	N	Y
4 Lucas	Y	Y	Y	Y	Y	Y
5 **Rogers**	Y	Y	Y	N	N	Y
6 **Fletcher**	Y	Y	Y	N	N	Y
LOUISIANA						
1 **Vitter**	Y	Y	Y	N	N	Y
2 Jefferson	Y	N	Y	Y	Y	Y
3 **Tauzin**	Y	Y	Y	N	N	Y
4 **McCrery**	?	?	Y	N	N	Y
5 **Cooksey**	Y	Y	Y	N	N	Y
6 **Baker**	Y	Y	Y	N	N	Y
7 John	Y	Y	Y	Y	Y	Y
MAINE						
1 Allen	Y	N	Y	Y	Y	?
2 Baldacci	Y	N	Y	Y	Y	Y
MARYLAND						
1 **Gilchrest**	Y	Y	Y	N	N	Y
2 **Ehrlich**	Y	Y	Y	N	N	?
3 Cardin	Y	Y	Y	Y	Y	Y
4 Wynn	Y	N	Y	Y	Y	Y
5 Hoyer	Y	N	Y	Y	Y	Y
6 **Bartlett**	Y	Y	Y	N	N	Y
7 Cummings	Y	N	Y	Y	Y	?
8 **Morella**	Y	Y	Y	Y	Y	?
MASSACHUSETTS						
1 Olver	Y	N	Y	Y	Y	Y
2 Neal	?	?	?	?	?	?
3 McGovern	Y	N	Y	Y	Y	Y
4 Frank	Y	Y	Y	?	?	?
5 Meehan	Y	Y	Y	Y	?	?
6 Tierney	Y	N	Y	Y	Y	Y
7 Markey	Y	?	Y	Y	Y	Y
8 Capuano	N	N	Y	Y	Y	N
9 Moakley	Y	N	Y	Y	Y	Y
10 Delahunt	?	?	?	Y	Y	?
MICHIGAN						
1 Stupak	N	Y	Y	Y	?	?
2 **Hoekstra**	Y	Y	Y	N	N	Y
3 **Ehlers**	Y	Y	Y	N	N	?
4 **Camp**	Y	Y	Y	N	N	Y
5 Barcia	Y	N	Y	Y	Y	Y
6 **Upton**	Y	Y	Y	N	N	Y
7 **Smith**	Y	Y	Y	N	N	?
8 Stabenow	Y	Y	Y	Y	Y	?
9 Kildee	Y	N	Y	Y	Y	Y
10 Bonior	Y	N	Y	Y	Y	Y
11 **Knollenberg**	Y	Y	Y	N	?	Y
12 Levin	Y	Y	Y	Y	Y	Y
13 Rivers	Y	N	Y	Y	Y	?
14 Conyers	?	?	?	?	?	?
15 Kilpatrick	Y	N	?	?	?	?
16 Dingell	?	?	?	?	?	?
MINNESOTA						
1 **Gutknecht**	Y	Y	Y	N	N	Y
2 Minge	Y	N	Y	Y	Y	Y
3 **Ramstad**	Y	Y	Y	N	N	Y
4 Vacant						
5 Sabo	Y	N	Y	?	Y	Y
6 Luther	Y	N	Y	Y	Y	Y
7 Peterson	Y	N	Y	N	Y	Y
8 Oberstar	Y	N	Y	Y	Y	?
MISSISSIPPI						
1 **Wicker**	Y	Y	Y	N	N	Y
2 Thompson	N	N	Y	Y	Y	Y
3 **Pickering**	Y	Y	Y	N	N	Y
4 Shows	Y	Y	Y	Y	Y	Y
5 Taylor	Y	N	Y	N	N	Y
MISSOURI						
1 Clay	Y	N	Y	?	Y	?
2 **Talent**	?	?	?	?	?	?
3 Gephardt	Y	N	Y	Y	Y	?
4 Skelton	Y	Y	Y	Y	Y	Y
5 McCarthy	Y	N	Y	Y	Y	Y
6 Danner	?	?	?	?	?	?
7 **Blunt**	Y	Y	Y	N	N	Y
8 **Emerson**	Y	?	?	?	?	?
9 **Hulshof**	Y	?	Y	N	N	Y
MONTANA						
AL **Hill**	?	?	?	?	?	?
NEBRASKA						
1 **Bereuter**	Y	Y	Y	N	N	?
2 **Terry**	Y	Y	Y	N	N	Y
3 **Barrett**	Y	Y	Y	N	N	Y
NEVADA						
1 Berkley	Y	N	Y	Y	Y	Y
2 **Gibbons**	Y	Y	Y	–	N	Y
NEW HAMPSHIRE						
1 **Sununu**	Y	Y	Y	N	N	Y
2 **Bass**	Y	Y	Y	N	N	Y
NEW JERSEY						
1 Andrews	Y	N	Y	Y	Y	Y
2 **LoBiondo**	Y	Y	Y	Y	Y	Y
3 **Saxton**	Y	Y	Y	+	N	Y
4 **Smith**	Y	Y	Y	Y	Y	Y
5 **Roukema**	Y	Y	Y	N	N	Y
6 Pallone	Y	N	Y	Y	Y	Y
7 **Franks**	?	?	?	?	?	?
8 Pascrell	Y	N	Y	Y	Y	Y
9 Rothman	Y	N	Y	Y	?	Y
10 Payne	Y	N	Y	Y	Y	?
11 **Frelinghuysen**	Y	Y	Y	N	N	Y
12 Holt	Y	Y	Y	Y	Y	Y
13 Menendez	Y	N	Y	Y	Y	?
NEW MEXICO						
1 **Wilson**	Y	Y	Y	N	N	Y
2 **Skeen**	Y	Y	Y	N	N	Y
3 Udall	Y	Y	Y	Y	Y	Y
NEW YORK						
1 Forbes	Y	?	?	?	?	?
2 **Lazio**	?	?	?	?	?	?
3 **King**	Y	Y	Y	N	?	Y
4 McCarthy	Y	N	Y	Y	Y	Y
5 Ackerman	Y	N	Y	?	?	?
6 Meeks	Y	Y	Y	Y	?	?
7 Crowley	Y	N	Y	Y	Y	?
8 Nadler	Y	N	Y	Y	Y	Y
9 Weiner	Y	N	Y	Y	Y	?
10 Towns	Y	N	Y	Y	Y	?
11 Owens	Y	N	Y	Y	Y	?
12 Velázquez	Y	N	?	Y	Y	?
13 **Fossella**	Y	Y	Y	N	N	Y
14 Maloney	Y	N	Y	Y	Y	?
15 Rangel	Y	Y	Y	Y	Y	Y
16 Serrano	Y	Y	Y	Y	Y	Y
17 Engel	Y	Y	Y	Y	Y	Y
18 Lowey	Y	N	Y	Y	Y	Y
19 **Kelly**	Y	Y	Y	N	N	Y
20 **Gilman**	Y	Y	Y	N	N	Y
21 McNulty	Y	N	Y	Y	Y	Y
22 **Sweeney**	Y	Y	Y	N	Y	Y
23 **Boehlert**	Y	Y	?	?	?	Y
24 **McHugh**	Y	Y	Y	Y	Y	Y
25 **Walsh**	Y	Y	Y	N	N	Y
26 Hinchey	Y	N	Y	Y	Y	?
27 **Reynolds**	Y	Y	Y	N	N	Y
28 Slaughter	Y	N	Y	Y	Y	Y
29 LaFalce	N	N	Y	Y	?	N
30 **Quinn**	Y	Y	Y	Y	Y	Y
31 **Houghton**	Y	Y	Y	N	N	Y
NORTH CAROLINA						
1 Clayton	Y	N	Y	Y	Y	?
2 Etheridge	Y	Y	Y	Y	Y	?
3 **Jones**	Y	Y	Y	N	N	Y
4 Price	Y	N	Y	Y	Y	?
5 **Burr**	Y	Y	Y	N	N	Y
6 **Coble**	Y	Y	Y	N	N	Y
7 McIntyre	Y	N	Y	Y	Y	Y
8 **Hayes**	Y	Y	?	?	?	Y
9 **Myrick**	Y	Y	Y	N	N	Y
10 **Ballenger**	Y	Y	Y	N	N	Y
11 **Taylor**	Y	Y	Y	N	N	Y
12 Watt	Y	N	Y	Y	Y	Y
NORTH DAKOTA						
AL Pomeroy	Y	Y	Y	Y	?	?
OHIO						
1 **Chabot**	Y	Y	Y	N	N	Y
2 **Portman**	Y	Y	Y	N	N	Y
3 Hall	Y	N	Y	Y	Y	?
4 **Oxley**	Y	Y	Y	N	N	Y
5 **Gillmor**	Y	Y	Y	N	N	Y
6 Strickland	Y	N	Y	Y	Y	Y
7 **Hobson**	Y	Y	Y	N	N	Y
8 **Boehner**	Y	Y	Y	N	N	Y
9 Kaptur	Y	N	Y	Y	Y	Y
10 Kucinich	Y	N	P	Y	Y	Y
11 Jones	Y	?	Y	Y	Y	?
12 **Kasich**	?	?	?	?	?	?
13 Brown	?	?	?	?	?	Y
14 Sawyer	Y	Y	Y	Y	Y	Y
15 **Pryce**	Y	Y	Y	N	N	?
16 **Regula**	Y	Y	Y	N	N	Y
17 Traficant	Y	Y	Y	N	N	Y
18 **Ney**	Y	Y	Y	Y	?	Y
19 **LaTourette**	Y	Y	Y	N	N	Y
OKLAHOMA						
1 **Largent**	Y	Y	Y	N	?	Y
2 **Coburn**	Y	Y	Y	N	N	?
3 **Watkins**	Y	Y	Y	N	N	Y
4 **Watts**	?	?	?	?	?	?
5 **Istook**	Y	Y	?	N	N	Y
6 **Lucas**	Y	Y	Y	?	N	Y
OREGON						
1 Wu	Y	Y	Y	Y	Y	Y
2 **Walden**	Y	Y	Y	N	N	Y
3 Blumenauer	Y	N	Y	Y	Y	?
4 DeFazio	N	N	Y	Y	Y	N
5 Hooley	Y	N	Y	Y	Y	Y
PENNSYLVANIA						
1 Brady	Y	Y	Y	Y	Y	Y
2 Fattah	Y	N	Y	Y	Y	?
3 Borski	Y	Y	Y	Y	Y	Y
4 Klink	?	?	?	?	?	?
5 **Peterson**	Y	?	Y	?	?	Y
6 Holden	Y	N	Y	Y	Y	Y
7 **Weldon**	Y	Y	Y	?	N	Y
8 **Greenwood**	?	?	?	?	?	?
9 **Shuster**	Y	Y	Y	N	N	Y
10 **Sherwood**	Y	Y	Y	N	N	Y
11 Kanjorski	Y	Y	Y	Y	Y	Y
12 Murtha	Y	Y	Y	Y	?	Y
13 Hoeffel	Y	Y	Y	Y	Y	Y
14 Coyne	Y	N	Y	Y	Y	Y
15 **Toomey**	Y	Y	Y	N	N	Y
16 **Pitts**	Y	Y	?	N	N	?
17 **Gekas**	Y	Y	Y	N	N	Y
18 Doyle	Y	N	Y	Y	Y	Y
19 **Goodling**	Y	Y	Y	N	N	?
20 Mascara	Y	N	Y	Y	Y	Y
21 **English**	Y	Y	Y	N	?	Y
RHODE ISLAND						
1 Kennedy	?	?	?	?	Y	?
2 Weygand	Y	N	Y	Y	?	?
SOUTH CAROLINA						
1 **Sanford**	Y	Y	Y	N	N	Y
2 **Spence**	Y	Y	Y	N	N	Y
3 **Graham**	Y	Y	Y	N	?	Y
4 **DeMint**	Y	Y	Y	N	N	Y
5 Spratt	Y	N	Y	?	?	?
6 Clyburn	Y	N	Y	Y	Y	Y
SOUTH DAKOTA						
AL **Thune**	Y	Y	Y	N	N	Y
TENNESSEE						
1 **Jenkins**	Y	?	Y	?	?	Y
2 **Duncan**	Y	Y	Y	N	N	Y
3 **Wamp**	Y	Y	Y	?	?	Y
4 **Hilleary**	Y	Y	Y	N	N	Y
5 Clement	Y	Y	Y	Y	Y	?
6 Gordon	Y	Y	Y	Y	Y	Y
7 **Bryant**	Y	Y	Y	N	N	Y
8 Tanner	Y	N	Y	Y	Y	Y
9 Ford	N	N	Y	?	Y	N
TEXAS						
1 Sandlin	Y	N	Y	Y	Y	Y
2 Turner	?	?	?	?	?	?
3 **Johnson, Sam**	Y	Y	Y	N	N	Y
4 Hall	Y	Y	Y	N	Y	Y
5 **Sessions**	Y	Y	Y	N	N	Y
6 **Barton**	N	Y	Y	N	N	?
7 **Archer**	?	?	?	?	?	Y
8 **Brady**	Y	Y	Y	?	?	Y
9 Lampson	Y	N	Y	Y	Y	Y
10 Doggett	Y	N	Y	Y	Y	Y
11 Edwards	Y	N	Y	Y	Y	Y
12 **Granger**	Y	Y	Y	N	N	?
13 **Thornberry**	Y	Y	Y	N	N	Y
14 **Paul**	Y	Y	N	N	N	Y
15 Hinojosa	Y	?	?	?	?	?
16 Reyes	Y	N	Y	Y	Y	?
17 Stenholm	Y	N	Y	N	Y	N
18 Jackson-Lee	+	–	+	+	?	Y
19 **Combest**	Y	Y	Y	N	N	Y
20 Gonzalez	Y	N	Y	Y	Y	Y
21 **Smith**	Y	Y	Y	N	N	Y
22 **DeLay**	Y	Y	Y	N	N	Y
23 **Bonilla**	Y	Y	Y	N	N	Y
24 Frost	Y	N	Y	Y	Y	Y
25 Bentsen	Y	N	Y	Y	Y	?
26 **Armey**	Y	Y	Y	N	N	Y
27 Ortiz	Y	N	Y	Y	Y	Y
28 Rodriguez	Y	N	Y	Y	Y	?
29 Green	Y	N	Y	Y	+	Y
30 Johnson, E.B.	Y	N	Y	Y	Y	Y
UTAH						
1 **Hansen**	?	?	?	?	?	?
2 **Cook**	Y	Y	Y	N	N	Y
3 **Cannon**	Y	Y	Y	N	?	Y
VERMONT						
AL *Sanders*	Y	N	Y	Y	Y	Y
VIRGINIA						
1 Vacant						
2 Pickett	Y	N	Y	?	?	?
3 Scott	?	?	?	?	?	Y
4 Sisisky	Y	Y	Y	Y	?	Y
5 *Goode*	Y	Y	Y	N	N	Y
6 **Goodlatte**	Y	Y	Y	N	N	Y
7 **Bliley**	Y	Y	?	N	?	Y
8 Moran	Y	N	Y	Y	Y	Y
9 Boucher	?	?	?	?	?	?
10 **Wolf**	Y	Y	Y	N	N	Y
11 **Davis**	Y	Y	Y	N	N	Y
WASHINGTON						
1 Inslee	Y	N	Y	Y	Y	Y
2 **Metcalf**	Y	N	N	N	N	Y
3 Baird	N	?	Y	Y	Y	?
4 **Hastings**	Y	Y	Y	N	N	Y
5 **Nethercutt**	Y	Y	Y	N	N	?
6 Dicks	?	?	?	?	?	?
7 McDermott	Y	N	Y	Y	Y	Y
8 **Dunn**	?	?	?	?	?	?
9 Smith	Y	?	Y	Y	N	?
WEST VIRGINIA						
1 Mollohan	?	?	?	?	?	?
2 Wise	?	?	?	?	?	?
3 Rahall	Y	N	Y	Y	Y	Y
WISCONSIN						
1 **Ryan**	Y	Y	Y	N	N	Y
2 Baldwin	Y	N	Y	Y	Y	Y
3 Kind	Y	N	Y	Y	Y	Y
4 Kleczka	Y	Y	Y	Y	Y	Y
5 Barrett	Y	N	Y	Y	Y	?
6 **Petri**	Y	Y	Y	N	N	Y
7 Obey	Y	N	Y	Y	Y	Y
8 **Green**	Y	Y	Y	N	N	Y
9 **Sensenbrenner**	Y	Y	Y	N	N	Y
WYOMING						
AL **Cubin**	Y	Y	Y	N	N	Y

Southern states - Ala., Ark., Fla., Ga., Ky., La., Miss., N.C., Okla., S.C., Tenn., Texas, Va.

593. Procedural Motion/Journal. Approval of the House Journal of Thursday, Nov. 2, 2000. Approved 253-46: R 158-10; D 94-36 (ND 66-29, SD 28-7); I 1-0. Nov. 3, 2000.

594. S 2796. Water Resources/Conference Report. Adoption of the conference report on the bill that would authorize Army Corps of Engineers' water projects for flood and beach erosion, navigation, and environmental restoration. It also would authorize $7.8 billion for the 35-year Everglades restoration project. Adopted (thus cleared for the president) 312-2: R 179-2; D 131-0 (ND 96-0, SD 35-0); I 2-0. Nov. 3, 2000.

595. S 2594. Mancos Water Project/Passage. Doolittle, R-Calif., motion to suspend the rules and pass the bill that would authorize the Interior Department to contract with the Mancos Water Conservancy District in Colorado to use its facilities for impounding, storing, diverting and carrying non-project water for irrigation purposes and domestic, municipal and industrial uses. Motion rejected 201-151: R 190-0; D 10-150 (ND 5-111, SD 5-39); I 1-1. A two-thirds majority of those present and voting (235 in this case) is required for passage under suspension of the rules. Nov. 13, 2000.

596. S 1972. Joe Rowell Park/Passage. Doolittle, R-Calif., motion to suspend the rules and pass the bill that would direct the Agriculture Department to convey the site of the Joe Rowell Park to the town of Dolores, Colo. Motion rejected 201-145: R 186-0; D 14-144 (ND 9-107, SD 5-37); I 1-1. A two-thirds majority of those present and voting (231 in this case) is required for passage under suspension of the rules. Nov. 13, 2000.

597. HR 4986. Foreign Income Tax Exemption/Passage. Archer, R-Texas, motion to suspend the rules and pass the bill that would exempt from federal taxes most income earned abroad and repeal portions of PL 98-369 that created foreign sales corporations (FSCs) at a cost of approximately $1.5 billion over five years. The bill would treat all foreign sales alike as long as at least 50 percent of the content of the goods sold was produced in the United States. Additionally, current FSCs would be abolished on Sept. 30 and certain products, including oil, gas and unprocessed softwood timber, would not receive the benefit. Motion agreed to (thus clearing the bill for the president) 316-72: R 197-6; D 118-65 (ND 74-58, SD 44-7); I 1-1. A two-thirds majority of those present and voting (259 in this case) is required for passage under suspension of the rules. Nov. 14, 2000. A "yea" was a vote in support of the president's position.

Key

- Y Voted for (yea).
- # Paired for.
- + Announced for.
- N Voted against (nay).
- X Paired against.
- – Announced against.
- P Voted "present."
- C Voted "present" to avoid possible conflict of interest.
- ? Did not vote or otherwise make a position known.

•

Democrats ***Republicans***
Independents

	593	594	595	596	597
ALABAMA					
1 ***Callahan***	Y	Y	Y	Y	Y
2 ***Everett***	Y	Y	Y	Y	Y
3 ***Riley***	?	?	Y	Y	+
4 ***Aderholt***	N	Y	?	?	Y
5 Cramer	Y	Y	N	N	Y
6 ***Bachus***	Y	Y	Y	Y	Y
7 Hilliard	N	Y	N	N	Y
ALASKA					
AL ***Young***	?	Y	Y	Y	Y
ARIZONA					
1 ***Salmon***	?	?	Y	Y	Y
2 Pastor	N	Y	N	N	Y
3 ***Stump***	Y	Y	Y	Y	Y
4 ***Shadegg***	Y	Y	Y	Y	Y
5 ***Kolbe***	Y	Y	Y	Y	Y
6 ***Hayworth***	Y	Y	Y	Y	Y
ARKANSAS					
1 Berry	N	Y	N	N	Y
2 Snyder	Y	Y	N	N	Y
3 ***Hutchinson***	?	?	Y	Y	Y
4 ***Dickey***	?	?	?	?	?
CALIFORNIA					
1 Thompson	N	Y	N	N	Y
2 ***Herger***	Y	Y	Y	Y	Y
3 ***Ose***	?	?	Y	Y	Y
4 ***Doolittle***	?	Y	Y	Y	Y
5 Matsui	Y	Y	N	N	Y
6 Woolsey	Y	Y	N	N	N
7 Miller, George	?	?	N	N	N
8 Pelosi	?	?	N	N	Y
9 Lee	?	?	N	N	N
10 Tauscher	N	Y	N	N	Y
11 ***Pombo***	?	Y	Y	Y	Y
12 Lantos	?	?	N	N	Y
13 Stark	?	?	?	?	N
14 Eshoo	Y	Y	N	N	Y
15 ***Campbell***	?	?	Y	Y	Y
16 Lofgren	?	?	N	N	Y
17 Farr	?	?	?	?	?
18 Condit	N	Y	N	N	N
19 ***Radanovich***	Y	Y	Y	Y	Y
20 Dooley	?	?	N	N	Y
21 ***Thomas***	Y	Y	Y	Y	Y
22 Capps	+	+	N	N	Y
23 ***Gallegly***	Y	Y	Y	Y	Y
24 Sherman	Y	Y	N	N	Y
25 ***McKeon***	Y	Y	Y	Y	Y
26 Berman	?	?	N	N	Y
27 ***Rogan***	Y	Y	?	?	Y
28 ***Dreier***	Y	Y	Y	Y	Y
29 Waxman	?	?	N	N	N
30 Becerra	+	+	–	–	+
31 ***Martinez***	?	Y	Y	Y	Y
32 Dixon	?	Y	N	N	Y
33 Roybal-Allard	Y	Y	N	N	N
34 Napolitano	Y	Y	N	N	Y
35 Waters	?	?	N	N	N
36 ***Kuykendall***	Y	Y	Y	Y	Y
37 Millender-McD.	Y	Y	?	?	?
38 ***Horn***	Y	Y	Y	Y	Y
39 ***Royce***	Y	Y	Y	Y	Y
40 ***Lewis***	Y	Y	Y	Y	Y
41 ***Miller, Gary***	?	?	Y	Y	Y
42 Baca	Y	Y	N	N	Y
43 ***Calvert***	?	?	Y	Y	Y
44 ***Bono***	Y	Y	Y	Y	Y
45 ***Rohrabacher***	Y	Y	Y	Y	Y
46 Sanchez	+	+	N	N	Y
47 ***Cox***	Y	Y	Y	Y	Y
48 ***Packard***	Y	Y	Y	Y	Y
49 ***Bilbray***	?	?	Y	Y	Y
50 Filner	–	+	–	–	–
51 ***Cunningham***	Y	Y	Y	Y	Y
52 ***Hunter***	Y	Y	Y	Y	Y
COLORADO					
1 DeGette	?	?	N	Y	N
2 Udall	N	Y	N	Y	N
3 ***McInnis***	Y	Y	Y	Y	Y
4 ***Schaffer***	?	?	Y	Y	Y
5 ***Hefley***	?	?	?	?	?
6 ***Tancredo***	?	?	Y	Y	Y
CONNECTICUT					
1 Larson	Y	Y	N	N	Y
2 Gejdenson	?	?	N	N	?
3 DeLauro	Y	Y	N	N	Y
4 ***Shays***	?	?	Y	Y	Y
5 Maloney	Y	Y	N	N	N
6 ***Johnson***	Y	Y	Y	Y	Y
DELAWARE					
AL ***Castle***	Y	Y	Y	Y	Y
FLORIDA					
1 ***Scarborough***	Y	Y	Y	Y	Y
2 Boyd	Y	Y	–	–	Y
3 Brown	?	Y	?	?	?
4 ***Fowler***	?	?	Y	Y	Y
5 Thurman	Y	Y	N	N	N
6 ***Stearns***	Y	Y	Y	Y	Y
7 ***Mica***	Y	Y	Y	Y	Y
8 ***McCollum***	?	?	Y	Y	Y
9 ***Bilirakis***	Y	Y	Y	Y	Y
10 ***Young***	Y	Y	Y	Y	Y
11 Davis	Y	Y	N	N	Y
12 ***Canady***	Y	Y	Y	Y	?
13 ***Miller***	Y	Y	?	?	Y
14 ***Goss***	Y	Y	Y	Y	Y
15 ***Weldon***	?	?	Y	?	Y
16 ***Foley***	Y	Y	Y	Y	Y
17 Meek	?	?	N	N	Y
18 ***Ros-Lehtinen***	Y	Y	Y	Y	Y
19 Wexler	?	?	?	?	Y
20 Deutsch	Y	Y	–	–	Y
21 ***Diaz-Balart***	Y	Y	?	?	Y
22 ***Shaw***	Y	Y	Y	Y	Y
23 Hastings	?	?	N	N	Y
GEORGIA					
1 ***Kingston***	Y	Y	Y	Y	Y
2 Bishop	?	?	?	?	Y
3 ***Collins***	?	?	Y	Y	Y
4 McKinney	Y	?	N	N	N
5 Lewis	N	Y	N	N	N
6 ***Isakson***	Y	Y	Y	Y	Y
7 ***Barr***	Y	Y	Y	Y	Y
8 ***Chambliss***	Y	?	Y	Y	Y
9 ***Deal***	Y	Y	Y	Y	Y
10 ***Norwood***	Y	Y	Y	Y	Y
11 ***Linder***	Y	Y	Y	Y	Y
HAWAII					
1 Abercrombie	Y	Y	N	N	Y
2 Mink	Y	?	N	N	Y
IDAHO					
1 ***Chenoweth-Hage***	Y	N	Y	Y	N
2 ***Simpson***	Y	Y	Y	Y	Y
ILLINOIS					
1 Rush	?	?	?	?	N
2 Jackson	Y	Y	N	N	N
3 Lipinski	N	Y	N	N	N
4 Gutierrez	?	?	N	N	N
5 Blagojevich	N	Y	N	Y	Y
6 ***Hyde***	Y	Y	Y	Y	Y
7 Davis	?	?	N	N	N
8 ***Crane***	N	Y	Y	Y	Y
9 Schakowsky	Y	Y	N	N	N
10 ***Porter***	?	Y	Y	Y	?
11 ***Weller***	N	Y	Y	Y	Y
12 Costello	N	Y	N	N	N
13 ***Biggert***	Y	Y	Y	Y	Y

ND Northern Democrats SD Southern Democrats

	593	594	595	596	597
14 ***Hastert***	Y	Y			
15 ***Ewing***	?	?	Y	Y	Y
16 ***Manzullo***	Y	Y	Y	Y	Y
17 Evans	Y	Y	N	N	N
18 ***LaHood***	Y	Y	Y	Y	Y
19 Phelps	Y	Y	N	N	Y
20 ***Shimkus***	Y	Y	Y	Y	Y
INDIANA					
1 Visclosky	?	?	N	N	N
2 ***McIntosh***	?	?	?	?	?
3 Roemer	Y	Y	N	N	Y
4 ***Souder***	Y	Y	?	?	Y
5 ***Buyer***	Y	Y	Y	Y	Y
6 ***Burton***	?	Y	Y	Y	Y
7 ***Pease***	Y	Y	Y	Y	Y
8 ***Hostettler***	?	Y	Y	Y	N
9 Hill	Y	Y	N	N	Y
10 Carson	?	?	–	+	N
IOWA					
1 ***Leach***	?	Y	Y	Y	Y
2 ***Nussle***	Y	Y	Y	Y	Y
3 Boswell	?	?	?	?	Y
4 ***Ganske***	?	?	?	?	?
5 ***Latham***	N	Y	?	?	Y
KANSAS					
1 ***Moran***	N	Y	Y	Y	Y
2 ***Ryun***	Y	Y	Y	Y	Y
3 Moore	N	Y	N	N	Y
4 ***Tiahrt***	Y	Y	Y	Y	Y
KENTUCKY					
1 ***Whitfield***	?	?	Y	?	Y
2 ***Lewis***	Y	Y	Y	Y	Y
3 ***Northup***	Y	Y	Y	Y	Y
4 Lucas	Y	Y	Y	Y	Y
5 ***Rogers***	Y	Y	Y	Y	Y
6 ***Fletcher***	Y	Y	Y	Y	Y
LOUISIANA					
1 ***Vitter***	Y	Y	Y	Y	Y
2 Jefferson	N	Y	?	?	?
3 ***Tauzin***	?	Y	Y	Y	Y
4 ***McCrery***	Y	Y	Y	?	Y
5 ***Cooksey***	Y	Y	?	?	Y
6 ***Baker***	Y	Y	Y	Y	Y
7 John	Y	Y	?	?	Y
MAINE					
1 Allen	?	?	N	N	Y
2 Baldacci	Y	Y	N	N	N
MARYLAND					
1 ***Gilchrest***	Y	Y	?	?	Y
2 ***Ehrlich***	Y	Y	?	?	Y
3 Cardin	Y	Y	N	N	Y
4 Wynn	Y	Y	N	N	Y
5 Hoyer	Y	Y	N	N	Y
6 ***Bartlett***	Y	Y	Y	Y	Y
7 Cummings	Y	Y	N	Y	Y
8 ***Morella***	Y	?	Y	Y	Y
MASSACHUSETTS					
1 Olver	N	Y	N	N	N
2 Neal	?	?	?	?	Y
3 McGovern	N	Y	N	N	N
4 Frank	?	?	?	?	Y
5 Meehan	?	?	?	?	?
6 Tierney	?	?	N	N	N
7 Markey	N	Y	N	N	N
8 Capuano	N	Y	N	N	N
9 Moakley	Y	Y	?	?	?
10 Delahunt	?	?	N	N	Y
MICHIGAN					
1 Stupak	?	?	N	N	N
2 ***Hoekstra***	Y	Y	Y	Y	Y
3 ***Ehlers***	?	?	Y	Y	Y
4 ***Camp***	Y	Y	Y	Y	Y
5 Barcia	Y	Y	N	N	Y
6 ***Upton***	Y	Y	Y	Y	Y
7 ***Smith***	Y	Y	Y	Y	Y
8 Stabenow	?	Y	Y	Y	Y
9 Kildee	Y	Y	Y	N	Y
10 Bonior	Y	Y	N	N	N
11 ***Knollenberg***	Y	Y	Y	Y	Y
12 Levin	Y	Y	N	Y	Y
13 Rivers	Y	Y	N	N	N
14 Conyers	?	?	N	N	N
15 Kilpatrick	?	?	N	N	N
16 Dingell	?	?	N	N	N
MINNESOTA					
1 ***Gutknecht***	Y	Y	Y	Y	Y
2 Minge	Y	Y	N	N	Y
3 ***Ramstad***	N	Y	Y	Y	Y
4 Vacant					
5 Sabo	N	Y	N	N	Y
6 Luther	Y	Y	N	N	N
7 Peterson	N	Y	?	?	N
8 Oberstar	?	?	N	N	N
MISSISSIPPI					
1 ***Wicker***	N	Y	Y	Y	Y
2 Thompson	?	?	N	N	Y
3 ***Pickering***	Y	Y	Y	Y	Y
4 Shows	Y	Y	N	Y	N
5 Taylor	N	Y	Y	Y	N
MISSOURI					
1 Clay	?	?	?	?	Y
2 ***Talent***	?	?	?	?	?
3 Gephardt	?	?	N	N	Y
4 Skelton	Y	Y	Y	Y	Y
5 McCarthy	+	+	N	N	Y
6 Danner	?	?	?	?	?
7 ***Blunt***	Y	Y	Y	Y	Y
8 ***Emerson***	?	?	Y	Y	Y
9 ***Hulshof***	N	Y	?	?	?
MONTANA					
AL ***Hill***	?	?	Y	Y	Y
NEBRASKA					
1 ***Bereuter***	Y	Y	Y	Y	Y
2 ***Terry***	Y	Y	Y	Y	Y
3 ***Barrett***	Y	Y	Y	Y	Y
NEVADA					
1 Berkley	Y	Y	N	N	Y
2 ***Gibbons***	Y	Y	Y	Y	Y
NEW HAMPSHIRE					
1 ***Sununu***	Y	Y	Y	Y	Y
2 ***Bass***	Y	Y	Y	Y	Y
NEW JERSEY					
1 Andrews	Y	Y	?	?	N
2 ***LoBiondo***	N	Y	Y	Y	N
3 ***Saxton***	Y	Y	Y	Y	N
4 ***Smith***	Y	Y	Y	Y	Y
5 ***Roukema***	Y	Y	Y	Y	Y
6 Pallone	N	Y	N	N	N
7 ***Franks***	?	?	Y	Y	Y
8 Pascrell	N	Y	?	?	?
9 Rothman	N	Y	?	?	N
10 Payne	Y	Y	N	N	N
11 ***Frelinghuysen***	Y	Y	?	?	Y
12 Holt	N	Y	N	N	N
13 Menendez	N	Y	N	N	N
NEW MEXICO					
1 ***Wilson***	Y	Y	+	+	Y
2 ***Skeen***	Y	Y	Y	Y	Y
3 Udall	Y	Y	N	N	N
NEW YORK					
1 Forbes	?	?	?	?	?
2 ***Lazio***	?	?	Y	Y	Y
3 ***King***	?	?	Y	Y	Y
4 McCarthy	Y	Y	?	?	?
5 Ackerman	?	?	?	?	?
6 Meeks	N	Y	N	N	Y
7 Crowley	N	Y	N	N	Y
8 Nadler	Y	Y	N	N	N
9 Weiner	Y	Y	?	?	?
10 Towns	?	?	N	N	Y
11 Owens	?	?	N	N	Y
12 Velázquez	Y	Y	?	?	N
13 ***Fossella***	Y	Y	?	?	Y
14 Maloney	+	+	–	–	+
15 Rangel	Y	Y	N	N	Y
16 Serrano	?	?	N	N	N
17 Engel	Y	Y	N	N	Y
18 Lowey	Y	Y	?	?	Y
19 ***Kelly***	Y	Y	Y	Y	Y
20 ***Gilman***	Y	Y	Y	Y	Y
21 McNulty	Y	Y	?	?	Y
22 ***Sweeney***	?	Y	Y	Y	Y
23 ***Boehlert***	Y	Y	Y	Y	Y
24 ***McHugh***	Y	Y	Y	Y	Y
25 ***Walsh***	Y	Y	?	Y	Y
26 Hinchey	?	Y	N	N	N
27 ***Reynolds***	Y	Y	Y	Y	Y
28 Slaughter	+	+	N	N	N
29 LaFalce	N	Y	N	N	N
30 ***Quinn***	Y	Y	Y	Y	Y
31 ***Houghton***	Y	Y	Y	Y	Y
NORTH CAROLINA					
1 Clayton	?	?	N	N	Y
2 Etheridge	Y	Y	N	N	Y
3 ***Jones***	Y	Y	Y	Y	Y
4 Price	?	?	?	?	Y
5 ***Burr***	Y	Y	?	?	?
6 ***Coble***	Y	Y	Y	Y	Y
7 McIntyre	N	Y	N	N	Y
8 ***Hayes***	Y	Y	Y	Y	Y
9 ***Myrick***	Y	Y	Y	Y	Y
10 ***Ballenger***	?	?	?	?	?
11 ***Taylor***	?	?	?	?	?
12 Watt	Y	Y	N	N	N
NORTH DAKOTA					
AL Pomeroy	?	?	N	N	Y
OHIO					
1 ***Chabot***	Y	Y	Y	Y	N
2 ***Portman***	Y	Y	Y	Y	Y
3 Hall	?	?	?	?	Y
4 ***Oxley***	Y	Y	Y	Y	Y
5 ***Gillmor***	Y	Y	Y	Y	Y
6 Strickland	N	Y	?	?	N
7 ***Hobson***	Y	Y	Y	Y	Y
8 ***Boehner***	Y	Y	Y	Y	Y
9 Kaptur	Y	Y	?	?	?
10 Kucinich	Y	Y	N	N	N
11 Jones	Y	?	N	N	N
12 ***Kasich***	?	?	?	?	?
13 Brown	Y	Y	N	N	N
14 Sawyer	Y	Y	N	N	Y
15 ***Pryce***	?	Y	Y	Y	Y
16 ***Regula***	Y	Y	Y	Y	Y
17 Traficant	Y	Y	Y	Y	Y
18 ***Ney***	Y	Y	Y	Y	Y
19 ***LaTourette***	Y	Y	Y	Y	Y
OKLAHOMA					
1 ***Largent***	Y	Y	?	?	?
2 ***Coburn***	Y	Y	?	?	?
3 ***Watkins***	Y	Y	Y	Y	Y
4 ***Watts***	?	+	Y	Y	Y
5 ***Istook***	Y	Y	Y	Y	Y
6 ***Lucas***	Y	Y	Y	Y	Y
OREGON					
1 Wu	Y	Y	N	Y	Y
2 ***Walden***	Y	Y	Y	Y	Y
3 Blumenauer	?	?	N	N	Y
4 DeFazio	N	Y	?	?	N
5 Hooley	Y	Y	N	N	Y
PENNSYLVANIA					
1 Brady	N	Y	N	N	N
2 Fattah	?	?	N	N	?
3 Borski	N	Y	?	?	Y
4 Klink	?	?	?	?	?
5 ***Peterson***	?	Y	?	?	?
6 Holden	Y	Y	?	?	?
7 ***Weldon***	Y	Y	Y	Y	Y
8 ***Greenwood***	?	?	Y	Y	Y
9 ***Shuster***	Y	Y	Y	Y	Y
10 ***Sherwood***	Y	Y	Y	Y	Y
11 Kanjorski	Y	Y	N	N	Y
12 Murtha	Y	Y	N	N	Y
13 Hoeffel	Y	Y	?	?	Y
14 Coyne	Y	Y	?	?	?
15 ***Toomey***	Y	Y	Y	Y	Y
16 ***Pitts***	Y	Y	?	?	Y
17 ***Gekas***	Y	Y	Y	Y	Y
18 Doyle	Y	Y	Y	N	Y
19 ***Goodling***	Y	Y	Y	Y	Y
20 Mascara	Y	Y	N	N	Y
21 ***English***	N	Y	Y	Y	Y
RHODE ISLAND					
1 Kennedy	+	+	–	–	?
2 Weygand	?	?	?	?	?
SOUTH CAROLINA					
1 ***Sanford***	Y	N	Y	Y	Y
2 ***Spence***	Y	Y	Y	Y	Y
3 ***Graham***	Y	Y	Y	Y	Y
4 ***DeMint***	Y	Y	Y	Y	Y
5 Spratt	?	?	N	N	Y
6 Clyburn	?	?	N	N	Y
SOUTH DAKOTA					
AL ***Thune***	Y	Y	Y	Y	Y
TENNESSEE					
1 ***Jenkins***	Y	Y	Y	Y	Y
2 ***Duncan***	Y	Y	Y	Y	Y
3 ***Wamp***	Y	Y	?	?	Y
4 ***Hilleary***	Y	Y	Y	Y	Y
5 Clement	?	?	N	N	Y
6 Gordon	Y	Y	N	N	Y
7 ***Bryant***	Y	Y	Y	Y	Y
8 Tanner	Y	Y	N	N	Y
9 Ford	?	Y	N	N	Y
TEXAS					
1 Sandlin	Y	Y	N	N	Y
2 Turner	?	?	N	N	Y
3 ***Johnson, Sam***	?	Y	Y	Y	Y
4 Hall	Y	Y	Y	Y	Y
5 ***Sessions***	Y	Y	Y	Y	Y
6 ***Barton***	?	Y	Y	Y	Y
7 ***Archer***	?	?	Y	Y	Y
8 ***Brady***	Y	Y	Y	Y	Y
9 Lampson	Y	Y	N	N	Y
10 Doggett	Y	Y	N	N	N
11 Edwards	Y	Y	N	?	Y
12 ***Granger***	?	?	Y	Y	Y
13 ***Thornberry***	Y	Y	Y	Y	Y
14 ***Paul***	Y	?	Y	Y	P
15 Hinojosa	Y	Y	N	N	Y
16 Reyes	?	?	N	N	Y
17 Stenholm	N	Y	?	?	?
18 Jackson-Lee	?	?	N	N	Y
19 ***Combest***	Y	Y	Y	Y	Y
20 Gonzalez	Y	Y	N	N	Y
21 ***Smith***	Y	Y	Y	Y	Y
22 ***DeLay***	Y	Y	Y	Y	Y
23 ***Bonilla***	Y	Y	Y	Y	Y
24 Frost	Y	Y	N	N	Y
25 Bentsen	?	?	N	N	Y
26 ***Armey***	Y	Y	Y	?	Y
27 Ortiz	Y	Y	N	N	Y
28 Rodriguez	?	?	N	N	Y
29 Green	Y	Y	?	?	Y
30 Johnson, E.B.	Y	Y	N	N	Y
UTAH					
1 ***Hansen***	?	?	?	?	Y
2 ***Cook***	?	Y	Y	Y	N
3 ***Cannon***	Y	Y	Y	Y	Y
VERMONT					
AL *Sanders*	?	Y	N	N	N
VIRGINIA					
1 Vacant					
2 Pickett	?	?	Y	Y	Y
3 Scott	Y	Y	N	N	Y
4 Sisisky	Y	Y	Y	?	Y
5 *Goode*	Y	Y	Y	Y	Y
6 ***Goodlatte***	Y	Y	?	?	?
7 ***Bliley***	Y	Y	Y	Y	Y
8 Moran	Y	?	N	N	Y
9 Boucher	?	?	N	N	Y
10 ***Wolf***	?	Y	Y	Y	Y
11 ***Davis, T.***	Y	Y	Y	Y	Y
WASHINGTON					
1 Inslee	Y	Y	N	N	Y
2 ***Metcalf***	Y	Y	Y	Y	Y
3 Baird	?	?	N	N	Y
4 ***Hastings***	Y	Y	Y	Y	Y
5 ***Nethercutt***	?	?	Y	Y	Y
6 Dicks	?	?	N	N	Y
7 McDermott	N	Y	N	N	Y
8 ***Dunn***	?	?	?	?	Y
9 Smith	?	?	?	?	Y
WEST VIRGINIA					
1 Mollohan	?	?	N	N	Y
2 Wise	?	?	?	?	?
3 Rahall	Y	Y	N	N	N
WISCONSIN					
1 ***Ryan***	Y	Y	Y	Y	Y
2 Baldwin	Y	Y	N	N	N
3 Kind	Y	Y	N	N	Y
4 Kleczka	Y	Y	N	N	?
5 Barrett	Y	Y	N	N	Y
6 ***Petri***	Y	Y	Y	Y	Y
7 Obey	N	Y	N	N	N
8 ***Green***	Y	Y	Y	Y	Y
9 ***Sensenbrenner***	Y	Y	Y	Y	Y
WYOMING					
AL ***Cubin***	Y	Y	Y	?	Y

Southern states - Ala., Ark., Fla., Ga., Ky., La., Miss., N.C., Okla., S.C., Tenn., Texas, Va.

598. S 3137. James Madison Commemoration/Passage. Biggert, R-Ill., motion to suspend the rules and pass the bill that would establish the James Madison Commemoration Commission and authorize $250,000 for its activities. Motion agreed to 359-3: R 179-3; D 178-0 (ND 128-0, SD 50-0); I 2-0. A two-thirds majority of those present and voting (242 in this case) is required for passage under suspension of the rules. Dec. 4, 2000.

599. S 1761. Rio Grande Valley Water/Passage. Gibbons, R-Nev., motion to suspend the rules and pass the bill that would authorize the Interior Department to improve the water supply for the counties of Hudspeth and El Paso and counties in the Rio Grande Regional Water Planning Area in Texas. It would authorize $2 million for a feasibility study. Motion agreed to 348-6: R 173-6; D 173-0 (ND 124-0, SD 49-0); I 2-0. A two-thirds majority of those present and voting (236 in this case) is required for passage under suspension of the rules. Dec. 4, 2000.

600. H J Res 126. Continuing Resolution/Passage. Passage of the joint resolution that would provide temporary funding authority, at current levels, until Dec. 7, for the departments and programs for which regular fiscal 2001 appropriations are not enacted by Dec. 5. Passed 378-6: R 193-2; D 184-4 (ND 133-4, SD 51-0); I 1-0. Dec. 5, 2000.

601. H J Res 127. Continuing Resolution/Passage. Passage of the joint resolution that would provide temporary funding authority, at current levels, until Dec. 8, for the departments and programs for which regular fiscal 2001 appropriations will not be enacted by Dec. 7. Passed 359-11: R 178-2; D 179-9 (ND 130-9, SD 49-0); I 2-0. Dec. 7, 2000.

602. H J Res 128. Continuing Resolution/Passage. Passage of the joint resolution that would provide temporary funding authority, at current levels, until Dec. 11, for the departments and programs for which regular fiscal 2001 appropriations will not be enacted by Dec. 8. Passed 284-37: R 160-2; D 123-34 (ND 83-29, SD 40-5); I 1-1. Dec. 8, 2000.

603. HR 4577. Labor-HHS-Education Fiscal 2001 Appropriations/Conference Report. Adoption of the conference report on the bill that would appropriate $108.9 billion in fiscal 2001 for the departments of Labor, Health and Human Services, and Education. The report also incorporates by reference bills that would appropriate $30.4 billion for the Treasury Department and Postal Service and $2.5 billion for the legislative branch. Other bills incorporated in the report would rewrite commodity exchange laws; provide tax incentives to encourage investment in low-income communities; reauthorize medical savings accounts for two years; and allocate approximately $35 billion in additional Medicare payments to health care providers. Adopted (thus sent to the Senate) 292-60: R 133-51; D 157-9 (ND 114-8, SD 43-1); I 2-0. Dec. 15, 2000.

[1] *Rep. Julian C. Dixon, D-Calif., died on Dec. 8, 2000. The last vote for which he was eligible was 601.*

Key

- Y Voted for (yea).
- # Paired for.
- + Announced for.
- N Voted against (nay).
- X Paired against.
- – Announced against.
- P Voted "present."
- C Voted "present" to avoid possible conflict of interest.
- ? Did not vote or otherwise make a position known.

•

Democrats ***Republicans***
Independents

	598	599	600	601	602	603
ALABAMA						
1 ***Callahan***	Y	Y	Y	Y	Y	?
2 ***Everett***	Y	Y	Y	Y	Y	?
3 ***Riley***	Y	Y	Y	Y	Y	N
4 ***Aderholt***	Y	Y	Y	Y	Y	N
5 Cramer	Y	Y	Y	Y	?	Y
6 ***Bachus***	Y	Y	Y	Y	Y	Y
7 Hilliard	?	?	Y	Y	Y	Y
ALASKA						
AL ***Young***	Y	Y	Y	?	?	Y
ARIZONA						
1 ***Salmon***	Y	Y	Y	Y	Y	N
2 Pastor	Y	?	Y	Y	Y	Y
3 ***Stump***	Y	Y	Y	Y	Y	Y
4 ***Shadegg***	Y	Y	Y	Y	Y	?
5 ***Kolbe***	Y	Y	Y	Y	Y	?
6 ***Hayworth***	Y	Y	Y	Y	Y	N
ARKANSAS						
1 Berry	Y	Y	Y	Y	Y	Y
2 Snyder	Y	Y	Y	Y	Y	?
3 ***Hutchinson***	Y	Y	Y	?	Y	Y
4 ***Dickey***	?	?	?	?	?	Y
CALIFORNIA						
1 Thompson	Y	Y	Y	Y	Y	Y
2 ***Herger***	Y	Y	Y	Y	Y	N
3 ***Ose***	Y	Y	Y	Y	Y	Y
4 ***Doolittle***	?	?	?	Y	Y	Y
5 Matsui	Y	Y	Y	Y	Y	Y
6 Woolsey	?	?	?	N	N	Y
7 Miller, George	?	?	Y	N	?	?
8 Pelosi	?	?	Y	Y	N	?
9 Lee	Y	Y	Y	Y	Y	Y
10 Tauscher	Y	Y	Y	Y	Y	Y
11 ***Pombo***	Y	Y	Y	Y	Y	N
12 Lantos	?	?	?	?	?	?
13 Stark	?	?	?	N	N	N
14 Eshoo	Y	Y	Y	Y	?	?
15 ***Campbell***	Y	N	Y	Y	Y	?
16 Lofgren	Y	Y	Y	Y	?	?
17 Farr	Y	Y	Y	Y	N	?
18 Condit	Y	Y	Y	Y	Y	Y
19 ***Radanovich***	?	?	Y	Y	Y	N
20 Dooley	Y	Y	?	Y	Y	+
21 ***Thomas***	Y	Y	Y	Y	Y	Y
22 Capps	Y	Y	Y	Y	Y	Y
23 ***Gallegly***	Y	Y	Y	?	?	Y
24 Sherman	Y	Y	Y	Y	Y	Y
25 ***McKeon***	Y	Y	Y	Y	Y	?
26 Berman	Y	Y	Y	Y	?	?
27 ***Rogan***	Y	?	Y	?	?	Y
28 ***Dreier***	Y	Y	Y	Y	Y	Y
29 Waxman	Y	?	Y	Y	?	?
30 Becerra	+	+	Y	Y	?	Y
31 ***Martinez***	?	?	Y	?	?	Y
32 Dixon [1]	?	?	?	?		
33 Roybal-Allard	Y	Y	Y	Y	Y	Y
34 Napolitano	Y	Y	Y	Y	Y	?
35 Waters	Y	Y	?	Y	N	?
36 ***Kuykendall***	Y	Y	Y	Y	Y	Y
37 Millender-McD.	Y	Y	Y	Y	Y	?
38 ***Horn***	Y	Y	Y	Y	Y	Y
39 ***Royce***	N	N	Y	Y	Y	N
40 ***Lewis***	Y	?	Y	Y	?	Y
41 ***Miller, Gary***	?	?	Y	?	?	?
42 Baca	Y	Y	Y	Y	?	Y
43 ***Calvert***	?	?	Y	Y	Y	?
44 ***Bono***	Y	Y	Y	?	?	?
45 ***Rohrabacher***	Y	Y	Y	Y	?	N
46 Sanchez	Y	Y	Y	Y	Y	?
47 ***Cox***	?	?	Y	Y	Y	N
48 ***Packard***	Y	Y	Y	?	?	Y
49 ***Bilbray***	?	?	Y	?	?	?
50 Filner	Y	Y	Y	+	+	–
51 ***Cunningham***	Y	Y	Y	Y	?	Y
52 ***Hunter***	Y	Y	Y	Y	Y	Y
COLORADO						
1 DeGette	Y	Y	Y	Y	N	Y
2 Udall	Y	Y	Y	Y	Y	Y
3 ***McInnis***	Y	Y	Y	Y	?	?
4 ***Schaffer***	Y	Y	Y	Y	Y	?
5 ***Hefley***	Y	Y	Y	Y	?	?
6 ***Tancredo***	Y	Y	Y	Y	?	N
CONNECTICUT						
1 Larson	Y	Y	Y	Y	Y	Y
2 Gejdenson	?	?	?	Y	?	?
3 DeLauro	Y	Y	Y	Y	N	Y
4 ***Shays***	Y	Y	Y	Y	Y	Y
5 Maloney	Y	?	Y	Y	Y	Y
6 ***Johnson***	?	?	?	Y	Y	Y
DELAWARE						
AL ***Castle***	?	?	Y	Y	Y	Y
FLORIDA						
1 ***Scarborough***	Y	Y	Y	?	?	?
2 Boyd	+	+	Y	Y	Y	Y
3 Brown	Y	Y	Y	Y	Y	+
4 ***Fowler***	?	?	Y	Y	?	Y
5 Thurman	Y	Y	Y	Y	N	N
6 ***Stearns***	Y	Y	Y	Y	Y	N
7 ***Mica***	Y	Y	Y	Y	Y	?
8 ***McCollum***	Y	Y	Y	Y	?	Y
9 ***Bilirakis***	Y	Y	Y	Y	Y	Y
10 ***Young***	Y	Y	Y	Y	Y	?
11 Davis	Y	?	Y	Y	Y	Y
12 ***Canady***	Y	Y	Y	Y	Y	Y
13 ***Miller***	?	?	?	?	?	Y
14 ***Goss***	Y	Y	Y	Y	Y	Y
15 ***Weldon***	Y	Y	?	Y	Y	N
16 ***Foley***	Y	Y	Y	Y	Y	Y
17 Meek	Y	Y	Y	Y	Y	?
18 ***Ros-Lehtinen***	Y	Y	Y	?	?	?
19 Wexler	?	?	?	Y	Y	Y
20 Deutsch	Y	Y	Y	Y	Y	Y
21 ***Diaz-Balart***	Y	Y	Y	?	Y	Y
22 ***Shaw***	Y	Y	Y	Y	Y	Y
23 Hastings	Y	Y	Y	Y	?	?
GEORGIA						
1 ***Kingston***	Y	Y	Y	?	?	N
2 Bishop	Y	Y	Y	Y	Y	Y
3 ***Collins***	Y	Y	Y	Y	Y	Y
4 McKinney	Y	Y	Y	Y	?	?
5 Lewis	Y	Y	Y	Y	?	Y
6 ***Isakson***	Y	Y	Y	Y	Y	Y
7 ***Barr***	Y	Y	Y	?	Y	N
8 ***Chambliss***	Y	Y	Y	Y	Y	Y
9 ***Deal***	?	?	?	Y	?	N
10 ***Norwood***	Y	Y	Y	Y	Y	?
11 ***Linder***	?	?	Y	Y	Y	Y
HAWAII						
1 Abercrombie	Y	Y	Y	Y	Y	Y
2 Mink	?	?	Y	Y	N	Y
IDAHO						
1 ***Chenoweth-Hage***	?	?	?	?	?	N
2 ***Simpson***	Y	Y	Y	Y	Y	Y
ILLINOIS						
1 Rush	Y	Y	Y	?	?	Y
2 Jackson	Y	Y	Y	Y	Y	Y
3 Lipinski	?	?	?	?	?	Y
4 Gutierrez	Y	?	Y	Y	Y	?
5 Blagojevich	Y	Y	Y	?	?	Y
6 ***Hyde***	Y	Y	Y	Y	?	Y
7 Davis	Y	Y	Y	?	?	Y
8 ***Crane***	Y	Y	Y	Y	Y	N
9 Schakowsky	Y	Y	Y	Y	N	Y
10 ***Porter***	Y	Y	Y	Y	Y	Y
11 ***Weller***	Y	Y	Y	Y	Y	Y
12 Costello	Y	Y	N	?	?	Y

ND Northern Democrats SD Southern Democrats

	598	599	600	601	602	603
13 ***Biggert***	Y	Y	Y	Y	Y	Y
14 ***Hastert***						Y
15 ***Ewing***	Y	Y	Y	Y	Y	Y
16 ***Manzullo***	Y	Y	Y	Y	Y	N
17 Evans	Y	Y	Y	Y	Y	Y
18 ***LaHood***	Y	Y	Y	Y	?	Y
19 Phelps	Y	Y	Y	Y	?	Y
20 ***Shimkus***	Y	Y	Y	Y	Y	Y
INDIANA						
1 Visclosky	Y	Y	N	N	N	Y
2 ***McIntosh***	Y	Y	Y	Y	?	?
3 Roemer	Y	Y	Y	Y	Y	Y
4 ***Souder***	Y	Y	Y	Y	Y	?
5 ***Buyer***	Y	Y	Y	Y	Y	Y
6 ***Burton***	Y	Y	?	Y	+	N
7 ***Pease***	Y	Y	Y	Y	Y	Y
8 ***Hostettler***	Y	N	Y	Y	Y	N
9 Hill	Y	Y	Y	Y	Y	Y
10 Carson	?	?	Y	Y	Y	Y
IOWA						
1 ***Leach***	Y	Y	Y	Y	Y	Y
2 ***Nussle***	Y	Y	Y	Y	Y	Y
3 Boswell	Y	Y	Y	Y	Y	N
4 ***Ganske***	Y	Y	Y	Y	Y	Y
5 ***Latham***	Y	Y	Y	Y	Y	?
KANSAS						
1 ***Moran***	Y	Y	Y	Y	Y	Y
2 ***Ryun***	Y	Y	Y	Y	Y	N
3 Moore	Y	Y	Y	Y	Y	Y
4 ***Tiahrt***	Y	Y	Y	Y	Y	Y
KENTUCKY						
1 ***Whitfield***	?	?	Y	Y	Y	Y
2 ***Lewis***	Y	Y	Y	Y	Y	Y
3 ***Northup***	?	?	Y	Y	Y	Y
4 Lucas	Y	Y	Y	Y	Y	Y
5 ***Rogers***	Y	Y	Y	Y	Y	?
6 ***Fletcher***	Y	Y	Y	Y	Y	Y
LOUISIANA						
1 ***Vitter***	?	?	?	Y	Y	N
2 Jefferson	?	?	?	Y	Y	Y
3 ***Tauzin***	Y	Y	Y	Y	Y	Y
4 ***McCrery***	Y	Y	Y	?	?	Y
5 ***Cooksey***	?	?	Y	Y	Y	Y
6 ***Baker***	Y	Y	Y	Y	?	?
7 John	Y	Y	Y	Y	?	Y
MAINE						
1 Allen	Y	Y	?	Y	Y	Y
2 Baldacci	Y	Y	Y	Y	Y	Y
MARYLAND						
1 ***Gilchrest***	Y	Y	Y	Y	Y	Y
2 ***Ehrlich***	Y	Y	Y	Y	?	Y
3 Cardin	Y	Y	Y	Y	Y	Y
4 Wynn	Y	Y	Y	Y	Y	Y
5 Hoyer	Y	Y	Y	Y	?	Y
6 ***Bartlett***	Y	Y	Y	Y	?	N
7 Cummings	Y	Y	Y	Y	Y	Y
8 ***Morella***	Y	Y	Y	Y	Y	Y
MASSACHUSETTS						
1 Olver	Y	Y	Y	Y	N	Y
2 Neal	Y	Y	Y	Y	?	Y
3 McGovern	Y	Y	Y	Y	Y	Y
4 Frank	Y	Y	Y	Y	Y	N
5 Meehan	Y	Y	Y	Y	?	Y
6 Tierney	Y	Y	Y	Y	?	Y
7 Markey	Y	Y	Y	Y	Y	Y
8 Capuano	Y	Y	Y	N	N	Y
9 Moakley	?	?	?	Y	Y	?
10 Delahunt	?	?	?	Y	?	?
MICHIGAN						
1 Stupak	Y	Y	N	N	N	Y
2 ***Hoekstra***	Y	Y	?	Y	Y	N
3 ***Ehlers***	Y	Y	Y	Y	Y	Y
4 ***Camp***	Y	Y	Y	Y	Y	Y
5 Barcia	Y	Y	Y	Y	Y	Y
6 ***Upton***	Y	Y	Y	Y	Y	Y
7 ***Smith***	Y	Y	Y	?	Y	N
8 Stabenow	?	?	Y	Y	Y	Y
9 Kildee	Y	Y	Y	Y	Y	Y
10 Bonior	?	Y	Y	N	N	+
11 ***Knollenberg***	Y	Y	Y	Y	Y	Y
12 Levin	Y	Y	Y	Y	Y	Y
13 Rivers	Y	Y	Y	Y	Y	Y
14 Conyers	Y	Y	Y	Y	N	?
15 Kilpatrick	Y	Y	Y	Y	N	Y
16 Dingell	Y	Y	N	N	N	Y
MINNESOTA						
1 ***Gutknecht***	?	?	?	Y	Y	Y
2 Minge	Y	Y	Y	Y	Y	Y
3 ***Ramstad***	Y	Y	Y	Y	Y	Y
4 Vacant						
5 Sabo	Y	Y	Y	Y	Y	Y
6 Luther	Y	Y	Y	Y	Y	Y
7 Peterson	Y	Y	Y	Y	Y	Y
8 Oberstar	Y	Y	Y	Y	N	?
MISSISSIPPI						
1 ***Wicker***	Y	Y	Y	?	?	N
2 Thompson	Y	Y	Y	?	?	Y
3 ***Pickering***	Y	Y	Y	Y	Y	Y
4 Shows	Y	Y	Y	Y	Y	Y
5 Taylor	Y	Y	Y	Y	Y	Y
MISSOURI						
1 Clay	?	?	Y	?	?	?
2 ***Talent***	?	?	?	?	?	Y
3 Gephardt	?	?	Y	Y	Y	Y
4 Skelton	Y	Y	Y	Y	Y	Y
5 McCarthy	Y	Y	Y	Y	Y	Y
6 Danner	Y	Y	Y	?	?	?
7 ***Blunt***	Y	Y	Y	Y	Y	N
8 ***Emerson***	Y	Y	Y	?	?	Y
9 ***Hulshof***	?	?	?	Y	Y	Y
MONTANA						
AL ***Hill***	Y	Y	?	?	?	?
NEBRASKA						
1 ***Bereuter***	Y	Y	Y	Y	Y	Y
2 ***Terry***	Y	Y	Y	Y	Y	N
3 ***Barrett***	?	?	?	Y	Y	Y
NEVADA						
1 Berkley	Y	Y	Y	Y	Y	Y
2 ***Gibbons***	Y	Y	Y	Y	Y	Y
NEW HAMPSHIRE						
1 ***Sununu***	Y	Y	Y	Y	Y	Y
2 ***Bass***	Y	Y	Y	Y	Y	Y
NEW JERSEY						
1 Andrews	Y	Y	Y	Y	Y	Y
2 ***LoBiondo***	Y	Y	Y	Y	Y	Y
3 ***Saxton***	Y	Y	Y	Y	Y	Y
4 ***Smith***	Y	Y	Y	Y	Y	N
5 ***Roukema***	Y	Y	Y	Y	Y	Y
6 Pallone	Y	Y	Y	Y	Y	Y
7 ***Franks***	Y	Y	Y	Y	Y	Y
8 Pascrell	Y	Y	Y	Y	Y	Y
9 Rothman	Y	Y	?	Y	?	Y
10 Payne	Y	Y	Y	Y	Y	Y
11 ***Frelinghuysen***	Y	Y	Y	Y	Y	Y
12 Holt	Y	Y	Y	Y	Y	?
13 Menendez	Y	Y	Y	Y	Y	Y
NEW MEXICO						
1 ***Wilson***	Y	Y	Y	Y	Y	Y
2 ***Skeen***	Y	Y	Y	Y	Y	Y
3 Udall	Y	Y	Y	Y	Y	Y
NEW YORK						
1 Forbes	?	?	Y	Y	?	?
2 ***Lazio***	Y	Y	Y	Y	Y	Y
3 ***King***	Y	Y	Y	?	?	Y
4 McCarthy	Y	Y	Y	?	?	Y
5 Ackerman	Y	Y	Y	?	?	?
6 Meeks	Y	Y	Y	Y	Y	Y
7 Crowley	Y	Y	Y	Y	?	Y
8 Nadler	?	?	Y	Y	Y	Y
9 Weiner	Y	Y	Y	Y	?	Y
10 Towns	Y	Y	?	?	?	Y
11 Owens	?	?	Y	Y	N	Y
12 Velázquez	Y	Y	Y	Y	Y	Y
13 ***Fossella***	Y	Y	Y	?	?	Y
14 Maloney	Y	Y	Y	Y	Y	Y
15 Rangel	Y	Y	Y	Y	Y	Y
16 Serrano	Y	Y	Y	Y	Y	Y
17 Engel	Y	Y	Y	Y	?	Y
18 Lowey	Y	Y	?	Y	N	Y
19 ***Kelly***	Y	Y	Y	Y	Y	Y
20 ***Gilman***	Y	Y	Y	Y	Y	Y
21 McNulty	Y	Y	Y	Y	Y	Y
22 ***Sweeney***	Y	Y	Y	Y	Y	Y
23 ***Boehlert***	Y	Y	Y	Y	Y	?
24 ***McHugh***	Y	Y	Y	Y	Y	Y
25 ***Walsh***	Y	Y	Y	Y	Y	?
26 Hinchey	?	?	Y	Y	N	Y
27 ***Reynolds***	?	?	Y	Y	Y	Y
28 Slaughter	Y	Y	Y	Y	Y	Y
29 LaFalce	Y	?	Y	Y	?	?
30 ***Quinn***	?	?	Y	Y	Y	Y
31 ***Houghton***	Y	Y	Y	Y	?	?
NORTH CAROLINA						
1 Clayton	Y	Y	Y	Y	Y	Y
2 Etheridge	Y	Y	Y	Y	Y	Y
3 ***Jones***	?	?	?	Y	Y	N
4 Price	Y	Y	Y	?	Y	?
5 ***Burr***	Y	Y	Y	Y	Y	Y
6 ***Coble***	Y	N	Y	Y	Y	Y
7 McIntyre	Y	Y	Y	Y	Y	Y
8 ***Hayes***	Y	Y	Y	Y	Y	Y
9 ***Myrick***	Y	Y	Y	Y	Y	Y
10 ***Ballenger***	Y	Y	Y	Y	Y	?
11 ***Taylor***	Y	Y	Y	?	?	Y
12 Watt	Y	Y	Y	Y	Y	Y
NORTH DAKOTA						
AL Pomeroy	Y	Y	?	Y	?	Y
OHIO						
1 ***Chabot***	Y	Y	Y	Y	Y	N
2 ***Portman***	Y	Y	Y	Y	Y	+
3 Hall	Y	Y	Y	Y	?	Y
4 ***Oxley***	Y	Y	Y	Y	?	Y
5 ***Gillmor***	Y	Y	Y	?	?	?
6 Strickland	Y	Y	Y	Y	N	Y
7 ***Hobson***	Y	Y	Y	Y	Y	?
8 ***Boehner***	Y	Y	Y	Y	?	Y
9 Kaptur	Y	Y	Y	Y	?	Y
10 Kucinich	Y	Y	Y	Y	Y	N
11 Jones	Y	Y	Y	Y	Y	Y
12 ***Kasich***	Y	Y	Y	?	?	Y
13 Brown	Y	Y	Y	Y	N	Y
14 Sawyer	Y	Y	Y	Y	Y	Y
15 ***Pryce***	?	?	Y	Y	Y	Y
16 ***Regula***	Y	Y	Y	Y	Y	Y
17 Traficant	Y	Y	Y	Y	Y	Y
18 ***Ney***	Y	Y	Y	?	Y	Y
19 ***LaTourette***	Y	Y	Y	?	Y	Y
OKLAHOMA						
1 ***Largent***	?	?	Y	?	?	?
2 ***Coburn***	?	?	?	?	?	?
3 ***Watkins***	?	?	Y	Y	?	Y
4 ***Watts***	?	?	Y	Y	Y	Y
5 ***Istook***	Y	Y	Y	?	Y	Y
6 ***Lucas***	Y	Y	Y	Y	Y	Y
OREGON						
1 Wu	Y	Y	Y	Y	Y	Y
2 ***Walden***	Y	Y	Y	Y	Y	+
3 Blumenauer	Y	Y	Y	Y	Y	?
4 DeFazio	?	?	?	?	?	N
5 Hooley	Y	Y	Y	Y	Y	Y
PENNSYLVANIA						
1 Brady	Y	Y	Y	Y	?	Y
2 Fattah	?	?	Y	Y	?	?
3 Borski	Y	Y	Y	Y	?	Y
4 Klink	?	?	?	Y	Y	?
5 ***Peterson***	?	?	?	?	?	?
6 Holden	Y	Y	Y	Y	Y	Y
7 ***Weldon***	Y	Y	?	Y	Y	Y
8 ***Greenwood***	Y	Y	Y	Y	?	Y
9 ***Shuster***	Y	Y	Y	Y	?	?
10 ***Sherwood***	Y	Y	Y	Y	Y	Y
11 Kanjorski	Y	Y	Y	Y	Y	Y
12 Murtha	?	?	Y	Y	Y	Y
13 Hoeffel	Y	Y	Y	Y	Y	Y
14 Coyne	Y	Y	Y	Y	N	Y
15 ***Toomey***	Y	Y	Y	Y	Y	N
16 ***Pitts***	Y	Y	Y	Y	Y	N
17 ***Gekas***	Y	Y	?	Y	Y	Y
18 Doyle	Y	Y	Y	Y	Y	Y
19 ***Goodling***	Y	Y	Y	Y	Y	Y
20 Mascara	Y	Y	Y	Y	Y	Y
21 ***English***	Y	Y	Y	Y	Y	Y
RHODE ISLAND						
1 Kennedy	Y	Y	Y	Y	N	Y
2 Weygand	Y	Y	Y	Y	?	Y
SOUTH CAROLINA						
1 ***Sanford***	N	N	Y	?	?	N
2 ***Spence***	Y	Y	?	Y	Y	Y
3 ***Graham***	?	Y	Y	?	?	N
4 ***DeMint***	Y	Y	Y	Y	Y	N
5 Spratt	Y	Y	Y	Y	Y	Y
6 Clyburn	Y	Y	Y	Y	Y	Y
SOUTH DAKOTA						
AL ***Thune***	Y	Y	Y	Y	Y	Y
TENNESSEE						
1 ***Jenkins***	Y	Y	Y	Y	Y	Y
2 ***Duncan***	Y	?	Y	Y	Y	N
3 ***Wamp***	?	?	Y	Y	?	Y
4 ***Hilleary***	Y	Y	Y	Y	Y	Y
5 Clement	Y	Y	Y	Y	?	Y
6 Gordon	Y	Y	Y	Y	Y	Y
7 ***Bryant***	Y	Y	?	?	?	Y
8 Tanner	Y	Y	Y	Y	Y	Y
9 Ford	Y	Y	Y	Y	N	Y
TEXAS						
1 Sandlin	Y	Y	Y	Y	Y	?
2 Turner	Y	Y	Y	Y	Y	Y
3 ***Johnson, Sam***	Y	Y	Y	Y	Y	N
4 Hall	Y	Y	Y	Y	Y	Y
5 ***Sessions***	?	?	?	Y	Y	N
6 ***Barton***	Y	Y	N	N	N	N
7 ***Archer***	Y	Y	Y	?	?	Y
8 ***Brady***	?	?	Y	Y	Y	Y
9 Lampson	Y	Y	Y	Y	Y	Y
10 Doggett	Y	Y	Y	Y	Y	Y
11 Edwards	Y	Y	?	Y	Y	Y
12 ***Granger***	?	?	Y	?	?	N
13 ***Thornberry***	Y	Y	Y	Y	Y	Y
14 ***Paul***	N	N	N	N	N	N
15 Hinojosa	Y	Y	Y	Y	?	Y
16 Reyes	Y	Y	Y	Y	Y	Y
17 Stenholm	Y	Y	Y	Y	Y	Y
18 Jackson-Lee	Y	Y	Y	Y	N	Y
19 ***Combest***	Y	Y	Y	Y	Y	Y
20 Gonzalez	Y	Y	Y	Y	Y	Y
21 ***Smith***	Y	Y	Y	Y	Y	Y
22 ***DeLay***	Y	Y	?	Y	Y	N
23 ***Bonilla***	Y	Y	Y	Y	Y	?
24 Frost	Y	Y	Y	Y	Y	Y
25 Bentsen	Y	Y	Y	Y	Y	Y
26 ***Armey***	?	?	?	?	Y	Y
27 Ortiz	Y	Y	Y	Y	Y	?
28 Rodriguez	Y	Y	Y	Y	Y	Y
29 Green	Y	Y	Y	+	Y	Y
30 Johnson, E.B.	Y	Y	Y	Y	N	Y
UTAH						
1 ***Hansen***	Y	Y	Y	Y	?	?
2 ***Cook***	Y	Y	Y	Y	Y	N
3 ***Cannon***	Y	Y	Y	Y	Y	N
VERMONT						
AL *Sanders*	Y	Y	Y	Y	N	Y
VIRGINIA						
1 Vacant						
2 Pickett	Y	Y	Y	?	?	?
3 Scott	Y	Y	Y	Y	N	Y
4 Sisisky	Y	Y	Y	Y	Y	Y
5 *Goode*	Y	Y	?	Y	Y	Y
6 ***Goodlatte***	Y	Y	Y	Y	Y	N
7 ***Bliley***	Y	?	Y	Y	Y	Y
8 Moran	Y	Y	Y	Y	Y	?
9 Boucher	Y	Y	Y	?	Y	Y
10 ***Wolf***	Y	Y	Y	Y	Y	Y
11 ***Davis, T.***	Y	Y	Y	Y	Y	Y
WASHINGTON						
1 Inslee	Y	Y	Y	Y	Y	N
2 ***Metcalf***	Y	Y	Y	Y	Y	N
3 Baird	Y	Y	Y	N	N	Y
4 ***Hastings***	Y	Y	Y	Y	Y	Y
5 ***Nethercutt***	Y	Y	Y	Y	Y	Y
6 Dicks	Y	Y	Y	Y	Y	Y
7 McDermott	Y	Y	+	Y	N	–
8 ***Dunn***	Y	Y	Y	Y	Y	Y
9 Smith	Y	Y	Y	Y	?	N
WEST VIRGINIA						
1 Mollohan	?	?	Y	Y	Y	?
2 Wise	?	?	Y	?	?	Y
3 Rahall	Y	Y	Y	Y	Y	Y
WISCONSIN						
1 ***Ryan***	?	?	?	?	?	N
2 Baldwin	Y	Y	Y	Y	N	Y
3 Kind	Y	Y	Y	+	Y	N
4 Kleczka	Y	Y	Y	Y	Y	Y
5 Barrett	Y	Y	Y	Y	Y	Y
6 ***Petri***	Y	Y	Y	Y	?	Y
7 Obey	Y	Y	Y	Y	N	Y
8 ***Green***	Y	Y	Y	Y	Y	N
9 ***Sensenbrenner***	Y	Y	Y	Y	Y	N
WYOMING						
AL ***Cubin***	Y	Y	Y	Y	?	Y

Southern states - Ala., Ark., Fla., Ga., Ky., La., Miss., N.C., Okla., S.C., Tenn., Texas, Va.

House Roll Call Votes By Subject

G

H

I

K

L

M

N

P

R

S

T

U

V

Appendix S

SENATE ROLL CALL VOTES

Senate Roll Call Votes By Bill Number

Senate Bills

House Bills

Senate Votes 1, 2, 3, 4, 5, 6

	1	2	3	4	5	6
ALABAMA						
Shelby	Y	Y	Y	N	Y	Y
Sessions	Y	N	Y	N	Y	Y
ALASKA						
Stevens	Y	Y	Y	N	Y	?
Murkowski	Y	Y	Y	N	Y	Y
ARIZONA						
McCain	?	?	?	?	?	?
Kyl	Y	N	Y	N	Y	?
ARKANSAS						
Hutchinson	Y	N	Y	N	Y	Y
Lincoln	Y	Y	Y	N	Y	Y
CALIFORNIA						
Feinstein	N	Y	Y	Y	Y	Y
Boxer	N	Y	N	Y	N	+
COLORADO						
Campbell	Y	Y	Y	N	Y	Y
Allard	Y	N	Y	N	Y	Y
CONNECTICUT						
Dodd	N	Y	N	N	N	Y
Lieberman	N	Y	Y	N	Y	Y
DELAWARE						
Roth	Y	Y	Y	N	Y	Y
Biden	N	Y	N	Y	Y	Y
FLORIDA						
Graham	N	Y	N	Y	N	Y
Mack	Y	Y	Y	N	Y	Y
GEORGIA						
Coverdell	Y	Y	Y	N	Y	Y
Cleland	N	Y	N	Y	Y	Y
HAWAII						
Inouye	N	Y	N	Y	Y	Y
Akaka	N	Y	N	Y	Y	Y
IDAHO						
Craig	Y	Y	Y	N	Y	Y
Crapo	Y	Y	Y	N	Y	Y
ILLINOIS						
Durbin	N	Y	N	Y	Y	Y
Fitzgerald	C	C	C	C	C	Y
INDIANA						
Lugar	Y	N	Y	N	Y	Y
Bayh	N	Y	N	N	Y	Y
IOWA						
Grassley	Y	Y	Y	N	Y	Y
Harkin	N	Y	N	Y	N	N
KANSAS						
Brownback	Y	N	Y	N	N	Y
Roberts	Y	N	Y	N	Y	Y
KENTUCKY						
McConnell	Y	Y	Y	N	Y	Y
Bunning	Y	N	Y	N	Y	Y
LOUISIANA						
Breaux	N	Y	N	N	Y	Y
Landrieu	N	Y	N	N	Y	Y
MAINE						
Snowe	Y	Y	Y	N	Y	Y
Collins	Y	Y	Y	N	Y	Y
MARYLAND						
Sarbanes	N	Y	N	Y	N	Y
Mikulski	N	Y	N	Y	Y	Y
MASSACHUSETTS						
Kennedy	N	Y	N	Y	N	Y
Kerry	N	Y	N	Y	Y	Y
MICHIGAN						
Levin	N	Y	N	Y	Y	Y
Abraham	Y	Y	Y	N	Y	Y
MINNESOTA						
Wellstone	N	Y	N	Y	N	N
Grams	Y	N	Y	N	Y	Y
MISSISSIPPI						
Cochran	Y	Y	Y	N	Y	Y
Lott	Y	Y	Y	N	Y	Y
MISSOURI						
Bond	Y	Y	Y	N	Y	Y
Ashcroft	Y	Y	Y	N	Y	Y
MONTANA						
Baucus	N	Y	N	N	Y	Y
Burns	Y	–	+	–	+	+
NEBRASKA						
Kerrey	N	Y	N	N	Y	Y
Hagel	Y	Y	Y	N	Y	?
NEVADA						
Reid	N	Y	N	Y	Y	N
Bryan	N	Y	N	N	Y	Y
NEW HAMPSHIRE						
Smith	Y	N	Y	N	Y	Y
Gregg	?	Y	Y	N	Y	Y
NEW JERSEY						
Lautenberg	N	Y	N	Y	N	Y
Torricelli	N	Y	N	Y	Y	Y
NEW MEXICO						
Domenici	Y	Y	Y	N	Y	Y
Bingaman	N	Y	N	N	Y	Y
NEW YORK						
Moynihan	N	Y	N	Y	N	Y
Schumer	N	Y	N	Y	N	Y
NORTH CAROLINA						
Helms	Y	N	Y	N	Y	Y
Edwards	N	Y	N	N	Y	Y
NORTH DAKOTA						
Conrad	N	Y	Y	N	Y	Y
Dorgan	N	Y	N	N	Y	N
OHIO						
DeWine	Y	N	Y	N	Y	Y
Voinovich	Y	N	Y	N	Y	Y
OKLAHOMA						
Nickles	Y	N	Y	N	Y	Y
Inhofe	Y	Y	Y	N	Y	Y
OREGON						
Wyden	N	Y	N	Y	Y	Y
Smith	Y	Y	Y	N	Y	Y
PENNSYLVANIA						
Specter	Y	Y	N	N	Y	Y
Santorum	Y	Y	Y	N	Y	Y
RHODE ISLAND						
Reed	N	Y	N	Y	N	+
Chafee	Y	Y	Y	Y	Y	Y
SOUTH CAROLINA						
Thurmond	Y	Y	Y	N	Y	Y
Hollings	N	Y	N	Y	Y	Y
SOUTH DAKOTA						
Daschle	N	Y	N	Y	Y	Y
Johnson	Y	Y	N	Y	Y	Y
TENNESSEE						
Thompson	Y	N	Y	N	Y	Y
Frist	Y	Y	Y	N	Y	Y
TEXAS						
Gramm	Y	N	Y	N	Y	Y
Hutchison	Y	Y	Y	N	N	Y
UTAH						
Hatch	Y	Y	Y	N	Y	Y
Bennett	Y	Y	Y	N	Y	Y
VERMONT						
Leahy	N	Y	N	N	Y	Y
Jeffords	N	Y	N	N	Y	Y
VIRGINIA						
Warner	Y	Y	Y	N	Y	Y
Robb	N	Y	N	N	Y	Y
WASHINGTON						
Gorton	Y	Y	Y	N	Y	Y
Murray	N	Y	N	Y	Y	Y
WEST VIRGINIA						
Byrd	N	Y	N	N	Y	Y
Rockefeller	N	Y	N	Y	Y	Y
WISCONSIN						
Kohl	N	Y	N	Y	Y	Y
Feingold	N	Y	N	N	N	Y
WYOMING						
Thomas	Y	Y	Y	N	Y	Y
Enzi	Y	N	Y	N	Y	Y

ND Northern Democrats SD Southern Democrats

Southern states - Ala., Ark., Fla., Ga., Ky., La., Miss., N.C., Okla., S.C., Tenn., Texas, Va.

Key

- Y Voted for (yea).
- # Paired for.
- \+ Announced for.
- N Voted against (nay).
- X Paired against.
- – Announced against.
- P Voted "present."
- C Voted "present" to avoid possible conflict of interest.
- ? Did not vote or otherwise make a position known.

Democrats • ***Republicans***
Independents

1. S 625. Bankruptcy Overhaul/Debt Collection Practices. Hatch, R-Utah, motion to table (kill) the Wellstone, D-Minn., amendment that would prevent lenders who charge an annual interest rate above 100 percent from collecting from debtors in bankruptcy proceedings. It would also seek to expand protections from coercive debt collection practices. Motion agreed to 53-44: R 51-1; D 2-43 (ND 1-36, SD 1-7). Feb. 1, 2000.

2. S 625. Bankruptcy Overhaul/Abortion Clinics. Schumer, D-N.Y., amendment that would prohibit debtors from discharging debts, such as damages, court fines, penalties, citations or attorney fees, incurred from acts of violence or potential acts of violence against abortion clinics or their workers. Adopted 80-17: R 35-17; D 45-0 (ND 37-0, SD 8-0). Feb. 2, 2000.

3. S 625. Bankruptcy Overhaul/Eviction Stays. Grassley, R-Iowa, motion to table (kill) Feingold, D-Wis., amendment that would allow renters to stay in their apartments during a bankruptcy proceeding if they can pay the rent during that time, unless the debtor has endangered property or used an illegal drug. Motion agreed to 54-43: R 50-2; D 4-41 (ND 3-34, SD 1-7). Feb. 2, 2000.

4. S 625. Bankruptcy Overhaul/Gun Manufacturer Debts. Levin, D-Mich., amendment that would bar gun manufacturers from discharging debts caused by fraud, recklessness, misrepresentation, nuisance, negligence or product liability such as lawsuits filed by municipalities. Rejected 29-68: R 1-51; D 28-17 (ND 25-12, SD 3-5). Feb. 2, 2000.

5. HR 833. Bankruptcy Overhaul/Passage. Passage of the bill that would revise bankruptcy laws to make it easier for courts to move debtors from Chapter 7 of the bankruptcy code, which allows most debts to be discharged, to Chapter 13, which requires a reorganization of debts under a repayment plan. It also would increase the minimum wage, currently $5.15 an hour, by $1 over three years. Passed 83-14: R 50-2; D 33-12 (ND 26-11, SD 7-1). (Before passage, the Senate struck all after the enacting clause and inserted the text of S 625, as amended.) Feb. 2, 2000.

6. Greenspan Nomination/Confirmation. Confirmation of President Clinton's nomination of Alan Greenspan of New York to be chairman of the Board of Governors of the Federal Reserve System. Confirmed 89-4: R 50-0; D 39-4 (ND 31-4, SD 8-0). Feb. 3, 2000. A "yea" was a vote in support of the president's position.

Senate Votes 7, 8, 9, 10, 11

	7	8	9	10	11
ALABAMA					
Shelby	Y	Y	N	Y	Y
Sessions	Y	Y	Y	Y	Y
ALASKA					
Stevens	Y	Y	Y	Y	Y
Murkowski	Y	Y	N	Y	Y
ARIZONA					
McCain	?	?	?	?	?
Kyl	Y	Y	Y	Y	Y
ARKANSAS					
Hutchinson	Y	Y	Y	Y	Y
Lincoln	Y	Y	Y	Y	Y
CALIFORNIA					
Feinstein	Y	N	Y	Y	Y
Boxer	N	N	Y	Y	Y
COLORADO					
Campbell	Y	N	Y	Y	Y
Allard	Y	Y	N	Y	Y
CONNECTICUT					
Dodd	Y	N	Y	Y	Y
Lieberman	Y	N	Y	Y	Y
DELAWARE					
Roth	Y	Y	Y	Y	Y
Biden	Y	N	Y	Y	Y
FLORIDA					
Graham	Y	Y	Y	Y	Y
Mack	Y	Y	Y	Y	?
GEORGIA					
Coverdell	Y	Y	Y	Y	Y
Cleland	Y	Y	Y	Y	Y
HAWAII					
Inouye	Y	N	Y	Y	Y
Akaka	Y	N	Y	Y	Y
IDAHO					
Craig	Y	Y	N	Y	Y
Crapo	Y	Y	N	Y	Y
ILLINOIS					
Durbin	Y	N	Y	Y	Y
Fitzgerald	Y	Y	Y	Y	Y
INDIANA					
Lugar	Y	Y	Y	Y	Y
Bayh	Y	N	Y	Y	Y
IOWA					
Grassley	Y	Y	N	Y	Y
Harkin	Y	N	Y	Y	Y
KANSAS					
Brownback	Y	Y	Y	Y	Y
Roberts	Y	Y	Y	Y	Y
KENTUCKY					
McConnell	Y	Y	N	Y	Y
Bunning	Y	Y	N	Y	Y
LOUISIANA					
Breaux	Y	Y	Y	Y	Y
Landrieu	Y	Y	Y	Y	Y
MAINE					
Snowe	Y	Y	Y	Y	Y
Collins	Y	Y	Y	Y	Y
MARYLAND					
Sarbanes	Y	N	Y	Y	Y
Mikulski	Y	N	Y	Y	Y
MASSACHUSETTS					
Kennedy	+	–	+	+	+
Kerry	Y	N	Y	Y	Y
MICHIGAN					
Levin	Y	Y	Y	Y	Y
Abraham	Y	Y	Y	Y	Y
MINNESOTA					
Wellstone	Y	N	Y	Y	Y
Grams	Y	Y	N	Y	Y
MISSISSIPPI					
Cochran	Y	Y	Y	Y	Y
Lott	Y	Y	Y	Y	Y
MISSOURI					
Bond	Y	Y	Y	Y	Y
Ashcroft	Y	Y	Y	Y	Y
MONTANA					
Baucus	Y	N	Y	Y	Y
Burns	Y	Y	N	Y	Y
NEBRASKA					
Kerrey	?	Y	Y	Y	Y
Hagel	Y	Y	Y	Y	Y
NEVADA					
Reid	N	N	Y	Y	Y
Bryan	N	N	Y	Y	Y
NEW HAMPSHIRE					
Smith	Y	Y	N	N	N
Gregg	Y	Y	N	Y	Y
NEW JERSEY					
Lautenberg	Y	N	Y	Y	Y
Torricelli	Y	N	Y	Y	Y
NEW MEXICO					
Domenici	Y	Y	N	Y	Y
Bingaman	Y	N	Y	Y	Y
NEW YORK					
Moynihan	Y	N	Y	Y	Y
Schumer	Y	N	Y	Y	Y
NORTH CAROLINA					
Helms	Y	Y	N	Y	Y
Edwards	Y	N	Y	Y	Y
NORTH DAKOTA					
Conrad	Y	N	Y	Y	Y
Dorgan	Y	N	Y	Y	Y
OHIO					
DeWine	Y	Y	Y	Y	Y
Voinovich	Y	Y	Y	Y	Y
OKLAHOMA					
Nickles	Y	Y	Y	Y	Y
Inhofe	Y	Y	N	N	N
OREGON					
Wyden	Y	N	Y	Y	Y
Smith	Y	Y	Y	Y	Y
PENNSYLVANIA					
Specter	Y	Y	Y	Y	Y
Santorum	Y	Y	Y	Y	Y
RHODE ISLAND					
Reed	Y	N	Y	Y	Y
Chafee, L.	Y	N	Y	Y	Y
SOUTH CAROLINA					
Thurmond	Y	Y	N	Y	Y
Hollings	Y	Y	Y	Y	Y
SOUTH DAKOTA					
Daschle	Y	N	Y	Y	Y
Johnson	Y	N	Y	Y	Y
TENNESSEE					
Thompson	Y	Y	Y	Y	Y
Frist	Y	Y	Y	Y	Y
TEXAS					
Gramm	Y	Y	N	Y	Y
Hutchison	Y	Y	Y	Y	Y
UTAH					
Hatch	Y	Y	Y	Y	Y
Bennett	Y	Y	Y	Y	Y
VERMONT					
Leahy	Y	Y	Y	Y	Y
Jeffords	Y	Y	Y	Y	Y
VIRGINIA					
Warner	Y	Y	Y	Y	Y
Robb	Y	Y	Y	Y	Y
WASHINGTON					
Gorton	Y	Y	Y	Y	Y
Murray	Y	Y	Y	Y	Y
WEST VIRGINIA					
Byrd	Y	N	Y	Y	Y
Rockefeller	Y	N	Y	Y	Y
WISCONSIN					
Kohl	Y	Y	Y	Y	Y
Feingold	Y	N	Y	Y	Y
WYOMING					
Thomas	Y	Y	N	Y	Y
Enzi	Y	Y	N	Y	Y

ND Northern Democrats SD Southern Democrats

Southern states - Ala., Ark., Fla., Ga., Ky., La., Miss., N.C., Okla., S.C., Tenn., Texas, Va.

Key

- Y Voted for (yea).
- \# Paired for.
- \+ Announced for.
- N Voted against (nay).
- X Paired against.
- – Announced against.
- P Voted "present."
- C Voted "present" to avoid possible conflict of interest.
- ? Did not vote or otherwise make a position known.

•

Democrats ***Republicans***
Independents

7. S 1287. Nuclear Waste Storage/Cloture. Motion to invoke cloture (thus limiting debate) on Murkowski, R-Alaska, substitute amendment that would authorize the Energy Department to take title of spent nuclear fuel at reactor sites. The EPA could set radiation protection standards before June 1, 2001, only if it had consulted with the National Academy of Sciences (NAS) and reached an agreement with the Nuclear Regulatory Commission (NRC) by that date. The NAS and NRC would be required to report to Congress by April 1, 2001, on the EPA's rule-making process for Yucca Mountain. Motion agreed to 94-3: R 54-0; D 40-3 (ND 32-3, SD 8-0). Three-fifths of the total Senate (60) is required to invoke cloture. Feb. 8, 2000.

8. S 1287. Nuclear Waste Storage/Passage. Passage of the bill that would allow the Environmental Protection Agency (EPA) to continue to set radiation protection standards at the proposed Yucca Mountain disposal site in Nevada, but not before June 1, 2001. It also would require the EPA to provide the Nuclear Regulatory Commission (NRC) and the National Academy of Sciences (NAS) with a detailed written comparison of its proposals and the academy's recommendations within 30 days of enactment, and require the NAS and the NRC to evaluate for Congress by April 1, 2001, EPA's rule-making process for Yucca Mountain. It also would authorize the NRC to make the final decision on whether to authorize construction of a repository at the proposed site by Jan. 31, 2006. Passed 64-34: R 52-2; D 12-32 (ND 5-31, SD 7-1). Feb. 10, 2000. A "nay" was a vote in support of the president's position.

9. Ambro Nomination/Motion to Proceed. Motion to proceed to executive session to consider President Clinton's nomination of Thomas L. Ambro, of Delaware, to be a judge for the Third U.S. Circuit Court. Motion agreed to 79-19: R 35-19; D 44-0 (ND 36-0, SD 8-0). Feb. 10, 2000.

10. Ambro Nomination/Confirmation. Confirmation of President Clinton's nomination of Thomas L. Ambro of Delaware, to be a judge for the Third U.S. Circuit Court. Confirmed 96-2: R 52-2; D 44-0 (ND 36-0, SD 8-0). Feb. 10, 2000. A "yea" was a vote in support of the president's position.

11. Pisano Nomination/Confirmation. Confirmation of President Clinton's nomination of Joel A. Pisano of New Jersey to be a judge for the U.S. District Court of New Jersey. Confirmed 95-2: R 51-2; D 44-0 (ND 36-0, SD 8-0). Feb. 10, 2000. A "yea" was a vote in support of the president's position.

	12	13	14
ALABAMA			
Shelby	Y	Y	Y
Sessions	Y	Y	Y
ALASKA			
Stevens	Y	Y	Y
Murkowski	Y	Y	Y
ARIZONA			
McCain	?	?	?
Kyl	Y	Y	Y
ARKANSAS			
Hutchinson	Y	Y	Y
Lincoln	Y	Y	Y
CALIFORNIA			
Feinstein	Y	Y	Y
Boxer	Y	Y	Y
COLORADO			
Campbell	Y	Y	Y
Allard	Y	Y	Y
CONNECTICUT			
Dodd	Y	Y	Y
Lieberman	Y	Y	Y
DELAWARE			
Roth	Y	Y	Y
Biden	Y	Y	Y
FLORIDA			
Graham	Y	Y	Y
Mack	Y	Y	Y
GEORGIA			
Coverdell	Y	Y	Y
Cleland	Y	Y	Y
HAWAII			
Inouye	Y	Y	Y
Akaka	Y	Y	Y
IDAHO			
Craig	Y	Y	Y
Crapo	Y	Y	Y
ILLINOIS			
Durbin	Y	Y	Y
Fitzgerald	Y	Y	Y
INDIANA			
Lugar	Y	Y	Y
Bayh	Y	Y	Y
IOWA			
Grassley	Y	Y	Y
Harkin	Y	Y	Y
KANSAS			
Brownback	Y	Y	Y
Roberts	Y	Y	Y
KENTUCKY			
McConnell	Y	Y	Y
Bunning	Y	Y	Y
LOUISIANA			
Breaux	Y	Y	Y
Landrieu	Y	Y	Y
MAINE			
Snowe	Y	Y	Y
Collins	Y	Y	Y
MARYLAND			
Sarbanes	Y	Y	Y
Mikulski	Y	Y	Y
MASSACHUSETTS			
Kennedy	Y	Y	Y
Kerry	Y	Y	Y
MICHIGAN			
Levin	Y	Y	Y
Abraham	Y	Y	Y
MINNESOTA			
Wellstone	Y	Y	Y
Grams	Y	Y	Y
MISSISSIPPI			
Cochran	Y	Y	Y
Lott	Y	Y	Y
MISSOURI			
Bond	Y	Y	Y
Ashcroft	Y	Y	Y
MONTANA			
Baucus	+	+	+
Burns	Y	Y	Y
NEBRASKA			
Kerrey	Y	Y	Y
Hagel	Y	Y	Y
NEVADA			
Reid	Y	Y	Y
Bryan	Y	Y	Y
NEW HAMPSHIRE			
Smith	Y	Y	Y
Gregg	Y	Y	Y
NEW JERSEY			
Lautenberg	Y	Y	Y
Torricelli	Y	Y	Y
NEW MEXICO			
Domenici	Y	Y	Y
Bingaman	Y	Y	Y
NEW YORK			
Moynihan	Y	Y	Y
Schumer	Y	Y	Y
NORTH CAROLINA			
Helms	Y	Y	Y
Edwards	Y	Y	Y
NORTH DAKOTA			
Conrad	Y	Y	Y
Dorgan	Y	Y	Y
OHIO			
DeWine	Y	Y	Y
Voinovich	Y	Y	Y
OKLAHOMA			
Nickles	Y	Y	Y
Inhofe	Y	Y	Y
OREGON			
Wyden	Y	Y	Y
Smith	Y	Y	Y
PENNSYLVANIA			
Specter	Y	Y	Y
Santorum	Y	Y	Y
RHODE ISLAND			
Reed	Y	Y	Y
Chafee, L.	Y	Y	Y
SOUTH CAROLINA			
Thurmond	Y	Y	Y
Hollings	Y	Y	Y
SOUTH DAKOTA			
Daschle	Y	Y	Y
Johnson	Y	Y	Y
TENNESSEE			
Thompson	Y	Y	Y
Frist	Y	Y	Y
TEXAS			
Gramm	Y	Y	Y
Hutchison	Y	Y	Y
UTAH			
Hatch	Y	Y	Y
Bennett	Y	Y	Y
VERMONT			
Leahy	Y	Y	Y
Jeffords	Y	Y	Y
VIRGINIA			
Warner	Y	Y	Y
Robb	Y	Y	Y
WASHINGTON			
Gorton	Y	Y	Y
Murray	Y	Y	Y
WEST VIRGINIA			
Byrd	Y	Y	Y
Rockefeller	Y	Y	Y
WISCONSIN			
Kohl	Y	Y	Y
Feingold	Y	Y	Y
WYOMING			
Thomas	Y	Y	Y
Enzi	Y	Y	Y

Key

- Y Voted for (yea).
- # Paired for.
- \+ Announced for.
- N Voted against (nay).
- X Paired against.
- – Announced against.
- P Voted "present."
- C Voted "present" to avoid possible conflict of interest.
- ? Did not vote or otherwise make a position known.

•

Democrats ***Republicans***
Independents

ND Northern Democrats SD Southern Democrats

Southern states - Ala., Ark., Fla., Ga., Ky., La., Miss., N.C., Okla., S.C., Tenn., Texas, Va.

12. HR 1883. Iran Nonproliferation/Passage. Passage of a bill that would require the president to submit a report to Congress identifying foreign entities that have transferred missile components or technology to Iran since January 1999. The bill as amended would also authorize, but not require, the president to impose sanctions against entities that transfer the components or technology. The bill would also prohibit the United States from making "extraordinary" payments to the Russian space agency for the international space station unless Russia demonstrates a sustained commitment to prevent weapons proliferation in Iran. Passed 98-0: R 54-0; D 44-0 (ND 36-0, SD 8-0). Feb. 24, 2000.

13. Bye Nomination/Confirmation. Confirmation of President Clinton's nomination of Kermit Bye of North Dakota to be a judge for the 8th U.S. Circuit Court of Appeals. Confirmed 98-0: R 54-0; D 44-0 (ND 36-0, SD 8-0). Feb. 24, 2000. A "yea" was a vote in support of the president's position.

14. Daniels Nomination/Confirmation. Confirmation of President Clinton's nomination of George B. Daniels of New York to be U.S. District judge for the Southern District of New York. Confirmed 98-0: R 54-0; D 44-0 (ND 36-0, SD 8-0). Feb. 24, 2000. A "yea" was a vote in support of the president's position.

Senate Votes 15, 16, 17, 18, 19, 20, 21

	15	16	17	18	19	20	21
ALABAMA							
Shelby	N	Y	Y	Y	Y	Y	N
Sessions	N	Y	Y	Y	Y	Y	N
ALASKA							
Stevens	N	Y	Y	Y	Y	Y	N
Murkowski	?	?	Y	Y	Y	Y	N
ARIZONA							
McCain	?	?	?	?	?	?	?
Kyl	N	Y	Y	Y	Y	Y	N
ARKANSAS							
Hutchinson	N	Y	Y	Y	Y	Y	N
Lincoln	Y	Y	N	Y	N	Y	Y
CALIFORNIA							
Feinstein	Y	Y	N	Y	N	Y	Y
Boxer	Y	Y	N	Y	N	Y	Y
COLORADO							
Campbell	N	Y	Y	Y	Y	Y	N
Allard	N	Y	Y	Y	Y	Y	N
CONNECTICUT							
Dodd	Y	Y	N	Y	N	Y	Y
Lieberman	Y	Y	Y	Y	Y	Y	N
DELAWARE							
Roth	N	Y	Y	Y	Y	Y	N
Biden	N	Y	N	Y	Y	Y	Y
FLORIDA							
Graham	Y	Y	N	Y	Y	Y	Y
Mack	N	Y	Y	Y	Y	Y	N
GEORGIA							
Coverdell	N	Y	Y	Y	Y	Y	N
Cleland	Y	Y	N	Y	N	Y	Y
HAWAII							
Inouye	Y	Y	N	Y	N	Y	Y
Akaka	Y	Y	N	Y	N	Y	Y
IDAHO							
Craig	N	Y	Y	Y	Y	N	N
Crapo	N	Y	Y	Y	Y	Y	N
ILLINOIS							
Durbin	Y	Y	N	Y	N	Y	Y
Fitzgerald	N	Y	Y	Y	Y	Y	N
INDIANA							
Lugar	N	Y	Y	Y	Y	Y	N
Bayh	Y	Y	N	Y	N	Y	Y
IOWA							
Grassley	N	Y	Y	Y	Y	Y	N
Harkin	Y	Y	N	Y	N	Y	Y
KANSAS							
Brownback	N	Y	Y	Y	Y	Y	N
Roberts	N	Y	Y	Y	Y	Y	N
KENTUCKY							
McConnell	N	Y	Y	Y	Y	Y	N
Bunning	N	Y	Y	Y	Y	Y	N
LOUISIANA							
Breaux	N	Y	N	Y	Y	Y	Y
Landrieu	Y	Y	N	Y	N	Y	Y
MAINE							
Snowe	N	Y	Y	Y	Y	Y	N
Collins	Y	Y	Y	Y	Y	Y	N
MARYLAND							
Sarbanes	Y	Y	N	Y	N	Y	Y
Mikulski	Y	Y	N	Y	N	Y	Y
MASSACHUSETTS							
Kennedy	Y	Y	N	Y	N	Y	Y
Kerry	Y	Y	N	Y	N	Y	Y
MICHIGAN							
Levin	Y	Y	N	Y	N	Y	Y
Abraham	N	Y	Y	Y	Y	Y	N
MINNESOTA							
Wellstone	Y	Y	N	Y	N	Y	Y
Grams	N	Y	Y	Y	Y	Y	N
MISSISSIPPI							
Cochran	N	Y	Y	Y	Y	Y	N
Lott	N	Y	Y	Y	Y	Y	N
MISSOURI							
Bond	N	Y	Y	?	?	?	?
Ashcroft	N	Y	Y	Y	Y	Y	N
MONTANA							
Baucus	Y	Y	N	Y	N	Y	Y
Burns	N	Y	Y	Y	Y	Y	N
NEBRASKA							
Kerrey	Y	Y	N	Y	N	Y	Y
Hagel	N	Y	Y	Y	Y	Y	N
NEVADA							
Reid	Y	Y	N	Y	N	Y	Y
Bryan	Y	Y	N	Y	N	Y	Y
NEW HAMPSHIRE							
Smith	N	Y	Y	Y	Y	N	N
Gregg	N	Y	Y	Y	Y	Y	N
NEW JERSEY							
Lautenberg	Y	Y	N	Y	N	Y	Y
Torricelli	N	Y	Y	Y	Y	Y	N
NEW MEXICO							
Domenici	N	Y	Y	Y	Y	Y	N
Bingaman	Y	Y	N	Y	N	Y	Y
NEW YORK							
Moynihan	Y	Y	N	Y	N	Y	Y
Schumer	Y	Y	N	Y	N	Y	Y
NORTH CAROLINA							
Helms	N	Y	Y	Y	Y	Y	N
Edwards	Y	Y	N	Y	N	Y	Y
NORTH DAKOTA							
Conrad	Y	Y	N	N	N	Y	Y
Dorgan	Y	Y	N	Y	N	Y	Y
OHIO							
DeWine	N	Y	Y	Y	Y	Y	N
Voinovich	N	Y	Y	Y	Y	N	N
OKLAHOMA							
Nickles	N	Y	Y	N	Y	N	N
Inhofe	N	Y	Y	Y	Y	N	N
OREGON							
Wyden	Y	Y	N	Y	N	Y	Y
Smith	N	Y	Y	Y	Y	Y	N
PENNSYLVANIA							
Specter	N	Y	N	Y	Y	Y	N
Santorum	N	Y	Y	Y	Y	Y	N
RHODE ISLAND							
Reed	Y	Y	N	Y	N	Y	Y
Chafee, L.	Y	Y	Y	Y	N	Y	N
SOUTH CAROLINA							
Thurmond	N	Y	Y	Y	Y	Y	N
Hollings	Y	Y	N	Y	N	Y	Y
SOUTH DAKOTA							
Daschle	Y	Y	N	Y	N	Y	Y
Johnson	Y	Y	N	Y	N	Y	Y
TENNESSEE							
Thompson	N	Y	Y	Y	Y	N	N
Frist	N	Y	Y	Y	Y	Y	N
TEXAS							
Gramm	N	Y	Y	Y	Y	N	N
Hutchison	N	Y	Y	Y	Y	Y	N
UTAH							
Hatch	N	Y	Y	Y	Y	Y	N
Bennett	N	Y	Y	Y	Y	Y	N
VERMONT							
Leahy	Y	Y	N	Y	N	Y	Y
Jeffords	Y	Y	Y	Y	Y	Y	N
VIRGINIA							
Warner	N	Y	Y	Y	Y	Y	N
Robb	Y	Y	N	Y	N	Y	Y
WASHINGTON							
Gorton	N	Y	Y	Y	Y	Y	N
Murray	Y	Y	N	Y	N	Y	Y
WEST VIRGINIA							
Byrd	N	Y	Y	Y	Y	Y	N
Rockefeller	Y	Y	N	Y	N	Y	Y
WISCONSIN							
Kohl	Y	Y	N	Y	N	Y	Y
Feingold	Y	Y	Y	Y	N	Y	Y
WYOMING							
Thomas	N	Y	Y	Y	Y	N	N
Enzi	N	Y	Y	Y	Y	N	N

ND Northern Democrats SD Southern Democrats

Southern states - Ala., Ark., Fla., Ga., Ky., La., Miss., N.C., Okla., S.C., Tenn., Texas, Va.

Key

Y Voted for (yea).
\# Paired for.
\+ Announced for.
N Voted against (nay).
X Paired against.
– Announced against.
P Voted "present."
C Voted "present" to avoid possible conflict of interest.
? Did not vote or otherwise make a position known.

•

Democrats ***Republicans***
Independents

15. S 1134. Education Savings Accounts/Special Education. Dodd, D-Conn., motion to waive the Budget Act with respect to the Coverdell, R-Ga., point of order against the Dodd amendment. The Dodd amendment would eliminate the education savings accounts provision of the bill and instead provide $1.2 billion over five years to states for special education programs. Motion rejected 44-54: R 3-50; D 41-4 (ND 34-3, SD 7-1). A three-fifths majority vote (60) of the total Senate is required to waive the Budget Act. (Subsequently, the chair upheld the point of order, and the amendment fell.) Feb. 29, 2000.

16. S 1134. Education Savings Accounts/Teacher Tax Credits. Collins, R-Maine, amendment to eliminate the 2 percent floor on miscellaneous itemized tax deductions for qualified professional development expenses, such as tuition, fees and books, for elementary and secondary school teachers. Elementary and secondary school teachers who purchase classroom materials, such as books, supplies and computer equipment, would also be eligible for a tax credit of up to $100 per year. Both provisions would be effective after Dec. 31, 2000. Adopted 98-0: R 53-0; D 45-0 (ND 37-0, SD 8-0). Feb. 29, 2000.

17. S 1134. Education Savings Accounts/School Construction Bonds. Roth, R-Del., motion to table (kill) the Robb, D-Va., amendment that would provide approximately $25 billion in tax credits for modernization bonds for public school construction. The amendment also would authorize approximately $1.3 billion each year for five years in grants and a zero-interest loan program to make urgent school repairs. Motion agreed to 57-42: R 53-1; D 4-41 (ND 4-33, SD 0-8). March 1, 2000.

18. S 1134. Education Savings Accounts/Computer Donations. Abraham, R-Mich., amendment to increase the age limit for donated computer equipment eligible for a tax deduction from two to three years and allow a tax credit for computers donated to schools and senior centers. Adopted 96-2: R 52-1; D 44-1 (ND 36-1, SD 8-0). March 1, 2000.

19. S 1134. Education Savings Accounts/School Improvement. Coverdell, R-Ga., motion to table (kill) the Bingaman, D-N.M., amendment that would eliminate the education savings accounts provision of the bill and instead authorize $275 million for fiscal 2001 and subsequent sums for the next four years to states for local districts to improve poor-performing schools. The amendment would require states to allot at least 70 percent of the funds to local districts. Motion agreed to 58-40: R 52-1; D 6-39 (ND 4-33, SD 2-6). March 1, 2000.

20. S 1134. Education Savings Accounts/Child Poverty. Wellstone, D-Minn., amendment to require the Health and Human Services secretary to submit a report to Congress on the extent and severity of child poverty before June 1, 2001, and prior to any reauthorization of the Temporary Assistance to Needy Families program. Adopted 89-9: R 44-9; D 45-0 (ND 37-0, SD 8-0). March 1, 2000.

21. S 1134. Education Savings Accounts/Class Size. Murray, D-Wash., amendment to strike the education savings account provision of the bill and insert a proposal to authorize $1.2 billion in fiscal 2001 to fund measures aimed at reducing class size, such as the recruiting and hiring of new teachers, testing new teachers, and providing professional development for teachers. The funds would go to local agencies based 80 percent on poverty and 20 percent on school enrollment. Rejected 42-56: R 0-53; D 42-3 (ND 34-3, SD 8-0). March 1, 2000.

	22	23	24	25	26	27	28
ALABAMA							
Shelby	Y	N	Y	N	Y	N	N
Sessions	Y	N	Y	N	Y	N	N
ALASKA							
Stevens	Y	N	Y	N	Y	N	N
Murkowski	Y	N	Y	N	Y	N	N
ARIZONA							
McCain	?	?	?	?	?	?	?
Kyl	Y	N	Y	N	Y	N	N
ARKANSAS							
Hutchinson	Y	N	Y	N	Y	N	N
Lincoln	N	N	N	Y	Y	Y	Y
CALIFORNIA							
Feinstein	N	N	Y	Y	Y	Y	Y
Boxer	N	Y	N	Y	Y	Y	Y
COLORADO							
Campbell	Y	N	Y	N	Y	N	N
Allard	Y	N	Y	N	Y	N	N
CONNECTICUT							
Dodd	N	Y	N	Y	Y	Y	Y
Lieberman	N	Y	Y	N	Y	Y	Y
DELAWARE							
Roth	Y	N	Y	N	Y	Y	Y
Biden	N	Y	Y	N	Y	Y	Y
FLORIDA							
Graham	N	Y	N	Y	Y	Y	Y
Mack	Y	N	Y	N	Y	N	N
GEORGIA							
Coverdell	Y	N	Y	N	Y	N	N
Cleland	N	Y	N	Y	Y	Y	Y
HAWAII							
Inouye	N	Y	N	Y	?	?	?
Akaka	N	Y	N	Y	Y	Y	Y
IDAHO							
Craig	Y	N	Y	N	Y	N	N
Crapo	Y	N	Y	N	Y	N	N
ILLINOIS							
Durbin	N	N	N	Y	Y	Y	Y
Fitzgerald	Y	N	Y	N	Y	Y	Y
INDIANA							
Lugar	Y	N	Y	N	Y	N	N
Bayh	N	N	N	Y	Y	Y	Y
IOWA							
Grassley	Y	N	Y	N	Y	N	N
Harkin	N	N	N	Y	Y	Y	Y
KANSAS							
Brownback	Y	N	Y	N	Y	N	N
Roberts	Y	N	Y	N	Y	N	N
KENTUCKY							
McConnell	Y	N	Y	N	Y	N	N
Bunning	Y	N	Y	N	Y	N	N
LOUISIANA							
Breaux	N	Y	Y	N	Y	Y	Y
Landrieu	N	N	N	Y	Y	Y	Y
MAINE							
Snowe	Y	N	Y	N	Y	N	N
Collins	Y	N	Y	N	Y	N	N
MARYLAND							
Sarbanes	N	N	N	Y	Y	Y	Y
Mikulski	N	Y	N	Y	?	Y	Y
MASSACHUSETTS							
Kennedy	N	N	N	Y	Y	Y	Y
Kerry	N	N	N	Y	Y	Y	Y
MICHIGAN							
Levin	N	Y	N	Y	Y	Y	Y
Abraham	Y	N	Y	N	Y	Y	Y
MINNESOTA							
Wellstone	N	N	N	Y	Y	Y	Y
Grams	Y	N	Y	N	Y	N	N
MISSISSIPPI							
Cochran	Y	N	Y	N	Y	N	N
Lott	Y	N	Y	N	Y	N	N
MISSOURI							
Bond	?	N	Y	N	Y	N	N
Ashcroft	Y	N	Y	N	Y	Y	Y
MONTANA							
Baucus	N	Y	N	Y	Y	Y	Y
Burns	Y	N	Y	N	Y	N	N
NEBRASKA							
Kerrey	N	Y	N	Y	Y	Y	Y
Hagel	Y	N	Y	N	Y	N	N
NEVADA							
Reid	N	N	N	Y	Y	Y	Y
Bryan	N	Y	N	Y	Y	Y	Y
NEW HAMPSHIRE							
Smith	Y	N	Y	N	Y	N	N
Gregg	Y	N	Y	N	Y	N	N
NEW JERSEY							
Lautenberg	N	Y	N	Y	Y	Y	Y
Torricelli	Y	Y	Y	N	Y	Y	Y
NEW MEXICO							
Domenici	Y	N	Y	N	Y	N	N
Bingaman	N	N	N	Y	Y	Y	Y
NEW YORK							
Moynihan	?	?	N	Y	Y	Y	Y
Schumer	N	N	N	Y	Y	Y	Y
NORTH CAROLINA							
Helms	Y	N	Y	N	Y	N	N
Edwards	N	N	N	Y	Y	Y	Y
NORTH DAKOTA							
Conrad	N	N	N	Y	Y	Y	Y
Dorgan	N	N	N	Y	Y	Y	Y
OHIO							
DeWine	Y	N	Y	N	Y	N	N
Voinovich	Y	Y	Y	N	Y	N	N
OKLAHOMA							
Nickles	Y	N	Y	N	Y	N	N
Inhofe	Y	N	Y	N	Y	N	N
OREGON							
Wyden	N	Y	N	Y	Y	Y	Y
Smith	Y	N	Y	N	Y	N	N
PENNSYLVANIA							
Specter	Y	N	Y	N	Y	N	N
Santorum	Y	N	Y	N	Y	N	N
RHODE ISLAND							
Reed	N	N	N	Y	Y	Y	Y
Chafee, L.	Y	N	Y	N	Y	Y	Y
SOUTH CAROLINA							
Thurmond	Y	N	Y	N	Y	N	N
Hollings	N	Y	N	Y	Y	Y	Y
SOUTH DAKOTA							
Daschle	N	Y	N	Y	Y	Y	Y
Johnson	N	N	N	Y	Y	Y	Y
TENNESSEE							
Thompson	Y	N	Y	N	N	N	N
Frist	Y	N	Y	N	Y	N	N
TEXAS							
Gramm	Y	N	Y	N	Y	N	N
Hutchison	Y	N	Y	N	Y	N	N
UTAH							
Hatch	Y	N	Y	N	Y	N	N
Bennett	Y	N	Y	N	Y	N	N
VERMONT							
Leahy	N	Y	N	Y	Y	Y	Y
Jeffords	Y	N	Y	N	Y	N	N
VIRGINIA							
Warner	Y	N	Y	N	Y	N	N
Robb	N	Y	N	Y	Y	Y	Y
WASHINGTON							
Gorton	Y	N	Y	N	Y	N	N
Murray	N	N	N	Y	Y	Y	Y
WEST VIRGINIA							
Byrd	N	Y	N	N	Y	Y	Y
Rockefeller	N	Y	N	Y	Y	Y	Y
WISCONSIN							
Kohl	N	Y	N	N	Y	Y	Y
Feingold	N	N	N	Y	Y	Y	Y
WYOMING							
Thomas	Y	N	Y	N	Y	N	N
Enzi	Y	N	Y	N	Y	N	N

ND Northern Democrats SD Southern Democrats

Southern states - Ala., Ark., Fla., Ga., Ky., La., Miss., N.C., Okla., S.C., Tenn., Texas, Va.

Key

- Y Voted for (yea).
- \# Paired for.
- \+ Announced for.
- N Voted against (nay).
- X Paired against.
- – Announced against.
- P Voted "present."
- C Voted "present" to avoid possible conflict of interest.
- ? Did not vote or otherwise make a position known.

•

Democrats ***Republicans***
Independents

22. S 1134. Education Savings Accounts/'Marriage Penalty' Tax. Mack, R-Fla., amendment that would allow married couples with combined incomes of up to $190,000 to make full contributions to the accounts, with eligibility phasing out completely at $220,000. Adopted 54-43: R 53-0; D 1-43 (ND 1-35, SD 0-8). March 2, 2000.

23. S 1134. Education Savings Accounts/Budgetary Offsets. Graham, D-Fla., amendment to the Roth, R-Del., amendment. The Graham amendment would reinstate approximately $5.5 billion of the budgetary offsets initially provided for in the underlying bill. The Roth amendment would remove these offsets. Rejected 25-73: R 1-53; D 24-20 (ND 19-17, SD 5-3). March 2, 2000.

24. S 1134. Education Savings Accounts/Sunset Provisions. Roth, R-Del., substitute amendment that would remove the sunset provisions from the bill and make permanent the increase from $500 to $2,000 in the annual contribution limit to the educational savings account, the provision to allow withdrawals for pre-kindergarten through college expenses and the exemption for employer-provided expenses for graduate and undergraduate education. The bill would have sunset these provisions after 2003. The amendment would also eliminate $5.5 billion in budgetary offsets provided in the underlying bill and fund the program using the surplus. Adopted 59-40: R 54-0; D 5-40 (ND 4-33, SD 1-7). March 2, 2000.

25. S 1134. Education Savings Accounts/Teacher Training Programs. Kennedy, D-Mass., amendment that would strike the education savings account provision and insert a provision to authorize $1.2 billion over five years for teacher training programs, including two national teacher recruitment programs, local professional development programs, teacher mentoring programs and local recruitment programs. The amendment specifies that states are held accountable for having a qualified teacher in classrooms within four years of enactment of the legislation. Rejected 39-60: R 0-54; D 39-6 (ND 32-5, SD 7-1). March 2, 2000.

26. S 1134. Education Savings Accounts/Safe Schools. Coverdell, R-Ga., amendment that would express the sense of the Senate that the reauthorization of the Safe and Drug Free Schools program should target the elimination of illegal drugs and violence in schools and should encourage local schools to insist on zero-tolerance policies toward violence and illegal drug use. Motion agreed to 96-1: R 53-1; D 43-0 (ND 35-0, SD 8-0). March 2, 2000.

27. S 1134. Education Savings Accounts/Gun Violence Reduction Policies. Boxer, D-Calif., amendment that would express the sense of the Senate that Congress should implement policies that will reduce the threat of gun violence in schools before April 20, 2000. Rejected 49-49: R 5-49; D 44-0 (ND 36-0, SD 8-0). (The chair incorrectly announced that the amendment was adopted 49-48. Subsequently, the chair announced that the amendment had actually been rejected 49-49.) March 2, 2000.

28. S 1134. Education Savings Accounts/Gun Violence Reduction Policies. Boxer, D-Calif., amendment that expresses the sense of the Senate that Congress implement policies that will reduce the threat of gun violence in schools before April 20, 2000. Rejected 49-49: R 5-49; D 44-0 (ND 36-0, SD 8-0). (Vote 28 was taken to clarify the tally on Vote 27. The amendment was unchanged.) March 2, 2000.

Senate Votes 29, 30, 31, 32, 33

	29	30	31	32	33
ALABAMA					
Shelby	N	N	Y	Y	Y
Sessions	N	N	Y	Y	Y
ALASKA					
Stevens	N	N	N	Y	Y
Murkowski	N	N	N	Y	Y
ARIZONA					
McCain	?	?	?	?	?
Kyl	N	N	N	Y	Y
ARKANSAS					
Hutchinson	N	N	Y	Y	Y
Lincoln	Y	N	Y	Y	N
CALIFORNIA					
Feinstein	Y	N	Y	Y	Y
Boxer	Y	Y	Y	Y	N
COLORADO					
Campbell	N	N	N	Y	Y
Allard	N	N	N	Y	Y
CONNECTICUT					
Dodd	Y	N	Y	Y	N
Lieberman	N	N	Y	Y	Y
DELAWARE					
Roth	N	N	N	Y	Y
Biden	N	Y	N	Y	Y
FLORIDA					
Graham	Y	Y	N	Y	N
Mack	N	N	N	Y	Y
GEORGIA					
Coverdell	N	N	Y	Y	Y
Cleland	Y	N	Y	Y	Y
HAWAII					
Inouye	?	?	?	?	?
Akaka	Y	Y	N	Y	N
IDAHO					
Craig	N	N	N	Y	Y
Crapo	N	N	N	Y	Y
ILLINOIS					
Durbin	Y	N	Y	Y	N
Fitzgerald	N	N	N	Y	Y
INDIANA					
Lugar	N	N	Y	Y	Y
Bayh	Y	N	N	Y	N
IOWA					
Grassley	N	N	N	Y	Y
Harkin	Y	Y	N	Y	N
KANSAS					
Brownback	N	N	N	Y	Y
Roberts	N	N	N	Y	Y
KENTUCKY					
McConnell	N	N	Y	Y	Y
Bunning	N	N	N	Y	Y
LOUISIANA					
Breaux	N	N	Y	Y	Y
Landrieu	Y	Y	N	Y	N
MAINE					
Snowe	N	N	N	Y	Y
Collins	Y	N	N	Y	Y
MARYLAND					
Sarbanes	Y	Y	N	Y	N
Mikulski	Y	Y	N	Y	N
MASSACHUSETTS					
Kennedy	Y	Y	N	Y	N
Kerry	Y	N	N	Y	N
MICHIGAN					
Levin	Y	Y	Y	Y	N
Abraham	N	N	N	Y	Y
MINNESOTA					
Wellstone	Y	Y	N	Y	N
Grams	N	N	N	Y	Y
MISSISSIPPI					
Cochran	N	N	N	Y	Y
Lott	N	N	Y	Y	Y
MISSOURI					
Bond	N	N	N	Y	Y
Ashcroft	N	N	N	Y	Y
MONTANA					
Baucus	Y	Y	Y	Y	N
Burns	N	N	N	Y	Y
NEBRASKA					
Kerrey	Y	Y	N	Y	Y
Hagel	N	N	Y	Y	Y
NEVADA					
Reid	Y	Y	N	Y	N
Bryan	Y	N	Y	Y	N
NEW HAMPSHIRE					
Smith	N	N	N	N	Y
Gregg	N	N	N	N	Y
NEW JERSEY					
Lautenberg	Y	Y	N	Y	N
Torricelli	N	Y	Y	Y	Y
NEW MEXICO					
Domenici	N	N	N	Y	Y
Bingaman	Y	Y	N	Y	N
NEW YORK					
Moynihan	Y	Y	Y	Y	N
Schumer	Y	N	Y	Y	N
NORTH CAROLINA					
Helms	N	N	N	N	Y
Edwards	Y	N	N	Y	N
NORTH DAKOTA					
Conrad	Y	Y	N	Y	N
Dorgan	Y	Y	Y	Y	N
OHIO					
DeWine	N	N	N	Y	Y
Voinovich	N	N	N	N	Y
OKLAHOMA					
Nickles	N	N	N	N	Y
Inhofe	N	N	N	N	Y
OREGON					
Wyden	Y	N	Y	Y	N
Smith	N	N	N	Y	Y
PENNSYLVANIA					
Specter	N	N	N	Y	Y
Santorum	N	N	N	Y	Y
RHODE ISLAND					
Reed	Y	Y	N	Y	N
Chafee, L.	Y	N	N	Y	N
SOUTH CAROLINA					
Thurmond	N	N	N	Y	Y
Hollings	Y	Y	N	Y	N
SOUTH DAKOTA					
Daschle	Y	Y	Y	Y	N
Johnson	Y	Y	N	Y	N
TENNESSEE					
Thompson	N	N	N	N	Y
Frist	N	N	N	Y	Y
TEXAS					
Gramm	N	N	N	Y	Y
Hutchison	N	N	N	Y	Y
UTAH					
Hatch	N	N	N	Y	Y
Bennett	N	N	N	Y	Y
VERMONT					
Leahy	Y	Y	N	Y	N
Jeffords	N	N	N	Y	N
VIRGINIA					
Warner	N	N	Y	Y	Y
Robb	Y	Y	Y	Y	N
WASHINGTON					
Gorton	N	N	N	Y	Y
Murray	Y	Y	N	Y	N
WEST VIRGINIA					
Byrd	N	N	Y	Y	Y
Rockefeller	Y	Y	Y	Y	N
WISCONSIN					
Kohl	Y	N	Y	Y	Y
Feingold	Y	Y	N	Y	N
WYOMING					
Thomas	N	N	N	Y	Y
Enzi	N	N	N	Y	Y

ND Northern Democrats SD Southern Democrats

Southern states - Ala., Ark., Fla., Ga., Ky., La., Miss., N.C., Okla., S.C., Tenn., Texas, Va.

Key

- Y Voted for (yea).
- # Paired for.
- + Announced for.
- N Voted against (nay).
- X Paired against.
- – Announced against.
- P Voted "present."
- C Voted "present" to avoid possible conflict of interest.
- ? Did not vote or otherwise make a position known.

Democrats ***Republicans***
Independents

29. S 1134. Education Savings Accounts/Pell Grants. Kennedy, D-Mass., motion to waive the Budget Act with respect to the Coverdell, R-Ga., point of order against the Bingaman, D-N.M., amendment, which would strike the educational savings accounts provision from the underlying bill and use the projected revenue from the bill to increase federal Pell grants by $1.2 billion. Motion rejected 41-57: R 2-52; D 39-5 (ND 32-4, SD 7-1). A three-fifths majority vote (60) of the total Senate is required to waive the Budget Act. (Subsequently the chairman upheld the point of order, and the amendment was rejected.) March 2, 2000.

30. S 1134. Education Savings Accounts/Achievement Standards. Wellstone, D-Minn., amendment to the Feinstein, D-Calif., amendment. The Wellstone amendment would exclude students who were not afforded the opportunity to learn material necessary to meet the state achievement standards from being subject to the standards. Rejected 29-69: R 0-54; D 29-15 (ND 25-11, SD 4-4). March 2, 2000.

31. S 1134. Education Savings Accounts/Social Promotion. Feinstein, D-Calif., amendment that would require local and state education agencies that receive funding under the Elementary and Secondary Education Act of 1965 to subject elementary and secondary school students to state achievement standards in the core curriculum as determined by the state. Agencies would also be required to assess student performance according to state achievement standards at key grades, such as fourth, eighth and twelfth, before promoting students to the next grade. The amendment would also require local education agencies to demonstrate that the state has adopted a policy prohibiting social promotion. Rejected 30-68: R 9-45; D 21-23 (ND 17-19, SD 4-4). March 2, 2000.

32. S 1134. Education Savings Accounts/Gun Violence. Durbin, D-Ill., amendment that would authorize up to $7 million for fiscal year 2001 and subsequent sums as necessary for four succeeding fiscal years for grants to elementary and secondary schools to develop programs to reduce violence in schools, educate students about the dangers associated with guns, and provide violence prevention information to children and their parents. Adopted 91-7: R 47-7; D 44-0 (ND 36-0, SD 8-0). March 2, 2000.

33. S 1134. Education Savings Accounts/Passage. Passage of the bill that would allow families to deposit up to $2,000 per child annually into tax-free accounts for elementary, secondary and higher education in private or public schools. The annual limit for the accounts would increase from $500 to $2,000; married couples with combined income of up to $190,000 would be allowed to make full contributions to the accounts. The bill would also make permanent a tax exemption for employer-provided higher education expenses, and would extend the exemption to graduate courses. Passed 61-37: R 52-2; D 9-35 (ND 7-29, SD 2-6). March 2, 2000. A "nay" was a vote in support of the president's position.

	34	35	36	37	38	39	40
ALABAMA							
Shelby	Y	Y	N	N	N	Y	N
Sessions	Y	N	Y	Y	N	Y	N
ALASKA							
Stevens	Y	Y	Y	Y	Y	N	Y
Murkowski	Y	Y	N	N	N	Y	N
ARIZONA							
McCain	?	?	?	?	?	?	?
Kyl	Y	N	Y	Y	Y	Y	N
ARKANSAS							
Hutchinson	Y	Y	N	N	N	Y	N
Lincoln	Y	Y	Y	Y	Y	N	Y
CALIFORNIA							
Feinstein	?	Y	Y	Y	Y	N	Y
Boxer	Y	Y	Y	Y	Y	N	Y
COLORADO							
Campbell	Y	Y	Y	Y	?	?	?
Allard	Y	Y	N	N	N	Y	N
CONNECTICUT							
Dodd	Y	Y	Y	Y	Y	N	Y
Lieberman	Y	Y	Y	Y	Y	N	Y
DELAWARE							
Roth	Y	Y	Y	Y	Y	N	Y
Biden	+	Y	Y	Y	Y	N	Y
FLORIDA							
Graham	Y	Y	Y	Y	Y	N	Y
Mack	Y	Y	Y	Y	Y	N	Y
GEORGIA							
Coverdell	?	Y	Y	Y	N	Y	N
Cleland	Y	Y	Y	Y	Y	N	Y
HAWAII							
Inouye	Y	Y	Y	Y	Y	N	Y
Akaka	Y	Y	Y	Y	Y	N	Y
IDAHO							
Craig	Y	N	N	N	N	Y	N
Crapo	Y	N	Y	Y	N	Y	N
ILLINOIS							
Durbin	Y	Y	Y	Y	Y	N	Y
Fitzgerald	Y	N	Y	Y	Y	Y	N
INDIANA							
Lugar	Y	Y	Y	Y	Y	N	Y
Bayh	Y	N	Y	Y	Y	N	Y
IOWA							
Grassley	Y	Y	Y	Y	N	Y	N
Harkin	Y	Y	Y	Y	Y	N	Y
KANSAS							
Brownback	Y	Y	N	N	N	Y	N
Roberts	Y	Y	Y	Y	N	N	N
KENTUCKY							
McConnell	Y	Y	Y	Y	N	Y	N
Bunning	Y	Y	N	N	N	N	N
LOUISIANA							
Breaux	Y	Y	Y	Y	Y	N	Y
Landrieu	Y	Y	Y	Y	Y	N	Y
MAINE							
Snowe	Y	Y	Y	Y	Y	N	Y
Collins	Y	Y	Y	Y	Y	N	Y
MARYLAND							
Sarbanes	Y	Y	Y	Y	Y	N	Y
Mikulski	Y	Y	Y	Y	Y	N	Y
MASSACHUSETTS							
Kennedy	Y	Y	Y	Y	Y	N	Y
Kerry	Y	Y	Y	Y	Y	N	Y
MICHIGAN							
Levin	Y	Y	Y	Y	Y	N	Y
Abraham	Y	Y	Y	Y	N	N	N
MINNESOTA							
Wellstone	+	Y	Y	Y	Y	N	Y
Grams	Y	N	Y	Y	N	Y	N
MISSISSIPPI							
Cochran	Y	Y	Y	Y	N	Y	N
Lott	Y	Y	Y	Y	N	Y	N
MISSOURI							
Bond	?	Y	Y	Y	N	Y	N
Ashcroft	Y	Y	Y	Y	N	Y	N
MONTANA							
Baucus	Y	Y	Y	Y	Y	N	Y
Burns	Y	N	Y	Y	Y	Y	N
NEBRASKA							
Kerrey	?	Y	Y	Y	Y	N	Y
Hagel	Y	Y	Y	Y	N	N	N
NEVADA							
Reid	Y	Y	Y	Y	Y	N	Y
Bryan	Y	Y	Y	Y	Y	N	Y
NEW HAMPSHIRE							
Smith	Y	Y	N	N	N	Y	N
Gregg	Y	N	Y	Y	N	Y	N
NEW JERSEY							
Lautenberg	Y	N	Y	Y	Y	N	Y
Torricelli	Y	Y	Y	Y	Y	N	Y
NEW MEXICO							
Domenici	Y	Y	Y	Y	N	N	Y
Bingaman	Y	Y	Y	Y	Y	N	Y
NEW YORK							
Moynihan	Y	N	Y	Y	Y	N	Y
Schumer	Y	Y	Y	Y	Y	N	Y
NORTH CAROLINA							
Helms	Y	Y	N	N	N	Y	N
Edwards	Y	N	Y	Y	Y	N	Y
NORTH DAKOTA							
Conrad	Y	Y	Y	Y	Y	N	Y
Dorgan	Y	Y	Y	Y	Y	N	Y
OHIO							
DeWine	Y	Y	N	N	N	Y	N
Voinovich	Y	N	Y	Y	N	N	N
OKLAHOMA							
Nickles	Y	N	Y	Y	N	Y	N
Inhofe	Y	Y	N	N	N	Y	N
OREGON							
Wyden	Y	Y	Y	Y	Y	N	Y
Smith	Y	Y	Y	Y	Y	N	Y
PENNSYLVANIA							
Specter	Y	Y	Y	Y	Y	N	Y
Santorum	Y	Y	Y	Y	Y	Y	N
RHODE ISLAND							
Reed	Y	Y	Y	Y	Y	N	Y
Chafee, L.	Y	Y	Y	Y	Y	N	Y
SOUTH CAROLINA							
Thurmond	Y	Y	Y	Y	N	Y	N
Hollings	Y	Y	Y	Y	Y	N	Y
SOUTH DAKOTA							
Daschle	Y	Y	Y	Y	Y	N	Y
Johnson	Y	Y	Y	Y	Y	N	Y
TENNESSEE							
Thompson	Y	Y	Y	Y	Y	N	N
Frist	Y	N	Y	N	Y	Y	N
TEXAS							
Gramm	Y	N	N	N	N	Y	N
Hutchison	Y	Y	Y	Y	N	N	N
UTAH							
Hatch	Y	Y	Y	Y	Y	N	Y
Bennett	Y	Y	Y	Y	Y	N	Y
VERMONT							
Leahy	Y	Y	Y	Y	Y	N	Y
Jeffords	Y	Y	Y	Y	Y	N	Y
VIRGINIA							
Warner	Y	Y	Y	Y	Y	Y	N
Robb	Y	N	Y	Y	Y	N	Y
WASHINGTON							
Gorton	Y	Y	Y	Y	N	N	Y
Murray	Y	Y	Y	Y	Y	N	Y
WEST VIRGINIA							
Byrd	Y	Y	Y	Y	Y	N	Y
Rockefeller	Y	Y	Y	Y	Y	N	Y
WISCONSIN							
Kohl	Y	Y	Y	Y	Y	N	Y
Feingold	Y	Y	Y	Y	Y	N	Y
WYOMING							
Thomas	Y	Y	Y	Y	N	Y	N
Enzi	Y	Y	N	N	N	N	N

ND Northern Democrats SD Southern Democrats

Southern states - Ala., Ark., Fla., Ga., Ky., La., Miss., N.C., Okla., S.C., Tenn., Texas, Va.

Key

- Y Voted for (yea).
- # Paired for.
- + Announced for.
- N Voted against (nay).
- X Paired against.
- – Announced against.
- P Voted "present."
- C Voted "present" to avoid possible conflict of interest.
- ? Did not vote or otherwise make a position known.

•

Democrats ***Republicans***
Independents

34. Fuentes Nomination/Confirmation. Confirmation of President Clinton's nomination of Julio M. Fuentes of New Jersey to be a judge for the 3rd U.S. Circuit Court of Appeals. Confirmed 93-0: R 52-0; D 41-0 (ND 33-0, SD 8-0). A "yea" was a vote in support of the president's position. March 7, 2000.

35. HR 1000. Federal Aviation Administration Reauthorization/Conference Report. Adoption of the conference report on the bill that would authorize $40 billion for aviation programs in fiscal years 2001 through 2003. The agreement would provide $3.2 billion in fiscal 2001, $3.3 billion in fiscal 2002 and $3.4 billion in fiscal 2003 for airport construction grants. Airports would be allowed to increase the local fee on an airline ticket from $3 to $4.50 per segment. The bill would also allow additional flights into Chicago O'Hare International, John F. Kennedy International, LaGuardia and Ronald Reagan Washington National airports. Adopted 82-17: R 42-12; D 40-5 (ND 34-3, SD 6-2). March 8, 2000.

36. Berzon Nomination/Cloture. Motion to invoke cloture (thus limiting debate) on the confirmation of President Clinton's nomination of Marsha L. Berzon of California to be a judge for the 9th U.S. Circuit Court of Appeals. Motion agreed to 86-13: R 41-13; D 45-0 (ND 37-0, SD 8-0). Three-fifths of the total Senate (60) is required to invoke cloture. March 8, 2000.

37. Paez Nomination/Cloture. Motion to invoke cloture (thus limiting debate) on the confirmation of President Clinton's nomination of Richard A. Paez of California to be a judge for the 9th U.S. Circuit Court of Appeals. Motion agreed to 85-14: R 40-14; D 45-0 (ND 37-0, SD 8-0). Three-fifths of the total Senate (60) is required to invoke cloture. March 8, 2000.

38. Berzon Nomination/Confirmation. Confirmation of President Clinton's nomination of Marsha L. Berzon of California to be a judge for the 9th U.S. Circuit Court of Appeals. Confirmed 64-34: R 19-34; D 45-0 (ND 37-0, SD 8-0). A "yea" was a vote in support of the president's position. March 9, 2000.

39. Paez Nomination/Motion to Postpone. Sessions, R-Ala., motion to postpone indefinitely the confirmation of President Clinton's nomination of Richard A. Paez of California to be a judge for the 9th U.S. Circuit Court of Appeals. Motion rejected 31-67: R 31-22; D 0-45 (ND 0-37, SD 0-8). March 9, 2000.

40. Paez Nomination/Confirmation. Confirmation of President Clinton's nomination of Richard A. Paez of California to be a judge for the 9th U.S. Circuit Court of Appeals. Confirmed 59-39: R 14-39; D 45-0 (ND 37-0, SD 8-0). A "yea" was a vote in support of the president's position. March 9, 2000.

	41	42	43	44
ALABAMA				
Shelby	Y	Y	Y	Y
Sessions	Y	Y	Y	Y
ALASKA				
Stevens	Y	Y	Y	Y
Murkowski	Y	Y	Y	Y
ARIZONA				
McCain	N	Y	Y	N
Kyl	Y	Y	Y	N
ARKANSAS				
Hutchinson	Y	Y	Y	Y
Lincoln	N	Y	Y	Y
CALIFORNIA				
Feinstein	N	Y	Y	Y
Boxer	N	Y	Y	Y
COLORADO				
Campbell	Y	Y	Y	Y
Allard	Y	Y	Y	Y
CONNECTICUT				
Dodd	N	Y	Y	Y
Lieberman	N	Y	Y	Y
DELAWARE				
Roth	Y	Y	Y	Y
Biden	N	Y	Y	Y
FLORIDA				
Graham	N	Y	Y	Y
Mack	Y	Y	Y	Y
GEORGIA				
Coverdell	Y	Y	Y	Y
Cleland	N	Y	Y	Y
HAWAII				
Inouye	N	Y	Y	Y
Akaka	N	Y	Y	Y
IDAHO				
Craig	Y	Y	Y	Y
Crapo	Y	Y	Y	Y
ILLINOIS				
Durbin	N	Y	Y	Y
Fitzgerald	Y	Y	Y	Y
INDIANA				
Lugar	Y	Y	Y	Y
Bayh	N	Y	Y	Y
IOWA				
Grassley	Y	Y	Y	Y
Harkin	N	Y	Y	Y
KANSAS				
Brownback	Y	Y	Y	Y
Roberts	Y	Y	Y	Y
KENTUCKY				
McConnell	Y	Y	Y	Y
Bunning	Y	Y	Y	Y
LOUISIANA				
Breaux	N	Y	Y	Y
Landrieu	N	Y	Y	Y
MAINE				
Snowe	Y	Y	Y	Y
Collins	Y	Y	Y	Y
MARYLAND				
Sarbanes	N	Y	Y	Y
Mikulski	N	Y	Y	Y
MASSACHUSETTS				
Kennedy	N	Y	Y	Y
Kerry	N	Y	Y	Y
MICHIGAN				
Levin	N	Y	Y	Y
Abraham	Y	Y	Y	Y
MINNESOTA				
Wellstone	Y	Y	Y	Y
Grams	Y	Y	Y	Y
MISSISSIPPI				
Cochran	Y	Y	Y	N
Lott	Y	Y	Y	N
MISSOURI				
Bond	Y	Y	Y	Y
Ashcroft	Y	Y	Y	Y
MONTANA				
Baucus	N	Y	Y	Y
Burns	Y	Y	Y	Y
NEBRASKA				
Kerrey	N	Y	Y	Y
Hagel	N	Y	Y	Y
NEVADA				
Reid	N	Y	Y	Y
Bryan	N	Y	Y	Y
NEW HAMPSHIRE				
Smith	Y	Y	Y	Y
Gregg	?	Y	Y	N
NEW JERSEY				
Lautenberg	N	Y	Y	Y
Torricelli	N	Y	Y	Y
NEW MEXICO				
Domenici	Y	Y	Y	Y
Bingaman	Y	Y	Y	Y
NEW YORK				
Moynihan	N	Y	Y	Y
Schumer	N	Y	Y	Y
NORTH CAROLINA				
Helms	Y	Y	Y	Y
Edwards	N	Y	Y	Y
NORTH DAKOTA				
Conrad	Y	Y	Y	Y
Dorgan	N	Y	Y	Y
OHIO				
DeWine	Y	Y	Y	Y
Voinovich	Y	Y	Y	Y
OKLAHOMA				
Nickles	Y	Y	Y	Y
Inhofe	Y	Y	Y	Y
OREGON				
Wyden	N	Y	Y	Y
Smith	Y	Y	Y	Y
PENNSYLVANIA				
Specter	Y	Y	Y	Y
Santorum	Y	Y	Y	Y
RHODE ISLAND				
Reed	N	Y	Y	Y
Chafee, L.	Y	Y	Y	Y
SOUTH CAROLINA				
Thurmond	Y	Y	Y	Y
Hollings	N	Y	Y	Y
SOUTH DAKOTA				
Daschle	N	Y	Y	Y
Johnson	N	Y	Y	Y
TENNESSEE				
Thompson	Y	Y	N	Y
Frist	Y	Y	Y	Y
TEXAS				
Gramm	Y	Y	Y	Y
Hutchison	Y	Y	Y	Y
UTAH				
Hatch	Y	Y	Y	Y
Bennett	Y	Y	Y	Y
VERMONT				
Leahy	N	Y	Y	Y
Jeffords	Y	Y	Y	Y
VIRGINIA				
Warner	Y	Y	Y	Y
Robb	N	Y	Y	Y
WASHINGTON				
Gorton	Y	Y	Y	Y
Murray	N	Y	Y	Y
WEST VIRGINIA				
Byrd	N	Y	Y	Y
Rockefeller	N	Y	Y	Y
WISCONSIN				
Kohl	N	Y	Y	Y
Feingold	N	Y	Y	Y
WYOMING				
Thomas	Y	Y	Y	Y
Enzi	Y	Y	Y	Y

ND Northern Democrats SD Southern Democrats

Southern states - Ala., Ark., Fla., Ga., Ky., La., Miss., N.C., Okla., S.C., Tenn., Texas, Va.

Key

- Y Voted for (yea).
- \# Paired for.
- \+ Announced for.
- N Voted against (nay).
- X Paired against.
- – Announced against.
- P Voted "present."
- C Voted "present" to avoid possible conflict of interest.
- ? Did not vote or otherwise make a position known.

Democrats • ***Republicans***
Independents

41. HR 5. Eliminate Social Security Earnings Test/Retirement Language. Roth, R-Del., motion to table (kill) the Kerrey, D-Neb., amendment that would strike the term "retirement age" from the Social Security Act and replace it with "the age of eligibility for full, unreduced old-age benefits." Also, the phrase "early retirement age" would be replaced with "the age of earliest eligibility for old-age benefits"; the phrase "delayed retirement" would be replaced with "delayed entitlement for old-age benefits." Motion agreed to 55-44: R 52-2; D 3-42 (ND 3-34, SD 0-8). March 21, 2000.

42. HR 5. Eliminate Social Security Earnings Test/Passage. Passage of the bill that would allow senior citizens ages 65 through 69 to earn money without having their Social Security benefits reduced. Under current law, retirees ages 65 through 69 lose $1 in Social Security benefits for every $3 they earn each year above a certain level (currently $17,000). Passed 100-0: R 55-0; D 45-0 (ND 37-0, SD 8-0). A " yea" was a vote in support of the president's position. March 22, 2000.

43. S 2251. Crop Insurance/Rural Policy Reform. Wellstone, D-Minn., amendment that would express the sense of Congress that the participants in the Rally for Rural America are commended and that Congress should respond with a "clear and strong" message that Congress is committed to giving the agriculture crisis its full attention by reforming rural policies in a way that will alleviate the agricultural price crisis, ensure competitive markets, invest in rural education and health care, protect natural resources and ensure a secure food supply. Adopted 99-1: R 54-1; D 45-0 (ND 37-0, SD 8-0). March 23, 2000.

44. HR 2559. Crop Insurance/Passage. Passage of a bill that would provide approximately $6 billion over the next four years to revise the federal crop insurance program. The bill would mandate approximately $5 billion in funding to modify current risk management programs and about $1 billion to fund research and development and pilot programs. Under the bill, the federal government would pay a higher share of the annual crop insurance premium, from 45 percent to 60 percent, compared with the current range of 13 percent to 57 percent. The bill, as amended, includes a $126 million provision for specialty crops and states with low-participation rates in risk management programs. Passed 95-5: R 50-5; D 45-0 (ND 37-0, SD 8-0). (Before passage, the Senate struck all after the enacting clause and inserted the text of S 2251, as amended.) March 23, 2000.

Senate Votes 45, 46, 47, 48, 49, 50, 51

	45	46	47	48	49	50	51
ALABAMA							
Shelby	N	Y	Y	Y	Y	Y	Y
Sessions	N	Y	Y	Y	Y	Y	Y
ALASKA							
Stevens	N	Y	Y	Y	Y	Y	Y
Murkowski	N	Y	Y	Y	Y	Y	Y
ARIZONA							
McCain	N	N	Y	Y	Y	Y	Y
Kyl	N	Y	Y	Y	Y	Y	Y
ARKANSAS							
Hutchinson	N	Y	Y	Y	Y	Y	Y
Lincoln	N	N	Y	Y	Y	Y	N
CALIFORNIA							
Feinstein	N	N	Y	Y	Y	Y	N
Boxer	Y	N	Y	N	?	?	?
COLORADO							
Campbell	N	Y	Y	Y	Y	Y	Y
Allard	N	Y	Y	Y	Y	Y	Y
CONNECTICUT							
Dodd	Y	N	Y	N	Y	Y	Y
Lieberman	Y	N	Y	N	Y	Y	Y
DELAWARE							
Roth	N	N	Y	Y	Y	Y	Y
Biden	Y	N	Y	N	Y	Y	Y
FLORIDA							
Graham	Y	N	Y	Y	Y	Y	Y
Mack	N	Y	Y	Y	Y	P	Y
GEORGIA							
Coverdell	N	Y	Y	Y	Y	Y	Y
Cleland	N	N	Y	Y	Y	Y	Y
HAWAII							
Inouye	Y	N	Y	N	Y	Y	Y
Akaka	Y	Y	Y	N	Y	Y	Y
IDAHO							
Craig	N	Y	Y	Y	Y	Y	Y
Crapo	N	Y	Y	Y	Y	Y	Y
ILLINOIS							
Durbin	Y	N	Y	N	Y	Y	Y
Fitzgerald	N	Y	Y	Y	Y	Y	Y
INDIANA							
Lugar	N	Y	Y	Y	Y	Y	Y
Bayh	N	N	Y	Y	Y	Y	Y
IOWA							
Grassley	N	Y	Y	Y	Y	Y	Y
Harkin	Y	N	Y	N	Y	Y	N
KANSAS							
Brownback	N	Y	Y	Y	Y	Y	Y
Roberts	N	Y	Y	Y	Y	Y	N
KENTUCKY							
McConnell	Y	Y	Y	N	Y	Y	Y
Bunning	N	Y	Y	Y	Y	Y	Y
LOUISIANA							
Breaux	N	N	Y	Y	Y	Y	Y
Landrieu	N	N	Y	Y	Y	Y	Y
MAINE							
Snowe	N	Y	Y	Y	Y	Y	Y
Collins	N	Y	Y	Y	Y	Y	Y
MARYLAND							
Sarbanes	Y	N	Y	N	Y	Y	Y
Mikulski	Y	N	Y	N	Y	Y	Y
MASSACHUSETTS							
Kennedy	N	Y	Y	N	Y	Y	Y
Kerry	Y	N	Y	N	Y	Y	Y
MICHIGAN							
Levin	Y	N	Y	N	Y	Y	Y
Abraham	N	Y	Y	Y	Y	Y	Y
MINNESOTA							
Wellstone	N	Y	Y	N	Y	Y	Y
Grams	N	Y	Y	Y	Y	Y	Y
MISSISSIPPI							
Cochran	N	Y	Y	Y	Y	Y	Y
Lott	N	Y	Y	Y	Y	Y	Y
MISSOURI							
Bond	N	Y	Y	Y	Y	Y	N
Ashcroft	N	Y	Y	Y	Y	Y	Y
MONTANA							
Baucus	N	N	Y	Y	Y	Y	N
Burns	N	Y	Y	Y	Y	Y	Y
NEBRASKA							
Kerrey	N	Y	Y	N	Y	Y	Y
Hagel	N	Y	Y	Y	Y	Y	Y
NEVADA							
Reid	N	N	Y	Y	Y	Y	Y
Bryan	Y	N	Y	N	Y	Y	Y
NEW HAMPSHIRE							
Smith	N	Y	Y	Y	Y	Y	Y
Gregg	N	Y	Y	Y	Y	Y	Y
NEW JERSEY							
Lautenberg	Y	Y	Y	N	Y	Y	Y
Torricelli	Y	Y	Y	N	Y	Y	Y
NEW MEXICO							
Domenici	N	Y	Y	Y	Y	?	?
Bingaman	Y	N	Y	N	Y	Y	Y
NEW YORK							
Moynihan	Y	Y	Y	N	Y	Y	Y
Schumer	Y	Y	Y	N	Y	Y	Y
NORTH CAROLINA							
Helms	N	Y	Y	Y	Y	Y	Y
Edwards	Y	Y	Y	N	Y	Y	Y
NORTH DAKOTA							
Conrad	Y	Y	Y	N	Y	Y	Y
Dorgan	Y	Y	Y	N	Y	Y	Y
OHIO							
DeWine	N	Y	Y	Y	Y	Y	Y
Voinovich	N	Y	Y	Y	Y	Y	Y
OKLAHOMA							
Nickles	Y	Y	Y	Y	Y	Y	Y
Inhofe	N	Y	Y	Y	Y	Y	?
OREGON							
Wyden	Y	N	Y	N	Y	Y	Y
Smith	Y	Y	Y	Y	Y	Y	Y
PENNSYLVANIA							
Specter	N	N	Y	Y	Y	Y	Y
Santorum	N	Y	Y	Y	Y	Y	Y
RHODE ISLAND							
Reed	N	N	Y	N	Y	Y	Y
Chafee, L.	Y	Y	Y	N	Y	Y	Y
SOUTH CAROLINA							
Thurmond	N	Y	Y	Y	Y	Y	Y
Hollings	N	N	Y	Y	Y	Y	Y
SOUTH DAKOTA							
Daschle	Y	N	Y	N	Y	Y	Y
Johnson	Y	N	Y	Y	Y	Y	Y
TENNESSEE							
Thompson	N	Y	Y	Y	Y	Y	Y
Frist	N	Y	Y	Y	Y	Y	Y
TEXAS							
Gramm	N	Y	Y	Y	Y	Y	Y
Hutchison	N	Y	Y	Y	Y	Y	Y
UTAH							
Hatch	N	Y	Y	Y	Y	Y	Y
Bennett	Y	Y	Y	N	Y	Y	Y
VERMONT							
Leahy	Y	Y	Y	N	Y	Y	Y
Jeffords	Y	Y	Y	N	Y	Y	Y
VIRGINIA							
Warner	N	Y	Y	Y	Y	Y	N
Robb	N	N	Y	N	Y	Y	N
WASHINGTON							
Gorton	Y	Y	Y	Y	Y	Y	Y
Murray	Y	Y	Y	N	Y	Y	Y
WEST VIRGINIA							
Byrd	Y	N	Y	N	Y	Y	N
Rockefeller	N	N	Y	Y	Y	Y	Y
WISCONSIN							
Kohl	Y	Y	Y	N	Y	Y	Y
Feingold	N	Y	Y	N	Y	Y	Y
WYOMING							
Thomas	N	Y	Y	Y	Y	Y	N
Enzi	N	Y	Y	Y	Y	Y	N

ND Northern Democrats SD Southern Democrats

Southern states - Ala., Ark., Fla., Ga., Ky., La., Miss., N.C., Okla., S.C., Tenn., Texas, Va.

Key

Y Voted for (yea).
\# Paired for.
\+ Announced for.
N Voted against (nay).
X Paired against.
– Announced against.
P Voted "present."
C Voted "present" to avoid possible conflict of interest.
? Did not vote or otherwise make a position known.

Democrats ***Republicans***
Independents

45. S J Res 14. Flag Desecration/Statutory Proposal. McConnell, R-Ky., substitute amendment to protect the U.S. flag by statute rather than through a constitutional amendment. The statute would impose fines of up to $100,000 and/or up to one year in prison for destroying or damaging a U.S. flag with a clear intent to incite violence or breach of peace. It also would impose fines of up to $250,000 or up to two years in prison, or both, for stealing and damaging a flag on federal land or one belonging to the federal government. Rejected 36-64: R 7-48; D 29-16 (ND 27-10, SD 2-6). March 28, 2000.

46. S J Res 14. Flag Desecration/Campaign Finance. Hatch, R-Utah, motion to table (kill) the Hollings, D-S.C., amendment, which would propose a constitutional amendment to grant Congress and individual states the power to set "reasonable" limits on contributions to and expenditures by campaigns in support of or opposition to candidates seeking election to federal office. Motion agreed to 67-33: R 52-3; D 15-30 (ND 14-23, SD 1-7). March 28, 2000.

47. S J Res 14. Flag Desecration/Cloture. Motion to invoke cloture (thus limiting debate) on the joint resolution to propose a constitutional amendment to grant Congress the power to prohibit the physical desecration of the U.S. flag. Motion agreed to 100-0: R 55-0; D 45-0 (ND 37-0, SD 8-0). Three-fifths of the total Senate (60) is required to invoke cloture. March 29, 2000.

48. S J Res 14. Flag Desecration/Passage. Passage of the joint resolution to propose a constitutional amendment to grant Congress the power to prohibit the physical desecration of the U.S. flag. Rejected 63-37: R 51-4; D 12-33 (ND 6-31, SD 6-2). A two-thirds majority vote of those present and voting (67 in this case) is required to pass a joint resolution proposing an amendment to the Constitution. March 29, 2000.

49. S 2097. Satellite Loan Guarantee Program/Nonprofit Financing Institutions. Johnson, D-S.D., amendment to insert language to allow certain nonprofit financing institutions not insured by the Federal Deposit Insurance Corporation, including the National Rural Utilities Cooperative Finance Corporation, to issue the loans. Adopted 99-0: R 55-0; D 44-0 (ND 36-0, SD 8-0). March 30, 2000.

50. S 2097. Satellite Loan Guarantee Program/Passage. Passage of the bill that would establish a $1.25 billion loan guarantee program to facilitate access to local television broadcast signals in unserved or underserved areas. The bill would allow the approval of loans up to $20 million to organizations such as direct-broadcast satellite services, cable TV operators or rural phone cooperatives. As amended, it would give extra additional consideration to loan proposals on projects that incorporate broadband and high-speed Internet access, as well as national weather service warnings. It also would allow certain nonprofit, non-FDIC-insured financing institutions to issue the loans. Passed 97-0: R 53-0; D 44-0 (ND 36-0, SD 8-0). March 30, 2000.

51. S 2285. Gas Tax Suspension/Cloture. Motion to invoke cloture (thus limiting debate) on the motion to proceed to the bill that would suspend the 4.3 cents-a-gallon portion of the federal gas tax from April 15 through Jan. 1, 2001. It also would suspend the remainder of the 18.4 cents-per-gallon federal tax if the national average price of gasoline reached $2 a gallon. It would provide a similar tax suspension for diesel fuel, kerosene and aviation fuel. Motion agreed to 86-11: R 48-5; D 38-6 (ND 32-4, SD 6-2). Three-fifths of the total Senate (60) is required to invoke cloture. March 30, 2000.

Senate Votes 52, 53, 54, 55, 56, 57, 58

	52	53	54	55	56	57	58
ALABAMA							
Shelby	N	Y	Y	Y	N	N	Y
Sessions	N	Y	Y	Y	N	N	Y
ALASKA							
Stevens	N	Y	Y	Y	N	Y	Y
Murkowski	N	Y	Y	Y	N	N	Y
ARIZONA							
McCain	N	Y	Y	N	Y	N	Y
Kyl	N	Y	Y	Y	N	N	Y
ARKANSAS							
Hutchinson	N	Y	Y	Y	Y	Y	Y
Lincoln	Y	Y	N	N	N	Y	N
CALIFORNIA							
Feinstein	Y	Y	N	N	N	Y	N
Boxer	Y	Y	N	N	N	Y	N
COLORADO							
Campbell	N	Y	Y	Y	Y	N	Y
Allard	N	Y	Y	Y	Y	Y	Y
CONNECTICUT							
Dodd	Y	Y	N	N	N	Y	N
Lieberman	Y	Y	N	N	N	Y	N
DELAWARE							
Roth	N	Y	Y	Y	N	N	N
Biden	Y	Y	N	N	N	N	N
FLORIDA							
Graham	Y	Y	N	N	N	Y	N
Mack	N	Y	Y	Y	N	N	Y
GEORGIA							
Coverdell	N	Y	Y	Y	N	N	Y
Cleland	Y	Y	N	N	N	Y	N
HAWAII							
Inouye	Y	Y	N	N	N	Y	Y
Akaka	Y	Y	N	N	N	Y	Y
IDAHO							
Craig	N	Y	Y	Y	Y	N	Y
Crapo	N	Y	Y	Y	Y	N	Y
ILLINOIS							
Durbin	Y	Y	N	N	N	Y	N
Fitzgerald	Y	Y	Y	Y	Y	N	N
INDIANA							
Lugar	N	Y	Y	Y	N	N	N
Bayh	Y	Y	N	N	N	Y	N
IOWA							
Grassley	N	Y	Y	Y	N	Y	Y
Harkin	Y	Y	N	N	N	Y	N
KANSAS							
Brownback	N	Y	Y	Y	N	N	Y
Roberts	N	Y	Y	Y	N	Y	Y
KENTUCKY							
McConnell	N	Y	Y	Y	N	N	Y
Bunning	N	Y	Y	Y	N	N	Y
LOUISIANA							
Breaux	Y	Y	N	N	N	Y	Y
Landrieu	Y	Y	N	N	N	Y	N
MAINE							
Snowe	N	Y	Y	Y	N	N	N
Collins	N	Y	Y	N	Y	N	N
MARYLAND							
Sarbanes	Y	Y	N	N	N	Y	N
Mikulski	Y	Y	N	N	N	Y	N
MASSACHUSETTS							
Kennedy	Y	Y	N	N	N	Y	N
Kerry	Y	Y	N	N	N	Y	N
MICHIGAN							
Levin	Y	Y	N	N	N	Y	N
Abraham	Y	Y	Y	Y	N	N	Y
MINNESOTA							
Wellstone	Y	Y	N	N	N	Y	N
Grams	N	Y	Y	Y	Y	N	Y
MISSISSIPPI							
Cochran	N	Y	Y	Y	N	N	Y
Lott	N	Y	Y	Y	N	N	Y
MISSOURI							
Bond	N	Y	Y	Y	N	Y	Y
Ashcroft	N	Y	Y	Y	Y	Y	Y
MONTANA							
Baucus	Y	Y	N	N	N	Y	N
Burns	Y	Y	Y	Y	N	Y	Y
NEBRASKA							
Kerrey	Y	Y	N	N	N	Y	N
Hagel	N	Y	Y	Y	N	Y	Y
NEVADA							
Reid	Y	Y	N	N	N	Y	N
Bryan	Y	Y	N	N	N	Y	N
NEW HAMPSHIRE							
Smith	N	Y	Y	Y	Y	N	N
Gregg	N	Y	Y	Y	N	N	Y
NEW JERSEY							
Lautenberg	Y	Y	N	N	N	Y	N
Torricelli	Y	Y	N	Y	N	Y	N
NEW MEXICO							
Domenici	N	Y	Y	Y	N	Y	Y
Bingaman	Y	Y	N	N	N	Y	N
NEW YORK							
Moynihan	Y	Y	N	N	N	Y	Y
Schumer	Y	Y	N	N	N	Y	N
NORTH CAROLINA							
Helms	N	Y	Y	Y	N	Y	Y
Edwards	Y	Y	N	N	N	Y	N
NORTH DAKOTA							
Conrad	Y	Y	N	N	N	Y	N
Dorgan	Y	Y	N	N	N	Y	N
OHIO							
DeWine	Y	Y	Y	Y	N	Y	Y
Voinovich	N	N	Y	Y	Y	Y	Y
OKLAHOMA							
Nickles	N	Y	Y	Y	N	N	Y
Inhofe	N	Y	Y	Y	Y	N	Y
OREGON							
Wyden	Y	Y	N	N	N	Y	N
Smith	N	Y	Y	Y	N	N	Y
PENNSYLVANIA							
Specter	Y	Y	Y	N	N	N	Y
Santorum	N	Y	Y	Y	N	N	Y
RHODE ISLAND							
Reed	Y	Y	N	N	N	Y	N
Chafee, L.	Y	Y	N	N	N	Y	N
SOUTH CAROLINA							
Thurmond	N	Y	Y	Y	N	N	Y
Hollings	Y	Y	N	N	N	Y	N
SOUTH DAKOTA							
Daschle	Y	Y	N	N	N	Y	N
Johnson	Y	Y	N	N	N	Y	N
TENNESSEE							
Thompson	N	Y	Y	Y	N	Y	Y
Frist	N	Y	Y	Y	N	Y	Y
TEXAS							
Gramm	N	Y	Y	Y	N	N	Y
Hutchison	N	Y	Y	Y	Y	N	Y
UTAH							
Hatch	N	Y	Y	Y	N	N	Y
Bennett	N	Y	Y	Y	N	Y	Y
VERMONT							
Leahy	Y	Y	N	N	N	Y	N
Jeffords	N	Y	Y	Y	N	Y	N
VIRGINIA							
Warner	N	Y	Y	Y	N	Y	Y
Robb	Y	Y	N	N	N	Y	N
WASHINGTON							
Gorton	N	Y	Y	Y	N	N	Y
Murray	Y	Y	N	N	N	Y	N
WEST VIRGINIA							
Byrd	Y	Y	N	N	N	Y	N
Rockefeller	Y	Y	N	N	N	Y	N
WISCONSIN							
Kohl	Y	Y	N	N	N	Y	N
Feingold	Y	Y	N	N	N	Y	N
WYOMING							
Thomas	N	Y	Y	Y	Y	Y	Y
Enzi	N	Y	Y	Y	Y	Y	Y

ND Northern Democrats SD Southern Democrats

Southern states - Ala., Ark., Fla., Ga., Ky., La., Miss., N.C., Okla., S.C., Tenn., Texas, Va.

Key

- Y Voted for (yea).
- \# Paired for.
- \+ Announced for.
- N Voted against (nay).
- X Paired against.
- – Announced against.
- P Voted "present."
- C Voted "present" to avoid possible conflict of interest.
- ? Did not vote or otherwise make a position known.

•

Democrats ***Republicans***
Independents

52. S Con Res 101. Fiscal 2001 Budget Resolution/Medicare Prescription Drug Benefit Program. Robb, D-Va., motion to waive the Budget Act with respect to the Domenici, R-N.M., point of order against the Robb amendment to the Hutchison, R-Texas, amendment. The Robb amendment would create a 60-vote point of order against any budget-reconciliation bill that resulted in net reduction of revenues in the absence of enacted legislation providing a Medicare prescription drug benefit program. Motion rejected 51-49: R 6-49; D 45-0 (ND 37-0, SD 8-0). A three-fifths majority vote (60) of the total Senate is require to waive the Budget Act. (Subsequently the chair upheld the point of order, and the amendment fell.) April 5, 2000.

53. S Con Res 101. Fiscal 2001 Budget Resolution/'Marriage Penalty' Tax. Hutchison, R-Texas, amendment that would express the sense of the Senate that it should consider legislation to relieve the so-called marriage penalty tax before April 15, 2000. Adopted 99-1: R 54-1; D 45-0 (ND 37-0, SD 8-0). April 5, 2000.

54. S Con Res 101. Fiscal 2001 Budget Resolution/Education Programs. Domenici, R-N.M., motion to table (kill) the Bingaman, D-N.M., amendment that would redirect $28.1 billion of the tax cut provision toward education programs and increase the total amount for education over a five-year period by $34.7 billion. Motion agreed to 54-46: R 54-1; D 0-45 (ND 0-37, SD 0-8). April 5, 2000.

55. S Con Res 101. Fiscal 2001 Budget Resolution/Debt Reduction. Domenici, R-N.M., motion to table (kill) the Conrad, D-N.D., amendment to the Allard, R-Colo., amendment. The Conrad amendment would strike the text of the Allard amendment and insert language to increase the amount of debt reduction in the resolution by $75 billion over five years, offset by reducing the tax cut from $150 billion to $75 billion over five years. Motion agreed to 52-48: R 51-4; D 1-44 (ND 1-36, SD 0-8). April 5, 2000.

56. S Con Res 101. Fiscal 2001 Budget Resolution/Debt Reduction. Allard, R-Colo., motion to waive the Budget Act with respect to the Domenici, R-N.M., point of order against the Allard amendment. The Allard amendment would require an annual budget surplus large enough to reduce the public debt by $15 billion in fiscal 2001 and by an additional $15 billion each year until the entire debt has been paid. The amendment also would require that, until a major Social Security overhaul is enacted, the Social Security surplus be used to reduce the publicly held portion of the federal debt. Motion rejected 16-84: R 16-39; D 0-45 (ND 0-37, SD 0-8). A three-fifths majority vote (60) of the total Senate is required to waive the Budget Act. (Subsequently, the chairman upheld the point of order, and the amendment fell.) April 5, 2000.

57. S Con Res 101. Fiscal 2001 Budget Resolution/Federal Gas Tax. Byrd, D-W.Va., amendment that would express the sense of the Senate that the functional totals in the budget resolution do not assume the reduction of any federal gas taxes on either a temporary or permanent basis. Adopted 65-35: R 21-34; D 44-1 (ND 36-1, SD 8-0). April 6, 2000.

58. S Con Res 101. Fiscal 2001 Budget Resolution/ANWR. Murkowski, R-Alaska, motion to table (kill) the Roth, R-Del., amendment that would strike from the budget resolution the assumption that $1.2 billion in revenue will result from oil exploration in the Arctic National Wildlife Refuge. Motion agreed to 51-49: R 47-8; D 4-41 (ND 3-34, SD 1-7). April 6, 2000.

	59	60	61	62	63	64
ALABAMA						
Shelby	Y	Y	Y	Y	N	N
Sessions	Y	Y	Y	?	N	N
ALASKA						
Stevens	Y	Y	Y	Y	Y	N
Murkowski	Y	Y	Y	Y	Y	N
ARIZONA						
McCain	Y	Y	Y	Y	N	Y
Kyl	Y	Y	Y	Y	N	N
ARKANSAS						
Hutchinson	Y	Y	Y	Y	N	N
Lincoln	Y	Y	Y	N	N	Y
CALIFORNIA						
Feinstein	Y	Y	Y	N	N	Y
Boxer	Y	Y	Y	N	N	Y
COLORADO						
Campbell	Y	Y	Y	Y	Y	N
Allard	Y	Y	Y	Y	N	N
CONNECTICUT						
Dodd	Y	Y	Y	N	N	Y
Lieberman	Y	Y	Y	N	N	Y
DELAWARE						
Roth	?	?	?	Y	N	Y
Biden	Y	Y	Y	N	Y	Y
FLORIDA						
Graham	Y	Y	Y	N	N	Y
Mack	Y	Y	Y	Y	N	N
GEORGIA						
Coverdell	Y	Y	Y	Y	N	N
Cleland	Y	Y	Y	N	Y	Y
HAWAII						
Inouye	Y	Y	Y	N	Y	Y
Akaka	Y	Y	Y	N	Y	Y
IDAHO						
Craig	Y	Y	Y	Y	N	N
Crapo	Y	Y	Y	Y	N	N
ILLINOIS						
Durbin	Y	Y	Y	N	N	Y
Fitzgerald	Y	Y	Y	Y	N	Y
INDIANA						
Lugar	Y	Y	Y	Y	N	Y
Bayh	Y	Y	Y	N	N	Y
IOWA						
Grassley	Y	Y	Y	Y	N	N
Harkin	Y	Y	Y	N	N	Y
KANSAS						
Brownback	Y	Y	Y	Y	N	N
Roberts	Y	Y	Y	Y	N	N
KENTUCKY						
McConnell	Y	Y	Y	Y	N	N
Bunning	Y	Y	Y	Y	N	N
LOUISIANA						
Breaux	Y	Y	Y	N	N	Y
Landrieu	Y	Y	Y	N	N	Y
MAINE						
Snowe	Y	Y	Y	Y	N	N
Collins	Y	Y	Y	Y	N	N
MARYLAND						
Sarbanes	Y	Y	Y	N	N	Y
Mikulski	Y	Y	Y	N	N	Y
MASSACHUSETTS						
Kennedy	Y	Y	Y	N	N	Y
Kerry	Y	Y	Y	N	N	Y
MICHIGAN						
Levin	Y	Y	Y	N	Y	Y
Abraham	Y	Y	Y	Y	N	Y
MINNESOTA						
Wellstone	Y	Y	Y	N	Y	Y
Grams	Y	Y	Y	Y	N	N
MISSISSIPPI						
Cochran	Y	Y	Y	Y	N	N
Lott	Y	Y	Y	Y	N	N
MISSOURI						
Bond	Y	Y	Y	Y	N	N
Ashcroft	Y	Y	Y	Y	N	N
MONTANA						
Baucus	Y	Y	Y	N	N	N
Burns	Y	Y	Y	Y	N	N
NEBRASKA						
Kerrey	Y	Y	Y	N	N	Y
Hagel	Y	Y	Y	Y	N	N
NEVADA						
Reid	Y	Y	Y	N	Y	Y
Bryan	Y	Y	Y	N	N	Y
NEW HAMPSHIRE						
Smith	Y	Y	Y	Y	N	N
Gregg	Y	Y	Y	Y	N	N
NEW JERSEY						
Lautenberg	Y	Y	Y	N	N	Y
Torricelli	Y	Y	Y	N	N	Y
NEW MEXICO						
Domenici	Y	Y	Y	Y	N	N
Bingaman	Y	Y	Y	N	N	Y
NEW YORK						
Moynihan	Y	Y	Y	N	Y	Y
Schumer	Y	Y	Y	N	N	Y
NORTH CAROLINA						
Helms	Y	Y	Y	Y	Y	N
Edwards	Y	Y	Y	N	Y	Y
NORTH DAKOTA						
Conrad	Y	Y	Y	N	N	Y
Dorgan	Y	Y	Y	N	N	Y
OHIO						
DeWine	Y	Y	Y	Y	N	Y
Voinovich	Y	Y	Y	Y	N	N
OKLAHOMA						
Nickles	Y	Y	Y	Y	N	N
Inhofe	Y	Y	Y	Y	N	N
OREGON						
Wyden	Y	Y	Y	N	N	Y
Smith	Y	Y	Y	Y	N	Y
PENNSYLVANIA						
Specter	Y	Y	Y	Y	N	N
Santorum	Y	Y	Y	Y	N	N
RHODE ISLAND						
Reed	Y	Y	Y	N	N	Y
Chafee, L.	Y	Y	Y	Y	N	Y
SOUTH CAROLINA						
Thurmond	Y	Y	Y	Y	N	N
Hollings	Y	Y	Y	N	Y	Y
SOUTH DAKOTA						
Daschle	Y	Y	Y	N	Y	Y
Johnson	Y	Y	Y	N	N	Y
TENNESSEE						
Thompson	Y	Y	Y	Y	N	N
Frist	Y	Y	Y	Y	N	N
TEXAS						
Gramm	Y	Y	Y	Y	N	N
Hutchison	Y	Y	Y	Y	N	N
UTAH						
Hatch	Y	Y	Y	Y	N	N
Bennett	Y	Y	Y	Y	N	N
VERMONT						
Leahy	Y	Y	Y	N	N	Y
Jeffords	Y	Y	Y	Y	N	N
VIRGINIA						
Warner	Y	Y	Y	Y	Y	Y
Robb	Y	Y	Y	N	Y	Y
WASHINGTON						
Gorton	Y	Y	Y	Y	N	N
Murray	Y	Y	Y	N	Y	Y
WEST VIRGINIA						
Byrd	Y	Y	Y	N	N	Y
Rockefeller	Y	Y	Y	N	Y	Y
WISCONSIN						
Kohl	Y	Y	Y	N	N	Y
Feingold	Y	Y	Y	N	N	Y
WYOMING						
Thomas	Y	Y	Y	Y	N	N
Enzi	Y	Y	Y	Y	N	N

ND Northern Democrats SD Southern Democrats

Southern states - Ala., Ark., Fla., Ga., Ky., La., Miss., N.C., Okla., S.C., Tenn., Texas, Va.

Key

Y Voted for (yea).
\# Paired for.
\+ Announced for.
N Voted against (nay).
X Paired against.
– Announced against.
P Voted "present."
C Voted "present" to avoid possible conflict of interest.
? Did not vote or otherwise make a position known.

•

Democrats **Republicans**
Independents

59. S Con Res 101. Fiscal 2001 Budget Resolution/Bush Tax Plan. Domenici, R-N.M., motion to table (kill) the Reid, D-Nev., perfecting amendment to the Durbin, D-Ill., amendment. The Reid amendment would revert the Durbin amendment to its original text, to provide for a $483 billion tax cut over five years, the plan proposed by Republican presidential candidate Texas Gov. George W. Bush. Motion agreed to 99-0: R 54-0; D 45-0 (ND 37-0, SD 8-0). April 6, 2000.

60. S Con Res 101. Fiscal 2001 Budget Resolution/Fuel Tax. Gramm, R-Texas, amendment to the Durbin, D-Ill., amendment. The Gramm amendment would strike the text of the Durbin amendment and replace it with language that would express the sense of the Senate that the Senate will not increase gasoline and diesel fuel taxes by $1.50 per gallon effective July 1, 2000, and by an additional $1.50 per gallon in fiscal year 2005 in order to eliminate the internal combustion engine. The Durbin amendment would provide for a $483 billion tax cut over five years, the plan proposed by Republican presidential candidate Texas Gov. George W. Bush. Adopted 99-0: R 54-0; D 45-0 (ND 37-0, SD 8-0). (Subsequently, the Durbin amendment as amended was adopted by voice vote.) April 6, 2000.

61. S Con Res 101. Fiscal 2001 Budget Resolution/Military Food Stamps. McCain, R-Ariz., amendment that would increase defense spending by $28 million over five years to pay for an additional allowance to military families that are eligible for food stamps. Adopted 99-0: R 54-0; D 45-0 (ND 37-0, SD 8-0). April 6, 2000.

62. S Con Res 101. Fiscal 2001 Budget Resolution/School Modernization Projects. Domenici, R-N.M., motion to table (kill) the Robb, D-Va., amendment that would redirect $5.9 billion in revenue from tax cuts over the next five years to fund school modernization projects. Motion agreed to 54-45: R 54-0; D 0-45 (ND 0-37, SD 0-8). April 6, 2000.

63. S Con Res 101. Fiscal 2001 Budget Resolution/Smoke Shops. Inouye, D-Hawaii, motion to table the Bond, R-Mo., amendment that would express the sense of the Senate that the budget levels in the resolution assume that no federal funds may be used by the Department of Housing and Urban Development to provide any grant or other assistance to construct, operate or otherwise benefit a smoke shop or other tobacco outlet. Motion rejected 19-81: R 5-50; D 14-31 (ND 10-27, SD 4-4). (Subsequently, the Bond amendment was adopted by voice vote.) April 6, 2000.

64. S Con Res 101. Fiscal 2001 Budget Resolution/Juvenile Justice. Reed, D-R.I., amendment that would express the sense of the Senate that Congress should pass the conference report on the juvenile justice bill (HR 1501), including the Senate-passed provisions, and consider the bill no later than April 20, 2000. Adopted 53-47: R 9-46; D 44-1 (ND 36-1, SD 8-0). April 6, 2000.

Senate Votes 65, 66, 67, 68, 69, 70, 71

State / Senator	65	66	67	68	69	70	71
ALABAMA							
Shelby	N	Y	N	N	N	N	N
Sessions	N	Y	N	N	N	Y	N
ALASKA							
Stevens	N	Y	N	N	N	N	N
Murkowski	N	Y	N	N	N	N	N
ARIZONA							
McCain	N	Y	N	Y	Y	Y	N
Kyl	N	Y	N	N	N	Y	N
ARKANSAS							
Hutchinson	N	Y	N	N	N	Y	N
Lincoln	Y	Y	Y	Y	Y	N	Y
CALIFORNIA							
Feinstein	Y	Y	Y	Y	Y	N	Y
Boxer	Y	Y	Y	Y	Y	N	Y
COLORADO							
Campbell	N	Y	N	N	N	Y	N
Allard	N	Y	N	N	N	Y	N
CONNECTICUT							
Dodd	Y	Y	Y	Y	Y	N	Y
Lieberman	Y	Y	Y	Y	Y	N	Y
DELAWARE							
Roth	N	Y	N	N	N	N	N
Biden	Y	Y	Y	Y	Y	N	Y
FLORIDA							
Graham	Y	Y	Y	Y	Y	N	Y
Mack	N	Y	N	N	N	N	N
GEORGIA							
Coverdell	N	Y	N	N	N	N	N
Cleland	Y	Y	Y	Y	Y	N	Y
HAWAII							
Inouye	Y	Y	Y	Y	Y	N	Y
Akaka	Y	Y	Y	Y	Y	N	Y
IDAHO							
Craig	N	Y	N	N	N	Y	N
Crapo	N	Y	N	N	N	Y	N
ILLINOIS							
Durbin	Y	Y	Y	Y	Y	N	Y
Fitzgerald	N	Y	N	N	N	Y	N
INDIANA							
Lugar	N	Y	Y	N	N	N	N
Bayh	Y	Y	Y	N	Y	N	Y
IOWA							
Grassley	N	Y	N	N	N	N	N
Harkin	Y	Y	Y	Y	Y	N	Y
KANSAS							
Brownback	N	Y	N	N	N	Y	N
Roberts	N	Y	N	N	N	Y	N
KENTUCKY							
McConnell	N	Y	N	N	N	Y	N
Bunning	N	Y	N	N	N	Y	N
LOUISIANA							
Breaux	Y	Y	Y	N	Y	N	Y
Landrieu	Y	Y	Y	Y	Y	N	Y
MAINE							
Snowe	N	Y	N	N	Y	N	N
Collins	N	Y	N	N	Y	N	N
MARYLAND							
Sarbanes	Y	Y	Y	Y	Y	N	Y
Mikulski	Y	Y	Y	Y	Y	N	Y
MASSACHUSETTS							
Kennedy	Y	Y	Y	Y	Y	N	Y
Kerry	Y	Y	Y	Y	Y	N	Y
MICHIGAN							
Levin	Y	Y	Y	Y	Y	N	Y
Abraham	N	Y	N	N	N	Y	N
MINNESOTA							
Wellstone	Y	Y	Y	Y	Y	N	Y
Grams	N	Y	N	N	N	Y	N
MISSISSIPPI							
Cochran	N	Y	N	N	N	N	N
Lott	N	Y	N	N	N	N	N
MISSOURI							
Bond	N	Y	N	N	N	Y	N
Ashcroft	N	Y	N	N	N	Y	N
MONTANA							
Baucus	Y	Y	Y	Y	Y	N	Y
Burns	N	Y	N	N	N	N	N
NEBRASKA							
Kerrey	N	Y	Y	N	Y	N	Y
Hagel	N	Y	N	N	N	Y	N
NEVADA							
Reid	Y	Y	Y	Y	Y	N	Y
Bryan	Y	Y	Y	Y	Y	N	Y
NEW HAMPSHIRE							
Smith	N	Y	N	N	N	Y	N
Gregg	N	Y	N	N	N	N	N
NEW JERSEY							
Lautenberg	Y	Y	Y	Y	Y	N	Y
Torricelli	Y	Y	Y	N	Y	N	Y
NEW MEXICO							
Domenici	N	Y	N	N	N	N	N
Bingaman	Y	Y	Y	N	Y	N	Y
NEW YORK							
Moynihan	Y	Y	Y	Y	Y	N	Y
Schumer	Y	Y	Y	N	Y	N	Y
NORTH CAROLINA							
Helms	N	Y	N	N	N	Y	N
Edwards	Y	Y	Y	Y	Y	N	N
NORTH DAKOTA							
Conrad	Y	Y	Y	Y	Y	N	Y
Dorgan	Y	Y	Y	Y	Y	N	Y
OHIO							
DeWine	N	Y	N	N	N	N	N
Voinovich	N	Y	N	Y	N	Y	N
OKLAHOMA							
Nickles	N	Y	N	N	N	N	N
Inhofe	N	Y	N	N	N	Y	N
OREGON							
Wyden	Y	Y	Y	Y	Y	N	Y
Smith	N	Y	N	N	N	N	N
PENNSYLVANIA							
Specter	N	Y	N	Y	Y	Y	N
Santorum	N	Y	N	N	N	Y	N
RHODE ISLAND							
Reed	Y	Y	Y	Y	Y	N	Y
Chafee, L.	N	Y	N	Y	Y	N	Y
SOUTH CAROLINA							
Thurmond	N	Y	N	N	N	N	N
Hollings	Y	Y	Y	Y	Y	N	Y
SOUTH DAKOTA							
Daschle	Y	Y	Y	Y	Y	N	Y
Johnson	Y	Y	Y	Y	Y	Y	Y
TENNESSEE							
Thompson	N	Y	N	N	N	N	N
Frist	N	Y	N	N	N	N	N
TEXAS							
Gramm	N	Y	N	N	N	N	N
Hutchison	N	Y	N	N	N	Y	N
UTAH							
Hatch	N	Y	N	N	N	Y	N
Bennett	N	Y	N	N	N	N	N
VERMONT							
Leahy	Y	Y	Y	Y	Y	N	Y
Jeffords	N	Y	N	Y	Y	Y	N
VIRGINIA							
Warner	N	Y	N	N	N	N	N
Robb	Y	Y	Y	Y	Y	N	Y
WASHINGTON							
Gorton	N	Y	N	N	N	N	N
Murray	Y	Y	Y	Y	Y	N	Y
WEST VIRGINIA							
Byrd	Y	Y	Y	Y	Y	N	Y
Rockefeller	Y	Y	Y	Y	Y	N	Y
WISCONSIN							
Kohl	Y	Y	Y	Y	Y	N	Y
Feingold	Y	Y	Y	Y	Y	Y	Y
WYOMING							
Thomas	N	Y	N	N	N	N	N
Enzi	N	Y	N	N	N	Y	N

ND Northern Democrats SD Southern Democrats

Southern states - Ala., Ark., Fla., Ga., Ky., La., Miss., N.C., Okla., S.C., Tenn., Texas, Va.

Key

- Y Voted for (yea).
- \# Paired for.
- \+ Announced for.
- N Voted against (nay).
- X Paired against.
- – Announced against.
- P Voted "present."
- C Voted "present" to avoid possible conflict of interest.
- ? Did not vote or otherwise make a position known.

Democrats **•** ***Republicans***
Independents

65. S Con Res 101. Fiscal 2001 Budget Resolution/Medicare Surplus. Conrad, D-N.D., motion to waive the Budget Act with respect to the Domenici, R-N.M., point of order against the Conrad amendment. The Conrad amendment would establish several points of order against legislation that would reduce the budget surplus below the levels of the Medicare surplus reserve. Motion rejected 44-56: R 0-55; D 44-1 (ND 36-1, SD 8-0). A three-fifths majority vote (60) of the total Senate is required to waive the Budget Act. (Subsequently the chairman upheld the point of order, and the amendment fell.) April 7, 2000.

66. S Con Res 101. Fiscal 2001 Budget Resolution/Veterans' Health Care. Craig, R-Idaho, amendment to the Johnson, D-S.D., amendment. The Craig amendment would replace the text of the Johnson amendment with language that would express the sense of the Senate that if the Congressional Budget Office determines there is an on-budget surplus in fiscal 2001, then $500 million of that surplus would be used for veterans' health care programs. Adopted 100-0: R 55-0; D 45-0 (ND 37-0, SD 8-0). (Subsequently, the Johnson amendment as amended was adopted by voice vote.) April 7, 2000.

67. S Con Res 101. Fiscal 2001 Budget Resolution/Reserve Fund. Graham, D-Fla., motion to waive the Budget Act with respect to the Domenici, R-N.M., point of order against the Graham amendment. The Graham amendment would create a reserve fund that would allow discretionary funding to be increased by $15 billion for fiscal 2001 through 2005, once the Senate acts on legislation to reauthorize the Elementary and Secondary Education Act. Motion rejected 46-54: R 1-54; D 45-0 (ND 37-0, SD 8-0). A three-fifths majority vote (60) of the total Senate is required to waive the Budget Act. (Subsequently the chairman upheld the point of order, and the amendment fell.) April 7, 2000.

68. S Con Res 101. Fiscal 2001 Budget Resolution/Tax Cuts. Voinovich, R-Ohio, amendment that would strike the tax cut provision in the resolution. Rejected 44-56: R 5-50; D 39-6 (ND 32-5, SD 7-1). April 7, 2000.

69. S Con Res 101. Fiscal 2001 Budget Resolution/Pell Grants. Kennedy, D-Mass., amendment that would increase the maximum Pell grant by $400, raising the basic Pell grant from the current $3,300 to $3,700. The amendment also would reduce the tax cut provision in the resolution by less than 1 percent in fiscal 2001, and 1.8 percent over five years. Adopted 51-49: R 6-49; D 45-0 (ND 37-0, SD 8-0). April 7, 2000.

70. S Con Res 101. Fiscal 2001 Budget Resolution/Medicare Surplus. Ashcroft, R-Mo., motion to waive the Budget Act with respect to the Domenici, R-N.M., point of order against the Ashcroft amendment. The Ashcroft amendment would establish a point of order against consideration of concurrent resolutions on the budget or conference reports that would set an on-budget deficit for any fiscal year or subsequent legislation if it would cause or increase an on-budget deficit. The net surplus of any trust fund for Part A of Medicare would not be counted as a net surplus. Motion rejected 30-70: R 28-27; D 2-43 (ND 2-35, SD 0-8). A three-fifths majority vote (60) of the total Senate is required to waive the Budget Act. (Subsequently the chairman upheld the point of order, and the amendment fell.) April 7, 2000.

71. S Con Res 101. Fiscal 2001 Budget Resolution/Democratic Alternative. Lautenberg, D-N.J., amendment that would provide for $616 billion in discretionary spending in fiscal 2001. The amendment would also create a reserve fund of $1.3 billion in 2001 and $40 billion over five years for a Medicare prescription drug benefit, pending Senate action on such legislation. The amendment would allocate $4.9 billion in fiscal 2001 and $58.9 billion over five years for tax cuts. Rejected 45-55: R 1-54; D 44-1 (ND 37-0, SD 7-1). April 7, 2000.

	72	73	74	75	76	77	78
ALABAMA							
Shelby	N	Y	Y	Y	N	Y	N
Sessions	N	Y	Y	Y	N	Y	N
ALASKA							
Stevens	N	Y	Y	Y	N	Y	N
Murkowski	N	Y	Y	Y	N	Y	N
ARIZONA							
McCain	N	N	Y	Y	N	?	?
Kyl	N	Y	Y	Y	N	Y	N
ARKANSAS							
Hutchinson	N	Y	Y	Y	N	Y	N
Lincoln	Y	N	N	N	Y	N	Y
CALIFORNIA							
Feinstein	Y	N	N	N	Y	N	Y
Boxer	Y	N	N	N	Y	N	Y
COLORADO							
Campbell	N	Y	Y	Y	N	Y	N
Allard	N	Y	Y	Y	N	Y	N
CONNECTICUT							
Dodd	Y	N	N	N	Y	N	Y
Lieberman	Y	N	N	N	Y	N	Y
DELAWARE							
Roth	N	Y	Y	Y	Y	Y	N
Biden	Y	N	N	N	Y	N	Y
FLORIDA							
Graham	Y	N	N	N	Y	N	Y
Mack	N	N	Y	Y	N	Y	N
GEORGIA							
Coverdell	N	Y	Y	Y	N	Y	N
Cleland	Y	N	N	N	Y	N	Y
HAWAII							
Inouye	Y	N	N	N	Y	N	Y
Akaka	Y	N	N	N	Y	N	Y
IDAHO							
Craig	N	Y	Y	Y	N	Y	N
Crapo	N	Y	Y	Y	N	Y	N
ILLINOIS							
Durbin	Y	N	N	N	Y	N	Y
Fitzgerald	N	Y	Y	Y	Y	Y	N
INDIANA							
Lugar	N	Y	Y	Y	N	Y	N
Bayh	Y	N	N	N	Y	N	Y
IOWA							
Grassley	N	Y	Y	Y	N	Y	N
Harkin	Y	N	N	N	Y	N	Y
KANSAS							
Brownback	N	Y	Y	Y	N	Y	N
Roberts	N	Y	Y	Y	N	Y	N
KENTUCKY							
McConnell	N	Y	Y	Y	N	Y	N
Bunning	N	Y	Y	Y	N	Y	N
LOUISIANA							
Breaux	N	N	N	N	Y	N	Y
Landrieu	Y	N	N	N	Y	N	Y
MAINE							
Snowe	Y	N	Y	Y	Y	N	Y
Collins	Y	N	Y	Y	N	N	Y
MARYLAND							
Sarbanes	Y	N	N	N	Y	N	Y
Mikulski	Y	N	N	N	Y	N	Y
MASSACHUSETTS							
Kennedy	Y	N	N	N	Y	N	Y
Kerry	Y	N	N	N	Y	N	Y
MICHIGAN							
Levin	Y	N	N	N	Y	N	Y
Abraham	N	N	Y	Y	N	Y	N
MINNESOTA							
Wellstone	Y	N	N	N	Y	N	Y
Grams	N	Y	Y	Y	N	Y	N
MISSISSIPPI							
Cochran	N	Y	Y	Y	N	Y	N
Lott	N	Y	Y	Y	N	Y	N
MISSOURI							
Bond	N	Y	Y	Y	N	Y	N
Ashcroft	N	Y	Y	Y	N	Y	N
MONTANA							
Baucus	Y	N	N	N	Y	N	Y
Burns	N	Y	Y	Y	N	Y	N
NEBRASKA							
Kerrey	Y	N	N	N	Y	N	Y
Hagel	N	Y	Y	Y	N	Y	N
NEVADA							
Reid	Y	N	N	N	Y	N	Y
Bryan	Y	N	N	N	Y	N	Y
NEW HAMPSHIRE							
Smith	N	Y	Y	Y	N	Y	N
Gregg	N	Y	Y	Y	N	Y	N
NEW JERSEY							
Lautenberg	Y	N	N	N	Y	N	Y
Torricelli	Y	N	N	N	Y	N	Y
NEW MEXICO							
Domenici	N	Y	Y	Y	N	Y	N
Bingaman	Y	N	N	N	Y	N	Y
NEW YORK							
Moynihan	Y	N	N	N	Y	N	Y
Schumer	Y	N	N	N	Y	N	Y
NORTH CAROLINA							
Helms	N	Y	Y	Y	N	Y	N
Edwards	Y	N	N	N	Y	N	Y
NORTH DAKOTA							
Conrad	Y	N	N	N	Y	N	Y
Dorgan	Y	N	N	N	Y	N	Y
OHIO							
DeWine	N	N	Y	Y	N	Y	N
Voinovich	N	Y	Y	N	N	Y	N
OKLAHOMA							
Nickles	N	Y	Y	Y	N	Y	N
Inhofe	N	Y	Y	Y	N	Y	N
OREGON							
Wyden	Y	N	N	N	Y	N	Y
Smith	N	Y	Y	Y	N	Y	N
PENNSYLVANIA							
Specter	N	N	Y	N	Y	Y	N
Santorum	N	N	Y	Y	N	Y	N
RHODE ISLAND							
Reed	Y	N	N	N	Y	N	Y
Chafee, L.	Y	N	N	N	Y	N	Y
SOUTH CAROLINA							
Thurmond	N	Y	Y	Y	N	Y	N
Hollings	Y	N	N	N	Y	N	Y
SOUTH DAKOTA							
Daschle	Y	N	N	N	Y	N	Y
Johnson	Y	N	N	N	Y	N	Y
TENNESSEE							
Thompson	N	Y	Y	Y	N	Y	N
Frist	N	Y	Y	Y	N	Y	N
TEXAS							
Gramm	N	Y	Y	Y	N	Y	N
Hutchison	N	Y	Y	Y	N	Y	N
UTAH							
Hatch	N	Y	Y	Y	N	Y	N
Bennett	N	Y	Y	Y	?	?	?
VERMONT							
Leahy	Y	N	N	N	Y	N	Y
Jeffords	Y	N	Y	N	Y	N	Y
VIRGINIA							
Warner	N	Y	Y	Y	N	Y	N
Robb	Y	N	N	N	Y	N	Y
WASHINGTON							
Gorton	N	Y	Y	Y	N	Y	N
Murray	Y	N	N	N	Y	N	Y
WEST VIRGINIA							
Byrd	N	N	N	N	Y	N	Y
Rockefeller	Y	N	N	N	Y	N	Y
WISCONSIN							
Kohl	Y	N	N	N	Y	N	Y
Feingold	Y	N	N	N	Y	N	Y
WYOMING							
Thomas	N	Y	Y	Y	N	Y	N
Enzi	N	Y	Y	Y	N	Y	N

ND Northern Democrats   SD Southern Democrats

Southern states - Ala., Ark., Fla., Ga., Ky., La., Miss., N.C., Okla., S.C., Tenn., Texas, Va.

Key

- Y Voted for (yea).
- # Paired for.
- + Announced for.
- N Voted against (nay).
- X Paired against.
- – Announced against.
- P Voted "present."
- C Voted "present" to avoid possible conflict of interest.
- ? Did not vote or otherwise make a position known.

•

Democrats   ***Republicans***
Independents

72. S Con Res 101. Fiscal 2001 Budget Resolution/IDEA Funding. Jeffords, R-Vt., motion to table (kill) the Voinovich, R-Ohio, amendment to the Jeffords amendment. The Voinovich amendment would express the sense of the Senate that the budget resolution assumes that Congress' first priority should be to fully fund the programs under Part B of the Individuals with Disabilities Education Act. It also would eliminate the increase for IDEA funding in the Jeffords amendment. Motion rejected 47-53: R 4-51; D 43-2 (ND 36-1, SD 7-1). (Subsequently, the Voinovich amendment was agreed to by voice vote. The Jeffords amendment as amended was also agreed to by voice vote.) April 7, 2000.

73. S Con Res 101. Fiscal 2001 Budget Resolution/Discretionary Health Funding. Domenici, R-N.M., amendment to the Specter, R-Pa., amendment. The Domenici amendment would increase discretionary health funding by $1.6 billion. The Specter amendment would increase funding to the National Institutes of Health by $1.6 billion. Rejected 45-55: R 45-10; D 0-45 (ND 0-37, SD 0-8). (Subsequently, the Senate adopted the Specter amendment by voice vote.) April 7, 2000.

74. S Con Res 101. Fiscal 2001 Budget Resolution/Gun Law Enforcement. Craig, R-Idaho, to the Durbin, D-Ill., amendment that would express the sense of the Senate that the budget resolution assumes that federal funds will be used for a law enforcement strategy requiring a commitment to enforce existing federal firearm laws by designating at least one assistant U.S. attorney in each district to prosecute federal gun law violations, upgrade the national instant criminal background system and provide incentive grants to encourage states to impose minimum sentence requirements for gun law offenses. Adopted 54-46: R 54-1; D 0-45 (ND 0-37, SD 0-8). April 7, 2000.

75. S Con Res 101. Fiscal 2001 Budget Resolution/Minimum Wage. Nickles, R-Okla., amendment to the Kennedy, D-Mass., amendment. The Nickles amendment would strike the text of the Kennedy amendment and insert language that would express the sense of the Senate that the minimum wage should be increased as provided in the bankruptcy legislation (S 625) passed by the Senate, which would increase the minimum wage by $1 over three years. The Kennedy amendment would express the sense of the Senate that Congress should enact legislation to increase the minimum wage by $1 over one year — 50 cents on May 1, 2000, and another 50 cents on May 1, 2001. Approved 51-49: R 51-4; D 0-45 (ND 0-37, SD 0-8). April 7, 2000.

76. S Con Res 101. Fiscal 2001 Budget Resolution/Minimum Wage. Kennedy, D-Mass., amendment to the Kennedy amendment that would express the sense of the Senate that the minimum wage should be increased by $1 over one year — 50 cents on May 2, 2000, and another 50 cents on May 2, 2001. Adopted 51-48: R 6-48; D 45-0 (ND 37-0, SD 8-0). (Subsequently, Kennedy's amendment, as amended by the Nickles and Kennedy amendments, was adopted by voice vote.) April 7, 2000.

77. S Con Res 101. Fiscal 2001 Budget Resolution/Medicaid. Domenici, R-N.M., motion to table (kill) the Kennedy, D-Mass., amendment that would redirect $11.2 billion of the resolution's proposed tax cut to expand Medicaid and S-CHIP coverage to low-income families over five years. Motion rejected 49-49: R 49-4; D 0-45 (ND 0-37, SD 0-8). April 7, 2000.

78. S Con Res 101. Fiscal 2001 Budget Resolution/Medicaid. Kennedy, D-Mass., amendment that would redirect $11.2 billion of the resolution's proposed tax cut to expand Medicaid and S-CHIP coverage to low-income families over five years. Rejected 49-49: R 4-49; D 45-0 (ND 37-0, SD 8-0). April 7, 2000.

Senate Votes 79, 80, 81, 82, 83, 84, 85

	79	80	81	82	83	84	85
ALABAMA							
Shelby	Y	Y	Y	Y	Y	Y	Y
Sessions	Y	Y	Y	Y	Y	Y	Y
ALASKA							
Stevens	Y	Y	Y	Y	Y	Y	Y
Murkowski	Y	Y	Y	Y	Y	Y	Y
ARIZONA							
McCain	?	Y	Y	Y	Y	Y	N
Kyl	Y	Y	Y	Y	Y	Y	Y
ARKANSAS							
Hutchinson	Y	N	Y	Y	Y	Y	Y
Lincoln	N	N	Y	N	N	N	N
CALIFORNIA							
Feinstein	N	N	Y	N	N	N	N
Boxer	N	N	Y	N	N	N	N
COLORADO							
Campbell	Y	Y	Y	Y	Y	Y	Y
Allard	Y	Y	Y	Y	Y	Y	Y
CONNECTICUT							
Dodd	N	N	Y	N	N	N	N
Lieberman	N	N	Y	N	N	N	N
DELAWARE							
Roth	Y	Y	?	?	?	?	?
Biden	N	N	Y	N	N	N	N
FLORIDA							
Graham	N	N	Y	N	N	N	N
Mack	Y	Y	Y	Y	Y	Y	Y
GEORGIA							
Coverdell	Y	Y	Y	Y	Y	Y	Y
Cleland	N	N	Y	N	N	N	N
HAWAII							
Inouye	N	N	Y	N	N	N	N
Akaka	N	N	Y	N	N	N	N
IDAHO							
Craig	Y	Y	Y	Y	Y	Y	Y
Crapo	Y	Y	Y	Y	Y	Y	Y
ILLINOIS							
Durbin	N	N	Y	N	N	N	N
Fitzgerald	Y	Y	Y	Y	Y	Y	Y
INDIANA							
Lugar	Y	Y	Y	Y	Y	Y	Y
Bayh	N	N	Y	N	N	N	N
IOWA							
Grassley	Y	Y	Y	Y	Y	Y	Y
Harkin	N	N	Y	N	N	N	N
KANSAS							
Brownback	Y	Y	Y	Y	Y	Y	Y
Roberts	Y	N	Y	Y	Y	Y	Y
KENTUCKY							
McConnell	Y	Y	Y	Y	Y	Y	Y
Bunning	Y	Y	Y	Y	Y	Y	Y
LOUISIANA							
Breaux	N	N	Y	N	N	N	N
Landrieu	N	N	Y	N	N	N	N
MAINE							
Snowe	Y	Y	?	Y	Y	Y	Y
Collins	Y	Y	Y	Y	Y	Y	Y
MARYLAND							
Sarbanes	N	N	Y	N	N	N	N
Mikulski	N	N	Y	N	N	N	N
MASSACHUSETTS							
Kennedy	N	N	Y	N	N	N	N
Kerry	N	N	?	N	N	N	N
MICHIGAN							
Levin	N	N	Y	N	N	N	N
Abraham	Y	Y	Y	Y	Y	Y	Y
MINNESOTA							
Wellstone	N	N	Y	N	N	N	N
Grams	Y	Y	Y	Y	Y	Y	Y
MISSISSIPPI							
Cochran	Y	Y	Y	Y	Y	Y	Y
Lott	Y	Y	Y	Y	Y	Y	Y
MISSOURI							
Bond	Y	N	Y	Y	Y	Y	Y
Ashcroft	Y	N	Y	Y	Y	Y	Y
MONTANA							
Baucus	N	N	Y	N	N	N	N
Burns	Y	Y	Y	Y	Y	Y	Y
NEBRASKA							
Kerrey	N	N	Y	N	N	N	N
Hagel	Y	Y	Y	Y	Y	Y	Y
NEVADA							
Reid	X	N	Y	N	N	N	N
Bryan	N	N	Y	N	N	N	N
NEW HAMPSHIRE							
Smith	Y	Y	Y	Y	Y	Y	Y
Gregg	Y	Y	Y	Y	Y	Y	Y
NEW JERSEY							
Lautenberg	N	N	Y	N	N	N	N
Torricelli	N	N	Y	N	N	Y	N
NEW MEXICO							
Domenici	Y	Y	Y	Y	Y	Y	Y
Bingaman	N	N	Y	N	N	N	N
NEW YORK							
Moynihan	?	N	?	?	?	?	?
Schumer	N	N	Y	N	N	N	N
NORTH CAROLINA							
Helms	Y	Y	Y	Y	Y	Y	Y
Edwards	N	N	Y	N	N	N	N
NORTH DAKOTA							
Conrad	N	N	Y	N	N	N	N
Dorgan	N	N	Y	N	N	N	N
OHIO							
DeWine	Y	Y	Y	Y	Y	Y	Y
Voinovich	N	N	Y	N	N	Y	Y
OKLAHOMA							
Nickles	Y	Y	Y	Y	Y	Y	Y
Inhofe	Y	Y	Y	Y	Y	Y	Y
OREGON							
Wyden	N	N	Y	N	N	N	N
Smith	Y	Y	Y	Y	Y	Y	Y
PENNSYLVANIA							
Specter	Y	Y	Y	Y	Y	Y	N
Santorum	Y	Y	Y	Y	Y	Y	Y
RHODE ISLAND							
Reed	N	N	Y	N	N	N	N
Chafee, L.	N	N	Y	Y	Y	Y	N
SOUTH CAROLINA							
Thurmond	Y	Y	Y	Y	Y	Y	Y
Hollings	N	N	Y	N	N	N	N
SOUTH DAKOTA							
Daschle	N	N	Y	N	N	N	N
Johnson	N	N	Y	N	N	N	N
TENNESSEE							
Thompson	Y	Y	Y	Y	Y	Y	Y
Frist	Y	N	Y	Y	Y	Y	Y
TEXAS							
Gramm	Y	Y	Y	Y	Y	Y	Y
Hutchison	Y	Y	Y	Y	Y	Y	Y
UTAH							
Hatch	Y	Y	Y	Y	Y	Y	Y
Bennett	#	N	Y	Y	Y	Y	Y
VERMONT							
Leahy	N	N	Y	N	N	N	N
Jeffords	Y	N	Y	Y	Y	Y	N
VIRGINIA							
Warner	Y	N	Y	Y	Y	Y	Y
Robb	N	N	Y	N	N	N	N
WASHINGTON							
Gorton	Y	Y	Y	Y	Y	Y	Y
Murray	N	N	Y	N	N	N	N
WEST VIRGINIA							
Byrd	N	N	Y	N	N	N	N
Rockefeller	N	?	?	N	N	N	N
WISCONSIN							
Kohl	N	N	Y	N	N	N	N
Feingold	N	N	Y	N	N	N	N
WYOMING							
Thomas	Y	N	Y	Y	Y	Y	Y
Enzi	Y	N	Y	Y	Y	Y	Y

ND Northern Democrats SD Southern Democrats

Southern states - Ala., Ark., Fla., Ga., Ky., La., Miss., N.C., Okla., S.C., Tenn., Texas, Va.

Key

- Y Voted for (yea).
- # Paired for.
- \+ Announced for.
- N Voted against (nay).
- X Paired against.
- – Announced against.
- P Voted "present."
- C Voted "present" to avoid possible conflict of interest.
- ? Did not vote or otherwise make a position known.

•

Democrats **_Republicans_**
Independents

79. H Con Res 290. Fiscal 2001 Budget Resolution/Adoption. Adoption of the fiscal 2001 concurrent resolution on the budget. The resolution calls for $147.1 billion in tax cuts over five years. The resolution would create a reserve fund of up to $40 billion over five years for a Medicare prescription drug benefit and allow $600.5 billion in discretionary budget authority in fiscal 2001. It would establish 60-vote points of order against legislation that would exceed the $289.9 billion recommended for non-defense programs and $310.8 billion for defense. Adopted 51-45: R 51-2; D 0-43 (ND 0-35, SD 0-8). (Before passage, the Senate struck all after the enacting clause and inserted the text of S Con Res 101 as amended.) April 7, 2000.

80. S 2285. Gas Tax Suspension/Cloture. Motion to invoke cloture (thus limiting debate) on the bill that would suspend the 4.3-cents-a-gallon portion of the federal gas tax from April 15 through Dec. 31, 2000. The bill would also suspend the remainder of the 18.4-cents-a-gallon federal tax if the national average price of gasoline reaches $2 a gallon and would provide a similar tax suspension for diesel fuel, kerosene and aviation fuel. Motion rejected 43-56: R 43-12; D 0-44 (ND 0-36, SD 0-8). Three-fifths of the total Senate (60) is required to invoke cloture. April 11, 2000.

81. S 2323. Employee Stock Options/Passage. Passage of a bill that would amend the Fair Labor Standards Act to exclude stock options, stock appreciation rights or bona fide stock purchase programs from an employee's regular rate, which is used to calculate overtime pay. The aim is to encourage employers to offer these programs to hourly wage employees. Passed 95-0: R 53-0; D 42-0 (ND 34-0, SD 8-0). April 12, 2000.

82. HR 6. 'Marriage Penalty' Tax/Cloture. Motion to invoke cloture (thus limiting debate) on the Roth, R-Del., substitute amendment that would increase the standard deduction available to married couples filing jointly and increase the upper boundaries of the 15 percent and 28 percent tax brackets for couples. The amendment would increase the cost of the bill to $248 billion over 10 years. The amendment also includes language that would exempt several family-oriented tax credits including the $500-per-child tax credit from the alternative minimum tax. Motion rejected 53-45: R 53-1; D 0-44 (ND 0-36, SD 0-8). Three-fifths of the total Senate (60) is required to invoke cloture. April 13, 2000.

83. HR 6. 'Marriage Penalty' Tax/Cloture. Motion to invoke cloture (thus limiting debate) on the bill that would increase the standard deduction available to married couples filing jointly and eventually raise the 15 percent tax bracket for married couples to double that for singles. The measure would cost an estimated $182 billion over the next 10 years. Motion rejected 53-45: R 53-1; D 0-44 (ND 0-36, SD 0-8). Three-fifths of the total Senate (60) is required to invoke cloture. April 13, 2000.

84. H Con Res 303. Adjournment Resolution/Adoption. Adoption of the concurrent resolution to adjourn the House from April 13 or April 14, 2000, until 12:30 p.m on May 2, 2000, or until noon on the second day after members are notified to reassemble, whichever occurs first. The resolution also adjourns or recesses the Senate from April 13 or April 14, 2000, until noon on April 25, 2000, or until a time the majority leader specifies, or until noon on the second day after members are notified to reassemble, whichever occurs first. Adopted 55-43: R 54-0; D 1-43 (ND 1-35, SD 0-8). April 13, 2000.

85. H Con Res 290. Fiscal 2001 Budget Resolution/Conference Report. Adoption of the conference report on the fiscal 2001 concurrent resolution on the budget. The resolution calls for cutting taxes by $150 billion over five years and creates a "reserve fund" of $25 billion that could also be used for tax cuts. It also would establish a $40 billion reserve fund for Medicare overhaul and to provide prescription drug coverage for seniors. The plan calls for $600.3 billion in discretionary spending and allows for $310.8 billion in defense appropriations. It would set non-defense discretionary spending at $289.5 billion. Adopted 50-48: R 50-4; D 0-44 (ND 0-36, SD 0-8). April 13, 2000.

Senate Votes 86, 87, 88, 89, 90, 91

	86	87	88	89	90	91
ALABAMA						
Shelby	Y	Y	Y	Y	N	N
Sessions	Y	Y	Y	Y	N	N
ALASKA						
Stevens	Y	Y	Y	Y	N	N
Murkowski	Y	Y	Y	Y	N	N
ARIZONA						
McCain	?	?	Y	Y	N	N
Kyl	Y	Y	Y	Y	N	N
ARKANSAS						
Hutchinson	Y	Y	Y	Y	N	N
Lincoln	Y	?	Y	Y	Y	Y
CALIFORNIA						
Feinstein	Y	N	N	Y	Y	Y
Boxer	Y	N	N	Y	Y	Y
COLORADO						
Campbell	Y	Y	N	Y	N	N
Allard	Y	Y	Y	Y	N	N
CONNECTICUT						
Dodd	N	N	N	Y	Y	Y
Lieberman	Y	N	N	Y	Y	Y
DELAWARE						
Roth	?	?	?	?	?	?
Biden	?	N	N	Y	Y	Y
FLORIDA						
Graham	Y	N	Y	Y	Y	Y
Mack	Y	?	Y	Y	N	N
GEORGIA						
Coverdell	Y	Y	Y	Y	N	N
Cleland	Y	N	Y	Y	Y	Y
HAWAII						
Inouye	Y	N	N	Y	Y	Y
Akaka	Y	N	N	Y	Y	Y
IDAHO						
Craig	Y	Y	Y	Y	N	N
Crapo	Y	Y	Y	Y	N	N
ILLINOIS						
Durbin	N	N	N	Y	Y	Y
Fitzgerald	Y	Y	Y	Y	N	N
INDIANA						
Lugar	Y	Y	Y	Y	N	N
Bayh	Y	N	N	Y	Y	Y
IOWA						
Grassley	Y	Y	Y	Y	N	N
Harkin	N	N	N	Y	Y	Y
KANSAS						
Brownback	Y	Y	Y	Y	N	N
Roberts	Y	Y	Y	Y	N	N
KENTUCKY						
McConnell	Y	Y	Y	Y	N	N
Bunning	Y	Y	Y	Y	N	N
LOUISIANA						
Breaux	Y	N	Y	Y	Y	+
Landrieu	Y	N	Y	Y	Y	Y
MAINE						
Snowe	Y	Y	Y	Y	N	N
Collins	Y	Y	Y	Y	N	N
MARYLAND						
Sarbanes	Y	N	N	Y	Y	Y
Mikulski	?	N	N	Y	Y	Y
MASSACHUSETTS						
Kennedy	Y	N	N	Y	Y	Y
Kerry	Y	?	N	Y	Y	Y
MICHIGAN						
Levin	Y	N	Y	Y	Y	Y
Abraham	Y	Y	Y	Y	N	N
MINNESOTA						
Wellstone	Y	N	N	Y	Y	Y
Grams	Y	Y	Y	Y	N	N
MISSISSIPPI						
Cochran	Y	Y	Y	Y	N	N
Lott	Y	Y	N	Y	N	N
MISSOURI						
Bond	Y	Y	Y	Y	N	N
Ashcroft	Y	Y	Y	Y	N	N
MONTANA						
Baucus	N	N	N	Y	Y	Y
Burns	Y	Y	Y	Y	N	N
NEBRASKA						
Kerrey	?	N	Y	Y	Y	Y
Hagel	Y	Y	Y	Y	N	N
NEVADA						
Reid	Y	N	N	Y	Y	Y
Bryan	Y	N	N	Y	Y	Y
NEW HAMPSHIRE						
Smith	Y	Y	Y	Y	N	N
Gregg	Y	Y	Y	Y	N	N
NEW JERSEY						
Lautenberg	N	N	N	Y	Y	Y
Torricelli	Y	N	N	Y	Y	Y
NEW MEXICO						
Domenici	Y	Y	Y	?	N	N
Bingaman	N	N	N	Y	Y	Y
NEW YORK						
Moynihan	N	N	N	Y	Y	Y
Schumer	N	N	N	Y	Y	Y
NORTH CAROLINA						
Helms	Y	Y	Y	Y	N	N
Edwards	Y	N	Y	Y	Y	Y
NORTH DAKOTA						
Conrad	Y	N	N	Y	Y	Y
Dorgan	N	N	N	Y	Y	Y
OHIO						
DeWine	Y	Y	Y	Y	N	N
Voinovich	Y	N	Y	Y	N	N
OKLAHOMA						
Nickles	Y	Y	Y	Y	N	N
Inhofe	Y	Y	Y	Y	N	N
OREGON						
Wyden	Y	N	N	Y	Y	Y
Smith	Y	Y	Y	Y	N	N
PENNSYLVANIA						
Specter	Y	Y	Y	Y	N	N
Santorum	Y	Y	Y	Y	N	N
RHODE ISLAND						
Reed	Y	N	N	Y	Y	Y
Chafee, L.	Y	Y	N	Y	N	Y
SOUTH CAROLINA						
Thurmond	Y	Y	Y	Y	N	N
Hollings	N	N	Y	Y	Y	Y
SOUTH DAKOTA						
Daschle	Y	N	N	Y	Y	Y
Johnson	Y	N	N	Y	Y	Y
TENNESSEE						
Thompson	Y	Y	Y	Y	N	N
Frist	Y	Y	Y	Y	N	N
TEXAS						
Gramm	Y	Y	Y	Y	N	N
Hutchison	Y	Y	Y	Y	N	N
UTAH						
Hatch	Y	Y	Y	Y	N	N
Bennett	Y	Y	Y	Y	N	N
VERMONT						
Leahy	Y	N	Y	Y	Y	Y
Jeffords	?	Y	Y	Y	N	N
VIRGINIA						
Warner	Y	Y	Y	Y	N	N
Robb	Y	N	Y	Y	Y	Y
WASHINGTON						
Gorton	Y	Y	Y	Y	N	N
Murray	Y	N	Y	Y	Y	Y
WEST VIRGINIA						
Byrd	N	N	N	Y	Y	N
Rockefeller	Y	N	N	Y	Y	Y
WISCONSIN						
Kohl	Y	N	Y	Y	Y	?
Feingold	N	N	N	Y	Y	Y
WYOMING						
Thomas	Y	Y	Y	Y	N	N
Enzi	Y	Y	Y	Y	N	N

ND Northern Democrats SD Southern Democrats

Southern states - Ala., Ark., Fla., Ga., Ky., La., Miss., N.C., Okla., S.C., Tenn., Texas, Va.

Key

- Y Voted for (yea).
- # Paired for.
- + Announced for.
- N Voted against (nay).
- X Paired against.
- – Announced against.
- P Voted "present."
- C Voted "present" to avoid possible conflict of interest.
- ? Did not vote or otherwise make a position known.

•

Democrats ***Republicans***
Independents

86. S J Res 3. Victims' Rights/Cloture. Motion to invoke cloture (thus limiting debate) on the motion to proceed to the resolution to propose a constitutional amendment that would give victims the right to be notified of and attend all proceedings related to the crime; the right to speak or submit statements at each public hearing in the case, including parole or other early release hearings; the right to reasonable notice if those convicted in their cases are released or escape; and the right to restitution. Motion agreed to 82-12: R 52-0; D 30-12 (ND 23-11, SD 7-1). Three-fifths of the total Senate (60) is required to invoke cloture. April 25, 2000.

87. HR 6. 'Marriage Penalty' Tax/Cloture. Motion to invoke cloture (thus limiting debate) on the Roth, R-Del., substitute amendment that would increase the standard deduction available to married couples filing jointly and increase the upper boundaries of the 15 percent and 28 percent tax brackets for couples. The amendment would increase the cost of the bill to $248 billion over 10 years. Motion rejected 51-44: R 51-1; D 0-43 (ND 0-36, SD 0-7). Three-fifths of the total Senate (60) is required to invoke cloture. April 27, 2000.

88. S 1287. Nuclear Waste Storage/Veto Override. Passage, over President Clinton's April 25, 2000 veto, of the bill that would provide for the completion of siting and licensing activities for a permanent nuclear waste repository at Yucca Mountain, Nev., and establish a timetable for the development of the proposed site. Rejected 64-35: R 51-3; D 13-32 (ND 5-32, SD 8-0). A two-thirds majority of those present and voting (66 in this case) of both houses is required to override a veto. May 2, 2000. A "nay" was a vote in support of the president's position.

89. S 2. Elementary and Secondary Education Reauthorization/Achievement Gap. Gorton, R-Wash., amendment that would require that the 15 states taking part in the "Straight A's" pilot program reduce the achievement gap between the highest and lowest performing students under Title I, by 10 percent over a five-year period. Adopted 98-0: R 53-0; D 45-0 (ND 37-0, SD 8-0). May 3, 2000.

90. S 2. Elementary and Secondary Education Reauthorization/Democratic Substitute. Daschle, D-S.D., substitute amendment that would require states that receive assistance under the bill to craft an accountability plan for increasing student performance and achievement for the most disadvantaged students. It would hold schools accountable for increased student performance by requiring schools to ensure that all students meet or exceed state proficiency standards within 10 years. The amendment also would provide $2 billion to help schools recruit and train teachers. It would provide $1.75 billion to fund President Clinton's proposal to hire 100,000 new teachers to reduce class size and authorize $1.3 billion in grants and loans for emergency school repairs and renovations. Rejected 45-54: R 0-54; D 45-0 (ND 37-0, SD 8-0). May 3, 2000.

91. S 2. Elementary and Secondary Education Reauthorization/Student Achievement. Kennedy, D-Mass., amendment to the Abraham, R-Mich., amendment. The Kennedy amendment would strike the text of the Abraham amendment and insert language that would authorize funds to implement merit school programs for rewarding all teachers in schools that improve student achievement for all students, including the lowest achieving students. The amendment also would provide incentives and subsidies for helping teachers gain advanced degrees in the fields they teach; implement peer review, evaluation and recertification programs for teachers; and provide incentives for highly qualified teachers to teach in the neediest schools. Rejected 43-54: R 1-53; D 42-1 (ND 35-1, SD 7-0). May 4, 2000.

	92	93	94	95	96	97
ALABAMA						
Shelby	Y	N	Y	N	Y	Y
Sessions	Y	N	Y	N	Y	Y
ALASKA						
Stevens	Y	N	Y	N	Y	Y
Murkowski	Y	N	Y	N	Y	Y
ARIZONA						
McCain	Y	N	Y	N	Y	Y
Kyl	Y	N	Y	N	Y	Y
ARKANSAS						
Hutchinson	Y	N	Y	N	Y	Y
Lincoln	N	Y	Y	Y	Y	?
CALIFORNIA						
Feinstein	Y	Y	Y	Y	Y	Y
Boxer	N	Y	Y	N	Y	N
COLORADO						
Campbell	Y	N	Y	N	Y	Y
Allard	Y	N	Y	N	Y	Y
CONNECTICUT						
Dodd	N	Y	Y	N	Y	Y
Lieberman	N	Y	Y	Y	Y	Y
DELAWARE						
Roth	?	?	?	?	?	?
Biden	N	Y	Y	N	Y	Y
FLORIDA						
Graham	N	Y	Y	Y	Y	Y
Mack	Y	N	Y	N	Y	Y
GEORGIA						
Coverdell	Y	N	Y	N	Y	Y
Cleland	N	Y	Y	N	Y	N
HAWAII						
Inouye	N	Y	Y	N	Y	Y
Akaka	N	Y	Y	N	Y	Y
IDAHO						
Craig	Y	N	Y	N	Y	Y
Crapo	Y	N	Y	N	Y	Y
ILLINOIS						
Durbin	N	Y	Y	N	Y	Y
Fitzgerald	Y	N	Y	N	Y	Y
INDIANA						
Lugar	Y	N	Y	N	Y	Y
Bayh	N	Y	Y	Y	Y	Y
IOWA						
Grassley	Y	N	Y	N	Y	Y
Harkin	N	Y	Y	N	Y	Y
KANSAS						
Brownback	Y	N	Y	N	Y	Y
Roberts	Y	N	Y	N	Y	Y
KENTUCKY						
McConnell	Y	N	Y	N	Y	Y
Bunning	+	-	Y	N	N	N
LOUISIANA						
Breaux	-	Y	Y	Y	Y	Y
Landrieu	N	Y	Y	Y	Y	?
MAINE						
Snowe	N	N	Y	N	Y	N
Collins	Y	N	Y	N	Y	N
MARYLAND						
Sarbanes	N	Y	Y	N	Y	Y
Mikulski	N	Y	Y	N	Y	Y
MASSACHUSETTS						
Kennedy	N	Y	Y	N	Y	N
Kerry	N	Y	Y	N	Y	Y
MICHIGAN						
Levin	N	Y	Y	N	Y	Y
Abraham	Y	N	Y	N	Y	Y
MINNESOTA						
Wellstone	N	Y	Y	N	Y	N
Grams	Y	N	Y	N	Y	Y
MISSISSIPPI						
Cochran	Y	N	Y	N	Y	Y
Lott	Y	N	Y	N	Y	Y
MISSOURI						
Bond	Y	N	Y	N	Y	Y
Ashcroft	Y	N	Y	N	Y	Y
MONTANA						
Baucus	N	Y	Y	N	Y	Y
Burns	Y	N	Y	N	Y	Y
NEBRASKA						
Kerrey	N	Y	Y	N	Y	Y
Hagel	Y	N	?	?	?	Y
NEVADA						
Reid	N	Y	Y	N	Y	Y
Bryan	N	Y	Y	Y	Y	?
NEW HAMPSHIRE						
Smith	Y	N	Y	N	N	N
Gregg	Y	N	Y	N	Y	Y
NEW JERSEY						
Lautenberg	N	Y	Y	N	Y	Y
Torricelli	N	Y	Y	N	Y	Y
NEW MEXICO						
Domenici	Y	N	Y	N	Y	?
Bingaman	N	Y	Y	N	Y	?
NEW YORK						
Moynihan	N	Y	Y	Y	Y	Y
Schumer	N	Y	Y	N	Y	Y
NORTH CAROLINA						
Helms	Y	N	Y	N	?	N
Edwards	N	Y	Y	Y	Y	N
NORTH DAKOTA						
Conrad	N	Y	Y	N	Y	N
Dorgan	N	Y	Y	N	N	N
OHIO						
DeWine	Y	N	Y	N	Y	Y
Voinovich	N	N	Y	N	Y	Y
OKLAHOMA						
Nickles	Y	N	Y	N	Y	Y
Inhofe	Y	N	Y	N	Y	Y
OREGON						
Wyden	N	Y	Y	N	Y	Y
Smith	Y	N	Y	N	Y	Y
PENNSYLVANIA						
Specter	Y	N	Y	N	Y	Y
Santorum	Y	N	Y	N	Y	Y
RHODE ISLAND						
Reed	N	Y	Y	N	N	N
Chafee, Lincoln	Y	N	Y	N	Y	Y
SOUTH CAROLINA						
Thurmond	Y	N	Y	N	?	N
Hollings	Y	Y	Y	N	N	N
SOUTH DAKOTA						
Daschle	N	Y	Y	N	Y	Y
Johnson	N	Y	Y	Y	Y	Y
TENNESSEE						
Thompson	Y	N	?	?	Y	Y
Frist	Y	N	Y	N	Y	Y
TEXAS						
Gramm	Y	N	Y	N	Y	Y
Hutchison	Y	N	Y	N	Y	Y
UTAH						
Hatch	Y	N	Y	N	Y	Y
Bennett	Y	N	Y	N	Y	Y
VERMONT						
Leahy	N	Y	Y	N	Y	N
Jeffords	Y	N	Y	N	Y	Y
VIRGINIA						
Warner	Y	N	Y	N	Y	Y
Robb	N	Y	Y	Y	Y	Y
WASHINGTON						
Gorton	Y	N	Y	N	Y	Y
Murray	N	Y	Y	N	Y	Y
WEST VIRGINIA						
Byrd	Y	Y	Y	N	N	N
Rockefeller	N	Y	Y	N	Y	Y
WISCONSIN						
Kohl	?	?	Y	Y	Y	Y
Feingold	N	Y	Y	N	Y	N
WYOMING						
Thomas	Y	N	Y	N	Y	Y
Enzi	Y	N	Y	N	Y	Y

ND Northern Democrats SD Southern Democrats

Southern states - Ala., Ark., Fla., Ga., Ky., La., Miss., N.C., Okla., S.C., Tenn., Texas, Va.

Key

- Y Voted for (yea).
- # Paired for.
- \+ Announced for.
- N Voted against (nay).
- X Paired against.
- – Announced against.
- P Voted "present."
- C Voted "present" to avoid possible conflict of interest.
- ? Did not vote or otherwise make a position known.

Democrats **_Republicans_**
Independents

92. S 2. Elementary and Secondary Education Reauthorization/Teacher Merit Increases. Abraham, R-Mich., amendment that would authorize the use of state and local funds to overhaul teacher tenure systems, establish teacher compensation systems based on merit and proven performance, and test teachers periodically in the academic subjects they teach. Adopted 54-42: R 51-2; D 3-40 (ND 2-34, SD 1-6). May 4, 2000.

93. S 2. Elementary and Secondary Education Reauthorization/Class Size Reduction. Murray, D-Wash., amendment that would provide $1.75 billion in fiscal 2001 to fund measures aimed at reducing class size, such as the recruiting and hiring of new teachers, testing new teachers, and providing professional development for teachers. The amendment would also provide that funds go to local agencies based 80 percent on need and 20 percent on school enrollment. Rejected 44-53: R 0-53; D 44-0 (ND 36-0, SD 8-0). A "yea" was a vote in support of the president's position. May 4, 2000.

94. S 2. Elementary and Secondary Education Act Reauthorization/Teacher Quality. Lott, R-Miss., amendment that would allow states and local communities to use their portion of professional development and class-size reduction funds to address the shortage of high-quality teachers. School districts receiving the money would be required to demonstrate improvements in student achievement. The amendment would authorize a new $50 million program to provide teacher certification training. It would also provide liability protection to teachers, principals and other school personnel who take reasonable action to maintain order or discipline a student. Adopted 97-0: R 52-0; D 45-0 (ND 37-0, SD 8-0). May 9, 2000.

95. S 2. Elementary and Secondary Education Act Reauthorization/Centrist Democratic Alternative. Lieberman, D-Conn., substitute amendment that would increase federal spending on public schools by $35 billion over five years. Grant programs under Title I for disadvantaged students would be consolidated and authorized at $12 billion. Various teacher and professional development programs would be combined into a single grant, with funding increased to $1.6 billion annually. The amendment would peg program funding to academic performance standards, authorize $100 million for a new public school choice program and continue President Clinton's program to hire 100,000 new teachers. Rejected 13-84: R 0-52; D 13-32 (ND 7-30, SD 6-2). May 9, 2000.

96. HR 434. Africa, Caribbean Trade/Motion to Proceed. Motion to proceed to the conference report on the bill that would extend certain tariff benefits to the nations of the Caribbean, Central America and sub-Saharan Africa. Motion agreed to 90-6: R 49-2; D 41-4 (ND 34-3, SD 7-1). May 10, 2000.

97. HR 434. Africa, Caribbean Trade/Cloture. Motion to invoke cloture (thus limiting debate) on the conference report on the bill that would extend certain tariff benefits to the nations of the Caribbean, Central America and sub-Saharan Africa. Motion agreed to 76-18: R 47-6; D 29-12 (ND 26-9, SD 3-3). Three-fifths of the total Senate (60) is required to invoke cloture. May 11, 2000.

Senate Votes 98, 99, 100, 101, 102, 103, 104

	98	99	100	101	102	103	104
ALABAMA							
Shelby	Y	Y	N	N	N	Y	N
Sessions	Y	Y	N	N	N	Y	N
ALASKA							
Stevens	Y	Y	N	N	N	Y	N
Murkowski	Y	Y	N	N	N	Y	N
ARIZONA							
McCain	Y	Y	N	N	N	Y	N
Kyl	Y	Y	N	N	N	Y	N
ARKANSAS							
Hutchinson	Y	Y	N	N	N	Y	N
Lincoln	Y	Y	Y	Y	Y	Y	Y
CALIFORNIA							
Feinstein	Y	Y	Y	Y	Y	N	Y
Boxer	N	Y	Y	Y	Y	N	Y
COLORADO							
Campbell	Y	Y	N	N	N	Y	N
Allard	Y	Y	N	N	N	Y	N
CONNECTICUT							
Dodd	Y	Y	Y	Y	+	+	+
Lieberman	Y	Y	Y	Y	Y	Y	Y
DELAWARE							
Roth	?	Y	N	N	N	Y	Y
Biden	Y	?	?	?	Y	N	Y
FLORIDA							
Graham	Y	Y	Y	Y	Y	N	Y
Mack	Y	Y	N	N	N	Y	N
GEORGIA							
Coverdell	Y	Y	N	N	N	Y	N
Cleland	N	Y	Y	Y	Y	Y	Y
HAWAII							
Inouye	Y	Y	Y	Y	Y	N	Y
Akaka	Y	Y	Y	Y	Y	N	Y
IDAHO							
Craig	Y	Y	N	N	N	Y	N
Crapo	Y	Y	N	N	N	Y	N
ILLINOIS							
Durbin	Y	Y	Y	Y	Y	N	Y
Fitzgerald	Y	Y	Y	N	N	Y	Y
INDIANA							
Lugar	Y	Y	N	N	N	Y	Y
Bayh	Y	Y	Y	Y	Y	N	Y
IOWA							
Grassley	Y	Y	N	N	N	Y	N
Harkin	Y	Y	Y	Y	Y	N	Y
KANSAS							
Brownback	Y	Y	N	N	N	Y	N
Roberts	Y	Y	N	N	N	Y	N
KENTUCKY							
McConnell	Y	Y	N	N	N	Y	N
Bunning	N	Y	N	N	N	Y	N
LOUISIANA							
Breaux	Y	N	Y	Y	Y	Y	Y
Landrieu	Y	Y	Y	Y	Y	Y	Y
MAINE							
Snowe	N	Y	N	N	N	Y	N
Collins	N	Y	N	N	N	Y	N
MARYLAND							
Sarbanes	Y	Y	Y	Y	Y	N	Y
Mikulski	Y	Y	Y	Y	Y	N	Y
MASSACHUSETTS							
Kennedy	N	Y	Y	Y	Y	N	Y
Kerry	Y	Y	Y	Y	Y	Y	Y
MICHIGAN							
Levin	Y	Y	Y	Y	Y	N	Y
Abraham	Y	Y	N	N	N	Y	N
MINNESOTA							
Wellstone	N	Y	Y	Y	Y	N	Y
Grams	Y	Y	N	N	N	Y	N
MISSISSIPPI							
Cochran	Y	Y	N	N	N	Y	N
Lott	Y	Y	N	N	N	Y	N
MISSOURI							
Bond	Y	Y	N	N	N	Y	N
Ashcroft	Y	Y	N	N	N	Y	N
MONTANA							
Baucus	Y	Y	N	Y	Y	Y	N
Burns	Y	Y	N	N	N	Y	N
NEBRASKA							
Kerrey	Y	Y	Y	Y	Y	N	Y
Hagel	Y	Y	N	N	N	Y	N
NEVADA							
Reid	N	Y	Y	Y	Y	N	Y
Bryan	?	Y	Y	Y	Y	Y	Y
NEW HAMPSHIRE							
Smith	N	Y	N	N	N	Y	N
Gregg	Y	Y	N	N	N	Y	N
NEW JERSEY							
Lautenberg	Y	Y	Y	Y	Y	N	Y
Torricelli	Y	Y	Y	Y	Y	N	Y
NEW MEXICO							
Domenici	?	Y	N	N	N	Y	N
Bingaman	?	Y	Y	Y	Y	Y	Y
NEW YORK							
Moynihan	Y	?	?	?	Y	N	Y
Schumer	Y	?	?	?	Y	N	Y
NORTH CAROLINA							
Helms	N	Y	N	N	N	Y	N
Edwards	N	Y	Y	Y	Y	Y	Y
NORTH DAKOTA							
Conrad	N	Y	Y	Y	Y	Y	Y
Dorgan	N	Y	Y	Y	Y	Y	Y
OHIO							
DeWine	Y	Y	N	N	N	Y	Y
Voinovich	Y	Y	N	N	N	N	N
OKLAHOMA							
Nickles	Y	Y	N	N	N	Y	N
Inhofe	Y	Y	N	N	N	Y	N
OREGON							
Wyden	Y	Y	Y	Y	Y	Y	Y
Smith	Y	?	?	?	N	Y	N
PENNSYLVANIA							
Specter	Y	Y	N	N	N	Y	N
Santorum	Y	Y	N	N	N	Y	N
RHODE ISLAND							
Reed	N	Y	Y	Y	Y	N	Y
Chafee, L.	Y	Y	N	N	Y	N	Y
SOUTH CAROLINA							
Thurmond	N	Y	N	N	N	Y	N
Hollings	N	Y	Y	Y	Y	N	Y
SOUTH DAKOTA							
Daschle	Y	Y	Y	Y	Y	N	Y
Johnson	Y	Y	Y	Y	Y	N	Y
TENNESSEE							
Thompson	Y	Y	N	N	N	N	N
Frist	Y	Y	N	N	N	Y	N
TEXAS							
Gramm	Y	Y	N	N	N	Y	N
Hutchison	Y	Y	N	N	N	Y	N
UTAH							
Hatch	Y	Y	N	N	N	Y	N
Bennett	Y	Y	N	N	N	Y	N
VERMONT							
Leahy	N	Y	Y	Y	Y	Y	Y
Jeffords	Y	Y	N	N	N	Y	Y
VIRGINIA							
Warner	Y	Y	N	N	N	Y	Y
Robb	Y	Y	Y	Y	Y	N	Y
WASHINGTON							
Gorton	Y	Y	N	?	N	Y	N
Murray	Y	Y	Y	Y	Y	Y	Y
WEST VIRGINIA							
Byrd	N	Y	Y	N	Y	Y	Y
Rockefeller	Y	Y	Y	Y	Y	N	Y
WISCONSIN							
Kohl	Y	Y	Y	Y	Y	N	Y
Feingold	N	Y	Y	Y	Y	Y	Y
WYOMING							
Thomas	Y	N	N	N	N	Y	N
Enzi	Y	Y	N	N	N	Y	N

ND Northern Democrats SD Southern Democrats

Southern states - Ala., Ark., Fla., Ga., Ky., La., Miss., N.C., Okla., S.C., Tenn., Texas, Va.

Key

- Y Voted for (yea).
- # Paired for.
- \+ Announced for.
- N Voted against (nay).
- X Paired against.
- – Announced against.
- P Voted "present."
- C Voted "present" to avoid possible conflict of interest.
- ? Did not vote or otherwise make a position known.

Democrats ***Republicans***
Independents

98. HR 434. Africa, Caribbean Trade/Conference Report. Adoption of the conference report on the bill that would extend certain tariff benefits to the nations of the Caribbean, Central America and sub-Saharan Africa. Adopted (thus cleared for the president) 77-19: R 47-6; D 30-13 (ND 25-10, SD 5-3). A "yea" was a vote in support of the president's position. May 11, 2000.

99. Procedural Motion/Require Attendance. Lott, R-Miss., motion to instruct the sergeant-at-arms to request the attendance of absent senators. Motion agreed to 94-2: R 53-1; D 41-1 (ND 34-0, SD 7-1). May 16, 2000.

100. S 2521. Fiscal 2001 Military Construction Appropriations/Juvenile Justice. Motion to table (kill) the Lott, R-Miss., point of order against the Daschle, D-S.D., amendment for not being germane. The Daschle amendment would express the sense of the Senate that organizers of the Million Mom March should be commended and that Congress should adopt the conference report on the juvenile justice bill (HR 1501), including the Senate-passed provisions, before the Memorial Day recess. Motion rejected 42-54: R 1-53; D 41-1 (ND 33-1, SD 8-0). May 16, 2000.

101. Hamilton Nomination/Motion to Proceed. Motion to proceed to executive session to consider President Clinton's nomination of E. Douglas Hamilton of Kentucky to be a U.S. marshal for the Western District of Kentucky. Motion rejected 41-54: R 0-53; D 41-1 (ND 33-1, SD 8-0). May 16, 2000.

102. S 2521. Fiscal 2001 Military Construction Appropriations/Ruling of the Chair. Judgment of the Senate to affirm the ruling of the chair against the Lott, R-Miss., point of order against the Lott amendment, thus establishing a Senate precedent that sense-of-the-Senate amendments, like all other amendments to appropriations bills, must be germane. The Lott amendment would express the sense of the Senate that the right of a law-abiding citizen to own firearms for a legitimate purpose should not be infringed, and that any juvenile crime conference report should designate at least one assistant U.S. attorney in each district to prosecute federal gun violations, upgrade the national instant criminal background system, and provide incentive grants to encourage states to impose mandatory minimum sentences for gun offenses. Ruling of the chair rejected 45-54: R 1-54; D 44-0 (ND 36-0, SD 8-0). May 17, 2000.

103. S 2521. Fiscal 2001 Military Construction Appropriations/Juvenile Justice. Lott, R-Miss., amendment that would express the sense of the Senate that the right of each law-abiding citizen to own firearms for a legitimate purpose should not be infringed, and any juvenile crime conference report should include designating at least one assistant U.S. attorney in each district to prosecute federal gun violations, upgrading the national instant criminal background system and providing incentive grants to encourage states to impose mandatory minimum sentences for gun offenses. Adopted 69-30: R 52-3; D 17-27 (ND 12-24, SD 5-3). May 17, 2000.

104. S 2521. Fiscal 2001 Military Construction Appropriations/Juvenile Justice. Daschle, D-S.D., amendment that would express the sense of the Senate that organizers of the Million Mom March should be commended and that Congress should pass the conference report to accompany the juvenile justice bill (HR 1501), including the Senate-passed provisions, before the Memorial Day recess. Adopted 50-49: R 7-48; D 43-1 (ND 35-1, SD 8-0). May 17, 2000.

Senate Votes 105, 106, 107, 108, 109, 110

State / Senator	105	106	107	108	109	110
ALABAMA						
Shelby	N	Y	Y	Y	N	Y
Sessions	N	Y	Y	Y	N	N
ALASKA						
Stevens	N	Y	Y	Y	Y	Y
Murkowski	N	Y	Y	Y	N	N
ARIZONA						
McCain	Y	N	N	N	Y	N
Kyl	N	Y	Y	Y	N	N
ARKANSAS						
Hutchinson	N	Y	Y	Y	N	N
Lincoln	Y	Y	N	Y	Y	Y
CALIFORNIA						
Feinstein	Y	Y	N	Y	Y	Y
Boxer	Y	Y	N	Y	Y	Y
COLORADO						
Campbell	N	Y	Y	Y	Y	N
Allard	N	Y	Y	Y	N	N
CONNECTICUT						
Dodd	Y	Y	Y	Y	Y	Y
Lieberman	Y	Y	N	Y	Y	Y
DELAWARE						
Roth	Y	Y	Y	Y	Y	Y
Biden	Y	Y	?	?	?	?
FLORIDA						
Graham	Y	Y	Y	Y	Y	Y
Mack	Y	Y	Y	Y	Y	N
GEORGIA						
Coverdell	N	Y	Y	Y	N	N
Cleland	N	Y	N	Y	Y	Y
HAWAII						
Inouye	N	Y	Y	Y	Y	Y
Akaka	Y	Y	N	Y	Y	Y
IDAHO						
Craig	N	Y	Y	Y	N	N
Crapo	N	Y	Y	Y	N	N
ILLINOIS						
Durbin	Y	Y	N	Y	Y	Y
Fitzgerald	N	Y	Y	Y	Y	Y
INDIANA						
Lugar	Y	Y	Y	Y	Y	Y
Bayh	Y	Y	N	Y	Y	Y
IOWA						
Grassley	N	Y	Y	Y	N	N
Harkin	Y	Y	N	Y	Y	Y
KANSAS						
Brownback	N	Y	Y	Y	N	N
Roberts	N	Y	Y	Y	N	N
KENTUCKY						
McConnell	N	Y	Y	Y	N	N
Bunning	N	Y	Y	Y	N	N
LOUISIANA						
Breaux	Y	Y	Y	Y	Y	Y
Landrieu	Y	Y	N	Y	Y	Y
MAINE						
Snowe	N	Y	Y	Y	Y	Y
Collins	N	Y	Y	Y	Y	Y
MARYLAND						
Sarbanes	Y	Y	N	Y	Y	Y
Mikulski	Y	Y	N	Y	Y	Y
MASSACHUSETTS						
Kennedy	Y	Y	N	Y	Y	Y
Kerry	Y	Y	N	Y	Y	Y
MICHIGAN						
Levin	Y	Y	N	Y	Y	Y
Abraham	Y	Y	Y	Y	Y	N
MINNESOTA						
Wellstone	Y	Y	N	Y	Y	Y
Grams	N	Y	Y	Y	Y	N
MISSISSIPPI						
Cochran	Y	Y	Y	Y	N	N
Lott	N	Y	Y	Y	N	N
MISSOURI						
Bond	N	Y	Y	Y	Y	N
Ashcroft	N	Y	Y	Y	N	N
MONTANA						
Baucus	Y	Y	Y	Y	Y	Y
Burns	N	Y	Y	Y	Y	N
NEBRASKA						
Kerrey	Y	Y	N	Y	Y	Y
Hagel	Y	Y	Y	Y	Y	N
NEVADA						
Reid	Y	Y	Y	Y	Y	Y
Bryan	Y	Y	Y	Y	Y	Y
NEW HAMPSHIRE						
Smith	N	Y	Y	Y	N	N
Gregg	N	Y	Y	Y	N	N
NEW JERSEY						
Lautenberg	Y	Y	N	Y	Y	Y
Torricelli	N	Y	Y	Y	Y	Y
NEW MEXICO						
Domenici	N	Y	Y	Y	Y	Y
Bingaman	Y	Y	N	Y	Y	Y
NEW YORK						
Moynihan	Y	Y	Y	Y	Y	Y
Schumer	Y	Y	N	Y	Y	Y
NORTH CAROLINA						
Helms	N	Y	Y	Y	N	N
Edwards	Y	Y	N	Y	Y	Y
NORTH DAKOTA						
Conrad	Y	Y	N	Y	Y	Y
Dorgan	Y	Y	N	Y	Y	Y
OHIO						
DeWine	Y	Y	Y	Y	Y	N
Voinovich	Y	Y	Y	Y	Y	Y
OKLAHOMA						
Nickles	N	Y	Y	Y	Y	N
Inhofe	N	Y	Y	Y	N	N
OREGON						
Wyden	Y	Y	N	Y	Y	Y
Smith	Y	Y	Y	Y	Y	Y
PENNSYLVANIA						
Specter	N	Y	Y	Y	Y	Y
Santorum	N	Y	Y	Y	Y	N
RHODE ISLAND						
Reed	Y	Y	N	Y	Y	Y
Chafee, L.	Y	Y	Y	Y	Y	Y
SOUTH CAROLINA						
Thurmond	N	Y	Y	Y	N	Y
Hollings	N	Y	N	Y	Y	Y
SOUTH DAKOTA						
Daschle	Y	Y	N	Y	Y	Y
Johnson	Y	Y	N	Y	Y	Y
TENNESSEE						
Thompson	Y	Y	Y	Y	Y	Y
Frist	Y	Y	Y	Y	Y	N
TEXAS						
Gramm	N	Y	Y	Y	N	N
Hutchison	N	Y	Y	Y	Y	N
UTAH						
Hatch	Y	Y	Y	Y	Y	Y
Bennett	N	Y	Y	Y	Y	Y
VERMONT						
Leahy	Y	Y	Y	Y	Y	Y
Jeffords	Y	Y	Y	Y	Y	Y
VIRGINIA						
Warner	N	Y	Y	Y	Y	Y
Robb	Y	Y	N	Y	Y	Y
WASHINGTON						
Gorton	N	N	Y	Y	Y	Y
Murray	Y	Y	N	Y	Y	Y
WEST VIRGINIA						
Byrd	N	Y	N	Y	Y	Y
Rockefeller	Y	Y	N	Y	Y	Y
WISCONSIN						
Kohl	N	Y	N	Y	Y	Y
Feingold	N	N	N	Y	Y	Y
WYOMING						
Thomas	N	N	Y	Y	N	N
Enzi	N	Y	Y	Y	N	N

ND Northern Democrats SD Southern Democrats

Southern states - Ala., Ark., Fla., Ga., Ky., La., Miss., N.C., Okla., S.C., Tenn., Texas, Va.

Key

- Y Voted for (yea).
- # Paired for.
- + Announced for.
- N Voted against (nay).
- X Paired against.
- – Announced against.
- P Voted "present."
- C Voted "present" to avoid possible conflict of interest.
- ? Did not vote or otherwise make a position known.

•

Democrats ***Republicans***
Independents

105. S 2521. Fiscal 2001 Military Construction Appropriations/U.S. Troops in Kosovo. Levin, D-Mich., amendment that would strike the provision in the bill that would terminate funding for continued deployment of U.S. ground troops in Kosovo after July 1, 2001, unless Congress authorizes the deployment. The provision would also state that not more than 75 percent of the fiscal 2000 supplemental spending for Kosovo could be obligated until the president certifies that European allies are paying 33 percent of reconstruction assistance, 75 percent of humanitarian assistance, 75 percent of general administrative costs and 75 percent of the civilian police force. If the administration did not certify those requirements by July 15, the remaining money could be used only to withdraw troops from Kosovo. Adopted 53-47: R 15-40; D 38-7 (ND 32-5, SD 6-2). A "yea" was a vote in support of the president's position. May 18, 2000.

106. HR 4425. Fiscal 2001 Military Construction Appropriations/Passage. Passage of the bill that would provide $8.6 billion for military construction projects, such as the construction of barracks, base facilities and family housing, for fiscal year 2001, about $260 million more than current spending. The bill also would provide $4.7 billion for Defense Department-related emergency supplemental funding for fiscal 2000, such as counternarcotics activities and peacekeeping operations. Passed 96-4: R 52-3; D 44-1 (ND 36-1, SD 8-0). Before passage, the Senate struck all after the enacting clause and inserted the text of S 2521 as amended. May 18, 2000.

107. Smith Nomination/Confirmation. Confirmation of President Clinton's nomination of Bradley A. Smith of Ohio to be a member of the Federal Election Commission. Confirmed 64-35: R 54-1; D 10-34 (ND 8-28, SD 2-6). A "yea" was a vote in support of the president's position. May 24, 2000.

108. McDonald Nomination/Confirmation. Confirmation of President Clinton's nomination of Danny Lee McDonald of Oklahoma to be a member of the Federal Election Commission. Confirmed 98-1: R 54-1; D 44-0 (ND 36-0, SD 8-0). A "yea" was a vote in support of the president's position. May 24, 2000.

109. Dyk Nomination/Confirmation. Confirmation of President Clinton's nomination of Timothy B. Dyk of the District of Columbia to be a judge for the U.S. Federal Circuit Court. Confirmed 74-25: R 30-25; D 44-0 (ND 36-0, SD 8-0). A "yea" was a vote in support of the president's position. May 24, 2000.

110. Lynch Nomination/Confirmation. Confirmation of President Clinton's nomination of Gerard E. Lynch of New York to be U.S. District judge for the Southern District of New York. Confirmed 63-36: R 19-36; D 44-0 (ND 36-0, SD 8-0). A "yea" was a vote in support of the president's position. May 24, 2000.

Senate Votes 111, 112, 113, 114, 115

	111	112	113	114	115
ALABAMA					
Shelby	Y	Y	Y	Y	Y
Sessions	Y	Y	Y	Y	Y
ALASKA					
Stevens	Y	Y	Y	Y	Y
Murkowski	Y	Y	Y	Y	?
ARIZONA					
McCain	N	Y	Y	Y	N
Kyl	N	Y	Y	Y	N
ARKANSAS					
Hutchinson	Y	Y	Y	Y	Y
Lincoln	Y	Y	Y	Y	Y
CALIFORNIA					
Feinstein	Y	Y	Y	Y	Y
Boxer	Y	Y	Y	Y	Y
COLORADO					
Campbell	Y	Y	Y	Y	Y
Allard	N	N	Y	Y	Y
CONNECTICUT					
Dodd	Y	Y	Y	Y	?
Lieberman	Y	Y	Y	Y	Y
DELAWARE					
Roth	Y	Y	Y	Y	Y
Biden	?	Y	Y	Y	Y
FLORIDA					
Graham	Y	Y	Y	Y	Y
Mack	N	Y	Y	Y	N
GEORGIA					
Coverdell	Y	Y	Y	Y	Y
Cleland	Y	Y	Y	Y	Y
HAWAII					
Inouye	Y	Y	Y	Y	?
Akaka	Y	Y	Y	Y	Y
IDAHO					
Craig	Y	Y	Y	Y	Y
Crapo	Y	Y	Y	Y	Y
ILLINOIS					
Durbin	Y	Y	Y	Y	Y
Fitzgerald	Y	N	Y	Y	Y
INDIANA					
Lugar	Y	Y	Y	Y	Y
Bayh	Y	Y	Y	Y	Y

	111	112	113	114	115
IOWA					
Grassley	Y	Y	Y	Y	Y
Harkin	Y	Y	Y	Y	Y
KANSAS					
Brownback	Y	N	Y	N	Y
Roberts	N	N	Y	Y	Y
KENTUCKY					
McConnell	Y	Y	Y	Y	Y
Bunning	N	N	Y	Y	Y
LOUISIANA					
Breaux	Y	Y	Y	Y	Y
Landrieu	Y	Y	Y	Y	Y
MAINE					
Snowe	Y	Y	Y	Y	Y
Collins	Y	Y	Y	Y	Y
MARYLAND					
Sarbanes	Y	Y	Y	Y	Y
Mikulski	Y	Y	Y	Y	Y
MASSACHUSETTS					
Kennedy	Y	Y	Y	Y	Y
Kerry	Y	Y	Y	Y	Y
MICHIGAN					
Levin	Y	Y	Y	Y	Y
Abraham	Y	Y	Y	Y	Y
MINNESOTA					
Wellstone	Y	Y	Y	Y	Y
Grams	N	N	Y	Y	Y
MISSISSIPPI					
Cochran	Y	Y	Y	Y	Y
Lott	Y	Y	Y	Y	Y
MISSOURI					
Bond	Y	Y	Y	Y	Y
Ashcroft	Y	Y	Y	Y	Y
MONTANA					
Baucus	Y	Y	Y	Y	Y
Burns	Y	Y	Y	Y	Y
NEBRASKA					
Kerrey	Y	Y	Y	Y	Y
Hagel	Y	Y	Y	Y	Y
NEVADA					
Reid	Y	Y	Y	Y	Y
Bryan	Y	Y	Y	Y	Y

	111	112	113	114	115
NEW HAMPSHIRE					
Smith	N	N	Y	N	Y
Gregg	Y	Y	Y	Y	?
NEW JERSEY					
Lautenberg	Y	Y	Y	Y	Y
Torricelli	Y	Y	Y	Y	Y
NEW MEXICO					
Domenici	Y	Y	Y	Y	Y
Bingaman	Y	Y	Y	Y	Y
NEW YORK					
Moynihan	Y	Y	Y	Y	Y
Schumer	Y	Y	Y	Y	Y
NORTH CAROLINA					
Helms	N	N	Y	Y	Y
Edwards	Y	Y	Y	Y	Y
NORTH DAKOTA					
Conrad	Y	Y	Y	Y	Y
Dorgan	Y	Y	Y	Y	Y
OHIO					
DeWine	Y	N	Y	Y	Y
Voinovich	Y	N	Y	Y	?
OKLAHOMA					
Nickles	N	N	Y	Y	N
Inhofe	N	N	Y	Y	Y
OREGON					
Wyden	Y	Y	Y	Y	Y
Smith	Y	Y	Y	Y	Y
PENNSYLVANIA					
Specter	Y	Y	Y	Y	Y
Santorum	Y	Y	Y	Y	Y
RHODE ISLAND					
Reed	Y	Y	Y	Y	Y
Chafee, L.	Y	Y	Y	Y	Y
SOUTH CAROLINA					
Thurmond	Y	Y	Y	Y	Y
Hollings	Y	Y	Y	Y	Y
SOUTH DAKOTA					
Daschle	Y	Y	Y	Y	Y
Johnson	Y	Y	Y	Y	Y
TENNESSEE					
Thompson	N	Y	Y	Y	Y
Frist	Y	Y	Y	Y	Y

Key

- Y Voted for (yea).
- \# Paired for.
- \+ Announced for.
- N Voted against (nay).
- X Paired against.
- – Announced against.
- P Voted "present."
- C Voted "present" to avoid possible conflict of interest.
- ? Did not vote or otherwise make a position known.

Democrats • ***Republicans*** *Independents*

	111	112	113	114	115
TEXAS					
Gramm	N	N	Y	Y	Y
Hutchison	N	Y	Y	Y	Y
UTAH					
Hatch	Y	Y	Y	Y	Y
Bennett	Y	Y	Y	Y	Y
VERMONT					
Leahy	Y	Y	Y	Y	Y
Jeffords	Y	Y	Y	Y	Y
VIRGINIA					
Warner	Y	Y	Y	Y	Y
Robb	Y	Y	Y	Y	Y
WASHINGTON					
Gorton	N	Y	Y	Y	Y
Murray	Y	Y	Y	Y	Y
WEST VIRGINIA					
Byrd	Y	Y	Y	Y	Y
Rockefeller	Y	Y	Y	Y	Y
WISCONSIN					
Kohl	Y	Y	Y	Y	Y
Feingold	Y	Y	Y	Y	Y
WYOMING					
Thomas	Y	Y	Y	Y	Y
Enzi	N	N	Y	Y	Y

ND Northern Democrats SD Southern Democrats

Southern states - Ala., Ark., Fla., Ga., Ky., La., Miss., N.C., Okla., S.C., Tenn., Texas, Va.

111. Brady Nomination/Confirmation. Confirmation of President Clinton's nomination of James J. Brady of Louisiana to be U.S. District judge for the Middle District of Louisiana. Confirmed 83-16: R 39-16; D 44-0 (ND 36-0, SD 8-0). A "yea" was a vote in support of the president's position. May 24, 2000.

112. McLaughlin Nomination/Confirmation. Confirmation of President Clinton's nomination of Mary A. McLaughlin of Pennsylvania to be U.S. District judge for the Eastern District of Pennsylvania. Confirmed 86-14: R 41-14; D 45-0 (ND 37-0, SD 8-0). A "yea" was a vote in support of the president's position. May 24, 2000.

113. S 2603. Fiscal 2001 Legislative Branch Appropriations/Capitol Police. Mikulski, D-Md., amendment that would express the sense of the Senate that Capitol police and all legislative employees should be commended and that conferees should maintain the funding provisions for the Capitol police and all legislative branch employees in the Senate bill. Adopted 100-0: R 55-0; D 45-0 (ND 37-0, SD 8-0). May 25, 2000.

114. S 2603. Fiscal 2001 Legislative Branch Appropriations/Question of Engrossment and Third Reading. Question of engrossment and third reading of the bill to provide $2.5 billion in fiscal 2001 funds for the legislative branch of government. Ordered engrossed and read a third time 98-2: R 53-2; D 45-0 (ND 37-0, SD 8-0). May 25, 2000.

115. HR 2559. Crop Insurance/Conference Report. Adoption of the conference report on the bill that would provide approximately $8.2 billion over the next five years to revise the federal crop insurance program. Under the bill, the federal government would pay a higher share of the annual crop insurance premium, from 38 percent to 67 percent, compared with the current range of 13 percent to 57 percent. The bill also would provide $7.1 billion in fiscal 2000 and fiscal 2001 for economic assistance to farmers. Adopted (thus cleared for the president) 91-4: R 48-4; D 43-0 (ND 35-0, SD 8-0). May 25, 2000.

Senate Votes 116, 117, 118, 119, 120, 121, 122

	116	117	118	119	120	121	122
ALABAMA							
Shelby	Y	Y	Y	Y	N	Y	Y
Sessions	Y	Y	N	Y	N	Y	Y
ALASKA							
Stevens	Y	Y	N	Y	N	Y	Y
Murkowski	Y	Y	N	Y	N	Y	Y
ARIZONA							
McCain	Y	Y	Y	Y	Y	N	N
Kyl	Y	Y	N	Y	Y	Y	Y
ARKANSAS							
Hutchinson	Y	Y	N	Y	N	Y	Y
Lincoln	Y	Y	Y	N	Y	N	N
CALIFORNIA							
Feinstein	Y	Y	Y	N	N	N	N
Boxer	Y	Y	Y	N	N	N	N
COLORADO							
Campbell	Y	Y	N	Y	N	Y	Y
Allard	Y	Y	N	Y	N	Y	Y
CONNECTICUT							
Dodd	?	Y	N	N	N	N	N
Lieberman	Y	Y	Y	N	Y	N	N
DELAWARE							
Roth	Y	Y	Y	Y	Y	Y	Y
Biden	?	Y	Y	N	Y	N	N
FLORIDA							
Graham	Y	Y	N	N	N	N	N
Mack	Y	Y	N	Y	N	Y	Y
GEORGIA							
Coverdell	Y	Y	N	Y	N	Y	Y
Cleland	Y	Y	Y	N	N	N	N
HAWAII							
Inouye	Y	Y	N	N	N	N	N
Akaka	Y	Y	Y	N	N	N	N
IDAHO							
Craig	Y	Y	N	Y	N	Y	Y
Crapo	?	?	?	?	?	Y	Y
ILLINOIS							
Durbin	Y	Y	Y	N	N	N	N
Fitzgerald	Y	Y	N	Y	N	N	Y
INDIANA							
Lugar	Y	Y	N	Y	Y	Y	N
Bayh	Y	Y	Y	N	Y	N	N
IOWA							
Grassley	Y	Y	N	Y	Y	Y	Y
Harkin	Y	?	Y	N	Y	N	N
KANSAS							
Brownback	Y	Y	N	Y	N	Y	Y
Roberts	Y	Y	N	Y	N	Y	Y
KENTUCKY							
McConnell	Y	Y	N	Y	N	Y	Y
Bunning	Y	Y	N	Y	N	Y	Y
LOUISIANA							
Breaux	?	Y	Y	N	N	N	N
Landrieu	?	Y	Y	N	Y	N	N
MAINE							
Snowe	Y	Y	Y	Y	N	Y	N
Collins	Y	Y	Y	Y	N	Y	N
MARYLAND							
Sarbanes	Y	Y	Y	N	N	N	N
Mikulski	Y	Y	Y	N	N	N	N
MASSACHUSETTS							
Kennedy	Y	Y	Y	N	Y	N	N
Kerry	Y	Y	Y	N	Y	N	N
MICHIGAN							
Levin	Y	Y	N	N	Y	N	N
Abraham	Y	Y	Y	Y	N	Y	N
MINNESOTA							
Wellstone	Y	Y	Y	N	Y	N	N
Grams	Y	Y	Y	Y	N	Y	Y
MISSISSIPPI							
Cochran	Y	Y	N	Y	N	Y	Y
Lott	Y	Y	N	Y	N	Y	Y
MISSOURI							
Bond	Y	Y	N	Y	N	Y	Y
Ashcroft	Y	Y	Y	Y	N	Y	Y
MONTANA							
Baucus	Y	Y	N	N	N	N	N
Burns	Y	Y	Y	Y	N	Y	N
NEBRASKA							
Kerrey	Y	N	N	N	Y	N	N
Hagel	Y	Y	N	Y	Y	Y	N
NEVADA							
Reid	Y	Y	Y	N	Y	N	N
Bryan	Y	Y	Y	N	Y	N	N
NEW HAMPSHIRE							
Smith	Y	Y	Y	Y	N	Y	Y
Gregg	Y	Y	N	Y	N	Y	Y
NEW JERSEY							
Lautenberg	?	Y	N	N	N	N	N
Torricelli	Y	Y	Y	N	N	N	N
NEW MEXICO							
Domenici	?	?	?	?	?	Y	Y
Bingaman	Y	Y	Y	N	N	N	N
NEW YORK							
Moynihan	Y	Y	Y	N	Y	N	Y
Schumer	Y	Y	Y	N	N	N	N
NORTH CAROLINA							
Helms	Y	Y	N	Y	N	Y	Y
Edwards	Y	Y	Y	N	N	N	N
NORTH DAKOTA							
Conrad	Y	Y	Y	Y	N	?	?
Dorgan	Y	Y	Y	N	N	N	N
OHIO							
DeWine	Y	Y	Y	Y	Y	Y	N
Voinovich	Y	Y	N	Y	Y	Y	Y
OKLAHOMA							
Nickles	Y	Y	N	Y	N	Y	Y
Inhofe	Y	Y	N	Y	N	Y	Y
OREGON							
Wyden	Y	Y	Y	N	Y	N	N
Smith	Y	Y	N	N	Y	Y	N
PENNSYLVANIA							
Specter	Y	Y	N	Y	N	N	N
Santorum	Y	Y	Y	Y	N	Y	Y
RHODE ISLAND							
Reed	Y	Y	N	N	Y	N	N
Chafee, L.	Y	Y	N	N	Y	N	N
SOUTH CAROLINA							
Thurmond	Y	Y	N	Y	N	Y	Y
Hollings	Y	Y	Y	N	N	N	N
SOUTH DAKOTA							
Daschle	Y	Y	Y	N	N	N	N
Johnson	Y	Y	Y	N	N	N	N
TENNESSEE							
Thompson	Y	Y	N	Y	Y	Y	N
Frist	Y	Y	N	Y	N	Y	Y
TEXAS							
Gramm	Y	Y	N	Y	Y	Y	Y
Hutchison	Y	Y	N	Y	N	Y	N
UTAH							
Hatch	Y	Y	Y	Y	N	Y	Y
Bennett	Y	Y	Y	Y	N	Y	Y
VERMONT							
Leahy	Y	Y	Y	N	Y	N	N
Jeffords	Y	Y	Y	N	Y	Y	N
VIRGINIA							
Warner	Y	Y	N	Y	N	Y	Y
Robb	Y	Y	Y	N	Y	N	N
WASHINGTON							
Gorton	Y	Y	Y	Y	N	Y	Y
Murray	Y	Y	Y	N	N	N	N
WEST VIRGINIA							
Byrd	Y	Y	N	N	Y	N	N
Rockefeller	Y	Y	Y	N	Y	N	N
WISCONSIN							
Kohl	Y	Y	Y	N	Y	N	N
Feingold	Y	Y	N	N	Y	N	N
WYOMING							
Thomas	Y	Y	Y	Y	N	Y	Y
Enzi	Y	Y	N	Y	N	Y	Y

ND Northern Democrats   SD Southern Democrats

Southern states - Ala., Ark., Fla., Ga., Ky., La., Miss., N.C., Okla., S.C., Tenn., Texas, Va.

Key

- Y Voted for (yea).
- # Paired for.
- + Announced for.
- N Voted against (nay).
- X Paired against.
- – Announced against.
- P Voted "present."
- C Voted "present" to avoid possible conflict of interest.
- ? Did not vote or otherwise make a position known.

•

Democrats   ***Republicans***
Independents

116. S 2549. Fiscal 2001 Defense Authorization/Subsistence Allowance. McCain, R-Ariz., amendment that would provide that an enlisted service member who is eligible for food stamp assistance is entitled to receive a subsistence allowance of $180 per month. Adopted 93-0: R 53-0; D 40-0 (ND 34-0, SD 6-0). June 6, 2000.

117. S 2549. Fiscal 2001 Defense Authorization/Military Retiree Health Benefits. Warner, R-Va., amendment that would extend eligibility for medical care under the CHAMPUS and the TRICARE programs to persons over the age of 64, beginning Oct. 1, 2001, through Sept. 30, 2003. Adopted 96-1: R 53-0; D 43-1 (ND 35-1, SD 8-0). June 7, 2000.

118. S 2549. Fiscal 2001 Defense Authorization/Military Retiree Health Benefits. Johnson, D-S.D., motion to waive the Budget Act with respect to the Gramm, R-Texas, point of order against the Johnson amendment. The Johnson amendment would allow military retirees who joined the services before June 7, 1956, to enroll in the Federal Employees Health Benefits Program, with the federal government paying 100 percent. It also would allow retirees who joined the services after June 7, 1956, to enroll in the federal health program if they paid the same fees as federal employees. Motion rejected 52-46: R 17-36; D 35-10 (ND 28-9, SD 7-1). A three-fifths majority vote (60) of the total Senate is required to waive the Budget Act. (Subsequently the chair upheld the point of order and the amendment fell.) June 7, 2000.

119. S 2549. Fiscal 2001 Defense Authorization/Strategic Nuclear Weapons Systems. Warner, R-Va., amendment to the Kerrey, D-Neb., amendment. The Warner amendment would replace the language of the Kerrey amendment with language that would require a nuclear overview study to be completed by December 2001, at the same time as the Defense Department's quadrennial review, before the president could waive current restrictions on dismantling strategic nuclear weapons systems. The Kerrey amendment would repeal the current restrictions. Adopted 51-47: R 50-3; D 1-44 (ND 1-36, SD 0-8). (Subsequently, the Kerrey amendment, as amended, was adopted by voice vote.) A "nay" was a vote in support of the president's position. June 7, 2000.

120. S 2549. Fiscal 2001 Defense Authorization/Military Base Closures and Realignments. McCain, R-Ariz., amendment that would authorize two rounds of military base closures and realignments, one in 2003 and another in 2005. Rejected 35-63: R 13-40; D 22-23 (ND 19-18, SD 3-5). June 7, 2000.

121. S 2549. Fiscal 2001 Defense Authorization/Managed Care. Nickles, R-Okla., motion to table (kill) the Daschle, D-S.D., amendment that would enact tax provisions designed to improve access to health care. The amendment is the same language as the House-passed managed-care bill (HR 2990). Motion agreed to 51-48: R 51-4; D 0-44 (ND 0-36, SD 0-8). June 8, 2000.

122. S 2549. Fiscal 2001 Defense Authorization/Campaign Finance Disclosures. Warner, R-Va., point of order that the McCain, R-Ariz., amendment to the Smith, R-N.H., amendment is out of order because the Constitution requires that revenue provisions must originate in the House. The McCain amendment would include language to require Section 527 organizations to disclose their existence to the Internal Revenue Service, to file publicly available tax returns with the IRS and make public reports specifying annual expenditures of more than $500 and identify those who contribute more than $200 annually to the organization. The Smith amendment would prohibit granting Defense Department security clearances to employees or contractors who are convicted felons, or have been declared mentally incompetent, or have used controlled substances illegally or been dishonorably discharged. Rejected 42-57: R 41-14; D 1-43 (ND 1-35, SD 0-8). (Subsequently, the McCain amendment was adopted by voice vote.) June 8, 2000.

Senate Votes 123, 124, 125, 126, 127

	123	124	125	126	127
ALABAMA					
Shelby	Y	Y	Y	Y	Y
Sessions	Y	N	N	Y	Y
ALASKA					
Stevens	Y	Y	Y	Y	Y
Murkowski	Y	Y	Y	Y	Y
ARIZONA					
McCain	?	Y	Y	Y	Y
Kyl	Y	N	Y	Y	Y
ARKANSAS					
Hutchinson	Y	N	Y	Y	Y
Lincoln	Y	Y	N	Y	Y
CALIFORNIA					
Feinstein	Y	Y	N	Y	Y
Boxer	Y	Y	N	N	N
COLORADO					
Campbell	Y	Y	Y	Y	Y
Allard	Y	N	Y	Y	Y
CONNECTICUT					
Dodd	Y	Y	Y	N	Y
Lieberman	Y	Y	Y	Y	Y
DELAWARE					
Roth	Y	Y	Y	Y	Y
Biden	Y	Y	Y	Y	Y
FLORIDA					
Graham	Y	Y	N	Y	Y
Mack	Y	Y	Y	Y	Y
GEORGIA					
Coverdell	Y	Y	Y	Y	Y
Cleland	Y	Y	Y	Y	Y
HAWAII					
Inouye	Y	Y	Y	Y	Y
Akaka	Y	Y	Y	Y	Y
IDAHO					
Craig	Y	Y	Y	Y	Y
Crapo	Y	Y	Y	Y	Y
ILLINOIS					
Durbin	Y	Y	N	N	Y
Fitzgerald	Y	Y	Y	Y	Y
INDIANA					
Lugar	Y	Y	Y	Y	Y
Bayh	Y	Y	N	Y	Y
IOWA					
Grassley	Y	Y	N	Y	Y
Harkin	Y	Y	N	N	Y
KANSAS					
Brownback	Y	Y	Y	Y	Y
Roberts	Y	Y	Y	Y	Y
KENTUCKY					
McConnell	Y	Y	Y	Y	Y
Bunning	+	Y	Y	Y	Y
LOUISIANA					
Breaux	Y	Y	Y	Y	Y
Landrieu	Y	N	Y	Y	Y
MAINE					
Snowe	Y	Y	Y	Y	Y
Collins	Y	Y	Y	Y	Y
MARYLAND					
Sarbanes	Y	Y	N	Y	Y
Mikulski	Y	Y	N	Y	Y
MASSACHUSETTS					
Kennedy	Y	Y	N	Y	Y
Kerry	?	Y	Y	Y	Y
MICHIGAN					
Levin	Y	Y	N	Y	Y
Abraham	Y	Y	N	Y	Y
MINNESOTA					
Wellstone	?	Y	N	N	N
Grams	Y	Y	N	Y	Y
MISSISSIPPI					
Cochran	Y	Y	Y	Y	Y
Lott	Y	Y	Y	Y	Y
MISSOURI					
Bond	Y	N	Y	Y	Y
Ashcroft	Y	Y	Y	Y	Y
MONTANA					
Baucus	Y	Y	N	Y	Y
Burns	Y	Y	Y	Y	Y
NEBRASKA					
Kerrey	Y	Y	Y	Y	Y
Hagel	Y	N	Y	Y	Y
NEVADA					
Reid	Y	Y	N	N	Y
Bryan	Y	Y	N	Y	Y
NEW HAMPSHIRE					
Smith	Y	N	Y	Y	Y
Gregg	Y	Y	Y	Y	Y
NEW JERSEY					
Lautenberg	Y	Y	N	N	Y
Torricelli	?	Y	N	N	Y
NEW MEXICO					
Domenici	?	Y	?	Y	Y
Bingaman	Y	Y	Y	Y	Y
NEW YORK					
Moynihan	Y	Y	Y	Y	Y
Schumer	Y	Y	N	N	Y
NORTH CAROLINA					
Helms	Y	Y	Y	Y	Y
Edwards	Y	Y	N	Y	Y
NORTH DAKOTA					
Conrad	?	Y	N	Y	Y
Dorgan	Y	Y	N	Y	Y
OHIO					
DeWine	Y	Y	Y	Y	Y
Voinovich	?	N	Y	Y	Y
OKLAHOMA					
Nickles	?	N	Y	Y	Y
Inhofe	Y	N	Y	Y	Y
OREGON					
Wyden	Y	Y	N	N	Y
Smith	Y	Y	Y	Y	Y
PENNSYLVANIA					
Specter	Y	?	?	?	?
Santorum	Y	Y	Y	Y	Y
RHODE ISLAND					
Reed	Y	Y	Y	N	Y
Chafee, L.	Y	Y	Y	Y	Y
SOUTH CAROLINA					
Thurmond	Y	Y	Y	Y	Y
Hollings	?	Y	Y	Y	Y
SOUTH DAKOTA					
Daschle	Y	Y	Y	N	Y
Johnson	Y	Y	N	Y	Y
TENNESSEE					
Thompson	Y	N	Y	Y	Y
Frist	Y	Y	Y	Y	Y
TEXAS					
Gramm	Y	N	Y	Y	Y
Hutchison	Y	Y	Y	Y	Y
UTAH					
Hatch	Y	Y	Y	Y	Y
Bennett	Y	Y	Y	Y	Y
VERMONT					
Leahy	Y	Y	Y	N	Y
Jeffords	Y	Y	Y	Y	Y
VIRGINIA					
Warner	Y	Y	Y	Y	Y
Robb	Y	Y	N	Y	Y
WASHINGTON					
Gorton	Y	Y	Y	Y	Y
Murray	?	Y	N	N	Y
WEST VIRGINIA					
Byrd	Y	Y	N	Y	Y
Rockefeller	?	?	?	?	?
WISCONSIN					
Kohl	Y	Y	N	Y	Y
Feingold	Y	Y	N	N	N
WYOMING					
Thomas	Y	Y	Y	Y	Y
Enzi	Y	N	Y	Y	Y

ND Northern Democrats SD Southern Democrats

Southern states - Ala., Ark., Fla., Ga., Ky., La., Miss., N.C., Okla., S.C., Tenn., Texas, Va.

Key

Y Voted for (yea).
\# Paired for.
\+ Announced for.
N Voted against (nay).
X Paired against.
– Announced against.
P Voted "present."
C Voted "present" to avoid possible conflict of interest.
? Did not vote or otherwise make a position known.

Democrats ***Republicans***
Independents

123. HR 4576. Fiscal 2001 Defense Appropriations/Accounting Method. Grassley, R-Iowa, amendment that would require the Defense Department to match certain disbursements with obligations prior to payment. Adopted 88-0: R 50-0; D 38-0 (ND 31-0, SD 7-0). June 9, 2000.

124. HR 4576. Fiscal 2001 Defense Appropriations/Pesticides. Boxer, D-Calif., amendment that would prohibit the use of funds in the bill for the routine use of dangerous pesticides, such as known or probable carcinogens, in areas owned or managed by the Defense Department that may be used by children, including base housing, parks, recreation centers or day care facilities. Adopted 84-14: R 41-13; D 43-1 (ND 36-0, SD 7-1). June 13, 2000.

125. HR 4576. Fiscal 2001 Defense Appropriations/Corporate Jets. Stevens, R-Alaska, motion to table (kill) the Boxer, D-Calif., amendment that would strike a section in the bill that allows the Army and Navy secretaries to lease special aircraft. Motion agreed to 65-32: R 49-4; D 16-28 (ND 12-24, SD 4-4). June 13, 2000.

126. HR 4576. Fiscal 2001 Defense Appropriations/Education Funding. Stevens, R-Alaska, motion to table (kill) the Wellstone, D-Minn., amendment that would reduce Defense Department procurement spending by approximately $1 billion and appropriate an additional $922 million for Title 1 funding under the Elementary and Secondary Education Act. Motion agreed to 83-15: R 54-0; D 29-15 (ND 21-15, SD 8-0). June 13, 2000.

127. HR 4576. Fiscal 2001 Defense Appropriations/Passage. Passage of the bill that would provide $287.6 billion for the Defense Department for fiscal 2001, including $57.9 billion for procurement, $39.6 billion for research and development and $96.7 billion for operations and maintenance. The bill would provide approximately $20 billion more than Congress appropriated in fiscal 2000. Passed 95-3: R 54-0; D 41-3 (ND 33-3, SD 8-0). June 13, 2000.

Senate Votes 128, 129, 130, 131, 132

	128	129	130	131	132
ALABAMA					
Shelby	Y	Y	N	Y	Y
Sessions	Y	Y	N	Y	Y
ALASKA					
Stevens	Y	Y	N	Y	Y
Murkowski	Y	Y	Y	Y	Y
ARIZONA					
McCain	Y	Y	N	Y	Y
Kyl	Y	Y	N	Y	Y
ARKANSAS					
Hutchinson	Y	Y	N	Y	Y
Lincoln	Y	Y	N	Y	Y
CALIFORNIA					
Feinstein	Y	Y	Y	Y	Y
Boxer	Y	Y	Y	Y	Y
COLORADO					
Campbell	Y	Y	N	Y	Y
Allard	Y	Y	N	Y	Y
CONNECTICUT					
Dodd	Y	Y	Y	Y	Y
Lieberman	Y	Y	Y	Y	Y
DELAWARE					
Roth	Y	Y	Y	Y	Y
Biden	Y	Y	Y	Y	Y
FLORIDA					
Graham	Y	Y	Y	Y	Y
Mack	Y	Y	N	Y	Y
GEORGIA					
Coverdell	Y	Y	Y	Y	Y
Cleland	Y	Y	Y	Y	Y
HAWAII					
Inouye	Y	Y	Y	Y	Y
Akaka	Y	Y	Y	Y	Y
IDAHO					
Craig	Y	Y	N	Y	Y
Crapo	Y	Y	N	Y	Y
ILLINOIS					
Durbin	Y	Y	Y	Y	Y
Fitzgerald	Y	Y	N	Y	Y
INDIANA					
Lugar	Y	Y	Y	Y	Y
Bayh	Y	Y	Y	Y	Y

	128	129	130	131	132
IOWA					
Grassley	Y	Y	N	Y	Y
Harkin	Y	Y	N	Y	Y
KANSAS					
Brownback	Y	Y	N	Y	Y
Roberts	Y	Y	N	Y	Y
KENTUCKY					
McConnell	Y	Y	N	Y	Y
Bunning	Y	Y	N	Y	Y
LOUISIANA					
Breaux	Y	Y	N	Y	Y
Landrieu	Y	Y	Y	Y	Y
MAINE					
Snowe	Y	Y	Y	Y	Y
Collins	Y	Y	N	Y	Y
MARYLAND					
Sarbanes	Y	Y	Y	Y	Y
Mikulski	Y	Y	Y	Y	Y
MASSACHUSETTS					
Kennedy	Y	Y	Y	Y	Y
Kerry	Y	Y	Y	Y	Y
MICHIGAN					
Levin	Y	Y	Y	Y	Y
Abraham	Y	Y	N	Y	Y
MINNESOTA					
Wellstone	Y	Y	Y	N	Y
Grams	Y	Y	N	Y	Y
MISSISSIPPI					
Cochran	Y	Y	N	Y	Y
Lott	Y	Y	N	Y	Y
MISSOURI					
Bond	Y	Y	N	Y	Y
Ashcroft	Y	Y	N	Y	Y
MONTANA					
Baucus	Y	Y	N	Y	Y
Burns	Y	Y	N	Y	Y
NEBRASKA					
Kerrey	Y	Y	N	Y	Y
Hagel	Y	Y	N	Y	Y
NEVADA					
Reid	Y	Y	Y	Y	Y
Bryan	Y	Y	Y	Y	Y

	128	129	130	131	132
NEW HAMPSHIRE					
Smith	Y	Y	N	Y	Y
Gregg	Y	Y	N	Y	Y
NEW JERSEY					
Lautenberg	Y	Y	Y	Y	Y
Torricelli	Y	Y	Y	Y	Y
NEW MEXICO					
Domenici	Y	?	?	?	Y
Bingaman	Y	Y	N	Y	Y
NEW YORK					
Moynihan	?	?	Y	Y	Y
Schumer	Y	Y	Y	Y	Y
NORTH CAROLINA					
Helms	Y	Y	N	Y	Y
Edwards	Y	Y	Y	Y	Y
NORTH DAKOTA					
Conrad	Y	Y	N	Y	Y
Dorgan	Y	Y	N	Y	Y
OHIO					
DeWine	Y	Y	Y	Y	Y
Voinovich	Y	Y	Y	Y	Y
OKLAHOMA					
Nickles	Y	Y	Y	Y	Y
Inhofe	Y	Y	N	Y	Y
OREGON					
Wyden	Y	Y	Y	Y	Y
Smith	Y	Y	N	Y	Y
PENNSYLVANIA					
Specter	Y	Y	Y	Y	Y
Santorum	Y	Y	Y	Y	Y
RHODE ISLAND					
Reed	?	Y	Y	Y	Y
Chafee, L.	Y	Y	Y	Y	Y
SOUTH CAROLINA					
Thurmond	Y	Y	N	Y	Y
Hollings	Y	Y	Y	N	Y
SOUTH DAKOTA					
Daschle	Y	Y	N	Y	Y
Johnson	Y	Y	Y	Y	Y
TENNESSEE					
Thompson	Y	Y	N	Y	Y
Frist	Y	Y	N	Y	Y

Key

Y Voted for (yea).
\# Paired for.
\+ Announced for.
N Voted against (nay).
X Paired against.
– Announced against.
P Voted "present."
C Voted "present" to avoid possible conflict of interest.
? Did not vote or otherwise make a position known.

•

Democrats ***Republicans***
Independents

	128	129	130	131	132
TEXAS					
Gramm	Y	Y	N	Y	Y
Hutchison	Y	Y	Y	Y	Y
UTAH					
Hatch	Y	Y	N	Y	Y
Bennett	Y	Y	N	Y	Y
VERMONT					
Leahy	Y	Y	Y	Y	Y
Jeffords	Y	Y	Y	Y	Y
VIRGINIA					
Warner	Y	Y	N	Y	Y
Robb	Y	Y	Y	Y	Y
WASHINGTON					
Gorton	Y	Y	N	Y	Y
Murray	Y	Y	Y	Y	Y
WEST VIRGINIA					
Byrd	Y	Y	N	N	Y
Rockefeller	?	?	?	?	?
WISCONSIN					
Kohl	Y	Y	Y	Y	Y
Feingold	Y	Y	N	Y	Y
WYOMING					
Thomas	Y	Y	N	Y	Y
Enzi	Y	Y	N	Y	Y

ND Northern Democrats SD Southern Democrats

Southern states - Ala., Ark., Fla., Ga., Ky., La., Miss., N.C., Okla., S.C., Tenn., Texas, Va.

128. Gordon Nomination/Confirmation. Confirmation of President Clinton's nomination of Gen. John A. Gordon to be undersecretary for nuclear security at the Department of Energy. Confirmed 97-0: R 55-0; D 42-0 (ND 34-0, SD 8-0). A "yea" was a vote in support of the president's position. June 14, 2000.

129. HR 4475. Fiscal 2001 Transportation Appropriations/Iowa Construction Project. Harkin, D-Iowa, amendment that would redesignate a portion of a highway construction project in Iowa. Adopted 97-0: R 54-0; D 43-0 (ND 35-0, SD 8-0). June 14, 2000.

130. HR 4475. Fiscal 2001 Transportation Appropriations/Highway Funds. Judgment of the Senate on the germaneness of the Voinovich, R-Ohio, amendment that would give states flexibility on spending highway funds. The amendment would allow states to use highway funds for rails. Ruled not germane 46-52: R 13-41; D 33-11 (ND 27-9, SD 6-2). (Subsequently, the Voinovich amendment fell.) June 15, 2000.

131. HR 4475. Fiscal 2001 Transportation Appropriations/Debt Reduction. Allard, R-Colo., amendment that would allocate $12.2 billion in fiscal 2000 for paying down the national debt. Adopted 95-3: R 54-0; D 41-3 (ND 34-2, SD 7-1). June 15, 2000.

132. HR 4475. Fiscal 2001 Transportation Appropriations/Passage. Passage of the bill to provide $54.8 billion in new budget authority for the Department of Transportation (DOT) and related programs in fiscal 2001. The measure would provide funding levels totaling $12.4 billion for the Federal Aviation Administration, $30.7 billion for the Federal Highway Administration and $4.4 billion for the Coast Guard. The bill also would prohibit the Federal Motor Carrier Safety Administration from implementing proposed rules covering hours of driving and required rest for commercial drivers and would require states to establish 0.08 blood alcohol content for drunken driving or face sanctions. Passed 99-0: R 55-0; D 44-0 (ND 36-0, SD 8-0). June 15, 2000.

	133	134	135	136	137	138
ALABAMA						
Shelby	Y	Y	Y	N	Y	Y
Sessions	Y	Y	Y	N	Y	Y
ALASKA						
Stevens	Y	Y	Y	Y	Y	Y
Murkowski	Y	Y	Y	N	Y	Y
ARIZONA						
McCain	Y	Y	Y	N	Y	Y
Kyl	Y	Y	Y	N	Y	Y
ARKANSAS						
Hutchinson	Y	Y	Y	N	Y	Y
Lincoln	Y	N	N	Y	N	Y
CALIFORNIA						
Feinstein	Y	N	N	Y	N	Y
Boxer	?	N	N	Y	N	N
COLORADO						
Campbell	+	Y	Y	N	Y	Y
Allard	Y	Y	Y	N	Y	Y
CONNECTICUT						
Dodd	Y	N	N	Y	N	Y
Lieberman	Y	N	N	Y	Y	Y
DELAWARE						
Roth	Y	Y	Y	Y	Y	Y
Biden	Y	N	N	Y	N	Y
FLORIDA						
Graham	Y	N	N	Y	Y	Y
Mack	Y	Y	Y	Y	Y	Y
GEORGIA						
Coverdell	Y	Y	Y	N	Y	Y
Cleland	Y	N	N	Y	N	Y
HAWAII						
Inouye	Y	N	N	Y	N	Y
Akaka	Y	N	N	Y	N	Y
IDAHO						
Craig	Y	Y	Y	N	Y	Y
Crapo	Y	Y	Y	N	Y	Y
ILLINOIS						
Durbin	Y	N	N	Y	N	Y
Fitzgerald	Y	Y	N	N	N	Y
INDIANA						
Lugar	Y	Y	Y	Y	Y	Y
Bayh	Y	N	N	Y	N	Y
IOWA						
Grassley	Y	Y	Y	N	Y	Y
Harkin	+	N	N	Y	N	N
KANSAS						
Brownback	Y	Y	Y	N	Y	Y
Roberts	Y	Y	Y	N	Y	Y
KENTUCKY						
McConnell	+	Y	Y	N	Y	Y
Bunning	+	Y	Y	N	Y	Y
LOUISIANA						
Breaux	Y	Y	N	Y	N	Y
Landrieu	Y	N	N	Y	N	Y
MAINE						
Snowe	Y	N	N	Y	Y	Y
Collins	Y	N	Y	Y	Y	Y
MARYLAND						
Sarbanes	Y	N	N	Y	N	Y
Mikulski	Y	N	N	Y	N	N
MASSACHUSETTS						
Kennedy	Y	N	N	Y	N	Y
Kerry	Y	N	N	Y	N	Y
MICHIGAN						
Levin	Y	N	N	Y	N	Y
Abraham	Y	Y	Y	N	Y	Y
MINNESOTA						
Wellstone	Y	N	N	Y	N	N
Grams	Y	Y	Y	N	N	N
MISSISSIPPI						
Cochran	Y	Y	Y	N	Y	Y
Lott	Y	Y	Y	N	Y	Y
MISSOURI						
Bond	Y	Y	Y	N	Y	Y
Ashcroft	Y	Y	Y	N	Y	Y
MONTANA						
Baucus	Y	N	N	Y	N	Y
Burns	Y	Y	Y	Y	Y	Y
NEBRASKA						
Kerrey	Y	N	N	Y	N	Y
Hagel	Y	Y	Y	N	Y	Y
NEVADA						
Reid	Y	Y	N	Y	Y	Y
Bryan	Y	N	N	Y	Y	Y
NEW HAMPSHIRE						
Smith	Y	Y	Y	N	Y	Y
Gregg	Y	Y	Y	N	Y	Y
NEW JERSEY						
Lautenberg	Y	N	N	Y	N	Y
Torricelli	Y	N	N	Y	Y	Y
NEW MEXICO						
Domenici	Y	Y	Y	N	Y	Y
Bingaman	Y	N	N	Y	N	Y
NEW YORK						
Moynihan	Y	N	Y	Y	N	Y
Schumer	Y	N	N	Y	N	Y
NORTH CAROLINA						
Helms	Y	Y	Y	N	Y	Y
Edwards	Y	N	N	Y	N	Y
NORTH DAKOTA						
Conrad	?	N	N	Y	N	Y
Dorgan	?	N	N	Y	N	N
OHIO						
DeWine	Y	Y	Y	Y	Y	Y
Voinovich	Y	Y	N	Y	Y	Y
OKLAHOMA						
Nickles	Y	Y	Y	N	Y	Y
Inhofe	?	?	?	?	Y	Y
OREGON						
Wyden	Y	N	N	Y	N	Y
Smith	Y	Y	Y	Y	Y	Y
PENNSYLVANIA						
Specter	Y	N	N	Y	Y	N
Santorum	Y	Y	Y	N	Y	Y
RHODE ISLAND						
Reed	Y	N	N	Y	N	Y
Chafee, L.	Y	N	N	Y	Y	Y
SOUTH CAROLINA						
Thurmond	Y	Y	Y	N	Y	Y
Hollings	Y	N	N	Y	N	Y
SOUTH DAKOTA						
Daschle	Y	N	N	Y	N	Y
Johnson	Y	N	N	Y	N	Y
TENNESSEE						
Thompson	Y	Y	Y	N	Y	Y
Frist	Y	Y	Y	N	Y	Y
TEXAS						
Gramm	Y	Y	Y	N	Y	Y
Hutchison	Y	Y	Y	N	Y	Y
UTAH						
Hatch	+	Y	Y	N	Y	Y
Bennett	Y	Y	Y	N	Y	Y
VERMONT						
Leahy	+	N	N	Y	N	N
Jeffords	Y	N	N	Y	N	Y
VIRGINIA						
Warner	?	Y	Y	N	Y	Y
Robb	?	N	N	Y	Y	Y
WASHINGTON						
Gorton	Y	N	Y	N	Y	Y
Murray	Y	N	N	Y	N	N
WEST VIRGINIA						
Byrd	Y	N	Y	N	N	N
Rockefeller	Y	N	N	Y	N	Y
WISCONSIN						
Kohl	Y	N	N	Y	Y	Y
Feingold	Y	N	N	Y	N	N
WYOMING						
Thomas	?	Y	Y	N	Y	Y
Enzi	Y	Y	Y	N	Y	Y

ND Northern Democrats SD Southern Democrats

Southern states - Ala., Ark., Fla., Ga., Ky., La., Miss., N.C., Okla., S.C., Tenn., Texas, Va.

Key

- Y Voted for (yea).
- # Paired for.
- + Announced for.
- N Voted against (nay).
- X Paired against.
- – Announced against.
- P Voted "present."
- C Voted "present" to avoid possible conflict of interest.
- ? Did not vote or otherwise make a position known.

Democrats ***Republicans***
Independents

133. S 761. Electronic Signatures/Conference Report. Adoption of the conference report on the bill to promote electronic commerce and establish a minimum federal standard for the use and recognition of electronic signatures. The bill would ensure that electronic signatures are given the same legal validity and enforceability as written ones. Consumers would have to consent to the use of electronic records and be provided with information on how to access those records. Adopted (thus cleared for the president) 87-0: R 48-0; D 39-0 (ND 32-0, SD 7-0). June 16, 2000.

134. S 2549. Fiscal 2001 Defense Authorization/Military Abortions. Hutchinson, R-Ark., motion to table (kill) the Murray, D-Wash., amendment that would allow military women and dependents of military personnel to obtain patient-funded abortions at overseas military hospitals. Motion agreed to 50-49: R 48-6; D 2-43 (ND 1-36, SD 1-7). June 20, 2000.

135. S 2549. Fiscal 2001 Defense Authorization/Hate Crimes. Hatch, R-Utah, amendment that would authorize $5 million per year for fiscal 2001 and 2002 for the Justice Department to assist state and local authorities in investigating and prosecuting hate crimes. The amendment also would authorize the Justice Department to conduct a study on hate crimes and require the comptroller general to report to Congress on hate crime activity. Adopted 50-49: R 48-6; D 2-43 (ND 2-35, SD 0-8). June 20, 2000.

136. S 2549. Fiscal 2001 Defense Authorization/Hate Crimes. Kennedy, D-Mass., amendment that would broaden the categories covered by hate crimes to include crimes related to gender, sexual orientation and disability and would make it easier for the federal government to get involved in the investigation and prosecution of hate crimes. The amendment would authorize $5 million per year for fiscal 2001 and 2002 to assist states and local authorities in investigating and prosecuting hate crimes. Adopted 57-42: R 13-41; D 44-1 (ND 36-1, SD 8-0). A "yea" was a vote in support of the president's position. June 20, 2000.

137. S 2549. Fiscal 2001 Defense Authorization/Cuba Commission. Mack, R-Fla., motion to table (kill) the Dodd, D-Conn., amendment that would establish a 12-member bipartisan commission to examine U.S. relations with Cuba. Motion agreed to 59-41: R 52-3; D 7-38 (ND 5-32, SD 2-6). June 20, 2000.

138. S 2522. Fiscal 2001 Foreign Operations Appropriations/Substance Abuse Programs. Biden, D-Del., motion to table (kill) the Wellstone, D-Minn., amendment that would reallocate $225 million designated for military purposes in emergency funding for Colombia to funding for domestic substance abuse and treatment programs. Motion agreed to 89-11: R 53-2; D 36-9 (ND 28-9, SD 8-0). June 21, 2000.

	139	140	141	142	143	144
ALABAMA						
Shelby	N	N	Y	Y	Y	N
Sessions	N	N	Y	Y	Y	N
ALASKA						
Stevens	N	N	Y	Y	Y	N
Murkowski	N	N	Y	N	Y	N
ARIZONA						
McCain	N	Y	Y	Y	Y	N
Kyl	N	N	Y	Y	Y	N
ARKANSAS						
Hutchinson	Y	N	Y	Y	Y	N
Lincoln	N	Y	Y	Y	Y	Y
CALIFORNIA						
Feinstein	N	Y	Y	Y	N	Y
Boxer	Y	Y	Y	?	?	?
COLORADO						
Campbell	N	N	Y	Y	Y	?
Allard	Y	N	Y	Y	Y	N
CONNECTICUT						
Dodd	N	Y	Y	Y	N	Y
Lieberman	N	Y	Y	Y	N	Y
DELAWARE						
Roth	N	N	Y	Y	Y	N
Biden	N	Y	Y	Y	N	Y
FLORIDA						
Graham	N	Y	Y	Y	N	Y
Mack	N	Y	Y	Y	Y	N
GEORGIA						
Coverdell	N	N	Y	Y	Y	N
Cleland	N	Y	Y	Y	N	Y
HAWAII						
Inouye	?	?	Y	?	?	?
Akaka	N	Y	Y	Y	N	Y
IDAHO						
Craig	Y	N	Y	Y	Y	N
Crapo	Y	N	Y	Y	Y	N
ILLINOIS						
Durbin	N	Y	Y	Y	N	Y
Fitzgerald	Y	N	Y	Y	Y	Y
INDIANA						
Lugar	N	N	Y	Y	Y	N
Bayh	N	Y	Y	Y	N	Y
IOWA						
Grassley	N	N	Y	Y	Y	N
Harkin	Y	Y	Y	Y	N	Y
KANSAS						
Brownback	N	N	Y	Y	Y	N
Roberts	N	N	Y	Y	Y	N
KENTUCKY						
McConnell	N	N	Y	Y	Y	N
Bunning	N	N	Y	Y	Y	N
LOUISIANA						
Breaux	N	Y	Y	N	Y	N
Landrieu	N	Y	Y	Y	N	Y
MAINE						
Snowe	N	Y	Y	Y	Y	N
Collins	Y	N	Y	Y	Y	N
MARYLAND						
Sarbanes	N	Y	Y	Y	N	Y
Mikulski	Y	N	Y	Y	N	Y
MASSACHUSETTS						
Kennedy	N	Y	Y	Y	N	Y
Kerry	N	Y	Y	Y	N	Y
MICHIGAN						
Levin	N	Y	Y	Y	N	Y
Abraham	N	N	Y	Y	Y	N
MINNESOTA						
Wellstone	N	Y	N	Y	N	Y
Grams	Y	Y	Y	Y	Y	N
MISSISSIPPI						
Cochran	N	N	Y	Y	Y	N
Lott	N	N	Y	Y	Y	N
MISSOURI						
Bond	N	N	Y	Y	Y	N
Ashcroft	N	N	Y	Y	Y	N
MONTANA						
Baucus	N	Y	Y	Y	N	Y
Burns	N	N	Y	Y	Y	N
NEBRASKA						
Kerrey	N	Y	Y	Y	N	Y
Hagel	N	Y	Y	Y	Y	N
NEVADA						
Reid	N	Y	Y	Y	N	Y
Bryan	N	Y	Y	Y	N	Y
NEW HAMPSHIRE						
Smith	N	N	N	Y	Y	N
Gregg	Y	N	Y	Y	Y	N
NEW JERSEY						
Lautenberg	N	Y	Y	Y	N	Y
Torricelli	N	Y	Y	Y	N	Y
NEW MEXICO						
Domenici	?	?	Y	Y	Y	N
Bingaman	N	N	Y	Y	N	Y
NEW YORK						
Moynihan	N	Y	Y	Y	N	Y
Schumer	N	Y	Y	Y	N	Y
NORTH CAROLINA						
Helms	N	N	Y	Y	Y	N
Edwards	N	Y	Y	Y	N	Y
NORTH DAKOTA						
Conrad	N	Y	Y	N	N	Y
Dorgan	N	N	Y	Y	N	Y
OHIO						
DeWine	N	N	Y	Y	Y	N
Voinovich	N	N	Y	Y	Y	N
OKLAHOMA						
Nickles	N	N	Y	Y	Y	N
Inhofe	N	N	Y	Y	Y	N
OREGON						
Wyden	N	N	Y	Y	N	Y
Smith	N	Y	Y	Y	Y	N
PENNSYLVANIA						
Specter	Y	Y	Y	Y	N	N
Santorum	N	Y	Y	Y	Y	N
RHODE ISLAND						
Reed	N	Y	Y	Y	N	Y
Chafee, L.	N	N	Y	Y	Y	Y
SOUTH CAROLINA						
Thurmond	N	N	Y	Y	Y	N
Hollings	N	Y	Y	Y	Y	Y
SOUTH DAKOTA						
Daschle	N	Y	Y	Y	N	Y
Johnson	N	Y	?	?	N	Y
TENNESSEE						
Thompson	N	N	Y	Y	Y	N
Frist	N	N	Y	Y	Y	N
TEXAS						
Gramm	Y	N	Y	Y	Y	N
Hutchison	N	N	Y	Y	Y	N
UTAH						
Hatch	N	N	Y	Y	Y	N
Bennett	N	N	Y	Y	Y	N
VERMONT						
Leahy	Y	Y	Y	Y	N	Y
Jeffords	N	N	Y	Y	Y	N
VIRGINIA						
Warner	N	N	Y	Y	Y	N
Robb	N	Y	Y	Y	N	Y
WASHINGTON						
Gorton	Y	N	Y	Y	Y	N
Murray	Y	Y	Y	Y	N	Y
WEST VIRGINIA						
Byrd	N	Y	Y	Y	N	Y
Rockefeller	N	Y	Y	Y	N	Y
WISCONSIN						
Kohl	Y	N	Y	Y	N	Y
Feingold	N	Y	N	Y	N	Y
WYOMING						
Thomas	Y	N	N	Y	Y	N
Enzi	Y	N	Y	Y	Y	N

Key

- Y Voted for (yea).
- # Paired for.
- + Announced for.
- N Voted against (nay).
- X Paired against.
- – Announced against.
- P Voted "present."
- C Voted "present" to avoid possible conflict of interest.
- ? Did not vote or otherwise make a position known.

Democrats ***Republicans*** *Independents*

ND Northern Democrats SD Southern Democrats

Southern states - Ala., Ark., Fla., Ga., Ky., La., Miss., N.C., Okla., S.C., Tenn., Texas, Va.

139. **S 2522. Fiscal 2001 Foreign Operations Appropriations/Counternarcotics Funding Reduction.** Gorton, R-Wash., amendment that would reduce the $934 million for South American and Caribbean counternarcotics activities to approximately $200 million. Rejected 19-79: R 13-41; D 6-38 (ND 6-30, SD 0-8). June 21, 2000.

140. **S 2522. Fiscal 2001 Foreign Operations Appropriations/Helicopter Procurement.** Dodd, D-Conn., amendment that would strike language in the bill that would require $110 million to be spent for the procurement, refurbishment and support for UH-1H Huey II helicopters and insert language that would require $110 million to be spent on the most effective aircraft to use for anti-drug trafficking missions as determined by the Defense Department in consultation with the Colombian military. Rejected 47-51: R 8-46; D 39-5 (ND 31-5, SD 8-0). June 21, 2000.

141. **S 2522. Fiscal 2001 Foreign Operations Appropriations/Question of Engrossment and Third Reading.** Question of engrossment and third reading of the bill to provide approximately $13.4 billion in new budget authority for foreign aid programs for fiscal 2001. The bill also would provide $934 million in fiscal 2000 supplemental money for anti-drug efforts in South America. Ordered engrossed and read a third time 95-4: R 53-2; D 42-2 (ND 34-2, SD 8-0). June 22, 2000.

142. **Procedural Motion/Require Attendance.** Lott, R-Miss., motion to instruct the sergeant-at-arms to request the attendance of absent senators. Motion agreed to 94-3: R 54-1; D 40-2 (ND 33-1, SD 7-1). June 22, 2000.

143. **HR 4577. Fiscal 2001 Labor-HHS-Education Appropriations/Ergonomic Standard.** Enzi, R-Wyo., amendment that would prohibit the use of funds in the bill to be used by the Occupational Safety and Health Administration to promulgate, issue, implement, administer or enforce any proposed, temporary or final ergonomic standard. Adopted 57-41: R 54-1; D 3-40 (ND 0-35, SD 3-5). June 22, 2000. A "nay" was a vote in support of the president's position.

144. **HR 4577. Fiscal 2001 Labor-HHS-Education Appropriations/Prescription Drugs.** Robb, D-Va., amendment that would add language to the bill to establish a Medicare prescription drug benefit program. Under the program, Medicare would contribute at least 50 percent of the cost of premiums for beneficiaries, and beneficiaries would pay a $250 deductible. Rejected 44-53: R 2-52; D 42-1 (ND 35-0, SD 7-1). June 22, 2000.

Senate Votes 145, 146, 147, 148, 149, 150, 151, 152

	145	146	147	148	149	150	151	152
ALABAMA								
Shelby	Y	N	N	N	Y	Y	Y	Y
Sessions	Y	N	N	N	Y	Y	Y	Y
ALASKA								
Stevens	Y	N	N	N	Y	Y	Y	Y
Murkowski	Y	N	N	N	Y	Y	Y	Y
ARIZONA								
McCain	Y	N	N	N	Y	N	Y	Y
Kyl	Y	N	N	N	Y	N	Y	Y
ARKANSAS								
Hutchinson	Y	N	N	N	Y	N	Y	Y
Lincoln	Y	Y	Y	Y	Y	Y	Y	Y
CALIFORNIA								
Feinstein	Y	Y	Y	Y	Y	Y	Y	Y
Boxer	Y	Y	Y	Y	Y	Y	Y	Y
COLORADO								
Campbell	Y	N	N	N	Y	Y	Y	Y
Allard	Y	N	N	N	Y	Y	Y	N
CONNECTICUT								
Dodd	Y	Y	Y	Y	Y	Y	Y	Y
Lieberman	Y	Y	Y	Y	Y	N	Y	Y
DELAWARE								
Roth	Y	N	N	N	Y	Y	Y	Y
Biden	Y	Y	Y	Y	Y	Y	Y	Y
FLORIDA								
Graham	Y	Y	Y	Y	Y	Y	Y	Y
Mack	Y	N	N	N	Y	Y	Y	Y
GEORGIA								
Coverdell	Y	N	N	N	Y	Y	Y	Y
Cleland	Y	Y	Y	Y	Y	N	Y	Y
HAWAII								
Inouye	?	?	?	?	?	?	?	?
Akaka	Y	Y	Y	Y	Y	Y	Y	Y
IDAHO								
Craig	Y	N	N	N	Y	Y	Y	Y
Crapo	Y	N	N	N	Y	Y	Y	Y
ILLINOIS								
Durbin	Y	Y	Y	Y	Y	Y	Y	Y
Fitzgerald	Y	N	N	N	Y	N	Y	Y
INDIANA								
Lugar	Y	Y	Y	N	Y	N	Y	Y
Bayh	Y	Y	Y	Y	Y	N	Y	Y
IOWA								
Grassley	Y	N	N	N	Y	N	Y	Y
Harkin	Y	Y	Y	Y	Y	Y	Y	Y
KANSAS								
Brownback	Y	N	N	N	Y	N	Y	Y
Roberts	Y	N	N	N	Y	Y	Y	Y
KENTUCKY								
McConnell	Y	N	N	N	Y	Y	Y	Y
Bunning	Y	N	N	N	Y	Y	Y	Y
LOUISIANA								
Breaux	Y	Y	Y	Y	Y	Y	Y	Y
Landrieu	Y	Y	Y	Y	Y	Y	Y	Y
MAINE								
Snowe	Y	N	Y	N	Y	Y	Y	Y
Collins	Y	N	Y	N	Y	Y	Y	Y
MARYLAND								
Sarbanes	Y	Y	Y	Y	Y	Y	Y	Y
Mikulski	Y	Y	Y	Y	Y	Y	Y	Y
MASSACHUSETTS								
Kennedy	Y	Y	Y	Y	Y	Y	Y	Y
Kerry	Y	Y	Y	Y	Y	Y	Y	Y
MICHIGAN								
Levin	Y	Y	Y	Y	Y	Y	Y	Y
Abraham	Y	N	N	N	Y	N	Y	Y
MINNESOTA								
Wellstone	Y	Y	Y	Y	Y	Y	Y	Y
Grams	Y	N	N	N	Y	Y	Y	Y
MISSISSIPPI								
Cochran	Y	N	N	N	Y	Y	Y	Y
Lott	Y	N	N	N	Y	Y	Y	Y
MISSOURI								
Bond	Y	N	N	N	Y	Y	Y	Y
Ashcroft	Y	N	N	N	Y	Y	Y	Y
MONTANA								
Baucus	+	Y	Y	Y	Y	Y	Y	Y
Burns	Y	N	N	N	Y	Y	Y	Y
NEBRASKA								
Kerrey	Y	Y	Y	Y	N	Y	Y	Y
Hagel	Y	N	N	N	Y	Y	Y	Y
NEVADA								
Reid	Y	Y	Y	Y	Y	Y	Y	Y
Bryan	Y	Y	Y	Y	Y	Y	Y	Y
NEW HAMPSHIRE								
Smith	Y	N	N	N	Y	N	Y	Y
Gregg	Y	N	N	N	Y	Y	Y	Y
NEW JERSEY								
Lautenberg	Y	Y	Y	Y	N	Y	Y	Y
Torricelli	Y	Y	Y	Y	Y	Y	Y	Y
NEW MEXICO								
Domenici	Y	N	N	N	Y	Y	Y	Y
Bingaman	Y	Y	Y	Y	Y	Y	Y	Y
NEW YORK								
Moynihan	?	Y	Y	Y	Y	Y	Y	Y
Schumer	?	Y	Y	Y	Y	Y	Y	Y
NORTH CAROLINA								
Helms	Y	N	N	N	Y	Y	Y	Y
Edwards	Y	Y	Y	Y	Y	Y	Y	Y
NORTH DAKOTA								
Conrad	Y	Y	Y	Y	Y	N	Y	Y
Dorgan	Y	Y	Y	Y	Y	N	Y	Y
OHIO								
DeWine	Y	N	N	N	Y	N	Y	Y
Voinovich	Y	N	N	N	Y	Y	Y	Y
OKLAHOMA								
Nickles	Y	N	N	N	Y	N	Y	Y
Inhofe	Y	N	N	N	Y	N	Y	Y
OREGON								
Wyden	Y	Y	Y	Y	Y	Y	Y	Y
Smith	Y	N	N	N	Y	Y	Y	Y
PENNSYLVANIA								
Specter	Y	N	N	N	Y	Y	Y	Y
Santorum	Y	N	N	N	Y	Y	Y	Y
RHODE ISLAND								
Reed	Y	Y	Y	Y	Y	Y	Y	Y
Chafee, L.	Y	Y	Y	N	Y	Y	Y	Y
SOUTH CAROLINA								
Thurmond	Y	N	N	N	Y	Y	Y	Y
Hollings	Y	Y	Y	Y	Y	N	Y	Y
SOUTH DAKOTA								
Daschle	Y	Y	Y	Y	Y	Y	Y	Y
Johnson	Y	Y	Y	Y	?	Y	Y	Y
TENNESSEE								
Thompson	Y	N	N	N	Y	N	Y	Y
Frist	Y	N	N	N	Y	Y	Y	Y
TEXAS								
Gramm	Y	N	N	N	Y	N	Y	Y
Hutchison	Y	N	N	N	Y	N	Y	Y
UTAH								
Hatch	Y	N	N	N	Y	N	Y	Y
Bennett	Y	N	N	N	Y	N	Y	Y
VERMONT								
Leahy	Y	Y	Y	Y	Y	Y	Y	Y
Jeffords	Y	Y	Y	N	Y	Y	Y	Y
VIRGINIA								
Warner	Y	N	N	N	Y	Y	Y	Y
Robb	Y	Y	Y	Y	Y	Y	Y	Y
WASHINGTON								
Gorton	Y	N	N	N	Y	Y	Y	Y
Murray	Y	Y	Y	Y	Y	Y	Y	Y
WEST VIRGINIA								
Byrd	Y	Y	Y	Y	Y	N	Y	Y
Rockefeller	Y	Y	Y	Y	Y	Y	Y	Y
WISCONSIN								
Kohl	Y	Y	Y	Y	Y	Y	Y	Y
Feingold	Y	Y	Y	Y	N	Y	Y	Y
WYOMING								
Thomas	Y	N	N	N	Y	Y	Y	Y
Enzi	Y	N	N	N	Y	Y	Y	Y

ND Northern Democrats SD Southern Democrats

Southern states - Ala., Ark., Fla., Ga., Ky., La., Miss., N.C., Okla., S.C., Tenn., Texas, Va.

Key

- Y Voted for (yea).
- # Paired for.
- + Announced for.
- N Voted against (nay).
- X Paired against.
- – Announced against.
- P Voted "present."
- C Voted "present" to avoid possible conflict of interest.
- ? Did not vote or otherwise make a position known.

•

Democrats ***Republicans***
Independents

145. HR 4577. Fiscal 2001 Labor-HHS-Education Appropriations/Antimicrobial Resistance Detection Pilot Programs. Cochran, R-Miss., amendment that would provide $25 million to agencies such as the Centers for Disease Control and Prevention to establish partnerships between the federal government, academic institutions and state and local public health departments to carry out pilot programs for antimicrobial resistance detection, surveillance, education and prevention, and to conduct research on resistance mechanisms and new or more effective antimicrobial compounds. Adopted 96-0: R 55-0; D 41-0 (ND 33-0, SD 8-0). June 27, 2000.

146. HR 4577. Fiscal 2001 Labor-HHS-Education Appropriations/Education Funding. Wellstone, D-Minn., motion to waive the Budget Act with respect to the Gregg, R-N.H., point of order against the amendment that would require $10 billion to be provided for Title 1 education grants. Motion rejected 47-52: R 3-52; D 44-0 (ND 36-0, SD 8-0). A three-fifths majority vote (60) of the total Senate is required to waive the Budget Act. (Subsequently the chair upheld the point of order, and the amendment fell.) June 27, 2000.

147. HR 4577. Fiscal 2001 Labor-HHS-Education Appropriations/Education Funding. Bingaman, D-N.M., motion to waive the Budget Act with respect to the Gregg, R-N.H., point of order against the Bingaman amendment that would provide $250 million to ensure accountability in Title 1 programs and assist state efforts to improve failing schools. Motion rejected 49-50: R 5-50; D 44-0 (ND 36-0, SD 8-0). A three-fifths majority vote (60) of the total Senate is required to waive the Budget Act. (Subsequently, the chair upheld the point of order, and the amendment fell.) A "yea" was a vote in support of the president's position. June 27, 2000.

148. HR 4577. Fiscal 2001 Labor-HHS-Education Appropriations/Class Size Reduction. Murray, D-Wash., motion to waive the Budget Act with respect to the Specter, R-Pa., point of order against the Murray amendment that would provide $1.75 billion for class-size reduction programs. Motion rejected 44-55: R 0-55; D 44-0 (ND 36-0, SD 8-0). A three-fifths majority vote (60) of the total Senate is required to waive the Budget Act. (Subsequently, the chair upheld the point of order, and the amendment fell.) A "yea" was a vote in support of the president's position. June 27, 2000.

149. HR 4577. Fiscal 2001 Labor-HHS-Education Appropriations/Internet Access For Minors. McCain, R-Ariz., amendment that would require elementary and secondary schools and libraries with Internet access that receive universal service discounts to certify that they have selected technology to filter or block on all computers Internet access to child pornography and other obscene material by minors under the age of 17. Adopted 95-3: R 55-0; D 40-3 (ND 32-3, SD 8-0). June 27, 2000.

150. HR 4577. Fiscal 2001 Labor-HHS-Education Appropriations/Internet Access For Minors. Santorum, R-Pa., amendment that would prohibit the availability of universal service discounts to schools or libraries unless they certify that they have met certain provisions, including installing a system to filter or block Internet access to inappropriate materials, and adopted an Internet policy that includes addressing the safety and security of minors when using e-mail, chatrooms and other forms of direct communication, and the unauthorized disclosure or dissemination of personal identification information regarding minors. Adopted 75-24: R 38-17; D 37-7 (ND 31-5, SD 6-2). June 27, 2000.

151. HR 4577. Fiscal 2001 Labor-HHS-Education Appropriations/Same Gender Schools. Hutchison, R-Texas, amendment that would specify that funding under the bill may be used for education projects that provide same gender schools and classrooms. Adopted 99-0: R 55-0; D 44-0 (ND 36-0, SD 8-0). June 28, 2000.

152. HR 4577. Fiscal 2001 Labor-HHS-Education Appropriations/Fetal Alcohol Syndrome. Daschle, D-S.D., amendment that would allocate a total of $25 million to be used for the fetal alcohol syndrome prevention and service program. Adopted 98-1: R 54-1; D 44-0 (ND 36-0, SD 8-0). June 28, 2000.

Senate Votes 153, 154, 155, 156, 157, 158, 159, 160

	153	154	155	156	157	158	159	160
ALABAMA								
Shelby	N	N	N	N	N	Y	N	Y
Sessions	N	N	N	N	N	Y	N	Y
ALASKA								
Stevens	N	N	N	N	N	Y	Y	Y
Murkowski	N	N	N	N	N	Y	N	Y
ARIZONA								
McCain	N	N	N	N	N	N	N	Y
Kyl	N	N	N	N	N	N	N	Y
ARKANSAS								
Hutchinson	N	N	N	N	N	Y	N	Y
Lincoln	Y	Y	Y	Y	Y	N	Y	Y
CALIFORNIA								
Feinstein	Y	Y	Y	Y	Y	N	Y	Y
Boxer	Y	Y	Y	Y	Y	Y	Y	Y
COLORADO								
Campbell	N	N	N	N	N	Y	N	Y
Allard	N	N	N	N	N	Y	N	Y
CONNECTICUT								
Dodd	Y	Y	Y	Y	Y	Y	Y	Y
Lieberman	Y	Y	Y	Y	Y	N	Y	Y
DELAWARE								
Roth	Y	N	N	N	N	Y	Y	Y
Biden	Y	Y	Y	Y	Y	N	Y	Y
FLORIDA								
Graham	Y	Y	Y	Y	Y	N	Y	Y
Mack	N	N	N	N	N	Y	N	N
GEORGIA								
Coverdell	N	N	N	N	N	Y	N	N
Cleland	Y	Y	Y	Y	Y	N	Y	Y
HAWAII								
Inouye	?	?	?	?	?	?	?	?
Akaka	Y	Y	Y	Y	Y	Y	Y	Y
IDAHO								
Craig	N	N	N	N	N	Y	N	Y
Crapo	N	N	N	N	N	Y	N	Y
ILLINOIS								
Durbin	Y	Y	Y	Y	Y	N	Y	Y
Fitzgerald	N	N	N	N	N	Y	N	Y
INDIANA								
Lugar	N	N	N	N	N	Y	N	Y
Bayh	Y	Y	Y	Y	Y	N	Y	Y
IOWA								
Grassley	N	N	N	N	N	Y	N	Y
Harkin	Y	Y	Y	Y	Y	Y	Y	Y
KANSAS								
Brownback	N	N	N	N	N	Y	N	Y
Roberts	N	N	N	N	N	Y	N	Y
KENTUCKY								
McConnell	N	N	N	N	N	N	N	N
Bunning	N	N	N	N	N	N	N	Y
LOUISIANA								
Breaux	Y	Y	Y	Y	Y	N	Y	Y
Landrieu	Y	Y	Y	Y	Y	N	Y	Y
MAINE								
Snowe	Y	Y	Y	N	Y	Y	N	Y
Collins	Y	N	N	Y	N	Y	N	Y
MARYLAND								
Sarbanes	Y	Y	Y	Y	Y	Y	Y	Y
Mikulski	Y	Y	Y	Y	Y	Y	Y	Y
MASSACHUSETTS								
Kennedy	Y	Y	Y	Y	Y	Y	Y	Y
Kerry	Y	Y	Y	Y	Y	Y	Y	Y
MICHIGAN								
Levin	Y	Y	Y	Y	Y	Y	Y	Y
Abraham	N	N	Y	N	Y	Y	N	Y
MINNESOTA								
Wellstone	Y	Y	Y	Y	Y	Y	Y	Y
Grams	N	N	N	N	N	Y	N	Y
MISSISSIPPI								
Cochran	N	N	N	N	N	Y	N	Y
Lott	N	N	N	N	N	Y	N	Y
MISSOURI								
Bond	N	N	N	N	N	Y	N	Y
Ashcroft	N	N	N	N	N	Y	N	Y
MONTANA								
Baucus	Y	Y	Y	Y	Y	Y	Y	Y
Burns	N	N	N	N	N	Y	N	Y
NEBRASKA								
Kerrey	Y	Y	Y	Y	Y	N	Y	Y
Hagel	N	N	N	N	N	Y	N	Y
NEVADA								
Reid	Y	Y	Y	Y	Y	Y	Y	Y
Bryan	Y	Y	Y	Y	Y	N	Y	Y
NEW HAMPSHIRE								
Smith	N	N	N	N	N	Y	N	Y
Gregg	N	N	N	N	N	?	?	?
NEW JERSEY								
Lautenberg	Y	Y	Y	Y	Y	Y	Y	Y
Torricelli	Y	Y	Y	Y	Y	N	Y	Y
NEW MEXICO								
Domenici	N	N	N	N	N	Y	N	Y
Bingaman	Y	Y	Y	Y	Y	Y	Y	Y
NEW YORK								
Moynihan	Y	Y	Y	Y	Y	N	Y	Y
Schumer	Y	Y	Y	Y	Y	Y	Y	Y
NORTH CAROLINA								
Helms	N	N	N	N	N	N	N	N
Edwards	Y	Y	Y	Y	Y	N	Y	Y
NORTH DAKOTA								
Conrad	Y	Y	Y	Y	Y	Y	Y	Y
Dorgan	Y	Y	Y	Y	Y	Y	Y	Y
OHIO								
DeWine	Y	N	N	N	Y	N	N	Y
Voinovich	N	N	N	N	N	Y	N	Y
OKLAHOMA								
Nickles	N	N	N	N	N	Y	N	N
Inhofe	N	N	N	N	N	Y	N	N
OREGON								
Wyden	Y	Y	Y	Y	Y	Y	Y	Y
Smith	Y	Y	N	N	N	Y	N	Y
PENNSYLVANIA								
Specter	N	N	N	N	N	Y	Y	Y
Santorum	N	N	N	N	N	Y	N	Y
RHODE ISLAND								
Reed	Y	Y	Y	Y	Y	Y	Y	Y
Chafee, L.	Y	Y	Y	Y	Y	Y	N	Y
SOUTH CAROLINA								
Thurmond	N	N	N	N	N	Y	N	Y
Hollings	Y	Y	Y	Y	Y	Y	Y	Y
SOUTH DAKOTA								
Daschle	Y	Y	Y	Y	Y	Y	Y	Y
Johnson	Y	Y	Y	Y	Y	Y	Y	Y
TENNESSEE								
Thompson	N	N	N	N	N	Y	Y	Y
Frist	N	N	N	N	N	Y	N	Y
TEXAS								
Gramm	N	N	N	N	N	Y	N	Y
Hutchison	N	N	N	N	N	Y	N	Y
UTAH								
Hatch	N	N	N	N	N	Y	Y	Y
Bennett	N	N	N	N	N	Y	Y	Y
VERMONT								
Leahy	Y	Y	Y	Y	Y	N	N	Y
Jeffords	Y	Y	Y	Y	Y	Y	N	Y
VIRGINIA								
Warner	N	N	N	N	N	Y	Y	Y
Robb	Y	Y	Y	Y	Y	Y	Y	Y
WASHINGTON								
Gorton	N	N	N	N	N	Y	Y	Y
Murray	Y	Y	Y	Y	Y	Y	Y	Y
WEST VIRGINIA								
Byrd	Y	Y	Y	Y	Y	Y	Y	Y
Rockefeller	Y	Y	Y	Y	Y	Y	Y	Y
WISCONSIN								
Kohl	Y	Y	Y	Y	Y	N	Y	Y
Feingold	Y	Y	Y	Y	Y	Y	Y	Y
WYOMING								
Thomas	N	N	N	N	N	Y	N	Y
Enzi	N	N	N	N	N	Y	N	Y

Key

- Y Voted for (yea).
- # Paired for.
- \+ Announced for.
- N Voted against (nay).
- X Paired against.
- – Announced against.
- P Voted "present."
- C Voted "present" to avoid possible conflict of interest.
- ? Did not vote or otherwise make a position known.

Democrats **Republicans**
Independents

ND Northern Democrats SD Southern Democrats

Southern states - Ala., Ark., Fla., Ga., Ky., La., Miss., N.C., Okla., S.C., Tenn., Texas, Va.

153. HR 4577. Fiscal 2001 Labor-HHS-Education Appropriations/ Teacher Training. Dodd, D-Conn., motion to waive the Budget Act with respect to the Specter, R-Pa., point of order against the Kennedy amendment that would provide an additional $202 million in funding for teacher training. Motion rejected 51-48: R 7-48; D 44-0 (ND 36-0, SD 8-0). A three-fifths majority vote (60) of the total Senate is required to waive the Budget Act. (Subsequently the chair upheld the point of order, and the amendment fell.) June 28, 2000.

154. HR 4577. Fiscal 2001 Labor-HHS-Education Appropriations/ Community Learning Centers. Dodd, D-Conn., motion to waive the Budget Act with respect to the Specter, R-Pa., point of order against the Dodd amendment that would provide an increase from $600 million to $1 billion for 21st Century Community Learning Centers. Motion rejected 48-51: R 4-51; D 44-0 (ND 36-0, SD 8-0). A three-fifths majority vote (60) of the total Senate is required to waive the Budget Act. (Subsequently, the chair upheld the point of order, and the amendment fell.) A "yea" was a vote in support of the president's position. June 28, 2000.

155. HR 4577. Fiscal 2001 Labor-HHS-Education Appropriations/ Technology Literacy. Kerry, D-Mass., motion to waive the Budget Act with respect to the Specter, R-Pa., point of order against the Kerry amendment that would provide an increase of $92 million for the technology literacy challenge fund. Motion rejected 48-51: R 4-51; D 44-0 (ND 36-0, SD 8-0). A three-fifths majority vote (60) of the total Senate is required to waive the Budget Act. (Subsequently, the chair upheld the point of order, and the amendment fell.) June 28, 2000.

156. HR 4577. Fiscal 2001 Labor-HHS-Education Appropriations/ GEAR UP Funding. Reed, D-R.I., motion to waive the Budget Act with respect to the Specter, R-Pa., point of order against the Reed amendment that would provide an additional $100 million for the GEAR UP program. Motion rejected 47-52: R 3-52; D 44-0 (ND 36-0, SD 8-0). A three-fifths majority vote (60) of the total Senate is required to waive the Budget Act. (Subsequently, the chair upheld the point of order, and the amendment fell.) June 28, 2000.

157. HR 4577. Fiscal 2001 Labor-HHS-Education Appropriations/Employment Training. Kennedy, D-Mass., motion to waive the Budget Act with respect to the Gorton, R-Wash., point of order against the Kennedy amendment that would provide that $1 billion be available for training and employment services funded under the bill. Motion rejected 49-50: R 5-50; D 44-0 (ND 36-0, SD 8-0). A three-fifths majority vote (60) of the total Senate is required to waive the Budget Act. (Subsequently, the chair upheld the point of order, and the amendment fell.) June 28, 2000.

158. HR 4577. Fiscal 2001 Labor-HHS-Education Appropriations/Targeted Education Grants. Specter, R-Pa., motion to table (kill) the Landrieu, D-La., amendment that would provide an increase of $750 million in targeted Title I grants under the Elementary and Secondary Education Act. Motion agreed to 75-23: R 48-6; D 27-17 (ND 25-11, SD 2-6). June 28, 2000.

159. HR 4577. Fiscal 2001 Labor-HHS-Education Appropriations/ IDEA Funding. Specter, R-Pa., motion to table (kill) the Jeffords, R-Vt., amendment that would increase funding for the Individuals with Disabilities Education Act by $2.6 billion. Motion agreed to 51-47: R 8-46; D 43-1 (ND 35-1, SD 8-0). June 28, 2000.

160. HR 4762. Campaign Finance Disclosure/Passage. Passage of the bill that would require groups organized under section 527 of the tax code to disclose contribution and expenditure information with the Treasury Department. Passed (thus cleared for the president) 92-6: R 48-6; D 44-0 (ND 36-0, SD 8-0). June 29, 2000.

	161	162	163	164	165	166	167
ALABAMA							
Shelby	Y	N	Y	N	Y	Y	N
Sessions	Y	N	Y	N	Y	Y	N
ALASKA							
Stevens	Y	N	N	N	Y	Y	N
Murkowski	Y	N	Y	N	Y	Y	N
ARIZONA							
McCain	Y	N	Y	N	Y	N	Y
Kyl	Y	N	Y	N	Y	Y	N
ARKANSAS							
Hutchinson	Y	N	Y	N	Y	Y	N
Lincoln	Y	Y	N	Y	N	N	Y
CALIFORNIA							
Feinstein	Y	Y	N	Y	Y	N	Y
Boxer	Y	Y	N	Y	N	N	Y
COLORADO							
Campbell	Y	Y	Y	N	Y	Y	N
Allard	Y	N	Y	N	Y	Y	N
CONNECTICUT							
Dodd	Y	Y	N	Y	N	N	Y
Lieberman	Y	Y	N	Y	Y	N	Y
DELAWARE							
Roth	Y	Y	Y	N	Y	Y	N
Biden	Y	Y	N	Y	N	N	Y
FLORIDA							
Graham	Y	Y	N	Y	N	N	Y
Mack	Y	N	Y	N	Y	Y	N
GEORGIA							
Coverdell	Y	N	Y	N	Y	Y	N
Cleland	Y	Y	N	Y	N	N	Y
HAWAII							
Inouye	?	?	?	?	?	?	?
Akaka	Y	Y	N	Y	N	N	Y
IDAHO							
Craig	Y	N	Y	N	Y	Y	N
Crapo	Y	N	Y	N	Y	Y	N
ILLINOIS							
Durbin	Y	Y	N	Y	N	N	Y
Fitzgerald	Y	Y	Y	N	Y	N	Y
INDIANA							
Lugar	Y	N	Y	N	Y	Y	N
Bayh	Y	Y	N	Y	N	N	Y
IOWA							
Grassley	Y	N	Y	N	Y	Y	N
Harkin	Y	Y	N	Y	N	N	Y
KANSAS							
Brownback	Y	N	Y	N	Y	Y	N
Roberts	Y	N	Y	N	Y	Y	N
KENTUCKY							
McConnell	Y	?	Y	N	Y	Y	N
Bunning	Y	N	Y	N	Y	Y	N
LOUISIANA							
Breaux	Y	Y	N	Y	N	N	Y
Landrieu	Y	Y	N	Y	N	N	Y
MAINE							
Snowe	Y	Y	Y	N	Y	Y	N
Collins	Y	Y	Y	N	Y	Y	N
MARYLAND							
Sarbanes	Y	Y	N	Y	N	N	Y
Mikulski	Y	Y	N	Y	N	N	Y
MASSACHUSETTS							
Kennedy	Y	Y	N	Y	N	N	Y
Kerry	Y	Y	N	Y	N	N	Y
MICHIGAN							
Levin	Y	Y	N	Y	N	N	Y
Abraham	Y	Y	Y	N	Y	Y	N
MINNESOTA							
Wellstone	Y	Y	N	Y	N	N	Y
Grams	Y	N	Y	N	Y	Y	N
MISSISSIPPI							
Cochran	Y	N	Y	N	Y	Y	N
Lott	Y	N	Y	N	Y	Y	N
MISSOURI							
Bond	Y	N	Y	N	Y	Y	N
Ashcroft	Y	Y	Y	N	Y	Y	N
MONTANA							
Baucus	Y	Y	N	Y	N	N	Y
Burns	Y	Y	Y	N	Y	Y	N
NEBRASKA							
Kerrey	Y	Y	N	Y	N	N	Y
Hagel	Y	N	Y	N	Y	Y	N
NEVADA							
Reid	Y	Y	N	Y	N	N	Y
Bryan	Y	Y	N	Y	N	N	Y
NEW HAMPSHIRE							
Smith	Y	N	Y	N	Y	Y	N
Gregg	?	?	?	N	Y	Y	N
NEW JERSEY							
Lautenberg	Y	Y	N	Y	N	N	Y
Torricelli	Y	Y	N	Y	N	N	Y
NEW MEXICO							
Domenici	Y	N	Y	N	Y	Y	N
Bingaman	Y	Y	N	Y	N	N	Y
NEW YORK							
Moynihan	Y	Y	N	Y	N	N	Y
Schumer	Y	Y	N	Y	N	N	Y
NORTH CAROLINA							
Helms	Y	N	Y	N	Y	Y	N
Edwards	Y	Y	N	Y	N	N	Y
NORTH DAKOTA							
Conrad	Y	Y	N	Y	N	N	Y
Dorgan	Y	Y	N	Y	N	N	Y
OHIO							
DeWine	Y	Y	Y	N	Y	Y	N
Voinovich	Y	Y	Y	N	Y	Y	N
OKLAHOMA							
Nickles	Y	N	Y	N	Y	Y	N
Inhofe	Y	N	Y	N	Y	Y	N
OREGON							
Wyden	Y	Y	N	Y	N	N	Y
Smith	Y	Y	Y	N	Y	Y	N
PENNSYLVANIA							
Specter	Y	Y	Y	Y	Y	N	Y
Santorum	Y	N	Y	N	Y	Y	N
RHODE ISLAND							
Reed	Y	Y	N	Y	N	N	Y
Chafee, L.	Y	Y	Y	N	Y	N	Y
SOUTH CAROLINA							
Thurmond	Y	N	Y	N	Y	Y	N
Hollings	Y	Y	N	Y	N	N	Y
SOUTH DAKOTA							
Daschle	Y	Y	N	Y	N	N	Y
Johnson	Y	Y	N	Y	N	N	Y
TENNESSEE							
Thompson	Y	N	Y	N	Y	Y	N
Frist	Y	N	Y	N	Y	Y	N
TEXAS							
Gramm	Y	N	Y	N	Y	Y	N
Hutchison	Y	Y	Y	N	Y	Y	N
UTAH							
Hatch	Y	N	Y	N	Y	Y	N
Bennett	Y	N	Y	N	Y	Y	N
VERMONT							
Leahy	Y	Y	?	?	?	?	?
Jeffords	Y	Y	Y	N	Y	Y	N
VIRGINIA							
Warner	Y	N	Y	N	Y	Y	N
Robb	Y	Y	N	Y	N	N	Y
WASHINGTON							
Gorton	Y	Y	Y	N	Y	Y	N
Murray	Y	Y	N	Y	N	N	Y
WEST VIRGINIA							
Byrd	Y	Y	N	Y	Y	N	Y
Rockefeller	Y	Y	N	Y	N	N	Y
WISCONSIN							
Kohl	Y	Y	N	Y	N	N	Y
Feingold	Y	Y	Y	Y	N	N	Y
WYOMING							
Thomas	Y	N	Y	N	Y	Y	N
Enzi	Y	N	Y	N	Y	Y	N

ND Northern Democrats SD Southern Democrats

Southern states - Ala., Ark., Fla., Ga., Ky., La., Miss., N.C., Okla., S.C., Tenn., Texas, Va.

Key

- Y Voted for (yea).
- # Paired for.
- + Announced for.
- N Voted against (nay).
- X Paired against.
- – Announced against.
- P Voted "present."
- C Voted "present" to avoid possible conflict of interest.
- ? Did not vote or otherwise make a position known.

•

Democrats **Republicans**
Independents

161. HR 4577. Fiscal 2001 Labor-HHS-Education Appropriations/Education Research Funding. Frist, R-Tenn., amendment that would increase funding for the Interagency Education Research Initiative by $10 million. The funding increase would be offset by making an across-the-board funding cut in administrative or related expenses. Adopted 98-0: R 54-0; D 44-0 (ND 36-0, SD 8-0). June 29, 2000.

162. HR 4577. Fiscal 2001 Labor-HHS-Education Appropriations/Medicare 'Lockbox.' Conrad, D-N.D., amendment that would create a Medicare and Social Security "lockbox." It would take the Medicare Part A off-budget; establish a 60-vote point of order against a budget resolution, conference report, bill or amendment that would reduce the Medicare Part A surplus or create an on-budget deficit; require Social Security and Medicare revenue outlays to be set every fiscal year in a budget resolution; and enforce points of order against reducing Social Security surpluses in every year covered by the budget resolution. Adopted 60-37: R 16-37; D 44-0 (ND 36-0, SD 8-0). June 29, 2000.

163. HR 4577. Fiscal 2001 Labor-HHS-Education Appropriations/Medicare 'Lockbox.' Ashcroft, R-Mo., amendment that would create a Medicare and Social Security "lockbox." It would take the Medicare Part A surplus off-budget and establish a 60-vote point of order against the consideration of a concurrent budget resolution, conference report, or subsequent legislation that would create an on-budget deficit for any fiscal year. Adopted 54-43: R 53-1; D 1-42 (ND 1-34, SD 0-8). June 29, 2000.

164. HR 4577. Fiscal 2001 Labor-HHS-Education Appropriations/Genetic Discrimination. Daschle, D-S.D., amendment that would prohibit health insurers and employers from using predictive genetic information to discriminate in the health care system and the workplace, including for use in hiring, advancement, salary or other workplace rights. It would prohibit insurance companies from raising or denying patients' health care coverage based on the results of genetic tests, as well as requiring such tests as a condition of coverage. It also would prevent the disclosure of genetic information to health insurers and employers. Rejected 44-54: R 1-54; D 43-0 (ND 35-0, SD 8-0). June 29, 2000.

165. HR 4577. Fiscal 2001 Labor-HHS-Education Appropriations/Genetic Discrimination. Jeffords, R-Vt., amendment that would prohibit health insurers from using predictive genetic information to discriminate in the health care system. It also would prohibit insurance companies from raising or denying patients' health care coverage based on the results of genetic tests. Adopted 58-40: R 55-0; D 3-40 (ND 3-32, SD 0-8). June 29, 2000.

166. HR 4577. Fiscal 2001 Labor-HHS-Education Appropriations/Managed Care. Nickles, R-Okla., amendment that would provide federal protections, such as access to emergency care, internal and external appeals, specialists and out-of-network doctors, primarily for the 56 million Americans in self-insured health plans. It also would prohibit denials based on predictive genetic information for patients in self-insured and employer plans, and allow patients to sue in federal court for harm caused by the failure to comply with the external medical review or harm caused due to delay in providing care. Adopted 51-47: R 51-4; D 0-43 (ND 0-35, SD 0-8). June 29, 2000.

167. HR 4577. Fiscal 2001 Labor-HHS-Education Appropriations/Managed Care. Dorgan, D-N.D., amendment that would provide that any bill on managed care passed by Congress shall provide a floor of federal protection to all Americans with private health insurance. Rejected 47-51: R 4-51; D 43-0 (ND 35-0, SD 8-0). A "yea" was a vote in support of the president's position. June 29, 2000.

	168	169	170	171
ALABAMA				
Shelby	Y	N	N	Y
Sessions	Y	N	N	N
ALASKA				
Stevens	Y	N	N	Y
Murkowski	Y	N	N	Y
ARIZONA				
McCain	Y	N	N	Y
Kyl	Y	N	N	Y
ARKANSAS				
Hutchinson	Y	N	N	Y
Lincoln	N	Y	Y	Y
CALIFORNIA				
Feinstein	N	Y	Y	N
Boxer	?	?	?	?
COLORADO				
Campbell	Y	Y	N	Y
Allard	Y	N	N	N
CONNECTICUT				
Dodd	Y	Y	Y	N
Lieberman	Y	Y	Y	N
DELAWARE				
Roth	N	N	N	Y
Biden	Y	Y	Y	N
FLORIDA				
Graham	N	Y	N	N
Mack	Y	N	N	Y
GEORGIA				
Coverdell	Y	N	N	Y
Cleland	N	Y	Y	Y
HAWAII				
Inouye	?	?	?	?
Akaka	N	Y	Y	N
IDAHO				
Craig	Y	N	N	Y
Crapo	Y	N	N	Y
ILLINOIS				
Durbin	N	Y	Y	N
Fitzgerald	Y	N	N	Y
INDIANA				
Lugar	Y	N	N	Y
Bayh	N	Y	Y	N
IOWA				
Grassley	N	N	N	Y
Harkin	N	Y	Y	Y
KANSAS				
Brownback	Y	N	N	N
Roberts	Y	N	N	Y
KENTUCKY				
McConnell	Y	N	N	Y
Bunning	Y	N	N	N
LOUISIANA				
Breaux	Y	N	Y	Y
Landrieu	Y	Y	Y	N
MAINE				
Snowe	Y	Y	Y	Y
Collins	Y	Y	Y	Y
MARYLAND				
Sarbanes	N	Y	Y	N
Mikulski	N	Y	Y	N
MASSACHUSETTS				
Kennedy	N	Y	Y	N
Kerry	N	Y	Y	N
MICHIGAN				
Levin	N	Y	Y	N
Abraham	Y	N	N	Y
MINNESOTA				
Wellstone	N	Y	Y	N
Grams	Y	N	N	N
MISSISSIPPI				
Cochran	Y	N	N	Y
Lott	Y	N	N	Y
MISSOURI				
Bond	Y	N	N	Y
Ashcroft	Y	N	N	Y
MONTANA				
Baucus	N	Y	Y	N
Burns	Y	N	N	Y
NEBRASKA				
Kerrey	Y	Y	Y	Y
Hagel	Y	N	N	Y
NEVADA				
Reid	N	Y	Y	N
Bryan	N	Y	Y	N
NEW HAMPSHIRE				
Smith	Y	N	N	N
Gregg	N	N	N	Y
NEW JERSEY				
Lautenberg	Y	Y	Y	N
Torricelli	Y	Y	Y	N
NEW MEXICO				
Domenici	Y	N	N	Y
Bingaman	N	Y	Y	N
NEW YORK				
Moynihan	?	?	?	?
Schumer	N	Y	N	N
NORTH CAROLINA				
Helms	Y	N	N	N
Edwards	N	Y	Y	N
NORTH DAKOTA				
Conrad	N	N	N	N
Dorgan	N	N	Y	N
OHIO				
DeWine	Y	N	N	Y
Voinovich	N	N	N	N
OKLAHOMA				
Nickles	Y	N	N	N
Inhofe	Y	N	N	Y
OREGON				
Wyden	N	Y	Y	N
Smith	Y	N	N	Y
PENNSYLVANIA				
Specter	Y	Y	N	Y
Santorum	Y	N	N	Y
RHODE ISLAND				
Reed	N	N	Y	N
Chafee, L.	N	Y	Y	Y
SOUTH CAROLINA				
Thurmond	Y	N	N	Y
Hollings	N	Y	Y	Y
SOUTH DAKOTA				
Daschle	N	Y	Y	N
Johnson	N	N	Y	N
TENNESSEE				
Thompson	Y	N	N	Y
Frist	Y	N	N	Y
TEXAS				
Gramm	Y	N	N	N
Hutchison	Y	N	N	Y
UTAH				
Hatch	+	–	–	+
Bennett	Y	N	N	Y
VERMONT				
Leahy	?	?	?	–
Jeffords	N	Y	Y	Y
VIRGINIA				
Warner	Y	N	N	Y
Robb	N	Y	Y	N
WASHINGTON				
Gorton	Y	N	N	Y
Murray	N	Y	Y	N
WEST VIRGINIA				
Byrd	N	Y	N	Y
Rockefeller	N	Y	Y	N
WISCONSIN				
Kohl	N	N	Y	Y
Feingold	N	Y	N	N
WYOMING				
Thomas	Y	N	N	Y
Enzi	Y	N	N	Y

Key

- Y Voted for (yea).
- # Paired for.
- + Announced for.
- N Voted against (nay).
- X Paired against.
- – Announced against.
- P Voted "present."
- C Voted "present" to avoid possible conflict of interest.
- ? Did not vote or otherwise make a position known.

Democrats ***Republicans***
Independents

ND Northern Democrats SD Southern Democrats

Southern states - Ala., Ark., Fla., Ga., Ky., La., Miss., N.C., Okla., S.C., Tenn., Texas, Va.

168. HR 4577. Fiscal 2001 Labor-HHS-Education Appropriations/ Prescription Drug Prices. Specter, R-Pa., motion to table (kill) the Wellstone, D-Minn., amendment that would require prescription drug producers to sign an agreement to sell products that are patented by the National Institutes of Health at a price determined by the Secretary of Health and Human Services. Motion agreed to 56-39: R 48-6, D 8-33 (ND 6-27, SD 2-6). June 30, 2000.

169. HR 4577. Fiscal 2001 Labor-HHS-Education Appropriations/ Morning After Pill. Specter, R-Pa., motion to table (kill) the Helms, R-N.C., amendment that would prohibit the use of funds under the bill for the distribution of the "morning after" pill on school grounds. Motion rejected 41-54: R 6-48; D 35-6 (ND 28-5, SD 7-1). (Subsequently the Helms amendment was adopted by voice vote.) June 30, 2000.

170. HR 4577. Fiscal 2001 Labor-HHS-Education Appropriations/ IDEA Funding. Harkin, D-Iowa, motion to waive the Budget Act with respect to the Specter, R-Pa., point of order against the Harkin amendment. The amendment would provide $15.8 billion in funding for the Individuals with Disabilities Education Act. Motion rejected 40-55: R 4-50: D 36-5 (ND 29-4, SD 7-1). A three-fifths majority vote (60) of the total Senate is required to waive the Budget Act. (Subsequently, the chair upheld the point of order and the amendment fell.) June 30, 2000.

171. HR 4577. Fiscal 2001 Labor-HHS-Education Appropriations/Passage. Passage of the bill that would appropriate approximately $354.6 billion for the Labor, Health and Human Services, and Education departments and related agencies. The bill, as amended, would prohibit health insurers from using predictive genetic information to discriminate in the health care system, and prohibit insurance companies from raising or denying patients' health care coverage based on the results of genetic tests. The measure also would prohibit the Occupational Safety and Health Administration from using funds to issue or propose any standards on ergonomic protection. Passed: 52-43: R 44-10; D 8-33 (ND 4-29, SD 4-4). June 30, 2000.

Senate Votes 172, 173, 174, 175, 176, 177

	172	173	174	175	176	177
ALABAMA						
Shelby	N	Y	N	N	Y	Y
Sessions	N	Y	N	N	Y	Y
ALASKA						
Stevens	Y	Y	Y	N	N	Y
Murkowski	?	Y	Y	N	Y	Y
ARIZONA						
McCain	?	Y	Y	N	Y	Y
Kyl	N	Y	N	N	Y	Y
ARKANSAS						
Hutchinson	N	Y	Y	N	Y	Y
Lincoln	?	Y	Y	Y	N	N
CALIFORNIA						
Feinstein	Y	Y	Y	N	N	Y
Boxer	Y	Y	Y	Y	N	N
COLORADO						
Campbell	N	Y	Y	N	N	Y
Allard	N	Y	Y	N	Y	Y
CONNECTICUT						
Dodd	Y	Y	?	N	N	Y
Lieberman	Y	Y	Y	Y	N	Y
DELAWARE						
Roth	Y	Y	Y	N	N	Y
Biden	?	Y	Y	Y	N	Y
FLORIDA						
Graham	Y	Y	Y	Y	N	Y
Mack	N	Y	Y	N	Y	Y
GEORGIA						
Coverdell	N	Y	Y	N	Y	Y
Cleland	Y	Y	Y	Y	N	Y
HAWAII						
Inouye	Y	Y	Y	N	N	Y
Akaka	?	Y	Y	Y	N	Y
IDAHO						
Craig	N	Y	Y	N	N	Y
Crapo	N	Y	Y	N	N	Y
ILLINOIS						
Durbin	?	Y	Y	Y	N	N
Fitzgerald	?	Y	Y	N	Y	Y
INDIANA						
Lugar	Y	Y	Y	N	N	Y
Bayh	Y	Y	Y	Y	N	Y
IOWA						
Grassley	N	Y	Y	N	N	N
Harkin	?	Y	Y	Y	N	N
KANSAS						
Brownback	N	Y	Y	N	Y	Y
Roberts	N	Y	Y	N	Y	Y
KENTUCKY						
McConnell	N	Y	Y	N	Y	Y
Bunning	N	Y	N	N	Y	Y
LOUISIANA						
Breaux	Y	Y	Y	N	N	Y
Landrieu	Y	Y	Y	Y	N	Y
MAINE						
Snowe	Y	Y	N	Y	N	Y
Collins	Y	Y	N	Y	N	Y
MARYLAND						
Sarbanes	Y	Y	Y	Y	N	Y
Mikulski	?	Y	Y	Y	N	?
MASSACHUSETTS						
Kennedy	Y	Y	Y	Y	N	Y
Kerry	?	Y	Y	Y	N	Y
MICHIGAN						
Levin	Y	Y	Y	Y	N	Y
Abraham	Y	Y	Y	N	Y	Y
MINNESOTA						
Wellstone	Y	Y	Y	Y	N	N
Grams	N	Y	Y	N	Y	Y
MISSISSIPPI						
Cochran	N	Y	Y	N	N	Y
Lott	N	Y	Y	N	N	Y
MISSOURI						
Bond	Y	Y	Y	N	N	Y
Ashcroft	Y	Y	Y	N	Y	Y
MONTANA						
Baucus	Y	Y	Y	N	N	Y
Burns	Y	Y	Y	N	Y	Y
NEBRASKA						
Kerrey	Y	Y	Y	N	N	N
Hagel	Y	Y	Y	N	Y	Y
NEVADA						
Reid	Y	Y	Y	Y	N	N
Bryan	Y	Y	Y	Y	N	Y
NEW HAMPSHIRE						
Smith	N	Y	N	N	Y	Y
Gregg	N	Y	?	N	N	Y
NEW JERSEY						
Lautenberg	Y	Y	Y	Y	N	N
Torricelli	?	Y	Y	Y	N	Y
NEW MEXICO						
Domenici	Y	Y	Y	N	N	Y
Bingaman	Y	Y	Y	N	N	Y
NEW YORK						
Moynihan	Y	Y	Y	Y	N	Y
Schumer	Y	Y	Y	Y	N	Y
NORTH CAROLINA						
Helms	N	Y	?	N	Y	Y
Edwards	Y	Y	Y	Y	N	Y
NORTH DAKOTA						
Conrad	Y	Y	Y	N	N	Y
Dorgan	Y	Y	Y	N	N	N
OHIO						
DeWine	Y	Y	N	N	N	Y
Voinovich	?	Y	Y	N	N	Y
OKLAHOMA						
Nickles	N	Y	Y	N	Y	Y
Inhofe	?	Y	Y	N	Y	Y
OREGON						
Wyden	Y	Y	Y	Y	N	N
Smith	N	Y	Y	N	N	Y
PENNSYLVANIA						
Specter	?	Y	N	N	N	Y
Santorum	?	Y	Y	N	N	Y
RHODE ISLAND						
Reed	Y	Y	Y	Y	N	Y
Chafee, L.	Y	Y	Y	Y	N	Y
SOUTH CAROLINA						
Thurmond	Y	Y	Y	N	Y	Y
Hollings	Y	N	Y	Y	N	Y
SOUTH DAKOTA						
Daschle	Y	Y	Y	N	N	Y
Johnson	Y	Y	Y	Y	N	N
TENNESSEE						
Thompson	N	Y	N	N	N	Y
Frist	N	Y	Y	N	N	Y
TEXAS						
Gramm	N	Y	Y	N	Y	Y
Hutchison	Y	Y	Y	N	N	Y
UTAH						
Hatch	N	Y	Y	N	N	Y
Bennett	N	Y	Y	N	N	Y
VERMONT						
Leahy	?	Y	Y	Y	N	N
Jeffords	Y	Y	Y	Y	N	N
VIRGINIA						
Warner	Y	Y	Y	N	N	Y
Robb	Y	Y	Y	Y	N	Y
WASHINGTON						
Gorton	Y	Y	Y	N	N	Y
Murray	Y	Y	Y	Y	N	N
WEST VIRGINIA						
Byrd	Y	Y	Y	N	N	Y
Rockefeller	Y	Y	Y	Y	N	N
WISCONSIN						
Kohl	Y	Y	Y	Y	N	N
Feingold	Y	Y	N	Y	N	N
WYOMING						
Thomas	N	Y	Y	N	Y	Y
Enzi	N	Y	Y	N	Y	Y

Key

- Y Voted for (yea).
- # Paired for.
- + Announced for.
- N Voted against (nay).
- X Paired against.
- – Announced against.
- P Voted "present."
- C Voted "present" to avoid possible conflict of interest.
- ? Did not vote or otherwise make a position known.

•

Democrats **Republicans**
Independents

ND Northern Democrats SD Southern Democrats

Southern states - Ala., Ark., Fla., Ga., Ky., La., Miss., N.C., Okla., S.C., Tenn., Texas, Va.

172. Creedon Nomination/Confirmation. Confirmation of President Clinton's nomination of Madelyn R. Creedon, of Indiana, to be deputy administrator for defense programs at the National Nuclear Security Administration. Confirmed 54-30: R 18-30; D 36-0 (ND 29-0, SD 7-0). A "yea" was a vote in support of the president's position. July 10, 2000.

173. HR 8. Estate Tax Repeal/Cloture. Motion to invoke cloture (thus limiting debate) on the motion to proceed to the bill that would amend the Internal Revenue Code of 1986 to reduce and ultimately repeal the estate and gift tax by 2010. Motion agreed to 99-1: R 55-0; D 44-1 (ND 37-0, SD 7-1). Three-fifths of the total Senate (60) is required to invoke cloture. July 11, 2000.

174. S 2549. Fiscal 2001 Defense Authorization/Computer Exports. Bennett, R-Utah, amendment that would shorten the period for Congress to review changes on regulations for the export of high performance computers from 180 days to 60 days. Adopted 86-11: R 43-10; D 43-1 (ND 35-1, SD 8-0). July 12, 2000.

175. HR 4578. Fiscal 2001 Interior Appropriations/Grazing Permits. Durbin, D-Ill., amendment that would strike language in the bill that would require the Bureau of Land Management to renew expiring grazing permits under the same terms and conditions as the old permit, before environmental reviews are complete. Rejected 38-62: R 4-51; D 34-11 (ND 27-10, SD 7-1). A "yea" was a vote in support of the president's position. July 12, 2000.

176. HR 4578. Fiscal 2001 Interior Appropriations/Indian Health Services Funding. Inhofe, R-Okla., amendment that would reallocate $7.37 million designated for the National Endowment for the Arts (NEA) to funding for the Indian Health Services for diabetes treatment, prevention and research. Rejected 27-73: R 27-28; D 0-45 (ND 0-37, SD 0-8). July 12, 2000.

177. S 2549. Fiscal 2001 Defense Authorization/Submarine Missile Program. Allard, R-Colo., motion to table (kill) the Feingold, D-Wis., amendment that would terminate further production under the Trident II (D-5) submarine-launched missile program. The amendment would reduce funding in the bill for fiscal 2001 by $462.7 million. Motion agreed to 81-18: R 53-2; D 28-16 (ND 21-15, SD 7-1). July 13, 2000.

	178	179	180	181	182	183
ALABAMA						
Shelby	Y	Y	N	Y	N	Y
Sessions	Y	Y	N	Y	N	Y
ALASKA						
Stevens	Y	Y	N	Y	N	Y
Murkowski	Y	Y	N	Y	N	Y
ARIZONA						
McCain	Y	Y	N	Y	N	Y
Kyl	Y	Y	N	Y	N	Y
ARKANSAS						
Hutchinson	Y	Y	N	Y	N	N
Lincoln	N	Y	Y	Y	Y	N
CALIFORNIA						
Feinstein	N	Y	Y	Y	Y	N
Boxer	N	N	Y	Y	Y	N
COLORADO						
Campbell	Y	Y	N	Y	N	Y
Allard	Y	Y	N	Y	N	Y
CONNECTICUT						
Dodd	N	Y	?	?	?	?
Lieberman	N	Y	Y	Y	Y	N
DELAWARE						
Roth	Y	Y	N	Y	N	Y
Biden	N	Y	Y	Y	Y	N
FLORIDA						
Graham	N	Y	Y	Y	Y	N
Mack	Y	Y	N	Y	?	Y
GEORGIA						
Coverdell	Y	Y	N	Y	N	Y
Cleland	N	Y	Y	Y	Y	N
HAWAII						
Inouye	N	Y	Y	Y	Y	N
Akaka	N	Y	Y	Y	Y	N
IDAHO						
Craig	Y	Y	N	Y	N	Y
Crapo	Y	Y	N	Y	N	Y
ILLINOIS						
Durbin	N	Y	Y	Y	Y	N
Fitzgerald	Y	Y	N	Y	N	Y
INDIANA						
Lugar	Y	Y	N	Y	N	Y
Bayh	N	Y	Y	Y	Y	N
IOWA						
Grassley	Y	Y	N	Y	N	Y
Harkin	N	Y	Y	Y	Y	N
KANSAS						
Brownback	Y	Y	N	Y	N	Y
Roberts	Y	Y	N	Y	N	N
KENTUCKY						
McConnell	Y	Y	N	Y	N	Y
Bunning	Y	Y	N	Y	N	Y
LOUISIANA						
Breaux	N	Y	Y	Y	Y	N
Landrieu	N	Y	Y	Y	Y	N
MAINE						
Snowe	N	Y	N	Y	N	Y
Collins	N	Y	N	Y	N	N
MARYLAND						
Sarbanes	N	Y	Y	Y	Y	N
Mikulski	N	Y	Y	Y	Y	N
MASSACHUSETTS						
Kennedy	N	Y	Y	Y	Y	N
Kerry	N	Y	Y	Y	Y	N
MICHIGAN						
Levin	N	Y	Y	Y	Y	N
Abraham	Y	Y	N	Y	N	Y
MINNESOTA						
Wellstone	N	N	N	Y	Y	N
Grams	Y	Y	N	Y	N	Y
MISSISSIPPI						
Cochran	Y	Y	N	Y	N	N
Lott	Y	Y	N	Y	N	Y
MISSOURI						
Bond	Y	Y	N	Y	N	N
Ashcroft	Y	Y	N	Y	N	Y
MONTANA						
Baucus	N	Y	Y	Y	Y	N
Burns	Y	Y	N	Y	N	N
NEBRASKA						
Kerrey	N	Y	Y	Y	Y	N
Hagel	Y	Y	N	Y	N	N
NEVADA						
Reid	N	Y	Y	Y	Y	N
Bryan	N	Y	Y	Y	Y	N
NEW HAMPSHIRE						
Smith	Y	Y	N	Y	N	Y
Gregg	Y	Y	N	Y	N	Y
NEW JERSEY						
Lautenberg	N	Y	Y	Y	Y	N
Torricelli	N	Y	Y	Y	Y	N
NEW MEXICO						
Domenici	Y	Y	N	Y	N	N
Bingaman	N	Y	Y	Y	Y	N
NEW YORK						
Moynihan	N	Y	Y	Y	Y	N
Schumer	N	Y	Y	Y	Y	N
NORTH CAROLINA						
Helms	Y	Y	N	Y	N	Y
Edwards	N	Y	Y	Y	Y	N
NORTH DAKOTA						
Conrad	N	Y	Y	Y	Y	N
Dorgan	N	Y	Y	Y	Y	N
OHIO						
DeWine	Y	Y	N	Y	N	N
Voinovich	Y	Y	N	N	N	N
OKLAHOMA						
Nickles	Y	Y	N	Y	N	Y
Inhofe	Y	Y	N	Y	N	Y
OREGON						
Wyden	N	Y	Y	Y	Y	N
Smith	Y	Y	N	Y	N	Y
PENNSYLVANIA						
Specter	Y	Y	Y	Y	Y	Y
Santorum	Y	Y	N	Y	N	Y
RHODE ISLAND						
Reed	N	Y	Y	Y	Y	N
Chafee, L.	Y	Y	Y	Y	Y	N
SOUTH CAROLINA						
Thurmond	Y	Y	N	Y	N	Y
Hollings	N	Y	Y	Y	Y	N
SOUTH DAKOTA						
Daschle	N	Y	Y	Y	Y	N
Johnson	N	Y	Y	Y	Y	N
TENNESSEE						
Thompson	Y	Y	N	Y	N	Y
Frist	Y	Y	N	Y	N	Y
TEXAS						
Gramm	Y	Y	N	Y	N	Y
Hutchison	Y	Y	N	Y	N	Y
UTAH						
Hatch	Y	Y	N	Y	N	Y
Bennett	Y	Y	N	Y	N	Y
VERMONT						
Leahy	N	Y	Y	Y	Y	N
Jeffords	N	Y	Y	Y	N	N
VIRGINIA						
Warner	Y	Y	N	Y	N	N
Robb	N	Y	Y	Y	Y	N
WASHINGTON						
Gorton	Y	Y	N	Y	N	Y
Murray	N	Y	Y	Y	Y	N
WEST VIRGINIA						
Byrd	N	Y	Y	Y	Y	N
Rockefeller	N	Y	Y	Y	Y	N
WISCONSIN						
Kohl	N	Y	Y	Y	Y	N
Feingold	N	N	Y	Y	Y	N
WYOMING						
Thomas	Y	Y	N	Y	N	N
Enzi	Y	Y	N	Y	N	N

ND Northern Democrats SD Southern Democrats

Southern states - Ala., Ark., Fla., Ga., Ky., La., Miss., N.C., Okla., S.C., Tenn., Texas, Va.

Key

- Y Voted for (yea).
- # Paired for.
- + Announced for.
- N Voted against (nay).
- X Paired against.
- – Announced against.
- P Voted "present."
- C Voted "present" to avoid possible conflict of interest.
- ? Did not vote or otherwise make a position known.

Democrats ***Republicans*** *Independents*

178. S 2549. Fiscal 2001 Defense Authorization/Missile Defense System Testing. Cochran, R-Miss., motion to table (kill) the Durbin, D-Ill., amendment that would require the Pentagon to test the national missile defense system against reasonable decoys and countermeasures that the system could encounter in a launch, and establish an independent panel to review the testing. Motion agreed to 52-48: R 52-3; D 0-45 (ND 0-37, SD 0-8). July 13, 2000.

179. HR 4205. Fiscal 2001 Defense Authorization/Passage. Passage of the bill to authorize $309.8 billion for defense-related activities in fiscal 2001. The bill contains language that would shorten the period for Congress to review changes on regulations for the export of high performance computers from 180 days to 60 days, and broaden the categories covered by hate crimes to include gender, sexual orientation and disability. It also would require a nuclear overview study to be completed by December 2001, at the same time as the Defense Department's quadrennial review, before the president could waive current restrictions on dismantling strategic nuclear weapons systems. Passed 97-3: R 55-0; D 42-3 (ND 34-3, SD 8-0). (Before passage, the Senate struck all after the enacting clause and inserted the text of S 2549 as amended.) July 13, 2000.

180. HR 8. Estate Tax Repeal/Democratic Substitute. Moynihan, D-N.Y., substitute amendment that would increase the general estate tax exemption to $2 million, and the exemption for a family-owned business to $3.375 million, by 2009. Rejected 46-53: R 3-52; D 43-1 (ND 35-1, SD 8-0). July 13, 2000.

181. HR 8. Estate Tax Repeal/Research Tax Credit. Hatch, R-Utah, amendment that would provide a permanent extension of the research and experimentation tax credit. Adopted 98-1: R 54-1; D 44-0 (ND 36-0, SD 8-0). July 13, 2000.

182. HR 8. Estate Tax Repeal/College Tuition Tax Credit. Schumer, D-N.Y., amendment that would replace the language of the bill with the text of the Democratic substitute amendment, which would increase the general estate tax exemption to $2 million, and the exemption for a family-owned business to $3.375 million, by 2009. It would also allow taxpayers with adjusted gross incomes of $62,540 ($104,050 for joint filers) to deduct up to $12,000 per year for college tuition. Rejected 46-52: R 2-52; D 44-0 (ND 36-0, SD 8-0). July 13, 2000.

183. HR 8. Estate Tax Repeal/Gas Tax Suspension. Abraham, R-Mich., motion to waive the Budget Act with respect to the Reid, D-Nev., point of order against the Abraham amendment. The Abraham amendment would suspend the 18.4 cents-per-gallon federal gas tax for 150 days. Motion rejected 40-59: R 40-15; D 0-44 (ND 0-36, SD 0-8). A three-fifths majority vote (60) of the total Senate is required to waive the Budget Act. (Subsequently, the chair upheld the point of order, and the amendment fell.) July 13, 2000.

	184	185	186	187	188
ALABAMA					
Shelby	N	Y	N	N	Y
Sessions	N	Y	N	N	Y
ALASKA					
Stevens	N	Y	N	N	Y
Murkowski	N	Y	N	N	Y
ARIZONA					
McCain	N	Y	N	N	Y
Kyl	N	Y	N	N	Y
ARKANSAS					
Hutchinson	N	Y	N	N	Y
Lincoln	Y	Y	Y	Y	N
CALIFORNIA					
Feinstein	Y	Y	Y	Y	Y
Boxer	Y	Y	Y	Y	N
COLORADO					
Campbell	N	Y	N	N	Y
Allard	N	Y	N	N	Y
CONNECTICUT					
Dodd	Y	Y	Y	Y	N
Lieberman	Y	Y	Y	Y	N
DELAWARE					
Roth	N	Y	N	N	Y
Biden	Y	Y	Y	Y	N
FLORIDA					
Graham	Y	N	Y	Y	N
Mack	N	Y	N	N	Y
GEORGIA					
Coverdell	N	Y	N	N	Y
Cleland	Y	Y	N	Y	N
HAWAII					
Inouye	Y	Y	Y	Y	N
Akaka	Y	Y	Y	Y	N
IDAHO					
Craig	N	Y	N	N	Y
Crapo	N	Y	N	N	Y
ILLINOIS					
Durbin	Y	Y	Y	Y	N
Fitzgerald	N	Y	N	N	Y
INDIANA					
Lugar	N	Y	N	N	Y
Bayh	Y	Y	Y	Y	N
IOWA					
Grassley	N	Y	N	N	Y
Harkin	Y	Y	Y	Y	N
KANSAS					
Brownback	N	Y	N	N	Y
Roberts	N	Y	N	N	Y
KENTUCKY					
McConnell	N	Y	N	N	Y
Bunning	N	Y	N	N	Y
LOUISIANA					
Breaux	Y	Y	Y	Y	N
Landrieu	Y	Y	Y	Y	N
MAINE					
Snowe	N	Y	Y	N	Y
Collins	N	Y	N	N	Y
MARYLAND					
Sarbanes	Y	Y	Y	Y	N
Mikulski	Y	Y	Y	Y	N
MASSACHUSETTS					
Kennedy	Y	Y	Y	Y	N
Kerry	Y	Y	Y	Y	N
MICHIGAN					
Levin	Y	Y	Y	Y	N
Abraham	N	Y	N	N	Y
MINNESOTA					
Wellstone	Y	Y	Y	Y	N
Grams	N	Y	N	N	Y
MISSISSIPPI					
Cochran	N	Y	N	N	Y
Lott	N	Y	N	N	Y
MISSOURI					
Bond	N	Y	N	N	Y
Ashcroft	N	Y	N	N	Y
MONTANA					
Baucus	Y	Y	Y	Y	N
Burns	N	Y	N	N	Y
NEBRASKA					
Kerrey	Y	Y	Y	Y	N
Hagel	N	Y	N	N	Y
NEVADA					
Reid	Y	Y	Y	Y	N
Bryan	Y	Y	Y	Y	N
NEW HAMPSHIRE					
Smith	N	Y	N	N	Y
Gregg	N	Y	N	N	Y
NEW JERSEY					
Lautenberg	Y	Y	Y	Y	N
Torricelli	Y	Y	?	?	?
NEW MEXICO					
Domenici	N	Y	N	N	Y
Bingaman	Y	Y	Y	Y	N
NEW YORK					
Moynihan	Y	Y	Y	Y	N
Schumer	Y	Y	Y	Y	N
NORTH CAROLINA					
Helms	N	Y	N	N	Y
Edwards	Y	Y	Y	Y	N
NORTH DAKOTA					
Conrad	Y	Y	Y	Y	Y
Dorgan	Y	Y	Y	Y	Y
OHIO					
DeWine	N	Y	N	N	Y
Voinovich	N	N	N	N	N
OKLAHOMA					
Nickles	N	Y	N	N	Y
Inhofe	N	Y	N	N	Y
OREGON					
Wyden	Y	Y	Y	Y	N
Smith	N	Y	N	N	Y
PENNSYLVANIA					
Specter	Y	Y	N	N	Y
Santorum	N	Y	N	N	Y
RHODE ISLAND					
Reed	Y	Y	Y	Y	N
Chafee, L.	Y	Y	Y	Y	Y
SOUTH CAROLINA					
Thurmond	N	Y	N	N	Y
Hollings	Y	N	Y	Y	N
SOUTH DAKOTA					
Daschle	Y	Y	Y	Y	N
Johnson	Y	Y	Y	Y	Y
TENNESSEE					
Thompson	N	Y	N	N	Y
Frist	N	Y	N	N	Y
TEXAS					
Gramm	N	Y	N	N	Y
Hutchison	N	Y	N	N	Y
UTAH					
Hatch	N	Y	N	N	Y
Bennett	N	Y	N	N	Y
VERMONT					
Leahy	Y	Y	Y	Y	N
Jeffords	N	Y	Y	N	Y
VIRGINIA					
Warner	N	Y	N	N	Y
Robb	Y	Y	Y	Y	N
WASHINGTON					
Gorton	N	Y	N	N	Y
Murray	Y	Y	Y	Y	N
WEST VIRGINIA					
Byrd	Y	Y	Y	N	N
Rockefeller	Y	Y	Y	Y	N
WISCONSIN					
Kohl	Y	Y	Y	Y	N
Feingold	Y	Y	Y	Y	N
WYOMING					
Thomas	N	Y	N	N	Y
Enzi	N	Y	N	N	Y

ND Northern Democrats SD Southern Democrats

Southern states - Ala., Ark., Fla., Ga., Ky., La., Miss., N.C., Okla., S.C., Tenn., Texas, Va.

Key

- Y Voted for (yea).
- \# Paired for.
- \+ Announced for.
- N Voted against (nay).
- X Paired against.
- – Announced against.
- P Voted "present."
- C Voted "present" to avoid possible conflict of interest.
- ? Did not vote or otherwise make a position known.

•

Democrats ***Republicans***
Independents

184. HR 8. Estate Tax Repeal/Education Funding. Bingaman, D-N.M., motion to waive the Budget Act with respect to the Hutchinson, R-Ark., point of order against the Bingaman amendment. The Bingaman amendment would replace the language of the bill with the text of the Democratic substitute amendment, which would increase the general estate tax exemption to $2 million, and the exemption for a family-owned business to $3.375 million, by 2009. Projected savings would be used to fund various education programs, including $1.3 billion for repairs for schools in high-needs areas, and $2.2 billion for the recruitment, mentoring and professional development of qualified teachers. Motion rejected 47-53: R 2-53; D 45-0 (ND 37-0, SD 8-0). A three-fifths majority vote (60) of the total Senate is required to waive the Budget Act. (Subsequently, the chair upheld the point of order and the amendment fell.) July 13, 2000.

185. HR 8. Estate Tax Repeal/Telephone Tax Repeal. Roth, R-Del., amendment that would repeal the 3 percent excise tax on telecommunications services. Adopted 97-3: R 54-1; D 43-2 (ND 37-0, SD 6-2). July 13, 2000.

186. HR 8. Estate Tax Repeal/Medicare Prescription Drug Benefits. Graham, D-Fla., motion to waive the Budget Act with respect to the Domenici, R-N.M., point of order against the Graham amendment. The Graham amendment would replace the language of the bill with the text of the Democratic substitute amendment, which would increase the general estate tax exemption to $2 million, and the exemption for a family-owned business to $3.375 million, by 2009. The first $40 billion of the additional projected savings would be reserved for a Medicare prescription drug benefit program. Motion rejected 46-53: R 3-52; D 43-1 (ND 36-0, SD 7-1). A three-fifths majority vote (60) of the total Senate is required to waive the Budget Act. (Subsequently, the chair upheld the point of order and the amendment fell.) July 13, 2000.

187. HR 8. Estate Tax Repeal/KidSave Accounts. Baucus, D-Mont., motion to waive the Budget Act with respect to the Roth, R-Del., point of order against the Baucus amendment. The Baucus amendment would replace the language of the bill with the text of the Democratic substitute amendment, which would increase the general estate tax exemption to $2 million, and the exemption for a family-owned business to $3.375 million, by 2009. It would also create a Social Security KidSave account, to which the Treasury Department would set aside $1,000 for every newborn, and provide tax credits to small businesses to establish and maintain qualified pension plans. Motion rejected 44-55: R 1-54; D 43-1 (ND 35-1, SD 8-0). A three-fifths majority vote (60) of the total Senate is required to waive the Budget Act. (Subsequently, the chair upheld the point of order and the amendment fell.) July 13, 2000.

188. HR 8. Estate Tax Repeal/Taxable Social Security Benefits. Grams, R-Minn., amendment that would reduce the percentage of Social Security benefits that are taxable from 85 percent to 50 percent, effective after Dec. 31, 2000. Adopted 58-41: R 54-1; D 4-40 (ND 4-32, SD 0-8). July 13, 2000.

Senate Votes 189, 190, 191, 192, 193, 194, 195

	189	190	191	192	193	194	195
ALABAMA							
Shelby	N	Y	N	N	N	N	N
Sessions	N	Y	N	N	N	N	N
ALASKA							
Stevens	N	Y	N	N	N	N	N
Murkowski	N	Y	N	N	N	N	N
ARIZONA							
McCain	N	Y	N	N	N	N	Y
Kyl	N	N	N	N	N	N	N
ARKANSAS							
Hutchinson	N	Y	N	?	?	?	?
Lincoln	Y	N	Y	Y	Y	N	Y
CALIFORNIA							
Feinstein	Y	Y	Y	Y	Y	N	Y
Boxer	Y	N	Y	Y	Y	N	Y
COLORADO							
Campbell	N	Y	N	N	N	N	N
Allard	N	Y	N	N	N	N	N
CONNECTICUT							
Dodd	+	–	+	+	+	N	Y
Lieberman	Y	Y	Y	Y	Y	N	Y
DELAWARE							
Roth	N	N	N	N	N	Y	N
Biden	Y	N	Y	Y	Y	Y	Y
FLORIDA							
Graham	Y	N	Y	Y	Y	N	N
Mack	N	Y	N	N	N	N	N
GEORGIA							
Coverdell	N	Y	N	N	N	N	N
Cleland	Y	Y	Y	Y	Y	N	N
HAWAII							
Inouye	Y	N	Y	Y	Y	N	Y
Akaka	Y	N	Y	Y	Y	N	Y
IDAHO							
Craig	N	Y	N	N	N	N	N
Crapo	N	Y	N	N	N	N	N
ILLINOIS							
Durbin	Y	N	Y	Y	Y	N	Y
Fitzgerald	N	Y	N	N	N	Y	N
INDIANA							
Lugar	N	Y	N	N	N	N	N
Bayh	Y	N	Y	Y	Y	N	Y
IOWA							
Grassley	N	Y	N	N	N	N	N
Harkin	Y	N	Y	Y	Y	N	Y
KANSAS							
Brownback	N	Y	N	N	N	N	N
Roberts	N	Y	N	N	N	N	N
KENTUCKY							
McConnell	N	Y	N	N	N	N	N
Bunning	N	Y	N	N	N	N	N
LOUISIANA							
Breaux	Y	Y	N	Y	Y	Y	Y
Landrieu	Y	Y	Y	Y	Y	N	Y
MAINE							
Snowe	N	Y	N	N	N	Y	N
Collins	N	Y	N	N	N	Y	N
MARYLAND							
Sarbanes	Y	N	Y	Y	Y	N	Y
Mikulski	Y	N	Y	Y	Y	N	Y
MASSACHUSETTS							
Kennedy	Y	N	Y	Y	Y	N	Y
Kerry	Y	Y	?	Y	Y	N	Y
MICHIGAN							
Levin	Y	N	Y	Y	Y	N	Y
Abraham	N	Y	N	N	N	Y	N
MINNESOTA							
Wellstone	Y	N	Y	Y	Y	N	Y
Grams	N	Y	N	N	N	N	N
MISSISSIPPI							
Cochran	N	Y	N	N	N	N	N
Lott	N	Y	N	N	N	N	N
MISSOURI							
Bond	N	Y	N	N	N	N	N
Ashcroft	N	Y	N	N	N	Y	N
MONTANA							
Baucus	Y	N	Y	Y	Y	N	Y
Burns	N	Y	N	N	N	N	N
NEBRASKA							
Kerrey	Y	N	N	N	Y	N	Y
Hagel	N	Y	N	N	N	N	N
NEVADA							
Reid	Y	N	Y	Y	Y	N	Y
Bryan	Y	N	Y	Y	Y	N	Y
NEW HAMPSHIRE							
Smith	N	Y	N	N	N	N	N
Gregg	N	Y	N	N	N	N	N
NEW JERSEY							
Lautenberg	Y	N	Y	Y	Y	N	Y
Torricelli	N	N	Y	Y	Y	Y	Y
NEW MEXICO							
Domenici	?	N	N	N	N	N	N
Bingaman	Y	N	Y	Y	Y	N	N
NEW YORK							
Moynihan	Y	N	Y	Y	Y	N	Y
Schumer	Y	N	Y	Y	Y	N	Y
NORTH CAROLINA							
Helms	N	Y	N	N	N	N	N
Edwards	Y	N	Y	Y	Y	N	Y
NORTH DAKOTA							
Conrad	Y	Y	Y	Y	Y	N	Y
Dorgan	Y	N	Y	Y	Y	N	Y
OHIO							
DeWine	N	Y	N	N	N	Y	N
Voinovich	N	N	N	N	N	N	N
OKLAHOMA							
Nickles	N	N	N	N	N	N	N
Inhofe	N	Y	N	N	N	N	N
OREGON							
Wyden	Y	N	Y	Y	Y	N	Y
Smith	N	Y	N	N	N	Y	N
PENNSYLVANIA							
Specter	Y	?	Y	N	Y	Y	N
Santorum	N	Y	N	N	N	Y	N
RHODE ISLAND							
Reed	Y	N	Y	Y	Y	N	Y
Chafee, L.	Y	N	Y	N	Y	N	Y
SOUTH CAROLINA							
Thurmond	N	Y	N	N	N	N	N
Hollings	Y	N	N	Y	Y	N	Y
SOUTH DAKOTA							
Daschle	+	–	+	+	+	–	+
Johnson	Y	Y	Y	Y	Y	N	Y
TENNESSEE							
Thompson	N	Y	N	N	N	N	N
Frist	N	Y	N	N	N	N	Y
TEXAS							
Gramm	N	N	N	N	N	N	N
Hutchison	N	Y	N	N	N	N	N
UTAH							
Hatch	N	Y	N	N	N	N	N
Bennett	N	Y	N	N	N	N	N
VERMONT							
Leahy	Y	N	Y	Y	Y	N	Y
Jeffords	Y	Y	Y	?	Y	N	N
VIRGINIA							
Warner	N	Y	N	N	N	N	N
Robb	Y	N	Y	Y	Y	N	Y
WASHINGTON							
Gorton	N	Y	N	N	N	Y	N
Murray	Y	N	Y	Y	Y	N	Y
WEST VIRGINIA							
Byrd	Y	Y	N	Y	Y	N	Y
Rockefeller	Y	N	Y	Y	Y	N	Y
WISCONSIN							
Kohl	Y	Y	Y	Y	Y	N	Y
Feingold	Y	N	Y	Y	Y	N	Y
WYOMING							
Thomas	N	Y	N	N	N	N	N
Enzi	N	Y	N	N	N	N	N

Key

- Y Voted for (yea).
- # Paired for.
- \+ Announced for.
- N Voted against (nay).
- X Paired against.
- – Announced against.
- P Voted "present."
- C Voted "present" to avoid possible conflict of interest.
- ? Did not vote or otherwise make a position known.

Democrats ***Republicans*** *Independents*

ND Northern Democrats SD Southern Democrats

Southern states - Ala., Ark., Fla., Ga., Ky., La., Miss., N.C., Okla., S.C., Tenn., Texas, Va.

189. HR 8. Estate Tax Repeal/Affordable Housing. Kerry, D-Mass., amendment that would replace the language of the bill with the text of the Democratic substitute and establish a National Affordable Housing Trust Fund for the production of affordable housing. Rejected 45-52: R 3-51; D 42-1 (ND 34-1, SD 8-0). July 14, 2000.

190. HR 8. Estate Tax Repeal/Economic Incentives. Santorum, R-Pa., motion to waive the Budget Act with respect to the Robb, D-Va., point of order against the Santorum amendment. The Santorum amendment would offer tax breaks, regulatory relief, and other incentives to attract economic development to inner cities and rural areas. Motion rejected 57-40: R 47-7; D 10-33 (ND 7-28, SD 3-5). A three-fifths majority vote (60) of the total Senate is required to waive the Budget Act. (Subsequently, the chair upheld the point of order and the amendment fell.) July 14, 2000.

191. HR 8. Estate Tax Repeal/Dependent Care Tax Credit. Wellstone, D-Minn., motion to waive the Budget Act with respect to the Domenici, R-N.M., point of order against the Dodd, D-Conn., amendment. The Dodd amendment would replace the language of the bill with the text of the Democratic substitute. It would also increase the dependent care tax credit for families earning under $60,000, make it refundable, and allow stay-at-home parents with children under age 1 to claim a portion of the credit. Motion rejected 41-56: R 3-52; D 38-4 (ND 32-2, SD 6-2). A three-fifths majority vote (60) of the total Senate is required to waive the Budget Act. (Subsequently, the chair upheld the point of order and the amendment fell.) July 14, 2000.

192. HR 8. Estate Tax Repeal/Social Security Benefits. Harkin, D-Iowa, amendment that would replace the language of the bill with the text of the Democratic substitute. It would also increase the Social Security survivors' benefit to at least 75 percent of a couple's combined benefits, allow workers to take up to five years off to raise a child or care for a dependent relative without affecting future Social Security benefits, and dedicate interest savings from paying off the national debt to Social Security. Rejected 42-54: R 0-53; D 42-1 (ND 34-1, SD 8-0). July 14, 2000.

193. HR 8. Estate Tax Repeal/Long-Term Care. Bayh, D-Ind., amendment would replace the language of the bill with the text of the Democratic substitute. It also would allow a $3,000 tax credit to taxpayers needing long-term care for themselves, their spouses or their dependents; it would make health insurance for the self-employed 100 percent deductible in 2001. Rejected 46-51: R 3-51; D 43-0 (ND 35-0, SD 8-0). July 14, 2000.

194. HR 8. Estate Tax Repeal/Education Savings Accounts. Lott, R-Miss., motion to waive the Budget Act with respect to the Reid, D-Nev., point of order against the Lott amendment. The Lott amendment would increase the annual contribution to education savings accounts to $2,000; provide a college tuition tax deduction of up to $12,000; allow a tax credit of up to $1,500 for student loan interest; provide 100 percent deductibility for long-term care insurance expenses; make medical savings accounts permanent; expand the dependent care tax credit; and create a credit for employer provided child care facilities. Motion rejected 14-84: R 11-43; D 3-41 (ND 2-34, SD 1-7). A three-fifths majority vote (60) of the total Senate is required to waive the Budget Act. (Subsequently, the chair upheld the point of order and the amendment fell.) July 14, 2000.

195. HR 8. Estate Tax Repeal/Tax Repeal Limits. Feingold, D-Wis., amendment that would limit the repeal of the estate tax to those estates up to $100 million. Rejected 44-54: R 3-51; D 41-3 (ND 35-1, SD 6-2). July 14, 2000.

	196	197	198	199	200	201
ALABAMA						
Shelby	Y	Y	N	Y	N	N
Sessions	Y	Y	N	Y	N	N
ALASKA						
Stevens	Y	Y	N	Y	N	N
Murkowski	Y	Y	N	Y	N	N
ARIZONA						
McCain	Y	Y	N	Y	N	N
Kyl	Y	Y	N	Y	N	N
ARKANSAS						
Hutchinson	?	?	?	?	?	?
Lincoln	N	Y	Y	N	Y	Y
CALIFORNIA						
Feinstein	N	Y	Y	N	Y	Y
Boxer	N	N	Y	N	Y	Y
COLORADO						
Campbell	Y	Y	N	Y	N	N
Allard	Y	Y	N	Y	N	N
CONNECTICUT						
Dodd	N	N	Y	N	Y	Y
Lieberman	N	N	Y	N	Y	Y
DELAWARE						
Roth	Y	Y	N	Y	N	N
Biden	N	N	Y	N	Y	N
FLORIDA						
Graham	Y	N	Y	N	Y	Y
Mack	Y	Y	N	Y	N	N
GEORGIA						
Coverdell	Y	Y	?	?	?	?
Cleland	N	Y	Y	N	Y	Y
HAWAII						
Inouye	N	N	Y	N	Y	Y
Akaka	N	N	Y	N	Y	Y
IDAHO						
Craig	Y	Y	N	Y	N	N
Crapo	Y	Y	N	Y	N	N
ILLINOIS						
Durbin	N	N	Y	N	Y	Y
Fitzgerald	Y	Y	N	Y	N	N
INDIANA						
Lugar	Y	Y	N	Y	N	N
Bayh	N	N	Y	N	Y	N

	196	197	198	199	200	201
IOWA						
Grassley	Y	Y	N	Y	N	N
Harkin	N	N	Y	N	Y	Y
KANSAS						
Brownback	Y	Y	N	Y	N	N
Roberts	Y	Y	N	Y	N	N
KENTUCKY						
McConnell	Y	Y	N	Y	N	N
Bunning	Y	Y	N	Y	N	N
LOUISIANA						
Breaux	N	Y	Y	N	Y	Y
Landrieu	N	Y	N	N	Y	Y
MAINE						
Snowe	Y	Y	N	Y	N	N
Collins	Y	Y	N	Y	N	N
MARYLAND						
Sarbanes	N	N	Y	N	Y	Y
Mikulski	N	N	Y	N	Y	Y
MASSACHUSETTS						
Kennedy	N	N	Y	N	Y	Y
Kerry	N	N	Y	N	Y	Y
MICHIGAN						
Levin	N	N	Y	N	Y	Y
Abraham	Y	Y	N	Y	N	N
MINNESOTA						
Wellstone	N	N	Y	N	Y	Y
Grams	Y	Y	N	Y	N	N
MISSISSIPPI						
Cochran	Y	Y	N	Y	N	N
Lott	Y	Y	N	Y	N	N
MISSOURI						
Bond	Y	Y	N	Y	N	N
Ashcroft	Y	Y	N	Y	N	N
MONTANA						
Baucus	N	N	Y	N	Y	N
Burns	Y	Y	N	Y	N	N
NEBRASKA						
Kerrey	N	N	Y	N	Y	Y
Hagel	Y	Y	N	Y	N	N
NEVADA						
Reid	N	N	Y	N	Y	Y
Bryan	N	N	Y	N	Y	N

	196	197	198	199	200	201
NEW HAMPSHIRE						
Smith	Y	Y	N	Y	N	N
Gregg	Y	Y	N	Y	N	N
NEW JERSEY						
Lautenberg	N	N	Y	N	Y	Y
Torricelli	N	Y	Y	N	Y	Y
NEW MEXICO						
Domenici	Y	Y	N	Y	N	N
Bingaman	N	N	Y	N	Y	N
NEW YORK						
Moynihan	N	N	Y	N	Y	Y
Schumer	N	N	Y	N	Y	Y
NORTH CAROLINA						
Helms	Y	Y	N	Y	N	N
Edwards	N	N	Y	N	Y	Y
NORTH DAKOTA						
Conrad	N	N	Y	N	Y	N
Dorgan	N	N	Y	N	Y	Y
OHIO						
DeWine	Y	Y	N	Y	N	N
Voinovich	Y	N	Y	N	N	N
OKLAHOMA						
Nickles	Y	Y	N	Y	N	N
Inhofe	Y	Y	–	+	–	–
OREGON						
Wyden	N	Y	Y	N	Y	Y
Smith	Y	Y	N	Y	N	N
PENNSYLVANIA						
Specter	Y	N	N	Y	N	N
Santorum	Y	Y	N	Y	N	N
RHODE ISLAND						
Reed	N	N	Y	N	Y	Y
Chafee, L.	N	N	Y	N	Y	Y
SOUTH CAROLINA						
Thurmond	Y	Y	N	Y	N	N
Hollings	N	N	Y	N	Y	Y
SOUTH DAKOTA						
Daschle	–	–	Y	N	Y	Y
Johnson	N	N	Y	N	Y	Y
TENNESSEE						
Thompson	Y	Y	N	Y	N	N
Frist	Y	Y	N	Y	N	N

Key

- Y Voted for (yea).
- # Paired for.
- + Announced for.
- N Voted against (nay).
- X Paired against.
- – Announced against.
- P Voted "present."
- C Voted "present" to avoid possible conflict of interest.
- ? Did not vote or otherwise make a position known.

Democrats • ***Republicans***
Independents

	196	197	198	199	200	201
TEXAS						
Gramm	Y	Y	N	Y	N	N
Hutchison	Y	Y	?	?	?	?
UTAH						
Hatch	Y	Y	N	Y	N	N
Bennett	Y	Y	N	Y	N	N
VERMONT						
Leahy	N	N	Y	N	Y	Y
Jeffords	N	N	N	Y	N	N
VIRGINIA						
Warner	Y	Y	?	?	N	N
Robb	N	Y	Y	N	Y	Y
WASHINGTON						
Gorton	Y	Y	N	Y	N	N
Murray	N	Y	Y	N	Y	Y
WEST VIRGINIA						
Byrd	N	N	Y	N	Y	Y
Rockefeller	N	N	+	N	Y	Y
WISCONSIN						
Kohl	N	N	Y	N	Y	Y
Feingold	N	N	Y	N	Y	Y
WYOMING						
Thomas	Y	Y	N	Y	N	N
Enzi	Y	Y	N	Y	N	N

ND Northern Democrats SD Southern Democrats

Southern states - Ala., Ark., Fla., Ga., Ky., La., Miss., N.C., Okla., S.C., Tenn., Texas, Va.

196. HR 8. Estate Tax Repeal/Motion to Commit. Lott, R-Miss., motion to commit the bill to the Senate Finance Committee with instructions to report it back with the text of the House-passed version. Motion agreed to 53-45: R 52-2; D 1-43 (ND 0-36, SD 1-7). July 14, 2000.

197. HR 8. Estate Tax Repeal/Passage. Passage of the bill that would amend the Internal Revenue Code to reduce and ultimately repeal the estate and gift tax by 2010. Passed (thus cleared for the president) 59-39: R 50-4; D 9-35 (ND 4-32, SD 5-3). July 14, 2000. A "nay" was a vote in support of the president's position.

198. HR 4810. Alleviate 'Marriage Penalty' Tax/Motion to Commit. Feingold, D-Wis., motion to commit the bill to the Senate Finance Committee with instructions to add legislation that would extend the solvency of Medicare and Social Security. Motion rejected 45-49: R 2-48; D 43-1 (ND 36-0, SD 7-1). July 17, 2000.

199. HR 4810. Alleviate 'Marriage Penalty' Tax/Sunset Provision. Roth, R-Del., motion to waive the Budget Act with respect to the Roth amendments that would strike the sunset provisions in the underlying bill and in the Democratic alternative. Motion rejected 48-47: R 48-2; D 0-45 (ND 0-37, SD 0-8). A three-fifths majority vote (60) of the total Senate is required to waive the Budget Act. (Subsequently, the chair upheld the point of order and the amendments fell.) July 17, 2000.

200. HR 4810. Alleviate 'Marriage Penalty' Tax/Democratic Substitute. Moynihan, D-N.Y., amendment that would strike the text of the bill and insert language to allow married couples to calculate income tax as two single filers or as a married couple. The plan would be capped at $100,000 per couple and gradually phased-out for couples with an adjusted gross income of more than $150,000. Rejected 46-50: R 1-50; D 45-0 (ND 37-0, SD 8-0). July 17, 2000.

201. HR 4810. Alleviate 'Marriage Penalty' Tax/Standard Deduction Increase. Feingold, D-Wis., amendment that would strike the provision in the bill that would increase the 15 percent and 28 percent tax brackets and insert language to provide an increase in the standard deduction to $4,750 for individuals and $7,500 for heads of households. Rejected 40-56: R 1-50; D 39-6 (ND 31-6, SD 8-0). July 17, 2000.

	202	203	204	205	206	207
ALABAMA						
Shelby	N	N	N	N	N	N
Sessions	N	N	N	N	N	N
ALASKA						
Stevens	N	N	N	N	N	N
Murkowski	N	N	N	N	N	N
ARIZONA						
McCain	N	N	N	N	N	N
Kyl	N	N	N	N	N	N
ARKANSAS						
Hutchinson	?	?	?	N	N	N
Lincoln	N	Y	Y	Y	Y	N
CALIFORNIA						
Feinstein	N	Y	Y	Y	Y	Y
Boxer	Y	Y	Y	Y	Y	Y
COLORADO						
Campbell	N	N	N	N	N	N
Allard	N	N	N	N	N	N
CONNECTICUT						
Dodd	Y	Y	Y	Y	Y	Y
Lieberman	Y	Y	Y	Y	Y	Y
DELAWARE						
Roth	N	N	N	N	N	Y
Biden	Y	Y	Y	Y	Y	Y
FLORIDA						
Graham	Y	Y	Y	Y	Y	Y
Mack	N	N	N	N	N	N
GEORGIA						
Coverdell	?	?	?	?	?	?
Cleland	N	Y	Y	Y	Y	Y
HAWAII						
Inouye	N	Y	Y	Y	Y	Y
Akaka	Y	Y	Y	Y	Y	Y
IDAHO						
Craig	N	N	N	N	N	N
Crapo	N	N	N	N	N	N
ILLINOIS						
Durbin	Y	Y	Y	Y	Y	Y
Fitzgerald	N	N	N	N	N	Y
INDIANA						
Lugar	N	N	N	N	N	N
Bayh	N	Y	Y	Y	Y	Y

	202	203	204	205	206	207
IOWA						
Grassley	N	N	N	N	N	N
Harkin	Y	Y	Y	Y	Y	Y
KANSAS						
Brownback	N	N	N	N	N	Y
Roberts	N	N	N	N	N	N
KENTUCKY						
McConnell	N	N	N	N	N	N
Bunning	N	N	N	N	N	N
LOUISIANA						
Breaux	Y	Y	Y	Y	Y	Y
Landrieu	Y	Y	Y	Y	Y	N
MAINE						
Snowe	Y	N	Y	Y	Y	N
Collins	Y	N	Y	Y	N	N
MARYLAND						
Sarbanes	Y	Y	Y	Y	Y	Y
Mikulski	Y	Y	Y	Y	Y	Y
MASSACHUSETTS						
Kennedy	Y	Y	Y	Y	Y	Y
Kerry	Y	Y	Y	Y	Y	Y
MICHIGAN						
Levin	Y	Y	Y	Y	Y	Y
Abraham	N	N	N	N	Y	N
MINNESOTA						
Wellstone	Y	Y	Y	Y	Y	Y
Grams	N	N	N	N	N	N
MISSISSIPPI						
Cochran	N	N	N	N	N	N
Lott	N	N	N	N	N	N
MISSOURI						
Bond	N	N	N	N	N	N
Ashcroft	N	N	N	N	N	N
MONTANA						
Baucus	N	Y	Y	Y	Y	N
Burns	N	N	N	N	N	N
NEBRASKA						
Kerrey	N	Y	Y	Y	Y	Y
Hagel	N	N	N	N	N	N
NEVADA						
Reid	N	Y	Y	Y	Y	Y
Bryan	N	Y	Y	Y	Y	Y

	202	203	204	205	206	207
NEW HAMPSHIRE						
Smith	N	N	N	N	N	N
Gregg	N	N	N	N	N	N
NEW JERSEY						
Lautenberg	Y	Y	Y	Y	Y	Y
Torricelli	Y	Y	Y	?	N	Y
NEW MEXICO						
Domenici	N	N	N	N	N	N
Bingaman	N	Y	Y	Y	Y	Y
NEW YORK						
Moynihan	N	Y	Y	Y	Y	Y
Schumer	Y	Y	Y	Y	Y	Y
NORTH CAROLINA						
Helms	N	N	N	N	N	N
Edwards	Y	Y	Y	Y	Y	Y
NORTH DAKOTA						
Conrad	N	Y	Y	Y	Y	Y
Dorgan	N	Y	Y	Y	Y	Y
OHIO						
DeWine	N	N	Y	N	N	Y
Voinovich	N	N	N	N	N	N
OKLAHOMA						
Nickles	N	N	N	N	N	N
Inhofe	N	N	N	N	N	N
OREGON						
Wyden	Y	Y	Y	Y	Y	Y
Smith	N	N	N	N	N	N
PENNSYLVANIA						
Specter	N	N	Y	Y	Y	Y
Santorum	N	N	N	N	N	N
RHODE ISLAND						
Reed	Y	Y	Y	Y	Y	Y
Chafee, L.	N	N	Y	Y	Y	Y
SOUTH CAROLINA						
Thurmond	N	N	N	N	N	N
Hollings	N	Y	Y	Y	Y	Y
SOUTH DAKOTA						
Daschle	Y	Y	Y	Y	Y	N
Johnson	Y	Y	Y	Y	Y	N
TENNESSEE						
Thompson	N	N	N	N	N	N
Frist	N	N	N	N	N	N

Key

- Y Voted for (yea).
- # Paired for.
- + Announced for.
- N Voted against (nay).
- X Paired against.
- – Announced against.
- P Voted "present."
- C Voted "present" to avoid possible conflict of interest.
- ? Did not vote or otherwise make a position known.

Democrats **Republicans**
Independents

	202	203	204	205	206	207
TEXAS						
Gramm	N	N	N	N	N	N
Hutchison	N	N	N	N	N	N
UTAH						
Hatch	N	N	N	N	N	N
Bennett	N	N	N	N	N	N
VERMONT						
Leahy	Y	Y	Y	Y	Y	Y
Jeffords	N	N	Y	Y	Y	Y
VIRGINIA						
Warner	N	N	N	N	N	N
Robb	Y	Y	Y	Y	Y	Y
WASHINGTON						
Gorton	N	N	N	N	N	N
Murray	Y	Y	Y	Y	Y	N
WEST VIRGINIA						
Byrd	N	Y	Y	Y	Y	N
Rockefeller	N	Y	Y	Y	Y	Y
WISCONSIN						
Kohl	N	Y	Y	Y	Y	Y
Feingold	Y	Y	Y	Y	Y	Y
WYOMING						
Thomas	N	N	N	N	N	N
Enzi	N	N	N	N	N	N

ND Northern Democrats SD Southern Democrats

Southern states - Ala., Ark., Fla., Ga., Ky., La., Miss., N.C., Okla., S.C., Tenn., Texas, Va.

202. HR 4810. Alleviate 'Marriage Penalty' Tax/COBRA Tax Credit. Feingold, D-Wis., motion to waive the Budget Act with respect to the Reid, D-Nev., point of order against the Feingold amendment. The Feingold amendment would create a 25 percent tax credit for COBRA premiums and expand COBRA to cover retirees whose employer-sponsored coverage is terminated. The amendment would be offset by eliminating the depletion allowance for hard rock minerals mined on federal lands. Motion rejected 30-68: R 2-51; D 28-17 (ND 23-14, SD 5-3). A three-fifths majority vote (60) of the total Senate is required to waive the Budget Act. (Subsequently, the chair upheld the point of order and the amendment fell.) July 17, 2000.

203. HR 4810. Alleviate 'Marriage Penalty' Tax/Wage Discrimination. Harkin, D-Iowa, motion to waive the Budget Act with respect to the Nickles, R-Okla., point of order against the Harkin amendment. Harkin's amendment would allow workers who won wage discrimination claims in court to collect punitive and compensatory damages in addition to back wages. Motion rejected 45-53: R 0-53; D 45-0 (ND 37-0, SD 8-0). A three-fifths majority vote (60) of the total Senate is required to waive the Budget Act. (Subsequently, the chair upheld the point of order and the amendment fell.) July 17, 2000.

204. HR 4810. Alleviate 'Marriage Penalty' Tax/S-CHIP Coverage. Kennedy, D-Mass., motion to waive the Budget Act with respect to the Roth, R-Del., point of order against the Kennedy amendment. The Kennedy amendment would allow states to expand coverage under Medicaid and the State Children's Health Insurance Program (S-CHIP) to the parents of the children enrolled in the programs. Motion rejected 51-47: R 6-47; D 45-0 (ND 37-0, SD 8-0). A three-fifths majority vote (60) of the total Senate is required to waive the Budget Act. (Subsequently, the chair upheld the point of order and the amendment fell.) July 17, 2000.

205. HR 4810. Alleviate 'Marriage Penalty' Tax/Health Insurance. Durbin, D-Ill., motion to waive the Budget Act with respect to the Nickles, R-Okla., point of order against the Durbin amendment. The Durbin amendment would allow businesses with up to 25 employees to receive a tax credit for employee health insurance for low-income workers. Motion rejected 49-49: R 5-49; D 44-0 (ND 36-0, SD 8-0). A three-fifths majority vote (60) of the total Senate is required to waive the Budget Act. (Subsequently, the chair upheld the point of order and the amendment fell.) July 17, 2000.

206. HR 4810. Alleviate 'Marriage Penalty' Tax/Prescription Drug Benefit. Robb, D-Va., motion to waive the Budget Act with respect to the Roth, R-Del., point of order against the Robb amendment. The Robb amendment would postpone enactment of the so-called marriage penalty provisions until enactment of a Medicare prescription drug benefit program. Motion rejected 49-50: R 5-49; D 44-1 (ND 36-1, SD 8-0). A three-fifths majority vote (60) of the total Senate is required to waive the Budget Act. (Subsequently, the chair upheld the point of order and the amendment fell.) July 17, 2000.

207. HR 4578. Fiscal 2001 Interior Appropriations/Wildland Fire Management. Bryan, D-Nev., amendment to reduce funding for the National Forest System's timber sales program by $30 million, redirecting $15 million to wildfire management and the remaining funds to debt reduction. Rejected 45-54: R 7-47; D 38-7 (ND 32-5, SD 6-2). July 18, 2000.

	208	209	210	211	212	213
ALABAMA						
Shelby	Y	Y	N	Y	Y	N
Sessions	Y	Y	N	Y	Y	N
ALASKA						
Stevens	Y	Y	N	Y	Y	N
Murkowski	Y	Y	N	Y	Y	N
ARIZONA						
McCain	Y	Y	N	Y	Y	N
Kyl	Y	Y	N	Y	Y	N
ARKANSAS						
Hutchinson	Y	Y	N	Y	Y	N
Lincoln	N	Y	N	Y	Y	Y
CALIFORNIA						
Feinstein	N	Y	Y	Y	Y	N
Boxer	N	Y	Y	Y	Y	Y
COLORADO						
Campbell	Y	Y	N	Y	Y	N
Allard	Y	Y	N	Y	Y	N
CONNECTICUT						
Dodd	N	Y	Y	Y	Y	Y
Lieberman	N	Y	Y	Y	Y	N
DELAWARE						
Roth	N	Y	N	Y	Y	N
Biden	N	Y	N	Y	Y	N
FLORIDA						
Graham	N	Y	Y	Y	Y	N
Mack	Y	Y	N	Y	Y	N
GEORGIA						
Coverdell	?	?	?	?	?	?
Cleland	N	Y	Y	Y	Y	N
HAWAII						
Inouye	N	Y	Y	Y	Y	Y
Akaka	N	Y	Y	Y	Y	Y
IDAHO						
Craig	Y	Y	N	Y	Y	N
Crapo	Y	Y	N	Y	Y	N
ILLINOIS						
Durbin	N	Y	Y	Y	Y	N
Fitzgerald	N	Y	Y	Y	Y	N
INDIANA						
Lugar	N	Y	Y	Y	Y	N
Bayh	N	Y	Y	Y	Y	N
IOWA						
Grassley	Y	Y	N	Y	Y	N
Harkin	N	Y	Y	Y	Y	Y
KANSAS						
Brownback	Y	Y	N	Y	Y	N
Roberts	Y	Y	N	Y	Y	N
KENTUCKY						
McConnell	Y	Y	N	Y	Y	N
Bunning	Y	Y	N	Y	Y	N
LOUISIANA						
Breaux	N	Y	N	Y	Y	N
Landrieu	N	Y	N	Y	Y	N
MAINE						
Snowe	Y	Y	Y	Y	Y	N
Collins	Y	Y	Y	Y	Y	N
MARYLAND						
Sarbanes	N	Y	Y	Y	Y	N
Mikulski	N	Y	Y	Y	Y	N
MASSACHUSETTS						
Kennedy	N	Y	Y	Y	Y	Y
Kerry	N	Y	Y	Y	Y	Y
MICHIGAN						
Levin	N	Y	Y	Y	Y	Y
Abraham	Y	Y	N	Y	Y	N
MINNESOTA						
Wellstone	N	Y	Y	N	Y	Y
Grams	Y	Y	N	Y	Y	N
MISSISSIPPI						
Cochran	Y	Y	N	Y	Y	N
Lott	Y	Y	N	Y	Y	N
MISSOURI						
Bond	Y	Y	N	Y	Y	N
Ashcroft	Y	Y	N	Y	Y	N
MONTANA						
Baucus	N	Y	N	Y	Y	N
Burns	Y	Y	N	Y	Y	N
NEBRASKA						
Kerrey	N	Y	N	Y	Y	N
Hagel	Y	Y	N	Y	Y	N
NEVADA						
Reid	N	Y	Y	Y	Y	N
Bryan	N	Y	Y	Y	Y	N
NEW HAMPSHIRE						
Smith	Y	Y	N	Y	Y	N
Gregg	Y	Y	N	Y	Y	N
NEW JERSEY						
Lautenberg	N	Y	Y	Y	Y	Y
Torricelli	N	Y	Y	Y	Y	N
NEW MEXICO						
Domenici	Y	Y	N	Y	Y	N
Bingaman	N	Y	Y	Y	Y	N
NEW YORK						
Moynihan	N	Y	Y	Y	Y	Y
Schumer	N	Y	Y	Y	Y	N
NORTH CAROLINA						
Helms	Y	Y	N	Y	Y	N
Edwards	N	Y	N	Y	Y	N
NORTH DAKOTA						
Conrad	N	Y	Y	Y	Y	N
Dorgan	N	Y	Y	Y	Y	N
OHIO						
DeWine	N	Y	N	Y	Y	N
Voinovich	Y	Y	N	Y	Y	Y
OKLAHOMA						
Nickles	Y	Y	N	Y	Y	N
Inhofe	Y	Y	N	Y	Y	N
OREGON						
Wyden	N	Y	Y	Y	Y	N
Smith	Y	Y	N	Y	Y	N
PENNSYLVANIA						
Specter	Y	Y	N	Y	Y	N
Santorum	Y	Y	N	Y	Y	N
RHODE ISLAND						
Reed	N	Y	Y	Y	Y	Y
Chafee, L.	N	Y	N	Y	Y	N
SOUTH CAROLINA						
Thurmond	Y	Y	N	Y	Y	N
Hollings	N	Y	Y	Y	Y	Y
SOUTH DAKOTA						
Daschle	N	Y	Y	Y	Y	Y
Johnson	N	Y	N	Y	Y	N
TENNESSEE						
Thompson	Y	Y	N	Y	Y	N
Frist	Y	Y	N	Y	Y	N
TEXAS						
Gramm	Y	Y	N	Y	Y	N
Hutchison	Y	Y	N	Y	Y	N
UTAH						
Hatch	Y	Y	N	Y	Y	N
Bennett	Y	Y	N	Y	Y	N
VERMONT						
Leahy	N	Y	Y	Y	Y	Y
Jeffords	N	Y	N	Y	Y	N
VIRGINIA						
Warner	Y	Y	N	Y	Y	N
Robb	N	Y	Y	Y	Y	Y
WASHINGTON						
Gorton	Y	Y	N	Y	Y	N
Murray	N	Y	Y	Y	Y	N
WEST VIRGINIA						
Byrd	Y	Y	Y	Y	Y	N
Rockefeller	N	Y	Y	Y	Y	Y
WISCONSIN						
Kohl	N	Y	Y	Y	Y	N
Feingold	N	Y	Y	N	Y	Y
WYOMING						
Thomas	Y	Y	N	Y	Y	N
Enzi	Y	Y	N	Y	Y	N

ND Northern Democrats SD Southern Democrats

Southern states - Ala., Ark., Fla., Ga., Ky., La., Miss., N.C., Okla., S.C., Tenn., Texas, Va.

Key

- Y Voted for (yea).
- # Paired for.
- + Announced for.
- N Voted against (nay).
- X Paired against.
- – Announced against.
- P Voted "present."
- C Voted "present" to avoid possible conflict of interest.
- ? Did not vote or otherwise make a position known.

Democrats ***Republicans***
Independents

208. HR 4578. Fiscal 2001 Interior Appropriations/National Monuments. Nickles, R-Okla., amendment that would prohibit the use of funds to designate national monuments without congressional approval. Rejected 49-50: R 48-6; D 1-44 (ND 1-36, SD 0-8). A "nay" was a vote in support of the president's position. July 18, 2000.

209. HR 4578. Fiscal 2001 Interior Appropriations/Pesticide Use. Bond, R-Mo., amendment to the Boxer, D-Calif., amendment. The Bond amendment would substitute language to bar the use of funds to apply a pesticide that is not approved by the EPA in any area owned or managed by the Interior Department that may be used by children, including national parks. Adopted 99-0: R 54-0; D 45-0 (ND 37-0, SD 8-0). July 18, 2000.

210. HR 4578. Fiscal 2001 Interior Appropriations/Pesticide Use. Boxer, D-Calif., amendment to the Boxer amendment. The amendment would add back language in the underlying Boxer amendment to prohibit application of certain toxic pesticides in national parks and national monuments, where children may be present. Rejected 41-58: R 4-50; D 37-8 (ND 33-4, SD 4-4). (Subsequently, the Boxer amendment, as amended, was adopted by voice vote.) July 18, 2000.

211. HR 4578. Fiscal 2001 Interior Appropriations/Passage. Passage of the bill to provide $15.5 billion for the Department of the Interior and related agencies. The bill would prohibit the use of funds to implement the 1997 Kyoto Protocol and would require that expiring grazing permits be renewed under the same terms as the old permits, before environmental reviews are complete. Passed 97-2: R 54-0; D 43-2 (ND 35-2, SD 8-0). July 18, 2000.

212. HR 4810. Alleviate 'Marriage Penalty' Tax/Accounting Method. Burns, R-Mont., amendment that would repeal the modification of the installment method of accounting. Adopted 99-0: R 54-0; D 45-0 (ND 37-0, SD 8-0). July 18, 2000.

213. HR 4810. Alleviate 'Marriage Penalty' Tax/Strike All Provisions. Hollings, D-S.C., amendment that would strike all provisions in the bill. Rejected 20-79: R 1-53; D 19-26 (ND 16-21, SD 3-5). July 18, 2000.

	214	215	216	217	218	219
ALABAMA						
Shelby	Y	Y	Y	Y	Y	Y
Sessions	Y	Y	Y	Y	Y	Y
ALASKA						
Stevens	Y	Y	Y	Y	Y	Y
Murkowski	Y	Y	Y	Y	Y	Y
ARIZONA						
McCain	Y	Y	Y	Y	Y	N
Kyl	Y	Y	Y	Y	Y	N
ARKANSAS						
Hutchinson	Y	Y	Y	N	Y	N
Lincoln	N	N	Y	Y	Y	Y
CALIFORNIA						
Feinstein	N	Y	Y	Y	N	N
Boxer	N	N	Y	Y	N	Y
COLORADO						
Campbell	Y	Y	Y	Y	Y	Y
Allard	Y	Y	Y	Y	Y	Y
CONNECTICUT						
Dodd	N	N	Y	Y	N	Y
Lieberman	N	N	Y	Y	N	Y
DELAWARE						
Roth	Y	Y	Y	Y	Y	N
Biden	N	Y	?	?	N	N
FLORIDA						
Graham	N	N	Y	Y	N	Y
Mack	Y	Y	Y	N	Y	Y
GEORGIA						
Coverdell[1]	?	?				
Cleland	N	Y	Y	Y	N	Y
HAWAII						
Inouye	N	N	Y	Y	N	Y
Akaka	N	N	Y	Y	N	Y
IDAHO						
Craig	Y	Y	Y	Y	Y	Y
Crapo	Y	Y	Y	Y	Y	Y
ILLINOIS						
Durbin	N	N	Y	Y	N	Y
Fitzgerald	Y	Y	Y	Y	N	N
INDIANA						
Lugar	Y	Y	Y	Y	N	N
Bayh	N	N	Y	N	N	Y
IOWA						
Grassley	Y	Y	Y	Y	N	Y
Harkin	N	N	Y	Y	N	Y
KANSAS						
Brownback	Y	Y	Y	Y	Y	N
Roberts	Y	Y	Y	Y	Y	Y
KENTUCKY						
McConnell	Y	Y	Y	N	Y	Y
Bunning	Y	Y	Y	N	?	?
LOUISIANA						
Breaux	N	N	Y	N	N	Y
Landrieu	N	Y	Y	Y	N	Y
MAINE						
Snowe	Y	Y	Y	Y	Y	N
Collins	Y	Y	Y	Y	Y	N
MARYLAND						
Sarbanes	N	N	Y	Y	N	N
Mikulski	N	N	Y	Y	N	N
MASSACHUSETTS						
Kennedy	N	N	Y	Y	N	N
Kerry	N	N	Y	Y	N	N
MICHIGAN						
Levin	N	N	Y	Y	N	Y
Abraham	Y	Y	Y	Y	N	Y
MINNESOTA						
Wellstone	N	N	Y	Y	N	Y
Grams	Y	Y	Y	Y	Y	Y
MISSISSIPPI						
Cochran	Y	Y	Y	N	Y	Y
Lott	Y	Y	Y	?	Y	Y
MISSOURI						
Bond	Y	Y	Y	N	Y	Y
Ashcroft	Y	Y	Y	Y	Y	Y
MONTANA						
Baucus	N	N	Y	Y	N	Y
Burns	Y	Y	Y	Y	N	Y
NEBRASKA						
Kerrey	N	Y	Y	Y	Y	Y
Hagel	Y	Y	Y	N	Y	Y
NEVADA						
Reid	N	N	Y	Y	N	Y
Bryan	N	N	Y	Y	N	Y
NEW HAMPSHIRE						
Smith	Y	Y	Y	Y	Y	N
Gregg	Y	Y	Y	Y	Y	N
NEW JERSEY						
Lautenberg	N	N	Y	Y	N	Y
Torricelli	N	Y	?	?	N	Y
NEW MEXICO						
Domenici	Y	Y	Y	Y	Y	Y
Bingaman	N	N	Y	Y	N	Y
NEW YORK						
Moynihan	N	N	Y	Y	N	Y
Schumer	N	N	Y	Y	N	N
NORTH CAROLINA						
Helms	Y	Y	Y	N	Y	Y
Edwards	N	N	Y	Y	N	Y
NORTH DAKOTA						
Conrad	N	N	Y	Y	N	Y
Dorgan	N	N	Y	Y	N	Y
OHIO						
DeWine	Y	Y	Y	Y	Y	N
Voinovich	Y	N	Y	N	Y	N
OKLAHOMA						
Nickles	Y	Y	Y	N	Y	N
Inhofe	Y	Y	Y	N	Y	Y
OREGON						
Wyden	N	N	Y	Y	N	Y
Smith	Y	Y	Y	Y	Y	Y
PENNSYLVANIA						
Specter	Y	Y	Y	Y	N	N
Santorum	Y	Y	Y	N	Y	N
RHODE ISLAND						
Reed	N	N	Y	Y	N	N
Chafee, L.	Y	Y	Y	Y	Y	N
SOUTH CAROLINA						
Thurmond	Y	Y	Y	Y	Y	Y
Hollings	N	N	?	?	N	Y
SOUTH DAKOTA						
Daschle	N	N	Y	Y	N	Y
Johnson	N	N	Y	Y	N	Y
TENNESSEE						
Thompson	Y	Y	Y	N	Y	N
Frist	Y	Y	Y	N	Y	N
TEXAS						
Gramm	Y	Y	Y	N	Y	N
Hutchison	Y	Y	Y	N	Y	Y
UTAH						
Hatch	Y	Y	Y	N	Y	Y
Bennett	Y	Y	Y	N	Y	Y
VERMONT						
Leahy	N	N	Y	Y	N	Y
Jeffords	Y	Y	Y	Y	Y	Y
VIRGINIA						
Warner	Y	Y	Y	Y	Y	Y
Robb	N	N	Y	Y	N	Y
WASHINGTON						
Gorton	Y	Y	Y	Y	Y	N
Murray	N	N	Y	Y	N	Y
WEST VIRGINIA						
Byrd	N	Y	Y	Y	N	N
Rockefeller	N	N	Y	Y	N	+
WISCONSIN						
Kohl	N	Y	Y	Y	N	N
Feingold	N	N	Y	Y	N	N
WYOMING						
Thomas	Y	Y	Y	Y	Y	Y
Enzi	Y	Y	Y	N	Y	Y

ND Northern Democrats SD Southern Democrats

Southern states - Ala., Ark., Fla., Ga., Ky., La., Miss., N.C., Okla., S.C., Tenn., Texas, Va.

Key

- Y Voted for (yea).
- # Paired for.
- \+ Announced for.
- N Voted against (nay).
- X Paired against.
- – Announced against.
- P Voted "present."
- C Voted "present" to avoid possible conflict of interest.
- ? Did not vote or otherwise make a position known.

•

Democrats ***Republicans***
Independents

214. HR 4810. Alleviate 'Marriage Penalty' Tax/Committee Bill. Lott, R-Miss., amendment that would strike all after the first word and insert the text of the bill as reported by the Senate Finance Committee. The bill would increase the standard deduction for married couples to twice that of single taxpayers, and expand the income limits on both the 15 percent and 28 percent tax brackets for married couples to twice that of singles. Adopted 54-45: R 54-0; D 0-45 (ND 0-37, SD 0-8). July 18, 2000.

215. HR 4810. Alleviate 'Marriage Penalty' Tax/Passage. Passage of the bill that would increase the standard deduction for married couples to twice that of single taxpayers and expand the income limits on both the 15 percent and 28 percent tax brackets for married couples to twice that of singles. Passed 61-38: R 53-1; D 8-37 (ND 6-31, SD 2-6). July 18, 2000. A "nay" was a vote in support of the president's position.

216. HR 4461. Fiscal 2001 Agriculture Appropriations/Prescription Drugs. Cochran, R-Miss., amendment to the Jeffords, R-Vt., amendment. The Cochran amendment would specify that the provisions of the Jeffords amendment could only take effect after the secretary of Health and Human Services certified to Congress that they would pose no risk to the public's health and safety and would result in a significant cost reduction of prescription drugs for consumers. The Jeffords amendment would permit licensed pharmacists or wholesalers to import prescription drugs made in the United States or at facilities approved by the Food and Drug Administration if they comply with certain conditions. Adopted 96-0: R 54-0; D 42-0 (ND 35-0, SD 7-0). July 19, 2000.

217. HR 4461. Fiscal 2001 Agriculture Appropriations/Prescription Drugs. Jeffords, R-Vt., amendment that would permit licensed pharmacists or wholesalers to import prescription drugs made in the United States or at facilities approved by the Food and Drug Administration if they comply with certain conditions. The provisions could only take effect after the secretary of Health and Human Services certified to Congress that they would pose no risk to the public's health and safety and would result in a cost reduction of prescription drugs for consumers. Adopted 74-21: R 34-19; D 40-2 (ND 34-1, SD 6-1). July 19, 2000.

218. HR 4461. Fiscal 2001 Agriculture Appropriations/Pathogen Standards. Cochran, R-Miss., motion to table (kill) the Harkin, D-Iowa, amendment that would clarify the Agriculture Department's authority to enforce standards for pathogens in meat and poultry products. Motion rejected 49-49: R 47-6; D 2-43 (ND 1-36, SD 1-7). July 20, 2000.

219. HR 4461. Fiscal 2001 Agriculture Appropriations/Sugar Program. Craig, R-Idaho, motion to table (kill) the McCain, R-Ariz., amendment that would prohibit the use of any funds by the Agriculture Department to implement the sugar program. Motion agreed to 65-32: R 32-21; D 33-11 (ND 25-11, SD 8-0). July 20, 2000.

[1] *Sen. Paul Coverdell, R-Ga., died July 18, 2000. The last vote for which he was eligible was 215.*

	220	221	222	223	224	225
ALABAMA						
Shelby	Y	N	Y	N	N	Y
Sessions	Y	N	N	N	N	Y
ALASKA						
Stevens	Y	N	Y	Y	N	Y
Murkowski	Y	N	Y	Y	N	Y
ARIZONA						
McCain	Y	N	Y	N	N	N
Kyl	Y	N	Y	N	N	N
ARKANSAS						
Hutchinson	Y	N	Y	Y	N	Y
Lincoln	Y	N	Y	Y	Y	Y
CALIFORNIA						
Feinstein	N	Y	Y	Y	Y	Y
Boxer	N	Y	Y	Y	?	?
COLORADO						
Campbell	Y	N	Y	N	N	Y
Allard	Y	N	Y	N	N	N
CONNECTICUT						
Dodd	N	Y	Y	Y	Y	Y
Lieberman	N	Y	Y	Y	Y	N
DELAWARE						
Roth	Y	N	Y	Y	Y	Y
Biden	Y	Y	Y	Y	Y	Y
FLORIDA						
Graham	N	Y	Y	Y	Y	N
Mack	Y	N	Y	N	N	N
GEORGIA						
Vacant						
Cleland	Y	Y	Y	Y	Y	Y
HAWAII						
Inouye	N	Y	Y	Y	?	?
Akaka	N	Y	Y	Y	Y	Y
IDAHO						
Craig	Y	N	Y	N	N	Y
Crapo	Y	N	Y	Y	N	Y
ILLINOIS						
Durbin	N	Y	Y	Y	Y	Y
Fitzgerald	Y	Y	Y	N	Y	Y
INDIANA						
Lugar	Y	Y	Y	Y	N	Y
Bayh	N	Y	Y	Y	Y	Y
IOWA						
Grassley	N	Y	Y	Y	N	Y
Harkin	N	Y	Y	Y	Y	Y
KANSAS						
Brownback	Y	N	Y	N	N	Y
Roberts	Y	N	Y	Y	N	Y
KENTUCKY						
McConnell	Y	N	Y	Y	N	Y
Bunning	?	?	?	?	?	?
LOUISIANA						
Breaux	Y	Y	Y	Y	N	Y
Landrieu	N	Y	Y	Y	Y	Y
MAINE						
Snowe	Y	N	Y	Y	Y	Y
Collins	Y	N	Y	Y	Y	Y
MARYLAND						
Sarbanes	N	Y	Y	Y	Y	Y
Mikulski	N	Y	Y	Y	N	Y
MASSACHUSETTS						
Kennedy	N	Y	Y	Y	?	?
Kerry	N	Y	?	?	?	?
MICHIGAN						
Levin	N	Y	Y	Y	Y	Y
Abraham	N	Y	Y	Y	N	Y
MINNESOTA						
Wellstone	N	Y	Y	Y	Y	Y
Grams	Y	N	Y	N	N	Y
MISSISSIPPI						
Cochran	Y	N	Y	Y	N	Y
Lott	Y	N	Y	Y	N	Y
MISSOURI						
Bond	N	N	Y	N	N	Y
Ashcroft	N	N	Y	N	N	Y
MONTANA						
Baucus	N	Y	Y	Y	N	Y
Burns	N	Y	Y	Y	N	Y
NEBRASKA						
Kerrey	N	N	Y	Y	?	?
Hagel	N	N	Y	N	N	Y
NEVADA						
Reid	N	Y	Y	Y	N	Y
Bryan	N	Y	Y	Y	N	Y
NEW HAMPSHIRE						
Smith	Y	N	N	N	N	N
Gregg	Y	N	Y	N	Y	Y
NEW JERSEY						
Lautenberg	N	Y	Y	Y	Y	Y
Torricelli	N	Y	Y	Y	Y	N
NEW MEXICO						
Domenici	Y	N	Y	Y	N	Y
Bingaman	N	Y	Y	Y	N	Y
NEW YORK						
Moynihan	N	Y	Y	Y	N	Y
Schumer	N	Y	Y	Y	Y	Y
NORTH CAROLINA						
Helms	Y	N	N	Y	N	Y
Edwards	N	Y	Y	Y	Y	Y
NORTH DAKOTA						
Conrad	N	Y	Y	Y	N	Y
Dorgan	N	Y	Y	Y	N	Y
OHIO						
DeWine	Y	N	Y	Y	N	Y
Voinovich	N	N	N	Y	Y	N
OKLAHOMA						
Nickles	Y	N	Y	Y	N	N
Inhofe	Y	N	Y	N	N	Y
OREGON						
Wyden	N	Y	Y	N	Y	Y
Smith	N	N	Y	N	N	Y
PENNSYLVANIA						
Specter	Y	Y	Y	Y	Y	Y
Santorum	Y	N	Y	Y	N	Y
RHODE ISLAND						
Reed	N	Y	Y	Y	Y	Y
Chafee, L.	Y	N	Y	Y	Y	Y
SOUTH CAROLINA						
Thurmond	Y	N	Y	Y	N	Y
Hollings	N	Y	Y	Y	N	Y
SOUTH DAKOTA						
Daschle	N	Y	Y	Y	N	Y
Johnson	N	Y	Y	Y	Y	Y
TENNESSEE						
Thompson	Y	N	N	Y	N	Y
Frist	Y	N	Y	N	N	Y
TEXAS						
Gramm	Y	N	Y	N	N	N
Hutchison	Y	N	Y	Y	N	Y
UTAH						
Hatch	Y	N	Y	Y	N	Y
Bennett	Y	N	Y	Y	N	Y
VERMONT						
Leahy	N	Y	Y	Y	Y	Y
Jeffords	Y	N	Y	Y	Y	Y
VIRGINIA						
Warner	Y	N	Y	Y	N	Y
Robb	N	Y	Y	Y	Y	Y
WASHINGTON						
Gorton	Y	N	Y	N	N	Y
Murray	N	?	?	?	?	?
WEST VIRGINIA						
Byrd	Y	Y	Y	Y	N	Y
Rockefeller	N	Y	Y	Y	Y	Y
WISCONSIN						
Kohl	Y	Y	Y	Y	Y	Y
Feingold	N	Y	Y	Y	Y	N
WYOMING						
Thomas	Y	N	N	N	N	Y
Enzi	Y	N	Y	N	N	N

ND Northern Democrats SD Southern Democrats

Southern states - Ala., Ark., Fla., Ga., Ky., La., Miss., N.C., Okla., S.C., Tenn., Texas, Va.

Key

- Y Voted for (yea).
- # Paired for.
- \+ Announced for.
- N Voted against (nay).
- X Paired against.
- – Announced against.
- P Voted "present."
- C Voted "present" to avoid possible conflict of interest.
- ? Did not vote or otherwise make a position known.

•

Democrats ***Republicans***
Independents

220. HR 4461. Fiscal 2001 Agriculture Appropriations/GIPSA Funding. Cochran, R-Miss., motion to table (kill) the Wellstone, D-Minn., amendment that would increase funding for the Grain Inspection, Packers and Stockyards Administration (GIPSA) by $3.95 million to fund programs including investigations of anti-competitive behavior practices, the Hog Contract Library, and civil rights activities. Motion agreed to 51-47: R 45-8; D 6-39 (ND 3-34, SD 3-5). July 20, 2000.

221. HR 4461. Fiscal 2001 Agriculture Appropriations/Pathogen Standards. Harkin, D-Iowa, amendment that would clarify the Agriculture Department's authority to enforce standards for pathogens in meat and poultry products. Rejected 48-49: R 6-47; D 42-2 (ND 35-1, SD 7-1). July 20, 2000.

222. HR 4461. Fiscal 2001 Agriculture Appropriations/Food Stamp Program. Wellstone, D-Minn., amendment that would require the Agriculture Department to conduct a study and report back to Congress on any problems that households with eligible children have experienced in obtaining food stamps, and reasons for the decline in participation in the food stamp program. Adopted 90-6: R 47-6; D 43-0 (ND 35-0, SD 8-0). July 20, 2000.

223. HR 4461. Fiscal 2001 Agriculture Appropriations/Amtrak Authority. Specter, R-Pa., amendment that would authorize Amtrak to lease motor vehicles from the General Services Administration. Adopted 72-24: R 30-23; D 42-1 (ND 34-1, SD 8-0). July 20, 2000.

224. HR 4461. Fiscal 2001 Agriculture Appropriations/Hardrock Mining Regulations. Judgment of the Senate on the germaneness on the Durbin, D-Ill., amendment that would clarify that language in the bill would not limit the authority of the secretary to promulgate final rules or amend certain regulations on hardrock mining. Ruled not germane 36-56: R 9-44; D 27-12 (ND 21-10, SD 6-2). July 20, 2000.

225. HR 4461. Fiscal 2001 Agriculture Appropriations/Passage. Final passage of the bill that would provide fiscal 2001 funding for the Department of Agriculture and related agencies. It also would provide emergency spending for agriculture, including money for natural disasters such as flooding and drought. Passed 79-13: R 44-9; D 35-4 (ND 28-3, SD 7-1). July 20, 2000.

	226	227	228	229	230	231
ALABAMA						
Shelby	Y	Y	Y	Y	Y	Y
Sessions	Y	Y	Y	Y	Y	Y
ALASKA						
Stevens	Y	Y	Y	Y	Y	Y
Murkowski	Y	Y	Y	Y	Y	Y
ARIZONA						
McCain	Y	Y	Y	Y	N	Y
Kyl	Y	Y	Y	Y	Y	Y
ARKANSAS						
Hutchinson	Y	Y	Y	Y	Y	Y
Lincoln	N	Y	Y	Y	Y	Y
CALIFORNIA						
Feinstein	Y	Y	Y	Y	Y	Y
Boxer	?	Y	Y	Y	N	Y
COLORADO						
Campbell	Y	Y	Y	Y	Y	N
Allard	Y	Y	Y	Y	N	Y
CONNECTICUT						
Dodd	N	Y	Y	Y	Y	Y
Lieberman	N	Y	Y	Y	Y	Y
DELAWARE						
Roth	Y	Y	Y	Y	Y	Y
Biden	Y	Y	Y	Y	Y	Y
FLORIDA						
Graham	N	Y	Y	Y	Y	Y
Mack	Y	Y	Y	Y	Y	Y
GEORGIA						
Cleland	Y	Y	Y	Y	Y	Y
Miller [1]				Y	Y	Y
HAWAII						
Inouye	?	Y	Y	Y	Y	Y
Akaka	N	Y	Y	Y	Y	Y
IDAHO						
Craig	Y	Y	Y	Y	Y	Y
Crapo	Y	Y	Y	Y	Y	Y
ILLINOIS						
Durbin	N	Y	Y	Y	Y	Y
Fitzgerald	Y	Y	Y	Y	Y	Y
INDIANA						
Lugar	Y	Y	Y	Y	Y	Y
Bayh	N	Y	Y	Y	Y	Y
IOWA						
Grassley	Y	Y	Y	Y	Y	Y
Harkin	N	Y	Y	Y	Y	Y
KANSAS						
Brownback	Y	Y	Y	Y	Y	Y
Roberts	Y	Y	Y	Y	Y	Y
KENTUCKY						
McConnell	Y	Y	Y	Y	Y	Y
Bunning	Y	Y	Y	Y	Y	N
LOUISIANA						
Breaux	N	Y	Y	Y	Y	Y
Landrieu	Y	Y	Y	Y	Y	Y
MAINE						
Snowe	Y	Y	Y	Y	Y	Y
Collins	Y	Y	Y	Y	Y	Y
MARYLAND						
Sarbanes	N	Y	Y	Y	Y	N
Mikulski	N	Y	Y	Y	Y	N
MASSACHUSETTS						
Kennedy	N	Y	Y	Y	Y	Y
Kerry	?	Y	Y	Y	Y	Y
MICHIGAN						
Levin	N	Y	Y	Y	Y	Y
Abraham	Y	Y	Y	Y	Y	Y
MINNESOTA						
Wellstone	N	Y	+	Y	N	N
Grams	Y	Y	Y	Y	Y	Y
MISSISSIPPI						
Cochran	Y	Y	Y	Y	Y	Y
Lott	Y	Y	Y	Y	Y	Y
MISSOURI						
Bond	Y	Y	Y	Y	Y	Y
Ashcroft	Y	Y	Y	Y	Y	Y
MONTANA						
Baucus	N	Y	Y	Y	Y	Y
Burns	Y	Y	Y	Y	Y	Y
NEBRASKA						
Kerrey	?	Y	Y	Y	Y	Y
Hagel	Y	Y	Y	Y	N	Y
NEVADA						
Reid	N	Y	Y	Y	Y	Y
Bryan	N	Y	Y	Y	Y	Y
NEW HAMPSHIRE						
Smith	Y	Y	Y	Y	Y	N
Gregg	Y	Y	Y	Y	Y	Y
NEW JERSEY						
Lautenberg	N	Y	Y	Y	Y	Y
Torricelli	Y	?	Y	Y	Y	Y
NEW MEXICO						
Domenici	Y	Y	Y	Y	Y	?
Bingaman	N	Y	Y	Y	Y	Y
NEW YORK						
Moynihan	N	Y	Y	Y	Y	Y
Schumer	N	Y	Y	Y	Y	Y
NORTH CAROLINA						
Helms	Y	Y	Y	Y	Y	N
Edwards	N	Y	Y	Y	Y	Y
NORTH DAKOTA						
Conrad	N	Y	Y	Y	Y	Y
Dorgan	N	Y	Y	Y	Y	Y
OHIO						
DeWine	Y	Y	Y	Y	Y	Y
Voinovich	N	Y	Y	Y	N	Y
OKLAHOMA						
Nickles	Y	Y	Y	Y	Y	Y
Inhofe	Y	Y	Y	Y	Y	N
OREGON						
Wyden	N	Y	Y	Y	Y	Y
Smith	Y	Y	Y	Y	Y	Y
PENNSYLVANIA						
Specter	Y	Y	Y	Y	Y	N
Santorum	Y	Y	Y	Y	Y	Y
RHODE ISLAND						
Reed	N	Y	Y	Y	Y	Y
Chafee, L.	Y	Y	Y	Y	Y	Y
SOUTH CAROLINA						
Thurmond	Y	Y	Y	Y	Y	N
Hollings	N	Y	Y	Y	Y	N
SOUTH DAKOTA						
Daschle	N	Y	Y	Y	Y	Y
Johnson	N	Y	Y	Y	Y	Y
TENNESSEE						
Thompson	Y	Y	Y	Y	Y	Y
Frist	Y	Y	Y	Y	Y	?
TEXAS						
Gramm	Y	Y	Y	Y	N	Y
Hutchison	Y	Y	Y	Y	Y	Y
UTAH						
Hatch	Y	Y	Y	Y	Y	Y
Bennett	Y	Y	Y	Y	Y	Y
VERMONT						
Leahy	N	Y	Y	Y	Y	Y
Jeffords	Y	Y	Y	Y	Y	Y
VIRGINIA						
Warner	Y	Y	Y	Y	Y	Y
Robb	N	Y	Y	Y	Y	Y
WASHINGTON						
Gorton	Y	Y	N	Y	Y	Y
Murray	?	Y	Y	Y	Y	Y
WEST VIRGINIA						
Byrd	Y	Y	Y	Y	Y	N
Rockefeller	N	Y	Y	Y	Y	Y
WISCONSIN						
Kohl	Y	Y	Y	Y	Y	Y
Feingold	N	Y	Y	Y	N	Y
WYOMING						
Thomas	Y	?	?	Y	Y	Y
Enzi	Y	Y	Y	Y	N	Y

ND Northern Democrats SD Southern Democrats

Southern states - Ala., Ark., Fla., Ga., Ky., La., Miss., N.C., Okla., S.C., Tenn., Texas, Va.

Key

- Y Voted for (yea).
- # Paired for.
- + Announced for.
- N Voted against (nay).
- X Paired against.
- – Announced against.
- P Voted "present."
- C Voted "present" to avoid possible conflict of interest.
- ? Did not vote or otherwise make a position known.

•

Democrats ***Republicans***
Independents

226. HR 4810. Alleviate 'Marriage Penalty' Tax/Conference Report. Adoption of the conference report on the bill that would reduce taxes for married couples by approximately $89.8 billion over five years. The measure would increase the standard deduction claimed by married couples to twice the amount claimed by single taxpayers. The upper boundary of the 15 percent tax bracket would gradually increase to twice the limit for singles. The measure also would allow couples to earn an additional $2,000 before being disqualified from receiving the earned income tax credit. The bill would also allow couples to use certain tax credits without paying the alternative minimum tax. Adopted (thus cleared for the president) 60-34: R 53-1; D 7-33 (ND 5-27, SD 2-6). July 21, 2000. A "nay" was a vote in support of the president's position.

227. HR 4871. Fiscal 2001 Treasury Appropriations/Cloture. Motion to invoke cloture (thus limiting debate) on the motion to proceed to the bill that would appropriate about $29 billion in fiscal 2001 for the Treasury Department, U.S. Postal Service, Executive Office of the President and certain independent agencies. Motion agreed to 97-0: R 53-0; D 44-0 (ND 36-0, SD 8-0). Three-fifths of the total Senate (60) is required to invoke cloture. July 26, 2000.

228. S 2507. Fiscal 2001 Intelligence Authorization/Cloture. Motion to invoke cloture (thus limiting debate) on the motion to proceed to the bill that would authorize fiscal 2001 spending levels for the government's intelligence activities. Motion agreed to 96-1: R 52-1; D 44-0 (ND 36-0, SD 8-0). Three-fifths of the total Senate (60) is required to invoke cloture. July 26, 2000.

229. HR 4733. Fiscal 2001 Energy and Water Appropriations/Cloture. Motion to invoke cloture (thus limiting debate) on the motion to proceed to the bill that would appropriate $22.5 billion for fiscal 2001 for energy and water resources development, including programs in the Energy Department, the Army Corps of Engineers, some Interior Department programs, and other independent agencies. Motion agreed to 100-0: R 54-0; D 46-0 (ND 37-0, SD 9-0). Three-fifths of the total Senate (60) is required to invoke cloture. July 27, 2000.

230. HR 4576. Fiscal 2001 Defense Appropriations/Conference Report. Adoption of the conference report on the bill to appropriate $287.8 billion in defense spending for fiscal 2001. The measure would provide $3.3 billion more than President Clinton's request and $21.7 billion more than appropriated in fiscal 2000. The measure includes $3.9 million for production of the F-22 fighter jet and $689 million for the development of a joint strike fighter jet for the Air Force, Navy and Marine Corps. Adopted (thus cleared for the president) 91-9: R 48-6; D 43-3 (ND 34-3, SD 9-0). July 27, 2000.

231. HR 4444. China Trade/Cloture. Motion to invoke cloture (thus limiting debate) on the motion to proceed to the bill that would make normal trade relations with the People's Republic of China permanent. Motion agreed to 86-12: R 45-7; D 41-5 (ND 33-4, SD 8-1). Three-fifths of the total Senate (60) is required to invoke cloture. July 27, 2000.

[1] *Sen. Zell Miller, D-Ga., was sworn in July 27, 2000, to replace Republican Paul Coverdell, who died July 18. The first vote for which Miller was eligible was 229.*

	232	233	234	235	236	237
ALABAMA						
Shelby	N	Y	Y	N	N	Y
Sessions	N	Y	Y	N	N	Y
ALASKA						
Stevens	N	Y	N	Y	N	Y
Murkowski	?	?	?	?	?	?
ARIZONA						
McCain	N	Y	N	N	?	?
Kyl	N	Y	N	N	N	Y
ARKANSAS						
Hutchinson	N	Y	Y	N	Y	Y
Lincoln	N	Y	N	N	N	Y
CALIFORNIA						
Feinstein	Y	Y	N	N	?	?
Boxer	Y	Y	Y	?	–	?
COLORADO						
Campbell	N	N	Y	Y	Y	Y
Allard	N	Y	N	N	N	Y
CONNECTICUT						
Dodd	Y	Y	Y	N	N	Y
Lieberman	?	?	?	?	?	?
DELAWARE						
Roth	Y	Y	N	N	N	Y
Biden	Y	Y	N	N	N	Y
FLORIDA						
Graham	Y	Y	N	N	N	Y
Mack	N	Y	N	N	N	Y
GEORGIA						
Miller	Y	Y	N	N	N	Y
Cleland	Y	Y	N	N	N	Y
HAWAII						
Inouye	Y	Y	N	N	N	Y
Akaka	?	?	?	?	?	?
IDAHO						
Craig	N	Y	Y	Y	N	Y
Crapo	N	Y	N	N	N	Y
ILLINOIS						
Durbin	Y	Y	N	N	N	Y
Fitzgerald	N	Y	N	N	N	Y
INDIANA						
Lugar	N	Y	N	N	N	Y
Bayh	Y	Y	N	N	N	Y
IOWA						
Grassley	N	Y	N	N	N	Y
Harkin	Y	Y	Y	Y	N	Y
KANSAS						
Brownback	N	Y	N	N	N	Y
Roberts	N	Y	N	N	N	Y
KENTUCKY						
McConnell	N	Y	N	Y	N	Y
Bunning	N	N	Y	Y	Y	Y
LOUISIANA						
Breaux	Y	Y	N	N	N	Y
Landrieu	Y	Y	N	N	N	Y
MAINE						
Snowe	N	Y	Y	Y	N	Y
Collins	N	Y	Y	Y	N	Y
MARYLAND						
Sarbanes	Y	Y	Y	Y	Y	Y
Mikulski	Y	Y	Y	Y	Y	Y
MASSACHUSETTS						
Kennedy	Y	Y	Y	Y	N	Y
Kerry	Y	Y	N	N	N	Y
MICHIGAN						
Levin	Y	Y	N	N	N	Y
Abraham	N	Y	N	N	N	Y
MINNESOTA						
Wellstone	Y	Y	Y	Y	Y	Y
Grams	N	Y	N	N	N	Y
MISSISSIPPI						
Cochran	N	Y	N	N	N	Y
Lott	N	Y	N	N	N	Y
MISSOURI						
Bond	N	Y	N	N	N	Y
Ashcroft	N	Y	Y	N	N	Y
MONTANA						
Baucus	Y	Y	N	N	N	N
Burns	N	Y	N	Y	N	Y
NEBRASKA						
Kerrey	Y	Y	N	N	N	Y
Hagel	N	Y	N	N	N	Y
NEVADA						
Reid	Y	Y	Y	N	N	Y
Bryan	Y	Y	N	N	N	Y
NEW HAMPSHIRE						
Smith	N	N	Y	Y	Y	Y
Gregg	N	Y	Y	Y	N	Y
NEW JERSEY						
Lautenberg	Y	Y	N	N	N	Y
Torricelli	Y	Y	Y	Y	N	Y
NEW MEXICO						
Domenici	N	Y	N	N	N	Y
Bingaman	Y	Y	N	N	N	Y
NEW YORK						
Moynihan	Y	Y	N	N	N	Y
Schumer	Y	Y	N	N	N	Y
NORTH CAROLINA						
Helms	N	Y	Y	Y	Y	Y
Edwards	Y	Y	N	Y	N	Y
NORTH DAKOTA						
Conrad	Y	Y	N	N	N	Y
Dorgan	Y	Y	Y	Y	N	Y
OHIO						
DeWine	N	Y	N	N	N	Y
Voinovich	N	Y	N	N	N	Y
OKLAHOMA						
Nickles	N	Y	N	N	N	Y
Inhofe	N	N	Y	Y	Y	Y
OREGON						
Wyden	Y	Y	N	N	N	Y
Smith	N	Y	N	N	N	Y
PENNSYLVANIA						
Specter	N	Y	Y	Y	Y	Y
Santorum	N	Y	Y	Y	N	Y
RHODE ISLAND						
Reed	Y	Y	Y	N	N	Y
Chafee, L.	Y	Y	N	N	N	Y
SOUTH CAROLINA						
Thurmond	N	Y	N	Y	N	Y
Hollings	Y	Y	Y	Y	Y	Y
SOUTH DAKOTA						
Daschle	Y	Y	N	Y	N	Y
Johnson	Y	Y	N	N	N	Y
TENNESSEE						
Thompson	N	Y	N	Y	N	Y
Frist	N	Y	N	N	N	Y
TEXAS						
Gramm	N	Y	N	N	N	Y
Hutchison	N	Y	N	N	N	Y
UTAH						
Hatch	N	Y	N	N	N	Y
Bennett	N	Y	N	N	N	Y
VERMONT						
Leahy	Y	Y	Y	Y	N	Y
Jeffords	N	N	N	Y	N	Y
VIRGINIA						
Warner	N	Y	N	N	N	Y
Robb	Y	Y	N	N	N	Y
WASHINGTON						
Gorton	N	Y	N	N	N	Y
Murray	Y	Y	N	N	N	Y
WEST VIRGINIA						
Byrd	Y	Y	Y	Y	Y	Y
Rockefeller	Y	Y	N	Y	N	Y
WISCONSIN						
Kohl	Y	Y	N	Y	N	Y
Feingold	Y	Y	Y	Y	Y	Y
WYOMING						
Thomas	N	Y	N	N	N	Y
Enzi	N	Y	N	N	N	Y

Key

- Y Voted for (yea).
- \# Paired for.
- \+ Announced for.
- N Voted against (nay).
- X Paired against.
- – Announced against.
- P Voted "present."
- C Voted "present" to avoid possible conflict of interest.
- ? Did not vote or otherwise make a position known.

•

Democrats ***Republicans***
Independents

ND Northern Democrats SD Southern Democrats

Southern states - Ala., Ark., Fla., Ga., Ky., La., Miss., N.C., Okla., S.C., Tenn., Texas, Va.

232. HR 4733. Fiscal 2001 Energy and Water Appropriations/Missouri River. Daschle, D-S.D., amendment that would strike language in the bill that would prohibit the use of funds for the Army Corps of Engineers to revise the Missouri River water control manual when such a revision provides for an increase in the springtime flows below Gavins Point Dam. Rejected 45-52: R 2-51; D 43-1 (ND 35-0, SD 8-1). Sept. 7, 2000. A "yea" was a vote in support of the president's position.

233. HR 4444. China Trade/Motion to Proceed. Motion to proceed to the bill that would make normal trade relations with the People's Republic of China permanent. Motion agreed to 92-5: R 48-5; D 44-0 (ND 35-0, SD 9-0). Sept. 7, 2000.

234. HR 4444. China Trade/Religious Freedom. Wellstone, D-Minn., amendment that would delay the effective date of permanent normal trade relations status with China until the president certifies that China has made substantial changes with respect to religious freedom, by demonstrating that China has: agreed to establish an ongoing and high-level dialogue with the U.S. government on religious freedom; ratified the International Convention on Civil and Political Rights; agreed to permit the U.S. Commission on International Religious Freedom and international human rights organizations unhindered access to religious leaders; responded to inquiries regarding people imprisoned, detained or under house arrest for religious reasons; and released prisoners incarcerated because of religious reasons. Rejected 30-67: R 15-38; D 15-29 (ND 14-21, SD 1-8). Sept. 7, 2000.

235. HR 4444. China Trade/Energy Technology. Byrd, D-W.Va., amendment that would require any U.S. government entity involved in any environmental and energy assistance programs in China to support the transfer of U.S. clean energy technology as part of that program, and authorize such sums as necessary to support the transfer of technology. Rejected 32-64: R 17-36; D 15-28 (ND 12-22, SD 2-7). Sept. 7, 2000.

236. HR 4444. China Trade/Annual Certification. Hollings, D-S.C., amendment that would strike language in the bill that would establish permanent normal trade relations with the People's Republic of China. The amendment would reinstate annual presidential certification and congressional review of normal trade relations with China and provide for the accession of China to the World Trade Organization. Rejected 13-81: R 7-45; D 6-36 (ND 5-28, SD 1-8). Sept. 7, 2000.

237. HR 4733. Fiscal 2001 Energy and Water Appropriations/Passage. Passage of the bill that would appropriate about $22.9 billion for the Energy Department, the Army Corps of Engineers, water projects, parts of the Interior Department, and other independent agencies for fiscal 2001, including $13.4 billion for defense-related activities, and $4.1 billion for the Corps of Engineers. Passed 93-1: R 52-0; D 41-1 (ND 32-1, SD 9-0). Sept. 7, 2000.

	238	239	240	241	242	243	244
ALABAMA							
Shelby	N	N	Y	N	N	Y	Y
Sessions	Y	Y	Y	Y	N	Y	Y
ALASKA							
Stevens	N	N	N	N	Y	N	N
Murkowski	N	N	N	N	Y	N	N
ARIZONA							
McCain	N	N	?	?	N	N	N
Kyl	N	Y	N	Y	N	Y	N
ARKANSAS							
Hutchinson	Y	Y	Y	Y	N	Y	N
Lincoln	N	N	N	N	Y	N	N
CALIFORNIA							
Feinstein	N	N	N	N	Y	N	N
Boxer	Y	Y	N	N	Y	Y	N
COLORADO							
Campbell	Y	Y	Y	N	Y	Y	Y
Allard	N	N	N	N	Y	N	N
CONNECTICUT							
Dodd	N	Y	N	N	Y	Y	N
Lieberman	?	?	?	?	?	?	?
DELAWARE							
Roth	N	N	N	N	Y	N	N
Biden	N	N	N	N	Y	N	N
FLORIDA							
Graham	N	N	N	N	Y	N	N
Mack	N	N	N	N	Y	N	N
GEORGIA							
Miller	N	N	N	N	Y	N	N
Cleland	N	N	N	N	Y	N	N
HAWAII							
Inouye	N	N	N	N	Y	N	N
Akaka	?	?	?	?	?	?	?
IDAHO							
Craig	N	Y	N	Y	Y	N	N
Crapo	N	N	N	N	Y	N	N
ILLINOIS							
Durbin	N	N	N	N	Y	N	N
Fitzgerald	N	N	N	N	Y	N	N
INDIANA							
Lugar	N	N	N	N	Y	N	N
Bayh	Y	N	Y	N	Y	Y	N
IOWA							
Grassley	N	N	N	N	Y	N	N
Harkin	Y	Y	N	N	Y	Y	N
KANSAS							
Brownback	N	N	N	N	Y	N	N
Roberts	N	N	N	N	Y	N	N
KENTUCKY							
McConnell	N	N	N	N	N	Y	N
Bunning	Y	Y	Y	Y	N	Y	N
LOUISIANA							
Breaux	N	N	N	N	Y	Y	N
Landrieu	N	N	N	N	Y	N	N
MAINE							
Snowe	Y	Y	Y	Y	N	Y	Y
Collins	Y	Y	Y	Y	N	Y	Y
MARYLAND							
Sarbanes	Y	Y	Y	Y	N	Y	Y
Mikulski	Y	Y	Y	Y	N	Y	Y
MASSACHUSETTS							
Kennedy	Y	Y	Y	Y	Y	?	?
Kerry	N	N	N	N	Y	Y	N
MICHIGAN							
Levin	N	N	Y	N	Y	N	N
Abraham	N	N	Y	Y	N	Y	N
MINNESOTA							
Wellstone	Y	Y	Y	N	N	Y	Y
Grams	N	?	N	N	Y	N	N
MISSISSIPPI							
Cochran	N	N	N	N	Y	N	N
Lott	N	Y	N	N	N	N	N
MISSOURI							
Bond	N	N	N	N	Y	N	N
Ashcroft	Y	Y	Y	Y	N	Y	Y
MONTANA							
Baucus	N	N	N	N	Y	N	N
Burns	N	Y	N	Y	Y	Y	N
NEBRASKA							
Kerrey	N	N	N	N	Y	N	N
Hagel	N	N	N	N	Y	N	N
NEVADA							
Reid	N	N	N	N	Y	Y	N
Bryan	N	N	N	N	Y	N	N
NEW HAMPSHIRE							
Smith	Y	Y	Y	Y	N	Y	Y
Gregg	Y	Y	Y	Y	N	Y	N
NEW JERSEY							
Lautenberg	Y	?	N	N	Y	N	Y
Torricelli	Y	Y	Y	Y	N	N	Y
NEW MEXICO							
Domenici	N	N	N	N	Y	N	N
Bingaman	N	N	N	N	Y	N	N
NEW YORK							
Moynihan	N	N	N	N	Y	N	N
Schumer	N	N	N	N	Y	N	N
NORTH CAROLINA							
Helms	Y	Y	Y	Y	N	Y	Y
Edwards	Y	N	Y	N	Y	Y	Y
NORTH DAKOTA							
Conrad	N	N	N	N	N	Y	N
Dorgan	Y	N	N	Y	Y	Y	N
OHIO							
DeWine	N	Y	Y	Y	N	Y	N
Voinovich	N	N	N	N	Y	Y	N
OKLAHOMA							
Nickles	N	N	N	N	Y	N	N
Inhofe	Y	Y	Y	Y	N	Y	Y
OREGON							
Wyden	N	N	N	N	Y	N	N
Smith	N	N	N	N	Y	N	N
PENNSYLVANIA							
Specter	Y	Y	Y	Y	N	Y	N
Santorum	Y	N	Y	Y	N	Y	N
RHODE ISLAND							
Reed	Y	Y	N	N	Y	Y	N
Chafee, L.	N	N	N	N	Y	N	N
SOUTH CAROLINA							
Thurmond	N	Y	Y	N	N	Y	Y
Hollings	Y	Y	Y	Y	N	Y	Y
SOUTH DAKOTA							
Daschle	N	N	N	N	Y	N	N
Johnson	N	N	N	N	Y	N	N
TENNESSEE							
Thompson	N	Y	Y	Y	N	Y	Y
Frist	N	N	N	N	N	N	N
TEXAS							
Gramm	N	N	N	N	Y	N	N
Hutchison	N	N	Y	N	N	N	N
UTAH							
Hatch	N	N	N	Y	Y	N	Y
Bennett	N	N	N	N	Y	N	N
VERMONT							
Leahy	Y	Y	Y	Y	Y	Y	N
Jeffords	?	?	?	?	Y	Y	Y
VIRGINIA							
Warner	N	N	N	N	Y	Y	N
Robb	N	N	N	N	Y	N	N
WASHINGTON							
Gorton	N	N	?	?	?	?	?
Murray	N	N	N	N	Y	N	N
WEST VIRGINIA							
Byrd	Y	Y	Y	Y	N	Y	Y
Rockefeller	N	N	Y	N	Y	N	N
WISCONSIN							
Kohl	N	N	Y	Y	N	Y	Y
Feingold	Y	Y	Y	Y	N	Y	Y
WYOMING							
Thomas	N	N	N	N	Y	N	N
Enzi	N	N	N	N	Y	N	N

ND Northern Democrats SD Southern Democrats

Southern states - Ala., Ark., Fla., Ga., Ky., La., Miss., N.C., Okla., S.C., Tenn., Texas, Va.

Key

Y Voted for (yea).
\# Paired for.
\+ Announced for.
N Voted against (nay).
X Paired against.
– Announced against.
P Voted "present."
C Voted "present" to avoid possible conflict of interest.
? Did not vote or otherwise make a position known.

•

Democrats ***Republicans***
Independents

238. HR 4444. China Trade/Prison Labor Products. Wellstone, D-Minn., amendment that would delay the effective date of permanent normal trade relations status for China until the president certifies that China is in compliance with various agreements prohibiting the import and export of prison labor products, and that China is fully cooperating with all outstanding U.S. requests for visitation and investigation of "reeducation through labor" facilities. Rejected 29-68: R 13-40; D 16-28 (ND 14-21, SD 2-7). Sept. 12, 2000.

239. HR 4444. China Trade/Human Rights. Helms, R-N.C., amendment that would delay the effective date of permanent normal trade relations status for China until the president certifies that China has ratified the International Covenant on Civil and Political Rights and is carrying out a number of specific reforms related to religious and human rights. Rejected 32-63: R 19-33; D 13-30 (ND 12-22, SD 1-8). Sept. 12, 2000.

240. HR 4444. China Trade/Import Relief. Byrd, D-W.Va., amendment that would establish a 15-day timetable, after a recommendation by the U.S. trade representative, for the president to provide import relief in the event of a market disruption, unless the president certifies to Congress that such relief is not in the U.S. national economic interest or that such action would cause serious harm to national security. Rejected 33-62: R 19-32; D 14-30 (ND 12-23, SD 2-7). Sept. 13, 2000.

241. HR 4444. China Trade/Organ Harvesting. Smith, R-N.H., amendment that would require the Congressional-Executive Commission, which would be created under the bill, to monitor China's cooperation in eliminating the harvesting and transporting of organs for profit from prisoners that it executes. The amendment would require the commission to issue an annual report on the results of the monitoring, including what actions China has taken to eliminate the harvesting of organs for profit. Rejected 29-66: R 19-32; D 10-34 (ND 9-26, SD 1-8). Sept. 13, 2000.

242. HR 4444. China Trade/Nonproliferation of Weapons. Roth, R-Del., motion to table (kill) the Thompson, R-Tenn., amendment that would provide for sanctions against China and other countries for selling illicit weapons of mass destruction. The proposal would establish an annual review process and would require the president to impose non-trade related sanctions on individuals, companies and groups found to be spreading weapons of mass destruction. The president also would be authorized to impose additional sanctions on key supplier countries. Motion agreed to 65-32: R 30-23; D 35-9 (ND 27-8, SD 8-1). Sept. 13, 2000.

243. HR 4444. China Trade/Forced Abortions. Helms, R-N.C. amendment that would express the sense of Congress that the president should urge China to cease forced abortion and sterilization policies and practices, and to cease its detention of those who resist. Rejected 43-53: R 24-29; D 19-24 (ND 16-18, SD 3-6). Sept. 13, 2000.

244. HR 4444. China Trade/U.S. Businesses. Helms, R-N.C., amendment that would express the sense of the Senate that the secretary of Commerce should encourage U.S. businesses with interests in China to adopt a voluntary code of conduct that "reflects basic American values of democracy, individual liberty and justice." Rejected 23-73: R 13-40; D 10-33 (ND 8-26, SD 2-7). Sept. 13, 2000.

Senate Votes 245, 246, 247, 248, 249, 250

	245	246	247	248	249	250
ALABAMA						
Shelby	N	N	N	Y	N	Y
Sessions	N	N	N	Y	N	Y
ALASKA						
Stevens	N	N	N	N	N	N
Murkowski	N	N	N	N	N	N
ARIZONA						
McCain	N	N	N	N	N	N
Kyl	N	N	N	N	N	N
ARKANSAS						
Hutchinson	Y	Y	N	Y	N	N
Lincoln	N	N	N	N	N	N
CALIFORNIA						
Feinstein	N	N	–	N	N	N
Boxer	N	Y	N	N	N	N
COLORADO						
Campbell	N	N	N	Y	Y	Y
Allard	N	N	N	N	N	N
CONNECTICUT						
Dodd	N	N	N	N	N	N
Lieberman	?	?	?	?	?	?
DELAWARE						
Roth	N	N	N	N	N	N
Biden	N	N	N	N	N	N
FLORIDA						
Graham	N	N	N	N	N	N
Mack	N	N	N	N	N	N
GEORGIA						
Miller	N	N	N	N	N	N
Cleland	N	N	N	N	N	N
HAWAII						
Inouye	N	N	N	N	N	N
Akaka	?	?	?	?	?	?
IDAHO						
Craig	N	N	N	N	N	N
Crapo	N	N	N	N	N	N
ILLINOIS						
Durbin	N	N	N	N	N	N
Fitzgerald	N	N	N	N	N	N
INDIANA						
Lugar	N	N	N	N	N	N
Bayh	N	Y	N	N	N	N
IOWA						
Grassley	N	N	N	N	N	N
Harkin	Y	Y	N	N	Y	Y
KANSAS						
Brownback	N	N	N	N	N	N
Roberts	N	N	N	N	N	N
KENTUCKY						
McConnell	N	N	N	N	N	N
Bunning	N	N	N	Y	N	N
LOUISIANA						
Breaux	N	N	N	N	N	N
Landrieu	N	N	N	N	N	N
MAINE						
Snowe	Y	Y	N	Y	Y	N
Collins	Y	Y	N	Y	Y	N
MARYLAND						
Sarbanes	Y	Y	N	Y	Y	Y
Mikulski	Y	Y	Y	Y	Y	Y
MASSACHUSETTS						
Kennedy	?	?	N	Y	Y	N
Kerry	N	N	N	N	N	N
MICHIGAN						
Levin	N	N	N	N	N	N
Abraham	N	N	N	N	N	N
MINNESOTA						
Wellstone	Y	Y	Y	Y	Y	Y
Grams	N	N	N	N	N	N
MISSISSIPPI						
Cochran	N	N	N	N	N	N
Lott	N	N	N	N	N	N
MISSOURI						
Bond	N	N	N	N	N	N
Ashcroft	N	Y	N	Y	Y	N
MONTANA						
Baucus	N	N	N	N	N	N
Burns	N	N	N	N	N	N
NEBRASKA						
Kerrey	N	N	?	N	N	N
Hagel	N	N	N	N	N	N
NEVADA						
Reid	N	N	N	N	N	N
Bryan	N	N	N	N	N	N
NEW HAMPSHIRE						
Smith	Y	Y	N	Y	Y	Y
Gregg	N	Y	N	N	N	N
NEW JERSEY						
Lautenberg	Y	N	N	N	Y	N
Torricelli	N	Y	N	N	Y	N
NEW MEXICO						
Domenici	N	N	N	N	N	N
Bingaman	N	N	N	N	N	N
NEW YORK						
Moynihan	N	N	N	N	N	N
Schumer	N	N	N	N	N	N
NORTH CAROLINA						
Helms	Y	Y	Y	Y	Y	Y
Edwards	N	N	N	N	Y	N
NORTH DAKOTA						
Conrad	N	N	N	Y	N	N
Dorgan	N	Y	N	Y	N	Y
OHIO						
DeWine	Y	N	N	Y	Y	N
Voinovich	N	N	N	Y	N	N
OKLAHOMA						
Nickles	N	N	N	N	N	N
Inhofe	N	Y	N	Y	Y	Y
OREGON						
Wyden	N	N	N	N	N	N
Smith	N	N	N	N	N	N
PENNSYLVANIA						
Specter	N	Y	N	Y	Y	Y
Santorum	N	N	N	Y	N	N
RHODE ISLAND						
Reed	Y	Y	N	N	Y	N
Chafee, L.	N	N	N	N	N	N
SOUTH CAROLINA						
Thurmond	N	N	N	Y	N	N
Hollings	Y	Y	Y	Y	Y	Y
SOUTH DAKOTA						
Daschle	N	N	N	N	N	N
Johnson	N	N	N	N	N	N
TENNESSEE						
Thompson	Y	N	N	Y	Y	N
Frist	N	N	N	N	N	N
TEXAS						
Gramm	N	N	N	N	N	N
Hutchison	N	N	N	N	N	Y
UTAH						
Hatch	N	N	N	Y	N	–
Bennett	N	N	N	N	N	N
VERMONT						
Leahy	Y	Y	N	Y	N	N
Jeffords	N	N	N	Y	Y	N
VIRGINIA						
Warner	N	N	N	Y	N	N
Robb	N	N	N	N	N	N
WASHINGTON						
Gorton	?	?	N	N	N	N
Murray	N	N	N	N	N	N
WEST VIRGINIA						
Byrd	Y	Y	Y	N	Y	Y
Rockefeller	N	N	N	N	N	N
WISCONSIN						
Kohl	Y	N	N	Y	Y	N
Feingold	Y	Y	Y	Y	Y	Y
WYOMING						
Thomas	N	N	N	N	N	N
Enzi	N	N	N	N	N	N

ND Northern Democrats SD Southern Democrats

Southern states - Ala., Ark., Fla., Ga., Ky., La., Miss., N.C., Okla., S.C., Tenn., Texas, Va.

Key

- Y Voted for (yea).
- # Paired for.
- + Announced for.
- N Voted against (nay).
- X Paired against.
- – Announced against.
- P Voted "present."
- C Voted "present" to avoid possible conflict of interest.
- ? Did not vote or otherwise make a position known.

•

Democrats ***Republicans***
Independents

245. HR 4444. China Trade/Congressional-Executive Commission. Feingold, D-Wis., amendment that would require the Congressional-Executive Commission, which would be created under the bill, to make recommendations for legislative and executive action, report annually to the House and Senate, and provide expedited procedures for considering a resolution implementing the commission's recommendations. Rejected 18-78: R 7-46; D 11-32 (ND 10-24, SD 1-8). Sept. 13, 2000.

246. HR 4444. China Trade/Union Organization. Wellstone, D-Minn., amendment that would delay permanent normal trade relations status for China until China has provided a detailed response to inquiries regarding the number of persons who are imprisoned, detained, or under house arrest for organizing unions, and has made substantial progress in releasing prisoners incarcerated for organizing independent trade unions. Rejected 22-74: R 9-44; D 13-30 (ND 12-22, SD 1-8). Sept. 13, 2000.

247. HR 4444. China Trade/Foreign Investment Information. Hollings, D-S.C., amendment that would direct the Securities and Exchange Commission to amend its regulations to require corporations to disclose foreign investment information in 10-K reports filed with the commission. Rejected 6-90: R 1-53; D 5-37 (ND 4-29, SD 1-8);. Sept. 14, 2000.

248. HR 4444. China Trade/Missing Prisoners of War. Smith, R-N.H., amendment that would require the Congressional-Executive Commission, which would be created under the bill, to monitor and encourage China in accounting for POWs and MIAs from the Korean War, Vietnam War, and the Cold War, and to report annually on China's cooperation. Rejected 30-68: R 20-34; D 10-34 (ND 9-26, SD 1-8). Sept. 14, 2000.

249. HR 4444. China Trade/Environmental Protection. Smith, R-N.H., amendment that would require the Congressional-Executive Commission, which would be created under the bill, to monitor and encourage China's cooperation in implementing and enforcing effective laws for the protection of human health and the environment. Rejected 24-74: R 11-43; D 13-31 (ND 11-24, SD 2-7). Sept. 14, 2000.

250. HR 4444. China Trade/Cereal and Soybean Trade Imbalance. Hollings, D-S.C., amendment that would require the president to report annually, beginning January 2001, on the balance of trade between the U.S. and China in cereals (wheat, corn and rice) and in soybeans. If there were a trade deficit, the president would be authorized to initiate negotiations to reduce or eliminate the imbalance. Rejected 16-81: R 8-45; D 8-36 (ND 7-28, SD 1-8). Sept. 14, 2000.

	251	252	253	254
ALABAMA				
Shelby	Y	Y	Y	Y
Sessions	Y	Y	N	Y
ALASKA				
Stevens	Y	Y	N	Y
Murkowski	Y	Y	Y	Y
ARIZONA				
McCain	Y	Y	N	N
Kyl	Y	Y	Y	Y
ARKANSAS				
Hutchinson	N	Y	Y	Y
Lincoln	Y	Y	N	N
CALIFORNIA				
Feinstein	Y	Y	?	?
Boxer	Y	Y	N	?
COLORADO				
Campbell	N	Y	Y	Y
Allard	Y	Y	Y	Y
CONNECTICUT				
Dodd	Y	Y	N	N
Lieberman	?	?	?	?
DELAWARE				
Roth	Y	Y	N	N
Biden	Y	Y	N	N
FLORIDA				
Graham	Y	Y	N	N
Mack	Y	Y	Y	N
GEORGIA				
Miller	Y	Y	N	N
Cleland	Y	Y	N	N
HAWAII				
Inouye	Y	Y	N	N
Akaka	?	?	?	?
IDAHO				
Craig	Y	Y	Y	N
Crapo	Y	Y	Y	?
ILLINOIS				
Durbin	Y	Y	N	N
Fitzgerald	Y	Y	Y	N
INDIANA				
Lugar	Y	Y	Y	N
Bayh	Y	Y	N	N

	251	252	253	254
IOWA				
Grassley	Y	Y	Y	Y
Harkin	Y	Y	N	N
KANSAS				
Brownback	Y	Y	N	N
Roberts	Y	Y	N	Y
KENTUCKY				
McConnell	Y	Y	Y	Y
Bunning	N	Y	N	Y
LOUISIANA				
Breaux	Y	Y	N	N
Landrieu	Y	Y	N	N
MAINE				
Snowe	Y	Y	N	N
Collins	Y	Y	N	N
MARYLAND				
Sarbanes	N	Y	N	N
Mikulski	N	Y	N	N
MASSACHUSETTS				
Kennedy	Y	Y	N	N
Kerry	Y	Y	N	N
MICHIGAN				
Levin	Y	Y	N	N
Abraham	Y	Y	N	N
MINNESOTA				
Wellstone	N	Y	N	N
Grams	Y	Y	N	N
MISSISSIPPI				
Cochran	Y	Y	Y	Y
Lott	Y	Y	Y	N
MISSOURI				
Bond	Y	Y	Y	N
Ashcroft	Y	Y	N	N
MONTANA				
Baucus	Y	Y	N	N
Burns	Y	Y	N	Y
NEBRASKA				
Kerrey	Y	Y	N	N
Hagel	Y	Y	Y	Y
NEVADA				
Reid	N	Y	N	N
Bryan	Y	Y	N	N

	251	252	253	254
NEW HAMPSHIRE				
Smith	N	Y	N	N
Gregg	Y	Y	Y	N
NEW JERSEY				
Lautenberg	Y	Y	N	N
Torricelli	Y	Y	N	N
NEW MEXICO				
Domenici	Y	Y	Y	N
Bingaman	Y	Y	N	N
NEW YORK				
Moynihan	Y	Y	N	N
Schumer	Y	Y	N	N
NORTH CAROLINA				
Helms	N	Y	N	Y
Edwards	Y	Y	N	N
NORTH DAKOTA				
Conrad	Y	Y	N	N
Dorgan	Y	Y	N	N
OHIO				
DeWine	Y	Y	N	N
Voinovich	Y	Y	N	Y
OKLAHOMA				
Nickles	Y	Y	Y	Y
Inhofe	N	Y	Y	Y
OREGON				
Wyden	Y	Y	N	N
Smith	Y	Y	Y	N
PENNSYLVANIA				
Specter	N	Y	Y	Y
Santorum	Y	Y	N	N
RHODE ISLAND				
Reed	Y	Y	N	N
Chafee, L.	Y	Y	N	N
SOUTH CAROLINA				
Thurmond	Y	Y	Y	N
Hollings	N	N	N	N
SOUTH DAKOTA				
Daschle	Y	Y	N	N
Johnson	Y	Y	N	N
TENNESSEE				
Thompson	Y	Y	N	N
Frist	Y	Y	N	N

Key

- Y Voted for (yea).
- # Paired for.
- + Announced for.
- N Voted against (nay).
- X Paired against.
- – Announced against.
- P Voted "present."
- C Voted "present" to avoid possible conflict of interest.
- ? Did not vote or otherwise make a position known.

Democrats ***Republicans***
Independents

	251	252	253	254
TEXAS				
Gramm	Y	Y	N	Y
Hutchison	Y	Y	N	Y
UTAH				
Hatch	Y	Y	N	N
Bennett	Y	Y	Y	N
VERMONT				
Leahy	Y	Y	N	N
Jeffords	N	Y	N	N
VIRGINIA				
Warner	Y	Y	N	Y
Robb	Y	Y	N	N
WASHINGTON				
Gorton	Y	Y	Y	N
Murray	Y	Y	N	N
WEST VIRGINIA				
Byrd	N	Y	N	N
Rockefeller	Y	Y	N	N
WISCONSIN				
Kohl	Y	Y	N	N
Feingold	N	Y	N	N
WYOMING				
Thomas	Y	Y	Y	Y
Enzi	Y	Y	Y	N

ND Northern Democrats SD Southern Democrats

Southern states - Ala., Ark., Fla., Ga., Ky., La., Miss., N.C., Okla., S.C., Tenn., Texas, Va.

251. HR 4444. China Trade/Passage. Passage of the bill that would make normal trade relations with the People's Republic of China permanent. The bill includes provisions to protect U.S. businesses and workers from import surges; establish a commission to monitor human rights, labor standards and religious freedom in China; require the administration to report annually on China's compliance with trade agreements; and express the sense of Congress that Taiwan should be admitted to the World Trade Organization.The measure would also authorize $99 million for Radio Free Asia and the Voice of America to expand broadcasts to China and neighboring countries. Passed (thus cleared for the president) 83-15: R 46-8; D 37-7 (ND 29-6, SD 8-1). Sept. 19, 2000. A "yea" was a vote in support of the president's position.

252. S 2045. H-1B Visas/Cloture. Motion to invoke cloture (thus limiting debate) on the motion to proceed to the bill that would increase the number of H-1B visas from 115,000 in fiscal 2000, to 195,000 annually in fiscal 2000-2002. Motion agreed to 97-1: R 54-0; D 43-1 (ND 35-0, SD 8-1). Sept. 19, 2000.

253. HR 4516. Fiscal 2001 Legislative Branch, Treasury-Postal Service Appropriations/Conference Report. Adoption of the conference report on the bill that would appropriate $2.5 billion in fiscal 2001 for the legislative branch; appropriate $30.4 billion for the Treasury Department, Postal Service, executive office of the president and certain independent agencies; and repeal the 3 percent federal excise tax on telecommunications services by the end of 2002. Rejected 28-69: R 28-26; D 0-43 (ND 0-34, SD 0-9). Sept. 20, 2000.

254. S 2796. Water Resources Development/Everglades Operation and Maintenance Costs. Warner, R-Va., amendment that would strike the provision in the bill that would require the federal government to finance half of the annual operation and management costs of the Everglades Restoration Project and require the state of Florida to be responsible for those costs. Rejected 24-71: R 24-29; D 0-42 (ND 0-33, SD 0-9). Sept. 21, 2000.

	255	256	257	258	259	260
ALABAMA						
Shelby	Y	Y	N	Y	Y	Y
Sessions	Y	Y	N	Y	Y	Y
ALASKA						
Stevens	Y	Y	N	Y	Y	Y
Murkowski	Y	Y	N	Y	Y	Y
ARIZONA						
McCain	?	Y	N	Y	?	?
Kyl	Y	Y	N	Y	Y	Y
ARKANSAS						
Hutchinson	Y	Y	N	Y	Y	Y
Lincoln	Y	Y	Y	Y	Y	Y
CALIFORNIA						
Feinstein	?	?	?	?	?	?
Boxer	Y	Y	Y	Y	Y	Y
COLORADO						
Campbell	Y	Y	N	Y	Y	Y
Allard	Y	Y	N	Y	Y	Y
CONNECTICUT						
Dodd	Y	Y	Y	Y	Y	Y
Lieberman	?	?	?	?	?	?
DELAWARE						
Roth	Y	Y	N	Y	Y	Y
Biden	Y	Y	Y	Y	Y	Y
FLORIDA						
Graham	Y	Y	Y	Y	Y	Y
Mack	Y	Y	N	Y	Y	Y
GEORGIA						
Miller	?	Y	Y	Y	Y	Y
Cleland	Y	Y	Y	Y	Y	Y
HAWAII						
Inouye	Y	Y	Y	Y	Y	Y
Akaka	?	?	Y	Y	Y	Y
IDAHO						
Craig	Y	Y	N	Y	Y	Y
Crapo	Y	Y	N	Y	Y	Y
ILLINOIS						
Durbin	Y	Y	Y	Y	Y	Y
Fitzgerald	Y	Y	N	Y	Y	Y
INDIANA						
Lugar	Y	Y	N	Y	Y	Y
Bayh	Y	Y	Y	Y	Y	Y

	255	256	257	258	259	260
IOWA						
Grassley	Y	Y	N	Y	Y	Y
Harkin	Y	Y	Y	Y	Y	Y
KANSAS						
Brownback	Y	Y	N	Y	Y	Y
Roberts	Y	Y	N	Y	Y	Y
KENTUCKY						
McConnell	?	Y	N	Y	Y	Y
Bunning	Y	Y	N	Y	Y	Y
LOUISIANA						
Breaux	Y	Y	Y	Y	Y	Y
Landrieu	Y	Y	Y	Y	Y	Y
MAINE						
Snowe	Y	Y	N	Y	Y	Y
Collins	Y	Y	N	Y	Y	Y
MARYLAND						
Sarbanes	Y	Y	Y	Y	Y	Y
Mikulski	Y	Y	Y	Y	Y	Y
MASSACHUSETTS						
Kennedy	Y	Y	Y	Y	Y	Y
Kerry	Y	Y	Y	Y	Y	Y
MICHIGAN						
Levin	Y	Y	Y	Y	Y	Y
Abraham	Y	Y	N	Y	Y	Y
MINNESOTA						
Wellstone	Y	Y	Y	N	Y	N
Grams	Y	Y	N	Y	Y	Y
MISSISSIPPI						
Cochran	Y	Y	N	Y	Y	Y
Lott	Y	Y	N	Y	Y	Y
MISSOURI						
Bond	Y	Y	N	Y	Y	Y
Ashcroft	Y	Y	N	Y	Y	Y
MONTANA						
Baucus	Y	Y	Y	Y	Y	Y
Burns	Y	Y	N	Y	Y	Y
NEBRASKA						
Kerrey	Y	Y	Y	Y	Y	Y
Hagel	Y	Y	N	Y	Y	Y
NEVADA						
Reid	Y	Y	Y	Y	Y	Y
Bryan	Y	Y	Y	Y	Y	Y

	255	256	257	258	259	260
NEW HAMPSHIRE						
Smith	Y	Y	N	Y	Y	Y
Gregg	Y	Y	N	Y	Y	Y
NEW JERSEY						
Lautenberg	?	Y	Y	Y	Y	Y
Torricelli	Y	Y	Y	Y	Y	Y
NEW MEXICO						
Domenici	Y	Y	N	Y	Y	Y
Bingaman	?	Y	Y	Y	Y	Y
NEW YORK						
Moynihan	Y	Y	Y	Y	Y	Y
Schumer	?	Y	Y	Y	Y	Y
NORTH CAROLINA						
Helms	Y	Y	N	Y	Y	Y
Edwards	Y	Y	Y	Y	Y	Y
NORTH DAKOTA						
Conrad	Y	Y	Y	Y	Y	Y
Dorgan	Y	Y	Y	Y	Y	Y
OHIO						
DeWine	Y	Y	N	Y	Y	Y
Voinovich	Y	Y	N	Y	Y	Y
OKLAHOMA						
Nickles	Y	Y	N	Y	Y	Y
Inhofe	N	Y	N	Y	Y	Y
OREGON						
Wyden	Y	Y	Y	Y	Y	Y
Smith	?	Y	N	Y	Y	Y
PENNSYLVANIA						
Specter	Y	Y	N	Y	Y	Y
Santorum	Y	Y	N	Y	Y	Y
RHODE ISLAND						
Reed	Y	N	Y	Y	Y	N
Chafee, L.	Y	N	N	Y	Y	Y
SOUTH CAROLINA						
Thurmond	Y	Y	N	Y	Y	Y
Hollings	Y	N	Y	N	Y	N
SOUTH DAKOTA						
Daschle	Y	Y	Y	Y	Y	Y
Johnson	Y	Y	Y	Y	Y	Y
TENNESSEE						
Thompson	Y	Y	N	Y	Y	Y
Frist	Y	Y	N	Y	Y	Y

Key

- Y Voted for (yea).
- # Paired for.
- \+ Announced for.
- N Voted against (nay).
- X Paired against.
- – Announced against.
- P Voted "present."
- C Voted "present" to avoid possible conflict of interest.
- ? Did not vote or otherwise make a position known.

•

Democrats ***Republicans***
Independents

	255	256	257	258	259	260
TEXAS						
Gramm	Y	Y	N	Y	Y	Y
Hutchison	Y	Y	N	Y	Y	Y
UTAH						
Hatch	Y	Y	N	Y	Y	Y
Bennett	Y	Y	N	Y	Y	Y
VERMONT						
Leahy	Y	Y	Y	Y	Y	Y
Jeffords	?	Y	N	Y	Y	Y
VIRGINIA						
Warner	Y	Y	N	Y	Y	Y
Robb	Y	Y	Y	Y	Y	Y
WASHINGTON						
Gorton	?	Y	N	Y	Y	Y
Murray	Y	Y	Y	Y	Y	+
WEST VIRGINIA						
Byrd	Y	Y	N	Y	Y	Y
Rockefeller	Y	Y	Y	Y	Y	Y
WISCONSIN						
Kohl	Y	Y	Y	Y	Y	Y
Feingold	Y	Y	Y	Y	Y	Y
WYOMING						
Thomas	?	Y	N	Y	?	?
Enzi	?	Y	N	Y	Y	Y

ND Northern Democrats SD Southern Democrats

Southern states - Ala., Ark., Fla., Ga., Ky., La., Miss., N.C., Okla., S.C., Tenn., Texas, Va.

255. S 2796. Water Resources Development/Passage. Passage of the bill that would authorize the first phase of a project to restore the Everglades ecosystem at a cost of $1.4 billion, to be jointly funded by the state of Florida and the federal government. The bill would also authorize dozens of other water projects and feasibility studies. Passed 85-1: R 46-1; D 39-0 (ND 31-0, SD 8-0). Sept. 25, 2000.

256. S 2045. H-1B Visas/Cloture. Motion to invoke cloture (thus limiting debate) on the Lott, R-Miss., amendment to the Lott amendment. Both amendments would increase the number of H-1B visas from 115,000 in fiscal 2000 to 195,000 annually for fiscal 2000-2002. Motion agreed to 94-3: R 53-1; D 41-2 (ND 33-1, SD 8-1). Sept. 26, 2000.

257. S 2045. H-1B Visas/Suspend Rule XXII. Daschle, D-S.D., motion to suspend Rule XXII to permit the consideration of the Kennedy, D-Mass., amendment that would create a set of procedures to allow certain immigrants from Central America, Haiti, Liberia and eastern Europe and former Soviet bloc countries to apply for permanent residence. It also would change the registry date from 1972 to 1986, and restore a provision in immigration law that would allow immigrants to remain in the United States while applying for permanent residence. Motion rejected 43-55: R 0-54; D 43-1 (ND 34-1, SD 9-0). A two-thirds majority of those voting (66 in this case), a quorum being present, is required to suspend the rules of the Senate. Sept. 27, 2000.

258. S 2045. H-1B Visas/Increase in Visas. Lott, R-Miss., amendment to the Lott amendment. Both amendments would increase the number of H-1B visas from 115,000 in fiscal 2000 to 195,000 annually for fiscal 2000-2002. Adopted 96-2: R 54-0; D 42-2 (ND 34-1, SD 8-1). Sept. 27, 2000.

259. H J Res 109. Continuing Resolution/Passage. Passage of the joint resolution that would provide temporary funding authority, at current levels, until Oct. 6, for the departments, agencies and programs for which regular fiscal year 2001 appropriations bills will not be enacted by Oct. 1. Passed (thus cleared for the president) 96-0: R 52-0; D 44-0 (ND 35-0, SD 9-0). Sept. 28, 2000.

260. S 2045. H-1B Visas/Cloture. Motion to invoke cloture (thus limiting debate) on the Lott, R-Miss., amendment to the committee substitute. Both would increase the number of H-1B visas from 115,000 in fiscal 2000 to 195,000 annually for fiscal 2000-2002. Motion agreed to 92-3: R 52-0; D 40-3 (ND 32-2, SD 8-1). Three-fifths of the total Senate (60) is required to invoke cloture. Sept. 28, 2000.

	261	262	263	264	265	266
ALABAMA						
Shelby	Y	Y	Y	Y	Y	Y
Sessions	Y	Y	Y	Y	Y	N
ALASKA						
Stevens	Y	Y	Y	Y	Y	Y
Murkowski	Y	Y	Y	Y	Y	Y
ARIZONA						
McCain	N	Y	Y	Y	N	N
Kyl	Y	Y	Y	Y	Y	Y
ARKANSAS						
Hutchinson	Y	Y	Y	Y	Y	Y
Lincoln	Y	Y	?	Y	Y	Y
CALIFORNIA						
Feinstein	?	?	?	?	?	?
Boxer	N	Y	Y	Y	Y	Y
COLORADO						
Campbell	Y	Y	Y	Y	Y	Y
Allard	Y	Y	Y	Y	Y	Y
CONNECTICUT						
Dodd	N	Y	Y	Y	Y	Y
Lieberman	?	?	?	?	?	?
DELAWARE						
Roth	Y	Y	Y	Y	Y	Y
Biden	N	Y	Y	Y	Y	Y
FLORIDA						
Graham	N	Y	Y	Y	N	N
Mack	Y	Y	Y	Y	Y	Y
GEORGIA						
Miller	Y	Y	Y	Y	Y	Y
Cleland	N	Y	Y	Y	Y	Y
HAWAII						
Inouye	N	Y	Y	Y	Y	Y
Akaka	N	Y	Y	Y	Y	Y
IDAHO						
Craig	Y	Y	Y	Y	Y	Y
Crapo	Y	Y	Y	Y	Y	Y
ILLINOIS						
Durbin	N	Y	Y	Y	Y	Y
Fitzgerald	Y	Y	Y	Y	N	N
INDIANA						
Lugar	Y	Y	Y	Y	Y	Y
Bayh	N	Y	Y	Y	Y	Y

	261	262	263	264	265	266
IOWA						
Grassley	Y	Y	Y	Y	Y	Y
Harkin	N	Y	Y	Y	Y	Y
KANSAS						
Brownback	Y	Y	Y	Y	Y	N
Roberts	Y	Y	Y	Y	Y	Y
KENTUCKY						
McConnell	Y	Y	Y	Y	Y	Y
Bunning	Y	Y	Y	Y	Y	Y
LOUISIANA						
Breaux	N	Y	Y	Y	N	N
Landrieu	N	Y	Y	Y	N	N
MAINE						
Snowe	Y	Y	Y	Y	Y	Y
Collins	Y	Y	Y	Y	Y	Y
MARYLAND						
Sarbanes	N	Y	Y	Y	Y	Y
Mikulski	N	Y	Y	Y	Y	Y
MASSACHUSETTS						
Kennedy	–	+	?	Y	Y	+
Kerry	N	Y	Y	Y	Y	Y
MICHIGAN						
Levin	N	Y	Y	Y	Y	Y
Abraham	Y	Y	Y	Y	Y	Y
MINNESOTA						
Wellstone	N	Y	Y	Y	Y	Y
Grams	?	Y	Y	Y	Y	Y
MISSISSIPPI						
Cochran	Y	Y	Y	Y	Y	Y
Lott	Y	Y	Y	Y	Y	Y
MISSOURI						
Bond	Y	Y	Y	Y	Y	Y
Ashcroft	Y	Y	Y	Y	Y	Y
MONTANA						
Baucus	N	Y	Y	Y	Y	Y
Burns	Y	Y	Y	Y	Y	Y
NEBRASKA						
Kerrey	N	Y	Y	Y	Y	Y
Hagel	Y	Y	Y	Y	Y	Y
NEVADA						
Reid	N	Y	Y	Y	Y	Y
Bryan	N	Y	Y	Y	Y	Y

	261	262	263	264	265	266
NEW HAMPSHIRE						
Smith	Y	Y	Y	Y	N	N
Gregg	Y	Y	?	Y	Y	Y
NEW JERSEY						
Lautenberg	N	Y	Y	Y	Y	Y
Torricelli	N	Y	Y	Y	Y	Y
NEW MEXICO						
Domenici	Y	Y	Y	Y	Y	Y
Bingaman	Y	Y	Y	Y	Y	Y
NEW YORK						
Moynihan	N	Y	Y	Y	Y	Y
Schumer	N	Y	Y	Y	Y	Y
NORTH CAROLINA						
Helms	Y	Y	Y	?	Y	N
Edwards	Y	Y	Y	Y	Y	Y
NORTH DAKOTA						
Conrad	N	Y	Y	Y	Y	Y
Dorgan	N	Y	Y	Y	Y	Y
OHIO						
DeWine	Y	Y	Y	Y	Y	Y
Voinovich	Y	Y	Y	Y	Y	N
OKLAHOMA						
Nickles	Y	Y	Y	Y	Y	Y
Inhofe	Y	Y	Y	Y	N	N
OREGON						
Wyden	?	Y	Y	Y	Y	Y
Smith	Y	Y	Y	Y	Y	Y
PENNSYLVANIA						
Specter	Y	Y	Y	Y	Y	Y
Santorum	Y	Y	Y	Y	Y	Y
RHODE ISLAND						
Reed	N	Y	Y	Y	Y	Y
Chafee, L.	Y	Y	Y	Y	Y	Y
SOUTH CAROLINA						
Thurmond	Y	Y	Y	Y	Y	Y
Hollings	N	N	Y	Y	Y	Y
SOUTH DAKOTA						
Daschle	N	Y	Y	Y	Y	Y
Johnson	N	Y	Y	Y	Y	Y
TENNESSEE						
Thompson	Y	Y	Y	Y	Y	Y
Frist	Y	Y	Y	Y	Y	Y

Key

- Y Voted for (yea).
- # Paired for.
- \+ Announced for.
- N Voted against (nay).
- X Paired against.
- – Announced against.
- P Voted "present."
- C Voted "present" to avoid possible conflict of interest.
- ? Did not vote or otherwise make a position known.

Democrats **Republicans**
Independents

	261	262	263	264	265	266
TEXAS						
Gramm	Y	Y	Y	Y	Y	N
Hutchison	Y	Y	Y	Y	Y	Y
UTAH						
Hatch	+	Y	Y	Y	Y	Y
Bennett	Y	Y	Y	Y	Y	Y
VERMONT						
Leahy	N	Y	Y	N	Y	Y
Jeffords	Y	Y	Y	?	?	?
VIRGINIA						
Warner	Y	Y	Y	Y	Y	Y
Robb	N	Y	Y	Y	Y	Y
WASHINGTON						
Gorton	Y	Y	Y	Y	Y	Y
Murray	Y	Y	Y	Y	Y	Y
WEST VIRGINIA						
Byrd	Y	Y	Y	Y	Y	Y
Rockefeller	N	Y	Y	Y	Y	Y
WISCONSIN						
Kohl	N	Y	Y	Y	Y	Y
Feingold	N	Y	Y	Y	N	N
WYOMING						
Thomas	Y	Y	Y	Y	Y	Y
Enzi	Y	Y	Y	Y	Y	Y

ND Northern Democrats SD Southern Democrats

Southern states - Ala., Ark., Fla., Ga., Ky., La., Miss., N.C., Okla., S.C., Tenn., Texas, Va.

261. HR 4733. Fiscal 2001 Energy-Water Appropriations/Conference Report. Adoption of the conference report on the bill that would appropriate $23.6 billion in fiscal 2001 for the Energy Department, the Army Corps of Engineers and other agencies, an 11 percent increase over current levels and $890 million more than the president requested. Adopted (thus cleared for the president) 57-37: R 51-1; D 6-36 (ND 3-30, SD 3-6). Oct. 2, 2000.

262. S 2045. H-1B Visas/Passage. Passage of the bill that would increase the number of H-1B visas from 115,000 in fiscal 2000, to 195,000 annually for fiscal 2001-2003. It would exclude from the cap foreign workers who sign up to work for government or nonprofit research organizations. Passed 96-1: R 54-0; D 42-1 (ND 34-0, SD 8-1). Oct. 3, 2000.

263. Teilborg Nomination/Confirmation. Confirmation of President Clinton's nomination of James A. Teilborg of Arizona to be U.S. District judge for the District of Arizona. Confirmed 95-0: R 53-0; D 42-0 (ND 34-0, SD 8-0). A "yea" was a vote in support of the president's position. Oct. 3, 2000.

264. H J Res 110. Continuing Resolution/Passage. Passage of the joint resolution that would provide temporary funding authority, at current levels until Oct. 14, for the departments, agencies and programs for which regular fiscal year 2001 appropriations bills will not be enacted by Oct. 6. Passed (thus cleared for the president) 95-1: R 52-0; D 43-1 (ND 34-1, SD 9-0). Oct. 5, 2000.

265. HR 4578. Fiscal 2001 Interior Appropriations/Cloture. Motion to invoke cloture (thus limiting debate) on the conference report on the bill that would appropriate $18.8 billion to the Interior Department and related agencies. Motion agreed to 89-8: R 49-4; D 40-4 (ND 34-1, SD 6-3). Three-fifths of the total Senate (60) is required to invoke cloture. Oct. 5, 2000.

266. HR 4578. Fiscal 2001 Interior Appropriations/Conference Report. Adoption of the conference report on the bill that would appropriate $18.8 billion for the Interior Department and related agencies. The bill includes an additional $1.6 billion in emergency funds and would provide $12 billion over six years for a land conservation and maintenance fund. Adopted (thus cleared for the president) 83-13: R 44-9; D 39-4 (ND 33-1, SD 6-3). Oct. 5, 2000.

	267	268	269	270	271
ALABAMA					
Shelby	Y	Y	Y	Y	Y
Sessions	Y	Y	Y	Y	Y
ALASKA					
Stevens	Y	Y	Y	Y	Y
Murkowski	?	Y	Y	Y	Y
ARIZONA					
McCain	N	Y	Y	Y	Y
Kyl	?	Y	Y	Y	Y
ARKANSAS					
Hutchinson	Y	Y	Y	Y	Y
Lincoln	Y	Y	Y	Y	N
CALIFORNIA					
Feinstein	?	?	?	?	?
Boxer	?	Y	Y	N	N
COLORADO					
Campbell	?	Y	Y	Y	Y
Allard	N	Y	Y	Y	Y
CONNECTICUT					
Dodd	Y	Y	Y	N	N
Lieberman	?	?	?	?	?
DELAWARE					
Roth	Y	Y	Y	N	N
Biden	Y	Y	Y	N	N
FLORIDA					
Graham	N	Y	Y	N	N
Mack	Y	Y	Y	Y	Y
GEORGIA					
Miller	Y	Y	Y	Y	Y
Cleland	Y	Y	Y	Y	Y
HAWAII					
Inouye	Y	Y	Y	Y	Y
Akaka	Y	Y	Y	N	N
IDAHO					
Craig	Y	Y	Y	Y	Y
Crapo	Y	Y	Y	Y	Y
ILLINOIS					
Durbin	+	Y	Y	N	N
Fitzgerald	Y	Y	Y	N	N
INDIANA					
Lugar	Y	Y	Y	Y	Y
Bayh	Y	Y	Y	Y	N

	267	268	269	270	271
IOWA					
Grassley	Y	Y	Y	Y	Y
Harkin	Y	Y	Y	Y	N
KANSAS					
Brownback	Y	Y	Y	Y	Y
Roberts	Y	Y	Y	Y	Y
KENTUCKY					
McConnell	Y	Y	Y	Y	Y
Bunning	Y	Y	Y	Y	Y
LOUISIANA					
Breaux	Y	Y	Y	Y	Y
Landrieu	Y	Y	Y	Y	N
MAINE					
Snowe	Y	Y	Y	N	N
Collins	Y	Y	Y	N	N
MARYLAND					
Sarbanes	Y	Y	Y	N	Y
Mikulski	Y	Y	Y	Y	Y
MASSACHUSETTS					
Kennedy	+	Y	Y	–	–
Kerry	Y	?	?	N	N
MICHIGAN					
Levin	Y	Y	Y	Y	N
Abraham	Y	Y	Y	Y	N
MINNESOTA					
Wellstone	Y	Y	Y	N	N
Grams	Y	Y	Y	?	?
MISSISSIPPI					
Cochran	Y	Y	Y	Y	Y
Lott	Y	Y	Y	Y	Y
MISSOURI					
Bond	?	N	Y	Y	Y
Ashcroft	Y	Y	Y	Y	Y
MONTANA					
Baucus	N	Y	Y	N	N
Burns	Y	Y	Y	Y	Y
NEBRASKA					
Kerrey	Y	Y	Y	N	N
Hagel	Y	N	Y	Y	Y
NEVADA					
Reid	Y	Y	Y	N	N
Bryan	Y	Y	Y	N	N

	267	268	269	270	271
NEW HAMPSHIRE					
Smith	N	Y	Y	Y	Y
Gregg	Y	Y	Y	Y	Y
NEW JERSEY					
Lautenberg	Y	Y	Y	N	N
Torricelli	Y	Y	Y	N	N
NEW MEXICO					
Domenici	Y	Y	Y	Y	Y
Bingaman	Y	Y	Y	Y	N
NEW YORK					
Moynihan	Y	Y	Y	Y	N
Schumer	Y	Y	Y	N	N
NORTH CAROLINA					
Helms	Y	?	?	?	?
Edwards	Y	Y	Y	N	N
NORTH DAKOTA					
Conrad	Y	Y	Y	Y	N
Dorgan	+	Y	Y	Y	Y
OHIO					
DeWine	Y	Y	Y	Y	Y
Voinovich	N	N	Y	Y	Y
OKLAHOMA					
Nickles	N	Y	Y	Y	Y
Inhofe	Y	+	+	Y	Y
OREGON					
Wyden	Y	Y	Y	N	N
Smith	Y	Y	Y	Y	Y
PENNSYLVANIA					
Specter	Y	Y	Y	N	N
Santorum	Y	Y	Y	Y	Y
RHODE ISLAND					
Reed	Y	Y	Y	N	N
Chafee, L.	Y	Y	Y	N	N
SOUTH CAROLINA					
Thurmond	Y	Y	Y	Y	Y
Hollings	Y	Y	Y	N	Y
SOUTH DAKOTA					
Daschle	Y	Y	Y	Y	Y
Johnson	Y	Y	Y	N	N
TENNESSEE					
Thompson	Y	N	Y	Y	Y
Frist	Y	Y	Y	Y	Y

Key

Y	Voted for (yea).
#	Paired for.
+	Announced for.
N	Voted against (nay).
X	Paired against.
–	Announced against.
P	Voted "present."
C	Voted "present" to avoid possible conflict of interest.
?	Did not vote or otherwise make a position known.

•

Democrats ***Republicans***
Independents

	267	268	269	270	271
TEXAS					
Gramm	N	Y	Y	Y	Y
Hutchison	Y	Y	Y	Y	Y
UTAH					
Hatch	Y	Y	Y	Y	Y
Bennett	Y	Y	Y	Y	Y
VERMONT					
Leahy	Y	Y	Y	N	N
Jeffords	Y	Y	Y	N	N
VIRGINIA					
Warner	Y	Y	Y	Y	Y
Robb	Y	Y	Y	N	N
WASHINGTON					
Gorton	Y	Y	Y	Y	Y
Murray	+	Y	Y	N	N
WEST VIRGINIA					
Byrd	Y	Y	Y	Y	Y
Rockefeller	Y	Y	Y	Y	Y
WISCONSIN					
Kohl	Y	Y	Y	Y	Y
Feingold	N	N	Y	N	N
WYOMING					
Thomas	N	Y	Y	Y	Y
Enzi	?	Y	Y	Y	Y

ND Northern Democrats SD Southern Democrats

Southern states - Ala., Ark., Fla., Ga., Ky., La., Miss., N.C., Okla., S.C., Tenn., Texas, Va.

267. HR 4475. Fiscal 2001 Transportation Appropriations/Conference Report. Adoption of the conference report on the bill that would provide $58 billion for the Transportation Department and related agencies in fiscal 2001, including $31.4 billion in highway funding. Adopted (thus cleared for the president) 78-10: R 42-7; D 36-3 (ND 28-2, SD 8-1). Oct. 6, 2000.

268. HR 3244. Human Trafficking/Ruling of the Chair. Judgment of the Senate to affirm the ruling of the chair against the Thompson, R-Tenn., point of order against the conference report on the bill that would combat human trafficking. Ruling of the chair upheld 90-5: R 48-4; D 42-1 (ND 33-1, SD 9-0). Oct. 11, 2000.

269. HR 3244. Human Trafficking/Conference Report. Adoption of the conference report on the bill to combat human trafficking, including those forced into sexual slavery, and establish a new visa for aliens who are victims of human trafficking. The bill also would: reauthorize the Violence Against Women Act and authorize $3.3 billion in fiscal 2001-2005 to carry it out; strengthen enforcement of state laws outlawing direct sales of alcohol over the Internet; require states releasing violent sexual offenders who commit similar crimes in another state to reimburse the second state for costs related to the incarceration, prosecution and apprehension of the criminal; and allow terrorism victims to recover judgments from frozen assets of countries listed by the State Department as terrorism sponsors. Adopted (thus cleared for the president) 95-0: R 52-0; D 43-0 (ND 34-0, SD 9-0). A "yea" was a vote in support of the president's position. Oct. 11, 2000.

270. HR 4635. Fiscal 2001 VA-HUD Appropriations/Drinking Water. Bond, R-Mo., motion to table (kill) the Boxer, D-Calif., amendment that would strike the provisions in the bill that would move by 6 months the effective date of the EPA's new drinking water standard for arsenic and prohibit the EPA from designating communities that do not meet smog standards under the Clean Air Act, until June 15, 2001, or until the Supreme Court acts. Motion agreed to 63-32: R 45-7; D 18-25 (ND 13-21, SD 5-4). Oct. 12, 2000.

271. HR 4635. Fiscal 2001 VA-HUD Appropriations/Clean Rivers. Bond, R-Mo., motion to table (kill) the Boxer, D-Calif., amendment that would express the sense of Congress that the EPA should move quickly to clean up U.S. rivers and ocean sites that have been contaminated with DDT, PCBs, dioxins, metals or other pollutants to protect the public health and environment. Motion agreed to 56-39: R 44-8; D 12-31 (ND 8-26, SD 4-5). Oct. 12, 2000.

Senate Votes 272, 273, 274, 275, 276

	272	273	274	275	276
ALABAMA					
Shelby	Y	Y	Y	Y	Y
Sessions	Y	N	Y	Y	Y
ALASKA					
Stevens	Y	Y	Y	Y	Y
Murkowski	Y	Y	Y	Y	Y
ARIZONA					
McCain	N	N	?	?	?
Kyl	N	Y	Y	Y	Y
ARKANSAS					
Hutchinson	Y	Y	Y	Y	Y
Lincoln	Y	N	Y	Y	Y
CALIFORNIA					
Feinstein	?	?	?	?	?
Boxer	Y	Y	Y	Y	Y
COLORADO					
Campbell	Y	Y	Y	Y	Y
Allard	N	N	Y	Y	Y
CONNECTICUT					
Dodd	Y	Y	Y	Y	Y
Lieberman	?	?	?	?	?
DELAWARE					
Roth	Y	Y	Y	Y	Y
Biden	Y	N	Y	Y	Y
FLORIDA					
Graham	N	N	N	Y	Y
Mack	Y	Y	N	Y	Y
GEORGIA					
Miller	Y	N	Y	Y	Y
Cleland	Y	N	Y	Y	Y
HAWAII					
Inouye	Y	Y	Y	Y	Y
Akaka	Y	Y	Y	Y	Y
IDAHO					
Craig	Y	Y	Y	Y	Y
Crapo	Y	Y	Y	Y	Y
ILLINOIS					
Durbin	Y	Y	Y	Y	Y
Fitzgerald	Y	Y	Y	Y	Y
INDIANA					
Lugar	Y	Y	Y	Y	Y
Bayh	Y	N	Y	Y	Y
IOWA					
Grassley	Y	Y	Y	Y	Y
Harkin	Y	N	Y	Y	Y
KANSAS					
Brownback	Y	N	Y	Y	?
Roberts	Y	N	Y	Y	Y
KENTUCKY					
McConnell	Y	Y	Y	Y	Y
Bunning	Y	N	Y	Y	Y
LOUISIANA					
Breaux	Y	Y	Y	Y	Y
Landrieu	Y	Y	Y	Y	Y
MAINE					
Snowe	Y	N	Y	Y	Y
Collins	Y	N	Y	Y	Y
MARYLAND					
Sarbanes	Y	Y	Y	Y	Y
Mikulski	Y	Y	Y	Y	Y
MASSACHUSETTS					
Kennedy	+	+	+	+	+
Kerry	Y	Y	Y	Y	Y
MICHIGAN					
Levin	Y	Y	Y	Y	Y
Abraham	Y	N	Y	Y	Y
MINNESOTA					
Wellstone	Y	N	Y	N	Y
Grams	?	?	?	?	?
MISSISSIPPI					
Cochran	Y	Y	Y	Y	Y
Lott	Y	Y	Y	Y	Y
MISSOURI					
Bond	Y	Y	Y	Y	Y
Ashcroft	Y	N	Y	Y	Y
MONTANA					
Baucus	Y	N	Y	Y	Y
Burns	Y	N	Y	Y	?
NEBRASKA					
Kerrey	Y	Y	N	N	Y
Hagel	Y	Y	Y	Y	Y
NEVADA					
Reid	Y	Y	Y	Y	Y
Bryan	Y	N	N	Y	Y
NEW HAMPSHIRE					
Smith	Y	N	Y	Y	Y
Gregg	Y	Y	N	Y	Y
NEW JERSEY					
Lautenberg	Y	Y	Y	Y	Y
Torricelli	Y	Y	?	?	?
NEW MEXICO					
Domenici	Y	Y	N	Y	Y
Bingaman	Y	N	Y	Y	Y
NEW YORK					
Moynihan	Y	Y	Y	Y	Y
Schumer	Y	N	Y	Y	Y
NORTH CAROLINA					
Helms	?	?	?	?	?
Edwards	Y	N	Y	Y	Y
NORTH DAKOTA					
Conrad	Y	N	Y	Y	Y
Dorgan	Y	Y	Y	Y	Y
OHIO					
DeWine	Y	N	Y	Y	Y
Voinovich	N	N	Y	Y	Y
OKLAHOMA					
Nickles	Y	Y	N	Y	Y
Inhofe	N	Y	Y	Y	Y
OREGON					
Wyden	Y	N	Y	Y	Y
Smith	Y	Y	Y	Y	Y
PENNSYLVANIA					
Specter	Y	Y	Y	Y	Y
Santorum	Y	N	Y	Y	Y
RHODE ISLAND					
Reed	Y	Y	Y	Y	Y
Chafee, L.	Y	Y	Y	Y	Y
SOUTH CAROLINA					
Thurmond	Y	Y	Y	Y	Y
Hollings	Y	Y	Y	Y	Y
SOUTH DAKOTA					
Daschle	Y	Y	Y	Y	Y
Johnson	Y	N	Y	Y	Y
TENNESSEE					
Thompson	Y	Y	Y	Y	Y
Frist	Y	N	Y	Y	Y
TEXAS					
Gramm	N	N	N	Y	Y
Hutchison	Y	N	Y	Y	Y
UTAH					
Hatch	Y	Y	Y	Y	Y
Bennett	Y	Y	Y	Y	Y
VERMONT					
Leahy	Y	Y	Y	Y	N
Jeffords	Y	Y	Y	Y	Y
VIRGINIA					
Warner	Y	N	Y	Y	Y
Robb	Y	Y	Y	Y	Y
WASHINGTON					
Gorton	Y	Y	Y	Y	Y
Murray	Y	Y	Y	Y	Y
WEST VIRGINIA					
Byrd	Y	N	Y	Y	Y
Rockefeller	Y	Y	Y	Y	Y
WISCONSIN					
Kohl	Y	Y	Y	Y	Y
Feingold	N	N	N	N	Y
WYOMING					
Thomas	Y	Y	Y	Y	Y
Enzi	Y	Y	Y	Y	Y

Key

- Y Voted for (yea).
- # Paired for.
- + Announced for.
- N Voted against (nay).
- X Paired against.
- – Announced against.
- P Voted "present."
- C Voted "present" to avoid possible conflict of interest.
- ? Did not vote or otherwise make a position known.

Democrats ***Republicans***
Independents

ND Northern Democrats SD Southern Democrats

Southern states - Ala., Ark., Fla., Ga., Ky., La., Miss., N.C., Okla., S.C., Tenn., Texas, Va.

272. HR 4635. Fiscal 2001 VA-HUD Appropriations/Passage. Passage of a bill that would provide $105.8 billion for departments of Veterans Affairs, Housing and Urban Development, NASA, EPA, National Science Foundation and related agencies. It includes $453 million for new rental assistance vouchers. The bill also includes language that incorporates a slightly amended version of the fiscal 2001 energy and water appropriations bill. Passed 87-8: R 46-6; D 41-2 (ND 33-1, SD 8-1). Oct. 12, 2000.

273. HR 4516. Fiscal 2001 Legislative Branch and Treasury-Postal Service Appropriations/Conference Report. Adoption of the conference report on the bill that would appropriate $2.5 billion in fiscal 2001 for the legislative branch; appropriate $30.4 billion for the Treasury Department, Postal Service, executive office of the president and certain independent agencies, and repeal the 3 percent federal excise tax on telecommunications services by the end of 2002. Adopted (thus cleared for the president) 58-37: R 33-19; D 25-18 (ND 21-13, SD 4-5). Oct. 12, 2000.

274. HR 4205. Fiscal 2001 Defense Department Authorization/Budget Act Waiver. Warner, R-Va., motion to waive the Budget Act with respect to the Kerrey, D-Neb., point of order against the conference report on the bill to authorize $309.9 billion for the Defense Department for fiscal 2001, including $4.8 billion for ballistic missile defense programs. It also would entitle military retirees to lifetime health care benefits and would restore prescription drug coverage to most Medicare-eligible retirees. Motion agreed to 84-9: R 46-5; D 38-4 (ND 30-3, SD 8-1). A three-fifths majority (60) of the total Senate is required to waive the Budget Act. (Subsequently, the Kerrey point of order failed.) Oct. 12, 2000.

275. HR 4205. Fiscal 2001 Defense Department Authorization/Conference Report. Adoption of the conference report on the bill that would authorize $309.9 billion for the Defense Department, including $4.8 billion for ballistic missile defense programs. It also would entitle military retirees to lifetime health care benefits and would restore prescription coverage to most Medicare-eligible retirees. Adopted (thus cleared for the president) 90-3: R 51-0; D 39-3 (ND 30-3, SD 9-0). Oct. 12, 2000.

276. H J Res 111. Continuing Resolution/Passage. Passage of the joint resolution that would provide temporary funding authority at current levels through Oct. 20, for the departments, agencies and programs for which regular fiscal year 2001 appropriations bills will not be enacted by Oct. 14. Passed (thus cleared for the president) 90-1: R 49-0; D 41-1 (ND 32-1, SD 9-0). Oct. 12, 2000.

Senate Votes 277, 278, 279

	277	278	279
ALABAMA			
Shelby	Y	Y	Y
Sessions	Y	Y	Y
ALASKA			
Stevens	Y	Y	Y
Murkowski	Y	Y	Y
ARIZONA			
McCain	N	?	?
Kyl	N	N	Y
ARKANSAS			
Hutchinson	Y	Y	Y
Lincoln	Y	Y	Y
CALIFORNIA			
Feinstein	?	?	?
Boxer	Y	Y	Y
COLORADO			
Campbell	Y	Y	Y
Allard	N	N	Y
CONNECTICUT			
Dodd	Y	Y	Y
Lieberman	?	?	?
DELAWARE			
Roth	Y	Y	Y
Biden	?	Y	Y
FLORIDA			
Graham	Y	N	Y
Mack	Y	Y	Y
GEORGIA			
Miller	Y	Y	Y
Cleland	Y	Y	Y
HAWAII			
Inouye	Y	?	?
Akaka	Y	Y	Y
IDAHO			
Craig	Y	Y	Y
Crapo	Y	Y	?
ILLINOIS			
Durbin	Y	Y	Y
Fitzgerald	Y	Y	C
INDIANA			
Lugar	Y	Y	Y
Bayh	Y	Y	Y
IOWA			
Grassley	Y	N	Y
Harkin	Y	Y	Y
KANSAS			
Brownback	Y	Y	Y
Roberts	Y	Y	Y
KENTUCKY			
McConnell	Y	Y	Y
Bunning	Y	Y	Y
LOUISIANA			
Breaux	Y	Y	Y
Landrieu	Y	Y	Y
MAINE			
Snowe	Y	Y	Y
Collins	Y	Y	Y
MARYLAND			
Sarbanes	Y	Y	Y
Mikulski	Y	Y	Y
MASSACHUSETTS			
Kennedy	?	Y	Y
Kerry	Y	?	?
MICHIGAN			
Levin	Y	Y	Y
Abraham	Y	Y	Y
MINNESOTA			
Wellstone	Y	Y	Y
Grams	?	?	?
MISSISSIPPI			
Cochran	Y	Y	Y
Lott	Y	Y	Y
MISSOURI			
Bond	Y	Y	Y
Ashcroft	Y	Y	Y
MONTANA			
Baucus	Y	Y	Y
Burns	Y	Y	?
NEBRASKA			
Kerrey	Y	Y	Y
Hagel	Y	Y	Y
NEVADA			
Reid	Y	Y	Y
Bryan	Y	Y	Y
NEW HAMPSHIRE			
Smith	N	Y	Y
Gregg	Y	Y	Y
NEW JERSEY			
Lautenberg	Y	Y	Y
Torricelli	Y	Y	Y
NEW MEXICO			
Domenici	Y	Y	Y
Bingaman	Y	Y	Y
NEW YORK			
Moynihan	Y	Y	Y
Schumer	Y	Y	Y
NORTH CAROLINA			
Helms	?	?	?
Edwards	Y	Y	Y
NORTH DAKOTA			
Conrad	Y	Y	Y
Dorgan	Y	Y	Y
OHIO			
DeWine	Y	Y	Y
Voinovich	N	N	Y
OKLAHOMA			
Nickles	N	Y	Y
Inhofe	Y	N	Y
OREGON			
Wyden	Y	Y	Y
Smith	Y	Y	Y
PENNSYLVANIA			
Specter	Y	Y	Y
Santorum	Y	Y	Y
RHODE ISLAND			
Reed	Y	Y	Y
Chafee, L.	Y	Y	Y
SOUTH CAROLINA			
Thurmond	Y	Y	Y
Hollings	Y	Y	Y
SOUTH DAKOTA			
Daschle	Y	Y	Y
Johnson	Y	Y	Y
TENNESSEE			
Thompson	Y	Y	Y
Frist	Y	Y	Y

Key

- Y Voted for (yea).
- # Paired for.
- \+ Announced for.
- N Voted against (nay).
- X Paired against.
- – Announced against.
- P Voted "present."
- C Voted "present" to avoid possible conflict of interest.
- ? Did not vote or otherwise make a position known.

Democrats ***Republicans***
Independents

	277	278	279
TEXAS			
Gramm	N	N	Y
Hutchison	Y	Y	Y
UTAH			
Hatch	Y	Y	Y
Bennett	Y	Y	Y
VERMONT			
Leahy	Y	Y	Y
Jeffords	Y	Y	Y
VIRGINIA			
Warner	Y	Y	Y
Robb	Y	Y	Y
WASHINGTON			
Gorton	Y	Y	Y
Murray	Y	Y	?
WEST VIRGINIA			
Byrd	Y	Y	Y
Rockefeller	Y	Y	Y
WISCONSIN			
Kohl	Y	Y	Y
Feingold	N	N	Y
WYOMING			
Thomas	Y	Y	Y
Enzi	Y	Y	Y

ND Northern Democrats SD Southern Democrats

Southern states - Ala., Ark., Fla., Ga., Ky., La., Miss., N.C., Okla., S.C., Tenn., Texas, Va.

277. HR 4461. Fiscal 2001 Agriculture Appropriations/Conference Report. Adoption of the conference report on the bill that would appropriate $78.5 billion for the Agriculture Department and related agencies. The agreement includes $3.6 billion in emergency aid for farmers and a deal that would allow the sale of food and medicine to five nations, including Cuba, but bar public or private U.S. financing of Cuban purchases. It also would codify an executive order restricting travel to Cuba. U.S. pharmacies and wholesalers would be allowed to re-import U.S.-made prescription drugs that are sold abroad for less than they cost in the United States. Adopted (thus cleared for the president) 86-8: R 45-7; D 41-1 (ND 32-1, SD 9-0). Oct. 18, 2000.

278. HR 4635. Fiscal 2001 VA-HUD and Energy-Water Appropriations/Conference Report. Adoption of the conference report on the bill that would appropriate $107.3 billion in fiscal 2001 for the Veterans Affairs and Housing and Urban Development departments and independent agencies. The bill also includes a slightly revised version of a bill (HR 4733) to appropriate $23.6 billion for the Energy Department and Army Corps of Engineers, and other independent agencies. Adopted (thus cleared for the president) 85-8: R 45-6; D 40-2 (ND 32-1, SD 8-1). Oct. 19, 2000.

279. HR 2415. Bankruptcy Overhaul/Motion to Proceed. Motion to proceed to the conference report on the bill that would overhaul the nation's bankruptcy laws. Motion agreed to 89-0: R 48-0; D 41-0 (ND 32-0, SD 9-0). Oct. 19, 2000.

Senate Votes 280, 281, 282, 283, 284, 285, 286, 287

	280	281	282	283	284	285	286	287
ALABAMA								
Shelby	Y	Y	Y	Y	Y	Y	Y	Y
Sessions	N	Y	Y	Y	Y	Y	Y	Y
ALASKA								
Stevens	Y	Y	Y	Y	N	Y	Y	Y
Murkowski	Y	Y	Y	Y	Y	Y	Y	Y
ARIZONA								
McCain	N	N	Y	Y	N	Y	Y	Y
Kyl	N	Y	Y	Y	Y	Y	Y	Y
ARKANSAS								
Hutchinson	Y	Y	Y	Y	N	Y	Y	Y
Lincoln	N	Y	Y	Y	N	Y	N	Y
CALIFORNIA								
Feinstein	?	?	?	?	?	?	?	?
Boxer	Y	N	N	Y	N	Y	N	Y
COLORADO								
Campbell	Y	Y	Y	Y	Y	Y	Y	Y
Allard	N	Y	Y	Y	Y	Y	Y	Y
CONNECTICUT								
Dodd	Y	N	Y	Y	N	Y	N	Y
Lieberman	?	?	?	?	?	?	?	?
DELAWARE								
Roth	Y	?	?	?	N	Y	Y	Y
Biden	Y	N	Y	Y	N	Y	N	Y
FLORIDA								
Graham	N	N	Y	Y	N	Y	N	Y
Mack	Y	Y	Y	Y	Y	Y	Y	Y
GEORGIA								
Miller	N	Y	Y	Y	N	Y	Y	Y
Cleland	N	N	Y	Y	N	Y	N	Y
HAWAII								
Inouye	Y	Y	Y	Y	N	Y	N	Y
Akaka	?	?	?	?	N	Y	N	Y
IDAHO								
Craig	N	Y	Y	Y	Y	Y	Y	Y
Crapo	Y	Y	Y	Y	N	Y	Y	Y
ILLINOIS								
Durbin	Y	N	N	Y	N	Y	N	Y
Fitzgerald	N	N	Y	Y	Y	Y	Y	Y
INDIANA								
Lugar	Y	Y	Y	Y	N	Y	Y	Y
Bayh	N	N	Y	Y	N	Y	N	Y

	280	281	282	283	284	285	286	287
IOWA								
Grassley	Y	Y	Y	Y	N	Y	Y	Y
Harkin	Y	N	Y	Y	N	Y	N	Y
KANSAS								
Brownback	Y	Y	Y	Y	Y	Y	Y	Y
Roberts	Y	Y	Y	Y	N	Y	Y	Y
KENTUCKY								
McConnell	Y	Y	Y	Y	Y	Y	Y	Y
Bunning	Y	Y	Y	Y	Y	Y	Y	Y
LOUISIANA								
Breaux	N	Y	Y	Y	N	Y	N	Y
Landrieu	N	Y	Y	Y	N	Y	N	Y
MAINE								
Snowe	Y	N	Y	Y	N	Y	Y	Y
Collins	Y	N	Y	Y	N	Y	Y	Y
MARYLAND								
Sarbanes	Y	N	Y	Y	N	Y	N	Y
Mikulski	Y	N	Y	Y	N	Y	N	Y
MASSACHUSETTS								
Kennedy	Y	N	Y	Y	N	Y	N	Y
Kerry	Y	N	Y	Y	N	Y	N	Y
MICHIGAN								
Levin	Y	N	Y	Y	N	Y	N	Y
Abraham	Y	Y	Y	Y	N	Y	Y	Y
MINNESOTA								
Wellstone	Y	N	Y	Y	N	Y	N	Y
Grams	?	?	?	?	?	?	?	?
MISSISSIPPI								
Cochran	Y	Y	Y	Y	N	Y	Y	Y
Lott	Y	Y	Y	Y	Y	Y	Y	Y
MISSOURI								
Bond	Y	Y	Y	Y	Y	Y	Y	Y
Ashcroft	?	?	?	?	Y	Y	Y	Y
MONTANA								
Baucus	Y	Y	Y	N	N	Y	N	Y
Burns	+	?	?	+	N	Y	Y	Y
NEBRASKA								
Kerrey	N	Y	Y	Y	N	Y	N	Y
Hagel	Y	Y	Y	Y	N	Y	Y	Y
NEVADA								
Reid	Y	N	Y	Y	N	Y	N	Y
Bryan	N	N	Y	Y	N	Y	N	Y

	280	281	282	283	284	285	286	287
NEW HAMPSHIRE								
Smith	N	Y	Y	Y	Y	Y	Y	Y
Gregg	Y	Y	Y	Y	Y	Y	Y	Y
NEW JERSEY								
Lautenberg	Y	N	N	Y	N	Y	N	Y
Torricelli	Y	Y	Y	Y	N	Y	N	Y
NEW MEXICO								
Domenici	Y	Y	Y	Y	N	Y	Y	Y
Bingaman	Y	Y	Y	Y	N	Y	Y	Y
NEW YORK								
Moynihan	Y	Y	Y	Y	N	Y	Y	Y
Schumer	Y	N	Y	Y	N	Y	N	Y
NORTH CAROLINA								
Helms	?	+	+	?	?	?	?	?
Edwards	N	N	Y	Y	N	Y	N	Y
NORTH DAKOTA								
Conrad	N	Y	Y	Y	N	Y	N	Y
Dorgan	Y	Y	Y	Y	N	Y	N	Y
OHIO								
DeWine	Y	Y	Y	Y	N	Y	Y	Y
Voinovich	N	Y	Y	Y	N	Y	Y	Y
OKLAHOMA								
Nickles	Y	Y	Y	Y	Y	Y	Y	Y
Inhofe	Y	Y	Y	Y	Y	Y	Y	Y
OREGON								
Wyden	Y	N	Y	Y	N	Y	N	Y
Smith	Y	Y	Y	Y	N	Y	Y	Y
PENNSYLVANIA								
Specter	Y	N	Y	Y	?	?	Y	Y
Santorum	Y	Y	Y	Y	N	Y	Y	Y
RHODE ISLAND								
Reed	Y	N	Y	Y	N	Y	N	Y
Chafee, L.	Y	N	N	Y	N	Y	Y	Y
SOUTH CAROLINA								
Thurmond	Y	Y	Y	Y	N	Y	Y	Y
Hollings	Y	Y	Y	Y	N	Y	N	Y
SOUTH DAKOTA								
Daschle	Y	Y	Y	Y	N	Y	N	Y
Johnson	N	Y	Y	Y	N	Y	N	Y
TENNESSEE								
Thompson	Y	Y	Y	Y	Y	Y	Y	Y
Frist	?	?	?	?	Y	Y	Y	Y

Key

- Y Voted for (yea).
- \# Paired for.
- \+ Announced for.
- N Voted against (nay).
- X Paired against.
- – Announced against.
- P Voted "present."
- C Voted "present" to avoid possible conflict of interest.
- ? Did not vote or otherwise make a position known.

•

Democrats ***Republicans***
Independents

	280	281	282	283	284	285	286	287
TEXAS								
Gramm	N	Y	Y	Y	Y	Y	N	Y
Hutchison	Y	Y	Y	Y	Y	Y	Y	Y
UTAH								
Hatch	Y	Y	Y	Y	N	Y	Y	Y
Bennett	Y	Y	Y	Y	N	Y	Y	Y
VERMONT								
Leahy	Y	N	Y	N	N	Y	N	N
Jeffords	Y	N	Y	?	N	Y	Y	Y
VIRGINIA								
Warner	Y	Y	Y	Y	Y	Y	Y	Y
Robb	N	N	Y	Y	N	Y	Y	Y
WASHINGTON								
Gorton	Y	+	+	+	?	?	?	?
Murray	Y	Y	Y	Y	N	Y	N	Y
WEST VIRGINIA								
Byrd	N	N	Y	Y	N	Y	N	Y
Rockefeller	Y	N	Y	Y	N	Y	N	Y
WISCONSIN								
Kohl	N	N	Y	Y	N	Y	Y	Y
Feingold	N	N	N	Y	N	Y	N	Y
WYOMING								
Thomas	N	Y	Y	Y	N	Y	Y	Y
Enzi	N	Y	Y	Y	Y	Y	Y	Y

ND Northern Democrats SD Southern Democrats

Southern states - Ala., Ark., Fla., Ga., Ky., La., Miss., N.C., Okla., S.C., Tenn., Texas, Va.

280. HR 4811. Fiscal 2001 Foreign Operations Appropriations/Conference Report. Adoption of the conference report on the bill that would appropriate $14.9 billion in fiscal year 2001 for foreign operations. It includes $2.9 billion for Israel, almost $2 billion for Egypt, $1.1 billion for international financial institutions and $435 million to restructure and forgive the debt of the world's poorest nations. Adopted (thus cleared for the president) 65-27: R 38-11; D 27-16 (ND 26-8, SD 1-8). Oct. 25, 2000.

281. S 2508. Colorado Ute Indian Water Rights/Animas-La Plata Project. Campbell, R-Colo., motion to table (kill) the Feingold, D-Wis., amendment to the Campbell substitute amendment. The Feingold amendment would clarify that the legislation would grant congressional approval only for the scaled-back version of the Animas-La Plata project and would require non-tribal water users to pay recreation, fish and wildlife costs. The Campbell amendment would scale back the water project to consist of the facilities needed to divert and impound water in an off-stream reservoir. Motion agreed to 56-34: R 40-7; D 16-27 (ND 11-23, SD 5-4). (Subsequently, the Campbell amendment was adopted by voice vote.) Oct. 25, 2000.

282. S 2508. Colorado Ute Indian Water Rights Settlement/Passage. Passage of a bill that would authorize the creation of a scaled-back version of the Animas-La Plata project, consisting of facilities needed to divert and impound water in an off-stream reservoir. The bill would settle the Southern Ute and Mountain Ute Indian tribes' water rights claims. Passed 85-5: R 46-1; D 39-4 (ND 30-4, SD 9-0). Oct. 25, 2000.

283. H J Res 115. Continuing Resolution/Passage. Passage of the joint resolution that would provide temporary funding authority, at current levels, through Oct. 26, for the departments, agencies and programs for which regular fiscal year 2001 appropriations bills have not been enacted by Oct. 25. Passed (thus cleared for the president) 87-2: R 46-0; D 41-2 (ND 32-2, SD 9-0). Oct. 25, 2000.

284. HR 782. Older Americans Act/Background Checks. Gregg, R-N.H., amendment that would require background checks for organizations applying for federal grants. Rejected 25-69: R 25-25; D 0-44 (ND 0-35, SD 0-9). Oct. 26, 2000.

285. HR 782. Older Americans Act/Passage. Passage of the bill that would reauthorize programs under the Older Americans Act and set aside $125 million for a new family caregiver program. Passed (thus cleared for the president) 94-0: R 50-0; D 44-0 (ND 35-0, SD 9-0). Oct. 26, 2000.

286. HR 2614. Tax Cut Package/Motion to Proceed. Motion to proceed to the conference report on the bill to reduce taxes and other measures that would decrease federal revenue by $240.4 billion over 10 years. Motion agreed to 55-40: R 50-1; D 5-39 (ND 3-32, SD 2-7). Oct. 26, 2000.

287. H J Res 116. Continuing Resolution/Passage. Passage of the joint resolution that would provide temporary funding authority, at current levels, until Oct. 27, for the departments, agencies and programs for which regular fiscal year 2001 appropriations bills have not been enacted by Oct. 26. Passed (thus cleared for the president) 94-1: R 51-0; D 43-1 (ND 34-1, SD 9-0). Oct. 26, 2000.

Senate Votes 288, 289, 290, 291, 292, 293, 294

	288	289	290	291	292	293	294
ALABAMA							
Shelby	Y	N	Y	Y	Y	Y	Y
Sessions	Y	N	?	?	Y	Y	Y
ALASKA							
Stevens	Y	Y	N	N	N	N	Y
Murkowski	Y	Y	Y	Y	?	Y	Y
ARIZONA							
McCain	?	?	?	?	?	?	?
Kyl	Y	Y	Y	?	?	Y	Y
ARKANSAS							
Hutchinson	Y	Y	Y	Y	Y	Y	Y
Lincoln	Y	Y	Y	Y	Y	Y	Y
CALIFORNIA							
Feinstein	?	?	?	?	?	?	?
Boxer	Y	N	Y	?	?	?	N
COLORADO							
Campbell	Y	Y	Y	?	?	Y	Y
Allard	Y	N	Y	Y	Y	Y	Y
CONNECTICUT							
Dodd	Y	N	Y	Y	Y	Y	N
Lieberman	?	?	?	?	?	?	?
DELAWARE							
Roth	Y	?	?	?	?	?	Y
Biden	+	N	Y	Y	Y	?	Y
FLORIDA							
Graham	Y	N	Y	Y	Y	Y	Y
Mack	Y	Y	Y	Y	?	?	Y
GEORGIA							
Miller	Y	Y	Y	Y	Y	Y	Y
Cleland	Y	N	Y	Y	?	Y	Y
HAWAII							
Inouye	Y	N	Y	Y	Y	Y	N
Akaka	Y	N	Y	Y	Y	Y	N
IDAHO							
Craig	Y	Y	Y	Y	Y	?	Y
Crapo	Y	Y	Y	?	?	?	Y
ILLINOIS							
Durbin	+	–	+	+	Y	Y	N
Fitzgerald	C	Y	Y	Y	Y	Y	C
INDIANA							
Lugar	Y	Y	Y	?	?	Y	Y
Bayh	Y	N	Y	Y	Y	Y	Y
IOWA							
Grassley	Y	N	Y	Y	Y	Y	Y
Harkin	Y	N	Y	Y	Y	Y	N
KANSAS							
Brownback	Y	Y	Y	Y	?	?	Y
Roberts	Y	Y	Y	Y	Y	Y	Y
KENTUCKY							
McConnell	Y	Y	Y	?	?	?	Y
Bunning	Y	Y	Y	Y	Y	Y	Y
LOUISIANA							
Breaux	Y	Y	Y	?	Y	Y	Y
Landrieu	Y	N	Y	Y	Y	Y	N
MAINE							
Snowe	Y	Y	Y	Y	Y	Y	Y
Collins	Y	Y	Y	Y	Y	Y	Y
MARYLAND							
Sarbanes	Y	N	Y	Y	Y	Y	N
Mikulski	Y	N	Y	Y	Y	Y	N
MASSACHUSETTS							
Kennedy	Y	N	Y	Y	Y	?	N
Kerry	Y	N	Y	Y	Y	Y	N
MICHIGAN							
Levin	Y	N	Y	Y	Y	Y	N
Abraham	Y	Y	Y	Y	Y	Y	Y
MINNESOTA							
Wellstone	Y	N	Y	?	?	Y	N
Grams	?	?	?	?	?	?	?
MISSISSIPPI							
Cochran	Y	Y	Y	?	Y	Y	Y
Lott	Y	Y	Y	Y	Y	Y	N
MISSOURI							
Bond	Y	Y	Y	?	?	?	Y
Ashcroft	?	?	?	?	?	?	?
MONTANA							
Baucus	Y	Y	Y	Y	Y	Y	N
Burns	?	+	?	+	+	+	+
NEBRASKA							
Kerrey	Y	N	Y	Y	Y	Y	N
Hagel	Y	Y	Y	Y	Y	?	Y
NEVADA							
Reid	Y	N	Y	Y	Y	Y	N
Bryan	Y	N	Y	?	Y	Y	N
NEW HAMPSHIRE							
Smith	Y	Y	Y	Y	Y	Y	Y
Gregg	Y	Y	Y	Y	Y	Y	Y
NEW JERSEY							
Lautenberg	Y	N	Y	?	?	Y	?
Torricelli	Y	N	Y	?	Y	Y	Y
NEW MEXICO							
Domenici	Y	Y	Y	Y	Y	Y	Y
Bingaman	Y	N	Y	Y	Y	Y	?
NEW YORK							
Moynihan	Y	N	Y	Y	Y	Y	N
Schumer	Y	N	Y	Y	Y	Y	N
NORTH CAROLINA							
Helms	+	+	+	+	+	+	+
Edwards	Y	N	Y	Y	Y	Y	N
NORTH DAKOTA							
Conrad	Y	N	Y	Y	?	Y	N
Dorgan	Y	N	Y	Y	Y	+	N
OHIO							
DeWine	Y	Y	Y	Y	Y	Y	Y
Voinovich	Y	Y	Y	Y	Y	Y	Y
OKLAHOMA							
Nickles	Y	Y	N	?	Y	Y	Y
Inhofe	Y	Y	Y	?	?	?	?
OREGON							
Wyden	Y	N	Y	Y	Y	Y	N
Smith	Y	Y	Y	Y	Y	Y	Y
PENNSYLVANIA							
Specter	Y	Y	Y	Y	Y	?	?
Santorum	?	Y	Y	Y	Y	?	?
RHODE ISLAND							
Reed	Y	N	Y	Y	Y	Y	N
Chafee, L.	Y	Y	Y	Y	Y	Y	Y
SOUTH CAROLINA							
Thurmond	Y	Y	Y	Y	Y	Y	Y
Hollings	Y	N	Y	?	?	Y	N
SOUTH DAKOTA							
Daschle	Y	N	Y	Y	Y	Y	Y
Johnson	Y	N	Y	Y	Y	Y	Y
TENNESSEE							
Thompson	Y	Y	Y	Y	?	Y	Y
Frist	Y	Y	Y	Y	?	Y	?
TEXAS							
Gramm	Y	Y	Y	Y	Y	Y	Y
Hutchison	Y	Y	?	?	Y	Y	Y
UTAH							
Hatch	Y	Y	Y	Y	Y	Y	Y
Bennett	Y	Y	Y	Y	Y	Y	Y
VERMONT							
Leahy	Y	N	N	N	?	?	?
Jeffords	Y	Y	Y	?	?	?	?
VIRGINIA							
Warner	Y	Y	Y	Y	Y	?	Y
Robb	Y	N	Y	Y	Y	Y	Y
WASHINGTON							
Gorton	Y	Y	Y	?	?	?	?
Murray	Y	N	Y	Y	Y	Y	N
WEST VIRGINIA							
Byrd	Y	Y	Y	Y	Y	Y	Y
Rockefeller	?	N	Y	Y	Y	Y	N
WISCONSIN							
Kohl	N	N	Y	?	?	?	N
Feingold	Y	N	Y	Y	Y	Y	N
WYOMING							
Thomas	Y	Y	Y	?	?	?	Y
Enzi	Y	Y	Y	Y	?	?	Y

Key

- Y Voted for (yea).
- \# Paired for.
- \+ Announced for.
- N Voted against (nay).
- X Paired against.
- – Announced against.
- P Voted "present."
- C Voted "present" to avoid possible conflict of interest.
- ? Did not vote or otherwise make a position known.

•

Democrats ***Republicans***
Independents

ND Northern Democrats SD Southern Democrats

Southern states - Ala., Ark., Fla., Ga., Ky., La., Miss., N.C., Okla., S.C., Tenn., Texas, Va.

288. HR 2415. Bankruptcy Overhaul/Motion to Proceed. Motion to proceed to the conference report on the bill that would overhaul the nation's bankruptcy laws. Motion agreed to 87-1: R 47-0; D 40-1 (ND 31-1, SD 9-0). Oct. 27, 2000.

289. HR 4942. Fiscal 2001 Commerce-Justice-State and District of Columbia Appropriations/Conference Report. Adoption of the conference report on the bill that would appropriate $445 million in federal funds for the District of Columbia and approve the expenditure of $6.67 billion of District funds. It also would appropriate $39.9 billion for the departments of Commerce, Justice, State and other independent agencies. It would allow certain illegal aliens to seek legal status through the courts and permit the families of legal resident aliens to remain in the United States while their applications for permanent residency are being processed. Adopted (thus cleared for the president) 49-42: R 44-4; D 5-38 (ND 2-32, SD 3-6). Oct. 27, 2000.

290. H J Res 117. Continuing Resolution/Passage. Passage of the joint resolution that would provide temporary funding authority, at current levels, until Oct. 28, for the departments, agencies and programs for which regular fiscal year 2001 appropriations bills are not enacted by Oct. 27. Passed (thus cleared for the president) 86-3: R 44-2; D 42-1 (ND 33-1, SD 9-0). Oct. 27, 2000.

291. H J Res 118. Continuing Resolution/Passage. Passage of the joint resolution that would provide temporary funding authority, at current levels, until Oct. 29, for the departments and programs for which regular fiscal 2001 appropriations are not enacted by Oct. 28. Passed (thus cleared for the president) 67-2: R 33-1; D 34-1 (ND 27-1, SD 7-0). Oct. 28, 2000.

292. H J Res 119. Continuing Resolution/Passage. Passage of the joint resolution that would provide temporary funding authority, at current levels, until Oct. 30, for the departments and programs for which regular fiscal 2001 appropriations are not enacted by Oct. 29. Passed (thus cleared for the president) 67-1: R 31-1; D 36-0 (ND 29-0, SD 7-0). Oct. 29, 2000.

293. H J Res 120. Continuing Resolution/Passage. Passage of the joint resolution that would provide temporary funding authority, at current levels, until Oct. 31, for the departments and programs for which regular fiscal 2001 appropriations are not enacted by Oct. 30. Passed (thus cleared for the president) 70-1: R 32-1; D 38-0 (ND 29-0, SD 9-0). Oct. 30, 2000.

294. HR 2415. Bankruptcy Overhaul/Cloture. Motion to invoke cloture (thus limiting debate) on the conference report on the bill that would overhaul the nation's bankruptcy laws. Motion rejected 53-30: R 41-1; D 12-29 (ND 6-26, SD 6-3). Three-fifths of the total Senate (60) is required to invoke cloture. Nov. 1, 2000.

	295	296	297	298
ALABAMA				
Shelby	Y	Y	Y	Y
Sessions	Y	Y	Y	Y
ALASKA				
Stevens	Y	Y	Y	Y
Murkowski	Y	Y	Y	Y
ARIZONA				
McCain	Y	Y	Y	Y
Kyl	Y	Y	Y	?
ARKANSAS				
Hutchinson	Y	Y	Y	Y
Lincoln	Y	Y	Y	Y
CALIFORNIA				
Feinstein	Y	N	N	Y
Boxer	Y	N	N	Y
COLORADO				
Campbell	Y	Y	Y	Y
Allard	Y	Y	Y	Y
CONNECTICUT				
Dodd	Y	N	N	Y
Lieberman	Y	N	N	Y
DELAWARE				
Roth	Y	Y	Y	Y
Biden	Y	Y	Y	Y
FLORIDA				
Graham	Y	Y	Y	Y
Mack	Y	Y	Y	Y
GEORGIA				
Miller	Y	Y	Y	Y
Cleland	Y	Y	Y	Y
HAWAII				
Inouye	Y	N	N	Y
Akaka	Y	N	N	Y
IDAHO				
Craig	Y	Y	Y	Y
Crapo	Y	Y	Y	Y
ILLINOIS				
Durbin	Y	N	N	Y
Fitzgerald	Y	C	C	Y
INDIANA				
Lugar	Y	Y	Y	Y
Bayh	Y	Y	Y	Y
IOWA				
Grassley	Y	Y	Y	Y
Harkin	Y	N	N	Y
KANSAS				
Brownback	Y	Y	Y	Y
Roberts	Y	Y	Y	Y
KENTUCKY				
McConnell	Y	Y	Y	Y
Bunning	Y	Y	Y	Y
LOUISIANA				
Breaux	Y	Y	Y	Y
Landrieu	Y	N	?	?
MAINE				
Snowe	Y	Y	Y	Y
Collins	Y	Y	Y	Y
MARYLAND				
Sarbanes	Y	N	N	Y
Mikulski	Y	N	N	Y
MASSACHUSETTS				
Kennedy	Y	N	N	Y
Kerry	Y	N	N	Y
MICHIGAN				
Levin	Y	N	N	Y
Abraham	Y	Y	Y	Y
MINNESOTA				
Wellstone	Y	N	N	Y
Grams	Y	Y	Y	Y
MISSISSIPPI				
Cochran	Y	Y	Y	Y
Lott	Y	Y	Y	Y
MISSOURI				
Bond	Y	Y	Y	Y
Ashcroft	Y	Y	Y	Y
MONTANA				
Baucus	Y	N	N	Y
Burns	Y	Y	Y	Y
NEBRASKA				
Kerrey	Y	Y	Y	Y
Hagel	Y	Y	Y	Y
NEVADA				
Reid	Y	N	N	Y
Bryan	Y	N	Y	Y
NEW HAMPSHIRE				
Smith	Y	Y	Y	Y
Gregg	Y	Y	Y	Y
NEW JERSEY				
Lautenberg	Y	N	N	Y
Torricelli	Y	Y	Y	Y
NEW MEXICO				
Domenici	Y	Y	Y	Y
Bingaman	Y	Y	Y	Y
NEW YORK				
Moynihan	Y	N	N	Y
Schumer	Y	N	N	Y
NORTH CAROLINA				
Helms	Y	Y	Y	Y
Edwards	Y	N	N	Y
NORTH DAKOTA				
Conrad	Y	N	Y	Y
Dorgan	Y	N	Y	Y
OHIO				
DeWine	Y	Y	Y	Y
Voinovich	Y	Y	Y	Y
OKLAHOMA				
Nickles	Y	Y	Y	Y
Inhofe	Y	Y	Y	Y
OREGON				
Wyden	Y	N	N	Y
Smith	Y	Y	Y	Y
PENNSYLVANIA				
Specter	Y	Y	Y	?
Santorum	Y	Y	Y	Y
RHODE ISLAND				
Reed	Y	N	N	Y
Chafee, L.	Y	Y	Y	Y
SOUTH CAROLINA				
Thurmond	Y	Y	Y	Y
Hollings	Y	N	Y	Y
SOUTH DAKOTA				
Daschle	Y	Y	N	Y
Johnson	Y	Y	Y	Y
TENNESSEE				
Thompson	Y	Y	Y	Y
Frist	Y	Y	Y	Y
TEXAS				
Gramm	Y	Y	Y	Y
Hutchison	Y	Y	Y	Y
UTAH				
Hatch	Y	Y	Y	Y
Bennett	Y	Y	Y	Y
VERMONT				
Leahy	?	?	N	N
Jeffords	Y	Y	Y	Y
VIRGINIA				
Warner	Y	Y	Y	Y
Robb	Y	Y	Y	Y
WASHINGTON				
Gorton	Y	Y	Y	Y
Murray	Y	N	N	Y
WEST VIRGINIA				
Byrd	Y	Y	Y	Y
Rockefeller	Y	N	N	Y
WISCONSIN				
Kohl	Y	N	N	Y
Feingold	Y	N	N	Y
WYOMING				
Thomas	Y	Y	Y	Y
Enzi	Y	Y	Y	Y

Key

- Y Voted for (yea).
- # Paired for.
- + Announced for.
- N Voted against (nay).
- X Paired against.
- – Announced against.
- P Voted "present."
- C Voted "present" to avoid possible conflict of interest.
- ? Did not vote or otherwise make a position known.

•

Democrats ***Republicans***
Independents

ND Northern Democrats SD Southern Democrats

Southern states - Ala., Ark., Fla., Ga., Ky., La., Miss., N.C., Okla., S.C., Tenn., Texas, Va.

295. H J Res 126. Continuing Resolution/Passage. Passage of the joint resolution that would provide temporary funding authority, at current levels, until Dec. 7, for the departments and programs for which regular fiscal 2001 appropriations are not enacted by Dec. 5. Passed (thus cleared for the president) 99-0: R 54-0; D 45-0 (ND 36-0, SD 9-0). Dec. 5, 2000.

296. HR 2415. Bankruptcy Overhaul/Cloture. Motion to invoke cloture (thus limiting debate) on the conference report on the bill that would overhaul the nation's bankruptcy laws. Motion agreed to 67-31: R 53-0; D 14-31 (ND 8-28, SD 6-3). Dec. 5, 2000.

297. HR 2415. Bankruptcy Overhaul/Conference Report. Adoption of the conference report on the bill that would require debtors able to repay $10,000 or 25 percent of their debts over five years to file under Chapter 13, which requires a reorganization of debts under a repayment plan, instead of seeking to discharge their debts under Chapter 7. The bill would cap the "homestead exemption" at $100,000 on homes purchased within two years of a bankruptcy filing. Adopted (thus cleared for the president) 70-28: R 53-0; D 17-28 (ND 10-27, SD 7-1). Dec. 7, 2000.

298. H J Res 127. Continuing Resolution/Passage. Passage of the joint resolution that would provide temporary funding authority, at current levels, until Dec. 8, for the departments and programs for which regular fiscal 2001 appropriations will not be enacted by Dec. 7. Passed (thus cleared for the president) 96-1: R 52-0; D 44-1 (ND 36-1, SD 8-0). Dec. 7, 2000.

Senate Roll Call Votes By Subject

A

B

C

D

E

F

G

H

I

K

L

M

N

P

R

S

T

V

W

Appendix I

GENERAL INDEX

General Index

General Index

B

D

E

F

H

M

Q

R

U

V

W

X

Y

Z